C0-AFI-922

Carmen Julia Martinez

HEBREW-GREEK

KEY WORD®

STUDY BIBLE

KEY INSIGHTS INTO GOD'S WORD

KING JAMES VERSION

AUTHORIZED VERSION

Robbie Lewis

Presented to

From

Occasion

2009

Date

HEBREW-GREEK

KEY WORD®

STUDY BIBLE

KEY INSIGHTS INTO GOD'S WORD

KING JAMES VERSION

AUTHORIZED VERSION

HEBREW-GREEK

KEY WORD®

STUDY BIBLE

KEY INSIGHTS INTO GOD'S WORD

KJV

KING JAMES VERSION

AUTHORIZED VERSION

Key words in the text numerically coded to James Strong's **Exhaustive Concordance of the Bible**, Introduction to each book, Exegetical Notes, Center column references, Words of Christ in Red, Grammatical helps to the New Testament, AMG's Bible Concordance, AMG's Annotated Strong's Dictionaries, and color maps.

Executive Editor
Hebrew-Greek Key Word Study Bibles
Spiros Zodhiates, Th.D.

Managing Editor, KJV edition
Warren Baker, D.R.E.

Chattanooga, TN

The Hebrew-Greek Key Word Study Bible
King James Version
Second Revised Edition

Study helps edited by Warren Baker
Cover and packaging design by Daryle Beam
Typesetting of Bible pages by the Allentown Digital Services Division of R. R. Donnelley & Sons
Typesetting of study helps by Warren Baker

Edition	*ISBN Number*
Hardbound	978-0-89957-745-6
Bonded Leather Black	978-0-89957-746-3
Bonded Leather Burgundy	978-0-89957-747-0
Genuine Leather Black	978-0-89957-748-7
Genuine Leather Burgundy	978-0-89957-749-4

Printed in South Korea
08 09 10 11 12 13 14 –SW– 6 5 4 3 2 1

A PERSONAL WORD FROM THE EXECUTIVE EDITOR

The Hebrew-Greek Key Word Study Bible is the result of years of study in the original languages and countless hours of editorial work by those engaged in it's production. The result is a Bible that provides key insights into the Hebrew, Aramaic, and Greek languages, the languages in which the original writings of the prophets and apostles were penned.

There are times when words cannot be translated accurately because of the lack of corresponding words in English. For instance, there are three words in the Greek New Testament that are translated with the English word "love." Each of these words—*agapē, philia,* and *storgē* (root of *astorgoi*)—has a distinct meaning that seriously affects the proper interpretation of Scripture. When you come across the word "love" in the English New Testament, unless you are familiar with the Greek language, you will not be able to determine which word was used in the original text or the differences between these words.

This Bible identifies the key words of the original languages and gives clear, precise explanations of their meaning and usage. Those who love God's Word, whether they are or are not trained in the biblical languages, will treasure this Bible, for it contains a whole library of biblical helps within its covers.

I would like to express my thanks to those who worked so hard to make the revisions and additions to this unique Bible possible. I would particularly like to thank the staff of the AMG Editorial Division, under the direction of Dr. Warren Baker: Jim Gee, David Gray, Joel Kletzing, Trevor Overcash, Alma Stewart, Sam Wallace, Todd Williams, and Mark Oshman. These people are responsible for the research and editorial work that has made this revised edition of the Hebrew-Greek Key Word Study Bible possible.

It is with an awesome sense of responsibility that my coworkers and I commit this Bible to you with the prayer that it will enhance your knowledge of God's Word and that the presence of Jesus Christ in your heart will be made more real and satisfying.

ON THE SECOND REVISED EDITION

I would like to express my thanks to Dr. Warren Baker, who is responsible for the research and editorial work that has made this second revised edition of the Hebrew-Greek Key Word Study Bible possible.

SPIROS ZODHIATES
Chattanooga, TN

The Hebrew-Greek

THE ACTS

of the Apostles

The Book of Acts was written by Luke, the physician, to Theophilus as a supplement to the Gospel of Luke (Acts 1:1, cf. Luke 1:1–3). The Gospel of Luke relates "all that Jesus began both to do and teach" (Acts 1:1). The Acts of the Apostles, on the other hand, begins with the Ascension of Jesus and tells the story of how the gospel was spread far beyond the confines of the Jewish community to the whole world. The statement of Jesus in Acts 1:8, "and ye shall be witnesses unto me both in Jerusalem, and in all Judea, and in Samaria, and unto the uttermost part of the earth," provides an excellent outline for the book.

The Book of Acts concludes rather abruptly with Paul's imprisonment in Rome. It is assumed that the reason for this unexpected closing is that Luke had recorded all the significant events known to him at that time. Hence, the date for the writing of the book is generally agreed to be about A.D. 61. It is clear from certain passages within the Book of Acts that the author was with the Apostle Paul on several occasions (Acts 16:10–17; 20:5—21:18; 27:1—28:16). In fact, many believe that Paul was referring to Luke in 2 Corinthians 8:18 when he mentions "the brother" who was praised "throughout all the churches."

Luke's purpose in writing Acts was not to give a complete history of the growth of the church, but only to list those events with which he was familiar. He does not record how the gospel spread to the east and south of Palestine, or why there were already believers in Damascus before Paul arrived. Nevertheless, the lives and ministries of the prominent individuals that Luke does include sufficiently demonstrate the shift of the evangelical concerns of Christianity from Jews to Gentiles.

AN INTRODUCTION is given for each book.

UNDERLINING identifies key words or phrases that may be studied further by looking up the attached number(s) in the appropriate dictionary.

SINGLE ITALICIZED SUPERIOR LETTERS preceding a word refer to cross references.

1 The former treatise[3056] [aom]have I made,[4160] O [a]Theophilus, of all that Jesus began both [pinf]to do[4160] and [pinf]teach,[1321]

2 [a]Until the day in which he [aop]was taken up,[353] after that he through the [an]Holy Ghost[4151] [apt][b]had given commandments unto the apostles[652] whom he [ao]had chosen:[1586]

3 [a]To whom also he shewed himself alive[2198] after his [aime]passion[3958] by many infallible proofs,[5039] [ppt]being seen of them forty days, and speaking of the things pertaining to the kingdom[932] of God:[2316]

4 [a]And, being assembled together with *them,* commanded them that they should not depart from Jerusalem, but [pinf]wait for[4037] the promise[1860] of the Father,[3962] [b]which, *saith he,* ye [ao]have heard of me.

🔑 5 [a]For John truly [ao]baptized[907] with water; [b]but ye [fp]shall be baptized with the [an]Holy Ghost not many days hence.

The Holy Spirit Will Come

6 When they therefore [apt]were come together,[4905] they [ipf]asked of him, saying,

1 [a]Luke 1:3
2 [a]Mark 16:19; Luke 9:51; 24:51; Acts 1:9; 1Tim. 3:16 [b]Matt. 28:19; Mark 16:15; John 20:21; Acts 10:41, 42
3 [a]Mark 16:14; Luke 24:36; John 20:19, 26; 21:1, 14; 1Cor. 15:5
4 [a]Luke 24:43, 49 [b]Luke 24:49; John 14:16, 26, 27; 15:26; 16:7; Acts 2:33
5 [a]Matt. 3:11; Acts 11:16; 19:4 [b]Joel 3:18; Acts 2:4; 11:15

🔑 **1:5** Many times this is interpreted to mean that the Holy Spirit did the baptizing. The correct understanding of this, however, is that the Holy Spirit is the element of the baptism just as water was the element of the baptism of John. This is the fifth time that the phrase, "baptized with the Holy Ghost," occurs in the New Testament. In each of the previous four instances Jesus Christ is the One being baptized (see Matt. 3:11; Mark 1:8; Luke 3:16; John 1:33).

MULTIPLE SUPERIOR LETTERS or f, m, and n (not italicized), preceding a word in the New Testament refer to the grammatical structure of the Greek word and are explained in the GRAMMATICAL NOTATIONS section.

KEYS identify explanatory notes at the bottom of the page.

Key Word Study Bible

[a]Lord, wilt thou at this time[5550] [b]restore
again[600] the kingdom[932] to Israel?
7 And he said unto them, [a]It is not
for you [ainf]to know the times[5550] or the
seasons,[2540] which the Father [aom]hath put
in his own power.[1849]
8 [a]But ye shall receive [I]power,[1411]
[b]after that the Holy Ghost [apt]is come
upon you: and [c]ye shall be witnesses[3144]
unto me both in Jerusalem, and in all
Judaea, and in Samaria, and unto the
uttermost part[2078] of the earth.
9 [a]And when he had spoken these
things, while they [ppt]beheld, [b]he [aop]was
taken up;1869 and a cloud received5274
him out of their sight.
10 And while they looked stedfastly
toward heaven[3772] as he [ppt]went up, behold,
two men[435] stood by them [a]in white
apparel;
🗝 11 Which also said, [a]Ye men of
Galilee, why stand ye gazing up1689 into
heaven?[3772] this same Jesus, which is
taken up from you into heaven, [b]shall so
come in like manner as ye [aom]have seen
him [ppt]go into heaven.

Matthias Replaces Judas

12 [a]Then returned they unto
Jerusalem from the mount called Olivet,
which is from Jerusalem a sabbath
day's4521 journey.[3598]
13 And when they were come in,
they went up [a]into an upper room, where
abode2258,2650 both [b]Peter, and James, and
John, and Andrew, Philip, and Thomas,
Bartholomew, and Matthew, James *the*
son of Alphaeus, and [c]Simon Zelotes, and
[d]Judas *the brother* of James.
14 [a]These all continued[4342]2258 with one
accord in prayer[4335] and supplication,[1162]
with [b]the women, and Mary the mother
of Jesus, and with [c]his brethren.[80]
15 And in those days Peter stood up
in the midst of the disciples,[3101] and said,
(the number [a]of names[3686] together were
about[5613] an hundred and twenty,)

6 [a]Matt. 24:3 [b]Isa. 1:26; Dan. 7:27; Amos 9:11
7 [a]Matt. 24:36; Mark 13:32; 1Thess. 5:1
8 [I]Or, *the power of the Holy Ghost coming upon you* [a]Acts 2:1, 4 [b]Luke 24:49 [c]Luke 24:48; John 15:27; Acts 1:22; 2:32
9 [a]Luke 24:51; John 6:32 [b]Acts 1:2
10 [a]Matt. 28:3; Mark 16:5; Luke 24:4; John 20:12; Acts 10:3, 30
11 [a]Acts 2:7; 13:31 [b]Dan. 7:13; Matt. 24:30; Mark 13:26; Luke 21:27; John 14:3; 1Thess. 1:10; 4:16; 2Thess. 1:10; Rev. 1:7
12 [a]Luke 24:52
13 [a]Acts 9:37, 39; 20:8 [b]Matt. 10:2-4 [c]Luke 6:15 [d]Jude 1:1
14 [a]Acts 2:1, 46 [b]Luke 23:49, 55; 24:10 [c]Matt. 13:55
15 [a]Rev. 3:4
16 [a]Ps. 41:9; John 13:18 [b]Luke 22:47; John 18:3
17 [a]Matt. 10:4; Luke 6:16 [b]Acts 1:25; 12:25; 20:24; 21:19
18 [a]Matt. 27:5, 7, 8 [b]Matt. 26:15; 2Pet. 2:15
20 [I]Or, *office,* or, *charge* [a]Ps. 69:25 [b]Ps. 109:8
22 [a]Mark 1:1 [b]Acts 1:9 [c]John 15:27; Acts 1:8; 4:33
23 [a]Acts 15:22
24 [a]1Sam. 16:7; 1Chr. 28:9; 29:17; Jer. 11:20; 17:10; Acts 15:8; Rev. 2:23
25 [a]Acts 1:17

16 Men *and* brethren, this scripture[1124]
must needs [aifp]have been fulfilled,[4137]
[a]which the Holy Ghost[4151] by
the mouth of David spake before concerning
Judas, [b]which was guide to them
that took Jesus.
17 For [a]he was numbered with us,
and had obtained part[2819] of [b]this ministry.
18 [a]Now this man purchased a field
with [b]the reward[3408] of iniquity;[93] and
falling headlong, he burst asunder2997 in
the midst,[3319] and all his bowels4698
gushed out.
19 And it was known[1110] unto all the
dwellers[2730] at Jerusalem; insomuch as
that field is called in their proper[2398]
tongue, Aceldama, that is to say, The
field of blood.[129]
20 For it is written in the book of
Psalms, [a]Let his habitation1886 be desolate,2048
and let no man dwell therein:
and [b]his [I]bishopric[1984] let another
take.
21 Wherefore of these men which
have companied with us all the time[5550]
that the Lord Jesus went in and out
among us,
22 [a]Beginning from the baptism[908] of
John, unto that same day that [b]he was
taken up from us, must one be ordained
[c]to be a witness[3144] with us of his resurrection.[386]
23 And they appointed[2476] two,
Joseph called [a]Barsabas, who was surnamed
Justus, and Matthias.
24 And they prayed, and said, Thou,
Lord, [a]which knowest the hearts[2589] of
all *men,* shew whether of these two thou
hast chosen,
25 [a]That he may take part[2819] of this
ministry[1248] and apostleship,[651] from
which Judas by transgression fell,[3845]
that he might go to his own place.
26 And they gave forth their lots;[2819]
and the lot fell[4098] upon Matthias; and he
was numbered with the eleven apostles.[652]

🗝 **1:11** See notes on 1 Thessalonians 1:10; 2:19.

RED LETTER type is used to indicate the words of Jesus.

ITALICIZED MARGINAL NOTES signify alternate readings for the biblical text.

INFERIOR NUMBERS indicate that the entry in the dictionary for the corresponding Hebrew, Aramaic, or Greek word contains only Strong's definition(s).

SUPERIOR NUMBERS indicate that the entry in the dictionary for the corresponding Hebrew, Aramaic, or Greek word has additional information taken from AMG's Complete Word Study dictionaries.

SUPERIOR ROMAN NUMERALS signify that literal renderings, alternate translations, or explanations are given in the cross references.

SUBJECT HEADINGS are provided throughout the biblical text.

MULTIPLE NUMBERS indicate that an underlined word or phrase is translated from more than one word in the original language.

ITALICS are used in the text to indicate words that are not found in the original Hebrew, Aramaic, or Greek text, but are implied by it.

SPECIAL FEATURES

KEY WORD STUDY BIBLE
King James Version

INTRODUCTIONS to each book of the Old and New Testaments cover Bible history, archaeology, and customs that are important in understanding the significance of the book in relationship to the whole Bible.

EXPLANATORY NOTES are placed at the lower section of the page, and each note identifies the chapter and verse(s) to which it refers.

BIBLE STUDY HELPS appear after the book of Revelation.
These include:

NEW TESTAMENT GRAMMATICAL CODES AND NOTATIONS. Multiple superior letters or f, m, and n, preceding a word in the text of the New Testament refer to the grammatical structure of the Greek word and are clarified in this section.

THE AMG BIBLE CONCORDANCE.

A GUIDE TO TRANSLITERATION FROM HEBREW TO ENGLISH with modern pronunciation guidelines.

AMG'S ANNOTATED STRONG'S HEBREW DICTIONARY is an adaptation of the dictionary by James Strong. Numbers in the text of the Old Testament refer to entries in this dictionary. Bold numbers identify entries that have been expanded by the addition of material from AMG's *Complete Word Study Dictionary: Old Testament.*

A GUIDE TO TRANSLITERATION FROM GREEK TO ENGLISH with modern pronunciation guidelines.

AMG'S ANNOTATED STRONG'S GREEK DICTIONARY is an adaptation of the dictionary by James Strong. Numbers in the text of the New Testament refer to entries in this dictionary. Bold numbers identify entries that have been expanded by the addition of material from AMG's *Complete Word Study Dictionary: New Testament.*

THE BOOKS OF THE BIBLE

THE OLD TESTAMENT

Book	*Abbrev.*	*Book*	*Abbrev.*	*Book*	*Abbrev.*
Genesis	Gen.	2 Chronicles	2 Chr.	Daniel	Dan.
Exodus	Ex.	Ezra	Ezra	Hosea	Hos.
Leviticus	Lev.	Nehemiah	Neh.	Joel	Joel
Numbers	Num.	Esther	Esth.	Amos	Amos
Deuteronomy	Deut.	Job	Job	Obadiah	Obad.
Joshua	Josh.	Psalms	Ps.	Jonah	Jon.
Judges	Judg.	Proverbs	Prov.	Micah	Mic.
Ruth	Ruth	Ecclesiastes	Eccl.	Nahum	Nah.
1 Samuel	1 Sam.	Song of Solomon	Song	Habakkuk	Hab.
2 Samuel	2 Sam.	Isaiah	Is.	Zephaniah	Zeph.
1 Kings	1 Kgs.	Jeremiah	Jer.	Haggai	Hag.
2 Kings	2 Kgs.	Lamentations	Lam.	Zechariah	Zech.
1 Chronicles	1 Chr.	Ezekiel	Ezek.	Malachi	Mal.

THE NEW TESTAMENT

Book	*Abbrev.*	*Book*	*Abbrev.*	*Book*	*Abbrev.*
Matthew	Matt.	Ephesians	Eph.	Hebrews	Heb.
Mark	Mark	Philippians	Phil.	James	James
Luke	Luke	Colossians	Col.	1 Peter	1 Pet.
John	John	1 Thessalonians	1 Thess.	2 Peter	2 Pet.
The Acts	Acts	2 Thessalonians	2 Thess.	1 John	1 John
Romans	Rom.	1 Timothy	1 Tim.	2 John	2 John
1 Corinthians	1 Cor.	2 Timothy	2 Tim.	3 John	3 John
2 Corinthians	2 Cor.	Titus	Titus	Jude	Jude
Galatians	Gal.	Philemon	Phile.	Revelation	Rev.

ABBREVIATIONS

accus.	accusative
act.	active
adj.	adjective
adv.	adverb
ant.	antonym
aor.	aorist
Aram.	Aramaic
art.	article
cf.	compare
chap.	chapter
Class.	Classical
coll.	collective
comp.	compound
conj.	conjunction
contr.	contrast, contrasted, contraction, contracted
dat.	dative
deriv.	derivative, derivation
DSS	Dead Sea Scrolls
e.g.	for example
emph.	emphatic
f.	singular following
fem.	feminine
ff.	plural following
fut.	future
gen.	genitive
Gr.	Greek translation of O.T. (Septuagint or LXX) or Greek text of N.T.
Heb.	Hebrew text, usually M.T.
i.e.	that is
imper.	imperative
inf.	infinitive
inten.	intensive
intrans.	intransitive
K.J.V.	King James Version
Lat.	Latin
Lit.	A literal translation
mas.	masculine
mid.	middle
Mod.	Modern
ms.	manuscript
mss.	manuscripts
M.T.	Masoretic text
neg.	negative
neut.	neuter
N.T.	New Testament
obj.	object, objective, objectivity
opp.	opposed, opposite
Or	An alternate translation justified by the Hebrew, Aramaic, or Greek
O.T.	Old Testament
p.	page
part.	participle
pass.	passively
perf.	perfect
pl.	plural
poss.	possessive
pp.	pages
prep.	preposition
priv.	privative
pron.	pronoun
sing.	singular
sub.	substantive
subj.	subject
syn.	synonym, synonymous
Syr.	Syriac
T.R.	Textus Receptus
trans.	transitive
U.B.S.	United Bible Society
v.	verse
vol.	volume
vv.	verses
Wisd.	Wisdom
[ ]	In text, brackets indicate words probably not in the original writings.
[ ]	In margin, brackets indicate references to a name, place or thing similar to, but not identical with that in the text.

CONTENTS

THE OLD TESTAMENT

THE NEW TESTAMENT

BIBLE STUDY HELPS

The
OLD TESTAMENT

GENESIS

The name "Genesis" comes from a Greek word meaning "beginning." This word was the title of the book in the Septuagint, the ancient Greek translation of the Old Testament. The Hebrew name for Genesis was *bᵉrē'shith*, "in the beginning." The Hebrews often identified the books of the Old Testament by the first word of the text. In this way when a scroll was unrolled they were able to tell immediately which book it contained.

Aside from Genesis, there are no other writings that inform us of the events which predated Moses. The first part of the book describes the key events in the early history of man. The remainder of the book records the history of the patriarchs.

Genesis was written in a prescientific age and was not meant to be a scientific document. Consequently, only divine inspiration can account for the perfect accuracy of its technical information. In Genesis, it is made clear that all things were designed and created by God and continue to operate within the boundaries of His purpose. Although the human race departed from God's original plan, God has lovingly provided a way for men to be reconciled to Him.

Though the Book of Genesis contains no express record as to who wrote the book, there are no logical reasons for denying that Moses is the author, not only of Genesis, but of all five books of the Pentateuch. The unity of the Pentateuch is attested to in various portions of the Old Testament, as well as in portions of the New Testament. Even the opening phrase of the Book of Exodus, "Now these are the names," provides clear evidence to that unity. The Hebrew prefix that is translated "now" is the common form of the conjunction in Hebrew (most often translated "and" or "but") and indicates that there was some other book which preceded the Book of Exodus. Jesus refers to Moses as an author of Scripture in Luke 16:31; 24:44; and John 5:46, 47. In John 7:23, the New Testament refers to circumcision as a part of the Law of Moses (see Gen. 17:12; Ex. 12:48; Lev. 12:3).

It has also been suggested that Moses made use of certain documents and oral traditions to write the book. Certain terms have been cited as proof of the previous authorship of certain portions. For instance, the term *tōlᵉdōth* (8435) generations, is said to be used to identify the author or the possessor of certain portions (Gen. 6:9, 11:27). The "looking over" or "familiarity with" other writings is not unheard of among the biblical writers, nor is it contrary to biblical inspiration (see Luke 1:1–4). However, it must be remembered that the actual writing of the Book of Genesis was done by Moses, under the inspiration of the Holy Spirit.

The Book of Genesis is an appropriate introduction to the entire Bible. It provides answers for the universal questions of the origin of all living things, the universe, sin, and evil in the world. More than half of human history is covered in its fifty chapters. However, the Book of Genesis is not merely the introductory book of the Pentateuch, but rather the foundation of it, of the whole Old Testament, yea of the whole of the Scriptures. Without the Book of Genesis, what would be known of the creation of the universe, the fall of man, God's judgment of man, or the promise of redemption? Since God is invisible, man may know of Him only through His works, which are seen in nature, revealed in Scripture, and accomplished in the life of the believer. And how deficient would our knowledge of God be without this book! Are not "his eternal power and Godhead" displayed in His creation (Ps. 19:1; Rom. 1:20)?

Yet the creation, in all that it portrays of the divine Creator, is not sufficient in its instruction to provide man with the knowledge necessary to attain salvation. At this point as well, however, the Book of Genesis lays the foundation of all the Scripture. For the book is not limited to the account of creation, but rather emphasizes the fact that the world was founded by God, that man was created in righteousness and true holiness, but that man fell by his own disobedience, and therefore was cursed by God. Furthermore, the first promise of a Redeemer, by whom the curse of death would be vanquished, is found in this book (Gen. 3:15, 16). The remainder of the Book of Genesis is in fact the first chapter of the history of redemption, in which God chose the seed of Abraham to be the line of the Messiah and the heirs of the promise (Gen. 12:1–3; Matt. 1:17; Gal. 3:6–9, 29).

Creation

1 In the [a]beginning[7225] [b]God[430]
created[1254] the heaven[8064] and the
earth.[776]
2 And the earth was[1961] without
form,[8414] and void; and darkness[2822] *was*
upon the face of the deep. [a]And the
Spirit[7307] of God moved[7363] upon the face
of the waters.
3 [a]And God said, [b]Let there be[1961]
light:[216] and there was light.
4 And God saw[7200] the light, that *it*
was good:[2896] and God divided[914] [I]the
light from the darkness.
5 And God called the light [a]Day,[3117]
and the darkness he called[7121] Night.[3915]
[I]And the evening[6153] and the morning[1242]
were the first day.
6 And God said, [a]Let there be a

1 [a]John 1:1, 2; Heb. 1:10 [b]Ps. 8:3; 33:6; 89:11, 12; 102:25; 136:5; 146:6; Isa. 44:24; Jer. 10:12; 51:15; Zech. 12:1; Acts 14:15; 17:24; Col. 1:16, 17; Heb. 11:3; Rev. 4:11; 10:6
2 [a]Ps. 33:6; Isa. 40:13, 14
3 [a]Ps. 33:9 [b]2Cor. 4:6

4 [I]Hebr. *between the light and between the darkness*
5 [I]Hebr. *And the evening was, and the morning was* [a]Ps. 74:16; 104:20
6 [a]Job 37:18; Ps. 136:5; Jer. 10:12; 51:15

1:1–2:4 The chronology which one often finds in the marginal notes of many of the older Bibles, notably in the Authorized Version of King James, is *not* a part of the Bible itself by any means! Archbishop Usher arrived at the date of 4004 B.C. by using his calculations of the years in the patriarchal genealogies (Gen. 5, 11). A comparison of these genealogies with those in the Gospels will reveal that biblical genealogies are not necessarily complete by design nor were they given to allow us to calculate the span of time between various events in the early history of man. They present certain significant names and omit others. Therefore, they cannot be used to establish the date of creation. The earliest time from which we can calculate calendar years with approximate accuracy is the time of Abraham. The age which one prescribes for the earth is extremely dependent on one's view of creation.

There are five major theories on the interpretation of the six days of creation. The pictorial day theory claims that the six days mentioned in Genesis are the six days during which God revealed to Moses the events of creation. But the Bible relates the creation as clearly, simply, and historically as it does any other events. To interpret the text in this manner requires the abandonment of all exegetical principles.

The gap view claims that Genesis 1:1 describes an original creation which was followed by the fall of Satan and great judgment. Genesis 1:2 is then supposed to be a description of the re-creation or restoration that took place (see footnote below on Genesis 1:2). Exodus 20:11 teaches that all the universe, including the heavens and the earth (Gen. 1:1), was created in the six day period mentioned in the first chapter of Genesis.

The intermittent day view claims that the days mentioned are literal days, but that they are separated by long periods of time. However, unless all the creative activity is limited to the literal days, this view is in direct contradiction to Exodus 20:11.

The day-age theory claims that the word *yōm* (3117), which is the Hebrew word for "day," is used to refer to periods of indefinite length, not to literal days. While this is a viable meaning of the word (Lev. 14:2, 9, 10) it is not the common meaning, nor is the meaning of the word sufficient foundation for the theory.

The literal day theory accepts the clear meaning of the text: the universe was created in six literal days. The various attempts to join together the biblical account of creation and evolution are not supportable even by the various gap theories because the order of creation is in direct opposition to the views of modern science (e.g., the creation of trees before light). The phrase "evening and morning" indicates literal days (cf. Dan. 8:14 where the same phrase in the Hebrew is translated "day").

1:1 God of His own free will and by His absolute power called the universe into being, creating it out of nothing (see Ex. 20:11; Ps. 33:6, 9; 102:25; Is. 45:12; Jer. 10:12; John 1:3; Acts 14:15; 17:24; Rom. 4:17; Col. 1:15–17; Heb. 3:4; 11:3; Rev. 4:11). When one acknowledges the absolute power of God, he must accept His power to create and destroy as stated in the Scriptures. There are many concepts such as this in Scripture which the finite mind cannot completely grasp. The believer must accept those things by faith (Heb. 11:3).

1:2 The Old Scofield Bible maintains that the condition of the earth in verse two is the result of judgment, and therefore interprets the verb *hāyāh* (1961) as "became." However, the Hebrew construction of verse two is disjunctive, describing the result of the creation described in verse one. The phrase "without form and void" is often misunderstood because of this rendering. These words are found only in a few other places (Is. 34:11; 45:18; Jer. 4:23). They do not describe chaos, but rather emptiness. A better translation would be "unformed and unfilled." See footnote on Genesis 1:1—2:4.

[I]firmament[7549] in the midst of the waters, and let it divide the waters from the waters.

7 And God made[6213] the firmament, [a]and divided the waters which *were* under the firmament from the waters which *were* [b]above the firmament: and it was so.

8 And God called the firmament[7549] Heaven.8064 And the evening and the morning were the second day.

9 And God said, [a]Let the waters under the heaven be gathered together[6960] unto one place, and let the dry[3004] *land* appear:[7200] and it was so.

10 And God called the dry *land* Earth;[776] and the gathering together[4723] of the waters called he Seas:3220 and God saw that *it was* good.

11 And God said, Let the earth [a]bring forth[1876] [I]grass, the herb yielding2232 seed,[2233] *and* the fruit tree yielding [b]fruit after his kind, whose seed *is* in itself, upon the earth: and it was so.

12 And the earth brought forth3318 grass, *and* herb yielding seed after his kind,[4327] and the tree yielding fruit, whose seed *was* in itself, after his kind: and God saw that *it was* good.[2896]

13 And the evening and the morning were the third day.

14 And God said, Let there be [a]lights[3974] in the firmament of the heaven8064 to divide[914] [I]the day from the night; and let them be for signs,[226] and [b]for seasons,[4150] and for days,[3117] and years:

15 And let them be for lights in the firmament of the heaven to give light upon the earth: and it was so.

16 And God [a]made two great1419 lights; the greater light [I]to rule[4475] the day, and [b]the lesser light to rule the night: *he made* [c]the stars also.

17 And God set5414 them in the firmament of the heaven to give light upon the earth,

18 And to [a]rule[4910] over the day and over the night, and to divide the light from the darkness: and God saw that *it was* good.

19 And the evening and the morning were the fourth day.

20 And God said, Let the waters bring forth abundantly8317 the [I]moving8318 creature that hath [II]life,[2416] and [III]fowl *that* may fly above the earth in the [IV]open firmament of heaven.

21 And [a]God created great whales,[8577] and every living[2416] creature[5315] that moveth, which the waters brought forth abundantly, after their kind, and every winged fowl after his kind: and God saw that *it was* good.

22 And God blessed[1288] them, saying, [a]Be fruitful, and multiply,7325 and fill the waters in the seas, and let fowl multiply in the earth.

23 And the evening and the morning were the fifth day.

24 And God said, Let the earth[776] bring forth the living creature after his kind, cattle, and creeping thing,7431 and beast[2416] of the earth after his kind: and it was so.

25 And God made the beast of the earth[776] after his kind, and cattle after their kind, and every thing that creepeth upon the earth after his kind: and God saw that *it was* good.

26 And God[430] said, [a]Let us make[6213] man[120] in our image,[6754] after our likeness:[1823] and [b]let them have dominion[7287] over the fish1710 of the sea, and over the fowl of the air,8064 and over the cattle,

6 [I]Hebr. *expansion*

7 [a]Prov. 8:28 [b]Ps. 148:4

9 [a]Job 26:10; 38:8; Ps. 33:7; 95:5; 104:9; 136:6; Prov. 8:29; Jer. 5:22; 2Pet. 3:5

11 [I]Hebr. *tender grass* [a]Heb. 6:7 [b]Luke 6:44

14 [I]Hebr. *between the day and between the night* [a]Deut. 4:19; Ps. 74:16; 136:7 [b]Ps. 74:17; 104:19

16 [I]Hebr. *for the rule of the day* [a]Ps. 136:7, 8, 9; 148:3, 5 [b]Ps. 8:3 [c]Job 38:7

18 [a]Jer. 31:35

20 [I]Or, *creeping* [II]Hebr. *soul* [III]Hebr. *let fowl fly* [IV]Hebr. *face of the firmament of heaven*

21 [a]Gen. 6:20; 7:14; 8:19; Ps. 104:26

22 [a]Gen. 8:17

26 [a]Gen. 5:1; 9:6; Ps. 100:3; Eccl. 7:29; Acts 17:26, 28, 29; 1Cor. 11:7; Eph. 4:24; Col. 3:10; James 3:9 [b]Gen. 9:2; Ps. 8:6

1:26, 27 Is God a singular entity (Deut. 6:4; 32:39; Is. 45:5, 6; John 17:3; 1 Cor. 8:6) or a plural entity (Gen. 3:22; 11:7; 18:1–3; Is. 6:8; 48:16; John 10:30, 34–38)? The Hebrew word for God is *'Elōhīm* (430), a plural noun. In Genesis 1:1, it is used in grammatical agreement with a singular verb *bārā'* (1254), "created." When plural pronouns are used, "Let us make man in our image after our likeness," does it denote a plural of number or the concept of excellence or majesty which may be indicated in such a way in Hebrew? Could God be speaking to the angels, the earth, or nature thus denoting Himself in relation to one of these? Or is this a germinal hint of a distinction

(continued on next page)

and over all the earth, and over every creeping thing that creepeth upon the earth.[776]

27 So God created[1254] man in his *own* image, [a]in the image of God created he him; [b]male[2145] and female[5347] created he them.

28 And God blessed them, and God said unto them, [a]Be fruitful, and multiply, and replenish[4390] the earth, and subdue it: and have dominion[7287] over the fish of the sea, and over the fowl of the air, and over every living thing[2416] that [I]moveth upon the earth.

29 And God said, Behold, I have given you every herb [I]bearing seed, which *is* upon the face of all the earth, and every tree, in the which *is* the fruit of a tree yielding seed; [a]to you it shall be for meat.[402]

30 And to [a]every beast of the earth, and to every [b]fowl of the air, and to every thing that creepeth upon the earth, wherein *there is* [I]life,[5315] *I have given* every green herb for meat: and it was so.

31 And [a]God saw every thing that he had made,[6213] and, behold, *it was* very[3966] [b]good. And the evening and the morning were the sixth day.

2 Thus the heavens[8064] and the earth[776] were finished,[3615] and [a]all the host[6635] of them.

2 [a]And on the seventh day God[430] ended[3615] his work[4399] which he had made;[6213] and he rested[7673] on the seventh day from all his work which he had made.

3 And God [a]blessed[1288] the seventh day, and sanctified[6942] it: because that in it he had rested from all his work which God [I]created[1254] and made.

Adam and Eve In the Garden

🗝 4 [a]These *are* the generations[8435] of the heavens and of the earth when they were created, in the day[3117] that the LORD[3068] God made the earth and the heavens,

5 And every [a]plant[7880] of the field[7704] before it was in the earth,[776] and every herb of the field before it grew: for the LORD had not [b]caused it to rain upon the earth, and *there was* not a man [c]to till[5647] the ground.[127]

6 But [I]there went up a mist from the earth, and watered the whole face of the ground.

27 [a]1Cor. 11:7 [b]Gen. 5:2; Mal. 2:15; Matt. 19:4; Mark 10:6
28 [I]Hebr. *creepeth* [a]Gen. 9:1, 7; Lev. 26:9; Ps. 127:3; 128:3, 4
29 [I]Hebr. *seeding seed* [a]Gen. 9:3; Job 36:31; Ps. 104:14, 15; 136:25; 146:7; Acts 14:17
30 [I]Hebr. *a living soul* [a]Ps. 145:15, 16; 147:9 [b]Job 38:41
31 [a]Ps. 104:24 [b]1Tim. 4:4

1 [a]Ps. 33:6
2 [a]Ex. 20:11; 31:17; Deut. 5:14; Heb. 4:4
3 [I]Hebr. *created to make* [a]Neh. 9:14; Isa. 58:13
4 [a]Gen. 1:1; Ps. 90:1, 2
5 [a]Gen. 1:12; Ps. 104:14 [b]Job 38:26–28 [c]Gen. 3:23
6 [I]Or, *a mist which went up from*

(continued from previous page)
in the divine personality? One cannot be certain. Until Jesus came, the essential (internal) unity of the Godhead was not understood to a great extent, though it was intimated (Is. 48:16).

God is essentially Spirit (John 4:24). Therefore, man, who is similar to God, possesses an immortal spirit. Men resemble God in certain respects (Gen. 1:26) without being equal with Him (Is. 40:25). Man's likeness to God is what truly distinguishes him from the rest of creation. Man is a personal being with the power to think, feel, and decide. He has the ability to make moral choices and the capacity for spiritual growth or decline. In the beginning, man loved God and was a holy creature. The Fall changed this. His spirit was so altered by sin that he fled from God and now loves evil more than righteousness (John 3:19, 20). After Adam's time, only those who lived uprightly before God were considered to be His offspring (see Matt. 3:7–10; 13:38; John 12:36; Acts 13:10; Col. 3:6). Man is no longer in the perfect state of innocence as at the time of his creation. Therefore, he does not have the same spiritual, God-like attributes and qualities of that original state. Jesus, the second Adam (1 Cor. 15:45), came to undo Satan's works (1 John 3:8) and to restore a spiritual likeness to God (2 Cor. 3:18; Eph. 4:24; Col. 3:10)

🗝 **2:4** It is well known that there seem to be two different accounts of creation in the first two chapters of Genesis, but this need not cause us to conclude that they are incompatible, as some have suggested. The two sections actually complement each other. Genesis 1:1—2:4a presents a wide-angle view of all seven days of creation and deals with the creation of man and woman as a single act. Then in 2:4b–24, the author focuses on the sixth day, giving details which were not mentioned in the overview in chapter one. The separate origins of man and woman are brought into sharp focus. Therefore, chapters one and two are not in chronological sequence, but Genesis 2:4b–24 presents in greater detail some of what Genesis 1:11, 12, 24–31 merely summarizes.

🔑 7 And the LORD God[430] formed man[120] [I]*of* the [a]dust[6083] of the ground, and [b]breathed[5301] into his [c]nostrils[639] the breath[5397] of life;[2416] and [d]man became a living[2416] soul.[5315]

🔑 8 And the LORD God planted [a]a garden [b]eastward in [c]Eden; and there [d]he put[7760] the man whom he had formed.[3335]

9 And out of the ground made the LORD God to grow [a]every tree that is pleasant[2530] to the sight, and good[2896] for food; [b]the tree of life[2416] also in the midst of the garden, [c]and the tree of knowledge[1847] of good[2896] and evil.[7451]

10 And a river went out of Eden to water the garden; and from thence it was parted, and became into four heads.

11 The name of the first *is* Pison: that *is* it which compasseth [a]the whole land[776] of Havilah, where *there is* gold;

12 And the gold of that land *is* good: [a]there *is* bdellium[916] and the onyx stone.

13 And the name of the second river *is* Gihon: the same *is* it that compasseth[5437] the whole land of [I]Ethiopia.

14 And the name of the third river *is* [a]Hiddekel: that *is* it which goeth [I]toward the east of Assyria. And the fourth river *is* Euphrates.

🔑 15 And the LORD God took [I]the man, and [a]put him into the garden of Eden to dress[5647] it and to keep[8104] it.

16 And the LORD God commanded[6680] the man, saying, Of every tree of the garden [I]thou mayest freely eat:

17 [a]But of the tree of the knowledge of good and evil, [b]thou shalt not eat of it: for in the day[3117] that thou eatest thereof [I][c]thou shalt surely die.[4191]

18 And the LORD God said, *It is* not good[2896] that the man[120] should be[1961] alone; [a]I will make[6213] him an help [I]meet[5048] for him.

19 [a]And out of the ground[127] the LORD God formed every beast[2416] of the field, and every fowl of the air;[8064] and [b]brought *them* unto [I]Adam[121] to see what

7 [I]Hebr. *dust of the ground* [a]Gen. 3:19, 23; Ps. 103:14; Eccl. 12:7; Isa. 64:8; 1Cor. 15:47 [b]Job 33:4; Acts 17:25 [c]Gen. 7:22; Isa. 2:22 [d]1Cor. 15:45
8 [a]Gen. 13:10; Isa. 51:3; Ezek. 28:13; Joel 2:3 [b]Gen. 3:24 [c]Gen. 4:16; 2Kgs. 19:12; Ezek. 27:23 [d]Gen. 2:15
9 [a]Ezek. 31:8 [b]Gen. 3:22; Prov. 3:18; 11:30; Rev. 2:7; 22:2, 14 [c]Gen. 1:17
11 [a]Gen. 25:18
12 [a]Num. 11:7
13 [I]Hebr. *Cush*
14 [I]Or, *eastward to Assyria* [a]Dan. 10:4
15 [I]Or, *Adam* [a]Gen. 1:8
16 [I]Hebr. *eating thou shalt eat*
17 [I]Hebr. *dying thou shalt die* [a]Gen. 1:9 [b]Gen. 3:1, 3, 11, 17 [c]Gen. 3:3, 19; Rom. 6:23; 1Cor. 15:56; James 1:15; 1John 5:16
18 [I]Hebr. *as before him* [a]Gen. 3:12; 1Cor. 11:9; 1Tim. 2:13
19 [I]Or, *The man* [a]Gen. 1:20, 24 [b]Ps. 8:6, See Gen. 6:20

🔑 **2:7** The term "soul" has been used in a variety of senses by different writers in the Bible. The Hebrew word is *nephesh* (5315) which means "that which breathes." It corresponds to the Greek word *psuchē* (5590), which is usually translated "soul" or "life" (see the annotated Strong's dictionaries for more complete definitions). The term "living soul" does not refer to Adam's spirit as immortal, but simply to the fact that he was a living, physical being. The same term is used in Genesis 1:20, 21 with reference to flying and swimming creatures. It merely signifies that Adam became alive; it denies the possibility of theistic evolution (the soul being breathed into a living animal form). The immortality of the human spirit is taught, however, in Genesis 1:26, 27.

🔑 **2:8, 9** Although there may have been other purposes for the tree of the knowledge of good and evil that are not mentioned in Scripture, it functioned as a test of obedience. Adam and Eve had to choose whether to obey God or break His commandment. There is conjecture as to what would have become of the tree and what other purpose it may have served, but these views should be recognized as conjecture. When they actually ate the forbidden fruit, the consequences of their actions became self-evident. They found themselves in a different relationship to God because of sin. Access to the tree of life was based upon a proper relationship with God. The real questions which faced Adam and Eve are the same ones that face people today: Which path should be chosen? What kind of relationship does one want with God?

🔑 **2:15–17** Man was always meant to accomplish work, but God intended man to enjoy it. Work only became drudgery after the Fall (Gen. 3:17–19). Is it possible for anyone to live sinlessly as Adam did prior to the Fall? The Bible explicitly pronounces all human beings to be sinners (Ps. 14:1–3; Rom. 3:9–23; 5:12–15), and cites the origin of their sin in Adam. Because of Adam's disobedience, all men are made sinners. But how is the sin of Adam imputed to the rest of mankind? Some people say that Adam's state of corruption and guilt is transmitted to his descendants. Others feel that Adam acted as the federal representative of the human race (Rom. 5:12–20; 10:5). The fact remains that all humans are now hopelessly lost and in need of a Savior. That is why Jesus came (Luke 19:10).

he would call[7121] them: and whatsoever Adam called every living creature,[5315] that *was* the name thereof.

20 And Adam [I]gave[7121] names to all cattle, and to the fowl of the air, and to every beast of the field; but for Adam there was not found an help meet for him.

🔑 21 And the LORD God caused a [a]deep sleep[8639] to fall upon Adam,[121] and he slept: and he took one of his ribs, and closed up the flesh[1320] instead thereof;

22 And the rib, which the LORD God had taken from man,[120] [I]made[1129] he a woman, and [a]brought her unto the man.

23 And Adam said, This *is* now [a]bone[6106] of my bones, and flesh[1320] of my flesh: she shall be called[7121] [I]Woman,[802] because she was [b]taken out of [II]Man.[376]

24 [a]Therefore shall a man leave[5800] his father[1] and his mother,[517] and shall cleave unto his wife:[802] and they shall be one flesh.[1320]

🔑 25 [a]And they were both naked,[6174] the man[120] and his wife, and were not [b]ashamed.[954]

Man Falls

3 🔑 Now the [a]serpent[5175] was [b]more subtil[6175] than any beast[2416] of the field[7704] which the LORD God[430] had made.[6213] And he said[559] unto the woman,[802] [I]Yea, hath God said, Ye shall not eat of every tree of the garden?

2 And the woman said unto the serpent, We may eat of the fruit of the trees of the garden:

3 [a]But of the fruit of the tree which *is* in the midst of the garden, God hath said, Ye shall not eat of it, neither shall ye touch[5060] it, lest ye die.[4191]

4 [a]And the serpent said unto the woman, Ye shall not surely die:

5 For God doth know that in the day ye eat thereof, then [a]your eyes shall be opened, and ye shall be as gods, knowing[3045] good[2896] and evil.[7451]

6 And when the woman saw[7200] that the tree *was* good for food, and that it *was* [I]pleasant to the eyes, and a tree to be desired[2530] to make *one* wise,[7919] she took of the fruit thereof, [a]and did eat, and gave also unto her husband[376] with her; [b]and he did eat.

7 And [a]the eyes of them both were opened, [b]and they knew that they *were* naked; and they sewed fig leaves together, and made[6213] themselves [I]aprons.

🔑 8 And they heard[8085] [a]the voice of the LORD God walking in the garden in the [I]cool[7307] of the day:[3117] and Adam and his wife[802] [b]hid themselves from the

20 IHebr. *called*
21 [a]Gen. 15:12; 1Sam. 26:12
22 IHebr. *builded* [a]Prov. 18:22; Heb. 13:4
23 IHebr. *Isha* IIHebr. *Ish* [a]Gen. 29:14; Judg. 9:2; 2Sam. 5:1; 19:13; Eph. 5:30 [b]1Cor. 11:8
24 [a]Gen. 31:15; Ps. 45:10; Matt. 19:5; Mark 10:7; 1Cor. 6:16; Eph. 5:31
25 [a]Gen. 3:7, 10, 11 [b]Ex. 32:25; Isa. 47:3

1 IHebr. *Yea, because* [a]Rev. 12:9; 20:2 [b]Matt. 10:16; 2Cor. 11:3
3 [a]Gen. 2:17
4 [a]Gen. 3:13; 2Cor. 11:3; 1Tim. 2:14
5 [a]Gen. 3:7; Acts 26:18
6 IHebr. *a desire* [a]1Tim. 2:14 [b]Gen. 3:12, 17
7 IOr, *things to gird about* [a]Gen. 3:5 [b]Gen. 2:25
8 IHebr. *wind* [a]Job 38:1 [b]Job 31:33; Jer. 23:24; Amos 9:3

🔑 **2:21–24** Monogamy for a lifetime was and is God's original plan. The Lord Jesus reemphasized this principle in Matthew 19:3–9.

🔑 **2:25** There was no shame before sin entered into the world. Only after Adam and Eve sinned did they become self-conscious of their naked bodies (Gen. 3:7, 10, 21). God intends for intimate, sexual joys to be fulfilled only within the bonds of marriage, and there without shame (Heb. 13:4).

🔑 **3:1–7** The idea that the fruit mentioned in this passage was an apple could have come from the similarity of the Latin words *malam* (apple) and *malum* (evil). Whatever the fruit was, eating it was a clear violation of the divine prohibition. The seriousness of the offense lies in Adam and Eve's deliberate, willful rejection of God's explicit command.

Satan's temptation of Eve begins by planting the seed of doubt, "Yea, hath God said . . .?" Notice how Satan negatively restates the prohibition that God made in Genesis 2:16, 17. And Eve belies her desire for the fruit and her hatred of God's command by adding the phrase "neither shall ye touch it" to God's prohibition.

Satan did not attempt to explain why "Ye shall not surely die," he merely affirmed it! He said it so convincingly that Eve believed it. Then the serpent went on to slander God's motives. He claimed God was keeping something from them. Once Eve "accepted" these assumptions, her desire for the fruit grew until she took of it and ate.

🔑 **3:8** God is omnipresent (2 Chr. 16:9; Ps. 34:15; 139:7–10; Jer. 23:23, 24; Amos 9:2, 3; Zech. 4:10). In this instance the presence of God from which Adam and Eve fled was the visible and spe-

(continued on next page)

presence of the LORD God amongst the trees of the garden.

9 And the LORD God called[7121] unto Adam, and said unto him, Where *art* thou?

10 And he said, I heard[8085] thy voice in the garden, [a]and I was afraid,[3372] because I *was* naked; and I hid myself.

11 And he said, Who told[5046] thee that thou *wast* naked? Hast thou eaten of the tree, whereof I commanded[6680] thee that thou shouldest not eat?

12 And the man[120] said, [a]The woman[802] whom thou gavest *to be* with me, she gave me of the tree, and I did eat.

13 And the LORD God said unto the woman, What *is* this *that* thou hast done?[6213] And the woman said, [a]The serpent beguiled[5377] me, and I did eat.

God Judges

14 And the LORD God said [a]unto the serpent, Because thou hast done this, thou *art* cursed[779] above all cattle, and above every beast of the field; upon thy belly shalt thou go, and [b]dust[6083] shalt thou eat all the days[3117] of thy life:[2416]

15 And I will put enmity[342] between thee and the woman,[802] and between [a]thy seed[2233] and [b]her seed; [c]it shall bruise thy head,[7218] and thou shalt bruise[7779] his heel.[6119]

16 Unto the woman he said, I will greatly multiply[7235] thy sorrow[6093] and thy conception; [a]in sorrow[6089] thou shalt bring forth children;[1121] [b]and thy desire[8669] *shall be* [I]to thy husband,[376] and he shall [c]rule[4910] over thee.

17 And unto Adam[121] he said, [a]Because thou hast hearkened[8085] unto the voice of thy wife,[802] [b]and hast eaten of the tree, [c]of which I commanded thee, saying, Thou shalt not eat of it: [d]cursed *is* the ground[127] for thy sake; [e]in sorrow shalt thou eat *of* it all the days of thy life;

18 [a]Thorns also and thistles shall it [I]bring forth[6779] to thee; and [b]thou shalt eat the herb of the field;

19 [a]In the sweat of thy face[639] shalt thou eat bread, till thou return[7725] unto the ground; for out of it wast thou taken: [b]for dust[6083] thou *art,* and [c]unto dust shalt thou return.

🗝 20 And Adam called his wife's name Eve;[2332] because she was the mother[517] of all living.[2416]

21 Unto Adam also and to his wife did the LORD God make[6213] coats[3801] of skins,[5785] and clothed them.

Adam and Eve Leave Eden

22 And the LORD God said, [a]Behold, the man is become as one of us, to know[3045] good and evil:[7451] and now, lest he put forth his hand,[3027] [b]and take also of the tree of life, and eat, and live[2425] for ever:[5769]

23 Therefore the LORD God sent him forth from the garden of Eden, [a]to till[5647] the ground from whence he was taken.

24 So he drove out[1644] the man; and he placed[7931] [a]at the east of the garden of Eden [b]Cherubims,[3742] and a flam-

10 [a]Gen. 2:25; Ex. 3:6; 1John 3:20
12 [a]Gen. 2:18; Job 31:33; Prov. 28:13
13 [a]Gen. 3:4; 2Cor. 11:3; 1Tim. 2:14
14 [a]Ex. 21:29, 32 [b]Isa. 65:25; Mic. 7:17
15 [a]Matt. 3:7; 13:38; 23:33; John 8:44; Acts 13:10; 1John 3:8 [b]Ps. 132:11; Isa. 7:14; Mic. 5:3; Matt. 1:23, 25; Luke 1:31, 34, 35; Gal. 4:4 [c]Rom. 16:20; Col. 2:15; Heb. 2:14; 1John 5:5; Rev. 12:7, 17
16 [I]Or, *subject to thy husband* [a]Ps. 48:6; Isa. 13:8; 21:3; John 16:21; 1Tim. 2:15 [b]Gen. 4:7 [c]1Cor. 11:3; 14:34; Eph. 5:22, 23, 24; 1Tim. 2:11, 12; Titus 2:5; 1Pet. 3:1, 5, 6
17 [a]1Sam. 15:23 [b]Gen. 3:6 [c]Gen. 2:17 [d]Eccl. 1:2, 3; Isa. 24:5, 6; Rom. 8:20 [e]Job 5:7; Eccl. 2:23
18 [I]Hebr. *cause to bud* [a]Job 31:40 [b]Ps. 104:14
19 [a]Eccl. 1:13; 2Thess. 3:10 [b]Gen. 2:7 [c]Job 21:26; 34:15; Ps. 104:29; Eccl. 3:20; 12:7; Rom. 5:12; Heb. 9:27
22 [a]Gen. 3:5; Isa. 19:12; 47:12, 13; Jer. 22:23 [b]Gen. 2:9
23 [a]Gen. 4:2; 9:20 **24** [a]Gen. 2:8 [b]Ps. 104:4; Heb. 1:7

(continued from previous page)

cial manifestation to them at that time. These manifestations are called "theophanies," appearances of God in human form. They are instances where God became man to relate to human weaknesses so that he might communicate with man in a more personal way. However, God is not a man, and He does not look like man or think like man (Is. 55:8, 9). But God is a personal being who seeks to fellowship with man, like a loving father.

🗝 **3:20** The name "Eve" (Hebrew *chawwāh*, [2332]) means "life." The fact that "Eve" is a Hebrew name does not mean that Hebrew was the original language. As thoughts were conveyed from one language to another, proper nouns were adjusted to carry their original meaning.

ing sword[2719] which turned every
way,[2015] to keep[8104] the way[1870] of the
tree of life.

Cain and Abel

4 🔑 And Adam[121] knew[3045] Eve his
wife;[802] and she conceived,[2029] and
bare [I]Cain,[7014] and said, I have gotten[7069]
a man[376] from the LORD.
2 And she again bare his brother[251]
[I]Abel.[1893] And Abel was [II]a keeper[7462] of
sheep, but Cain was [a]a tiller[5647] of the
ground.[127]
🔑 3 And [I]in process of time[3117] it came
to pass, that Cain brought [a]of the fruit of
the ground an offering[4503] unto the LORD.
4 And Abel, he also brought of [a]the
firstlings[1062] of his [I]flock and of the fat
thereof. And the LORD had [b]respect[8159]
unto Abel and to his offering:
5 But unto Cain and to his offering
he had not respect. And Cain was very
wroth,[2734] [a]and his countenance[6440] fell.
6 And the LORD said unto Cain, Why
art thou wroth? and why is thy countenance fallen?[5307]
7 If thou doest well,[3190] shalt thou
not [I][a]be accepted?[7613] and if thou doest
not well, sin[2403] lieth[7257] at the door. And
[II][b]unto thee *shall be* his desire,[8669] and
thou shalt rule[4910] over him.
🔑 8 And Cain talked with Abel his
brother: and it came to pass, when they
were in the field,[7704] that Cain rose up
against Abel his brother, and [a]slew[2026]
him.
9 And the LORD said unto Cain,
[a]Where *is* Abel thy brother? And he said,
[b]I know[3045] not: *Am* I my brother's
keeper?[8104]
10 And he said, What hast thou
done?[6213] the voice of thy brother's
[I]blood[1818] [a]crieth unto me from the ground.
11 And now *art* thou cursed[779] from
the earth,[127] which hath opened her
mouth to receive thy brother's blood from
thy hand;[3027]
12 When thou tillest[5647] the ground,
it shall not henceforth yield unto thee her
strength; a fugitive[5128] and a vagabond[5110] shalt thou be in the earth.[776]
🔑 13 And Cain said unto the LORD, [I]My
punishment[5771] *is* greater than I can
bear.[5375]
14 [a]Behold, thou hast driven me out
this day[3117] from the face of the earth;
and [b]from thy face shall I be hid;[5640] and

1 [I]That is, *Gotten,* or, *Acquired*
2 [I]Hebr. *Hebel* [II]Hebr. *a feeder* [a]Gen. 3:23; 9:20
3 [I]Hebr. *at the end of days* [a]Num. 18:12
4 [I]Hebr. *sheep,* or, *goats* [a]Num. 18:17; Prov. 3:9 [b]Heb. 11:4
5 [a]Gen. 31:2
7 [I]Or, *have the excellency?* [II]Or, *subject unto thee* [a]Heb. 11:4 [b]Gen. 3:16
8 [a]Matt. 23:35; 1John 3:12; Jude 11
9 [a]Ps. 9:12 [b]John 8:44
10 [I]Hebr. *bloods* [a]Heb. 12:24; Rev. 6:10
13 [I]Or, *Mine iniquity is greater than that it may be forgiven*
14 [a]Job 15:20-24 [b]Ps. 51:11

🔑 **4:1, 2** The Hebrew word *yāda'* (3045) indicates the most intimate relationship between a man and a woman, the sexual bond. Its basic meaning is "to know," but it could be translated "and Adam experienced Eve." Cain and Abel may have been twins, since conception is only mentioned once.

🔑 **4:3–7** Is God a respecter of persons (Ex. 2:25; Lev. 26:9; 2 Kgs. 13:23; Ps. 138:6), or is He completely impartial (Deut. 10:17; 2 Chr. 19:7; Acts 10:34; Rom. 2:11; Gal. 2:6; Eph. 6:9; 1 Pet. 1:17)? The first series of texts implies a righteous and benevolent "respect" based on a proper discrimination as to character which God exercises toward man. The second series of biblical references denotes a "respect" which is partial, arising out of selfish and unworthy considerations which God does not exercise because He is impartial.

That God accepted Abel's sacrifice and rejected Cain's was not based on the fact that Cain's sacrifice was bloodless. Many of the required OT offerings were bloodless (as meal and meat offerings). The difference was in the hearts of the two men. Abel offered in faith (Heb. 11:4), while Cain did not. This basic difference is indicated by the wording of the passage: God "had respect unto Abel and to his offering; but unto Cain and to his offering he had not respect." Only when they are offered in faith do the sacrifices and service of men please God (Is. 1:11–17; Eph. 6:5–7).

🔑 **4:8** The Septuagint, the Samaritan Pentateuch, and the Syriac Version add the phrase, "Let us go out to the field," after the phrase "and Cain talked with Abel his brother."

🔑 **4:13, 14** Cain's cry was one of remorse, not true repentance. He was overwhelmed by the severity of the sentence, but he was not sorry for his crime. There was no plea for pardon, or expression of sorrow or regret. He was a selfish person who was about to be deprived of all material belongings and driven into the wilderness. Cain was afraid that some of the relatives of Abel would

(continued on next page)

I shall be a fugitive and a vagabond in
the earth; and it shall come to pass,[1961]
[c]*that* every one that findeth me shall
slay[2026] me.
15 And the LORD said unto him,
Therefore whosoever slayeth[2026] Cain,
vengeance[5358] shall be taken on him [a]sev-
enfold. And the LORD [b]set[7760] a mark[226]
upon Cain, lest any finding him should
kill[5221] him.
16 And Cain [a]went out from the presence of the LORD, and dwelt in the
land[776] of Nod, on the east of Eden.
🗝 17 And Cain knew his wife; and she
conceived, and bare[3205] [I]Enoch: and he
builded a city, [a]and called the name of
the city, after the name of his son,[1121]
Enoch.
18 And unto Enoch was born Irad:
and Irad begat Mehujael: and Mehujael
begat Methusael: and Methusael begat
[I]Lamech.
19 And Lamech took unto him two
wives: the name of the one *was* Adah,
and the name of the other Zillah.
20 And Adah bare Jabal: he was the
father[1] of such as dwell in tents,[168] and
of such as have cattle.
21 And his brother's name *was* Jubal:
he was the [a]father of all such as handle
the harp and organ.
22 And Zillah, she also bare Tubal–
cain, an [I]instructer of every artificer[2794]
in brass and iron: and the sister of
Tubal–cain *was* Naamah.
🗝 23 And Lamech said unto his wives,
Adah and Zillah, Hear[8085] my voice; ye
wives of Lamech, hearken unto[238] my
speech:[565] for [II]I have slain[2026] a man[376]
to my wounding, and a young man [II]to
my hurt.[2250]
24 [a]If Cain shall be avenged[5358] sevenfold, truly Lamech seventy and sevenfold.

Another Son

25 And Adam knew his wife again;
and she bare a son, and [a]called his name
[I]Seth:[8352] For God,[430] *said she,* hath
appointed[7896] me another seed[2233] instead
of Abel, whom Cain slew.
🗝 26 And to Seth, [a]to him also there
was born a son; and he called his name
[I]Enos: then began men [IIa]to call[7121] upon
the name of the LORD.[3068]

Adam's Family Record

5 🗝 This *is* the [a]book[5612] of the generations of Adam. In the day[3117]

14 [c]Gen. 9:6; Num. 35:19, 21, 27
15 [a]Ps. 79:12 [b]Ezek. 9:4, 6
16 [a]2Kgs. 13:23; 24:20; Jer. 23:39; 52:3
17 [I]Hebr. *Chanoch* [a]Ps. 49:11
18 [I]Hebr. *Lemech*
21 [a]Rom. 4:11, 12
22 [I]Hebr. *whetter*
23 [I]Or, *I would slay a man in my wound* [II]Or, *in my hurt*
24 [a]Gen. 4:15
25 [I]That is, *Appointed,* or, *Put,* Hebr. *Sheth* [a]Gen. 5:3
26 [I]Hebr. *Enosh* [II]Or, *to call themselves by the name of the LORD* [a]Gen. 5:6 [b]1Kgs. 18:24; Ps. 116:17; Joel 2:32; Zeph. 3:9; 1Cor. 1:2
1 [a]1Chr. 1:1; Luke 3:38

(continued from previous page)
find him and kill him in revenge. Thus, it is logical to assume that the population of the world had already multiplied considerably since the expulsion of Adam and Eve from the garden of Eden.

🗝 **4:17** The origin of Cain's wife has perplexed many people. Genesis does not answer the question directly, but Genesis 5:4 asserts that Adam had other sons and daughters besides the three sons whose names appear in the text. Given the longevity of people at that time, Cain could have married one of his own sisters or even a more distant relative.

🗝 **4:23** This particular outburst of Lamech showed a proud and presumptuous self-confidence. This was the boast of a bold, bad man who was elated with the possession of arms which his son Tubal–cain had invented. He felt he could take a human life at will.

🗝 **4:26** The phrase "men began to call on the name of the Lord" denotes that worship, consisting perhaps only of a mute adoration, already existed (Gen. 4:3, 4). This passage may refer to the first instance of regular, solemn, public worship of God. Men were beginning to address God formally in prayer and thanksgiving in the time of Enos.

🗝 **5:1–32** In this chapter Moses gives a ten-person genealogy of the people of the pre-flood era, and in chapter eleven there is a similar listing of ten post-flood persons which ended with Terah, Abraham's father. In both lists, the longevity of these men is far beyond anything in our own day. Yet Moses, who himself lived to be 120 years of age (Deut. 34:7), intended that these figures be taken literally. This was a time when men were capable of procreation at 182 years of age (v. 28). Since it is impossible to accurately assess past conditions based upon existing conditions, these statements should be taken literally.

that God created man,[120] in [b]the likeness[1823] of God made[6213] he him;
2 [a]Male[2145] and female[5347] created[1254] he them; and blessed[1288] them,
and called[7121] their name Adam, in the
day when they were created.
3 And Adam[121] lived[2421] an hundred
and thirty years, and begat *a son* in his
own likeness,[1823] after his image;[6754] and
[a]called his name Seth:
4 [a]And the days[3117] of Adam after
he had begotten[3205] Seth were eight hundred years: [b]and he begat sons and
daughters:
5 And all the days that Adam
lived[2425] were nine hundred and thirty
years: [a]and he died.
6 And Seth lived an hundred and five
years, and [a]begat Enos:
7 And Seth lived after he begat Enos
eight hundred and seven years, and begat
sons and daughters:
8 And all the days of Seth were
nine hundred and twelve years: and he
died.
9 And Enos lived ninety years, and
begat [‖]Cainan:
10 And Enos lived after he begat
Cainan eight hundred and fifteen years,
and begat sons and daughters:
11 And all the days of Enos were
nine hundred and five years: and he died.
12 And Cainan lived seventy years,
and begat [‖]Mahalaleel:
13 And Cainan lived after he begat
Mahalaleel eight hundred and forty years,
and begat sons and daughters:
14 And all the days of Cainan were
nine hundred and ten years: and he died.
15 And Mahalaleel lived sixty and
five years, and begat [‖]Jared:
16 And Mahalaleel lived after he
begat Jared eight hundred and thirty
years, and begat sons and daughters:
17 And all the days of Mahalaleel
were eight hundred ninety and five years:
and he died.
18 And Jared lived an hundred sixty
and two years, and he begat [a]Enoch:
19 And Jared lived after he begat
Enoch eight hundred years, and begat
sons and daughters:
20 And all the days of Jared were
nine hundred sixty and two years: and he
died.
21 And Enoch lived sixty and five
years, and begat Methuselah:
🔑 22 And Enoch [a]walked with God[430]
after he begat Methuselah three hundred
years, and begat sons and daughters:
23 And all the days of Enoch were
three hundred sixty and five years:
🔑 24 And [a]Enoch walked with God:
and he *was* not; for God took him.
25 And Methuselah lived an hundred
eighty and seven years, and begat
Lamech:
26 And Methuselah lived after he
begat Lamech seven hundred eighty and
two years, and begat sons and daughters:
27 And all the days of Methuselah
were nine hundred sixty and nine years:
and he died.
28 And Lamech lived an hundred
eighty and two years, and begat a son:
29 And he called his name [‖a]Noah,
saying, This *same* shall comfort[5162] us
concerning our work[4639] and toil[6093] of
our hands, because of the ground[127]
[b]which the LORD hath cursed.[779]
30 And Lamech lived after he begat
Noah five hundred ninety and five years,
and begat sons and daughters:

1 [b]Gen. 1:26; Eph. 4:24; Col. 3:10
2 [a]Gen. 1:27
3 [a]Gen. 4:25
4 [a]1Chr. 1:1 [b]Gen. 1:28
5 [a]Gen. 3:19; Heb. 9:27
6 [a]Gen. 4:26
9 [‖]Hebr. *Kenan*
12 [‖]Gr. *Maleleel*
15 [‖]Hebr. *Jered*
18 [a]Jude 1:14, 15
22 [a]Gen. 6:9; 17:1; 24:40; 2Kgs. 20:3; Ps. 16:8; 116:9; 128:1; Mic. 6:8; Mal. 2:6
24 [a]2Kgs. 2:11; Heb. 11:5
29 [‖]That is, *Rest*, or, *Comfort* [a]Luke 3:36; Heb. 11:7; 1Pet. 3:20 [b]Gen. 3:17; 4:11

🔑 **5:22, 24** The original Hebrew adds the definite article before "God" in both of these verses. Perhaps this is an indication that idolatry was emerging, but Enoch lived in accordance with the will of the true God. By so doing, he had recorded of him the testimony that he pleased God (Heb. 11:5). This verse puts forth one of the first hints of the belief of immortality in the Old Testament. The bodies of both Enoch and Elijah (2 Kgs. 2:11) were doubtless transformed (see 1 Cor. 15:51, 52). They may have been given spiritual bodies similar to that of the resurrected Christ (Luke 24:38–43; John 20:19). Enoch is also the speaker of a prophecy (Jude 1:14, 15). The reference to him is said to have been a part of an apocryphal book containing various prophecies given by Enoch. It is more likely that Enoch merely spoke these words and the Lord preserved them through Jude.

31 And all the days of Lamech were
seven hundred seventy and seven years:
and he died.
32 And Noah was five hundred years
old: and Noah begat [a]Shem, Ham, [b]and
Japheth.

Evil Rules Over Mankind

6 ⚿ And it came to pass, [a]when
men[120] began to multiply on the face
of the earth,[127] and daughters were born
unto them,
2 That the sons of God[430] saw[7200]
the daughters of men that they *were*
fair;[2896] and they [a]took them wives of all
which they chose.[977]

32 [a]Gen. 6:10 [b]Gen. 10:21

1 [a]Gen. 1:28
2 [a]Deut. 7:3, 4
3 [a]Gal. 5:16, 17; 1Pet. 3:19, 20 [b]Ps. 78:39
5 [I]Or, *the whole imagination:* The Hebrew word signifies not only *the imagination,* but also *the purposes and desires* [II]Hebr. *everyday* [a]Gen. 8:21; Deut. 29:19; Prov. 6:18; Matt. 15:19
6 [a]Num. 23:19; 1Sam. 15:11, 29; 2Sam. 24:16; Mal. 3:6; James 1:17

3 And the LORD said, [a]My spirit[7307]
shall[1777] not always[5769] strive[1777] with
man, [b]for that he also *is* flesh:[1320] yet his
days shall be an hundred and twenty
years.
4 There were giants[5303] in the
earth[776] in those days; and also after that,
when the sons of God came in unto the
daughters of men, and they bare *children*
to them, the same *became* mighty men[1368]
which *were* of old,[5769] men[582] of renown.
5 And GOD saw that the wick-
edness[7451] of man *was* great in the earth,
and *that* [I]every [a]imagination[3336] of the
thoughts[4284] of his heart[3820] *was* only
evil[7451] [II]continually.[3117]
⚿ 6 And [a]it repented[5162] the LORD that

⚿ **6:1–4** The identity of the "sons of God" is uncertain. Three main theories are advanced to identify the "sons of God" and the "daughters of men." The first theory is that the "sons of God" are fallen angels and the "daughters of men" are mortals. The wickedness for which they are condemned is the unlawful marriage between those who are supernatural and those who are mortal. This ancient viewpoint hinges in part on the assumption that Jude 1:6, 7 refer to these angels. The proponents of this view insist, perhaps with some Scriptural backing, that the term "sons of God" refers only to angels (Job 1:6–12). However, there is no precedent at this point from which we can conclude this idea. And if this sin is, at least to a large extent, the fault of the angels, why is man punished by the Flood? When the proponents of this theory are reminded of the fact that Christ, in Matthew 22:30, says that angels do not marry, they answer that He only said that they do not, not that they could not or did not. Besides the mythological quality which this viewpoint brings to the text, there is considerable theological difficulty with the existence of human beings who are, at least in part, not descended from Adam (Acts 17:26).

The second theory as to their identity is the one most often held to within conservative scholarship. The "sons of God" are reckoned to be the godly line of Seth while the "daughters of men" are of the line of Cain. Thus the sin with which they are charged is one which is common to the whole of Scripture, and especially of the Pentateuch: the intermarriage of the chosen people of God (the believers) with those who are unholy. How can these men be considered holy when the Bible states that only Noah was holy (Gen. 6:8, 9)? And why is the term "sons of God" not used with this meaning in any other place? Other people also question why only sons and not daughters are associated with the line of Seth.

The last theory is one that is gaining popularity among conservatives. Recent archaeological evidence has suggested that the phrase "sons of God" was sometimes used to describe kings (Ex. 21:6; 22:8; Ps. 82:6, 7). Therefore the "sons of God" are immoral human kings who use their power to take as many women and whatever women they choose. It must be noted that the Scripture never describes human rulers as deities. This theory rests upon the conjecture that the "giants" of verse four are the children of the union described in the preceding verses. The word "giant" comes from the Septuagint rendering of the Hebrew *nephilim* ("the fallen ones") which comes from *nāphal* (5307), "to fall." It is often associated with violence, and so translated "overthrow, fall upon." The term emphasizes their violence and lack of respect for others. However, neither the text nor the fact that they were "giants" supports the idea that they are the result of a union between angels and human beings. No one believes that because the children of Anak, Goliath and his brothers, were giants that they were necessarily the offspring of some supernatural union.

⚿ **6:6** This verse has puzzled students of the Bible for many years. The phrase "it repented the LORD does not mean that God changed (Num. 23:19; 1 Sam. 15:29; Mal. 3:6; James 1:17), or that

(continued on next page)

he had made[6213] man on the earth, and it [b]grieved[6087] him at his heart.

7 And the LORD said, I will destroy[4229] man whom I have created[1254] from the face of the earth; [I]both man, and beast, and the creeping thing, and the fowls of the air;8064 for it repenteth me that I have made them.

8 But Noah [a]found grace[2580] in the eyes of the LORD.

Noah

🔑 9 These *are* the generations[8435] of Noah: [a]Noah was a just[6662] man *and* perfect[8549] in his generations,[1755] *and* Noah [b]walked with God.

10 And Noah begat three sons, [a]Shem, Ham, and Japheth.

11 The earth also was corrupt[7843] [a]before God, and the earth was [b]filled with violence.[2555]

12 And God [a]looked upon the earth, and, behold, it was corrupt; for all flesh[1320] had corrupted his way[1870] upon the earth.

13 And God said unto Noah, [a]The end of all flesh is come before me; for the earth is filled with violence through them; [b]and, behold, I will destroy[7843] them [I]with the earth.

14 Make thee an ark of gopher1613 wood; [I]rooms shalt thou make in the ark, and shalt pitch it within and without with pitch.

🔑 15 And this *is the fashion* which thou shalt make it *of*: The length[753] of the ark *shall be* three hundred cubits, the breadth of it fifty cubits, and the height of it thirty cubits.

16 A window shalt thou make to the ark, and in a cubit shalt thou finish it above; and the door of the ark shalt thou set in the side thereof; *with* lower, second, and third *stories* shalt thou make it.

17 [a]And, behold, I, even I, do bring a flood3999 of waters upon the earth, to destroy[7843] all flesh, wherein *is* the breath[7307] of life,[2416] from under heaven;8064 *and* every thing that *is* in the earth shall die.[1478]

18 But with thee will I establish my covenant;[1285] and [a]thou shalt come into the ark, thou, and thy sons, and thy wife,[802] and thy sons' wives with thee.

19 And of every living thing[2416] of all flesh, [a]two of every *sort* shalt thou bring into the ark, to keep *them* alive[2421] with thee; they shall be male2145 and female.[5347]

20 Of fowls after their kind, and of cattle after their kind, of every creeping thing of the earth after his kind, two of every *sort* [a]shall come unto thee, to keep *them* alive.

21 And take thou unto thee of all food that is eaten, and thou shalt gather[622] *it* to thee; and it shall be for food for thee, and for them.

6 [b]Isa. 63:10; Eph. 4:30

7 [I]Hebr. *from man unto beast*

8 [a]Gen. 19:19; Ex. 33:12, 13, 16, 17; Luke 1:30; Acts 7:46

9 [a]Gen. 7:1; Ezek. 14:14, 20; Rom. 1:17; Heb. 11:7; 2Pet. 2:5 [b]Gen. 5:22

10 [a]Gen. 5:32

11 [a]Gen. 7:1; 10:9; 13:13; 2Chr. 34:27; Luke 1:6; Rom. 2:13; 3:19 [b]Ezek. 8:17; 28:16; Hab. 2:8, 17

12 [a]Gen. 18:21; Ps. 14:2; 33:13, 14; 53:2, 3

13 [I]Or, *from the earth* [a]Jer. 51:13; Ezek. 7:2, 3, 6; Amos 8:2; 1Pet. 4:7 [b]Gen. 6:1

14 [I]Hebr. *nests*

17 [a]Gen. 6:13; 7:4, 21-23; 2Pet. 2:5

18 [a]Gen. 7:1, 7, 13; 1Pet. 3:20; 2Pet. 2:5

19 [a]Gen. 7:8, 9, 15, 16

20 [a]Gen. 2:19; 7:9, 15

(continued from previous page)

He is affected by sorrow or other feelings which are common to humanity. However, it was necessary for the inspired biblical writers to use terms which were comprehensible to the minds of human beings. A person cannot conceive of God except in human terms and concepts.

🔑 **6:9** How could Noah be called "perfect" (blameless) when no one is perfect (1 Kgs. 8:46; Ps. 14:1–3; Prov. 20:9; Eccl. 7:20; Mark 10:18; Rom. 3:23; 1 John 1:8)? In both the Old and New Testaments, the words translated "perfect" refer to completeness and maturity rather than to sinlessness. Some have suggested that "perfect in his generations" (lit., "blameless in his time") refers to Noah's having an ancestry from the line of Seth, free from the mixing with the worldly line of Cain which ruined the rest of the race (see footnote above on Gen. 6:1–4). It is also possible that Noah is called "blameless" by comparison to the wicked mass of humanity. Noah is recorded in the list of the heroes of faith (Heb. 11:7) as one who stood alone for righteousness.

🔑 **6:15** The dimensions of the ark present an interesting contrast when set beside the Sumerian account of the flood. In the longest and most famous of these accounts, the Akkadian Epic of Gilgamesh, the ark was a perfect cube, 200 feet long on each side. On the other hand the relative dimensions of Noah's ark are not only seaworthy, but those of modern ships are very similar.

22 [a]Thus did Noah; [b]according to all that God commanded[6680] him, so did he.

The Flood

7 And the LORD said unto Noah, [a]Come thou and all thy house[1004] into the ark; for [b]thee have I seen[7200] righteous[6662] before me in this generation.[1755]

2 Of every [a]clean[2889] beast thou shalt take to thee by sevens, the male[376] and his female:[802] [b]and of beasts that *are* not clean by two, the male and his female.

3 Of fowls also of the air[8064] by sevens, the male[2145] and the female;[5347] to keep seed[2233] alive upon the face of all the earth.[776]

4 For yet seven days, and I will cause it to rain upon the earth [a]forty days and forty nights; and every living substance that I have made will I [I]destroy[4229] from off the face of the earth.[127]

5 [a]And Noah did according unto all that the LORD commanded[6680] him.

6 And Noah *was* six hundred years old when the flood of waters was upon the earth.

7 [a]And Noah went in, and his sons,[1121] and his wife,[802] and his sons' wives with him, into the ark, because of the waters of the flood.

8 Of clean beasts, and of beasts that *are* not clean, and of fowls, and of every thing that creepeth upon the earth,

9 There went in two and two unto Noah into the ark, the male and the female, as God[430] had commanded Noah.

10 And it came to pass [I]after seven days, that the waters of the flood were upon the earth.

11 In the six hundredth year of Noah's life,[2416] in the second month, the seventeenth day of the month, the same day were[1234] all [a]the fountains of the great deep[8415] broken up,[1234] and the [I][b]windows of heaven[8064] were opened.

🔑 12 [a]And the rain was upon the earth forty days and forty nights.

13 In the selfsame day [a]entered Noah, and Shem, and Ham, and Japheth, the sons of Noah, and Noah's wife, and the three wives of his sons with them, into the ark;

14 [a]They, and every beast[2416] after his kind, and all the cattle after their kind, and every creeping thing that creepeth upon the earth after his kind, and every fowl[5775] after his kind, every bird[6833] of every [I]sort.

15 And they [a]went in unto Noah into the ark, two and two of all flesh,[1320] wherein *is* the breath[7307] of life.

16 And they that went in, went in male and female of all flesh, [a]as God had commanded him: and the LORD shut him in.

17 [a]And the flood was forty days upon the earth; and the waters increased, and bare up[5375] the ark, and it was lift up[7311] above the earth.

18 And the waters prevailed,[1396] and were increased greatly upon the earth; [a]and the ark went upon the face of the waters.

19 And the waters prevailed exceedingly upon the earth; [a]and all the high hills, that *were* under the whole heaven, were covered.

20 Fifteen cubits upward did the waters prevail; and the mountains were covered.

21 [a]And all flesh died[1478] that moved upon the earth, both of fowl, and of cattle, and of beast, and of every creeping thing that creepeth upon the earth, and every man:[120]

22 All in [a]whose nostrils *was* [I]the breath[5397] of life,[2416] of all that *was* in the dry[2724] *land,* died.[4191]

22 [a]Ex. 40:16; Heb. 11:7; [b]Gen. 7:5, 9, 16

1 [a]Gen. 7:7, 13; Matt. 24:38; Luke 17:26; Heb. 11:7; 1Pet. 3:20; 2Pet. 2:5 [b]Gen. 6:9; Ps. 33:18, 19; Prov. 10:9; 2Pet. 2:9

2 [a]Gen. 7:8; Lev. 11:2-4 [b]Lev. 10:10; Ezek. 44:23

4 [I]Hebr. *blot out* [a]Gen. 7:12, 17

5 [a]Gen. 6:22

7 [a]Gen. 7:1

10 [I]Or, *on the seventh day*

11 [I]Or, *floodgates* [a]Gen. 8:2; Prov. 8:28; Ezek. 26:19 [b]Gen. 1:7; 8:2; Ps. 78:23

12 [a]Gen. 7:4, 17

13 [a]Gen. 2:1, 7; Gen. 6:18; Heb. 11:7; 1Pet. 3:20; 2Pet. 2:5

14 [I]Hebr. *wing* [a]Gen. 7:2, 3, 8, 9

15 [a]Gen. 6:20

16 [a]Gen. 7:2, 3

17 [a]Gen. 7:4, 12

18 [a]Ps. 104:26

19 [a]Ps. 104:6; Jer. 3:23

21 [a]Gen. 6:13, 17; 7:4; Job 22:16; Matt. 24:39; Luke 17:27; 2Pet. 3:6

22 [I]Hebr. *the breath of the spirit of life* [a]Gen. 2:7

🔑 **7:12** The number forty is not merely an arbitrary period nor a rounded figure of the period during which it rained. The number forty is used repeatedly in Scripture to signify periods of testing, sometimes of judgmental testing. Other prominent references involving the number forty are: Noah's waiting after the tops of the mountains appeared (Gen. 8:6); Moses' forty days on Mount Sinai (Ex. 24:18; Deut. 19:9); the spies' forty days searching out Canaan (Num. 13:25); the forty years in the wilderness (Num. 14:33); the forty days Nineveh was given until judgment (Jon. 3:4).

23 And every living substance was destroyed which was upon the face of the ground,[127] both man, and cattle, and the creeping things, and the fowl of the heaven; and they were destroyed from the earth: and [a]Noah only remained[7604] *alive,* and they that *were* with him in the ark.

24 [a]And the waters prevailed upon the earth an hundred and fifty days.

The Flood Ends

8 And God[430] [a]remembered[2142] Noah, and every living thing,[2416] and all the cattle that *was* with him in the ark: [a]and God made[5674] a wind[7307] to pass[5674] over the earth,[776] and the waters asswaged;[7918]

2 [a]The fountains also of the deep and the windows of heaven[8064] were stopped, and [b]the rain from heaven was restrained;[3607]

3 And the waters returned[7725] from off the earth [I]continually: and after the end [a]of the hundred and fifty days the waters were abated.[2637]

4 And the ark rested in the seventh month, on the seventeenth day of the month, upon the mountains of Ararat.

5 And the waters [I]decreased continually until the tenth month: in the tenth *month,* on the first *day* of the month, were the tops[7218] of the mountains seen.

6 And it came to pass at the end of forty days, that Noah opened [a]the window of the ark which he had made:

7 And he sent forth a raven, which went forth [I]to and fro, until the waters were dried up[3001] from off the earth.

8 Also he sent forth a dove from him, to see[7200] if the waters were abated[7043] from off the face of the ground;[127]

9 But the dove found no rest for the sole[3709] of her foot, and she returned unto him into the ark, for the waters *were* on the face of the whole earth: then he put forth his hand, and took her, and [I]pulled her in unto him into the ark.

23 [a]1Pet. 3:20; 2Pet. 2:5; 3:6

24 [a]Gen. 8:3, 4; cf. Gen. 7:11

1 [a]Gen. 19:29; Ex. 2:24; 1Sam. 1:19 [b]Ex. 14:21

2 [a]Gen. 7:11 [b]Job 38:37

3 [I]Hebr. *in going and returning* [a]Gen. 7:24

5 [I]Hebr. *were in going and decreasing*

6 [a]Gen. 6:16

7 [I]Hebr. *in going forth and returning*

9 [I]Hebr. *caused her to come*

16 [a]Gen. 7:13

17 [a]Gen. 7:15 [b]Gen. 1:22

19 [I]Hebr. *families*

20 [a]Lev. 11:1-47

21 [I]Hebr. *a savor of rest* [II]Or, *though* [a]Lev. 1:9; Ezek. 20:41; 2Cor. 2:15; Eph. 5:2 [b]Gen. 3:17; 6:17

10 And he stayed yet other seven days; and again he sent forth the dove out of the ark;

11 And the dove came in to him in the evening; and, lo, in her mouth *was* an olive leaf pluckt off: so Noah knew that the waters were abated from off the earth.

12 And he stayed yet other seven days; and sent forth the dove; which returned not again unto him any more.

13 And it came to pass in the six hundredth and first year, in the first *month,* the first *day* of the month, the waters were dried up from off the earth: and Noah removed[5493] the covering of the ark, and looked,[7200] and, behold, the face of the ground was dry.[2717]

14 And in the second month, on the seven and twentieth day of the month, was the earth dried.[3001]

15 And God spake unto Noah, saying,

16 Go forth of the ark, [a]thou, and thy wife,[802] and thy sons, and thy sons' wives with thee.

17 Bring forth with thee [a]every living thing that *is* with thee, of all flesh,[1320] *both* of fowl, and of cattle, and of every creeping thing that creepeth upon the earth; that they may breed abundantly in the earth, and [b]be fruitful, and multiply upon the earth.

18 And Noah went forth, and his sons, and his wife, and his sons' wives with him:

19 Every beast,[2416] every creeping thing, and every fowl, *and* whatsoever creepeth upon the earth, after their [I]kinds,[4940] went forth out of the ark.

20 And Noah builded an altar[4196] unto the LORD; and took of [a]every clean beast, and of every clean[2889] fowl, and offered[5927] burnt offerings[5930] on the altar.

🔑 21 And the LORD smelled[7306] [I][a]a sweet savour; and the LORD said in his heart,[3820] I will not again [b]curse[7043] the ground any more for man's[120] sake; [II]for

---

🔑 **8:21, 22** Contained in this promise is a stipulation that is easy to miss. Day, night, and the seasons will continue as seen in the phrase "while the earth remaineth." The earth was not intended

(continued on next page)

the [c]imagination[3336] of man's heart *is* evil[7451] from his youth; [d]neither will I again smite[5221] any more every thing living, as I have done.[6213]

22 [1][a]While the earth remaineth,[3117,3605] seedtime[2233] and harvest, and cold and heat, and summer and winter, and [b]day and night shall not cease.

Noahic Covenant

9 And God[430] blessed[1288] Noah and his sons, and said unto them, [a]Be fruitful, and multiply, and replenish the earth.[776]

2 [a]And the fear[4172] of you and the dread of you shall be upon every beast of the earth, and upon every fowl of the air, upon all that moveth *upon* the earth,[127] and upon all the fishes[1709] of the sea; into your hand are they delivered.

3 [a]Every moving thing that liveth[2416] shall be meat for you; even as the [b]green herb have I given you [c]all things.

4 [a]But flesh[1320] with the life[5315] thereof, *which is* the blood[1818] thereof, shall ye not eat.

5 And surely your blood of your lives[5315] will I require;[1875] [a]at the hand of every beast will I require it, and [b]at the hand of man;[120] at the hand of every [c]man's brother[251] will I require the life of man.

6 [a]Whoso sheddeth[8210] man's blood, by man shall his blood be shed: [b]for in the image[6754] of God[430] made he man.

7 And you, [a]be ye fruitful, and multiply; bring forth abundantly in the earth, and multiply therein.

🔑 8 And God spake unto Noah, and to his sons with him, saying,

9 And I, [a]behold, I establish [b]my covenant[1285] with you, and with your seed[2233] after you;

10 [a]And with every living[2416] creature[5315] that *is* with you, of the fowl, of the cattle, and of every beast[2416] of the earth with you; from all that go out of the ark, to every beast of the earth.

11 And [a]I will establish[6965] my covenant with you; neither shall all flesh be cut off[3772] any more by the waters of a flood; neither shall there any more be a flood to destroy[7843] the earth.

12 And God said, [a]This *is* the token[226] of the covenant which I make between me and you and every living creature that *is* with you, for perpetual[5769] generations:[1755]

13 I do set [a]my bow in the cloud,[6051] and it shall be for a token of a covenant between me and the earth.

14 And it shall come to pass, when I bring a cloud over the earth, that the bow shall be seen in the cloud:

15 And [a]I will remember[2142] my covenant, which *is* between me and you and every living creature of all flesh; and the waters shall no more become a flood to destroy all flesh.

16 And the bow shall be in the cloud; and I will look upon[7200] it, that I may remember[2142] [a]the everlasting[5769] covenant between God and every living

21 [c]Gen. 6:5; Job 14:4; 15:14; Ps. 51:5; Jer. 17:9; Matt. 15:19; Rom. 1:21; 3:23 [d]Gen. 9:11, 15
22 [1]Hebr. *As yet all the days of the earth* [a]Isa. 54:9 [b]Jer. 33:20, 25
1 [a]Gen. 1:28; 9:7, 19; 10:32
2 [a]Gen. 1:28; Hos. 2:18
3 [a]Deut. 12:15; 14:3, 9, 11; Acts 10:12, 13 [b]Gen. 1:29 [c]Rom. 14:14, 20; 1Cor. 10:23, 26; Col. 2:16; 1Tim. 4:3, 4
4 [a]Lev. 17:10, 11, 14; 19:26; Deut. 12:23; 1Sam. 14:33, 34; Acts 15:20, 29
5 [a]Ex. 21:28 [b]Gen. 4:9, 10; Ps. 9:12 [c]Acts 17:26
6 [a]Ex. 21:12, 14; Lev. 24:17; Matt. 26:52; Rev. 13:10 [b]Gen. 1:27
7 [a]Gen. 1:28; 8:1, 19
9 [a]Gen. 6:18 [b]Isa. 54:9
10 [a]Ps. 145:9
11 [a]Isa. 54:9
12 [a]Gen. 17:11
13 [a]Rev. 4:3
15 [a]Ex. 28:12; Lev. 26:42, 45; Ezek. 16:60
16 [a]Gen. 17:13, 19

(continued from previous page)
by God to be eternal. Its final destruction is described in Psalm 102:26 (quoted in Heb. 1:11, 12). The most graphic account of the end of the world, indeed of the entire physical universe, is found in 2 Peter 3:10.

🔑 **9:8–17** Throughout history God has dealt with man through covenants or agreements. Later, the Jews regarded this covenant between God and Noah as the basis of the relationship between God and all mankind, but the covenants with Abraham (chap. 15) and with Moses at Mount Sinai were seen as forming the basis of God's special relationship with Israel. Some believe that the stipulations laid on the Gentiles in Acts 15:20, 29 find validity here in the covenant between God and Noah. In spite of the fact that the distinction between clean and unclean animals existed (Gen. 7:2), God allowed the eating of any plant or animal. The only restriction was the eating of animal blood, for that is where the life of the animal resided (Gen. 9:4). Later, Israel was forbidden to eat not only blood but also the flesh of certain animals. The Lord removed the clean–unclean distinction from food altogether under the New Covenant (Mark 7:15; Acts 10:15; 1 Tim. 4:4, 5; Titus 1:15).

creature of all flesh that *is* upon the earth.

17 And God said unto Noah, This *is* the token of the covenant, which I have established between me and all flesh that *is* upon the earth.

Noah's Sons

18 And the sons of Noah, that went forth of the ark, were Shem, and Ham, and Japheth: [a]and Ham *is* the father of Canaan.

19 [a]These *are* the three sons of Noah: [b]and of them was the whole earth overspread.[5310]

🔑 20 And Noah began *to be* an [a]husbandman,[376,127] and he planted a vineyard:

21 And he drank[8354] of the wine, [a]and was drunken;[7937] and he was uncovered within his tent.[168]

22 And Ham, the father of Canaan, saw the nakedness[6172] of his father, and told[5046] his two brethren without.

23 [a]And Shem and Japheth took a garment, and laid *it* upon both their shoulders, and went backward, and covered[3680] the nakedness of their father; and their faces *were* backward, and they saw not their father's nakedness.

24 And Noah awoke from his wine, and knew what his younger son had done unto him.

25 And he said, [a]Cursed[779] *be* Canaan; [b]a servant of servants[5650] shall he be unto his brethren.

26 And he said, [a]Blessed[1288] *be* the LORD God of Shem; and Canaan shall be [I]his servant.

27 God shall [I]enlarge Japheth, [a]and he shall dwell in the tents of Shem; and Canaan shall be his servant.

28 And Noah lived[2421] after the flood three hundred and fifty years.

29 And all the days[3117] of Noah were nine hundred and fifty years: and he died.[4191]

Noah's Family Record

10 Now these *are* the generations[8435] of the sons of Noah, Shem, Ham, and Japheth: [a]and unto them were sons born after the flood.

2 [a]The sons of Japheth; Gomer, and Magog, and Madai, and Javan, and Tubal, and Meshech, and Tiras.

3 And the sons of Gomer; Ashkenaz, and Riphath, and Togarmah.

4 And the sons of Javan; Elishah, and Tarshish, Kittim, and Dodanim.

5 By these were [a]the isles of the Gentiles[1471] divided in their lands;[776] every one[376] after his tongue, after their families,[4940] in their nations.

6 [a]And the sons of Ham; Cush, and Mizraim, and Phut, and Canaan.

7 And the sons of Cush; Seba, and Havilah, and Sabtah, and Raamah, and Sabtechah: and the sons of Raamah; Sheba, and Dedan.

8 And Cush begat Nimrod: he began to be a mighty one in the earth.[776]

9 He was a mighty[1368] [a]hunter[6718] [b]before the LORD: wherefore it is said, Even as Nimrod the mighty hunter before the LORD.

10 [a]And the beginning[7225] of his kingdom[4467] was [I]Babel, and Erech, and Accad, and Calneh, in the land of Shinar.

18 [a]Gen. 10:6
19 [a]Gen. 5:32 [b]Gen. 10:32; 1Chr. 1:4
20 [a]Gen. 3:19, 23; 4:2; Prov. 12:11
21 [a]Prov. 20:1; 1Cor. 10:12
23 [a]Ex. 20:12; Gal. 6:1
25 [a]Deut. 27:16 [b]Josh. 9:23; 1Kgs. 9:20, 21
26 [I]Or, *servant to them* [a]Ps. 144:15; Heb. 11:16
27 [I]Or, *persuade* [a]Eph. 2:13, 14; 3:6
1 [a]Gen. 9:1, 7, 19
2 [a]1Chr. 1:5
5 [a]Ps. 72:10; Jer. 2:10; 25:22; Zeph. 2:11
6 [a]1Chr. 1:8
9 [a]Jer. 16:16; Mic. 7:2 [b]Gen. 6:11
10 [I]Gr. *Babylon* [a]Mic. 5:6

🔑 **9:20–27** The Hebrew word for "nakedness" (*'erwāh* [6172]) actually means "shameful nakedness" and is often used to describe immoral behavior. A different word (*'ēyrōm* [5903]) is used to describe simple nakedness or bareness.

The statement in verse twenty-two that Ham was the father of Canaan, and the fact that Noah's curse is directed against Canaan (v. 25), indicate that Canaan was somehow involved in immoral and indecent behavior with his drunken grandfather. Ham was indirectly to blame because he had allowed Canaan to grow up with this character and because he evidently did not treat Noah with respect when he found him.

The prophecy of Noah was to a large extent fulfilled when the Canaanites became "hewers of wood and drawers of water" for the Israelites (v. 25, cf. Josh. 9:23).

11 Out of that land [I]went forth Asshur, and builded Nineveh, and [II]the city Rehoboth, and Calah,

12 And Resen between Nineveh and Calah: the same *is* a great city.

13 And Mizraim begat Ludim, and Anamim, and Lehabim, and Naphtuhim,

14 And Pathrusim, and Casluhim, ([a]out of whom came Philistim,) and Caphtorim.

🔑 15 And Canaan begat Sidon his firstborn,[1060] and Heth,

16 And the Jebusite, and the Amorite, and the Girgasite,

🔑 17 And the Hivite, and the Arkite, and the Sinite,

18 And the Arvadite, and the Zemarite, and the Hamathite: and afterward were the families of the Canaanites spread abroad.

19 [a]And the border of the Canaanites was from Sidon, as thou comest to Gerar, unto Gaza; as thou goest, unto Sodom, and Gomorrah, and Admah, and Zeboim, even unto Lasha.

20 These *are* the sons of Ham, after their families, after their tongues, in their countries,[776] *and* in their nations.

21 Unto Shem also, the father of all the children[1121] of Eber, the brother of Japheth the elder, even to him were *children* born.

22 The [a]children of Shem; Elam, and Asshur, and Arphaxad, and Lud, and Aram.

23 And the children of Aram; Uz, and Hul, and Gether, and Mash.

24 And Arphaxad begat [a]Salah; and Salah begat Eber.

25 [a]And unto Eber were born two sons: the name of one *was* [I]Peleg; for in his days[3117] was[6385] the earth[776] divided;[6385] and his brother's name *was* Joktan.

26 And Joktan begat Almodad, and Sheleph, and Hazarmaveth, and Jerah,

27 And Hadoram, and Uzal, and Diklah,

28 And Obal, and Abimael, and Sheba,

29 And Ophir, and Havilah, and Jobab: all these *were* the sons of Joktan.

30 And their dwelling[4186] was from Mesha, as thou goest unto Sephar a mount of the east.

31 These *are* the sons of Shem, after their families, after their tongues, in their lands, after their nations.

32 [a]These *are* the families of the sons of Noah, after their generations,[8435] in their nations: [b]and by these were the nations divided[6504] in the earth after the flood.

The Tower of Babel

11 🔑 And the whole earth[776] was of one [I]language,[8193] and of one [II]speech.[1697]

2 And it came to pass, as they journeyed [I][a]from the east, that they found a plain in the land[776] of Shinar; and they dwelt there.

3 And [I]they said one[376] to another,[7453] Go to, let us make[3835] brick, and [II]burn[8313] them throughly.[8316] And they had brick for stone, and slime had they for morter.

4 And they said, Go to,[3051] let us build us a city and a tower, whose [a]top[7218] *may reach* unto heaven;[8064] and let us make[6213] us a name, lest we be scattered abroad upon the face of the whole earth.

11 [I]Or, *he went out* into *Assyria* [II]Or, *the streets of the city*
14 [a]1Chr. 1:12
19 [a]Gen. 13:12, 14, 15, 17; 15:18-21; Num. 34:2-12; Josh. 12:7, 8
22 [a]1Chr. 1:17
24 [a]Gen. 11:12
25 [I]That is, *Division* [a]1Chr. 1:19
32 [a]Gen. 10:1 [b]Gen. 9:19
1 [I]Hebr. *lip* [II]Hebr. *words*
2 [I]Or, *eastward* [a]Gen. 13:11; 2Sam. 6:2; 1Chr. 13:6
3 [I]Hebr. *a man said to his neighbor* [II]Hebr. *burn them to a burning*
4 [a]Deut. 1:28

🔑 **10:15, 17** The Hivites were one of the seven nations descended from Canaan (Gen. 10:17; Deut. 7:1). They were present in Shechem, Gibeon, and Lebanon (Gen. 34:2; Josh. 9:3–7; Judg. 3:3). Israel was commanded to destroy them, but they failed to obey, and some were still present in Solomon's day (1 Kgs. 9:20, 21).

🔑 **11:1–9** Josephus, the Jewish historian, places Babel in the days of Nimrod. Babel was a pointed rejection of God's instruction to "replenish the earth" (Gen. 9:1). It was a flagrant example of the corporate pride and willfulness of man. The intent of the tower may not have been to reach heaven; the expression can refer to a tower with an idolatrous "temple for heaven" on its top.

5 [a]And the LORD came down to see[7200] the city and the tower, which the children[1121] of men[120] builded.

6 And the LORD said, Behold, [a]the people[5971] *is* one, and they have all [b]one language; and this they begin to do:[6213] and now nothing will be restrained[1219] from them, which they have [c]imagined[2161] to do.

7 Go to, [a]let us go down, and there confound[1101] their language, that they may [b]not understand[8085] one another's speech.[8193]

8 So [a]the LORD scattered them abroad from thence [b]upon the face of all the earth: and they left off[2308] to build the city.

9 Therefore is the name of it called[7121] [I]Babel;[894] [a]because the LORD did there confound[1101] the language of all the earth: and from thence did the LORD scatter them abroad[6327] upon the face of all the earth.

Shem's Family Record

10 [a]These *are* the generations[8435] of Shem: Shem *was* an hundred years old, and begat Arphaxad two years after the flood:

11 And Shem lived[2421] after he begat Arphaxad five hundred years, and begat sons and daughters.

12 And Arphaxad lived[2425] five and thirty years, [a]and begat Salah:

13 And Arphaxad lived after he begat Salah four hundred and three years, and begat sons and daughters.

14 And Salah lived[2425] thirty years, and begat Eber:

15 And Salah lived[2421] after he begat Eber four hundred and three years, and begat sons and daughters.

16 [a]And Eber lived four and thirty years, and begat [b]Peleg:

17 And Eber lived after he begat Peleg four hundred and thirty years, and begat sons and daughters.

18 And Peleg lived thirty years, and begat Reu:

19 And Peleg lived after he begat Reu two hundred and nine years, and begat sons and daughters.

20 And Reu lived two and thirty years, and begat [a]Serug:

21 And Reu lived after he begat Serug two hundred and seven years, and begat sons and daughters.

22 And Serug lived thirty years, and begat Nahor:

23 And Serug lived after he begat Nahor two hundred years, and begat sons and daughters.

24 And Nahor lived nine and twenty years, and begat [a]Terah:

25 And Nahor lived after he begat Terah an hundred and nineteen years, and begat sons and daughters.

26 And Terah lived seventy years, and [a]begat Abram, Nahor, and Haran.

27 Now these *are* the generations[8435] of Terah: Terah begat Abram, Nahor, and Haran; and Haran begat Lot.

28 And Haran died[4191] before his father Terah in the land[776] of his nativity, in Ur of the Chaldees.

29 And Abram and Nahor took them wives: the name of Abram's wife[802] *was* [a]Sarai; and the name of Nahor's wife, [b]Milcah, the daughter of Haran, the father of Milcah, and the father of Iscah.

30 But [a]Sarai was barren;[6135] she *had* no child.

31 And Terah [a]took Abram his son, and Lot the son of Haran his son's son, and Sarai his daughter in law, his son

5 [a]Gen. 18:21
6 [a]Gen. 9:19; Acts 17:26 [b]Gen. 11:1 [c]Ps. 2:1
7 [a]Gen. 1:26; Ps. 2:4; Acts 2:4-6 [b]Gen. 42:23; Deut. 28:49; Jer. 5:15; 1Cor. 14:2, 11
8 [a]Luke 1:51 [b]Gen. 10:25, 32
9 [I]That is, *Confusion* [a]1Cor. 14:23
10 [a]Gen. 10:22; 1Chr. 1:17
12 [a]Luke 3:36
16 [a]1Chr. 1:19 [b]Luke 3:35, *Phalec*
20 [a]Luke 3:35, *Saruch*
24 [a]Luke 3:34, *Thara*
26 [a]Josh. 24:2; 1Chr. 1:26
29 [a]Gen. 17:15; 20:12 [b]Gen. 22:20
30 [a]Gen. 16:1, 2; 18:11, 12
31 [a]Gen. 12:1

11:10–27 Note the steadily decreasing lifespan (Gen. 5:1–32).

11:31 The statement that "Terah took Abram" is worded in that way because of Oriental propriety. Even though Abram was the practical leader of the family (Gen. 12:4, 5), his old and probably infirm father still occupied the place of honor. When Abram took this step, he was motivated by faith in the promise of God and did not even know his ultimate destination (Heb. 11:31; Gal. 3:6–9). The phrase "to go into the land of Canaan" in Genesis 11:31 is an infinitive of result, not of purpose.

Abram's wife; and they went forth with them from [b]Ur of the Chaldees, to go into [c]the land of Canaan; and they came unto Haran, and dwelt there.

32 And the days of Terah were two hundred and five years: and Terah died in Haran.

God Calls Abram

12 Now the [a]LORD had said unto Abram, Get thee out of thy country,[776] and from thy kindred,[4138] and from thy father's house,[1004] unto a land that I will shew[7200] thee:

2 [a]And I will make[6213] of thee a great nation,[1471] [b]and I will bless[1288] thee, and make thy name great; [c]and thou shalt be a blessing:[1293]

3 [a]And I will bless them that bless thee, and curse[779] him that curseth[7043] thee: [b]and in thee shall[1288] all families[4940] of the earth[127] be blessed.[1288]

4 So Abram departed, as the LORD had spoken[1696] unto him; and Lot went with him: and Abram *was* seventy and five years old when he departed out of Haran.

5 And Abram took Sarai his wife, and Lot his brother's son, and all their substance[7399] that they had gathered, and [a]the souls[5315] that they had gotten[6213] [b]in Haran; and they went forth to go into the land of Canaan; and into the land of Canaan they came.

6 And Abram [a]passed through[5674] the land unto the place of Sichem, [b]unto the plain of Moreh. [c]And the Canaanite *was* then[227] in the land.

7 [a]And the LORD appeared[7200] unto Abram, and said, [b]Unto thy seed[2233] will I give this land: and there builded he an [c]altar[4196] unto the LORD, who appeared unto him.

8 And he removed from thence unto a mountain on the east of Bethel, and pitched his tent,[168] *having* Bethel on the west, and Hai on the east: and there he builded an altar unto the LORD, and [a]called[7121] upon the name of the LORD.

9 And Abram journeyed, [1][a]going on still toward the south.

Abram Goes to Egypt

10 And there was [a]a famine in the land: and Abram [b]went down into Egypt to sojourn[1481] there; for the famine *was* [c]grievous[3515] in the land.

11 And it came to pass, when he was come near to enter into Egypt, that he said unto Sarai his wife,[802] Behold now,[4994] I know that thou *art* [a]a fair woman[802] to look upon:

12 Therefore it shall come to pass, when the Egyptians shall see[7200] thee, that they shall say,[559] This *is* his wife: and they [a]will kill[2026] me, but they will save thee alive.[2421]

13 [a]Say, I pray thee,[4994] thou *art* my sister:[269] that it may be well[3190] with me for thy sake; and my soul shall live[2421] because of thee.

14 And it came to pass, that, when Abram was come into Egypt, the Egyptians [a]beheld[7200] the woman that she *was* very fair.

15 The princes[8269] also of Pharaoh

31 [b]Neh. 9:7; Acts 7:4 [c]Gen. 10:19
1 [a]Gen. 15:7; Neh. 9:7; Isa. 41:2; Acts 7:3; Heb. 11:8
2 [a]Gen. 17:6; 18:18; Deut. 26:5; 1Kgs. 3:8 [b]Gen. 24:35 [c]Gen. 28:4; Gal. 3:14
3 [a]Gen. 27:29; Ex. 23:22; Num. 24:9 [b]Gen. 18:18; 22:18; 26:4; Ps. 72:17; Acts 3:25; Gal. 3:8
5 [a]Gen. 14:14 [b]Gen. 11:31
6 [a]Heb. 11:9 [b]Deut. 11:30; Judg. 7:1 [c]Gen. 10:18, 19; 13:7
7 [a]Gen. 17:1 [b]Gen. 13:15; 17:8; Ps. 105:9, 11 [c]Gen. 13:4
8 [a]Gen. 13:4
9 [1]Hebr. *in going and journeying* [a]Gen. 13:3
10 [a]Gen. 26:1 [b]Ps. 105:13 [c]Gen. 43:1
11 [a]Gen. 12:14; 26:7
12 [a]Gen. 20:11; 26:7
13 [a]Gen. 20:5, 13; 26:7
14 [a]Gen. 39:7; Matt. 5:28

12:1–3 This promise to Abraham is one of the most significant passages in the entire Bible. It points ultimately to the redemption of the whole world. Abraham's family became a divinely appointed channel through which blessing would come to all men. This promise was formalized in a covenant (Gen. 15:18–21), and was repeated four additional times: twice to Abraham (Gen. 17:6–8; 22:16–18); once to Isaac (Gen. 26:3, 4); and once to Jacob (Gen. 28:13, 14). Note the critical circumstances for the family in each case. This promise is emphasized in the New Testament in Acts 3:25, Romans 4:13, Galatians 3:8, 29, and Ephesians 2:12. Galatians calls it "the gospel." Its importance to the Gentiles is stressed in Galatians as well as Ephesians where it is clearly stated that Gentiles who were "far off" and "strangers to the covenant of promise" have been brought to it by the blood of Christ.

12:11–20 See note on Genesis 20:2–18.

saw her, and commended[1984] her before Pharaoh: and the woman was [a]taken into Pharaoh's house.[1004]

16 And he [a]entreated Abram well[3190] for her sake: and he had sheep, and oxen, and he asses, and menservants,[5650] and maidservants, and she asses, and camels.

17 And the Lord [a]plagued[5060] Pharaoh and his house with great plagues[5061] because of Sarai Abram's wife.

18 And Pharaoh called[7121] Abram, and said, [a]What *is* this *that* thou hast done[6213] unto me? why didst thou not tell[5046] me that she *was* thy wife?

19 Why saidst thou, She *is* my sister? so I might have taken her to me to wife: now therefore behold thy wife, take *her,* and go thy way.

20 [a]And Pharaoh commanded[6680] *his* men[582] concerning him: and they sent him away, and his wife, and all that he had.

Abram and Lot Separate

13 And Abram went up out of Egypt, he, and his wife,[802] and all that he had, and Lot with him, [a]into the south.

2 [a]And Abram *was* very rich[3513] in cattle, in silver, and in gold.

3 And he went on his journeys [a]from the south even to Bethel, unto the place where his tent[168] had been at the beginning, between Bethel and Hai;

4 Unto the [a]place of the altar,[4196] which he had made[6213] there at the first:[7223] and there Abram [b]called[7121] on the name of the Lord.

5 And Lot also, which went with Abram, had flocks, and herds, and tents.

6 And [a]the land was not able to bear[5375] them, that they might dwell together: for their substance was great, so that they could not dwell together.

7 And there was [a]a strife[7379] between the herdmen of Abram's cattle and the herdmen of Lot's cattle: [b]and the Canaanite and the Perizzite dwelled then in the land.

8 And Abram said unto Lot, [a]Let there be[1961] no strife, I pray thee, between me and thee, and between my herdmen and thy herdmen; for we *be* [I]brethren.[251]

9 [a]*Is* not the whole land before thee? separate thyself, I pray thee, from me: [b]if *thou wilt take* the left hand, then I will go to the right; or if *thou depart* to the right hand, then I will go to the left.

10 And Lot lifted up his eyes, and beheld[7200] all [a]the plain of Jordan, that it *was* well watered every where, before the Lord [b]destroyed[7843] Sodom and Gomorrah, [c]*even* as the garden of the Lord, like the land of Egypt, as thou comest unto [d]Zoar.

11 Then Lot chose[977] him all the plain of Jordan; and Lot journeyed east: and they separated themselves the one[376] from the other.

12 Abram dwelled in the land of Canaan, and Lot [a]dwelled in the cities of the plain, and [b]pitched *his* tent toward Sodom.

13 But the men[582] of Sodom [a]*were* wicked[7451] and [b]sinners[2400] before the Lord exceedingly.

Abram Moves to Hebron

14 And the Lord said unto Abram, after that Lot [a]was separated from him, Lift up[5375] now thine eyes, and look[7200] from the place where thou art [b]northward, and southward, and eastward, and westward:

🔑 15 For all the land which thou seest, [a]to thee will I give it, and [b]to thy seed[2233] for ever.5704,5769

16 And [a]I will make[7760] thy seed as the dust[6083] of the earth:[776] so that if a man[376] can number the dust of the earth, *then* shall thy seed also be numbered.

15 [a]Gen. 20:2
16 [a]Gen. 20:14
17 [a]Gen. 20:18; 1Chr. 16:21; Ps. 105:14; Heb. 13:4
18 [a]Gen. 20:9; 26:10
20 [a]Prov. 21:1

1 [a]Gen. 12:9
2 [a]Gen. 24:35; Ps. 112:3; Prov. 10:22
3 [a]Gen. 12:8, 9
4 [a]Gen. 12:7, 8 [b]Ps. 116:17
6 [a]Gen. 36:7
7 [a]Gen. 26:20 [b]Gen. 12:6
8 [I]Hebr. *men brethren.* See Gen. 11:27, 31; Ex. 2:13; Ps. 133:1; Acts 7:26 [a]1Cor. 6:7
9 [a]Gen. 20:15; 34:10 [b]Rom. 12:18; Heb. 12:14; James 3:17
10 [a]Gen. 19:17; Deut. 34:3; Ps. 107:34 [b]Gen. 19:24, 25 [c]Gen. 2:10; Isa. 51:3 [d]Gen. 14:2, 8; 19:22
12 [a]Gen. 19:29 [b]Gen. 14:12; 19:1; 2Pet. 2:7, 8
13 [a]Gen. 18:20; Ezek. 16:49; 2Pet. 2:7, 8 [b]Gen. 6:11
14 [a]Gen. 13:11 [b]Gen. 28:14
15 [a]Gen. 12:7; 15:18; 17:8; 24:7; 26:4; Num. 34:12; Deut. 34:4; Acts 7:5 [b]2Chr. 20:7; Ps. 37:22, 29; 112:2
16 [a]Gen. 15:5; 22:17; 26:4; 28:14; 32:12; Ex. 32:13; Num. 23:10; Deut. 1:10; 1Kgs. 4:20; 1Chr. 27:23; Isa. 48:19; Jer. 33:22; Rom. 4:16-18; Heb. 11:12

🔑 **13:15** Here and in Genesis 15:18 God's gift was not given to Abraham personally (Acts 7:5), but to him as the founder and representative of the nation. The land was given to him "in trust."

17 Arise, walk through the land in
the length of it and in the breadth of it;
for I will give it unto thee.
18 Then Abram removed *his* tent,
and came [a]and dwelt in the plain of
Mamre, [b]which *is* in Hebron, and built
there an altar unto the LORD.

Abram Rescues Lot

14 And it came to pass in the days
of Amraphel king[4428] [a]of Shinar,
Arioch king of Ellasar, Chedorlaomer
king of [b]Elam, and Tidal king of nations;[1471]
🗝 2 *That these* made war with Bera
king of Sodom, and with Birsha king of
Gomorrah, Shinab king of [a]Admah, and
Shemeber king of Zeboiim, and the king
of Bela, which is [b]Zoar.
3 All these were joined together in
the vale[6010] of Siddim, [a]which is the salt
sea.
4 Twelve years [a]they served[5647]
Chedorlaomer, and in the thirteenth year
they rebelled.[4775]
5 And in the fourteenth year came
Chedorlaomer, and the kings that *were*
with him, and smote[5221] [a]the Rephaims[7497] [b]in Ashteroth Karnaim, and [c]the
Zuzims in Ham, [d]and the Emims in
[I]Shaveh Kiriathaim,
6 [a]And the Horites in their mount
Seir, unto [I]El–paran, which *is* by the
wilderness.
7 And they returned, and came to
Enmishpat, which *is* Kadesh, and smote
all the country[7704] of the Amalekites,
and also the Amorites, that dwelt [a]in
Hazezon–tamar.
8 And there went out the king of
Sodom, and the king of Gomorrah, and
the king of Admah, and the king of
Zeboiim, and the king of Bela (the same
is Zoar;) and they joined[6186] battle with
them in the vale of Siddim;
9 With Chedorlaomer the king of
Elam, and with Tidal king of nations,
and Amraphel king of Shinar, and
Arioch king of Ellasar; four kings with
five.
10 And the vale of Siddim *was full
of* [a]slime[2564] pits; and the kings of
Sodom and Gomorrah fled, and fell[5307]
there; and they that remained[7604] fled [b]to
the mountain.
11 And they took [a]all the goods of
Sodom and Gomorrah, and all their victuals,[400] and went their way.
12 And they took Lot, Abram's
[a]brother's son, [b]who dwelt in Sodom, and
his goods, and departed.
🗝 13 And there came one that had escaped, and told[5046] Abram the
Hebrew;[5680] for [a]he dwelt in the plain of
Mamre the Amorite, brother of Eshcol,
and brother of Aner: [b]and these *were*
confederate[1167] with Abram.
14 And when Abram heard that [a]his
brother was taken captive,[7617] he [I]armed
his [II]trained *servants,* [b]born in his own
house,[1004] three hundred and eighteen,
and pursued *them* [c]unto Dan.
15 And he divided himself[2505]
against them, he and his servants,[5650] by
night, and [a]smote them, and pursued
them unto Hobah, which *is* on the left
hand of Damascus.
16 And he brought back [a]all the
goods, and also brought again his brother
Lot, and his goods, and the women also,
and the people.[5971]

18 [a]Gen. 14:13 [b]Gen. 35:27; 37:14
1 [a]Gen. 10:10; 11:2 [b]Isa. 11:11
2 [a]Deut. 29:23 [b]Gen. 19:22
3 [a]Num. 34:12; Deut. 3:17; Josh. 3:16; Ps. 107:34
4 [a]Gen. 9:26
5 [I]Or, *The plain of Kiriathaim* [a]Gen. 15:20; Deut. 3:11 [b]Josh. 12:4; 13:12 [c]Deut. 2:20 [d]Deut. 2:10, 11
6 [I]Or, *The plain of Paran,* Gen. 21:21; Num. 12:16; 13:3 [a]Deut. 2:12, 22
7 [a]2Chr. 20:2
10 [a]Gen. 11:3 [b]Gen. 19:17, 30
11 [a]Gen. 14:16, 21
12 [a]Gen. 12:5 [b]Gen. 13:12
13 [a]Gen. 13:18 [b]Gen. 14:24
14 [I]Or, *led forth* [II]Or, *instructed* [a]Gen. 13:8 [b]Gen. 15:3; 17:12, 27; Eccl. 2:7 [c]Deut. 34:1; Judg. 18:29
15 [a]Isa. 41:2, 3
16 [a]Gen. 14:11, 12

🗝 **14:2** According to Josephus, the affairs of the country of Sodom were controlled by the five kings listed in this verse. Small but populous, the country of Sodom was rich and flourishing. However, their wickedness and sexual sin was so persistent that God decided to destroy them (or at least the major cities, Sodom and Gomorrah). Fire and brimstone from the hand of God made them a lasting example of the wages of sin (Gen. 19:12, 13; 2 Pet. 2:6–8).

🗝 **14:13** Abram (Abraham) was the first to be called a Hebrew (from the root *'āvar* [5674], "to cross over"). Presumably, it was used in the sense of an immigrant. The name is seldom used of the Israelites in the Old Testament, except when the speaker is a foreigner, or when the Israelites speak of themselves to one from another nation.

Melchizedek Blesses Abram

17 And the king of Sodom [a]went out to meet him [b]after his return from the slaughter[5221] of Chedorlaomer, and of the kings that *were* with him, at the valley of Shaveh, which *is* the [c]king's dale.

⊶ 18 And [a]Melchizedek[4442] king of Salem brought forth bread and wine: and he *was* [b]the priest[3548] of [c]the most high[5945] God.[410]

19 And he blessed[1288] him, and said, [a]Blessed *be* Abram of the most high God, [b]possessor[7069] of heaven[8064] and earth:[776]

20 And [a]blessed be the most high God, which hath delivered thine enemies into thy hand.[3027] And he gave him tithes[4643] [b]of all.

21 And the king of Sodom said unto Abram, Give me the [I]persons,[5315] and take the goods to thyself.

22 And Abram said to the king of Sodom, I [a]have lift up mine hand unto the LORD, the most high God, [b]the possessor of heaven and earth,

23 That [a]I will not *take* from a thread even to a shoelatchet,[8288] and that I will not take any thing that *is* thine, lest thou shouldest say, I have made Abram rich:

24 Save only that which the young men[5288] have eaten, and the portion of the men [a]which went with me, Aner, Eshcol, and Mamre; let them take their portion.

Abrahamic Covenant

15 After these things the word[1697] of the LORD came[1961] unto Abram [a]in a vision,[4236] saying, [b]Fear[3372] not, Abram: I *am* thy [c]shield, *and* thy exceeding [d]great reward.[7939]

2 And Abram said, Lord[136] GOD, what wilt thou give me, [a]seeing I go childless, and the steward[1121] of my house[1004] *is* this Eliezer of Damascus?

3 And Abram said, Behold, to me thou hast given no seed:[2233] and, lo, [a]one born[1121] in my house is mine heir.[3423]

4 And, behold, the word of the LORD

17 [a]Judg. 11:34; 1Sam. 18:6 [b]Heb. 7:1 [c]2Sam. 18:18
18 [a]Heb. 7:1 [b]Ps. 110:4; Heb. 5:6 [c]Mic. 6:6; Acts 16:17
19 [a]Ruth 3:10; 2Sam. 2:5 [b]Gen. 14:22; Matt. 11:25
20 [a]Gen. 24:27 [b]Heb. 7:4
21 [I]Hebr. *souls*
22 [a]Ex. 6:8; Dan. 12:7; Rev. 10:5, 6 [b]Gen. 14:19; 21:33
23 [a]Esth. 9:15, 16
24 [a]Gen. 14:13
1 [a]Dan. 10:1; Acts 10:10, 11 [b]Gen. 26:24; Dan. 10:12; Luke 1:13, 30 [c]Ps. 3:3; 5:12; 84:11; 91:4; 119:114 [d]Ps. 16:5; 58:11; Prov. 11:18
2 [a]Acts 7:5
3 [a]Gen. 14:14

⊶ **14:18–20** Abram gave Melchizedek a tithe because, as priest of the most high God, Melchizedek was a representative of God. This brief encounter was the foundation of a messianic prophecy (Ps. 110:4, cf. Heb. 5:10; 6:10; 7:1–28 [see note on this passage]). Melchizedek's identity has been hotly debated over the centuries. There are three main viewpoints: (1) Melchizedek was the preincarnate Christ. It has been contended that the titles "King of Peace" and "King of Righteousness" ascribed to Melchizedek (Heb. 7:2) rightfully belong only to Jesus Christ (cf. 1 Cor. 1:30; Eph. 2:14). Neither would it be improper for the Son of God to both bless Abram and receive tithes from him (Gen. 14:19, 20). Nevertheless, the language of Hebrews 7:3 undermines this position. The Greek word *aphōmoiōmenos* (871), is a masculine present participle which means "making similar or alike." This implies that a comparison is being made between two persons. It would be strange to compare Melchizedek to the Son of God if he were the preincarnate Christ. (2) Melchizedek was the patriarch of Shem. The blessing given by Melchizedek to Abram in Genesis 14:19, 20 certainly has overtones of the blessing given by Noah to Shem in Genesis 9:26. Abram, the lesser, was blessed by Melchizedek, the better (Heb. 7:6, 7). Who would be greater than Shem, Abram's ancestor, the one who had received the promises? However, the identification of Melchizedek is described as being "without father, without mother, having neither beginning of days, nor end of life" (Heb. 7:3). Shem's parentage (Gen. 6:10; 10:1) and lifespan (Gen. 11:10, 11) are known. In addition, Shem's descendants are listed as inhabitants of the Mesopotamian and Arabian areas (Gen. 10:21–31). What would Shem be doing in Canaan, a land inhabited by Ham's posterity (Gen. 10:6, 15–20)? Why would Shem be mentioned by another name? (3) Melchizedek was a Canaanite priest-king. There would be nothing unusual about a Canaanite ruler meeting a victorious Abram in conjunction with the king of Sodom (Gen. 14:17, 18). In the light of the degrading nature of Canaanite religious practices, however, it would be unusual to find a Canaanite priest who worshiped the true God. In addition, Abram was known for building altars of worship (e.g., Gen. 12:7, 8; 13:18). Why would not he worship with Melchizedek, whom he acknowledged as being greater than himself? The problem of Melchizedek's identity is a perplexing one. Each view has its strengths and weaknesses, so the question remains open to debate.

came unto him, saying, This shall not be
thine heir; but he that [a]shall come forth
out of thine own bowels[4578] shall be
thine heir.
5 And he brought him forth abroad,
and said, Look now toward heaven, and
[a]tell[5608] the [b]stars, if thou be able to
number[5608] them: and he said unto him,
[c]So shall thy seed be.
🔑 6 And he [a]believed[539] in the LORD;
and he [b]counted[2803] it to him for
righteousness.[6666]
7 And he said unto him, I *am* the
LORD that [a]brought thee out of [b]Ur of
the Chaldees, [c]to give thee this land[776] to
inherit[3423] it.
8 And he said, Lord GOD, [a]whereby
shall I know that I shall inherit it?
9 And he said unto him, Take me an
heifer of three years old, and a she goat
of three years old, and a ram of three
years old, and a turtledove, and a young
pigeon.
10 And he took unto him all these,
and [a]divided[1334] them in the midst, and
laid each[376] piece one against another:
but [b]the birds divided he not.
11 And when the fowls came down
upon the carcases,[6297] Abram drove them
away.
12 And when the sun was going
down, [a]a deep sleep[8639] fell upon Abram;

4 [a]2Sam. 7:12; 16:11; 2Chr. 32:21
5 [a]Ps. 147:4 [b]Jer. 33:22 [c]Gen. 13:16; 22:17; Ex. 32:13; Deut. 1:10; 10:22; 1Chr. 27:23; Rom. 4:18; Heb. 11:12
6 [a]Rom. 4:3, 9, 22; Gal. 3:6; James 2:23 [b]Ps. 106:31
7 [a]Gen. 12:1 [b]Gen. 11:28, 31 [c]Ps. 105:42, 44; Rom. 4:13
8 [a]Gen. 24:13, 14; Judg. 6:17, 37; 1Sam. 14:9, 10; 2Kgs. 20:8; Luke 1:18
10 [a]Jer. 34:18, 19 [b]Lev. 1:17
12 [a]Gen. 2:21; Job 4:13
13 [a]Ex. 12:40; Ps. 105:23; Acts 7:6 [b]Ex. 1:11; Ps. 105:25
14 [a]Ex. 6:6; Deut. 6:22 [b]Ex. 12:36; Ps. 105:37
15 [a]Job 5:26 [b]Acts 13:36 [c]Gen. 25:8
16 [a]Ex. 12:40 [b]1Kgs. 21:26 [c]Dan. 8:23; Matt. 23:32; 1Thess. 2:16

and, lo, an horror[367] of great darkness[2825] fell upon him.
🔑 13 And he said unto Abram, Know
of a surety [a]that thy seed shall be
a stranger[1616] in a land *that is* not
theirs, and shall serve[5647] them; and
[b]they shall afflict[6031] them four hundred
years;
14 And also that nation,[1471] whom
they shall serve,[5647] [a]will I judge: and afterward [b]shall they come out with great
substance.
15 And [a]thou shalt go [b]to thy
fathers[1] in peace;[7965] [c]thou shalt be
buried[6912] in a good[2896] old age.[7872]
🔑 16 But [a]in the fourth generation[1755]
they shall come hither again: for the
iniquity[5771] [b]of the Amorites [c]*is* not yet
full.[8003]
17 And it came to pass, that, when
the sun went down, and it was dark, behold a smoking furnace, and [I]a burning
lamp that [a]passed[5674] between those
pieces.[1506]
18 In the same day[3117] the LORD
[a]made[3772] a covenant[1285] with Abram,
saying, [b]Unto thy seed have I given this

17 [I]Hebr. *a lamp of fire* [a]Jer. 34:18, 19
18 [a]Gen. 24:7 [b]Gen. 12:7; 13:15; 26:4; Ex. 23:31; Num. 34:3; Deut. 1:7; 11:24; 34:4; Josh. 1:4; 1Kgs. 4:21; 2Chr. 9:26; Neh. 9:8; Ps. 105:11; Isa. 27:12

🔑 **15:6** This verse is believed by some to be the key verse of the entire Old Testament. It is an important witness to the doctrine of justification by faith and to the doctrine of the unity of believers in both dispensations. Abraham's faith was accounted to him for righteousness before he was circumcised and more than four hundred years before the law was given to his descendants. Therefore, neither circumcision nor the law had a part in Abraham's righteousness. Paul proves that Abraham's faith was not merely confidence in God nor simple obedience to God's command, but that it was indeed faith in the promise of redemption through Christ (Rom. 3:21, 22; 4:18–25; Gal. 3:14).

🔑 **15:13–16** God gave Abraham a preview of events in his family's future up to the point of their possession of the land which He had promised. They would first be temporary residents in a strange land for four hundred years and become slaves. Their bondage in Egypt was certainly a part of God's overall plan. Four hundred years is a round figure. There is no conflict with the 430 years mentioned in Exodus 12:40, 41. The four generations of their sojourn should be understood as four lifetimes. One hundred years would have been a conservative estimate for one lifetime in patriarchal times.

🔑 **15:16** The Amorite nation was one of the seven nations of Canaan and was governed by many independent kings (Josh. 5:1; 9:10). Originally they inhabited a mountain district in the south (Num. 13:29), but later they acquired an extensive tract of land from Moab, east of Jordan (Num. 21:26). They had many strong cities (Num. 32:17, 33). They were profane, wicked, and idolatrous (Josh. 24:15). They interfered with Israel at times (Num. 21:24), again were peaceful, but were finally brought into bondage by Solomon (1 Kgs. 9:20, 21).

land, from the river of Egypt unto the great river, the river Euphrates:

19 The Kenites, and the Kenizzites, and the Kadmonites,

20 And the Hittites, and the Perizzites, and the Rephaims,[7497]

21 And the Amorites, and the Canaanites, and the Girgashites, and the Jebusites.

Hagar and Ishmael

16 Now Sarai Abram's wife[802] [a]bare him no children: and she had an handmaid,8198 [b]an Egyptian, whose name *was* [c]Hagar.

2 [a]And Sarai said unto Abram, Behold now, the LORD [b]hath restrained6113 me from bearing: I pray thee, [c]go in unto my maid; it may be that I may [I]obtain children by her. And Abram [d]hearkened[8085] to the voice of Sarai.

3 And Sarai Abram's wife took Hagar her maid the Egyptian, after Abram [a]had dwelt ten years in the land[776] of Canaan, and gave her to her husband[376] Abram to be his wife.

4 And he went in unto Hagar, and she conceived: and when she saw[7200] that she had conceived, her mistress[1404] was [a]despised[7043] in her eyes.

5 And Sarai said unto Abram, My wrong[2555] *be* upon thee: I have given my maid into thy bosom; and when she saw that she had conceived, I was despised in her eyes: [a]the LORD judge between me and thee.

6 [a]But Abram said unto Sarai, [b]Behold, thy maid *is* in thy hand;[3027] do to her [I]as it pleaseth[2896] thee. And when Sarai [II]dealt hardly6031 with her, [c]she fled from her face.

7 And the angel of the LORD found her by a fountain of water in the wilderness, [a]by the fountain in the way to [b]Shur.

8 And he said, Hagar, Sarai's maid, whence camest thou? and whither wilt thou go? And she said, I flee from the face of my mistress Sarai.

9 And the angel of the LORD said unto her, Return to thy mistress, and [a]submit thyself6031 under her hands.

10 And the angel of the LORD said unto her, [a]I will multiply thy seed[2233] exceedingly, that it shall not be numbered[5608] for multitude.

11 And the angel of the LORD said unto her, Behold, thou *art* with child, [a]and shalt bear a son, and shalt call[7121] his name [I]Ishmael; because the LORD hath heard[8085] thy affliction.6040

12 [a]And he will be a wild man;[120] his hand[3027] *will be* against every man, and every man's hand against him; [b]and he shall dwell[7931] in the presence of all his brethren.

13 And she called[7121] the name of the LORD that spake[1696] unto her, Thou God[410] seest[7210] me: for she said, Have I also here looked[7200] after him [a]that seeth[7210] me?

14 Wherefore the well was called [I][a]Beer–lahai–roi;883 behold, *it is* [b]between Kadesh and Bered.

🗝 15 And [a]Hagar bare Abram a son: and Abram called his son's name, which Hagar bare, [b]Ishmael.3458

16 And Abram *was* fourscore and six years old, when Hagar bare Ishmael to Abram.

1 [a]Gen. 15:2, 3 [b]Gen. 21:9 [c]Gal. 4:24

2 [I]Hebr. *be built by her* [a]Gen. 30:3 [b]Gen. 20:18; 30:2; 1Sam. 1:5, 6 [c]Gen. 30:3, 9 [d]Gen. 3:17

3 [a]Gen. 12:5

4 [a]2Sam. 6:16; Prov. 30:21, 23

5 [a]Gen. 31:53; 1Sam. 24:12

6 [I]Hebr. that which is *good in thine eyes* [II]Hebr. *afflicted her* [a]Prov. 15:1; 1Pet. 3:7 [b]Job 2:6; Ps. 106:41, 42; Jer. 38:5 [c]Ex. 2:15

7 [a]Gen. 25:18 [b]Ex. 15:22

9 [a]Titus 2:9; 1Pet. 2:18

10 [a]Gen. 17:20; 21:18, 25:12

11 [I]That is, *God shall hear* [a]Gen. 17:19; Matt. 1:21; Luke 1:13, 31

12 [a]Gen. 21:20 [b]Gen. 25:18

13 [a]Gen. 31:42

14 [I]That is, *The well of him that liveth* and *seeth me* [a]Gen. 24:62; 25:11 [b]Num. 13:26

15 [a]Gal. 4:22 [b]Gen. 16:11

🗝 **16:15, 16** The Ishmaelites were the descendants of Ishmael and were divided into twelve tribes (Gen. 25:16). They were also called Hagarites, Hagarenes, and Arabians (1 Chr. 5:10; Ps. 83:6; Is. 13:20). They lived in tents and traveled around in large caravans (Gen. 37:25; Is. 13:20; Jer. 25:24). They were rich in cattle, but a great portion of their wealth may have been gained by lawless activity (1 Chr. 5:21; Jer. 3:2). After harassing Israel for a time, they were overcome by Gideon (Judg. 8:10–21). During the reign of the more powerful kings they became more peacefully inclined to the Israelites; they even sent sent presents to King Solomon and King Jehoshaphat (1 Kgs. 10:15; 2 Chr. 17:11). However, these peaceful inclinations did not endure for long for some Midianite tribes fought against King Uzziah (2 Chr. 26:7).

Circumcision Is the Sign Of the Covenant

17 And when Abram was ninety years old and nine, the LORD [a]appeared[7200] to Abram, and said unto him, [b]I *am* the Almighty[7706] God;[410] [c]walk before me, and be thou [I][d]perfect.[8549]

2 And I will make my covenant[1285] between me and thee, and [a]will multiply thee exceedingly.

3 And Abram [a]fell on his face: and God[430] talked with him, saying,

4 As for me, behold, my covenant *is* with thee, and thou shalt be [a]a father[1] of [I]many nations.[1471]

🔑 5 Neither shall thy name any more be called[7121] Abram,[87] but [a]thy name shall be [I]Abraham;[85] [b]for a father of many nations have I made thee.

6 And I will make thee exceeding fruitful, and I will make [a]nations of thee, and [b]kings[4428] shall come out of thee.

7 And I will [a]establish my covenant between me and thee and thy seed[2233] after thee in their generations[1755] for an everlasting[5769] covenant, [b]to be a God unto thee, and to [c]thy seed after thee.

8 And [a]I will give unto thee, and to thy seed after thee, the land[776] [I][b]wherein thou art a stranger,[4033] all the land of Canaan, for an everlasting possession;[272] and [c]I will be their God.[430]

9 And God said unto Abraham, Thou shalt keep[8104] my covenant therefore, thou, and thy seed after thee in their generations.

10 This *is* my covenant, which ye shall keep, between me and you and thy seed after thee; [a]Every man child[2145] among you shall be circumcised.[4135]

11 And ye shall circumcise[5243] the flesh[1320] of your foreskin;[6190] and it shall be [a]a token[226] of the covenant betwixt me and you.

12 And [I]he that is eight days[3117] old [a]shall be circumcised[4135] among you, every man child in your generations, he that is born in the house,[1004] or bought with money of any stranger,[1121,5236] which *is* not of thy seed.

13 He that is born in thy house, and he that is bought with thy money, must needs be circumcised: and my covenant shall be in your flesh for an everlasting covenant.

14 And the uncircumcised[6189] man child whose flesh of his foreskin is not circumcised, that soul[5315] [a]shall be cut off[3772] from his people;[5971] he hath broken[6565] my covenant.

15 And God said unto Abraham, As for Sarai[8297] thy wife, thou shalt not call[7121] her name Sarai, but [I]Sarah[8283] *shall* her name *be.*

16 And I will bless[1288] her, [a]and give thee a son[1121] also of her: yea, I will bless her, and [I]she shall be *a mother* [b]of nations; kings of people shall be of her.

17 Then Abraham fell upon his face, [a]and laughed,[6711] and said in his heart,[3820] Shall *a child* be born unto him that is an hundred years old? and shall Sarah, that is ninety years old, bear?

18 And Abraham said unto God, O that Ishmael might live[2421] before thee!

🔑 19 And God said, [a]Sarah thy wife shall bear thee a son indeed; and thou shalt call[7121] his name Isaac:[3327] and I will establish[6965] my covenant with him for an everlasting covenant, *and* with his seed after him.

20 And as for Ishmael, I have heard[8085] thee: Behold, I have blessed him, and will make him fruitful, and [a]will multiply him exceedingly; [b]twelve princes[5387] shall he beget, [c]and I will make him a great nation.[1471]

21 But my covenant will I establish with Isaac, [a]which Sarah shall bear unto thee at this set time[4150] in the next year.

1 IOr, *upright,* or, *sincere* [c]Gen. 12:1 [d]Gen. 28:3; 35:11; Ex. 6:3; Deut. 10:17 [e]Gen. 5:22; 48:15; 1Kgs. 2:4; 8:25; 2Kgs. 20:3 [f]Gen. 6:9; Deut. 18:13; Job 1:1; Matt. 5:48
2 [a]Gen. 12:2; 13:16; 22:17
3 [a]Gen. 17:17
4 IHebr. *multitude of nations* [a]Rom. 4:11, 12, 16; Gal. 3:29
5 IThat is, *Father of a great multitude* [a]Neh. 9:7 [b]Rom. 4:17
6 [a]Gen. 35:11 [b]Gen. 17:16; 35:11; Matt. 1:6
7 [a]Gal. 3:17 [b]Gen. 26:24; 28:13; Heb. 11:16 [c]Rom. 9:8
8 IHebr. *of thy sojournings* [a]Gen. 12:7; 13:15; Ps. 105:9, 11 [b]Gen. 23:4; 28:4 [c]Ex. 6:7; Lev. 26:12; Deut. 4:37; 14:2; 26:18; 29:13
10 [a]Acts 7:8
11 [a]Acts 7:8; Rom. 4:11
12 IHebr. *a son of eight days* [a]Lev. 12:3; Luke 2:21; John 7:22; Phil. 3:5
14 [a]Ex. 4:24
15 IThat is, *Princess*
16 IHebr. *she shall become nations* [a]Gen. 18:10 [b]Gen. 35:11; Gal. 4:31; 1Pet. 3:6
17 [a]Gen. 18:12; 21:6
19 [a]Gen. 18:10; 21:2; Gal. 4:28
20 [a]Gen. 16:10 [b]Gen. 25:12, 16 [c]Gen. 21:18
21 [a]Gen. 21:2

🔑 **17:5, 6** In Hebrew, the name Abram means "exalted father" (87), and the name Abraham means "father of a multitude" (85).

🔑 **17:19** In Hebrew, the name Isaac means "laughter" (3327). Both Abraham and Sarah laughed when they thought of the apparent impossibility of this birth (Gen. 17:17; 21:6).

22 And he left off talking with him, and God went up from Abraham.

23 And Abraham took Ishmael his son, and all that were born in his house, and all that were bought with his money, every male[2145] among the men[582] of Abraham's house; and circumcised[4135] the flesh of their foreskin in the selfsame day, as God had said unto him.

24 And Abraham *was* ninety years old and nine, when he was circumcised in the flesh of his foreskin.

25 And Ishmael his son *was* thirteen years old, when he was circumcised in the flesh of his foreskin.

26 In the selfsame day was Abraham circumcised, and Ishmael his son.

27 And [a]all the men of his house, born in the house, and bought with money of the stranger, were circumcised with him.

The Promise of a Son

18 🔑 And the LORD appeared[7200] unto him in the [a]plains of Mamre: and he sat in the tent[168] door in the heat of the day;

2 [a]And he lift up[5375] his eyes and looked,[7200] and, lo, three men[582] stood[5324] by him: [b]and when he saw *them,* he ran to meet them from the tent door, and bowed[7812] himself toward the ground,[776]

3 And said, My Lord,[136] if now I have found favour[2580] in thy sight, pass not away,[5674] I pray thee, from thy servant:[5650]

4 Let [a]a little water, I pray you,[4994] be fetched, and wash your feet, and rest yourselves under the tree:

5 And [a]I will fetch a morsel of bread, and [I][b]comfort[5582] ye your hearts;[3820] after that ye shall pass on: [c]for therefore [II]are ye come[5674] to your servant. And they said,[1696] So do, as thou hast said.

6 And Abraham hastened into the tent unto Sarah, and said, Make ready quickly[4116] three measures of fine meal, knead *it,* and make[6213] cakes upon the hearth.

7 And Abraham ran unto the herd, and fetcht a calf tender and good,[2896] and gave *it* unto a young man; and he hasted to dress[6213] it.

8 And [a]he took butter, and milk, and the calf which he had dressed, and set *it* before them; and he stood by them under the tree, and they did eat.

9 And they said unto him, Where *is* Sarah thy wife? And he said, Behold, [a]in the tent.

10 And he said, I [a]will certainly return[7725] unto thee [b]according to the time[6256] of life; and, lo, [c]Sarah thy wife shall have a son. And Sarah heard[8085] *it* in the tent door, which *was* behind him.

11 Now [a]Abraham and Sarah *were* old[2205] *and* well stricken in age;[3117] *and* it ceased to be with Sarah [b]after the manner[734] of women.

🔑 12 Therefore Sarah [a]laughed[6711] within herself, saying, [b]After I am waxed old shall I have pleasure, my [c]lord[113] being old[2204] also?

13 And the LORD said unto Abraham, Wherefore did Sarah laugh, saying, Shall I of a surety[637,552] bear a child, which am old?

14 [a]Is[6381] any thing[1697] too hard[6381] for the LORD? [b]At the time appointed[4150]

27 [a]Gen. 18:19

1 [a]Gen. 13:18; 14:13

2 [a]Heb. 13:2 [b]Gen. 19:1; 1Pet. 4:9

4 [a]Gen. 19:2; 43:24

5 [I]Hebr. *stay* [II]Hebr. *you have passed* [a]Judg. 6:18; 13:15 [b]Judg. 19:5; Ps. 104:15 [c]Gen. 19:8; 33:10

8 [a]Gen. 19:3

9 [a]Gen. 24:67

10 [a]Gen. 19:4 [b]2Kgs. 4:16 [c]Gen. 17:19, 21; 21:2; Rom. 9:9

11 [a]Gen. 17:17; Rom. 4:19; Heb. 11:11, 12, 19 [b]Gen. 31:35

12 [a]Gen. 17:17 [b]Luke 1:18 [c]1Pet. 3:6

14 [a]Jer. 32:17; Zech. 8:6; Matt. 3:9; 19:26; Luke 1:37 [b]Gen. 17:21; 19:10; 2Kgs. 4:16

🔑 **18:1–33** Did Abraham actually see and talk with God? Does this contradict John 1:18, "No man hath seen God at any time"? This theophany (appearance of God to man) in the Old Testament is believed to have been Christ. The New Testament teaches that Christ existed co-eternally with God the Father (John 1:1; 8:56–58; 10:30; 17:5; Col. 1:15–17), and it is not inconceivable that He would at times take the appearance of humanity prior to His incarnation. For verily, Jesus Christ is the personal manifestation of God to man (John 14:9).

🔑 **18:12** There are several different kinds of laughter in the Bible: (1) the laughter of incredulity (Gen. 17:17; 18:12); (2) the laughter of joyful wonder (Gen. 21:6); (3) the laughter of defiance (Job 5:22); (4) the laughter of approbation (Job 29:24); (5) hollow laughter with undertones of sorrow (Prov. 14:13); (6) the laughter of scorn (Ps. 2:4); (7) the laughter of rapturous delight (Ps. 126:2).

I will return unto thee, according to the
time of life, and Sarah shall have a son.
15 Then Sarah denied, saying, I
laughed not; for she was afraid.[3372] And
he said, Nay; but thou didst laugh.

Abraham Begs for Sodom

16 And the men rose up from thence,
and looked8259 toward Sodom: and
Abraham went with them [a]to bring them
on the way.
17 And the LORD said, [a]Shall I
hide[3680] from Abraham that thing which
I do;
18 Seeing that Abraham shall surely
become a great and mighty nation,[1471]
and all the nations of the earth[776] shall
be [a]blessed[1288] in him?
19 For I know him, [a]that he will command his children[1121] and his household[1004] after him, and they shall
keep[8104] the way[1870] of the LORD, to
do[6213] justice[6666] and judgment;[4941] that
the LORD may bring upon Abraham that
which he hath spoken[1696] of him.
20 And the LORD said, Because
[a]the cry2201 of Sodom and Gomorrah is
great, and because their sin[2403] is very
grievous;[3513]
21 [a]I will go down now, and see
whether they have done altogether according to the cry6818 of it, which is
come unto me; and if not, [b]I will know.
22 And the men turned their faces
from thence, [a]and went toward Sodom:
but Abraham [b]stood yet before the
LORD.
23 And Abraham [a]drew near, and
said, [b]Wilt[5595] thou also637 destroy[5595] the
righteous[6662] with the wicked?[7563]
24 [a]Peradventure194 there be fifty
righteous within the city: wilt thou also

16 [a]Rom. 15:24; 3John 1:6
17 [a]Ps. 25:14; Amos 3:7; John 15:15
18 [a]Gen. 12:3; 22:18; Acts 3:25; Gal. 3:8
19 [a]Deut. 4:9, 10; 6:7; Josh. 24:15; Eph. 6:4
20 [a]Gen. 4:10; 19:13; James 5:4
21 [a]Gen. 11:5; Ex. 3:8 [b]Deut. 8:2; 13:3; Josh. 22:22; Luke 16:15; 2Cor. 11:11
22 [a]Gen. 19:1 [b]Gen. 18:1
23 [a]Heb. 10:22 [b]Num. 16:22; 2Sam. 24:17
24 [a]Jer. 5:1
25 [a]Job 8:20; Isa. 3:10, 11 [b]Job 8:3; 34:17; Ps. 58:11; 94:2; Rom. 3:6
26 [a]Jer. 5:1; Ezek. 22:30
27 [a]Luke 18:1 [b]Gen. 3:19; Job 4:19; Eccl. 12:7; 1Cor. 15:47, 48; 2Cor. 5:1
32 [a]Judg. 6:39 [b]James 5:16

destroy and not spare the place for the
fifty righteous that *are* therein?
25 That be far from thee to do after
this manner,[1697] to slay the righteous
with the wicked: and [a]that the righteous
should be as the wicked, that be far from
thee: [b]Shall not the Judge[8199] of all the
earth do right?[4941]
26 And the LORD said, [a]If I find in
Sodom fifty righteous within the city, then
I will spare[5375] all the place for their sakes.
27 And Abraham answered and said,
[a]Behold now, I have taken upon me to
speak[1696] unto the Lord, which *am but*
[b]dust[6083] and ashes:
28 Peradventure there shall lack
five of the fifty righteous: wilt thou
destroy[7843] all the city for *lack of* five?
And he said, If I find there forty and
five, I will not destroy *it.*
29 And he spake unto him yet again,
and said, Peradventure there shall be
forty found there. And he said, I will not
do *it* for forty's sake.
30 And he said *unto him,* Oh[4994] let
not the Lord be angry,[2734] and I will
speak: Peradventure there shall thirty be
found there. And he said, I will not do *it,*
if I find thirty there.
31 And he said, Behold now, I have
taken upon me[2974] to speak unto the
Lord: Peradventure there shall be twenty
found there. And he said, I will not destroy *it* for twenty's sake.
32 And he said, [a]Oh let not the Lord
be angry, and I will speak yet but this
once: Peradventure ten shall be found
there. [b]And he said, I will not destroy *it*
for ten's sake.
33 And the LORD went his way, as
soon as he had left communing[1696] with
Abraham: and Abraham returned unto
his place.

18:16–33 Abraham's intercession for Sodom, and in reality for Lot, was based on the principle in verse twenty-five, "Shall not the Judge of all the earth do right?" He succeeded in postponing the judgment for the sake of a few righteous persons: 50, 45, 40, 30, 20, and finally only 10. But Lot had been an even poorer missionary than Abraham supposed, failing even to witness to his own family (Gen. 19:14, 26, 30–36); the ten righteous persons could not be found. Yet the Lord spared Lot and his family on Abraham's behalf (see note on Gen. 19:26).

God Destroys Sodom and Gomorrah

19 And there [a]came two angels[4397] to Sodom at even; and Lot sat in the gate of Sodom: and [b]Lot seeing *them* rose up to meet them; and he bowed[7812] himself with his face[639] toward the ground;[776]

2 And he said, Behold now, my lords,[113] [a]turn in, I pray you, into your servant's[5650] house,[1004] and tarry all night, and [b]wash your feet, and ye shall rise up early, and go on your ways.[1870] And they said, [c]Nay; but we will abide 3885 in the street all night.

3 And he pressed 6484 upon them greatly; and they turned in unto him, and entered into his house; [a]and he made them a feast,[4960] and did bake unleavened bread,[4682] and they did eat.

4 But before they lay down, the men[582] of the city, *even* the men of Sodom, compassed the house round, both old[2205] and young, all the people[5971] from every quarter:

5 [a]And they called[7121] unto Lot, and said unto him, Where *are* the men which came in to thee this night? [b]bring them out unto us, that we [c]may know them.

6 And [a]Lot went out at the door unto them, and shut the door after him,

7 And said, I pray you, brethren,[251] do not so wickedly.[7489]

8 [a]Behold now, I have two daughters which have not known[3045] man;[376] let me, I pray you, bring them out unto you, and do[6213] ye to them as *is* good[2896] in your eyes: only unto these men do nothing; [b]for therefore came they under the shadow of my roof.

9 And they said, Stand back. And they said *again,* This one *fellow* [a]came in to sojourn,[1481] [b]and he will needs be a judge: now will we deal worse[7489] with thee, than with them. And they pressed sore upon the man, *even* Lot, and came near to break[7665] the door.

10 But the men put forth their hand,[3027] and pulled Lot into the house to them, and shut to the door.

11 And they smote[5221] the men [a]that *were* at the door of the house with blindness, both small and great: so that they wearied[3811] themselves to find the door.

12 And the men said unto Lot, Hast thou here any besides? son in law, and thy sons, and thy daughters, and whatsoever thou hast in the city, [a]bring *them* out of this place:

13 For we will destroy[7843] this place, because the [a]cry of them is waxen great before the face of the LORD; and [b]the LORD hath sent us to destroy it.

14 And Lot went out, and spake unto his sons in law, [a]which married his daughters, and said, [b]Up, get you out of this place; for the LORD will destroy this city. [c]But he seemed as one that mocked 6711 unto his sons in law.

15 And when the morning arose, then the angels hastened[213] Lot, saying, [a]Arise, take thy wife, and thy two daughters, which [I]are here; lest thou be consumed[5595] in the [II]iniquity[5771] of the city.

16 And while he lingered,[4102] the men laid hold[2388] upon his hand, and upon the hand of his wife, and upon the hand of his two daughters; [a]the LORD being merciful[2551] unto him: [b]and they brought him forth, and set him without the city.

17 And it came to pass, when they had brought them forth abroad, that he said, [a]Escape[4422] for thy life;[5315] [b]look not behind thee, neither stay thou in all the plain; escape to the mountain, lest thou be consumed.

18 And Lot said unto them, Oh, [a]not so, my Lord:[113]

19 Behold now, thy servant hath found grace[2580] in thy sight, and thou hast magnified thy mercy,[2617] which thou hast shewed[6213] unto me in saving[2421] my life; and I cannot escape to the mountain, lest some evil[7451] take me, and I die:[4191]

20 Behold now, this city *is* near to flee unto, and it *is* a little one: Oh, let me escape thither, (*is* it not a little one?) and my soul[5315] shall live.[2421]

21 And he said unto him, See, [a]I have accepted[5375] [I]thee concerning this

1 [a]Gen. 18:22 [b]Gen. 18:1
2 [a]Heb. 13:2 [b]Gen. 18:4 [c]Luke 24:28
3 [a]Gen. 18:8
5 [a]Isa. 3:9 [b]Judg. 19:22 [c]Gen. 4:1; Rom. 1:24, 27; Jude 7
6 [a]Judg. 19:23
8 [a]Judg. 19:24 [b]Gen. 18:5
9 [a]2Pet. 2:7, 8 [b]Ex. 2:14
11 [a]2Kgs. 6:18; Acts 13:11
12 [a]Gen. 7:1; 2Pet. 2:7, 9
13 [a]Gen. 18:20 [b]1Chr. 21:15
14 [a]Matt. 1:18 [b]Num. 16:21, 45 [c]Ex. 9:21; Luke 17:28; 24:11
15 [I]Hebr. *are found* [II]Or, *punishment* [a]Num. 16:24, 26; Rev. 18:4
16 [a]Luke 18:13; Rom. 9:15, 16 [b]Ps. 34:22
17 [a]1Kgs. 19:3; Gen. 19:26 [b]Matt. 24:16, 17, 18; Luke 9:62; Phil. 3:13, 14
18 [a]Acts 10:14
21 [I]Hebr. *thy face* [a]Job 42:8, 9; Ps. 145:19

thing[1697] also, that I will not overthrow[2015] this city, for the which thou hast spoken.

22 Haste thee, escape thither; for [a]I cannot do any thing[1697] till thou be come thither. Therefore [b]the name of the city was called[7121] [I][c]Zoar.

23 The sun was [I]risen upon the earth[776] when Lot entered into Zoar.

24 Then [a]the LORD rained upon Sodom and upon Gomorrah brimstone[1614] and fire from the LORD out of heaven;[8064]

25 And he overthrew[2015] those cities, and all the plain, and all the inhabitants of the cities, and [a]that which grew upon the ground.[127]

🗝 26 But his wife looked back[5027] from behind him, and she became [a]a pillar of salt.

27 And Abraham gat up early in the morning to the place where [a]he stood before the LORD:

28 And he looked toward Sodom and Gomorrah, and toward all the land[776] of the plain, and beheld, and, lo, [a]the smoke of the country[776] went up as the smoke of a furnace.

29 And it came to pass, when God[430] destroyed the cities of the plain, that God [a]remembered[2142] Abraham, and sent Lot out of the midst of the overthrow, when he overthrew the cities in the which Lot dwelt.

Incest

30 And Lot went up out of Zoar, and [a]dwelt in the mountain, and his two daughters with him; for he feared[3372] to dwell in Zoar: and he dwelt in a cave, he and his two daughters.

31 And the firstborn said unto the younger, Our father *is* old,[2204] and *there is* not a man[376] in the earth [a]to come in unto us after the manner[1870] of all the earth:

32 Come, let us make our father drink wine,[3196] and we will lie with him, that we [a]may preserve[2421] seed[2233] of our father.

33 And they made their father drink wine that night: and the firstborn went in, and lay[7901] with her father; and he perceived[3045] not when she lay down, nor when she arose.

34 And it came to pass on the morrow, that the firstborn said unto the younger, Behold, I lay yesternight with my father: let us make him drink[8248] wine this night also; and go thou in, *and* lie with him, that we may preserve seed of our father.

35 And they made their father drink wine that night also: and the younger arose, and lay with him; and he perceived not when she lay down, nor when she arose.

36 Thus were both the daughters of Lot with child by their father.

🗝 37 And the firstborn bare a son, and called his name Moab:[4124] [a]the same *is*

22 [I]That is, *Little* [a]Gen. 32:25, 26; Ex. 32:10; Deut. 9:14; Mark 6:5 [b]Gen. 13:10; 14:2 [c]Gen. 19:20

23 [I]Hebr. *gone forth*

24 [a]Deut. 29:23; Isa. 13:19; Jer. 20:16; 50:40; Ezek. 16:49, 50; Hos. 11:8; Amos 4:11; Zeph. 2:9; Luke 17:29; 2Pet. 2:6; Jude 1:7

25 [a]Gen. 14:3; Ps. 107:34

26 [a]Luke 17:32

27 [a]Gen. 18:22

28 [a]Rev. 18:9

29 [a]Gen. 8:1; 18:23

30 [a]Gen. 19:17, 19

31 [a]Gen. 16:2, 4; 38:8, 9; Deut. 25:5

32 [a]Mark 12:19

37 [a]Deut. 2:9

🗝 **19:26** There was for centuries a peculiar formation of crumbling, crystalline rock that was associated by tradition with the story of Lot's wife. Josephus (Antiquities I.11.4) declared that this pillar still remained in his day and that he had seen it. Clement of Rome, Irenaeus, and Benjamin of Tudela also wrote of this strange formation as visible in their day, but later writers stated that it had ceased to exist. Perhaps the existence of this pillar was used as an object lesson for the admonition of Christ to His disciples (Luke 17:32).

🗝 **19:37** The Moabites were the descendants of Lot and were neighbors of the Amorites on the opposite side of the Arnon River (Num. 21:13). They possessed many great cities (Num. 21:28–30; 23:7; Is. 15:1), and were prosperous, arrogant, and idolatrous. They were mighty men of war (Is. 16:6). The Amorites deprived them of a large part of their territory (Num. 21:26). The Moabites refused to let Israel pass through their country and were so greatly impressed and alarmed by the multitude of the Israelite army that, along with Midian, they sent Balaam to curse it (Num. 22—24). Subsequently, Israel was enticed into idolatry and even intermarried with them. They were always hostile to Israel until King Saul subdued them (1 Sam. 14:47). Later they became tributary to David and succeeding Jewish kings (2 Sam. 8:2, 12; 2 Kgs. 3:4), but they finally joined Babylon against Judah (2 Kgs. 24:2). On several occasions, God pronounced judgments against Moab (Is. 15:1—16:14; Jer. 48:1–47; Amos 2:1–3).

the father of the Moabites unto this
day.[3117]
🔑 38 And the younger, she also bare a
son, and called his name Ben–ammi:[1151]
[a]the same *is* the father of the children of
Ammon unto this day.

Abraham and Abimelech

20 And Abraham journeyed from
[a]thence toward the south coun-
try,[776] and dwelled between [b]Kadesh and
Shur, and [c]sojourned[1481] in Gerar.
🔑 2 And Abraham said of Sarah his
wife,[802] [a]She *is* my sister:[269] and
Abimelech king of Gerar sent, and [b]took
Sarah.
3 But [a]God[430] came to Abimelech [b]in
a dream by night, and said to him,
[c]Behold, thou *art but* a dead man, for the
woman[802] which thou hast taken; for she
is [I]a man's wife.[1166,1167]
4 But Abimelech had not come near
her: and he said, Lord,[136] [a]wilt thou
slay[2026] also a righteous[6662] nation?[1471]
5 Said[559] he not unto me, She *is* my
sister? and she, even she herself said, He
is my brother:[251] [a]in the [I]integrity[8537] of
my heart[3824] and innocency[5356] of my
hands[3709] have I done[6213] this.
6 And God said unto him in a dream,
Yea, I know[3045] that thou didst this in the
integrity of thy heart; for [a]I also withheld
thee from sinning[2398] [b]against me: therefore suffered I thee not to touch[5060] her.

38 [a]Deut. 2:19

1 [a]Gen. 18:1 [b]Gen. 16:7, 14 [c]Gen. 26:6

2 [a]Gen. 12:13; 26:7 [b]Gen. 12:15

3 [I]Hebr. *married to a husband* [a]Ps. 105:14 [b]Job 33:15 [c]Gen. 20:7

4 [a]Gen. 18:23; 20:18

5 [I]Or, *simplicity, or, sincerity* [a]2Kgs. 20:3; 2Cor. 1:12

6 [a]Gen. 31:7; 35:5; Ex. 34:24; 1Sam. 25:26, 34 [b]Gen. 39:9; Lev. 6:2; Ps. 51:4

7 [a]1Sam. 7:5; 2Kgs. 5:11; Job 42:8; James 5:14, 15; 1John 5:16 [b]Gen. 2:17 [c]Num. 16:32, 33

9 [a]Gen. 26:10; Ex. 32:21; Josh. 7:25 [b]Gen. 34:7

11 [a]Gen. 42:18; Ps. 36:1; Prov. 16:6 [b]Gen. 12:12; 26:7

12 [a]Gen. 11:29

13 [a]Gen. 12:1, 9, 11; Heb. 11:8 [b]Gen. 12:13

7 Now therefore restore[7725] the
man[376] *his* wife; [a]for he *is* a prophet,[5030]
and he shall pray[6419] for thee, and thou
shalt live:[2421] and if thou restore *her* not,
[b]know thou that thou shalt surely die,[4191]
thou, [c]and all that *are* thine.
8 Therefore Abimelech rose early in
the morning, and called[7121] all his
servants,[5650] and told all these things in
their ears:[241] and the men[582] were sore
afraid.[3372]
9 Then Abimelech called Abraham,
and said unto him, What hast thou done
unto us? and what have I offended[2398]
thee, [a]that thou hast brought on me and
on my kingdom[4467] a great sin?[2401] thou
hast done deeds[4639] unto me [b]that ought
not to be done.
10 And Abimelech said unto
Abraham, What sawest[7200] thou, that
thou hast done this thing?
11 And Abraham said, Because I
thought,[559] Surely [a]the fear[3374] of God[430]
is not in this place; and [b]they will slay[2026]
me for my wife's sake.
🔑 12 And yet indeed [a]*she is* my sister;
she *is* the daughter of my father, but not
the daughter of my mother; and she became my wife.
13 And it came to pass, when [a]God
caused me to wander[8582] from my father's
house,[1004] that I said unto her, This *is* thy
kindness[2617] which thou shalt shew unto
me; at every place whither we shall come,
[b]say of me, He *is* my brother.

🔑 **19:38** The Ammonites were the children of Lot (Deut. 2:19). They were a cruel, covetous, proud, vindictive, and idolatrous nation (see Judg. 10:6; Ezek. 25:3, 6; Amos 1:13; Zeph. 2:10). Their chief city was Rabbah (2 Sam. 12:26, 27), from which they were governed by hereditary kings (Jer. 27:3). They had various encounters with Israel. With the Philistines they oppressed Israel for eighteen years (Judg. 10:7–9). King Saul succeeded against them (1 Sam. 11:11). David and Joab also overcame them (2 Sam. 10:7–14), but Solomon intermarried with their women and introduced their idols into Israel (1 Kgs. 11:1–5).

🔑 **20:2–18** How does this section relate to Genesis 12:11–20? There were two American Presidents named Roosevelt who were in office within a few years of one another. Hence, similar events are not necessarily identical. The cases of Pharaoh and Abimelech were distinctly different but similar circumstances. In the first instance, Pharaoh was quite taken with the beautiful sixty-five-year-old princess. Abimelech merely wanted a political alliance with a rich, nomadic chieftain. The text does not say that this ninety-year-old woman was beautiful to Abimelech. The case of Isaac in Genesis 26:6–11 is only similar in the use of Abimelech, a mere title of the kings of Gerar.

🔑 **20:12** Abraham speaks of Sarah as his half-sister. The common Jewish tradition referred to by Josephus (Antiquities I.6.6) and also by Jerome is that Sarah was identical with Iscah (see Gen. 11:29), daughter of Haran and sister of Lot, who is called Abraham's "brother" (Gen. 13:8).

14 And Abimelech [a]took sheep, and oxen, and menservants,[5650] and womenservants, and gave *them* unto Abraham, and restored him Sarah his wife.

15 And Abimelech said, Behold, [a]my land[776] *is* before thee: dwell [I]where it pleaseth[2896] thee.

16 And unto Sarah he said, Behold, I have given [a]thy brother a thousand *pieces* of silver: [b]behold, he *is* to thee [c]a covering3682 of the eyes, unto all that *are* with thee, and with all *other*: thus she was reproved.

17 So Abraham [a]prayed unto God: and God healed Abimelech, and his wife, and his maidservants; and they bare *children.*

18 For the LORD [a]had fast closed up6113 all the wombs of the house of Abimelech, because of Sarah Abraham's wife.

Isaac Is Born

21 And the LORD [a]visited[6485] Sarah as he had said, and the LORD did6213 unto Sarah [b]as he had spoken.[1696]

2 For Sarah [a]conceived, and bare Abraham a son in his old age,[2208] [b]at the set time[4150] of which God[430] had spoken to him.

3 And Abraham called the name of his son that was born unto him, whom Sarah bare to him, [a]Isaac.

4 And Abraham [a]circumcised[4135] his son Isaac being eight days old, [b]as God had commanded[6680] him.

5 And [a]Abraham was an hundred years old, when his son Isaac[3327] was born unto him.

6 And Sarah said, [a]God hath made me to laugh,6711 *so that* all that hear[8085] [b]will laugh with me.

7 And she said, Who would have said unto Abraham, that Sarah should have given children[1121] suck? [a]for I have born *him* a son in his old age.

Hagar and Ishmael Are Sent Away

8 And the child grew, and was weaned: and Abraham made a great feast[4960] the *same* day that Isaac was weaned.

9 And Sarah saw the son of Hagar [a]the Egyptian, [b]which she had born unto Abraham, [c]mocking.6711

10 Wherefore she said unto Abraham, [a]Cast out this bondwoman519 and her son: for the son of this bondwoman shall not be heir[3423] with my son, *even* with Isaac.[3327]

11 And the thing[1697] was very grievous[7489] in Abraham's sight [a]because of his son.

12 And God said unto Abraham, Let it not be grievous in thy sight because of the lad, and because of thy bondwoman; in all that Sarah hath said unto thee, hearken[8085] unto her voice; for [a]in Isaac shall[7121] thy seed[2233] be called.[7121]

13 And also of the son of the bondwoman will I make [a]a nation,[1471] because he *is* thy seed.

14 And Abraham rose up early in the morning, and took bread, and a bottle of water, and gave *it* unto Hagar, putting *it* on her shoulder, and the child, and [a]sent her away: and she departed, and wandered in the wilderness of Beer–sheba.

15 And the water was spent in the bottle, and she cast the child3206 under one of the shrubs.[7880]

16 And she went, and sat her down over against *him* a good way off, as it were a bowshot: for she said, Let me not see the death[4194] of the child. And she sat over against *him,* and lift up[5375] her voice, and wept.

17 And [a]God heard[8085] the voice of the lad; and the angel of God called to Hagar out of heaven,8064 and said unto her, What aileth thee, Hagar? fear[3372] not; for God hath heard the voice of the lad5288 where he *is.*

18 Arise, lift up[5375] the lad, and hold[2388] him in thine hand; for [a]I will make[7760] him a great nation.

19 And [a]God opened her eyes, and she saw a well of water; and she went, and filled the bottle with water, and gave the lad drink.

20 And God [a]was with the lad; and

14 [a]Gen. 12:16
15 [I]Hebr. *as is good in thine eyes* [a]Gen. 13:9
16 [a]Gen. 20:5 [b]Gen. 26:11 [c]Gen. 24:65
17 [a]Job 42:9, 10
18 [a]Gen. 12:17
1 [a]1Sam. 2:21 [b]Gen. 17:19; 18:10, 14; Gal. 4:23, 28
2 [a]Acts 7:8; Gal. 4:22; Heb. 11:11 [b]Gen. 17:21
3 [a]Gen. 17:19
4 [a]Acts 7:8 [b]Gen. 17:10, 12
5 [a]Gen. 17:1, 17
6 [a]Ps. 126:2; Isa. 54:1; Gal. 4:27 [b]Luke 1:58
7 [a]Gen. 18:11, 12
9 [a]Gen. 16:1 [b]Gen. 16:15 [c]Gal. 4:29
10 [a]Gal. 4:30; Gen. 25:6; 36:6, 7
11 [a]Gen. 17:18
12 [a]Rom. 9:7, 8; Heb. 11:18
13 [a]Gen. 16:20; 17:2; 21:18
14 [a]John 8:35
17 [a]Ex. 3:7
18 [a]Gen. 21:13
19 [a]Num. 22:31; 2Kgs. 6:17, 18, 20; Luke 24:16, 31
20 [a]Gen. 28:15; 39:2, 3, 21

he grew, and dwelt in the wilderness, [b]and became an archer.

21 And he dwelt in the wilderness of Paran: and his mother[517] [a]took him a wife out of the land[776] of Egypt.

Abraham Makes an Agreement With Abimelech

22 And it came to pass at that time,[6256] that [a]Abimelech and Phichol the chief captain[8269] of his host[6635] spake unto Abraham, saying, [b]God *is* with thee in all that thou doest:

23 Now therefore [a]swear[7650] unto me here by God [I]that thou wilt not deal falsely[8266] with me, nor with my son, nor with my son's son: *but* according to the kindness[2617] that I have done unto thee, thou shalt do unto me, and to the land wherein thou hast sojourned.[1481]

24 And Abraham said, I will swear.

25 And Abraham reproved[3198] Abimelech because of a well of water, which Abimelech's servants[5650] [a]had violently taken away.[1497]

26 And Abimelech said, I wot[3045] not who hath done this thing: neither didst thou tell[5046] me, neither yet heard I *of it,* but to day.

27 And Abraham took sheep and oxen, and gave them unto Abimelech; and both of them [a]made[3772] a covenant.[1285]

28 And Abraham set seven ewe lambs[3525] of the flock by themselves.

29 And Abimelech said unto Abraham, [a]What *mean* these seven ewe lambs which thou hast set[5324] by themselves?

30 And he said, For *these* seven ewe lambs shalt thou take of my hand, that [a]they may be a witness[5713] unto me, that I have digged this well.[875]

31 Wherefore he [a]called[7121] that place [I]Beer–sheba;[884] because there they sware[7650] both of them.

32 Thus they made a covenant at Beer–sheba: then Abimelech rose up, and Phichol the chief captain of his host, and they returned into the land of the Philistines.

33 And *Abraham* planted a [I]grove[815] in Beer–sheba, and [a]called there on the name of the LORD,[3068] the [b]everlasting[5769] God.[410]

34 And Abraham sojourned[1481] in the Philistines' land many days.

God Tests Abraham

22 🔑 And it came to pass after these things, that [a]God[430] did tempt[5254] Abraham, and said unto him, Abraham: and he said, [I]Behold, *here* I *am.*

2 And he said, Take now thy son, [a]thine only[3173] *son* Isaac, whom thou lovest,[157] and get thee [b]into the land[776] of Moriah; and offer[5927] him there for a burnt offering[5930] upon one of the mountains which I will tell thee of.

3 And Abraham rose up early in the morning, and saddled his ass, and took two of his young men with him, and Isaac his son, and clave the wood for the burnt offering, and rose up, and went unto the place of which God had told[559] him.

4 Then on the third day Abraham lifted up his eyes, and saw the place afar off.

5 And Abraham said unto his young men, Abide ye here with the ass; and I and the lad will go yonder and worship,[7812] and come again to you.

6 And Abraham took the wood of the burnt offering, and [a]laid[7760] *it* upon Isaac his son; and he took the fire in his

20 [b]Gen. 16:12
21 [a]Gen. 24:4
22 [a]Gen. 20:2; 26:26 [b]Gen. 26:28
23 [I]Hebr. *if thou shalt lie unto me* [a]Josh. 2:12; 1Sam. 24:21
25 [a]Gen. 26:15, 18, 20-22
27 [a]Gen. 26:31
29 [a]Gen. 33:8
30 [a]Gen. 31:48, 52
31 [I]That is, *The well of the oath* [a]Gen. 26:33
33 [I]Or, *tree* [a]Gen. 4:26 [b]Deut. 33:27; Isa. 40:28; Rom. 16:26; 1Tim. 1:17
1 [I]Hebr. *Behold me* [a]1Cor. 10:13; Heb. 11:17; James 1:12; 1Pet. 1:7
2 [a]Heb. 11:17 [b]2Chr. 3:1
6 [a]John 19:17

🔑 **22:1** Some versions translate Genesis 22:1 as God "tempting" Abraham. The Hebrew word in question is *nissah* (5254), which means to "put to the test." See the Annotated Strong's Old Testament Dictionary for a more detailed definition. God may allow us to be tested, but He will never place inducements before us to lead us into temptation that are more than we can bear (1 Cor. 10:13). Abraham proved faithful to the test for he believed that God would bring Isaac back to life to keep His promise even if Abraham had killed him (Heb. 11:17–19).

hand, and a knife; and they went both of them together.

7 And Isaac spake unto Abraham his father, and said, My father: and he said, [I]Here *am* I, my son. And he said, Behold the fire and the wood: but where *is* the lamb for a burnt offering?

8 And Abraham said, My son, God will provide[7200] himself a lamb for a burnt offering: so they went both of them together.

9 And they came to the place which God had told him of; and Abraham built an altar[4196] there, and [a]laid the wood in order, and bound Isaac his son, and laid him on the altar upon the wood.

10 And Abraham stretched forth his hand, and took the knife to slay[7819] his son.

11 And the angel of the LORD called[7121] unto him out of heaven,[8064] and said, Abraham, Abraham: and he said, Here *am* I.

🗝 12 And he said, [a]Lay not thine hand upon the lad, neither do thou any thing unto him: for [b]now I know[3045] that thou fearest[3373] God, seeing thou hast not withheld thy son, thine only *son* from me.

13 And Abraham lifted up his eyes, and looked,[7200] and behold behind *him* a ram caught in a thicket by his horns: and Abraham went and took the ram, and offered him up for a burnt offering in the stead of his son.

14 And Abraham called the name of that place [I]Jehovah–jireh:[3070] as it is said *to* this day,[3117] In the mount of the LORD it shall be seen.[7200]

15 And the angel of the LORD called unto Abraham out of heaven the second time,

16 And said, [a]By myself have I sworn,[7650] saith the LORD, for because thou hast done[6213] this thing,[1697] and hast not withheld thy son, thine only *son:*

17 That in blessing[1288] I will bless thee, and in multiplying I will multiply thy seed[2233] [a]as the stars of the heaven,[8064] [b]and as the sand which *is* upon the [I]sea shore;[8193][3220] and [c]thy seed shall possess[3423] [d]the gate of his enemies;

18 [a]And in thy seed shall all the nations[1471] of the earth[776] be blessed; [b]because thou hast obeyed[8085] my voice.

19 So Abraham returned unto his young men, and they rose up and went together to [a]Beer–sheba; and Abraham dwelt at Beer–sheba.

Nahor's Family

20 And it came to pass[1961] after these things, that it was told[5046] Abraham, saying, Behold, [a]Milcah, she hath also born children[1121] unto thy brother Nahor;

21 [a]Huz his firstborn, and Buz his brother, and Kemuel the father [b]of Aram,

22 And Chesed, and Hazo, and Pildash, and Jidlaph, and Bethuel.

23 And [a]Bethuel begat [b]Rebekah: these eight Milcah did bear to Nahor, Abraham's brother.

24 And his concubine, whose name *was* Reumah, she bare also Tebah, and Gaham, and Thahash, and Maachah.

Sarah Dies

23 And Sarah was an hundred and seven and twenty years old:[2416] *these were* the years of the life of Sarah.

7 [I]Hebr. *Behold me*

9 [a]Heb. 11:17; James 2:21

12 [a]1Sam. 15:22; Mic. 6:7, 8 [b]Gen. 26:5; James 2:22

14 [I]That is, *The LORD will see, or, provide*

16 [a]Ps. 105:9; Luke 1:73; Heb. 6:13, 14

17 [I]Hebr. *lip* [a]Gen. 15:5; Jer. 33:22 [b]Gen. 13:16 [c]Gen. 24:60 [d]Mic. 1:9

18 [a]Gen. 12:3; 18:18; 26:4; Acts 3:25; Gal. 3:8, 9, 16, 18 [b]Gen. 22:3, 10; 26:5

19 [a]Gen. 21:31

20 [a]Gen. 11:29

21 [a]Job 1:1 [b]Job 32:2

23 [a]Gen. 24:15 [b]Rom. 9:10, *Rebecca*

🗝 **22:12** Since God is all-knowing, some question how He could say, "For now I know that you fear God." One cannot profitably discuss God's foreknowledge, because it is clearly a part of God's thoughts that are higher than man's (Is. 55:9). In one sense, this use of "know" may parallel the use suggested in the note on Genesis 4:1, God "experienced" Abraham's fear of Him. The test of Abraham's faith was a valid one, truly reflecting his absolute trust in God. Abraham was not imitating idolatrous neighbors who practiced child sacrifice (Lev. 18:21; Deut. 18:10). On the contrary, God commanded Abraham to sacrifice his son. Abraham did not have to give up his beloved son, but he was fully prepared to kill Isaac when God's angel suddenly intervened. God's provision of a substitute animal showed that He did not want human sacrifices. The only human sacrifice approved by God was that of His Son, the sinless Lamb of God (John 1:29).

🔑 2 And Sarah died in [a]Kirjath–arba;
the same *is* [b]Hebron in the land of
Canaan: and Abraham came to mourn
for Sarah, and to weep for her.
3 And Abraham stood up from before his dead, and spake unto the
sons[1121] of Heth, saying,
4 [a]I *am* a stranger[1616] and a
sojourner[8453] with you: [b]give me a
possession[272] of a buryingplace[6913] with
you, that I may bury[6912] my dead out of
my sight.
5 And the children[1121] of Heth answered Abraham, saying unto him,
6 Hear us, my lord:[113] thou *art* [I][a]a
mighty prince[5387] among us: in the choice
of our sepulchres[6913] bury thy dead; none
of us shall withhold from thee his sepulchre, but that thou mayest bury thy dead.
7 And Abraham stood up, and
bowed[7812] himself to the people[5971] of
the land, *even* to the children of Heth.
8 And he communed with them, saying, If it be your mind[5315] that I should
bury my dead out of my sight; hear me,
and intreat[6293] for me to Ephron the son
of Zohar,
9 That he may give me the cave of
Machpelah, which he hath, which *is* in
the end of his field;[7704] for [I]as much
money as it is worth he shall give it me
for a possession of a buryingplace
amongst you.
10 And Ephron dwelt among the
children of Heth: and Ephron the Hittite
answered Abraham in the [I]audience[241] of
the children of Heth, *even* of all that
[a]went in at the gate of his city, saying,
11 [a]Nay, my lord, hear me: the field
give I thee, and the cave that *is* therein, I
give it thee; in the presence of the sons
of my people give I it thee: bury thy dead.
12 And Abraham bowed down him-
self before the people of the land.

2 [a]Josh. 14:15; Judg. 1:10 [b]Gen. 13:18; 23:19

4 [a]Gen. 17:8; 1Chr. 29:15; Ps. 105:12; Heb. 11:9, 13 [b]Acts 7:5

6 [I]Hebr. *a prince of God* [a]Gen. 13:2; 14:14; 24:35

9 [I]Hebr. *full money*

10 [I]Hebr. *ears* [a]Gen. 34:20, 24; Ruth 4:4

11 [a]2Sam. 24:21-24

15 [a]Ex. 30:13; Ezek. 45:12

16 [a]Jer. 32:9

17 [a]Gen. 25:9; 49:30-32; 50:13; Acts 7:16

20 [a]Ruth 4:7-10; Jer. 32:10, 11

1 [I]Hebr. *gone into days* [a]Gen. 18:11; 21:5 [b]Gen. 13:2; 24:35; Ps. 112:3; Prov. 10:22

13 And he spake unto Ephron in the
audience of the people of the land, saying, But if thou *wilt give it,* I pray thee,
hear[8085] me: I will give thee money for
the field; take *it* of me, and I will bury
my dead there.
14 And Ephron answered Abraham,
saying unto him,
15 My lord, hearken unto me: the
land *is worth* four hundred [a]shekels of
silver; what *is* that betwixt me and thee?
bury therefore thy dead.
16 And Abraham hearkened[8085] unto
Ephron; and Abraham [a]weighed to
Ephron the silver, which he had
named[1696] in the audience of the sons of
Heth, four hundred shekels of silver,
current[2316] *money* with the merchant.
17 And [a]the field of Ephron, which
was in Machpelah, which *was* before
Mamre, the field, and the cave which *was*
therein, and all the trees that *were* in the
field, that *were* in all the borders round
about, were made sure
18 Unto Abraham for a possession
in the presence of the children of Heth,
before all that went in at the gate of his
city.
🔑 19 And after this, Abraham
buried[6912] Sarah his wife in the cave of
the field of Machpelah before Mamre:
the same *is* Hebron in the land of
Canaan.
20 And the field, and the cave that *is*
therein, [a]were made sure[6965] unto Abraham for a possession of a buryingplace
by the sons of Heth.

Isaac Marries Rebekah

24 And Abraham [a]was old,[2204] *and*
[I]well stricken in age:[3117] and the
LORD [b]had blessed[1288] Abraham in all
things.

🔑 **23:2, 3, 19** The Hittites were descendants of Canaan's son, Heth, and one of the seven Canaanite nations. They dwelt in Hebron (Deut. 7:1; 1 Kgs. 10:29). They were warlike people and made many conquests. Their land was promised to Israel and the Israelites were commanded to destroy them, but Israel did not destroy them entirely (Deut. 7:1, 2, 24; Judg. 3:5). Among their prominent leaders were Ephron, Ahimelech, and Uriah (Gen. 49:30; 1 Sam. 26:6; 2 Sam. 11:6, 21). Esau, Solomon, and many other Israelites intermarried with the Hittites.

2 And Abraham said [a]unto his eldest[2205] servant[5650] of his house, that [b]ruled[4910] over all that he had, [c]Put,[7760] I pray thee, thy hand under my thigh:[3409]

3 And I will make thee [a]swear[7650] by the LORD, the God[430] of heaven,[8064] and the God of the earth,[776] that [b]thou shalt not take a wife[802] unto my son of the daughters of the Canaanites, among whom I dwell:

4 [a]But thou shalt go [b]unto my country,[776] and to my kindred,[4138] and take a wife unto my son Isaac.

5 And the servant said unto him, Peradventure the woman[802] will not be willing to follow me unto this land: must I needs bring thy son again unto the land from whence thou camest?

6 And Abraham said unto him, Beware[8104] thou that thou bring not my son thither again.

7 The LORD God of heaven, which [a]took me from my father's house, and from the land of my kindred, and which spake unto me, and that sware[7650] unto me, saying, [b]Unto thy seed[2233] will I give this land; [c]he shall send his angel[4397] before thee, and thou shalt take a wife unto my son from thence.

8 And if the woman will not be willing to follow thee, then [a]thou shalt be clear[5352] from this my oath:[7621] only bring not my son thither again.

9 And the servant put his hand under the thigh of Abraham his master,[113] and sware to him concerning that matter.[1697]

10 And the servant took ten camels of the camels of his master, and [1a]departed; for all the goods[2898] of his master *were* in his hand: and he arose, and went to Mesopotamia, unto [b]the city of Nahor.

11 And he made his camels to kneel down[1288] without the city by a well of water at the time[6256] of the evening, *even* the time [1a]that women go out to draw *water.*

12 And he said, [a]O LORD God of my master Abraham, I pray thee, [b]send me good speed this day,[3117] and shew[6213] kindness[2617] unto my master Abraham.

2 [a]Gen. 15:2 [b]Gen. 24:10; 39:4-6 [c]Gen. 47:29; 1Chr. 29:24; Lam. 5:6

3 [a]Gen. 14:22; Deut. 6:13; Josh. 2:12 [b]Gen. 26:35; 27:46; 28:2; Ex. 34:16; Deut. 7:3

4 [a]Gen. 28:2 [b]Gen. 12:1

7 [a]Gen. 12:1 [b]Gen. 12:7; 13:15; 15:18; 17:8; Ex. 32:13; Deut. 1:8; 34:4; Acts 7:5 [c]Ex. 23:20, 23; 33:2; Heb. 1:14

8 [a]Josh. 2:17, 20

10 [1]Or, *and* [a]Gen. 24:2 [b]Gen. 27:43

11 [1]Hebr. *that women which draw water go forth* [a]Ex. 2:16; 1Sam. 9:11

12 [a]Gen. 24:27; 26:24; 28:13; 32:9; Ex. 3:6, 15 [b]Neh. 1:11; Ps. 37:5

13 [a]Gen. 24:43 [b]Gen. 29:9; Ex. 2:16

14 [a]Judg. 6:17, 37; 1Sam. 6:7; 14:10; 20:7

15 [a]Gen. 11:29; 22:23

16 [1]Hebr. *good of countenance* [a]Gen. 26:7

18 [a]1Pet. 3:8; 4:9

21 [a]Gen. 24:12, 56

22 [1]Or, *jewel for the forehead* [a]Ex. 32:2, 3; Isa. 3:19-21; Ezek. 16:11, 12; 1Pet. 3:3

24 [a]Gen. 22:23

13 Behold, [a]I stand[5324] *here* by the well of water; and [b]the daughters of the men[582] of the city come out to draw water:

14 And let it come to pass, that the damsel to whom I shall say, Let down thy pitcher, I pray thee, that I may drink; and she shall say, Drink, and I will give thy camels drink also: *let the same be* she *that* thou hast appointed[3414] for thy servant Isaac; and [a]thereby shall I know that thou hast shewed[6213] kindness unto my master.

15 And it came to pass, before he had done speaking, that, behold, Rebekah came out, who was born to Bethuel, son of [a]Milcah, the wife of Nahor, Abraham's brother, with her pitcher upon her shoulder.

16 And the damsel [a]*was* [1]very fair[2896] to look upon, a virgin,[1330] neither had any man[376] known[3045] her: and she went down to the well, and filled her pitcher, and came up.

17 And the servant ran to meet her, and said, Let me, I pray thee, drink a little water of thy pitcher.

18 [a]And she said, Drink, my lord:[113] and she hasted, and let down her pitcher upon her hand, and gave him drink.

19 And when she had done giving him drink, she said, I will draw *water* for thy camels also, until they have done drinking.

20 And she hasted, and emptied her pitcher into the trough, and ran again unto the well to draw *water,* and drew for all his camels.

21 And the man wondering at her held his peace, to wit[3045] whether [a]the LORD had made his journey[1870] prosperous or not.

22 And it came to pass, as the camels had done drinking, that the man took a golden [1a]earring of half a shekel weight, and two bracelets for her hands of ten *shekels* weight of gold;

23 And said, Whose daughter *art* thou? tell[5046] me, I pray thee: is there room *in* thy father's house for us to lodge in?

24 And she said unto him, [a]I *am* the

daughter of Bethuel the son of Milcah,
which she bare unto Nahor.
25 She said moreover unto him, We
have both straw and provender4554
enough, and room to lodge in.
26 And the man [a]bowed down his
head, and worshipped[7812] the LORD.
27 And he said, [a]Blessed[1288] *be* the
LORD God of my master Abraham, who
hath not left destitute[5800] my master of
[b]his mercy[2617] and his truth:[571] I *being* in
the way, the LORD [c]led[5148] me to the
house of my master's brethren.
28 And the damsel ran, and told[5046]
them of her mother's house these
things.[1697]
29 And Rebekah had a brother, and
his name *was* Laban: and [a]Laban ran out
unto the man, unto the well.
30 And it came to pass, when he saw
the earring and bracelets upon his sister's
hands, and when he heard the words[1697]
of Rebekah his sister, saying, Thus
spake[1696] the man unto me; that he came
unto the man; and, behold, he stood by
the camels at the well.
31 And he said, Come in, [a]thou
blessed of the LORD; wherefore standest
thou without? for I have prepared the
house, and room for the camels.
32 And the man came into the house:
and he ungirded6605 his camels, and [a]gave
straw and provender for the camels, and
water to wash his feet, and the men's feet
that *were* with him.
33 And there was set[7760] *meat* before
him to eat: but he said, [a]I will not eat,
until I have told[1696] mine errand.[1697] And
he said, Speak on.
34 And he said, I *am* Abraham's servant.
35 And the LORD [a]hath blessed my
master greatly; and he is become great:
and he hath given him flocks, and herds,
and silver, and gold, and menservants,[5650] and maidservants, and camels,
and asses.
36 And Sarah my master's wife [a]bare
a son to my master when she was
old:[2209] and [b]unto him hath he given all
that he hath.
37 And my master [a]made me swear,
saying, Thou shalt not take a wife to my
son of the daughters of the Canaanites,
in whose land I dwell:
38 [a]But thou shalt go unto my father's house, and to my kindred,[4940] and
take a wife unto my son.
39 [a]And I said unto my master,
Peradventure the woman will not follow
me.
40 [a]And he said unto me, The LORD,
[b]before whom I walk, will send his angel
with thee, and prosper thy way; and thou
shalt take a wife for my son of my kindred, and of my father's house:
41 [a]Then shalt thou be clear[5352] from
this my oath,[423] when thou comest to my
kindred; and if they give not thee *one,*
thou shalt be clear from my oath.
42 And I came this day unto the
well, and said, [a]O LORD God of my master Abraham, if now thou do prosper my
way which I go:
43 [a]Behold, I stand by the well of
water; and it shall come to pass, that
when the virgin[5959] cometh forth to draw
water, and I say to her, Give me, I pray
thee, a little water of thy pitcher to drink;
44 And she say to me, Both drink
thou, and I will also draw for thy camels:
let the same *be* the woman whom the
LORD hath appointed out[3198] for my master's son.
45 [a]And before I had done [b]speaking
in mine heart,[3820] behold, Rebekah came
forth with her pitcher on her shoulder;
and she went down unto the well, and
drew *water:* and I said unto her, Let me
drink, I pray thee.
46 And she made haste, and let
down her pitcher from her *shoulder,* and
said, Drink, and I will give thy camels
drink also: so I drank, and she made the
camels drink also.
47 And I asked[7592] her, and said,
Whose daughter *art* thou? And she said,
The daughter of Bethuel, Nahor's son,
whom Milcah bare unto him: and I [a]put
the earring upon her face,[639] and the
bracelets upon her hands.
48 [a]And I bowed down my head, and
worshipped the LORD, and blessed[1288] the
LORD God of my master Abraham, which

26 [a]Gen. 24:52; Ex. 4:31
27 [a]Ex. 18:10; Ruth 4:14; 1Sam. 25:32, 39; 2Sam. 18:28; Luke 1:68 [b]Gen. 32:20; Ps. 98:3 [c]Gen. 24:48
29 [a]Gen. 29:5
31 [a]Gen. 26:29; Judg. 17:2; Ruth 3:10; Ps. 115:15
32 [a]Gen. 43:24; Judg. 19:21
33 [a]Job 23:12; John 4:34; Eph. 6:5-7
35 [a]Gen. 13:2; 24:1
36 [a]Gen. 21:2 [b]Gen. 21:10; 25:5
37 [a]Gen. 24:3
38 [a]Gen. 24:4
39 [a]Gen. 24:5
40 [a]Gen. 24:7 [b]Gen. 17:1
41 [a]Gen. 24:8
42 [a]Gen. 24:12
43 [a]Gen. 24:13
45 [a]Gen. 24:15-28 [b]1Sam. 1:13
47 [a]Ezek. 16:11, 12
48 [a]Gen. 24:26

had led[5148] me in the right[571] way[1870] to take [b]my master's brother's daughter unto his son.

49 And now if ye will [a]deal[6213] kindly[2617] and truly[571] with my master, tell me: and if not, tell me; that I may turn to the right hand, or to the left.

50 Then Laban and Bethuel answered and said, [a]The thing[1697] proceedeth from the LORD: we cannot [b]speak unto thee bad[7451] or good.[2896]

51 Behold, Rebekah [a]*is* before thee, take *her,* and go, and let her be thy master's son's wife, as the LORD hath spoken.[1696]

52 And it came to pass, that, when Abraham's servant heard their words,[1697] he [a]worshipped the LORD, *bowing himself* to the earth.[776]

53 And the servant brought forth [1][a]jewels of silver, and jewels of gold, and raiment, and gave *them* to Rebekah: he gave also to her brother and to her mother [b]precious things.

54 And they did eat and drink, he and the men that *were* with him, and tarried all night; and they rose up in the morning, and he said, [a]Send me away unto my master.

55 And her brother and her mother said, Let the damsel abide with us [1][a]*a few* days, at the least ten; after that she shall go.

56 And he said unto them, Hinder me not, seeing the LORD hath prospered my way; send me away that I may go to my master.

57 And they said, We will call[7121] the damsel, and enquire[7592] at her mouth.

58 And they called Rebekah, and said unto her, Wilt thou go with this man? And she said, I will go.

59 And they sent away Rebekah their sister, and [a]her nurse, and Abraham's servant, and his men.

60 And they blessed[1288] Rebekah, and said unto her, Thou *art* our sister,[269] be thou [a]*the mother* of thousands[505] of millions, and [b]let thy seed possess the gate of those which hate[8130] them.

61 And Rebekah arose, and her damsels, and they rode upon the camels, and followed the man: and the servant took Rebekah, and went his way.

62 And Isaac came from the way of the [a]well Lahai–roi; for he dwelt in the south country.[776]

63 And Isaac went out [1][a]to meditate[7742] in the field[7704] at the eventide:[6256] and he lifted up his eyes, and saw, and, behold, the camels *were* coming.

64 And Rebekah lifted up her eyes, and when she saw Isaac, [a]she lighted off[5307][4480] the camel.

65 For she *had* said unto the servant, What man *is* this that walketh in the field to meet us? And the servant *had* said, It *is* my master: therefore she took a vail, and covered[3680] herself.

66 And the servant told[5608] Isaac all things[1697] that he had done.

67 And Isaac brought her into his mother[517] Sarah's tent,[168] and took Rebekah, and she became his wife; and he loved[157] her: and Isaac [a]was comforted[5162] after his mother's *death.*

Abraham's Other Family

25 ⊶ Then again Abraham took a wife,[802] and her name *was* Keturah.

2 And [a]she bare him Zimran, and Jokshan, and Medan, and Midian, and Ishbak, and Shuah.

3 And Jokshan begat Sheba, and Dedan. And the sons of Dedan were Asshurim, and Letushim, and Leummim.

4 And the sons of Midian; Ephah, and Epher, and Hanoch, and Abidah, and Eldaah. All these *were* the children of Keturah.

48 [b]Gen. 22:23
49 [a]Gen. 47:29; Josh. 2:14
50 [a]Ps. 118:23; Matt. 21:42; Mark 12:11 [b]Gen. 31:24
51 [a]Gen. 20:15
52 [a]Gen. 24:26
53 [1]Hebr. *vessels* [a]Ex. 3:22; 11:2; 12:35 [b]2Chr. 21:3; Ezra 1:6
54 [a]Gen. 24:56, 59
55 [1]Or, *a full year, or, ten months* [a]Judg. 14:8
59 [a]Gen. 35:8
60 [a]Gen. 17:16 [b]Gen. 22:17
62 [a]Gen. 16:14; 25:11
63 [1]Or, *to pray* [a]Josh. 1:8; Ps. 1:2; 77:12; 119:15; 143:5
64 [a]Josh. 15:18
67 [a]Gen. 38:12
2 [a]1Chr. 1:32

⊶ **25:1, 2** How can this fact be reconciled with Genesis 17:17 and Hebrews 11:12? These verses speak of Abraham's condition before the miracle of God that allowed the birth of Isaac. The great age of Abraham at death suggests that the miraculous quickening of his virile powers, by which he was enabled to become the father of Isaac, continued for some years.

5 And [a]Abraham gave all that he had unto Isaac.

6 But unto the sons of the concubines, which Abraham had, Abraham gave gifts, and [a]sent them away from Isaac his son, while he yet lived,[2416] eastward, unto [b]the east country.[776]

Abraham Dies

7 And these *are* the days of the years of Abraham's life which he lived,[2425] an hundred threescore and fifteen years.

8 Then Abraham gave up the ghost,[1478] and [a]died[4191] in a good[2896] old age,[7872] an old man,[2205] and full *of years;* and [b]was gathered to his people.[5971]

9 And [a]his sons Isaac and Ishmael buried[6912] him in the cave of Machpelah, in the field of Ephron the son of Zohar the Hittite, which *is* before Mamre;

10 [a]The field[7704] which Abraham purchased of the sons of Heth: [b]there was Abraham buried,[6912] and Sarah his wife.

11 And it came to pass after the death[4194] of Abraham, that God[430] blessed[1288] his son Isaac; and Isaac dwelt by the [a]well Lahai–roi.

Ishmael's Family

12 Now these *are* the generations[8435] of Ishmael, Abraham's son, [a]whom Hagar the Egyptian, Sarah's handmaid, bare unto Abraham:

13 And [a]these *are* the names of the sons of Ishmael, by their names, according to their generations: the firstborn of Ishmael, Nebajoth; and Kedar, and Adbeel, and Mibsam,

14 And Mishma, and Dumah, and Massa,

15 [I][a]Hadar, and Tema, Jetur, Naphish, and Kedemah:

16 These *are* the sons of Ishmael, and these *are* their names, by their towns,[2691] and by their castles;[2918] [a]twelve princes[5387] according to their nations.[523]

17 And these *are* the years of the life of Ishmael, an hundred and thirty and seven years: and [a]he gave up the ghost and died;[4191] and was gathered unto his people.

18 [a]And they dwelt from Havilah unto Shur, that *is* before Egypt, as thou goest toward Assyria: *and* he [I][b]died[5307] [c]in the presence of all his brethren.

Isaac's Twin Boys

19 And these *are* the generations[8435] of Isaac, Abraham's son: [a]Abraham begat Isaac:

20 And Isaac was forty years old when he took Rebekah to wife, [a]the daughter of Bethuel the Syrian of Padan–aram, [b]the sister to Laban the Syrian.

21 And Isaac intreated[6279] the LORD for his wife, because she *was* barren:[6135] [a]and the LORD was intreated of him, and [b]Rebekah his wife conceived.

22 And the children[1121] struggled together within her; and she said, If *it be* so, why *am* I thus? [a]And she went to enquire[1875] of the LORD.

23 And the LORD said unto her, [a]Two nations[1471] *are* in thy womb,[990] and two manner of people[3816] shall be separated from thy bowels;[4578] and [b]*the one* people shall be stronger than *the other* people; and the [c]elder shall serve[5647] the younger.

24 And when her days[3117] to be delivered were fulfilled, behold, *there were* twins in her womb.

25 And the first[7223] came out red,[132] [a]all over like an hairy[8181] garment; and they called his name Esau.[6215]

26 And after that came his brother out, and [a]his hand[3027] took hold on Esau's heel;[6119] and [b]his name was called Jacob:[3290] and Isaac *was* threescore years old when she bare them.

🔑 27 And the boys grew: and Esau was [a]a cunning hunter, a man[376] of the field;[7704] and Jacob *was* [b]a plain[8535] man, [c]dwelling in tents.[168]

5 [a]Gen. 24:36
6 [a]Gen. 21:14 [b]Judg. 6:3
8 [a]Gen. 15:15; 49:29 [b]Gen. 35:29; 49:33
9 [a]Gen. 35:29; 50:13
10 [a]Gen. 23:16 [b]Gen. 49:31
11 [a]Gen. 16:14; 24:62
12 [a]Gen. 16:15
13 [a]1Chr. 1:29
15 [I]Or, *Hadad* [a]1Chr. 1:30
16 [a]Gen. 17:20
17 [a]Gen. 25:8
18 [I]Hebr. *fell* [a]1Sam. 15:7; [b]Ps. 78:64; [c]Gen. 16:12
19 [a]Matt. 1:2
20 [a]Gen. 22:23 [b]Gen. 24:29
21 [a]1Chr. 5:20; 2Chr. 33:13; Ezra 8:23 [b]Rom. 9:10
22 [a]1Sam. 9:9; 10:22
23 [a]Gen. 17:16; 24:60 [b]2Sam. 8:14 [c]Gen. 27:29; Mal. 1:3; Rom. 9:12
25 [a]Gen. 27:11, 16, 23
26 [a]Hos. 12:3 [b]Gen. 27:36
27 [a]Gen. 27:3, 5 [b]Job 1:1, 8; 2:3; Ps. 37:37 [c]Heb. 11:9

🔑 **25:27** The strife between Rebekah's twin sons Jacob and Esau began even before their birth (vv. 22, 23) and continued not only throughout their lives but between their descendants. Much of

(continued on next page)

28 And Isaac loved[157] Esau, because Ihe did [a]eat of *his* venison: [b]but Rebekah loved Jacob.

🗝 29 And Jacob sod[2102] pottage:5138 and Esau came from the field, and he *was* faint:

30 And Esau said to Jacob, Feed me, I pray thee, Iwith that same red122 *pottage;* for I *am* faint: therefore was his name called[7121] IIEdom.

31 And Jacob said, Sell me this day thy birthright.[1062]

32 And Esau said, Behold, I *am* Iat the point to die: and what profit shall this birthright do to me?

33 And Jacob said, Swear[7650] to me this day; and he sware unto him: and [a]he sold his birthright unto Jacob.

34 Then Jacob gave Esau bread and pottage of lentiles; and [a]he did eat and drink, and rose up, and went his way: thus Esau despised959 *his* birthright.

Isaac Moves to Gerar

26 And there was a famine in the land,[776] beside [a]the first famine that was in the days[3117] of Abraham. And Isaac went unto [b]Abimelech king of the Philistines unto Gerar.

2 And the LORD appeared[7200] unto him, and said, Go not down into Egypt; dwell in [a]the land which I shall tell thee of:

3 [a]Sojourn[1481] in this land, and [b]I will be with thee, and [c]will bless[1288] thee; for unto thee, and unto thy seed,[2233] [d]I will give all these countries,[776] and I will perform [e]the oath[7621] which I sware[7650] unto Abraham thy father;

4 And [a]I will make thy seed to multiply as the stars of heaven,8064 and will give unto thy seed all these countries; [b]and in thy seed shall all the nations[1471] of the earth[776] be blessed;

5 [a]Because that Abraham obeyed my voice, and kept[8104] my charge,[4931] my commandments,[4687] my statutes,[2708] and my laws.[8451]

6 And Isaac dwelt in Gerar:

7 And the men[582] of the place asked *him* of his wife; and [a]he said, She *is* my sister: for [b]he feared[3372] to say, *She is* my wife; lest, *said he,* the men of the place should kill[2026] me for Rebekah; because she [c]*was* fair[2896] to look upon.

8 And it came to pass, when he had been there a long time, that Abimelech king of the Philistines looked out at a window, and saw, and, behold, Isaac *was* sporting6711 with Rebekah his wife.

9 And Abimelech called Isaac, and said, Behold, of a surety she *is* thy wife: and how saidst[559] thou, She *is* my sister? And Isaac said unto him, Because I said, Lest I die[4191] for her.

10 And Abimelech said, What *is* this thou hast done[6213] unto us? one of the people[5971] might lightly have lien with thy wife, and [a]thou shouldest have brought guiltiness[817] upon us.

11 And Abimelech charged[6680] all *his* people, saying, He that [a]toucheth[5060] this man[376] or his wife shall surely be put to death.

12 Then Isaac sowed in that land,[776] and Ireceived in the same year an [a]hundredfold: and the LORD [b]blessed[1288] him.

13 And the man [a]waxed great, and Iwent forward,3212 and grew until he became very great:

14 For he had possession of flocks, and possession of herds, and great store of Iservants:[5657] and the Philistines [a]envied[7065] him.

15 For all the wells [a]which his father's servants[5650] had digged in the days of Abraham his father, the Philistines had stopped them, and filled them with earth.[6083]

16 And Abimelech said unto Isaac,

28 IHebr. *venison was in his mouth* [a]Gen. 27:19, 25, 31 [b]Gen. 27:6
30 IHebr. *with that red,* with that *red* pottage IIThat is, *Red*
32 IHebr. *going to die*
33 [a]Heb. 12:16
34 [a]Eccl. 8:15; Isa. 22:13; 1Cor. 15:32
1 [a]Gen. 12:10 [b]Gen. 20:2
2 [a]Gen. 12:1
3 [a]Gen. 20:1; Ps. 39:12; Heb. 11:9 [b]Gen. 28:15 [c]Gen. 12:2 [d]Gen. 13:15; 15:18 [e]Gen. 22:16; Ps. 105:9
4 [a]Gen. 15:5; 22:17 [b]Gen. 12:3; 22:18
5 [a]Gen. 22:16, 18
7 [a]Gen. 12:13; 20:2, 13 [b]Prov. 29:25 [c]Gen. 24:16
10 [a]Gen. 20:9
11 [a]Ps. 105:15
12 IHebr. *found* [a]Matt. 13:8; Mark 4:8 [b]Gen. 24:1, 35; 25:3; Job 42:12
13 IHebr. *went going* [a]Gen. 24:35; Ps. 112:3; Prov. 10:22
14 IOr, *husbandry* [a]Gen. 37:11; Eccl. 4:4
15 [a]Gen. 21:30

(continued from previous page)
the suffering of the Israelites (Jacob) came at the hands of the Edomites (Esau) as is noted throughout the Old Testament (Num. 20:20, 21; 2 Sam. 8:13, 14; Ps. 137:7; Joel 3:19).

🗝 **25:29–34** See note on Genesis 27:1–38.

Go from us; for [a]thou art much mightier
than we.
17 And Isaac departed thence, and
pitched his tent2583 in the valley of Gerar,
and dwelt there.
18 And Isaac digged again the wells of
water, which they had digged in the days
of Abraham his father; for the Philistines
had stopped them after the death[4194] of
Abraham: [a]and he called[7121] their names
after the names by which his father had
called them.
19 And Isaac's servants digged in the
valley, and found there a well of
[I]springing[2416] water.
20 And the herdmen of Gerar [a]did
strive[7378] with Isaac's herdmen, saying,
The water *is* ours: and he called the name
of the well [I]Esek;6230 because they
strove6229 with him.
21 And they digged another well,
and strove[7378] for that also: and he called
the name of it [I]Sitnah.7856
22 And he removed from thence, and
digged another well; and for that they
strove not: and he called the name of it
[I]Rehoboth;7344 and he said, For now the
LORD hath made room7337 for us, and we
shall [a]be fruitful in the land.
23 And he went up from thence to
Beer–sheba.
24 And the LORD appeared unto him
the same night, and said, [a]I *am* the
God[430] of Abraham thy father: [b]fear[3372]
not, for [c]I *am* with thee, and will
bless[1288] thee, and multiply thy seed for
my servant Abraham's sake.
25 And he [a]builded an altar[4196] there,
and [b]called upon the name of the LORD,
and pitched his tent[168] there: and there
Isaac's servants digged a well.

Isaac Makes an Agreement With Abimelech

26 Then Abimelech went to him
from Gerar, and Ahuzzath one of his

16 [a]Ex. 1:9
18 [a]Gen. 21:31
19 [I]Hebr. *living*
20 [I]That is, *Contention* [a]Gen. 21:25
21 [I]That is, *Hatred*
22 [I]That is, *Room* [a]Gen. 17:6; 28:3; 41:52; Ex. 1:7
24 [a]Gen. 17:7; 24:12; 28:13; Ex. 3:6; Acts 7:32 [b]Gen. 15:1 [c]Gen. 26:3, 4
25 [a]Gen. 12:7; 13:18 [b]Ps. 116:17
26 [a]Gen. 21:22
27 [a]Judg. 11:7 [b]Gen. 26:16
28 [I]Hebr. *Seeing we saw* [a]Gen. 21:22, 23
29 [I]Hebr. *If thou shalt* [a]Gen. 24:31; Ps. 115:15
30 [a]Gen. 19:3
31 [a]Gen. 21:31
33 [I]That is, *An oath* [II]That is, *The well of the oath* [a]Gen. 21:31
34 [a]Gen. 36:2
35 [I]Hebr. *bitterness of spirit* [a]Gen. 27:46; 28:1, 8
1 [a]Gen. 48:10; 1Sam. 3:2
2 [a]Prov. 27:1; James 4:14

friends, [a]and Phichol the chief captain[8269]
of his army.[6635]
27 And Isaac said unto them,
Wherefore come ye to me, seeing [a]ye
hate[8130] me, and have [b]sent me away
from you?
28 And they said, [I]We saw certainly
that the LORD [a]was with thee: and we
said, Let there be now an oath[423] betwixt
us, *even* betwixt us and thee, and let us
make[3772] a covenant[1285] with thee;
29 [I]That thou wilt do us no hurt,[7451]
as we have not touched thee, and as we
have done unto thee nothing but good,[2896]
and have sent thee away in peace:[7965]
[a]thou *art* now the blessed[1288] of the LORD.
30 [a]And he made them a feast,[4960]
and they did eat and drink.
31 And they rose up betimes7925 in
the morning, and [a]sware[7650] one to another: and Isaac sent them away, and
they departed from him in peace.
32 And it came to pass the same day,
that Isaac's servants came, and told[5046]
him concerning the well875 which they
had digged, and said unto him, We have
found water.
33 And he called it [I]Shebah:7656
[a]therefore the name of the city *is*
[II]Beer–sheba884 unto this day.
34 [a]And Esau was forty years old
when he took to wife Judith the daughter of Beeri the Hittite, and Bashemath
the daughter of Elon the Hittite:
35 Which [a]were [I]a grief4786 of
mind[7307] unto Isaac and to Rebekah.

Jacob Steals Isaac's Blessing

27 🗝 And it came to pass,[1961] that
when Isaac was old,[2204] and [a]his
eyes were dim, so that he could not see,
he called Esau his eldest son, and said
unto him, My son: and he said unto him,
Behold, *here am* I.
2 And he said, Behold now, I am old,
I [a]know not the day[3117] of my death:[4194]

🗝 **27:1–38** There is often confusion about the difference between the birthright and the blessing in the narrative about Jacob and Esau. The birthright is related to the order of birth of sons. The

(continued on next page)

3 [a]Now therefore take,[5375] I pray
thee, thy weapons, thy quiver and thy
bow, and go out to the field, and [I]take me
some venison;
4 And make[6213] me savoury meat,
such as I love,[157] and bring *it* to me, that
I may eat; that my soul[5315] [a]may bless[1288]
thee before I die.[4191]
5 And Rebekah heard when Isaac
spake to Esau his son. And Esau went to
the field[7704] to hunt *for* venison, *and* to
bring *it*.
6 And Rebekah spake[559] unto Jacob
her son, saying, Behold, I heard[8085] thy
father speak unto Esau thy brother, saying,
7 Bring me venison, and make me
savoury meat, that I may eat, and bless
thee before the LORD before my death.
8 Now therefore, my son, [a]obey[8085]
my voice according to that which I
command[6680] thee.
9 Go now to the flock, and fetch me
from thence two good kids of the goats;
and I will make them [a]savoury meat[4303]
for thy father, such as he loveth:
10 And thou shalt bring *it* to thy father, that he [a]may eat, and that he may
bless thee before his death.
11 And Jacob said to Rebekah his
mother,[517] Behold, [a]Esau my brother *is* a
hairy[8163] man,[376] and I *am* a smooth
man:
12 My father peradventure will [a]feel
me, and I shall seem to him as a deceiver; and I shall bring [b]a curse[7045] upon
me, and not a blessing.[1293]
13 And his mother said unto him,
[a]Upon me *be* thy curse, my son: only
obey my voice, and go fetch me *them*.
14 And he went, and fetched, and
brought *them* to his mother: and his
mother [a]made savoury meat, such as his
father loved.
15 And Rebekah took [I][a]goodly raiment of her eldest son Esau, which *were*
with her in the house,[1004] and put them
upon Jacob her younger son:
16 And she put the skins[5785] of the
kids of the goats upon his hands, and
upon the smooth of his neck:
17 And she gave the savoury meat
and the bread, which she had prepared,[6213] into the hand of her son Jacob.
18 And he came unto his father, and
said, My father: and he said, Here *am* I;
who *art* thou, my son?

3 [I]Hebr. *hunt* [a]Gen. 25:27, 28
4 [a]Gen. 27:27; 48:9, 15; 49:28; Deut. 33:1
8 [a]Gen. 27:13
9 [a]Gen. 27:4
10 [a]Gen. 27:4
11 [a]Gen. 25:25
12 [a]Gen. 27:22 [b]Gen. 9:25; Deut. 27:18
13 [a]Gen. 43:9; 1Sam. 25:24; 2Sam. 14:9; Matt. 27:25
14 [a]Gen. 27:4, 9
15 [I]Hebr. *desirable* [a]Gen. 27:27

(continued from previous page)
firstborn son was given the title to the family name and a double portion of his father's inheritance. In this case Esau foolishly gave in to Jacob's extortion and sold his birthright to Jacob. Yet despite Jacob's wickedness and Esau's foolishness, the agreement over the birthright was binding. The regulation was later given that the father could not alter the birthright nor give it to another (Deut. 21:17).

None of this had anything to do with the blessing of Isaac upon Esau. As Esau himself recognized a father could bless his son in any way he saw fit (Gen. 27:36). Therefore, when Jacob deceived his father and got Esau's blessing, he stole something from his brother to which he had no right.

Esau had already sold his birthright to Jacob. Jacob was now seeking to secure Isaac's final blessing as well, which would additionally constitute an acknowledgement of Jacob's possession of the birthright. Jacob realized that once the blessing had been given, it could not be withdrawn (27:33). In this act, Jacob revealed the true meaning of his name, "one who supplants." While God had previously recognized Jacob to be in the line of promise, He did not approve of Jacob's conduct. Jacob's scheming bore terrible fruits throughout his life. He was banished from home never to see his mother again, he was tricked by his uncle Laban repeatedly (chaps. 29—30), and he lived in fear of Esau for years (chap. 31). His dishonesty also affected his children, who not only dealt treacherously with the Shechemites (chap. 34), but also deceived their own father regarding the alleged death of his favorite son, Joseph (chap. 37). These results show not only God's disapproval, but also the bitter harvest that sin can bring in one's life. Jacob ultimately repented of his conduct and finished his years as a changed man (chap. 32). In spite of his weaknesses, God chose to confirm the blessing of Abraham to him (Gen. 28:12–15).

19 And Jacob said unto his father, I
am Esau thy firstborn; I have done according as thou badest[1696] me: arise, I
pray thee, sit and eat of my venison,
[a]that thy soul may bless me.
20 And Isaac said unto his son, How
is it that thou hast found *it* so quickly,
my son? And he said, Because the
LORD[3068] thy God[430] brought *it* [I]to me.
21 And Isaac said unto Jacob, Come
near, I pray thee, that I [a]may feel thee,
my son, whether thou *be* my very son
Esau or not.
22 And Jacob went near unto Isaac
his father; and he felt him, and said, The
voice *is* Jacob's voice, but the hands *are*
the hands of Esau.
23 And he discerned[5234] him not, because [a]his hands[3027] were hairy, as his
brother Esau's hands: so he blessed[1288]
him.
24 And he said, *Art* thou my very
son Esau? And he said, I *am.*
25 And he said, Bring *it* near to me,
and I will eat of my son's venison, [a]that
my soul may bless thee. And he brought
it near to him, and he did eat: and he
brought him wine, and he drank.
26 And his father Isaac said unto
him, Come near now, and kiss[2726] me,
my son.
27 And he came near, and kissed
him: and he smelled[7306] the smell of his
raiment, and blessed him, and said, See,
[a]the smell of my son *is* as the smell of a
field which the LORD hath blessed:
28 Therefore [a]God give thee of [b]the
dew of heaven,[8064] and [c]the fatness of
the earth,[776] and [d]plenty of corn and
wine:
29 [a]Let people[5971] serve[5647] thee, and
nations[3816] bow down to thee: be lord[1376]
over thy brethren, and [b]let thy mother's
sons bow down[7812] to thee: [c]cursed[779] *be*
every one that curseth thee, and
blessed[1288] *be* he that blesseth thee.
30 And it came to pass, as soon as
Isaac had made an end of blessing Jacob,
and Jacob was yet scarce gone out from
the presence of Isaac his father, that
Esau his brother came in from his hunting.
31 And he also had made savoury
meat, and brought it unto his father, and
said unto his father, Let my father arise,
and [a]eat of his son's venison, that thy
soul may bless me.
32 And Isaac his father said unto
him, Who *art* thou? And he said, I *am*
thy son, thy firstborn Esau.
33 And Isaac [I]trembled very exceedingly, and said, Who? where *is* he that
hath [II]taken venison, and brought *it* me,
and I have eaten of all before thou
camest, and have blessed him? yea, [a]and
he shall be blessed.
34 And when Esau heard the
words[1697] of his father, [a]he cried[6817] with
a great and exceeding bitter[4751] cry, and
said unto his father, Bless[1288] me, *even*
me also, O my father.
35 And he said, Thy brother came
with subtilty,[4820] and hath taken away
thy blessing.[1293]
36 And he said, [a]Is not he rightly
named[7121] [I]Jacob? for he hath supplanted[6117] me these two times: [b]he took
away my birthright;[1062] and, behold, now
he hath taken away my blessing. And he
said, Hast thou not reserved a blessing
for me?
37 And Isaac answered and said unto
Esau, [a]Behold, I have made[7760] him thy
lord, and all his brethren have I given to
him for servants;[5650] and [b]with corn and
wine have I [I]sustained him: and what
shall I do now unto thee, my son?
38 And Esau said unto his father,
Hast thou but one blessing, my father?
bless me, *even* me also, O my father. And
Esau lifted up his voice, [a]and wept.
🗝 39 And Isaac his father answered
and said unto him, Behold, [a]thy
dwelling[4186] shall be [I]the fatness[4924] of

19 [a]Gen. 27:4
20 [I]Hebr. *before me*
21 [a]Gen. 27:12
23 [a]Gen. 27:16
25 [a]Gen. 27:4
27 [a]Hos. 14:6
28 [a]Heb. 11:20 [b]Deut. 33:13, 28; 2Sam. 1:21 [c]Gen. 45:18 [d]Deut. 33:28
29 [a]Gen. 9:25; 25:23 [b]Gen. 49:8 [c]Gen. 12:3; Num. 24:9
31 [a]Gen. 27:4
33 [I]Hebr. *trembled with a great trembling greatly* [II]Hebr. *hunted* [a]Gen. 28:3, 4; Rom. 11:29
34 [a]Heb. 12:17
36 [I]That is, *A supplanter* [a]Gen. 25:26 [b]Gen. 25:33
37 [I]Or, *supported* [a]2Sam. 8:14; Gen. 27:29 [b]Gen. 27:28
38 [a]Heb. 12:17
39 [I]Or, *of the fatness* [a]Gen. 27:28; Heb. 11:20

🗝 **27:39, 40** The Edomites were the descendants of Esau. They inhabited a rich, fertile country which was given especially to them (Deut. 2:5). Their country was traversed by roads, though it

(continued on next page)

the earth, and of the dew of heaven from above;

40 And by thy sword shalt thou live, and [a]shalt serve thy brother; and [b]it shall come to pass when thou shalt have the dominion,[7300] that thou shalt break his yoke from off thy neck.

Jacob Runs Away From Esau

41 And Esau [a]hated[7852] Jacob because of the blessing wherewith his father blessed him: and Esau said in his heart,[3820] [b]The days of mourning for my father are at hand; [c]then will I slay[2026] my brother[251] Jacob.

42 And these words of Esau her elder son were told[5046] to Rebekah: and she sent and called Jacob her younger son, and said unto him, Behold, thy brother Esau, as touching thee, doth [a]comfort[5162] himself, *purposing* to kill[2026] thee.

43 Now therefore, my son, obey my voice; and arise, flee thou to Laban my brother [a]to Haran;

44 And tarry with him a few days,[3117] until thy brother's fury[2534] turn away;

45 Until thy brother's anger[639] turn away[7725] from thee, and he forget *that* which thou hast done to him: then I will send, and fetch thee from thence: why should I be deprived also of you both in one day?

46 And Rebekah said to Isaac, [a]I am weary[6973] of my life[2416] because of the daughters of Heth: [b]if Jacob take a wife of the daughters of Heth, such as these *which are* of the daughters of the land,[776] what good shall my life do me?

40 [a]Gen. 25:23; 2Sam. 8:14; Obad. 1:18, 19, 20 [b]2Kgs. 8:20

41 [a]Gen. 37:4, 8 [b]Gen. 50:3, 4, 10 [c]Obad. 1:10

42 [a]Ps. 64:5

43 [a]Gen. 11:31

46 [a]Gen. 26:35; 28:8 [b]Gen. 24:3

1 [a]Gen. 27:33 [b]Gen. 24:3

2 [a]Hos. 12:12 [b]Gen. 25:20 [c]Gen. 22:23 [d]Gen. 24:29

3 [I]Hebr. *an assembly of people* [a]Gen. 17:1, 6

4 [I]Hebr. *of thy sojournings* [a]Gen. 12:2 [b]Gen. 17:8

8 [a]Gen. 24:3; 26:35 [I]Hebr. *were evil in the eyes*

9 [a]Gen. 36:3, *she is called Bashemath* [b]Gen. 25:13

28 And Isaac called Jacob, and [a]blessed him, and charged[6680] him, and said unto him, [b]Thou shalt not take a wife[802] of the daughters of Canaan.

2 [a]Arise, go to [b]Padan–aram, to the house[1004] of [c]Bethuel thy mother's father; and take thee a wife from thence of the daughters of [d]Laban thy mother's brother.

3 [a]And God[410] Almighty[7706] bless thee, and make thee fruitful, and multiply thee, that thou mayest be [I]a multitude[6951] of people;[5971]

4 And give thee the [a]blessing[1293] of Abraham, to thee, and to thy seed[2233] with thee; that thou mayest inherit the land [I][b]wherein thou art a stranger,[4033] which God[430] gave unto Abraham.

5 And Isaac sent away Jacob: and he went to Padan–aram unto Laban, son of Bethuel the Syrian, the brother of Rebekah, Jacob's and Esau's mother.[517]

6 When Esau saw[7200] that Isaac had blessed[1288] Jacob, and sent him away to Padan–aram, to take him a wife from thence; and that as he blessed him he gave him a charge, saying, Thou shalt not take a wife of the daughters of Canaan;

7 And that Jacob obeyed[8085] his father and his mother, and was gone to Padan–aram;

8 And Esau seeing[7200] [a]that the daughters of Canaan [I]pleased not[7451][1323] Isaac his father;

9 Then went Esau unto Ishmael, and took unto the wives which he had [a]Mahalath the daughter of Ishmael Abraham's son, [b]the sister of Nebajoth, to be his wife.

(continued from previous page)

was mountainous and rocky (Num. 20:17; Jer. 49:16). In character they are said to have been shrewd, proud and self-confident, strong, cruel, and idolatrous (Jer. 27:3; 49:7, 16, 19; Ezek. 25:12; 2 Chr. 25:14, 20). They inhabited the cities of Avith, Pau, Bozrah, and Teman and and were implacable enemies of Israel. It was forbidden to hate them and they could be received into the congregation (Deut. 23:7, 8). King Saul made war against them and David conquered them (1 Sam. 14:47; 2 Sam. 8:14). They took refuge in Egypt and returned after David's death (1 Kgs. 11:17–22). They were again overthrown by Israel (2 Chr. 20:22, 23) but finally aided Babylon against Judah (Ps. 137:7; Obad. 1:11). God pronounced special judgment against Edom (Ezek. 35).

Jacob Has a Dream at Bethel

⊶ 10 And Jacob [a]went out from Beer–sheba, and went toward [b]Haran.

11 And he lighted upon a certain place, and tarried there all night,[3885] because the sun was set; and he took of the stones of that place, and put[7760] *them for* his pillows, and lay down in that place to sleep.

12 And he [a]dreamed, and behold a ladder set up[5324] on the earth,[776] and the top[7218] of it reached[5060] to heaven:[8064] and behold [b]the angels of God ascending[5927] and descending[3381] on it.

13 [a]And, behold, the LORD stood[5324] above it, and said, [b]I *am* the LORD God of Abraham thy father, and the God of Isaac: [c]the land whereon thou liest, to thee will I give it, and to thy seed;

14 And [a]thy seed shall be as the dust[6083] of the earth, and thou shalt [I]spread abroad [b]to the west, and to the east, and to the north, and to the south: and in thee and [c]in thy seed shall[1288] all the families[4940] of the earth be blessed.[1288]

15 And, behold, [a]I *am* with thee, and will [b]keep[8104] thee in all *places* whither thou goest, and will [c]bring thee again[7725] into this land;[127] for [d]I will not leave[5800] thee, [e]until I have done *that* which I have spoken to thee of.

16 And Jacob awaked out of his sleep, and he said, Surely the LORD is in [a]this place; and I knew[3045] *it* not.

17 And he was afraid,[3372] and said, How dreadful[3372] *is* this place! this *is* none other but the house[1004] of God,[430] and this *is* the gate of heaven.

18 And Jacob rose up early in the morning, and took the stone that he had put[7760] *for* his pillows, and [a]set it up *for* a pillar,[4676] [b]and poured oil[8081] upon the top of it.

19 And he called the name of [a]that place [I]Bethel:[1008] but the name of that city *was called* Luz at the first.

10 [a]Hos. 12:12 [b]Acts 7:2, *Charran*

12 [a]Gen. 41:1; Job 33:15 [b]John 1:51; Heb. 1:14

13 [a]Gen. 35:1; 48:3 [b]Gen. 26:24 [c]Gen. 13:15; 35:12

14 [I]Hebr. *break forth* [a]Gen. 13:16 [b]Gen. 13:14; Deut. 12:20 [c]Gen. 12:3; 18:18; 22:18; 26:4

15 [a]Gen. 28:20, 21; 26:24; 31:3 [b]Gen. 48:16; Ps. 121:5, 7, 8 [c]Gen. 35:6 [d]Deut. 31:6, 8; Josh. 1:5; 1Kgs. 8:57; Heb. 13:5 [e]Num. 23:19

16 [a]Ex. 3:5; Josh. 5:15

18 [a]Gen. 31:13, 45; 35:14 [b]Lev. 8:10-12; Num. 7:1

19 [I]That is, *The house of God* [a]Judg. 1:23, 26; Hos. 4:15

20 [a]Gen. 31:13; Judg. 11:30; 2Sam. 15:8 [b]Gen. 28:15 [c]1Tim. 6:8

21 [a]Judg. 11:31; 2Sam. 19:24, 30 [b]Deut. 26:17; 2Sam. 15:8; 2Kgs. 5:17

22 [a]Gen. 35:7, 14 [b]Lev. 27:30

1 [I]Hebr. *lifted up his feet* [II]Hebr. *children* [a]Num. 23:7; Hos. 12:12

6 [I]Hebr. Is there *peace to him?* [a]Gen. 43:27

7 [I]Hebr. *yet the day is great*

20 [a]And Jacob vowed[5087] a vow,[5088] saying, If [b]God will be with me, and will keep me in this way[1870] that I go, and will give me [c]bread to eat, and raiment to put on,

21 So that [a]I come again to my father's house in peace;[7965] [b]then shall the LORD be my God:

22 And this stone, which I have set[7760] *for* a pillar, [a]shall be God's house: [b]and of all that thou shalt give me I will surely give the tenth[6237] unto thee.

Jacob Arrives at Laban's House

29 Then Jacob [I]went on his journey, [a]and came into the land[776] of the [II]people[1121] of the east.

2 And he looked, and behold a well in the field, and, lo, there *were* three flocks of sheep lying by it; for out of that well they watered[8248] the flocks: and a great stone *was* upon the well's mouth.[6310]

3 And thither were all the flocks gathered: and they rolled[1556] the stone from the well's mouth, and watered the sheep, and put the stone again upon the well's mouth in his place.

4 And Jacob said unto them, My brethren, whence *be* ye? and they said, Of Haran *are* we.

5 And he said unto them, Know[3045] ye Laban the son[1121] of Nahor? And they said, We know *him.*

6 And he said unto them, [Ia]*Is* he well?[7965] And they said, *He is* well: and, behold, Rachel his daughter cometh with the sheep.

7 And he said, Lo, [I]*it is* yet high day,[3117] neither *is it* time[6256] that the cattle should be gathered together: water ye the sheep, and go *and* feed *them.*

⊶ **28:10–22** God promised Jacob two things: he assured Jacob that he was the promised carrier of both the seed and the covenant of Abraham, and he assured him of his personal safety and blessing. Jacob accepted these promises by faith and desires to commune with and to serve God. Many look upon this passage as the time of Jacob's conversion.

8 And they said, We cannot, until all the flocks be gathered together,[622] and *till* they roll the stone from the well's mouth; then we water the sheep.

9 And while he yet spake with them, [a]Rachel came with her father's sheep: for she kept them.

10 And it came to pass, when Jacob saw[7200] Rachel the daughter of Laban his mother's brother, and the sheep of Laban his mother's brother, that Jacob went near,[5066] and [a]rolled the stone from the well's mouth, and watered the flock of Laban his mother's brother.

11 And Jacob [a]kissed[5401] Rachel, and lifted up his voice, and wept.

12 And Jacob told[5046] Rachel that he *was* [a]her father's brother, and that he *was* Rebekah's son: [b]and she ran and told her father.

13 And it came to pass, when Laban heard the [I]tidings[8088] of Jacob his sister's son, that [a]he ran to meet him, and embraced him, and kissed him, and brought him to his house. And he told[5608] Laban all these things.

14 And Laban said to him, [a]Surely thou *art* my bone[6106] and my flesh.[1320] And he abode with him [I]the space of a month.[2320,3117]

Jacob Works to Pay For Two Wives

15 And Laban said unto Jacob, Because thou *art* my brother,[251] shouldest thou therefore serve[5647] me for nought?[2600] tell[5046] me, what *shall* thy wages *be?*

16 And Laban had two daughters: the name of the elder *was* Leah, and the name of the younger *was* Rachel.

17 Leah *was* tender[7390] eyed; but Rachel was beautiful[3303,8389] and well favoured.[3303,4758]

18 And Jacob loved[157] Rachel; and said, [a]I will serve thee seven years for Rachel thy younger daughter.

19 And Laban said, *It is* better[2896] that I give her to thee, than that I should give her to another man:[376] abide with me.

9 [a]Ex. 2:16
10 [a]Ex. 2:17
11 [a]Gen. 33:4; 45:14, 15
12 [a]Gen. 13:8; 14:14, 16 [b]Gen. 24:28
13 [I]Hebr. *hearing* [a]Gen. 24:29
14 [I]Hebr. *a month of days* [a]Gen. 2:23; Judg. 9:2; 2Sam. 5:1; 19:12, 13
18 [a]Gen. 31:41; 2Sam. 3:14
20 [a]Gen. 30:26; Hos. 12:12
21 [a]Judg. 15:1
22 [a]Judg. 14:10; John 2:1, 2
26 [I]Hebr. *place*
27 [a]Judg. 14:12
30 [a]Gen. 29:20; Deut. 21:15 [b]Gen. 30:26; 31:41; Hos. 12:12
31 [a]Ps. 127:3 [b]Gen. 30:1
32 [I]That is, *See a son* [a]Ex. 3:7; 4:31; Deut. 26:7; Ps. 25:18; 106:44

20 And Jacob [a]served seven years for Rachel; and they seemed unto him *but* a few days, for the love[160] he had to her.

21 And Jacob said unto Laban, Give *me* my wife, for my days are fulfilled, that I may [a]go in unto her.

22 And Laban gathered together all the men[582] of the place, and [a]made a feast.[4960]

23 And it came to pass in the evening, that he took Leah his daughter, and brought her to him; and he went in unto her.

24 And Laban gave unto his daughter Leah Zilpah his maid *for* an handmaid.

25 And it came to pass, that in the morning, behold, it *was* Leah: and he said to Laban, What *is* this thou hast done[6213] unto me? did not I serve with thee for Rachel? wherefore then hast thou beguiled me?

26 And Laban said, It must not be so done in our [I]country, to give the younger before the firstborn.

27 [a]Fulfil her week,[7620] and we will give thee this also for the service[5656] which thou shalt serve with me yet seven other years.

28 And Jacob did so, and fulfilled her week: and he gave him Rachel his daughter to wife also.

29 And Laban gave to Rachel his daughter Bilhah his handmaid to be her maid.

30 And he went in also unto Rachel, and he [a]loved also Rachel more than Leah, and served with him [b]yet seven other years.

Jacob's Family Record

31 And when the LORD [a]saw[7200] that Leah *was* hated,[8130] he [b]opened her womb: but Rachel *was* barren.[6135]

32 And Leah conceived,[2029] and bare a son, and she called his name [I]Reuben:[7205] for she said, Surely the LORD hath [a]looked[7200] upon my affliction; now therefore my husband[376] will love me.

33 And she conceived again, and bare a son; and said, Because the LORD

hath heard[8085] that I *was* hated, he hath therefore given me this *son* also: and she called his name [I]Simeon.[8095]

34 And she conceived again, and bare a son; and said, Now this time will my husband be joined[3867] unto me, because I have born him three sons: therefore was his name called [Ia]Levi.[3878]

35 And she conceived again, and bare a son: and she said, Now will I praise[3034] the LORD: therefore she called his name [Ia]Judah;[3063] and [II]left[5975] bearing.

30 And when Rachel saw that [a]she bare Jacob no children,[3205] Rachel [b]envied[7065] her sister;[269] and said unto Jacob, Give me children, [c]or else I die.

2 And Jacob's anger[639] was kindled[2734] against Rachel: and he said, [a]*Am* I in God's stead, who hath withheld from thee the fruit of the womb?[990]

3 And she said, Behold [a]my maid Bilhah, go in unto her; [b]and she shall bear upon my knees, [c]that I may also [I]have children[1129] by her.

4 And she gave him Bilhah her handmaid [a]to wife: and Jacob went in unto her.

5 And Bilhah conceived, and bare Jacob a son.

6 And Rachel said, God[430] hath [a]judged[1777] me, and hath also heard[8085] my voice, and hath given me a son: therefore called[7121] she his name [I]Dan.[1835]

7 And Bilhah Rachel's maid conceived again, and bare Jacob a second son.

8 And Rachel said, With [I]great[430] wrestlings[5319] have I wrestled[6617] with my sister, and I have prevailed: and she called his name [IIa]Naphtali.[5321]

9 When Leah saw that she had left bearing, she took Zilpah her maid, and [a]gave her Jacob to wife.

10 And Zilpah Leah's maid bare Jacob a son.

11 And Leah said, A troop[1409] cometh: and she called his name [Ia]Gad.[1410]

12 And Zilpah Leah's maid bare Jacob a second son.

13 And Leah said, [I]Happy[837] am I, for the daughters [a]will call me blessed:[833] and she called his name [II]Asher.[836]

14 And Reuben went in the days[3117] of wheat harvest, and found mandrakes[1736] in the field,[7704] and brought them unto his mother Leah. Then Rachel said to Leah, [a]Give me, I pray thee, of thy son's mandrakes.

15 And she said unto her, [a]*Is it* a small matter that thou hast taken my husband?[376] and wouldest thou take away my son's mandrakes also? And Rachel said, Therefore he shall lie[7901] with thee to night for thy son's mandrakes.

16 And Jacob came out of the field in the evening, and Leah went out to meet him, and said, Thou must come in unto me; for surely I have hired thee with my son's mandrakes. And he lay with her that night.

17 And God hearkened[8085] unto Leah, and she conceived, and bare Jacob the fifth son.

18 And Leah said, God hath given me my hire, because I have given my maiden to my husband: and she called his name [I]Issachar.[3485]

19 And Leah conceived again, and bare Jacob the sixth son.

20 And Leah said, God hath endued me *with* a good dowry;[2065] now will my husband dwell[2082] with me, because I have born him six sons: and she called his name [Ia]Zebulun.[2074]

21 And afterwards she bare a daughter, and called her name [I]Dinah.

22 And God [a]remembered[2142] Rachel, and God hearkened to her, and [b]opened her womb.

23 And she conceived, and bare a son; and said, God hath taken away[622] [a]my reproach:[2781]

24 And she called his name [I]Joseph;[3130] and said, [a]The LORD shall add[3254] to me another son.

Jacob's Bargain

25 And it came to pass, when Rachel had born Joseph, that Jacob said unto

33 [I]That is, *Hearing*

34 [I]That is, *Joined* [a]Num. 18:2, 4

35 [I]That is, *Praise* [II]Hebr. *stood from bearing* [a]Matt. 1:2

1 [a]Gen. 29:31 [b]Gen. 37:11 [c]Job 5:2

2 [a]Gen. 16:2; 1Sam. 1:5

3 [I]Hebr. *be built by her* [a]Gen. 16:2 [b]Gen. 50:23; Job 3:12 [c]Gen. 16:2

4 [a]Gen. 16:3; 35:22

6 [I]That is, *Judging* [a]Ps. 35:24; 43:1; Lam. 3:59

8 [I]Hebr. *wrestlings of God,* Gen. 23:6 [II]That is, *My wrestling* [a]Matt. 4:13, *Nephthalim*

9 [a]Gen. 30:4

11 [I]That is, *A troop,* or, *company* [a]Isa. 65:11

13 [I]Hebr. *In my happiness* [II]That is, *Happy* [a]Prov. 31:28; Luke 1:48

14 [a]Gen. 25:30

15 [a]Num. 16:9, 13

18 [I]That is, *A hire*

20 [I]That is, *Dwelling* [a]Matt. 4:13, *Zabulon*

21 [I]That is, *Judgment*

22 [a]Gen. 8:1; 1Sam. 1:19 [b]Gen. 29:31

23 [a]1Sam. 1:6; Isa. 4:1; Luke 1:25

24 [I]That is, *Adding* [a]Gen. 35:17

Laban, [a]Send me away, that I may go unto [b]mine own place, and to my country.[776]

26 Give *me* my wives and my children, [a]for whom I have served[5647] thee, and let me go: for thou knowest my service[5656] which I have done[5647] thee.

27 And Laban said unto him, I pray thee, if I have found favour[2580] in thine eyes, *tarry: for* [a]I have learned by experience[5172] that the LORD hath blessed[1288] me [b]for thy sake.

28 And he said, [a]Appoint[5344] me thy wages, and I will give *it.*

29 And he said unto him, [a]Thou knowest how I have served thee, and how thy cattle was with me.

30 For *it was* little which thou hadst before I *came,* and it is *now* [I][a]increased unto a multitude; and the LORD hath blessed thee [II]since my coming: and now when shall I [b]provide[6213] for mine own house[1004] also?

31 And he said, What shall I give thee? And Jacob said, Thou shalt not give me anything:3972 if thou wilt do this thing for me, I will again feed *and* keep[8104] thy flock.

32 I will pass[5674] through all thy flock to day, removing from thence all the speckled and spotted cattle, and all the brown cattle among the sheep, and the spotted and speckled among the goats: and [a]*of such* shall be my hire.

33 So shall my [a]righteousness[6666] answer for me [I][b]in time to come, when it shall come for my hire before thy face: every one that *is* not speckled and spotted among the goats, and brown among the sheep, that shall be counted stolen with me.

34 And Laban said, Behold, I would it might be according to thy word.[1697]

35 And he removed that day the he goats that were ringstraked6124 and spotted, and all the she goats that were speckled and spotted, *and* every one that had *some* white in it, and all the brown among the sheep, and gave *them* into the hand[3027] of his sons.

36 And he set three days'[3117] journey[1870] betwixt himself and Jacob: and Jacob fed the rest[3498] of Laban's flocks.

37 And [a]Jacob took him rods of green poplar, and of the hazel and chestnut tree; and pilled6478 white strakes in them, and made the white appear which *was* in the rods.

38 And he set the rods which he had pilled before the flocks in the gutters7298 in the watering troughs when the flocks came to drink, that they should conceive when they came to drink.

39 And the flocks conceived before the rods, and brought forth cattle ringstraked, speckled, and spotted.

40 And Jacob did separate the lambs, and set the faces of the flocks toward the ringstraked, and all the brown in the flock of Laban; and he put his own flocks by themselves, and put them not unto Laban's cattle.

41 And it came to pass, whensoever the stronger cattle did conceive, that Jacob laid[7760] the rods before the eyes of the cattle in the gutters, that they might conceive among the rods.

42 But when the cattle were feeble, he put *them* not in: so the feebler were Laban's, and the stronger Jacob's.

43 And the man[376] [a]increased exceedingly, and [b]had much cattle, and maidservants, and menservants,[5650] and camels, and asses.

Jacob Runs Away From His Uncle

31 And he heard the words of Laban's sons, saying, Jacob hath taken away all that *was* our father's;[1] and of *that* which *was* our father's hath he gotten[6213] all this [a]glory.[3519]

2 And Jacob beheld[7200] [a]the countenance of Laban, and, behold, it *was* not [a]toward him [I][b]as before.

3 And the LORD said unto Jacob, [a]Return[7725] unto the land[776] of thy fathers,[1] and to thy kindred; and I will be with thee.

4 And Jacob sent and called Rachel and Leah to the field unto his flock.

25 [a]Gen. 24:54, 56 [b]Gen. 18:33; 31:55
26 [a]Gen. 29:20, 30
27 [a]Gen. 39:3, 5 [b]Gen. 26:24
28 [a]Gen. 29:15
29 [a]Gen. 31:6, 38-40; Matt. 24:45; Titus 2:10
30 [I]Hebr. *broken forth* [II]Hebr. *at my foot* [a]Gen. 30:43 [b]1Tim. 5:8
32 [a]Gen. 31:8
33 [I]Hebr. *tomorrow* [a]Ps. 37:6 [b]Ex. 13:14
37 [a]Gen. 31:9-12
43 [a]Gen. 30:30 [b]Gen. 13:2; 24:35; 26:13, 14
1 [a]Ps. 49:16
2 [I]Hebr. *as yesterday and the day before* [a]Gen. 4:5 [b]Deut. 28:54 [c]1Sam. 19:7
3 [a]Gen. 28:15, 20, 21; 32:9

5 And said unto them, [a]I see your father's countenance, that it *is* not toward me as before; but the God[430] of my father [b]hath been with me.

6 And [a]ye know that with all my power I have served[5647] your father.

7 And your father hath deceived me, and [a]changed my wages [b]ten times; but God [c]suffered him not to hurt[7489] me.

8 If he said thus, [a]The speckled shall be thy wages; then all the cattle bare speckled: and if he said thus, The ringstraked[6124] shall be thy hire; then bare all the cattle ringstraked.

9 Thus God hath [a]taken away the cattle of your father, and given *them* to me.

10 And it came to pass at the time[6256] that the cattle conceived, that I lifted up mine eyes, and saw[7200] in a dream, and, behold, the [1]rams which leaped[5927] upon the cattle *were* ringstraked, speckled, and grisled.

11 And [a]the angel of God spake unto me in a dream, *saying,* Jacob: and I said, Here *am* I.

12 And he said, Lift up[5375] now thine eyes, and see, all the rams which leap upon the cattle *are* ringstraked, speckled, and grisled: for [a]I have seen all that Laban doeth unto thee.

13 I *am* the God[410] of Bethel, [a]where thou anointedst[4886] the pillar,[4676] *and* where thou vowedst[5087] a vow[5088] unto me: now [b]arise, get thee out from this land, and return unto the land of thy kindred.

14 And Rachel and Leah answered and said unto him, [a]*Is there* yet any portion or inheritance[5159] for us in our father's house?[1004]

15 Are we not counted[2803] of him strangers?[5237] for [a]he hath sold us, and hath quite devoured[398] also our money.

16 For all the riches which God hath taken from our father, that *is* ours, and our children's:[1121] now then, whatsoever God hath said unto thee, do.

17 Then Jacob rose up, and set his sons[1121] and his wives upon camels;

18 And he carried away all his cattle, and all his goods which he had gotten, the cattle of his getting, which he had gotten in Padan–aram, for to go to Isaac his father in the land of Canaan.

19 And Laban went to shear his sheep: and Rachel had stolen the [a]images[8655] that *were* her father's.

20 And Jacob stole away[1589] [1]unawares to Laban the Syrian, in that he told[5046] him not that he fled.

21 So he fled with all that he had; and he rose up, and passed over[5674] the river, and [a]set his face *toward* the mount Gilead.

Laban Pursues Jacob

22 And it was told[5046] Laban on the third day[3117] that Jacob was fled.

23 And he took [a]his brethren with him, and pursued after him seven days' journey; and they overtook him in the mount Gilead.

24 And God [a]came to Laban the Syrian in a dream by night, and said unto him, Take heed[8104] that thou [b]speak not to Jacob [1]either good[2896] or bad.[7451]

25 Then Laban overtook Jacob. Now Jacob had pitched his tent[168] in the mount: and Laban with his brethren pitched in the mount of Gilead.

26 And Laban said to Jacob, What hast thou done, that thou hast stolen away[1589] unawares to me, and [a]carried away my daughters, as captives[7617] *taken* with the sword?

27 Wherefore didst thou flee away[1272] secretly, and [1]steal away from me; and didst not tell me, that I might have sent thee away with mirth, and with songs,[7892] with tabret,[8596] and with harp?

28 And hast not suffered me [a]to kiss my sons[1121] and my daughters? [b]thou hast now done foolishly in *so* doing.

29 It is in the power[410] of my hand[3027] to do you hurt:[7451] but the [a]God[430] of your father[1] spake unto me [b]yesternight, saying, Take thou heed that thou speak not to Jacob either good or bad.

30 And now, *though* thou wouldest needs be gone, because thou sore longedst[3700] after thy father's house, *yet* wherefore hast thou [a]stolen my gods?[430]

---

5 [a]Gen. 31:2 [b]Gen. 31:3
6 [a]Gen. 30:29; Gen. 31:38-41
7 [a]Gen. 31:41 [b]Num. 14:22; Neh. 4:12; Job 19:3; Zech. 8:23 [c]Gen. 20:6; Ps. 105:14
8 [a]Gen. 30:32
9 [a]Gen. 31:1, 16
10 [1]Or, *he goats*
11 [a]Gen. 48:16
12 [a]Ex. 3:7
13 [a]Gen. 28:18-20 [b]Gen. 31:3; Gen. 32:9
14 [a]Gen. 2:24
15 [a]Gen. 29:15, 27
19 [a]Gen. 35:2; Judg. 17:5; 1Sam. 19:13; Hos. 3:4
20 [1]Hebr. *the heart of Laban*
21 [a]Gen. 46:28; 2Kgs. 12:17; Luke 9:51, 53
23 [a]Gen. 13:8
24 [1]Hebr. *from good to bad* [a]Gen. 20:3; Job 33:15; Matt. 1:20 [b]Gen. 24:50
26 [a]1Sam. 30:2
27 [1]Hebr. *hast stolen me*
28 [a]Gen. 31:5; Ruth 1:9, 14; 1Kgs. 19:20; Acts 20:37 [b]1Sam. 13:13; 2Chr. 16:9
29 [a]Gen. 28:13; 31:53 [b]Gen. 31:24
30 [a]Gen. 31:19; Judg. 18:24

31 And Jacob answered and said to Laban, Because I was afraid:[3372] for I said, Peradventure6435 thou wouldest take by force thy daughters from me.

32 With whomsoever thou findest thy gods, [a]let him not live: before our brethren discern[5234] thou what *is* thine with me, and take *it* to thee. For Jacob knew[3045] not that Rachel had stolen them.

33 And Laban went into Jacob's tent, and into Leah's tent, and into the two maidservants' tents; but he found *them* not. Then went he out of Leah's tent, and entered into Rachel's tent.

34 Now Rachel had taken the images, and put them in the camel's furniture, and sat upon them. And Laban [I]searched all the tent, but found *them* not.

35 And she said to her father, Let it not displease my lord[113] that I cannot [a]rise up before thee; for the custom[1870] of women *is* upon me. And he searched, but found not the images.

36 And Jacob was wroth,[2734] and chode[7378] with Laban: and Jacob answered and said to Laban, What *is* my trespass?[6588] what *is* my sin,[2403] that thou hast so hotly pursued after me?

37 Whereas thou hast [I]searched all my stuff, what hast thou found of all thy household[1004] stuff? set[7760] *it* here before my brethren and thy brethren, that they may judge[3198] betwixt us both.

38 This twenty years *have* I *been* with thee; thy ewes7353 and thy she goats have not cast their young, and the rams of thy flock have I not eaten.

39 [a]That which was torn *of beasts* I brought not unto thee; I bare the loss[2398] of it; of [b]my hand didst thou require it, *whether* stolen by day, or stolen by night.

40 *Thus* I was; in the day the drought consumed me, and the frost by night; and my sleep departed from mine eyes.

41 Thus have I been twenty years in thy house; I [a]served thee fourteen years for thy two daughters, and six years for thy cattle: and [b]thou hast changed my wages ten times.

42 [a]Except the God of my father, the God of Abraham, and [b]the fear[6343] of Isaac, had been with me, surely thou hadst sent me away now empty. [c]God hath seen mine affliction6040 and the labour of my hands,[3709] and [d]rebuked *thee* yesternight.

Jacob's New Agreement With Laban

43 And Laban answered and said unto Jacob, *These* daughters *are* my daughters, and *these* children[1121] *are* my children, and *these* cattle *are* my cattle, and all that thou seest *is* mine: and what can I do[6213] this day[3117] unto these my daughters, or unto their children which they have born?

44 Now therefore come thou, let us [a]make[3772] a covenant,[1285] I and thou; [b]and let it be for a witness5707 between me and thee.

45 And Jacob [a]took a stone, and set it up *for* a pillar.

46 And Jacob said unto his brethren, Gather[3950] stones; and they took stones, and made[6213] an heap:1530 and they did eat there upon the heap.

47 And Laban called it [I]Jegar–sahadutha:3026 but Jacob called[7121] it [II]Galeed.1567

48 And Laban said, [a]This heap *is* a witness betwixt me and thee this day. Therefore was the name of it called Galeed;

49 And [Ia]Mizpah; for he said, The LORD watch between me and thee, when we are absent5641 one[376] from another.[7453]

50 If thou shalt afflict my daughters, or if thou shalt take *other* wives beside my daughters, no man[376] *is* with us; see, God *is* witness betwixt me and thee.

51 And Laban said to Jacob, Behold this heap, and behold *this* pillar, which I have cast betwixt me and thee:

52 This heap *be* witness,5707 and *this* pillar *be* witness, that I will not pass over this heap to thee, and that thou shalt not pass over this heap and this pillar unto me, for harm.[7451]

53 The God of Abraham, and the

---

32 [a]Gen. 44:9

34 [I]Hebr. *felt*

35 [a]Ex. 20:12; Lev. 19:32

37 [I]Hebr. *felt*

39 [a]Ex. 22:10-13 [b]Ex. 22:12

41 [a]Gen. 29:27, 28 [b]Gen. 31:7

42 [a]Ps. 124:1, 2 [b]Gen. 31:53; Isa. 8:13 [c]Gen. 29:32; Ex. 3:7 [d]1Chr. 12:17; Jude 1:9

44 [a]Gen. 26:28 [b]Josh. 24:27

45 [a]Gen. 28:18

47 [I]That is, *The heap of witness.* Aram. [II]That is, *The heap of witness.* Hebr.

48 [a]Josh. 24:27

49 [I]That is, *A beacon,* or *watchtower* [a]Judg. 11:29; 1Sam. 7:5

God of Nahor, the God of their father, [a]judge betwixt us. And Jacob [b]sware[7650] by [c]the fear[6343] of his father Isaac.

54 Then Jacob [I]offered sacrifice[2077] upon the mount, and called[7121] his brethren to eat bread: and they did eat bread, and tarried all night in the mount.

55 And early in the morning Laban rose up, and kissed his sons[1121] and his daughters, and [a]blessed[1288] them: and Laban departed, and [b]returned unto his place.

Jacob Prepares to Meet Esau

32 And Jacob went on his way, and [a]the angels of God[430] met him.

2 And when Jacob saw them, he said, This *is* God's [a]host:[4264] and he called the name of that place [I]Mahanaim.[4266]

3 And Jacob sent messengers before him to Esau his brother [a]unto the land of Seir, [b]the [I]country[7704] of Edom.

4 And he commanded[6680] them, saying, [a]Thus shall ye speak unto my lord[113] Esau; Thy servant[5650] Jacob saith thus, I have sojourned[1481] with Laban, and stayed there until now:

5 And [a]I have oxen, and asses, flocks, and menservants,[5650] and womenservants:[8198] and I have sent to tell[5046] my lord, that [b]I may find grace[2580] in thy sight.

6 And the messengers returned to Jacob, saying, We came to thy brother Esau, and also [a]he cometh to meet thee, and four hundred men[376] with him.

7 Then Jacob was greatly afraid[3372] and [a]distressed: and he divided the people[5971] that *was* with him, and the flocks, and herds, and the camels, into two bands;[4264]

8 And said, If Esau come to the one company,[4264] and smite[5221] it, then the other company which is left[7604] shall escape.[6413]

9 [a]And Jacob said, [b]O God of my father[1] Abraham, and God of my father Isaac, the LORD [c]which saidst unto me, Return[7725] unto thy country,[776] and to thy kindred, and I will deal well[3190] with thee:

10 [I]I am not worthy[6994] of the least of all the [a]mercies,[2617] and of all the truth,[571] which thou hast shewed[6213] unto thy servant; for with [b]my staff I passed over[5674] this Jordan; and now I am become two bands.

11 [a]Deliver[5337] me, I pray thee, from the hand[3027] of my brother, from the hand of Esau: for I fear[3373] him, lest he will come and smite me, *and* [b]the mother [I]with the children.[1121]

12 And [a]thou saidst, I will surely do thee good,[3190] and make[7760] thy seed[2233] as the sand of the sea, which cannot be numbered[5608] for multitude.

13 And he lodged there that same night; and took of that which came to his hand [a]a present[4503] for Esau his brother;

14 Two hundred she goats, and twenty he goats, two hundred ewes,[7353] and twenty rams,

15 Thirty milch camels with their colts,[1121] forty kine,[6510] and ten bulls, twenty she asses, and ten foals.

16 And he delivered *them* into the hand of his servants, every drove by themselves; and said unto his servants, Pass over before me, and put a space[7305] betwixt drove and drove.

17 And he commanded the foremost,[7223] saying, When Esau my brother meeteth thee, and asketh[7592] thee, saying, Whose *art* thou? and whither goest thou? and whose *are* these before thee?

18 Then thou shalt say, *They be* thy servant Jacob's; it *is* a present[4503] sent unto my lord Esau: and, behold, also he *is* behind us.

19 And so commanded he the second, and the third, and all that followed the droves, saying, On this manner shall ye speak unto Esau, when ye find him.

20 And say ye moreover, Behold, thy servant Jacob *is* behind us. For he said, I will [a]appease[3722,6440] him with the present that goeth before me, and afterward I will see his face; peradventure[194] he will accept[5375] [I]of me.

21 So went the present over[5674] before him: and himself lodged that night in the company.

---

53 [a]Gen. 16:5 [b]Gen. 21:23 [c]Gen. 31:42

54 [I]Or, *killed beasts*

55 [a]Gen. 28:1 [b]Gen. 18:33; 30:25

1 [a]Ps. 91:11; Heb. 1:14

2 [I]That is, *Two hosts,* or *camps* [a]Josh. 5:14; Ps. 103:21; 148:2; Luke 2:13

3 [I]Hebr. *field* [a]Gen. 33:14, 16 [b]Gen. 36:6-8; Deut. 2:5; Josh. 24:4

4 [a]Prov. 15:1

5 [a]Gen. 30:43 [b]Gen. 33:8, 15

6 [a]Gen. 33:1

7 [a]Gen. 35:3

9 [a]Ps. 50:15 [b]Gen. 28:13 [c]Gen. 31:3, 13

10 [I]Hebr. *I less than all* [a]Gen. 24:27 [b]Job 8:7

11 [I]Hebr. *upon* [a]Ps. 59:1, 2 [b]Hos. 10:14

12 [a]Gen. 28:13-15

13 [a]Gen. 43:11; Prov. 18:16

20 [I]Hebr. *my face* [a]Prov. 21:14 [b]Job 42:8, 9

Jacob Wrestles With God

🔑22 And he rose up that night, and took his two wives, and his two womenservants, and his eleven sons, [a]and passed over[5674] the ford Jabbok.

23 And he took them, and ǀsent them over the brook, and sent over that he had.

24 And Jacob was left[3498] alone; and there [a]wrestled a man[376] with him until the ǀbreaking of the day.

25 And when he saw that he prevailed not against him, he touched[5060] the hollow[3709] of his thigh; and [a]the hollow of Jacob's thigh was out of joint, as he wrestled with him.

26 And [a]he said, Let me go, for the day breaketh.[5927] And he said, [b]I will not let thee go, except thou bless[1288] me.

27 And he said unto him, What is thy name? And he said, Jacob.

28 And he said, [a]Thy name shall be called no more Jacob,3290 but ǀIsrael:3478 for as a prince hast thou [b]power[8280] with God and [c]with men,[582] and hast prevailed.

29 And Jacob asked *him,* and said, Tell[5046] *me,* I pray thee, thy name. And he said, [a]Wherefore *is* it *that* thou dost ask after my name? And he blessed him there.

30 And Jacob called the name of the place ǀPeniel:6439 for [a]I have seen God[430] face to face, and my life[5315] is preserved.[5337]

31 And as he passed over[5674] Penuel the sun rose upon him, and he halted upon his thigh.

32 Therefore the children[1121] of Israel eat not *of* the sinew which shrank,5384 which *is* upon the hollow of the thigh, unto this day: because he touched the hollow of Jacob's thigh in the sinew that shrank.

Jacob Meets Esau

33 And Jacob lifted up his eyes and looked,[7200] and, behold, [a]Esau came, and with him four hundred men.[376] And he divided the children unto Leah, and unto Rachel, and unto the two handmaids.

2 And he put the handmaids and their children foremost,[7223] and Leah and her children after, and Rachel and Joseph hindermost.[314]

3 And he passed over[5674] before them, and [a]bowed[7812] himself to the ground[776] seven times, until he came near to his brother.

4 And Esau ran to meet him, and [a]embraced him, and fell on his neck, and kissed him: and they wept.

5 And he lifted up his eyes, and saw the women and the children; and said, Who *are* those ǀwith thee? And he said, The children [a]which God[430] hath graciously given[2603] thy servant.[5650]

6 Then the handmaidens came near, they and their children, and they bowed themselves.

7 And Leah also with her children came near, and bowed themselves: and after came Joseph near and Rachel, and they bowed themselves.

8 And he said, ǀWhat *meanest* thou by [a]all this drove[4264] which I met? And he said, *These are* [b]to find grace[2580] in the sight of my lord.[113]

9 And Esau said, I have enough, my brother; ǀkeep that thou hast unto thyself.

10 And Jacob said, Nay, I pray thee, if now I have found grace in thy sight, then receive my present[4503] at my hand: for therefore I [a]have seen thy face, as though I had seen the face of God, and thou wast pleased[7521] with me.

11 Take, I pray thee, [a]my blessing[1293] that is brought to thee; because

22 [a]Deut. 3:16
23 ǀHebr. *caused to pass*
24 ǀHebr. *ascending of the morning* [a]Hos. 12:3, 4; Eph. 6:12
25 [a]Matt. 26:41; 2Cor. 12:7
26 [a]Luke 24:28 [b]Hos. 12:4
28 ǀThat is, *A prince of God* [a]Gen. 35:10; 2Kgs. 17:34 [b]Hos. 12:3, 4 [c]Gen. 25:31; 27:33
29 [a]Judg. 13:18
30 ǀThat is, *The face of God* [a]Gen. 16:13; Ex. 24:11; 33:20; Deut. 5:24; Judg. 6:22; 13:22; Isa. 6:5
1 [a]Gen. 32:6
3 [a]Gen. 18:2; 42:6; 43:26
4 [a]Gen. 45:14, 15
5 ǀHebr. *to thee?* [a]Gen. 48:9; Ps. 127:3; Isa. 8:18
8 ǀHebr. *What is all this band to thee?* [a]Gen. 32:16 [b]Gen. 32:5
9 ǀHebr. *be that to thee that is thine*
10 [a]Gen. 43:3; 2Sam. 3:13; 14:24, 28, 32; Matt. 18:10
11 [a]Judg. 1:15; 1Sam. 25:27; 30:26; 2Kgs. 5:15

🔑 **32:22–32** The events at the ford Jabbok represent a climactic point in Jacob's spiritual growth. He proved that he could persevere and overcome without cheating. He saw that his own strength was futile and he humbly sought help from God. From his salvation at Bethel (see note on Genesis 28:10–22) to this point, Jacob had undergone tremendous spiritual growth. He was a different man that the one who had supplanted his brother through deceit. Therefore, God gave to him a new name, Israel ("he who strives with God").

God hath dealt graciously with me, and because I have [Ib]enough. [c]And he urged[6484] him, and he took *it.*

12 And he said, Let us take our journey, and let us go, and I will go before thee.

13 And he said unto him, My lord knoweth that the children *are* tender, and the flocks and herds with young *are* with me: and if men should overdrive[1849] them one day,[3117] all the flock will die.

14 Let my lord, I pray thee, pass over[5674] before his servant: and I will lead on softly,[5095,328] [I]according as the cattle[4399] that goeth before me and the children be able to endure, until I come unto my lord [a]unto Seir.

15 And Esau said, Let me now [I]leave with thee *some* of the folk[5971] that *are* with me. And he said, [II]What needeth it? [a]let me find grace in the sight of my lord.

16 So Esau returned that day on his way unto Seir.

17 And Jacob journeyed to [a]Succoth, and built him an house,[1004] and made[6213] booths[5521] for his cattle: therefore the name of the place is called[7121] [I]Succoth.[5523]

18 And Jacob came to [a]Shalem, a city of [Ib]Shechem, which *is* in the land[776] of Canaan, when he came from Padan–aram; and pitched his tent before the city.

19 And [a]he bought a parcel of a field,[7704] where he had spread his tent,[168] at the hand of the children[1121] of [I]Hamor, Shechem's father, for an hundred [II]pieces of money.

20 And he erected there an altar,[4196] and [a]called it [I]El–elohe–Israel.[415]

Dinah Is Raped

34 And [a]Dinah the daughter of Leah, which she bare unto Jacob, [a]went out to see the daughters of the land.[776]

2 And when Shechem the son of Hamor the Hivite, prince[5387] of the country,[776] [a]saw her, he [b]took her, and lay with her, and [Ic]defiled her.

3 And his soul[5315] clave unto Dinah the daughter of Jacob, and he loved the damsel, and spake [Ia]kindly[3820] unto the damsel.

4 And Shechem [a]spake unto his father Hamor, saying, Get me this damsel to wife.

5 And Jacob heard that he had defiled[2930] Dinah his daughter: now his sons were with his cattle in the field:[7704] and Jacob [a]held his peace until they were come.

6 And Hamor the father of Shechem went out unto Jacob to commune with him.

7 And the sons of Jacob came out of the field when they heard *it:* and the men[582] were grieved, and they [a]were very wroth,[2734] because he [b]had wrought[6213] folly[5039] in Israel in lying with Jacob's daughter; [c]which thing ought not to be done.

8 And Hamor communed with them, saying, The soul of my son Shechem longeth[2836] for your daughter: I pray you give her him to wife.

9 And make ye marriages with us, *and* give your daughters unto us, and take our daughters unto you.

10 And ye shall dwell with us: and [a]the land shall be before you; dwell and [b]trade ye therein, and [c]get you possessions therein.

11 And Shechem said unto her father and unto her brethren, Let me find grace[2580] in your eyes, and what ye shall say unto me I will give.

12 Ask me never so much [a]dowry[4119] and gift, and I will give according as ye shall say unto me: but give me the damsel to wife.

13 And the sons of Jacob answered Shechem and Hamor his father [a]deceitfully,[4820] and said, because he had defiled Dinah their sister:

14 And they said unto them, We cannot do this thing,[1697] to give our sister to one[376] that is uncircumcised;[6190] for [a]that *were* a reproach[2781] unto us:

15 But in this will we consent unto you: If ye will be as we *be,* that every male[2145] of you be circumcised;

16 Then will we give our daughters

11 [I]Hebr. *all things* [b]Phil. 4:18 [c]2Kgs. 5:23

14 [I]Hebr. *according to the foot of the work . . . and according to the foot of the children* [a]Gen. 32:3

15 [I]Hebr. *set,* or, *place* [II]Hebr. *Wherefore is this?* [a]Gen. 34:11; 47:25; Ruth 2:13

17 [I]That is, *Booths* [a]Josh. 13:27; Judg. 8:5; Ps. 60:6

18 [I]Acts 7:16, *Sychem* [a]John 3:23 [b]Josh. 24:1; Judg. 9:1

19 [I]Acts 7:16, *Emmor* [II]Or, *lambs* [a]Josh. 24:32; John 4:5

20 [I]That is, *God the God of Israel* [a]Gen. 35:7

1 [a]Gen. 30:21 [b]Titus 2:5

2 [I]Hebr. *humbled her* [a]Gen. 6:2; Judg. 14:1 [b]Gen. 20:2; [c]Deut. 22:29

3 [I]Hebr. *to the heart of the damsel* [a]Isa. 40:2; Hos. 2:14

4 [a]Judg. 14:2

5 [a]1Sam. 10:27; 2Sam. 13:22

7 [a]Gen. 49:7; 2Sam. 13:21 [b]Josh. 7:15; Judg. 20:6 [c]Deut. 23:17; 2Sam. 13:12

10 [a]Gen. 13:9; 20:15 [b]Gen. 42:34 [c]Gen. 47:27

12 [a]Ex. 22:16, 17; Deut. 22:29; 1Sam. 18:25

13 [a]2Sam. 13:24-33

14 [a]Josh. 5:9

unto you, and we will take your daughters to us, and we will dwell with you, and we will become one people.[5971]

17 But if ye will not hearken[8085] unto us, to be circumcised; then will we take our daughter, and we will be gone.

18 And their words[1697] pleased[3190] Hamor, and Shechem Hamor's son.

19 And the young man deferred not to do the thing, because he had delight[2654] in Jacob's daughter: and he *was* [a]more honourable[3513] than all the house[1004] of his father.

20 And Hamor and Shechem his son came unto the gate of their city, and communed with the men of their city, saying,

21 These men *are* peaceable[8003] with us; therefore let them dwell in the land, and trade therein; for the land, behold, *it is* large enough for them; let us take their daughters to us for wives, and let us give them our daughters.

22 Only herein will the men consent unto us for to dwell[3427] with us, to be one people, if every male among us be circumcised, as they *are* circumcised.

23 *Shall* not their cattle and their substance and every beast of theirs *be* ours? only let us consent unto them, and they will dwell with us.

24 And unto Hamor and unto Shechem his son hearkened all that [a]went out of the gate of his city; and every male was circumcised, all that went out of the gate of his city.

25 And it came to pass on the third day, when they were sore, that two of the sons of Jacob, [a]Simeon and Levi, Dinah's brethren,[251] took each man[376] his sword, and came upon the city boldly, and slew[2026] all the males.

26 And they slew Hamor and Shechem his son with the [I]edge[6310] of the sword, and took Dinah out of Shechem's house, and went out.

27 The sons of Jacob came upon the slain,[2491] and spoiled the city, because they had defiled their sister.

28 They took their sheep, and their oxen, and their asses, and that which *was* in the city, and that which *was* in the field,

29 And all their wealth,[2428] and all their little ones,[2945] and their wives took they captive,[7617] and spoiled even all that *was* in the house.

30 And Jacob said to Simeon and Levi, [a]Ye have [b]troubled me [c]to make me to stink[887] among the inhabitants of the land, among the Canaanites and the Perizzites: [d]and I *being* few in number, they shall gather themselves together against me, and slay[5221] me; and I shall be destroyed,[8045] I and my house[1004].

31 And they said, Should he deal[6213] with our sister as with an harlot?[2181]

Jacob Returns to Bethel

35 And God[430] said unto Jacob, Arise, go up to [a]Bethel, and dwell there: and make[6213] there an altar[4196] unto God,[410] [b]that appeared unto thee [c]when thou fleddest from the face of Esau thy brother.

2 Then Jacob said unto his [a]household,[1004] and to all that *were* with him, Put away[5493] [b]the strange[5236] gods[430] that *are* among you, and [c]be clean, and change your garments:

3 And let us arise, and go up to Bethel; and I will make there an altar unto God, [a]who answered me in the day[3117] of my distress, [b]and was with me in the way which I went.

4 And they gave unto Jacob all the strange gods which *were* in their hand, and *all their* [a]earrings which *were* in their ears; and Jacob hid them under [b]the oak which *was* by Shechem.

5 And they journeyed: and [a]the terror[2847] of God was upon the cities that *were* round about them, and they did not pursue after the sons of Jacob.

6 So Jacob came to [a]Luz, which *is* in the land[776] of Canaan, that *is,* Bethel, he and all the people[5971] that *were* with him.

7 And he [a]built there an altar, and called the place [I]El–beth–el:[416] because [b]there God[430] appeared unto him, when he fled from the face of his brother.

8 But [a]Deborah Rebekah's nurse died,[4191] and she was buried beneath Bethel under an oak: and the name of it was called [I]Allon–bachuth.

19 [a]1Chr. 4:9
24 [a]Gen. 23:10
25 [a]Gen. 49:5-7
26 [I]Hebr. *mouth*
30 [a]Gen. 49:6 [b]Josh. 7:25 [c]Ex. 5:21; 1Sam. 13:4 [d]Deut. 4:27; Ps. 105:12
1 [a]Gen. 28:19 [b]Gen. 28:13 [c]Gen. 27:43
2 [a]Gen. 18:19; Josh. 24:15 [b]Gen. 31:19, 34; Josh. 24:2, 23; 1Sam. 7:3 [c]Ex. 19:10
3 [a]Gen. 32:7, 24; Ps. 107:6 [b]Gen. 28:20; 31:3, 42
4 [a]Hos. 2:13 [b]Josh. 24:26; Judg. 9:6
5 [a]Ex. 15:16; 23:27; 34:24; Deut. 11:25; Josh. 2:9; 5:1; 1Sam. 14:15; 2Chr. 14:14
6 [a]Gen. 28:19, 22
7 [I]That is, *The God of Beth-el* [a]Eccl. 5:4 [b]Gen. 28:13
8 [I]That is, *The oak of weeping* [a]Gen. 24:59

9 And [a]God appeared[7200] unto Jacob again, when he came out of Padan–aram, and blessed[1288] him.

10 And God said unto him, Thy name *is* Jacob: [a]thy name shall not be called[7121] any more Jacob, [b]but Israel shall be thy name: and he called his name Israel.3478

11 And God said unto him, [a]I *am* God[410] Almighty:[7706] be fruitful and multiply; [b]a nation[1471] and a company[6951] of nations shall be of thee, and kings[4428] shall come out of thy loins;

12 And the land [a]which I gave Abraham and Isaac, to thee I will give it, and to thy seed[2233] after thee will I give the land.

13 And God [a]went up from him in the place where he talked[1696] with him.

14 And Jacob [a]set up[5324] a pillar[4676] in the place where he talked with him, *even* a pillar of stone: and he poured[5258] a drink offering[5262] thereon, and he poured oil[8081] thereon.

15 And Jacob called the name of the place where God spake[1696] with him, [a]Bethel.1008

Rachel Dies

16 And they journeyed from Bethel; and there was but [I]a little way to come to Ephrath: and Rachel travailed,3205 and she had hard labour.

17 And it came to pass, when she was in hard labour, that the midwife said unto her, Fear[3372] not; [a]thou shalt have this son[1121] also.

18 And it came to pass, as her soul[5315] was in departing, (for she died[4191]) that she called[7121] his name [I]Ben–oni:1126 but his father[1] called him [II]Benjamin.1144

19 And [a]Rachel died, and was buried[6912] in the way to [a]Ephrath, which *is* Bethlehem.

20 And Jacob set a pillar upon her grave: that *is* the pillar of Rachel's grave[6900] [a]unto this day.[3117]

21 And Israel journeyed, and spread his tent[168] beyond [a]the tower of Edar.

Jacob's Sons

22 And it came to pass, when Israel dwelt in that land, that Reuben went and [a]lay with Bilhah his father's concubine: and Israel heard *it*. Now the sons of Jacob were twelve:

23 The sons of Leah; [a]Reuben, Jacob's firstborn, and Simeon, and Levi, and Judah, and Issachar, and Zebulun:

24 The sons of Rachel; Joseph, and Benjamin:

25 And the sons of Bilhah, Rachel's handmaid; Dan, and Naphtali:

26 And the sons of Zilpah, Leah's handmaid; Gad, and Asher: these *are* the sons of Jacob, which were born to him in Padan–aram.

Isaac Dies

27 And Jacob came unto Isaac his father unto [a]Mamre, unto the [b]city of Arbah, which *is* Hebron, where Abraham and Isaac sojourned.[1481]

28 And the days[3117] of Isaac were an hundred and fourscore years.

29 And Isaac gave up the ghost,[1478]

9 [a]Hos. 12:4
10 [a]Gen. 17:5 [b]Gen. 32:28
11 [a]Gen. 17:1; 48:3, 4; Ex. 6:3 [b]Gen. 17:5, 6, 16; 28:3; 48:4
12 [a]Gen. 12:7; 13:15; 26:3, 4; 28:13
13 [a]Gen. 17:22
14 [a]Gen. 28:18
15 [a]Gen. 28:19
16 [I]Hebr. *a little piece of ground*
17 [a]Gen. 30:24; 1Sam. 4:20
18 [I]That is, *The son of my sorrow* [II]That is, *The son of the right hand*
19 [a]Gen. 48:7 [b]Ruth 1:2; 4:11; Mic. 5:2; Matt. 2:6
20 [a]1Sam. 10:2; 2Sam. 18:18
21 [a]Mic. 4:8
22 [a]Gen. 49:4; 1Chr. 5:1; 2Sam. 16:22; 20:3; 1Cor. 5:1
23 [a]Gen. 46:8; Ex. 1:2
27 [a]Gen. 13:18; 23:2, 19 [b]Josh. 14:15; 15:13

35:23–26 This brief listing of Jacob's twelve sons and their mothers follows a longer account of the circumstances of their births. Although later there would be twelve tribes of Israel, Jacob's sons and the heads of those twelve tribes are not the same in every case. Ten of the sons, excluding Levi and Joseph, were the heads of tribes named for them. God later claimed the tribe of Levi as an exchange for the firstborn sons to which he had right because of the Passover in Egypt. Therefore, they had no portion of the inheritance of Israel. Joseph was Jacob's favorite son and was afforded the honor of having two tribes come from him. Jacob formally adopted his two grandsons, Ephraim and Manasseh, as his own sons. Through them Joseph received a double portion of his father's inheritance. With the double portion of Joseph there remained twelve tribes to share the inheritance which God promised to Israel.

and died,[4191] and [a]was gathered unto his people, *being* old[2205] and full of days:[3117] and [b]his sons Esau and Jacob buried[6912] him.

Esau's Family Record

36 Now these *are* the generations[8435] of Esau, [a]who is Edom.[123]

2 [a]Esau took his wives of the daughters of Canaan; Adah the daughter of Elon the Hittite, and [a]Aholibamah the daughter of Anah the daughter of Zibeon the Hivite;

3 And [a]Bashemath Ishmael's daughter, sister of Nebajoth.

4 And [a]Adah bare to Esau Eliphaz; and Bashemath bare Reuel;

5 And Aholibamah bare Jeush, and Jaalam, and Korah: these *are* the sons of Esau, which were born unto him in the land of Canaan.

6 And Esau took his wives, and his sons, and his daughters, and all the [I]persons[5315] of his house, and his cattle, and all his beasts, and all his substance, which he had got in the land[776] of Canaan; and went into the country[776] from the face of his brother Jacob.

7 [a]For their riches were more than that they might dwell together; and [b]the land wherein they were strangers[4033] could not bear[5375] them because of their cattle.

8 Thus dwelt Esau in [a]mount Seir: [b]Esau *is* Edom.

9 And these *are* the generations of Esau the father[1] of [I]the Edomites in mount Seir:

10 These *are* the names of Esau's sons; [a]Eliphaz the son of Adah the wife of Esau, Reuel the son of Bashemath the wife of Esau.

11 And the sons of Eliphaz were Teman, Omar, [Ia]Zepho, and Gatam, and Kenaz.

12 And Timna was concubine to Eliphaz Esau's son; and she bare to Eliphaz [a]Amalek: these *were* the sons of Adah Esau's wife.

13 And these *are* the sons of Reuel; Nahath, and Zerah, Shammah, and

29 [a]Gen. 15:15; 25:8 [b]Gen. 25:9; 49:31
1 [a]Gen. 25:30
2 [a]Gen. 26:34 [b]Gen. 36:25
3 [a]Gen. 28:9
4 [a]1Chr. 1:35
6 [I]Hebr. *souls*
7 [a]Gen. 13:6, 11 [b]Gen. 17:8; 28:4
8 [a]Gen. 32:3; Deut. 2:5; Josh. 24:4 [b]Gen. 36:1
9 [I]Hebr. *Edom*
10 [a]1Chr. 1:35-37
11 [I]Or, *Zephi* [a]1Chr. 1:36
12 [a]Ex. 17:8, 14; Num. 24:20; 1Sam. 15:2-9
20 [a]1Chr. 1:38 [b]Gen. 14:6; Deut. 2:12, 22
22 [I]Or, *Homam* [a]1Chr. 1:39
23 [I]Or, *Alian* [II]Or, *Shephi* [a]1Chr. 1:40 [b]1Chr. 1:40
24 [a]Lev. 19:19
26 [I]Or, *Amram* [a]1Chr. 1:41

Mizzah: these were the sons of Bashemath Esau's wife.

14 And these were the sons of Aholibamah, the daughter of Anah the daughter of Zibeon, Esau's wife: and she bare to Esau Jeush, and Jaalam, and Korah.

15 These *were* dukes[441] of the sons of Esau: the sons of Eliphaz the firstborn *son* of Esau; duke Teman, duke Omar, duke Zepho, duke Kenaz,

16 Duke Korah, duke Gatam, *and* duke Amalek: these *are* the dukes *that came* of Eliphaz in the land of Edom; these *were* the sons of Adah.

17 And these *are* the sons of Reuel Esau's son; duke Nahath, duke Zerah, duke Shammah, duke Mizzah: these *are* the dukes *that came* of Reuel in the land of Edom; these *are* the sons of Bashemath Esau's wife.

18 And these *are* the sons of Aholibamah Esau's wife; duke Jeush, duke Jaalam, duke Korah: these *were* the dukes *that came* of Aholibamah the daughter of Anah, Esau's wife.

19 These are the sons of Esau, who *is* Edom, and these *are* their dukes.

20 [a]These *are* the sons of Seir [b]the Horite, who inhabited[3427] the land; Lotan, and Shobal, and Zibeon, and Anah.

21 And Dishon, and Ezer, and Dishan: these *are* the dukes of the Horites, the children[1121] of Seir in the land of Edom.

22 And the children of Lotan were Hori and [Ia]Hemam; and Lotan's sister *was* Timna.

23 And the children of Shobal *were* these; [Ia]Alvan, and Manahath, and Ebal, [IIb]Shepho, and Onam.

24 And these *are* the children of Zibeon; both Ajah, and Anah: this *was that* Anah that found [a]the mules in the wilderness, as he fed the asses of Zibeon his father.

25 And the children of Anah *were* these; Dishon, and Aholibamah the daughter of Anah.

26 And these *are* the children of Dishon; [Ia]Hemdan, and Eshban, and Ithran, and Cheran.

27 The children of Ezer *are* these; Bilhan, and Zaavan, and [I][a]Akan.

28 The children of Dishan *are* these; Uz, and Aran.

29 These *are* the dukes *that came* of the Horites; duke Lotan, duke Shobal, duke Zibeon, duke Anah.

30 Duke Dishon, duke Ezer, duke Dishan: these *are* the dukes *that came* of Hori, among their dukes in the land of Seir.

31 And [a]these *are* the kings that reigned[4427] in the land of Edom, before there reigned any king over the children of Israel.

32 And Bela the son of Beor reigned in Edom: and the name of his city *was* Dinhabah.

33 And Bela died,[4191] and Jobab the son of Zerah of Bozrah reigned in his stead.

34 And Jobab died, and Husham of the land of Temani reigned in his stead.

35 And Husham died, and Hadad the son of Bedad, who smote[5221] Midian in the field of Moab, reigned in his stead: and the name of his city *was* Avith.

36 And Hadad died, and Samlah of Masrekah reigned in his stead.

37 And Samlah died, and Saul of Rehoboth *by* the river reigned in his stead.

38 And Saul died, and Baal–hanan the son of Achbor reigned in his stead.

39 And Baal–hanan the son of Achbor died, and [a]Hadar reigned in his stead: and the name of his city *was* Pau; and his wife's name *was* Mehetabel, the daughter of Matred, the daughter of Mezahab.

40 And these *are* the names of [a]the dukes *that came* of Esau, according to their families,[4940] after their places,[4725] by their names; duke Timnah, duke [I]Alvah, duke Jetheth,

41 Duke Aholibamah, duke Elah, duke Pinon,

42 Duke Kenaz, duke Teman, duke Mibzar,

43 Duke Magdiel, duke Iram: these *be* the dukes of Edom, according to their habitations[4186] in the land of their possession:[272] he *is* Esau the father of [I]the Edomites.

Joseph Has a Dream

37 ⊶ And Jacob dwelt in the land[776] [I][a]wherein his father[1] was a stranger,[4033] in the land of Canaan.

2 These *are* the generations[8435] of Jacob. Joseph, *being* seventeen years old, was feeding the flock with his brethren; and the lad *was* with the sons of Bilhah, and with the sons of Zilpah, his father's wives: and Joseph brought unto his father [a]their evil[7451] report.

3 Now Israel loved[157] Joseph more than all his children,[1121] because he *was* [a]the son[1121] of his old age:[2208] and he made[6213] him a coat of *many* [I][b]colours.[6446]

4 And when his brethren saw[7200] that their father loved him more than all his brethren, they [a]hated[8130] him, and could not speak peaceably[7965] unto him.

5 And Joseph dreamed a dream, and he told[5046] *it* his brethren: and they hated him yet the more.

6 And he said unto them, Hear, I pray you, this dream which I have dreamed:

7 For, [a]behold, we *were* binding sheaves in the field,[7704] and, lo, my sheaf

27 [I]Or, *Jakan* [a]1Chr. 1:42
31 [a]1Chr. 1:43
39 [a]1Chr. 1:50
40 [I]Or, *Aliah* [a]1Chr. 1:51
43 [I]Hebr. *Edom*
1 [I]Hebr. *of his father's sojournings* [a]Gen. 17:8; 23:4; 28:4; 36:7; Heb. 11:9
2 [a]1Sam. 2:22-24
3 [I]Or, *pieces* [a]Gen. 44:20 [b]Judg. 5:30; 2Sam. 13:18
4 [a]Gen. 27:41; 49:23
7 [a]Gen. 42:6, 9; 43:26; 44:14

⊶ **37:1–11** Joseph was singled out by God from his conception. His very birth was an answer to his mother Rachel's prayers. His father's preferential treatment of him, his special coat being an emblem of this, caused his brothers to envy him and Joseph's prophetic dreams only intensified their feelings. Yet these dreams, and Joseph's ability to interpret them, were a sign of God's special blessing on Joseph. They would be the means of his advancement in Egypt and the preservation of God's people. Joseph's personal faith and obedience never wavered, whether he was in a prison or a palace. His clever suggestions to Pharaoh would provide a place for Jacob's family to grow into a nation. They would also usher in a time of prosperity for Egypt—God is willing to bless others so that His people may prosper.

arose, and also stood upright;[5324] and, behold, your sheaves stood round about, and made obeisance[7812] to my sheaf.

8 And his brethren said to him, Shalt thou indeed reign[4427] over us? or shalt thou indeed have dominion[4910] over us? And they hated him yet the more for his dreams, and for his words.

9 And he dreamed yet another dream, and told[5608] it his brethren, and said, Behold, I have dreamed a dream more; and, behold, [a]the sun and the moon and the eleven stars made obeisance to me.

10 And he told *it* to his father, and to his brethren: and his father rebuked[1605] him, and said unto him, What *is* this dream that thou hast dreamed? Shall I and thy mother and [a]thy brethren indeed come to bow down[7812] ourselves to thee to the earth?[776]

11 And [a]his brethren[251] envied[7065] him; but his father [b]observed[8104] the saying.[1697]

Joseph Becomes a Slave

12 And his brethren went to feed their father's flock in Shechem.

13 And Israel said unto Joseph, Do not thy brethren feed *the flock* in Shechem? come, and I will send thee unto them. And he said to him, Here *am I.*

14 And he said to him, Go, I pray thee, [I][a]see whether it be well[7965] with thy brethren, and well with the flocks; and bring me word[1697] again. So he sent him out of the vale[6010] of [b]Hebron, and he came to Shechem.

15 And a certain man[376] found him, and, behold, *he was* wandering in the field: and the man asked him, saying, What seekest thou?

16 And he said, I seek my brethren: [a]tell[5046] me, I pray thee, where they feed *their flocks.*

17 And the man said, They are departed hence; for I heard them say, Let us go to Dothan. And Joseph went after his brethren, and found them in [a]Dothan.

18 And when they saw him afar off, even before he came near unto them, [a]they conspired against him to slay him.

19 And they said one to another, Behold, this [I]dreamer[1167,2472] cometh.

20 [a]Come now therefore, and let us slay[2026] him, and cast him into some pit,[953] and we will say, Some evil[7451] beast[2416] hath devoured him: and we shall see[7200] what will become of his dreams.

21 And [a]Reuben heard *it,* and he delivered him out of their hands;[3027] and said, Let us not kill[5221] him.

22 And Reuben said unto them, Shed[8210] no blood,[1818] *but* cast him into this pit that *is* in the wilderness, and lay no hand upon him; that he might rid[5337] him out of their hands, to deliver him to his father again.

23 And it came to pass, when Joseph was come unto his brethren, that they stript Joseph out of his coat, *his* coat of *many* [I]colours that *was* on him;

24 And they took him, and cast him into a pit: and the pit *was* empty, *there was* no water in it.

🗝 25 [a]And they sat down to eat bread: and they lifted up their eyes and looked, and, behold, a company of [b]Ishmeelites came from Gilead with their camels bearing[5375] spicery and [c]balm and myrrh,[3910] going to carry *it* down to Egypt.

26 And Judah said unto his brethren, What profit[1215] *is it* if we slay our brother, and [a]conceal[3680] his blood?

27 Come, and let us sell him to the Ishmeelites, and [a]let not our hand be upon him; for he *is* [b]our brother *and* [c]our flesh.[1320] And his brethren [I]were content.

9 [a]Gen. 45:9

10 [a]Gen. 27:29

11 [a]Acts 7:9 [b]Dan. 7:28; Luke 2:19, 51

14 [I]Hebr. *see the peace of thy brethren* [a]Gen. 29:6 [b]Gen. 35:27

16 [a]Song 1:7

17 [a]2Kgs. 6:13

18 [a]1Sam. 19:1; Ps. 31:13; 37:12, 32; 94:21; Matt. 27:1; Mark 14:1; John 11:53; Acts 23:12

19 [I]Hebr. *master of dreams*

20 [a]Prov. 1:11, 16; 6:17; 27:4

21 [a]Gen. 42:22

23 [I]Or, *pieces*

25 [a]Prov. 30:20; Amos 6:6 [b]Gen. 37:28, 36 [c]Jer. 8:22

26 [a]Gen. 4:10; Gen. 37:20; Job 16:18

27 [I]Hebr. *hearkened* [a]1Sam. 18:17 [b]Gen. 42:21 [c]Gen. 29:14

🗝 **37:25, 28, 36** It is possible that the Ishmaelites may have been the owners of the caravan, which was made up of other peoples. Another possibility is the term "Midianites" is only given as a geographical reference. However, it is most likely that several different groups traveled together in the caravan to help ward off robbers.

🔑 28 Then there passed by[5674] [a]Midianites merchantmen; and they drew and lifted up[5927] Joseph out of the pit, [b]and sold Joseph to the Ishmeelites for [c]twenty *pieces* of silver: and they brought Joseph into Egypt.

29 And Reuben returned unto the pit; and, behold, Joseph *was* not in the pit; and he [a]rent his clothes.

30 And he returned unto his brethren, and said, The child [a]is not; and I, whither shall I go?

31 And they took [a]Joseph's coat, and killed[7819] a kid[8163] of the goats, and dipped[2881] the coat in the blood;[1818]

32 And they sent the coat of *many* colours, and they brought *it* to their father; and said, This have we found: know[5234] now whether it *be* thy son's coat or no.

33 And he knew it, and said, *It is* my son's coat; an [a]evil beast hath devoured him; Joseph is without doubt rent in pieces.

34 And Jacob [a]rent his clothes, and put sackcloth[8242] upon his loins, and mourned for his son many days.

35 And all his sons and all his daughters [a]rose up to comfort[5162] him; but he refused[3985] to be comforted; and he said, For [b]I will go down into the grave[7585] unto my son mourning. Thus his father wept for him.

🔑 36 And [a]the Midianites sold him into Egypt unto Potiphar, an [I][b]officer[5631] of Pharaoh's, *and* [II]captain[8269] of the guard.

Judah and Tamar

38 And it came to pass at that time,[6256] that Judah went down from his brethren, and [a]turned in to a certain[376] Adullamite, whose name *was* Hirah.

2 And Judah [a]saw there a daughter of a certain[376] Canaanite, whose name *was* [b]Shuah; and he took her, and went in unto her.

3 And she conceived, and bare a son; and he called his name [a]Er.

4 And she conceived again, and bare a son; and she called his name [a]Onan.

5 And she yet again conceived, and bare a son; and called his name [a]Shelah: and he was at Chezib, when she bare him.

6 And Judah [a]took a wife for Er his firstborn, whose name *was* Tamar.

7 And [a]Er, Judah's firstborn, was wicked[7451] in the sight of the LORD; [b]and the LORD slew[4191] him.

🔑 8 And Judah said unto Onan, Go in unto [a]thy brother's[251] wife, and marry her, and raise up seed[2233] to thy brother.

9 And Onan knew that the seed should not be [a]his; and it came to pass, when he went in unto his brother's wife, that he spilled[7843] *it* on the ground,[776] lest that he should give seed to his brother.

10 And the thing which he did[6213] [I]displeased[3411,5869] the LORD: wherefore he slew [a]him also.

11 Then said Judah to Tamar his daughter in law, [a]Remain a widow[490] at thy father's house, till Shelah my son be grown: for he said, Lest peradventure he die[4191] also, as his brethren *did*. And Tamar went and dwelt [b]in her father's house.

12 And [I]in process of time[7235,3117] the daughter of Shuah Judah's wife died; and Judah [a]was comforted, and went up unto his sheepshearers to Timnath, he and his friend[7453] Hirah the Adullamite.

13 And it was told[5046] Tamar, saying, Behold thy father in law goeth up [a]to Timnath to shear his sheep.

14 And she put her widow's garments off from her, and covered[3680] her with a vail, and wrapped herself, and [a]sat in [I]an open place, which *is* by the way to Timnath; for she saw [b]that Shelah was grown, and she was not given unto him to wife.[802]

15 When Judah saw[7200] her, he

28 [a]Judg. 6:3 [b]Gen. 45:4, 5; Ps. 105:17; Acts 7:9 [c]Matt. 27:9
29 [a]Job 1:20
30 [a]Gen. 42:13, 36; Jer. 31:15
31 [a]Gen. 37:23
33 [a]Gen. 37:20; 44:28
34 [a]Gen. 37:29; 2Sam. 3:31
35 [a]2Sam. 12:17 [b]Gen. 42:38; 44:29, 31
36 [I]Hebr. *eunuch:* But the word doth signify not only *eunuchs,* but also *chamberlains, courtiers,* and *officers* [II]Hebr. *chief of the slaughtermen, or executioners* [a]Gen. 39:1 [b]Esth. 1:10

1 [a]Gen. 19:3; 2Kgs. 4:8
2 [a]Gen. 34:2 [b]1Chr. 2:3
3 [a]Gen. 46:12; Num. 26:19
4 [a]Gen. 46:12; Num. 26:19
5 [a]Gen. 46:12; Num. 26:20
6 [a]Gen. 21:21
7 [a]Gen. 46:12; Num. 26:19 [b]1Chr. 2:3
8 [a]Deut. 25:5; Matt. 22:24
9 [a]Deut. 25:6
10 [I]Hebr. *was evil in the eyes of the LORD* [a]Gen. 46:12; Num. 26:19
11 [a]Ruth 1:13 [b]Lev. 22:13
12 [I]Hebr. *the days were multiplied* [a]2Sam. 13:39
13 [a]Josh. 15:10, 57; Judg. 14:1
14 [I]Hebr. *the door of eyes,* or, *of Enaji* [a]Prov. 7:12 [b]Gen. 38:11, 26

🔑 **38:8** See note on Ruth 4:1–8, on kinsman redeemer.

thought[2803] her *to be* an harlot;[2181] because she had covered her face.

16 And he turned unto her by the way, and said, Go to, I pray thee, let me come in unto thee; (for he knew[3045] not that she *was* his daughter in law.) And she said, What wilt thou give me, that thou mayest come in unto me?

17 And he said, [a]I will send *thee* [I]a kid from the flock. And she said, [b]Wilt thou give *me* a pledge,[6162] till thou send *it?*

18 And he said, What pledge shall I give thee? And she said, [a]Thy signet, and thy bracelets, and thy staff[4294] that *is* in thine hand. And he gave *it* her, and came in unto her, and she conceived by him.

19 And she arose, and went away, and [a]laid by her vail from her, and put on the garments of her widowhood.

20 And Judah sent the kid by the hand of his friend the Adullamite, to receive *his* pledge from the woman's[802] hand: but he found her not.

21 Then he asked[7592] the men[582] of that place, saying, Where *is* the harlot,[6948] that *was* openly by the way side? And they said, There was no harlot in this *place.*

22 And he returned to Judah, and said, I cannot find her; and also the men of the place said, *that* there was no harlot in this *place.*

23 And Judah said, Let her take *it* to her, lest we [I]be shamed: behold, I sent this kid, and thou hast not found her.

24 And it came to pass about three months after, that it was told Judah, saying, Tamar thy daughter in law hath [a]played the harlot;[2181] and also, behold, she *is* with child by whoredom.[2183] And Judah said, Bring her forth, [b]and let her be burnt.

25 When she *was* brought forth, she sent to her father in law, saying, By the man,[376] whose these *are, am* I with child: and she said, [a]Discern,[5234] I pray thee, whose *are* these, [b]the signet, and bracelets, and staff.

26 And Judah [a]acknowledged[5234] *them,* and said, [b]She hath been more righteous[6663] than I; because that [c]I gave her not to Shelah my son. And he knew her again [d]no more.

27 And it came to pass in the time[6256] of her travail, that, behold, twins *were* in her womb.[990]

28 And it came to pass, when she travailed,[3205] that *the one* put out *his* hand: and the midwife took and bound upon his hand[3027] a scarlet thread, saying, This came out first.[7223]

29 And it came to pass, as he drew back his hand, that, behold, his brother came out: and she said, [I]How hast thou broken forth?[6555] *this* breach[6556] *be* upon thee: therefore his name was called [II][a]Pharez.[6557]

30 And afterward came out his brother, that had the scarlet thread upon his hand: and his name was called Zarah.

Joseph and Potiphar's Wife

39 And Joseph was brought down[3381] to Egypt; and [a]Potiphar, an officer[5631] of Pharoah, captain[8269] of the guard, an Egyptian, [b]bought him of the hands of the Ishmeelites, which had brought him down thither.

2 And [a]the LORD was with Joseph, and he was a prosperous man;[376] and he was in the house[1004] of his master[113] the Egyptian.

3 And his master saw[7200] that the LORD *was* with him, and that the LORD [a]made all that he did[6213] to prosper in his hand.

4 And Joseph [a]found grace[2580] in his sight, and he served[8334] him: and he made him [b]overseer[6485] over his house, and all *that* he had he put into his hand.

5 And it came to pass from the time[227] *that* he had made him overseer in his house, and over all that he had, that [a]the LORD blessed[1288] the Egyptian's house for Joseph's sake; and the blessing[1293] of the LORD was upon all that he had in the house, and in the field.

6 And he left[5800] all that he had in Joseph's hand;[3027] and he knew[3045] not ought he had, save the bread which he did eat. And Joseph [a]was a goodly *person,* and well favoured.

17 [I]Hebr. *a kid of the goats* [a]Ezek. 16:33 [b]Gen. 38:20

18 [a]Gen. 38:25

19 [a]Gen. 38:14

23 [I]Hebr. *become a contempt*

24 [a]Judg. 19:2 [b]Lev. 21:9; Deut. 22:21

25 [a]Gen. 37:32 [b]Gen. 38:18

26 [a]Gen. 37:33 [b]1Sam. 24:17 [c]Gen. 38:14 [d]Job 34:31, 32

29 [I]Or, *Wherefore hast thou made* this *breach against thee?* [II]That is, *A breach* [a]Gen. 46:12; Num. 26:20; 1Chr. 2:4; Matt. 1:3

1 [a]Gen. 37:36; Ps. 105:17 [b]Gen. 37:28

2 [a]Gen. 21:22; 26:24, 28; 28:15; 1Sam. 3:19; 16:18; 18:14, 28; Acts 7:9

3 [a]Ps. 1:3

4 [a]Gen. 18:3; 19:19; 39:21 [b]Gen. 24:2

5 [a]Gen. 30:27

6 [a]1Sam. 16:12

7 And it came to pass after these things, that his master's wife[802] cast her eyes upon Joseph; and she said, [a]Lie7901 with me.

8 But he refused,[3985] and said unto his master's wife, Behold, my master wotteth[3045] not what *is* with me in the house, and he hath committed all that he hath to my hand;

9 *There is* none greater in this house than I; neither hath he kept back any thing from me but thee, because thou *art* his wife: [a]how then can I do[6213] this great wickedness,[7451] and [b]sin[2398] against God?[430]

10 And it came to pass, as she spake to Joseph day by day, that he hearkened[8085] not unto her, to lie by her, *or* to be with her.

11 And it came to pass about this time,[3117] that *Joseph* went into the house to do his business;[4399] and *there was* none of the men[582] of the house there within.

12 And [a]she caught him by his garment, saying, Lie with me: and he left his garment in her hand, and fled, and got him out.

13 And it came to pass, when she saw that he had left[5800] his garment in her hand, and was fled forth,

14 That she called[7121] unto the men of her house, and spake unto them, saying, See,[7200] he hath brought in an Hebrew5680 unto us to mock6711 us; he came in unto me to lie with me, and I cried with a [I]loud voice:

15 And it came to pass, when he heard that I lifted up my voice and cried, that he left his garment with me, and fled, and got him out.

16 And she laid up his garment by her, until his lord[113] came home.

17 And she [a]spake unto him according to these words, saying, The Hebrew servant,[5650] which thou hast brought unto us, came in unto me to mock me:

18 And it came to pass, as I lifted up my voice and cried, that he left his garment with me, and fled out.

19 And it came to pass, when his master heard the words of his wife,

7 [a]2Sam. 13:11
9 [a]Prov. 6:29, 32 [b]Gen. 20:6; Lev. 6:2; 2Sam. 12:13; Ps. 51:4
12 [a]Prov. 7:13-20
14 [I]Hebr. *great*
17 [a]Ex. 23:1; Ps. 120:3
19 [a]Prov. 6:34, 35
20 [a]Ps. 105:18; 1Pet. 2:19 [b]Gen. 40:3, 15; 41:14
21 [I]Hebr. *extended kindness unto him* [a]Ex. 3:21; 11:3; 12:36; Ps. 106:46; Prov. 16:7; Dan. 1:9; Acts 7:9, 10
22 [a]Gen. 40:3, 4
23 [a]Gen. 39:2, 3
1 [a]Neh. 1:11
2 [a]Prov. 16:14
3 [a]Gen. 39:20, 23

which she spake unto him, saying, After this manner did thy servant to me; that his [a]wrath[639] was kindled.[2734]

20 And Joseph's master took him, and [a]put him into the [b]prison, a place where the king's prisoners615 *were* bound: and he was there in the prison.

21 But the LORD was with Joseph, and [I]shewed him mercy,[2617] and [a]gave him favour[2580] in the sight of the keeper[8269] of the prison.

22 And the keeper of the prison [a]committed to Joseph's hand all the prisoners that *were* in the prison;[1004,5470] and whatsoever they did there, he was the doer *of it*.

23 The keeper of the prison looked not to any thing *that was* under his hand; because [a]the LORD was with him, and *that* which he did, the LORD made *it* to prosper.6743

Joseph Explains the Prisoners' Dreams

40 And it came to pass after these things, *that* the [a]butler4945 of the king of Egypt and *his* baker644 had offended[2398] their lord[113] the king of Egypt.

2 And Pharaoh was [a]wroth against two *of* his officers,[5631] against the chief[8269] of the butlers, and against the chief of the bakers.

3 [a]And he put them in ward4929 in the house of the captain[8269] of the guard, into the prison, the place where Joseph *was* bound.

4 And the captain of the guard charged[6485] Joseph with them, and he served[8334] them: and they continued a season[3117] in ward.

5 And they dreamed a dream both of them, each man his dream in one night, each man[376] according to the interpretation of his dream, the butler and the baker of the king of Egypt, which *were* bound in the prison.

6 And Joseph came in unto them in the morning, and looked[7200] upon them, and, behold, they *were* sad.[2196]

7 And he asked Pharaoh's officers

that *were* with him in the ward of his lord's house, saying, Wherefore [I][a]look ye *so* sadly[7451] to day?

8 And they said unto him, [a]We have dreamed a dream, and *there is* no interpreter[6622] of it. And Joseph said unto them, [b]*Do* not interpretations *belong* to God?[430] tell[5608] me *them,* I pray you.

9 And the chief butler told his dream to Joseph, and said to him, In my dream, behold, a vine *was* before me;

10 And in the vine *were* three branches: and it *was* as though it budded, *and* her blossoms shot forth; and the clusters thereof brought forth ripe grapes:

11 And Pharaoh's cup *was* in my hand:[3027] and I took the grapes, and pressed them into Pharaoh's cup, and I gave the cup into Pharaoh's hand.

12 And Joseph said unto him, [a]This *is* the interpretation of it: The three branches [b]*are* three days:[3117]

13 Yet within three days shall Pharaoh [I][a]lift up[5375] thine head, and restore thee unto thy place: and thou shalt deliver Pharaoh's cup into his hand, after the former manner when thou wast his butler.

14 But [I][a]think on[2142] me when it shall be well[3190] with thee, and [b]shew[6213] kindness,[2617] I pray thee, unto me, and make mention[2142] of me unto Pharaoh, and bring me out of this house:

15 For indeed I was stolen away out of the land[776] of the Hebrews: [a]and here also have I done nothing that they should put[7760] me into the dungeon.[953]

16 When the chief baker saw[7200] that the interpretation was good,[2896] he said unto Joseph, I also *was* in my dream, and, behold, I *had* three [I]white baskets on my head:

17 And in the uppermost[5945] basket *there was* of all manner of [I]bakemeats[3978,4639,644] for Pharaoh; and the birds did eat them out of the basket upon my head.

18 And Joseph answered and said, [a]This *is* the interpretation thereof: The three baskets *are* three days:

19 [a]Yet within three days shall Pharaoh [I]lift up thy head from off thee, and shall hang thee on a tree; and the birds shall eat thy flesh[1320] from off thee.

20 And it came to pass the third day, *which was* Pharaoh's [a]birthday, that he [b]made a feast[4960] unto all his servants: and he [I][c]lifted up the head of the chief butler and of the chief baker among his servants.

21 And he [a]restored the chief butler unto his butlership again; and [b]he gave the cup into Pharaoh's hand:

22 But he [a]hanged the chief baker: as Joseph had interpreted to them.

23 Yet did not the chief butler remember Joseph, but [a]forgat him.

Joseph Explains Pharaoh's Dream

41 And it came to pass at the end of two full years, that Pharaoh dreamed: and, behold, he stood by the river.

2 And, behold, there came up out of the river seven well favoured[4758][3303] kine[6510] and fatfleshed;[1320][1277] and they fed in a meadow.

3 And, behold, seven other kine came up after them out of the river, ill favoured[4758,7451] and leanfleshed;[1320][1851] and stood by the *other* kine upon the brink[8193] of the river.

4 And the ill favoured and leanfleshed kine did eat up the seven well favoured and fat kine. So Pharaoh awoke.

5 And he slept and dreamed the second time: and, behold, seven ears of corn came up upon one stalk, [I]rank[1277] and good.[2896]

6 And, behold, seven thin[1851] ears and blasted[7710] with the east wind sprung up after them.

7 And the seven thin ears devoured the seven rank and full ears. And Pharaoh awoke, and, behold, *it was* a dream.

8 And it came to pass in the morning [a]that his spirit[7307] was troubled; and he sent and called[7121] for all [b]the magicians[2748] of Egypt, and all the [c]wise men[2450] thereof: and Pharaoh told[5608]

7 [I]Hebr. are *your faces evil?* [a]Neh. 2:2

8 [a]Gen. 41:15 [b]Gen. 41:16; Dan. 2:11, 28, 47

12 [a]Gen. 40:18; 41:12, 25; Judg. 7:14; Dan. 2:36; 4:19 [b]Gen. 41:26

13 [I]Or, *reckon* [a]2Kgs. 25:27; Ps. 3:3; Jer. 52:31

14 [I]Hebr. *remember me with thee* [a]Luke 23:42 [b]Josh. 2:12; 1Sam. 20:14, 15; 2Sam. 9:1; 1Kgs. 2:7

15 [a]Gen. 39:20

16 [I]Or, *full of holes*

17 [I]Hebr. *meat of Pharaoh, the work of a baker, or cook*

18 [a]Gen. 40:12

19 [I]Or, *reckon thee,* and take thy office *from thee* [a]Gen. 40:13

20 [a]Matt. 14:6 [b]Mark 6:21 [I]Or, *reckoned* [c]Gen. 40:13, 19

21 [a]Gen. 40:13 [b]Neh. 2:1

22 [a]Gen. 40:19

23 [a]Job 19:14; Ps. 31:12; Eccl. 9:15, 16; Amos 6:6

5 [I]Hebr. *fat*

8 [a]Dan. 2:1; 4:5, 19 [b]Ex. 7:11, 22; Isa. 29:14; Dan. 1:20; 2:2; 4:7 [c]Matt. 2:1

them his dream; but *there was* none that could interpret them unto Pharaoh.

9 Then spake the chief[8269] butler unto Pharaoh, saying, I do remember[2142] my faults[2399] this day:

10 Pharaoh was [a]wroth[7107] with his servants,[5650] [b]and put me in ward in the captain[8269] of the guard's house, *both* me and the chief baker:

11 And [a]we dreamed a dream in one night, I and he; we dreamed each man according to the interpretation of his dream.

12 And *there was* there with us a young man, an Hebrew,5680 [a]servant to the captain of the guard; and we told him, and he [b]interpreted to us our dreams; to each man according to his dream he did interpret.

13 And it came to pass, [a]as he interpreted to us, so it was; me he restored unto mine office, and him he hanged.

14 [a]Then Pharaoh sent and called Joseph, and they [I][b]brought him hastily [c]out of the dungeon:[953] and he shaved *himself,* and changed his raiment, and came in unto Pharaoh.

15 And Pharaoh said unto Joseph, I have dreamed a dream, and *there is* none that can interpret it: [a]and I have heard say of thee, *that* [I]thou canst understand[8085] a dream to interpret it.

16 And Joseph answered Pharaoh, saying, [a]*It is* not in me: [b]God[430] shall give Pharaoh an answer of peace.[7965]

17 And Pharaoh said unto Joseph, [a]In my dream, behold, I stood upon the bank[8193] of the river:

18 And, behold, there came up out of the river seven kine, fatfleshed and well favoured; and they fed in a meadow:

19 And, behold, seven other kine came up after them, poor and very ill favoured and leanfleshed, such as I never saw in all the land[776] of Egypt for badness:[7455]

20 And the lean and the ill favoured kine did eat up the first seven fat kine:

21 And when they had [I]eaten them up, it could not be known that they had eaten them; but they *were* still ill favoured, as at the beginning. So I awoke.

22 And I saw[7200] in my dream, and, behold, seven ears came up in one stalk, full and good:

23 And, behold, seven ears, [I]withered, thin, *and* blasted with the east wind, sprung up after them:

24 And the thin ears devoured the seven good ears: and [a]I told *this* unto the magicians; but *there was* none that could declare[5046] *it* to me.

25 And Joseph said unto Pharaoh, The dream of Pharaoh *is* one: [a]God hath showed[5046] Pharaoh what he *is* about to do[6213].

26 The seven good[2896] kine *are* seven years; and the seven good ears *are* seven years: the dream *is* one.

27 And the seven thin and ill favoured kine that came up after them *are* seven years; and the seven empty ears blasted with the east wind shall be [a]seven years of famine.

28 [a]This *is* the thing[1697] which I have spoken unto Pharaoh: What God *is* about to do he sheweth[7200] unto Pharaoh.

29 Behold, there come [a]seven years of great plenty throughout all the land of Egypt:

30 And there shall [a]arise after them seven years of famine; and all the plenty shall be forgotten in the land of Egypt; and the famine [b]shall consume the land;

31 And the plenty shall not be known in the land by reason of that famine following; for it *shall be* very [I]grievous.

32 And for that the dream was doubled unto Pharaoh twice; *it is* because the [a]thing *is* [I]established by God, and God will shortly bring it to pass.[6213]

33 Now therefore let Pharaoh look out[7200] a man[376] discreet[995] and wise,[2450] and set him over the land of Egypt.

34 Let Pharaoh do[6213] *this,* and let him appoint[6485] [I]officers[6496] over the land, and [a]take up the fifth part of the land of Egypt in the seven plenteous years.

35 And [a]let them gather[6908] all the food of those good years that come, and lay up corn under the hand of Pharaoh, and let them keep[8104] food in the cities.

36 And that food shall be for

10 [a]Gen. 40:2, 3 [b]Gen. 39:20
11 [a]Gen. 40:5
12 [a]Gen. 37:36 [b]Gen. 40:12-23
13 [a]Gen. 40:22
14 [I]Hebr. *made him run* [a]Ps. 105:20 [b]Dan. 2:25 [c]1Sam. 2:8; Ps. 113:7, 8
15 [I]Or, *when thou hearest a dream thou canst interpret it* [a]Gen. 41:12; Ps. 25:14; Dan. 5:16
16 [a]Dan. 2:30; Acts 3:12; 2Cor. 3:5 [b]Gen. 40:8; Dan. 2:22, 28, 47; 4:2
17 [a]Gen. 41:1
21 [I]Hebr. *come to the inward parts of them*
23 [I]Or, *small*
24 [a]Gen. 41:8; Dan. 4:7
25 [a]Dan. 2:28, 29, 45; Rev. 4:1
27 [a]2Kgs. 8:1
28 [a]Gen. 41:25
29 [a]Gen. 41:47
30 [a]Gen. 41:54 [b]Gen. 47:13
31 [I]Hebr. *heavy*
32 [I]Or, *prepared of God* [a]Num. 23:19; Isa. 46:10, 11
34 [I]Or, *overseers* [a]Prov. 6:6-8
35 [a]Gen. 41:48

store[6487] to the land against the seven years of famine, which shall be in the land of Egypt; that the land [I][a]perish[3772] not through the famine.

Pharaoh Makes Joseph A Ruler

37 And [a]the thing was good[3190] in the eyes of Pharaoh, and in the eyes of all his servants.

38 And Pharaoh said unto his servants, Can we find *such a one* as this *is,* a man [a]in whom the Spirit[7307] of God *is?*

39 And Pharaoh said unto Joseph, Forasmuch as God hath shewed thee all this, *there is* none so discreet and wise as thou *art:*

40 [a]Thou shalt be[1961] over my house,[1004] and according unto thy word[6310] shall all my people[5971] [I]be ruled: only in the throne[3678] will I be greater than thou.

41 And Pharaoh said unto Joseph, See, I have [a]set thee over all the land of Egypt.

🔑42 And Pharaoh [a]took off his ring[2885] from his hand, and put it upon Joseph's hand, and [b]arrayed him in vestures[899] of [I]fine linen, [c]and put a gold chain about his neck;

43 And he made him to ride in the second chariot which he had; [a]and they cried[7121] before him, [I][b]Bow the knee: and he made him *ruler* [c]over all the land of Egypt.

44 And Pharaoh said unto Joseph, I *am* Pharaoh, and without thee shall no man lift up his hand or foot in all the land of Egypt.

45 And Pharaoh called Joseph's name [I]Zaphnath–paaneah; and he gave him to wife Asenath the daughter of Poti–pherah [II][a]priest[3548] of On. And Joseph went out over *all* the land of Egypt.

46 And Joseph *was* thirty years old when he [a]stood before Pharaoh king[4428] of Egypt. And Joseph went out from the presence of Pharaoh, and went throughout all the land of Egypt.

47 And in the seven plenteous years the earth brought forth by handfuls.

48 And he gathered up all the food of the seven years, which were in the land of Egypt, and laid up the food in the cities: the food of the field, which *was* round about every city, laid he up in the same.

49 And Joseph gathered corn [a]as the sand of the sea, very much, until he left numbering;[5608] for *it was* without number.

50 [a]And unto Joseph were born two sons[1121] before the years of famine came, which Asenath the daughter of Poti–pherah [I][b]priest of On bare unto him.

51 And Joseph called the name of the firstborn [I]Manasseh:[4519] For God, *said he,* hath made me forget[5382] all my toil,[5999] and all my father's house.

52 And the name of the second called[7121] he [I]Ephraim:[669] For God hath caused me to be [a]fruitful[6509] in the land of my affliction.

53 And the seven years of plenteousness, that was in the land of Egypt, were ended.

54 [a]And the seven years of dearth[7458] began to come, [b]according as Joseph had said: and the dearth was in all lands;[776] but in all the land of Egypt there was bread.

55 And when all the land of Egypt was famished, the people cried to Pharaoh for bread: and Pharaoh said unto all the Egyptians, Go unto Joseph; what he saith to you, do.

36 IHebr. *be not cut off* aGen. 47:15, 19
37 aPs. 105:19; Acts 7:10
38 aNum. 27:18; Job 32:8; Prov. 2:6; Dan. 4:8, 18; 5:11, 14; 6:3
40 IHebr. *be armed,* or, *kiss* aPs. 105:21, 22; Acts 7:10
41 aDan. 6:3
42 IOr, *silk* aEsth. 3:10; 8:2, 8 bEsth. 8:15 cDan. 5:7, 29
43 IOr, *Tender father* aEsth. 6:9 bGen. 45:8 cGen. 42:6; 45:8, 26; Acts 7:10
45 IWhich in the Coptic signifies, *A revealer of secrets,* or, *The man to whom secrets are revealed* IIOr, *prince* aEx. 2:16; 2Sam. 8:18; 20:26
46 a1Sam. 16:21; 1Kgs. 12:6, 8; Dan. 1:19
49 aGen. 22:17; Judg. 7:12; 1Sam. 13:5; Ps. 78:27
50 IOr, *prince,* aGen. 46:20; 48:5 bGen. 41:45; 2Sam. 8:18
51 IThat is, *Forgetting*
52 IThat is, *Fruitful* aGen. 49:22
54 aPs. 105:16; Acts 7:11 bGen. 41:30

🔑 **41:42–49** Joseph was at the summit of political power. The ring and necklace were symbols of his office; riding in the second chariot suggests that Joseph was second in command over the whole kingdom. Joseph's service in the house of Potiphar and in the prison was divinely ordained preparation for directing the most populous nation in the ancient world. His scheme of gathering grain directly under Pharaoh's control (41:35, 48), undermined the power of the provincial nobles, and gives us reason to believe that he served under Pharaoh Sesostris III.

56 And the famine was over all the face of the earth:[776] And Joseph opened [I]all the storehouses, and [a]sold unto the Egyptians; and the famine waxed sore[2388] in the land of Egypt.

57 [a]And all countries[776] came into Egypt to Joseph for to buy *corn;* because that the famine was *so* sore[2388] in all lands.

Joseph's Brothers Come To Buy Food

42 Now when [a]Jacob saw that there was corn[7668] in Egypt, Jacob said unto his sons, Why do ye look one upon another?

2 And he said, Behold, I have heard that there is corn in Egypt: get you down thither, and buy for us from thence; that we may [a]live,[2421] and not die.[4191]

3 And Joseph's ten brethren went down to buy corn in Egypt.

4 But Benjamin, Joseph's brother, Jacob sent not with his brethren; for he said,[559] [a]Lest peradventure mischief befall him.

5 And the sons of Israel came to buy *corn* among those that came: for the famine was [a]in the land[776] of Canaan.

6 And Joseph *was* the governor[7989] [a]over the land, *and* he *it was* that sold to all the people[5971] of the land: and Joseph's brethren came, and [b]bowed down themselves[7812] before him *with* their faces[639] to the earth.

7 And Joseph saw his brethren, and he knew[5234] them, but made himself strange[5234] unto them, and spake [I]roughly[7186] unto them; and he said unto them, Whence come ye? And they said, From the land of Canaan to buy food.

8 And Joseph knew[5234] his brethren, but they knew not him.

9 And Joseph [a]remembered[2142] the dreams which he dreamed of them, and said unto them, Ye *are* spies; to see[7200] the nakedness[6172] of the land ye are come.

10 And they said unto him, Nay, my lord,[113] but to buy food are thy servants[5650] come.

11 We *are* all one man's[376] sons; we *are* true[3651] *men,* thy servants are no spies.

12 And he said unto them, Nay, but to see the nakedness of the land ye are come.

13 And they said, Thy servants *are* twelve brethren, the sons of one man in the land of Canaan; and, behold, the youngest *is* this day with our father, and one [a]*is* not.

14 And Joseph said unto them, That *is it* that I spake unto you, saying, Ye *are* spies:

15 Hereby ye shall be proved:[974] [a]By the life[2416] of Pharaoh ye shall not go forth hence, except your youngest brother come hither.

16 Send one of you, and let him fetch your brother, and ye shall be [I]kept in prison, that your words[1697] may be proved, whether *there be any* truth[571] in you: or else by the life of Pharaoh surely ye *are* spies.

17 And he [I]put them all together into ward three days.

18 And Joseph said unto them the third day, This do,[6213] and live;[2421] [a]*for* I fear[3373] God:[430]

19 If ye *be* true *men,* let one of your brethren be bound in the house of your prison: go ye, carry corn for the famine of your houses:

56 IHebr. *all wherein* was [a]Gen. 42:6; 47:14, 24
57 [a]Deut. 9:28
1 [a]Acts 7:12
2 [a]Gen. 43:8; Ps. 118:17; Isa. 38:1
4 [a]Gen. 42:38
5 [a]Acts 7:11
6 [a]Gen. 41:41 [b]Gen. 37:7
7 IHebr. *hard things with them*
9 [a]Gen. 37:5, 9
13 [a]Gen. 37:30; 44:20; Lam. 5:7
15 [a]1Sam. 1:26; 17:55
16 IHebr. *bound*
17 IHebr. *gathered*
18 [a]Lev. 25:43; Neh. 5:15

42:8 Why did Joseph's brothers not recognize him? To begin with, Joseph had been a teenager when he was sold into slavery. Almost twenty years had elapsed since that time. His brothers had never expected to see him again; as far as they were concerned, he was dead. In fact, both because of regret and because Jacob had most likely lamented over the loss of Joseph for all these years, his brothers had likely done all they could to forget Joseph. As an Egyptian leader, he would have been clean-shaven and well-dressed. And lastly, Joseph, whose voice was probably much different now, spoke to them through an interpreter. They would never have dreamed that it could be Joseph.

20 But [a]bring your youngest brother unto me; so shall your words be verified,[539] and ye shall not die. And they did so.

21 And they said one[376] to another,[251] [a]We *are* verily guilty[816] concerning our brother,[251] in that we saw the anguish6869 of his soul,[5315] when he besought[2603] us, and we would not hear; [b]therefore is this distress come upon us.

22 And Reuben answered them, saying, [a]Spake[559] I not unto you, saying, Do not sin[2398] against the child; and ye would not hear? therefore, behold, also his blood[1818] is [b]required.

23 And they knew[3045] not that Joseph understood[8085] *them;* for [I]he spake unto them by an interpreter.[3887]

24 And he turned himself about[5347] from them, and wept; and returned to them again, and communed with them, and took from them Simeon, and bound him before their eyes.

25 Then Joseph commanded[6680] to fill their sacks with corn, and to restore every man's money into his sack, and to give them provision for the way:[1870] and [a]thus did he unto them.

26 And they laded[5375] their asses with the corn, and departed thence.

27 And as [a]one of them opened his sack to give his ass provender4554 in the inn, he espied[7200] his money; for, behold, it *was* in his sack's mouth.[6310]

28 And he said unto his brethren, My money is restored;[7725] and, lo, *it is* even in my sack: and their heart[3820] [I]failed *them,* and they were afraid,[2729] saying one to another, What *is* this *that* God hath done[6213] unto us?

29 And they came unto Jacob their father unto the land of Canaan, and told[5046] him all that befell unto them; saying,

30 This man, *who is* the lord of the land,[776] [a]spake [I]roughly to us, and took us for spies of the country.[776]

31 And we said unto him, We *are* true *men;* we are no spies:

32 We *be* twelve brethren, sons of our father; one *is* not, and the youngest

20 [a]Gen. 42:34; 43:5; 44:23
21 [a]Job 36:8, 9; Hos. 5:15 [b]Prov. 21:13; Matt. 7:2
22 [a]Gen. 37:21 [b]Gen. 9:5; 1Kgs. 2:32; 2Chr. 24:22; Ps. 9:12; Luke 11:50, 51
23 [I]Hebr. *an interpreter was between them*
25 [a]Matt. 5:44; Rom. 12:17, 20, 21
27 [a]Gen. 43:21
28 [I]Hebr. *went forth*
30 [I]Hebr. *with us hard things* [a]Gen. 42:7
33 [a]Gen. 42:15, 19, 20
34 [a]Gen. 34:10
35 [a]Gen. 43:21
36 [a]Gen. 43:14
38 [a]Gen. 37:33; 42:13; 44:28 [b]Gen. 42:4; 44:29
1 [a]Gen. 41:54, 57
3 [I]Hebr. *protesting protested* [a]Gen. 42:20; 44:23

is this day with our father in the land of Canaan.

33 And the man, the lord of the country, said unto us, [a]Hereby shall I know that ye *are* true *men;* leave one of your brethren *here* with me, and take *food for* the famine of your households, and be gone:

34 And bring your youngest brother unto me: then shall I know that ye *are* no spies, but *that* ye *are* true *men: so* will I deliver you your brother, and ye shall [a]traffick5503 in the land.

35 And it came to pass as they emptied their sacks, that, behold, [a]every man's bundle of money *was* in his sack: and when *both* they and their father saw the bundles of money, they were afraid.[3372]

36 And Jacob their father said unto them, Me have ye [a]bereaved7921 *of my children:* Joseph *is* not, and Simeon *is* not, and ye will take Benjamin *away:* all these things are against me.

37 And Reuben spake unto his father, saying, Slay my two sons, if I bring him not to thee: deliver him into my hand,[3027] and I will bring him to thee again.

38 And he said, My son shall not go down with you; for [a]his brother is dead,[4191] and he is left[7604] alone: [b]if mischief[611] befall him by the way in the which ye go, then shall ye [c]bring down my gray hairs[7872] with sorrow to the grave.[7585]

The Brothers' Second Trip to Egypt

43 And the famine *was* [a]sore in the land.[776]

2 And it came to pass, when they had eaten up the corn[7668] which they had brought out of Egypt, their father said unto them, Go again, buy us a little food.

3 And Judah spake unto him, saying, The man[376] [I]did solemnly protest[5749] unto us, saying, Ye shall not see my face, except your [a]brother[251] *be* with you.

4 If thou wilt send our brother with us, we will go down and buy thee food:

5 But if thou wilt not send *him,* we will not go down: for the man said[559] unto us, Ye shall not see my face, except your brother *be* with you.

6 And Israel said, Wherefore dealt ye *so* ill[7489] with me, *as* to tell[5046] the man whether ye had yet a brother?

7 And they said, The man [I]asked[7592] us straitly of our state, and of our kindred, saying, *Is* your father yet alive?[2416] have ye *another* brother? and we told him according to the [II]tenor of these words: [III]could we certainly know that he would say, Bring your brother down?

8 And Judah said unto Israel his father, Send the lad with me, and we will arise and go; that we may live, and not die,[4191] both we, and thou, *and* also our little ones.[2945]

9 I will be surety[6148] for him; of my hand[3027] shalt thou require him: [a]if I bring him not unto thee, and set him before thee, then let me bear the blame[2398] for ever:[3117] [3605]

10 For except we had lingered, surely now we had returned [I]this second time.

11 And their father Israel said unto them, If *it must be* so now, do[6213] this; take of the best fruits in the land in your vessels, and [a]carry down the man a present,[4503] a little [b]balm, and a little honey, spices, and myrrh,[3910] nuts, and almonds:

12 And take double money in your hand; and the money [a]that was brought again in the mouth of your sacks, carry *it* again in your hand; peradventure[194] it *was* an oversight:

13 Take also your brother, and arise, go again unto the man:

14 And God[410] Almighty[7706] give you mercy[7356] before the man, that he may send away your other brother, and Benjamin. [Ia]If I be bereaved *of my children,* I am bereaved.

15 And the men[582] took that present, and they took double money in their hand, and Benjamin; and rose up, and went down to Egypt, and stood before Joseph.

16 And when Joseph saw[7200] Benjamin with them, he said to the [a]ruler of his house,[1004] Bring *these* men home,[1004] and [Ib]slay,[2873] and make ready; for *these* men shall [II]dine with me at noon.

17 And the man[376] did as Joseph bade;[559] and the man brought the men into Joseph's house.

18 And the men were afraid,[3372] because they were brought unto Joseph's house; and they said, Because of the money that was returned in our sacks at the first time are we brought in; that he may [I]seek occasion[1556] against us, and fall upon us, and take us for bondmen,[5650] and our asses.

19 And they came near to the steward of Joseph's house, and they communed with him at the door of the house,

20 And said, O sir,[113] [Ia]we came indeed down at the first time to buy food:

21 And [a]it came to pass, when we came to the inn, that we opened our sacks, and, behold, *every* man's money *was* in the mouth of his sack, our money in full weight: and we have brought it again in our hand.

22 And other money have we brought down in our hands to buy food: we cannot tell[3045] who put[7760] our money in our sacks.

23 And he said, Peace[7965] *be* to you, fear[3372] not: your God,[430] and the God of your father,[1] hath given you treasure in your sacks: [I]I had your money. And he brought Simeon out unto them.

24 And the man brought the men into Joseph's house, and [a]gave *them* water, and they washed[7364] their feet; and he gave their asses provender.[4554]

25 And they made ready the present against Joseph came at noon: for they heard that they should eat bread there.

26 And when Joseph came home, they brought him the present which *was* in their hand into the house, and [a]bowed[7812] themselves to him to the earth.[776]

27 And he asked[7592] them of *their* [Ia]welfare,[7965] and said, [II]*Is* your father well,[7965] the old man[2205] [b]of whom ye spake?[559] *Is* he yet alive?

7 [I]Hebr. *asking asked us* [II]Hebr. *mouth* [III]Hebr. *Knowing could we know?*

9 [a]Gen. 44:32; Phile. 1:18, 19

10 [I]Or, *twice by this*

11 [a]Gen. 32:20; Prov. 18:16 [b]Gen. 37:25; Jer. 8:22

12 [a]Gen. 42:25, 35

14 [I]Or, *And I, as I have been* [a]Esth. 4:16

16 [I]Hebr. *kill a killing* [II]Hebr. *eat* [a]Gen. 24:2; 39:4; 44:1 [b]1Sam. 25:11

18 [I]Hebr. *roll himself upon us* [a]Job 30:14

20 [I]Hebr. *coming down we came down* [a]Gen. 42:3, 10

21 [a]Gen. 42:27, 35

23 [I]Hebr. *your money came to me*

24 [a]Gen. 18:4; 24:32

26 [a]Gen. 37:7, 10

27 [I]Hebr. *peace,* [II]Hebr. Is there *peace to your father* [a]Gen. 37:14 [b]Gen. 42:11, 13

28 And they answered, Thy servant[5650] our father *is* in good health, he *is* yet alive. [a]And they bowed down their heads, and made obeisance.[7812]

29 And he lifted up his eyes, and saw his brother Benjamin, [a]his mother's son, and said, *Is* this your younger brother, [b]of whom ye spake unto me? And he said, God be gracious[2603] unto thee, my son.

30 And Joseph made haste; for [a]his bowels[7356] did yearn[3648] upon his brother: and he sought *where* to weep; and he entered into *his* chamber, and [b]wept there.

31 And he washed his face, and went out, and refrained himself, and said, Set on [a]bread.

32 And they set on for him by himself, and for them by themselves, and for the Egyptians, which did eat with him, by themselves: because the Egyptians might not eat bread with the Hebrews; for that *is* [a]an abomination[8441] unto the Egyptians.

33 And they sat before him, the firstborn according to his birthright,[1062] and the youngest according to his youth: and the men marvelled one at another.[7453]

34 And he took *and sent* messes[4864] unto them from before him: but Benjamin's mess was [a]five times so much as any of theirs. And they drank, and [I][b]were merry[7937] with him.

Joseph's Silver Cup Is Missing

44 And he commanded[6680] [I]the steward of his house, saying, Fill the men's[582] sacks *with* food, as much as they can carry,[5375] and put every man's[376] money in his sack's mouth.

2 And put[7760] my cup, the silver cup, in the sack's mouth of the youngest, and his corn[7668] money. And he did[6213] according to the word[1697] that Joseph had spoken.

28 [a]Gen. 37:7, 10
29 [a]Gen. 35:17, 18 [b]Gen. 42:13
30 [a]1Kgs. 3:26 [b]Gen. 42:24
31 [a]Gen. 43:25
32 [a]Gen. 46:34; Ex. 8:26
34 [I]Hebr. *drank largely* [a]Gen. 45:22 [b]Hag. 1:6; John 2:10
1 [I]Hebr. him *that was over his house*
5 [I]Or, *maketh trial?*
8 [a]Gen. 43:21
9 [a]Gen. 31:32
13 [a]Gen. 37:29, 34; Num. 14:6; 2Sam. 1:11
14 [a]Gen. 37:7

3 As soon as the morning was light, the men were sent away, they and their asses.

4 *And* when they were gone out of the city, *and* not *yet* far off, Joseph said unto his steward, Up, follow after the men; and when thou dost overtake them, say unto them, Wherefore have ye rewarded evil[7451] for good?[2896]

5 *Is* not this *it* in which my lord[113] drinketh, and whereby indeed he [I]divineth?[5172] ye have done evil[7489] in so doing.[6213]

6 And he overtook them, and he spake unto them these same words.

7 And they said unto him, Wherefore saith my lord these words? God forbid that thy servants[5650] should do according to this thing:

8 Behold, [a]the money, which we found in our sacks' mouths, we brought again unto thee out of the land[776] of Canaan: how then should we steal out of thy lord's house silver or gold?

9 With whomsoever of thy servants it be found, [a]both let him die,[4191] and we also will be my lord's bondmen.[5650]

10 And he said, Now also *let* it *be* according unto your words: he with whom it is found shall be my servant; and ye shall be blameless.[5355]

11 Then they speedily took down every man his sack to the ground,[776] and opened every man his sack.

12 And he searched, *and* began at the eldest, and left at the youngest: and the cup was found in Benjamin's sack.

13 Then they [a]rent their clothes, and laded every man his ass, and returned to the city.

14 And Judah and his brethren came to Joseph's house; for he *was* yet there: and they [a]fell[5307] before him on the ground.

🗝 15 And Joseph said unto them, What deed *is* this that ye have done? wot[3045] ye

🗝 **44:15** Divination, or foretelling the future, was a common practice in ancient Egypt. Joseph here is speaking in his role as an Egyptian. Joseph did receive information from God concerning the future, but he did not practice the idolatrous divinations of the Egyptians.

not that such a man as I can certainly [I][a]divine?[5172]

16 And Judah said, What shall we say unto my lord? what shall we speak? or how shall we clear ourselves?[6663] God[430] hath found out the iniquity[5771] of thy servants: behold, [a]we *are* my lord's servants, both we, and *he* also with whom the cup is found.

17 And he said, [a]God forbid that I should do so: *but* the man in whose hand the cup is found, he shall be my servant; and as for you, get you up in peace[7965] unto your father.

18 Then Judah came near unto him, and said, Oh my lord, let thy servant, I pray thee, speak a word[1697] in my lord's ears,[241] and [a]let not thine anger[639] burn[2734] against thy servant: for thou *art* even as Pharaoh.

19 My lord asked[7592] his servants, saying, Have ye a father, or a brother?

20 And we said unto my lord, We have a father, an old man,[2205] and [a]a child of his old age,[2208] a little one; and his brother is dead,[4191] and he alone is left[3498] of his mother,[517] and his father loveth[157] him.

21 And thou saidst unto thy servants, [a]Bring him down unto me, that I may set mine eyes upon him.

22 And we said unto my lord, The lad cannot leave[5800] his father: for *if* he should leave his father, *his father* would die.

23 And thou saidst unto thy servants, [a]Except your youngest brother come down with you, ye shall see[7200] my face no more.

24 And it came to pass when we came up unto thy servant my father, we told[5046] him the words of my lord.

25 And [a]our father said, Go again, *and* buy us a little food.

26 And we said, We cannot go down: if our youngest brother be with us, then will we go down: for we may not see the man's face, except our youngest brother *be* with us.

27 And thy servant my father said unto us, Ye know[3045] that [a]my wife bare me two *sons:*

28 And the one went out from me, and I said, [a]Surely he is torn in pieces;[2963] and I saw him not since:

29 And if ye [a]take this also from me, and mischief befall him, ye shall bring down my gray hairs[7872] with sorrow[7451] to the grave.[7585]

30 Now therefore when I come to thy servant my father, and the lad *be* not with us; seeing that [a]his life is bound up in the lad's life;[5315]

31 It shall come to pass, when he seeth that the lad is not *with us,* that he will die: and thy servants shall bring down the gray hairs of thy servant our father with sorrow to the grave.

32 For thy servant became surety[6148] for the lad unto my father, saying, [a]If I bring him not unto thee, then I shall bear the blame[2398] to my father for ever.[3117][3605]

33 Now therefore, I pray thee, [a]let thy servant abide instead of the lad a bondman to my lord; and let the lad go up with his brethren.

34 For how shall I go up to my father, and the lad *be* not with me? lest peradventure I see[7200] the evil[7451] that shall [I][a]come on my father.

Joseph Reveals Himself To His Brothers

45 Then Joseph could not refrain himself before all them that stood[5324] by him; and he cried,[7121] Cause every[3605] man[376] to go out from me. And there stood no man with him, while Joseph made himself known unto his brethren.

2 And he [I][a]wept aloud: and the Egyptians and the house[1004] of Pharaoh heard.

3 And Joseph said unto his brethren, [a]I *am* Joseph; doth my father yet live?[2416] And his brethren could not answer him; for they were [I][b]troubled[926] at his presence.

4 And Joseph said unto his brethren, Come near to me, I pray you. And they came near. And he said, I *am* Joseph your brother, [a]whom ye sold into Egypt.

---

15 [I]Or, *make trial?* [a]Gen. 44:5

16 [a]Gen. 44:9

17 [a]Prov. 17:15

18 [a]Gen. 18:30, 32; Ex. 32:22

20 [a]Gen. 37:3

21 [a]Gen. 42:15, 20

23 [a]Gen. 43:3, 5

25 [a]Gen. 43:2

27 [a]Gen. 46:19

28 [a]Gen. 37:33

29 [a]Gen. 42:36, 38

30 [a]1Sam. 18:1

32 [a]Gen. 43:9

33 [a]Ex. 32:32

34 [I]Hebr. *find my father* [a]Ex. 18:8; Job 31:29; Ps. 116:3; 119:143

2 [I]Hebr. *gave forth his voice in weeping* [a]Num. 14:1

3 [I]Or, *terrified* [a]Acts 7:13 [b]Job 4:5; 23:15; Matt. 14:26; Mark 6:50

4 [a]Gen. 37:28

5 Now therefore [a]be not grieved,[6087] [I]nor angry[2734] with yourselves, that ye sold me hither: [b]for God[430] did send me before you to preserve life.[4241]

6 For these two years *hath* the famine *been* in the land:[776] and yet *there are* five years, in the which *there shall* neither *be* earing nor harvest.

7 And God sent me before you [I]to preserve[7760] you a posterity[7611] in the earth,[776] and to save your lives[2421] by a great deliverance.[6413]

8 So now *it was* not you *that* sent me hither, but God: and he hath made[7760] me [a]a father to Pharaoh, and lord[113] of all his house, and a ruler[4910] throughout all the land of Egypt.

9 Haste ye, and go up to my father, and say unto him, Thus saith thy son[1121] Joseph, God hath made[7760] me lord of all Egypt: come down unto me, tarry not:

10 And [a]thou shalt dwell in the land of Goshen, and thou shalt be near unto me, thou, and thy children, and thy children's children, and thy flocks, and thy herds, and all that thou hast:

11 And there will I nourish thee; for yet *there are* five years of famine; lest thou, and thy household,[1004] and all that thou hast, come to poverty.

12 And, behold, your eyes see,[7200] and the eyes of my brother Benjamin, that *it is* [a]my mouth[6310] that speaketh unto you.

13 And ye shall tell[5046] my father of all my glory[3519] in Egypt, and of all that ye have seen; and ye shall haste and [a]bring down my father hither.

14 And he fell upon his brother Benjamin's neck, and wept; and Benjamin wept upon his neck.

15 Moreover he kissed all his brethren, and wept upon them: and after that his brethren talked[1696] with him.

16 And the fame[6963] thereof was heard[8085] in Pharaoh's house, saying, Joseph's brethren are come: and it [Ia]pleased Pharaoh well, and his servants.[5650]

5 [I]Hebr. *neither let there be anger in your eyes* [a]Isa. 40:2; 2Cor. 2:7 [b]Gen. 50:20; Ps. 105:16, 17; 2Sam. 16:10, 11; Acts 4:27, 28

7 [I]Hebr. *to put for you a remnant*

8 [a]Gen. 41:43; Judg. 17:10; Job 29:16

10 [a]Gen. 47:1

12 [a]Gen. 42:23

13 [a]Acts 7:14

16 [I]Hebr. *was good in the eyes of Pharaoh* [a]Gen. 41:33

18 [a]Gen. 27:28; Num. 18:12, 29

20 [I]Hebr. *let not your eye spare*

21 [I]Hebr. *mouth* [a]Num. 3:16

22 [a]Gen. 43:34

23 [I]Hebr. *carrying*

26 [I]Hebr. *his* [a]Job 29:24; Ps. 126:1; Luke 24:11, 41

17 And Pharaoh said unto Joseph, Say unto thy brethren, This do[6213] ye; lade your beasts, and go, get you unto the land of Canaan;

18 And take your father and your households, and come unto me: and I will give you the good[2898] of the land of Egypt, and ye shall eat [a]the fat of the land.

19 Now thou art commanded,[6680] this do ye; take you wagons out of the land of Egypt for your little ones,[2945] and for your wives, and bring[5375] your father, and come.

20 Also [I]regard not your stuff; for the good of all the land of Egypt *is* yours.

21 And the children of Israel did so: and Joseph gave them wagons, according to the [Ia]commandment[6310] of Pharaoh, and gave them provision for the way.

22 To all of them he gave each man[376] changes of raiment; but to Benjamin he gave three hundred *pieces* of silver, and [a]five changes of raiment.

23 And to his father he sent after this *manner;* ten asses [I]laden[5375] with the good things[2898] of Egypt, and ten she asses laden with corn and bread and meat for his father by the way.

24 So he sent his brethren away, and they departed: and he said unto them, See that ye fall not out[7264] by the way.

25 And they went up out of Egypt, and came into the land of Canaan unto Jacob their father,

26 And told[5046] him, saying, Joseph *is* yet alive, and he *is* governor[4910] over all the land of Egypt. [a]And [I]Jacob's heart[3820] fainted, for he believed[539] them not.

27 And they told him all the words[1697] of Joseph, which he had said[1696] unto them: and when he saw the wagons which Joseph had sent to carry him, the spirit[7307] of Jacob their father revived:[2421]

28 And Israel said, *It is* enough; Joseph my son *is* yet alive: I will go and see him before I die.[4191]

Jacob and His Family Move to Egypt

46 And Israel took his journey with
all that he had, and came to
[a]Beer–sheba, and offered sacrifices[2077]
[b]unto the God[430] of his father[1] Isaac.
2 And God spake unto Israel [a]in the
visions[4759] of the night, and said, Jacob,
Jacob. And he said, Here *am* I.
3 And he said, I *am* God,[410] [a]the God
of thy father: fear[3372] not to go down
into Egypt; for I will there [b]make[7760] of
thee a great nation:[1471]
4 [a]I will go down with thee into
Egypt; and I will also surely [b]bring thee
up *again:* and [c]Joseph shall put his
hand[3027] upon thine eyes.
5 And [a]Jacob rose up from Beer–
sheba: and the sons of Israel carried
Jacob their father, and their little ones,[2945]
and their wives, in the wagons [b]which
Pharaoh had sent to carry[5375] him.
6 And they took their cattle, and
their goods, which they had gotten in
the land[776] of Canaan, and came into
Egypt, [a]Jacob, and all his seed[2233] with
him:
7 His sons, and his sons' sons with
him, his daughters, and his son's daughters, and all his seed brought he with
him into Egypt.
8 And [a]these *are* the names of the
children[1121] of Israel, which came into
Egypt, Jacob and his sons:[1121] [b]Reuben,
Jacob's firstborn.
9 And the sons of Reuben; Hanoch,
and Phallu, and Hezron, and Carmi.
10 And [a]the sons of Simeon; [I]Jemuel,
and Jamin, and Ohad, and [II]Jachin, and
[III][b]Zohar, and Shaul the son of a
Canaanitish women.
11 And the sons of [a]Levi; [I]Gershon,
Kohath, and Merari.
12 And the sons of [a]Judah; Er, and
Onan, and Shelah, and Pharez, and Zarah: but [b]Er and Onan died[4191] in the
land of Canaan. And [c]the sons of Pharez
were Hezron and Hamul.
13 [a]And the sons of Issachar; Tola,
and [I]Phuvah, and Job, and Shimron.
14 And the sons of Zebulun; Sered,
and Elon, and Jahleel.
15 These *be* the sons[1121] of Leah,
which she bare unto Jacob in Padan–
aram, with his daughter Dinah: all the
souls[5315] of his sons and his daughters
were thirty and three.
16 And the sons of Gad; [a]Ziphion,
and Haggi, Shuni, and [I]Ezbon, Eri, and
[II]Arodi, and Areli.
17 [a]And the sons of Asher; Jimnah,
and Ishuah, and Isui, and Beriah, and
Serah their sister: and the sons of Beriah;
Heber, and Malchiel.
18 [a]These *are* the sons of Zilpah,
[b]whom Laban gave to Leah his daughter,
and these she bare unto Jacob, *even* sixteen souls.
19 The sons of Rachel [a]Jacob's wife;
Joseph, and Benjamin.
20 [a]And unto Joseph in the land of
Egypt were born Manasseh and Ephraim,
which Asenath the daughter of Poti–
pherah [I]priest[3548] of On bare unto him.
21 [a]And the sons of Benjamin *were*
Belah, and Becher, and Ashbel, Gera, and
Naaman, Ehi, and Rosh, Muppim, and
Huppim, and Ard.
22 These *are* the sons of Rachel,
which were born to Jacob: all the souls
were fourteen.
23 [a]And the sons of Dan; Hushim.
24 [a]And the sons of Naphtali;
Jahzeel, and Guni, and Jezer, and Shillem.
25 [a]These *are* the sons of Bilhah,
[b]which Laban gave unto Rachel his
daughter, and she bare these unto Jacob:
all the souls *were* seven.
🗝 26 [a]All the souls that came with
Jacob into Egypt, which came out of his
[I][b]loins,[3409] besides Jacob's sons' wives, all
the souls *were* threescore and six;

1 [a]Gen. 21:31, 33; 28:10 [b]Gen. 26:24, 25; 28:13; 31:42
2 [a]Gen. 15:1; Job 33:14, 15
3 [a]Gen. 28:13 [b]Gen. 12:2; Deut. 26:5
4 [a]Gen. 28:15; 48:21 [b]Gen. 15:16; 50:13, 24, 25; Ex. 3:8 [c]Gen. 50:1
5 [a]Acts 7:15 [b]Gen. 45:19, 21
6 [a]Deut. 26:5; Josh. 24:4; Ps. 105:23; Isa. 52:4
8 [a]Ex. 1:1; 6:14 [b]Num. 26:5; 1Chr. 5:1
10 [I]Or, *Nemuel* [II]Or, *Jarib* [III]Or, *Zerah* [a]Ex. 6:15; 1Chr. 4:24 [b]1Chr. 4:24
11 [I]Or, *Gershom* [a]1Chr. 6:1, 16
12 [a]1Chr. 2:3; 4:21 [b]Gen. 38:3, 7, 10 [c]Gen. 38:29; 1Chr. 2:5
13 [I]Or, *Puah, and Jashub* [a]1Chr. 7:1
16 [I]Or, *Ozni* [II]Or, *Arod* [a]Num. 26:15, *Zephon*
17 [a]1Chr. 7:30
18 [a]Gen. 30:10 [b]Gen. 29:24
19 [a]Gen. 44:27
20 [I]Or, *prince* [a]Gen. 41:50
21 [a]1Chr. 7:6; 8:1
23 [a]1Chr. 7:12
24 [a]1Chr. 7:13
25 [a]Gen. 30:5, 7 [b]Gen. 29:29
26 [I]Hebr. *thigh* [a]Ex. 1:5 [b]Gen. 35:14

🗝 **46:26, 27** The differences between this and other passages (Ex. 1:1–5; Acts 7:14) as to the number who migrated to Egypt are due to the point of reference and method of calculation, not

(continued on next page)

27 And the sons of Joseph, which were born him in Egypt, *were* two souls: [a]all the souls of the house[1004] of Jacob, which came into Egypt, *were* threescore and ten.

28 And he sent Judah before him unto Joseph, [a]to direct[3384] his face unto Goshen; and they came [b]into the land of Goshen.

29 And Joseph made ready[631] his chariot, and went up to meet Israel his father, to Goshen, and presented himself[7200] unto him; and he [a]fell on his neck, and wept on his neck a good while.

30 And Israel said unto Joseph, [a]Now let me die, since I have seen thy face, because thou *art* yet alive.

31 And Joseph said unto his brethren,[251] and unto his father's house, [a]I will go up, and shew[5046] Pharaoh, and say unto him, My brethren, and my father's house, which *were* in the land of Canaan, are come unto me;

32 And the men[582] *are* shepherds, for [I]their trade hath been to feed cattle; and they have brought their flocks, and their herds, and all that they have.

33 And it shall come to pass, when Pharaoh shall call[7121] you, and shall say, [a]What *is* your occupation?[4639]

34 That ye shall say, Thy servants'[5650] [a]trade hath been about cattle [b]from our youth even until now, both we, *and* also our fathers: that ye may dwell in the land of Goshen; for every shepherd *is* [c]an abomination[8441] unto the Egyptians.

47

Then Joseph [a]came and told[5046] Pharaoh, and said, My father and my brethren,[251] and their flocks, and their herds, and all that they have, are come out of the land[776] of Canaan; and, behold, they *are* in [a]the land of Goshen.

2 And he took some of his brethren, *even* five men,[582] and [a]presented them unto Pharaoh.

3 And Pharaoh said unto his brethren, [a]What *is* your occupation? And they said unto Pharaoh, [b]Thy servants[5650] *are* shepherds, both we, *and* also our fathers.

4 They said moreover unto Pharaoh, [a]For to sojourn[1481] in the land are we come; for thy servants have no pasture

27 [a]Deut. 10:22; Acts 7:14
28 [a]Gen. 31:21 [b]Gen. 47:1
29 [a]Gen. 45:14
30 [a]Luke 2:29, 30
31 [a]Gen. 47:1
32 [I]Hebr. *they are men of cattle* [a]Gen. 47:2, 3
34 [a]Gen. 46:32 [b]Gen. 30:35; 34:5; 37:12 [c]Gen. 43:32; Ex. 8:26
1 [a]Gen. 46:31 [b]Gen. 45:10; 46:28
2 [a]Acts 7:13
3 [a]Gen. 46:33 [b]Gen. 46:34
4 [a]Gen. 15:13; Deut. 26:5

(continued from previous page)

to contradiction or error. Jacob's direct descendants in Canaan, his children, grandchildren, and great-grandchildren, amounted to sixty-six persons (Gen. 46:8–26). The seventy souls of the house of Jacob mentioned in verse twenty-seven and in Exodus 1:5 adds to the sixty-six above Jacob himself, Joseph, and Joseph's two sons. In Acts 7:14 Stephen states that the number of Joseph's kindred who came to Egypt was seventy-five. Jacob, who is mentioned separately, and Joseph and his family who were already in Egypt, were not a part of this number. But remember that the sixty-six persons mentioned elsewhere included only the direct descendants of Jacob. The number mentioned in Acts also includes those who came with Jacob, but who were not his direct descendants, that is his son's wives. Since Judah's wives and Simeon's wives were dead, there were only nine of the wives who made the trip with Jacob. These nine, plus his sixty-six direct descendants made up the seventy-five persons who traveled with Jacob from Egypt.

46:34 Throughout its history, Egypt had a hatred for foreign things. Their very language depicts foreigners as a lower class of human. In addition, the particular manners and customs of the Jews were totally disgusting to the Egyptians. The Jews had hair and beards, while the Egyptians, both men and women, shaved all their body hair off (41:14). This attitude of superiority is reflected in Pharaoh's instructions to basically "leave everything behind because we will give you good Egyptian stuff" (45:20). God had carefully chosen Egypt as the one place where Israel could grow into a nation. The Egyptian abhorrence for the Jews would limit the danger of intermingling, either racially or religiously (a problem which would lead to much trouble in Canaan). The size and prosperity of Egypt would allow the Hebrew people to become numerous while still being a minority in the country. The later invasion of the Hyksos, an eastern people, led to the enslavement of the Jews, which served to make them physically strong.

for their flocks; [b]for the famine *is* sore in the land of Canaan: now therefore, we pray thee, let thy servants [c]dwell in the land of Goshen.

5 And Pharaoh spake unto Joseph, saying, Thy father and thy brethren are come unto thee:

6 [a]The land of Egypt *is* before thee; in the best of the land make thy father and brethren to dwell; [b]in the land of Goshen let them dwell: and if thou knowest *any* men of activity[2428] among them, then make[7760] them rulers[8269] over my cattle.

7 And Joseph brought in Jacob his father, and set him before Pharaoh: and Jacob blessed[1288] Pharaoh.

8 And Pharaoh said unto Jacob, [I]How old *art* thou?

9 And Jacob said unto Pharaoh, [a]The days[3117] of the years of my pilgrimage[4033] *are* an hundred and thirty years: [b]few and evil[7451] have the days of the years of my life been, and [c]have not attained unto the days of the years of the life of my fathers in the days of their pilgrimage.

10 And Jacob [a]blessed Pharaoh, and went out from before Pharaoh.

11 And Joseph placed his father and his brethren, and gave them a possession[272] in the land of Egypt, in the best of the land, in the land of [a]Rameses, [b]as Pharaoh had commanded.[6680]

12 And Joseph nourished his father, and his brethren, and all his father's household,[1004] with bread, [Ia]according to *their* families.[2945]

The Seven Years of Famine

13 And *there was* no bread in all the land; for the famine *was* very sore, [a]so that the land of Egypt and *all* the land of Canaan fainted by reason of the famine.

14 [a]And Joseph gathered up[3950] all the money that was found in the land of Egypt, and in the land of Canaan, for the corn[7668] which they bought: and Joseph brought the money into Pharaoh's house.[1004]

15 And when money failed[8552] in the land of Egypt, and in the land of Canaan, all the Egyptians came unto Joseph, and said, Give us bread: for [a]why should we die in thy presence? for the money faileth.[656]

16 And Joseph said, Give your cattle; and I will give you for your cattle, if money fail.

17 And they brought their cattle unto Joseph: and Joseph gave them bread *in exchange* for horses, and for the flocks, and for the cattle of the herds, and for the asses: and he [I]fed them with bread for all their cattle for that year.

18 When that year was ended,[8552] they came unto him the second year, and said unto him, We will not hide *it* from my lord,[113] how that our money is spent;[8552] my lord also hath our herds of cattle; there is not aught left in the sight of my lord, but our bodies,[1472] and our lands:[127]

19 Wherefore shall we die before thine eyes, both we and our land? buy us and our land for bread, and we and our land will be servants unto Pharaoh: and give *us* seed,[2233] that we may live,[2421] and not die, that the land be not desolate.[3456]

20 And Joseph bought all the land of Egypt for Pharaoh; for the Egyptians sold every man[376] his field, because the famine prevailed[2388] over them: so the land became Pharaoh's.

21 And as for the people,[5971] he removed[5674] them to cities from *one* end of the borders of Egypt even to the *other* end thereof.

22 [a]Only the land of the [Ib]priests[3548] bought he not; for the priests had a portion[2706] *assigned them* of Pharaoh, and did eat their portion which Pharaoh gave them: wherefore they sold not their lands.

23 Then Joseph said unto the people, Behold, I have bought you this day[3117] and your land for Pharaoh: lo, *here is* seed for you, and ye shall sow the land.

24 And it shall come to pass in the increase, that ye shall give the fifth *part*

4 [b]Gen. 43:1; Acts 7:11 [c]Gen. 46:34
6 [a]Gen. 20:15 [b]Gen. 47:4
8 [I]Hebr. *How many are the days of the years of thy life?*
9 [a]Ps. 39:12; Heb. 11:9, 13 [b]Job 14:1 [c]Gen. 25:7; 35:28
10 [a]Gen. 47:7
11 [a]Ex. 1:11; 12:37 [b]Gen. 47:6
12 [I]Hebr. *according to the little ones* [a]Gen. 50:21
13 [a]Gen. 41:30; Acts 7:11
14 [a]Gen. 41:56
15 [a]Gen. 47:19
17 [I]Hebr. *led them*
22 [I]Or, *princes,* [a]Ezra 7:24 [b]Gen. 41:45; 2Sam. 8:18

unto Pharaoh, and four parts shall be your own, for seed of the field, and for your food, and for them of your households, and for food for your little ones.

25 And they said, Thou hast saved[2421] our lives:[2421] [a]let us find grace[2580] in the sight of my lord, and we will be Pharaoh's servants.

26 And Joseph made[7760] it a law[2706] over the land of Egypt unto this day, *that* Pharaoh should have the fifth *part;* [a]except the land of the [I]priests only, *which* became not Pharaoh's.

Jacob's Last Wish

27 And Israel [a]dwelt in the land of Egypt, in the country of Goshen; and they had possessions therein, and [b]grew, and multiplied exceedingly.

28 And Jacob lived[2421] in the land of Egypt seventeen years: so [I]the whole age of Jacob was an hundred forty and seven years.

29 And the time[3117] [a]drew nigh that Israel must die: and he called his son Joseph, and said unto him, If now I have found grace in thy sight, [b]put,[7760] I pray thee, thy hand under my thigh,[3409] and [c]deal[6213] kindly[2617] and truly[571] with me; [d]bury[6912] me not, I pray thee, in Egypt:

30 But [a]I will lie with my fathers, and thou shalt carry[5375] me out of Egypt, and [b]bury[6912] me in their buryingplace.[6913] And he said,[559] I will do[6213] as thou hast said:

🔑 31 And he said, Swear[7650] unto me. And he sware unto him. And [a]Israel bowed[7812] himself upon the bed's head.[7218]

25 [a]Gen. 33:15
26 [I]Or, *princes* [a]Gen. 47:22
27 [a]Gen. 47:11 [b]Gen. 46:3
28 [I]Hebr. *the days of the years of his life*
29 [a]Deut. 31:14; 1Kgs. 2:1 [b]Gen. 24:2 [c]Gen. 24:49 [d]Gen. 50:25
30 [a]2Sam. 19:37 [b]Gen. 49:29; 50:5, 13
31 [a]Gen. 48:2; 1Kgs. 1:47; Heb. 11:21
3 [a]Gen. 28:13, 19; 35:6, 9-15
4 [a]Gen. 17:8
5 [a]Gen. 41:50; 46:20; Josh. 13:7; 14:4
7 [a]Gen. 35:9, 16, 19
9 [a]Gen. 33:5

Jacob Gives His Blessing To Joseph's Two Sons

48 And it came to pass after these things,[1697] that *one* told Joseph, Behold, thy father *is* sick: and he took with him his two sons, Manasseh and Ephraim.

2 And *one* told[5046] Jacob, and said, Behold, thy son Joseph cometh unto thee: and Israel strengthened himself,[2388] and sat upon the bed.

3 And Jacob said unto Joseph, God[410] Almighty[7706] appeared unto me at [a]Luz in the land of Canaan, and blessed[1288] me,

4 And said unto me, Behold, I will make thee fruitful, and multiply thee, and I will make of thee a multitude[6951] of people;[5971] and will give this land[776] to thy seed[2233] after thee [a]*for* an everlasting[5769] possession.[272]

🔑 5 And now thy [a]two sons, Ephraim and Manasseh, which were born unto thee in the land of Egypt before I came unto thee into Egypt, *are* mine; as Reuben and Simeon, they shall be mine.

6 And thy issue,[4138] which thou begettest after them, shall be thine, *and* shall be called[7121] after the name of their brethren[251] in their inheritance.[5159]

7 And as for me, when I came from Padan, [a]Rachel died[4191] by me in the land of Canaan in the way, when yet *there was* but a little way to come unto Ephrath: and I buried[6912] her there in the way[1870] of Ephrath; the same *is* Bethlehem.

8 And Israel beheld[7200] Joseph's sons, and said, Who *are* these?

9 And Joseph said unto his father, [a]They *are* my sons, whom God[430] hath

---

🔑 **47:31** Did Jacob support himself on the head of his bed or did he support himself by his staff (Heb. 11:21)? The present Hebrew vocalization (*mittah*) is translated as "bed, " while the Septuagint and the Epistle to the Hebrews follow a different vocalization (*matteh*), which is translated as "staff." Since the Hebrew vowels were not inserted into the Hebrew consonantal text until much later, one cannot be sure which vocalization is correct. However, the meaning and context of the passage are unaffected regardless of which is chosen. In addition, there is the possibility that the two passages may not be referring to the same incident.

🔑 **48:5** See note on Genesis 35:23–26.

given me in this *place.* And he said, Bring them, I pray thee, unto me, and [b]I will bless them.

10 Now [a]the eyes of Israel were [I][b]dim[3513] for age,[2207] *so that* he could not see.[7200] And he brought them near unto him; and [c]he kissed them, and embraced them.

11 And Israel said unto Joseph, [a]I had not thought[6419] to see thy face: and, lo, God hath shewed[7200] me also thy seed.

12 And Joseph brought them out from between his knees, and he bowed[7812] himself with his face[639] to the earth.[776]

13 And Joseph took them both, Ephraim in his right hand toward Israel's left hand, and Manasseh in his left hand toward Israel's right hand, and brought *them* near unto him.

14 And Israel stretched out his right hand,3225 and laid *it* upon Ephraim's head, who *was* the younger, and his left hand upon Manasseh's head, [a]guiding his hands wittingly;[7919] for Manasseh *was* the firstborn.

15 And [a]he blessed[1288] Joseph, and said, God, [b]before whom my fathers Abraham and Isaac did walk, the God which fed me all my life long unto this day,[3117]

16 The Angel [a]which redeemed[1350] me from all evil,[7451] bless the lads; and let [b]my name be named on them, and the name of my fathers Abraham and Isaac; and let them [I][c]grow[1711] into a multitude in the midst of the earth.

17 And when Joseph saw that his father [a]laid his right hand upon the head of Ephraim, it [I][b]displeased him: and he held up his father's hand, to remove it from Ephraim's head unto Manasseh's head.

18 And Joseph said unto his father, Not so, my father: for this *is* the firstborn; put[7760] thy right hand upon his head.

19 And his father refused,[3985] and said, [a]I know[3045] *it,* my son, I know *it:* he also shall become a people, and he also shall be great: but truly [b]his younger

9 [b]Gen. 27:4
10 [I]Hebr. *heavy* [a]Gen. 27:1 [b]Isa. 6:10; 59:1 [c]Gen. 27:27
11 [a]Gen. 45:26
14 [a]Gen. 48:19
15 [a]Heb. 11:21 [b]Gen. 17:1; 24:40
16 [I]Hebr. *as fishes do increase* [a]Gen. 28:15; 31:11, 13, 24; Ps. 34:22; 121:7 [b]Amos 9:12; Acts 15:17 [c]Num. 26:34, 37
17 [I]Or, *was evil in his eyes* [a]Gen. 48:14 [b]Gen. 28:8
19 [I]Hebr. *fulness* [a]Gen. 48:14 [b]Num. 1:33, 35; 2:19, 21; Deut. 33:17; Rev. 7:6, 8
20 [a]Ruth 4:11, 12
21 [a]Gen. 46:4; 50:24
22 [a]Josh. 24:32; 1Chr. 5:2; John 4:5 [b]Gen. 15:16; 34:28; Josh. 17:14-18

1 [a]Deut. 33:1; Amos 3:7 [b]Num. 24:14; Deut. 4:30; Isa. 2:2; 39:6; Jer. 23:20; Dan. 2:28, 29; Acts 2:17; Heb. 1:2
2 [a]Ps. 34:11
3 [a]Gen. 29:32 [b]Deut. 21:17; Ps. 78:51
4 [I]Hebr. *do not thou excel* [II]Or, *my couch is gone* [a]1Chr. 5:1 [b]Gen. 35:22; Deut. 27:20; 1Chr. 5:1
5 [I]Or, *their swords* are *weapons of violence* [a]Gen. 29:33, 34 [b]Prov. 18:9 [c]Gen. 34:25
6 [I]Or, *houghed oxen* [a]Prov. 1:15, 16 [b]Ps. 26:9; Eph. 5:11 [c]Ps. 16:9; 30:12; 57:8 [d]Gen. 34:26
7 [a]Josh. 19:1; 21:5-7; 1Chr. 4:24, 39
8 [a]Gen. 29:35; Deut. 33:7 [b]Ps. 18:40 [c]Gen. 27:29; 1Chr. 5:2

brother shall be greater than he, and his seed shall become a [I]multitude of nations.[1471]

20 And he blessed them that day, saying, [a]In thee shall Israel bless, saying, God make thee as Ephraim and as Manasseh: and he set Ephraim before Manasseh.

21 And Israel said unto Joseph, Behold, I die: but [a]God shall be with you, and bring you again[7725] unto the land of your fathers.

22 Moreover [a]I have given to thee one portion above thy brethren, which I took out of the hand [b]of the Amorite with my sword and with my bow.

Jacob Gives a Blessing To All His Sons

49 And Jacob called[7121] unto his sons,[1121] and said, Gather yourselves together, that I may [a]tell[5046] you *that* which shall befall you [b]in the last[319] days.[3117]

2 Gather yourselves together, and hear, ye sons of Jacob; and [a]hearken unto Israel your father.[1]

3 Reuben, thou *art* [a]my firstborn, my might, [b]and the beginning[7225] of my strength, the excellency[3499] of dignity, and the excellency of power:

4 Unstable as water, thou [I][a]shalt not excel;[3498] because thou [b]wentest up to thy father's bed; then defiledst[2490] thou *it:* [II]he went up to my couch.

5 [a]Simeon and Levi *are* [b]brethren; [I][c]instruments of cruelty[2555] *are in* their habitations.

6 O my soul,[5315] [a]come not thou into their secret;[5475] [b]unto their assembly,[6951] [c]mine honour,[3519] be not thou united: for [d]in their anger[639] they slew[2026] a man,[376] and in their selfwill[7522] they [I]digged down6131 a wall.

7 Cursed[779] *be* their anger, for *it was* fierce; and their wrath,[5678] for it was cruel: [a]I will divide2505 them in Jacob, and scatter6327 them in Israel.

8 [a]Judah, thou *art he* whom thy brethren shall praise: [b]thy hand *shall be* in the neck of thine enemies; [c]thy father's

children[1121] shall bow down[7812] before thee.

9 Judah *is* [a]a lion's whelp:[1482] from the prey, my son, thou art gone up: [b]he stooped down,[3766] he couched as a lion, and as an old lion; who shall rouse him up?

🗝 10 [a]The sceptre[7626] shall not depart from Judah, nor [b]a lawgiver[2710] [c]from between his feet, [d]until Shiloh7886 come; [e]and unto him *shall* the gathering of the people[5971] *be.*

11 [a]Binding his foal unto the vine, and his ass's colt[1121] unto the choice vine; he washed[3526] his garments in wine, and his clothes in the blood[1818] of grapes:

12 His [a]eyes *shall be* red with wine, and his teeth white with milk.

13 [a]Zebulun shall dwell at the haven[2348] of the sea; and he *shall be* for an haven of ships; and his border *shall be* unto Zidon.

14 Issachar *is* a strong ass couching down between two burdens:

15 And he saw[7200] that rest *was* good,[2896] and the land that *it was* pleasant; and bowed [a]his shoulder to bear, and became a servant[5647] unto tribute.

16 [a]Dan shall judge his people, as one of the tribes[7626] of Israel.

17 [a]Dan shall be a serpent[5175] by the way, [I]an adder8207 in the path,[734] that biteth the horse heels,[6119] so that his rider shall fall backward.

18 I [a]have waited[6960] for thy salvation,[3444] O LORD.

19 [a]Gad, a troop[1416] shall overcome him: but he shall overcome at the last.[6119]

20 [a]Out of Asher his bread *shall be* fat, and he shall yield royal dainties.

21 [a]Naphtali *is* a hind355 let loose: he giveth goodly words.[561]

22 Joseph *is* a fruitful bough,[1121] 6509 *even* a fruitful bough by a well; *whose* [I]branches run over the wall:

23 The archers[1167] have [a]sorely4843 grieved him, and shot *at him,* and hated7852 him:

24 But his [a]bow abode in strength,[386] and the arms of his hands were made strong by the hands[3027] of [b]the mighty *God* of Jacob; ([c]from thence [d]*is* the shepherd, [e]the stone68 of Israel:)

25 [a]*Even* by the God[410] of thy father, who shall help thee; [b]and by the Almighty,[7706] [c]who shall bless[1288] thee with blessings[1293] of heaven above, blessings of the deep8415 that lieth under, blessings of the breasts, and of the womb:

26 The blessings of thy father have prevailed above the blessings of my progenitors [a]unto the utmost bound of the everlasting[5769] hills: [b]they shall be on the head of Joseph, and on the crown of the head of him that was separate[5139] from his brethren.

27 Benjamin shall [a]ravin[2963] *as* a wolf: in the morning he shall devour the prey, [b]and at night he shall divide the spoil.

28 All these *are* the [a]twelve tribes of Israel: and this *is it* that their father spake[1696] unto them, and blessed them; every one[376] according to his blessing he blessed them.

Jacob Dies

29 And he charged[6680] them, and said unto them, I [a]am to be gathered unto my people: [b]bury me with my fathers [c]in the cave that *is* in the field[7704] of Ephron the Hittite,

30 In the cave that *is* in the field of Machpelah, which *is* before Mamre, in the land of Canaan, [a]which Abraham bought with the field of Ephron the Hittite for a possession[272] of a buryingplace.[6913]

31 [a]There they buried[6912] Abraham and Sarah his wife; [b]there they buried

9 [a]Hos. 5:14; Rev. 5:5 [b]Num. 23:24; 24:9
10 [a]Num. 24:17; Jer. 30:21; Zech. 10:11 [b]Ps. 60:7; 108:8; Num. 21:18 [c]Deut. 28:57 [d]Isa. 11:1; 62:11; Ezek. 21:27; Dan. 9:25; Matt. 21:9; Luke 1:32, 33 [e]Isa. 2:2; 11:10; 42:1, 4; 49:6, 7, 22, 23; 55:4, 5; 60:1, 3-5; Hag. 2:7; Luke 2:30-32
11 [a]2Kgs. 18:32
12 [a]Prov. 23:29
13 [a]Deut. 33:18, 19; Josh. 19:10, 11
15 [a]Matt. 23:4
16 [a]Deut. 33:22; Judg. 18:1, 2
17 [I]Hebr. *an arrowsnake* [a]Judg. 18:27
18 [a]Ps. 25:5; 119:166, 174; Isa. 25:9
19 [a]Deut. 33:20; 1Chr. 5:18
20 [a]Deut. 33:24; Josh. 19:24
21 [a]Deut. 33:23
22 [I]Hebr. *daughters*
23 [a]Gen. 37:4, 24, 28; 39:20; 42:21; Ps. 118:13
24 [a]Job 29:20; Ps. 37:15 [b]Ps. 132:2, 5 [c]Gen. 45:11; 47:12; 50:21 [d]Ps. 80:1 [e]Isa. 28:16
25 [a]Gen. 28:13, 21; 35:3; 43:23 [b]Gen. 17:1; 35:11 [c]Deut. 33:13
26 [a]Deut. 33:15; Hab. 3:6 [b]Deut. 33:16
27 [a]Judg. 20:21, 25; Ezek. 22:25, 27 [b]Num. 23:24
28 [a]Esth. 8:11; Ezek. 39:10; Zech. 14:1, 7
29 [a]Gen. 15:15; 25:8 [b]Gen. 47:30; 2Sam. 19:37 [c]Gen. 50:13
30 [a]Gen. 23:16
31 [a]Gen. 23:19; 25:9 [b]Gen. 35:29

🗝 **49:10** This does not mean that there will be a continuous sovereignty by the descendants of Judah, but merely that their line will retain a permanent right to rule. Note that the scepter and staff represent only the right to rule. This verse is normally regarded as a messianic prophecy.

Isaac and Rebekah his wife; and there I buried Leah.

32 The purchase of the field and of the cave that *is* therein *was* from the children of Heth.

33 And when Jacob had made an end of commanding[6680] his sons, he gathered up his feet into the bed, and yielded up the ghost,[1478] and [a]was gathered unto his people.

Joseph Comforts His Brothers

50 And Joseph [a]fell upon his father's[1] face, and [b]wept upon him, and kissed him.

2 And Joseph commanded[6680] his servants[5650] the physicians to [a]embalm his father: and the physicians embalmed Israel.

3 And forty days were fulfilled for him; for so are fulfilled the days[3117] of those which are embalmed: and the Egyptians [I][a]mourned for him threescore and ten days.

4 And when the days of his mourning were past,[5674] Joseph spake unto [a]the house[1004] of Pharaoh, saying, If now I have found grace[2580] in your eyes, speak, I pray you, in the ears[241] of Pharaoh, saying,

5 [a]My father made me swear,[7650] saying, Lo, I die: in my grave[6913] [b]which I have digged for me in the land[776] of Canaan, there shalt thou bury[6912] me. Now therefore let me go up, I pray thee, and bury my father, and I will come again.[7725]

6 And Pharaoh said, Go up, and bury thy father, according as he made thee swear.

7 And Joseph went up to bury his father: and with him went up all the servants of Pharaoh, the elders[2205] of his house, and all the elders of the land of Egypt,

8 And all the house of Joseph, and his brethren,[251] and his father's house: only their little ones,[2945] and their flocks, and their herds, they left[5800] in the land of Goshen.

9 And there went up with him both chariots and horsemen: and it was a very great company.[4264]

10 And they came to the threshingfloor of Atad, which *is* beyond Jordan, and there they [a]mourned with a great and very sore lamentation: [b]and he made[6213] a mourning for his father seven days.

11 And when the inhabitants of the land, the Canaanites, saw[7200] the mourning in the floor of Atad, they said, This *is* a grievous mourning[60] to the Egyptians: wherefore the name of it was called[7121] [I]Abel–mizraim,[67] which *is* beyond Jordan.

12 And his sons[1121] did unto him according as he commanded[6680] them:

13 For [a]his sons carried[5375] him into the land of Canaan, and buried him in the cave of the field[7704] of Machpelah, which Abraham [b]bought with the field for a possession[272] of a buryingplace[6913] of Ephron the Hittite, before Mamre.

14 And Joseph returned[7725] into Egypt, he, and his brethren, and all that went up with him to bury his father, after he had buried his father.

Joseph Dies

15 And when Joseph's brethren saw that their father was dead,[4191] [a]they said, Joseph will[7852] peradventure[3863] hate[7852] us, and will certainly requite[7725] us all the evil[7451] which we did[1580] unto him.

16 And they [I]sent a messenger[6680] unto Joseph, saying, Thy father did command before he died,[4194] saying,

17 So shall ye say unto Joseph, Forgive,[5375] I pray thee[577] now, the trespass[6588] of thy brethren, and their sin;[2403] [a]for they did unto thee evil: and now, we pray thee, forgive the trespass of the servants of [b]the God[430] of thy father. And Joseph wept when they spake unto him.

18 And his brethren also went and [a]fell down before his face; and they said, Behold, we *be* thy servants.

19 And Joseph said unto them, [a]Fear[3372] not: [b]for *am* I in the place of God?

33 [a]Gen. 49:29

1 [a]Gen. 46:4 [b]2Kgs. 13:14

2 [a]Gen. 50:26; 2Chr. 16:14; Matt. 26:12; Mark 14:8; 16:1; Luke 24:1; John 12:7; 19:39, 40

3 [I]Hebr. *wept* [a]Num. 20:29; Deut. 34:8

4 [a]Esth. 4:2

5 [a]Gen. 47:29 [b]2Chr. 16:14; Isa. 22:16; Matt. 27:60

10 [a]2Sam. 1:17; Acts 8:2 [b]1Sam. 31:13; Job 2:13

11 [I]That is, *The mourning of the Egyptians*

13 [a]Gen. 49:29, 30; Acts 7:16 [b]Gen. 23:16

15 [a]Job 15:21, 22

16 [I]Hebr. *charged*

17 [a]Prov. 28:13 [b]Gen. 49:25

18 [a]Gen. 37:7, 10

19 [a]Gen. 45:5 [b]Deut. 32:35; 2Kgs. 5:7; Job 34:29; Rom. 12:19; Heb. 10:30

20 [a]But as for you, ye thought[2803] evil against me; *but* [b]God meant it unto good,[2896] to bring to pass,[6213] as *it is* this day, to save[2421] much people[5971] alive.[2421]

21 Now therefore fear ye not: [a]I will nourish[3557] you, and your little ones. And he comforted[5162] them, and spake [I][b]kindly[3820][5921] unto them.

22 And Joseph dwelt in Egypt, he, and his father's house:[1004] and Joseph lived[2421] an hundred and ten years.

23 And Joseph saw Ephraim's children[1121] [a]of the third *generation:* [b]the children also of Machir the son of Manasseh [c]were [I]brought up upon Joseph's knees.

24 And Joseph said unto his brethren, I die: and [a]God will surely visit[6485] you, and bring you out of this land unto the land [b]which he sware[7650] to Abraham, to Isaac, and to Jacob.

25 And [a]Joseph took an oath[7650] of the children of Israel, saying, God will surely visit you, and ye shall carry up my bones[6106] from hence.

26 So Joseph died, *being* an hundred and ten years old: and they [a]embalmed him, and he was put in a coffin[727] in Egypt.

20 [a]Ps. 56:5; Isa. 10:7 [b]Gen. 45:5, 7; Acts 3:13-15
21 [I]Hebr. *to their hearts* [a]Gen. 47:12; Matt. 5:44 [b]Gen. 34:3
23 [I]Hebr. *borne* [a]Job 42:16 [b]Num. 32:39 [c]Gen. 30:3
24 [a]Gen. 15:14; 46:4; 48:21; Ex. 3:16, 17; Heb. 11:22 [b]Gen. 15:18; 26:3; 35:12; 46:4
25 [a]Ex. 13:19; Josh. 24:32; Acts 7:16
26 [a]Gen. 50:2

EXODUS

Exodus is a Greek word which means "departure" and is derived from *ek* (1537), "out of," and *hodós* (3598), "road." The Hebrew title (the first words of the Hebr. text) means "and these are the names of."

The Book of Exodus describes the deliverance of the Israelites from Egypt, their journey to Mount Sinai, and the events that occurred during their sojourn there.

The patriarch Jacob had brought his family to Egypt to avoid starvation (see Gen. 46:1–27). When the Hyksos invaded Egypt and gained political power, the descendants of Jacob were forced into slavery (Ex. 1:8, 10). Despite the bitterness of their bondage, Jacob's descendants grew from a family of seventy (see note on Gen. 46:26, 27) into a nation of about two million (based on the figure of six hundred thousand men over twenty years of age, Ex. 12:37). The primary emphasis in Genesis was on the family of Abraham, but the Book of Exodus focuses on the developing nation of Israel.

The main theme of Exodus is redemption. The deliverance of the children of Israel from bondage in Egypt is a type of all redemption, and Moses who led them is a type of Christ.

A New King in Egypt

1 🔑 Now [a]these *are* the names of the
children[1121] of Israel, which came
into Egypt; every man[376] and his household[1004] came with Jacob.
2 Reuben, Simeon, Levi, and Judah,
3 Issachar, Zebulun, and Benjamin,
4 Dan, and Naphtali, Gad, and Asher.
5 And all the souls[5315] that came out
of the [I]loins[3409] of Jacob were [a]seventy
souls: for Joseph was in Egypt *already*.
🔑 6 And [a]Joseph died, and all his
brethren,[251] and all that generation.[1755]
7 [a]And the children of Israel were
fruitful, and increased abundantly,
and multiplied, and waxed exceeding
mighty; and the land[776] was filled with
them.

🔑 8 Now there [a]arose up a new king[4428]
over Egypt, which knew[3045] not Joseph.
9 And he said[559] unto his people,[5971]
Behold, [a]the people of the children of
Israel *are* more and mightier than we:
10 [a]Come on, let us [b]deal wisely[2449]
with them; lest they multiply, and it come
to pass, that, when there falleth out[7122]
any war, they join also unto our
enemies,[8130] and fight against us, and *so*
get them up[5927] out of the land.
11 Therefore they did set over them
taskmasters[8269] [a]to afflict them with their
[b]burdens. And they built for Pharaoh
treasure[4543] cities, Pithom [c]and Raamses.
12 [I]But the more they afflicted them,
the more they multiplied and grew. And
they were grieved[6973] because of the children of Israel.

1 [a]Gen. 46:8; Ex. 6:14
5 [I]Hebr. *thigh* [a]Gen. 46:26, 27; Ex. 1:20; Deut. 10:22
6 [a]Gen. 50:26; Acts 7:15
7 [a]Gen. 46:3; Deut. 26:5; Ps. 105:24; Acts 7:17
8 [a]Acts 7:18
9 [a]Ps. 105:24
10 [a]Ps. 10:2; 83:3, 4 [b]Job 5:13; Ps. 105:25; Prov. 16:25; 21:30; Acts 7:19
11 [a]Gen. 15:13; Ex. 3:7; Deut. 26:6 [b]Ex. 2:11; 5:4, 5; Ps. 81:6 [c]Gen. 47:11
12 [I]Hebr. *And as they afflicted them, so they multiplied*

🔑 **1:1–5** See note on Genesis 46:26, 27.

🔑 **1:6** The word "generation" is used in a variety of ways in the Scriptures. In some cases it refers to an unspecified period of time (Ps. 102:24), while at other times it is used as a simple reference to the past (Is. 51:8) or the future (Ps. 100:5). It is also used to designate men who belonged to a certain class in society. In this verse it refers to all those in a particular class living at a designated time.

🔑 **1:8** The expression "arose over Egypt" could better be translated "arose against Egypt." This probably refers to the invasion of the Hyksos, a people related to the Hebrews, who conquered Egypt. The Hyksos were never numerous, so the growing nation of Israel posed a threat to them (Ex. 1:9). This threat ultimately led the Hyksos rulers to enslave the Jews. When the Hyksos were later driven out, all of the hatred which the native Egyptians had for foreigners was focused on the Hebrews. Because the native Egyptians also feared they would become too numerous, they made the Israelite servitude more harsh (Ex. 1:13) and attempted to control the population by killing the male babies (see note on Ex. 1:17–20).

13 And the Egyptians made the children of Israel to serve with rigour:[6531]

14 And they [a]made their lives[2416] bitter with hard bondage,[5656] [b]in morter, and in brick, and in all manner of service[5656] in the field:[7704] all their service, wherein they made them serve,[5647] *was* with rigour.

15 And the king of Egypt spake to the Hebrew midwives, of which the name of the one *was* Shiphrah, and the name of the other Puah:

16 And he said, When ye do the office of a midwife to the Hebrew women, and see[7200] *them* upon the stools; if it *be* a son, then ye shall kill him: but if it *be* a daughter, then she shall live.[2425]

17 But the midwives [a]feared[3372] God,[430] and did[6213] not [b]as the king of Egypt commanded[1696] them, but saved the men children alive.[2421]

18 And the king of Egypt called[7121] for the midwives, and said unto them, Why have ye done this thing,[1697] and have saved the men children alive?

19 And [a]the midwives said unto Pharaoh, Because the Hebrew women *are* not as the Egyptain women; for they *are* lively,[2422] and are delivered ere[2962] the midwives come in unto them.

20 [a]Therefore God dealt well with the midwives: and the people multiplied, and waxed very mighty.

21 And it came to pass, because the midwives feared God, [a]that he made[6213] them houses.[1004]

22 And Pharaoh charged[6680] all his people, saying,[559] [a]Every son that is born ye shall cast into the river,[2975] and every daughter ye shall save alive.

Moses Is Born

2 And there went [a]a man[376] of the house[1004] of Levi, and took *to wife* a daughter of Levi.

2 And the woman[802] conceived, and bare a son: and [a]when she saw[7200] him that he *was a* goodly[2896] *child,* she hid him three months.

3 And when she could not longer hide him, she took for him an ark[8392] of bulrushes,[1573] and daubed it with slime and with pitch, and put the child therein; and she laid *it* in the flags[5488] by the river's brink.[8193]

4 [a]And his sister stood afar off, to wit[3045] what would be done[6213] to him.

5 And the [a]daughter of Pharaoh came down to wash *herself* at the river; and her maidens walked along by the river's side;[3027] and when she saw the ark among the flags, she sent her maid to fetch it.

6 And when she had opened *it,* she saw the child: and, behold, the babe wept. And she had compassion on him, and said, This *is one* of the Hebrews' children.

7 Then said his sister to Pharaoh's daughter, Shall I go and call[7121] to thee a nurse of the Hebrew women, that she may nurse the child for thee?

8 And Pharaoh's daughter said to her, Go. And the maid[5959] went and called the child's mother.[517]

9 And Pharaoh's daughter said unto her, Take this child away, and nurse[3243] it for me, and I will give *thee* thy wages. And the woman took the child, and nursed[5134] it.

10 And the child grew, and she

14 [a]Ex. 2:23; 6:9; Num. 20:15; Acts 7:19, 34 [b]Ps. 81:6
17 [a]Prov. 16:6 [b]Dan. 3:16, 18; 6:13; Acts 5:29
19 [a]2Sam. 17:19, 20
20 [a]Prov. 11:18; Eccl. 8:12; Isa. 3:10; Heb. 6:10
21 [a]1Sam. 2:35; 2Sam. 7:11, 13, 27, 29; 1Kgs. 2:24; 11:38; Ps. 127:1
22 [a]Acts 7:19
1 [a]Ex. 6:20; Num. 26:59; 1Chr. 23:14
2 [a]Acts 7:20; Heb. 11:23
4 [a]Ex. 15:20; Num. 26:59
5 [a]Acts 7:21

1:17–20 God has instituted civil government for the good of all people (Rom. 13:1–5). Throughout Scripture, He instructs His people to be in submission to the powers of government (Eccl. 8:2; 1 Pet. 2:13, 14). However, the governments were not granted the right to compel men to do things which are contrary to God's law (Dan. 3:16, 18; Acts 4:19; 5:29). The question arises here whether the midwives were blessed for lying and refusing obedience to the king. The fact was that God blessed the midwives, not for their lying, but for their obedience to God. See note on Joshua 2:1.

2:10 It is likely that the name given him by the Egyptian princess was a compound of an Egyptian river-god's name (such as Hapi or Osiris) and the Egyptian word *mos* meaning "child" (i.e.

(continued on next page)

brought him unto Pharaoh's daughter, and he became [a]her son. And she called his name [I]Moses:[4872] and she said, Because I drew him out[4871] of the water.

Moses Runs Away

11 And it came to pass in those days,[3117] [a]when Moses was grown, that he went out unto his brethren,[251] and looked on their [b]burdens: and he spied an Egyptian smiting[5221] an Hebrew, one of his brethren.

12 And he looked this way and that way, and when he saw that *there was* no man, he [a]slew[5221] the Egyptian, and hid him in the sand.

13 And [a]when he went out the second day, behold, two men[582] of the Hebrews strove together: and he said to him that did the wrong,[7563] Wherefore smitest thou thy fellow?[7453]

14 And he said, [a]Who made[7760] thee [Ib]a prince[8269] and a judge[8199] over us? intendest[559] thou to kill[2026] me, as thou killedst the Egyptian? And Moses feared,[3372] and said, Surely this thing[1697] is known.

🔑 15 Now when Pharaoh heard[8085] this thing, he sought to slay[2026] Moses. But [a]Moses fled from the face of Pharaoh, and dwelt in the land of Midian: and he sat down by [b]a well.

🔑 16 [a]Now the [I]priest[3548] of Midian had seven daughters: [b]and they came and drew *water,* and filled the troughs to water their father's flock.

17 And the shepherds came and drove them away: but Moses stood up and helped them, and [a]watered their flock.

18 And when they came to [a]Reuel their father, he said, How *is it that* ye are come so soon to day?[3117]

19 And they said, An Egyptian delivered us out[5337] of the hand[3027] of the shepherds, and also drew *water* enough for us, and watered the flock.

20 And he said unto his daughters, And where *is* he? why *is* it *that* ye have left[5800] the man? call[7121] him, that he may [a]eat bread.

🔑 21 And Moses was content[2974] to dwell with the man: and he gave Moses [a]Zipporah his daughter.

🔑 22 And she bare *him* a son,[1121] and he called his name [Ia]Gershom: for he said, I have been [b]a stranger[1616] in a strange[5237] land.[776]

23 And it came to pass [a]in process of time, that the king[4428] of Egypt died: and the children of Israel [b]sighed by reason of the bondage,[5656] and they cried, and [c]their cry came up[5927] unto God[430] by reason of the bondage.

24 And God [a]heard their groaning, and God [b]remembered his [c]covenant[1285] with Abraham, with Isaac, and with Jacob.

10 [I]That is, *Drawn out* [a]Acts 7:21
11 [a]Acts 7:23, 24; Heb. 11:24-26 [b]Ex. 1:11
12 [a]Acts 7:24
13 [a]Acts 7:26
14 [I]Hebr. *a man, a prince* [a]Gen. 13:8 [b]Acts 7:27, 28
15 [a]Acts 7:29; Heb. 11:27 [b]Gen. 24:11; 29:2
16 [I]Or, *prince* [a]Ex. 3:1 [b]Gen. 24:11; 29:10; 1Sam. 9:11
17 [a]Gen. 29:10
18 [a]Num. 10:29; Ex. 3:1; 4:18; 18:1
20 [a]Gen. 31:54; 43:25
21 [a]Ex. 4:25; 18:2
22 [I]That is, *A stranger here* [a]Ex. 18:3 [b]Acts 7:29; Heb. 11:13, 14
23 [a]Ex. 7:7; Acts 7:30 [b]Num. 20:16; Deut. 26:7; Ps. 12:5 [c]Gen. 18:20; Ex. 3:9; 22:23, 27; Deut. 24:15; James 5:4
24 [a]Ex. 6:5 [b]Ex. 6:5; Ps. 105:8, 42; 106:45 [c]Gen. 15:14; 46:4

(continued from previous page)
Hapimos). To the Egyptian princess, drawing Moses out of the water meant that a river-god had given birth to him. Moses may have thereafter dropped the false god's name and used the Hebrew name *Mosheh* (4872), "Moses" from the Hebrew word *māshāh* (4871), "to draw out." The text here could also mean that Moses' mother named him since the Hebrew does not specify which "she," Pharaoh's daughter or Moses' mother, actually named him.

🔑 **2:15** The Midianites were descendants of Abraham by another wife, Keturah, whom he married after Sarah died (Gen. 25:1).

🔑 **2:16, 21** In Numbers 12:1, Moses' wife is said to be an Ethiopian. Since Ethiopia was settled by descendants of Cush, they can be referred to as both. It can also be seen from Habakkuk 3:7 that "Cushan" and "Midian" are either interchangeable names or that Midian is the place where these people lived. Therefore, Zipporah was most likely the Ethiopian wife. Another possibility is that, at the point of Numbers 12:1, Moses' first wife Zipporah had died, and he married an Ethiopian woman (just as Abraham had married Keturah after the death of Sarah; see note on Gen. 2:15–17).

🔑 **2:22** In Hebrew the name "Gershom" suggests a foreigner who was banished into exile. Moses' second son, Eliezer ("God is a Helper"), is mentioned in Exodus 18:4.

25 And God [a]looked upon the children of Israel, and God [1][b]had respect unto[3045] *them.*

God Sends Moses to Egypt

3 Now Moses kept the flock of Jethro his father in law, [a]the priest[3548] of Midian: and he led the flock to the backside of the desert, and came to [b]the mountain of God,[430] *even* to Horeb.

🔑 2 And [a]the angel of the LORD appeared[7200] unto him in a flame of fire out of the midst of a bush: and he looked,[7200] and, behold, the bush burned with fire, and the bush *was* not consumed.

3 And Moses said, I will now turn aside, and see this [a]great sight, why the bush is not burnt.

4 And when the LORD saw that he turned aside[5493] to see, God called[7121] [a]unto him out of the midst of the bush, and said, Moses, Moses. And he said, Here *am* I.

5 And he said, Draw not nigh[7126] hither: [a]put off thy shoes from off thy feet, for the place whereon thou standest is holy[6944] ground.[127]

6 Moreover he said, [a]I *am* the God[430] of thy father,[1] the God of Abraham, the God of Isaac, and the God of Jacob. And Moses hid his face; for [b]he was afraid[3372] to look[5027] upon God.

7 And the LORD said, [a]I have surely seen[7200] the affliction[6040] of my people[5971] which *are* in Egypt, and have heard[8085] their cry [b]by reason of their taskmasters; for [c]I know[3045] their sorrows;

8 And [a]I am come down to [b]deliver them out of the hand[3027] of the Egyptians, and to bring them up[5927] out of that land[776] [c]unto a good[2896] land and a large,[7342] unto a land [d]flowing[2100] with milk and honey; unto the place of [e]the Canaanites, and the Hittites, and the Amorites,[567] and the Perizzites, and the Hivites, and the Jebusites.

9 Now therefore, behold, [a]the cry of the children[1121] of Israel is come unto me: and I have also seen the [b]oppression wherewith the Egyptians oppress them.

10 [a]Come now therefore, and I will send thee unto Pharaoh, that thou mayest bring forth my people the children of Israel out of Egypt.

11 And Moses said unto God, [a]Who *am* I, that I should go unto Pharaoh, and that I should bring forth the children of Israel out of Egypt?

12 And he said, [a]Certainly I will be with thee; and this *shall be* a token[226] unto thee, that I have sent thee: When thou hast brought forth the people out of Egypt, ye shall serve God upon this mountain.

13 And Moses said unto God, Behold, *when* I come unto the children of Israel, and shall say unto them, The God of your fathers hath sent me unto you; and they shall say to me, What *is* his name? what shall I say unto them?

🔑 14 And God said unto Moses, I AM THAT I AM:[1961] and he said, Thus shalt thou say unto the children of Israel, [a]I AM hath sent me unto you.

15 And God said moreover unto Moses, Thus shalt thou say unto the children of Israel, the LORD God of your fathers, the God of Abraham, the God of Isaac, and the God of Jacob, hath sent me unto you: this *is* [a]my name for ever,[5769]

25 [1]Hebr. *knew* [a]Ex. 4:31; 1Sam. 1:11; 2Sam. 16:12; Luke 1:25 [b]Ex. 3:7
1 [a]Ex. 2:16 [b]Ex. 18:5; 1Kgs. 19:8
2 [a]Deut. 33:16; Isa. 63:9; Acts 7:30
3 [a]Ps. 111:2; Acts 7:31
4 [a]Deut. 33:16
5 [a]Ex. 19:12–21; Josh. 5:15; Acts 7:33
6 [a]Gen. 28:13; Ex. 3:15; 4:5; Matt. 22:32; Mark 12:26; Luke 20:37; Acts 7:32 [b]1Kgs. 19:13; Isa. 6:1, 5
7 [a]Ex. 2:23-25; Neh. 9:9; Ps. 106:44; Acts 7:34 [b]Ex. 1:11 [c]Gen. 18:21; Ex. 2:25
8 [a]Gen. 11:5, 7; 18:21; 50:24 [b]Ex. 6:6, 8; 12:51 [c]Deut. 1:25; 8:7-9 [d]Ex. 3:17; 13:5; 33:3; Num. 13:27; Deut. 26:9, 15; Jer. 11:5; 32:22; Ezek. 20:6 [e]Gen. 15:18
9 [a]Ex. 2:23 [b]Ex. 1:11, 13, 14, 22
10 [a]Ps. 105:26; Mic. 6:4
11 [a]Ex. 6:12; 1Sam. 18:18; Isa. 6:5, 8; Jer. 1:6
12 [a]Gen. 31:3; Deut. 31:23; Josh. 1:5; Rom. 8:31
14 [a]Ex. 6:3; John 8:58; 2Cor. 1:20; Heb. 13:8; Rev. 1:4
15 [a]Ps. 135:13; Hos. 12:5

🔑 **3:2–6** See note on Exodus 23:20–23.

🔑 **3:14** The phrase "I AM" in Hebrew appears to be closely related to God's personal name of Jehovah (Ex. 6:3; or Yahweh or YHWH) which occurs more than 6,000 times in the Old Testament. However, the abbreviated form of Yahweh is *Yāh* ([3050] Ps. 68:4; and in the word hallelujah). Hence, the meaning of Jehovah is not completely clear to biblical scholars, though it seems to suggest the timelessness of God, who is the very foundation of all existence. Perhaps there is a hint of this understanding of the name in Revelation 1:4 where it is said of Christ, "Him which is, and which was, and which is to come" (see also Heb. 13:8). Jesus probably alluded to this name of God in John 8:58, "Before Abraham was, I AM."

and this *is* my memorial[2146] unto all generations.[1755]

16 Go, and [a]gather[622] the elders[2205] of Israel together, and say unto them, The LORD God of your fathers,[1] the God of Abraham, of Isaac, and of Jacob, appeared unto me, saying, [b]I have surely visited[6485] you, and *seen* that which is done to you in Egypt:

17 And I have said, [a]I will bring you up out of the affliction of Egypt unto the land of the Canaanites, and the Hittites, and the Amorites, and the Perizzites, and the Hivites, and the Jebusites, unto a land flowing with milk and honey.

18 And [a]they shall hearken[8085] to thy voice: and [b]thou shalt come, thou and the elders of Israel, unto the king of Egypt, and ye shall say unto him, The LORD God of the Hebrews hath [c]met with us: and now let us go, we beseech thee, three days' journey[1870] into the wilderness, that we may sacrifice[2076] to the LORD our God.

19 And I am sure[3045] that the king of Egypt [a]will not let you go, [I]no, not by a mighty[2389] hand.

20 And I will [a]stretch out my hand, and smite Egypt with [b]all my wonders[6381] which I will do in the midst thereof: and [c]after that he will let you go.

21 And [a]I will give this people favour[2580] in the sight of the Egyptians: and it shall come to pass, that, when ye go, ye shall not go empty:

22 [a]But every woman[802] shall borrow[7592] of her neighbour,[7934] and of her that sojourneth[1481] in her house,[1004] jewels of silver, and jewels of gold, and raiment: and ye shall put *them* upon your sons, and upon your daughters; and [b]ye shall spoil[5337] [I]the Egyptians.

God Gives Power To Moses

4 And Moses answered and said, But, behold, they will not believe[539] me, nor hearken[8085] unto my voice: for they will say, The LORD hath not appeared unto thee.

16 [a]Ex. 4:29 [b]Gen. 50:24; Ex. 2:25; 4:31; Luke 1:68

17 [a]Gen. 15:14, 16; Ex. 3:8

18 [a]Ex. 4:31 [b]Ex. 5:1, 3 [c]Num. 23:3, 4, 15, 16

19 [I]Or, *but by strong hand* [a]Ex. 5:2; 7:4

20 [a]Ex. 6:6; 7:5; 9:15 [b]Ex. 7:3; 11:9; Deut. 6:22; Neh. 9:10; Ps. 105:27; 135:9; Jer. 32:20; Acts 7:36; [c]Ex. 7:1—13:22; 12:31

21 [a]Ex. 11:3; 12:36; Ps. 106:46; Prov. 16:7

22 [I]Or, *Egypt* [a]Gen. 15:14; Ex. 11:2; 12:35, 36 [b]Job 27:17; Prov. 13:22; Ezek. 39:10

2 [a]Ex. 4:17, 20

5 [a]Ex. 19:9 [b]Ex. 3:15

6 [a]Num. 12:10; 2Kgs. 5:27

7 [a]Num. 12:13, 14; Deut. 32:39; 2Kgs. 5:14; Matt. 8:3

9 [I]Hebr. *shall be and shall be* [a]Ex. 7:19

10 [I]Hebr. *a man of words* [II]Hebr. *since yesterday, nor since the third day* [a]Ex. 6:12; Jer. 1:6

11 [a]Ps. 94:9

12 [a]Isa. 50:4; Jer. 1:9; Matt. 10:19; Mark 13:11; Luke 12:11, 12; 21:14, 15

2 And the LORD said unto him, What *is* that in thine hand? And he said, [a]A rod.[4294]

3 And he said, Cast it on the ground.[776] And he cast it on the ground, and it became a serpent;[5175] and Moses fled from before it.

4 And the LORD said unto Moses, Put forth thine hand, and take it by the tail. And he put forth his hand, and caught it, and it became a rod in his hand:

5 That they may [a]believe that [b]the LORD[3068] God[430] of their fathers,[1] the God of Abraham, the God of Isaac, and the God of Jacob, hath appeared unto thee.

6 And the LORD said furthermore unto him, Put now thine hand into thy bosom. And he put his hand into his bosom: and when he took it out, behold, his hand *was* leprous as [a]snow.

7 And he said, Put thine hand into thy bosom again.[7725] And he put his hand into his bosom again; and plucked it out of his bosom, and, behold, [a]it was turned again[7725] as his *other* flesh.[1320]

8 And it shall come to pass, if they will not believe thee, neither hearken to the voice of the first[7223] sign,[226] that they will believe the voice of the latter sign.

9 And it shall come to pass, if they will not believe also these two signs, neither hearken unto thy voice, that thou shalt take of the water of the river, and pour[8210] *it* upon the dry *land:* and [a]the water which thou takest out of the river [I]shall become blood[1818] upon the dry *land.*

10 And Moses said unto the LORD, O my Lord,[136] I *am* not [I]eloquent,[376,1697] neither [II]heretofore, nor since thou hast spoken unto thy servant:[5650] but [a]I *am* slow of speech,[6310] and of a slow tongue.

11 And the LORD said unto him, [a]Who hath made[7760] man's[120] mouth?[6310] or who maketh the dumb, or deaf, or the seeing, or the blind? have not I the LORD?

12 Now therefore go, and I will be [a]with thy mouth, and teach thee what thou shalt say.[1696]

🔑 13 And he said, O my Lord, [a]send, I pray thee, by the hand *of him whom* thou [I]wilt send.

14 And the anger[639] of the LORD was kindled[2734] against Moses, and he said, *Is* not Aaron the Levite thy brother?[251] I know[3045] that he can speak well. And also, behold, [a]he cometh forth to meet thee: and when he seeth[7200] thee, he will be glad in his heart.[3820]

15 And [a]thou shalt speak[1696] unto him, and [b]put[7760] words[1697] in his mouth: and I will be with thy mouth, and with his mouth, and [c]will teach you what ye shall do.[6213]

16 And he shall be thy spokesman[1696] unto the people:[5971] and he shall be, *even* he shall be to thee instead of a mouth, and [a]thou shalt be to him instead of God.

17 And thou shalt take [a]this rod in thine hand, wherewith thou shalt do signs.

Moses Returns to Egypt

18 And Moses went and returned[7725] to [I]Jethro his father in law, and said unto him, Let me go, I pray thee, and return unto my brethren[251] which *are* in Egypt, and see whether they be yet alive.[2416] And Jethro said to Moses, Go in peace.[7965]

19 And the LORD said unto Moses in Midian, Go, return into Egypt: for [a]all the men[582] are dead[4191] which sought thy life.[5315]

20 And Moses took his wife[802] and his sons, and set them upon an ass, and he returned to the land[776] of Egypt: and Moses took [a]the rod of God[430] in his hand.

21 And the LORD said unto Moses, When thou goest to return into Egypt, see[7200] that thou do all those [a]wonders[4159] before Pharaoh, which I have put in thine hand: but [b]I will harden[2388] his heart, that he shall not let the people go.

22 And thou shalt say unto Pharaoh, Thus saith the LORD, [a]Israel *is* my son, [b]*even* my firstborn:

23 And I say unto thee, Let my son go, that he may serve me: and if thou refuse to let him go, behold, [a]I will slay[2026] thy son, *even* thy firstborn.

24 And it came to pass by the way[1870] in the inn, that the LORD [a]met him, and sought to [b]kill[4191] him.

25 Then Zipporah took [a]a sharp [I]stone, and cut off[3772] the foreskin[6190] of her son, and [II]cast[5060] *it* at his feet, and said, Surely a bloody[1818] husband *art* thou to me.

26 So he let him go:[7503] then she said, A bloody husband *thou art,* because of the circumcision.[4150]

27 And the LORD said to Aaron, Go into the wilderness [a]to meet Moses. And he went and met him in [b]the mount of God, and kissed him.

28 And Moses [a]told[5046] Aaron all the words of the LORD who had sent him, and all the [b]signs which he had commanded[6680] him.

29 And Moses and Aaron [a]went and gathered together[622] all the elders[2205] of the children[1121] of Israel:

30 [a]And Aaron spake[1696] all the words which the LORD had spoken unto Moses, and did the signs in the sight of the people.

31 And the people [a]believed:[539] and when they heard[8085] that the LORD had [b]visited[6485] the children of Israel, and that he [c]had looked upon[7200] their affliction, then [d]they bowed their heads and worshipped.[7812]

Moses and Aaron Meet Pharaoh

5 And afterward Moses and Aaron went in, and told Pharaoh, Thus

13 [I]Or, *shouldest* [a]Jon. 1:3
14 [a]Ex. 4:27; 1Sam. 10:2, 3, 5
15 [a]Ex. 7:1, 2 [b]Num. 22:38; 23:5, 12, 16; Deut. 18:18; Isa. 51:16; Jer. 1:9 [c]Deut. 5:31
16 [a]Ex. 7:1; 18:19
17 [a]Ex. 4:2
18 [I]Hebr. *Jether*
19 [a]Ex. 2:15, 23; Matt. 2:20
20 [a]Ex. 17:9; Num. 20:8, 9
21 [a]Ex. 3:20 [b]Ex. 7:3, 13; 9:12, 35; 10:1; 14:8; Deut. 2:30; Josh. 11:20; Isa. 63:17; John 12:40; Rom. 9:18
22 [a]Hos. 11:1; Rom. 9:4; 2Cor. 6:18 [b]Jer. 31:9; James 1:18
23 [a]Ex. 11:5; 12:29
24 [a]Num. 22:22 [b]Gen. 17:14
25 [I]Or, *knife* [II]Hebr. *made it touch* [a]Josh. 5:2, 3
27 [a]Ex. 4:14 [b]Ex. 3:1
28 [a]Ex. 4:15, 16 [b]Ex. 4:8, 9
29 [a]Ex. 3:16
30 [a]Ex. 4:16
31 [a]Ex. 3:18; 4:8, 9 [b]Ex. 3:16 [c]Ex. 2:25; 3:7 [d]Gen. 24:26; Ex. 12:27; 1Chr. 29:20

🔑 **4:13** God desires obedience exclusively, and He can give whatever skill is needed. This is the fifth and last time that Moses objects to being made the leader of the exodus (see Ex. 3:11; 3:13; 4:1; 4:10).

saith[559] the LORD God[430] of Israel, Let my people[5971] go, that they may hold [a]a feast unto me in the wilderness.

2 And Pharaoh said, [a]Who *is* the LORD, that I should obey[8085] his voice to let Israel go? I know[3045] not the LORD, [b]neither will I let Israel go.

3 And they said, [a]The God of the Hebrews hath met with us: let us go, we pray thee, three days' journey into the desert, and sacrifice[2076] unto the LORD our God; lest he fall upon us with pestilence,[1698] or with the sword.

4 And the king[4428] of Egypt said unto them, Wherefore do ye, Moses and Aaron, let[6544] the people from their works? get you unto your [a]burdens.

5 And Pharaoh said, Behold, the people of the land now *are* [a]many, and ye make them rest[7673] from their burdens.

6 And Pharaoh commanded[6680] the same day[3117] the [a]taskmasters of the people, and their officers,[7860] saying,

7 Ye shall no more give the people straw to make brick, as heretofore: let them go and gather straw for themselves.

8 And the tale[4971] of the bricks, which they did make heretofore, ye shall lay upon them; ye shall not diminish *ought* thereof: for they *be* idle;[7503] therefore they cry, saying, Let us go *and* sacrifice to our God.

9 [I]Let there more work[5656] be laid upon the men,[582] that they may labour[6213] therein; and let them not regard vain[8267] words.

10 And the taskmasters of the people went out, and their officers, and they spake to the people, saying, Thus saith Pharaoh, I will not give you straw.

11 Go ye, get you straw where ye can find it: yet not ought of your work shall be diminished.

12 So the people were scattered abroad throughout all the land of Egypt to gather stubble instead of straw.

13 And the taskmasters hasted *them,* saying, Fulfil[3615] [I]your works,[4639] *your* daily tasks,[1697] as when there was straw.

14 And the officers of the children of Israel, which Pharaoh's taskmasters had set[7760] over them, were beaten,[5221] *and* demanded,[559] Wherefore have ye not fulfilled[3615] your task[2706] in making brick both yesterday and to day,[3117] as heretofore?

15 Then the officers of the children of Israel came and cried unto Pharaoh, saying, Wherefore dealest[6213] thou thus with thy servants?[5650]

16 There is no straw given unto thy servants, and they say to us, Make brick: and, behold, thy servants *are* beaten; but the fault[2398] *is* in thine own people.

17 But he said, Ye *are* idle, *ye are* idle: therefore ye say, Let us go *and* do sacrifice to the LORD.

18 Go therefore now, *and* work; for there shall no straw be given you, yet shall ye deliver the tale[8506] of bricks.

19 And the officers of the children of Israel did see[7200] *that* they *were* in evil[7451] *case,* after it was said, Ye shall not minish *ought* from your bricks of your daily task.

20 And they met Moses and Aaron, who stood[5324] in the way, as they came forth from Pharaoh:

21 [a]And they said unto them, The LORD look upon you, and judge;[8199] because ye have made our savour [I]to be abhorred[887] in the eyes of Pharaoh, and in the eyes of his servants, to put a sword[2719] in their hand to slay[2026] us.

God Promises to Deliver Israel

22 And Moses returned[7725] unto the LORD, and said, Lord,[136] wherefore hast thou *so* evil entreated[7489] this people? why *is* it *that* thou hast sent me?

23 For since I came to Pharaoh to speak[1696] in thy name, he hath done evil to this people; [I]neither hast thou delivered thy people at all.

6 Then the LORD said unto Moses, Now shalt thou see what I will do to Pharaoh: for [a]with a strong[2389] hand shall he let them go, and with a strong hand[3027] [b]shall he drive them out[1644] of his land.

5:1 [a]Ex. 10:9
5:2 [a]2Kgs. 18:35; Job 21:15 [b]Ex. 3:19
5:3 [a]Ex. 3:18
5:4 [a]Ex. 1:11
5:5 [a]Ex. 1:7, 9
5:6 [a]Ex. 1:11
5:9 [I]Hebr. *Let the work be heavy upon the men*
5:13 [I]Hebr. *a matter of a day in his day*
5:21 [I]Hebr. *to stink* [a]Gen. 34:30; Ex. 6:9; 1Sam. 13:4; 27:12; 2Sam. 10:6; 1Chr. 19:6
5:23 [I]Hebr. *delivering thou hast not delivered*
6:1 [a]Ex. 3:19 [b]Ex. 11:1; 12:31, 33, 39

2 And God[430] spake[1696] unto Moses, and said unto him, I *am* [I]the LORD:

🔑 3 And I appeared[7200] unto Abraham, unto Isaac, and unto Jacob, by *the name of* [a]God[410] Almighty,[7706] but by my name [b]JEHOVAH[3068] was I not known to them.

4 [a]And I have also established my covenant[1285] with them, [b]to give them the land of Canaan, the land of their pilgrimage,[4033] wherein they were strangers.[1481]

5 And [a]I have also heard[8085] the groaning of the children[1121] of Israel, whom the Egyptians keep in bondage; and I have remembered my covenant.

6 Wherefore say unto the children of Israel, [a]I *am* the LORD, and [b]I will bring you out from under the burdens of the Egyptians, and I will rid you out of their bondage,[5656] and I will [c]redeem[1350] you with a stretched out arm, and with great judgments:[8201]

7 And I will [a]take you to me for a people,[5971] and [b]I will be to you a God: and ye shall know[3045] that I *am* the LORD your God, which bringeth you out [c]from under the burdens of the Egyptians.

8 And I will bring you in unto the land, concerning the which I did [Ia]swear to give it to Abraham, to Isaac, and to Jacob; and I will give it you for an heritage:[4181] I *am* the LORD.

9 And Moses spake so unto the children of Israel: [a]but they hearkened[8085] not unto Moses for [I]anguish[7115] of spirit,[7307] and for cruel bondage.

10 And the LORD spake unto Moses, saying,

11 Go in, speak[1696] unto Pharaoh

2 IOr, *JEHOVAH*

3 [a]Gen. 17:1; 35:11; 48:3 [b]Ex. 3:14; Ps. 68:4; 83:18; John 8:58; Rev. 1:4

4 [a]Gen. 15:18; 17:4, 7 [b]Gen. 17:8; 28:4

5 [a]Ex. 2:24

6 [a]Ex. 6:2, 8, 29 [b]Ex. 3:17; 7:4; Deut. 26:8; Ps. 81:6; 136:11, 12 [c]Ex. 15:13; Deut. 7:8; 1Chr. 17:21; Neh. 1:10

7 [a]Deut. 4:20; 7:6; 14:2; 26:18; 2Sam. 7:24 [b]Gen. 17:7, 8; Ex. 29:45, 46; Deut. 29:13; Rev. 21:7 [c]Ex. 5:4, 5; Ps. 81:6

8 IHebr. *lift up my hand* [a]Gen. 15:18; 26:3; 28:13; 35:12

9 IHebr. *shortness*, or, *straitness* [a]Ex. 5:21

12 [a]Ex. 6:12 [b]Ex. 4:10; 6:30; Jer. 1:6

14 [a]Gen. 46:9; 1Chr. 5:3

15 [a]Gen. 46:10; 1Chr. 4:24

16 [a]Gen. 46:11; Num. 3:17; 1Chr. 6:1, 16

17 [a]1Chr. 6:17; 23:7

18 [a]Num. 26:57; 1Chr. 6:2, 18

king of Egypt, that he let the children of Israel go out of his land.

12 And Moses spake before the LORD, saying, Behold, the children of Israel have [a]not hearkened unto me; how then shall Pharaoh hear me, [b]who *am* of uncircumcised[6189] lips?[8193]

13 And the LORD spake unto Moses and unto Aaron, and gave them a charge[6680] unto the children of Israel, and unto Pharaoh king of Egypt, to bring the children of Israel out of the land of Egypt.

Moses' and Aaron's Family Record

14 These *be* the heads[7218] of their fathers'[1] houses:[1004] [a]The sons of Reuben the firstborn of Israel; Hanoch, and Pallu, Hezron, and Carmi: these *be* the families[4940] of Reuben.

15 [a]And the sons of Simeon; Jemuel, and Jamin, and Ohad, and Jachin, and Zohar, and Shaul the son of a Canaanitish woman: these *are* the families of Simeon.

16 And these *are* the names of [a]the sons of Levi according to their generations;[8435] Gershon, and Kohath, and Merari: and the years of the life[2416] of Levi *were* an hundred thirty and seven years.

17 [a]The sons of Gershon; Libni, and Shimi, according to their families.

18 And [a]the sons of Kohath; Amram, and Izhar, and Hebron, and Uzziel: and the years of the life of Kohath *were* an hundred thirty and three years.

🔑 **6:3** In light of such passages as Genesis 12:8 and 14:18, 22 in which LORD is equivalent to JEHOVAH in this verse, this name of God was evidently known among the patriarchs. Some scholars have suggested that Moses, because of his personal knowledge of the Lord at this time, inserted the name in the passages in Genesis when he wrote it at a later time. However, the key to this problem probably lies in a proper understanding of the Hebrew word *yādāh* (3034), "known." One meaning of this word is "to know by instruction or experience." Israel was about to witness the events of their exodus from Egypt, a more graphic demonstration of God's power than their forefathers had ever seen. It was by this name, Jehovah, that God's powerful works of salvation would be done. Israel would know by experience the full meaning of His name. Though they knew He was called "LORD," the patriarchs had not seen such a demonstration of power. Therefore, they had not known all the implications of that name.

19 And [a]the sons of Merari; Mahali
and Mushi: these *are* the families of Levi
according to their generations.
20 And [a]Amram took him Jochebed
his father's sister to wife; and she bare
him Aaron and Moses: and the years of
the life of Amram *were* an hundred and
thirty and seven years.
21 And [a]the sons of Izhar; Korah,
and Nepheg, and Zichri.
22 And [a]the sons of Uzziel; Mishael,
and Elzaphan, and Zithri.
23 And Aaron took him Elisheba,
daughter of [a]Amminadab, sister of
Naashon, to wife; and she bare him
[b]Nadab, and Abihu, Eleazar, and Ithamar.
24 And the [a]sons of Korah; Assir,
and Elkanah, and Abiasaph: these *are* the
families of the Korhites.
25 And Eleazar Aaron's son took him
one of the daughters of Putiel to wife;
and [a]she bare him Phinehas: these *are*
the heads of the fathers of the Levites
according to their families.
26 These *are* that Aaron and Moses,
[a]to whom the LORD said, Bring out the
children of Israel from the land of Egypt
according to their [b]armies.[6635]
27 These *are* they which [a]spake to
Pharaoh king of Egypt, [b]to bring out the
children of Israel from Egypt: these *are*
that Moses and Aaron.

Moses and Aaron Return to Pharaoh

28 And it came to pass on the day
when the LORD spake unto Moses in the
land of Egypt,
29 That the LORD spake[1696] unto
Moses, saying, [a]I *am* the LORD: [b]speak
thou unto Pharaoh king of Egypt all that
I say[1696] unto thee.
30 And Moses said before the LORD,
Behold, [a]I *am* of uncircumcised lips,
and how shall Pharaoh hearken[8085] unto
me?

7 And the LORD said unto Moses, See,
I have made thee [a]a god[430] to
Pharaoh: and Aaron thy brother shall be
[b]thy prophet.[5030]
2 Thou [a]shalt speak all that I command[6680] thee: and Aaron thy brother
shall speak unto Pharaoh, that he send
the children[1121] of Israel out of his
land.[776]
3 And [a]I will harden Pharaoh's
heart,[3820] and [b]multiply my [c]signs[226] and
my wonders[4159] in the land of Egypt.
4 But Pharaoh shall not hearken[8085]
unto you, [a]that I may lay my hand[3027]
upon Egypt, and bring forth mine
armies,[6635] *and* my people[5971] the children of Israel, out of the land of Egypt
[b]by great judgments.[8201]
5 And the Egyptians [a]shall know[3045]
that I *am* the LORD, when I [b]stretch forth
mine hand upon Egypt, and bring
out the children of Israel from among
them.
6 And Moses and Aaron [a]did as the
LORD commanded them, so did they.
7 And Moses *was* [a]fourscore years
old, and Aaron fourscore and three years
old, when they spake unto Pharaoh.
8 And the LORD spake unto Moses
and unto Aaron, saying,
9 When Pharaoh shall speak unto
you, saying, [a]Shew a miracle[4159] for you:
then thou shalt say unto Aaron, [b]Take

19 [a]1Chr. 6:19; 23:21
20 [a]Ex. 2:1, 2; Num. 26:59
21 [a]Num. 16:1; 1Chr. 6:37, 38
22 [a]Lev. 10:4; Num. 3:30
23 [a]Ruth 4:19, 20; 1Chr. 2:10; Matt. 1:4 [b]Lev. 10:1; Num. 3:2; 26:60; 1Chr. 6:3; 24:1
24 [a]Num. 26:11
25 [a]Num. 25:7, 11; Josh. 24:33
26 [a]Ex. 6:13 [b]Ex. 7:4; 12:17, 51; Num. 33:1
27 [a]Ex. 5:1, 3; 7:10 [b]Ex. 6:13; 32:7; 33:1; Ps. 77:20
29 [a]Ex. 6:2 [b]Ex. 6:11; 7:2
30 [a]Ex. 4:10; 6:12

1 [a]Ex. 4:16; Jer. 1:10 [b]Ex. 4:16
2 [a]Ex. 4:15
3 [a]Ex. 4:21 [b]Ex. 11:9 [c]Ex. 4:7
4 [a]Ex. 10:1; 11:9 [b]Ex. 6:6
5 [a]Ex. 7:17; 8:22; 14:4, 18; Ps. 9:16 [b]Ex. 3:20
6 [a]Ex. 7:2
7 [a]Deut. 29:5; 31:2; 34:7; Acts 7:23, 30
9 [a]Isa. 7:11; John 2:18; 6:30 [b]Ex. 4:2, 17

6:20 Variant readings in the Septuagint, the Syriac, and the Latin Vulgate indicate that Jochebed was actually Amram's paternal cousin.

7:3 Compare this verse to Exodus 8:15, where Pharaoh is said to have hardened his own heart. Scripture indicates that the natural inclination of man is to oppose God (Rom. 3:9–23; 5:10). Furthermore, Romans 1:24 reveals that God, in certain cases, allows men to follow the evil desires of their own hearts. God may have simply allowed Pharaoh, in his pride and sinfulness, to do as he desired. This would account for God "hardening" his heart in that God could have softened Pharaoh's heart had he chosen to intervene.

thy rod,[4294] and cast *it* before Pharaoh, *and* it shall become a serpent.[8577]

10 And Moses and Aaron went in unto Pharaoh, and they did so [a]as the LORD had commanded: and Aaron cast down his rod before Pharaoh, and before his servants,[5650] and it [b]became a serpent.

11 Then Pharaoh also [a]called[7121] the wise men[2450] and [b]the sorcerers:[3784] now the magicians[2748] of Egypt, they also [c]did in like manner with their enchantments.[3858]

12 For they cast down every man his rod, and they became serpents: but Aaron's rod swallowed up their rods.

13 And he hardened[2388] Pharaoh's heart, that he hearkened[8085] not unto them; [a]as the LORD had said.[1696]

The Waters Turned to Blood

14 And the LORD said unto Moses, [a]Pharaoh's heart *is* hardened, he refuseth[3985] to let the people go.

15 Get thee unto Pharaoh in the morning; lo, he goeth out3318 unto the water; and thou shalt stand[5324] by the river's brink[8193] against he come; and [a]the rod which was turned[2015] to a serpent[5175] shalt thou take in thine hand.

16 And thou shalt say unto him, [a]The LORD[3068] God[430] of the Hebrews hath sent me unto thee, saying, Let my people go, [b]that they may serve me in the wilderness: and, behold, hitherto thou wouldest not hear.[8085]

17 Thus saith[559] the LORD, In this [a]thou shalt know[3045] that I *am* the LORD: behold, I will smite with the rod that *is* in mine hand upon the waters which *are* in the river, and [b]they shall be turned[2015] [c]to blood.[1818]

18 And the fish1710 that *is* in the river shall die, and the river shall stink;[887] and the Egyptians shall [a]lothe3811 to drink of the water of the river.

19 And the LORD spake unto Moses, Say unto Aaron, Take thy rod, and [a]stretch out thine hand upon the waters of Egypt, upon their streams, upon their rivers, and upon their ponds, and upon all their [I]pools[4723] of water, that they may become blood; and *that* there may be blood throughout all the land of Egypt, both in *vessels of* wood, and in *vessels of* stone.

20 And Moses and Aaron did so, as the LORD commanded; and he [a]lifted up the rod, and smote[5221] the waters that *were* in the river, in the sight of Pharaoh, and in the sight of his servants; and all the [b]waters that *were* in the river were turned[2015] to blood.

21 And the fish that *was* in the river died;[4191] and the river stank, and the Egyptians [a]could not drink of the water of the river; and there was blood throughout all the land of Egypt.

22 [a]And the magicians of Egypt did so with their enchantments:[3909] and Pharaoh's heart was hardened, neither did he hearken unto them; [b]as the LORD had said.

23 And Pharaoh turned and went into his house,[1004] neither did he set his heart[3820] to this also.

24 And all the Egyptians digged round about the river for water to drink; for they could not drink of the water of the river.

25 And seven days were fulfilled, after that the LORD had smitten the river.

The Plague of Frogs

8 And the LORD spake[559] unto Moses, Go unto Pharaoh, and say unto him, Thus saith the LORD, Let my people go, [a]that they may serve me.

2 And if thou [a]refuse[3985] to let *them* go, behold, I will smite all thy borders with [b]frogs:

3 And the river shall bring forth frogs abundantly, which shall go up[5927] and come into thine house, and into [a]thy bedchamber, and upon thy bed, and into the house of thy servants,[5650] and upon thy people,[5971] and into thine ovens, and into thy [I]kneadingtroughs:

4 And the frogs shall come up both on thee, and upon thy people, and upon all thy servants.

10 [a]Ex. 7:9 [b]Ex. 4:3
11 [a]Gen. 41:8 [b]2Tim. 3:8 [c]Ex. 7:22; 8:7, 18
13 [a]Ex. 4:21; 7:4
14 [a]Ex. 8:15; 10:1, 20, 27
15 [a]Ex. 4:2, 3; 7:10
16 [a]Ex. 3:18 [b]Ex. 3:12, 18; 5:1, 3
17 [a]Ex. 5:2; 7:5 [b]Ex. 4:9 [c]Rev. 16:4, 6
18 [a]Ex. 7:24
19 [I]Hebr. *gathering of their waters* [a]Ex. 8:5, 6, 16; 9:22; 10:12, 21; 14:21, 26
20 [a]Ex. 17:5 [b]Ps. 78:44; 105:29
21 [a]Ex. 7:18
22 [a]Ex. 7:11 [b]Ex. 7:3
1 [a]Ex. 3:12, 18
2 [a]Ex. 7:14; 9:2 [b]Rev. 16:13
3 [I]Or, *dough* [a]Ps. 105:30

5 And the LORD spake unto Moses, Say unto Aaron, [a]Stretch forth thine hand with thy rod[4294] over the streams, over the rivers, and over the ponds, and cause frogs to come up upon the land of Egypt.

6 And Aaron stretched out his hand over the waters of Egypt; and [a]the frogs came up, and covered[3680] the land of Egypt.

7 [a]And the magicians[2748] did so with their enchantments,[3909] and brought up frogs upon the land of Egypt.

8 Then Pharaoh called[7121] for Moses and Aaron, and said, [a]Intreat[6279] the LORD, that he may take away the frogs from me, and from my people; and I will let the people go, that they may do sacrifice[2076] unto the LORD.

9 And Moses said unto Pharaoh, [I]Glory[6286] over me: [II]when shall I intreat for thee, and for thy servants, and for thy people, [III]to destroy[3772] the frogs from thee and thy houses, *that* they may remain[7604] in the river only?

10 And he said, [I]To morrow. And he said, *Be it* according to thy word:[1697] that thou mayest know[3045] that [a]*there is* none like unto the LORD our God.[430]

11 And the frogs shall depart[5493] from thee, and from thy houses, and from thy servants, and from thy people; they shall remain in the river only.

12 And Moses and Aaron went out from Pharaoh: and Moses [a]cried unto the LORD because of the frogs which he had brought against Pharaoh.

13 And the LORD did according to the word of Moses; and the frogs died out of the houses, out of the villages, and out of the fields.

14 And they gathered them together upon heaps: and the land stank.

15 But when Pharaoh saw that there was [a]respite,[7309] [b]he hardened his heart,[3820] and hearkened[8085] not unto them; as the LORD had said.[1696]

The Plague of Lice

16 And the LORD said unto Moses, Say unto Aaron, Stretch out thy rod, and smite[5221] the dust[6083] of the land, that it may become lice[3654] throughout all the land of Egypt.

17 And they did so; for Aaron stretched out his hand with his rod, and smote the dust of the earth, and [a]it became lice in man,[120] and in beast; all the dust of the land became lice throughout all the land of Egypt.

18 And [a]the magicians did so with their enchantments to bring forth lice, but they [b]could not: so there were lice upon man, and upon beast.

19 Then the magicians said unto Pharaoh, This *is* [a]the finger of God: and Pharaoh's [b]heart was hardened, and he hearkened not unto them; as the LORD had said.

Swarms of Flies

20 And the LORD said unto Moses, [a]Rise up early in the morning, and stand before Pharaoh; lo, he cometh forth to the water; and say unto him, Thus saith the LORD, [b]Let my people go, that they may serve me.

21 Else, if thou wilt not let my people go, behold, I will send [I]swarms *of flies* upon thee, and upon thy servants, and upon thy people, and into thy houses: and the houses of the Egyptians shall be full of swarms *of flies,* and also the ground[127] whereon they *are.*

22 And [a]I will sever in that day the land[776] of Goshen, in which my people dwell, that no swarms *of flies* shall be there; to the end thou mayest know that I *am* the LORD in the midst of the earth.[776]

23 And I will put [I]a division[6304] between my people and thy people: [II]to morrow shall this sign[226] be.

24 And the LORD did so; and [a]there came a grievous[3515] swarm *of flies* into the house of Pharaoh, and *into* his servants' houses, and into all the land of Egypt: the land was [I]corrupted[7843] by reason of the swarm *of flies.*

25 And Pharaoh called for Moses and for Aaron, and said, Go ye, sacrifice to your God in the land.

5 [a]Ex. 7:19
6 [a]Ps. 78:45; 105:30
7 [a]Ex. 7:11
8 [a]Ex. 9:28; 10:17; Num. 21:7; 1Kgs. 13:6; Acts 8:24
9 [I]Or, *Have this honor over me* [II]Or, *against when* [III]Hebr. *to cut off*
10 [I]Or, *Against tomorrow* [a]Ex. 9:14; Deut. 33:26; 2Sam. 7:22; 1Chr. 17:20; Ps. 86:8; Isa. 46:9; Jer. 10:6, 7
12 [a]Ex. 8:30; 9:33; 10:18; 32:11; James 5:16-18
15 [a]Eccl. 8:11 [b]Ex. 7:14
17 [a]Ps. 105:31
18 [a]Ex. 7:11 [b]Luke 10:18; 2Tim. 3:8, 9
19 [a]1Sam. 6:3, 9; Ps. 8:3; Matt. 12:28; Luke 11:20 [b]Ex. 8:15
20 [a]Ex. 7:15 [b]Ex. 8:1
21 [I]Or, *a mixture of noisome beasts*
22 [a]Ex. 9:4, 6, 26; 10:23; 11:6, 7; 12:13
23 [I]Hebr. *a redemption* [II]Or, *by tomorrow*
24 [I]Or, *destroyed* [a]Ps. 78:45; 105:31

26 And Moses said,[559] It is not meet so to do, for we shall sacrifice[2076] [a]the abomination[8841] of the Egyptians to the LORD our God: lo, shall we sacrifice the abomination of the Egyptians before their eyes, and will they not stone us?

27 We will go [a]three days' journey into the wilderness, and sacrifice to the LORD our God, as [b]he shall command[559] us.

28 And Pharaoh said, I will let you go, that ye may sacrifice to the LORD your God in the wilderness; only ye shall not go very far away: [a]intreat for me.

29 And Moses said, Behold, I go out from thee, and I will intreat[6279] the LORD that the swarms *of flies* may depart from Pharaoh, from his servants, and from his people, to morrow: but let not Pharaoh [a]deal deceitfully[2048] any more[3254] in not letting the people go to sacrifice to the LORD.

30 And Moses went out from Pharaoh, and [a]intreated the LORD.

31 And the LORD did according to the word of Moses; and he removed the swarms *of flies* from Pharaoh, from his servants, and from his people; there remained[7604] not one.

32 And Pharaoh [a]hardened his heart at this time also, neither would he let the people go.

The Animals Die

9 Then the LORD said unto Moses, [a]Go in unto Pharaoh, and tell[1696] him, Thus saith[559] the LORD God[430] of the Hebrews, Let my people[5971] go, that they may serve me.

2 For if thou [a]refuse to let *them* go, and wilt hold[2388] them still,

3 Behold, the [a]hand[3027] of the LORD is upon thy cattle which *is* in the field,[7704] upon the horses, upon the asses, upon the camels, upon the oxen, and upon the sheep: *there shall be* a very grievous murrain.[1698]

4 And [a]the LORD shall sever[6395] between the cattle of Israel and the cattle of Egypt: and there shall nothing die of all *that is* the children's of Israel.

26 [a]Gen. 43:32; 46:34; Deut. 7:25, 26; 12:31
27 [a]Ex. 3:18 [b]Ex. 3:12
28 [a]Ex. 8:8; 9:28; 1Kgs. 13:6
29 [a]Ex. 8:15
30 [a]Ex. 8:12
32 [a]Ex. 4:21; 8:15
1 [a]Ex. 8:1
2 [a]Ex. 8:2
3 [a]Ex. 7:4
4 [a]Ex. 8:22
6 [a]Ps. 78:50
7 [a]Ex. 7:14; 8:32
9 [a]Rev. 16:2
10 [a]Deut. 28:27
11 [a]Ex. 8:18, 19; 2Tim. 3:9
12 [a]Ex. 4:21
13 [a]Ex. 8:20
14 [a]Ex. 8:10

5 And the LORD appointed a set time,[4150] saying, To morrow the LORD shall do this thing in the land.

6 And the LORD did that thing on the morrow, and [a]all the cattle of Egypt died: but of the cattle of the children of Israel died not one.

7 And Pharaoh sent, and, behold, there was not one of the cattle of the Israelites dead. And [a]the heart[3820] of Pharaoh was hardened, and he did not let the people go.

The Boils

8 And the LORD said unto Moses and unto Aaron, Take to you handfuls of ashes of the furnace, and let Moses sprinkle[2236] it toward the heaven[8064] in the sight of Pharaoh.

9 And it shall become small dust[80] in all the land of Egypt, and shall be [a]a boil breaking forth *with* blains[76] upon man,[120] and upon beast, throughout all the land of Egypt.

10 And they took ashes of the furnace, and stood before Pharaoh; and Moses sprinkled it up toward heaven; and it became [a]a boil breaking forth *with* blains upon man, and upon beast.

11 And the [a]magicians[2748] could not stand before Moses because of the boils; for the boil was upon the magicians, and upon all the Egyptians.

12 And the LORD hardened[2388] the heart of Pharaoh, and he hearkened not unto them; [a]as the LORD had spoken[1696] unto Moses.

The Plague of Hail

13 And the LORD said unto Moses, [a]Rise up early in the morning, and stand before Pharaoh, and say unto him, Thus saith the LORD God of the Hebrews, Let my people go, that they may serve me.

14 For I will at this time send all my plagues upon thine heart, and upon thy servants,[5650] and upon thy people; [a]that thou mayest know that *there is* none like me in all the earth.[776]

15 For now I will [a]stretch out my hand, that I may smite[5221] thee and thy people with pestilence;[1698] and thou shalt be cut off from the earth.

16 And in very deed for [a]this *cause* have I [I]raised thee up, for to shew[7200] *in* thee my power; and that my name may be declared[5608] throughout all the earth.

17 As yet exaltest[5549] thou thyself against my people, that thou wilt not let them go?

18 Behold, to morrow about this time[6256] I will cause it to rain a very grievous hail, such as hath not been in Egypt since the foundation[3245] thereof even until now.

19 Send therefore now, *and* gather thy cattle, and all that thou hast in the field; *for upon* every man and beast which shall be found in the field, and shall not be brought[622] home,[1004] the hail shall come down upon them, and they shall die.[4191]

20 He that feared the word[1697] of the LORD among the servants of Pharaoh made his servants and his cattle flee into the houses:

21 And he that [Ia]regarded not the word of the LORD left[5800] his servants and his cattle in the field.

22 And the LORD said unto Moses, Stretch forth thine hand toward heaven, that there may be [a]hail in all the land[776] of Egypt, upon man, and upon beast, and upon every herb[6212] of the field, throughout the land of Egypt.

23 And Moses stretched forth his rod[4294] toward heaven: and [a]the LORD sent thunder and hail, and the fire ran along upon the ground;[776] and the LORD rained hail upon the land of Egypt.

24 So there was hail, and fire mingled with the hail, very grievous, such as there was none like it in all the land of Egypt since it became a nation.[1471]

25 And the hail smote throughout all the land of Egypt all that *was* in the field, both man and beast; and the hail [a]smote every herb of the field, and brake[7665] every tree of the field.

26 [a]Only in the land[776] of Goshen, where the children of Israel *were,* was there no hail.

27 And Pharaoh sent, and called[7121] for Moses and Aaron, and said unto them, [a]I have sinned[2398] this time: [b]the LORD *is* righteous,[6662] and I and my people *are* wicked.[7563]

28 [a]Intreat[6279] the LORD (for *it is* enough) that there be no *more* [Ib]mighty[430] thunderings and hail; and I will let you go, and ye shall stay no longer.

29 And Moses said unto him, As soon as I am gone out of the city, I will [a]spread abroad my hands[3709] unto the LORD; *and* the thunder shall cease, neither shall there be any more hail; that thou mayest know how that the [b]earth[776] *is* the LORD's.

30 But as for thee and thy servants, [a]I know[3045] that ye will not yet fear[3372] the LORD God.

31 And the flax and the barley was smitten: [a]for the barley *was* in the ear,[24] and the flax *was* bolled.[1392]

🔑 32 But the wheat and the rie were not smitten: for they *were* [I]not grown up.

33 And Moses went out of the city from Pharaoh, and [a]spread abroad his hands[3709] unto the LORD: and the thunders and hail ceased, and the rain was not poured[5413] upon the earth.

34 And when Pharaoh saw[7200] that the rain and the hail and the thunders were ceased, he sinned[2398] yet more, and hardened his heart, he and his servants.

35 And [a]the heart of Pharaoh was hardened,[2388] neither would he let the children of Israel go; as the LORD had spoken [Ib]by Moses.

15 [a]Ex. 3:20
16 [I]Hebr. *made thee stand* [a]Ex. 14:17; Prov. 16:4; Rom. 9:17; 1Pet. 2:9
21 [I]Hebr. *set not his heart unto* [a]Ex. 7:23
22 [a]Rev. 16:21
23 [a]Josh. 10:11; Ps. 18:13; 78:47; 105:32; 148:8; Isa. 30:30; Ezek. 38:22; Rev. 8:7
25 [a]Ps. 105:33
26 [a]Ex. 8:22; 9:4, 6; 10:23; 11:7; 12:13; Isa. 32:18, 19
27 [a]Ex. 10:16 [b]2Chr. 12:6; Ps. 129:4; 145:17; Lam. 1:18; Dan. 9:14
28 [I]Hebr. *voices of God* [a]Ex. 8:8, 28; 10:17; Acts 8:24 [b]Ps. 29:3, 4
29 [a]1Kgs. 8:22, 38; Ps. 143:6; Isa. 1:15 [b]Ps. 24:1; 1Cor. 10:26, 28
30 [a]Isa. 26:10
31 [a]Ruth 1:22; 2:23
32 [I]Hebr. *hidden, or, dark*
33 [a]Ex. 8:12; 9:29
35 [I]Hebr. *by the hand of Moses,* [a]Ex. 4:21 [b]Ex. 4:13

🔑 **9:32** Rye or spelt was a wild wheat which was more edible than barley, but it was not as good as wheat. It was harvested later than barley and was difficult to separate from its chaff. The Egyptians used it to make their basic bread.

Locusts

10 And the LORD said unto Moses, Go in unto Pharaoh: [a]for I have hardened his heart,[3820] and the heart of his servants,[5650] [b]that I might shew these my signs[226] before him:

2 And that [a]thou mayest tell in the ears[241] of thy son,[1121] and of thy son's son, what things I have wrought in Egypt, and my signs which I have done[7760] among them; that ye may know[3045] how that I *am* the LORD.

3 And Moses and Aaron came in unto Pharaoh, and said unto him, Thus saith[559] the LORD God[430] of the Hebrews, How long wilt thou refuse[3985] to [a]humble thyself before me? let my people[5971] go, that they may serve me.

4 Else, if thou refuse to let my people go, behold, to morrow will I bring the [a]locusts into thy coast:

5 And they shall cover[3680] the [I][a]face of the earth,[776] that one cannot be able to see the earth: and [b]they shall eat the residue[3499] of that which is escaped,[6413] which remaineth[7604] unto you from the hail, and shall eat every tree which groweth for you out of the field:[7704]

6 And they [a]shall fill thy houses, and the houses of all thy servants, and the houses of all the Egyptians; which neither thy fathers,[1] nor thy fathers' fathers have seen, since the day[3117] that they were upon the earth[127] unto this day. And he turned himself, and went out from Pharaoh.

7 And Pharaoh's servants said unto him, How long shall this man be [a]a snare[4170] unto us? let the men[582] go, that they may serve the LORD their God: knowest thou not yet that Egypt is destroyed?[6]

8 And Moses and Aaron were brought again unto Pharaoh: and he said unto them, Go, serve the LORD your God: *but* [I]who *are* they that shall go?

1 [a]Ex. 4:21; 7:14 [b]Ex. 7:4
2 [a]Deut. 4:9; Ps. 44:1; 71:18; 78:5; Joel 1:3
3 [a]1Kgs. 21:29; 2Chr. 7:14; 34:27; Job 42:6; Jer. 13:18; James 4:10; 1Pet. 5:6
4 [a]Prov. 30:27; Rev. 9:3
5 [I]Hebr. *eye* [a]Ex. 10:15 [b]Ex. 9:32; Joel 1:4; 2:25
6 [a]Ex. 8:3, 21
7 [a]Ex. 23:33; Josh. 23:13; 1Sam. 18:21; Eccl. 7:26; 1Cor. 7:35
8 [I]Hebr. *who, and who*
9 [a]Ex. 5:1
12 [a]Ex. 7:19 [b]Ex. 10:5
14 [a]Ps. 78:46; 105:34 [b]Joel 2:2
15 [a]Ex. 10:5 [b]Ps. 105:35
16 [I]Hebr. *hastened to call* [a]Ex. 9:27
17 [a]Ex. 9:28; 1Kgs. 13:6

9 And Moses said, We will go with our young and with our old,[2205] with our sons and with our daughters, with our flocks and with our herds will we go; for [a]we *must hold* a feast[2282] unto the LORD.

10 And he said unto them, Let the LORD be so with you, as I will let you go, and your little ones:[2945] look[7200] *to it*; for evil[7451] *is* before you.

11 Not so: go now ye *that are* men,[1397] and serve the LORD; for that ye did desire. And they were driven out from Pharaoh's presence.

12 And the LORD said unto Moses, [a]Stretch out thine hand[3027] over the land[776] of Egypt for the locusts, that they may come up upon the land of Egypt, and [b]eat every herb of the land, *even* all that the hail hath left.[7604]

13 And Moses stretched forth his rod[4294] over the land of Egypt, and the LORD brought an east wind[7307] upon the land all that day, and all *that* night;[3915] *and* when it was morning, the east wind brought the locusts.

14 And [a]the locusts went up over all the land of Egypt, and rested in all the coasts of Egypt: very grievous *were they*; [b]before them there were no such locusts as they, neither after them shall be such.

15 For they [a]covered[3680] the face of the whole earth, so that the land was darkened; and they [b]did eat every herb of the land, and all the fruit of the trees which the hail had left:[3498] and there remained[3498] not any green thing in the trees, or in the herbs of the field, through all the land of Egypt.

16 Then Pharaoh [I]called[7121] for Moses and Aaron in haste; and he said, [a]I have sinned[2398] against the LORD your God, and against you.

17 Now therefore forgive, I pray thee, my sin[2403] only this once, and [a]intreat[6279] the LORD your God, that he may take away from me this death[4194] only.

10:1–20 See note on Joel 1:4 regarding locusts.

18 And he [a]went out from Pharaoh, and intreated the LORD.

19 And the LORD turned[2015] a mighty strong[2389] west wind, which took away the locusts, and [I]cast them [a]into the Red[5488] sea; there remained not one locust in all the coasts of Egypt.

20 But the LORD [a]hardened[2388] Pharaoh's heart, so that he would not let the children of Israel go.

Three Days of Darkness

21 And the LORD said[559] unto Moses, [a]Stretch out thine hand toward heaven,[8064] that there may be darkness[2822] over the land of Egypt, [I]even darkness *which* may be felt.

22 And Moses stretched forth his hand toward heaven; and there was a [a]thick[653] darkness in all the land of Egypt three days:

23 They saw not one another, neither rose any from his place for three days: [a]but all the children of Israel had light[216] in their dwellings.[4186]

24 And Pharaoh called[7121] unto Moses, and [a]said, Go ye, serve the LORD; only let your flocks and your herds be stayed: let your [b]little ones also go with you.

25 And Moses said, Thou must give [I]us also sacrifices[2077] and burnt offerings,[5930] that we may sacrifice[6213] unto the LORD our God.

26 Our cattle[4735] also shall go with us; there shall not an hoof be left behind; for thereof must we take to serve the LORD our God; and we know not with what we must serve the LORD, until we come thither.

27 But the LORD [a]hardened Pharaoh's heart, and he would not let them go.

28 And Pharaoh said unto him, Get thee from me, take heed[8104] to thyself, see my face no more; for in *that* day[3117] thou seest my face thou shalt die.

29 And Moses said, Thou hast spoken[1696] well, [a]I will see thy face again no more.

All Firstborn Must Die

11 And the LORD said unto Moses, Yet will I bring one plague[5061] *more* upon Pharaoh, and upon Egypt; afterwards he will let you go hence: [a]when he shall let *you* go, he shall surely thrust you out hence altogether.[3617]

2 Speak[1696] now in the ears of the people,[5971] and let every man borrow[7592] of his neighbour,[7453] and every woman[802] of her neighbour,[7468] [a]jewels of silver, and jewels of gold.

3 [a]And the LORD gave the people favour[2580] in the sight of the Egyptians. Moreover the man[376] [b]Moses *was* very great in the land[776] of Egypt, in the sight of Pharaoh's servants,[5650] and in the sight of the people.

4 And Moses said, Thus saith[559] the LORD, [a]About midnight will I go out into the midst of Egypt:

5 And [a]all the firstborn in the land of Egypt shall die,[4191] from the firstborn of Pharaoh that sitteth upon his throne,[3678] even unto the firstborn of the maidservant that *is* behind the mill; and all the firstborn of beasts.

6 [a]And there shall be a great cry throughout all the land of Egypt, such as there was none like it, nor shall be like it any more.

7 [a]But against any of the children[1121] of Israel [b]shall not a dog move his tongue, against man[376] or beast: that ye may know[3045] how that the LORD doth put a difference[6395] between the Egyptians and Israel.

8 And [a]all these thy servants shall come down unto me, and bow down[7812] themselves unto me, saying, Get thee out, and all the people [Ib]that follow thee: and after that I will go out. And he went out from Pharaoh in [II]a great anger.[639]

9 And the LORD said unto Moses, [a]Pharaoh shall not hearken unto you; that [b]my wonders[4159] may be multiplied in the land of Egypt.

10 And Moses and Aaron did all these wonders before Pharaoh: [a]and the LORD hardened Pharaoh's heart, so that

18 [a]Ex. 8:30
19 [I]Hebr. *fastened* [a]Joel 2:20
20 [a]Ex. 4:21; 11:10
21 [I]Hebr. *that* one *may feel darkness* [a]Ex. 9:22
22 [a]Ps. 105:28
23 [a]Ex. 8:22
24 [a]Ex. 10:8 [b]Ex. 10:10
25 [I]Hebr. *into our hands*
27 [a]Ex. 4:21; 10:20; 14:4, 8
29 [a]Heb. 11:27

1 [a]Ex. 12:31, 33, 39
2 [a]Ex. 3:22; 12:35
3 [a]Ex. 3:21; 12:36; Ps. 106:46 [b]2Sam. 7:9; Esth. 9:4
4 [a]Ex. 12:12, 23, 29; Amos 5:17
5 [a]Ex. 12:12, 29; Amos 4:10
6 [a]Ex. 12:30; Amos 5:17
7 [a]Ex. 8:22 [b]Josh. 10:21
8 [I]Hebr. *that is at thy feet* [II]Hebr. *heat of anger* [a]Ex. 12:33 [b]Judg. 4:10; 8:5; 1Kgs. 20:10
9 [a]Ex. 3:19; 7:4; 10:1 [b]Ex. 7:3
10 [a]Ex. 10:20, 27; Rom. 2:5; 9:22

he would not let the children of Israel go out of his land.

The Passover

12 And the LORD spake unto Moses and Aaron in the land[776] of Egypt, saying,

🔑 2 [a]This month *shall be* unto you the beginning[7218] of months: it *shall be* the first[7223] month of the year to you.

3 Speak[1696] ye unto all the congregation[5712] of Israel, saying, In the tenth *day* of this month they shall take to them every man a [I]lamb, according to the house[1004] of *their* fathers,[1] a lamb for an house:

4 And if the household[1004] be too little for the lamb, let him and his neighbour[7934] next unto his house take *it* according to the number of the souls;[5315] every man according to his eating shall make your count for the lamb.

5 Your lamb shall be [a]without blemish,[8549] a male[2145] [Ib]of the first year: ye shall take *it* out from the sheep, or from the goats:

6 And ye shall keep[4931] it up until the [a]fourteenth day of the same month: and the whole assembly[6951] of the congregation of Israel shall kill[7819] it [Ib]in the evening.

7 And they shall take of the blood,[1818] and strike *it* on the two side posts and on the upper door post of the houses, wherein they shall eat it.

8 And they shall eat the flesh[1320] in that night,[3915] roast with fire, and [a]unleavened bread;[4682] *and* with bitter *herbs* they shall eat it.

9 Eat not of it raw, nor sodden[1310] at all with water, but [a]roast *with* fire; his head with his legs, and with the purtenance[7130] thereof.

10 [a]And ye shall let nothing of it remain[3498] until the morning; and that which remaineth of it until the morning ye shall burn with fire.

11 And thus shall ye eat it; *with* your loins girded, your shoes on your feet, and your staff in your hand; and ye shall eat it in haste: [a]it *is* the LORD'S passover.[6453]

12 For I [a]will pass through[5674] the land of Egypt this night, and will smite all the firstborn in the land of Egypt, both man and beast; and [b]against all the [Ic]gods[430] of Egypt I will execute[6213] judgment:[8201] [d]I *am* the LORD.

13 And the blood shall be to you for a token[226] upon the houses where ye *are:* and when I see[7200] the blood, I will pass over[6452] you, and the plague[5063] shall not be upon you [I]to destroy[4889] *you,* when I smite[5221] the land of Egypt.

14 And this day[3117] shall be unto you [a]for a memorial;[2146] and ye shall keep it a [b]feast[2282] to the LORD throughout your generations;[1755] ye shall keep it a feast [c]by an ordinance[2708] for ever.[5769]

15 [a]Seven days shall ye eat unleavened bread;[2557] even the first day ye shall put away[7673] leaven out of your houses: for whosoever eateth leavened bread from the first day until the seventh day, [b]that soul shall be cut off[3772] from Israel.

16 And in the first day *there shall be* [a]an holy[6944] convocation,[4744] and in the seventh day there shall be an holy convocation to you; no manner of work[4399] shall be done[6213] in them, save *that* which every [I]man[5315] must eat, that only may be done of you.

17 And ye shall observe[8104] *the feast of* unleavened bread; for [a]in this selfsame day have I brought your armies[6635] out of the land of Egypt: therefore shall ye observe this day in your generations by an ordinance for ever.

18 [a]In the first *month,* on the four-

2 [a]Ex. 13:4; Deut. 16:1

3 [I]Or, *kid*

5 [I]Hebr. *son of a year* [a]Lev. 22:19-21; Mal. 1:8, 14; Heb. 9:14; 1Pet. 1:19 [b]Lev. 23:12

6 [I]Hebr. *between the two evenings* [a]Lev. 23:5; Num. 9:3; 28:16; Deut. 16:1, 6 [b]Ex. 16:12

8 [a]Ex. 34:25; Num. 9:11; Deut. 16:3; 1Cor. 5:8

9 [a]Deut. 16:7

10 [a]Ex. 23:18; 34:25

11 [a]Deut. 16:5

12 [I]Or, *princes* [a]Ex. 11:4, 5; Amos 5:17 [b]Num. 33:4 [c]Ex. 21:6; 22:28; Ps. 82:1, 6; John 10:34, 35 [d]Ex. 6:2

13 [I]Hebr. *for a destruction*

14 [a]Ex. 13:9 [b]Lev. 23:4, 5; 2Kgs. 23:21 [c]Ex. 12:24, 43; 13:10

15 [a]Ex. 13:6, 7; 23:15; 34:18, 25; Lev. 23:5, 6; Num. 28:17; Deut. 16:3, 8; 1Cor. 5:7 [b]Gen. 17:14; Num. 9:13

16 [I]Hebr. *soul* [a]Lev. 23:7, 8; Num. 28:18, 25

17 [a]Ex. 13:3

18 [a]Lev. 23:5; Num. 28:16

🔑 **12:2** The Jewish calendar, which is based on lunar months, had its beginning at this time. The first month was called Abib (Ex. 13:4) up until the Babylonian Captivity. After that time it was called Nisan (see Neh. 2:1; Esth. 3:7). On modern calendars it corresponds to the latter part of March and the first part of April.

teenth day of the month at even, ye shall eat unleavened bread, until the one and twentieth day of the month at even.

19 [a]Seven days shall there be no leaven found in your houses: for whosoever eateth that which is leavened, [b]even that soul shall be cut off from the congregation of Israel, whether he be a stranger,[1616] or born in the land.

20 Ye shall eat nothing leavened; in all your habitations[4186] shall ye eat unleavened bread.

21 Then Moses called[7121] for all the elders[2205] of Israel, and said unto them, [a]Draw out and take you a [I]lamb according to your families,[4940] and kill[7819] the passover.

22 [a]And ye shall take a bunch of hyssop,[231] and dip[2881] *it* in the blood that *is* in the bason,[5592] and [b]strike[5060] the lintel[4947] and the two side posts[4201] with the blood that *is* in the bason: and none of you shall go out at the door of his house until the morning.

23 [a]For the LORD will pass through[5674] to smite[5062] the Egyptians; and when he seeth the blood upon the lintel, and on the two side posts, the LORD will pass over the door, and [b]will not suffer[5414] [c]the destroyer[7843] to come in unto your houses to smite *you.*

24 And ye shall observe this thing[1697] for an ordinance[2706] to thee and to thy sons[1121] for ever.

25 And it shall come to pass, when ye be come to the land which the LORD will give you, [a]according as he hath promised,[1696] that ye shall keep[8104] this service.[5656]

26 [a]And it shall come to pass, when your children shall say unto you, What mean ye by this service?

27 That ye shall say, [a]It *is* the sacrifice[2077] of the LORD's passover, who passed over the houses of the children of Israel in Egypt, when he smote the Egyptians, and delivered our houses. And the people[5971] [b]bowed the head and worshipped.[7812]

28 And the children of Israel went away, and [a]did as the LORD had commanded[6680] Moses and Aaron, so did they.

The Death of the Firstborn

29 [a]And it came to pass, that at midnight [b]the LORD smote all the firstborn in the land of Egypt, [c]from the firstborn of Pharaoh that sat on his throne[3678] unto the firstborn of the captive[7628] that *was* in the [I]dungeon;[953] and all the firstborn of cattle.

30 And Pharaoh rose up in the night,[3915] he, and all his servants,[5650] and all the Egyptians; and there was a [a]great cry in Egypt; for *there was* not an house where *there was* not one dead.

31 And [a]he called for Moses and Aaron by night, and said, Rise up, *and* get you forth from among my people, [b]both ye and the children of Israel; and go, serve the LORD, as ye have said.

32 [a]Also take your flocks and your herds, as ye have said,[1696] and be gone; and [b]bless[1288] me also.

33 [a]And the Egyptians were urgent[2388] upon the people, that they might send them out of the land in haste; for they said, [b]We *be* all dead *men.*

34 And the people took their dough before it was leavened,[2556] their [I][a]kneadingtroughs being bound up in their clothes upon their shoulders.

35 And the children of Israel did according to the word[1697] of Moses; and they borrowed[7592] of the Egyptians

19 [a]Ex. 23:15; 34:18; Deut. 16:3; 1Cor. 5:7, 8 [b]Num. 9:13
21 [I]Or, *kid* [a]Ex. 12:3; Num. 9:4; Josh. 5:10; 2Kgs. 23:21; Ezra 6:20; Matt. 26:18, 19; Mark 14:12-16; Luke 22:7
22 [a]Heb. 11:28 [b]Ex. 12:7
23 [a]Ex. 12:13 [b]Ezek. 9:6; Rev. 7:3; 9:4 [c]2Sam. 24:16; 1Cor. 10:10; Heb. 11:28
25 [a]Ex. 3:8, 17
26 [a]Ex. 13:8, 14; Deut. 32:7; Josh. 4:6; Ps. 78:6
27 [a]Ex. 12:11 [b]Ex. 4:31
28 [a]Heb. 11:28
29 [I]Hebr. *house of the pit* [a]Ex. 11:4 [b]Num. 8:17; 33:4; Ps. 78:51; 105:36; 135:8; 136:10 [c]Ex. 4:23; 11:5
30 [a]Ex. 11:6; Prov. 21:13; Amos 5:17; James 2:13
31 [a]Ex. 11:1; Ps. 105:38 [b]Ex. 10:9
32 [a]Ex. 10:26 [b]Gen. 27:34
33 [a]Ex. 11:8; Ps. 105:38 [b]Gen. 20:3
34 [I]Or, *dough* [a]Ex. 8:3

12:22 Hyssop most likely refers to a group of plants such as Egyptian marjoram and thyme. The hairy stems of these plants would serve well as a brush.

12:35 It was customary at the parting of friends or departure of a servant to give a gift. The Israelites had long been servants of the Egyptians. Probably in a state of panic which followed these events, the Egyptians were willing to give them anything if they would leave and do so quickly. This is a fulfillment of Genesis 15:14.

[a]jewels of silver, and jewels of gold, and raiment:

36 [a]And the LORD gave the people favour[2580] in the sight of the Egyptians, so that they lent[7592] unto them *such things as they required.* And [b]they spoiled[5337] the Egyptians.

The Long Trip Begins

37 And [a]the children[1121] of Israel journeyed from [b]Rameses to Succoth, about [c]six hundred thousand on foot *that were* men,[1397] beside children.[2945]

38 And [I][a]a mixed[6154] multitude went up[5927] also with them; and flocks, and herds, *even* very much cattle.

39 And they baked unleavened cakes of the dough which they brought forth out of Egypt, for it was not leavened; because [a]they were thrust out of Egypt, and could not tarry, neither had they prepared[6213] for themselves any victual.[6720]

40 Now the sojourning[4186] of the children of Israel, who dwelt in Egypt, *was* [a]four hundred and thirty years.

41 And it came to pass at the end of the four hundred and thirty years, even the selfsame day it came to pass, that all [a]the hosts[6635] of the LORD went out from the land of Egypt.

42 It *is* [I][a]a night to be much observed unto the LORD for bringing them out from the land of Egypt: this *is* that night of the LORD to be observed of all the children of Israel in their generations.

43 And the LORD said unto Moses and Aaron, This *is* [a]the ordinance[2708] of the passover: There shall no stranger[5236] eat thereof:

44 But every man's servant that is bought for money, when thou hast [a]circumcised him, then shall he eat thereof.

45 [a]A foreigner[8453] and an hired servant shall not eat thereof.

46 In one house shall it be eaten; thou shalt not carry forth ought of the flesh abroad out of the house; [a]neither shall ye break[7665] a bone[6106] thereof.

47 [a]All the congregation of Israel shall [I]keep[6213] it.

48 And [a]when a stranger shall sojourn[1481] with thee, and will keep the passover to the LORD, let all his males be circumcised,[4135] and then let him come near[7126] and keep it; and he shall be as one that is born in the land: for no uncircumcised[6189] person shall eat thereof.

49 [a]One law[8451] shall be to him that is homeborn,[249] and unto the stranger that sojourneth among you.

50 Thus did all the children of Israel; as the LORD commanded Moses and Aaron, so did they.

51 [a]And it came to pass the selfsame day, *that* the LORD did bring the children of Israel out of the land of Egypt [b]by their armies.

The Consecration of the Firstborn

13 And the LORD spake[1696] unto Moses, saying,

2 [a]Sanctify[6942] unto me all the firstborn, whatsoever openeth the womb among the children of Israel, *both* of man[120] and of beast: it *is* mine.

3 And Moses said unto the people,[5971] [a]Remember this day,[3117] in which ye came out from Egypt, out of the house[1004] of [I]bondage;[5650] for [b]by strength[2392] of hand[3027] the LORD brought you out from this *place*: [c]there shall no leavened bread[2557] be eaten.

35 [a]Ex. 3:22; 11:2

36 [a]Ex. 3:21; 11:3 [b]Gen. 15:14; Ex. 3:22; Ps. 105:37

37 [a]Num. 33:3, 5 [b]Gen. 47:11; [c]Gen. 12:2; 46:3; Ex. 38:26; Num. 1:46; 11:21

38 [I]Hebr. *a great mixture* [a]Num. 11:4

39 [a]Ex. 6:1; 11:1; 12:33

40 [a]Gen. 15:13; Acts 7:6; Gal. 3:17

41 [a]Ex. 7:4; 12:51

42 [I]Hebr. *a night of observations* [a]Deut. 16:6

43 [a]Num. 9:14

44 [a]Gen. 17:12, 13

45 [a]Lev. 22:10

46 [a]Num. 9:12; John 19:33, 36

47 [I]Hebr. *do it* [a]Ex. 12:6; Num. 9:13

48 [a]Num. 9:14

49 [a]Num. 9:14; 15:15, 16; Gal. 3:28

51 [a]Ex. 12:41 [b]Ex. 6:26

2 [a]Ex. 13:12, 13, 15; 22:29, 30; 34:19; Lev. 27:26; Num. 3:13; 8:16, 17; 18:15; Deut. 15:19; Luke 2:23

3 [I]Hebr. *servants* [a]Ex. 12:42; Deut. 16:3 [b]Ex. 6:1 [c]Ex. 12:8

12:40 The Samaritan Pentateuch and the Septuagint add the words "and in the land of Canaan" after "Egypt." See note on Genesis 15:13–16.

12:46 In this verse and in Numbers 9:12, the breaking of the lamb's bones is forbidden. This passage, not Psalm 34:20, is the reference that is fulfilled in John 19:36, where Jesus' legs were not broken. In a passage reminiscent of Exodus chapter twelve, Paul refers to Jesus as the Christians' Passover Lamb (1 Cor. 5:7).

4 [a]This day came ye out in the month Abib.

5 And it shall be when the LORD shall [a]bring thee into the land[776] of the Canaanites, and the Hittites, and the Amorites, and the Hivites, and the Jebusites, which he [b]sware[7650] unto thy fathers[1] to give thee, a land flowing with milk and honey, [c]that thou shalt keep[5647] this service[5656] in this month.

6 [a]Seven days thou shalt eat unleavened bread, and in the seventh day *shall be* a feast[2282] to the LORD.

7 Unleavened bread shall be eaten seven days; and there shall [a]no leavened bread be seen[7200] with thee, neither shall there be leaven seen with thee in all thy quarters.

8 And thou shalt [a]shew[5046] thy son[1121] in that day, saying, *This is done* because of that *which* the LORD did[6213] unto me when I came forth out of Egypt.

9 And it shall be for [a]a sign[226] unto thee upon thine hand, and for a memorial[2146] between thine eyes, that the LORD's law[8451] may be in thy mouth:[6310] for with a strong[2389] hand hath the LORD brought thee out of Egypt.

10 [a]Thou shalt therefore keep[8104] this ordinance[2708] in his season[4150] from year to year.

11 And it shall be when the LORD shall bring thee into the land of the Canaanites, as he sware unto thee and to thy fathers, and shall give it thee,

12 [a]That thou shalt [I]set apart[5674] unto the LORD all that openeth the matrix,[7358] and every firstling that cometh of a beast which thou hast; the males[2145] *shall be* the LORD's.

13 And [a]every firstling of an ass thou shalt redeem[6299] with a [I]lamb; and if thou wilt not redeem it, then thou shalt break his neck: and all the firstborn of man among thy children [b]shalt thou redeem.

14 [a]And it shall be when thy son asketh[7592] thee [I]in time to come, saying, What *is* this? that thou shalt say unto him, [b]By strength[2392] of hand the LORD brought us out from Egypt, from the house of bondage:

15 And it came to pass, when Pharaoh would hardly let us go, that [a]the LORD slew[2026] all the firstborn in the land of Egypt, both the firstborn of man, and the firstborn of beast: therefore I sacrifice[2076] to the LORD all that openeth the matrix, being males; but all the firstborn of my children I redeem.

16 And it shall be for [a]a token[226] upon thine hand, and for frontlets[2903] between thine eyes: for by strength of hand the LORD brought us forth out of Egypt.

God Leads Them

17 And it came to pass, when Pharaoh had let the people go, that God[430] led[5148] them not *through* the way[1870] of the land of the Philistines, although that *was* near; for God said, Lest peradventure the people [a]repent[5162] when they see[7200] war, and [b]they return[7725] to Egypt:

18 But God [a]led the people about, *through* the way of the wilderness of the Red sea: and the children of Israel went up[5927] [I]harnessed out of the land of Egypt.

19 And Moses took the bones[6106] of Joseph with him: for he had straitly sworn[7650] the children of Israel, saying, [a]God will surely visit[6485] you; and ye shall carry up[5927] my bones away hence with you.

20 And [a]they took their journey from Succoth, and encamped in Etham, in the edge of the wilderness.

21 And [a]the LORD went before them by day in a pillar of a cloud,[6051] to lead them the way; and by night[3915] in a

4 [a]Ex. 23:15; 34:18; Deut. 16:1
5 [a]Ex. 3:8 [b]Ex. 6:8 [c]Ex. 12:25, 26
6 [a]Ex. 12:15, 16
7 [a]Ex. 12:19
8 [a]Ex. 12:26; 13:14
9 [a]Ex. 12:14; 13:16; Num. 15:39; Deut. 6:8; 11:18; Prov. 1:9; Isa. 49:16; Jer. 22:24; Matt. 23:5
10 [a]Ex. 12:14, 24
12 [I]Hebr. *cause to pass over* [a]Ex. 13:2; 22:29; 34:19; Lev. 27:26; Num. 8:17; 18:15; Deut. 15:19; Ezek. 44:30
13 [I]Or, *kid* [a]Ex. 34:20; Num. 18:15, 16 [b]Num. 3:46, 47; 18:15, 16
14 [I]Hebr. *tomorrow* [a]Ex. 12:26; Deut. 6:20; Josh. 4:6, 21 [b]Ex. 13:3
15 [a]Ex. 12:29
16 [a]Ex. 13:9
17 [a]Ex. 14:11, 12; Num. 14:1-4 [b]Deut. 17:16
18 [I]Or, *by five in a rank* [a]Ex. 14:2; Num. 33:6
19 [a]Gen. 50:25; Josh. 24:32; Acts 7:16
20 [a]Num. 33:6
21 [a]Ex. 14:19, 24; 40:38; Num. 9:15; 10:34; 14:14; Deut. 1:33; Neh. 9:12, 19; Ps. 78:14; 99:7; 105:39; Isa. 4:5; 1Cor. 10:1

13:4 Abib is the first month of the Hebrew year. Since they used the lunar calendar, the equivalent date in our solar calendar changes. This is also the reason that the date of the observance of Easter varies (see note on Ex. 12:12).

pillar[5982] of fire, to give them light; to go
by day and night:
22 He took not away the pillar of the
cloud by day, nor the pillar of fire by
night, *from* before the people.

God Divides the Waters

14 And the LORD spake[1696] unto
Moses, saying,
2 Speak unto the children of Israel,
[a]that they turn[7725] and encamp before
[b]Pi–hahiroth, between [c]Migdol and the
sea, over against Baal–zephon: before it
shall ye encamp by the sea.
3 For Pharaoh will say[559] of the children of Israel, [a]They *are* entangled[943] in
the land,[776] the wilderness hath shut
them in.
4 And [a]I will harden[2388] Pharaoh's
heart,[3820] that he shall follow after them;
and I [b]will be honoured upon Pharaoh,
and upon all his host;[2428] [c]that the
Egyptians may know[3045] that I *am* the
LORD. And they did[6213] so.
5 And it was told[5046] the king[4428]
of Egypt that the people[5971] fled: and
[a]the heart of Pharaoh and of his servants[5650] was turned[2015] against the people, and they said, Why have we done
this, that we have let Israel go from serving us?
6 And he made ready his chariot,
and took his people with him:
7 And he took [a]six hundred chosen
chariots, and all the chariots of Egypt,
and captains[7991] over every one of them.
8 And the LORD [a]hardened[2388] the
heart of Pharaoh king of Egypt, and he
pursued after the children of Israel: and
[b]the children of Israel went out with an
high hand.[3027]
9 But the [a]Egyptians pursued after
them, all the horses *and* chariots of
Pharaoh, and his horsemen,[6571] and his
army,[2428] and overtook them encamping
by the sea, beside Pi–hahiroth, before
Baal–zephon.
10 And when Pharaoh drew nigh, the
children of Israel lifted up[5375] their eyes,
and, behold, the Egyptians marched after
them; and they were sore afraid:[3372] and

2 [a]Ex. 13:18; [b]Num. 33:7 [c]Jer. 44:1
3 [a]Ps. 71:11
4 [a]Ex. 4:21; 7:3 [b]Ex. 9:16; 14:17, 18; Rom. 9:17, 22, 23 [c]Ex. 7:5
5 [a]Ps. 105:25
7 [a]Ex. 15:4
8 [a]Ex. 14:4 [b]Ex. 6:1; 13:9; Num. 33:3
9 [a]Ex. 15:9; Josh. 24:6
10 [a]Josh. 24:7; Neh. 9:9; Ps. 34:17; 107:6
11 [a]Ps. 106:7, 8
12 [a]Ex. 5:21; 6:9
13 [I]Or, *for whereas ye have seen the Egyptians today* [a]2Chr. 20:15, 17; Isa. 41:10-14
14 [a]Ex. 14:25; Deut. 1:30; 3:22; 20:4; Josh. 10:14, 42; 23:3; 2Chr. 20:29; Neh. 4:20; Isa. 31:4 [b]Isa. 30:15
16 [a]Ex. 7:19; 14:21, 26
17 [a]Ex. 7:3; 14:8 [b]Ex. 14:4
18 [a]Ex. 14:4
19 [a]Ex. 13:21; 23:20; 32:34; Num. 20:16; Isa. 63:9
20 [a]Isa. 8:14; 2Cor. 4:3

the children of Israel [a]cried out unto the
LORD.
11 [a]And they said unto Moses,
Because *there were* no graves[6913] in
Egypt, hast thou taken us away to die in
the wilderness? wherefore hast thou dealt
thus with us, to carry us forth out of
Egypt?
12 [a]*Is* not this the word[1697] that we
did tell[1696] thee in Egypt, saying, Let us
alone, that we may serve the Egyptians?
For *it had been* better[2896] for us to serve
the Egyptians, than that we should die in
the wilderness.
13 And Moses said unto the people,
[a]Fear[3372] ye not, stand still,[3320] and see
the salvation[3444] of the LORD, which he
will shew[6213] to you to day:[3117] [I]for the
Egyptians whom ye have seen to day, ye
shall see[7200] them again no more for
ever.[5769]
14 [a]The LORD shall fight for you, and
ye shall [b]hold your peace.[2790]
15 And the LORD said unto Moses,
Wherefore criest thou unto me? speak
unto the children of Israel, that they go
forward:[5265]
16 But [a]lift thou up thy rod,[4294] and
stretch out thine hand over the sea, and
divide it: and the children of Israel shall
go on dry[3004] *ground* through the midst
of the sea.
17 And I, behold, I will [a]harden[2388]
the hearts[3820] of the Egyptians, and they
shall follow them: and I will [b]get me honour upon Pharaoh, and upon all his
host, upon his chariots, and upon his
horsemen.
18 And the Egyptians [a]shall know
that I *am* the LORD, when I have gotten
me honour upon Pharaoh, upon his chariots, and upon his horsemen.
19 And the angel of God,[430] [a]which
went before the camp[4264] of Israel,
removed and went behind them; and
the pillar of the cloud[6051] went from
before their face, and stood behind
them:
20 And it came between the camp of
the Egyptians and the camp of Israel;
and [a]it was a cloud and darkness[2822] *to
them,* but it gave light by night *to these:*

so that the one came not near[7126] the other all the night.[3915]

21 And Moses [a]stretched out his hand over the sea; and the LORD caused the sea to go *back* by a strong east wind[7307] all that night, and [b]made the sea dry[2724] *land,* and the waters were [c]divided.

22 And [a]the children of Israel went into the midst of the sea upon the dry[3004] *ground:* and the waters *were* [b]a wall unto them on their right hand, and on their left.

23 And the Egyptians pursued, and went in after them to the midst of the sea, *even* all Pharaoh's horses, his chariots, and his horsemen.

24 And it came to pass, that in the morning watch [a]the LORD looked unto the host of the Egyptians through the pillar of fire and of the cloud, and troubled[2000] the host of the Egyptians,

25 And took off their chariot wheels,[212] [I]that they drave them heavily: so that the Egyptians said, Let us flee from the face of Israel; for the LORD [a]fighteth for them against the Egyptians.

26 And the LORD said unto Moses, [a]Stretch out thine hand over the sea, that the waters may come again[7725] upon the Egyptians, upon their chariots, and upon their horsemen.

27 And Moses stretched forth his hand over the sea, and the sea [a]returned[7725] to his strength when the morning appeared; and the Egyptians fled against it; and the LORD [I][b]overthrew[5287] the Egyptians in the midst of the sea.

28 And [a]the waters returned, and [b]covered[3680] the chariots, and the horsemen, *and* all the host of Pharaoh that came into the sea after them; there remained not so much as one of them.

29 But [a]the children of Israel walked upon dry *land* in the midst of the sea; and the waters *were* a wall unto them on their right hand, and on their left.

🔑 30 Thus the LORD [a]saved Israel that day[3117] out of the hand of the Egyptians; and Israel [b]saw[7200] the Egyptians dead upon the sea shore.[8193]

31 And Israel saw that great [I]work[3027] which the LORD did upon the Egyptians: and the people feared[3372] the LORD, and [a]believed[539] the LORD, and his servant Moses.

Moses' Song

15 Then sang[7891] [a]Moses and the children[1121] of Israel this song[7892] unto the LORD, and spake, saying, I will [b]sing unto the LORD, for he hath triumphed[1342] gloriously: the horse and his rider hath he thrown into the sea.

2 The LORD *is* my strength and [a]song, and he is become my salvation:[3444] he *is* my God,[410] and I will prepare him [b]an habitation; my [c]father's[1] God,[430] and I [d]will exalt him.

3 The LORD *is* a man[376] of [a]war: the LORD *is* his [b]name.

4 [a]Pharaoh's chariots and his host[2428] hath he cast[3384] into the sea: [b]his chosen captains[7991] also are drowned in the Red sea.

5 [a]The depths have covered[3680] them: [b]they sank into the bottom as a stone.

6 [a]Thy right hand, O LORD, is become glorious[142] in power: thy right

21 [a]Ex. 14:16 [b]Ps. 66:6 [c]Ex. 15:8; Josh. 3:16; 4:23; Neh. 9:11; Ps. 74:13; 106:9; 114:3; Isa. 63:12
22 [a]Ex. 14:29; 15:19; Num. 33:8; Ps. 66:6; 78:13; Isa. 63:13; 1Cor. 10:1; Heb. 11:29 [b]Hab. 3:10
24 [a]Ps. 77:17
25 [I]Or, *and made them to go heavily* [a]Ex. 14:14
26 [a]Ex. 14:16
27 [I]Hebr. *shook off* [a]Josh. 4:18 [b]Ex. 15:1, 7; Deut. 11:4; Neh. 9:11; Ps. 78:53; Heb. 11:29
28 [a]Hab. 3:8–10 [b]Ps. 106:11
29 [a]Ex. 14:22; Ps. 77:20; 78:52, 53
30 [a]Ps. 106:8, 10 [b]Ps. 58:10; 59:10
31 [I]Hebr. *hand* [a]Ex. 4:31; 19:9; Ps. 106:12; John 2:11; 11:45

1 [a]Judg. 5:1; 2Sam. 22:1; Ps. 106:12 [b]Ex. 15:21
2 [a]Deut. 10:21; Ps. 18:2; 22:3; 59:17; 62:6; 109:1; 118:14, 140:7; Isa. 12:2; Hab. 3:18, 19 [b]Gen. 28:21, 22; 2Sam. 7:5; Ps. 132:5; [c]Ex. 3:15, 16 [d]2Sam. 22:47; Ps. 99:5; 118:28; Isa. 25:1
3 [a]Ps. 24:8; Rev. 19:11 [b]Ex. 6:3; Ps. 83:18
4 [a]Ex. 14:28 [b]Ex. 14:7
5 [a]Ex. 14:28 [b]Neh. 9:11
6 [a]Ps. 118:15, 16

🔑 **14:30, 31** Moses had commanded Israel in verse thirteen to "stand still, and see the salvation of the LORD." The confirmation is now made that on the day that God saved them, they saw His great work and believed. He had led them into a position in which they were not able to save themselves, and they could only depend upon Him for that salvation. The deliverance of the Israelites from Egypt is a central theme throughout the Old Testament. Throughout their history the descendants of these Israelites remembered the events of that day (2 Kgs. 17:7; 2 Chr. 6:4, 5). In times of apostasy, the Lord called upon Israel to remember that work of salvation (Jer. 11:3, 4; Hos. 12:13). Forty years later, as they marched forward to possess Canaan, their adversaries remembered the demonstration of the power of their God in their flight from Egypt (Josh. 2:10).

hand, O LORD, hath dashed in pieces the enemy.

7 And in the greatness of thine [a]excellency[1347] thou hast overthrown them that rose up against thee: thou sentest forth thy wrath, *which* [b]consumed them [c]as stubble.

8 And [a]with the blast[7307] of thy nostrils[639] the waters were gathered together,[6192] [b]the floods stood upright[5324] as an heap, *and* the depths were congealed in the heart[3820] of the sea.

9 [a]The enemy said,[559] I will pursue, I will overtake, I will [b]divide the spoil; my lust[5315] shall be satisfied upon them; I will draw my sword, my hand[3027] shall [1]destroy[3423] them.

10 Thou didst [a]blow with thy wind,[7307] [b]the sea covered them: they sank as lead in the mighty[117] waters.

11 [a]Who *is* like unto thee, O LORD, among the [1]gods?[410] who *is* like thee, [b]glorious in holiness,[6944] fearful[3372] *in* praises,[8416] [c]doing[6213] wonders?[6382]

12 Thou stretchedst out [a]thy right hand, the earth[776] swallowed them.

13 Thou in thy mercy[2617] hast [a]led forth[5148] the people[5971] *which* thou hast redeemed:[1350] thou hast guided *them* in [b]thy strength unto thy holy[6944] habitation.

14 [a]The people shall hear,[8085] *and* be afraid:[7264] [b]sorrow shall take hold on the inhabitants of Palestina.

15 [a]Then [b]the dukes[441] of Edom shall be amazed;[926] [c]the mighty men of Moab, trembling[7461] shall take hold upon them; [d]all the inhabitants of Canaan shall melt away.

16 [a]Fear[367] and dread[6343] shall fall[5307] upon them; by the greatness of thine arm they shall be *as* still [b]as a stone; till thy people pass over,[5674] O LORD, till the people pass over, [c]*which* thou hast purchased.

17 Thou shalt bring them in, and [a]plant them in the mountain of thine inheritance,[5159] *in* the place, O LORD, *which* thou hast made for thee to dwell in, *in* the [b]Sanctuary,[4720] O LORD,[136] *which* thy hands have established.

18 [a]The LORD shall reign[4427] for ever[5769] and ever.[5703]

Miriam's Song

19 For the [a]horse of Pharaoh went in with his chariots and with his horsemen into the sea, and [b]the LORD brought again[7725] the waters of the sea upon them; but the children of Israel went on dry *land* in the midst of the sea.

20 And Miriam [a]the prophetess, [b]the sister[269] of Aaron, [c]took a timbrel[8596] in her hand; and all the women went out after her [d]with timbrels and with dances.

21 And Miriam [a]answered them, [b]Sing ye to the LORD, for he hath triumphed gloriously; the horse and his rider hath he thrown into the sea.

The Bitter Water at Marah

22 So Moses brought Israel from the Red sea, and they went out into the wilderness of [a]Shur; and they went three days in the wilderness, and found no water.

🔑 23 And when they came to [a]Marah, they could not drink of the waters of Marah, for they *were* bitter:[4751] therefore the name of it was called [1][b]Marah.

24 And the people [a]murmured against Moses, saying, What shall we drink?

25 And he [a]cried unto the LORD; and

7 [a]Deut. 33:26 [b]Ps. 59:13 [c]Isa. 5:24; 47:14
8 [a]Ex. 14:21; 2Sam. 22:16; Job 4:9; 2Thess. 2:8 [b]Ps. 78:13; Hab. 3:10
9 [1]Or, *repossess* [a]Judg. 5:30 [b]Gen. 49:27; Isa. 53:12; Luke 11:22
10 [a]Ex. 14:21; Ps. 147:18 [b]Ex. 14:28; 15:5
11 [1]Or, *mighty ones?* [a]2Sam. 7:22; 1Kgs. 8:23; Ps. 71:19; 86:8; 89:6, 8; Jer. 10:6; 49:19 [b]Isa. 6:3 [c]Ps. 77:14
12 [a]Ex. 15:6
13 [a]Ps. 77:15, 20; 78:52; 80:1; 106:9; Isa. 63:12, 13; Jer. 2:6 [b]Ps. 78:54
14 [a]Num. 14:14; Deut. 2:25; Josh. 2:9, 10 [b]Ps. 48:6
15 [a]Gen. 36:40 [b]Deut. 2:4 [c]Num. 22:3; Hab. 3:7 [d]Josh. 5:1
16 [a]Deut. 2:25; 11:25; Josh. 2:9 [b]1Sam. 25:37 [c]Ex. 19:5; Deut. 32:9; 2Sam. 7:23; Ps. 74:2; Isa. 43:1, 3; 51:10; Jer. 31:11; Titus 2:14; 1Pet. 2:9; 2Pet. 2:1
17 [a]Ps. 44:2; 80:8 [b]Ps. 78:54
18 [a]Ps. 10:16; 29:10; 146:10; Isa. 57:15
19 [a]Ex. 14:23; Prov. 21:31 [b]Ex. 14:28, 29
20 [a]Judg. 4:4; 1Sam. 10:5 [b]Num. 26:59 [c]1Sam. 18:6 [d]Judg. 11:34; 21:21; 2Sam. 6:16; Ps. 68:11–25; 149:3; 150:4

21 [a]1Sam. 18:7 [b]Ex. 15:1 **22** [a]Gen. 16:7; 25:18
23 [1]That is *Bitterness* [a]Ruth 1:20 [b]Num. 33:8
24 [a]Ex. 16:2; 17:3 **25** [a]Ex. 14:10; 17:4; Ps. 50:15

🔑 **15:23–25** The Lord did not take Israel to Canaan by the most direct route. The people needed not only to observe the mighty works of His power, but also to depend upon Him in a practical way for the necessities of life. Ultimately, they needed to understand that all would be accomplished by God's own power and not by their own ability. At Marah they needed water, but that which was available was not fit for drinking until God acted. Thus, God was instructing them that even though they had been brought out of bondage and had witnessed the defeat of the Egyptian army, they must still depend on Him.

the LORD shewed[3384] him a tree, [b]*which* when he had cast into the waters, the waters were made[7760] sweet: there he [c]made for them a statute[2706] and an ordinance,[4941] and there [d]he proved[5254] them,

26 And said, [a]If thou wilt diligently hearken[8085] to the voice of the LORD thy God, and wilt do[6213] that which is right in his sight, and wilt give ear[238] to his commandments,[4687] and keep[8104] all his statutes, I will put none of these [b]diseases[4245] upon thee, which I have brought upon the Egyptians: for I *am* the LORD [c]that healeth thee.

27 [a]And they came to Elim, where *were* twelve wells of water, and threescore and ten palm trees: and they encamped there by the waters.

Manna and Quail

16 And they [a]took their journey from Elim, and all the congregation[5712] of the children[1121] of Israel came unto the wilderness of [b]Sin, which *is* between Elim and Sinai, on the fifteenth day of the second month after their departing out of the land[776] of Egypt.

2 And the whole congregation of the children of Israel [a]murmured against Moses and Aaron in the wilderness:

3 And the children of Israel said unto them, [a]Would to God we had died by the hand[3027] of the LORD in the land of Egypt, [b]when we sat by the flesh[1320] pots, *and* when we did eat bread to the full; for ye have brought us forth into this wilderness, to kill this whole assembly[6951] with hunger.

4 Then said the LORD unto Moses, Behold, I will rain [a]bread from heaven[8064] for you; and the people[5971] shall go out and gather[3950] [I][b]a certain rate[1697] every day,[3117] that I may [c]prove[5254] them, whether they will walk in my law,[8451] or no.

5 And it shall come to pass, that on the sixth day they shall prepare[3559] *that* which they bring in; and [a]it shall be twice as much as they gather daily.

6 And Moses and Aaron said unto all the children of Israel, [a]At even, then ye shall know[3045] that the LORD hath brought you out from the land of Egypt:

7 And in the morning, then ye shall see[7200] [a]the glory[3519] of the LORD; for that he heareth[8085] your murmurings against the LORD: and [b]what *are* we, that ye murmur against us?

8 And Moses said, *This shall be,* when the LORD shall give you in the evening flesh to eat, and in the morning bread to the full; for that the LORD heareth your murmurings which ye murmur against him: and what *are* we? your murmurings *are* not against us, but [a]against the LORD.

9 And Moses spake unto Aaron, Say unto all the congregation of the children of Israel, [a]Come near[7126] before the LORD: for he hath heard your murmurings.

10 And it came to pass, as Aaron spake unto the whole congregation of the children of Israel, that they looked toward the wilderness, and, behold, the glory of the LORD [a]appeared in the cloud.[6051]

11 And the LORD spake[1696] unto Moses, saying,

12 [a]I have heard the murmurings of the children of Israel: speak unto them, saying, [b]At even ye shall eat flesh,[1320] and [c]in the morning ye shall be filled with bread; and ye shall know that I *am* the LORD your God.[430]

🔑 13 And it came to pass, that at even [a]the quails came up, and covered[3680] the

25 [b]2Kgs. 2:21; 4:41 [c]Josh. 24:25 [d]Ex. 16:4; Deut. 8:2, 16; Judg. 2:22; 3:1, 4; Ps. 66:10; 81:7
26 [a]Deut. 7:12, 15 [b]Deut. 28:27, 60 [c]Ex. 23:25; Ps. 41:3, 4; 103:3; 147:3
27 [a]Num. 33:9
1 [a]Num. 33:10, 11 [b]Ezek. 30:15
2 [a]Ex. 15:24; Ps. 106:25; 1Cor. 10:10
3 [a]Lam. 4:9 [b]Num. 11:4, 5
4 [I]Hebr. *the portion of a day in his day* [a]Ps. 78:24, 25; 105:40; John 6:31, 32; 1Cor. 10:3 [b]Ex. 15:25; Deut. 8:2, 16 [c]Prov. 30:8; Matt. 6:11
5 [a]Ex. 16:22; Lev. 25:21
6 [a]Ex. 6:7; 16:12, 13; Num. 16:28, 29, 30
7 [a]Ex. 16:10; Isa. 35:2; 40:5; John 11:4, 40 [b]Num. 16:11
8 [a]1Sam. 8:7; Luke 10:16; Rom. 13:2
9 [a]Num. 16:16
10 [a]Ex. 13:21; 16:7; Num. 16:19; 1Kgs. 8:10, 11
12 [a]Ex. 16:8 [b]Ex. 16:6 [c]Ex. 16:7
13 [a]Num. 11:31; Ps. 78:27, 28; 105:40

🔑 **16:13–15** The events of this passage were another of the steps in building the faith of Israel. There were no facilities in the Sinai wilderness to feed several million people, let alone their herds and flocks. God had provided water; He would now provide food. The provision of quail was miraculous—the birds were native to the region, but normally they could only be found in small and scattered numbers. God brought multitudes of quail, though the text does not tell how frequently this

(continued on next page)

camp:[4264] and in the morning [b]the dew lay round about the host.[4264]

14 And when the dew that lay was gone up, behold, upon the face of the wilderness *there lay* [a]a small round thing, *as* small as the hoar frost[3713] on the ground.[776]

15 And when the children of Israel saw *it,* they said one[376] to another, [I]It *is* manna:[4478] for they wist[3045] not what it *was.* And Moses said unto them, [a]This *is* the bread which the LORD hath given you to eat.

16 This *is* the thing[1697] which the LORD hath commanded,[6680] Gather of it every man[376] according to his eating, [a]an omer[6016] [I]for every man, *according to* the number of your [II]persons;[5315] take ye every man for *them* which *are* in his tents.[168]

17 And the children of Israel did so, and gathered, some more, some less.

18 And when they did mete[4058] *it* with an omer, [a]he that gathered much had nothing over, and he that gathered little had no lack; they gathered every man according to his eating.

19 And Moses said, Let no man leave[3498] of it till the morning.

20 Notwithstanding they hearkened[8085] not unto Moses; but some of them left of it until the morning, and it bred worms, and stank: and Moses was wroth[7107] with them.

21 And they gathered it every morning, every man according to his eating: and when the sun waxed hot, it melted.

22 And it came to pass, *that* on the sixth day they gathered twice as much bread, two omers[6016] for one *man:* and all the rulers[5387] of the congregation came and told[5046] Moses.

23 And he said[1696] unto them, This *is that* which the LORD[3068] hath said, To morrow *is* [a]the rest[7677] of the holy[6944] sabbath[7676] unto the LORD: bake *that* which ye will bake *to day,* and seethe that ye will seethe; and that which remaineth over lay up for you to be kept[4931] until the morning.

24 And they laid it up till the morning, as Moses bade: and it did not [a]stink, neither was there any worm therein.

25 And Moses said, Eat that to day; for to day *is* a sabbath unto the LORD: to day ye shall not find it in the field.[7704]

26 [a]Six days ye shall gather it; but on the seventh day, *which is* the sabbath, in it there shall be none.

27 And it came to pass, *that* there went out *some* of the people on the seventh day for to gather, and they found none.

28 And the LORD said unto Moses, How long [a]refuse[3985] ye to keep[8104] my commandments[4687] and my laws?

29 See,[7200] for that the LORD hath given you the sabbath, therefore he giveth you on the sixth day the bread of two days; abide ye every man in his place, let no man go out of his place on the seventh day.

30 So the people rested[7673] on the seventh day.

31 And the house[1004] of Israel called[7121] the name thereof Manna: and [a]it *was* like coriander seed,[2233] white; and the taste[2940] of it *was* like wafers *made* with honey.

32 And Moses said, This *is* the thing which the LORD commandeth,[6680] Fill an omer of it to be kept for your generations;[1755] that they may see the bread wherewith I have fed you in the wilderness, when I brought you forth from the land of Egypt.

33 And Moses said unto Aaron,

13 [b]Num. 11:9

14 [a]Num. 11:7; Deut. 8:3; Neh. 9:15; Ps. 78:24; 105:40

15 [I]Or, *What is this?* or, *It is a portion* [a]John 6:31, 49, 58; 1Cor. 10:3

16 [I]Hebr. *by the poll,* or, *head* [II]Hebr. *souls* [a]Ex. 16:36

18 [a]2Cor. 8:15

23 [a]Gen. 2:3; Ex. 20:8; 31:15; 35:3; Lev. 23:3

24 [a]Ex. 16:20

26 [a]Ex. 20:9, 10

28 [a]2Kgs. 17:14; Ps. 78:10, 22; 106:13

31 [a]Num. 11:7, 8

(continued from previous page)

occurred. Manna differed in that it was God's daily provision from this time until Israel entered the promised land and was able to eat its crops (Josh. 5:12). Gathering the manna each day would increase Israel's dependence upon God. The amount gathered would be just sufficient (Ex. 16:18), confirming God's personal care. There is no natural way to explain the nature of manna; it was truly "bread from heaven." Manna was a type of Jesus, who is "the bread of life" (John 6:32–35).

[a]Take a pot, and put an omer full of manna therein, and lay it up before the LORD, to be kept for your generations.

34 As the LORD commanded Moses, so Aaron laid it up [a]before the Testimony,[5715] to be kept.

35 And the children of Israel did eat manna [a]forty years, [b]until they came to a land inhabited; they did eat manna, until they came unto the borders of the land of Canaan.

36 Now an omer *is* the tenth *part* of an ephah.

Water Flows From the Rock

17 And [a]all the congregation[5712] of the children[1121] of Israel journeyed from the wilderness of Sin, after their journeys, according to the commandment[6310] of the LORD, and pitched in Rephidim: and *there was* no water for the people[5971] to drink.

2 [a]Wherefore the people did chide[7378] with Moses, and said, Give us water that we may drink. And Moses said unto them, Why chide ye with me? wherefore do ye [b]tempt[5254] the LORD?

3 And the people thirsted there for water; and the people [a]murmured against Moses, and said, Wherefore *is* this *that* thou hast brought us up[5927] out of Egypt, to kill us and our children and our cattle with thirst?

4 And Moses [a]cried unto the LORD, saying, What shall I do[6213] unto this people? they be almost ready to [b]stone me.

5 And the LORD said unto Moses, [a]Go on[5674] before the people, and take with thee of the elders[2205] of Israel; and thy rod,[4294] wherewith [b]thou smotest[5221] the river, take in thine hand,[3027] and go.

6 [a]Behold, I will stand before thee there upon the rock in Horeb; and thou shalt smite the rock, and there shall come water out of it, that the people may drink. And Moses did so in the sight of the elders of Israel.

7 And he called[7121] the name of the place [I][a]Massah,[4531] and [II]Meribah, because of the chiding[7379] of the children of Israel, and because they tempted the LORD, saying, Is the LORD among us, or not?

The First Battle

8 [a]Then came Amalek, and fought with Israel in Rephidim.

9 And Moses said unto [a]Joshua, Choose us out men,[582] and go out, fight with Amalek: to morrow I will stand[5324] on the top[7218] of the hill with [b]the rod of God[430] in mine hand.

10 So Joshua did as Moses had said[559] to him, and fought with Amalek: and Moses, Aaron, and Hur went up[5927] to the top of the hill.

11 And it came to pass, when Moses [a]held up his hand, that Israel prevailed:[1396] and when he let down his hand, Amalek prevailed.

12 But Moses' hands *were* heavy; and they took a stone, and put *it* under him, and he sat thereon; and Aaron and Hur stayed up[8551] his hands, the one on the one side, and the other on the other side; and his hands were steady[530] until the going down of the sun.

13 And Joshua discomfited[2522]

33 [a]Heb. 9:4

34 [a]Ex. 25:16, 21; 40:20; Num. 17:10; Deut. 10:5; 1Kgs. 8:9

35 [a]Num. 33:38; Deut. 8:2, 3; Neh. 9:20, 21; John 6:31, 49 [b]Josh. 5:12; Neh. 9:15

1 [a]Ex. 16:1; Num. 33:12, 14

2 [a]Num. 20:3, 4 [b]Deut. 6:16; Ps. 78:18, 41; Isa. 7:12; Matt. 4:7; 1Cor. 10:9

3 [a]Ex. 16:2

4 [a]Ex. 14:15 [b]1Sam. 30:6; John 8:59; 10:31

5 [a]Ezek. 2:6 [b]Ex. 7:20; Num. 20:8

6 [a]Num. 20:10, 11; Ps. 78:15, 20; 105:41; 114:8; 1Cor. 10:4

7 [I]That is, *Temptation* [II]That is, *Water of Strife* [a]Num. 20:13; Ps. 81:7; 95:8; Heb. 3:8

8 [a]Gen. 36:12; Num. 24:20; Deut. 25:17; 1Sam. 15:2

9 [a]Acts 7:45; Heb. 4:8 [b]Ex. 4:20

11 [a]James 5:16

17:6 This passage is one of the ones that Paul referenced in 1 Corinthians 10:4 (others include Num. 20:8–11; Ps. 78:15, 16). Paul affirms that the rock "was Christ." He does this in much the same sense that Jesus says that the bread "is my body" (Matt. 26:26). The relationship is a symbolic one, not referring to His essence. The rock provided water for Israel, and it was smitten in the process, just as Jesus was smitten in His work of providing salvation. This correspondence between historical events and the ultimate, greater truths to which they point is called typology. While this concept is a genuine part of the method of God's Old Testament revelation, it is a concept that interpreters often carry to extremes.

17:8–13 This is the first reference to Joshua, Moses' successor (see note on Num. 27:18–23).

Amalek and his people with the edge[6310] of the sword.

14 And the LORD said unto Moses, [a]Write this *for* a memorial[2146] in a book,[5612] and rehearse *it* in the ears of Joshua: for [b]I will utterly put out[4229] the remembrance[2143] of Amalek from under heaven.[8064]

15 And Moses built an altar,[4196] and called the name of it [I][a]Jehovah–nissi:

16 For he said, [I]Because the LORD hath sworn *that* the LORD *will have* war with Amalek from generation[1755] to generation.

The First Judges

18 When [a]Jethro, the priest[3548] of Midian, Moses' father in law, heard of all that [b]God[430] had done[6213] for Moses, and for Israel his people,[5971] *and* that the LORD had brought Israel out of Egypt;

2 Then Jethro, Moses' father in law, took Zipporah, Moses' wife,[802] [a]after he had sent her back,

3 And her [a]two sons;[1121] of which the [b]name of the one *was* [I]Gershom; for he said, I have been an alien[1616] in a strange[5237] land:[776]

4 And the name of the other *was* [I]Eliezer; for the God of my father,[1] *said he, was* mine help, and delivered[5337] me from the sword[2719] of Pharaoh:

5 And Jethro, Moses' father in law, came with his sons and his wife unto Moses into the wilderness, where he encamped at [a]the mount of God:

6 And he said unto Moses, I thy father in law Jethro am come unto thee, and thy wife, and her two sons with her.

7 And Moses [a]went out to meet his father in law, and did obeisance,[7812] and [b]kissed him; and they asked[7592] each[376] other[7453] of *their* [I][c]welfare;[7965] and they came into the tent.[168]

8 And Moses told his father in law all that the LORD had done unto Pharaoh and to the Egyptians for Israel's sake, *and* all the travail[8513] that had [I][a]come upon them by the way, and *how* the LORD [b]delivered them.

9 And Jethro rejoiced for all the goodness[2896] which the LORD had done to Israel, whom he had delivered out of the hand[3027] of the Egyptians.

10 And Jethro said, [a]Blessed[1288] *be* the LORD, who hath delivered you out of the hand of the Egyptians, and out of the hand of Pharaoh, who hath delivered the people from under the hand of the Egyptians.

11 Now I know[3045] that the LORD *is* [a]greater than all gods:[430] [b]for in the thing[1697] wherein they dealt [c]proudly *he was* above them.

12 And Jethro, Moses' father in law, took a burnt offering[5930] and sacrifices[2077] for God: and Aaron came, and all the elders[2205] of Israel, to eat bread with Moses' father in law [a]before God.

13 And it came to pass on the morrow, that Moses sat to judge[8199] the people: and the people stood by Moses from the morning unto the evening.

14 And when Moses' father in law saw[7200] all that he did to the people, he said, What *is* this thing that thou doest to the people? why sittest thou thyself alone, and all the people stand[5324] by thee from morning unto even?

15 And Moses said unto his father in law, Because [a]the people come unto me to enquire of God:

16 When they have [a]a matter,[1697] they come unto me; and I judge between [I]one and another,[7453] and I do [b]make *them* know the statutes[2706] of God, and his laws.[8451]

17 And Moses' father in law said unto him, The thing that thou doest *is* not good.[2896]

18 [I]Thou wilt surely wear away, both thou, and this people that *is* with thee: for this thing *is* too heavy for thee; [a]thou art not able to perform[6213] it thyself alone.

19 Hearken[8085] now unto my voice, I will give thee counsel,[3289] and [a]God shall

14 [a]Ex. 34:27 [b]Num. 24:20; Deut. 25:19; 1Sam. 5:3, 7; 30:1, 17; 2Sam. 8:12; Ezra 9:14
15 [I]That is, *The LORD my banner* [a]Judg. 6:24
16 [I]Or, *Because the hand of Amalek is against the throne of the LORD*

1 [a]Ex. 2:16; 3:1 [b]Ps. 44:1; 77:14, 15; 78:4; 105:5, 43; 106:2, 8
2 [a]Ex. 4:26
3 [I]That is, *A stranger there* [a]Acts 7:29 [b]Ex. 2:22
4 [I]That is, *My God is a help*
5 [a]Ex. 3:1, 12
7 [I]Hebr. *peace* [a]Gen. 14:17; 18:2; 19:1; 1Kgs. 2:19 [b]Gen. 29:13; 33:4 [c]Gen. 43:27; 2Sam. 11:7
8 [I]Hebr. *found them* [a]Gen. 44:34; Num. 20:14 [b]Ps. 78:42; 81:7; 106:10; 107:2
10 [a]Gen. 14:20; 2Sam. 18:28; Luke 1:68
11 [a]2Chr. 2:5; Ps. 95:3; 97:9; 135:5 [b]Ex. 1:10, 16, 22; 5:2, 7; 14:8, 18 [c]1Sam. 2:3; Neh. 9:10, 16, 29; Job 40:11, 12; Ps. 31:23; 119:21; Luke 1:51
12 [a]Deut. 12:7; 1Chr. 29:22; 1Cor. 10:18, 21, 31
15 [a]Lev. 24:12; Num. 15:34
16 [I]Hebr. *a man and his fellow* [a]Ex. 23:7; 24:14; Deut. 17:8; 2Sam. 15:3; Job 31:13; Acts 18:15; 1Cor. 6:1 [b]Lev. 24:15; Num. 15:35; 27:6; 36:6-9

18 [I]Hebr. *Fading thou wilt fade* [a]Num. 11:14, 17; Deut. 1:9, 12 **19** [a]Ex. 3:12

be with thee: Be thou [b]for the people to God-ward, that thou mayest [c]bring the causes[1697] unto God:

20 And thou shalt [a]teach[2094] them ordinances[2706] and laws, and shalt shew them [b]the way wherein they must walk, and [c]the work that they must do.

21 Moreover thou shalt provide[2372] out of all the people [a]able[2428] men,[582] such as [b]fear[3373] God, [c]men of truth,[571] [d]hating covetousness;1215 and place[7760] *such* over them, *to be* rulers[8269] of thousands, *and* rulers of hundreds, rulers of fifties, and rulers of tens:

22 And let them judge the people [a]at all seasons:[6256] [b]and it shall be, *that* every great matter they shall bring unto thee, but every small matter they shall judge: so shall it be easier[7043] for thyself, and [c]they shall bear[5375] *the burden* with thee.

23 If thou shalt do this thing, and God command[6680] thee *so,* then thou shalt be [a]able to endure, and all this people shall also go to [b]their place in peace.

24 So Moses hearkened to the voice of his father in law, and did all that he had said.

25 And [a]Moses chose able men out of all Israel, and made them heads[7218] over the people, rulers of thousands, rulers of hundreds, rulers of fifties, and rulers of tens.

26 And they [a]judged the people at all seasons: the [b]hard causes[1697] they brought unto Moses, but every small matter[1697] they judged themselves.

27 And Moses let his father in law depart; and [a]he went his way into his own land.

19 [b]Ex. 4:16; 20:19; Deut. 5:5 [c]Num. 27:5 **20** [a]Deut. 4:1, 5; 5:1; 6:1, 2; 7:11 [b]Ps. 143:8 [c]Deut. 1:18 **21** [a]Ex. 18:25; Deut. 1:15, 16; 16:18; 2Chr. 19:5-10; Acts 6:3 [b]Gen. 42:18; 2Sam. 23:3; 2Chr. 19:9 [c]Ezek. 18:8 [d]Deut. 16:19 **22** [a]Ex. 18:26 [b]Ex. 18:26; Lev. 24:11; Num. 15:33; 27:2; 36:1; Deut. 1:17; 17:8 [c]Num. 11:17 **23** [a]Ex. 18:18 [b]Gen. 18:33; 30:25; Ex. 16:29; 2Sam. 19:39 **25** [a]Deut. 1:15; Acts 6:5 **26** [a]Ex. 18:22 [b]Job 29:16 **27** [a]Num. 10:29, 30

1 [a]Num. 33:15 **2** [a]Ex. 17:1, 8 [b]Ex. 3:1, 12 **3** [a]Ex. 20:21; Acts 7:38 [b]Ex. 3:4 **4** [a]Deut. 29:2 [b]Deut. 32:11; Isa. 63:9; Rev. 12:14 **5** [a]Deut. 5:2 [b]Deut. 4:20; 7:6; 14:2, 21; 26:18; 32:8, 9; 1Kgs. 8:53; Ps. 135:4; Song 8:12; Isa. 41:8; 43:1; Jer. 10:16; Mal. 3:17; Titus 2:14 [c]Ex. 9:29; Deut. 10:14; Job 41:11; Ps. 24:1; 50:12; 1Cor. 10:26, 28 **6** [a]Deut. 33:2, 3, 4; 1Pet. 2:5, 9; Rev. 1:6; 5:10;

Mount Sinai

19 In the third month, when the children[1121] of Israel were gone forth out of the land[776] of Egypt, the same day[3117] [a]came they *into* the wilderness of Sinai.

2 For they were departed from [a]Rephidim, and were come *to* the desert of Sinai, and had pitched in the wilderness; and there Israel camped before [b]the mount.

3 And [a]Moses went up[5927] unto God, and the LORD [b]called[7121] unto him out of the mountain, saying, Thus shalt thou say to the house[1004] of Jacob, and tell[5046] the children of Israel;

4 [a]Ye have seen[7200] what I did[6213] unto the Egyptians, and *how* [b]I bare[5375] you on eagles' wings, and brought you unto myself.

5 Now [a]therefore, if ye will obey[8085] my voice indeed, and keep[8104] my covenant,[1285] then [b]ye shall be a peculiar treasure[5459] unto me above all people:[5971] for [c]all the earth[776] *is* mine:

6 And ye shall be unto me a [a]kingdom[4467] of priests,[3548] and an [b]holy[6918] nation. These *are* the words[1697] which thou shalt speak[1696] unto the children of Israel.

7 And Moses came and called for the elders[2205] of the people, and laid before their faces all these words which the LORD commanded[6680] him.

8 And [a]all the people answered together, and said, All that the LORD hath spoken we will do.[6213] And Moses

20:6 [b]Lev. 20:24, 26; Deut. 7:6; 26:19; 28:9; Isa. 62:12; 1Cor. 3:17; 1Thess. 5:27 **8** [a]Ex. 24:3, 7; Deut. 5:27; 26:17

19:1 Israel had now arrived at Mount Sinai where they would remain for almost a year (Ex. 19:1, cf. Num. 10:11). Some of the high points and low points of their history occurred here. At Sinai, they rebelled against God and made an idol of gold (Ex. 32), but also at this holy mountain they received and ratified the Ten Commandments and most of the Law of Moses (Ex. 19—24).

19:5, 6 God here makes a conditional promise to Israel that if they would obey Him and keep His covenant, He would regard and treat them in a special way. The people chose instead to make a golden calf and forsake the God who had rescued them from Egyptian slavery (Ex. 32). This event, as well as persistent idolatry throughout most of their history, greatly limited the extent to which Israel could realize these promises. This passage is applied to Christians in 1 Peter 2:9, 10, showing how a believer's obedience will benefit him (see also Is. 43:20, 21).

returned[7725] the words of the people unto the LORD.

9 And the LORD said unto Moses, Lo, I come unto thee [a]in a thick cloud,[6051] [b]that the people may hear when I speak with thee, and [c]believe[539] thee for ever.[5769] And Moses told the words of the people unto the LORD.

10 And the LORD said unto Moses, Go unto the people, and [a]sanctify[6942] them to day and to morrow, and let them [b]wash[3526] their clothes,

11 And be ready[3559] against the third day: for the third day the LORD [a]will come down in the sight of all the people upon mount Sinai.

12 And thou shalt set bounds unto the people round about, saying, Take heed[8104] to yourselves, *that ye* go *not* up into the mount, or touch[5060] the border of it: [a]whosoever toucheth the mount shall be surely put to death:

13 There shall not an hand[3027] touch it, but he shall surely be stoned, or shot through;[3384] whether *it be* beast or man,[376] it shall not live:[2421] when the [I][a]trumpet soundeth long, they shall come up to the mount.

14 And Moses went down from the mount unto the people, and [a]sanctified the people; and they washed their clothes.

15 And he said unto the people, [a]Be ready against the third day: [b]come[5066] not at *your* wives.

16 And it came to pass on the third day in the morning, that there were [a]thunders and lightnings, and a [b]thick cloud upon the mount, and the [c]voice of the trumpet exceeding loud;[2389] so that all the people that *was* in the camp[4264] [d]trembled.[2729]

17 And [a]Moses brought forth the people out of the camp to meet with God; and they stood at the nether[8482] part of the mount.

18 And [a]mount Sinai *was* altogether on a smoke,[6225] because the LORD descended upon it [b]in fire: [c]and the smoke thereof ascended as the smoke of a furnace, and [d]the whole mount quaked[2729] greatly.

19 And [a]when the voice of the trumpet sounded long, and waxed louder and louder,[2390] [3966] [b]Moses spake, and [c]God answered him by a voice.

20 And the LORD came down upon mount Sinai, on the top[7218] of the mount: and the LORD called Moses *up* to the top of the mount; and Moses went up.

21 And the LORD said unto Moses, Go down, [I]charge the people, lest they break through unto the LORD [a]to gaze,[7200] and many of them perish.[5307]

22 And let the priests[3548] also, which come near[5066] to the LORD, [a]sanctify themselves,[6942] lest the LORD [b]break forth upon them.

23 And Moses said unto the LORD, The people cannot come up to mount Sinai: for thou chargedst us, saying, [a]Set bounds about the mount, and sanctify it.

24 And the LORD said unto him, Away, get thee down, and thou shalt come up, thou, and Aaron with thee: but let not the priests and the people break through[2040] to come up unto the LORD, lest he break forth upon them.

25 So Moses went down unto the people, and spake unto them.

The Ten Commandments

20 And God[430] spake[1696] [a]all these words,[1697] saying,

9 [a]Ex. 19:16; 20:21; 24:15, 16; Deut. 4:11; Ps. 18:11, 12; 97:2; Matt. 17:5 [b]Deut. 4:12, 36; John 12:29, 30 [c]Ex. 14:31
10 [a]Lev. 11:44, 45; Heb. 10:22 [b]Ex. 19:14; Gen. 35:2; Lev. 15:5
11 [a]Ex. 19:16, 18; 34:5; Deut. 33:2
12 [a]Heb. 12:20
13 [I]Or, *cornet* [a]Ex. 19:16, 19
14 [a]Ex. 19:10
15 [a]Ex. 19:11 [b]1Sam. 21:4, 5; Zech. 7:3; 1Cor. 7:5
16 [a]Ps. 77:18; Heb. 12:18, 19; Rev. 4:5; 8:5; 11:19 [b]Ex. 19:19; 40:34; 2Chr. 5:14 [c]Rev. 1:10; 4:1 [d]Heb. 12:21
17 [a]Deut. 4:10
18 [a]Deut. 4:11; 33:2; Judg. 5:5; Ps. 68:7, 8; Isa. 6:4; Hab. 3:3 [b]Ex. 3:2; 24:17; 2Chr. 7:1, 2, 3 [c]Gen. 15:17; Ps. 144:5; Rev. 15:8 [d]Ps. 68:8; 77:18; 114:7; Jer. 4:24; Heb. 12:26
19 [a]Ex. 19:13 [b]Heb. 12:21 [c]Neh. 9:13; Ps. 81:7
21 [I]Hebr. *contest* [a]Ex. 3:5; 1Sam. 6:19
22 [a]Lev. 10:3 [b]2Sam. 6:7, 8
23 [a]Ex. 19:12; Josh. 3:4
1 [a]Deut. 5:22

20:1–17 With these Ten Commandments the covenant with Israel begins. The ancient rabbis isolated 613 separate commandments in the entire Law of Moses, but these ten are the principles upon which the rest are based. By themselves they are called "the words of the covenant" (Ex. 34:28). The first four commandments deal with reverence for God directly, while the latter six refer to human relationships. The first four have as their theme total love for God, as expressed in Deuteronomy 6:5. The last six are summarized in the statement in Leviticus 19:18: "You shall love your neighbor as yourself." Therefore, Jesus took 613 commandments which had been condensed to ten in the Law of Moses and reduced them to two (see Matt. 22:35–40). All of God's com-

(continued on next page)

2 [a]I *am* the LORD thy God, which
have brought thee out of the land[776] of
Egypt, [b]out of the house[1004] of [I]bond-
age.[5650]
3 [a]Thou shalt have no other gods[430]
before me.
4 [b]Thou shalt not make[6213] unto
thee any graven image,[6459] or any likeness[8544] *of any thing* that *is* in
heaven8064 above, or that *is* in the
earth[776] beneath, or that *is* in the water
under the earth:
5 [a]Thou shalt not bow down[7812] thyself to them, nor serve them: for I the
LORD thy God[430] *am* [b]a jealous[7067]
God,[410] [c]visiting[6485] the iniquity[5771] of
the fathers[1] upon the children[1121] unto
the third and fourth *generation* of them
that hate me;
6 And [a]shewing[6213] mercy[2617] unto
thousands of them that love[157] me, and
keep[8104] my commandments.[4687]
7 [a]Thou shalt not take[5375] the name
of the LORD thy God in vain;[7723] for the
LORD [b]will not hold him guiltless[5352] that
taketh his name in vain.
8 [a]Remember the sabbath[7676] day, to
keep it holy.[6942]
9 [a]Six days shalt thou labour, and
do[6213] all thy work:[4399]
10 But the [a]seventh day *is* the
sabbath of the LORD thy God: *in it* thou
shalt not do any work, thou, nor thy
son,[1121] nor thy daughter, thy manservant,[5650] nor thy maidservant, nor thy
cattle, [b]nor thy stranger[1616] that *is* within
thy gates:
11 For [a]*in* six days the LORD made
heaven and earth, the sea, and all that in
them *is,* and rested the seventh day:
wherefore the LORD blessed[1288] the sabbath day, and hallowed[6942] it.
12 [a]Honour thy father[1] and thy
mother:[517] that thy days may be long[748]
upon the land[127] which the LORD thy God
giveth thee.
13 [a]Thou shalt not kill.[7523]
14 [a]Thou shalt not commit adul-
tery.5003
15 [a]Thou shalt not steal.
16 [a]Thou shalt not bear false[8267] witness against thy neighbour.[7453]
17 [a]Thou shalt not covet[2530] thy
neighbour's house,[1004] [b]thou shalt not
covet thy neighbour's wife,[802] nor his
manservant, nor his maidservant, nor his
ox, nor his ass, nor any thing that *is* thy
neighbour's.
18 And [a]all the people[5971] [b]saw[7200]
the thunderings, and the lightnings, and
the noise of the trumpet, and the mountain [c]smoking: and when the people saw
it, they removed,5128 and stood afar off.
19 And they said unto Moses,
[a]Speak[1696] thou with us, and we will
hear:[8085] but [b]let not God speak with us,
lest we die.
20 And Moses said unto the people,
[a]Fear[3372] not: [b]for God[430] is come to
prove[5254] you, and [c]that his fear may be
before your faces, that ye sin[2398] not.
21 And the people stood afar off, and
Moses drew near[5066] unto [a]the thick
darkness[6205] where God *was.*

Instructions for Building An Altar

22 And the LORD said unto Moses,
Thus thou shalt say unto the children of
Israel, Ye have seen that I have talked[1696]
with you [a]from heaven.
23 Ye shall not make [a]with me
gods[430] of silver, neither shall ye make
unto you gods of gold.

2 [I]Hebr. *servants* [a]Lev. 26:1, 13; Deut. 5:6; Ps. 81:10; Hos. 13:4 [b]Ex. 13:3
3 [a]Deut. 5:7; 6:14; 2Kgs. 17:35; Jer. 25:6; 35:15
4 [a]Lev. 26:1; Deut. 4:16; 5:8; 27:15; Ps. 97:7
5 [a]Ex. 23:24; Josh. 23:7; 2Kgs. 17:35; Isa. 44:15, 19 [b]Ex. 34:14; Deut. 4:24; 6:15; Josh. 24:19; Nah. 1:2 [c]Ex. 34:7; Lev. 20:5; 26:39, 40; Num. 14:18, 33; 1Kgs. 21:29; Job 5:4; 21:19; Ps. 79:8; 109:14; Isa. 14:20, 21; 65:6, 7; Jer. 2:9; 32:18
6 [a]Ex. 34:7; Deut. 7:9; Ps. 89:34; Rom. 11:28
7 [a]Ex. 23:1; Lev. 19:12; Deut. 5:11; Ps. 15:4; Matt. 5:33 [b]Mic. 6:11
8 [a]Ex. 31:13, 14; Lev. 19:3, 30; 26:2; Deut. 5:12
9 [a]Ex. 23:12; 31:15; 34:21; Lev. 23:3; Ezek. 20:12; Luke 13:14
10 [a]Gen. 2:2, 3; Ex. 16:26; 31:15 [b]Neh. 13:16-19
11 [a]Gen. 2:2
12 [a]Ex. 23:26; Lev. 19:3; Deut. 5:16; Jer. 35:7, 18, 19; Matt. 15:4; 19:19; Mark 7:10; 10:19; Luke 18:20; Eph. 6:2
13 [a]Deut. 5:17; Matt. 5:21; Rom. 13:9
14 [a]Deut. 5:18; Matt. 5:27
15 [a]Lev. 19:11; Deut. 5:19; Matt. 19:18; Rom. 13:9; 1Thess. 4:6
16 [a]Ex. 23:1; Deut. 5:20; 19:16; Matt. 19:18
17 [a]Deut. 5:21; Mic. 2:2; Hab. 2:9; Luke 12:15; Acts 20:33; Rom. 7:7; 13:9; Eph. 5:3, 5; Heb. 13:5 [b]Job 31:9; Prov. 6:29; Jer. 5:8; Matt. 5:28
18 [a]Heb. 12:18 [b]Rev. 1:10, 12 [c]Ex. 19:18
19 [a]Deut. 5:27; 18:16; Gal. 3:19, 20; Heb. 12:19 [b]Deut. 5:25
20 [a]1Sam. 12:20; Isa. 41:10, 13 [b]Gen. 22:1; Deut. 13:3 [c]Deut. 4:10; 6:2; 10:12; 17:13, 19; 19:20; 28:58; Prov. 3:7; 16:6; Isa. 8:13
21 [a]Ex. 19:16; Deut. 5:5; 1Kgs. 8:12
22 [a]Deut. 4:36; Neh. 9:13
23 [a]Ex. 32:1, 2, 4; 1Sam. 5:4, 5; 2Kgs. 17:33; Ezek. 20:39; 43:8; Dan. 5:4, 23; Zeph. 1:5; 2Cor. 6:14-16

(continued from previous page)
mandments in the Old Testament dealing with how His people should live may be abbreviated simply to have love for God and for man.

24 An altar[4196] of earth[127] thou shalt make unto me, and shalt sacrifice[2076] thereon thy burnt offerings,[5930] and thy peace offerings,[8002] [a]thy sheep, and thine oxen: in all [b]places where I record my name I will come unto thee, and I will [c]bless thee.

25 And [a]if thou wilt make me an altar of stone, thou shalt not [I]build it of hewn1496 stone: for if thou lift up[5130] thy tool[2719] upon it, thou hast polluted it.

26 Neither shalt thou go up by steps unto mine altar, that thy nakedness[6172] be not discovered[1540] thereon.

The Treatment of Servants

21 Now these *are* the judgments[4941] which thou shalt [a]set before them.

2 [a]If thou buy an Hebrew servant,[5650] six years he shall serve: and in the seventh he shall go out free for nothing.

3 If he came in [I]by himself, he shall go out by himself: if he were married,[1167] then his wife shall go out with him.

4 If his master[113] have given him a wife, and she have born him sons[1121] or daughters; the wife and her children shall be her master's, and he shall go out by himself.

5 [a]And if the servant [I]shall plainly say, I love[157] my master, my wife, and my children;[1121] I will not go out free:

6 Then his master shall bring[5066] him unto the [a]judges;[430] he shall also bring him to the door, or unto the door post; and his master shall [b]bore his ear through with an aul;4836 and he shall serve[5647] him for ever.[5769]

7 And if a man[376] [a]sell his daughter to be a maidservant, she shall not go out [b]as the menservants do.

8 If she [I]please not[7451,5869] her master, who hath betrothed[3259] her to himself, then shall he let her be redeemed:[6299] to sell her unto a strange[5237] nation[5971] he shall have no power,[4910] seeing he hath dealt deceitfully[898] with her.

9 And if he have betrothed her unto his son, he shall deal[6213] with her after the manner[4941] of daughters.

10 If he take him another *wife*; her food,[7606] her raiment, [a]and her duty of marriage,5772 shall he not diminish.

11 And if he do not these three unto her, then shall she go out free without money.

Laws Against Violence

12 [a]He that smiteth[5221] a man, so that he die,[4191] shall be surely put to death.

13 And [a]if a man lie not in wait,[6658] but God[430] [b]deliver *him* into his hand;[3027] then [c]I will appoint[7760] thee a place whither he shall flee.

14 But if a man come [a]presumptuously upon his neighbour,[7453] to slay[2026] him with guile;[6195] [b]thou shalt take him from mine altar,[4196] that he may die.

15 And he that smiteth his father,[1] or his mother,[517] shall be surely put to death.

16 And [a]he that stealeth a man, and [b]selleth him, or if he be [c]found in his hand, he shall surely be put to death.

17 And [a]he that [I]curseth[7043] his father, or his mother, shall surely be put to death.

18 And if men[582] strive together,[7378] and one smite [I]another with a stone, or with *his* fist, and he die not, but keepeth *his* bed:

19 If he rise again, and walk abroad [a]upon his staff, then shall he that smote *him* be quit:[5352] only he shall pay *for* [I]the loss of his time, and shall cause *him* to be thoroughly healed.

20 And if a man smite his servant, or his maid, with a rod,[7626] and he die under his hand; he shall be surely [Ia]punished.[5358]

21 Notwithstanding, if he continue a day or two, he shall not be punished: for [a]he *is* his money.

22 If men strive, and hurt[5062] a woman with child, so that her fruit depart *from her,* and yet no mischief[611] follow: he shall be surely punished, accord-

---

24 [a]Lev. 1:2 [b]Deut. 12:5, 11, 21; 14:23; 16:6, 11; 26:2; 1Kgs. 8:43; 9:3; 2Chr. 6:6; 7:16; 12:13; Ezra 6:12; Neh. 1:9; Ps. 74:7; Jer. 7:10, 12 [c]Gen. 12:2; Deut. 7:13
25 [I]Hebr. *build them* with *hewing* [a]Deut. 27:5; Josh. 8:31

1 [a]Ex. 24:3, 4; Deut. 4:14; 6:1
2 [a]Lev. 25:39, 40, 41; Deut. 15:12; Jer. 34:14
3 [I]Hebr. *with his body*
5 [I]Hebr. *saying shall say* [a]Deut. 15:16, 17
6 [a]Ex. 12:12; 22:8, 28 [b]Ps. 40:6
7 [a]Neh. 5:5 [b]Ex. 21:2, 3
8 [I]Hebr. *be evil in the eyes of*
10 [a]1Cor. 7:5
12 [a]Gen. 9:6; Lev. 24:17; Num. 35:30, 31; Matt. 26:52
13 [a]Num. 35:22; Deut. 19:4, 5 [b]1Sam. 24:4, 10, 18 [c]Num. 35:11; Deut. 19:3; Josh. 20:2
14 [a]Num. 15:30; 35:20; Deut. 19:11, 12; Heb. 10:26 [b]1Kgs. 2:28-34; 2Kgs. 11:15
16 [a]Deut. 24:7 [b]Gen. 37:28 [c]Ex. 22:4
17 [I]Or, *reviletth* [a]Lev. 20:9; Prov. 20:20; Matt. 15:4; Mark 7:10
18 [I]Or, *his neighbor*
19 [I]Hebr. *his ceasing* [a]2Sam. 3:29
20 [I]Hebr. *avenged* [a]Gen. 4:15, 24; Rom. 13:4
21 [a]Lev. 25:45, 46

ing as the woman's husband[1167] will lay upon him; and he shall [a]pay as the judges[6414] *determine.*

23 And if *any* mischief follow, then thou shalt give life[5315] for life,

24 [a]Eye for eye, tooth for tooth, hand for hand, foot for foot,

25 Burning for burning, wound for wound, stripe for stripe.

26 And if a man smite the eye of his servant, or the eye of his maid, that it perish;[7843] he shall let him go free for his eye's sake.

27 And if he smite out[5307] his manservant's tooth, or his maidservant's tooth; he shall let him go free for his tooth's sake.

28 If an ox gore a man or a woman, that they die: then [a]the ox shall be surely stoned, and his flesh[1320] shall not be eaten; but the owner[1167] of the ox *shall be* quit.[5355]

29 But if the ox were wont[5056] to push with his horn in time past, and it hath been testified to his owner, and he hath not kept him in,[8104] but that he hath killed a man or a woman; the ox shall be stoned, and his owner also shall be put to death.

30 If there be laid on him a sum of money,[3724] then he shall give for [a]the ransom[6306] of his life whatsoever is laid upon him.

31 Whether he have gored a son, or have gored a daughter, according to this judgment shall it be done unto him.

32 If the ox shall push a manservant or a maidservant; he shall give unto their master [a]thirty shekels of silver, and the [b]ox shall be stoned.

33 And if a man shall open a pit,[953] or if a man shall dig a pit, and not cover[3680] it, and an ox or an ass fall therein;

34 The owner of the pit shall make *it* good, *and* give money unto the owner of them; and the dead *beast* shall be his.

35 And if one man's ox hurt another's, that he die; then they shall sell the live[2416] ox, and divide the money of it; and the dead *ox* also they shall divide.

36 Or if it be known that the ox hath used to push in time past, and his owner hath not kept him in; he shall surely pay[7999] ox for ox; and the dead shall be his own.

Laws About Repayment

22 If a man[376] shall steal an ox, or a [I]sheep, and kill[2873] it, or sell it; he shall restore five oxen for an ox, and [a]four sheep for a sheep.

2 If a thief be found [a]breaking up, and be smitten[5221] that he die,[4191] *there shall* [b]no blood[1818] *be shed* for him.

3 If the sun be risen upon him, *there shall be* blood *shed* for him; *for* he should make full restitution;[7999] if he have nothing, then he shall be [a]sold for his theft.

4 If the theft be certainly [a]found in his hand[3027] alive,[2416] whether it be ox, or ass, or sheep; he shall [b]restore double.

5 If a man shall cause a field or vineyard to be eaten, and shall put in his beast, and shall feed in another man's field;[7704] of the best of his own field, and of the best of his own vineyard, shall he make restitution.

6 If fire break out, and catch in thorns, so that the stacks of corn, or the standing corn, or the field, be consumed *therewith;* he that kindled the fire shall surely make restitution.

7 If a man shall deliver unto his neighbour[7453] money or stuff to keep,[8104] and it be stolen out of the man's house; [a]if the thief be found, let him pay double.

8 If the thief be not found, then the master[1167] of the house shall be brought unto the [a]judges,[430] *to see* whether he have put his hand unto his neighbour's goods.[4399]

9 For all manner[1697] of trespass,[6588] *whether it be* for ox, for ass, for sheep, for raiment, *or* for any manner of lost thing, which *another* challengeth[559] to be his, the [a]cause[1697] of both parties shall come before the judges; *and* whom the judges shall condemn,[7561] he shall pay double unto his neighbour.

10 If a man deliver[5414] unto his

22 [a]Ex. 21:30; Deut. 22:18, 19
24 [a]Lev. 24:20; Deut. 19:21; Matt. 5:38
28 [a]Gen. 9:5
30 [a]Ex. 21:22; Num. 35:31
32 [a]Zech. 11:12, 13; Matt. 26:15; Phil. 2:7 [b]Ex. 21:28
1 [I]Or, *goat* [a]2Sam. 12:6; Luke 19:8; Prov. 6:31
2 [a]Matt. 24:43 [b]Num. 35:27
3 [a]Ex. 21:2
4 [a]Ex. 21:16 [b]Ex. 22:1, 7; Prov. 6:31
7 [a]Ex. 22:4
8 [a]Ex. 21:6; 22:28
9 [a]Deut. 25:1; 2Chr. 19:10

neighbour an ass, or an ox, or a sheep, or any beast, to keep; and it die, or be hurt,[7665] or driven away,[7617] no man seeing[7200] *it:*

11 *Then* shall an [a]oath[7621] of the LORD be between them both, that he hath not put his hand unto his neighbour's goods; and the owner[1167] of it shall accept *thereof,* and he shall not make *it* good.[7999]

12 And [a]if it be stolen from him, he shall make restitution unto the owner thereof.

13 If it be torn in pieces, *then* let him bring it *for* witness, *and* he shall not make good that which was torn.

14 And if a man borrow[7592] *ought* of his neighbour, and it be hurt, or die, the owner thereof *being* not with it, he shall surely make *it* good.

15 *But* if the owner thereof *be* with it, he shall not make *it* good: if it *be* an hired *thing,* it came for his hire.

Laws of Human Relations

16 And [a]if a man entice6601 a maid[1330] that is not betrothed,781 and lie with her, he shall surely endow her to be his wife.

17 If her father[1] utterly refuse to give her unto him, he shall [I][a]pay money according to the [b]dowry4119 of virgins.[1330]

18 [a]Thou shalt not suffer[2421] a witch[3784] to live.[2421]

19 [a]Whosoever lieth with a beast shall surely be put to death.

20 [a]He that sacrificeth[2076] unto *any* god, save unto the LORD only, he shall be utterly destroyed.[2763]

21 [a]Thou shalt neither vex[3238] a stranger,[1616] nor oppress him: for ye were strangers in the land of Egypt.

22 [a]Ye shall not afflict any widow, or fatherless child.

23 If thou afflict them in any wise, and they [a]cry at all unto me, I will surely [b]hear[8085] their cry;

24 And my [a]wrath[639] shall wax hot,[2734] and I will kill[2026] you with the sword; and [b]your wives shall be widows, and your children[1121] fatherless.

25 [a]If thou lend money to *any of* my people[5971] *that is* poor by thee, thou shalt not be to him as an usurer, neither shalt thou lay upon him usury.

26 [a]If thou at all take thy neighbour's raiment to pledge,[2254] thou shalt deliver[7725] it unto him by that the sun goeth down:

27 For that *is* his covering only, it *is* his raiment for his skin:[5785] wherein shall he sleep? and it shall come to pass, when he [a]crieth unto me, that I will hear; for I *am* [b]gracious.[2587]

28 [a]Thou shalt not revile[7043] the [I][b]gods,[430] nor curse[779] the ruler[5387] of thy people.

29 Thou shalt not delay *to offer* [I][a]the first of thy ripe fruits, and of thy [II]liquors: [b]the firstborn of thy sons[1121] shalt thou give unto me.

30 [a]Likewise shalt thou do with thine oxen, *and* with thy sheep: [b]seven days it shall be with his dam;[517] on the eighth day thou shalt give it me.

31 And ye shall be [a]holy[6944] men[582] unto me: [b]neither shall ye eat *any* flesh[1320] *that is* torn of beasts in the field; ye shall cast it to the dogs.

23

Thou [a]shalt not [I]raise[5375] a false[7723] report:[8088] put not thine hand[3027] with the wicked[7563] to be an [b]unrighteous[2555] witness.

2 [a]Thou shalt not follow a multitude to *do* evil;[7451] [b]neither shalt thou [I]speak[1696] in a cause[7379] to decline5186 after many to wrest *judgment:*

3 Neither shalt thou countenance a poor man in his cause.

4 [a]If thou meet thine enemy's ox or his ass going astray,[8582] thou shalt surely bring it back to him again.[7725]

---

11 [a]Heb. 6:16 **12** [a]Gen. 31:39 **16** [a]Deut. 22:28, 29 **17** [I]Hebr. *weigh* [a]Gen. 23:16 [b]Gen. 34:12; Deut. 22:29; 1Sam. 18:25 **18** [a]Lev. 19:26, 31; 20:27; Deut. 18:10, 11; 1Sam. 28:3, 9 **19** [a]Lev. 18:23; 20:15 **20** [a]Num. 25:2, 7, 8; Deut. 13:1, 2, 5, 6, 9, 13-15; 17:2, 3, 5 **21** [a]Ex. 23:9; Lev. 19:33; 25:35; Deut. 10:19; Jer. 7:6; Zech. 7:10; Mal. 3:5 **22** [a]Deut. 10:18; 24:17; 27:19; Ps. 94:6; Isa. 1:17, 23; 10:2; Ezek. 22:7; Zech. 7:10; James 1:27 **23** [a]Deut. 15:9; 24:15; Job 35:9; Luke 18:7 [b]Ex. 22:27; Job 34:28; Ps. 18:6; 145:19; James 5:4 **24** [a]Job 31:23; Ps. 69:24 [b]Ps. 109:9; Lam. 5:3 **25** [a]Lev. 25:35-37; Deut. 23:19, 20; Neh. 5:7; Ps. 15:5; Ezek. 18:8, 17 **26** [a]Deut. 24:6, 10, 13, 17; Job 22:6; 24:3, 9; Prov. 20:16; 22:27; Ezek. 18:7, 16; Amos 2:8 **27** [a]Ex. 22:23 [b]Ex. 34:6; 2Chr. 30:9; Ps. 86:15 **28** [I]Or, *judges* [a]Eccl. 10:20; Acts 23:5; Jude 8 [b]Ex. 22:8, 9 **29** [I]Hebr. *thy fullness* [II]Hebr. *tear* [a]Ex. 23:16, 19; Prov. 3:9 [b]Ex. 13:2, 12; 34:19 **30** [a]Deut. 15:19 [b]Lev. 22:27 **31** [a]Ex. 19:6; Lev. 19:2; Deut. 14:21 [b]Lev. 22:8; Ezek. 4:14; 44:31

1 [I]Or, *receive* [a]Ex. 22:7; Lev. 19:16; Ps. 15:3; 101:5; Prov. 10:18; 2Sam. 19:27 [b]Ex. 20:16; Deut. 19:16-18; Ps. 35:11; Prov. 19:5, 9, 28; 24:28; 1Kgs. 21:10, 13; Matt. 26:59-61; Acts 6:11, 13 **2** [I]Hebr. *answer* [a]Gen. 7:1; 19:4, 7; Ex. 32:1, 2; Josh. 24:15; 1Sam. 15:9; 1Kgs. 19:10; Job 31:34; Prov. 1:10, 11, 15; 4:14; Matt. 27:24, 26; Mark 15:15; Luke 23:23; Acts 24:27; 25:9 [b]Ex. 23:6, 7; Lev. 19:15; Deut. 1:17; Ps. 72:2 **4** [a]Deut. 22:1; Job 31:29; Prov. 24:17; 25:21; Matt. 5:44; Rom. 12:20; 1Thess. 5:15

5 [a]If thou see the ass of him that
hateth thee lying under his burden,[4853]
[I]and wouldest forbear[2308] to help him,
thou shalt surely help with him.
6 [a]Thou shalt not wrest the
judgment[4941] of thy poor in his cause.
7 [a]Keep thee far from a false[8267]
matter;[1697] [b]and the innocent[5355] and
righteous[6662] slay[2026] thou not: for [c]I will
not justify[6663] the wicked.
8 And [a]thou shalt take no gift: for
the gift blindeth [I]the wise, and perverteth
the words[1697] of the righteous.
9 Also [a]thou shalt not oppress a
stranger:[1616] for ye know[3045] the
[I]heart[5315] of a stranger, seeing ye were
strangers in the land of Egypt.

The Seventh Day

10 And [a]six years thou shalt sow thy
land,[776] and shalt gather in[622] the fruits
thereof:
11 But the seventh *year* thou shalt
let it rest and lie still; that the poor of
thy people[5971] may eat: and what they
leave[3499] the beasts[2416] of the field[7704]
shall eat. In like manner thou shalt
deal[6213] with thy vineyard, *and* with thy
[I]olive yard.
12 [a]Six days thou shalt do[6213] thy
work, and on the seventh day thou shalt
rest:[7673] that thine ox and thine ass may
rest, and the son of thy handmaid, and
the stranger, may be refreshed.
13 And in all *things* that I have said
unto you [a]be circumspect:[8104] and [b]make
no mention[2142] of the name of other
gods,[430] neither let it be heard[8085] out of
thy mouth.[6310]

Three Festivals Each Year

14 [a]Three times thou shalt keep a
feast unto me in the year.
15 [a]Thou shalt keep[8104] the feast[2282]
of unleavened bread: (thou shalt eat unleavened bread seven days, as I
commanded[6680] thee, in the time
appointed[4150] of the month Abib; for in
it thou camest out from Egypt: [b]and none
shall appear[7200] before me empty:)
16 [a]And the feast of harvest, the
firstfruits[1061] of thy labours, which thou
hast sown in the field: and [b]the feast of
ingathering, *which is* in the end of the
year, when thou hast gathered[622] in thy
labours out of the field.
17 [a]Three times in the year all thy
males[2138] shall appear before the Lord[113]
GOD.
18 [a]Thou shalt not offer[2076] the
blood[1818] of my sacrifice[2077] with
leavened bread;[2557] neither shall the fat of
my [I]sacrifice remain until the morning.
19 [a]The first[7225] of the firstfruits of
thy land[127] thou shalt bring into the
house[1004] of the LORD thy God.[430] [b]Thou
shalt not seethe a kid in his mother's[517]
milk.

5 [I]Or, *wilt thou cease to help him? or, and wouldest cease to leave* thy business *for him; thou shalt surely leave* it to join *with him* [a]Deut. 22:1
6 [a]Ex. 23:2; Deut. 27:19; Job 31:13, 21; Eccl. 5:8; Isa. 10:1, 2; Jer. 5:28; 7:6; Amos 5:12; Mal. 3:5
7 [a]Ex. 23:1; Lev. 19:11; Luke 3:14; Eph. 4:25 [b]Deut. 27:25; Ps. 94:21; Prov. 17:15, 26; Jer. 7:6; Matt. 27:4 [c]Ex. 34:7; Rom. 1:18
8 [I]Hebr. *the seeing* [a]Deut. 16:19; 1Sam. 8:3; 12:3; 2Chr. 19:7; Ps. 26:10; Prov. 15:27; 17:8, 23; 29:4; Isa. 1:23; 5:23; 33:15; Ezek. 22:12; Amos 5:12; Acts 24:26
9 [I]Hebr. *soul* [a]Ex. 22:21; Deut. 10:19; 24:14, 17; 27:19; Ps. 94:6; Ezek. 22:7; Mal. 3:5
10 [a]Lev. 25:3, 4
11 [a]Or, *olive trees*
12 [a]Ex. 20:8, 9; Deut. 5:13; Luke 13:14
13 [a]Deut. 4:9; Josh. 22:5; Ps. 39:1; Hos. 2:17; Eph. 5:15; 1Tim. 4:16 [b]Num. 32:38; Deut. 12:3; Josh. 23:7; Ps. 16:4; Zech. 13:2
14 [a]Ex. 34:23; Lev. 23:4; Deut. 16:16
15 [a]Ex. 12:15; 13:6; 34:18; Lev. 23:6; Deut. 16:8 [b]Ex. 34:20; Deut. 16:16
16 [a]Ex. 34:22; Lev. 23:10; [b]Deut. 16:13
17 [a]Ex. 34:23; Deut. 16:16
18 [I]Or, *feast* [a]Ex. 12:8; 34:25; Lev. 2:11; Deut. 16:4
19 [a]Ex. 22:29; 34:26; Lev. 23:10, 17; Num. 18:12, 13; Deut. 26:10; Neh. 10:35; [b]Ex. 34:26; Deut. 14:21

23:11 This was a sabbath rest for the land. A fuller form of this law of the sabbatical year is found in Leviticus 25:1–7. Though it followed sound agricultural principles (restoring fertility to the soil), this was not the purpose stated for its observance. The natural uncultivated growth of the grain and fruit would be a much needed resource for the poor and even provide food for the wild animals.

23:14–17 These three appearances before God by the people were three of the seven annual feasts of the Jews (see Lev. 23:16, 17, 33–36). They are listed as the Feast of Unleavened Bread (which was closely associated with the Passover; see Ex. 12:1–11, 14–20; Lev. 23:4–8; Deut. 16:1–8), the Feast of Harvest or Firstfruits (later called the Feast of Weeks and in New Testament times known as Pentecost [see Lev. 23:9–14; Deut. 16:9–12]), and the Feast of Ingathering (later called the Feast of Tabernacles; see Lev. 23:33–36, 39–43; Deut. 16:13–15). At the time of each of these feasts, all males were to make a pilgrimage to the sanctuary, which was at this time the Tabernacle and later became the temple after its construction.

God's Angel

⊶ 20 [a]Behold, I send an Angel before thee, to keep[8104] thee in the way,[1870] and to bring thee into the place which I have prepared.

21 Beware[8104] of him, and obey[8085] his voice, [a]provoke him not; for he will [b]not pardon[5375] your transgressions:[6588] for [c]my name *is* in him.

22 But if thou shalt indeed obey his voice, and do[6213] all that I speak; then [a]I will be an enemy unto thine enemies, and [I]an adversary unto thine adversaries.

23 [a]For mine Angel shall go before thee, and [b]bring thee in unto the Amorites, and the Hittites, and the Perizzites, and the Canaanites, the Hivites, and the Jebusites: and I will cut them off.

24 Thou shalt not [a]bow down[7812] to their gods, nor serve them, [b]nor do after their works: [c]but thou shalt utterly overthrow them, and quite break down[7665] their images.[4676]

25 And ye shall [a]serve[5647] the LORD your God, and [b]he shall bless[1288] thy bread, and thy water; and [c]I will take sickness away from the midst of thee.

26 [a]There shall nothing cast their young, nor be barren,6135 in thy land: the number of thy days[3117] I will [b]fulfil.

27 I will send [a]my fear[367] before thee, and will [b]destroy[2000] all the people to whom thou shalt come, and I will make all thine enemies turn their [Ic]backs unto thee.

28 And [a]I will send hornets before thee, which shall drive out the Hivite, the Canaanite, and the Hittite, from before thee.

29 [a]I will not drive them out from before thee in one year; lest the land become desolate,[8077] and the beast of the field multiply against thee.

30 By little and little I will drive them out from before thee, until thou be increased, and inherit[5157] the land.

31 And [a]I will set thy bounds from the Red sea even unto the sea of the Philistines, and from the desert unto the river: for I will [b]deliver the inhabitants of the land into your hand; and thou shalt drive them out before thee.

32 [a]Thou shalt make[3772] no covenant[1285] with them, nor with their gods.

33 They shall not dwell in thy land, lest they make thee sin[2398] against me: for if thou serve their gods, [a]it will surely be a snare[4170] unto thee.

The Agreement Is Signed

24 And he said unto Moses, Come up unto the LORD, thou, and Aaron, [a]Nadab, and Abihu, [b]and seventy of the elders[2205] of Israel; and worship[7812] ye afar off.

2 And Moses [a]alone shall come near the LORD: but they shall not come nigh;[5066] neither shall[5927] the people[5971] go up[5927] with him.

3 And Moses came and told the people all the words[1697] of the LORD, and all the judgments:[4941] and all the people answered with one voice, and said,[1696]

20 [a]Ex. 14:19; 32:34; 33:2, 14; Num. 20:16; Josh. 5:13; 6:2; Ps. 91:11; Isa. 63:9 **21** [a]Num. 14:11; Ps. 78:40, 56; Eph. 4:30; Heb. 3:10, 16; [b]Ex. 32:34; Num. 14:35; Deut. 18:19; Josh. 24:10; Jer. 5:7; Heb. 3:11; 1John 5:16 [c]Isa. 9:6; Jer. 23:6; John 10:30, 38 **22** [I]Or, *I will afflict them that afflict thee* [a]Gen. 12:3; Deut. 30:7; Jer. 30:20 **23** [a]Ex. 23:20; 33:2; [b]Josh. 24:8, 11 **24** [a]Ex. 20:5; [b]Lev. 18:3; Deut. 12:30, 31 [c]Ex. 34:13; Num. 33:52; Deut. 7:5, 25; 12:3 **25** [a]Deut. 6:13; 10:12, 20; 11:13, 14; 13:4; Josh. 22:5; 24:14, 15, 21, 24; 1Sam. 7:3; 12:20, 24; Matt. 4:10 [b]Deut. 7:13; 28:5, 8 [c]Ex. 15:26; Deut. 7:15 **26** [a]Deut. 7:14; 28:4; Job 21:10; Mal. 3:10, 11 [b]Gen. 25:8; 35:29; 1Chr. 23:1; Job 5:26; 42:17; Ps. 55:23; 90:10 **27** [I]Hebr. *neck* [a]Gen. 35:5; Ex. 15:14, 16; Deut. 2:25; 11:25; Josh. 2:9, 11; 1Sam. 14:15; 2Chr. 14:14 [b]Deut. 7:23 [c]Ps. 18:40 **28** [a]Deut. 7:20; Josh. 24:12 **29** [a]Deut. 7:22

31 [a]Gen. 15:18; Num. 34:3; Deut. 11:24; Josh. 1:4; 1Kgs. 4:21, 24; Ps. 72:8 [b]Josh. 21:44; Judg. 1:4; 11:21 **32** [a]Ex. 34:12, 15; Deut. 7:2 **33** [a]Ex. 34:12; Deut. 7:16; 12:30; Josh. 23:13; Judg. 2:3; 1Sam. 18:21; Ps. 106:36 **1** [a]Ex. 28:1; Lev. 10:1, 2 [b]Ex. 1:5; Num. 11:16 **2** [a]Ex. 24:13, 15, 18

⊶ **23:20–23** There is strong evidence that the appearances of the "angel of the LORD" are in fact preincarnate appearances of Christ, the Son of God. Things are said of the angel of the LORD that go beyond the category of angels, and are applicable only to Christ. Hagar called Him by the name of God (Gen. 16:13). When the angel of the LORD appeared to Moses from within the burning bush, the text of the Scripture, the angel Himself, and Moses all affirm that the angel is God (Ex. 3:2–6). Here in Exodus chapter twenty-three it is said of angel of the LORD that He has the power to forgive sins and that He has the name of God in Him. (cf. Luke 7:49; Mark 2:7). No man could see God and live, but the Son of God, who is the fullness of the Godhead bodily, has declared Him (Ex. 33:20; John 1:18; Col. 2:9).

[a]All the words which the LORD hath said will we do.[6213]

4 And Moses [a]wrote all the words of the LORD, and rose up early in the morning, and builded an altar[4196] under the hill, and twelve [b]pillars,[4676] according to the twelve tribes[7626] of Israel.

5 And he sent young men of the children[1121] of Israel, which offered[5927] burnt offerings,[5930] and sacrificed[2076] peace[8002] offerings[2077] of oxen unto the LORD.

6 And Moses [a]took half of the blood,[1818] and put *it* in basons;[101] and half of the blood he sprinkled[2236] on the altar.

7 And he [a]took the book[5612] of the covenant,[1285] and read in the audience[241] of the people: and they said, [b]All that the LORD hath said will we do, and be obedient.[8085]

8 And Moses took the blood, and sprinkled *it* on the people, and said, Behold [a]the blood of the covenant, which the LORD hath made[3772] with you concerning all these words.

9 Then [a]went up Moses, and Aaron, Nadab, and Abihu, and seventy of the elders of Israel:

10 And they [a]saw[7200] the God[430] of Israel: and *there was* under his feet as it were a paved[3840] work of a [b]sapphire stone, and as it were the [c]body of heaven[8064] in *his* clearness.[2892]

11 And upon the nobles[678] of the children of Israel he [a]laid not his hand:[3027] also [b]they saw[2372] God, and did [c]eat and drink.

The Tablets of Stone

12 And the LORD said unto Moses, [a]Come up to me into the mount, and be there: and I will give thee [b]tables of stone, and a law,[8451] and commandments[4687] which I have written; that thou mayest teach[3384] them.

3 [a]Ex. 19:8; 24:7; Deut. 5:27; Gal. 3:19, 20
4 [a]Deut. 31:9 [b]Gen. 28:18; 31:45
6 [a]Heb. 9:18
7 [a]Heb. 9:19 [b]Ex. 24:3
8 [a]Heb. 9:20; 13:20; 1Pet. 1:2
9 [a]Ex. 24:1
10 [a]Gen. 32:30; Ex. 3:6; Judg. 13:22; Isa. 6:1, 5; John 1:18; 1Tim. 6:16; 1John 4:12 [b]Ezek. 1:26; 10:1; Rev. 4:3 [c]Matt. 17:2
11 [a]Ex. 19:21 [b]Gen. 16:13; 32:30; Ex. 24:10; 33:20; Deut. 4:33; Judg. 13:22 [c]Gen. 31:54; Ex. 18:12; 1Cor. 10:18
12 [a]Ex. 24:2, 15, 18 [b]Ex. 31:18; 32:15, 16; Deut. 5:22
13 [a]Ex. 32:17; 33:11 [b]Ex. 24:2
15 [a]Ex. 19:9; 16; Matt. 17:5
16 [a]Ex. 16:10; Num. 14:10
17 [a]Ex. 3:2; 19:18; Deut. 4:36; Heb. 12:18, 29
18 [a]Ex. 34:28; Deut. 9:9
2 IHebr. *take for me* IIOr, *heave offering* [a]Ex. 35:5, 21; 1Chr. 29:3, 5, 9, 14; Ezra 2:68; 3:5; 7:16; Neh. 11:2; 2Cor. 8:12; 9:7
4 IOr, *silk* [a]Gen. 41:42
6 [a]Ex. 27:20 [b]Ex. 30:23 [c]Ex. 30:34
7 [a]Ex. 28:4, 6 [b]Ex. 28:15

🔑 13 And Moses rose up, and [a]his minister[8334] Joshua: and Moses [b]went up into the mount of God.

14 And he said unto the elders, Tarry ye here for us, until we come again unto you: and, behold, Aaron and Hur *are* with you: if any man have any matters[1697] to do, let him come unto them.

15 And Moses went up into the mount, and [a]a cloud[6051] covered the mount.

16 And [a]the glory[3519] of the LORD abode[7931] upon mount Sinai, and the cloud covered it six days: and the seventh day he called[7121] unto Moses out of the midst of the cloud.

17 And the sight of the glory of the LORD *was* like [a]devouring fire on the top of the mount in the eyes of the children of Israel.

18 And Moses went into the midst of the cloud, and gat him up[5927] into the mount: and [a]Moses was in the mount forty days and forty nights.

Gifts for the Tent

25 And the LORD spake[1696] unto Moses, saying,

2 Speak unto the children[1121] of Israel, that they Ibring me an IIoffering:[8641] [a]of every man that giveth it willingly[5068] with his heart[3820] ye shall take my offering.

3 And this *is* the offering which ye shall take of them; gold, and silver, and brass,

4 And blue, and purple, and scarlet, and I[a]fine linen, and goats' *hair,*

5 And rams' skins[5785] dyed red, and badgers' skins, and shittim wood,

6 [a]Oil[8081] for the light,[3974] [b]spices for anointing[4888] oil, and for [c]sweet incense,[7004]

🔑 7 Onyx stones, and stones to be set in the [a]ephod, and in the [b]breastplate.[2833]

🔑 **24:13** See note on Numbers 27:18–23, concerning Joshua, Moses' "minister."

🔑 **25:7** The word "ephod" (646) is a Hebrew name for the sacred upper garment of the priest. Made of plain linen for the regular priest, it was multi-colored and specially embroidered for the

(continued on next page)

🔑 8 And let them make[6213] me a [a]sanctuary;[4720] that [b]I may dwell[7931] among them.

9 [a]According to all that I shew[7200] thee, *after* the pattern of the tabernacle,[4908] and the pattern[8403] of all the instruments thereof, even so shall ye make *it*.

The Ark of the Covenant

10 [a]And they shall make an ark[727] *of* shittim wood: two cubits and a half *shall be* the length[753] thereof, and a cubit and a half the breadth thereof, and a cubit and a half the height thereof.

11 And thou shalt overlay it with pure[2889] gold, within and without shalt thou overlay it, and shalt make upon it a crown of gold round about.

12 And thou shalt cast four rings of gold for it, and put *them* in the four corners thereof; and two rings *shall be* in the one side of it, and two rings in the other side of it.

13 And thou shalt make staves *of* shittim wood, and overlay them with gold.

14 And thou shalt put the staves into the rings by the sides of the ark, that the ark may be borne[5375] with them.

15 [a]The staves shall be in the rings of the ark: they shall not be taken from it.

16 And thou shalt put into the ark [a]the testimony[5715] which I shall give thee.

17 And [a]thou shalt make a mercy seat[3727] *of* pure gold: two cubits and a half *shall be* the length thereof, and a cubit and a half the breadth thereof.

18 And thou shalt make two cherubims[3742] *of* gold, *of* beaten work shalt thou make them, in the two ends of the mercy seat.

19 And make one cherub on the one end, and the other cherub on the other end: *even* [1]of the mercy seat shall ye make the cherubims on the two ends thereof.

20 And [a]the cherubims shall stretch forth *their* wings on high, covering the mercy seat with their wings, and their faces *shall look* one to another; toward the mercy seat shall the faces of the cherubims be.

21 [a]And thou shalt put the mercy seat above upon the ark; and [b]in the ark thou shalt put the testimony that I shall give thee.

22 And [a]there I will meet with thee, and I will commune[1696] with thee from above the mercy seat, from [b]between the two cherubims which *are* upon the ark of the testimony, of all *things* which I will give thee in commandment[6680] unto the children of Israel.

The Table for the Shewbread

23 [a]Thou shalt also make a table *of* shittim wood: two cubits *shall be* the length thereof, and a cubit the breadth thereof, and a cubit and a half the height thereof.

24 And thou shalt overlay it with pure gold, and make thereto a crown of gold round about.

25 And thou shalt make unto it a border of an hand breadth round about,

8 [a]Ex. 36:1, 3, 4; Lev. 4:6; 10:4; 21:12; Heb. 9:1, 2 [b]Ex. 29:45; 1Kgs. 6:13; 2Cor. 6:16; Heb. 3:6; Rev. 21:3
9 [a]Ex. 25:40
10 [a]Ex. 37:1; Deut. 10:3; Heb. 9:4
15 [a]1Kgs. 8:8
16 [a]Ex. 16:34; 31:18; Deut. 10:2, 5; 31:26; 1Kgs. 8:9; 2Kgs. 11:12; Heb. 9:4
17 [a]Ex. 37:6; Rom. 3:25; Heb. 9:5
19 [1]Or, *of the* matter *of the mercy seat*
20 [a]1Kgs. 8:7; 1Chr. 28:18; Heb. 9:5
21 [a]Ex. 26:34 [b]Ex. 25:16
22 [a]Ex. 29:42, 43; 30:6, 36; Lev. 16:2; Num. 17:4 [b]Num. 7:89; 1Sam. 4:4; 2Sam. 6:2; 2Kgs. 19:15; Ps. 80:1; 90:1; Isa. 37:16
23 [a]Ex. 37:10; 1Kgs. 7:48; 2Chr. 4:8; Heb. 9:2

(continued from previous page)
high priest. The breastplate, which was worn by the high priest alone, went on top of the ephod or upper garment. It was square and contained twelve inset precious stones, one for each of the twelve tribes. It extended from the waist to the shoulders and was connected at the shoulders by a gem. The robe was sleeveless under the ephod and came down to the ankles.

🔑 **25:8, 9** The Lord commanded Moses to build a sanctuary. It was to be a tabernacle or moveable tent which would be suitable for Israel's nomadic lifestyle. The Levites would have responsibility for it (Num. 18:2–4). It was to be a dwelling place for the Lord among His people (v. 8) and a depository for the tables of the law or testimony, hence it was called "the tabernacle of testimony" (Ex. 38:21). Also, it was known as the "tent of meeting" (Ex. 40:34), because the Lord met His people there. Its general designation was "the house of the LORD" (Ex. 34:26), and it was to be filled with "the glory of the LORD" (Ex. 40:36–38) and by His presence. From there He would lead the children of Israel on their journey.

and thou shalt make a golden crown to the border thereof round about.

26 And thou shalt make for it four rings of gold, and put the rings in the four corners that *are* on the four feet thereof.

27 Over against the border shall the rings be for places of the staves to bear the table.

28 And thou shalt make the staves *of* shittim wood, and overlay them with gold, that the table may be borne with them.

29 And thou shalt make [a]the dishes thereof, and spoons[3709] thereof, and covers thereof, and bowls thereof, [I]to cover withal: *of* pure gold shalt thou make them.

30 And thou shalt set upon the table [a]shewbread[6440][3899] before me alway.[8548]

31 [a]And thou shalt make a candlestick *of* pure gold: *of* beaten work shall the candlestick be made: his shaft,[3409] and his branches, his bowls, his knops, and his flowers, shall be of the same.

32 And six branches[7070] shall come out of the sides of it; three branches of the candlestick out of the one side, and three branches of the candlestick out of the other side:

33 Three bowls[1375] made like unto almonds, *with* a knop and a flower in one branch; and three bowls made like almonds in the other branch, *with* a knop and a flower: so in the six branches that come out of the candlestick.

34 And in the candlestick *shall be* four bowls made like unto almonds, *with* their knops and their flowers.

35 And *there shall be* a knop under two branches of the same, and a knop under two branches of the same, and a knop under two branches of the same, according to the six branches that proceed[3318] out of the candlestick.

36 Their knops and their branches shall be of the same: all it *shall be* one beaten work *of* pure gold.

37 And thou shalt make the seven lamps[5216] thereof: and [a]they shall [I]light the lamps thereof, that they may [b]give light over against [II]it.

29 [I]Or, *to pour out withal* [a]Ex. 37:16; Num. 4:7

30 [a]Lev. 24:5, 6

31 [a]Ex. 37:17; 1Kgs. 7:49; Zech. 4:2; Heb. 9:2; Rev. 1:12; 4:5

37 [I]Or, *cause to ascend* [II]Hebr. *the face of it* [a]Ex. 27:21; 30:8; Lev. 24:3, 4; 2Chr. 13:11 [b]Num. 8:2

40 [I]Hebr. *which thou wast caused to see* [a]Ex. 26:30; Num. 8:4; 1Chr. 28:11, 19; Acts 7:44; Heb. 8:5

1 [I]Hebr. *the work of a cunning workman,* or, *embroiderer* [a]Ex. 36:8

7 [a]Ex. 36:14

38 And the tongs thereof, and the snuffdishes thereof, *shall be of* pure gold.

39 *Of* a talent of pure gold shall he make it, with all these vessels.

40 And [a]look[7200] that thou make *them* after their pattern, [I]which was shewed[7200] thee in the mount.

The Tabernacle

26 Moreover [a]thou shalt make[6213] the tabernacle[4908] *with* ten curtains *of* fine twined linen, and blue, and purple, and scarlet: *with* cherubims[3742] [I]of cunning[2803] work shalt thou make them.

2 The length of one curtain *shall be* eight and twenty cubits, and the breadth of one curtain four cubits: and every one of the curtains shall have one measure.

3 The five curtains shall be coupled together one[802] to another;[269] and *other* five curtains *shall be* coupled one to another.

4 And thou shalt make loops of blue upon the edge[8193] of the one curtain from the selvedge[7098] in the coupling; and likewise shalt thou make in the uttermost edge of *another* curtain, in the coupling of the second.

5 Fifty loops shalt thou make in the one curtain, and fifty loops shalt thou make in the edge of the curtain that *is* in the coupling of the second; that the loops may take hold one of another.

6 And thou shalt make fifty taches[7165] of gold, and couple the curtains together with the taches: and it shall be one tabernacle.

7 And [a]thou shalt make curtains *of* goats' *hair* to be a covering[168] upon the tabernacle: eleven curtains shalt thou make.

8 The length of one curtain *shall be* thirty cubits, and the breadth of one curtain four cubits: and the eleven curtains *shall be all* of one measure.

9 And thou shalt couple five curtains by themselves, and six curtains by themselves, and shalt double the sixth curtain in the forefront of the tabernacle.[168]

10 And thou shalt make fifty loops on the edge of the one curtain *that is* outmost in the coupling, and fifty loops in the edge of the curtain which coupleth the second.

11 And thou shalt make fifty taches of brass, and put the taches into the loops, and couple the [I]tent[168] together, that it may be one.

12 And the remnant that remaineth of the curtains of the tent, the half curtain that remaineth, shall hang over the backside of the tabernacle.

13 And a cubit on the one side, and a cubit on the other side [I]of that which remaineth in the length of the curtains of the tent, it shall hang over the sides of the tabernacle on this side and on that side, to cover[3680] it.

14 And [a]thou shalt make a covering for the tent *of* rams' skins dyed red, and a covering above *of* badgers' skins.

15 And thou shalt make boards for the tabernacle *of* shittim wood standing up.

16 Ten cubits *shall be* the length of a board, and a cubit and a half *shall be* the breadth of one board.

17 Two [I]tenons[3027] *shall there be* in one board, set in order one against another: thus shalt thou make for all the boards of the tabernacle.

18 And thou shalt make the boards for the tabernacle, twenty boards on the south side southward.

19 And thou shalt make forty sockets[134] of silver under the twenty boards; two sockets under one board for his two tenons, and two sockets under another board for his two tenons.

20 And for the second side of the tabernacle on the north side *there shall be* twenty boards:

21 And their forty sockets *of* silver; two sockets under one board, and two sockets under another board.

22 And for the sides of the tabernacle westward thou shalt make six boards.

23 And two boards shalt thou make for the corners of the tabernacle in the two sides.

24 And they shall be [I]coupled together[8382] beneath, and they shall be coupled together above the head[7218] of it unto one ring: thus shall it be for them both; they shall be for the two corners.

25 And they shall be eight boards, and their sockets *of* silver, sixteen sockets; two sockets under one board, and two sockets under another board.

26 And thou shalt make bars *of* shittim wood; five for the boards of the one side of the tabernacle,

27 And five bars for the boards of the other side of the tabernacle, and five bars for the boards of the side of the tabernacle, for the two sides westward.

28 And the middle bar in the midst of the boards shall reach from end to end.

29 And thou shalt overlay the boards with gold, and make their rings *of* gold *for* places for the bars: and thou shalt overlay the bars with gold.

30 And thou shalt rear up the tabernacle [a]according to the fashion[4941] thereof which was shewed thee in the mount.

🗝 31 And [a]thou shalt make a vail *of* blue, and purple, and scarlet, and fine twined linen of cunning work: with cherubims shall it be made:

11 IOr, *covering*

13 IHebr. *in the remainder,* or, *surplusage*

14 [a]Ex. 36:19

17 IHebr. *hands*

24 IHebr. *twinned*

30 [a]Ex. 25:9, 40; 27:8; Acts 7:44; Heb. 8:5

31 [a]Ex. 36:35; Lev. 16:2; 2Chr. 3:14; Matt. 27:51; Heb. 9:3

🗝 **26:31–35** The vail, literally "a separation," was hung between the Holy of Holies and the Holy Place. Its function was to separate all men, even the priests, from the presence of God. Only one man, the high priest, went beyond that vail and he was permitted to do so only once a year, on the Day of Atonement (Lev. 16:1–19). His purpose was to take the blood of the bull and the goat to atone for his sins and the sins of the people. The meaning was clear: man was separated from God by reason of sin and could approach Him only through blood which was presented by a priest. When Jesus died on the cross, the vail hanging in the temple was torn in two (Matt. 27:51). Jesus went beyond that vail (Heb. 9:12, 24) as high priest (Heb. 9:11; 7:23–28) taking His own blood (Heb. 9:12), and making full atonement (Heb. 10:10, 12).

32 And thou shalt hang it upon four pillars of shittim *wood* overlaid with gold: their hooks *shall be of* gold, upon the four sockets of silver.

33 And thou shalt hang up the vail under the taches, that thou mayest bring in thither within the vail [a]the ark[727] of the testimony:[5715] and the vail shall divide unto you between [b]the holy[6944] *place* and the most holy.

34 And [a]thou shalt put the mercy seat[3727] upon the ark of the testimony in the most holy *place.*

35 And [a]thou shalt set the table without the vail, and [b]the candlestick over against the table on the side of the tabernacle toward the south: and thou shalt put the table on the north side.

36 And [a]thou shalt make an hanging[4539] for the door of the tent, *of* blue, and purple, and scarlet, and fine twined linen, wrought with needlework.

37 And thou shalt make for the hanging [a]five pillars *of* shittim *wood,* and overlay them with gold, *and* their hooks *shall be of* gold: and thou shalt cast five sockets of brass for them.

The Altar of Burnt Offering

27 And thou shalt make[6213] [a]an altar[4196] *of* shittim wood, five cubits long,[753] and five cubits broad; the altar shall be foursquare: and the height thereof *shall be* three cubits.

2 And thou shalt make the horns[7161] of it upon the four corners thereof: his horns shall be of the same: and [a]thou shalt overlay it with brass.

3 And thou shalt make his pans to receive his ashes, and his shovels, and his basons,[4219] and his fleshhooks, and his firepans: all the vessels thereof thou shalt make *of* brass.

4 And thou shalt make for it a grate of network *of* brass; and upon the net shalt thou make four brasen rings in the four corners thereof.

5 And thou shalt put it under the compass of the altar beneath, that the net may be even to the midst of the altar.

6 And thou shalt make staves for the altar, staves *of* shittim wood, and overlay them with brass.

7 And the staves shall be put into the rings, and the staves shall be upon the two sides of the altar, to bear[5375] it.

8 Hollow with boards shalt thou make it: [a]as [I]it was shewed[7200] thee in the mount, so shall they make *it.*

The Enclosure of the Tabernacle

9 And [a]thou shalt make the court of the tabernacle:[4908] for the south side southward *there shall be* hangings for the court *of* fine twined linen of an hundred cubits long for one side:

10 And the twenty pillars thereof and their twenty sockets *shall be of* brass; the hooks of the pillars and their fillets[2838] *shall be of* silver.

11 And likewise for the north side in length *there shall be* hangings of an hundred *cubits* long, and his twenty pillars and their twenty sockets *of* brass; the hooks of the pillars and their fillets *of* silver.

12 And *for* the breadth of the court[2691] on the west side *shall be* hangings of fifty cubits: their pillars ten, and their sockets ten.

13 And the breadth of the court on the east side eastward *shall be* fifty cubits.

14 The hangings of one side *of the gate shall be* fifteen cubits: their pillars three, and their sockets three.

15 And on the other side *shall be* hangings fifteen *cubits:* their pillars three, and their sockets three.

16 And for the gate of the court *shall be* an hanging of twenty cubits, *of* blue, and purple, and scarlet, and fine twined linen, wrought with needlework: *and* their pillars *shall be* four, and their sockets four.

17 All the pillars round about the court *shall be* filleted[2836] with silver; their

33 [a]Ex. 25:16; 40:21 [b]Lev. 16:2; Heb. 9:2, 3
34 [a]Ex. 25:21; 40:20; Heb. 9:5
35 [a]Ex. 40:22; Heb. 9:2 [b]Ex. 40:24
36 [a]Ex. 36:37
37 [a]Ex. 36:38
1 [a]Ex. 38:1; Ezek. 43:13
2 [a]Num. 16:38
8 [I]Hebr. *he showed* [a]Ex. 25:40; 26:30
9 [a]Ex. 38:9

hooks *shall be of* silver, and their sockets *of* brass.
18 The length of the court *shall be*
an hundred cubits, and the breadth [I]fifty
every where, and the height five cubits *of*
fine twined linen, and their sockets *of*
brass.
19 All the vessels of the tabernacle
in all the service[5656] thereof, and all the
pins thereof, and all the pins of the court,
shall be of brass.

Taking Care of the Lamp

20 And [a]thou shalt command[6680] the
children[1121] of Israel, that they bring thee
pure[2134] oil[8081] olive beaten for the
light,[3974] to cause[5927] the lamp[5216] [I]to
burn[5927] always.[8548]
21 In the tabernacle[168] of the
congregation[4150] [a]without the vail, which
is before the testimony,[5715] [b]Aaron and
his sons[1121] shall order it from evening to
morning before the LORD: [c]*it shall be* a
statute[2708] for ever[5769] unto their generations[1755] on the behalf of the children of
Israel.

The Priests' Clothes

28 🔑 And take thou unto thee
[a]Aaron thy brother, and his
sons[1121] with him, from among the children[1121] of Israel, that he may minister
unto me in the priest's office,[3547] *even*
Aaron, Nadab and Abihu, Eleazar and
Ithamar, Aaron's sons.
2 And [a]thou shalt make[6213] holy[6944]
garments for Aaron thy brother for
glory[3519] and for beauty.[8597]
3 And [a]thou shalt speak[1696] unto all
that are wise hearted,[2450,3820] [b]whom I
have filled with the spirit[7307] of wisdom,[2451] that they may make Aaron's garments to consecrate[6942] him, that he may
minister unto me in the priest's office.
4 And these *are* the garments which
they shall make; [a]a breastplate,[2833] and
[b]an ephod,[646] and [c]a robe, and [d]an broi-

18 [I]Hebr. *fifty by fifty*

20 [I]Hebr. *to ascend up* [a]Lev. 24:2

21 [a]Ex. 26:31, 33 [b]Ex. 30:8; 1Sam. 3:3; 2Chr. 13:11 [c]Ex. 28:43; 29:9, 28; Lev. 3:17; 16:34; 24:9; Num. 18:23; 19:21; 1Sam. 30:25

1 [a]Num. 18:7; Heb. 5:1, 4

2 [a]Ex. 29:5, 29; 31:10; 39:1, 2; Lev. 8:7, 30; Num. 20:26, 28

3 [a]Ex. 31:6; 36:1 [b]Ex. 31:3; 35:30, 31

4 [a]Ex. 28:15 [b]Ex. 28:6 [c]Ex. 28:31 [d]Ex. 28:39

6 [a]Ex. 39:2

8 [I]Or, *embroidered*

12 [a]Ex. 28:29; 39:7 [b]Josh. 4:7; Zech. 6:14

15 [a]Ex. 39:8

dered coat, a mitre,[4701] and a girdle:[73]
and they shall make holy garments for
Aaron thy brother, and his sons, that he
may minister unto me in the priest's office.
5 And they shall take gold, and
blue, and purple, and scarlet, and fine
linen.
6 [a]And they shall make the ephod
of gold, *of* blue, and *of* purple, *of* scarlet, and fine twined linen, with cunning
work.
7 It shall have the two shoulderpieces
thereof joined at the two edges thereof;
and *so* it shall be joined together.
8 And the [I]curious girdle[2805] of the
ephod, which *is* upon it, shall be of the
same, according to the work thereof; *even*
of gold, *of* blue, and purple, and scarlet,
and fine twined linen.
9 And thou shalt take two onyx
stones, and grave on them the names of
the children of Israel:
10 Six of their names on one stone,
and *the other* six names of the rest[3498]
on the other stone, according to their
birth.[8435]
11 With the work of an engraver in
stone, *like* the engravings of a signet,
shalt thou engrave the two stones with
the names of the children of Israel: thou
shalt make them to be set in ouches[4865]
of gold.
12 And thou shalt put the two stones
upon the shoulders of the ephod *for*
stones of memorial[2146] unto the children
of Israel: and [a]Aaron shall bear[5375] their
names before the LORD upon his two
shoulders [b]for a memorial.
13 And thou shalt make ouches *of*
gold;
14 And two chains *of* pure[2889] gold
at the ends; *of* wreathen[5688] work shalt
thou make them, and fasten the wreathen chains to the ouches.
15 And [a]thou shalt make the breastplate of judgment[4941] with cunning work;
after the work of the ephod thou shalt
make it; *of* gold, *of* blue, and *of* purple,

🔑 **28:1–5** See note on Exodus 32:25–29, concerning the priesthood.

and *of* scarlet, and *of* fine twined linen, shalt thou make it.

16 Foursquare it shall be *being* doubled; a span *shall be* the length thereof, and a span *shall be* the breadth thereof.

17 [a]And thou shalt [I]set in it settings of stones, *even* four rows of stones: *the first* row *shall be* a [II]sardius, a topaz, and a carbuncle: *this shall be* the first row.

18 And the second row *shall be* an emerald, a sapphire, and a diamond.

19 And the third row a ligure, an agate, and an amethyst.

20 And the fourth row a beryl, and an onyx, and a jasper: they shall be set in gold in their [I]inclosings.

21 And the stones shall be with the names of the children of Israel, twelve, according to their names, *like* the engravings of a signet; every one with his name shall they be according to the twelve tribes.[7626]

22 And thou shalt make upon the breastplate chains at the ends *of* wreathen work *of* pure gold.

23 And thou shalt make upon the breastplate two rings of gold, and shalt put the two rings on the two ends of the breastplate.

24 And thou shalt put the two wreathen *chains* of gold in the two rings *which are* on the ends of the breastplate.

25 And *the other* two ends of the two wreathen *chains* thou shalt fasten in the two ouches, and put *them* on the shoulderpieces of the ephod before it.

26 And thou shalt make two rings of gold, and thou shalt put them upon the two ends of the breastplate in the border[8193] thereof, which *is* in the side of the ephod inward.[1004]

17 [I]Hebr. *fill in it fillings of stone* [II]Or, *ruby* [a]Ex. 39:10-14

20 [I]Hebr. *fillings*

29 [a]Ex. 28:12

30 [a]Lev. 8:8; Num. 27:21; Deut. 33:8; 1Sam. 28:6; Ezra 2:63; Neh. 7:65

31 [a]Ex. 39:22

33 [I]Or, *skirts*

27 And two *other* rings of gold thou shalt make, and shalt put them on the two sides of the ephod underneath, toward the forepart thereof, over against the *other* coupling thereof, above the curious girdle of the ephod.

28 And they shall bind the breastplate by the rings thereof unto the rings of the ephod with a lace of blue, that *it* may be above the curious girdle of the ephod, and that the breastplate be not loosed from the ephod.

29 And Aaron shall bear the names of the children of Israel in the breastplate of judgment upon his heart, when he goeth in unto the holy *place,* [a]for a memorial before the LORD continually.[8548]

30 And [a]thou shalt put in the breastplate of judgment the Urim[224] and the Thummim;[8550] and they shall be upon Aaron's heart, when he goeth in before the LORD: and Aaron shall bear the judgment of the children of Israel upon his heart before the LORD continually.

31 And [a]thou shalt make the robe of the ephod all[3632] *of* blue.

32 And there shall be an hole[6310] in the top[7218] of it, in the midst thereof: it shall have a binding[8193] of woven work round about the hole of it, as it were the hole of a habergeon,[8473] that it be not rent.

33 And *beneath* upon the [I]hem of it thou shalt make pomegranates *of* blue, and *of* purple, and *of* scarlet, round about the hem thereof; and bells of gold between them round about:

34 A golden bell and a pomegranate, a golden bell and a pomegranate, upon the hem of the robe round about.

28:30 This is the first mention of these sacred objects called the "Urim and Thummim." They were used by the priests to receive divine messages and were kept in the high priest's breastplate. The mention of the ephod in connection with simple oracles (1 Sam. 23:6, 9–12) suggests that at times these objects may have been associated with the priest's ephod. No one knows what the Urim and Thummim looked like or how they worked, but it appears that they provided only yes or no answers. Sometimes there was no answer given at all. This would help explain King Saul's inability to get an answer from God on two different occasions (1 Sam. 14:36, 37; 28:6). The Urim and Thummim are not mentioned in the Old Testament between the early monarchy and post-exilic times. This was the period of the prophets, when God revealed Himself much more fully than in the simple answers to questions posed by priests. Quite possibly the lack of description of the Urim and Thummim is deliberate, in order to prevent copies from being made.

35 And it shall be upon Aaron to minister:[8334] and his sound shall be heard[8085] when he goeth in unto the holy *place* before the LORD, and when he cometh out, that he die not.

36 And [a]thou shalt make a plate *of* pure gold, and grave upon it, *like* the engravings of a signet, HOLINESS[6944] TO THE LORD.

37 And thou shalt put it on a blue lace, that it may be upon the mitre; upon the forefront of the mitre it shall be.

38 And it shall be upon Aaron's forehead, that Aaron may [a]bear the iniquity[5771] of the holy things,[6944] which the children of Israel shall hallow[6942] in all their holy gifts; and it shall be always[8548] upon his forehead, that they may be [b]accepted[7522] before the LORD.

39 And thou shalt embroider the coat of fine linen, and thou shalt make the mitre *of* fine linen, and thou shalt make the girdle[73] *of* needlework.

40 [a]And for Aaron's sons thou shalt make coats, and thou shalt make for them girdles, and bonnets shalt thou make for them, for glory and for beauty.

41 And thou shalt put them upon Aaron thy brother, and his sons with him; and shalt [a]anoint[4886] them, and [I][b]consecrate[3027,4390] them, and sanctify[6942] them, that they may minister unto me in the priest's office.

42 And thou shalt make them [a]linen breeches to cover[3680] [I]their nakedness;[6172] from the loins even unto the thighs[3409] they shall [II]reach:

43 And they shall be upon Aaron, and upon his sons, when they come in unto the tabernacle[168] of the congregation,[4150] or when they come near[5066] [a]unto the altar[4196] to minister in the holy *place;* that they [b]bear[5375] not iniquity, and die:[4191] [c]*it shall be* a statute[2708] for ever unto him and his seed[2233] after him.

The Dedication of Aaron And His Sons

29 And this *is* the thing[1697] that thou shalt do unto them to hallow[6942] them, to minister unto me in the priest's office: [a]Take one young bullock, and two rams without blemish,[8549]

2 And [a]unleavened bread, and cakes unleavened tempered with oil,[8081] and wafers unleavened anointed with oil: *of* wheaten[2406] flour shalt thou make them.

3 And thou shalt put them into one basket, and bring them in the basket, with the bullock and the two rams.

4 And Aaron and his sons thou shalt bring[7126] unto the door of the tabernacle[168] of the congregation,[4150] [a]and shalt wash[7364] them with water.

5 [a]And thou shalt take the garments, and put upon Aaron the coat, and the robe of the ephod, and the ephod, and the breastplate, and gird him with [b]the curious girdle[2805] of the ephod:

6 [a]And thou shalt put the mitre upon his head,[7218] and put the holy[6944] crown[5145] upon the mitre.[4701]

7 Then shalt thou take the anointing[4888] [a]oil, and pour *it* upon his head, and anoint[4886] him.

8 And [a]thou shalt bring his sons, and put coats upon them.

9 And thou shalt gird them with girdles,[73] Aaron and his sons, and [I]put the bonnets on them: and [a]the priest's office[3550] shall be theirs for a perpetual[5769] statute:[2708] and thou shalt [II][b]consecrate[3027,4390] Aaron and his sons.

10 And thou shalt cause a bullock to be brought[7126] before the tabernacle of the congregation: and [a]Aaron and his sons shall put their hands[3027] upon the head of the bullock.

11 And thou shalt kill[7819] the bullock before the LORD, *by* the door of the tabernacle of the congregation.

12 And thou [a]shalt take of the blood[1818] of the bullock, and put *it* upon [b]the horns of the altar[4196] with thy finger, and pour[8210] all the blood beside the bottom[3247] of the altar.

13 And [a]thou shalt take all the fat that covereth[3680] the inwards,[7130] and [I]the caul *that is* above the liver, and the two kidneys, and the fat that *is* upon them, and burn[6999] *them* upon the altar.

36 [a]Ex. 39:30; Zech. 14:20

38 [a]Ex. 28:43; Lev. 10:17; 22:9; Num. 18:1; Isa. 53:11; Ezek. 4:4-6; John 1:29; Heb. 9:28; 1Pet. 2:24 [b]Lev. 1:4; 22:27; 23:11; Isa. 56:7

40 [a]Ex. 28:4; 39:27-29, 41; Ezek. 44:17, 18

41 [I]Hebr. *fill their hand* [a]Ex. 29:7; 30:30; 40:15; Lev. 10:7 [b]Ex. 29:9-35; Lev. 8:1-30; Heb. 7:28

42 [I]Hebr. *flesh of their nakedness* [II]Hebr. *be* [a]Ex. 39:28; Lev. 6:10; 16:4; Ezek. 44:18

43 [a]Ex. 20:26 [b]Lev. 5:1, 17; 20:19, 20; 22:9; Num. 9:13; 18:22 [c]Ex. 27:21; Lev. 17:7

1 [a]Lev. 8:2

2 [a]Lev. 2:4; 6:20-22

4 [a]Ex. 40:12; Lev. 8:6; Heb. 10:22

5 [a]Ex. 28:2; Lev. 8:7 [b]Ex. 28:8

6 [a]Lev. 8:9

7 [a]Ex. 28:41; 30:25; Lev. 8:12; 10:7; 21:10; Num. 35:25

8 [a]Lev. 8:13

9 [I]Hebr. *bind* [II]Hebr. *fill the hand of* [a]Num. 18:7 [b]Ex. 28:41; Lev. 8:22; Heb. 7:28

10 [a]Lev. 1:4; 8:14

12 [a]Lev. 8:15 [b]Ex. 27:2; 30:2

13 [I]It seems by anatomy, and the Hebrew doctors, to be *the midriff* [a]Lev. 3:3

14 But [a]the flesh[1320] of the bullock, and his skin,[5785] and his dung, shalt thou burn with fire without the camp:[4264] it *is* a sin offering.[2403]

15 [a]Thou shalt also take one ram; and Aaron and his sons shall [b]put their hands upon the head of the ram.

16 And thou shalt slay the ram, and thou shalt take his blood, and sprinkle[2236] *it* round about upon the altar.

17 And thou shalt cut the ram in pieces, and wash the inwards of him, and his legs, and put *them* unto his pieces, and [I]unto his head.

18 And thou shalt burn the whole ram upon the altar: it *is* a burnt offering[5930] unto the LORD: it *is* a [a]sweet savour, an offering made by fire[801] unto the LORD.

19 [a]And thou shalt take the other ram; and Aaron and his sons shall put their hands upon the head of the ram.

20 Then shalt thou kill the ram, and take of his blood, and put *it* upon the tip of the right ear of Aaron, and upon the tip of the right ear of his sons, and upon the thumb of their right hand, and upon the great toe of their right foot, and sprinkle the blood upon the altar round about.

21 And thou shalt take of the blood that *is* upon the altar, and of [a]the anointing oil, and sprinkle *it* upon Aaron, and upon his garments, and upon his sons, and upon the garments of his sons with him: and [b]he shall be hallowed,[6942] and his garments, and his sons, and his sons' garments with him.

22 Also thou shalt take of the ram the fat and the rump, and the fat that covereth the inwards, and the caul *above* the liver, and the two kidneys, and the fat that *is* upon them, and the right shoulder; for it *is* a ram of consecration:[4394]

23 [a]And one loaf of bread, and one cake of oiled bread, and one wafer out of the basket of the unleavened bread that *is* before the LORD:

24 And thou shalt put all in the hands[3709] of Aaron, and in the hands of his sons; and shalt [I][a]wave[5130] them *for* a wave offering[8573] before the LORD.

14 [a]Lev. 4:11, 12, 21; Heb. 13:11
15 [a]Lev. 8:18 [b]Lev. 1:4-9
17 [I]Or, *upon*
18 [a]Gen. 8:21
19 [a]Ex. 29:3; Lev. 8:22
21 [a]Ex. 30:25, 31; Lev. 8:30 [b]Ex. 29:1; Heb. 9:22
23 [a]Lev. 8:26
24 [I]Or, *shake to and fro* [a]Lev. 7:30
25 [a]Lev. 8:28
26 [a]Lev. 8:29 [b]Ps. 99:6
27 [a]Lev. 7:31, 34; Num. 18:11, 18; Deut. 18:3
28 [a]Lev. 10:15 [b]Lev. 7:34
29 [a]Num. 20:26, 28 [b]Num. 18:8; 35:25
30 [I]Hebr. *he of his sons* [a]Num. 20:28 [b]Lev. 8:35; 9:1, 8
31 [a]Lev. 8:31
32 [a]Matt. 12:4
33 [a]Lev. 10:14, 15, 17 [b]Lev. 22:10
34 [a]Lev. 8:32

25 [a]And thou shalt receive them of their hands, and burn *them* upon the altar for a burnt offering, for a sweet savour before the LORD: it *is* an offering made by fire unto the LORD.

26 And thou shalt take [a]the breast of the ram of Aaron's consecration, and wave it *for* a wave offering before the LORD: and [b]it shall be thy part.

27 And thou shalt sanctify[6942] the [a]breast of the wave offering, and the shoulder of the heave offering,[8641] which is waved, and which is heaved up,[7311] of the ram of the consecration, *even* of *that* which *is* for Aaron, and of *that* which is for his sons:

28 And it shall be Aaron's and his sons'[1121] [a]by a statute[2706] for ever[5769] from the children[1121] of Israel: for it *is* an heave offering: and [b]it shall be an heave offering from the children of Israel of the sacrifice[2077] of their peace offerings,[8002] *even* their heave offering unto the LORD.

29 And the holy garments of Aaron [a]shall be his sons' after him, [b]to be anointed[4888] therein, and to be consecrated in them.

30 *And* [I][a]that son that is priest[3548] in his stead shall put them on [b]seven days, when he cometh into the tabernacle of the congregation to minister[8334] in the holy *place*.

31 And thou shalt take the ram of the consecration, and [a]seethe his flesh in the holy[6918] place.

32 And Aaron and his sons shall eat the flesh of the ram, and the [a]bread that *is* in the basket, *by* the door of the tabernacle of the congregation.

33 And [a]they shall eat those things wherewith the atonement was made,[3722] to consecrate *and* to sanctify[6942] them: [b]but a stranger[2114] shall not eat *thereof*, because they *are* holy.

34 And if ought of the flesh of the consecrations, or of the bread, remain[3498] unto the morning, then [a]thou shalt burn[8313] the remainder[3498] with fire: it shall not be eaten, because it *is* holy.

35 And thus shalt thou do[6213] unto

Aaron, and to his sons, according to all *things* which I have commanded[6680] thee: [a]seven days shalt thou consecrate them.

36 And thou shalt [a]offer every day[3117] a bullock *for* a sin offering for atonement:[3725] and thou shalt cleanse[2398] the altar, when thou hast made an atonement[3722] for it, [b]and thou shalt anoint it, to sanctify it.

37 Seven days thou shalt make an atonement for the altar, and sanctify it; [a]and it shall be an altar most holy:[6942] [b]whatsoever toucheth[5060] the altar shall be holy.

Two Lambs Every Day

38 Now this *is that* which thou shalt offer upon the altar; [a]two lambs of the first year [b]day by day continually.[8548]

39 The one lamb thou shalt offer [a]in the morning; and the other lamb thou shalt offer at even:

40 And with the one lamb a tenth deal of flour mingled with the fourth part of an hin of beaten oil; and the fourth part of an hin of wine *for* a drink offering.[5262]

41 And the other lamb thou shalt [a]offer at even, and shalt do thereto according to the meat offering[4503] of the morning, and according to the drink offering thereof, for a sweet savour, an offering made by fire unto the LORD.

42 *This shall be* [a]a continual burnt offering throughout your generations[1755] *at* the door of the tabernacle of the congregation before the LORD: [b]where I will meet you, to speak there unto thee.

43 And there I will meet with the children of Israel, and [I]*the tabernacle* [a]shall be sanctified[6942] by my glory.[3519]

44 And I will sanctify the tabernacle of the congregation, and the altar: I will [a]sanctify also both Aaron and his sons, to minister to me in the priest's office.

45 And [a]I will dwell among the children of Israel, and will be their God.[430]

46 And they shall know[3045] that [a]I *am* the LORD their God, that brought them forth out of the land[776] of Egypt, that I may dwell[7931] among them: I *am* the LORD their God.

The Incense Altar

30 And thou shalt make[6213] [a]an altar[4196] [b]to burn incense[7004] upon: *of* shittim wood shalt thou make it.

2 A cubit *shall be* the length thereof, and a cubit the breadth thereof; foursquare shall it be: and two cubits *shall be* the height thereof: the horns thereof *shall be* of the same.

3 And thou shalt overlay it with pure[2889] gold, the [I]top thereof, and the [II]sides thereof round about, and the horns thereof; and thou shalt make unto it a crown of gold round about.

4 And two golden rings shalt thou make to it under the crown of it, by the two [I]corners thereof, upon the two sides of it shalt thou make *it;* and they shall be for places for the staves to bear[5375] it withal.

5 And thou shalt make the staves *of* shittim wood, and overlay them with gold.

6 And thou shalt put it before the vail that *is* by the ark[727] of the testimony,[5715] before the [a]mercy seat[3727] that *is* over the testimony, where I will meet with thee.

7 And Aaron shall burn[6999] thereon [I][a]sweet incense every morning: when [b]he dresseth the lamps,[5216] he shall burn incense upon it.

8 And when Aaron [I]lighteth[5927] the lamps [II][a]at even, he shall burn incense upon it, a perpetual[8548] incense before the LORD throughout your generations.[1755]

9 Ye shall offer[5927] no [a]strange[2114] incense thereon, nor burnt sacrifice,[5930] nor meat offering,[4503] neither shall ye pour drink offering[5262] thereon.

10 And [a]Aaron shall make an atonement[3722] upon the horns of it once in a year with the blood[1818] of the sin offering[2403] of atonements:[3725] once in the year shall he make atonement upon it

---

35 [a]Ex. 40:12; Lev. 8:33-35
36 [a]Heb. 10:11 [b]Ex. 30:26, 28, 29; 40:10
37 [a]Ex. 40:10 [b]Ex. 30:29; Matt. 23:19
38 [a]Num. 28:3; 1Chr. 16:40; 2Chr. 2:4; 13:11; 31:3; Ezra 3:3 [b]Dan. 9:27; 12:11
39 [a]2Kgs. 16:15; Ezek. 46:13-15
41 [a]1Kgs. 18:29, 36; 2Kgs. 16:15; Ezra 9:4, 5; Ps. 141:2; Dan. 9:21
42 [a]Ex. 29:38; 30:8; Num. 28:6; Dan. 8:11-13 [b]Ex. 25:22; 30:6, 36; Num. 17:4
43 [I]Or, Israel [a]Ex. 40:34; 1Kgs. 8:11; 2Chr. 5:14; 7:1-3; Ezek. 43:5; Hag. 2:7, 9; Mal. 3:1
44 [a]Lev. 21:15; 22:9, 16
45 [a]Ex. 25:8; Lev. 26:12; Zech. 2:10; John 14:17, 23; 2Cor. 6:16; Rev. 21:3
46 [a]Ex. 20:2
1 [a]Ex. 37:25; 40:5 [b]Ex. 30:7, 8, 10; Lev. 4:7, 18; Rev. 8:3
3 [I]Hebr. *roof* [II]Hebr. *walls*
4 [I]Hebr. *ribs*
6 [a]Ex. 25:21, 22
7 [I]Hebr. *incense of spices* [a]Ex. 30:34; 1Sam. 2:28; 1Chr. 23:13; Luke 1:9 [b]Ex. 27:21
8 [I]Or, *setteth up* [II]Hebr. *between two evens* [a]Ex. 12:6
9 [a]Lev. 10:1
10 [a]Lev. 16:18; 23:27

throughout your generations: it *is* most holy[6944] unto the LORD.

A Tax for the Tent

11 And the LORD spake unto Moses, saying,

12 [a]When thou takest the sum[7218] of the children[1121] of Israel after [I]their number, then shall they give every man[376] [b]a ransom[3724] for his soul[5315] unto the LORD, when thou numberest[6485] them; that there be no [c]plague[5063] among them, when *thou* numberest them.

13 [a]This they shall give, every one that passeth[5674] among them that are numbered, half a shekel after the shekel of the sanctuary: ([b]a shekel *is* twenty gerahs:1626) [c]an half shekel *shall be* the offering[8641] of the LORD.

14 Every one that passeth among them that are numbered, from twenty years old and above, shall give an offering unto the LORD.

15 The [a]rich shall not [I]give more, and the poor shall not [II]give less than half a shekel, when *they* give an offering unto the LORD, to make an [b]atonement for your souls.

16 And thou shalt take the atonement[3725] money of the children of Israel, and [a]shalt appoint it for the service[5656] of the tabernacle[168] of the congregation;[4150] that it may be [b]a memorial[2146] unto the children of Israel before the LORD, to make an atonement for your souls.

The Brass Bason

17 And the LORD spake unto Moses, saying,

18 [a]Thou shalt also make a laver3595 *of* brass, and his foot *also of* brass, to wash *withal:* and thou shalt [b]put it between the tabernacle of the congregation and the altar, and thou shalt put water therein.

19 For Aaron and his sons[1121] [a]shall wash[7364] their hands[3027] and their feet thereat:

20 When they go into the tabernacle of the congregation, they shall wash with water, that they die not; or when they come near[5066] to the altar to minister,[8334] to burn offering made by fire unto the LORD:

21 So they shall wash their hands and their feet, that they die not: and [a]it shall be a statute[2706] for ever[5769] to them, *even* to him and to his seed[2233] throughout their generations.

How to Make the Oil

22 Moreover the LORD spake unto Moses, saying,

23 Take thou also unto thee [a]principal[7218] spices, of pure [b]myrrh4753 five hundred *shekels,* and of sweet cinnamon half so much, *even* two hundred and fifty *shekels,* and of sweet [c]calamus7070 two hundred and fifty *shekels,*

24 And of [a]cassia6916 five hundred *shekels,* after the shekel of the sanctuary, and of oil[8081] olive an [b]hin:

25 And thou shalt make it an oil of holy ointment,[4888] an ointment compound after the art of the [I]apothecary: it shall be an [a]holy anointing oil.

26 [a]And thou shalt anoint[4886] the tabernacle of the congregation therewith, and the ark of testimony,

27 And the table and all his vessels, and the candlestick and his vessels, and the altar of incense,

28 And the altar of burnt offering with all his vessels, and the laver and his foot.

29 And thou shalt sanctify[6942] them, that they may be most holy: [a]whatsoever toucheth[5060] them shall be holy.

30 [a]And thou shalt anoint Aaron and his sons, and consecrate[6942] them, that *they* may minister unto me in the priest's office.

31 And thou shalt speak unto the children of Israel, saying, This shall be an holy anointing oil unto me throughout your generations.

32 Upon man's[120] flesh[1320] shall it not be poured, neither shall ye make *any other* like it, after the composition of

---

12 [I]Hebr. *them that are to be numbered* [a]Ex. 38:25; Num. 1:2, 5; 26:2; 2Sam. 24:2 [b]Num. 31:50; Job 33:24; 36:18; Ps. 49:7; Matt. 20:28; Mark 10:45; 1Tim. 2:6; 1Pet. 1:18, 19 [c]2Sam. 24:15

13 [a]Matt. 17:24 [b]Lev. 27:25; Num. 3:47; Ezek. 45:12 [c]Ex. 38:26

15 [I]Hebr. *multiply* [II]Hebr. *diminish* [a]Job 34:19; Prov. 22:2; Eph. 6:9; Col. 3:25 [b]Ex. 30:12

16 [a]Ex. 38:25 [b]Num. 16:40

18 [a]Ex. 38:8; 1Kgs. 7:38 [b]Ex. 40:7, 30

19 [a]Ex. 40:31, 32; Ps. 26:6; Isa. 52:11; John 13:10; Heb. 10:22

21 [a]Ex. 28:43

23 [a]Song 4:14; Ezek. 27:22 [b]Ps. 45:8; Prov. 7:17 [c]Song 4:14; Jer. 6:20

24 [a]Ps. 45:8 [b]Ex. 29:40

25 [I]Or, *perfumer* [a]Ex. 37:29; Num. 35:25; Ps. 89:20; 133:2

26 [a]Ex. 40:9; Lev. 8:10; Num. 7:1

29 [a]Ex. 29:37

30 [a]Ex. 29:7-14; Lev. 8:12, 30

it: [a]it *is* holy, *and* it shall be holy unto you.

33 [a]Whosoever compoundeth *any* like it, or whosoever putteth *any* of it upon a stranger,[2114] [b]shall even be cut off[3772] from his people.[5971]

How to Make the Incense

34 And the LORD said unto Moses, [a]Take unto thee sweet spices, stacte,[5198] and onycha, and galbanum;[2464] *these* sweet spices with pure[2134] frankincense:[3828] of each shall there be a like *weight:*

35 And thou shalt make it a perfume,[7004] a confection[7545] [a]after the art of the apothecary, [I][b]tempered together,[4414] pure *and* holy:

36 And thou shalt beat[7833] *some* of it very small, and put of it before the testimony in the tabernacle of the congregation, [a]where I will meet with thee: [b]it shall be unto you most holy.

37 And *as for* the perfume which thou shalt make, [a]ye shall not make to yourselves according to the composition thereof: it shall be unto thee holy for the LORD.

38 [a]Whosoever shall make like unto that, to smell[7306] thereto, shall even be cut off from his people.

God Appoints the Builders

31 And the LORD spake[1696] unto Moses, saying,

2 [a]See,[7200] I have called by name Bezaleel the [b]son of Uri, the son of Hur, of the tribe[4294] of Judah:

3 And I have [a]filled him with the spirit[7307] of God,[430] in wisdom,[2451] and in understanding,[8394] and in knowledge,[1847] and in all manner of workmanship,[4399]

4 To devise[2803] cunning works,[4284] to work[6213] in gold, and in silver, and in brass,

5 And in cutting of stones, to set *them,* and in carving of timber, to work in all manner of workmanship.

6 And I, behold, I have given with him [a]Aholiab, the son of Ahisamach, of the tribe of Dan: and in the hearts[3820] of all that are [b]wise hearted[2450,3820] I have put wisdom, that they may make[6213] all that I have commanded[6680] thee;

7 [a]The tabernacle[168] of the congregation,[4150] and [b]the ark[727] of the testimony,[5715] and [c]the mercy seat[3727] that *is* thereupon, and all the [I]furniture of the tabernacle,

8 And [a]the table and his furniture, and [b]the pure candlestick with all his furniture, and the altar[4196] of incense,[7004]

9 And [a]the altar of burnt offering with all his furniture, and [b]the laver[3595] and his foot,

10 And [a]the cloths of service, and the holy[6944] garments for Aaron the priest,[3548] and the garments of his sons, to minister in the priest's office,

11 [a]And the anointing[4888] oil,[8081] and [b]sweet incense for the holy *place:* according to all that I have commanded thee shall they do.

Rest on the Seventh Day

12 And the LORD spake unto Moses, saying,

13 Speak[1696] thou also unto the children[1121] of Israel, saying, [a]Verily my sabbaths[7676] ye shall keep:[8104] for it *is* a sign[226] between me and you throughout your generations;[1755] that *ye* may know[3045] that I *am* the LORD that doth sanctify[6942] you.

14 [a]Ye shall keep the sabbath therefore; for it *is* holy unto you: every one that defileth[2490] it shall surely be put to death: for [b]whosoever doeth *any* work therein, that soul[5315] shall be cut off[3772] from among his people.[5971]

15 [a]Six days may work be done;[6213] but in the [b]seventh *is* the sabbath of rest,[7677] [I]holy to the LORD: whosoever doeth *any* work in the sabbath day, he shall surely be put to death.

16 Wherefore the children of Israel shall keep the sabbath, to observe[6213] the sabbath throughout their generations, *for* a perpetual[5769] covenant.[1285]

---

32 [a]Ex. 30:25, 37

33 [a]Ex. 30:38 [b]Gen. 17:14; Ex. 12:15; Lev. 7:20, 21

34 [a]Ex. 25:6; 37:29

35 [I]Hebr. *salted* [a]Ex. 30:25 [b]Lev. 2:13

36 [a]Ex. 29:42; Lev. 16:2 [b]Ex. 29:37; 30:32; Lev. 2:3

37 [a]Ex. 30:32

38 [a]Ex. 30:33

2 [a]Ex. 35:30; 36:1 [b]1Chr. 2:20

3 [a]Ex. 35:31; 1Kgs. 7:14

6 [a]Ex. 35:34 [b]Ex. 28:3; 35:10, 35; 36:1

7 [I]Hebr. *vessels* [a]Ex. 36:8 [b]Ex. 37:1 [c]Ex. 37:6

8 [a]Ex. 37:10 [b]Ex. 37:17

9 [a]Ex. 38:1 [b]Ex. 38:8

10 [a]Ex. 39:1, 41; Num. 4:5-15

11 [a]Ex. 30:25, 31; 37:29 [b]Ex. 30:34; 37:29

13 [a]Lev. 19:3, 30; 26:2; Ezek. 20:12, 20; 44:24

14 [a]Ex. 20:8; Deut. 5:12; Ezek. 20:12 [b]Ex. 35:2; Num. 15:35

15 [I]Hebr. *holiness* [a]Ex. 20:9 [b]Gen. 2:2; Ex. 16:23; 20:10

17 It *is* [a]a sign between me and the children of Israel for ever:[5769] for [b]*in* six days the LORD made[6213] heaven[8064] and earth,[776] and on the seventh day he rested,[7673] and was refreshed.

18 And he gave unto Moses, when he had made an end[3615] of communing[1696] with him upon mount Sinai, [a]two tables of testimony, tables of stone, written with the finger of God.

The Golden Calf

32 And when the people[5971] saw[7200] that Moses [a]delayed to come down out of the mount, the people gathered themselves together[6950] unto Aaron, and said unto him, [b]Up, make us gods,[430] which shall [c]go before us; for *as for* this Moses, the man[376] that brought us up[5927] out of the land[776] of Egypt, we wot[3045] not what is become of him.

2 And Aaron said unto them, Break off[6561] the [a]golden earrings, which *are* in the ears of your wives, of your sons, and of your daughters, and bring *them* unto me.

3 And all the people brake off the golden earrings which *were* in their ears, and brought *them* unto Aaron.

4 [a]And he received *them* at their hand,[3027] and fashioned it with a graving tool,[2747] after he had made it a molten[4541] calf: and they said, These *be* thy gods, O Israel, which brought thee up out of the land of Egypt.

5 And when Aaron saw *it,* he built an altar[4196] before it; and Aaron made [a]proclamation,[7121] and said, To morrow *is* a feast[2282] to the LORD.

6 And they rose up early on the morrow, and offered[5927] burnt offerings,[5930] and brought[5066] peace offerings;[8002] and the [a]people sat down to eat and to drink, and rose up to play.

7 And the LORD[3068] said[1696] unto Moses, [a]Go, get thee down; for thy people, which thou broughtest out of the land of Egypt, [b]have corrupted[7843] *themselves:*

8 They have turned aside[5493] quickly out of the way[1870] which [a]I commanded[6680] them: they have made them a molten calf, and have worshipped[7812] it, and have sacrificed[2076] thereunto, and said, [b]These *be* thy gods, O Israel, which have brought thee up out of the land of Egypt.

9 And the LORD said unto Moses, [a]I have seen this people, and, behold, it *is* a stiffnecked people:

10 Now therefore [a]let me alone, that [b]my wrath[639] may wax hot[2734] against them, and that I may consume[3615] them: and [c]I will make[6213] of thee a great nation.[1471]

11 [a]And Moses besought [I]the LORD his God,[430] and said, LORD, why doth thy wrath wax hot against thy people, which thou hast brought forth out of the land of Egypt with great power, and with a mighty[2389] hand?

12 [a]Wherefore should the Egyptians speak, and say, For mischief[7451] did he bring them out, to slay[2026] them in the mountains, and to consume[3615] them from the face of the earth?[127] Turn[7725] from thy fierce wrath, and [b]repent[5162] of this evil[7451] against thy people.

13 Remember Abraham, Isaac, and Israel, thy servants,[5650] to whom thou [a]swarest[7650] by thine own self, and saidst unto them, [b]I will multiply your seed[2233] as the stars of heaven,[8064] and all this land that I have spoken[559] of will I give unto your seed, and they shall inherit[5157] *it* for ever.[5769]

14 And the LORD [a]repented of the evil which he thought[1696] to do unto his people.

15 And [a]Moses turned, and went down from the mount, and the two tables of the testimony[5715] *were* in his hand: the tables *were* written on both their sides; on the one side and on the other *were* they written.

16 And the [a]tables *were* the work of God, and the writing *was* the writing of God, graven upon the tables.

17 And when Joshua heard[8085] the noise of the people as they shouted, he said unto Moses, *There is* a noise of war in the camp.[4264]

17 [a]Ex. 31:13; Ezek. 20:12, 20 [b]Gen. 1:31; 2:2

18 [a]Ex. 24:12; 32:15, 16; 34:28, 29; Deut. 4:13; 5:22; 9:10, 11; 2Cor. 3:3

1 [a]Ex. 24:18; Deut. 9:9 [b]Acts 7:40 [c]Ex. 13:21

2 [a]Judg. 8:24-27

4 [a]Ex. 20:23; Deut. 9:16; Judg. 17:3, 4; 1Kgs. 12:28; Neh. 9:18; Ps. 106:19; Isa. 46:6; Acts 7:41; Rom. 1:23

5 [a]Lev. 23:2, 4, 21, 37; 2Kgs. 10:20; 2Chr. 30:5

6 [a]1Cor. 10:7

7 [a]Ex. 32:1; 33:1; Deut. 9:12; Dan. 9:24 [b]Gen. 6:11, 12; Deut. 4:16; 32:5; Judg. 2:19; Hos. 9:9

8 [a]Ex. 20:3, 4, 23; Deut. 9:16 [b]1Kgs. 12:28

9 [a]Ex. 33:3, 5; 34:9; Deut. 9:6, 13; 31:27; 2Chr. 30:8; Isa. 48:4; Acts 7:51

10 [a]Deut. 9:14, 19 [b]Ex. 22:24 [c]Num. 14:12

11 [I]Hebr. *the face of the LORD* [a]Deut. 9:18, 26-29; Ps. 74:1, 2; 106:23

12 [a]Num. 14:13; Deut. 9:28; 32:27 [b]Ex. 32:14

13 [a]Gen. 22:16; Heb. 6:13 [b]Gen. 12:7; 13:15; 15:7, 18; 26:4; 28:13; 35:11, 12

14 [a]Deut. 32:26; 2Sam. 24:16; 1Chr. 21:15; Ps. 106:45; Jer. 18:8; 26:13, 19; Joel 2:13; Jon. 3:10; 4:2

15 [a]Deut. 9:15

16 [a]Ex. 31:18

18 And he said, *It is* not the voice of *them that* shout for mastery, neither *is it* the voice of *them that* cry for [I]being overcome: *but* the noise of *them that* sing do I hear.[8085]

19 And it came to pass, as soon as he came nigh[7126] unto the camp, that [a]he saw the calf, and the dancing: and Moses' anger[639] waxed hot, and he cast the tables out of his hands, and brake[7665] them beneath the mount.

20 [a]And he took the calf which they had made, and burnt *it* in the fire, and ground *it* to powder, and strawed[2219] *it* upon the water, and made the children[1121] of Israel drink *of it*.

21 And Moses said unto Aaron, [a]What did this people unto thee, that thou hast brought so great a sin[2401] upon them?

22 And Aaron said, Let not the anger of my lord[113] wax hot: [a]thou knowest[3045] the people, that they *are set* on mischief.

23 For they said unto me, [a]Make us gods, which shall go before us: for *as for* this Moses, the man that brought us up out of the land of Egypt, we wot not what is become of him.

24 And I said unto them, Whosoever hath any gold, let them break *it* off. So they gave *it* me: then I cast[7993] it into the fire, and there [a]came out[3423] this calf.

🗝 25 And when Moses saw that the people *were* [a]naked; (for Aaron [b]had made them naked[6544] unto *their* shame among [I]their enemies:)

🗝 26 Then Moses stood in the gate of the camp, and said, Who *is* on the LORD's side? *let him come* unto me. And all the sons[1121] of Levi gathered themselves together[622] unto him.

27 And he said unto them, Thus saith[559] the LORD God of Israel, Put every man his sword by his side,[3409] *and* go in[5674] and out[7725] from gate to gate throughout the camp, and [a]slay[2026] every man his brother,[251] and every man his companion, and every man his neighbour.[7138]

28 And the children of Levi did according to the word[1697] of Moses: and there fell[5307] of the people that day[3117] about three thousand men.[376]

29 [I][a]For Moses had said, [II]Consecrate[3027][4390] yourselves to day to the LORD, even every man upon his son, and upon his brother; that he may bestow upon you a blessing[1293] this day.

30 And it came to pass on the morrow, that Moses said unto the people, [a]Ye have sinned[2398] a great sin:[2401] and now I will go up[5927] unto the LORD; [b]peradventure[194] I shall [c]make an atonement[3722] for your sin.[2403]

31 And Moses [a]returned[7725] unto the LORD, and said, Oh, this people have sinned a great sin, and have [b]made them gods of gold.

18 [I]Hebr. *weakness*
19 [a]Deut. 9:16, 17
20 [a]Deut. 9:21
21 [a]Gen. 20:9; 26:10
22 [a]Ex. 14:11; 15:24; 16:2, 20, 28; 17:2, 4
23 [a]Ex. 32:1
24 [a]Ex. 32:4
25 [I]Hebr. *those that rose up against them* [a]Ex. 33:4, 5 [b]2Chr. 28:19
27 [a]Num. 25:5; Deut. 33:9
29 [I]Or, *And Moses said, Consecrate yourselves to day to the LORD, because every man hath* been *against his son, and against his brother* [II]Hebr. *Fill your hands* [a]Num. 25:11-13; Deut. 13:6-11; 33:9, 10; 1Sam. 15:18, 22; Prov. 21:3; Zech. 13:3; Matt. 10:37
30 [a]1Sam. 12:20, 23; Luke 15:18 [b]2Sam. 16:12; Amos 5:15 [c]Num. 25:13
31 [a]Deut. 9:18 [b]Ex. 20:23

🗝 **32:25–29** This passage describe how the Levites won the privilege of serving the Lord in the Tabernacle. Apparently some of the people were still rebellious. The Levites responded immediately when Moses asked the question, "Who is on the LORD's side?" They were then commissioned by Moses to go throughout the camp executing the rebels. For their loyalty to God, they became His special ministers. The priests were a special class within the tribe of Levi whose ministry included the more sacred functions, which functions other members of the tribe were not permitted to perform. For even though, in a general sense, God wanted all Israel to be a "kingdom of priests" (Ex. 19:6), a special priesthood already existed (Ex. 19:22, 24). Only Aaron and his sons could be priests (Ex. 28:1; Num. 3:10). The choice of Aaron's line was made a hereditary appointment after Phinehas' act of zealous loyalty to God (Num. 25:6–13).

🗝 **32:26, 27** The Law had just been given to Moses by God and it strictly forbade both the worship of false gods and murder. In this passage, God commanded that the people who were guilty of breaking the Law were to be put to death. Even though the Israelites had promised earlier, "all the words which the Lord hath said will we do" (Ex. 24:3), these had forsaken God. In His sovereignty, God required that this sin be judged. The children of Israel were merely the means that God chose to carry out His judgment.

32 Yet now, if thou wilt forgive[5375] their sin—; and if not, [a]blot me, I pray thee, [b]out of thy book[5612] which thou hast written.

33 And the LORD said unto Moses, [a]Whosoever hath sinned against me, him will I blot out[4229] of my book.

34 Therefore now go, lead[5148] the people unto *the place* of which I have spoken[1696] unto thee: [a]behold, mine Angel shall go before thee: nevertheless [b]in the day when I visit[6485] I will visit their sin upon them.

35 And the LORD plagued[5062] the people, because [a]they made the calf, which Aaron made.

God Gives the Orders To March

33 And the LORD said[1696] unto Moses, Depart, *and* go up hence, thou [a]and the people[5971] which thou hast brought up[5927] out of the land[776] of Egypt, unto the land which I sware[7650] unto Abraham, to Isaac, and to Jacob, saying, [b]Unto thy seed[2233] will I give it:

2 [a]And I will send an angel before thee; [b]and I will drive out the Canaanite, the Amorite, and the Hittite, and the Perizzite, the Hivite, and the Jebusite:

3 [a]Unto a land flowing with milk and honey: [b]for I will not go up[5927] in the midst of thee; for thou *art* a [c]stiffnecked people: lest [d]I consume[3615] thee in the way.

4 And when the people heard[8085] these evil[7451] tidings,[1697] [a]they mourned: [b]and no man did put on him his ornaments.

5 For the LORD had said unto Moses, Say unto the children[1121] of Israel, [a]Ye *are* a stiffnecked people: I will come up [b]into the midst of thee in a moment, and consume[3615] thee: therefore now put off thy ornaments from thee,

32 [a]Ps. 69:28; Rom. 9:3 [b]Ps. 56:8; 139:16; Dan. 12:1; Phil. 4:3; Rev. 3:5; 13:8; 17:8; 20:12, 15; 21:27; 22:19
33 [a]Lev. 23:30; Ezek. 18:4
34 [a]Ex. 33:2, 14; Num. 20:16 [b]Deut. 32:35; Amos 3:14; Rom. 2:5, 6
35 [a]2Sam. 12:9; Acts 7:41
1 [a]Ex. 32:7 [b]Gen. 12:7; Ex. 32:13
2 [a]Ex. 32:34; 34:11 [b]Deut. 7:22; Josh. 24:11
3 [a]Ex. 3:8 [b]Ex. 33:15, 17 [c]Ex. 32:9; 34:9; Deut. 9:6, 13 [d]Ex. 23:21; 32:10; Num. 16:21, 45
4 [a]Num. 14:1, 39 [b]Lev. 10:6; 2Sam. 19:24; 1Kgs. 21:27; 2Kgs. 19:1; Ezra 9:3; Esth. 4:1, 4; Job 1:20; 2:12; Isa. 32:11; Ezek. 24:17, 23; 26:16
5 [a]Ex. 33:3 [b]Num. 16:45, 46 [c]Deut. 8:2; Ps. 139:23
7 [a]Ex. 29:42, 43 [b]Deut. 4:29; 2Sam. 21:1
8 [a]Num. 16:27
9 [a]Ex. 25:22; 31:18; Ps. 99:7
10 [a]Ex. 4:31
11 [a]Gen. 32:30; Num. 12:8; Deut. 34:10 [b]Ex. 24:13
12 [a]Ex. 32:34 [b]Gen. 18:19; Ex. 33:17; Ps. 1:6; Jer. 1:5; John 10:14, 15; 2Tim. 2:19
13 [a]Ex. 34:9 [b]Ps. 25:4; 27:11; 86:11; 119:33

that I may [c]know[3045] what to do[6213] unto thee.

6 And the children of Israel stripped themselves[5337] of their ornaments by the mount Horeb.

7 And Moses took the tabernacle, and pitched it without the camp,[4264] afar off from the camp, [a]and called[7121] it the Tabernacle[168] of the congregation.[4150] And it came to pass, *that* every one which [b]sought the LORD went out unto the tabernacle of the congregation, which *was* without the camp.

8 And it came to pass, when Moses went out unto the tabernacle, *that* all the people rose up, and stood[5324] every man[376] [a]*at* his tent door, and looked after Moses, until he was gone into the tabernacle.

9 And it came to pass, as Moses entered into the tabernacle, the cloudy[6051] pillar descended, and stood *at* the door of the tabernacle, and *the LORD* [a]talked[1696] with Moses.

10 And all the people saw[7200] the cloudy pillar stand *at* the tabernacle door: and all the people rose up and [a]worshipped,[7812] every man *in* his tent[168] door.

⊶11 And [a]the LORD spake[1696] unto Moses face to face, as a man speaketh unto his friend.[7453] And he turned again[7725] into the camp: but [b]his servant[8334] Joshua, the son of Nun, a young man, departed not out of the tabernacle.

12 And Moses said unto the LORD, See,[7200] [a]thou sayest unto me, Bring up this people: and thou hast not let me know whom thou wilt send with me. Yet thou hast said, [b]I know[3045] thee by name, and thou hast also found grace[2580] in my sight.

13 Now therefore, I pray thee, [a]if I have found grace in thy sight, [b]shew[3045] me now thy way,[1870] that I may know thee, that I may find grace in thy sight:

⊶ **33:11** See note on Num. 27:18–23, on Joshua.

and consider[7200] that this nation[1471] *is* [c]thy people.

14 And he said, [a]My presence shall go *with thee,* and I will give thee [b]rest.

15 And he said unto him, [a]If thy presence go not *with me,* carry us not up hence.

16 For wherein shall it be known[3045] here that I and thy people have found grace in thy sight? [a]*is it* not in that thou goest with us? so [b]shall we be separated, I and thy people, from all the people that *are* upon the face of the earth.[127]

17 And the LORD said unto Moses, [a]I will do this thing[1697] also that thou hast spoken: for [b]thou hast found grace in my sight, and I know thee by name.

18 And he said, I beseech thee,[4994] shew[7200] me [a]thy glory.[3519]

19 And he said, [a]I will make[5674] all my goodness[2896] pass[5674] before thee, and I will proclaim[7121] the name of the LORD before thee; [b]and will be [c]gracious[2603] to whom I will be gracious, and will shew mercy[7355] on whom I will shew mercy.

20 And he said, Thou canst not see[7200] my face: for [a]there shall no man[120] see me, and live.[2425]

21 And the LORD said, Behold, *there is* a place by me, and thou shalt stand upon a rock:

22 And it shall come to pass, while my glory passeth by,[5674] that I will put[7760] thee [a]in a clift of the rock, and will [b]cover thee with my hand[3709] while I pass by:

23 And I will take away mine hand, and thou shalt see my back parts: but my face shall [a]not be seen.

The New Tablets

34 And the LORD said unto Moses, [a]Hew[6458] thee two tables of stone like unto the first:[7223] [b]and I will write upon *these* tables the words[1697] that were in the first tables, which thou brakest.[7665]

2 And be ready[3559] in the morning, and come up in the morning unto mount Sinai, and present thyself[5324] there to me [a]in the top[7218] of the mount.

3 And no man shall [a]come up with thee, neither let any man be seen[7200] throughout all the mount; neither let the flocks nor herds feed before that mount.

4 And he hewed two tables of stone like unto the first; and Moses rose up early in the morning, and went up[5927] unto mount Sinai, as the LORD had commanded[6680] him, and took in his hand[3027] the two tables of stone.

5 And the LORD descended in the cloud,[6051] and stood with him there, and [a]proclaimed[7121] the name of the LORD.

6 And the LORD passed by[5674] before him, and proclaimed, The LORD, The LORD [a]God,[410] merciful and gracious,[2587] longsuffering,[639] and abundant[7227] in [b]goodness[2617] and [c]truth,[571]

7 [a]Keeping[5341] mercy[2617] for thousands, [b]forgiving iniquity[5771] and transgression[6588] and sin,[2403] and [c]that will by no means clear *the guilty;* visiting[6485] the iniquity of the fathers[1] upon the children,[1121] and upon the children's children, unto the third and to the fourth *generation.*

8 And Moses made haste, and [a]bowed his head toward the earth,[776] and worshipped.[7812]

9 And he said, If now I have found grace[2580] in thy sight, O Lord,[136] [a]let my Lord, I pray thee, go among us; for [b]it *is* a stiffnecked people;[5971] and pardon[5545] our iniquity and our sin, and take us for [c]thine inheritance.[5157]

God's Agreement

10 And he said, Behold, [a]I make[3772] a covenant:[1285] before all thy people I will [b]do[6213] marvels,[6381] such as have not been done in all the earth, nor in any nation:[1471] and all the people among which thou *art* shall see[7200] the work of the LORD: for it *is* [c]a terrible thing[3372] that I will do with thee.

11 [a]Observe[8104] thou that which I

---

13 [c]Deut. 9:26, 29; Joel 2:17
14 [a]Ex. 13:21; 40:34-38; Isa. 63:9 [b]Deut. 3:20; Josh. 21:44; 22:4; 23:1; Ps. 95:11
15 [a]Ex. 33:3; 34:9
16 [a]Num. 14:14 [b]Ex. 34:10; Deut. 4:7, 34; 2Sam. 7:23; 1Kgs. 8:53; Ps. 147:20
17 [a]Gen. 19:21; James 5:16 [b]Ex. 33:12
18 [a]Ex. 33:20; 1Tim. 6:16
19 [a]Ex. 34:5-7; Jer. 31:14 [b]Rom. 9:15, 16, 18 [c]Rom. 4:4, 16
20 [a]Gen. 32:30; Deut. 5:24; Judg. 6:22; 13:22; Isa. 6:5; Rev. 1:16, 17; Ex. 24:10
22 [a]Isa. 2:21 [b]Ps. 91:1, 4
23 [a]Ex. 33:20; John 1:18

1 [a]Ex. 32:16, 19; Deut. 10:1 [b]Ex. 34:28; Deut. 10:2, 4
2 [a]Ex. 19:20; 24:12
3 [a]Ex. 19:12, 13, 21
5 [a]Ex. 33:19; Num. 14:17
6 [a]Num. 14:18; 2Chr. 30:9; Neh. 9:17; Ps. 86:15; 103:8; 111:4; 112:4; 116:5; 145:8; Joel 2:13 [b]Ps. 31:19; Rom. 2:4 [c]Ps. 57:10; 108:4
7 [a]Ex. 20:6; Deut. 5:10; Ps. 86:15; Jer. 32:18; Dan. 9:4 [b]Ps. 103:3; 130:4; Dan. 9:9; Eph. 4:32; 1John 1:9 [c]Ex. 23:7, 21; Josh. 24:19; Job 10:14; Mic. 6:11; Nah. 1:3
8 [a]Ex. 4:31
9 [a]Ex. 33:15, 16 [b]Ex. 33:3 [c]Deut. 32:9; Ps. 28:9; 33:12; 78:62; 94:14; Jer. 10:16; Zech. 2:12
10 [a]Deut. 5:2; 29:12, 14 [b]Deut. 4:32; 2Sam. 7:23; Ps. 77:14; 78:12; 147:20 [c]Deut. 10:21; Ps. 145:6; Isa. 64:3
11 [a]Deut. 5:32; 6:3, 25; 12:28, 32; 28:1

command[6680] thee this day:[3117] behold, [b]I drive out before thee the Amorite, and the Canaanite, and the Hittite, and the Perizzite, and the Hivite, and the Jebusite.

12 [a]Take heed[8104] to thyself, lest thou make[3772] a covenant with the inhabitants of the land[776] whither thou goest, lest it be for [b]a snare[4170] in the midst of thee:

13 But ye shall [a]destroy[5422] their altars,[4196] break[7665] their [I]images,[4676] and [b]cut down[3772] their groves:[842]

14 For thou shalt worship [a]no other god:[410] for the LORD, whose [b]name *is* Jealous,[7067] *is* a [c]jealous God:[410]

15 [a]Lest thou make a covenant with the inhabitants of the land, and they [b]go a whoring[2181] after their gods,[430] and do sacrifice[2076] unto their gods, and *one* [c]call thee, and thou [d]eat of his sacrifice;[2077]

🔑 16 And thou take of [a]their daughters unto thy sons, and their daughters [b]go a whoring after their gods, and make thy sons go a whoring after their gods.

17 [a]Thou shalt make thee no molten gods.

18 The feast[2282] of [a]unleavened bread shalt thou keep.[8104] Seven days thou shalt eat unleavened bread, as I commanded thee, in the time[4150] of the [b]month Abib: for in the month Abib thou camest out from Egypt.

19 [a]All that openeth the matrix[7358] *is* mine; and every firstling among thy cattle, *whether* ox or sheep, *that is male.*

20 But [a]the firstling of an ass thou shalt redeem[6299] with a [I]lamb: and if thou redeem *him* not, then shalt thou break his neck. All the firstborn of thy sons thou shalt redeem. And none shall appear[7200] before me [b]empty.

21 [a]Six days thou shalt work, but on the seventh day thou shalt rest:[7673] in earing time and in harvest thou shalt rest.

22 [a]And thou shalt observe the feast of weeks, of the firstfruits of wheat harvest, and the feast of ingathering at the [I]year's end.

23 [a]Thrice in the year shall all your menchildren appear before the Lord[113] GOD, the God[430] of Israel.

24 For I will [a]cast out the nations[1471] before thee, and [b]enlarge thy borders: [c]neither shall any man desire[2530] thy land, when thou shalt go up to appear before the LORD thy God thrice in the year.

25 [a]Thou shalt not offer the blood[1818] of my sacrifice with leaven;[2557] [b]neither shall the sacrifice of the feast of the passover[6453] be left unto the morning.

26 [a]The first[7225] of the firstfruits of thy land[127] thou shalt bring unto the house[1004] of the LORD thy God. [b]Thou shalt not seethe a kid in his mother's milk.

27 And the LORD said unto Moses, Write thou [a]these words: for after the tenor of these words I have made[3772] a covenant with thee and with Israel.

28 [a]And he was there with the LORD forty days and forty nights; he did neither eat bread, nor drink water. And [b]he wrote upon the tables the words of the covenant, the ten [I]commandments.[1697]

29 And it came to pass, when Moses came down from mount Sinai with the [a]two tables of testimony[5715] in Moses' hand, when he came down from the mount, that Moses wist[3045] not that [b]the skin[5785] of his face shone while he talked[1696] with him.

30 And when Aaron and all the children of Israel saw[7200] Moses, behold, the skin of his face shone; and they were afraid[3372] to come nigh[5066] him.

31 And Moses called[7121] unto them; and Aaron and all the rulers[5387] of the

11 [b]Ex. 33:2
12 [a]Ex. 23:32; Deut. 7:2; Judg. 2:2 [b]Ex. 23:33
13 [I]Hebr. *statues* [a]Ex. 23:24; Deut. 12:3; Judg. 2:2 [b]Deut. 7:5; 12:2; Judg. 6:25; 2Kgs. 18:4; 23:14; 2Chr. 31:1; 34:3, 4
14 [a]Ex. 20:3, 5 [b]Isa. 9:6; 57:15 [c]Ex. 20:5
15 [a]Ex. 33:12 [b]Deut. 31:16; Judg. 2:17; Jer. 3:9; Ezek. 6:9 [c]Num. 25:2; 1Cor. 10:27 [d]Ps. 106:28; 1Cor. 8:4, 7, 10
16 [a]Deut. 7:3; 1Kgs. 11:2; Ezra 9:2; Neh. 13:25 [b]Num. 25:1, 2; 1Kgs. 11:4
17 [a]Ex. 32:8; Lev. 19:4
18 [a]Ex. 12:15; 23:15 [b]Ex. 13:4
19 [a]Ex. 13:2, 12; 22:29; Ezek. 44:30; Luke 2:23
20 [I]Or, *kid* [a]Ex. 13:13; Num. 18:15 [b]Ex. 23:15; Deut. 16:16; 1Sam. 9:7, 8; 2Sam. 24:24
21 [a]Ex. 20:9; 23:12; 35:2; Deut. 5:12, 13; Luke 13:14
22 [I]Hebr. *revolution of the year* [a]Ex. 23:16; Deut. 16:10, 13
23 [a]Ex. 23:14, 17; Deut. 16:16
24 [a]Ex. 33:2; Lev. 18:24; Deut. 7:1; Ps. 78:55; 80:8 [b]Deut. 12:20; 19:8 [c]Gen. 35:5; 2Chr. 17:10; Prov. 16:7; Acts 18:10
25 [a]Ex. 23:18 [b]Ex. 12:10
26 [a]Ex. 23:19; Deut. 26:2, 10 [b]Ex. 23:19; Deut. 14:21
27 [a]Ex. 33:10; Deut. 4:13; 31:9
28 [I]Hebr. *words* [a]Ex. 24:18; Deut. 9:9, 18 [b]Ex. 31:18; 32:16; 33:1; Deut. 4:13; 10:2, 4
29 [a]Ex. 32:15 [b]Matt. 17:2; 2Cor. 3:7, 13

🔑 **34:16** In much of the Old Testament Israel is referred to as the bride of the Lord (see Is. 54:5, 6; 62:5; Jer. 31:33). Idolatry was equivalent to adultery (see Jer. 3:8, 9, 20; Ezek. 16:20–34; 23:37).

congregation[5712] returned unto him: and Moses talked[1696] with them.

32 And afterward all the children of Israel came nigh: [a]and he gave them in commandment[6680] all that the LORD had spoken[1696] with him in mount Sinai.

33 And *till* Moses had done[3615] speaking[1696] with them, he put [a]a vail on his face.

34 But [a]when Moses went in before the LORD to speak with him, he took the vail off, until he came out. And he came out, and spake unto the children of Israel *that* which he was commanded.

35 And the children of Israel saw the face of Moses, that the skin of Moses' face shone: and Moses put[7725] the vail upon his face again, until he went in to speak with him.

Regulations for the Sabbath

35 And Moses gathered[6950] all the congregation[5712] of the children[1121] of Israel together,[6950] and said unto them, [a]These *are* the words[1697] which the LORD hath commanded,[6680] that *ye* should do them.

2 [a]Six days[3117] shall work[4399] be done, but on the seventh day[3117] there shall be to you [1]an holy day,[6944] a sabbath[7676] of rest[7677] to the LORD: whosoever doeth work therein shall be put to death.

3 [a]Ye shall kindle no fire throughout your habitations[4186] upon the sabbath day.

Collecting the Building Materials

4 And Moses spake unto all the congregation of the children of Israel, saying, [a]This *is* the thing[1697] which the LORD commanded, saying,

5 Take ye from among you an offering[8641] unto the LORD: [a]whosoever *is* of a willing[5081] heart,[3820] let him bring it, an offering of the LORD: gold, and silver, and brass,

6 And blue, and purple, and scarlet, and fine linen, and goats' *hair,*

7 And rams' skins dyed red, and badgers' skins, and shittim wood,

8 And oil[8081] for the light,[3974] [a]and spices for anointing[4888] oil, and for the sweet incense,[7004]

9 And onyx stones, and stones to be set for the ephod, and for the breastplate.

10 And [a]every wise hearted[2450,3820] among you shall come, and make[6213] all that the LORD hath commanded;

11 [a]The tabernacle,[4908] his tent,[168] and his covering, his taches,7165 and his boards, his bars, his pillars, and his sockets,

12 [a]The ark,[727] and the staves thereof, *with* the mercy seat,[3727] and the vail of the covering,

13 The [a]table, and his staves, and all his vessels, [b]and the shewbread,

14 [a]The candlestick also for the light, and his furniture, and his lamps,[5216] with the oil for the light,

15 [a]And the incense altar,[4196] and his staves, [b]and the anointing oil, and [c]the sweet incense, and the hanging for the door at the entering in of the tabernacle,

16 [a]The altar of burnt offering,[5930] with his brasen grate, his staves, and all his vessels, the laver3595 and his foot,

17 [a]The hangings of the court, his pillars, and their sockets, and the hanging for the door of the court,

18 The pins of the tabernacle, and the pins of the court, and their cords,

19 [a]The cloths of service, to do service[8334] in the holy[6944] *place,* the holy garments for Aaron the priest,[3548] and the garments of his sons, to minister in the priest's office.

20 And all the congregation of the children of Israel departed from the presence of Moses.

21 And they came, every one[376] [a]whose heart stirred him up, and every one whom his spirit[7307] made willing,[5068] *and* they brought the LORD's offering to the work of the tabernacle[168] of the congregation,[4150] and for all his service,[5656] and for the holy garments.

22 And they came, both men[582] and

32 [a]Ex. 24:3
33 [a]2Cor. 3:13
34 [a]2Cor. 3:16
1 [a]Ex. 34:32
2 [1]Hebr. *holiness* [a]Ex. 20:9; 31:14, 15; Lev. 23:3; Num. 15:32; Deut. 5:12; Luke 13:14
3 [a]Ex. 16:23
4 [a]Ex. 25:1, 2
5 [a]Ex. 25:2
8 [a]Ex. 25:6
10 [a]Ex. 31:6
11 [a]Ex. 26:1—27:21
12 [a]Ex. 25:10-22
13 [a]Ex. 25:23 [b]Ex. 25:30; Lev. 24:5, 6
14 [a]Ex. 25:31-40
15 [a]Ex. 30:1 [b]Ex. 30:23 [c]Ex. 30:34
16 [a]Ex. 27:1
17 [a]Ex. 27:9
19 [a]Ex. 31:10; 39:1, 41; Num. 4:5, 6
21 [a]Ex. 25:2; 35:5, 22, 26, 29; 36:2; 1Chr. 28:2, 9; 29:9; Ezra 7:27; 2Cor. 8:12; 9:7

women, as many as were willing hearted, *and* brought bracelets, and earrings, and rings, and tablets,[3558] all jewels of gold: and every man[376] that offered[5130] *offered* an offering of gold unto the LORD.

23 And [a]every man, with whom was found blue, and purple, and scarlet, and fine linen, and goats' *hair,* and red skins of rams, and badgers' skins, brought *them.*

24 Every one that did offer an offering of silver and brass brought the LORD's offering: and every man, with whom was found shittim wood for any work of the service, brought *it.*

25 And all the women that were [a]wise hearted did spin with their hands,[3027] and brought that which they had spun, *both* of blue, and of purple, *and* of scarlet, and of fine linen.

26 And all the women whose heart stirred them up in wisdom[2451] spun goats' *hair.*

27 And [a]the rulers[5387] brought onyx stones, and stones to be set, for the ephod, and for the breastplate;

28 And [a]spice, and oil for the light, and for the anointing oil, and for the sweet incense.

29 The children of Israel brought a [a]willing offering[5071] unto the LORD, every man and woman, whose heart made them willing[5068] to bring for all manner of work, which the LORD had commanded to be made by the hand of Moses.

30 And Moses said unto the children of Israel, See,[7200] [a]the LORD hath called by name Bezaleel the son of Uri, the son of Hur, of the tribe[4294] of Judah;

31 And he hath filled him with the spirit of God,[430] in wisdom, in understanding,[8394] and in knowledge,[1847] and in all manner of workmanship;

32 And to devise curious works,[4284] to work in gold, and in silver, and in brass,

33 And in the cutting of stones, to set *them,* and in carving of wood, to make any manner of cunning[4284] work.

34 And he hath put in his heart that he may teach,[3384] *both* he, and [a]Aholiab, the son of Ahisamach, of the tribe of Dan.

35 Them hath he [a]filled with wisdom of heart, to work all manner of work, of the engraver, and of the cunning workman,[2803] and of the embroiderer, in blue, and in purple, in scarlet, and in fine linen, and of the weaver, *even* of them that do any work, and of those that devise[2803] cunning work.

36 Then wrought[6213] Bezaleel and Aholiab, and every [a]wise hearted[2450,3820] man, in whom the LORD put wisdom[2451] and understanding[8394] to know[3045] how to work[6213] all manner of work[4399] for the service[5656] of the [b]sanctuary, according to all that the LORD had commanded.[6680]

2 And Moses called Bezaleel and Aholiab, and every wise hearted man, in [a]whose heart the LORD had put wisdom, *even* every one whose heart stirred him up to come unto the work to do it:

3 And they received of Moses all the offering,[8641] which the children[1121] of Israel [a]had brought for the work of the service of the sanctuary,[6944] to make it *withal.* And they brought yet unto him free offerings[5071] every morning.

4 And all the wise men, that wrought[6213] all the work of the sanctuary, came every man from his work which they made;

5 And they spake unto Moses, saying, [a]The people[5971] bring much more than enough for the service of the work, which the LORD commanded to make.

6 And Moses gave commandment,[6680] and they caused it to be proclaimed[5674][6963] throughout the camp, saying, Let neither man nor woman make[6213] any more work for the offering of the sanctuary. So the people were restrained from bringing.

7 For the stuff they had was sufficient for all the work to make it, and too much.

23 [a]1Chr. 29:8
25 [a]Ex. 28:3; 31:6; 36:1; 2Kgs. 23:7; Prov. 31:19, 22, 24
27 [a]1Chr. 29:6; Ezra 2:68
28 [a]Ex. 30:23
29 [a]Ex. 35:21; 1Chr. 29:9
30 [a]Ex. 31:2-5
34 [a]Ex. 31:6
35 [a]Ex. 31:3, 6; 35:31; 1Kgs. 7:14; 2Chr. 2:14; Isa. 28:26
1 [a]Ex. 28:3; 31:6; 35:10, 35 [b]Ex. 25:8
2 [a]Ex. 35:21, 26; 1Chr. 29:5
3 [a]Ex. 35:27
5 [a]2Cor. 8:2, 3

The Making of the Tabernacle

8 [a]And every wise hearted man among them that wrought the work of the tabernacle[4908] made ten curtains *of* fine twined linen, and blue, and purple, and scarlet: *with* cherubims[3742] of cunning work[4399] made he them.

9 The length of one curtain *was* twenty and eight cubits, and the breadth of one curtain four cubits: the curtains *were* all of one size.

10 And he coupled the five curtains one unto another: and *the other* five curtains he coupled one unto another.

11 And he made loops of blue on the edge[8193] of one curtain from the selvedge[7098] in the coupling: likewise he made in the uttermost side of *another* curtain, in the coupling of the second.

12 [a]Fifty loops made he in one curtain, and fifty loops made he in the edge of the curtain which *was* in the coupling of the second: the loops held one *curtain* to another.

13 And he made fifty taches[7165] of gold, and coupled the curtains one unto another with the taches: so it became one tabernacle.

14 [a]And he made curtains *of* goats' *hair* for the tent[168] over the tabernacle: eleven curtains he made them.

15 The length of one curtain *was* thirty cubits, and four cubits *was* the breadth of one curtain: the eleven curtains *were* of one size.

16 And he coupled five curtains by themselves, and six curtains by themselves.

17 And he made fifty loops upon the uttermost edge of the curtain in the coupling, and fifty loops made he upon the edge of the curtain which coupleth the second.

18 And he made fifty taches *of* brass to couple the tent together,[2266] that it might be one.

19 [a]And he made a covering for the tent *of* rams' skins dyed red, and a covering *of* badgers' skins above *that.*

20 [a]And he made boards for the tabernacle *of* shittim wood, standing up.

21 The length of a board *was* ten cubits, and the breadth of a board one cubit and a half.

22 One board had two tenons,[3027] equally distant one from another: thus did he make for all the boards of the tabernacle.

23 And he made boards for the tabernacle; twenty boards for the south side southward:

24 And forty sockets of silver he made under the twenty boards; two sockets under one board for his two tenons, and two sockets under another board for his two tenons.

25 And for the other side of the tabernacle, *which is* toward the north corner, he made twenty boards,

26 And their forty sockets of silver; two sockets under one board, and two sockets under another board.

27 And for the sides of the tabernacle westward he made six boards.

28 And two boards made he for the corners of the tabernacle in the two sides.

29 And they were [I]coupled[8382] beneath, and coupled together[1961,8549] at the head[7218] thereof, to one ring: thus he did to both of them in both the corners.

30 And there were eight boards; and their sockets *were* sixteen sockets of silver, [I]under every board two sockets.

31 And he made [a]bars of shittim wood; five for the boards of the one side of the tabernacle,

32 And five bars for the boards of the other side of the tabernacle, and five bars for the boards of the tabernacle for the sides westward.

33 And he made the middle bar to shoot through the boards from the one end to the other.

34 And he overlaid the boards with gold, and made their rings *of* gold *to be* places for the bars, and overlaid the bars with gold.

35 And he made [a]a vail *of* blue, and purple, and scarlet, and fine twined linen: *with* cherubims made he it of cunning work.

---

8 [a]Ex. 26:1

12 [a]Ex. 26:5

14 [a]Ex. 26:7

19 [a]Ex. 26:14

20 [a]Ex. 26:15

29 [I]Hebr. *twinned*

30 [I]Hebr. *two sockets, two sockets under one board*

31 [a]Ex. 26:26

35 [a]Ex. 26:31

36 And he made thereunto four pillars *of* shittim *wood,* and overlaid them with gold: their hooks *were of* gold; and he cast for them four sockets of silver.

37 And he made an [a]hanging for the tabernacle[168] door *of* blue, and purple, and scarlet, and fine twined linen, [I]of needlework;

38 And the five pillars of it with their hooks: and he overlaid their chapiters[7218] and their fillets[2838] with gold: but their five sockets *were of* brass.

Making the Ark of God

37 And Bezaleel made[6213] [a]the ark[727] *of* shittim wood: two cubits and a half *was* the length of it, and a cubit and a half the breadth of it, and a cubit and a half the height of it:

2 And he overlaid it with pure[2889] gold within and without, and made a crown of gold to it round about.

3 And he cast for it four rings of gold, *to be set* by the four corners of it; even two rings upon the one side of it, and two rings upon the other side of it.

4 And he made staves *of* shittim wood, and overlaid them with gold.

5 And he put the staves into the rings by the sides of the ark, to bear[5375] the ark.

6 And he made the [a]mercy seat[3727] *of* pure gold: two cubits and a half *was* the length thereof, and one cubit and a half the breadth thereof.

7 And he made[6213] two cherubims *of* gold, beaten out of one piece made he them, on the two ends of the mercy seat;

8 One cherub[3742] [I]on the end on this side, and another cherub [II]on the *other* end on that side: out of the mercy seat made he the cherubims on the two ends thereof.

9 And the cherubims spread out *their* wings on high, *and* covered with their wings over the mercy seat, with their faces one to another; *even* to the mercy seatward were the faces of the cherubims.

Making the Table

10 And he made [a]the table *of* shittim wood: two cubits *was* the length thereof, and a cubit the breadth thereof, and a cubit and a half the height thereof:

11 And he overlaid it with pure gold, and made thereunto a crown of gold round about.

12 Also he made thereunto a border[4526] of an handbreadth round about; and made a crown of gold for the border thereof round about.

13 And he cast for it four rings of gold, and put the rings upon the four corners that *were* in the four feet thereof.

14 Over against the border were the rings, the places for the staves to bear the table.

15 And he made the staves *of* shittim wood, and overlaid them with gold, to bear the table.

16 And he made the vessels which *were* upon the table, his [a]dishes, and his spoons,[3709] and his bowls, and his covers [I]to cover withal, *of* pure gold.

Making the Lampstand

17 And he made the [a]candlestick *of* pure gold: *of* beaten work made he the candlestick; his shaft,[3409] and his branch, his bowls, his knops, and his flowers, were of the same:

18 And six branches going out of the sides thereof; three branches of the candlestick out of the one side thereof, and three branches of the candlestick out of the other side thereof:

19 Three bowls made after the fashion of almonds in one branch, a knop and a flower; and three bowls made like almonds in another branch, a knop and a flower: so throughout the six branches going out of the candlestick.

20 And in the candlestick *were* four bowls made like almonds, his knops, and his flowers:

21 And a knop under two branches of the same, and a knop under two branches of the same, and a knop under

37 [I]Hebr. *the work of a needle-worker, or, embroiderer* [a]Ex. 26:36

1 [a]Ex. 25:10

6 [a]Ex. 25:17

8 [I]Or, *out of* [II]Or, *out of*

10 [a]Ex. 25:23

16 [I]Or, *to pour out withal* [a]Ex. 25:29

17 [a]Ex. 25:31

two branches of the same, according to the six branches going out of it.

22 Their knops and their branches were of the same: all of it *was* one beaten work *of* pure gold.

23 And he made his seven lamps,[5216] and his snuffers, and his snuffdishes, *of* pure gold.

24 *Of* a talent of pure gold made he it, and all the vessels thereof.

Making the Incense Altar

25 [a]And he made the incense[7004] altar[4196] *of* shittim wood: the length of it *was* a cubit, and the breadth of it a cubit; *it was* foursquare; and two cubits *was* the height of it; the horns thereof were of the same.

26 And he overlaid it with pure gold, *both* the top of it, and the sides thereof round about, and the horns of it: also he made unto it a crown of gold round about.

27 And he made two rings of gold for it under the crown thereof, by the two corners of it, upon the two sides thereof, to be places for the staves to bear it withal.

28 And he made the staves *of* shittim wood, and overlaid them with gold.

29 And he made [a]the holy[6944] anointing[4888] oil,[8081] and the pure incense of sweet spices, according to the work of the apothecary.[7543]

Making the Altar And the Bason

38 And [a]he made[6213] the altar[4196] of burnt offering[5930] *of* shittim wood: five cubits *was* the length thereof, and five cubits the breadth thereof; *it was* foursquare; and three cubits the height thereof.

2 And he made the horns thereof on the four corners of it; the horns thereof were of the same: and he overlaid it with brass.

3 And he made all the vessels of the altar, the pots, and the shovels, and the basons,[4219] *and* the fleshhooks, and the firepans: all the vessels thereof made he *of* brass.

4 And he made for the altar a brasen grate of network under the compass thereof beneath unto the midst of it.

5 And he cast four rings for the four ends of the grate of brass, *to be* places[1004] for the staves.

6 And he made the staves *of* shittim wood, and overlaid them with brass.

7 And he put the staves into the rings on the sides of the altar, to bear[5375] it withal; he made the altar hollow with boards.

8 And he made [a]the laver[3595] *of* brass, and the foot of it *of* brass, of the [I]lookingglasses[4759] of *the women* [II][b]assembling,[6633] which assembled *at* the door of the tabernacle[168] of the congregation.[4150]

Making the Enclosure

9 And he made [a]the court: on the south side southward the hangings of the court *were of* fine twined linen, an hundred cubits:

10 Their pillars *were* twenty, and their brasen sockets twenty; the hooks of the pillars and their fillets[2838] *were of* silver.

11 And for the north side *the hangings were* an hundred cubits, their pillars *were* twenty, and their sockets of brass twenty; the hooks of the pillars and their fillets *of* silver.

12 And for the west side *were* hangings of fifty cubits, their pillars ten, and their sockets ten; the hooks of the pillars and their fillets *of* silver.

13 And for the east side eastward fifty cubits.

14 The hangings of the one side *of the gate were* fifteen cubits; their pillars three, and their sockets three.

15 And for the other side of the court gate, on this hand and that hand, *were* hangings of fifteen cubits; their pillars three, and their sockets three.

16 All the hangings of the court round about *were* of fine twined linen.

17 And the sockets for the pillars

25 [a]Ex. 30:1

29 [a]Ex. 30:23, 34

1 [a]Ex. 27:1

8 [I]Or, *brazen glasses* [II]Hebr. *assembling by troops* [a]Ex. 30:18 [b]1Sam. 2:22

9 [a]Ex. 27:9

were of brass; the hooks of the pillars and their fillets *of* silver; and the overlaying of their chapiters[7218] *of* silver; and all the pillars of the court *were* filleted[2836] with silver.

18 And the hanging for the gate of the court *was* needlework, *of* blue, and purple, and scarlet, and fine twined linen: and twenty cubits *was* the length, and the height in the breadth *was* five cubits, answerable to the hangings of the court.

19 And their pillars *were* four, and their sockets *of* brass four; their hooks *of* silver, and the overlaying of their chapiters and their fillets *of* silver.

20 And all the [a]pins of the tabernacle,[4908] and of the court round about, *were of* brass.

"The Sum of the Tabernacle"

21 This is the sum of the tabernacle, *even* of [a]the tabernacle of testimony,[5715] as it was counted,[6485] according to the commandment[6310] of Moses, *for* the service[5656] of the Levites, [b]by the hand[3027] of Ithamar, son to Aaron the priest.[3548]

22 And [a]Bezaleel the son of Uri, the son of Hur, of the tribe[4294] of Judah, made all that the LORD commanded[6680] Moses.

23 And with him *was* Aholiab, son of Ahisamach, of the tribe of Dan, an engraver, and a cunning workman, and an embroiderer in blue, and in purple, and in scarlet, and fine linen.

24 All the gold that was occupied[6213] for the work in all the work of the holy[6944] *place,* even the gold of the offering, was twenty and nine talents, and seven hundred and thirty shekels, after [a]the shekel of the sanctuary.

25 And the silver of them that were numbered[6485] of the congregation[5712] *was* an hundred talents, and a thousand seven hundred and threescore and fifteen shekels, after the shekel of the sanctuary:[6944]

26 [a]A bekah for [I]every man, *that is,* half a shekel, after the shekel of the sanctuary, for every one that went[5674] to be numbered, from twenty years old and upward, for [b]six hundred thousand and three thousand and five hundred and fifty *men.*

27 And of the hundred talents of silver were cast [a]the sockets of the sanctuary, and the sockets of the vail; an hundred sockets of the hundred talents, a talent for a socket.

28 And of the thousand seven hundred seventy and five *shekels* he made hooks for the pillars, and overlaid their chapiters, and filleted them.

29 And the brass of the offering *was* seventy talents, and two thousand and four hundred shekels.

30 And therewith he made the sockets to the door of the tabernacle of the congregation, and the brasen altar, and the brasen grate for it, and all the vessels of the altar,

31 And the sockets of the court round about, and the sockets of the court gate, and all the pins of the tabernacle, and all the pins of the court round about.

The Making of the Priests' Clothes

39 And of [a]the blue, and purple, and scarlet, they made [b]cloths of service, to do service[8334] in the holy[6944] *place,* and made[6213] the holy garments for Aaron; [c]as the LORD commanded[6680] Moses.

2 [a]And he made the ephod *of* gold, blue, and purple, and scarlet, and fine twined linen.

3 And they did beat the gold into thin plates, and cut *it into* wires, to work[6213] *it* in the blue, and in the purple, and in the scarlet, and in the fine linen, *with* cunning work.

4 They made shoulderpieces for it, to couple *it* together: by the two edges was it coupled together.

5 And the curious girdle[2805] of his ephod, that *was* upon it, *was* of the same, according to the work thereof; *of* gold, blue, and purple, and scarlet, and fine twined linen; as the LORD commanded Moses.

20 [a]Ex. 27:19
21 [a]Num. 1:50, 53; 9:15; 10:11; 17:7, 8; 18:2; 2Chr. 24:6; Acts 7:44 [b]Num. 4:28, 33
22 [a]Ex. 31:2, 6
24 [a]Ex. 30:13, 24; Lev. 5:15; 27:3, 25; Num. 3:47; 18:16
26 [I]Hebr. *a poll* [a]Ex. 30:13, 15 [b]Num. 1:46
27 [a]Ex. 26:19, 21, 25, 32
1 [a]Ex. 35:23 [b]Ex. 31:10; 35:19 [c]Ex. 28:4
2 [a]Ex. 28:6

6 [a]And they wrought onyx stones inclosed in ouches[4865] of gold, graven, as signets are graven, with the names of the children[1121] of Israel.

7 And he put them on the shoulders of the ephod, *that they should be* stones for a [a]memorial[2146] to the children of Israel; as the LORD commanded Moses.

8 [a]And he made the breastplate *of* cunning work, like the work of the ephod; *of* gold, blue, and purple, and scarlet, and fine twined linen.

9 It was foursquare; they made the breastplate double: a span *was* the length thereof, and a span the breadth thereof, *being* doubled.

10 [a]And they set in it four rows of stones: *the first* row *was* a [I]sardius, a topaz, and a carbuncle: this *was* the first row.

11 And the second row, an emerald, a sapphire, and a diamond.

12 And the third row, a ligure, an agate, and an amethyst.

13 And the fourth row, a beryl, an onyx, and a jasper: *they were* enclosed in ouches of gold in their inclosings.

14 And the stones *were* according to the names of the children of Israel, twelve, according to their names, *like* the engravings of a signet, every one with his name, according to the twelve tribes.[7626]

15 And they made upon the breastplate chains at the ends, *of* wreathen[5688] work *of* pure[2889] gold.

16 And they made two ouches *of* gold, and two gold rings; and put the two rings in the two ends of the breastplate.

17 And they put the two wreathen chains of gold in the two rings on the ends of the breastplate.

18 And the two ends of the two wreathen chains they fastened in the two ouches, and put them on the shoulderpieces of the ephod, before it.

19 And they made two rings of gold, and put *them* on the two ends of the breastplate, upon the border[8193] of it, which *was* on the side of the ephod inward.[1004]

20 And they made two *other* golden rings, and put them on the two sides of the ephod underneath, toward the forepart of it, over against the *other* coupling thereof, above the curious girdle of the ephod.

21 And they did bind the breastplate by his rings unto the rings of the ephod with a lace of blue, that it might be above the curious girdle of the ephod, and that the breastplate might not be loosed from the ephod; as the LORD commanded Moses.

22 [a]And he made the robe of the ephod *of* woven work, all[3632] *of* blue.

23 And *there was* an hole[6310] in the midst of the robe, as the hole of a habergeon,[8473] *with* a band[8193] round about the hole, that it should not rend.

24 And they made upon the hems of the robe pomegranates *of* blue, and purple, and scarlet, *and* twined *linen.*

25 And they made [a]bells *of* pure gold, and put the bells between the pomegranates upon the hem of the robe, round about between the pomegranates;

26 A bell and a pomegranate, a bell and a pomegranate, round about the hem of the robe to minister[8334] *in;* as the LORD commanded Moses.

27 [a]And they made coats *of* fine linen *of* woven work for Aaron, and for his sons,

28 [a]And a mitre[4701] *of* fine linen, and goodly bonnets *of* fine linen, and [b]linen breeches *of* fine twined linen,

29 [a]And a girdle[73] *of* fine twined linen, and blue, and purple, and scarlet, *of* needlework; as the LORD commanded Moses.

30 [a]And they made the plate of the holy crown[5145] *of* pure gold, and wrote upon it a writing, *like to* the engravings of a signet, HOLINESS[6944] TO THE LORD.

31 And they tied unto it a lace of blue, to fasten *it* on high upon the mitre; as the LORD commanded Moses.

The Tabernacle Is Completed!

32 Thus was[3615] all the work[5656] of the tabernacle[4908] of the tent[168] of the

6 [a]Ex. 28:9
7 [a]Ex. 28:12
8 [a]Ex. 28:15
10 [I]Or, *ruby* [a]Ex. 28:17, 21
22 [a]Ex. 28:31
25 [a]Ex. 28:33
27 [a]Ex. 28:39, 40
28 [a]Ex. 28:4, 39; Ezek. 44:18 [b]Ex. 28:42
29 [a]Ex. 28:39
30 [a]Ex. 28:36, 37

congregation[4150] finished:[3615] and the children of Israel did [a]according to all that the LORD commanded Moses, so did they.

33 And they brought the tabernacle unto Moses, the tent, and all his furniture, his taches,[7165] his boards, his bars, and his pillars, and his sockets,

34 And the covering of rams' skins dyed red, and the covering of badgers' skins, and the vail of the covering,

35 The ark[727] of the testimony,[5715] and the staves thereof, and the mercy seat,[3727]

36 The table, *and* all the vessels thereof, and the shewbread,

37 The pure candlestick, *with* the lamps[5216] thereof, *even with* the lamps to be set in order, and all the vessels thereof, and the oil[8081] for light,[3974]

38 And the golden altar,[4196] and the anointing[4888] oil, and [I]the sweet incense,[7004] and the hanging for the tabernacle[168] door,

39 The brasen altar, and his grate of brass, his staves, and all his vessels, the laver[3595] and his foot,

40 The hangings of the court, his pillars, and his sockets, and the hanging for the court gate, his cords, and his pins, and all the vessels of the service[5656] of the tabernacle, for the tent of the congregation,

41 The cloths of service to do service in the holy *place,* and the holy garments for Aaron the priest,[3548] and his sons' garments, to minister in the priest's office.

42 According to all that the LORD commanded Moses, so the children of Israel [a]made all the work.

43 And Moses did look[7200] upon all the work,[4399] and, behold, they had done it as the LORD had commanded, even so had they done it: and Moses [a]blessed[1288] them.

Setting Up the Tabernacle

40 And the LORD spake[1696] unto Moses, saying,

2 On the first day of the [a]first month shalt thou set up [b]the tabernacle[4908] of the tent[168] of the congregation.[4150]

3 And [a]thou shalt put therein the ark[727] of the testimony,[5715] and cover the ark with the vail.

4 And [a]thou shalt bring in the table, and [b]set in order [I]the things that are to be set in order upon it; [c]and thou shalt bring in the candlestick, and light the lamps[5216] thereof.

5 [a]And thou shalt set the altar[4196] of gold for the incense[7004] before the ark of the testimony, and put the hanging of the door to the tabernacle.

6 And thou shalt set the altar of the burnt offering[5930] before the door of the tabernacle of the tent of the congregation.

7 And [a]thou shalt set the laver[3595] between the tent of the congregation and the altar, and shalt put water therein.

8 And thou shalt set up the court round about, and hang up the hanging at the court gate.

9 And thou shalt take the anointing[4888] oil,[8081] and [a]anoint[4886] the tabernacle, and all that *is* therein, and shalt hallow[6942] it, and all the vessels thereof: and it shall be holy.[6944]

10 And thou shalt anoint the altar of the burnt offering, and all his vessels, and sanctify[6942] the altar: and [a]it shall be an altar [I]most holy.

11 And thou shalt anoint the laver and his foot, and sanctify it.

12 [a]And thou shalt bring[7126] Aaron and his sons[1121] unto the door of the tabernacle[168] of the congregation, and wash[7464] them with water.

13 And thou shalt put upon Aaron the holy garments, [a]and anoint him, and sanctify him; that he may minister unto me in the priest's office.

14 And thou shalt bring his sons, and clothe them with coats:

15 And thou shalt anoint them, as thou didst anoint their father,[1] that they may minister unto me in the priest's office:[3547] for their anointing shall surely be [a]an everlasting[5769] priesthood throughout their generations.[1755]

---

32 [a]Ex. 25:40; 39:42, 43
38 [I]Hebr. *the incense of sweet spices*
42 [a]Ex. 35:10
43 [a]Lev. 9:22, 23; Num. 6:23; Josh. 22:6; 2Sam. 6:18; 1Kgs. 8:14; 2Chr. 30:27
2 [a]Ex. 12:2; 13:4 [b]Ex. 26:1, 30; 40:17
3 [a]Ex. 26:33; 40:21; Num. 4:5
4 [I]Hebr. *the order thereof* [a]Ex. 26:35; 40:22 [b]Ex. 25:30; 40:23 [c]Ex. 40:24, 25
5 [a]Ex. 40:26
7 [a]Ex. 30:18; 40:30
9 [a]Ex. 30:26
10 [I]Hebr. *holiness of holinesses* [a]Ex. 29:36, 37
12 [a]Lev. 8:1-13
13 [a]Ex. 28:41
15 [a]Num. 25:13

16 Thus did[6213] Moses: according to all that the LORD commanded[6680] him, so did he.

17 And it came to pass in the first month in the second year, on the first *day* of the month, *that* the [a]tabernacle was reared up.

18 And Moses reared up the tabernacle, and fastened his sockets, and set up the boards thereof, and put in the bars thereof, and reared up his pillars.

19 And he spread abroad the tent over the tabernacle, and put the covering of the tent above upon it; as the LORD commanded Moses.

20 And he took and put [a]the testimony into the ark, and set the staves on the ark, and put the mercy seat[3727] above upon the ark:

21 And he brought the ark into the tabernacle, and [a]set up the vail of the covering, and covered the ark of the testimony; as the LORD commanded Moses.

22 [a]And he put the table in the tent of the congregation, upon the side[3409] of the tabernacle northward, without the vail.

23 [a]And he set the bread in order upon it before the LORD; as the LORD had commanded Moses.

24 [a]And he put the candlestick in the tent of the congregation, over against the table, on the side of the tabernacle southward.

25 And [a]he lighted[5927] the lamps before the LORD; as the LORD commanded Moses.

26 [a]And he put the golden altar in the tent of the congregation before the vail:

27 [a]And he burnt[6999] sweet incense thereon; as the LORD commanded Moses.

28 [a]And he set up the hanging *at* the door of the tabernacle.

29 [a]And he put the altar of burnt offering *by* the door of the tabernacle of the tent of the congregation, and [b]offered[5927] upon it the burnt offering and the meat offering;[4503] as the LORD commanded Moses.

30 [a]And he set the laver between the tent of the congregation and the altar, and put water there, to wash *withal*.

31 And Moses and Aaron and his sons washed their hands[3027] and their feet thereat:

32 When they went into the tent of the congregation, and when they came near[7126] unto the altar, they washed; [a]as the LORD commanded Moses.

33 [a]And he reared up the court round about the tabernacle and the altar, and set up the hanging of the court gate. So Moses finished[3615] the work.[4399]

The Glory of the Lord Fills the Tabernacle

🗝 34 [a]Then a cloud[6051] covered[3680] the tent of the congregation, and the glory[3519] of the LORD filled the tabernacle.

35 And Moses [a]was not able to enter into the tent of the congregation, because the cloud abode thereon, and the glory of the LORD filled the tabernacle.

36 [a]And when the cloud was taken up from over the tabernacle, the

17 [a]Ex. 40:1; Num. 7:1
20 [a]Ex. 25:16
21 [a]Ex. 26:33; 35:12
22 [a]Ex. 26:35
23 [a]Ex. 40:4
24 [a]Ex. 26:35
25 [a]Ex. 25:37; 40:4
26 [a]Ex. 30:6; 40:5
27 [a]Ex. 30:7
28 [a]Ex. 26:36; 40:5
29 [a]Ex. 40:6 [b]Ex. 29:38-42
30 [a]Ex. 30:18; 40:7
32 [a]Ex. 30:19, 20
33 [a]Ex. 27:9, 16; 40:8
34 [a]Ex. 29:43; Lev. 16:2; Num. 9:15; 1Kgs. 8:10, 11; 2Chr. 5:13; 7:2; Isa. 6:4; Hag. 2:7, 9; Rev. 15:8
35 [a]Lev. 16:2; 1Kgs. 8:11; 2Chr. 5:14
36 [a]Num. 9:17; 10:11; Neh. 9:19

🗝 **40:34** The phrase "the glory of the LORD filled the tabernacle," indicated that He approved of their work. Evidently, this glory appeared before Israel in the form of a cloud, the same cloud by which the Lord Himself went before the people when they came out of Egypt. At night it took the form of a pillar of fire (Ex. 13:21, 22). In these forms, He led them throughout their journey (Ex. 40:38). When Solomon had completed building the temple (2 Chr. 5:13, 14) it was also filled with the glory of the Lord in the form of a cloud. During the time of Zedekiah that glory departed (Ezek. 11:22, 23) and will not return until it fills the millennial Temple (Ezek. 43:1–9). When this Temple is built, God promises that the "latter glory of this house shall be greater than the former . . . and in this place I shall give peace" (see note on Hag. 2:6–9).

children[1121] of Israel [I]went onward in all their journeys:

37 But [a]if the cloud were not taken up, then they journeyed not till the day that it was taken up.

38 For [a]the cloud of the LORD *was* upon the tabernacle by day, and fire was on it by night,[3915] in the sight of all the house[1004] of Israel, throughout all their journeys.

36 [I]Hebr. *journeyed*

37 [a]Num. 9:19-22

38 [a]Ex. 13:21; Num. 9:15

LEVITICUS

The title "Leviticus" is a transliteration of the title in the Septuagint (the ancient Greek translation of the Old Testament). It is so named because it records the duties of the Levites. The Hebrew name for the book (the first word of the Hebrew text) means "and He called." This title is representative of the content and purpose of the book, namely the calling of God's people, and in particular the calling of the Levites to minister before Him.

This third book of Moses is a primer for the moral and ethical instruction of the chosen people of God. As such, it contains civil, sanitary, ceremonial, moral, and religious regulations for the nation of Israel. All the offerings, as well as the ceremonies and laws, served to constantly remind Israel that God was eminently holy. God could be approached only by the priests, and then only in strict obedience to the detailed instructions for purification. God required the sacrifice of innocent animals for the covering of man's sin. These sacrifices were symbolic of the ultimate sacrifice which would take away the sin of the whole world (John 1:29).

Burnt Offerings

1 ⚿ And the LORD [a]called[7121] unto Moses, and spake unto him [b]out of the tabernacle[168] of the congregation,[4150] saying,[559]

2 Speak[1696] unto the children[1121] of Israel, and say unto them, [a]If any man[120] of you bring an offering[7133] unto the Lord, ye shall bring your offering of the cattle, *even* of the herd, and of the flock.

3 If his offering *be* a burnt sacrifice[5930] of the herd, let him offer a male[2145] [a]without blemish:[8549] he shall offer it of his own voluntary will[7522] at the door of the tabernacle of the congregation before the LORD.

4 [a]And he shall put his hand[3027] upon the head[7218] of the burnt offering;[5930] and it shall be [b]accepted[7521] for him [c]to make atonement[3722] for him.

5 And he shall kill[7819] the [a]bullock before the LORD: [b]and the priests,[3548] Aaron's sons,[1121] shall bring[7126] the blood,[1818] [c]and sprinkle[2236] the blood round about upon the altar[4196] that *is by* the door of the tabernacle of the congregation.

6 And he shall flay[6584] the burnt offering, and cut it into his pieces.

1 [a]Ex. 19:3 [b]Ex. 40:34, 35; Num. 12:4, 5

2 [a]Lev. 22:18, 19

3 [a]Ex. 12:5; 3:1; 22:20, 21; Deut. 15:21; Mal. 1:14; Eph. 5:27; Heb. 9:14; 1Pet. 1:19

4 [a]Ex. 29:10, 15, 19; Lev. 3:2, 8, 13; 4:15; 8:14, 22; 16:21 [b]Lev. 22:21, 27; Isa. 56:7; Rom. 12:1; Phil. 4:18 [c]Lev. 4:20, 26, 31, 35; 9:7; 16:24; Num. 15:25; 2Chr. 29:23, 24; Rom. 5:11

5 [a]Mic. 6:6 [b]2Chr. 35:11; Heb. 10:11 [c]Lev. 3:8; Heb. 12:24; 1Pet. 1:2

7 [a]Gen. 22:9

9 [a]Gen. 8:21; Ezek. 20:28, 41; 2Cor. 2:15; Eph. 5:2; Phil. 4:18

10 [a]Lev. 1:3

11 [a]Lev. 1:5

7 And the sons of Aaron the priest shall put fire upon the altar, and [a]lay the wood in order upon the fire:

8 And the priests, Aaron's sons, shall lay the parts, the head, and the fat, in order upon the wood that *is* on the fire which *is* upon the altar:

9 But his inwards and his legs shall he wash[7364] in water: and the priest shall burn[6999] all on the altar, *to be* a burnt sacrifice, an offering made by fire,[801] of a [a]sweet savour unto the LORD.

10 And if his offering *be* of the flocks, *namely,* of the sheep, or of the goats, for a burnt sacrifice; he shall bring it a male [a]without blemish.

11 [a]And he shall kill it on the side[3409] of the altar northward before the LORD: and the priests, Aaron's sons, shall sprinkle his blood round about upon the altar.

12 And he shall cut it into his pieces, with his head and his fat: and the priest shall lay them in order[6186] on the wood that *is* on the fire which *is* upon the altar:

13 But he shall wash the inwards and the legs with water: and the priest shall bring *it* all, and burn *it* upon the

---

⚿ **1:1** The Book of Leviticus emphasizes the fact that God was speaking directly to Moses. In fact, this is recorded no less than fifty times in the book. In this verse He speaks to Moses from the Holy of Holies above the ark of the covenant. This speaking face-to-face with God distinguished Moses even from the prophets who followed him (Deut. 34:10).

altar: it *is* a burnt sacrifice, an offering made by fire, of a sweet savour unto the LORD.

14 And if the burnt sacrifice for his offering to the LORD *be* of fowls, then he shall bring his offering of [a]turtledoves, or of young pigeons.

15 And the priest shall bring it unto the altar, and [I]wring off[4454] his head, and burn *it* on the altar; and the blood thereof shall be wrung out[4680] at the side of the altar:

16 And he shall pluck away[5493] his crop with [I]his feathers, and cast it [a]beside the altar on the east part, by the place of the ashes:

17 And he shall cleave it with the wings thereof, *but* [a]shall not divide *it* asunder:[914] and the priest shall burn it upon the altar, upon the wood that *is* upon the fire: [b]it *is* a burnt sacrifice, an offering made by fire, of a sweet savour unto the LORD.

Meat Offerings

2 And when any[5315] will offer [a]a meat[4503] offering[7133] unto the LORD, his offering shall be *of* fine flour; and he shall pour oil[8081] upon it, and put frankincense[3828] thereon:

2 And he shall bring it to Aaron's sons[1121] the priests:[3548] and he shall take thereout his handful of the flour thereof, and of the oil thereof, with all the frankincense thereof; and the priest shall burn[6999] [a]the memorial of it upon the altar,[4196] *to be* an offering made by fire, of a sweet savour unto the LORD:

3 And [a]the remnant[3498] of the meat offering[4503] *shall be* Aaron's and his sons': [b]*it is* a thing most holy of the offerings of the LORD made by fire.[801]

4 And if thou bring an oblation[7133] of a meat offering baken in the oven, *it shall be* unleavened cakes of fine flour mingled[1101] with oil, or unleavened wafers [a]anointed[4886] with oil.

5 And if thy oblation *be* a meat offering *baken* [I]in a pan, it shall be *of* fine flour unleavened, mingled with oil.

6 Thou shalt part it in pieces, and pour oil thereon: it *is* a meat offering.

7 And if thy oblation *be* a meat offering *baken* in the fryingpan, it shall be made *of* fine flour with oil.

8 And thou shalt bring[5066] the meat offering that is made of these things unto the LORD: and when it is presented[7126] unto the priest, he shall bring it unto the altar.

9 And the priest shall take from the meat offering [a]a memorial thereof, and shall burn *it* upon the altar: *it is* an [b]offering made by fire, of a sweet savour unto the LORD.

10 And [a]that which is left[3498] of the meat offering *shall be* Aaron's and his sons': *it is* a thing most holy of the offerings of the LORD made by fire.

11 No meat offering, which ye shall bring unto the LORD, shall be made with [a]leaven:[2557] for ye shall burn no leaven, nor any honey, in any offering of the LORD made by fire.

12 [a]As for the oblation of the firstfruits,[7225] ye shall offer them unto the LORD: but they shall not [I]be burnt[5927] on the altar for a sweet savour.

13 And every oblation of thy meat offering [a]shalt thou season with salt; neither shalt thou suffer [b]the salt of the covenant[1285] of thy God[430] to be lacking[7673] from thy meat offering: [c]with all thine offerings thou shalt offer salt.

14 And if thou offer a meat offering of thy firstfruits unto the LORD, [a]thou shalt offer for the meat offering of thy firstfruits green ears of corn dried by the fire, *even* corn beaten out of [b]full ears.

15 And [a]thou shalt put oil upon it, and lay[7760] frankincense thereon: it *is* a meat offering.

16 And the priest shall burn [a]the memorial of it, *part* of the beaten corn thereof, and *part* of the oil thereof, with all the frankincense thereof: *it is* an offering made by fire unto the LORD.

14 [a]Lev. 5:7; 12:8; Luke 2:24
15 [a]Or, *pinch off the head with the nail*
16 [I]Or, *the filth thereof* [a]Lev. 6:10
17 [a]Gen. 15:10 [b]Lev. 1:9, 13
1 [a]Lev. 6:14–18; 9:17; Num. 15:4
2 [a]Lev. 2:9; 5:12; 6:15; 24:7; Isa. 66:3; Acts 10:4
3 [a]Lev. 7:9; 10:12, 13 [b]Ex. 29:37; Num. 18:9
4 [a]Ex. 29:2
5 [I]Or, *on a flat plate, or, slice*
9 [a]Lev. 2:2 [b]Ex. 29:18
10 [a]Lev. 2:3
11 [a]Lev. 6:17; Matt. 16:12; Mark 8:15; Luke 12:1; 1Cor. 5:8; Gal. 5:9
12 [I]Hebr. *ascend* [a]Ex. 22:29; Lev. 23:10, 11
13 [a]Mark 9:49; Col. 4:6 [b]Num. 18:19 [c]Ezek. 43:24
14 [a]Lev. 23:10, 14 [b]2Kgs. 4:42
15 [a]Lev. 2:1
16 [a]Lev. 2:2

Peace Offerings

3 And if his oblation[7133] *be* a [a]sacrifice[2077] of peace offering,[8002] if he offer *it* of the herd; whether *it be* a male[2145] or female,[5347] he shall offer it [b]without blemish[8549] before the LORD.

2 And [a]he shall lay his hand[3027] upon the head of his offering,[7133] and kill[7819] it *at* the door of the tabernacle[168] of the congregation:[4150] and Aaron's sons[1121] the priests[3548] shall sprinkle[2236] the blood[1818] upon the altar[4196] round about.

3 And he shall offer[7126] of the sacrifice of the peace offering an offering made by fire unto the LORD; [a]the [I]fat that covereth[3680] the inwards, and all the fat that *is* upon the inwards,

4 And the two kidneys, and the fat that *is* on them, which *is* by the flanks, and the [I]caul[3508] above the liver, with the kidneys, it shall he take away.[5493]

5 And Aaron's sons [a]shall burn[6999] it on the altar upon the burnt sacrifice,[5930] which *is* upon the wood that *is* on the fire: *it is* an offering made by fire,[801] of a sweet savour unto the LORD.

6 And if his offering for a sacrifice of peace offering unto the LORD *be* of the flock; male or female, [a]he shall offer it without blemish.

7 If he offer a lamb for his offering, then shall he offer it before the LORD.

8 And he shall lay his hand upon the head of his offering, and kill it before the tabernacle of the congregation: and Aaron's sons shall sprinkle[2236] the blood thereof round about upon the altar.

9 And he shall offer of the sacrifice of the peace offering an offering made by fire unto the LORD; the fat thereof, *and* the whole rump, it shall he take off hard by the backbone; and the fat that covereth the inwards, and all the fat that *is* upon the inwards,

10 And the two kidneys, and the fat that *is* upon them, which *is* by the flanks, and the caul above the liver, with the kidneys, it shall he take away.

11 And the priest shall burn it upon the altar: *it is* [a]the food of the offering made by fire unto the LORD.

12 And if his offering *be* a goat, then [a]he shall offer it before the LORD.

13 And he shall lay his hand upon the head of it, and kill it before the tabernacle of the congregation: and the sons of Aaron shall sprinkle the blood thereof upon the altar round about.

14 And he shall offer thereof his offering, *even* an offering made by fire unto the LORD; the fat that covereth the inwards,[7130] and all the fat that *is* upon the inwards,

15 And the two kidneys, and the fat that *is* upon them, which *is* by the flanks, and the caul above the liver, with the kidneys, it shall he take away.

16 And the priest shall burn them upon the altar: *it is* the food of the offering made by fire for a sweet savour: [a]all the fat *is* the LORD's.

17 *It shall be* a [a]perpetual[5769] statute[2708] for your generations[1755] throughout all your dwellings,[4186] that ye eat neither [b]fat nor [c]blood.

Sin Offerings

4 And the LORD spake unto Moses, saying,[559]

2 Speak[1696] unto the children[1121] of Israel, saying, [a]If a soul[5315] shall sin through ignorance[7684] against any of the commandments[4687] of the LORD *concerning things* which ought not to be done, and shall do against any of them:

3 [a]If the priest that is anointed[4399] do sin according to the sin[819] of the people;[5971] then let him bring[7126] for his sin,[2403] which he hath sinned,[2398] [b]a young bullock without blemish[8549] unto the LORD for a sin offering.[2403]

4 And he shall bring the bullock [a]unto the door of the tabernacle[168] of the congregation[4150] before the LORD; and shall lay his hand[3027] upon the bullock's head, and kill[7819] the bullock before the LORD.

5 And the priest that is anointed [a]shall take of the bullock's blood,[1818] and

---

1 [a]Lev. 7:11, 29; 22:21 [b]Lev. 1:3
2 [a]Ex. 29:10; Lev. 1:4, 5
3 [I]Or, *suet* [a]Ex. 29:13, 22; Lev. 4:8, 9
4 [I]Or, *midriff over the liver, and over the kidneys*
5 [a]Ex. 29:13; Lev. 6:12
6 [a]Lev. 3:1
11 [a]Lev. 21:6, 8, 17, 21, 22; 22:25; Ezek. 44:7; Mal. 1:7, 12
12 [a]Lev. 3:1, 7
16 [a]Lev. 7:23, 25; 1Sam. 2:15; 2Chr. 7:7
17 [a]Lev. 6:18; 7:36; 17:7; 23:14 [b]Lev. 3:16; cf. Deut. 32:14; Neh. 8:10 [c]Gen. 9:4; Lev. 7:23, 26; 17:10, 14; Deut. 12:16; 1Sam. 14:33; Ezek. 44:7, 15
2 [a]Lev. 5:15, 17; Num. 15:22-29; 1Sam. 14:27; Ps. 19:12
3 [a]Lev. 8:12 [b]Lev. 9:2
4 [a]Lev. 1:3, 4
5 [a]Lev. 16:14; Num. 19:4

bring it to the tabernacle of the congregation:

6 And the priest shall dip[2881] his finger in the blood, and sprinkle of the blood seven times before the LORD, before the vail of the sanctuary.[6944]

7 And the priest shall [a]put *some* of the blood upon the horns of the altar[4196] of sweet incense[7004] before the LORD, which *is* in the tabernacle of the congregation; and shall pour[8210] [b]all the blood of the bullock at the bottom[3247] of the altar of the burnt offering,[5930] which *is at* the door of the tabernacle of the congregation.

8 And he shall take off from it all the fat of the bullock for the sin offering; the fat that covereth[3680] the inwards, and all the fat that *is* upon the inwards,

9 And the two kidneys, and the fat that *is* upon them, which *is* by the flanks, and the caul[3508] above the liver, with the kidneys, it shall he take away,[5493]

10 [a]As it was taken off from the bullock of the sacrifice[2077] of peace offerings:[8002] and the priest shall burn[6999] them upon the altar of the burnt offering.

11 [a]And the skin[5785] of the bullock, and all his flesh,[1320] with his head, and with his legs, and his inwards, and his dung,

12 Even the whole bullock shall he carry forth [I]without the camp[4264] unto a clean[2889] place, [a]where the ashes are poured out, and [b]burn[8313] him on the wood with fire: [II]where the ashes are poured out shall he be burnt.

13 And [a]if the whole congregation[5712] of Israel sin through ignorance,[7686] [b]and the thing[1697] be hid from the eyes of the assembly,[6951] and they have done *somewhat against* any of the commandments of the LORD *concerning things* which should not be done, and are guilty;[816]

14 When the sin, which they have sinned against it, is known, then the congregation[6951] shall offer a young bullock for the sin, and bring him before the tabernacle of the congregation.

15 And the elders[2205] of the congregation [a]shall lay their hands upon the head of the bullock before the LORD: and the bullock shall be killed before the LORD.

16 [a]And the priest that is anointed shall bring of the bullock's blood to the tabernacle of the congregation:

17 And the priest shall dip his finger *in some* of the blood, and sprinkle *it* seven times before the LORD, *even* before the vail.

18 And he shall put *some* of the blood upon the horns of the altar which *is* before the LORD, that *is* in the tabernacle of the congregation, and shall pour out all the blood at the bottom of the altar of the burnt offering, which *is at* the door of the tabernacle of the congregation.

19 And he shall take all his fat from him, and burn *it* upon the altar.

20 And he shall do with the bullock as he did [a]with the bullock for a sin offering, so shall he do with this: [b]and the priest shall make an atonement[3722] for them, and it shall be forgiven[5545] them.

21 And he shall carry forth the bullock without the camp, and burn him as he burned the first bullock: it *is* a sin offering for the congregation.

22 When a ruler[5387] hath sinned, and [a]done *somewhat* through ignorance *against* any of the commandments of the LORD his God[430] *concerning things* which should not be done, and is guilty;

23 Or [a]if his sin, wherein he hath sinned, come to his knowledge;[3045] he shall bring his offering,[7133] a kid of the goats, a male[2145] without blemish:

24 And [a]he shall lay his hand upon the head of the goat, and kill it in the place where they kill the burnt offering before the LORD: it *is* a sin offering.

25 [a]And the priest shall take of the blood of the sin offering with his finger, and put *it* upon the horns of the altar of burnt offering, and shall pour out his blood at the bottom of the altar of burnt offering.

7 [a]Lev. 8:15; 9:9; 16:18 [b]Lev. 5:9
10 [a]Lev. 3:3-5
11 [a]Ex. 29:14; Num. 19:5
12 [I]Hebr. *to without the camp* [II]Hebr. *at the pouring out of the ashes* [a]Lev. 6:11 [b]Heb. 13:11
13 [a]Num. 15:24; Josh. 7:11 [b]Lev. 5:2-4, 17
15 [a]Lev. 1:4
16 [a]Lev. 4:5; Heb. 9:12, 13, 14
20 [a]Lev. 4:3 [b]Num. 15:25; Dan. 9:24; Rom. 5:11; Heb. 2:17; 10:10-12; 1John 1:7; 2:2
22 [a]Lev. 4:2, 13
23 [a]Lev. 4:14
24 [a]Lev. 4:4-7
25 [a]Lev. 4:30

26 And he shall burn all his fat upon the altar, as [a]the fat of the sacrifice of peace offerings: [b]and the priest shall make an atonement for him as concerning his sin, and it shall be forgiven him.

27 And [a]if [I]any one of the [II]common people sin through ignorance, while he doeth *somewhat against* any of the commandments of the LORD *concerning things* which ought not to be done, and be guilty;

28 Or [a]if his sin, which he hath sinned, come to his knowledge: then he shall bring his offering, a kid of the goats, a female[5347] without blemish, for his sin which he hath sinned.

29 [a]And he shall lay his hand upon the head of the sin offering, and slay the sin offering in the place of the burnt offering.

30 And the priest shall take of the blood thereof with his finger, and put *it* upon the horns of the altar of burnt offering, and shall pour out all the blood thereof at the bottom of the altar.

31 And [a]he shall take away all the fat thereof, [b]as the fat is taken away[5493] from off the sacrifice of peace offerings; and the priest shall burn *it* upon the altar for a [c]sweet savour unto the LORD; [d]and the priest shall make an atonement for him, and it shall be forgiven him.

32 And if he bring a lamb for a sin offering, [a]he shall bring it a female without blemish.

33 And he shall lay his hand upon the head of the sin offering, and slay[7819] it for a sin offering in the place where they kill the burnt offering.

34 And the priest shall take of the blood of the sin offering with his finger, and put *it* upon the horns of the altar of burnt offering, and shall pour out all the blood thereof at the bottom of the altar:

35 And he shall take away all the fat thereof, as the fat of the lamb is taken away from the sacrifice of the peace offerings; and the priest shall burn them upon the altar, [a]according to the offerings made by fire[801] unto the LORD: [b]and the priest shall make an atonement for his sin that he hath committed, and it shall be forgiven him.

Situations

5 And if a soul sin, [a]and hear[8085] the voice of swearing,[423] and *is* a witness, whether he hath seen[7200] or known[3045] *of it;* if he do not utter[5046] *it,* then he shall [b]bear[5375] his iniquity.[5771]

2 Or [a]if a soul touch[5060] any unclean[2931] thing,[1697] whether *it be* a carcase of an unclean beast,[2416] or a carcase[5038] of unclean cattle, or the carcase of unclean creeping things, and *if* it be hidden from him; he also shall be unclean, and [b]guilty.[816]

3 Or if he touch [a]the uncleanness[2932] of man, whatsoever uncleanness *it be* that a man[120] shall be defiled[2930] withal, and it be hid from him; when he knoweth *of it,* then he shall be guilty.

4 Or if a soul swear, pronouncing with *his* lips[8193] [a]to do evil,[7489] or [b]to do good, whatsoever *it be* that a man shall pronounce with an oath,[7621] and it be hid from him; when he knoweth *of it,* then he shall be guilty in one of these.

5 And it shall be, when he shall be guilty in one of these *things,* that he shall [a]confess[3034] that he hath sinned[2398] in that *thing:*

6 And he shall bring his trespass offering[817] unto the LORD for his sin[2403] which he hath sinned, a female[5347] from the flock, a lamb or a kid of the goats, for a sin offering;[2403] and the priest[3548]

26 [a]Lev. 3:5 [b]Lev. 4:20; Num. 15:28
27 [I]Hebr. *any soul* [II]Hebr. *people of the land* [a]Lev. 4:2; Num. 15:27
28 [a]Lev. 4:23
29 [a]Lev. 4:4, 24
31 [a]Lev. 3:14 [b]Lev. 3:3 [c]Ex. 29:18; Lev. 1:9 [d]Lev. 4:26
32 [a]Lev. 4:28
35 [a]Lev. 3:5 [b]Lev. 4:26, 31
1 [a]1Kgs. 8:31; Matt. 26:63 [b]Lev. 5:17; 7:18; 17:16; 19:8; 20:17; Num. 9:13
2 [a]Lev. 11:24, 28, 31, 39; Num. 19:11, 13, 16 [b]Lev. 5:17
3 [a]Lev. 12:1; 13:59; 15:1-33
4 [a]1Sam. 25:22 [b]Acts 23:12; Mark 6:23
5 [a]Lev. 16:21; 26:40; Num. 5:7; Ezra 10:11, 12

4:26 This passage might seem to suggest that forgiveness and atonement came about through the act of the sacrifice. However, the Scriptures deny that animal sacrifices can take away sin (Heb. 10:4, 11). Transgressions were not forgiven under the Law through the shedding of the blood of animals, because their blood could offer no real atonement. The sacrifices made under the Law were symbolical and typical of the atonement of Christ. Therefore, forgiveness in the Old Testament was granted in anticipation of and by faith in Jesus' final offering (Heb. 9:15).

shall make an atonement[3722] for him concerning his sin.
7 And [a]if [I]he be not able to bring[5060]
a lamb, then he shall bring for his
trespass,[817] which he hath committed,[2398]
two [b]turtledoves, or two young pigeons,
unto the LORD; one for a sin offering, and
the other for a burnt offering.[5930]
8 And he shall bring them unto the
priest, who shall offer[7126] *that* which *is*
for the sin offering first, and [a]wring
off[4454] his head from his neck, but shall
not divide *it* asunder:
9 And he shall sprinkle of the
blood[1818] of the sin offering upon the
side of the altar;[4196] and [a]the rest[7604] of
the blood shall be wrung out[4680] at the
bottom[3247] of the altar: it *is* a sin offering.
10 And he shall offer the second *for*
a burnt offering, according to the
[Ia]manner:[4941] [b]and the priest shall make
an atonement for him for his sin which
he hath sinned, and it shall be forgiven[5545] him.
11 But if he be not able to bring two
turtledoves, or two young pigeons, then
he that sinned shall bring for his
offering[7133] the tenth part of an ephah of
fine flour for a sin offering; [a]he shall put
no oil[8081] upon it, neither shall he put *any*
frankincense[3828] thereon: for it *is* a sin offering.
12 Then shall he bring it to the
priest, and the priest shall take his handful of it, [a]*even* a memorial thereof, and
burn[6999] *it* on the altar, [b]according to the
offerings made by fire unto the LORD: it
is a sin offering.
13 [a]And the priest shall make an
atonement for him as touching his sin
that he hath sinned in one of these, and
it shall be forgiven him: and [b]*the remnant*
shall be the priest's, as a meat offering.[4503]

Trespass Offerings

14 And the LORD spake unto Moses,
saying,[559]
15 [a]If a soul commit a trespass,[4604]
and sin through ignorance,[7684] in the holy
things[6944] of the LORD; then [b]he shall
bring for his trespass unto the LORD a
ram without blemish[8549] out of the
flocks, with thy estimation by shekels of
silver, after [c]the shekel of the sanctuary,[6944] for a trespass offering:
16 And he shall make amends for the
harm that he hath done in the holy thing,
and [a]shall add the fifth part thereto, and
give it unto the priest: [b]and the priest
shall make an atonement for him with
the ram of the trespass offering, and it
shall be forgiven him.
17 And if a [a]soul sin, and commit[6213]
any of these things which are forbidden
to be done by the commandments[4687]
of the LORD; [b]though he wist[3045] *it* not,
yet is he [c]guilty, and shall bear his
iniquity.
18 [a]And he shall bring a ram without blemish out of the flock, with thy estimation, for a trespass offering, unto the
priest: [b]and the priest shall make an
atonement for him concerning his ignorance wherein he erred[7683] and wist *it*
not, and it shall be forgiven him.
19 It *is* a trespass offering: [a]he hath
certainly trespassed[816] against the LORD.

6 And the LORD spake unto Moses,
saying,[559]
2 If a soul[5315] sin, and [a]commit[4603] a
trespass against the LORD, and [b]lie unto
his neighbour in that [c]which was delivered him to keep,[6487] or in [Id]fellowship, or
in a thing taken away by violence, or
hath [e]deceived his neighbour;
3 Or [a]have found that which was
lost,[9] and lieth concerning it, and
[b]sweareth[7650] falsely;[8267] in any of all
these that a man[120] doeth, sinning
therein:
4 Then it shall be, because he hath
sinned, and is guilty,[816] that he shall
restore[7725] that which he took violently
away, or the thing which he hath deceitfully gotten, or that which was delivered
him to keep, or the lost thing which he
found,
5 Or all that about which he hath
sworn falsely; he shall even [a]restore it in

7 [I]Hebr. *his hand cannot reach to the sufficiency of a lamb* [a]Lev. 12:8; 14:21 [b]Lev. 1:14
8 [a]Lev. 1:15
9 [a]Lev. 4:7, 18, 30, 34
10 [I]Or, *ordinance* [a]Lev. 1:14 [b]Lev. 4:26
11 [a]Num. 5:15
12 [a]Lev. 2:2 [b]Lev. 4:35
13 [a]Lev. 4:26 [b]Lev. 2:3
15 [a]Lev. 22:14 [b]Ezra 10:19 [c]Ex. 30:13; Lev. 27:25
16 [a]Lev. 6:5; 22:14; 27:13, 15, 27, 31; Num. 5:7 [b]Lev. 4:26
17 [a]Lev. 4:2 [b]Lev. 4:2, 13, 22, 27; 5:15; Ps. 19:12; Luke 12:48 [c]Lev. 5:1, 2
18 [a]Lev. 5:15 [b]Lev. 5:16
19 [a]Ezra 10:2
2 [I]Or, *in dealing* [a]Num. 5:6 [b]Lev. 19:11; Acts 5:4; Col. 3:9 [c]Ex. 22:7, 10 [d]Prov. 24:28; 26:19
3 [a]Deut. 22:1, 2, 3 [b]Ex. 22:11; Lev. 19:12; Jer. 7:9; Zech. 5:4
5 [a]Lev. 5:16; Num. 5:7; 2Sam. 12:6; Luke 19:8

the principal, and shall add the fifth part more thereto, *and* give it unto him to whom it appertaineth, [I]in the day[3117] of his trespass offering.[819]

6 And he shall bring his trespass offering[817] unto the LORD, [a]a ram without blemish[8549] out of the flock, with thy estimation, for a trespass offering, unto the priest:[3548]

7 [a]And the priest shall make an atonement for him before the LORD: and it shall be forgiven him for any thing of all that he hath done in trespassing therein.

The Law of the Offerings

8 And the LORD spake unto Moses, saying,

9 Command[6680] Aaron and his sons,[1121] saying, This *is* the law[8451] of the burnt offering:[5930] It *is* the burnt offering, [I]because of the burning upon the altar[4196] all night[3915] unto the morning, and the fire of the altar shall be burning in it.

10 [a]And the priest shall put on[7760] his linen garment, and his linen breeches shall he put upon his flesh,[1320] and take up the ashes which the fire hath consumed with the burnt offering on the altar, and he shall put them [b]beside the altar.

11 And [a]he shall put off his garments, and put on other garments, and carry forth the ashes without the camp[4264] [b]unto a clean place.

12 And the fire upon the altar shall be burning in it; it shall not be put out: and the priest shall burn[6999] wood on it every morning, and lay the burnt offering in order upon it; and he shall burn thereon [a]the fat of the peace offerings.[8002]

13 The fire shall ever[8548] be burning upon the altar; it shall never go out.

Grain Offerings

14 [a]And this *is* the law of the meat offering:[4503] the sons of Aaron shall offer[7126] it before the LORD, before the altar.

15 And he shall take of it his handful, of the flour of the meat offering, and of the oil[8081] thereof, and all the frankincense[3828] which *is* upon the meat offering, and shall burn *it* upon the altar *for* a sweet savour, *even* the [a]memorial of it, unto the LORD.

16 And [a]the remainder[3498] thereof shall Aaron and his sons eat: [b]with unleavened bread shall it be eaten in the holy[6918] place; in the court of the tabernacle[168] of the congregation[4150] they shall eat it.

17 [a]It shall not be baken with leaven.[2557] [b]I have given it *unto them for* their portion of my offerings made by fire;[801] [c]it *is* most holy,[6944] as *is* the sin offering,[2403] and as the trespass offering.

18 [a]All the males[2145] among the children[1121] of Aaron shall eat of it. [b]*It shall be* a statute[2706] for ever[5769] in your generations[1755] concerning the offerings of the LORD made by fire: [c]every one that toucheth[5060] them shall be holy.[6942]

19 And the LORD spake unto Moses, saying,

20 [a]This *is* the offering[7133] of Aaron and of his sons, which they shall offer unto the LORD in the day when he is anointed; the tenth part of an [b]ephah of fine flour for a meat offering perpetual,[8548] half of it in the morning, and half thereof at night.

21 In a pan it shall be made with oil; *and when it is* baken, thou shalt bring it in: *and* the baken pieces of the meat offering shalt thou offer *for* a sweet savour unto the LORD.

22 And the priest of his sons [a]that is anointed[4899] in his stead shall offer it: *it is* a statute for ever unto the LORD; [b]it shall be wholly[3632] burnt.

23 For every meat offering for the priest shall be wholly burnt: it shall not be eaten.

Sin Offerings

24 And the LORD spake unto Moses, saying,

25 Speak[1696] unto Aaron and to his

5 [I]Or, *in the day of his being found guilty*
6 [a]Lev. 5:15
7 [a]Lev. 4:26
9 [I]Or, *for the burning*
10 [a]Ex. 28:39, 40, 41, 43; Lev. 16:4; Ezek. 44:17, 18 [b]Lev. 1:16
11 [a]Ezek. 44:19 [b]Lev. 4:12
12 [a]Lev. 3:3, 9, 14
14 [a]Lev. 2:1; Num. 15:4
15 [a]Lev. 2:2, 9
16 [a]Lev. 2:3; Ezek. 44:29 [b]Lev. 6:26; 10:12, 13; Num. 18:10
17 [a]Lev. 2:11 [b]Num. 18:9, 10 [c]Ex. 29:37; Lev. 2:3; 6:25; 7:1
18 [a]Lev. 6:29; Num. 18:10 [b]Lev. 3:17 [c]Ex. 29:37; Lev. 22:3-7
20 [a]Ex. 29:2 [b]Ex. 16:36
22 [a]Lev. 4:3 [b]Ex. 29:25

sons, saying, [a]This *is* the law of the sin offering: [b]In the place where the burnt offering is killed shall the sin offering be killed before the LORD: [c]it *is* most holy.

26 [a]The priest that offereth it for sin shall eat it: [b]in the holy place shall it be eaten, in the court of the tabernacle of the congregation.

27 [a]Whatsoever shall touch the flesh thereof shall be holy: and when there is sprinkled[5137] of the blood[1818] thereof upon any garment, thou shalt wash[3526] that whereon it was sprinkled in the holy place.

28 But the earthen[2789] vessel wherein it is sodden1310 [a]shall be broken:[7665] and if it be sodden in a brasen pot, it shall be both scoured, and rinsed in water.

29 [a]All the males among the priests shall eat thereof: [b]it *is* most holy.

30 [a]And no sin offering, whereof *any* of the blood is brought into the tabernacle of the congregation to reconcile[3722] *withal* in the holy *place,* shall be eaten: it shall be burnt[8313] in the fire.

Regulations for Repayment Offerings

7 Likewise [a]this *is* the law[8451] of the trespass offering:[817] [b]it *is* most holy.[6944]

2 [a]In the place where they kill[7819] the burnt offering[5930] shall they kill the trespass offering: and the blood[1818] thereof shall he sprinkle round about upon the altar.[4196]

3 And he shall offer of it [a]all the fat thereof; the rump, and the fat that covereth[3680] the inwards,

4 And the two kidneys, and the fat that *is* on them, which *is* by the flanks, and the caul3508 *that is* above the liver, with the kidneys, it shall he take away:[5493]

5 And the priest[3548] shall burn[6999] them upon the altar *for* an offering made by fire[801] unto the LORD: it *is* a trespass offering.

25 [a]Lev. 4:2 [b]Lev. 1:3, 5, 11; 4:24, 29, 33 [c]Lev. 6:17; 21:22

26 [a]Lev. 10:17, 18; Num. 18:9, 10; Ezek. 44:28, 29 [b]Lev. 6:16

27 [a]Ex. 29:37; 30:29

28 [a]Lev. 11:33; 15:12

29 [a]Lev. 6:18; Num. 18:10 [b]Lev. 6:25

30 [a]Lev. 4:7, 11, 12, 18, 21; 10:18; 16:27; Heb. 13:11

1 [a]Lev. 5:1-19; 6:1-7 [b]Lev. 6:17, 25; 21:22

2 [a]Lev. 1:3, 5, 11; 4:24, 29, 33

3 [a]Ex. 29:13; Lev. 3:4, 9, 10, 14-16; 4:8-9

6 [a]Lev. 6:16-18; Num. 18:9, 10 [b]Lev. 2:3

7 [a]Lev. 6:25, 26; 14:13

9 [I]Or, *on the flat plate,* or, *slice* [a]Lev. 2:3, 10; Num. 18:9; Ezek. 44:29

11 [a]Lev. 3:1; 22:18, 21

12 [a]Lev. 2:4; Num. 6:15

13 [a]Amos 4:5

14 [a]Num. 18:8, 11, 19

15 [a]Lev. 22:30

16 [a]Lev. 19:6-8

6 [a]Every male2145 among the priests shall eat thereof: it shall be eaten in the holy[6918] place: [b]it *is* most holy.

7 As the sin offering[2403] *is,* so *is* [a]the trespass offering: *there is* one law for them: the priest that maketh atonement therewith shall have *it.*

8 And the priest that offereth any man's burnt offering, *even* the priest shall have to himself the skin[5785] of the burnt offering which he hath offered.[7126]

9 And [a]all the meat offering[4503] that is baken in the oven, and all that is dressed in the fryingpan, and [I]in the pan, shall be the priest's that offereth it.

10 And every meat offering, mingled[1101] with oil,[8081] and dry,[2720] shall all the sons[1121] of Aaron have, one[376] *as much* as another.[251]

Peace Offerings

11 And [a]this *is* the law of the sacrifice[2077] of peace offerings,[8002] which he shall offer unto the LORD.

12 If he offer it for a thanksgiving,[8426] then he shall offer with the sacrifice of thanksgiving unleavened cakes mingled with oil, and unleavened wafers [a]anointed[4886] with oil, and cakes mingled with oil, of fine flour, fried.

13 Besides the cakes, he shall offer *for* his offering[7133] [a]leavened[2557] bread with the sacrifice of thanksgiving of his peace offerings.

14 And of it he shall offer one out of the whole oblation[7133] *for* an heave offering[8641] unto the LORD, [a]*and* it shall be the priest's that sprinkleth the blood of the peace offerings.

15 [a]And the flesh[1320] of the sacrifice of his peace offerings for thanksgiving shall be eaten the same day[3117] that it is offered; he shall not leave any of it until the morning.

16 But [a]if the sacrifice of his offering *be* a vow,[5088] or a voluntary offering,[5071] it shall be eaten the same day that he offereth[7126] his sacrifice: and on

the morrow also the remainder[3498] of it shall be eaten:

17 But the remainder of the flesh of the sacrifice on the third day shall be burnt with fire.

18 And if *any* of the flesh of the sacrifice of his peace offerings be eaten at all on the third day, it shall not be accepted,[7521] neither shall it be [a]imputed[2803] unto him that offereth it: it shall be an [b]abomination,[6292] and the soul[5315] that eateth of it shall bear[5375] his iniquity.[5771]

19 And the flesh that toucheth[5060] any unclean[2931] *thing* shall not be eaten; it shall be burnt with fire: and as for the flesh, all that be clean[2889] shall eat thereof.

20 But the soul that eateth *of* the flesh of the sacrifice of peace offerings, that *pertain* unto the LORD, [a]having his uncleanness[2932] upon him, even that soul [b]shall be cut off[3772] from his people.[5971]

21 Moreover the soul that shall touch any unclean *thing, as* [a]the uncleanness of man,[120] or *any* [b]unclean beast, or any [c]abominable unclean *thing,* and eat of the flesh of the sacrifice of peace offerings, which *pertain* unto the LORD, even that soul [d]shall be cut off from his people.

22 And the LORD spake unto Moses, saying,[559]

23 Speak[1696] unto the children[1121] of Israel, saying, [a]Ye shall eat no manner of fat, of ox, or of sheep, or of goat.

24 And the fat of the [1a]beast that dieth of itself,[5038] and the fat of that which is torn with beasts, may be used in any other use:[4399] but ye shall in no wise eat of it.

25 For whosoever eateth the fat of the beast, of which men offer an offering made by fire unto the LORD, even the soul that eateth *it* shall be cut off from his people.

26 [a]Moreover ye shall eat[398] no manner of blood, *whether it be* of fowl or of beast, in any of your dwellings.[4186]

27 Whatsoever soul *it be* that eateth any manner of blood, even that soul shall be cut off from his people.

18 [a]Num. 18:27 [b]Lev. 11:10, 11, 41; 19:7

20 [a]Lev. 15:3 [b]Gen. 17:14

21 [a]Lev. 12:1-3; 13:59; 15:1-33 [b]Lev. 11:24, 28 [c]Ezek. 4:14 [d]Lev. 7:20

23 [a]Lev. 3:17

24 [1]Hebr. *carcass* [a]Lev. 17:15; Deut. 14:21; Ezek. 4:14; 44:31

26 [a]Gen. 9:4; Lev. 3:17; 17:10-14

29 [a]Lev. 3:1

30 [a]Lev. 3:3, 4, 9, 14 [b]Ex. 29:24, 27; Lev. 8:27; 9:21; Num. 6:20

31 [a]Lev. 3:5, 11, 16 [b]Lev. 7:34

32 [a]Lev. 7:34; 9:21; Num. 6:20

34 [a]Ex. 29:28; Lev. 10:14, 15; Num. 18:18, 19; Deut. 18:3

36 [a]Ex. 40:13, 15; Lev. 8:12, 30

37 [a]Lev. 6:9 [b]Lev. 6:14 [c]Lev. 6:25 [d]Lev. 7:1 [e]Ex. 29:1; 6:20 [f]Lev. 7:11

38 [a]Lev. 1:2

28 And the LORD spake unto Moses, saying,

29 Speak unto the children of Israel, saying, [a]He that offereth the sacrifice of his peace offerings unto the LORD shall bring his oblation unto the LORD of the sacrifice of his peace offerings.

30 [a]His own hands[3027] shall bring the offerings of the LORD made by fire, the fat with the breast, it shall he bring, that [b]the breast may be waved *for* a wave offering before the LORD.

31 [a]And the priest shall burn the fat upon the altar: [b]but the breast shall be Aaron's and his sons'.

32 And [a]the right shoulder shall ye give unto the priest *for* an heave offering of the sacrifices of your peace offerings.

33 He among the sons of Aaron, that offereth the blood of the peace offerings, and the fat, shall have the right shoulder for *his* part.

34 For [a]the wave breast and the heave shoulder have I taken of the children of Israel from off the sacrifices of their peace offerings, and have given them unto Aaron the priest and unto his sons by a statute[2706] forever[5769] from among the children of Israel.

35 This *is the portion* of the anointing[4886] of Aaron, and of the anointing of his sons, out of the offerings of the LORD made by fire, in the day *when* he presented them to minister unto the LORD in the priest's office;[3547]

36 Which the LORD commanded[6680] to be given them of the children of Israel, [a]in the day that he anointed[4886] them, *by* a statute[2708] for ever throughout their generations.[1755]

37 This *is* the law [a]of the burnt offering, [b]of the meat offering, [c]and of the sin offering, [d]and of the trespass offering, [e]and of the consecrations,[4394] and [f]of the sacrifice of the peace offerings;

38 Which the LORD commanded Moses in mount Sinai, in the day that he commanded the children of Israel [a]to offer their oblations[7133] unto the LORD, in the wilderness of Sinai.

Aaron and His Sons Are Ordained

8 And the LORD spake unto Moses, saying,

2 [a]Take Aaron and his sons[1121] with him, and [b]the garments, and [c]the anointing[4886] oil,[8081] and a bullock for the sin offering,[2403] and two rams, and a basket of unleavened bread;

3 And gather thou all the congregation[5712] together unto the door of the tabernacle[168] of the congregation.[4150]

4 And Moses did as the LORD commanded[6680] him; and the assembly[5712] was gathered together[6950] unto the door of the tabernacle of the congregation.

5 And Moses said unto the congregation, [a]This *is* the thing[1697] which the LORD commanded to be done.[6213]

6 And Moses brought Aaron and his sons, [a]and washed[7364] them with water.

7 [a]And he put upon him the [b]coat, and girded him with the girdle,[73] and clothed him with the robe, and put the ephod upon him, and he girded him with the curious girdle[2805] of the ephod, and bound *it* unto him therewith.

8 And he put the breastplate[2833] upon him: also he [a]put[7760] in the breastplate the Urim[217] and the Thummim.[8537]

9 [a]And he put the mitre[4701] upon his head; also upon the mitre, *even* upon his forefront, did he put the golden plate, the holy[6944] crown;[5145] as the LORD [b]commanded Moses.

10 [a]And Moses took the anointing oil, and anointed[4886] the tabernacle[4908] and all that *was* therein, and sanctified[6942] them.

11 And he sprinkled thereof upon the altar[4196] seven times, and anointed the altar and all his vessels, both the laver[3595] and his foot, to sanctify them.

12 And he [a]poured of the anointing oil upon Aaron's head, and anointed him, to sanctify him.

13 [a]And Moses brought Aaron's sons, and put coats upon them, and girded them with girdles,[73] and [I]put bonnets upon them; as the LORD commanded Moses.

14 [a]And he brought[5066] the bullock for the sin offering: and Aaron and his sons [b]laid their hands[3027] upon the head of the bullock for the sin offering.

15 And he slew *it;* [a]and Moses took the blood,[1818] and put *it* upon the horns of the altar round about with his finger, and purified the altar, and poured the blood at the bottom[3247] of the altar, and sanctified it, to make reconciliation[3722] upon it.

16 [a]And he took all the fat that *was* upon the inwards, and the caul *above* the liver, and the two kidneys, and their fat, and Moses burned[6999] *it* upon the altar.

17 But the bullock, and his hide,[5785] his flesh,[1320] and his dung, he burnt[8313] with fire without the camp[4264] as the LORD [a]commanded Moses.

18 [a]And he brought the ram for the burnt offering:[5930] and Aaron and his sons laid their hands upon the head of the ram.

19 And he killed *it;* and Moses sprinkled the blood upon the altar round about.

20 And he cut the ram into pieces; and Moses burnt the head, and the pieces, and the fat.

21 And he washed[7364] the inwards and the legs in water; and Moses burnt the whole ram upon the altar: it *was* a burnt sacrifice for a sweet savour, *and* an offering made by fire[801] unto the LORD; [a]as the LORD commanded Moses.

22 And [a]he brought the other ram, the ram of consecration: and Aaron and his sons laid their hands upon the head of the ram.

23 And he slew *it;* and Moses took of the blood of it, and put *it* upon the tip of Aaron's right ear,[241] and upon the thumb of his right hand, and upon the great toe of his right foot.

24 And he brought Aaron's sons, and Moses put of the blood upon the tip of their right ear, and upon the thumbs of their right hands, and upon the great toes of their right feet: and Moses sprinkled the blood upon the altar round about.

2 [a]Ex. 29:1-3 [b]Ex. 28:2, 4 [c]Ex. 30:24, 25
5 [a]Ex. 29:4
6 [a]Ex. 29:4
7 [a]Ex. 29:5 [b]Ex. 28:4
8 [a]Ex. 28:30
9 [a]Ex. 29:6 [b]Ex. 28:36-43
10 [a]Ex. 30:26-29
12 [a]Ex. 29:7; 30:30; Lev. 21:10, 12; Ps. 133:2
13 [I]Hebr. *bound* [a]Ex. 29:8, 9
14 [a]Ex. 29:10; Ezek. 43:19 [b]Lev. 4:4
15 [a]Ex. 29:12, 36; Lev. 4:7; Ezek. 43:20, 26; Heb. 9:22
16 [a]Ex. 29:13; Lev. 4:8
17 [a]Ex. 29:14; Lev. 4:11, 12
18 [a]Ex. 29:15
21 [a]Ex. 29:18
22 [a]Ex. 29:19, 31

25 [a]And he took the fat, and the rump, and all the fat that *was* upon the inwards, and the caul *above* the liver, and the two kidneys, and their fat, and the right shoulder:

26 [a]And out of the basket of unleavened bread, that *was* before the LORD, he took one unleavened cake, and a cake of oiled bread, and one wafer, and put *them* on the fat, and upon the right shoulder:

27 And he put all [a]upon Aaron's hands,[3709] and upon his son's hands, and waved them *for* a wave offering before the LORD.

28 [a]And Moses took them from off their hands, and burnt *them* on the altar upon the burnt offering: they *were* consecrations for a sweet savour: it *is* an offering made by fire unto the LORD.

29 And Moses took the breast, and waved it *for* a wave offering before the LORD: *for* of the ram of consecration it was Moses' [a]part; as the LORD commanded Moses.

30 And [a]Moses took of the anointing oil, and of the blood which *was* upon the altar, and sprinkled *it* upon Aaron, *and* upon his garments, and upon his sons, and upon his sons' garments with him; and sanctified Aaron, *and* his garments, and his sons, and his sons' garments with him.

31 And Moses said unto Aaron and to his sons, [a]Boil the flesh *at* the door of the tabernacle of the congregation: and there eat it with the bread that *is* in the basket of consecrations, as I commanded, saying, Aaron and his sons shall eat it.

32 [a]And that which remaineth[3498] of the flesh and of the bread shall ye burn with fire.

33 And ye shall not go out of the door of the tabernacle of the congregation *in* seven days, until the days of your consecration be at an end: for [a]seven days shall he consecrate you.

34 [a]As he hath done this day, *so* the LORD hath commanded to do, to make an atonement[3722] for you.

35 Therefore shall ye abide *at* the door of the tabernacle of the congregation day[3119] and night[3915] seven days, and [a]keep[8104] the charge[4931] of the LORD, that ye die[4191] not: for so I am commanded.

36 So Aaron and his sons did all things which the LORD commanded by the hand of Moses.

Aaron Offers Sacrifices

9 And [a]it came to pass on the eighth day, *that* Moses called Aaron and his sons,[1121] and the elders[2205] of Israel;

2 And he said unto Aaron, [a]Take thee a young calf for a sin offering,[2403] [b]and a ram for a burnt offering,[5930] without blemish,[8549] and offer[7126] *them* before the LORD.

3 And unto the children[1121] of Israel thou shalt speak, saying, [a]Take ye a kid of the goats for a sin offering; and a calf and a lamb, *both* of the first[1121] year, without blemish, for a burnt offering;

4 Also a bullock and a ram for peace offerings,[8002] to sacrifice before the LORD; and [a]a meat offering[4503] mingled[1101] with oil:[8081] for [b]to day[3117] the LORD will appear[7200] unto you.

5 And they brought *that* which Moses commanded[6680] before the tabernacle[168] of the congregation:[4150] and all the congregation[5712] drew near[7126] and stood before the LORD.

6 And Moses said, This *is* the thing[1697] which the LORD commanded that ye should do:[6213] and [a]the glory[3519] of the LORD shall appear unto you.

7 And Moses said unto Aaron, Go[7126] unto the altar,[4196] and [a]offer[6213] thy sin offering,[7133] and thy burnt offering, and make an atonement for thyself, and for the people:[5971] and [b]offer the offering of the people, and make an atonement for them; as the LORD commanded.

8 Aaron therefore went unto the altar, and slew the calf of the sin offering, which *was* for himself.

9 [a]And the sons of Aaron brought the blood[1818] unto him: and he dipped[2881] his finger in the blood, and [b]put *it* upon

25 [a]Ex. 29:22
26 [a]Ex. 29:23
27 [a]Ex. 29:24, 28
28 [a]Ex. 29:25
29 [a]Ex. 29:26
30 [a]Ex. 29:21; 30:30; Num. 3:3
31 [a]Ex. 29:31, 32
32 [a]Ex. 29:34
33 [a]Ex. 29:30, 35; Ezek. 43:25, 26
34 [a]Heb. 7:16
35 [a]Num. 3:7; 9:19; Deut. 11:1; 1Kgs. 2:3
1 [a]Ezek. 43:27
2 [a]Ex. 29:1; Lev. 4:3; 8:14 [b]Lev. 8:18
3 [a]Lev. 4:23; Ezra 6:17; 10:19
4 [a]Lev. 2:4 [b]Ex. 29:43; Lev. 9:6, 23
6 [a]Ex. 24:16; Lev. 9:23
7 [a]Lev. 4:3; 1Sam. 3:14; Heb. 5:3; 7:27; 9:7 [b]Lev. 4:16, 20; Heb. 5:1
9 [a]Lev. 8:15 [b]Lev. 4:7

the horns of the altar, and poured out the blood at the bottom[3247] of the altar:

10 [a]But the fat, and the kidneys, and the caul[3508] above the liver of the sin offering, he burnt[6999] upon the altar; [b]as the LORD commanded Moses.

11 [a]And the flesh[1320] and the hide[5785] he burnt[8313] with fire without the camp.[4264]

12 And he slew the burnt offering; and Aaron's sons presented unto him the blood, [a]which he sprinkled round about upon the altar.

13 [a]And they presented the burnt offering unto him, with the pieces thereof, and the head: and he burnt *them* upon the altar.

14 [a]And he did wash[7364] the inwards and the legs, and burnt *them* upon the burnt offering on the altar.

15 [a]And he brought the people's offering,[7133] and took the goat, which *was* the sin offering for the people, and slew it, and offered it for sin, as the first.

16 And he brought the burnt offering, and offered[6213] it [a]according to the [I]manner.

17 And he brought [a]the meat offering, and [I]took an handful[3709] thereof, and burnt *it* upon the altar, [b]beside the burnt sacrifice of the morning.

18 He slew also the bullock and the ram *for* [a]a sacrifice[2077] of peace offerings, which *was* for the people: and Aaron's sons presented unto him the blood, which he sprinkled upon the altar round about,

19 And the fat of the bullock and of the ram, the rump, and that which covereth *the inwards,* and the kidneys, and the caul *above* the liver:

20 And they put the fat upon the breasts, [a]and he burnt the fat upon the altar:

21 And the breasts and the right shoulder Aaron waved [a]*for* a wave offering before the LORD; as Moses commanded.

22 And Aaron lifted up[5375] his hand[3027] toward the people, and [a]blessed[1288] them, and came down from offering[6213] of the sin offering, and the burnt offering, and peace offerings.

23 And Moses and Aaron went into the tabernacle of the congregation, and came out, and blessed the people: [a]and the glory of the LORD appeared unto all the people.

24 And [a]there came a fire out from before the LORD, and consumed upon the altar the burnt offering and the fat: *which* when all the people saw,[7200] [b]they shouted, and fell[5347] on their faces.

Nadab and Abihu Sin

10 And [a]Nadab and Abihu, the sons of Aaron, [b]took either of them his censer, and put fire therein, and put incense[7004] thereon, and offered [c]strange[2114] fire before the LORD, which he commanded[6680] them not.

2 And there [a]went out fire from the LORD, and devoured them, and they died[4191] before the LORD.

3 Then Moses said unto Aaron, This *is it* that the LORD spake,[1696] saying, I will be sanctified[6942] in them [a]that come

10 [a]Lev. 8:16 [b]Lev. 4:8
11 [a]Lev. 4:11; 8:17
12 [a]Lev. 1:5; 8:19
13 [a]Lev. 8:20
14 [a]Lev. 8:21
15 [a]Lev. 9:3; Isa. 53:10; Heb. 2:17; 5:3
16 [I]Or, *ordinance* [a]Lev. 1:3, 10
17 [I]Hebr. *filled his hand out of it* [a]Lev. 2:1, 2; 9:4 [b]Ex. 29:38
18 [a]Lev. 3:1-17
20 [a]Lev. 3:5, 16
21 [a]Ex. 29:24, 26; Lev. 7:30-34
22 [a]Num. 6:23; Deut. 21:5; Luke 24:50
23 [a]Lev. 9:6; Num. 14:10; 16:19, 42
24 [a]Gen. 4:4; Judg. 6:21; 1Kgs. 18:38; 2Chr. 7:1; Ps. 20:3 [b]1Kgs. 18:39; 2Chr. 7:3; Ezra 3:11

1 [a]Lev. 16:1; 22:9; Num. 3:3, 4; 26:61; 1Chr. 24:2 [b]Lev. 16:12; Num. 16:18 [c]Ex. 30:9
2 [a]Lev. 9:24; Num. 16:35; 2Sam. 6:7
3 [a]Ex. 19:22; 29:43; Lev. 21:6, 17, 21; Isa. 52:11; Ezek. 20:41; 42:13

10:1–3 Nadab and Abihu's sin in offering "strange fire" to Yahweh is not defined in the text. It is most likely that they performed some ceremony in a forbidden manner. Some have suggested that these newly consecrated priests were anxious to begin the more honorable portion of their duty, and so they proceeded to offer incense when they had not been commanded to do so. Special incense had been prepared for such an offering (Ex. 39:38). However, this incense was likely kept in the custody of Moses or Aaron, requiring Nadab and Abihu to use common incense. Hence, they were guilty of offering strange incense (Ex. 30:9). They may also have been drunk (see Lev. 10:9). Whatever their sinful action may have been, the punishment for it was swift and complete; another fire came forth from God and consumed them. There is a similar instance in the New Testament where Ananias and Sapphira died immediately after lying to God, and it had a beneficial sobering effect upon all who heard about it (Acts 5:1–11).

nigh me, and before all the people[5971] I will be [b]glorified.[3513] [c]And Aaron held his peace.

4 And Moses called Mishael and Elzaphan, the sons of [a]Uzziel the uncle of Aaron, and said unto them, Come near,[7126] [b]carry your brethren[251] from before the sanctuary[6944] out of the camp.[4264]

5 So they went near, and carried[5375] them in their coats out of the camp; as Moses had said.[1696]

6 And Moses said unto Aaron, and unto Eleazar and unto Ithamar, his sons, [a]Uncover[6544] not your heads,[7218] neither rend 6533 your clothes; lest ye die, and lest [b]wrath come upon all the people:[5712] but let your brethren, the whole house[1004] of Israel, bewail 1058 the burning which the LORD hath kindled.[8313]

7 [a]And ye shall not go out from the door of the tabernacle[168] of the congregation,[4150] lest ye die: [b]for the anointing[4886] oil[8081] of the LORD *is* upon you. And they did[6213] according to the word[1697] of Moses.

Rules for Priests

8 And the LORD spake unto Aaron, saying,

9 [a]Do not drink wine 3196 nor strong drink, 7941 thou, nor thy sons with thee, when ye go into the tabernacle of the congregation, lest ye die: *it shall be* a statute[2708] forever[5769] throughout your generations:[1755]

10 And that ye may [a]put difference between holy and unholy, and between unclean[2931] and clean;[2889]

11 [a]And that ye may teach[3384] the children of Israel all the statutes[2706] which the LORD hath spoken unto them by the hand[3027] of Moses.

12 And Moses spake[1696] unto Aaron, and unto Eleazar and unto Ithamar, his sons that were left, Take [a]the meat offering[4503] that remaineth[3498] of the offerings of the LORD made by fire,[801] and eat it without leaven beside the altar:[4196] for [b]it *is* most holy:

13 And ye shall eat it in the holy[6918] place, because it *is* thy due,[2706] and thy sons' due, of the sacrifices of the LORD made by fire: for [a]so I am commanded.

14 And [a]the wave breast and heave[8641] shoulder shall ye eat in a clean place; thou, and thy sons, and thy daughters with thee: for *they be* thy due, and thy sons' due, *which* are given out of the sacrifices[2077] of peace offerings[8002] of the children of Israel.

15 [a]The heave shoulder and the wave breast shall they bring with the offerings made by fire of the fat, to wave *it for* a wave offering before the LORD; and it shall be thine, and thy sons' with thee, by a statute for ever; as the LORD hath commanded.

16 And Moses diligently sought [a]the goat of the sin offering,[2403] and, behold, it was burnt: and he was angry with Eleazar and Ithamar, the sons of Aaron *which were* left *alive,* saying,

17 [a]Wherefore have ye not eaten the sin offering in the holy place, seeing it *is* most holy, and *God* hath given it you to bear[5375] the iniquity[5771] of the congregation,[5712] to make atonement[3722] for them before the LORD?

18 Behold, [a]the blood[1818] of it was not brought in within the holy *place:* ye should indeed have eaten it in the holy *place,* [b]as I commanded.

19 And Aaron said[1696] unto Moses, Behold, [a]this day have they offered[7126] their sin offering and their burnt offering[5930] before the LORD; and such things have befallen me: and *if* I had eaten the sin offering to day, [b]should it have been accepted[3190] in the sight of the LORD?

20 And when Moses heard *that,* he was content.

Clean and Unclean Animals

11 And the LORD spake unto Moses and to Aaron, saying unto them,

2 Speak[1696] unto the children[1121] of Israel, saying,[559] [a]These *are* the beasts[2416] which ye shall eat among all the beasts that *are* on the earth.[776]

3 [b]Isa. 49:3; Ezek. 28:22; John 13:31, 32; 14:13; 2Thess. 1:10 [c]Ps. 39:9

4 [a]Ex. 6:18, 22; Num. 3:19, 30 [b]Luke 7:12; Acts 5:6, 9, 10; 8:2

6 [a]Ex. 33:5; Lev. 13:45; 21:1, 10; Num. 6:6, 7; Deut. 33:9; Ezek. 24:16, 17 [b]Num. 16:22, 46; Josh. 7:1; 22:18, 20; 2Sam. 24:1

7 [a]Lev. 21:12 [b]Ex. 28:41; Lev. 8:30

9 [a]Ezek. 44:21; Luke 1:15; 1Tim. 3:3; Titus 1:7

10 [a]Lev. 11:47; 20:25; Jer. 15:19; Ezek. 22:6; 44:23

11 [a]Deut. 24:8; Neh. 8:2, 8, 9, 13; Jer. 18:18; Mal. 2:7

12 [a]Ex. 29:2; Lev. 6:16; Num. 18:9, 10 [b]Lev. 21:22

13 [a]Lev. 2:3; 6:16

14 [a]Ex. 29:24, 26, 27; Lev. 7:31, 34; Num. 18:11

15 [a]Lev. 7:29, 30, 34

16 [a]Lev. 9:3, 15

17 [a]Lev. 6:26, 29

18 [a]Lev. 6:30 [b]Lev. 6:26

19 [a]Lev. 9:8, 12 [b]Jer. 6:20; 14:12; Hos. 9:4; Mal. 1:10, 13

2 [a]Deut. 14:4; Acts 10:12, 14

3 Whatsoever parteth the hoof, and is clovenfooted, *and* cheweth[5927] the cud, among the beasts, that shall ye eat.

4 Nevertheless these shall ye not eat of them that chew the cud, or of them that divide the hoof: *as* the camel, because he cheweth the cud, but divideth not the hoof; he *is* unclean[2931] unto you.

5 And the coney, because he cheweth the cud, but divideth not the hoof; he *is* unclean unto you.

6 And the hare, because he cheweth the cud, but divideth not the hoof; he *is* unclean unto you.

7 And the swine, though he divide the hoof, and be clovenfooted, yet he cheweth not the cud; [a]he *is* unclean to you.

8 Of their flesh[1320] shall ye not eat, and their carcase[5038] shall ye not touch;[5060] [a]they *are* unclean to you.

9 [a]These shall ye eat of all that *are* in the waters: whatsoever hath fins and scales in the waters, in the seas, and in the rivers, them shall ye eat.

10 And all that have not fins and scales in the seas, and in the rivers, of all that move in the waters, and of any living thing[5315] which *is* in the waters, they *shall be* an [a]abomination unto you:

11 They shall be even an abomination unto you; ye shall not eat of their flesh, but ye shall have their carcases in abomination.[8262]

12 Whatsoever hath no fins nor scales in the waters, that *shall be* an abomination unto you.

13 [a]And these *are they which* ye shall have in abomination among the fowls; they shall not be eaten, they *are* an abomination: the eagle, and the ossifrage, and the ospray,

14 And the vulture, and the kite after his kind;

15 Every raven after his kind;

16 And the owl, and the night hawk, and the cuckow, and the hawk after his kind,

17 And the little owl, and the cormorant, and the great owl,

18 And the swan, and the pelican, and the gier eagle,

7 [a]Isa. 65:4; 66:3, 17

8 [a]Isa. 52:11; Matt. 15:11, 20; Mark 7:2, 15, 18; Acts 10:14, 15; 15:29; Rom. 14:14, 17; 1Cor. 8:8; Col. 2:16, 21; Heb. 9:10

9 [a]Deut. 14:9

10 [a]Lev. 7:18; Deut. 14:3

13 [a]Deut. 14:12

22 [a]Matt. 3:4; Mark 1:6

25 [a]Lev. 14:8; 15:5; Num. 19:10, 22; 31:24

29 [a]Isa. 66:17

19 And the stork, the heron after her kind, and the lapwing, and the bat.

20 All fowls that creep, going upon *all* four, *shall be* an abomination unto you.

21 Yet these may ye eat of every flying creeping thing that goeth upon *all* four, which have legs above their feet, to leap withal upon the earth;

22 *Even* these of them ye may eat; [a]the locust after his kind, and the bald locust after his kind, and the beetle after his kind, and the grasshopper after his kind.

23 But all *other* flying creeping things, which have four feet, *shall be* an abomination unto you.

24 And for these ye shall be unclean:[2930] whosoever toucheth the carcase of them shall be unclean until the even.

25 And whosoever beareth *ought* of the carcase of them [a]shall wash[3526] his clothes, and be unclean[2930] until the even.

26 *The carcases* of every beast which divideth[6536] the hoof, and *is* not clovenfooted, nor cheweth the cud, *are* unclean unto you: every one that toucheth them shall be unclean.

27 And whatsoever goeth upon his paws,[3709] among all manner of beasts that go on *all* four, those *are* unclean unto you: whoso toucheth their carcase shall be unclean until the even.

28 And he that beareth the carcase of them shall wash his clothes, and be unclean until the even: they *are* unclean unto you.

29 These also *shall be* unclean unto you among the creeping things that creep upon the earth; the weasel, and [a]the mouse, and the tortoise after his kind,

30 And the ferret, and the chame leon, and the lizard, and the snail, and the mole.

31 These *are* unclean to you among all that creep: whosoever doth touch them, when they be dead,[4194] shall be unclean until the even.

32 And upon whatsoever *any* of them, when they are dead, doth fall,[5307] it shall be unclean; whether *it be* any vessel of wood, or raiment, or skin,[5785] or

sack, whatsoever vessel *it be,* wherein *any* work[4399] is done, [a]it must be put into water, and it shall be unclean until the even; so it shall be cleansed.[2891]

33 And every earthen[2789] vessel, whereinto *any* of them falleth, whatsoever *is* in it shall be unclean; and [a]ye shall break[7665] it.

34 Of all meat which may be eaten, *that* on which *such* water cometh shall be unclean: and all drink that may be drunk in every *such* vessel shall be unclean.

35 And every *thing* whereupon *any part* of their carcase falleth shall be unclean; *whether it be* oven, or ranges for pots, they shall be broken down:[5422] *for* they *are* unclean, and shall be unclean unto you.

36 Nevertheless a fountain or pit,[953] *wherein there is* [I]plenty[4723] of water, shall be clean:[2889] but that which toucheth their carcase shall be unclean.

37 And if *any part* of their carcase fall upon any sowing seed[2233] which is to be sown, it *shall be* clean.

38 But if *any* water be put upon the seed, and *any part* of their carcase fall thereon, it *shall be* unclean unto you.

39 And if any beast, of which ye may eat, die;[4191] he that toucheth the carcase thereof shall be unclean until the even.

40 And [a]he that eateth of the carcase of it shall wash his clothes, and be unclean until the even: he also that beareth the carcase of it shall wash his clothes, and be unclean until the even.

41 And every creeping thing that creepeth upon the earth *shall be* an abomination; it shall not be eaten.

42 Whatsoever goeth upon the belly, and whatsoever goeth upon *all* four, or

32 [a]Lev. 15:12

33 [a]Lev. 6:28; 15:12

36 [I]Hebr. *a gathering together of waters*

40 [a]Lev. 17:15; 22:8; Deut. 14:21; Ezek. 4:14; 44:31

42 [I]Hebr. *doth multiply feet*

43 [I]Hebr. *souls* [a]Lev. 20:25

44 [a]Ex. 19:6; Lev. 19:2; 20:7, 26; 1Thess. 4:7; 1Pet. 1:15, 16

45 [a]Ex. 6:7 [b]Lev. 11:44

47 [a]Lev. 10:10

2 [a]Lev. 15:19 [b]Luke 2:22 [c]Lev. 15:19

3 [a]Gen. 17:12; Luke 1:59; 2:21; John 7:22, 23

whatsoever [I]hath more feet among all creeping things that creep upon the earth, them ye shall not eat; for they *are* an abomination.

43 [a]Ye shall not make [I]yourselves abominable with any creeping thing that creepeth, neither shall ye make yourselves unclean with them, that ye should be defiled[2933] thereby.

🗝 44 For I *am* the LORD your God:[430] ye shall therefore sanctify yourselves, and [a]ye shall be holy;[6918] for I *am* holy: neither shall ye defile yourselves with any manner of creeping thing that creepeth upon the earth.

45 [a]For I *am* the LORD that bringeth you up out of the land of Egypt, to be your God: [b]ye shall therefore be holy, for I *am* holy.

46 This *is* the law[8451] of the beasts, and of the fowl, and of every living[2416] creature that moveth in the waters, and of every creature that creepeth upon the earth:

47 [a]To make a difference[914] between the unclean and the clean, and between the beast that may be eaten and the beast that may not be eaten.

The Purification of Women After Childbirth

12 And the LORD spake unto Moses, saying,

2 Speak unto the children of Israel, saying,[559] If a [a]woman[802] have conceived seed, and born a man child:[2145] then [b]she shall be unclean[2930] seven days; [c]according to the days of the separation[5079] for her infirmity shall she be unclean.[2930]

3 And in the [a]eighth day the flesh[1320] of his foreskin[6190] shall be circumcised.[4135]

🗝 **11:44, 45** The holiness of God is a major theme throughout the whole Old Testament, and particularly in the Book of Leviticus. God commands His people to reflect His holiness in their lives. Peter quotes these verses (see also Lev. 19:2; 20:26) to challenge his readers to live pure lives (1 Pet. 1:15, 16). God's people are to live holy lives because they have been separated from the world unto God (2 Cor. 6:17, quoted from Is. 52:11).

4 And she shall then continue in the blood[1818] of her purifying[2892] three and thirty days; she shall touch[5060] no hallowed thing,[6944] nor come into the sanctuary,[4720] until the days of her purifying be fulfilled.

5 But if she bear a maid child,[5347] then she shall be unclean two weeks, as in her separation: and she shall continue in the blood of her purifying threescore and six days.

6 And [a]when the days of her purifying are fulfilled, for a son, or for a daughter, she shall bring a lamb [I]of the first year for a burnt offering,[5930] and a young pigeon, or a turtledove, for a sin offering,[2403] unto the door of the tabernacle[168] of the congregation,[4150] unto the priest:[3548]

7 Who shall offer[7126] it before the LORD, and make an atonement[3722] for her; and she shall be cleansed[2891] from the issue of her blood. This *is* the law[8451] for her that hath born a male[2145] or a female.[5347]

8 [a]And if [I]she be not able to bring a lamb, then she shall bring two turtles, or two young pigeons; the one for the burnt offering, and the other for a sin offering: [b]and the priest shall make an atonement for her, and she shall be clean.

Laws About Leprosy

13 And the LORD spake unto Moses and Aaron, saying,

2 When a man[120] shall have in the skin[5785] of his flesh[1320] a [I]rising, [a]a scab, or bright spot, and it be in the skin of his flesh *like* the plague[5061] of leprosy; [b]then he shall be brought unto Aaron the priest,[3548] or unto one of his sons[1121] the priests:

3 And the priest shall look on[7200] the plague in the skin of the flesh: and *when* the hair in the plague is turned[2015] white, and the plague in sight *be* deeper than the skin of his flesh, it *is* a plague of leprosy: and the priest shall look on him, and pronounce him unclean.

4 If the bright spot *be* white in the skin of his flesh, and in sight *be* not deeper than the skin, and the hair thereof be not turned white; then the priest shall shut up *him that hath* the plague seven days:

5 And the priest shall look on him the seventh day: and, behold, *if* the plague in his sight be at a stay,[5975] *and* the plague spread not in the skin; then the priest shall shut him up seven days more:

6 And the priest shall look on him again the seventh day: and, behold, *if* the plague *be* somewhat dark, *and* the plague spread not in the skin, the priest shall pronounce him clean:[2891] it *is but* a scab: and he [a]shall wash[3526] his clothes, and be clean.

7 But if the scab spread much abroad in the skin, after that he hath been seen of the priest for his cleansing,[2893] he shall be seen of the priest again:

8 And *if* the priest see that, behold, the scab spreadeth in the skin, then the priest shall pronounce him unclean: it *is* a leprosy.

9 When the plague of leprosy is in a man, then he shall be brought unto the priest;

10 [a]And the priest shall see *him:* and, behold, *if* the rising *be* white in the skin, and it have turned the hair white, and *there be* [I]quick[4241] raw[2416] flesh in the rising;

11 It *is* an old leprosy in the skin of his flesh, and the priest shall pronounce him unclean,[2931] and shall not shut him up: for he *is* unclean.

12 And if a leprosy break out abroad in the skin, and the leprosy cover[3680] all the skin of *him that hath* the plague from

6 [I]Hebr. *a son of his year* [a]Luke 2:22

8 [I]Hebr. *her hand find not sufficiency of* [a]Lev. 5:7; Luke 2:24 [b]Lev. 4:26

2 [I]Or, *swelling* [a]Deut. 28:27; Isa. 3:17 [b]Deut. 17:8, 9; 24:8; Luke 17:14

6 [a]Lev. 11:25; 14:8

10 [I]Hebr. *the quickening of living flesh* [a]Num. 12:10, 12; 2Kgs. 5:27; 2Chr. 26:20

12:6–8 Compare the offering brought by Mary and Joseph to the temple soon after Jesus was born (Luke 2:24).

his head[7218] even to his foot, wheresoever the priest looketh;

13 Then the priest shall consider: and, behold, *if* the leprosy have covered all his flesh, he shall pronounce *him* clean[2889] *that hath* the plague: it is all turned white: he *is* clean.

14 But when raw flesh appeareth[7200] in him, he shall be unclean.[2930]

15 And the priest shall see the raw flesh, and pronounce him to be unclean: *for* the raw flesh *is* unclean: it *is* a leprosy.

16 Or if the raw flesh turn again,[7725] and be changed[2015] unto white, he shall come unto the priest;

17 And the priest shall see him: and, behold, *if* the plague be turned into white; then the priest shall pronounce *him* clean *that hath* the plague: he *is* clean.

18 The flesh also, in which, *even* in the skin thereof, was a [a]boil, and is healed,

19 And in the place of the boil there be a white rising, or a bright spot, white, and somewhat reddish,[125] and it be shewed to the priest;

20 And if, when the priest seeth it, behold, it *be* in sight lower than the skin, and the hair thereof be turned white; the priest shall pronounce him unclean: it *is* a plague of leprosy broken out of the boil.

21 But if the priest look on it, and, behold, *there be* no white hairs therein, and *if* it *be* not lower than the skin, but *be* somewhat dark; then the priest shall shut him up seven days:

22 And if it spread much abroad in the skin, then the priest shall pronounce him unclean: it *is* a plague.

23 But if the bright spot stay in his place, *and* spread not, it *is* a burning boil; and the priest shall pronounce him clean.

24 Or if there be *any* flesh, in the skin whereof *there is* [l]a hot burning, and the quick *flesh* that burneth have a white bright spot, somewhat reddish, or white;

25 Then the priest shall look upon it: and, behold, *if* the hair in the bright spot be turned[2015] white, and it *be in* sight deeper than the skin; it *is* a leprosy broken out of the burning: wherefore the priest shall pronounce him unclean: it *is* the plague of leprosy.

26 But if the priest look on it, and, behold, *there be* no white hair in the bright spot, and it *be* no lower than the *other* skin, but *be* somewhat dark; then the priest shall shut him up seven days:

27 And the priest shall look upon him the seventh day: *and* if it be spread much abroad in the skin, then the priest shall pronounce him unclean: it *is* the plague of leprosy.

28 And if the bright spot stay in his place, *and* spread not in the skin, but it *be* somewhat dark; it *is* a rising of the burning, and the priest shall pronounce him clean: for it *is* an inflammation of the burning.

29 If a man[376] or woman[802] have a plague upon the [a]head or the beard;[2206]

30 Then the priest shall see the plague: and, behold, if it *be* in sight deeper than the skin; *and there be* in it a yellow thin hair; then the priest shall pronounce him unclean: it *is* a dry scall,[5424] *even* a leprosy upon the head or beard.

31 And if the priest look on the plague of the scall, and, behold, it *be* not in sight deeper than the skin, and *that there is* no black hair in it; then the priest shall shut up *him that hath* the plague of the scall seven days:

32 And in the seventh day the priest shall look on the plague: and, behold, *if* the scall spread not, and there be in it no yellow hair, and the scall *be* not in sight deeper than the skin;

33 He shall be shaven, but the scall shall he not shave; and the priest shall shut up *him that hath* the scall seven days more:

34 And in the seventh day the priest shall look on the scall: and, behold, *if* the scall be not spread in the skin, nor *be* in sight deeper than the skin; then the priest shall pronounce him clean: and he shall wash his clothes, and be clean.

35 But if the scall spread much in the skin after his cleansing;

18 [a]Ex. 9:9

24 [l]Hebr. *a burning of fire*

29 [a]Isa. 1:5; 3:17

36 Then the priest shall look on him: and, behold, if the scall be spread in the skin, the priest shall not seek for yellow hair; he *is* unclean.

37 But if the scall be in his sight at a stay, and *that* there is black hair grown up therein; the scall is healed, he *is* clean: and the priest shall pronounce him clean.

38 If a man also or a woman have in the skin of their flesh bright spots, *even* white bright spots;

39 Then the priest shall look: and, behold, *if* the bright spots in the skin of their flesh *be* darkish white; it *is* a freckled spot *that* groweth in the skin; he *is* clean.

40 And the man whose [I]hair is fallen off his head, he is bald; *yet is* he clean.

41 And he that hath his hair fallen off from the part of his head toward his face, he *is* forehead bald: *yet is* he clean.

42 And if there be in the bald head, or bald forehead, a white reddish sore; it *is* a leprosy sprung up in his bald head, or his bald forehead.

43 Then the priest shall look upon it: and, behold, *if* the rising of the sore *be* white reddish in his bald head, or in his bald forehead, as the leprosy appeareth in the skin of the flesh;

44 He is a leprous man, he *is* unclean: the priest shall pronounce him utterly unclean; his plague *is* in his head.

45 And the leper in whom the plague *is,* his clothes shall be rent, and his head bare, and he shall [a]put a covering upon his upper lip, and shall cry,[7121] [b]Unclean, unclean.

46 All the days wherein the plague *shall be* in him he shall be defiled; he *is* unclean: he shall dwell alone; [a]without the camp[4264] *shall* his habitation[4186] *be.*

Cleansing a Leper's Garment

47 The garment also that the plague of leprosy is in, *whether it be* a woollen garment, or a linen garment;

48 Whether *it be* in the warp,[8359] or woof;[6154] of linen, or of woollen; whether in a skin, or in any [I]thing made of skin;[4399,5785]

49 And if the plague be greenish or reddish in the garment, or in the skin, either in the warp, or in the woof, or in any [I]thing of skin; it *is* a plague of leprosy, and shall be shewed unto the priest:

50 And the priest shall look upon the plague, and shut up *it that hath* the plague seven days:

51 And he shall look on the plague on the seventh day: if the plague be spread in the garment, either in the warp, or in the woof, or in a skin, *or* in any work that is made of skin; the plague *is* [a]a fretting[3992] leprosy; it *is* unclean.

52 He shall therefore burn[8313] that garment, whether warp or woof, in woollen or in linen, or any thing of skin, wherein the plague is: for it *is* a fretting leprosy; it shall be burnt in the fire.

53 And if the priest shall look, and, behold, the plague be not spread in the garment, either in the warp, or in the woof, or in any thing of skin;

54 Then the priest shall command[6680] that they wash *the thing* wherein the plague *is,* and he shall shut it up seven days more:

55 And the priest shall look on the plague, after that it is washed: and, behold, *if* the plague have not changed[2015] his colour, and the plague be not spread; it *is* unclean; thou shalt burn it in the fire; it *is* fret inward,[6356] [I]*whether* it *be* bare within or without.

56 And if the priest look, and, behold, the plague *be* somewhat dark after the washing of it; then he shall rend[7167] it out of the garment, or out of the skin, or out of the warp, or out of the woof:

57 And if it appear[7200] still in the garment, either in the warp, or in the woof, or in any thing of skin; it *is* a spreading *plague:* thou shalt burn that wherein the plague *is* with fire.

58 And the garment, either warp, or woof, or whatsoever thing of skin *it be,* which thou shalt wash,[3526] if the plague be departed[5493] from them, then it shall

40 [I]Hebr. *head is pilled*

45 [a]Ezek. 24:17, 22; Mic. 3:7 [b]Lam. 4:15

46 [a]Num. 5:2; 12:14; 2Kgs. 7:3; 15:5; 2Chr. 26:21; Luke 17:12

48 [I]Hebr. *work of*

49 [I]Hebr. *vessel,* or, *instrument*

51 [a]Lev. 14:44

55 [I]Hebr. whether *it be bald in the head thereof, or in the forehead thereof*

be washed the second time, and shall be
clean.
59 This *is* the law[8451] of the plague
of leprosy in a garment of woollen or
linen, either in the warp, or woof, or any
thing of skins, to pronounce it clean, or
to pronounce it unclean.

Purification of a Leper

14 And the LORD spake unto Moses,
saying,[559]
2 This shall be the law[8451] of the
leper in the day of his cleansing:[2893] He
[a]shall be brought unto the priest:[3548]
3 And the priest shall go forth out of
the camp;[4264] and the priest shall
look,[7200] and, behold, *if* the plague[5061] of
leprosy be healed in the leper;
4 Then shall the priest command[6680]
to take for him that is to be cleansed[2891]
two [I]birds alive[2416] *and* clean,[2889] and
[a]cedar wood, and [b]scarlet, and [c]hyssop:[231]
5 And the priest shall command that
one of the birds be killed[7819] in an
earthen[2789] vessel over running water:
6 As for the living[2416] bird, he shall
take it, and the cedar wood, and the scarlet, and the hyssop, and shall dip[2881]
them and the living bird in the blood[1818]
of the bird *that was* killed over the running water:
7 And he shall [a]sprinkle upon him
that is to be cleansed from the leprosy
[b]seven times, and shall pronounce him
clean, and shall let the living bird loose
[I]into the open field.
8 And he that is to be cleansed [a]shall
wash[3526] his clothes, and shave off all his
hair, [b]and wash[7364] himself in water, that
he may be clean:[2891] and after that he
shall come into the camp, and [c]shall tarry
abroad out of his tent[168] seven days.
9 But it shall be on the seventh day,
that he shall shave all his hair off his
head[7218] and his beard[2206] and his eye-
brows, even all his hair he shall shave off:
and he shall wash his clothes, also he
shall wash his flesh[1320] in water, and he
shall be clean.
10 And on the eighth day [a]he shall
take two he lambs without blemish,[8549]
and one ewe lamb[3535] [I]of the first year
without blemish, and three tenth deals of
fine flour *for* [b]a meat offering,[4503] mingled with oil,[8081] and one log of oil.
11 And the priest that maketh *him*
clean shall present the man[376] that is to
be made clean, and those things, before
the LORD, *at* the door of the tabernacle of
the congregation:[4150]
12 And the priest shall take one he
lamb, and [a]offer[7126] him for a trespass
offering,[817] and the log of oil, and
[b]wave them *for* a wave offering before
the LORD:
13 And he shall slay the lamb [a]in the
place where he shall kill the sin offering[2403] and the burnt offering,[5930] in the
holy[6944] place: for [b]as the sin offering *is*
the priest's, *so is* the trespass offering:
[c]it *is* most holy:
14 And the priest shall take *some* of
the blood of the trespass offering, and
the priest shall put *it* [a]upon the tip
of the right ear[241] of him that is to be
cleansed, and upon the thumb of his
right hand, and upon the great toe of his
right foot:
15 And the priest shall take *some* of
the log of oil, and pour *it* into the
palm[3709] of his own left hand:
16 And the priest shall dip his right
finger in the oil that *is* in his left hand,
and shall sprinkle of the oil with his finger seven times before the LORD:
17 And of the rest[3499] of the oil that
is in his hand shall the priest put upon
the tip of the right ear of him that is to
be cleansed, and upon the thumb of his
right hand, and upon the great toe of his
right foot, upon the blood of the trespass
offering:
18 And the remnant[3498] of the oil
that *is* in the priest's hand he shall pour
upon the head of him that is to be
cleansed: [a]and the priest shall make
an atonement[3722] for him before the
LORD.
19 And the priest shall offer[6213] [a]the
sin offering, and make an atonement for
him that is to be cleansed from his
uncleanness;[2932] and afterward he shall
kill the burnt offering:

2 [a]Matt. 8:2, 4; Mark 1:40, 44; Luke 5:12, 14; 17:14

4 [I]Or, *sparrows* [a]Num. 19:6 [b]Heb. 9:19 [c]Ps. 51:7

7 [I]Hebr. *upon the face of the field* [a]Heb. 9:13 [b]2Kgs. 5:10, 14

8 [a]Lev. 13:6 [b]Lev. 13:6 [c]Num. 12:15

10 [I]Hebr. *the daughter of her year* [a]Matt. 8:4; Mark 1:44; Luke 5:14 [b]Lev. 2:1; Num. 15:4, 15

12 [a]Lev. 5:2, 18; 6:6, 7 [b]Ex. 29:24

13 [a]Ex. 29:11; Lev. 1:5, 11; 4:4, 24 [b]Lev. 7:7 [c]Lev. 2:3; 7:6; 21:22

14 [a]Ex. 29:20; Lev. 8:23

18 [a]Lev. 4:26

19 [a]Lev. 5:1, 6; 12:7

20 And the priest shall offer[5927] the burnt offering and the meat offering upon the altar:[4196] and the priest shall make an atonement for him, and he shall be clean.

21 And [a]if he *be* poor, and [I]cannot get so much; then he shall take one lamb *for* a trespass offering [II]to be waved, to make an atonement[3722] for him, and one tenth deal of fine flour mingled[1101] with oil for a meat offering, and a log of oil;

22 [a]And two turtledoves, or two young pigeons, such as he is able to get; and the one shall be a sin offering, and the other a burnt offering.

23 [a]And he shall bring them on the eighth day for his cleansing unto the priest, unto the door of the tabernacle of the congregation, before the LORD.

24 [a]And the priest shall take the lamb of the trespass offering, and the log of oil, and the priest shall wave[5130] them *for* a wave offering[8573] before the LORD:

25 And he shall kill the lamb of the trespass offering, [a]and the priest shall take *some* of the blood of the trespass offering, and put *it* upon the tip of the right ear of him that is to be cleansed, and upon the thumb of his right hand, and upon the great toe of his right foot:

26 And the priest shall pour of the oil into the palm of his own left hand:

27 And the priest shall sprinkle with his right finger *some* of the oil that *is* in his left hand seven times before the LORD:

28 And the priest shall put of the oil that *is* in his hand upon the tip of the right ear of him that is to be cleansed, and upon the thumb of his right hand, and upon the great toe of his right foot, upon the place of the blood of the trespass offering:

29 And the rest[3498] of the oil that *is* in the priest's hand he shall put upon the head of him that is to be cleansed, to make an atonement for him before the LORD.

30 And he shall offer the one of [a]the turtledoves, or of the young pigeons, such as he can get;[5381]

31 *Even* such as he is able to get, the one *for* a sin offering, and the other *for* a burnt offering, with the meat offering: and the priest shall make an atonement for him that is to be cleansed before the LORD.

32 This *is* the law *of him* in whom *is* the plague of leprosy, whose hand is not able to get [a]*that which pertaineth* to his cleansing.

Cleansing Infected Houses

33 And the LORD spake unto Moses and unto Aaron, saying,

34 [a]When ye be come into the land[776] of Canaan, which I give to you for a possession,[272] and I put the plague of leprosy in an house[1004] of the land of your possession;

35 And he that owneth the house shall come and tell[5046] the priest, saying, It seemeth to me *there is* as it were [a]a plague in the house:

36 Then the priest shall command that they [I]empty the house, before the priest go *into it* to see the plague, that all that *is* in the house be not made unclean:[2930] and afterward the priest shall go in to see the house:

37 And he shall look on the plague, and, behold, *if* the plague *be* in the walls of the house with hollow strakes, greenish or reddish,[125] which in sight *are* lower than the wall;

38 Then the priest shall go out of the house to the door of the house, and shut up the house seven days:

39 And the priest shall come again[7725] the seventh day, and shall look: and, behold, *if* the plague be spread in the walls of the house;

40 Then the priest shall command that they take away the stones in which the plague *is,* and they shall cast them into an unclean[2931] place without the city:

41 And he shall cause the house to be scraped within round about, and they shall pour out[8210] the dust[6083] that they

21 [I]Hebr. *his hand reach not* [II]Hebr. *for a waving* [a]Lev. 5:7; 12:8
22 [a]Lev. 12:8; 15:14, 15
23 [a]Lev. 14:10, 11
24 [a]Lev. 14:12
25 [a]Lev. 14:14
30 [a]Lev. 14:22; 15:15
32 [a]Lev. 14:10
34 [a]Gen. 17:8; Num. 32:22; Deut. 7:1; 32:49
35 [a]Ps. 91:10; Prov. 3:33; Zech. 5:4
36 [I]Or, *prepare*

scrape off without the city into an unclean place:

42 And they shall take other stones, and put *them* in the place of those stones; and he shall take other morter,[6083] and shall plaister the house.

43 And if the plague come again, and break out in the house, after that he hath taken away the stones, and after he hath scraped the house, and after it is plaistered;

44 Then the priest shall come and look, and, behold, *if* the plague be spread in the house, it *is* [a]a fretting leprosy in the house: it *is* unclean.

45 And he shall break down[5422] the house, the stones of it, and the timber thereof, and all the morter of the house; and he shall carry *them* forth out of the city into an unclean place.

46 Moreover he that goeth into the house all the while that it is shut up shall be unclean until the even.

47 And he that lieth in the house shall wash[3526] his clothes; and he that eateth in the house shall wash his clothes.

48 And if the priest [I]shall come in, and look *upon it,* and, behold, the plague hath not spread in the house, after the house was plaistered: then the priest shall pronounce the house clean, because the plague is healed.

49 And [a]he shall take to cleanse the house two birds, and cedar wood, and scarlet, and hyssop:

50 And he shall kill the one of the birds in an earthen vessel over running water:

51 And he shall take the cedar wood, and the hyssop, and the scarlet, and the living bird, and dip them in the blood of the slain bird, and in the running water, and sprinkle[5137] the house seven times:

52 And he shall cleanse the house with the blood of the bird, and with the running water, and with the living bird, and with the cedar wood, and with the hyssop, and with the scarlet:

53 But he shall let go the living bird out of the city into the open fields, and [a]make an atonement for the house: and it shall be clean.

44 [a]Lev. 13:51; Zech. 5:4

48 [I]Hebr. *in coming in shall come in*

49 [a]Lev. 14:4

53 [a]Lev. 14:20

54 [a]Lev. 13:30

55 [a]Lev. 13:47 [b]Lev. 14:34

56 [a]Lev. 13:2

57 [I]Hebr. *in the day of the unclean, and in the day of the clean* [a]Deut. 24:8; Ezek. 44:23

2 [I]Or, *running of the reins* [a]Lev. 22:4; Num. 5:2; 2Sam. 3:29; Matt. 9:20; Mark 5:25; Luke 8:43

4 [I]Hebr. *vessel*

5 [a]Lev. 11:25; 17:15

54 This *is* the law for all manner of plague of leprosy, and [a]scall,[5424]

55 And for the [a]leprosy of a garment, [b]and of an house,

56 And [a]for a rising, and for a scab, and for a bright spot:

57 To [a]teach[3384] [I]when *it is* unclean, and when *it is* clean: this *is* the law of leprosy.

Unclean Discharges From the Body

15 And the LORD spake unto Moses and to Aaron, saying,

2 Speak[1696] unto the children[1121] of Israel, and say[559] unto them, [a]When any man[376] hath a [I]running issue out of his flesh,[1320] *because of* his issue he *is* unclean.[2931]

3 And this shall be his uncleanness[2932] in his issue: whether his flesh run with his issue, or his flesh be stopped from his issue, it *is* his uncleanness.

4 Every bed, whereon he lieth that hath the issue, is unclean:[2930] and every [I]thing, whereon he sitteth, shall be unclean.

5 And whosoever toucheth[5060] his bed shall wash[3526] his clothes, [a]and bathe[7364] *himself* in water, and be unclean until the even.

6 And he that sitteth on *any* thing whereon he sat that hath the issue shall wash his clothes, and bathe *himself* in water, and be unclean until the even.

7 And he that toucheth the flesh of him that hath the issue shall wash his clothes, and bathe *himself* in water, and be unclean until the even.

8 And if he that hath the issue spit upon him that is clean;[2889] then he shall wash[3526] his clothes, and bathe *himself* in water, and be unclean until the even.

9 And what saddle soever he rideth upon that hath the issue shall be unclean.

10 And whosoever toucheth any thing that was under him shall be unclean until the even: and he that beareth *any of* those things shall wash his clothes, and bathe *himself* in water, and be unclean until the even.

11 And whomsoever he toucheth that hath the issue, and hath not rinsed[7857] his hands[3027] in water, he shall wash his clothes, and bathe *himself* in water, and be unclean until the even.

12 And the [a]vessel of earth,[2789] that he toucheth which hath the issue, shall be broken:[7665] and every vessel of wood shall be rinsed in water.

13 And when he that hath an issue is cleansed[2891] of his issue; then [a]he shall number[5608] to himself seven days for his cleansing,[2893] and wash his clothes, and bathe his flesh in running[2416] water, and shall be clean.

14 And on the eighth day he shall take to him [a]two turtledoves, or two young pigeons, and come before the LORD unto the door of the tabernacle of the congregation, and give them unto the priest:[3548]

15 And the priest shall offer[6213] them, [a]the one *for* a sin offering, and the other *for* a burnt offering;[5930] [b]and the priest shall make an atonement[3722] for him before the LORD for his issue.

16 And [a]if any man's seed[2233] of copulation[7902] go out from him, then he shall wash all his flesh in water, and be unclean until the even.

17 And every garment, and every skin,[5785] whereon is the seed of copulation, shall be washed with water, and be unclean until the even.

18 The woman[802] also with whom man shall lie *with* seed of copulation, they shall *both* bathe *themselves* in water, and [a]be unclean until the even.

19 And [a]if a woman have an issue, *and* her issue in her flesh be blood,[1818] she shall be ‖put apart seven days: and whosoever toucheth her shall be unclean until the even.

20 And every thing that she lieth upon in her separation shall be unclean: every thing also that she sitteth upon shall be unclean.

21 And whosoever toucheth her bed shall wash his clothes, and bathe *himself* in water, and be unclean until the even.

22 And whosoever toucheth any thing that she sat upon shall wash his clothes, and bathe *himself* in water, and be unclean until the even.

23 And if it *be* on *her* bed, or on any thing whereon she sitteth, when he toucheth it, he shall be unclean until the even.

24 And [a]if any man lie with her at all, and her flowers[5079] be upon him, he shall be unclean seven days; and all the bed whereon he lieth shall be unclean.

25 And if [a]a woman have an issue of her blood many days out of the time[6256] of her separation, or if it run beyond the time of her separation; all the days of the issue of her uncleanness shall be as the days of her separation: she *shall be* unclean.

26 Every bed whereon she lieth all the days of her issue shall be unto her as the bed of her separation: and whatsoever she sitteth upon shall be unclean, as the uncleanness of her separation.

27 And whosoever toucheth those things shall be unclean, and shall wash[3526] his clothes, and bathe *himself* in water, and be unclean until the even.

28 But [a]if she be cleansed[2891] of her issue, then she shall number to herself seven days, and after that she shall be clean.

29 And on the eighth day she shall take unto her two turtles, or two young pigeons, and bring them unto the priest, to the door of the tabernacle of the congregation.

30 And the priest shall offer the one *for* a sin offering, and the other *for* a burnt offering; and the priest shall make an atonement for her before the LORD for the issue of her uncleanness.

31 Thus shall ye [a]separate[5144] the children[1121] of Israel from their uncleanness; that they die[4191] not in their uncleanness, when they [b]defile my tabernacle[4908] that *is* among them.

32 [a]This *is* the law[8451] of him that hath an issue, [b]and *of him* whose seed goeth from him, and is defiled[2930] therewith;

33 [a]And of her that is sick of her flowers, and of him that hath an issue,

12 [a]Lev. 6:28; 11:32, 33
13 [a]Lev. 14:8; 15:28
14 [a]Lev. 14:22, 23
15 [a]Lev. 14:30, 31 [b]Lev. 14:19, 31
16 [a]Lev. 22:4; Deut. 23:10
18 [a]1Sam. 21:4
19 ‖Hebr. *in her separation* [a]Lev. 12:2
24 [a]Lev. 20:18
25 [a]Matt. 9:20; Mark 5:25; Luke 8:43
28 [a]Lev. 15:13
31 [a]Lev. 11:47; Deut. 24:8; Ezek. 44:23 [b]Num. 5:3; 19:13, 20; Ezek. 5:11; 23:38
32 [a]Lev. 15:2 [b]Lev. 15:16
33 [a]Lev. 15:19

of the man,[2145] [b]and of the woman,[5347] [c]and of him that lieth with her that is unclean.

The Day of Atonement

16 And the LORD spake unto Moses after [a]the death[4194] of the two sons[1121] of Aaron, when they offered[7126] before the LORD, and died;[4191]

2 And the LORD said unto Moses, Speak[1696] unto Aaron thy brother,[251] that he [a]come not at all times[6256] into the holy[6944] *place* within[1004] the vail before the mercy seat,[3727] which *is* upon the ark;[727] that he die not: for [b]I will appear[7200] in the cloud[6051] upon the mercy seat.

3 Thus shall Aaron [a]come into the holy *place:* [b]with a young bullock for a sin offering,[2403] and a ram for a burnt offering.[5930]

4 He shall put on [a]the holy linen coat, and he shall have the linen breeches upon his flesh,[1320] and shall be girded with a linen girdle,[73] and with the linen mitre[4701] shall he be attired: these *are* holy garments; therefore [b]shall he wash[7364] his flesh in water, and *so* put them on.

5 And he shall take of [a]the congregation[5712] of the children[1121] of Israel two kids of the goats for a sin offering, and one ram for a burnt offering.

6 And Aaron shall offer[7126] his bullock of the sin offering, which *is* for himself, and [a]make an atonement[3722] for himself, and for his house.[1004]

7 And he shall take the two goats, and present them before the LORD *at* the door of the tabernacle of the congregation.[4150]

8 And Aaron shall cast lots upon the two goats; one lot for the LORD, and the other lot for the [I]scapegoat.[5799]

9 And Aaron shall bring the goat upon which the LORD's lot [I]fell,[5927] and offer[6213] him *for* a sin offering.

10 But the goat, on which the lot fell to be the scapegoat, shall be presented alive[2416] before the LORD, to make [a]an atonement[3722] with him, *and* to let him go for a scapegoat into the wilderness.

11 And Aaron shall bring the bullock of the sin offering, which *is* for himself, and shall make an atonement for himself, and for his house, and shall kill[7819] the bullock of the sin offering which *is* for himself:

12 And he shall take [a]a censer full of burning coals of fire from off the altar[4196] before the LORD, and his hands full of [b]sweet incense[7004] beaten small, and bring *it* within the vail:

13 [a]And he shall put the incense upon the fire before the LORD, that the cloud of the incense may cover[3680] the [b]mercy seat that *is* upon the testimony,[5715] that he die not:

14 And [a]he shall take of the blood[1818] of the bullock, and [b]sprinkle *it* with his finger upon the mercy seat eastward; and before the mercy seat shall he sprinkle of the blood with his finger seven times.

15 [a]Then shall he kill the goat of the sin offering, that *is* for the people,[5971] and bring his blood [b]within the vail, and do with that blood as he did with the blood of the bullock, and sprinkle it upon the mercy seat, and before the mercy seat:

16 And he shall [a]make an atonement for the holy *place,* because of the uncleanness[2932] of the children of Israel, and because of their transgressions[6588] in all their sins: and so shall he do for the tabernacle[168] of the congregation, that [I]remaineth among them in the midst of their uncleanness.

17 [a]And there shall be no man[120] in the tabernacle of the congregation[6951] when he goeth in to make an atonement in the holy *place,* until he come out, and have made an atonement for himself, and for his household, and for all the congregation of Israel.

33 [b]Lev. 15:25 [c]Lev. 15:24

1 [a]Lev. 10:1, 2

2 [a]Ex. 30:10; Lev. 23:27; Heb. 9:7; 10:19 [b]Ex. 25:22; 40:34; 1Kgs. 8:10-12

3 [a]Heb. 9:7, 12, 24, 25 [b]Lev. 4:3

4 [a]Ex. 28:39, 42, 43; Lev. 6:10; Ezek. 44:17, 18 [b]Ex. 30:20; Lev. 8:6, 7

5 [a]Lev. 4:14; Num. 29:11; 2Chr. 29:21; Ezra 6:17; Ezek. 45:22, 23

6 [a]Lev. 9:7; Heb. 5:2; 7:27, 28; 9:7

8 [I]Hebr. *Azazel*

9 [I]Hebr. *went up*

10 [a]1John 2:2

12 [a]Lev. 10:1; Num. 16:18, 46; Rev. 8:5 [b]Ex. 30:34

13 [a]Ex. 30:1, 7, 8; Num. 16:7, 18, 46; Rev. 8:3, 4 [b]Ex. 25:21

14 [a]Lev. 4:5; Heb. 9:13, 25; 10:4 [b]Lev. 4:6

15 [a]Heb. 2:17; 5:2; 9:7, 28 [b]Lev. 16:2; Heb. 6:19; 9:3, 7, 12

16 [I]Hebr. *dwelleth* [a]Ex. 29:36; Ezek. 45:18; Heb. 9:22, 23

17 [a]Ex. 34:3; Luke 1:10

16:2, 14 See note on Exodus 26:31–35 concerning the "vail" and "most holy place."

18 And he shall go out unto the altar that *is* before the LORD, and [a]make an atonement for it; and shall take of the blood of the bullock, and of the blood of the goat, and put *it* upon the horns of the altar round about.

19 And he shall sprinkle of the blood upon it with his finger seven times, and cleanse it, and [a]hallow[6942] it from the uncleanness of the children of Israel.

The Scapegoat

20 And when he hath made an end[3615] of [a]reconciling the holy *place,* and the tabernacle of the congregation, and the altar, he shall bring the live[2416] goat:

21 And Aaron shall lay both his hands[3027] upon the head[7218] of the live goat, and confess[3034] over him all the iniquities[5771] of the children of Israel, and all their transgressions in all their sins, [a]putting them upon the head of the goat, and shall send *him* away by the hand of [I]a fit man into the wilderness:

22 And the goat shall [a]bear[5375] upon him all their iniquities unto a land[776] [I]not inhabited: and he shall let go the goat in the wilderness.

23 And Aaron shall come into the tabernacle of the congregation, [a]and shall put off the linen garments, which he put on when he went into the holy *place,* and shall leave them there:

24 And he shall wash his flesh with water in the holy[6918] place, and put on his garments, and come forth, [a]and offer his burnt offering, and the burnt offering of the people, and make an atonement for himself, and for the people.

25 And [a]the fat of the sin offering shall he burn[6999] upon the altar.

26 And he that let go the goat for the scapegoat shall wash[3526] his clothes, [a]and bathe his flesh in water, and afterward come into the camp.

27 [a]And the bullock *for* the sin offering, and the goat *for* the sin offering, whose blood was brought in to make atonement in the holy *place,* shall *one* carry forth without the camp;[4264] and they shall burn[8313] in the fire their skins,[5785] and their flesh, and their dung.

28 And he that burneth them shall wash his clothes, and bathe his flesh in water, and afterward he shall come into the camp.

Regulations for The Day of Atonement

🗝 29 And *this* shall be a statute[2708] for ever[5769] unto you: *that* [a]in the seventh month, on the tenth *day* of the month, ye shall afflict your souls,[5315] and do no work[4399] at all, *whether it be* one of your own country, or a stranger[1616] that sojourneth[1481] among you:

30 For on that day[3117] shall *the priest* make an atonement for you, to [a]cleanse you, *that* ye may be clean from all your sins[2403] before the LORD.

31 [a]It *shall be* a sabbath[7676] of rest[7677] unto you, and ye shall afflict your souls, by a statute for ever.

32 [a]And the priest,[3548] whom he shall anoint, and whom he shall [I][b]consecrate to minister in the priest's office[3547] in his father's[1] stead, shall make the atonement, and [c]shall put on the linen clothes, *even* the holy garments:

33 And [a]he shall make an atonement for the holy sanctuary,[4720] and he shall make an atonement for the tabernacle of the congregation, and for the altar, and he shall make an atonement for the priests, and for all the people of the congregation.

18 [a]Ex. 30:10; Lev. 4:7, 18; Heb. 9:22, 23
19 [a]Ezek. 43:20
20 [a]Lev. 16:16; Ezek. 45:20
21 [I]Hebr. *a man of opportunity* [a]Isa. 53:6
22 [I]Hebr. *of separation* [a]Isa. 53:11, 12; John 1:29; Heb. 9:28; 1Pet. 2:24
23 [a]Ezek. 42:14; 44:19
24 [a]Lev. 16:3, 5
25 [a]Lev. 4:10
26 [a]Lev. 15:5
27 [a]Lev. 4:12, 21; 6:30; Heb. 13:11
29 [a]Ex. 30:10; Lev. 23:27; Num. 29:7; Isa. 58:3, 5; Dan. 10:3, 12
30 [a]Ps. 51:2; Jer. 33:8; Eph. 5:26; Heb. 9:13, 14; 10:1, 2; 1John 1:7, 9
31 [a]Lev. 23:32
32 [I]Hebr. *fill his hand* [a]Lev. 4:3, 5, 16 [b]Ex. 29:29, 30; Num. 20:26, 28 [c]Lev. 16:4
33 [a]Lev. 16:6, 16-18, 24

🗝 **16:29** Here the Day of Atonement is said to be on the tenth day of the seventh month, whereas Leviticus 23:32 specifies the ninth day of the month. The latter passage provides the solution to this apparent discrepancy. It says that the rest is to begin on the ninth day of the month "at evening." For the Hebrews, the tenth day began on the evening of the ninth day.

34 [a]And this shall be an everlasting statute unto you, to make an atonement for the children of Israel for all their sins [b]once a year. And he did as the LORD commanded[6680] Moses.

Blood Is Sacred

17 And the LORD spake unto Moses, saying,

2 Speak[1696] unto Aaron, and unto his sons,[1121] and unto all the children[1121] of Israel, and say[559] unto them; This *is* the thing[1697] which the LORD hath commanded,[6680] saying,

3 What man[376] soever *there be* of the house[1004] of Israel, [a]that killeth an ox, or lamb, or goat, in the camp, or that killeth[7819] *it* out of the camp,[4264]

4 [a]And bringeth it not unto the door of the tabernacle[4908] of the congregation,[4150] to offer[7126] an offering[7133] unto the LORD before the tabernacle[168] of the LORD; blood[1818] shall be [b]imputed[2803] unto that man; he hath shed[8210] blood; and that man [c]shall be cut off[3772] from among his people:[5971]

5 To the end that the children of Israel may bring their sacrifices,[2077] [a]which they offer[2076] in the open field, even that they may bring them unto the LORD, unto the door of the tabernacle of the congregation, unto the priest,[3548] and offer them *for* peace offerings[8002] unto the LORD.

6 And the priest [a]shall sprinkle[2236] the blood upon the altar[4196] of the LORD *at* the door of the tabernacle of the congregation, and [b]burn[6999] the fat for a sweet savour unto the LORD.

7 And they shall no more offer their sacrifices [a]unto devils,[8163] after whom they [b]have gone a whoring.[2181] This shall be a statute[2708] for ever[5769] unto them throughout their generations.[1755]

8 And thou shalt say unto them, Whatsoever man *there be* of the house of Israel, or of the strangers[1616] which sojourn[1481] among you, [a]that offereth[5927] a burnt offering[5930] or sacrifice,

9 And [a]bringeth it not unto the door of the tabernacle of the congregation, to offer[6213] it unto the LORD; even that man shall be cut off from among his people.

10 [a]And whatsoever man *there be* of the house of Israel, or of the strangers that sojourn among you, that eateth any manner of blood; [b]I will even set my face against that soul[5315] that eateth blood, and will cut him off from among his people.

11 [a]For the life[5315] of the flesh[1320] *is* in the blood: and I have given it to you upon the [b]altar to make an atonement[3722] for your souls: for [c]it *is* the blood *that* maketh an atonement for the soul.

12 Therefore I said unto the children of Israel, No soul of you shall eat blood, neither shall any stranger that sojourneth among you eat blood.

13 And whatsoever man *there be* of the children of Israel, or of the strangers that sojourn among you, [I]which [a]hunteth and catcheth[6679] any beast[2416] or fowl that may be eaten; he shall even [b]pour out the blood thereof, and [c]cover[3680] it with dust.[6083]

14 [a]For *it is* the life of all flesh; the blood of it *is* for the life thereof: therefore I said unto the children of Israel, Ye shall eat the blood of no manner of flesh: for the life of all flesh *is* the blood thereof: whosoever eateth it shall be cut off.

15 [a]And every soul that eateth [I]that which died[5038] *of itself,* or that which was torn *with beasts, whether it be* one of your own country, or a stranger, [b]he shall both wash[3526] his clothes, [c]and bathe[7364] *himself* in water, and be unclean[2930] until the even: then shall he be clean.[2891]

16 But if he wash[3526] *them* not, nor bathe his flesh; then [a]he shall bear[5375] his iniquity.[5771]

Forbidden Sexual Practices

18 And the LORD spake unto Moses, saying,

2 Speak[1696] unto the children[1121] of Israel, and say[559] unto them, [a]I am the LORD[3068] your God.[430]

34 [a]Lev. 23:31; Num. 29:7 [b]Ex. 30:10; Heb. 9:7, 25
3 [a]Deut. 12:5, 15, 21
4 [a]Deut. 12:5, 6, 13, 14 [b]Rom. 5:13 [c]Gen. 17:14
5 [a]Gen. 21:33; 22:2; 31:54; Deut. 12:2; 1Kgs. 14:23; 2Kgs. 16:4; 17:10; 2Chr. 28:4; Ezek. 20:28; 22:9
6 [a]Lev. 3:2 [b]Ex. 29:18; Lev. 3:5, 11, 16; 4:31; Num. 18:17
7 [a]Deut. 32:17; 2Chr. 11:15; Ps. 106:37; 1Cor. 10:20; Rev. 9:20 [b]Ex. 34:15; Lev. 20:5; Deut. 31:16; Ezek. 23:8
8 [a]Lev. 1:2, 3
9 [a]Lev. 17:4
10 [a]Gen. 9:4; Lev. 3:17; 7:26, 27; 19:26; Deut. 12:16, 23; 15:23; 1Sam. 14:33; Ezek. 44:7 [b]Lev. 20:3, 5, 6; 26:17; Jer. 44:11; Ezek. 14:8; 15:7
11 [a]Lev. 17:14 [b]Matt. 26:28; Mark 14:24; Rom. 3:25; 5:9; Eph. 1:7; Col. 1:14, 20; Heb. 13:12; 1Pet. 1:2; 1John 1:7; Rev. 1:5 [c]Heb. 9:22
13 [I]Hebr. *that hunteth any hunting* [a]Lev. 7:26 [b]Deut. 12:16, 24; 15:23 [c]Ezek. 24:7
14 [a]Lev. 17:11, 12; Gen. 9:4; Deut. 12:23
15 [I]Hebr. *a carcass* [a]Ex. 22:31; Lev. 22:8; Deut. 14:21; Ezek. 4:14; 44:31 [b]Lev. 11:25 [c]Lev. 15:5
16 [a]Lev. 5:1; 7:18; 19:8; Num. 19:20
2 [a]Ex. 6:7; 18:4; Lev. 11:44; 19:4, 10, 34; 20:7; Ezek. 20:5, 7, 19, 20

3 [a]After the doings of the land[776] of Egypt, wherein ye dwelt, shall ye not do:[6213] and [b]after the doings of the land of Canaan, whither I bring you, shall ye not do: neither shall ye walk in their ordinances.[2708]

4 [a]Ye shall do my judgments,[4941] and keep[8104] mine ordinances, to walk therein: I *am* the LORD your God.

5 Ye shall therefore keep[8104] my statutes,[2708] and my judgments: [a]which if a man[120] do, he shall live[2425] in them: [b]I *am* the LORD.

6 None of you shall approach[7126] to any that is [1]near[7607] of kin[1320] to him, to uncover[1540] *their* nakedness:[6172] I *am* the LORD.

7 [a]The nakedness of thy father,[1] or the nakedness of thy mother,[517] shalt thou not uncover: she *is* thy mother; thou shalt not uncover her nakedness.

8 [a]The nakedness of thy father's wife[802] shalt thou not uncover: it *is* thy father's nakedness.

9 [a]The nakedness of thy sister,[269] the daughter of thy father, or daughter of thy mother, *whether she be* born at home,[1004] or born abroad, *even* their nakedness thou shalt not uncover.

10 The nakedness of thy son's[1121] daughter, or of thy daughter's daughter, *even* their nakedness thou shalt not uncover: for theirs *is* thine own nakedness.

11 The nakedness of thy father's wife's daughter, begotten[4138] of thy father, she *is* thy sister, thou shalt not uncover her nakedness.

12 [a]Thou shalt not uncover the nakedness of thy father's sister: she *is* thy father's near kinswoman.

13 Thou shalt not uncover the nakedness of thy mother's sister: for she *is* thy mother's near kinswoman.

14 [a]Thou shalt not uncover the nakedness of thy father's brother,[251] thou shalt not approach to his wife: she *is* thine aunt.

15 [a]Thou shalt not uncover the nakedness of thy daughter in law: she *is* thy son's wife; thou shalt not uncover her nakedness.

16 [a]Thou shalt not uncover the nakedness of thy brother's wife: it *is* thy brother's nakedness.

17 [a]Thou shalt not uncover the nakedness of a woman[802] and her daughter, neither shalt thou take her son's daughter, or her daughter's daughter, to uncover her nakedness; *for* they *are* her near kinswomen: it *is* wickedness.[2154]

18 Neither shalt thou take [1]a wife to her sister, [a]to vex[6887] *her,* to uncover her nakedness, beside the other in her life[2416] *time.*

19 [a]Also thou shalt not approach unto a woman to uncover her nakedness, as long as she is put apart[5079] for her uncleanness.[2932]

20 Moreover [a]thou shalt not lie carnally[2233][5414,7903] with thy neighbour's wife, to defile[2930] thyself with her.

21 And thou shalt[5674] not let any of thy seed[2233] [a]pass through[5674] *the fire* to [b]Molech, neither shalt thou [c]profane[2490] the name of thy God: I *am* the LORD.

22 [a]Thou shalt not lie[7901] with mankind as with womankind: it *is* abomination.[8441]

23 [a]Neither shalt thou lie with any beast to defile thyself therewith: neither shall any woman stand before a beast to lie down thereto: it *is* [b]confusion.[8397]

3 [a]Ezek. 20:7, 8; 23:8 [b]Ex. 23:24; Lev. 20:23; Deut. 12:4, 30, 31
4 [a]Deut. 4:1, 2; 6:1; Ezek. 20:19
5 [a]Ezek. 20:11, 13, 21; Luke 10:28; Rom. 10:5; Gal. 3:12 [b]Ex. 6:2, 6, 29; Mal. 3:6
6 [1]Hebr. *remainder of his flesh*
7 [a]Lev. 20:11
8 [a]Gen. 49:4; Lev. 20:11; Deut. 22:30; 27:20; Ezek. 22:10; Amos 2:7; 1Cor. 5:1
9 [a]Lev. 20:17; 2Sam. 13:12; Ezek. 22:11
12 [a]Lev. 20:19
14 [a]Lev. 20:20
15 [a]Gen. 38:18, 26; Lev. 20:12; Ezek. 22:11
16 [a]Lev. 20:21; Deut. 25:5; Matt. 14:4; 22:14; Mark 12:19
17 [a]Lev. 20:14
18 [1]Or, one *wife to another* [a]1Sam. 1:6, 8
19 [a]Lev. 20:18; Ezek. 18:6; 22:10
20 [a]Ex. 20:14; Lev. 20:10; Deut. 5:18; 22:22; Prov. 6:29, 32; Mal. 3:5; Matt. 5:27; Rom. 2:22; 1Cor. 6:9; Heb. 13:4
21 [a]Lev. 20:2; 2Kgs. 16:3; 21:6; 23:10; Jer. 19:5; Ezek. 20:31; 23:37, 39 [b]1Kgs. 11:7, 33 [c]Lev. 19:12; 20:3; 21:6; 22:2, 32; Ezek. 36:20; Mal. 1:12
22 [a]Lev. 20:13; Rom. 1:27; 1Cor. 6:9; 1Tim. 1:10
23 [a]Ex. 22:19; Lev. 20:15, 16 [b]Lev. 20:12

18:21 Perhaps one of the most atrocious elements of the religion of Israel's neighbors in Canaan was the practice of human sacrifice. This passage and others (Lev. 20:2; Deut. 18:10) show how God hates this practice. Yet, some of the kings of Judah sacrificed their sons to Molech, the Ammonite national deity (2 Kgs. 16:3; 21:6; see note on 2 Kgs. 23:10). The people of Judah even built a special high place where they could sacrifice their sons and daughters (Jer. 7:31). All of this was done in the worship of foreign gods, which only served to intensify God's hatred of it.

24 [a]Defile not ye yourselves in any of these things: [b]for in all these the nations[1471] are defiled which I cast out before you:

25 And [a]the land is defiled:[2930] therefore I do [b]visit[6485] the iniquity[5771] thereof upon it, and the land itself [c]vomiteth out her inhabitants.

26 [a]Ye shall therefore keep my statutes and my judgments, and shall not commit *any* of these abominations; *neither* any of your own nation, nor any stranger[1616] that sojourneth[1481] among you:

27 (For all these abominations have[6213] the men[582] of the land done,[6213] which *were* before you, and the land is defiled;)

28 That [a]the land spue not you out also, when ye defile it, as it spued out the nations that *were* before you.

29 For whosoever shall commit any of these abominations, even the souls[5315] that commit *them* shall be cut off[3772] from among their people.[5971]

30 Therefore shall ye keep mine ordinance,[4931] [a]that *ye* commit[6213] not *any one* of these abominable customs, which were committed before you, and that ye [b]defile not yourselves therein: [c]I *am* the LORD your God.

Laws of Holiness and Justice

19 And the LORD spake unto Moses, saying,

2 Speak[1696] unto all the congregation[5712] of the children[1121] of Israel, and say[559] unto them, [a]Ye shall be holy:[6918] for I the LORD your God[430] *am* holy.

3 [a]Ye shall fear[3372] every man[376] his mother,[517] and his father,[1] and [b]keep my sabbaths:[7676] I *am* the LORD your God.

4 [a]Turn ye not unto idols,[457] [b]nor make[6213] to yourselves molten[4541] gods: I *am* the LORD your God.

5 And [a]if ye offer[2076] a sacrifice[2077] of peace offerings[8002] unto the LORD, ye shall offer it at your own will.[7522]

6 It shall be eaten the same day ye offer it, and on the morrow: and if ought remain[3498] until the third day, it shall be burnt[8313] in the fire.

7 And if it be eaten at all on the third day, it *is* abominable;[6292] it shall not be accepted.[7521]

8 Therefore *every one* that eateth it shall bear[5375] his iniquity,[5771] because he hath profaned the hallowed thing[6944] of the LORD: and that soul[5315] shall be cut off[3772] from among his people.[5971]

🔑 9 And [a]when ye reap the harvest of your land,[776] thou shalt not wholly reap[3615] the corners of thy field,[7704] neither shalt thou gather the gleanings of thy harvest.

10 And thou shalt not glean thy vineyard, neither shalt thou gather *every* grape of thy vineyard; thou shalt leave[5800] them for the poor and stranger:[1616] I *am* the LORD your God.

11 [a]Ye shall not steal, neither deal falsely, [b]neither lie one to another.

12 And ye shall not [a]swear by my name falsely,[8267] [b]neither shalt thou profane the name of thy God: I *am* the LORD.

13 [a]Thou shalt not defraud thy neighbour,[7453] neither rob *him:* [b]the wages of him that is hired shall not abide with thee all night until the morning.

14 Thou shalt not curse[7043] the deaf, [a]nor put a stumblingblock[4383] before the blind, but shalt [b]fear[3372] thy God: I *am* the LORD.

24 [a]Lev. 18:30; Matt. 15:18, 19, 20; Mark 7:21, 22, 23; 1Cor. 3:17 [b]Lev. 20:23; Deut. 18:12
25 [a]Num. 35:34; Jer. 2:7; 16:18; Ezek. 36:17 [b]Ps. 89:32; Isa. 26:21; Jer. 5:9, 29; 9:9; 14:10; 23:2; Hos. 2:13; 8:13; 9:9 [c]Lev. 18:28
26 [a]Lev. 18:5, 30
28 [a]Lev. 20:22; Jer. 9:19; Ezek. 36:13, 17
30 [a]Lev. 18:3, 26; 20:23; Deut. 18:9 [b]Lev. 18:24 [c]Lev. 18:2, 4
2 [a]Lev. 11:44; 20:7, 26; 1Pet. 1:16
3 [a]Ex. 20:12 [b]Ex. 20:8; 31:13
4 [a]Ex. 20:4; Lev. 26:1; 1Cor. 10:14; 1John 5:21; [b]Ex. 34:17; Deut. 27:15
5 [a]Lev. 7:16
9 [a]Lev. 23:22; Deut. 24:19-21; Ruth 2:15, 16
11 [a]Ex. 20:15; 22:1, 7, 10-12; Deut. 5:19 [b]Lev. 6:2; Eph. 4:25; Col. 3:9
12 [a]Ex. 20:7; Lev. 6:3; Deut. 5:11; Matt. 5:33; James 5:12 [b]Lev. 18:21
13 [a]Mark 10:19; 1Thess. 4:6 [b]Deut. 24:14, 15; Mal. 3:5; James 5:4
14 [a]Deut. 27:18; Rom. 14:13 [b]Gen. 42:18; Lev. 19:32; 25:17; Eccl. 5:7; 1Pet. 2:17

🔑 **19:9, 10** The Law of Moses contains numerous laws that protect poor people and foreigners. These verses, along with Leviticus 23:22, put restrictions on how closely crops could be harvested, so the poor would have something to glean. That the law was being followed during the period of the Judges is evident from the fact that Ruth gleaned in the field of Boaz, her future husband (Ruth 2:2–7).

15 [a]Ye shall do no unrighteousness[5766] in judgment:[4941] thou shalt not respect the person of the poor, nor honour[1921] the person of the mighty: *but* in righteousness[6664] shalt thou judge[8199] thy neighbour.

16 [a]Thou shalt not go up and down *as* a talebearer among thy people: neither shalt thou [b]stand against the blood[1818] of thy neighbour: I *am* the LORD.

17 [a]Thou shalt not hate[8130] thy brother[251] in thine heart:3824 [b]thou shalt in any wise rebuke[3198] thy neighbour, [I]and not suffer[5375] sin upon him.

🔑 18 [a]Thou shalt not avenge,[5358] nor bear any grudge against the children of thy people, [b]but thou shalt love[157] thy neighbour as thyself: I *am* the LORD.

19 Ye shall keep my statutes.[2708] Thou shalt not let thy cattle gender7250 with a diverse kind: [a]thou shalt not sow thy field with mingled seed: [b]neither shall a garment mingled of linen and woollen come upon thee.

20 And whosoever lieth carnally[2233] 7901,7902 with a woman,[802] that *is* a bondmaid, [I]betrothed2778 to an husband,[376] and not at all redeemed,[6299] nor freedom given her; [II]she shall be scourged;1244 they shall not be put to death,[4191] because she was not free.

21 And [a]he shall bring his trespass offering[817] unto the LORD, unto the door of the tabernacle of the congregation,[4150] *even* a ram for a trespass offering.

22 And the priest[3548] shall make an atonement[3722] for him with the ram of the trespass offering before the LORD for his sin[2403] which he hath done:[2398] and the sin which he hath done shall be forgiven[5545] him.

23 And when ye shall come into the land, and shall have planted all manner of trees for food, then ye shall count the fruit thereof as uncircumcised:[6189] three years shall it be as uncircumcised unto you: it shall not be eaten of.

24 But in the fourth year all the fruit thereof shall be [I]holy [a]to praise the LORD *withal.*

25 And in the fifth year shall ye eat of the fruit thereof, that it may yield unto you the increase thereof: I *am* the LORD your God.

26 [a]Ye shall not eat *any thing* with the blood: [b]neither shall ye use enchantment,[5172] nor observe times.[6049]

27 [a]Ye shall not round[5362] the corners of your heads, neither shalt thou mar[7843] the corners of thy beard.[2206]

28 Ye shall not [a]make any cuttings in your flesh[1320] for the dead,[5315] nor print any marks upon you: I *am* the LORD.

29 [a]Do not [I]prostitute[2490] thy daughter, to cause her to be a whore; lest the land fall to whoredom,[2181] and the land become full of wickedness.[2154]

30 [a]Ye shall keep my sabbaths, and [b]reverence[3372] my sanctuary:[4720] I *am* the LORD.

31 [a]Regard not them that have familiar spirits,[178] neither seek after wizards,[3049] to be defiled[2930] by them: I *am* the LORD your God.

32 [a]Thou shalt rise up before the hoary head,[7872] and honour the face of the old man,[2205] and [b]fear thy God: I *am* the LORD.

🔑 33 And [a]if a stranger sojourn[1481]

15 [a]Ex. 23:2, 3; Deut. 1:17; 16:19; 27:19; Ps. 82:2; Prov. 24:23; James 2:9
16 [a]Ex. 23:1; Ps. 15:3; 50:20; Prov. 11:13; 20:19; Ezek. 22:9 [b]Ex. 23:1, 7; 1Kgs. 21:13; Matt. 26:60, 61; 27:4
17 [I]Or, *that thou bear not sin for him* [a]1John 2:9, 11; 3:15 [b]Matt. 18:15; Luke 17:3; Gal. 6:1; Eph. 5:11; 1Tim. 5:20; 2Tim. 4:2; Titus 1:13; 2:15
18 [a]2Sam. 13:22; Prov. 20:22; Rom. 12:17, 19; Gal. 5:20; Eph. 4:31; James 5:9; 1Pet. 2:1 [b]Matt. 5:43; 22:39; Rom. 13:9; Gal. 5:14; James 2:8
19 [a]Deut. 22:9, 10 [b]Deut. 22:11
20 [I]Hebr. *reproached by, or, for man* [II]Hebr. *there shall be a scourging*
21 [a]Lev. 5:15; 6:6
24 [I]Hebr. *holiness of praises to the LORD* [a]Deut. 12:17, 18; Prov. 3:9
26 [a]Lev. 17:10-14; Deut. 12:23 [b]Deut. 18:10, 11, 14; 1Sam. 15:23; 2Kgs. 17:17; 21:6; 2Chr. 33:6; Mal. 3:5
27 [a]Lev. 21:5; Isa. 15:2; Jer. 9:26; 48:37
28 [a]Lev. 21:5; Deut. 14:1; Jer. 16:6; 48:37
29 [I]Hebr. *profane* [a]Deut. 23:17
30 [a]Lev. 19:3; 26:2 [b]Eccl. 5:1
31 [a]Ex. 22:18; Lev. 20:6, 27; Deut. 18:10; 1Sam. 28:7; 1Chr. 10:13; Isa. 8:19; Acts 16:16
32 [a]Prov. 20:29; 1Tim. 5:1 [b]Lev. 19:14
33 [a]Ex. 22:21; 23:9

🔑 **19:18** See note on Exodus 20:1–17.

🔑 **19:33, 34** This did not eliminate all the distinctions between the Israelites and the foreigners living among them. In certain contexts, especially in the lending of money, the foreigners were to be treated differently. The usual reason to lend to a fellow countryman was to help a poor man get back on his feet, and no interest was to be exacted (Lev. 25:35–38). The case was different for foreigners, who could be charged interest (Deut. 23:20) and whose debts were not cancelled on the Sabbatical Year (Deut. 15:1–3). Nevertheless, Leviticus 19:33, 34 expresses the overriding ethical concern, and it is based on the fact that they themselves had been foreigners in Egypt.

with thee in your land, ye shall not [I]vex[3238] him.

34 [a]*But* the stranger that dwelleth[1481] with you shall be unto you as one born among you, and [b]thou shalt love him as thyself; for ye were strangers in the land of Egypt: I *am* the LORD your God.

35 [a]Ye shall do no unrighteousness in judgment, in meteyard, in weight, or in measure.

36 [a]Just[6664] balances, just [I]weights, a just ephah, and a just hin, shall ye have: I *am* the LORD your God, which brought you out of the land of Egypt.

37 [a]Therefore shall ye observe[8104] all my statutes, and all my judgments, and do[6213] them: I *am* the LORD.

The Penalties for Sin

20 And the LORD spake unto Moses, saying,

2 [a]Again, thou shalt say to the children[1121] of Israel, [b]Whosoever *he be* of the children of Israel, or of the strangers[1616] that sojourn[1481] in Israel, that giveth *any* of his seed[2233] unto Molech; he shall surely be put to death:[4191] the people[5971] of the land[776] shall stone him with stones.

3 And [a]I will set my face against that man, and will cut him off[3772] from among his people; because he hath given of his seed unto Molech, to [b]defile my sanctuary,[4720] and [c]to profane[2490] my holy[6944] name.

4 And if the people of the land do any ways hide their eyes from the man, when he giveth of his seed unto Molech, and [a]kill[4191] him not:

5 Then [a]I will set my face against that man, and [b]against his family,[4940] and will cut him off, and all that [c]go a whoring[2181] after him, to commit whoredom[2181] with Molech, from among their people.

6 And [a]the soul[5315] that turneth after such as have familiar spirits,[178] and after wizards,[3049] to go a whoring[2181] after them, I will even set my face against that soul, and will cut him off from among his people.

7 [a]Sanctify yourselves therefore, and be ye holy: for I *am* the LORD your God.[430]

8 [a]And ye shall keep[8104] my statutes,[2708] and do[6213] them: [b]I *am* the LORD which sanctify[6942] you.

9 [a]For every one that curseth[7043] his father[1] or his mother[517] shall be surely put to death: he hath cursed his father or his mother; [b]his blood[1818] *shall be* upon him.

10 And [a]the man that committeth adultery with *another* man's wife,[802] *even he* that committeth adultery[5003] with his neighbour's[7453] wife, the adulterer[5003] and the adulteress[5003] shall surely be put to death.

11 [a]And the man that lieth with his father's wife hath uncovered[1540] his father's nakedness:[6172] both of them shall surely be put to death; their blood *shall be* upon them.

12 [a]And if a man lie with his daughter in law, both of them shall surely be put to death: [b]they have wrought confusion; their blood *shall be* upon them.

13 [a]If a man also lie with mankind,[2145] as he lieth with a woman,[802] both of them have committed an abomination:[8441] they shall surely be put to death; their blood *shall be* upon them.

14 [a]And if a man take a wife and her mother, it *is* wickedness:[2154] they shall be burnt[8313] with fire, both he and they; that there be no wickedness among you.

15 [a]And if a man lie with a beast, he shall surely be put to death: and ye shall slay[2026] the beast.

16 And if a woman approach unto any beast, and lie down thereto, thou shalt kill[2026] the woman, and the beast: they shall surely be put to death; their blood *shall be* upon them.

17 [a]And if a man shall take his sister,[269] his father's daughter, or his mother's daughter, and see[7200] her nakedness, and she see his nakedness; it *is* a wicked thing;[2617] and they shall be cut off[3772] in the sight of their people: he hath uncovered his sister's nakedness; he shall bear[5375] his iniquity.[5771]

---

33 [I]Or, *oppress*
34 [a]Ex. 12:48, 49 [b]Deut. 10:19
35 [a]Lev. 19:15
36 [I]Hebr. *stones* [a]Deut. 25:13, 15; Prov. 11:1; 16:11; 20:10
37 [a]Lev. 18:4, 5; Deut. 4:5, 6; 5:1; 6:25

2 [a]Lev. 18:2 [b]Lev. 18:21; Deut. 12:31; 18:10; 2Kgs. 17:17; 23:10; 2Chr. 33:6; Jer. 7:31; 32:35; Ezek. 20:26, 31
3 [a]Lev. 17:10 [b]Ezek. 5:11; 23:38, 39 [c]Lev. 18:21
4 [a]Deut. 17:2, 3, 5
5 [a]Lev. 17:10 [b]Ex. 20:5 [c]Lev. 17:7
6 [a]Lev. 19:31
7 [a]Lev. 11:44; 19:2; 1Pet. 1:16
8 [a]Lev. 19:37 [b]Ex. 31:13; Lev. 21:8; Ezek. 37:28
9 [a]Ex. 21:17; Deut. 27:16; Prov. 20:20; Matt. 15:4 [b]Lev. 20:11-13, 16, 27; 2Sam. 1:16
10 [a]Lev. 18:20; Deut. 22:22; John 8:4, 5
11 [a]Lev. 18:8; Deut. 27:23
12 [a]Lev. 18:15 [b]Lev. 18:23
13 [a]Gen. 19:5 [b]Lev. 18:22; Deut. 23:17; Judg. 19:22
14 [a]Lev. 18:17; Deut. 27:23
15 [a]Lev. 18:23; Deut. 27:21
17 [a]Gen. 20:12; Lev. 18:9; Deut. 27:22

18 [a]And if a man shall lie with a woman having her sickness,[1739] and shall uncover her nakedness; he hath [I]discovered her fountain, and she hath uncovered the fountain of her blood: and both of them shall be cut off from among their people.

19 [a]And thou shalt not uncover the nakedness of thy mother's sister, nor of thy father's sister: [b]for he uncovereth his near kin:[7607] they shall bear their iniquity.

20 [a]And if a man shall lie with his uncle's wife, he hath uncovered his uncle's nakedness: they shall bear their sin; they shall die[4191] childless.

21 [a]And if a man shall take his brother's[251] wife, it *is* [I]an unclean thing: he hath uncovered his brother's nakedness; they shall be childless.

22 Ye shall therefore keep all my [a]statutes, and all my judgments, and do them: that the land, whither I bring you to dwell therein, [b]spue you not out.

23 [a]And ye shall not walk in the manners[2708] of the nation,[1471] which I cast out before you: for they committed all these things, and [b]therefore I abhorred[6973] them.

24 But [a]I have said unto you, Ye shall inherit[3423] their land,[127] and I will give it unto you to possess[3423] it, a land that floweth with milk and honey: I *am* the LORD your God, [b]which have separated[914] you from *other* people.

25 [a]Ye shall therefore put difference[914] between clean[2889] beasts and unclean, and between unclean[2931] fowls and clean: [b]and ye shall not make your souls abominable by beast, or by fowl, or by any manner of living thing that [I]creepeth on the ground, which I have separated from you as unclean.

🔑 26 And ye shall be holy unto me: [a]for I the LORD *am* holy, and [b]have severed[914] you from *other* people, that ye should be mine.

27 [a]A man also or woman that hath a familiar spirit, or that is a wizard, shall surely be put to death: they shall stone them with stones: [b]their blood *shall be* upon them.

The Holiness of the Priests

21 And the LORD said unto Moses, Speak unto the priests[3548] the sons[1121] of Aaron, and say unto them, [a]There shall none be defiled for the dead[5315] among his people:[5971]

2 But for his kin,[7607] that is near unto him, *that is,* for his mother,[517] and for his father,[1] and for his son, and for his daughter, and for his brother,[251]

3 And for his sister[269] a virgin,[1330] that is nigh unto him, which hath had no husband;[376] for her may he be defiled.

4 *But* [I]he shall not defile himself, *being* a chief man[1167] among his people, to profane himself.

5 [a]They shall not make baldness upon their head, neither shall they shave off the corner of their beard,[2206] nor make any cuttings in their flesh.[1320]

6 They shall be holy[6918] unto their God,[430] and [a]not profane[2490] the name of their God: for the offerings of the LORD made by fire,[801] *and* [b]the bread of their God, they do offer: therefore they shall be holy.[6944]

7 [a]They shall not take a wife[802] *that is* a whore,[2181] or profane;[2490] neither shall they take a woman[802] [b]put away from her husband: for he *is* holy unto his God.

8 Thou shalt sanctify[6942] him therefore; for he offereth the bread of thy God: he shall be holy unto thee: [a]for I the LORD, which sanctify you, *am* holy.

9 [a]And the daughter of any priest, if she profane herself by playing the whore,[2181] she profaneth her father: she shall be burnt[8313] with fire.

10 [a]And *he that is* the high priest among his brethren, upon whose head the anointing[4886] oil[8081] was poured, and

18 [I]Hebr. *made naked* [a]Lev. 15:24; 18:19
19 [a]Lev. 18:12, 13 [b]Lev. 18:6
20 [a]Lev. 18:14
21 [I]Hebr. *a separation* [a]Lev. 18:16
22 [a]Lev. 18:26; 19:37 [b]Lev. 18:25, 28
23 [a]Lev. 18:3, 24, 30 [b]Lev. 18:27; Deut. 9:5
24 [a]Ex. 3:17; 6:8 [b]Ex. 19:5; 33:16; Lev. 20:26; Deut. 7:6; 14:2; 1Kgs. 8:53
25 [I]Or, *moveth* [a]Lev. 11:47; Deut. 14:4 [b]Lev. 11:43
26 [a]Lev. 19:2; 20:7; 1Pet. 1:16 [b]Lev. 20:24; Titus 2:14
27 [a]Ex. 22:18; Lev. 19:31; Deut. 18:10, 11; 1Sam. 28:7, 8 [b]Lev. 20:9

1 [a]Ezek. 44:25
4 [I]Or, *being a husband among his people, he shall not defile himself* for his wife
5 [a]Lev. 19:27, 28; Deut. 14:1; Ezek. 44:20
6 [a]Lev. 18:21; 19:12 [b]Lev. 3:11
7 [a]Ezek. 44:22 [b]Deut. 24:1, 2
8 [a]Lev. 20:7, 8
9 [a]Gen. 38:24
10 [a]Ex. 29:29, 30; Lev. 8:12, 16:32; Num. 35:25

🔑 **20:26** See note on Leviticus 11:44, 45.

[b]that is consecrated to put on the garments, [c]shall not uncover[6544] his head, nor rend6533 his clothes;

11 Neither shall he [a]go in to any dead[4191] body,[5315] nor defile himself for his father, or for his mother;

12 [a]Neither shall he go out of the sanctuary,[4720] nor profane the sanctuary of his God; for [b]the crown[5145] of the anointing oil of his God *is* upon him: I *am* the LORD.

13 And [a]he shall take a wife in her virginity.[1331]

14 A widow, or a divorced woman,1644 or profane,2491 *or* an harlot,[2181] these shall he not take: but he shall take a virgin of his own people to wife.

15 Neither shall he profane his seed[2233] among his people: for [a]I the LORD do sanctify him.

16 And the LORD spake unto Moses, saying,

17 Speak[1696] unto Aaron, saying,[559] Whosoever[376] *he be* of thy seed in their generations[1755] that hath *any* blemish,[3971] let him not [a]approach to offer[7126] the [I]bread of his God.

18 For whatsoever man *he be* that hath a blemish, he shall not approach: a blind man, or a lame, or he that hath a flat nose,[2763] or any thing [a]superfluous,

19 Or a man that is brokenfooted,[7667] or brokenhanded,

20 Or crookbackt, or [I]a dwarf, or that hath a blemish[8400] in his eye, or be scurvy,1618 or scabbed, or [a]hath his stones broken;

21 No man that hath a blemish of the seed of Aaron the priest shall come nigh[5066] to [a]offer the offerings of the LORD made by fire: he hath a blemish; he shall not come nigh to offer the bread of his God.

22 He shall eat the bread of his God, *both* of the [a]most holy, and of the [b]holy.[6944]

23 Only he shall not go in unto the vail, nor come nigh unto the altar,[4196] because he hath a blemish; that [a]he profane not my sanctuaries: for I the LORD do sanctify them.

24 And Moses told[1696] *it* unto Aaron, and to his sons, and unto all the children of Israel.

The Holiness of the Offerings

22 And the LORD spake unto Moses, saying,

2 Speak unto Aaron and to his sons,[1121] that they [a]separate[5144] themselves from the holy things of the children of Israel, and that they [b]profane[2490] not my holy name *in those things* which they [c]hallow[6942] unto me: I *am* the LORD.

3 Say unto them, Whosoever *he be* of all your seed[2233] among your generations,[1755] that goeth[7126] unto the holy things, which the children of Israel hallow unto the LORD, [a]having his uncleanness[2932] upon him, that soul[5315] shall be cut off[3772] from my presence: I *am* the LORD.

4 What man soever of the seed of Aaron *is* a leper, or hath [a]a [I]running issue; he shall not eat of the holy things, [b]until he be clean. And [c]whoso toucheth[5060] any thing *that is* unclean[2931] *by* the dead,[5315] or [d]a man whose seed goeth from him;

5 Or [a]whosoever toucheth any creeping thing, whereby he may be made unclean,[2930] or [b]a man[120] of whom he may take uncleanness, whatsoever uncleanness he hath;

6 The soul which hath touched any such shall be unclean[2930] until even, and shall not eat of the holy things, unless he [a]wash[7364] his flesh[1320] with water.

7 And when the sun is down, he shall be clean,[2891] and shall afterward eat of the holy things; because [a]it *is* his food.

8 [a]That which dieth of itself,[5038] or is torn *with beasts,* he shall not eat to defile[2930] himself therewith: I *am* the LORD.

9 They shall therefore keep[8104] mine ordinance,[4931] [a]lest they bear[5375] sin for it, and die[4191] therefore, if they profane it: I the LORD do sanctify them.

10 [a]There shall no stranger[2114] eat *of*

10 [b]Ex. 28:2; Lev. 16:32 [c]Lev. 10:6
11 [a]Lev. 21:1, 2; Num. 19:14
12 [a]Lev. 10:7 [b]Ex. 28:36; Lev. 8:9, 12, 30
13 [a]Lev. 21:7; Ezek. 44:22
15 [a]Lev. 21:8
17 [I]Or, *food* [a]Lev. 10:3; Num. 16:5; Ps. 65:4
18 [a]Lev. 22:23
20 [I]Or, *too slender* [a]Deut. 23:1
21 [a]Lev. 21:6
22 [a]Lev. 2:3, 10; 6:17, 29; 7:1; 24:9; Num. 18:9 [b]Lev. 22:10, 11, 12; Num. 18:19
23 [a]Lev. 21:12
2 [a]Num. 6:3 [b]Lev. 18:21 [c]Ex. 28:38; Num. 18:32; Deut. 15:19
3 [a]Lev. 7:20
4 [I]Hebr. *running of the reins* [a]Lev. 15:2 [b]Lev. 14:2; 15:13 [c]Num. 19:11, 22 [d]Lev. 15:16
5 [a]Lev. 11:24, 43, 44 [b]Lev. 15:7, 19
6 [a]Lev. 15:5; Heb. 10:22
7 [a]Lev. 21:22; Num. 18:11, 13
8 [a]Ex. 22:31; Lev. 17:15; Ezek. 44:31
9 [a]Ex. 28:43; Num. 18:22, 32
10 [a]1Sam. 21:6

the holy thing: a sojourner[8453] of the priest,[3548] or an hired servant, shall not eat *of* the holy thing.

11 But if the priest buy *any* soul [I]with his money, he shall eat of it, and he that is born in his house:[1004] [a]they shall eat of his meat.

12 If the priest's daughter also be *married* unto [I]a stranger, she may not eat of an offering[8641] of the holy things.

13 But if the priest's daughter be a widow, or divorced,1644 and have no child, and is [a]returned[7725] unto her father's[1] house, [b]as in her youth, she shall eat of her father's meat: but there shall no stranger eat thereof.

14 [a]And if a man eat *of* the holy thing unwittingly,[7684] then he shall put the fifth *part* thereof unto it, and shall give *it* unto the priest with the holy thing.

15 And [a]they shall not profane the holy things of the children of Israel, which they offer unto the LORD;

16 Or [I]suffer them [a]to bear the iniquity[5771] of trespass,[819] when they eat their holy things: for I the LORD do sanctify them.

17 And the LORD spake unto Moses, saying,

18 Speak unto Aaron, and to his sons, and unto all the children of Israel, and say unto them, [a]Whatsoever *he be* of the house of Israel, or of the strangers[1616] in Israel, that will offer his oblation[7133] for all his vows,[5088] and for all his freewill offerings,[5071] which they will offer unto the LORD for a burnt offering;[5930]

19 [a]Ye shall offer at your own will[7522] a male2145 without blemish,[8549] of the beeves, of the sheep, or of the goats.

20 [a]*But* whatsoever hath a blemish,[3971] *that* shall ye not offer: for it shall not be acceptable[7522] for you.

21 And [a]whosoever offereth a sacrifice[2077] of peace offerings[8002] unto the LORD [b]to accomplish[6381] *his* vow, or a freewill offering in beeves or [I]sheep, it shall be perfect to be accepted;[7522] there shall be no blemish therein.

22 [a]Blind, or broken,[7665] or maimed, or having a wen, or scurvy,[1618] or

11 [I]Hebr. *with the purchase of his money* [a]Num. 18:11, 13

12 [I]Hebr. *a man a stranger*

13 [a]Gen. 38:11 [b]Lev. 10:14; Num. 18:11, 19

14 [a]Lev. 5:15, 16

15 [a]Num. 18:32

16 [I]Or, *lade themselves with the iniquity of trespass in their eating* [a]Lev. 22:9

18 [a]Lev. 1:2, 3, 10; Num. 15:14

19 [a]Lev. 1:3

20 [a]Deut. 15:21; 17:1; Mal. 1:8, 14; Eph. 5:27; Heb. 9:14; 1Pet. 1:19

21 [I]Or, *goats* [a]Lev. 3:1, 6 [b]Lev. 7:16; Num. 15:3, 8; Deut. 23:21, 23; Ps. 61:8; 65:1; Eccl. 5:4, 5

22 [a]Lev. 22:20; Mal. 1:8 [b]Lev. 1:9, 13; 3:3, 5

23 [I]Or, *kid* [a]Lev. 21:18

25 [a]Num. 15:14–16 [b]Lev. 21:6, 17 [c]Mal. 1:14

27 [a]Ex. 22:30

28 [I]Or, *she-goat* [a]Deut. 22:6

29 [a]Lev. 7:12; Ps. 107:22; 116:17; Amos 4:5

30 [a]Lev. 7:15

31 [a]Lev. 19:37; Num. 15:40; Deut. 4:40

32 [a]Lev. 18:21 [b]Lev. 10:3; Matt. 6:9; Luke 11:2; [c]Lev. 20:8

33 [a]Ex. 6:7; Lev. 11:45; 19:36; 25:38; Num. 15:41

scabbed, ye shall not offer these unto the LORD, nor make [b]an offering by fire[801] of them upon the altar[4196] unto the LORD.

23 Either a bullock or a [I]lamb that hath any thing [a]superfluous or lacking in his parts, that mayest thou offer *for* a freewill offering; but for a vow it shall not be accepted.[7521]

24 Ye shall not offer unto the LORD that which is bruised, or crushed,[3807] or broken, or cut;[3772] neither shall ye make *any offering thereof* in your land.[776]

25 Neither [a]from a stranger's[5236] hand[3027] shall ye offer [b]the bread of your God[430] of any of these; because their [c]corruption *is* in them, *and* blemishes *be* in them: they shall not be accepted[7521] for you.

26 And the LORD spake unto Moses, saying,

27 [a]When a bullock, or a sheep, or a goat, is brought forth, then it shall be seven days under the dam;[517] and from the eighth day and thenceforth it shall be accepted for an offering[7133] made by fire unto the LORD.

28 And *whether it be* cow or [I]ewe,7716 ye shall not kill[7819] it [a]and her young both in one day.

29 And when ye will [a]offer[2076] a sacrifice of thanksgiving[8426] unto the LORD, offer *it* at your own will.

30 On the same day it shall be eaten up; ye shall leave [a]none of it until the morrow: I *am* the LORD.

31 [a]Therefore shall ye keep my commandments,[4687] and do[6213] them: I *am* the LORD.

32 [a]Neither shall ye profane my holy name; but [b]I will be hallowed[6942] among the children of Israel: I *am* the LORD which [c]hallow[6942] you,

33 [a]That brought you out of the land of Egypt, to be your God: I *am* the LORD.

The Appointed Festivals

23 And the LORD spake unto Moses, saying,

2 Speak unto the children[1121] of Israel, and say unto them, *Concerning*

[a]the feasts[4150] of the LORD, which ye shall [b]proclaim[7121] *to be* holy[6944] convocations,[4744] *even* these *are* my feasts.

3 [a]Six days shall work[4399] be done: but the seventh day *is* the sabbath[7676] of rest,[7677] an holy convocation;[4744] ye shall do[6213] no work *therein:* it *is* the sabbath of the LORD in all your dwellings.[4186]

4 [a]These *are* the feasts of the LORD, *even* holy convocations, which ye shall proclaim in their seasons.

5 [a]In the fourteenth *day* of the first month at even *is* the LORD'S passover.[6453]

6 And on the fifteenth day of the same month *is* the feast[2282] of unleavened bread unto the LORD: seven days ye must eat unleavened bread.

7 [a]In the first day ye shall have an holy convocation: ye shall do no servile[5656] work therein.

8 But ye shall offer[7126] an offering made by fire[801] unto the LORD seven days: in the seventh day *is* an holy convocation: ye shall do no servile work *therein.*

9 And the LORD spake unto Moses, saying,

10 Speak unto the children of Israel, and say unto them, [a]When ye be come into the land[776] which I give unto you, and shall reap the harvest thereof, then ye shall bring a [I]sheaf of [b]the firstfruits[7225] of your harvest unto the priest:[3548]

11 And he shall [a]wave the sheaf before the LORD, to be accepted[7522] for you: on the morrow after the sabbath the priest shall wave it.

12 And ye shall offer[6213] that day when ye wave the sheaf an he lamb without blemish[8549] of the first year for a burnt offering[5930] unto the LORD.

13 [a]And the meat offering[4503] thereof *shall be* two tenth deals of fine flour mingled[1101] with oil,[8081] an offering made by fire unto the LORD *for* a sweet savour: and the drink offering[5262] thereof *shall be* of wine, the fourth *part* of an hin.

14 And ye shall eat neither bread, nor parched corn, nor green ears, until the selfsame day that ye have brought an offering[7133] unto your God:[430] *it shall be* a statute[2708] for ever[5769] throughout your generations[1755] in all your dwellings.

15 And [a]ye shall count[5608] unto you from the morrow after the sabbath, from the day that ye brought the sheaf of the wave offering; seven sabbaths shall be complete:[8549]

16 Even unto the morrow after the seventh sabbath shall ye number[5608] [a]fifty days; and ye shall offer [b]a new meat offering unto the LORD.

17 Ye shall bring out of your habitations[4186] two wave loaves of two tenth deals: they shall be of fine flour; they shall be baken with leaven;[2557] *they are* [a]the firstfruits unto the LORD.

18 And ye shall offer with the bread seven lambs without blemish of the first year, and one young bullock, and two rams: they shall be *for* a burnt offering unto the LORD, with their meat offering, and their drink offerings, *even* an offering made by fire, of sweet savour unto the LORD.

19 Then ye shall sacrifice[6213] [a]one kid of the goats for a sin offering,[2398] and two lambs of the first year for a sacrifice[2077] of [b]peace offerings.[8002]

20 And the priest shall wave them with the bread of the firstfruits *for* a wave offering before the LORD, with the two lambs: [a]they shall be holy to the LORD for the priest.

21 And ye shall proclaim on the selfsame day, *that* it may be an holy convocation unto you: ye shall do no servile work *therein: it shall be* a statute for ever in all your dwellings throughout your generations.

⊶ 22 And [a]when ye reap the harvest of your land, thou shalt not make clean riddance[3615] of the corners of thy field[7704] when thou reapest, [b]neither shalt thou gather any gleaning of thy harvest:

2 [a]Lev. 23:4, 37 [b]Ex. 32:5; 2Kgs. 10:20; Ps. 81:3
3 [a]Ex. 20:9; 23:12; 31:15; 34:21; Lev. 19:3; Deut. 5:13; Luke 13:14
4 [a]Ex. 23:14; Lev. 23:2, 37
5 [a]Ex. 12:6, 14, 18; 13:3, 10; 23:15; 34:18; Num. 9:2, 3; 28:16, 17; Deut. 16:1-8; Josh. 5:10
7 [a]Ex. 12:16; Num. 28:18, 25
10 IHebr. *omer* [a]Ex. 23:16, 19; 34:22, 26; Num. 15:2, 18; 28:26; Deut. 16:9; Josh. 3:15 [b]Rom. 11:16; 1Cor. 15:20; James 1:18; Rev. 14:4
11 [a]Ex. 29:24
13 [a]Lev. 2:14-16
15 [a]Ex. 34:22; Lev. 25:8; Deut. 16:9
16 [a]Acts 2:1 [b]Num. 28:26
17 [a]Ex. 23:16, 19; 22:29; 34:22, 26; Num. 15:17-21; 28:26; Deut. 26:1
19 [a]Lev. 4:23, 28; Num. 28:30 [b]Lev. 3:1
20 [a]Num. 18:12; Deut. 18:4
22 [a]Lev. 19:9 [b]Deut. 24:19

⊶ **23:22** See note on Leviticus 19:9, 10.

thou shalt leave[5800] them unto the poor, and to the stranger:[1616] I *am* the LORD your God.

23 And the LORD spake unto Moses, saying,

24 Speak unto the children of Israel, saying, In the [a]seventh month, in the first *day* of the month, shall ye have a sabbath,[7677] [b]a memorial[2146] of blowing of trumpets, an holy convocation.

25 Ye shall do no servile work *therein:* but ye shall offer an offering made by fire unto the LORD.

26 And the LORD spake unto Moses, saying,

27 [a]Also on the tenth *day* of this seventh month *there shall be* a day of atonement:[3725] it shall be an holy convocation unto you; and ye shall afflict your souls,[5315] and offer an offering made by fire unto the LORD.

28 And ye shall do no work in that same day: for it *is* a day of atonement, to make an atonement[3722] for you before the LORD your God.

29 For whatsoever soul *it be* that shall not be afflicted in that same day, [a]he shall be cut off[3772] from among his people.[5971]

30 And whatsoever soul *it be* that doeth any work in that same day, [a]the same soul will I destroy from among his people.

31 Ye shall do no manner of work: *it shall be* a statute for ever throughout your generations in all your dwellings.

⊶ 32 It *shall be* unto you a sabbath of rest, and ye shall afflict your souls: in the ninth *day* of the month at even, from even unto even, shall ye [I]celebrate[7673] your sabbath.

33 And the LORD spake unto Moses, saying,

34 Speak unto the children of Israel, saying, [a]The fifteenth day of this seventh month *shall be* the feast of tabernacles[5521] *for* seven days unto the LORD.

35 On the first day *shall be* an holy convocation: ye shall do no servile work *therein.*

36 Seven days ye shall offer an offering made by fire unto the LORD: [a]on the eighth day shall be an holy convocation unto you; and ye shall offer an offering made by fire unto the LORD: it *is* a [I][b]solemn assembly;[6116] *and* ye shall do no servile work *therein.*

37 [a]These *are* the feasts of the LORD, which ye shall proclaim *to be* holy convocations, to offer an offering made by fire unto the LORD, a burnt offering, and a meat offering, a sacrifice, and drink offerings, every thing[1697] upon his day:

38 [a]Beside the sabbaths of the LORD, and beside your gifts, and beside all your vows,[5088] and beside all your freewill offerings,[5071] which ye give unto the LORD.

39 Also in the fifteenth day of the seventh month, when ye have [a]gathered in the fruit of the land, ye shall keep a feast unto the LORD seven days: on the first day *shall be* a sabbath, and on the eighth day *shall be* a sabbath.

40 And [a]ye shall take you on the first day the [I]boughs of goodly[1926] trees, branches of palm trees, and the boughs of thick trees, and willows of the brook; [b]and ye shall rejoice before the LORD your God seven days.

41 [a]And ye shall keep it a feast unto the LORD seven days in the year. *It shall be* a statute for ever in your generations: ye shall celebrate it in the seventh month.

42 [a]Ye shall dwell in booths seven days; all that are Israelites born shall dwell in booths:[5521]

43 [a]That your generations may know[3045] that I made the children of Israel to dwell in booths, when I brought them out of the land of Egypt: I *am* the LORD your God.

44 And Moses [a]declared[1696] unto the children of Israel the feasts of the LORD.

24 [a]Num. 29:1 [b]Lev. 25:9
27 [a]Lev. 16:30; Num. 29:7
29 [a]Gen. 17:14
30 [a]Lev. 20:3, 5, 6
32 [I]Hebr. *rest*
34 [a]Ex. 23:16; Num. 29:12; Deut. 16:13; Ezra 3:4; Neh. 8:14; Zech. 14:16; John 7:2
36 [I]Hebr. day of *restraint* [a]Num. 29:35; Neh. 8:18; John 7:37 [b]Deut. 16:8; 2Chr. 7:9; Neh. 8:18; Joel 1:14; 2:15
37 [a]Lev. 23:2, 4
38 [a]Num. 29:39
39 [a]Ex. 23:16; Deut. 16:13
40 [I]Hebr. *fruit* [a]Neh. 8:15 [b]Deut. 16:14, 15
41 [a]Num. 29:12; Neh. 8:18
42 [a]Neh. 8:14-16
43 [a]Deut. 31:13; Ps. 78:5, 6
44 [a]Lev. 23:2

⊶ **23:32** See note on Leviticus 16:29.

Taking Care of the Lamp

24 And the LORD spake unto Moses, saying,

2 [a]Command the children of Israel, that they bring unto thee pure[2114] oil[8081] olive beaten for the light,[3974] [I]to cause[5927] the lamps[5216] to burn[5927] continually.[8548]

3 Without the vail of the testimony,[5715] in the tabernacle[168] of the congregation,[4150] shall Aaron order it from the evening unto the morning before the LORD continually: *it shall be* a statute[2708] for ever in your generations.[1755]

4 He shall order the lamps upon [a]the pure[2889] candlestick before the LORD continually.

The Shewbread

5 And thou shalt take fine flour, and bake twelve [a]cakes thereof: two tenth deals shall be in one cake.

6 And thou shalt set[7760] them in two rows, six on a row,[4635] [a]upon the pure table before the LORD.

7 And thou shalt put pure frankincense[3828] upon *each* row, that it may be on the bread for a memorial, *even* an offering made by fire[801] unto the LORD.

8 [a]Every sabbath[7676] he shall set it in order before the LORD continually, *being taken* from the children of Israel by an everlasting[5769] covenant.[1285]

9 And [a]it shall be Aaron's and his sons'; [b]and they shall eat it in the holy[6918] place: for it *is* most holy[6944] unto him of the offerings of the LORD made by fire by a perpetual[5769] statute.[2706]

The Punishment for Blasphemy

10 And the son of an Israelitish woman,[802] whose father *was* an Egyptian, went out among the children of Israel: and this son of the Israelitish *woman* and a man of Israel strove together in the camp;[4264]

11 And the Israelitish woman's son [a]blasphemed[5344] the name *of the LORD, and* [b]cursed.[7043] And they [c]brought him unto Moses: (and his mother's name *was* Shelomith, the daughter of Dibri, of the tribe[4294] of Dan:)

12 And they [a]put him in ward, [Ib]that the mind[6310] of the LORD might be shewed them.

13 And the LORD spake unto Moses, saying,

14 Bring forth him that hath cursed without the camp; and let all that heard[8085] *him* [a]lay their hands[3027] upon his head,[7218] and let all the congregation[5712] stone him.

15 And thou shalt speak unto the children of Israel, saying, Whosoever curseth[7043] his God[430] [a]shall bear[5375] his sin.

16 And he that [a]blasphemeth the name of the LORD, he shall surely be put to death, *and* all the congregation shall certainly stone him: as well the stranger,[1616] as he that is born in the land, when he blasphemeth[5344] the name *of the LORD,* shall be put to death.[4191]

17 [a]And he that [I]killeth any man[120] shall surely be put to death.

18 [a]And he that killeth a beast shall make it good; [I]beast for beast.

19 And if a man cause a blemish[3971] in his neighbour; as [a]he hath done,[6213] so shall it be done to him;

20 Breach[7667] for breach, eye for eye, tooth for tooth: as he hath caused a blemish in a man, so shall it be done to him *again.*

21 [a]And he that killeth a beast, he shall restore it: [b]and he that killeth a man, he shall be put to death.

22 Ye shall have [a]one manner of law,[4941] as well for the stranger, as for one of your own country: for I *am* the LORD your God.

23 And Moses spake to the children of Israel, [a]that they should bring forth him that had cursed out of the camp, and stone him with stones. And the children of Israel did as the LORD commanded[6680] Moses.

---

2 [I]Hebr. *to cause to ascend* [a]Ex. 27:20, 21

4 [a]Ex. 31:8; 39:37

5 [a]Ex. 25:30

6 [a]1Kgs. 7:48; 2Chr. 4:19; 13:1; Heb. 9:2

8 [a]Num. 4:7; 1Chr. 9:32; 2Chr. 2:4

9 [a]1Sam. 21:6; Matt. 12:4; Mark 2:26; Luke 6:4 [b]Ex. 20:33; Lev. 8:31; 21:22

11 [a]Lev. 24:16 [b]Job 1:5, 11, 22; 2:5, 9, 10; Isa. 8:21 [c]Ex. 18:22, 26

12 [I]Hebr. *to expound unto them according to the mouth of the LORD* [a]Num. 15:34 [b]Ex. 18:15, 16; Num. 27:5; 36:5, 6

14 [a]Deut. 13:9; 17:7

15 [a]Lev. 5:1; 20:17; Num. 9:13

16 [a]1Kgs. 21:10, 13; Ps. 74:10, 18; Matt. 12:31; Mark 3:28; James 2:7

17 [I]Hebr. *smiteth the life of a man* [a]Ex. 21:12; Num. 35:31; Deut. 19:11, 12

18 [I]Hebr. *life for life* [a]Lev. 24:21

19 [a]Ex. 21:24; Deut. 19:21; Matt. 5:38; 7:2

21 [a]Ex. 21:33; Lev. 24:18 [b]Lev. 24:17

22 [a]Ex. 12:49; Lev. 19:34; Num. 15:16

23 [a]Lev. 24:14

Sabbath Years and the Year Of Jubile

25 ⊶ And the LORD spake unto Moses in Mount Sinai, saying,

2 Speak unto the children[1121] of Israel, and say unto them, When ye come into the land[776] which I give you, then shall the land [I]keep[7673] [a]a sabbath[7676] unto the LORD.

3 Six years thou shalt sow thy field,[7704] and six years thou shalt prune thy vineyard, and gather[622] in the fruit thereof;

4 But in the seventh year shall be a sabbath of rest[7677] unto the land, a sabbath for the LORD: thou shalt neither sow thy field, nor prune thy vineyard.

5 [a]That which groweth of its own accord[5599] of thy harvest thou shalt not reap, neither gather the grapes [I]of thy vine undressed:[5139] *for* it is a year of rest unto the land.

6 And the sabbath of the land shall be meat for you; for thee, and for thy servant,[5650] and for thy maid, and for thy hired servant, and for thy stranger[8453] that sojourneth[1481] with thee,

7 And for thy cattle, and for the beast[2416] that *are* in thy land, shall all the increase thereof be meat.

8 And thou shalt number[5608] seven sabbaths of years unto thee, seven times seven years; and the space of the seven sabbaths of years shall be unto thee forty and nine years.

9 Then shalt thou cause[5674] the trumpet [I]of the jubile[8643] to sound[5674] on the tenth *day* of the seventh month, [a]in the day of atonement[3725] shall ye make the trumpet sound throughout all your land.

10 And ye shall hallow[6942] the fiftieth year, and [a]proclaim[7121] liberty throughout *all* the land unto all the inhabitants thereof: it shall be a jubile[3104] unto you; [b]and ye shall return[7725] every man unto his possession,[272] and ye shall return every man unto his family.[4940]

11 A jubile shall that fiftieth year be unto you: [a]ye shall not sow, neither reap that which groweth of itself in it, nor gather *the grapes* in it of thy vine undressed.

12 For it *is* the jubile; it shall be holy[6944] unto you: [a]ye shall eat the increase thereof out of the field.

13 [a]In the year of this jubile ye shall return every man unto his possession.

14 And if thou sell ought unto thy neighbour, or buyest *ought* of thy neighbour's hand, [a]ye shall not oppress[3238] one another:

15 [a]According to the number of years after the jubile thou shalt buy of thy neighbour, *and* according unto the

2 [I]Hebr. *rest* [a]Ex. 23:10; Lev. 26:34, 35; 2Chr. 36:21

5 [I]Hebr. *of thy separation* [a]2Kgs. 19:29

9 [I]Hebr. *loud of sound* [a]Lev. 23:24, 27

10 [a]Isa. 61:2; 63:4; Jer. 34:8, 15, 17; Luke 4:19 [b]Lev. 25:13; Num. 36:4

11 [a]Lev. 25:5

12 [a]Lev. 25:6, 7

13 [a]Lev. 25:10; Num. 36:4

14 [a]Lev. 19:13; 25:17; 1Sam. 12:3, 4; Mic. 2:2; 1Cor. 6:8

15 [a]Lev. 27:18, 23

⊶ **25:1–55** The provisions of this chapter prevent overworking the land, call for regular land redistribution, and forbid perpetual servitude. These actions may have been intended to eliminate poverty (Deut. 15:4, 5). Years are divided into groups of seven, with the seventh designated as the Sabbatical Year (year of rest). In that year no farming was to be done (Lev. 25:3–5), debts among the Israelites were to be cancelled (Deut. 15:2), and indentured servants were to be set free (Deut. 15:12). This cycle was to repeat itself seven times, for a total of forty-nine years. The fiftieth year was set aside as the Year of Jubilee (Lev. 25:8, 9). The regulations for the Year of Jubilee were identical to those of the Sabbatical Year, with one exception. In the Year of Jubilee all real estate, except that within walled cities, automatically reverted to the family to which it had originally been assigned (Lev. 25:13).

These things were not proposed merely as sound social legislation, for each one had a specific theological cause as well. Servants were to be released in the Year of Jubilee because God had rescued the Israelites from Egypt and they were all His servants (Lev. 25:55). The land was to be redeemed regularly, because it actually belonged to God, not Israel (Lev. 25:23, 24). Even centuries later, the duty of keeping ancestral real estate in the family was Naboth's reason for refusing to sell his vineyard to King Ahab (1 Kgs. 21:3). For an example of the influence of these regulations during the period of the judges, see the note on Ruth 4:1–8.

number of years of the fruits he shall
sell unto thee:
16 According to the multitude of
years thou shalt increase the price
thereof, and according to the fewness of
years thou shalt diminish the price of it:
for *according* to the number *of the years*
of the fruits doth he sell unto thee.
17 [a]Ye shall not therefore oppress one
another; [b]but thou shalt fear[3372] thy
God:[430] for I *am* the LORD your God.
18 [a]Wherefore ye shall do[6213] my
statutes,[2708] and keep my judgments,[4941]
and do them; [b]and ye shall dwell in the
land in safety.[983]
19 And the land shall yield her fruit,
and [a]ye shall eat your fill, and dwell
therein in safety.
20 And if ye shall say, [a]What
shall we eat the seventh year? behold,
[b]we shall not sow, nor gather in our increase:
21 Then I will [a]command[6680] my
blessing[1293] upon you in the sixth year,
and it shall bring forth fruit for three
years.
22 [a]And ye shall sow the eighth year,
and eat *yet* of [b]old fruit until the ninth
year; until her fruits come in ye shall eat
of the old *store*.
23 The land shall not be sold
[I]for ever:[6783] for [a]the land *is* mine; for ye
are [b]strangers[1616] and sojourners with
me.
24 And in all the land of your possession ye shall grant a redemption[1353]
for the land.
25 [a]If thy brother[251] be waxen poor,
and hath sold away *some* of his possession, and if [b]any of his kin come to
redeem[1350] it, then shall he redeem that
which his brother sold.
26 And if the man have none to redeem it, and [I]himself be able to redeem
it;
27 Then [a]let him count[2803] the years
of the sale thereof, and restore[7725] the
overplus[5736] unto the man to whom he

17 [a]Lev. 25:14 [b]Lev. 19:14, 32; 25:45
18 [a]Lev. 19:37 [b]Lev. 26:5; Deut. 12:10; Ps. 4:8; Prov. 1:33; Jer. 23:6
19 [a]Lev. 26:5; Ezek. 34:25, 27, 28
20 [a]Matt. 6:25, 31 [b]Lev. 25:4, 5
21 [a]Ex. 16:29; Deut. 28:8
22 [a]2Kgs. 19:29 [b]Josh. 5:11, 12
23 [I]Or, *to be quite cut off* [a]Deut. 32:43; 2Chr. 7:20; Ps. 85:1; Joel 2:18; 3:2 [b]1Chr. 29:15; Ps. 39:12; 119:19; 1Pet. 2:11
25 [a]Ruth 2:20; 4:4, 6 [b]Ruth 3:2, 9, 12; Jer. 32:7, 8
26 [I]Hebr. *his hand hath attained and found sufficiency*
27 [a]Lev. 25:50-52
28 [a]Lev. 25:13
31 [I]Hebr. *redemption belongeth unto it*
32 [a]Num. 35:2; Josh. 21:2, 3
33 [I]Or, *one of the Levites redeem them* [a]Lev. 25:28
34 [a]Acts 4:36, 37
35 [I]Hebr. *his hand faileth* [II]Hebr. *strengthen* [a]Deut. 15:7, 8; Ps. 37:26; 41:1; 112:5, 9; Prov. 14:31; Luke 6:35; Acts 11:29; Rom. 12:10; 1John 3:17
36 [a]Ex. 22:25; Deut. 23:19; Neh. 5:7; Ps. 15:5; Prov. 28:8; Ezek. 18:8, 13, 17; 22:12 [b]Lev. 25:17; Neh. 5:9

sold it; that he may return unto his possession.
28 But if he be not able to restore *it*
to him, then that which is sold shall remain in the hand of him that hath
bought it until the year of jubile: [a]and in
the jubile it shall go out, and he shall return unto his possession.
29 And if a man sell a dwelling[4186]
house[1004] in a walled city, then he may
redeem it within a whole[8552] year after it
is sold; *within* a full year may he redeem
it.
30 And if it be not redeemed within
the space of a full[8549] year, then the
house that *is* in the walled city shall be
established for ever to him that bought it
throughout his generations:[1755] it shall
not go out in the jubile.
31 But the houses of the villages
which have no wall round about them
shall be counted[2803] as the fields of the
country:[776] [I]they may be redeemed, and
they shall go out in the jubile.
32 Notwithstanding [a]the cities of the
Levites, *and* the houses of the cities of
their possession, may the Levites redeem
at any time.[5769]
33 And if [I]a man purchase of the
Levites, then the house that was sold,
and the city of his possession, [a]shall go
out in *the year of* jubile: for the houses
of the cities of the Levites *are* their possession among the children of Israel.
34 But [a]the field of the suburbs of
their cities may not be sold; for it *is* their
perpetual[5769] possession.
🔑35 And if thy brother be waxen
poor, and [I]fallen in decay with thee; then
thou shalt [II][a]relieve[2388] him: *yea, though*
he be a stranger, or a sojourner; that he
may live with thee.
36 [a]Take thou no usury of him, or
increase: but [b]fear thy God; that thy
brother may live with thee.
37 Thou shalt not give him thy
money upon usury, nor lend him thy
victuals[400] for increase.

🔑 **25:35–38** See note on Leviticus 19:33, 34.

38 [a]I *am* the LORD your God, which brought you forth out of the land of Egypt, to give you the land of Canaan, *and* to be your God.

39 And [a]if thy brother *that dwelleth* by thee be waxen poor, and be sold unto thee; thou shalt not [I]compel[5647] him to serve as a bondservant:

40 *But* as an hired servant, *and* as a sojourner, he shall be with thee, *and* shall serve[5647] thee unto the year of jubile:

41 And *then* shall he depart from thee, *both* he and his children [a]with him, and shall return unto his own family, and [b]unto the possession of his fathers[1] shall he return.

42 For they *are* [a]my servants, which I brought forth out of the land of Egypt: they shall not be sold [I]as bondmen.

43 [a]Thou shalt not rule[7287] over him [b]with rigour; but [c]shalt fear thy God.

44 Both thy bondmen, and thy bondmaids, which thou shalt have, *shall be* of the heathen[1471] that are round about you; of them shall ye buy bondmen[5650] and bondmaids.

45 Moreover of [a]the children of the strangers[8453] that do sojourn among you, of them shall ye buy, and of their families that *are* with you, which they begat in your land: and they shall be your possession.

46 And [a]ye shall take them as an inheritance for your children after you, to inherit[3423] *them for* a possession; [I]they shall be your bondmen[5647] for ever:[5769] but over your brethren the children of Israel, [b]ye shall not rule one over another with rigour.

47 And if a sojourner or stranger [I]wax rich by thee, and [a]thy brother *that dwelleth* by him wax poor, and sell himself unto the stranger *or* sojourner[1616] by thee, or to the stock of the stranger's family:

48 After that he is sold he may be redeemed again; one of his brethren may [a]redeem him:

49 Either his uncle, or his uncle's son, may redeem him, or *any* that is nigh of kin[7607] unto him of his family may redeem him; or if [a]he be able, he may redeem himself.

50 And he shall reckon[2803] with him that bought him from the year that he was sold to him unto the year of jubile: and the price of his sale shall be according unto the number of years, [a]according to the time of an hired servant shall it be with him.

51 If *there be* yet many years *behind,* according unto them he shall give again[7725] the price of his redemption[1353] out of the money that he was bought for.

52 And if there remain but few years unto the year of jubile, then he shall count with him, *and* according unto his years shall he give him again the price of his redemption.

53 *And* as a yearly hired servant shall he be with him: *and the other* shall not rule with rigour over him in thy sight.

54 And if he be not redeemed [I]in these *years,* then [a]he shall go out in the year of jubile, *both* he, and his children with him.

55 For [a]unto me the children of Israel *are* servants; they *are* my servants whom I brought forth out of the land of Egypt: I *am* the LORD your God.

Blessings for Obedience

26 Ye shall make you [a]no idols nor graven image,[6459] neither rear you up a [I]standing image,[4676] neither shall ye set up *any* [II]image of stone in your land, to bow down[7812] unto it: for I *am* the LORD your God.[430]

2 [a]Ye shall keep my sabbaths,[7676] and reverence[3372] my sanctuary:[4720] I *am* the LORD.

3 [a]If ye walk in my statutes,[2708] and keep my commandments,[4687] and do them;

4 [a]Then I will give you rain in due season,[6256] [b]and the land shall yield her increase, and the trees of the field shall yield their fruit.

5 And [a]your threshing shall reach unto the vintage, and the vintage shall

38 [a]Lev. 22:32, 33

39 [I]Hebr. *serve thyself with him with the service* [a]Ex. 21:2; Deut. 15:12; 1Kgs. 9:22; 2Kgs. 4:1; Neh. 5:5; Jer. 34:14

41 [a]Ex. 21:3 [b]Lev. 25:28

42 [I]Hebr. *with the sale of a bondman* [a]Lev. 25:55; Rom. 6:22; 1Cor. 7:23

43 [a]Eph. 6:9; Col. 4:1 [b]Ex. 1:13; Lev. 23:46 [c]Ex. 1:17, 21; Lev. 25:17; Deut. 25:18; Mal. 3:5

45 [a]Isa. 56:3, 6

46 [I]Hebr. *ye shall serve yourselves with them* [a]Isa. 14:2 [b]Lev. 25:43

47 [I]Hebr. *his hand obtain* [a]Lev. 25:25, 35

48 [a]Neh. 5:5

49 [a]Lev. 25:26

50 [a]Job 7:1; Isa. 16:14; 21:16

54 [I]Or, *by these* means [a]Ex. 21:2, 3; Lev. 25:41

55 [a]Lev. 25:42

1 [I]Or, *pillar* [II]Hebr. *a stone of picture* [a]Ex. 20:4, 5; Deut. 5:8; 16:22; 27:15; Ps. 97:7

2 [a]Lev. 19:30

3 [a]Deut. 11:13; 14:15; 28:1-14

4 [a]Isa. 30:23; Ezek. 34:26; Joel 2:23, 24 [b]Ps. 67:7; 85:12; Ezek. 34:27; 36:30; Zech. 8:12

5 [a]Amos 9:13

reach unto the sowing time:[2233] and [b]ye
shall eat your bread to the full, and
[c]dwell in your land safely.[983]
6 And [a]I will give peace[7965] in the
land, and [b]ye shall lie down, and none
shall make *you* afraid: and I will [I]rid[7673]
[c]evil[7451] beasts[2416] out of the land, neither shall[5674] [d]the sword[2719] go[5674]
through your land.
7 And ye shall chase your enemies,
and they shall fall[5307] before you by the
sword.
8 And [a]five of you shall chase an
hundred, and an hundred of you shall
put ten thousand to flight: and your enemies shall fall before you by the sword.
9 For I will [a]have respect unto you,
and [b]make you fruitful, and multiply
you, and establish my covenant[1285] with
you.
10 And ye shall eat [a]old store, and
bring forth the old because of the new.
11 [a]And I will set my tabernacle[4908]
among you: and my soul[5315] shall not
[b]abhor you.
12 [a]And I will walk among you, and
[b]will be your God, and ye shall be my
people.[5971]
13 [a]I *am* the LORD your God, which
brought you forth out of the land of
Egypt, that ye should not be their bondmen; [b]and I have broken the bands of
your yoke, and made you go upright.

Punishment for Disobedience

14 [a]But if ye will not hearken unto
me, and will not do all these commandments;
15 And if ye shall [a]despise[3988] my
statutes, or if your soul abhor[1602] my
judgments,[4941] so that ye will not do[6213]
all my commandments, *but* that ye
break[6565] my covenant:
16 I also will do this unto you; I will
even appoint[6485] [I]over you [a]terror,[928]
[b]consumption, and the burning ague, that
shall [c]consume[3615] the eyes, and cause
sorrow of heart: and [d]ye shall sow your
seed in vain, for your enemies shall eat
it.
17 And [a]I will set my face against
you, and [b]ye shall be slain before your enemies: [c]they that hate[8130] you shall
reign[7287] over you; and [d]ye shall flee
when none pursueth you.
18 And if ye will not yet for all
this hearken unto me, then I will punish[3256] you [a]seven times more for your
sins.[2403]
19 And I will [a]break[7665] the pride of
your power; and I [b]will make your
heaven[8064] as iron, and your earth as
brass:
20 And your [a]strength shall be
spent[8552] in vain: for [b]your land shall not
yield her increase, neither shall the trees
of the land yield their fruits.
21 And if ye walk [I]contrary unto me,
and will not hearken[8085] unto me; I will
bring seven times more plagues[4347] upon
you according to your sins.
22 [a]I will also send wild beasts
among you, which shall rob you of your
children, and destroy[3772] your cattle, and
make you few in number; and [b]your *high*
ways[1870] shall be desolate.
23 And if ye [a]will not be
reformed[3256] by me by these things, but
will walk contrary unto me;
24 [a]Then will I also walk contrary
unto you, and will punish you yet seven
times for your sins.
25 And [a]I will bring a sword upon
you, that shall avenge[5358] the quarrel[5359]
of *my* covenant: and when ye are gathered together within your cities, [b]I will

5 [b]Lev. 25:19; Deut. 11:15; Joel 2:19, 26 [c]Lev. 25:18; Job 11:18; Ezek. 34:25, 27, 28
6 [I]Hebr. *cause to cease* [a]1Chr. 22:9; Ps. 29:11; 147:14; Isa. 45:7; Hag. 2:9 [b]Job 11:19; Ps. 3:5; 4:8; Isa. 35:9; Jer. 30:10; Ezek. 34:25; Hos. 2:18; Zeph. 3:13 [c]2Kgs. 0:25; Ezek. 5:17; 14:15 [d]Ezek. 14:17
8 [a]Deut. 32:30; Josh. 23:10
9 [a]Ex. 2:25; 2Kgs. 13:23 [b]Gen. 17:6, 7; Neh. 9:23; Ps. 107:38
10 [a]Lev. 25:22
11 [a]Ex. 25:8; 29:45; Josh. 22:19; Ps. 76:2; Ezek. 37:26-28; Rev. 21:3 [b]Lev. 20:23; Deut. 32:19
12 [a]2Cor. 6:16 [b]Ex. 6:7; Jer. 7:23; 11:4; 30:22; Ezek. 11:20; 36:28
13 [a]Lev. 25:38, 42, 55 [b]Jer. 2:20; Ezek. 34:27
14 [a]Deut. 28:15; Lam. 2:17; Mal. 2:2
15 [a]Lev. 26:43; 2Kgs. 17:15
16 [I]Hebr. *upon you* [a]Deut. 28:65-67; 32:25; Jer. 15:8 [b]Deut. 28:22 [c]1Sam. 2:33 [d]Deut. 28:33, 51; Job 31:8; Jer. 5:17; 12:13; Mic. 6:15
17 [a]Lev. 17:10 [b]Deut. 28:25; Judg. 2:14; Jer. 19:7 [c]Ps. 106:41 [d]Lev. 26:36; Ps. 53:5; Prov. 28:1
18 [a]1Sam. 2:5; Ps. 119:164; Prov. 24:16
19 [a]Isa. 25:11; 26:5; Ezek. 7:24; 30:6 [b]Deut. 28:23
20 [a]Ps. 127:1; Isa. 49:4 [b]Deut. 11:17; 28:18; Hag. 1:10 **21** [I]Or, *at all adventures with me*
22 [a]Deut. 32:24; 2Kgs. 17:25; Ezek. 5:17; 14:15 [b]Judg. 5:6; 2Chr. 15:5; Isa. 33:8; Lam. 1:4; Zech. 7:14
23 [a]Jer. 2:30; 5:3; Amos 4:6-12 **24** [a]2Sam. 22:27; Ps. 18:26 **25** [a]Ezek. 5:17; 6:3; 14:17; 29:8; 33:2 [b]Num. 14:12; Deut. 28:21; Jer. 14:12; 24:10; 29:17, 18; Amos 4:10

26:9 This conditional statement is built upon the promises to Abraham (Gen. 12:1–3; 13:16; 15:5; 17:5, 6; 18:18; 22:17, 18), but it does not change those unconditional promises (Gal. 3:17).

send the pestilence[1698] among you; and ye shall be delivered into the hand[3027] of the enemy.

26 [a]*And* when I have broken the staff[4294] of your bread, ten women shall bake your bread in one oven, and they shall deliver *you* your bread again[7725] by weight: and [b]ye shall eat, and not be satisfied.

27 And [a]if ye will not for all this hearken unto me, but walk contrary unto me;

28 Then I will walk contrary unto you also [a]in fury;[2534] and I, even I, will chastise[3256] you seven times for your sins.

29 [a]And ye shall eat the flesh[1320] of your sons,[1121] and the flesh of your daughters shall ye eat.

30 And [a]I will destroy[8045] your high places,[1116] and cut down[3772] your images,[2553] and [b]cast your carcases[6297] upon the carcases of your idols,[1544] and my soul shall [c]abhor[1602] you.

31 [a]And I will make your cities waste,[2723] and [b]bring your sanctuaries unto desolation, and I will not smell[7306] the savour of your sweet odours.

32 [a]And I will bring the land into desolation: and your enemies which dwell therein shall be [b]astonished at it.

33 And [a]I will scatter you among the heathen,[1471] and will draw out a sword after you: and your land shall be desolate,[8077] and your cities waste.

34 [a]Then shall the land enjoy[7521] her sabbaths, as long as[3117] [3605] it lieth desolate, and ye *be* in your enemies' land; *even* then shall the land rest, and enjoy her sabbaths.

35 As long as it lieth desolate it shall rest; because it did not rest[7673] in your [a]sabbaths, when ye dwelt upon it.

36 And upon them that are left[7604] *alive* of you [a]I will send a faintness into their hearts[3824] in the lands of their enemies; and [b]the sound of a [I]shaken leaf shall chase them; and they shall flee, as fleeing from a sword; and they shall fall when none pursueth.

37 And [a]they shall fall one[376] upon another, as it were before a sword, when none pursueth: and [b]ye shall have no power to stand before your enemies.

38 And ye shall perish[6] among the heathen, and the land of your enemies shall eat you up.

39 And they that are left of you [a]shall pine away[4743] in their iniquity[5771] in your enemies' lands; and also in the iniquities of their fathers[1] shall they pine away with them.

40 [a]If they shall confess[3034] their iniquity, and the iniquity of their fathers, with their trespass which they trespassed[4603] against me, and that also they have walked contrary unto me;

41 And *that* I also have walked contrary unto them, and have brought them into the land of their enemies; if then their [a]uncircumcised[6189] hearts be [b]humbled, and they then accept[7521] of the punishment of their iniquity:

42 Then will I [a]remember[2142] my covenant with Jacob, and also my covenant with Isaac, and also my covenant with Abraham will I remember; and I will [b]remember the land.

43 [a]The land also shall be left[5800] of them, and shall enjoy her sabbaths, while she lieth desolate without them: and they shall accept of the punishment of their iniquity: because, even because they [b]despised[3988] my judgments, and because their soul abhorred my statutes.

44 And yet for all that, when they be in the land of their enemies, [a]I will not cast them away, neither will I abhor them, to destroy them utterly,[3615] and to break my covenant with them: for I *am* the LORD their God.

45 But I will [a]for their sakes remember the covenant of their ancestors,[7223] [b]whom I brought forth out of the land of Egypt [c]in the sight of the heathen, that I might be their God: I *am* the LORD.

46 [a]These *are* the statutes[2706] and

26 [a]Ps. 105:16; Isa. 3:1; Ezek. 4:16; 5:16; 14:13 [b]Isa. 9:20; Mic. 6:14; Hag. 1:6
27 [a]Lev. 26:21, 24
28 [a]Isa. 59:18; 63:3; 66:15; Jer. 21:5; Ezek. 5:13, 15; 8:18
29 [a]Deut. 28:53; 2Kgs. 6:29; Lam. 4:10; Ezek. 5:10
30 [a]2Chr. 34:3, 4, 7; Isa. 27:9; Ezek. 6:3-6, 13 [b]2Kgs. 23:20; 2Chr. 34:5 [c]Lev. 20:23; Ps. 78:59; 89:38; Jer. 14:19
31 [a]Neh. 2:3; Jer. 4:7; Ezek. 6:6 [b]Ps. 74:7; Lam. 1:10; Ezek. 9:6; 21:2
32 [a]Jer. 9:11; 25:11, 18 [b]Deut. 28:37; 1Kgs. 9:8; Jer. 18:16; 19:8; Ezek. 5:15
33 [a]Deut. 4:27; 28:64; Ps. 44:11; Jer. 9:16; Ezek. 12:15; 20:23; 22:15; Zech. 7:14
34 [a]2Chr. 36:21
35 [a]Lev. 25:2
36 [I]Hebr. *driven* [a]Ezek. 21:7, 12, 15 [b]Lev. 26:17; Job 15:21; Prov. 28:1
37 [a]Judg. 7:22; 1Sam. 14:15, 16; Isa. 10:4 [b]Josh. 7:12, 13; Judg. 2:14
39 [a]Deut. 4:27; 28:65; Neh. 1:8; Jer. 3:25; 29:12, 13; Ezek. 4:17; 6:9; 20:43; 24:23; 33:10; 36:31; Hos. 5:15; Zech. 10:9
40 [a]Num. 5:7; 1Kgs. 8:33, 35, 47; Neh. 9:2; Prov. 28:13; Dan. 9:3, 4; Luke 15:18; 1John 1:9
41 [a]Jer. 6:10; 9:25, 26; Ezek. 44:7; Acts 7:51; Rom. 2:29; Col. 2:11 [b]1Kgs. 21:29; 2Chr. 12:6, 7, 12; 32:26; 33:12, 13

42 [a]Ex. 2:24; 6:5; Ps. 106:45; Ezek. 16:60 [b]Ps. 136:23 **43** [a]Lev. 26:34, 35 [b]Lev. 26:15
44 [a]Deut. 4:31; 2Kgs. 13:23; Rom. 11:2
45 [a]Rom. 11:28 [b]Lev. 22:33; 25:38 [c]Ps. 98:2; Ezek. 20:9, 14, 22 **46** [a]Lev. 27:34; Deut. 6:1; 12:1; 33:4; John 1:17

judgments and laws,[8451] which the LORD made between him and the children[1121] of Israel [b]in mount Sinai by the hand of Moses.

Laws About Dedications

27 And the LORD spake unto Moses, saying,

2 Speak unto the children[1121] of Israel, and say unto them, [a]When a man shall make a singular[6381] vow,[5088] the persons[5315] *shall be* for the LORD by thy estimation.

3 And thy estimation shall be of the male[2145] from twenty years old even unto sixty years old, even thy estimation[6187] shall be fifty shekels of silver, [a]after the shekel of the sanctuary.[6944]

4 And if it *be* a female,[5347] then thy estimation shall be thirty shekels.

5 And if *it be* from five years old even unto twenty years old, then thy estimation shall be of the male twenty shekels, and for the female ten shekels.

6 And if *it be* from a month old even unto five years old, then thy estimation shall be of the male five shekels of silver, and for the female thy estimation *shall be* three shekels of silver.

7 And if *it be* from sixty years old and above; if *it be* a male, then thy estimation shall be fifteen shekels, and for the female ten shekels.

8 But if he be poorer than thy estimation, then he shall present himself before the priest,[3548] and the priest shall value him; according to his ability that vowed[5087] shall the priest value him.

9 And if *it be* a beast, whereof men bring an offering[7133] unto the LORD, all that *any man* giveth of such unto the LORD shall be holy.[6944]

10 He shall not alter[2498] it, nor change it, a good[2896] for a bad,[7451] or a bad for a good: and if he shall at all change beast for beast, then it and the exchange[8545] thereof shall be holy.

11 And if *it be* any unclean[2931] beast, of which they do not offer a sacrifice unto the LORD, then he shall present the beast before the priest:

12 And the priest shall value it, whether it be good or bad: [l]as thou valuest it, *who art* the priest, so shall it be.

13 [a]But if he will at all redeem[1350] it, then he shall add a fifth *part* thereof unto thy estimation.

14 And when a man shall sanctify his house[1004] *to be* holy unto the LORD, then the priest shall estimate it, whether it be good or bad: as the priest shall estimate it, so shall it stand.

15 [a]And if he that sanctified it will redeem his house, then he shall add the fifth *part* of the money of thy estimation unto it, and it shall be his.

16 And if a man shall sanctify unto the LORD *some part* of a field[7704] of his possession,[272] then thy estimation shall be according to the seed[2233] thereof: [l]an homer[2563] of barley seed *shall be valued* at fifty shekels of silver.

17 If he sanctify his field from the year of jubile,[3104] according to thy estimation it shall stand.

18 But if he sanctify his field after the jubile, then the priest shall [a]reckon[2803] unto him the money according to the years that remain,[3498] even unto the year of the jubile, and it shall be abated[1639] from thy estimation.

19 [a]And if he that sanctified the field will in any wise redeem it, then he shall add the fifth *part* of the money of thy estimation unto it, and it shall be assured to him.

20 And if he will not redeem the field, or if he have sold the field to another man, it shall not be redeemed any more.

21 But the field, [a]when it goeth out in the jubile, shall be holy unto the LORD, as a field [b]devoted;[2764] [c]the possession thereof shall be the priest's.

22 And if *a man* sanctify unto the LORD a field which he hath bought, which *is* not of the fields of [a]his possession;

23 [a]Then the priest shall reckon unto him the worth of thy estimation, *even* unto the year of the jubile: and he shall give thine estimation in that day, *as* an holy thing unto the LORD.

46 [b]Lev. 25:1

2 [a]Num. 6:2; Judg. 11:30, 31, 39; 1Sam. 1:11, 28

3 [a]Ex. 30:13

12 [l]Hebr. *according to thy estimation, O priest*

13 [a]Lev. 27:15, 19

15 [a]Lev. 27:13

16 [l]Or, the land *of a homer*

18 [a]Lev. 25:15, 16

19 [a]Lev. 27:13

21 [a]Lev. 25:10, 28, 31 [b]Lev. 27:28 [c]Num. 18:14; Ezek. 44:29

22 [a]Lev. 25:10, 25

23 [a]Lev. 27:18

24 [a]In the year of the jubile the field shall return[7725] unto him of whom it was bought, *even* to him to whom the possession of the land[776] *did belong.*

25 And all thy estimations shall be according to the shekel of the sanctuary: [a]twenty gerahs[1626] shall be the shekel.

26 Only the [I][a]firstling of the beasts, which should be the LORD's firstling, no man shall sanctify it; whether *it be* ox, or sheep: it *is* the LORD's.

27 And if *it be* of an unclean beast, then he shall redeem[6299] *it* according to thine estimation, [a]and shall add a fifth *part* of it thereto: or if it be not redeemed, then it shall be sold according to thy estimation.

28 [a]Notwithstanding no devoted thing, that a man[120] shall devote[2763] unto the LORD of all that he hath, *both* of man and beast, and of the field of his possession, shall be sold or redeemed: every devoted thing *is* most holy unto the LORD.

29 [a]None devoted, which shall be devoted[2763] of men, shall be redeemed; *but* shall surely be put to death.[4191]

30 And [a]all the tithe[4643] of the land, *whether* of the seed of the land, *or* of the fruit of the tree, *is* the LORD's: *it is* holy unto the LORD.

31 [a]And if a man will at all redeem *ought* of his tithes, he shall add thereto the fifth *part* thereof.

32 And concerning the tithe of the herd, or of the flock, *even* of whatsoever [a]passeth under the rod,[7626] the tenth shall be holy unto the LORD.

33 He shall not search whether it be good or bad, [a]neither shall he change it: and if he change it at all, then both it and the change thereof shall be holy; it shall not be redeemed.

34 [a]These *are* the commandments,[4687] which the LORD commanded[6680] Moses for the children of Israel in mount Sinai.

24 [a]Lev. 25:28
25 [a]Ex. 30:13; Num. 3:47; 18:16
26 IHebr. *firstborn* [a]Ex. 13:2, 12; 22:30; Num. 18:17; Deut. 15:19
27 [a]Lev. 27:11-13
28 [a]Lev. 27:21; Josh. 6:17-19
29 [a]Num. 21:2, 3
30 [a]Gen. 28:22; Num. 18:21, 24; 2Chr. 31:5, 6, 12; Neh. 13:12; Mal. 3:8, 10
31 [a]Lev. 27:13
32 [a]Jer. 33:13; Ezek. 20:37; Mic. 7:14
33 [a]Lev. 27:10
34 [a]Lev. 26:46

NUMBERS

The Book of Numbers is so named because it records several occasions where the people were counted or numbered (chaps. 1, 3, 4, 26). The Hebrew title (the first word in the Hebrew text) means "in the wilderness," and appropriately gives the setting for the events in this book. The Book of Numbers relates the earliest experiences of Israel under the theocracy. When the people were obedient to God, they enjoyed His blessing and protection (Num. 21:21–35), but their disobedience brought His judgment (Num. 21:4–9). Despite the wonders that God performed on Israel's behalf, the people were ready to return to Egypt on several occasions (Num. 11:4–6; 14:2–4; 20:4, 5; 21:5) because of their unbelief—it was easier to get Israel out of Egypt than to get Egypt out of the Israelites!

A large portion of the forty years that Israel spent in the wilderness is covered in this book. During this time God removed the generation that failed to trust Him (all but Joshua and Caleb, Num. 14:30) and molded the new generation into a unified nation, prepared to conquer the land He had promised them.

Census of Israel at Sinai

1 🔑 And the LORD spake[1696] unto
Moses [a]in the wilderness of Sinai, [b]in
the tabernacle[168] of the congregation,[4150]
on the first *day* of the second month, in
the second year after they were come out
of the land of Egypt, saying,
🔑 2 [a]Take[5375] ye the sum[7218] of all the
congregation[5712] of the children[1121] of
Israel, after their families,[4940] by the
house[1004] of their fathers,[1] with the number of *their* names, every male by their
polls;[1538]
3 From twenty years old and up
ward, all that are able to go forth to
war[6635] in Israel: thou and Aaron shall
number[6485] them by their armies.[6635]
4 And with you there shall be a
man[376] of every tribe;[4294] every one[376]
head[7218] of the house of his fathers.
5 And these *are* the names of the
men[582] that shall stand with you: of *the*
tribe of Reuben; Elizur the son[1121] of
Shedeur.

1 [a]Ex. 19:1; Num. 10:11, 12 [b]Ex. 25:22
2 [a]Ex. 30:12; 38:26; Num. 26:2, 63, 64; 2Sam. 24:2; 1Chr. 21:2
14 [a]Num. 2:14, he is called *Reuel*
16 [a]Num. 7:2; 1Chr. 27:16

6 Of Simeon; Shelumiel the son of
Zurishaddai.
7 Of Judah; Nahshon the son of
Amminadab.
8 Of Issachar; Nethaneel the son of
Zuar.
9 Of Zebulun; Eliab the son of Helon.
10 Of the children of Joseph: of
Ephraim; Elishama the son of Ammihud:
of Manasseh; Gamaliel the son of Pedahzur.
11 Of Benjamin; Abidan the son of
Gideoni.
12 Of Dan; Ahiezer the son of
Ammishaddai.
13 Of Asher; Pagiel the son of Ocran.
14 Of Gad; Eliasaph the son of
[a]Deuel.
15 Of Naphtali; Ahira the son of
Enan.
16 [a]These *were* the renowned[7121] of the
congregation, princes[5387] of the tribes[4294]

🔑 **1:1** God speaks with Moses one month after the construction of the Tabernacle was completed (Ex. 40:17) and one year and fifteen days after the original Passover, when Israel began its journey from Egypt (Ex. 12:6; Num. 33:3).

🔑 **1:2** The Book of Numbers, as its name suggests, records the taking of two censuses (numberings) of Israel. The first census was taken just before Israel left Mount Sinai, because their intention was to conquer Canaan immediately. Unfortunately, the people sinned at Kadesh-barnea, and had to spend a total of forty years in the wilderness, until all the men who rebelled against God had died. This was a military census, counting only the males at the military age of twenty years old and older. For a discussion of the procedure used for counting the tribe of Levi, see the note on Numbers 3:39.

of their fathers, [b]heads[7218] of thousands[505] in Israel.

17 And Moses and Aaron took these men which are expressed[5344] by *their* names:

18 And they assembled all the congregation together[6950] on the first *day* of the second month, and they declared their pedigrees3205 after their families, by the house of their fathers, according to the number of the names, from twenty years old and upward, by their polls.

19 As the LORD commanded[6680] Moses, so he numbered[6485] them in the wilderness of Sinai.

20 And the children of Reuben, Israel's eldest son, by their generations,[8435] after their families, by the house of their fathers, according to the number of the names, by their polls, every male from twenty years old and upward, all that were able to go forth to war;

21 Those that were numbered of them, *even* of the tribe of Reuben, *were* forty and six thousand and five hundred.

22 Of the children of Simeon, by their generations, after their families, by the house of their fathers, those that were numbered of them, according to the number of the names, by their polls, every male from twenty years old and upward, all that were able to go forth to war;

23 Those that were numbered of them, *even* of the tribe of Simeon, *were* fifty and nine thousand and three hundred.

24 Of the children of Gad, by their generations, after their families, by the house of their fathers, according to the number of the names, from twenty years old and upward, all that were able to go forth to war;

25 Those that were numbered of them, *even* of the tribe of Gad, *were* forty and five thousand six hundred and fifty.

26 Of the [a]children of Judah, by their generations, after their families, by the house of their fathers, according to the number of the names, from twenty years old and upward, all that were able to go forth to war;

27 Those that were numbered of them, *even* of the tribe of Judah, *were* threescore and fourteen thousand and six hundred.

28 Of the children of Issachar, by their generations,[8435] after their families, by the house of their fathers, according to the number of the names, from twenty years old and upward, all that were able to go forth to war;

29 Those that were numbered of them, *even* of the tribe of Issachar, *were* fifty and four thousand and four hundred.

30 Of the children of Zebulun, by their generations, after their families,[4940] by the house of their fathers, according to the number of the names, from twenty years old and upward, all that were able to go forth to war;

31 Those that were numbered of them, *even* of the tribe of Zebulun, *were* fifty and seven thousand and four hundred.

32 Of the [a]children of Joseph, *namely,* of the children of Ephraim, by their generations, after their families, by the house of their fathers, according to the number of the names, from twenty years old and upward, all that were able to go forth to war;

33 Those that were numbered of them, *even* of the tribe of Ephraim, *were* forty thousand and five hundred.

34 Of the children of Manasseh, by their generations, after their families, by the house of their fathers, according to the number of the names, from twenty years old and upward, all that were able to go forth to war;

35 Those that were numbered of them, *even* of the tribe of Manasseh, *were* thirty and two thousand and two hundred.

36 Of the children of Benjamin, by their generations, after their families, by the house of their fathers, according to the number of the names, from twenty years old and upward, all that were able to go forth to war;

16 [b]Ex. 18:21, 25
26 [a]2Sam. 24:9
32 [a]Gen. 48:8-22

37 Those that were numbered of them, *even* of the tribe of Benjamin, *were* thirty and five thousand and four hundred.

38 Of the children of Dan, by their generations,[8435] after their families, by the house of their fathers, according to the number of the names, from twenty years old and upward, all that were able to go forth to war;

39 Those that were numbered of them, *even* of the tribe of Dan, *were* threescore and two thousand and seven hundred.

40 Of the children of Asher, by their generations, after their families, by the house of their fathers, according to the number of the names, from twenty years old and upward, all that were able to go forth to war;

41 Those that were numbered of them, *even* of the tribe of Asher, *were* forty and one thousand and five hundred.

42 Of the children of Naphtali, throughout their generations, after their families,[4940] by the house of their fathers, according to the number of the names, from twenty years old and upward, all that were able to go forth to war;

43 Those that were numbered of them, *even* of the tribe of Naphtali, *were* fifty and three thousand and four hundred.

44 [a]These *are* those that were numbered, which Moses and Aaron numbered, and the princes of Israel, *being* twelve men:[376] each one was for the house of his fathers.

45 So were all those that were numbered of the children of Israel, by the house of their fathers, from twenty years old and upward, all that were able to go forth to war in Israel;

46 Even all they that were numbered were [a]six hundred thousand and three thousand and five hundred and fifty.

The Levites Are Exempted

47 But [a]the Levites after the tribe of their fathers were not numbered among them.

44 [a]Num. 26:64
46 [a]Ex. 12:37; 38:26; Num. 2:32; 26:51
47 [a]Num. 2:33; 3:4; 26:57; 1Chr. 21:6
49 [a]Num. 2:33; 26:62
50 [a]Ex. 38:21; Num. 3:7, 8; 4:15, 25-27, 33 [b]Num. 3:23, 29, 35, 38
51 [a]Num. 10:17, 21 [b]Num. 3:10, 38; 18:22
52 [a]Num. 2:2, 34
53 [a]Num. 1:50 [b]Lev. 10:6; Num. 8:19; 16:46; 18:5; 1Sam. 6:19 [c]Num. 3:7, 8; 8:24-26; 18:3-5; 31:30, 47; 1Chr. 23:32; 2Chr. 13:11
2 [l]Hebr. *over against* [a]Num. 1:52 [b]Josh. 3:4
3 [a]Num. 10:14; Ruth 4:20; 1Chr. 2:10; Matt. 1:4; Luke 3:32, 33

48 For the LORD had spoken[1696] unto Moses, saying,

49 [a]Only thou shalt not number the tribe of Levi, neither take the sum of them among the children of Israel:

50 [a]But thou shalt appoint[6485] the Levites over the tabernacle[4908] of testimony,[5715] and over all the vessels thereof, and over all things that *belong* to it: they shall bear[5375] the tabernacle, and all the vessels thereof; and they shall minister[8334] unto it, [b]and shall encamp round about the tabernacle.

51 [a]And when the tabernacle setteth forward,[5265] the Levites shall take it down: and when the tabernacle is to be pitched, the Levites shall set it up: [b]and the stranger[2114] that cometh nigh shall be put to death.[4191]

52 And the children of Israel shall pitch their tents, [a]every man by his own camp,[4264] and every man by his own standard, throughout their hosts.[6635]

53 [a]But the Levites shall pitch round about the tabernacle of testimony, that there be no [b]wrath[7110] upon the congregation of the children of Israel: [c]and the Levites shall keep[8104] the charge[4931] of the tabernacle of testimony.

54 And the children of Israel did[6213] according to all that the LORD commanded Moses, so did they.

Tribal Arrangement of the Camp

2 And the LORD spake unto Moses and unto Aaron, saying,

2 [a]Every man[376] of the children[1121] of Israel shall pitch by his own standard, with the ensign[226] of their father's[1] house:[1004] [l][b]far off about the tabernacle[168] of the congregation[4150] shall they pitch.

3 And on the east side toward the rising of the sun shall they of the standard of the camp of Judah pitch throughout their armies:[6635] and [a]Nahshon the son[1121] of Amminadab *shall be* captain[5387] of the children of Judah.

4 And his host, and those that were numbered[6485] of them, *were* threescore and fourteen thousand and six hundred.

5 And those that do pitch next unto him *shall be* the tribe[4294] of Issachar: and Nethaneel the son of Zuar *shall be* captain of the children of Issachar.

6 And his host, and those that were numbered thereof, *were* fifty and four thousand and four hundred.

7 *Then* the tribe of Zebulun: and Eliab the son of Helon *shall be* captain of the children of Zebulun.

8 And his host, and those that were numbered thereof, *were* fifty and seven thousand and four hundred.

9 All that were numbered in the camp of Judah *were* an hundred thousand and fourscore thousand and six thousand and four hundred, throughout their armies. [a]These shall first[7223] set forth.

10 On the south side *shall be* the standard of the camp of Reuben according to their armies: and the captain of the children of Reuben *shall be* Elizur the son of Shedeur.

11 And his host, and those that were numbered thereof, *were* forty and six thousand and five hundred.

12 And those which pitch[2583] by him *shall be* the tribe of Simeon: and the captain of the children of Simeon *shall be* Shelumiel the son of Zurishaddai.

13 And his host, and those that were numbered of them, *were* fifty and nine thousand and three hundred.

14 Then the tribe of Gad: and the captain of the sons[1121] of Gad *shall be* Eliasaph the son of [1a]Reuel.

15 And his host, and those that were numbered of them, *were* forty and five thousand and six hundred and fifty.

16 All that were numbered in the camp of Reuben *were* an hundred thousand and fifty and one thousand and four hundred and fifty, throughout their armies. [a]And they shall set forth in the second rank.

17 [a]Then the tabernacle of the congregation shall set forward with the camp of the Levites in the midst[8432] of the camp: as they encamp, so shall they set forward, every man in his place by their standards.

9 [a]Num. 10:14

14 [1]*Deuel* [a]Num. 1:14; 7:42, 47; 10:20

16 [a]Num. 10:18

17 [a]Num. 10:17, 21

24 [a]Num. 10:22

31 [a]Num. 10:25

18 On the west side *shall be* the standard of the camp of Ephraim according to their armies: and the captain of the sons of Ephraim *shall be* Elishama the son of Ammihud.

19 And his host, and those that were numbered of them, *were* forty thousand and five hundred.

20 And by him *shall be* the tribe of Manasseh: and the captain of the children of Manasseh *shall be* Gamaliel the son of Pedahzur.

21 And his host, and those that were numbered of them, *were* thirty and two thousand and two hundred.

22 Then the tribe of Benjamin: and the captain of the sons of Benjamin *shall be* Abidan the son of Gideoni.

23 And his host, and those that were numbered of them, *were* thirty and five thousand and four hundred.

24 All that were numbered of the camp of Ephraim *were* an hundred thousand and eight thousand and an hundred, throughout their armies. [a]And they shall go forward[5265] in the third rank.

25 The standard of the camp of Dan *shall be* on the north side by their armies: and the captain of the children of Dan *shall be* Ahiezer the son of Ammishaddai.

26 And his host, and those that were numbered of them, *were* threescore and two thousand and seven hundred.

27 And those that encamp by him *shall be* the tribe of Asher: and the captain of the children of Asher *shall be* Pagiel the son of Ocran.

28 And his host, and those that were numbered of them, *were* forty and one thousand and five hundred.

29 Then the tribe of Naphtali: and the captain of the children of Naphtali *shall be* Ahira the son of Enan.

30 And his host,[6635] and those that were numbered of them, *were* fifty and three thousand and four hundred.

31 All they that were numbered in the camp of Dan *were* an hundred thousand and fifty and seven thousand and six hundred. [a]They shall go hindmost[314] with their standards.

32 These *are* those which were numbered of the children of Israel by the
house of their fathers:[1] [a]all those that
were numbered of the camps[4264] throughout their hosts[6635] *were* six hundred thousand and three thousand and five hundred and fifty.
33 But [a]the Levites were not numbered among the children of Israel; as
the LORD commanded[6680] Moses.
34 And the children of Israel did[6213]
according to all that the LORD commanded Moses: [a]so they pitched by their
standards, and so they set forward, every
one[376] after their families,[4940] according
to the house of their fathers.

The Levites Are Set Apart

3 These also *are* the generations[8435] of
Aaron and Moses in the day[3117] *that*
the LORD spake[1696] with Moses in mount
Sinai.
2 And these *are* the names of the
sons[1121] of Aaron; Nadab the [a]firstborn,
and Abihu, Eleazar, and Ithamar.
3 These *are* the names of the sons of
Aaron, [a]the priests[3548] which were
anointed,[4886] [I]whom he consecrated to
minister in the priest's office.[3547]
4 [a]And Nadab and Abihu died before
the LORD, when they offered[7126]
strange[2114] fire before the LORD, in the
wilderness of Sinai, and they had no
children:[1121] and Eleazar and Ithamar
ministered in the priest's office in the
sight of Aaron their father.[1]
5 And the LORD spake unto Moses,
saying,
6 [a]Bring[7126] the tribe[4294] of Levi
near,[7126] and present them before Aaron

32 [a]Ex. 38:26; Num. 1:46; 11:21
33 [a]Num. 1:47
34 [a]Num. 24:2, 5, 6
2 [a]Ex. 6:23
3 [I]Hebr. *whose hand he filled* [a]Ex. 28:41; Lev. 8
4 [a]Lev. 10:1; Num. 26:61; 1Chr. 24:2
6 [a]Num. 8:6; 18:2
7 [a]Num. 1:50; 8:11, 15, 24, 26
9 [a]Num. 8:19; 18:6
10 [a]Num. 18:7 [b]Num. 1:51; 3:38; 16:40
12 [a]Num. 3:41; 8:16; 18:6
13 [a]Ex. 13:2; Lev. 27:26; Num. 8:16; Luke 2:23 [b]Ex. 13:12, 15; Num. 8:17

the priest, that they may minister unto
him.
7 And they shall keep[8104] his
charge,[4931] and the charge of the whole
congregation before the tabernacle[168] of
the congregation,[4150] to do[5647] [a]the
service[5656] of the tabernacle.[4908]
8 And they shall keep all the instruments[3627] of the tabernacle of the congregation, and the charge of the children
of Israel, to do the service of the tabernacle.
9 And [a]thou shalt give the Levites
unto Aaron and to his sons: they *are*
wholly given unto him out of the children of Israel.
10 And thou shalt appoint[6485] Aaron
and his sons, [a]and they shall wait[8104] on
their priest's office:[3550] [b]and the
stranger[2114] that cometh nigh shall be
put to death.[4191]

The Redemption of the Firstborn

11 And the LORD spake unto Moses,
saying,
12 And I, behold, [a]I have taken
the Levites from among the children of
Israel instead of all the firstborn that
openeth the matrix[7358] among the children of Israel: therefore the Levites shall
be mine;
13 Because [a]all the firstborn *are*
mine; [b]*for* on the day that I smote[5221] all
the firstborn in the land of Egypt I hallowed unto me all the firstborn in Israel,
both man[120] and beast: mine shall they
be: I *am* the LORD.
14 And the LORD spake unto Moses
in the wilderness of Sinai, saying,
15 Number the children of Levi after

3:10 See note on Exodus 32:25–29.

3:12, 13 In the time of the patriarchs, the firstborn son had a position of special honor and responsibility in the family structure. God proclaimed Israel to be His firstborn (Ex. 4:22). With the death of the Egyptians' firstborn sons, all the firstborn sons of Israel who had been saved on the night of the Passover were to be sanctified unto the Lord (Ex. 11:4, 5; 12:21–29; 13:2, 11–16). These were set apart for the Lord and it was necessary to make a sacrifice for their redemption (Ex. 22:29). Now all the male members of the tribe of Levi, from one month old and above, were substituted for the firstborn males of the rest of the tribes of Israel (see vv. 41, 45). Thus, the Levites were to be consecrated for the Lord's service. See the note on Num. 3:46–51.

the house[1004] of their fathers,[1] by their families:[4940] [a]every male from a month old and upward shalt thou number them.

16 And Moses numbered[6485] them according to the [I]word of the LORD, as he was commanded.[6680]

17 [a]And these were the sons of Levi by their names; Gershon, and Kohath, and Merari.

Duties of the Gershonites

18 And these *are* the names of the sons of Gershon by their families; [a]Libni, and Shimei.

19 And the sons of Kohath by their families; [a]Amram, and Izehar, Hebron, and Uzziel.

20 [a]And the sons of Merari by their families; Mahli, and Mushi. These *are* the families of the Levites according to the house of their fathers.

21 Of Gershon *was* the family of the Libnites, and the family of the Shimites: these *are* the families of the Gershonites.

22 Those that were numbered of them, according to the number of all the males,[2145] from a month old and upward, *even* those that were numbered of them *were* seven thousand and five hundred.

23 [a]The families of the Gershonites shall pitch behind the tabernacle westward.

24 And the chief of the house of the father of the Gershonites *shall be* Eliasaph the son[1121] of Lael.

25 And [a]the charge of the sons of Gershon in the tabernacle of the congregation *shall be* [b]the tabernacle, and [c]the tent,[168] [d]the covering thereof, and [e]the hanging for the door of the tabernacle of the congregation,

26 And [a]the hangings of the court, and [b]the curtain for the door of the court, which *is* by the tabernacle, and by the altar[4196] round about, and [c]the cords of it for all the service thereof.

Duties of the Kohathites

27 [a]And of Kohath *was* the family of the Amramites, and the family of the Izeharites, and the family of the Hebronites, and the family of the Uzzielites: these *are* the families of the Kohathites.

28 In the number of all the males, from a month old and upward, *were* eight thousand and six hundred, keeping[8104] the charge of the sanctuary.[6944]

29 [a]The families of the sons of Kohath shall pitch on the side[3409] of the tabernacle southward.

30 And the chief of the house of the father of the families of the Kohathites *shall be* Elizaphan the son of Uzziel.

31 And [a]their charge *shall be* [b]the ark,[727] and [c]the table, and [d]the candlestick, and [e]the altars, and the vessels of the sanctuary wherewith they minister, and [f]the hanging, and all the service thereof.

32 And Eleazar the son of Aaron the priest *shall be* chief over the chief of the Levites, *and have* the oversight[6486] of them that keep the charge of the sanctuary.

Duties of the Sons of Merari

33 Of Merari *was* the family of the Mahlites, and the family of the Mushites: these *are* the families of Merari.

34 And those that were numbered of them, according to the number of all the males, from a month old and upward, *were* six thousand and two hundred.

35 And the chief of the house of the father of the families of Merari *was* Zuriel the son of Abihail: [a]*these* shall pitch on the side of the tabernacle northward.

36 And [Ia]*under* the custody[6486] and charge of the sons of Merari *shall be* the boards of the tabernacle, and the bars thereof, and the pillars thereof, and the sockets thereof, and all the vessels thereof, and all that serveth thereto,

37 And the pillars of the court round about, and their sockets, and their pins, and their cords.

38 [a]But those that encamp before the tabernacle toward the east, *even* before the tabernacle of the congregation eastward, *shall be* Moses, and Aaron and his

---

15 [a]Num. 3:39; 26:62
16 [I]Hebr. *mouth*
17 [a]Gen. 46:11; Ex. 6:16; Num. 26:57; 1Chr. 6:1, 16; 23:6
18 [a]Ex. 6:17
19 [a]Ex. 6:18
20 [a]Ex. 6:19
23 [a]Num. 1:53
25 [a]Num. 4:24-26 [b]Ex. 25:9 [c]Ex. 26:1 [d]Ex. 26:7, 14 [e]Ex. 26:36
26 [a]Ex. 27:9 [b]Ex. 27:16 [c]Ex. 35:18
27 [a]1Chr. 26:23
29 [a]Num. 1:53
31 [a]Num. 4:15 [b]Ex. 25:10 [c]Ex. 25:23 [d]Ex. 25:31 [e]Ex. 27:1; 30:1 [f]Ex. 26:32
35 [a]Num. 1:53
36 [I]Hebr. *the office of the charge* [a]Num. 4:31, 32
38 [a]Num. 1:53

sons, [b]keeping the charge of the sanctuary[4720] [c]for the charge of the children of Israel; and [d]the stranger that cometh nigh shall be put to death.

🔑 39 [a]All that were numbered of the Levites, which Moses and Aaron numbered at the commandment[6310] of the LORD, throughout their families, all the males from a month old and upward, *were* twenty and two thousand.

40 And the LORD said[559] unto Moses, [a]Number[6485] all the firstborn of the males of the children of Israel from a month old and upward, and take[5375] the number of their names.

41 [a]And thou shalt take the Levites for me (I *am* the LORD) instead of all the firstborn among the children of Israel; and the cattle of the Levites instead of all the firstlings among the cattle of the children of Israel.

42 And Moses numbered, as the LORD commanded him, all the firstborn among the children of Israel.

43 And all the firstborn males[2145] by the number of names, from a month old and upward, of those that were numbered of them, were twenty and two thousand two hundred and threescore and thirteen.

44 And the LORD spake unto Moses, saying,

45 [a]Take the Levites instead of all the firstborn among the children of Israel, and the cattle of the Levites instead of their cattle; and the Levites shall be mine: I *am* the LORD.

38 [b]Num. 18:5 [c]Num. 3:7, 8 [d]Num. 3:10
39 [a]Num. 26:62
40 [a]Num. 3:15
41 [a]Num. 3:12, 45
45 [a]Num. 3:12, 41
46 [a]Ex. 13:13; Num. 18:15 [b]Num. 3:39, 43
47 [a]Lev. 27:6; Num. 18:16 [b]Ex. 30:13; Lev. 27:25; Num. 18:16; Ezek. 45:12
50 [a]Num. 3:46, 47
51 [a]Num. 3:48
3 [a]Num. 8:24; 1Chr. 23:3, 24, 27

🔑 46 And for those that are to be [a]redeemed of the two hundred and threescore and thirteen of the firstborn of the children of Israel, [b]which are more than the Levites;

47 Thou shalt even take [a]five shekels apiece by the poll,[1538] after the shekel of the sanctuary shalt thou take *them:* ([b]the shekel *is* twenty gerahs:[1626])

48 And thou shalt give the money, wherewith the odd number of them is to be redeemed, unto Aaron and to his sons.

49 And Moses took the redemption[6306] money of them that were over and above them that were redeemed[6302] by the Levites:

50 Of the firstborn of the children of Israel took he the money; [a]a thousand three hundred and threescore and five *shekels,* after the shekel of the sanctuary:

51 And Moses [a]gave the money of them that were redeemed unto Aaron and to his sons, according to the word of the LORD, as the LORD commanded Moses.

Further Duties of the Levites

4 And the LORD spake[1696] unto Moses and unto Aaron, saying,

2 Take[5375] the sum[7218] of the sons[1121] of Kohath from among the sons of Levi, after their families,[4940] by the house[1004] of their fathers,[1]

3 [a]From thirty years old and upward even until fifty years old, all that enter

---

🔑 **3:39** A different method was used to number those of the tribe of Levi than was used to number the rest of Israel. All males as old as one month were counted, and the total for the census before Israel left Mount Sinai was 22,000. Using the same method, 23,000 were recorded at the second census, about thirty-seven years later (Num. 26:26). Since Levi was not to be given a separate tribal territory, the figures were kept separate from the number of the rest of Israel.

🔑 **3:46–51** The firstborn of Israel were numbered at 22,273 and the Levites at 22,000 (v. 39), a difference of 273. In the substitution of the Levites for the firstborn these 273 extra among the firstborn were to be redeemed by a contribution of five shekels of silver apiece which were to be given to Aaron and his sons, the priestly family. The shekel of silver was to weigh 20 gerahs (Ex. 30:12–16). A gerah has been estimated to have been slightly less than six tenths of a gram. Therefore, the shekel would have weighed approximately eleven and one-half grams or four-tenths of an ounce. Hence, the redemption price for each of the 273 extra among the firstborn was two ounces of silver.

into the host,[6635] to do[6213] the work in the tabernacle[168] of the congregation.[4150]

4 [a]This *shall be* the service[5656] of the sons of Kohath in the tabernacle of the congregation, *about* [b]the most holy things:[6944]

5 And when the camp[4264] setteth forward, Aaron shall come, and his sons, and they shall take down [a]the covering vail, and cover[3680] the [b]ark[727] of testimony[5715] with it:

6 And shall put thereon the covering of badgers' skins, and shall spread over *it* a cloth wholly[3632] of blue, and shall put[7760] in the [a]staves thereof.

7 And upon the [a]table of shewbread[6440] they shall spread a cloth of blue, and put thereon the dishes, and the spoons,[3709] and the bowls, and covers to [I]cover[5258] withal: and the continual[8548] bread shall be thereon:

8 And they shall spread upon them a cloth of scarlet, and cover the same with a covering of badgers' skins, and shall put in the staves thereof.

9 And they shall take a cloth of blue, and cover the [a]candlestick of the light,[3974] [b]and his lamps,[5216] and his tongs, and his snuffdishes, and all the oil[8081] vessels thereof, wherewith they minister[8334] unto it:

10 And they shall put it and all the vessels thereof within a covering of badgers' skins, and shall put *it* upon a bar.

11 And upon [a]the golden altar[4196] they shall spread a cloth of blue, and cover it with a covering of badgers' skins, and shall put to the staves thereof:

12 And they shall take all the instruments of ministry,[8335] wherewith they minister in the sanctuary,[6944] and put *them* in a cloth of blue, and cover them with a covering of badgers' skins, and shall put *them* on a bar:

13 And they shall take away the ashes from the altar, and spread a purple cloth thereon:

14 And they shall put upon it all the vessels thereof, wherewith they minister about it, *even* the censers, the fleshhooks, and the shovels, and the [I]basons,[4219] all the vessels of the altar; and they shall spread upon it a covering of badgers' skins, and put to the staves of it.

15 And when Aaron and his sons have made an end[3615] of covering[3680] the sanctuary, and all the vessels of the sanctuary, as the camp is to set forward; after that, [a]the sons of Kohath shall come to bear[5375] *it*: [b]but they shall not touch[5060] *any* holy thing,[6944] lest they die.[4191] [c]These *things are* the burden[4853] of the sons of Kohath in the tabernacle of the congregation.

16 And to the office[6486] of Eleazar the son[1121] of Aaron the priest[3548] *pertaineth* [a]the oil for the light, and the [b]sweet incense,[7004] and [c]the daily[8548] meat offering,[4503] and the [d]anointing[4888] oil, *and* the oversight[6486] of all the tabernacle,[4908] and of all that therein *is,* in the sanctuary, and in the vessels thereof.

17 And the LORD spake unto Moses and unto Aaron, saying,

18 Cut ye not off[3772] the tribe[7626] of the families of the Kohathites from among the Levites:

19 But thus do unto them, that they may live,[2421] and not die, when they approach unto [a]the most holy things: Aaron and his sons shall go in, and appoint[7760] them every one[376] to his service and to his burden:

20 [a]But they shall not go in to see when the holy things are covered,[1104] lest they die.

21 And the LORD spake unto Moses, saying,

22 Take also the sum of the sons of Gershon, throughout the houses[1004] of their fathers, by their families;

23 [a]From thirty years old and upward until fifty years old shalt thou number[6485] them; all that enter in [I]to perform[6633] the service, to do[5647] the work in the tabernacle of the congregation.

24 This *is* the service of the families of the Gershonites, to serve,[5647] and for [I]burdens:

25 And [a]they shall bear the curtains of the tabernacle, and the tabernacle of the congregation, his covering, and the

4 [a]Num. 4:15 [b]Num. 4:19
5 [a]Ex. 26:31 [b]Ex. 25:10, 16
6 [a]Ex. 25:13
7 [I]Or, *pour out withal* [a]Ex. 25:23, 29, 30; Lev. 24:6, 8
9 [a]Ex. 25:31 [b]Ex. 25:37, 38
11 [a]Ex. 30:1, 3
14 [I]Or, *bowls*
15 [a]Num. 7:9; 10:21; Deut. 31:9; 2Sam. 6:13; 1Chr. 15:2, 15 [b]2Sam. 6:6, 7; 1Chr. 13:9, 10 [c]Num. 3:31
16 [a]Ex. 25:6; Lev. 24:2 [b]Ex. 30:34 [c]Ex. 29:40 [d]Ex. 30:23
19 [a]Num. 4:4
20 [a]Ex. 19:21; 1Sam. 6:19
23 [I]Hebr. *to war the warfare* [a]Num. 4:3
24 [I]Or, *carriage*
25 [a]Num. 3:25, 26

covering of the badgers' skins that *is* above upon it, and the hanging for the door of the tabernacle of the congregation,

26 And the hangings of the court, and the hanging for the door of the gate of the court, which *is* by the tabernacle and by the altar round about, and their cords, and all the instruments of their service, and all that is made[6213] for them: so shall they serve.

27 At the [I]appointment[6310] of Aaron and his sons shall be all the service of the sons of the Gershonites, in all their burdens, and in all their service: and ye shall appoint[6485] unto them in charge[4931] all their burdens.

28 This *is* the service of the families of the sons of Gershon in the tabernacle of the congregation: and their charge *shall be* under the hand[3027] of Ithamar the son of Aaron the priest.

29 As for the sons of Merari, thou shalt number them after their families, by the house of their fathers;

30 [a]From thirty years old and upward even unto fifty years old shalt thou number them, every one that entereth into the [I]service, to do the work of the tabernacle of the congregation.

31 And [a]this *is* the charge of their burden, according to all their service in the tabernacle of the congregation; [b]the boards of the tabernacle, and the bars thereof, and the pillars thereof, and sockets thereof,

32 And the pillars of the court round about, and their sockets, and their pins, and their cords, with all their instruments, and with all their service: and by name ye shall [a]reckon the instruments of the charge of their burden.

33 This *is* the service of the families of the sons of Merari, according to all their service, in the tabernacle of the congregation, under the hand of Ithamar the son of Aaron the priest.

The Number of Levites Eligible for Service

34 [a]And Moses and Aaron and the chief of the congregation[5712] numbered the sons of the Kohathites after their families, and after the house of their fathers,

35 From thirty years old and upward even unto fifty years old, every one that entereth into the service, for the work in the tabernacle of the congregation:

36 And those that were numbered of them by their families were two thousand seven hundred and fifty.

37 These *were* they that were numbered of the families of the Kohathites, all that might do service in the tabernacle of the congregation, which Moses and Aaron did number according to the commandment[6310] of the LORD by the hand of Moses.

38 And those that were numbered of the sons of Gershon, throughout their families, and by the house of their fathers,

39 From thirty years old and upward even unto fifty years old, every one that entereth into the service, for the work in the tabernacle of the congregation,

40 Even those that were numbered of them, throughout their families, by the house of their fathers, were two thousand and six hundred and thirty.

41 [a]These *are* they that were numbered of the families of the sons of Gershon, of all that might do service[5647] in the tabernacle of the congregation, whom Moses and Aaron did number according to the commandment of the LORD.

42 And those that were numbered of the families of the sons of Merari, throughout their families, by the house of their fathers,

43 From thirty years old and upward even unto fifty years old, every one that entereth into the service, for the work in the tabernacle of the congregation,

44 Even those that were numbered of them after their families, were three thousand and two hundred.

45 These *be* those that were numbered of the families of the sons of Merari, whom Moses and Aaron numbered [a]according to the word of the LORD by the hand of Moses.

46 All those that were numbered of

27 [I]Hebr. *mouth*
30 [I]Hebr. *warfare* [a]Num. 4:3
31 [a]Num. 3:36, 37 [b]Ex. 26:15
32 [a]Ex. 38:21
34 [a]Num. 4:2
41 [a]Num. 4:22
45 [a]Num. 4:29

the Levites, whom Moses and Aaron and the chief of Israel numbered, after their families, and after the house of their fathers,

47 [a]From thirty years old and upward even unto fifty years old, every one that came to do the service of the ministry,[5656] and the service of the burden in the tabernacle of the congregation,

48 Even those that were numbered of them, were eight thousand and five hundred and fourscore.

49 According to the commandment of the LORD they were numbered by the hand of Moses, [a]every one[376] according to his service, and according to his burden: thus were they numbered of him, [b]as the LORD commanded Moses.

Unclean People

5 🗝 And the LORD spake[1696] unto Moses, saying,

2 Command[6680] the children[1121] of Israel, that they put out of the camp[4264] every [a]leper, and every one that hath an [b]issue, and whosoever is defiled[2931] by the [c]dead:

3 Both male and female[5347] shall ye put out, without the camp shall ye put them; that they defile[2930] not their camps, [a]in the midst whereof I dwell.[7931]

4 And the children of Israel did[6213] so, and put them out without the camp: as the LORD spake unto Moses, so did the children of Israel.

Restitution for Wrongs

5 And the LORD spake unto Moses, saying,

6 Speak unto the children of Israel, [a]When a man[376] or woman[802] shall commit[6213] any sin that men commit to do[6213] a trespass[4604] against the LORD, and that person[5315] be guilty;[816]

7 [a]Then they shall confess[3034] their sin which they have done: and he shall recompense[7725] his trespass [b]with the principal[7218] thereof, and add unto it the fifth *part* thereof, and give *it* unto *him* against whom he hath trespassed.[816]

8 But if the man have no kinsman[1350] to recompense the trespass unto, let the trespass be recompensed unto the LORD, *even* to the priest;[3548] beside [a]the ram of the atonement,[3725] whereby an atonement shall be made for him.

9 And every [I][a]offering[8641] of all the holy things of the children of Israel, which they bring[7126] unto the priest, shall be his.

10 And every man's hallowed things[6944] shall be his: whatsoever any man giveth the priest, it shall be [a]his.

Wives Suspected of Adultery

🗝 11 And the LORD spake unto Moses, saying,

12 Speak unto the children of Israel, and say unto them, If any man's wife[802] go aside, and commit a trespass against him,

13 And a man [a]lie with her carnally,[2233] [7902] and it be hid from the eyes of her husband,[376] and be kept close, and she be defiled,[2930] and *there be* no witness against her, neither she be taken *with the manner;*

14 And the spirit[7307] of jealousy[7068] come upon him, and he be jealous of his wife, and she be defiled: or if the spirit of jealousy come upon him, and he be jealous of his wife, and she be not defiled:

47 [a]Num. 4:3, 23, 30
49 [a]Num. 4:15, 24, 31 [b]Num. 4:1, 21
2 [a]Lev. 13:3, 46; Num. 12:14 [b]Lev. 15:2 [c]Lev. 21:1; Num. 9:6, 10; 19:11, 13; 31:19
3 [a]Lev. 26:11, 12; 2Cor. 6:16
6 [a]Lev. 6:2, 3
7 [a]Lev. 5:5; 26:40; Josh. 7:19 [b]Lev. 6:5
8 [a]Lev. 6:6, 7; 7:7
9 IOr, *heave offering* [a]Ex. 29:28; Lev. 6:17, 18, 26; 7:6, 7, 9, 10, 14; Num. 18:8, 9, 19; Deut. 18:3, 4; Ezek. 44:29, 30
10 [a]Lev. 10:13
13 [a]Lev. 18:20

🗝 **5:1–4** This is an application of some of the laws which appear in Leviticus chapters fourteen and fifteen.

🗝 **5:11–31** When a married woman was suspected of sexual infidelity, God's personal judgment was to be sought in the matter. The punishment for such unfaithfulness was death (Lev. 20:10). Sometimes called the "law of jealousy," this passage contains the prescribed ritual by which the priest was to ask God to reveal whether this woman was guilty or innocent.

15 Then shall the man bring his wife unto the priest, and he shall bring her offering[7133] for her, the tenth *part* of an ephah of barley meal; he shall pour no oil[8081] upon it, nor put frankincense[3828] thereon; for it *is* an offering[4503] of jealousy, an offering of memorial, [a]bringing iniquity to remembrance.[2142]

16 And the priest shall bring her near, and set her before the LORD:

17 And the priest shall take holy[6918] water in an earthen[2789] vessel; and of the dust[6083] that is in the floor of the tabernacle[4908] the priest shall take, and put *it* into the water:

18 And the priest shall set the woman before the LORD, and uncover[6544] the woman's[802] head,[7218] and put the offering of memorial in her hands,[3709] which *is* the jealousy offering: and the priest shall have in his hand[3027] the bitter[4751] water that causeth the curse:[779]

19 And the priest shall charge her by an oath, and say unto the woman, If no man have lain with thee, and if thou hast not gone aside to uncleanness[2932] [I]*with another* instead of thy husband, be thou free[5352] from this bitter water that causeth the curse:

20 But if thou hast gone aside *to another* instead of thy husband, and if thou be defiled, and some man have lain with thee beside thine husband:

21 Then the priest shall [a]charge the woman with an oath[7621] of cursing,[423] and the priest shall say unto the woman, [b]The LORD make thee a curse and an oath among thy people,[5971] when the LORD doth make thy thigh[3409] to [I]rot,[5307] and thy belly[990] to swell;

22 And this water that causeth the curse [a]shall go into thy bowels,[4578] to make *thy* belly to swell, and *thy* thigh to rot: [b]And the woman shall say, Amen,[543] amen.

23 And the priest shall write these curses[423] in a book,[5612] and he shall blot *them* out[4229] with the bitter water:

24 And he shall cause the woman to drink the bitter water that causeth the curse: and the water that causeth the curse shall enter into her, *and become* bitter.

25 Then the priest shall take the jealousy offering out of the woman's hand, and shall [a]wave[5130] the offering before the LORD, and offer it upon the altar:[4196]

26 [a]And the priest shall take an handful of the offering, *even* the memorial thereof, and burn[6999] *it* upon the altar, and afterward shall cause the woman to drink the water.

27 And when he hath made her to drink the water, then it shall come to pass, *that,* if she be defiled, and have done trespass against her husband, that the water that causeth the curse shall enter into her, *and become* bitter, and her belly shall swell, and her thigh shall rot: and the woman [a]shall be a curse among[7130] her people.

28 And if the woman be not defiled, but be clean;[2889] then she shall be free, and shall conceive seed.[2233]

29 This *is* the law[8451] of jealousies,[7068] when a wife goeth aside *to another* [a]instead of her husband, and is defiled;

30 Or when the spirit of jealousy cometh upon him, and he be jealous over his wife, and shall set the woman before the LORD, and the priest shall execute upon her all this law.

31 Then shall the man be guiltless[5352] from iniquity, and this woman [a]shall bear[5375] her iniquity.

The Nazarite Vow

6 And the LORD spake unto Moses, saying,

2 Speak[1696] unto the children[1121] of Israel, and say unto them, When either

15 [a]1Kgs. 17:18; Ezek. 29:16
19 [I]Or, being *in the power of thy husband;* Hebr. *under thy husband*
21 [I]Hebr. *fall* [a]Josh. 6:26; 1Sam. 14:24; Neh. 10:29 [b]Jer. 29:22
22 [a]Ps. 109:18 [b]Deut. 27:15
25 [a]Lev. 8:27
26 [a]Lev. 2:2, 9
27 [a]Deut. 28:37; Ps. 83:9, 11; Jer. 24:9; 29:18, 22; 42:18; Zech. 8:13
29 [a]Num. 5:19
31 [a]Lev. 20:17, 19, 20

6:2–21 The word Nazarite, not to be confused with Nazarene, means "separated," and in this context means specifically "one who was separated unto the Lord." It was probably similar to a

(continued on next page)

man[376] or woman[802] shall [I][a]separate *themselves* to vow[5087] a vow[5088] of a Nazarite,[5139] to separate[5144] *themselves* unto the LORD:

3 [a]He shall separate *himself* from wine and strong drink, and shall drink no vinegar of wine, or vinegar of strong drink, neither shall he drink any liquor of grapes, nor eat moist grapes, or dried.[3002]

4 All the days of his [I]separation[5145] shall he eat nothing that is made of the [II]vine tree, from the kernels even to the husk.

5 All the days of the vow of his separation there shall no [a]razor come upon his head:[7218] until the days be fulfilled, in the which he separateth *himself* unto the LORD, he shall be holy, *and* shall let the locks of the hair of his head grow.

6 All the days that he separateth *himself* unto the LORD [a]he shall come at no dead body.[5315]

7 [a]He shall not make himself unclean[2930] for his father, or for his mother,[517] for his brother,[251] or for his sister,[269] when they die:[4194] because the [I]consecration[5145] of his God *is* upon his head.

8 All the days of his separation he *is* holy unto the LORD.

9 And if any man die very suddenly by him, and he hath defiled[2930] the head of his consecration; then he shall [a]shave his head in the day of his cleansing,[2893] on the seventh day shall he shave it.

10 And [a]on the eighth day he shall bring two turtles, or two young pigeons, to the priest,[3548] to the door of the tabernacle[168] of the congregation:[4150]

11 And the priest shall offer[6213] the one for a sin offering,[2403] and the other for a burnt offering,[5930] and make an atonement[3722] for him, for that he sinned[2398] by the dead, and shall hallow[6942] his head that same day.

12 And he shall consecrate[5144] unto the LORD the days of his separation, and shall bring a lamb of the first[1121] year [a]for a trespass offering:[817] but the days that were before[7223] shall [I]be lost, because his separation was defiled.

13 And this *is* the law[8451] of the Nazarite, [a]when the days of his separation are fulfilled: he shall be brought unto the door of the tabernacle of the congregation:

14 And he shall offer[7126] his offering[7133] unto the LORD, one he lamb of the first year without blemish[8549] for a burnt offering, and one ewe lamb[3535] of the first year without blemish [a]for a sin offering, and one ram without blemish [b]for peace offerings,

15 And a basket of unleavened bread,[4682] [a]cakes of fine flour mingled[1101] with oil,[8081] and wafers of unleavened bread [b]anointed[4886] with oil, and their meat offering, and their [c]drink offerings.[5262]

16 And the priest shall bring[7126] *them* before the LORD, and shall offer his sin offering, and his burnt offering:

17 And he shall offer the ram *for* a sacrifice[2077] of peace offerings unto the LORD, with the basket of unleavened bread: the priest shall offer also his meat offering, and his drink offering.

18 [a]And the Nazarite shall shave the head of his separation *at* the door of the tabernacle of the congregation, and shall take the hair of the head of his separation, and put *it* in the fire which *is* under the sacrifice of the peace offerings.

19 And the priest shall take the

2 [I]Or, *make themselves Nazarites* [a]Lev. 27:2; Judg. 13:5; Acts 21:23; Rom. 1:1

3 [a]Amos 2:12; Luke 1:15

4 [I]Or, *Nazariteship* [II]Hebr. *vine of the wine*

5 [a]Judg. 13:5; 16:17; 1Sam. 1:11

6 [a]Lev. 21:11; Num. 19:11, 16

7 [I]Hebr. *separation* [a]Lev. 21:1, 2, 11; Num. 9:6

9 [a]Acts 18:18; 21:24

10 [a]Lev. 5:7; 14:22; 15:14, 29

12 [I]Hebr. *fall* [a]Lev. 5:6

13 [a]Acts 21:26

14 [a]Lev. 4:2, 27, 32 [b]Lev. 3:6

15 [a]Lev. 2:4 [b]Ex. 29:2 [c]Num. 15:5, 7, 10

18 [a]Acts 21:24

(continued from previous page)

vow which existed among the Hebrews prior to Mount Sinai, but in this passage, it is brought under the regulation of the law. By the terms of the vow, a man or woman could voluntarily separate themselves unto the Lord for a specific period of time, even for life. They did not, however, become hermits, separating himself from society. Samson (Judg. 13:5) and Samuel (1 Sam. 1:11, 28) are two of the Nazarites mentioned in the Bible. It is also thought that John the Baptist may have been a Nazarite (Luke 1:15) and that perhaps this is the vow associated with the Apostle Paul (Acts 21:23–26).

[a]sodden[1311] shoulder of the ram, and one unleavened cake out of the basket, and one unleavened wafer, and [b]shall put *them* upon the hands[3709] of the Nazarite, after *the hair of* his separation is shaven:

20 And the priest shall wave[5130] them *for* a wave offering[8573] before the LORD: [a]this *is* holy[6944] for the priest, with the wave breast[8573] and heave[8641] shoulder: and after that the Nazarite may drink wine.

21 This *is* the law of the Nazarite who hath vowed, *and of* his offering unto the LORD for his separation, beside *that* that his hand[3027] shall get: according to the vow which he vowed, so he must do[6213] after the law of his separation.

The Priestly Blessing

22 And the LORD spake unto Moses, saying,

23 Speak unto Aaron and unto his sons,[1121] saying, On this wise [a]ye shall bless[1288] the children of Israel, saying unto them,

24 The LORD bless thee, and [a]keep[8104] thee:

25 The LORD [a]make his face shine upon thee, and [b]be gracious[2603] unto thee:

26 [a]The LORD lift up his countenance upon thee, and [b]give[7760] thee peace.[7965]

27 [a]And they shall put my name upon the children of Israel; and [b]I will bless them.

Offerings at the Tabernacle Dedication

7 And it came to pass on the day that Moses had fully [a]set up the tabernacle,[4908] and had anointed[4886] it, and sanctified[6942] it, and all the instruments thereof, both the altar[4106] and all the vessels thereof, and had anointed them, and sanctified them;

2 That [a]the princes[5387] of Israel, heads[7218] of the house of their fathers, who *were* the princes of the tribes,[4294] [I]and were over them that were numbered,[6485] offered:[7126]

3 And they brought[7126] their offering before the LORD, six covered wagons, and twelve oxen; a wagon for two of the princes, and for each one[259] an ox: and they brought them before the tabernacle.

4 And the LORD spake unto Moses, saying,

5 Take *it* of them, that they may be to do[5647] the service[5656] of the tabernacle[168] of the congregation;[4150] and thou shalt give them unto the Levites, to every man[376] according to his service.

6 And Moses took the wagons and the oxen, and gave them unto the Levites.

7 Two wagons and four oxen [a]he gave unto the sons[1121] of Gershon, according to their service:

8 [a]And four wagons and eight oxen he gave unto the sons of Merari, according unto their service, [b]under the hand[3027] of Ithamar the son of Aaron the priest.[3548]

9 But unto the sons of Kohath he gave none: because [a]the service of the sanctuary[6944] belonging unto them [b]*was that* they should bear[5375] upon their shoulders.

10 And the princes offered for [a]dedicating[2598] of the altar in the day that it was anointed, even the princes offered their offering before the altar.

🗝 11 And the LORD said unto Moses, They shall offer[7126] their offering, each prince[5387] on his day, for the dedicating of the altar.

12 And he that offered his offering the first[7223] day was [a]Nahshon the son of Amminadab, of the tribe[4294] of Judah:

19 [a]1Sam. 2:15 [b]Ex. 29:23, 24
20 [a]Ex. 29:27, 28
23 [a]Lev. 9:22; 1Chr. 23:13
24 [a]Ps. 121:7; John 17:11
25 [a]Ps. 31:16; 67:1; 80:3, 7, 19; 119:135; Dan. 9:17 [b]Gen. 43:29
26 [a]Ps. 4:6 [b]John 14:27; 2Thess. 3:16
27 [a]Deut. 28:10; 2Chr. 7:14; Isa. 43:7; Dan. 9:18, 19 [b]Ps. 115:12
1 [a]Ex. 40:18; Lev. 8:10, 11
2 [I]Hebr. *who stood* [a]Num. 1:4
7 [a]Num. 4:25
8 [a]Num. 4:31 [b]Num. 4:28, 33
9 [a]Num. 4:15 [b]Num. 4:6, 8, 10, 12, 14; 2Sam. 6:13
10 [a]Deut. 20:5; 1Kgs. 8:63; 2Chr. 7:5, 9; Ezra 6:16; Neh. 12:27
12 [a]Num. 2:3

🗝 **7:11** The space in the courtyard was too limited for all the offerings of all the leaders to be made in one day. There simply was not enough room to allow the receiving, slaughtering, and preparation of 252 animals in one day in that one area, not to mention the 36 whole animals and the fat parts of 216 animals on the altar.

13 And his offering[4503] *was* one silver charger, the weight thereof *was* an hundred and thirty *shekels,* one silver bowl of seventy shekels, after [a]the shekel of the sanctuary; both of them *were* full of fine flour mingled[1101] with oil[8081] for a [b]meat offering:

14 One spoon of ten *shekels* of gold, full of [a]incense:[7004]

15 [a]One young bullock, one ram, one lamb of the first[1121] year, for a burnt offering:[5930]

16 One kid[8163] of the goats for a [a]sin offering:[2403]

17 And for [a]a sacrifice[2077] of peace offerings,[8002] two oxen, five rams, five he goats, five lambs of the first year: this *was* the offering[7133] of Nahshon the son of Amminadab.

18 On the second day Nethaneel the son of Zuar, prince of Issachar, did offer:

19 He offered *for* his offering one silver charger, the weight whereof *was* an hundred and thirty *shekels,* one silver bowl of seventy shekels, after the shekel of the sanctuary; both of them full of fine flour mingled with oil for a meat offering:

20 One spoon of gold of ten *shekels,* full of incense:

21 One young bullock, one ram, one lamb of the first year, for a burnt offering:

22 One kid of the goats for a sin offering:

23 And for a sacrifice of peace offerings, two oxen, five rams, five he goats, five lambs of the first year: this *was* the offering of Nethaneel the son of Zuar.

24 On the third day Eliab the son of Helon, prince of the children[1121] of Zebulun, *did offer:*

25 His offering *was* one silver charger, the weight whereof *was* an hundred and thirty *shekels,* one silver bowl of seventy shekels, after the shekel of the sanctuary; both of them full of fine flour mingled with oil for a meat offering:

26 One golden spoon of ten *shekels,* full of incense:

13 [a]Ex. 30:13 [b]Lev. 2:1
14 [a]Ex. 30:34
15 [a]Lev. 1:2
16 [a]Lev. 4:23
17 [a]Lev. 3:1

27 One young bullock, one ram, one lamb of the first year, for a burnt offering:

28 One kid of the goats for a sin offering:

29 And for a sacrifice of peace offerings, two oxen, five rams, five he goats, five lambs of the first year: this *was* the offering of Eliab the son of Helon.

30 On the fourth day Elizur the son of Shedeur, prince of the children of Reuben, *did offer:*

31 His offering *was* one silver charger of the weight of an hundred and thirty *shekels,* one silver bowl of seventy shekels, after the shekel of the sanctuary; both of them full of fine flour mingled with oil for a meat offering:

32 One golden spoon of ten *shekels,* full of incense:

33 One young bullock, one ram, one lamb of the first year, for a burnt offering:

34 One kid of the goats for a sin offering:

35 And for a sacrifice of peace offerings, two oxen, five rams, five he goats, five lambs[3532] of the first year: this *was* the offering of Elizur the son of Shedeur.

36 On the fifth day Shelumiel the son of Zurishaddai, prince of the children of Simeon, *did offer:*

37 His offering *was* one silver charger, the weight whereof *was* an hundred and thirty *shekels,* one silver bowl of seventy shekels, after the shekel of the sanctuary; both of them full of fine flour mingled with oil for a meat offering:

38 One golden spoon of ten *shekels,* full of incense:

39 One young bullock, one ram, one lamb of the first year, for a burnt offering:

40 One kid of the goats for a sin offering:

41 And for a sacrifice[2077] of peace offerings, two oxen, five rams, five he goats, five lambs of the first year: this *was* the offering of Shelumiel the son of Zurishaddai.

42 On the sixth day Eliasaph the son of Deuel, prince of the children of Gad, *offered:*

43 His [a]offering *was* one silver charger of the weight of an hundred and thirty *shekels,* a silver bowl of seventy shekels, after the shekel of the sanctuary; both of them full of fine flour mingled with oil for a meat offering:

44 One golden spoon of ten *shekels,* full of incense:

45 One young bullock, one ram, one lamb of the first year, for a burnt offering:

46 One kid of the goats for a sin offering:

47 And for a sacrifice of peace offerings, two oxen, five rams, five he goats, five lambs of the first year: this *was* the offering of Eliasaph the son of Deuel.

48 On the seventh day Elishama the son of Ammihud, prince of the children of Ephraim, *offered:*

49 His offering[7133] *was* one silver charger, the weight whereof *was* an hundred and thirty *shekels,* one silver bowl of seventy shekels, after the shekel of the sanctuary; both of them full of fine flour mingled with oil for a [a]meat offering:

50 One golden spoon of ten *shekels,* full of incense:

51 One young bullock, one ram, one lamb of the first year, for a burnt offering:

52 One kid of the goats for a sin offering:

53 And for a sacrifice of peace offerings, two oxen, five rams, five he goats, five lambs of the first year: this *was* the offering of Elishama the son of Ammihud.

54 On the eighth day *offered* Gamaliel the son of Pedahzur, prince of the children of Manasseh:

55 His offering *was* one silver charger of the weight of an hundred and thirty *shekels,* one silver bowl of seventy shekels, after the shekel of the sanctuary; both of them full of fine flour mingled with oil for a meat offering:[4503]

56 One golden spoon of ten *shekels,* full of incense:

57 One young bullock, one ram, one lamb of the first year, for a [a]burnt offering:

58 One kid of the goats for a sin offering:

59 And for a sacrifice of peace offerings, two oxen, five rams, five he goats, five lambs of the first year: this *was* the offering of Gamaliel the son of Pedahzur.

60 On the ninth day Abidan the son of Gideoni, prince[5387] of the children of Benjamin, *offered:*

61 His offering *was* one silver charger, the weight whereof *was* an hundred and thirty *shekels,* one silver bowl of seventy shekels, after the shekel of the sanctuary; both of them full of fine flour mingled with oil for a meat offering:

62 One golden spoon of ten *shekels,* full of incense:

63 One young bullock, one ram, one lamb of the first year, for a burnt offering:

64 One kid of the goats for a [a]sin offering:

65 And for a sacrifice of peace offerings,[8002] two oxen, five rams, five he goats, five lambs of the first year: this *was* the offering of Abidan the son of Gideoni.

66 On the tenth day Ahiezer the son of Ammishaddai, prince of the children of Dan, *offered:*

67 His offering *was* one silver charger, the weight whereof *was* an hundred and thirty *shekels,* one silver bowl of seventy shekels, after the shekel of the sanctuary;[6944] both of them full of fine flour mingled with oil for a meat offering:

68 One golden spoon of ten *shekels,* full of incense:

69 One young bullock, one ram, one lamb of the first year, for a burnt offering:

70 One kid of the goats for a sin offering:

71 And for a sacrifice[2077] of [a]peace

43 [a]Num. 1:4-16
49 [a]Lev. 6:14-23
57 [a]Lev. 6:9-13
64 [a]Lev. 6:25-30
71 [a]Lev. 7:11-34; 1Kgs. 8:63

offerings, two oxen, five rams, five he goats, five lambs of the first year: this *was* the offering of Ahiezer the son of Ammishaddai.

72 On the eleventh day Pagiel the son of Ocran, prince of the children of Asher, *offered*:

73 His offering *was* one silver charger, the weight whereof *was* an hundred and thirty *shekels,* one silver bowl of seventy shekels, after the shekel of the sanctuary; both of them full of fine flour mingled with oil for a meat offering:

74 One golden spoon of ten *shekels,* full of incense:

75 One young bullock, one ram, one lamb of the first year, for a burnt offering:

76 One kid of the goats for a sin offering:

77 And for a sacrifice of peace offerings, two oxen, five rams, five he goats, five lambs of the first year: this *was* the offering of Pagiel the son of Ocran.

78 On the twelfth day Ahira the son of Enan, prince of the children of Naphtali, *offered:*

79 His offering *was* one silver charger, the weight whereof *was* an hundred and thirty *shekels,* one silver bowl of seventy shekels, after the shekel of the sanctuary; both of them full of fine flour mingled with oil for a meat offering:

80 One golden spoon of ten *shekels,* full of incense:

81 One young bullock, one ram, one lamb of the first year, for a burnt offering:

82 One kid of the goats for a sin offering:

83 And for a sacrifice of peace offerings, two oxen, five rams, five he goats, five lambs of the first year: this *was* the offering of Ahira the son of Enan.

84 This *was* the dedication[2598] of the altar, in the day when it was anointed, by the princes of Israel: twelve chargers of silver, twelve silver bowls, twelve spoons[3709] of gold:

85 Each charger of silver *weighing* an hundred and thirty *shekels,* each bowl seventy: all the silver vessels *weighed* two thousand and four hundred *shekels,* after the shekel of the sanctuary:

86 The golden spoons *were* twelve, full of incense, *weighing* ten *shekels* apiece, after the shekel of the sanctuary: all the gold of the spoons *was* an hundred and twenty *shekels.*

87 All the oxen for the burnt offering *were* twelve bullocks, the rams twelve, the lambs of the first year twelve, with their meat offering: and the kids[8163] of the goats for sin offering twelve.

88 And all the oxen for the sacrifice of the peace offerings *were* twenty and four bullocks, the rams sixty, the he goats sixty, the lambs of the first year sixty. This *was* the dedication of the altar, after that it was [a]anointed.

89 And when Moses was gone into the tabernacle of the congregation [a]to speak[1696] with [I]him, then he heard[8085] [b]the voice of one speaking unto him from off the mercy seat that *was* upon the ark[727] of testimony,[5715] from between the two cherubims:[3742] and he spake unto him.

The Seven Lamps

8 And the LORD spake unto Moses, saying,

2 Speak[1696] unto Aaron, and say[559] unto him, When thou [a]lightest[5927] the lamps,[5216] the seven lamps shall give light[215] over against the candlestick.

3 And Aaron did so; he lighted the lamps thereof over against the candlestick, as the LORD commanded[6680] Moses.

4 [a]And this work of the candlestick *was of* beaten gold, unto the shaft[3409] thereof, unto the flowers thereof, *was* [b]beaten work: [c]according unto the pattern which the LORD had shewed[7200] Moses, so he made the candlestick.

The Levites Are Purified

5 And the LORD spake unto Moses, saying,

6 Take the Levites from among the

88 [a]Num. 7:1

89 [I]That is, *God* [a]Ex. 33:9, 11; Num. 12:8 [b]Ex. 25:22

2 [a]Ex. 25:37; 40:25

4 [a]Ex. 25:31 [b]Ex. 25:18 [c]Ex. 25:40

children[1121] of Israel, and cleanse[2891] them.

7 And thus shalt thou do[6213] unto them, to cleanse them: Sprinkle[5137] [a]water of purifying upon them, and [I][b]let them shave all their flesh,[1320] and let them wash[3526] their clothes, and *so* make themselves clean.[2891]

8 Then let them take a young bullock with [a]his meat offering,[4503] *even* fine flour mingled[1101] with oil,[8081] and another young bullock shalt thou take for a sin offering.[2403]

9 [a]And thou shalt bring the Levites before the tabernacle[168] of the congregation:[4150] [b]and thou shalt gather the whole assembly[5712] of the children of Israel together:

10 And thou shalt bring the Levites before the LORD: and the children of Israel [a]shall put their hands[3027] upon the Levites:

11 And Aaron shall [I]offer the Levites before the LORD *for* an [II]offering of the children of Israel, that [III]they may execute the service[5656] of the LORD.

12 [a]And the Levites shall lay their hands upon the heads[7218] of the bullocks: and thou shalt offer[6213] the one *for* a sin offering, and the other *for* a burnt offering,[5930] unto the LORD, to make an atonement[3722] for the Levites.

13 And thou shalt set the Levites before Aaron, and before his sons,[1121] and offer them *for* an offering unto the LORD.

14 Thus shalt thou separate[914] the Levites from among the children of Israel: and the Levites shall be [a]mine.

15 And after that shall the Levites go in to do[5647] the service of the tabernacle of the congregation: and thou shalt cleanse them, and [a]offer them *for* an offering.

16 For they *are* wholly given unto me from among the children of Israel; [a]instead of such as open every womb, *even instead of* the firstborn of all the children of Israel, have I taken them unto me.

17 [a]For all the firstborn[1060] of the children of Israel *are* mine, *both* man[120] and beast: on the day[3117] that I smote[5221] every firstborn in the land of Egypt I sanctified[6942] them for myself.

18 And I have taken the Levites for all the firstborn of the children of Israel.

19 And [a]I have given the Levites *as* [I]a gift to Aaron and to his sons from among the children of Israel, to do the service of the children of Israel in the tabernacle of the congregation, and to make an atonement for the children of Israel: [b]that there be no plague[5063] among the children of Israel, when the children of Israel come nigh[5066] unto the sanctuary.[6944]

20 And Moses, and Aaron, and all the congregation[5712] of the children of Israel, did to the Levites according unto all that the LORD commanded Moses concerning the Levites, so did the children of Israel unto them.

21 [a]And the Levites were purified,[2398] and they washed[3526] their clothes; [b]and Aaron offered[5130] them *as* an offering before the LORD; and Aaron made an atonement for them to cleanse them.

22 [a]And after that went the Levites in to do their service in the tabernacle of the congregation before Aaron, and before his sons: [b]as the LORD had commanded Moses concerning the Levites, so did they unto them.

23 And the LORD spake unto Moses, saying,

24 This *is it* that *belongeth* unto the Levites: [a]from twenty and five years old and upward they shall go in [I][b]to wait upon[6633] the service of the tabernacle of the congregation:

25 And from the age of fifty years they shall [I]cease waiting upon the service *thereof,* and shall serve[5647] no more:

26 But shall minister[8334] with their brethren[251] in the tabernacle of the congregation, [a]to keep[8104] the charge,[4931] and shall do no service. Thus shalt thou do unto the Levites touching their charge.

The Passover

9 And the LORD spake[1696] unto Moses in the wilderness of Sinai, in the

7 [I]Hebr. *let them cause a razor to pass over* [a]Num. 19:9, 17, 18 [b]Lev. 14:8, 9
8 [a]Lev. 2:1
9 [a]Ex. 29:4; 40:12 [b]Lev. 8:3
10 [a]Lev. 1:4
11 [I]Hebr. *wave* [II]Hebr. *wave offering* [III]Hebr. *they may be to execute*
12 [a]Ex. 29:10
14 [a]Num. 3:45; 16:9
15 [a]Num. 8:11, 13
16 [a]Num. 3:12, 45
17 [a]Ex. 13:2, 12, 13, 15; 3:13; Luke 2:23
19 [I]Hebr. *given* [a]Num. 3:9 [b]Num. 1:53; 16:46; 18:5; 2Chr. 26:16
21 [a]Num. 8:7 [b]Num. 8:11, 12
22 [a]Num. 8:22 [b]Num. 8:5-22
24 [I]Hebr. *to war the warfare of* [a]Num. 4:3; 1Chr. 23:3, 24, 27 [b]1Tim. 1:18
25 [I]Hebr. *return from the warfare of the service*
26 [a]Num. 1:53

first[7223] month of the second year after they were come out of the land of Egypt, saying,

2 Let the children[1121] of Israel also keep [a]the passover[6453] at his appointed season.[4150]

3 In the fourteenth day[3117] of this month, [I][a]at even, ye shall keep it in his appointed season: according to all the rites of it, and according to all the ceremonies[4941] thereof, shall ye keep it.

4 And Moses spake unto the children of Israel, that they should keep the passover.

5 And [a]they kept[6213] the passover on the fourteenth day of the first month at even in the wilderness of Sinai: according to all that the LORD commanded[6680] Moses, so did[6213] the children of Israel.

6 And there were certain men,[582] who were [a]defiled[2931] by the dead body[5315] of a man,[376] that they could not keep the passover on that day: [b]and they came before Moses and before Aaron on that day:

7 And those men said[559] unto him, We *are* defiled by the dead body of a man: wherefore are we kept back, that we may not offer[7126] an offering[7133] of the LORD in his appointed season among the children of Israel?

8 And Moses said unto them, Stand still, and [a]I will hear[8085] what the LORD will command[6680] concerning you.

9 And the LORD spake unto Moses, saying,

10 Speak unto the children of Israel, saying, If any man of you or of your posterity shall be unclean[2931] by reason of a dead body, or *be* in a journey afar off, yet he shall keep the passover unto the LORD.

11 [a]The fourteenth day of the second month at even they shall keep it, *and* [b]eat it with unleavened bread[4682] and bitter *herbs*.

12 [a]They shall leave[7604] none of it unto the morning, [b]nor break[7665] any bone[6106] of it: [c]according to all the ordinances[2708] of the passover they shall keep it.

13 But the man that *is* clean,[2889] and is not in a journey, and forbeareth to keep the passover, even the same soul[5315] [a]shall be cut off[3772] from among his people:[5971] because he [b]brought[7126] not the offering of the LORD in his appointed season, that man shall [c]bear[5375] his sin.[2399]

14 And if a stranger[1616] shall sojourn[1481] among you, and will keep the passover unto the LORD; according to the ordinance[2708] of the passover, and according to the manner[4941] thereof, so shall he do: [a]ye shall have one ordinance, both for the stranger, and for him that was born in the land.

The Cloud Over the Tabernacle

15 And [a]on the day that the tabernacle[4908] was reared up the cloud[6051] covered[3680] the tabernacle, *namely,* the tent[168] of the testimony:[5715] and [b]at even there was upon the tabernacle as it were the appearance of fire, until the morning.

16 So it was alway:[8548] the cloud covered it *by day,* and the appearance of fire by night.[3915]

17 And when the cloud [a]was taken up[5927] from the tabernacle,[168] then after that the children of Israel journeyed: and in the place where the cloud abode,[7931] there the children of Israel pitched their tents.

18 At the commandment[6310] of the LORD the children of Israel journeyed, and at the commandment of the LORD they pitched: [a]as long as the cloud abode

2 [a]Ex. 12:1, 14-17; Lev. 23:5; Num. 28:16; Deut. 16:1, 2

3 [I]Hebr. *between the two evenings* [a]Ex. 12:6

5 [a]Josh. 5:10

6 [a]Num. 5:2; 19:11, 16; John 18:28 [b]Ex. 18:15, 19, 26; Num. 27:2

8 [a]Num. 27:5

11 [a]2Chr. 30:2, 15 [b]Ex. 12:8

12 [a]Ex. 12:10 [b]Ex. 12:46; John 19:36 [c]Ex. 12:43

13 [a]Gen. 17:14; Ex. 12:15 [b]Num. 8:13 [c]Num. 5:31

14 [a]Ex. 12:49

15 [a]Ex. 40:34; Neh. 9:12, 19; Ps. 78:14 [b]Ex. 13:21; 40:38

17 [a]Ex. 40:36; Num. 10:11, 33, 34; Ps. 80:1

18 [a]1Cor. 10:1

9:6 An unclean person could not participate in a sacrificial meal (Lev. 7:20, 21, cf. 1 Cor. 11:28, 29).

9:10, 11 If for some reason a man could not observe the Passover, or be present at the sanctuary at the prescribed time, provisions were made for him to keep it one month later.

upon the tabernacle they rested in their tents.

19 And when the cloud [I]tarried long upon the tabernacle many days,[3117] then the children of Israel [a]kept[8104] the charge[4931] of the LORD, and journeyed not.

20 And *so* it was, when the cloud was a few days upon the tabernacle; according to the commandment of the LORD they abode in their tents, and according to the commandment of the LORD they journeyed.

21 And *so* it was, when the cloud [I]abode from even unto the morning, and *that* the cloud was taken up in the morning, then they journeyed: whether *it was* by day[3119] or by night that the cloud was taken up, they journeyed.

22 Or *whether it were* two days, or a month, or a year, that the cloud tarried upon the tabernacle, remaining[7931] thereon, the children of Israel [a]abode in their tents, and journeyed not: but when it was taken up, they journeyed.

23 At the commandment of the LORD they rested in the tents,[2583] and at the commandment of the LORD they journeyed: they [a]kept the charge of the LORD, at the commandment of the LORD by the hand[3027] of Moses.

The Silver Trumpets

10 And the LORD spake unto Moses, saying,

2 Make[6213] thee two trumpets of silver; of a whole piece shalt thou make them: that thou mayest use them for the [a]calling[4744] of the assembly,[712] and for the journeying of the camps.[4264]

3 And when [a]they shall blow[8628] with them, all the assembly shall assemble themselves[3259] to thee at the door of the tabernacle[168] of the congregation.[4150]

4 And if they blow *but* with one *trumpet,* then the princes,[5387] *which are* [a]heads[7218] of the thousands[505] of Israel, shall gather themselves[3259] unto thee.

5 When ye blow an alarm, then [a]the camps that lie on the east parts shall go forward.

6 When ye blow an alarm[8643] the second time, then the camps that lie [a]on the south side shall take their journey: they shall blow an alarm for their journeys.

7 But when the congregation[6951] is to be gathered together,[6950] [a]ye shall blow, but ye shall not [b]sound an alarm.[7321]

8 [a]And the sons of Aaron, the priests,[3548] shall blow with the trumpets; and they shall be to you for an ordinance[2708] for ever[5769] throughout your generations.[1755]

9 And [a]if ye go to war in your land against the enemy that [b]oppresseth you, then ye shall blow an alarm[7321] with the trumpets; and ye shall be [c]remembered[2142] before the LORD your God,[430] and ye shall be saved from your enemies.

🔑 10 Also [a]in the day of your gladness, and in your solemn days,[4150] and in the beginnings[7218] of your months, ye shall blow with the trumpets over your burnt offerings,[5930] and over the sacrifices[2077] of your peace offerings;[8002] that they may be to you [b]for a memorial before your God: I *am* the LORD your God.

The Israelites Leave Sinai

11 And it came to pass on the twentieth *day* of the second month, in the second year, that the cloud[6051] [a]was taken up from off the tabernacle[4908] of the testimony.[5715]

12 And the children[1121] of Israel took [a]their journeys out of the [b]wilderness of Sinai: and the cloud rested[7931] in the [c]wilderness of Paran.

13 And they first[7223] took their journey [a]according to the command-

19 [I]Hebr. *prolonged* [a]Num. 1:53; 3:8
21 [I]Hebr. *was*
22 [a]Ex. 40:36, 37
23 [a]Num. 9:19
2 [a]Isa. 1:13
3 [a]Jer. 4:5; Joel 2:15
4 [a]Ex. 18:21; Num. 1:16; 7:2
5 [a]Num. 2:3
6 [a]Num. 2:10
7 [a]Num. 10:3 [b]Joel 2:1
8 [a]Num. 31:6; Josh. 6:4; 1Chr. 15:24; 2Chr. 13:12
9 [a]Num. 31:6; Josh. 6:5; 2Chr. 13:14 [b]Judg. 2:18; 4:3; 6:9; 10:8, 12; 1Sam. 10:18; Ps. 106:42 [c]Gen. 8:1; Ps. 106:4
10 [a]Num. 29:1; Lev. 23:24; 1Chr. 15:24; 2Chr. 5:12; 7:6; 29:26; Ezra 3:10; Neh. 12:35; Ps. 81:3 [b]Num. 10:9
11 [a]Num. 9:17
12 [a]Ex. 40:36; Num. 2:9, 16, 24, 31 [b]Ex. 19:1; Num. 1:1; 9:5 [c]Gen. 21:21; 12:16; 13:3, 26; Deut. 1:1
13 [a]Num. 2:34; 10:5, 6

🔑 **10:10** For a discussion of the phrase "the beginnings of your months," see note on Numbers 28:11–15.

ment[6310] of the LORD by the hand[3027] of Moses.

14 [a]In the first *place* went the standard of the camp[4264] of the children of Judah according to their armies:[6635] and over his host[6635] *was* [b]Nahshon the son[1121] of Amminadab.

15 And over the host of the tribe[4294] of the children of Issachar *was* Nethaneel the son of Zuar.

16 And over the host of the tribe of the children of Zebulun *was* Eliab the son of Helon.

17 And [a]the tabernacle was taken down; and the sons of Gershon and the sons of Merari set forward, [b]bearing[5375] the tabernacle.

18 And [a]the standard of the camp of Reuben set forward according to their armies: and over his host *was* Elizur the son of Shedeur.

19 And over the host of the tribe of the children of Simeon *was* Shelumiel the son of Zurishaddai.

20 And over the host of the tribe of the children of Gad *was* Eliasaph the son of Deuel.

21 And the Kohathites set forward, bearing the [a]sanctuary:[4720] and [1b]*the other* did set up the tabernacle against they came.

22 And [a]the standard of the camp of the children of Ephraim set forward according to their armies: and over his host *was* Elishama the son of Ammihud.

23 And over the host of the tribe of the children of Manasseh *was* Gamaliel the son of Pedahzur.

24 And over the host of the tribe of the children of Benjamin *was* Abidan the son of Gideoni.

25 And [a]the standard of the camp of the children of Dan set forward, *which was* the rereward[622] of all the camps throughout their hosts:[6635] and over his host *was* Ahiezer the son of Ammishaddai.

14 [a]Num. 2:3, 9 [b]Num. 1:7
17 [a]Num. 1:51 [b]Num. 4:24, 31; 7:6-8
18 [a]Num. 2:10, 16
21 [1]That is, *the Gershonites and the Merarites* [a]Num. 4:4, 15; 7:9 [b]Num. 1:51; 10:17
22 [a]Num. 2:18, 24
25 [a]Num. 2:25, 31; Josh. 6:9
28 [1]Hebr. *These* [a]Num. 2:34
29 [a]Ex. 2:18 [b]Gen. 12:7 [c]Judg. 1:16; 4:11 [d]Gen. 32:12; Ex. 3:8; 6:7, 8
31 [a]Job 29:15
32 [a]Judg. 1:16
33 [a]Ex. 3:1 [b]Deut. 1:33; Josh. 3:3, 4, 6; Ps. 132:8; Jer. 31:2; Ezek. 20:6
34 [a]Ex. 13:21; Neh. 9:12, 19 [b]Ps. 68:1, 2; 132:8
36 [1]Hebr. *ten thousand thousands*

26 And over the host of the tribe of the children of Asher *was* Pagiel the son of Ocran.

27 And over the host of the tribe of the children of Naphtali *was* Ahira the son of Enan.

28 [1a]Thus *were* the journeyings[4550] of the children of Israel according to their armies, when they set forward.

29 And Moses said[559] unto Hobab, the son of [a]Raguel the Midianite, Moses' father in law, We are journeying unto the place of which the LORD said, [b]I will give it you: come thou with us, and [c]we will do thee good:[2895] for [d]the LORD hath spoken[1696] good[2896] concerning Israel.

30 And he said unto him, I will not go; but I will depart to mine own land, and to my kindred.

31 And he said, Leave[5800] us not, I pray thee;[4994] forasmuch as thou knowest[3045] how we are to encamp in the wilderness, and thou mayest be to us [a]instead of eyes.

🔑 32 And it shall be, if thou go with us, yea, it shall be, that [a]what goodness[2896] the LORD shall do unto us, the same will we do unto thee.

33 And they departed from [a]the mount of the LORD three days'[3117] journey:[1870] and the ark[727] of the covenant[1285] [b]went before them in the three days' journey, to search out a resting place for them.

34 And [a]the cloud of the LORD *was* upon them by day,[3119] when they went out of the camp.

35 And it came to pass, when the ark set forward, that Moses said, [a]Rise up, LORD, and let thine enemies be scattered; and let them that hate[8130] thee flee before thee.

36 And when it rested, he said, Return,[7725] O LORD, unto the [1]many thousands of Israel.

🔑 **10:32** Since Hobab's descendants are later said to live in Canaan (Judg. 1:16; 1 Sam. 15:6), he must have complied with Moses' request, although his decision was not recorded.

God Sends Fire

11 And [a]*when* the people[5971] complained, it [I]displeased the LORD: and the LORD heard[8085] *it;* [b]and his anger[639] was kindled;[2734] and the [c]fire of the LORD burnt among them, and consumed *them that were* in the uttermost parts of the camp.[4264]

2 And the people cried unto Moses; and when Moses [a]prayed[6419] unto the LORD, the fire [I]was quenched.

3 And he called[7121] the name of the place [Ia]Taberah: because the fire of the LORD burnt among them.

God Sends Quail

4 And the [a]mixt multitude[628] that *was* among[7130] them [I]fell a lusting: and the children[1121] of Israel also [II]wept again, and said, [b]Who shall give us flesh[1320] to eat?

5 [a]We remember[2142] the fish,[1710] which we did eat in Egypt freely; the cucumbers, and the melons, and the leeks,[2682] and the onions, and the garlick:

6 But now [a]our soul[5315] *is* dried away:[3001] *there is* nothing at all, beside this manna,[4478] *before* our eyes.

7 And [a]the manna *was* as coriander seed,[2233] and the [I]colour thereof as the colour of [b]bdellium.

8 *And* the people went about, and gathered[3950] *it,* and ground *it* in mills, or beat *it* in a mortar, and baked *it* in pans, and made[6213] cakes of it: and [a]the taste[2940] of it was as the taste of fresh oil.[8081]

9 And [a]when the dew fell upon the camp in the night,[3915] the manna fell upon it.

10 Then Moses heard the people weep throughout their families,[4940] every man[376] in the door of his tent:[168] and [a]the anger of the LORD was kindled greatly; Moses also was displeased.

11 [a]And Moses said unto the LORD, Wherefore hast thou afflicted[7489] thy servant?[5650] and wherefore have I not found favour[2580] in thy sight, that thou layest the burden[4853] of all this people upon me?

12 Have I conceived all this people? have I begotten[3205] them, that thou shouldest say unto me, [a]Carry[5375] them in thy bosom, as a [b]nursing father[539] beareth the sucking child, unto the land[127] which thou [c]swarest[7650] unto their fathers?[1]

13 [a]Whence should I have flesh to give unto all this people? for they weep unto me, saying, Give us flesh, that we may eat.

14 [a]I am not able to bear[5375] all this people alone, because *it is* too heavy for me.

15 And if thou deal[6213] thus with me, [a]kill me, I pray thee,[4994] out of hand, if I have found favour in thy sight; and let me not [b]see my wretchedness.[7451]

16 And the LORD said unto Moses, Gather[622] unto me [a]seventy men[376] of the elders[2205] of Israel, whom thou knowest[3045] to be the elders of the people, and [b]officers over them; and bring them unto the tabernacle[168] of the congregation,[4150] that they may stand there with thee.

17 And I will [a]come down and talk[1696] with thee there: and [b]I will take of the spirit[7307] which *is* upon thee, and will put *it* upon them; and they shall bear the burden of the people with thee, that thou bear *it* not thyself alone.

1 [I]Hebr. *it was evil in the ears of* [a]Deut. 9:22 [b]Ps. 78:21 [c]Lev. 10:2; Num. 16:35; 2Kgs. 1:12; Ps. 106:18
2 [I]Hebr. *sunk* [a]James 5:16
3 [I]That is, *A burning* [a]Deut. 9:22
4 [I]Hebr. *lusted a lust* [II]Hebr. *returned and wept* [a]Ex. 12:38 [b]Ps. 78:18; 106:14; 1Cor. 10:6
5 [a]Ex. 16:3
6 [a]Num. 21:5
7 [I]Hebr. *eye of it as the eye of* [a]Ex. 16:14, 31 [b]Gen. 2:12
8 [a]Ex. 16:31
9 [a]Ex. 16:13, 14
10 [a]Ps. 78:21
11 [a]Deut. 1:12
12 [a]Isa. 40:11 [b]Isa. 49:23; 1Thess. 2:7 [c]Gen. 26:3; 50:24; Ex. 13:5
13 [a]Matt. 15:33; Mark 8:4
14 [a]Ex. 18:18
15 [a]1Kgs. 19:4; Jon. 4:3 [b]Zeph. 3:15
16 [a]Ex. 24:1, 9 [b]Deut. 16:18
17 [a]Num. 11:25; Gen. 11:5; 18:21; Ex. 19:20 [b]1Sam. 10:6; 2Kgs. 2:15; Neh. 9:20; Isa. 44:3; Joel 2:28

11:1–5 The source of discontent and complaint is described as "the mixed multitude," which is rendered in other versions as "rabble" and "foreigners." These people had come out of Egypt with Israel (Ex. 12:38). Since they were not Hebrews, they had no personal attachment either to the promise or to God. They were tired of the manna and, forgetting all of the reasons for fleeing from Egypt, they remembered only the fish, onions, and garlic which were formerly available to them. They were held in low esteem by the Israelites although Israel allowed themselves to be influenced by their grumbling.

18 And say thou unto the people, [a]Sanctify yourselves[6942] against to morrow, and ye shall eat flesh: for ye have wept [b]in the ears[241] of the LORD, saying, Who shall give us flesh to eat? [c]for *it was* well[2895] with us in Egypt: therefore the LORD will give you flesh, and ye shall eat.

19 Ye shall not eat one day,[3117] nor two days, nor five days, neither ten days, nor twenty days;

🔑 20 [a]*But* even a [I]whole[3117] month, until it come out at your nostrils,[639] and it be loathsome unto you: because that ye have despised[3988] the LORD which *is* among you, and have wept before him, saying, [b]Why came we forth out of Egypt?

21 And Moses said, [a]The people, among whom I *am, are* six hundred thousand footmen; and thou hast said, I will give them flesh, that they may eat a whole month.

22 [a]Shall the flocks and the herds be slain[7819] for them, to suffice them? or shall[622] all the fish[1709] of the sea be gathered together[622] for them, to suffice them?

23 And the LORD said unto Moses, [a]Is the LORD's hand[3027] waxed short? thou shalt see now whether [b]my word[1697] shall come to pass unto thee or not.

24 And Moses went out, and told the people the words[1697] of the LORD, and [a]gathered the seventy men of the elders of the people, and set them round about the tabernacle.

25 And the LORD [a]came down in a cloud,[6051] and spake[1696] unto him, and took of the spirit that *was* upon him, and gave *it* unto the seventy elders: and it came to pass, *that,* [b]when the spirit rested upon them, [c]they prophesied,[5012] and did not cease.

26 But there remained two *of the* men in the camp, the name of the one *was* Eldad, and the name of the other Medad: and the spirit rested upon them; and they *were* of them that were written, but [a]went not out unto the tabernacle: and they prophesied in the camp.

27 And there ran a young man, and told[5046] Moses, and said, Eldad and Medad do prophesy[5012] in the camp.

28 And Joshua the son[1121] of Nun, the servant[8334] of Moses, *one* of his young men, answered and said, My lord[113] Moses, [a]forbid them.

29 And Moses said unto him, Enviest[7065] thou for my sake? [a]would God that all the LORD's people were prophets,[5030] *and* that the LORD would put his spirit upon them

30 And Moses gat him into the camp, he and the elders of Israel.

31 And there went forth a [a]wind[7307] from the LORD, and brought quails from the sea, and let *them* fall by the camp, [I]as it were a day's journey[1870] on this side, and as it were a day's journey on the other side, round about the camp, and as it were two cubits *high* upon the face of the earth.[776]

32 And the people stood up all that day, and all *that* night, and all the next day, and they gathered the quails: he that gathered least gathered ten [a]homers:[2563] and they spread *them* all abroad for themselves round about the camp.

33 And while the [a]flesh *was* yet between their teeth, ere[2962] it was chewed,[3772] the wrath[639] of the LORD was kindled against the people, and the LORD smote[5221] the people with a very great plague.[4347]

34 And he called the name of that [I][a]place Kibroth–hattaavah: because there they buried[6912] the people that lusted.[183]

35 [a]And the people journeyed from Kibroth–hattaavah unto Hazeroth; and [I]abode at Hazeroth.

18 [a]Ex. 19:10 [b]Ex. 16:7 [c]Num. 11:5; Acts 7:39

20 [I]Hebr. *month of days* [a]Ps. 78:29; 106:15 [b]Num. 21:5

21 [a]Gen. 12:2; Ex. 12:37; 38:26; Num. 1:46

22 [a]2Kgs. 7:2; Matt. 15:33; Mark 8:4; John 6:7, 9

23 [a]Isa. 50:2; 59:1 [b]Num. 23:19; Ezek. 12:25; 24:14

24 [a]Num. 11:16

25 [a]Num. 11:17; 12:5 [b]2Kgs. 2:15 [c]1Sam. 10:5, 6, 10; 19:20, 21, 23; Joel 2:28; Acts 2:17, 18; 1Cor. 14:1-6

26 [a]1Sam. 20:26; Jer. 36:5

28 [a]Mark 9:38; Luke 9:49; John 3:26

29 [a]1Cor. 14:5

31 [I]Hebr. *as it were the way of a day* [a]Ex. 16:13; Ps. 78:26-28; 105:40

32 [a]Ex. 16:36; Ezek. 45:11

33 [a]Ps. 78:30, 31

34 [I]That is, *The graves of lust* [a]Deut. 9:22

35 [I]Hebr. *they were in* [a]Num. 33:17

🔑 **11:20** God will hold people accountable for the words which they speak, just as He did here (Prov. 5:21; Matt. 12:36, 37; Heb. 4:13).

Miriam Is Punished

12 And Miriam and Aaron spake against Moses because of the [I]Ethiopian woman[802] whom he had married: for [a]he had [II]married an Ethiopian woman.

2 And they said,[559] Hath the LORD indeed spoken[1696] only by Moses? [a]hath he not spoken also by us? And the LORD [b]heard[8085] *it.*

🗝 3 (Now the man[376] Moses *was* very meek, above all the men[120] which *were* upon the face of the earth.[127])

4 [a]And the LORD spake suddenly unto Moses, and unto Aaron, and unto Miriam, Come out ye three unto the tabernacle[168] of the congregation. And they three came out.

5 [a]And the LORD came down in the pillar of the cloud,[6051] and stood *in* the door of the tabernacle, and called[7121] Aaron and Miriam: and they both came forth.

6 And he said, Hear[8085] now my words:[1697] If there be a prophet[5030] among you, *I* the LORD will make myself known[3045] unto him [a]in a vision, *and* will speak[1696] unto him [b]in a dream.

🗝 7 [a]My servant[5650] Moses *is* not so, [b]who *is* faithful[539] in all [c]mine house.[1004]

8 With him will I speak [a]mouth[6310] to mouth, even [b]apparently, and not in dark speeches;[2420] and [c]the similitude of the LORD[3068] shall he behold: wherefore then [d]were ye not afraid[3372] to speak against my servant Moses?

9 And the anger[639] of the LORD was kindled[2734] against them; and he departed.

🗝 10 And the cloud departed[5493] from off the tabernacle; and, [a]behold, Miriam *became* [b]leprous, *white* as snow: and Aaron looked upon Miriam, and, behold, *she was* leprous.

11 And Aaron said unto Moses, Alas, my lord,[113] I beseech thee,[4994] [a]lay not the sin[2403] upon us, wherein we have done foolishly, and wherein we have sinned.[2398]

12 Let her not be [a]as one dead,[4191] of whom the flesh[1320] is half consumed when he cometh out of his mother's[517] womb.

13 And Moses cried unto the LORD, saying, Heal her now, O God,[410] I beseech thee.

14 And the LORD said unto Moses, [a]If her father[1] had but spit in her face, should she not be ashamed[3637] seven days? let her be [b]shut out from the camp[4264] seven days, and after that let her be received in *again.*

15 [a]And Miriam was shut out from the camp seven days: and the people[5971] journeyed not till Miriam was brought in *again.*

16 And afterward the people removed from [a]Hazeroth, and pitched in the wilderness of Paran.

1 IOr, *Cushite* IIHebr. *taken* [a]Ex. 2:21
2 [a]Ex. 15:20; Mic. 6:4 [b]Gen. 29:33; Num. 11:1; 2Kgs. 19:4; Isa. 37:4; Ezek. 35:12, 13
4 [a]Ps. 76:9
5 [a]Num. 11:25; 16:19
6 [a]Gen. 15:1; 46:2; Job 33:15; Ezek. 1:1; Dan. 8:2; 10:8, 16, 17; Luke 1:11, 22; Acts 10:11, 17; 22:17, 18 [b]Gen. 31:10, 11; 1Kgs. 3:5; Matt. 1:20
7 [a]Ps. 105:26 [b]Heb. 3:2, 5 [c]1Tim. 3:15
8 [a]Ex. 33:11; Deut. 34:10 [b]1Cor. 13:12 [c]Ex. 33:19 [d]2Pet. 2:10; Jude 1:8
10 [a]Deut. 24:9 [b]2Kgs. 5:27; 15:5; 2Chr. 26:19, 20
11 [a]2Sam. 19:19; 24:10; Prov. 30:32
12 [a]Ps. 88:4
14 [a]Heb. 12:9 [b]Lev. 13:46; Num. 5:2, 3
15 [a]Deut. 24:9; 2Chr. 26:20, 21
16 [a]Num. 11:35; 33:18

🗝 **12:3** Some scholars have thought it necessary to consider this verse a later insertion in the text, possibly by Joshua, as it did not seem proper for Moses (the author) to glorify himself. However, the purpose of the statement was not to glorify Moses but to explain why he took no steps to justify himself when Miriam and Aaron questioned his authority as God's spokesman. The book was written by Moses under the inspiration of the Holy Spirit. The same objectivity that allowed him to record his spiritual successes also allowed for the recording of his own faults and sins.

🗝 **12:7** Moses was more than just the leader of Israel or a well-known prophet. The writer of Hebrews describes him as a type of Christ (Heb. 3:2–6). He was chosen by God to be a deliverer (Ex. 3:1–10) and was designated as a prophet (Deut. 18:15). As a servant in God's house, he was considered faithful and trustworthy (Heb. 3:5, 6). Moses was a mediator between Jehovah and Israel (Ex. 17:1–7; 32:30–35) as Christ is for His church (see 1 John 2:1, 2).

🗝 **12:10** Miriam had apparently initiated this insurrection against Moses (v. 1), and was therefore punished. Aaron was again showing his lack of spiritual backbone, just as he did in the incident of the golden calf (Ex. 32:1–6; 21–24).

The Spies Explore Canaan

13 And the LORD spake[1696] unto Moses, saying,

2 [a]Send thou men,[582] that they may search the land[776] of Canaan, which I give unto the children[1121] of Israel: of every tribe[4294] of their fathers[1] shall ye send a man,[376] every one a ruler[5387] among them.

3 And Moses by the commandment[6310] of the LORD sent them [a]from the wilderness of Paran: all those men *were* heads[7218] of the children of Israel.

4 And these *were* their names: of the tribe of Reuben, Shammua the son[1121] of Zaccur.

5 Of the tribe of Simeon, Shaphat the son of Hori.

6 [a]Of the tribe of Judah, [b]Caleb the son of Jephunneh.

7 Of the tribe of Issachar, Igal the son of Joseph.

8 Of the tribe of Ephraim, [a]Oshea the son of Nun.

9 Of the tribe of Benjamin, Palti the son of Raphu.

10 Of the tribe of Zebulun, Gaddiel the son of Sodi.

11 Of the tribe of Joseph, *namely,* of the tribe of Manasseh, Gaddi the son of Susi.

12 Of the tribe of Dan, Ammiel the son of Gemalli.

13 Of the tribe of Asher, Sethur the son of Michael.

14 Of the tribe of Naphtali, Nahbi the son of Vophsi.

15 Of the tribe of Gad, Geuel the son of Machi.

🔑16 These *are* the names of the men which Moses sent to spy out the land. And Moses called[7121] [a]Oshea the son of Nun Jehoshua.

🔑17 And Moses sent them to spy out the land of Canaan, and said[559] unto them, Get you up this *way* [a]southward, and go up[5927] into [b]the mountain:

18 And see the land, what it *is;* and the people[5971] that dwelleth therein, whether they *be* strong[2389] or weak, few or many;

19 And what the land *is* that they dwell in, whether it *be* good[2896] or bad;[7451] and what cities *they be* that they dwell in, whether in tents,[4264] or in strong holds;

20 And what the land *is,* whether it *be* [a]fat or lean, whether there be wood therein, or not. And [b]be ye of good courage,[2388] and bring of the fruit of the land. Now the time[3117] *was* the time of the firstripe grapes.

21 So they went up,[5927] and searched the land [a]from the wilderness of Zin unto [b]Rehob, as men come to Hamath.

🔑22 And they ascended by the south, and came unto Hebron; where [a]Ahiman, Sheshai, and Talmai, the [b]children of Anak, *were.* (Now [c]Hebron was built seven years before [d]Zoan in Egypt.)

2 [a]Num. 32:8; Deut. 1:22
3 [a]Num. 12:16; 32:8; Deut. 1:19; 9:23
6 [a]Num. 34:19; 1Chr. 4:15 [b]Num. 13:30; 14:6, 30; Josh. 14:6, 7, 13, 14; Judg. 1:12
8 [a]Num. 13:16
16 [a]Num. 13:8; Ex. 17:9; Num. 14:6, 30
17 [a]Num. 13:21 [b]Gen. 14:10; Judg. 1:9, 19
20 [a]Neh. 9:25, 35; Ezek. 34:14 [b]Deut. 31:6, 7, 23
21 [a]Num. 34:3; Josh. 15:1 [b]Josh. 19:28
22 [a]Josh. 11:21, 22; 15:13, 14; Judg. 1:10 [b]Num. 13:33 [c]Josh. 21:11 [d]Ps. 78:12; Isa. 19:11; 30:4

🔑 **13:16** See note on Numbers 27:18–23.

🔑 **13:17** The word *Negev* (5045), translated "southward," is better translated "south country." The south country was a well-defined territory forming the southernmost and least fertile part of Canaan and was subsequently a part of Judah's inheritance. It extended northward from Kadesh to within a few miles of Hebron and from the Dead Sea westward to the Mediterranean.

The word *har* (2022), translated "mountain," may also be used to refer to a range of hills or mountains. This was a description of the country of southern and central Canaan, mostly within the borders of the inheritance of Judah and Ephraim. It began a few miles south of Hebron and extended northward to the plain of Jezreel continuing northwest to the sea just above Mount Carmel.

🔑 **13:22** Until recently, Zoan was identified with Tanis and Avaris, later Egyptian cities. More recent archaeological evidence has again affirmed the biblical account, suggesting that a city in the area of modern Qantir is Zoan. Moreover, this city is doubtless the cite of "Raamses," mentioned in Exodus 1:11. This would seem to confirm that the Hyksos rulers began the oppression of Israel in Egypt. It was near Hebron that the Hebrew patriarchs had been buried (Gen. 23:19; 49:31).

23 [a]And they came unto the [I][b]brook
of Eshcol, and cut down[3772] from thence
a branch with one cluster of grapes, and
they bare[5375] it between two upon a staff;
and *they brought* of the pomegranates,
and of the figs.
24 The place was called the [I]brook
[II]Eshcol, because of the cluster of grapes
which the children of Israel cut down
from thence.
25 And they returned[7725] from
searching of the land after forty days.[3117]
26 And they went and came to
Moses, and to Aaron, and to all the
congregation[5712] of the children of Israel,
[a]unto the wilderness of Paran, to
[b]Kadesh; and brought back word[1697] unto
them, and unto all the congregation, and
shewed[7200] them the fruit of the land.
27 And they told[5608] him, and said,
We came unto the land whither thou
sentest us, and surely it floweth with
[a]milk and honey; [b]and this *is* the fruit
of it.
28 Nevertheless [a]the people *be* strong
that dwell in the land, and the cities *are*
walled, *and* very great: and moreover we
saw[7200] [b]the children of Anak there.
29 [a]The Amalekites dwell in the land
of the south: and the Hittites, and the
Jebusites, and the Amorites, dwell in the
mountains: and the Canaanites dwell by
the sea, and by the coast of Jordan.
30 And [a]Caleb stilled the people before Moses, and said, Let us go up at
once, and possess[3423] it; for we are
well[2895] able to overcome it.
31 [a]But the men that went up with
him said, We be not able to go up against
the people; for they *are* stronger[2389] than
we.
32 And they [a]brought up an evil report of the land which they had searched
unto the children of Israel, saying, The
land, through which we have gone to
search it, *is* a land that eateth up the inhabitants thereof; and [b]all the people that
we saw in it *are* [I]men of a great stature.

23 [I]Or, *valley* [a]Deut. 1:24, 25 [b]Num. 32:9; Judg. 16:4
24 [I]Or, *valley* [II]That is, *A cluster of grapes*
26 [a]Num. 13:3 [b]Num. 20:1, 16; 32:8; 33:36; Deut. 1:19; Josh. 14:6
27 [a]Ex. 3:8; 33:3 [b]Deut. 1:25
28 [a]Deut. 1:28; 9:1, 2 [b]Num. 13:33
29 [a]Ex. 17:8; Num. 14:43; Judg. 6:3; 1Sam. 14:48; 15:3
30 [a]Num. 14:6, 24; Josh. 14:7
31 [a]Num. 32:9; Deut. 1:28; Josh. 14:8
32 [I]Hebr. *men of statures* [a]Num. 14:36, 37 [b]Amos 2:9

13:26 Kadesh, also known as Kadesh-Barnea, was an oasis in the wilderness just south of Canaan proper. It was often a place of defeat, failure, and death for the nation of Israel during their years of wandering. The people rebelled when the twelve spies returned to Kadesh (Num. 14:1–10); they were repulsed in their rash attack from Kadesh (Num. 14:40–45); Miriam, Moses' sister, died and was buried at Kadesh (Num. 20:1); and the great sin of Moses in smiting the rock occurred at Kadesh (Num. 20:11, 12). Aaron soon died on Mount Hor (Num. 20:23–29), and Moses died on Mount Nebo (Deut. 34:1–5).

The rebellion at Kadesh is expounded upon in Psalm 95:7b–11. The psalmist attributed Israel's loss of God's "rest" to this rebellion. In addition, the Book of Hebrews affirms that the loss was only temporary, and that God's "rest" was still available if God's people in the New Testament did not "fall after the same example of unbelief" (Heb. 4:9, 11).

13:28 Regarding the cities that were "walled and very great," modern archaeologists have found that there were indeed numerous walled fortresses throughout Canaan even in 1440 B.C. These cities made invasion by foreign armies difficult for some time, until the science of siege warfare was as well developed as the techniques of fortification.

13:30–33 The spies reported that the people of the land were large: "men of great stature" and "giants." The Hebrew word for "giant" is *nephilim* (5303), which appears elsewhere only in Genesis 6:4 (see note). Obviously these people have no connection to those in Genesis chapter six, since that was before the flood. The emphasis of this passage may be that these sons of Anak were not only large, but violent and evil as well (see Deut. 2:10, 11 where "giant" is a translation of *rephaim* [7497]). Caleb and Joshua were the spies who brought back the faithful report that, with the Lord's help, Canaan could easily be taken (Num. 14:6–9). For their faithfulness, God allowed them to survive the wilderness experience and enter Canaan (Num. 14:30). When the second census was taken as preparations were being made to move into Canaan (see note on Num. 26:52–56), Caleb and Joshua were the only ones from the original group that were still alive. After the major campaigns of the conquest were completed, Joshua divided the land of Canaan by lot. In keeping with God's promise forty-five years earlier, Caleb was the first to be given his land (Num. 14:24; Josh. 14:6–15). He was allotted Hebron, near the cave of Machpelah, where the patriarchs had been buried.

33 And there we saw the giants,[5303] [a]the sons[1121] of Anak, *which come* of the giants: and we were in our own sight [b]as grasshoppers, and so we were [c]in their sight.

The People Rebel

14 🔑 And all the congregation[5712] lifted up their voice, and cried; and the [a]people[5971] wept that night.[3915]

2 [a]And all the children[1121] of Israel murmured against Moses and against Aaron: and the whole congregation said[559] unto them, Would God that we had died in the land[776] of Egypt! or [b]would God we had died in this wilderness!

3 And wherefore hath the LORD brought us unto this land, to fall by the sword,[2719] that our wives[802] and our children[2945] should be a prey? were it not better[2896] for us to return[7725] into Egypt?

4 And they said one[376] to another, [a]Let us make a captain, and [b]let us return into Egypt.

5 Then [a]Moses and Aaron fell[5307] on their faces before all the assembly[6951] of the congregation of the children of Israel.

🔑 6 [a]And Joshua the son[1121] of Nun, and Caleb the son of Jephunneh, *which were* of them that searched the land, rent their clothes:

7 And they spake[559] unto all the company[5712] of the children of Israel, saying, [a]The land, which we passed through[5674] to search it, *is* an exceeding good[2896] land.

8 If the LORD [a]delight[2654] in us, then he will bring us into this land, and give it us; [b]a land which floweth with milk and honey.

9 Only [a]rebel[4775] not ye against the LORD, [b]neither fear[3372] ye the people of the land; for [c]they *are* bread for us: their [I]defence is departed[5493] from them, [d]and the LORD *is* with us: fear them not.

10 [a]But all the congregation bade stone them with stones. And the [b]glory[3519] of the LORD appeared[7200] in the tabernacle[168] of the congregation[4150] before all the children of Israel.

11 And the LORD said unto Moses, How long will this people [a]provoke[5006] me? and how long will it be ere[3808] they [b]believe[539] me, for all the signs[226] which I have shewed[6213] among[7130] them?

12 I will smite[5221] them with the pestilence,[1698] and disinherit them, and [a]will make[6213] of thee a greater nation[1471] and mightier than they.

13 And [a]Moses said unto the LORD, Then the Egyptians shall hear[8085] *it*, (for thou broughtest up[5927] this people in thy might from among them;)

14 And they will tell[559] *it* to the inhabitants of this land: [a]*for* they have heard[8085] that thou LORD *art* among this people, that thou LORD art seen[7200] face to face, and *that* [b]thy cloud[6051] standeth over them, and *that* thou goest before them, by day time[3119] in a pillar of a cloud, and in a pillar of fire by night.

15 Now *if* thou shalt kill[4191] *all* this people as one man,[376] then the nations[3816] which have heard the fame[8088] of thee will speak,[559] saying,

16 Because the LORD was not [a]able to bring this people into the land which he sware[7650] unto them, therefore he hath slain[7819] them in the wilderness.

17 And now, I beseech thee,[4994] let the power of my Lord[136] be great, according as thou hast spoken, saying,

18 The LORD *is* [a]longsuffering, and of great mercy,[2617] forgiving[5375] iniquity[5771] and transgression,[6588] and by no means clearing *the guilty,* [b]visiting the iniquity of the fathers[1] upon the children[1121] unto the third and fourth *generation.*

33 [a]Deut. 1:28; 2:10; 9:2 [b]Isa. 40:22 [c]1Sam. 17:42
1 [a]Num. 11:4
2 [a]Ex. 16:2; 17:3; Num. 16:41; Ps. 106:25 [b]Num. 14:28, 29
4 [a]Neh. 9:17 [b]Deut. 17:16; Acts 7:39
5 [a]Num. 16:4, 22
6 [a]Num. 13:6, 8; 14:24, 30, 38
7 [a]Num. 13:27; Deut. 1:25
8 [a]Deut. 10:15; 2Sam. 15:25, 26; 22:20; 1Kgs. 10:9; Ps. 22:8; 147:10, 11; Isa. 62:4 [b]Num. 13:27
9 [I]Hebr. *shadow* Ps. 121:5; Isa. 30:2, 3; Jer. 48:45 [a]Deut. 9:7, 23, 24 [b]Deut. 7:18; 20:3 [c]Num. 24:8 [d]Gen. 48:21; Ex. 33:16; Deut. 20:1, 3, 4; 31:6, 8; Josh. 1:5; Judg. 1:22; 2Chr. 13:12; 15:2; 20:17; 32:8; Ps. 46:7, 11; Isa. 41:10; Amos 5:14; Zech. 8:23
10 [a]Ex. 17:4 [b]Ex. 16:10; 24:16, 17; 40:34; Lev. 9:23; Num. 16:19, 42; 20:6
11 [a]Num. 14:23; Deut. 9:7, 8, 22; Ps. 95:8; Heb. 3:8, 16 [b]Deut. 1:32; 9:23; Ps. 78:22, 32, 42; 106:24; John 12:37; Heb. 3:18
12 [a]Ex. 32:10
13 [a]Ex. 32:12; Deut. 9:26-28; 32:27; Ps. 106:23; Ezek. 20:9, 14
14 [a]Ex. 15:14; Josh. 2:9, 10; 5:1 [b]Ex. 13:21; 40:38; Num. 10:34; Neh. 9:12; Ps. 78:14; 105:39
16 [a]Deut. 9:28; Josh. 7:9
18 [a]Ex. 34:6, 7; Ps. 103:8; 145:8; Jon. 4:2 [b]Ex. 20:5; 34:7

🔑 **14:1–10** See note on Numbers 13:26.

🔑 **14:6–9** See note on Numbers 13:30–33.

19 [a]Pardon,[5545] I beseech thee, the iniquity of this people [b]according unto the greatness of thy mercy, and [c]as thou hast forgiven[5375] this people, from Egypt even [I]until now.

God Punishes Israel

20 And the LORD said, I have pardoned[5545] [a]according to thy word:[1697]

21 But *as* truly *as* I live,[2416] [a]all the earth[776] shall be filled with the glory of the LORD.

🔑 22 [a]Because all those men[582] which have seen my glory, and my miracles,[226] which I did[6213] in Egypt and in the wilderness, and have tempted[5254] me now [b]these ten times, and have not hearkened[8085] to my voice;

23 [I][a]Surely they shall not see the land which I sware unto their fathers, neither shall any of them that provoked[5006] me see it:

🔑 24 But my servant[5650] [a]Caleb, because he had another spirit[7307] with him, and [b]hath followed me fully, him will I bring into the land whereinto he went; and his seed[2233] shall possess[3423] it.

🔑 25 (Now the Amalekites and the Canaanites dwelt in the valley.) To morrow turn you, [a]and get you into the wilderness by the way[1870] of the Red sea.

26 And the LORD spake[1696] unto Moses and unto Aaron, saying,

27 [a]How long *shall I bear with* this evil[7451] congregation, which murmur against me? [b]I have heard the murmurings of the children of Israel, which they murmur against me.

28 Say[559] unto them, [a]*As truly as* I live, saith the LORD, [b]as ye have spoken in mine ears,[241] so will I do[6213] to you:

29 Your carcases[6297] shall fall in this wilderness; and [a]all that were numbered[6485] of you, according to your whole number, from twenty years old and upward, which have murmured against me,

🔑 30 Doubtless ye shall not come into the land, *concerning* which I [I][a]sware to make you dwell[7931] therein, [b]save Caleb the son of Jephunneh, and Joshua the son of Nun.

31 [a]But your little ones,[2945] which ye said should be a prey, them will I bring in, and they shall know[3045] the land which [b]ye have despised.[3988]

32 But *as for* you, [a]your carcases, they shall fall in this wilderness.

33 And your children shall [I][a]wander in the wilderness [b]forty years, and [c]bear your whoredoms,[2184] until your carcases be wasted[8552] in the wilderness.

34 [a]After the number of the days[3117] in which ye searched the land, *even* [b]forty days, each day for a year, shall ye bear your iniquities,[5771] *even* forty years, [c]and ye shall know my [I]breach of promise.

35 [a]I the LORD have said,[1696] I will surely do it unto all [b]this evil congregation, that are gathered together[3259] against me: in this wilderness they shall be consumed, and there they shall die.[4191]

36 [a]And the men, which Moses sent to search the land, who returned,[7725] and made all the congregation to murmur against him, by bringing up a slander upon the land,

19 [I]Or, *hitherto* [a]Ex. 34:9 [b]Ps. 106:45 [c]Ps. 78:38
20 [a]Ps. 106:23; James 5:16; 1John 5:14-16
21 [a]Ps. 72:19
22 [a]Deut. 1:35; Ps. 95:11; 106:26; Heb. 3:17, 18 [b]Gen. 31:7
23 [I]Hebr. *If they see the land* [a]Num. 32:11; Ezek. 20:15
24 [a]Deut. 1:36; Josh. 14:6, 8, 9, 14 [b]Num. 32:12
25 [a]Deut. 1:40
27 [a]Num. 14:11; Ex. 16:28; Matt. 17:17 [b]Ex. 16:12
28 [a]Num. 14:23; 26:65; 32:11; Deut. 1:35; Heb. 3:17 [b]Num. 14:2
29 [a]Num. 1:45; 26:64
30 [I]Hebr. *lifted up my hand* [a]Gen. 14:22 [b]Num. 14:38; 26:65; 32:12; Deut. 1:36, 38
31 [a]Deut. 1:39 [b]Ps. 106:24
32 [a]1Cor. 10:5; Heb. 3:17
33 [I]Or, *feed* [a]Num. 32:13; Ps. 107:40 [b]Deut. 2:14 [c]Ezek. 23:35
34 [I]Or, *altering of my purpose* [a]Num. 13:25 [b]Ps. 95:10; Ezek. 4:6 [c]1Kgs. 8:56; Ps. 77:8; 105:42; Heb. 4:1
35 [a]Num. 23:19 [b]Num. 14:27, 29; 26:65; 1Cor. 10:5
36 [a]Num. 13:31, 32

🔑 **14:22** There are two views concerning Israel having tempted God "ten times." Some scholars hold that there are actually ten instances recorded in Scripture which involve Israel and their exodus from Egypt. They were the two temptations at the Red Sea (Ex. 14:11; Ps. 106:7); demanding water twice (Ex. 15:23; 17:2); demanding food twice (Ex. 16:20, 27); demanding flesh twice (Ex.16:3; Num. 11:4); the incident with the golden calf (Ex. 32); and the incident with the twelve spies (Ex. 13). Others say that the number "ten" times that Israel tempted God is not to be taken literally. They say it is symbolic of completeness. In either case it refers to Israel's frequent acts of rebellion, of which the Lord had grown weary.

🔑 **14:24, 30** See note on Numbers 13:30–33 regarding Joshua and Caleb.

🔑 **14:25** This verse notes the beginning of the wilderness wanderings. Unbelief had cost a whole generation the blessings of the Promised Land that God desired to give them.

37 Even those men that did bring up the evil report upon the land, [a]died by the plague before the LORD.

38 [a]But Joshua the son of Nun, and Caleb the son of Jephunneh, *which were* of the men that went to search the land, lived[2421] *still.*

39 And Moses told these sayings[1697] unto all the children of Israel: [a]and the people mourned greatly.

40 And they rose up early in the morning, and gat them up into the top[7218] of the mountain, saying, Lo, [a]we *be here,* and will go up[5927] unto the place which the LORD hath promised:[559] for we have sinned.[2398]

41 And Moses said, Wherefore now do ye transgress[5674] [a]the commandment[6310] of the LORD? but it shall not prosper.

42 [a]Go not up, for the LORD *is* not among you; that ye be not smitten[5062] before your enemies.

43 For the Amalekites and the Canaanites *are* there before you, and ye shall fall by the sword: [a]because ye are turned away from the LORD, therefore the LORD will not be with you.

🔑 44 [a]But they presumed6075 to go up unto the hill top: nevertheless the ark[727] of the covenant[1285] of the LORD, and Moses, departed not out of the camp.[4264]

45 [a]Then the Amalekites came down, and the Canaanites which dwelt in that hill, and smote[5221] them, and discomfited[3807] them, *even* unto [b]Hormah.

Laws About Offerings

15 And the LORD spake[1696] unto Moses, saying,

2 [a]Speak unto the children[1121] of Israel, and say[559] unto them, When ye be come into the land of your habitations,[4186] which I give unto you,

3 And [a]will make[6213] an offering by fire unto the LORD, a burnt offering,[5930] or a sacrifice[2077] [b]in [1]performing[6381] a vow,[5088] or in a freewill offering,[5071] or [c]in your solemn feasts,[4150] to make a [d]sweet savour unto the LORD, of the herd, or of the flock:

4 Then [a]shall he that offereth his offering[7133] unto the LORD bring[7126] [b]a meat offering[4503] of a tenth deal6241 of flour mingled[1101] [c]with the fourth *part* of an hin of oil.[8081]

5 [a]And the fourth *part* of an hin of wine for a drink offering[5262] shalt thou prepare with the burnt offering or sacrifice, for one lamb.

6 [a]Or for a ram, thou shalt prepare *for* a meat offering two tenth deals of flour mingled with the third *part* of an hin of oil.

7 And for a drink offering thou shalt offer the third *part* of an hin of wine, *for* a sweet savour unto the LORD.

8 And when thou preparest a bullock *for* a burnt offering, or *for* a sacrifice in performing a vow, or [a]peace offerings[8002] unto the LORD:

9 Then shall he bring [a]with a bullock a meat offering of three tenth deals of flour mingled with half an hin of oil.

10 And thou shalt bring for a drink offering half an hin of wine, *for* an offering made by fire, of a sweet savour unto the LORD.

11 Thus shall it be done[6213] for one bullock, or for one ram, or for a lamb, or a kid.

12 According to the number that ye shall prepare, so shall ye do to every one according to their number.

13 All that are born of the country shall do these things after this manner, in offering an offering made by fire, of a sweet savour unto the LORD.

14 And if a stranger[1616] sojourn[1481] with you, or whosoever *be* among you in your generations,[1755] and will offer[6213] an offering made by fire, of a sweet savour unto the LORD; as ye do, so he shall do.

37 [a]1Cor. 10:10; Heb. 3:17; Jude 1:5
38 [a]Num. 26:65; Josh. 14:6, 10
39 [a]Ex. 33:4
40 [a]Deut. 1:41
41 [a]Num. 14:25; 2Chr. 24:20
42 [a]Deut. 1:42
43 [a]2Chr. 15:2
44 [a]Deut. 1:43
45 [a]Num. 14:43; Deut. 1:44 [b]Num. 21:3; Judg. 1:17
2 [a]Num. 15:18; Lev. 23:10; Deut. 7:1
3 [1]Hebr. *separating* [a]Lev. 1:2, 3 [b]Lev. 7:16; 22:18, 21 [c]Lev. 23:8, 12, 36; Num. 28:19, 27; 29:2, 8, 13; Deut. 16:10 [d]Gen. 8:21; Ex. 29:18
4 [a]Lev. 2:1; 6:14 [b]Ex. 20:40; Lev. 23:13 [c]Lev. 14:10; Num. 28:5
5 [a]Num. 28:7, 14
6 [a]Num. 28:12, 14
8 [a]Lev. 7:11
9 [a]Num. 28:12, 14

🔑 **14:44** The children of Israel were adding the sin of presumptuous self-confidence to their sin of unbelief (vv. 1–4).

15 [a]One ordinance[2708] *shall be both* for you of the congregation,[6951] and also for the stranger that sojourneth[1481] *with you,* an ordinance for ever[5769] in your generations: as ye *are,* so shall the stranger be before the LORD.

16 One law[8451] and one manner[4941] shall be for you, and for the stranger that sojourneth with you.

17 And the LORD spake unto Moses, saying,

18 [a]Speak unto the children of Israel, and say unto them, When ye come into the land whither I bring you,

19 Then it shall be, that, when ye eat of [a]the bread of the land, ye shall offer up an heave offering[8641] unto the LORD.

20 [a]Ye shall offer up a cake of the first[7225] of your dough *for* an heave offering: as *ye do* [b]the heave offering of the threshingfloor, so shall ye heave[7311] it.

21 Of the first of your dough ye shall give unto the LORD an heave offering in your generations.

22 And [a]if ye have erred,[7683] and not observed all these commandments, which the LORD hath spoken[1696] unto Moses,

23 *Even* all that the LORD hath commanded[6680] you by the hand[3027] of Moses, from the day[3117] that the LORD commanded *Moses,* and henceforward among your generations;

24 Then it shall be, [a]if *ought* be committed by ignorance[7684] [I]without the knowledge of the congregation,[5712] that all the congregation shall offer one young bullock for a burnt offering, for a sweet savour unto the LORD, [b]with his meat offering, and his drink offering,[5262] according to the [II]manner, and [c]one kid[8163] of the goats for a sin offering.

25 [a]And the priest[3548] shall make an atonement[3722] for all the congregation of the children of Israel, and it shall be forgiven[5545] them; for it *is* ignorance: and they shall bring their offering, a sacrifice made by fire[801] unto the LORD, and their sin offering before the LORD, for their ignorance:

26 And it shall be forgiven all the congregation of the children of Israel, and the stranger that sojourneth among them; seeing all the people[5971] *were* in ignorance.

27 And [a]if any soul[5315] sin[2398] through ignorance, then he shall bring a she goat of the first year for a sin offering.[2403]

28 [a]And the priest shall make an atonement for the soul that sinneth ignorantly,[7683] when he sinneth[2398] by ignorance before the LORD, to make an atonement for him; and it shall be forgiven him.

29 [a]Ye shall have one law for him that [I]sinneth[6213] through ignorance, *both for* him that is born among the children of Israel, and for the stranger that sojourneth among them.

30 [a]But the soul that doeth[6213] *ought* [I]presumptuously, *whether he be* born in the land, or a stranger, the same reproacheth the LORD; and that soul shall be cut off[3772] from among[7130] his people.

31 Because he hath [a]despised the word[1697] of the LORD, and hath broken[6565] his commandment,[4687] that soul shall utterly be cut off; [b]his iniquity[5771] *shall be* upon him.

A Sabbath Breaker Is Punished

32 And while the children of Israel were in the wilderness, [a]they found a man[376] that gathered sticks upon the sabbath[7676] day.

33 And they that found him gathering sticks brought[7126] him unto Moses and Aaron, and unto all the congregation.

34 And they put him [a]in ward, because it was not declared what should be done to him.

35 And the LORD said[559] unto Moses, [a]The man shall be surely put to death:[4191] all the congregation shall [b]stone him with stones without the camp.[4264]

36 And all the congregation brought him without the camp, and stoned him with stones, and he died; as the LORD commanded Moses.

15 [a]Ex. 12:49; Num. 9:14; 15:29
18 [a]Num. 15:2; Deut. 26:1
19 [a]Josh. 5:11, 12
20 [a]Deut. 26:2, 10; Prov. 3:9, 10 [b]Lev. 2:14; 23:10, 16
22 [a]Lev. 4:2
24 [I]Hebr. *from the eyes* [II]Or, *ordinance* [a]Lev. 4:13 [b]Num. 15:8-10 [c]Lev. 4:23; Num. 28:15; Ezra 6:17; 8:35
25 [a]Lev. 4:20
27 [a]Lev. 4:27, 28
28 [a]Lev. 4:35
29 [I]Hebr. *doth* [a]Num. 15:15
30 [I]Hebr. *with a high hand* [a]Deut. 17:12; Ps. 19:13; Heb. 10:26; 2Pet. 2:10
31 [a]2Sam. 12:9; Prov. 13:13 [b]Lev. 5:1; Ezek. 18:20
32 [a]Ex. 31:14, 15; 35:2, 3
34 [a]Lev. 24:12
35 [a]Ex. 31:14, 15 [b]Lev. 24:14; 1Kgs. 21:13; Acts 7:58

Fringes of Their Garments

37 And the LORD spake[559] unto Moses, saying,

38 Speak unto the children of Israel, and bid[559] [a]them that they make[6213] them fringes in the borders of their garments throughout their generations, and that they put upon the fringe of the borders a ribband of blue:

39 And it shall be unto you for a fringe, that ye may look upon it, and remember[2142] all the commandments of the LORD, and do them; and that ye [a]seek not after your own heart[3824] and your own eyes, after which ye use [b]to go a whoring:[2181]

40 That ye may remember, and do all my commandments, and be [a]holy[6918] unto your God.

41 I *am* the LORD your God,[430] which brought you out of the land[776] of Egypt, to be your God: I *am* the LORD your God.

Korah's Rebellion

16 Now [a]Korah, the son[1121] of Izhar, the son of Kohath, the son of Levi, and Dathan and Abiram, the sons of Eliab, and On, the son of Peleth, sons of Reuben, took *men:*

2 And they rose up before Moses, with certain[582] of the children[1121] of Israel, two hundred and fifty princes[5387] of the assembly,[712] [a]famous in the congregation,[4150] men[582] of renown:

3 And [a]they gathered themselves together[6950] against Moses and against Aaron, and said[559] unto them, [I]*Ye take* too much upon you, seeing [b]all the congregation[5712] *are* holy,[6918] every one of them, [c]and the LORD *is* among them: wherefore then lift ye up yourselves above the congregation[6951] of the LORD?

4 And when Moses heard[8085] *it,* [a]he fell[5307] upon his face:

38 [a]Deut. 22:12; Matt. 23:5

39 [a]Deut. 29:19; Job 31:7; Jer. 9:14; Ezek. 6:9 [b]Ps. 73:27; 106:39; James 4:4

40 [a]Lev. 11:44, 45; Rom. 12:1; Col. 1:22; 1Pet. 1:15, 16

1 [a]Ex. 6:21; Num. 26:9; 27:3; Jude 1:11

2 [a]Num. 26:9

3 [I]Hebr. It is *much for you* [a]Ps. 106:16 [b]Ex. 19:6 [c]Ex. 29:45; Num. 14:14; 35:34

4 [a]Num. 14:5; 20:6

5 [a]Num. 16:3; Lev. 21:6-8, 12, 15 [b]Ex. 28:1; Num. 17:5; 1Sam. 2:28; Ps. 105:26 [c]Num. 3:10; Lev. 10:3; 21:17, 18; Ezek. 40:46; 44:15, 16

9 [a]1Sam. 18:23; Isa. 7:13 [b]Num. 3:41, 45; 8:14; Deut. 10:8

11 [a]Ex. 16:8; 1Cor. 3:5

13 [a]Num. 16:9 [b]Ex. 2:14; Acts 7:27, 35

14 [I]Hebr. *bore out* [a]Ex. 3:8; Lev. 20:24

5 And he spake[1696] unto Korah and unto all his company,[5712] saying, Even to morrow the LORD will shew[3045] who *are* his, and *who is* [a]holy; and will cause *him* to come near[7126] unto him: even *him* whom he hath [b]chosen[977] will he cause to [c]come near unto him.

6 This do;[6213] Take you censers, Korah, and all his company;

7 And put fire therein, and put incense[7004] in them before the LORD to morrow: and it shall be *that* the man[376] whom the LORD doth choose,[977] he *shall be* holy: *ye take* too much upon you, ye sons of Levi.

8 And Moses said unto Korah, Hear,[8085] I pray you,[4994] ye sons of Levi:

9 *Seemeth it but* [a]a small thing unto you, that the God[430] of Israel hath [b]separated[914] you from the congregation of Israel, to bring you near[7126] to himself to do[5647] the service[5656] of the tabernacle[4908] of the LORD, and to stand before the congregation to minister[8334] unto them?

10 And he hath brought thee near *to him,* and all thy brethren[251] the sons of Levi with thee: and seek ye the priesthood[3550] also?

11 For which cause *both* thou and all thy company *are* gathered together[3259] against the LORD: [a]and what *is* Aaron, that ye murmur against him?

12 And Moses sent to call[7121] Dathan and Abiram, the sons of Eliab: which said, We will not come up:[5927]

13 [a]*Is it* a small thing that thou hast brought us up[5927] out of a land[776] that floweth with milk and honey, to kill us in the wilderness, except thou [b]make thyself altogether a prince[8323] over us?

14 Moreover thou hast not brought us into [a]a land that floweth with milk and honey, or given us inheritance[5159] of fields[7704] and vineyards: wilt thou [I]put

15:37–40 These blue fringes placed upon the borders of their garments were to be a daily reminder to Israel of the Lord's commandments and of the fact that they were a holy or separated people. Jesus accused some Jewish leaders of making their fringes extremely long in order to make a show of their religion, without being committed to the Lord's commandments (Matt. 23:5).

out the eyes of these men? we will not come up.

15 And Moses was very wroth,[2734] and said unto the LORD, [a]Respect not thou their offering:[4503] [b]I have not taken[5375] one ass from them, neither have I hurt[7489] one of them.

16 And Moses said unto Korah, [a]Be thou and all thy company [b]before the LORD, thou, and they, and Aaron, to morrow:

17 And take every man his censer, and put incense in them, and bring ye before the LORD every man his censer, two hundred and fifty censers; thou also, and Aaron, each[376] *of you* his censer.

18 And they took every man his censer, and put fire in them, and laid[7760] incense thereon, and stood in the door of the tabernacle[168] of the congregation with Moses and Aaron.

19 And Korah gathered all the congregation against them unto the door of the tabernacle of the congregation: and [a]the glory[3519] of the LORD appeared[7200] unto all the congregation.

20 And the LORD spake unto Moses and unto Aaron, saying,

21 [a]Separate yourselves[914] from among this congregation, that I may [b]consume[3615] them in a moment.

22 And they [a]fell upon their faces, and said, O God,[410] [b]the God of the spirits[7307] of all flesh,[1320] shall one man sin,[2398] and wilt thou be wroth[7107] with all the congregation?

23 And the LORD spake unto Moses, saying,

24 Speak[1696] unto the congregation, saying, Get you up from about the tabernacle of Korah, Dathan, and Abiram.

25 And Moses rose up and went unto Dathan and Abiram; and the elders[2205] of Israel followed him.

26 And he spake unto the congregation, saying, [a]Depart,[5493] I pray you, from the tents[168] of these wicked[7563] men, and touch[5060] nothing of theirs, lest ye be consumed[5595] in all their sins.

27 So they gat up from the tabernacle of Korah, Dathan, and Abiram, on every side: and Dathan and Abiram came out, and stood[5324] in the door of their tents, and their wives,[802] and their sons, and their little children.[2945]

28 And Moses said, [a]Hereby ye shall know[3045] that the LORD hath sent me to do all these works; for *I have* not *done them* [b]of mine own mind.[3820]

29 If these men[120] die[4191] [I]the common death[4194] of all men, or if they be [a]visited[6485] after the visitation[6486] of all men; *then* the LORD hath not sent me.

30 But if the LORD [I]make [a]a new thing, and the earth[127] open her mouth,[6310] and swallow them up,[1104] with all that *appertain* unto them, and they [b]go down quick[2416] into the pit;[7585] then ye shall understand that these men have provoked[5006] the LORD.

31 [a]And it came to pass, as he had made an end[3615] of speaking[1696] all these words,[1697] that the ground[127] clave asunder that *was* under them.

🗝 32 And the earth[776] opened her mouth, and swallowed them up, and their houses,[1004] and [a]all the men that *appertained* unto Korah, and all *their* goods.

33 They, and all that *appertained* to them, went down alive[2416] into the pit, and the earth closed upon them: and they perished[6] from among the congregation.

34 And all Israel that *were* round about them fled at the cry of them: for they said, Lest the earth swallow us up *also*.

35 And there [a]came out a fire from the LORD, and consumed [b]the two hundred and fifty men[376] that offered[7126] incense.

15 [a]Gen. 4:4, 5 [b]1Sam. 12:3; Acts 20:33; 2Cor. 7:2

16 [a]Num. 16:6, 7 [b]1Sam. 12:3, 7

19 [a]Ex. 16:7, 10; Lev. 9:6, 23; Num. 14:10; 16:42

21 [a]Gen. 19:17, 22; Jer. 51:6; Acts 2:40; Rev. 18:4 [b]Ex. 32:10; 33:5

22 [a]Num. 14:5; 16:45 [b]Num. 27:16; Job 12:10; Eccl. 12:7; Isa. 57:16; Zech. 12:1; Heb. 12:9

26 [a]Gen. 19:12, 14; Isa. 52:11; 2Cor. 6:17; Rev. 18:4

28 [a]Ex. 3:12; Deut. 18:22; Zech. 2:9, 11; 4:9; John 5:36 [b]Num. 24:13; Jer. 23:16; Ezek. 13:17; John 5:30; 6:38

29 [I]Hebr. *as every man dieth* [a]Ex. 20:5; 32:34; Job 35:15; Isa. 10:3; Jer. 5:9

30 [I]Hebr. *create a creature* [a]Job 31:3; Isa. 28:21 [b]Num. 16:33; Ps. 55:15

31 [a]Num. 26:10; 27:3; Deut. 11:6; Ps. 106:17

32 [a]Num. 16:17; 26:11; 1Chr. 6:22, 37

35 [a]Lev. 10:2; Num. 11:1; Ps. 106:18 [b]Num. 16:17

🗝 **16:32** The phrase "and all that appertained unto them" does not refer to their possessions nor to the children of Korah, but to all those (whether of Korah's house or not) who had taken part in the crime. Korah's children did not perish as a result of his sin (Numbers 26:11). Some of his descendants are mentioned in Numbers 26:58; 1 Chronicles 9:19; and in the titles of Psalms 84, 85, 87, 88.

36 And the LORD spake unto Moses, saying,

37 Speak[559] unto Eleazar the son of Aaron the priest,[3548] that he take up the censers out of the burning,[8316] and scatter thou the fire yonder; for [a]they are hallowed.[6942]

38 The censers of these [a]sinners[2400] against their own souls,[5315] let them make them broad[7555] plates[6341] *for* a covering of the altar:[4196] for they offered them before the LORD, therefore they are hallowed: [b]and they shall be a sign[226] unto the children of Israel.

39 And Eleazar the priest took the brasen censers, wherewith they that were burnt[8313] had offered; and they were made broad *plates for* a covering of the altar:

40 *To be* a memorial unto the children of Israel, [a]that no stranger,[2114] which *is* not of the seed[2233] of Aaron, come near to offer incense before the LORD; that he be not as Korah, and as his company: as the LORD said[1696] to him by the hand[3027] of Moses.

Others Complain and Die

41 But on the morrow [a]all the congregation of the children of Israel murmured against Moses and against Aaron, saying, Ye have killed the people[5971] of the LORD.

42 And it came to pass, when the congregation was gathered against Moses and against Aaron, that they looked toward the tabernacle of the con gregation: and, behold, [a]the cloud[6051] covered[1642] it, and [b]the glory of the LORD appeared.

43 And Moses and Aaron came before the tabernacle of the congregation.

44 And the LORD spake unto Moses, saying,

45 [a]Get you up from among this congregation, that I may consume them as in a moment. And [b]they fell upon their faces.

46 And Moses said unto Aaron, Take a censer, and put fire therein from off the altar, and put on incense, and go quickly unto the congregation, and make an atonement[3722] for them: [a]for there is wrath[7110] gone out from the LORD; the plague[5063] is begun.

47 And Aaron took as Moses commanded,[1696] and ran into the midst of the congregation; and, behold, the plague was begun among the people: and he put on incense, and made an atonement for the people.

48 And he stood between the dead[4191] and the living;[2416] and the plague was stayed.[6113]

49 Now they that died in the plague were fourteen thousand and seven hundred, beside them that died about the matter[1697] of Korah.

50 And Aaron returned[7725] unto Moses unto the door of the tabernacle of the congregation: and the plague was stayed.

Aaron's Rod Buds

17 And the LORD spake[1696] unto Moses, saying,

2 Speak unto the children[1121] of Israel, and take of every one of them a rod[4294] according to the house[1004] of *their* fathers,[1] of all their princes[5387] according to the house of their fathers twelve rods:[4294] write thou every man's name upon his rod.

3 And thou shalt write Aaron's name upon the rod of Levi: for one rod *shall be* for the head[7218] of the house of their fathers.

4 And thou shalt lay them up in the tabernacle[168] of the congregation[4150] before the testimony,[5715] [a]where I will meet[3259] with you.

5 And it shall come to pass, *that* the man's rod, [a]whom I shall choose,[977] shall blossom: and I will make to cease from me the murmurings of the children of Israel, [b]whereby they murmur against you.

6 And Moses spake unto the children of Israel, and every one of their princes gave him [1]a rod apiece, for each[376] prince[5387] one, according to their fathers'[1] houses,[1004] *even* twelve rods: and the rod of Aaron *was* among their rods.

37 [a]Lev. 27:28
38 [a]Prov. 20:2; Hab. 2:10 [b]Num. 17:10; 26:10; Ezek. 14:8
40 [a]Num. 3:10; 2Chr. 26:18
41 [a]Num. 14:2; Ps. 106:25
42 [a]Ex. 40:34 [b]Num. 16:19; 20:6
45 [a]Num. 16:21, 24 [b]Num. 16:22; 20:6
46 [a]Lev. 10:6; Num. 1:53; 8:19; 11:33; 18:5; 1Chr. 27:24; Ps. 106:29
4 [a]Ex. 25:22; 29:42, 43; 30:36
5 [a]Num. 16:5 [b]Num. 16:11
6 [1]Hebr. *a rod for one prince, a rod for one prince*

7 And Moses laid up the rods before the LORD in [a]the tabernacle of witness.[5715]

🗝 8 And it came to pass, that on the morrow Moses went into the tabernacle of witness; and, behold, the rod of Aaron for the house of Levi was budded, and brought forth buds, and bloomed blossoms, and yielded[1580] almonds.

9 And Moses brought out all the rods from before the LORD unto all the children of Israel: and they looked,[7200] and took every man[376] his rod.

10 And the LORD said unto Moses, Bring [a]Aaron's rod again before the testimony, to be kept[4931] [b]for a token[226] against the [I]rebels;[4805] [c]and thou shalt quite take away their murmurings from me, that they die[4191] not.

11 And Moses did[6213] *so:* as the LORD commanded[6680] him, so did he.

12 And the children of Israel spake[559] unto Moses, saying, Behold, we die,[1478] we perish, we all perish.

13 [a]Whosoever cometh any thing near unto the tabernacle[4908] of the LORD shall die: shall we be consumed with dying?[1478]

The Priests' and Levites' Duties

18 And the LORD said[559] unto Aaron, [a]Thou and thy sons[1121] and thy father's[1] house[1004] with thee shall [b]bear[5375] the iniquity[5771] of the sanctuary:[4720] and thou and thy sons with thee shall bear the iniquity of your priesthood.[3550]

2 And thy brethren[251] also of the tribe[4294] of Levi, the tribe[7626] of thy father, bring[7126] thou with thee, that they may be [a]joined unto thee, and [b]minister[8334] unto thee: but [c]thou and thy sons with thee *shall minister* before the tabernacle[168] of witness.[5715]

3 And they shall keep[8104] thy charge,[4931] and [a]the charge of all the tabernacle: [b]only they shall not come nigh the vessels of the sanctuary[6944] and the altar,[4196] [c]that neither they, nor ye also, die.[4191]

4 And they shall be joined unto thee, and keep the charge of the tabernacle of the congregation,[4250] for all the service[5656] of the tabernacle: [a]and a stranger[2114] shall not come nigh unto you.

🗝 5 And ye shall keep [a]the charge of the sanctuary, and the charge of the altar: [b]that there be no wrath[7110] any more upon the children[1121] of Israel.

6 And I, behold, I have [a]taken your brethren the Levites from among the children of Israel: [b]to you *they are* given *as* a gift for the LORD, to do[5647] the service of the tabernacle of the congregation.

7 Therefore [a]thou and thy sons with thee shall keep your priest's office[3550] for every thing[1697] of the altar, and [b]within[1004] the vail; and ye shall serve:[5647] I have given your priest's office *unto you as* a service of gift: and the stranger that cometh nigh shall be put to death.[4191]

The Priests' and Levites' Shares

8 And the LORD spake[1696] unto Aaron, Behold, [a]I also have given thee the charge of mine heave offerings[8641] of all the hallowed things[6944] of the children of Israel; unto thee have I given

7 [a]Ex. 38:21; Num. 18:2; Acts 7:44
10 [I]Hebr. *children of rebellion* [a]Heb. 9:4 [b]Num. 16:38 [c]Num. 17:5
13 [a]Num. 1:51, 53; 18:4, 7
1 [a]Num. 17:13 [b]Ex. 28:38
2 [a]Gen. 29:34 [b]Num. 3:6, 7 [c]Num. 3:10
3 [a]Num. 3:25, 31, 36 [b]Num. 16:40 [c]Num. 4:15
4 [a]Num. 3:10
5 [a]Ex. 27:21; 30:7; Lev. 24:3; Num. 8:2 [b]Num. 16:46
6 [a]Num. 3:12, 45 [b]Num. 3:9; 8:19
7 [a]Num. 3:10; 18:5 [b]Heb. 9:3, 6
8 [a]Lev. 6:16, 18, 26; 7:6, 32; Num. 5:9

🗝 **17:8** God used Aaron's rod as an answer to Israel who complained against Moses and Aaron after many unfaithful people had been killed during the rebellion of Korah. Each of the rods were alike in that they had long been severed from the parent tree, but God chose the rod of Aaron and caused it to bloom blossoms and yield almonds as a sign of His approval. Aaron's rod was to be placed in front of the ark (later within the ark, Heb. 9:4) of the covenant as a sign to those who would rebel and complain against God and His spokesman. Apparently, both the pot of manna (Ex. 16:33, 34) and Aaron's rod were lost when the ark was held by the Philistines (1 Kgs. 8:9).

🗝 **18:5** God's wrath had consumed men as a result of an unlawful offering twice before (Lev. 10:2 and Num. 16:35).

them [b]by reason of the anointing,[4888] and to thy sons, by an ordinance[2706] for ever.[5769]

9 This shall be thine of the most holy things,[6944] *reserved* from the fire: every oblation[7133] of theirs, every [a]meat offering of theirs, and every [b]sin offering[2403] of theirs, and every [c]trespass offering[817] of theirs which they shall render[7725] unto me, *shall be* most holy[6944] for thee and for thy sons.

10 [a]In the most holy *place* shalt thou eat it; every male shall eat it: it shall be holy unto thee.

11 And this *is* thine; [a]the heave offering[8641] of their gift, with all the wave offerings[8573] of the children of Israel: I have given them unto [b]thee, and to thy sons and to thy daughters with thee, by a statute[2706] for ever: [c]every one that is clean[2889] in thy house shall eat of it.

12 [a]And the [I][b]best of the oil,[8081] and all the best of the wine, and of the wheat, [c]the firstfruits[7225] of them which they shall offer unto the LORD, them have I given thee.

13 *And* whatsoever is first ripe in the land,[776] [a]which they shall bring unto the LORD, shall be thine; [b]every one that is clean in thine house shall eat *of* it.

14 [a]Every thing devoted[2764] in Israel shall be thine.

15 Every thing that openeth [a]the matrix[7358] in all flesh,[1320] which they bring unto the LORD, *whether it be* of men[120] or beasts, shall be thine: nevertheless [b]the firstborn of man shalt thou surely redeem, and the firstling of unclean[2931] beasts shalt thou redeem.[6299]

16 And those that are to be redeemed[6299] from a month old shalt thou redeem, [a]according to thine estimation, for the money of five shekels, after the shekel of the sanctuary, [b]which *is* twenty gerahs.[1626]

17 [a]But the firstling of a cow, or the firstling of a sheep, or the firstling of a goat, thou shalt not redeem; they *are* holy: [b]thou shalt sprinkle[2236] their blood[1818] upon the altar, and shalt burn[6999] their fat *for* an offering made by fire, for a sweet savour unto the LORD.

18 And the flesh of them shall be thine, as the [a]wave breast and as the right shoulder are thine.

19 [a]All the heave offerings of the holy things, which the children of Israel offer unto the LORD, have I given thee, and thy sons and thy daughters with thee, by a statute for ever: [b]it *is* a covenant[1285] of salt for ever before the LORD unto thee and to thy seed[2233] with thee.

20 And the LORD spake[559] unto Aaron, Thou shalt have no inheritance[5157] in their land, neither shalt thou have any part among them: [a]I *am* thy part and thine inheritance[5159] among the children of Israel.

21 And, behold, [a]I have given the children of Levi all the tenth[4643] in Israel for an inheritance, for their service which they serve, *even* [b]the service of the tabernacle of the congregation.

22 [a]Neither must the children of Israel henceforth come nigh the tabernacle of the congregation, [b]lest they bear sin,[2399] [I]and die.

23 [a]But the Levites shall do the service of the tabernacle of the congregation, and they shall bear their iniquity: *it shall be* a statute[2708] for ever throughout your generations,[1755] that among the children of Israel they have no inheritance.

24 [a]But the tithes[4643] of the children of Israel, which they offer *as* an heave offering[8641] unto the LORD, I have given to the Levites to inherit:[5159] therefore I have said unto them, [b]Among the children of Israel they shall have no inheritance.

25 And the LORD spake unto Moses, saying,

26 Thus speak[1696] unto the Levites, and say[559] unto them, When ye take of the children of Israel the tithes which I have given you from them for your inheritance, then ye shall offer up an heave offering of it for the LORD, *even* [a]a tenth *part* of the tithe.[4643]

8 [b]Ex. 29:29; 40:13, 15
9 [a]Lev. 2:2, 3; 10:12, 13 [b]Lev. 4:22, 27; 6:25, 26 [c]Lev. 5:1; 7:7; 10:12; 14:13
10 [a]Lev. 6:16, 18, 26, 29; 7:6
11 [a]Ex. 29:27, 28; Lev. 7:30, 34 [b]Lev. 10:14; Deut. 18:3 [c]Lev. 22:2, 3, 11-13
12 [I]Hebr. *fat* [a]Num. 18:29 [b]Ex. 23:19; Deut. 18:4; Neh. 10:35, 36 [c]Ex. 22:29
13 [a]Ex. 22:29; 23:19; 34:26; Lev. 2:14; Num. 15:19; Deut. 26:2 [b]Num. 18:11
14 [a]Lev. 27:28
15 [a]Ex. 13:2; 22:29; Lev. 27:26; Num. 3:13 [b]Ex. 13:13; 34:20
16 [a]Lev. 27:2, 6; Num. 3:47 [b]Ex. 30:13; Lev. 27:25; Num. 3:47; Ezek. 45:12
17 [a]Deut. 15:19 [b]Lev. 3:2, 5
18 [a]Ex. 29:26, 28; Lev. 7:31, 32, 34
19 [a]Num. 18:11 [b]Lev. 2:13; 2Chr. 13:5
20 [a]Deut. 10:9; 12:12; 14:27, 29; 18:1, 2; Josh. 13:14, 33; 14:3; 18:7; Ps. 16:5; Ezek. 44:28
21 [a]Num. 18:24, 26; Lev. 27:30, 32; Neh. 10:37; 12:44; Heb. 7:5, 8, 9 [b]Num. 3:7, 8
22 [I]Hebr. *to die* [a]Num. 1:51 [b]Lev. 22:9
23 [a]Num. 3:7
24 [a]Num. 18:21 [b]Num. 18:20; Deut. 10:9; 14:27, 29; 18:1
26 [a]Neh. 10:38

27 [a]And *this* your heave offering shall be reckoned[2803] unto you, as though *it were* the corn of the threshingfloor, and as the fulness of the winepress.

28 Thus ye also shall offer an heave offering unto the LORD of all your tithes, which ye receive of the children of Israel; and ye shall give thereof the LORD's heave offering to Aaron the priest.[3548]

29 Out of all your gifts ye shall offer every heave offering of the LORD, of all the [I][a]best thereof, *even* the hallowed part[4720] thereof out of it.

30 Therefore thou shalt say unto them, When ye have heaved[7311] the best thereof from it, [a]then it shall be counted[2803] unto the Levites as the increase of the threshingfloor, and as the increase of the winepress.

31 And ye shall eat it in every place, ye and your households:[1004] for it *is* [a]your reward for your service in the tabernacle of the congregation.

32 And ye shall [a]bear no sin by reason of it, when ye have heaved from it the best of it: neither shall ye [b]pollute[2490] the holy things of the children of Israel, lest ye die.

Purifying an Unclean Person

19 And the LORD spake[1696] unto Moses and unto Aaron, saying,

2 This *is* the ordinance[2708] of the law[8451] which the LORD hath commanded,[6680] saying, Speak unto the children[1121] of Israel, that they bring thee a red[122] heifer without spot,[8549] wherein *is* no blemish,[3971] [a]*and* upon which never came yoke:

3 And ye shall give her unto Eleazar the priest,[3548] that he may bring her [a]forth without the camp,[4264] and *one* shall slay[7819] her before his face:

4 And Eleazar the priest shall take of her blood[1818] with his finger, and [a]sprinkle[5137] of her blood directly before the tabernacle[168] of the congregation[4150] seven times:

5 And *one* shall burn[8316] the heifer in his sight; [a]her skin,[5785] and her flesh,[1320] and her blood, with her dung, shall he burn:

6 And the priest shall take [a]cedar wood, and hyssop,[231] and scarlet, and cast *it* into the midst of the burning[8316] of the heifer.

7 [a]Then the priest shall wash[3526] his clothes, and he shall bathe[7364] his flesh in water, and afterward he shall come into the camp, and the priest shall be unclean[2930] until the even.

8 And he that burneth[8313] her shall wash his clothes in water, and bathe his flesh in water, and shall be unclean until the even.

9 And a man[376] *that is* clean[2889] shall gather up[622] [a]the ashes of the heifer, and lay *them* up without the camp in a clean place, and it shall be kept for the congregation[5712] of the children of Israel [b]for a water of separation: it *is* a purification for sin.[2403]

10 And he that gathereth[622] the ashes of the heifer shall wash his clothes, and be unclean until the even: and it shall be unto the children of Israel, and unto the stranger[1616] that sojourneth[1481] among them, for a statute[2708] for ever.[5769]

11 [a]He that toucheth[5060] the dead[4191] body[5315] of any [I]man[120] shall be unclean seven days.[3117]

12 [a]He shall purify[2398] himself with it on the third day,[3117] and on the seventh day he shall be clean:[2891] but if he purify not himself the third day, then the seventh day he shall not be clean.

13 Whosoever toucheth the dead body of any man that is dead, and purifieth not himself, [a]defileth[2930] the tabernacle[4908] of the LORD; and that soul[5315] shall be cut off[3772] from Israel: because [b]the water of separation was not sprinkled[2236] upon him, he shall be unclean;[2931] [c]his uncleanness[2932] *is* yet upon him.

14 This *is* the law, when a man dieth[4191] in a tent:[168] all that come into the tent, and all that *is* in the tent, shall be unclean seven days.

15 And every [a]open vessel, which hath no covering bound upon it, *is* unclean.

16 And [a]whosoever toucheth one that is slain[2491] with a sword[2719] in the open

---

27 [a]Num. 18:30
29 [I]Hebr. *fat* [a]Num. 18:12
30 [a]Num. 18:27
31 [a]Matt. 10:10; Luke 10:7; 1Cor. 9:13; 1Tim. 5:18
32 [a]Lev. 19:8; 22:16 [b]Lev. 22:2, 15
2 [a]Deut. 21:3; 1Sam. 6:7
3 [a]Lev. 4:12, 21; 16:27; Heb. 13:11
4 [a]Lev. 4:6; 16:14, 19; Heb. 9:13
5 [a]Ex. 29:14; Lev. 4:11, 12
6 [a]Lev. 14:4, 6, 49
7 [a]Lev. 11:25; 15:5
9 [a]Heb. 9:13 [b]Num. 19:13, 20, 21; 31:23
11 [I]Hebr. *soul of man* [a]Num. 19:16; Lev. 21:1; Num. 5:2; 9:6, 10; 31:19; Lam. 4:14; Hag. 2:13
12 [a]Num. 31:19
13 [a]Lev. 15:31 [b]Num. 8:7; 19:9 [c]Lev. 7:20; 22:3
15 [a]Lev. 11:32; Num. 31:20
16 [a]Num. 19:11

fields,[7704] or a dead body, or a bone[6106] of a man, or a grave,[6913] shall be unclean seven days.

17 And for an unclean *person* they shall take of the [I][a]ashes[6083] of the burnt[8316] heifer of purification for sin, and [II][b]running[2416] water shall be put thereto in a vessel:

18 And a clean[2889] person shall take [a]hyssop, and dip[2881] *it* in the water, and sprinkle *it* upon the tent, and upon all the vessels, and upon the persons[5315] that were there, and upon him that touched[5060] a bone, or one slain, or one dead, or a grave:

19 And the clean *person* shall sprinkle upon the unclean on the third day, and on the seventh day: [a]and on the seventh day he shall purify himself, and wash his clothes, and bathe himself in water, and shall be clean at even.

20 But the man that shall be unclean, and shall not purify himself, that soul shall be cut off from among the congregation,[6951] because he hath [a]defiled[2930] the sanctuary[4720] of the LORD: the water of separation hath not been sprinkled upon him; he *is* unclean.

21 And it shall be a perpetual[5769] statute unto them, that he that sprinkleth[5137] the water of separation shall wash his clothes; and he that toucheth the water of separation shall be unclean until even.

22 And [a]whatsoever the unclean *person* toucheth shall be unclean; and [b]the soul that toucheth *it* shall be unclean until even.

Moses and Aaron Sin

20 Then [a]came the children[1121] of Israel, *even* the whole congregation,[5712] into the desert of Zin in the first[7223] month: and the people[5971] abode in Kadesh; and [b]Miriam died there, and was buried[6912] there.

2 [a]And there was no water for the congregation: [b]and they gathered themselves together[6950] against Moses and against Aaron.

3 And the people [a]chode[7378] with Moses, and spake[559] saying, Would God that we had died[1478] [b]when our brethren[251] died before the LORD!

4 And [a]why have ye brought up the congregation[6951] of the LORD into this wilderness, that we and our cattle should die[4191] there?

5 And wherefore have ye made us to come up[5927] out of Egypt, to bring us in unto this evil[7451] place? it *is* no place of seed,[2233] or of figs, or of vines, or of pomegranates; neither *is* there any water to drink.

6 And Moses and Aaron went from the presence of the assembly[6951] unto the door of the tabernacle[168] of the congregation,[4150] and [a]they fell[5307] upon their faces: and [b]the glory[3519] of the LORD appeared[7200] unto them.

7 And the LORD spake[1696] unto Moses, saying,

8 [a]Take the rod,[4294] and gather thou the assembly[5712] together, thou, and Aaron thy brother,[251] and speak[1696] ye unto the rock before their eyes; and it shall give forth his water, and [b]thou shalt bring forth to them water out of the rock: so thou shalt give the congregation and their beasts drink.

9 And Moses took the rod [a]from before the LORD, as he commanded[6680] him.

10 And Moses and Aaron gathered the congregation together before the rock, and he said[559] unto them, [a]Hear[8085] now, ye rebels;[4784] must we fetch you water out of this rock?

11 And Moses lifted up his hand,[3027] and with his rod he smote[5221] the rock twice: and [a]the water came out abundantly, and the congregation drank, and their beasts *also*.

12 And the LORD spake unto Moses

17 [I]Hebr. *dust* [II]Hebr. *living waters shall be given* [a]Gen. 26:19 [b]Num. 19:9
18 [a]Ps. 51:7
19 [a]Lev. 14:9
20 [a]Num. 19:13
22 [a]Hag. 2:13 [b]Lev. 15:5
1 [a]Num. 33:36 [b]Ex. 15:20; Num. 26:59
2 [a]Ex. 17:1 [b]Num. 16:19, 42
3 [a]Ex. 17:2; Num. 14:2 [b]Num. 11:1, 33; 14:37; 16:32, 35, 49
4 [a]Ex. 17:3
6 [a]Num. 14:5; 16:4, 22, 45 [b]Num. 14:10
8 [a]Ex. 17:5 [b]Neh. 9:15; Ps. 78:15, 16; 105:41; 114:8; Isa. 43:20; 48:21
9 [a]Num. 17:10
10 [a]Ps. 106:33
11 [a]Ex. 17:6; Deut. 8:15; 1Cor. 10:4

20:12 This sin of unbelief caused Moses to be excluded from entering Canaan. His sin is seen in his attitude and in his action of striking the rock, because Moses did not credit God's ability to

(continued on next page)

and Aaron, Because [a]ye believed[539] me not, to [b]sanctify[6942] me in the eyes of the children of Israel, therefore ye shall not bring this congregation into the land which I have given them.

13 [a]This *is* the water of [I]Meribah; because the children of Israel strove[7378] with the LORD, and he was sanctified[6942] in them.

Edom Refuses Passage to Israel

14 [a]And Moses sent messengers[4397] from Kadesh unto the king[4428] of Edom, [b]Thus saith thy brother Israel, Thou knowest[3045] all the travail that hath [Ic]befallen us:

15 [a]How our fathers[1] went down into Egypt, [b]and we have dwelt in Egypt a long time; [c]and the Egyptians vexed[7489] us, and our fathers:

16 And [a]when we cried unto the LORD, he heard[8085] our voice, and [b]sent an angel,[4397] and hath brought us forth out of Egypt: and, behold, we *are* in Kadesh, a city in the uttermost of thy border:

🔑 17 [a]Let us pass, I pray thee,[4994] through thy country:[776] we will not pass[5674] through the fields,[7704] or through the vineyards, neither will we drink *of* the water of the wells: we will go by the king's[4428] *high* way,[1870] we will not turn to the right hand nor to the left, until we have passed thy borders.

18 And Edom said unto him, Thou shalt not pass by me, lest I come out against thee with the sword.[2719]

19 And the children of Israel said unto him, We will go by the high way: and if I and my cattle drink of thy water, [a]then I will pay for it: I will only, without *doing* anything *else,* go through on my feet.

20 And he said, [a]Thou shalt not go through. And Edom came out against him with much people, and with a strong[2389] hand.

21 Thus Edom [a]refused[3985] to give Israel passage[5674] through his border: wherefore Israel [b]turned away from him.

Aaron's Death

22 And the children of Israel, *even* the whole congregation, journeyed from [a]Kadesh, [b]and came unto mount Hor.

23 And the LORD spake unto Moses and Aaron in mount Hor, by the coast[1366] of the land of Edom, saying,

24 Aaron shall be [a]gathered[622] unto his people: for he shall not enter into the land which I have given unto the children of Israel, because [b]ye rebelled[4784] against my [I]word at the water of Meribah.

25 [a]Take Aaron and Eleazar his son,[1121] and bring them up unto mount Hor:

26 And strip Aaron of his garments, and put them upon Eleazar his son: and Aaron shall be gathered *unto his people,* and shall die there.

27 And Moses did[6213] as the LORD commanded: and they went up[5927] into mount Hor in the sight of all the congregation.

12 [a]Num. 27:14; Deut. 1:37; 3:26; 32:51 [b]Lev. 10:3; Ezek. 20:41; 36:23; 38:16; 1Pet. 3:15

13 [I]That is, *Strife* [a]Deut. 33:8; Ps. 95:8; 106:32-43

14 [I]Hebr. *found us* [a]Judg. 11:16, 17 [b]Deut. 2:4-9; 23:7; Obad. 1:10, 12 [c]Ex. 18:8

15 [a]Gen. 46:6; Acts 7:15 [b]Ex. 12:40 [c]Ex. 1:11; Deut. 26:6; Acts 7:19

16 [a]Ex. 2:23; 3:7 [b]Ex. 3:2; 14:19; 23:20; 33:2

17 [a]Num. 21:22; Deut. 2:27

19 [a]Deut. 2:6, 28

20 [a]Judg. 11:17

21 [a]Deut. 2:27, 29 [b]Deut. 2:4, 5, 8; Judg. 11:18

22 [a]Num. 33:37 [b]Num. 21:4

24 [I]Hebr. *mouth* [a]Gen. 25:8; Num. 27:13; 31:2; Deut. 32:50 [b]Num. 20:12

25 [a]Num. 33:38; Deut. 32:50

(continued from previous page)
bring forth water by him simply speaking. In Numbers 27:14, the sin is called rebellion, while in Deuteronomy 32:51 it is described as trespassing and failing to sanctify God, breaking faith and failing to hold God in reverence. Both of these aspects can be seen in Moses' refusal to do what God had commanded him to do.

🔑 **20:17** The "king's highway," was the direct road from the Gulf of Aqabah to Syria on the east side of the Dead Sea and Jordan valley. Its entire length has been a valuable source of archaeological information for modern scholars. Ruins found there indicate that it was in use as early as the twenty-third century B.C. During Solomon's reign it was part of the commercial trade route from Ezion-geber to Judah and Syria. Recovered Roman milestones indicate that Trajan had used part of it in his road system in the second century A.D. Today a modern highway covers a part of that route.

28 [a]And Moses stripped Aaron of his garments, and put them upon Eleazar his son; and [b]Aaron died there in the top[7218] of the mount: and Moses and Eleazar came down from the mount.

29 And when all the congregation saw[7200] that Aaron was dead,[1478] they mourned for Aaron [a]thirty days,[3117] *even* all the house[1004] of Israel.

Victory Over Canaanites

21 And *when* [a]king[4428] Arad the Canaanite, which dwelt in the south, heard tell[8085] that Israel came [b]by the way[1870] of the spies; then he fought against Israel, and took *some* of them prisoners.[7628]

2 [a]And Israel vowed a vow[5088] unto the LORD, and said, If thou wilt indeed deliver this people[5971] into my hand,[3027] then [b]I will utterly destroy[2763] their cities.

3 And the LORD hearkened[8085] to the voice of Israel, and delivered up the Canaanites; and they utterly destroyed them and their cities: and he called[7121] the name of the place [I]Hormah.

The Bronze Snake

🗝 4 And [a]they journeyed from mount Hor by the way of the Red sea, to [b]compass the land of Edom: and the soul[5315] of the people was much [I c]discouraged[7114] because of the way.

5 And the people [a]spake[1696] against God,[430] and against Moses, [b]Wherefore have ye brought us up[5927] out of Egypt to die[4191] in the wilderness? for *there is* no bread, neither *is there any* water; and [c]our soul loatheth[6973] this light bread.

6 And [a]the LORD sent [b]fiery[8314] serpents[5175] among the people, and they bit the people; and much people of Israel died.

7 [a]Therefore the people came to Moses, and said, We have sinned,[2398] for [b]we have spoken[1696] against the LORD, and against thee; [c]pray[6419] unto the LORD, that he take away the serpents from us. And Moses prayed[6419] for the people.

8 And the LORD said unto Moses, Make[6213] thee a fiery serpent, and set[7760] it upon a pole: and it shall come to pass, that every one that is bitten, when he looketh upon[7200] it, shall live.[2425]

9 And [a]Moses made a serpent[5175] of brass, and put it upon a pole, and it came to pass, that if a serpent had bitten any man,[376] when he beheld the serpent of brass, he lived.

Israel Moves to East of the Jordan

10 And the children[1121] of Israel set forward, and [a]pitched in Oboth.

11 And they journeyed from Oboth, and [a]pitched at [I]Ije–abarim, in the wilderness which *is* before Moab, toward the sunrising.

12 [a]From thence they removed, and pitched in the valley of Zared.

13 From thence they removed, and pitched on the other side of Arnon, which *is* in the wilderness that cometh out of the coasts of the Amorites: for [a]Arnon *is* the border of Moab, between Moab and the Amorites.

14 Wherefore it is said in the book[5612] of the wars of the LORD, [I]What he did in the Red sea, and in the brooks of Arnon,

28 [a]Ex. 29:29, 30 [b]Num. 33:38; Deut. 10:6; 32:50
29 [a]Deut. 34:8
1 [a]Num. 33:40; Judg. 1:16 [b]Num. 13:21
2 [a]Gen. 28:20; Judg. 11:30 [b]Lev. 27:28
3 [I]That is, *Utter destruction*
4 [I]Or, *grieved* [a]Num. 20:22; 33:41 [b]Judg. 11:18 [c]Ex. 6:9
5 [a]Ps. 78:19 [b]Ex. 16:3; 17:3 [c]Num. 11:6
6 [a]1Cor. 10:9 [b]Deut. 8:15
7 [a]Ps. 78:34 [b]Num. 21:5 [c]Ex. 8:8, 28; 1Sam. 12:19; 1Kgs. 13:6; Acts 8:24
9 [a]2Kgs. 18:4; John 3:14, 15
10 [a]Num. 33:43
11 [I]Or, *Heaps of Abarim* [a]Num. 33:44
12 [a]Deut. 2:13
13 [a]Num. 22:36; Judg. 11:18
14 [I]Or, *Vaheb in Suphah*

🗝 **21:4–9** Since it appears that the people were plagued by serpents for some time (the Lord did not take away the serpents as they had requested), it is likely that they carried the brazen serpent with them, setting it up wherever they camped, and that it was fixed in a permanent location once they were in the land. It was later destroyed by King Hezekiah because the people had begun to worship it (2 Kgs. 18:4).

The brazen serpent is a type of Christ (John 3:14, 15), and since a crossbeam was likely needed to support the snake, the pole is considered by some to be a symbol of the Cross. The Jews themselves claim that faith in God, not the mere sight of the brazen serpent, was what healed. Both testaments affirm that such faith in the Lord Jesus is the way of salvation (Is. 45:22; Heb. 12:2).

15 And at the stream of the brooks that goeth down to the dwelling of Ar, [a]and [I]lieth[8172] upon the border of Moab.

16 And from thence *they went* [a]to Beer: that *is* the well whereof the LORD spake unto Moses, Gather the people together,[622] and I will give them water.

17 [a]Then Israel sang[7891] this song,[7892] [I]Spring up,[5927] O well; [II]sing ye unto it:

18 The princes[8269] digged the well, the nobles[5081] of the people digged it, by *the direction of* [a]the lawgiver,[2710] with their staves. And from the wilderness *they went* to Mattanah:

19 And from Mattanah to Nahaliel: and from Nahaliel to Bamoth:

20 And from Bamoth *in* the valley, that *is* in the [I]country[7704] of Moab, to the top[7218] of [II]Pisgah, which looketh [a]toward [III]Jeshimon.

21 And [a]Israel sent messengers[4397] unto Sihon king of the Amorites, saying,

22 [a]Let me pass[5674] through thy land: we will not turn into the fields,[7704] or into the vineyards; we will not drink *of* the waters of the well: *but* we will go along by the king's[4428] *high* way, until we be past thy borders.

23 [a]And Sihon would not suffer Israel to pass through his border: but Sihon gathered all his people together, and went out against Israel into the wilderness: [b]and he came to Jahaz, and fought against Israel.

24 And [a]Israel smote[5221] him with the edge[6310] of the sword,[2719] and possessed[3423] his land from Arnon unto Jabbok, even unto the children of Ammon: for the border of the children of Ammon *was* strong.

25 And Israel took all these cities: and Israel dwelt in all the cities of the Amorites, in Heshbon, and in all the [I]villages thereof.

26 For Heshbon *was* the city of Sihon the king of the Amorites, who had fought against the former king of Moab, and taken all his land out of his hand, even unto Arnon.

27 Wherefore they that speak in proverbs[4911] say,[559] Come into Heshbon, let the city of Sihon be built and prepared:[3559]

28 For there is [a]a fire gone out of Heshbon, a flame from the city of Sihon: it hath consumed [b]Ar of Moab, *and* the lords[1167] of the high places[1116] of Arnon.

29 Woe to thee, Moab! thou art undone, O people of [a]Chemosh: he hath given his sons[1121] that escaped, and his daughters, into captivity[7628] unto Sihon king of the Amorites.

30 We have shot[3384] at them; Heshbon is perished[6] even [a]unto Dibon, and we have laid them waste[8074] even unto Nophah, which *reacheth* unto [b]Medeba.

31 Thus Israel dwelt in the land of the Amorites.

32 And Moses sent to spy out [a]Jaazer, and they took the villages thereof, and drove out the Amorites that *were* there.

33 [a]And they turned and went up[5927] by the way of Bashan: and Og the king of Bashan went out against them, he, and all his people, to the battle [b]at Edrei.

34 And the LORD said unto Moses, [a]Fear[3372] him not: for I have delivered him into thy hand, and all his people, and his land; and [b]thou shalt do[6213] to him as thou didst unto Sihon king of the Amorites, which dwelt at Heshbon.

35 [a]So they smote him, and his sons, and all his people, until there was none left[7604] him alive:[8300] and they possessed his land.

Balak Sends for Balaam

22 And [a]the children[1121] of Israel set forward, and pitched in the plains[6160] of Moab on this side Jordan *by* Jericho.

2 And [a]Balak the son[1121] of Zippor saw[7200] all that Israel had done[6213] to the Amorites.

3 And [a]Moab was sore afraid[1481] of the people,[5971] because they *were* many: and Moab was distressed[6973] because of the children of Israel.

---

15 [I]Hebr. *leaneth* [a]Deut. 2:18, 29
16 [a]Judg. 9:21
17 [I]Hebr. *Ascend* [II]Or, *answer* [a]Ex. 15:1; Ps. 105:2; 106:12
18 [a]Isa. 33:22
20 [I]Hebr. *field* [II]Or, *The hill* [III]Or, *The wilderness* [a]Num. 23:28
21 [a]Deut. 2:26, 27; Judg. 11:19
22 [a]Num. 20:17
23 [a]Deut. 29:7 [b]Deut. 2:32; Judg. 11:20
24 [a]Deut. 2:33; 29:7; Josh. 12:1, 2; 24:8; Neh. 9:22; Ps. 135:10, 11; 136:19; Amos 2:9
25 [I]Hebr. *daughters*
28 [a]Jer. 48:45, 46 [b]Deut. 2:9, 18; Isa. 15:1
29 [a]Judg. 11:24; 1Kgs. 11:7, 33; 2Kgs. 23:13; Jer. 48:7, 13
30 [a]Jer. 48:18, 22 [b]Isa. 15:2
32 [a]Num. 32:1; Jer. 48:32
33 [a]Deut. 3:1; 29:7 [b]Josh. 13:12
34 [a]Deut. 3:2 [b]Num. 21:24; Ps. 135:10, 11; 136:20
35 [a]Deut. 3:3, 4
1 [a]Num. 33:48
2 [a]Judg. 11:25
3 [a]Ex. 15:15

4 And Moab said[559] unto [a]the
elders[2205] of Midian, Now shall this
company[6951] lick up all *that are* round
about us, as the ox licketh up the grass
of the field.[7704] And Balak the son of
Zippor *was* king[4428] of the Moabites at
that time.[6256]
🗝 5 [a]He sent messengers[4397] therefore
unto Balaam the son of Beor to [b]Pethor,
which *is* by the river of the land of the
children of his people, to call[7121] him,
saying, Behold, there is a people come
out from Egypt: behold, they cover[3680]
the [I]face of the earth,[776] and they abide
over against me:
6 Come now therefore, I pray
thee,[4994] [a]curse[779] me this people; for they
are too mighty for me: peradventure[194] I
shall prevail, *that* we may smite[5221] them,
and *that* I may drive them out of the
land: for I wot[3045] that he whom thou
blessest *is* blessed,[1288] and he whom thou
cursest is cursed.
7 And the elders of Moab and the
elders of Midian departed with [a]the
rewards of divination[7081] in their hand;
and they came unto Balaam, and
spake[1696] unto him the words[1697] of
Balak.
8 And he said unto them, [a]Lodge
here this night,[3915] and I will bring you
word again, as the LORD shall speak unto
me: and the princes[8269] of Moab abode
with Balaam.
9 [a]And God[430] came unto Balaam,
and said, What men[582] *are* these with
thee?

4 [a]Num. 31:8; Josh. 13:21

5 [I]Hebr. *eye* [a]Deut. 23:4; Josh. 13:22; 24:9; Neh. 13:1, 2; Mic. 6:5; 2Pet. 2:15; Jude 1:11; Rev. 2:14 [b]Num. 23:7; Deut. 23:4

6 [a]Num. 23:7

7 [a]1Sam. 9:7, 8

8 [a]Num. 22:19

9 [a]Gen. 20:3; Num. 22:20

11 [I]Hebr. *I shall prevail in fighting against him*

12 [a]Num. 23:20; Rom. 11:29

16 [I]Hebr. *Be not thou letted from*

17 [a]Num. 22:6

18 [a]Num. 24:13 [b]1Kgs. 22:14; 2Chr. 18:13

10 And Balaam said unto God, Balak
the son of Zippor, king of Moab, hath
sent unto me, *saying,*
11 Behold, *there is* a people come out
of Egypt, which covereth[3680] the face of
the earth: come now, curse[6895] me them;
peradventure [I]I shall be able to overcome
them, and drive them out.
12 And God said unto Balaam,
Thou shalt not go with them; thou shalt
not curse the people: for [a]they *are*
blessed.
13 And Balaam rose up in the morning, and said unto the princes of Balak,
Get you into your land: for the LORD
refuseth[3985] to give me leave to go with
you.
14 And the princes of Moab rose up,
and they went unto Balak, and said,
Balaam refuseth to come with us.
15 And Balak sent yet again princes,
more, and more honourable[3513] than they.
16 And they came to Balaam, and
said to him, Thus saith Balak the son of
Zippor, [I]Let nothing, I pray thee, hinder
thee from coming unto me:
17 For I will promote thee unto
very great honour,[3513] and I will do
whatsoever thou sayest[1697] unto me:
[a]come therefore, I pray thee, curse me
this people.
18 And Balaam answered and said
unto the servants[5650] of Balak, [a]If Balak
would give me his house[1004] full of silver and gold, [b]I cannot go beyond[5674] the
word of the LORD my God, to do less or
more.

🗝 **22:5–24:25** Balaam lived a long distance away from Moab, yet he must have been quite famous for Balak to have known of him and sent for him. Balak was motivated by his fear of Israel (22:5, 6). Balaam refers to his activity as divination (Num. 22:7; 23:23: 24:1), but in this he may have been reflecting on a foreign custom, as did Joseph (Gen. 44:15). Certainly Balaam's response to Balak was done in accordance with the Lord's instructions. However, a comparison of 22:20 and 22:22 suggests that Balaam may have been going with motives other than obeying God. Certainly Balaam's later suggestions to the Midianites were opposed to God's plans, and brought about his own death, judgment on Israel, and the destruction of Midian (Num. 25:1–9; 31:2, 8, 15–17). Balaam's prophecies of blessing on Israel and judgment on Israel's enemies, especially the messianic reference (Num. 24:17), are indeed remarkable.

Archaeological evidence from Deir Alla indicates that Balaam was highly regarded by pagans 500 years after his death. Two New Testament writers tell us that Balaam is an example of those who sin for personal gain (2 Pet. 2:15; Jude 1:11). John uses Balaam as an example of one who taught others how to sin (Rev. 2:14).

19 Now therefore, I pray you, [a]tarry ye also here this night, that I may know[3045] what the LORD will say[1696] unto me more.

20 [a]And God came unto Balaam at night, and said unto him, If the men come to call thee, rise up, *and* go with them; but [b]yet the word which I shall say unto thee, that shalt thou do.

Balaam Meets the Angel of the LORD

21 And Balaam rose up in the morning, and saddled[2280] his ass, and went with the princes of Moab.

22 And God's anger[639] was kindled[2734] because he went: [a]and the angel[4397] of the LORD stood in the way[1870] for an adversary[7854] against him. Now he was riding upon his ass, and his two servants *were* with him.

23 And [a]the ass saw the angel of the LORD standing[5324] in the way, and his sword[2719] drawn in his hand: and the ass turned aside out of the way, and went into the field: and Balaam smote[5221] the ass, to turn her into the way.

24 But the angel of the LORD stood in a path of the vineyards, a wall *being* on this side, and a wall on that side.

25 And when the ass saw the angel of the LORD, she thrust herself[3905] unto the wall, and crushed Balaam's foot against the wall: and he smote her again.

26 And the angel of the LORD went further, and stood in a narrow place, where *was* no way to turn either to the right hand or to the left.

27 And when the ass saw the angel of the LORD, she fell down under Balaam: and Balaam's anger was kindled, and he smote the ass with a staff.

28 And the LORD [a]opened the mouth[6310] of the ass, and she said unto Balaam, What have I done unto thee, that thou hast smitten[5221] me these three times?

29 And Balaam said unto the ass, Because thou hast mocked me: I would there were a sword in mine hand, [a]for now would I kill[2026] thee.

30 [a]And the ass said[559] unto Balaam, *Am* not I thine ass, [I]upon which thou hast ridden [II]ever since *I* was thine unto this day?[3117] was I ever wont[5532] to do so unto thee? And he said, Nay.

31 Then the LORD [a]opened the eyes of Balaam, and he saw the angel of the LORD standing in the way, and his sword drawn in his hand: and he [b]bowed down his head,[7218] and [I]fell flat[7812] on his face.[639]

32 And the angel of the LORD said unto him, Wherefore hast thou smitten thine ass these three times? behold, I went out [I]to withstand[7854] thee, because *thy* way is [a]perverse before me:

33 And the ass saw me, and turned from me these three times: unless she had turned from me, surely now also I had slain[2026] thee, and saved her alive.

34 And Balaam said unto the angel of the LORD, [a]I have sinned;[2398] for I knew[3045] not that thou stoodest[5324] in the way against me: now therefore, if it [I]displease thee, I will get me back again.

35 And the angel of the LORD said unto Balaam, Go with the men: [a]but only the word that I shall speak unto thee, that thou shalt speak. So Balaam went with the princes of Balak.

Balaam Arrives and Blesses Israel

36 And when Balak heard[8085] that Balaam was come, [a]he went out to meet him unto a city of Moab, [b]which *is* in the border of Arnon, which *is* in the utmost coast.

37 And Balak said unto Balaam, Did I not earnestly send unto thee to call thee? wherefore camest thou not unto me? am I not able indeed[552] [a]to promote thee to honour?

38 And Balaam said unto Balak, Lo, I am come unto thee: have I now any power at all to say any thing? [a]the word that God putteth[7760] in my mouth, that shall I speak.

39 And Balaam went with Balak, and they came unto [I]Kirjath–huzoth.

40 And Balak offered[2076] oxen and

---

19 [a]Num. 22:8
20 [a]Num. 22:9 [b]Num. 22:35; 23:12, 26; 24:13
22 [a]Ex. 4:24
23 [a]2Kgs. 6:17; Dan. 10:7; Acts 22:9; 2Pet. 2:16; Jude 1:11
28 [a]2Pet. 2:16
29 [a]Prov. 12:10
30 [I]Hebr. *who hast ridden upon me* [II]Or, *ever since thou wast* [a]2Pet. 2:16
31 [I]Or, *bowed himself* [a]Gen. 21:19; 2Kgs. 6:17; Luke 24:16, 31 [b]Ex. 34:8
32 [I]Hebr. *to be an adversary unto thee* [a]2Pet. 2:14, 15
34 [I]Hebr. *be evil in thine eyes* [a]1Sam. 15:24, 30; 26:21; 2Sam. 12:13; Job 34:31, 32
35 [a]Num. 22:20
36 [a]Gen. 14:17 [b]Num. 21:13
37 [a]Num. 22:17; 24:11
38 [a]Num. 23:26; 24:13; 1Kgs. 22:14; 2Chr. 18:13
39 [I]Or, *A city of streets*

sheep, and sent to Balaam, and to the princes that *were* with him.

41 And it came to pass on the morrow, that Balak took Balaam, and brought him up[5927] into the [a]high places[1116] of Baal, that thence he might see the uttermost *part* of the people.

23

And Balaam said[559] unto Balak, [a]Build me here seven altars,[4196] and prepare[3559] me here seven oxen and seven rams.

2 And Balak did as Balaam had spoken;[1696] and Balak and Balaam [a]offered[5927] on *every* altar[4196] a bullock and a ram.

3 And Balaam said unto Balak, [a]Stand by thy burnt offering,[5930] and I will go: peradventure[194] the LORD will come [b]to meet me: and whatsoever he sheweth me I will tell[5046] thee. And [I]he went to an high place.[8205]

4 [a]And God[430] met Balaam: and he said unto him, I have prepared seven altars, and I have offered upon *every* altar a bullock and a ram.

5 And the LORD [a]put a word[1697] in Balaam's mouth,[6310] and said, Return[7725] unto Balak, and thus thou shalt speak.[1696]

6 And he returned unto him, and, lo, he stood[5324] by his burnt sacrifice,[5930] he, and all the princes[8269] of Moab.

7 And he [a]took up his parable, and said, Balak the king of Moab hath brought[5148] me from Aram, out of the mountains of the east, *saying,* [b]Come, curse[779] me Jacob, and come, [c]defy[2194] Israel.

8 [a]How shall I curse, whom God[410] hath not cursed?[6895] or how shall I defy, *whom* the LORD hath not defied?[2194]

9 For from the top[7218] of the rocks I see him, and from the hills I behold him: lo, [a]the people[5971] shall dwell alone, and [b]shall not be reckoned[2803] among the nations.[1471]

10 [a]Who can count the dust[6083] of Jacob, and the number of the fourth *part* of Israel? Let [I]me die[4191] [b]the death[4194] of the righteous, and let my last end[319] be like his!

11 And Balak said unto Balaam, What hast thou done unto me? [a]I took thee to curse[6895] mine enemies, and, behold, thou hast blessed[1288] *them* altogether.

12 And he answered and said, [a]Must I not take heed to speak that which the LORD hath put in my mouth?

13 And Balak said unto him, Come, I pray thee,[4994] with me unto another place, from whence thou mayest see them: thou shalt see but the utmost part of them, and shalt not see them all: and curse me them from thence.

14 And he brought him into the field[7704] of Zophim, to the top of [I]Pisgah, [a]and built seven altars, and offered a bullock and a ram on *every* altar.

15 And he said unto Balak, Stand here by thy burnt offering, while I meet *the LORD* yonder.

16 And the LORD met Balaam, and [a]put a word in his mouth, and said, Go again[7725] unto Balak, and say[1696] thus.

17 And when he came to him, behold, he stood by his burnt offering, and the princes of Moab with him. And Balak said unto him, What hath the LORD spoken?

18 And he took up[5375] his parable, and said, [a]Rise up, Balak, and hear;[8085] hearken unto me, thou son[1121] of Zippor:

19 [a]God *is* not a man,[376] that he should lie;[3576] neither the son of man,[120] that he should repent:[5162] hath he said, and shall he not do *it*? or hath he spoken, and shall he not make it good?

20 Behold, I have received *commandment* to bless:[1288] and [a]he hath blessed; and I cannot reverse it.

21 [a]He hath not beheld iniquity[205] in Jacob, neither hath he seen[7200] perverseness[5999] in Israel: [b]the LORD his God *is* with him, [c]and the shout of a king *is* among them.

22 [a]God brought them out of Egypt; he hath as it were [b]the strength[8443] of an unicorn.

23 Surely *there is* no enchantment[5172]

---

41 [a]Deut. 12:2

1 [a]Num. 23:29

2 [a]Num. 23:14, 30

3 [I]Or, *he went solitary* [a]Num. 23:15 [b]Num. 24:1

4 [a]Num. 23:16

5 [a]Num. 22:35; 23:16; Deut. 18:18; Jer. 1:9

7 [a]Num. 23:18; 24:3, 15, 23; Job 27:1; 29:1; Ps. 78:2; Ezek. 17:2; Mic. 2:4; Hab. 2:6 [b]Num. 22:6, 11, 17 [c]1Sam. 17:10

8 [a]Isa. 47:12, 13

9 [a]Deut. 33:28 [b]Ex. 33:16; Ezra 9:2; Eph. 2:14

10 [I]Hebr. *my soul,* or, *my life* [a]Gen. 13:16; 22:17 [b]Ps. 116:15

11 [a]Num. 22:11, 17; 24:10

12 [a]Num. 22:38

14 [I]Or, *The hill* [a]Num. 23:14

16 [a]Num. 22:35; 23:5

18 [a]Judg. 3:20

19 [a]1Sam. 15:29; Mal. 3:6; Rom. 11:29; Titus 1:2; James 1:17

20 [a]Gen. 12:2; 22:17; Num. 22:12

21 [a]Rom. 4:7, 8 [b]Ex. 13:21; 29:45, 46; 33:14 [c]Ps. 89:15

22 [a]Num. 24:8 [b]Deut. 33:17; Job 39:10, 11

[I]against Jacob, neither *is there* any divination[7081] against Israel: according to this time it shall be said of Jacob and of Israel, [a]What hath God wrought!

24 Behold, the people shall rise up [a]as a great lion, and lift up himself as a young lion: [b]he shall not lie down until he eat *of* the prey, and drink the blood[1818] of the slain.[2491]

25 And Balak said unto Balaam, Neither curse them at all, nor bless them at all.

26 But Balaam answered and said unto Balak, Told not I thee, saying, [a]All that the LORD speaketh, that I must do?

27 And Balak said unto Balaam, [a]Come, I pray thee, I will bring thee unto another place; peradventure it will please God that thou mayest curse me them from thence.

28 And Balak brought Balaam unto the top of Peor, that looketh [a]toward Jeshimon.

29 And Balaam said unto Balak, [a]Build me here seven altars, and prepare me here seven bullocks and seven rams.

30 And Balak did as Balaam had said, and offered a bullock and a ram on *every* altar.

24 And when Balaam saw[7200] that it pleased[2895,5869] the LORD to bless[1288] Israel, he went not, as at [a]other times, [I]to seek for enchantments,[5172] but he set his face toward the wilderness.

2 And Balaam lifted up his eyes, and he saw Israel [a]abiding[7931] *in his tents* according to their tribes;[7626] and [b]the spirit[7307] of God[430] came upon him.

3 [a]And he took up his parable, and said,[559] Balaam the son[1121] of Beor hath said, and the man [I]whose eyes are open hath said:

4 He hath said, which heard[8085] the words[561] of God,[410] which saw[2372] the vision[4236] of the Almighty,[7706] [a]falling *into a trance,* but having his eyes open:[1540]

5 How goodly[2896] are thy tents,[168] O Jacob, *and* thy tabernacles,[4908] O Israel!

6 As the valleys are they spread forth, as gardens by the river's side, [a]as the trees of lign aloes[174] [b]which the LORD hath planted, *and* as cedar trees beside the waters.

7 He shall pour the water out of his buckets, and his seed[2233] *shall be* [a]in many waters, and his king[4428] shall be higher than [b]Agag, and his [c]kingdom[4438] shall be exalted.[5375]

8 [a]God brought him forth out of Egypt; he hath as it were the strength of an unicorn: he shall [b]eat up the nations[1471] his enemies, and shall [c]break their bones,[6106] and [d]pierce *them* through[4272] with his arrows.

9 [a]He couched,[3766] he lay down as a lion, and as a great lion: who shall stir him up? [b]Blessed[1288] *is* he that blesseth thee, and cursed[779] *is* he that curseth thee.

Balaam's Prophecy

10 And Balak's anger[639] was kindled[2734] against Balaam, and he [a]smote[5606] his hands[3709] together: and Balak said unto Balaam, [b]I called[7121] thee to curse[6895] mine enemies, and, behold, thou hast altogether blessed *them* these three times.

11 Therefore now flee thou to thy place: I [a]thought[559] to promote thee unto great honour;[3513] but, lo, the LORD hath kept thee back from honour.[3519]

12 And Balaam said unto Balak, Spake[1696] I not also to thy messengers[4397] which thou sentest unto me, saying,

13 [a]If Balak would give me his house[1004] full of silver and gold, I cannot

23 IOr, *in* [a]Ps. 31:19; 44:1
24 [a]Gen. 49:9 [b]Gen. 49:27
26 [a]Num. 22:38; 23:12; 1Kgs. 22:14
27 [a]Num. 23:13
28 [a]Num. 21:20
29 [a]Num. 23:1
1 IHebr. *to the meeting of enchantments* [a]Num. 23:3, 15
2 [a]Num. 2:2 [b]Num. 11:25; 1Sam. 10:10; 19:20, 23; 2Chr. 15:1
3 IHebr. *who had his eyes shut,* but now opened [a]Num. 23:7, 18
4 [a]1Sam. 19:24; Ezek. 1:28; Dan. 8:18; 10:15, 16; 2Cor. 12:2, 3, 4; Rev. 1:10, 17
6 [a]Ps. 1:3; Jer. 17:8 [b]Ps. 104:16
7 [a]Jer. 51:13; Rev. 17:1, 15 [b]1Sam. 15:9 [c]2Sam. 5:12; 1Chr. 14:2
8 [a]Num. 23:22 [b]Num. 14:9; 23:24 [c]Ps. 2:9; Isa. 38:13; Jer. 50:17 [d]Ps. 45:5; Jer. 50:9
9 [a]Gen. 49:9 [b]Gen. 12:3; 27:29
10 [a]Ezek. 21:14, 17; 22:13 [b]Num. 23:11; Deut. 23:4, 5; Josh. 24:9, 10; Neh. 13:2
11 [a]Num. 22:17, 37
13 [a]Num. 22:18

24:7 Perhaps Agag was a general title given to the Amalekite kings, just as Pharaoh was the general title for the king of Egypt.

go beyond[5674] the commandment[6310] of the LORD, to do[6213] *either* good[2896] or bad[7451] of mine own mind;[3820] *but* what the LORD saith,[1696] that will I speak?[1696]

14 And now, behold, I go unto my people:[5971] come *therefore, and* [a]I will advertise[3289] thee what this people shall do to thy people [b]in the latter[319] days.[3117]

15 [a]And he took up his parable, and said, Balaam the son of Beor hath said, and the man whose eyes are open hath said:

16 He hath said, which heard the words of God, and knew[3045] the knowledge[1847] of the most High,[5945] *which* saw the vision of the Almighty, falling *into a trance,* but having his eyes open:

17 [a]I shall see him, but not now: I shall behold him, but not nigh: there shall come [b]a Star out of Jacob, and [c]a Sceptre[7626] shall rise out of Israel, and shall [I][d]smite[4272] the corners of Moab, and destroy all the children[1121] of Sheth.

18 And [a]Edom shall be a possession,[3424] Seir also shall be a possession for his enemies; and Israel shall do valiantly.[2428]

19 [a]Out of Jacob shall come he that shall have dominion,[7287] and shall destroy[6] him that remaineth[8300] of the city.

20 And when he looked on[7200] Amalek, he took up his parable, and said, Amalek *was* [I][a]the first[7225] of the nations; but his latter end [II][b]*shall be* that he perish[8] for ever.

21 And he looked on the Kenites, and took up his parable, and said, Strong is thy dwellingplace, and thou puttest[7760] thy nest in a rock.

22 Nevertheless [I][a]the Kenite shall be wasted, [II]until Asshur shall carry thee away captive.[7617]

23 And he took up his parable, and said, Alas, who shall live[2421] when God doeth this!

24 And ships *shall come* from the coast of [a]Chittim, and shall afflict Asshur, and shall afflict [b]Eber, and he also shall perish for ever.

25 And Balaam rose up, and went and [a]returned[7725] to his place: and Balak also went his way.[1870]

Moabite Women Seduce Israel

25 And Israel abode in [a]Shittim, and [b]the people[5971] began to commit whoredom[2181] with the daughters of Moab.

2 And [a]they called[7121] the people unto [b]the sacrifices[2077] of their gods:[430] and the people did eat, and [c]bowed down[7812] to their gods.

3 And Israel joined himself unto Baal–peor: and [a]the anger[639] of the LORD was kindled[2734] against Israel.

4 And the LORD said unto Moses, [a]Take all the heads[7218] of the people, and hang them up before the LORD against the sun, [b]that the fierce anger of the LORD may be turned away from Israel.

5 And Moses said unto [a]the judges[8199] of Israel, [b]Slay[2026] ye every one[376] his men[582] that were joined unto Baal–peor.

🗝 6 And, behold, one of the children of Israel came and brought[7126] unto his brethren[251] a Midianitish woman in the sight of Moses, and in the sight of all the congregation of the children of Israel, [a]who *were* weeping *before* the door of the tabernacle[168] of the congregation.[4150]

7 And [a]when Phinehas, [b]the son[1121] of Eleazar, the son of Aaron the priest,[3548] saw[7200] *it,* he rose up from among the congregation,[5712] and took a javelin in his hand;[3027]

8 And he went after the man[376] of Israel into the tent,[6898] and thrust both of them through, the man of Israel, and the woman[802] through her belly. So [a]the plague was stayed from the children of Israel.

14 [a]Mic. 6:5; Rev. 2:14 [b]Gen. 49:1; Dan. 2:28; 10:14
15 [a]Num. 24:3, 4
17 [I]Or, *smite through the princes of Moab* [a]Rev. 1:7 [b]Matt. 2:2; Rev. 22:16 [c]Gen. 49:10; Ps. 110:2 [d]2Sam. 8:2; Jer. 48:45
18 [a]2Sam. 8:14; Ps. 60:8, 9, 12
19 [a]Gen. 49:10
20 [I]Or, *the first of the nations that warred against Israel* [II]Or, shall be *even to destruction* [a]Ex. 17:8 [b]Ex. 17:14; 1Sam. 15:3, 8
22 [I]Hebr. *Kain* [II]Or, *how long shall it be ere Asshur carry thee away captive?* [a]Gen. 15:19
24 [a]Gen. 10:4; Dan. 11:30 [b]Gen. 10:21, 25
25 [a]Num. 31:8

1 [a]Num. 33:49; Josh. 2:1; Mic. 6:5 [b]Num. 31:16; 1Cor. 10:8
2 [a]Josh. 22:17; Ps. 106:28; Hos. 9:10 [b]Ex. 34:15, 16; 1Cor. 10:20 [c]Ex. 20:5
3 [a]Ps. 106:29
4 [a]Deut. 4:3; Josh. 22:17 [b]Num. 25:11; Deut. 13:17
5 [a]Ex. 18:21, 25 [b]Ex. 32:27; Deut. 13:6, 9, 13, 15
6 [a]Joel 2:17
7 [a]Ps. 106:30 [b]Ex. 6:25
8 [a]Ps. 106:30

🗝 **25:6–13** See note on Exodus 32:25–29.

9 And [a]those that died in the plague were twenty and four thousand.

10 And the LORD spake[1696] unto Moses, saying,

11 [a]Phinehas, the son of Eleazar, the son of Aaron the priest, hath turned my wrath[2534] away from the children of Israel, while he was zealous[7065] [I][b]for my sake[7068] among them, that I consumed[3615] not the children of Israel in [c]my jealousy.[7068]

12 Wherefore say, [a]Behold, I give unto him my covenant[1285] of peace:[7965]

13 And he shall have it, and [a]his seed[2233] after him, *even* the covenant of [b]an everlasting[5769] priesthood;[3550] because he was [c]zealous for his God,[430] and [d]made an atonement[3722] for the children of Israel.

14 Now the name of the Israelite that was slain,[5221] *even* that was slain with the Midianitish woman, *was* Zimri, the son of Salu, a prince[5387] of a [I]chief house[1004] among the Simeonites.

15 And the name of the Midianitish woman that was slain *was* Cozbi, the daughter of [a]Zur; he *was* head[7218] over a people,[523] *and* of a chief house in Midian.

16 And the LORD spake unto Moses, saying,

17 [a]Vex[6887] the Midianites, and smite[5221] them:

18 For they vex you with their [a]wiles, wherewith they have beguiled you in the matter[1697] of Peor, and in the matter of Cozbi, the daughter of a prince of Midian, their sister,[269] which was slain in the day[3117] of the plague for Peor's sake.

The Second Census

26 And it came to pass after the plague, that the LORD spake unto Moses and unto Eleazar the son of Aaron the priest,[3548] saying,

2 [a]Take[5375] the sum[7218] of all the congregation[5712] of the children[1121] of Israel, [b]from twenty years old and upward, throughout their fathers'[1] house,[1004] all that are able to go to war[6635] in Israel.

3 And Moses and Eleazar the priest spake with them [a]in the plains[6160] of Moab by Jordan *near* Jericho, saying,

4 *Take the sum of the people,* from twenty years old and upward; as the LORD [a]commanded[6680] Moses and the children of Israel, which went forth out of the land of Egypt.

5 [a]Reuben, the eldest son of Israel: the children of Reuben; Hanoch, *of whom cometh* the family[4940] of the Hanochites: of Pallu, the family of the Palluites:

6 Of Hezron, the family of the Hezronites: of Carmi, the family of the Carmites.

7 These *are* the families of the Reubenites: and they that were numbered[6485] of them were forty and three thousand and seven hundred and thirty.

8 And the sons[1121] of Pallu; Eliab.

9 And the sons of Eliab; Nemuel, and Dathan, and Abiram. This *is that* Dathan and Abiram, *which were* [a]famous[7121] in the congregation, who strove against Moses and against Aaron in the company[5712] of Korah, when they strove against the LORD:

10 [a]And the earth[776] opened her mouth,[6310] and swallowed them up together with Korah, when that company died,[4194] what time the fire devoured two hundred and fifty men:[376] [b]and they became a sign.

11 Notwithstanding [a]the children of Korah died not.

12 The sons of Simeon after their families: of [a]Nemuel, the family of the Nemuelites: of Jamin, the family of the Jaminites: of [b]Jachin, the family of the Jachinites:

13 Of [a]Zerah, the family of the Zarhites: of Shaul, the family of the Shaulites.

14 These *are* the families of the Simeonites, twenty and two thousand and two hundred.

15 The children of Gad after their families:[4940] of [a]Zephon, the family of the Zephonites: of Haggi, the family of the Haggites: of Shuni, the family of the Shunites:

9 [a]Deut. 4:3; 1Cor. 10:8

11 [I]Hebr. *with my zeal* [a]Ps. 106:23 [b]2Cor. 11:2 [c]Ex. 20:5; Deut. 32:16, 21; 1Kgs. 14:22; Ps. 78:58; Ezek. 16:38; Zeph. 1:18; 3:8

12 [a]Mal. 2:4, 5; 3:1

13 [a]1Chr. 6:4 [b]Ex. 40:15 [c]Acts 22:3; Rom. 10:2 [d]Heb. 2:17

14 [I]Hebr. *house of a father*

15 [a]Num. 31:8; Josh. 13:21

17 [a]Num. 31:2

18 [a]Num. 31:16; Rev. 2:14

2 [a]Ex. 30:12; 38:25, 26; Num. 1:2 [b]Num. 1:3

3 [a]Num. 22:1; 26:63; 31:12; 33:48; 35:1

4 [a]Num. 1:1

5 [a]Gen. 46:8; Ex. 6:14; 1Chr. 5:1

9 [a]Num. 16:1, 2

10 [a]Num. 16:32, 35 [b]Num. 16:38; 1Cor. 10:6; 2Pet. 2:6

11 [a]Ex. 6:24; 1Chr. 6:22

12 [a]Gen. 46:10; Ex. 6:15, *Jemuel* [b]1Chr. 4:24, *Jarib*

13 [a]Gen. 46:10, *Zohar*

15 [a]Gen. 46:16, *Ziphion*

16 Of [I][a]Ozni, the family of the Oznites: of Eri, the family of the Erites:

17 Of [a]Arod, the family of the Arodites: of Areli, the family of the Arelites.

18 These *are* the families of the children of Gad according to those that were numbered of them, forty thousand and five hundred.

19 [a]The sons of Judah *were* Er and Onan: and Er and Onan died in the land of Canaan.

20 And [a]the sons of Judah after their families were; of Shelah, the family of the Shelanites: of Pharez, the family of the Pharzites: of Zerah, the family of the Zarhites.

21 And the sons of Pharez were; of Hezron, the family of the Hezronites: of Hamul, the family of the Hamulites.

22 These *are* the families of Judah according to those that were numbered of them, threescore and sixteen thousand and five hundred.

23 [a]*Of* the sons of Issachar after their families: *of* Tola, the family of the Tolaites: of [I]Pua, the family of the Punites:

24 Of [I]Jashub, the family of the Jashubites: of Shimron, the family of the Shimronites.

25 These *are* the families of Issachar according to those that were numbered[6485] of them, threescore and four thousand and three hundred.

26 [a]*Of* the sons of Zebulun after their families: of Sered, the family of the Sardites: of Elon, the family of the Elonites: of Jahleel, the family of the Jahleelites.

27 These *are* the families of the Zebulunites according to those that were numbered of them, threescore thousand and five hundred.

28 [a]The sons of Joseph after their families *were* Manasseh and Ephraim.

29 Of the sons of Manasseh: of [a]Machir, the family of the Machirites: and Machir begat Gilead: of Gilead *come* the family of the Gileadites.

30 These *are* the sons of Gilead: *of* [a]Jeezer, the family of the Jeezerites: of Helek, the family of the Helekites:

31 And *of* Asriel, the family of the Asrielites: and *of* Shechem, the family of the Shechemites:

32 And *of* Shemida, the family of the Shemidaites: and *of* Hepher, the family of the Hepherites.

33 And [a]Zelophehad the son of Hepher had no sons, but daughters:[1323] and the names of the daughters of Zelophehad *were* Mahlah, and Noah, Hoglah, Milcah, and Tirzah.

34 These *are* the families of Manasseh, and those that were numbered of them, fifty and two thousand and seven hundred.

35 These *are* the sons of Ephraim after their families: of Shuthelah, the family of the Shuthalhites: of [a]Becher, the family of the Bachrites: of Tahan, the family of the Tahanites.

36 And these *are* the sons of Shuthelah: of Eran, the family of the Eranites.

37 These *are* the families of the sons[1121] of Ephraim according to those that were numbered of them, thirty and two thousand and five hundred. These *are* the sons of Joseph after their families.

38 [a]The sons of Benjamin after their families: of Bela, the family of the Belaites: of Ashbel, the family of the Ashbelites: of [b]Ahiram, the family of the Ahiramites:

39 Of [a]Shupham, the family of the Shuphamites: of Hupham, the family of the Huphamites.

40 And the sons of Bela were [a]Ard and Naaman: *of Ard,* the family of the Ardites: *and* of Naaman, the family of the Naamites.

41 These *are* the sons of Benjamin after their families: and they that were numbered of them *were* forty and five thousand and six hundred.

42 [a]These *are* the sons of Dan after their families: of [I]Shuham, the family of the Shuhamites. These *are* the families of Dan after their families.

43 All the families[4940] of the Shuhamites, according to those that were numbered of them, *were* threescore and four thousand and four hundred.

16 [I]Or, *Ezbon* [a]Gen. 46:16
17 [a]Gen. 46:16, *Arodi*
19 [a]Gen. 38:2-10; 46:12
20 [a]1Chr. 2:3
23 [I]Or, *Phuvah* [a]Gen. 46:13; 1Chr. 7:1
24 [I]Or, *Job*
26 [a]Gen. 46:14
28 [a]Gen. 46:20
29 [a]Josh. 17:1; 1Chr. 7:14, 15
30 [a]Josh. 17:2; Judg. 6:11, 24, 34, *Abiezer*
33 [a]Num. 27:1; 36:11
35 [a]1Chr. 7:20, *Bered*
38 [a]Gen. 46:21; 1Chr. 7:6 [b]Gen. 46:21, *Ehi;* 1Chr. 8:1, *Aharah*
39 [a]Gen. 46:21, *Muppim and Huppim*
40 [a]1Chr. 8:3, *Addar*
42 [I]Or, *Hushim* [a]Gen. 46:23

44 [a]*Of* the children of Asher after their families: of Jimna, the family of the Jimnites: of Jesui, the family of the Jesuites: of Beriah, the family of the Beriites.

45 Of the sons of Beriah: of Heber, the family of the Heberites: of Malchiel, the family of the Malchielites.

46 And the name of the daughter of Asher *was* Sarah.

47 These are the families of the sons of Asher according to those that were numbered of them; *who were* fifty and three thousand and four hundred.

48 [a]*Of* the sons of Naphtali after their families: of Jahzeel, the family of the Jahzeelites: of Guni, the family of the Gunites:

49 Of Jezer, the family[4940] of the Jezerites: of [a]Shillem, the family of the Shillemites.

50 These *are* the families of Naphtali according to their families: and they that were numbered[6485] of them *were* forty and five thousand and four hundred.

51 [a]These *were* the numbered of the children of Israel, six hundred thousand and a thousand seven hundred and thirty.

52 And the LORD spake unto Moses, saying,

53 [a]Unto these the land shall be divided for an inheritance[5159] according to the number of names.

54 [a]To many thou shalt [I]give the more inheritance, and to few thou shalt [II]give the less inheritance: to every one shall his inheritance be given according to those that were numbered of him.

44 [a]Gen. 46:17; 1Chr. 7:30
48 [a]Gen. 46:24; 1Chr. 7:13
49 [a]1Chr. 7:13, *Shallum*
51 [a]Num. 1:46
53 [a]Josh. 11:23; 14:1
54 [I]Hebr. *multiply his inheritance* [II]Hebr. *diminish his inheritance* [a]Num. 33:54
55 [a]Num. 33:54; 34:13; Josh. 11:23; 14:2
57 [a]Gen. 46:11; Ex. 6:16-19; 1Chr. 6:1, 16
59 [a]Ex. 2:1, 2; 6:20
60 [a]Num. 3:2
61 [a]Lev. 10:1, 2; Num. 3:4; 1Chr. 24:2
62 [a]Num. 3:39 [b]Num. 1:49 [c]Num. 18:20, 23, 24; Deut. 10:9; Josh. 13:14, 33; 14:3
63 [a]Num. 26:3

55 Notwithstanding the land shall be [a]divided by lot: according to the names of the tribes[4294] of their fathers[1] they shall inherit.[5157]

56 According to the lot shall the possession thereof be divided between many and few.

57 [a]And these *are* they that were numbered of the Levites after their families: of Gershon, the family of the Gershonites: of Kohath, the family of the Kohathites: of Merari, the family of the Merarites.

58 These *are* the families of the Levites: the family of the Libnites, the family of the Hebronites, the family of the Mahlites, the family of the Mushites, the family of the Korathites. And Kohath begat Amram.

59 And the name of Amram's wife[802] *was* [a]Jochebed, the daughter of Levi, whom *her mother* bare to Levi in Egypt: and she bare unto Amram Aaron and Moses, and Miriam their sister.[269]

60 [a]And unto Aaron was born Nadab, and Abihu, Eleazar, and Ithamar.

61 And [a]Nadab and Abihu died, when they offered[7126] strange[2114] fire before the LORD.

62 [a]And those that were numbered of them were twenty and three thousand, all males[2145] from a month old and upward: [b]for they were not numbered among the children of Israel, because there was [c]no inheritance given them among the children of Israel.

63 These *are* they that were numbered by Moses and Eleazar the priest, who numbered the children of Israel [a]in

---

26:52–56 Approximately thirty-seven years after the first census, a second one was taken following the same procedure (Num. 26:1–51). These figures were to be used in determining the size of the territory allotted to each tribe (Num. 26:52–56). When the figures from the two censuses are compared, some interesting facts emerge. Only Joshua and Caleb, the two men who had not rebelled at Kadesh-barnea, were counted in both censuses. The first numbering found 603,550 fighting men in the twelve tribes (Num. 1:46), a remarkable number for Moses to have led through the wilderness. The totals for the second census were 601,730 (Num. 26:51), which reflects almost no change in thirty-seven years. The composition of the two groups was, however, totally different. Had the 24,000 who were killed just before the second census because of their sin at Baal-peor (Num. 25:9) still been alive, the adult male population would have shown a modest increase. See note on Numbers 1:2.

the plains of Moab by Jordan *near* Jericho.

🔑 64 [a]But among these there was not a man[376] of them whom Moses and Aaron the priest numbered, when they numbered the children of Israel in the wilderness of Sinai.

65 For the LORD had said[559] of them, They [a]shall surely die[4191] in the wilderness. And there was not left[3498] a man of them, [b]save Caleb the son of Jephunneh, and Joshua the son of Nun.

The Law of Inheritance

27 Then came the daughters of [a]Zelophehad, the son of Hepher, the son of Gilead, the son of Machir, the son of Manasseh, of the families of Manasseh the son of Joseph: and these *are* the names of his daughters; Mahlah, Noah, and Hoglah, and Milcah, and Tirzah.

2 And they stood before Moses, and before Eleazar the priest,[3548] and before the princes[3548] and all the congregation,[5712] *by* the door of the tabernacle[168] of the congregation,[4150] saying,

3 Our father[1] [a]died in the wilderness, and he was not in the company[5712] of them that gathered themselves together[3259] against the LORD [b]in the company of Korah; but died in his own sin,[2399] and had no sons.[1121]

4 Why should the name of our father be [I]done away from among his family,[4940] because he hath no son? [a]Give unto us *therefore* a possession[272] among the brethren[251] of our father.

5 And Moses [a]brought[7126] their cause before the LORD.

6 And the LORD spake[559] unto Moses, saying,

7 The daughters of Zelophehad speak[1696] right: [a]thou shalt surely give them a possession of an inheritance[5159] among their father's[1] brethren; and thou shalt cause the inheritance of their father to pass unto them.

8 And thou shalt speak unto the children[1121] of Israel, saying, If a man[376] die,[4191] and have no son, then ye shall cause his inheritance to pass unto his daughter.

9 And if he have no daughter, then ye shall give his inheritance unto his brethren.

10 And if he have no brethren, then ye shall give his inheritance unto his father's brethren.

11 And if his father have no brethren, then ye shall give his inheritance unto his kinsman[7607] that is next to him of his family, and he shall possess[3423] it: and it shall be unto the children of Israel [a]a statute[2708] of judgment,[4941] as the LORD commanded[6680] Moses.

Joshua Named to Succeed Moses

12 And the LORD said unto Moses, [a]Get thee up into this mount Abarim, and see the land which I have given unto the children of Israel.

13 And when thou hast seen[7200] it, thou also [a]shalt be gathered[622] unto thy people,[5971] as Aaron thy brother[251] was gathered.

14 For ye [a]rebelled[4784] against my commandment[6310] in the desert of Zin, in the strife of the congregation, to sanctify[6942] me at the [b]water before their eyes: that *is* the water of Meribah in Kadesh in the wilderness of Zin.

15 And Moses spake[1696] unto the LORD, saying,

16 Let the LORD, [a]the God[430] of the spirits[7307] of all flesh,[1320] set a man over the congregation,

17 [a]Which may go out before them, and which may go in before them, and which may lead them out, and which may bring them in; that the congregation

64 [a]Deut. 2:14, 15
65 [a]Num. 14:28, 29; 1Cor. 10:5, 6 [b]Num. 14:30
1 [a]Num. 26:33; 36:1, 11; Josh. 17:3
3 [a]Num. 14:35; 26:64, 65 [b]Num. 16:1, 2
4 [I]Hebr. *diminished* [a]Josh. 17:4
5 [a]Ex. 18:15, 19
7 [a]Num. 36:2
11 [a]Num. 35:29
12 [a]Num. 33:47; Deut. 3:27; 32:49; 34:1
13 [a]Num. 20:24, 28; 31:2; Deut. 10:6
14 [a]Num. 20:12, 24; Deut. 1:37; 32:51; Ps. 106:32 [b]Ex. 17:7
16 [a]Num. 16:22; Heb. 12:9
17 [a]Deut. 31:2; 1Sam. 8:20; 18:13; 2Chr. 1:10

🔑 **26:64, 65** See note on Numbers 13:30–33.

of the LORD be not [b]as sheep which have no shepherd.

🔑 18 And the LORD said unto Moses, Take thee Joshua the son of Nun, a man [a]in whom *is* the spirit,[7307] and [b]lay thine hand[3027] upon him;

19 And set him before Eleazar the priest, and before all the congregation; and [a]give him a charge[6680] in their sight.

20 And [a]thou shalt put *some* of thine honour[1935] upon him, that all the congregation of the children of Israel [b]may be obedient.[8085]

21 [a]And he shall stand before Eleazar the priest, who shall ask[7592] *counsel* for him [b]after the judgment of Urim before the LORD: [c]at his word shall they go out, and at his word they shall come in, *both* he, and all the children of Israel with him, even all the congregation.

22 And Moses did as the LORD commanded him: and he took Joshua, and set him before Eleazar the priest, and before all the congregation:

23 And he laid his hands[3027] upon him, [a]and gave him a charge, as the LORD commanded[1696] by the hand of Moses.

Laws for Offerings

28 And the LORD spake[1696] unto Moses, saying,

2 Command[6680] the children[1121] of Israel, and say[559] unto them, My offering,[7133] *and* [a]my bread for my sacrifices made by fire, *for* [I]a sweet savour unto me, shall ye observe[8104] to offer[7126] unto me in their due season.[4150]

3 And thou shalt say unto them, [a]This *is* the offering made by fire which ye shall offer unto the LORD; two lambs of the first year without spot[8549] [I]day by day, *for* a continual[8548] burnt offering.[5930]

4 The one lamb shalt thou offer[6213] in the morning, and the other lamb shalt thou offer [I]at even;

🔑 5 And [a]a tenth *part* of an ephah of flour for a [b]meat offering,[4503] mingled[1101] with the fourth *part* of an [c]hin of beaten oil.[8081]

6 *It is* [a]a continual burnt offering, which was ordained in mount Sinai for a sweet savour, a sacrifice made by fire[801] unto the LORD.

🔑 7 And the drink offering[5262] thereof *shall be* the fourth *part* of an hin for the one lamb: [a]in the holy[6944] *place* shalt thou cause the strong wine to be poured[5258] unto the LORD *for* a drink offering.

8 And the other lamb shalt thou offer at even: as the meat offering of the morning, and as the drink offering thereof, thou shalt offer *it,* a sacrifice made by fire, of a sweet savour unto the LORD.

9 And on the sabbath[7676] day two lambs of the first year without spot, and two tenth deals of flour *for* a meat offering, mingled with oil, and the drink offering thereof:

10 *This is* [a]the burnt offering of every sabbath, beside the continual burnt offering, and his drink offering.

🔑 11 And [a]in the beginnings[7218] of your months ye shall offer[7126] a burnt of-

17 [b]1Kgs. 22:17; Zech. 10:2; Matt. 9:36; Mark 6:34
18 [a]Gen. 41:38; Judg. 3:10; 11:29; 1Sam. 16:13, 18 [b]Deut. 34:9
19 [a]Deut. 31:7
20 [a]Num. 11:17, 28; 1Sam. 10:6, 9; 2Kgs. 2:15 [b]Josh. 1:16, 17
21 [a]Josh. 9:14; Judg. 1:1; 20:18, 23, 26; 1Sam. 23:9; 30:7 [b]Ex. 28:30 [c]Josh. 9:14; 1Sam. 22:10, 13, 15
23 [a]Deut. 3:28; 31:7

2 [I]Hebr. *a savor of my rest* [a]Lev. 3:11; 21:6, 8; Mal. 1:7, 12
3 [I]Hebr. *in a day* [a]Ex. 29:38
4 [I]Hebr. *between the two evenings*
5 [a]Ex. 16:36; Num. 15:4 [b]Lev. 2:1 [c]Ex. 29:40
6 [a]Ex. 29:42; Amos 5:25
7 [a]Ex. 29:42
10 [a]Ezek. 46:4
11 [a]Num. 10:10; 1Sam. 20:5; 1Chr. 23:31; 2Chr. 2:4; Ezra 3:5; Neh. 10:33; Isa. 1:13, 14; Ezek. 45:17; 46:6; Hos. 2:11; Col. 2:16

🔑 **27:18–23** Knowing that it would not be long before he would die, Moses asked God to choose a successor to lead Israel in his place (v. 16). God selected Joshua, a man who had been Moses' close associate and servant since the time when Israel was still at Mount Sinai (Ex. 24:13; 32:17; 33:11). Even before their arrival at Sinai, Moses had appointed Joshua to be the leader of the army against Amalek (Ex. 17:8–13). His public commissioning involved more than the role of military leader, but it was in this area that he was to make his greatest contribution. Joshua is mentioned twice in the New Testament (Acts 7:45; Heb. 4:8).

🔑 **28:5, 7** The "ephah" and "hin" are Egyptian measures, which reveal the influence of Israel's sojourn in Egypt.

🔑 **28:11–15** The phrase "beginnings of your months" refers to the observance of the new moon (1 Chr. 23:31; Ezra 3:5). Though it was characterized by the blowing of trumpets, it is not to be

(continued on next page)

fering unto the LORD; two young bullocks, and one ram, seven lambs of the first year without spot;

12 And [a]three tenth deals of flour *for* a meat offering, mingled with oil, for one bullock; and two tenth deals of flour *for* a meat offering, mingled with oil, for one ram;

13 And a several tenth deal[6241] of flour mingled with oil *for* a meat offering unto one lamb; *for* a burnt offering of a sweet savour, a sacrifice made by fire unto the LORD.

14 And their drink offerings shall be half an hin of wine unto a bullock, and the third *part* of an hin unto a ram, and a fourth *part* of an hin unto a lamb: this *is* the burnt offering of every month throughout the months of the year.

15 And [a]one kid[8163] of the goats for a sin offering[2403] unto the LORD shall be offered,[6213] beside the continual burnt offering, and his drink offering.

Offerings at the Annual Assemblies

16 [a]And in the fourteenth day of the first[7223] month *is* the passover[6453] of the LORD.

17 [a]And in the fifteenth day of this month *is* the feast: seven days[3117] shall unleavened bread[4682] be eaten.

18 In the [a]first day *shall be* an holy convocation;[4744] ye shall do[6213] no manner of servile[5656] work *therein:*

19 But ye shall offer a sacrifice made by fire *for* a burnt offering unto the LORD; two young bullocks, and one ram, and seven lambs of the first year: [a]they shall be unto you without blemish:[8549]

20 And their meat offering *shall be of* flour mingled with oil: three tenth deals shall ye offer for a bullock, and two tenth deals for a ram;

21 A several tenth deal shalt thou offer for every lamb, throughout the seven lambs:

22 And [a]one goat *for* a sin offering, to make an atonement[3722] for you.

23 Ye shall offer these beside the burnt offering in the morning, which *is* for a continual burnt offering.

24 After this manner ye shall offer daily,[3117] throughout the seven days, the meat of the sacrifice made by fire, of a sweet savour unto the LORD: it shall be offered beside the continual burnt offering, and his drink offering.

25 And [a]on the seventh day ye shall have an holy convocation; ye shall do no servile work.

26 Also [a]in the day of the firstfruits, when ye bring[7126] a new meat offering unto the LORD, after your weeks *be out,* ye shall have an holy convocation; ye shall do no servile work:

27 But ye shall offer the burnt offering for a sweet savour unto the LORD; [a]two young bullocks, one ram, seven lambs of the first year;

28 And their meat offering of flour mingled with oil, three tenth deals unto one bullock, two tenth deals unto one ram,

29 A several tenth deal unto one lamb, throughout the seven lambs;

30 *And* one kid of the goats, to make an atonement for you.

31 Ye shall offer *them* beside the continual burnt offering, and his meat offering, ([a]they shall be unto you without blemish) and their drink offerings.

12 [a]Num. 15:4-12
15 [a]Num. 15:24; 28:22
16 [a]Ex. 12:6, 18; Lev. 23:5; Num. 9:3; Deut. 16:1; Ezek. 45:21
17 [a]Lev. 23:6
18 [a]Ex. 12:16; Lev. 23:7
19 [a]Num. 28:31; 29:8; Lev. 22:20; Deut. 15:21
22 [a]Num. 28:15
25 [a]Ex. 12:16; 13:6; Lev. 23:8
26 [a]Ex. 23:16; 34:22; Lev. 23:10, 15; Deut. 16:10; Acts 2:1
27 [a]Lev. 23:18, 19
31 [a]Num. 28:19

(continued from previous page)
confused with the Feast of Trumpets (Num. 29:1–6). The Feast of Trumpets was celebrated at the beginning of the seventh month, not the first day of every month as is the case with these observances. Special sacrifices were offered, and it was a time of inquiring of God's messengers and worshiping at God's house, as well as a time for fellowship (1 Sam. 20:5, 18; 2 Kgs. 4:23). The observance was one of great solemnity; all business and work was to cease. When Israel began to approach it with insincerity and treated it as a mere ritual, God condemned its observance (Is. 1:13, 14).

29 And in the seventh month, on the first *day* of the month, ye shall have an holy[6944] convocation;[4744] ye shall do no servile[5656] work: [a]it is a day of blowing the trumpets unto you.

2 And ye shall offer a burnt offering[5930] for a sweet savour unto the LORD; one young bullock, one ram, *and* seven lambs of the first year without blemish:[8549]

3 And their meat offering[4503] *shall be of* flour mingled[1101] with oil,[8081] three tenth deals for a bullock, *and* two tenth deals for a ram,

4 And one tenth deal[6241] for one lamb, throughout the seven lambs:

5 And one kid[8163] of the goats *for* a sin offering,[2403] to make an atonement[3722] for you:

6 Beside [a]the burnt offering of the month, and his meat offering, and [b]the daily[8548] burnt offering, and his meat offering, and their drink offerings,[5262] [c]according unto their manner,[4941] for a sweet savour, a sacrifice made by fire[801] unto the LORD.

7 And [a]ye shall have on the tenth *day* of this seventh month an holy convocation; and ye shall [b]afflict your souls:[5315] ye shall not do any work *therein:*

8 But ye shall offer[7126] a burnt offering unto the LORD *for* a sweet savour; one young bullock, one ram, *and* seven lambs of the first year; [a]they shall be unto you without blemish:

9 And their meat offering *shall be of* flour mingled with oil, three tenth deals to a bullock, *and* two tenth deals to one ram,

10 A several tenth deal for one lamb, throughout the seven lambs:

11 One kid of the goats *for* a sin offering; beside [a]the sin offering of atonement, and the continual[4744] burnt offering, and the meat offering of it, and their drink offerings.

12 And [a]on the fifteenth day of the seventh month ye shall have an holy convocation; ye shall do no servile work, and ye shall keep a feast unto the LORD seven days:[3117]

13 And [a]ye shall offer a burnt offering, a sacrifice made by fire, of a sweet savour unto the LORD; thirteen young bullocks, two rams, *and* fourteen lambs of the first year; they shall be without blemish:

14 And their meat offering *shall be of* flour mingled with oil, three tenth deals unto every bullock of the thirteen bullocks, two tenth deals to each ram of the two rams,

15 And a several tenth deal to each lamb of the fourteen lambs:

16 And one kid of the goats *for* a sin offering; beside the continual burnt offering, his meat offering, and his drink offering.

17 And on the second day *ye shall offer* twelve young bullocks, two rams, fourteen lambs of the first year without spot:[8549]

18 And their meat offering and their drink offerings for the bullocks, for the rams, and for the lambs, *shall be* according to their number, [a]after the manner:

19 And one kid of the goats *for* a sin offering; beside the continual burnt offering, and the meat offering thereof, and their drink offerings.

20 And on the third day eleven bullocks, two rams, fourteen lambs of the first year without blemish;

21 And their meat offering and their drink offerings for the bullocks, for the rams, and for the lambs, *shall be* according to their number, [a]after the manner:

22 And one goat *for* a sin offering; beside the continual burnt offering, and his meat offering, and his drink offering.

23 And on the fourth day ten bullocks, two rams, *and* fourteen lambs of the first year without blemish:

24 Their meat offering and their drink offerings for the bullocks, for the rams, and for the lambs, *shall be* according to their number,[4557] after the manner:

25 And one kid of the goats *for* a sin offering; beside the continual burnt offering, his meat offering, and his drink offering.

1 [a]Lev. 23:24
6 [a]Num. 28:11 [b]Num. 28:3 [c]Num. 15:11, 12
7 [a]Lev. 16:29; 23:27 [b]Ps. 35:13; Isa. 58:5
8 [a]Num. 28:19
11 [a]Lev. 16:3, 5
12 [a]Lev. 23:34; Deut. 16:13; Ezek. 45:25
13 [a]Ezra 3:4
18 [a]Num. 15:12; 28:7, 14; 29:3, 4, 9, 10
21 [a]Num. 29:18

26 And on the fifth day nine bullocks, two rams, *and* fourteen lambs of the first year without spot:

27 And their meat offering and their drink offerings for the bullocks, for the rams, and for the lambs, *shall be* according to their number, after the manner:

28 And one goat *for* a sin offering; beside the continual burnt offering, and his meat offering, and his drink offering.[5262]

29 And on the sixth day eight bullocks, two rams, *and* fourteen lambs of the first year without blemish:

30 And their meat offering and their drink offerings for the bullocks, for the rams, and for the lambs, *shall be* according to their number, after the manner:

31 And one goat *for* a sin offering; beside the continual burnt offering, his meat offering, and his drink offering.

32 And on the seventh day seven bullocks, two rams, *and* fourteen lambs of the first year without blemish:

33 And their meat offering and their drink offerings for the bullocks, for the rams, and for the lambs, *shall be* according to their number, after the manner:

34 And one goat *for* a sin offering; beside the continual burnt offering, his meat offering, and his drink offering.

35 On the eighth day ye shall have a [a]solemn assembly:[6116] ye shall do no servile work *therein*:

36 But ye shall offer a burnt offering, a sacrifice made by fire, of a sweet savour unto the LORD: one bullock, one ram, seven lambs of the first year without blemish:

37 Their meat offering and their drink offerings for the bullock, for the ram, and for the lambs, *shall be* according to their number, after the manner:

38 And one goat *for* a sin offering; beside the continual burnt offering, and his meat offering, and his drink offering.

39 These *things* ye shall [I]do unto the LORD in your [a]set feasts,[4150] beside your [b]vows,[5088] and your freewill offerings,[5071] for your burnt offerings, and for your meat offerings,[4503] and for your drink offerings, and for your peace offerings.[8002]

40 And Moses told the children[1121] of Israel according to all that the LORD commanded[6680] Moses.

Women's Vows

30 And Moses spake[1696] unto [a]the heads[7218] of the tribes[4294] concerning the children[1121] of Israel, saying, This *is* the thing[1697] which the LORD hath commanded.[6680]

2 [a]If a man[376] vow[5087] a vow[5088] unto the LORD, or [b]swear[7650] an oath[7621] to bind his soul[5315] with a bond; he shall not [I][c]break[2490] his word,[1697] he shall [d]do[6213] according to all that proceedeth out of his mouth.[6310]

3 If a woman[802] also vow a vow unto the LORD, and bind *herself* by a bond, *being* in her father's[1] house[1004] in her youth;

4 And her father hear[8085] her vow, and her bond wherewith she hath bound her soul, and her father shall hold his peace at her: then all her vows[5088] shall stand, and every bond wherewith she hath bound her soul shall stand.

5 But if her father disallow her in the day[3117] that he heareth;[8085] not any of her vows, or of her bonds wherewith she hath bound her soul, shall stand: and the LORD shall forgive[5545] her, because her father disallowed her.

6 And if she had at all an husband,[376] when [I][a]she vowed, or uttered ought out of her lips,[8193] wherewith she bound her soul;

7 And her husband heard[8085] *it,* and held his peace[2790] at her in the day that he heard *it:* then her vows shall stand, and her bonds wherewith she bound her soul shall stand.

8 But if her husband [a]disallowed her on the day that he heard *it;* then he shall make her vow which she vowed, and that which she uttered with her lips, wherewith she bound her soul, of none effect: and the LORD shall forgive her.

9 But every vow of a widow, and of her that is divorced,[1644] wherewith they

29:35 [a]Lev. 23:36

39 [I]Or, *offer* [a]Lev. 23:2; 1Chr. 23:31; 2Chr. 31:3; Ezra 3:5; Neh. 10:33; Isa. 1:14 [b]Lev. 7:11, 16; 22:21, 23

30:1 [a]Num. 1:4, 16; 7:2

2 [I]Hebr. *profane* [a]Lev. 27:2; Deut. 23:21; Judg. 11:30, 35; Eccl. 5:4 [b]Lev. 5:4; Matt. 14:9; Acts 23:14 [c]Job 22:27; Ps. 22:25; 50:14; 66:13, 14; 116:14, 18; Nah. 1:15 [d]Ps. 55:20

6 [I]Hebr. *her vows were upon her* [a]Ps. 56:12

8 [a]Gen. 3:16

have bound their souls,[5315] shall stand against her.

10 And if she vowed in her husband's house, or bound her soul by a bond with an oath;

11 And her husband heard *it,* and held his peace at her, *and* disallowed her not: then all her vows shall stand, and every bond wherewith she bound her soul shall stand.

12 But if her husband hath utterly made them void[6565] on the day he heard *them; then* whatsoever proceeded out of her lips concerning her vows, or concerning the bond of her soul, shall not stand: her husband hath made them void; and the LORD shall forgive her.

13 Every vow, and every binding oath to afflict the soul, her husband may establish it, or her husband may make it void.

14 But if her husband altogether hold his peace at her from day to day; then he establisheth[6965] all her vows, or all her bonds, which *are* upon her: he confirmeth them, because he held his peace at her in the day that he heard *them.*

15 But if he shall any ways make them void after that he hath heard *them;* then he shall bear[5375] her iniquity.[5771]

16 These *are* the statutes,[2706] which the LORD commanded Moses, between a man and his wife,[802] between the father and his daughter, *being yet* in her youth in her father's house.

War Against Midian

31 And the LORD spake[1696] unto Moses, saying,

2 [a]Avenge the children[1121] of Israel of the Midianites: afterward shalt thou [b]be gathered[622] unto thy people.[5971]

3 And Moses spake unto the people, saying, Arm some of yourselves unto the war,[6635] and let them go against the Midianites, and avenge the LORD of Midian.

4 [l]Of every tribe[4294] a thousand, throughout all the tribes[4294] of Israel, shall ye send to the war.

5 So there were delivered out of the thousands[505] of Israel, a thousand of *every* tribe, twelve thousand armed for war.

6 And Moses sent them to the war, a thousand of *every* tribe, them and Phinehas the son[1121] of Eleazar the priest,[3548] to the war, with the holy[6944] instruments, and [a]the trumpets to blow in his hand.[3027]

7 And they warred[6633] against the Midianites, as the LORD commanded[6680] Moses; and [a]they slew[2026] all the [b]males.[2145]

8 And they slew the kings of Midian, beside the rest of them that were slain;[2491] *namely,* [a]Evi, and Rekem, and Zur, and Hur, and Reba, five kings[4428] of Midian: [b]Balaam also the son of Beor they slew with the sword.[2719]

9 And the children of Israel took *all* the women of Midian captives,[7617] and their little ones,[2945] and took the spoil of all their cattle, and all their flocks, and all their goods.

10 And they burnt[8313] all their cities wherein they dwelt, and all their goodly[2896] castles, with fire.

11 And [a]they took all the spoil, and all the prey, *both* of men[120] and of beasts.

12 And they brought the captives,[7628] and the prey, and the spoil, unto Moses, and Eleazar the priest, and unto the congregation[5712] of the children of Israel, unto the camp[4264] at the plains[6160] of Moab, which *are* by Jordan *near* Jericho.

13 And Moses, and Eleazar the priest, and all the princes[5387] of the congregation, went forth to meet them without the camp.

14 And Moses was wroth[7107] with the officers[6485] of the host,[2428] *with* the captains over thousands, and captains over hundreds, which came from the [l]battle.

15 And Moses said[559] unto them, Have ye saved [a]all the women alive?

16 Behold, [a]these caused the children of Israel, through the [b]counsel[1697] of Balaam, to commit trespass[4604] against the LORD in the matter[1697] of Peor, and

2 [a]Num. 25:17 [b]Num. 27:13

4 [l]Hebr. *A thousand of a tribe*

6 [a]Num. 10:9

7 [a]Deut. 20:13; Judg. 21:11; 1Sam. 27:9; 1Kgs. 11:15, 16 [b]Judg. 6:1, 2, 33

8 [a]Josh. 13:21 [b]Josh. 13:22

11 [a]Deut. 20:14

14 [l]Hebr. *host of war*

15 [a]Deut. 20:14; 1Sam. 15:3

16 [a]Num. 25:2 [b]Num. 24:14; 2Pet. 2:15; Rev. 2:14

[c]there was a plague among the congregation of the LORD.

17 Now therefore [a]kill every male among the little ones, and kill every woman[802] that hath known[3045] man by lying with ǀhim.

18 But all the women children,[2945] that have not known a man by lying with him, keep alive for yourselves.

19 And [a]do ye abide without the camp seven days: whosoever hath killed[2026] any person,[5315] and [b]whosoever hath touched[5060] any slain, purify[2398] *both* yourselves and your captives on the third day,[3117] and on the seventh day.

20 And purify all *your* raiment, and all ǀthat is made of skins, and all work of goats' *hair,* and all things made of wood.

Division of the Booty

21 And Eleazar the priest said unto the men[582] of war which went to the battle, This *is* the ordinance[2708] of the law which the LORD commanded Moses;

22 Only the gold, and the silver, the brass, the iron, the tin, and the lead,

23 Every thing[1697] that may abide the fire, ye shall make *it* go through the fire, and it shall be clean:[2891] nevertheless it shall be purified[2398] [a]with the water of separation: and all that abideth not the fire ye shall make go through the water.

24 [a]And ye shall wash[3526] your clothes on the seventh day, and ye shall be clean, and afterward ye shall come into the camp.

25 And the LORD spake[559] unto Moses, saying,

26 Take[5375] the sum[7218] of the prey ǀthat was taken, *both* of man[120] and of beast, thou, and Eleazar the priest, and the chief[7218] fathers[1] of the congregation:

27 And [a]divide the prey into two parts; between them that took the war upon them, who went out to battle,[6635] and between all the congregation:

28 And levy a tribute unto the LORD of the men of war which went out to battle; [a]one soul[5315] of five hundred, *both* of the persons,[120] and of the beeves, and of the asses, and of the sheep:

29 Take *it* of their half, and give *it* unto Eleazar the priest, *for* an heave offering[8641] of the LORD.

30 And of the children of Israel's half, thou shalt take [a]one portion of fifty, of the persons, of the beeves, of the asses, and of the ǀflocks, of all manner of beasts, and give them unto the Levites, [b]which keep[8104] the charge[4931] of the tabernacle[4908] of the LORD.

31 And Moses and Eleazar the priest did[6213] as the LORD commanded Moses.

32 And the booty,[4455] *being* the rest[3499] of the prey which the men of war had caught, was six hundred thousand and seventy thousand and five thousand sheep,

33 And threescore and twelve thousand beeves,

34 And threescore and one thousand asses,

35 And thirty and two thousand persons in all, of women that had not known man by lying with him.

36 And the half, *which was* the portion of them that went out to war, was in number three hundred thousand and seven and thirty thousand and five hundred sheep:

37 And the LORD's tribute[4371] of the sheep was six hundred and threescore and fifteen.

38 And the beeves *were* thirty and six thousand; of which the LORD's tribute *was* threescore and twelve.

39 And the asses *were* thirty thousand and five hundred; of which the LORD's tribute *was* threescore and one.

40 And the persons *were* sixteen thousand; of which the LORD's tribute *was* thirty and two persons.

41 And Moses gave the tribute, *which was* the LORD's heave offering, unto Eleazar the priest, [a]as the LORD commanded Moses.

42 And of the children of Israel's half, which Moses divided from the men that warred,

43 (Now the half *that pertained unto* the congregation was three hundred thou-

16 [c]Num. 25:9
17 ǀHebr. *a male* [a]Judg. 21:11
19 [a]Num. 5:2 [b]Num. 19:11
20 ǀHebr. *instrument,* or, *vessel of skins*
23 [a]Num. 19:9, 17
24 [a]Lev. 11:25
26 ǀHebr. *of the captivity*
27 [a]Josh. 22:8; 1Sam. 30:24
28 [a]Num. 18:26; 31:30, 47
30 ǀOr, *goats* [a]Num. 31:42-47 [b]Num. 3:7, 8, 25, 31, 36; 18:3, 4
41 [a]Num. 18:8, 19

sand and thirty thousand *and* seven thousand and five hundred sheep,

44 And thirty and six thousand beeves,

45 And thirty thousand asses and five hundred,

46 And sixteen thousand persons;)

47 Even [a]of the children of Israel's half, Moses took one portion of fifty, *both* of man[120] and of beast, and gave them unto the Levites, which kept[8104] the charge of the tabernacle of the LORD; as the LORD commanded Moses.

48 And the officers which *were* over thousands of the host,[6635] the captains of thousands, and captains of hundreds, came near[5066] unto Moses:

49 And they said unto Moses, Thy servants[5650] have taken the sum of the men of war which *are* under our [I]charge, and there lacketh[6485] not one man[376] of us.

50 We have therefore brought[7126] an oblation[7133] for the LORD, what every man hath [I]gotten, of jewels of gold, chains, and bracelets, rings, earrings, and tablets,[3558] [a]to make an atonement[3722] for our souls[5315] before the LORD.

51 And Moses and Eleazar the priest took the gold of them, *even* all wrought jewels.

52 And all the gold of the [I]offering that they offered up to the LORD, of the captains of thousands, and of the captains of hundreds, was sixteen thousand seven hundred and fifty shekels.

53 (*For* [a]the men of war had taken spoil, every man for himself.)

54 And Moses and Eleazar the priest took the gold of the captains[8269] of thousands and of hundreds, and brought it into the tabernacle[168] of the congregation,[4150] [a]*for* a memorial for the children of Israel before the LORD.

Three Tribes Settle East of the Jordan

32 Now the children[1121] of Reuben and the children of Gad had a very great multitude of cattle: and when they saw[7200] the land of [a]Jazer, and the land of Gilead, that, behold, the place *was* a place for cattle;

2 The children of Gad and the children of Reuben came and spake[559] unto Moses, and to Eleazar the priest,[3548] and unto the princes[5387] of the congregation,[5712] saying,

3 Ataroth, and Dibon, and Jazer, and [a]Nimrah, and Heshbon, and Elealeh, and [b]Shebam, and Nebo, and [c]Beon,

4 *Even* the country[776] [a]which the LORD smote[5221] before the congregation of Israel, *is* a land for cattle, and thy servants[5650] have cattle:

5 Wherefore, said[559] they, if we have found grace[2580] in thy sight, let this land be given unto thy servants for a possession,[272] *and* bring us not over Jordan.

6 And Moses said unto the children of Gad and to the children of Reuben, Shall your brethren[251] go to war, and shall ye sit here?

7 And wherefore [I]discourage[5106] ye the heart[3820] of the children of Israel from going over[5674] into the land which the LORD hath given them?

8 Thus did[6213] your fathers,[1] [a]when I sent them from Kadesh–barnea [b]to see the land.

9 For [a]when they went up[5927] unto the valley of Eshcol, and saw the land, they discouraged the heart of the children of Israel, that they should not go into the land which the LORD had given them.

10 [a]And the LORD's anger[639] was kindled[2734] the same time, and he sware,[7650] saying,

11 Surely none of the men[582] that came up[5927] out of Egypt, [a]from twenty years old and upward, shall see the land which I sware unto Abraham, unto Isaac, and unto Jacob; because [b]they have not [I]wholly followed me:

12 Save Caleb the son[1121] of Jephunneh the Kenezite, and Joshua the son of Nun: [a]for they have wholly followed[4390,310] the LORD.

13 And the LORD's anger was kindled against Israel, and he made them [a]wander in the wilderness forty years, until

47 [a]Num. 31:30
49 [I]Hebr. *hand*
50 [I]Hebr. *found* [a]Ex. 30:12, 16
52 [I]Hebr. *heave offering*
53 [a]Deut. 20:14
54 [a]Ex. 30:16
1 [a]Num. 21:32; Josh. 13:25; 2Sam. 24:5
3 [a]Num. 32:36, *Beth-nimrah* [b]Num. 32:38, *Shibmah* [c]Num. 32:38, *Baal-meon*
4 [a]Num. 21:24, 34
7 [I]Hebr. *break*
8 [a]Num. 13:3, 26 [b]Deut. 1:22
9 [a]Num. 13:24, 31; Deut. 1:24, 28
10 [a]Num. 14:11, 21; Deut. 1:34
11 [I]Hebr. *fulfilled after me* [a]Num. 14:28, 29; Deut. 1:35 [b]Num. 14:24, 30
12 [a]Num. 14:24; Deut. 1:36; Josh. 14:8, 9
13 [a]Num. 14:33-35

[b]all the generation,[1755] that had done[6213] evil[7451] in the sight of the LORD, was consumed.[8552]

14 And, behold, ye are risen up in your fathers'[1] stead, an increase of sinful[2400] men, to augment yet the [a]fierce anger of the LORD toward Israel.

15 For if ye [a]turn away[7725] from after him, he will yet again leave them in the wilderness; and ye shall destroy[7843] all this people.[5971]

16 And they came near[5066] unto him, and said, We will build sheepfolds here for our cattle, and cities for our little ones:[2945]

17 But [a]we ourselves will go ready armed before the children of Israel, until we have brought them unto their place: and our little ones shall dwell in the fenced cities because of the inhabitants of the land.

18 [a]We will not return[7725] unto our houses,[1004] until the children of Israel have inherited every man[376] his inheritance.[5159]

19 For we will not inherit[5157] with them on yonder side Jordan, or forward; [a]because our inheritance is fallen to us on this side Jordan eastward.

20 And [a]Moses said unto them, If ye will do[6213] this thing,[1697] if ye will go armed before the LORD to war,

21 And will go all of you armed over Jordan before the LORD, until he hath driven out his enemies from before him,

22 And [a]the land be subdued before the LORD: then afterward [b]ye shall return, and be guiltless[5355] before the LORD, and before Israel; and [c]this land shall be your possession before the LORD.

23 But if ye will not do so, behold, ye have sinned[2398] against the LORD: and be sure[3045] [a]your sin[2403] will find you out.

24 [a]Build you cities for your little ones, and folds for your sheep; and do that which hath proceeded out of your mouth.[6310]

25 And the children of Gad and the children of Reuben spake unto Moses, saying, Thy servants will do as my lord[113] commandeth.[6680]

26 [a]Our little ones, our wives,[802] our flocks, and all our cattle, shall be there in the cities of Gilead:

27 [a]But thy servants will pass over, every man armed for war,[6635] before the LORD to battle, as my lord saith.

28 So [a]concerning them Moses commanded[6680] Eleazar the priest, and Joshua the son of Nun, and the chief[7218] fathers of the tribes[4294] of the children of Israel:

29 And Moses said unto them, If the children of Gad and the children of Reuben will pass with you over Jordan, every man armed to battle, before the LORD, and the land shall be subdued before you; then ye shall give them the land of Gilead for a possession:

30 But if they will not pass over with you armed, they shall have possessions among you in the land of Canaan.

31 And the children of Gad and the children of Reuben answered, saying, As the LORD hath said[1696] unto thy servants, so will we do.

32 We will pass over armed before the LORD into the land of Canaan, that the possession of our inheritance on this side Jordan *may be* ours.

33 And [a]Moses gave unto them, *even* to the children of Gad, and to the children of Reuben, and unto half the tribe[7626] of Manasseh the son of Joseph, [b]the kingdom[4467] of Sihon king of the Amorites, and the kingdom of Og king[4428] of Bashan, the land, with the cities thereof in the coasts, *even* the cities of the country round about.

34 And the children of Gad built [a]Dibon, and Ataroth, and [b]Aroer,

35 And Atroth, Shophan, and [a]Jaazer, and Jogbehah,

36 And [a]Beth–nimrah, and Beth–haran, [b]fenced cities: and folds for sheep.

37 And the children of Reuben [a]built Heshbon, and Elealeh, and Kirjathaim,

38 And [a]Nebo, and [b]Baal–meon ([c]their names being changed), and Shibmah: and [I]gave other names unto the cities which they builded.

39 And the children of [a]Machir the son of Manasseh went to Gilead, and

13 [b]Num. 26:64, 65
14 [a]Deut. 1:34
15 [a]Deut. 30:17; Josh. 22:16, 18; 2Chr. 7:19; 15:2
17 [a]Josh. 4:12, 13
18 [a]Josh. 22:4
19 [a]Num. 32:33; Josh. 12:1; 13:8
20 [a]Deut. 3:18; Josh. 1:14; 4:12, 13
22 [a]Deut. 3:20; Josh. 11:23; 18:1 [b]Josh. 22:4 [c]Deut. 3:12, 15, 16, 18; Josh. 1:15; 13:8, 32; 22:4, 9
23 [a]Gen. 4:7; 44:16; Isa. 59:12
24 [a]Num. 32:16, 34-42
26 [a]Josh. 1:14
27 [a]Josh. 4:12
28 [a]Josh. 1:13
33 [a]Deut. 3:12-17; 29:8; Josh. 12:6; 13:8; 22:4 [b]Num. 21:24, 33, 35
34 [a]Num. 33:45, 46 [b]Deut. 2:36
35 [a]Num. 32:1, 3, *Jazer*
36 [a]Num. 32:3, *Nimrah* [b]Num. 32:24
37 [a]Num. 21:27
38 [I]Hebr. *they called by names the names of the cities* [a]Isa. 46:1 [b]Num. 22:41 [c]Num. 32:3; Ex. 23:13; Josh. 23:7
39 [a]Gen. 50:23

took it, and dispossessed[3423] the Amorite which *was* in it.

40 And Moses [a]gave Gilead unto Machir the son of Manasseh; and he dwelt therein.

41 And [a]Jair the son of Manasseh went and took the small towns thereof, and called[7121] them [b]Havoth–jair.

42 And Nobah went and took Kenath, and the villages thereof, and called it Nobah, after his own name.

Israel's Wilderness Itinerary

33 These *are* the journeys of the children[1121] of Israel, which went forth out of the land of Egypt with their armies[6635] under the hand[3027] of Moses and Aaron.

2 And Moses wrote their goings out according to their journeys by the commandment[6310] of the LORD: and these *are* the journeys according to their goings out.

3 And they [a]departed from Rameses in [b]the first[7223] month, on the fifteenth day of the first month; on the morrow after the passover[6453] the children of Israel went out [c]with an high hand in the sight of all the Egyptians.

4 For the Egyptians buried[6912] all *their* firstborn, [a]which the LORD had smitten[5221] among them: [b]upon their gods[430] also the LORD executed[6213] judgments.[8201]

5 [a]And the children of Israel removed from Rameses, and pitched in Succoth.

6 And they departed from [a]Succoth, and pitched in Etham, which *is* in the edge of the wilderness.

7 And [a]they removed from Etham, and turned again[7725] unto Pi–hahiroth, which *is* before Baal–zephon: and they pitched before Migdol.

8 And they departed from before Pi–hahiroth, and [a]passed[5674] through the midst of the sea into the wilderness, and went three days'[3117] journey in the wilderness of Etham, and pitched in Marah.

9 And they removed from Marah, and [a]came unto Elim: and in Elim *were* twelve fountains of water, and threescore and ten palm trees; and they pitched there.

10 And they removed from Elim, and encamped by the Red sea.

11 And they removed from the Red sea, and encamped in the [a]wilderness of Sin.

12 And they took their journey out of the wilderness of Sin, and encamped in Dophkah.

13 And they departed from Dophkah, and encamped in Alush.

14 And they removed from Alush, and encamped at [a]Rephidim, where was no water for the people[5971] to drink.

15 And they departed from Rephidim, and pitched in the [a]wilderness of Sinai.

16 And they removed from the desert of Sinai, and pitched [a]at [I]Kibroth– hattaavah.

17 And they departed from Kibroth–hattaavah, and [a]encamped at Hazeroth.

18 And they departed from Hazeroth, and pitched in [a]Rithmah.

19 And they departed from Rithmah, and pitched at Rimmon–parez.

20 And they departed from Rimmon–parez, and pitched in Libnah.

21 And they removed from Libnah, and pitched at Rissah.

22 And they journeyed[5265] from Rissah and pitched in Kehelathah.

23 And they went from Kehelathah, and pitched in mount Shapher.

24 And they removed from mount Shapher, and encamped in Haradah.

25 And they removed from Haradah, and pitched in Makheloth.

26 And they removed from Makheloth, and encamped at Tahath.

27 And they departed from Tahath, and pitched at Tarah.

28 And they removed from Tarah, and pitched in Mithcah.

29 And they went from Mithcah, and pitched in Hashmonah.

30 And they departed from Hashmonah, and [a]encamped at Moseroth.

40 [a]Deut. 3:12, 13, 15; Josh. 13:31; 17:1
41 [a]Deut. 3:14; Josh. 13:30; 1Chr. 2:21-23 [b]Judg. 10:4; 1Kgs. 4:13
3 [a]Ex. 12:37 [b]Ex. 12:2; 13:4 [c]Ex. 14:8
4 [a]Ex. 12:29 [b]Ex. 12:12; 18:11; Isa. 19:1; Rev. 12:8
5 [a]Ex. 12:37
6 [a]Ex. 13:20
7 [a]Ex. 14:2, 9
8 [a]Ex. 14:22; 15:22, 23
9 [a]Ex. 15:27
11 [a]Ex. 16:1
14 [a]Ex. 17:1; 19:2
15 [a]Ex. 16:1; 19:1, 2
16 [I]That is, *The graves of lust* [a]Num. 11:34
17 [a]Num. 11:35
18 [a]Num. 12:16
30 [a]Deut. 10:6

31 And they departed from Moseroth, and pitched in Bene–jaakan.

32 And they removed from [a]Bene–jaakan, and [b]encamped[2583] at Hor–hagidgad.

33 And they went from Hor–hagidgad, and pitched in Jotbathah.

34 And they removed from Jotbathah, and encamped at Ebronah.

35 And they departed from Ebronah, [a]and encamped at Ezion–gaber.

36 And they removed from Ezion–gaber, and pitched in the [a]wilderness of Zin, which *is* Kadesh.

37 And they removed from [a]Kadesh, and pitched in mount Hor, in the edge of the land of Edom.

38 And [a]Aaron the priest[3548] went up[5927] into mount Hor at the commandment of the LORD, and died there, in the fortieth year after the children of Israel were come out of the land of Egypt, in the first *day* of the fifth month.

39 And Aaron *was* an hundred and twenty and three years old when he died[4194] in mount Hor.

40 And [a]king[4428] Arad the Canaanite, which dwelt in the south in the land of Canaan, heard[8085] of the coming of the children of Israel.

41 And they departed from mount [a]Hor, and pitched in Zalmonah.

42 And they departed from Zalmonah, and pitched in Punon.

43 And they departed from Punon, and [a]pitched in Oboth.

44 And [a]they departed from Oboth, and [I][b]pitched in Ije–abarim, in the border of Moab.

45 And they departed from Iim, and pitched [a]in Dibon–gad.

46 And they removed from Dibon–gad, and encamped in Almon–[a]diblathaim.

47 And they removed from Almon–diblathaim, [a]and pitched in the mountains of Abarim, before Nebo.

48 And they departed from the mountains of Abarim, and [a]pitched in the plains[6160] of Moab by Jordan *near* Jericho.

49 And they pitched by Jordan, from

32 [a]Gen. 36:27; Deut. 10:6; 1Chr. 1:42 [b]Deut. 10:7

35 [a]Deut. 2:8; 1Kgs. 9:26; 22:48

36 [a]Num. 20:1; 27:14

37 [a]Num. 20:22, 23; 21:4

38 [a]Num. 20:25, 28; Deut. 10:6; 32:50

40 [a]Num. 21:1-3

41 [a]Num. 21:4

43 [a]Num. 21:10

44 [I]Or, *Heaps of Abarim* [a]Num. 21:11 [b]Num. 21:11

45 [a]Num. 32:34

46 [a]Jer. 48:22; Ezek. 6:14

47 [a]Num. 21:20; Deut. 32:49

48 [a]Num. 22:1

49 [I]Or, *The plains of Shittim* [a]Num. 25:1; Josh. 2:1

51 [a]Deut. 7:1, 2; 9:1; Josh. 3:17

52 [a]Ex. 23:24, 33; 34:13; Deut. 7:2, 5; 12:3; Josh. 11:12; Judg. 2:2

54 [I]Hebr. *multiply his inheritance* [II]Hebr. *diminish his inheritance* [a]Num. 26:53-55

55 [a]Josh. 23:13; Judg. 2:3; Ps. 106:34, 36; Ezek. 28:24

2 [a]Gen. 17:8; Deut. 1:7; Ps. 78:55; 105:11; Ezek. 47:14

Beth–jesimoth *even* [I][a]unto Abel–shittim in the plains of Moab.

Instructions for Taking Over Canaan

50 And the LORD spake[1696] unto Moses in the plains of Moab by Jordan *near* Jericho, saying,

51 Speak unto the children of Israel, and say[559] unto them, [a]When ye are passed over Jordan into the land of Canaan;

52 [a]Then ye shall drive out[3423] all the inhabitants of the land from before you, and destroy[6] all their pictures,[4906] and destroy all their molten images, and quite pluck down[8045] all their high places:[1116]

53 And ye shall dispossess[3423] *the inhabitants of* the land, and dwell therein: for I have given you the land to possess[3423] it.

54 And [a]ye shall divide the land by lot for an inheritance[5157] among your families:[4940] *and* to the more ye shall [I]give the more inheritance,[5159] and to the fewer ye shall [II]give the less inheritance: every man's *inheritance* shall be in the place where his lot falleth; according to the tribes[4294] of your fathers[1] ye shall inherit.

55 But if ye will not drive out the inhabitants of the land from before you; then it shall come to pass, that those which ye let remain of them *shall be* [a]pricks in your eyes, and thorns in your sides, and shall vex[6887] you in the land wherein ye dwell.

56 Moreover it shall come to pass, *that* I shall do unto you, as I thought to do unto them.

34 And the LORD spake[1696] unto Moses, saying,

2 Command[6680] the children[1121] of Israel, and say[559] unto them, When ye come into [a]the land of Canaan; (this *is* the land that shall fall unto you for an inheritance,[5159] *even* the land of Canaan with the coasts thereof:)

3 Then [a]your south quarter shall be from the wilderness of Zin along by the coast of Edom, and your south border shall be the outmost coast of [b]the salt sea eastward:

4 And your border shall turn from the south [a]to the ascent of Akrabbim, and pass on to Zin: and the going forth thereof shall be from the south [b]to Kadesh–barnea, and shall go on to [c]Hazar– addar, and pass on to Azmon:

5 And the border shall fetch a compass[5437] from Azmon [a]unto the river of Egypt, and the goings out of it shall be at the sea.

6 And *as for* the western border, ye shall even have the great sea for a border: this shall be your west border.

7 And this shall be your north border: from the great sea ye shall point out for you [a]mount Hor:

8 From mount Hor ye shall point out *your border* [a]unto the entrance of Hamath; and the goings forth of the border shall be to [b]Zedad:

9 And the border shall go on to Ziphron, and the goings out of it shall be at [a]Hazar–enan: this shall be your north border.

10 And ye shall point out your east border from Hazar–enan to Shepham:

11 And the coast shall go down from Shepham [a]to Riblah, on the east side of Ain; and the border shall descend, and shall reach unto the [I]side of the sea [b]of Chinnereth eastward:

12 And the border shall go down to Jordan, and the goings out of it shall be at [a]the salt sea: this shall be your land with the coasts thereof round about.

13 And Moses commanded[6680] the children of Israel, saying, [a]This *is* the land which ye shall inherit[5157] by lot, which the LORD commanded to give unto the nine tribes,[4294] and to the half tribe:

14 [a]For the tribe of the children of Reuben according to the house[1004] of their fathers,[1] and the tribe of the children of Gad according to the house of their fathers, have received *their inheritance;* and half the tribe of Manasseh have received their inheritance:

3 [a]Josh. 15:1; Ezek. 47:13 [b]Gen. 14:3; Josh. 15:2

4 [a]Josh. 15:3 [b]Num. 13:26; 32:8 [c]Josh. 15:3, 4

5 [a]Gen. 15:18; Josh. 15:4, 47; 1Kgs. 8:65; Isa. 27:12

7 [a]Num. 33:37

8 [a]Num. 13:21; 2Kgs. 14:25 [b]Ezek. 47:15

9 [a]Ezek. 47:17

11 [I]Hebr. *shoulder* [a]2Kgs. 23:33; Jer. 39:5, 6 [b]Deut. 3:17; Josh. 11:2; 19:35; Matt. 14:34; Luke 5:1

12 [a]Num. 34:3

13 [a]Num. 34:1; Josh. 14:1, 2

14 [a]Num. 32:33; Josh. 14:2, 3

17 [a]Josh. 14:1; 19:51

18 [a]Num. 1:4, 16

15 The two tribes and the half tribe have received their inheritance on this side Jordan *near* Jericho eastward, toward the sunrising.

16 And the LORD spake unto Moses, saying,

17 These *are* the names of the men[582] which shall divide[5157] the land unto you: [a]Eleazar the priest,[3548] and Joshua the son[1121] of Nun.

18 And ye shall take one [a]prince[5387] of every tribe, to divide the land by inheritance.[5157]

19 And the names of the men *are* these: Of the tribe of Judah, Caleb the son of Jephunneh.

20 And of the tribe of the children of Simeon, Shemuel the son of Ammihud.

21 Of the tribe of Benjamin, Elidad the son of Chislon.

22 And the prince[5387] of the tribe of the children of Dan, Bukki the son of Jogli.

23 The prince of the children of Joseph, for the tribe of the children of Manasseh, Hanniel the son of Ephod.

24 And the prince of the tribe of the children of Ephraim, Kemuel the son of Shiphtan.

25 And the prince of the tribe of the children of Zebulum, Elizaphan the son of Parnach.

26 And the prince of the tribe of the children of Issachar, Paltiel the son of Azzan.

27 And the prince of the tribe of the children of Asher, Ahihud the son of Shelomi.

28 And the prince of the tribe of the children of Naphtali, Pedahel the son of Ammihud.

29 These *are they* whom the LORD commanded to divide the inheritance unto the children of Israel in the land of Canaan.

Cities for the Levites

35 And the LORD spake[1696] unto Moses in the plains[6160] of Moab by Jordan *near* Jericho, saying,

2 [a]Command[6680] the children[1121] of Israel, that they give unto the Levites of the inheritance[5159] of their pos session[272] cities to dwell in; and ye shall give *also* unto the Levites suburbs for the cities round about them.

3 And the cities shall they have to dwell in; and the suburbs of them shall be for their cattle, and for their goods, and for all their beasts.[2416]

4 And the suburbs of the cities, which ye shall give unto the Levites, *shall reach* from the wall of the city and outward a thousand cubits round about.

5 And ye shall measure from without the city on the east side two thousand cubits, and on the south side two thousand cubits, and on the west side two thousand cubits, and on the north side two thousand cubits; and the city *shall be* in the midst: this shall be to them the suburbs of the cities.

6 And among the cities which ye shall give unto the Levites *there shall be* [a]six cities for refuge, which ye shall appoint for the manslayer,[7523] that he may flee thither: and [I]to them ye shall add forty and two cities.

7 *So* all the cities which ye shall give to the Levites *shall be* [a]forty and eight cities: them *shall ye give* with their suburbs.

8 And the cities which ye shall give *shall be* [a]of the possession of the children of Israel: from *them that have* many ye shall give many; but [b]from *them that have* few ye shall give few: every one[376] shall give of his cities unto the Levites accord ing to his inheritance which [I]he inheriteth.

The Cities of Refuge

9 And the LORD spake unto Moses, saying,

10 Speak[1696] unto the children of Israel, and say[559] unto them, [a]When ye be come over[5674] Jordan into the land of Canaan;

11 Then [a]ye shall appoint you cities to be cities of refuge for you; that the slayer[7523] may flee thither, which killeth[5221] any person[5315] [I]at unawares.[7684]

12 [a]And they shall be unto you cities for refuge from the avenger;[1350] that the manslayer die[4191] not, until he stand before the congregation[5712] in judgment.[4941]

13 And of these cities which ye shall give [a]six cities shall ye have for refuge.

14 [a]Ye shall give three cities on this side Jordan, and three cities shall ye give in the land of Canaan, *which* shall be cities of refuge.

15 These six cities shall be a refuge, *both* for the children of Israel, and [a]for the stranger,[1616] and for the sojourner[8453] among them: that every one that killeth any person unawares may flee thither.

16 [a]And if he smite[5221] him with an instrument of iron, so that he die, he *is* a murderer: the murderer shall surely be put to death.[4191]

17 And if he smite him [I]with throwing a stone, wherewith he may die, and he die, he *is* a murderer: the murderer shall surely be put to death.

18 Or *if* he smite him with an hand[3027] weapon of wood, wherewith he may die, and he die, he *is* a murderer: the murderer shall surely be put to death.

19 [a]The revenger[1350] of blood[1818] himself shall slay[4191] the murderer: when he meeteth him, he shall slay him.

20 But [a]if he thrust him of hatred, or hurl at him [b]by laying of wait, that he die;

21 Or in enmity[342] smite him with his hand, that he die: he that smote *him* shall surely be put to death; *for* he *is* a murderer: the revenger of blood shall slay the murderer, when he meeteth him.

22 But if he thrust him suddenly [a]without enmity, or have cast upon him any thing without laying of wait,

23 Or with any stone, wherewith a man may die, seeing[7200] *him* not, and cast[5307] *it* upon him, that he die, and *was* not his enemy, neither sought his harm:[7451]

2 [a]Josh. 14:3, 4; 21:2; Ezek. 45:1-5; 48:8-10

6 [I]Hebr. *above them ye shall give* [a]Num. 35:13; Deut. 4:41; Josh. 20:2, 7, 8; 21:3, 13, 21, 27, 32, 36, 38

7 [a]Josh. 21:41

8 [I]Hebr. *they inherit* [a]Josh. 21:3 [b]Num. 26:54

10 [a]Deut. 19:2; Josh. 20:2

11 [I]Hebr. *by error* [a]Ex. 21:13

12 [a]Deut. 19:6; Josh. 20:3, 5, 6

13 [a]Num. 35:6

14 [a]Deut. 4:41; Josh. 20:8

15 [a]Num. 15:16

16 [a]Ex. 21:12, 14; Lev. 24:17; Deut. 19:11, 12

17 [I]Hebr. *with a stone of the hand*

19 [a]Num. 35:21, 24, 27; Deut. 19:6, 12; Josh. 20:3, 5

20 [a]Gen. 4:8; 2Sam. 3:27; 20:10; 1Kgs. 2:31, 32 [b]Ex. 21:14; Deut. 19:11

22 [a]Ex. 21:13

24 Then [a]the congregation shall judge[8199] between the slayer and the revenger of blood according to these judgments:[4941]

25 And the congregation shall deliver[5337] the slayer out of the hand of the revenger of blood, and the congregation shall restore[7725] him to the city of his refuge, whither he was fled: and [a]he shall abide in it unto the death[4194] of the high priest,[3548] [b]which was anointed[4886] with the holy[6944] oil.[8081]

26 But if the slayer shall at any time come without the border of the city of his refuge, whither he was fled;

27 And the revenger of blood find him without the borders of the city of his refuge, and the revenger of blood kill[7523] the slayer; [I][a]he shall not be guilty of blood:

28 Because he should have remained in the city of his refuge until the death of the high priest: but after the death of the high priest the slayer shall return into the land of his possession.

29 So these *things* shall be for [a]a statute[2708] of judgment unto you throughout your generations[1755] in all your dwellings.[4186]

30 Whoso killeth any person, the murderer shall be put to death by the [a]mouth[6310] of witnesses: but one witness shall not testify against any person *to cause him* to die.

31 Moreover ye shall take no satisfaction[3724] for the life[5315] of a murderer, which *is* [I]guilty[7563] of death: but he shall be surely put to death.[4191]

32 And ye shall take no satisfaction for him that is fled to the city of his refuge, that he should come again[7725] to dwell in the land, until the death of the priest.

33 So ye shall not pollute[2610] the land wherein ye *are:* for blood [a]it defileth[2610] [I]the land: and the land cannot be cleansed[3722] of the blood that is shed[8210] therein, but [b]by the blood of him that shed it.

34 [a]Defile[2930] not therefore the land which ye shall inhabit, wherein I dwell:[7931] for [b]I the LORD dwell among the children of Israel.

24 [a]Num. 35:12; Josh. 20:6

25 [a]Josh. 20:6 [b]Ex. 29:7; Lev. 4:3; 21:10

27 [I]Hebr. *no blood shall be to him* [a]Ex. 22:2

29 [a]Num. 27:11

30 [a]Deut. 17:6; 19:15; Matt. 18:16; 2Cor. 13:1; Heb. 10:28

31 [I]Hebr. *faulty to die*

33 [I]Hebr. *there can be no expiation for the land* [a]Ps. 106:38; Mic. 4:11 [b]Gen. 9:6

34 [a]Lev. 18:25; Deut. 21:23 [b]Ex. 29:45, 46

1 [a]Num. 26:29

2 [a]Num. 26:55; 33:54; Josh. 17:3 [b]Num. 27:1, 7; Josh. 17:3, 4

3 [I]Hebr. *unto whom they shall be*

4 [a]Lev. 25:10

5 [a]Num. 27:7

6 [I]Hebr. *be wives* [a]Num. 36:12

7 [I]Hebr. *cleave to the* [a]1Kgs. 21:3

8 [a]1Chr. 23:22

Further Instructions on Inheritance

36 And the chief[7218] fathers[1] of the families[4940] of the [a]children[1121] of Gilead, the son[1121] of Machir, the son of Manasseh, of the families of the sons of Joseph, came near,[7126] and spake[1696] before Moses, and before the princes,[5387] the chief fathers of the children of Israel:

2 And they said,[559] [a]The LORD[113] commanded[6680] my lord to give the land for an inheritance[5159] by lot to the children of Israel: and [b]my lord was commanded by the LORD to give the inheritance of Zelophehad our brother[251] unto his daughters.

3 And if they be married to any of the sons of the *other* tribes[7626] of the children of Israel, then shall their inheritance be taken from the inheritance of our fathers, and shall be put to the inheritance of the tribe [I]whereunto they are received: so shall it be taken from the lot of our inheritance.

4 And when [a]the jubile[3104] of the children of Israel shall be, then shall their inheritance be put unto the inheritance of the tribe whereunto they are received: so shall their inheritance be taken away from the inheritance of the tribe of our fathers.

5 And Moses commanded the children of Israel according to the word of the LORD, saying, The tribe of the sons of Joseph [a]hath said[1696] well.

6 This *is* the thing[1697] which the LORD doth command[6680] concerning the daughters of Zelophehad, saying, Let them [I]marry to whom they think best;[2896,5869] [a]only to the family[4940] of the tribe of their father[1] shall they marry.

7 So shall not the inheritance of the children of Israel remove from tribe to tribe: for every one[376] of the children of Israel [I][a]shall keep himself to the inheritance of the tribe of his fathers.

8 And [a]every daughter, that possesseth[3423] an inheritance in any tribe of the children of Israel, shall be wife[802] unto one of the family of the tribe of her fa-

ther, that the children of Israel may enjoy every man the inheritance of his fathers.

9 Neither shall the inheritance remove from *one* tribe to another tribe; but every one of the tribes[4294] of the children of Israel shall keep himself to his own inheritance.

10 Even as the LORD commanded Moses, so did[6213] the daughters[1121] of Zelophehad:

11 [a]For Mahlah, Tirzah, and Hoglah, and Milcah, and Noah, the daughters of Zelophehad, were married unto their father's brothers' sons:

12 *And* they were married [l]into the families of the sons of Manasseh the son of Joseph, and their inheritance remained in the tribe of the family of their father.

13 These *are* the commandments and the judgments,3613 which the LORD commanded by the hand[3027] of Moses unto the children of Israel [a]in the plains of Moab by Jordan *near* Jericho.

11 [a]Num. 27:1

12 [l]Hebr. to some that were *of the families*

13 [a]Num. 26:3; 33:50

DEUTERONOMY

"Deuteronomy" is a transliteration from a Greek word which means "second law." This title for the book is derived from the incorrect translation of Deuteronomy 17:18 in the Septuagint (the ancient Greek translation of the Old Testament). The Hebrew text is properly translated in the KJV, "that he shall write him a copy of this law in a book." Deuteronomy is not a "second Law," but merely a repetition and expansion of the laws contained in the first books of the Pentateuch. The Hebrew title (the first words of the text) means "these are the words."

Deuteronomy is the fifth and final book of the Pentateuch or Law of Moses. The three final discourses of Moses which are recorded in this book (Deut. 1:6—4:43; 4:44—26:19; 27—31) were given while the Israelites were encamped in the plains of Moab. These discourses reviewed the history of the Israelites up to that time, repeated and expanded upon the laws that God had given, and listed the promised blessings for obedience and cursings for disobedience. Moses was addressing the children of Israel only two months before they would cross the Jordan into Canaan (Deut. 1:3; cf. Josh. 4:19).

The form of the Book of Deuteronomy is very similar to that of the vassal-treaties written prior to 1000 B.C. It contains a historical introduction, an enumeration of laws, and concluding threats and promises. Unfortunately, Israel did not take heed to this or subsequent warnings that they would be judged for their disobedience. They were commanded not to do that which was right in their own eyes (Deut. 12:8), but this later became a characteristic of the entire nation (Judg. 17:6; 21:25). They were also given instructions which specified what kind of king should rule over them and outlined his responsibilities, but these directives were often forgotten or ignored (Deut. 17:14–20, cf. 1 Sam. 8:7–9; 1 Kgs. 10:26; 11:1–8).

Sections of Deuteronomy are strongly prophetic in nature. For example, the discourse on the prophet who would be like Moses (Deut. 18) is a prophecy of the Messiah. Likewise, certain portions of the book have great significance to the history of Israel. Consequently, words and phrases from Deuteronomy appear throughout the Old Testament. The prophets in particular sought to call the people back to the standards found in this book.

The New Testament writers quoted from the Book of Deuteronomy nearly two hundred times. Christ Himself quoted from it exclusively in his answers to Satan's temptations (Matt. 4:1–11, cf. Deut. 6:13, 16; 8:3).

Israel at Horeb

1 🔑 These *be* the words[1697] which
Moses spake[1696] unto all Israel [a]on
this side Jordan in the wilderness, in the
plain[6160] over against [1]the Red *sea,* between Paran, and Tophel, and Laban, and
Hazeroth, and Dizahab.

2 (*There are* eleven days'[3117] *journey*
from Horeb by the way[1870] of mount Seir
[a]unto Kadesh–barnea.)

3 And it came to pass [a]in the fortieth year, in the eleventh month, on the
first *day* of the month, *that* Moses spake
unto the children[1121] of Israel, according
unto all that the LORD had given him in
commandment unto them;

4 [a]After he had slain[5221] Sihon the
king[4428] of the Amorites, which dwelt in
Heshbon, and Og the king of Bashan,
which dwelt at Astaroth [b]in Edrei:

5 On this side Jordan, in the land of
Moab, began Moses to declare this
law,[8451] saying,

6 The LORD our God[430] spake unto
us [a]in Horeb, saying, Ye have dwelt long
[b]enough in this mount:

1 [1]Or, *Zuph* [a]Josh. 9:1, 10; 22:4, 7

2 [a]Num. 13:26; Deut. 9:23

3 [a]Num. 33:38

4 [a]Num. 21:24, 33 [b]Num. 21:33; Josh. 13:12

6 [a]Ex. 3:1 [b]Ex. 19:1; Num. 10:11

🔑 **1:1** The phrase "on this side Jordan" should read "beyond Jordan" as it does in Deuteronomy 3:20, 25. This was the common term used for land east of the Jordan River. Later, the land was inhabited by Greeks, who named the area Perea. The "wilderness" is a general reference to the region southeast of Jordan; the "plain over against the Red Sea" is more specifically the land along the Rift Valley from the Dead Sea to the Gulf of Aqabah.

7 Turn you, and take your journey,
and go to the mount of the Amorites,
and unto [I]all *the places* nigh thereunto, in
the plain, in the hills, and in the vale,[8219]
and in the south, and by the sea side, to
the land of the Canaanites, and unto
Lebanon, unto the great river, the river
Euphrates.
8 Behold, I have [I]set the land before
you: go in and possess the land which the
LORD sware[7650] unto your fathers,
[a]Abraham, Isaac, and Jacob, to give unto
them and to their seed[2233] after them.
9 And I [a]spake[559] unto you at that
time,[6256] saying, I am not able to bear[5375]
you myself alone:
10 The LORD your God hath multiplied you, and, behold, [a]ye *are* this
day as the stars of heaven[8064] for multitude.
11 ([a]The LORD God of your fathers
make you a thousand times so many
more as ye *are*, and bless[1288] you, [b]as he
hath promised[1696] you!)
12 [a]How can I myself alone bear
your cumbrance,[2960] and your burden,[4853]
and your strife?[7379]
13 [I][a]Take you wise men,[2450] and
understanding,[995] and known[3045] among
your tribes,[7626] and I will make[7760] them
rulers[7218] over you.
14 And ye answered me, and said,[559]
The thing[1697] which thou hast spoken[1696]
is good[2896] *for us* to do.
15 So I took the chief[7218] of your
tribes, wise men, [a]and [I]known, and made
them heads[7218] over you, captains[8269]
over thousands,[505] and captains over hundreds, and captains over fifties, and captains over tens, and officers[7860] among
your tribes.
🔑 16 And I charged[6680] your judges[8199]
at that time, saying, Hear[8085] *the causes*
between your brethren,[251] and [a]judge[8199]
righteously[6664] between *every* man[376] and
his [b]brother,[251] and the stranger[1616] *that
is* with him.
17 [a]Ye shall not [I]respect persons in
judgment;[4941] *but* ye shall hear the small
as well as the great; ye shall not be
afraid[1481] of the face of man; for [b]the
judgment *is* God's: and the cause[1697] that
is too hard for you, [c]bring[7126] *it* unto me,
and I will hear it.
18 And I commanded[6680] you at that
time all the things which ye should do.

The Spies and God's Punishment

19 And when we departed from
Horeb, [a]we went through all that great
and terrible[3372] wilderness, which ye saw
by the way of the mountain of the
Amorites, as the LORD our God commanded us; and [b]we came to Kadesh–
barnea.
20 And I said unto you, Ye are come
unto the mountain of the Amorites,
which the LORD our God doth give unto
us.
21 Behold, the LORD thy God hath set
the land before thee: go up[5927] *and* possess *it*, as the LORD God of thy fathers
hath said unto thee; [a]fear[3372] not, neither
be discouraged.[2865]
22 And ye came near unto me every
one of you, and said, We will send men
before us, and they shall search us out
the land, and bring us word[1697] again by
what way we must go up, and into what
cities we shall come.
23 And the saying pleased me well:
and [a]I took twelve men of you, one of a
tribe:[7626]
24 And [a]they turned and went up[5927]
into the mountain, and came unto the valley of Eshcol, and searched it out.
25 And they took of the fruit of the
land in their hands,[3027] and brought *it*
down unto us, and brought us word

7 [I]Hebr. *all his neighbors*
8 [I]Hebr. *given* [a]Gen. 12:7; 15:18; 17:7, 8; 26:4; 28:13
9 [a]Ex. 18:18; Num. 11:14
10 [a]Gen. 15:5; Deut. 10:22; 28:62
11 [a]2Sam. 24:3 [b]Gen. 15:5; 22:17; 26:4; Ex. 32:13
12 [a]1Kgs. 3:8, 9
13 [I]Hebr. *Give* [a]Ex. 18:21; Num. 11:16, 17
15 [I]Hebr. *gave* [a]Ex. 18:25
16 [a]Deut. 16:18; John 7:24 [b]Lev. 24:22
17 [I]Hebr. *acknowledge faces* [a]Lev. 19:15; Deut. 16:19; 1Sam. 16:7; Prov. 24:23; James 2:1 [b]2Chr. 19:6 [c]Ex. 18:22, 26
19 [a]Num. 10:12; Deut. 8:15; Jer. 2:6 [b]Num. 13:26
21 [a]Josh. 1:9
23 [a]Num. 13:3
24 [a]Num. 13:22-24

🔑 **1:16** In Hebrew *gēr* (1616) is translated as "stranger," meaning a "sojourner," "immigrant," or "alien." These were non-Israelites who, for the most part, enjoyed equal rights under the Law of Moses while residing with their Hebrew neighbors. If they were poor, they were provided for along with the Levites, the orphans, and the widows. However, they were required to be circumcised and conform to the Law of Moses.

again, and said, [a]*It is* a good land which
the LORD our God doth give us.
26 [a]Notwithstanding ye would[14] not
go up, but rebelled[4784] against the
commandment[6310] of the LORD your God:
27 And ye murmured in your
tents,[168] and said, Because the LORD
[a]hated us, he hath brought us forth out
of the land of Egypt, to deliver us into
the hand of the Amorites, to destroy[8045]
us.
28 Whither shall we go up? our
brethren have [I]discouraged our heart,[3824]
saying, [a]The people[5971] *is* greater and
taller than we; the cities *are* great and
walled up to heaven; and moreover we
have seen[7200] the sons[1121] of the
[b]Anakims there.
29 Then I said unto you, Dread[6206]
not, neither be afraid of them.
30 [a]The LORD your God which goeth
before you, he shall fight for you, according to all that he did[6213] for you in
Egypt before your eyes;
31 And in the wilderness, where thou
hast seen how that the LORD thy God
[a]bare[5375] thee, as a man doth bear his
son, in all the way that ye went, until ye
came into this place.
32 Yet in this thing [a]ye did not
believe[539] the LORD your God,
33 [a]Who went in the way before you,
[b]to search you out a place to pitch your
tents *in,* in fire by night, to shew[7200] you
by what way ye should go, and in a
cloud[6051] by day.[3119]
34 And the LORD heard[8085] the voice
of your words, and was wroth,[7107] [a]and
sware, saying,
35 [a]Surely there shall not one[376] of
these men of this evil[7451] generation[1755]
see that good land, which I sware to give
unto your fathers,
36 [a]Save Caleb the son[1121] of
Jephunneh; he shall see it, and to him
will I give the land that he hath trodden
upon, and to his children, because [b]he
hath [I]wholly followed the LORD.

25 [a]Num. 13:27
26 [a]Num. 14:1-4; Ps. 106:24, 25
27 [a]Deut. 9:28
28 [I]Hebr. *melted* [a]Num. 13:28, 31-33; Deut. 9:1, 2 [b]Num. 13:28
30 [a]Ex. 14:14, 25; Neh. 4:20
31 [a]Ex. 19:4; Deut. 32:11, 12; Isa. 46:3, 4; 63:9; Hos. 11:3; Acts 13:18
32 [a]Ps. 106:24; Jude 1:5
33 [a]Ex. 13:21; Ps. 78:14 [b]Num. 10:33; Ezek. 20:6
34 [a]Deut. 2:14, 15
35 [a]Num. 14:22, 23; Ps. 95:11
36 [I]Hebr. *fulfilled to go after* [a]Num. 14:24, 30; Josh. 14:9 [b]Num. 14:24
37 [a]Num. 20:12; 27:14; Deut. 3:26; 4:21; 34:4; Ps. 106:32
38 [a]Num. 14:30 [b]Ex. 24:13; 33:11; 1Sam. 16:22 [c]Num. 27:18, 19; Deut. 31:7, 23
39 [a]Num. 14:31 [b]Num. 14:3 [c]Isa. 7:15, 16; Rom. 9:11
40 [a]Num. 14:25
41 [a]Num. 14:40
42 [a]Num. 14:42
43 [I]Hebr. *ye were presumptuous, and went up* [a]Num. 14:44, 45
44 [a]Ps. 118:12
46 [a]Num. 13:25; 20:1, 22; Judg. 11:17
1 [a]Num. 14:25; Deut. 1:40

🗝 37 [a]Also the LORD was angry[599] with
me for your sakes, saying, Thou also
shalt not go in thither.
38 [a]*But* Joshua the son of Nun,
[b]which standeth before thee, he shall go
in thither: [c]encourage[2388] him: for he shall
cause Israel to inherit it.
39 [a]Moreover your little ones,[2945]
which [b]ye said should be a prey, and your
children, which in that day [c]had no
knowledge[3045] between good and evil,
they shall go in thither, and unto them
will I give it, and they shall possess it.
40 [a]But *as for* you, turn you, and
take your journey into the wilderness by
the way of the Red sea.
41 Then ye answered and said unto
me, [a]We have sinned[2398] against the
LORD, we will go up and fight, according
to all that the LORD our God commanded
us. And when ye had girded on every
man his weapons of war, ye were ready
to go up into the hill.
42 And the LORD said unto me, Say
unto them, [a]Go not up, neither fight; for
I *am* not among[7130] you; lest ye be smitten[5062] before your enemies.
43 So I spake unto you; and ye would
not hear, but rebelled against the commandment of the LORD, and went
[Ia]presumptuously up into the hill.
44 And the Amorites, which dwelt in
that mountain, came out against you, and
chased you, [a]as bees do, and destroyed[3807]
you in Seir, *even* unto Hormah.
45 And ye returned[7725] and wept before the LORD; but the LORD would not
hearken[8085] to your voice, nor give ear[238]
unto you.
46 [a]So ye abode in Kadesh many
days,[3117] according unto the days that ye
abode *there.*

The Journey in the Wilderness

2 Then we turned, and took our journey into the wilderness by the
way[1870] of the Red sea, [a]as the LORD

🗝 **1:37** See note on Numbers 20:12.

spake[1696] unto me: and we compassed mount Seir many days.

2 And the LORD spake[559] unto me, saying,

3 Ye have compassed this mountain [a]long enough: turn you northward.

4 And command[6680] thou the people,[5971] saying, [a]Ye *are* to pass through[5674] the coast of your brethren[251] the children[1121] of Esau, which dwell in Seir; and they shall be afraid of you: take ye good heed unto yourselves therefore:

5 Meddle[1624] not with them; for I will not give you of their land, [I]no, not so much as a foot breadth; [a]because I have given mount Seir unto Esau *for* a possession.[3425]

6 Ye shall buy meat of them for money, that ye may eat; and ye shall also buy water of them for money, that ye may drink.

7 For the LORD thy God[430] hath blessed[1288] thee in all the works of thy hand:[3027] he knoweth thy walking through this great wilderness: [a]these forty years the LORD thy God *hath been* with thee; thou hast lacked nothing.

8 [a]And when we passed by[5674] from our brethren the children of Esau, which dwelt in Seir, through the way of the plain[6160] from [b]Elath, and from Ezion–gaber, we turned and passed by the way of the wilderness of Moab.

9 And the LORD said unto me, [I]Distress[6696] not the Moabites, neither contend with them in battle: for I will not give thee of their land *for* a possession; because I have given [a]Ar unto [b]the children of Lot *for* a possession.

🔑 10 [a]The Emims dwelt therein in times past, a people great, and many, and tall, as [b]the Anakims;

11 Which also were accounted[2803] giants,[7497] as the Anakims; but the Moabites call[7121] them Emims.

12 [a]The Horims also dwelt in Seir beforetime; but the children of Esau [I]succeeded them, when they had destroyed[8045] them from before them, and dwelt in their [II]stead; as Israel did[6213] unto the land of his possession, which the LORD gave unto them.

13 Now rise up, *said I,* and get you over [a]the [I]brook Zered. And we went over[5674] the brook Zered.

14 And the space[3117] in which we came [a]from Kadesh–barnea, until we were come over[5674] the brook Zered, *was* thirty and eight years; [b]until all the generation[1755] of the men of war were wasted[8552] out from among[7130] the host,[4264] [c]as the LORD sware[7650] unto them.

15 For indeed the [a]hand of the LORD was against them, to destroy[2000] them from among the host, until they were consumed.

16 So it came to pass, when all the men of war were consumed and dead[4191] from among the people,

17 That the LORD spake unto me, saying,

18 Thou art to pass over through Ar, the coast of Moab, this day:[3117]

19 And *when* thou comest nigh[7126] over against the children of Ammon, distress them not, nor meddle with them: for I will not give thee of the land of the children of Ammon *any* possession; because I have given it unto [a]the children of Lot *for* a possession.

20 (That also was accounted a land of giants: giants dwelt therein in old time; and the Ammonites call them [a]Zamzummims:

21 [a]A people great, and many, and tall, as the Anakims; but the LORD destroyed them before them; and they succeeded[3423] them, and dwelt in their stead:

22 As he did to the children of Esau, [a]which dwelt in Seir, when he destroyed [b]the Horims from before them; and they succeeded them, and dwelt in their stead even unto this day:

3 [a]Deut. 2:7, 14

4 [a]Num. 20:14

5 [I]Hebr. *even to the treading of the sole of the foot* [a]Gen. 36:8; Josh. 24:4

7 [a]Deut. 8:2-4

8 [a]Judg. 11:18 [b]1Kgs. 9:26

9 [I]Or, *Use no hostility against Moab* [a]Num. 21:28 [b]Gen. 19:36, 37

10 [a]Gen. 14:5 [b]Num. 13:22, 33; Deut. 9:2

12 [I]Hebr. *inherited them* [II]Or, *room* [a]Gen. 14:6; 36:20; Deut. 2:22

13 [I]Or, *valley* [a]Num. 21:12

14 [a]Num. 13:26 [b]Num. 14:33; 26:64 [c]Num. 14:25; Deut. 1:34, 35; Ezek. 20:15

15 [a]Ps. 78:33; 106:26

19 [a]Gen. 19:38

20 [a]Gen. 14:5; *Zuzim*

21 [a]Deut. 2:10

22 [a]Gen. 36:8 [b]Gen. 14:6; 36:20-30; Deut. 2:12

🔑 **2:10, 11** See note on Numbers 13:30–33.

23 And [a]the Avims which dwelt in
Hazerim, *even* unto [b]Azzah, [c]the
Caphtorims, which came forth out of
Caphtor, destroyed them, and dwelt in
their stead.)
24 Rise ye up, take your journey, and
[a]pass over the river Arnon: behold,[7200] I
have given into thine hand Sihon the
Amorite, king[4428] of Heshbon, and his
land: [I]begin to possess *it,* and contend
with him in battle.
25 [a]This day will I begin to put the
dread[6343] of thee and the fear[3374] of thee
upon the nations[5971] *that are* under the
whole heaven,8064 who shall hear[8085]
report[8088] of thee, and shall tremble, and
be in anguish[2342] because of thee.

Israel Defeats Sihon

26 And I sent messengers[4397] out of
the wilderness of Kedemoth unto Sihon
king of Heshbon [a]with words[1697] of
peace,[7965] saying,
27 [a]Let me pass through thy land: I
will go along by the high way, I will neither turn unto the right hand nor to the
left.
28 Thou shalt sell me meat for
money, that I may eat; and give me water
for money, that I may drink: [a]only I will
pass through on my feet;
29 ([a]As the children of Esau which
dwell in Seir, and the Moabites which
dwell in Ar, did unto me;) until I shall
pass over Jordan into the land which the
LORD our God giveth us.
30 [a]But Sihon king of Heshbon
would[14] not let us pass by him: for [b]the
LORD thy God [c]hardened his spirit,[7307]
and made his heart obstinate, that he
might deliver him into thy hand, as *appeareth* this day.
31 And the LORD said unto me,
Behold, I have begun to [a]give Sihon and
his land before thee: begin to possess,
that thou mayest inherit[3423] his land.
32 [a]Then Sihon came out against
us, he and all his people, to fight at
Jahaz.
33 And [a]the LORD our God delivered
him before us; and [b]we smote[5221] him,
and his sons,[1121] and all his people.
34 And we took all his cities at that
time,[6256] and [a]utterly destroyed[2763] [I]the
men, and the women,[802] and the little
ones,[2945] of every city, we left[7604] none to
remain:[8300]
35 Only the cattle we took for a prey
unto ourselves, and the spoil of the cities
which we took.
36 [a]From Aroer, which *is* by the
brink[8193] of the river of Arnon, and *from*
the city that *is* by the river, even unto
Gilead, there was not one city too strong
for us: [b]the LORD our God delivered all
unto us:
37 Only unto the land of the children of Ammon thou camest not, *nor*
unto any place of the river [a]Jabbok,
nor unto the cities in the mountains, nor
unto [b]whatsoever the LORD our God forbad us.

Israel Defeats Og

3 Then we turned, and went up[5927] the
way[1870] to Bashan: and [a]Og the
king[4428] of Bashan came out against us,
he and all his people,[5971] to battle [b]at
Edrei.
2 And the LORD said[559] unto me,
Fear[3372] him not: for I will deliver him,
and all his people, and his land, into thy
hand;[3027] and thou shalt do unto him as
thou didst[6213] unto [a]Sihon king of the
Amorites, which dwelt at Heshbon.
3 So the LORD our God[430] delivered
into our hands Og also, the king of
Bashan, and all his people: [a]and we

23 [a]Josh. 13:3 [b]Jer. 25:20 [c]Gen. 10:14; Amos 9:7
24 [I]Hebr. *begin, possess* [a]Num. 21:13, 14; Judg. 11:18, 21
25 [a]Ex. 15:14, 15; Deut. 11:25; Josh. 2:9, 10
26 [a]Deut. 20:10
27 [a]Num. 21:21, 22; Judg. 11:19
28 [a]Num. 20:19
29 [a]Num. 20:18; Deut. 23:3, 4; Judg. 11:17, 18
30 [a]Num. 21:23 [b]Josh. 11:20 [c]Ex. 4:21
31 [a]Deut. 1:8
32 [a]Num. 21:23
33 [a]Deut. 7:2; 20:16 [b]Num. 21:24; Deut. 29:7
34 [I]Hebr. *every city of men, and women, and little ones* [a]Lev. 27:28; Deut. 7:2, 26
36 [a]Deut. 3:12; 4:48; Josh. 13:9 [b]Ps. 44:3
37 [a]Gen. 32:22; Num. 21:24; Deut. 3:16 [b]Deut. 2:5, 9, 19
1 [a]Num. 21:33-35; Deut. 29:7 [b]Deut. 1:4
2 [a]Num. 21:34
3 [a]Num. 21:35

2:23 "Hazerim" is not a proper noun but a word that means "villages" or "enclosures." The Avim mentioned in this verse are called Avites in Joshua 13:3. They were the scattered remnant of a people conquered by the Caphtorim, a tribe descended from the Egyptians (Gen. 10:14; 1 Chr. 1:12). Their name means "ruins" and seems to be a statement about their fallen state. "Azzah" refers to Gaza of the New Testament and modern times.

smote[5221] him until none was left[7604] to him remaining.[8300]

4 And we took all his cities at that time,[6256] there was not a city which we took not from them, threescore cities, [a]all the region[2256] of Argob, the kingdom[4467] of Og in Bashan.

5 All these cities *were* fenced with high walls, gates, and bars; beside unwalled towns a great many.

6 And we utterly destroyed them, as we did unto Sihon king [a]of Heshbon, utterly destroying[2763] the men, women,[802] and children,[2945] of every city.

7 But all the cattle, and the spoil of the cities, we took for a prey to ourselves.

8 And we took at that time out of the hand of the two kings of the Amorites the land that *was* on this side Jordan, from the river of Arnon unto mount Hermon;

9 (*Which* [a]Hermon the Sidonians call[7121] Sirion; and the Amorites call it [b]Shenir;)

10 [a]All the cities of the plain, and all Gilead, and [b]all Bashan, unto Salchah and Edrei, cities of the kingdom of Og in Bashan.

11 [a]For only Og king of Bashan remained[7604] of the remnant[3499] of [b]giants;[7497] behold, his bedstead *was* a bedstead of iron; *is* it not in [c]Rabbath of the children[1121] of Ammon? nine cubits *was* the length thereof, and four cubits the breadth of it, after the cubit of a man.[376]

The Transjordanic Tribes

12 And this land, *which* we possessed[3423] at that time, [a]from Aroer, which *is* by the river Arnon, and half mount Gilead, and [b]the cities thereof, gave I unto the Reubenites and to the Gadites.

13 [a]And the rest of Gilead, and all Bashan, *being* the kingdom of Og, gave I unto the half tribe[7626] of Manasseh; all the region of Argob, with all Bashan, which was called[7121] the land of giants.

14 [a]Jair the son[1121] of Manasseh took all the country[2256] of Argob [b]unto the coasts of Geshuri and Maachathi; and [c]called them after his own name, Bashan–havoth–jair, unto this day.[3117]

15 [a]And I gave Gilead unto Machir.

16 And unto the Reubenites [a]and unto the Gadites I gave from Gilead even unto the river Arnon half the valley, and the border even unto the river Jabbok, [b]*which is* the border of the children of Ammon;

17 The plain[6160] also, and Jordan, and the coast *thereof,* from [a]Chinnereth [b]even unto the sea of the plain, [c]*even* the salt sea, [I]under Ashdoth–pisgah eastward.

18 And I commanded[6680] you at that time, saying, The LORD your God hath given you this land to possess it: [a]ye shall pass over armed before your brethren[251] the children of Israel, all *that are* [I]meet for the war.

19 But your wives,[802] and your little ones,[2945] and your cattle, (*for* I know[3045] that ye have much cattle,) shall abide in your cities which I have given you;

20 Until the LORD have given rest unto your brethren, as well as unto you, and *until* they also possess the land which the LORD your God hath given them beyond Jordan: and *then* shall ye [a]return[7725] every man unto his possession,[3425] which I have given you.

21 And [a]I commanded Joshua at that time, saying, Thine eyes have seen[7200] all that the LORD your God hath done[6213] unto these two kings: so shall the LORD do unto all the kingdoms[4467] whither thou passest.[5674]

22 Ye shall not fear them: for [a]the LORD your God he shall fight for you.

Moses Is Forbidden to Enter Canaan

23 And [a]I besought[2603] the LORD at that time, saying,

24 O Lord[136] GOD, thou hast begun to shew[7200] thy servant[5650] [a]thy greatness, and thy mighty[2389] hand: for [b]what God[410] *is there* in heaven[8064] or in

4 [a]1Kgs. 4:13
6 [a]Deut. 2:24; Ps. 135:10-12; 136:19-21
9 [a]Deut. 4:48; Ps. 29:6 [b]1Chr. 5:23
10 [a]Deut. 4:49 [b]Josh. 12:5; 13:11
11 [a]Amos 2:9 [b]Gen. 14:5 [c]2Sam. 12:26; Jer. 49:2; Ezek. 21:20
12 [a]Deut. 2:36; Josh. 12:2 [b]Num. 32:33; Josh. 12:6; 13:8
13 [a]Josh. 13:29
14 [a]1Chr. 2:22 [b]Josh. 13:13; 2Sam. 3:3; 10:6 [c]Num. 32:41
15 [a]Num. 32:39
16 [a]2Sam. 24:5 [b]Num. 21:24; Josh. 12:2
17 [I]Or, *under the springs of Pisgah,* or, *the hill* [a]Num. 34:11 [b]Num. 34:12; Deut. 4:49; Josh. 12:3 [c]Gen. 14:3
18 [I]Hebr. *sons of power* [a]Num. 32:20-33
20 [a]Josh. 22:4
21 [a]Num. 27:18
22 [a]Ex. 14:14; Deut. 1:30; 20:4
23 [a]2Cor. 12:8, 9
24 [a]Deut. 11:2 [b]Ex. 15:11; 2Sam. 7:22; Ps. 71:19; 86:8; 89:6, 8

earth,[776] that can do according to thy works, and according to thy might?

25 I pray thee,[4994] let me go over,[5674] and see [a]the good land that *is* beyond Jordan, that goodly[2896] mountain, and Lebanon.

26 But the LORD [a]was wroth[5674] with me for your sakes, and would not hear[8085] me: and the LORD said unto me, Let it suffice thee; speak[1696] no more unto me of this matter.[1697]

27 [a]Get thee up into the top[7218] of [I]Pisgah, and lift up[5375] thine eyes westward, and northward, and southward, and eastward, and behold[7200] *it* with thine eyes: for thou shalt not go over this Jordan.

28 But [a]charge[6680] Joshua, and encourage[2388] him, and strengthen him: for he shall go over before this people, and he shall cause them to inherit[5157] the land which thou shalt see.

29 So we abode in [a]the valley over against Beth–peor.

Moses Urges Obedience

4 Now therefore hearken,[8085] O Israel, unto [a]the statutes[2706] and unto the judgments,[4941] which I teach[3925] you, for to do *them,* that ye may live,[2421] and go in and possess the land which the LORD God[430] of your fathers giveth you.

2 [a]Ye shall not add unto the word[1697] which I command[6680] you, neither shall ye diminish *ought* from it, that ye may keep[8104] the commandments of the LORD your God which I command you.

3 Your eyes have seen[7200] what the LORD did because of [a]Baal–peor: for all the men[376] that followed Baal–peor, the LORD thy God hath destroyed[8045] them from among[7130] you.

4 But ye that did cleave unto the LORD your God *are* alive[2416] every one of you this day.[3117]

25 [a]Ex. 3:8; Deut. 4:22
26 [a]Num. 20:12; 27:14; Deut. 1:37; 31:2; 32:51, 52; 34:4; Ps. 106:32
27 [I]Or, *The hill* [a]Num. 27:12
28 [a]Num. 27:18, 23; Deut. 1:38; 31:3, 7
29 [a]Deut. 4:46; 34:6

1 [a]Lev. 19:37; 20:8; 22:31; Deut. 5:1; 8:1; Ezek. 20:11; Rom. 10:5
2 [a]Deut. 12:32; Josh. 1:7; Prov. 30:6; Eccl. 12:13; Rev. 22:18, 19
3 [a]Num. 25:4, 5; Josh. 22:17; Ps. 106:28, 29
6 [a]Job 28:28; Ps. 19:7; 111:10; Prov. 1:7
7 [a]2Sam. 7:23 [b]Ps. 46:1; 145:18; 148:14; Isa. 55:6
9 [a]Prov. 4:23 [b]Prov. 3:1, 3; 4:21 [c]Gen. 18:19; Deut. 6:7; 11:19; Ps. 78:5, 6; Eph. 6:4
10 [a]Ex. 19:9, 16; 20:18; Heb. 12:18, 19
11 [I]Hebr. *heart* [a]Ex. 19:18; Deut. 5:23
12 [I]Hebr. *save a voice* [a]Deut. 5:4, 22 [b]Deut. 4:33, 36 [c]Ex. 20:22; 1Kgs. 19:12
13 [a]Deut. 9:9, 11

5 Behold,[7200] I have taught[3925] you statutes and judgments, even as the LORD my God commanded me, that ye should do so in the land whither ye go to possess it.

6 Keep therefore and do *them;* for this *is* [a]your wisdom[2451] and your understanding[998] in the sight of the nations,[4171] which shall hear[8085] all these statutes, and say, Surely this great nation *is* a wise[2450] and understanding[995] people.[5971]

7 For [a]what nation *is there so* great, who *hath* [b]God *so* nigh unto them, as the LORD our God *is* in all *things that* we call[7121] upon him *for?*

8 And what nation *is there so* great, that hath statutes and judgments *so* righteous as all this law,[8451] which I set before you this day?

9 Only take heed to thyself, and [a]keep thy soul[5315] diligently, [b]lest thou forget the things[1697] which thine eyes have seen, and lest they depart[5493] from thy heart all the days of thy life:[2416] but [c]teach[3045] them thy sons, and thy sons' sons;

10 *Specially* [a]the day that thou stoodest before the LORD thy God in Horeb, when the LORD said unto me, Gather me the people together, and I will make them hear my words,[1697] that they may learn[3925] to fear[3372] me all the days that they shall live[2416] upon the earth,[127] and *that* they may teach their children.[1121]

11 And ye came near and stood under the mountain; and the [a]mountain burned with fire unto the [I]midst[3820] of heaven, with darkness,[2822] clouds,[6051] and thick darkness.[6205]

12 [a]And the LORD spake unto you out of the midst of the fire: [b]ye heard[8085] the voice of the words, but saw[7200] no similitude;[8544] [Ic]only *ye heard* a voice.

🔑 13 [a]And he declared[5046] unto you his covenant,[1285] which he commanded you

🔑 **4:13, 14** This was the covenant that the people entered into at Mount Horeb. It was based on the Ten Commandments, but included much additional material incorporated into Exodus, Leviticus,
(continued on next page)

to perform,[6213] *even* [b]ten commandments;
and [c]he wrote them upon two tables of
stone.
14 And [a]the LORD commanded me
at that time[6256] to teach you statutes
and judgments, that ye might do them
in the land whither ye go over[5647] to possess it.

Idolatry and Its Consequences

15 [a]Take ye therefore good heed unto
yourselves; for ye saw no manner of
[b]similitude on the day *that* the LORD
spake unto you in Horeb out of the midst
of the fire:
16 Lest ye [a]corrupt[7843] *yourselves,*
and [b]make[6213] you a graven image,[6459]
the similitude of any figure,[5566] [c]the likeness[8403] of male$_{2145}$ or female,[5347]
17 The likeness of any beast that *is*
on the earth,[776] the likeness of any
winged fowl that flieth in the air,$_{8064}$
18 The likeness of any thing that
creepeth on the ground,[127] the likeness of
any fish$_{1710}$ that *is* in the waters beneath
the earth:
19 And lest thou [a]lift up thine eyes
unto heaven, and when thou seest the
sun, and the moon, and the stars, *even*
[b]all the host[6635] of heaven, shouldest be
driven to [c]worship[7812] them, and
serve[5647] them, which the LORD thy God
hath [I]divided unto all nations under the
whole heaven.
20 But the LORD hath taken you, and
[a]brought you forth out of the iron furnace, *even* out of Egypt, [b]to be unto him
a people of inheritance,[5159] as *ye are* this
day.
21 Furthermore [a]the LORD was
angry[599] with me for your sakes, and
sware[7650] that I should not go over
Jordan, and that I should not go in unto
that good land, which the LORD thy God
giveth thee *for* an inheritance:
22 But [a]I must die[4191] in this land, [b]I
must not go over Jordan: but ye shall go
over, and possess [c]that good land.
23 Take heed unto yourselves, [a]lest
ye forget the covenant of the LORD your
God, which he made with you, [b]and make
you a graven image, *or* the likeness[8544] of
any *thing,* which the LORD thy God hath
forbidden[6680] thee.
24 For [a]the LORD thy God *is* a consuming fire, *even* [b]a jealous God.[410]
25 When thou shalt beget children,
and children's children, and ye shall
have remained long in the land, and
[a]shall corrupt *yourselves,* and make a
graven image, *or* the likeness of any
thing, and [b]shall do evil[7451] in the sight
of the LORD thy God, to provoke him to
anger:[3707]
26 [a]I call heaven and earth to
witness[5749] against you this day, that
ye shall soon utterly perish[6] from off
the land whereunto ye go over Jordan to
possess it; ye shall not prolong[748] *your*
days upon it, but shall utterly be destroyed.
27 And the LORD [a]shall scatter you
among the nations, and ye shall be
left[7604] few in number among the heathen,[1471] whither the LORD shall lead you.
28 And [a]there ye shall serve gods,[430]
the work of men's[120] hands,[3027] wood
and stone, [b]which neither see, nor hear,
nor eat, nor smell.[7306]
29 [a]But if from thence thou shalt
seek the LORD thy God, thou shalt find
him, if thou seek him with all thy heart
and with all thy soul.
30 When thou art in tribulation, and
all these things [I]are come upon thee,
[a]*even* in the latter days, if thou [b]turn[7725]
to the LORD thy God, and shalt be
obedient[8085] unto his voice;

13 [b]Ex. 34:28 [c]Ex. 24:12; 31:18
14 [a]Ex. 21:1; 22:1—23:33
15 [a]Josh. 23:11 [b]Isa. 40:18 [c]Ex. 32:7 [d]Ex. 20:4, 5; Deut. 4:23; 5:8 [e]Rom. 1:23
19 [I]Or, *imparted* [a]Deut. 17:3; Job 31:26, 27 [b]Gen. 2:1; 2Kgs. 17:16; 21:3 [c]Rom. 1:25
20 [a]1Kgs. 8:51; Jer. 11:4 [b]Ex. 19:5; Deut. 9:29; 32:9
21 [a]Num. 20:12; Deut. 1:37; 3:26
22 [a]2Pet. 1:13-15 [b]Deut. 3:27 [c]Deut. 3:25
23 [a]Deut. 4:9 [b]Ex. 20:4, 5; Deut. 4:16
24 [a]Ex. 24:17; Deut. 9:3; Isa. 33:14; Heb. 12:29 [b]Ex. 20:5; Deut. 6:15; Isa. 42:8
25 [a]Deut. 4:16 [b]2Kgs. 17:17
26 [a]Deut. 30:18, 19; Isa. 1:2; Mic. 6:2
27 [a]Lev. 26:33; Deut. 28:62, 64; Neh. 1:8
28 [a]Deut. 28:64; 1Sam. 26:19; Jer. 16:13 [b]Ps. 115:4, 5; 135:15, 16; Isa. 44:9; 46:7
29 [a]Lev. 26:39, 40; Deut. 30:1, 2, 3; 2Chr. 15:4; Neh. 1:9; Isa. 55:6, 7; Jer. 29:12-14
30 [I]Hebr. *have found thee* [a]Gen. 49:1; Deut. 31:29; Jer. 23:20; Hos. 3:5 [b]Joel 2:12

(continued from previous page)
and Numbers. After the people became fearful, they were sent to their tents, while God delivered the remainder of the instruction directly to Moses. This part of Deuteronomy is called a "historical prologue." It parallels similar prologues in treaties of Moses' day.

31 (For the LORD thy God *is* [a]a merciful God;) he will not forsake[7503] thee, neither destroy[7843] thee, nor forget the covenant of thy fathers which he sware unto them.

Exhortation to Keep God's Law

32 For [a]ask[7592] now of the days that are past, which were before thee, since the day that God created[1254] man[120] upon the earth, and *ask* [b]from the one side of heaven unto the other, whether there hath been *any such thing* as this great thing *is,* or hath been heard like it?

33 [a]Did *ever* people hear the voice of God speaking[1696] out of the midst of the fire, as thou hast heard, and live?

34 Or hath God assayed[5254] to go *and* take him a nation from the midst[7130] of *another* nation, [a]by temptations,[4531] [b]by signs,[226] and by wonders,[4159] and by war, and [c]by a mighty[2389] hand, and [d]by a stretched out arm, [e]and by great terrors,[4172] according to all that the LORD your God did for you in Egypt before your eyes?

35 Unto thee it was shewed,[7200] that thou mightest know[3045] that the LORD he *is* God; [a]*there is* none else beside him.

36 [a]Out of heaven he made thee to hear his voice, that he might instruct[3256] thee: and upon earth he shewed thee his great fire; and thou heardest[8085] his words out of the midst of the fire.

37 And because [a]he loved[157] thy fathers,[1] therefore he chose[977] their seed[2233] after them, and [b]brought thee out in his sight with his mighty power out of Egypt;

38 [a]To drive out[3423] nations[1471] from before thee greater and mightier than thou *art,* to bring thee in, to give thee their land *for* an inheritance, as *it is* this day.

39 Know therefore this day, and consider *it* in thine heart, that [a]the LORD he *is* God in heaven above, and upon the earth beneath: *there is* none else.

40 [a]Thou shalt keep therefore his statutes, and his commandments, which I command thee this day, [b]that it may go well[3190] with thee, and with thy children after thee, and that thou mayest prolong *thy* days upon the earth, which the LORD thy God giveth thee, for ever.

Eastern Cities of Refuge

41 Then Moses [a]severed[914] three cities on this side Jordan toward the sunrising;

42 [a]That the slayer[7523] might flee thither, which should kill his neighbour unawares,[1097][1847] and hated[8130] him not in times past; and that fleeing unto one of these cities he might live:

43 *Namely,* [a]Bezer in the wilderness, in the plain country,[776] of the Reubenites; and Ramoth in Gilead, of the Gadites; and Golan in Bashan, of the Manassites.

Moses Reiterates the Law

44 And this *is* the law which Moses set[7760] before the children of Israel:

45 These *are* the testimonies,[5713] and the statutes, and the judgments, which Moses spake unto the children of Israel, after they came forth out of Egypt,

46 On this side Jordan, [a]in the valley over against Beth–peor, in the land of Sihon king[4428] of the Amorites, who dwelt at Heshbon, whom Moses and the children of Israel [b]smote,[5221] after they were come forth out of Egypt:

47 And they possessed[3423] his land, and the land [a]of Og king of Bashan, two kings of the Amorites, which *were* on this side Jordan toward the sunrising;

48 [a]From Aroer, which *is* by the bank[8143] of the river Arnon, even unto mount Sion, which *is* [b]Hermon,

49 And all the plain[6160] on this side Jordan eastward, even unto the sea of the plain, under the [a]springs of Pisgah.

The Ten Commandments

5 And Moses called[7121] all Israel, and said[559] unto them, Hear,[8085] O Israel, the statutes[2706] and judgments[4941] which I speak[1696] in your ears[241] this day,[3117]

31 [a]2Chr. 30:9; Neh. 9:31; Ps. 116:5; Jon. 4:2
32 [a]Job 8:8 [b]Matt. 24:31
33 [a]Ex. 24:11; 33:20; Deut. 5:24, 26
34 [a]Deut. 7:19; 29:3 [b]Ex. 7:3 [c]Ex. 13:3 [d]Ex. 6:6 [e]Deut. 26:8; 34:12
35 [a]Deut. 32:39; 1Sam. 2:2; Isa. 45:5, 18, 22; Mark 12:29, 32
36 [a]Ex. 19:9, 19; 20:18, 22; 24:16; Heb. 12:18
37 [a]Deut. 10:15 [b]Ex. 13:3, 9, 14
38 [a]Deut. 7:1; 9:1, 4, 5
39 [a]Deut. 4:35; Josh. 2:11
40 [a]Lev. 22:31 [b]Deut. 5:16; 6:3, 18; 12:25, 28; 22:7; Eph. 6:3
41 [a]Num. 35:6, 14
42 [a]Deut. 19:4
43 [a]Josh. 20:8
46 [a]Deut. 3:29 [b]Num. 21:24; Deut. 1:4
47 [a]Num. 21:35; Deut. 3:3, 4
48 [a]Deut. 2:36; 3:12 [b]Deut. 3:9; Ps. 133:3
49 [a]Deut. 3:17

that ye may learn[3925] them, and [I]keep,[8104] and do them.

2 [a]The LORD our God[430] made[3772] a covenant[1285] with us in Horeb.

3 The LORD [a]made not this covenant with our fathers,[1] but with us, *even* us, who *are* all of us here alive[2416] this day.

4 [a]The LORD talked[1696] with you face to face in the mount out of the midst of the fire,

5 ([a]I stood between the LORD and you at that time,[6256] to shew[5046] you the word[1697] of the LORD: for [b]ye were afraid by reason of the fire, and went not up into the mount;) saying,

6 [a]I *am* the LORD thy God, which brought thee out of the land of Egypt, from the house[1004] of [I]bondage.[5650]

7 [a]Thou shalt have none other gods[430] before me.

8 [a]Thou shalt not make thee *any* graven image,[6459] *or* any likeness[8544] *of any thing* that *is* in heaven[8064] above, or that *is* in the earth[776] beneath, or that *is* in the waters beneath the earth:

9 Thou shalt not bow down thyself[7812] unto them, nor serve[5647] them: for I the LORD thy God *am* a jealous God,[410] [a]visiting the iniquity[5771] of the fathers upon the children[1121] unto the third and fourth *generation* of them that hate[8130] me,

10 [a]And shewing mercy[2617] unto thousands[505] of them that love[157] me and keep my commandments.

11 [a]Thou shalt not take[5375] the name of the LORD thy God in vain:[7723] for the LORD will not hold *him* guiltless[5352] that taketh his name in vain.

12 [a]Keep the sabbath[7676] day to sanctify[6942] it, as the LORD thy God hath commanded[6680] thee.

13 [a]Six days thou shalt labour,[5647] and do all thy work:

14 But the seventh day *is* the [a]sabbath of the LORD thy God: *in it* thou shalt not do any work, thou, nor thy son,[1121] nor thy daughter, nor thy manservant,[5650] nor thy maidservant, nor thine ox, nor

1 [I]Hebr. *keep to do them*
2 [a]Ex. 19:5; Deut. 4:23
3 [a]Matt. 13:17; Heb. 8:9
4 [a]Ex. 19:9, 19; 20:22; Deut. 4:33, 36; 34:10
5 [a]Ex. 20:21; Gal. 3:19 [b]Ex. 19:16; 20:18; 24:2
6 [I]Hebr. *servants* [a]Ex. 20:2; Lev. 26:1; Deut. 6:4; Ps. 81:10
7 [a]Ex. 20:3
8 [a]Ex. 20:4
9 [a]Ex. 34:7
10 [a]Jer. 32:18; Dan. 9:4
11 [a]Ex. 20:7; Lev. 19:12; Matt. 5:33
12 [a]Ex. 20:8
13 [a]Ex. 23:12; 35:2; Ezek. 20:12
14 [a]Gen. 2:2; Ex. 16:29, 30; Heb. 4:4
15 [a]Deut. 15:15; 16:12; 24:18, 22 [b]Deut. 4:34, 37
16 [a]Ex. 20:12; Lev. 19:3; Deut. 27:16; Eph. 6:2, 3; Col. 3:20 [b]Deut. 4:40
17 [a]Ex. 20:13; Matt. 5:21
18 [a]Ex. 20:14; Luke 18:20; James 2:11
19 [a]Ex. 20:15; Rom. 13:9
20 [a]Ex. 20:16
21 [a]Ex. 20:17; Mic. 2:2; Hab. 2:9; Luke 12:15; Rom. 7:7; 13:9
22 [a]Ex. 24:12; 31:18; Deut. 4:13
23 [a]Ex. 20:18, 19
24 [a]Ex. 19:19 [b]Deut. 4:33; Judg. 13:22

thine ass, nor any of thy cattle, nor thy stranger[1616] that *is* within thy gates; that thy manservant and thy maidservant may rest as well as thou.

15 [a]And remember[2142] that thou wast a servant[5650] in the land of Egypt, and *that* the LORD thy God brought thee out thence [b]through a mighty[2389] hand and by a stretched out arm: therefore the LORD thy God commanded thee to keep[6213] the sabbath day.

16 [a]Honour thy father[1] and thy mother, as the LORD thy God hath commanded thee; [b]that thy days may be prolonged,[748] and that it may go well[3190] with thee, in the land[127] which the LORD thy God giveth thee.

17 [a]Thou shalt not kill.

18 [a]Neither shalt thou commit adultery.[5003]

19 [a]Neither shalt thou steal.

20 [a]Neither shalt thou bear false[7723] witness against thy neighbour.

21 [a]Neither shalt thou desire thy neighbour's wife,[802] neither shalt thou covet[183] thy neighbour's house, his field,[7704] or his manservant, or his maidservant, his ox, or his ass, or any *thing* that *is* thy neighbour's.

22 These words[1697] the LORD spake[1696] unto all your assembly[6951] in the mount out of the midst of the fire, of the cloud,[6051] and of the thick darkness,[6205] with a great voice: and he added no more. And [a]he wrote them in two tables of stone, and delivered them unto me.

23 [a]And it came to pass, when ye heard[8085] the voice out of the midst of the darkness,[2822] (for the mountain did burn with fire,) that ye came near unto me, *even* all the heads[7218] of your tribes,[7626] and your elders:[2205]

24 And ye said, Behold, the LORD our God hath shewed[7200] us his glory[3519] and his greatness, and [a]we have heard his voice out of the midst of the fire: we have seen[7200] this day that God doth talk[1696] with man, and he [b]liveth.[2425]

5:9 See note on Ezekiel 18:1–32.

25 Now therefore why should we
die?[4191] for this great fire will consume
us: [a]if we [I]hear the voice of the LORD our
God any more, then we shall die.
26 [a]For who *is there of* all flesh,[1320]
that hath heard the voice of the living[2416]
God speaking[1696] out of the midst of the
fire, as we *have,* and lived?[2421]
27 Go thou near,[7126] and hear all that
the LORD our God shall say:[559] and
[a]speak thou unto us all that the LORD our
God shall speak unto thee; and we will
hear *it,* and do *it.*
28 And the LORD heard the voice of
your words, when ye spake unto me; and
the LORD said unto me, I have heard the
voice of the words of this people,[5971]
which they have spoken[1696] unto thee:
[a]they have well said all that they have
spoken.
29 [a]O that there were such an
heart[3824] in them, that they would
fear[3372] me, and [b]keep all my commandments always, [c]that it might be well with
them, and with their children for ever![5769]
30 Go say to them, Get you into your
tents[168] again.
31 But as for thee, stand thou here
by me, [a]and I will speak unto thee all
the commandments, and the statutes,
and the judgments, which thou shalt
teach[3925] them, that they may do *them*
in the land[776] which I give them to possess it.
32 Ye shall observe[8104] to do therefore as the LORD your God hath commanded you: [a]ye shall not turn aside to
the right hand or to the left.
33 Ye shall walk in [a]all the ways[1870]
which the LORD your God hath commanded you, that ye may live,[2421] [b]and
that it may be well[2895] with you, and *that*

25 [I]Hebr. *add to hear* [a]Deut. 18:16
26 [a]Deut. 4:33
27 [a]Ex. 20:19; Heb. 12:19
28 [a]Deut. 18:17
29 [a]Deut. 32:29; Ps. 81:13; Isa. 48:18; Matt. 23:37; Luke 19:42 [b]Deut. 11:1 [c]Deut. 4:40
31 [a]Gal. 3:19
32 [a]Deut. 17:20; 28:14; Josh. 1:7; 23:6; Prov. 4:27
33 [a]Deut. 10:12; Ps. 119:6; Jer. 7:23; Luke 1:6; Deut. 4:40

1 [I]Hebr. *pass over* [a]Deut. 4:1; 5:31; 12:1
2 [a]Ex. 20:20; Deut. 10:12, 13; Ps. 111:10; 128:1; Eccl. 12:13 [b]Deut. 4:40; Prov. 3:1, 2
3 [a]Gen. 15:5; 22:17 [b]Ex. 3:8
4 [a]Isa. 42:8; Mark 12:29, 32; John 17:3; 1Cor. 8:4, 6
5 [a]Deut. 10:12; Matt. 22:37; Mark 12:30; Luke 10:27 [b]2Kgs. 23:25
6 [a]Deut. 11:18; 32:46; Ps. 37:31; 40:8; 119:11, 98; Prov. 3:3; Isa. 51:7
7 [I]Hebr. *whet, or, sharpen* [a]Deut. 4:9; 11:19; Ps. 78:4-6; Eph. 6:4
8 [a]Ex. 13:9, 16; Deut. 11:18; Prov. 3:3; 6:21; 7:3

ye may prolong[748] *your* days in the land
which ye shall possess.

Remember God Every Day

6 Now these *are* [a]the commandments,
the statutes,[2706] and the judgments,[4941] which the LORD your God[430]
commanded[6680] to teach[3925] you, that ye
might do *them* in the land whither ye [I]go
to possess it:
2 [a]That thou mightest fear[3372] the
LORD thy God, to keep[8104] all his
statutes[2708] and his commandments,
which I command thee, thou, and thy
son,[1121] and thy son's son, all the
days[3117] of thy life;[2416] [b]and that thy
days may be prolonged.[748]
3 Hear[8085] therefore, O Israel, and
observe[8104] to do *it;* that it may be
well[3190] with thee, and that ye may increase mightily, [a]as the LORD God of thy
fathers[1] hath promised[1696] thee, in [b]the
land that floweth with milk and honey.
🔑 4 [a]Hear, O Israel: The LORD our God
is one LORD:
5 And [a]thou shalt love[157] the LORD
thy God [b]with all thine heart,[3824] and
with all thy soul,[5315] and with all thy
might.[3966]
6 And [a]these words,[1697] which I command thee this day,[3117] shall be in thine
heart:
7 And [a]thou shalt [I]teach them diligently[8150] unto thy children,[1121] and shalt
talk[1696] of them when thou sittest in
thine house,[1004] and when thou walkest
by the way,[1870] and when thou liest
down, and when thou risest up.
8 [a]And thou shalt bind them for a
sign[226] upon thine hand,[3027] and they

🔑 **6:4–9** To the Jew, this is the most important text in the Old Testament. Jesus Himself called the injunction in 6:5 "the first and great commandment" (Matt. 22:36–38; see note on Ex. 20:1–17). The Jews refer to Deuteronomy 6:4–9 as the "Shema," naming it after the first word in the text. This word means to hear in the sense of obeying. Moses is teaching not only the priority of belief in one God, but also a means to preserve that belief. As time went on, the proper understanding of the Shema with its spiritual implications was no longer grasped by the people (Zech. 7:12–14; James 1:22–25). This absence of saving knowledge became a factor in their spiritual downfall (Hos. 4:6), which ultimately led to the deportation of Israel and the exile of Judah.

shall be as frontlets[2903] between thine
eyes.
9 [a]And thou shalt write them upon
the posts of thy house, and on thy gates.
10 And it shall be, when the LORD
thy God shall have brought thee into the
land which he sware[7650] unto thy fathers,
to Abraham, to Isaac, and to Jacob, to
give thee great and goodly[2896] cities,
[a]which thou buildedst not,
11 And houses full of all good
things, which thou filledst not, and
wells[953] digged, which thou diggedst not,
vineyards and olive trees, which thou
plantedst not; [a]when thou shalt have
eaten and be full;
12 *Then* beware[8104] lest thou forget
the LORD, which brought thee forth out of
the land of Egypt, from the house of
[I]bondage.[5650]
🔑 13 Thou shalt [a]fear the LORD thy
God, and serve[5647] him, and [b]shalt
swear[7650] by his name.
14 Ye shall not [a]go after other
gods,[430] [b]of the gods of the people[5971]
which *are* round about you;
15 (For [a]the LORD thy God *is* a jealous God[410] among[7130] you) [b]lest the
anger of the LORD thy God be kindled[2734]
against thee, and destroy[8045] thee from
off the face of the earth.[127]
🔑 16 [a]Ye shall not tempt[5254] the LORD
your God, [b]as ye tempted *him* in Massah.
17 Ye shall [a]diligently keep[8104] the
commandments of the LORD your God,
and his testimonies,[5713] and his statutes,
which he hath commanded thee.
18 And thou [a]shalt do *that which is*
right and good[2896] in the sight of the
LORD: that it may be well with thee, and
that thou mayest go in and possess the
good land which the LORD sware unto
thy fathers,
19 [a]To cast out all thine enemies
from before thee, as the LORD hath
spoken.[1696]
20 *And* [a]when thy son asketh[7592]
thee [I]in time to come, saying, What *mean*
the testimonies, and the statutes, and the
judgments, which the LORD our God hath
commanded you?
21 Then thou shalt say[559] unto thy
son, We were Pharaoh's bondmen[5650] in
Egypt; and the LORD brought us out of
Egypt [a]with a mighty[2389] hand:
22 [a]And the LORD shewed signs[226]
and wonders,[4159] great and [I]sore,[7451]
upon Egypt, upon Pharaoh, and upon all
his household,[1004] before our eyes:
23 And he brought us out from
thence, that he might bring us in, to give
us the land which he sware unto our fathers.
24 And the LORD commanded us to
do all these statutes, [a]to fear the LORD
our God, [b]for our good always, that [c]he
might preserve us alive,[2421] as *it is* at
this day.
25 And [a]it shall be our righteousness,[6666] if we observe to do all these
commandments before the LORD our God,
as he hath commanded us.

Totally Destroy the Canaanite Culture

7 When the [a]LORD thy God[430] shall
bring thee into the land whither thou
goest to possess it, and hath cast out
many nations[1471] before thee, [b]the Hittites,
and the Girgashites, and the Amor-
ites, and the Canaanites, and the Perizzites, and the Hivites, and the Jebusites,
seven nations [c]greater and mightier than
thou;
2 And when the LORD thy God shall
[a]deliver them before thee; thou shalt
smite[5221] them, *and* [b]utterly destroy[2763]

9 [a]Deut. 11:20; Isa. 57:8
10 [a]Josh. 24:13; Ps. 105:44
11 [a]Deut. 8:10-20
12 [I]Hebr. *bondmen,* or, *servants*
13 [a]Deut. 10:12, 20; 13:4; Matt. 4:10; Luke 4:8 [b]Ps. 63:11; Isa. 45:23; 65:16; Jer. 4:2; 5:7; 12:16
14 [a]Deut. 8:19; 11:28; Jer. 25:6 [b]Deut. 13:7
15 [a]Ex. 20:5; Deut. 4:24 [b]Deut. 7:4; 11:17
16 [a]Matt. 4:7; Luke 4:12 [b]Ex. 17:2, 7; Num. 20:3, 4; 21:4, 5; 1Cor. 10:9
17 [a]Deut. 11:13, 22; Ps. 119:4
18 [a]Ex. 15:26; Deut. 12:28; 13:18
19 [a]Num. 33:52, 53
20 [I]Hebr. *tomorrow* [a]Ex. 13:14
21 [a]Ex. 3:19; 13:3
22 [I]Hebr. *evil* [a]Ex. 7:1—12:51; Ps. 135:9
24 [a]Deut. 6:2 [b]Deut. 10:13; Job 35:7, 8; Jer. 32:39 [c]Deut. 4:1; 8:1; Ps. 41:2; Luke 10:28
25 [a]Lev. 18:5; Deut. 24:13; Rom. 10:3, 5

1 [a]Deut. 31:3; Ps. 44:2, 3 [b]Gen. 15:18–21; Ex. 33:2 [c]Deut. 4:38; 9:1
2 [a]Deut. 7:23; 23:14 [b]Lev. 27:28, 29; Num. 33:52; Deut. 20:16, 17; Josh. 6:17; 8:24; 9:24; 10:28, 40; 11:11, 12

🔑 **6:13, 16** Jesus quoted part of verse thirteen and Deuteronomy 10:20 in response to one of Satan's temptations (Matt. 4:10; Luke 4:8). In fact, the early part of this book, which was spoken by Moses while Israel was still in the period of her wilderness wanderings, formed the basis of all three of Jesus' responses to Satan. "Thou shalt not tempt the Lord thy God" (Matt. 4:7; Luke 4:12) comes from Deuteronomy 6:16, and "Man shall not live by bread alone" (Matt. 4:4; Luke 4:4) is a quotation of Deuteronomy 8:3.

them; [c]thou shalt make no covenant[1285]
with them, nor shew mercy unto them:
3 [a]Neither shalt thou make marriages
with them; thy daughter thou shalt not
give unto his son,[1121] nor his daughter
shalt thou take unto thy son.
4 For they will turn away thy son
from following me, that they may
serve[5647] other gods:[430] [a]so will the anger
of the LORD be kindled[2734] against you,
and destroy[8045] thee suddenly.
5 But thus shall ye deal[6213] with
them; ye shall [a]destroy[5422] their altars,
and break down[7665] their [I]images, and
cut down their groves,[842] and burn[8313]
their graven images[6456] with fire.
6 [a]For thou *art* an holy[6918] people[5971]
unto the LORD thy God: [b]the LORD thy
God hath chosen[977] thee to be a
special[5459] people unto himself, above all
people that *are* upon the face of the
earth.
7 The LORD did not set his love[2836]
upon you, nor choose[977] you, because
ye were more in number than any
people; for ye *were* [a]the fewest of all
people:
8 But [a]because the LORD loved[160] you,
and because he would keep[8104] [b]the
oath[7621] which he had sworn[7650] unto
your fathers,[1] [c]hath the LORD brought you
out with a mighty[2389] hand,[3027] and redeemed[6299] you out of the house[1004] of
bondmen,[5650] from the hand of Pharaoh
king[4428] of Egypt.
9 Know[3045] therefore that the LORD
thy God, he *is* God, [a]the faithful[539]
God,[410] [b]which keepeth[8104] covenant and
mercy[2617] with them that love[157] him
and keep his commandments to a thousand generations;[1755]
10 And [a]repayeth them that hate[8130]
him to their face, to destroy[6] them:
[b]he will not be slack309 to him that
hateth[8130] him, he will repay[7999] him to
his face.
11 Thou shalt therefore keep the
commandments, and the statutes,[2706] and
the judgments,[4941] which I command[6680]
thee this day,[3117] to do them.
12 [a]Wherefore it shall come to pass,
[I]if ye hearken[8085] to these judgments, and
keep, and do them, that the LORD thy
God shall keep unto thee [b]the covenant
and the mercy which he sware[7650] unto
thy fathers:
13 And he will [a]love thee, and
bless[1288] thee, and multiply thee: [b]he will
also bless the fruit of thy womb,[990] and
the fruit of thy land,[127] thy corn, and
thy wine, and thine oil,[3323] the increase of
thy kine,504 and the flocks of thy sheep,
in the land which he sware unto thy fathers to give thee.
14 Thou shalt be blessed[1288] above
all people: [a]there shall not be male or female barren[6135] among you, or among
your cattle.
15 And the LORD will take away from
thee all sickness, and will put none of the
[a]evil[7451] diseases4064 of Egypt, which
thou knowest,[3045] upon thee; but will lay
them upon all *them* that hate thee.
16 And [a]thou shalt consume all the
people which the LORD thy God shall deliver thee; [b]thine eye shall have no pity
upon them: neither shalt thou serve their
gods; for that *will be* [c]a snare[4170] unto
thee.
17 If thou shalt say[559] in thine
heart,3824 These nations *are* more than I;
how can I [a]dispossess[3423] them?
18 [a]Thou shalt not be afraid of them:
but shalt well [b]remember[2142] what the
LORD thy God did[6213] unto Pharaoh, and
unto all Egypt;
19 [a]The great temptations[4531] which
thine eyes saw,[7200] and the signs,[226] and
the wonders,[4159] and the mighty hand,
and the stretched out arm, whereby the
LORD thy God brought thee out: so shall
the LORD thy God do unto all the people
of whom thou art afraid.[3373]
20 [a]Moreover the LORD thy God will
send the hornet among them, until they
that are left,[7604] and hide themselves
from thee, be destroyed.[6]
21 Thou shalt not be affrighted[6206]
at them: for the LORD thy God *is*
[a]among[7130] you, [b]a mighty God and
terrible.[3372]
22 [a]And the LORD thy God will [I]put
out those nations before thee by little and
little: thou mayest not consume[3615] them

2 [c]Ex. 23:32; 34:12, 15, 16; Deut. 20:10; Josh. 2:14; 9:18; Judg. 1:24; 2:2
3 [a]Josh. 23:12; 1Kgs. 11:2; Ezra 9:2
4 [a]Deut. 6:15
5 [I]Hebr. *statues, or, pillars* [a]Ex. 23:24; 34:13; Deut. 12:2, 3
6 [a]Ex. 19:6; Deut. 14:2; 26:19; Ps. 50:5; Jer. 2:3 [b]Ex. 19:5; Amos 3:2; 1Pet. 2:9
7 [a]Deut. 10:22
8 [a]Deut. 10:15 [b]Ex. 32:13; Ps. 105:8, 9, 10; Luke 1:55, 72, 73 [c]Ex. 13:3, 14
9 [a]Isa. 49:7; 1Cor. 1:9; 10:13; 2Cor. 1:18; 1Thess. 5:24; 2Thess. 3:3; 2Tim. 2:13; Heb. 11:11; 1John 1:9 [b]Ex. 20:6; Deut. 5:10; Neh. 1:5; Dan. 9:4
10 [a]Isa. 59:18; Nah. 1:2 [b]Deut. 32:35
12 [I]Hebr. *because* [a]Lev. 26:3; Deut. 28:1 [b]Ps. 105:8, 9; Luke 1:55, 72, 73
13 [a]John 14:21 [b]Deut. 28:4
14 [a]Ex. 23:26
15 [a]Ex. 9:14; 15:26; Deut. 28:27, 60
16 [a]Deut. 7:2 [b]Deut. 13:8; 19:13, 21; 25:12 [c]Ex. 23:33; Deut. 12:30; Judg. 8:27; Ps. 106:36
17 [a]Num. 33:53
18 [a]Deut. 31:6 [b]Ps. 105:5
19 [a]Deut. 4:34; 29:3
20 [a]Ex. 23:28; Josh. 24:12
21 [a]Num. 11:20; 14:9, 14, 42; 16:3; Josh. 3:10 [b]Deut. 10:17; Neh. 1:5; 4:14; 9:32
22 [I]Hebr. *pluck off* [a]Ex. 23:29, 30

at once, lest the beasts[2416] of the field[7704]
increase upon thee.
23 But the LORD thy God shall deliver them [I]unto thee, and shall
destroy[2000] them with a mighty destruction,[4103] until they be destroyed.[8045]
24 And [a]he shall deliver their
kings[4428] into thine hand, and thou shalt
destroy their name [b]from under
heaven:[8064] [c]there shall no man be able to
stand before thee, until thou have destroyed them.
25 The graven images of their gods
[a]shall ye burn with fire: thou [b]shalt not
desire the silver or gold *that is* on them,
nor take *it* unto thee, lest thou be
[c]snared[3369] therein: for it *is* [d]an abomination[8441] to the LORD thy God.
26 Neither shalt thou bring an
abomination into thine house, lest thou
be a cursed thing[2764] like it: *but* thou
shalt utterly detest[8262] it, and thou shalt
utterly abhor[8581] it; [a]for it *is* a cursed
thing.

Remember God in Canaan

8 All the commandments which I
command[6680] thee this day[3117] [a]shall
ye observe[8104] to do, that ye may live,[2421]
and multiply, and go in and possess the
land[776] which the LORD sware[7650] unto
your fathers.[1]
2 And thou shalt remember[2142] all
the way[1870] which the LORD thy God[430]
[a]led thee these forty years in the wilderness, to humble thee, *and* [b]to prove[5254]
thee, [c]to know[3045] what *was* in thine
heart, whether thou wouldest keep[8104] his
commandments, or no.
🗝 3 And he humbled thee, and [a]suf-
fered thee to hunger, and [b]fed thee with
manna,[4478] which thou knewest[3045] not,
neither did thy fathers know; that he
might make thee know that man[120] doth
[c]not live by bread only, but by every
word that proceedeth out of the
mouth[6310] of the LORD doth man live.
4 [a]Thy raiment waxed not old upon
thee, neither did thy foot swell, these
forty years.
5 [a]Thou shalt also consider[3045] in
thine heart, that, as a man[376] chasteneth
his son,[1121] *so* the LORD thy God chasteneth thee.
6 Therefore thou shalt keep the
commandments of the LORD thy God,
[a]to walk in his ways,[1870] and to fear[3372]
him.
7 For the LORD thy God bringeth thee
into a good[2896] land, [a]a land of brooks of
water, of fountains and depths that
spring out of valleys and hills;
8 A land of wheat, and barley, and
vines, and fig trees, and pomegranates; a
land [I]of oil[8081] olive, and honey;
9 A land wherein thou shalt eat
bread without scarceness, thou shalt not
lack any *thing* in it; a land [a]whose stones
are iron, and out of whose hills thou
mayest dig brass.
10 [a]When thou hast eaten and art
full, then thou shalt bless[1288] the LORD
thy God for the good land which he hath
given thee.
11 Beware[8104] that thou forget not
the LORD thy God, in not keeping[8104] his
commandments, and his judgments, and
his statutes,[2708] which I command thee
this day:
12 [a]Lest *when* thou hast eaten and
art full, and hast built goodly[2896]
houses,[1004] and dwelt *therein;*
13 And *when* thy herds and thy
flocks multiply, and thy silver and thy
gold is multiplied, and all that thou hast
is multiplied;
14 [a]Then thine heart be lifted up, and
thou [b]forget the LORD thy God, which
brought thee forth out of the land of
Egypt, from the house[1004] of
bondage;[5650]
15 Who [a]led thee through that great
and terrible[3372] wilderness, [b]*wherein were*
fiery[8314] serpents,[5175] and scorpions, and
drought, where *there was* no water; [c]who
brought thee forth water out of the rock
of flint;

23 [I]Hebr. *before thy face*
24 [a]Josh. 10:24, 25, 42; 12:1 [b]Ex. 17:14; Deut. 9:14; 25:19; 29:20 [c]Deut. 11:25; Josh. 1:5; 10:8; 23:9
25 [a]Ex. 32:20; Deut. 12:3; 1Chr. 14:12 [b]Josh. 7:1, 21 [c]Judg. 8:27; Zeph. 1:3 [d]Deut. 17:1
26 [a]Lev. 27:28; Deut. 13:17; Josh. 6:17, 18; 7:1
1 [a]Deut. 4:1; 5:32, 33; 6:1-3
2 [a]Deut. 1:3; 2:7; 29:5; Ps. 136:16; Amos 2:10 [b]Ex. 16:4; Deut. 13:3 [c]2Chr. 32:31; John 2:25
3 [a]Ex. 16:2, 3 [b]Ex. 16:12, 14, 35 [c]Ps. 104:29; Matt. 4:4; Luke 4:4
4 [a]Deut. 29:5; Neh. 9:21
5 [a]2Sam. 7:14; Ps. 89:32; Prov. 3:12; Heb. 12:5, 6; Rev. 3:19
6 [a]Deut. 5:33
7 [a]Deut. 11:10-12
8 [I]Hebr. *of olive tree of oil*
9 [a]Deut. 33:25
10 [a]Deut. 6:11, 12
12 [a]Deut. 28:47; 32:15; Prov. 30:9; Hos. 13:6
14 [a]1Cor. 4:7 [b]Ps. 106:21
15 [a]Isa. 63:12, 13, 14; Jer. 2:6 [b]Num. 21:6; Hos. 13:5 [c]Num. 20:11; Ps. 78:15; 114:8

🗝 **8:3** See note on Deuteronomy 6:13, 16.

16 Who fed thee in the wilderness with [a]manna, which thy fathers knew[3045] not, that he might humble thee, and that he might prove thee, [b]to do thee good[3190] at thy latter end;

17 [a]And thou say in thine heart, My power and the might of *mine* hand[3027] hath gotten[6213] me this wealth.[2428]

18 But thou shalt remember the LORD thy God: [a]for *it is* he that giveth thee power to get wealth, [b]that he may establish his covenant[1285] which he sware unto thy fathers, as *it is* this day.

19 And it shall be, if thou do at all forget the LORD thy God, and walk after other gods,[430] and serve[5647] them, and worship[7812] them, [a]I testify[5749] against you this day that ye shall surely perish.[6]

20 As the nations which the LORD destroyeth before your face, [a]so shall ye perish; because ye would not be obedient[8085] unto the voice of the LORD your God.

God Will Destroy the Canaanites

9 Hear[8085] O Israel: Thou *art* to [a]pass over Jordan this day, to go in to possess nations[1471] [b]greater and mightier than thyself, cities great and [c]fenced up to heaven,8064

2 A people[5971] great and tall, [a]the children[1121] of the Anakims, whom thou knowest,[3045] and *of whom* thou hast heard[8085] *say,* Who can stand before the children of Anak!

3 Understand therefore this day, that the LORD thy God[430] *is* he which [a]goeth over before thee; *as* a [b]consuming fire [c]he shall destroy[8045] them, and he shall bring them down before thy face: [d]so shalt thou drive them out, and destroy[6] them quickly, as the LORD hath said[1696] unto thee.

4 [a]Speak[559] not thou in thine heart, after that the LORD thy God hath cast them out from before thee, saying, For my righteousness[6666] the LORD hath brought me in to possess this land: but [b]for the wickedness[7564] of these nations the LORD doth drive them out from before thee.

16 [a]Ex. 16:15; Deut. 8:3 [b]Jer. 24:5, 6; Heb. 12:11
17 [a]Deut. 9:4; 1Cor. 4:7
18 [a]Prov. 10:22; Hos. 2:8 [b]Deut. 7:8, 12
19 [a]Deut. 4:26; 30:18
20 [a]Dan. 9:11, 12
1 [a]Deut. 11:31; Josh. 3:16; 4:19 [b]Deut. 4:38; 7:1; 11:23 [c]Deut. 1:28
2 [a]Num. 13:22, 28, 32, 33
3 [a]Deut. 31:3; Josh. 3:11 [b]Deut. 4:24; Heb. 12:29 [c]Deut. 7:23 [d]Ex. 23:31; Deut. 7:24
4 [a]Deut. 8:17; Rom. 11:6, 20; 1Cor. 4:4, 7 [b]Gen. 15:16; Lev. 18:24, 25; Deut. 18:12
5 [a]Titus 3:5 [b]Gen. 12:7; 13:15; 15:7; 17:8; 26:4; 28:13
6 [a]Ex. 32:9; 33:3; 34:9; Deut. 9:3
7 [a]Ex. 14:11; 16:2; 17:2; Num. 11:4; 20:2; 25:2; Deut. 31:27
8 [a]Ex. 32:4; Ps. 106:19
9 [a]Ex. 24:12, 15 [b]Ex. 24:18; 34:28
10 [a]Ex. 31:18 [b]Ex. 19:17; 20:1; Deut. 4:10; 10:4; 18:16
12 [a]Ex. 32:7 [b]Deut. 31:29; Judg. 2:17

5 [a]Not for thy righteousness, or for the uprightness[3476] of thine heart, dost thou go to possess their land: but for the wickedness of these nations the LORD thy God doth drive them out from before thee, and that he may perform [b]the word[1697] which the LORD sware[7650] unto thy fathers,[1] Abraham, Isaac, and Jacob.

Remember the Rebellions in the Wilderness

6 Understand therefore, that the LORD thy God giveth thee not this good[2896] land to possess it for thy righteousness; for thou *art* [a]a stiffnecked people.

7 Remember,[2142] *and* forget not, how thou provokedst the LORD thy God to wrath[7107] in the wilderness: [a]from the day that thou didst depart out of the land of Egypt, until ye came unto this place, ye have been rebellious against the LORD.

8 Also [a]in Horeb ye provoked the LORD to wrath, so that the LORD was angry[599] with you to have destroyed[8045] you.

9 [a]When I was gone up[5927] into the mount to receive the tables of stone, *even* the tables of the covenant[1285] which the LORD made with you, then [b]I abode in the mount forty days[3117] and forty nights,[3915] I neither did eat bread nor drink water:

10 [a]And the LORD delivered unto me two tables of stone written with the finger of God; and on them *was written* according to all the words, which the LORD spake with you in the mount out of the midst of the fire [b]in the day of the assembly.[6951]

11 And it came to pass at the end of forty days and forty nights, *that* the LORD gave me the two tables of stone, *even* the tables of the covenant.

12 And the LORD said unto me, [a]Arise, get thee down quickly from hence; for thy people which thou hast brought forth out of Egypt have corrupted[7843] *themselves;* they are [b]quickly turned aside out of the way[1870] which I com-

manded[6680] them; they have made[6213] them a molten image.

13 Furthermore [a]the LORD spake unto me, saying, I have seen[7200] this people, and, behold, [b]it *is* a stiffnecked people:

14 [a]Let me alone,[7503] that I may destroy them, and [b]blot out[4229] their name from under heaven: [c]and I will make of thee a nation mightier and greater than they.

15 [a]So I turned and came down from the mount, and [b]the mount burned with fire: and the two tables of the covenant *were* in my two hands.[3027]

16 And [a]I looked,[7200] and, behold, ye had sinned[2398] against the LORD your God, *and* had made you a molten calf: ye had turned aside[5493] quickly out of the way which the LORD had commanded you.

17 And I took the two tables, and cast them out of my two hands, and brake[7665] them before your eyes.

18 And I [a]fell down[5307] before the LORD, as at the first,[7223] forty days and forty nights: I did neither eat bread, nor drink water, because of all your sins which ye sinned, in doing[6213] wickedly[7451] in the sight of the LORD, to provoke him to anger.[3707]

19 [a]For I was afraid[3025] of the anger and hot displeasure,[2534] wherewith the LORD was wroth[7107] against you to destroy you. [b]But the LORD hearkened[8085] unto me at that time also.

20 And the LORD was very angry[599] with Aaron to have destroyed him: and I prayed[6419] for Aaron also the same time.[6256]

21 And [a]I took your sin,[2403] the calf which ye had made, and burnt[8313] it with fire, and stamped[3807] it, *and* ground *it* very small, *even* until it was as small as dust:[6083] and I cast the dust thereof into the brook that descended out of the mount.

13 [a]Ex. 32:9 [b]Deut. 9:10; 10:16; 31:27; 2Kgs. 17:14
14 [a]Ex. 32:10 [b]Deut. 29:20; Ps. 9:5; 109:13 [c]Num. 14:12
15 [a]Ex. 32:15 [b]Ex. 19:18; Deut. 4:11; 5:23
16 [a]Ex. 32:19
18 [a]Ex. 34:28; Ps. 106:23
19 [a]Ex. 32:10, 11 [b]Ex. 32:14; 33:17; Deut. 10:10; Ps. 106:23
21 [a]Ex. 32:20; Isa. 31:7
22 [a]Num. 11:1, 3; 5 [b]Ex. 17:7 [c]Num. 11:4, 34
23 [a]Num. 13:3; 14:1 [b]Ps. 106:24, 25
24 [a]Deut. 31:27
25 [a]Deut. 9:18
26 [a]Ex. 32:11-13
28 [a]Gen. 41:57; 1Sam. 14:25 [b]Ex. 32:12; Num. 14:16
29 [a]Deut. 4:20; 1Kgs. 8:51; Neh. 1:10; Ps. 95:7 [b]Ex. 34:1, 2 [c]Ex. 25:10

22 And at [a]Taberah, and at [b]Massah, and at [c]Kibroth–hattaavah, ye provoked the LORD to wrath.

23 Likewise [a]when the LORD sent you from Kadesh–barnea, saying, Go up[5927] and possess the land which I have given you; then ye rebelled[4784] against the commandment[6310] of the LORD your God, and [b]ye believed[539] him not, nor hearkened to his voice.

24 [a]Ye have been rebellious against the LORD from the day that I knew[3045] you.

25 [a]Thus I fell down before the LORD forty days and forty nights, as I fell down *at the first*; because the LORD had said he would destroy you.

26 [a]I prayed therefore unto the LORD, and said, O Lord[136] GOD, destroy[7843] not thy people and thine inheritance,[5159] which thou hast redeemed[6299] through thy greatness, which thou hast brought forth out of Egypt with a mighty hand.

27 Remember thy servants,[5650] Abraham, Isaac, and Jacob; look not unto the stubbornness of this people, nor to their wickedness,[7562] nor to their sin:

28 Lest [a]the land whence thou broughtest us out say, [b]Because the LORD was not able to bring them into the land which he promised[1696] them, and because he hated them, he hath brought them out to slay[4191] them in the wilderness.

29 [a]Yet they *are* thy people and thine inheritance, which thou broughtest out by thy mighty power and by thy stretched out arm.

The Second Set of Stone Tablets

10 At that time the LORD said unto me, [a]Hew[6458] thee two tables of stone like unto the first,[7223] and come up[5927] unto me into the mount, and [b]make thee an ark[727] of wood.

2 And I will write on the tables the words[1697] that were in the first tables

10:1–5 God's rewriting of His Law was a demonstration of His forgiveness. The ark of the covenant, made of wood (humanity) and covered with gold (deity), is believed by some to be a symbol of Jesus, in whom full humanity and full deity were combined (Col. 2:9).

which thou brakest,[7665] and [a]thou shalt
put them in the ark.
3 And I made[6213] an ark *of* [a]shittim
wood, and [b]hewed two tables of stone
like unto the first, and went up into the
mount, having the two tables in mine
hand.[3027]
4 And [a]he wrote on the tables, according to the first writing, the ten
[I]commandments, [b]which the LORD spake
unto you in the mount out of the midst
of the fire [c]in the day of the assembly:[6951] and the LORD gave them unto me.
5 And I turned myself and [a]came
down from the mount, and [b]put the tables
in the ark which I had made; [c]and there
they be, as the LORD commanded[6680] me.
6 And the children[1121] of Israel took
their journey from Beeroth [a]of the children of Jaakan to [b]Mosera: [c]there Aaron
died,[4191] and there he was buried;[6912] and
Eleazar his son[1121] ministered in the
priest's office[3547] in his stead.
7 [a]From thence they journeyed unto
Gudgodah; and from Gudgodah to
Jotbath, a land of rivers of waters.
8 At that time[6256] [a]the LORD[3068]
separated[914] the tribe[7626] of Levi, [b]to
bear[5375] the ark[727] of the covenant[1285] of
the LORD, [c]to stand before the LORD to
minister[8334] unto him, and [d]to bless[1288] in
his name, unto this day.
9 [a]Wherefore Levi hath no part nor
inheritance[5159] with his brethren;[251] the
LORD *is* his inheritance, according as the
LORD thy God[430] promised[1696] him.
10 And [a]I stayed in the mount, according to the [I]first time, forty days[3117]
and forty nights;[3915] and [b]the LORD
hearkened[8085] unto me at that time also,
and the LORD would[14] not destroy[7843] thee.
11 [a]And the LORD said unto me,
Arise, [I]take *thy* journey before the
people,[5971] that they may go in and possess the land, which I sware[7650] unto
their fathers[1] to give unto them.

What God Requires

12 And now, Israel, [a]what doth the
LORD thy God require of thee, but [b]to
fear[3372] the LORD thy God, [c]to walk in all
his ways,[1870] and [d]to love[157] him, and to
serve[5647] the LORD thy God with all thy
heart[3824] and with all thy soul,[5315]
13 To keep[8104] the commandments of
the LORD, and his statutes, which I
command[6680] thee this day [a]for thy
good?[2896]
14 Behold, [a]the heaven[8064] and the
heaven of heavens *is* the LORD's thy
God, [b]the earth[776] *also,* with all that
therein *is.*
15 [a]Only the LORD had a delight[2836]
in thy fathers to love them, and he
chose[977] their seed[2233] after them, *even*
you above all people, as *it is* this day.
🗝 16 Circumcise[4135] therefore [a]the
foreskin[6190] of your heart, and be no
more [b]stiffnecked.
17 For the LORD your God *is* [a]God of
gods,[430] and [b]Lord[113] of lords, a great
God,[410] [c]a mighty, and a terrible,[3372]
which [d]regardeth[5375] not persons,[6440] nor
taketh reward:
18 [a]He doth execute the judgment[4941] of the fatherless and widow,
and loveth[157] the stranger,[1616] in giving
him food and raiment.
19 [a]Love ye therefore the stranger:
for ye were strangers in the land of
Egypt.
🗝 20 [a]Thou shalt fear the LORD thy

2 [a]Ex. 25:16, 21
3 [a]Ex. 25:5, 10; 37:1 [b]Ex. 34:4
4 [I]Hebr. *words* [a]Ex. 34:28 [b]Ex. 20:1 [c]Ex. 19:17; 9:10; 18:16
5 [a]Ex. 34:29 [b]Ex. 40:20 [c]1Kgs. 8:9
6 [a]Num. 33:31 [b]Num. 33:30 [c]Num. 20:28; 33:38
7 [a]Num. 33:32, 33
8 [a]Num. 3:6; 4:4; 8:14; 16:9 [b]Num. 4:15 [c]Deut. 18:5 [d]Lev. 9:22; Num. 6:23; Deut. 21:5
9 [a]Num. 18:20, 24; Deut. 18:1, 2; Ezek. 44:28
10 [I]Or, *former days* [a]Ex. 34:28; Deut. 9:18, 25 [b]Ex. 32:14, 33, 34; 33:17; Deut. 9:10
11 [I]Hebr. *go in journey* [a]Ex. 32:34; 33:1
12 [a]Mic. 6:8 [b]Deut. 6:13 [c]Deut. 5:33 [d]Deut. 6:5; 11:13; 30:16, 20; Matt. 22:37
13 [a]Deut. 6:24
14 [a]1Kgs. 8:27; Ps. 115:16; 148:4 [b]Gen. 14:19; Ex. 19:5; Ps. 24:1
15 [a]Deut. 4:37
16 [a]Lev. 26:41; Deut. 30:6; Jer. 4:4; Rom. 2:28, 29; Col. 2:11 [b]Deut. 9:6, 13
17 [a]Josh. 22:22; Ps. 136:2; Dan. 2:47; 11:36 [b]Rev. 17:14; 19:16 [c]Deut. 7:21 [d]2Chr. 19:7; Job 34:19; Acts 10:34; Rom. 2:11; Gal. 2:6; Eph. 6:9; Col. 3:25; 1Pet. 1:17
18 [a]Ps. 68:5; 146:9 **19** [a]Lev. 19:33, 34
20 [a]Deut. 6:13; Matt. 4:10; Luke 4:8

🗝 **10:16** Circumcision had been instituted as an outward sign of obedience and of relationship to God (Gen. 17:9–14). The citizen of a country has certain rights because of that citizenship. Circumcision was a sign, not that one was a citizen of the nation of Israel, but that he had certain rights under the covenant. In this verse the figure of circumcision is used to call for a change of heart. The circumcision of the flesh could not create a saving relationship with God. Indeed, the circumcision of the heart (repentance unto salvation) was that by which an Israelite (male or female) was made an heir to the promise of eternal life (Gal. 3:29).

🗝 **10:20** See note on Deuteronomy 6:13, 16.

God; him shalt thou serve, and to him shalt thou [b]cleave, [c]and swear by his name.

21 [a]He *is* thy praise,[8416] and he *is* thy God, [b]that hath done[6213] for thee these great and terrible things,[3372] which thine eyes have seen.[7200]

22 Thy fathers went down into Egypt [a]with threescore and ten persons;[5315] and now the LORD thy God hath made[7760] thee [b]as the stars of heaven for multitude.

God's Great Acts

11 Therefore thou shalt [a]love[157] the LORD thy God,[430] and [b]keep[8104] his charge,[4931] and his statutes, and his judgments,[4941] and his commandments, alway.

2 And know[3045] ye this day:[3117] for *I speak* not with your children[1121] which have not known, and which have not seen[7200] [a]the chastisement of the LORD your God, [b]his greatness, [c]his mighty[2389] hand,[3027] and his stretched out arm,

3 [a]And his miracles,[226] and his acts, which he did[6213] in the midst of Egypt unto Pharaoh the king[4428] of Egypt, and unto all his land;

4 And what he did unto the army[2428] of Egypt, unto their horses, and to their chariots; [a]how he made the water of the Red sea to overflow them as they pursued after you, and *how* the LORD hath destroyed[6] them unto this day;

5 And what he did unto you in the wilderness, until ye came into this place;

6 And [a]what he did unto Dathan and Abiram, the sons[1121] of Eliab, the son of Reuben: how the earth[776] opened her mouth,[6310] and swallowed them up, and their households,[1004] and their tents,[168] and all the [I]substance that [II]*was* in their possession, in the midst[7130] of all Israel:

7 But [a]your eyes have seen all the great acts of the LORD which he did.

New Life in the New Land

8 Therefore shall ye keep all the commandments which I command[6680] you this day, that ye may [a]be strong,[2388] and go in and possess the land, whither ye go to possess it;

9 And [a]that ye may prolong[748] *your* days in the land,[127] [b]which the LORD sware[7650] unto your fathers[1] to give unto them and to their seed,[2233] [c]a land[776] that floweth with milk and honey.

10 For the land, whither thou goest in to possess it, *is* not as the land of Egypt, from whence ye came out, [a]where thou sowedst thy seed, and wateredst *it* with thy foot, as a garden of herbs:

11 [a]But the land, whither ye go to possess it, *is* a land of hills and valleys, *and* drinketh water of the rain of heaven:[8064]

12 A land which the LORD thy God [I]careth for: [a]the eyes of the LORD thy God *are* always upon it, from the beginning[7225] of the year even unto the end[319] of the year.

13 And it shall come to pass, if ye shall hearken[8085] [a]diligently unto my commandments which I command you this day, [b]to love the LORD your God, and to serve[5647] him with all your heart[3824] and with all your soul,[5315]

14 That [a]I will give *you* the rain of your land in his due season,[6256] [b]the first rain and the latter rain, that thou mayest gather in[622] thy corn, and thy wine, and thine oil.[3323]

15 [a]And I will [I]send grass in thy fields[7704] for thy cattle, that thou mayest [b]eat and be full.

16 Take heed to yourselves, [a]that your heart be not deceived, and ye turn aside, and [b]serve other gods,[430] and worship[7812] them;

17 And *then* [a]the LORD's wrath[639] be kindled[2734] against you, and he [b]shut up the heaven, that there be no rain, and that the land yield not her fruit; and *lest* [c]ye perish[6] quickly from off the good[2896] land which the LORD giveth you.

18 Therefore [a]shall ye lay up[7760] these my words[1697] in your heart and in your soul, and [b]bind them for a sign[226] upon your hand, that they may be as frontlets[2903] between your eyes.

19 [a]And ye shall teach[3925] them your

---

20 [b]Deut. 11:22; 13:4 [c]Ps. 63:11
21 [a]Ex. 15:2; Ps. 22:3; Jer. 17:14 [b]1Sam. 12:24; 2Sam. 7:23; Ps. 106:21, 22
22 [a]Gen. 46:27; Ex. 1:5; Acts 7:14 [b]Gen. 15:5; Deut. 1:10; 28:62

1 [a]Deut. 10:12; 30:16, 20 [b]Zech. 3:7
2 [a]Deut. 8:5 [b]Deut. 5:24 [c]Deut. 7:19
3 [a]Ps. 78:12; 135:9
4 [a]Ex. 14:27, 28; 15:9, 10; Ps. 106:11
6 [I]Or, *living substance which followed them* [II]Hebr. *was at their feet* [a]Num. 16:1, 31; 27:3; Ps. 106:17
7 [a]Deut. 5:3; 7:19
8 [a]Josh. 1:6, 7
9 [a]Deut. 4:40; 5:16; Prov. 10:27 [b]Deut. 9:5 [c]Ex. 3:8
10 [a]Zech. 14:18
11 [a]Deut. 8:7
12 [I]Hebr. *seeketh* [a]1Kgs. 9:3
13 [a]Deut. 6:17; 11:22 [b]Deut. 10:12
14 [a]Lev. 26:4; Deut. 28:12 [b]Joel 2:23; James 5:7
15 [I]Hebr. *give* [a]Ps. 104:14 [b]Deut. 6:11; Joel 2:19
16 [a]Deut. 29:18; Job 31:27 [b]Deut. 8:19; 30:17
17 [a]Deut. 6:15 [b]1Kgs. 8:35; 2Chr. 6:26; 7:13 [c]Deut. 4:26; 8:19, 20; 30:18; Josh. 23:13, 15, 16
18 [a]Deut. 6:6; 32:46 [b]Deut. 6:8
19 [a]Deut. 4:9, 10; 6:7

children, speaking[1696] of them when thou sittest in thine house,[1004] and when thou walkest by the way,[1870] when thou liest down, and when thou risest up.

20 [a]And thou shalt write them upon the door posts of thine house, and upon thy gates:

21 That [a]your days may be multiplied, and the days of your children, in the land which the LORD sware unto your fathers to give them, [b]as the days of heaven upon the earth.

22 For if [a]ye shall diligently keep[8104] all these commandments which I command you, to do them, to love the LORD your God, to walk in all his ways, and [b]to cleave unto him;

23 Then will the LORD [a]drive out[3423] all these nations[1471] from before you, and ye shall [b]possess greater nations and mightier than yourselves.

24 [a]Every place whereon the soles[3709] of your feet shall tread shall be yours: [b]from the wilderness and Lebanon, from the river, the river Euphrates, even unto the uttermost sea shall your coast be.

25 [a]There shall no man[376] be able to stand before you: *for* the LORD your God shall [b]lay the fear[6343] of you and the dread[4172] of you upon all the land that ye shall tread upon, [c]as he hath said[1696] unto you.

26 [a]Behold,[7200] I set before you this day a blessing[1293] and a curse;[7045]

27 [a]A blessing, if ye obey[8085] the commandments of the LORD your God, which I command you this day:

28 And a [a]curse, if ye will not obey the commandments of the LORD your God, but turn aside out of the way which I command you this day, to go after other gods, which ye have not known.

29 And it shall come to pass, when the LORD thy God hath brought thee in unto the land whither thou goest to possess it, that thou shalt put [a]the blessing upon mount Gerizim, and the curse upon mount Ebal.

30 *Are* they not on the other side Jordan, by the way where the sun goeth down, in the land of the Canaanites, which dwell in the champaign[6160] over against Gilgal, [a]beside the plains of Moreh?

31 [a]For ye shall pass over Jordan to go in to possess the land which the LORD your God giveth you, and ye shall possess it, and dwell therein.

32 And ye shall observe [a]to do all the statutes and judgments which I set before you this day.

Worship Only in the Special Place

12 [a]These *are* the statutes[2706] and judgments,[4941] which ye shall observe[8104] to do in the land, which the LORD God[430] of thy fathers[1] giveth thee to possess it, [b]all the days[3117] that ye live[2416] upon the earth.[127]

2 [a]Ye shall utterly destroy[6] all the places, wherein the nations[1471] which ye shall [I]possess served[5647] their gods,[430] [b]upon the high mountains, and upon the hills, and under every green tree:

3 And [a]ye shall [I]overthrow[5422] their altars, and break[7665] their pillars, and burn[8313] their groves[842] with fire; and ye shall hew down[1438] the graven images[6456] of their gods, and destroy the names of them out of that place.

4 [a]Ye shall not do so unto the LORD your God.

⊶ 5 But unto the place which the LORD your God shall [a]choose[977] out of all your tribes[7626] to put his name there, *even* unto his habitation shall ye seek, and thither thou shalt come:

6 And [a]thither ye shall bring your

20 [a]Deut. 6:9
21 [a]Deut. 4:40; 6:2; Prov. 3:2; 4:10; 9:11 [b]Ps. 72:5; 89:29
22 [a]Deut. 6:17; 11:13 [b]Deut. 10:20; 30:20
23 [a]Deut. 4:38; 9:5 [b]Deut. 9:1
24 [a]Josh. 1:3; 14:9 [b]Gen. 15:18; Ex. 23:31; Num. 34:3-15
25 [a]Deut. 7:24 [b]Deut. 2:25 [c]Ex. 23:27
26 [a]Deut. 30:1, 15, 19
27 [a]Deut. 28:2
28 [a]Deut. 28:15
29 [a]Deut. 27:12, 13; Josh. 8:33
30 [a]Gen. 12:6; Judg. 7:1
31 [a]Deut. 9:1; Josh. 1:11
32 [a]Deut. 5:32; 12:32

1 [a]Deut. 6:1 [b]Deut. 4:10; 1Kgs. 8:40
2 [I]Or, *inherit* [a]Ex. 34:13; Deut. 7:5 [b]2Kgs. 16:4; 17:10, 11; Jer. 3:6
3 [I]Hebr. *break down* [a]Num. 33:52; Judg. 2:2
4 [a]Deut. 12:31
5 [a]Deut. 12:11; 26:2; Josh. 9:27; 1Kgs. 8:29; 2Chr. 7:12; Ps. 78:68
6 [a]Lev. 17:3, 4

⊶ **12:5** "The place . . . God shall choose" is the prophetic reference to God's selecting one place in the Promised Land for a fixed central sanctuary to which all Israel would be related. This was necessary since the people would no longer be camped around the Tabernacle, but would be dispersed into the towns of Canaan.

burnt offerings,[5930] and your sacrifices,[2077] and your [b]tithes,[4643] and heave offerings[8641] of your hand, and your vows,[5088] and your freewill offerings,[5071] and the firstlings of your herds and of your flocks:

7 And [a]there ye shall eat before the LORD your God, and [b]ye shall rejoice in all that ye put your hand unto, ye and your households,[1004] wherein the LORD thy God hath blessed[1288] thee.

8 Ye shall not do after all *the things* that we do here this day, [a]every man[376] whatsoever *is* right in his own eyes.

9 For ye are not as yet come to the rest and to the inheritance,[5159] which the LORD your God giveth you.

10 But *when* [a]ye go over[5647] Jordan, and dwell in the land which the LORD your God giveth you to inherit,[5157] and *when* he giveth you rest from all your enemies round about, so that ye dwell in safety;

11 Then there shall be [a]a place which the LORD your God shall choose to cause his name to dwell[7931] there; thither shall ye bring all that I command[6680] you; your burnt offerings, and your sacrifices, your tithes, and the heave offering[8641] of your hand, and all [I]your choice vows which ye vow[5087] unto the LORD:

12 And [a]ye shall rejoice before the LORD your God, ye, and your sons,[1121] and your daughters, and your menservants,[5650] and your maidservants, and the Levite that *is* within your gates; forasmuch as [b]he hath no part nor inheritance with you.

13 [a]Take heed to thyself that thou offer not thy burnt offerings in every place that thou seest:

14 [a]But in the place which the LORD shall choose in one of thy tribes, there thou shalt offer thy burnt offerings, and there thou shalt do all that I command thee.

15 Notwithstanding [a]thou mayest kill[2076] and eat flesh[1320] in all thy gates, whatsoever thy soul[5315] lusteth after, according to the blessing[1293] of the LORD thy God which he hath given thee: [b]the unclean[2931] and the clean[2889] may eat thereof, [c]as of the roebuck,[6643] and as of the hart.

16 [a]Only ye shall not eat the blood; ye shall pour[8210] it upon the earth[776] as water.

17 Thou mayest not eat within thy gates the tithe[4643] of thy corn, or of thy wine, or of thy oil,[3233] or the firstlings of thy herds or of thy flock, nor any of thy vows which thou vowest,[5087] nor thy freewill offerings, or heave offering of thine hand:

18 [a]But thou must eat them before the LORD thy God in the place which the LORD thy God shall choose, thou, and thy son, and thy daughter, and thy manservant,[5650] and thy maidservant, and the Levite that *is* within thy gates: and thou shalt rejoice before the LORD thy God in all that thou puttest thine hands[3027] unto.

19 [a]Take heed to thyself that thou forsake[5800] not the Levite [I]as long as thou livest upon the earth.

20 When the LORD thy God shall enlarge thy border, [a]as he hath promised[1696] thee, and thou shalt say,[559] I will eat flesh, because thy soul longeth to eat flesh; thou mayest eat flesh, whatsoever thy soul lusteth after.

21 If the place which the LORD thy God hath chosen to put his name there be too far from thee, then thou shalt kill of thy herd and of thy flock, which the LORD hath given thee, as I have commanded thee, and thou shalt eat in thy gates whatsoever thy soul lusteth after.

22 [a]Even as the roebuck and the hart is eaten, so thou shalt eat them: the unclean and the clean shall eat *of* them alike.

23 [a]Only [I]be sure[2388] that thou eat not the blood: [b]for the blood *is* the life;[5315] and thou mayest not eat the life with the flesh.

24 Thou shalt not eat it; thou shalt pour it upon the earth as water.

25 Thou shalt not eat it; [a]that it may go well[3190] with thee, and with thy children[1121] after thee, [b]when thou shalt do *that which is* right in the sight of the LORD.

6 [b]Deut. 12:17; 14:22, 23; 15:19, 20

7 [a]Deut. 14:26 [b]Lev. 23:40; Deut. 12:12, 18; 16:11, 14, 15; 26:11; 27:7

8 [a]Judg. 17:6; 21:25

10 [a]Deut. 11:31

11 [I]Hebr. *the choice of your vows* [a]Deut. 12:5, 14, 18, 21, 26; 14:23; 15:20; 16:2; 17:8; 18:6; 23:16; 26:2; 31:11; Josh. 18:1; 1Kgs. 8:29; Ps. 78:68

12 [a]Deut. 12:7 [b]Deut. 10:9; 14:29

13 [a]Lev. 17:4

14 [a]Deut. 12:11

15 [a]Deut. 12:21 [b]Deut. 12:22 [c]Deut. 14:5; 15:22

16 [a]Gen. 9:4; Lev. 7:26; 17:10; Deut. 12:23, 24; 15:23

18 [a]Deut. 12:11, 12; 14:23

19 [I]Hebr. *all thy days* [a]Deut. 14:27

20 [a]Gen. 15:18; 28:14; Ex. 34:24; Deut. 11:24; 19:8

22 [a]Deut. 12:15

23 [I]Hebr. *be strong* [a]Deut. 12:16 [b]Gen. 9:4; Lev. 17:11, 14

25 [a]Deut. 4:40; Isa. 3:10 [b]Ex. 15:26; Deut. 13:18; 1Kgs. 11:38

26 Only thy [a]holy things[6944] which thou hast, and [b]thy vows, thou shalt take, and go unto the place which the LORD shall choose:

27 And [a]thou shalt offer[6213] thy burnt offerings, the flesh and the blood, upon the altar of the LORD thy God: and the blood of thy sacrifices shall be poured out[8210] upon the altar[4196] of the LORD thy God, and thou shalt eat the flesh.

28 Observe and hear[8085] all these words[1697] which I command thee, [a]that it may go well with thee, and with thy children after thee for ever, when thou doest[6213] *that which is* good[2896] and right in the sight of the LORD thy God.

Destroy All Idol Worship

29 When [a]the LORD thy God shall cut off[3772] the nations from before thee, whither thou goest to possess them, and thou [I]succeedest[3423] them, and dwellest in their land;

30 Take heed to thyself [a]that thou be not snared[3369] [I]by following them, after that they be destroyed[8045] from before thee; and that thou enquire not after their gods, saying, How did these nations serve their gods? even so will I do likewise.

31 [a]Thou shalt not do so unto the LORD thy God: for every [I]abomination to the LORD, which he hateth,[8130] have they done[6213] unto their gods; for [b]even their sons and their daughters they have burnt[8313] in the fire to their gods.

32 What thing[1697] soever I command you, observe to do it: [a]thou shalt not add thereto, nor diminish from it.

13 If there arise among[7130] you a prophet,[5030] or a [a]dreamer of dreams, [b]and giveth thee a sign[226] or a wonder,

2 And [a]the sign or the wonder come to pass, whereof he spake[1696] unto thee, saying, Let us go after other gods,[430] which thou hast not known,[3045] and let us serve[5647] them;

3 Thou shalt not hearken[8085] unto the words[1697] of that prophet, or that dreamer of dreams: for the LORD your God[430] [a]proveth[5254] you, to know whether ye love[157] the LORD your God with all your heart[3824] and with all your soul.[5315]

4 Ye shall [a]walk after the LORD your God, and fear[3372] him, and keep[8104] his commandments, and obey[8085] his voice, and ye shall serve him, and [b]cleave unto him.

5 And [a]that prophet, or that dreamer of dreams, shall be put to death;[4191] because he hath [I]spoken[1696] to turn *you* away[5627] from the LORD your God, which brought you out of the land of Egypt, and redeemed[6299] you out of the house[1004] of bondage,[5650] to thrust thee out of the way[1870] which the LORD thy God commanded[6680] thee to walk in. [b]So shalt thou put the evil[7451] away from the midst of thee.

6 [a]If thy brother,[251] the son[1121] of thy mother, or thy son, or thy daughter, or [b]the wife[802] of thy bosom, or thy friend,[7453] [c]which *is* as thine own soul, entice[5496] thee secretly, saying, Let us go and serve other gods, which thou hast not known, thou, nor thy fathers;[1]

7 *Namely,* of the gods of the people[5971] which *are* round about you, nigh unto thee, or far off from thee, from the *one* end of the earth[776] even unto the *other* end of the earth;

8 Thou shalt [a]not consent[14] unto him, nor hearken[8085] unto him; neither shall thine eye pity him, neither shalt thou spare, neither shalt thou conceal[3680] him:

9 But [a]thou shalt surely kill him; [b]thine hand[3027] shall be first[7223] upon him to put him to death, and afterwards the hand of all the people.

10 And thou shalt stone him with stones, that he die;[4191] because he hath

26 [a]Num. 5:9, 10; 18:19 [b]1Sam. 1:21, 22, 24

27 [a]Lev. 1:5, 9, 13; 17:11

28 [a]Deut. 12:25

29 [I]Hebr. *inheritest,* or, *possessest them* [a]Ex. 23:23; Deut. 19:1; Josh. 23:4

30 [I]Hebr. *after them* [a]Deut. 7:16

31 [I]Hebr. *abomination of the* [a]Lev. 18:3, 26, 30; Deut. 12:4; 2Kgs. 17:15 [b]Lev. 18:21; 20:2; Deut. 18:10; Jer. 32:35; Ezek. 23:37

32 [a]Deut. 4:2; 13:18; Josh. 1:7; Prov. 30:6; Rev. 22:18

1 [a]Zech. 10:2 [b]Matt. 24:24; 2Thess. 2:9

2 [a]Deut. 18:22; Jer. 28:9; Matt. 7:22

3 [a]Deut. 8:2; Matt. 24:24; 1Cor. 11:19; 2Thess. 2:11; Rev. 13:14

4 [a]2Kgs. 23:3; 2Chr. 34:31 [b]Deut. 10:20; 30:20

5 [I]Hebr. *spoken revolt against the LORD* [a]Deut. 18:20; Jer. 14:15; Zech. 13:3 [b]Deut. 17:7; 22:21, 22, 24; 1Cor. 5:13

6 [a]Deut. 17:2 [b]Gen. 16:5; Deut. 28:54; Prov. 5:20; Mic. 7:5 [c]1Sam. 18:1, 3; 20:17

8 [a]Prov. 1:10

9 [a]Deut. 17:5 [b]Deut. 17:7; Acts 7:58

13:1–5 See note on Deuteronomy 18:20–22.

sought to thrust thee away from the LORD thy God, which brought thee out of the land of Egypt, from the house of [I]bondage.

11 And [a]all Israel shall hear,[8085] and fear, and shall do no more any such wickedness[7451] as this is among you.

12 [a]If thou shalt hear *say* in one of thy cities, which the LORD thy God hath given thee to dwell there, saying,

13 *Certain* men,[582] [Ia]the children[1121] of Belial,[1100] [b]are gone out from among you, and have [c]withdrawn the inhabitants of their city, saying, [d]Let us go and serve other gods, which ye have not known;

14 Then shalt thou enquire, and make search, and ask[7592] diligently,[3190] and, behold, *if it be* truth,[571] *and* the thing[1697] certain, *that* such abomination is wrought[6213] among[7130] you;

15 Thou shalt surely smite[5221] the inhabitants of that city with the edge[6310] of the sword,[2719] [a]destroying it utterly,[2763] and all that *is* therein, and the cattle thereof, with the edge of the sword.

16 And thou shalt gather[6908] all the spoil of it into the midst of the street thereof, and shalt [a]burn[8313] with fire the city, and all the spoil thereof every whit,[3632] for the LORD thy God: and it shall be [b]an heap for ever;[5769] it shall not be built again.

17 And [a]there shall cleave nought[3972] of the [I]cursed thing[2764] to thine hand: that the LORD may [b]turn from the fierceness of his anger, and shew thee mercy, and have compassion[7355] upon thee, and multiply thee, [c]as he hath sworn[7650] unto thy fathers;

18 When thou shalt hearken to the voice of the LORD thy God, [a]to keep all his commandments which I command[6680] thee this day,[3117] to do *that which is* right in the eyes of the LORD thy God.

14 Ye *are* [a]the children of the LORD your God:[430] [b]ye shall not cut[1413] yourselves, nor make[7760] any baldness between your eyes for the dead.[4191]

2 [a]For thou *art* an holy[6918] people[5971] unto the LORD thy God, and the LORD hath chosen[977] thee to be a peculiar[5459] people unto himself, above all the nations[5971] that *are* upon the earth.[127]

Clean and Unclean Food

3 [a]Thou shalt not eat any abominable thing.[8441]

4 [a]These *are* the beasts which ye shall eat: the ox, the sheep, and the goat,

5 The hart, and the roebuck,[6643] and the fallow deer, and the wild goat, and the [I]pygarg,[1788] and the wild ox, and the chamois.

6 And every beast that parteth the hoof, and cleaveth the cleft into two claws, *and* cheweth[5927] the cud among the beasts, that ye shall eat.

7 Nevertheless these ye shall not eat of them that chew the cud, or of them that divide the cloven hoof; *as* the camel, and the hare, and the coney: for they chew the cud, but divide not the hoof; *therefore* they *are* unclean[2931] unto you.

8 And the swine, because it divideth the hoof, yet cheweth not the cud, it *is* unclean unto you: ye shall not eat of their flesh,[1320] [a]nor touch[5060] their dead carcase.[5038]

9 [a]These ye shall eat of all that *are* in the waters: all that have fins and scales shall ye eat:

10 And whatsoever hath not fins and scales ye may not eat; it *is* unclean unto you.

11 *Of* all clean[2889] birds ye shall eat.

10 [I]Hebr. *bondmen*
11 [a]Deut. 17:13; 19:20
12 [a]Josh. 22:11; Judg. 20:1, 2
13 [I]Or, *naughty men* [a]Judg. 19:22; 1Sam. 2:12; 25:17, 25; 1Kgs. 21:10, 13; 2Cor. 6:15 [b]1John 2:19; Jude 19 [c]2Kgs. 17:21 [d]Deut. 13:26
15 [a]Ex. 22:20; Lev. 27:28; Josh. 6:17, 21
16 [a]Josh. 6:24 [b]Josh. 8:28; Isa. 17:1; 25:2; Jer. 49:2
17 [I]Or, *devoted* [a]Deut. 7:26; Josh. 6:18 [b]Josh. 6:26 [c]Gen. 22:17; 26:4, 24; 28:14
18 [a]Deut. 12:25, 28, 32
1 [a]Rom. 8:16; 9:8, 26; Gal. 3:26 [b]Lev. 19:28; 21:5; Jer. 16:6; 41:5; 47:5; 1Thess. 4:13
2 [a]Lev. 20:26; Deut. 7:6; 26:18, 19
3 [a]Ezek. 4:14; Acts 10:13, 14
4 [a]Lev. 11:2
5 [I]Or, *bison*
8 [a]Lev. 11:26, 27
9 [a]Lev. 11:9

14:3–21 In this passage God declares certain animals to be "unclean," thereby making it unlawful for the Israelites to eat them. They were, however, free to partake of those animals which are declared to be "clean." There are three views as to why God established this system. Some believe that the "unclean" animals were designated as such for hygienic purposes. They speculate that these animals posed certain health risks for those who would eat them, even after the animals

(continued on next page)

12 [a]But these *are they* of which ye shall not eat: the eagle, and the ossifrage, and the ospray,

13 And the glede,[7201] and the kite, and the vulture after his kind,

14 And every raven after his kind,

15 And the owl, and the night hawk, and the cuckow, and the hawk after his kind,

16 The little owl, and the great owl, and the swan,

17 And the pelican, and the gier eagle, and the cormorant,

18 And the stork, and the heron after her kind, and the lapwing, and the bat.

19 And [a]every creeping thing that flieth *is* unclean unto you: [b]they shall not be eaten.

20 *But of* all clean fowls ye may eat.

21 [a]Ye shall not eat *of* any thing that dieth of itself: thou shalt give it unto the stranger[1616] that *is* in thy gates, that he may eat it; or thou mayest sell it unto an alien:[5237] [b]for thou *art* an holy people unto the LORD thy God. [c]Thou shalt not seethe a kid in his mother's[517] milk.

Tithing

22 [a]Thou shalt truly tithe all the increase of thy seed,[2233] that the field[7704] bringeth forth year by year.

23 [a]And thou shalt eat before the LORD thy God, in the place which he shall choose[977] to place his name there, the tithe[4643] of thy corn, of thy wine, and of thine oil,[3323] and [b]the firstlings of thy herds and of thy flocks; that thou mayest learn[3925] to fear[3372] the LORD thy God always.

24 And if the way[1870] be too long for thee, so that thou art not able to carry[5375] it; *or* [a]if the place be too far from thee, which the LORD thy God shall choose to set[7760] his name there, when the LORD thy God hath blessed[1288] thee:

25 Then shalt thou turn *it* into money, and bind up the money in thine hand,[3027] and shalt go unto the place which the LORD thy God shall choose:

26 And thou shalt bestow that money for whatsoever thy soul[5315] lusteth after,[183] for oxen, or for sheep, or for wine, or for strong drink, or for whatsoever thy soul [I]desireth: [a]and thou shalt eat there before the LORD thy God, and thou shalt rejoice, thou, and thine household,[1004]

27 And [a]the Levite that *is* within thy gates; thou shalt not forsake[5800] him; for [b]he hath no part nor inheritance[5159] with thee.

28 [a]At the end of three years thou shalt bring forth all the tithe of thine increase the same year, and shalt lay *it* up within thy gates:

29 [a]And the Levite, (because [b]he hath no part nor inheritance with thee,) and the stranger, and the fatherless, and the widow, which *are* within thy gates, shall come, and shall eat and be satisfied; that [c]the LORD thy God may bless[1288] thee in all the work of thine hand which thou doest.[6213]

The Seventh Year

15 ⚿ At the end of [a]*every* seven years thou shalt make[6213] a release.[8059]

12 [a]Lev. 11:13
19 [a]Lev. 11:20 [b]Lev. 11:21
21 [a]Lev. 17:15; 22:8; Ezek. 4:14 [b]Deut. 14:2 [c]Ex. 23:19; 34:26
22 [a]Lev. 27:30; Deut. 12:6, 17; Neh. 10:37
23 [a]Deut. 12:5-7, 17, 18 [b]Deut. 15:19, 20
24 [a]Deut. 12:21
26 [I]Hebr. *asketh of thee* [a]Deut. 12:7, 18; 26:11
27 [a]Deut. 12:12, 18, 19 [b]Num. 18:20; Deut. 18:1, 2
28 [a]Deut. 26:12; Amos 4:4
29 [a]Deut. 26:12 [b]Deut. 12:12; 14:27 [c]Deut. 15:10; Prov. 3:9, 10; Mal. 3:10
1 [a]Ex. 21:2; 23:10, 11; Lev. 25:2, 4; Deut. 31:10; Jer. 34:14

(continued from previous page)

had been properly cooked and prepared. Others have suggested that since the Israelites would soon be entering the Promised Land, this system was intended to distinguish God's people from the religions and practices of their pagan neighbors. Therefore, certain pagan practices were not allowed, such as eating or drinking blood and the boiling of a calf or small animal in its mother's milk (see v. 21), since those things were part of the idolatrous rituals of the heathen people living around them. Finally, others contend that there was nothing in the animals themselves that warranted their designation as clean or unclean, but that God established the system as a test of Israel's obedience and loyalty to Him. Notice that the last two views are not necessarily mutually exclusive.

⚿ **15:1–18** See note on Leviticus 25:1–55, on the Sabbatical Year and the Year of Jubile.

⚿ **15:1–3** See note on Leviticus 19:33, 34.

2 And this *is* the manner of the release: Every [I]creditor that lendeth *ought* unto his neighbour shall release *it;* he shall not exact *it* of his neighbour, or of his brother;[251] because it is called[7121] the LORD's release.

3 [a]Of a foreigner[5237] thou mayest exact *it again:* but *that* which is thine with thy brother thine hand[3027] shall release;

4 [I]Save when there shall be no poor among[7130] you; [a]for the LORD shall greatly bless[1288] thee in the land which the LORD thy God[430] giveth thee *for* an inheritance[5159] to possess it:

5 Only [a]if thou carefully hearken[8085] unto the voice of the LORD thy God, to observe[8104] to do all these commandments which I command[6680] thee this day.[3117]

6 For the LORD thy God blesseth thee, as he promised[1696] thee: and [a]thou shalt lend unto many nations,[1471] but thou shalt not borrow; and [b]thou shalt reign[4910] over many nations, but they shall not reign over thee.

7 If there be among you a poor man of one of thy brethren within any of thy gates in thy land which the LORD thy God giveth thee, [a]thou shalt not harden thine heart,[3824] nor shut thine hand from thy poor brother:

8 [a]But thou shalt open thine hand wide unto him, and shalt surely lend him sufficient for his need, *in that* which he wanteth.

9 Beware[8104] that there be not a [I]thought[1697] in thy [II]wicked[1100] heart, saying, The seventh year, the year of release, is at hand;[7126] and thine [a]eye be evil[7489] against thy poor brother, and thou givest him nought;[3808] and [b]he cry unto the LORD against thee, and [c]it be sin[2403] unto thee.

10 Thou shalt surely give him, and [a]thine heart shall not be grieved when thou givest unto him: because that [b]for this thing[1697] the LORD thy God shall bless thee in all thy works, and in all that thou puttest thine hand unto.

11 For [a]the poor shall never cease out of the land: therefore I command thee, saying, Thou shalt open thine hand wide unto thy brother, to thy poor, and to thy needy, in thy land.

12 *And* [a]if thy brother, an Hebrew man, or an Hebrew woman, be sold unto thee, and serve[5647] thee six years; then in the seventh year thou shalt let him go free from thee.

13 And when thou sendest him out free from thee, thou shalt not let him go away empty:

14 Thou shalt furnish him liberally[6059] out of thy flock, and out of thy floor, and out of thy winepress: *of that* wherewith the LORD thy God hath [a]blessed thee thou shalt give unto him.

15 And [a]thou shalt remember[2142] that thou wast a bondman[5650] in the land of Egypt, and the LORD thy God redeemed[6299] thee: therefore I command thee this thing to day.

16 And it shall be, [a]if he say[559] unto thee, I will not go away from thee; because he loveth[157] thee and thine house,[1004] because he is well[2895] with thee;

17 Then thou shalt take an aul,[4836] and thrust *it* through his ear[241] unto the door, and he shall be thy servant[5650] for ever.[5769] And also unto thy maidservant thou shalt do likewise.

18 It shall not seem hard unto thee, when thou sendest him away free from thee; for he hath been worth [a]a double hired servant *to thee,* in serving thee six years: and the LORD thy God shall bless thee in all that thou doest.[6213]

Firstborn Animals

19 [a]All the firstling males[2145] that come of thy herd and of thy flock thou shalt sanctify[6942] unto the LORD thy God: thou shalt do no work with the firstling of thy bullock, nor shear the firstling of thy sheep.

20 [a]Thou shalt eat *it* before the LORD thy God year by year in the place which the LORD shall choose,[977] thou and thy household.[1004]

21 [a]And if there be *any* blemish[3971] therein, *as if it be* lame, or blind, *or have*

---

2 [I]Hebr. *master of the lending of his hand*
3 [a]Deut. 23:20
4 [I]Or, *To the end that there be no poor among you* [a]Deut. 28:8
5 [a]Deut. 28:1
6 [a]Deut. 28:12, 44 [b]Deut. 28:13; Prov. 22:7
7 [a]1John 3:17
8 [a]Lev. 25:35; Matt. 5:42; Luke 6:34, 35
9 [I]Hebr. *word* [II]Hebr. *Belial* [a]Deut. 28:54, 56; Prov. 23:6; 28:22; Matt. 20:15 [b]Deut. 24:15 [c]Matt. 25:41, 42
10 [a]2Cor. 9:5, 7 [b]Deut. 14:29; 24:19; Ps. 41:1; Prov. 22:9
11 [a]Matt. 26:11; Mark 14:7; John 12:8
12 [a]Ex. 21:2; Lev. 25:39; Jer. 34:14
14 [a]Prov. 10:22
15 [a]Deut. 5:15; 16:12
16 [a]Ex. 21:5, 6
18 [a]Isa. 16:14; 21:16
19 [a]Ex. 13:2; 34:19; Lev. 27:26; Num. 3:13
20 [a]Deut. 12:5, 6, 7, 17; 14:23; 16:11, 14
21 [a]Lev. 22:20; Deut. 17:1

any ill blemish, thou shalt not sacrifice[2076] it unto the LORD thy God.

22 Thou shalt eat it within thy gates: [a]the unclean[2931] and the clean[2889] *person shall eat it* alike, as the roebuck,[6643] and as the hart.

23 [a]Only thou shalt not eat the blood thereof; thou shalt pour[8210] it upon the ground[776] as water.

Three Festivals Each Year

16 🔑 Observe[8104] the [a]month of Abib, and keep[6213] the passover[6453] unto the LORD thy God:[430] for [b]in the month of Abib the LORD thy God brought thee forth out of Egypt [c]by night.[3915]

2 Thou shalt therefore sacrifice[2076] the passover unto the LORD thy God, of the flock and [a]the herd, in the [b]place which the LORD shall choose[977] to place his name there.

3 [a]Thou shalt eat no leavened bread[2557] with it; seven days[3117] shalt thou eat unleavened bread[4682] therewith, *even* the bread of affliction; for thou camest forth out of the land of Egypt in haste: that thou mayest remember[2142] the day when thou camest forth out of the land of Egypt all the days of thy life.[2416]

4 [a]And there shall be no leavened bread seen[7200] with thee in all thy coast seven days; [b]neither shall there *any thing* of the flesh,[1320] which thou sacrificedst the first[7223] day at even, remain all night until the morning.

5 Thou mayest not [I]sacrifice the passover within any of thy gates, which the LORD thy God giveth thee:

6 But at the place which the LORD thy God shall choose to place his name in, there thou shalt sacrifice the passover [a]at even, at the going down of the sun, at the season[4150] that thou camest forth out of Egypt.

7 And thou shalt [a]roast and eat *it* [b]in the place which the LORD thy God shall choose: and thou shalt turn in the morning, and go unto thy tents.[168]

8 Six days thou shalt eat unleavened bread: and [a]on the seventh day *shall be* a [I]solemn assembly[6116] to the LORD thy God: thou shalt do no work *therein.*

9 [a]Seven weeks shalt thou number[5608] unto thee: begin to number the seven weeks from *such time as* thou beginnest *to put* the sickle to the corn.

10 And thou shalt keep the feast of weeks unto the LORD thy God with [I]a tribute of a freewill offering[5071] of thine hand,[3027] which thou shalt give *unto the LORD thy God,* [a]according as the LORD thy God hath blessed[1288] thee:

11 And [a]thou shalt rejoice before the LORD thy God, thou, and thy son,[1121] and thy daughter, and thy manservant,[5650] and thy maidservant, and the Levite that *is* within thy gates, and the stranger,[1616] and the fatherless, and the widow, that *are* among[7130] you, in the place which the LORD thy God hath chosen to place his name there.

12 [a]And thou shalt remember that thou wast a bondman[5650] in Egypt: and thou shalt observe and do these statutes.[2706]

13 [a]Thou shalt observe the feast of tabernacles[5521] seven days, after that thou hast gathered in[622] thy [I]corn and thy wine:

14 And [a]thou shalt rejoice in thy feast, thou, and thy son, and thy daughter, and thy manservant, and thy maidservant, and the Levite, the stranger, and the fatherless, and the widow, that *are* within thy gates.

15 [a]Seven days shalt thou keep a solemn feast[2287] unto the LORD thy God in the place which the LORD shall choose: because the LORD thy God shall bless thee in all thine increase, and in all the works of thine hands, therefore thou shalt surely rejoice.

16 [a]Three times in a year shall all

22 [a]Deut. 12:15, 22

23 [a]Deut. 12:16, 23

1 [a]Ex. 12:2 [b]Ex. 13:4; 34:18 [c]Ex. 12:29, 42

2 [a]Num. 28:19; [b]Deut. 12:5, 26

3 [a]Ex. 12:15, 19, 39; 13:3, 6, 7; 34:18

4 [a]Ex. 13:7 [b]Ex. 12:10; 34:25

5 [I]Or, *kill*

6 [a]Ex. 12:6

7 [a]Ex. 12:8, 9; 2Chr. 35:13 [b]2Kgs. 23:23; John 2:13, 23; 11:55

8 [I]Hebr. *restraint* [a]Ex. 12:16; 13:6; Lev. 23:8

9 [a]Ex. 23:16; 34:22; Lev. 23:15; Num. 28:26; Acts 2:1

10 [I]Or, *sufficiency* [a]Deut. 16:17; 1Cor. 16:2

11 [a]Deut. 12:7, 12, 18; 16:14

12 [a]Deut. 15:15

13 [I]Hebr. *floor, and thy winepress* [a]Ex. 23:16; Lev. 23:34; Num. 29:12

14 [a]Neh. 8:9

15 [a]Lev. 23:39, 40

16 [a]Ex. 23:14, 17; 34:23

🔑 **16:1–12** See note on Exodus 23:14–17.

thy males appear[7200] before the LORD thy God in the place which he shall choose; in the feast of unleavened bread, and in the feast of weeks, and in the feast of tabernacles: and [b]they shall not appear before the LORD empty:

17 Every man[376] *shall give* [I]as he is able, [a]according to the blessing[1288] of the LORD thy God which he hath given thee.

The Legal System

18 [a]Judges[8199] and officers[7860] shalt thou make thee in all thy gates, which the LORD thy God giveth thee, throughout thy tribes:[7626] and they shall judge[8199] the people[5971] with just[6664] judgment.[4941]

19 [a]Thou shalt not wrest judgment; [b]thou shalt not respect persons, [c]neither take a gift: for a gift doth blind the eyes of the wise,[2450] and pervert the [I]words[1697] of the righteous.

20 [I]That which is altogether just[6664] shalt thou follow, that thou mayest [a]live,[2421] and inherit[3423] the land which the LORD thy God giveth thee.

21 [a]Thou shalt not plant thee a grove[842] of any trees near unto the altar[4196] of the LORD thy God, which thou shalt make[6213] thee.

22 [a]Neither shalt thou set thee up *any* [I]image; which the LORD thy God hateth.[8130]

17 Thou [a]shalt not sacrifice[2076] unto the LORD thy God[430] *any* bullock, or [I]sheep, wherein *is* blemish,[3971] *or* any evilfavouredness: for that *is* an abomination unto the LORD thy God.

2 [a]If there be found among[7130] you, within any of thy gates which the LORD thy God giveth thee, man[376] or woman,[802] that hath wrought[6213] wickedness[7451] in the sight of the LORD thy God, [b]in transgressing[5674] his covenant,[1285]

3 And hath gone and served[5647] other gods,[430] and worshipped[7812] them, either [a]the sun, or moon, or any of the host[6635] of heaven,[8064] [b]which I have not commanded;[6680]

4 [a]And it be told[5046] thee, and thou hast heard[8085] *of it,* and enquired diligently,[3190] and, behold, *it be* true, *and* the thing certain, *that* such abomination is wrought in Israel:

5 Then shalt thou bring forth that man or that woman, which have committed that wicked[7451] thing, unto thy gates, *even* that man or that woman, and [a]shalt stone them with stones, till they die.[4191]

6 [a]At the mouth[6310] of two witnesses, or three witnesses, shall he that is worthy of death[4191] be put to death; *but* at the mouth of one witness he shall not be put to death.

7 [a]The hands[3027] of the witnesses shall be first[7223] upon him to put him to death, and afterward the hands of all the people.[5971] So [b]thou shalt put the evil[7451] away from among you.

8 [a]If there arise a matter too hard[6381] for thee in judgment,[4941] [b]between blood and blood, between plea[1779] and plea, and between stroke[5061] and stroke, *being* matters of controversy[7379] within thy gates: then shalt thou arise, [c]and get thee up into the place which the LORD thy God shall choose;[977]

9 And [a]thou shalt come unto the priests[3548] the Levites, and [b]unto the judge[8199] that shall be in those days, and enquire; [c]and they shall shew[5046] thee the sentence[1697] of judgment:

10 And thou shalt do according to the sentence, which they of that place which the LORD shall choose shall shew thee; and thou shalt observe to do according to all that they inform[3384] thee:

11 According to the sentence[6310] of the law[8451] which they shall teach[3384] thee, and according to the judgment which they shall tell[559] thee, thou shalt do: thou shalt not decline from the sentence which they shall shew thee, *to* the right hand, nor *to* the left.

12 And [a]the man that will do presumptuously,[2087] [I]and will not hearken[8085] unto the priest [b]that standeth to minister[8334] there before the LORD thy God, or unto the judge, even that man

16 [b]Ex. 23:15; 34:20
17 IHebr. *according to the gift of his hand* [a]Deut. 16:10
18 [a]Deut. 1:16; 1Chr. 23:4; 26:29; 2Chr. 19:5, 8
19 IOr, *matters* [a]Ex. 23:2, 6; Lev. 19:15 [b]Deut. 1:17; Prov. 24:23 [c]Ex. 23:8; Prov. 17:23; Eccl. 7:7
20 IHebr. *Justice, justice* [a]Ezek. 18:5, 9
21 [a]Ex. 34:13; 1Kgs. 14:15; 16:33; 2Kgs. 17:16; 21:3; 2Chr. 33:3
22 IOr, *statue, or, pillar* [a]Lev. 26:1

1 IOr, *goat* [a]Deut. 15:21; Mal. 1:8, 13, 14
2 [a]Deut. 13:6 [b]Josh. 7:11, 15; 23:16; Judg. 2:20; 2Kgs. 18:12; Hos. 8:1
3 [a]Deut. 4:19; Job 31:26 [b]Jer. 7:22, 23, 31; 19:5; 32:35
4 [a]Deut. 13:12, 14
5 [a]Lev. 24:14, 16; Deut. 13:10; Josh. 7:25
6 [a]Num. 35:30; Deut. 19:15; Matt. 18:16; John 8:17; 2Cor. 13:1; 1Tim. 5:19; Heb. 10:28
7 [a]Deut. 13:9; Acts 7:58 [b]Deut. 13:5; 17:12; 19:19
8 [a]2Chr. 19:10; Hag. 2:11; Mal. 2:7 [b]Ex. 21:13, 20, 22, 28; 22:2; Num. 35:11, 16, 19; Deut. 19:4, 10, 11 [c]Deut. 12:5; 19:17; Ps. 122:5
9 [a]Jer. 18:18 [b]Deut. 19:17 [c]Ezek. 44:24
12 IHebr. *not to hearken* [a]Num. 15:30; Ezra 10:8; Hos. 4:4 [b]Deut. 18:5, 7

shall die: and [c]thou shalt put away the
evil from Israel.
13 [a]And all the people shall hear,[8085]
and fear,[3372] and do no more presumptuously.

The Future King

🔑 14 When thou art come unto the land
which the LORD thy God giveth thee, and
shalt possess it, and shalt dwell therein,
and shalt say, [a]I will set a king[4428] over
me, like as all the nations[1471] that *are*
about me;
15 Thou shalt in any wise set *him*
king over thee, [a]whom the LORD thy God
shall choose: *one* [b]from among[7130] thy
brethren[251] shalt thou set king over thee:
thou mayest not set a stranger over thee,
which *is* not thy brother.[251]
🔑 16 But he shall not multiply [a]horses
to himself, nor cause the people [b]to
return[7725] to Egypt, to the end that he
should multiply horses: forasmuch as [c]the
LORD hath said unto you, [d]Ye shall henceforth return no more that way.[1870]
17 Neither shall he multiply wives[802]
to himself, that [a]his heart[3824] turn not
away: neither shall he greatly multiply to
himself silver and gold.
18 [a]And it shall be, when he sitteth
upon the throne[3678] of his kingdom,[4467]
that he shall write him a copy of this law
in a book[5612] out of [b]*that which is* before
the priests the Levites:
19 And [a]it shall be with him, and he
shall read[7121] therein all the days of his
life:[2416] that he may learn[3925] to fear the
LORD his God, to keep[8104] all the
words[1697] of this law and these
statutes,[2706] to do them:
20 That his heart be not lifted up
above his brethren, and that he [a]turn not
aside from the commandment,[4687] *to* the
right hand, or *to* the left: to the end that
he may prolong[748] *his* days in his kingdom, he, and his children, in the midst of
Israel.

The Priests' and Levites' Shares

18 The priests[3548] the Levites, *and*
all the tribe[7626] of Levi, [a]shall
have no part nor inheritance[5159] with
Israel: they [b]shall eat the offerings of the
LORD made by fire, and his inheritance.
2 Therefore shall they have no inheritance among[7130] their brethren:[251] the
LORD *is* their inheritance, as he hath
said[1696] unto them.
3 And this shall be the priest's[3548]
due[4941] from the people,[5971] from them
that offer[2076] a sacrifice,[2077] whether *it be*
ox or sheep; and [a]they shall give unto the
priest the shoulder, and the two cheeks,
and the maw.[6896]
4 [a]The firstfruit *also* of thy corn, of
thy wine, and of thine oil,[3323] and the
first[7225] of the fleece of thy sheep, shalt
thou give him.
5 For [a]the LORD thy God hath chosen[977] him out of all thy tribes,[7626]

12 [c]Deut. 13:5
13 [a]Deut. 13:11; 19:20
14 [a]1Sam. 8:5, 19, 20
15 [a]1Sam. 9:15; 10:24; 16:12; 1Chr. 22:10 [b]Jer. 30:21
16 [a]1Kgs. 4:26; 10:26, 28; Ps. 20:7 [b]Isa. 31:1; Ezek. 17:15 [c]Ex. 13:17; Num. 14:3, 4 [d]Deut. 28:68; Hos. 11:5; Jer. 42:15
17 [a]1Kgs. 11:3, 4
18 [a]2Kgs. 11:12 [b]Deut. 31:9, 26; 2Kgs. 22:8
19 [a]Josh. 1:8; Ps. 119:97, 98
20 [a]Deut. 5:32; 1Kgs. 15:5
1 [a]Num. 18:20; 26:62; Deut. 10:9 [b]Num. 18:8, 9; 1Cor. 9:13
3 [a]Lev. 7:30-34
4 [a]Ex. 22:29; Num. 18:12, 24
5 [a]Ex. 28:1; Num. 3:10

🔑 **17:14–20** See note on 1 Samuel 8:5–7.

🔑 **17:16** The regulations mentioned in this verse, namely the multiplying of horses and wives, were set up so that the king's attention would not be turned from God to a reliance on himself, or worse yet, on idols. God specifically commanded that the children of Israel rely on Him when it came to military endeavors, not on horses or chariots (Josh. 11:4, 6). Israel's kings would be tempted to amass as much protection as they thought they needed; in doing so, however, their hearts would be turned away from God. The example of God destroying the Egyptians in the Red Sea was intended to show Israel that the accumulating of horses for the purpose of building military strength was unnecessary as long as they trusted exclusively in God (Ex. 15:19, 21; Deut. 11:4). When Elisha and his servant were surrounded by the armies of Aram, God opened the eyes of the servant so that he could see God's army of chariots surrounding the Aramean forces. God was providing His watchcare over his servants. God wanted Israel to depend on Him, not on what man could do (Ps. 33:17; 147:10). David and Solomon are examples of kings who disobeyed this command (2 Sam. 8:4; 1 Kgs. 4:26; 10:25).

[b]to stand to minister[8334] in the name of
the LORD, him and his sons[1121] for ever.
6 And if a Levite come from any of
thy gates out of all Israel, where he
[a]sojourned,[1481] and come with all the
desire[183] of his mind[5315] [b]unto the place
which the LORD shall choose;
7 Then he shall minister in the name
of the LORD his God, [a]as all his brethren
the Levites *do,* which stand there before
the LORD.
8 They shall have like [a]portions to
eat, beside [I]that which cometh of the sale
of his patrimony.

Forbidden Practices

9 When thou art come into the land
which the LORD thy God giveth thee,
[a]thou shalt not learn[3925] to do after the
abominations of those nations.[1471]
🔑 10 There shall not be found among
you *any one* that maketh his son or his
daughter [a]to pass[5674] through the fire, [b]*or*
that useth divination,[7081] *or* an observer
of times, or an enchanter,[5172] or a
witch,[3784]
11 [a]Or a charmer,[2267] or a consulter[7592] with familiar spirits, or a wizard,[3049] or a [b]necromancer.[4191]
12 For all that do these things *are* an
abomination unto the LORD: and [a]because
of these abominations the LORD thy God
doth drive them out from before thee.
13 Thou shalt be [I]perfect[8549] with the
LORD thy God.
14 For these nations, which thou
shalt [I]possess, hearkened[8085] unto observers of times, and unto diviners:[7080]
but as for thee, the LORD thy God hath
not suffered thee so *to do.*

The Prophet Like Moses

🔑 15 [a]The LORD thy God[430] will raise
up unto thee a Prophet[5030] from the
midst of thee, of thy brethren, like unto
me; unto him ye shall hearken;[8085]
16 According to all that thou desiredst of the LORD thy God in Horeb [a]in
the day[3117] of the assembly,[6951] saying,
[b]Let me not hear[8085] again the voice of
the LORD my God, neither let me see this
great fire any more, that I die[4191] not.
17 And the LORD said[559] unto me,
[a]They have well[3190] *spoken that* which
they have spoken.[1696]
18 [a]I will raise them up a Prophet
from among their brethren, like unto thee,
and [b]will put my words[1697] in his
mouth;[6310] [c]and he shall speak unto them
all that I shall command[6680] him.
19 [a]And it shall come to pass, *that*
whosoever will not hearken unto my
words which he shall speak in my name,
I will require *it* of him.
🔑 20 But [a]the prophet, which shall presume to speak a word in my name,
which I have not commanded him to
speak, or [b]that shall speak in the name
of other gods,[430] even that prophet shall
die.

5 [b]Deut. 10:8; 17:12
6 [a]Num. 35:2, 3 [b]Deut. 12:5
7 [a]2Chr. 31:2
8 [I]Hebr. *his sales by the fathers* [a]2Chr. 31:4; Neh. 12:44, 47
9 [a]Lev. 18:26, 27, 30; Deut. 12:29-31
10 [a]Lev. 18:21; Deut. 12:31 [b]Lev. 19:26, 31; 20:27; Isa. 8:19
11 [a]Lev. 20:27 [b]1Sam. 28:7
12 [a]Lev. 18:24, 25; Deut. 9:4
13 [I]Or, *upright,* or, *sincere*
14 [I]Or, *inherit*
15 [a]Deut. 18:18; John 1:45; Acts 3:22; 7:37
16 [a]Deut. 9:10 [b]Ex. 20:19; Heb. 12:19
17 [a]Deut. 5:28
18 [a]Deut. 18:15; John 1:45; Acts 3:22; 7:37 [b]Isa. 51:16; John 17:8 [c]John 4:25; 8:28; 12:49, 50
19 [a]Acts 3:23
20 [a]Deut. 13:5; Jer. 14:14, 15; Zech. 13:3 [b]Deut. 13:1, 2; Jer. 2:8

🔑 **18:10** See note on Leviticus 18:21.

🔑 **18:15–19** The identity of this unnamed prophet is not revealed anywhere in the Old Testament. By Jesus' day, the Jews had developed a clear-cut expectation of a yet future figure who would fulfill Moses' words. Priests and Levites from Jerusalem asked John the Baptist if he was "the Prophet," and he denied it (John 1:21). It is elsewhere revealed that "the Prophet" spoken of in these verses is the Lord Jesus Christ (Acts 3:22, 23).

🔑 **18:20–22** The existence of prophets during the period of the monarchy presented a number of problems, one of which was how to distinguish between the true and false ones. Turbulent times, during which the people wanted to hear words of hope and security, produced the greatest outbreak of prophets for hire and seers with optimistic lies. Shortly after Judah started going into exile in Babylon, but before the fall of Jerusalem, Jeremiah and Ezekiel had to contend with a rash of these charlatans, upon whom they issued stern denunciations (Jer. 23:9–32; Ezek. 13:1–23). The penalty for being a false prophet was death (Deut. 13:5; 18:20; see Jer. 28:16).

In this passage in Deuteronomy chapter eighteen, Moses gave one of the tests by which the

(continued on next page)

21 And if thou say[559] in thine heart,
How shall we know[3045] the word which
the LORD hath not spoken?
22 [a]When a prophet speaketh in the
name of the LORD, [b]if the thing follow
not, nor come to pass,[935] that *is* the thing
which the LORD hath not spoken, *but* the
prophet hath spoken it [c]presumptu-
ously:[2087] thou shalt not be afraid[1481] of
him.

The Cities of Refuge

19 [key] When the LORD thy God[430]
[a]hath cut off[3772] the nations,[1471]
whose land the LORD thy God giveth thee,
and thou [I]succeedest[3423] them, and
dwellest in their cities, and in their
houses;[1004]
2 [a]Thou shalt separate[914] three cities
for thee in the midst of thy land, which
the LORD thy God giveth thee to possess
it.
3 Thou shalt prepare thee a way,[1870]
and divide the coasts of thy land, which
the LORD thy God giveth thee to inherit,[5157] into three parts, that every
slayer[7523] may flee thither.

22 [a]Jer. 28:9 [b]Deut. 13:2 [c]Deut. 18:20

1 [I]Hebr. *inheritest, or, possessest* [a]Deut. 12:29

2 [a]Ex. 21:13; Num. 35:10, 14; Josh. 20:2

4 [I]Hebr. *from yesterday the third day* [a]Num. 35:15; Deut. 4:42

5 [I]Hebr. *iron* [II]Hebr. *wood* [III]Hebr. *findeth*

6 [I]Hebr. *smite him in life* [II]Hebr. *from yesterday the third day* [a]Num. 35:12

8 [a]Gen. 15:18; Deut. 12:20

4 And [a]this *is* the case of the slayer,
which shall flee thither, that he may live:
Whoso killeth[5221] his neighbour[7453] ignorantly,[1847] whom he hated[8130] not [I]in time
past;
5 As when a man[376] goeth into the
wood with his neighbour to hew2404
wood, and his hand[3027] fetcheth a stroke
with the axe to cut down[3772] the tree,
and the [I]head slippeth from the
[II]helve,6086 and [III]lighteth upon his neighbour, that he die;[4191] he shall flee unto
one of those cities, and live:
6 [a]Lest the avenger[1350] of the blood
pursue the slayer, while his heart3824 is
hot, and overtake him, because the way
is long, and [I]slay[5221] him; whereas he *was*
not worthy of death,[4194] inasmuch as he
hated him not [II]in time past.
7 Wherefore I command[6680] thee,
saying, Thou shalt separate three cities
for thee.
8 And if the LORD thy God [a]enlarge
thy coast, as he hath sworn[7650] unto thy
fathers,[1] and give thee all the land which
he promised[1696] to give unto thy fathers;
9 If thou shalt keep[8104] all these
commandments to do them, which I com-

(continued from previous page)
people could distinguish a true prophet from a false one. If the prophet's message did not come true as predicted, he was a false prophet (see 1 Kgs. 22:28). In his conflict with the false prophet Hananiah, Jeremiah expressed the test positively, so that if the prophecy came true, all would know that Hananiah was a true prophet (Jer. 28:9). This was only a general rule which applied to the case at hand, because it was possible for a false prophet to utter a true message, either as a guess or as a test from the Lord to see whether the people would obey (Deut. 13:1–3). Another test for a true prophet was that he had to have the ability, as a sign of God's calling, to perform miracles (Ex. 4:6). A third test, though it did not always apply, was that an easy message in hard times was often an unreliable one (Jer. 23:16, 17, 29; 28:8, 9; Ezek. 13:10–16). The most important test of a true prophet was that the content of his message had to be consistent with all prior revelation. Thus, if a prophet said that Israel should serve another god, he was obviously false (Deut. 13:1–3). Similarly, in the New Testament both Paul and John taught that the content of the message already received was the standard by which to measure any new message, even if it came from Paul himself, or an angel (Gal. 1:8), or a spirit masquerading as God's Spirit (1 John 4:1–3). By this test alone the claims of the false religions of the world, and of the cults in particular, are silenced.

[key] **19:1–10** This passage outlines how the Israelites were to establish "cities of refuge" when they had entered the Promised Land. These places were designed to take in those who were accused of accidental homicides (killing someone without malice). Provision was made for their safety until their case could be judged. In the Promised Land there were six such cities established. Three were located on the east side of the Jordan River, while three others were established on the west side. For an explanation of the Levitical cities, of which the six "cities of refuge" were a part, see note on Joshua 21:2.

mand thee this day,[3117] to love[157] the LORD thy God, and to walk ever in his ways;[1870] [a]then shalt thou add three cities more for thee, beside these three:

10 That innocent[5355] blood be not shed[8210] in thy land, which the LORD thy God giveth thee *for* an inheritance,[5159] and *so* blood be upon thee.

11 But [a]if any man hate[8130] his neighbour, and lie in wait for him, and rise up against him, and smite[5221] him mortally[5315] that he die, and fleeth into one of these cities:

12 Then the elders[2205] of his city shall send and fetch him thence, and deliver him into the hand of the avenger of blood, that he may die.

13 [a]Thine eye shall not pity him, [b]but thou shalt put away *the guilt of* innocent blood from Israel, that it may go well[2895] with thee.

14 [a]Thou shalt not remove thy neighbour's landmark, which they of old time[7223] have set in thine inheritance, which thou shalt inherit in the land that the LORD thy God giveth thee to possess it.

Witnesses

15 [a]One witness shall not rise up against a man for any iniquity,5571 or for any sin,[2403] in any sin[2399] that he sinneth:[2398] at the mouth of two witnesses, or at the mouth[6310] of three witnesses, shall the matter be established.

16 If a false[2555] witness [a]rise up against any man to testify against him [I]*that which is* wrong;[5627]

17 Then both the men, between whom the controversy[7379] *is,* shall stand before the LORD, [a]before the priests[3548] and the judges,[8199] which shall be in those days;

18 And the judges shall make1875 diligent[3190] inquisition:1875 and, behold, *if* the witness *be* a false witness, *and* hath testified falsely[8267] against his brother;[251]

19 [a]Then shall ye do unto him, as he had thought[2161] to have done[6213] unto his brother: so [b]shalt thou put the evil[7451] away from among you.

20 [a]And those which remain shall hear,[8085] and fear,[3372] and shall henceforth commit[6213] no more any such evil among you.

21 [a]And thine eye shall not pity; *but* [b]life *shall go* for life,[5315] eye for eye, tooth for tooth, hand for hand, foot for foot.

How to Wage War

20 When thou goest out to battle against thine enemies, and seest [a]horses, and chariots, *and* a people[5971] more than thou, be not afraid[3372] of them: for the LORD thy God[430] *is* [b]with thee, which brought thee up[5927] out of the land of Egypt.

2 And it shall be, when ye are come nigh unto the battle, that the priest shall approach and speak[1696] unto the people,

3 And shall say[559] unto them, Hear,[8085] O Israel, ye approach[7126] this day[3117] unto battle against your enemies: let not your hearts [I]faint, fear not, and do not [II]tremble, neither be ye terrified[6206] because of them;

4 For the LORD your God *is* he that goeth with you, [a]to fight for you against your enemies, to save[3467] you.

5 And the officers[7860] shall speak unto the people, saying, What man *is there* that hath built a new house,[1004] and hath not [a]dedicated[2596] it? let him go and return[7725] to his house, lest he die[4191] in the battle, and another man[376] dedicate[2596] it.

6 And what man *is he* that hath planted a vineyard, and hath not *yet* [Ia]eaten[2490] of it? let him *also* go and return unto his house, lest he die in the battle, and another man eat of it.

7 [a]And what man *is there* that hath betrothed781 a wife,[802] and hath not taken her? let him go and return unto his house, lest he die in the battle, and another man take her.

8 And the officers shall speak further unto the people, and they shall say, [a]What man *is there that is* fearful[3373] and fainthearted? let him go and return unto

9 [a]Josh. 20:7, 8
11 [a]Ex. 21:12; Num. 35:16, 24; Deut. 27:24; Prov. 28:17
13 [a]Deut. 13:8; 25:12 [b]Num. 35:33, 34; Deut. 21:9; 1Kgs. 2:31
14 [a]Deut. 27:17; Job 24:2; Prov. 22:28; Hos. 5:10
15 [a]Num. 35:30; Deut. 17:6; Matt. 18:16; John 8:17; 2Cor. 13:1; 1Tim. 5:19; Heb. 10:28
16 [I]Or, *falling away* [a]Ps. 27:12; 35:11
17 [a]Deut. 17:9; 21:5
19 [a]Prov. 19:5, 9; Dan. 6:24 [b]Deut. 13:5; 17:7; 21:21; 22:21, 24; 24:7
20 [a]Deut. 17:13; 21:21
21 [a]Deut. 19:13 [b]Ex. 21:23, 24; Lev. 24:20; Matt. 5:38
1 [a]Ps. 20:7; Isa. 31:1 [b]Num. 23:21; Deut. 31:6, 8; 2Chr. 13:12; 32:7, 8
3 [I]Hebr. *be tender* [II]Hebr. *make haste*
4 [a]Deut. 1:30; 3:22; Josh. 23:10
5 [a]Neh. 12:27
6 [I]Hebr. *made it common* [a]Lev. 19:23, 24; Deut. 28:30
7 [a]Deut. 24:5
8 [a]Judg. 7:3

his house, lest his brethren's heart [I]faint as well as his heart.[3824]

9 And it shall be, when the officers have made an end[3615] of speaking[1696] unto the people, that they shall make captains[8269] of the armies[6635] [I]to lead the people.

10 When thou comest nigh[7126] unto a city to fight against it, [a]then proclaim[7121] peace unto it.

11 And it shall be, if it make thee answer of peace, and open unto thee, then it shall be, *that* all the people *that is* found therein shall be tributaries unto thee, and they shall serve[5647] thee.

12 And if it will make no peace with thee, but will make war against thee, then thou shalt besiege it:

13 And when the LORD thy God hath delivered it into thine hands,[3027] [a]thou shalt smite[5221] every male thereof with the edge[6310] of the sword:

14 But the women,[802] and the little ones,[2945] and [a]the cattle, and all that is in the city, *even* all the spoil thereof, shalt thou [I]take unto thyself; and [b]thou shalt eat the spoil of thine enemies, which the LORD thy God hath given thee.

15 Thus shalt thou do unto all the cities *which are* very far off from thee, which *are* not of the cities of these nations.[1471]

🔑 16 But [a]of the cities of these people, which the LORD thy God doth give thee *for* an inheritance,[5159] thou shalt save alive[2421] nothing that breatheth:

17 But thou shalt utterly destroy[2763] them; *namely,* the Hittites, and the Amorites, the Canaanites, and the Perizzites, the Hivites, and the Jebusites; as the LORD thy God hath commanded[6680] thee:

18 That [a]they teach[3925] you not to do after all their abominations, which they have done unto their gods; so should ye [b]sin[2398] against the LORD your God.

19 When thou shalt besiege a city a long time, in making war against it to take it, thou shalt not destroy[7843] the trees thereof by forcing an axe against them: for thou mayest eat of them, and thou shalt not cut them down[3772] ([I]for the tree of the field[7704] *is* man's[120] *life*) [II]to employ *them* in the siege:

20 Only the trees which thou knowest[3045] that they *be* not trees for meat, thou shalt destroy and cut them down; and thou shalt build bulwarks against the city that maketh[6213] war with thee, until [I]it be subdued.

Expiation for Innocent Blood

21 If *one* be found slain in the land[127] which the LORD thy God giveth thee to possess it, lying[5307] in the field,[7704] *and* it be not known[3045] who hath slain[2491] him:

2 Then thy elders[2205] and thy judges[8199] shall come forth, and they shall measure unto the cities which *are* round about him that is slain:

3 And it shall be, *that* the city *which is* next unto the slain man,[376] even the elders of that city shall take an heifer, which hath not been wrought[5647] with, *and* which hath not drawn in the yoke;

4 And the elders of that city shall bring down the heifer unto a rough valley, which is neither eared[5647] nor sown,

8 [I]Hebr. *melt*

9 [I]Hebr. to be *in the head of the people*

10 [a]2Sam. 20:18, 20

13 [a]Num. 31:7

14 [I]Hebr. *spoil* [a]Josh. 8:2 [b]Josh. 22:8

16 [a]Num. 21:2, 3, 35; 33:52; Deut. 7:1, 2; Josh. 11:14

18 [a]Deut. 7:4; 12:30, 31; 18:9 [b]Ex. 23:33

19 [I]Or, *for, O man, the tree of the field is to be employed in the siege* [II]Hebr. *to go from before thee*

20 [I]Hebr. *it come down*

🔑 **20:16–18** This is the final statement of God's justice on these seven peoples listed in this passage. Five hundred years before, God had stated that "their iniquity was not yet full" (Gen. 15:16), but it was now full to overflowing. Archaeological evidence reveals how incredibly depraved these tribes were. They practiced human sacrifice and every sort of sexual perversion. Because of the multitude and grievous nature of their sins, it is said that the land "vomiteth out her inhabitants" (Lev. 18:21–25). The sinfulness of these tribes would present a strong temptation to Israel; they must therefore be wiped out. As the incident with the Moabites revealed (Num. 25:1–3), Israel was all too prone to adopt the idolatrous and inhuman practices of her neighbors. In fact, the inhabitants of Canaan that Israel did not destroy according to God's command are described as being "snares" to Israel (Ex. 23:33; 34:12; Deut. 7:16; 12:30).

and shall strike off the heifer's neck there in the valley:

5 And the priests[3548] the sons[1121] of Levi shall come near;[5066] for [a]them the LORD thy God hath chosen[977] to minister[8334] unto him, and to bless[1288] in the name of the LORD; and [b]by their [I]word shall every controversy[7379] and every stroke be *tried:*

6 And all the elders of that city, *that are* next unto the slain *man,* [a]shall wash[7364] their hands[3027] over the heifer that is beheaded in the valley:

7 And they shall answer and say,[559] Our hands have not shed[8210] this blood, neither have our eyes seen[7200] *it.*

8 Be merciful,[3722] O LORD, unto thy people[5971] Israel, whom thou hast redeemed,[6299] [a]and lay not innocent[5355] blood [I]unto thy people of Israel's charge. And the blood shall be forgiven[3722] them.

9 So [a]shalt thou put away the *guilt of* innocent blood from among you, when thou shalt do *that which is* right in the sight of the LORD.

Laws Pertaining to the Family

10 When thou goest forth to war against thine enemies, and the LORD thy God hath delivered them into thine hands, and thou hast taken them captive,[7617]

11 And seest among the captives[7633] a beautiful woman,[802] and hast a desire[2836] unto her, that thou wouldest have her to thy wife;[802]

12 Then thou shalt bring her home to thine house;[1004] and she shall shave her head,[7218] and [I]pare her nails;

13 And she shall put the raiment of her captivity[7633] from off her, and shall remain in thine house, and [a]bewail[1058] her father[1] and her mother a full[3117] month: and after that thou shalt go in unto her, and be her husband,[1167] and she shall be thy wife.

14 And it shall be, if thou have no delight[2654] in her, then thou shalt let her go whither she will; but thou shalt not sell her at all for money, thou shalt not make merchandise of her, because thou hast [a]humbled her.

15 If a man have two wives,[802] one beloved,[157] [a]and another[259] hated,[8130] and they have born him children,[1121] *both* the beloved and the hated;[8130] and *if* the firstborn son[1121] be hers that was hated:[8146]

16 Then it shall be, [a]when he maketh his sons to inherit[5157] *that* which he hath, *that* he may not make the son of the beloved[157] firstborn before the son of the hated, *which is indeed* the firstborn:

17 But he shall acknowledge[5234] the son of the hated *for* the firstborn, [a]by giving him a double portion of all [I]that he hath: for he *is* [b]the beginning[7225] of his strength; [c]the right[4941] of the firstborn *is* his.

18 If a man have a stubborn[5637] and rebellious son, which will not obey[8085] the voice of his father, or the voice of his mother, and *that,* when they have chastened him, will not hearken[8085] unto them:

19 Then shall his father and his mother lay hold on him, and bring him out unto the elders of his city, and unto the gate of his place;

20 And they shall say unto the elders of his city, This our son *is* stubborn and rebellious, he will not obey our voice; *he is* a glutton, and a drunkard.

21 And all the men of his city shall stone him with stones, that he die:[4191] [a]so shalt thou put evil[7451] away from among you; [b]and all Israel shall hear,[8085] and fear.[3372]

Various Laws

22 And if a man have committed[1961] a sin[2399] [a]worthy of death,[4194] and he be to be put to death,[4191] and thou hang him on a tree:

23 [a]His body shall not remain all night[3915] upon the tree, but thou shalt in any wise bury[6912] him that day;[3117] (for [b]he that is hanged *is* [I]accursed[7045] of God;) that [c]thy land be not defiled, which the LORD thy God giveth thee *for* an inheritance.[5159]

---

5 [I]Hebr. *mouth* [a]Deut. 10:8; 1Chr. 23:13 [b]Deut. 17:8, 9

6 [a]Ps. 19:12; 26:6; Matt. 27:24

8 [I]Hebr. *in the midst* [a]Jon. 1:14

9 [a]Deut. 19:13

12 [I]Hebr. *make, or, dress*

13 [a]Ps. 45:10

14 [a]Gen. 34:2; Deut. 22:29; Judg. 19:24

15 [a]Gen. 29:33

16 [I]Hebr. *that is found with him* [a]1Chr. 5:2; 26:10; 2Chr. 11:19, 22 [b]1Chr. 5:1 [c]Gen. 49:3 [d]Gen. 25:31, 33

21 [a]Deut. 13:5; 19:19, 20; 22:21, 24 [b]Deut. 13:11

22 [a]Deut. 19:6; 22:26; Acts 23:29; 25:11, 25; 26:31

23 [I]Hebr. *the curse of God* [a]Josh. 8:29; 10:26, 27; John 19:31 [b]Gal. 3:13 [c]Lev. 18:25; Num. 35:34

22 Thou [a]shalt not see thy brother's[251] ox or his sheep go astray, and hide thyself from them: thou shalt in any case bring them again unto thy brother.

2 And if thy brother *be* not nigh unto thee, or if thou know[3045] him not, then thou shalt bring[622] it unto thine own house,[1004] and it shall be with thee until thy brother seek after it, and thou shalt restore it to him again.[7725]

3 In like manner shalt thou do with his ass; and so shalt thou do with his raiment; and with all lost thing[9] of thy brother's, which he hath lost, and thou hast found, shalt thou do likewise: thou mayest not hide thyself.

4 [a]Thou shalt not see thy brother's ass or his ox fall down by the way,[1870] and hide thyself from them: thou shalt surely help him to lift *them* up again.

5 The woman[802] shall not wear that which pertaineth unto a man,[1397] neither shall a man put on a woman's garment: for all that do so *are* abomination unto the LORD thy God.[430]

6 If a bird's nest chance to be before thee in the way in any tree, or on the ground,[776] *whether they be* young ones, or eggs, and the dam[517] sitting upon the young, or upon the eggs, [a]thou shalt not take the dam with the young:[1121]

7 *But* thou shalt in any wise let the dam go, and take the young to thee; [a]that it may be well[3190] with thee, and *that* thou mayest prolong[748] *thy* days.[3117]

8 When thou buildest[1129] a new house, then thou shalt make[6213] a battlement for thy roof, that thou bring not blood upon thine house, if any man fall from thence.

9 [a]Thou shalt not sow thy vineyard with divers seeds: lest the [I]fruit of thy seed[2233] which thou hast sown, and the fruit of thy vineyard, be defiled.[6942]

10 [a]Thou shalt not plow with an ox and an ass together.

11 [a]Thou shalt not wear a garment of divers sorts, *as* of woollen and linen together.

12 Thou shalt make thee [a]fringes upon the four [I]quarters of thy vesture, wherewith thou coverest *thyself.*

Sexual Matters

13 If any man[376] take a wife,[802] and [a]go in unto her, and hate[8130] her,

14 And give[7760] occasions[5949] of speech[1697] against her, and bring up an evil[7451] name upon her, and say, I took this woman, and when I came to her, I found her not a maid:[1331]

15 Then shall the father[1] of the damsel,[5291] and her mother, take and bring forth *the tokens of* the damsel's virginity[1331] unto the elders[2205] of the city in the gate:

16 And the damsel's father shall say unto the elders, I gave my daughter unto this man to wife, and he hateth her;

17 And, lo, he hath given occasions of speech *against her,* saying, I found not thy daughter a maid; and yet these *are the tokens of* my daughter's virginity. And they shall spread the cloth before the elders of the city.

18 And the elders of that city shall take that man and chastise[3256] him;

19 And they shall amerce[6064] him in an hundred *shekels* of silver, and give *them* unto the father of the damsel, because he hath brought up an evil name upon a virgin[1330] of Israel: and she shall be his wife; he may not put her away all his days.

20 But if this thing[1697] be true, *and the tokens of* virginity be not found for the damsel:

21 Then they shall bring out the damsel to the door of her father's[1] house, and the men of her city shall stone her with stones that she die:[4191] because she hath [a]wrought[6213] folly in Israel, to play the whore[2181] in her father's house: [b]so shalt thou put evil away from among you.

22 [a]If a man be found lying with a woman married[1166] to an husband,[1167] then they shall both of them die, *both* the man that lay with the woman, and the woman: so shalt thou put away evil from Israel.

1 [a]Ex. 23:4
4 [a]Ex. 23:5
6 [a]Lev. 22:28
7 [a]Deut. 4:40
9 [I]Hebr. *fullness of thy seed* [a]Lev. 19:19
10 [a]2Cor. 6:14-16
11 [a]Lev. 19:19
12 [I]Hebr. *wings* [a]Num. 15:38; Matt. 23:5
13 [a]Gen. 29:21; Judg. 15:1
21 [a]Gen. 34:7; Judg. 20:6, 10; 2Sam. 13:12, 13 [b]Deut. 13:5
22 [a]Lev. 20:10; John 8:5

23 If a damsel *that is* a virgin be [a]betrothed[781] unto an husband,[376] and a man find her in the city, and lie with her;

24 Then ye shall bring them both out unto the gate of that city, and ye shall stone them with stones that they die; the damsel, because she cried not, *being* in the city; and the man, because he hath [a]humbled his neighbour's wife: [b]so thou shalt put away evil from among you.

25 But if a man find a betrothed damsel in the field,[7704] and the man [I]force her, and lie with her: then the man only that lay with her shall die:

26 But unto the damsel thou shalt do nothing; *there is* in the damsel no sin[2399] *worthy* of death:[4194] for as when a man riseth against his neighbour, and slayeth[7523] him, even so *is* this matter:[1697]

27 For he found her in the field, *and* the betrothed damsel cried, and *there was* none to save her.

28 [a]If a man find a damsel *that is* a virgin, which is not betrothed, and lay hold on her, and lie with her, and they be found;

29 Then the man that lay with her shall give unto the damsel's father fifty *shekels* of silver, and she shall be his wife; [a]because he hath humbled her, he may not put her away all his days.

30 [a]A man shall not take his father's wife, nor [b]discover[1540] his father's skirt.

Persons Excluded From the Congregation

23 He that is wounded in the stones, or hath his privy member cut off,[3772] shall not enter[935] into the congregation[6951] of the LORD.

2 A bastard shall not enter into the congregation of the LORD; even to his tenth generation[1755] shall he not enter into the congregation of the LORD.

3 [a]An Ammonite or Moabite shall not enter into the congregation of the LORD; even to their tenth generation shall they not enter into the congregation of the LORD for ever:[5769]

4 [a]Because they met you not with bread and with water in the way,[1870] when ye came forth out of Egypt; and [b]because they hired against thee Balaam the son[1121] of Beor of Pethor of Mesopotamia, to curse[7043] thee.

5 Nevertheless the LORD thy God[430] would[14] not hearken[8085] unto Balaam; but the LORD thy God turned[2015] the curse[7045] into a blessing[1288] unto thee, because the LORD thy God loved[157] thee.

6 [a]Thou shalt not seek their peace[7965] nor their [I]prosperity[2896] all thy days[3117] for ever.

7 Thou shalt not abhor[8581] an Edomite; [a]for he *is* thy brother:[251] thou shalt not abhor an Egyptian; because [b]thou wast a stranger[1616] in his land.[776]

8 The children[1121] that are begotten[3205] of them shall enter into the congregation of the LORD in their third generation.

Purity During War

9 When the host[4264] goeth forth against thine enemies, then keep[8104] thee from every wicked[4751] thing.

10 [a]If there be among you any man,[376] that is not clean[2889] by reason of uncleanness that chanceth[7137] him by night,[3915] then shall he go abroad out of the camp,[4264] he shall not come within the camp:

11 But it shall be, when evening [I]cometh on, [a]he shall wash[7364] *himself* with water: and when the sun is down, he shall come into the camp *again.*

12 Thou shalt have a place also without the camp, whither thou shalt go forth abroad:

13 And thou shalt have a paddle[3489] upon thy weapon; and it shall be, when thou [I]wilt ease thyself abroad, thou shalt dig therewith, and shalt turn back[7725] and cover[3680] that which cometh from thee:

14 For the LORD thy God [a]walketh in the midst[7130] of thy camp, to

---

23 [a]Matt. 1:18, 19
24 [a]Deut. 21:14 [b]Deut. 22:21, 22
25 [I]Or, *take strong hold of her*
28 [a]Ex. 22:16, 17
29 [a]Deut. 22:21
30 [a]Lev. 18:8; 20:11; Deut. 27:20; 1Cor. 5:1 [b]Ruth 3:9; Ezek. 16:8
3 [a]Neh. 13:1, 2
4 [a]Deut. 2:29 [b]Num. 22:5, 6
6 [I]Hebr. *good* [a]Ezra 9:12
7 [a]Gen. 25:24-26; Obad. 1:10, 12 [b]Ex. 22:21; 23:9; Lev. 19:34; Deut. 10:19
10 [a]Lev. 15:16
11 [I]Hebr. *turneth toward* [a]Lev. 15:5
13 [I]Hebr. *sittest down*
14 [a]Lev. 26:12

deliver[5337] thee, and to give up thine enemies before thee; therefore shall thy camp be holy:[6918] that he see no [I]unclean[6172] thing in thee, and turn away[7725] from thee.

Various Laws

15 [a]Thou shalt not deliver unto his master[113] the servant[5650] which is escaped[5337] from his master unto thee:

16 He shall dwell with thee, *even* among you, in that place which he shall choose[977] in one of thy gates, where it [I]liketh him best: [a]thou shalt not oppress[3238] him.

17 There shall be no [I]whore[6948] [a]of the daughters of Israel, nor [b]a sodomite[6945] of the sons[1121] of Israel.

🔑 18 Thou shalt not bring the hire of a whore,[2181] or the price of a dog, into the house[1004] of the LORD thy God for any vow:[5088] for even both these *are* abomination unto the LORD thy God.

🔑 19 [a]Thou shalt not lend upon usury to thy brother; usury of money, usury of victuals,400 usury of any thing that is lent upon usury:

20 [a]Unto a stranger thou mayest lend upon usury; but unto thy brother thou shalt not lend upon usury: [b]that the LORD thy God may bless[1288] thee in all that thou settest thine hand[3027] to in the land whither thou goest to possess it.

21 [a]When thou shalt vow a vow unto the LORD thy God, thou shalt not slack309 to pay it: for the LORD thy God will surely require it of thee; and it would be sin[2399] in thee.

22 But if thou shalt forbear to vow, it shall be no sin in thee.

23 [a]That which is gone out of thy lips[8193] thou shalt keep and perform;[6213] *even* a freewill offering,[5071] according as thou hast vowed unto the LORD thy God, which thou hast promised[1696] with thy mouth.[6310]

14 [I]Hebr. *nakedness of anything*

15 [a]1Sam. 30:15

16 [I]Hebr. *is good for him* [a]Ex. 22:21

17 [I]Or, *sodomitess* [a]Lev. 19:29; Prov. 2:16 [b]Gen. 19:5; 2Kgs. 23:7

19 [a]Ex. 22:25; Lev. 25:36, 37; Neh. 5:2, 7; Ps. 15:5; Luke 6:34, 35

20 [a]Lev. 19:34; Deut. 15:3 [b]Deut. 15:10

21 [a]Num. 30:2; Eccl. 5:4, 5

23 [a]Num. 30:2; Ps. 66:13, 14

25 [a]Matt. 12:1; Mark 2:23; Luke 6:1

1 [I]Hebr. *matter of nakedness* [II]Hebr. *Cutting off* [a]Matt. 5:31; 19:7; Mark 10:4

4 [a]Jer. 3:1

5 [I]Hebr. *not any thing shall pass upon hi* [a]Deut. 20:7 [b]Prov. 5:18

7 [a]Ex. 21:16

24 When thou comest into thy neighbour's vineyard, then thou mayest eat grapes thy fill at thine own pleasure;[5315] but thou shalt not put *any* in thy vessel.

25 When thou comest into the standing corn of thy neighbour, [a]then thou mayest pluck the ears with thine hand; but thou shalt not move[5130] a sickle unto thy neighbour's standing corn.

24

When a [a]man[376] hath taken a wife,[802] and married[1166] her, and it come to pass that she find no favour[2580] in his eyes, because he hath found [I]some uncleanness in her: then let him write her a bill[5612] of [II]divorcement,[3748] and give *it* in her hand,[3027] and send her out of his house.[1004]

2 And when she is departed out of his house, she may go and be another man's *wife.*

3 And *if* the latter husband[376] hate[8130] her, and write her a bill of divorcement, and giveth *it* in her hand, and sendeth her out of his house; or if the latter husband die,[4191] which took her *to be* his wife;

4 [a]Her former husband,[1167] which sent her away, may not take her again to be his wife, after that she is defiled; for that *is* abomination before the LORD: and thou shalt not cause the land to sin,[2398] which the LORD thy God[430] giveth thee *for* an inheritance.[5159]

5 [a]When a man hath taken a new wife, he shall not go out to war,[6635] [I]neither shall he be charged with any business:[1697] *but* he shall be free[5355] at home[1004] one year, and shall [b]cheer up his wife which he hath taken.

6 No man shall take the nether7347 or the upper millstone to pledge: for he taketh *a man's* life[5315] to pledge.[2254]

7 [a]If a man be found stealing any of

🔑 **23:18** The word "dog" here means a male prostitute (see v. 17).

🔑 **23:19, 20** See note on Leviticus 19:33, 34.

his brethren[251] of the children[1121] of Israel, and maketh merchandise of him, or selleth him; then that thief shall die; [b]and thou shalt put evil[7451] away from among you.

8 Take heed in [a]the plague[5061] of leprosy, that thou observe diligently, and do according to all that the priests the Levites shall teach[3384] you: as I commanded[6680] them, *so* ye shall observe to do.

9 [a]Remember[2142] what the LORD thy God did[6213] [b]unto Miriam by the way,[1870] after that ye were come forth out of Egypt.

10 When thou dost [I]lend thy brother[7453] any thing, thou shalt not go into his house to fetch his pledge.

11 Thou shalt stand abroad, and the man to whom thou dost lend shall bring out the pledge abroad unto thee.

12 And if the man *be* poor, thou shalt not sleep with his pledge:

13 [a]In any case thou shalt deliver him the pledge again[7225] when the sun goeth down, that he may sleep in his own raiment, and [b]bless[1288] thee: and [c]it shall be righteousness[6666] unto thee before the LORD thy God.

14 Thou shalt not [a]oppress an hired servant *that is* poor and needy, *whether he be* of thy brethren, or of thy strangers[1616] that *are* in thy land within thy gates:

15 At his day[3117] [a]thou shalt give *him* his hire, neither shall the sun go down upon it; for he *is* poor, and [I][b]setteth his heart[5315] upon it: [c]lest he cry against thee unto the LORD, and it be sin[2399] unto thee.

🔑 16 [a]The fathers[1] shall not be put to death[4191] for the children, neither shall the children be put to death for the fathers: every man shall be put to death for his own sin.

17 [a]Thou shalt not pervert the judgment[4941] of the stranger,[1616] *nor* of the

7 [b]Deut. 19:19
8 [a]Lev. 13:2; 14:2
9 [a]Luke 17:32; 1Cor. 10:6 [b]Num. 12:10
10 [I]Hebr. *lend the loan of any thing to*
13 [a]Ex. 22:26 [b]Job 29:11, 13; 31:20; 2Cor. 9:13; 2Tim. 1:18 [c]Deut. 6:25; Ps. 106:31; 112:9; Dan. 4:27
14 [a]Mal. 3:5
15 [I]Hebr. *lifteth his soul unto it* [a]Lev. 19:13; Jer. 22:13 [b]Ps. 25:1; 86:4 [c]James 5:4
16 [a]2Kgs. 14:6; 2Chr. 25:4; Jer. 31:29, 30; Ezek. 18:20
17 [a]Ex. 22:21, 22; Prov. 22:22; Isa. 1:23; Jer. 5:28; 22:3; Ezek. 22:29; Zech. 7:10; Mal. 3:5 [b]Ex. 22:26
18 [a]Deut. 16:12; 24:22
19 [a]Lev. 19:9, 10; 23:22 [b]Deut. 15:10; Ps. 41:1; Prov. 19:17
20 [I]Hebr. *thou shalt not bough it after thee*
21 [I]Hebr. *after thee*
22 [a]Deut. 24:18
1 [a]Deut. 19:17; Ezek. 44:24 [b]Prov, 17:15
2 [a]Luke 12:48 [b]Matt. 10:17
3 [a]2Cor. 11:24 [b]Job 18:3
4 [I]Hebr. *thresheth* [a]Prov. 12:10; 1Cor. 9:9; 1Tim. 5:18

fatherless; [b]nor take a widow's raiment to pledge:

18 But [a]thou shalt remember that thou wast a bondman[5650] in Egypt, and the LORD thy God redeemed[6299] thee thence: therefore I command[6680] thee to do this thing.[1697]

19 [a]When thou cuttest down thine harvest in thy field,[7704] and hast forgot a sheaf in the field, thou shalt not go again to fetch it: it shall be for the stranger, for the fatherless, and for the widow: that the LORD thy God may [b]bless thee in all the work of thine hands.[3027]

20 When thou beatest thine olive tree, [I]thou shalt not go over the boughs[6286] again: it shall be for the stranger, for the fatherless, and for the widow.

21 When thou gatherest the grapes[1219] of thy vineyard, thou shalt not glean *it* [I]afterward: it shall be for the stranger, for the fatherless, and for the widow.

22 And [a]thou shalt remember that thou wast a bondman in the land of Egypt: therefore I command thee to do this thing.

25 If there be a [a]controversy[7379] between men, and they come unto judgment,[4941] that *the judges* may judge[8199] them; then they [b]shall justify[6663] the righteous, and condemn[7561] the wicked.[7563]

2 And it shall be, if the wicked man *be* [a]worthy to be beaten,[5221] that the judge shall cause him to lie down,[5307] [b]and to be beaten before his face, according to his fault,[7564] by a certain number.

3 [a]Forty stripes[5221] he may give him, *and* not exceed: lest, *if* he should exceed, and beat him above these with many stripes,[4347] then thy brother[251] should [b]seem vile[7043] unto thee.

4 [a]Thou shalt not muzzle the ox when he [I]treadeth out *the corn.*

🔑 **24:16** See note on Ezekiel 18:1–32.

🔑 5 [a]If brethren[251] dwell together, and one of them die,[4191] and have no child, the wife[802] of the dead[4191] shall not marry without unto a stranger:[2114] her [I]husband's brother shall go in unto her, and take her to him to wife, and perform the duty of an husband's brother[2992] unto her.

6 And it shall be, *that* the firstborn which she beareth [a]shall succeed in the name of his brother *which is* dead, that [b]his name be not put out[4229] of Israel.

7 And if the man[376] like[2654] not to take his [I]brother's wife, then let his brother's wife go up[5927] to the [a]gate unto the elders,[2205] and say,[559] My husband's brother refuseth[3985] to raise up unto his brother a name in Israel, he will not perform the duty of my husband's brother.

8 Then the elders of his city shall call[7121] him, and speak[1696] unto him: and *if* he stand *to it,* and say, [a]I like not to take her;

9 Then shall his brother's wife[2994] come unto him in the presence of the elders, and [a]loose his shoe from off his foot, and spit in his face, and shall answer and say, So shall it be done[6213] unto that man that will not [b]build up his brother's house.[1004]

10 And his name shall be called[7121] in Israel, The house of him that hath his shoe loosed.

11 When men strive together one with another, and the wife of the one draweth near[7126] for to deliver[5337] her husband[376] out of the hand[3027] of him that smiteth him, and putteth forth her hand, and taketh[2388] him by the secrets:

12 Then thou shalt cut off her hand,[3709] [a]thine eye shall not pity *her.*

13 [a]Thou shalt not have in thy bag [I]divers weights, a great and a small.

14 Thou shalt not have in thine house [I]divers measures, a great and a small.

15 *But* thou shalt have a perfect[8003] and just[6664] weight, a perfect and just measure shalt thou have: [a]that thy days[3117] may be lengthened in the land[127] which the LORD thy God[430] giveth thee.

16 For [a]all that do such things, *and* all that do unrighteously,[5766] *are* an abomination unto the LORD thy God.

Destroy Amalek

17 [a]Remember[2142] what Amalek did unto thee by the way,[1870] when ye were come forth out of Egypt;

18 How he met thee by the way, and smote[5221] the hindmost[2179] of thee, *even* all *that were* feeble behind thee, when thou *wast* faint and weary; and he [a]feared[3373] not God.

19 Therefore it shall be, [a]when the LORD thy God hath given thee rest from all thine enemies round about, in the land[127] which the LORD thy God giveth thee *for* an inheritance[5159] to possess it, *that* thou shalt [b]blot out[4229] the remembrance[2143] of Amalek from under heaven;[8064] thou shalt not forget *it.*

Harvest Offerings

26 And it shall be, when thou *art* come in unto the land which the LORD thy God[430] giveth thee *for* an inheritance,[5159] and possessest it, and dwellest therein;

2 [a]That thou shalt take of the first[7225] of all the fruit of the earth,[127] which thou shalt bring of thy land that the LORD thy God giveth thee, and shalt put *it* in a basket, and shalt [b]go unto the place which the LORD thy God shall choose[977] to place[7931] his name there.

3 And thou shalt go unto the priest that shall be in those days,[3117] and say[559] unto him, I profess[5046] this day unto the LORD thy God, that I am come unto the country[776] which the LORD sware[7650] unto our fathers[1] for to give us.

5 [I]Or, *next kinsman* [a]Matt. 22:24; Mark 12:19; Luke 20:28

6 [a]Gen. 38:9 [b]Ruth 4:10

7 [I]Or, *next kinsman's wife* [a]Ruth 4:1, 2

8 [a]Ruth 4:6

9 [a]Ruth 4:7 [b]Ruth 4:11

12 [a]Deut. 19:13

13 [I]Hebr. *a stone and a stone* [a]Lev. 19:35, 36; Prov. 11:1; Ezek. 45:10; Mic. 6:11

14 [I]Hebr. *an ephah and an ephah*

15 [a]Ex. 20:12

16 [a]Prov. 11:1; 1Thess. 4:6

17 [a]Ex. 17:8

18 [a]Ps. 36:1; Prov. 16:6; Rom. 3:18

19 [a]1Sam. 15:3; [b]Ex. 17:14

2 [a]Ex. 23:19; 34:26; Num. 18:13; Deut. 16:10; Prov. 3:9 [b]Deut. 12:5

🔑 **25:5–10** For an application of these regulations, see note on Ruth 4:1–8.

4 And the priest shall take the basket out of thine hand,[3027] and set it down before the altar[4196] of the LORD thy God.

5 And thou shalt speak and say before the LORD thy God, [a]A Syrian [b]ready to perish[6] *was* my father,[1] and [c]he went down into Egypt, and sojourned[1481] there with a [d]few, and became there a nation,[1471] great, mighty, and populous:

6 And [a]the Egyptians evil[7489] entreated us, and afflicted us, and laid upon us hard[7186] bondage:

7 And [a]when we cried unto the LORD God of our fathers, the LORD heard[8085] our voice, and looked on[7200] our affliction, and our labour,[5999] and our oppression:

8 And [a]the LORD brought us forth out of Egypt with a mighty[2389] hand, and with an outstretched arm, and [b]with great terribleness,[4172] and with signs,[226] and with wonders:[4159]

9 And he hath brought us into this place, and hath given us this land, *even* [a]a land that floweth with milk and honey.

10 And now, behold, I have brought the firstfruits[7225] of the land,[127] which thou, O LORD, hast given me. And thou shalt set it before the LORD thy God, and worship[7812] before the LORD thy God:

11 And [a]thou shalt rejoice in every good[2896] *thing* which the LORD thy God hath given unto thee, and unto thine house,[1004] thou, and the Levite, and the stranger[1616] that *is* among you.

12 When thou hast made an end[3615] of tithing[6237] all the [a]tithes[4643] of thine increase the third year, *which is* [b]the year of tithing, and hast given *it* unto the Levite, the stranger, the fatherless, and the widow, that they may eat within thy gates, and be filled;

13 Then thou shalt say before the LORD thy God, I have brought away the hallowed things[6944] out of *mine* house, and also have given them unto the Levite, and unto the stranger, to the fatherless, and to the widow, according to all thy commandments which thou hast commanded[6680] me: I have not transgressed[5674] thy commandments, [a]neither have I forgotten *them:*

14 [a]I have not eaten thereof in my mourning, neither have I taken away *ought* thereof for *any* unclean[2931] *use,* nor given *ought* thereof for the dead:[4191] *but* I have hearkened[8085] to the voice of the LORD my God, *and* have done[6213] according to all that thou hast commanded me.

15 [a]Look down from thy holy[6944] habitation, from heaven, and bless[1288] thy people[5971] Israel, and the land[776] which thou hast given us, as thou swarest unto our fathers, a land that floweth with milk and honey.

Concluding Charge

16 This day the LORD thy God hath commanded thee to do these statutes[2706] and judgments:[4941] thou shalt therefore keep[8104] and do them with all thine heart,[3824] and with all thy soul.[5315]

17 Thou hast [a]avouched[559] the LORD this day to be thy God, and to walk in his ways,[1870] and to keep his statutes, and his commandments, and his judgments, and to hearken[8085] unto his voice:

18 And [a]the LORD hath avouched thee this day to be his peculiar[5459] people, as he hath promised[1696] thee, and that *thou* shouldest keep all his commandments;

19 And to make thee [a]high[5945] above all nations[1471] which he hath made,[6213] in praise,[8416] and in name, and in honour;[8597] and that thou mayest be [b]an holy people unto the LORD thy God, as he hath spoken.[1696]

The Law at Mount Ebal

27 And Moses with the elders[2205] of Israel commanded the people, saying, Keep[8104] all the commandments which I command you this day.[3117]

2 And it shall be on the day [a]when ye shall pass over Jordan unto the land which the LORD thy God[430] giveth thee, that [b]thou shalt set thee up great stones, and plaister them with plaister:

3 And thou shalt write upon them all the words[1697] of this law,[8451] when

5 [a]Hos. 12:12 [b]Gen. 43:1, 2; 45:7, 11 [c]Gen. 46:1, 6; Acts 7:15; [d]Gen. 46:27; Deut. 10:22
6 [a]Ex. 1:11, 14
7 [a]Ex. 2:23-25; 3:9; 4:31
8 [a]Ex. 12:37, 51; 13:3, 14, 16; Deut. 5:15 [b]Deut. 4:34
9 [a]Ex. 3:8
11 [a]Deut. 12:7, 12, 18; 16:11
12 [a]Lev. 27:30; Num. 18:24 [b]Deut. 14:28, 29
13 [a]Ps. 119:141, 153, 176
14 [a]Lev. 7:20; 21:1, 11; Hos. 9:4
15 [a]Isa. 63:15; Zech. 2:13
17 [a]Ex. 20:19
18 [a]Ex. 6:7; 19:5; Deut. 7:6; 14:2; 28:9
19 [a]Deut. 4:7, 8; 28:1; Ps. 148:14 [b]Ex. 19:6; Deut. 7:6; 28:9; 1Pet. 2:9
2 [a]Josh. 4:1 [b]Josh. 8:32

thou art passed over,[5674] that thou mayest go in unto the land which the LORD thy God giveth thee, a land that floweth with milk and honey; as the LORD God of thy fathers[1] hath promised[1696] thee.

4 Therefore it shall be when ye be gone over Jordan, *that* ye shall set up these stones, which I command you this day, [a]in mount Ebal, and thou shalt plaister them with plaister.

5 And there shalt thou build an altar[4196] unto the LORD thy God, an altar of stones: [a]thou shalt not lift up[5130] *any* iron *tool* upon them.

6 Thou shalt build the altar of the LORD thy God of whole[8003] stones: and thou shalt offer burnt offerings[5930] thereon unto the LORD thy God:

7 And thou shalt offer peace offerings,[8002] and shalt eat there, and rejoice before the LORD thy God.

8 And thou shalt write upon the stones all the words of this law very plainly.

9 And Moses and the priests[3548] the Levites spake[1696] unto all Israel, saying, Take heed, and hearken,[8085] O Israel; [a]this day thou art become[1961] the people of the LORD thy God.

10 Thou shalt therefore obey[8085] the voice of the LORD thy God, and do his commandments and his statutes,[2706] which I command thee this day.

The Curses at Mount Ebal

11 And Moses charged[6680] the people the same day, saying,

12 These shall stand [a]upon mount Gerizim to bless[1288] the people, when ye are come over[5674] Jordan; Simeon, and Levi, and Judah, and Issachar, and Joseph, and Benjamin:

13 And [a]these shall stand upon mount Ebal [1]to curse;[7045] Reuben, Gad, and Asher, and Zebulun, Dan, and Naphtali.

14 And [a]the Levites shall speak, and say unto all the men[376] of Israel with a loud voice,

15 [a]Cursed[779] *be* the man that maketh *any* graven or molten image, an abomination unto the LORD, the work of the hands[3027] of the craftsman, and putteth[7760] *it* in *a* secret *place.* [b]And all the people shall answer and say, Amen.[543]

16 [a]Cursed *be* he that setteth light by his father[1] or his mother. And all the people shall say, Amen.

17 [a]Cursed *be* he that removeth his neighbour's landmark. And all the people shall say, Amen.

18 [a]Cursed *be* he that maketh the blind to wander[7686] out of the way.[1870] And all the people shall say, Amen.

19 [a]Cursed *be* he that perverteth the judgment[4941] of the stranger,[1616] fatherless, and widow. And all the people shall say, Amen.

20 [a]Cursed *be* he that lieth with his father's[1] wife;[802] because he uncovereth his father's skirt. And all the people shall say, Amen.

21 [a]Cursed *be* he that lieth with any manner of beast. And all the people shall say, Amen.

22 [a]Cursed *be* he that lieth with his sister,[269] the daughter of his father, or the daughter of his mother. And all the people shall say, Amen.

23 [a]Cursed *be* he that lieth with his mother in law. And all the people shall say, Amen.

24 [a]Cursed *be* he that smiteth his neighbour secretly. And all the people shall say, Amen.

25 [a]Cursed *be* he that taketh reward to slay[5221] an innocent[5355] person.[5315] And all the people shall say, Amen.

26 [a]Cursed *be* he that confirmeth not *all* the words of the law[8451] to do them. And all the people shall say, Amen.

The Blessings for Obedience

28 And it shall come to pass, [a]if thou shalt hearken diligently[8085] unto the voice of the LORD thy God,[430] to observe *and* to do all his commandments which I command[6680] thee this day,[3117]

---

4 [a]Deut. 11:29; Josh. 8:30

5 [a]Ex. 20:25; Josh. 8:31

9 [a]Deut. 26:18

12 [a]Deut. 11:29; Josh. 8:33; Judg. 9:7

13 [1]Hebr. *for a cursing* [a]Deut. 11:29; Josh. 8:33

14 [a]Deut. 33:10; Josh. 8:33; Dan. 9:11

15 [a]Ex. 20:4, 23; 34:17; Lev. 19:4; 26:1; Deut. 4:16, 23; 5:8; Isa. 44:9; Hos. 13:2 [b]Num. 5:22; Jer. 11:5; 1Cor. 14:16

16 [a]Ex. 20:12; 21:17; Lev. 19:3; Deut. 21:18

17 [a]Deut. 19:14; Prov. 22:28

18 [a]Lev. 19:14

19 [a]Ex. 22:21, 22; Deut. 10:18; 24:17; Mal. 3:5

20 [a]Lev. 18:8; 20:11; Deut. 22:30

21 [a]Lev. 18:23; 20:15

22 [a]Lev. 18:9; 20:17

23 [a]Lev. 18:17; 20:14

24 [a]Ex. 20:13; 21:12, 14; Lev. 24:17; Num. 35:31; Deut. 19:11

25 [a]Ex. 23:7, 8; Deut. 10:17; 16:19; Ezek. 22:12

26 [a]Deut. 28:15; Ps. 119:21; Jer. 11:3; Gal. 3:10

1 [a]Ex. 15:26; Lev. 26:3; Isa. 55:2

that the LORD thy God [b]will set thee on high[5945] above all nations[1471] of the earth:[776]

2 And all these blessings[1293] shall come on thee, and [a]overtake thee, if thou shalt hearken unto the voice of the LORD thy God.

3 [a]Blessed[1288] *shalt* thou *be* in the city, and blessed *shalt* thou *be* [b]in the field.[7704]

4 Blessed *shall be* [a]the fruit of thy body,[990] and the fruit of thy ground,[127] and the fruit of thy cattle, the increase of thy kine,504 and the flocks of thy sheep.

5 Blessed *shall be* thy basket and thy [I]store.

6 [a]Blessed *shalt* thou *be* when thou comest in, and blessed *shalt* thou *be* when thou goest out.

7 The LORD [a]shall cause thine enemies that rise up against thee to be smitten[5062] before thy face: they shall come out against thee one way, and flee before thee seven ways.[1870]

8 The LORD shall [a]command the blessing[1293] upon thee in thy [I]storehouses, and in all that thou [b]settest thine hand[3027] unto; and he shall bless[1288] thee in the land[127] which the LORD thy God giveth thee.

9 [a]The LORD shall establish thee an holy[6918] people[5971] unto himself, as he hath sworn[7650] unto thee, if thou shalt keep[8104] the commandments of the LORD thy God, and walk in his ways.

10 And all the people of the earth shall see that thou art [a]called[7121] by the name of the LORD; and they shall be [b]afraid of thee.

11 And [a]the LORD shall make thee plenteous [I]in goods, in the fruit of thy [II]body, and in the fruit of thy cattle, and in the fruit of thy ground, in the land which the LORD sware[7650] unto thy fathers[1] to give thee.

12 The LORD shall open unto thee his good[2896] treasure, the heaven8064 [a]to give the rain unto thy land[776] in his season,[6256] and [b]to bless all the work of thine hand: and [c]thou shalt lend unto many nations, and thou shalt not borrow.

13 And the LORD shall make thee [a]the head,[7218] and not the tail; and thou shalt be above only, and thou shalt not be beneath; if that thou hearken unto the commandments of the LORD thy God, which I command thee this day, to observe and to do *them:*

14 [a]And thou shalt not go aside from any of the words[1697] which I command thee this day, *to* the right hand, or *to* the left, to go after other gods[430] to serve[5647] them.

The Punishment for Disobedience

15 But it shall come to pass, [a]if thou wilt not hearken unto the voice of the LORD thy God, to observe to do all his commandments and his statutes[2708] which I command thee this day; that all these curses[7045] shall come upon thee, and [b]overtake thee:

16 Cursed[779] *shalt* thou *be* [a]in the city, and cursed *shalt* thou *be* in the field.

17 Cursed *shall be* thy basket and thy store.

18 Cursed *shall be* the fruit of thy body, and the fruit of thy land, the increase of thy kine, and the flocks of thy sheep.

19 Cursed *shalt* thou *be* when thou comest in, and cursed *shalt* thou *be* when thou goest out.

20 The LORD shall send upon thee [a]cursing,3994 [b]vexation,[4103] and [c]rebuke, in all that thou settest thine hand unto [I]for to do, until thou be destroyed,[8045] and until thou perish[6] quickly; because of the wickedness[7455] of thy doings, whereby thou hast forsaken[5800] me.

21 The LORD shall make [a]the pestilence[1698] cleave unto thee, until he have consumed[3615] thee from off the land, whither thou goest to possess it.

22 The [a]LORD shall smite[5221] thee with a consumption, and with a fever, and with an inflammation, and with an extreme burning, and with the [I]sword,[2719] and with [b]blasting, and with mildew; and they shall pursue thee until thou perish.

23 And [a]thy heaven that *is* over thy

1 [b]Deut. 26:19
2 [a]Deut. 28:15; Zech. 1:6
3 [a]Ps. 128:1, 4 [b]Gen. 39:5
4 [a]Gen. 22:17; 49:25; Deut. 7:13; 28:11; Ps. 107:38; 127:3; 128:3; Prov. 10:22; 1Tim. 4:8
5 IOr, *dough,* or, *kneading trough*
6 [a]Ps. 121:8
7 [a]Lev. 26:7, 8; 2Sam. 22:38-41; Ps. 89:23, 25
8 IOr, *barns* [a]Lev. 25:21 [b]Deut. 15:10
9 [a]Ex. 19:5, 6; Deut. 7:6; 26:18, 19; 29:13
10 [a]Num. 6:27; 2Chr. 7:14; Isa. 63:19; Dan. 9:18, 19 [b]Deut. 11:25
11 IOr, *for good* IIHebr. *belly* [a]Deut. 28:4; 30:9; Prov. 10:22
12 [a]Lev. 26:4; Deut. 11:14 [b]Deut. 14:29 [c]Deut. 15:6
13 [a]Isa. 9:14, 15
14 [a]Deut. 5:32; 11:16
15 [a]Lev. 26:14; Lam. 2:17; Dan. 9:11, 13; Mal. 2:2 [b]Deut. 28:2
16 [a]Deut. 28:3
20 IHebr. *which thou wouldest do* [a]Mal. 2:2 [b]1Sam. 14:20; Zech. 14:13 [c]Ps. 80:16; Isa. 30:17; 51:20; 66:15
21 [a]Lev. 26:25; Jer. 24:10
22 IOr, *drought* [a]Lev. 26:16 [b]Amos 4:9
23 [a]Lev. 26:19

head shall be brass, and the earth that *is* under thee *shall be* iron.

24 The LORD shall make the rain of thy land powder[80] and dust:[6083] from heaven shall it come down upon thee, until thou be destroyed.

25 [a]The LORD shall cause thee to be smitten before thine enemies: thou shalt go out one way against them, and flee seven ways before them: and [b]shalt be [I]removed into all the kingdoms[4467] of the earth.

26 And [a]thy carcase[5038] shall be meat unto all fowls of the air, and unto the beasts of the earth, and no man shall fray *them* away.

27 The LORD will smite thee with [a]botch[7822] of Egypt, and with [b]the emerods,[6076] and with the scab, and with the itch, whereof thou canst not be healed.

28 The LORD shall smite thee with madness, and blindness, and [a]astonishment of heart:[3824]

29 And thou shalt [a]grope at noonday, as the blind gropeth in darkness,[653] and thou shalt not prosper in thy ways: and thou shalt be only oppressed and spoiled evermore, and no man shall save *thee.*

30 [a]Thou shalt betroth[781] a wife,[802] and another man shall lie with her: [b]thou shalt build an house,[1004] and thou shalt not dwell therein: [c]thou shalt plant a vineyard, and shalt not [I]gather the grapes thereof.

31 Thine ox *shall be* slain[2873] before thine eyes, and thou shalt not eat thereof: thine ass *shall be* violently taken away from before thy face, and [I]shall not be restored[7725] to thee: thy sheep *shall be* given unto thine enemies, and thou shalt have none to rescue *them.*

32 Thy sons[1121] and thy daughters *shall be* given unto another people, and thine eyes shall look, and [a]fail[3615] *with longing* for them all the day long: and *there shall be* no might in thine hand.

33 [a]The fruit of thy land, and all thy labours, shall a nation[5971] which thou knowest[3045] not eat up; and thou shalt be only oppressed and crushed alway:

34 So that thou shalt be mad [a]for the sight of thine eyes which thou shalt see.

35 The LORD shall [a]smite thee in the knees, and in the legs, with a sore[7451] botch that cannot be healed, from the sole[3709] of thy foot unto the top of thy head.

36 The LORD shall [a]bring thee, and thy king[4428] which thou shalt set over thee, unto a nation[1471] which neither thou nor thy fathers have known;[3045] and [b]there shalt thou serve other gods, wood and stone.

37 And thou shalt become[1961] [a]an astonishment, a proverb, [b]and a byword, among all nations[5971] whither the LORD shall lead thee.

38 [a]Thou shalt carry much seed[2233] out into the field, and shalt gather *but* little in;[622] for [b]the locust shall consume it.

39 Thou shalt plant vineyards, and dress[5647] *them,* but shalt neither drink *of* the wine, nor gather *the grapes;* for the worms shall eat them.

40 Thou shalt have olive trees throughout all thy coasts, but thou shalt not anoint[5480] *thyself* with the oil;[8081] for thine olive shall cast *his fruit.*

41 Thou shalt beget sons and daughters, but [I]thou shalt not enjoy them; for [a]they shall go into captivity.[7628]

42 And thy trees and fruit of thy land shall the locust [I]consume.[3423]

43 The stranger[1616] that *is* within[7130] thee shall get up above thee very high; and thou shalt come down very low.

44 [a]He shall lend to thee, and thou shalt not lend to him: [b]he shall be the head, and thou shalt be the tail.

45 Moreover [a]all these curses shall come upon thee, and shall pursue thee, and overtake thee, till thou be de stroyed; because thou hearkenedst[8085] not unto the voice of the LORD thy God, to keep his commandments and his statutes which he commanded[6680] thee:

46 And they shall be upon thee [a]for a sign[226] and for a wonder, and upon thy seed for ever.[5769]

47 [a]Because thou servedst[5647] not the LORD thy God with joyfulness, and with

25 [I]Hebr. *for a removing* [a]Lev. 26:17, 37; Deut. 28:7; 32:30; Isa. 30:17 [b]Jer. 15:4; 24:9; Ezek. 23:46

26 [a]1Sam. 17:44, 46; Ps. 79:2; Jer. 7:33; 16:4; 34:20

27 [a]Ex. 9:9; 15:26; Deut. 28:35 [b]1Sam. 5:6; Ps. 78:66

28 [a]Jer. 4:9

29 [a]Job 5:14; Isa. 59:10

30 [I]Hebr. *profane, or, use it as common meat* [a]Job 31:10; Jer. 8:10 [b]Job 31:8; Jer. 12:13; Amos 5:11; Mic. 6:15; Zeph. 1:13 [c]Deut. 20:6

31 [I]Hebr. *shall not return to thee*

32 [a]Ps. 119:82

33 [a]Deut. 28:51; Lev. 26:16; Jer. 5:17

34 [a]Deut. 28:67

35 [a]Deut. 28:27

36 [a]2Kgs. 17:4, 6; 24:12, 14; 25:7, 11; 2Chr. 33:11; 36:6, 20 [b]Deut. 4:28; 28:64; Jer. 16:13

37 [a]1Kgs. 9:7, 8; Jer. 24:9; 25:9; Zech. 8:13 [b]Ps. 44:14

38 [a]Mic. 6:15; Hag. 1:6 [b]Joel 1:4

41 [I]Hebr. *they shall not be thine* [a]Lam. 1:5

42 [I]Or, *possess*

44 [a]Deut. 28:12 [b]Deut. 28:13; Lam. 1:5

45 [a]Deut. 28:15

46 [a]Isa. 8:18; Ezek. 14:8

47 [a]Neh. 9:35-37

gladness[2898] of heart, [b]for the abundance of all *things;*

48 Therefore shalt thou serve thine enemies which the LORD shall send against thee, in hunger, and in thirst, and in nakedness, and in want of all *things:* and he [a]shall put a yoke of iron upon thy neck, until he have destroyed thee.

49 [a]The LORD shall bring[5375] a nation against thee from far, from the end of the earth, [b]*as swift* as the eagle flieth; a nation whose tongue thou shalt not [I]understand;[8085]

50 A nation [I][a]of fierce countenance, [b]which shall not regard[5375] the person of the old,[2205] nor shew favour[2603] to the young:

51 And he shall [a]eat the fruit of thy cattle, and the fruit of thy land, until thou be destroyed:[6] which *also* shall not leave[7604] thee *either* corn, wine, or oil,[3323] *or* the increase of thy kine, or flocks of thy sheep, until he have destroyed thee.

52 And he shall [a]besiege thee in all thy gates, until thy high and fenced walls come down, wherein thou trustedst,[982] throughout all thy land: and he shall besiege thee in all thy gates throughout all thy land, which the LORD thy God hath given thee.

53 And [a]thou shalt eat the fruit of thine own [I]body, the flesh[1320] of thy sons and of thy daughters, which the LORD thy God hath given thee, in the siege, and in the straitness, wherewith thine enemies shall distress thee:

54 *So that* the man *that is* tender among you, and very delicate, [a]his eye shall be evil[7489] toward his brother,[251] and toward [b]the wife of his bosom, and toward the remnant[3499] of his children which he shall leave:[3498]

55 So that he will not give to any of them of the flesh of his children whom he shall eat: because he hath nothing left[7604] him in the siege, and in the straitness, wherewith thine enemies shall distress thee in all thy gates.

56 The tender and delicate woman among you, which would not adventure[5254] to set the sole of her foot upon the ground[776] for delicateness and tenderness, [a]her eye shall be evil toward the husband[376] of her bosom, and toward her son,[1121] and toward her daughter,

57 And toward her [I]young one that cometh out [a]from between her feet, and toward her children which she shall bear: for she shall eat them for want of all *things* secretly in the siege and straitness, wherewith thine enemy shall distress thee in thy gates.

58 If thou wilt not observe to do all the words of this law[8451] that are written in this book,[5612] that thou mayest fear[3372] [a]this glorious[3513] and fearful[3372] name, THE LORD THY GOD;

59 Then the LORD will make thy plagues [a]wonderful,[6381] and the plagues of thy seed, *even* great plagues, and of long continuance,[539] and sore sicknesses, and of long continuance.

60 Moreover he will bring upon thee all [a]the diseases[4064] of Egypt, which thou wast afraid of; and they shall cleave unto thee.

61 Also every sickness, and every plague,[4347] which *is* not written in the book of this law, them will the LORD [I]bring upon thee, until thou be destroyed.

62 And ye [a]shall be left few in number, whereas ye were [b]as the stars of heaven for multitude; because thou wouldest not obey[8085] the voice of the LORD thy God.

63 And it shall come to pass, *that* as the LORD [a]rejoiced[7797] over you to do you good,[3190] and to multiply you; so the LORD [b]will rejoice over you to destroy[6] you, and to bring you to nought;[8045] and ye shall be plucked from off the land whither thou goest to possess it.

64 And the LORD [a]shall scatter thee among all people, from the one end of the earth even unto the other; and [b]there thou shalt serve other gods, which neither thou nor thy fathers have known, *even* wood and stone.

65 And [a]among these nations shalt thou find no ease, neither shall the sole of thy foot have rest: [b]but the LORD shall give thee there a trembling[7626] heart, and failing of eyes, and [c]sorrow of mind:[5315]

---

47 [b]Deut. 32:15

48 [a]Jer. 28:14

49 [I]Hebr. *hear* [a]Jer. 5:15; 6:22, 23; Luke 19:43 [b]Jer. 48:40; 49:22; Lam. 4:19; Ezek. 17:3, 12; Hos. 8:1

50 [I]Hebr. *strong of face* [a]Prov. 7:13; Eccl. 8:1; Dan. 8:23 [b]2Chr. 36:17; Isa. 47:6

51 [a]Deut. 28:33; Isa. 1:7; 62:8

52 [a]2Kgs. 25:1, 2, 4

53 [I]Hebr. *belly* [a]Lev. 26:29; 2Kgs. 6:28, 29; Jer. 19:9; Lam. 2:20; 4:10

54 [a]Deut. 15:9 [b]Deut. 13:6

56 [a]Deut. 28:54

57 [I]Hebr. *afterbirth* [a]Gen. 49:10

58 [a]Ex. 6:3

59 [a]Dan. 9:12

60 [a]Deut. 7:15

61 [I]Hebr. *cause to ascend*

62 [a]Deut. 4:27 [b]Deut. 10:22; Neh. 9:23

63 [a]Deut. 30:9; Jer. 32:41 [b]Prov. 1:26; Isa. 1:24

64 [a]Lev. 26:33; Deut. 4:27, 28; Neh. 1:8; Jer. 16:13 [b]Deut. 28:36

65 [a]Amos 9:4 [b]Lev. 26:36 [c]Lev. 26:16

66 And thy life[2416] shall hang in doubt before thee; and thou shalt fear[6342] day[3119] and night,[3915] and shalt have none assurance[539] of thy life:

67 [a]In the morning thou shalt say,[559] Would God it were even! and at even thou shalt say, Would God it were morning! for the fear[6343] of thine heart wherewith thou shalt fear, and [b]for the sight of thine eyes which thou shalt see.

🔑 68 And the LORD [a]shall bring thee into Egypt again with ships, by the way whereof I spake[559] unto thee, [b]Thou shalt see it no more again: and there ye shall be sold unto your enemies for bondmen[5650] and bondwomen, and no man shall buy *you.*

Covenant Renewal

29 These *are* the words[1697] of the covenant,[1285] which the LORD commanded[6680] Moses to make with the children[1121] of Israel in the land[776] of Moab, beside [a]the covenant which he made[3772] with them in Horeb.

2 And Moses called[7121] unto all Israel, and said[559] unto them, [a]Ye have seen[7200] all that the LORD did before your eyes in the land of Egypt unto Pharaoh, and unto all his servants, and unto all his land;

3 [a]The great temptations[4531] which thine eyes have seen, the signs,[226] and those great miracles:

4 Yet [a]the LORD hath not given you an heart3920 to perceive,[3045] and eyes to see, and ears[241] to hear,[8085] unto this day.[3117]

5 [a]And I have led you forty years in the wilderness: [b]your clothes are not waxen old upon you, and thy shoe is not waxen old upon thy foot.

6 [a]Ye have not eaten bread, neither have ye drunk wine or strong drink: that ye might know[3045] that I *am* the LORD your God.[430]

7 And when ye came unto this place, [a]Sihon the king[4428] of Heshbon, and Og the king of Bashan, came out against us unto battle, and we smote[5221] them:

8 And we took their land, and [a]gave it for an inheritance[5159] unto the Reubenites, and to the Gadites, and to the half tribe[7626] of Manasseh.

9 [a]Keep[8104] therefore the words of this covenant, and do them, that ye may [b]prosper in all that ye do.

10 Ye stand[5324] this day all of you before the LORD your God; your captains[7218] of your tribes, your elders, and your officers,[7860] *with* all the men[376] of Israel,

🔑 11 Your little ones,[2945] your wives,[802] and thy stranger[1616] that *is* in thy camp,[4264] from [a]the hewer2404 of thy wood unto the drawer of thy water:

12 That thou shouldest [I]enter[5674] into covenant with the LORD thy God, and [a]into his oath, which the LORD thy God maketh[3772] with thee this day:

13 That he may [a]establish thee to day for a people[5971] unto himself, and *that* he may be unto thee a God, [b]as he hath said unto thee, and [c]as he hath sworn[7650] unto thy fathers,[1] to Abraham, to Isaac, and to Jacob.

14 Neither with you only [a]do I make this covenant and this oath;

15 But with *him* that standeth here with us this day before the LORD our God, [a]and also with *him* that *is* not here with us this day:

16 (For ye know how we have dwelt in the land of Egypt; and how we came through the nations[1471] which ye passed by;[5674]

17 And ye have seen their abominations, and their [I]idols,[1544] wood and stone, silver and gold, which *were* among them:)

18 Lest there should be among you man,[376] or woman,[802] or family,7940 or tribe, [a]whose heart turneth away this day from the LORD our God, to go *and*

67 [a]Job 7:4 [b]Deut. 28:34
68 [a]Jer. 43:7; Hos. 8:13; 9:3 [b]Deut. 17:16
1 [a]Deut. 5:2, 3
2 [a]Ex. 19:4
3 [a]Deut. 4:34; 7:19
4 [a]Isa. 6:9, 10; 63:17; John 8:43; Acts 28:26, 27; Eph. 4:18; 2Thess. 2:11, 12
5 [a]Deut. 1:3; 8:2 [b]Deut. 8:4
6 [a]Ex. 16:12; Deut. 8:3; Ps. 78:24, 25
7 [a]Num. 21:23, 24, 33; Deut. 2:32; 3:1
8 [a]Num. 32:33; Deut. 3:12, 13
9 [a]Deut. 4:6; Josh. 1:7; 1Kgs. 2:3 [b]Josh. 1:7 [c]Josh. 9:21, 23, 27
12 [I]Hebr. *pass* [a]Neh. 10:29
13 [a]Deut. 28:9; [b]Ex. 6:7 [c]Gen. 17:7
14 [a]Jer. 31:31-33; Heb. 8:7, 8
15 [a]Acts 2:39; 1Cor. 7:14
17 [I]Hebr. *dungy gods*
18 [a]Deut. 11:16

🔑 **28:68** See note on Jeremiah 18:7–10.
🔑 **29:11** See note on Numbers 11:1–5.

serve[5647] the gods[430] of these nations;
[b]lest there should be among you a root
that beareth [I]gall[7219] and wormwood;[3939]
19 And it come to pass, when he
heareth[8085] the words of this curse,[423]
that he bless himself[1288] in his heart, saying, I shall have peace,[7965] though I walk
[a]in the [I]imagination[8307] of mine heart, [b]to
add [II]drunkenness[7302] to thirst:
20 [a]The LORD will not spare him, but
then [b]the anger of the LORD and [c]his jealousy[7068] shall smoke[6225] against that
man, and all the curses[423] that are written in this book[5612] shall lie upon him,
and the LORD [d]shall blot out[4229] his name
from under heaven.[8064]
21 And the LORD [a]shall separate[914]
him unto evil[7451] out of all the tribes of
Israel, according to all the curses of the
covenant that [I]are written in this book of
the law:[8451]
22 So that the generation[1755] to come
of your children that shall rise up after
you, and the stranger that shall come
from a far land, shall say,[559] when they
see the plagues of that land, and the
sicknesses [I]which the LORD hath laid
upon it;
23 *And that* the whole land thereof *is*
brimstone,[1614] [a]and salt, *and* burning,[8316]
that it is not sown, nor beareth, nor any
grass groweth therein, [b]like the overthrow
of Sodom, and Gomorrah, Admah, and
Zeboim, which the LORD overthrew[2015] in
his anger, and in his wrath:[2534]
24 Even all nations shall say,
[a]Wherefore hath the LORD done[6213] thus
unto this land? what *meaneth* the heat of
this great anger?
25 Then men shall say, Because they
have forsaken[5800] the covenant of the
LORD God of their fathers, which he
made with them when he brought them
forth out of the land of Egypt:
26 For they went and served[5647]
other gods, and worshipped[7812] them,
gods whom they knew[3045] not, and
[I]*whom* he had not [II]given unto them:
27 And the anger of the LORD was
kindled[2734] against this land, [a]to bring
upon it all the curses[7045] that are written
in this book:

18 [I]Or, *a poisonous herb* [b]Acts 8:23; Heb. 12:15

19 [I]Or, *stubbornness* [II]Hebr. *the drunken to the thirsty* [a]Num. 15:39; Eccl. 11:9 [b]Isa. 30:1

20 [a]Ezek. 14:7, 8 [b]Ps. 74:1 [c]Ps. 79:5; Ezek. 23:25 [d]Deut. 9:14

21 [I]Hebr. *is written* [a]Matt. 24:51

22 [I]Hebr. *wherewith the LORD hath made it sick*

23 [a]Ps. 107:34; Jer. 17:6; Zeph. 2:9 [b]Gen. 19:24, 25; Jer. 20:16

24 [a]1Kgs. 9:8, 9; Jer. 22:8, 9

26 [I]Or, *who had not given to them any portion* [II]Hebr. *divided*

27 [a]Dan. 9:11, 13, 14

28 [a]1Kgs. 14:15; 2Chr. 7:20; Ps. 52:5; Prov. 2:22

1 [a]Lev. 26:40 [b]Deut. 28 [c]Deut. 4:29, 30; 1Kgs. 8:47, 48

2 [a]Neh. 1:9; Isa. 55:7; Lam. 3:40; Joel 2:12, 13

3 [a]Ps. 106:45; 126:1, 4; Jer. 29:14; Lam. 3:22, 32 [b]Ps. 147:2; Jer. 32:37; Ezek. 34:13; 36:24

4 [a]Deut. 28:64; Neh. 1:9

6 [a]Deut. 10:16; Jer. 32:39; Ezek. 11:19; 36:26

28 And the LORD [a]rooted them out of
their land[127] in anger, and in wrath, and
in great indignation,[7110] and cast them
into another land, as *it is* this day.
29 The secret *things belong* unto the
LORD our God: but those *things which are*
revealed[1540] *belong* unto us and to our
children for ever,[5769] that *we* may do all
the words of this law.

God's Promise Remains Constant

30 And [a]it shall come to pass, when
[b]all these things[1697] are come
upon thee, the blessing[1293] and the
curse,[7045] which I have set before thee,
and [c]thou shalt call *them* to mind[3824]
among all the nations,[1471] whither the
LORD thy God[430] hath driven thee,
2 And shalt [a]return[7725] unto the
LORD thy God, and shalt obey[8085] his
voice according to all that I command[6680]
thee this day,[3117] thou and thy children,[1121] with all thine heart,[3824] and
with all thy soul;[5315]
3 [a]That then the LORD thy God will
turn thy captivity,[7622] and have compassion[7355] upon thee, and will return and
[b]gather[6908] thee from all the nations,[5971]
whither the LORD thy God hath scattered
thee.
4 [a]If *any* of thine be driven out unto
the outmost *parts* of heaven,[8064] from
thence will the LORD thy God gather thee,
and from thence will he fetch thee:
5 And the LORD thy God will bring
thee into the land which thy fathers[1]
possessed,[3423] and thou shalt possess it;
and he will do thee good,[3190] and multiply thee above thy fathers.
6 And [a]the LORD thy God will
circumcise[4135] thine heart, and the heart
of thy seed,[2233] to love[157] the LORD thy
God with all thine heart, and with all thy
soul, that thou mayest live.[2416]
7 And the LORD thy God will put all
these curses[423] upon thine enemies, and
on them that hate[8130] thee, which persecuted thee.
8 And thou shalt return and obey the
voice of the LORD, and do all his com-

mandments which I command thee this day.

9 [a]And the LORD thy God will make thee plenteous in every work of thine hand,[3027] in the fruit of thy body,[990] and in the fruit of thy cattle, and in the fruit of thy land,[127] for good:[2896] for the LORD will again [b]rejoice over thee for good, as he rejoiced over thy fathers:

10 If thou shalt hearken[8085] unto the voice of the LORD thy God, to keep[8104] his commandments and his statutes which are written in this book[5612] of the law,[8451] *and* if thou turn unto the LORD thy God with all thine heart, and with all thy soul.

11 For this commandment[4687] which I command thee this day, [a]it *is* not hidden[6381] from thee, neither *is* it far off.

12 [a]It *is* not in heaven, that thou shouldest say,[559] Who shall go up[5927] for us to heaven, and bring it unto us, that we may hear[8085] it, and do it?

13 Neither *is* it beyond the sea, that thou shouldest say, Who shall go over[5674] the sea for us, and bring it unto us, that we may hear it, and do it?

14 But the word[1697] *is* very nigh unto thee, in thy mouth,[6310] and in thy heart, that thou mayest do it.

Choose Life

15 See, [a]I have set before thee this day life[2416] and good, and death[4191] and evil;[7451]

16 In that I command thee this day to love the LORD thy God, to walk in his ways,[1870] and to keep his commandments and his statutes and his judgments, that thou mayest live[2421] and multiply: and the LORD thy God shall bless[1288] thee in the land whither thou goest to possess it.

17 But if thine heart turn away, so that thou wilt not hear, but shalt be drawn away, and worship[7812] other gods,[430] and serve[5647] them;

18 [a]I denounce[5046] unto you this day,[3117] that ye shall surely perish,[6] *and that* ye shall not prolong[748] *your* days upon the land, whither thou passest over[5674] Jordan to go to possess it.

19 [a]I call heaven and earth[776] to record this day against you, *that* [b]I have set before you life and death, blessing and cursing:[7045] therefore choose[977] life, that both thou and thy seed may live:

20 That thou mayest love the LORD thy God, *and* that thou mayest obey his voice, and that thou mayest cleave unto him: for he *is* thy [a]life, and the length of thy days: that thou mayest dwell in the land which the LORD sware[7650] unto thy fathers, to Abraham, to Isaac, and to Jacob, to give them.

Joshua Is Appointed the New Leader

31 And Moses went and spake[1696] these words[1697] unto all Israel.

2 And he said[559] unto them, I [a]*am* an hundred and twenty years old this day;[3117] I can no more [b]go out and come in: also the LORD hath said unto me, [c]Thou shalt not go over[5647] this Jordan.

3 The LORD thy God,[430] [a]he will go over before thee, *and* he will destroy[8045] these nations[1471] from before thee, and thou shalt possess them: *and* Joshua, he shall go over before thee, [b]as the LORD hath said.[1696]

4 [a]And the LORD shall do unto them [b]as he did[6213] to Sihon and to Og, kings[4428] of the Amorites, and unto the land[776] of them, whom he destroyed.[8045]

5 And [a]the LORD shall give them up before your face, that ye may do unto them according unto all the commandments which I have commanded[6680] you.

6 [a]Be strong[2388] and of a good courage,[553] [b]fear[3372] not, nor be afraid[6206] of them: for the LORD thy God, [c]he *it is* that doth go with thee; [d]he will not fail[7503] thee, nor forsake[5800] thee.

7 And Moses called[7121] unto Joshua, and said unto him in the sight of all Israel, [a]Be strong and of a good courage: for thou must go with this people[5971] unto the land which the LORD hath sworn[7650] unto their fathers[1] to give

---

9 [a]Deut. 28:11 [b]Deut. 28:63; Jer. 32:41

11 [a]Isa. 45:19

12 [a]Rom. 10:6

15 [a]Deut. 11:26; 30:1, 19

18 [a]Deut. 4:26; 8:19

19 [a]Deut. 4:26; 31:28 [b]Deut. 30:15

20 [a]Ps. 27:1; 66:9; John 11:25

2 [a]Ex. 7:7; Deut. 34:7 [b]Num. 27:17; 1Kgs. 3:7 [c]Num. 20:12; 27:13; Deut. 3:27

3 [a]Deut. 9:3 [b]Num. 27:21; Deut. 3:28

4 [a]Deut. 3:21 [b]Num. 21:24, 33

5 [a]Deut. 7:2

6 [a]Josh. 10:25; 1Chr. 22:13 [b]Deut. 1:29; 7:18 [c]Deut. 20:4 [d]Josh. 1:5; Heb. 13:5

7 [a]Deut. 1:38; 3:28; 31:23; Josh. 1:6

them; and thou shalt cause them to inherit[5157] it.

8 And the LORD, [a]he *it is* that doth go before thee; [b]he will be with thee, he will not fail thee, neither forsake thee: fear not, neither be dismayed.[2865]

9 And Moses wrote this law,[8451] [a]and delivered it unto the priests[3548] the sons[1121] of Levi, [b]which bare[5375] the ark[727] of the covenant[1285] of the LORD, and unto all the elders[2205] of Israel.

10 And Moses commanded them, saying, At the end of *every* seven years, in the solemnity[4150] of the [a]year of release,[8059] [b]in the feast of tabernacles,[5521]

11 When all Israel is come to [a]appear[7200] before the LORD thy God in the place which he shall choose,[977] [b]thou shalt read[7121] this law before all Israel in their hearing.[241]

12 [a]Gather the people together, men,[582] and women,[802] and children,[2945] and thy stranger[1616] that *is* within thy gates, that they may hear,[8085] and that they may learn,[3925] and fear the LORD your God, and observe to do all the words of this law:

13 And *that* their children,[1121] [a]which have not known[3045] *any thing,* [b]may hear, and learn to fear the LORD your God, as long as ye live[2416] in the land[127] whither ye go over Jordan to possess it.

14 And the LORD said unto Moses, [a]Behold, thy days[3117] approach[7126] that thou must die:[4191] call[7121] Joshua, and present yourselves in the tabernacle[168] of the congregation,[4150] that [b]I may give him a charge.[6680] And Moses and Joshua went, and presented themselves in the tabernacle of the congregation.

15 And [a]the LORD appeared[7200] in the tabernacle in a pillar of a cloud:[6051] and the pillar of the cloud stood over the door of the tabernacle.

16 And the LORD said unto Moses, Behold, thou shalt [I]sleep with thy fathers; and this people will [a]rise up, and [b]go a whoring[2181] after the gods[430] of the strangers of the land, whither they go *to be* among them, and will [c]forsake me, and [d]break[6565] my covenant which I have made with them.

17 Then my anger shall be kindled[2734] against them in that day, and [a]I will forsake them, and I will [b]hide my face from them, and they shall be devoured, and many evils and troubles shall [I][c]befall them; so that they will say[559] in that day, [d]Are not these evils come upon us, because our God *is* [e]not among us?

18 And [a]I will surely hide my face in that day for all the evils which they shall have wrought,[6213] in that they are turned unto other gods.

19 Now therefore write ye this song[7892] for you, and teach[3925] it the children of Israel: put it in their mouths,[6310] that this song may be [a]a witness for me against the children of Israel.

20 For when I shall have brought them into the land which I sware[7650] unto their fathers, that floweth with milk and honey; and they shall have eaten and filled themselves, [a]and waxen fat;[1878] [b]then will they turn unto other gods, and serve[5647] them, and provoke[5006] me, and break my covenant.

21 And it shall come to pass, [a]when many evils and troubles are befallen them, that this song shall testify [I]against them as a witness; for it shall not be forgotten out of the mouths of their seed:[2233] for [b]I know[3045] their imagination[3336] [c]which they [II]go about, even now, before I have brought them into the land which I sware.

22 Moses therefore wrote this song the same day, and taught[3925] it the children of Israel.

23 [a]And he gave Joshua the son[1121] of Nun a charge, and said, [b]Be strong and of a good courage: for thou shalt bring the children of Israel into the land which I sware unto them: and I will be with thee.

Moses Speaks to the Levites

24 And it came to pass, when Moses had made an end[3615] of [a]writing the words of this law in a book,[5612] until they were finished,[8552]

25 That Moses commanded the

---

8 [a]Ex. 13:21, 22; 33:14; Deut. 9:3 [b]Josh. 1:5, 9; 1Chr. 28:20

9 [a]Deut. 17:18; 31:25 [b]Num. 4:15; Josh. 3:3; 1Chr. 15:12, 15

10 [a]Deut. 15:1 [b]Lev. 23:34

11 [a]Deut. 16:16 [b]Josh. 8:34, 35; 2Kgs. 23:2; Neh. 8:1-3

12 [a]Deut. 4:10

13 [a]Deut. 11:2 [b]Ps. 78:6, 7

14 [a]Num. 27:13; Deut. 34:5 [b]Deut. 31:28; Num. 27:19

15 [a]Ex. 33:9

16 [I]Hebr. *lie down* [a]Ex. 32:6 [b]Ex. 34:15; Judg. 2:17 [c]Deut. 32:15; Judg. 2:12; 10:6, 13 [d]Judg. 2:20

17 [I]Hebr. *find them* [a]2Chr. 15:2 [b]Deut. 32:20; Ps. 104:29; Isa. 8:17; 64:7; Ezek. 39:23 [c]Neh. 9:32 [d]Judg. 6:13 [e]Num. 14:42

18 [a]Deut. 31:17

19 [a]Deut. 31:26

20 [a]Deut. 32:15; Neh. 9:25, 26; Hos. 13:6 [b]Deut. 31:16

21 [I]Hebr. *before* [II]Hebr. *do* [a]Deut. 31:17 [b]Hos. 5:3; 13:5, 6 [c]Amos 5:25, 26

23 [a]Deut. 31:14 [b]Deut. 31:7; Josh. 1:6

24 [a]Deut. 31:9

Levites, which bare the ark[727] of the covenant of the LORD, saying,

26 Take this book of the law, [a]and put it in the side of the ark[727] of the covenant of the LORD your God, that it may be there [b]for a witness against thee.

27 [a]For I know thy rebellion, and thy [b]stiff[7186] neck: behold, while I am yet alive[2416] with you this day, ye have been rebellious against the LORD; and how much more after my death?[4194]

28 Gather unto me all the elders of your tribes,[7626] and your officers,[7860] that I may speak[1696] these words in their ears,[241] [a]and call heaven8064 and earth[776] to record against them.

29 For I know that after my death ye will utterly [a]corrupt[7843] *yourselves,* and turn aside[5493] from the way[1870] which I have commanded you; and [b]evil[7451] will befall you [c]in the latter days; because ye will do evil in the sight of the LORD, to provoke him to anger[3707] through the work of your hands.[3027]

30 And Moses spake in the ears of all the congregation[6951] of Israel the words of this song, until they were ended.[8552]

Moses' Song

32 Give [a]ear,[238] O ye heavens, and I will speak;[1696] and hear,[8085] O earth,[776] the words[561] of my mouth.[6310]

2 [a]My doctrine[3948] shall drop[6201] as the rain, my speech[565] shall distil5140 as the dew, [b]as the small rain upon the tender herb, and as the showers upon the grass:

3 Because I will publish the name of the LORD: [a]ascribe ye greatness unto our God.[430]

4 *He is* [a]the Rock, [b]his work *is* perfect:[8549] for [c]all his ways[1870] *are* judgment:[4941] [d]a God[410] of truth[530] and [e]without iniquity,[5766] just[6662] and right *is* he.

5 [I][a]They have corrupted[7843] themselves, [II]their spot[3971] *is* not *the spot* of his children:[1121] *they are* a [b]perverse and crooked generation.[1755]

6 Do ye thus [a]requite[1580] the LORD, O foolish people[5971] and unwise? *is* not he [b]thy father[1] *that* hath [c]bought thee? hath he not [d]made[6213] thee, and established[3559] thee?

7 Remember[2142] the days[3117] of old,[5769] consider[995] the years of [I]many generations:[1755] [a]ask[7592] thy father, and he will shew[5046] thee; thy elders,[2205] and they will tell[559] thee.

8 When the Most High[5945] [a]divided to the nations[1471] their inheritance,[5157] when he [b]separated the sons[1121] of Adam, he set the bounds of the people according to the number of the children of Israel.

9 For [a]the LORD's portion *is* his people; Jacob *is* the [I]lot[2256] of his inheritance.[5159]

10 He found him [a]in a desert land, and in the waste[8414] howling wilderness; he [I]led him about, he [b]instructed[995] him, he [c]kept[5341] him as the apple of his eye.

11 [a]As an eagle stirreth up her nest, fluttereth over her young, spreadeth abroad her wings, taketh them, beareth them on her wings:

12 *So* the LORD alone did lead[5148] him, and *there was* no strange[5236] god with him.

13 [a]He made him ride on the high places of the earth, that he might eat the increase of the fields; and he made him to suck [b]honey out of the rock, and oil[8081] out of the flinty rock;

14 Butter of kine,1241 and milk of sheep, with fat of lambs,[3733] and rams of the breed of Bashan, and goats, [a]with the fat of kidneys of wheat; and thou didst drink the pure [b]blood of the grape.

15 But [a]Jeshurun waxed fat, and [b]kicked: [c]thou art waxen fat, thou art grown thick, thou art covered *with fatness;* then he [d]forsook[5203] God *which* [e]made him, and lightly esteemed the [f]Rock of his salvation.[3444]

16 [a]They provoked him to jeal-

26 [a]2Kgs. 22:8 [b]Deut. 31:19
27 [a]Deut. 9:24; 32:20 [b]Ex. 32:9; Deut. 9:6
28 [a]Deut. 30:19; 32:1
29 [a]Deut. 32:5; Judg. 2:19; Hos. 9:9 [b]Deut. 28:15 [c]Gen. 49:1; Deut. 4:30

1 [a]Deut. 4:26; 30:19; 31:28; Ps. 50:4; Isa. 1:2; Jer. 2:12; 6:19
2 [a]Isa. 55:10, 11; 1Cor. 3:6-8 [b]Ps. 72:6; Mic. 5:7
3 [a]1Chr. 29:11
4 [a]2Sam. 22:3; 23:3; Ps. 18:2, 31, 46; Hab. 1:12 [b]2Sam. 22:31 [c]Dan. 4:37; Rev. 15:3 [d]Jer. 10:10 [e]Job 34:10; Ps. 92:15
5 [I]Hebr. *He hath corrupted to himself* [II]Or, that *they are not his children,* that is *their blot* [a]Deut. 31:29 [b]Matt. 17:17; Luke 9:41; Phil. 2:15
6 [a]Ps. 116:12 [b]Isa. 63:16 [c]Ps. 74:2 [d]Deut. 32:15; Isa. 27:11; 44:2
7 [I]Hebr. *generation and generation* [a]Ex. 13:14; Ps. 44:1; 78:3, 4
8 [a]Zech. 9:2; Acts 17:26 [b]Gen. 11:8
9 [I]Hebr. *cord* [a]Ex. 15:16; 19:5; 1Sam. 10:1; Ps. 78:71
10 [I]Or, *compassed him about* [a]Deut. 8:15; Jer. 2:6; Hos. 13:5 [b]Deut. 4:36 [c]Ps. 17:8; Prov. 7:2; Zech. 2:8
11 [a]Ex. 19:4; Deut. 1:31; Isa. 31:5; 46:4; 63:9; Heb. 11:3
13 [a]Deut. 33:29; Isa. 58:14; Ezek. 36:2 [b]Job 29:6; Ps. 81:16
14 [a]Ps. 81:16; 147:14 [b]Gen. 49:11
15 [a]Deut. 33:5, 26; Isa. 44:2 [b]1Sam. 2:29 [c]Deut. 31:20; Neh. 9:25; Ps. 17:10; Jer. 2:7; 5:7, 28; Hos. 13:6 [d]Deut. 31:16; Isa. 1:4 [e]Deut. 32:6; Isa. 51:13 [f]2Sam. 22:47; Ps. 89:26; 95:1
16 [a]1Kgs. 14:22; 1Cor. 10:22

ousy[7065] with strange[2114] *gods,* with
abominations provoked they him to
anger.[3707]
17 [a]They sacrificed[2076] unto devils,[7700]
[I][b]not to God; to gods[430] whom they
knew[3045] not, to new *gods that* came
newly up, whom your fathers[1] feared[8175]
not.
18 [a]Of the Rock *that* begat thee thou
art unmindful, and hast [b]forgotten God
that formed[2342] thee.
19 [a]And when the LORD saw[7200] *it,* he
[I]abhorred[5006] *them,* [b]because of the provoking of his sons, and of his daughters.
20 And he said,[559] [a]I will hide my
face from them, I will see what their
end[319] *shall be:* for they *are* a very
froward[8419] generation, [b]children in whom
is no faith.
21 [a]They have moved me to jealousy
with *that which is* not God; they have
provoked me to anger[3707] [b]with their vanities: and [c]I will move them to jealousy[7065] with *those which are* not a people; I will provoke them to anger with a
foolish nation.[1471]
22 For [a]a fire is kindled in mine
anger, and [I]shall burn unto the lowest
hell, and [II]shall consume the earth with
her increase, and set on fire the foundations[4146] of the mountains.
23 I will [a]heap[5595] mischiefs[7451] upon
them; [b]I will spend[3615] mine arrows upon
them.
24 *They shall be* burnt with hunger,
and devoured with [I]burning heat, and
with bitter destruction:[6986] I will also
send [a]the teeth of beasts upon them, with
the poison[2534] of serpents[2119] of the
dust.[6083]
25 [a]The sword[2719] without, and ter-
ror[367] [I]within, shall [II]destroy[7921] both the
young man and the virgin,[1330] the suckling *also* with the man of gray hairs.[7872]
26 [a]I said, I would scatter them into
corners, I would make[7673] the remembrance[2143] of them to cease[7673] from
among men:[582]
27 Were it not that I feared the
wrath[3708] of the enemy, lest their adversaries [a]should behave themselves
strangely,[5234] *and* lest they should
[b]say,[559] [I]Our hand[3027] *is* high, and the
LORD hath not done[6213] all this.
28 For they *are* a nation void of
counsel,[6098] [a]neither *is there any* understanding[8394] in them.
29 [a]O that they were wise,[2449] *that*
they understood this, [b]*that* they would
consider their latter end30 How should
[a]one chase a thousand, and two put ten
thousand to flight, except their Rock [b]had
sold them, and the LORD had shut them
up?
31 For [a]their rock *is* not as our Rock,
[b]even our enemies themselves *being*
judges.[6414]
32 For [a]their vine [I]*is* of the vine of
Sodom, and of the fields of Gomorrah:
their grapes *are* grapes of gall,[7219] their
clusters *are* bitter:
33 Their wine *is* [a]the poison of dragons,[8577] and the cruel [b]venom of asps.[6620]
34 *Is* not this [a]laid up in store with
me, *and* sealed up among my treasures?
35 [a]To me *belongeth* vengeance,[5359]
and recompence; their foot shall slide in
due time:[6256] for [b]the day[3117] of their
calamity[343] *is* at hand, and the things
that shall come upon them make haste.
36 [a]For the LORD shall judge[1777] his
people, [b]and repent himself[5162] for his
servants,[5650] when he seeth[7200] that *their*
[I]power[3027] is gone, and [c]*there is* none
shut up, or left.[5800]
37 And he shall say, [a]Where *are* their
gods, *their* rock in whom they trusted,[2620]
38 Which did eat the fat of their
sacrifices,[2077] *and* drank the wine of their
drink offerings?[5257] let them rise up and
help you, *and* be [I]your protection.
39 See now that [a]I, *even* I, *am* he,
and [b]*there is* no god with me: [c]I kill, and
I make alive; I wound, and I heal: neither
is there any that can deliver[5337] out of
my hand.
40 [a]For I lift up[5375] my hand to
heaven,[8064] and say, I live[2416] for ever.[5769]

17 [I]Or, which were *not God* [a]Lev. 17:7; Ps. 106:37; 1Cor. 10:20; Rev. 9:20 [b]Deut. 32:2
18 [a]Isa. 17:10 [b]Jer. 2:32
19 [I]Or, *despised* [a]Judg. 2:14 [b]Isa. 1:2
20 [a]Deut. 31:17 [b]Isa. 30:9; Matt. 17:17
21 [a]Deut. 32:16; Ps. 78:58 [b]1Sam. 12:21; 1Kgs. 16:13, 26; Ps. 31:6; Jer. 8:19; 10:8; 14:22; Jon. 2:8; Acts 14:15 [c]Hos. 1:10; Rom. 10:19
22 [I]Or, *hath burned* [II]Or, *hath consumed* [a]Jer. 15:14; 17:4; Lam. 4:11
23 [a]Isa. 26:15 [b]Ps. 7:12, 13; Ezek. 5:16
24 [I]Hebr. *burning coals* [a]Lev. 26:22
25 [I]Hebr. *from the chambers* [II]Hebr. *bereave* [a]Lam. 1:20; Ezek. 7:15; 2Cor. 7:5
26 [a]Ezek. 20:13, 14, 23
27 [I]Or, *Our high hand, and not the* LORD, *hath done all this* [a]Jer. 19:4 [b]Ps. 140:8
28 [a]Isa. 27:11; Jer. 4:22
29 [a]Deut. 5:29; Ps. 81:13; 107:43; Luke 19:42 [b]Isa. 47:7; Lam. 1:9
30 [a]Lev. 26:8; Josh. 23:10; 2Chr. 24:24; Isa. 30:17 [b]Ps. 44:12; Isa. 50:1; 52:3
31 [a]1Sam. 2:2 [b]1Sam. 4:8; Jer. 40:3
32 [I]Or, *is worse than the vine of Sodom* [a]Isa. 1:10
33 [a]Ps. 58:4 [b]Ps. 140:3; Rom. 3:13
34 [a]Job 14:17; Jer. 2:22; Hos. 13:12; Rom. 2:5
35 [a]Ps. 94:1; Rom. 12:19; Heb. 10:30 [b]2Pet. 2:3

36 [I]Hebr. *hand* [a]Ps. 135:14 [b]Judg. 2:18; Ps. 106:45; Jer. 31:20; Joel 2:14 [c]1Kgs. 14:10; 21:21; 2Kgs. 9:8; 14:26 **37** [a]Judg. 10:14; Jer. 2:28 **38** [I]Hebr. *a hiding for you* **39** [a]Ps. 102:27; Isa. 41:4; 48:12 [b]Deut. 4:35; Isa. 45:5, 18, 22 [c]1Sam. 2:6; 2Kgs. 5:7; Job 5:18; Ps. 68:20; Hos. 6:1 **40** [a]Gen. 14:22; Ex. 6:8; Num. 14:30

41 [a]If I whet[8150] my glittering sword, and mine hand take hold on judgment; [b]I will render[7725] vengeance to mine enemies, and will reward[7999] them that hate[8130] me.

42 I will make mine arrows [a]drunk with blood, and my sword shall devour flesh;[1320] *and that* with the blood of the slain[2491] and of the captives,[7633] from the beginning[7218] of [b]revenges[6546] upon the enemy.

43 [I][a]Rejoice, O ye nations, *with* his people: for he will [b]avenge the blood of his servants, and [c]will render vengeance to his adversaries, and [d]will be merciful[3722] unto his land,[127] *and* to his people.

44 And Moses came and spake[1696] all the words[1697] of this song in the ears[241] of the people, he, and [I]Hoshea the son[1121] of Nun.

45 And Moses made an end[3615] of speaking all these words to all Israel:

46 And he said unto them, [a]Set[7760] your hearts unto all the words which I testify[5749] among you this day, which ye shall command[6680] your children to observe to do, all the words of this law.[8451]

47 For it *is* not a vain thing[1697] for you; [a]because it *is* your life:[2416] and through this thing ye shall prolong[748] *your* days in the land, whither ye go over[5674] Jordan to possess it.

God Prepares Moses for Death

48 [a]And the LORD spake unto Moses that selfsame day, saying,

49 Get thee up into this [a]mountain Abarim, *unto* mount Nebo, which *is* in the land[776] of Moab, that *is* over against Jericho; and behold[7200] the land of Canaan, which I give unto the children of Israel for a possession:[272]

50 And die[4191] in the mount whither thou goest up, and be gathered unto thy people; as [a]Aaron thy brother[251] died[4191] in mount Hor, and was gathered[622] unto his people:

51 Because [a]ye trespassed[4603] against me among the children of Israel at the waters of [I]Meribah–Kadesh, in the wilderness of Zin; because ye [b]sanctified[6942] me not in the midst of the children of Israel.

52 [a]Yet thou shalt see the land before *thee;* but thou shalt not go thither unto the land which I give the children of Israel.

Moses Blesses Israel

33 And this *is* [a]the blessing,[1293] wherewith Moses the man of God[430] blessed[1288] the children[1121] of Israel before his death.[4194]

2 And he said,[559] [a]The LORD came from Sinai, and rose up from Seir unto them; he shined forth from mount Paran, and he came with [b]ten thousands of saints: from his right hand *went* [I]a fiery law[1881] for them.

3 Yea, [a]he loved[2245] the people;[5971] [b]all his saints[6918] *are* in thy hand:[3027] and they [c]sat down at thy feet; *every one* shall [d]receive[5375] of thy words.[1703]

4 [a]Moses commanded[6680] us a law,[8451] [b]*even* the inheritance of the congregation[6952] of Jacob.

5 And he was [a]king[4428] in [b]Jeshurun, when the heads[7218] of the people *and* the tribes[7626] of Israel were gathered together.[622]

6 Let Reuben live,[2421] and not die;[4191] and let *not* his men be few.

7 And this *is the blessing* of Judah: and he said, Hear,[8085] LORD, the voice of Judah, and bring him unto his people: [a]let his hands[3027] be sufficient for him; and be thou [b]an help *to him* from his enemies.

8 And of Levi he said, [a]*Let* thy Thummim and thy Urim *be* with thy holy one,[2623] [b]whom thou didst prove at Massah,[5254] *and with* whom thou didst strive[7378] at the waters of Meribah;

9 Who said unto his father[1] and to his mother, I have not [a]seen[7200] him; [b]neither did he acknowledge[5234] his brethren,[251] nor knew[3045] his own children: for [c]they have observed[8104] thy word,[565] and kept[5341] thy covenant.[1285]

---

41 [a]Isa. 27:1; 34:5; 66:16; Ezek. 21:9, 10, 14, 20 [b]Isa. 1:24; Nah. 1:2
42 [a]Jer. 46:10 [b]Job 13:24; Jer. 30:14; Lam. 2:5
43 [I]Or, *Praise his people, ye nations:* or, *Sing ye* [a]Rom. 15:10 [b]Rev. 6:10; 19:2 [c]Deut. 32:41 [d]Ps. 85:1
44 [I]Or, *Joshua*
46 [a]Deut. 6:6; 11:18; Ezek. 40:4
47 [a]Lev. 18:5; Deut. 30:19; Prov. 3:2, 22; 4:22; Rom. 10:5
48 [a]Num. 27:12, 13
49 [a]Num. 33:47, 48; Deut. 34:1
50 [a]Num. 20:25, 28; 33:38
51 [I]Or, *Strife at Kadesh* [a]Num. 20:11-13; 27:14; [b]Lev. 10:3
52 [a]Num. 27:12; Deut. 34:4

1 [a]Gen. 49:28
2 [I]Hebr. *a fire of law* [a]Ex. 19:18, 20; Judg. 5:4, 5; Hab. 3:3 [b]Ps. 68:17; Dan. 7:10; Acts 7:53; Gal. 3:19; Heb. 2:2; Rev. 5:11; 9:16
3 [a]Ex. 19:5; Deut. 7:7, 8; Ps. 47:4; Hos. 11:1; Mal. 1:2 [b]Deut. 7:6; 1Sam. 2:9; Ps. 50:5 [c]Luke 10:39; Acts 22:3 [d]Prov. 2:1
4 [a]John 1:17; 7:19 [b]Ps. 119:111
5 [a]Gen. 36:31; Judg. 9:2; 17:6 [b]Deut. 32:15
7 [a]Gen. 49:8 [b]Ps. 146:5
8 [a]Ex. 28:30 [b]Ex. 17:7; Num. 20:13; Deut. 8:2, 3, 16; Ps. 81:7
9 [a]Gen. 29:32; 1Chr. 17:17; Job 37:24 [b]Ex. 32:26-28 [c]Jer. 18:18; Mal. 2:5, 6

10 [I][a]They shall teach Jacob thy judgments,[4941] and Israel thy law: [II][b]they shall put incense[7004] [III]before thee, [c]and whole burnt sacrifice[3632] upon thine altar.[4196]

11 Bless,[1288] LORD, his substance, and [a]accept[7521] the work of his hands: smite through the loins of them that rise against him, and of them that hate[8130] him, that they rise not again.

12 *And* of Benjamin he said, The beloved[3039] of the LORD shall dwell[7931] in safety by him; *and the LORD* shall cover him all the day long, and he shall dwell between his shoulders.

13 And of Joseph he said, [a]Blessed of the LORD *be* his land,[776] for the precious things of heaven,[8064] for [b]the dew, and for the deep that coucheth beneath,

14 And for the precious fruits *brought forth* by the sun, and for the precious things [I]put forth by the [II]moon,

15 And for the chief things[7218] of [a]the ancient[6924] mountains, and for the precious things [b]of the lasting[5769] hills,

16 And for the precious things of the earth[776] and fulness thereof, and *for* the good will[7522] of [a]him that dwelt[7931] in the bush: let *the blessing* [b]come upon the head[7218] of Joseph, and upon the top of the head of him *that was* separated from his brethren.

17 His glory[1926] *is like* the [a]firstling of his bullock, and his horns *are like* [b]the horns of [I]unicorns: with them [c]he shall push the people together to the ends of the earth: and [d]they *are* the ten thousands[505] of Ephraim, and they *are* the thousands of Manasseh.

18 And of Zebulun he said, [a]Rejoice, Zebulun, in thy going out; and, Issachar, in thy tents.[168]

19 They shall [a]call[7121] the people unto the mountain; there [b]they shall offer sacrifices[2077] of righteousness:[6664] for they shall suck *of* the abundance of the seas, and *of* treasures hid in the sand.

20 And of Gad he said, Blessed *be* he that [a]enlargeth Gad: he dwelleth[7931] as a lion, and teareth the arm with the crown of the head.

21 And [a]he provided[7200] the first part[7225] for himself, because there, *in* a portion of the lawgiver,[2710] *was he* [I]seated; and [b]he came with the heads of the people, he executed[6213] the justice[6666] of the LORD, and his judgments with Israel.

22 And of Dan he said, Dan *is* a lion's whelp:[1482] [a]he shall leap from Bashan.

23 And of Naphtali he said, O Naphtali, [a]satisfied with favour,[7522] and full with the blessing of the LORD: [b]possess thou the west and the south.

24 And of Asher he said, [a]*Let* Asher *be* blessed with children; let him be acceptable[7522] to his brethren, and let him [b]dip[2881] his foot in oil.

25 [I]Thy shoes *shall be* [a]iron and brass; and as thy days,[3117] *so shall* thy strength *be.*

26 There is [a]none like unto the God[410] of [b]Jeshurun, [c]*who* rideth upon the heaven in thy help, and in his excellency on the sky.[7834]

27 The eternal[6924] God *is thy* [a]refuge, and underneath *are* the everlasting[5769] arms: and [b]he shall thrust out the enemy from before thee; and shall say,[559] Destroy[8045] *them.*

28 [a]Israel then shall dwell in safety alone: [b]the fountain of Jacob *shall be* upon a land of corn and wine; also his [c]heavens[8064] shall drop down[6201] dew.

29 [a]Happy[835] *art* thou, O Israel: [b]who *is* like unto thee, O people saved by the LORD, [c]the shield of thy help, and who *is* the sword[2719] of thy excellency! and thine enemies [I][d]shall be found liars unto thee; and [e]thou shalt tread upon their high places.[1116]

Moses' Death

34 And Moses went up[5927] from the plains[6160] of Moab [a]unto the mountain of Nebo, to the top[7218] of [I]Pisgah, that *is* over against Jericho. And the LORD [b]shewed him all the land[776] of Gilead, [c]unto Dan,

2 And all Naphtali, and the land of

10 [I]Or, *Let them teach* [II]Or *let them put incense* [III]Hebr. *at thy nose* [a]Lev. 10:11; Deut. 17:9, 10, 11; 24:8; Ezek. 44:23, 24; Mal. 2:7 [b]Ex. 30:7, 8; Num. 16:40; 1Sam. 2:28 [c]Lev. 1:9, 13, 17; Ps. 51:19; Ezek. 43:27
11 [a]2Sam. 24:23; Ps. 20:3; Ezek. 20:40, 41; 43:27
13 [a]Gen. 49:25 [b]Gen. 27:28
14 [I]Hebr. *thrust forth* [II]Hebr. *moons*
15 [a]Gen. 49:26 [b]Hab. 3:6
16 [a]Ex. 3:2, 4; Acts 7:30, 35 [b]Gen. 49:26
17 [I]Hebr. *a unicorn* [a]1Chr. 5:1 [b]Num. 23:22; Ps. 92:10 [c]1Kgs. 22:11; Ps. 44:5 [d]Gen. 48:19
18 [a]Gen. 49:13-15
19 [a]Isa. 2:3 [b]Ps. 4:5
20 [a]Josh. 13:10; 1Chr. 12:8
21 [I]Hebr. *ceiled* [a]Num. 32:16, 17 [b]Josh. 4:12
22 [a]Josh. 19:47; Judg. 18:27
23 [a]Gen. 49:21 [b]Josh. 19:32
24 [a]Gen. 49:20 [b]Job 29:6
25 [I]Or, *Under thy shoes* shall be *iron* [a]Deut. 8:9
26 [a]Ex. 15:11; Ps. 86:8; Jer. 10:6 [b]Deut. 32:15 [c]Ps. 68:4, 33, 34; 104:3; Hab. 3:8
27 [a]Ps. 90:1 [b]Deut. 9:3-5
28 [a]Num. 23:9; Jer. 23:6; 33:16 [b]Deut. 8:7, 8 [c]Gen. 27:28; Deut. 11:11
29 [I]Or, *shall be subdued* [a]Ps. 144:15 [b]2Sam. 7:23 [c]Ps. 115:9, 10, 11 [d]2Sam. 22:45; Ps. 18:44; 66:3; 81:15 [e]Deut. 32:13

1 [I]Or, *The hill* [a]Num. 27:12; 33:47; Deut. 32:49 [b]Deut. 3:27 [c]Gen. 14:14

Ephraim, and Manasseh, and all the land
of Judah, [a]unto the utmost sea,
3 And the south, and the plain of the
valley of Jericho, [a]the city of palm trees,
unto Zoar.
4 And the LORD said[559] unto him,
[a]This *is* the land which I sware[7650] unto
Abraham, unto Isaac, and unto Jacob,
saying, I will give it unto thy seed:[2233] [b]I
have caused thee to see *it* with thine eyes,
but thou shalt not go over[5674] thither.
🗝 5 [a]So Moses the servant[5650] of the
LORD died[4191] there in the land of Moab,
according to the word of the LORD.
6 And he buried[6912] him in a valley
in the land of Moab, over against Beth–
peor: but [a]no man[376] knoweth of his
sepulchre[6900] unto this day.
7 [a]And Moses *was* an hundred and
twenty years old when he died:[4194] [b]his
eye was not dim, nor his [I]natural force
[II]abated.[5127]

8 And the children[1121] of Israel
wept for Moses in the plains of Moab
[a]thirty days:[3117] so the days of weeping *and* mourning for Moses were
ended.[8552]
9 And Joshua the son[1121] of Nun
was full of the [a]spirit[7307] of wisdom;[2451]
for [b]Moses had laid his hands[3027] upon
him: and the children of Israel hearkened[8085] unto him, and did[6213] as the
LORD commanded[6680] Moses.
10 And there [a]arose not a prophet[5030]
since in Israel like unto Moses, [b]whom
the LORD knew[3045] face to face,
11 In all [a]the signs[226] and the
wonders,[4159] which the LORD sent him
to do in the land of Egypt to Pharaoh,
and to all his servants,[5650] and to all his
land,
12 And in all that mighty hand,[3027]
and in all the great terror[4172] which
Moses shewed in the sight of all Israel.

2 [a]Deut. 11:24
3 [a]Judg. 1:16; 3:13; 2Chr. 28:15
4 [a]Gen. 12:7; 13:15; 15:18; 26:3; 28:13 [b]Deut. 3:27; 32:52
5 [a]Deut. 32:50; Josh. 1:1, 2
6 [a]Jude 1:9
7 [I]Hebr. *moisture* [II]Hebr. *fled* [a]Deut. 31:2 [b]Gen. 27:1; 48:10; Josh. 14:10, 11
8 [a]Gen. 50:3, 10; Num. 20:29
9 [a]Isa. 11:2; Dan. 6:3 [b]Num. 27:18, 23
10 [a]Deut. 18:15, 18 [b]Ex. 33:11; Num. 12:6, 8; Deut. 5:4
11 [a]Deut. 4:34; 7:19

🗝 **34:5–7** The life of Moses may be divided into three periods of forty years each. The first forty years were spent in Egypt as a member of Pharaoh's household (Acts 7:21–23). Next, he lived a private family life in the land of Midian (Acts 7:29, 30). Finally, he lived forty years from God's call at the burning bush until his death, during which time he led the children of Israel out of Egypt. See note on Jude 1:9, on the dispute over Moses' burial place.

The Book of
JOSHUA

This book describes the conquest of the land of Canaan under the leadership of Joshua, the successor of Moses. His name means "Jehovah saves" or "Jehovah is salvation." The Greek transliteration of his name is "Jesus" (see Heb. 4:8).

Joshua had worked with Moses since the giving of the Ten Commandments at Mount Sinai. He continued to serve with Moses throughout the wilderness wanderings (Ex. 24:13), and became a strong leader who was full of faith and courage. Joshua and Caleb were in favor of conquering the land of Canaan in spite of the height and agressive nature of the people there. Consequently, they were the only two of their generation that God permitted to cross the Jordan River (Num. 14:29, 30, 38; Deut. 1:35, 36).

The theme of the Book of Joshua is "victory through faith" (see Josh. 1:6–9). The land that God promised to Abraham (Gen. 15:18) was now being conquered. Joshua began by attacking a few key cities (e.g., Jericho and Ai) and breaking up dangerous coalitions among the Canaanites (Josh. 10:2–5). The conquest of the Promised Land under Joshua, however, was not complete. The Israelites continued to encounter resistance after they had settled in the land. In accordance with God's plan, it was left up to the individual tribes to slowly displace the remaining strong holds (Ex. 23:27–31; Josh. 13:1–6; Judg. 3:1, 2).

God's Charge to Joshua

1 🔑 Now after the death[4194] of Moses
the servant[5650] of the LORD it came
to pass, that the LORD spake[559] unto
Joshua the son[1121] of Nun, Moses'
[a]minister,[8334] saying,
2 [a]Moses my servant is dead;[4191] now
therefore arise, go over this Jordan, thou,
and all this people,[5971] unto the land[776]
which I do give to them, *even* to the children[1121] of Israel.
🔑 3 [a]Every place that the sole[3709] of
your foot shall tread upon, that have I
given unto you, as I said[1696] unto Moses.
4 [a]From the wilderness and this
Lebanon even unto the great river, the
river Euphrates, all the land of the
Hittites, and unto the great sea toward
the going down of the sun, shall be your
coast.
5 [a]There shall not any man[376] be able
to stand before thee all the days[3117] of
thy life:[2416] [b]as I was with Moses, *so* [c]I
will be with thee: [d]I will not fail[7503] thee,
nor forsake[5800] thee.
6 [a]Be strong[2388] and of a good
courage: for [1]unto this people shalt thou
divide for an inheritance[5157] the land,
which I sware[7650] unto their fathers[1] to
give them.

1 [a]Ex. 24:13; Deut. 1:38
2 [a]Deu**1** [a]Ex. 24:13; Deut. 1:38
2 [a]Deut. 34:5
3 [a]Deut. 11:24; Josh. 14:9
4 [a]Gen. 15:18; Ex. 23:31; Num. 34:3-12
5 [a]Deut. 7:24 [b]Ex. 3:12 [c]Deut. 31:8, 23; Josh. 1:9, 17; 3:7; 6:27; Isa. 43:2, 5 [d]Deut. 31:6, 8; Heb. 13:5
6 [1]Or, *thou shalt cause this people to inherit the land* [a]Deut. 31:7, 23

🔑 **1:1** Joshua is introduced as Moses' servant, which is seen in the Hebrew word *meshareth* (8334), a participle meaning "one who ministers." Joshua's name had been changed from Oshea (Num. 13:16). He had been previously commissioned by God to be Moses' successor (Num. 27:16–23). This commission included instructions to inquire through the priests, via the Urim and Thummim, for answers from God. However, on this occasion of Joshua's charge to take command, God appeared directly to Joshua as He had with Moses (Num. 12:8) and would later do with the prophets.

🔑 **1:3–6** This passage amplifies the physical nature of the land promised to the children of Israel, as had been affirmed before (Gen. 15:7–21; 28:13, 14). Many scholars deny any unconditional promise of a physical land to Israel; they are hard put to explain these references to places where the "sole of your foot shall tread," and to specific geographic features. There remains as yet an unfulfilled promise of this land to the descendants of Israel.

🔑 7 Only be thou strong and very courageous, that thou mayest observe to do[6213] according to all the law,[8451] [a]which Moses my servant commanded[6680] thee: [b]turn not from it *to* the right hand or *to* the left, that thou mayest [I]prosper whithersoever thou goest.

8 [a]This book[5612] of the law shall not depart out of thy mouth;[6310] but [b]thou shalt meditate[1897] therein day[3119] and night,[3915] that thou mayest observe to do according to all that is written therein: for then thou shalt make thy way[1870] prosperous, and then thou shalt [I]have good success.[7919]

9 [a]Have not I commanded thee? Be strong and of a good courage; [b]be not afraid,[6206] neither be thou dismayed:[2865] for the LORD thy God[430] *is* with thee whithersoever thou goest.

10 Then Joshua commanded the officers[7860] of the people, saying,

11 Pass[5674] through the host,[4264] and command[6680] the people, saying, Prepare[3559] you victuals;[6720] for [a]within three days ye shall pass over this Jordan, to go in to possess[3423] the land, which the LORD your God giveth you to possess it.

12 And to the Reubenites, and to the Gadites, and to half the tribe[7626] of Manasseh, spake Joshua, saying,

🔑 13 Remember [a]the word[1697] which Moses the servant of the LORD commanded you, saying, The LORD your God hath given you rest, and hath given you this land.

14 Your wives,[802] your little ones,[2945] and your cattle, shall remain in the land which Moses gave you on this side Jordan; but ye shall pass before your brethren[251] [I]armed, all the mighty men of valour,[2428] and help them;

15 Until the LORD have given your brethren rest, as *he hath given* you, and they also have possessed[3423] the land which the LORD your God giveth them: [a]then ye shall return[7725] unto the land of your possession,[3425] and enjoy it, which Moses the LORD's servant gave you on this side Jordan toward the sunrising.

16 And they answered Joshua, saying, All that thou commandest[6680] us we will do, and whithersoever thou sendest us, we will go.

17 According as we hearkened[8085] unto Moses in all things, so will we hearken unto thee: only the LORD thy God [a]be with thee, as he was with Moses.

18 Whosoever *he be* that doth rebel against thy commandment,[6310] and will not hearken unto thy words[1697] in all that thou commandest him, he shall be put to death:[4191] only be strong and of a good courage.

Joshua Sends Spies

2 🔑 And Joshua the son[1121] of Nun [I]sent [a]out of Shittim two men to spy

7 [I]Or, *do wisely* [a]Num. 27:23; Deut. 31:7; Josh. 11:15 [b]Deut. 5:32; 28:14

8 [I]Or, *do wisely* [a]Deut. 17:18, 19 [b]Ps. 1:2

9 [a]Deut. 31:7, 8, 23 [b]Ps. 27:1; Jer. 1:8

11 [a]Deut. 9:1; 11:31; Josh. 3:2

13 [a]Num. 32:20-28; Josh. 22:2-4

14 [I]Hebr. *marshalled by five*

15 [a]Josh. 22:4-6

17 [a]Josh. 1:5; 1Sam. 20:13; 1Kgs. 1:37

1 [I]Or, *had sent* [a]Num. 25:1

🔑 **1:7** The call to courage is really a call to faith. Believing God's promise would lead both to courage and to obedience to the Law. God's promises must be appropriated in the same way today—by faith.

🔑 **1:13** It is important to realize that the term "rest," as used elsewhere, does not mean total peace; it is a relative term.

🔑 **2:1** Some have tried to render this passage "the house of a woman" or "house of an innkeeper," but the translation "harlot's house" is the correct one. The Hebrew term *zānāh* (2181) is the common word for an "adulterer" or "prostitute" (Lev. 21:7; Jer. 5:7). Both the Old and New Testaments affirm that such a woman can be pardoned (Luke 7:37). Rahab was not only pardoned, but raised to a position of honor. She married into an Israelite family, and was blessed by being the ancestor of David (Ruth 4:21, 22), thus placing her in the line of Jesus, the Messiah (Matt. 1:5). Moreover, she is enshrined in the New Testament "hall of faith" (Heb. 11:31; James 2:25). It was not unusual for strangers and foreigners to go to Rahab's house, thus the spies would not represent any unusual activity there. Also, the traffic through a harlot's house would provide information on the local situation. Rahab is another case in which God did not bless someone for lying, but for her faith in the report that the spies gave (see note on Ex. 1:17–20). Note that in this case as well, the issue was the loss of human life.

secretly, saying, Go view the land,[776] even
Jericho. And they went, and [b]came into
an harlot's[2181] house,[1004] named [c]Rahab,
and [II]lodged there.
2 And [a]it was told the king of
Jericho, saying, Behold, there came men
in hither to night of the children[1121] of
Israel to search out the country.[776]
3 And the king of Jericho sent unto
Rahab, saying, Bring forth the men that
are come to thee, which are entered into
thine house: for they be come to search
out all the country.
4 [a]And the woman[802] took the two
men, and hid them, and said[559] thus,
There came men unto me, but I wist[3045]
not whence they *were:*
5 And it came to pass *about the time*
of shutting of the gate, when it was
dark,[2822] that the men went out: whither
the men went I wot[3045] not: pursue after
them quickly; for ye shall overtake them.
6 But [a]she had brought them up[5927]
to the roof of the house, and hid them
with the stalks of flax, which she had
laid in order upon the roof.
7 And the men pursued after them
the way[1870] to Jordan unto the fords: and
as soon as they which pursued after them
were gone out, they shut the gate.
8 And before they were laid down,
she came up[5927] unto them upon the roof;
9 And she said unto the men, I
know[3045] that the LORD hath given you
the land, and that [a]your terror[367] is
fallen[5307] upon us, and that all the inhabitants of the land [I]faint because of you.
10 For we have heard[8085] how the
LORD [a]dried up[3001] the water of the Red
sea for you, when ye came out of Egypt;
and [b]what ye did[6213] unto the two
kings[4428] of the Amorites, that *were* on
the other side Jordan, Sihon and Og,
whom ye utterly destroyed.[2763]
11 And as soon as we had [a]heard
these things, [b]our hearts[3824] did melt,
neither [I]did there remain any more courage in any man,[376] because of you: for
[c]the LORD your God,[430] he *is* God in
heaven[8064] above, and in earth[776] beneath.
12 Now therefore, I pray you,[4994]
[a]swear[7650] unto me by the LORD, since I
have shewed[6213] you kindness,[2617] that
ye will also shew kindness unto [b]my father's house, and [c]give me a true[571]
token:[226]
13 And *that* ye will save alive[2421] my
father,[1] and my mother,[517] and my
brethren,[251] and my sisters,[269] and all
that they have, and deliver[5337] our
lives[5315] from death.[4194]
14 And the men answered[559] her, Our
life[5315] [I]for yours, if ye utter[5046] not this
our business.[1697] And it shall be, when
the LORD hath given us the land, that [a]we
will deal kindly[2617] and truly[571] with
thee.
15 Then she [a]let them down by a
cord[2256] through the window: for her
house *was* upon the town wall, and she
dwelt upon the wall.
16 And she said unto them, Get you
to the mountain, lest the pursuers meet
you; and hide yourselves there three
days,[3117] until the pursuers be returned:[7725] and afterward may ye go your
way.
17 And the men said unto her, We
will be [a]blameless[5355] of this thine
oath[7621] which thou hast made us swear.
18 [a]Behold, *when* we come into the
land, thou shalt bind this line of scarlet
thread in the window which thou didst
let us down by: [b]and thou shalt [I]bring[622]
thy father, and thy mother, and thy
brethren, and all thy father's household,[1004] home[1004] unto thee.

1 [II]Hebr. *lay* [b]Heb. 11:31; James 2:25 [c]Matt. 1:5
2 [a]Ps. 127:1; Prov. 21:30
4 [a]2Sam. 17:19, 20
6 [a]Ex. 1:17; 2Sam. 17:19
9 [I]Hebr. *melt* [a]Gen. 35:5; Ex. 23:27; Deut. 2:25; 11:25
10 [a]Ex. 14:21; Josh. 4:23 [b]Num. 21:24, 34, 35
11 [I]Hebr. *rose up* [a]Ex. 15:14, 15 [b]Josh. 5:1; 7:5; Isa. 13:7 [c]Deut. 4:39
12 [a]1Sam. 20:14, 15, 17 [b]1Tim. 5:8 [c]Josh. 2:18
14 [I]Hebr. *instead of you to die* [a]Judg. 1:24; Matt. 5:7
15 [a]Acts 9:25
17 [a]Ex. 20:7
18 [I]Hebr. *gather* [a]Josh. 2:21 [b]Josh. 6:23

2:18 Many writers have said that throughout Scripture this concept of the "scarlet thread" can be found: the line of blood atonement began in the Garden of Eden (Gen. 3:21), was exemplified in the Passover (Ex. 12:1–28), and was finally fulfilled in Christ's sacrifice on the cross (Heb. 9:22; 1 Pet. 1:19, 20). Here the thread was the means of deliverance for Rahab and her family. All who were to be delivered had to trust Rahab and stay in her house.

19 And it shall be, *that* whosoever shall go out of the doors of thy house into the street, his blood[1818] *shall be* upon his head, and we *will be* guiltless:[5355] and whosoever shall be with thee in the house, [a]his blood *shall be* on our head, if *any* hand[3027] be upon him.

20 And if thou utter this our business, then we will be quit[5355] of thine oath which thou hast made us to swear.

21 And she said, According unto your words,[1697] so *be* it. And she sent them away, and they departed: and she bound the scarlet line in the window.

22 And they went, and came unto the mountain, and abode there three days, until the pursuers were returned: and the pursuers sought *them* throughout all the way, but found *them* not.

23 So the two men returned, and descended from the mountain, and passed over,[5674] and came to Joshua the son of Nun, and told[5608] him all *things* that befell them:

24 And they said unto Joshua, Truly [a]the LORD hath delivered into our hands[3027] all the land; for even all the inhabitants of the country do [I]faint because of us.

Israel Crosses the Jordan

3 And Joshua rose early in the morning; and they removed [a]from Shittim, and came to Jordan, he and all the children[1121] of Israel, and lodged there before they passed over.[5674]

2 And it came to pass [a]after three days,[3117] that the officers[7860] went through the host;[4264]

3 And they commanded[6680] the people,[5971] saying, [a]When ye see the ark[727] of the covenant[1285] of the LORD your God,[430] [b]and the priests[3548] the Levites bearing[5375] it, then ye shall remove from your place, and go after it.

4 [a]Yet there shall be a space between you and it, about two thousand cubits by measure: come not near unto it, that ye may know[3045] the way[1870] by which ye must go: for ye have not passed *this* way [I]heretofore.

5 And Joshua said[559] unto the people, [a]Sanctify yourselves:[6942] for to morrow the LORD will do[6213] wonders[6381] among[7130] you.

6 And Joshua spake[559] unto the priests, saying, [a]Take up[5375] the ark[727] of the covenant, and pass over before the people. And they took up the ark of the covenant, and went before the people.

7 And the LORD said unto Joshua, This day[3117] will I begin to [a]magnify thee in the sight of all Israel, that they may know that, [b]as I was with Moses, *so* I will be with thee.

8 And thou shalt command[6680] [a]the priests that bear the ark[727] of the covenant, saying, When ye are come to the brink of the water of Jordan, [b]ye shall stand still in Jordan.

9 And Joshua said unto the children of Israel, Come hither, and hear[7181] the words[1697] of the LORD your God.

10 And Joshua said, Hereby ye shall know that [a]the living[2416] God[410] *is* among[7130] you, and *that* he will without fail [b]drive out[3423] from before you the Canaanites, and the Hittites, and the Hivites, and the Perizzites, and the Girgashites, and the Amorites, and the Jebusites.

11 Behold, the ark[727] of the covenant of [a]the Lord[113] of all the earth[776] passeth over[5674] before you into Jordan.

12 Now therefore [a]take you twelve men out of the tribes[7626] of Israel, out of every tribe a man.[376]

13 And it shall come to pass, [a]as soon as the soles[3709] of the feet of the priests that bear the ark of the LORD, [b]the Lord of all the earth, shall rest in the waters of Jordan, *that* the waters of Jordan shall be cut off[3772] *from* the waters that come down from above; and they [c]shall stand upon an heap.

14 And it came to pass, when the people removed from their tents,[168] to pass over Jordan, and the priests bearing the [a]ark of the covenant before the people;

19 [a]Matt. 27:25
24 [I]Hebr. *melt* [a]Ex. 23:31; Josh. 6:2; 21:44
1 [a]Josh. 2:1
2 [a]Josh. 1:10, 11
3 [a]Num. 10:33 [b]Deut. 31:9, 25
4 [I]Hebr. *since yesterday, and the third day* [a]Ex. 19:12
5 [a]Ex. 19:10, 14, 15; Lev. 20:7; Num. 11:18; Josh. 7:13; 1Sam. 16:5; Joel 2:16
6 [a]Num. 4:15
7 [a]Josh. 4:14; 1Chr. 29:25; 2Chr. 1:1 [b]Josh. 1:5
8 [a]Josh. 3:3 [b]Josh. 3:17
10 [a]Deut. 5:26; 1Sam. 17:26; 2Kgs. 19:4; Hos. 1:10; Matt. 16:16; 1Thess. 1:9 [b]Ex. 33:2; Deut. 7:1; Ps. 44:2
11 [a]Josh. 3:13; Mic. 4:13; Zech. 4:14; 6:5
12 [a]Josh. 4:2
13 [a]Josh. 3:15, 16 [b]Josh. 3:11 [c]Ps. 78:13; 114:3
14 [a]Acts 7:45

15 And as they that bare[5375] the ark[727] were come unto Jordan, and [a]the feet of the priests that bare the ark were dipped[2881] in the brim of the water, (for [b]Jordan overfloweth all his banks [c]all the time[3117] of harvest,)

16 That the waters which came down from above stood *and* rose up upon an heap very far from the city Adam, that *is* beside [a]Zaretan: and those that came down [b]toward the sea of the plain,[6160] *even* [c]the salt sea, failed,[8552] *and* were cut off: and the people passed over right against Jericho.

17 And the priests that bare the ark[727] of the covenant of the LORD stood firm[3559] on dry ground[2724] in the midst of Jordan, [a]and all the Israelites passed over on dry ground, until all the people[1471] were passed clean[8552] over Jordan.

Stone Monument Set Up at Gilgal

4 And it came to pass, when all the people were[5674] clean[8552] passed [a]over[5674] Jordan, that the LORD spake[559] unto Joshua, saying,

2 [a]Take you twelve men out of the people,[5971] out of every tribe[7626] a man,[376]

3 And command[6680] ye them, saying, Take[5375] you hence out of the midst of Jordan, out of the place where [a]the priests'[3548] feet stood firm,[3559] twelve stones, and ye shall carry them over with you, and leave them in [b]the lodging place, where ye shall lodge this night.[3915]

4 Then Joshua called[7121] the twelve men, whom he had prepared of the children[1121] of Israel, out of every tribe a man:

5 And Joshua said[559] unto them, Pass over before the ark[727] of the LORD your God[430] into the midst of Jordan, and take you up every man of you a stone upon his shoulder, according unto the number of the tribes of the children of Israel:

6 That this may be a sign[226] among[7130] you, *that* [a]when your children ask[7592] *their fathers* [1]in time to come, saying, What *mean* ye by these stones?

7 Then ye shall answer[559] them, That [a]the waters of Jordan were cut off[3772] before the ark[727] of the covenant[1285] of the LORD; when it passed over Jordan, the waters of Jordan were cut off: and these stones shall be for [b]a memorial unto the children of Israel for ever.[5769]

8 And the children of Israel did[6213] so as Joshua commanded,[6680] and took up[5375] twelve stones out of the midst of Jordan, as the LORD spake[1696] unto Joshua, according to the number of the tribes of the children of Israel, and carried them over[5674] with them unto the place where they lodged, and laid them down there.

9 And Joshua set up twelve stones in the midst of Jordan, in the place where the feet of the priests[3548] which bare[5375] the ark[727] of the covenant stood: and they are there unto this day.[3117]

15 [a]Josh. 3:13 [b]1Chr. 12:15; Jer. 12:5; 49:19 [c]Josh. 4:18; 5:10, 12

16 [a]1Kgs. 4:12; 7:46 [b]Deut. 3:17 [c]Gen. 14:3; Num. 34:3

17 [a]Ex. 14:29

1 [a]Deut. 27:2; Josh. 3:17

2 [a]Josh. 3:12

3 [a]Josh. 3:13 [b]Josh. 4:19, 20

6 [1]Hebr. *tomorrow* [a]Ex. 12:26; 13:14; Deut. 6:20; Josh. 4:21; Ps. 44:1; 78:3-6

7 [a]Josh. 3:13, 16 [b]Ex. 12:14; Num. 16:40

3:15–17 Notice that the Lord did not stop the flow of the Jordan until the priests' feet were actually in the water. They were called upon to exercise their faith first. The swollen condition of the Jordan River at that time of the year emphasizes God's miraculous provision for Israel. The Jordan lies in a deep valley, and so does not spread out when it is flooded. It merely goes over its normal banks, and further up the valley sides. When it is flooded, the only way to get across the water is to swim or sail, but neither of these methods would have been possible for several million Israelites with children, livestock, and household goods. Since irrigation now drains off much of its water, the Jordan no longer floods as it once did. Some scholars have suggested that an earthquake or landslide stopped the flow, but the text of Scripture refutes any attempt at explaining away God's supernatural intervention.

4:9 The phrase "unto this day" signifies that when Joshua wrote this book at the end of his life (Josh. 24:26), these two pillars were still standing. For most of the year, the Jordan is a shallow river so the pillar of stones in the center of it would be visible as a sign.

10 For the priests which bare the ark
stood in the midst of Jordan, until every
thing was finished[8552] that the LORD commanded Joshua to speak[1696] unto the people, according to all that Moses commanded Joshua: and the people hasted
and passed over.
11 And it came to pass, when all the
people were clean passed over, that the
ark of the LORD passed over, and the
priests, in the presence of the people.
12 And [a]the children of Reuben, and
the children of Gad, and half the tribe of
Manasseh, passed over armed before the
children of Israel, as Moses spake unto
them:
13 About forty thousand [I]prepared
for war[6635] passed over before the LORD
unto battle, to the plains[6160] of Jericho.
14 On that day the LORD [a]magnified
Joshua in the sight of all Israel; and they
feared[3372] him, as they feared Moses, all
the days[3117] of his life.[2416]
15 And the LORD spake unto Joshua,
saying,
16 Command the priests that bear
the [a]ark[727] of the testimony,[5715] that they
come up[5927] out of Jordan.
17 Joshua therefore commanded the
priests, saying, Come ye up out of Jordan.
18 And it came to pass, when the
priests that bare the ark of the covenant
of the LORD were come up out of the
midst of Jordan, *and* the soles[3709] of the
priests' feet were [I]lifted up unto the dry
land,[2724] that the waters of Jordan
returned[7725] unto their place, [a]and
[II]flowed over all his banks, as *they did* before.
19 And the people came up[5927] out of
Jordan on the tenth *day* of the first[7223]
month, and encamped [a]in Gilgal, in the
east border of Jericho.
20 And [a]those twelve stones, which
they took out of Jordan, did Joshua pitch
in Gilgal.
21 And he spake unto the children of
Israel, saying, [a]When your children shall
ask[7592] their fathers [I]in time to come, saying, What *mean* these stones?
22 Then ye shall let your children
know,[3045] saying, [a]Israel came over[5674]
this Jordan on dry land.[3004]
23 For the LORD your God dried
up[3001] the waters of Jordan from before
you, until ye were passed over, as the
LORD your God did to the Red sea, [a]which
he dried up from before us, until we were
gone over:[5674]
24 [a]That all the people of the
earth[776] might know the hand[3027] of the
LORD, that it *is* [b]mighty:[2389] that ye might
[c]fear[3372] the LORD your God [I]for ever.

Circumcision and Passover At Gilgal

5 And it came to pass, when all the
kings[4428] of the Amorites, which
were on the side of Jordan westward, and
all the kings of the Canaanites, [a]which
were by the sea, [b]heard[8085] that the LORD
had dried up the waters of Jordan from
before the children[1121] of Israel, until we
were passed over,[5674] that their heart[3824]
melted, [c]neither was there spirit[7307] in
them any more, because of the children
of Israel.
2 At that time the LORD said[559] unto
Joshua, Make[6213] thee [I][a]sharp knives,[2719]

12 [a]Num. 32:20, 27, 28
13 [I]Or, *ready armed*
14 [a]Josh. 3:7
16 [a]Ex. 25:16, 22
18 [I]Hebr. *plucked up* [II]Hebr. *went* [a]Josh. 3:15
19 [a]Josh. 5:9
20 [a]Josh. 4:3
21 [I]Hebr. *tomorrow* [a]Josh. 4:6
22 [a]Josh. 3:17
23 [a]Ex. 14:21
24 [I]Hebr. *all days* [a]1Kgs. 8:42, 43; 2Kgs. 19:19; Ps. 106:8 [b]Ex. 15:16; 1Chr. 29:12; Ps. 89:13 [c]Ex. 14:31; Deut. 6:2; Ps. 89:7; Jer. 10:7
1 [a]Num. 13:29 [b]Ex. 15:14, 15; Josh. 2:9-11; Ps. 48:6; Ezek. 21:7 [c]1Kgs. 10:5
2 [I]Or, *knives of flints* [a]Ex. 4:25

4:10 Moses told Joshua that God would speak through him to the people and that God would be with him (see Deut. 31:7, 8).

4:19 After crossing the Jordan, Israel camped at Gilgal for a while before the conquest of Canaan began. Several things happened at Gilgal which signified that the wilderness wanderings were over and that Israel was embarking on a new phase of her national history. First, Joshua had the people set up twelve stones as a monument to the miraculous drying up of the Jordan for their crossing (Josh. 4:19–24). Next, the young males were circumcised, which reinstituted a practice that had not been kept for nearly forty years (5:2–9). With that accomplished (see Ex. 12:48), they could then observe the Passover (5:10). Finally, and probably most indicative of the end of their wanderings, on the day after the Passover, the manna stopped, and they ate from the produce of Canaan (5:11, 12).

and circumcise[4135] again the children of Israel the second time.

3 And Joshua made him sharp knives, and circumcised[4135] the children of Israel at [I]the hill of the foreskins.[6190]

4 And this *is* the cause[1697] why Joshua did circumcise: [a]All the people that came out of Egypt, *that were* males,[2145] *even* all the men of war, died[4191] in the wilderness by the way,[1870] after they came out of Egypt.

5 Now all the people that came out were circumcised: but all the people *that were* born in the wilderness by the way as they came forth out of Egypt, *them* they had not circumcised.

6 For the children of Israel walked [a]forty years in the wilderness, till all the people[1471] *that were* men of war, which came out of Egypt, were consumed,[8552] because they obeyed[8085] not the voice of the LORD: unto whom the LORD sware[7650] that [b]he would not shew[7200] them the land,[776] which the LORD sware unto their fathers[1] that he would give us, [c]a land that floweth with milk and honey.

7 And [a]their children, *whom* he raised up in their stead, them Joshua circumcised: for they were uncircumcised,[6189] because they had not circumcised them by the way.

8 And it came to pass, [I]when they had done circumcising[4135] all the people, that they abode in their places in the camp,[4264] [a]till they were whole.[2421]

9 And the LORD said unto Joshua, This day[3117] have I rolled away[1556] [a]the reproach[2781] of Egypt from off you. Wherefore the name of the place is called[7121] [Ib]Gilgal unto this day.

10 And the children of Israel encamped in Gilgal, and kept[6213] the passover[6453] [a]on the fourteenth day of the month at even in the plains[6160] of Jericho.

11 And they did eat of the old corn of the land on the morrow after the passover, unleavened cakes,[4682] and parched *corn* in the selfsame day.

12 And [a]the manna[4478] ceased[7673] on the morrow after they had eaten of the old corn of the land; neither had the children of Israel manna any more; but they did eat of the fruit of the land of Canaan that year.

🔑 13 And it came to pass, when Joshua was by Jericho, that he lifted up[5375] his eyes and looked,[7200] and, behold, there stood [a]a man[376] over against him [b]with his sword[2719] drawn in his hand:[3027] and Joshua went unto him, and said unto him, *Art* thou for us, or for our adversaries?

14 And he said, Nay; but *as* [Ia]captain[8269] of the host[6635] of the LORD am I now come. And Joshua [b]fell[5307] on his face to the earth,[776] and did worship,[7812] and said unto him, What saith[1696] my lord[113] unto his servant?[5650]

15 And the captain of the LORD's host said unto Joshua, [a]Loose thy shoe from off thy foot; for the place whereon thou standest *is* holy.[6944] And Joshua did so.

Jericho Falls

6 🔑 Now Jericho [I]was straitly shut up because of the children of Israel: none went out, and none came in.

2 And the LORD said[559] unto Joshua,

3 IOr, *Gibeah-haaraloth*

4 aNum. 14:29; 26:64, 65; Deut. 2:16

6 aNum. 14:33; Deut. 1:3; 2:7, 14; Ps. 95:10 bNum. 14:23; Ps. 95:11; Heb. 3:11 cEx. 3:8

7 aNum. 14:31; Deut. 1:39

8 IHebr. *when the people had made an end to be circumcised* aGen. 34:25

9 IThat is, *Rolling* aGen. 34:14; Lev. 18:3; Josh. 24:14; 1Sam. 14:6; Ezek. 20:7; 23:3, 8 bJosh. 4:19

10 aEx. 12:6; Num. 9:5

12 aEx. 16:35

13 aGen. 18:2; 32:24; Ex. 23:23; Zech. 1:8; Acts 1:10 bNum. 22:23

14 IOr, *prince* aEx. 23:20; Dan. 10:13, 21; 12:1; Rev. 12:7; 19:11, 14 bGen. 17:3

15 aEx. 3:5; Acts 7:33

1 IHebr. *it did shut up, and was shut up*

🔑 **5:13–15** The man who is called "the captain of the host of the LORD" is actually the Angel of the LORD, a preincarnate appearance of Jesus Christ (Ex. 3:2–6; Judg. 6:12, 16). This is seen in the use of the phrase in verse fifteen: "Loose thy shoe from off thy foot; for the place whereon thou standest is holy." No man or angel could pronounce a place "holy." The angel of the LORD also appeared to Moses in the burning bush and used this phrase commanding Moses to take his shoes off (Ex. 3:5).

🔑 **6:1–7** This was not a mere military confrontation with people who were entrenched in a formidable stronghold. The implications are more spiritual than political. While God was bringing judgment upon those who had long refused Him, He was working on behalf of the people with whom

(continued on next page)

See, [a]I have given into thine hand[3027]
Jericho, and the [b]king thereof, *and* the
mighty men of valour.[2428]
3 And ye shall compass the city, all
ye men of war, *and* go round about[5362]
the city once. Thus shalt thou do[6213] six
days.[3117]
4 And seven priests shall bear before
the ark[727] seven [a]trumpets of rams' horns:
and the seventh day ye shall compass the
city seven times, and [b]the priests[3548] shall
blow[8628] with the trumpets.
5 And it shall come to pass, that
when they make a long *blast* with the
ram's horn, *and* when ye hear[7181] the
sound of the trumpet, all the people[5971]
shall shout[7321] with a great shout; and
the wall of the city shall fall down [I]flat,
and the people shall ascend up every
man[376] straight before him.
6 And Joshua the son[1121] of Nun
called[7121] the priests, and said unto them,
Take up[5375] the ark[727] of the covenant,[1285] and let seven priests bear
seven trumpets of rams' horns before the
ark of the LORD.
7 And he said unto the people, Pass
on, and compass the city, and let him
that is armed pass on before the ark of
the LORD.
8 And it came to pass, when Joshua
had spoken[559] unto the people, that the
seven priests bearing[5375] the seven trumpets of rams' horns passed on[5674] before
the LORD, and blew[8628] with the trumpets: and the ark of the covenant of the
LORD followed them.
9 And the armed men went before
the priests that blew with the trumpets,
[a]and the [I]rereward[622] came after the ark,
the priests going on, and blowing[8628] with
the trumpets.
10 And Joshua had commanded[6680]
the people, saying, Ye shall not shout,
nor [I]make any noise with your voice, neither shall *any* word[1697] proceed out of
your mouth,[6310] until the day I bid[559] you
shout; then shall ye shout.
11 So the ark[727] of the LORD compassed the city, going about *it* once: and
they came into the camp,[4264] and lodged
in the camp.
12 And Joshua rose early in the
morning, [a]and the priests took up[5375] the
ark of the LORD.
13 And seven priests bearing seven
trumpets of rams' horns before the ark
of the LORD went on continually, and
blew with the trumpets: and the armed
men went before them; but the rereward
came after the ark of the LORD, *the
priests* going on, and blowing with the
trumpets.
14 And the second day they compassed the city once, and returned[7725]
into the camp: so they did[6213] six days.
15 And it came to pass on the seventh day, that they rose early about the
dawning of the day, and compassed the
city after the same manner[4941] seven
times: only on that day they compassed
the city seven times.
16 And it came to pass at the seventh time, when the priests blew with the
trumpets, Joshua said unto the people,
Shout; for the LORD hath given you the
city.
🔑 17 And the city shall be[1961]
[I][a]accursed,[2764] *even* it, and all that *are*
therein, to the LORD: only Rahab the

2 [a]Josh. 2:9, 24; 8:1 [b]Deut. 7:24
4 [a]Judg. 7:16, 22 [b]Num. 10:8
5 [I]Hebr. *under it*
9 [I]Hebr. *gathering* host [a]Num. 10:25
10 [I]Hebr. *make your voice to be heard*
12 [a]Deut. 31:25
17 [I]Or, *devoted* [a]Lev. 27:28; Mic. 4:13

(continued from previous page)
He had just renewed His covenant. The fall of Jericho sent a powerful message to the Canaanites that Israel's successes were not mere human victories of man against man, but victories by the true God of Israel over their gods. This event, following closely upon the crossing of the Jordan by miraculous means, impressed upon the people that the same God who had led their fathers out of Egypt and through the Red Sea was with Joshua just as surely as He had been with Moses. The most recent archaeological research at Jericho has affirmed the Bible's account that the city was destroyed around 1400 B.C.

🔑 **6:17** The order from the Lord regarding the plunder of Jericho treated it as the first fruits of Canaan, and this did not apply to other cities they would conquer (Deut. 20:10–18). Whatever they took from Jericho was "reserved" exclusively for God, because the firstfruits belonged to Him (Ex. 23:19).

harlot[2181] shall live,[2421] she and all that
are with her in the house,[1004] because
[b]she hid the messengers[4397] that we sent.
18 And ye, [a]in any wise[7535] keep[8104]
yourselves from the accursed thing, lest ye
make *yourselves* accursed,[2763] when ye
take of the accursed thing,[2764] and make
the camp of Israel a curse, [b]and trouble it.
19 But all the silver, and gold, and
vessels of brass and iron, *are* [I]conse-
crated unto the LORD: they shall come
into the treasury of the LORD.
20 So the people shouted[7321] when
the priests blew with the trumpets: and
it came to pass, when the people
heard[8085] the sound of the trumpet, and
the people shouted with a great shout,
that [a]the wall fell down[5307] [I]flat, so that
the people went up[5927] into the city, every
man straight before him, and they took
the city.
21 And they [a]utterly destroyed[2763] all
that *was* in the city, both man and
woman,[802] young and old, and ox, and
sheep, and ass, with the edge[6310] of the
sword.[2719]
22 But Joshua had said unto the two
men that had spied out the country,[776]
Go into the harlot's[2181] house, and bring
out thence the woman, and all that she
hath, [a]as ye sware[7650] unto her.
23 And the young men that were
spies went in, and brought out Rahab,
[a]and her father,[1] and her mother,[517] and
her brethren,[251] and all that she had; and
they brought out all her [I]kindred,[4940] and
left them without the camp of Israel.
24 And they burnt[8313] the city with
fire, and all that *was* therein: [a]only the silver, and the gold, and the vessels of
brass and of iron, they put into the treasury of the house of the LORD.
25 And Joshua saved Rahab the harlot alive, and her father's household,[1004]
and all that she had; and [a]she dwelleth in
Israel *even* unto this day; because she hid
the messengers, which Joshua sent to spy
out Jericho.
26 And Joshua adjured[7650] *them* at
that time, saying, [a]Cursed[779] *be* the man
before the LORD, that riseth up and
buildeth this city Jericho: he shall lay the
foundation[3245] thereof in his firstborn,
and in his youngest *son* shall he set
up[5324] the gates of it.
27 [a]So the LORD was with Joshua;
and [b]his fame was *noised* throughout all
the country.

Achan's Sin

7 But the children of Israel committed a trespass[4604] in the accursed
thing:[2764] [Ia]for Achan, the son of Carmi,

17 [b]Josh. 2:4
18 [a]Deut. 7:26; 13:17; Josh. 7:1, 11, 12 [b]Josh. 7:25; 1Kgs. 18:17, 18; Jon. 1:12
19 [I]Hebr. *holiness*
20 [I]Hebr. *under it* [a]Josh. 6:5; Heb. 11:30
21 [a]Deut. 7:2
22 [a]Josh. 2:14; Heb. 11:31
23 [I]Hebr. *families* [a]Josh. 2:13
24 [a]Josh. 6:19
25 [a]Matt. 1:5
26 [a]1Kgs. 16:34
27 [a]Deut. 1:5 [b]Deut. 9:1, 3
1 [I]*Achar* [a]Josh. 22:20; 1Chr. 2:7

6:21 This severe measure of killing every living thing was taken to prevent alien elements of Canaanite culture and worship, on the basis of their total corruption before God, from infecting Israel (see Rom. 1:18–32). Later, instructions like those given to Israel at Jericho were ignored in other campaigns (1 Sam. 15:3, 13–22).

6:26 This curse fell upon Hiel the Bethelite in the early days of King Ahab (1 Kgs. 16:34). It was a local custom to dedicate the gates and walls of a new city by burying children inside the foundations.

7:1 The sin of Achan stands as a lesson to all Israel of the consequences to one who breaks faith with God. The nation as a collective whole was in a covenant relationship with God and was dealt with by Him not merely as a group of people living together under a common law for their own protection and to accomplish their own goals. Instead, He treated them as a whole. Understanding this concept is essential to understanding the words of Paul in Romans 5:12–21. Achan had defiled not only himself, but all of Israel. They were no longer acceptable to God because they, in the person of Achan, had broken the covenant. Therefore, God would no longer work for them in driving out the Canaanites. Only after Achan (and his family, because of their connection with him in the deed) had been dealt with did God release Israel from their guilt in the matter. Achan's sin was not simply one of stealing goods or even of covetousness. He clearly defied God by disobeying His command (vv. 1, 11). Achan's punishment (Josh. 22:20) was a warning to all that they should never allow their greed to cause them to defy God's will.

the son of ‖Zabdi, the son of Zerah, of the tribe[4294] of Judah, took of the accursed thing: and the anger[639] of the LORD was kindled[2734] against the children of Israel.

🔑 2 And Joshua sent men from Jericho to Ai, which *is* beside Beth–aven, on the east side of Bethel, and spake[559] unto them, saying, Go up[5927] and view the country.[776] And the men went up and viewed Ai.

3 And they returned[7725] to Joshua, and said[559] unto him, Let not all the people[5971] go up; but let about two or three thousand men go up and smite Ai; *and* make not all the people to labour thither; for they *are but* few.

4 So there went up thither of the people about three thousand men: [a]and they fled before the men of Ai.

5 And the men of Ai smote[5221] of them about thirty and six men: for they chased them *from* before the gate *even* unto Shebarim, and smote them |in the going down: wherefore [a]the hearts[3824] of the people melted, and became as water.

6 And Joshua [a]rent his clothes, and fell[5307] to the earth[776] upon his face before the ark[727] of the LORD until the eventide,[6153] he and the elders[2205] of Israel, and [b]put dust[5083] upon their heads.[7218]

7 And Joshua said, Alas, O Lord[136] God, [a]wherefore hast thou at all brought this people over Jordan, to deliver us into the hand[3027] of the Amorites, to destroy[6] us? would to God we had been content,[2974] and dwelt on the other side Jordan!

8 O Lord, what shall I say,[559] when Israel turneth[2015] their |backs before their enemies!

9 For the Canaanites and all the inhabitants of the land[776] shall hear[7181] *of it,* and shall environ us round, and [a]cut off[3772] our name from the earth: and [b]what wilt thou do[6213] unto thy great name?

10 And the LORD said unto Joshua, Get thee up; wherefore |liest[5307] thou thus upon thy face?

11 [a]Israel hath sinned,[2398] and they have also transgressed[5674] my covenant[1285] which I commanded[6680] them: [b]for they have even taken of the accursed thing,[2764] and have also stolen, and [c]dissembled also, and they have put *it* even among[7130] their own stuff.

12 [a]Therefore the children of Israel could not stand before their enemies, *but* turned *their* backs before their enemies, because [b]they were accursed:[2764] neither will I be with you any more, except ye destroy[8045] the accursed from among[7130] you.

13 Up, [a]sanctify[6942] the people, and say, [b]Sanctify yourselves against to morrow: for thus saith[559] the LORD God[430] of Israel, *There* is an accursed thing[2764] in the midst[7130] of thee, O Israel: thou canst not stand before thine enemies, until ye take away the accursed thing from among you.

14 In the morning therefore ye shall be brought[7126] according to your tribes:[7626] and it shall be, *that* the tribe[7626] which [a]the LORD taketh shall come according to the families[4940] *thereof;* and the family which the LORD shall take shall come by households;[1004] and the household which the LORD shall take shall come man by man.[1397]

15 [a]And it shall be, *that* he that is taken with the accursed thing[2764] shall be burnt[8313] with fire, he and all that he hath: because he hath [b]transgressed the covenant of the LORD, and because he [c]hath wrought[6213] |folly in Israel.

16 So Joshua rose up early in the morning, and brought Israel by their tribes; and the tribe of Judah was taken:

17 And he brought the family of

---

1 ‖Or, *Zimri*

4 [a]Lev. 26:17; Deut. 28:25

5 |Or, *in Morad* [a]Lev. 26:36; Josh. 2:9, 11; Ps. 22:14

6 [a]Gen. 37:29, 34 [b]1Sam. 4:12; 2Sam. 1:2; 13:19; Neh. 9:1; Job 2:12

7 [a]Ex. 5:22; 2Kgs. 3:10

8 |Hebr. *necks*

9 [a]Ps. 83:4 [b]Ex. 32:12; Num. 14:13

10 |Hebr. *fallest*

11 [a]Josh. 7:1 [b]Josh. 6:17, 18 [c]Acts 5:1, 2

12 [a]Num. 14:45; Judg. 2:14 [b]Deut. 7:26; Josh. 6:18

13 [a]Ex. 19:10 [b]Josh. 3:5

14 [a]Prov. 16:33

15 |Or, *wickedness* [a]1Sam. 14:38, 39 [b]Josh. 7:11 [c]Gen. 34:7; Judg. 20:6

🔑 **7:2–5** This unsuccessful first battle at Ai illustrates the partnership between God and Israel during the conquest of Canaan. When the people presumed upon the power of God and fought without consulting Him, they were not victorious. What should have been an easy victory turned into a painful defeat, because God was not with them.

Judah; and he took the family of the Zarhites: and he brought the family of the Zarhites man by man; and Zabdi was taken:

18 And he brought his household man by man; and Achan, the son of Carmi, the son of Zabdi, the son of Zerah, of the tribe of Judah, [a]was taken.

19 And Joshua said unto Achan, My son, [a]give,[7760] I pray thee,[4994] glory[3519] to the LORD God of Israel, [b]and make confession[8426] unto him; and [c]tell[5046] me now what thou hast done;[6213] hide *it* not from me.

20 And Achan answered Joshua, and said, Indeed[546] I have sinned against the LORD God of Israel, and thus and thus have I done:

21 When I saw[7200] among the spoils a goodly[2896] Babylonish garment, and two hundred shekels of silver, and a [I]wedge of gold of fifty shekels weight, then I coveted[2530] them, and took them; and, behold, they *are* hid in the earth in the midst of my tent,[168] and the silver under it.

22 So Joshua sent messengers,[4397] and they ran unto the tent; and, behold, *it was* hid in his tent, and the silver under it.

23 And they took them out of the midst of the tent, and brought them unto Joshua, and unto all the children of Israel, and [I]laid them out before the LORD.

24 And Joshua, and all Israel with him, took Achan the son of Zerah, and the silver, and the garment, and the wedge of gold, and his sons,[1121] and his daughters, and his oxen, and his asses, and his sheep, and his tent, and all that he had: and they brought[5927] them unto [a]the valley of Achor.

🔑 25 And Joshua said, [a]Why hast thou troubled us? the LORD shall trouble thee this day.[3117] [b]And all Israel stoned him with stones, and burned[8313] them with fire, after they had stoned them with stones.

26 And they [a]raised over him a great heap of stones unto this day. So [b]the LORD turned from the fierceness of his anger.[639] Wherefore the name of that place was called,[7121] [c]The valley of [I]Achor, unto this day.

Ai Falls

8 And the LORD said[559] unto Joshua, [a]Fear[3372] not, neither be thou dismayed:[2865] take all the people[5971] of war with thee, and arise, go up[5927] to Ai: see, [b]I have given into thy hand[3027] the king of Ai, and his people, and his city, and his land:[776]

2 And thou shalt do[6213] to Ai and her king as thou didst unto [a]Jericho and her king: only [b]the spoil thereof, and the cattle thereof, shall ye take for a prey unto yourselves: lay[7760] thee an ambush for the city behind it.

3 So Joshua arose, and all the people of war, to go up against Ai: and Joshua chose[977] out thirty thousand mighty men of valour,[2428] and sent them away by night.[3915]

4 And he commanded[6680] them, saying, Behold,[7200] [a]ye shall lie in wait against the city, *even* behind the city: go not very far from the city, but be ye all ready:[3559]

5 And I, and all the people that *are* with me, will approach[7126] unto the city: and it shall come to pass, when they come out against us, as at the first,[7223] that [a]we will flee before them,

6 (For they will come out after us) till we have [I]drawn them from the city; for they will say,[559] They flee before us, as at the first: therefore we will flee before them.

7 Then ye shall rise up from the ambush, and seize upon the city: for the LORD your God[430] will deliver it into your hand.

8 And it shall be, when ye have taken the city, *that* ye shall set the city

18 [a]1Sam. 14:42

19 [a]1Sam. 6:5; Jer. 13:16; John 9:24 [b]Num. 5:6, 7; 2Chr. 30:22; Ps. 51:3; Dan. 9:4 [c]1Sam. 14:43

21 [I]Hebr. *tongue*

23 [I]Hebr. *poured*

24 [a]Josh. 7:26; 15:7

25 [a]Josh. 6:18; 1Chr. 2:7; Gal. 5:12 [b]Deut. 17:5

26 [I]That is *Trouble* [a]Josh. 8:29; 2Sam. 18:17; Lam. 3:53 [b]Deut. 13:17; 2Sam. 21:14 [c]Josh. 7:24; Isa. 65:10; Hos. 2:15

1 [a]Deut. 1:21; 7:18; 31:8; Josh. 1:9 [b]Josh. 6:2

2 [a]Josh. 6:21 [b]Deut. 20:14

4 [a]Judg. 20:29

5 [a]Judg. 20:32

6 [I]Hebr. *pulled*

🔑 **7:25** Since Deuteronomy 24:16 prohibited the execution of children for the sins of their fathers, it is evident that Achan's children must have condoned or assisted him in what he did.

on fire: according to the commandment[1697] of the LORD shall ye do. [a]See, I have commanded you.

9 Joshua therefore sent them forth: and they went to lie in ambush, and abode between Bethel and Ai, on the west side of Ai: but Joshua lodged that night among the people.

10 And Joshua rose up early in the morning, and numbered[6485] the people, and went up,[5927] he and the elders[2205] of Israel, before the people to Ai.

11 [a]And all the people, *even the people* of war that *were* with him, went up, and drew nigh, and came before the city, and pitched on the north side of Ai: now *there was* a valley between them and Ai.

12 And he took about five thousand men, and set[7760] them to lie in ambush between Bethel and Ai, on the west side [I]of the city.

13 And when they had set the people, *even* all the host[4264] that *was* on the north of the city, and [Ia]their liers in wait on the west of the city, Joshua went that night into the midst of the valley.

14 And it came to pass, when the king of Ai saw[7200] *it,* that they hasted and rose up early, and the men of the city went out against Israel to battle, he and all his people, at a time appointed,[4150] before the plain;[6160] but he [a]wist[3045] not that *there were* liers in ambush against him behind the city.

15 And Joshua and all Israel [a]made as if they were beaten[5060] before them, and fled by the way[1870] of the wilderness.

16 And all the people that *were* in Ai were called together[2199] to pursue after them: and they pursued after Joshua, and were drawn away from the city.

17 And there was[7604] not a man[376] left[7604] in Ai or Bethel, that went not out after Israel: and they left[5800] the city open, and pursued after Israel.

18 And the LORD said unto Joshua, Stretch out the spear that *is* in thy hand toward Ai; for I will give it into thine hand. And Joshua stretched out the spear that *he had* in his hand toward the city.

19 And the ambush arose quickly out of their place, and they ran as soon as he had stretched out his hand: and they entered into the city, and took it, and hasted and set the city on fire.

20 And when the men[582] of Ai looked behind them, they saw, and, behold, the smoke of the city ascended up[5927] to heaven,[8064] and they had no [I]power[3027] to flee this way or that way: and the people that fled to the wilderness turned back[2015] upon the pursuers.

21 And when Joshua and all Israel saw that the ambush had taken the city, and that the smoke of the city ascended, then they turned again,[7725] and slew[5221] the men of Ai.

22 And the other issued out of the city against them; so they were in the midst of Israel, some on this side, and some on that side: and they smote[5221] them, so that they [a]let none of them remain[8300] or escape.

23 And the king of Ai they took alive,[2416] and brought[7126] him to Joshua.

24 And it came to pass, when Israel had made an end[3615] of slaying all the inhabitants of Ai in the field,[7704] in the wilderness wherein they chased them, and when they were all fallen[5307] on the edge[6310] of the sword,[2719] until they were consumed,[8552] that all the Israelites returned[7725] unto Ai, and smote it with the edge of the sword.

25 And *so* it was, *that* all that fell that day,[3117] both of men[376] and women,[802] *were* twelve thousand, *even* all the men of Ai.

26 For Joshua drew not his hand back, wherewith he stretched out the spear, until he had utterly destroyed[2763] all the inhabitants of Ai.

27 [a]Only the cattle and the spoil of that city Israel took for a prey unto themselves, according unto the word[1697] of the LORD which he [b]commanded Joshua.

28 And Joshua burnt[8313] Ai, and made[7760] it [a]an heap for ever,[5769] *even* a desolation[8077] unto this day.

29 [a]And the king of Ai he hanged on a tree until eventide:[6153] [b]and as soon as the sun was down, Joshua commanded

8 [a]2Sam. 13:28
11 [a]Josh. 8:5
12 [I]Or, *of Ai*
13 [I]Hebr. *their lying in wait* [a]Josh. 8:4
14 [a]Judg. 20:34; Eccl. 9:12
15 [a]Judg. 20:36
20 [I]Hebr. *hand*
22 [a]Deut. 7:2
27 [a]Num. 31:22, 26 [b]Josh. 8:2
28 [a]Deut. 13:16
29 [a]Josh. 10:26; Ps. 107:40; 110:5 [b]Deut. 21:23; Josh. 10:27

that they should take his carcase[5038]
down from the tree, and cast it at the entering of the gate of the city, and [c]raise
thereon a great heap of stones, *that remaineth* unto this day.

The Ceremony at Mount Ebal

30 Then Joshua built an altar[4196]
unto the LORD God of Israel [a]in mount
Ebal,
31 As Moses the servant[5650] of the
LORD commanded the children[1121] of
Israel, as it is written in the [a]book[5612]
of the law[8451] of Moses, an altar of
whole[8003] stones, over which no man hath
lift up[5130] *any* iron: and [b]they offered[5927]
thereon burnt offerings[5930] unto the LORD,
and sacrificed[2076] peace offerings.[8002]
32 And [a]he wrote there upon the
stones a copy of the law of Moses, which
he wrote in the presence of the children
of Israel.
33 And all Israel, and their elders,
and officers,[7860] and their judges,[8199]
stood on this side the ark[727] and on that
side before the priests the Levites, [a]which
bare[5375] the ark of the covenant[1285] of
the LORD, as well [b]the stranger,[1616] as he
that was born among them; half of them
over against mount Gerizim, and half of
them over against mount Ebal; [c]as Moses
the servant of the LORD had commanded
before,[7223] that they should bless[1288] the
people of Israel.
34 And afterward [a]he read[7121] all the
words[1697] of the law, [b]the blessings[1293]
and cursings,[7045] according to all that is
written in the book of the law.
35 There was not a word of all that
Moses commanded, which Joshua read
not before all the congregation[6951] of
Israel, [a]with the women, and [b]the little
ones,[2945] and the strangers[1616] that [I]were
conversant[1980] among[7130] them.

The Gibeonites Deceive Joshua

9 And it came to pass, when all the
kings[4428] which *were* on this side
Jordan, in the hills, and in the valleys,
and in all the coasts of [a]the great sea
over against Lebanon, [b]the Hittite, and
the Amorite, the Canaanite, the Perizzite,
the Hivite, and the Jebusite, heard[8085]
thereof;
2 That they [a]gathered themselves together, to fight with Joshua and with
Israel, with one [I]accord.[6310]
3 And when the inhabitants of
[a]Gibeon [b]heard what Joshua had done[6213]
unto Jericho and to Ai,
4 They did work[6213] wilily,[6195] and
went and made as if they had been
ambassadors,[6735] and took old sacks
upon their asses, and wine bottles, old,
and rent, and bound up;
5 And old shoes and clouted[2921]
upon their feet, and old garments upon
them; and all the bread of their provision
was dry[3001] *and* mouldy.
6 And they went to Joshua [a]unto the
camp[4264] at Gilgal, and said[559] unto him,
and to the men[376] of Israel, We be come
from a far country:[776] now therefore
make ye a league[1285] with us.
7 And the men of Israel said unto
the [a]Hivites, Peradventure[194] ye dwell
among[7130] us; and [b]how shall we make a
league with you?
8 And they said unto Joshua, [a]We *are*
thy servants.[5650] And Joshua said unto
them, Who *are* ye? and from whence
come ye?
9 And they said unto him, [a]From a
very far country thy servants are come
because of the name of the LORD thy
God:[430] for we have [b]heard the fame of
him, and all that he did in Egypt,
10 And [a]all that he did to the two
kings of the Amorites, that *were* beyond
Jordan, to Sihon king of Heshbon, and
to Og king of Bashan, which *was* at
Ashtaroth.
11 Wherefore our elders[2205] and all
the inhabitants of our country spake[559]
to us, saying, Take victuals[6720] [I]with you
for the journey,[1870] and go to meet them,
and say[559] unto them, We *are* your servants: therefore now make ye a league
with us.
12 This our bread we took hot *for*
our provision out of our houses[1004] on
the day[3117] we came forth to go unto you;

29 [c]Josh. 7:26; 10:27
30 [a]Deut. 27:4, 5
31 [a]Ex. 20:25; Deut. 27:5, 6 [b]Ex. 20:24
32 [a]Deut. 27:2, 8
33 [a]Deut. 31:9, 25 [b]Deut. 31:12 [c]Deut. 11:29; 27:12
34 [a]Deut. 31:11; Neh. 8:3 [b]Deut. 28:2, 15, 45; 29:20, 21; 30:19
35 [I]Hebr. *walked* [a]Deut. 31:12 [b]Josh. 8:33
1 [a]Num. 34:6 [b]Ex. 3:17; 23:23
2 [I]Hebr. *mouth* [a]Ps. 83:3, 5
3 [a]Josh. 10:2; 2Sam. 21:1, 2 [b]Josh. 6:27
6 [a]Josh. 5:10
7 [a]Josh. 11:19 [b]Ex. 23:32; Deut. 7:2; 20:16; Judg. 2:2
8 [a]Deut. 20:11; 2Kgs. 10:5
9 [a]Deut. 20:15 [b]Ex. 15:14; Josh. 2:10
10 [a]Num. 21:24, 33
11 [I]Hebr. *in your hand*

but now, behold, it is dry, and it is
mouldy:
13 And these bottles of wine, which
we filled, *were* new; and, behold, they be
rent: and these our garments and our
shoes are become old by reason of the
very long journey.
14 And [I]the men[582] took of their victuals, [a]and asked[7592] not *counsel* at the
mouth[6310] of the LORD.
15 And Joshua [a]made peace[7965] with
them, and made[6213] a league with them,
to let them live:[2421] and the princes[5387]
of the congregation[5712] sware[7650] unto
them.
16 And it came to pass at the end of
three days[3117] after they had made[3772] a
league[1285] with them, that they heard
that they *were* their neighbours, and *that*
they dwelt among[7130] them.
17 And the children[1121] of Israel
journeyed, and came unto their cities on
the third day. Now their cities *were*
[a]Gibeon, and Chephirah, and Beeroth, and
Kirjath–jearim.
18 And the children of Israel
smote[5221] them not, [a]because the princes
of the congregation had sworn[7650] unto
them by the LORD God of Israel. And all
the congregation murmured against the
princes.
19 But all the princes said unto all
the congregation, We have sworn unto
them by the LORD God of Israel:
now therefore we may not touch[5060]
them.
20 This we will do[6213] to them; we
will even let them live, lest [a]wrath[7110] be
upon us, because of the oath[7621] which
we sware unto them.
21 And the princes said unto them,
Let them live;[2421] but let them be
[a]hewers[2404] of wood and drawers of
water unto all the congregation; as the
princes had [b]promised[1696] them.
22 And Joshua called[7121] for them,
and he spake[1696] unto them, saying,
Wherefore have ye beguiled us, saying,
[a]We *are* very far from you; when [b]ye
dwell among[7130] us?
23 Now therefore ye *are* [a]cursed,[779]
and there shall [I]none of you be freed[3772]
from being bondmen,[5650] and [b]hewers of
wood and drawers of water for the
house[1004] of my God.
24 And they answered Joshua, and
said, Because it was certainly told[5046] thy
servants, how that the LORD thy God
[a]commanded[6680] his servant[5650] Moses to
give you all the land,[776] and to
destroy[8045] all the inhabitants of the land
from before you, therefore [b]we were sore
afraid[3372] of our lives[5315] because of you,
and have done this thing.[1697]
25 And now, behold, we *are* [a]in thine
hand:[3027] as it seemeth good[2896] and right
unto thee to do unto us, do.
26 And so did he unto them, and
delivered[5337] them out of the hand of the
children of Israel, that they slew[2026] them
not.
🗝 27 And Joshua [I][a]made them that day
[b]hewers of wood and drawers of water
for the congregation, and for the altar[4196]
of the LORD, even unto this day, [c]in the
place which he should choose.[977]

The Amorites Are Defeated

10 Now it came to pass, when
Adoni–zedec king of Jerusalem
had heard[8085] how Joshua had taken Ai,
and had utterly destroyed[2763] it; [a]as he
had done[6213] to Jericho and her king, so
he had done to [b]Ai and her king; and
[c]how the inhabitants of Gibeon had made
peace with Israel, and were among[7130]
them;
2 That they [a]feared[3372] greatly, because Gibeon *was* a great city, as one of
the [I]royal[4467] cities, and because it *was*
greater than Ai, and all the men[582]
thereof *were* mighty.
3 Wherefore Adoni–zedec king of

14 [I]Or, *they received the men by reason of their victuals* [a]Num. 27:21; Judg. 1:1; 1Sam. 22:10; 23:10, 11; 30:8; 2Sam. 2:1; 5:19; Isa. 30:1, 2

15 [a]Josh. 11:19; 2Sam. 21:2

17 [a]Josh. 18:25, 26, 28; Ezra 2:25

18 [a]Ps. 15:4; Eccl. 5:2

20 [a]2Sam. 21:1, 2, 6; Ezek. 17:13, 15, 18, 19; Zech. 5:3, 4; Mal. 3:5

21 [a]Deut. 29:11 [b]Josh. 9:15

22 [a]Josh. 9:6, 9 [b]Josh. 9:16

23 [I]Hebr. *not be cut off from you* [a]Gen. 9:25 [b]Josh. 9:21, 27

24 [a]Ex. 23:32; Deut. 7:1, 2 [b]Ex. 15:14

25 [a]Gen. 16:6

27 [I]Hebr. *gave, or, delivered to be* [a]1Chr. 9:2; Ezra 8:20 [b]Josh. 9:21, 23 [c]Deut. 12:5

1 [a]Josh. 6:21 [b]Josh. 8:22, 26, 28 [c]Josh. 9:15

2 [I]Hebr. *cities of the kingdom* [a]Ex. 15:14-16; Deut. 11:25

🗝 **9:27** The Gibeonites were among those who rebuilt the walls of Jerusalem after the return of Israel from Exile (Neh. 7:25). The irony is seen in that Solomon received a message from God in a dream at Gibeon (1 Kgs. 3:5–15).

Jerusalem sent unto Hoham king of Hebron, and unto Piram king of Jarmuth, and unto Japhia king of Lachish, and unto Debir king of Eglon, saying,

4 Come up[5927] unto me, and help me, that we may smite Gibeon: [a]for it hath made peace with Joshua and with the children[1121] of Israel.

5 Therefore the five kings[4428] of the Amorites, the king of Jerusalem, the king of Hebron, the king of Jarmuth, the king of Lachish, the king of Eglon, [a]gathered themselves together,[622] and went up,[5927] they and all their hosts,[4264] and encamped before Gibeon, and made war against it.

6 And the men of Gibeon sent unto Joshua [a]to the camp[4264] to Gilgal, saying, Slack[7503] not thy hand[3027] from thy servants;[5650] come up to us quickly, and save[3467] us, and help us: for all the kings of the Amorites that dwell in the mountains are gathered together[6908] against us.

7 So Joshua ascended from Gilgal, he, and [a]all the people[5971] of war with him, and all the mighty men of valour.[2428]

8 And the LORD said[559] unto Joshua, [a]Fear[3372] them not: for I have delivered them into thine hand; [b]there shall not a man[376] of them stand before thee.

9 Joshua therefore came unto them suddenly, *and* went up from Gilgal all night.[3915]

10 And the LORD [a]discomfited them before Israel, and slew[5221] them with a great slaughter[4347] at Gibeon, and chased them along the way[1870] that goeth up [b]to Beth–horon, and smote[5221] them to [c]Azekah, and unto Makkedah.

11 And it came to pass, as they fled from before Israel, *and* were in the going down to Beth–horon, [a]that the LORD cast down great stones from heaven[8064] upon them unto Azekah, and they died: *they were* more which died[4191] with hailstones than *they* whom the children of Israel slew[2026] with the sword.[2719]

🗝 12 Then spake[1696] Joshua to the LORD in the day[3117] when the LORD delivered up the Amorites before the children of Israel, and he said in the sight of Israel, [a]Sun, [I]stand thou still[1826] upon Gibeon; and thou, Moon, in the valley of [b]Ajalon.

13 And the sun stood still, and the moon stayed, until the people[1471] had avenged[5358] themselves upon their enemies. [a]*Is* not this written in the book[5612] of [I]Jasher?[3477] So the sun stood still in the midst of heaven, and hasted not to go down about a whole[8549] day.

14 And there was [a]no day like that before it or after it, that the LORD hearkened[8085] unto the voice of a man: for [b]the LORD fought for Israel.

15 [a]And Joshua returned,[7725] and all Israel with him, unto the camp to Gilgal.

16 But these five kings fled, and hid themselves in a cave at Makkedah.

17 And it was told[5046] Joshua, saying, The five kings are found hid in a cave at Makkedah.

18 And Joshua said, Roll[1556] great stones upon the mouth[6310] of the cave, and set men by it for to keep[8104] them:

19 And stay ye not, *but* pursue after your enemies, and [I]smite the hindmost[2179] of them; suffer[5414] them not to enter into their cities: for the LORD your God[430] hath delivered them into your hand.

20 And it came to pass, when Joshua and the children of Israel had made an end[3615] of slaying[5221] them with a very great slaughter,[4347] till they were consumed,[8552] that the rest[8300] *which* remained of them entered into fenced cities.

21 And all the people returned to the camp to Joshua at Makkedah in peace:[7965] [a]none moved his tongue against any of the children of Israel.

4 [a]Josh. 9:15; 10:1
5 [a]Josh. 9:2
6 [a]Josh. 5:10; 9:6
7 [a]Josh. 8:1
8 [a]Josh. 11:6; Judg. 4:14 [b]Josh. 1:5
10 [a]Judg. 4:15; 1Sam. 7:10, 12; Ps. 18:14; Isa. 28:21 [b]Josh. 16:3, 5 [c]Josh. 15:35
11 [a]Ps. 18:13, 14; 77:17; Isa. 30:30; Rev. 16:21
12 [I]Hebr. *be silent* [a]Isa. 28:21; Hab. 3:11 [b]Judg. 12:12
13 [I]Or, *The upright* [a]2Sam. 1:18
14 [a]Isa. 38:8 [b]Deut. 1:30; Josh. 10:42; 23:3
15 [a]Josh. 10:43
19 [I]Hebr. *cut off the tail*
21 [a]Ex. 11:7

🗝 **10:12–14** At Joshua's request, God caused the sun to stand still for 12 or 24 hours so that Israel could achieve a greater victory. This is one of the two times recorded in the Old Testament when God interrupted time as a favor or a sign to a man. The other occasion was the turning back of the sundial ten points for the benefit of Hezekiah (Is. 38:7, 8).

22 Then said Joshua, Open the mouth of the cave, and bring out those five kings unto me out of the cave.

23 And they did[6213] so, and brought forth those five kings unto him out of the cave, the king of Jerusalem, the king of Hebron, the king of Jarmuth, the king of Lachish, *and* the king of Eglon.

24 And it came to pass, when they brought out those kings unto Joshua, that Joshua called[7121] for all the men[376] of Israel, and said unto the captains[8269] of the men of war which went with him, Come near,[7126] [a]put your feet upon the necks of these kings. And they came near, and put their feet upon the necks of them.

25 And Joshua said unto them, [a]Fear not, nor be dismayed,[2865] be strong[2388] and of good courage:[553] for [b]thus shall the LORD do to all your enemies against whom ye fight.

26 And afterward Joshua smote them, and slew[4191] them, and hanged them on five trees: and they [a]were hanging upon the trees until the evening.

27 And it came to pass at the time of the going down of the sun, *that* Joshua commanded,[6680] and they [a]took them down off the trees, and cast them into the cave wherein they had been hid, and laid[7760] great stones in the cave's mouth, *which remain* until this very day.

Joshua Smites the Southern Cities

28 And that day Joshua took Makkedah, and smote it with the edge[6310] of the sword, and the king thereof he utterly destroyed, them, and all the souls[5315] that *were* therein; he let none remain:[8300] and he did to the king of Makkedah [a]as he did unto the king of Jericho.

29 Then Joshua passed[5674] from Makkedah, and all Israel with him, unto Libnah, and fought against Libnah:

30 And the LORD delivered it also, and the king thereof, into the hand of Israel; and he smote it with the edge of the sword, and all the souls that *were* therein; he let none remain in it; but did unto the king thereof as he did unto the king of Jericho.

31 And Joshua passed from Libnah, and all Israel with him, unto Lachish, and encamped against it, and fought against it:

32 And the LORD delivered Lachish into the hand of Israel, which took it on the second day, and smote it with the edge of the sword, and all the souls that *were* therein, according to all that he had done to Libnah.

🔑 33 Then Horam king of Gezer came up[5927] to help Lachish; and Joshua smote him and his people, until he had left[7604] him none remaining.[8300]

34 And from Lachish Joshua passed unto Eglon, and all Israel with him; and they encamped against it, and fought against it:

35 And they took it on that day, and smote it with the edge of the sword, and all the souls that *were* therein he utterly destroyed that day, according to all that he had done to Lachish.

36 And Joshua went up from Eglon, and all Israel with him, unto [a]Hebron; and they fought against it:

37 And they took it, and smote it with the edge of the sword, and the king thereof, and all the cities thereof, and all the souls that *were* therein; he left none remaining, according to all that he had done to Eglon; but destroyed it utterly, and all the souls that *were* therein.

38 And Joshua returned, and all Israel with him, to [a]Debir; and fought against it:

39 And he took it, and the king thereof, and all the cities thereof; and they smote them with the edge of the sword, and utterly destroyed all the souls that

24 [a]Ps. 107:40; 110:5; 149:8, 9; Isa. 26:5, 6; Mal. 4:3

25 [a]Deut. 31:6, 8; Josh. 1:9 [b]Deut. 3:21; 7:19

26 [a]Josh. 8:29

27 [a]Deut. 21:23; Josh. 8:29

28 [a]Josh. 6:21

36 [a]Josh. 14:13; 15:13; Judg. 1:10

38 [a]Josh. 15:15; Judg. 1:11

🔑 **10:33** Because Gezer remained a Canaanite stronghold long after Joshua's time (Josh. 16:10; Judg. 1:29), one can assume that Joshua did not attempt to destroy it.

were therein; he left none remaining: as he had done to Hebron, so he did to Debir, and to the king thereof; as he had done also to Libnah, and to her king.

40 So Joshua smote all the country[776] of the hills, and of the south, and of the vale,[8219] and of the springs, and all their kings: he left none remaining, but utterly destroyed all that breathed, as the LORD God of Israel [a]commanded.

41 And Joshua smote them from Kadesh–barnea even unto [a]Gaza, [b]and all the country of Goshen, even unto Gibeon.

42 And all these kings and their land[776] did Joshua take at one time, [a]because the LORD God of Israel fought for Israel.

43 And Joshua returned, and all Israel with him, unto the camp to Gilgal.

Northern Kings Are Defeated

11 And it came to pass, when Jabin king of Hazor had heard[8085] *those things,* that he [a]sent to Jobab king of Madon, and to the king [b]of Shimron, and to the king of Achshaph,

2 And to the kings[4428] that *were* on the north of the mountains, and of the plains[6160] south of [a]Chinneroth, and in the valley, and in the borders [b]of Dor on the west,

3 *And to* the Canaanite on the east and on the west, and *to* the Amorite, and the Hittite, and the Perizzite, and the Jebusite in the mountains, [a]and *to* the Hivite under [b]Hermon [c]in the land[776] of Mizpeh.

4 And they went out, they and all their hosts[4264] with them, much people,[5971] [a]even as the sand that *is* upon the sea shore[8193] in multitude, with horses and chariots very many.

5 And when all these kings were [I]met together, they came and pitched together at the waters of Merom, to fight against Israel.

🔑 6 And the LORD said[559] unto Joshua, [a]Be not afraid[3372] because of them: for to morrow about this time will I deliver them up all slain[2491] before Israel: thou shalt [b]hough[6131] their horses, and burn[8313] their chariots with fire.

7 So Joshua came, and all the people of war with him, against them by the waters of Merom suddenly; and they fell[5307] upon them.

8 And the LORD delivered them into the hand[3027] of Israel, who smote[5221] them, and chased them unto [I]great Zidon, and unto [II][a]Misrephoth–maim, and unto the valley of Mizpeh eastward; and they smote them, until they left[7604] them none remaining.[8300]

9 And Joshua did[6213] unto them [a]as the LORD bade him: he houghed[6131] their horses, and burnt[8313] their chariots with fire.

10 And Joshua at that time turned back, and took Hazor, and smote the king thereof with the sword: for Hazor beforetime was the head[7218] of all those kingdoms.[4467]

11 And they smote all the souls[5315] that *were* therein with the edge[6310] of the sword, utterly destroying[2763] *them:* there was not [I]any left[3498] to breathe: and he burnt Hazor with fire.

12 And all the cities of those kings, and all the kings of them, did Joshua take, and smote them with the edge of the sword, *and* he utterly destroyed them, [a]as Moses the servant[5650] of the LORD commanded.[6680]

13 But *as for* the cities that stood still [I]in their strength, Israel burned[8313] none of them, save Hazor only; *that* did Joshua burn.

14 And all the spoil of these cities,

40 [a]Deut. 20:16, 17

41 [a]Gen. 10:19 [b]Josh. 11:16

42 [a]Josh. 10:14

1 [a]Josh. 10:3 [b]Josh. 19:15

2 [a]Num. 34:11 [b]Josh. 17:11; Judg. 1:27; 1Kgs. 4:11

3 [a]Judg. 3:3 [b]Josh. 13:11 [c]Gen. 31:49

4 [a]Gen. 22:17; 32:12; Judg. 7:12; 1Sam. 13:5

5 [I]Hebr. *assembled by appointment*

6 [a]Josh. 10:8 [b]2Sam. 8:4

8 [I]Or, *Zidonrabbah* [II]Hebr. *Burnings of waters* [a]Josh. 13:6

9 [a]Josh. 11:6

11 [I]Hebr. *any breath*

12 [a]Num. 33:52; Deut. 7:2; 20:16, 17

13 [I]Hebr. *on their heap*

🔑 **11:6** Cutting the tendons of the legs rendered the horses unfit for military service. This is illustrated in the word translated "hough." Israel herself was forbidden by God to develop a cavalry (Deut. 17:16), because God wanted them to depend upon Him, not the strength of horses (Is. 31:1, 3).

and the cattle, the children[1121] of Israel took for a prey unto themselves; but every man they smote with the edge of the sword, until they had destroyed[8045] them, neither left they any to breathe.

15 [a]As the LORD commanded Moses his servant, so [b]did Moses command[6680] Joshua, and [c]so did Joshua; [I]he left[5493] nothing[3808,1697] undone[5493] of all that the LORD commanded Moses.

Summary of Joshua's Victories

16 So Joshua took all that land, [a]the hills, and all the south country, [b]and all the land of Goshen, and the valley, and the plain,[6160] and the mountain of Israel, and the valley of the same;

17 [a]*Even* from [I]the mount Halak, that goeth up to Seir, even unto Baal–gad in the valley of Lebanon under mount Hermon: and [b]all their kings he took, and smote them, and slew[4191] them.

18 Joshua made[6213] war a long time[3117] with all those kings.

19 There was not a city that made peace with the children of Israel, save [a]the Hivites the inhabitants of Gibeon: all *other* they took in battle.

20 For [a]it was of the LORD to harden their hearts,[3820] that they should come against Israel in battle, that he might destroy them utterly,[2763] *and* that they might have no favour,[8467] but that he might destroy[8045] them, [b]as the LORD commanded Moses.

21 And at that time came Joshua, and cut off[3772] [a]the Anakims from the mountains, from Hebron, from Debir, from Anab, and from all the mountains of Judah, and from all the mountains of Israel: Joshua destroyed them utterly with their cities.

22 There was none of the Anakims left in the land of the children of Israel: only in Gaza, in [a]Gath, [b]and in Ashdod, there remained.[7604]

23 So Joshua took the whole land, [a]according to all that the LORD said[1696] unto Moses; and Joshua gave it for an inheritance[5159] unto Israel [b]according to their divisions by their tribes.[7626] [c]And the land rested[8252] from war.

The Kings Defeated Under Moses

12 Now these *are* the kings[4428] of the land,[776] which the children[1121] of Israel smote,[5221] and possessed[3423] their land on the other side Jordan toward the rising of the sun, [a]from the river Arnon [b]unto mount Hermon, and all the plain[6160] on the east:

2 [a]Sihon king of the Amorites, who dwelt in Heshbon, *and* ruled[4910] from Aroer, which *is* upon the bank[8193] of the river Arnon, and from the middle of the river, and from half Gilead, even unto the river Jabbok, *which is* the border of the children of Ammon;

3 And [a]from the plain to the sea of Chinneroth on the east, and unto the sea of the plain, *even* the salt sea on the east, [b]the way to Beth–jeshimoth; and from [I]the south, under [II][c]Ashdoth–pisgah:

4 And [a]the coast of Og king of Bashan, *which was* of [b]the remnant[3499] of the giants,[7497] [c]that dwelt at Ashtaroth and at Edrei,

15 [I]Hebr. *he removed nothing* [a]Ex. 34:11, 12 [b]Deut. 7:2 [c]Josh. 1:7
16 [a]Josh. 12:8 [b]Josh. 10:41
17 [I]Or, *the smooth mountain* [a]Josh. 12:7 [b]Deut. 7:24; Josh. 12:7
19 [a]Josh. 9:3, 7
20 [a]Deut. 2:30; Judg. 14:4; 1Sam. 2:25; 1Kgs. 12:15; Rom. 9:18 [b]Deut. 20:16, 17
21 [a]Num. 13:22, 33; Deut. 1:28; Josh. 15:13, 14
22 [a]1Sam. 17:4 [b]Josh. 15:46
23 [a]Num. 34:2 [b]Num. 26:53; Josh. 14; 15; 16; 17; 18; 19 [c]Josh. 11:18; 14:15; 21:44; 22:4; 23:1
1 [a]Num. 21:24 [b]Deut. 3:8, 9
2 [a]Num. 21:24; Deut. 2:33, 36; 3:6, 16
3 [a]Deut. 3:17 [b]Josh. 13:20 [I]Or, *Teman* [II]Or, *The springs of Pisgah,* or, *The hill* [c]Deut. 3:17; 4:49
4 [a]Num. 21:35; Deut. 3:4, 10 [b]Deut. 3:11; Josh. 13:12; [c]Deut. 1:4

11:21 The Anakim were the giants of whom the ten spies were so afraid (Num. 13:33). Caleb conquered them (Josh. 15:14). Caleb's action is probably in view here under Joshua's name as part of the larger campaign.

11:23 See introduction to the Book of Joshua.

12:1 The extent of the conquest under Joshua's leadership was vast, but the task was too large to have been completed in his life time (Deut 7:22; Josh. 13:1–6). During the nearly seven-year military campaign (see Josh. 14:7–10), the borders of Israel were expanded from Kadesh-barnea in the south (Josh. 10:41) to the foothills of Mount Hermon in the north (Josh. 11:17). Joshua's task now was to distribute the land among the tribes and leave the further conquest to God (Josh. 13:6, 7). The details of that distribution are given in chapters 13—21.

5 And reigned[4910] in [a]mount Hermon, [b]and in Salcah, and in all Bashan, [c]unto the border of the Geshurites, and the Maachathites, and half Gilead, the border of Sihon king of Heshbon.

6 [a]Them did[5221] Moses the servant[5650] of the LORD and the children of Israel smite:[5221] and [b]Moses the servant of the LORD gave it *for* a possession[3425] unto the Reubenites, and the Gadites, and the half tribe[7626] of Manasseh.

The Kings Defeated Under Joshua

7 And these *are* the kings of the country[776] [a]which Joshua and the children of Israel smote on this side Jordan on the west, from Baal–gad in the valley[1237] of Lebanon even unto the mount Halak, that goeth up to [b]Seir; which Joshua [c]gave unto the tribes of Israel *for* a possession according to their divisions;

8 [a]In the mountains, and in the valleys,8219 and in the plains,[6160] and in the springs, and in the wilderness, and in the south country; [b]the Hittites, the Amorites, and the Canaanites, the Perizzites, the Hivites, and the Jebusites:

9 [a]The king of Jericho, one; [b]the king of Ai, which *is* beside Bethel, one;

10 [a]The king of Jerusalem, one; the king of Hebron, one;

11 The king of Jarmuth, one; the king of Lachish, one;

12 The king of Eglon, one; [a]the king of Gezer, one;

13 [a]The king of Debir, one; the king of Geder, one;

14 The king of Hormah, one; the king of Arad, one;

15 [a]The king of Libnah, one; the king of Adullam, one;

5 [a]Deut. 3:8 [b]Deut. 3:10; Josh. 13:11 [c]Deut. 3:14
6 [a]Num. 21:24, 33 [b]Num. 32:29, 33; Deut. 3:11, 12; Josh. 13:8
7 [a]Josh. 11:17 [b]Gen. 14:6; 32:3; Deut. 2:1, 4 [c]Josh. 11:23
8 [a]Josh. 10:40; 11:16 [b]Ex. 3:8; 23:23; Josh. 9:1
9 [a]Josh. 6:2 [b]Josh. 8:29
10 [a]Josh. 10:23
12 [a]Josh. 10:33
13 [a]Josh. 10:38
15 [a]Josh. 10:29
16 [a]Josh. 10:28 [b]Josh. 8:17; Judg. 1:22
17 [a]1Kgs. 4:10
18 [I]Or, *Sharon*
19 [a]Josh. 11:10
20 [a]Josh. 11:1; 19:15
22 [a]Josh. 19:37
23 [a]Josh. 11:2 [b]Gen. 14:1, 2; Isa. 9:1
1 [I]Hebr. *to possess it* [a]Josh. 14:10; 23:1
2 [a]Judg. 3:1 [b]Joel 3:4 [c]Josh. 13:13; 2Sam. 3:3; 13:37, 38
3 [a]Jer. 2:18 [b]Judg. 3:3; 1Sam. 6:4, 16; Zeph. 2:5 [c]Deut. 2:23
4 [I]Or, *The cave* [a]Josh. 19:30 [b]Judg. 1:34
5 [a]1Kgs. 5:18; Ps. 83:7; Ezek. 27:9 [b]Josh. 12:7

16 [a]The king of Makkedah, one; [b]the king of Bethel, one;

17 The king of Tappuah, one; [a]the king of Hepher, one;

18 The king of Aphek, one; the king of [I]Lasharon, one;

19 The king of Madon, one; [a]the king of Hazor, one;

20 The king of [a]Shimron–meron, one; the king of Achshaph, one;

21 The king of Taanach, one; the king of Megiddo, one;

22 [a]The king of Kedesh, one; the king of Jokneam of Carmel, one;

23 The king of Dor in the [a]coast of Dor, one; the king of [b]the nations[1471] of Gilgal, one;

24 The king of Tirzah, one: all the kings thirty and one.

The Unconquered Territory

13 Now Joshua [a]was old[2204] *and* stricken in years; and the LORD said[559] unto him, Thou art old *and* stricken in years, and there remaineth[7604] yet very much land[776] [I]to be possessed.[3423]

2 [a]This *is* the land that yet remaineth: [b]all the borders of the Philistines, and all [c]Geshuri,

3 [a]From Sihor, which *is* before Egypt, even unto the borders of Ekron northward, *which* is counted[2803] to the Canaanite: [b]five lords[5633] of the Philistines; the Gazathites, and the Ashdothites, the Eshkalonites, the Gittites, and the Ekronites; also [c]the Avites:

4 From the south, all the land of the Canaanites, and [I]Mearah that *is* beside the Sidonians, [a]unto Aphek, to the borders of [b]the Amorites:

5 And the land of [a]the Giblites, and all Lebanon, toward the sunrising, [b]from

---

12:23 This is not the same Gilgal which is mentioned as being near Jericho or the one which was near Bethel. This Gilgal was probably located about 42 miles north of Jerusalem, just south of Carmel.

13:1–7 See note on Joshua 12:1, on the territories that remained unconquered.

13:3 See note on Deuteronomy 2:23.

Baal–gad under mount Hermon unto the entering into Hamath.

6 All the inhabitants of the hill country from Lebanon unto [a]Misrephoth–maim, *and* all the Sidonians, them [b]will I drive out[3423] from before the children[1121] of Israel: only [c]divide thou it by lot unto the Israelites for an inheritance, as I have commanded[6680] thee.

Division of the Land East of the Jordan

🗝 7 Now therefore divide this land for an inheritance unto the nine tribes,[7626] and the half tribe of Manasseh,

8 With whom the Reubenites and the Gadites have received their inheritance, [a]which Moses gave them, beyond Jordan eastward, *even* as Moses the servant[5650] of the LORD gave them;

9 From Aroer, that *is* upon the bank of the river Arnon, and the city that *is* in the midst of the river, [a]and all the plain of Medeba unto Dibon;

10 And [a]all the cities of Sihon king of the Amorites, which reigned[4427] in Heshbon, unto the border of the children of Ammon;

11 [a]And Gilead, and the border of the Geshurites and Maachathites, and all mount Hermon, and all Bashan unto Salcah;

12 All the kingdom[4468] of Og in Bashan, which reigned in Ashtaroth and in Edrei, who remained[7604] of [a]the remnant[3499] of the giants:[7497] [b]for these did Moses smite,[5221] and cast them out.[3423]

13 Nevertheless the children of Israel expelled[3423] [a]not the Geshurites, nor the Maachathites: but the Geshurites and the Maachathites dwell among[7130] the Israelites until this day.[3117]

14 [a]Only unto the tribe of Levi he gave none inheritance; the sacrifices[2077] of the LORD God[430] of Israel made by fire *are* their inheritance, [b]as he said[1696] unto them.

15 And Moses gave unto the tribe[4294] of the children of Reuben *inheritance* according to their families.[4940]

16 And their coast was [a]from Aroer, that *is* on the bank of the river Arnon, [b]and the city that *is* in the midst of the river, [c]and all the plain[4334] by Medeba;

17 Heshbon, and all her cities that *are* in the plain; Dibon, and [I]Bamoth–baal, and Beth–baal–meon,

18 [a]And Jahaza, and Kedemoth, and Mephaath,

19 [a]And Kirjathaim, and [b]Sibmah, and Zareth–shahar in the mount of the valley,

20 And Beth–peor, and [Ia]Ashdoth–pisgah, and Beth–jeshimoth,

21 [a]And all the cities of the plain, and all the kingdom of Sihon king of the Amorites, which reigned in Heshbon, [b]whom Moses smote[5221] [c]with the princes[5387] of Midian, Evi, and Rekem, and Zur, and Hur, and Reba, *which were* dukes[5257] of Sihon, dwelling in the country.[776]

22 [a]Balaam also the son[1121] of Beor, the [I]soothsayer,[7080] did the children of Israel slay[2026] with the sword[2719] among them that were slain[2491] by them.

23 And the border of the children of Reuben was Jordan, and the border *thereof.* This *was* the inheritance of the children of Reuben after their families, the cities and the villages thereof.

24 And Moses gave *inheritance* unto the tribe of Gad, *even* unto the children of Gad according to their families.

25 [a]And their coast was Jazer, and all the cities of Gilead, [b]and half the land of the children of Ammon, unto Aroer that *is* before [c]Rabbah;

26 And from Heshbon unto Ramath–mizpeh, and Betonim; and from Mahanaim unto the border of Debir;

6 [a]Josh. 11:8 [b]Josh. 23:13; Judg. 2:21, 23 [c]Josh. 14:1, 2
8 [a]Num. 32:33; Deut. 3:12, 13; Josh. 22:4
9 [a]Num. 21:30; Josh. 13:16
10 [a]Num. 21:24, 25
11 [a]Josh. 12:5
12 [a]Deut. 3:11; Josh. 12:4 [b]Num. 21:24, 35
13 [a]Josh. 13:11
14 [a]Num. 18:20, 23, 24; Josh. 14:3, 4 [b]Josh. 13:33
16 [a]Josh. 12:2 [b]Num. 21:28 [c]Num. 21:30; Josh. 13:9
17 [I]Or, *The high places of Baal, and house of Baalmeon*
18 [a]Num. 21:23
19 [a]Num. 32:37 [b]Num. 32:38
20 [I]Or, *Springs of Pisgah,* or, *The hill* [a]Deut. 3:17; Josh. 12:3
21 [a]Deut. 3:10 [b]Num. 21:24 [c]Num. 31:8
22 [I]Or, *diviner* [a]Num. 22:5; 31:8
25 [a]Num. 32:35 [b]Num. 21:26, 28, 29; Deut. 2:19; Judg. 11:13, 15 [c]2Sam. 11:1; 12:26

🗝 **13:7** Although the conquest of Canaan was still incomplete, God intended that each tribe should complete the occupation of their allotment as their numbers increased to fill it.

27 And in the valley, [a]Beth–aram, and Beth–nimrah, [b]and Succoth, and Zaphon, the rest[3499] of the kingdom of Sihon king of Heshbon, Jordan and *his* border, *even* unto the edge [c]of the sea of Chinnereth on the other side Jordan eastward.

28 This *is* the inheritance of the children of Gad after their families, the cities, and their villages.

29 And Moses gave *inheritance* unto the half tribe of Manasseh: and *this* was *the possession* of the half tribe of the children of Manasseh by their families.

30 And their coast was from Mahanaim, all Bashan, all the kingdom of Og king of Bashan, and [a]all the towns of Jair, which *are* in Bashan, threescore cities:

31 And half Gilead, and [a]Ashtaroth, and Edrei, cities of the kingdom of Og in Bashan, *were pertaining* unto the children of Machir the son of Manasseh, *even* to the one half of the [b]children of Machir by their families.

32 These *are the countries* which Moses did distribute for inheritance[5157] in the plains[6160] of Moab, on the other side Jordan, by Jericho, eastward.

33 [a]But unto the tribe of Levi Moses gave not *any* inheritance: the LORD God of Israel *was* their inheritance, [b]as he said unto them.

Division of Canaan

14 And these *are the countries* which the children of Israel inherited in the land[776] of Canaan, [a]which Eleazar the priest, and Joshua the son of Nun, and the heads[7218] of the fathers[1] of the tribes[4294] of the children of Israel, distributed for inheritance to them.

2 [a]By lot *was* their inheritance,[5159] as the LORD commanded[6680] by the hand[3027] of Moses, for the nine tribes, and *for* the half tribe.

3 [a]For Moses had given the inheritance of two tribes and an half tribe on the other side Jordan: but unto the Levite he gave none inheritance among them.

4 For [a]the children of Joseph were two tribes, Manasseh and Ephraim: therefore they gave no part unto the Levites in the land, save cities to dwell *in*, with their suburbs for their cattle and for their substance.

5 [a]As the LORD commanded Moses, so the children of Israel did,[6213] and they divided the land.

Caleb's Inheritance

6 Then the children of Judah came unto Joshua in Gilgal: and Caleb the son of Jephunneh the [a]Kenezite said[559] unto him, Thou knowest[3045] [b]the thing[1697] that the LORD said[1696] unto Moses the man[376] of God[430] concerning me and thee [c]in Kadesh–barnea.

7 Forty years old *was* I when Moses the servant[5650] of the LORD [a]sent me from Kadesh–barnea to espy out the land; and I brought him word[1697] again as *it was* in mine heart.[3824]

8 Nevertheless [a]my brethren[251] that went up[5927] with me made the heart[3820] of the people[5971] melt: but I wholly [b]followed[4390,310] the LORD my God.

9 And Moses sware[7650] on that day,[3117] saying, [a]Surely the land [b]whereon thy feet have trodden shall be thine inheritance, and thy children's for ever,[5769] because thou hast wholly followed the LORD my God.

10 And now, behold, the LORD hath kept me alive, [a]as he said, these forty

27 [a]Num. 32:36 [b]Gen. 33:17; 1Kgs. 7:46 [c]Num. 34:11
30 [a]Num. 32:41; 1Chr. 2:23
31 [a]Josh. 12:4 [b]Num. 32:39, 40
33 [a]Josh. 13:14; 18:7 [b]Num. 18:20; Deut. 10:9; 18:1, 2
1 [a]Num. 34:17, 18
2 [a]Num. 26:55; 33:54; 34:13
3 [a]Josh. 13:8, 32, 33
4 [a]Gen. 48:5; 1Chr. 5:1, 2
5 [a]Num. 35:2; Josh. 21:2
6 [a]Num. 32:12; Josh. 15:17 [b]Num. 14:24, 30; Deut. 1:36, 38 [c]Num. 13:26
7 [a]Num. 13:6; 14:6
8 [a]Num. 13:31, 32; Deut. 1:28 [b]Num. 14:24; Deut. 1:36
9 [a]Num. 14:23, 24; Deut. 1:36; Josh. 1:3 [b]Num. 13:22
10 [a]Num. 14:30

14:6–15 See note on Numbers 13:30–33, concerning Caleb's allotment.

14:6 Kenaz was an Edomite tribe. Caleb was of the tribe of Judah (Num. 13:6; 34:19). This was a result of the Kenizzite and Judahite lineages being blended by marriage (cf. 1 Chr. 2:4, 5, 18, 19; 4:13–15).

14:9 When Caleb explored the land of Canaan as one of the twelve spies, he visited the people known as Anakim (Deut. 1:28). Moses promised him this same region for a possession (Deut. 1:36).

and five years, even since the LORD
spake[1696] this word unto Moses, while
the children of Israel [I]wandered in the
wilderness: and now, lo, I *am* this day
fourscore and five years old.
11 [a]As yet I *am as* strong[2389] this
day as *I was* in the day that Moses sent
me: as my strength *was* then, even so *is*
my strength now, for war, both [b]to go
out, and to come in.
12 Now therefore give me this mountain, whereof the LORD spake in that day;
for thou heardest[8085] in that day how [a]the
Anakims *were* there, and *that* the cities
were great *and* fenced: [b]if so be the LORD
will be with me, then [c]I shall be able to
drive them out, as the LORD said.
13 And Joshua [a]blessed[1288] him, [b]and
gave unto Caleb the son of Jephunneh
Hebron for an inheritance.
14 [a]Hebron therefore became the inheritance of Caleb the son of Jephunneh
the Kenezite unto this day, because that
he [b]wholly followed the LORD God of
Israel.
15 And [a]the name of Hebron before
was Kirjath–arba; *which Arba was* a
great man[120] among the Anakims. [b]And
the land had rest[8252] from war.

Judah's Portion

15 *This* then was the lot of the
tribe[4294] of the children[1121] of
Judah by their families;[4940] [a]*even* to the
border of Edom the [b]wilderness of Zin
southward *was* the uttermost part of the
south coast.
2 And their south border was from
the shore of the salt sea, from the [I]bay
that looketh southward:
3 And it went out to the south
side [a]to [I]Maaleh–acrabbim, and passed
along[5674] to Zin, and ascended up on the
south side unto Kadesh–barnea, and
passed along to Hezron, and went up[5927]
to Adar, and fetched a compass[5437] to
Karkaa:
4 *From thence* it passed [a]toward
Azmon, and went out unto the river of
Egypt; and the goings out of that coast
were at the sea: this shall be your south
coast.
5 And the east border *was* the salt
sea, *even* unto the end of Jordan. And
their border in the north quarter *was*
from the bay of the sea at the uttermost
part of Jordan:
6 And the border went up to [a]Beth–
hogla, and passed along by the north
of Beth–arabah; and the border went
up [b]to the stone of Bohan the son[1121] of
Reuben:
🗝 7 And the border went up toward
Debir from [a]the valley of Achor, and so
northward, looking toward Gilgal, that *is*
before the going up to Adummim, which
is on the south side of the river: and the
border passed toward the waters of
En–shemesh, and the goings out thereof
were at [b]En–rogel:
🗝 8 And the border went up [a]by the
valley of the son of Hinnom unto the
south side of the [b]Jebusite; the same *is*
Jerusalem: and the border went up to the
top[7218] of the mountain that *lieth* before
the valley of Hinnom westward, which *is*
at the end [c]of the valley of the giants[7497]
northward:
9 And the border was drawn from
the top of the hill unto [a]the fountain of
the water of Nephtoah, and went out
to the cities of mount Ephron; and the
border was drawn [b]to Baalah, which *is*
[c]Kirjath–jearim:
10 And the border compassed from

10 [I]Heb. *walked*
11 [a]Deut. 31:7 [b]Deut. 31:2
12 [a]Num. 13:28, 33 [b]Ps. 18:32, 34; 60:12; Rom. 8:31 [c]Josh. 15:14; Judg. 1:20
13 [a]Josh. 22:6 [b]Josh. 10:37; 15:13; 21:11, 12; Judg. 1:20; 1Chr. 6:55, 56
14 [a]Josh. 21:12 [b]Josh. 14:8, 9
15 [a]Gen. 23:2; Josh. 15:13 [b]Josh. 11:23
1 [a]Num. 34:3 [b]Num. 33:36
2 [I]Hebr. *tongue*
3 [I]Or, *The going up to Acrabbim* [a]Num. 34:4
4 [a]Num. 34:5
6 [a]Josh. 18:19 [b]Josh. 18:17
7 [a]Josh. 7:26 [b]2Sam. 17:17; 1Kgs. 1:9
8 [a]Josh. 18:16; 2Kgs. 23:10; Jer. 19:2, 6 [b]Josh. 18:28; Judg. 1:21; 19:10 [c]Josh. 18:16
9 [a]Josh. 18:15 [b]1Chr. 13:6 [c]Judg. 18:12

🗝 **15:7** This was not the Gilgal which was Israel's first campsite (Josh. 4:19). It is the Geliloth mentioned in Joshua 18:17.

🗝 **15:8** Later, the valley of Hinnom was the site for human sacrifices in the worship of Molech (see note on 2 Kgs. 23:10 for a further discussion of this pagan practice). The Hebrew phrase *gē ben hinnōm* ([2011] or "valley of Tophet") was transliterated to the Greek word, *Geénna* (NT 1067), which was the word for "hell" in the New Testament (Matt. 5:29, 30).

Baalah westward unto mount Seir, and passed along unto the side of mount Jearim, which *is* Chesalon, on the north side, and went down to Beth–shemesh, and passed on to [a]Timnah:

11 And the border went out unto the side of [a]Ekron northward: and the border was drawn to Shicron, and passed along to mount Baalah, and went out unto Jabneel; and the goings out of the border were at the sea.

12 And the west border *was* [a]to the great sea, and the coast *thereof.* This *is* the coast of the children of Judah round about according to their families.

13 [a]And unto Caleb the son of Jephunneh he gave a part among the children of Judah, according to the commandment[6310] of the LORD to Joshua, *even* [I][b]the city of Arba the father[1] of Anak, which *city is* Hebron.

14 And Caleb drove thence [a]the three sons[1121] of Anak, [b]Sheshai, and Ahiman, and Talmai, the children of Anak.

15 And [a]he went up thence to the inhabitants of Debir: and the name of Debir before *was* Kirjath–sepher.

16 [a]And Caleb said,[559] He that smiteth Kirjath–sepher, and taketh it, to him will I give Achsah my daughter to wife.[802]

17 And [a]Othniel the [b]son of Kenaz, the brother[251] of Caleb, took it: and he gave him Achsah his daughter to wife.

18 And [a]it came to pass, as she came *unto him,* that she moved him to ask[7592] of her father a field:[7704] and [b]she lighted off *her* ass; and Caleb said unto her, What wouldest thou?

19 Who answered,[559] Give me a [a]blessing;[1293] for thou hast given me a south land;[776] give me also springs of water. And he gave her the upper springs, and the nether[8482] springs.

20 This *is* the inheritance of the tribe of the children of Judah according to their families.

21 And the uttermost cities of the tribe of the children of Judah toward the coast of Edom southward were Kabzeel, and Eder, and Jagur,

22 And Kinah, and Dimonah, and Adadah,

23 And Kedesh, and Hazor, and Ithnan,

24 Ziph, and Telem, and Bealoth,

25 And Hazor, Hadattah, and Kerioth, *and* Hezron, which *is* Hazor,

26 Amam, and Shema, and Moladah,

27 And Hazar–gaddah, and Heshmon, and Beth–palet,

28 And Hazar–shual, and Beer–sheba, and Bizjothjah,

29 Baalah, and Iim, and Azem,

30 And Eltolad, and Chesil, and Hormah,

31 And [a]Ziklag, and Madmannah, and Sansannah.

32 And Lebaoth, and Shilhim, and Ain, and Rimmon: all the cities *are* twenty and nine, with their villages:[2691]

33 *And* in the valley, [a]Eshtaol, and Zoreah, and Ashnah,

34 And Zanoah, and En–gannim, Tappuah, and Enam,

35 Jarmuth, and Adullam, Socoh, and Azekah,

36 And Sharaim, and Adithaim, and Gederah, [I]and Gederothaim; fourteen cities with their villages:

37 Zenan, and Hadashah, and Migdal–gad,

38 And Dilean, and Mizpeh, [a]and Joktheel,

39 Lachish, and Bozkath, and Eglon,

40 And Cabbon, and Lahmam, and Kithlish,

41 And Gederoth, Beth–dagon, and Naamah, and Makkedah; sixteen cities with their villages:

42 Libnah, and Ether, and Ashan,

43 And Jiphtah, and Ashnah, and Nezib,

44 And Keilah, and Achzib, and Mareshah; nine cities with their villages:

45 Ekron, with her towns[1323] and her villages:

46 From Ekron even unto the sea, all that *lay* [I]near Ashdod, with their villages:

47 Ashdod with her towns and her villages, Gaza with her towns and her villages, unto [a]the river of Egypt, and [b]the great sea, and the border *thereof:*

10 [a]Gen. 38:13; Judg. 14:1
11 [a]Josh. 19:43
12 [a]Num. 34:6, 7; Josh. 15:47
13 [I]Or, *Kirjath-arba* [a]Josh. 14:13 [b]Josh. 14:15
14 [a]Judg. 1:10, 20 [b]Num. 13:22
15 [a]Josh. 10:38; Judg. 1:11
16 [a]Judg. 1:12
17 [a]Judg. 1:13; 3:9 [b]Num. 32:12; Josh. 14:6
18 [a]Judg. 1:14 [b]Gen. 24:64; 1Sam. 25:23
19 [a]Gen. 33:11
31 [a]1Sam. 27:6
33 [a]Num. 13:23
36 [I]Or, *or*
38 [a]2Kgs. 14:7
46 [I]Hebr. *by the place of*
47 [a]Josh. 15:4 [b]Num. 34:6

48 And in the mountains, Shamir,
and Jattir, and Socoh,
49 And Dannah, and Kirjath–sannah,
which *is* Debir,
50 And Anab, and Eshtemoh, and
Anim,
51 [a]And Goshen, and Holon, and
Giloh; eleven cities with their villages:
52 Arab, and Dumah, and Eshean,
53 And [I]Janum, and Beth–tappuah,
and Aphekah,
54 And Humtah, and [a]Kirjath–arba,
which *is* Hebron, and Zior; nine cities
with their villages:
55 Maon, Carmel, and Ziph, and
Juttah,
56 And Jezreel, and Jokdeam, and
Zanoah,
57 Cain, Gibeah, and Timnah; ten
cities with their villages:
58 Halhul, Beth–zur, and Gedor,
59 And Maarath, and Beth–anoth,
and Eltekon; six cities with their villages:
60 [a]Kirjath–baal, which *is* Kirjath–
jearim, and Rabbah; two cities with their
villages:
61 In the wilderness,[4057] Beth–
arabah, Middin, and Secacah,
62 And Nibshan, and the city of Salt,
and En–gedi; six cities with their villages.
63 As for the Jebusites the inhabitants of Jerusalem, [a]the children of Judah
could not drive them out: [b]but the
Jebusites dwell with the children of Judah
at Jerusalem unto this day.[3117]

Ephraim's and Manasseh's Portions

16 And the lot of the children[1121] of
Joseph [I]fell from Jordan by
Jericho, unto the water of Jericho on the
east, to the wilderness that goeth up from
Jericho throughout mount Bethel,
2 And goeth out from Bethel to [a]Luz,
and passeth along[5674] unto the borders of
Archi to Ataroth,
3 And goeth down westward to the
coast of Japhleti, [a]unto the coast of Beth–
horon the nether,[8481] and to [b]Gezer: and
the goings out thereof are at the sea.
4 [a]So the children of Joseph,
Manasseh and Ephraim, took their
inheritance.[5157]
5 And the border of the children of
Ephraim according to their families[4940]
was *thus:* even the border of their
inheritance[5159] on the east side was
[a]Ataroth–addar, [b]unto Beth–horon the
upper;[5945]
6 And the border went out toward
the sea to [a]Michmethah on the north side;
and the border went about eastward unto
Taanath–shiloh, and passed by[5674] it on
the east to Janohah;
7 And it went down from Janohah to
Ataroth, [a]and to Naarath, and came[6293] to
Jericho, and went out at Jordan.
8 The border went out from Tappuah
westward unto the [a]river Kanah; and the
goings out thereof were at the sea. This
is the inheritance of the tribe[4294] of the
children of Ephraim by their families.
9 And [a]the separate cities for the
children of Ephraim *were* among the inheritance of the children of Manasseh, all
the cities with their villages.
10 [a]And they drave not out the
Canaanites that dwelt in Gezer: but
the Canaanites dwell among[7130] the
Ephraimites unto this day, and serve[5647]
under tribute.

17 There was also a lot for the
tribe[4294] of Manasseh; for he *was*
the [a]firstborn of Joseph; *to wit,* for

51 [a]Josh. 10:41; 11:16
53 [I]Or, *Janus*
54 [a]Josh. 14:15; 15:13
60 [a]Josh. 18:14
63 [a]Judg. 1:8, 21; 2Sam. 5:6 [b]Judg. 1:21
1 [I]Hebr. *went forth*
2 [a]Josh. 18:13; Judg. 1:26
3 [a]Josh. 18:13; 2Chr. 8:5 [b]1Chr. 7:28; 1Kgs. 9:15
4 [a]Josh. 17:14
5 [a]Josh. 18:13 [b]2Chr. 8:5
6 [a]Josh. 17:7
7 [a]1Chr. 7:28
8 [a]Josh. 17:9
9 [a]Josh. 17:9
10 [a]Judg. 1:29; 1Kgs. 9:16
1 [a]Gen. 41:51; 46:20; 48:18

15:63 Jerusalem was located along the borders of the land that was allotted to both the tribe of Judah and the tribe of Benjamin (cf. Josh. 18:28). Both tribes attempted to drive out the Jebusites who inhabited the city, but they were unsuccessful on two consecutive campaigns (Judg. 1:8, 21). The city remained occupied by the Jebusites until David conquered them (2 Sam. 5:6–10).

16:2 The city of Bethel was formerly known as Luz (Gen. 28:19; Josh. 18:13; Judg. 1:23).

16:10 The city of Gezer was later conquered by the king of Egypt, who gave it to Solomon as a dowry (1 Kgs. 9:16).

[b]Machir the firstborn of Manasseh, the father[1] of Gilead: because he was a man[376] of war, therefore he had [c]Gilead and Bashan.

2 There was also *a lot* for [a]the rest[3498] of the children[1121] of Manasseh by their families;[4940] [b]for the children of [I]Abiezer, and for the children of Helek, [c]and for the children of Asriel, and for the children of Shechem, [d]and for the children of Hepher, and for the children of Shemida: these *were* the male[2145] children of Manasseh the son of Joseph by their families.

3 But [a]Zelophehad, the son of Hepher, the son of Gilead, the son of Machir, the son of Manasseh, had no sons,[1121] but daughters: and these *are* the names of his daughters, Mahlah, and Noah, Hoglah, Milcah, and Tirzah.

4 And they came near before [a]Eleazar the priest, and before Joshua the son of Nun, and before the princes,[5387] saying, [b]The LORD commanded[6680] Moses to give us an inheritance among our brethren.[251] Therefore according to the commandment[6310] of the LORD he gave them an inheritance among the brethren of their father.

5 And there fell[5307] ten portions[2256] to Manasseh, beside the land[776] of Gilead and Bashan, which *were* on the other side Jordan;

6 Because the daughters of Manasseh had an inheritance[5157] among his sons: and the rest of Manasseh's sons had the land of Gilead.

7 And the coast of Manasseh was from Asher to [a]Michmethah, that *lieth* before Shechem; and the border went along on the right hand unto the inhabitants of En–tappuah.

8 *Now* Manasseh had the land of Tappuah: but [a]Tappuah on the border of Manasseh *belonged* to the children of Ephraim;

9 And the coast descended [a]unto the [I]river Kanah, southward of the river: [b]these cities of Ephraim *are* among the cities of Manasseh: the coast of Manasseh also *was* on the north side of the river, and the outgoings of it were at the sea:

10 Southward *it was* Ephraim's, and northward *it was* Manasseh's, and the sea is his border; and they met together[6293] in Asher on the north, and in Issachar on the east.

11 [a]And Manasseh had in Issachar and in Asher [b]Beth–shean and her towns, and Ibleam and her towns, and the inhabitants of Dor and her towns, and the inhabitants of Endor and her towns, and the inhabitants of Taanach and her towns, and the inhabitants of Megiddo and her towns, *even* three countries.

12 Yet [a]the children of Manasseh could not drive out[3423] *the inhabitants of* those cities; but the Canaanites would dwell in that land.

13 Yet it came to pass, when the children of Israel were waxen strong,[2388] that they put the Canaanites to [a]tribute, but did not utterly drive them out.

14 [a]And the children of Joseph spake[1696] unto Joshua, saying, Why hast thou given me *but* [b]one lot and one portion to inherit, seeing I *am* [c]a great people,[5971] forasmuch as the LORD hath blessed[1288] me hitherto?

15 And Joshua answered[559] them, If thou *be* a great people, *then* get thee up to the wood *country,* and cut down for thyself there in the land of the Perizzites and of the [I]giants,[7497] if mount Ephraim be too narrow for thee.

16 And the children of Joseph said,[559] The hill is not enough for us: and all the Canaanites that dwell in the land of the valley have [a]chariots of iron, *both they* who *are* of Beth–shean and her towns, and *they* who *are* [b]of the valley of Jezreel.

1 [b]Gen. 50:23; Num. 26:29; 32:39, 40; 1Chr. 7:14 [c]Deut. 3:15
2 [I]Num. 26:30, *Jeezer* [a]Num. 26:29-32 [b]1Chr. 7:18 [c]Num. 26:31 [d]Num. 26:32
3 [a]Num. 26:33; 27:1; 36:2
4 [a]Josh. 14:1 [b]Num. 27:6, 7
7 [a]Josh. 16:6
8 [a]Josh. 16:8
9 [I]Or, *brook of reeds* [a]Josh. 16:8 [b]Josh. 16:9
11 [a]1Chr. 7:29 [b]1Sam. 31:10; 1Kgs. 4:12
12 [a]Judg. 1:27, 28
13 [a]Josh. 16:10
14 [a]Josh. 16:4 [b]Gen. 48:22 [c]Gen. 48:19; Num. 26:34, 37
15 [I]Or, *Rephaim*
16 [a]Judg. 1:19; 4:3 [b]Josh. 19:18; 1Kgs. 4:12

17:3 Approximately 400 years had elapsed between the lifetimes of Manasseh and the daughters of Zelophehad.

17 And Joshua spake[559] unto the
house[1004] of Joseph, *even* to Ephraim and
to Manasseh, saying, Thou *art* a great
people, and hast great power: thou shalt
not have one lot *only:*
18 But the mountain shall be thine;
for it *is* a wood, and thou shalt cut it
down: and the outgoings of it shall be
thine: for thou shalt drive out the
Canaanites, [a]though they have iron chariots, *and* though they *be* strong.[2389]

The Remaining Land Is Divided

18 And the whole congregation[5712] of the children of Israel
assembled together[6950] [a]at Shiloh, and
[b]set up[7931] the tabernacle[168] of the
congregation[4150] there. And the land[776]
was subdued before them.
2 And there remained[3498] among
the children of Israel seven tribes,[7626]
which had not yet received their inheritance.[5159]
3 And Joshua said[559] unto the children of Israel, [a]How long *are* ye slack[7503]
to go to possess[3423] the land, which the
LORD God[430] of your fathers[1] hath given
you?
4 Give out from among you three
men[582] for *each* tribe: and I will send
them, and they shall rise, and go through
the land, and describe it according to the
inheritance of them; and they shall come
again to me.
5 And they shall divide it into seven
parts: [a]Judah shall abide in their coast on
the south, and [b]the house of Joseph shall
abide in their coasts on the north.
6 Ye shall therefore describe the land
into seven parts, and bring *the description* hither to me, [a]that I may cast[3384]
lots for you here before the LORD our
God.
7 [a]But the Levites have no part
among[7130] you; for the priesthood[3550] of
the LORD *is* their inheritance: [b]and Gad,
and Reuben, and half the tribe of
Manasseh, have received their inheritance beyond Jordan on the east, which
Moses the servant[5650] of the LORD gave
them.
8 And the men arose, and went
away: and Joshua charged[6680] them that
went to describe the land, saying, Go and
walk through the land, and describe it,
and come again[7725] to me, that I may
here cast lots for you before the LORD in
Shiloh.
9 And the men went and passed
through[5674] the land, and described[3789] it
by cities into seven parts in a book,[5612]
and came *again* to Joshua to the host[4264]
at Shiloh.
10 And Joshua cast lots for them in
Shiloh before the LORD: and there Joshua
divided the land unto the children of
Israel according to their divisions.

Benjamin's Portion

11 And the lot of the tribe[4294] of
the children of Benjamin came up[5927]
according to their families:[4940] and the
coast of their lot came forth between the
children of Judah and the children of
Joseph.
12 [a]And their border on the north
side was from Jordan; and the border
went up[5927] to the side of Jericho on the
north side, and went up through the
mountains westward; and the goings out
thereof were at the wilderness of Beth–
aven.
13 And the border went over[5674]
from thence toward Luz, to the side of
Luz, [a]which *is* Bethel, southward; and the
border descended to Ataroth–adar, near

18 [a]Deut. 20:1

1 [a]Josh. 19:51; 21:2; 22:9; Jer. 7:12 [b]Judg. 18:31; 1Sam. 1:3, 24; 4:3, 4

3 [a]Judg. 18:9

5 [a]Josh. 15:1 [b]Josh. 16:1, 4

6 [a]Josh. 14:2; 18:10

7 [a]Josh. 13:33 [b]Josh. 13:8

12 [a]Josh. 16:1

13 [a]Gen. 28:19; Judg. 1:23

18:1 The Tabernacle had been standing at Gilgal. Shiloh was a strategic site in the hill country which could be defended better, and it was more centrally located for all the tribes. Israel was a large, religious congregation, not just a nation. This holy tent was of natural importance to them because it was where they met with God (Ex. 29:42–46).

18:7 The Levites were scattered throughout the Israelites in order to minister to them.

the hill that *lieth* on the south side [b]of the
nether[8481] Beth–horon.
14 And the border was drawn *thence,*
and compassed the corner of the sea
southward, from the hill that *lieth* before Beth–horon southward; and the goings out thereof were at [a]Kirjath–baal,
which *is* Kirjath–jearim, a city of the
children of Judah: this *was* the west quarter.
15 And the south quarter *was* from
the end of Kirjath–jearim, and the border
went out on the west, and went out to
[a]the well of waters of Nephtoah:
16 And the border came down to the
end of the mountain that *lieth* before [a]the
valley of the son[1121] of Hinnom, *and*
which *is* in the valley of the giants[7497]
on the north, and descended to the
valley of Hinnom, to the side of Jebusi
on the south, and descended to [b]En–
rogel,
17 And was drawn from the north,
and went forth to En–shemesh, and went
forth toward Geliloth, which *is* over
against the going up of Adummim, and
descended to [a]the stone of Bohan the son
of Reuben,
18 And passed along[5674] toward the
side over against [Ia]Arabah northward,
and went down unto Arabah:
19 And the border passed along
to the side of Beth–hoglah northward:
and the outgoings of the border were
at the north [I]bay of the salt sea at the
south end of Jordan: this *was* the south
coast.
20 And Jordan was the border of it
on the east side. This *was* the inheritance
of the children of Benjamin, by the
coasts thereof round about, according to
their families.
21 Now the cities of the tribe of the
children of Benjamin according to their
families were Jericho, and Beth–hoglah,
and the valley of Keziz,
22 And Beth–arabah, and Zemaraim,
and Bethel,
23 And Avim, and Parah, and
Ophrah,
24 And Chephar–haammonai, and
Ophni, and Gaba; twelve cities with their
villages:[2691]
25 Gibeon, and Ramah, and Beeroth,
26 And Mizpeh, and Chephirah, and
Mozah,
27 And Rekem, and Irpeel, and
Taralah,
28 And Zelah, Eleph, and [a]Jebusi,
which *is* Jerusalem, Gibeath, *and* Kirjath;
fourteen cities with their villages. This
is the inheritance of the children of
Benjamin according to their families.

Simeon's Portion

19 🗝 And the second lot came
forth to Simeon, *even* for the tribe
of the children[1121] of Simeon according
to their families:[4940] [a]and their inheritance
was within the inheritance of the children
of Judah.
2 And [a]they had in their inheritance Beer–sheba, or Sheba, and
Moladah,
3 And Hazar–shual, and Balah, and
Azem,
4 And Eltolad, and Bethul, and
Hormah,
5 And Ziklag, and Beth–marcaboth,
and Hazar–susah,
6 And Beth–lebaoth, and Sharuhen;
thirteen cities and their villages:
7 Ain, Remmon, and Ether, and
Ashan; four cities and their villages:
8 And all the villages that *were*
round about these cities to Baalath–beer,
Ramath of the south. This *is* the inheri-

13 [b]Josh. 16:3
14 [a]Josh. 15:9
15 [a]Josh. 15:9
16 [a]Josh. 15:8 [b]Josh. 15:7
17 [a]Josh. 15:6
18 [I]Or, *The plain* [a]Josh. 15:6
19 [I]Hebr. *tongue*
28 [a]Josh. 15:8
1 [a]Josh. 19:9
2 [a]1Chr. 4:28

🗝 **19:1–9** Simeon's allotment was in the extreme south in the territory which was already given to Judah, because Judah was not large enough to fill all of her land. This had consequences for later times. During the period of the divided monarchy, although the tribe of Simeon was politically a part of the ten tribes of Israel, the tribe's proximity to Judah led to its eventual assimilation into Judah.

tance of the tribe of the children of Simeon according to their families.

9 Out of the portion of the children of Judah *was* the inheritance[5159] of the children of Simeon: for the part of the children of Judah was too much for them: [a]therefore the children of Simeon had their inheritance[5157] within the inheritance of them.

Zebulun's Portion

10 And the third lot came up[5927] for the children of Zebulun according to their families: and the border of their inheritance was unto Sarid:

11 [a]And their border went up[5927] toward the sea, and Maralah, and reached[6293] to Dabbasheth, and reached to the river that *is* [b]before Jokneam;

12 And turned from Sarid eastward toward the sunrising unto the border of Chisloth–tabor, and then goeth out to Daberath, and goeth up to Japhia,

13 And from thence passeth on[5674] along on the east to Gittah–hepher, to Ittah–kazin, and goeth out to Remmon–[I]methoar to Neah;

14 And the border compasseth it on the north side to Hannathon: and the outgoings thereof are in the valley of Jiphthah–el:

15 And Kattath, and Nahallal, and Shimron, and Idalah, and Bethlehem: twelve cities with their villages.

16 This *is* the inheritance of the children of Zebulun according to their families, these cities with their villages.

Issachar's Portion

17 *And* the fourth lot came out to Issachar, for the children of Issachar according to their families.

18 And their border was toward Jezreel, and Chesulloth, and Shunem,

19 And Haphraim, and Shion, and Anaharath,

20 And Rabbith, and Kishion, and Abez,

21 And Remeth, and En–gannim, and En–haddah, and Beth–pazzez;

22 And the coast reacheth[6293] to Tabor, and Shahazimah, and Beth–shemesh; and the outgoings of their border were at Jordan: sixteen cities with their villages.

23 This *is* the inheritance of the tribe of the children of Issachar according to their families, the cities and their villages.

Asher's Portion

24 And the fifth lot came out for the tribe of the children of Asher according to their families.

25 And their border was Helkath, and Hali, and Beten, and Achshaph,

26 And Alammelech, and Amad, and Misheal; and reacheth to Carmel westward, and to Shihor–libnath;

27 And turneth[7725] toward the sunrising to Beth–dagon, and reacheth to Zebulun, and to the valley of Jiphthah–el toward the north side of Beth–emek, and Neiel, and goeth out to Cabul on the left hand,

28 And Hebron, and Rehob, and Hammon, and Kanah, [a]*even* unto great Zidon;

29 And *then* the coast[2256] turneth to Ramah, and to the strong city [I]Tyre; and the coast turneth to Hosah; and the outgoings thereof are at the sea from the coast to [a]Achzib:

30 Ummah also, and Aphek, and Rehob; twenty and two cities with their villages.

31 This *is* the inheritance of the tribe of the children of Asher according to their families, these cities with their villages.

Naphtali's Portion

32 The sixth lot came out to the children of Naphtali, *even* for the children of Naphtali according to their families.

33 And their coast was from Heleph, from Allon to Zaanannim, and Adami, Nekeb, and Jabneel, unto Lakum; and the outgoings thereof were at Jordan:

34 And *then* [a]the coast turneth westward to Aznoth–tabor, and goeth out

9 [a]Josh. 19:1

11 [a]Gen. 49:13 [b]Josh. 12:22

13 [I]Or, *which is drawn*

28 [a]Josh. 11:8; Judg. 1:31

29 [I]Hebr. *Tzor* [a]Gen. 38:5; Judg. 1:31; Mic. 1:14

34 [a]Deut. 33:23

from thence to Hukkok, and reacheth to Zebulun on the south side, and reacheth to Asher on the west side, and to Judah upon Jordan toward the sunrising.

35 And the fenced[4013] cities *are* Ziddim, Zer, and Hammath, Rakkath, and Chinnereth,

36 And Adamah, and Ramah, and Hazor,

37 And Kedesh, and Edrei, and En–hazor,

38 And Iron, and Migdal–el, Horem, and Beth–anath, and Beth–shemesh; nineteen cities with their villages.

39 This *is* the inheritance of the tribe of the children of Naphtali according to their families, the cities and their villages.

Dan's Portion

40 *And* the seventh lot came out for the tribe of the children of Dan according to their families.

41 And the coast of their inheritance was Zorah, and Eshtaol, and Ir–shemesh,

42 And [a]Shaalabbin, and Ajalon, and Jethlah,

43 And Elon, and Thimnathah, and Ekron,

44 And Eltekeh, and Gibbethon, and Baalath,

45 And Jehud, and Bene–berak, and Gath–rimmon,

46 And Me–jarkon, and Rakkon, with the border[1366] [I]before [II]Japho.

47 And the coast of the children of Dan went out *too little* for them: therefore the children of Dan went up to fight against Leshem, and took it, and smote[5221] it with the edge[6310] of the sword,[2719] and possessed[3423] it, and dwelt therein, and called[7121] Leshem, [a]Dan, after the name of Dan their father.[1]

48 This *is* the inheritance of the tribe of the children of Dan according to their families, these cities with their villages.

Joshua's Portion

49 When they had made an end[3615] of dividing the land[776] for inheritance by their coasts, the children of Israel gave an inheritance to Joshua the son[1121] of Nun among them:

50 According to the word of the LORD they gave him the city which he asked,[7592] *even* [a]Timnath–[b]serah in mount Ephraim: and he built the city, and dwelt therein.

51 [a]These *are* the inheritances, which Eleazar the priest, and Joshua the son of Nun, and the heads[7218] of the fathers[1] of the tribes[4294] of the children of Israel, divided for an inheritance by lot [b]in Shiloh before the LORD, at the door of the tabernacle[168] of the congregation. So they made an end of dividing the country.[776]

The Cities of Refuge

20 The LORD also spake[1696] unto Joshua, saying,

2 Speak to the children[1121] of Israel, saying, [a]Appoint out for you cities of

42 [a]Judg. 1:35
46 [I]Or, *over against* [II]Or, *Joppa*
47 [a]Judg. 18:29
50 [a]Josh. 24:30 [b]1Chr. 7:24
51 [a]Num. 34:17; Josh. 14:1 [b]Josh. 18:1, 10
2 [a]Ex. 21:13; Num. 35:6, 11, 14; Deut. 19:2, 9

19:40–48 Dan's inheritance was on the coastal plain south of the territory given to Ephraim, but she was unable to possess it. Therefore, the tribe took the city of Leshem above the Sea of Galilee in the extreme north and settled it and the surrounding territory (Judg. 18:27–29). The tribe renamed the city "Dan," and it became a popular designation of the northern extremity of Israel (note the phrase "from Dan to Beersheba" in Judg. 20:1).

19:49, 50 There is no information in the Book of Numbers regarding a special allotment for Joshua, as is done for Caleb (Num. 14:6–9, 24; Josh. 14:6–15). The name of the city given Joshua was Timnath-serah which means "abundant or extra portion." In Judges 2:9 the Septuagint and the KJV call it Timnath-heres which means "portion of the sun" (Judg. 2:9). Ancient tradition says this new name was given to commemorate Joshua's calling on God to make the sun to stand still (Josh. 10:12–14). Others believe that "heres" is a scribal error, "serah" written backwards.

20:2–4 See note on Deuteronomy 19:1–10 on the "cities of refuge."

refuge, whereof I spake unto you by the hand[3027] of Moses:

3 That the slayer[7523] that killeth[5221] *any* person[5315] unawares[7684] *and* unwittingly[1097,1847] may flee thither: and they shall be your refuge from the avenger[1350] of blood.[1818]

4 And when he that doth flee unto one of those cities shall stand at the entering of [a]the gate of the city, and shall declare[1696] his cause[1697] in the ears[241] of the elders[2205] of that city, they shall take him into the city unto them, and give him a place, that he may dwell among them.

5 [a]And if the avenger of blood pursue after him, then they shall not deliver the slayer up into his hand; because he smote[5221] his neighbour unwittingly, and hated[8130] him not beforetime.

6 And he shall dwell in that city, [a]until he stand before the congregation[5712] for judgment,[4941] *and* until the death[4194] of the high priest that shall be in those days:[3117] then shall the slayer return,[7725] and come unto his own city, and unto his own house,[1004] unto the city from whence he fled.

7 And they [I]appointed[6942] [a]Kedesh in Galilee in mount Naphtali, and [b]Shechem in mount Ephraim, and [c]Kirjath–arba, which *is* Hebron, in [d]the mountain of Judah.

8 And on the other side Jordan by Jericho eastward, they assigned [a]Bezer in the wilderness upon the plain out of the tribe of Reuben, and [b]Ramoth in Gilead out of the tribe of Gad, and [c]Golan in Bashan out of the tribe of Manasseh.

9 [a]These were the cities appointed for all the children of Israel, and for the stranger[1616] that sojourneth[1481] among them, that whosoever killeth *any* person at unawares might flee thither, and not die[4191] by the hand of the avenger of blood, [b]until he stood before the congregation.

4 [a]Ruth 4:1, 2

5 [a]Num. 35:12

6 [a]Num. 35:12, 25

7 [I]Hebr. *sanctified* [a]Josh. 21:32; 1Chr. 6:76 [b]Josh. 21:21; 2Chr. 10:1 [c]Josh. 14:15; 21:11, 13 [d]Luke 1:39

8 [a]Deut. 4:43; Josh. 21:36; 1Chr. 6:78 [b]Josh. 21:38; 1Kgs. 22:3 [c]Josh. 21:27 [a]Num. 35:15 [b]Josh. 20:6

1 [a]Josh. 14:1; 17:4

2 [a]Josh. 18:1 [b]Num. 35:2

4 [a]Josh. 21:8, 19 [b]Josh. 24:33

5 [a]Josh. 21:20-26

6 [a]Josh. 21:27-33

7 [a]Josh. 21:34-42

8 [a]Josh. 21:3

The Levites' Cities

21 Then came near[5066] the heads[7218] of the fathers[1] of the Levites unto [a]Eleazar the priest, and unto Joshua the son[1121] of Nun, and unto the heads of the fathers of the tribes of the children[1121] of Israel;

🔑 2 And they spake[1696] unto them at [a]Shiloh in the land[776] of Canaan, saying, [b]The LORD commanded[6680] by the hand[3027] of Moses to give us cities to dwell in, with the suburbs thereof for our cattle.

3 And the children of Israel gave unto the Levites out of their inheritance,[5159] at the commandment[6310] of the LORD, these cities and their suburbs.

4 And the lot came out for the families[4940] of the Kohathites: and [a]the children of Aaron the priest, *which were* of the Levites, [b]had by lot out of the tribe of Judah, and out of the tribe of Simeon, and out of the tribe of Benjamin, thirteen cities.

5 And [a]the rest[3498] of the children of Kohath *had* by lot out of the families of the tribe of Ephraim, and out of the tribe of Dan, and out of the half tribe of Manasseh, ten cities.

6 And [a]the children of Gershon *had* by lot out of the families of the tribe of Issachar, and out of the tribe of Asher, and out of the tribe of Naphtali, and out of the half tribe of Manasseh in Bashan, thirteen cities.

7 [a]The children of Merari by their families *had* out of the tribe of Reuben, and out of the tribe of Gad, and out of the tribe of Zebulun, twelve cities.

8 [a]And the children of Israel gave by lot unto the Levites these cities with their

---

🔑 **21:2** These were cities that the children of Israel gave to the Levites so they would have places to live and raise cattle (v. 3). There was a total of forty-eight cities which were given to the tribe of Levi and distributed throughout the land so there would be four cities for each tribe of Israel.

suburbs,[4054] [b]as the LORD commanded by the hand of Moses.

9 And they gave out of the tribe of the children of Judah, and out of the tribe of the children of Simeon, these cities which are *here* [I]mentioned by name,

10 [a]Which the children of Aaron, *being* of the families of the Kohathites, *who were* of the children of Levi, had: for theirs was the first[7223] lot.

11 [a]And they gave them [I]the city of Arba the father[1] of [b]Anak, which *city is* Hebron, [c]in the hill *country* of Judah, with the suburbs thereof round about it.

12 But [a]the fields[7704] of the city, and the villages thereof, gave they to Caleb the son of Jephunneh for his possession.[272]

13 Thus [a]they gave to the children of Aaron the priest [b]Hebron with her suburbs, *to be* a city of refuge for the slayer;[7523] [c]and Libnah with her suburbs,

14 And [a]Jattir with her suburbs, [b]and Eshtemoa with her suburbs,

15 And [a]Holon with her suburbs, [b]and Debir with her suburbs,

16 And [a]Ain with her suburbs, [b]and Juttah with her suburbs, *and* [c]Beth–shemesh with her suburbs; nine cities out of those two tribes.[7626]

17 And out of the tribe of Benjamin, [a]Gibeon with her suburbs, [b]Geba with her suburbs,

🗝 18 Anathoth with her suburbs, and [a]Almon with her suburbs; four cities.

19 All the cities of the children of Aaron, the priests,[3548] *were* thirteen cities with their suburbs.

20 [a]And the families of the children of Kohath, the Levites which remained[3498] of the children of Kohath, even they had the cities of their lot out of the tribe of Ephraim.

21 For they gave them [a]Shechem with her suburbs in mount Ephraim, *to be* a city of refuge for the slayer; and Gezer with her suburbs,

22 And Kibzaim with her suburbs, and Beth–horon with her suburbs; four cities.

23 And out of the tribe of Dan, Eltekeh with her suburbs, Gibbethon with her suburbs,

24 Aijalon with her suburbs, Gath–rimmon with her suburbs; four cities.

25 And out of the half tribe of Manasseh, Tanach with her suburbs, and Gath–rimmon with her suburbs; two cities.

26 All the cities *were* ten with their suburbs for the families of the children of Kohath that remained.

27 [a]And unto the children of Gershon, of the families of the Levites, out of the *other* half tribe of Manasseh *they gave* [b]Golan in Bashan with her suburbs, *to be* a city of refuge for the slayer;[7523] and Beesh–terah with her suburbs; two cities.

28 And out of the tribe of Issachar, Kishon with her suburbs, Dabareh with her suburbs,

29 Jarmuth with her suburbs, En–gannim with her suburbs; four cities.

30 And out of the tribe of Asher, Mishal with her suburbs, Abdon with her suburbs,

31 Helkath with her suburbs, and Rehob with her suburbs; four cities.

32 And out of the tribe of Naphtali, [a]Kedesh in Galilee with her suburbs, *to be* a city of refuge[4733] for the slayer; and Hammoth–dor with her suburbs, and Kartan with her suburbs; three cities.

33 All the cities of the Gershonites according to their families *were* thirteen cities with their suburbs.

34 [a]And unto the families of the children of Merari, the rest of the Levites, out of the tribe of Zebulun, Jokneam with her suburbs,[4054] and Kartah with her suburbs,

8 [b]Num. 35:2
9 [I]Hebr. *called*
10 [a]Josh. 21:4
11 [I]Or, *Kirjath-arba* [a]1Chr. 6:55 [b]Josh. 15:13, 14 [c]Josh. 20:7; Luke 1:39
12 [a]Josh. 14:14; 1Chr. 6:56
13 [a]1Chr. 6:57 [b]Josh. 15:54; 20:7 [c]Josh. 15:42
14 [a]Josh. 15:48 [b]Josh. 15:50
15 [a]Josh. 15:51; 1Chr. 6:58, *Hillen* [b]Josh. 15:49
16 [a]Josh. 15:42; 1Chr. 6:59, *Ashan* [b]Josh. 15:55 [c]Josh. 15:10
17 [a]Josh. 18:25 [b]Josh. 18:24, *Gaba*
18 [a]1Chr. 6:60, *Alemeth*
20 [a]Josh. 21:5; 1Chr. 6:66
21 [a]Josh. 20:7
27 [a]Josh. 21:6; 1Chr. 6:71 [b]Josh. 20:8
32 [a]Josh. 20:7
34 [a]Josh. 21:7; 1Chr. 6:77

🗝 **21:18** See note on Jeremiah 1:1, regarding Anathoth.

35 Dimnah with her suburbs, Nahalal
with her suburbs; four cities.
36 And out of the tribe of Reuben,
[a]Bezer with her suburbs, and Jahazah
with her suburbs,
37 Kedemoth with her suburbs,
and Mephaath with her suburbs; four
cities.
38 And out of the tribe of Gad,
[a]Ramoth in Gilead with her suburbs, *to*
be a city of refuge for the slayer; and
Mahanaim with her suburbs,
39 Heshbon with her suburbs, Jazer
with her suburbs; four cities in all.
40 So all the cities for the children of
Merari by their families, which were remaining of the families of the Levites,
were *by* their lot twelve cities.
41 [a]All the cities of the Levites
within the possession of the children of
Israel *were* forty and eight cities with
their suburbs.
42 These cities were every one with
their suburbs round about them: thus
were all these cities.

Israel Settles the Land

43 And the LORD gave unto Israel [a]all
the land which he sware[7650] to give unto
their fathers; and they possessed[3423] it,
and dwelt therein.
44 [a]And the LORD gave them rest
round about, according to all that he
sware unto their fathers: and [b]there stood
not a man[376] of all their enemies before
them; the LORD delivered all their enemies into their hand.
45 [a]There failed[5307] not ought of any
good[2896] thing[1697] which the LORD had
spoken[1696] unto the house[1004] of Israel;
all came to pass.

Eastern Tribes Are Sent Home

22 Then Joshua called[7121] the
Reubenites, and the Gadites, and
the half tribe[4294] of Manasseh,
2 And said unto them, Ye have
kept[8104] [a]all that Moses the servant[5650] of
the LORD commanded[6680] you, [b]and have
obeyed[8085] my voice in all that I commanded you:
3 Ye have not left[5800] your
brethren[251] these many days[3117] unto this
day, but have kept the charge[4931] of the
commandment[6310] of the LORD your
God.[430]
4 And now the LORD your God
hath given rest unto your brethren, as
he promised[1696] them: therefore now return ye, and get you unto your tents,[168]
and unto the land[776] of your possession,[272] [a]which Moses the servant of
the LORD gave you on the other side
Jordan.
5 But [a]take diligent heed to do[6213]
the commandment and the law,[8451] which
Moses the servant of the LORD
charged[6680] you, [b]to love[157] the LORD your
God, and to walk in all his ways,[1870] and
to keep[8104] his commandments, and to
cleave unto him, and to serve[5647] him
with all your heart[3824] and with all your
soul.[5315]
6 So Joshua [a]blessed[1288] them, and
sent them away: and they went unto their
tents.
7 Now to the *one* half of the tribe[7626]
of Manasseh Moses had given *possession*
in Bashan: [a]but unto the *other* half
thereof gave Joshua among their brethren
on this side Jordan westward. And when
Joshua sent them away also unto their
tents, then he blessed them,
8 And he spake[559] unto them, saying,
Return[7725] with much riches unto your
tents, and with very much cattle, with silver, and with gold, and with brass, and
with iron, and with very much raiment:
[a]divide the spoil of your enemies with
your brethren.
9 And the children[1121] of Reuben
and the children of Gad and the half
tribe of Manasseh returned, and departed
from the children of Israel out of Shiloh,
which *is* in the land of Canaan, to go
unto [a]the country[776] of Gilead, to the
land of their possession, whereof they
were possessed,[3423] according to the
word of the LORD by the hand[3027] of
Moses.

36 [a]Josh. 20:8
38 [a]Josh. 20:8
41 [a]Num. 35:7
43 [a]Gen. 13:15; 15:18; 26:3; 28:4, 13
44 [a]Josh. 11:23; 22:4 [b]Deut. 7:24
45 [a]Josh. 23:14
2 [a]Num. 32:20; Deut. 3:18 [b]Josh. 1:16, 17
4 [a]Num. 32:33; Deut. 29:8; Josh. 13:8
5 [a]Deut. 6:6, 17; 11:22 [b]Deut. 10:12
6 [a]Gen. 47:7; Ex. 39:43; Josh. 14:13; 2Sam. 6:18; Luke 24:50
7 [a]Josh. 17:5
8 [a]Num. 31:27; 1Sam. 30:24
9 [a]Num. 32:1, 26, 29

⊶10 And when they came unto the borders of Jordan, that *are* in the land of Canaan, the children of Reuben and the children of Gad and the half tribe of Manasseh built there an altar[4196] by Jordan, a great altar to see to.

11 And the children of Israel [a]heard[8085] say,[559] Behold, the children of Reuben and the children of Gad and the half tribe of Manasseh have built an altar over against the land of Canaan, in the borders of Jordan, at the passage of the children of Israel.

12 And when the children of Israel heard *of it,* [a]the whole congregation[5712] of the children of Israel gathered themselves together[6950] at Shiloh, to go up[5927] to war[6635] aganst them.

13 And the children of Israel [a]sent unto the children of Reuben, and to the children of Gad, and to the half tribe of Manasseh, into the land of Gilead, [b]Phinehas the son[1121] of Eleazar the priest,

14 And with him ten princes,[5387] of each [I]chief house[1004] a prince throughout all the tribes[4294] of Israel; and [a]each one[376] *was* an head[7218] of the house of their fathers[1] among the thousands[505] of Israel.

15 And they came unto the children of Reuben, and to the children of Gad, and to the half tribe of Manasseh, unto the land of Gilead, and they spake[1696] with them, saying,

⊶16 Thus saith[559] the whole congregation of the LORD, What trespass[4604] *is* this that ye have committed against the God of Israel, to turn away[7725] this day from following the LORD, in that ye have builded you an altar,[4196] [a]that ye might rebel[4775] this day against the LORD?

17 *Is* the iniquity[5771] [a]of Peor too little for us, from which we are not cleansed[2891] until this day, although there was a plague[5063] in the congregation of the LORD,

18 But that ye must turn away this day from following the LORD? and it will be, *seeing* ye rebel to day[3117] against the LORD, that to morrow [a]he will be wroth with the whole congregation of Israel.

19 Notwithstanding, if the land of your possession *be* unclean,[2931] *then* pass ye over unto the land of the possession of the LORD, [a]wherein the LORD's tabernacle[4908] dwelleth,[7931] and take possession among us: but rebel not against the LORD, nor rebel against us, in building you an altar[4196] beside the altar of the LORD our God.

20 [a]Did not Achan the son of Zerah commit a trespass in the accursed thing,[2764] and wrath[7110] fell[1961] on all the congregation of Israel? and that man[376] perished[1478] not alone in his iniquity.

21 Then the children of Reuben and the children of Gad and the half tribe of Manasseh answered, and said[1696] unto the heads[7218] of the thousands of Israel,

22 The LORD [a]God[410] of gods,[430] the LORD God of gods, he [b]knoweth, and Israel he shall know;[3045] if *it be* in rebellion,[4777] or if in transgression[4604] against the LORD, (save[3467] us not this day,)

23 That we have built us an altar[4196] to turn from following the LORD, or if to offer thereon burnt offering[5930] or meat offering,[4503] or if to offer[6213] peace offerings[8002] thereon, let the LORD himself [a]require *it;*

24 And if we have not *rather* done[6213] it for fear[1674] of *this* thing,[1697] saying, [I]In time to come your children might speak[559] unto our children, saying, What have ye to do with the LORD God of Israel?

25 For the LORD hath made Jordan a border between us and you, ye children of Reuben and children of Gad; ye have

11 [a]Deut. 13:12; Judg. 20:12
12 [a]Judg. 20:1
13 [a]Deut. 13:14; Judg. 20:12 [b]Ex. 6:25; Num. 25:7
14 [I]Hebr. *house of the father* [a]Num. 1:4
16 [a]Lev. 17:8, 9; Deut. 12:13, 14
17 [a]Num. 25:3, 4; Deut. 4:3
18 [a]Num. 16:22
19 [a]Josh. 18:1
20 [a]Josh. 7:1, 5
22 [a]Deut. 10:17 [b]1Kgs. 8:39; Job 10:7; 23:10; Ps. 44:21; 139:1, 2; Jer. 12:3; 2Cor. 11:11, 31
23 [a]Deut. 18:19; 1Sam. 20:16
24 [I]Hebr. *Tomorrow*

⊶ **22:10, 16** The word that is translated "altar" in these verses should have been rendered "monument." When the tribes of Reuben, Gad and the half-tribe of Manasseh returned to the east side of the Jordan River, they built a monument for a testimony to God of all that He had done for them (see vv. 21–29).

no part in the LORD: so shall your children make our children cease[7673] from fearing[3372] the LORD.

26 Therefore we said, Let us now prepare to build us an altar, not for burnt offering, nor for sacrifice:[2077]

27 But *that* it *may be* [a]a witness between us, and you, and our generations[1755] after us, that we might [b]do[5647] the service[5656] of the LORD before him with our burnt offerings, and with our sacrifices,[2077] and with our peace offerings; that your children may not say to our children in time to come, Ye have no part in the LORD.

28 Therefore said we, that it shall be, when they should *so* say to us or to our generations in time to come, that we may say *again,* Behold[7200] the pattern of the altar[4196] of the LORD, which our fathers made, not for burnt offerings, nor for sacrifices; but it *is* a witness between us and you.

29 God forbid that we should rebel against the LORD, and turn this day from following the LORD, [a]to build an altar for burnt offerings, for meat offerings,[4503] or for sacrifices, beside the altar of the LORD our God that *is* before his tabernacle.

30 And when Phinehas the priest, and the princes of the congregation and heads of the thousands of Israel which *were* with him, heard the words[1697] that the children of Reuben and the children of Gad and the children of Manasseh spake, [I]it pleased them.

31 And Phinehas the son of Eleazar the priest said unto the children of Reuben, and to the children of Gad, and to the children of Manasseh, This day we perceive that the LORD *is* [a]among us, because ye have not committed this trespass against the LORD: [I]now ye have delivered[5337] the children of Israel out of the hand of the LORD.

32 And Phinehas the son of Eleazar the priest, and the princes, returned from the children of Reuben, and from the children of Gad, out of the land of Gilead, unto the land of Canaan, to the children of Israel, and brought them word[1697] again.

33 And the thing pleased the children of Israel; and the children of Israel [a]blessed God, and did not intend[559] to go up against them in battle,[6635] to destroy[7843] the land wherein the children of Reuben and Gad dwelt.

34 And the children of Reuben and the children of Gad called the altar[4196] *Ed:* for it *shall be* a witness between us that the LORD *is* God.

Joshua's Charge to the People

23 And it came to pass a long[7227] time[3117] after that the LORD [a]had given rest unto Israel from all their enemies round about, that Joshua [b]waxed old[2204] *and* [I]stricken in age.

2 And Joshua [a]called[7121] for all Israel, *and* for their elders,[2205] and for their heads,[7218] and for their judges,[8199] and for their officers,[7860] and said unto them, I am old *and* stricken in age:

3 And ye have seen[7200] all that the LORD your God[430] hath done unto all these nations[1471] because of you; for the [a]LORD your God *is* he that hath fought for you.

4 Behold,[7200] [a]I have divided unto you by lot these nations that remain, to be an inheritance[5159] for your tribes,[7626] from Jordan, with all the nations that I have cut off,[3772] even unto the great sea [I]westward.

5 And the LORD your God, [a]he shall expel them from before you, and drive them from out of your sight; and ye shall possess[3423] their land,[776] [b]as the LORD your God hath promised[1696] unto you.

6 [a]Be ye therefore very courageous[2388] to keep[8104] and to do[6213] all that is written in the book[5612] of the law[8451] of Moses, [b]that ye turn not aside therefrom *to* the right hand or *to* the left;

7 That ye [a]come not among these nations, these that remain among you; neither [b]make mention of[2142] the name of their gods,[430] nor cause to swear[7650] *by them,* neither serve[5647] them, nor bow yourselves unto them:

8 [I]But [a]cleave unto the LORD your God, as ye have done unto this day.

27 [a]Gen. 31:48; Josh. 22:34; 24:37 [b]Deut. 12:5, 6, 11, 12, 17, 18, 26, 27

29 [a]Deut. 12:13, 14

30 [I]Hebr. *it was good in their eyes*

31 [I]Hebr. *then* [a]Lev. 26:11, 12; 2Chr. 15:2

33 [a]1Chr. 29:20; Neh. 8:6; Dan. 2:19; Luke 2:28

1 [I]Hebr. *come into days* [a]Josh. 21:44; 22:4 [b]Josh. 13:1

2 [a]Deut. 31:28; Josh. 24:1; 1Chr. 28:1

3 [a]Ex. 14:14; Josh. 10:14, 42

4 [I]Hebr. *at the sunset* [a]Josh. 13:2, 6; 18:10

5 [a]Ex. 23:30; 33:2; 34:11; Deut. 11:23; Josh. 13:6 [b]Num. 33:53

6 [a]Josh. 1:7 [b]Deut. 5:32; 28:14

7 [a]Ex. 23:33; Deut. 7:2, 3; Prov. 4:14; Eph. 5:11 [b]Ex. 23:13; Num. 32:38; Ps. 16:4; Jer. 5:7; Zeph. 1:5

8 [I]Or, *For if ye will cleave* [a]Deut. 10:20; 11:22; 13:4; Josh. 22:5

9 [1][a]For the LORD hath driven out from before you great nations and strong: but *as for* you, [b]no man hath been able to stand before you unto this day.

10 [a]One man of you shall chase a thousand: for the LORD your God, he *it is* that fighteth for you, [b]as he hath promised you.

11 [a]Take good heed therefore unto [1]yourselves, that ye love[157] the LORD your God.

⊶ 12 Else if ye do in any wise [a]go back, and cleave unto the remnant[3499] of these nations, *even* these that remain among you, and shall [b]make marriages with them, and go in unto them, and they to you:

13 Know[3045] for a certainty that [a]the LORD your God will no more drive out *any of* these nations from before you; [b]but they shall be snares[6341] and traps[4170] unto you, and scourges[7850] in your sides, and thorns in your eyes, until ye perish[6] from off this good[2896] land[127] which the LORD your God hath given you.

14 And, behold, this day [a]I *am* going the way[1870] of all the earth:[776] and ye know in all your hearts[3824] and in all your souls,[5315] that [b]not one thing hath failed[5307] of all the good things which the LORD your God spake concerning you; all are come to pass unto you, *and* not one thing hath failed thereof.

15 [a]Therefore it shall come to pass, *that* as all good things are come upon you, which the LORD your God promised you; so shall the LORD bring upon you [b]all evil[7451] things, until he have destroyed[8045] you from off this good land which the LORD your God hath given you.

9 [1]Or, *Then the LORD will drive* [a]Deut. 11:23 [b]Josh. 1:5
10 [a]Lev. 26:8; Deut. 32:30; Judg. 3:31; 15:15; 2Sam. 23:8 [b]Ex. 14:14; 23:27; Deut. 3:22
11 [1]Hebr. *your souls* [a]Josh. 22:5
12 [a]Heb. 10:38, 39; 2Pet. 2:20, 21 [b]Deut. 7:3
13 [a]Judg. 2:3 [b]Ex. 23:33; Num. 33:55; Deut. 7:16; 1Kgs. 11:4
14 [a]1Kgs. 2:2; Heb. 9:27 [b]Josh. 21:45; Luke 21:33
15 [a]Deut. 28:63 [b]Lev. 26:16; Deut. 28:15, 16
1 [a]Gen. 35:4 [b]Josh. 23:2 [c]1Sam. 10:19
2 [a]Gen. 11:26, 31 [b]Gen. 31:53
3 [a]Gen. 12:1; Acts 7:2, 3 [b]Gen. 21:2, 3; Ps. 127:3
4 [a]Gen. 25:24-26 [b]Gen. 36:8; Deut. 2:5 [c]Gen. 46:1, 6; Acts 7:15
5 [a]Ex. 3:10

16 When ye have transgressed[5674] the covenant[1285] of the LORD your God, which he commanded[6680] you, and have gone and served[5647] other gods, and bowed[7812] yourselves to them; then shall[2734] the anger[639] of the LORD be kindled[2734] against you, and ye shall perish quickly from off the good land which he hath given unto you.

Joshua's Farewell Address at Shechem

24 ⊶ And Joshua gathered[622] all the tribes[7626] of Israel to [a]Shechem, and [b]called[7121] for the elders[2205] of Israel, and for their heads,[7218] and for their judges,[8199] and for their officers;[7860] and they [c]presented themselves before God.[430]

⊶ 2 And Joshua said unto all the people,[5971] Thus saith[559] the LORD God of Israel, [a]Your fathers[1] dwelt on the other side of the flood in old time, *even* Terah, the father of Abraham, and the father of Nachor: and [b]they served[5647] other gods.[430]

3 And [a]I took your father Abraham from the other side of the flood, and led him throughout all the land of Canaan, and multiplied his seed,[2233] and [b]gave him Isaac.

4 And I gave unto Isaac [a]Jacob and Esau: and I gave unto [b]Esau mount Seir, to possess[3423] it; [c]but Jacob and his children[1121] went down into Egypt.

5 [a]I sent Moses also and Aaron, and I plagued Egypt, according to that which I did among[7130] them: and afterward I brought you out.

⊶ **23:12–16** In the last two chapters of the book, Joshua addressed Israel twice. One of the features of this first speech was a stern warning about the consequences of apostasy. Although God intended to drive out the remaining Canaanites (Josh. 13:2–6), He would not do it if Israel was unfaithful to Him. The Book of Judges reveals the tragic story of Israel's infidelity and the consequences that followed.

⊶ **24:1** Shechem was a historic site for the people of Israel. It was there that the Lord first promised the land of Canaan to Abram (Gen. 12:6, 7), and where Jacob destroyed the idols which had been brought from Mesopotamia (Gen. 35:2–5).

⊶ **24:2** Actually, Terah had three sons (Gen. 11:27), but only Abraham and Nahor were mentioned because they were direct ancestors of Israel. Nahor was the grandfather of Rebekah, Isaac's wife (Gen. 22:20–23) and the great-grandfather of Rachel and Leah, who were Jacob's wives (Gen. 29:10, 16).

6 And I [a]brought your fathers out of Egypt: and [b]ye came unto the sea; [c]and the Egyptians pursued after your fathers with chariots and horsemen unto the Red sea.

7 And when they [a]cried unto the LORD, [b]he put darkness between you and the Egyptians, [c]and brought the sea upon them, and covered[3680] them; and [d]your eyes have seen[7200] what I have done in Egypt: and ye dwelt in the wilderness [e]a long[7227] season.[3117]

8 And I brought you into the land of the Amorites, which dwelt on the other side Jordan; [a]and they fought with you: and I gave them into your hand,[3027] that ye might possess their land; and I destroyed[8045] them from before you.

9 Then [a]Balak the son[1121] of Zippor, king of Moab, arose and warred against Israel, and [b]sent and called Balaam the son of Beor to curse[7043] you:

10 [a]But I would[14] not hearken[8085] unto Balaam; [b]therefore he blessed[1288] you still: so I delivered[5337] you out of his hand.

11 And [a]ye went over[5674] Jordan, and came unto Jericho: and [b]the men[1167] of Jericho fought against you, the Amorites, and the Perizzites, and the Canaanites, and the Hittites, and the Girgashites, the Hivites, and the Jebusites; and I delivered them into your hand.

12 And [a]I sent the hornet before you, which drave them out from before you, *even* the two kings[4428] of the Amorites; *but* [b]not with thy sword,[2719] nor with thy bow.

13 And I have given you a land for which ye did not labour, and [a]cities which ye built not, and ye dwell in them; of the vineyards and oliveyards which ye planted not do ye eat.

14 [a]Now therefore fear[3372] the LORD, and serve[5647] him in [b]sincerity[8549] and in truth:[571] and [c]put away[5493] the gods which your fathers served on the other side of the flood, and [d]in Egypt; and serve ye the LORD.

🔑 15 And if it seem evil[7489] unto you to serve the LORD, [a]choose[977] you this day[3117] whom ye will serve; whether [b]the gods which your fathers served that *were* on the other side of the flood, or [c]the gods of the Amorites, in whose land ye dwell: [d]but as for me and my house,[1004] we will serve the LORD.

16 And the people answered and said, God forbid that we should forsake[5800] the LORD, to serve other gods;

17 For the LORD our God, he *it is* that brought us up and our fathers out of the land of Egypt, from the house of bondage,[5650] and which did those great signs[226] in our sight, and preserved[8104] us in all the way[1870] wherein we went, and among all the people through[7130] whom we passed:[5674]

18 And the LORD drave out from before us all the people, even the Amorites which dwelt in the land: *therefore* will we also serve the LORD; for he *is* our God.

6 [a]Ex. 12:37, 51 [b]Ex. 14:2 [c]Ex. 14:9
7 [a]Ex. 14:10 [b]Ex. 14:20 [c]Ex. 14:27, 28 [d]Deut. 4:34; 29:2 [e]Josh. 5:6
8 [a]Num. 21:21, 33; Deut. 2:32; 3:1
9 [a]Judg. 11:25 [b]Num. 22:5; Deut. 23:4
10 [a]Deut. 23:5 [b]Num. 23:11, 20; 24:10
11 [a]Josh. 3:14, 17; 4:10, 11, 12 [b]Josh. 6:1; 10:1; 11:1
12 [a]Ex. 23:28; Deut. 7:20 [b]Ps. 44:3, 6
13 [a]Deut. 6:10, 11; Josh. 11:13
14 [a]Deut. 10:12; 1Sam. 12:24 [b]Gen. 17:1; 20:5; Deut. 18:13; Ps. 119:1; 2Cor. 1:12; Eph. 6:24 [c]Josh. 24:2, 23; Lev. 17:7; Ezek. 20:18 [d]Ezek. 20:7, 8; 23:3
15 [a]Ruth 1:15; 1Kgs. 18:21; Ezek. 20:39; John 6:67 [b]Josh. 24:14 [c]Ex. 23:24, 32, 33; 34:15; Deut. 13:7; 29:18; Judg. 6:10 [d]Gen. 18:19

🔑 **24:15, 16** This invitation of Joshua is similar to that extended by Moses to Israel on the other side of the Jordan (Deut. 30:15–20). He recognized that one can only serve God in sincerity and truth if he has freely and willingly pledged in his heart to do so. He summarizes the options that are open to Israel: (1) They could return to serve the gods of their ancestors. "On the other side of the flood" would be better translated "on the other side of the river," that is, the river Euphrates (the same meaning is true of vv. 2, 14). "The gods which your fathers served" is a reference to the ones that Terah, Abraham's father worshiped (see v. 2). These were similar to the "images" or "teraphim" which Laban called "his gods" (Gen. 31:19, 30, 34). Perhaps there were some people who secretly worshiped these gods among the children of Israel (see vv. 14–23). (2) They could serve the gods of the Amorites. Although the term "Amorites" referred to a specific people, it was also used in a generic sense for all people living in Canaan. Hence, the reference is made to Baalim and Ashteroth in Judges 10:6. (3) They could follow the example of Joshua and his family, that is, to serve the Lord. This statement of Joshua's stands as one of the greatest affirmations of faith in all the Bible.

19 And Joshua said unto the people,
[a]Ye cannot serve the LORD: for he *is* an
[b]holy[6918] God; he *is* [c]a jealous God;[410] [d]he
will not forgive[5375] your transgres-
sions[6588] nor your sins.
20 [a]If ye forsake the LORD, and serve
strange[5236] gods, [b]then he will turn[7725]
and do you hurt,[7489] and consume[3615]
you, after that he hath done you good.[3190]
21 And the people said unto Joshua,
Nay; but we will serve the LORD.
22 And Joshua said unto the people,
Ye *are* witnesses against yourselves that
[a]ye have chosen[977] you the LORD, to serve
him. And they said, *We are* witnesses.
23 Now therefore [a]put away, *said he,*
the strange gods which *are* among[7130]
you, and incline your heart[3824] unto the
LORD God of Israel.
24 And the people said unto Joshua,
The LORD our God will we serve, and his
voice will we obey.[8085]
25 So Joshua [a]made[3772] a covenant[1285] with the people that day, and
set[7760] them a statute[2706] and an ordinance[4941] [b]in Shechem.
26 And Joshua [a]wrote these
words[1697] in the book[5612] of the law[8451]
of God, and took [b]a great stone, and [c]set
it up there [d]under an oak, that *was* by the
sanctuary[4720] of the LORD.
27 And Joshua said unto all the people, Behold, this stone shall be [a]a
witness[5713] unto us; for [b]it hath heard[8085]
all the words[561] of the LORD which he
spake[1696] unto us: it shall be therefore a
witness unto you, lest ye deny your God.
28 So [a]Joshua let the people depart,
every man unto his inheritance.[5159]

The Leaders' Deaths

29 [a]And it came to pass after these
things, that Joshua the son of Nun, the
servant[5650] of the LORD, died,[4191] *being*
an hundred and ten years old.
30 And they buried[6912] him in the
border of his inheritance in [a]Timnath–
serah, which *is* in mount Ephraim, on the
north side of the hill of Gaash.
31 And [a]Israel served the LORD all
the days[3117] of Joshua, and all the days
of the elders that [I]overlived Joshua,
and which had [b]known[3045] all the
works of the LORD, that he had done for
Israel.
32 And [a]the bones[6106] of Joseph,
which the children of Israel brought up
out of Egypt, buried they in Shechem, in
a parcel of ground [b]which Jacob bought
of the sons[1121] of Hamor the father of
Shechem for an hundred [I]pieces of silver:
and it became the inheritance of the children of Joseph.
33 And Eleazar the son of Aaron
died; and they buried him in a hill *that*
pertained to [a]Phinehas his son, which
was given him in mount Ephraim.

19 [a]Matt. 6:24 [b]Lev. 19:2; 1Sam. 6:20; Ps. 99:5, 9; Isa. 5:16 [c]Ex. 20:5 [d]Ex. 23:21
20 [a]1Chr. 28:9; 2Chr. 15:2; Ezra 8:22; Isa. 1:28; 65:11, 12; Jer. 17:13 [b]Josh. 23:15; Isa. 63:10; Acts 7:42
22 [a]Ps. 119:173
23 [a]Gen. 35:2; Josh. 24:14; Judg. 10:16; 1Sam. 7:3
25 [a]Ex. 15:25; 2Kgs. 11:17 [b]Josh. 24:26
26 [a]Deut. 31:24 [b]Judg. 9:6 [c]Gen. 28:18; Josh. 4:3 [d]Gen. 35:4
27 [a]Gen. 31:48, 52; Deut. 31:19, 21, 26; Josh. 22:27, 28, 34 [b]Deut. 32:1
28 [a]Judg. 2:6
29 [a]Judg. 2:8
30 [a]Josh. 19:50; Judg. 2:9
31 [I]Hebr. *prolonged* their *days after Joshua* [a]Judg. 2:7 [b]Deut. 11:2; 31:13
32 [I]Or, *lambs* [a]Gen. 50:25; Ex. 13:19 [b]Gen. 33:19
33 [a]Ex. 6:25; Judg. 20:28

24:31 Moses had trained Joshua to be his successor, but Joshua and the elders of Israel failed to train their own successors, and to thoroughly ground new leaders in the faith of Israel. As a result, the next generation succumbed to Canaanite idolatry. God's people are always just one generation away from apostasy. Therefore, young people must be trained to walk in the fear of the Lord today so that they become the proper, godly leaders of tomorrow.

The Book of

JUDGES

"Judges" is the Hebrew term used to refer to those whom God raised up to lead His people during the period between the conquest of Canaan and the monarchy. There were thirteen judges during this period, but only eleven are mentioned in the Book of Judges (the ministries of Eli and Samuel are recorded in 1 Samuel). Although these eleven judges had a tremendous impact on the nation of Israel, none of them ruled over all of the twelve tribes. In fact, some of them were at work at the same time in different areas of the country. For this reason, the length of time that the judges ruled could not be arrived at by simply adding the number of years that each judge ruled. The most commonly accepted figure for this is 350 years (see note on Gen. 15:13–16).

The Book of Judges contains an introduction (chaps. 1, 2), narrative accounts of the judges who led the people (chaps. 3—16), and a conclusion which describes the social and spiritual state of the people (chaps. 17—21). The introduction and conclusion are not chronologically linked to the narrative accounts.

Samuel is considered the most likely one to have written the Book of Judges, and internal evidence points to its being written during his lifetime. It is inferred from the phrase, "in those days there was no king in Israel" (Judg. 17:6; 18:1; 19:1; 21:25), that at the time of the writing, there was a king. Thus, it is obvious that it was written after Saul took the throne. Also, one can be sure that this book was written before Solomon's reign because the Canaanites had not yet been driven out of Gezer (Judg. 1:29, cf. 1 Kgs. 9:16). Furthermore, it may be concluded that it was written before David conquered Jerusalem (Judg. 1:21, cf. 1 Chr. 11:4–7). This is supported by the implication in the Book of Judges that Sidon, rather than Tyre, was still considered the capital of Phoenicia (Judg. 1:31; 3:3; 10:6; 18:28, cf. 2 Sam. 5:11).

The Book of Judges recounts the sad events of Israel's apostasy. It was common in Israel during the time of the judges for every man to do "that which was right in his own eyes" (Judg. 17:6; 21:25). God had to remind them again and again that He was the one true God, because they repeatedly indulged in the idolatry and immorality of the Canaanites among whom they lived. The main section of the book reflects a cycle from which Israel seemed unable to escape—Israel falls into apostasy, God sends an oppressor, Israel repents, God sends a deliverer, there is peace and prosperity, and then Israel falls away again. During the times of "rest" that Israel experienced, the Lord caused Israel's enemies to fight among themselves.

Additional Land Is Conquered

1 🔑 Now after the death of Joshua it came to pass, that the children[1121] of Israel [a]asked[7592] the LORD, saying, Who shall go up[5927] for us against the Canaanites first, to fight against them?

2 And the LORD said,[559] [a]Judah shall go up: behold, I have delivered the land[776] into his hand.[3027]

3 And Judah said unto Simeon his brother, Come up with me into my lot, that we may fight against the Canaanites; and [a]I likewise will go with thee into thy lot. So Simeon went with him.

4 And Judah went up;[5927] and the LORD delivered the Canaanites and the Perizzites into their hand: and they slew[5221] of them in [a]Bezek ten thousand men.[376]

5 And they found Adoni–bezek in Bezek: and they fought against him, and

1 [a]Num. 27:21; 20:18
2 [a]Gen. 49:8
3 [a]Judg. 1:17
4 [a]1Sam. 11:8

🔑 **1:1** The phrase "asked the LORD" is found only in the books of Samuel and Judges. The civil ruler of Israel had the right to ask the high priest to consult the Urim and the Thummim for him (Num. 27:21). This was the means which God set up for the judges, and later the kings, to know His judgment on any particular matter.

they slew the Canaanites and the Perizzites.

6 But Adoni–bezek fled; and they pursued after him, and caught him, and cut off his thumbs and his great toes.

7 And Adoni–bezek said, Threescore and ten kings,[4428] having [I]their thumbs and their great toes cut off, [II]gathered[3950] *their meat* under my table: [a]as I have done,[6213] so God[430] hath requited[7999] me. And they brought him to Jerusalem, and there he died.

🗝 8 Now [a]the children of Judah had fought against Jerusalem, and had taken it, and smitten[5221] it with the edge[6310] of the sword,[2719] and set the city on fire.

9 [a]And afterward the children of Judah went down to fight against the Canaanites, that dwelt in the mountain, and in the south, and in the [I]valley.

10 And Judah went against the Canaanites that dwelt in Hebron: (now the name of Hebron before *was* [a]Kirjath–arba:) and they slew Sheshai, and Ahiman, and Talmai.

11 [a]And from thence he went against the inhabitants of Debir: and the name of Debir before *was* Kirjath–sepher:

12 [a]And Caleb said, He that smiteth Kirjath–sepher, and taketh it, to him will I give Achsah my daughter to wife.[802]

13 And Othniel the son[1121] of Kenaz, [a]Caleb's younger brother, took it: and he gave him Achsah his daughter to wife.

14 [a]And it came to pass, when she came *to him,* that she moved him to ask[7592] of her father[1] a field:[7704] and she lighted from off *her* ass; and Caleb said unto her, What wilt thou?

15 And she said unto him, [a]Give me a blessing:[1293] for thou has given me a south land; give me also springs of water. And Caleb gave her the upper springs and the nether[8482] springs.

16 [a]And the children of the Kenite, Moses' father in law, went up out [b]of the city of palm trees with the children of Judah into the wilderness of Judah, which *lieth* in the south of [c]Arad; [d]and they went and dwelt among the people.

17 [a]And Judah went with Simeon his brother, and they slew the Canaanites that inhabited Zephath, and utterly destroyed[2763] it. And the name of the city was called[7121] [b]Hormah.

18 Also Judah took [a]Gaza with the coast thereof, and Askelon with the coast thereof, and Ekron with the coast thereof.

19 And [a]the LORD was with Judah; and [I]he drave out *the inhabitants of* the mountain; but could not drive out the inhabitants of the valley, because they had [b]chariots of iron.

20 [a]And they gave Hebron unto Caleb, as Moses said:[1696] and he expelled[3423] thence the three sons[1121] of Anak.

21 [a]And the children of Benjamin did not drive out the Jebusites that inhabited Jerusalem; but the Jebusites dwell with the children of Benjamin in Jerusalem unto this day.[3117]

22 And the house of Joseph, they also went up against Bethel: [a]and the LORD *was* with them.

23 And the house of Joseph [a]sent to descry Bethel. (Now the name of the city before *was* [b]Luz.)

24 And the spies[8104] saw[7200] a man[376] come forth out of the city, and they said unto him, Shew[7200] us, we pray thee,[4994] the entrance into the city, and [a]we will shew[6213] thee mercy.[2617]

7 [I]Hebr. *the thumbs of their hands and of their feet* [II]Or, *gleaned* [a]Lev. 24:19; 1Sam. 15:33; James 2:13

8 [a]Josh. 15:63

9 [I]Or, *low country* [a]Josh. 10:36; 11:21; 15:13

10 [a]Josh. 14:15; 15:13, 14

11 [a]Josh. 15:15

12 [a]Josh. 15:16, 17

13 [a]Judg. 3:9

14 [a]Josh. 15:18, 19

15 [a]Gen. 33:11

16 [a]Judg. 4:11, 17; 1Sam. 15:6; 1Chr. 2:55; Jer. 35:2 [b]Deut. 34:3 [c]Num. 21:1 [d]Num. 10:32

17 [a]Judg. 1:3 [b]Num. 21:3; Josh. 19:4

18 [a]Josh. 11:22

19 [I]Or, *he possessed the mountain* [a]Judg. 1:2; 2Kgs. 18:7 [b]Josh. 17:16, 18

20 [a]Num. 14:24; Deut. 1:36; Josh. 14:9, 13; 15:13, 14

21 [a]Josh. 15:63; 18:28

22 [a]Judg. 1:19

23 [a]Josh. 2:1; 7:2; Judg. 18:2 [b]Gen. 28:19

24 [a]Josh. 2:12, 14

🗝 **1:8** The early history of the city of Jerusalem is not certain, because it was known by several different names during its history. Also, it is difficult to determine which name applied at what time. This city is called Salem in Psalm 76:2. Therefore, if the Salem mentioned in Genesis 14:18 is the same site, Melchizedek was one of its early kings. It did not become the capital of Israel until David drove out the Jebusites from the fortified southern hill known as Mount Zion (see note on 2 Sam. 5:6–10), because members of the tribe of Benjamin and the Jebusites are said to have "inhabited Jerusalem" together (Judg. 1:21).

25 And when he shewed[7200] them the entrance into the city, they smote[5221] the city with the edge of the sword; but they let go the man and all his family.[4940]

26 And the man went into the land of the Hittites, and built a city, and called the name thereof Luz: which *is* the name thereof unto this day.

Some Land Is Not Conquered

27 [a]Neither did Manasseh drive out *the inhabitants of* Beth–shean and her towns, nor Taanach and her towns, nor the inhabitants of Dor and her towns, nor the inhabitants of Ibleam and her towns, nor the inhabitants of Megiddo and her towns: but the Canaanites would dwell in that land.

28 And it came to pass, when Israel was strong,[2388] that they put the Canaanites to tribute, and did not utterly drive them out.

29 [a]Neither did Ephraim drive out the Canaanites that dwelt in Gezer; but the Canaanites dwelt in Gezer among[7130] them.

30 Neither did Zebulun drive out the inhabitants of Kitron, nor the [a]inhabitants of Nahalol; but the Canaanites dwelt among them, and became tributaries.

31 [a]Neither did Asher drive out the inhabitants of Accho, nor the inhabitants of Zidon, nor of Ahlab, nor of Achzib, nor of Helbah, nor of Aphik, nor of Rehob:

32 But the Asherites [a]dwelt among the Canaanites, the inhabitants of the land: for they did not drive them out.

33 [a]Neither did Naphtali drive out the inhabitants of Beth–shemesh, nor the inhabitants of Beth–anath; but he [b]dwelt among the Canaanites, the inhabitants of the land: nevertheless the inhabitants of Beth–shemesh and of Beth–anath [c]became tributaries unto them.

34 And the Amorites forced the children of Dan into the mountain: for they would not suffer them to come down to the valley:

35 But the Amorites would dwell in mount Heres [a]in Aijalon, and in Shaalbim: yet the hand of the house of Joseph [I]prevailed,[3513] so that they became tributaries.

36 And the coast of the Amorites *was* [a]from [I]the going up to Akrabbim, from the rock, and upward.

God Sends His Angel

2 And an [I]angel[4397] of the LORD came up[5927] from Gilgal [a]to Bochim, and said,[559] I made you to go up[5927] out of Egypt, and have brought you unto the land[776] which I sware[7650] unto your fathers;[1] and [b]I said, I will never break[6565] my covenant[1285] with you.

2 And [a]ye shall make no league[1285] with the inhabitants of this land; [b]ye shall throw down[5422] their altars:[4196] [c]but ye have not obeyed[8085] my voice: why have ye done[6213] this?

3 Wherefore I also said, I will not drive them out from before you; but they shall be [a]*as thorns* in your sides, and [b]their gods[430] shall be a [c]snare[4170] unto you.

4 And it came to pass, when the angel of the LORD spake[1696] these words[1697] unto all the children of Israel, that the people lifted up[5375] their voice, and wept.

5 And they called[7121] the name of that place [I]Bochim: and they sacrificed[2076] there unto the LORD.

Joshua's Death

6 And when [a]Joshua had let the people go, the children of Israel went every man[376] unto his inheritance[5159] to possess[3423] the land.

7 [a]And the people served[5647] the LORD all the days of Joshua, and all the days of the elders[2205] that [I]outlived Joshua, who had seen[7200] all the great works of the LORD, that he did for Israel.

8 And [a]Joshua the son[1121] of Nun, the servant[5650] of the LORD, died, *being* an hundred and ten years old.

27 [a]Josh. 17:11-13

29 [a]Josh. 16:10; 1Kgs. 9:16

30 [a]Josh. 19:15

31 [a]Josh. 19:24-30

32 [a]Ps. 106:34, 35

33 [a]Josh. 19:38 [b]Judg. 1:32 [c]Judg. 1:30

35 [I]Hebr. *was heavy* [a]Josh. 19:42

36 [I]Or, *Maaleh-akrabbim* [a]Num. 34:4; Josh. 15:3

1 [I]Or, *messenger* [a]Judg. 2:5 [b]Gen. 17:7

2 [a]Deut. 7:2 [b]Deut. 12:3 [c]Judg. 2:20; Ps. 106:34

3 [a]Josh. 23:13 [b]Judg. 3:6 [c]Ex. 23:33; 34:12; Deut. 7:16; Ps. 106:36

5 [I]That is, *Weepers*

6 [a]Josh. 22:6; 24:28

7 [I]Hebr. *prolonged days after Joshua* [a]Josh. 24:31 [b]Josh. 24:29

9 [a]And they buried[6912] him in the border of his inheritance in [b]Timnath–heres, in the mount of Ephraim, on the north side of the hill Gaash.

10 And also all that generation[1755] were gathered[622] unto their fathers: and there arose another generation after them, which [a]knew[3045] not the LORD, nor yet the works which he had done[6213] for Israel.

Preview of Israel's Sin

11 And the children of Israel did evil[7451] in the sight of the LORD, and served Baalim:

12 And they [a]forsook[5800] the LORD God[430] of their fathers, which brought them out of the land of Egypt, and followed [b]other gods, of the gods of the people that *were* round about them, and [c]bowed themselves[7812] unto them, and provoked the LORD to anger.[3707]

🔑 13 And they forsook the LORD, [a]and served Baal and Ashtaroth.

14 [a]And the anger[639] of the LORD was hot[2734] against Israel, and he [b]delivered them into the hands of spoilers[8154] that spoiled them, and [c]he sold them into the hands of their enemies round about, so that they [d]could not any longer stand before their enemies.

15 Whithersoever they went out, the hand[3027] of the LORD was against them for evil, as the LORD had said,[1696] and as the LORD had sworn[7650] unto them: and they were greatly distressed.[3334]

🔑 16 Nevertheless [a]the LORD raised up judges,[8199] which [I]delivered[3467] them out of the hand of those that spoiled[8154] them.

17 And yet they would not hearken unto their judges, but they [a]went a whoring[2181] after other gods, and bowed themselves unto them: they turned quickly out of the way[1870] which their fathers walked in, obeying the commandments of the LORD; *but* they did not so.

18 And when the LORD raised them up judges, then [a]the LORD was with the judge,[8199] and delivered them out of the hand of their enemies all the days of the judge: [b]for it repented[5162] the LORD because of their groanings by reason of them that oppressed them and vexed[1766] them.

19 And it came to pass, [a]when the judge was dead,[4191] *that* they returned,[7725] and [I]corrupted[7843] *themselves* more than their fathers, in following other gods to serve[5647] them, and to bow down unto them; [II]they ceased not from their own doings, nor from their stubborn[7186] way.

20 [a]And the anger of the LORD was hot against Israel; and he said, Because that this people[1471] hath [b]transgressed[5674]

9 [a]Josh. 24:30 [b]Josh. 19:50; 24:30, *Timnath-serah*

10 [a]Ex. 5:2; 1Sam. 2:12; 1Chr. 28:9; Jer. 9:3; 22:16; Gal. 4:8; 2Thess. 1:8; Titus 1:16

12 [a]Deut. 31:16 [b]Deut. 6:14 [c]Ex. 20:5

13 [a]Judg. 3:7; 10:6; Ps. 106:36

14 [a]Judg. 3:8; Ps. 106:40-42 [b]2Kgs. 17:20 [c]Judg. 3:8; 4:2; Ps. 44:12; Isa. 50:1 [d]Lev. 26:37; Josh. 7:12, 13

16 [I]Hebr. *saved* [a]Judg. 3:9, 10, 15; 1Sam. 12:11; Acts 13:20

17 [a]Ex. 34:15, 16; Lev. 17:7

18 [a]Josh. 1:5 [b]Gen. 6:6; Deut. 32:36; Ps. 106:44, 45

19 [I]Or, *were corrupt* [II]Hebr. *they let nothing fall of their* [a]Judg. 3:12; 4:1; 8:33

20 [a]Judg. 2:14 [b]Josh. 23:16

🔑 **2:13** These Canaanite deities, Baal and Ashtaroth, remained a problem for Judah until the Babylonian Exile (two other Canaanite deities noted in Judges are Asherah [Judg. 3:7] and Dagon [Judg. 16:23]). Only the seventy years in captivity finally cured Israel of its idolatrous ways. Recent archaeological discoveries have helped to clarify the facts about the religion of Canaan in the days of the judges. Baal and Ashtaroth are the names of two individual gods in a much larger and complicated system of polytheism. Moreover, they were also community gods whose names differed from region to region. For instance, Baal was called Baal-Peor, Baal-Berith, and Baal-zebub (Num. 25:3; Judg. 8:33; 2 Kgs. 1:2). It is for this reason that Scripture describes Israel as serving "Baal" or "Baalim" ("im" is the Hebrew plural ending). Overall, the religion of the Canaanites was extremely corrupt. It was characterized by the practices of human sacrifice, ritual prostitution and homosexuality, and self-mutilation. These religions taught that these practices were prevalent among their gods as well, so it is not surprising that the people became equally debased. The many gods were particularly connected with agriculture (the seasons, weather, and grain) and many of God's judgments against these people would ultimately discredit the supposed abilities of these Canaanite "gods" (1 Kgs. 18:20–40; Hos. 2:8–13; Amos 4:4–11).

🔑 **2:16** See the introduction to the Book of Judges.

my covenant which I commanded[6680] their fathers, and have not hearkened[8085] unto my voice;

21 [a]I also will not henceforth drive out any from before them of the nations[1471] which Joshua left[5800] when he died:

22 [a]That through them I may [b]prove[5254] Israel, whether they will keep[8104] the way of the LORD to walk therein, as their fathers did keep *it,* or not.

23 Therefore the LORD [I]left those nations, without driving them out hastily; neither delivered he them into the hand of Joshua.

The Nations Left Unconquered

3 Now these *are* [a]the nations[1471] which the LORD left, to prove[5254] Israel by them, *even* as many *of Israel* as had not known[3045] all the wars of Canaan;

2 Only that the generations[1755] of the children[1121] of Israel might know, to teach[3925] them war, at the least such as before knew nothing thereof;

3 *Namely,* [a]five lords[5633] of the Philistines, and all the Canaanites, and the Sidonians, and the Hivites that dwelt in mount Lebanon, from mount Baal– hermon unto the entering in of Hamath.

4 [a]And they were to prove Israel by them, to know whether they would hearken[8085] unto the commandments of the LORD, which he commanded[6680] their fathers[1] by the hand[3027] of Moses.

5 [a]And the children of Israel dwelt among[7130] the Canaanites, Hittites, and Amorites, and Perizzites, and Hivites, and Jebusites:

6 And [a]they took their daughters to be their wives, and gave their daughters to their sons,[1121] and served[5647] their gods.[430]

Othniel

7 [a]And the children of Israel did evil[7451] in the sight of the LORD, and forgat the LORD their God,[430] [b]and served Baalim and [c]the groves.[842]

8 Therefore the anger[639] of the LORD was hot[2734] against Israel, and he [a]sold them into the hand of [b]Chushan–rishathaim king[4428] of [I]Mesopotamia: and the children of Israel served Chushan–rishathaim eight years.

9 And when the children of Israel [a]cried[2199] unto the LORD, the LORD [b]raised up a [I]deliverer[3467] to the children of Israel, who delivered them, *even* [c]Othniel the son[1121] of Kenaz, Caleb's younger brother.[251]

10 And [a]the Spirit[7307] of the LORD [I]came upon him, and he judged[8199] Israel, and went out to war: and the LORD delivered Chushan–rishathaim king of [II]Mesopotamia into his hand; and his hand prevailed against Chushan–rishathaim.

11 And the land[776] had rest[8252] forty years. And Othniel the son of Kenaz died.

Ehud

12 [a]And the children of Israel did evil again in the sight of the LORD: and the LORD strengthened[2388] [b]Eglon the king of Moab against Israel, because they had done[6213] evil in the sight of the LORD.

13 And he gathered[622] unto him the children of Ammon and [a]Amalek, and went and smote[5221] Israel, and possessed[3423] [b]the city of palm trees.

14 So the children of Israel [a]served Eglon the king of Moab eighteen years.

15 But when the children of Israel [a]cried unto the LORD, the LORD raised them up a deliverer, Ehud the son of

21 [a]Josh. 23:13
22 [a]Judg. 3:1, 4 [b]Deut. 8:2, 16; 13:3
23 [I]Or, *suffered*
1 [a]Judg. 2:21, 22
3 [a]Josh. 13:3
4 [a]Judg. 2:22
5 [a]Ps. 106:35
6 [a]Ex. 34:16; Deut. 7:3
7 [a]Judg. 2:11 [b]Judg. 2:13 [c]Ex. 34:13; Deut. 16:21; Judg. 6:25
8 [I]Hebr. *Aram-naharaim* [a]Judg. 2:14 [b]Hab. 3:7
9 [I]Hebr. *savior* [a]Judg. 3:15; 4:3; 6:7; 10:10; 1Sam. 12:10; Neh. 9:27; Ps. 22:5; 106:44; 107:13, 19 [b]Judg. 2:16 [c]Judg. 1:13
10 [I]Hebr. *was* [II]Hebr. *Aram* [a]Num. 27:18; Judg. 6:34; 11:29; 13:25; 14:6, 19; 1Sam. 11:6; 2Chr. 15:1
12 [a]Judg. 2:19 [b]1Sam. 12:9
13 [a]Judg. 5:14 [b]Judg. 1:16
14 [a]Deut. 28:48
15 [a]Judg. 3:9; Ps. 78:34

3:7 The word translated "groves" refers to the shrines of the Canaanite goddess, Asherah. See note on Judges 2:13.

Gera, [I]a Benjamite, a man[376] [II][b]left-handed: and by him the children of Israel sent a present[4503] unto Eglon the king of Moab.

16 But Ehud made[6213] him a dagger which had two edges, of a cubit length;[753] and he did gird it under his raiment upon his right thigh.[3409]

17 And he brought[7126] the present unto Eglon king of Moab: and Eglon *was* a very fat man.

18 And when he had made an end[3615] to offer the present, he sent away the people[5971] that bare[5375] the present.

19 But he himself turned again[7725] [a]from the [I]quarries[6456] that *were* by Gilgal, and said,[559] I have a secret errand unto thee, O king: who said, Keep silence.[2013] And all that stood by him went out from him.

20 And Ehud came unto him; and he was sitting in [I][a]a summer parlour, which he had for himself alone. And Ehud said, I have a message from God unto thee. And he arose out of *his* seat.[3678]

21 And Ehud put forth his left hand, and took the dagger from his right thigh, and thrust it into his belly:[990]

22 And the haft also went in after the blade; and the fat closed upon the blade, so that he could not draw the dagger out of his belly; and [I]the dirt came out.

23 Then Ehud went forth through the porch, and shut the doors of the parlour upon him, and locked them.

24 When he was gone out, his servants[5650] came; and when they saw[7200] that, behold, the doors of the parlour *were* locked, they said, Surely he [I][a]covereth his feet in his summer chamber.

25 And they tarried[2342] till they were ashamed:[954] and, behold, he opened not the doors of the parlour; therefore they took a key, and opened *them*: and, behold,

15 [I]Or, *the son of Gemini* [II]Hebr. *shut of his right hand* [b]Judg. 20:16

19 [I]Or, *graven images* [a]Josh. 4:20

20 [I]Hebr. *a parlor of cooling* [a]Amos 3:15

22 [I]Or, *it came out at the fundament*

24 [I]Or, *doeth his easement* [a]1Sam. 24:3

27 [a]Judg. 5:14; 6:34; 1Sam. 13:3 [b]Josh. 17:15; Judg. 7:24; 17:1; 19:1

28 [a]Judg. 7:9, 15; 1Sam. 17:47 [b]Josh. 2:7; Judg. 12:5

29 [I]Hebr. *fat*

30 [a]Judg. 3:11

31 [a]Judg. 5:6, 8; 1Sam. 13:19, 22; it seems to concern only the country next to the Philistines [b]1Sam. 17:47, 50 [c]Judg. 2:16 [d]Judg. 4:1, 3-10; 10:7, 17; 11:4; 1Sam. 4:1

1 [a]Judg. 2:19

2 [a]Judg. 2:14 [b]Josh. 11:1, 10; 19:36 [c]1Sam. 12:9; Ps. 83:9; it seems to concern only North Israel [d]Judg. 4:13, 16

3 [a]Judg. 1:19 [b]Judg. 5:8; Ps. 106:42

their lord[113] *was* fallen down[5307] dead[4191] on the earth.[776]

26 And Ehud escaped[4422] while they tarried, and passed beyond[5674] the quarries, and escaped unto Seirath.

27 And it came to pass, when he was come, that [a]he blew[8628] a trumpet in the [b]mountain of Ephraim, and the children of Israel went down with him from the mount, and he before them.

28 And he said unto them, Follow after me: for [a]the LORD hath delivered your enemies the Moabites into your hand. And they went down after him, and took [b]the fords of Jordan toward Moab, and suffered not a man to pass over.

29 And they slew[5221] of Moab at that time[6256] about ten thousand men,[376] all [I]lusty, and all men of valour;[2428] and there escaped not a man.

30 So Moab was subdued that day[3117] under the hand of Israel. And [a]the land had rest fourscore years.

Shamgar

31 And after him was [a]Shamgar the son of Anath, which slew of the Philistines six hundred men [b]with an ox goad:[4451] [c]and he also delivered[3647] [d]Israel.

Deborah

4 And [a]the children[1121] of Israel again did evil[7451] in the sight of the LORD, when Ehud was dead.[4191]

🗝 2 And the LORD [a]sold them into the hand[3027] of Jabin king[4428] of Canaan, that reigned in [b]Hazor; the captain[8269] of whose host[6635] *was* [c]Sisera, which dwelt in [d]Harosheth of the Gentiles.[1471]

3 And the children of Israel cried unto the LORD: for he had nine hundred [a]chariots of iron; and twenty years [b]he mightily oppressed the children of Israel.

🗝 **4:2** "Jabin" was probably a title for a Canaanite king (Josh. 11:1; Judg. 4:23, 24), just as Pharaoh was a title for the kings of Egypt.

🔑 4 And Deborah, a prophetess,[5031] the wife[802] of Lapidoth, she judged[8199] Israel at that time.[6256]

5 [a]And she dwelt under the palm tree of Deborah between Ramah and Bethel in mount Ephraim: and the children of Israel came up[5927] to her for judgment.[4941]

🔑 6 And she sent and called[7121] [a]Barak the son[1121] of Abinoam out [b]of Kedesh–naphtali, and said[559] unto him, Hath[6680] not the LORD God[430] of Israel commanded,[6680] *saying,* Go and draw toward mount Tabor, and take with thee ten thousand men[376] of the children of Naphtali and of the children of Zebulun?

7 And [a]I will draw unto thee to the [b]river Kishon Sisera, the captain of Jabin's army,[6635] with his chariots and his multitude; and I will deliver him into thine hand.

🔑 8 And Barak said unto her, If thou wilt go with me, then I will go: but if thou wilt not go with me, *then* I will not go.

9 And she said, I will surely go with thee: notwithstanding the journey that thou takest shall not be for thine honour;[8597] for the LORD shall [a]sell Sisera into the hand of a woman.[802] And Deborah arose, and went with Barak to Kedesh.

10 And Barak called [a]Zebulun and Naphtali to Kedesh; and he went up[5927] with ten thousand men [b]at his feet: and Deborah went up with him.

11 Now Heber [a]the Kenite, *which was* of the children of [b]Hobab the father in law of Moses, had severed himself from the Kenites, and pitched his tent[168] unto the plain of Zaanaim, [c]which *is* by Kedesh.

12 And they shewed[5046] Sisera that Barak the son of Abinoam was gone up[5927] to mount Tabor.

13 And Sisera [1]gathered together[2199] all his chariots, *even* nine hundred chariots of iron, and all the people that *were* with him, from Haro sheth of the Gentiles unto the river of Kishon.

14 And Deborah said unto Barak, Up; for this *is* the day[3117] in which the LORD hath delivered Sisera into thine hand: [a]is not the LORD gone out before thee? So Barak went down from mount Tabor, and ten thousand men after him.

15 And [a]the LORD discomfited[2000] Sisera, and all *his* chariots, and all *his* host,[4264] with the edge[6310] of the sword[2719] before Barak; so that Sisera lighted down off *his* chariot, and fled away on his feet.

16 But Barak pursued after the chariots, and after the host, unto Harosheth of the Gentiles: and all the host of Sisera fell[5307] upon the edge of the sword; *and* there was not [1]a man left.[7604]

17 Howbeit Sisera fled away on his feet to the tent of Jael the wife of Heber the Kenite: for *there was* peace[7965] between Jabin the king of Hazor and the house[1004] of Heber the Kenite.

18 And Jael went out to meet Sisera, and said unto him, Turn in, my lord,[113] turn in to me; fear[3372] not. And when he had turned in[5493] unto her into the tent, she covered[3680] him with a [1]mantle.[8063]

19 And he said unto her, Give me, I pray thee,[4994] a little water to drink; for I am thirsty. And she opened [a]a bottle of milk, and gave him drink, and covered him.

20 Again he said unto her, Stand in the door of the tent, and it shall be, when any man[376] doth come and enquire[7592] of

5 [a]Gen. 35:8
6 [a]Heb. 11:32 [b]Josh. 19:37
7 [a]Ex. 14:4 [b]Judg. 5:21; 1Kgs. 18:40; Ps. 83:9, 10
9 [a]Judg. 2:14
10 [a]Judg. 5:18 [b]Ex. 11:8; 1Kgs. 20:10
11 [a]Judg. 1:16 [b]Num. 10:29 [c]Judg. 4:6
13 [1]Hebr. *gathered by cry,* or, *proclamation*
14 [a]Deut. 9:3; 2Sam. 5:24; Ps. 68:7; Isa. 52:12
15 [a]Ps. 83:9, 10; Josh. 10:10
16 [1]Hebr. *unto one*
18 [1]Or, *rug,* or, *blanket*
19 [a]Judg. 5:25

🔑 **4:4** The name Deborah means "bee," perhaps emphasizing the organized life of that insect. She is also called a "prophetess" (Judg. 4:1) and examples of her prophetic gift are seen in verses six, nine, and fourteen. Samuel (1 Sam. 3:20) is the only other judge who was expressly called a prophet, though all of the judges received information from the Lord through some special means.

🔑 **4:6, 8** Barak wisely hesitated to lead the armies of Israel without receiving guidance from God through Deborah. He is listed as one of the "heroes of faith" (Heb. 11:32) because he trusted God and depended upon God's spokesperson.

thee, and say,[559] Is there any man here?
that thou shalt say, No.
21 Then Jael Heber's wife [a]took a nail
of the tent, and [I]took an hammer in her
hand, and went softly unto him, and
smote the nail into his temples, and fastened it into the ground:[776] for he was
fast asleep and weary. So he died.
22 And, behold, as Barak pursued
Sisera, Jael came out to meet him, and
said unto him, Come, and I will shew[7200]
thee the man whom thou seekest. And
when he came into her *tent,* behold,
Sisera lay dead, and the nail *was* in his
temples.
23 So [a]God subdued on that day
Jabin the king of Canaan before the children of Israel.
24 And the hand of the children of
Israel [I]prospered, and prevailed against
Jabin the king of Canaan, until they had
destroyed[3772] Jabin king of Canaan.

Deborah's Song

5 Then [a]sang[7891] Deborah and Barak
the son[1121] of Abinoam on that
day,[3117] saying,
2 Praise[1288] ye the LORD for the
[a]avenging of Israel, [b]when the people
willingly offered themselves.[5068]
3 [a]Hear, O ye kings;[4428] give ear,[238] O
ye princes;[7336] I, *even* I, will sing[7891] unto
the LORD; I will sing[2167] *praise* to the
LORD God[430] of Israel.
4 LORD, [a]when thou wentest out of
Seir, when thou marchedst out of the
field[7704] of Edom, [b]the earth[776] trembled,[7493] and the heavens[8064] dropped, the
clouds also dropped water.
5 [a]The mountains [I]melted from before the LORD, *even* [b]that Sinai from before the LORD God of Israel.
6 In the days of [a]Shamgar the son of
Anath, in the days of [b]Jael, [c]the highways[734] were unoccupied,[2308] and the
[I]travellers walked through [II]byways.
7 *The inhabitants of* the villages
ceased, they ceased in Israel, until that I
Deborah arose, that I arose [a]a mother[517]
in Israel.
8 They [a]chose[977] new gods;[430] then
was war in the gates: [b]was there a shield
or spear seen[7200] among forty thousand
in Israel?
9 My heart[3820] *is* toward the governors[2710] of Israel, that [a]offered themselves willingly[5068] among the people.
Bless[1288] ye the LORD.
10 [Ia]Speak,[7878] ye [b]that ride on white
asses, [c]ye that sit in judgment, and walk
by the way.[1870]
11 *They that are delivered* from the
noise of archers in the places of drawing
water, there shall they rehearse the
[Ia]righteous acts[6666] of the LORD, *even* the
righteous acts *toward the inhabitants* of
his villages in Israel: then shall the people of the LORD go down to the gates.
12 [a]Awake, awake, Deborah: awake,
awake, utter a song:[7892] arise, Barak, and
[b]lead[7617] thy captivity,[7628] captive,[7617]
thou son of Abinoam.
13 Then he made him that remaineth[8300] [a]have dominion[7287] over
the nobles[117] among the people: the
LORD made me have dominion over the
mighty.
14 [a]Out of Ephraim *was there* a root
of them [b]against Amalek; after thee,
Benjamin, among thy people; out of
[c]Machir came down governors, and out of
Zebulun they that [I]handle the pen of the
writer.[5608]
15 And the princes[8269] of Issachar
were with Deborah; even Issachar, and
also [a]Barak: he was sent on [I]foot into
the valley. [II]For the divisions[6391] of
Reuben *there were* great [III]thoughts[2711] of
heart.
16 Why abodest[3427] thou [a]among the
sheepfolds, to hear the bleatings[8292] of
the flocks? [I]For the divisions of Reuben
there were great searchings of heart.
17 [a]Gilead abode[7931] beyond Jordan:
and why did Dan remain in ships? [b]Asher
continued on the sea [I]shore, and abode in
his [II]breaches.
18 [a]Zebulun and Naphtali *were* a
people *that* [I]jeoparded their lives unto
the death[4191] in the high places of the
field.
19 The kings came *and* fought, then
fought the kings of Canaan in Taanach

21 [I]Hebr. *put* [a]Judg. 5:26
23 [a]Ps. 18:47
24 [I]Hebr. *going went and was hard*

1 [a]Ex. 15:1
2 [a]Ps. 18:47 [b]2Chr. 17:16
3 [a]Deut. 32:1, 3; Ps. 2:10
4 [a]Deut. 33:2; Ps. 68:7 [b]2Sam. 22:8; Ps. 68:8; Isa. 64:3; Hab. 3:3, 10
5 [I]Hebr. *flowed* [a]Deut. 4:11; Ps. 97:5 [b]Ex. 19:18
6 [I]Hebr. *walkers of paths* [II]Hebr. *crooked ways* [a]Judg. 3:31 [b]Judg. 4:17 [c]Lev. 26:22; 2Chr. 15:5; Isa. 33:8; Lam. 1:4; 4:18
7 [a]Isa. 49:23
8 [a]Deut. 32:16; Judg. 2:12, 17 [b]1Sam. 13:19, 22; Judg. 4:3
9 [a]Judg. 5:2
10 [I]Or, *Meditate* [a]Ps. 105:2; 145:5 [b]Judg. 10:4; 12:14 [c]Ps. 107:32
11 [I]Hebr. *righteousnesses of the LORD* [a]1Sam. 12:7; Ps. 145:7
12 [a]Ps. 57:8 [b]Ps. 68:18
13 [a]Ps. 49:14
14 [I]Hebr. *draw with the pen* [a]Judg. 3:27 [b]Judg. 3:13 [c]Num. 32:39, 40
15 [I]Hebr. *his feet* [II]Or, *In the divisions* [III]Hebr. *impressions* [a]Judg. 4:14
16 [I]Or, *In* [a]Num. 32:1
17 [I]Or, *port* [II]Or, *creeks* [a]Josh. 13:25, 31 [b]Josh. 19:29, 31
18 [I]Hebr. *exposed to reproach* [a]Judg. 4:10

by the waters of Megiddo; [a]they took no gain of money.

20 [a]They fought from *heaven*;[8064] [b]the stars in their [I]courses fought against Sisera.

21 [a]The river of Kishon swept them away, that ancient river, the river Kishon. O my soul,[5315] thou hast trodden down strength.

22 Then were the horsehoofs broken[1986] by the means of the [I]prancings, the prancings of their mighty ones.[47]

23 Curse[779] ye Meroz, said[559] the angel[4397] of the LORD, curse ye bitterly the inhabitants thereof; [a]because they came not to the help [b]of the LORD, to the help of the LORD against the mighty.

24 Blessed[1288] above women[802] shall [a]Jael the wife[802] of Heber the Kenite be, [b]blessed shall she be above women in the tent.[168]

25 [a]He asked[7592] water, *and* she gave *him* milk; she brought forth[7126] butter in a lordly[117] dish.

26 [a]She put her hand[3027] to the nail, and her right hand to the workmen's hammer; and [I]with the hammer she smote[1986] Sisera, she smote off[4277] his head,[7218] when she had pierced[4272] and stricken through his temples.

27 [I]At her feet he bowed,[3766] he fell, he lay down: at her feet he bowed, he fell: where he bowed, there he fell down[5307] [II]dead.[7703]

28 The mother of Sisera looked out at a window, and cried[2980] through the lattice,[822] Why is his chariot *so* long in coming? why tarry the wheels of his chariots?

29 Her wise[2450] ladies[8282] answered her, yea, she returned[7725] [I]answer[559] to herself,

30 [a]Have they not sped? have they *not* divided the prey; [I]to every man[1397] a damsel *or* two; to Sisera a prey of divers colours, a prey of divers colours of needlework, of divers colours of needlework on both sides, *meet* for the necks of *them that take* the spoil?

31 [a]So let all thine enemies perish,[6] O LORD: but *let* them that love[157] him *be* [b]as the sun [c]when he goeth forth in his might. And the land[776] had rest[8252] forty years.

Gideon's Call

6 [a]And the children[1121] of Israel did evil[7451] in the sight of the LORD: and the LORD delivered them into the hand[3027] [b]of Midian seven years.

2 And the hand of Midian [I]prevailed against Israel: *and* because of the Midianites the children of Israel made[6213] them [a]the dens which *are* in the mountains, and caves, and strong holds.

3 And *so* it was, when Israel had sown, that the Midianites came up,[5927] and [a]the Amalekites, [b]and the children of the east, even they came up against them;

4 And they encamped against them, and [a]destroyed[7843] the increase of the earth,[776] till thou come unto Gaza, and left no sustenance[4241] for Israel, neither [I]sheep, nor ox, nor ass.

5 For they came up with their cattle and their tents,[168] and they came [a]as grasshoppers for multitude; *for* both they and their camels were without number: and they entered into the land[776] to destroy[7843] it.

6 And Israel was greatly impoverished because of the Midianites; and the children of Israel [a]cried[2199] unto the LORD.

7 And it came to pass, when the children of Israel cried unto the LORD because of the Midianites,

8 That the LORD sent [I]a prophet[5030] unto the children of Israel, which said unto them, Thus saith[559] the LORD God[430] of Israel, I brought you up[5927] from Egypt, and brought you forth out of the house[1004] of bondage;[5650]

9 And I delivered[5337] you out of the hand of the Egyptians, and out of the hand of all that oppressed[3905] you, and [a]drave them out from before you, and gave you their land;

10 And I said unto you, I *am* the LORD your God; [a]fear[3372] not the gods[430]

---

19 [a]Gen. 4:16; Ps. 44:12; Judg. 5:30
20 [I]Hebr. *paths* [a]Josh. 10:11; Ps. 77:17, 18 [b]Judg. 4:15
21 [a]Judg. 4:7
22 [I]Or, *tramplings*, or, *plungings*
23 [a]Judg. 21:9, 10; Neh. 3:5 [b]1Sam. 17:47; 18:17; 25:28
24 [a]Judg. 4:17 [b]Luke 1:28
25 [a]Judg. 4:19
26 [I]Hebr. *she hammered* [a]Judg. 4:21
27 [I]Hebr. *Between* [II]Hebr. *destroyed*
29 [I]Hebr. *her words*
30 [I]Hebr. *to the head of a man* [a]Ex. 15:9
31 [a]Ps. 83:9, 10 [b]2Sam. 23:4 [c]Ps. 19:5
1 [a]Judg. 2:19 [b]Hab. 3:7
2 [I]Hebr. *was strong* [a]1Sam. 13:6; Heb. 11:38
3 [a]Judg. 3:13 [b]Gen. 29:1; Judg. 7:12; 8:10; 1Kgs. 4:30; Job 1:3
4 [I]Or, *goat* [a]Lev. 26:16; Deut. 28:30, 33, 51; Mic. 6:15
5 [a]Judg. 7:12
6 [a]Judg. 3:15; Hos. 5:15
8 [I]Hebr. *a man a prophet*
9 [a]Ps. 44:2, 3
10 [a]2Kgs. 17:35, 37, 38; Jer. 10:2

of the Amorites, in whose land ye dwell: but ye have not obeyed[8085] my voice.

11 And there came an angel[4397] of the LORD, and sat under an oak which *was* in Ophrah, that *pertained* unto Joash [a]the Abi–ezrite: and his son[1121] [b]Gideon threshed wheat by the winepress, [I]to hide *it* from the Midianites.

12 And the [a]angel of the LORD appeared[7200] unto him, and said unto him, The LORD *is* [b]with thee, thou mighty man of valour.[2428]

13 And Gideon said unto him, Oh my Lord,[113] if the LORD be with us, why then is all this befallen us? and [a]where *be* all his miracles[6381] [b]which our fathers[1] told[5046] us of, saying, Did not the LORD bring us up from Egypt? but now the LORD hath [c]forsaken[5203] us, and delivered us into the hands[3709] of the Midianites.

14 And the LORD looked upon him, and said, [a]Go in this thy might, and thou shalt save[3467] Israel from the hand of the Midianites: [b]have not I sent thee?

15 And he said unto him, Oh my Lord, wherewith shall I save Israel? behold, [Ia]my family *is* poor in Manasseh, and I *am* the least in my father's[1] house.

16 And the LORD said unto him, [a]Surely I will be with thee, and thou shalt smite[5221] the Midianites as one man.[376]

17 And he said unto him, If now I have found grace[2580] in thy sight, then [a]shew[6213] me a sign[226] that thou talkest[1696] with me.

18 [a]Depart not hence, I pray thee,[4994] until I come unto thee, and bring forth my [I]present,[4503] and set *it* before thee. And he said, I will tarry until thou come again.[7725]

19 [a]And Gideon went in, and made ready [I]a kid, and unleavened cakes[4682] of an ephah of flour: the flesh[1320] he put in a basket, and he put the broth in a pot, and brought *it* out unto him under the oak, and presented[5066] *it.*

20 And the angel of God said unto him, Take the flesh and the unleavened cakes, and [a]lay *them* upon this rock, and [b]pour out[8210] the broth. And he did so.

21 Then the angel of the LORD put forth the end of the staff that *was* in his hand, and touched[5060] the flesh and the unleavened cakes; and [a]there rose up[5927] fire out of the rock, and consumed the flesh and the unleavened cakes. Then the angel of the LORD departed out of his sight.

22 And when Gideon [a]perceived[7200] that he *was* an angel of the LORD,[3068] Gideon said, Alas, O Lord[136] GOD! [b]for because I have seen[7200] an angel of the LORD face to face.

23 And the LORD said unto him, [a]Peace[7965] *be* unto thee; fear not: thou shalt not die.[4191]

24 Then Gideon built an altar there unto the LORD, and called it [Ia]Jehovah–shalom: unto this day[3117] it *is* yet in Ophrah of the Abi–ezrites.

Gideon Destroys Altar of Baal

25 And it came to pass the same night,[3915] that the LORD said unto him, Take thy father's young bullock, [I]even the second bullock of seven years old, and throw down[2040] the altar of Baal that thy father[1] hath, and [a]cut down[3772] the grove[842] that *is* by it:

26 And build an altar unto the LORD thy God upon the top[7248] of this [I]rock, [II]in the ordered place, and take the second bullock, and offer a burnt sacrifice[5930] with the wood of the grove which thou shalt cut down.

27 Then Gideon took ten men[582] of his servants,[5650] and did as the LORD had said unto him: and *so* it was, because he feared[3372] his father's household,[1004] and the men of the city, that he could not do *it* by day,[3119] that he did *it* by night.

28 And when the men of the city arose early in the morning, behold, the altar of Baal was cast down,[5422] and the grove was cut down that *was* by it, and the second bullock was offered[5927] upon the altar *that was* built.

29 And they said one[376] to another,[7453] Who hath done[6213] this thing?[1697] And when they enquired and

---

11 [I]Hebr. *to cause it to flee* [a]Josh. 17:2 [b]Heb. 11:32

12 [a]Judg. 13:3; Luke 1:11, 28 [b]Josh. 1:5

13 [a]Ps. 89:49; Isa. 59:1; 63:15 [b]Ps. 44:1 [c]2Chr. 15:2

14 [a]1Sam. 12:11; Heb. 11:32, 34 [b]Josh. 1:9; Judg. 4:6

15 [I]Hebr. *my thousand* is the *meanest* [a]Ex. 18:21, 25; 1Sam. 9:21; Mic. 5:2

16 [a]Ex. 3:12; Josh. 1:5

17 [a]Ex. 4:1-8; Judg. 6:36, 37; 2Kgs. 20:8; Ps. 86:17; Isa. 7:11

18 [I]Or, *meat offering* [a]Gen. 18:3, 5; Judg. 13:15

19 [I]Hebr. *a kid of the goats* [a]Gen. 18:6-8

20 [a]Judg. 13:19 [b]1Kgs. 18:33, 34

21 [a]Lev. 9:24; 1Kgs. 18:38; 2Chr. 7:1

22 [a]Judg. 13:21 [b]Gen. 16:13; 32:30; Ex. 33:20; Judg. 13:22

23 [a]Dan. 10:19

24 [I]That is, *The LORD* send *peace* [a]Gen. 22:14; Ex. 17:15; Jer. 33:16; Ezek. 48:35 [b]Judg. 8:32

25 [I]Or, *and* [a]Ex. 34:13; Deut. 7:5

26 [I]Hebr. *strong place* [II]Or, *in an orderly manner*

asked, they said, Gideon the son of Joash hath done this thing.

30 Then the men of the city said unto Joash, Bring out thy son, that he may die: because he hath cast down the altar of Baal, and because he hath cut down the grove that *was* by it.

31 And Joash said unto all that stood against him, Will ye plead[7378] for Baal? will ye save him? he that will plead for him, let him be put to death[4191] whilst *it is yet* morning: if he *be* a god, let him plead for himself, because *one* hath cast down his altar.

32 Therefore on that day he called him [I][a]Jerubbaal, saying, Let Baal plead against him, because he hath thrown down[5422] his altar.

Gideon Prepares for Battle

33 Then all [a]the Midianites and the Amalekites and the children of the east were gathered[622] together, and went over,[5674] and pitched in [b]the valley of Jezreel.

34 But [a]the Spirit[7307] of the LORD [I]came upon Gideon, and he [b]blew[8628] a trumpet; and Abi–ezer [II]was gathered[2199] after him.

35 And he sent messengers[4397] throughout all Manasseh; who also was gathered after him: and he sent messengers unto Asher, and unto Zebulun, and unto Naphtali; and they came up to meet them.

🗝 36 And Gideon said unto God, If thou wilt save Israel by mine hand, as thou hast said,

37 [a]Behold, I will put a fleece of wool in the floor; *and* if the dew be on the fleece only, and *it be* dry upon all the earth *beside,* then shall I know[3045] that thou wilt save Israel by mine hand, as thou hast said.

38 And it was so: for he rose up early on the morrow, and thrust the fleece together, and wringed the dew out of the fleece, a bowl full of water.

39 And Gideon said unto God, [a]Let not thine anger[639] be hot[2734] against me, and I will speak[1696] but this once: let me prove,[5254] I pray thee, but this once with the fleece; let it now be dry only upon the fleece, and upon all the ground[776] let there be dew.

40 And God did so that night: for it was dry upon the fleece only, and there was dew on all the ground.

7 Then [a]Jerubbaal, who *is* Gideon, and all the people[5971] that *were* with him, rose up early, and pitched beside the well of Harod: so that the host[4264] of the Midianites were on the north side of them, by the hill of Moreh, in the valley.

2 And the LORD said[559] unto Gideon, The people that *are* with thee *are* too many for me to give the Midianites into their hands,[3027] lest Israel [a]vaunt themselves[6286] against me, saying, Mine own hand hath saved me.

3 Now therefore go to,[4994] proclaim[7121] in the ears[241] of the people, saying, [a]Whosoever *is* fearful[3373] and afraid,[2730] let him return[7725] and depart early from mount Gilead. And there returned of the people twenty and two thousand; and there remained[7604] ten thousand.

4 And the LORD said unto Gideon, The people *are* yet *too* many; bring them down unto the water, and I will try[6884] them for thee there: and it shall be, *that* of whom I say[559] unto thee, This shall go with thee, the same shall go with thee; and of whomsoever I say unto thee, This shall not go with thee, the same shall not go.

32 [I]That is, *Let Baal plead* [a]1Sam. 12:11; 2Sam. 11:21, *Jerub-besheth*

33 [a]Judg. 6:3 [b]Josh. 17:16

34 [I]Hebr. *clothed* [II]Hebr. *was called after him* [a]Judg. 3:10; 1Chr. 12:18; 2Chr. 24:20 [b]Num. 10:3; Judg. 3:27

37 [a]Ex. 4:3, 4, 6, 7

39 [a]Gen. 18:32

1 [a]Judg. 6:32

2 [a]Deut. 8:17; Isa. 10:13; 1Cor. 1:29; 2Cor. 4:7

3 [a]Deut. 20:8

🗝 **6:36, 37** In humility, Gideon desired a tangible sign to reassure him of God's leading. God does not condemn Gideon, but graciously gives him repeated signs to confirm the divine call (vv. 36–40). These two signs involving the "fleece of wool" provided an increased assurance that it was God's supernatural working. From that point on, Gideon never wavered in his trust in God, even when God sent him into battle with only three hundred men. Because of his faith, Gideon is included among God's "heroes of faith" (Heb. 11:32).

5 So he brought down the people unto the water: and the LORD said unto Gideon, Every one that lappeth of the water with his tongue, as a dog lappeth, him shalt thou set by himself; likewise every one that boweth down[3766] upon his knees to drink.

6 And the number of them that lapped, *putting* their hand to their mouth,[6310] were three hundred men:[376] but all the rest[3499] of the people bowed down[3766] upon their knees to drink water.

7 And the LORD said unto Gideon, [a]By the three hundred men that lapped will I save[3467] you, and deliver the Midianites into thine hand: and let all the *other* people go every man[376] unto his place.

8 So the people took victuals[6720] in their hand, and their trumpets: and he sent all *the rest of* Israel every man unto his tent,[168] and retained those three hundred men: and the host of Midian was beneath him in the valley.

The Battle

9 And it came to pass the same [a]night,[3915] that the LORD said unto him, Arise, get thee down unto the host; for I have delivered it into thine hand.

10 But if thou fear[3373] to go down, go thou with Phurah thy servant down to the host:

11 And thou shalt [a]hear[8085] what they say;[1696] and afterward shall thine hands be strengthened[2388] to go down unto the host. Then went he down with Phurah his servant unto the outside of the [I][b]armed men that *were* in the host.

12 And the Midianites and the Amalekites and [a]all the children[1121] of the east lay along in the valley like grasshoppers for multitude; and their camels *were* without number, as the sand by the sea side[8193] for multitude.

13 And when Gideon was come, behold, *there was* a man that told[5608] a dream unto his fellow,[7453] and said, Behold, I dreamed a dream, and, lo, a cake of barley bread tumbled[2015] into the host of Midian, and came unto a tent, and smote[5221] it that it fell,[5307] and overturned it, that the tent lay along.

14 And his fellow answered and said, This *is* nothing else save the sword[2719] of Gideon the son[1121] of Joash, a man of Israel: *for* into his hand hath God[430] delivered Midian, and all the host.

15 And it was *so,* when Gideon heard[8085] the telling of the dream, and [I]the interpretation[7667] thereof, that he worshipped,[7812] and returned into the host of Israel, and said, Arise; for the LORD hath delivered into your hand the host of Midian.

16 And he divided the three hundred men *into* three companies,[7218] and he put [I]a trumpet in every man's hand, with empty pitchers, and [II]lamps within the pitchers.

17 And he said unto them, Look on me, and do likewise: and, behold, when I come to the outside of the camp,[4264] it shall be *that,* as I do, so shall ye do.

18 When I blow with a trumpet, I and all that *are* with me, then blow[8628] ye the trumpets also on every side of all the camp, and say, *The sword* of the LORD, and of Gideon.

19 So Gideon, and the hundred men that *were* with him, came unto the outside of the camp in the beginning[7218] of the middle watch; and they had but

7 [a]1Sam. 14:6

9 [a]Gen. 46:2, 3

11 [I]Or, *ranks by five* [a]Judg. 7:13-15; Gen. 24:14; 1Sam. 14:9, 10 [b]Ex. 13:18

12 [a]Judg. 6:5, 33; 8:10

15 [I]Hebr. *the breaking thereof*

16 [I]Hebr. *trumpets in the hand of all of them* [II]Or, *firebrands,* or, *torches*

7:5 There are two views in regard to the reason for God's choice of Gideon's men which are based on the events of this verse. Some scholars hold that the way the men drank the water served no real purpose as far as God was concerned. It was merely one final way that God used to reduce the number of men. Others believe that because some of the men knelt and scooped the water in their hands to drink it, they were more prepared for battle than those who lapped the water with their tongues like a dog, thus revealing themselves as easy targets for the enemy. Therefore, the latter ones were sent home as unfit for war.

newly set the watch:[8104] and they blew[8628] the trumpets, and brake the pitchers that *were* in their hands.

20 And the three companies blew the trumpets, and brake[7665] the pitchers, and held[2388] the lamps in their left hands, and the trumpets in their right hands to blow *withal:* and they cried,[7121] The sword of the LORD, and of Gideon.

21 And they [a]stood every man in his place round about the camp: [b]and all the host ran, and cried,[7321] and fled.

22 And the three hundred [a]blew the trumpets, and [b]the LORD set[7760] [c]every man's sword against his fellow, even throughout all the host: and the host fled to Beth–shittah [I]in Zererath, *and* to the [II]border[8193] of Abel–meholah, unto Tabbath.

23 And the men of Israel gathered themselves together out of Naphtali, and out of Asher, and out of all Manasseh, and pursued after the Midianites.

24 And Gideon sent messengers[4397] throughout all [a]mount Ephraim, saying, Come down against the Midianites, and take before them the waters unto Beth–barah and Jordan. Then all the men of Ephraim gathered themselves together, and [b]took the waters unto [c]Beth–barah and Jordan.

25 And they took [a]two princes[8269] of the Midianites, Oreb and Zeeb; and they slew[2026] Oreb upon [b]the rock Oreb, and Zeeb they slew at the winepress of Zeeb, and pursued Midian, and brought the heads[7218] of Oreb and Zeeb to Gideon on the [c]other side Jordan.

Gideon Pursues the Escaping Kings

8 And [a]the men[376] of Ephraim said unto him, [I]Why hast thou served us thus, that thou calledst[7121] us not, when thou wentest to fight with the Midianites? And they did[6213] chide[7378] with him [II]sharply.[2394]

2 And he said unto them, What have I done now in comparison of you? *Is* not the gleaning of the grapes of Ephraim better[2896] than the vintage of Abi–ezer?

3 [a]God[430] hath delivered into your hands[3027] the princes[8269] of Midian, Oreb and Zeeb: and what was I able to do in comparison of you? Then their [I][b]anger was abated[7503] toward him, when he had said[1696] that.

4 And Gideon came to Jordan, *and* passed over,[5674] he, and the three hundred men that *were* with him, faint, yet pursuing *them.*

5 And he said unto the men[582] of [a]Succoth, Give, I pray you,[4994] loaves of bread unto the people[5971] that follow me; for they *be* faint, and I am pursuing after Zebah and Zalmunna, kings[4428] of Midian.

6 And the princes of Succoth said, [a]*Are* the hands[3709] of Zebah and Zalmunna now in thine hand,[3027] that [b]we should give bread unto thine army?[6635]

7 And Gideon said, Therefore when the LORD hath delivered Zebah and Zalmunna into mine hand, [a]then I will [I]tear your flesh[1320] with the thorns of the wilderness and with briers.

8 And he went up[5927] thence [a]to Penuel, and spake[1696] unto them likewise: and the men of Penuel answered him as the men of Succoth had answered *him.*

9 And he spake[559] also unto the men of Penuel, saying, When I [a]come again[7725] in peace,[7965] [b]I will break down[5422] this tower.

10 Now Zebah and Zalmunna *were* in Karkor, and their hosts[4264] with them, about fifteen thousand *men,* all that were left[3498] of [a]all the hosts of the children[1121] of the east: for there fell[5307] [I][b]an hundred and twenty thousand men that drew sword.[2719]

11 And Gideon went up by the way[1870] of them that dwelt[7931] in tents[168] on the east of [a]Nobah and Jogbehah, and smote[5221] the host:[4264] for the host was [b]secure.

12 And when Zebah and Zalmunna fled, he pursued after them, and [a]took the two kings of Midian, Zebah and

---

21 [a]Ex. 14:13, 14; 2Chr. 20:17 [b]2Kgs. 7:7

22 [I]Or, *towards* [II]Hebr. *lip* [a]Josh. 6:4, 16, 20; 2Cor. 4:7 [b]Ps. 83:9; Isa. 9:4 [c]1Sam. 14:20; 2Chr. 20:23

24 [a]Judg. 3:27 [b]Judg. 3:28 [c]John 1:28

25 [a]Judg. 8:3; Ps. 83:11 [b]Isa. 10:26 [c]Judg. 8:4

1 [I]Hebr. *What thing is this thou hast done unto us?* [II]Hebr. *strongly* [a]Judg. 12:1; 2Sam. 19:41

3 [I]Hebr. *spirit* [a]Judg. 7:24, 25; Phil. 2:3 [b]Prov. 15:1

5 [a]Gen. 33:17; Ps. 60:6

6 [a]1Kgs. 20:11 [b]1Sam. 25:11

7 [I]Hebr. *thresh* [a]Judg. 8:16

8 [a]Gen. 32:30; 1Kgs. 12:25

9 [a]1Kgs. 22:27 [b]Judg. 8:17

10 [I]Or, *a hundred and twenty thousand, every one drawing a sword* [a]Judg. 7:12 [b]20:2, 15, 17, 25 [c]2Kgs. 3:26

11 [a]Num. 32:35, 42 [b]Judg. 18:27; 1Thess. 5:3

12 [a]Ps. 83:11

Zalmunna, and [I]discomfited[2729] all the host.

13 And Gideon the son[1121] of Joash returned[7725] from battle before the sun *was up,*

14 And caught a young man of the men of Succoth, and enquired[7592] of him: and he described unto him the princes of Succoth, and the elders[2205] thereof, *even* threescore and seventeen men.

15 And he came unto the men of Succoth, and said, Behold Zebah and Zalmunna, with whom ye did [a]upbraid[2778] me, saying, *Are* the hands of Zebah and Zalmunna now in thine hand, that we should give bread unto thy men *that are* weary?

16 [a]And he took the elders of the city, and thorns of the wilderness and briers, and with them he [I]taught[3045] the men of Succoth.

17 [a]And he beat down[5422] the tower of [b]Penuel, and slew[2026] the men of the city.

18 Then said he unto Zebah and Zalmunna, What manner of men *were they* whom ye slew at [a]Tabor? And they answered,[559] As thou *art,* so *were* they; each one [I]resembled the children of a king.[4428]

19 And he said, They *were* my brethren,[251] *even* the sons[1121] of my mother:[517] *as* the LORD liveth,[2416] if ye had saved them alive, I would not slay[2026] you.

20 And he said unto Jether his firstborn, Up, *and* slay them. But the youth drew not his sword: for he feared,[3372] because he *was* yet a youth.

21 Then Zebah and Zalmunna said, Rise thou, and fall upon us: for as the man[376] *is, so is* his strength. And Gideon arose, and [a]slew Zebah and Zalmunna, and took away the [I]ornaments that *were* on their camels' necks.

Gideon's Later Years

22 Then the men of Israel said unto Gideon, Rule[4910] thou over us, both thou, and thy son, and thy son's son also: for thou hast delivered[3467] us from the hand of Midian.

23 And Gideon said unto them, I will not rule over you, neither shall my son rule over you: [a]the LORD shall rule over you.

24 And Gideon said unto them, I would desire[7592] a request[7596] of you, that ye would give me every man the earrings of his prey. (For they had golden earrings, [a]because they *were* Ishmaelites.)

25 And they answered, We will willingly give *them.* And they spread a garment, and did cast therein every man the earrings of his prey.

26 And the weight of the golden earrings that he requested[7592] was a thousand and seven hundred *shekels* of gold; beside ornaments, and [I]collars, and purple raiment that *was* on the kings of Midian, and beside the chains that *were* about their camels' necks.

🗝 27 And Gideon [a]made[6213] an ephod thereof, and put it in his city, *even* [b]in Ophrah: and all Israel [c]went thither a whoring[2181] after it: which thing became [d]a snare[4170] unto Gideon, and to his house.[1004]

28 Thus was Midian subdued before the children of Israel, so that they lifted up[5375] their heads[7218] no more. [a]And the country[776] was in quietness[8252] forty years in the days of Gideon.

29 And Jerubbaal the son of Joash went and dwelt in his own house.

30 And Gideon had [a]threescore and ten sons [I]of his body begotten:[3318] for he had many wives.[802]

31 [a]And his concubine that *was* in Shechem, she also bare him a son, whose name he [I]called Abimelech.

12 [I]Hebr. *terrified*
15 [a]Judg. 8:6
16 [I]Hebr. *made to know* [a]Judg. 8:7
17 [a]Judg. 8:9 [b]1Kgs. 12:25
18 [I]Hebr. *according to the form* [a]Judg. 4:6; Ps. 89:12
21 [I]Or, *ornaments like the moon* [a]Ps. 83:11
23 [a]1Sam. 8:7; 10:19; 12:12
24 [a]Gen. 25:13; 37:25, 28
26 [I]Or, *sweet jewels*
27 [a]Judg. 17:5 [b]Judg. 6:24 [c]Ps. 106:39 [d]Deut. 7:16
28 [a]Judg. 5:31
30 [I]Hebr. *going out of his thigh* [a]Judg. 9:2, 5
31 [I]Hebr. *set* [a]Judg. 9:1

🗝 **8:27** The "ephod" mentioned here may have varied from the priestly ephod (Ex. 28:5–30) or been a mere copy of the breastplate of Aaron's ephod. It seems to represent man's attempt to achieve a standing with God on his own (see Judg. 17:5), and could be considered a form of their idolatry which was prevalent during this time because the objects themselves were worshiped, not God.

32 And Gideon the son of Joash died [a]in a good[2896] old age,[7872] and was buried[6912] in the sepulchre[6913] of Joash his father,[1] [b]in Ophrah of the Abi–ezrites.

🔑 33 And it came to pass, [a]as soon as Gideon was dead,[4191] that the children of Israel turned again,[7725] and [b]went a whoring[2181] after Baalim, [c]and made[7760] Baal–berith their god.

34 And the children of Israel [a]remembered[2142] not the LORD their God, who had delivered[5337] them out of the hands of all their enemies on every side:

35 [a]Neither shewed[6213] they kindness[2617] to the house of Jerubbaal, *namely,* Gideon, according to all the goodness[2896] which he had shewed unto Israel.

Abimelech

9 And Abimelech the son[1121] of Jerubbaal went to Shechem unto [a]his mother's[517] brethren,[251] and communed with them, and with all the family[4940] of the house[1004] of his mother's father,[1] saying,

2 Speak,[1696] I pray you,[4994] in the ears[241] of all the men[1167] of Shechem, [I]Whether *is* better[2896] for you, either that all the sons of Jerubbaal, *which are* [a]threescore and ten persons,[376] reign[4910] over you, or that one reign over you? remember[2142] also that I *am* [b]your bone[6106] and your flesh.[1320]

3 And his mother's brethren spake[1696] of him in the ears of all the men of Shechem all these words:[1697] and their hearts[3820] inclined [I]to follow Abimelech; for they said,[559] He *is* our [a]brother.

4 And they gave him threescore and ten *pieces* of silver out of the house of [a]Baal–berith, wherewith Abimelech hired [b]vain and light persons,[582] which followed him.

5 And he went unto his father's[1] house [a]at Ophrah, and [b]slew[2026] his brethren the sons of Jerubbaal, *being* threescore and ten persons, upon one stone: notwithstanding yet Jotham the youngest son of Jerubbaal was left;[3498] for he hid himself.

6 And all the men of Shechem gathered together,[622] and all the house of Millo, and went, and made Abimelech king,[4427] [I][a]by the plain of the pillar[5324] that *was* in Shechem.

🔑 7 And when they told[5046] *it* to Jotham, he went and stood in the top[7218] of [a]mount Gerizim, and lifted up[5375] his voice, and cried,[7121] and said unto them, Hearken[8085] unto me, ye men of Shechem, that God[430] may hearken unto you.

8 [a]The trees went forth *on a time* to anoint[4886] a king over them; and they said unto the olive tree, [b]Reign[4427] thou over us.

9 But the olive tree said unto them, Should I leave my fatness, [a]wherewith by me they honour[3513] God and man,[376] and [I]go to be promoted over the trees?

10 And the trees said to the fig tree, Come thou, *and* reign over us.

11 But the fig tree said unto them, Should I forsake my sweetness, and my good[2896] fruit, and go to be promoted over the trees?

12 Then said the trees unto the vine, Come thou, *and* reign over us.

13 And the vine said unto them, Should I leave my wine, [a]which cheereth God and man, and go to be promoted over the trees?

14 Then said all the trees unto the [I]bramble, Come thou, *and* reign over us.

15 And the bramble said unto the

32 [a]Gen. 25:8; Job 5:26 [b]Judg. 6:24; 8:27
33 [a]Judg. 2:19 [b]Judg. 2:17 [c]Judg. 9:4, 46
34 [a]Ps. 78:11-42; 106:18-21
35 [a]Judg. 9:16-18; Eccl. 9:14, 15
1 [a]Judg. 8:31
2 [I]Hebr. *What is good? whether* [a]Judg. 8:30 [b]Gen. 29:14
3 [I]Hebr. *after* [a]Gen. 29:15
4 [a]Judg. 8:33 [b]Judg. 11:3; 2Chr. 13:7; Prov. 12:11; Acts 17:5
5 [a]Judg. 6:24 [b]2Kgs. 11:1, 2
6 [I]Or, *by the oak of the pillar* [a]Josh. 24:26
7 [a]Deut. 11:29; 27:12; Josh. 8:33; John 4:20
8 [a]2Kgs. 14:9 [b]Judg. 8:22, 23
9 [I]Hebr. *go up and down for other trees* [a]Ps. 104:15
13 [a]Ps. 104:15
14 [I]Or, *thistle*

🔑 **8:33** A strange contrast is made in this verse between Baal-berith, which means "Baal (the lord) of the covenant," and Jehovah, with whom Israel had made their covenant. They were in fact exchanging one covenant for the other! This apostasy was centered in Shechem, and no doubt Gideon had opened the way for this apostasy by making the ephod (see note on Judg. 8:27).

🔑 **9:7–15** This is one of the few parables in the Old Testament.

trees, If in truth[571] ye anoint me king over you, *then* come *and* put your trust[2620] in my [a]shadow: and if not, [b]let fire come out of the bramble, and devour the [c]cedars of Lebanon.

16 Now therefore, if ye have done[6213] truly and sincerely,[8549] in that ye have made Abimelech king,[4427] and if ye have dealt[6213] well[2895] with Jerubbaal and his house, and have done unto him [a]according to the deserving of his hands;[3027]

17 (For my father fought for you, and [I]adventured[7993] his life[5315] far, and delivered you out of the hand[3027] of Midian:

18 [a]And ye are risen up against my father's house this day,[3117] and have slain[2026] his sons, threescore and ten persons, upon one stone, and have made Abimelech, the son of his maidservant, king over the men of Shechem, because he *is* your brother;)

19 If ye then have dealt truly and sincerely with Jerubbaal and with his house this day, *then* [a]rejoice ye in Abimelech, and let him also rejoice in you:

20 But if not, [a]let fire come out from Abimelech, and devour the men of Shechem, and the house of Millo; and let fire come out from the men of Shechem, and from the house of Millo, and devour Abimelech.

21 And Jotham ran away, and fled, and went to [a]Beer, and dwelt there, for fear of Abimelech his brother.

22 When Abimelech had reigned[7786] three years over Israel,

23 Then [a]God sent an evil[7451] spirit[7307] between Abimelech and the men of Shechem; and the men of Shechem [b]dealt treacherously[898] with Abimelech:

24 [a]That the cruelty[2555] *done* to the threescore and ten sons of Jerubbaal might come, and their blood be laid[7760] upon Abimelech their brother, which slew them; and upon the men of Shechem, which [I]aided him in the killing of his brethren.

25 And the men of Shechem set liers in wait for him in the top of the mountains, and they robbed all that came along that way[1870] by them: and it was told Abimelech.

26 And Gaal the son of Ebed came with his brethren, and went over[5674] to Shechem: and the men of Shechem put their confidence in him.

27 And they went out into the fields,[7704] and gathered their vineyards, and trode *the grapes,* and made[6213] [I][a]merry,1974 and went into [b]the house of their god, and did[6213] eat and drink, and cursed[7043] Abimelech.

28 And Gaal the son of Ebed said, [a]Who *is* Abimelech, and who *is* Shechem, that we should serve[5647] him? *is* not *he* the son of Jerubbaal? and Zebul his officer? serve the men[582] of [b]Hamor the father of Shechem: for why should we serve him?

29 And [a]would to God this people[5971] were under my hand! then would I remove Abimelech. And he said to Abimelech, Increase thine army,[6635] and come out.

30 And when Zebul the ruler[8269] of the city heard[8085] the words of Gaal the son of Ebed, his anger[639] was [I]kindled.[2734]

31 And he sent messengers[4397] unto Abimelech [I]privily,8649 saying, Behold, Gaal the son of Ebed and his brethren be come to Shechem; and, behold, they fortify the city against thee.

32 Now therefore up by night,[3915] thou and the people that *is* with thee, and lie in wait in the field:[7704]

33 And it shall be, *that* in the morning, as soon as the sun is up, thou shalt rise early, and set upon the city: and, behold, *when* he and the people that *is* with him come out against thee, then mayest thou do[6213] to them [I][a]as thou shalt find occasion.

34 And Abimelech rose up, and all the people that *were* with him, by night, and they laid wait against Shechem in four companies.[7218]

35 And Gaal the son of Ebed went out, and stood in the entering of the gate of the city: and Abimelech rose up, and

15 [a]Isa. 30:2; Dan. 4:12; Hos. 14:7 [b]Judg. 9:20; Num. 21:28; Ezek. 19:14 [c]2Kgs. 14:9; Ps. 104:16; Isa. 2:13; 37:24; Ezek. 31:3

16 [a]Judg. 8:35

17 [I]Hebr. *cast his life*

18 [a]Judg. 9:5, 6

19 [a]Isa. 8:6; Phil. 3:3

20 [a]Judg. 9:15, 56, 57

21 [a]2Sam. 20:14

23 [a]1Sam. 16:14; 18:9, 10; 1Kgs. 12:15; 22:22; 2Chr. 10:15; 18:19-34; Isa. 19:2, 14 [b]Isa. 33:1

24 [I]Hebr. *strengthened his hands to kill* [a]1Kgs. 2:32; Esth. 9:25; Ps. 7:16; Matt. 23:35, 36

27 [I]Or, *songs* [a]Isa. 16:9, 10; Jer. 25:30; [b]Judg. 9:4

28 [a]1Sam. 25:10; 1Kgs. 12:16 [b]Gen. 34:2, 6

29 [a]2Sam. 15:4

30 [I]Or, *hot*

31 [I]Hebr. *craftily,* or, *to Tormah*

33 [I]Hebr. *as thy hand shall find* [a]1Sam. 10:7; 25:8; Eccl. 9:10

the people that *were* with him, from lying in wait.

36 And when Gaal saw[7200] the people, he said to Zebul, Behold, there come people down from the top of the mountains. And Zebul said unto him, Thou seest the shadow of the mountains as *if they were* men.

37 And Gaal spake again and said, See there come people down by the [I]middle of the land,[776] and another company come along by the plain of [II][a]Meonenim.[6049]

38 Then said Zebul unto him, Where *is* now thy mouth,[6310] wherewith thou [a]saidst,[559] Who *is* Abimelech, that we should serve him? *is* not this the people that thou hast despised?[3988] go out, I pray now, and fight with them.

39 And Gaal went out before the men of Shechem, and fought with Abimelech.

40 And Abimelech chased him, and he fled before him, and many were overthrown[5307] *and* wounded,[2491] *even* unto the entering of the gate.

41 And Abimelech dwelt at Arumah: and Zebul thrust out Gaal and his brethren, that they should not dwell in Shechem.

42 And it came to pass on the morrow, that the people went out into the field; and they told Abimelech.

43 And he took the people, and divided them into three companies, and laid wait in the field, and looked,[7200] and, behold, the people *were* come forth out of the city; and he rose up against them, and smote[5221] them.

44 And Abimelech, and the company that *was* with him, rushed forward, and stood in the entering of the gate of the city: and the two *other* companies ran upon all *the people* that *were* in the fields, and slew[5221] them.

45 And Abimelech fought against the city all that day; and [a]he took the city, and slew the people that *was* therein, and [b]beat down[5422] the city, and sowed it with salt.

46 And when all the men of the tower of Shechem heard *that,* they entered into an hold[6877] of the house [a]of the god[410] Berith.

47 And it was told Abimelech, that all the men of the tower of Shechem were gathered together.[6908]

48 And Abimelech gat him up to mount [a]Zalmon, he and all the people that *were* with him; and Abimelech took an axe in his hand, and cut down[3772] a bough from the trees, and took[5375] it, and laid *it* on his shoulder, and said unto the people that *were* with him, What ye have seen[7200] [I]me do, make haste, *and* do as I *have done.*

49 And all the people likewise cut down every man his bough, and followed Abimelech, and put *them* to the hold, and set the hold on fire upon them; so that all the men[376] of the tower of Shechem died also, about a thousand men and women.[802]

50 Then went Abimelech to Thebez, and encamped against Thebez, and took it.

51 But there was a strong tower within the city, and thither fled all the men and women, and all they of the city, and shut *it* to them, and gat them up to the top of the tower.

52 And Abimelech came unto the tower, and fought against it, and went hard unto the door of the tower to burn[8313] it with fire.

53 And a certain woman[802] [a]cast a piece of a millstone upon Abimelech's head,[7218] and all to brake his skull.

54 Then [a]he called[7121] hastily unto the young man his armourbearer, and said unto him, Draw thy sword,[2719] and slay[4191] me, that men say[559] not of me, A woman slew him. And his young man thrust him through, and he died.

55 And when the men of Israel saw that Abimelech was dead,[4191] they departed every man unto his place.

56 [a]Thus God rendered[7725] the wickedness[7451] of Abimelech, which he did unto his father, in slaying his seventy brethren:

57 And all the evil of the men of Shechem did God render upon their

37 [I]Hebr. *navel* [II]Or, *The regarders of times* [a]Deut. 18:14

38 [a]Judg. 9:28, 29

45 [a]Judg. 9:20 [b]Deut. 29:23; 1Kgs. 12:25; 2Kgs. 3:25

46 [a]Judg. 8:33

48 [I]Hebr. *I have done* [a]Ps. 68:14

53 [a]2Sam. 11:21

54 [a]1Sam. 31:4

56 [a]Judg. 9:24; Job 31:3; Ps. 94:23; Prov. 5:22

heads:[7218] and upon them came [a]the curse[7045] of Jotham the son of Jerubbaal.

Tola

10 And after Abimelech there [a]arose to [I]defend[3467] Israel Tola the son[1121] of Puah, the son of Dodo, a man[376] of Issachar; and he dwelt in Shamir in mount Ephraim.

2 And he judged[8199] Israel twenty and three years, and died, and was buried[6912] in Shamir.

Jair

3 And after him arose Jair, a Gileadite, and judged Israel twenty and two years.

4 And he had thirty sons[1121] that [a]rode on thirty ass colts, and they had thirty cities, [b]which are called[7121] [I][c]Havoth–jair unto this day,[3117] which *are* in the land[776] of Gilead.

5 And Jair died, and was buried in Camon.

6 And [a]the children[1121] of Israel did[6213] evil[7451] again in the sight of the LORD, and [b]served[5647] Baalim, and Ashtaroth, and [c]the gods[430] of Syria, and the gods of [d]Zidon, and the gods of Moab, and the gods of the children of Ammon, and the gods of the Philistines, and forsook[5800] the LORD, and served not him.

7 And the anger of the LORD was hot[2734] against Israel, and he [a]sold them into the hands[3027] of the Philistines, and into the hands of the children of Ammon.

8 And that year they vexed[7492] and [I]oppressed the children of Israel: eighteen years, all the children of Israel that *were* on the other side Jordan in the land of the Amorites, which *is* in Gilead.

9 Moreover the children of Ammon passed over[5674] Jordan to fight also against Judah, and against Benjamin, and against the house[1004] of Ephraim; so that Israel was sore distressed.

10 [a]And the children of Israel cried[2199] unto the LORD, saying, We have sinned[2398] against thee, both because we have forsaken[5800] our God,[430] and also served Baalim.

11 And the LORD said[559] unto the children of Israel, *Did* not *I deliver you* [a]from the Egyptians, and [b]from the Amorites, [c]from the children of Ammon, [d]and from the Philistines?

12 [a]The Zidonians also, [b]and the Amalekites, and the Maonites, [c]did oppress you; and ye cried to me, and I delivered[3467] you out of their hand.

13 [a]Yet ye have forsaken me, and served other gods: wherefore I will deliver you no more.

14 Go and [a]cry[2199] unto the gods which ye have chosen;[977] let them deliver you in the time[6256] of your tribulation.

15 And the children of Israel said unto the LORD, We have sinned: [a]do[6213] thou unto us whatsoever [I]seemeth good[2896] unto thee; deliver[5337] us only, we pray thee,[4994] this day.

16 [a]And they put away[5493] the [I]strange[5236] gods from among them, and served the LORD: and [b]his soul[5315] [II]was grieved for the misery[5999] of Israel.

17 Then the children of Ammon were [I]gathered together,[6817] and encamped in Gilead. And the children of Israel assembled themselves together,[622] and encamped in [a]Mizpeh.

18 And the people *and* princes[8269] of Gilead said one[376] to another,[7453] What man *is he* that will begin to fight against the children of Ammon? he shall [a]be head[7218] over all the inhabitants of Gilead.

Jephthah Is Asked to Lead Gilead's Army

11 Now [a]Jephthah the Gileadite was [b]a mighty man of valour,[2428] and he *was* the son[1121] of [I]an harlot:[2181] and Gilead begat Jephthah.

2 And Gilead's wife[802] bare him sons; and his wife's sons grew up, and they thrust out Jephthah, and said[559] unto him, Thou shalt not inherit[5157] in our father's[1] house;[1004] for thou *art* the son of a strange woman.[802]

---

57 [a]Judg. 9:20

1 [I]Or, *deliver* [a]Judg. 2:16

4 [I]Or, *The villages of Jair* [a]Judg. 5:10; 12:14; [b]Deut. 3:14 [c]Num. 32:41

6 [a]Judg. 2:11; 3:7; 4:1; 6:1; 13:1 [b]Judg. 2:13 [c]Judg. 2:12 [d]1Kgs. 11:33; Ps. 106:36

7 [a]Judg. 2:14; 1Sam. 12:9

8 [I]Hebr. *crushed*

10 [a]1Sam. 12:10

11 [a]Ex. 14:30 [b]Num. 21:21; 24, 25 [c]Judg. 3:12, 13 [d]Judg. 3:31

12 [a]Judg. 5:19 [b]Judg. 6:3 [c]Ps. 106:42, 43

13 [a]Deut. 32:15; Jer. 2:13

14 [a]Deut. 32:37, 38; 2Kgs. 3:13; Jer. 2:28

15 [I]Hebr. *is good in thine eyes* [a]1Sam. 3:18; 2Sam. 15:26

16 [I]Hebr. *gods of strangers* [II]Hebr. *was shortened* [a]2Chr. 7:14; 15:8; Jer. 18:7, 8 [b]Ps. 106:44, 45; Isa. 63:9

17 [I]Hebr. *cried together* [a]Gen. 31:49; Judg. 11:11, 29

18 [a]Judg. 11:8, 11

1 [I]Hebr. *a woman a harlot* [a]Heb. 11:32 [b]Judg. 6:12; 2Kgs. 5:1

3 Then Jephthah fled [I]from his brethren,[251] and dwelt in the land[776] of Tob: and there were gathered[3850] [a]vain men to Jephthah, and went out with him.

4 And it came to pass [I]in process of time,[3117] that the children of Ammon made war against Israel.

5 And it was so, that when the children of Ammon made war against Israel, the elders[2205] of Gilead went to fetch Jephthah out of the land of Tob:

6 And they said unto Jephthah, Come, and be our captain, that we may fight with the children of Ammon.

7 And Jephthah said unto the elders of Gilead, [a]Did not ye hate[8130] me, and expel me out of my father's house? and why are ye come unto me now when ye are in distress?

8 [a]And the elders of Gilead said unto Jephthah, Therefore we [b]turn again[7725] to thee now, that thou mayest go with us, and fight against the children of Ammon, and be [c]our head[7218] over all the inhabitants of Gilead.

9 And Jephthah said unto the elders of Gilead, If ye bring me home again to fight against the children of Ammon, and the LORD deliver them before me, shall I be your head?

10 And the elders of Gilead said unto Jephthah, [a]The LORD [I]be witness[8085] between us, if we do[6213] not so according to thy words.[1697]

11 Then Jephthah went with the elders of Gilead, and the people[5271] made[7760] him [a]head and captain over them: and Jephthah uttered all his words [b]before the LORD in Mizpeh.

12 And Jephthah sent messengers[4397] unto the king[4428] of the children of Ammon, saying, What hast thou to do with me, that thou art come against me to fight in my land?

13 And the king of the children of Ammon answered[559] unto the messengers of Jephthah, [a]Because Israel took away my land, when they came up[5927] out of Egypt, from Arnon even unto [b]Jabbok, and unto Jordan: now therefore restore[7725] those *lands* again peaceably.

14 And Jephthah sent messengers again unto the king of the children of Ammon:

15 And said unto him, Thus saith[559] Jephthah, [a]Israel took not away the land of Moab, nor the land of the children of Ammon:

16 But when Israel came up from Egypt, and [a]walked through the wilderness unto the Red sea, and [b]came to Kadesh;

17 Then [a]Israel sent messengers unto the king of Edom, saying, Let me, I pray thee,[4994] pass[5674] through thy land: [b]but the king of Edom would not hearken[8085] *thereto.* And in like manner they sent unto the king of Moab: but he would[14] not *consent:* and Israel [c]abode in Kadesh.

18 Then they went along through the wilderness, and [a]compassed the land of Edom, and the land of Moab, and [b]came by the east side of the land of Moab, [c]and pitched on the other side of Arnon, but came not within the border of Moab: for Arnon *was* the border of Moab.

19 And [a]Israel sent messengers unto Sihon king of the Amorites, the king of Heshbon; and Israel said unto him, [b]Let us pass, we pray thee, through thy land into my place.

20 [a]But Sihon trusted not Israel to pass through his coast: but Sihon gathered all his people together,[622] and pitched in Jahaz, and fought against Israel.

21 And the LORD God[430] of Israel delivered Sihon and all his people into the hand of Israel, and they [a]smote[5221] them: so Israel possessed[3423] all the land of the Amorites, the inhabitants of that country.[776]

22 And they possessed [a]all the coasts of the Amorites, from Arnon even unto Jabbok, and from the wilderness even unto Jordan.

23 So now the LORD God of Israel hath dispossessed[3423] the Amorites from before his people Israel, and shouldest thou possess[3423] it?

24 Wilt not thou possess that which [a]Chemosh thy god giveth thee to possess?

3 [I]Hebr. *from the face* [a]Judg. 9:4; 1Sam. 22:2
4 [I]Hebr. *after days*
7 [a]Gen. 26:27
8 [a]Judg. 10:18 [b]Luke 17:4 [c]Judg. 10:18
10 [I]Hebr. *be the hearer between us* [a]Jer. 42:5
11 [a]Judg. 11:8 [b]Judg. 10:17; 20:1; 1Sam. 10:17; 11:15
13 [a]Num. 21:24-26 [b]Gen. 32:22
15 [a]Deut. 2:9, 19
16 [a]Num. 14:25; Deut. 1:40; Josh. 5:6 [b]Num. 13:26; 20:1; Deut. 1:46
17 [a]Num. 20:14 [b]Num. 20:18, 21; [c]Num. 20:1
18 [a]Num. 21:4; Deut. 2:1-8 [b]Num. 21:11 [c]Num. 21:13; 22:36
19 [a]Num. 21:21; Deut. 2:26 [b]Num. 21:22; Deut. 2:27
20 [a]Num. 21:23; Deut. 2:32
21 [a]Num. 21:24, 25; Deut. 2:33, 34
22 [a]Deut. 2:36
24 [a]Num. 21:29; 1Kgs. 11:7; Jer. 48:7

So whomsoever [b]the LORD our God shall
drive out from before us, them will we
possess.
25 And now *art* thou any thing
better[2896] than [a]Balak the son of Zippor,
king of Moab? did he ever strive[7378]
against Israel, or did he ever fight against
them,
26 While Israel dwelt in [a]Heshbon
and her towns, and in [b]Aroer and her
towns, and in all the cities that *be* along
by the coasts of Arnon, three hundred
years? why therefore did ye not
recover[5337] *them* within that time?[6256]
27 Wherefore I have not sinned[2398]
against thee, but thou doest[6213] me
wrong[7451] to war against me: the LORD
[a]the Judge[8199] [b]be judge this day[3117] between the children of Israel and the children of Ammon.
28 Howbeit the king of the children
of Ammon hearkened[8085] not unto the
words of Jephthah which he sent him.

Jephthah's Vow

🔑29 Then [a]the Spirit[7307] of the LORD
came upon [I]Jephthah, and he passed
over[5674] Gilead, and Manasseh, and
passed over Mizpeh of Gilead, and from
Mizpeh of Gilead he passed over *unto* the
children of Ammon.
30 And Jephthah [a]vowed a vow[5088]
unto the LORD, and said, If thou shalt
without fail deliver the children of
Ammon into mine hands,[3027]
31 Then it shall be, that [I]whatso-
ever cometh forth of the doors of
my house to meet me, when I return[7725]
in peace[7965] from the children of Ammon, [a]shall surely be the LORD's, [IIb]and
I will offer it up for a burnt offering.[5930]
32 So Jephthah passed over unto the
children of Ammon to fight against
them; and the LORD delivered them into
his hands.

24 [b]Deut. 9:4, 5; 18:12; Josh. 3:10

25 [a]Num. 22:2; Josh. 24:9

26 [a]Num. 21:25; [b]Deut. 2:36

27 [a]Gen. 18:25; [b]Gen. 16:5; 31:53; 1Sam. 24:12, 15

29 [I]Jephthah seems to have been Judge only of Northeast Israel [a]Judg. 3:10

30 [a]Gen. 28:20; 1Sam. 1:11

31 [I]Hebr. *that which cometh forth, which shall come forth* [II]Or, *or I will offer it* [a]Lev. 27:2, 3; 1Sam. 1:11, 28; 2:18 [b]Ps. 66:13; Lev. 27:11, 12

🔑 **11:29–33** This vow of Jephthah has caused much concern for many Bible scholars. If no other considerations are brought into the discussion, the language of this passage would naturally lead one to believe that Jephthah actually did offer his daughter as a sacrifice to the Lord. Most conservative commentators, on the contrary, hold that Jephthah did not actually put his daughter to death, but dedicated her to the service of the Lord.

There are two major areas of discussion relative to the vow. The first deals with whether Jephthah actually intended a human sacrifice when he made the vow. Some would attempt to prove by the choice of words used in the vow that he did intend a human sacrifice. However, it must be pointed out that this was only one of the possibilities according to the usage of the word "whatsoever." Otherwise, if he had intended a human sacrifice, why would he have been so surprised and distraught when his daughter became the object of the vow (v. 35). Also, Jephthah knew the Law well enough that he could not have been ignorant of the fact that God did not allow human sacrifice. Furthermore, he would have been doubly guilty since he had no other children, and he knew that sacrifices to Jehovah were to be exclusively of the male gender (v. 34). Jephthah's apprehension concerning the coming battle with the children of Ammon caused him to word his vow hastily and leave open the possibility of a human sacrifice.

The second problem is whether Jephthah actually did take his own daughter's life. It would have been next to impossible for Jephthah to have found a priest who would perform such a sacrifice. The idea expressed by conservative scholars is that if this were true, Jephthah would not have been included in the "heroes of the faith" (Heb. 11:32). Furthermore, would it be proper to commend Jephthah if he had broken God's laws in such a serious matter? To say that his daughter spent her last two months of life up in the mountains with her friends rather than with her mourning father would have been peculiar. In addition to this, why is it that she bemoans her virginity rather than her short life? The phrase "and she knew no man" would be meaningless if her life was taken. It would seem more logical to assume that she was to be wholly given to the service of the Lord where she must continue in her virginity.

The most sensible explanation of these events then would be that Jephthah did not actually perform a human sacrifice because he knew and obeyed God's laws even though, according to his original vow, this would have been the result. The phrase stating that he "did with her according to his vow" does not actually state that he took her life, but that Jephthah dedicated her to the Lord.

33 And he smote them from Aroer, even till thou come to [a]Minnith, *even* twenty cities, and unto [I]the plain of the vineyards, with a very great slaughter.[4347] Thus the children of Ammon were subdued before the children of Israel.

34 And Jephthah came to [a]Mizpeh unto his house, and, behold, [b]his daughter came out to meet him with timbrels8596 and with dances: and she *was his* only child;[3173] [I]beside her he had neither son nor daughter.

35 And it came to pass, when he saw her, that he [a]rent his clothes, and said, Alas, my daughter! thou hast brought me very low,3766 and thou art one of them that trouble5916 me: for I [b]have opened my mouth unto the LORD, and [c]I cannot go back.

36 And she said unto him, My father,[1] *if* thou hast opened thy mouth unto the LORD, [a]do to me according to that which hath proceeded out of thy mouth; forasmuch as [b]the LORD hath taken vengeance[5360] for thee of thine enemies, *even* of the children of Ammon.

37 And she said unto her father, Let this thing[1697] be done[6213] for me: let me alone[7503] two months, that I may [I]go up and down upon the mountains, and bewail my virginity,[1331] I and my fellows.

38 And he said, Go. And he sent her away *for* two months: and she went with her companions, and bewailed1058 her virginity upon the mountains.

39 And it came to pass at the end of two months, that she returned[7725] unto her father, who [a]did[6213] with her *according* to his vow which he had vowed: and she knew[3045] no man.[376] And it was a [I]custom[2706] in Israel,

40 *That* the daughters of Israel went [I]yearly [II]to lament the daughter of Jephthah the Gileadite four days in a year.

33 [I]Or, *Abel* [a]Ezek. 27:17

34 [I]Hebr. *of himself* [a]Judg. 10:17; 11:11; [b]Ex. 15:20; 1Sam. 18:6; Ps. 68:25; Jer. 31:4

35 [a]Gen. 37:29; 34 [b]Eccl. 5:2 [c]Num. 30:2; Ps. 15:4; Eccl. 5:4, 5

36 [a]Num. 30:2; [b]2Sam. 18:19, 31

37 [I]Hebr. *go and go down*

39 [I]Or, *ordinance* [a]Judg. 11:31; 1Sam. 1:22, 24; 2:18

40 [I]Hebr. *from year to year* [II]Or, to talk with [a]Judg. 5:11

1 [I]Hebr. *were called* [a]Judg. 8:1

3 [a]1Sam. 19:5; 28:21; Job 13:14; Ps. 119:109

4 [a]1Sam. 25:10; Ps. 78:9

5 [a]Josh. 22:11; Judg. 3:28; 7:24

6 [I]Which signifieth *a stream,* or, *flood* [a]Ps. 69:2, 15; Isa. 27:12

Jephthah Defeats Ephraim

12 And [a]the men[376] of Ephraim [I]gathered themselves together, and went northward, and said[559] unto Jephthah, Wherefore passedst thou over to fight against the children[1121] of Ammon, and didst not call[7121] us to go with thee? we will burn[8313] thine house[1004] upon thee with fire.

2 And Jephthah said unto them, I and my people[5971] were at great strife[7379] with the children of Ammon; and when I called you, ye delivered[3467] me not out of their hands.[3027]

3 And when I saw[7200] that ye delivered *me* not, I [a]put my life[5315] in my hands,[3709] and passed over[5674] against the children of Ammon, and the LORD delivered them into my hand:[3027] wherefore then are ye come up[5927] unto me this day,[3117] to fight against me?

4 Then Jephthah gathered together[6908] all the men[582] of Gilead, and fought with Ephraim: and the men of Gilead smote[5221] Ephraim, because they said, Ye Gileadites [a]*are* fugitives of Ephraim among the Ephraimites, *and* among the Manassites.

5 And the Gileadites took the [a]passages of Jordan before the Ephraimites: and it was *so,* that when those Ephraimites which were escaped said, Let me go over;[5674] that the men of Gilead said unto him, *Art* thou an Ephraimite? If he said, Nay;

🗝 6 Then said they unto him, Say[559] now [Ia]Shibboleth: and he said Sibboleth: for he could not frame to pronounce *it* right. Then they took him, and slew[7819] him at the passages of Jordan: and there fell[5307] at that time[6256] of the Ephraimites forty and two thousand.

7 And Jephthah judged[8199] Israel six years. Then died Jephthah the Gileadite,

🗝 **12:6** This was a linguistic test given in order to tell whether or not a man was an Ephraimite. The word "Shibboleth" meant "a stream in flood time." However, an Ephraimite, because of the nature of his dialect, said "Sibboleth," substituting the "s" sound for the "sh" sound. Even though he denied being an Ephraimite his tongue would betray him, resulting in his certain death.

and was buried[6912] in *one of* the cities of Gilead.

Ibzan

8 And after him [I]Ibzan of Bethlehem judged Israel.

9 And he had thirty sons,[1121] and thirty daughters, *whom* he sent abroad, and took in thirty daughters from abroad for his sons. And he judged Israel seven years.

10 Then died Ibzan, and was buried at Bethlehem.

Elon

11 And after him [I]Elon, a Zebulonite, judged Israel; and he judged Israel ten years.

12 And Elon the Zebulonite died, and was buried in Aijalon in the country[776] of Zebulun.

Abdon

13 And after him [I]Abdon the son[1121] of Hillel, a Pirathonite, judged Israel.

14 And he had forty sons and thirty [I]nephews, that [a]rode on threescore and ten ass colts: and he judged Israel eight years.

15 And Abdon the son of Hillel the Pirathonite died, and was buried in Pirathon in the land[776] of Ephraim, [a]in the mount of the Amalekites.

Samson's Birth

13 ⚿ And the children[1121] of Israel [I][a]did[6213] evil[7451] again in the sight of the LORD; [II]and the LORD delivered them [b]into the hand[3027] of the Philistines forty years.

2 And there was a certain man[376] of [a]Zorah, of the family[4940] of the Danites, whose name *was* Manoah; and his wife[802] *was* barren,[6135] and bare not.

3 And the [a]angel[4397] of the LORD appeared[7200] unto the woman,[802] and said[559] unto her, Behold now, thou *art* barren, and bearest not: but thou shalt conceive, and bear a son.[1121]

4 Now therefore beware,[8104] I pray thee,[4994] and [a]drink not wine nor strong drink, and eat not any unclean[2931] *thing:*

⚿ 5 For, lo, thou shalt conceive, and bear a son; and no [a]razor shall come on his head:[7218] for the child shall be [b]a Nazarite[5139] unto God[430] from the womb:[990] and he shall [c]begin to deliver Israel out of the hand of the Philistines.

6 Then the woman came and told[5046] her husband,[376] saying, [a]A man of God came unto me, and his [b]countenance *was* like the countenance of an angel of God, very terrible:[3372] but I [c]asked[7592] him not whence he *was,* neither told he me his name:

7 But he said unto me, Behold, thou shalt conceive, and bear a son; and now drink no wine nor strong drink, neither eat any unclean[2932] *thing:* for the child shall be a Nazarite to God from the womb to the day[3117] of his death.[4191]

8 Then Manoah intreated[6279] the LORD, and said, O my Lord, let the man of God which thou didst send come again unto us, and teach[3384] us what we shall do[6213] unto the child that shall be born.

9 And God hearkened[8085] to the voice of Manoah; and the angel of God came again unto the woman as she sat in the field:[7704] but Manoah her husband *was* not with her.

10 And the woman made haste, and ran, and shewed[5046] her husband, and said unto him, Behold, the man hath ap-

8 [I]He seems to have been only a civil judge in Northeast *Israel*

11 [I]A civil Judge in Northeast *Israel*

13 [I]A civil Judge in Northeast *Israel*

14 [I]Hebr. *sons' sons* [a]Judg. 5:10; 10:4

15 [a]Judg. 3:13, 27; 5:14

1 [I]Hebr. *added to commit* [II]This seems a partial captivity [a]Judg. 2:11; 3:7; 4:1; 6:1; 10:6 [b]1Sam. 12:9

2 [a]Josh. 19:41

3 [a]Judg. 6:12; Luke 1:11, 13, 28, 31

4 [a]Num. 6:2, 3; Judg. 13:14; Luke 1:15

5 [a]Num. 6:5; 1Sam. 1:11 [b]Num. 6:2 [c]1Sam. 7:13; 2Sam. 8:1; 1Chr. 18:1

6 [a]Deut. 33:1; 1Sam. 2:27; 9:6; 1Kgs. 17:24 [b]Matt. 28:3; Luke 9:29; Acts 6:15 [c]Judg. 13:17, 18

⚿ **13:1** The Philistines were a group of people from the Aegean Sea area. Called "the sea people," they had been present in Canaan for centuries in small numbers (Gen. 20, 21, 26). In the thirteenth century B.C., a large number of these "sea people" attempted to conquer Egypt, but were defeated and afterward settled on the coast of Canaan. Even Samson's victory against them (Judg. 16:30) was not the final time that the Philistines were mentioned in regards to Israel. They were evidently still a plague to Israel even in David's day (2 Sam. 5:17–25).

⚿ **13:5** See note on Numbers 6:2–21, on Nazarite.

peared unto me, that came unto me the *other* day.

11 And Manoah arose, and went after his wife, and came to the man, and said unto him, *Art* thou the man that spakest[1696] unto the woman? And he said, I *am*.

12 And Manoah said, Now let thy words[1697] come to pass. [I]How shall we order[4941] the child, and [II]*how* shall we do unto him?

13 And the angel of the LORD said unto Manoah, Of all that I said unto the woman let her beware.

14 She may not eat of any *thing* that cometh of the vine, [a]neither let her drink wine or strong drink, nor eat any unclean *thing:* all that I commanded[6680] her let her observe.[8104]

15 And Manoah said unto the angel of the LORD, I pray thee, [a]let us detain thee, until we shall have made ready[6213] a kid [I]for thee.

16 And the angel of the LORD said unto Manoah, Though thou detain me, I will not eat of thy bread: and if thou wilt offer a burnt offering,[5930] thou must offer[6213] it unto the LORD. For Manoah knew[3045] not that he *was* an angel of the LORD.

17 And Manoah said unto the angel of the LORD, What *is* thy name, that when thy sayings[1697] come to pass we may do thee honour?[3513]

18 And the angel of the LORD said unto him, [a]Why askest thou thus after my name, seeing it *is* [I][b]secret?[6383]

19 So Manoah took a kid with a meat offering,[4503] [a]and offered[5922] *it* upon a rock unto the LORD: and *the angel* did wonderously; and Manoah and his wife looked on.[7200]

20 For it came to pass, when the flame went up[5927] toward heaven[8064] from off the altar, that the angel of the LORD ascended in the flame of the altar. And Manoah and his wife looked on *it,* and [a]fell[5307] on their faces to the ground.[776]

21 But the angel of the LORD did no more appear[7200] to Manoah and to his wife. [a]Then Manoah knew that he *was* an angel of the LORD.

22 And Manoah said unto his wife, [a]We shall surely die,[4191] because we have seen[7200] God.

23 But his wife said unto him, If the LORD were pleased[2654] to kill us, he would not have received a burnt offering and a meat offering at our hands,[3027] neither would he have shewed us all these *things,* nor would as at this time[6256] have told[8085] us *such things* as these.

24 And the woman bare a son, and called[7121] his name [a]Samson: and [b]the child grew, and the LORD blessed[1288] him.

25 [a]And the Spirit[7307] of the LORD began to move him at times in [I][b]the camp[4264] of Dan [c]between Zorah and Eshtaol.

Samson's First Wife

14 And Samson went down [a]to Timnath, and [b]saw[7200] a woman[802]

12 [I]Hebr. *What shall be the manner of the child* [II]Hebr. *what shall be his work?*
14 [a]Judg. 13:4
15 [I]Hebr. *before thee* [a]Gen. 18:5; Judg. 6:18
18 [I]Or, *wonderful* [a]Gen. 32:29 [b]Isa. 9:6
19 [a]Judg. 6:19, 20
20 [a]Lev. 9:24; 1Chr. 21:16; Ezek. 1:28; Matt. 17:6
21 [a]Judg. 6:22
22 [a]Gen. 32:30; Ex. 33:20; Deut. 5:26; Judg. 6:22
24 [a]Heb. 11:32 [b]1Sam. 3:19; Luke 1:80; 2:52
25 [I]Hebr. *Mahanehdan* [a]Judg. 3:10; 1Sam. 11:6; Matt. 4:1 [b]Judg. 18:12 [c]Josh. 15:33; Judg. 18:11
1 [a]Gen. 38:13; Josh. 15:10 [b]Gen. 34:2

13:18, 19 The Hebrew word translated "secret" (*pali* [6383]) should be translated "wonderful." This is the adjectival form of the noun *peli* (6382) which occurs in the Messianic prophecy in Isaiah 9:6, where it is translated "Wonderful." This, plus the angel's willingness to accept offerings, indicate that this was a Christophany, an appearance of Jesus Christ before His incarnation.

13:22 See note on Exodus 23:20–23.

13:24 Samson was a Danite, living adjacent to the Philistines. He was selected before birth as the one who would begin to deliver Israel from the Philistines (Judg. 13:5). God gave him superhuman strength to achieve this, but Samson's whole life was filled with compromise in his repeated refusal to control his sensual desires and whims. His physical blinding by the Philistines (Judg. 16:21) seemingly brought about the opening of his spiritual eyes; for he gave his life for his people, and is included with the "heroes of faith" in the New Testament (Heb. 11:32). His last act of killing the Philistines' leaders did more to defeat them than all his earlier conquests combined (Judg. 16:30).

in Timnath of the daughters of the Philistines.

2 And he came up,[5927] and told[5046] his father[1] and his mother,[517] and said,[559] I have seen a woman in Timnath of the daughters of the Philistines: now therefore [a]get her for me to wife.[802]

3 Then his father and his mother said unto him, *Is there* never a woman among the daughters of [a]thy brethren,[251] or among all my people,[5971] that thou goest to take a wife of the [b]uncircumcised[6189] Philistines? And Samson said unto his father, Get her for me; for [I]she pleaseth[3477] me well.[5869]

4 But his father and his mother knew[3045] not that it *was* [a]of the LORD, that he sought an occasion against the Philistines: for at that time[6256] [b]the Philistines had dominion[7287] over Israel.

5 Then went Samson down, and his father and his mother, to Timnath, and came to the vineyards of Timnath: and, behold, a young lion roared [I]against him.

6 And [a]the Spirit[7307] of the LORD came mightily upon him, and he rent him as he would have rent a kid, and *he had* nothing in his hand:[3027] but he told not his father or his mother what he had done.[6213]

7 And he went down, and talked[1696] with the woman; and she pleased[3477] Samson well.

8 And after a time[3117] he returned[7725] to take her, and he turned aside[5493] to see the carcase[4658] of the lion: and, behold, *there was* a swarm of bees and honey in the carcase[1472] of the lion.

9 And he took thereof in his hands,[3709] and went on eating, and came to his father and mother, and he gave them, and they did eat: but he told not them that he had taken the honey out of the carcase of the lion.

10 So his father went down unto the woman: and Samson made there a feast;[4960] for so used the young men to do.[6213]

11 And it came to pass, when they saw him, that they brought thirty companions to be with him.

12 And Samson said unto them, I will now [a]put forth a riddle[2420] unto you: if ye can certainly declare[5046] it me [b]within the seven days of the feast, and find *it* out, then I will give you thirty [I]sheets and thirty [c]change of garments:

13 But if ye cannot declare *it* me, then shall ye give me thirty sheets and thirty change of garments. And they said unto him, Put forth thy riddle, that we may hear[8085] it.

14 And he said unto them, Out of the eater came forth meat, and out of the strong came forth sweetness. And they could not in three days expound[5046] the riddle.

15 And it came to pass on the seventh day,[3117] that they said unto Samson's wife, [a]Entice[6601] thy husband,[376] that he may declare unto us the riddle, [b]lest we burn[8313] thee and thy father's[1] house[1004] with fire: have ye called[7121] us [I]to take that we have? *is it* not *so?*

16 And Samson's wife wept before him, and said, [a]Thou dost but hate[8130] me, and lovest me not: thou hast put forth a riddle unto the children[1121] of my people, and hast not told *it* me. And he said unto her, Behold, I have not told *it* my father nor my mother, and shall I tell[5046] *it* thee?

17 And she wept before him [I]the seven days, while their feast lasted: and it came to pass on the seventh day, that he told her, because she lay sore upon him: and she told the riddle to the children of her people.

18 And the men[582] of the city said

2 [a]Gen. 21:21; 34:4

3 [I]Hebr. *she is right in mine eyes* [a]Gen. 24:3, 4 [b]Gen. 34:14; Ex. 34:16; Deut. 7:3

4 [a]Josh. 11:20; 1Kgs. 12:15; 2Kgs. 6:33; 2Chr. 10:15; 22:7; 25:20 [b]Judg. 13:1; Deut. 28:48

5 [I]Hebr. *in meeting him*

6 [a]Judg. 3:10; 13:25; 1Sam. 11:6

12 [I]Or, *shirts* [a]1Kgs. 10:1; Ezek. 17:2; Luke 14:7 [b]Gen. 29:27 [c]Gen. 45:22; 2Kgs. 5:22

15 [I]Hebr. *to possess us,* or, *to impoverish us?* [a]Judg. 16:5; [b]Judg. 15:6

16 [a]Judg. 16:15

17 [I]Or, *the rest of the seven days*

14:3, 4 Mixed marriages by Israelites with other races were forbidden (Deut. 7:3). Samson's parents were right to oppose his marriage to a heathen woman from the Philistine people who constantly oppressed Israel. It should not be understood here that God forced Samson into this marriage, but that he made his own decision. Though it was not right, God used it to accomplish His will in spite of the lack of wisdom on Samson's part. It proved to be the crucial link in the liberation of Israel from the Philistines (Judg. 15:1–8).

unto him on the seventh day before the
sun went down, What *is* sweeter than
honey? and what *is* stronger than a lion?
And he said unto them, If ye had not
plowed with my heifer, ye had not found
out my riddle.
19 And [a]the Spirit of the LORD came
upon him, and he went down to
Ashkelon, and slew[5221] thirty men[376] of
them, and took their [I]spoil, and gave
change of garments unto them which expounded the riddle. And his anger was
kindled,[2734] and he went up[5927] to his father's house.
20 But Samson's wife [a]was *given* to
his companion, whom he had used as
[b]his friend.

15

15 But it came to pass within a
while after, in the time[3117] of
wheat harvest, that Samson visited[6485]
his wife[802] with a kid; and he said,[559] I
will go in to my wife into the chamber.
But her father[1] would not suffer him to
go in.
2 And her father said, I verily
thought[559] that thou hadst utterly
[a]hated[8130] her; therefore I gave her to thy
companion: *is* not her younger sister[269]
fairer[2896] than she? [I]take her, I pray
thee,[4994] instead of her.
3 And Samson said concerning them,
[I]Now shall I be more blameless[5352] than
the Philistines, though I do[6213] them a
displeasure.[7451]
4 And Samson went and caught
three hundred foxes, and took [I]firebrands,
and turned tail to tail, and put a firebrand in the midst between two tails.
5 And when he had set the brands
on fire, he let *them* go into the standing
corn of the Philistines, and burnt up
both the shocks, and also the standing
corn, with the vineyards *and* olives.
6 Then the Philistines said, Who
hath done this? And they answered,[559]
Samson, the son in law of the Timnite,
because he had taken his wife, and given
her to his companion. [a]And the Philistines came up,[5927] and burnt[8313] her and
her father with fire.
7 And Samson said unto them,
Though ye have done this, yet will I be
avenged[5358] of you, and after that I will
cease.
8 And he smote[5221] them hip[7785] and
thigh[3409] with a great slaughter:[4347] and
he went down and dwelt in the top of the
rock Etam.

Samson Kills a Thousand Philistines

9 Then the Philistines went up,[5927]
and pitched in Judah, and spread themselves[5203] [a]in Lehi.
10 And the men[376] of Judah said,
Why are ye come up[5927] against us? And
they answered, To bind Samson are we
come up, to do to him as he hath done
to us.
11 Then three thousand men of
Judah [I]went to the top of the rock Etam,
and said to Samson, Knowest[3045] thou
not that the Philistines *are* [a]rulers[4910]
over us? what *is* this *that* thou hast done
unto us? And he said unto them, As
they did unto me, so have I done unto
them.
12 And they said unto him, We are
come down to bind thee, that we may deliver thee into the hand of the Philistines.
And Samson said unto them, Swear[7650]
unto me, that ye will not fall upon me
yourselves.
13 And they spake[559] unto him, saying, No; but we will bind thee fast, and
deliver thee into their hand: but surely we
will not kill thee. And they bound him
with two new cords, and brought him
up[5927] from the rock.
14 *And* when he came unto Lehi, the
Philistines shouted[7321] against him: and

19 [I]Or, *apparel* [a]Judg. 3:10; 13:25
20 [a]Judg. 15:2 [b]John 3:29
2 [I]Hebr. *let her be thine* [a]Judg. 14:20
3 [I]Or, *Now shall I be blameless from the Philistines, though*
4 [I]Or, *torches*
9 [a]Judg. 15:19
11 [I]Hebr. *went down* [a]Judg. 14:4

15:14, 15 The great statement of these verses is that the true source of Samson's strength was not merely in his long hair or in abstaining from strong drink. It was provided by God to accomplish His will. For a contrasting look at Samson's life, see note on Judges 16:17.

[a]the Spirit[7307] of the LORD came mightily upon him, and the cords that *were* upon his arms became as flax that was burnt with fire, and his bands [I]loosed from off his hands.[3027]

15 And he found a [I]new jawbone of an ass, and put forth his hand, and took it, and [a]slew[5221] a thousand men therewith.

16 And Samson said, With the jawbone of an ass, [I]heaps upon heaps, with the jaw of an ass have I slain[5221] a thousand men.

17 And it came to pass, when he had made an end[3615] of speaking,[1696] that he cast away the jawbone out of his hand, and called[7121] that place [I]Ramath–lehi.

18 And he was sore athirst, and called on the LORD, and said, [a]Thou hast given this great deliverance[8668] into the hand of thy servant:[5650] and now shall I die[4191] for thirst, and fall into the hand of the uncircumcised?[6189]

19 But God[430] clave an hollow place that *was* in [I]the jaw, and there came water thereout; and when he had drunk, [a]his spirit came again, and he revived: wherefore he called the name thereof [II]En–hakkore, which *is* in Lehi unto this day.[3117]

20 [I]And he judged[8199] Israel [a]in the days of the Philistines twenty years.

Samson Removes Gaza's City Gates

16 Then went Samson to Gaza, and saw[7200] there [I]an harlot,[2181] and went in unto her.

2 *And it was told* the Gazites, saying, Samson is come hither. And they [a]compassed *him* in, and laid wait for him all night[3915] in the gate of the city, and were [I]quiet all the night, saying, In the morning, when it is day, we shall kill him.

3 And Samson lay till midnight, and arose at midnight, and took the doors of the gate of the city, and the two posts, and went away with them, [I]bar and all, and put *them* upon his shoulders, and carried them up to the top[7218] of an hill that *is* before Hebron.

Samson and Delilah

4 And it came to pass afterward, that he loved[157] a woman[802] [I]in the valley of Sorek, whose name *was* Delilah.

5 And the lords[5633] of the Philistines came up[5927] unto her, and said[559] unto her, [a]Entice[6601] him, and see wherein his great strength *lieth,* and by what *means* we may prevail against him, that we may bind him to [I]afflict him: and we will give thee every one[376] of us eleven hundred *pieces* of silver.

6 And Delilah said to Samson, Tell[5046] me, I pray thee,[4994] wherein thy great strength *lieth,* and wherewith thou mightest be bound to afflict thee.

7 And Samson said unto her, If they bind me with seven [I]green withs that were never dried, then shall I be weak, and be as [II]another man.[120]

8 Then the lords of the Philistines brought up[5927] to her seven green withs which had not been dried, and she bound him with them.

9 Now *there were* men lying in wait, abiding with her in the chamber. And she said unto him, The Philistines *be* upon thee, Samson. And he brake the withs, as a thread of tow is broken when it [I]toucheth[7306] the fire. So his strength was not known.[3045]

10 And Delilah said unto Samson, Behold, thou hast mocked[2048] me, and told me lies: now tell me, I pray thee, wherewith thou mightest be bound.

11 And he said unto her, If they bind me fast with new ropes [I]that never were occupied, then shall I be weak, and be as another man.

12 Delilah therefore took new ropes, and bound him therewith, and said unto him, The Philistines *be* upon thee, Samson. And *there were* liers in wait abiding in the chamber. And he brake them from off his arms like a thread.

---

14 [I]Hebr. *were melted* [a]Judg. 3:10; 14:6

15 [I]Hebr. *moist* [a]Lev. 26:8; Josh. 23:10; Judg. 3:31

16 [I]Hebr. *a heap, two heaps*

17 [I]That is, *The lifting up of the jawbone,* or, *casting away of the jawbone*

18 [a]Ps. 3:7

19 [I]Or, *Lehi* [II]That is, *The well of him that called,* or, *cried* Ps. 34:6 [a]Gen. 45:27; Isa. 40:29

20 [I]He seems to have judged Southwest Israel during twenty years of their servitude of the Philistines [a]Judg. 13:1

1 [I]Hebr. *a woman a harlot*

2 [I]Hebr. *silent* [a]1Sam. 23:26; Ps. 118:10-12; Acts 9:24

3 [I]Hebr. *with the bar*

4 [I]Or, *by the brook*

5 [I]Or, *humble* [a]Judg. 14:15; Prov. 2:16-19; 5:3-11; 6:24-26; 7:21-23

7 [I]Or, *new cords* [II]Hebr. *one*

9 [I]Hebr. *smelleth*

11 [I]Hebr. *wherewith work hath not been done*

13 And Delilah said unto Samson,
Hitherto thou hast mocked me, and told
me lies: tell me wherewith thou mightest
be bound. And he said unto her, If thou
weavest the seven locks of my head[7218]
with the web.
14 And she fastened[8628] *it* with the
pin, and said unto him, The Philistines *be*
upon thee, Samson. And he awaked out
of his sleep, and went away with the pin
of the beam, and with the web.
15 And she said unto him, [a]How
canst thou say,[559] I love[157] thee, when
thine heart[3820] *is* not with me? thou hast
mocked me these three times, and hast
not told[5046] me wherein thy great
strength *lieth.*
16 And it came to pass, when she
pressed him daily with her words,[1697]
and urged him, *so* that his soul[5315] was
[I]vexed[7114] unto death;
17 That he [a]told her all his heart,
and said unto her, [b]There hath not come
a razor upon mine head; for I *have been*
a Nazarite[5139] unto God[430] from my
mother's[517] womb:[990] if I be shaven, then
my strength will go from me, and I shall
become weak, and be like any *other* man.
18 And when Delilah saw that he
had told her all his heart, she sent and
called[7121] for the lords of the Philistines,
saying, Come up this once, for he hath
shewed[5046] me all his heart. Then the
lords of the Philistines came up unto
her, and brought money in their
hand.[3027]
19 [a]And she made him sleep upon
her knees; and she called for a man,[376]
and she caused him to shave off the
seven locks of his head; and she began

15 [a]Judg. 14:16
16 [I]Hebr. *shortened*
17 [a]Mic. 7:5; [b]Num. 6:5; Judg. 13:5
19 [a]Prov. 7:26, 27
20 [a]Num. 14:9, 42, 43; Josh. 7:12; 1Sam. 16:14; 18:12; 28:15, 16; 2Chr. 15:2
21 [I]Hebr. *bored out*
22 [I]Or, *as when he was shaven*
24 [I]Hebr. *and who multiplied our slain* [a]Dan. 5:4
25 [I]Hebr. *before them* [a]Judg. 9:27

to afflict him, and his strength went from
him.
20 And she said, The Philistines *be*
upon thee, Samson. And he awoke out of
his sleep, and said, I will go out as at
other times before, and shake myself.[5287]
And he wist[3045] not that the LORD [a]was
departed[5493] from him.
21 But the Philistines took him, and
[I]put out his eyes, and brought him down
to Gaza, and bound him with fetters of
brass; and he did grind in the prison
house.[1004]
22 Howbeit the hair of his head
began to grow [I]again after he was
shaven.

Samson's Death

23 Then the lords of the Philistines
gathered them together[622] for to offer[2076]
a great sacrifice[2077] unto Dagon their
god, and to rejoice: for they said, Our
god hath delivered Samson our enemy
into our hand.
24 And when the people[5971] saw him,
they [a]praised[1984] their god: for they said,
Our god hath delivered into our hands[3027]
our enemy, and the destroyer of our
country,[776] [I]which slew[2491] many of us.
25 And it came to pass, when their
hearts[3820] were [a]merry, that they said,
Call[7121] for Samson, that he may make us
sport.[7832] And they called for Samson out
of the prison house; and he made [I]them
sport: and they set him between the pillars.
26 And Samson said unto the lad
that held him by the hand, Suffer me that
I may feel the pillars whereupon the

16:13 The "web" mentioned here was undoubtedly the cloth which Delilah was weaving in a loom. The pin was the object with which the braided locks were fastened to the web. She probably wove Samson's hair into the cloth.

16:17 Samson's admission to Delilah here should be interpreted then as a denial of that trust and a breaking of his covenant, the Nazarite vow, for which God left him (Judg. 16:20). However, his strength returned one more time, allowing him to decimate the Philistine leaders. This came about only after he made a statement of repentance and admitted that God was the true Source of his strength (Judg. 16:28).

16:23 The Philistines were a sea people. Therefore, it is not surprising that one of their gods was Dagon, the fish god. See note on Judges 2:13.

house standeth,[3559] that I may lean[8172] upon them.

27 Now the house was full of men[582] and women;[802] and all the lords of the Philistines *were* there; and *there were* upon the [a]roof about three thousand men[376] and women, that beheld while Samson made sport.

28 And Samson called unto the LORD, and said, O Lord[136] GOD, [a]remember[2142] me, I pray thee, and strengthen[2388] me, I pray thee, only this once, O God, that I may be at once avenged[5358] of the Philistines for my two eyes.

29 And Samson took hold of the two middle pillars upon which the house stood, and [I]on which it was borne up, of the one with his right hand, and of the other with his left.

30 And Samson said, Let [I]me die[4191] with the Philistines. And he bowed himself with *all his* might; and the house fell[5307] upon the lords, and upon all the people that *were* therein. So the dead[4191] which he slew at his death were more than *they* which he slew in his life.[2416]

31 Then his brethren[251] and all the house of his father[1] came down, and took[5375] him, and brought *him* up, and [a]buried[6912] him between Zorah and Eshtaol in the buryingplace[6913] of Manoah his father. And he judged[8199] Israel twenty years.

Micah's Idols

17 And there was a man[376] of mount Ephraim, whose name *was* Micah.

2 And he said[559] unto his mother,[517] The eleven hundred *shekels* of silver that were taken from thee, about which thou cursedst,[422] and spakest[559] of also in mine ears,[241] behold, the silver *is* with me; I took it. And his mother said, [a]Blessed[1288] *be thou* of the LORD, my son.[1121]

3 And when he had restored[7725] the eleven hundred *shekels* of silver to his mother, his mother said, I had wholly dedicated[6942] the silver unto the LORD from my hand[3027] for my son, to [a]make a graven image[6459] and a molten image: now therefore I will restore[7725] it unto thee.

4 Yet he restored the money unto his mother; and his mother [a]took two hundred *shekels* of silver, and gave them to the founder,[6884] who made thereof a graven image and a molten image: and they were in the house[1004] of Micah.

5 And the man Micah had an house of gods,[430] and made an [a]ephod, and [b]teraphim,[8655] and [Ic]consecrated one of his sons,[1121] who became his priest.

6 [a]In those days *there was* no king[4428] in Israel, [b]*but* every man did[6213] *that which was* right in his own eyes.

Micah's Priest

7 And there was a young man out of [a]Bethlehem–judah of the family[4940] of Judah, who *was* a Levite, and he sojourned[1481] there.

8 And the man departed out of the city from Bethlehem–judah to sojourn where he could find *a place:* and he came to mount Ephraim to the house of Micah, [I]as he journeyed.

9 And Micah said unto him, Whence comest thou? And he said unto him, I *am* a Levite of Bethlehem–judah, and I go to sojourn where I may find *a place.*

10 And Micah said unto him, Dwell with me, [a]and be unto me a [b]father[1] and a priest, and I will give thee ten *shekels* of silver by the year, and [Ic]a suit of apparel, and thy victuals.[4241] So the Levite went in.

11 And the Levite was content[2974] to dwell with the man; and the young man was unto him as one of his sons.

12 And Micah [a]consecrated the Levite; and the young man [b]became his priest, and was in the house of Micah.

13 Then said Micah, Now know[3045] I that the LORD will do me good,[3190] seeing I have a Levite to *my* priest.

Micah and the Tribe of Dan

18 In [a]those days *there was* no king in Israel: and in those days [b]the

---

27 [a]Deut. 22:8

28 [a]Jer. 15:15

29 [I]Or, *he leaned on them*

30 [I]Hebr. *my soul*

31 [a]Judg. 13:25

2 [a]Gen. 14:19; Ruth 3:10

3 [a]Ex. 20:4, 23; Lev. 19:4

4 [a]Isa. 46:6

5 [I]Hebr. *filled the hand* [a]Ex. 29:9; 1Kgs. 13:33 [b]Judg. 8:27 [c]Gen. 31:19, 30; Hos. 3:4

6 [a]Judg. 18:1; 19:1; 21:25; Deut. 33:5; [b]Deut. 12:8

7 [a]Josh. 19:15; Judg. 19:1; Ruth 1:1, 2; Mic. 5:2; Matt. 2:1, 5, 6

8 [I]Hebr. *in making his way*

10 [I]Or, *a double suit* [II]Hebr. *an order of garments* [a]Judg. 18:19 [b]Gen. 45:8; Job 29:16

12 [a]Judg. 17:5; [b]Judg. 18:30

1 [a]Judg. 17:6; 21:25 [b]Josh. 19:47

tribe[7626] of the Danites sought them an inheritance to dwell in; for unto that day[3117] *all their* inheritance[5159] had not fallen[5307] unto them among the tribes of Israel.

2 And the children[1121] of Dan sent of their family[4940] five men[582] from their coasts, [I]men of valour,[2428] from [a]Zorah, and from Eshtaol, [b]to spy out the land,[776] and to search it; and they said[559] unto them, Go, search the land: who when they came to mount Ephraim, to the [c]house[1004] of Micah, they lodged there.

3 When they *were* by the house of Micah, they knew[5234] the voice of the young man the Levite: and they turned in[5493] thither, and said unto him, Who brought thee hither? and what makest[6213] thou in this *place*? and what hast thou here?

4 And he said unto them, Thus and thus dealeth Micah with me, and hath [a]hired me, and I am his priest.

5 And they said unto him, [a]Ask counsel,[7592] we pray thee,[4994] [b]of God,[430] that we may know[3045] whether our way[1870] which we go shall be prosperous.

6 And the priest said unto them, [a]Go in peace:[7965] before the LORD *is* your way wherein ye go.

7 Then the five men departed, and came to [a]Laish, and saw[7200] the people[5971] that *were* therein,[7130] [b]how they dwelt careless,[983] after the manner[4941] of the Zidonians, quiet[8252] and secure;[982] and *there was* no [I]magistrate in the land, that might put *them* to shame in *any* thing; and they *were* far from the Zidonians, and had no business[1697] with *any* man.[120]

8 And they came unto their brethren[251] to [a]Zorah and Eshtaol: and their brethren said unto them, What *say* ye?

9 And they said, [a]Arise, that we may go up[5927] against them: for we have seen[7200] the land, and, behold, it *is* very good:[2896] and *are* ye [b]still? be not slothful to go, *and* to enter to possess[3423] the land.

10 When ye go, ye shall come unto a people [a]secure, and to a large land: for God hath given it into your hands;[3027] [b]a place where *there is* no want of any thing that *is* in the earth.[776]

11 And there went from thence of the family of the Danites, out of Zorah and out of Eshtaol, six hundred men[376] [I]appointed with weapons of war.

12 And they went up,[5927] and pitched in [a]Kirjath–jearim, in Judah: wherefore they called[7121] that place [b]Mahaneh–dan unto this day: behold, *it is* behind Kirjath–jearim.

13 And they passed[5674] thence unto mount Ephraim, and came unto [a]the house of Micah.

14 [a]Then answered the five men that went to spy out the country[776] of Laish, and said unto their brethren, Do ye know that [b]there is in these houses[1004] an ephod, and teraphim,[8655] and a graven image,[6459] and a molten image? now therefore consider[3045] what ye have to do.

15 And they turned thitherward, and came to the house of the young man the Levite, *even* unto the house of Micah, and [I]saluted[7965] him.

16 And the [a]six hundred men appointed with their weapons of war, which *were* of the children of Dan, stood[5324] by the entering of the gate.

17 And [a]the five men that went to spy out the land went up, *and* came in thither, *and* took [b]the graven image, and the ephod, and the teraphim, and the molten image: and the priest stood in the entering of the gate with the six hundred men *that were* appointed with weapons of war.

18 And these went into Micah's house, and fetched the carved image,[6459] the ephod, and the teraphim, and the molten image. Then said the priest unto them, What do ye?

19 And they said unto him, Hold thy peace, [a]lay[7760] thine hand[3027] upon thy mouth,[6310] and go with us, [b]and be to us a father[1] and a priest: *is it* better[2896] for thee to be a priest unto the house of one man,[376] or that thou be a priest unto a tribe and a family in Israel?

---

2 [I]Hebr. *sons* [a]Judg. 13:25 [b]Num. 13:17; Josh. 2:1 [c]Judg. 17:1

4 [a]Judg. 17:10

5 [a]1Kgs. 22:5; Isa. 30:1; Hos. 4:12 [b]Judg. 17:5; 18:14

6 [a]1Kgs. 22:6

7 [I]Hebr. *possessor, or, heir of restraint* [a]Josh. 19:47, called, *Leshem* [b]Judg. 18:27, 28

8 [a]Judg. 18:2

9 [a]Num. 13:30; Josh. 2:23, 24 [b]1Kgs. 22:3

10 [a]Judg. 18:7, 27 [b]Deut. 8:9

11 [I]Hebr. *girded*

12 [a]Josh. 15:60 [b]Judg. 13:25

13 [a]Judg. 18:2

14 [a]1Sam. 14:28; [b]Judg. 17:5

15 [I]Hebr. *asked him of peace,* Gen. 43:27; 1Sam. 17:22

16 [a]Judg. 18:11

17 [a]Judg. 18:2, 14 [b]Judg. 17:4, 5

19 [a]Job 21:5; 29:9; 40:4; Prov. 30:32; Mic. 7:16; [b]Judg. 17:10

20 And the priest's[3548] heart[3820] was glad,[3190] and he took the ephod, and the teraphim, and the graven image, and went in the midst[7130] of the people.

21 So they turned and departed, and put the little ones[2945] and the cattle and the carriage before them.

22 *And* when they were a good way from the house of Micah, the men that *were* in the houses near to Micah's house were gathered together,[2199] and overtook the children of Dan.

23 And they cried[7121] unto the children of Dan. And they turned their faces, and said unto Micah, What aileth thee, [I]that thou comest with such a company?

24 And he said, Ye have taken away my gods[430] which I made,[6213] and the priest, and ye are gone away: and what have I more? and what *is* this *that* ye say unto me, What aileth thee?

25 And the children of Dan said unto him, Let not thy voice be heard[8085] among us, lest [I][a]angry[4751,5315] fellows run upon thee, and thou lose thy life,[5315] with the lives of thy household.[1004]

26 And the children of Dan went their way: and when Micah saw that they *were* too strong[2389] for him, he turned and went back unto his house.

27 And they took *the things* which Micah had made, and the priest which he had, and [a]came unto Laish, unto a people *that were* at quiet and secure: [b]and they smote[5221] them with the edge[6310] of the sword,[2719] and burnt[8313] the city with fire.

28 And *there was* no deliverer, because it *was* [a]far from Zidon, and they had no business with *any* man; and it was in the valley that *lieth* [b]by Beth–rehob. And they built a city, and dwelt therein.

29 And [a]they called the name of the city Dan, after the name of [b]Dan their father, who was born unto Israel: howbeit the name of the city *was* Laish at the first.[7223]

30 And the children of Dan set up the graven image: and Jonathan, the son of Gershom, the son of Manasseh, he and his sons were priests[3548] to the tribe of Dan [a]until the day of the captivity[1546] of the land.

31 And they set them up[7760] Micah's graven image, which he made, [a]all the time that the house of God was in Shiloh.

The Levite and His Concubine

19 And it came to pass in those days, [a]when *there was* no king[4428] in Israel, that there was a certain[376] Levite sojourning on the side of mount Ephraim, who took to him [I]a concubine out of [b]Bethlehem–judah.

2 And his concubine played the whore[2181] against him, and went away from him unto her father's[1] house[1004] to Bethlehem–judah, and was there [I]four whole months.

3 And her husband[376] arose, and went after her, to speak[1696] [I][a]friendly[3820] unto her, *and* to bring her again, having his servant with him, and a couple of asses: and she brought him into her father's house: and when the father[1] of the damsel saw[7200] him, he rejoiced to meet him.

4 And his father in law, the damsel's father, retained him; and he abode with him three days: so they did eat and drink, and lodged there.

5 And it came to pass on the fourth day, when they arose early in the morning, that he rose up to depart: and the damsel's father said unto his son in law, [I][a]Comfort thine heart[3820] with a morsel of bread, and afterward go your way.[1870]

6 And they sat down, and did eat and drink both of them together: for the damsel's father had said unto the man,[376] Be content,[2974] I pray thee,[4994] and tarry all night,[3915] and let thine heart be merry.[3190]

7 And when the man rose up to depart, his father in law urged him: therefore he lodged there again.

8 And he arose early in the morning on the fifth day to depart: and the damsel's father said, Comfort thine heart, I pray thee. And they tarried [I]until afternoon, and they did eat both of them.

23 [I]Hebr. *that thou art gathered together?*

25 [I]Hebr. *bitter of soul* [a]2Sam. 17:8

27 [a]Judg. 18:7, 10; Deut. 33:22 [b]Josh. 19:47

28 [a]Judg. 18:7 [b]Num. 13:21; 2Sam. 10:6

29 [a]Josh. 19:47; [b]Gen. 14:14; Judg. 20:1; 1Kgs. 12:29, 30; 15:20

30 [a]Judg. 13:1; 1Sam. 4:2, 3, 10, 11; Ps. 78:60, 61

31 [a]Josh. 18:1; Judg. 19:18; 21:12-21

1 [I]Hebr. *a woman a concubine,* or, *a wife a concubine* [a]Judg. 17:6; 18:1; 21:25 [b]Judg. 17:7

2 [I]Or, *a year and four months* [II]Hebr. *days four months*

3 [I]Hebr. *to her heart* [a]Gen. 34:3

5 [I]Hebr. *Strengthen* [a]Gen. 18:5

8 [I]Hebr. *till the day declined*

9 And when the man rose up[6965] to
depart, he, and his concubine, and his
servant, his father in law, the damsel's father, said unto him, Behold,2009 now the
day [I]draweth[7503] toward evening, I pray
you tarry all night: behold, [II]the day
groweth to an end, lodge here, that thine
heart may be merry; and to morrow get
you early on your way, that thou mayest
go [III]home.
10 But the man would[14] not tarry
that night, but he rose up and departed,
and came [I]over against [a]Jebus, which *is*
Jerusalem; and *there were* with him two
asses saddled,[2280] his concubine also *was*
with him.
11 *And* when they *were* by Jebus, the
day was far spent; and the servant said
unto his master,[113] Come, I pray thee,
and let us turn in into this city [a]of the
Jebusites, and lodge in it.
12 And his master said unto him, We
will not turn aside[5493] hither into the city
of a stranger, that *is* not of the children[1121] of Israel; we will pass over [a]to
Gibeah.
13 And he said unto his servant,
Come, and let us draw near to one of
these places to lodge all night, in Gibeah,
or in [a]Ramah.
14 And they passed on[5674] and went
their way; and the sun went down upon
them *when they were* by Gibeah, which
belongeth to Benjamin.
15 And they turned aside[5493] thither,
to go in *and* to lodge in Gibeah: and
when he went in, he sat him down in
a street of the city: for *there was* no
man that [a]took them into his house to
lodging.
16 And, behold, there came an old[2205]
man from [a]his work out of the field[7704]
at even, which *was* also of mount
Ephraim; and he sojourned[1481] in Gibeah:
but the men[582] of the place *were*
Benjamites.
17 And when he had lifted up[5375] his
eyes, he saw a wayfaring[732] man in the
street of the city: and the old man said,
Whither goest thou? and whence comest
thou?
18 And he said unto him, We *are*

9 [I]Hebr. *is weak* [II]Hebr. it is *the pitching* time of *the day* [III]Hebr. *to thy tent*

10 [I]Hebr. *to over against* [a]Josh. 18:28

11 [a]Josh. 15:8, 63; Judg. 1:21; 2Sam. 5:6

12 [a]Josh. 18:28

13 [a]Josh. 18:25

15 [a]Matt. 25:43; Heb. 13:2

16 [a]Ps. 104:23

18 [I]Hebr. *gathereth,* Judg. 19:18 [a]Josh. 18:1; 18:31; Judg. 20:18; 1Sam. 1:3, 7

20 [a]Gen. 43:23; Judg. 6:23 [b]Gen. 19:2

21 [a]Gen. 24:32; 43:24 [b]Gen. 18:4; John 13:5

22 [a]Gen. 19:4; Judg. 20:5; Hos. 9:9; 10:9 [b]Deut. 13:13; [c]Gen. 19:5; Rom. 1:26, 27

23 [a]Gen. 19:6, 7; [b]2Sam. 13:12

24 [I]Hebr. *the matter of this folly* [a]Gen. 19:8 [b]Gen. 34:2; Deut. 21:14

25 [a]Gen. 4:1

passing[5674] from Bethlehem–judah toward the side of mount Ephraim; from
thence *am* I: and I went to Bethlehem–
judah, but I *am now* going to [a]the house
of the LORD; and there *is* no man that
[Ib]receiveth me to house.
19 Yet there is both straw and
provender4554 for our asses; and there is
bread and wine also for me, and for thy
handmaid, and for the young man *which*
is with thy servants:[5650] *there is* no want
of any thing.
20 And the old man said, [a]Peace[7965]
be with thee; howsoever *let* all thy wants
lie upon me; [b]only lodge not in the street.
21 [a]So he brought him into his house,
and gave provender[1101] unto the asses:
[b]and they washed[7364] their feet, and did
eat and drink.
22 *Now* as they were making their
hearts[3820] merry, behold, [a]the men of
the city, certain[582] [b]sons[1121] of Belial,[1100]
beset the house round about, *and* beat
at the door, and spake[559] to the
master[1167] of the house, the old man,
saying, [c]Bring forth the man that came
into thine house, that we may know[3045]
him.
23 And [a]the man, the master of the
house, went out unto them, and said unto
them, Nay, my brethren,[251] *nay,* I pray
you, do not *so* wickedly;[7489] seeing that
this man is come into mine house, [b]do not
this folly.
24 [a]Behold, *here is* my daughter a
maiden, and his concubine; them I will
bring out now, and [b]humble ye them, and
do with them what seemeth good[2896]
unto you: but unto this man do not [I]so
vile5039 a thing.
25 But the men would not hearken
to him: so the man took[2388] his concubine, and brought her forth unto them;
and they [a]knew[3045] her, and abused5953
her all the night until the morning: and
when the day began to spring, they let
her go.
26 Then came the woman[802] in the
dawning of the day, and fell down[5307] at
the door of the man's house where her
lord[113] *was,* till it was light.[216]
27 And her lord rose up6965 in the

morning, and opened the doors of the house, and went out to go his way: and, behold, the woman his concubine was fallen down *at* the door of the house, and her hands[3027] *were* upon the threshold.

28 And he said unto her, Up, and let us be going. But [a]none answered. Then the man took her *up* upon an ass, and the man rose up, and gat him unto his place.

29 And when he was come into his house, he took a knife, and laid hold on his concubine, and [a]divided her, *together* with her bones,[6106] into twelve pieces, and sent her into all the coasts of Israel.

30 And it was so, that all that saw it said, There was no such deed done[1961] nor seen[7200] from the day that the children of Israel came up out of the land[776] of Egypt unto this day: consider[7760] of it, [a]take advice, and speak *your minds.*

Israel Punishes Benjamin For Its Sin

20 Then [a]all the children[1121] of Israel went out, and the congregation[5712] was gathered together as one man,[376] from [b]Dan even to Beer–sheba, with the land[776] of Gilead, unto the LORD [c]in Mizpeh.

2 And the chief of all the people,[5971] *even* of all the tribes[7626] of Israel, presented themselves in the assembly[6951] of the people of God,[430] four hundred thousand footmen [a]that drew sword.[2719]

3 (Now the children of Benjamin heard[8085] that the children of Israel were gone up[5927] to Mizpeh.) Then said[559] the children of Israel, Tell[1696] *us,* how was this wickedness?[7451]

4 And [I]the Levite, the husband[376] of the woman[802] that was slain,[7523] answered and said, [a]I came into Gibeah that *belongeth* to Benjamin, I and my concubine, to lodge.

5 [a]And the men[1167] of Gibeah rose against me, and beset the house[1004] round about upon me by night,[3915] *and* thought to have slain[2026] me: [b]and my concubine have they [I]forced, that she is dead.[4191]

6 And [a]I took my concubine, and cut her in pieces, and sent her throughout all the country[7704] of the inheritance[5159] of Israel: for they [b]have committed[6213] lewdness[2154] and folly in Israel.

7 Behold, ye *are* all children of Israel; [a]give here your advice[1697] and counsel.[6098]

8 And all the people arose as one man, saying, We will not any *of us* go to his tent,[168] neither will we any *of us* turn into his house.

9 But now this *shall be* the thing which we will do to Gibeah; *we will go up* by lot[1486] against it;

10 And we will take ten men[582] of an hundred throughout all the tribes of Israel, and an hundred of a thousand, and a thousand out of ten thousand, to fetch victual[6720] for the people, that they may do, when they come to Gibeah of Benjamin, according to all the folly that they have wrought[6213] in Israel.

11 So all the men[376] of Israel were gathered[622] against the city, [I]knit together as one man.

12 [a]And the tribes of Israel sent men through all the tribe[7626] of Benjamin, saying, What wickedness *is* this that is done among you?

13 Now therefore deliver *us* the men, [a]the children of Belial,[1100] which *are* in Gibeah, that we may put them to death,[4191] and [b]put away evil[7451] from Israel. But the children of Benjamin would[14] not hearken[8085] to the voice of their brethren[251] the children of Israel:

14 But the children of Benjamin gathered themselves together out of the cities unto Gibeah, to go out to battle against the children of Israel.

15 And the children of Benjamin

28 [a]Judg. 20:5
29 [a]Judg. 20:6; 1Sam. 11:7
30 [a]Judg. 20:7; Prov. 13:10
1 [a]Deut. 13:12; Josh. 22:12; Judg. 21:5; 1Sam. 11:7 [b]Judg. 18:29; 1Sam. 3:20; 2Sam. 3:10; 24:2; [c]Judg. 10:17; 11:11; 1Sam. 7:5; 10:17
2 [a]Judg. 8:10
4 [I]Hebr. *the man the Levite* [a]Judg. 19:15
5 [I]Hebr. *humbled* [a]Judg. 19:22 [b]Judg. 19:25, 26
6 [a]Judg. 19:29 [b]Josh. 7:15
7 [a]Judg. 19:30
11 [I]Hebr. *fellows*
12 [a]Deut. 13:14; Josh. 22:13, 16
13 [a]Deut. 13:13; Judg. 19:22 [b]Deut. 17:12

20:1 The phrase "from Dan to Beersheba" does not imply that Dan's settlement of its portion, recorded in chapter eighteen, had already been completed. It only shows that "from Dan to Beersheba" had become a proverbial expression for all the land of Israel (see note on Josh. 19:40–48).

were numbered[6485] at that time out of the cities twenty and six thousand men that drew sword, beside the inhabitants of Gibeah, which were numbered seven hundred chosen men.

16 Among all this people *there were* seven hundred chosen men [a]lefthanded; every one could sling stones at an hair *breadth,* and not miss.[2398]

17 And the men of Israel, beside Benjamin, were numbered four hundred thousand men that drew sword: all these *were* men of war.

18 And the children of Israel arose, and [a]went up[5927] to the house of God, and [b]asked counsel[7592] of God, and said, Which of us shall go up first to the battle against the children of Benjamin? And the LORD said, Judah *shall go up* first.

19 And the children of Israel rose up in the morning, and encamped against Gibeah.

20 And the men of Israel went out to battle against Benjamin; and the men of Israel put themselves in array to fight against them at Gibeah.

21 And [a]the children of Benjamin came forth out of Gibeah, and destroyed[7843] down to the ground[776] of the Israelites that day[3117] twenty and two thousand men.

22 And the people the men of Israel encouraged themselves,[2388] and set their battle again in array in the place where they put themselves in array the first[7223] day.

23 ([a]And the children of Israel went up and wept before the LORD until even, and asked counsel of the LORD, saying, Shall I go up[5066] again to battle against the children of Benjamin my brother?[251] And the LORD said, Go up against him.)

24 And the children of Israel came near against the children of Benjamin the second day.

25 And [a]Benjamin went forth against them out of Gibeah the second day, and destroyed down to the ground of the children of Israel again eighteen thousand men; all these drew the sword.

26 Then all the children of Israel, and all the people, [a]went up, and came unto the house of God, and wept, and sat there before the LORD, and fasted that day until even, and offered[5927] burnt offerings[5930] and peace offerings[8002] before the LORD.

27 And the children of Israel enquired[7592] of the LORD, (for [a]the ark of the covenant[1285] of God *was* there in those days,

28 [a]And Phinehas, the son of Eleazar, the son of Aaron, [b]stood before it in those days,) saying, Shall I yet again go out to battle against the children of Benjamin my brother, or shall I cease? And the LORD said, Go up; for to morrow I will deliver them into thine hand.[3027]

29 And Israel [a]set[7760] liers in wait round about Gibeah.

30 And the children of Israel went up against the children of Benjamin on the third day, and put themselves in array against Gibeah, as at other times.

31 And the children of Benjamin went out against the people, *and* were drawn away from the city; and they began [I]to smite[5221] of the people, *and* kill,[2491] as at other times, in the highways, of which one goeth up to [II]the house of God, and the other to Gibeah in the field,[7704] about thirty men of Israel.

32 And the children of Benjamin said, They *are* smitten down[5062] before us, as at the first. But the children of Israel said, Let us flee, and draw them from the city unto the highways.

33 And all the men of Israel rose up out of their place, and put themselves in array at Baal–tamar: and the liers in wait of Israel came forth out of their places, *even* out of the meadows of Gibeah.

16 [a]Judg. 3:15; 1Chr. 12:2
18 [a]Judg. 20:23, 26 [b]Num. 27:21; Judg. 1:1
21 [a]Gen. 49:27
23 [a]Judg. 20:26, 27
25 [a]Judg. 20:21
26 [a]Judg. 20:18
27 [a]Josh. 18:1; 1Sam. 4:3, 4
28 [a]Josh. 24:33 [b]Deut. 10:8; 18:5
29 [a]Josh. 8:4
31 [I]Hebr. *to smite of the people wounded as at* [II]Or, *Bethel*

20:23 Apparently the Israelites trusted in their army and the righteousness of their cause. They did not include God in their planning. All Israel needed a strong disciplinary lesson, and God used their enemies to teach it to them.

34 And there came against Gibeah ten thousand chosen men out of all Israel, and the battle was sore:[3513] [a]but they knew[3045] not that evil *was* near them.

35 And the LORD smote[5062] Benjamin before Israel: and the children of Israel destroyed of the Benjamites that day twenty and five thousand and an hundred men: all these drew the sword.

36 So the children of Benjamin saw[7200] that they were smitten: [a]for the men of Israel gave place to the Benjamites, because they trusted[982] unto the liers in wait which they had set beside Gibeah.

37 [a]And the liers in wait hasted, and rushed upon Gibeah; and the liers in wait [I][b]drew *themselves* along, and smote[5221] all the city with the edge of the sword.

38 Now there was an appointed [I]sign[226] between the men of Israel [II]and the liers in wait, that they should make a great [III]flame with smoke rise up[5927] out of the city.

39 And when the men of Israel retired in the battle, Benjamin began [I]to smite *and* kill of the men of Israel about thirty persons: for they said, Surely they are smitten down before us, as *in* the first battle.

40 But when the flame began to arise up out of the city with a pillar of smoke, the Benjamites [a]looked behind them, and, behold, [I]the flame of the city ascended up to heaven.

41 And when the men of Israel turned again,[2015] the men of Benjamin were amazed:[926] for they saw that evil [I]was come upon them.

42 Therefore they turned *their backs* before the men of Israel unto the way[1870] of the wilderness; but the battle overtook them; and them which *came* out of the cities they destroyed in the midst of them.

43 *Thus* they inclosed the Benjamites round about, *and* chased them, *and* trode them down [I]with ease [II]over against Gibeah toward the sunrising.

44 And there fell[5307] of Benjamin eighteen thousand men; all these *were* men of valour.[2428]

45 And they turned and fled toward the wilderness unto the rock of [a]Rimmon: and they gleaned of them in the highways five thousand men; and pursued hard after them unto Gidom, and slew[5221] two thousand men of them.

46 So that all which fell that day of Benjamin were twenty and five thousand men that drew the sword; all these *were* men of valour.

47 [a]But six hundred men turned and fled to the wilderness unto the rock Rimmon, and abode in the rock Rimmon four months.

48 And the men of Israel turned again[7725] upon the children of Benjamin, and smote them with the edge of the sword, as well the men of *every* city, as the beast, and all that [I]came to hand: also they set on fire all the cities that [II]they came to.

Wives for the Tribe of Benjamin

21 Now [a]the men[376] of Israel had sworn[7650] in Mizpeh, saying, There shall not any of us give his daughter unto Benjamin to wife.[802]

2 And the people[5971] came [a]to the house[1004] of God,[430] and abode there till even before God, and lifted up[5375] their voices, and wept sore;

3 And said,[559] O LORD God of Israel, why is this come to pass in Israel, that there should be[6485] to day one tribe[7626] lacking[6485] in Israel?

4 And it came to pass on the morrow, that the people rose early, and [a]built there an altar, and offered[5927] burnt offerings[5930] and peace offerings.

5 And the children[1121] of Israel said, Who *is there* among all the tribes of Israel that came not up with the congregation[6951] unto the LORD? [a]For they had made a great oath[7621] concerning him that came not up to the LORD to Mizpeh, saying, He shall surely be put to death.[4191]

6 And the children of Israel repented[5162] them for Benjamin their

34 [a]Josh. 8:14; Isa. 47:11
36 [a]Josh. 8:15
37 [I]Or, *made a long* sound with the trumpet; [a]Josh. 8:19 [b]Josh. 6:5
38 [I]Or, *time* [II]Hebr. *with* [III]Hebr. *elevation*
39 [I]Hebr. *to smite the wounded*
40 [I]Hebr. *the whole consumption* [a]Josh. 8:20
41 [I]Hebr. *touched them*
43 [I]Or, from *Menuchah* [II]Hebr. *unto over against*
45 [a]Josh. 15:32
47 [a]Judg. 21:13
48 [I]Hebr. *was found* [II]Hebr. *were found*
1 [a]Judg. 20:1
2 [a]Judg. 20:18, 26
4 [a]2Sam. 24:25
5 [a]Judg. 5:23

brother,[251] and said, There is one tribe cut off from Israel this day.

7 How shall we do[6213] for wives[802] for them that remain,[3498] seeing we have sworn by the LORD that we will not give them of our daughters to wives?

8 And they said, What one *is there* of the tribes[7626] of Israel that came not up to Mizpeh to the LORD? And, behold, there came none to the camp[4264] from [a]Jabesh–gilead to the assembly.[6951]

9 For the people were numbered,[6485] and, behold, *there were* none of the inhabitants of Jabesh–gilead there.

10 And the congregation[5712] sent thither twelve thousand men of the valiantest, and commanded[6680] them, saying, [a]Go and smite[5221] the inhabitants of Jabesh–gilead with the edge[6310] of the sword,[2719] with the women[802] and the children.[2945]

11 And this *is* the thing that ye shall do, [a]Ye shall utterly destroy[2763] every male,[2145] and every woman[802] that [I]hath lain by man.

12 And they found among the inhabitants of Jabesh–gilead four hundred [I]young virgins,[1330] that had known[3045] no man[376] by lying with any male: and they brought them unto the camp to [a]Shiloh, which *is* in the land[776] of Canaan.

13 And the whole congregation sent *some* [I]to speak to the children of Benjamin [a]that *were* in the rock Rimmon, and to [II]call[7121] peaceably unto them.

14 And Benjamin came again at that time;[6256] and they gave them wives which they had saved alive of the women of Jabesh–gilead: and yet so they sufficed them not.

15 And the people [a]repented them for Benjamin, because that the LORD had made[6213] a breach in the tribes of Israel.

🔑 16 Then the elders[2205] of the congregation said, How shall we do for wives for them that remain, seeing the women are destroyed[8045] out of Benjamin?

17 And they said, *There must be* an inheritance[3425] for them that be escaped of Benjamin, that a tribe be not destroyed[4229] out of Israel.

18 Howbeit we may not give them wives of our daughters: [a]for the children of Israel have sworn, saying, Cursed[779] *be* he that giveth a wife to Benjamin.

19 Then they said, Behold, *there is* a feast[2282] of the LORD in Shiloh [I]yearly *in a place* which *is* on the north side of Bethel, [II]on the east side [III]of the highway that goeth up from Bethel to Shechem, and on the south of Lebonah.

20 Therefore they commanded the children of Benjamin, saying, Go and lie in wait in the vineyards;

21 And see, and, behold, if the daughters of Shiloh come out [a]to dance in dances, then come ye out of the vineyards, and catch you every man his wife of the daughters of Shiloh, and go to the land[776] of Benjamin.

22 And it shall be, when their fathers[1] or their brethren[251] come unto us to complain,[7378] that we will say unto

8 [a]1Sam. 11:1; 31:11
10 [a]Judg. 21:5; 5:23; 1Sam. 11:7
11 [I]Hebr. *knoweth the lying* with *man* [a]Num. 31:17
12 [I]Hebr. *young women virgins* [a]Josh. 18:1
13 [I]Hebr. *and spake and called* [II]Or, *proclaim peace* [a]Deut. 20:10; Judg. 20:47
15 [a]Judg. 21:6
18 [a]Judg. 11:35; 21:1
19 [I]Hebr. *from year to year* [II]Or, *toward the sunrising* [III]Or, *on*
21 [a]Judg. 11:34; 1Sam. 18:6; Jer. 31:13

🔑 **21:16–24** The "feast" spoken of in verse nineteen probably refers to the Passover or one of the three great Jewish feasts (Ex. 23:14–17). In these unsettled times the men went up to Shiloh only once a year instead of three times (1 Sam. 1:3). Only the males kept the feasts, therefore the virgins of Shiloh would naturally be the only maidens present. The public festival would be a likely occasion for their festive dances. It is possible that this was simply a local festival which was peculiar to Shiloh, like the yearly sacrifice by David's family at Bethlehem (1 Sam. 20:29). The men of Israel had made a hasty oath in the heat of anger (Judg. 21:1). Later, when they saw the plight of Benjamin, that without wives the tribe would soon cease to exist, they felt compassion for them (Judg. 21:13, 14). However, the terms of their oath stood; though they would not give their daughters as wives to the Benjamites, they instructed them in detail how to go up to Shiloh and carry off the girls at the festival. In their minds, they would not be guilty of breaking the oath, and the Benjamites would have wives and be preserved as a tribe even though the women were gained by violent means.

them, [I]Be favourable[2603] unto them for
our sakes: because we reserved not to
each man his wife in the war: for ye did
not give unto them at this time,[6256] *that*
ye should be guilty.[816]
23 And the children of Benjamin
did[6213] so, and took[5375] *them* wives, according to their number, of them that
danced,[2342] whom they caught: and they
went and returned[7725] unto their inheritance,[5159] and [a]repaired the cities, and
dwelt in them.
24 And the children of Israel departed thence at that time, every man to
his tribe and to his family,[4940] and they
went out from thence every man to his
inheritance.
25 [a]In those days *there was* no
king[4428] in Israel: [b]every man did *that*
which was right in his own eyes.

22 [I]Or, *Gratify us in them*

23 [a]Judg. 20:48

25 [a]Judg. 17:6; 18:1; 19:1 [b]Deut. 12:8; Judg. 17:6

The Book of
RUTH

The Book of Ruth is an inspiring love story which demonstrates God's providential care. The name of the author is not given, but traditionally the book is credited to Samuel. The Book of Ruth was originally part of the Book of Judges. However, by New Testament times it was included on a scroll with four other books that were read publicly at the feasts of Israel. These books were known as the Five Megilloth (scrolls) and were arranged in the following order: Song of Solomon, Ruth, Lamentations, Ecclesiastes, Esther. The Book of Ruth was read at the Feast of Harvest (Pentecost) because much of the story is set in the harvest fields.

Ruth is one of the four women named in the genealogy of Jesus (Matt. 1:5). The genealogy at the end of the book is very important because it shows that God chose Ruth, a woman from the heathen land of Moab, to be an ancestor of King David.

The story of Ruth probably took place during the time of Gideon (ca. 1130 B.C.). The famine mentioned in Ruth seems to correspond to the oppression by the Midianites and Israel's subsequent deliverance (Ruth 1:1, 6, cf. Judg. 6:3, 4). Jewish tradition holds that Ruth lived at the same time as Eli the priest. Since she was at least the great-grandmother of David, she must have lived around the twelfth century B.C.

Several laws and customs were involved in the proceedings which led to the marriage of Boaz and Ruth. According to Deuteronomy 25:5, if a woman's husband died and she was left without children, her husband's brother was required to marry her so that there could be an heir to carry on the name of the man who had died. Since Ruth's deceased husband, Mahlon, had no other living brothers, she would most likely have remained unmarried. However, Naomi and Ruth decided to sell the land that belonged to Elimelech, Mahlon, and Chilion. The historian Josephus explains that in this case, the nearest kinsman would customarily have the first option to buy the land, but he would also be expected to marry Ruth (Antiquities V. 9. 4.). The nearest kinsman to Ruth refused to buy the land because in raising up heirs to Mahlon he would have marred his own inheritance (Ruth 4:6). In other words, any children born to him and Ruth would be the heirs to all his fortune, making it impossible for him to give an inheritance to those of his own family name.

Ruth and Naomi

1 Now it came to pass in the days[3117]
when [a]the judges [I]ruled, that there
was [b]a famine in the land.[776] And a
certain man of [c]Bethlehem–judah
went to sojourn[1481] in the country[7704] of
Moab, he, and his wife,[802] and his two
sons.[1121]
2 And the name of the man *was*
Elimelech, and the name of his wife
Naomi, and the name of his two sons
Mahlon and Chilion, [a]Ephrathites of
Bethlehem–judah. And they came [b]into
the country of Moab, and [I]continued
there.
3 And Elimelech Naomi's husband
died; and she was left,[7604] and her two
sons.
4 And they took them wives of the
women of Moab; the name of the one
was Orpah, and the name of the other
Ruth: and they dwelled there about ten
years.
5 And Mahlon and Chilion died also
both of them; and the woman[802] was left
of her two sons and her husband.
6 Then she arose with her daughters in law, that she might return from
the country of Moab: for she had
heard[8085] in the country of Moab how
that the LORD had [a]visited[6485] his people[5971] in [b]giving them bread.
7 Wherefore she went forth out of
the place where she was, and her two
daughters in law with her; and they went
on the way[1870] to return[7725] unto the
land[776] of Judah.
8 And Naomi said unto her two

1 [I]Hebr. *judged* [a]Judg. 2:16 [b]Gen. 12:10; 26:1; 2Kgs. 8:1 [c]Judg. 17:8

2 [I]Hebr. *were* [a]Gen. 35:19 [b]Judg. 3:30

6 [a]Ex. 4:31; Luke 1:68 [b]Ps. 132:15; Matt. 6:11

daughters in law, [a]Go, return each[802] to her mother's[517] house:[1004] [b]the LORD deal[6213] kindly[2617] with you, as ye have dealt with [c]the dead, and with me.

9 The LORD grant you that ye may find [a]rest, each *of you* in the house of her husband. Then she kissed them; and they lifted up[5375] their voice, and wept.

10 And they said unto her, Surely we will return[7725] with thee unto thy people.

11 And Naomi said, Turn again,[7725] my daughters: why will ye go with me? *are* there yet *any more* sons in my womb,[4578] [a]that they may be your husbands?[582]

12 Turn again, my daughters, go *your way;* for I am too old[2204] to have an husband. If I should say,[559] I have hope, [I]*if* I should have an husband also to night, and should also bear sons;

13 Would ye [I]tarry for them till they were grown? would ye stay for them from having husbands? nay, my daughters; for [II]it grieveth me much for your sakes that [a]the hand[3027] of the LORD is gone out against me.

14 And they lifted up their voice, and wept again: and Orpah kissed her mother in law; but Ruth [a]clave unto her.

15 And she said, Behold, thy sister in law is gone back[7725] unto her people, and unto [a]her gods:[430] [b]return[7725] thou after thy sister in law.

16 And Ruth said, [Ia]Intreat[6293] me not to leave[5800] thee, *or* to return from following after thee: for whither thou goest, I will go; and where thou lodgest, I will lodge: [b]thy people[5971] *shall be* my people, and thy God[430] my God:

17 Where thou diest, will I die, and there will I be buried:[6912] [a]the LORD do[6213] so to me, and more also, *if ought* but death[4194] part thee and me.

18 [a]When she saw[7200] that she [I]was stedfastly minded to go with her, then she left speaking unto her.

19 So they two went until they came to Bethlehem. And it came to pass, when they were come to Bethlehem, that [a]all the city was moved[1949] about them, and they said, [b]*Is* this Naomi?

20 And she said unto them, Call me not [I]Naomi, call me [II]Mara:[4751] for the Almighty[7706] hath dealt very bitterly[4843] with me.

21 I went out full, [a]and the LORD hath brought me home again[7725] empty: why *then* call ye me Naomi, seeing the LORD hath testified against me, and the Almighty hath afflicted[7489] me?

22 So Naomi returned, and Ruth the Moabitess, her daughter in law, with her, which returned out of the country of Moab: and they came to Bethlehem [a]in the beginning of barley harvest.

Ruth Works in the Field of Boaz

2 And Naomi had a [a]kinsman[1350] of her husband's, a mighty man of wealth,[2428] of the family of Elimelech; and his name *was* [b]Boaz.

2 And Ruth the Moabitess said unto Naomi, Let me now go to the field,[7704] and [a]glean[3950] ears of corn after *him* in whose sight I shall find grace.[2580] And she said unto her, Go, my daughter.

3 And she went, and came, and gleaned in the field after the reapers: and her [I]hap[4745] was to light on[7136] a part of the field *belonging* unto Boaz, who *was* of the kindred of Elimelech.

4 And, behold, Boaz came from

8 [a]Josh. 24:15 [b]2Tim. 1:16-18 [c]Ruth 1:5; Ruth 2:20
9 [a]Ruth 3:1
11 [a]Gen. 38:11; Deut. 25:5
12 [I]Or, *if I were with a husband*
13 [I]Hebr. *hope* [II]Hebr. *I have much bitterness* [a]Judg. 2:15; Job 19:21; Ps. 32:4; 38:2; 39:9, 10
14 [a]Prov. 17:17; 18:24
15 [a]Judg. 11:24 [b]Josh. 24:15, 19; 2Kgs. 2:2; Luke 24:28
16 [I]Or, *Be not against me* [a]2Kgs. 2:2, 4, 6 [b]Ruth 2:11, 12
17 [a]1Sam. 3:17; 25:22; 2Sam. 19:13; 2Kgs. 6:31
18 [I]Hebr. *strengthened herself* [a]Acts 21:14
19 [a]Matt. 21:10 [b]Isa. 23:7; Lam. 2:15
20 [I]That is, *Pleasant* [II]That is, *Bitter*
21 [a]Job 1:21
22 [a]Ex. 9:31, 32; Ruth 2:23; 2Sam. 21:9

1 [a]Ruth 3:2, 12 [b]Ruth 4:21
2 [a]Lev. 19:9; Deut. 24:19
3 [I]Hebr. *hap happened*

2:1 See note on Ruth 4:17–22, on the lineage of Boaz.

2:2, 3 The field of Boaz was near the city of Bethlehem and was the place where Ruth gleaned corn for herself and Naomi. It is also in this area that David would tend his father's sheep, and that Joseph would bring his young wife, Mary, to deliver her baby, the Lord Jesus Christ. It is possible that in the hills above these fields the shepherds were tending to their flocks on the night when Christ was born.

2:2–7 See note on Leviticus 19:9, 10.

Bethlehem, and said unto the reapers, [a]The LORD *be* with you. And they answered him, The LORD bless[1288] thee.

5 Then said Boaz unto his servant that was set over[5324] the reapers, Whose damsel *is* this?

6 And the servant that was set over the reapers answered and said, It *is* the Moabitish damsel [a]that came back[7725] with Naomi out of the country[7704] of Moab:

7 And she said, I pray you, let me glean and gather[622] after the reapers among the sheaves: so she came, and hath continued even from the morning until now, that she tarried a little in the house.[1004]

8 Then said Boaz unto Ruth, Hearest[8085] thou not, my daughter? Go not to glean[3950] in another field, neither go[5674] from hence, but abide here fast[1692] by my maidens:

9 *Let* thine eyes *be* on the field that they do reap, and go thou after them: have I not charged[6680] the young men that they shall not touch thee? and when thou art athirst, go unto the vessels, and drink of *that* which the young men have drawn.

10 Then she [a]fell on her face, and bowed herself[7812] to the ground,[776] and said unto him, Why have I found grace in thine eyes, that thou shouldest take knowledge[5234] of me, seeing I *am* a stranger?[5237]

11 And Boaz answered and said unto her, It hath fully been shewed me, [a]all that thou hast done unto thy mother in law since the death[4194] of thine husband: and *how* thou hast left[5800] thy father[1] and thy mother,[517] and the land[776] of thy nativity, and art come unto a people[5971] which thou knewest[3045] not heretofore.

12 [a]The LORD recompense thy work, and a full[8003] reward be given thee of the LORD God of Israel, [b]under whose wings thou art come to trust.[2620]

13 Then she said, [I][a]Let me find favour[2580] in thy sight, my lord;[113] for that thou hast comforted[5162] me, and for that thou hast spoken[1696] [II][b]friendly[3820] unto thine handmaid, [c]though I be not like unto one of thine handmaidens.

14 And Boaz said unto her, At mealtime[6256][400] come[5066] thou hither, and eat of the bread, and dip[2881] thy morsel in the vinegar. And she sat beside the reapers: and he reached[6642] her parched *corn,* and she did eat, and [a]was sufficed, and left.

15 And when she was risen up to glean, Boaz commanded[6680] his young men, saying, Let her glean[3950] even among the sheaves, and [I]reproach her not:

16 And let fall also *some* of the handfuls of purpose[7997] for her, and leave[5800] *them,* that she may glean *them,* and rebuke[1605] her not.

17 So she gleaned in the field until even, and beat out that she had gleaned: and it was about an ephah of barley.

18 And she took *it* up,[5375] and went into the city: and her mother in law saw[7200] what she had gleaned: and she brought forth, and gave to her [a]that she had reserved after she was sufficed.

19 And her mother in law said unto her, Where hast thou gleaned to day? and where wroughtest[6213] thou? blessed[1288] be he that did [a]take knowledge of thee. And she shewed her mother in law with whom she had wrought, and said, The man's name with whom I wrought to day *is* Boaz.

🔑 20 And Naomi said unto her daughter in law, [a]Blessed *be* he of the LORD, who [b]hath not left off his kindness[2617] to

4 [a]Ps. 129:7, 8; Luke 1:28; 2Thess. 3:16
6 [a]Ruth 1:22
10 [a]1Sam. 25:23
11 [a]Ruth 1:14, 16, 17
12 [a]1Sam. 24:19 [b]Ruth 1:16; Ps. 17:8; 36:7; 57:1; 63:7
13 [I]Or, *I find favor* [II]Hebr. *to the heart* [a]Gen. 33:15; 1Sam. 1:18 [b]Gen. 34:3; Judg. 19:3 [c]1Sam. 25:41
14 [a]Ruth 2:18
15 [I]Hebr. *shame her not*
18 [a]Ruth 2:14
19 [a]Ruth 2:10; Ps. 41:1
20 [a]Ruth 3:10; 2Sam. 2:5; Job 29:13 [b]Prov. 17:17

🔑 **2:20** The three requirements to be a kinsman-redeemer were: relationship, financial ability, and willingness (Lev. 25:25, 48, 49). Boaz fulfilled all three requirements, after the nearest kin was unwilling (see introduction to Ruth and note on Ruth 4:1–8). These requirements help us understand why Christ, as our kinsman-redeemer, had to come as a man (relationship) who was also fully God (ability), and voluntarily accept the cost (Matt. 26:39, 42) of redeeming His people (willingness).

the living[2416] and to the dead. And Naomi said unto her, The man *is* near of kin unto us, [I][c]one of our next kinsmen.[1350]

21 And Ruth the Moabitess said, He said[559] unto me also, Thou shalt keep fast by my young men, until they have ended[3615] all my harvest.

22 And Naomi said unto Ruth her daughter in law, *It is* good,[2896] my daughter, that thou go out with his maidens, that they [I]meet thee not in any other field.

23 So she kept fast by the maidens of Boaz to glean unto the end[3615] of barley harvest and of wheat harvest; and dwelt with her mother in law.

Naomi Finds a Husband For Ruth

3 Then Naomi her mother in law said unto her, My daughter, [a]shall I not seek [b]rest for thee, that it may be well[3190] with thee?

2 And now *is* not Boaz of our kindred, [a]with whose maidens thou wast? Behold, he winnoweth[2219] barley to night in the threshingfloor.

3 Wash thyself[7364] therefore, [a]and anoint[5480] thee, and put thy raiment upon thee, and get thee down to the floor: *but* make not thyself known[3045] unto the man, until he shall have done[3615] eating and drinking.

4 And it shall be, when he lieth down, that thou shalt mark[3045] the place where he shall lie, and thou shalt go in, and [I]uncover[1540] his feet, and lay thee down; and he will tell thee what thou shalt do.

5 And she said unto her, All that thou sayest unto me I will do.

6 And she went down unto the floor, and did according to all that her mother in law bade[6680] her.

7 And when Boaz had eaten and drunk, and [a]his heart was merry,[3190] he went to lie down at the end of the heap of corn: and she came softly, and uncovered his feet, and laid her down.

8 And it came to pass at midnight, that the man was afraid,[2729] and [I]turned himself: and, behold, a woman[802] lay at his feet.

9 And he said, Who *art* thou? And she answered, I *am* Ruth thine handmaid: [a]spread therefore thy skirt over thine handmaid; for thou *art* [I][b]a near kinsman.[1350]

10 And he said, [a]Blessed[1288] *be* thou of the LORD, my daughter: *for* thou hast shewed[3190] more kindness[2617] in the latter end than [b]at the beginning,[7223] inasmuch as thou followedst not young men, whether poor or rich.

11 And now, my daughter, fear not; I will do to thee all that thou requirest: for all the [I]city of my people[5971] doth know[3045] that thou *art* [a]a virtuous[2428] woman.

12 And now *it is* true[551] that I *am thy* [a]near kinsman: howbeit [b]there is a kinsman nearer than I.

13 Tarry this night, and it shall be in the morning, *that* if he will [a]perform unto thee the part of a kinsman, well;[2896] let him do the kinsman's part: but if he will[2654] not do the part of a kinsman[1350] to thee, then will I do the part of a kinsman to thee, [b]*as* the LORD liveth:[2416] lie down until the morning.

14 And she lay at his feet until the morning: and she rose up before one could know[5234] another.[7453] And he said, [a]Let it not be known[3045] that a woman came into the floor.

15 Also he said, Bring the [I]vail that *thou hast* upon thee, and hold it. And when she held it, he measured six *measures* of barley, and laid *it* on her: and she went into the city.

16 And when she came to her mother in law, she said, Who *art* thou, my daughter? And she told her all that the man had done to her.

17 And she said, These six *measures* of barley gave he me; for he said[559] to me, Go not empty unto thy mother in law.

18 Then said she, [a]Sit still, my daughter, until thou know[3045] how the matter[1697] will fall: for the man will not

---

20 IOr, *one that hath right to redeem* [c]Lev. 25:25; Ruth 3:9; 4:6
22 IOr, *fall upon thee*
1 [a]1Cor. 7:36; 1Tim. 5:8 [b]Ruth 1:9
2 [a]Ruth 2:8
3 [a]2Sam. 14:2
4 IOr, *lift up the clothes that are on his feet*
7 [a]Judg. 19:6, 9, 22; 2Sam. 13:28; Esth. 1:10
8 IOr, *took hold on*
9 IOr, *one that hath right to redeem* [a]Ezek. 16:8 [b]Ruth 2:20; 3:12
10 [a]Ruth 2:20 [b]Ruth 1:8
11 IHebr. *gate* [a]Prov. 12:4
12 [a]Ruth 3:9 [b]Ruth 4:1
13 [a]Deut. 25:5; Ruth 4:5; Matt. 22:24 [b]Judg. 8:19; Jer. 4:2
14 [a]Rom. 12:17; 14:16; 1Cor. 10:32; 2Cor. 8:21; 1Thess. 5:22
15 IOr, *sheet,* or, *apron*
18 [a]Ps. 37:3, 5

be in rest,[8252] until he have finished[3615] the thing[1697] this day.[3117]

Boaz Marries Ruth

4 🗝 Then went Boaz up[5927] to the gate, and sat him down there: and, behold, [a]the kinsman[1350] of whom Boaz spake[1696] came by; unto whom he said, Ho, such a one! turn aside, sit down here. And he turned aside, and sat down.

2 And he took ten men[582] of [a]the elders[2205] of the city, and said, Sit ye down here. And they sat down.

3 And he said unto the kinsman, Naomi, that is come again[7725] out of the country[7704] of Moab, selleth a parcel of land,[7704] which *was* our brother[251] Elimelech's:

4 And [I]I thought[559] to advertise[1540] thee, saying, [a]Buy *it* [b]before the inhabitants, and before the elders of my people.[5971] If thou wilt redeem[1350] *it,* redeem *it:* but if thou wilt not redeem *it, then* tell me, that I may know:[3045] [c]for *there is* none to redeem *it* beside thee; and I *am* after thee. And he said, I will redeem *it.*

5 Then said Boaz, What day[3117] thou buyest the field[7704] of the hand[3027] of Naomi, thou must buy *it* also of Ruth the Moabitess, the wife[802] of the dead, [a]to raise up the name of the dead upon his inheritance.[5159]

6 [a]And the kinsman said, I cannot redeem *it* for myself, lest I mar[7843] mine own inheritance: redeem thou my right[1353] to thyself; for I cannot redeem *it.*

7 [a]Now this *was the manner* in former time in Israel concerning redeeming[1353] and concerning changing,[8545] for to confirm all things;[1697] a man plucked off his shoe, and gave *it* to his neighbour: and this *was* a testimony[8584] in Israel.

8 Therefore the kinsman said unto Boaz, Buy *it* for thee. So he drew off his shoe.

9 And Boaz said unto the elders, and *unto* all the people,[5971] Ye *are* witnesses this day, that I have bought[7069] all that *was* Elimelech's, and all that *was* Chilion's and Mahlon's, of the hand of Naomi.

10 Moreover Ruth the Moabitess, the wife of Mahlon, have I purchased to be my wife, to raise up the name of the dead upon his inheritance, [a]that the name of the dead be not cut off[3772] from among his brethren,[251] and from the gate of his place: ye *are* witnesses this day.

11 And all the people that *were* in the gate, and the elders, said, *We are* witnesses. [a]The LORD make the woman[802] that is come into thine house[1004] like Rachel and like Leah, which two did [b]build the house of Israel: and [I]do[6213] thou worthily[2428] in [c]Ephratah, and [II]be famous in Bethlehem:

12 And let thy house be like the house of Pharez, [a]whom Tamar bare unto Judah, of [b]the seed[2233] which the LORD shall give thee of this young woman.

The Genealogy of Boaz

13 So Boaz [a]took Ruth, and she was his wife:[802] and when he went in unto

1 [a]Ruth 3:12

2 [a]1Kgs. 21:8; Prov. 31:23

4 [I]Hebr. *I said I will reveal* in *thine ear* [a]Jer. 32:7, 8 [b]Gen. 23:18 [c]Lev. 25:25

5 [a]Gen. 38:8; Deut. 25:5, 6; Ruth 3:13; Matt. 22:24

6 [a]Ruth 3:12, 13

7 [a]Deut. 25:7, 9

10 [a]Deut. 25:6

11 [I]Or, *get thee riches,* or *power* [II]Hebr. *proclaim thy name* [a]Ps. 127:3; 128:3 [b]Deut. 25:9; [c]Gen. 35:16, 19

12 [a]Gen. 38:29; 1Chr. 2:4; Matt. 1:3 [b]1Sam. 2:20

13 [a]Ruth 3:11

🗝 **4:1–8** Boaz was willing to perform the duty of next of kin to redeem a piece of land so it could stay in the family (see Lev. 25:25), but there was a man who was a closer relative. However, the plans of the closer relative were complicated by the need to contract a "levirate marriage." Therefore, the other relative deferred to Boaz, who willingly married Ruth. The legal basis for this practice is found in Deuteronomy 25:5–10, but the obligation dates back to the patriarchs (Gen. 38:8). The legal ramifications of such cases were still being discussed in Jesus' day (Matt. 22:23–28).

It is to be noted that Ruth did not shame the relative who refused to perform his duty. According to Deuteronomy, she was supposed to take off his sandal and spit in his face, yet it appears that she was not even present with Boaz at the time. Some have suggested that Ruth was not able to do so because she was a Moabitess. Others say that because of her love for Boaz, Ruth did not want to marry the person who was the closest relative. See introduction to the Book of Ruth.

her, [b]the LORD gave her conception, and she bare a son.[1121]

14 And [a]the women said unto Naomi, Blessed[1288] *be* the LORD, which hath not [I]left[7673] thee this day without a [II]kinsman, that his name may be famous[7121] in Israel.

15 And he shall be unto thee a restorer[7725] of *thy* life,[5315] and [Ia]a nourisher of [II]thine old age:[7872] for thy daughter in law, which loveth[157] thee, which is [b]better[2896] to thee than seven sons, hath born him.

16 And Naomi took the child, and laid it in her bosom, and became nurse[539] unto it.

🗝 17 [a]And the women her neighbours[7934] gave it a name, saying, There is a son born to Naomi; and they called his name Obed: he *is* the father[1] of Jesse, the father of David.

18 Now these *are* the generations[8435] of Pharez: [a]Pharez begat Hezron,

19 And Hezron begat Ram, and Ram begat Amminadab,

20 And Amminadab begat [a]Nahshon, and Nahshon begat [Ib]Salmon,

21 And Salmon begat Boaz, and Boaz begat Obed,

22 And Obed begat Jesse, and Jesse begat [a]David.

13 [b]Gen. 29:31; 33:5
14 [I]Hebr. *caused to cease unto thee* [II]Or, *redeemer* [a]Luke 1:58; Rom. 12:15
15 [I]Hebr. *to nourish* [II]Hebr. *thy gray hairs* [a]Gen. 45:11; Ps. 55:22 [b]1Sam. 1:8
17 [a]Luke 1:58, 59
18 [a]1Chr. 2:4; Matt. 1:3
20 [I]Or, *Salmah* [a]Num. 1:7 [b]Matt. 1:4
22 [a]1Chr. 2:15; Matt. 1:6

🗝 **4:17–22** Boaz was a descendant of Salmon who married Rahab the harlot of Jericho (Josh. 2:1–21; Matt. 1:5). Since the purpose of Hebrew genealogies was to show lineage rather than to list each particular descendant, it is possible that some generations are missing in both Ruth 4:18–22 or Matthew 1:4–6. Assuming that the generations from Ruth to David are complete, Ruth and Boaz were King David's great-grandparents.

The First Book of
SAMUEL

The books of 1 and 2 Samuel made up one book originally. It remained so in the Hebrew text until the publishing of the Hebrew Bible in A.D. 1517 where it appeared as 1 and 2 Samuel. The Septuagint and other translations of the Old Testament that followed divided the books of Samuel and Kings into First Kings through Fourth Kings. The principal characters of 1 Samuel are Samuel, Saul, and David.

Furthermore, the Book of 1 Samuel presents in detail the transitional phase between the period of the judges and the period of the kings. During this time God instituted the offices of prophet and king, the latter replacing the office of the judge as Israel's political leader. It is important to note that the prophetic function did not originate at this time. Moses and Deborah are examples of those who were both political leaders over Israel and prophets (Ex. 3:11–22; Judg. 4:4, 5). These should be distinguished from the prophets from this time forward who were not rulers used in a prophetic capacity, but those who held the office of prophet. It is not until Samuel organized the "company of the prophets" (1 Sam. 19:20) that the office seems to have been formally established in Israel. Samuel bridged the gap between the periods of the judges and kings in that he was the last one to serve as a judge in all Israel (see note on 1 Sam. 8:5–7) and that he anointed the first two kings of Israel, Saul and David.

The book is divided into two sections: the first seven chapters outline the life and ministry of Samuel, and the remainder of the book describes the events during the reign of Saul. The climax is reached when God rejects Saul from being king for disobeying His command, and instructed Samuel to anoint David, the son of Jesse, as the next king (1 Sam. 15:26).

Samuel's Birth

1 Now there was a certain man of Ramathaim–zophim, of mount Ephraim, and his name *was* [a]Elkanah, the son of Jeroham, the son of Elihu, the son of Tohu, the son of Zuph, [b]an Ephrathite:

2 And he had two wives;[802] the name of the one *was* Hannah, and the name of the other Peninnah: and Peninnah had children, but Hannah had no children.

3 And this man went up out of his city [1a]yearly [b]to worship[7812] and to sacrifice[2076] unto the LORD of hosts in [c]Shiloh. And the two sons[1121] of Eli, Hophni and Phinehas, the priests[3548] of the LORD, *were* there.

4 And when the time was that Elkanah [a]offered,[2076] he gave to Peninnah his wife, and to all her sons and her daughters, portions:

5 But unto Hannah he gave [1]a worthy[639] portion; for he loved[157] Hannah: [a]but the LORD had shut up her womb.

6 And her adversary also [1a]provoked[3707] her sore,[3708] for to make her fret,[7481] because the LORD had shut up her womb.

7 And *as* he did so year by year, [1]when she went up to the house of the LORD, so she provoked her; therefore she wept, and did not eat.

8 Then said Elkanah her husband to her, Hannah, why weepest thou? and why eatest thou not? and why is thy heart grieved? *am* not I [a]better[2896] to thee than ten sons?

9 So Hannah rose up after they had eaten in Shiloh, and after they had drunk. Now Eli the priest[3548] sat upon a seat[3678] by a post of [a]the temple of the LORD.

10 [a]And she *was* [1]in bitterness[4751] of

1 [a]1Chr. 6:27, 34 [b]Ruth 1:2
3 [1]Hebr. *from year to year* [a]Ex. 23:14; Deut. 16:16; Luke 2:41; [b]Deut. 12:5-7; [c]Josh. 18:1
4 [a]Deut. 12:17, 18; 16:11
5 [1]Or, *a double portion* [a]Gen. 30:2
6 [1]Hebr. *angered her* [a]Job 6:14; 24:21
7 [1]Hebr. *from her going up*
8 [a]Ruth 4:15
9 [a]1Sam. 3:3
10 [1]Hebr. *bitter of soul* [a]Job 7:11; 10:1

soul,[5315] and prayed[6419] unto the LORD, and wept sore.

🗝 11 And she [a]vowed[5087] a vow, and said, O LORD of hosts, if thou wilt indeed [b]look on the affliction of thine handmaid, and [c]remember me, and not forget thine handmaid, but wilt give unto thine handmaid [I]a man child,[2233] then I will give him unto the LORD all the days[3117] of his life,[2416] and [d]there shall no razor come upon his head.

12 And it came to pass, as she [I]continued praying[6419] before the LORD, that Eli marked[8104] her mouth.

13 Now Hannah, she spake[1696] in her heart; only her lips[8193] moved, but her voice was not heard: therefore Eli thought she had been drunken.

14 And Eli said unto her, How long wilt thou be drunken? put away thy wine from thee.

15 And Hannah answered and said, No, my lord,[113] I *am* a woman[802] [I]of a sorrowful[7186] spirit:[7307] I have drunk neither wine nor strong drink, but have [a]poured out[8210] my soul before the LORD.

16 Count not thine handmaid for a daughter of [a]Belial:[1100] for out of the abundance of my [I]complaint[7878] and grief[3708] have I spoken[1696] hitherto.

17 Then Eli answered and said, [a]Go in peace:[7965] and [b]the God[430] of Israel grant *thee* thy petition[7596] that thou hast asked[7592] of him.

18 And she said, [a]Let thine handmaid find grace[2580] in thy sight. So the woman [b]went her way,[1870] and did eat, and her countenance was no more *sad.*

19 And they rose up in the morning early, and worshipped[7812] before the LORD, and returned, and came to their house to Ramah: and Elkanah [a]knew[3045] Hannah his wife; and [b]the LORD remembered her.

20 Wherefore it came to pass, [I]when the time was come about after Hannah had conceived, that she bare a son, and called[7121] his name [II]Samuel, *saying,* Because I have asked him of the LORD.

21 And the man Elkanah, and all his house, [a]went up to offer[2076] unto the LORD the yearly sacrifice,[2077] and his vow.

22 But Hannah went not up; for she said unto her husband, *I will not go up* until the child be weaned,[1580] and *then* I will [a]bring him, that he may appear[7200] before the LORD, and there [b]abide [c]for ever.

23 And [a]Elkanah her husband said unto her, Do what seemeth thee good;[2896] tarry until thou have weaned him; [b]only the LORD establish his word.[1697] So the woman abode, and gave her son suck until she weaned him.

24 And when she had weaned him, she [a]took him up with her, with three bullocks, and one ephah of flour, and a bottle[5035] of wine, and brought him unto [b]the house of the LORD in Shiloh: and the child *was* young.

25 And they slew[2819] a bullock, and [a]brought the child to Eli.

26 And she said, Oh my lord, [a]*as* thy soul liveth,[2416] my lord, I *am* the woman that stood[5324] by thee here, praying unto the LORD.

27 [a]For this child I prayed;[6419] and the LORD hath given me my petition which I asked of him:

28 [a]Therefore also I have [I]lent[7592] him to the LORD; as long as he liveth [II]he shall be lent to the LORD. And he [b]worshipped the LORD there.

Hannah's Prayer

2 And Hannah [a]prayed,[6419] and said, [b]My heart rejoiceth in the LORD, [c]mine horn is exalted in the LORD: my

11 [I]Hebr. *seed of men* [a]Gen. 28:20; Num. 30:3; Judg. 11:30 [b]Gen. 29:32; Ex. 4:31; 2Sam. 16:12; Ps. 25:18 [c]Gen. 8:1; 30:22 [d]Num. 6:5; Judg. 13:5
12 [I]Hebr. *multiplied to pray*
15 [I]Hebr. *hard of spirit* [a]Ps. 62:8; 142:2
16 [I]Or, *meditation* [a]Deut. 13:13
17 [a]Judg. 18:6; Mark 5:34; Luke 7:50; 8:48 [b]Ps. 20:4, 5
18 [a]Gen. 33:15; Ruth 2:13 [b]Eccl. 9:7
19 [a]Gen. 4:1 [b]Gen. 30:22
20 [I]Hebr. *in revolution of days* [II]That is, *Asked of God*
21 [a]1Sam. 1:3
22 [a]Luke 2:22 [b]1Sam. 1:11, 28; 2:11, 18; 3:1 [c]Ex. 21:6
23 [a]Num. 30:7 [b]2Sam. 7:25
24 [a]Deut. 12:5, 6, 11 [b]Josh. 18:1
25 [a]Luke 2:22
26 [a]Gen. 42:15; 2Kgs. 2:2, 4, 6
27 [a]Matt. 7:7
28 [I]Or, *returned him, whom I have obtained by petition, to the LORD* [II]Or, *he whom I have obtained by petition, shall be returned* [a]1Sam. 1:11, 22 [b]Gen. 24:26, 52
1 [a]Phil. 4:6 [b]Luke 1:46 [c]Ps. 92:10; 112:9

🗝 **1:11** The outward sign of not shaving Samuel's head was associated with the Nazarite vow (see note on Num. 6:2–21). Apparently Samuel, like Samson (see Judg. 13:4, 5), was to be a Nazarite. The difference was that Samson was a Nazarite by God's instruction and Samuel's mother made the vow for her son. As a result of her faith toward God, Hannah's prayer was answered.

mouth is enlarged over mine enemies; because I [d]rejoice in thy salvation.

2 [a]*There is* none holy as the LORD: for *there is* [b]none beside thee: neither *is there* any rock like our God.[430]

3 Talk no more so exceeding proudly; [a]let *not* [I]arrogancy[6279] come out of your mouth: for the LORD *is* a God of knowledge,[1844] and by him actions are weighed.[8505]

4 [a]The bows of the mighty men *are* broken, and they that stumbled[3782] are girded with strength.[2428]

5 [a]*They that were* full have hired out themselves for bread; and *they that were* hungry ceased: so that [b]the barren[6135] hath born seven; and [c]she that hath many children[1121] is waxed feeble.[535]

6 [a]The LORD killeth,[4191] and maketh alive: he bringeth down to the grave,[7585] and bringeth up.

7 The LORD [a]maketh poor, and maketh rich: [b]he bringeth low, and lifteth up.

8 [a]He raiseth up the poor out of the dust,[6083] *and* lifteth up the beggar from the dunghill, [b]to set *them* among princes,[5081] and to make them inherit[5157] the throne of glory: for [c]the pillars of the earth[776] *are* the LORD's, and he hath set the world[8398] upon them.

9 [a]He will keep[8104] the feet of his saints,[2623] and the wicked[6563] shall be silent[1826] in darkness;[2822] for by strength shall no man prevail.

10 The adversaries[7378] of the LORD shall be [a]broken to pieces;[2865] [b]out of heaven shall he thunder upon them: [c]the LORD shall judge[1777] the ends of the earth; and he shall give strength unto his king,[4428] and [d]exalt the horn of his anointed.[4899]

11 And Elkanah went to Ramah to his house. [a]And the child did minister unto the LORD before Eli the priest.[3548]

Eli's Corrupt Sons

12 Now the sons[1121] of Eli *were* [a]sons of Belial;[1100] [b]they knew[3045] not the LORD.

13 And the priests'[3548] custom[4941] with the people[5971] *was, that,* when any man offered[2076] sacrifice,[2077] the priest's servant came, while the flesh[1320] was in seething, with a fleshhook[4207] of three teeth in his hand;

14 And he struck *it* into the pan, or kettle, or caldron, or pot; all that the fleshhook brought up[5927] the priest took for himself. So they did[6213] in Shiloh unto all the Israelites that came thither.

15 Also before they [a]burnt[6999] the fat, the priest's servant[5288] came, and said to the man that sacrificed,[2076] Give flesh to roast for the priest; for he will not have sodden[1310] flesh of thee, but raw.[2416]

16 And *if* any man said unto him, Let them not fail to burn the fat [I]presently, and *then* take *as much* as thy soul[5315] desireth; then he would answer[559] him, *Nay;* but thou shalt give *it me* now: and if not, I will take *it* by force.

17 Wherefore the sin[2403] of the young men was very great [a]before the LORD:[3068] for men [b]abhorred[5006] the offering[4503] of the LORD.

18 [a]But Samuel ministered[8334] before the LORD, *being* a child, [b]girded with a linen ephod.

19 Moreover his mother made him a little coat, and brought *it* to him from year to year, when she [a]came up with her husband to offer[2076] the yearly sacrifice.

20 And Eli [a]blessed[1288] Elkanah and his wife,[802] and said, The LORD give[7760] thee seed[2233] of this woman[802] for the [I]loan which is [b]lent[7592] to the LORD. And they went unto their own home.

21 And the LORD [a]visited[6485] Hannah, so that she conceived, and bare three sons and two daughters. And the child Samuel [b]grew before the LORD.

22 Now Eli was very old,[2204] and heard all that his sons did unto all Israel; and how they lay with [a]the women[802] that [I]assembled[6633] *at* the door of the tabernacle of the congregation.[4150]

23 And he said unto them, Why do ye such things? for [I]I hear of your evil[7451] dealings by all this people.

---

1 [d]Ps. 9:14; 13:5; 20:5; 35:9

2 [a]Ex. 15:11; Deut. 3:24; 32:4; Ps. 86:8; 89:6, 8 [b]Deut. 4:35; 2Sam. 22:32

3 [I]Hebr. *hard* [a]Ps. 94:4; Mal. 3:13; Jude 1:15

4 [a]Ps. 37:15, 17; 76:3

5 [a]Ps. 34:10; Luke 1:53 [b]Ps. 113:9 [c]Isa. 54:1; Jer. 15:9

6 [a]Deut. 32:39; Job 5:18; Hos. 6:1

7 [a]Job 1:21 [b]Ps. 75:7

8 [a]Ps. 113:7, 8; Dan. 4:17; Luke 1:52 [b]Job 36:7 [c]Job 38:4-6; Ps. 24:2; 102:25; 104:5; Heb. 1:3

9 [a]Ps. 91:11; 121:3

10 [a]Ps. 2:9 [b]1Sam. 7:10; Ps. 18:13 [c]Ps. 96:13; 98:9 [d]Ps. 89:24

11 [a]1Sam. 2:18; 3:1

12 [a]Deut. 13:13 [b]Judg. 2:10; Jer. 22:16; Rom. 1:28

15 [a]Lev. 3:3-5, 16

16 [I]Hebr. *as on the day*

17 [a]Gen. 6:11 [b]Mal. 2:8

18 [a]1Sam. 2:11 [b]Ex. 28:4; 2Sam. 6:14

19 [a]1Sam. 1:3, 7

20 [I]Or, *petition which she asked* [a]Gen. 14:19 [b]1Sam. 1:28

21 [a]Gen. 21:1 [b]Judg. 13:24; 1Sam. 2:26; 3:19; Luke 1:80; 2:40

22 [I]Hebr. *assembled by troops* [a]Ex. 38:8

23 [I]Or, *I hear evil words of you*

24 Nay, my sons; for *it is* no good[2896] report that I hear: ye make the LORD's people [I]to transgress.[5674]

25 If one man sin[2398] against another, the judge[430] shall judge him: but if a man [a]sin against the LORD, who shall intreat for him? Notwithstanding they hearkened not unto the voice of their father, [b]because the LORD would[2654] slay[4191] them.

26 And the child Samuel [a]grew on, and was [b]in favour[2896] both with the LORD, and also with men.

27 [a]And there came a man of God unto Eli, and said unto him, Thus saith the LORD, [b]Did I plainly appear[1540] unto the house of thy father, when they were in Egypt in Pharaoh's house?

28 And did I [a]choose[977] him out of all the tribes of Israel *to be* my priest, to offer upon mine altar,[4196] to burn incense,[7004] to wear an ephod before me? and [b]did I give unto the house of thy father all the offerings made by fire of the children of Israel?

29 Wherefore [a]kick[1163] ye at my sacrifice and at mine offering, which I have commanded[6680] *in my* [b]habitation; and honourest thy sons above me, to make yourselves fat with the chiefest[7225] of all the offerings of Israel my people?

30 Wherefore the LORD God of Israel saith,[5001] [a]I said indeed *that* thy house, and the house of thy father, should walk before me for ever: but now the LORD saith, [b]Be it far from me; for them that honour me [c]I will honour, and [d]they that despise me shall be lightly esteemed.[7043]

🔑 31 Behold, [a]the days[3117] come, that I will cut off thine arm, and the arm of thy father's[1] house, that there shall not be an old man[2205] in thine house.

32 And thou shalt see [I]an enemy[6862] *in my* habitation, in all *the wealth* which *God* shall give Israel: and there shall not be [a]an old man in thine house for ever.

33 And the man of thine, *whom* I shall not cut off[3772] from mine altar, *shall be* to consume[3615] thine eyes, and to grieve[109] thine heart: and all the increase of thine house shall die[4191] [I]in the flower of their age.

34 And this *shall be* [a]a sign[226] unto thee, that shall come upon thy two sons, on Hophni and Phinehas; [b]in one day[3117] they shall die both of them.

35 And [a]I will raise me up a faithful[539] priest, *that* shall do according to *that* which *is* in mine heart and in my mind: and [b]I will build him a sure[539] house; and he shall walk before [c]mine anointed for ever.

36 [a]And it shall come to pass, *that* every one that is left[3498] in thine house shall come *and* crouch[7812] to him for a piece of silver and a morsel of bread, and shall say, [I]Put me, I pray thee,[4994] into [II]one of the priests' offices, that I may eat a piece of bread.

Samuel's Call

3 And [a]the child Samuel ministered unto the LORD before Eli. And [b]the word[1697] of the LORD was precious in those days;[3117] *there was* no open[6555] vision.[2377]

2 And it came to pass at that time, when Eli *was* laid down in his place, [a]and his eyes began to wax dim,[3544] *that* he could not see;

3 And ere[2962] the [a]lamp[5216] of God[430] went out [b]in the temple of the LORD, where the ark[727] of God *was,* and Samuel was laid down *to sleep;*

4 That the LORD called[7121] Samuel: and he answered,[559] Here *am* I.

5 And he ran unto Eli, and said, Here *am* I; for thou calledst me. And he said, I called not; lie down again. And he went and lay down.

6 And the LORD called yet again, Samuel. And Samuel arose and went to Eli, and said, Here *am* I; for thou didst call me. And he answered, I called not, my son;[1121] lie down again.

24 [I]Or, *to cry out*
25 [a]Num. 15:30 [b]Josh. 11:20; Prov. 15:10
26 [a]1Sam. 2:21 [b]Prov. 3:4; Luke 2:52; Acts 2:47; Rom. 14:18
27 [a]1Kgs. 13:1 [b]Ex. 4:14, 27
28 [a]Ex. 28:1, 4; Num. 16:5; 18:1, 7 [b]Lev. 2:3, 10; 6:16; 7:7, 8, 34, 35; 10:14, 15; Num. 5:9, 10; 18:8-19
29 [a]Deut. 32:15 [b]Deut. 12:5, 6
30 [a]Ex. 29:9 [b]Jer. 18:9, 10 [c]Ps. 18:20; 91:14 [d]Mal. 2:9
31 [a]1Sam. 4:11; 14:3; 18:20; 22:18; 1Kgs. 2:27; Ezek. 44:10
32 [I]Or, *the affliction of the tabernacle, for all the wealth which God would have given Israel* [a]Zech. 8:4
33 [I]Hebr. *men*
34 [a]1Kgs. 13:3 [b]1Sam. 4:11
35 [a]1Kgs. 2:35; 1Chr. 29:22; Ezek. 44:15 [b]2Sam. 7:11, 27; 1Kgs. 11:38 [c]Ps. 2:2; 18:50
36 [I]Hebr. *Join* [II]Or, *somewhat about the priesthood* [a]1Kgs. 2:27

1 [a]1Sam. 2:11 [b]1Sam. 3:21; Ps. 74:9; Amos 8:11
2 [a]Gen. 27:1; 48:10; 1Sam. 2:22; 4:15
3 [a]Ex. 27:21; Lev. 24:3; 2Chr. 13:11 [b]1Sam. 1:9

🔑 **2:31–36** See note on 1 Kings 2:26, 27 regarding the fulfillment of this prophecy.

7 [I]Now Samuel [a]did not yet know[3045] the LORD, neither was the word of the LORD yet revealed unto him.

8 And the LORD called Samuel again the third time. And he arose and went to Eli, and said, Here *am* I; for thou didst call me. And Eli perceived[995] that the LORD had called the child.

9 Therefore Eli said unto Samuel, Go, lie down: and it shall be, if he call thee, that thou shalt say, Speak,[1696] LORD; for thy servant[5650] heareth. So Samuel went and lay down in his place.

10 And the LORD came, and stood, and called as at other times, Samuel, Samuel. Then Samuel answered, Speak; for thy servant heareth.

11 And the LORD said to Samuel, Behold, I will do[6213] a thing in Israel, [a]at which both the ears[241] of every one that heareth it shall tingle.

12 In that day[3117] I will perform against Eli [a]all *things* which I have spoken[1696] concerning his house: [I]when I begin, I will also make an end.[3615]

13 [I][a]For I have told him that I will [b]judge[8199] his house for ever for the iniquity[5771] which he knoweth; because [c]his sons[1121] made themselves [II]vile,[7043] and he [III][d]restrained them not.

14 And therefore I have sworn unto the house of Eli, that the iniquity of Eli's house [a]shall not be purged[3722] with sacrifice[2077] nor offering[4503] for ever.

15 And Samuel lay until the morning, and opened the doors of the house of the LORD. And Samuel feared[3372] to shew[5046] Eli the vision.

16 Then Eli called Samuel, and said, Samuel, my son. And he answered, Here *am* I.

17 And he said,[1696] What *is* the thing that *the LORD* hath said unto thee? I pray thee hide *it* not from me: [a]God do so to thee, and [I]more also, if thou hide *any* [II]thing from me of all the things that he said unto thee.

18 And Samuel told him [I]every whit,[1697] and hid nothing from him. And he said, [a]It *is* the LORD: let him do what seemeth him good.[2896]

19 And Samuel [a]grew, and [b]the LORD was with him, [c]and did let none of his words[1697] fall to the ground.[776]

20 And all Israel [a]from Dan even to Beer–sheba knew[3045] that Samuel *was* [I]established[539] *to be* a prophet[5030] of the LORD.

21 And the LORD appeared[7200] again in Shiloh: for the LORD revealed himself to Samuel in Shiloh by [a]the word of the LORD.

The Philistines Capture The Ark of God

4 And the word[1697] of Samuel [I]came to all Israel. Now Israel went out against the Philistines to battle, and pitched beside [a]Eben–ezer: and the Philistines pitched in Aphek.

2 And the Philistines put themselves in array[6186] against Israel: and when [I]they joined[5203] battle, Israel was smitten before the Philistines: and they slew[5221] of [II]the army in the field[7704] about four thousand men.

3 And when the people[5971] were come into the camp,[4264] the elders[2205] of Israel said, Wherefore hath the LORD smitten us to day before the Philistines? Let us [I]fetch the ark[727] of the covenant[1285] of the LORD out of Shiloh unto us, that, when it cometh among[7130] us, it may save[3467] us out of the hand of our enemies.

4 So the people sent to Shiloh, that they might bring[5375] from thence the ark of the covenant of the LORD[3068] of hosts, [a]which dwelleth[3427] *between* [b]the

7 [I]Or, *Thus did Samuel before he knew the LORD, and before the word of the LORD was revealed unto him* [a]Acts 19:2

11 [a]2Kgs. 21:12; Jer. 19:3

12 [I]Hebr. *beginning and ending* [a]1Sam. 2:30-36

13 [I]Or, *And I will tell him* [II]Or, *accursed* [III]Hebr. *frowned not upon them* [a]1Sam. 2:29-31 [b]Ezek. 7:3; 18:30 [c]1Sam. 2:12, 17, 22 [d]1Sam. 2:23, 25

14 [a]Num. 15:30, 31; Isa. 22:14

17 [I]Hebr. *so add* [II]Or, *word* [a]Ruth 1:17

18 [I]Hebr. *all the things or words* [a]Job 1:21; 2:10; Ps. 39:9; Isa. 39:8

19 [a]1Sam. 2:21 [b]Gen. 39:2, 21, 23 [c]1Sam. 9:6

20 [I]Or, *faithful* [a]Judg. 20:1

21 [a]1Sam. 3:1, 4

1 [I]Or, *came to pass* [a]1Sam. 5:1; 7:12

2 [I]Hebr. *the battle was spread* [II]Hebr. *the array*

3 [I]Hebr. *take unto us*

4 [a]2Sam. 6:2; Ps. 80:1; 99:1 [b]Ex. 25:18, 22; Num. 7:89

3:13 Eli had probably spoken to his sons about their bad behavior, but he had failed to discipline them effectively. The proper thing would have been for him to have administered correction in love at an early stage in their lives (see Eph. 6:4; Heb. 12:5–8).

4:3 The Israelites were treating the ark as a kind of magic charm instead of the testimony of God's power and presence. The mere presence of the ark would not bring victory in the battle.

cherubims:[3742] and the two sons[1121] of Eli, Hophni and Phinehas, *were* there with the ark of the covenant of God.[430]

5 And when the ark of the covenant of the LORD came into the camp, all Israel shouted[7321] with a great shout, so that the earth[776] rang again.

6 And when the Philistines heard the noise of the shout, they said, What *meaneth* the noise of this great shout in the camp of the Hebrews? And they understood[3045] that the ark of the LORD was come into the camp.

7 And the Philistines were afraid,[3372] for they said, God is come into the camp. And they said, Woe unto us! for there hath not been such a thing [I]heretofore.

8 Woe unto us! who shall deliver[5337] us out of the hand of these mighty Gods?[430] these *are* the Gods that smote[5221] the Egyptians with all the plagues[4347] in the wilderness.

9 [a]Be strong,[2388] and quit[1961] yourselves like men, O ye Philistines, that ye be not servants unto the Hebrews, [b]as they have been to you: [I]quit yourselves like men, and fight.

10 And the Philistines fought, and [a]Israel was smitten, and they fled every man into his tent: and there was a very great slaughter; for there fell[5307] of Israel thirty thousand footmen.

11 And [a]the ark of God was taken; and [b]the two sons of Eli, Hophni and Phinehas, [I]were slain.[4191]

Eli's Death

12 And there ran a man of Benjamin out of the army, and [a]came to Shiloh the same day[3117] with his clothes rent, and [b]with earth[127] upon his head.

13 And when he came, lo, Eli sat upon [a]a seat[3678] by the wayside watching: for his heart trembled[2730] for the ark of God. And when the man came into the city, and told *it,* all the city cried out.[2199]

14 And when Eli heard the noise of the crying, he said, What *meaneth* the noise of this tumult?[1995] And the man came in hastily, and told Eli.

15 Now Eli was ninety and eight years old; and [a]his eyes [I]were dim, that he could not see.

16 And the man said unto Eli, I *am* he that came out of the army, and I fled to day out of the army. And he said, [a]What [I]is there done, my son?[1121]

17 And the messenger[1319] answered and said, Israel is fled before the Philistines, and there hath been also a great slaughter among the people, and thy two sons also, Hophni and Phinehas, are dead,[4191] and the ark of God is taken.

18 And it came to pass, when he made mention of the ark of God, that he fell from off the seat backward by the side[3027] of the gate, and his neck brake,[7665] and he died: for he was an old[2204] man, and heavy. [I]And he had judged[8199] Israel forty years.

19 And his daughter in law, Phinehas' wife,[802] was with child, *near* [I]to be delivered: and when she heard the tidings that the ark of God was taken, and that her father in law and her husband were dead, she bowed herself[3766] and travailed;[3205] for her pains [II]came upon her.

20 And about the time of her death[4191] [a]the women that stood[5324] by her said[1696] unto her, Fear[3372] not; for thou hast born a son. But she answered not, [I]neither did she regard *it.*

21 And she named[7121] the child [I][a]I–chabod, saying, [b]The glory is departed[1540] from Israel: because the ark of God was taken, and because of her father in law and her husband.

22 And she said, The glory is departed from Israel: for the ark of God is taken.

God Judges the Philistines

5 And the Philistines took the ark[727] of God,[430] and brought it [a]from Eben–ezer unto Ashdod.

---

7 [I]Hebr. *yesterday,* or, *the third day*

9 [I]Hebr. *be men* [a]1Cor. 16:13 [b]Judg. 13:1

10 [a]Lev. 26:17; Deut. 28:25; 1Sam. 4:2; Ps. 78:9, 62

11 [I]Hebr. *died* [a]1Sam. 2:32; Ps. 78:61 [b]1Sam. 2:34; Ps. 78:64

12 [a]2Sam. 1:2 [b]Josh. 7:6; 2Sam. 13:19; 15:32; Neh. 9:1; Job 2:12

13 [a]1Sam. 1:9

15 [I]Hebr. *stood* [a]1Sam. 3:2

16 [I]Hebr. *is the thing* [a]2Sam. 1:4

18 [I]He seems to have been a judge to do justice only, and that in southwest *Israel*

19 [I]Or, *to cry out* [II]Hebr. *were turned*

20 [I]Hebr. *set not her heart* [a]Gen. 35:17

21 [I]That is, *Where is the glory?* or, There is *no glory* [a]1Sam. 14:3 [b]Ps. 26:8; 78:61

1 [a]1Sam. 4:1; 7:12

2 When the Philistines took the ark of God, they brought it into the house of [a]Dagon, and set it by Dagon.

3 And when they of Ashdod arose early on the morrow, behold, Dagon *was* [a]fallen[5307] upon his face to the earth[776] before the ark of the LORD. And they took Dagon, and [b]set him in his place again.

4 And when they arose early on the morrow morning, behold, Dagon *was* fallen upon his face to the ground[776] before the ark of the LORD; and [a]the head of Dagon and both the palms[3709] of his hands *were* cut off[3772] upon the threshold; only [I]*the stump of* Dagon was left[7604] to him.

5 Therefore neither the priests[3548] of Dagon, nor any that come into Dagon's house, [a]tread on the threshold of Dagon in Ashdod unto this day.[3117]

6 But [a]the hand of the LORD was heavy upon them of Ashdod, and he [b]destroyed[8074] them, and smote[5221] them with [c]emerods,[6076] *even* Ashdod and the coasts thereof.

7 And when the men of Ashdod saw[7200] that *it was* so, they said, The ark of the God of Israel shall not abide with us: for his hand is sore[7185] upon us, and upon Dagon our god.

8 They sent therefore and gathered[622] all the lords[5633] of the Philistines unto them, and said, What shall we do[6213] with the ark of the God of Israel? And they answered,[559] Let the ark of the God of Israel be carried about unto Gath. And they carried the ark of the God of Israel about *thither.*

9 And it was *so,* that, after they had carried it about, [a]the hand of the LORD was against the city [b]with a very great destruction:[4103] and [c]he smote the men of the city, both small and great, and they had emerods in their secret parts.

10 Therefore they sent the ark of God to Ekron. And it came to pass, as the ark of God came to Ekron, that the Ekronites cried out,[2199] saying, They have brought about the ark of the God of Israel to [I]us, to slay[4191] us and our people.[5971]

11 So they sent and gathered together all the lords of the Philistines, and said, Send away the ark of the God of Israel, and let it go again to his own place, that it slay [I]us not, and our people: for there was a deadly destruction throughout all the city; [a]the hand of God was very heavy there.

12 And the men that died[4191] not were smitten[5221] with the emerods: and the cry of the city went up to heaven.

The Philistines Return the Ark to Israel

6 And the ark[727] of the LORD was in the country[7704] of the Philistines seven months.

2 And the Philistines [a]called[7121] for the priests[3548] and the diviners,[7080] saying, What shall we do[6213] to the ark of the LORD? tell us wherewith we shall send it to his place.

3 And they said, If ye send away the ark of the God[430] of Israel, send it not [a]empty; but in any wise return him [b]a trespass offering: then ye shall be healed, and it shall [c]be known[3045] to you why his hand is not removed from you.

4 Then said they, What *shall be* the trespass offering which we shall return to him? They answered,[559] Five golden emerods,[6076] and five golden mice, [a]*according to* the number of the lords[5633] of the Philistines: for one plague[4046] *was* on [I]you all, and on your lords.

5 Wherefore ye shall make images[6754] of your emerods, and images of your mice that [a]mar[7843] the land;[776] and ye shall [b]give glory unto the God of Israel: peradventure[194] he will [c]lighten[7043] his hand from off you, and from off [d]your gods,[430] and from off your land.

6 Wherefore then do ye harden your hearts, [a]as the Egyptians and Pharaoh

2 [a]Judg. 16:23
3 [a]Isa. 19:1; 46:1, 2 [b]Isa. 46:7
4 [I]Or, the fishy part [a]Jer. 50:2; Ezek. 6:4, 6; Mic. 1:7
5 [a]Zeph. 1:9
6 [a]Ex. 9:3; 1Sam. 5:7, 11; Ps. 32:4; Acts 13:11 [b]1Sam. 6:5 [c]Deut. 28:27; Ps. 78:66
9 [a]Deut. 2:15; 1Sam. 7:13; 12:15 [b]1Sam. 5:11 [c]1Sam. 5:6; Ps. 78:66
10 [I]Hebr. *me, to slay me and my*
11 [I]Hebr. *me not, and my* [a]1Sam. 5:6, 9
2 [a]Gen. 41:8; Ex. 7:11; Dan. 2:2; 5:7; Matt. 2:4
3 [a]Ex. 23:15; Deut. 16:16 [b]Lev. 5:15, 16 [c]1Sam. 6:9
4 [I]Hebr. *them* [a]1Sam. 6:17, 18; Josh. 13:3; Judg. 3:3
5 [a]1Sam. 5:6 [b]Josh. 7:19; Isa. 42:12; Mal. 2:2; John 9:24 [c]1Sam. 5:6, 11; Ps. 39:10 [d]1Sam. 5:3, 4, 7
6 [a]Ex. 7:13; 8:15; 14:17

5:2 See note on Judges 2:13 on Dagon.

hardened their hearts? when he had wrought [I]wonderfully[5953] among them, [b]did they not let [II]the people go, and they departed?

🔑 7 Now therefore make [a]a new cart, and take two milch kine,[6510] [b]on which there hath come no yoke, and tie the kine to the cart, and bring their calves[1121] home from them:

8 And take the ark of the LORD, and lay it upon the cart; and put [a]the jewels of gold, which ye return him *for* a trespass offering, in a coffer by the side thereof; and send it away, that it may go.

9 And see, if it goeth up by the way of his own coast to [a]Beth–shemesh, *then* [I]he hath done us this great evil:[7451] but if not, then [b]we shall know[3045] that *it is* not his hand *that* smote[5060] us; it *was* a chance[4745] *that* happened to us.

10 And the men did[6213] so; and took two milch kine, and tied them to the cart, and shut up their calves at home:

11 And they laid[7760] the ark of the LORD upon the cart, and the coffer with the mice of gold and the images of their emerods.[2914]

12 And the kine took the straight[3474] way to the way of Beth–shemesh, *and* went along the highway, lowing[1600] as they went, and turned not aside *to* the right hand or *to* the left; and the lords of the Philistines went after them unto the border of Beth–shemesh.

13 And *they of* Beth–shemesh *were* reaping their wheat harvest in the valley: and they lifted up their eyes, and saw[7200] the ark, and rejoiced to see *it.*

14 And the cart came into the field[7704] of Joshua, a Beth–shemite, and stood there, where *there was* a great stone: and they clave[1234] the wood of the cart, and offered[5927] the kine a burnt offering unto the LORD.

6 [I]Or, *reproach fully* [II]Hebr. *them* [b]Ex. 12:31

7 [a]2Sam. 6:3 [b]Num. 19:2

8 [a]1Sam. 6:4, 5

9 [I]Or, *it* [a]Josh. 15:10 [b]1Sam. 6:3

16 [a]Josh. 13:3

17 [a]1Sam. 6:4

18 [I]Or, *great stone*

19 [a]Ex. 19:21; Num. 4:5, 15, 20; 2Sam. 6:7

20 [a]2Sam. 6:9; Mal. 3:2

21 [a]Josh. 18:14; Judg. 18:12; 1Chr. 13:5, 6

1 [a]1Sam. 6:21; Ps. 132:6

15 And the Levites took down the ark of the LORD, and the coffer that *was* with it, wherein the jewels of gold *were,* and put *them* on the great stone: and the men of Beth–shemesh offered burnt offerings and sacrificed[2076] sacrifices the same day[3117] unto the LORD.

16 And when [a]the five lords of the Philistines had seen[7200] *it,* they returned to Ekron the same day.

17 [a]And these *are* the golden emerods which the Philistines returned *for* a trespass offering unto the LORD; for Ashdod one, for Gaza one, for Askelon one, for Gath one, for Ekron one;

18 And the golden mice, *according to* the number of all the cities of the Philistines *belonging* to the five lords, *both* of fenced cities, and of country villages, even unto the [I]great *stone of* Abel, whereon they set down the ark of the LORD: *which stone remaineth* unto this day in the field of Joshua, the Beth–shemite.

19 And [a]he smote[5221] the men of Beth–shemesh, because they had looked[7200] into the ark of the LORD, even he smote of the people[5971] fifty thousand and threescore and ten men: and the people lamented, because the LORD had smitten[5221] *many* of the people with a great slaughter.[4347]

20 And the men of Beth–shemesh said, [a]Who is able to stand before this holy LORD God? and to whom shall he go up from us?

21 And they sent messengers[4397] to the inhabitants of [a]Kirjath–jearim, saying, The Philistines have brought again the ark of the LORD; come ye down, *and* fetch it up to you.

7

And the men of [a]Kirjath–jearim came, and fetched up[5927] the ark[727] of the LORD, and brought it into the

🔑 **6:7–12** Normally, it is difficult to drive even the best trained cows straight on a road when their calves have just been taken away from them. In this case, the cows did follow a straight line, carrying the ark back to Israel, which revealed that their behavior was being controlled by God (cf. Num. 22:22–31). God is all-powerful and is able to use all facets of His creation to accomplish His will.

house of [b]Abinadab in the hill, and sanctified[6942] Eleazar his son[1121] to keep[8104]
the ark of the LORD.
2 And it came to pass, while the ark
abode in Kirjath–jearim, that the time
was long; for it was twenty years: and
all the house of Israel lamented[5091] after
the LORD.

Samuel Leads Israel

3 And Samuel spake[559] unto all the
house of Israel, saying, If ye do [a]return
unto the LORD with all your hearts,
then [b]put away the strange[5236] gods[430]
and [c]Ashtaroth from among you, and
[d]prepare[3559] your hearts unto the LORD,
and [e]serve[5647] him only: and he will
deliver[5337] you out of the hand of the
Philistines.
🔑 4 Then the children[1121] of Israel did
put away [a]Baalim and Ashtaroth, and
served the LORD only.
5 And Samuel said, [a]Gather[6908] all
Israel to Mizpeh, and I will pray[6419] for
you unto the LORD.
6 And they gathered together to Miz-
peh, [a]and drew water, and poured *it* out[8210]
before the LORD, and [b]fasted on that
day,[3117] and said there, [c]We have
sinned[2398] against the LORD. And Samuel
judged[8199] the children of Israel in Mizpeh.
7 And when the Philistines heard
that the children of Israel were gathered
together to Mizpeh, the lords[5633] of the
Philistines went up against Israel. And
when the children of Israel heard *it,* they
were afraid of the Philistines.
8 And the children of Israel said to
Samuel, [1][a]Cease not to cry[2199] unto the
LORD our God[430] for us, that he will
save[3467] us out of the hand of the
Philistines.
9 And Samuel took a sucking lamb,
and offered[5927] *it for* a burnt offering
wholly[3632] unto the LORD: And [a]Samuel
cried[2199] unto the LORD for Israel; and
the LORD [1]heard him.
10 And as Samuel was offering
up[5927] the burnt offering, the Philistines drew near[5066] to battle against
Israel: [a]but the LORD thundered with
a great thunder on that day upon the
Philistines, and discomfited[2000] them;
and they were smitten[5062] before Israel.
11 And the men of Israel went out of
Mizpeh, and pursued the Philistines, and
smote[5221] them, until *they came* under
Beth–car.
12 Then Samuel [a]took a stone, and
set[7760] *it* between Mizpeh and Shen, and
called[7121] the name of it [1]Eben–ezer,
saying, Hitherto hath the LORD helped
us.
13 [a]So the Philistines were subdued,[3665] and they [b]came no more into
the coast of Israel: and the hand of the
LORD was against the Philistines all the
days[3117] of Samuel.
14 And the cities which the
Philistines had taken from Israel were restored to Israel from Ekron even unto
Gath; and the coasts thereof did Israel
deliver out of the hands of the
Philistines. And there was peace[7965] between Israel and the Amorites.
15 And Samuel [a]judged Israel all the
days of his life.[2416]
16 And he went from year to year [1]in
circuit[5437] to Bethel, and Gilgal, and
Mizpeh, and judged Israel in all those
places.
17 And [a]his return *was* to Ramah;
for there *was* his house; and there he
judged Israel; and there he [b]built an
altar[4196] unto the LORD.

Israel Asks for a King

8 And it came to pass, when Samuel
was old,[2204] that he [a]made his
[b]sons[1121] judges[8199] over Israel.
2 Now the name of his firstborn was
[1][a]Joel; and the name of his second, Abiah:
they were judges in Beer–sheba.

1 [b]2Sam. 6:4
3 [a]Deut. 30:2-10; 1Kgs. 8:48; Isa. 55:7; Hos. 6:1; Joel 2:12 [b]Gen. 35:2; Josh. 24:14, 23 [c]Judg. 2:13 [d]2Chr. 30:19; Job 11:13, 14 [e]Deut. 6:13; 10:20; 13:4; Matt. 4:10; Luke 4:8
4 [a]Judg. 2:11
5 [a]Judg. 20:1; 2Kgs. 25:23
6 [a]2Sam. 14:14 [b]Neh. 9:1, 2; Dan. 9:3-5; Joel 2:12 [c]Judg. 10:10; 1Kgs. 8:47; Ps. 106:6
8 [1]Hebr. *Be not silent from us from crying* [a]Isa. 37:4
9 [1]Or, *answered* [a]Ps. 99:6; Jer. 15:1
10 [a]Josh. 10:10; Judg. 4:15; 5:20; 1Sam. 2:10; 2Sam. 22:14, 15
12 [1]That is, *The stone of help* [a]Gen. 28:18; 31:45; 35:14; Josh. 4:9; 24:26
13 [a]Judg. 13:1 [b]Judg. 13:5
15 [a]Judg. 2:16; 1Sam. 7:6; 12:1
16 [1]Hebr. *and he circuited*
17 [a]1Sam. 8:4 [b]Judg. 21:4
1 [a]Deut. 16:18; 2Chr. 19:5 [b]Judg. 10:4; 12:14
2 [1]*Vashni* [a]1Chr. 6:28

🔑 **7:4** Concerning the Baalim and Ashtaroth, see note on Judges 2:13.

3 And his sons [a]walked not in his
ways,[1870] but turned aside [b]after
lucre,1215 and [c]took bribes,7810 and perverted judgment.[4941]
4 Then all the elders[2205] of Israel
gathered themselves together,[6908] and
came to Samuel unto Ramah,
5 And said unto him, Behold, thou
art old, and thy sons walk not in thy
ways: now [a]make us a king[4428] to
judge[8199] us like all the nations.[1471]
6 But the thing [I]displeased Samuel,
when they said, Give us a king to judge
us. And Samuel prayed[6419] unto the LORD.
7 And the LORD said unto Samuel,
Hearken unto the voice of the people[5971]
in all that they say unto thee: for [a]they
have not rejected[3988] thee, but [b]they have
rejected me, that I should not reign over
them.
8 According to all the works which
they have done[6213] since the day[3117] that
I brought them up[5927] out of Egypt even
unto this day, wherewith they have
forsaken[5800] me, and served other
gods,[430] so do[6213] they also unto thee.
9 Now therefore [I]hearken unto their
voice: [II]howbeit yet protest[5749] solemnly
unto them, and [a]shew[5046] them the
manner[4941] of the king that shall reign
over them.
10 And Samuel told all the words[1697]
of the LORD unto the people that
asked[7592] of him a king.
11 And he said, [a]This will be the
manner of the king that shall reign over
you: [b]He will take your sons, and
appoint[7760] *them* for himself, for his chariots, and *to be* his horsemen; and *some*
shall run before his chariots.
12 And he will appoint him captains[8269] over thousands, and captains
over fifties; and *will set them* to ear2790
his ground,[2758] and to reap his harvest,
and to make his instruments of war, and
instruments of his chariots.
13 And he will take your daughters
to be confectionaries,7543 and *to be* cooks,
and *to be* bakers.
14 And [a]he will take your fields,[7704]
and your vineyards, and your oliveyards,
even the best[2896] *of them,* and give *them*
to his servants.
15 And he will take the tenth of your
seed,[2233] and of your vineyards, and give
to his [Ia]officers,[5631] and to his servants.
16 And he will take your menser-
vants, and your maidservants, and your

3 [a]Jer. 22:15-17 [b]Ex. 18:21; 1Tim. 3:3; 6:10 [c]Deut. 16:19; Ps. 15:5
5 [a]Deut. 17:14; 1Sam. 8:19, 20; Hos. 13:10; Acts 13:21
6 [I]Hebr. *was evil in the eyes of Samuel*
7 [a]Ex. 16:8 [b]1Sam. 10:19; 12:17, 19; Hos. 13:10, 11
9 [I]Or, *obey* [II]Or, *notwithstanding when thou hast solemnly protested against them, then thou shalt show* [a]1Sam. 8:11
11 [a]Deut. 17:16; 1Sam. 10:25 [b]1Sam. 14:52
14 [a]1Kgs. 21:7; Ezek. 46:18
15 [I]Hebr. *eunuchs* [a]Gen. 37:36

8:3 Like Eli, Samuel neglected to discipline and teach his sons properly. Perhaps, like servants of God today, he was away from home too much and too occupied with helping others. Just as the personal failures of individual ministers lead many to reject the whole concept of the Church, the failure of Samuel's sons led the people to reject their authority as judges, as well as to reject God, who in His sovereignty set them up to rule over His people.

8:5–7 In this passage, the Israelites' request for a king is condemned by God. What is it that made this request a sin? It seems clear that there was nothing wrong with the desire for a monarchy. God knew that someday Israel would desire a king. In Deuteronomy 17:14–20, He had given guidelines that were to be followed by the people and by the kings that would reign over them (cf. Gen. 17:6, 16; 35:11). It seems equally clear that there was nothing wrong with the time of their request. Though some have suggested that the kingdom was not proper until the coming of the Messiah, there is nothing in the context of the passages in question that supports this view. Hence, it seems that the motive of the people in making the request was what made their actions sinful; though on the surface their motives seem to be justified. They wanted to avoid further military losses (1 Sam. 8:20) and to be rid of the corrupt leaders of the future, the sons of Samuel and of Eli.

Samuel saw their request to be a rejection of himself, but God affirmed that they had actually rejected Him. The people were no longer satisfied with the system of judges that had been established. They improperly attributed the failures during that time to the system itself, not to their sin. They rejected God because they wanted to be like the other nations, not a peculiar people, set apart as the chosen ones of God. What the people wanted was a visible deliverer, a man in whom they could place their trust (cf. Judg. 8:22, 23). They wanted to walk by sight, not by faith. In so doing, they thought to escape the moral demands of the Law by doing away with the theocracy under which they had been living.

goodliest[2896] young men, and your asses,
and put *them* to his work.[4399]
17 He will take the tenth of your
sheep: and ye shall be his servants.
18 And ye shall cry out[2199] in that
day because of your king which ye shall
have chosen[977] you; and the LORD [a]will
not hear you in that day.
19 Nevertheless the people [a]refused
to obey the voice of Samuel; and they
said, Nay; but we will have a king over
us;
20 That we also may be [a]like all the
nations; and that our king may judge us,
and go out before us, and fight our battles.
21 And Samuel heard all the words
of the people, and he rehearsed them in
the ears[241] of the LORD.
22 And the LORD said to Samuel,
[a]Hearken unto their voice, and make them
a king. And Samuel said unto the
men of Israel, Go ye every man unto his
city.

Samuel Anoints Saul King

9 Now there was a man of Benjamin,
whose name *was* [a]Kish, the son[1121]
of Abiel, the son of Zeror, the son of
Bechorath, the son of Aphiah, [I]a
Benjamite, a mighty man of [II]power.[2428]
2 And he had a son, whose name
was Saul, a choice young man, and a
goodly:[2896] and *there was* not among the
children[1121] of Israel a goodlier person[376]
than he: [a]from his shoulders and upward
he was higher than any of the people.[5971]
3 And the asses of Kish Saul's father
were lost.[6] And Kish said to Saul his son,
Take now one of the servants with thee,
and arise, go seek the asses.
4 And he passed through[5674] mount
Ephraim, and passed through the land[776]
of [a]Shalisha, but they found *them*
not: then they passed through the land
of Shalim, and *there they were* not:
and he passed through the land of
the Benjamites, but they found *them*
not.
5 *And* when they were come to the
land of Zuph, Saul said to his servant
that *was* with him, Come, and let us
return; lest my father leave[2308] *caring*
for the asses, and take thought[1672] for
us.
6 And he said unto him, Behold now,
there is in this city [a]a man of God,[430] and
he is an honourable man; [b]all that he
saith[1696] cometh surely to pass: now let
us go thither; peradventure[194] he can
shew[5046] us our way[1870] that we should
go.
7 Then said Saul to his servant, But,
behold, *if* we go, [a]what shall we bring
the man? for the bread [I]is spent[235] in
our vessels, and *there is* not a present
to bring to the man of God: what [II]have
we?
8 And the servant answered Saul
again, and said, Behold, [I]I have here at
hand the fourth part of a shekel of silver: *that* will I give to the man of God,
to tell us our way.
9 (Beforetime in Israel, when a man
[a]went to enquire of God, thus he spake,[559]
Come, and let us go to the seer:[7200] for
he that is now *called* a Prophet[5030] was
beforetime called[7121] [b]a Seer.)
10 Then said Saul to his servant,
[I]Well said; come, let us go. So they went
unto the city where the man of God
was.
11 *And* as they went up [I]the hill[4608]
to the city, [a]they found young maidens
going out to draw water, and said unto
them, Is the seer here?
12 And they answered them, and
said, He is; behold, *he is* before you: make
haste now, for he came to day to the city;
for [a]*there is* a [I]sacrifice[2077] of the people
to day [b]in the high place:
13 As soon as ye be come into the
city, ye shall straightway[3651] find him,
before he go up to the high place to eat:
for the people will not eat until he come,
because he doth bless[1288] the sacrifice;
and afterwards they eat that be bidden.[7121] Now therefore get you up; for
about [I]this time ye shall find him.
14 And they went up into the city:
and when they were come into the city,
behold, Samuel came out against them,
for to go up to the high place.

18 [a]Prov. 1:25-28; Isa. 1:15; Mic. 3:4
19 [a]Jer. 44:16
20 [a]1Sam. 8:5
22 [a]1Sam. 8:7; Hos. 13:11
1 [I]Or, *the son of a man of Jemini* [II]Or, *substance* [a]1Sam. 14:51; 1Chr. 8:33; 9:39
2 [a]1Sam. 10:23
4 [a]2Kgs. 4:42
6 [a]Deut. 33:1; 1Kgs. 13:1 [b]1Sam. 3:19
7 [I]Hebr. *is gone out of* [II]Hebr. *is with us* [a]Judg. 6:18; 13:17; 1Kgs. 14:3; 2Kgs. 4:42; 8:8
8 [I]Hebr. *there is found in my hand*
9 [a]Gen. 25:22 [b]2Sam. 24:11; 2Kgs. 17:13; 1Chr. 26:28; 29:29; 2Chr. 16:7, 10; Isa. 30:10; Amos 7:12
10 [I]Hebr. *Thy word is good*
11 [I]Hebr. *in the ascent of the city* [a]Gen. 24:11
12 [I]Or, *feast* [a]Gen. 31:54; 1Sam. 16:2 [b]1Kgs. 3:2
13 [I]Hebr. *today*

15 [a]Now the LORD had [I][b]told Samuel in his ear[241] a day[3117] before Saul came, saying,

16 To morrow about this time I will send thee a man out of the land of Benjamin, [a]and thou shalt anoint[4886] him *to be* captain[5057] over my people Israel, that he may save[3467] my people out of the hand of the Philistines: for I have [b]looked upon[7200] my people, because their cry is come unto me.

17 And when Samuel saw[7200] Saul, the LORD said unto him, [a]Behold the man whom I spake to thee of! this same shall [I]reign over my people.

18 Then Saul drew near[5066] to Samuel in the gate, and said, Tell me, I pray thee,[4994] where the seer's house *is.*

19 And Samuel answered Saul, and said, I *am* the seer: go up before me unto the high place; for ye shall eat with me to day, and to morrow I will let thee go, and will tell thee all that *is* in thine heart.

20 And as for [a]thine asses that were lost [I]three days ago, set[7760] not thy mind on them; for they are found. And on whom [b]*is* all the desire of Israel? *Is it* not on thee, and on all thy father's[1] house?

21 And Saul answered and said, [a]*Am* not I a Benjamite, of the [b]smallest of the tribes of Israel? and [c]my family[4940] the least of all the families of the tribe of Benjamin? wherefore then speakest[1696] thou [I]so to me?

22 And Samuel took Saul and his servant, and brought them into the parlour, and made them sit in the chiefest place among them that were bidden, which *were* about thirty persons.[376]

23 And Samuel said unto the cook,[2876] Bring the portion which I gave thee, of which I said unto thee, Set it by thee.

24 And the cook took up [a]the shoulder, and *that* which *was* upon it, and set *it* before Saul. And Samuel said, Behold that which is [I]left![7604] set *it* before thee, *and* eat: for unto this time hath it been kept[8104] for thee since I said, I have invited[7121] the people. So Saul did eat with Samuel that day.

25 And when they were come down from the high place into the city, *Samuel* communed with Saul upon [a]the top of the house.

26 And they arose early: and it came to pass about the spring[5927] of the day,[7837] that Samuel called Saul to the top of the house, saying, Up, that I may send thee away. And Saul arose, and they went out both of them, he and Samuel, abroad.

27 *And* as they were going down to the end of the city, Samuel said to Saul, Bid[559] the servant pass on[5674] before us, (and he passed on,) but stand thou still [I]a while, that I may shew thee the word[1697] of God.

10

Then [a]Samuel took a vial of oil,[8081] and poured *it* upon his head, [b]and kissed[5401] him, and said, *Is it* not because [c]the LORD hath anointed[4886] thee *to be* captain[5057] over [d]his inheritance?[5159]

2 When thou art departed from me to day, then thou shalt find two men by [a]Rachel's sepulchre[6900] in the border of Benjamin [b]at Zelzah; and they will say unto thee, The asses which thou wentest to seek are found: and, lo, thy father[1] hath left[5203] [I]the care[1697] of the asses, and sorroweth[1672] for you, saying, What shall I do for my son?[1121]

3 Then shalt thou go on forward from thence, and thou shalt come to the plain of Tabor, and there shall meet thee three men going up [a]to God[430] to Bethel, one carrying three kids, and another carrying three loaves of bread, and another carrying a bottle of wine:

4 And they will [I][a]salute thee, and give thee two *loaves* of bread; which thou shalt receive of their hands.

15 [I]Hebr. *revealed the ear of Samuel* [a]1Sam. 15:1; Acts 13:21 [b]1Sam. 20:2

16 [a]1Sam. 10:1 [b]Ex. 2:25; 3:7, 9

17 [I]Hebr. *restrain in* [a]1Sam. 16:12; Hos. 13:11

20 [I]Hebr. *today three days* [a]1Sam. 9:3 [b]1Sam. 8:5, 19; 12:13

21 [I]Hebr. *according to this word* [a]1Sam. 15:17 [b]Judg. 20:46-48; Ps. 68:27 [c]Judg. 6:15

24 [I]Or, *reserved* [a]Lev. 7:32, 33; Ezek. 24:4

25 [a]Deut. 22:8; 2Sam. 11:2; Acts 10:9

27 [I]Hebr. *today*

1 [a]1Sam. 9:16; 16:13; 2Kgs. 9:3, 6 [b]Ps. 2:12 [c]Acts 13:21 [d]Deut. 32:9; Ps. 78:71

2 [I]Hebr. *the business* [a]Gen. 35:19, 20 [b]Josh. 18:28

3 [a]Gen. 28:22; 35:1, 3, 7

4 [I]Hebr. *ask thee of peace* [a]Judg. 18:15

9:21 At one point the tribe of Benjamin had been reduced to only six hundred men (Judg. 20:47).

5 After that thou shalt come to
[a]the hill of God, [b]where *is* the garrison[5333] of the Philistines: and it shall
come to pass, when thou art come
thither to the city, that thou shalt meet a
company[2256] of prophets[5030] coming
down [c]from the high place with a
psaltery, and a tabret,[8596] and a pipe, and
a harp, before them; [d]and they shall
prophesy:[5012]
6 And [a]the Spirit[7307] of the LORD will
come upon thee, and [b]thou shalt prophesy with them, and shalt be turned[2015]
into another man.
7 And [I]let it be, when these [a]signs[226]
are come unto thee, [II][b]*that* thou do as occasion serve[5647] thee; for [c]God *is* with
thee.
8 And thou shalt go down before me
[a]to Gilgal; and, behold, I will come down
unto thee, to offer burnt offerings, *and* to
sacrifice[2076] sacrifices of peace offerings:
[b]seven days shalt thou tarry, till I come
to thee, and shew[3045] thee what thou
shalt do.

Saul Prophesies

9 And it was *so,* that when he had
turned his [I]back to go from Samuel, God
[II]gave him another heart: and all those
signs came to pass that day.[3117]
🗝 10 And [a]when they came thither to
the hill, behold, [b]a company of prophets
met him; and [c]the Spirit of God came
upon him, and he prophesied[5012] among
them.
11 And it came to pass, when all that
knew[3045] him beforetime saw[7200] that, behold, he prophesied among the prophets,
then the people[5971] said [I]one[376] to
another,[7453] What *is* this *that* is come
unto the son of Kish? [a]*Is* Saul also
among the prophets?
12 And one [I]of the same place answered and said, But [a]who *is* their father? Therefore it became a proverb, *Is*
Saul also among the prophets?
13 And when he had made an
end[3615] of prophesying, he came to the
high place.
14 And Saul's uncle said unto him
and to his servant, Whither went ye? And
he said, To seek the asses: and when we
saw that *they were* no where, we came to
Samuel.
15 And Saul's uncle said, Tell me, I
pray thee, what Samuel said unto you.
16 And Saul said unto his uncle, He
told[5046] us plainly that the asses were
found. But of the matter of the kingdom,
whereof Samuel spake,[559] he told him
not.

Saul Becomes King

17 And Samuel called the people together [a]unto the LORD [b]to Mizpeh;
18 And said unto the children[1121]
of Israel, [a]Thus saith the LORD God of
Israel, I brought up[5927] Israel out of
Egypt, and delivered[5337] you out of the
hand of the Egyptians, and out of the
hand of all kingdoms,[4467] *and* of them
that oppressed[3905] you:
19 [a]And ye have this day rejected
your God, who himself saved[3467] you out
of all your adversities[7451] and your
tribulations;[6869] and ye have said unto
him, *Nay,* but set[7760] a king[4428] over us.
Now therefore present yourselves before
the LORD by your tribes, and by your
thousands.
🗝 20 And when Samuel had [a]caused all

5 [a]1Sam. 10:10 [b]1Sam. 13:3 [c]1Sam. 9:12 [d]Ex. 15:20, 21; 2Kgs. 3:15
6 [a]Num. 11:25; 1Sam. 16:13 [b]1Sam. 10:10; 19:23, 24
7 [I]Hebr. *it shall come to pass, that when these signs* [II]Hebr. *do for thee as thine hand shall find* [a]Judg. 9:33 [b]Ex. 4:8; Luke 2:12 [c]Judg. 6:12
8 [a]1Sam. 11:14, 15; 13:4 [b]1Sam. 13:8
9 [I]Hebr. *shoulder* [II]Hebr. *turned*
10 [a]1Sam. 10:5 [b]1Sam. 19:20 [c]1Sam. 10:6
11 [I]Hebr. *a man to his neighbor* [a]1Sam. 19:24; Matt. 13:54, 55; John 7:15; Acts 4:13
12 [I]Hebr. *from thence* [a]Isa. 54:13; John 6:45; 7:16
17 [a]Judg. 11:11; 20:1; 1Sam. 11:15 [b]1Sam. 7:5, 6
18 [a]Judg. 6:8, 9
19 [a]1Sam. 8:7, 19; 12:12
20 [a]Josh. 7:14, 16, 17; Acts 1:24, 26

🗝 **10:10** See note on 2 Kings 2:3, 5 on the "sons of the prophets."

🗝 **10:20–24** That Saul was "taken" (*lakad* [3920]) means that lots were drawn, probably out of an urn. The selection was carried out by process of elimination, beginning with the selection of the tribe of Benjamin and ending with the selection of an individual of the clan of Matri and the family of Kish. The lot fell upon Saul. The Jews understood the drawing or casting of lots to be a means of discovering God's will. As to the necessity of the procedures carried on at Mizpeh, it may be observed that neither Saul nor Samuel had informed the people of Saul's prior anointing (v. 16),

(continued on next page)

the tribes of Israel to come near, the tribe of Benjamin was taken.

21 When he had caused the tribe of Benjamin to come near by their families,[4940] the family of Matri was taken, and Saul the son of Kish was taken: and when they sought him, he could not be found.

22 Therefore they [a]enquired[7592] of the LORD further, if the man should yet come thither. And the LORD answered,[559] Behold, he hath hid himself among the stuff.

23 And they ran and fetched him thence: and when he stood among the people, [a]he was higher than any of the people from his shoulders and upward.

24 And Samuel said to all the people, See ye him [a]whom the LORD hath chosen,[977] that *there is* none like him among all the people? And all the people shouted,[7321] and said, [I][b]God save[2421] the king.

25 Then Samuel told the people [a]the manner of the kingdom, and wrote *it* in a book,[5612] and laid *it* up before the LORD. And Samuel sent all the people away, every man to his house.

26 And Saul also went home [a]to Gibeah; and there went with him a band of men, whose hearts God had touched.[5060]

27 [a]But the [b]children of Belial[1100] said, How shall this man save us? And they despised him, [c]and brought him no presents.[4503] But [I]he held his peace.

22 [a]1Sam. 23:2, 4, 10, 11

23 [a]1Sam. 9:2

24 [I]Hebr. *Let the king live* [a]2Sam. 21:6 [b]1Kgs. 1:25, 39; 2Kgs. 11:12

25 [a]Deut. 17:14; 1Sam. 8:11

26 [a]Judg. 20:14; 1Sam. 11:4

27 [I]Or, *he was as though he had been deaf* [a]1Sam. 11:12 [b]Deut. 13:13 [c]2Sam. 8:2; 1Kgs. 4:21; 10:25; 2Chr. 17:5; Ps. 72:10; Matt. 2:11

1 [a]1Sam. 12:12 [b]Judg. 21:8 [c]Gen. 26:28; Ex. 23:32; 1Kgs. 20:34; Job 41:4; Ezek. 17:13

2 [a]Gen. 34:14; 1Sam. 17:26

3 [I]Hebr. *Forbear us*

4 [a]1Sam. 10:26; 15:34; 2Sam. 21:6 [b]Judg. 2:4; 21:2

6 [a]Judg. 3:10; 6:34; 11:29; 13:25; 14:6; 1Sam. 10:10; 16:13

7 [a]Judg. 19:29 [b]Judg. 21:5, 8, 10

Saul Rescues Jabesh-gilead

11 Then [a]Nahash the Ammonite came up, and encamped against [b]Jabesh–gilead: and all the men of Jabesh said unto Nahash, [c]Make a covenant[1285] with us, and we will serve[5647] thee.

2 And Nahash the Ammonite answered[559] them, On this *condition* will I make *a covenant* with you, that I may thrust out all your right eyes, and lay[7760] it *for* [a]a reproach upon all Israel.

3 And the elders[2205] of Jabesh said unto him, [I]Give us seven days'[3117] respite, that we may send messengers unto all the coasts of Israel: and then, if *there be* no man to save us, we will come out to thee.

4 Then came the messengers [a]to Gibeah of Saul, and told the tidings in the ears[241] of the people:[5971] and [b]all the people lifted up their voices, and wept.

5 And, behold, Saul came after the herd out of the field;[7704] and Saul said, What *aileth* the people that they weep? And they told him the tidings of the men of Jabesh.

6 [a]And the Spirit[7307] of God[430] came upon Saul when he heard those tidings, and his anger[639] was kindled[2734] greatly.

7 And he took a yoke of oxen, and [a]hewed them in pieces,[5408] and sent *them* throughout all the coasts of Israel by the hands of messengers, saying, [b]Whosoever cometh not forth after Saul and after Samuel, so shall it be done[6213] unto his oxen. And the fear of the LORD fell[5307] on

(continued from previous page)

making this action necessary to show the people that Saul was to be their king. It is likely that the days between the anointing and this ceremony at Mizpeh were intended for meditation and instruction (v. 8, cf. 1 Sam. 13:7, 8).

Only divine wisdom can fully understand the choice of Saul for king. Yet, it should be noted that Saul fully satisfied the desires of the people. He was a man of great stature from the most military tribe in all of Israel. Who better, they thought, to lead the people in battle against their enemies? Saul was also a man whose own spiritual life mirrored that of the majority of Israel: he was a house built upon the sand, whose lack of saving faith was made clear when the storms came. Any life or nation built upon such a foundation will surely fail.

Nevertheless, the purposes and design of God are never circumvented by the wickedness of men (Job 35:6). Soon after Saul's failure, David was chosen. Saul's reign revealed the motive of the people's demand for a king. Even if Saul had been obedient, his reign was destined to be temporary, for the tribe of Judah was the royal tribe, from which the King of Glory would come (Gen. 49:10).

the people, and they came out [I][c]with one consent.

8 And when he numbered them in [a]Bezek, the children[1121] [b]of Israel were three hundred thousand, and the men of Judah thirty thousand.

9 And they said unto the messengers that came, Thus shall ye say unto the men of Jabesh–gilead, To morrow, by *that time* the sun be hot, ye shall have [I]help. And the messengers came and shewed[5046] *it* to the men of Jabesh; and they were glad.

10 Therefore the men of Jabesh said, To morrow [a]we will come out unto you, and ye shall do[6213] with us all that seemeth good[2896] unto you.

11 And it was *so* on the morrow, that [a]Saul put the people [b]in three companies;[7128] and they came into the midst of the host in the morning watch, and slew[5221] the Ammonites until the heat of the day:[3117] and it came to pass, that they which remained were scattered, so that two of them were not left[7604] together.

12 And the people said unto Samuel, [a]Who *is* he that said, Shall Saul reign over us? [b]bring the men, that we may put them to death.[4191]

13 And Saul said, [a]There shall not a man be put to death this day: for to day [b]the LORD hath wrought salvation in Israel.

14 Then said Samuel to the people, Come, and let us go [a]to Gilgal, and renew the kingdom there.

15 And all the people went to Gilgal; and there they made Saul king[4427] [a]before the LORD in Gilgal; and [b]there they sacrificed[2076] sacrifices of peace offerings before the LORD; and there Saul and all the men of Israel rejoiced greatly.

Samuel Addresses Israel

12 And Samuel said unto all Israel, Behold, I have hearkened unto [a]your voice in all that ye said unto me, and [b]have made a king[4428] over you.

2 And now, behold, the king [a]walketh before you: [b]and I am old[2204] and gray-headed; and, behold, my sons[1121] *are* with you: and I have walked before you from my childhood unto this day.[3117]

3 Behold, here I *am:* witness against me before the LORD, and before [a]his anointed:[4899] [b]whose ox have I taken? or whose ass have I taken? or whom have I defrauded? whom have I oppressed? or of whose hand have I received *any* [I]bribe [II]to [c]blind mine eyes therewith? and I will restore it you.

4 And they said, Thou hast not defrauded us, nor oppressed us, neither hast thou taken ought of any man's hand.

5 And he said unto them, The LORD *is* witness against you, and his anointed *is* witness this day, [a]that ye have not found ought [b]in my hand. And they answered,[559] *He is* witness.

6 And Samuel said unto the people,[5971] [a]*It is* the LORD that [I]advanced Moses and Aaron, and that brought[5927] your fathers[1] up[5927] out of the land[776] of Egypt.

7 Now therefore stand still, that I may [a]reason[8199] with you before the LORD of all the [I][b]righteous acts of the LORD, which he did[6213] [II]to you and to your fathers.

8 [a]When Jacob was come into Egypt, and your fathers [b]cried[2199] unto the LORD, then the LORD [c]sent Moses and Aaron, which brought forth your fathers out of Egypt, and made them dwell in this place.

9 And when they [a]forgat the LORD their God,[430] [b]he sold them into the hand of Sisera, captain[8269] of the host of Hazor, and into the hand of [c]the Philistines, and into the hand of the king [d]of Moab, and they fought against them.

10 And they cried unto the LORD, and said, [a]We have sinned,[2398] because we have forsaken[5800] the LORD, [b]and have served Baalim and Ashtaroth: but now [c]deliver[5337] us out of the hand of our enemies, and we will serve thee.

11 And the LORD sent [a]Jerubbaal, and Bedan, and [b]Jephthah, and [c]Samuel, and delivered you out of the hand of your

---

7 IHebr. *as one man* cJudg. 20:1

8 aJudg. 1:5 b2Sam. 24:9

9 IOr, *deliverance*

10 a1Sam. 11:3

11 a1Sam. 13:17 bJudg. 7:16

12 a1Sam. 10:27 bLuke 19:27

13 a2Sam. 19:22 bEx. 14:13, 30; 1Sam. 19:5

14 a1Sam. 10:8

15 a1Sam. 10:17 b1Sam. 10:8

1 a1Sam. 8:5, 19, 20 b1Sam. 10:24; 11:14, 15

2 aNum. 27:17; 1Sam. 8:20 b1Sam. 8:1, 5

3 IHebr. *ransom* IIOr, *that I should hide mine eyes at him?* a1Sam. 10:1; 12:5; 24:6; 2Sam. 1:14, 16 bNum. 16:15; Acts 20:33; 1Thess. 2:5 cDeut. 16:19

5 aJohn 18:38; Acts 23:9; 24:16, 20 bEx. 22:4

6 IOr, *made* aMic. 6:4

7 IHebr. *righteousnesses, or, benefits* IIHebr. *with* aJudg. 5:11 bIsa. 1:18; 5:3, 4; Mic. 6:2, 3

8 aGen. 46:5, 6 bEx. 2:23 cEx. 3:10; 4:16

9 aJudg. 3:7 bJudg. 4:2 cJudg. 10:7; 13:1 dJudg. 3:12

10 aJudg. 10:10 bJudg. 2:13 cJudg. 10:15, 16

11 aJudg. 6:14, 32 bJudg. 11:1 c1Sam. 7:13

enemies on every side, and ye dwelled safe.[983]

12 And when ye saw[7200] that [a]Nahash the king of the children[1121] of Ammon came against you, [b]ye said unto me, Nay; but a king shall reign over us: when [c]the LORD your God *was* your king.

13 Now therefore [a]behold the king [b]whom ye have chosen,[977] *and* whom ye have desired[7592] and, behold, [c]the LORD hath set a king over you.

14 If ye will [a]fear[3372] the LORD, and serve him, and obey his voice, and not rebel against the [I]commandment[6310] of the LORD, then shall both ye and also the king that reigneth over you [II]continue following the LORD your God:

15 But if ye will [a]not obey the voice of the LORD, but rebel against the commandment of the LORD, then shall the hand of the LORD be against you, [b]as *it was* against your fathers.

16 Now therefore [a]stand and see this great thing, which the LORD will do[6213] before your eyes.

17 *Is it* not [a]wheat harvest to day? [b]I will call[7121] unto the LORD, and he shall send thunder and rain; that ye may perceive[3045] and see that [c]your wickedness[7451] *is* great, which ye have done in the sight of the LORD, in asking[7592] you a king.

18 So Samuel called unto the LORD; and the LORD sent thunder and rain that day: and [a]all the people greatly feared the LORD and Samuel.

19 And all the people said unto Samuel, [a]Pray[6419] for thy servants unto the LORD thy God, that we die[4191] not: for we have added unto all our sins *this* evil,[7451] to ask us a king.

20 And Samuel said unto the people, Fear not: ye have done all this wickedness: yet turn not aside from following the LORD, but serve the LORD with all your heart;

21 And [a]turn ye not aside: [b]for *then should ye go* after vain[8414] *things,* which cannot profit nor deliver; for they *are* vain.

22 For [a]the LORD will not forsake[5203] his people [b]for his great name's sake: because [c]it hath pleased[2974] the LORD to make you his people.

23 Moreover as for me, God forbid that I should sin[2398] against the LORD [I][a]in ceasing to pray for you: but [b]I will teach you the [c]good[2896] and the right way:[1870]

24 [a]Only fear the LORD, and serve him in truth with all your heart: for [b]consider[7200] [I]how [c]great *things* he hath done for you.

25 But if ye shall still do wickedly, [a]ye shall be consumed,[5595] [b]both ye and your king.

Saul's First Sin at Gilgal

13 Saul [I]reigned one year; and when he had reigned two years over Israel,

2 Saul chose[977] him three thousand *men* of Israel; *whereof* two thousand were with Saul in Michmash and in mount Bethel, and a thousand were with Jonathan in [a]Gibeah of Benjamin: and the rest of the people[5971] he sent every man to his tent.

3 And Jonathan smote[5221] [a]the garrison of the Philistines that *was* in [I]Geba, and the Philistines heard *of it.* And Saul blew[8628] the trumpet throughout all the land,[776] saying, Let the Hebrews hear.

4 And all Israel heard say *that* Saul had smitten a garrison of the Philistines, and *that* Israel also [I][a]was had in abomination[887] with the Philistines. And the people were called together after Saul to Gilgal.

5 And the Philistines gathered themselves together[622] to fight with Israel, thirty thousand chariots, and six thousand horsemen, and people as the sand which *is* on the sea shore in multitude: and they came up, and pitched in Michmash, eastward from Beth–aven.

6 When the men of Israel saw[7200] that they were in a strait,[6887] (for the people were distressed,) then the people [a]did hide themselves in caves, and in

---

12 [a]1Sam. 11:1 [b]1Sam. 8:5, 19 [c]Judg. 8:23; 1Sam. 8:7; 10:19
13 [a]1Sam. 10:24 [b]1Sam. 8:5; 9:20 [c]Hos. 13:11
14 [I]Hebr. *mouth* [II]Hebr. *be after* [a]Josh. 24:14; Ps. 81:13, 14
15 [a]Lev. 26:14, 15; Deut. 28:15; Josh. 24:20 [b]1Sam. 12:9
16 [a]Ex. 14:13, 31
17 [a]Prov. 26:1 [b]Josh. 10:12; 1Sam. 7:9, 10; James 5:16-18 [c]1Sam. 8:7
18 [a]Ex. 14:31; Ezra 10:9
19 [a]Ex. 9:28; 10:17; James 5:15; 1John 5:16
21 [a]Deut. 11:16 [b]Jer. 16:19; Hab. 2:18; 1Cor. 8:4
22 [a]1Kgs. 6:13; Ps. 94:14 [b]Josh. 7:9; Ps. 106:8; Jer. 14:21; Ezek. 20:9, 14 [c]Deut. 7:7, 8; 14:2; Mal. 1:2
23 [I]Hebr. *from ceasing* [a]Acts 12:5; Rom. 1:9; Col. 1:9; 2Tim. 1:3 [b]Ps. 34:11; Prov. 4:11 [c]1Kgs. 8:36; 2Chr. 6:27; Jer. 6:16
24 [I]Or, *what a great thing* [a]Eccl. 12:13 [b]Isa. 5:12 [c]Deut. 10:21; Ps. 126:2, 3
25 [a]Josh. 24:20 [b]Deut. 28:36

1 [I]Hebr. *the son of one year in his reigning*
2 [a]1Sam. 10:26
3 [I]Or, *The hill* [a]1Sam. 10:5
4 [I]Hebr. *did stink* [a]Gen. 34:30; Ex. 5:21
6 [a]Judg. 6:2

thickets, and in rocks, and in high places,
and in pits.[953]
7 And *some of* the Hebrews went
over Jordan to the land of Gad and
Gilead. As for Saul, he *was* yet in Gilgal,
and all the people [I]followed him trembling.[2729]
8 [a]And he tarried seven days,[3117] according to the set time[4150] that Samuel
had appointed: but Samuel came not to
Gilgal; and the people were scattered
from him.
9 And Saul said, Bring hither[5066] a
burnt offering to me, and peace offerings.[8002] And he offered[5927] the burnt offering.
10 And it came to pass, that as soon
as he had made an end[3615] of offering the
burnt offering,[5930] behold, Samuel came;
and Saul went out to meet him, that he
might [I]salute[1288] him.
11 And Samuel said, What hast thou
done?[6213] And Saul said, Because I saw
that the people were scattered from me,
and *that* thou camest not within the days
appointed,[4150] and *that* the Philistines
gathered themselves together at Michmash;
12 Therefore said I, The Philistines
will come down now upon me to Gilgal,
and I have not [I]made supplication[2470]
unto the LORD: I forced myself therefore,
and offered a burnt offering.
🗝 13 And Samuel said to Saul, [a]Thou
hast done foolishly: [b]thou hast not
kept[8104] the commandment[4687] of the
LORD thy God,[430] which he commanded[6680] thee: for now would the LORD
have established[3559] thy kingdom[4467]
upon Israel for ever.
14 [a]But now thy kingdom shall not
continue: [b]the LORD hath sought him a
man after his own heart, and the LORD
hath commanded him *to be* captain[5057]
over his people, because thou hast not
kept *that* which the LORD commanded
thee.
15 And Samuel arose, and gat him
up from Gilgal unto Gibeah of Benjamin.
And Saul numbered the people *that were*
[I]present with him, [a]about six hundred
men.
16 And Saul, and Jonathan his
son,[1121] and the people *that were* present
with them, abode in [I]Gibeah of Benjamin:
but the Philistines encamped in Michmash.
17 And the spoilers[7843] came out of
the camp[4264] of the Philistines in three
companies: one company[7218] turned unto
the way[1870] *that leadeth to* [a]Ophrah, unto
the land of Shual:
18 And another company turned the
way *to* [a]Beth–horon: and another company turned *to* the way of the border
that looketh to the valley of [b]Zeboim toward the wilderness.

Israel's Lack of Weapons

19 Now [a]there was no smith[2796]
found throughout all the land of Israel: for the Philistines said, Lest the
Hebrews make *them* swords[2719] or
spears:
20 But all the Israelites went down to
the Philistines, to sharpen every man his
share, and his coulter,[855] and his axe, and
his mattock.[4281]
21 Yet they had [I]a file for the mattocks, and for the coulters, and for the
forks, and for the axes, and to
[II]sharpen[5324] the goads.[1861]
22 So it came to pass in the day[3117]
of battle, that [a]there was neither
sword[2719] nor spear found in the hand of
any of the people that *were* with Saul

7 [I]Hebr. *trembled after him*
8 [a]1Sam. 10:8
10 [I]Hebr. *bless him*
12 [I]Hebr. *entreated the face*
13 [a]2Chr. 16:9 [b]1Sam. 15:11
14 [a]1Sam. 15:28 [b]Ps. 89:20; Acts 13:22
15 [I]Hebr. *found* [a]1Sam. 14:2
16 [I]Hebr. *Geba*
17 [a]Josh. 18:23
18 [a]Josh. 16:3; 18:13, 14 [b]Neh. 11:34
19 [a]2Kgs. 24:14; Jer. 24:1
21 [I]Hebr. *a file with mouths* [II]Hebr. *to set*
22 [a]Judg. 5:8

🗝 **13:13, 14** Saul showed himself to be a man who had no regard for God's will. Though Samuel affirmed that the kingdom would pass from him to another, Saul did not repent. He continued to disobey according to his own whims, especially in regard to the battle with the Amalekites. Later, when Samuel discovered that Saul had kept the sheep alive from the Amalekite victory (saying he would sacrifice them before the Lord) he stated, "to obey is better than sacrifice" (1 Sam. 15:22). Note that Samuel continued to pray for Saul even after God had rejected Saul from being king (1 Sam. 15:11).

and Jonathan: but with Saul and with Jonathan his son was there found.

23 [a]And the [I]garrison[4673] of the Philistines went out to the passage of Michmash.

Jonathan's Daring Attack

14 Now [I]it came to pass upon a day,[3117] that Jonathan the son of Saul said unto the young man that bare[5375] his armour, Come, and let us go over to the Philistines' garrison, that *is* on the other side. But he told not his father.

2 And Saul tarried in the uttermost part of Gibeah under a pomegranate tree which *is* in Migron: and the people[5971] that *were* with him *were* [a]about six hundred men;

3 And [a]Ahiah, the son of Ahitub, [b]I–chabod's brother, the son of Phinehas, the son of Eli, the LORD's priest[3548] in Shiloh, [c]wearing an ephod. And the people knew[3045] not that Jonathan was gone.

4 And between the passages, by which Jonathan sought to go over [a]unto the Philistines' garrison, *there was* a sharp[8127] rock on the one side, and a sharp rock on the other side: and the name of the one *was* Bozez, and the name of the other Seneh.

5 The [I]forefront of the one *was* situate northward over against Michmash, and the other southward over against Gibeah.

6 And Jonathan said to the young man that bare his armour, Come, and let us go over unto the garrison of these uncircumcised:[6189] it may be that the LORD will work[6213] for us: for *there is* no restraint to the LORD [a]to save by many or by few.

7 And his armourbearer said unto him, Do[6213] all that *is* in thine heart: turn thee; behold, I *am* with thee according to thy heart.

8 Then said Jonathan, Behold, we will pass over[5674] unto *these* men, and we will discover[1540] ourselves unto them.

9 If they say thus unto us, [I]Tarry until we come[5060] to you; then we will stand still in our place, and will not go up unto them.

10 But if they say thus, Come up unto us; then we will go up: for the LORD hath delivered them into our hand: and [a]this *shall be* a sign[226] unto us.

11 And both of them discovered themselves unto the garrison of the Philistines: and the Philistines said, Behold, the Hebrews come forth out of the holes where they had hid themselves.

12 And the men of the garrison answered Jonathan and his armourbearer, and said, Come up to us, and we will shew[3045] you a thing. And Jonathan said unto his armourbearer, Come up after me: for the LORD hath delivered them into the hand of Israel.

13 And Jonathan climbed up upon his hands and upon his feet, and his armourbearer after him: and they fell[5307] before Jonathan; and his armourbearer slew[4191] after him.

14 And that first slaughter,[4347] which Jonathan and his armourbearer made, was about twenty men, within as it were [I]an half acre of land, *which* a yoke[6776] *of oxen might plow.*

15 And [a]there was trembling in the host, in the field,[7704] and among all the people: the garrison, and [b]the spoilers,[7843] they also trembled, and the earth[776] quaked: so it was [Ic]a very great trembling.

Israel Defeats the Philistines

16 And the watchmen of Saul in Gibeah of Benjamin looked;[7200] and, behold, the multitude melted away, and they [a]went on beating down[1986] *one another.*

17 Then said Saul unto the people that *were* with him, Number[6485] now, and see who is gone from us. And when they had numbered, behold, Jonathan and his armourbearer *were* not *there.*

23 [I]Or, *standing camp* [a]1Sam. 14:1, 4

1 [I]Or, *there was a day*

2 [a]1Sam. 13:15

3 [a]1Sam. 22:9, 11, 20 [b]1Sam. 4:21 [c]1Sam. 2:28

4 [a]1Sam. 13:23

5 [I]Hebr. *tooth*

6 [a]Judg. 7:4, 7; 2Chr. 14:11

9 [I]Hebr. *Be still*

10 [a]Gen. 24:14; Judg. 7:11

14 [I]Or, *half a furrow of an acre of land*

15 [I]Hebr. *a trembling of God* [a]2Kgs. 7:7; Job 18:11 [b]1Sam. 13:17 [c]Gen. 35:5

16 [a]1Sam. 14:20

🔑 18 And Saul said unto Ahiah, Bring hither the ark[727] of God.[430] For the ark of God was at that time with the children[1121] of Israel.

19 And it came to pass, while Saul [a]talked unto the priest, that the [I]noise that *was* in the host of the Philistines went on and increased: and Saul said unto the priest, Withdraw[622] thine hand.

20 And Saul and all the people that *were* with him [I]assembled[2199] themselves, and they came to the battle: and, behold, [a]every man's sword[2719] was against his fellow,[7453] *and there was* a very great discomfiture.[4103]

21 Moreover the Hebrews *that* were with the Philistines before that time, which went up with them into the camp[4264] *from the country* round about, even they also *turned* to be with the Israelites that *were* with Saul and Jonathan.

22 Likewise all the men of Israel which [a]had hid themselves in mount Ephraim, *when* they heard that the Philistines fled, even they also followed hard after them in the battle.

23 [a]So the LORD saved[3467] Israel that day: and the battle passed over[5674] [b]unto Beth–aven.

Jonathan and Saul's Oath

24 And the men of Israel were distressed that day: for Saul had [a]adjured[422] the people, saying, Cursed[779] *be* the man that eateth *any* food until evening, that I may be avenged on mine enemies. So none of the people tasted *any* food.

25 [a]And all *they of* the land[776] came to a wood; and there was [b]honey upon the ground.[7704]

26 And when the people were come into the wood, behold, the honey dropped;[1982] but no man put his hand to his mouth: for the people feared[3372] the oath.[7621]

27 But Jonathan heard not when his father charged[7650] the people with the oath: wherefore he put forth the end of the rod that *was* in his hand, and dipped[2881] it in an honeycomb, and put his hand to his mouth; and his eyes were enlightened.[215]

28 Then answered one of the people, and said, Thy father straitly charged the people with an oath, saying, Cursed *be* the man that eateth *any* food this day. And the people were [I]faint.

29 Then said Jonathan, My father hath troubled the land: see, I pray you,[4994] how mine eyes have been enlightened, because I tasted a little of this honey.

30 How much more, if haply the people had eaten freely to day of the spoil of their enemies which they found? for had there not been now a much greater slaughter[4347] among the Philistines?

31 And they smote[5221] the Philistines that day from Michmash to Aijalon: and the people were very faint.

32 And the people flew[6213] upon the spoil, and took sheep, and oxen, and calves, and slew[7819] *them* on the ground:[776] and the people did eat *them* [a]with the blood.[1818]

33 Then they told Saul, saying, Behold, the people sin[2398] against the

19 [I]Or, *tumult* [a]Num. 27:21
20 [I]Hebr. *were cried together* [a]Judg. 7:22; 2Chr. 20:23
22 [a]1Sam. 13:6
23 [a]Ex. 14:30; Ps. 44:6, 7; Hos. 1:7 [b]1Sam. 13:5
24 [a]Josh. 6:26
25 [a]Deut. 9:28; Matt. 3:5 [b]Ex. 3:8; Num. 13:27; Matt. 3:4
28 [I]Or, *weary*
32 [a]Lev. 3:17; 7:26; 17:10; 19:26; Deut. 12:16, 23, 24
33 [I]Or, *dealt treacherously*

🔑 **14:18, 19** This passage states that Saul desired to know God's will by seeking the "ark of God." However, there is some controversy as to whether Saul was calling for the ark of the covenant to be brought from Kirjath-jearim (see 1 Chr. 13:5, 6), or simply asking the priest wearing the ephod to step forward. Some manuscripts have the word for "ark." There are certainly cases in Scripture where the ark of the covenant was taken along with the children of Israel when they went to battle (1 Sam. 4:3). Other Hebrew manuscripts have the word for "ephod." The Septuagint (the Greek translation of the Old Testament) also used the word "ephod." The ephod was already in Saul's camp at Gibeah (1 Sam. 14:3). It contained the Urim and Thummim and was used to receive guidance from God (1 Sam. 23:9; 30:7). Some speculate that the phrase "withdraw thy hand" is more appropriate in regard to the ephod (see 2 Sam. 6:6, 7). Still other Hebrew texts imply that Saul may have sought guidance through both methods.

LORD, in that they eat with the blood. And he said, Ye have [I]transgressed:[898] roll a great stone unto me this day.

34 And Saul said, Disperse yourselves among the people, and say unto them, Bring me hither every man his ox, and every man his sheep, and slay[7819] *them* here, and eat; and sin not against the LORD in eating with the blood. And all the people brought[5066] every man his ox [I]with him that night,[3915] and slew *them* there.

35 And Saul [a]built an altar[4196] unto the LORD: [I]the same was the first altar that he built unto the LORD.

🗝 36 And Saul said, Let us go down after the Philistines by night, and spoil them until the morning light,[216] and let us not leave[7604] a man of them. And they said, Do whatsoever seemeth good[2896] unto thee. Then said the priest, Let us draw near hither unto God.

37 And Saul asked[7592] counsel of God, Shall I go down after the Philistines? wilt thou deliver them into the hand of Israel? But [a]he answered him not that day.

38 And Saul said, [a]Draw ye near[5066] hither, all the chief of the people: and know[3045] and see wherein this sin[2403] hath been this day.

39 For, [a]*as* the LORD liveth,[2416] which saveth[3467] Israel, though it be in Jonathan my son, he shall surely die.[4191] But *there was* not a man among all the people *that* answered him.

40 Then said he unto all Israel, Be ye on one side, and I and Jonathan my son will be on the other side. And the people said unto Saul, Do what seemeth good unto thee.

41 Therefore Saul said unto the LORD God of Israel, [Ia]Give a perfect[8549] *lot.* [b]And Saul and Jonathan were taken: but the people [II]escaped.

42 And Saul said, Cast[5307] *lots* between me and Jonathan my son. And Jonathan was taken.

43 Then Saul said to Jonathan, [a]Tell me what thou hast done.[6213] And Jonathan told him, and said, [b]I did but taste a little honey with the end of the rod that *was* in mine hand, *and,* lo, I must die.

44 And Saul answered,[559] [a]God do so and more also: [b]for thou shalt surely die, Jonathan.

45 And the people said unto Saul, Shall Jonathan die, who hath wrought this great salvation[3444] in Israel? God forbid: [a]*as* the LORD liveth, there shall not one hair of his head fall to the ground; for he hath wrought with God this day. So the people rescued Jonathan, that he died[4191] not.

46 Then Saul went up from following the Philistines: and the Philistines went to their own place.

Summary of Saul's Military Leadership

47 So Saul took the kingdom over Israel, and fought against all his enemies on every side, against Moab, and against the children of [a]Ammon, and against Edom, and against the kings[4428] of [b]Zobah, and against the Philistines: and whithersoever he turned himself, he vexed[7561] *them.*

48 And he [I]gathered an host, and [a]smote the Amalekites, and delivered[5337] Israel out of the hands of them that spoiled[8154] them.

49 Now [a]the sons[1121] of Saul were Jonathan, and Ishui, and Melchishua: and the names of his two daughters *were these*; the name of the firstborn Merab, and the name of the younger Michal:

50 And the name of Saul's wife[802] *was* Ahinoam, the daughter of Ahimaaz: and the name of the captain[8269] of his host *was* [I]Abner, the son of Ner, Saul's uncle.

51 [a]And Kish *was* the father of Saul; and Ner the father of Abner *was* the son of Abiel.

52 And there was sore[2389] war

34 [I]Hebr. *in his hand*
35 [I]Hebr. *that altar he began to build unto the LORD* [a]1Sam. 7:17
37 [a]1Sam. 28:6
38 [a]Josh. 7:14; 1Sam. 10:19
39 [a]2Sam. 12:5
41 [I]Or, *Show the innocent* [II]Hebr. *went forth* [a]Prov. 16:33; Acts 1:24 [b]Josh. 7:16; Acts 10:20, 21
43 [a]Josh. 7:19 [b]1Sam. 14:27
44 [a]Ruth 1:17 [b]1Sam. 14:39
45 [a]2Sam. 14:11; 1Kgs. 1:52; Luke 21:18
47 [a]1Sam. 11:11 [b]2Sam. 10:6
48 [I]Or, *wrought mightily* [a]1Sam. 15:3, 7
49 [a]1Sam. 31:2; 1Chr. 8:33
50 [I]Hebr. *Abiner*
51 [a]1Sam. 9:1

🗝 **14:36, 37** See note on Exodus 28:30 concerning seeking direction from God.

against the Philistines all the days[3117] of Saul: and when Saul saw[7200] any strong man, or any valiant man, [a]he took him unto him.

Saul's Second Sin at Gilgal

15 Samuel also said unto Saul, [a]The LORD sent me to anoint[4886] thee *to be* king[4428] over his people,[5971] over Israel: now therefore hearken thou unto the voice of the words[1697] of the LORD.

2 Thus saith[559] the LORD of hosts, I remember *that* which Amalek did[6213] to Israel, [a]how he laid[7760] *wait* for him in the way,[1870] which he came up from Egypt.

3 Now go and smite[5221] Amalek, and [a]utterly destroy all that they have, and spare them not; but slay[4191] both man and woman,[802] infant and suckling, ox and sheep, camel and ass.

4 And Saul gathered the people together,[8085] and numbered them in Telaim, two hundred thousand footmen, and ten thousand men of Judah.

5 And Saul came to a city of Amalek, and [1]laid wait in the valley.

6 And Saul said unto [a]the Kenites, [b]Go, depart,[5493] get you down from among the Amalekites, lest I destroy you with them: for [c]ye shewed[6213] kindness[2617] to all the children[1121] of Israel, when they came up out of Egypt. So the Kenites departed from among the Amalekites.

7 [a]And Saul smote[5221] the Amalekites from [b]Havilah *until* thou comest to [c]Shur, that *is* over against Egypt.

🗝 8 And [a]he took Agag the king of the Amalekites alive,[2416] and [b]utterly destroyed[2763] all the people with the edge[6310] of the sword.[2719]

9 But Saul and the people [a]spared Agag, and the best of the sheep, and of the oxen, and [1]of the fatlings, and the lambs,[3733] and all *that was* good,[2896] and would[14] not utterly destroy them: but every thing *that was* vile[5240] and refuse, that they destroyed utterly.

10 Then came the word[1697] of the LORD unto Samuel, saying,

11 [a]It repenteth[5162] me that I have set up Saul *to be* king: for he is [b]turned back from following me, [c]and hath not performed my commandments.[1697] And it [d]grieved Samuel; and he cried[2199] unto the LORD all night.[3915]

🗝 12 And when Samuel rose early to meet Saul in the morning, it was told Samuel, saying, Saul came to [a]Carmel, and, behold, he set[5324] him up a place, and is gone about, and passed on,[5674] and gone down to Gilgal.

13 And Samuel came to Saul: and Saul said unto him, [a]Blessed[1288] *be* thou of the LORD: I have performed the commandment[1697] of the LORD.

14 And Samuel said, What *meaneth* then this bleating[6963] of the sheep in mine ears,[241] and the lowing[6963] of the oxen which I hear?

15 And Saul said, They have brought them from the Amalekites: [a]for the people spared the best of the sheep and of the oxen, to sacrifice[2076] unto the LORD thy God;[430] and the rest we have utterly destroyed.

16 Then Samuel said[1696] unto Saul, Stay, and I will tell thee what the LORD hath said to me this night. And he said unto him, Say on.

17 And Samuel said, [a]When thou *wast* little in thine own sight, *wast* thou not *made* the head of the tribes of Israel, and the LORD anointed[4886] thee king over Israel?

18 And the LORD sent thee on a journey,[1870] and said, Go and utterly destroy the sinners[2400] the Amalekites, and fight against them until [1]they be consumed.[3615]

52 [a]1Sam. 8:11

1 [a]1Sam. 9:16

2 [a]Ex. 17:8, 14; Num. 24:20; Deut. 25:17-19

3 [a]Lev. 27:28, 29; Josh. 6:17, 21

5 [1]Or, *fought*

6 [a]Num. 24:21; Judg. 1:16; 4:11 [b]Gen. 18:25; 19:12, 14; Rev. 18:14 [c]Ex. 18:10, 19; Num. 10:29, 32

7 [a]1Sam. 14:48 [b]Gen. 2:11; 25:18 [c]Gen. 16:7

8 [a]1Kgs. 20:34, 35 [b]1Sam. 30:1

9 [1]Or, *of the second sort* [a]1Sam. 15:3, 15

11 [a]1Sam. 15:35; Gen. 6:6, 7; 2Sam. 24:16 [b]Josh. 22:16; 1Kgs. 9:6 [c]1Sam. 13:13; 1Sam. 15:3, 9; [d]1Sam. 15:35; 1Sam. 16:1

12 [a]Josh. 15:55

13 [a]Gen. 14:19; Judg. 17:2; Ruth 3:10

15 [a]Gen. 3:12; 1Sam. 15:9, 21; Prov. 28:13

17 [a]1Sam. 9:21

18 [1]Hebr. *they consume them*

🗝 **15:8** Agag may have been a general title given to the Amalekite kings, just as Pharaoh was the general title for the King of Egypt (cf. Num. 24:7).

🗝 **15:12** Carmel (which means "garden") does not refer here to the famous mountain in the western part of Galilee but to a town in Judah which lay about seven miles south of Hebron.

19 Wherefore then didst[6213] thou not obey the voice of the LORD, but didst fly upon the spoil, and didst evil[7451] in the sight of the LORD?

20 And Saul said unto Samuel, Yea, [a]I have obeyed[8085] the voice of the LORD, and have gone the way which the LORD sent me, and have brought Agag the king of Amalek, and have utterly destroyed the Amalekites.

21 [a]But the people took of the spoil, sheep and oxen, the chief[7225] of the things which should have been utterly destroyed, to sacrifice unto the LORD thy God in Gilgal.

22 And Samuel said, [a]Hath the LORD *as great* delight[2656] in burnt offerings and sacrifices, as in obeying the voice of the LORD? Behold, [b]to obey *is* better[2896] than sacrifice,[2077] *and* to hearken than the fat of rams.

23 For rebellion *is as* the sin[2403] of [I]witchcraft, and stubbornness *is as* iniquity[205] and idolatry.[8655] Because thou hast rejected[3988] the word of the LORD, [a]he hath also rejected thee from *being* king.

24 [a]And Saul said unto Samuel, I have sinned:[2398] for I have transgressed the commandment[6310] of the LORD, and thy words: because I [b]feared[3372] the people, and obeyed their voice.

25 Now therefore, I pray thee, pardon[5374] my sin, and turn again with me, that I may worship[7812] the LORD.

26 And Samuel said unto Saul, I will not return with thee: [a]for thou hast rejected the word of the LORD, and the LORD hath rejected thee from being king over Israel.

27 And as Samuel turned about to go away, [a]he laid hold upon the skirt of his mantle,[4598] and it rent.

28 And Samuel said unto him, [a]The LORD hath rent the kingdom[4468] of Israel from thee this day, and hath given it to a neighbour[7453] of thine, *that is* better than thou.

29 And also the [I]Strength[5331] of Israel [a]will not lie[8266] nor repent: for he *is* not a man, that he should repent.

30 Then he said, I have sinned: *yet* [a]honour me now, I pray thee, before the elders[2205] of my people, and before Israel, and turn again with me, that I may worship the LORD thy God.

31 So Samuel turned again after Saul; and Saul worshipped[7812] the LORD.

32 Then said Samuel, Bring ye hither to me Agag the king of the Amalekites. And Agag came unto him delicately.[4574] And Agag said, Surely the bitterness[4751] of death[4194] is past.

33 And Samuel said, [a]As thy sword hath made women[802] childless, so shall thy mother be childless among women. And Samuel hewed Agag in pieces[8158] before the LORD in Gilgal.

34 Then Samuel went to Ramah; and Saul went up to his house to [a]Gibeah of Saul.

35 And [a]Samuel came no more to see Saul until the day of his death: nevertheless Samuel [b]mourned for Saul: and the LORD [c]repented that he had made Saul king[4427] over Israel.

Samuel Anoints David King

16 And the LORD said unto Samuel, [a]How long wilt thou mourn[56] for Saul, seeing [b]I have rejected him from reigning over Israel? [c]fill thine horn with oil,[8081] and go, I will send thee to Jesse the Bethlehemite: for [d]I have provided[7200] me a king[4428] among his sons.[1121]

2 And Samuel said, How can I go? if Saul hear *it,* he will kill[2026] me. And the LORD said, Take an heifer [I]with thee, and say,[559] [a]I am come to sacrifice[2076] to the LORD.

3 And call[7121] Jesse to the sacrifice,[2077] and [a]I will shew[3045] thee what thou shalt do:[6213] and [b]thou shalt anoint[4886] unto me *him* whom I name unto thee.

4 And Samuel did that which the LORD spake, and came to Bethlehem. And the elders[2205] of the town [a]trembled at his [I]coming, and said, [b]Comest thou peaceably?[7965]

5 And he said, Peaceably: I am come to sacrifice unto the LORD: [a]sanctify[6942]

20 [a]1Sam. 15:13
21 [a]1Sam. 15:15
22 [a]Ps. 50:8, 9; Prov. 21:3; Isa. 1:11-13, 16, 17; Jer. 7:22, 23; Mic. 6:6-8; Heb. 10:6-9 [b]Eccl. 5:1; Hos. 6:6; Matt. 5:24; 9:13; 12:7; Mark 12:33
23 [I]Hebr. *divination* [a]1Sam. 13:14
24 [a]2Sam. 12:13 [b]Ex. 23:2; Prov. 29:25; Isa. 51:12, 13
26 [a]1Sam. 2:30
27 [a]1Kgs. 11:30
28 [a]1Sam. 28:17, 18; 1Kgs. 11:31
29 [I]Or, *Eternity,* or, *Victory* [a]Num. 23:19; Ezek. 24:14; 2Tim. 2:13; Titus 1:2
30 [a]John 5:44; 12:43
33 [a]Ex. 17:11; Num. 14:45; Judg. 1:7
34 [a]1Sam. 11:4
35 [a]1Sam. 19:24; [b]1Sam. 15:11; 1Sam. 16:1; [c]1Sam. 15:11
1 [a]1Sam. 15:35 [b]1Sam. 15:23 [c]1Sam. 9:16; 2Kgs. 9:1 [d]Ps. 78:70; 89:19, 20; Acts 13:22
2 [I]Hebr. *in thine hand* [a]1Sam. 9:12; 20:29
3 [a]Ex. 4:15 [b]1Sam. 9:16
4 [I]Hebr. *meeting* [a]1Sam. 21:1 [b]1Kgs. 2:13; 2Kgs. 9:22
5 [a]Ex. 19:10, 14

yourselves, and come with me to the sacrifice. And he sanctified Jesse and his sons, and called them to the sacrifice.

6 And it came to pass, when they were come, that he looked on[7200] [a]Eliab, and [b]said, Surely the LORD's anointed[4899] *is* before him.

7 But the LORD said unto Samuel, Look not on [a]his countenance,[4758] or on the height of his stature; because I have refused him: [b]for *the LORD seeth* not as man seeth; for man [c]looketh[7200] on the [I]outward appearance, but the LORD looketh on the [d]heart.

8 Then Jesse called [a]Abinadab, and made him pass before Samuel. And he said, Neither hath the LORD chosen[977] this.

9 Then Jesse made [a]Shammah to pass by. And he said, Neither hath the LORD chosen this.

10 Again, Jesse made seven of his sons to pass before Samuel. And Samuel said unto Jesse, The LORD hath not chosen these.

11 And Samuel said unto Jesse, Are here all *thy* children? And he said, [a]There remaineth yet the youngest, and, behold, he keepeth the sheep. And Samuel said unto Jesse, [b]Send and fetch him: for we will not sit [I]down till he come hither.

12 And he sent, and brought him in. Now he *was* [a]ruddy, *and* withal [I]of a beautiful countenance,[5869] and goodly[2896] to look to. And the LORD said, Arise, anoint him: for this *is* he.

🔑 13 Then Samuel took the horn of oil, and [a]anointed[4886] him in the midst of his brethren:[251] and [b]the Spirit[7307] of the LORD came upon David from that day[3117] forward. So Samuel rose up, and went to Ramah.

6 [a]1Sam. 17:13; 1Chr. 27:18, *Elihu* [b]1Kgs. 12:26
7 [I]Hebr. *eyes* [a]Ps. 147:10, 11 [b]Isa. 55:8 [c]2Cor. 10:7 [d]1Kgs. 8:39; 1Chr. 28:9; Ps. 7:9; Jer. 11:20; 17:10; 20:12; Acts 1:24
8 [a]1Sam. 17:13
9 [a]1Sam. 17:13; 2Sam. 13:3, Shimeah; 1Chr. 2:13, Shimma
11 [I]Hebr. *round* [a]1Sam. 17:12 [b]2Sam. 7:8; Ps. 78:70
12 [I]Hebr. *fair of eyes* [a]1Sam. 17:42; Song 5:10
13 [a]1Sam. 10:1; Ps. 89:20 [b]Num. 27:18; Judg. 11:29; 13:25; 14:6; 1Sam. 10:6, 10
14 [I]Or, *terrified* [a]Judg. 16:20; 1Sam. 11:6; 18:12; 28:15; Ps. 51:11 [b]Judg. 9:23; 1Sam. 18:10; 19:9
16 [a]Gen. 41:46; 1Sam. 16:21, 22; 1Kgs. 10:8 [b]1Sam. 16:23; 2Kgs. 3:15
18 [I]Or, *speech* [a]1Sam. 17:32, 34-36 [b]1Sam. 3:19; 18:12, 14
19 [a]1Sam. 16:11; 17:15, 34
20 [a]1Sam. 10:27; 17:18; Gen. 43:11; Prov. 18:16
21 [a]Gen. 41:46; 1Kgs. 10:8; Prov. 22:29
23 [a]1Sam. 16:14, 16

David Becomes Saul's Musician

14 [a]But the Spirit of the LORD departed from Saul, and [b]an evil[7451] spirit from the LORD [I]troubled him.

15 And Saul's servants said unto him, Behold now, an evil spirit from God[430] troubleth thee.

16 Let our lord[113] now command thy servants, *which are* [a]before thee, to seek out a man, *who is* a cunning[3045] player on an harp: and it shall come to pass, when the evil spirit from God is upon thee, that he shall [b]play with his hand, and thou shalt be well.[2895]

17 And Saul said unto his servants, Provide[7200] me now a man that can play well,[3190] and bring *him* to me.

🔑 18 Then answered one of the servants, and said, Behold, I have seen[7200] a son[1121] of Jesse the Bethlehemite, *that is* cunning in playing, and [a]a mighty valiant man, and a man of war, and prudent[995] in [I]matters, and a comely[8389] person,[376] and [b]the LORD *is* with him.

19 Wherefore Saul sent messengers unto Jesse, and said, Send me David thy son, [a]which *is* with the sheep.

20 And Jesse [a]took an ass *laden* with bread, and a bottle of wine, and a kid, and sent *them* by David his son unto Saul.

21 And David came to Saul, and [a]stood before him: and he loved[157] him greatly; and he became his armourbearer.

22 And Saul sent to Jesse, saying, Let David, I pray thee, stand before me; for he hath found favour[2580] in my sight.

23 And it came to pass, when [a]the *evil* spirit from God was upon Saul, that David took an harp, and played with his

---

🔑 **16:13** The Jews recognized that the Messiah, the Christ, would come from David's descendants (John 7:42). One of the key titles given to Jesus during His earthly ministry was "Son of David" (Matt. 9:27; 12:23; 15:22), emphasizing His heirship of all of David's royal prerogatives, as well as His fulfillment of the messianic promises to David (2 Sam. 7:8–17, cf. Matt. 22:41–45; Luke 1:32, 69).

🔑 **16:18** It is interesting that David is called here a "mighty valiant man, and a man of war" when he had not yet had a chance to prove himself in battle (see 1 Sam. 17:33). It seems likely that David had exhibited these qualities in his experiences as a shepherd, and they were equated with valor in war situations.

hand: so Saul was refreshed,[7304] and was well, and the evil spirit departed from him.

David and Goliath

17 Now the Philistines [a]gathered together[622] their armies to battle, and were gathered together at [b]Shochoh, which *belongeth* to Judah, and pitched between Shochoh and Azekah, in [I][c]Ephesdammim.

2 And Saul and the men of Israel were gathered together, and pitched by the valley of Elah, and [I]set the battle in array[6186] against the Philistines.

3 And the Philistines stood on a mountain on the one side, and Israel stood on a mountain on the other side: and *there was* a valley between them.

4 And there went out a champion out of the camp[4264] of the Philistines named [a]Goliath, of [b]Gath, whose height *was* six cubits and a span.

5 And *he had* an helmet of brass upon his head, and he *was* [I]armed[3847] with a coat of mail; and the weight of the coat *was* five thousand shekels of brass.

6 And *he had* greaves[4697] of brass upon his legs, and a [I]target[3591] of brass between his shoulders.

7 And the [a]staff of his spear *was* like a weaver's beam; and his spear's head *weighed* six hundred shekels of iron: and one bearing[5375] a shield went before him.

8 And he stood and cried[7121] unto the armies of Israel, and said unto them, Why are ye come out to set *your* battle in array? *am* not I a Philistine, and ye [a]servants[5650] to Saul? choose you a man for you, and let him come down to me.

9 If he be able to fight with me, and to kill me, then will we be your servants: but if I prevail against him, and kill him, then shall ye be our servants, and [a]serve us.

10 And the Philistine said, I [a]defy the armies of Israel this day; give me a man, that we may fight together.

11 When Saul and all Israel heard those words of the Philistine, they were dismayed,[2865] and greatly afraid.[3372]

12 Now David *was* [a]the son of that [b]Ephrathite of Bethlehem–judah, whose name *was* Jesse; and he had [c]eight sons: and the man went among men *for* an old[2204] man in the days[3117] of Saul.

13 And the three eldest sons of Jesse went *and* followed Saul to the battle: and the [a]names of his three sons that went to the battle *were* Eliab the firstborn, and next unto him Abinadab, and the third Shammah.

14 And David *was* the youngest: and the three eldest followed Saul.

15 But David went and returned from Saul [a]to feed his father's[1] sheep at Bethlehem.

16 And the Philistine drew near[5066] morning and evening, and presented himself forty days.

17 And Jesse said unto David his son, Take now for thy brethren[251] an ephah of this parched *corn,* and these ten loaves, and run to the camp to thy brethren;

18 And carry these ten [I]cheeses unto the [II]captain[8269] of *their* thousand, and [a]look[6485] how thy brethren fare,[7965] and take their pledge.[6161]

19 Now Saul, and they, and all the men of Israel, *were* in the valley of Elah, fighting with the Philistines.

20 And David rose up early in the morning, and left[5203] the sheep with a keeper,[8104] and took, and went, as Jesse had commanded[6680] him; and he came to the [I][a]trench, as the host was going forth to the [II]fight, and shouted[7321] for the battle.

21 For Israel and the Philistines had put the battle in array, army against army.

22 And David left [I]his carriage in the hand of the keeper of the carriage, and ran into the army, and came and [II]saluted his brethren.

23 And as he talked with them, behold, there came up the champion, the Philistine of Gath, Goliath by name, out of the armies of the Philistines, and

1 [I]Or, *The coast of Dammim, called Pasdammim* [a]1Sam. 13:5 [b]Josh. 15:35; 2Chr. 28:18 [c]1Chr. 11:13

2 [I]Hebr. *ranged the battle*

4 [a]2Sam. 21:19 [b]Josh. 11:22

5 [I]Hebr. *clothed*

6 [I]Or, *gorget*

7 [a]2Sam. 21:19

8 [a]1Sam. 8:17

9 [a]1Sam. 11:1

10 [a]1Sam. 17:26; 2Sam. 21:21

12 [a]1Sam. 17:58; Ruth 4:22; 1Sam. 16:1, 18 [b]Gen. 35:19 [c]1Sam. 16:10, 11; 1Chr. 2:13-15

13 [a]1Sam. 16:6, 8, 9; 1Chr. 2:13

15 [a]1Sam. 16:19

18 [I]Hebr. *cheeses of milk* [II]Hebr. *captain of a thousand* [a]Gen. 37:14

20 [I]Or, *place of the carriage* [II]Or, *battle array, or place of fight* [a]1Sam. 26:5

22 [I]Hebr. *the vessels from upon him* [II]Hebr. *asked his brethren of peace*

spake[1696] [a]according to the same words: and David heard *them.*

24 And all the men of Israel, when they saw[7200] the man, fled [I]from him, and were sore afraid.

25 And the men of Israel said, Have ye seen this man that is come up? surely to defy[2778] Israel is he come up: and it shall be, *that* the man who killeth[5221] him, the king[4428] will enrich him with great riches, and [a]will give him his daughter, and make his father's house free in Israel.

26 And David spake[559] to the men that stood by him, saying, What shall be done[6213] to the man that killeth this Philistine, and taketh away [a]the reproach[2781] from Israel? for who *is* this [b]uncircumcised[6189] Philistine, that he should [c]defy the armies of [d]the living[2416] God?[430]

27 And the people[5971] answered[559] him after this manner, saying, [a]So shall it be done to the man that killeth him.

28 And Eliab his eldest brother[251] heard when he spake[1696] unto the men; and Eliab's [a]anger[639] was kindled[2734] against David, and he said, Why camest thou down hither? and with whom hast thou left those few sheep in the wilderness? I know[3045] thy pride,[2087] and the naughtiness[7455] of thine heart; for thou art come down that thou mightest see the battle.

29 And David said, What have I now done? [a]*Is there* not a cause?[1697]

30 And he turned from him toward another, and [a]spake after the same [I]manner: and the people answered him again after the former[7223] manner.

31 And when the words were heard which David spake, they rehearsed *them* before Saul: and he [I]sent for him.

32 And David said to Saul, [a]Let no man's heart fail because of him; [b]thy servant[5650] will go and fight with this Philistine.

🔑 33 And Saul said to David, [a]Thou art not able to go against this Philistine to

23 [a]1Sam. 17:8
24 [I]Hebr. *from his face*
25 [a]Josh. 15:16
26 [a]1Sam. 11:2 [b]1Sam. 14:6 [c]1Sam. 17:10 [d]Deut. 5:26
27 [a]1Sam. 17:25
28 [a]Gen. 37:4, 8, 11; Matt. 10:36
29 [a]1Sam. 17:17
30 [I]Hebr. *word* [a]1Sam. 17:26, 27
31 [I]Hebr. *took him*
32 [a]Deut. 20:1, 3 [b]1Sam. 16:18
33 [a]Num. 13:31; Deut. 9:2
34 [I]Or, *kid*
37 [a]Ps. 18:16, 17; 63:7; 77:11; 2Cor. 1:10; 2Tim. 4:17, 18 [b]1Sam. 20:13; 1Chr. 22:11, 16
38 [I]Hebr. *clothed David with his clothes*
40 [I]Or, *valley* [II]Hebr. *vessel*
42 [a]Ps. 123:3, 4; 1Cor. 1:27, 28 [b]1Sam. 16:12
43 [a]1Sam. 24:14; 2Sam. 3:8; 9:8; 16:9; 2Kgs. 8:13

fight with him: for thou *art but* a youth, and he a man of war from his youth.

34 And David said unto Saul, Thy servant kept his father's sheep, and there came a lion, and a bear, and took a [I]lamb out of the flock:

35 And I went out after him, and smote[5221] him, and delivered[5337] *it* out of his mouth: and when he arose against me, I caught[2388] *him* by his beard,[2206] and smote him, and slew[4191] him.

36 Thy servant slew[5221] both the lion and the bear: and this uncircumcised Philistine shall be as one of them, seeing he hath defied[2778] the armies of the living God.

37 David said moreover, [a]The LORD that delivered me out of the paw of the lion, and out of the paw of the bear, he will deliver[5337] me out of the hand of this Philistine. And Saul said unto David, Go, and [b]the LORD be with thee.

38 And Saul [I]armed David with his armour, and he put an helmet of brass upon his head; also he armed him with a coat of mail.

39 And David girded his sword[2719] upon his armour, and he assayed[2974] to go; for he had not proved[5254] *it.* And David said unto Saul, I cannot go with these; for I have not proved *them.* And David put them off him.

40 And he took his staff in his hand, and chose[977] him five smooth stones out of the [I]brook, and put them in a shepherd's [II]bag which he had, even in a scrip;[3219] and his sling *was* in his hand: and he drew near to the Philistine.

41 And the Philistine came on and drew near unto David; and the man that bare[5375] the shield *went* before him.

42 And when the Philistine looked about, and saw David, he [a]disdained[959] him: for he was *but* a youth, and [b]ruddy, and of a fair countenance.

43 And the Philistine said unto David, [a]*Am* I a dog, that thou comest to me with staves? and the Philistine cursed[7043] David by his gods.[430]

🔑 **17:33** See note on 1 Samuel 16:18.

44 And the Philistine [a]said to David, Come to me, and I will give thy flesh[1320] unto the fowls of the air,[8064] and to the beasts of the field.[7704]

45 Then said David to the Philistine, Thou comest to me with a sword, and with a spear, and with a shield: [a]but I come to thee in the name of the LORD of hosts, the God of the armies of Israel, whom thou hast [b]defied.

46 This day will the LORD [I]deliver thee into mine hand; and I will smite[5221] thee, and take thine head from thee; and I will give [a]the carcases[6297] of the host of the Philistines this day unto the fowls of the air, and to the wild beasts[2416] of the earth;[776] [b]that all the earth may know that there is a God in Israel.

47 And all this assembly[6951] shall know that the LORD [a]saveth[3467] not with sword and spear: for [b]the battle *is* the LORD's, and he will give you into our hands.

48 And it came to pass, when the Philistine arose, and came and drew nigh to meet David, that David hasted, and ran toward the army to meet the Philistine.

49 And David put his hand in his bag, and took thence a stone, and slang[7044] *it,* and smote the Philistine in his forehead, that the stone sunk into his forehead; and he fell[5307] upon his face to the earth.

50 So [a]David prevailed[2388] over the Philistine with a sling and with a stone, and smote the Philistine, and slew[4191] him; but *there was* no sword in the hand of David.

51 Therefore David ran, and stood upon the Philistine, and took his sword, and drew it out of the sheath thereof, and slew him, and cut off[3772] his head therewith. And when the Philistines saw their champion was dead,[4191] [a]they fled.

52 And the men of Israel and of Judah arose, and shouted, and pursued the Philistines, until thou come to the valley, and to the gates of Ekron. And the wounded[2491] of the Philistines fell down by the way[1870] to [a]Shaaraim, even unto Gath, and unto Ekron.

53 And the children[1121] of Israel returned from chasing after the Philistines, and they spoiled[8154] their tents.

54 And David took the head of the Philistine, and brought it to Jerusalem; but he put his armour in his tent.

🗝 55 And when Saul saw David go forth against the Philistine, he said unto Abner, the captain of the host, Abner, [a]whose son *is* this youth? And Abner said, *As* thy soul[5315] liveth,[2416] O king, I cannot tell.

56 And the king said, Enquire[7592] thou whose son the stripling[5958] *is.*

57 And as David returned from the slaughter[5221] of the Philistine, Abner took him, and brought him before Saul [a]with the head of the Philistine in his hand.

58 And Saul said to him, Whose son *art* thou, *thou* young man? And David answered, *I am* [a]the son of thy servant Jesse the Bethlehemite.

David and Jonathan Become Friends

18 And it came to pass, when he had made an end[3615] of speaking[1696] unto Saul, that [a]the soul[5315] of Jonathan was knit with the soul of David, [b]and Jonathan loved[157] him as his own soul.

2 And Saul took him that day,[3117] [a]and would let him go no more home to his father's[1] house.

3 Then Jonathan and David made a covenant,[1285] because he loved[160] him as his own soul.

4 And Jonathan stripped himself of the robe that *was* upon him, and gave it to David, and his garments, even to his

44 [a]1Kgs. 20:10, 11
45 [a]2Sam. 22:33, 35; Ps. 124:8; 125:1; 2Cor. 10:4; Heb. 11:33, 34 [b]1Sam. 17:10
46 [I]Hebr. *shut thee up* [a]Deut. 28:26 [b]Josh. 4:24; 1Kgs. 8:43; 18:36; 2Kgs. 19:19; Isa. 52:10
47 [a]Ps. 44:6, 7; Hos. 1:7; Zech. 4:6 [b]2Chr. 20:15
50 [a]1Sam. 21:9; Judg. 3:31; 15:15; 1Sam. 21:9
51 [a]Heb. 11:34
52 [a]Josh. 15:36
55 [a]1Sam. 16:21, 22
57 [a]1Sam. 17:54
58 [a]1Sam. 17:12
1 [a]Gen. 44:30 [b]Deut. 13:6; 1Sam. 19:2; 20:17; 2Sam. 1:26
2 [a]1Sam. 17:15

🗝 **17:55–58** It is of interest that Saul seemingly did not recognize David here. No one knows for what length of time or how frequently David played his musical instruments for King Saul. The incident with Goliath probably happened several years after David's service in the king's court.

sword,[2719] and to his bow, and to his girdle.2290

5 And David went out whithersoever Saul sent him, *and* [I][a]behaved himself wisely: and Saul set him over the men of war, and he was accepted[3190] in the sight of all the people,[5971] and also in the sight of Saul's servants.[5650]

Saul Becomes Jealous of David

6 And it came to pass as they came, when David was returned from the slaughter[5221] of the [I]Philistine, that [a]the women[802] came out of all cities of Israel, singing[7891] and dancing, to meet king[4428] Saul, with tabrets,8596 with joy, and with [II]instruments of musick.

7 And the women [a]answered *one another* as they played, and said, [b]Saul hath slain[5221] his thousands, and David his ten thousands.

8 And Saul was very wroth,[2734] and the saying[1697] [I][a]displeased[7489] him; and he said, They have ascribed unto David ten thousands, and to me they have ascribed *but* thousands: and *what* can he have more but [b]the kingdom?

9 And Saul eyed5770 David from that day and forward.

10 And it came to pass on the morrow, that [a]the evil[7451] spirit[7307] from God[430] came upon Saul, [b]and he prophesied[5012] in the midst of the house: and David played with his hand, as at other times: [c]and *there was* a javelin in Saul's hand.

11 And Saul [a]cast the javelin; for he said, I will smite[5221] David even to the wall *with it.* And David avoided out of his presence twice.

12 And Saul was [a]afraid[3372] of David, because [b]the LORD was with him, and was [c]departed from Saul.

13 Therefore Saul removed him from him, and made him his captain[8269] over a thousand; and [a]he went out and came in before the people.

14 And David [I][a]behaved himself wisely in all his ways;[1870] and [b]the LORD *was* with him.

15 Wherefore when Saul saw[7200] that he behaved himself very wisely, he was afraid[1481] of him.

16 But [a]all Israel and Judah loved David, because he went out and came in before them.

David Marries Saul's Daughter

17 And Saul said to David, Behold my elder daughter Merab, [a]her will I give thee to wife:[802] only be thou [I]valiant for me, and fight [b]the LORD's battles. For Saul said, [c]Let not mine hand be upon him, but let the hand of the Philistines be upon him.

18 And David said unto Saul, [a]Who *am* I? and what *is* my life,[2416] *or* my father's family[4940] in Israel, that I should be son in law to the king?

19 But it came to pass at the time when Merab Saul's daughter should have been given to David, that she was given unto [a]Adriel the [b]Meholathite to wife.

20 [a]And Michal Saul's daughter loved David: and they told Saul, and the thing [I]pleased him.

21 And Saul said, I will give him her, that she may be [a]a snare[4170] to him, and that [b]the hand of the Philistines may be against him. Wherefore Saul said to David, Thou shalt [c]this day be my son in law in *the one of* the twain.8147

22 And Saul commanded[6680] his servants, *saying,* Commune[1696] with David secretly, and say,[559] Behold, the king hath delight[2654] in thee, and all his servants love[157] thee: now therefore be the king's[4428] son in law.

23 And Saul's servants spake[1696] those words[1697] in the ears[241] of David. And David said, Seemeth it to you *a* light *thing* to be a king's son in law, seeing that I *am* a poor man, and lightly esteemed?

24 And the servants of Saul told him, saying, [I]On this manner spake David.

25 And Saul said, Thus shall ye say to David, The king desireth[2656] not any [a]dowry,4119 but an hundred foreskins[6190] of the Philistines, to be [b]avenged of the king's enemies. But Saul [c]thought to

5 [I]Or, *prospered* [a]1Sam. 18:14, 15, 30

6 [I]Or, *Philistines* [II]Hebr. *three-stringed instruments* [a]Ex. 15:20; Judg. 11:34

7 [a]Ex. 15:21 [b]1Sam. 21:11; 29:5

8 [I]Hebr. *was evil in his eyes* [a]Eccl. 4:4 [b]1Sam. 15:28

10 [a]1Sam. 16:14 [b]1Sam. 19:24; 1Kgs. 18:29; Acts 16:16 [c]1Sam. 19:9

11 [a]1Sam. 19:10; 20:33; Prov. 27:4

12 [a]1Sam. 18:15, 29 [b]1Sam. 16:13, 18 [c]1Sam. 16:14; 28:15

13 [a]Num. 27:17; 1Sam. 18:16; 2Sam. 5:2

14 [I]Or, *prospered* [a]1Sam. 18:5 [b]Gen. 39:2, 3, 23; Josh. 6:27

16 [a]1Sam. 18:5

17 [I]Hebr. *a son of valor* [a]1Sam. 17:25 [b]Num. 32:20, 27, 29; 1Sam. 25:28 [c]1Sam. 18:21, 25; 2Sam. 12:9

18 [a]1Sam. 18:23; 1Sam. 9:21; 2Sam. 7:18

19 [a]2Sam. 21:8 [b]Judg. 7:22

20 [I]Hebr. *was right in his eyes* [a]1Sam. 18:28

21 [a]Ex. 10:7 [b]1Sam. 18:17 [c]1Sam. 18:26

24 [I]Hebr. *According to these words*

25 [a]Gen. 34:12; Ex. 22:17 [b]1Sam. 14:24 [c]1Sam. 18:17

make David fall by the hand of the Philistines.

26 And when his servants told David these words, it pleased David well to be the king's son in law: and [a]the days[3117] were not [I]expired.

27 Wherefore David arose and went, he and [a]his men, and slew[5221] of the Philistines two hundred men; and [b]David brought their foreskins, and they gave them in full tale to the king, that he might be the king's son in law. And Saul gave him Michal his daughter to wife.

28 And Saul saw and knew[3045] that the LORD *was* with David, and *that* Michal Saul's daughter loved him.

29 And Saul was yet the more afraid of David; and Saul became David's enemy continually.

30 Then the princes[8269] of the Philistines [a]went forth: and it came to pass, after they went forth, *that* David [b]behaved himself more wisely than all the servants of Saul; so that his name was much [I]set by.[3365]

Saul Tries to Kill David

19 And Saul spake[1696] to Jonathan his son, and to all his servants,[5650] that they should kill[4191] David.

2 But Jonathan Saul's son [a]delighted[2654] much in David: and Jonathan told David, saying, Saul my father[1] seeketh to kill thee: now therefore, I pray thee,[4994] take heed to thyself until the morning, and abide in a secret *place,* and hide thyself:

3 And I will go out and stand beside my father in the field[7704] where thou *art,* and I will commune[1696] with my father of thee; and what I see, that I will tell thee.

4 And Jonathan [a]spake good[2896] of David unto Saul his father, and said unto him, Let not the king[4428] [b]sin against his servant,[5650] against David; because he hath not sinned[2398] against thee, and because his works *have been* to thee- ward very good:

26 [I]Hebr. *fulfilled* [a]1Sam. 18:21

27 [a]1Sam. 18:13 [b]2Sam. 3:14

30 [I]Hebr. *precious* [a]2Sam. 11:1 [b]1Sam. 18:5

2 [a]1Sam. 18:1

4 [a]Prov. 31:8, 9 [b]Gen. 42:22; Ps. 35:12; 109:5; Prov. 17:13; Jer. 18:20

5 [a]Judg. 9:17; 12:3; 1Sam. 28:21; Ps. 119:109 [b]1Sam. 17:49, 50 [c]1Sam. 11:13; 1Chr. 11:14 [d]1Sam. 20:32 [e]Matt. 27:4

7 [I]Hebr. *yesterday third day* [a]1Sam. 16:21; 18:2, 13

8 [I]Hebr. *his face*

9 [a]1Sam. 16:14; 18:10, 11

12 [a]Josh. 2:15; Acts 9:24, 25

13 [I]Hebr. *teraphim*

5 For he did put his [a]life[5315] in his hand, and [b]slew[5221] the Philistine, and [c]the LORD wrought a great salvation[8668] for all Israel: thou sawest[7200] *it,* and didst rejoice: [d]wherefore then wilt thou [e]sin against innocent[5355] blood,[1818] to slay[4191] David without a cause?

6 And Saul hearkened unto the voice of Jonathan: and Saul sware,[7650] *As* the LORD liveth,[2416] he shall not be slain.[4191]

7 And Jonathan called[7121] David, and Jonathan shewed[5046] him all those things. And Jonathan brought David to Saul, and he was in his presence, [a]as [I]in times past.

8 And there was war again: and David went out, and fought with the Philistines, and slew them with a great slaughter; and they fled from [I]him.

9 And [a]the evil[7451] spirit[7307] from the LORD was upon Saul, as he sat in his house with his javelin in his hand: and David played with *his* hand.

10 And Saul sought to smite[5221] David even to the wall with the javelin; but he slipped away out of Saul's presence, and he smote the javelin into the wall: and David fled, and escaped[4422] that night.[3915]

11 Saul also sent messengers unto David's house, to watch[8104] him, and to slay him in the morning: and Michal David's wife[802] told him, saying, If thou save[4422] not thy life to night, to morrow thou shalt be slain.

12 So Michal [a]let David down through a window: and he went, and fled, and escaped.

13 And Michal took an [I]image,[8655] and laid[7760] *it* in the bed, and put a pillow of goats' *hair* for his bolster,[4763] and covered[3680] *it* with a cloth.

14 And when Saul sent messengers to take David, she said, He *is* sick.

15 And Saul sent the messengers *again* to see David, saying, Bring him up to me in the bed, that I may slay him.

16 And when the messengers were come in, behold, *there was* an image in the bed, with a pillow of goats' *hair* for his bolster.

17 And Saul said unto Michal, Why
hast thou deceived me so, and sent away
mine enemy, that he is escaped? And
Michal answered[559] Saul, He said unto
me, Let me go; [a]why should I kill thee?
18 So David fled, and escaped, and
came to Samuel to Ramah, and told him
all that Saul had done to him. And he
and Samuel went and dwelt in Naioth.
19 And it was told Saul, saying,
Behold, David *is* at Naioth in Ramah.
20 And [a]Saul sent messengers to take
David: [b]and when they saw[7200] the company of the prophets[5030] prophesying,
and Samuel standing *as* appointed[5324]
over them, the Spirit of God[430] was upon
the messengers[4397] of Saul, and they also
[c]prophesied.[5012]
21 And when it was told Saul, he
sent other messengers. And they prophesied likewise, and Saul sent messengers
again the third time, and they prophesied also.
22 Then went he also to Ramah, and
came to a great well[953] that *is* in Sechu:
and he asked[7592] and said, Where *are*
Samuel and David? And *one* said, Behold,
they be at Naioth in Ramah.
23 And he went thither to Naioth
in Ramah: and [a]the Spirit of God was
upon him also, and he went on, and
prophesied, until he came to Naioth in
Ramah.
24 [a]And he stripped off his clothes
also, and prophesied before Samuel in
like manner, and [I]lay down [b]naked[6174] all
that day[3117] and all that night. Wherefore
they say, [c]*Is* Saul also among the
prophets?

Jonathan Helps David Escape

20 And David fled from Naioth in
Ramah, and came and said before
Jonathan, What have I done?[6213] what *is*
mine iniquity?[5771] and what *is* my sin before thy father,[1] that he seeketh my
life?[5315]
2 And he said unto him, God forbid;
thou shalt not die:[4191] behold, my father
will do nothing[3808,1697] either great or
small, but that he [I][a]will shew[1540] it me:
and why should my father hide this thing
from me? it *is* not *so*.
3 And David sware[7650] moreover, and
said, Thy father certainly knoweth[3045]
that I have found grace[2580] in thine eyes;
and he saith,[559] Let not Jonathan know
this, lest he be grieved: but truly *as* the
LORD liveth,[2416] and *as* thy soul[5315] liveth,
there is but a step between me and
death.[4194]
4 Then said Jonathan unto David,
[I]Whatsoever thy soul [II]desireth, I will
even do *it* for thee.
5 And David said unto Jonathan,
Behold, to morrow *is* the [a]new moon, and
I should not fail to sit with the king[4428]
at meat: but let me go, that I may [b]hide
myself in the field[7704] unto the third *day*
at even.
6 If thy father at all miss me, then
say,[559] David earnestly asked[7592] *leave* of
me that he might run [a]to Bethlehem his
city: for *there is* a yearly [I][b]sacrifice[2077]
there for all the family.[4940]
7 [a]If he say thus, *It is* well; thy
servant[5650] shall have peace:[7965] but if
he be very wroth,[2734] *then* be sure[3045]
that [b]evil[7451] is determined[3615] by him.
8 Therefore thou shalt [a]deal
kindly[2617] with thy servant; for [b]thou
hast brought thy servant into a
covenant[1285] of the LORD with thee:
notwithstanding, [c]if there be in me iniquity, slay[4191] me thyself; for why
shouldest thou bring me to thy father?
9 And Jonathan said, Far be it from
thee: for if I knew[3045] certainly that evil
were determined by my father to come
upon thee, then would not I tell it thee?
10 Then said David to Jonathan,
Who shall tell me? or what *if* thy father
answer thee roughly?[7186]
11 And Jonathan said unto David,
Come, and let us go out into the field.
And they went out both of them into the
field.

17 [a]2Sam. 2:22
20 [a]John 7:32, 45 [b]1Sam. 10:5, 6; 1Cor. 14:3, 24, 25 [c]Num. 11:25; Joel 2:28
23 [a]1Sam. 10:10
24 [I]Hebr. *fell,* Num. 24:4 [a]Isa. 20:2 [b]Mic. 1:8; 2Sam. 6:14, 20 [c]1Sam. 10:11
2 [I]Hebr. *uncover mine ear* [a]1Sam. 9:15; 20:12
4 [I]Or, *Say what is thy mind, and I will do* [II]Hebr. *speaketh,* or, *thinketh*
5 [a]Num. 10:10; 28:11 [b]1Sam. 19:2
6 [I]Or, *feast* [a]1Sam. 16:4 [b]1Sam. 9:12
7 [a]Deut. 1:23; 2Sam. 17:4 [b]1Sam. 25:17; Esth. 7:7
8 [a]Josh. 2:14 [b]1Sam. 18:3; 20:16; 23:18 [c]2Sam. 14:32

19:20 Concerning the phrase "sons of the prophets," see note on 2 Kings 2:3, 5.

12 And Jonathan said unto David, O LORD God of Israel, when I have [I]sounded my father about to morrow any time, *or* the third *day,* and, behold, *if there be* good[2896] toward David, and I then send not unto thee, and [II][a]shew it thee;

13 [a]The LORD do[6213] so and much more to Jonathan: but if it please[3190] my father *to do* thee evil, then I will shew it thee, and send thee away, that thou mayest go in peace: and [b]the LORD be with thee, as he hath been with my father.

14 And thou shalt not only while yet I live[2416] shew[6213] me the kindness[2617] of the LORD, that I die not:

15 But *also* [a]thou shalt not cut off[3772] thy kindness from my house for ever: no, not when the LORD hath cut off the enemies of David every one[376] from the face of the earth.[127]

16 So Jonathan [I]made *a covenant* with the house of David, *saying,* [a]Let the LORD even require *it* at the hand of David's enemies.

17 And Jonathan caused David to swear[7650] again, [I]because he loved[160] him: [a]for he loved[157] him as he loved his own soul.

18 Then Jonathan said to David, [a]To morrow *is* the new moon: and thou shalt be missed, because thy seat[4186] will be [I]empty.[6485]

19 And *when* thou hast stayed three days, *then* thou shalt go down [I]quickly, and come to [a]the place where thou didst hide thyself [II]when the business[4639] was *in hand,* and shalt remain by the stone [III]Ezel.

20 And I will shoot[3384] three arrows on the side *thereof,* as though I shot at a mark.

21 And, behold, I will send a lad, *saying,* Go, find out the arrows. If I expressly say unto the lad, Behold, the arrows *are* on this side of thee, take them; then come thou: for *there is* peace to thee, and [I]no hurt; [a]*as* the LORD liveth.

22 But if I say thus unto the young man, Behold, the arrows *are* beyond thee; go thy way:[3212] for the LORD hath sent thee away.

23 And *as touching* [a]the matter which thou and I have spoken[1696] of, behold, the LORD *be* between thee and me for ever.

24 So David hid himself in the field: and when the new moon was come, the king sat him down to eat meat.

25 And the king sat upon his seat, as at other times, *even* upon a seat by the wall: and Jonathan arose, and Abner sat by Saul's side, and David's place was empty.

26 Nevertheless Saul spake[1696] not any thing that day: for he thought, Something hath befallen him, he *is* [a]not clean; surely he *is* not clean.[2889]

27 And it came to pass on the morrow, *which was* the second *day* of the month, that David's place was empty: and Saul said unto Jonathan his son,[1121] Wherefore cometh not the son of Jesse to meat, neither yesterday, nor to day?

28 And Jonathan [a]answered Saul, David earnestly asked *leave* of me *to go* to Bethlehem:

29 And he said, Let me go, I pray thee; for our family hath a sacrifice in the city; and my brother,[251] he hath commanded[6680] me *to be there:* and now, if I have found favour[2580] in thine eyes, let me get away, I pray thee, and see my brethren.[251] Therefore he cometh not unto the king's[4428] table.

30 Then Saul's anger[639] was kindled[2734] against Jonathan, and he said unto him, [I]Thou son of the perverse[5753] rebellious[4780] *woman,* do not I know that thou hast chosen[977] the son of Jesse to thine own confusion, and unto the confusion of thy mother's nakedness?[6172]

31 For as long as the son of Jesse liveth[2425] upon the ground,[127] thou shalt not be established,[3559] nor thy kingdom.[4438] Wherefore now send and fetch him unto me, for he [I]shall surely die.

32 And Jonathan answered Saul his father, and said unto him, [a]Wherefore shall he be slain? what hath he done?

---

12 [I]Hebr. *searched* [II]Hebr. *uncover thine ear* [a]1Sam. 20:2
13 [a]Ruth 1:17 [b]Josh. 1:5; 1Sam. 17:37; 1Chr. 22:11, 16
15 [a]2Sam. 9:1, 3, 7; 21:7
16 [I]Hebr. *cut* [a]1Sam. 25:22; 1Sam. 31:2; 2Sam. 4:7; 21:8
17 [I]Or, *by his love toward him* [a]1Sam. 18:1
18 [I]Hebr. *missed* [a]1Sam. 20:5
19 [I]Hebr. *greatly* [II]Hebr. *in the day of the business* [III]Or, *That showeth the way* [a]1Sam. 19:2
21 [I]Hebr. *not any thing* [a]Jer. 4:2
23 [a]1Sam. 20:14, 15, 42
26 [a]Lev. 7:21; 15:5
28 [a]1Sam. 20:6
30 [I]Hebr. *son of perverse rebellion*
31 [I]Hebr. *is the son of death*
32 [a]1Sam. 19:5; Matt. 27:23; Luke 23:22

33 And Saul [a]cast a javelin at him to
smite[5221] him: [b]whereby Jonathan knew
that it was determined of his father to
slay David.
34 So Jonathan arose from the table
in fierce[2750] anger, and did eat no meat
the second day of the month: for he was
grieved for David, because his father had
done him shame.
35 And it came to pass in the morning,
that Jonathan went out into the field
at the time appointed[4150] with David, and
a little lad with him.
36 And he said unto his lad, Run,
find out now the arrows which I shoot.
And as the lad ran, he shot an arrow
[I]beyond him.
37 And when the lad was come to
the place of the arrow which Jonathan
had shot, Jonathan cried[7121] after the lad,
and said, *Is* not the arrow beyond thee?
38 And Jonathan cried after the lad,
Make speed, haste, stay not. And
Jonathan's lad gathered up[3950] the arrows,
and came to his master.
39 But the lad knew not any thing:
only Jonathan and David knew the matter.
40 And Jonathan gave his
[I]artillery[3627] unto his [II]lad, and said unto
him, Go, carry *them* to the city.
41 *And* as soon as the lad was gone,
David arose out of *a place* toward the
south, and fell[5307] on his face[639] to the
ground,[776] and bowed[7812] himself three
times: and they kissed[5401] one another,[7453]
and wept one with another,
until David exceeded.[1419]
42 And Jonathan said to David, [a]Go
in peace, [I][b]forasmuch as we have sworn
both of us in the name of the LORD, saying,
The LORD be between me and thee,
and between my seed[2233] and thy seed
for ever. And he arose and departed: and
Jonathan went into the city.

33 [a]1Sam. 18:11 [b]1Sam. 20:7

36 [I]Hebr. *to pass over him*

40 [I]Hebr. *instruments* [II]Hebr. *that was his*

42 [I]Or, the LORD be witness of that *which* [a]1Sam. 1:17; [b]1Sam. 20:23

1 [a]1Sam. 14:3, also called *Ahiah* or *Abiathar;* ark 2:26 [b]1Sam. 16:4

3 [I]Hebr. *found*

4 [a]Ex. 25:30; Lev. 24:5; Matt. 12:4 [b]Ex. 19:15; Zech. 7:3

David Gets Help From Ahimelech

21 Then came David to Nob to
[a]Ahimelech the priest:[3548] and
Ahimelech was [b]afraid[2729] at the meeting
of David, and said unto him, Why *art*
thou alone, and no man with thee?
2 And David said unto Ahimelech
the priest, The king hath commanded[6680]
me a business,[1697] and hath said unto
me, Let no man know[3045] any thing of
the business whereabout I send thee, and
what I have commanded thee: and I have
appointed[3045] *my* servants to such and
such a place.
3 Now therefore what is under thine
hand? give *me* five *loaves of* bread in
mine hand, or what there is [I]present.
4 And the priest answered David,
and said, *There is* no common[2455]
bread under mine hand, but there is
[a]hallowed bread; [b]if the young men

21:1–6 According to the levitical law, the hallowed bread was only to be eaten by the priests who lived in the sanctuary (Lev. 24:9). However, there is a higher law than the levitical ordinance. It is the law of love for one's neighbor (Lev. 19:18). In the New Testament, Jesus summarized the ten commandments in what He called the two greatest commandments: to love God with one's entire being and to love one's neighbor as oneself (Matt. 22:37–40). According to this principle, the pressing need of David and his men to obtain food warranted an overriding of the levitical law. A similar instance occurred with Christ and His disciples as they picked and ate corn on the Sabbath because they had no other food (Matt. 12:3, 4; Mark 2:25, 26; Luke 6:3, 4). When confronted by the Pharisees about this violation of the letter of the law, Christ referred back to David's actions as an example of how the Pharisees' misunderstood the whole point of the laws and the Sabbath. Mercy and necessity override the letter, but not the spirit of the law (cf. Hos. 6:6), as Christ illustrated by healing on the Sabbath (Matt. 12:10–13).

The only stipulation which the priest set forth was that the men who were to eat the consecrated bread were not levitically defiled (cf. Lev. 15:18). David responded that he and his men had indeed kept themselves clean because of the mission which they were performing. He proclaimed in verse five that even though the levitical law regarding who should eat the bread was being broken, he and his men, as instruments of God, would make the bread become holy as they carried out their task for God.

have kept themselves[8104] at least from women.[802]

5 And David answered the priest, and said unto him, Of a truth women *have been* kept from us about these three days, since I came out, and the [a]vessels of the young men are holy, and *the bread is* in a manner common, [I]yea, though it were sanctified[6942] this day[3117] [b]in the vessel.

6 So the priest [a]gave him hallowed *bread:* for there was no bread there but the shewbread, [b]that was taken from before the LORD, to put hot bread in the day when it was taken away.

7 Now a certain man of the servants of Saul *was* there that day, detained before the LORD; and his name *was* [a]Doeg, an Edomite, the chiefest[47] of the herdmen that *belonged* to Saul.

8 And David said unto Ahimelech, And is there not here under thine hand spear or sword?[2719] for I have neither brought my sword nor my weapons with me, because the king's[4428] business required haste.

9 And the priest said, The sword of Goliath the Philistine, whom thou slewest[5221] in [a]the valley of Elah, [b]behold, it *is here* wrapped in a cloth behind the ephod: if thou wilt take that, take *it:* for *there is* no other save that here. And David said, *There is* none like that; give it me.

David Acts Insane

10 And David arose, and fled that day for fear of Saul, and went to [I]Achish the king of Gath.

11 And the servants of Achish said unto him, *Is* not this David the king of the land?[776] did they not sing one[376] to another[7453] of him in dances, saying, [a]Saul hath slain his thousands, and David his ten thousands?

12 And David [a]laid up[7760] these words[1697] in his heart, and was sore afraid[3372] of Achish the king of Gath.

13 And he changed[8138] his behaviour[2940] before them, and feigned himself mad in their hands, and [I]scrabbled[8427] on the doors of the gate, and let his spittle fall down upon his beard.[2206]

14 Then said Achish unto his servants, Lo, ye see the man [I]is mad: wherefore *then* have ye brought him to me?

15 Have I need of mad men, that ye have brought this *fellow* to play the mad man in my presence? shall this *fellow* come into my house?

David Raises a Small Army

22 David therefore departed thence, and escaped[4422] [a]to the cave Adullam: and when his brethren[251] and all his father's[1] house heard *it,* they went down thither to him.

2 [a]And every one *that was* in distress, and every one that [I]*was* in debt, and every one *that was* [II]discontented,[4751] gathered themselves[6908] unto him; and he became a captain[8269] over them: and there were with him about four hundred men.

3 And David went thence to Mizpeh of Moab: and he said unto the king of Moab, Let my father and my mother, I pray thee, come forth, *and be* with you, till I know[3045] what God[430] will do for me.

4 And he brought[5148] them before the king of Moab: and they dwelt with him all the while that David was in the hold.

5 And the prophet[5030] [a]Gad said unto David, Abide not in the hold; depart, and get thee into the land[776] of Judah. Then David departed, and came into the forest of Hareth.

Saul Kills the Priests Who Helped David

6 When Saul heard that David was discovered,[3045] and the men that *were* with him, (now Saul abode in Gibeah under a [I]tree in Ramah, having his spear in his hand, and all his servants *were* standing[5324] about him;)

7 Then Saul said unto his servants that stood about him, Hear now, ye Benja-

---

5 [I]Or, *especially when this day there is other sanctified in the vessel* [a]1Thess. 4:4 [b]Lev. 8:26

6 [a]Matt. 12:3, 4; Mark 2:25, 26; Luke 6:3, 4 [b]Lev. 24:8, 9

7 [a]1Sam. 22:9

9 [a]1Sam. 17:2, 50 [b]1Sam. 31:10

10 [I]Or, *Abimelech*

11 [a]1Sam. 18:7; 29:5; 1Chr. 14:8

12 [a]Luke 2:19

13 [I]Or, *made marks*

14 [I]Or, *playeth the madman*

1 [a]2Sam. 23:13

2 [I]Hebr. *had a creditor* [II]Hebr. *bitter of soul* [a]Judg. 11:3

5 [a]2Sam. 24:11; 1Chr. 21:9; 2Chr. 29:25

6 [I]Or, *grove in a high place*

mites; will the son[1121] of Jesse [a]give every one of you fields[7704] and vineyards, *and* make you all captains of thousands, and captains of hundreds;

8 That all of you have conspired against me, and *there is* none that [I][a]sheweth[241] me that [b]my son hath made a league with the son of Jesse, and *there is* none of you that is sorry for me, or sheweth unto me that my son hath stirred up my servant[5650] against me, to lie in wait, as at this day?

9 Then answered [a]Doeg the Edomite, which was set[5324] over the servants of Saul, and said, I saw[7200] the son of Jesse coming to Nob, to [b]Ahimelech the son of [c]Ahitub.

10 [a]And he enquired[7592] of the LORD for him, and [b]gave him victuals,[6720] and gave him the sword[2719] of Goliath the Philistine.

11 Then the king sent to call[7121] Ahimelech the priest,[3548] the son of Ahitub, and all his father's house, the priests[3548] that *were* in Nob: and they came all of them to the king.

12 And Saul said, Hear now, thou son of Ahitub. And he answered,[559] [I]Here I *am*, my lord.[113]

13 And Saul said unto him, Why have ye conspired against me, thou and the son of Jesse, in that thou hast given him bread, and a sword, and hast enquired of God for him, that he should rise against me, to lie in wait, as at this day?

14 Then Ahimelech answered the king, and said, And who *is so* faithful[539] among all thy servants as David, which is the king's son in law, and goeth at thy bidding,[4928] and is honourable in thine house?

15 Did I then begin to enquire[7592] of God for him? be it far from me: let not the king impute[7760] *any* thing unto his servant, *nor* to all the house of my father: for thy servant knew[3045] nothing of all this, [I]less or more.

16 And the king said, Thou shalt surely die,[4191] Ahimelech, thou, and all thy father's house.

17 And the king said unto the [I]footmen that stood about him, Turn, and slay[4191] the priests of the LORD; because their hand also *is* with David, and because they knew when he fled, and did not shew[1540] it to me. But the servants of the king [a]would[14] not put forth their hand to fall upon the priests of the LORD.

18 And the king said to Doeg, Turn thou, and fall upon the priests. And Doeg the Edomite turned, and he fell upon the priests, and [a]slew on that day fourscore and five persons[376] that did wear a linen ephod.

19 [a]And Nob, the city of the priests, smote[5221] he with the edge[6310] of the sword, both men and women,[802] children and sucklings, and oxen, and asses, and sheep, with the edge of the sword.

20 [a]And one of the sons of Ahimelech the son of Ahitub, named Abiathar, [b]escaped, and fled after David.

21 And Abiathar shewed[5046] David that Saul had slain[2026] the LORD's priests.

22 And David said unto Abiathar, I knew *it* that day, when Doeg the Edomite *was* there, that he would surely tell Saul: I have occasioned *the death* of all the persons[5315] of thy father's house.

23 Abide thou with me, fear[3372] not: [a]for he that seeketh my life[5315] seeketh thy life: but with me thou *shalt* be in safeguard.[4931]

David Rescues Keilah

23 Then they told David, saying, Behold, the Philistines fight against [a]Keilah, and they rob the threshingfloors.

2 Therefore David [a]enquired[7592] of the LORD, saying, Shall I go and smite[5221] these Philistines? And the LORD said unto David, Go, and smite the Philistines, and save Keilah.

3 And David's men said unto him, Behold, we be afraid[3373] here in Judah: how much more then if we come to Keilah against the armies of the Philistines?

4 Then David enquired of the LORD

---

7 [a]1Sam. 8:14
8 [I]Hebr. *uncovereth mine ear* [a]1Sam. 20:2 [b]1Sam. 18:3; 20:30
9 [a]1Sam. 21:7; 22:1-3 [b]1Sam. 21:1 [c]1Sam. 14:3
10 [a]Num. 27:21 [b]1Sam. 21:6, 9
12 [I]Hebr. *Behold me*
15 [I]Hebr. *little or great*
17 [I]Or, *guard;* Hebr. *runners* [a]Ex. 1:17
18 [a]1Sam. 2:31
19 [a]1Sam. 22:9, 11
20 [a]1Sam. 23:6 [b]1Sam. 2:33
23 [a]1Kgs. 2:26
1 [a]Josh. 15:44
2 [a]1Sam. 23:4, 6, 9; 30:8; 2Sam. 5:19, 23

yet again. And the LORD answered him and said, Arise, go down to Keilah; for I will deliver the Philistines into thine hand.

5 So David and his men went to Keilah, and fought with the Philistines, and brought away their cattle, and smote them with a great slaughter.[4347] So David saved[3467] the inhabitants of Keilah.

Saul Pursues David

🗝 6 And it came to pass, when Abiathar the son of Ahimelech [a]fled to David to Keilah, *that* he came down *with* an ephod in his hand.

7 And it was told Saul that David was come to Keilah. And Saul said, God[430] hath delivered him into mine hand; for he is shut in, by entering into a town that hath gates and bars.

8 And Saul called[8085] all the people[5971] together to war, to go down to Keilah, to besiege David and his men.

9 And David knew[3045] that Saul secretly practised mischief against him; and [a]he said to Abiathar the priest,[3548] Bring[5066] hither the ephod.

10 Then said David, O LORD God of Israel, thy servant[5650] hath certainly heard that Saul seeketh to come to Keilah, [a]to destroy[7843] the city for my sake.

11 Will the men of Keilah deliver me up into his hand? will Saul come down, as thy servant hath heard? O LORD God of Israel, I beseech thee,[4994] tell thy servant. And the LORD said, He will come down.

12 Then said David, Will the men of Keilah [I]deliver me and my men into the hand of Saul? And the LORD said, They will deliver *thee* up.

13 Then David and his men, [a]*which were* about six hundred, arose and departed out of Keilah, and went whithersoever they could go. And it was told Saul that David was escaped[4422] from Keilah; and he forbare to go forth.

14 And David abode in the wilderness in strong holds,[4679] and remained in [a]a mountain in the wilderness of [b]Ziph. And Saul [c]sought him every day,[3117] but God delivered him not into his hand.

15 And David saw[7200] that Saul was come out to seek his life:[5315] and David *was* in the wilderness of Ziph in a wood.

16 And Jonathan Saul's son arose, and went to David into the wood, and strengthened[2388] his hand in God.

17 And he said unto him, Fear[3372] not: for the hand of Saul my father[1] shall not find thee; and thou shalt be king[4427] over Israel, and I shall be next unto thee; and [a]that also Saul my father knoweth.

18 And they two [a]made a covenant[1285] before the LORD: and David abode in the wood, and Jonathan went to his house.

19 Then [a]came up the Ziphites to Saul to Gibeah, saying, Doth not David hide himself with us in strong holds in the wood, in the hill of Hachilah, which *is* [I]on the south of [II]Jeshimon?

20 Now therefore, O king, come down according to all the desire[183] of thy soul[5315] to come down; and [a]our part *shall be* to deliver him into the king's hand.

21 And Saul said, Blessed[1288] *be* ye of the LORD; for ye have compassion[2550] on me.

22 Go, I pray you, prepare[3559] yet, and know[3045] and see his place where his [I]haunt is, *and* who hath seen him there: for it is told me *that* he dealeth very subtilly.[6191]

23 See therefore, and take knowledge[3045] of all the lurking places where he hideth himself, and come ye again to me with the certainty,[3559] and I will go with you: and it shall come to pass, if he be in the land,[776] that I will search him out throughout all the thousands of Judah.

24 And they arose, and went to Ziph

6 [a]1Sam. 22:20
9 [a]Num. 27:21; 1Sam. 30:7
10 [a]1Sam. 22:19
12 [I]Hebr. *shut up*
13 [a]1Sam. 22:2; 25:13
14 [a]Ps. 11:1 [b]Josh. 15:55 [c]Ps. 54:3, 4
17 [a]1Sam. 24:20
18 [a]1Sam. 18:3; 20:16, 42; 2Sam. 21:7
19 [I]Hebr. *on the right hand* [II]Or, *the wilderness* [a]1Sam. 26:1
20 [a]Ps. 54:3
22 [I]Hebr. *foot shall be*

🗝 **23:6** See note on Exodus 28:30 concerning the ephod.

before Saul: but David and his men *were* in the wilderness [a]of Maon, in the plain[6160] on the south of Jeshimon.

25 Saul also and his men went to seek *him.* And they told David: wherefore he came down [I]into a rock, and abode in the wilderness of Maon. And when Saul heard *that,* he pursued after David in the wilderness of Maon.

26 And Saul went on this side of the mountain, and David and his men on that side of the mountain: [a]and David made haste to get away for fear of Saul; for Saul and his men [b]compassed David and his men round about to take them.

27 [a]But there came a messenger unto Saul, saying, Haste thee, and come; for the Philistines have [I]invaded the land.

28 Wherefore Saul returned from pursuing after David, and went against the Philistines: therefore they called[7121] that place [I]Sela–hammahlekoth.

29 And David went up from thence, and dwelt in strong holds at [a]En–gedi.

David Spares Saul in a Cave

24 And it came to pass, [a]when Saul was returned from [I]following the Philistines, that it was told him, saying, Behold, David *is* in the wilderness of En–gedi.

2 Then Saul took three thousand chosen men out of all Israel, and [a]went to seek David and his men upon the rocks of the wild goats.

3 And he came to the sheepcotes[1448,6629] by the way,[1870] where *was* a cave; and [a]Saul went in to [b]cover his feet: and David and his men remained in the sides of the cave.

4 [a]And the men of David said[559] unto him, Behold the day[3117] of which the LORD said unto thee, Behold, I will deliver thine enemy into thine hand, that thou mayest do[6213] to him as it shall seem good[3190] unto thee. Then David arose, and cut off[3772] the skirt of [I]Saul's robe privily.[3909]

5 And it came to pass afterward, that [a]David's heart smote[5221] him, because he had cut off Saul's skirt.

6 And he said unto his men, [a]The LORD forbid that I should do this thing unto my master, the LORD's anointed,[4899] to stretch forth mine hand against him, seeing he *is* the anointed of the LORD.

7 So David [I][a]stayed[8156] his servants[582] with these words,[1697] and suffered them not to rise against Saul. But Saul rose up out of the cave, and went on *his* way.

8 David also arose afterward, and went out of the cave, and cried[7121] after Saul, saying, My lord[113] the king.[4428] And when Saul looked behind him, David stooped with his face[639] to the earth,[776] and bowed[7812] himself.

9 And David said to Saul, [a]Wherefore hearest thou men's words, saying, Behold, David seeketh thy hurt?

10 Behold, this day thine eyes have seen[7200] how that the LORD had delivered thee to day into mine hand in the cave: and *some* bade *me* kill[2026] thee: but *mine eye* spared thee; and I said, I will not put forth mine hand against my lord; for he *is* the LORD's anointed.

11 Moreover, my father,[1] see, yea, see the skirt of thy robe in my hand: for in that I cut off the skirt of thy robe, and killed thee not, know[3045] thou and see that *there is* [a]neither evil[7451] nor transgression[6588] in mine hand, and I have not sinned[2398] against thee; yet thou [b]huntest my soul[5315] to take it.

12 [a]The LORD judge[8199] between me and thee, and the LORD avenge[5358] me of thee: but mine hand shall not be upon thee.

13 As saith[559] the proverb of the ancients, Wickedness[7562] proceedeth from the wicked:[7563] but mine hand shall not be upon thee.

14 After whom is the king of Israel come out? after whom dost thou pursue? [a]after a dead[4191] dog, after [b]a flea.

15 [a]The LORD therefore be judge, and judge between me and thee, and [b]see, and [c]plead[7378] my cause,[7379] and [I]deliver[8199] me out of thine hand.

---

24 [a]Josh. 15:55; 1Sam. 25:2

25 [I]Or, *from the rock*

26 [a]Ps. 31:22 [b]Ps. 17:9

27 [I]Hebr. *spread themselves upon* [a]2Kgs. 19:9

28 [I]That is, *the rock of divisions*

29 [a]2Chr. 20:2

1 [I]Hebr. *after* [a]1Sam. 23:28

2 [a]Ps. 38:12

3 [a]Ps. 141:6 [b]Judg. 3:24

4 [I]Hebr. *the robe which* was *Saul's* [a]1Sam. 26:8

5 [a]2Sam. 24:10

6 [a]1Sam. 26:11

7 [I]Hebr. *cut off* [a]Ps. 7:4; Matt. 5:44; Rom. 12:17, 19

9 [a]Ps. 141:6; Prov. 16:28; 17:9

11 [a]Ps. 7:3; 35:7 [b]1Sam. 26:20

12 [a]Gen. 16:5; Judg. 11:27; 1Sam. 26:10; Job 5:8

14 [a]1Sam. 17:43; 2Sam. 9:8 [b]1Sam. 26:20

15 [I]Hebr. *judge* [a]1Sam. 24:12 [b]2Chr. 24:22 [c]Ps. 35:1; 43:1; 119:154; Mic. 7:9

16 And it came to pass, when David had made an end[3615] of speaking[1696] these words unto Saul, that Saul said, [a]*Is* this thy voice, my son[1121] David? And Saul lifted up his voice, and wept.

17 [a]And he said to David, Thou *art* [b]more righteous than I: for [c]thou hast rewarded me good,[2896] whereas I have rewarded thee evil.

18 And thou hast shewed[5046] this day how that thou hast dealt[6213] well with me: forasmuch as when [a]the LORD had [I]delivered me into thine hand, thou killedst[2026] me not.

19 For if a man find his enemy, will he let him go well away? wherefore the LORD reward thee good for that thou hast done[6213] unto me this day.

20 And now, behold, [a]I know well that thou shalt surely be king,[4427] and that the kingdom[4467] of Israel shall be established in thine hand.

21 [a]Swear[7650] now therefore unto me by the LORD, [b]that thou wilt not cut off my seed[2233] after me, and that thou wilt not destroy[8045] my name out of my father's house.

22 And David sware[7650] unto Saul. And Saul went home; but David and his men gat them up unto [a]the hold.

Samuel's Death

25 And [a]Samuel died;[4191] and all the Israelites were gathered together,[6908] and [b]lamented him, and buried[6912] him in his house at Ramah.

David and Abigail

And David arose, and went down [a]to the wilderness of Paran.

2 And *there was* a man [a]in Maon, whose [I]possessions *were* in [b]Carmel; and the man *was* very great, and he had three thousand sheep, and a thousand goats: and he was shearing his sheep in Carmel.

3 Now the name of the man *was* Nabal; and the name of his wife[802] Abigail: and *she was* a woman[802] of good[2896] understanding,[7922] and of a beautiful countenance: but the man *was* churlish[7186] and evil[7451] in his doings; and he *was* of the house of Caleb.

4 And David heard in the wilderness that Nabal did [a]shear his sheep.

5 And David sent out ten young men, and David said[559] unto the young men, Get you up to Carmel, and go to Nabal, and [I]greet him in my name:

6 And thus shall ye say to him that liveth[2416] *in prosperity,* [a]Peace[7965] *be* both to thee, and peace *be* to thine house, and peace *be* unto all that thou hast.

7 And now I have heard that thou hast shearers: now thy shepherds which were with us, we [I]hurt them not, [a]neither was there ought missing unto them, all the while they were in Carmel.

8 Ask[7592] thy young men, and they will shew[5046] thee. Wherefore let the young men find favour[2580] in thine eyes: for we come in [a]a good day:[3117] give, I pray thee, whatsoever cometh to thine hand unto thy servants, and to thy son[1121] David.

9 And when David's young men came, they spake[1696] to Nabal according to all those words[1697] in the name of David, and [I]ceased.

10 And Nabal answered David's servants, and said, [a]Who *is* David? and who *is* the son of Jesse? there be many servants now a days[3117] that break away every man from his master.

11 [a]Shall I then take my bread, and my water, and my [I]flesh[2878] that I have killed[2873] for my shearers, and give *it* unto men, whom I know[3045] not whence they *be?*

12 So David's young men turned their way,[1870] and went again, and came and told him all those sayings.[1697]

13 And David said unto his men, Gird ye on every man his sword.[2719] And they girded on every man his sword; and David also girded on his sword: and there went up after David about four hundred men; and two hundred [a]abode by the stuff.

14 But one of the young men told Abigail, Nabal's wife, saying, Behold, David sent messengers[4397] out of the

---

16 [a]1Sam. 26:17
17 [a]1Sam. 26:21 [b]Gen. 38:26 [c]Matt. 5:44
18 [I]Hebr. *shut up* [a]1Sam. 23:12; 26:8, 23
20 [a]1Sam. 23:17
21 [a]Gen. 21:23 [b]2Sam. 21:6, 8
22 [a]1Sam. 23:29
1 [a]1Sam. 28:3 [b]Num. 20:29; Deut. 34:8 [c]Gen. 21:21; Ps. 120:5
2 [I]Or, *business* [a]1Sam. 23:24 [b]Josh. 15:55
4 [a]Gen. 38:13; 2Sam. 13:23
5 [I]Hebr. *ask him in my name of peace*
6 [a]1Chr. 12:18; Ps. 122:7; Luke 10:5
7 [I]Hebr. *shamed* [a]1Sam. 25:15, 21
8 [a]Neh. 8:10; Esth. 9:19
9 [I]Hebr. *rested*
10 [a]Judg. 9:28; Ps. 73:7, 8; 123:3, 4
11 [I]Hebr. *slaughter* [a]Judg. 8:6
13 [a]1Sam. 30:24

wilderness to salute[1288] our master; and he [I]railed on them.

15 But the men *were* very good unto us, and [a]we were not [I]hurt, neither missed[6485] we any thing, as long as we were conversant with them, when we were in the fields:[7704]

16 They were [a]a wall unto us both by night[3915] and day,[3119] all the while we were with them keeping the sheep.

17 Now therefore know and consider[7200] what thou wilt do;[6213] for [a]evil is determined[3615] against our master, and against all his household: for he *is such* a son of [b]Belial,[1100] that *a man* cannot speak[1696] to him.

18 Then Abigail made haste, and [a]took two hundred loaves, and two bottles of wine, and five sheep ready dressed,[6213] and five measures of parched *corn,* and an hundred [I]clusters of raisins, and two hundred cakes of figs, and laid[7760] *them* on asses.

19 And she said unto her servants, [a]Go on before me; behold, I come after you. But she told not her husband Nabal.

20 And it was *so, as* she rode on the ass, that she came down by the covert[5643] of the hill, and, behold, David and his men came down against her; and she met them.

21 Now David had said, Surely in vain[8267] have I kept[8104] all that this *fellow* hath in the wilderness, so that nothing was missed of all that *pertained* unto him: and he hath [a]requited me evil for good.

22 [a]So and more also do God[430] unto the enemies of David, if I [b]leave[7604] of all that *pertain* to him by the morning light[216] [c]any that pisseth against the wall.

23 And when Abigail saw[7200] David, she hasted, and [a]lighted off the ass, and fell[5307] before David on her face, and bowed[7812] herself to the ground,[776]

24 And fell at his feet, and said, Upon me, my lord,[113] *upon* me *let this* iniquity[5771] *be*: and let thine handmaid, I pray thee, speak in thine [I]audience, and hear the words of thine handmaid.

25 Let not my lord, I pray thee, [I]regard this man of Belial, *even* Nabal: for as his name *is,* so *is* he; [II]Nabal *is* his name, and folly *is* with him: but I thine handmaid saw not the young men of my lord, whom thou didst send.

26 Now therefore, my lord, [a]*as* the LORD liveth, and *as* thy soul[5315] liveth, seeing the LORD hath [b]withholden[4513] thee from coming to *shed* blood,[1818] and from [I][c]avenging[3467] thyself with thine own hand, now [d]let thine enemies, and they that seek evil to my lord, be as Nabal.

27 And now [a]this [I]blessing[1293] which thine handmaid hath brought unto my lord, let it even be given unto the young men that [II]follow my lord.

28 I pray thee, forgive[5375] the trespass of thine handmaid: [a]for the LORD will certainly make my lord a sure house; because my lord [b]fighteth the battles of the LORD, and [c]evil hath not been found in thee *all* thy days.

29 Yet a man is risen to pursue thee, and to seek thy soul:[5315] but the soul of my lord shall be bound in the bundle of life[2416] with the LORD thy God; and the souls of thine enemies, them shall he [a]sling out, *as out* of the middle of a sling.

30 And it shall come to pass, when the LORD shall have done[6213] to my lord according to all the good that he hath spoken[1696] concerning thee, and shall have appointed[6680] thee ruler over Israel;

31 That this shall be no grief unto thee, nor offence[4385] of heart unto my lord, either that thou hast shed[8210] blood causeless,[2600] or that my lord hath avenged himself: but when the LORD shall have dealt[6213] well[3190] with my lord, then remember thine handmaid.

32 And David said to Abigail, [a]Blessed[1288] *be* the LORD God of Israel, which sent thee this day to meet me:

33 And blessed *be* thy advice,[2940] and blessed *be* thou, which hast [a]kept me this day from coming to *shed* blood, and from avenging myself with mine own hand.

34 For in very deed, *as* the LORD God

14 [I]Hebr. *flew upon them*

15 [I]Hebr. *shamed* [a]1Sam. 25:7

16 [a]Ex. 14:22; Job 1:10

17 [a]1Sam. 20:7 [b]Deut. 13:13; Judg. 19:22

18 [I]Or, *lumps* [a]Gen. 32:13; Prov. 18:16; 21:14

19 [a]Gen. 32:16, 20

21 [a]Ps. 109:5; Prov. 17:13

22 [a]Ruth 1:17; 1Sam. 3:17; 20:13, 16 [b]1Sam. 25:34 [c]1Kgs. 14:10; 21:21; 2Kgs. 9:8

23 [a]Josh. 15:18; Judg. 1:14

24 [I]Hebr. *ears*

25 [I]Hebr. *lay it to his heart* [II]That is, *Fool*

26 [I]Hebr. *saving thyself* [a]2Kgs. 2:2 [b]Gen. 20:6; 1Sam. 25:33 [c]Rom. 12:19 [d]2Sam. 18:32

27 [I]Or, *present* [II]Hebr. *walk at the feet of* [a]Gen. 33:11; 1Sam. 30:26; 2Kgs. 5:15

28 [a]2Sam. 7:11, 27; 1Kgs. 9:5; 1Chr. 17:10, 25; [b]1Sam. 18:17 [c]1Sam. 24:11

29 [a]Jer. 10:18

32 [a]Gen. 24:27; Ex. 18:10; Ps. 41:13; 72:18; Luke 1:68

33 [a]1Sam. 25:26

of Israel liveth, which hath [a]kept me
back from hurting thee, except thou
hadst hasted and come to meet me,
surely there had [b]not been left[3498] unto
Nabal by the morning light any that pisseth against the wall.
35 So David received of her hand
that which she had brought him, and said
unto her, [a]Go up in peace to thine house;
see, I have hearkened to thy voice, and
have [b]accepted[5375] thy person.
36 And Abigail came to Nabal; and,
behold, [a]he held a feast in his house, like
the feast[4960] of a king;[4428] and Nabal's
heart *was* merry within him, for he *was*
very drunken: wherefore she told him
nothing, less or more, until the morning
light.
37 But it came to pass in the morning, when the wine was gone out of
Nabal, and his wife had told him these
things, that his heart died within[7130] him,
and he became *as* a stone.
38 And it came to pass about ten
days *after,* that the LORD smote[5062] Nabal,
that he died.
39 And when David heard that Nabal
was dead,[4191] he said, [a]Blessed *be*
the LORD, that hath [b]pleaded[7378] the
cause[7379] of my reproach from the hand
of Nabal, and hath [c]kept his servant[5650]
from evil: for the LORD hath [d]returned
the wickedness[7451] of Nabal upon his
own head. And David sent and communed with Abigail, to take her to him
to wife.
40 And when the servants of David were come to Abigail to Carmel,
they spake unto her, saying, David
sent us unto thee, to take thee to him to
wife.
41 And she arose, and bowed herself
on *her* face[639] to the earth,[776] and said,
Behold, *let* [a]thine handmaid *be* a servant
to wash[7364] the feet of the servants of
my lord.

34 [a]1Sam. 25:26 [b]1Sam. 25:22

35 [a]1Sam. 20:42; 2Sam. 15:9; 2Kgs. 5:19; Luke 7:50; 8:48 [b]Gen. 19:21

36 [a]2Sam. 13:23

39 [a]1Sam. 25:32 [b]Prov. 22:23 [c]1Sam. 25:26; 34 [d]1Kgs. 2:44; Ps. 7:16

41 [a]Ruth 2:10, 13; Prov. 15:33

42 [1]Hebr. *at her feet*

43 [a]Josh. 15:56 [b]1Sam. 27:3; 30:5

44 [1]*Phaltiel* [a]2Sam. 3:15 [b]2Sam. 3:14 [c]Isa. 10:30

1 [a]1Sam. 23:19

5 [1]Or, *midst of his carriages* [a]1Sam. 14:50; 17:55 [b]1Sam. 17:20

6 [a]1Chr. 2:16 [b]Judg. 7:10, 11

42 And Abigail hasted, and arose,
and rode upon an ass, with five damsels
of hers that went [1]after her; and she went
after the messengers of David, and became his wife.
43 David also took Ahinoam [a]of
Jezreel; [b]and they were also both of them
his wives.[802]
🔑44 But Saul had given [a]Michal his
daughter, David's wife, to [1][b]Phalti the son
of Laish, which *was* of [c]Gallim.

David Spares Saul Again

26 And the Ziphites came unto Saul
to Gibeah, saying, [a]Doth not
David hide himself in the hill of
Hachilah, *which is* before Jeshimon?
2 Then Saul arose, and went down to
the wilderness of Ziph, having three
thousand chosen[977] men of Israel with
him, to seek David in the wilderness of
Ziph.
3 And Saul pitched in the hill of Hachilah, which *is* before Jeshimon, by the
way.[1870] But David abode in the wilderness, and he saw[7200] that Saul came after
him into the wilderness.
4 David therefore sent out spies, and
understood[3045] that Saul was come in
very deed.
5 And David arose, and came to the
place where Saul had pitched: and David
beheld[7200] the place where Saul lay, and
[a]Abner the son[1121] of Ner, the captain[8269]
of his host: and Saul lay in the [1][b]trench,
and the people[5971] pitched round about
him.
6 Then answered David and said[559]
to Ahimelech the Hittite, and to Abishai
[a]the son of Zeruiah, brother[251] to Joab,
saying, Who will [b]go down with me to
Saul to the camp?[4264] And Abishai said,
I will go down with thee.
7 So David and Abishai came to the
people by night:[3915] and, behold, Saul lay

🔑 **25:44** Saul's second daughter, Michal, had been given in marriage to David for slaying Goliath. However, Saul, while pursuing David, decided to give her to another man. Later, David demanded her back (2 Sam. 3:14), but she no longer loved him (2 Sam. 6:16). Shortly thereafter, Michal died childless (2 Sam. 6:23).

sleeping within the trench,4570 and his spear stuck in the ground[776] at his bolster:[4763] but Abner and the people lay round about him.

8 Then said Abishai to David, God[430] hath [I][a]delivered thine enemy into thine hand this day:[3117] now therefore let me smite[5221] him, I pray thee,[4994] with the spear even to the earth[776] at once, and I will not *smite* him the second time.

9 And David said to Abishai, Destroy[7843] him not: [a]for who can stretch forth his hand against the LORD's anointed, and be guiltless?[5352]

10 David said furthermore, *As* the LORD liveth,[2416] [a]the LORD shall smite[5062] him; or [b]his day shall come to die; or he shall [c]descend into battle, and perish.[5595]

11 [a]The LORD forbid that I should stretch forth mine hand against the LORD's anointed: but, I pray thee, take thou now the spear that *is* at his bolster, and the cruse6835 of water, and let us go.

12 So David took the spear and the cruse of water from Saul's bolster; and they gat them away, and no man saw *it,* nor knew[3045] *it,* neither awaked: for they *were* all asleep; because [a]a deep sleep from the LORD was fallen[5307] upon them.

13 Then David went over to the other side, and stood on the top of a hill afar off; a great space *being* between them:

14 And David cried[7121] to the people, and to Abner the son of Ner, saying, Answerest thou not, Abner? Then Abner answered and said, Who *art* thou *that* criest to the king?

15 And David said to Abner, *Art* not thou a *valiant* man? and who *is* like to thee in Israel? wherefore then hast thou not kept[8104] thy lord[113] the king? for there came one of the people in to destroy the king thy lord.

16 This thing *is* not good[2896] that thou hast done.[6213] *As* the LORD liveth, ye *are* [I][a]worthy to die, because ye have not kept your master, the LORD's anointed.[4899]

8 IHebr. *shut up* [a]1Sam. 24:18

9 [a]1Sam. 24:6, 7; 2Sam. 1:16

10 [a]1Sam. 25:38; Ps. 94:1, 2, 23; Luke 18:7; Rom. 12:19 [b]Gen. 47:29; Deut. 31:14; Job 7:1; 14:5; Ps. 37:13 [c]1Sam. 31:6

11 [a]1Sam. 24:6, 12

12 [a]Gen. 2:21; 15:12

16 IHebr. *the sons of death* [a]2Sam. 12:5

17 [a]1Sam. 24:16

18 [a]1Sam. 24:9, 11

19 IHebr. *smell* IIHebr. *cleaving* [a]2Sam. 16:11; 24:1 [b]Deut. 4:28; Ps. 120:5 [c]2Sam. 14:16; 20:19

20 [a]1Sam. 24:14

21 [a]1Sam. 15:24; 24:17 [b]1Sam. 18:30

23 [a]Ps. 7:8; 18:20

25 [a]Gen. 32:28

And now see where the king's[4428] spear *is,* and the cruse of water that *was* at his bolster.

17 And Saul knew[5234] David's voice, and said, [a]*Is* this thy voice, my son David? And David said, *It is* my voice, my lord, O king.

18 And he said, [a]Wherefore doth my lord thus pursue after his servant?[5650] for what have I done? or what evil[7451] *is* in mine hand?

19 Now therefore, I pray thee, let my lord the king hear the words[1697] of his servant. If the LORD have [a]stirred thee up5496 against me, let him [I]accept[7306] an offering:[4503] but if *they be* the children[1121] of men, cursed[779] *be* they before the LORD; [b]for they have driven me out this day from [II]abiding in the [c]inheritance[5159] of the LORD, saying, Go, serve other gods.[430]

20 Now therefore, let not my blood[1818] fall to the earth before the face of the LORD: for the king of Israel is come out to seek [a]a flea, as when one doth hunt a partridge in the mountains.

21 Then said Saul, [a]I have sinned:[2398] return, my son David: for I will no more do thee harm, because my soul[5315] was [b]precious in thine eyes this day: behold, I have played the fool, and have erred[7683] exceedingly.

22 And David answered and said, Behold the king's spear! and let one of the young men come over and fetch it.

23 [a]The LORD render to every man his righteousness and his faithfulness:[530] for the LORD delivered thee into *my* hand to day, but I would[14] not stretch forth mine hand against the LORD's anointed.

24 And, behold, as thy life[5315] was much set by this day in mine eyes, so let my life be much set by in the eyes of the LORD, and let him deliver[5337] me out of all tribulation.

25 Then Saul said to David, Blessed[1288] *be* thou, my son David: thou shalt both do[6213] great *things,* and also shalt still [a]prevail. So David went on his way, and Saul returned to his place.

David Returns to Gath

27 And David said[559] in his heart, I shall now [I]perish[5595] one day[3117] by the hand of Saul: *there is* nothing better[2896] for me than that I should speedily escape[4422] into the land[776] of the Philistines; and Saul shall despair[2976] of me, to seek me any more in any coast of Israel: so shall I escape out of his hand.

2 And David arose, [a]and he passed over[5674] with the six hundred men that *were* with him [b]unto Achish, the son[1121] of Maoch, king[4428] of Gath.

3 And David dwelt with Achish at Gath, he and his men, every man with his household, *even* David [a]with his two wives,[802] Ahinoam the Jezreelitess, and Abigail the Carmelitess, Nabal's wife.

4 And it was told Saul that David was fled to Gath: and he sought no more again for him.

5 And David said unto Achish, If I have now found grace[2580] in thine eyes, let them give me a place in some town in the country,[7704] that I may dwell there: for why should thy servant[5650] dwell in the royal city with thee?

6 Then Achish gave him Ziklag that day: wherefore [a]Ziklag pertaineth[1961] unto the kings of Judah unto this day.

7 And [I]the time that David dwelt in the country of the Philistines was [II][a]a full year and four months.

8 And David and his men went up, and invaded[6584] [a]the Geshurites, [b]and the [I]Gezrites, and the [c]Amalekites: for those *nations were* of old[5769] the inhabitants of the land, [d]as thou goest to Shur, even unto the land of Egypt.

9 And David smote[5221] the land, and left neither man[376] nor woman[802] alive, and took away the sheep, and the oxen, and the asses, and the camels, and the apparel, and returned, and came to Achish.

10 And Achish said, [I]Whither have ye made a road to day? And David said, Against the south of Judah, and against the south of [a]the Jerahmeelites, and against the south of [b]the Kenites.

11 And David saved[2421] neither man nor woman alive, to bring *tidings* to Gath, saying, Lest they should tell on us, saying, So did[6213] David, and so *will be* his manner all the while he dwelleth in the country of the Philistines.

12 And Achish believed[539] David, saying, He hath made his people[5971] Israel [I]utterly to abhor[887] him; therefore he shall be my servant for ever.

28 And [a]it came to pass in those days,[3117] that the Philistines gathered their armies together[6908] for warfare,[6635] to fight with Israel. And Achish said[559] unto David, Know[3045] thou assuredly, that thou shalt go out with me to battle, thou and thy men.

2 And David said to Achish, Surely thou shalt know what thy servant[5650] can do.[6213] And Achish said to David, Therefore will I make thee keeper[8104] of mine head for ever.

Saul and the Medium at Endor

3 Now [a]Samuel was dead,[4191] and all Israel had lamented him, and buried[6912] him in Ramah, even in his own city. And Saul had put away [b]those that had familiar spirits, and the wizards,[3049] out of the land.[776]

4 And the Philistines gathered themselves together, and came and pitched in [a]Shunem: and Saul gathered all Israel together, and they pitched in [b]Gilboa.

5 And when Saul saw[7200] the host of the Philistines, he was [a]afraid,[3372] and his heart greatly trembled.

🔑 6 And when Saul enquired[7592] of the LORD, [a]the LORD answered him not, neither by [b]dreams, nor [c]by Urim,[217] nor by prophets.[5030]

7 Then said Saul unto his servants,

27:1 [I]Hebr. *be consumed*
2 [a]1Sam. 25:13 [b]1Sam. 21:10
3 [a]1Sam. 25:43
6 [a]Josh. 15:31; 19:5
7 [I]Hebr. *the number of days* [II]Hebr. a year of *days* [a]1Sam. 29:3
8 [I]Or, *Gerzites* [a]Josh. 13:2 [b]Josh. 16:10; Judg. 1:29 [c]Ex. 17:16; 1Sam. 15:7, 8 [d]Gen. 25:18
10 [I]Or, *Did you not make a road* [a]1Chr. 2:9, 25 [b]Judg. 1:16
12 [I]Hebr. *to stink*

28:1 [a]1Sam. 29:1
3 [a]1Sam. 25:1 [b]1Sam. 28:9; Ex. 22:18; Lev. 19:31; 20:27; Deut. 18:10, 11
4 [a]Josh. 19:18; 2Kgs. 4:8 [b]1Sam. 31:1
5 [a]Job 18:11
6 [a]1Sam. 14:37; Prov. 1:28; Lam. 2:9 [b]Num. 12:6 [c]Ex. 28:30; Num. 27:21; Deut. 33:8

🔑 **28:6** See note on Exodus 28:30 concerning the Urim and Thummim.

Seek me a woman[802] that hath a familiar spirit,[178] that I may go to her, and enquire of her. And his servants said to him, Behold, *there is* a woman that hath a familiar spirit at Endor.

8 And Saul disguised himself, and put on other raiment, and he went, and two men with him, and they came to the woman by night:[3915] and [a]he said, I pray thee,[4994] divine[7080] unto me by the familiar spirit, and bring me *him* up, whom I shall name unto thee.

9 And the woman said unto him, Behold, thou knowest[3045] what Saul hath done, how he hath [a]cut off[3772] those that have familiar spirits, and the wizards, out of the land: wherefore then layest thou a snare[5367] for my life,[5315] to cause me to die?[4191]

10 And Saul sware[7650] to her by the LORD, saying, *As* the LORD liveth,[2416] there shall no punishment[5771] happen to thee for this thing.

11 Then said the woman, Whom shall I bring up unto thee? And he said, Bring me up Samuel.

12 And when the woman saw Samuel, she cried[2199] with a loud voice: and the woman spake[559] to Saul, saying, Why hast thou deceived me? for thou *art* Saul.

13 And the king said unto her, Be not afraid: for what sawest[7200] thou? And the woman said unto Saul, I saw [a]gods[430] ascending[5927] out of the earth.[776]

14 And he said unto her, [I]What form *is* he of? And she said, An old[2205] man cometh up; and he *is* covered with [a]a mantle.[4598] And Saul perceived[3045] that it *was* Samuel, and he stooped with *his* face[639] to the ground,[776] and bowed[7812] himself.

15 And Samuel said to Saul, Why hast thou disquieted[7264] me, to bring me up? And Saul answered, [a]I am sore distressed; for the Philistines make war against me, and [b]God[430] is departed from me, and [c]answereth me no more, neither by [I]prophets, nor by dreams: therefore I have called[7121] thee, that thou mayest make known[3045] unto me what I shall do.

16 Then said Samuel, Wherefore then dost thou ask[7592] of me, seeing the LORD is departed from thee, and is become[1961] thine enemy?

17 And the LORD hath done [I]to him, [a]as he spake[1696] by [II]me: for the LORD hath rent the kingdom out of thine hand, and given it to thy neighbour,[7453] *even* to David:

18 [a]Because thou obeyedst[8085] not the voice of the LORD, nor executedst[6213] his fierce wrath[639] upon Amalek, therefore hath the LORD done this thing unto thee this day.

19 Moreover the LORD will also deliver Israel with thee into the hand of the Philistines: and to morrow *shalt* thou and thy sons[1121] *be* with me: the LORD also shall deliver the host of Israel into the hand of the Philistines.

20 Then Saul [I]fell[5307] straightway[4116] all along on the earth, and was sore afraid, because of the words[1697] of Samuel: and there was no strength in him; for he had eaten no bread all the day, nor all the night.

21 And the woman came unto Saul, and saw that he was sore troubled, and said unto him, Behold, thine handmaid hath obeyed[8085] thy voice, and I have [a]put my life in my hand, and have harkened unto thy words which thou spakest[1696] unto me.

22 Now therefore, I pray thee, hearken thou also unto the voice of thine handmaid, and let me set a morsel of bread before thee; and eat, that thou mayest have strength, when thou goest on thy way.[1870]

23 But he refused, and said, I will not eat. But his servants, together with the woman, compelled him; and he hearkened unto their voice. So he arose from the earth, and sat upon the bed.

24 And the woman had a fat calf in the house; and she hasted, and killed[2076] it, and took flour, and kneaded *it,* and did bake unleavened bread[4682] thereof:

25 And she brought[5066] *it* before Saul, and before his servants; and they

---

8 [a]Deut. 18:11; 1Chr. 10:13; Isa. 8:19
9 [a]1Sam. 28:3
13 [a]Ex. 22:28
14 [I]Hebr. What is *his form?* [a]1Sam. 15:27; 2Kgs. 2:8, 13
15 [I]Hebr. *by the hand of prophets* [a]Prov. 5:11-13; 14:14 [b]1Sam. 18:12 [c]1Sam. 28:6
17 [I]Or, *for himself* [II]Hebr. *mine hand* [a]1Sam. 15:28
18 [a]1Sam. 15:9; 1Kgs. 20:42; 1Chr. 10:13; Jer. 48:10
20 [I]Hebr. *made haste, and fell with the fulness of his stature*
21 [a]Judg. 12:3; 1Sam. 19:5; Job 13:14

did eat. Then they rose up, and went away that night.

The Philistines Question David's Loyalty

29 Now [a]the Philistines gathered together[6908] all their armies [b]to Aphek: and the Israelites pitched by a fountain which *is* in Jezreel.

2 And the lords[5633] of the Philistines passed on[5674] by hundreds, and by thousands: but David and his men passed on in the rereward[314] [a]with Achish.

3 Then said[559] the princes[8269] of the Philistines, What *do* these Hebrews *here*? And Achish said unto the princes of the Philistines, *Is* not this David, the servant[5650] of Saul the king of Israel, which hath been with me [a]these days,[3117] or these years, and I have [b]found no fault in him since he fell[5307] *unto me* unto this day?

4 And the princes of the Philistines were wroth[7107] with him; and the princes of the Philistines said unto him, [a]Make this fellow[376] return, that he may go again to his place which thou hast appointed him, and let him not go down with us to battle, lest [b]in the battle he be an adversary[7854] to us: for wherewith should he reconcile[7521] himself unto his master? *should it* not *be* with the heads of these men?

5 *Is* not this David, of whom they sang one to another[7453] in dances, saying, [a]Saul slew[5221] his thousands, and David his ten thousands?

6 Then Achish called[7121] David, and said unto him, Surely, *as* the LORD liveth,[2416] thou hast been upright,[3477] and [a]thy going out and thy coming in with me in the host *is* good[2896] in my sight: for [b]I have not found evil[7451] in thee since the day of thy coming unto me unto this day: nevertheless [I]the lords favour thee not.

7 Wherefore now return, and go in peace, that thou [I]displease not the lords of the Philistines.

8 And David said unto Achish, But what have I done?[6213] and what hast thou found in thy servant so long as I have been [I]with thee unto this day, that I may not go fight against the enemies of my lord[113] the king?

9 And Achish answered and said to David, I know[3045] that thou *art* good in my sight, [a]as an angel[4397] of God:[430] notwithstanding [b]the princes of the Philistines have said, He shall not go up with us to the battle.

10 Wherefore now rise up early in the morning with thy master's servants that are come with thee: and as soon as ye be up early in the morning, and have light,[216] depart.

11 So David and his men rose up early to depart in the morning, to return into the land[776] of the Philistines. [a]And the Philistines went up to Jezreel.

David Defeats the Amalekites

30 And it came to pass, when David and his men were come to Ziklag on the third day, that the [a]Amalekites had invaded the south, and Ziklag, and smitten[5221] Ziklag, and burned[8313] it with fire;

2 And had taken the women captives,[7617] that *were* therein: they slew[4191] not any, either great or small, but carried *them* away, and went on their way.[1870]

3 So David and his men came to the city, and, behold, *it was* burned with fire; and their wives, and their sons,[1121] and their daughters, were taken captives.

4 Then David and the people[5971] that *were* with him lifted up their voice and wept, until they had no more power to weep.

5 And David's [a]two wives were taken captives, Ahinoam the Jezreelitess, and Abigail the wife[802] of Nabal the Carmelite.

6 And David was greatly distressed; [a]for the people spake[559] of stoning him, because the soul[5315] of all the people was [I]grieved, every man for his sons and for his daughters: [b]but David encouraged himself[2388] in the LORD his God.[430]

---

1 [a]1Sam. 28:1 [b]1Sam. 4:1
2 [a]1Sam. 28:1, 2
3 [a]1Sam. 27:7 [b]Dan. 6:5
4 [a]1Chr. 12:19 [b]1Sam. 14:21
5 [a]1Sam. 18:7; 21:11
6 [I]*thou art not good in the eyes of the lords* [a]2Sam. 3:25; 2Kgs. 19:27 [b]1Sam. 29:3
7 [I]Hebr. *do not evil in the eyes of the lords*
8 [I]Hebr. *before thee*
9 [a]2Sam. 14:17, 20; 19:27 [b]1Sam. 29:4
11 [a]2Sam. 4:4
1 [a]1Sam. 15:7; 27:8
5 [a]1Sam. 25:42, 43; 2Sam. 2:2
6 [I]Hebr. *bitter* [a]Ex. 17:4 [b]Ps. 42:5; 56:3, 4, 11; Hab. 3:17, 18

7 [a]And David said to Abiathar the priest,[3548] Ahimelech's son, I pray thee, bring me hither[5066] the ephod. And Abiathar brought thither the ephod to David.

8 [a]And David enquired[7592] at the LORD, saying, Shall I pursue after this troop? shall I overtake them? And he answered[559] him, Pursue: for thou shalt surely overtake *them,* and without fail recover *all.*

9 So David went, he and the six hundred men that *were* with him, and came to the brook Besor, where those that were left behind[3498] stayed.

10 But David pursued, he and four hundred men: [a]for two hundred abode behind, which were so faint that they could not go over the brook Besor.

11 And they found an Egyptian in the field,[7704] and brought him to David, and gave him bread, and he did eat; and they made him drink water;

12 And they gave him a piece of a cake of figs, and two clusters of raisins: and [a]when he had eaten, his spirit[7307] came again to him: for he had eaten no bread, nor drunk *any* water, three days[3117] and three nights.[3915]

13 And David said unto him, To whom *belongest* thou? and whence *art* thou? And he said, I *am* a young man of Egypt, servant[5650] to an Amalekite; and my master left[5800] me, because three days agone I fell sick.

14 We made an invasion *upon* the south of [a]the Cherethites, and upon *the coast* which *belongeth* to Judah, and upon the south of [b]Caleb; and we burned Ziklag with fire.

15 And David said to him, Canst thou bring me down to this company?[1466] And he said, Swear[7650] unto me by God, that thou wilt neither kill[4191] me, nor deliver me into the hands of my master, and I will bring thee down to this company.

16 And when he had brought him down, behold, *they were* spread abroad[5203] upon all the earth,[776] [a]eating and drinking, and dancing, because of all the great spoil that they had taken out of the land[776] of the Philistines, and out of the land of Judah.

17 And David smote[5221] them from the twilight even unto the evening of [I]the next day: and there escaped[4422] not a man of them, save four hundred young men, which rode upon camels, and fled.

18 And David recovered all that the Amalekites had carried away: and David rescued his two wives.

19 And there was nothing lacking to them, neither small nor great, neither sons nor daughters, neither spoil, nor any *thing* that they had taken to them: [a]David recovered all.

20 And David took all the flocks and the herds, *which* they drave before those *other* cattle, and said, This *is* David's spoil.

21 And David came to the [a]two hundred men, which were so faint that they could not follow David, whom they had made also to abide at the brook Besor: and they went forth to meet David, and to meet the people that *were* with him: and when David came near[5066] to the people, he [I]saluted them.

22 Then answered all the wicked[7451] men and *men* [a]of Belial,[1100] of [I]those that went with David, and said, Because they went not with us, we will not give them *ought* of the spoil that we have recovered, save to every man his wife and his children,[1121] that they may lead *them* away, and depart.

23 Then said David, Ye shall not do[6213] so, my brethren,[251] with that which the LORD hath given us, who hath preserved us, and delivered the company that came against us into our hand.

24 For who will hearken unto you in this matter? but [a]as his part[2506] *is* that goeth down to the battle, so *shall* his part *be* that tarrieth by the stuff: they shall part alike.

25 And it was *so* from that day [I]forward, that he made it a statute[2706] and an ordinance[4941] for Israel unto this day.

26 And when David came to Ziklag, he sent of the spoil unto the elders[2205] of Judah, *even* to his friends,[7453] saying,

7 [a]1Sam. 23:6, 9
8 [a]1Sam. 23:2, 4
10 [a]1Sam. 30:21
12 [a]Judg. 15:19; 1Sam. 14:27
14 [a]1Sam. 30:16; 2Sam. 8:18; 1Kgs. 1:38, 44; Ezek. 25:16; Zeph. 2:5 [b]Josh. 14:13; 15:13
16 [a]1Thess. 5:3
17 [I]Hebr. *their morrow*
19 [a]1Sam. 30:8
21 [I]Or, *asked the how they did* [a]1Sam. 30:10
22 [I]Hebr. *men* [a]Deut. 13:13; Judg. 19:22
24 [a]Num. 31:27; Josh. 22:8
25 [I]Hebr. *and forward*

Behold a [I]present[1293] for you of the spoil of the enemies of the LORD;

27 To *them* which *were* in Bethel, and to *them* which *were* in [a]south Ramoth, and to *them* which *were* in [b]Jattir,

28 And to *them* which *were* in [a]Aroer, and to *them* which *were* in Siphmoth, and to *them* which *were* in [b]Eshtemoa,

29 And to *them* which *were* in Rachal, and to *them* which *were* in the cities of [a]the Jerahmeelites, and to *them* which *were* in the cities of the [b]Kenites,

30 And to *them* which *were* in [a]Hormah, and to *them* which *were* in Chorashan, and to *them* which *were* in Athach,

31 And to *them* which *were* in [a]Hebron, and to all the places where David himself and his men were wont to haunt.[1980]

Saul's Death

31 Now [a]the Philistines fought against Israel: and the men of Israel fled from before the Philistines, and fell down[5307] [I]slain 2491 in mount [b]Gilboa.

2 And the Philistines followed hard upon 1692 Saul and upon his sons;[1121] and the Philistines slew[5221] [a]Jonathan, and Abinadab, and Melchishua, Saul's sons.

3 And [a]the battle went sore[3513] against Saul, and the [I]archers[3384] [II]hit him; and he was sore wounded[2342] of the archers.

4 [a]Then said[559] Saul unto his armourbearer, Draw thy sword,[2719] and thrust me through therewith; lest [b]these uncircumcised[6189] come and thrust me through, and [I]abuse 5953 me. But his armourbearer would[14] not; [c]for he was sore afraid.[3372] Therefore Saul took a sword, and [d]fell upon it.

5 And when his armourbearer saw[7200] that Saul was dead,[4191] he fell likewise upon his sword, and died with him.

6 So Saul died, and his three sons, and his armourbearer, and all his men, that same day[3117] together.

7 And when the men of Israel that *were* on the other side of the valley, and *they* that *were* on the other side Jordan, saw that the men of Israel fled, and that Saul and his sons were dead, they forsook[5800] the cities, and fled; and the Philistines came and dwelt in them.

8 And it came to pass on the morrow, when the Philistines came to strip the slain, that they found Saul and his three sons fallen in mount[5307] Gilboa.

9 And they cut off[3772] his head, and stripped off his armour, and sent into the land[776] of the Philistines round about, to [a]publish[1319] *it in* the house of their idols,[6091] and among the people.[5971]

10 [a]And they put his armour in the house of [b]Ashtaroth: and [c]they fastened[8628] his body[1472] to the wall of [d]Beth–shan.

11 [a]And when the inhabitants of Jabesh–gilead heard [I]of that which the Philistines had done[6213] to Saul;

12 [a]All the valiant men arose, and went all night,[3915] and took the body of Saul and the bodies of his sons from the wall of Beth–shan, and came to Jabesh, and [b]burnt[8313] them there.

13 And they took their bones,[6106] and [a]buried[6912] *them* under a tree at Jabesh, [b]and fasted seven days.

---

26 [I]Hebr. *blessing*
27 [a]Josh. 19:8 [b]Josh. 15:48
28 [a]Josh. 13:16 [b]Josh. 15:50
29 [a]1Sam. 27:10 [b]Judg. 1:16
30 [a]Judg. 1:17
31 [a]Josh. 14:13; 2Sam. 2:1
1 [I]Or, *wounded* [a]1Chr. 10:1-12 [b]1Sam. 28:4
2 [a]1Sam. 14:49; 1Chr. 8:33
3 [I]Hebr. *shooters, men with bows* [II]Hebr. *found him* [a]2Sam. 1:6
4 [I]Or, *mock me* [a]Judg. 9:54 [b]1Sam. 14:6; 17:26 [c]2Sam. 1:14 [d]2Sam. 1:10
9 [a]2Sam. 1:20
10 [a]1Sam. 21:9 [b]Judg. 2:13 [c]2Sam. 21:12 [d]Josh. 17:11; Judg. 1:27
11 [I]Or, *concerning him* [a]1Sam. 11:1-11
12 [a]2Sam. 2:4-7 [b]2Chr. 16:14; Jer. 34:5; Amos 6:10
13 [a]2Sam. 2:4, 5; 21:12-14 [b]Gen. 50:10

The Second Book of

SAMUEL

The Book of 2 Samuel was originally combined with 1 Samuel, making up one book. It remained one book in the Hebrew text until the printing of the Hebrew Bible in A.D. 1517 at which time it was separated from 1 Samuel. The Septuagint and other translations of the Old Testament that followed divided the books of Samuel and Kings into First Kings through Fourth Kings. God's reason for choosing David is clear from the statement, "the LORD hath sought him a man after his [God's] own heart" (1 Sam. 13:14). The psalms that David wrote reveal his passionate devotion to God. Despite this strong commitment, he was guilty of several great sins, the consequences of which affected not only him personally, but also the members of his family and the whole nation (2 Sam. 24:13–15).

The Book of 2 Samuel focuses on the reign of King David. Some commentators outline the book according to the political situation, dividing it into his rule over Judah (2 Sam. 1:1—4:12) and over all Israel (2 Sam. 5:1—12:31). Others divide the book by spiritual content, making note of two particular sections: David's triumphs (2 Sam. 1:1—12:31) and David's troubles (2 Sam. 13:1—24:25).

The prophetic blessing that God gave to David includes the promise that his kingdom would be established forever (chap. 7). This blessing, called the Davidic Covenant, is an expansion of God's promises to Abraham (Gen. 12:7; 15:18; 17:8; 22:17). The promise of an all-powerful king that would reign on the throne of David is repeated many times throughout Scripture (Is. 55:3; Jer. 23:5; 30:9; 33:15–26; Ezek. 34:23, 24; 37:24, 25; Acts 15:16). The kingship of David was enhanced by the prophetic ministries of Samuel, Nathan, and Gad. For this reason, it is very possible that Nathan and Gad also wrote portions of this book (1 Chr. 29:29).

David Learns of Saul's Death

1 🔑 Now it came to pass after the death[4194] of Saul, when David was returned from [a]the slaughter of the Amalekites, and David had abode two days in Ziklag;

2 It came even to pass on the third day, that, behold, [a]a man came out of the camp from Saul [b]with his clothes rent, and earth[127] upon his head: and *so* it was, when he came to David, that he fell[5307] to the earth,[776] and did obeisance.[7812]

3 And David said unto him, From whence comest thou? And he said unto him, Out of the camp of Israel am I escaped.[4422]

4 And David said unto him, [I]How went the matter? I pray thee, tell me. And he answered,[559] That the people are fled from the battle, and many of the people also are fallen[5307] and dead;[4191] and Saul and Jonathan his son are dead also.

5 And David said unto the young man that told him, How knowest[3045] thou that Saul and Jonathan his son be dead?

6 And the young man that told him said, As I happened[7136] by chance upon [a]mount Gilboa, behold, [b]Saul leaned[8172] upon his spear; and, lo, the chariots and horsemen followed hard after him.

7 And when he looked behind him, he saw me, and called[7121] unto me. And I answered, [I]Here *am* I.

8 And he said unto me, Who *art* thou? And I answered him, I *am* an Amalekite.

1 [a]1Sam. 30:17, 26

2 [a]2Sam. 4:10 [b]1Sam. 4:12

4 [I]Hebr. *What was*

6 [a]1Sam. 31:1 [b]1Sam. 31:2-4

7 [I]Hebr. *Behold me*

🔑 **1:1–10** The story the Amalekite told was different from the actual account in 1 Samuel 31:3–5. Apparently, this man discovered Saul's dead body and looted it. Some time later he told his own version to David, hoping that he would be rewarded for his "good news" (see 2 Sam. 4:10).

9 He said unto me again, Stand, I pray thee, upon me, and slay me: for [I]anguish[7661] is come upon me, because my life[5315] *is* yet whole in me.

10 So I stood upon him, and [a]slew him, because I was sure that he could not live[2421] after that he was fallen: and I took the crown[5145] that *was* upon his head, and the bracelet that *was* on his arm, and have brought them hither unto my lord.[113]

11 Then David took hold[2388] on his clothes, and [a]rent them; and likewise all the men that *were* with him:

12 And they mourned,[5594] and wept, and fasted until even, for Saul, and for Jonathan his son, and for the people of the LORD, and for the house of Israel; because they were fallen by the sword.

13 And David said unto the young man that told him, Whence *art* thou? And he answered, I *am* the son of a stranger, an Amalekite.

14 And David said unto him, [a]How wast thou not [b]afraid[3372] to [c]stretch forth thine hand to destroy[7843] the LORD's anointed?[4899]

15 And [a]David called one of the young men, and said, Go near, *and* fall upon him. And he smote him that he died.[4191]

16 And David said unto him, [a]Thy blood[1818] *be* upon thy head; for [b]thy mouth hath testified against thee, saying, I have slain the LORD's anointed.

David's Lament

17 And David lamented with this lamentation over Saul and over Jonathan his son:

🔑18 ([a]Also he bade them teach the children[1121] of Judah *the use of* the bow: behold, *it is* written [b]in the book[5612] [I]of Jasher.[3477])

19 The beauty[6643] of Israel is slain upon thy high places: [a]how are the mighty fallen!

20 [a]Tell *it* not in Gath, publish *it* not in the streets of Askelon; lest [b]the daughters of the Philistines rejoice, lest the daughters of [c]the uncircumcised[6189] triumph.

21 Ye [a]mountains of Gilboa, [b]*let there be* no dew, neither *let there be* rain, upon you, nor fields[7704] of offerings:[8641] for there the shield of the mighty is vilely cast away,[1602] the shield of Saul, *as though he had* not *been* [c]anointed with oil.[8081]

22 From the blood of the slain, from the fat of the mighty, [a]the bow of Jonathan turned not back, and the sword of Saul returned not empty.

23 Saul and Jonathan *were* lovely[157] and [I]pleasant[5273] in their lives, and in their death they were not divided: they were swifter than eagles, they were [a]stronger than lions.

24 Ye daughters of Israel, weep over Saul, who clothed you in scarlet, with *other* delights, who put on ornaments of gold upon your apparel.

25 How are the mighty fallen in the midst of the battle! O Jonathan, *thou wast* slain in thine high places.

🔑26 I am distressed for thee, my brother[251] Jonathan: very pleasant hast thou been unto me: [a]thy love[160] to me was wonderful,[6381] passing the love of women.[802]

27 [a]How are the mighty fallen, and the weapons of war perished!

9 [I]Or, *my coat of mail, or, my embroidered coat hindereth me, that my*
10 [a]Judg. 9:54
11 [a]2Sam. 3:31; 13:31
14 [a]Num. 12:8 [b]1Sam. 31:4 [c]1Sam. 24:6; 26:9; Ps. 105:15
15 [a]2Sam. 4:10, 12
16 [a]1Sam. 26:9; 1Kgs. 2:32, 33, 37 [b]2Sam. 1:10; Luke 19:22
18 [I]Or, *of the upright* [a]1Sam. 31:3 [b]Josh. 10:13
19 [a]2Sam. 1:27
20 [a]1Sam. 31:9; Mic. 1:10 [b]Ex. 15:20; Judg. 11:34; 1Sam. 18:6 [c]1Sam. 31:4
21 [a]1Sam. 31:1 [b]Judg. 5:23; Job 3:3, 4; Jer. 20:14 [c]1Sam. 10:1
22 [a]1Sam. 18:4
23 [I]Or, *sweet* [a]Judg. 14:18
26 [a]1Sam. 18:1, 3; 19:2; 20:17, 41; 23:16
27 [a]2Sam. 1:19

🔑 **1:18** A reference to the book of Jasher is also found in Joshua 10:13. It is apparently a historical book of military poetry, a collection of songs about heroes. It had more material added to it as the years went by, but it is now lost. Jasher is probably a name used to refer to Israel. It is seen in Deuteronomy 32:15 under the form "Jeshurun" which means "the righteous or upright one." The book printed under this name in modern times is spurious.

🔑 **1:26** David and Jonathan truly loved each other, and their relationship was one of loyalty to one another. Jonathan, the heir apparent to the throne of King Saul, was willing to take second place for the sake of David, his friend.

David Becomes Judah's King

2 And it came to pass after this, that
David [a]enquired[7592] of the LORD,
saying, Shall I go up into any of the
cities of Judah? And the LORD said
unto him, Go up. And David said,
Whither shall I go up? And he said, Unto
[b]Hebron.
2 So David went up thither, and his
[a]two wives[802] also, Ahinoam the Jezreelitess, and Abigail Nabal's wife the
Carmelite.
3 And [a]his men that *were* with him
did David bring up, every man with his
household: and they dwelt in the cities of
Hebron.
4 [a]And the men of Judah came, and
there they anointed[4886] David king[4428]
over the house of Judah. And they told
David, saying, *That* [b]the men of Jabesh–
gilead *were they* that buried[6912] Saul.
5 And David sent messengers unto
the men of Jabesh–gilead, and said unto
them, [a]Blessed[1288] *be* ye of the LORD, that
ye have shewed this kindness[2617] unto
your lord,[113] *even* unto Saul, and have
buried him.
6 And now [a]the LORD shew kindness
and truth unto you: and I also will requite you this kindness, because ye have
done this thing.
7 Therefore now let your hands be
strengthened, and [I]be ye valiant: for your
master Saul is dead,[4191] and also the
house of Judah have anointed me king
over them.

1 [a]Judg. 1:1; 1Sam. 23:2, 4, 9; 30:7, 8 [b]1Sam. 30:31; 2Sam. 2:11; 5:1, 3; 1Kgs. 2:11

2 [a]1Sam. 30:5

3 [a]1Sam. 27:2, 3; 30:1; 1Chr. 12:1

4 [a]2Sam. 2:11; 5:5 [b]1Sam. 31:11, 13

5 [a]Ruth 2:20; 3:10; Ps. 115:15

6 [a]2Tim. 1:16, 18

7 [I]Hebr. *be ye the sons of valor*

8 [I]Hebr. *the host which* was *Saul's* [II]Or, *Esh-baal* [a]1Sam. 14:50 [b]1Chr. 8:33; 9:39

11 [I]Hebr. *number of days* [a]2Sam. 5:5; 1Kgs. 2:11

12 [a]Josh. 18:25

13 [I]Hebr. *them together* [a]Jer. 41:12

Ish–bosheth Succeeds Saul

🔑 8 But [a]Abner the son of Ner,
captain[8269] of [I]Saul's host, took [II][b]Ish–
bosheth the son of Saul, and brought him
over to Mahanaim;
9 And made him king[4427] over
Gilead, and over the Ashurites, and over
Jezreel, and over Ephraim, and over
Benjamin, and over all Israel.
10 Ish–bosheth Saul's son *was* forty
years old when he began to reign over
Israel, and reigned two years. But the
house of Judah followed David.
11 And [a]the [I]time that David was
king in Hebron over the house of Judah
was seven years and six months.

War Between Israel and Judah

12 And Abner the son of Ner, and
the servants of Ish–bosheth the son of
Saul, went out from Mahanaim to
[a]Gibeon.
🔑 13 And Joab the son of Zeruiah, and
the servants of David, went out, and met
[I]together by [a]the pool of Gibeon: and
they sat down, the one on the one side of
the pool, and the other on the other side
of the pool.
🔑 14 And Abner said to Joab, Let the
young men now arise, and play[7832] before
us. And Joab said, Let them arise.
15 Then there arose and went over
by number twelve of Benjamin, which
pertained to Ish–bosheth the son of Saul,
and twelve of the servants of David.

🔑 **2:8–11** Abner was a close relative of Saul (1 Sam. 14:50) and wanted to gain as much control as possible after the death of Saul and Jonathan. This is why he set up Ish–bosheth as king of all the tribes except Judah, which was loyal to David. Up to this time David had been accepted as king only by his own tribe, Judah (v. 10). Hebron was the capital city for the first seven and one-half years of David's reign. Ish–bosheth, the son of Saul, was his rival for two years, reigning over all the other tribes of Israel (vv. 8–10). He depended upon Abner, who had been Saul's commander-in-chief. It was only after the death of Abner, who incidentally had already defected to David's side, that Israel's confidence in Ish-bosheth began to diminish (2 Sam. 3:1). After the death of Ish–bosheth, David was crowned king over all Israel and reigned for thirty-three and one-half years (2 Sam. 5:1–5). He was king for a total of forty years.

🔑 **2:13** Joab was the nephew of David. Zeruiah was David's half-sister (1 Chr. 2:16), probably through the marriage of his mother to Nahash (2 Sam. 17:25). This was before David's mother married Jesse, David's father.

🔑 **2:14** This is similar to the offer made by Goliath (1 Sam. 17:8, 9). It was hoped that a single contest between champions would avoid much bloodshed.

16 And they caught[2388] every one[376] his fellow[7453] by the head, and *thrust* his sword in his fellow's side; so they fell down[5307] together: wherefore that place was called[7121] [I]Helkath–hazzurim, which *is* in Gibeon.

17 And there was a very sore battle that day; and Abner was beaten,[5062] and the men of Israel, before the servants of David.

18 And there were [a]three sons of Zeruiah there, Joab, and Abishai, and Asahel: and Asahel *was as* [b]light[7031] [I]of foot [IIc]as a wild roe.

19 And Asahel pursued after Abner; and in going he turned not to the right hand nor to the left [I]from following Abner.

20 Then Abner looked behind him, and said, *Art* thou Asahel? And he answered,[559] I *am*.

21 And Abner said to him, Turn thee aside to thy right hand or to thy left, and lay thee hold on one of the young men, and take thee his [Ia]armour. But Asahel would[14] not turn aside from following of him.

22 And Abner said again to Asahel, Turn thee aside from following me: wherefore should I smite thee to the ground?[776] how then should I hold up my face to Joab thy brother?[251]

23 Howbeit he refused to turn aside: wherefore Abner with the hinder end of the spear smote him [a]under the fifth *rib*, that the spear came out behind him; and he fell down there, and died[4191] in the same place: and it came to pass, *that* as many as came to the place where Asahel fell down and died stood still.

24 Joab also and Abishai pursued after Abner: and the sun went down when they were come to the hill of Ammah, that *lieth* before Giah by the way[1870] of the wilderness of Gibeon.

25 And the children[1121] of Benjamin gathered themselves together after Abner, and became one troop,[92] and stood on the top of an hill.

26 Then Abner called to Joab, and said, Shall the sword devour for ever? knowest[3045] thou not that it will be bitterness[4751] in the latter end? how long shall it be then, ere thou bid[559] the people return from following their brethren?[251]

27 And Joab said, *As* God[430] liveth,[2416] unless [a]thou hadst spoken, surely then [I]in the morning the people had [II]gone up every one from following his brother.

28 So Joab blew[8628] a trumpet, and all the people stood still, and pursued after Israel no more, neither fought they any more.

29 And Abner and his men walked all that night through the plain,[6160] and passed over Jordan, and went through all Bithron, and they came to Mahanaim.

30 And Joab returned from following Abner: and when he had gathered all the people together, there lacked of David's servants nineteen men and Asahel.

31 But the servants of David had smitten of Benjamin, and of Abner's men, *so that* three hundred and threescore men died.

32 And they took up Asahel, and buried him in the sepulchre[6913] of his father,[1] which *was in* Bethlehem. And Joab and his men went all night, and they came to Hebron at break of day.

3 Now there was long[752] war between the house of Saul and the house of David: but David waxed stronger and stronger, and the house of Saul waxed weaker and weaker.

David's Sons Born at Hebron

🔑 2 And [a]unto David were sons born in Hebron: and his firstborn was Amnon, [b]of Ahinoam the Jezreelitess;

3 And his second, [Ia]Chileab, of Abigail the wife[802] of Nabal the Carmelite; and the third, Absalom the son of

16 [I]That is, *The field of strong men*

18 [I]Hebr. *of his feet* [II]Hebr. *as one of the roes that is in the field* [a]1Chr. 2:16 [b]1Chr. 12:8 [c]Ps. 18:33; Song 2:17; 8:14

19 [I]Hebr. *from after Abner*

21 [I]Or, *spoil* [a]Judg. 14:19

23 [a]2Sam. 3:27; 4:6; 20:10

27 [I]Hebr. *from the morning* [II]Or, *gone away* [a]2Sam. 2:14; Prov. 17:14

2 [a]1Chr. 3:1-4 [b]1Sam. 25:43

3 [I]Or, *Daniel* [a]1Chr. 3:1

🔑 **3:2–5** See 1 Chronicles 3:1–9 for an additional list of David's children.

Maacah the daughter of Talmai king[4428] [b]of Geshur;

4 And the fourth, [a]Adonijah the son of Haggith; and the fifth, Shephatiah the son of Abital;

5 And the sixth, Ithream, by Eglah David's wife. These were born to David in Hebron.

Abner Decides to Join David

6 And it came to pass, while there was war between the house of Saul and the house of David, that Abner made himself strong for the house of Saul.

🔑 7 And Saul had a concubine, whose name *was* [a]Rizpah, the daughter of Aiah: and *Ish–bosheth* said to Abner, Wherefore hast thou [b]gone in unto my father's[1] concubine?

8 Then was Abner very wroth[2734] for the words[1697] of Ish–bosheth, and said, *Am* I [a]a dog's head, which against Judah do shew[6213] kindness[2617] this day[3117] unto the house of Saul thy father, to his brethren,[251] and to his friends, and have not delivered thee into the hand of David, that thou chargest[6485] me to day with a fault concerning this woman?[802]

9 [a]So do God[430] to Abner, and more also, except, [b]as the LORD hath sworn to David, even so I do to him;

10 To translate[5674] the kingdom[4467] from the house of Saul, and to set up the throne of David over Israel and over Judah, [a]from Dan even to Beer–sheba.

11 And he could not answer[7725] Abner a word[1697] again,[7725] because he feared[3372] him.

12 And Abner sent messengers to David on his behalf, saying, Whose *is* the land?[776] saying *also,* Make thy league[1285]

3 [b]1Sam. 27:8; 2Sam. 13:27
4 [a]1Kgs. 1:5
7 [a]2Sam. 21:8, 10 [b]2Sam. 16:21
8 [a]Deut. 23:18; 1Sam. 24:14; 2Sam. 9:8; 16:9
9 [a]Ruth 1:17; 1Kgs. 19:2 [b]1Sam. 15:28; 16:1, 12; 28:17; 1Chr. 12:23
10 [a]Judg. 20:1; 2Sam. 17:11; 1Kgs. 4:25
13 [I]Hebr. *saying* [a]Gen. 43:3 [b]1Sam. 18:20
14 [a]1Sam. 18:25, 27
15 [a]1Sam. 25:44, *Phalti*
16 [I]Hebr. *going and weeping* [a]2Sam. 19:16
17 [I]Hebr. *both yesterday and the third day*
18 [a]2Sam. 3:9
19 [a]1Chr. 12:29
21 [a]2Sam. 3:10, 12

with me, and, behold, my hand *shall be* with thee, to bring about all Israel unto thee.

13 And he said, Well;[2896] I will make a league with thee: but one thing I require of thee, [I]that is, [a]Thou shalt not see my face, except thou first bring [b]Michal Saul's daughter, when thou comest to see my face.

14 And David sent messengers to Ish–bosheth Saul's son, saying, Deliver *me* my wife Michal, which I espoused[781] to me [a]for an hundred foreskins[6190] of the Philistines.

15 And Ish–bosheth sent, and took her from *her* husband, *even* from [a]Phaltiel the son of Laish.

16 And her husband went with her [I]along weeping behind her to [a]Bahurim. Then said Abner unto him, Go, return. And he returned.

17 And Abner had communication with the elders[2205] of Israel, saying, Ye sought for David [I]in times past *to be* king over you:

18 Now then do *it:* [a]for the LORD hath spoken of David, saying, By the hand of my servant David I will save my people Israel out of the hand of the Philistines, and out of the hand of all their enemies.

19 And Abner also spake in the ears[241] of [a]Benjamin: and Abner went also to speak in the ears of David in Hebron all that seemed good to Israel, and that seemed good[2895] to the whole house of Benjamin.

20 So Abner came to David to Hebron, and twenty men with him. And David made Abner and the men that *were* with him a feast.[4960]

21 And Abner said unto David, I will arise and go, and [a]will gather[5908] all

---

🔑 **3:7** A concubine was much more than a mistress. In a sense, she was a secondary "wife" (Ex. 21:8–10; Deut. 21:11–13). She was a member of the royal household, took her position by an official ceremony of appointment, and had the rights of a married woman. Unlike a true wife, concubines were usually acquired by purchase or were captives taken in war. She could be "divorced" summarily and then released, but never to be a slave (Gen. 16:2, 3; 21:10; Ex. 21 7, 8; Deut. 21:10–14; Mal. 2:14–16).

Abner was a powerful, ambitious man, and he knew that possessing one of the court women was equivalent to royal power.

Israel unto my lord[113] the king, that they may make a league with thee, and that thou mayest [b]reign over all that thine heart desireth. And David sent Abner away; and he went in peace.

Joab Kills Abner

22 And, behold, the servants of David and Joab came from *pursuing* a troop,[1416] and brought in a great spoil with them: but Abner *was* not with David in Hebron: for he had sent him away, and he was gone in peace.

23 When Joab and all the host that *was* with him were come, they told Joab, saying, Abner the son of Ner came to the king, and he hath sent him away, and he is gone in peace.

24 Then Joab came to the king, and said, What hast thou done?[6213] behold, Abner came unto thee; why *is* it *that* thou hast sent him away, and he is quite gone?

25 Thou knowest[3045] Abner the son of Ner, that he came to deceive thee, and to know [a]thy going out and thy coming in, and to know all that thou doest.

26 And when Joab was come out from David, he sent messengers after Abner, which brought him again from the well[953] of Sirah: but David knew *it* not.

27 And when Abner was returned to Hebron, Joab [a]took him aside in the gate to speak with him [I]quietly,[7987] and smote him there [b]under the fifth *rib,* that he died,[4191] for the blood[1818] of [c]Asahel his brother.

28 And afterward when David heard *it,* he said, I and my kingdom[4467] *are* guiltless[5355] before the LORD for ever from the [I]blood of Abner the son of Ner:

29 [a]Let it rest on the head of Joab, and on all his father's house; and let there not [I]fail from the house of Joab one [b]that hath an issue,[2100] or that is a leper, or that leaneth[2388] on a staff, or that falleth[5307] on the sword, or that lacketh bread.

30 So Joab and Abishai his brother slew Abner, because he had slain their brother [a]Asahel at Gibeon in the battle.

31 And David said to Joab, and to all the people that *were* with him, [a]Rend[7167] your clothes, and [b]gird you with sackcloth, and mourn before Abner. And king David *himself* followed the [I]bier.

32 And they buried[6912] Abner in Hebron: and the king lifted up his voice, and wept at the grave[6913] of Abner; and all the people wept.

33 And the king lamented over Abner, and said, Died Abner as a [a]fool[5036] dieth?[4194]

34 Thy hands *were* not bound, nor thy feet put into fetters: as a man falleth before [I]wicked men, *so* fellest[5307] thou. And all the people wept again over him.

35 And when all the people came [a]to cause David to eat meat while it was yet day, David sware, saying, [b]So do God to me, and more also, if I taste bread, or ought else, [c]till the sun be down.

36 And all the people took notice[5234] *of it,* and it [I]pleased them: as whatsoever the king did pleased all the people.

37 For all the people and all Israel understood[3045] that day that it was not of the king to slay Abner the son of Ner.

38 And the king said unto his servants, Know ye not that there is a prince and a great man fallen[5307] this day in Israel?

39 And I *am* this day [I]weak,[7390] though anointed[4886] king; and these men the sons of Zeruiah [a]*be* too hard[7186] for me: [b]the LORD shall reward the doer[6213] of evil[7451] according to his wickedness.[7451]

Ish–bosheth Is Assassinated

4 And when Saul's son heard that Abner was dead[4191] in Hebron, [a]his hands were feeble,[7503] and all the Israelites were [b]troubled.

2 And Saul's son had two men *that were* captains[8269] of bands:[1416] the name of the one *was* Baanah, and the name of the [I]other Rechab, the sons of Rimmon a

21 [b]1Kgs. 11:37

25 [a]1Sam. 29:6; Isa. 37:28

27 [I]Or, *peaceably* [a]2Sam. 20:9, 10; 1Kgs. 2:5 [b]2Sam. 4:6 [c]2Sam. 2:23

28 [I]Hebr. *bloods*

29 [I]Hebr. *be cut off* [a]1Kgs. 2:32, 33 [b]Lev. 15:2

30 [a]2Sam. 2:23

31 [I]Hebr. *bed* [a]Josh. 7:6; 2Sam. 1:2, 11 [b]Gen. 37:34

33 [a]2Sam. 13:12, 13

34 [I]Hebr. *children of iniquity*

35 [a]2Sam. 12:17; Jer. 16:7 [b]Ruth 1:17 [c]2Sam. 1:12

36 [I]Hebr. *was good in their eyes*

39 [I]Hebr. *tender* [a]2Sam. 19:7 [b]2Sam. 19:13; 1Kgs. 2:5, 6, 33, 34; Ps. 28:4; 62:12; 2Tim. 4:14

1 [a]Ezra 4:4; Isa. 13:7 [b]Matt. 2:3

2 [I]Hebr. *second*

Beerothite, of the children[1121] of Benjamin: (for [a]Beeroth also was reckoned to Benjamin.

3 And the Beerothites fled to [a]Gittaim, and were sojourners there until this day.[3117])

4 And [a]Jonathan, Saul's son, had a son *that was* lame[5223] of *his* feet. He was five years old when the tidings came of Saul and Jonathan [b]out of Jezreel, and his nurse took him up, and fled: and it came to pass, as she made haste to flee, that he fell,[5307] and became lame.[6452] And his name *was* [I]Mephibosheth.

5 And the sons of Rimmon the Beerothite, Rechab and Baanah, went, and came about the heat of the day to the house of Ish–bosheth, who lay on a bed at noon.

6 And they came thither into the midst of the house, *as though* they would have fetched wheat; and they smote him [a]under the fifth *rib:* and Rechab and Baanah his brother[251] escaped.[4422]

7 For when they came into the house, he lay on his bed in his bedchamber, and they smote him, and slew him, and beheaded him, and took his head, and gat them away through the plain all night.

8 And they brought the head of Ish–bosheth unto David to Hebron, and said to the king,[4428] Behold the head of Ish–bosheth the son of Saul thine enemy, [a]which sought thy life;[5315] and the LORD hath avenged my lord[113] the king this day of Saul, and of his seed.

9 And David answered Rechab and Baanah his brother, the sons of Rimmon the Beerothite, and said unto them, *As* the LORD liveth,[2416] [a]who hath redeemed my soul out of all adversity,[6869]

10 When [a]one told me, saying, Behold, Saul is dead, [I]thinking to have brought good tidings,[1319] I took hold of him, and slew him in Ziklag, [II]who *thought* that I would have given him a reward for his tidings:

11 How much more, when wicked[7563] men have slain a righteous person in his own house upon his bed? shall I not therefore now [a]require his blood[1818] of your hand, and take you away from the earth?[776]

12 And David [a]commanded[6680] his young men, and they slew them, and cut off their hands and their feet, and hanged *them* up over the pool in Hebron. But they took the head of Ish–bosheth, and buried[6912] *it* in the [b]sepulchre[6913] of Abner in Hebron.

David Becomes Israel's King

5 🔑 Then [a]came all the tribes[7626] of Israel to David unto Hebron, and spake, saying, Behold, [b]we *are* thy bone[6106] and thy flesh.[1320]

2 Also in time past, when Saul was king[4428] over us, [a]thou wast he that leddest out and broughtest in Israel: and the LORD said to thee, [b]Thou shalt feed my people Israel, and thou shalt be a captain[5057] over Israel.

3 [a]So all the elders[2205] of Israel came to the king to Hebron; [b]and king David made a league[1285] with them in Hebron [c]before the LORD: and they anointed[4886] David king over Israel.

4 David *was* thirty years old when he began to reign, [a]*and* he reigned forty years.

5 In Hebron he reigned over Judah [a]seven years and six months: and in Jerusalem he reigned thirty and three years over all Israel and Judah.

David Captures Zion

🔑 6 And the king and his men went [a]to Jerusalem unto [b]the Jebusites, the

---

2 [a]Josh. 18:25
3 [a]Neh. 11:33
4 [I]Or, *Meribbaal* [a]2Sam. 9:3; 1Sam. 29:1, 11 [b]1Chr. 8:34; 9:40
6 [a]2Sam. 2:23
8 [a]1Sam. 19:2, 10, 11; 23:15; 25:29
9 [a]Gen. 48:16; 1Kgs. 1:29; Ps. 31:7
10 [I]Hebr. *he was in his own eyes as a bringer* [II]Or, *which was the reward I gave him for his tidings* [a]2Sam. 1:2, 4, 15
11 [a]Gen. 9:5, 6
12 [a]2Sam. 1:15 [b]2Sam. 3:32
1 [a]1Chr. 11:1; 12:23 [b]Gen. 29:14
2 [a]1Sam. 18:13 [b]1Sam. 16:1, 12; 2Sam. 7:7; Ps. 78:71
3 [a]1Chr. 11:3 [b]2Kgs. 11:17 [c]Judg. 11:11; 1Sam. 23:18
4 [a]1Chr. 26:31; 29:27
5 [a]2Sam. 2:11; 1Chr. 3:4
6 [a]Judg. 1:21; [b]Josh. 15:63; Judg. 1:8; 19:11, 12

🔑 **5:1–5** Concerning David's rise to power over all Israel, see note on 2 Samuel 2:8–11.

🔑 **5:6–10** David's first undertaking, after being crowned king of all Israel, was to conquer the city of Jerusalem. The fortress of Zion (5:6b–7) was almost invulnerable, located as it was in the mountains

(continued on next page)

inhabitants of the land:[776] which spake unto David, saying, Except thou take away[5493] the blind and the lame, thou shalt not come in hither: [I]thinking, David cannot come in hither.

7 Nevertheless David took the strong hold of Zion: [a]the same *is* the city of David.

🔑 8 And David said on that day, Whosoever getteth up to the gutter,6794 and smiteth the Jebusites, and the lame and the blind, *that are* hated of David's soul, [a]*he shall be chief and captain.* [I]Wherefore they said, The blind and the lame shall not come into the house.

9 So David dwelt in the fort, and called[7121] it [a]the city of David. And David built round about from Millo and inward.

10 And David [I]went on, and grew great, and the LORD God[430] of hosts *was* with him.

David Prospers

11 And [a]Hiram king of Tyre sent messengers to David, and cedar trees, and carpenters,2796,6086 and [I]masons:[2796] and they built David an house.

12 And David perceived that the LORD had established[3559] him king over Israel, and that he had exalted his kingdom[4467] for his people Israel's sake.

13 And [a]David took *him* more concubines and wives[802] out of Jerusalem, after he was come from Hebron: and there were yet sons and daughters born to David.

14 And [a]these *be* the names of those that were born unto him in Jerusalem; [Ib]Shammuah, and Shobab, and Nathan, and Solomon,

6 [I]Or, *saying, David shall not*

7 [a]2Sam. 5:9; 1Kgs. 2, 10; 8:1

8 [I]Or, *Because they had said, even the blind and the lame, He shall not come into the house* [a]1Chr. 11:6-9

9 [a]2Sam. 5:7

10 [I]Hebr. *went going and growing*

11 [I]Hebr. *hewers of the stone of the wall* [a]1Kgs. 5:2; 1Chr. 14:1

13 [a]Deut. 17:17; 1Chr. 3:9; 14:3

14 [I]Or, *Shimea* [a]1Chr. 3:5; 14:4 [b]1Chr. 3:5

15 [I]Or, *Elishama* [a]1Chr. 3:6

16 [I]Or, *Beeliada* [a]1Chr. 14:7

17 [a]1Chr. 11:16; 14:8 [b]2Sam. 23:14

18 [a]Josh. 15:8; Isa. 17:5

19 [a]1Sam. 23:2, 4; 30:8; 2Sam. 2:1

20 [I]That is, *The plain of breaches* [a]Isa. 28:21

21 [I]Or, *took them away* [a]Deut. 7:5, 25; 1Chr. 14:12

22 [a]1Chr. 14:13

23 [a]2Sam. 5:19

24 [a]2Kgs. 7:6

15 Ibhar also and [Ia]Elishua, and Nepheg, and Japhia,

16 And Elishama, and [Ia]Eliada, and Eliphalet.

David Defeats the Philistines

17 [a]But when the Philistines heard that they had anointed David king over Israel, all the Philistines came up to seek David; and David heard *of it,* [b]and went down to the hold.4686

18 The Philistines also came and spread themselves[5203] in [a]the valley of Rephaim.

19 And David [a]enquired[7592] of the LORD, saying, Shall I go up to the Philistines? wilt thou deliver them into mine hand? And the LORD said unto David, Go up: for I will doubtless deliver the Philistines into thine hand.

20 And David came to [a]Baal–perazim, and David smote them there, and said, The LORD hath broken forth6555 upon mine enemies before me, as the breach of waters. Therefore he called the name of that place [I]Baal–perazim.

21 And there they left[5800] their images,[6091] and David and his men [Ia]burned[5375] them.

22 [a]And the Philistines came up yet again, and spread themselves in the valley of Rephaim.

23 And when [a]David enquired of the LORD, he said, Thou shalt not go up; *but* fetch a compass5437 behind them, and come upon them over against the mulberry trees.

24 And let it be, when thou [a]hearest the sound of a going6807 in the tops of the mulberry trees, that then thou shalt

---

(continued from previous page)
of Judah. It was a strategic military site, centrally located between Judah in the south and the rest of Israel in the north. It also dominated the main trade routes in the area. Salem was an early name for the city (see notes on Gen. 14:18–20; Judg. 1:8). Members of the nation of Israel had been living in the area, but the central fortress remained in the hands of a group of Amorite people called "Jebusites." After David captured the fortress, he began to rebuild and expand the city, making it the seat of his kingdom.

🔑 **5:8** The word "gutter" refers to a concealed passageway which was cut down through the rock under the city.

bestir thyself:[2782] for then [b]shall the LORD go out before thee, to smite the host of the Philistines.

25 And David did so, as the LORD had commanded[6680] him; and smote the Philistines from [a]Geba until thou come to [b]Gazer.

David Brings the Ark to Jerusalem

6 Again, David gathered together all *the* chosen *men* of Israel, thirty thousand.

🗝 2 And [a]David arose, and went with all the people that *were* with him from [I][b]Baale of Judah, to bring up from thence the ark[727] of God,[430] [II]whose name is called[7121] by the name of the LORD of hosts [c]that dwelleth *between* the cherubims.[3742]

3 And they [I]set the ark of God [a]upon a new cart, and brought[5375] it out of the house of Abinadab that *was* in [II]Gibeah: and Uzzah and Ahio, the sons of Abinadab, drave the new cart.

4 And they brought it out of [a]the house of Abinadab which *was* at Gibeah, [I]accompanying the ark of God: and Ahio went before the ark.

5 And David and all the house of Israel played[7832] before the LORD on all manner of *instruments made of* fir wood, even on harps, and on psalteries, and on timbrels,[8596] and on cornets, and on cymbals.

6 And when they came to [a]Nachon's threshingfloor, Uzzah [b]put forth *his hand* to the ark of God, and took hold of it; for the oxen [I]shook *it*.

🗝 7 And the anger[639] of the LORD was kindled[2734] against Uzzah; and [a]God smote him there for *his* [I]error;[7944] and there he died by the ark of God.

8 And David was displeased,[2734] because the LORD had [I]made a breach upon Uzzah: and he called the name of the place [II]Perez–uzzah to this day.[3117]

9 And [a]David was afraid[3372] of the LORD that day, and said, How shall the ark of the LORD come to me?

10 So David would[14] not remove the ark of the LORD unto him into the city of David: but David carried it aside into the house of Obed–edom [a]the Gittite.

11 [a]And the ark of the LORD continued in the house of Obed–edom the Gittite three months: and the LORD [b]blessed[1288] Obed–edom, and all his household.

12 And it was told king[4428] David, saying, The LORD hath blessed the house of Obed–edom, and all that *pertaineth* unto him, because of the ark of God. [a]So David went and brought up[5927] the ark of God from the house of Obed–edom into the city of David with gladness.

13 And it was *so*, that when [a]they that bare[5375] the ark of the LORD had gone six paces, he sacrificed [b]oxen and fatlings.

14 And David [a]danced before the LORD with all *his* might; and David *was* girded [b]with a linen ephod.

15 [a]So David and all the house of Israel brought up the ark of the LORD with shouting,[8643] and with the sound of the trumpet.

16 And [a]as the ark of the LORD came into the city of David, Michal Saul's daughter looked through a window, and saw king David leaping and dancing before the LORD; and she despised[959] him in her heart.

24 [b]Judg. 4:14
25 [a]1Chr. 14:16, *Gibeon* [b]Josh. 16:10
2 [I]Or, *Baalah, that is, Kirjathjearim* [II]Or, *at which the name, even the name of the LORD of hosts, was called upon* [a]1Chr. 13:5, 6 [b]1Sam. 4:4; Ps. 80:1 [c]Josh. 15:9, 60
3 [I]Hebr. *made to ride* [II]Or, *The hill* [a]Num. 7:9; 1Sam. 6:7
4 [I]Hebr. *with* [a]1Sam. 7:1
6 [I]Or, *stumbled* [a]1Chr. 13:9, *Chidon* [b]Num. 4:15
7 [I]Or, *rashness* [a]1Sam. 6:19
8 [I]Hebr. *broken* [II]That is, *The breach of Uzzah*
9 [a]Ps. 119:120; Luke 5:8, 9
10 [a]1Chr. 13:13
11 [a]1Chr. 13:14 [b]Gen. 30:27; 39:5
12 [a]1Chr. 15:25
13 [a]Num. 4:15; Josh. 3:3; 1Chr. 15:2, 15 [b]1Kgs. 8:5; 1Chr. 15:26
14 [a]Ex. 15:20; Ps. 30:11 [b]1Sam. 2:18; 1Chr. 15:27
15 [a]1Chr. 15:28
16 [a]1Chr. 15:29

🗝 **6:2** The ark of the covenant had stayed in the house of Abinadab for almost a century (cf. 1 Sam. 14:18), after its capture by the Philistines and subsequent return (1 Sam. 7:1).

🗝 **6:7** God's severity toward Uzzah served notice to the people of Israel that God must be revered and obeyed. Uzzah showed disrespect for God by touching the ark (Num 4:15). Furthermore, as one of the priests, he was disobeying God by letting the ark be carried on a cart. How true it is that by disobedience of God's specific instructions, one is often led into another error! The ark was supposed to be carried by the priests upon staves or poles (Ex. 25:12–15; Josh. 3:8). However, nowhere does the text indicate that Uzzah's personal, eternal salvation was involved; his intentions were good (Matt. 7:1).

17 And [a]they brought in the ark of the LORD, and set it in [b]his place, in the midst of the tabernacle that David had [I]pitched for it: and David [c]offered[5927] burnt offerings and peace offerings before the LORD.

18 And as soon as David had made an end[3615] of offering burnt offerings and peace offerings, [a]he blessed the people in the name of the LORD of hosts.

19 [a]And he dealt among all the people, *even* among the whole multitude of Israel, as well to the women[802] as men, to every one[376] a cake of bread, and a good piece *of flesh,* and a flagon[809] *of wine.* So all the people departed every one to his house.

20 Then David returned to bless[1288] his household. And Michal the daughter of Saul came out to meet David, and said, How glorious was the king of Israel to day, who [a]uncovered himself[1540] to day in the eyes of the handmaids of his servants, as one of the [b]vain fellows[7386] [I]shamelessly uncovereth himself!

21 And David said unto Michal, *It was* before the LORD, [a]which chose[977] me before thy father, and before all his house, to appoint[6680] me ruler over the people of the LORD, over Israel: therefore will I play before the LORD.

22 And I will yet be more vile[7043] than thus, and will be base[8217] in mine own sight: and [I]of the maidservants which thou hast spoken of, of them shall I be had in honour.

23 Therefore Michal the daughter of Saul had no child [a]unto the day of her death.

17 IHebr. *stretched* [a]1Chr. 16:1 [b]1Chr. 15:1; Ps. 132:8 [c]1Kgs. 8:5, 62, 63
18 [a]1Kgs. 8:55; 1Chr. 16:2
19 [a]1Chr. 16:3
20 IOr, *openly* [a]1Sam. 19:24; 2Sam. 6:14, 16 [b]Judg. 9:4
21 [a]1Sam. 13:14; 15:28
22 IOr, *of the handmaids* of my servants
23 [a]1Sam. 15:35; Isa. 22:14; Matt. 1:25

1 [a]1Chr. 17:1-15
2 [a]2Sam. 5:11 [b]Acts 7:46 [c]Ex. 26:1; 40:21
3 [a]1Kgs. 8:17, 18; 1Chr. 22:7; 28:2
5 IHebr. *to my servant, to David* [a]1Kgs. 5:3; 8:19; 1Chr. 22:8; 28:3
6 [a]1Kgs. 8:16 [b]Ex. 40:18, 19, 34
7 I*any of the judges,* [a]Lev. 26:11, 12; Deut. 23:14 [b]1Chr. 17:6 [c]2Sam. 5:2; Ps. 78:71, 72; Matt. 2:6; Acts 20:28
8 IHebr. *from after* [a]1Sam. 16:11, 12; Ps. 78:70
9 IHebr. *from thy face* [a]1Sam. 18:14; 2Sam. 5:10; 8:6, 14 [b]1Sam. 31:6; Ps. 89:23 [c]Gen. 12:2

God's Promise to David

7 And it came to pass, [a]when the king sat in his house, and the LORD had given him rest[5117] round about from all his enemies;

2 That the king said unto Nathan the prophet, See now, I dwell in [a]an house of cedar, [b]but the ark[727] of God[430] dwelleth within [c]curtains.

3 And Nathan said to the king, Go, do[6213] all that *is* [a]in thine heart; for the LORD *is* with thee.

🗝 4 And it came to pass that night, that the word[1697] of the LORD came unto Nathan, saying,

5 Go and tell [I]my servant David, Thus saith the LORD, [a]Shalt thou build me an house for me to dwell in?

6 Whereas I have not dwelt in *any* house [a]since the time that I brought up[5927] the children[1121] of Israel out of Egypt, even to this day,[3117] but have walked in [b]a tent and in a tabernacle.

7 In all *the places* wherein I have [a]walked with all the children of Israel spake I a word with [I][b]any of the tribes of Israel, whom I commanded[6680] [c]to feed[7462] my people Israel, saying, Why build ye not me a house of cedar?

8 Now therefore so shalt thou say unto my servant David, Thus saith the LORD of hosts, [a]I took thee from the sheepcote,[5116] [I]from following the sheep, to be ruler over my people, over Israel:

9 And [a]I was with thee whithersoever thou wentest, [b]and have cut off[3772] all thine enemies [I]out of thy sight, and have made thee [c]a great name, like unto

---

🗝 **7:4–16** David's desire to build a house for the Lord sets the stage for one of the key passages in Scripture relating to the coming Messiah (see note on 1 Sam. 16:13). God's message through Nathan (vv. 8–16) is called the Davidic Covenant. It is both an expansion and a clarification of God's promises to Abraham. It represents an unconditional promise to David that he would be the father of an everlasting kingdom (v. 16). David is also promised that his son would reign over Israel (v. 12), and that this son (Solomon) would be the one to build a house for the Lord (v. 13). Elsewhere, God's reasons for not allowing David to build the temple are spelled out: he was a man of war and bloodshed (1 Kgs. 5:3; 1 Chr. 22:8; 28:3), whereas his son would be a man of peace. It was also too early to build the temple—the city is not yet secure (1 Kgs. 5:3, 4). David was, however, permitted to begin stockpiling the materials Solomon would use to build the temple (1 Chr. 22:2–19).

the name of the great *men* that *are* in the earth.[776]

10 Moreover I will appoint[7760] a place for my people Israel, and will [a]plant them, that they may dwell[7931] in a place of their own, and move no more; [b]neither shall the children of wickedness[5766] afflict them any more, as beforetime,

11 And as [a]since the time that I commanded judges[8199] *to be* over my people Israel, and have [b]caused thee to rest from all thine enemies. Also the LORD telleth thee [c]that he will make thee an house.

12 And [a]when thy days be fulfilled, and thou [b]shalt sleep with thy fathers,[1] [c]I will set up thy seed after thee, which shall proceed out of thy bowels,[4578] and I will establish his kingdom.[4467]

13 [a]He shall build an house for my name, and I will [b]stablish the throne of his kingdom for ever.

14 [a]I will be his father,[1] and he shall be my son. [b]If he commit iniquity,[5753] I will chasten[3198] him with the rod of men, and with the stripes of the children[1121] of men:

15 But my mercy shall not depart[5493] away from him, [a]as I took *it* from Saul, whom I put away before thee.

16 And [a]thine house and thy kingdom shall be established[539] for ever before thee: thy throne shall be established[3559] for ever.

17 According to all these words,[1697] and according to all this vision,[2384] so did Nathan speak unto David.

David's Prayer of Appreciation

18 Then went king David in, and sat before the LORD, and he said, [a]Who *am* I, O Lord[136] God? and what *is* my house, that thou hast brought me hitherto?

19 And this was yet a small thing in thy sight, O Lord God; [a]but thou hast spoken also of thy servant's house for a great while to come. [b]And *is* this the [I]manner[8452] of man, O Lord God?

20 And what can David say more unto thee? for thou, Lord GOD, [a]knowest[3045] thy servant.

21 For thy word's sake, and according to thine own heart, hast thou done[6213] all these great things, to make thy servant know *them.*

22 Wherefore [a]thou art great, O LORD God: for [b]*there is* none like thee, neither *is there any* God beside thee, according to all that we have heard with our ears.[241]

23 And [a]what one nation in the earth *is* like thy people, *even* like Israel, whom God went to redeem[6299] for a people to himself, and to make him a name, and to do for you great things and terrible,[3372] for thy land,[776] before [b]thy people, which thou redeemedst to thee from Egypt, *from* the nations and their gods?

24 For [a]thou hast confirmed[3559] to thyself thy people Israel *to be* a people unto thee for ever: [b]and thou, LORD, art become[1961] their God.

25 And now, O LORD God, the word that thou hast spoken concerning thy servant, and concerning his house, establish *it* for ever, and do as thou hast said.

26 And let thy name be magnified for ever, saying, The LORD of hosts *is* the God over Israel: and let the house of thy servant David be established before thee.

27 For thou, O LORD of hosts, God of Israel, hast [I]revealed[1540] to thy servant, saying, I will build thee an house:

10 [a]Ps. 44:2; 80:8; Jer. 24:6; Amos 9:15 [b]Ps. 89:22

11 [a]Judg. 2:14-16; 1Sam. 12:9, 11; Ps. 106:42 [b]2Sam. 7:1 [c]Ex. 1:21; 2Sam. 7:27; 1Kgs. 11:38

12 [a]1Kgs. 2:1 [b]Deut. 31:16; 1Kgs. 1:21; Acts 13:36 [c]1Kgs. 8:20; Ps. 132:11

13 [a]1Kgs. 5:5; 6:12; 8:19; 1Chr. 22:10; 28:6 [b]2Sam. 7:16; Ps. 89:4, 29, 36, 37

14 [a]Ps. 89:26, 27; Heb. 1:5 [b]Ps. 89:30–33

15 [a]1Sam. 15:23, 28; 16:14; 1Kgs. 11:13, 34

16 [a]2Sam. 7:13; Ps. 89:36, 37; John 12:34

18 [a]Gen. 32:10

19 [I]Hebr. *law* [a]2Sam. 7:12, 13 [b]Isa. 55:8

20 [a]Gen. 18:19; Ps. 139:1

22 [a]1Chr. 16:25; 2Chr. 2:5; Ps. 48:1; 86:10; 96:4; 135:5; 145:3; Jer. 10:6 [b]Deut. 3:24; 4:35; 32:39; 1Sam. 2:2; Ps. 86:8; 89:6, 8; Isa. 45:5, 18, 22

23 [a]Deut. 4:7, 32, 34; 33:29; Ps. 147:20 [b]Deut. 9:26; Neh. 1:10

24 [a]Deut. 26:18 [b]Ps. 48:14

27 [I]Hebr. *opened the ear*

7:13 This refers initially to Solomon, but ultimately the reference is to Jesus Christ, the "Son of David" (Luke 1:31–33; Acts 2:25–35) who reigns at God's right hand (Ps. 2:7; Acts 13:33).

7:24 These words affirm a central promise of the Scriptures to the Jewish people that He would be their God and they would be His people eternally (Gen. 17:7; Ex. 6:7; Deut. 7:6–9; Rom. 11:1–26; Rev. 21:3).

therefore hath thy servant found in his heart to pray this prayer unto thee.

28 And now, O Lord GOD, thou *art* that God, and [a]thy words be true,[571] and thou hast promised this goodness unto thy servant:

29 Therefore now [I]let it please thee to bless[1288] the house of thy servant, that it may continue for ever before thee: for thou, O Lord GOD, hast spoken *it:* and with thy blessing[1293] let the house of thy servant be blessed[1288] [a]for ever.[5769]

David's Military Success

8 And [a]after this it came to pass, that David smote the Philistines, and subdued[3665] them: and David took [I]Metheg–ammah out of the hand of the Philistines.

2 And [a]he smote Moab, and measured[4058] them with a line,[2256] casting them down to the ground;[776] even with two lines[2256] measured he to put to death,[4191] and with one full line to keep alive. And *so* the Moabites [b]became David's servants, *and* [c]brought[5375] gifts.[4503]

3 David smote also [Ia]Hadadezer, the son of Rehob, king[4428] of [b]Zobah, as he went to recover [c]his border at the river Euphrates.

4 And David took [I]from him a thousand *chariots,* and seven hundred horsemen, and twenty thousand footmen: and David [a]houghed[6131] all the chariot *horses,* but reserved of them *for* an hundred chariots.

5 [a]And when the Syrians of Damascus came to succour[5826] Hadadezer king of Zobah, David slew of the Syrians two and twenty thousand men.

6 Then David put garrisons in Syria of Damascus: and the Syrians [a]became servants to David, *and* brought gifts. [b]And the LORD preserved David whithersoever he went.

7 And David took [a]the shields of gold that were on the servants of Hadadezer, and brought them to Jerusalem.

8 And from [I]Betah, and from [IIa]Berothai, cities of Hadadezer, king David took exceeding much brass.

9 When [Ia]Toi king of Hamath heard that David had smitten all the host of Hadadezer,

10 Then Toi sent [a]Joram his son unto king David, to [I]salute him, and to bless[1288] him, because he had fought against Hadadezer, and smitten him: for Hadadezer [II]had wars with Toi. And *Joram* [III]brought with him vessels of silver, and vessels of gold, and vessels of brass:

11 Which also king David [a]did dedicate[6942] unto the LORD, with the silver and gold that he had dedicated of all nations which he subdued;

12 Of Syria, and of Moab, and of the children of Ammon, and of the Philistines, and of Amalek, and of the spoil of Hadadezer, son of Rehob, king of Zobah.

13 And David gat *him* a name when he returned from [I]smiting[5221] of the Syrians in [a]the valley of salt, [IIb]*being* eighteen thousand *men.*

14 And he put garrisons in Edom; throughout all Edom put he garrisons, and [a]all they of Edom became David's servants. [b]And the LORD preserved David withersoever he went.

David's Officials

15 And David reigned over all Israel; and David executed[6213] judgment[4941] and justice[6666] unto all his people.

16 [a]And Joab the son of Zeruiah *was* over the host; and [b]Jehoshaphat the son of Ahilud *was* [I]recorder;[2142]

17 And [a]Zadok the son of Ahitub, and Ahimelech the son of Abiathar, *were* the priests; and Seraiah *was* the [I]scribe;[5608]

18 [a]And Benaiah the son of Jehoiada *was over* both the [b]Cherethites and the Pelethites; and David's sons were [Ic]chief rulers.[3548]

David's Kindness to Mephibosheth

9 And David said, Is there yet any that is left[3498] of the house of Saul,

---

28 [a]John 17:17
29 [I]Hebr. *be thou pleased and bless* [a]2Sam. 22:51
1 [I]Or, *The bridle of Ammah* [a]1Chr. 18:1
2 [a]Num. 24:17 [b]2Sam. 8:6 [c]1Sam. 10:27; Ps. 72:10
3 [I]Or, *Hadarezer* [a]1Chr. 18:3 [b]2Sam. 10:6 [c]Gen. 15:18
4 [I]Or, *of his* [a]Josh. 11:6, 9
5 [a]1Kgs. 11:23-25
6 [a]2Sam. 8:2 [b]2Sam. 7:9; 8:14
7 [a]1Kgs. 10:16
8 [I]Or, *Tibhath* [II]Or, *Chun* [a]1Chr. 18:8
9 [I]*Tou* [a]1Chr. 18:9
10 [I]Hebr. *ask him of peace* [II]Hebr. *was a man of wars with* [III]Hebr. *in his hand were* [a]1Chr. 18:10, *Hadoram*
11 [a]1Kgs. 7:51; 1Chr. 18:11; 26:26
13 [I]Hebr. *his smiting* [II]Or, *slaying* [a]2Kgs. 14:7 [b]1Chr. 18:12
14 [a]Gen. 27:29, 37, 40; Num. 24:18 [b]2Sam. 8:6
16 [I]Or, *remembrancer,* or, *writer of chronicles* [a]2Sam. 19:13; 20:23; 1Chr. 11:6; 18:15 [b]1Kgs. 4:3
17 [I]Or, *secretary* [a]1Chr. 24:3
18 [I]Or, *princes* [a]1Chr. 18:17 [b]1Sam. 30:14 [c]2Sam. 20:26

that I may [a]shew him kindness[2617] for Jonathan's sake?

2 And *there was* of the house of Saul a servant whose name *was* [a]Ziba. And when they had called[7121] him unto David, the king[4428] said unto him, *Art* thou Ziba? And he said, Thy servant *is he.*

3 And the king said, *Is* there not yet any of the house of Saul, that I may shew the [a]kindness of God[430] unto him? And Ziba said unto the king, Jonathan hath yet a son, *which is* [b]lame[5223] on *his* feet.

4 And the king said unto him, Where *is* he? And Ziba said unto the king, Behold, he *is* in the house of [a]Machir, the son of Ammiel, in Lo–debar.

5 Then king David sent, and fetched him out of the house of Machir, the son of Ammiel, from Lo–debar.

6 Now when [I][a]Mephibosheth, the son of Jonathan, the son of Saul, was come unto David, he fell[5307] on his face, and did reverence. And David said, Mephibosheth. And he answered,[559] Behold thy servant!

7 And David said unto him, Fear[3372] not: [a]for I will surely shew thee kindness for Jonathan thy father's sake, and will restore thee all the land of Saul thy father;[1] and thou shalt eat bread at my table continually.[8548]

8 And he bowed[7812] himself, and said, What *is* thy servant, that thou shouldest look upon such [a]a dead[4191] dog as I *am?*

9 Then the king called to Ziba, Saul's servant, and said unto him, [a]I have given unto thy master's son all that pertained to Saul and to all his house.

10 Thou therefore, and thy sons, and thy servants, shall till the land[127] for him, and thou shalt bring in *the fruits,* that thy master's son may have food to eat: but Mephibosheth thy master's son [a]shall eat bread alway[8548] at my table. Now Ziba had [b]fifteen sons and twenty servants.

11 Then said Ziba unto the king, According to all that my lord[113] the king hath commanded[6680] his servant, so shall thy servant do.[6213] As for Mephibo sheth, *said the king,* he shall eat at my table, as one of the king's[4428] sons.

12 And Mephibosheth had a young son, [a]whose name *was* Micha. And all that dwelt in the house of Ziba *were* servants unto Mephibosheth.

13 So Mephibosheth dwelt in Jerusalem: [a]for he did eat continually at the king's table; and [b]was lame on both his feet.

Israel Defeats the Ammonites And Syrians

10 And it came to pass after this, that the [a]king of the children[1121] of Ammon died,[4191] and Hanun his son reigned in his stead.

2 Then said David, I will shew kindness[2617] unto Hanun the son of Nahash, as his father[1] shewed kindness unto me. And David sent to comfort[5162] him by the hand of his servants for his father. And David's servants came into the land[776] of the children of Ammon.

3 And the princes of the children of Ammon said unto Hanun their lord,[113] [I]Thinkest thou that David doth honour thy father, that he hath sent comforters[5162] unto thee? hath not David *rather* sent his servants unto thee, to search the city, and to spy it out, and to overthrow[2015] it?

4 Wherefore Hanun took David's servants, and shaved off the one half of their beards,[2206] and cut off[3772] their garments in the middle, [a]*even* to their buttocks, and sent them away.

5 When they told *it* unto David, he sent to meet them, because the men were greatly ashamed: and the king said, Tarry at Jericho until your beards be grown, and *then* return.

6 And when the children of Ammon saw that they [a]stank[887] before David, the children of Ammon sent and hired [b]the Syrians of Beth–rehob, and the Syrians of Zoba, twenty thousand footmen, and of king Maacah a thousand men, and of [I][c]Ish–tob twelve thousand men.

7 And when David heard of *it,* he

---

1 [a]1Sam. 18:3; 20:14-17, 42; Prov. 27:10

2 [a]2Sam. 16:1; 19:17, 29

3 [a]1Sam. 20:14 [b]2Sam. 4:4

4 [a]2Sam. 17:27

6 [I]Called, *Meribbaal* [a]1Chr. 8:34

7 [a]2Sam. 9:1, 3

8 [a]1Sam. 24:14; 2Sam. 16:9

9 [a]2Sam. 16:4; 19:29

10 [a]2Sam. 9:7, 11, 13; 19:28 [b]2Sam. 19:17

12 [a]1Chr. 8:34

13 [a]2Sam. 9:7, 10 [b]2Sam. 9:3

1 [a]1Chr. 19:3

3 [I]Hebr. *In thine eyes doth David*

4 [a]Isa. 20:4; 47:2

6 [I]Or, *the men of Tob* [a]Gen. 34:30; Ex. 5:21; 1Sam. 13:4 [b]2Sam. 8:3, 5 [c]Judg. 11:3, 5 sent Joab, and all the host of [a]the mighty men.

8 And the children of Ammon came out, and put the battle in array at the entering in of the gate: and [a]the Syrians of Zoba, and of Rehob, and Ishtob, and Maacah, *were* by themselves in the field.[7704]

9 When Joab saw that the front of the battle was against him before and behind, he chose[977] of all the choice[977] *men* of Israel, and put *them* in array against the Syrians:

10 And the rest of the people he delivered into the hand of Abishai his brother,[251] that he might put *them* in array against the children of Ammon.

11 And he said, If the Syrians be too strong for me, then thou shalt help me: but if the children of Ammon be too strong for thee, then I will come and help thee.

12 [a]Be of good courage,[2388] and let us [b]play the men[2388] for our people, and for the cities of our God:[430] and [c]the LORD do[6213] that which seemeth him good.[2896]

13 And Joab drew nigh, and the people that *were* with him, unto the battle against the Syrians: and they fled before him.

14 And when the children of Ammon saw that the Syrians were fled, then fled they also before Abishai, and entered into the city. So Joab returned from the children of Ammon, and came to Jerusalem.

15 And when the Syrians saw that they were smitten before Israel, they gathered[622] themselves together.

16 And Hadarezer sent, and brought out the Syrians that *were* beyond [I]the river: and they came to Helam; and [II][a]Shobach the captain[8269] of the host of Hadarezer *went* before them.

17 And when it was told David, he gathered all Israel together, and passed over Jordan, and came to Helam. And the Syrians set themselves in array against David, and fought with him.

18 And the Syrians fled before Israel; and David slew *the men of* seven hundred chariots of the Syrians, and forty thousand [a]horsemen, and smote Shobach the captain of their host, who died there.

19 And when all the kings[4428] *that were* servants to Hadarezer saw that they were smitten before Israel, they made peace with Israel, and [a]served them. So the Syrians feared[3372] to help the children of Ammon any more.

David and Bath-sheba

11 And it came to pass, [I]after the year was expired, at the time when kings go forth *to battle,* that [a]David sent Joab, and his servants with him, and all Israel; and they destroyed[7843] the children[1121] of Ammon, and besieged Rabbah. But David tarried still at Jerusalem.

2 And it came to pass in an eveningtide,[6256][6153] that David arose from off his bed, [a]and walked upon the roof of the king's house: and from the roof he [b]saw a woman[802] washing[7364] herself; and the woman *was* very beautiful[2896] to look upon.

3 And David sent and enquired after the woman. And *one* said, *Is* not this [I][a]Bath-sheba, the daughter of [II]Eliam, the wife[802] [b]of Uriah the Hittite?

4 And David sent messengers, and took her; and she came in unto him, and he [a]lay with her; [I]for she was [b]purified from her uncleanness:[2932] and she returned unto her house.

5 And the woman conceived, and sent and told David, and said, I *am* with child.

6 And David sent to Joab, *saying,*

7 [a]2Sam. 23:8
8 [a]2Sam. 10:6
12 [a]Deut. 31:6 [b]1Sam. 4:9; 1Cor. 16:13 [c]1Sam. 3:18
16 [I]That is, *Euhphrates* [II]Or, *Shophach* [a]1Chr. 19:16
18 [a]1Chr. 19:18, *footmen*
19 [a]2Sam. 8:6
1 [I]Hebr. *at the return of the year* [a]1Chr. 20:1
2 [a]Deut. 22:8 [b]Gen. 34:2; Job 31:1; Matt. 5:28
3 [I]Or, *Bathshua* [II]Or, *Ammiel* [a]1Chr. 3:5 [b]2Sam. 23:39
4 [I]Or, *and when she had purified herself, she returned* [a]James 1:14 [b]Lev. 15:18

10:14 After the rainy season was over, Joab commenced the siege the next spring (2 Sam. 11:1). It was too late in the year to undertake a full-scale siege.

Send me Uriah the Hittite. And Joab sent Uriah to David.

7 And when Uriah was come unto him, David demanded[7592] *of him* [I]how Joab did, and how the people did, and how the war prospered.[7965]

8 And David said to Uriah, Go down to thy house, and [a]wash[7364] thy feet. And Uriah departed out of the king's house, and there [I]followed him a mess[4864] *of meat* from the king.

9 But Uriah slept at the door of the king's house with all the servants of his lord,[113] and went not down to his house.

10 And when they had told David, saying, Uriah went not down unto his house, David said unto Uriah, Camest thou not from *thy* journey?[1870] why *then* didst thou not go down unto thine house?

11 And Uriah said unto David, [a]The ark,[727] and Israel, and Judah, abide in tents; and [b]my lord Joab, and the servants of my lord, are encamped in the open fields;[7704] shall I then go into mine house, to eat and to drink, and to lie with my wife? *as* thou livest, and *as* thy soul liveth,[2416] I will not do[6213] this thing.

12 And David said to Uriah, Tarry here to day[3117] also, and to morrow I will let thee depart. So Uriah abode in Jerusalem that day, and the morrow.

13 And when David had called[7121] him, he did eat and drink before him; and he made him [a]drunk: and at even he went out to lie on his bed [b]with the servants of his lord, but went not down to his house.

14 And it came to pass in the morning, that David [a]wrote a letter[5612] to Joab, and sent *it* by the hand of Uriah.

15 And he wrote in the letter, saying, Set ye Uriah in the forefront of the [I]hottest battle, and retire ye [II]from him, that he may [a]be smitten, and die.[4191]

16 And it came to pass, when Joab observed[8104] the city, that he assigned Uriah unto a place where he knew[3045] that valiant men *were.*

17 And the men of the city went out, and fought with Joab: and there fell[5307] *some* of the people of the servants of David; and Uriah the Hittite died also.

18 Then Joab sent and told David all the things concerning the war;

19 And charged[6680] the messenger, saying, When thou hast made an end[3615] of telling the matters of the war unto the king,

20 And if so be that the king's wrath arise,[5927] and he say unto thee, Wherefore approached ye so nigh unto the city when ye did fight? knew ye not that they would shoot from the wall?

21 Who smote [a]Abimelech the son of [Ib]Jerubbesheth? did not a woman cast a piece of a millstone upon him from the wall, that he died in Thebez? why went ye nigh the wall? then say thou, Thy servant Uriah the Hittite is dead[4191] also.

22 So the messenger went, and came and shewed David all that Joab had sent him for.

23 And the messenger said unto David, Surely the men prevailed against us, and came out unto us into the field,[7704] and we were upon them even unto the entering of the gate.

24 And the shooters shot[3384] from off the wall upon thy servants; and *some* of the king's servants be dead, and thy servant Uriah the Hittite is dead also.

25 Then David said unto the messenger, Thus shalt thou say unto Joab, Let not this thing [I]displease thee, for the sword devoureth [II]one as well as another: make thy battle more strong against the city, and overthrow it: and encourage[2388] thou him.

26 And when the wife of Uriah heard that Uriah her husband was dead, she mourned for her husband.

27 And when the mourning was past, David sent and fetched[622] her to his house, and she [a]became his wife, and bare him a son. But the thing that David had done[6213] [I]displeased the LORD.

7 [I]Hebr. *of the peace of*

8 [I]Hebr. *went out after him* [a]Gen. 18:4; 19:2

11 [a]2Sam. 7:2, 6 [b]2Sam. 20:6

13 [a]Gen. 19:33, 35 [b]2Sam. 11:9

14 [a]1Kgs. 21:8, 9

15 [I]Hebr. *strong* [II]Hebr. *from after him* [a]2Sam. 12:9

21 [I]That is, *Let the shameful thing plead* [a]Judg. 9:53 [b]Judg. 6:32, *Jerubbaal*

25 [I]Hebr. *be evil in thine eyes* [II]Hebr. *so and such*

27 [I]Hebr. *was evil in the eyes of* [a]2Sam. 12:9

Nathan Confronts David

12 🔑 And the LORD sent Nathan unto David. And he came unto him, and [a]said unto him, There were two men in one city; the one rich, and the other poor.

2 The rich *man* had exceeding many flocks and herds:

3 But the poor *man* had nothing, save one little ewe lamb,[3535] which he had bought and nourished up: and it grew up together with him, and with his children;[1121] it did eat of his own [1]meat, and drank of his own cup, and lay in his bosom, and was unto him as a daughter.

4 And there came a traveller[1982] unto the rich man, and he spared[2550] to take of his own flock and of his own herd, to dress[6213] for the wayfaring man[732] that was come unto him; but took the poor man's lamb, and dressed[6213] it for the man that was come to him.

5 And David's anger[639] was greatly kindled[2734] against the man; and he said to Nathan, *As* the LORD liveth,[2416] the man that hath done[6213] this *thing* [1][a]shall surely die:[4194]

6 And he shall restore the lamb [a]fourfold, because he did this thing, and because he had no pity.[2550]

7 And Nathan said to David, Thou *art* the man. Thus saith the LORD God[430] of Israel, I [a]anointed[4886] thee king[4428] over Israel, and I delivered[5337] thee out of the hand of Saul;

8 And I gave thee thy master's house, and thy master's wives[802] into thy bosom, and gave thee the house of Israel and of Judah; and if *that had been* too little, I would moreover have given unto thee such and such things.

9 [a]Wherefore hast thou [b]despised the commandment[1697] of the LORD, to do evil[7451] in his sight? [c]thou hast killed[5221] Uriah the Hittite with the sword, and hast taken his wife *to be* thy wife, and hast slain him with the sword of the children of Ammon.

10 Now therefore [a]the sword shall never depart[5493] from thine house; because thou hast despised me, and hast taken the wife of Uriah the Hittite to be thy wife.

11 Thus saith the LORD, Behold, I will raise up evil against thee out of thine own house, and I will [a]take thy wives before thine eyes, and give *them* unto thy neighbour, and he shall lie with thy wives in the sight of this sun.

12 For thou didst *it* secretly: [a]but I will do this thing before all Israel, and before the sun.

13 [a]And David said unto Nathan, [b]I have sinned against the LORD. And Nathan said unto David, The LORD also hath [c]put away thy sin; thou shalt not die.[4191]

14 Howbeit, because by this deed thou hast given great occasion to the enemies of the LORD [a]to blaspheme,[5006] the child[1121] also *that is* born unto thee shall surely die.

The Child Dies

15 And Nathan departed unto his house. And the LORD struck[5062] the child

1 [a]2Sam. 14:5; 1Kgs. 20:35-41; Isa. 5:3
3 [1]Hebr. *morsel*
5 [1]Or, is *worthy to die,* or, is *a son of death* [a]1Sam. 26:16
6 [a]Ex. 22:1; Luke 19:8
7 [a]1Sam. 16:13
9 [a]1Sam. 15:19 [b]Num. 15:31 [c]2Sam. 11:15-17, 27
10 [a]Amos 7:9
11 [a]Deut. 28:30; 2Sam. 16:22
12 [a]2Sam. 16:22
13 [a]1Sam. 15:24 [b]2Sam. 24:10; Job 7:20; Ps. 32:5; 51:4; Prov. 28:13 [c]2Sam. 24:10; Job 7:21; Ps. 32:1; Mic. 7:18; Zech. 3:4
14 [a]Isa. 52:5; Ezek. 36:20, 23; Rom. 2:24

🔑 **12:1–14** Here the consequences of David's great sin became evident to him. Observe how skillfully Nathan used his parable (vv. 1–4) to bring David to condemn himself. David had violated four of the ten commandments in one rash sin: thou shalt not kill, thou shalt not steal, thou shalt not commit adultery, and thou shalt not covet your neighbor's wife. Although it was about a year later, David sincerely repented of his sin (see Ps. 32:3, 4; 51:1–19). While his repentance brought about forgiveness from God, it did not prevent him from suffering the consequences of his sin. God revealed that because of David's sin, the son born from his adulterous relationship would die (2 Sam. 12:14, 18), the sword would never depart from his house (v. 10), evil would come from his own family (v. 11; see chaps. 15–18), and his wives would be publicly shamed (v. 11; see 2 Sam. 16:22). The important lesson to learn from these events is that even the best of men can sin. Also, true repentance does bring forgiveness from God, but does not eliminate the consequences of sin.

that Uriah's wife bare unto David, and it
was very sick.
16 David therefore besought God for
the child; and David [I]fasted, and went in,
and [a]lay all night upon the earth.[776]
17 And the elders[2205] of his house
arose, *and went* to him, to raise him up
from the earth: but he would[14] not, neither did he eat bread with them.
18 And it came to pass on the seventh day, that the child died.[4191] And the
servants of David feared[3372] to tell him
that the child was dead: for they said,
Behold, while the child was yet alive,[2416]
we spake unto him, and he would not
hearken unto our voice: how will he then
[I]vex[7451] himself, if we tell him that the
child is dead?
19 But when David saw that his servants whispered,[3907] David perceived[995]
that the child was dead: therefore David
said unto his servants, Is the child dead?
And they said, He is dead.
20 Then David arose from the earth,
and washed,[7364] and [a]anointed[5480] *himself,* and changed his apparel, and came
into the house of the LORD, and
[b]worshipped:[7812] then he came to his own
house; and when he required, they set
bread before him, and he did eat.
21 Then said his servants unto him,
What thing *is* this that thou hast done?
thou didst fast and weep for the child,
while it was alive; but when the child
was dead, thou didst rise and eat bread.
22 And he said, While the child was
yet alive, I fasted and wept: [a]for I said,
Who can tell *whether* God will be
gracious[2603] to me, that the child may
live?[2416]
23 But now he is dead, wherefore
should I fast? can I bring him back
again? I shall go to him, but [a]he shall not
return to me.

Solomon Is Born

24 And David comforted[5162] Bath–
sheba his wife, and went in unto her, and
lay with her: and [a]she bare a son, and [b]he
called[7121] his name Solomon: and the
LORD loved[157] him.
25 And he sent by the hand of
Nathan the prophet; and he called his
name [I]Jedidiah,[3041] because of the LORD.

Another Victory Over the Ammonites

26 And [a]Joab fought against [b]Rabbah
of the children of Ammon, and took the
royal city.
27 And Joab sent messengers to
David, and said, I have fought against
Rabbah, and have taken[3920] the city of
waters.
28 Now therefore gather the rest of
the people together,[622] and encamp
against the city, and take it: lest I take
the city, and [I]it be called after my name.
29 And David gathered all the people
together, and went to Rabbah, and fought
against it, and took it.

16 [I]Hebr. *fasted a fast* [a]2Sam. 13:31
18 [I]Hebr. *do hurt*
20 [a]Ruth 3:3 [b]Job 1:20
22 [a]Isa. 38:1, 5; Jon. 3:9
23 [a]Job 7:8-10
24 [a]Matt. 1:6 [b]1Chr. 22:9
25 [I]That is, *Beloved of the LORD*
26 [a]1Chr. 20:1 [b]Deut. 3:11
28 [I]Hebr. *my name be called upon it*

12:23 The phrase in this verse "I shall go to him, but he shall not return to me" that David spoke after the child died should be understood to mean that David was aware previous to the death of the child of its inevitability; therefore, he no longer wept for the life of the child. In addition to this, David also realized that there would be a time in the future when he too would die, and there he would be joined to his son who had died. While the child was alive, David's prayer was for life; after the death of the child, he no longer saw the need to mourn for him, but rather he continued living with the expectancy of someday being with his child again. This verse has been used as a source of comfort for those who have lost infants or small children to early deaths.

12:24 Solomon's name appears fourth on the lists of Bathsheba's sons (2 Sam. 5:14–16; 1 Chr. 3:5; 14:4), but this does not necessarily mean that he was the fourth born. This verse seems to indicate that he was the oldest of David's and Bathsheba's sons. However, he was not David's firstborn, for it is clear from 2 Samuel 3:2–5 and 1 Chronicles 3:1–9 that David had six sons born to him in Hebron. Normally, the firstborn son would succeed the father a king; but in this case, God made Solomon his choice. In 1 Chronicles 28:4, 5, David says, "he [God] hath chosen Solomon my son"; and in 1 Chronicles 29:1, he says "Solomon my son, whom alone God hath chosen."

30 [a]And he took their king's[4428] crown from off his head, the weight whereof *was* a talent of gold with the precious stones: and it was *set* on David's head. And he brought forth the spoil of the city [I]in great abundance.

31 And he brought forth the people that *were* therein, and put *them* under saws, and under harrows[2757] of iron, and under axes of iron, and made them pass through[5674] the brickkiln: and thus did he unto all the cities of the children of Ammon. So David and all the people returned unto Jerusalem.

Amnon Rapes Tamar

13 And it came to pass after this, [a]that Absalom the son of David had a fair[3303] sister, whose name *was* [b]Tamar; and Amnon the son of David loved[157] her.

2 And Amnon was so vexed,[3334] that he fell sick for his sister Tamar; for she *was* a virgin;[1330] and [I]Amnon thought it hard for him to do[6213] any thing to her.

3 But Amnon had a friend,[7453] whose name *was* Jonadab, [a]the son of Shimeah David's brother: and Jonadab *was* a very subtil[2450] man.

4 And he said unto him, Why *art* thou, *being* the king's[4428] son, [I]lean [II]from day to day? wilt thou not tell me? And Amnon said unto him, I love Tamar, my brother Absalom's sister.

5 And Jonadab said unto him, Lay thee down on thy bed, and make thyself sick: and when thy father cometh to see thee, say unto him, I pray thee, let my sister Tamar come, and give me meat, and dress[6213] the meat in my sight, that I may see *it,* and eat *it* at her hand.

6 So Amnon lay down, and made himself sick: and when the king was come to see him, Amnon said unto the king, I pray thee, let Tamar my sister come, and [a]make[3823] me a couple of cakes in my sight, that I may eat at her hand.

7 Then David sent home to Tamar, saying, Go now to thy brother Amnon's house, and dress him meat.

8 So Tamar went to her brother Amnon's house; and he was laid down. And she took [I]flour, and kneaded *it,* and made cakes in his sight, and did bake[1310] the cakes.

9 And she took a pan, and poured *them* out before him; but he refused to eat. And Amnon said, [a]Have out all men from me. And they went out every man from him.

10 And Amnon said unto Tamar, Bring the meat into the chamber, that I may eat of thine hand. And Tamar took the cakes which she had made, and brought *them* unto the chamber to Amnon her brother.

11 And when she had brought[5066] *them* unto him to eat, he [a]took hold of her, and said unto her, Come lie with me, my sister.

12 And she answered[559] him, Nay, my brother, do not [I]force me; for [II][a]no such thing ought to be done in Israel: do not thou this [b]folly.[5039]

13 And I, whither shall I cause my shame to go? and as for thee, thou shalt be as one of the fools in Israel. Now therefore, I pray thee, speak unto the king; [a]for he will not withhold me from thee.

14 Howbeit he would[14] not hearken unto her voice: but, being stronger than she, [a]forced her, and lay with her.

🔑 15 Then Amnon hated her [I]exceedingly; so that the hatred wherewith he hated her *was* greater than the love wherewith he had loved her. And Amnon said unto her, Arise, be gone.

16 And she said unto him, *There is* no cause: this evil[7451] in sending me away *is* greater than the other that thou didst[6213] unto me. But he would not hearken unto her.

30 [I]Hebr. *very great* [a]1Chr. 20:2
1 [a]2Sam. 3:2, 3 [b]1Chr. 3:9
2 [I]Hebr. *it was marvelous,* or, *hidden in the eyes of Amnon*
3 [a]1Sam. 16:9
4 [I]Hebr. *thin* [II]Hebr. *morning by morning*
6 [a]Gen. 18:6
8 [I]Or, *paste*
9 [a]Gen. 45:1
11 [a]Gen. 39:12
12 [I]Hebr. *humble me* [II]Hebr. *it ought not so to be done* [a]Lev. 18:9, 11; 20:17 [b]Gen. 34:7; Judg. 19:23; 20:6
13 [a]Lev. 18:9, 11
14 [a]Deut. 22:25; 2Sam. 12:11
15 [I]Hebr. *with great hatred greatly*

🔑 **13:15** This verse shows how there can be consuming desire without love. Once Amnon used Tamar to satisfy his sinful lust, he was filled with a feeling of contempt.

17 Then he called[7121] his servant that ministered unto him, and said, Put now this *woman* out from me, and bolt the door after her.

18 And *she had* [a]a garment of divers colours[6446] upon her: for with such robes were the king's daughters *that were* virgins[1330] apparelled. Then his servant brought her out, and bolted the door after her.

19 And Tamar put [a]ashes on her head, and rent her garment[3801] of divers colours that *was* on her, and [b]laid[7760] her hand on her head, and went on crying.

Absalom Avenges Tamar

20 And Absalom her brother said unto her, Hath [I]Amnon thy brother been with thee? but hold now thy peace, my sister: he *is* thy brother; [II]regard not this thing. So Tamar remained [III]desolate[8076] in her brother Absalom's house.

21 But when king David heard of all these things, he was very wroth.[2734]

22 And Absalom spake unto his brother Amnon [a]neither good[2896] nor bad:[7451] for Absalom [b]hated Amnon, because he had forced his sister Tamar.

23 And it came to pass after two full years, that Absalom [a]had sheepshearers in Baalhazor, which *is* beside Ephraim: and Absalom invited[7121] all the king's sons.

24 And Absalom came to the king, and said, Behold now, thy servant hath sheepshearers; let the king, I beseech thee, and his servants go with thy servant.

25 And the king said to Absalom, Nay, my son, let us not all now go, lest we be chargeable[3513] unto thee. And he pressed[6555] him: howbeit he would not go, but blessed[1288] him.

26 Then said Absalom, If not, I pray thee, let my brother Amnon go with us. And the king said unto him, Why should he go with thee?

27 But Absalom pressed him, that he let Amnon and all the king's sons go with him.

28 Now Absalom had commanded his servants, saying, Mark ye now when Amnon's [a]heart is merry[2896] with wine, and when I say unto you, Smite Amnon; then kill[4191] him, fear[3372] not: [I][b]have not I commanded you? be courageous,[2388] and be [II]valiant.

29 And the servants of Absalom did[6213] unto Amnon as Absalom had commanded. Then all the king's sons arose, and every man [I]gat him up upon his mule, and fled.

30 And it came to pass, while they were in the way,[1870] that tidings came to David, saying, Absalom hath slain all the king's sons, and there is not one of them left.[3498]

31 Then the king arose, and [a]tare his garments, and [b]lay on the earth;[776] and all his servants stood by with their clothes rent.

32 And [a]Jonadab, the son of Shimeah David's brother, answered and said, Let not my lord[113] suppose *that* they have slain all the young men the king's sons; for Amnon only is dead:[4191] for by the [I]appointment[6310] of Absalom this hath been [II]determined[7760] from the day that he forced his sister Tamar.

33 Now therefore [a]let not my lord the king take the thing to his heart, to think that all the king's sons are dead: for Amnon only is dead.

Absalom Escapes

34 [a]But Absalom fled. And the young man that kept the watch lifted up his eyes, and looked,[7200] and, behold, there came much people by the way of the hill side behind him.

35 And Jonadab said unto the king, Behold, the king's sons come: [I]as thy servant said, so it is.

36 And it came to pass, as soon as he had made an end[3615] of speaking, that, behold, the king's sons came, and lifted up their voice and wept: and the king also and all his servants wept [I]very sore.

37 But Absalom fled, and went to [a]Talmai, the son of [I]Ammihud, king of Geshur. And *David* mourned for his son every day.

18 [a]Gen. 37:3; Judg. 5:30; Ps. 45:14

19 [a]Josh. 7:6; 2Sam. 1:2; Job 2:12 [b]Jer. 2:37

20 [I]Hebr. *Aminon* [II]Hebr. *set not thine heart* [III]Hebr. *and desolate*

22 [a]Gen. 24:50; 31:24 [b]Lev. 19:17, 18

23 [a]Gen. 38:12, 13; 1Sam. 25:4, 36

28 [I]Or, *will you not, since I have commanded you?* [II]Hebr. *sons of valor* [a]Judg. 19:6, 9, 22; Ruth 3:7; 1Sam. 25:36; Esth. 1:10; Ps. 104:15

29 [I]Hebr. *rode*

31 [a]2Sam. 1:11 [b]2Sam. 12:16

32 [I]Hebr. *mouth* [II]Or, *settled* [a]2Sam. 13:3

33 [a]2Sam. 19:19

34 [a]2Sam. 13:38

35 [I]Hebr. *according to the word of thy servant*

36 [I]Hebr. *with a great weeping greatly*

37 [I]Or, *Ammihur* [a]2Sam. 3:3

38 So Absalom fled, and went to [a]Geshur, and was there three years.

39 And *the soul of* king David [I][a]longed[3615] to go forth unto Absalom: for he was [b]comforted[5162] concerning Amnon, seeing he was dead.

Joab Plots Absalom's Return

14 Now Joab the son of Zeruiah perceived that the king's[4428] heart *was* [a]toward Absalom.

2 And Joab sent to [a]Tekoah, and fetched thence a wise[2450] woman,[802] and said unto her, I pray thee, feign thyself to be a mourner, [b]and put on now mourning apparel, and anoint[5480] not thyself with oil,[8081] but be as a woman that had a long time mourned for the dead:

3 And come to the king, and speak on this manner unto him. So Joab [a]put the words[1697] in her mouth.

4 And when the woman of Tekoah spake to the king, she [a]fell[5307] on her face[639] to the ground,[776] and did obeisance,[7812] and said, [I][b]Help, O king.

5 And the king said unto her, What aileth thee? And she answered,[559] [a]I *am* indeed a widow[490] woman, and mine husband is dead.

6 And thy handmaid had two sons, and they two strove together[5327] in the field,[7704] and *there was* [I]none to part them, but the one smote the other, and slew him.

7 And, behold, [a]the whole family[4940] is risen against thine handmaid, and they said, Deliver him that smote his brother,[251] that we may kill[4191] him, for the life[5315] of his brother whom he slew; and we will destroy[8045] the heir also: and so they shall quench[3518] my coal which is left,[7604] and shall not leave to my husband *neither* name nor remainder [I]upon the earth.[127]

8 And the king said unto the woman, Go to thine house, and I will give charge[6680] concerning thee.

🔑 9 And the woman of Tekoah said unto the king, My lord,[113] O king, [a]the iniquity[5771] *be* on me, and on my father's[1] house: [b]and the king and his throne *be* guiltless.[5355]

10 And the king said, Whosoever saith *ought* unto thee, bring him to me, and he shall not touch thee any more.

11 Then said she, I pray thee, let the king remember the LORD thy God,[430] [I]that thou wouldest not suffer [a]the revengers of blood[1818] to destroy[7843] any more, lest they destroy my son. And he said, [b]*As* the LORD liveth,[2416] there shall not one hair of thy son fall to the earth.[776]

12 Then the woman said, Let thine handmaid, I pray thee, speak *one* word[1697] unto my lord the king. And he said, Say on.

13 And the woman said, Wherefore then hast thou thought such a thing against [a]the people of God? for the king doth speak this thing as one which is faulty,[818] in that the king doth not fetch home again [b]his banished.

14 For we [a]must needs die, and *are* as water spilt on the ground, which cannot be gathered up again;[622] [I]neither doth God respect *any* person: yet doth he [b]devise[2803] means, that his banished[5080] be not expelled from him.

15 Now therefore that I am come to speak of this thing unto my lord the king, *it is* because the people have made me afraid:[3372] and thy handmaid said, I will now speak unto the king; it may be that the king will perform the request of his handmaid.

16 For the king will hear, to deliver[5337] his handmaid out of the hand of the man *that would* destroy me and my son together out of the inheritance[5159] of God.

38 [a]2Sam. 14:23, 32; 15:8
39 [I]Or, *was consumed* [a]Ps. 84:2 [b]Gen. 38:12
1 [a]2Sam. 13:39
2 [a]2Chr. 11:6 [b]Ruth 3:3
3 [a]Ex. 4:15; 2Sam. 14:19
4 [I]Hebr. *Save* [a]1Sam. 20:41; 2Sam. 1:2 [b]2Kgs. 6:26, 28
5 [a]2Sam. 12:1
6 [I]Hebr. *no deliverer between them*
7 [I]Hebr. *upon the face of the earth* [a]Num. 35:19; Deut. 19:12
9 [a]Gen. 27:13; 1Sam. 25:24; Matt. 27:25 [b]2Sam. 3:28, 29; 1Kgs. 2:33
11 [I]Hebr. *that the revenger of blood do not multiply to destroy* [a]Num. 35:19 [b]1Sam. 14:45; Acts 27:34
13 [a]Judg. 20:2 [b]2Sam. 13:37, 38
14 [I]Hebr. Or, *because God hath not taken away* his *life, he hath also devised means* [a]Job 34:15; Heb. 9:27 [b]Num. 35:15, 25, 28

🔑 **14:9** Joab here demonstrates his shrewdness by getting Absalom restored to his position in the king's family despite the fact that he murdered Amnon. Through the help of a "wise woman" (see note on 2 Sam. 20:16), Joab induced David to pardon an intentional killing and confirm it with an oath, so that David would have no excuse for not accepting Absalom back.

17 Then thine handmaid said, The word of my lord the king shall now be [I]comfortable: for [a]as an angel[4397] of God, so *is* my lord the king [II]to discern[8085] good[2896] and bad:[7451] therefore the LORD thy God will be with thee.

18 Then the king answered and said unto the woman, Hide not from me, I pray thee, the thing that I shall ask[7592] thee. And the woman said, Let my lord the king now speak.

19 And the king said, *Is not* the hand of Joab with thee in all this? And the woman answered and said, *As* thy soul liveth, my lord the king, none can turn to the right hand or to the left from ought that my lord the king hath spoken: for thy servant Joab, he bade me, and [a]he put all these words in the mouth of thine handmaid:

20 To fetch about this form of speech hath thy servant Joab done[6213] this thing: and my lord *is* wise, [a]according to the wisdom[2451] of an angel of God, to know[3045] all *things* that *are* in the earth.

21 And the king said unto Joab, Behold now, I have done this thing: go therefore, bring the young man Absalom again.

22 And Joab fell to the ground on his face, and bowed[7812] himself, and [I]thanked the king: and Joab said, To day[3117] thy servant knoweth that I have found grace[2580] in thy sight, my lord, O king, in that the king hath fulfilled[6213] the request of [II]his servant.

23 So Joab arose [a]and went to Geshur, and brought Absalom to Jerusalem.

24 And the king said, Let him turn to his own house, and let him [a]not see my face. So Absalom returned to his own house, and saw not the king's face.

Absalom Returns to Jerusalem

25 [I]But in all Israel there was none to be so much praised as Absalom for his beauty: [a]from the sole of his foot even to the crown of his head there was no blemish[3971] in him.

26 And when he polled[1548] his head, (for it was at every year's end that he polled *it:* because *the hair* was heavy on him, therefore he polled it:) he weighed the hair of his head at two hundred shekels after the king's weight.

27 And [a]unto Absalom there were born three sons, and one daughter, whose name *was* Tamar: she was a woman of a fair countenance.

28 So Absalom dwelt two full years in Jerusalem, [a]and saw not the king's face.

29 Therefore Absalom sent for Joab, to have sent him to the king; but he would[14] not come to him: and when he sent again the second time, he would not come.

30 Therefore he said unto his servants, See, Joab's field is [I]near mine, and he hath barley there; go and set it on fire. And Absalom's servants set the field on fire.

31 Then Joab arose, and came to Absalom unto *his* house, and said unto him, Wherefore have thy servants set my field on fire?

32 And Absalom answered Joab, Behold, I sent unto thee, saying, Come hither, that I may send thee to the king, to say, Wherefore am I come from Geshur? *it had been* good for me *to have been* there still: now therefore let me see the king's face; and if there be *any* iniquity[5771] in me, let him kill me.

33 So Joab came to the king, and told him: and when he had called[7121] for Absalom, he came to the king, and bowed himself on his face to the ground before the king: and the king [a]kissed[5401] Absalom.

Absalom Prepares for a Revolt

15 🗝 And [a]it came to pass after this, that Absalom [b]prepared[6213]

17 [I]Hebr. *for rest* [II]Hebr. *to hear* [a]2Sam. 14:20; 19:27

19 [a]2Sam. 14:3

20 [a]2Sam. 14:17; 19:27

22 [a]Hebr. *blessed* [I]Or, *thy*

23 [a]2Sam. 13:37

24 [a]Gen. 43:3; 2Sam. 3:13

25 [I]Hebr. *And as Absalom there was not a beautiful man in all Israel to praise greatly* [a]Isa. 1:6

27 [a]2Sam. 18:18

28 [a]2Sam. 14:24

30 [I]Hebr. *near my place*

33 [a]Gen. 33:4; 45:14; Luke 15:20

1 [a]2Sam. 12:11 [b]1Kgs. 1:5

🗝 **15:1–12** These verses describe the actions of Absalom by which he was attempting to assume royal power. David was showing weakness by allowing this to happen.

him chariots and horses, and fifty men to
run before him.
🔑 2 And Absalom rose up early, and
stood beside the way[1870] of the gate: and
it was *so,* that when any man that had a
controversy[7379] ǀcame to the king for
judgment,[4941] then Absalom called[7121]
unto him, and said, Of what city *art*
thou? And he said, Thy servant *is* of one
of the tribes of Israel.
3 And Absalom said unto him, See,
thy matters *are* good[2896] and right; but
ǀ*there is* no man *deputed* of the king to
hear thee.
4 Absalom said moreover, [a]Oh that I
were made judge[8199] in the land,[776] that
every man which hath any suit or
cause[4941] might come unto me, and I
would do him justice![6663]
5 And it was *so,* that when any man
came nigh *to him* to do him
obeisance,[7812] he put forth his hand, and
took him, and kissed[5401] him.
6 And on this manner did Absalom
to all Israel that came to the king for
judgment: [a]so Absalom stole[1589] the
hearts of the men of Israel.
7 And it came to pass [a]after forty
years, that Absalom said unto the king,
I pray thee, let me go and pay my vow,
which I have vowed[5087] unto the LORD, in
Hebron.
8 [a]For thy servant [b]vowed a vow
[c]while I abode at Geshur in Syria, saying,
If the LORD shall bring me again indeed
to Jerusalem, then I will serve the LORD.
9 And the king said unto him, Go
in peace. So he arose, and went to Hebron.
10 But Absalom sent spies[7270]
throughout all the tribes of Israel, saying,
As soon as ye hear the sound of the
trumpet, then ye shall say, Absalom
reigneth in Hebron.
11 And with Absalom went two hundred men out of Jerusalem, *that were*
[a]called; and they went [b]in their simplicity,[8537] and they knew[3045] not any thing.
🔑 12 And Absalom sent for Ahithophel
the Gilonite, [a]David's counselor,[3289] from
his city, *even* from [b]Giloh, while he
offered[2076] sacrifices. And the conspiracy[7195] was strong; for the people [c]in-
creased continually with Absalom.

David Escapes

13 And there came a messenger to
David, saying, [a]The hearts of the men of
Israel are after Absalom.
14 And David said unto all his servants that *were* with him at Jerusalem,
Arise, and let us [a]flee; for we shall not
else escape[6413] from Absalom: make
speed to depart, lest he overtake us suddenly, and ǀbring evil[7451] upon us, and
smite the city with the edge[6310] of the
sword.
15 And the king's[4428] servants said
unto the king, Behold, thy servants *are
ready to do* whatsoever my lord[113] the
king shall ǀappoint.[977]
16 And the king went forth, and all
his household ǀafter him. And the king
left[5800] [a]ten women,[802] *which were* concubines, to keep[8104] the house.
17 And the king went forth, and all
the people after him, and tarried in a
place that was far off.
🔑 18 And all his servants passed on
beside him; [a]and all the Cherethites, and
all the Pelethites, and all the Gittites, six
hundred men which came after him from
Gath, passed on before the king.

2 ǀHebr. *to come*
3 ǀOr, *none will hear thee from the king downward*
4 [a]Judg. 9:29
6 [a]Rom. 16:18
7 [a]1Sam. 16:1
8 [a]1Sam. 16:2 [b]Gen. 28:20, 21 [c]2Sam. 13:38
11 [a]1Sam. 9:13; 16:3, 5 [b]Gen. 20:5
12 [a]Ps. 41:9; 55:12, 13, 14 [b]Josh. 15:51 [c]Ps. 3:1
13 [a]Judg. 9:3; 2Sam. 15:6
14 ǀHebr. *thrust* [a]2Sam. 19:9
15 ǀHebr. *choose*
16 ǀHebr. *at his feet* [a]2Sam. 16:21, 22
18 [a]2Sam. 8:18

🔑 **15:2** Judicial cases in Jewish society were decided at the city gate (Deut. 21:19; 22:15).

🔑 **15:12** Ahithophel had been a member of David's cabinet as well as his chief counselor. Perhaps Ahithophel turned against David because of the events surrounding the death of Uriah the Hittite, the husband of Bathsheba. This would seem logical since Ahithophel was Bathsheba's grandfather (2 Sam. 11:3; 23:34).

🔑 **15:18** Originally, David's band of rebels that had fled with him from Saul to the Philistine city of Gath (1 Sam. 27:2) and continued with him in Ziklag, Hebron, and Jerusalem (1 Sam. 30:1; 2 Sam. 2:3; 5:6) was composed of six hundred men. Now, some thirty years later, these men were still together.

19 Then said the king to [a]Ittai the Gittite, Wherefore goest thou also with us? return to thy place, and abide with the king: for thou *art* a stranger,[5237] and also an exile.[1540]

20 Whereas thou camest *but* yesterday, should I this day[3117] [I]make thee go up and down with us? seeing I go [a]whither I may, return thou, and take back thy brethren:[251] mercy and truth *be* with thee.

21 And Ittai answered the king,[4428] and said, [a]*As* the LORD liveth,[2416] and *as* my lord the king liveth, surely in what place my lord the king shall be, whether in death[4194] or life,[2416] even there also will thy servant be.

22 And David said to Ittai, Go and pass over. And Ittai the Gittite passed over, and all his men, and all the little ones that *were* with him.

23 And all the country[776] wept with a loud voice, and all the people passed over: the king also himself passed over the brook [a]Kidron, and all the people passed over, toward the way of the [b]wilderness.

24 And lo Zadok also, and all the Levites *were* with him, [a]bearing[5375] the ark[727] of the covenant[1285] of God:[430] and they set down the ark of God; and Abiathar went up, until all the people had done[8552] passing out of the city.

25 And the king said unto Zadok, Carry back the ark of God into the city: if I shall find favour[2580] in the eyes of the LORD, he [a]will bring me again, and shew me *both* it, and his habitation:

26 But if he thus say, I have no [a]delight[2654] in thee; behold, *here am* I, [b]let him do to me as seemeth good unto him.

27 The king said also unto Zadok the priest, *Art not* thou a [a]seer?[7200] return into the city in peace, and [b]your two sons with you, Ahimaaz thy son, and Jonathan the son of Abiathar.

28 See, [a]I will tarry in the plain of the wilderness, until there come word[1697] from you to certify me.

29 Zadok therefore and Abiathar carried the ark of God again to Jerusalem: and they tarried there.

30 And David went up by the ascent of *mount* Olivet, [I]and wept as he went up, and [a]had his head covered, and he went [b]barefoot: and all the people that *was* with him [c]covered every man his head, and they went up, [d]weeping as they went up.

31 And *one* told David, saying [a]Ahithophel *is* among the conspirators with Absalom. And David said, O LORD, I pray thee, [b]turn the counsel[6098] of Ahithophel into foolishness.

32 And it came to pass, that *when* David was come to the top *of the mount,* where he worshipped[7812] God, behold, Hushai the [a]Archite came to meet him [b]with his coat rent, and earth[127] upon his head:

33 Unto whom David said, If thou passest on with me, then thou shalt be [a]a burden[4853] unto me:

34 But if thou return to the city, and say unto Absalom, [a]I will be thy servant, O king; *as* I *have been* thy father's[1] servant hitherto, so *will* I now also *be* thy servant: then mayest thou for me defeat[6565] the counsel of Ahithophel.

35 And *hast thou* not there with thee Zadok and Abiathar the priests? therefore it shall be, *that* what thing soever thou shalt hear out of the king's house, [a]thou shalt tell *it* to Zadok and Abiathar the priests.

36 Behold, *they have* there [a]with them their two sons, Ahimaaz Zadok's *son,* and Jonathan Abiathar's *son;* and by them ye shall send unto me every thing that ye can hear.

37 So Hushai [a]David's friend came into the city, [b]and Absalom came into Jerusalem.

16

And [a]when David was a little past the top *of the hill,* behold, [b]Ziba the servant of Mephibosheth met him, with a couple of asses saddled, and upon them two hundred *loaves* of bread, and an hundred bunches of raisins, and

19 [a]2Sam. 18:2
20 [I]Hebr. *make thee wander in going* [a]1Sam. 23:13
21 [a]Ruth 1:16, 17; Prov. 17:17; 18:24
23 [a]John 18:1, *Cedron* [b]2Sam. 16:2
24 [a]Num. 4:15
25 [a]Ps. 43:3
26 [a]Num. 14:8; 2Sam. 22:20; 1Kgs. 10:9; 2Chr. 9:8; Isa. 62:4 [b]1Sam. 3:18
27 [a]1Sam. 9:9 [b]2Sam. 17:17
28 [a]2Sam. 17:16
30 [I]Hebr. *going up, and weeping* [a]2Sam. 19:4; Esth. 6:12 [b]Isa. 20:2, 4 [c]Jer. 14:3, 4 [d]Ps. 126:6
31 [a]Ps. 3:1, 2; 55:12 [b]2Sam. 16:23; 17:14, 23
32 [a]Josh. 16:2 [b]2Sam. 1:2
33 [a]2Sam. 19:35
34 [a]2Sam. 16:19
35 [a]2Sam. 17:15, 16
36 [a]2Sam. 15:27
37 [a]2Sam. 16:16; 1Chr. 27:33 [b]2Sam. 16:15
1 [a]2Sam. 15:30, 32 [b]2Sam. 9:2

an hundred of summer fruits, and a bottle of wine.

2 And the king said unto Ziba, What meanest thou by these? And Ziba said, The asses *be* for the king's[4428] household to ride on; and the bread and summer fruit for the young men to eat; and the wine, [a]that such as be faint in the wilderness may drink.

3 And the king said, And where *is* thy master's son? [a]And Ziba said unto the king, Behold, he abideth at Jerusalem: for he said, To day[3117] shall the house of Israel restore me the kingdom[4468] of my father.[1]

4 [a]Then said the king to Ziba, Behold, thine *are* all that *pertained* unto Mephibosheth. And Ziba said, [I]I humbly beseech[7812] thee *that* I may find grace[2580] in thy sight, my lord,[113] O king.

5 And when king David came to Bahurim, behold, thence came out a man of the family[4940] of the house of Saul, whose name *was* [a]Shimei, the son of Gera: [I]he came forth, and cursed[7043] still as he came.

6 And he cast stones at David, and at all the servants of king David: and all the people and all the mighty men *were* on his right hand and on his left.

7 And thus said Shimei when he cursed, Come out, come out, thou [I]bloody[1818] man, and thou [a]man of Belial:[1100]

8 The LORD hath [a]returned upon thee all [b]the blood of the house of Saul, in whose stead thou hast reigned; and the LORD hath delivered the kingdom into the hand of Absalom thy son: and, [I]behold, thou *art taken* in thy mischief, because thou *art* a bloody man.

2 [a]2Sam. 15:28; 17:29

3 [a]2Sam. 19:27

4 [I]Hebr. *I do obeisance* [a]Prov. 18:13

5 [I]Or, *he still came forth and cursed* [a]2Sam. 19:16; 1Kgs. 2:8, 44

7 [I]Hebr. *man of blood* [a]Deut. 13:13

8 [I]Hebr. *behold thee in thy evil* [a]Judg. 9:24, 56, 57; 1Kgs. 2:32, 33 [b]2Sam. 1:16; 3:28, 29; 4:11, 12

9 [a]1Sam. 24:14; 2Sam. 9:8 [b]Ex. 22:28

10 [a]2Sam. 19:22; 1Pet. 2:23 [b]2Kgs. 18:25; Lam. 3:38 [c]Rom. 9:20

11 [a]2Sam. 12:11 [b]Gen. 15:4

12 [I]Hebr. *eye, as of tears* [a]Rom. 8:28

13 [I]Hebr. *dusted him with dust*

15 [a]2Sam. 15:37

16 [I]Hebr. *Let the king live* [a]2Sam. 15:37

9 Then said Abishai the son of Zeruiah unto the king, Why should[7043] this [a]dead[4191] dog [b]curse[7043] my lord the king? let me go over, I pray thee, and take off his head.

10 And the king said, [a]What have I to do with you, ye sons of Zeruiah? so let him curse, because [b]the LORD hath said unto him, Curse David. [c]Who shall then say, Wherefore hast thou done[6213] so?

11 And David said to Abishai, and to all his servants, Behold, [a]my son, which [b]came forth of my bowels,[4578] seeketh my life:[5315] how much more now *may this* Benjamite *do it?* let him alone, and let him curse; for the LORD hath bidden[559] him.

12 It may be that the LORD will look on mine [I]affliction, and that the LORD will [a]requite me good[2896] for his cursing[7045] this day.

13 And as David and his men went by the way,[1870] Shimei went along on the hill's side over against him, and cursed as he went, and threw stones at him, and [I]cast[6080] dust.[6083]

14 And the king, and all the people that *were* with him, came weary,[5889] and refreshed themselves there.

Absalom Returns to Jerusalem

15 And [a]Absalom, and all the people the men of Israel, came to Jerusalem, and Ahithophel with him.

16 And it came to pass, when Hushai the Archite, [a]David's friend, was come unto Absalom, that Hushai said unto Absalom, [I]God save the king, God save[2421] the king.

16:4 David's decision to trust the words of Ziba was too hasty. According to 2 Samuel 19:24–28, Ziba was lying, and Mephibosheth's loyalty to David had never changed.

16:8 In this verse Shimei was probably blaming David for the deaths of Abner (2 Sam. 3:27–39), and Ish–bosheth (2 Sam. 4:1–12) who, along with himself, were related to Saul. However, in these instances David was not guilty of any wrong. In fact, he had the men put to death that murdered Ish–bosheth. It was true that David was a man of war, but he was not necessarily the one responsible for eliminating the members of Saul's family.

16:14 He arrived at the fords of the Jordan River (2 Sam. 15:28). It is believed that David wrote Psalms 3 and 63 while fleeing through the wilderness of Judah.

17 And Absalom said to Hushai, *Is*
this thy kindness[2617] to thy friend?[7453]
[a]why wentest thou not with thy friend?
18 And Hushai said unto Absalom,
Nay; but whom the LORD, and this
people, and all the men of Israel,
choose,[977] his will I be, and with him will
I abide.
19 And again, [a]whom should I serve?
should I not *serve* in the presence of his
son? as I have served in thy father's presence, so will I be in thy presence.
20 Then said Absalom to Ahithophel,
Give counsel[6098] among you what we
shall do.
21 And Ahithophel said unto
Absalom, Go in unto thy father's [a]concu-
bines, which he hath left to keep[8104] the
house; and all Israel shall hear that thou
[b]art abhorred[887] of thy father: then shall
[c]the hands of all that *are* with thee be
strong.
22 So they spread Absalom a tent
upon the top of the house; and Absalom
went in unto his father's concubines [a]in
the sight of all Israel.
23 And the counsel of Ahithophel,
which he counselled[3289] in those days,
was as if a man had enquired[7592] at the
[I]oracle[1697] of God: so *was* all the counsel
of Ahithophel [a]both with David and with
Absalom.

Absalom Receives Counsel

17 Moreover Ahithophel said unto
Absalom, Let me now choose
out[977] twelve thousand men, and I
will arise and pursue after David this
night:
2 And I will come upon him while he
is [a]weary and weak handed, and will
make him afraid:[2729] and all the people
that *are* with him shall flee; and I will
[b]smite the king[4428] only:
3 And I will bring back all the people unto thee: the man whom thou seekest *is* as if all returned: *so* all the people
shall be in peace.
4 And the saying [I]pleased Absalom
well, and all the elders[2205] of Israel.
5 Then said Absalom, Call[7121] now
Hushai the Archite also, and let us hear
likewise [I]what he saith.
6 And when Hushai was come to
Absalom, Absalom spake unto him,
saying, Ahithophel hath spoken after this
manner: shall we do[6213] *after* his [I]saying?
if not; speak thou.
7 And Hushai said unto Absalom,
The counsel[6098] that Ahithophel hath
[I]given *is* not good[2896] at this time.
8 For, said Hushai, thou knowest[3045]
thy father and his men, that they *be*
mighty men, and they *be* [I]chafed[4751] in
their minds, as [a]a bear robbed of her
whelps in the field:[7704] and thy father *is*
a man of war, and will not lodge with the
people.
9 Behold, he is hid now in some pit,
or in some *other* place: and it will come
to pass, when some of them be
[I]overthrown[5307] at the first, that whosoever heareth it will say, There is a slaughter[4046] among the people that follow
Absalom.
10 And he also *that is* valiant, whose
heart *is* as the heart of a lion, shall utterly [a]melt: for all Israel knoweth that thy
father *is* a mighty man, and *they* which
be with him *are* valiant men.
11 Therefore I counsel[3289] that all
Israel be generally gathered[622] unto thee,
[a]from Dan even to Beer–sheba, [b]as the
sand that *is* by the sea for multitude; and
[I]that thou go to battle in thine own person.
12 So shall we come upon him in
some place where he shall be found, and
we will light upon him as the dew
falleth[5307] on the ground:[127] and of him
and of all the men that *are* with him

17 [a]2Sam. 19:25; Prov. 17:17
19 [a]2Sam. 15:34
21 [a]2Sam. 15:16; 20:3 [b]Gen. 34:30; 1Sam. 13:4 [c]2Sam. 2:7; Zech. 8:13
22 [a]2Sam. 12:11, 12
23 [I]Hebr. *word* [a]2Sam. 15:12
2 [a]Deut. 25:18; 2Sam. 16:14 [b]Zech. 13:7
4 [I]Hebr. *was right in the eyes of*
5 [I]Hebr. *what is in his mouth*
6 [I]Hebr. *word*
7 [I]Hebr. *counseled*
8 [I]Hebr. *bitter of soul* Judg. 18:25 [a]Hos. 13:8
9 [I]Hebr. *fallen*
10 [a]Josh. 2:11
11 [I]Hebr. *that thy face,* or, *presence go* [a]Judg. 20:1 [b]Gen. 22:17

16:22 This event was one of the things that Nathan predicted would happen as a result of David's sin with Bathsheba (see note on 2 Sam. 12:1–14). Absalom did so on the counsel of Ahithophel. Besides the fact that this was forbidden by God, it made Absalom's reconciliation with David impossible and forced the people to take sides between the two of them.

there shall not be left[3498] so much as one.

13 Moreover, if he be gotten into a city, then shall all Israel bring[5375] ropes to that city, and we will draw it into the river, until there be not one small stone found there.

14 And Absalom and all the men of Israel said, The counsel of Hushai the Archite *is* better[2896] than the counsel of Ahithophel. For [a]the LORD had [I]appointed[6680] to defeat[6565] the good counsel of Ahithophel, to the intent that the LORD might bring evil[7451] upon Absalom.

David Is Warned to Retreat

15 [a]Then said Hushai unto Zadok and to Abiathar the priests, Thus and thus did Ahithophel counsel Absalom and the elders of Israel; and thus and thus have I counselled.[3289]

16 Now therefore send quickly, and tell David, saying, Lodge not this night [a]in the plains of the wilderness, but speedily pass over; lest the king be swallowed up,[1104] and all the people that *are* with him.

17 [a]Now Jonathan and Ahimaaz [b]stayed by [c]En–rogel; for they might not be seen to come into the city: and a wench[8198] went and told them; and they went and told king David.

18 Nevertheless a lad saw them, and told Absalom: but they went both of them away quickly, and came to a man's house [a]in Bahurim, which had a well in his court; whither they went down.

19 And [a]the woman[802] took and spread a covering over the well's mouth, and spread ground corn thereon; and the thing was not known.[3045]

20 And when Absalom's servants came to the woman to the house, they said, Where *is* Ahimaaz and Jonathan? And [a]the woman said unto them, They be gone over the brook of water. And when they had sought and could not find *them,* they returned to Jerusalem.

21 And it came to pass, after they were departed, that they came up out of the well, and went and told king David, and said unto David, [a]Arise, and pass quickly over the water: for thus hath Ahithophel counselled against you.

22 Then David arose, and all the people that *were* with him, and they passed over Jordan: by the morning light[216] there lacked not one of them that was not gone over Jordan.

23 And when Ahithophel saw that his counsel was not [I]followed, he saddled *his* ass, and arose, and gat him home to his house, to [a]his city, and [II]put his household in order,[6680] and [b]hanged himself,[2614] and died,[4191] and was buried[6912] in the sepulchre[6913] of his father.

Absalom Advances on David

24 Then David came to [a]Mahanaim. And Absalom passed over Jordan, he and all the men of Israel with him.

25 And Absalom made Amasa captain of the host instead of Joab: which Amasa *was* a man's son, whose name *was* [I]Ithra an Israelite, that went in to [IIa]Abigail the daughter of [IIIb]Nahash, sister to Zeruiah Joab's mother.

26 So Israel and Absalom pitched in the land[776] of Gilead.

27 And it came to pass, when David was come to Mahanaim, that [a]Shobi the son of Nahash of Rabbah of the children[1121] of Ammon, and [b]Machir the son of Ammiel of Lo–debar, and [c]Barzillai the Gileadite of Rogelim,

28 Brought[5066] beds, and [I]basons,[5592] and earthen[3335] vessels, and wheat, and barley, and flour, and parched *corn,* and beans, and lentiles, and parched *pulse,*

🔑 29 And honey, and butter, and sheep, and cheese of kine,[1241] for David, and

14 [I]Hebr. *commanded* [a]2Sam. 15:31, 34
15 [a]2Sam. 15:35
16 [a]2Sam. 15:28
17 [a]2Sam. 15:27, 36 [b]Josh. 2:4 [c]Josh. 15:7; 18:16
18 [a]2Sam. 16:5
19 [a]Josh. 2:6
20 [a]Ex. 1:19; Josh. 2:4, 5
21 [a]2Sam. 17:15, 16
23 [I]Hebr. *done* [II]Hebr. *gave charge concerning his house* [a]2Sam. 15:12 [b]Matt. 27:5
24 [a]Gen. 32:2; Josh. 13:26; 2Sam. 2:8
25 [I]Or, *Jether an Ishmaelite* [II]Hebr. *Abigal* [III]Or, *Jesse* [a]1Chr. 2:13, 16 [b]1Chr. 2:16, 17
27 [a]2Sam. 10:1; 12:29 [b]2Sam. 9:4 [c]2Sam. 19:31, 32; 1Kgs. 2:7
28 [I]Or, *cups*

🔑 **17:29** David may have written Psalms 61 and 62 about the time the events of this verse took place.

for the people that *were* with him, to eat: for they said, The people *is* hungry, and weary, and thirsty, [a]in the wilderness.

Absalom's Death

18 And David numbered the people that *were* with him, and set captains[8269] of thousands and captains of hundreds over them.

2 And David sent forth a third part of the people under the hand of Joab, and a third part under the hand of Abishai the son of Zeruiah, Joab's brother,[251] [a]and a third part under the hand of Ittai the Gittite. And the king said unto the people, I will surely go forth with you myself also.

3 [a]But the people answered,[559] Thou shalt not go forth: for if we flee away, they will not [I]care for us; neither if half of us die, will they care for us: but now *thou art* [II]worth ten thousand of us: therefore now *it is* better[2896] that thou [III]succour[5826] us out of the city.

4 And the king said unto them, What seemeth you best I will do. And the king stood by the gate side, and all the people came out by hundreds and by thousands.

5 And the king commanded[6680] Joab and Abishai and Ittai, saying, *Deal* gently for my sake with the young man, *even* with Absalom. [a]And all the people heard when the king gave all the captains charge[6680] concerning Absalom.

6 So the people went out into the field[7704] against Israel: and the battle was in the [a]wood of Ephraim;

7 Where the people of Israel were slain before the servants of David, and there was there a great slaughter that day[3117] of twenty thousand *men.*

8 For the battle was there scattered over the face of all the country:[776] and the wood [I]devoured more people that day than the sword devoured.

9 And Absalom met the servants of David. And Absalom rode upon a mule, and the mule went under the thick boughs of a great oak, and his head caught hold[2388] of the oak, and he was taken up between the heaven and the earth;[776] and the mule that *was* under him went away.

10 And a certain man saw *it,* and told Joab, and said, Behold, I saw Absalom hanged[8518] in an oak.

11 And Joab said unto the man that told him, And, behold, thou sawest *him,* and why didst thou not smite him there to the ground? and I would have given thee ten *shekels* of silver, and a girdle.[2290]

12 And the man said unto Joab, Though I should [I]receive a thousand *shekels* of silver in mine hand, *yet* would I not put forth mine hand against the king's[4428] son: [a]for in our hearing the king charged[6680] thee and Abishai and Ittai, saying, [II]Beware[8104] that none *touch* the young man Absalom.

13 Otherwise I should have wrought falsehood[8267] against mine own life:[5315] for there is no matter hid from the king, and thou thyself wouldest have set thyself against *me.*

14 Then said Joab, I may not tarry[3176] thus [I]with thee. And he took three darts in his hand, and thrust them through the heart of Absalom, while he *was* yet alive[2416] in the [II]midst of the oak.

15 And ten young men that bare[5375] Joab's armour compassed about and smote Absalom, and slew him.

16 And Joab blew[8628] the trumpet, and the people returned from pursuing after Israel: for Joab held back the people.

17 And they took Absalom, and cast him into a great pit in the wood, and [a]laid[5324] a very great heap of stones upon him: and all Israel fled every one[376] to his tent.

18 Now Absalom in his lifetime[2416] had taken and reared up for himself a pillar, which *is* in [a]the king's dale:[6010] for he said, [b]I have no son to keep my name in remembrance: and he called[7121] the pillar after his own name: and it is called unto this day, Absalom's place.

19 Then said Ahimaaz the son of Zadok, Let me now run, and bear the

29 [a]2Sam. 16:2

2 [a]2Sam. 15:19

3 [I]Hebr. *set their heart on us* [II]Hebr. *as ten thousand of us* [III]Hebr. *be to succor* [a]2Sam. 21:17

5 [a]2Sam. 18:12

6 [a]Josh. 17:15, 18

8 [I]Hebr. *multiplied to devour*

12 [I]Hebr. *weigh upon mine hand* [II]Hebr. *Beware whosoever ye be of* [a]2Sam. 18:5

14 [I]Hebr. *before thee* [II]Hebr. *heart*

17 [a]Josh. 7:26

18 [a]Gen. 14:17 [b]2Sam. 14:27

king tidings, how that the LORD hath
avenged[8199] him of his enemies.
20 And Joab said unto him, Thou
shalt not [I]bear tidings[376,1319] this day, but
thou shalt bear tidings another day: but
this day thou shalt bear no tidings, because the king's son is dead.[4191]
21 Then said Joab to Cushi, Go tell
the king what thou hast seen. And Cushi
bowed[7812] himself unto Joab, and ran.
22 Then said Ahimaaz the son of
Zadok yet again to Joab, But [I]howsoever,
let me, I pray thee, also run after Cushi.
And Joab said, Wherefore wilt thou run,
my son, seeing that thou hast no tidings
[II]ready?
23 But howsoever, *said he,* let me
run. And he said unto him, Run. Then
Ahimaaz ran by the way[1870] of the plain,
and overran[5674] Cushi.
24 And David sat between the two
gates: and [a]the watchman went up to the
roof over the gate unto the wall, and
lifted up his eyes, and looked,[7200] and behold a man running alone.
25 And the watchman cried,[7121] and
told the king. And the king said, If he *be*
alone, *there is* tidings in his mouth. And
he came apace, and drew near.
26 And the watchman saw another
man running: and the watchman called
unto the porter,[7778] and said, Behold *another* man running alone. And the king
said, He also bringeth tidings.
27 And the watchman said, [I]Me thinketh the running of the foremost[7223] is
like the running of Ahimaaz the son of
Zadok. And the king said, He *is* a
good[2896] man, and cometh with good tidings.
28 And Ahimaaz called, and said
unto the king, [I]All is well.[7965] And he fell
down to the earth upon his face[639] before
the king, and said, Blessed[1288] *be* the
LORD thy God,[430] which hath [II]delivered
up the men that lifted up their hand
against my lord[113] the king.
29 And the king said, [I]Is the young
man Absalom safe?[7965] And Ahimaaz answered, When Joab sent the king's servant, and *me* thy servant, I saw a great
tumult, but I knew[3045] not what *it was.*

20 [I]Hebr. *be a man of tidings*

22 [I]Hebr. *be what may* [II]Or, *convenient*

24 [a]2Kgs. 9:17

27 [I]Hebr. *I see the running*

28 [I]Or, *Peace be to thee;* Hebr. *Peace* [II]Hebr. *shut up*

29 [I]Hebr. Is there *peace?*

31 [I]Hebr. *Tidings is brought*

33 [a]2Sam. 19:4

2 [I]Hebr. salvation, or, *deliverance*

3 [a]2Sam. 19:32

4 [a]2Sam. 15:30 [b]2Sam. 18:33

6 [I]Hebr. *By loving* [II]Hebr. *that princes or servants are not to thee*

30 And the king said *unto him,* Turn
aside, *and* stand here. And he turned
aside, and stood still.

David Mourns Absalom

31 And, behold, Cushi came; and
Cushi said, [I]Tidings, my lord the king: for
the LORD hath avenged thee this day of
all them that rose up against thee.
32 And the king said unto Cushi,
Is the young man Absalom safe? And
Cushi answered, The enemies of my
lord the king, and all that rise against
thee to do *thee* hurt, be as *that* young
man *is.*
33 And the king was much
moved,[7264] and went up to the chamber
over the gate, and wept: and as he went,
thus he said, [a]O my son Absalom, my
son, my son Absalom! would God I had
died[4191] for thee, O Absalom, my son,
my son!

19 And it was told Joab, Behold, the
king[4428] weepeth and mourneth
for Absalom.
2 And the [I]victory[8668] that day was
turned into mourning unto all the people:
for the people heard say that day how the
king was grieved for his son.
3 And the people gat them by
stealth[1589] that day [a]into the city, as people being ashamed steal away when they
flee in battle.
4 But the king [a]covered his face, and
the king cried[2199] with a loud voice, [b]O
my son Absalom, O Absalom, my son,
my son!
5 And Joab came into the house to
the king, and said, Thou hast shamed
this day the faces of all thy servants,
which this day have saved thy life,[5315]
and the lives of thy sons and of thy
daughters, and the lives of thy wives,[802]
and the lives of thy concubines;
6 [I]In that thou lovest[157] thine
enemies,[8130] and hatest thy friends.[157] For
thou hast declared this day, [II]that thou regardest neither princes nor servants: for
this day I perceive, that if Absalom had

lived,[2416] and all we had died this day, then it had pleased thee well.

7 Now therefore arise, go forth, and speak [I]comfortably unto thy servants: for I swear by the LORD, if thou go not forth, there will not tarry one[376] with thee this night: and that will be worse[7489] unto thee than all the evil[7451] that befell thee from thy youth until now.

8 Then the king arose, and sat in the gate. And they told unto all the people, saying, Behold, the king doth sit in the gate. And all the people came before the king: for Israel had fled every man to his tent.

David's Kingdom Is Restored

9 And all the people were at strife[1777] throughout all the tribes of Israel, saying, The king saved us out of the hand of our enemies, and he delivered[4422] us out of the hand of the Philistines; and now he is [a]fled out of the land[776] for Absalom.

10 And Absalom, whom we anointed[4886] over us, is dead[4191] in battle. Now therefore why [I]speak ye not a word of bringing the king back?

11 And king David sent to Zadok and to Abiathar the priests, saying, Speak unto the elders[2205] of Judah, saying, Why are ye the last to bring the king back to his house? seeing the speech of all Israel is come to the king, *even* to his house.

12 Ye *are* my brethren,[251] ye *are* [a]my bones[6106] and my flesh:[1320] wherefore then are ye the last to bring back the king?

13 [a]And say ye to Amasa, *Art* thou not of my bone, and of my flesh? [b]God[430] do[6213] so to me, and more also, if thou be not captain[8269] of the host before me continually in the room of Joab.

14 And he bowed[5186] the heart of all the men of Judah, [a]even as *the heart of* one man; so that they sent *this word* unto the king, Return thou, and all thy servants.

15 So the king returned, and came to Jordan. And Judah came to [a]Gilgal, to go to meet the king, to conduct the king over[5674] Jordan.

16 And [a]Shimei the son of Gera, a Benjamite, which *was* of Bahurim, hasted and came down with the men of Judah to meet king David.

17 And *there were* a thousand men of Benjamin with him, and [a]Ziba the servant of the house of Saul, and his fifteen sons and his twenty servants with him; and they went over Jordan before the king.

18 And there went over a ferry boat to carry over the king's[4428] household, and to do [I]what he thought good.[2896] And Shimei the son of Gera fell down[5307] before the king, as he was come over Jordan;

19 And said unto the king, [a]Let not my lord[113] impute[2803] iniquity[5771] unto me, neither do thou remember [b]that which thy servant did perversely[5753] the day that my lord the king went out of Jerusalem, that the king should [c]take it to his heart.

20 For thy servant doth know[3045] that I have sinned: therefore, behold, I am come the first[7223] this day of all [a]the house of Joseph to go down to meet my lord the king.

21 But Abishai the son of Zeruiah answered and said, Shall not Shimei be put to death[4191] for this, because he [a]cursed[7043] the LORD's anointed?[4899]

22 And David said, [a]What have I to do with you, ye sons of Zeruiah, that ye should this day be adversaries[7854] unto me? [b]shall there any man be put to death this day in Israel? for do not I know[3045] that I *am* this day king over Israel?

⊶ 23 Therefore [a]the king said unto

7 [I]Hebr. *to the heart of thy servants*

9 [a]2Sam. 15:14

10 [I]Hebr. are *ye silent?*

12 [a]2Sam. 5:1

13 [a]2Sam. 17:25 [b]Ruth 1:17

14 [a]Judg. 20:1

15 [a]Josh. 5:9

16 [a]2Sam. 16:5; 1Kgs. 2:8

17 [a]2Sam. 9:2, 10; 16:1, 2

18 [I]Hebr. *the good in his eyes*

19 [a]1Sam. 22:15; [b]2Sam. 16:5, 6 [c]2Sam. 13:33

20 [a]2Sam. 16:5

21 [a]Ex. 22:28

22 [a]2Sam. 16:10 [b]1Sam. 11:13

23 [a]1Kgs. 2:8, 9, 37, 46

⊶ **19:23** David had not really forgiven Shimei; it was only intended that Shimei think he had been forgiven (cf. 1 Kgs. 2:8, 9).

Shimei, Thou shalt not die. And the king
sware unto him.
24 And [a]Mephibosheth the son of
Saul came down to meet the king, and
had neither dressed[6213] his feet, nor
trimmed[6213] his beard,[8222] nor washed[3526]
his clothes, from the day the king departed until the day he came *again* in
peace.
25 And it came to pass, when he
was come to Jerusalem to meet the king,
that the king said unto him, [a]Wherefore
wentest not thou with me, Mephibosheth?
26 And he answered,[559] My lord,
O king, my servant deceived me: for
thy servant said, I will saddle me an
ass, that I may ride thereon, and go
to the king; because thy servant *is*
lame.
27 And [a]he hath slandered thy servant unto my lord the king; [b]but my lord
the king *is* as an angel[4397] of God: do
therefore *what is* good in thine eyes.
28 For all *of* my father's[1] house were
but [I]dead[4194] men before my lord the
king: [a]yet didst thou set thy servant
among them that did eat at thine own
table. What right therefore have I yet to
cry[2199] any more unto the king?
29 And the king said unto him, Why
speakest thou any more of thy matters?
I have said, Thou and Ziba divide the
land.
30 And Mephibosheth said unto the
king, Yea, let him take all, forasmuch as
my lord the king is come again in peace
unto his own house.
31 And [a]Barzillai the Gileadite came
down from Rogelim, and went over
Jordan with the king, to conduct him over
Jordan.
32 Now Barzillai was a very aged
man, *even* fourscore years old: and [a]he
had provided the king of sustenance[3557]
while he lay at Mahanaim; for he *was* a
very great man.

24 [a]2Sam. 9:6
25 [a]2Sam. 16:17
27 [a]2Sam. 16:3 [b]2Sam. 14:17, 20
28 [I]Hebr. *men of death* [a]2Sam. 9:7, 10, 13
31 [a]1Kgs. 2:7
32 [a]2Sam. 17:27
34 [I]Hebr. *How many days are the years of my life?*
35 [a]Ps. 90:10
37 [a]1Kgs. 2:7; Jer. 41:17
38 [I]Hebr. *choose*
39 [a]Gen. 31:55
40 [I]Hebr. *Chimhan*
41 [a]2Sam. 19:15

33 And the king said unto Barzillai,
Come thou over with me, and I will feed
thee with me in Jerusalem.
34 And Barzillai said unto the king,
[I]How long have I to live,[2416] that I
should go up with the king unto Jerusalem?
35 I *am* this day [a]fourscore years old:
and can I discern[3045] between good and
evil? can thy servant taste what I eat or
what I drink? can I hear any more the
voice of singing men and singing
women? wherefore then should thy servant be yet a burden[4853] unto my lord the
king?
36 Thy servant will go a little way
over Jordan with the king: and why
should the king recompense it me with
such a reward?
37 Let thy servant, I pray thee, turn
back again, that I may die in mine own
city, *and be buried* by the grave[6913] of
my father[1] and of my mother. But behold
thy servant [a]Chimham; let him go over
with my lord the king; and do to him
what shall seem good unto thee.
38 And the king answered, Chimham
shall go over with me, and I will do to
him that which shall seem good unto
thee: and whatsoever thou shalt [I]require
of me, *that* will I do for thee.
39 And all the people went over
Jordan. And when the king was come
over, the king [a]kissed[5401] Barzillai, and
blessed[1288] him; and he returned unto his
own place.
40 Then the king went on to Gilgal,
and [I]Chimham went on with him: and
all the people of Judah conducted[5674]
the king, and also half the people of Israel.
41 And, behold, all the men of Israel
came to the king, and said unto the king,
Why have our brethren the men of Judah
stolen thee away, and [a]have brought the
king, and his household, and all David's
men with him, over Jordan?

19:24 In this way, Mephibosheth mourned the fact that David had to flee from Absalom (Ezek. 24:17).

42 And all the men of Judah answered the men of Israel, Because the king *is* [a]near of kin[7138] to us: wherefore then be ye angry[2734] for this matter? have we eaten at all of the king's *cost*? or hath he given us any gift?

43 And the men of Israel answered the men of Judah, and said, We have ten parts in the king, and we have also more *right* in David than ye: why then did ye [I]despise[7043] us, that our advice[1697] should not be first had in bringing back our king? And [a]the words[1697] of the men of Judah were fiercer[7185] than the words of the men of Israel.

Sheba's Revolt

20 And there happened to be there a man of Belial,[1100] whose name *was* Sheba, the son of Bichri, a Benjamite: and he blew[8628] a trumpet, and said, [a]We have no part in David, neither have we inheritance[5159] in the son of Jesse: [b]every man to his tents, O Israel.

2 So every man of Israel went up from after David, *and* followed Sheba the son of Bichri: but the men of Judah clave[1692] unto their king,[4428] from Jordan even to Jerusalem.

3 And David came to his house at Jerusalem; and the king took the ten women[802] *his* [a]concubines, whom he had left to keep[8104] the house, and put them in [I]ward,[4931] and fed them, but went not in unto them. So they were [II]shut up unto the day[3117] of their death,[4191] [III]living[2424] in widowhood.

4 Then said the king to Amasa, [Ia]Assemble[2199] me the men of Judah within three days, and be thou here present.

5 So Amasa went to assemble *the men of* Judah: but he tarried longer than the set time which he had appointed[3259] him.

6 And David said to Abishai, Now shall Sheba the son of Bichri do us more harm than *did* Absalom: take thou [a]thy lord's servants, and pursue after him, lest he get him fenced cities, and [I]escape us.

7 And there went out after him Joab's men, and the [a]Cherethites, and the Pelethites, and all the mighty men: and they went out of Jerusalem, to pursue after Sheba the son of Bichri.

8 When they *were* at the great stone which *is* in Gibeon, Amasa went before them. And Joab's garment that he had put on was girded unto him, and upon it a girdle[2290] *with* a sword fastened upon his loins in the sheath thereof; and as he went forth it fell out.[5307]

9 And Joab said to Amasa, *Art* thou in health, my brother?[251] [a]And Joab took Amasa by the beard[2206] with the right hand to kiss[5401] him.

10 But Amasa took no heed to the sword that *was* in Joab's hand: so [a]he smote him therewith [b]in the fifth *rib,* and shed out his bowels[4578] to the ground,[776] and [I]struck him not again; and he died.[4191] So Joab and Abishai his brother pursued after Sheba the son of Bichri.

11 And one[376] of Joab's men[5288] stood by him, and said, He that favoureth[2654] Joab, and he that *is* for David, *let him go* after Joab.

12 And Amasa wallowed[1556] in blood in the midst of the highway. And when the man saw that all the people stood still, he removed Amasa out of the highway into the field,[7704] and cast a cloth upon him, when he saw that every one that came by him stood still.

13 When he was removed[3014] out of the highway, all the people went on after Joab, to pursue after Sheba the son of Bichri.

14 And he went through all the tribes of Israel unto [a]Abel, and to Beth–maachah, and all the Berites: and they were gathered together, and went also after him.

15 And they came and besieged him in Abel of Beth–maachah, and they [a]cast up[8210] a bank[5550] against the city, and [I]it stood in the trench: and all the people that *were* with Joab [II]battered the wall, to throw it down.

42 [a]2Sam. 19:12
43 [I]Hebr. *set us at light* [a]Judg. 8:1; 12:1
1 [a]2Sam. 19:43 [b]1Kgs. 12:16; 2Chr. 10:16
3 [I]Hebr. *a house of ward* [II]Hebr. *bound* [III]Hebr. *in widowhood of life* [a]2Sam. 15:16; 16:21, 22
4 [I]Hebr. *Call* [a]2Sam. 19:13
6 [I]Hebr. *deliver himself from our eyes* [a]2Sam. 11:11; 1Kgs. 1:33
7 [a]2Sam. 8:18; 1Kgs. 1:38
9 [a]Matt. 26:49; Luke 22:47
10 [I]Hebr. *doubled not his stroke* [a]1Kgs. 2:5 [b]2Sam. 2:23
14 [a]2Kgs. 15:29; 2Chr. 16:4
15 [I]Or, *it stood against the outmost wall* [II]Hebr. *marred to throw down* [a]2Kgs. 19:32

16 Then cried a wise[2450] woman[802]
out of the city, Hear, hear; say, I pray
you, unto Joab, Come near hither, that I
may speak with thee.
17 And when he was come near unto
her, the woman said, *Art* thou Joab? And
he answered,[559] I *am he.* Then she said
unto him, Hear the words[1697] of thine
handmaid. And he answered, I do hear.
18 Then she spake, saying, [I][a]They
were wont[1696] to speak in old time, saying, They shall surely ask[7592] *counsel* at
Abel: and so they ended[8552] *the matter.*
19 I *am one of them that are* peaceable *and* faithful[539] in Israel: thou seekest to destroy[4191] a city and a mother in
Israel: why wilt thou swallow up [a]the inheritance of the LORD?
20 And Joab answered and said, Far
be it, far be it from me, that I should
swallow up or destroy.[7843]
21 The matter *is* not so: but a man
of mount Ephraim, Sheba the son of
Bichri [I]by name, hath lifted up his hand
against the king, *even* against David: deliver him only, and I will depart from the
city. And the woman said unto Joab,
Behold, his head shall be thrown to thee
over the wall.
22 Then the woman went unto all
the people [a]in her wisdom.[2451] And they
cut off[3772] the head of Sheba the son
of Bichri, and cast *it* out to Joab. And
he blew a trumpet, and they [I]retired
from the city, every man to his tent. And
Joab returned to Jerusalem unto the
king.

David's Officials

23 Now [a]Joab *was* over all the host of
Israel: and Benaiah the son of Jehoiada
was over the Cherethites and over the
Pelethites:
24 And Adoram *was* [a]over the
tribute:[4522] and [b]Jehoshaphat the son of
Ahilud *was* [I]recorder:
25 And Sheva *was* scribe: and [a]Zadok
and Abiathar *were* the priests:
26 [a]And Ira also the Jairite was [I][b]a
chief ruler[3548] about David.

Gibeonites Are Avenged

21 Then there was a famine in the
days of David three years, year
after year; and David [I][a]enquired of the
LORD. And the LORD answered,[559] *It is*
for Saul, and for *his* bloody[1818] house,
because he slew the Gibeonites.
2 And the king called[7121] the
Gibeonites, and said unto them; (now the
Gibeonites *were* not of the children[1121] of
Israel, but [a]of the remnant of the
Amorites; and the children of Israel had
sworn unto them: and Saul sought to
slay[5221] them in his zeal[7065] to the children of Israel and Judah.)
3 Wherefore David said unto the Gibeonites, What shall I do[6213] for you? and
wherewith shall I make the atonement,[3722] that ye may bless[1288] [a]the
inheritance[5159] of the LORD?
4 And the Gibeonites said unto him,
[I]We will have no silver nor gold of Saul,
nor of his house; neither for us shalt thou
kill[4191] any man in Israel. And he said,
What ye shall say, *that* will I do for you.
5 And they answered the king, The
man that consumed[3615] us, and that
[I]devised against us *that* we should be
destroyed[8045] from remaining in any of
the coasts of Israel,
6 Let seven men of his sons be delivered unto us, and we will hang them
up unto the LORD [a]in Gibeah of Saul,
[I][b]*whom* the LORD did choose. And the
king said, I will give *them.*
7 But the king spared Mephibosheth,
the son of Jonathan the son of Saul,

18 [I]Or, *They plainly spake in the beginning, saying, Surely they will ask of Abel, and so make an end* [a]Deut. 20:11
19 [a]1Sam. 26:19; 2Sam. 21:3
21 [I]Hebr. *by his name*
22 [I]Hebr. *were scattered* [a]Eccl. 9:14, 15
23 [a]2Sam. 8:16, 18
24 [I]Or, *remembrancer* [a]1Kgs. 4:6 [b]2Sam. 8:16; 1Kgs. 4:3
25 [a]2Sam. 8:17; 1Kgs. 4:4
26 [I]Or, *a prince* [a]Gen. 41:45; Ex. 2:16; 2Sam. 8:18 [b]2Sam. 23:38
1 [I]Hebr. *sought the face* [a]Num. 27:21
2 [a]Josh. 9:3, 15-17
3 [a]2Sam. 20:19
4 [I]Or, It is *not silver nor gold that we have to do with Saul or his house, neither* pertains *it to us to kill*
5 [I]Or, *cut us off*
6 [I]Or, *chosen of the LORD* [a]1Sam. 10:26; 11:4 [b]1Sam. 10:24

20:16 The phrase "wise woman" used of the woman in this verse means that she was doing something extraordinary. The word translated "wise" is also used of Joseph when he was able to interpret the Pharaoh's dream (Gen. 41:33). In this verse, this woman is called "wise" because she did what was in the best interest of protecting her people.

because of [a]the LORD's oath[7621] that *was* between them, between David and Jonathan the son of Saul.

8 But the king took the two sons of [a]Rizpah the daughter of Aiah, whom she bare unto Saul, Armoni and Mephibosheth; and the five sons of [I]Michal the daughter of Saul, whom she [II]brought up for Adriel the son of Barzillai the Meholathite:

9 And he delivered them into the hands of the Gibeonites, and they hanged them in the hill [a]before the LORD: and they fell[5307] *all* seven together, and were put to death[4191] in the days of harvest, in the first[7223] *days,* in the beginning of barley harvest.

10 And [a]Rizpah the daughter of Aiah took sackcloth, and spread it for her upon the rock, [b]from the beginning of harvest until water dropped upon them out of heaven, and suffered neither the birds of the air[8064] to rest on them by day,[3119] nor the beasts[2416] of the field[7704] by night.

11 And it was told David what Rizpah the daughter of Aiah, the concubine of Saul, had done.[6213]

12 And David went and took the bones[6106] of Saul and the bones of Jonathan his son from the men of [a]Jabesh–gilead, which had stolen them from the street of Beth–shan, where the [b]Philistines had hanged them, when the Philistines had slain Saul in Gilboa:

13 And he brought up[5927] from thence the bones of Saul and the bones of Jonathan his son; and they gathered[622] the bones of them that were hanged.

14 And the bones of Saul and Jonathan his son buried[6912] they in the country[776] of Benjamin in [a]Zelah, in the sepulchre[6913] of Kish his father:[1] and they performed all that the king commanded.[6680] And after that [b]God[430] was intreated[6279] for the land.[776]

Philistine Giants Die in Battle

15 Moreover the Philistines had yet war again with Israel; and David went down, and his servants with him, and fought against the Philistines: and David waxed faint.[5774]

16 And Ishbi–benob, which *was* of the sons of [I]the giant,[7497] the weight of whose [II]spear *weighed* three hundred *shekels* of brass in weight, he being girded with a new *sword,* thought to have slain David.

17 But Abishai the son of Zeruiah succoured[5826] him, and smote the Philistine, and killed[4191] him. Then the men of David sware unto him, saying, [a]Thou shalt go no more out with us to battle, that thou quench not the [Ib]light[5216] of Israel.

18 [a]And it came to pass after this, that there was again a battle with the Philistines at Gob: then [b]Sibbechai the Hushathite slew [I]Saph, which *was* of the sons of [II]the giant.

19 And there was again a battle in Gob with the Philistines, where Elhanan the son of [I]Jaare–oregim, a Bethlehemite, slew [a]*the brother of* Goliath the Gittite, the staff of whose spear *was* like a weaver's beam.

20 And [a]there was yet a battle in Gath, where was a man of *great* stature, that had on every hand six fingers, and on every foot six toes, four and twenty in number; and he also was born to [I]the giant.

21 And when he [Ia]defied[2778] Israel, Jonathan the son of [b]Shimeah the brother of David slew him.

22 [a]These four were born to the giant in Gath, and fell by the hand of David, and by the hand of his servants.

David's Song

22 ⊶ And David [a]spake unto the LORD the words[1697] of this song

---

7 [a]1Sam. 18:3; 20:8, 15, 42; 23:18

8 [I]Or, *Michal's sister* [II]Hebr. *bare to Adriel* [a]2Sam. 3:7

9 [a]2Sam. 6:17

10 [a]2Sam. 3:7; 21:8 [b]Deut. 21:13

12 [a]1Sam. 31:11-13 [b]1Sam. 31:10

14 [a]Josh. 18:28 [b]Josh. 7:26; 2Sam. 24:25

16 [I]Or, *Rapha* [II]Hebr. *the staff,* or, *the head*

17 [I]Hebr. *candle,* or, *lamp* [a]2Sam. 18:3 [b]1Kgs. 11:36; 15:4; Ps. 132:17

18 [I]Or, *Sippai* [II]Or, *Rapha* [a]1Chr. 20:4 [b]1Chr. 11:29

19 [I]Or, *Jair* [a]1Chr. 20:5

20 [I]Or, *Rapha* [a]1Chr. 20:6

21 [I]Or, *reproached* [a]1Sam. 17:10, 25, 26 [b]1Sam. 16:9, *Shammah*

22 [a]1Chr. 20:8

1 [a]Ex. 15:1; Judg. 5:1

⊶ **22:1–51** This passage is a song of praise that is a personal expression of David's heart. David is praising God for deliverance, yet in his praise, he focuses strongly on the omnipotence of God.

(continued on next page)

in the day[3117] *that* the LORD had
[b]delivered[5337] him out of the hand of all
his enemies, and out of the hand of Saul:
2 And he said, [a]The LORD *is* my rock,
and my fortress,4686 and my deliverer;6403
3 The God[430] of my rock; [a]in him
will I trust:[2620] *he is* my [b]shield, and
the [c]horn of my salvation, my high
[d]tower,4869 and my [e]refuge, my saviour;[3467]
thou savest me from violence.[2555]
4 I will call[7121] on the LORD, *who is*
worthy to be praised: so shall I be saved
from mine enemies.
5 When the [I]waves of death[4194] compassed me, the floods of [II]ungodly
men[1100] made me afraid;[1204]
6 The [Ia]sorrows[2256] of hell[7585] compassed me about; the snares of death prevented me;
7 In my distress [a]I called upon[7121]
the LORD, and cried[7121] to my God: and
he did [b]hear my voice out of his temple,
and my cry *did enter* into his ears.[241]
8 Then [a]the earth[776] shook and trembled; [b]the foundations[4146] of heaven
moved and shook, because he was
wroth.[2734]
9 There went up a smoke [I]out of his
nostrils, and [a]fire out of his mouth devoured: coals were kindled by it.
10 He [a]bowed the heavens also, and
came down; and [b]darkness[6205] *was* under
his feet.
11 And he rode upon a cherub,[3742]
and did fly: and he was seen [a]upon the
wings of the wind.[7307]
12 And he made [a]darkness[2822] pavilions round about him, [I]dark[2841] waters,
and thick clouds of the skies.
13 Through the brightness before
him were [a]coals of fire kindled.
14 The LORD [a]thundered from
heaven, and the most High uttered his
voice.
15 And he sent out [a]arrows, and scattered them; lightning, and discomfited[2000]
them.
16 And the channels of the sea

1 [b]Ps. 34:19
2 [a]Deut. 32:4; Ps. 18:2; 31:3; 71:3; 91:2; 144:2
3 [a]Heb. 2:13 [b]Gen. 15:1 [c]Luke 1:69 [d]Prov. 18:10 [e]Ps. 9:9; 14:6; 59:16; 71:7; Jer. 16:19
5 IOr, *pangs* IIHebr. *Belial*
6 IOr, *cords* [a]Ps. 116:3
7 [a]Ps. 116:4; 120:1; Jon. 2:2 [b]Ex. 3:7; Ps. 34:6, 15, 17
8 [a]Judg. 5:4; Ps. 77:18; 97:4 [b]Job 26:11
9 IHebr. *by* [a]Ps. 97:3; Hab. 3:5; Heb. 12:29
10 [a]Ps. 144:5; Isa. 64:1 [b]Ex. 20:21; 1Kgs. 8:12; Ps. 97:2
11 [a]Ps. 104:3
12 IHebr. *binding of waters* [a]2Sam. 22:10; Ps. 97:2
13 [a]2Sam. 22:9
14 [a]Judg. 5:20; 1Sam. 2:10; 7:10; Ps. 29:3; Isa. 30:30
15 [a]Deut. 32:23; Ps. 7:13; 77:17; 144:6; Hab. 3:11
16 IOr, *anger* [a]Ps. 74:1 [b]Ex. 15:8; Ps. 106:9; Nah. 1:4; Matt. 8:26
17 IOr, *great* [a]Ps. 144:7
18 [a]2Sam. 22:1
20 [a]Ps. 31:8; 118:5 [b]2Sam. 15:26; Ps. 22:8
21 [a]1Sam. 26:23; 2Sam. 22:25; 1Kgs. 8:32; Ps. 7:8 [b]Ps. 24:4
22 [a]Gen. 18:19; Ps. 119:3; 128:1; Prov. 8:32
23 [a]Deut. 7:12; Ps. 119:30, 102
24 IHebr. *to him* [a]Gen. 6:9; 17:1; Job 1:1
25 IHebr. *before his eyes* [a]2Sam. 22:21

appeared,[7200] the foundations of the
world[8398] were discovered,[1540] at the [a]re-
buking of the LORD, at the blast of the
breath[7307] of his [I]nostrils.
17 [a]He sent from above, he took me;
he drew me out of [I]many waters;
18 [a]He delivered me from my strong
enemy, *and* from them that hated me: for
they were too strong for me.
19 They prevented me in the day of
my calamity:[343] but the LORD was my stay.
20 [a]He brought me forth also into a
large place: he delivered[2502] me, because
he [b]delighted[2654] in me.
21 [a]The LORD rewarded[1580] me according to my righteousness: according to
the [b]cleanness[1252] of my hands hath he
recompensed me.
22 For I have [a]kept[8104] the ways[1870]
of the LORD, and have not wickedly
departed[7561] from my God.
23 For all his [a]judgments[4941] *were* before me: and *as for* his statutes, I did not
depart[5493] from them.
24 I was also [a]upright[8549] [I]before
him, and have kept myself[8104] from mine
iniquity.[5771]
25 Therefore [a]the LORD hath recompensed me according to my righteousness; according to my cleanness[1252] [I]in
his eye sight.
26 With [a]the merciful thou wilt shew
thyself merciful, *and* with the upright[8552]
man thou wilt shew thyself upright.
27 With the pure thou wilt shew thyself pure; and [a]with the froward6141 thou
[Ib]wilt shew thyself unsavoury.6617
28 And the [a]afflicted people thou wilt
save: but thine eyes *are* upon [b]the
haughty, *that* thou mayest bring *them*
down.8213
29 For thou *art* my [Ia]lamp,[5216]
O LORD; and the LORD will lighten my
darkness.

26 [a]Matt. 5:7 **27** IOr, *wrestle* [a]Lev. 26:23, 24, [b]Ps. 18:26 **28** [a]Ex. 3:7, 8; Ps. 72:12, 13 [b]Job 40:11, 12; Isa. 2:11, 12, 17; 5:15; Dan. 4:37 **29** IOr, *candle* [a]Job 29:3; Ps. 27:1

(continued from previous page)
David's psalms help us to understand how, with all of his failings, he was indeed "a man after God's heart" (1 Sam. 13:14; 1 Kgs. 15:3).

30 For by thee I have [I]run through a troop: by my God have I leaped over a wall.

31 *As for* God,[410] [a]his way[1870] *is* perfect;[8549] [b]the word[565] of the LORD *is* [I]tried:[6884] he *is* a buckler[4043] to all them that trust in him.

32 For [a]who *is* God, save the LORD? and who *is* a rock, save our God?

33 God *is* my [a]strength *and* power: and he [I][b]maketh[5425] my way [c]perfect.

34 He [I]maketh my feet [a]like hinds'[355] *feet:* and [b]setteth me upon my high places.

35 [a]He teacheth my hands [I]to war; so that a bow of steel is broken by mine arms.

36 Thou hast also given me the shield of thy salvation: and thy gentleness hath [I]made me great.

37 Thou hast [a]enlarged my steps under me; so that my [I]feet did not slip.

38 I have pursued mine enemies, and destroyed them; and turned not again until I had consumed[3615] them.

39 And I have consumed them, and wounded[4272] them, that they could not arise: yea, they are fallen[5307] [a]under my feet.

40 For thou hast [a]girded me with strength to battle: [b]them that rose up against me hast thou [I]subdued under me.

41 Thou hast also given me the [a]necks of mine enemies, that I might destroy[6789] them that hate me.

42 They looked, but *there was* none to save; *even* [a]unto the LORD, but he answered them not.

43 Then did I beat[7833] them as small [a]as the dust[6083] of the earth, I did stamp them [b]as the mire of the street, *and* did spread them abroad.

44 [a]Thou also hast delivered[6403] me from the strivings of my people, thou hast kept me *to be* [b]head of the heathen: [c]a people *which* I knew not shall serve me.

45 [I]Strangers shall [II]submit[3584] themselves unto me: as soon as they hear, they shall be obedient[8085] unto me.

46 Strangers shall fade away,[5034] and they shall be afraid [a]out of their close places.

47 The LORD liveth;[2416] and blessed[1288] *be* my rock; and exalted be the God of the [a]rock of my salvation.

48 It *is* God that [I]avengeth[5360] me, and that [a]bringeth down the people under me,

49 And that bringeth me forth from mine enemies: thou also hast lifted me up on high above them that rose up against me: thou hast delivered me from the [a]violent[2555] man.

50 Therefore I will give thanks unto thee, O LORD, among [a]the heathen, and I will sing praises unto thy name.

51 [a]*He is* the tower of salvation for his king:[4428] and sheweth mercy to his [b]anointed,[4899] unto David, and [c]to his seed for evermore.[5704,5769]

David's Last Words

23 🔑 Now these *be* the last words[1697] of David. David the son of Jesse said,[5002] [a]and the man *who was* raised up on high, [b]the anointed[4899] of the God[430] of Jacob, and the sweet[5273] psalmist of Israel, said,

2 [a]The Spirit of the LORD spake by me, and his word[4405] *was* in my tongue.

3 The God of Israel said, [a]the Rock[6697] of Israel spake to me, [I][b]He that ruleth over men *must be* just,[6662] ruling [c]in the fear of God.

4 And [a]*he shall be* as the light[216] of the morning, *when* the sun riseth, *even* a morning without clouds; *as* the tender grass *springing* out of the earth[776] by clear shining after rain.

5 Although my house *be* not so with God;[410] [a]yet he hath made with me an

30 IOr, *broken a troop*
31 IOr, *refined* [a]Deut. 32:4; Dan. 4:37; Rev. 15:3 [b]Ps. 12:6; 119:140; Prov. 30:5
32 [a]1Sam. 2:2; Isa. 45:5, 6
33 IHebr. *riddeth,* or, *looseth* [a]Ex. 15:2; Ps. 27:1; 28:7, 8; 31:4; Isa. 12:2 [b]Heb. 13:21 [c]Deut. 18:13; Job 22:3; Ps. 101:2, 6; 119:1
34 IHebr. *equalleth* [a]2Sam. 2:18; Hab. 3:19 [b]Deut. 32:13; Isa. 33:16; 58:14
35 IHebr. *for the war* [a]Ps. 144:1
36 IHebr. *multiplied me*
37 IHebr. *ankles* [a]Prov. 4:12
39 [a]Mal. 4:3
40 IHebr. *caused to bow;* [a]Ps. 18:32, 39 [b]Ps. 44:5
41 [a]Gen. 49:8; Ex. 23:27; Josh. 10:24
42 [a]Job 27:9; Prov. 1:28; Isa. 1:15; Mic. 3:4
43 [a]2Kgs. 13:7; Ps. 35:5; Dan. 2:35 [b]Isa. 10:6; Mic. 7:10; Zech. 10:5
44 [a]2Sam. 3:1; 5:1; 19:9, 14; 20:1, 2, 22 [b]Deut. 28:13; 2Sam. 8:1-14; Ps. 2:8 [c]Isa. 55:5
45 IHebr. *Sons of the stranger* IIOr, *yield feigned obedience;* Hebr. *lie*
46 [a]Mic. 7:17
47 [a]Ps. 89:26
48 IHebr. *giveth avengement for me* [a]Ps. 144:2
49 [a]Ps. 140:1
50 [a]Rom. 15:9
51 [a]Ps. 144:10 [b]Ps. 89:20 [c]2Sam. 12:13; Ps. 89:29
1 [a]2Sam. 7:8, 9; Ps. 78:70, 71; 89:27 [b]1Sam. 16:12, 13; Ps. 89:20 **2** [a]2Pet. 1:21 **3** IOr, *Be thou ruler* [a]Deut. 32:4, 31; 2Sam. 22:2, 32 [b]Ex. 18:21; 2Chr. 19:7, 9; [c]Ps. 110:2 **4** [a]Judg. 5:31; Ps. 89:36; Prov. 4:18; Hos. 6:5 **5** [a]2Sam. 7:15, 16; Ps. 89:29; Isa. 55:3

🔑 **23:1–7** This song of David is a prophecy of the Messiah that would come and bring about God's new covenant of salvation.

everlasting[5769] covenant,[1285] ordered in all *things,* and sure:[8104] for *this is* all my salvation, and all *my* desire,[2656] although he make *it* not to grow.

6 But *the sons* of Belial[1100] *shall be* all of them as thorns thrust away, because they cannot be taken with hands:

7 But the man *that* shall touch them must be [I]fenced[4390] with iron and the staff of a spear; and they shall be utterly burned[8313] with fire in the *same* place.

David's Mighty Men

8 These *be* the names of the mighty men whom David had: [I]The Tachmonite that sat in the seat,3429 chief[7218] among the captains;7791 the same *was* Adino the Eznite: [a]*he lift up his spear* against eight hundred, [II]whom he slew at one time.

9 And after him *was* [a]Eleazar the son of Dodo the Ahohite, *one* of the three mighty men with David, when they defied2778 the Philistines *that* were there gathered together[622] to battle, and the men of Israel were gone away:[5927]

10 He arose, and smote the Philistines until his hand was weary, and his hand clave unto the sword: and the LORD wrought a great victory[8668] that day; and the people returned after him only to spoil.

11 And after him *was* [a]Shammah the son of Agee the Hararite. [b]And the Philistines were gathered [I]together into a troop, where was a piece of ground[7704] full of lentiles: and the people fled from the Philistines.

12 But he stood3320 in the midst of the ground, and defended[5337] it, and slew the Philistines: and the LORD wrought a great victory.

13 And [I][a]three of the thirty chief went down, and came to David in the harvest time unto [b]the cave of Adullam: and the troop of the Philistines pitched in [c]the valley of Rephaim.

14 And David *was* then in [a]an hold,4686 and the garrison of the Philistines *was* then *in* Bethlehem.

7 [I]Hebr. *filled*

8 [I]Or, *Joshebbassebet the Tachmonite, head of the three* [II]Hebr. *slain* [a]1Chr. 11:11; 27:2

9 [a]1Chr. 11:12; 27:4

11 [I]Or, *for foraging* [a]1Chr. 11:27 [b]1Chr. 11:13, 14

13 [I]Or, *the three captains over the thirty* [a]1Chr. 11:15 [b]1Sam. 22:1 [c]2Sam. 5:18

14 [a]1Sam. 22:4, 5

17 [a]Lev. 17:10

18 [I]Hebr. *slain* [a]1Chr. 11:20

20 [I]Hebr. *great of acts* [II]Hebr. *lions of God* [a]Josh. 15:21 [b]Ex. 15:15; 1Chr. 11:22

21 [I]Hebr. *a man of countenance,* or, *sight* [a]1Chr. 11:23, *a man of great stature*

23 [I]Or, *honorable among the thirty* [II]Or, *council;* Hebr. *at his command* [a]2Sam. 8:18; 20:23; [b]1Sam. 22:14

24 [a]2Sam. 2:18

25 [a]1Chr. 11:27

15 And David longed,[183] and said, Oh that one would give me drink of the water of the well[953] of Bethlehem, which *is* by the gate!

16 And the three mighty men brake through the host of the Philistines, and drew water out of the well of Bethlehem, that *was* by the gate, and took *it,* and brought *it* to David: nevertheless he would[14] not drink thereof, but poured it out unto the LORD.

17 And he said, Be it far from me, O LORD, that I should do[6213] this: *is not this* [a]the blood[1818] of the men that went in jeopardy of their lives?[5315] therefore he would not drink it. These things did these three mighty men.

18 And [a]Abishai, the brother of Joab, the son of Zeruiah, was chief among three. And he lifted up his spear against three hundred, [I]*and* slew *them,* and had the name among three.

19 Was he not most honourable of three? therefore he was their captain:[8269] howbeit he attained not unto the *first*[4928] three.

20 And Benaiah the son of Jehoiada, the son of a valiant man, of [a]Kabzeel, [I]who had done[6213] many acts, [b]he slew two [II]lionlike men[739] of Moab: he went down also and slew a lion in the midst of a pit in time of snow:

21 And he slew an Egyptian, a [I][a]goodly[4758] man: and the Egyptian had a spear in his hand; but he went down to him with a staff, and plucked the spear out of the Egyptian's hand, and slew him with his own spear.

22 These *things* did Benaiah the son of Jehoiada, and had the name among three mighty men.

23 He was [I]more honourable than the thirty, but he attained not to the *first* three. And David set him [a]over his [II]guard.[4928]

24 [a]Asahel the brother of Joab *was* one of the thirty; Elhanan the son of Dodo of Bethlehem,

25 [a]Shammah the Harodite, Elika the Harodite,

26 Helez the Paltite, Ira the son of Ikkesh the Tekoite,

27 Abiezer the Anethothite, Mebunnai the Hushathite,

28 Zalmon the Ahohite, Maharai the Netophathite,

29 Heleb the son of Baanah, a Netophathite, Ittai the son of Ribai out of Gibeah of the children[1121] of Benjamin,

30 Benaiah the Pirathonite, Hiddai of the [I][a]brooks of [b]Gaash,

31 Abi–albon the Arbathite, Azmaveth the Barhumite,

32 Eliahba the Shaalbonite, of the sons of Jashen, Jonathan,

33 Shammah the Hararite, Ahiam the son of Sharar the Hararite,

34 Eliphelet the son of Ahasbai, the son of the Maachathite, Eliam the son of Ahithophel the Gilonite,

35 Hezrai the Carmelite, Paarai the Arbite,

36 Igal the son of Nathan of Zobah, Bani the Gadite,

37 Zelek the Ammonite, Nahari the Beerothite, armourbearer[5375,3627] to Joab the son of Zeruiah,

38 [a]Ira an Ithrite, Gareb an Ithrite,

39 [a]Uriah the Hittite: thirty and seven in all.

David Takes a Census

24 And [a]again the anger[639] of the LORD was kindled[2734] against Israel, and [I][b]he moved[5496] David against them to say, [c]Go, number Israel and Judah.

2 For the king[4428] said to Joab the captain[8269] of the host, which *was* with him, [I]Go now through all the tribes of Israel, [a]from Dan even to Beer–sheba, and number ye the people, that [b]I may know[3045] the number of the people.

3 And Joab said unto the king, Now the LORD thy God[430] add unto the people, how many soever they be, an hundredfold, and that the eyes of my lord[113] the king may see *it:* but why doth my lord the king delight[2654] in this thing?

4 Notwithstanding the king's word[1697] prevailed against Joab, and against the captains of the host. And Joab and the captains of the host went out from the presence of the king, to number the people of Israel.

5 And they passed over Jordan, and pitched in [a]Aroer, on the right side of the city that *lieth* in the midst of the [I]river of Gad, and toward [b]Jazer:

6 Then they came to Gilead, and to the [I]land[776] of Tahtim–hodshi; and they came to [a]Dan–jaan, and about to [b]Zidon,

7 And came to the strong hold[4013] of Tyre, and to all the cities of the Hivites, and of the Canaanites: and they went out to the south of Judah, *even* to Beer–sheba.

8 So when they had gone through all the land, they came to Jerusalem at the end of nine months and twenty days.

9 And Joab gave up the sum[4557] of the number[4662] of the people unto the king: [a]and there were in Israel eight hundred thousand valiant men that drew the sword; and the men of Judah *were* five hundred thousand men.

David's Punishment

10 And [a]David's heart smote him after that he had numbered the people. And David said unto the LORD, [b]I have sinned greatly in that I have done:[6213] and now, I beseech thee, O LORD, take away the iniquity[5771] of thy servant; for I have [c]done very foolishly.

30 IOr, *valleys* [a]Deut. 1:24 [b]Judg. 2:9

38 [a]2Sam. 20:26

39 [a]2Sam. 11:3, 6

1 IOr, *Satan* [a]2Sam. 21:2 [b]1Chr. 21:1; James 1:13, 14 [c]1Chr. 27:23, 24

2 IOr, *Compass* [a]Judg. 20:1 [b]Jer. 17:5

5 IOr, *valley* [a]Deut. 2:36; Josh. 13:9, 16 [b]Num. 32:1, 3

6 IOr, *nether land newly inhabited* [a]Josh. 19:47; Judg. 18:29 [b]Josh. 19:28; Judg. 18:28

9 [a]1Chr. 21:5

10 [a]1Sam. 24:5; [b]2Sam. 12:13 [c]1Sam. 13:13

24:1–14 Opinions vary concerning the sin involved in this census. Josephus stated that David failed to collect the proper offering, which had been commanded in Exodus 30:12. Most scholars, however, feel that the sin was a result of David's attitude of pride and arrogance. Still others suggest that his intentions were to maximize military strength and to tax the people further. In any event, when he repented, God gave him three options for the consequences of his sin: famine, military defeat, or pestilence. David fully trusted in God even as he chose (v. 14). There is a lesson to be learned from David's action: while one may be experiencing God's chastening, he must still rely on His ultimate grace, trust Him fully, and be committed to Him.

11 For when David was up in the morning, the word of the LORD came unto the prophet [a]Gad, David's [b]seer, saying,

12 Go and say unto David, Thus saith the LORD, I offer thee three *things;* choose[977] thee one of them, that I may *do it* unto thee.

13 So Gad came to David, and told him, and said unto him, Shall [a]seven years of famine come unto thee in thy land? or wilt thou flee three months before thine enemies, while they pursue thee? or that there be three days'[3117] pestilence in thy land? now advise, and see what answer[1697] I shall return to him that sent me.

14 And David said unto Gad, I am in a great strait:[6887] let us fall now into the hand of the LORD; [a]for his mercies[7356] *are* [I]great: and [b]let me not fall into the hand of man.

15 So [a]the LORD sent a pestilence upon Israel from the morning even to the time appointed:[4150] and there died[4191] of the people from Dan even to Beer-sheba seventy thousand men.

16 [a]And when the angel stretched out his hand upon Jerusalem to destroy[7843] it, [b]the LORD repented[5162] him of the evil,[7451] and said to the angel that destroyed[7843] the people, It is enough: stay now thine hand. And the angel of the LORD was by the threshingplace of [c]Araunah the Jebusite.

17 And David spake unto the LORD when he saw the angel[4397] that smote the people, and said, Lo, [a]I have sinned, and I have done wickedly: but these sheep, what have they done?[6213] let thine hand, I pray thee, be against me, and against my father's[1] house.

11 [a]1Sam. 22:5 [b]1Sam. 9:9; 1Chr. 29:29

13 [a]1Chr. 21:12

14 [I]Or, *many* [a]Ps. 103:8, 13, 14; 119:156 [b]Isa. 47:6; Zech. 1:15

15 [a]1Chr. 21:14; 27:24

16 [a]Ex. 12:23; 1Chr. 21:15 [b]Gen. 6:6; 1Sam. 15:11; Joel 2:13, 14 [c]2Sam. 24:18; 1Chr. 21:15; 2Chr. 3:1, Ornan

17 [a]1Chr. 21:17

18 [I]Hebr. *Araniah* [a]1Chr. 21:18

21 [a]Gen. 23:8-16 [b]Num. 16:48, 50

22 [a]1Kgs. 19:21

23 [a]Ezek. 20:40, 41

24 [a]1Chr. 21:24, 25

25 [a]2Sam. 21:14 [b]2Sam. 24:2

David Offers Sacrifice

18 And Gad came that day[3117] to David, and said unto him, [a]Go up, rear an altar[4196] unto the LORD in the threshingfloor of [I]Araunah the Jebusite.

19 And David, according to the saying of Gad, went up as the LORD commanded.[6680]

20 And Araunah looked, and saw the king and his servants coming on toward him: and Araunah went out, and bowed himself before the king on his face[639] upon the ground.[776]

21 And Araunah said, Wherefore is my lord the king come to his servant? [a]And David said, To buy the threshingfloor of thee, to build an altar unto the LORD, that [b]the plague may be stayed[6113] from the people.

22 And Araunah said unto David, Let my lord the king take and offer up what *seemeth* good[2896] unto him: [a]behold,[7200] *here be* oxen for burnt sacrifice,[5930] and threshing instruments and *other* instruments of the oxen for wood.

23 All these *things* did Araunah, *as* a king, give unto the king. And Araunah said unto the king, The LORD thy God [a]accept[7521] thee.

24 And the king said unto Araunah, Nay; but I will surely buy *it* of thee at a price: neither will I offer burnt offerings unto the LORD my God of that which doth cost me nothing. So [a]David bought the threshingfloor and the oxen for fifty shekels of silver.

25 And David built there an altar unto the LORD, and offered[5927] burnt offerings and peace offerings. [a]So the LORD was intreated[6279] for the land, and [b]the plague was stayed from Israel.

The First Book of

KINGS

The books of 1 and 2 Kings originally made up only one volume in the Hebrew Scriptures. The Septuagint and the translations of the Old Testament that followed divided the books of Samuel and Kings into First Kings through Fourth Kings. These books were first divided in the Hebrew Bible in an edition that was published in A.D. 1517. The books of 1 and 2 Kings relate the history of the Jewish people from the death of David to the captivity of Judah (ca. 970 to 560 B.C.).

A recurring theme in both books involves the examples that each king chose to follow. Repeatedly, David is presented as the best example for kings (1 Kgs. 3:14; 11:4, 6; 15:3; 2 Kgs. 14:3; 16:2; 22:2) and Jeroboam as the worst (1 Kgs. 15:34; 16:2, 26, 31; 22:52; 2 Kgs. 3:3; 10:29, 31; 13:2, 6, 11).

The Talmud states that Jeremiah was the author of both books of the Kings. Nevertheless, the Holy Spirit directed him to use the records of contemporary prophets to complete the work. Some prophets who wrote during this time, but whose writings were not included in the canon of Scripture, are Jehu (1 Kgs. 16:1), Nathan, Ahijah, and Iddo (2 Chr. 9:29), Shemaiah (2 Chr. 12:15), and some other works of Isaiah (2 Chr. 26:22; 32:32).

The Book of 1 Kings covers the reign of Solomon, the division of the kingdom, and the reigns of the kings of Israel and Judah up through Jehoshaphat and Ahaziah respectively. The immense riches that Solomon accumulated and the tremendous advances that the nation made during his reign deteriorated under later kings. It was Solomon, however, who started the nation on this course. He brought disgrace on himself and all Israel by refusing to use discretion in his relationships with women (1 Kgs. 11:1–11). Solomon did well to ask God for wisdom to govern Israel (1 Kgs. 3:4–28), but he did not continue to act wisely. He ignored the last counsel that his father David had given him (1 Kgs. 2:2, 3) and began to trust in human means of government rather than on God. Solomon taxed the nation so heavily that the people were ready to rebel, and following his death, the nation permanently divided because his successor, Rehoboam, thought he could continue to tax the people as heavily as Solomon.

David Approaches Death

1 Now king David was old *and*
Istricken in years; and they covered[3680] him with clothes, but he gat no
heat.
2 Wherefore his servants said unto
him, ILet there be sought for my lord
the king IIa young virgin:[1330] and let her
stand before the king, and let her
IIIcherish[5532] him, and let her lie in thy
bosom, that my lord the king may get
heat.
3 So they sought for a fair
damsel[5291] throughout all the coasts
of Israel, and found Abishag a
aShunammite, and brought her to the
king.
4 And the damsel *was* very fair, and
cherished the king, and ministered[8334] to
him: but the king knew her not.

Adonijah Usurps David's Throne

5 Then aAdonijah the son of Haggith
exalted himself, saying, I will Ibe king:
and bhe prepared him chariots and horsemen, and fifty men to run before him.
6 And his father[1] had not displeased[6087] him Iat any time in saying,

1 IHebr. *entered into days*

2 IHebr. *Let them seek* IIHebr. *a damsel, a virgin* IIIHebr. *be a cherisher unto him*

3 aJosh. 19:18

5 IHebr. *reign* a2Sam. 3:4 b2Sam. 15:1

6 IHebr. *from his days*

1:5 According to the Jewish custom during this time, the birthright belonged to the oldest son in the family. In the case of royal families, this would include the accession to the throne. Though he was David's fourth son, Adonijah was the oldest living son, and thus he assumed he would be the next king. David had not informed him that this custom was not to be followed. He was wrong in seeking the throne (1 Kgs. 2:15).

Why hast thou done[6213] so? and he also *was a* very goodly[2896] [8389] *man;* [a]and *his mother* bare him after Absalom.

7 And [I]he conferred with Joab the son of Zeruiah, and with [a]Abiathar the priest: and [b]they [II]following Adonijah helped *him.*

8 But Zadok the priest, and Benaiah the son of Jehoiada, and Nathan the prophet, and [a]Shimei, and Rei, and [b]the mighty men which *belonged* to David, were not with Adonijah.

9 And Adonijah slew sheep and oxen and fat cattle by the stone of Zoheleth, which *is* by [Ia]En–rogel, and called[7121] all his brethren[251] the king's sons, and all the men of Judah the king's servants:

10 But Nathan the prophet, and Benaiah, and the mighty men, and Solomon his brother, he called not.

11 Wherefore Nathan spake unto Bath–sheba the mother of Solomon, saying, Hast thou not heard that Adonijah the son of [a]Haggith doth reign, and David our lord knoweth *it* not?

12 Now therefore come, let me, I pray thee, give thee counsel,[6098] that thou mayest save thine own life, and the life of thy son Solomon.

13 Go and get thee in unto king David, and say unto him, Didst not thou, my lord, O king, swear unto thine handmaid, saying, [a]Assuredly Solomon thy son shall reign after me, and he shall sit upon my throne? why then doth Adonijah reign?

14 Behold, while thou yet talkest there with the king, I also will come in after thee, and [I]confirm thy words.

15 And Bath–sheba went in unto the king into the chamber: and the king was very old; and Abishag the Shunammite ministered unto the king.

16 And Bath–sheba bowed, and did obeisance[7812] unto the king. And the king said, [I]What wouldest thou?

17 And she said unto him, My lord, [a]thou swarest by the LORD thy God[430] unto thine handmaid, *saying,* Assuredly Solomon thy son shall reign after me, and he shall sit upon my throne.

18 And now, behold, Adonijah reigneth; and now, my lord the king, thou knowest *it* not:

19 [a]And he hath slain oxen and fat cattle and sheep in abundance, and hath called all the sons of the king, and Abiathar the priest, and Joab the captain[8269] of the host: but Solomon thy servant hath he not called.

20 And thou, my lord, O king, the eyes of all Israel *are* upon thee, that thou shouldest tell them who shall sit on the throne of my lord the king after him.

21 Otherwise it shall come to pass, when my lord the king shall [a]sleep with his fathers,[1] that I and my son Solomon shall be counted [I]offenders.[2400]

22 And, lo, while she yet talked with the king, Nathan the prophet also came in.

23 And they told the king, saying, Behold Nathan the prophet. And when he was come in before the king, he bowed[7812] himself before the king with his face[639] to the ground.[776]

24 And Nathan said, My lord, O king, hast thou said, Adonijah shall reign after me, and he shall sit upon my throne?

25 [a]For he is gone down this day,[3117] and hath slain oxen and fat cattle and sheep in abundance, and hath called all the king's sons, and the captains[8269] of the host, and Abiathar the priest; and, behold, they eat and drink before him, and say, [Ib]God save king Adonijah.

26 But me, *even* me thy servant, and Zadok the priest, and Benaiah the son of Jehoiada, and thy servant Solomon, hath he not called.

27 Is this thing done by my lord the king, and thou hast not shewed *it* unto thy servant, who should sit on the throne of my lord the king after him?

David Has Solomon Anointed King

28 Then king David answered and said, Call[7121] me Bath–sheba. And she came [I]into the king's presence, and stood before the king.

29 And the king sware, and said,

6 [a]2Sam. 3:3, 4; 1Chr. 3:2

7 [I]Hebr. *his words were with Joab* [II]Hebr. *helped after Adonijah* [a]2Sam. 20:25 [b]1Kgs. 2:22, 28

8 [a]1Kgs. 4:18 [b]2Sam. 23:8

9 [I]Or, *The well Rogel* [a]2Sam. 17:17

11 [a]2Sam. 3:4

13 [a]1Chr. 22:9

14 [I]Hebr. *fill up*

16 [I]Hebr. *What to thee*

17 [a]1Kgs. 1:13, 30

19 [a]1Kgs. 1:7-9, 25

21 [I]Hebr. *sinners* [a]Deut. 31:16; 1Kgs. 2:10

25 [I]Hebr. *Let king Adonijah live* [a]1Kgs. 1:19 [b]1Sam. 10:24

28 [I]Hebr. *before the king*

[a]As the LORD liveth, that hath redeemed[6299] my soul out of all distress,

30 [a]Even as I sware unto thee by the LORD God of Israel, saying, Assuredly Solomon thy son shall reign after me, and he shall sit upon my throne in my stead; even so will I certainly do[6213] this day.

31 Then Bath–sheba bowed with *her* face to the earth,[776] and did reverence to the king, and said, [a]Let my lord king David live for ever.

32 And king David said, Call me Zadok the priest, and Nathan the prophet, and Benaiah the son of Jehoiada. And they came before the king.

33 The king also said unto them, [a]Take with you the servants of your lord, and cause Solomon my son to ride upon [I][b]mine own mule, and bring him down to [c]Gihon:

34 And let Zadok the priest and Nathan the prophet [a]anoint[4886] him there king over Israel: and [b]blow[8628] ye with the trumpet, and say, God save[2421] king Solomon.

35 Then ye shall come up after him, that he may come and sit upon my throne; for he shall be king in my stead: and I have appointed[6680] him to be ruler over Israel and over Judah.

36 And Benaiah the son of Jehoiada answered the king, and said, Amen:[543] the LORD God of my lord the king say so *too.*

37 [a]As the LORD hath been with my lord the king, even so be he with Solomon, and [b]make his throne greater than the throne of my lord king David.

38 So Zadok the priest, and Nathan the prophet, [a]and Benaiah the son of Jehoiada, and the Cherethites,[3746] and the Pelethites, went down, and caused Solomon to ride upon king David's mule, and brought him to Gihon.

39 And Zadok the priest took an horn of [a]oil out of the tabernacle, and [b]anointed[4886] Solomon. And they blew[8628] the trumpet; [c]and all the people said, God save king Solomon.

40 And all the people came up after him, and the people piped with [I]pipes,

29 [a]2Sam. 4:9

30 [a]1Kgs. 1:17

31 [a]Neh. 2:3; Dan. 2:4

33 [I]Hebr. *which* belongeth *to me* [a]2Sam. 20:6 [b]Esth. 6:8 [c]2Chr. 32:30

34 [a]1Sam. 10:1; 16:3, 12; 2Sam. 2:4; 5:3; 1Kgs. 19:16; 2Kgs. 9:3; 11:12 [b]2Sam. 15:10; 2Kgs. 9:13; 11:14

37 [a]Josh. 1:5, 17; 1Sam. 20:13 [b]1Kgs. 1:47

38 [a]2Sam. 8:18; 23:20-23

39 [a]Ex. 30:23, 25, 32; Ps. 89:20 [b]1Chr. 29:22 [c]1Sam. 10:24

40 [I]Or, *flutes*

42 [a]2Sam. 18:27

46 [a]1Chr. 29:23

47 [a]1Kgs. 1:37 [b]Gen. 47:31

48 [a]1Kgs. 3:6; Ps. 132:11, 12

50 [a]1Kgs. 2:28

and rejoiced with great joy, so that the earth rent[1234] with the sound of them.

41 And Adonijah and all the guests[7121] that *were* with him heard *it* as they had made an end[3615] of eating. And when Joab heard the sound of the trumpet, he said, Wherefore *is this* noise of the city being in an uproar?

42 And while he yet spake, behold, Jonathan the son of Abiathar the priest came; and Adonijah said unto him, Come in; for [a]thou *art* a valiant man, and bringest good[2896] tidings.

43 And Jonathan answered and said to Adonijah, Verily our lord king David hath made Solomon king.

44 And the king hath sent with him Zadok the priest, and Nathan the prophet, and Benaiah the son of Jehoiada, and the Cherethites, and the Pelethites, and they have caused him to ride upon the king's mule:

45 And Zadok the priest and Nathan the prophet have anointed him king in Gihon: and they are come up from thence rejoicing, so that the city rang again.[1949] This *is* the noise that ye have heard.

46 And also Solomon [a]sitteth on the throne of the kingdom.

47 And moreover the king's servants came to bless[1288] our lord king David, saying, [a]God make the name of Solomon better[3190] than thy name, and make his throne greater than thy throne. [b]And the king bowed himself upon the bed.

48 And also thus said the king, Blessed[1288] *be* the LORD God of Israel, which hath [a]given *one* to sit on my throne this day, mine eyes even seeing *it.*

49 And all the guests that *were* with Adonijah were afraid,[2729] and rose up, and went every man his way.

50 And Adonijah feared[3372] because of Solomon, and arose, and went, and [a]caught hold[2388] on the horns of the altar.[4196]

51 And it was told Solomon, saying, Behold, Adonijah feareth king Solomon: for, lo, he hath caught hold on the horns of the altar, saying, Let king Solomon swear unto me to day that he will not slay his servant with the sword.

52 And Solomon said, If he will shew himself a worthy man,[1121,2428] [a]there shall not an hair of him fall to the earth: but if wickedness[7451] shall be found in him, he shall die.[4191]

53 So king Solomon sent, and they brought him down from the altar. And he came and bowed himself to king Solomon: and Solomon said unto him, Go to thine house.

David Gives Instructions to Solomon

2 Now the [a]days[3117] of David drew nigh that he should die;[4191] and he charged[6680] Solomon his son, saying,

2 [a]I go the way of all the earth:[776] [b]be thou strong therefore, and shew thyself a man;

3 And keep[8104] the charge[4931] of the LORD thy God,[430] to walk in his ways, to keep his statutes, and his commandments,[4687] and his judgments,[4941] and his testimonies,[5715] as it is written in the law of Moses, that thou mayest [I][a]prosper[7919] in all that thou doest, and whithersoever thou turnest thyself:

4 That the LORD may [a]continue his word which he spake concerning me, saying, [b]If thy children[1121] take heed to their way, to [c]walk before me in truth with all their heart and with all their soul, [d]there shall not [I]fail thee (said he) a man on the throne of Israel.

5 Moreover thou knowest also what Joab the son of Zeruiah [a]did[6213] to me, *and* what he did to the two captains[8269] of the hosts of Israel, unto [b]Abner the son of Ner, and unto [c]Amasa the son of Jether, whom he slew, and [I]shed the blood[1818] of war in peace, and put the blood of war upon his girdle[2290] that *was* about his loins, and in his shoes that *were* on his feet.

6 Do therefore [a]according to thy wisdom, and let not his hoar head[7872] go down to the grave[7585] in peace.

7 But shew kindness unto the sons of [a]Barzillai the Gileadite, and let them be of those that [b]eat at thy table: for so [c]they came to me when I fled because of Absalom thy brother.[251]

8 And, behold, *thou hast* with thee [a]Shimei the son of Gera, a Benjamite of Bahurim, which cursed[7043] me with a [I]grievous curse[7045] in the day when I went to Mahanaim: but [b]he came down to meet me at Jordan, and [c]I sware to him by the LORD, saying, I will not put thee to death[4191] with the sword.

9 Now therefore [a]hold him not guiltless:[5352] for thou *art* a wise man, and knowest what thou oughtest to do unto him; but his hoar head [b]bring thou down to the grave with blood.

David's Death

10 So [a]David slept with his fathers,[1] and was buried[6912] in [b]the city of David.

11 And the days that David [a]reigned over Israel *were* forty years: seven years reigned he in Hebron, and thirty and three years reigned he in Jerusalem.

12 [a]Then sat Solomon upon the throne of David his father; and his kingdom was established[3559] greatly.

Solomon Consolidates His Rule

13 And Adonijah the son of Haggith came to Bath–sheba the mother of Solomon. And she said, [a]Comest thou peaceably? And he said, Peaceably.

14 He said moreover, I have somewhat to say unto thee. And she said, Say on.

15 And he said, Thou knowest that the kingdom was [a]mine, and *that* all Israel set their faces on me, that I should reign: howbeit the kingdom is turned about, and is become[1961] my brother's: for [b]it was his from the LORD.

16 And now I ask[7592] one petition of thee, [I][a]deny me not. And she said unto him, Say on.

17 And he said, Speak, I pray thee, unto Solomon the king, (for he will not say thee nay,) that he give me [a]Abishag the Shunammite to wife.

---

52 [a]1Sam. 14:45; 2Sam. 14:11; Acts 27:34

1 [a]Gen. 47:29; Deut. 31:14

2 [a]Josh. 23:14 [b]Deut. 17:19, 20

3 [I]Or, *do wisely* [a]Deut. 29:9; Josh. 1:7; 1Sam. 18:5, 14, 30; 1Chr. 22:12, 13

4 [I]Hebr. *be cut off from thee from the throne* [a]2Sam. 7:25 [b]Ps. 132:12 [c]2Kgs. 20:3 [d]2Sam. 7:12, 13; 1Kgs. 8:25

5 [I]Hebr. *put* [a]2Sam. 3:39; 18:5, 12, 14; 19:5-7 [b]2Sam. 3:27 [c]2Sam. 20:10

6 [a]1Kgs. 2:9; Prov. 20:26

7 [a]2Sam. 19:31, 38 [b]2Sam. 9:7, 10; 19:28 [c]2Sam. 17:27

8 [I]Hebr. *strong* [a]2Sam. 16:5 [b]2Sam. 19:18 [c]2Sam. 19:23

9 [a]Ex. 20:7; Job 9:28 [b]Gen. 42:38; 44:31

10 [a]1Kgs. 1:21; Acts 2:29; 13:36 [b]2Sam. 5:7

11 [a]2Sam. 5:4; 1Chr. 29:26, 27

12 [a]1Chr. 29:23; 2Chr. 1:1

13 [a]1Sam. 16:4, 5

15 [a]1Kgs. 1:5 [b]1Chr. 22:9, 10; 28:5-7; Prov. 21:30; Dan. 2:21

16 [I]Hebr. *turn not away my face* [a]Ps. 132:10

17 [a]1Kgs. 1:3, 4

18 And Bath–sheba said, Well;[2896] I will speak for thee unto the king.

19 Bath–sheba therefore went unto king Solomon, to speak unto him for Adonijah. And the king rose up to meet her, and [a]bowed[7812] himself unto her, and sat down on his throne, and caused a seat to be set for the king's mother; [b]and she sat on his right hand.

20 Then she said, I desire[7592] one small petition of thee; I *pray thee,* say me not nay. And the king said unto her, Ask on, my mother: for I will not say thee nay.

21 And she said, Let Abishag the Shunammite be given to Adonijah thy brother to wife.

22 And king Solomon answered and said unto his mother, And why dost thou ask Abishag the Shunammite for Adonijah? ask for him the kingdom also; for he *is* mine elder brother; even for him, and for [a]Abiathar the priest, and for Joab the son of Zeruiah.

23 Then king Solomon sware by the LORD, saying, [a]God do so to me, and more also, if Adonijah have not spoken this word against his own life.[5315]

24 Now therefore, *as* the LORD liveth, which hath established me, and set me on the throne of David my father, and who hath made me an house, as he [a]promised, Adonijah shall be put to death this day.

25 And king Solomon sent by the hand of Benaiah the son of Jehoiada; and he fell upon him that he died.[4191]

26 And unto Abiathar the priest said the king, Get thee to [a]Anathoth, unto thine own fields;[7704] for thou *art* Iworthy of death:[4194] but I will not at this time put thee to death, [b]because thou barest the ark[727] of the Lord GOD before David my father, and because [c]thou hast been afflicted in all wherein my father was afflicted.

27 So Solomon thrust out[1644] Abiathar from being priest unto the LORD; that he might [a]fulfil the word of the LORD, which he spake concerning the house of Eli in Shiloh.

28 Then tidings came to Joab: for Joab [a]had turned after Adonijah, though he turned not after Absalom. And Joab fled unto the tabernacle of the LORD, and [b]caught hold on the horns of the altar.[4196]

29 And it was told king Solomon that Joab was fled unto the tabernacle[168] of the LORD; and, behold, *he is* by the altar. Then Solomon sent Benaiah the son of Jehoiada, saying, Go, fall upon[6293] him.

30 And Benaiah came to the tabernacle of the LORD, and said unto him, Thus saith the king, Come forth. And he said, Nay; but I will die here. And Benaiah brought the king word again, saying, Thus said Joab, and thus he answered me.

31 And the king said unto him, [a]Do as he hath said, and fall upon him, and bury[6912] him; [b]that thou mayest take away the innocent blood, which Joab shed, from me, and from the house of my father.

32 And the LORD [a]shall return his blood upon his own head, who fell upon two men more righteous [b]and better[2896] than he, and slew them with the sword, my father David not knowing *thereof, to wit,* [c]Abner the son of Ner, captain[8269] of the host of Israel, and [d]Amasa the son of Jether, captain of the host of Judah.

33 Their blood shall therefore return upon the head of Joab, and [a]upon the head of his seed for ever: [b]but upon David, and upon his seed, and upon his

19 [a]Ex. 20:12 [b]Ps. 45:9
22 [a]1Kgs. 1:7
23 [a]Ruth 1:17
24 [a]2Sam. 7:11, 13; 1Chr. 22:10
26 IHebr. *a man of death* [a]Josh. 21:18 [b]1Sam. 23:6; 2Sam. 15:24, 29 [c]1Sam. 22:20, 23; 2Sam. 15:24
27 [a]1Sam. 2:31–35
28 [a]1Kgs. 1:7 [b]1Kgs. 1:50
31 [a]Ex. 21:14 [b]Num. 35:33; Deut. 19:13; 21:8, 9
32 [a]Judg. 9:24, 57; Ps. 7:16 [b]2Chr. 21:13 [c]2Sam. 3:27 [d]2Sam. 20:10
33 [a]2Sam. 3:29 [b]Prov. 25:5

2:22 Apparently Adonijah had not given up all aspirations of ascending to his father's throne. According to eastern customs, marrying any of a late king's wives or concubines was recognized as an attempt to claim the former king's rights.

2:26, 27 Solomon's actions fulfilled the prophecy of 1 Samuel 2:31–36 that the priesthood would depart from the family of Eli of which Abiathar was a descendant. When Zadok was appointed priest (v. 35), the priesthood was returned to its ancient lineage since Zadok was a descendant of Eleazar the son of Aaron (1 Chr. 6:1–8). See note on Jeremiah 1:1, with regard to Anathoth.

house, and upon his throne,[3678] shall there be peace for ever from the LORD.

34 So Benaiah the son of Jehoiada went up, and fell upon him, and slew him: and he was buried in his own house in the wilderness.

35 And the king put Benaiah the son of Jehoiada in his room over the host: and [a]Zadok the priest did the king put in the room of [b]Abiathar.

36 And the king sent and called[7121] for [a]Shimei, and said unto him, Build thee an house in Jerusalem, and dwell there, and go not forth thence any whither.

37 For it shall be, *that* on the day thou goest out, and passest over [a]the brook Kidron, thou shalt know for certain that thou shalt surely die: [b]thy blood shall be upon thine own head.

38 And Shimei said unto the king, The saying *is* good:[2896] as my lord the king hath said, so will thy servant do. And Shimei dwelt in Jerusalem many days.

39 And it came to pass at the end of three years, that two of the servants of Shimei ran away unto [a]Achish son of Maachah king of Gath. And they told Shimei, saying, Behold, thy servants *be* in Gath.

40 And Shimei arose, and saddled his ass, and went to Gath to Achish to seek his servants: and Shimei went, and brought his servants from Gath.

41 And it was told Solomon that Shimei had gone from Jerusalem to Gath, and was come again.

42 And the king sent and called for Shimei, and said unto him, Did I not make thee to swear[7650] by the LORD, and protested unto thee, saying, Know for a certain, on the day thou goest out, and walkest abroad any whither, that thou shalt surely die? and thou saidst unto me, The word *that* I have heard *is* good.

43 Why then hast thou not kept the oath of the LORD, and the commandment[4687] that I have charged thee with?

44 The king said moreover to Shimei, Thou knowest [a]all the wickedness which thine heart is privy to, that thou didst to David my father: therefore the LORD shall [b]return thy wickedness upon thine own head;

45 And king Solomon *shall be* blessed,[1288] and [a]the throne of David shall be established before the LORD for ever.

46 So the king commanded[6680] Benaiah the son of Jehoiada; which went out, and fell upon him, that he died. And the [a]kingdom was established in the hand of Solomon.

Solomon Marries Pharaoh's Daughter

3 And [a]Solomon made affinity[2859] with Pharaoh king of Egypt, and took Pharaoh's daughter, and brought her into the [b]city of David, until he had made an end[3615] of building his [c]own house, and the house of the LORD, and [d]the wall of Jerusalem round about.

2 [a]Only the people sacrificed in high places,[1116] because there was no house built unto the name of the LORD, until those days.[3117]

Solomon Asks for Wisdom

3 And Solomon [a]loved the LORD, [b]walking in the statutes of David his father:[1] only he sacrificed and burnt incense[6999] in high places.

4 And [a]the king went to Gibeon to sacrifice there; [b]for that *was* the great high place: a thousand burnt offerings did Solomon offer upon that altar.[4196]

5 [a]In Gibeon the LORD appeared[7200] to Solomon [b]in a dream by night: and God[430] said, Ask[7592] what I shall give thee.

6 [a]And Solomon said, Thou hast shewed unto thy servant David my father great [I]mercy, according as he [b]walked before thee in truth, and in righteousness, and in uprightness of heart with thee; and thou hast kept for him this great kindness, that thou [c]hast given him a son to sit on his throne, as *it is* this day.[3117]

7 And now, O LORD my God, thou

35 [a]Num. 25:11-13; 1Sam. 2:35; 1Chr. 6:53; 24:3 [b]1Kgs. 2:27

36 [a]2Sam. 16:5; 1Kgs. 2:8

37 [a]2Sam. 15:23 [b]Lev. 20:9; Josh. 2:19; 2Sam. 1:16

39 [a]1Sam. 27:2

44 [a]2Sam. 16:5 [b]Ps. 7:16; Ezek. 17:19

45 [a]Prov. 25:5

46 [a]1Kgs. 2:12; 2Chr. 1:1

1 [a]1Kgs. 7:8; 9:24 [b]2Sam. 5:7 [c]1Kgs. 7:1 [d]1Kgs. 9:15, 19

2 [a]Lev. 17:3, 4, 5; Deut. 12:2, 4, 5; 1Kgs. 22:43

3 [a]Deut. 6:5; 30:16, 20; Ps. 31:23; Rom. 8:28; 1Cor. 8:3 [b]1Kgs. 3:6, 14

4 [a]2Chr. 1:3 [b]1Chr. 16:39; 2Chr. 1:3

5 [a]1Kgs. 9:2; 2Chr. 1:7 [b]Num. 12:6; Matt. 1:20; 2:13, 19

6 [a]2Chr. 1:8-10 [I]Or, bounty [b]1Kgs. 2:4; 9:4; 2Kgs. 20:3; Ps. 15:2 [c]1Kgs. 1:48

hast made thy servant king instead of David my father: [a]and I *am but* a little child: I know not *how* [b]to go out or come in.

8 And thy servant *is* in the midst of thy people which thou [a]hast chosen,[977] a great people, [b]that cannot be numbered nor counted for multitude.

9 [a]Give therefore thy servant an [I]understanding[8085] heart [b]to judge[8199] thy people, that I may [c]discern[995] between good[2896] and bad:[7451] for who is able to judge this thy so great a people?

10 And the speech pleased the LORD, that Solomon had asked[7592] this thing.

11 And God said unto him, Because thou hast asked this thing, and hast [a]not asked for thyself [I]long life; neither hast asked riches for thyself, nor hast asked the life of thine enemies; but hast asked for thyself understanding [II]to discern[8085] judgment;[4941]

12 [a]Behold, I have done[6213] according to thy words: [b]lo, I have given thee a wise and an understanding heart; so that there was none like thee before thee, neither after thee shall any arise like unto thee.

13 And I have also [a]given thee that which thou hast not asked, both [b]riches, and honour: so that there [I]shall not be any among the kings like unto thee all thy days.

14 And if thou wilt walk in my ways, to keep my statutes and my commandments,[4687] [a]as thy father David did walk, then I will [b]lengthen thy days.

15 And Solomon [a]awoke; and, behold, *it was* a dream. And he came to Jerusalem, and stood before the ark[727] of the covenant[1285] of the LORD, and offered up burnt offerings,[5930] and offered peace offerings,[8002] and [b]made a feast to all his servants.

An Example of Solomon's Wisdom

16 Then came there two women, *that were* harlots,[2181] unto the king, and [a]stood before him.

17 And the one woman said, O my lord, I and this woman dwell in one house; and I was delivered of a child with her in the house.

18 And it came to pass the third day after that I was delivered, that this woman was delivered also: and we *were* together; *there was* no stranger[2114] with us in the house, save we two in the house.

19 And this woman's child[1121] died[4191] in the night; because she overlaid it.

20 And she arose at midnight, and took my son from beside me, while thine handmaid slept, and laid it in her bosom, and laid her dead child in my bosom.

21 And when I rose in the morning to give my child suck, behold, it was dead: but when I had considered[995] it in the morning, behold, it was not my son, which I did bear.

22 And the other woman said, Nay; but the living *is* my son, and the dead *is* thy son. And this said, No; but the dead *is* thy son, and the living *is* my son. Thus they spake before the king.

23 Then said the king, The one saith, This *is* my son that liveth, and thy son *is* the dead: and the other saith, Nay; but thy son *is* the dead, and my son *is* the living.

24 And the king said, Bring me a sword. And they brought a sword before the king.

25 And the king said, Divide[1504] the living child in two, and give half to the one, and half to the other.

26 Then spake the woman whose the living child *was* unto the king, for [a]her bowels[7356] [I]yearned upon her son, and she said, O my lord, give her the living child, and in no wise slay it. But the other said, Let it be neither mine nor thine, *but* divide *it*.

27 Then the king answered and said, Give her the living child, and in no wise slay it: she *is* the mother thereof.

28 And all Israel heard of the judgment which the king had judged;[8199] and they feared[3372] the king: for they saw that the [a]wisdom of God *was* [I]in him, to do[6213] judgment.

7 [a]1Chr. 29:1 [b]Num. 27:17

8 [a]Deut. 7:6 [b]Gen. 13:16; 15:5

9 [I]Hebr. *hearing* [a]2Chr. 1:10; Prov. 2:3-9; James 1:5 [b]Ps. 72:1, 2 [c]Heb. 5:14

11 [I]Hebr. *many days* [II]Hebr. *to hear* [a]James 4:3

12 [a]1John 5:14, 15 [b]1Kgs. 4:29, 30, 31; 5:12; 10:24; Eccl. 1:16

13 [I]Or, *hath not been* [a]Matt. 6:33; Eph. 3:20 [b]1Kgs. 4:21, 24; 10:23, 25; Prov. 3:16

14 [a]1Kgs. 15:5 [b]Ps. 91:16; Prov. 3:2

15 [a]Gen. 41:7 [b]Gen. 40:20; 1Kgs. 8:65; Esth. 1:3; Dan. 5:1; Mark 6:21

16 [a]Num. 27:2

26 [I]Hebr. *were hot* [a]Gen. 43:30; Isa. 49:15; Jer. 31:20; Hos. 11:8

28 [I]Hebr. *in the midst of him* [a]1Kgs. 3:9, 11, 12

Solomon's Officials

4 So king Solomon was king over all Israel.

2 And these *were* the princes[8269] which he had; Azariah the son of Zadok [I]the priest,

3 Elihoreph and Ahiah, the sons of Shisha, [I]scribes;[5608] [a]Jehoshaphat the son of Ahilud, the [II]recorder.

4 And [a]Benaiah the son of Jehoiada *was* over the host: and Zadok and [b]Abiathar *were* the priests:

5 And Azariah the son of Nathan *was* over [a]the officers:[5324] and Zabud the son of Nathan *was* [b]principal officer,[3548] *and* [c]the king's friend:

6 And Ahishar *was* over the household: and [a]Adoniram the son of Abda *was* over the [I]tribute.

7 And Solomon had twelve officers over all Israel, which provided victuals[3557] for the king and his household: each man his month in a year made provision.

8 And these *are* their names: [I]The son of Hur, in mount Ephraim:

9 [I]The son of Dekar, in Makaz, and in Shaalbim, and Beth–shemesh, and Elon–beth–hanan:

10 [I]The son of Hesed, in Aruboth; to him *pertained* Sochoh, and all the land of Hepher:

11 [I]The son of Abinadab, in all the region of Dor; which had Taphath the daughter of Solomon to wife:

12 Baana the son[1121] of Ahilud; *to him pertained* Taanach and Megiddo, and all Beth–shean, which *is* by Zartanah beneath Jezreel, from Beth–shean to Abel–meholah, *even* unto *the place that is* beyond Jokneam:

13 [I]The son of Geber, in Ramoth–gilead; to him *pertained* [a]the towns of Jair the son of Manasseh, which *are* in Gilead; to him *also pertained* the [b]region[2256] of Argob, which *is* in Bashan, threescore great cities with walls and brasen bars:

14 Ahinadab the son of Iddo *had* [I]Mahanaim:

15 Ahimaaz *was* in Naphtali; he also took Basmath the daughter of Solomon to wife:

16 Baanah the son of Hushai *was* in Asher and in Aloth:

17 Jehoshaphat the son of Paruah, in Issachar:

18 Shimei the son of Elah, in Benjamin:

19 Geber the son of Uri *was* in the country[776] of Gilead, *in* [a]the country of Sihon king of the Amorites, and of Og king of Bashan; and *he was* the only officer which *was* in the land.

Solomon Prospers

20 Judah and Israel *were* many, [a]as the sand which *is* by the sea in multitude, [b]eating and drinking, and making merry.[8056]

21 And [a]Solomon reigned over all kingdoms from [b]the river unto the land of the Philistines, and unto the border of Egypt: [c]they brought[5066] presents, and served Solomon all the days[3117] of his life.

22 And Solomon's [I]provision for one day was thirty [II]measures of fine flour, and threescore measures of meal,

23 Ten fat oxen, and twenty oxen out of the pastures, and an hundred sheep, beside harts, and roebucks,[6643] and fallowdeer, and fatted fowl.

24 For he had dominion[7287] over all *the region* on this side the river, from Tiphsah even to Azzah, over [a]all the kings on this side the river: and [b]he had peace on all sides round about him.

25 And Judah and Israel [a]dwelt [I]safely, [b]every man under his vine and under his fig tree, [c]from Dan even to Beersheba, all the days of Solomon.

26 And Solomon had forty thousand stalls of [a]horses for his chariots, and twelve thousand horsemen.

27 And [a]those officers provided victual[3557] for king Solomon, and for all that came unto king Solomon's table, every man in his month: they lacked nothing.

28 Barley also and straw for the horses and [I][a]dromedaries[7409] brought

---

2 [I]Or, *the chief officer*

3 [I]Or, *secretaries* [II]Or, *remembrancer* [a]2Sam. 8:16; 20:24

4 [a]1Kgs. 2:35 [b]1Kgs. 2:27

5 [a]1Kgs. 4:7 [b]2Sam. 8:18; 20:26 [c]2Sam. 15:37; 16:16; 1Chr. 27:33

6 [I]Or, *levy* [a]1Kgs. 5:14

8 [I]Or, *Benhur*

9 [I]Or, *Bendekar*

10 [I]Or, *Benhesed*

11 [I]Or, *Benabinadab*

13 [I]Or, *Bengeber* [a]Num. 32:41 [b]Deut. 3:4

14 [I]Or, *to Mahanai*

19 [a]Deut. 3:8

20 [a]Gen. 22:17; 1Kgs. 3:8; Prov. 14:28 [b]Ps. 72:3, 7; Mic. 4:4

21 [a]2Chr. 9:26; Ps. 72:8 [b]Gen. 15:18; Josh. 1:4 [c]Ps. 68:29; 72:10, 11

22 [I]Hebr. *bread* [II]Hebr. *cords*

24 [a]Ps. 72:11 [b]1Chr. 22:9

25 [I]Hebr. *confidently* [a]Jer. 23:6 [b]Mic. 4:4; Zech. 3:10 [c]Judg. 20:1

26 [a]1Kgs. 10:26; 2Chr. 1:14; 9:25 [b]Deut. 17:16

27 [a]1Kgs. 4:7-19

28 [I]Or, *mules, or, swift beasts* [a]Esth. 8:14; Mic. 1:13

they unto the place where *the officers* were, every man according to his charge.

29 And [a]God[430] gave Solomon wisdom and understanding[8394] exceeding much, and largeness of heart, even as the sand that *is* on the sea shore.

30 And Solomon's wisdom excelled the wisdom of all the children[1121] [a]of the east country, and all [b]the wisdom of Egypt.

31 For he was [a]wiser than all men; [b]than Ethan the Ezrahite, [c]and Heman, and Chalcol, and Darda, the sons of Mahol: and his fame was in all nations round about.

32 And [a]he spake three thousand proverbs;[4192] and his [b]songs were a thousand and five.

33 And he spake of trees, from the cedar tree that *is* in Lebanon even unto the hyssop[231] that springeth out of the wall: he spake also of beasts, and of fowl, and of creeping things, and of fishes.[1709]

34 And [a]there came of all people to hear the wisdom of Solomon, from all kings of the earth,[776] which had heard of his wisdom.

Solomon Prepares to Build The Temple

5 And [a]Hiram king of Tyre sent his servants unto Solomon; for he had heard that they had anointed[4886] him king in the room of his father:[1] [b]for Hiram was ever a lover of David.

2 And Solomon sent to Hiram, saying,

3 Thou knowest how that David my father could not build an house unto the name of the LORD his God[430] [a]for the wars which were about him on every side, until the LORD put them under the soles of his feet.

4 But now the LORD my God hath given me [a]rest on every side, *so that there is* neither adversary nor evil[7451] occurrent.[6294]

5 [a]And, behold, I [I]purpose[559] to build an house unto the name of the LORD my God, [b]as the LORD spake unto David my father, saying, Thy son, whom I will set upon thy throne in thy room, he shall build an house unto my name.

6 Now therefore command[6680] thou that they hew[3772] me [a]cedar trees out of Lebanon; and my servants shall be with thy servants: and unto thee will I give hire for thy servants according to all that thou shalt [I]appoint:[559] for thou knowest that *there is* not among us any that can skill to hew timber like unto the Sidonians.

7 And it came to pass, when Hiram heard the words of Solomon, that he rejoiced greatly, and said, Blessed[1288] *be* the LORD this day,[3117] which hath given unto David a wise son over this great people.

8 And Hiram sent to Solomon, saying, I have [I]considered[8085] the things which thou sentest to me for: *and* I will do[6213] all thy desire[2656] concerning timber of cedar, and concerning timber of fir.

9 My servants shall bring *them* down from Lebanon unto the sea: [a]and I will convey them by sea in floats unto the place that thou shalt [I]appoint me, and will cause them to be discharged there, and thou shalt receive *them:* and thou shalt accomplish[6213] my desire, [b]in giving food for my household.

10 So Hiram gave Solomon cedar trees and fir trees *according to* all his desire.

11 [a]And Solomon gave Hiram twenty thousand [I]measures of wheat *for* food to his household, and twenty measures of pure oil: thus gave Solomon to Hiram year by year.

12 And the LORD gave Solomon wisdom, [a]as he promised him: and there was

29 [a]1Kgs. 3:12
30 [a]Gen. 25:6 [b]Acts 7:22
31 [a]1Kgs. 3:12 [b]1Chr. 15:19 [c]1Chr. 2:6; 6:33; 15:19
32 [a]Prov. 1:1; Eccl. 12:9 [b]Song 1:1
34 [a]1Kgs. 10:1; 2Chr. 9:1, 23
1 [a]1Kgs. 5:10, 18; 2Chr. 2:3, Huram [b]2Sam. 5:11; 1Chr. 14:1; Amos 1:9
3 [a]1Chr. 22:8; 28:3
4 [a]1Kgs. 4:24; 1Chr. 22:9
5 [I]Hebr. *say* [a]2Chr. 2:4 [b]2Sam. 7:13; 1Chr. 17:12; 22:10
6 [I]Hebr. *say* [a]2Chr. 2:8, 10
8 [I]Hebr. *heard*
9 [I]Hebr. *send* [a]2Chr. 2:16 [b]Ezra 3:7; Ezek. 27:17; Acts 12:20
11 [I]Hebr. *cords* [a]2Chr. 2:10
12 [a]1Kgs. 3:12

4:31 Psalm 88 was written by Heman, and Psalm 89 was composed by Ethan. They were among five famous brothers listed in this verse who were from the tribe of Judah.

peace between Hiram and Solomon; and they two made a league together.

13 And king Solomon raised a [I]levy[4522] out of all Israel; and the levy was thirty thousand men.

14 And he sent them to Lebanon, ten thousand a month by courses: a month they were in Lebanon, *and* two months at home: and [a]Adoniram *was* over the levy.

15 [a]And Solomon had threescore and ten thousand that bare[5375] burdens, and fourscore thousand hewers[2672] in the mountains;

16 Beside the chief of Solomon's officers which *were* over the work, three thousand and three hundred, which ruled over the people that wrought in the work.

17 And the king commanded,[6680] and they brought[5265] great stones, costly stones, *and* [a]hewed[1496] stones, to lay the foundation[3245] of the house.

18 And Solomon's builders[1129] and Hiram's builders did hew[6458] *them,* and the [I]stonesquarers:[1382] so they prepared timber and stones to build the house.

Solomon Builds the Temple

6 And [a]it came to pass in the four hundred and eightieth year after the children[1121] of Israel were come out of the land of Egypt, in the fourth year of Solomon's reign over Israel, in the month Zif, which *is* the second month, that [b]he [I]began to build the house of the LORD.

🗝 2 And [a]the house which king Solomon built for the LORD, the length thereof *was* threescore cubits, and the breadth thereof twenty *cubits,* and the height thereof thirty cubits.

3 And the porch before the temple of the house, twenty cubits *was* the length thereof, according to the breadth of the house; *and* ten cubits *was* the breadth thereof before the house.

4 And for the house he made [Ia]windows of narrow lights.[8261]

5 And [I]against the wall of the house he built [IIa]chambers round about, *against* the walls of the house round about, *both* of the temple [b]and of the oracle: and he made [III]chambers round about:

6 The nethermost[8481] chamber *was* five cubits broad, and the middle *was* six cubits broad, and the third *was* seven cubits broad: for without *in the wall* of the house he made [I]narrowed rests round about, that *the beams* should not be fastened in the walls of the house.

7 And [a]the house, when it was in building, was built of stone made ready before it was brought[4551] thither: so that there was neither hammer nor axe *nor* any tool of iron heard in the house, while it was in building.

8 The door for the middle chamber *was* in the right [I]side of the house: and they went up with winding stairs into the middle *chamber,* and out of the middle into the third.

9 [a]So he built the house, and finished[3615] it; and covered the house [I]with beams and boards of cedar.

10 And *then* he built chambers against all the house, five cubits high: and they rested[270] on the house with timber of cedar.

11 And the word of the LORD came to Solomon, saying,

12 *Concerning* this house which thou art in building, [a]if thou wilt walk in my statutes, and execute my judgments,[4941] and keep all my commandments[4687] to

13 [I]Hebr. *tribute*
14 [a]1Kgs. 4:6
15 [a]1Kgs. 9:21; 2Chr. 2:17, 18
17 [a]1Chr. 22:2
18 [I]Or, *Giblites;* Ezek. 27:9
1 [I]Hebr. *built* [a]2Chr. 3:1, 2 [b]Acts 7:47
2 [a]Ezek. 41:1-15
4 [I]Or, *windows broad* within, and: *narrow* without; or, *skewed* and *closed* [a]Ezek. 40:16; 41:16
5 [I]Or, *upon,* or, *joining to* [II]Hebr. *floors* [III]Hebr. *ribs* [a]Ezek. 41:6 [b]1Kgs. 6:16; 19-21, 31
6 [I]Hebr. *narrowings,* or, *rebatements*
7 [a]Deut. 27:5, 6; 1Kgs. 5:18
8 [I]Hebr. *shoulder*
9 [I]Or, *the vault beams and the ceilings with cedar* [a]1Kgs. 6:14, 38
12 [a]1Kgs. 2:4; 9:4

🗝 **6:2** Exodus chapter twenty-six indicates that the Tabernacle proper had been thirty cubits by ten cubits. Solomon's Temple maintained the same proportions but was double the size (roughly 60 cubits by 20 cubits). This was large enough, for only the priests entered this central sanctuary. The rest of the temple complex was more magnificent and large enough for all the people to enter the outer courts. It was the richness of its furnishings, as much as the size, which distinguished Solomon's Temple from the Tabernacle that Moses had built.

walk in them; then will I perform my word with thee, [b]which I spake unto David thy father:[1]

13 And [a]I will dwell[7931] among the children of Israel, and will not [b]forsake[5800] my people Israel.

14 [a]So Solomon built the house, and finished it.

15 And he built the walls of the house within with boards of cedar, [I]both the floor of the house, and the walls of the cieling: *and* he covered *them* on the inside with wood, and covered the floor of the house with planks of fir.

16 And he built twenty cubits on the sides of the house, both the floor and the walls[7023] with boards of cedar: he even built *them* for it within, *even* for the oracle, *even* for the [a]most holy *place.*

17 And the house, that *is,* the temple[1964] before it, was forty cubits *long.*

18 And the cedar of the house within *was* carved with [I]knops6497 and open flowers: all *was* cedar; there was no stone seen.

19 And the oracle[1687] he prepared in the house within, to set there the ark[727] of the covenant[1285] of the LORD.

20 And the oracle in the forepart *was* twenty cubits in length, and twenty cubits in breadth, and twenty cubits in the height thereof: and he overlaid it with [I]pure gold; and *so* covered the altar[4196] *which was of* cedar.

21 So Solomon overlaid the house within with pure gold: and he made a partition[5674] by the chains of gold before the oracle; and he overlaid it with gold.

22 And the whole house he overlaid with gold, until he had finished[8552] all the house: also [a]the whole altar that *was* by the oracle he overlaid with gold.

23 And within the oracle [a]he made two cherubims[3742] *of* [I]olive tree, *each* ten cubits high.

24 And five cubits *was* the one wing of the cherub, and five cubits the other wing of the cherub: from the uttermost part7098 of the one wing unto the uttermost part of the other *were* ten cubits.

12 [b]2Sam. 7:13; 1Chr. 22:10

13 [a]Ex. 25:8; Lev. 26:11; 2Cor. 6:16; Rev. 21:3 [b]Deut. 31:6

14 [a]1Kgs. 6:38

15 [I]Or, *from the floor of the house unto the walls*

16 [a]Ex. 26:33; Lev. 16:2; 1Kgs. 8:6; 2Chr. 3:8; Ezek. 45:3; Heb. 9:3

18 [I]Hebr. *openings of flowers*

20 [I]Hebr. *shut up*

22 [a]Ex. 30:1, 3, 6

23 [I]Or, *oily* [II]Hebr. *trees of oil* [a]Ex. 37:7-9; 2Chr. 3:10-12

27 [I]Or, *the cherubim stretched forth their wings* [a]Ex. 25:20; 37:9; 2Chr. 5:8

29 [I]Hebr. *openings of flowers*

31 [I]Or, *five-square*

32 [I]Hebr. *openings of flowers*

33 [I]Or, *four-square*

34 [a]Ezek. 41:23-25

37 [a]1Kgs. 6:1

38 [I]Or, *with all the appurtenances thereof, and with all the ordinances thereof*

25 And the other cherub *was* ten cubits: both the cherubims *were* of one measure and one size.

26 The height of the one cherub *was* ten cubits, and so *was it* of the other cherub.

27 And he set the cherubims within the inner house: and [I][a]they stretched forth the wings of the cherubims, so that the wing of the one touched the *one* wall, and the wing of the other cherub touched the other wall; and their wings touched one another in the midst of the house.

28 And he overlaid the cherubims with gold.

29 And he carved all the walls of the house round about with carved figures of cherubims and palm trees and [I]open flowers, within and without.

30 And the floor of the house he overlaid with gold, within and without.

31 And for the entering of the oracle he made doors *of* olive tree: the lintel352 *and* side posts *were* [I]a fifth part *of the wall.*

32 The two doors also *were of* olive tree; and he carved upon them carvings of cherubims and palm trees and [I]open flowers, and overlaid *them* with gold, and spread gold upon the cherubims, and upon the palm trees.

33 So also made he for the door of the temple posts *of* olive tree, [I]a fourth part *of the wall.*

34 And the two doors *were of* fir tree: the [a]two leaves of the one door *were* folding, and the two leaves of the other door *were* folding.

35 And he carved *thereon* cherubims and palm trees and open flowers: and covered *them* with gold fitted[3474] upon the carved work.

36 And he built the inner court with three rows of hewed[1496] stone, and a row of cedar beams.

37 [a]In the fourth year was the foundation of the house of the LORD laid,[3245] in the month Zif:

38 And in the eleventh year, in the month Bul, which *is* the eighth month, was the house finished [I]throughout all

the parts thereof, and according to all the fashion[4941] of it. So was he [a]seven years in building it.

Solomon Completes Other Building Projects

7 But Solomon was building his own house [a]thirteen years, and he finished[3615] all his house.

2 He built also the house of the forest of Lebanon; the length thereof *was* an hundred cubits, and the breadth thereof fifty cubits, and the height thereof thirty cubits, upon four rows of cedar pillars, with cedar beams upon the pillars.

3 And *it was* covered with cedar above upon the [I]beams, that *lay* on forty five pillars, fifteen *in* a row.

4 And *there were* windows *in* three rows, and [I]light *was* against light *in* three ranks.

5 And all the [I]doors and posts *were* square, with the windows: and light *was* against light *in* three ranks.

6 And he made a porch of pillars; the length thereof *was* fifty cubits, and the breadth thereof thirty cubits: and the porch *was* [I]before them: and the *other* pillars and the thick beam *were* [II]before them.

7 Then he made a porch for the throne where he might judge,[8199] *even* the porch of judgment:[4941] and *it was* covered with cedar [I]from one side of the floor to the other.

8 And his house where he dwelt *had* another court within the porch, *which* was of the like work. Solomon made also an house for Pharaoh's daughter, [a]whom he had taken *to wife,* like unto this porch.

9 All these *were of* costly stones, according to the measures of hewed stones,[1496] sawed with saws, within and without, even from the foundation unto the coping,[2947] and *so* on the outside toward the great court.

10 And the foundation[3245] *was of* costly stones, even great stones, stones of ten cubits, and stones of eight cubits.

11 And above *were* costly stones, after the measures of hewed stones, and cedars.

12 And the great court round about *was* with three rows of hewed stones, and a row of cedar beams, both for the inner court of the house of the LORD, [a]and for the porch of the house.

13 And king Solomon sent and fetched [a]Hiram out of Tyre.

14 [a]He *was* [I]a widow's son of the tribe of Naphtali, and [b]his father[1] *was* a man of Tyre, a worker in brass: and [c]he was filled with wisdom, and understanding, and cunning[1847] to work all works in brass. And he came to king Solomon, and wrought all his work.

The Two Large Pillars

15 For he [I]cast [a]two pillars of brass, of eighteen cubits high apiece: and a line of twelve cubits did compass either of them about.

16 And he made two chapiters[3805] *of* molten brass, to set upon the tops of the pillars: the height of the one chapiter *was* five cubits, and the height of the other chapiter *was* five cubits:

17 *And* nets of checker work, and wreaths of chain work, for the chapiters which *were* upon the top of the pillars; seven for the one chapiter, and seven for the other chapiter.

18 And he made the pillars, and two rows round about upon the one network, to cover[3680] the chapiters that *were* upon the top, with pomegranates: and so did[6213] he for the other chapiter.

19 And the chapiters that *were* upon the top of the pillars *were* of lily work in the porch, four cubits.

20 And the chapiters upon the two pillars *had pomegranates* also above, over against the belly[990] which *was* by the

38 [a]1Kgs. 6:1
1 [a]1Kgs. 9:10; 2Chr. 8:1
3 [I]Hebr. *ribs*
4 [I]Hebr. *sight against sight*
5 [I]Or, *spaces and pillars* were *square in prospect*
6 [I]Or, *according to them* [II]Or, *according to them*
7 [I]Hebr. *from floor to floor*
8 [a]1Kgs. 3:1; 2Chr. 8:11
12 [a]John 10:23; Acts 3:11
13 [a]2Chr. 4:11, *Huram;* 1Kgs. 7:40
14 [I]Hebr. *the son of a widow woman* [a]2Chr. 2:14 [b]2Chr. 4:16 [c]Ex. 31:3; 36:1
15 [I]Hebr. *fashioned* [a]2Kgs. 25:17; 2Chr. 3:15; 4:12; Jer. 52:21

7:13 This Hiram is not to be confused with King Hiram of Tyre (1 Kgs. 5:1).

network: and the pomegranates *were* [a]two hundred in rows round about upon the other chapiter.

21 [a]And he set up the pillars in [b]the porch of the temple: and he set up the right pillar, and called[7121] the name thereof [I]Jachin: and he set up the left pillar, and called the name thereof [II]Boaz.

22 And upon the top of the pillars *was* lily work: so was the work of the pillars finished.[8552]

Furnishings for the Temple

23 And he made [a]a molten sea, ten cubits [I]from the one brim[8193] to the other: *it was* round all about, and his height *was* five cubits: and a line of thirty cubits did compass it round about.

24 And under the brim of it round about *there were* knops compassing[5362] it, ten in a cubit, [a]compassing the sea round about: the knops *were* cast in two rows, when it was cast.

25 It stood upon [a]twelve oxen, three looking toward the north, and three looking toward the west, and three looking toward the south, and three looking toward the east: and the sea *was set* above upon them, and all their hinder parts *were* inward.[1004]

26 And it *was* an hand breadth thick, and the brim thereof was wrought like the brim of a cup, with flowers of lilies: it contained [a]two thousand baths.

27 And he made ten bases of brass; four cubits *was* the length of one base, and four cubits the breadth thereof, and three cubits the height of it.

28 And the work of the bases *was* on this *manner:* they had borders, and the borders *were* between the ledges:

29 And on the borders that *were* between the ledges *were* lions, oxen, and cherubims:[3742] and upon the ledges *there was* a base above: and beneath the lions and oxen *were* certain additions made of thin work.

30 And every base had four brasen wheels, and plates of brass: and the four corners thereof had undersetters:[3802] under the laver[3595] *were* undersetters molten, at the side of every addition.

31 And the mouth of it within the chapiter[3805] and above *was* a cubit: but the mouth thereof *was* round *after* the work of the base, a cubit and an half: and also upon the mouth of it *were* gravings[4734] with their borders, foursquare, not round.

32 And under the borders *were* four wheels; and the axletrees of the wheels *were* [I]*joined* to the base: and the height of a wheel *was* a cubit and half a cubit.

33 And the work of the wheels *was* like the work of a chariot wheel: their axletrees, and their naves,[1354] and their felloes,[2839] and their spokes,[2840] *were* all molten.

34 And *there were* four undersetters to the four corners of one base: *and* the undersetters *were* of the very base itself.

35 And in the top of the base *was there* a round compass[5439] of half a cubit high: and on the top of the base the ledges thereof and the borders thereof *were* of the same.

36 For on the plates of the ledges thereof, and on the borders thereof, he graved[6605] cherubims, lions, and palm trees, according to the [I]proportion of every one, and additions round about.

37 After this *manner* he made the ten bases: all of them had one casting, one measure, *and* one size.

38 Then [a]made he ten lavers[3595] of brass: one laver contained forty baths: *and* every laver was four cubits: *and* upon every one of the ten bases one laver.

39 And he put five bases on the right [I]side of the house, and five on the left side of the house: and he set the sea on the right side of the house eastward over against the south.

40 And [I]Hiram made the lavers, and the shovels, and the basons.[4219] So Hiram made an end[3615] of doing[6213] all the work that he made king Solomon for the house of the LORD:

---

20 [a]2Chr. 3:16; 4:13; Jer. 52:23

21 [I]*He shall establish* [II]*In it is strength* [a]2Chr. 3:17 [b]1Kgs. 6:3

23 [I]Hebr. *from his brim to his brim* [a]2Kgs. 25:13; 2Chr. 4:2; Jer. 52:17

24 [a]2Chr. 4:3

25 [a]2Chr. 4:4, 5; Jer. 52:20

26 [a]2Chr. 4:5

32 [I]Hebr. *in the base*

36 [I]Hebr. *nakedness*

38 [a]2Chr. 4:6

39 [I]Hebr. *shoulder*

40 [I]Hebr. *Hirom* 1Kgs. 7:13

41 The two pillars, and the *two* bowls[1543] of the chapiters that *were* on the top of the two pillars; and the two [a]networks, to cover the two bowls of the chapiters which *were* upon the top of the pillars;

42 And four hundred pomegranates for the two networks, *even* two rows of pomegranates for one network, to cover the two bowls of the chapiters that *were* [I]upon the pillars;

43 And the ten bases,[4350] and ten lavers on the bases;

44 And one sea, and twelve oxen under the sea;

45 [a]And the pots, and the shovels, and the basons: and all these vessels, which Hiram made to king Solomon for the house of the LORD, *were of* [I]bright brass.

46 [a]In the plain of Jordan did the king cast them, [I]in the clay ground[127] between [b]Succoth and [c]Zarthan.

47 And Solomon left all the vessels *unweighed,* [I]because they were exceeding many: neither was the weight of the brass [IIa]found out.

48 And Solomon made all the vessels that *pertained* unto the house of the LORD: [a]the altar[4196] of gold, and [b]the table of gold, whereupon [c]the shew bread *was,*

49 And the candlesticks of pure gold, five on the right *side,* and five on the left, before the oracle, with the flowers, and the lamps, and the tongs *of* gold,

50 And the bowls, and the snuffers, and the basons, and the spoons, and the censers *of* pure gold; and the hinges *of* gold, *both* for the doors of the inner house, the most holy *place, and* for the doors of the house, *to wit,* of the temple.

51 So was ended[7999] all the work that king Solomon made for the house of the LORD. And Solomon brought in the [I]things [a]which David his father had dedicated;[6944] *even* the silver, and the gold, and the vessels, did he put among the treasures of the house of the LORD.

Solomon Brings the Ark of God Into the Temple

8 Then [a]Solomon assembled[6950] the elders[2205] of Israel, and all the heads of the tribes, the [I]chief[5387] of the fathers[1] of the children[1121] of Israel, unto king Solomon in Jerusalem, [b]that they might bring up the ark[727] of the covenant[1285] of the LORD [c]out of the city of David, which *is* Zion.

2 And all the men of Israel assembled themselves unto king Solomon at the [a]feast[2282] in the month Ethanim, which *is* the seventh month.

3 And all the elders of Israel came, [a]and the priests took up the ark.

4 And they brought up[5927] the ark of the LORD, [a]and the tabernacle of the congregation,[4150] and all the holy vessels that *were* in the tabernacle, even those did the priests and the Levites bring up.

5 And king Solomon, and all the congregation[5712] of Israel, that were assembled[3259] unto him, *were* with him before the ark, [a]sacrificing sheep and oxen, that could not be told nor numbered for multitude.

6 And the priests [a]brought in the ark of the covenant of the LORD unto [b]his place, into the oracle of the house, to the most holy *place, even* [c]under the wings of the cherubims.[3742]

7 For the cherubims spread forth *their* two wings over the place of the ark, and the cherubims covered the ark and the staves thereof above.

8 And they [a]drew out the staves, that the [I]ends of the staves were seen out in the [IIb]holy *place* before the oracle, and they were not seen without:[2351] and there they are unto this day.[3117]

9 [a]*There was* nothing in the ark [b]save the two tables of stone, which Moses [c]put there at Horeb, [Id]when the LORD made *a covenant* with the children of Israel, when they came out of the land of Egypt.

10 And it came to pass, when the priests were come out of the holy *place,* that the cloud[6051] [a]filled the house of the LORD,

41 [a]1Kgs. 7:17, 18

42 [I]Hebr. *upon the face of the pillars*

45 [I]Hebr. *made bright,* or, *scoured* [a]Ex. 27:3; 2Chr. 4:16

46 [I]Hebr. *in the thickness of the ground* [a]2Chr. 4:17 [b]Gen. 33:17 [c]Josh. 3:16

47 [I]Hebr. *for the exceeding multitude* [II]Hebr. *searched* [a]1Chr. 22:14

48 [a]Ex. 37:25-28 [b]Ex. 37:10-16 [c]Ex. 25:30; Lev. 24:5-8

51 [I]Hebr. *holy things of David* [a]2Sam. 8:11; 2Chr. 5:1

1 [I]Hebr. *princes* [a]2Chr. 5:2-5 [b]2Sam. 6:17 [c]2Sam. 5:7, 9; 6:12, 16

2 [a]Lev. 23:34; 2Chr. 7:8

3 [a]Num. 4:15; Deut. 31:9; Josh. 3:3, 6; 1Chr. 15:14, 15

4 [a]1Kgs. 3:4; 2Chr. 1:3

5 [a]2Sam. 6:13

6 [a]2Sam. 6:17 [b]Ex. 26:33, 34; 1Kgs. 6:19; [c]1Kgs. 6:27

8 [I]Hebr. *heads* [II]Or, *ark* [a]Ex. 25:14 [b]2Chr. 5:9

9 [I]Or, *where* [a]Ex. 25:21; Deut. 10:2 [b]Deut. 10:5; Heb. 9:4 [c]Ex. 40:20 [d]Ex. 34:27, 28; Deut. 4:13; 1Kgs. 8:21

10 [a]Ex. 40:34, 35; 2Chr. 5:13-14; 7:2

11 So that the priests could not stand
to minister because of the cloud: for the
glory of the LORD had filled the house of
the LORD.

Solomon Addresses the People

12 [a]Then spake Solomon, The LORD
said that he would dwell[7931] [b]in the thick
darkness.[6205]
13 [a]I have surely built thee an house
to dwell in, [b]a settled place for thee to
abide in for ever.
14 And the king turned his face
about, and [a]blessed[1288] all the congregation[6951] of Israel: (and all the congregation of Israel stood;)
15 And he said, [a]Blessed *be* the LORD
God[430] of Israel, which [b]spake with his
mouth unto David my father,[1] and hath
with his hand fulfilled *it,* saying,
16 [a]Since the day that I brought forth
my people Israel out of Egypt, I chose[977]
no city out of all the tribes of Israel to
build an house, that [b]my name might be
therein; but I chose [c]David to be over my
people Israel.
17 And [a]it was in the heart of David
my father to build an house for the name
of the LORD God of Israel.
18 [a]And the LORD said unto David
my father, Whereas it was in thine heart
to build an house unto my name, thou
didst well that it was in thine heart.
19 Nevertheless [a]thou shalt not build
the house; but thy son that shall come
forth out of thy loins, he shall build the
house unto my name.
20 And the LORD hath performed[6965]
his word that he spake, and I am risen
up[6965] in the room of David my father,
and sit on the throne of Israel, [a]as
the LORD promised, and have built an
house for the name of the LORD God of
Israel.
21 And I have set there a place for
the ark, wherein *is* [a]the covenant of the
LORD, which he made with our fathers,
when he brought them out of the land of
Egypt.

Solomon's Temple Prayer

22 And Solomon stood before [a]the
altar[4196] of the LORD in the presence of
all the congregation of Israel, and
[b]spread forth his hands toward heaven:
23 And he said, LORD God of Israel,
[a]*there is* no God like thee, in heaven
above, or on earth[776] beneath, [b]who
keepest covenant and mercy with thy servants that [c]walk before thee with all their
heart:
24 Who hast kept with thy servant
David my father that thou promisedst
him: thou spakest also with thy mouth,
and hast fulfilled *it* with thine hand, as
it is this day.
25 Therefore now, LORD God of
Israel, keep with thy servant David my
father that thou promisedst him, saying,
[I][a]There shall not fail thee a man in my
sight to sit on the throne of Israel; [II]so
that thy children take heed[8104] to their
way, that they walk before me as thou
hast walked before me.
26 [a]And now, O God of Israel, let thy
word, I pray thee, be verified,[539] which
thou spakest unto thy servant David my
father.
🔑 27 But [a]will God indeed[552] dwell
on the earth? behold, the heaven and
[b]heaven of heavens cannot contain thee;
how much less this house that I have
builded?
28 Yet have thou respect[6437] unto the
prayer of thy servant, and to his supplication, O LORD my God, to hearken unto
the cry and to the prayer, which thy servant prayeth before thee to day:
29 That thine eyes may be open
toward this house night and day, *even* to-

12 [a]2Chr. 6:1-6 [b]Lev. 16:2; Ps. 18:11; 97:2
13 [a]2Sam. 7:13 [b]Ps. 132:14
14 [a]2Sam. 6:18
15 [a]Luke 1:68 [b]2Sam. 7:5, 25
16 [a]2Sam. 7:6; 2Chr. 6:5-7 [b]Deut. 12:11; 1Kgs. 8:29 [c]1Sam. 16:1; 2Sam. 7:8; 1Chr. 28:4
17 [a]2Sam. 7:2; 1Chr. 17:1
18 [a]2Chr. 6:8, 9
19 [a]2Sam. 7:5, 12, 13; 1Kgs. 5:3, 5
20 [a]1Chr. 28:5, 6
21 [a]Deut. 31:26; 1Kgs. 8:9
22 [a]2Chr. 6:12-21 [b]Ex. 9:33; Ezra 9:5; Isa. 1:15
23 [a]Ex. 15:11; 2Sam. 7:22 [b]Deut. 7:9; Neh. 1:5; Dan. 9:4 [c]Gen. 17:1; 1Kgs. 3:6; 2Kgs. 20:3
25 [I]Hebr. *There shall not be cut off unto thee a man from my sight* [II]Hebr. *only if* [a]2Sam. 7:12, 16; 1Kgs. 2:4
26 [a]2Sam. 7:25
27 [a]2Chr. 2:6; Isa. 66:1; Jer. 23:24; Acts 7:49; 17:24 [b]2Cor. 12:2

🔑 **8:27** This is a key verse concerning God's transcendence. God is a Spirit (John 4:24). Therefore, he cannot be limited to time-space dimensions. Christians are themselves God's temples, and the Spirit of God dwells in them (1 Cor. 3:16, 17; 6:19, 20).

ward the place of which thou hast said, [a]My name shall be there: that thou mayest hearken unto the prayer[8605] which thy servant shall make [I][b]toward this place.

30 [a]And hearken thou to the supplication[8467] of thy servant, and of thy people Israel, when they shall pray [I]toward this place: and hear thou in heaven thy dwelling place: and when thou hearest, forgive.[5545]

31 If any man trespass against his neighbour, [I][a]and an oath be laid upon him to cause him to swear, and the oath come before thine altar in this house:

32 Then hear thou in heaven, and do,[6213] and judge[8199] thy servants, [a]condemning[7561] the wicked, to bring his way upon his head; and justifying[6663] the righteous, to give him according to his righteousness.

33 [a]When thy people Israel be smitten down before the enemy, because they have sinned against thee, and [b]shall turn again to thee, and confess[3034] thy name, and pray, and make supplication unto thee [I]in this house:

34 Then hear thou in heaven, and forgive the sin of thy people Israel, and bring them again unto the land which thou gavest unto their fathers.

35 [a]When heaven is shut up, and there is no rain, because they have sinned against thee; if they pray toward this place, and confess thy name, and turn from their sin, when thou afflictest them:

36 Then hear thou in heaven, and forgive the sin of thy servants, and of thy people Israel, that thou [a]teach them [b]the good[2896] way wherein they should walk, and give rain upon thy land, which thou hast given to thy people for an inheritance.[5159]

37 [a]If there be in the land famine, if there be pestilence, blasting, mildew, locust, *or* if there be caterpiller; if their enemy besiege them in the land of their [I]cities; whatsoever plague, whatsoever sickness *there be;*

38 What prayer and supplication soever be *made* by any man, *or* by all thy people Israel, which shall know every man the plague of his own heart, and spread forth his hands[3709] toward this house:

39 Then hear thou in heaven thy dwelling place, and forgive, and do, and give to every man according to his ways, whose heart thou knowest; (for thou, *even* thou only, [a]knowest the hearts of all the children of men;)

40 [a]That they may fear[3372] thee all the days[3117] that they live in the land which thou gavest unto our fathers.

41 Moreover concerning a stranger, that *is* not of thy people Israel, but cometh out of a far country[776] for thy name's sake;

42 (For they shall hear of thy great name, and of thy [a]strong hand, and of thy stretched out arm;) when he shall come and pray toward this house;

43 Hear thou in heaven thy dwelling place, and do[6213] according to all that the stranger calleth[7121] to thee for: [a]that all people of the earth may know thy name, to [b]fear thee, as *do* thy people Israel; and that they may know that [I]this house, which I have builded, is called by thy name.

44 If thy people go out to battle against their enemy, whithersoever thou shalt send them, and shall pray unto the LORD [I]toward the city which thou hast chosen,[977] and *toward* the house that I have built for thy name:

45 Then hear thou in heaven their prayer and their supplication, and maintain their [I]cause.[4941]

46 If they sin against thee, ([a]for *there is* no man that sinneth not,) and thou be angry[599] with them, and deliver them to the enemy, so that they carry them away captives[7617] [b]unto the land of the enemy, far or near;

47 [a]*Yet* if they shall [I]bethink[7725] themselves in the land whither they were carried captives, and repent, and make supplication unto thee in the land of them that carried them captives, [b]saying, We have sinned, and have done perversely, we have committed wickedness;

48 And *so* [a]return[7725] unto thee with

29 [I]Or, *in this place* [a]Deut. 12:11 [b]Dan. 6:10

30 [I]Or, *in this place* [a]2Chr. 20:9; Neh. 1:6

31 [I]Hebr. *and he require an oath of him* [a]Ex. 22:11; Lev. 5:1

32 [a]Deut. 25:1

33 [I]Or, *towards* [a]Lev. 26:17; Deut. 28:25 [b]Lev. 26:39, 40; Neh. 1:9

35 [a]Lev. 26:19; Deut. 28:23

36 [a]Ps. 25:4; 27:11; 94:12; 143:8 [b]1Sam. 12:23

37 [I]Or, *jurisdiction* [a]Lev. 26:16, 25, 26; Deut. 28:21, 22, 27, 38, 42, 52; 2Chr. 20:9

39 [a]1Sam. 16:7; 1Chr. 28:9; Ps. 11:4; Jer. 17:10; Acts 1:24

40 [a]Ps. 130:4

42 [a]Deut. 3:24

43 [I]Hebr. *thy name is called upon this house* [a]1Sam. 17:46; 2Kgs. 19:19; Ps. 67:2 [b]Ps. 102:15

44 [I]Hebr. the way of the city

45 [I]Or, *right*

46 [a]2Chr. 6:36; Prov. 20:9; Eccl. 7:20; James 3:2; 1John 1:8, 10 [b]Lev. 26:34, 44; Deut. 28:36, 64

47 [I]Hebr. *bring back to their heart* [a]Lev. 26:40 [b]Neh. 1:6; Ps. 106:6; Dan. 9:5

48 [a]Jer. 29:12-14

all their heart, and with all their soul, in
the land of their enemies, which led them
away captive,[7617] and [b]pray unto thee toward their land, which thou gavest unto
their fathers, the city which thou hast
chosen, and the house which I have built
for thy name:
49 Then hear thou their prayer and
their supplication in heaven thy dwelling
place, and maintain their [I]cause,[4941]
50 And forgive thy people that have
sinned against thee, and all their transgressions wherein they have transgressed
against thee, and [a]give them compassion[7356] before them who carried them
captive, that they may have compassion
on them:
51 For [a]they *be* thy people, and thine
inheritance, which thou broughtest forth
out of Egypt, [b]from the midst of the furnace of iron:
52 That thine eyes may be open unto
the supplication of thy servant, and unto
the supplication of thy people Israel, to
hearken unto them in all that they call[7121]
for unto thee.
53 For thou didst separate[914] them
from among all the people of the earth,
to be thine inheritance, [a]as thou spakest
by the hand of Moses thy servant, when
thou broughtest our fathers out of Egypt,
O Lord GOD.

Solomon Admonishes the People

54 And it was *so,* that when Solomon
had made an end[3615] of praying all this
prayer and supplication unto the LORD, he
arose from before the altar of the LORD,
from kneeling on his knees with his
hands spread up to heaven.
55 And he stood, [a]and blessed all the
congregation of Israel with a loud voice,
saying,
56 Blessed *be* the LORD, that hath
given rest unto his people Israel, according to all that he promised: [a]there hath
not [I]failed[5307] one word of all his good
promise, which he promised by the hand
of Moses his servant.
57 The LORD our God be with us, as
he was with our fathers: [a]let him not
leave us, nor forsake[5203] us:
58 That he may [a]incline our hearts
unto him, to walk in all his ways, and to
keep his commandments,[4687] and his
statutes,[2706] and his judgments,[4941] which
he commanded[6680] our fathers.
59 And let these my words, wherewith I have made supplication before the
LORD, be nigh unto the LORD our God
day[3119] and night, that he maintain the
cause of his servant, and the cause of his
people Israel [I]at all times, as the matter
shall require:
60 [a]That all the people of the earth
may know that [b]the LORD *is* God, *and
that there is* none else.
61 Let your [a]heart therefore be
perfect[8003] with the LORD our God, to
walk in his statutes, and to keep his commandments, as at this day.

Sacrifice and Celebration

62 And [a]the king, and all Israel with
him, offered sacrifice before the LORD.
63 And Solomon offered a sacrifice
of peace offerings, which he offered unto
the LORD, two and twenty thousand oxen,
and an hundred and twenty thousand
sheep. So the king and all the children
of Israel dedicated[2596] the house of the
LORD.
64 [a]The same day did the king
hallow[6942] the middle of the court that
was before the house of the LORD: for
there he offered burnt offerings, and meat
offerings,[4503] and the fat of the peace offerings: because [b]the brasen altar that
was before the LORD *was* too little to receive the burnt offerings, and meat offerings, and the fat of the peace offerings.
65 And at that time Solomon held [a]a
feast, and all Israel with him, a great
congregation, from [b]the entering in of
Hamath unto [c]the river of Egypt, before
the LORD our God, [d]seven days and seven
days, *even* fourteen days.
66 [a]On the eighth day he sent the
people away: and they [I]blessed the king,
and went unto their tents joyful and

48 [b]Dan. 6:10
49 [I]Or, *right*
50 [a]Ezra 7:6; Ps. 106:46
51 [a]Deut. 9:29; Neh. 1:10 [b]Deut. 4:20; Jer. 11:4
53 [a]Ex. 19:5; Deut. 9:26, 29; 14:2
55 [a]2Sam. 6:18
56 [I]Hebr. *fallen* [a]Deut. 12:10; Josh. 21:45; 23:14
57 [a]Deut. 31:6; Josh. 1:5
58 [a]Ps. 119:36
59 [I]Hebr. *the thing of a day in his day*
60 [a]Josh. 4:24; 1Sam. 17:46; 2Kgs. 19:19 [b]Deut. 4:35, 39
61 [a]1Kgs. 11:4; 15:3, 14; 2Kgs. 20:3
62 [a]2Chr. 7:4, 5
64 [a]2Chr. 7:7 [b]2Chr. 4:1
65 [a]Lev. 23:34; 1Kgs. 8:2 [b]Num. 34:8; Josh. 13:5; Judg. 3:3; 2Kgs. 14:25 [c]Gen. 15:18; Num. 34:5 [d]2Chr. 7:8
66 [I]Or, *thanked* [a]2Chr. 7:9, 10

glad[2896] of heart for all the goodness that the LORD had done[6213] for David his servant, and for Israel his people.

God Appears to Solomon

9 And [a]it came to pass, when Solomon had finished[3615] the building of the house of the LORD, [b]and the king's house, and [c]all Solomon's desire[2837] which he was pleased to do,[6213]

2 That the LORD appeared[7200] to Solomon the second time, [a]as he had appeared unto him at Gibeon.

3 And the LORD said unto him, [a]I have heard thy prayer and thy supplication, that thou hast made before me: I have hallowed this house, which thou hast built, [b]to put my name there for ever; [c]and mine eyes and mine heart shall be there perpetually.[3117][3605]

4 And if thou wilt [a]walk before me, [b]as David thy father[1] walked, in integrity[8537] of heart, and in uprightness, to do according to all that I have commanded[6680] thee, *and* wilt keep my statutes and my judgments:[4941]

5 Then I will establish the throne of thy kingdom upon Israel for ever, [a]as I promised to David thy father, saying, There shall not fail thee a man upon the throne of Israel.

6 [a]*But* if ye shall at all turn from following me, ye or your children,[1121] and will not keep my commandments[4687] *and* my statutes which I have set before you, but go and serve other gods,[430] and worship them:

7 [a]Then will I cut off[3772] Israel out of the land which I have given them; and this house, which I have hallowed [b]for my name, will I cast out of my sight; [c]and Israel shall be a proverb and a byword[8148] among all people:

8 And [a]at this house, *which* is high, every one that passeth by it shall be astonished,[8074] and shall hiss; and they shall say, [b]Why hath the LORD done thus unto this land, and to this house?

9 And they shall answer,[559] Because they forsook[5800] the LORD their God,[430] who brought forth their fathers[1] out of the land of Egypt, and have taken hold upon other gods, and have worshipped them, and served them: therefore hath the LORD brought upon them all this evil.[7451]

Solomon's Other Projects

10 And [a]it came to pass at the end of twenty years, when Solomon had built the two houses, the house of the LORD, and the king's house,

11 ([a]*Now* Hiram the king of Tyre had furnished[5375] Solomon with cedar trees and fir trees, and with gold, according to all his desire,[2656]) that then king Solomon gave Hiram twenty cities in the land of Galilee.

12 And Hiram came out from Tyre to see the cities which Solomon had given him; and they [I]pleased him not.

13 And he said, What cities *are* these which thou hast given me, my brother?[251] [a]And he called[7121] them the land of [I]Cabul unto this day.[3117]

14 And Hiram sent to the king sixscore talents of gold.

15 And this *is* the reason of [a]the levy which king Solomon raised; for to build the house of the LORD, and his own house, and [b]Millo, and the wall of Jerusalem, and [c]Hazor, and [d]Megiddo, and [e]Gezer.

16 *For* Pharaoh king of Egypt had gone up, and taken Gezer, and burnt[8313] it with fire, [a]and slain the Canaanites that dwelt in the city, and given it *for* a present unto his daughter, Solomon's wife.

17 And Solomon built Gezer, and [a]Beth–horon the nether,[8481]

18 And [a]Baalath, and Tadmor in the wilderness, in the land,

19 And all the cities of store[4543] that Solomon had, and cities for [a]his chariots, and cities for his horsemen, and [I]that which Solomon [b]desired[2836] to build in Jerusalem, and in Lebanon, and in all the land of his dominion.[4475]

20 [a]*And* all the people *that were* left of the Amorites, Hittites, Perizzites, Hivites, and Jebusites, which *were* not of the children of Israel,

1 [a]2Chr. 7:11 [b]1Kgs. 7:1 [c]2Chr. 8:6

2 [a]1Kgs. 3:5

3 [a]2Kgs. 20:5; Ps. 10:17 [b]1Kgs. 8:29 [c]Deut. 11:12

4 [a]Gen. 17:1 [b]1Kgs. 11:4, 6, 38; 14:8; 15:5

5 [a]2Sam. 7:12, 16; 1Kgs. 2:4; 6:12; 1Chr. 22:10; Ps. 132:12

6 [a]2Sam. 7:14; 2Chr. 7:19, 20; Ps. 89:30-32

7 [a]Deut. 4:26; 2Kgs. 17:23; 25:21 [b]Jer. 7:14 [c]Deut. 28:37; Ps. 44:14

8 [a]2Chr. 7:21 [b]Deut. 29:24-26; Jer. 22:8, 9

10 [a]1Kgs. 6:37, 38; 7:1; 2Chr. 8:1

11 [a]2Chr. 8:2

12 [I]Hebr. *were not right in his eyes*

13 [I]*Displeasing, or, Dirty* [a]Josh. 19:27

15 [a]1Kgs. 5:13 [b]2Sam. 5:9; 1Kgs. 9:24 [c]Josh. 19:36 [d]Josh. 17:11 [e]Josh. 16:10; Judg. 1:29

16 [a]Josh. 16:10

17 [a]Josh. 16:3; 21:22; 2Chr. 8:5

18 [a]Josh. 19:44; 2Chr. 8:4-6

19 [I]Hebr. *the desire of Solomon which he desired* [a]1Kgs. 4:26 [b]1Kgs. 9:1

20 [a]2Chr. 8:7-9

21 Their children [a]that were left after them in the land, [b]whom the children of Israel also were not able utterly to destroy,[2763] [c]upon those did Solomon levy a tribute of [d]bondservice[5647] unto this day.

22 But of the children of Israel did Solomon [a]make no bondmen:[5650] but they *were* men of war, and his servants, and his princes, and his captains,[7991] and rulers of his chariots, and his horsemen.

23 These *were* the chief of the officers that *were* over Solomon's work, [a]five hundred and fifty, which bare rule over the people that wrought in the work.

24 But [a]Pharaoh's daughter came up out of the city of David unto [b]her house which *Solomon* had built for her: [c]then did he build Millo.

25 [a]And three times in a year did Solomon offer burnt offerings[5930] and peace offerings upon the altar[4196] which he built unto the LORD, and he burnt incense[6999] [I]upon the altar that *was* before the LORD. So he finished[7999] the house.

26 And [a]king Solomon made a navy of ships in [b]Ezion-geber, which *is* beside Eloth, on the [I]shore of the Red sea, in the land of Edom.

27 [a]And Hiram sent in the navy his servants, shipmen that had knowledge of the sea, with the servants of Solomon.

28 And they came to [a]Ophir, and fetched from thence gold, four hundred and twenty talents, and brought *it* to king Solomon.

The Queen of Sheba Visits Solomon

10 🗝 And when the [a]queen of Sheba heard of the fame[8088] of Solomon concerning the name of the LORD, she came [b]to prove[5254] him with hard questions.

21 [a]Judg. 1:21, 27, 29; 3:1 [b]Josh. 15:63; 17:12 [c]Judg. 1:28 [d]Gen. 9:25, 26; Ezra 2:55, 58; Neh. 7:57; 11:3

22 [a]Lev. 25:39

23 [a]2Chr. 8:10

24 [a]1Kgs. 3:1; 2Chr. 8:11 [b]1Kgs. 7:8 [c]2Sam. 5:9; 11:27; 2Chr. 32:5

25 [I]Hebr. *upon it* [a]2Chr. 8:12, 13, 16

26 [I]Hebr. *lip* [a]2Chr. 8:17, 18 [b]Num. 33:35; Deut. 2:8; 22:48

27 [a]1Kgs. 10:11-22

28 [a]Job 22:24

1 [a]2Chr. 9:1-9; Matt. 12:42; Luke 11:31; [b]Judg. 14:12; Prov. 1:6

3 [I]Hebr. *words*

5 [I]Hebr. *standing* [II]Or, *butlers* [a]1Chr. 26:16

6 [I]Hebr. *word* [II]Or, *sayings*

7 [I]Hebr. *thou hast added wisdom and goodness to the fame*

8 [a]Prov. 8:34

9 [a]1Kgs. 5:7 [b]2Sam. 8:15; Ps. 72:2; Prov. 8:15

10 [a]Ps. 72:10, 15

11 [a]1Kgs. 9:27

2 And she came to Jerusalem with a very great train,[2428] with camels that bare[5375] spices, and very much gold, and precious stones: and when she was come to Solomon, she communed with him of all that was in her heart.

3 And Solomon told her all her [I]questions: there was not *any* thing hid from the king, which he told her not.

4 And when the queen of Sheba had seen all Solomon's wisdom, and the house that he had built,

5 And the meat of his table, and the sitting of his servants, and the [I]attendance of his ministers,[8334] and their apparel, and his [II]cupbearers, [a]and his ascent[5930] by which he went up unto the house of the LORD; there was no more spirit in her.

6 And she said to the king, It was a true [I]report that I heard in mine own land of thy [II]acts[1697] and of thy wisdom.

7 Howbeit I believed[539] not the words, until I came, and mine eyes had seen *it:* and, behold, the half was not told me: [I]thy wisdom and prosperity[2896] exceedeth the fame which I heard.

8 [a]Happy *are* thy men, happy *are* these thy servants, which stand continually[8548] before thee, *and* that hear thy wisdom.

9 [a]Blessed[1288] be the LORD thy God,[430] which delighted[2654] in thee, to set thee on the throne of Israel: because the LORD loved Israel for ever, therefore made he thee king, [b]to do[6213] judgment[4941] and justice.[6666]

10 And she [a]gave the king an hundred and twenty talents of gold, and of spices very great store, and precious stones: there came no more such abun dance of spices as these which the queen of Sheba gave to king Solomon.

11 [a]And the navy also of Hiram, that brought[5375] gold from Ophir, brought in

🗝 **10:1, 2** Sheba is a reference to Saba, the land of the Sabeans in southwestern Arabia. The Sabeans controlled the trade route by which precious spices, metals, and other commodities were transported from southern Arabia and beyond Palestine.

from Ophir great plenty of [I][b]almug[484] trees, and precious stones.

12 [a]And the king made of the almug trees [I]pillars for the house of the LORD, and for the king's house, harps also and psalteries for singers: there came no such [b]almug trees, nor were seen unto this day.[3117]

13 And king Solomon gave unto the queen of Sheba all her desire,[2656] whatsoever she asked,[7592] beside *that* which Solomon gave her [I]of his royal bounty.[3027] So she turned and went to her own country,[776] she and her servants.

Solomon's Wealth and Fame

14 Now the weight of gold that came to Solomon in one year was six hundred threescore and six talents of gold,

15 Beside *that he had* of the merchantmen, and of the traffick[4536] of the spice merchants, and [a]of all the kings of Arabia, and of the [I]governors[6346] of the country.

16 And king Solomon made two hundred targets *of* beaten[7820] gold: six hundred *shekels* of gold went to one target.

17 And *he made* [a]three hundred shields *of* beaten gold; three pound of gold went to one shield: and the king put them in the [b]house of the forest of Lebanon.

18 [a]Moreover the king made a great throne of ivory, and overlaid it with the best gold.

19 The throne had six steps, and the top of the throne *was* round [I]behind: and *there were* [II]stays[3027] on either side on the place of the seat, and two lions stood beside the stays.

20 And twelve lions stood there on the one side and on the other upon the six steps: there was not [I]the like made in any kingdom.

21 [a]And all king Solomon's drinking vessels *were of* gold, and all the vessels of the house of the forest of Lebanon *were of* pure gold; [I]none *were of* silver: it was nothing accounted of[2803] in the days[3117] of Solomon.

22 For the king had at sea a navy of [a]Tharshish with the navy of Hiram: once in three years came the navy of Tharshish, bringing[5375] gold, and silver, [I]ivory, and apes, and peacocks.

23 So [a]king Solomon exceeded all the kings of the earth[776] for riches and for wisdom.

24 And all the earth [I]sought to Solomon, to hear his wisdom,[2451] which God had put in his heart.

25 And they brought every man his present, vessels of silver, and vessels of gold, and garments, and armour,[5402] and spices, horses, and mules, a rate year by year.

26 [a]And Solomon [b]gathered together chariots and horsemen: and he had a thousand and four hundred chariots, and twelve thousand horsemen, whom he bestowed in the cities for chariots, and with the king at Jerusalem.

27 [a]And the king [I]made silver *to be* in Jerusalem as stones, and cedars made he *to be* as the sycomore trees that *are* in the vale,[8219] for abundance.

28 [I][a]And Solomon had horses brought out of Egypt, and linen yarn: the king's merchants received the [b]linen yarn at a price.

29 And a chariot came up and went out of Egypt for six hundred *shekels* of silver, and an horse for an hundred and fifty: [a]and so for all the kings of the Hittites, and for the kings of Syria, did they bring *them* out [I]by their means.

11 [I]*algum trees* [b]2Chr. 2:8; 9:10, 11

12 [I]Hebr. *a prop* [a]2Chr. 9:11 [b]2Chr. 9:10

13 [I]Hebr. *according to the hand of king Solomon*

15 [I]Or, *captains* [a]2Chr. 9:24; Ps. 72:10

17 [a]1Kgs. 14:26 [b]1Kgs. 7:2

18 [a]2Chr. 9:17-19

19 [I]Hebr. *on the hinder part thereof* [II]Hebr. *hands*

20 [I]Hebr. *so*

21 [I]Or, there was *no silver* in them [a]2Chr. 9:20-22

22 [I]Or, *elephants' teeth* [a]Gen. 10:4; 2Chr. 20:36

23 [a]1Kgs. 3:12, 13; 4:30

24 [I]Hebr. *sought the face of*

26 [a]1Kgs. 4:26; 2Chr. 1:14; 9:25 [b]Deut. 17:16

27 [I]Hebr. *gave* [a]2Chr. 1:15-17

28 [I]Hebr. *And the going forth of the horses* which were *Solomon's* [a]Deut. 17:16; 2Chr. 1:16; 9:28 [b]Ezek. 27:7

29 [I]Hebr. *by their hand* [a]Josh. 1:4; 2Kgs. 7:6

10:22 Recent studies suggest that this "navy of Tarshish" was a specialized "refinery fleet" primarily responsible for transporting refined metal from Solomon's mining operations. The "three years" journeys were the exceptions, when the ships went (probably) south along the African coast gathering the exotic cargoes mentioned, and trading the iron and copper of Solomon's mines.

Solomon Turns From God

11 But [a]king Solomon loved [b]many strange[5237] women, [I]together with the daughter of Pharaoh, women of the Moabites, Ammonites, Edomites, Zidonians, *and* Hittites;

2 Of the nations *concerning* which the LORD said unto the children[1121] of Israel, [a]Ye shall not go in to them, neither shall they come in unto you: *for* surely they will turn away your heart after their gods:[430] Solomon clave unto these in love.

3 And he had seven hundred wives, princesses, and three hundred concubines: and his wives turned away his heart.

4 For it came to pass, when Solomon was old, [a]*that* his wives turned away his heart after other gods: and his [b]heart was not perfect with the LORD his God,[430] [c]as *was* the heart of David his father.[1]

5 For Solomon went after [a]Ashtoreth the goddess[430] of the Zidonians, and after [I]Milcom the abomination[8251] of the Ammonites.

6 And Solomon did[6213] evil[7451] in the sight of the LORD, and [I][a]went not fully after the LORD, as *did* David his father.

7 [a]Then did Solomon build an high place for [b]Chemosh, the abomination of Moab, in [c]the hill that *is* before Jerusalem, and for Molech, the abomination of the children of Ammon.

8 And likewise did he for all his strange wives, which burnt incense[6999] and sacrificed unto their gods.

The Consequences of Solomon's Sins

9 And the LORD was angry[599] with Solomon, because [a]his heart was turned from the LORD God of Israel, [b]which had appeared[7200] unto him twice,

10 And [a]had commanded[6680] him concerning this thing, that he should not go after other gods: but he kept not that which the LORD commanded.

11 Wherefore the LORD said unto Solomon, Forasmuch as this [I]is done of thee, and thou hast not kept my covenant[1285] and my statutes, which I have commanded thee, [a]I will surely rend[7167] the kingdom from thee, and will give it to thy servant.

12 Notwithstanding in thy days[3117] I will not do[6213] it for David thy father's[1] sake: *but* I will rend it out of the hand of thy son.

13 [a]Howbeit I will not rend away all the kingdom; *but* will give [b]one tribe to thy son for David my servant's sake, and for Jerusalem's sake [c]which I have chosen.[977]

14 And the LORD [a]stirred up an adversary[7854] unto Solomon, Hadad the Edomite: he *was* of the king's seed in Edom.

15 [a]For it came to pass, when David was in Edom, and Joab the captain[8269] of the host was gone up to bury[6912] the slain, [b]after he had smitten every male in Edom;

16 (For six months did Joab remain there with all Israel, until he had cut off[3772] every male in Edom:)

17 That Hadad fled, he and certain[582] Edomites of his father's servants with him, to go into Egypt; Hadad *being* yet a little child.

18 And they arose out of Midian, and came to Paran: and they took men with them out of Paran, and they came to Egypt, unto Pharaoh king of Egypt; which gave him an house, and appointed[559] him victuals,[3899] and gave him land.

19 And Hadad found great favour[2580] in the sight of Pharaoh, so that he gave him to wife the sister of his own wife, the sister of Tahpenes the queen.

20 And the sister of Tahpenes bare him Genubath his son, whom Tahpenes weaned in Pharaoh's house: and Genubath was in Pharaoh's household among the sons of Pharaoh.

21 [a]And when Hadad heard in Egypt that David slept with his fathers,[1] and that Joab the captain of the host was dead,[4191] Hadad said to Pharaoh, [I]Let me depart, that I may go to mine own country.[776]

1 [I]Or, *besides* [a]Neh. 13:26 [b]Deut. 17:17

2 [a]Ex. 34:16; Deut. 7:3, 4

4 [a]Deut. 17:17; Neh. 13:26 [b]1Kgs. 8:61 [c]1Kgs. 9:4

5 [I]*Molech* [a]1Kgs. 11:33; Judg. 2:13; 2Kgs. 23:13

6 [I]Hebr. *fulfilled not after* [a]Num. 14:24

7 [a]Num. 33:52 [b]Num. 21:29; Judg. 11:24 [c]2Kgs. 23:13

9 [a]1Kgs. 11:2, 3 [b]1Kgs. 3:5; 9:2

10 [a]1Kgs. 6:12; 9:6

11 [I]Hebr. *is with thee* [a]1Kgs. 11:31; 12:15, 16

13 [a]2Sam. 7:15; Ps. 89:33 [b]1Kgs. 12:20 [c]Deut. 12:11

14 [a]1Chr. 5:26

15 [a]2Sam. 8:14; 1Chr. 18:12, 13 [b]Num. 24:19; Deut. 20:13

21 [I]Hebr. *Send me away* [a]1Kgs. 2:10, 34

22 Then Pharaoh said unto him, But what hast thou lacked with me, that, behold, thou seekest to go to thine own country? And he answered,[559] [I]Nothing: howbeit let me go in any wise.

23 And God stirred him up *another* adversary, Rezon the son of Eliadah, which fled from his lord [a]Hadadezer king of Zobah:

24 And he gathered[6908] men unto him, and became captain over a band,[1416] [a]when David slew them *of Zobah:* and they went to Damascus, and dwelt therein, and reigned in Damascus.

25 And he was an adversary to Israel all the days of Solomon, beside the mischief that Hadad *did:* and he abhorred[6973] Israel, and reigned over Syria.

Jeroboam Is Chosen to Rule Ten Tribes

26 And [a]Jeroboam the son of Nebat, an Ephrathite of Zereda, Solomon's servant, whose mother's name *was* Zeruah, a widow woman, even he [b]lifted up *his* hand against the king.

27 And this *was* the cause[1697] that he lifted up *his* hand against the king: [a]Solomon built Millo, *and* [I]repaired the breaches of the city of David his father.

28 And the man Jeroboam *was* a mighty man of valour: and Solomon seeing the young man that he [I]was industrious,[6213,4399] he made him ruler over all the [II]charge of the house of Joseph.

29 And it came to pass at that time when Jeroboam went out of Jerusalem, that the prophet [a]Ahijah the Shilonite found him in the way; and he had clad[3680] himself with a new garment; and they two *were* alone in the field:[7704]

30 And Ahijah caught the new garment that *was* on him, and [a]rent it *in* twelve pieces:

31 And he said to Jeroboam, Take thee ten pieces: for [a]thus saith the LORD, the God of Israel, Behold, I will rend[7167] the kingdom out of the hand of Solomon, and will give ten tribes to thee:

32 (But he shall have one tribe for my servant David's sake, and for Jerusalem's sake, the city which I have chosen out of all the tribes of Israel:)

33 [a]Because that they have forsaken[5800] me, and have worshipped Ashtoreth the goddess of the Zidonians, Chemosh the god of the Moabites, and Milcom the god of the children of Ammon, and have not walked in my ways, to do *that which is* right in mine eyes, and *to keep* my statutes and my judgments,[4941] as *did* David his father.

34 Howbeit I will not take the whole kingdom out of his hand: but I will make[7896] him prince all the days of his life for David my servant's sake, whom I chose,[977] because he kept my commandments[4687] and my statutes:[2708]

35 But [a]I will take the kingdom out of his son's hand, and will give it unto thee, *even* ten tribes.

36 And unto his son will I give one tribe, that [a]David my servant may have a [I]light alway before me in Jerusalem, the city which I have chosen me to put my name there.

37 And I will take thee, and thou shalt reign according to all that thy soul desireth, and shalt be king over Israel.

38 And it shall be, if thou wilt hearken unto all that I command[6680] thee, and wilt walk in my ways, and do *that is* right in my sight, to keep my statutes and my commandments, as David my servant did; that [a]I will be with thee, and

22 [I]Hebr. *Not*
23 [a]2Sam. 8:3
24 [a]2Sam. 8:3; 10:8, 18
26 [a]1Kgs. 12:2; 2Chr. 13:6 [b]2Sam. 20:21
27 [I]Hebr. *closed* [a]1Kgs. 9:24
28 [I]Hebr. *did work* [II]Hebr. *burden*
29 [a]1Kgs. 14:2
30 [a]1Sam. 15:27; 24:5
31 [a]1Kgs. 11:11, 13
33 [a]1Kgs. 11:5-7
35 [a]1Kgs. 12:16, 17
36 [I]Hebr. *lamp, or, candle* [a]1Kgs. 15:4; 2Kgs. 8:19; Ps. 132:17
38 [a]Josh. 1:5

11:31–35 Only eleven of the twelve pieces of the cloak are accounted for in this passage. What tribe was left out? The most reasonable response is that the tribe of Benjamin did not really have an independent existence at this time. Benjamin was still one of the twelve tribes, but one that did not figure into this prophecy concerning the division of the kingdom. The tribe of Benjamin was so small that it had all but disappeared into the tribe of Judah. In 1 Kings 12:21, the tribe of Benjamin is listed as the ally of the tribe of Judah when the latter is preparing to attack the Northern Kingdom.

[b]build thee a sure[539] house, as I built for David, and will give Israel unto thee.

39 And I will for this afflict the seed of David, but not for ever.

40 Solomon sought therefore to kill Jeroboam. And Jeroboam arose, and fled into Egypt, unto Shishak king of Egypt, and was in Egypt until the death[4194] of Solomon.

Solomon's Death

41 And [a]the rest of the [I]acts[1697] of Solomon, and all that he did, and his wisdom, *are* they not written in the book[5612] of the acts of Solomon?

42 [a]And the [I]time that Solomon reigned in Jerusalem over all Israel *was* forty years.

43 [a]And Solomon slept with his fathers, and was buried[6912] in the city of David his father: and [b]Rehoboam his son reigned in his stead.

The Northern Tribes Revolt

12 And [a]Rehoboam went to Shechem: for all Israel were come to Shechem to make him king.

2 And it came to pass, when [a]Jeroboam the son of Nebat, who was yet in [b]Egypt, heard *of it,* (for he was fled from the presence of king Solomon, and Jeroboam dwelt in Egypt;)

3 That they sent and called him. And Jeroboam and all the congregation[6951] of Israel came, and spake unto Rehoboam, saying,

4 Thy father made our [a]yoke grievous:[7186] now therefore make thou the grievous service of thy father, and his heavy yoke which he put upon us, lighter, and we will serve thee.

5 And he said unto them, Depart yet *for* three days, then come again to me. And the people departed.

6 And king Rehoboam consulted[3298] with the old men, that stood before Solomon his father while he yet lived, and said, How do ye advise that I may answer[7725,1697] this people?

7 And they spake unto him, saying, [a]If thou wilt be a servant unto this people this day,[3117] and wilt serve them, and answer them, and speak good[2896] words to them, then they will be thy servants for ever.

8 But he forsook[5800] the counsel[6098] of the old men, which they had given him, and consulted with the young men that were grown up with him, *and* which stood before him:

9 And he said unto them, What counsel[3289] give ye that we may answer this people, who have spoken to me, saying, Make the yoke which thy father did put upon us lighter?

10 And the young men that were grown up with him spake unto him, saying, Thus shalt thou speak unto this people that spake unto thee, saying, Thy father made our yoke heavy, but make thou *it* lighter unto us; thus shalt thou say unto them, My little *finger* shall be thicker than my father's[1] loins.

11 And now whereas my father did lade you with a heavy yoke, I will add to your yoke: my father hath chastised[3256] you with whips, but I will chastise you with scorpions.

12 So Jeroboam and all the people came to Rehoboam the third day, as the king had appointed,[1696] saying, Come to me again the third day.

13 And the king answered the people [I]roughly,[7186] and forsook the old men's counsel that they gave him;

14 And spake to them after the counsel of the young men, saying, My father made your yoke heavy, and I will add to your yoke: my father *also* chastised you with whips, but I will chastise you with scorpions.

15 Wherefore the king hearkened not unto the people; for [a]the cause[5438] was from the LORD, that he might perform his saying, which the LORD [b]spake by Ahijah the Shilonite unto Jeroboam the son of Nebat.

16 So when all Israel saw that the king hearkened not unto them, the people answered the king, saying, [a]What portion have we in David? neither *have we* inheritance[5159] in the son of Jesse: to

38 [b]2Sam. 7:11, 27
41 [I]Or, *words,* or, *things* [a]2Chr. 9:29
42 [I]Hebr. *days* [a]2Chr. 9:30
43 [a]2Chr. 9:31 [b]Matt. 1:7, called *Roboam*
1 [a]2Chr. 10:1-11
2 [a]1Kgs. 11:26 [b]1Kgs. 11:40
4 [a]1Sam. 8:11-18; 1Kgs. 4:7
7 [a]2Chr. 10:7; Prov. 15:1
13 [I]Hebr. *hardly*
15 [a]1Kgs. 12:24; Judg. 14:4; 2Chr. 10:15; 22:7; 25:20 [b]1Kgs. 11:11, 31
16 [a]2Sam. 20:1

your tents, O Israel: now see to thine own
house, David. So Israel departed unto
their tents.
17 But [a]*as for* the children[1121] of
Israel which dwelt in the cities of Judah,
Rehoboam reigned over them.
18 Then king Rehoboam [a]sent
Adoram, who *was* over the tribute; and
all Israel stoned him with stones, that he
died.[4191] Therefore king Rehoboam [I]made
speed to get him up to his chariot, to flee
to Jerusalem.
19 So [a]Israel [I]rebelled against the
house of David unto this day.
20 And it came to pass, when all
Israel heard that Jeroboam was come
again, that they sent and called him unto
the congregation,[5712] and made him king
over all Israel: there was none that followed the house of David, but the tribe
of Judah [a]only.

Civil War Is Averted

21 And when [a]Rehoboam was come
to Jerusalem, he assembled[6950] all the
house of Judah, with the tribe of
Benjamin, an hundred and fourscore
thousand chosen men, which were warriors, to fight against the house of Israel,
to bring the kingdom again to Rehoboam
the son of Solomon.
22 But [a]the word of God[430] came
unto Shemaiah the man of God, saying,
23 Speak unto Rehoboam, the son of
Solomon, king of Judah, and unto all the
house of Judah and Benjamin, and to the
remnant[3499] of the people, saying,
24 Thus saith the LORD, Ye shall not
go up, nor fight against your brethren[251]
the children of Israel: return every man
to his house; [a]for this thing is from me.
They hearkened therefore to the word of
the LORD, and returned to depart, according to the word of the LORD.

Jeroboam's Apostasy

25 Then Jeroboam [a]built Shechem in
mount Ephraim, and dwelt therein; and
went out from thence, and built [b]Penuel.
26 And Jeroboam said in his heart,
Now shall the kingdom return to the
house of David:
27 If this people [a]go up to do[6213] sacrifice in the house of the LORD at
Jerusalem, then shall the heart of this
people turn again unto their lord, *even*
unto Rehoboam king of Judah, and they
shall kill me, and go again to Rehoboam
king of Judah.
🗝 28 Whereupon the king took counsel,
and [a]made two calves *of* gold, and said
unto them, It is too much for you to go
up to Jerusalem: [b]behold thy gods,[430] O
Israel, which brought thee up[5927] out of
the land of Egypt.
29 And he set the one in [a]Bethel, and
the other put he in [b]Dan.
30 And this thing became [a]a sin:[2403]
for the people went *to worship* before the
one, *even* unto Dan.
31 And he made an [a]house of high
places,[1116] [b]and made priests of the lowest of the people, which were not of the
sons of Levi.
32 And Jeroboam ordained a feast[2282]
in the eighth month, on the fifteenth
day of the month, like unto [a]the feast
that *is* in Judah, and he [I]offered upon
the altar.[4196] So did[6213] he in Bethel,
[II]sacrificing unto the calves that he
had made: [b]and he placed in Bethel the
priests of the high places which he had
made.
33 So he [I]offered[5927] upon the altar
which he had made in Bethel the fifteenth
day of the eighth month, *even* in the
month which he had [a]devised of his own
heart; and ordained a feast unto the children of Israel: and he offered upon the
altar, [II]and [b]burnt incense.[6999]

17 [a]1Kgs. 11:13, 36
18 [I]Hebr. *strengthened himself* [a]1Kgs. 4:6; 5:14
19 [I]Or, *fell away* [a]2Kgs. 17:21
20 [a]1Kgs. 11:13, 32
21 [a]2Chr. 11:1
22 [a]2Chr. 11:2
24 [a]1Kgs. 12:15
25 [a]Judg. 9:45 [b]Judg. 8:17
27 [a]Deut. 12:5, 6
28 [a]2Kgs. 10:29; 17:16 [b]Ex. 32:4, 8
29 [a]Gen. 28:19; Hos. 4:15 [b]Judg. 18:29
30 [a]1Kgs. 13:34; 2Kgs. 17:21
31 [a]1Kgs. 13:32 [b]Num. 3:10; 1Kgs. 13:33; 2Kgs. 17:32; 2Chr. 11:14, 15; Ezek. 44:7, 8
32 [I]Or, *went up to the altar* [II]Or, *to sacrifice* [a]Lev. 23:33, 34; Num. 29:12; 1Kgs. 8:2, 5 [b]Amos 7:13
33 [I]Or, *went up to the altar* [II]Hebr. *to burn incense* [a]Num. 15:39 [b]1Kgs. 13:1

🗝 **12:28** "Behold thy gods, O Israel, which brought thee up out of Egypt" was the very phrase used by Aaron when he made the golden calf near Mount Sinai (Ex. 32:4). Jeroboam offered the people idolatry as an alternative to worshiping Jehovah.

A Judean Prophet Warns Jeroboam

13 And, behold, there [a]came a man of God[430] out of Judah by the word of the LORD unto Bethel: [b]and Jeroboam stood by the altar[4196] [1]to burn incense.

2 And he cried[7121] against the altar in the word of the LORD, and said, O altar, altar, thus saith the LORD; Behold, a child[1121] shall be born unto the house of David, [a]Josiah by name; and upon thee shall he offer the priests of the high places that burn incense upon thee, and men's bones[6106] shall be burnt[8313] upon thee.

3 And he gave [a]a sign[4159] the same day, saying, This *is* the sign which the LORD hath spoken; Behold, the altar shall be rent, and the ashes that *are* upon it shall be poured out.

4 And it came to pass, when king Jeroboam heard the saying of the man of God, which had cried against the altar in Bethel, that he put forth his hand from the altar, saying, Lay hold on[8610] him. And his hand, which he put forth against him, dried up,[3001] so that he could not pull it in again to him.

5 The altar also was rent, and the ashes poured out from the altar, according to the sign which the man of God had given by the word of the LORD.

6 And the king answered and said unto the man of God, [a]Intreat[2470] now the face of the LORD thy God, and pray for me, that my hand may be restored me again. And the man of God besought [1]the LORD, and the king's hand was restored him again, and became as *it was* before.[7223]

7 And the king said unto the man of God, Come home with me, and refresh[5582] thyself, and [a]I will give thee a reward.

8 And the man of God said unto the king, [a]If thou wilt give me half thine house, I will not go in with thee, neither will I eat bread nor drink water in this place:

9 For so was it charged[6680] me by the word of the LORD, saying, [a]Eat no bread, nor drink water, nor turn again by the same way that thou camest.

10 So he went another way, and returned not by the way that he came to Bethel.

The Prophet Disobeys and Dies

11 Now there dwelt an old prophet in Bethel; and his [1]sons came and told him all the works that the man of God had done[6213] that day in Bethel: the words which he had spoken unto the king, them they told also to their father.[1]

12 And their father said unto them, What way went he? For his sons had seen what way the man of God went, which came from Judah.

13 And he said unto his sons, Saddle me the ass. So they saddled him the ass: and he rode thereon,

14 And went after the man of God, and found him sitting under an oak: and he said unto him, *Art* thou the man of God that camest[935] from Judah? And he said, I *am*.

15 Then he said unto him, Come[3212] home with me, and eat bread.

16 And he said, [a]I may not return with thee, nor go in with thee: neither will I eat bread nor drink water with thee in this place:

17 For [1]it was said to me [a]by the word of the LORD, Thou shalt eat no bread nor drink water there, nor turn again to go by the way that thou camest.

18 He said unto him, I *am* a prophet also as thou *art;* and an angel[4397] spake unto me by the word of the LORD, saying, Bring him back with thee into thine house, that he may eat bread and drink water. *But* he lied unto him.

19 So he went back with him, and did eat bread in his house, and drank water.

20 And it came to pass, as they sat at the table, that the word of the LORD came unto the prophet that brought him back:

21 And he cried unto the man of God that came from Judah, saying, Thus saith the LORD, Forasmuch as thou hast

1 [1]Or, *to offer* [a]2Kgs. 23:17 [b]1Kgs. 12:32, 33
2 [a]2Kgs. 23:15, 16
3 [a]Isa. 7:14; John 2:18; 1Cor. 1:22
6 [1]Hebr. *the face of the LORD* [a]Ex. 8:8; 9:28; 10:17; Num. 21:7; Acts 8:24; James 5:16
7 [a]1Sam. 9:7; 2Kgs. 5:15
8 [a]Num. 22:18; 24:13
9 [a]1Cor. 5:11
11 [1]Hebr. *son*
16 [a]1Kgs. 13:8, 9
17 [1]Hebr. *a word was* [a]1Kgs. 20:35; 1Thess. 4:15

disobeyed[4784] the mouth of the LORD, and
hast not kept the commandment[4687]
which the LORD thy God commanded[6680]
thee,
22 But camest back, and hast eaten
bread and drunk water in the [a]place, of
the which *the LORD* did say to thee, Eat
no bread, and drink no water; thy
carcase[5038] shall not come unto the
sepulchre[6913] of thy fathers.[1]
23 And it came to pass, after he had
eaten bread, and after he had drunk, that
he saddled for him the ass, *to wit,* for the
prophet whom he had brought back.
24 And when he was gone, [a]a lion
met him by the way, and slew him: and
his carcase was cast in the way, and the
ass stood by it, the lion also stood by the
carcase.
25 And, behold, men passed by, and
saw the carcase cast in the way, and the
lion standing by the carcase: and they
came and told *it* in the city where the old
prophet dwelt.
26 And when the prophet that
brought him back from the way heard
thereof, he said, It *is* the man of God,
who was disobedient[4784] unto the word
of the LORD: therefore the LORD hath delivered him unto the lion, which hath
[I]torn him, and slain him, according to the
word of the LORD, which he spake unto
him.
27 And he spake to his sons, saying,
Saddle me the ass. And they saddled
him.
28 And he went and found his carcase cast in the way, and the ass and the
lion standing by the carcase: the lion had
not eaten the carcase, nor [I]torn[7665] the
ass.
29 And the prophet took up the carcase of the man of God, and laid it upon
the ass, and brought it back: and the old
prophet came to the city, to mourn and
to bury[6912] him.
30 And he laid his carcase in his own
grave;[6913] and they mourned over him,
saying, [a]Alas, my brother[251]
31 And it came to pass, after he had
buried him, that he spake to his sons,
saying, When I am dead,[4191] then bury
me in the sepulchre wherein the man of
God *is* buried; [a]lay my bones beside his
bones:
32 [a]For the saying which he cried[7121]
by the word of the LORD against the altar
in Bethel, and against all the houses of
the high places which *are* in the cities of
[b]Samaria, shall surely come to pass.
33 [a]After this thing Jeroboam returned not from his evil[7451] way, but
[I]made again of the lowest of the people
priests of the high places: whosoever
would, he [II]consecrated him, and he became *one* of the priests of the high
places.
34 [a]And this thing became sin unto
the house of Jeroboam, even [b]to cut *it* off,
and to destroy[8045] *it* from off the face of
the earth.[127]

Ahijah Prophesies Against Jeroboam

14 At that time Abijah the son of
Jeroboam fell sick.
2 And Jeroboam said to his wife,
Arise, I pray thee, and disguise thyself,
that thou be not known to be the wife of
Jeroboam; and get thee to Shiloh: behold,
there *is* Ahijah the prophet, which told
me that [a]*I should be* king over this people.
3 [a]And take [I]with thee ten loaves,
and [II]cracknels,[5350] and a [III]cruse[1228] of
honey, and go to him: he shall tell thee
what shall become[1961] of the child.
4 And Jeroboam's wife did[6213] so,
and arose, [a]and went to Shiloh, and came
to the house of Ahijah. But Ahijah could
not see; for his eyes [I]were set[6965] by reason of his age.
5 And the LORD said unto Ahijah,
Behold, the wife of Jeroboam cometh to
ask a thing of thee for her son; for he *is*
sick: thus and thus shalt thou say unto
her: for it shall be, when she cometh in,
that she shall feign herself *to be* another
woman.
6 And it was *so,* when Ahijah heard
the sound of her feet, as she came in at
the door, that he said, Come in, thou wife
of Jeroboam; why feignest thou thyself *to*

22 [a]1Kgs. 13:9
24 [a]1Kgs. 20:36
26 [I]Hebr. *broken*
28 [I]Hebr. *broken*
30 [a]Jer. 22:18
31 [a]2Kgs. 23:17, 18
32 [a]1Kgs. 13:2; 2Kgs. 23:16, 19 [b]1Kgs. 16:24
33 [I]Hebr. *returned and made* [II]Hebr. *filled his hand* Judg. 17:12 [a]1Kgs. 12:31, 32; 2Chr. 11:15; 13:9
34 [a]1Kgs. 12:30 [b]1Kgs. 14:10
2 [a]1Kgs. 11:31
3 [I]Hebr. *in thine hand* [II]Or, *cakes* [III]Or, *bottle* [a]1Sam. 9:7, 8
4 [I]Hebr. *stood for his hoariness* [a]1Kgs. 11:29

be another? for *I am* sent to thee *with* [I]heavy *tidings.*

7 Go, tell Jeroboam, Thus saith the LORD God[430] of Israel, [a]Forasmuch as I exalted thee from among the people, and made thee prince over my people Israel.

8 And [a]rent the kingdom away from the house of David, and gave it thee: and *yet* thou hast not been as my servant David, [b]who kept my commandments,[4687] and who followed me with all his heart, to do[6213] *that* only *which was* right in mine eyes;

9 But hast done evil[7489] above all that were before thee: [a]for thou hast gone and made thee other gods,[430] and molten images, to provoke me to anger,[3707] and [b]hast cast me behind thy back:

10 Therefore, behold, [a]I will bring evil[7451] upon the house of Jeroboam, and [b]will cut off[3772] from Jeroboam him that pisseth against the wall, [c]*and* him that is shut up and left[5800] in Israel, and will take away the remnant of the house of Jeroboam, as a man taketh away dung, till it be all gone.

11 [a]Him that dieth[4191] of Jeroboam in the city shall the dogs eat; and him that dieth in the field[7704] shall the fowls of the air[8064] eat: for the LORD hath spoken *it.*

12 Arise thou therefore, get thee to thine own house: *and* [a]when thy feet enter into the city, the child shall die.

13 And all Israel shall mourn for him, and bury[6912] him: for he only of Jeroboam shall come to the grave,[6913] because in him [a]there is found *some* good[2896] thing toward the LORD God of Israel in the house of Jeroboam.

14 [a]Moreover the LORD shall raise him up a king over Israel, who shall cut off the house of Jeroboam that day:[3117] but what? even now.

15 For the LORD shall smite Israel, as a reed is shaken in the water, and he shall [a]root up Israel out of this [b]good land, which he gave to their fathers,[1] and shall scatter them [c]beyond the river, [d]because they have made their groves,[842] provoking the LORD to anger.

16 And he shall give Israel up because of the sins of Jeroboam, [a]who did sin, and who made Israel to sin.

17 And Jeroboam's wife arose, and departed, and came to [a]Tirzah: *and* [b]when she came to the threshold of the door, the child died;[4191]

18 And they buried[6912] him; and all Israel mourned for him, [a]according to the word of the LORD, which he spake by the hand of his servant Ahijah the prophet.

Jeroboam's Death

19 And the rest of the acts[1697] of Jeroboam, how he [a]warred, and how he reigned, behold, they *are* written in the book[5612] of the chronicles of the kings of Israel.

20 And the days[3117] which Jeroboam reigned *were* two and twenty years: and he [I]slept with his fathers, and Nadab his son reigned in his stead.

Rehoboam Rules Judah

21 And Rehoboam the son of Solomon reigned in Judah. [a]Rehoboam *was* forty and one years old when he began to reign, and he reigned seventeen years in Jerusalem, the city [b]which the LORD did choose[977] out of all the tribes of Israel, to put his name there. [c]And his mother's name *was* Naamah an Ammonitess.

22 [a]And Judah did evil in the sight of the LORD, and they [b]provoked him to jealousy with their sins which they had committed,[2398] above all that their fathers had done.

23 For they also built them [a]high places, and [I]images,[4676] [b]and groves, on every high hill, and [c]under every green tree.

24 [a]And there were also sodomites[6945] in the land: *and* they did according to all the abominations[8441] of the nations which the LORD cast out[3423] before the children[1121] of Israel.

25 [a]And it came to pass in the fifth year of king Rehoboam, *that* Shishak

---

6 [I]Hebr. *hard*
7 [a]2Sam. 12:7, 8; 1Kgs. 16:2
8 [a]1Kgs. 11:31 [b]1Kgs. 11:33, 38; 15:5
9 [a]1Kgs. 12:28; 2Chr. 11:15 [b]Neh. 9:26; Ps. 50:17; Ezek. 23:35
10 [a]1Kgs. 15:29 [b]1Kgs. 21:21; 2Kgs. 9:8 [c]Deut. 32:36; 2Kgs. 14:26
11 [a]1Kgs. 16:4; 21:24
12 [a]1Kgs. 14:17
13 [a]2Chr. 12:12; 19:3
14 [a]1Kgs. 15:27-29
15 [a]2Kgs. 17:6; Ps. 52:5 [b]Josh. 23:15, 16 [c]2Kgs. 15:29 [d]Ex. 34:13; Deut. 12:3, 4
16 [a]1Kgs. 12:30; 13:34; 15:30, 34; 16:2
17 [a]1Kgs. 16:6, 8, 15, 23; Song 6:4 [b]1Kgs. 14:12
18 [a]1Kgs. 14:13
19 [a]2Chr. 13:2, 3
20 [I]Hebr. *lay down*
21 [a]2Chr. 12:13 [b]1Kgs. 11:36 [c]1Kgs. 14:31
22 [a]2Chr. 12:1 [b]Deut. 32:21; Ps. 78:58; 1Cor. 10:22
23 [I]Or, *standing images,* or, *statues* [a]Deut. 12:2; Ezek. 16:24, 25 [b]2Kgs. 17:9, 10 [c]Isa. 57:5
24 [a]Deut. 23:17; 1Kgs. 15:12; 22:46; 2Kgs. 23:7
25 [a]1Kgs. 11:40; 2Chr. 12:2

king of Egypt came up against Jerusalem:

26 [a]And he took away the treasures of the house of the LORD, and the treasures of the king's house; he even took away all: and he took away all the shields of gold [b]which Solomon had made.

27 And king Rehoboam made in their stead brasen shields, and committed[6485] *them* unto the hands of the chief of the [I]guard, which kept the door of the king's house.

28 And it was *so,* when the king went into the house of the LORD, that the guard bare[5375] them, and brought them back into the guard chamber.

29 [a]Now the rest of the acts of Rehoboam, and all that he did, *are* they not written in the book of the chronicles of the kings of Judah?

30 And there was [a]war between Rehoboam and Jeroboam all *their* days.

31 [a]And Rehoboam slept with his fathers, and was buried with his fathers in the city of David. [b]And his mother's name *was* Naamah an Ammonitess. And [c]Abijam his son reigned in his stead.

Abijam Rules Judah

15 Now [a]in the eighteenth year of king Jeroboam the son of Nebat reigned Abijam over Judah.

2 Three years reigned he in Jerusalem. [a]And his mother's name *was* [b]Maachah, the daughter of [c]Abishalom.

3 And he walked in all the sins of his father, which he had done before him: and [a]his heart was not perfect with the LORD his God,[430] as the heart of David his father.

4 Nevertheless [a]for David's sake did the LORD his God give him a [I]lamp[5216] in Jerusalem, to set up his son after him, and to establish Jerusalem.

5 Because David [a]did *that which was* right in the eyes of the LORD, and turned not aside from any *thing* that he commanded[6680] him all the days[3117] of his life, [b]save only in the matter of Uriah the Hittite.

6 [a]And there was war between Rehoboam and Jeroboam all the days of his life.

7 [a]Now the rest of the acts[1697] of Abijam, and all that he did, *are* they not written in the book[5612] of the chronicles of the kings of Judah? And there was war between Abijam and Jeroboam.

8 [a]And Abijam slept with his fathers;[1] and they buried[6912] him in the city of David: and Asa his son reigned in his stead.

Asa Rules Judah

9 And in the twentieth year of Jeroboam king of Israel reigned Asa over Judah.

10 And forty and one years reigned he in Jerusalem. And his [I][a]mother's name *was* Maachah, the daughter of Abishalom.

11 [a]And Asa did *that which was* right in the eyes of the LORD, as *did* David his father.

12 [a]And he took away the sodomites[6945] out of the land, and removed all the idols[1544] that his fathers had made.

13 And also [a]Maachah his mother, even her he removed from *being* queen, because she had made an idol[4656] in a grove;[842] and Asa [I]destroyed[3772] her idol, and [b]burnt[8313] *it* by the brook Kidron.

26 [a]2Chr. 12:9, 10, 11 [b]10:17
27 [I]Hebr. *runners*
29 [a]2Chr. 12:15
30 [a]1Kgs. 12:24; 15:6; 2Chr. 12:15
31 [a]2Chr. 12:16 [b]1Kgs. 14:21 [c]2Chr. 12:16, *Abijah*; Matt. 1:7, *Abia*
1 [a]2Chr. 13:1, 2
2 [a]2Chr. 11:20-22 [b]2Chr. 13:2, *Michaiah the daughter of Uriel* [c]2Chr. 11:21, *Absalom*
3 [a]1Kgs. 11:4; Ps. 119:80
4 [I]Or, *candle,* 1Kgs. 11:36 [a]1Kgs. 11:32, 36; 2Chr. 21:7
5 [a]1Kgs. 14:8 [b]2Sam. 11:4, 15; 12:9
6 [a]1Kgs. 14:30
7 [a]2Chr. 13:2, 3, 22
8 [a]2Chr. 14:1
10 [I]*grand-mother's* [a]1Kgs. 15:2
11 [a]2Chr. 14:2
12 [a]1Kgs. 14:24; 22:46
13 [I]Hebr. *cut off* [a]2Chr. 15:16 [b]Ex. 32:20

15:10 Maachah is called Asa's mother in verse ten though she was in fact his grandmother. This practice of skipping generations when recording a line of descendants was common among the Hebrews. It can also be seen in David's being called Asa's father, when he was really Asa's great-great-grandfather (v. 11). Rehoboam preferred Maachah over his other wives, and he intended that only children born to him by her would be in the line of succession to be king (2 Chr. 11:21, 22). As a result of being a direct descendant of Maachah, Asa could make a legitimate claim to the throne.

14 [a]But the high places were not removed: nevertheless Asa's [b]heart was
perfect[8003] with the LORD all his days.
15 And he brought in the [I]things
which his father had dedicated,[6944] and
the things which himself had dedicated,
into the house of the LORD, silver, and
gold, and vessels.
16 And there was war between Asa
and Baasha king of Israel all their days.
17 And [a]Baasha king of Israel went
up against Judah, and built [b]Ramah, [c]that
he might not suffer[5414] any to go out or
come in to Asa king of Judah.
18 Then Asa took all the silver and
the gold *that were* left in the treasures of
the house of the LORD, and the treasures
of the king's house, and delivered them
into the hand of his servants: and king
Asa sent them to [a]Ben–hadad, the son of
Tabrimon, the son of Hezion, king of
Syria, that dwelt at [b]Damascus, saying,
19 *There is* a league[1285] between me
and thee, *and* between my father and thy
father: behold, I have sent unto thee a
present of silver and gold; come and
break[6565] thy league with Baasha king of
Israel, that he may [I]depart from me.
20 So Ben–hadad hearkened unto
king Asa, and sent the captains[8269] of
the hosts which he had against the cities
of Israel, and smote [a]Ijon, and [b]Dan, and
[c]Abel–beth–maachah, and all Cinneroth,
with all the land of Naphtali.
21 And it came to pass, when
Baasha heard *thereof*, that he left off
building of Ramah, and dwelt in Tirzah.
22 [a]Then king Asa made a proclamation[8085] throughout all Judah; none
was [I]exempted:[5355] and they took away
the stones of Ramah, and the timber
thereof, wherewith Baasha had builded;
and king Asa built with them [b]Geba of
Benjamin, and [c]Mizpah.
23 The rest of all the acts of Asa,
and all his might, and all that he did, and
the cities which he built, *are* they not
written in the book of the chronicles of
the kings of Judah? Nevertheless [a]in the
time of his old age he was diseased[2470]
in his feet.
24 And Asa slept with his fathers,

14 [a]1Kgs. 22:43; 2Chr. 15:17, 18 [b]1Kgs. 15:3
15 [I]Hebr. *holy*
17 [a]2Chr. 16:1-6 [b]Josh. 18:25 [c]1Kgs. 12:27
18 [a]2Chr. 16:2 [b]1Kgs. 11:23, 24
19 [I]Hebr. *go up*
20 [a]2Kgs. 15:29 [b]Judg. 18:29 [c]2Sam. 20:14
22 [I]Hebr. *free* [a]2Chr. 16:6 [b]Josh. 21:17 [c]Josh. 18:26
23 [a]2Chr. 16:12
24 [a]2Chr. 17:1 [b]Matt. 1:8, called *Josaphat*
25 [I]Hebr. *reigned*
26 [a]1Kgs. 12:30; 14:16
27 [a]1Kgs. 14:14 [b]Josh. 19:44; 21:23; 1Kgs. 16:15
29 [a]1Kgs. 14:10, 14
30 [a]1Kgs. 14:9, 16
32 [a]1Kgs. 15:16
34 [a]1Kgs. 12:28, 29; 13:33; 14:16

and was buried with his fathers in the
city of David his father: [a]and [b]Jehosh-
aphat his son reigned in his stead.

Nadab Rules Israel

25 And Nadab the son of Jeroboam
[I]began to reign over Israel in the second
year of Asa king of Judah, and reigned
over Israel two years.
26 And he did evil[7451] in the sight of
the LORD, and walked in the way of his
father, and in [a]his sin wherewith he made
Israel to sin.
27 [a]And Baasha the son of Ahijah, of
the house of Issachar, conspired against
him; and Baasha smote him at [b]Gibbe-
thon, which *belonged* to the Philistines;
for Nadab and all Israel laid siege to
Gibbethon.
28 Even in the third year of Asa
king of Judah did Baasha slay him, and
reigned in his stead.
29 And it came to pass, when he
reigned, *that* he smote all the house of
Jeroboam; he left not to Jeroboam any
that breathed,[5397] until he had destroyed[8045] him, according unto [a]the saying of the LORD, which he spake by his
servant Ahijah the Shilonite:
30 [a]Because of the sins of Jeroboam
which he sinned, and which he made
Israel sin, by his provocation wherewith
he provoked the LORD God of Israel to
anger.[3707]
31 Now the rest of the acts of
Nadab, and all that he did, *are* they not
written in the book of the chronicles of
the kings of Israel?
32 [a]And there was war between Asa
and Baasha king of Israel all their days.

Baasha Rules Israel

33 In the third year of Asa king of
Judah began Baasha the son of Ahijah to
reign over all Israel in Tirzah, twenty and
four years.
34 And he did evil in the sight of
the LORD, and walked in [a]the way of
Jeroboam, and in his sin wherewith he
made Israel to sin.[2398]

16

Then the word of the LORD came to [a]Jehu the son of Hanani against Baasha, saying,

2 [a]Forasmuch as I exalted thee out of the dust,[6083] and made thee prince over my people Israel; and [b]thou hast walked in the way of Jeroboam, and hast made my people Israel to sin, to provoke me to anger[3707] with their sins;

3 Behold, I will [a]take away the posterity of Baasha, and the posterity of his house; and will make thy house like [b]the house of Jeroboam the son of Nebat.

4 [a]Him that dieth of Baasha in the city shall the dogs eat; and him that dieth of his in the fields[7704] shall the fowls of the air[8064] eat.

5 Now the rest of the acts[1697] of Baasha, and what he did, and his might, [a]*are* they not written in the book[5612] of the chronicles of the kings of Israel?

6 So Baasha slept with his fathers,[1] and was buried[6912] in [a]Tirzah: and Elah his son reigned in his stead.

7 And also by the hand of the prophet [a]Jehu the son of Hanani came the word of the LORD against Baasha, and against his house, even for all the evil[7451] that he did in the sight of the LORD, in provoking him to anger with the work of his hands, in being like the house of Jeroboam; and because [b]he killed him.

Elah Rules Israel

8 In the twenty and sixth year of Asa king of Judah began Elah the son of Baasha to reign over Israel in Tirzah, two years.

9 [a]And his servant Zimri, captain[8269] of half *his* chariots, conspired against him, as he was in Tirzah, drinking himself drunk in the house of Arza ǀsteward of *his* house in Tirzah.

10 And Zimri went in and smote him, and killed him, in the twenty and seventh year of Asa king of Judah, and reigned in his stead.

11 And it came to pass, when he began to reign, as soon as he sat on his throne, *that* he slew all the house of Baasha: he left him [a]not one that pisseth against a wall, ǀneither of his kinsfolks, nor of his friends.[7453]

12 Thus did Zimri destroy[8045] all the house of Baasha, [a]according to the word of the LORD, which he spake against Baasha ǀ[b]by Jehu the prophet,

13 For all the sins of Baasha, and the sins of Elah his son, by which they sinned, and by which they made Israel to sin, in provoking the LORD God[430] of Israel to anger [a]with their vanities.

14 Now the rest of the acts of Elah, and all that he did, *are* they not written in the book of the chronicles of the kings of Israel?

Zimri Rules Israel

15 In the twenty and seventh year of Asa king of Judah did Zimri reign seven days[3117] in Tirzah. And the people *were* encamped [a]against Gibbethon, which *belonged* to the Philistines.

16 And the people *that were* encamped heard say, Zimri hath conspired, and hath also slain the king: wherefore all Israel made Omri, the captain of the host, king over Israel that day in the camp.

17 And Omri went up from Gibbethon, and all Israel with him, and they besieged[6696] Tirzah.

18 And it came to pass, when Zimri saw that the city was taken, that he went into the palace of the king's house, and burnt[8313] the king's house over him with fire, and died,[4191]

19 For his sins which he sinned in doing[6213] evil in the sight of the LORD, [a]in walking in the way of Jeroboam, and in his sin which he did, to make Israel to sin.

20 Now the rest of the acts of Zimri, and his treason that he wrought, *are* they not written in the book of the chronicles of the kings of Israel?

Omri Rules Israel

21 Then were the people of Israel divided into two parts:[2677] half[2677] of the

---

1 [a]1Kgs. 16:7; 2Chr. 19:2; 20:34

2 [a]1Kgs. 14:7 [b]1Kgs. 15:34

3 [a]1Kgs. 16:11 [b]1Kgs. 14:10; 15:29

4 [a]1Kgs. 14:11

5 [a]2Chr. 16:1

6 [a]1Kgs. 14:7; 15:21

7 [a]1Kgs. 16:1 [b]1Kgs. 15:27, 29; Hos. 1:4

9 ǀHebr. *which was over* [a]2Kgs. 9:31

11 ǀOr, *both his kinsmen and his friends* [a]1Sam. 25:22

12 ǀHebr. *by the hand of* [a]1Kgs. 16:3 [b]1Kgs. 16:1

13 [a]Deut. 32:21; 1Sam. 12:21; Isa. 41:29; Jon. 2:8; 1Cor. 8:4; 10:19

15 [a]1Kgs. 15:27

19 [a]1Kgs. 12:28; 15:26, 34

people followed Tibni the son of Ginath, to make him king; and half[2677] followed Omri.

22 But the people that followed Omri prevailed against the people that followed Tibni the son of Ginath: so Tibni died, and Omri reigned.

23 In the thirty and first year of Asa king of Judah began Omri to reign over Israel, twelve years: six years reigned he in Tirzah.

24 And he bought the hill Samaria of Shemer for two talents of silver, and built on the hill, and called[7121] the name of the city which he built, after the name of Shemer, owner of the hill, [I][a]Samaria.

25 But [a]Omri wrought evil in the eyes of the LORD, and did worse than all that *were* before him.

26 For he walked in all the way of Jeroboam the son of Nebat, and in his sin wherewith he made Israel to sin, to provoke the LORD God of Israel to anger with their vanities.

27 Now the rest of the acts of Omri which he did, and his might that he shewed, *are* they not written in the book of the chronicles of the kings of Israel?

28 So Omri slept with his fathers, and was buried in Samaria: and Ahab his son reigned in his stead.

Ahab Rules Israel

29 And in the thirty and eighth year of Asa king of Judah began Ahab the son of Omri to reign over Israel: and Ahab the son of Omri reigned over Israel in Samaria twenty and two years.

30 And Ahab the son of Omri did evil in the sight of the LORD above all that *were* before him.

31 And it came to pass, [I]as if it had been a light thing[7043] for him to walk in the sins of Jeroboam the son of Nebat, [a]that he took to wife Jezebel the daughter of Ethbaal king of the [b]Zidonians, [c]and went and served Baal, and worshipped him.

32 And he reared up an altar[4196] for Baal in [a]the house of Baal, which he had built in Samaria.

33 [a]And Ahab made a grove;[842] and Ahab [b]did more to provoke the LORD God of Israel to anger than all the kings of Israel that were before him.

34 In his days did Hiel the Bethelite build Jericho: he laid the foundation[3245] thereof in Abiram his firstborn, and set up the gates thereof in his youngest *son* Segub, [a]according to the word of the LORD, which he spake by Joshua the son of Nun.

Elijah Warns Ahab of a Drought

17 And [I][a]Elijah the Tishbite, *who was* of the inhabitants[8453] of Gilead, said unto Ahab, [b]*As* the LORD God[430] of Israel liveth, [c]before whom I stand, [d]there shall not be dew nor rain [e]these years, but according to my word.

2 And the word of the LORD came unto him, saying,

3 Get thee hence, and turn thee eastward, and hide thyself by the brook Cherith, that *is* before Jordan.

4 And it shall be, *that* thou shalt drink of the brook; and I have commanded[6680] the ravens to feed thee there.

5 So he went and did[6213] according unto the word of the LORD; for he went and dwelt by the brook Cherith, that *is* before Jordan.

6 And the ravens brought him bread and flesh[1320] in the morning, and bread and flesh in the evening; and he drank of the brook.

24 [I]Hebr. *Shomeron* [a]1Kgs. 13:32; 2Kgs. 17:24; John 4:4
25 [a]Mic. 6:16
31 [I]Hebr. *was it a light thing* [a]Deut. 7:3 [b]Judg. 18:7 [c]1Kgs. 21:25, 26; 2Kgs. 10:18; 17:16
32 [a]2Kgs. 10:21, 26, 27
33 [a]2Kgs. 13:6; 17:11-16; 21:3; Jer. 17:2 [b]1Kgs. 16:30; 21:25
34 [a]Josh. 6:26
1 [I]Hebr. Elijahu [a]Luke 1:17; 4:25, he is called *Elias* [b]2Kgs. 3:14 [c]Deut. 10:8 [d]James 5:17 [e]Luke 4:25

17:1 God raised Elijah up at a time when the worship of Baal threatened the very existence of the worship of Jehovah in Israel. Elijah was perhaps associated with the schools of the prophets at Bethel, Jericho, and Gilgal (see note on 2 Kgs. 2:3–5). His prominence among the Old Testament prophets is seen in the fact that the forerunner of Christ, John the Baptist, was to come in the spirit and power of Elijah (Luke 1:17). It is also interesting that Elijah (representing the Prophets) and Moses (representing the Law), stood with Jesus on the Mount of Transfiguration.

7 And it came to pass [I]after a while, that the brook dried up,[3001] because there had been no rain in the land.

Elijah Raises the Widow's Son

8 And the word of the LORD came unto him, saying,

9 Arise, get thee to [a]Zarephath, which *belongeth* to Zidon, and dwell there: behold, I have commanded a widow woman there to sustain[3557] thee.

10 So he arose and went to Zarephath. And when he came to the gate of the city, behold, the widow woman *was* there gathering of sticks: and he called[7121] to her, and said, Fetch me, I pray thee, a little water in a vessel, that I may drink.

11 And as she was going to fetch *it,* he called to her, and said, Bring me, I pray thee, a morsel of bread in thine hand.

12 And she said, *As* the LORD thy God liveth, I have not a cake, but an handful of meal in a barrel, and a little oil in a cruse:[6835] and, behold, I *am* gathering two sticks, that I may go in and dress[6213] it for me and my son, that we may eat it, and die.

13 And Elijah said unto her, Fear[3372] not; go *and* do[6213] as thou hast said: but make me thereof a little cake first,[7223] and bring *it* unto me, and after make for thee and for thy son.

14 For thus saith the LORD God of Israel, The barrel of meal shall not waste, neither shall the cruse of oil fail, until the day[3117] *that* the LORD [I]sendeth rain upon the earth.[127]

15 And she went and did according to the saying of Elijah: and she, and he, and her house, did eat [I]*many* days.[3117]

16 *And* the barrel of meal wasted[3615] not, neither did the cruse of oil fail, according to the word of the LORD, which he spake [I]by Elijah.

17 And it came to pass after these things, *that* the son of the woman, the mistress of the house, fell sick; and his sickness was so sore, that there was no breath[5397] left in him.

18 And she said unto Elijah, [a]What have I to do with thee, O thou man of God? art thou come unto me to call my sin[5771] to remembrance, and to slay my son?

19 And he said unto her, Give me thy son. And he took him out of her bosom, and carried him up into a loft, where he abode, and laid him upon his own bed.

20 And he cried[7121] unto the LORD, and said, O LORD my God, hast thou also brought evil[7489] upon the widow with whom I sojourn, by slaying her son?

21 [a]And he [I]stretched himself upon the child three times, and cried unto the LORD, and said, O LORD my God, I pray thee, let this child's soul come [II]into him again.

22 And the LORD heard the voice of Elijah; and the soul of the child came into him again, and he [a]revived.[2421]

23 And Elijah took the child, and brought him down out of the chamber into the house, and delivered him unto his mother: and Elijah said, See, thy son liveth.

24 And the woman said to Elijah, Now by this [a]I know that thou *art* a man of God, *and* that the word of the LORD in thy mouth *is* truth.[571]

Elijah Confronts Ahab Again

18 And it came to pass *after* [a]many days,[3117] that the word of the LORD came to Elijah in the third year, saying, Go, shew thyself unto Ahab; and [b]I will send rain upon the earth.[127]

2 And Elijah went to shew himself unto Ahab. And *there was* a sore famine in Samaria.

🗝 3 And Ahab called[7121] [I]Obadiah, which *was* [II]the governor of *his* house.

7 [I]Hebr. *at the end of days*
9 [a]Obad. 20; Luke 4:26, called *Sarepta*
14 [I]Hebr. *giveth*
15 [I]Or, *a full year*
16 [I]Hebr. *by the hand of*
18 [a]Luke 5:8
21 [I]Hebr. *measured* [II]Hebr. *into his inward parts* [a]2Kgs. 4:34, 35
22 [a]Heb. 11:35
24 [a]John 3:2; 16:30
1 [a]Luke 4:25; James 5:17 [b]Deut. 28:12
3 [I]Hebr. *Obadiahu* [II]Hebr. *over his house*

🗝 **18:3** Obadiah was one of the seven thousand faithful men of God, of whom Elijah was unaware (1 Kgs. 19:18).

(Now Obadiah feared[3373] the LORD greatly:

4 For it was *so,* when [I]Jezebel cut off[3772] the prophets of the LORD, that Obadiah took an hundred prophets, and hid them by fifty in a cave, and fed them with bread and water.)

5 And Ahab said unto Obadiah, Go into the land, unto all fountains of water, and unto all brooks: peradventure[194] we may find grass to save the horses and mules alive, [I]that we lose not all the beasts.

6 So they divided the land between them to pass throughout it: Ahab went one way by himself, and Obadiah went another way by himself.

7 And as Obadiah was in the way, behold, Elijah met him: and he knew him, and fell[5307] on his face, and said, *Art* thou that my lord Elijah?

8 And he answered[559] him, I *am:* go, tell thy lord, Behold, Elijah *is here.*

9 And he said, What have I sinned, that thou wouldest deliver thy servant into the hand of Ahab, to slay me?

10 *As* the LORD thy God[430] liveth, there is no nation or kingdom, whither my lord hath not sent to seek thee: and when they said, *He is* not *there;* he took an oath of the kingdom and nation, that they found thee not.

11 And now thou sayest, Go, tell thy lord, Behold, Elijah *is here.*

12 And it shall come to pass, *as soon as* I am gone from thee, that [a]the Spirit of the LORD shall carry[5375] thee whither I know not; and *so* when I come and tell Ahab, and he cannot find thee, he shall slay me: but I thy servant fear[3372] the LORD from my youth.

13 Was it not told my lord what I did when Jezebel slew the prophets of the LORD, how I hid an hundred men of the LORD's prophets by fifty in a cave, and fed them with bread and water?

14 And now thou sayest, Go, tell thy lord, Behold, Elijah *is here:* and he shall slay me.

15 And Elijah said, *As* the LORD of hosts liveth, before whom I stand, I will surely shew myself unto him to day.[3117]

16 So Obadiah went to meet Ahab, and told him: and Ahab went to meet Elijah.

17 And it came to pass, when Ahab saw Elijah, that Ahab said unto him, [a]*Art* thou he that [b]troubleth[5916] Israel?

18 And he answered, I have not troubled Israel; but thou, and thy father's[1] house, [a]in that ye have forsaken[5800] the commandments[4687] of the LORD, and thou hast followed Baalim.

19 Now therefore send, *and* gather[6908] to me all Israel unto mount [a]Carmel, and the prophets of Baal four hundred and fifty, [b]and the prophets of the groves[842] four hundred, which eat at Jezebel's table.

Elijah at Mount Carmel

20 So Ahab sent unto all the children[1121] of Israel, and [a]gathered the prophets together unto mount Carmel.

21 And Elijah came unto all the people, and said, [a]How long halt[6452] ye between two [I]opinions? if the LORD *be* God, follow him: but if Baal, [b]*then* follow him. And the people answered him not a word.

22 Then said Elijah unto the people, [a]I, *even* I only, remain a prophet of the LORD; [b]but Baal's prophets *are* four hundred and fifty men.

23 Let them therefore give us two bullocks; and let them choose[977] one bullock for themselves, and cut it in pieces, and lay *it* on wood, and put no fire *under:* and I will dress[6213] the other bullock, and lay *it* on wood, and put no fire *under:*

24 And call[7121] ye on the name of your gods,[430] and I will call on the name of the LORD: and the God that [a]answereth by fire, let him be God. And all the people answered and said, [I]It is well spoken.

25 And Elijah said unto the prophets of Baal, Choose you one bullock for yourselves, and dress *it* first;[7223] for ye *are* many; and call on the name of your gods, but put no fire *under.*

26 And they took the bullock which was given them, and they dressed[6213] *it,* and called on the name of Baal from morning even until noon, saying, O Baal,

4 [I]Hebr. *Izebel*

5 [I]Hebr. *that we cut not off ourselves from the beasts*

12 [a]2Kgs. 2:16; Ezek. 3:12, 14; Matt. 4:1; Acts 8:39

17 [a]1Kgs. 21:20 [b]Josh. 7:25; Acts 16:20

18 [a]2Chr. 15:2

19 [a]Josh. 19:26 [b]1Kgs. 16:32

20 [a]1Kgs. 22:6

21 [I]Or, *thoughts* [a]2Kgs. 17:41; Matt. 6:24 [b]Josh. 24:15

22 [a]1Kgs. 19:10, 14 [b]1Kgs. 18:19

24 [I]Hebr. *The word is good* [a]1Kgs. 18:38; 1Chr. 21:26

[I]hear us. But *there was* [a]no voice, nor any that [II]answered. And they [III]leaped upon the altar[4196] which was made.

27 And it came to pass at noon, that Elijah mocked them, and said, Cry [I]aloud: for he *is* a god; either [II]he is talking, or he [III]is pursuing, or he is in a journey,[1870] *or* peradventure he sleepeth, and must be awaked.

28 And they cried[7121] aloud, and [a]cut themselves[1413] after their manner with knives and lancets, till [I]the blood[1818] gushed out upon them.

29 And it came to pass, when midday was past, [a]and they prophesied until the *time* of the [I]offering of the *evening* sacrifice, that *there was* [b]neither voice, nor any to answer, nor any [II]that regarded.

30 And Elijah said unto all the people, Come near unto me. And all the people came near unto him. [a]And he repaired the altar of the LORD *that was* broken down.

31 And Elijah took twelve stones, according to the number of the tribes of the sons of Jacob, unto whom the word of the LORD came, saying, [a]Israel shall be thy name:

32 And with the stones he built an altar [a]in the name of the LORD: and he made a trench about the altar, as great as would contain two measures of seed.

33 And he [a]put the wood in order, and cut the bullock in pieces, and laid *him* on the wood, and said, Fill four barrels with water, and [b]pour *it* on the burnt sacrifice, and on the wood.

34 And he said, Do *it* the second time. And they did *it* the second time. And he said, Do *it* the third time. And they did *it* the third time.

35 And the water [I]ran round about[5439] the altar; and he filled [a]the trench also with water.

36 And it came to pass at *the time of* the offering of the *evening* sacrifice, that Elijah the prophet came near, and said, LORD [a]God of Abraham, Isaac, and of Israel, [b]let it be known this day that thou *art* God in Israel, and *that I am* thy servant, and *that* [c]I have done[6213] all these things at thy word.

37 Hear me, O LORD, hear me, that this people may know that thou *art* the LORD God, and *that* thou hast turned their heart back again.

38 Then [a]the fire of the LORD fell, and consumed the burnt sacrifice,[5930] and the wood, and the stones, and the dust,[6083] and licked up the water that *was* in the trench.

39 And when all the people saw *it,* they fell on their faces: and they said, [a]The LORD, he *is* the God; the LORD, he *is* the God.

40 And Elijah said unto them, [Ia]Take the prophets of Baal; let not one of them escape.[4422] And they took them: and Elijah brought them down to the brook Kishon, and [b]slew them there.

The Drought Ends

41 And Elijah said unto Ahab, Get thee up, eat and drink; for *there is* [I]a sound of abundance of rain.

42 So Ahab went up to eat and to drink. And Elijah went up to the top of Carmel; [a]and he cast himself down upon the earth,[776] and put his face between his knees,

🗝 43 And said to his servant, Go up now, look toward the sea. And he went up, and looked, and said, *There is* nothing. And he said, Go again seven times.

44 And it came to pass at the seventh time, that he said, Behold, there ariseth a little cloud out of the sea, like a man's hand.[3709] And he said, Go up, say unto Ahab, [I]Prepare *thy chariot,* and get thee down, that the rain stop thee not.

45 And it came to pass in the mean while, that the heaven was black[6937]

26 [I]Or, *answer* [II]Or, *heard* [III]Or, *leaped up and down at the altar* [a]Ps. 115:5; Jer. 10:5; 1Cor. 8:4; 12:2

27 [I]Hebr. *with a great voice* [II]Or, *he meditateth* [III]Hebr. *hath a pursuit*

28 [I]Hebr. *poured out blood upon them* [a]Lev. 19:28; Deut. 14:1

29 [I]Hebr. *ascending* [II]Hebr. *attention* [a]1Cor. 14:4, 5 [b]1Kgs. 18:26

30 [a]1Kgs. 19:10

31 [a]Gen. 32:28; 35:10; 2Kgs. 17:34

32 [a]Col. 3:17

33 [a]Lev. 1:6–8 [b]Judg. 6:20

35 [I]Hebr. *went* [a]1Kgs. 18:32, 38

36 [a]Ex. 3:6 [b]1Kgs. 8:43; 2Kgs. 19:19; Ps. 83:18 [c]Num. 16:28

38 [a]Lev. 9:24; Judg. 6:21; 1Chr. 21:26; 2Chr. 7:1

39 [a]1Kgs. 18:24

40 [I]Or, *Apprehend* [a]2Kgs. 10:25 [b]Deut. 13:5; 18:20

41 [I]Or, *a sound of a noise of rain*

42 [a]James 5:17, 18

44 [I]Hebr. *Tie,* or, *Bind*

🗝 **18:43** This is an example of persistent prayer (see Luke 11:5–10; 18:1–8). When Elijah prayed, it rained (James 5:17, 18).

with clouds and wind, and there was a great rain. And Ahab rode, and went to Jezreel.

46 And the hand of the LORD was on Elijah; and he [a]girded up his loins, and ran before Ahab [I]to the entrance of Jezreel.

Elijah Flees to Mount Horeb

19 And Ahab told Jezebel all that Elijah had done, and withal how he had [a]slain all the prophets with the sword.

2 Then Jezebel sent a messenger unto Elijah, saying, [a]So let the gods[430] do *to me,* and more also, if I make not thy life as the life of one of them by to morrow about this time.

3 And when he saw *that,* he arose, and went for his life, and came to Beer–sheba, which *belongeth* to Judah, and left his servant there.

4 But he himself went a day's journey[1870] into the wilderness, and came and sat down under a juniper tree: and he [a]requested [I]for himself that he might die; and said, It is enough; now, O LORD, take away my life; for I *am* not better[2896] than my fathers.[1]

5 And as he lay and slept under a juniper tree, behold, then an angel[4397] touched him, and said unto him, Arise *and* eat.

6 And he looked, and, behold, *there was* a cake baken on the coals, and a cruse6835 of water at his [I]head. And he did eat and drink, and laid him down again.

7 And the angel of the LORD came again the second time, and touched him, and said, Arise *and* eat; because the journey *is* too great for thee.

8 And he arose, and did eat and drink, and went in the strength of that meat [a]forty days[3117] and forty nights unto [b]Horeb the mount of God.[430]

God Commissions Elijah

9 And he came thither unto a cave, and lodged there; and, behold, the word of the LORD *came* to him, and he said unto him, What doest thou here, Elijah?

10 And he said, [a]I have been very [b]jealous[7065] for the LORD God of hosts: for the children[1121] of Israel have forsaken[5800] thy covenant,[1285] thrown down thine altars,[4196] and [c]slain thy prophets with the sword; and [d]I, *even* I only, am left; and they seek my life, to take it away.

11 And he said, Go forth, and stand [a]upon the mount before the LORD. And, behold, the LORD passed by, and [b]a great and strong wind rent the mountains, and brake in pieces[7665] the rocks before the LORD; *but* the LORD *was* not in the wind: and after the wind an earthquake;7494 *but* the LORD *was* not in the earthquake:

12 And after the earthquake a fire; *but* the LORD *was* not in the fire: and after the fire a still1827 small1851 voice.

13 And it was *so,* when Elijah heard *it,* that [a]he wrapped his face in his mantle,[155] and went out, and stood in the entering in of the cave. [b]And, behold, *there came* a voice unto him, and said, What doest thou here, Elijah?

14 [a]And he said, I have been very jealous for the LORD God of hosts: because the children of Israel have forsaken thy covenant, thrown down thine altars, and slain thy prophets with the sword; and I, *even* I only, am left; and they seek my life, to take it away.

15 And the LORD said unto him, Go, return on thy way to the wilderness of Damascus: [a]and when thou comest, anoint[4886] Hazael *to be* king over Syria:

16 And [a]Jehu the son of Nimshi shalt thou anoint *to be* king over Israel: and [b]Elisha the son of Shaphat of Abel–meholah shalt thou anoint *to be* prophet in thy room.

17 And [a]it shall come to pass,[1961] *that* him that escapeth[4422] the sword of Hazael shall Jehu slay:[4191] and him that escapeth from the sword of Jehu [b]shall Elisha slay.

18 [a]Yet [I]I have left *me* seven thousand in Israel, all the knees which have not bowed[3766] unto Baal, [b]and every mouth which hath not kissed him.

46 [I]Hebr. *till thou come to Jezreel* [a]2Kgs. 4:29; 9:1

1 [a]1Kgs. 18:40

2 [a]Ruth 1:17; 1Kgs. 20:10; 2Kgs. 6:31

4 [I]Hebr. *for his life* [a]Num. 11:15; Jon. 4:3, 8

6 [I]Hebr. *bolster*

8 [a]Ex. 34:28; Deut. 9:9, 18; Matt. 4:2 [b]Ex. 3:1

10 [a]Rom. 11:3 [b]Num. 25:11, 13; Ps. 69:9 [c]1Kgs. 18:4 [d]1Kgs. 18:22; Rom. 11:3

11 [a]Ex. 24:12 [b]Ezek. 1:4; 37:7

13 [a]Ex. 3:6; Isa. 6:2 [b]1Kgs. 19:9

14 [a]1Kgs. 19:10

15 [a]2Kgs. 8:12, 13

16 [a]2Kgs. 9:1–3 [b]Luke 4:27, called *Eliseus*

17 [a]2Kgs. 8:12; 9:14; 10:6; 13:3 [b]Hos. 6:5

18 [I]Or, *I will leave* [a]Rom. 11:4 [b]Hos. 13:2

Elijah Calls Elisha

19 So he departed thence, and found Elisha the son of Shaphat, who *was* plowing *with* twelve yoke *of oxen* before him, and he with the twelfth: and Elijah passed by him, and cast his mantle upon him.

20 And he left the oxen, and ran after Elijah, and said, [a]Let me, I pray thee, kiss my father[1] and my mother, and *then* I will follow thee. And he said unto him, [I]Go back again: for what have I done to thee?

21 And he returned back from him, and took a yoke of oxen, and slew them, and [a]boiled their flesh[1320] with the instruments of the oxen, and gave unto the people, and they did eat. Then he arose, and went after Elijah, and ministered unto him.

The Syrian Army Surrounds Samaria

20 And Ben–hadad the king of Syria gathered all his host together: and *there were* thirty and two kings with him, and horses, and chariots: and he went up and besieged Samaria, and warred against it.

2 And he sent messengers to Ahab king of Israel into the city, and said unto him, Thus saith Ben–hadad,

3 Thy silver and thy gold *is* mine; thy wives also and thy children,[1121] *even* the goodliest,[2896] *are* mine.

4 And the king of Israel answered and said, My lord, O king, according to thy saying, I *am* thine, and all that I have.

5 And the messengers came again, and said, Thus speaketh Ben–hadad, saying, Although I have sent unto thee, saying, Thou shalt deliver me thy silver, and thy gold, and thy wives, and thy children;

6 Yet I will send my servants unto thee to morrow about this time, and they shall search thine house, and the houses of thy servants; and it shall be, *that* whatsoever is [I]pleasant[4261] in thine eyes, they shall put *it* in their hand, and take *it* away.

7 Then the king of Israel called[7121] all the elders[2205] of the land, and said, Mark, I pray you, and see how this *man* seeketh mischief: for he sent unto me for my wives, and for my children, and for my silver, and for my gold; and [I]I denied him not.

8 And all the elders and all the people said unto him, Hearken not *unto him,* nor consent.[14]

9 Wherefore he said unto the messengers of Ben–hadad, Tell my lord the king, All that thou didst send for to thy servant at the first[7223] I will do:[6213] but this thing I may not do. And the messengers departed, and brought him word again.

10 And Ben–hadad sent unto him, and said, [a]The gods[430] do so unto me, and more also, if the dust[6083] of Samaria shall suffice for handfuls for all the people that [I]follow me.

11 And the king of Israel answered and said, Tell *him,* Let not him that girdeth on *his harness* boast[1984] himself as he that putteth it off.

12 And it came to pass, when *Ben–hadad* heard this [I]message, as he *was* [a]drinking, he and the kings in the [II]pavilions, that he said unto his servants, [III]Set *yourselves in array.* And they set *themselves in array* against the city.

A Prophet Predicts Ahab's Victory

13 And, behold, there [I]came a prophet unto Ahab king of Israel, saying, Thus saith the LORD, Hast thou seen all this great multitude? behold, [a]I will deliver it into thine hand this day;[3117] and thou shalt know that I *am* the LORD.

14 And Ahab said, By whom? And he said, Thus saith the LORD, *Even* by the [I]young men of the princes of the provinces. Then he said, Who shall [II]order the battle? And he answered,[559] Thou.

15 Then he numbered[6485] the young men of the princes of the provinces, and they were two hundred and thirty two:

20 [I]Hebr. *Go return* [a]Matt. 8:21, 22; Luke 9:61, 62

21 [a]2Sam. 24:22

6 [I]Hebr. *desirable*

7 [I]Hebr. *I kept not back from him*

10 [I]Hebr. *are at my feet* [a]1Kgs. 19:2 [b]Ex. 11:8; Judg. 4:10

12 [I]Hebr. *word* [II]Or, *tents* [III]Or, *Place* the engines: *And they placed* engines [a]1Kgs. 20:16

13 [I]Hebr. *approached* [a]1Kgs. 20:28

14 [I]Or, *servants* [II]Hebr. *bind,* or, *tie*

and after them he numbered all the people, *even* all the children of Israel, *being* seven thousand.

16 And they went out at noon. But Ben–hadad *was* [a]drinking himself drunk in the pavilions, he and the kings, the thirty and two kings that helped him.

17 And the young men of the princes of the provinces went out first; and Ben–hadad sent out, and they told him, saying, There are men come out of Samaria.

18 And he said, Whether they be come out for peace, take them alive;[2416] or whether they be come out for war, take them alive.

19 So these young men of the princes of the provinces came out of the city, and the army[2428] which followed them.

20 And they slew every one his man: and the Syrians fled; and Israel pursued them: and Ben–hadad the king of Syria escaped[4422] on an horse with the horsemen.

21 And the king of Israel went out, and smote the horses and chariots, and slew the Syrians with a great slaughter.

22 And the prophet came to the king of Israel, and said unto him, Go, strengthen thyself, and mark,[3045] and see what thou doest: [a]for at the return of the year the king of Syria will come up against thee.

Ahab Defeats Syria Again

23 And the servants of the king of Syria said unto him, Their gods *are* gods of the hills; therefore they were stronger than we; but let us fight against them in the plain,[4334] and surely we shall be stronger than they.

24 And do this thing, Take the kings away, every man out of his place, and put captains[6346] in their rooms:

25 And number[4487] thee an army, like the army [I]that thou hast lost, horse for horse, and chariot for chariot: and we will fight against them in the plain, *and* surely we shall be stronger than they. And he hearkened unto their voice, and did so.

26 And it came to pass at the return of the year, that Ben–hadad numbered the Syrians, and went up to [a]Aphek, [I]to fight against Israel.

27 And the children of Israel were numbered, and [I]were all present, and went against them: and the children of Israel pitched before them like two little flocks of kids; but the Syrians filled the country.[776]

28 And there came a man of God,[430] and spake unto the king of Israel, and said, Thus saith the LORD, Because the Syrians have said, The LORD *is* God of the hills, but he *is* not God of the valleys, therefore [a]will I deliver all this great multitude into thine hand, and ye shall know that I *am* the LORD.

29 And they pitched one over against the other seven days.[3117] And *so* it was, that in the seventh day the battle was joined: and the children of Israel slew of the Syrians an hundred thousand footmen in one day.

30 But the rest fled to Aphek, into the city; and *there* a wall fell[5307] upon twenty and seven thousand of the men *that were* left. And Ben–hadad fled, and came into the city, [Ia]into an inner chamber.

31 And his servants said unto him, Behold now, we have heard that the kings of the house of Israel *are* merciful[2617] kings: let us, I pray thee, [a]put sackcloth on our loins, and ropes upon our heads, and go out to the king of Israel: peradventure[194] he will save thy life.

32 So they girded sackcloth on their loins, and *put* ropes on their heads, and came to the king of Israel, and said, Thy servant Ben–hadad saith, I pray thee, let me live. And he said, *Is* he yet alive? he *is* my brother.[251]

33 Now the men did diligently observe[5172] whether *any thing would come* from him, and did hastily catch *it:* and they said, Thy brother Ben–hadad. Then he said, Go ye, bring him. Then Ben–hadad came forth to him; and he caused him to come up into the chariot.

16 [a]1Kgs. 20:12; 1Kgs. 16:9
22 [a]2Sam. 11:1
25 [I]Hebr. *that was fallen*
26 [I]Hebr. *to the war with Israel* [a]Josh. 13:4
27 [I]Or, *were victualled*
28 [a]1Kgs. 20:13
30 [I]Hebr. *into a chamber within a chamber* [a]1Kgs. 22:25
31 [a]Gen. 37:34

34 And *Ben–hadad* said unto him, [a]The cities, which my father[1] took from thy father, I will restore; and thou shalt make streets for thee in Damascus, as my father made in Samaria. Then *said Ahab,* I will send thee away with this covenant.[1285] So he made a covenant with him, and sent him away.

A Prophet Condemns Ahab

35 And a certain man of [a]the sons of the prophets said unto his neighbour [b]in the word of the LORD, Smite me, I pray thee. And the man refused to smite him.

36 Then said he unto him, Because thou hast not obeyed the voice of the LORD, behold, as soon as thou art departed from me, a lion shall slay thee. And as soon as he was departed from him, [a]a lion found him, and slew him.

37 Then he found another man, and said, Smite me, I pray thee. And the man smote him, [I]so that in smiting[5221] he wounded *him.*

38 So the prophet departed, and waited for the king by the way, and disguised himself with ashes upon his face.

39 And as the king passed by, he cried unto the king: and he said, Thy servant went out into the midst of the battle; and, behold, a man turned aside,[5493] and brought a man unto me, and said, Keep this man: if by any means he be missing, then [a]shall thy life be for his life, or else thou shalt [I]pay a talent of silver.

40 And as thy servant was busy[6213] here and there, [I]he was gone. And the king of Israel said unto him, So *shall* thy judgment[4941] *be*; thyself hast decided *it.*

41 And he hasted, and took the ashes away from his face; and the king of Israel discerned[5234] him that he *was* of the prophets.

42 And he said unto him, Thus saith the LORD, [a]Because thou hast let go out of *thy* hand a man whom I appointed to utter destruction, therefore thy life shall go for his life, and thy people for his people.

43 And the king of Israel [a]went to his house heavy[5620] and displeased,[2198] and came to Samaria.

Naboth's Vineyard

21 And it came to pass after these things, *that* Naboth the Jezreelite had a vineyard, which *was* in Jezreel, hard by[681] the palace of Ahab king of Samaria.

2 And Ahab spake unto Naboth, saying, Give me thy [a]vineyard, that I may have it for a garden of herbs, because it *is* near unto my house: and I will give thee for it a better[2896] vineyard than it; *or,* if it [I]seem good[2896] to thee, I will give thee the worth of it in money.

⊶ 3 And Naboth said to Ahab, The LORD forbid it me, [a]that I should give the inheritance[5159] of my fathers[1] unto thee.

4 And Ahab came into his house heavy and displeased[2198] because of the word which Naboth the Jezreelite had spoken to him: for he had said, I will not give thee the inheritance of my fathers. And he laid him down upon his bed, and turned away his face, and would eat no bread.

5 But Jezebel his wife came to him, and said unto him, Why is thy spirit so sad,[5620] that thou eatest no bread?

6 And he said unto her, Because I spake unto Naboth the Jezreelite, and said unto him, Give me thy vineyard for money; or else, if it please thee, I will give thee *another* vineyard for it: and he answered,[559] I will not give thee my vineyard.

7 And Jezebel his wife said unto him, Dost thou now govern the kingdom of Israel? arise, *and* eat bread, and let thine

34 [a]1Kgs. 15:20
35 [a]2Kgs. 2:3, 5, 7, 15 [b]1Kgs. 13:17, 18
36 [a]1Kgs. 13:24
37 [I]Hebr. *smiting and wounding*
39 [I]Hebr. *weigh* [a]2Kgs. 10:24
40 [I]Hebr. *he was not*
42 [a]1Kgs. 22:31-37
43 [a]1Kgs. 21:4
2 [I]Hebr. be *good in thine eyes* [a]1Sam. 8:14
3 [a]Lev. 25:23; Num. 36:7; Ezek. 46:18

⊶ **21:3** See note on Leviticus 25:1–55 concerning Israel's property laws.

heart be merry:[3190] I will give thee the
vineyard of Naboth the Jezreelite.
8 So she wrote letters in Ahab's
name, and sealed *them* with his seal, and
sent the letters unto the elders[2205] and to
the nobles that *were* in his city, dwelling
with Naboth.
9 And she wrote in the letters, saying, Proclaim[7121] a fast, and set Naboth
[I]on high[7218] among the people:
10 And set two men, sons of
Belial,[1100] before him, to bear witness
against him, saying, Thou didst [a]blas-
pheme[1288] God and the king. And *then*
carry him out, and [b]stone him, that he
may die.[4191]
11 And the men of his city, *even* the
elders and the nobles who were the inhabitants in his city, did[6213] as Jezebel
had sent unto them, *and* as it *was* written in the letters which she had sent unto
them.
12 [a]They proclaimed a fast, and set
Naboth on high among the people.
13 And there came in two men,
children[1121] of Belial, and sat before him:
and the men of Belial witnessed against
him, *even* against Naboth, in the presence
of the people, saying, Naboth did blaspheme God and the king. [a]Then they carried him forth out of the city, and stoned
him with stones, that he died.
14 Then they sent to Jezebel, saying,
Naboth is stoned, and is dead.
15 And it came to pass, when Jezebel
heard that Naboth was stoned, and was
dead, that Jezebel said to Ahab, Arise,
take possession[3423] of the vineyard of
Naboth the Jezreelite, which he refused to
give thee for money: for Naboth is not
alive,[2416] but dead.
16 And it came to pass, when Ahab
heard that Naboth was dead, that Ahab
rose up to go down to the vineyard of
Naboth the Jezreelite, to take possession
of it.
17 [a]And the word of the LORD came
to Elijah the Tishbite, saying,
18 Arise, go down to meet Ahab king
of Israel, [a]which *is* in Samaria: behold, *he*
is in the vineyard of Naboth, whither he
is gone down to possess it.

9 [I]Hebr. *in the top of the people*
10 [a]Ex. 22:28; Lev. 24:15, 16; Acts 6:11 [b]Lev. 24:14
12 [a]Isa. 58:4
13 [a]2Kgs. 9:26
17 [a]Ps. 9:12
18 [a]1Kgs. 13:32; 2Chr. 22:9
19 [a]1Kgs. 22:38
20 [a]1Kgs. 18:17 [b]2Kgs. 17:17; Rom. 7:14
21 [a]1Kgs. 14:10; 2Kgs. 9:8 [b]1Sam. 25:22 [c]1Kgs. 14:10
22 [a]1Kgs. 15:29 [b]1Kgs. 16:3, 11
23 [I]Or, *ditch* [a]2Kgs. 9:36
24 [a]1Kgs. 14:11; 16:4
25 [I]Or, *incited* [a]1Kgs. 16:30, 31 [b]1Kgs. 16:31
26 [a]Gen. 15:16; 2Kgs. 21:11
27 [a]Gen. 37:34
29 [a]2Kgs. 9:25

19 And thou shalt speak unto him,
saying, Thus saith the LORD, Hast thou
killed,[7523] and also taken possession?
And thou shalt speak unto him, saying,
Thus saith the LORD, [a]In the place where
dogs licked the blood[1818] of Naboth shall
dogs lick thy blood, even thine.
20 And Ahab said to Elijah, [a]Hast
thou found me, O mine enemy? And he
answered, I have found *thee:* because
[b]thou hast sold thyself to work evil[7451] in
the sight of the LORD.
21 Behold, [a]I will bring evil upon
thee, and will take away thy posterity,
and will cut off[3772] from Ahab [b]him that
pisseth against the wall, and [c]him that is
shut up and left in Israel,
22 And will make thine house like
the house of [a]Jeroboam the son of Nebat,
and like the house of [b]Baasha the son of
Ahijah, for the provocation wherewith
thou hast provoked *me* to anger,[3707] and
made Israel to sin.
23 And [a]of Jezebel also spake the
LORD, saying, The dogs shall eat Jezebel
by the [I]wall of Jezreel.
24 [a]Him that dieth[4191] of Ahab in the
city the dogs shall eat; and him that dieth
in the field[7704] shall the fowls of the
air[8064] eat.
25 But [a]there was none like unto
Ahab, which did sell himself to work
wickedness in the sight of the LORD,
[b]whom Jezebel his wife [I]stirred up.[5496]
26 And he did very abominably[8581]
in following idols,[1544] according to all
things [a]as did[6213] the Amorites, whom
the LORD cast out[3423] before the children
of Israel.
27 And it came to pass, when Ahab
heard those words, that he rent his
clothes, and [a]put sackcloth upon his
flesh,[1320] and fasted, and lay in sackcloth,
and went softly.
28 And the word of the LORD came
to Elijah the Tishbite, saying,
29 Seest thou how Ahab humbleth
himself before me? because he humbleth
himself before me, I will not bring the
evil in his days:[3117] *but* [a]in his son's days
will I bring the evil upon his house.

Micaiah Predicts Ahab's Defeat

22 And they continued three years without war between Syria and Israel.

2 And it came to pass in the third year, that [a]Jehoshaphat the king of Judah came down to the king of Israel.

3 And the king of Israel said unto his servants, Know ye that [a]Ramoth in Gilead *is* ours, and we *be* [I]still, *and* take it not out of the hand of the king of Syria?

4 And he said unto Jehoshaphat, Wilt thou go with me to battle to Ramoth–gilead? And Jehoshaphat said to the king of Israel, [a]I *am* as thou *art,* my people as thy people, my horses as thy horses.

5 And Jehoshaphat said unto the king of Israel, Enquire, I pray thee, at the word of the LORD to day.[3117]

6 Then the king of Israel [a]gathered the prophets together,[6908] about four hundred men, and said unto them, Shall I go against Ramoth–gilead to battle, or shall I forbear?[2308] And they said, Go up; for the LORD shall deliver *it* into the hand of the king.

7 And [a]Jehoshaphat said, *Is there* not here a prophet of the LORD[3068] besides, that we might enquire of him?

8 And the king of Israel said unto Jehoshaphat, *There is* yet one man, Micaiah the son of Imlah, by whom we may enquire of the LORD: but I hate him; for he doth not prophesy good[2896] concerning me, but evil.[7451] And Jehoshaphat said, Let not the king say so.

9 Then the king of Israel called[7121] an [I]officer, and said, Hasten *hither* Micaiah the son of Imlah.

10 And the king of Israel and Jehoshaphat the king of Judah sat each[376] on his throne, having put on their robes, in a [I]void place[1637] in the entrance of the gate of Samaria; and all the prophets prophesied before them.

11 And Zedekiah the son of Chenaanah made him horns of iron: and he said, Thus saith the LORD, With these shalt thou push the Syrians, until thou have consumed[3615] them.

12 And all the prophets prophesied so, saying, Go up to Ramoth–gilead, and prosper: for the LORD shall deliver *it* into the king's hand.

13 And the messenger that was gone to call[7121] Micaiah spake unto him, saying, Behold now, the words of the prophets *declare* good unto the king with one mouth: let thy word, I pray thee, be like the word of one of them, and speak *that which is* good.

14 And Micaiah said, *As* the LORD liveth, [a]what the LORD saith unto me, that will I speak.

15 So he came to the king. And the king said unto him, Micaiah, shall we go against Ramoth–gilead to battle, or shall we forbear? And he answered[559] him, Go, and prosper: for the LORD shall deliver *it* into the hand of the king.

16 And the king said unto him, How many times shall I adjure[7650] thee that thou tell me nothing but *that which is* true in the name of the LORD?

17 And he said, I saw all Israel [a]scattered upon the hills, as sheep that have not a shepherd: and the LORD said, These have no master:[113] let them return every man to his house in peace.

18 And the king of Israel said unto Jehoshaphat, Did I not tell thee that he would prophesy no good concerning me, but evil?

19 And he said, Hear thou therefore the word of the LORD: [a]I saw the LORD sitting on his throne, [b]and all the host[6635] of heaven standing by him on his right hand and on his left.

20 And the LORD said, Who shall [I]persuade Ahab, that he may go up and fall at Ramoth–gilead? And one said on this manner, and another said on that manner.

21 And there came forth a spirit, and stood before the LORD, and said, I will persuade him.

22 And the LORD said unto him, Wherewith? And he said, I will go forth, and I will be a lying[8267] spirit in the mouth of all his prophets. And he said, [a]Thou shalt persuade *him,* and prevail also: go forth, and do[6213] so.

2 [a]2Chr. 18:2, 3
3 [I]Hebr. *silent from taking it* [a]Deut. 4:43
4 [a]2Kgs. 3:7
6 [a]1Kgs. 18:19
7 [a]2Kgs. 3:11
9 [I]Or, *eunuch*
10 [I]Hebr. *floor*
14 [a]Num. 22:38
17 [a]Matt. 9:36
19 [a]Isa. 6:1; Dan. 7:9 [b]Job 1:6; 2:1; Ps. 103:20, 21; Dan. 7:10; Zech. 1:10; Matt. 18:10; Heb. 1:7, 14
20 [I]Or, *deceive*
22 [a]Judg. 9:23; Job 12:16; Ezek. 14:9; 2Thess. 2:11

23 [a]Now therefore, behold, the LORD hath put a lying[8267] spirit[7307] in the mouth of all these thy prophets, and the LORD hath spoken evil[7451] concerning thee.

24 But Zedekiah the son of Chenaanah went near, and smote Micaiah on the cheek, and said, [a]Which way went[5674] the Spirit of the LORD from me to speak unto thee?

25 And Micaiah said, Behold, thou shalt see in that day, when thou shalt go [I]into [II][a]an inner chamber to hide thyself.

26 And the king of Israel said, Take Micaiah, and carry him back unto Amon the governor of the city, and to Joash the king's son;

27 And say, Thus saith the king, Put this *fellow* in the prison, and feed him with bread of affliction and with water of affliction, until I come in peace.

🔑 28 And Micaiah said, If thou return at all in peace, [a]the LORD hath not spoken by me. And he said, Hearken, O people, every one of you.

Ahab Dies in Battle

29 So the king of Israel and Jehoshaphat the king of Judah went up to Ramoth–gilead.

30 And the king of Israel said unto Jehoshaphat, [I]I will disguise myself, and enter into the battle; but put thou on thy robes. And the king of Israel [a]disguised himself, and went into the battle.

31 But the king[4430] of Syria commanded his thirty and two captains[8269] that had rule over his chariots, saying, Fight neither with small nor great, save only with the king of Israel.

32 And it came to pass, when the captains of the chariots saw Jehoshaphat, that they said, Surely it *is* the king of Israel. And they turned aside to fight against him: and Jehoshaphat [a]cried out.[2119]

33 And it came to pass, when the captains of the chariots perceived that it *was* not the king of Israel, that they turned back from pursuing him.

34 And a *certain* man drew a bow [I][a]at a venture,[8537] and smote the king of Israel between the [II]joints of the harness:[8302] wherefore he said unto the driver of his chariot, Turn thine hand, and carry me out of the host; for I am [III]wounded.

35 And the battle [I]increased[5927] that day: and the king was stayed up in his chariot against the Syrians, and died[4191] at even: and the blood[1818] ran out of the wound into the [II]midst of the chariot.

36 And there went a proclamation[7440] throughout the host about the going down of the sun, saying, Every man to his city, and every man to his own country.[776]

37 So the king died, and [I]was brought to Samaria; and [I]they buried[6912] the king in Samaria.

38 And *one* washed the chariot in the pool of Samaria; and the dogs licked up his blood; and they washed his armour; according [a]unto the word of the LORD which he spake.

39 Now the rest of the acts[1697] of Ahab, and all that he did,[6213] and [a]the ivory house which he made, and all the cities that he built, *are* they not written in the book[5612] of the chronicles of the kings of Israel?

40 So Ahab slept with his fathers; and Ahaziah his son reigned in his stead.

Jehoshaphat Rules Judah

41 And [a]Jehoshaphat the son of Asa began to reign over Judah in the fourth year of Ahab king of Israel.

42 Jehoshaphat *was* thirty and five years old when he began to reign; and he reigned twenty and five years in Jerusalem. And his mother's name *was* Azubah the daughter of Shilhi.

23 [a]Ezek. 14:9
24 [a]2Chr. 18:23
25 [I]Or, *from chamber to chamber* [II]Hebr. *a chamber in a chamber* [a]1Kgs. 20:30
28 [a]Num. 16:29; Deut. 18:20-22
30 [I]Or, *when he was to disguise himself, and enter into the battle* [a]2Chr. 35:22
32 [a]2Chr. 18:31; Prov. 13:20
34 [I]Hebr. *in his simplicity,* [II]Hebr. *joints and the breastplate* [III]Hebr. *made sick* [a]2Sam. 15:11
35 [I]Hebr. *ascended* [II]Hebr. *bosom*
37 [I]Hebr. *came*
38 [a]1Kgs. 21:19
39 [a]Amos 3:15
41 [a]2Chr. 20:31

🔑 **22:28** See note on Deuteronomy 18:20–22 regarding the tests of a true prophet.

43 And [a]he walked in all the ways of
Asa his father;[1] he turned not aside from
it, doing[6213] *that which was* right in the
eyes of the LORD: nevertheless [b]the high
places were not taken away; *for* the people offered and burnt incense[6999] yet in
the high places.
44 And [a]Jehoshaphat made peace
with the king of Israel.
45 Now the rest of the acts of
Jehoshaphat, and his might that he
shewed, and how he warred, *are* they not
written in the book of the chronicles of
the kings of Judah?
46 [a]And the remnant of the
sodomites,[6045] which remained in the
days[3117] of his father Asa, he took out of
the land.
47 [a]*There was* then no king in Edom:
a deputy[5324] *was* king.
48 [a]Jehoshaphat [1][b]made ships of
Tharshish to go to Ophir for gold: [c]but
they went not; for the ships were
broken[7665] at [d]Ezion–geber.

43 [a]2Chr. 17:3 [b]1Kgs. 14:23; 15:14; 2Kgs. 12:3
44 [a]2Chr. 19:2; 2Cor. 6:14
46 [a]1Kgs. 14:24; 15:12
47 [a]Gen. 25:23; 2Sam. 8:14; 2Kgs. 3:9; 8:20
48 [1]Or, had *ten ships* [a]2Chr. 20:35, 36 [b]1Kgs. 10:22 [c]2Chr. 20:37 [d]1Kgs. 9:26
50 [a]2Chr. 21:1
51 [a]1Kgs. 22:40
52 [a]1Kgs. 15:26
53 [a]Judg. 2:11; 1Kgs. 16:31

49 Then said Ahaziah the son of
Ahab unto Jehoshaphat, Let my servants
go with thy servants in the ships. But
Jehoshaphat would not.
50 And [a]Jehoshaphat slept[7901] with
his fathers, and was buried with his fathers in the city of David his father: and
Jehoram his son reigned in his stead.

Ahaziah Rules Israel

51 [a]Ahaziah the son of Ahab began
to reign over Israel in Samaria the seventeenth year of Jehoshaphat king of
Judah, and reigned two years over Israel.
52 And he did evil in the sight of
the LORD, and [a]walked in the way of his
father, and in the way of his mother, and
in the way of Jeroboam the son of Nebat,
who made Israel to sin:
53 For [a]he served Baal, and worshipped him, and provoked to anger[3707]
the LORD God[430] of Israel, according to
all that his father had done.

22:44 Jehoshaphat made peace with the Northern Kingdom by contracting a marriage between his son and Athaliah, the wicked daughter of Ahab and Jezebel. This turned out to be disastrous for Judah (2 Kgs. 11:1–3).

The Second Book of
KINGS

The books of 1 and 2 Kings, which made up only one volume in the Hebrew Scriptures, were divided in the edition of the Hebrew Bible that was published in A.D. 1517. The Septuagint and the translations of the Old Testament that followed divided the books of Samuel and Kings into First Kings through Fourth Kings. The Book of 2 Kings traces the history of the divided kingdoms from the reign of Solomon until the destruction of Jerusalem in 586 B.C. The fact is often overlooked that most of those who are now called the "writing prophets" ministered during this same period. This is likely because so few of them are named in the text of Kings and Chronicles. The prophets Elijah and Elisha also ministered during this time. Throughout this period, the ministry of the prophets had a great influence in the lives of the people of Israel.

In summary, the religious activity of the divided kingdoms of Israel and Judah was characterized by apostasy. On the one hand, all the kings of the Northern Kingdom (Israel) acted "according to the sins of Jeroboam the son of Nebat" (2 Kgs. 3:3; 9:9; 10:29, 31; 13:2; 14:24; 15:9, 18; 17:22). These sins, however, did not go unpunished. Eventually, the Northern Kingdom and its capital, Samaria, were destroyed by Assyria and the people deported (722 B.C.) as judgment from the Lord. On the other hand, although the Southern Kingdom (Judah) experienced periodic revivals under godly kings (2 Kgs. 14:3; 15:3; 18:3; 20:3; 22:2), the people always forgot God and returned to their wickedness. As a result, the Lord allowed Nebuchadnezzar to conquer them and carry them away into Babylon.

Elijah Predicts Ahaziah's Death

1 Then Moab [a]rebelled against Israel [b]after the death of Ahab.

🔑 2 And Ahaziah fell down through a lattice[7639] in his upper chamber that *was* in Samaria, and was sick: and he sent messengers, and said unto them, Go, enquire of Baal–zebub the god[430] of [a]Ekron whether I shall recover of this disease.[2483]

3 But the angel[4397] of the LORD said to Elijah the Tishbite, Arise, go up to meet the messengers of the king[4428] of Samaria, and say unto them, *Is it* not because *there is* not a God in Israel, *that* ye go to enquire of Baal–zebub the god of Ekron?

4 Now therefore thus saith the LORD, [I]Thou shalt not come down from that bed on which thou art gone up, but shalt surely die.[4191] And Elijah departed.

5 And when the messengers turned back unto him, he said unto them, Why are ye now turned back?

6 And they said unto him, There came a man up to meet us, and said unto us, Go, turn again unto the king that sent you, and say unto him, Thus saith the LORD, *Is it* not because *there is* not a God in Israel, *that* thou sendest to enquire of Baal–zebub the god of Ekron? therefore thou shalt not come down from that bed on which thou art gone up, but shalt surely die.

7 And he said unto them, [I]What manner of man *was he* which came up to meet you, and told you these words?[1697]

1 [a]2Sam. 8:2 [b]2Kgs. 3:5
2 [a]1Sam. 5:10
4 [I]Hebr. *The bed whither thou art gone up, thou shalt not come down from it*
7 [I]Hebr. *What was the manner of the man?*

🔑 **1:2** The actual name of this pagan god was "Baal-zebul," meaning "lord of life." The Hebrews mockingly changed it to Baal-zebub, "lord of flies." This derogative term later became a name for Satan, the prince of demons (Matt. 10:25; 12:24).

8 And they answered[559] him, *He was* [a]an hairy man, and girt with a girdle[232] of leather about his loins. And he said, It *is* Elijah the Tishbite.

9 Then the king sent unto him a captain[8269] of fifty with his fifty. And he went up to him: and, behold, he sat on the top of an hill. And he spake unto him, Thou man of God, the king hath said, Come down.

10 And Elijah answered and said to the captain of fifty, If I *be* a man of God, then [a]let fire come down from heaven, and consume thee and thy fifty. And there came down fire from heaven, and consumed him and his fifty.

11 Again also he sent unto him another captain of fifty with his fifty. And he answered and said unto him, O man of God, thus hath the king said, Come down quickly.

12 And Elijah answered and said unto them, If I *be* a man of God, let fire come down from heaven, and consume thee and thy fifty. And the fire of God came down from heaven, and consumed him and his fifty.

13 And he sent again a captain of the third fifty with his fifty. And the third captain of fifty went up, and came and [I]fell on his knees before Elijah, and besought[2603] him, and said unto him, O man of God, I pray thee,[4994] let my life,[5315] and the life of these fifty thy servants, [a]be precious in thy sight.

14 Behold, there came fire down from heaven, and burnt up the two captains[8269] of the former[7223] fifties with their fifties: therefore let my life now be precious in thy sight.

8 [a]Zech. 13:4; Matt. 3:4

10 [a]Luke 9:54

13 [I]Hebr. *bowed* [a]1Sam. 26:21; Ps. 72:14

17 [a]2Kgs. 3:1

1 [a]Gen. 5:24 [b]1Kgs. 19:21

2 [a]Ruth 1:15, 16 [b]1Sam. 1:26; 2Kgs. 2:4, 6; 4:30

3 [a]1Kgs. 20:35; 2Kgs. 2:5, 7, 15; 4:1, 38; 9:1

15 And the angel of the LORD said unto Elijah, Go down with him: be not afraid[3372] of him. And he arose, and went down with him unto the king.

16 And he said unto him, Thus saith the LORD, Forasmuch as thou hast sent messengers to enquire of Baal–zebub the God of Ekron, *is it* not because *there is* no God in Israel to enquire of his word?[1697] therefore thou shalt not come down off that bed on which thou art gone up, but shalt surely die.

17 So he died[4191] according to the word of the LORD which Elijah had spoken. And [a]Jehoram reigned in his stead in the second year of Jehoram the son of Jehoshaphat king of Judah; because he had no son.

18 Now the rest of the acts[1697] of Ahaziah which he did,[6213] *are* they not written in the book[5612] of the chronicles of the kings of Israel?

Elijah Is Taken Up to Heaven

2 And it came to pass, when the LORD would [a]take up Elijah into heaven by a whirlwind, that Elijah went with [b]Elisha from Gilgal.

2 And Elijah said unto Elisha, [a]Tarry here, I pray thee; for the LORD hath sent me to Bethel. And Elisha said *unto him, As* the LORD liveth,[2416] and [b]*as* thy soul liveth, I will not leave[5800] thee. So they went down to Bethel.

3 And [a]the sons of the prophets[5030] that *were* at Bethel came forth to Elisha, and said unto him, Knowest[3045] thou that

1:8 Elijah's clothing became symbolic of his power, and false prophets many times would copy it (Zech. 13:4). In the New Testament, John the Baptist appeared wearing clothing similar to Elijah's (Matt. 3:4; Mark 1:6), leading some to believe that he (John) was the one that was foretold to come in the "spirit and power of Elijah" (Luke 1:17, cf. Mal. 4:5).

2:3, 5 The phrase "sons of the prophets" is a reference to the organization of those who were true, God-called prophets into schools at Gibeah and Naioth where they could be supervised by Samuel (1 Sam.10:10; 19:20). Later, there is mention made of a group of one hundred prophets, members of such a school, who were hidden by Obadiah to keep them from being executed by Jezebel (1 Kgs. 18:4). The school set up in Gilgal (2 Kgs. 4:38–44) seems to indicate an atmosphere of a college where the prophets resided. In 2 Kings 6:1–4, there is an account of the building of such a school, and Elijah was the leader of this particular group.

the LORD will take away thy master from
thy head to day?[3117] And he said, Yea, I
know *it*; hold ye your peace.
4 And Elijah said unto him, Elisha,
tarry[3427] here, I pray thee; for the LORD
hath sent me to Jericho. And he said, *As*
the LORD liveth, and *as* thy soul liveth, I
will not leave thee. So they came to
Jericho.
5 And the sons of the prophets that
were at Jericho came to Elisha, and said
unto him, Knowest thou that the LORD
will take away thy master from thy head
to day? And he answered,[559] Yea, I know
it: hold ye your peace.
6 And Elijah said unto him, Tarry, I
pray thee, here; for the LORD hath sent
me to Jordan. And he said, *As* the LORD
liveth, and *as* thy soul liveth, I will not
leave thee. And they two went on.
7 And fifty men of the sons of the
prophets went, and stood [I]to view afar
off: and they two stood by Jordan.
8 And Elijah took his mantle,[155] and
wrapped *it* together, and smote the waters, and [a]they were divided hither and
thither, so that they two went over on dry
ground.[2724]
9 And it came to pass, when they
were gone over, that Elijah said unto
Elisha, Ask[7592] what I shall do[6213] for
thee, before I be taken away from
thee. And Elisha said, I pray thee, let
a double portion of thy spirit be upon
me.
10 And he said, [I]Thou hast asked[7592]
a hard thing: *nevertheless,* if thou see me
when I am taken from thee, it shall be
so unto thee; but if not, it shall not be
so.
11 And it came to pass, as they still
went on, and talked, that, behold, *there
appeared* [a]a chariot of fire, and horses of
fire, and parted them both asunder; and
Elijah went up by a whirlwind into
heaven.
12 And Elisha saw *it,* and he cried,
[a]My father,[1] my father, the chariot of
Israel, and the horsemen thereof. And he
saw him no more: and he took hold of
his own clothes, and rent them in two
pieces.

7 [I]Hebr. *in sight, or, over against*

8 [a]Ex. 14:21; Josh. 3:16; 2Kgs. 2:14

10 [I]Hebr. *Thou hast done hard in asking*

11 [a]2Kgs. 6:17

12 [a]2Kgs. 13:14

13 [I]Hebr. *lip*

14 [a]2Kgs. 2:8

15 [a]2Kgs. 2:7

16 [I]Hebr. *sons of strength* [II]Hebr. *one of the mountains* [a]1Kgs. 18:12; Ezek. 8:3; Acts 8:39

19 [I]Hebr. *causing to miscarry*

21 [a]Ex. 15:25; 2Kgs. 4:41; 6:6; John 9:6

Elisha Returns Without Elijah

13 He took up also the mantle[155] of
Elijah that fell[5307] from him, and went
back, and stood by the [I]bank[8193] of
Jordan;
14 And he took the mantle of Elijah
that fell from him, and smote the waters,
and said, Where *is* the LORD God[430] of
Elijah? and when he also had smitten the
waters, [a]they parted hither and thither:
and Elisha went over.
15 And when the sons of the
prophets which *were* [a]to view at Jericho
saw him, they said, The spirit of Elijah
doth rest on Elisha. And they came to
meet him, and bowed themselves[7812] to
the ground[776] before him.
16 And they said unto him, Behold
now, there be with thy servants fifty
[I]strong men; let them go, we pray thee,
and seek thy master: [a]lest peradventure[194] the Spirit of the LORD hath taken
him up, and cast him upon [II]some mountain, or into some valley. And he said, Ye
shall not send.
17 And when they urged him till he
was ashamed,[954] he said, Send. They sent
therefore fifty men; and they sought three
days,[3117] but found him not.
18 And when they came again to
him, (for he tarried at Jericho,) he said
unto them, Did I not say unto you, Go
not?

Elisha Purifies a Spring

19 And the men of the city said unto
Elisha, Behold, I pray thee, the situation[4186] of this city *is* pleasant,[2896] as my
lord[113] seeth: but the water *is* naught,[7451]
and the ground [I]barren.[7921]
20 And he said, Bring me a new
cruse,[6746] and put salt therein. And they
brought *it* to him.
21 And he went forth unto the spring
of the waters, and [a]cast the salt in there,
and said, Thus saith the LORD, I have
healed these waters; there shall not be
from thence any more death[4194] or barren *land.*
22 So the waters were healed unto

this day, according to the saying of
Elisha which he spake.

The Children Curse Elisha

23 And he went up from thence unto
Bethel: and as he was going up by the
way,[1870] there came forth little children[5288] out of the city, and mocked him,
and said unto him, Go up, thou bald
head; go up, thou bald head.
24 And he turned back, and
looked[7200] on them, and cursed[7043] them
in the name of the LORD. And there came
forth two she bears out of the wood, and
tare[1234] forty and two children[3206] of
them.
25 And he went from thence to
mount Carmel, and from thence he returned to Samaria.

Elisha Helps Jehoram Defeat Moab

3 Now [a]Jehoram the son of Ahab
began to reign over Israel in Samaria
the eighteenth year of Jehoshaphat
king[4428] of Judah, and reigned twelve
years.
2 And he wrought evil[7451] in the
sight of the LORD; but not like his father,[1]
and like his mother: for he put away
the [I]image of Baal [a]that his father had
made.
3 Nevertheless he cleaved unto [a]the
sins of Jeroboam the son of Nebat, which
made Israel to sin; he departed[5493] not
therefrom.
4 And Mesha king of Moab was a
sheepmaster,[5349] and rendered unto the
king of Israel an hundred thousand
[a]lambs,[3733] and an hundred thousand
rams, with the wool.
5 But it came to pass, when [a]Ahab
was dead,[4194] that the king of Moab rebelled against the king of Israel.
6 And king Jehoram went out of
Samaria the same time, and numbered
all Israel.
7 And he went and sent to
Jehoshaphat the king of Judah, saying,
The king of Moab hath rebelled[6586]
against me: wilt thou go with me against
Moab to battle? And he said, I will go up:
[a]I *am* as thou *art,* my people[5971] as thy
people, *and* my horses as thy horses.
8 And he said, Which way shall we
go up? And he answered,[559] the way[1870]
through the wilderness of Edom.
9 So the king of Israel went, and the
king of Judah, and the king of Edom:
and they fetched a compass[5437] of seven
days'[3117] journey:[1870] and there was no
water for the host, and for the cattle [I]that
followed them.
10 And the king of Israel said, Alas!
that the LORD hath called[7121] these three
kings[4428] together, to deliver them into
the hand of Moab!
11 But [a]Jehoshaphat said, *Is there* not
here a prophet[5030] of the LORD, that we
may enquire of the LORD by him? And
one of the king of Israel's servants answered and said, Here *is* Elisha the son
of Shaphat, which poured water on the
hands of Elijah.
12 And Jehoshaphat said, The
word[1697] of the LORD is with him. So
the king of Israel and Jehoshaphat and
the king of Edom [a]went down to him.
13 And Elisha said unto the king of
Israel, [a]What have I to do with thee? [b]get
thee to [c]the prophets of thy father, and
to the prophets of thy mother. And the
king of Israel said unto him, Nay: for
the LORD hath called these three kings together, to deliver them into the hand of
Moab.
14 And Elisha said, [a]*As* the LORD
of hosts liveth,[2416] before whom I
stand, surely, were it not that I regard the
presence of Jehoshaphat the king of
Judah, I would not look toward thee, nor
see thee.
15 But now bring me [a]a minstrel.[5059]
And it came to pass, when the minstrel
played, that [b]the hand of the LORD came
upon him.
16 And he said, Thus saith the LORD,
[a]Make this valley full of ditches.
17 For thus saith the LORD, Ye shall
not see wind,[7307] neither shall ye see rain;
yet that valley shall be filled with water,
that ye may drink, both ye, and your cattle, and your beasts.

1 [a]2Kgs. 1:17
2 [I]Hebr. *statue* [a]1Kgs. 16:31, 32
3 [a]1Kgs. 12:28, 31, 32
4 [a]Isa. 16:1
5 [a]2Kgs. 1:1
7 [a]1Kgs. 22:4
9 [I]Hebr. *at their feet* [a]Ex. 11:8
11 [a]1Kgs. 22:7
12 [a]2Kgs. 2:25
13 [a]Ezek. 14:3 [b]Judg. 10:14; Ruth 1:15 [c]1Kgs. 18:19
14 [a]1Kgs. 17:1; 2Kgs. 5:16
15 [a]1Sam. 10:5 [b]Ezek. 1:3; 3:14, 22; 8:1
16 [a]2Kgs. 4:3

18 And this is *but* a light thing in the
sight of the LORD: he will deliver the
Moabites also into your hand.
19 And ye shall smite every fenced
city, and every choice city, and shall
fell[5307] every good[2896] tree, and stop all
wells of water, and [I]mar every good piece
of land with stones.
20 And it came to pass in the morning, when [a]the meat offering was offered,
that, behold, there came water by the
way of Edom, and the country[776] was
filled with water.
21 And when all the Moabites heard
that the kings were come up to fight
against them, they [I]gathered all that were
able to [II]put on armour, and upward, and
stood in the border.
22 And they rose up early in the
morning, and the sun shone upon the
water, and the Moabites saw the water on
the other side *as* red as blood:[1818]
23 And they said, This *is* blood: the
kings are surely [I]slain, and they have
smitten one another: now therefore, Moab,
to the spoil.
24 And when they came to the
camp[4262] of Israel, the Israelites rose up
and smote the Moabites, so that they fled
before them: but [I]they went forward
smiting[5221] the Moabites, even in *their*
country.
25 And they beat down the cities,
and on every good piece of land cast
every man his stone, and filled it; and
they stopped all the wells of water, and
felled all the good trees: [I]only in
[a]Kirharaseth left[7604] they the stones
thereof; howbeit the slingers went
about[5437] *it,* and smote it.
26 And when the king of Moab
saw that the battle was too sore[2388] for
him, he took with him seven hundred
men that drew swords, to break through
even unto the king of Edom: but they
could not.
27 Then [a]he took his eldest son that
should have reigned in his stead, and offered him *for* a burnt offering upon the
wall. And there was great indignation[7110]
against Israel: [b]and they departed from
him, and returned to *their own* land.

19 [I]Hebr. *grieve*

20 [a]Ex. 29:39, 40

21 [I]Hebr. *were cried together* [II]Hebr. *gird himself with a girdle*

23 [I]Hebr. *destroyed*

24 [I]Or, *they smote in it even smiting*

25 [I]Hebr. *until he left the stones thereof in Kirhara-seth* [a]Isa. 16:7, 11

27 [a]Amos 2:1 [b]2Kgs. 8:20

1 [a]1Kgs. 20:35 [b]Lev. 25:39; Matt. 18:25

3 [I]Or, *scant not* [a]2Kgs. 3:16

7 [I]Or, *creditor*

8 [I]Hebr. *there was a day* [II]Hebr. *laid hold on him* [a]Josh. 19:18

Elisha Helps a Prophet's Widow

4 Now there cried a certain woman[802]
of the wives[802] of [a]the sons of the
prophets[5030] unto Elisha, saying, Thy servant my husband is dead;[4191] and thou
knowest[3045] that thy servant did fear[3373]
the LORD: and the creditor is come [b]to
take unto him my two sons to be bondmen.[5650]
2 And Elisha said unto her, What
shall I do[6213] for thee? tell me, what hast
thou in the house? And she said, Thine
handmaid hath not any thing in the
house, save a pot of oil.
3 Then he said, Go, borrow[7592] thee
vessels abroad of all thy neighbours,[7934]
even empty vessels; [I][a]borrow not a few.
4 And when thou art come in, thou
shalt shut the door upon thee and upon
thy sons, and shalt pour out into all those
vessels, and thou shalt set aside that
which is full.
5 So she went from him, and shut
the door upon her and upon her sons,
who brought[5066] *the vessels* to her; and
she poured out.
6 And it came to pass, when the vessels were full, that she said unto her son,
Bring me yet a vessel. And he said unto
her, *There is* not a vessel more. And the
oil stayed.
7 Then she came and told the man of
God.[430] And he said, Go, sell the oil, and
pay thy [I]debt,[2421] and live thou and thy
children[1121] of the rest.

Elisha and the Woman From Shunem

8 And it [I]fell[1961] on a day,[3117] that
Elisha passed[5674] to [a]Shunem, where *was*
a great woman; and she [II]constrained[2388]
him to eat bread. And *so* it was, *that* as
oft as he passed by, he turned in thither
to eat bread.
9 And she said unto her husband,
Behold now, I perceive that this *is* an
holy man of God, which passeth[5674] by
us continually.
10 Let us make a little chamber,[5944]
I pray thee,[4994] on the wall; and let us set

for him there a bed, and a table, and a stool, and a candlestick: and it shall be, when he cometh to us, that he shall turn in thither.

11 And it fell on a day, that he came thither, and he turned into the chamber, and lay there.

12 And he said to Gehazi his servant, Call[7121] this Shunammite. And when he had called her, she stood before him.

13 And he said unto him, Say now unto her, Behold, thou hast been careful[2729] for us with all this care;[2731] what *is* to be done[6213] for thee? wouldest thou be spoken for to the king,[4428] or to the captain[8269] of the host? And she answered,[559] I dwell among mine own people.[5971]

14 And he said, What then *is* to be done for her? and Gehazi answered, Verily she hath no child,[1121] and her husband is old.

15 And he said, Call her. And when he had called her, she stood in the door.

16 And he said, [a]About this [I]season, according to the time of life,[2416] thou shalt embrace a son. And she said, Nay, my lord,[113] *thou* man of God, [b]do not lie[3576] unto thine handmaid.

17 And the woman conceived, and bare a son at that season that Elisha had said unto her, according to the time of life.

Elisha Raises the Woman's Son

18 And when the child was grown, it fell on a day, that he went out to his father[1] to the reapers.

19 And he said unto his father, My head, my head. And he said to a lad, Carry[5375] him to his mother.

20 And when he had taken him, and brought him to his mother, he sat on her knees till noon, and *then* died.[4191]

21 And she went up, and laid him on the bed of the man of God, and shut *the door* upon him, and went out.

22 And she called unto her husband, and said, Send me, I pray thee, one of the young men, and one of the asses, that I may run to the man of God, and come again.

23 And he said, Wherefore wilt thou go to him to day? *it is* neither new moon, nor sabbath. And she said, *It shall be* [I]well.[7965]

24 Then she saddled an ass, and said to her servant, Drive, and go forward; [I]slack[6113] not *thy* riding for me, except I bid[559] thee.

25 So she went and came unto the man of God [a]to mount Carmel. And it came to pass, when the man of God saw her afar off, that he said to Gehazi his servant, Behold, *yonder is* that Shunammite:

26 Run now, I pray thee, to meet her, and say unto her, *Is it* well with thee? *is it* well with thy husband? *is it* well with the child? And she answered, *It is* well.

27 And when she came to the man of God to the hill, she caught[2388] [I]him by the feet: but Gehazi came near[5066] to thrust her away. And the man of God said, Let her alone;[7503] for her soul *is* [II]vexed[4843] within her: and the LORD[3068] hath hid *it* from me, and hath not told me.

28 Then she said, Did I desire[7592] a son of my lord? [a]did I not say, Do not deceive[7952] me?

29 Then he said to Gehazi, [a]Gird up thy loins, and take my staff in thine hand, and go thy way: if thou meet any man, [b]salute him not; and if any salute[1288] thee, answer him not again: and [c]lay[7760] my staff upon the face of the child.

30 And the mother of the child said, [a]*As* the LORD liveth,[2416] and *as* thy soul liveth, I will not leave[5800] thee. And he arose, and followed her.

31 And Gehazi passed on before them, and laid[7760] the staff upon the face of the child; but *there was* neither voice, nor [I]hearing.[7182] Wherefore he went again to meet him, and told him, saying, The child is [a]not awaked.

32 And when Elisha was come into the house, behold, the child was dead, *and* laid upon his bed.

16 [I]Hebr. *set time* [a]Gen. 18:10, 14 [b]2Kgs. 4:28

23 [I]Hebr. *peace*

24 [I]Hebr. *restrain not for me to ride*

25 [a]2Kgs. 2:25

27 [I]Hebr. *by his feet* [II]Hebr. *bitter*

28 [a]2Kgs. 4:16

29 [a]1Kgs. 18:46; 2Kgs. 9:1 [b]Luke 10:4 [c]Ex. 7:19; 14:16; 2Kgs. 2:8, 14; Acts 19:12

30 [a]2Kgs. 2:2

31 [I]Hebr. *attention* [a]John 11:11

33 He [a]went in therefore, and shut the door upon them twain,[8147] [b]and prayed[6419] unto the LORD.[3068]

34 And he went up, and lay[7901] upon the child, and put his mouth upon his mouth, and his eyes upon his eyes, and his hands upon his hands: and [a]he stretched himself upon the child; and the flesh[1320] of the child waxed warm.

35 Then he returned, and walked in the house [I]to and fro; and went up, [a]and stretched himself[1457] upon him: and [b]the child sneezed seven times, and the child opened his eyes.

36 And he called Gehazi, and said, Call this Shunammite. So he called her. And when she was come in unto him, he said, Take up thy son.

37 Then she went in, and fell[5307] at his feet, and bowed herself[7812] to the ground,[776] and [a]took up her son, and went out.

The Poison Food Is Made Edible

🔑 38 And Elisha came again to [a]Gilgal: and *there was* a [b]dearth in the land; and the sons of the prophets *were* [c]sitting before him: and he said unto his servant, Set on the great pot, and seethe pottage[5138] for the sons of the prophets.

39 And one went out into the field[7704] to gather[3950] herbs, and found a wild vine, and gathered thereof wild gourds his lap full, and came and shred *them* into the pot of pottage: for they knew[3045] *them* not.

40 So they poured out for the men to eat. And it came to pass, as they were eating of the pottage, that they cried out, and said, O *thou* man of God, *there is* [a]death[4194] in the pot. And they could not eat *thereof.*

41 But he said, Then bring meal.[7058] And [a]he cast *it* into the pot; and he said, Pour out for the people, that they may eat. And there was no [I]harm[1697,7451] in the pot.

42 And there came a man from [a]Baal–shalisha, [b]and brought the man of God bread of the firstfruits, twenty loaves of barley, and full ears of corn [I]in the husk thereof. And he said, Give unto the people, that they may eat.

43 And his servitor[8334] said, [a]What, should I set this before an hundred men? He said again, Give the people, that they may eat: for thus saith the LORD, [b]They shall eat, and shall leave[3498] *thereof.*

44 So he set *it* before them, and they did eat, [a]and left *thereof,* according to the word[1697] of the LORD.

Naaman Is Cured of Leprosy

5 Now [a]Naaman, captain[8269] of the host of the king[4428] of Syria, was [b]a great man [I]with his master, and [II]honourable, because by him the LORD had given [III]deliverance[8668] unto Syria: he was also a mighty man in valour,[2428] *but he was* a leper.

2 And the Syrians had gone out by companies,[1416] and had brought away captive out of the land of Israel a little maid; and she [I]waited on Naaman's wife.[802]

3 And she said unto her mistress, Would God my lord[113] *were* [I]with the prophet[5030] that *is* in Samaria! for he would [II]recover him of his leprosy.

4 And *one* went in, and told his lord, saying, Thus and thus said the maid that *is* of the land of Israel.

5 And the king of Syria said, Go to, go, and I will send a letter[5612] unto the king of Israel. And he departed, and [a]took [I]with him ten talents of silver, and six thousand *pieces* of gold, and ten changes of raiment.

6 And he brought the letter to the king of Israel, saying, Now when this letter is come unto thee, behold, I have *therewith* sent Naaman my servant to thee, that thou mayest recover him of his leprosy.

---

33 [a]2Kgs. 4:4; Matt. 6:6 [b]1Kgs. 17:20
34 [a]1Kgs. 17:21; Acts 20:10
35 [I]Hebr. *once hither, and once thither* [a]1Kgs. 17:21 [b]2Kgs. 8:1, 5
37 [a]1Kgs. 17:23; Heb. 11:35
38 [a]2Kgs. 2:1 [b]2Kgs. 8:1 [c]2Kgs. 2:3; Luke 10:39; Acts 22:3
40 [a]Ex. 10:17
41 [I]Hebr. *evil thing* [a]Ex. 15:25; 2Kgs. 2:21; 5:10; John 9:6
42 [I]Or, *in his scrip,* or, *garment* [a]1Sam. 9:4 [b]1Sam. 9:7; 1Cor. 9:11; Gal. 6:6
43 [a]Luke 9:13; John 6:9 [b]Luke 9:17; John 6:11
44 [a]Matt. 14:20; 15:37; John 6:13
1 [I]Hebr. *before* [II]Hebr. *lifted up,* or, *accepted in countenance* [III]Or, *victory* [a]Luke 4:27 [b]Ex. 11:3
2 [I]Hebr. *was before*
3 [I]Hebr. *before* [II]Hebr. *gather in*
5 [I]Hebr. *in his hand* [a]1Sam. 9:8; 2Kgs. 8:8, 9

🔑 **4:38** For a discussion of the "sons of the prophets" see note on 2 Kings 2:3, 5.

7 And it came to pass, when the king
of Israel had read the letter, that he rent
his clothes, and said, *Am* I [a]God, to
kill[4191] and to make alive, that this man
doth send unto me to recover a man of
his leprosy? wherefore consider,[3045] I
pray you, and see how he seeketh a quarrel against me.
8 And it was *so,* when Elisha the
man of God had heard that the king of
Israel had rent his clothes, that he sent
to the king saying, Wherefore hast thou
rent thy clothes? let him come now to
me, and he shall know[3045] that there is a
prophet in Israel.
9 So Naaman came with his horses
and with his chariot, and stood at the
door of the house of Elisha.
10 And Elisha sent a messenger
unto him, saying, Go and [a]wash[7364] in
Jordan seven times, and thy flesh[1320]
shall come again to thee, and thou shalt
be clean.[2891]
11 But Naaman was wroth,[7107] and
went away, and said, Behold, [I]I thought,
He will surely come out to me, and stand,
and call[7121] on the name of the LORD his
God, and [II]strike[5130] his hand over the
place, and recover the leper.
12 *Are* not [I]Abana and Pharpar,
rivers of Damascus, better[2896] than all
the waters of Israel? may I not wash in
them, and be clean? So he turned and
went away in a rage.
13 And his servants came near,[5066]
and spake unto him, and said, My
father,[1] *if* the prophet had bid thee
do some great thing, wouldest thou not
have done[6213] *it?* how much rather then,
when he saith to thee, Wash, and be
clean?
14 Then went he down, and
dipped[2881] himself seven times in Jordan,
according to the saying of the man of
God: and [a]his flesh came again like unto
the flesh of a little child, and [b]he was
clean.
15 And he returned to the man of
God, he and all his company,[4264] and
came, and stood before him: and he said,
Behold, now I know that *there is* [a]no God
in all the earth,[776] but in Israel: now
therefore, I pray thee, take [b]a blessing[1293]
of thy servant.
16 But he said, [a]*As* the LORD
liveth,[2416] before whom I stand, [b]I will receive none. And he urged6484 him to take
it; but he refused.
17 And Naaman said, Shall there not
then, I pray thee, be given to thy servant
two mules' burden[4853] of earth?[127] for
thy servant will henceforth offer neither
burnt offering nor sacrifice unto other
gods,[430] but unto the LORD.[3068]
18 In this thing the LORD pardon[5545]
thy servant, *that* when my master goeth
into the house of Rimmon to worship[7812]
there, and [a]he leaneth[8172] on my hand,
and I bow myself in the house of
Rimmon: when I bow down myself in
the house of Rimmon, the LORD pardon
thy servant in this thing.
19 And he said unto him, Go in
peace.[7965] So he departed from him [I]a little way.

Gehazi Gets Naaman's Leprosy

20 But Gehazi, the servant5288 of
Elisha the man of God, said, Behold, my
master hath spared Naaman this Syrian,
in not receiving at his hands that which
he brought: but, *as* the LORD liveth, I will
run after him, and take somewhat of
him.
21 So Gehazi followed after Naaman.
And when Naaman saw *him* running
after him, he lighted down[5307] from the
chariot to meet him, and said, [I]*Is* all
well?[7965]
22 And he said, All *is* well. My master hath sent me, saying, Behold, even
now there be come to me from mount
Ephraim two young men of the sons of
the prophets:[5030] give them, I pray thee,
a talent of silver, and two changes of
garments.
23 And Naaman said, Be content,[2974]
take two talents. And he urged6555 him,
and bound two talents of silver in two
bags, with two changes of garments, and
laid *them* upon two of his servants; and
they bare[5375] *them* before him.
24 And when he came to the

7 [a]Gen. 30:2; Deut. 32:39; 1Sam. 2:6

10 [a]2Kgs. 4:41; John 9:7

11 [I]Or, *I said with myself, He will surely come out;* Hebr. *I said* [II]Hebr. *move up and down*

12 [I]Or, *Amana*

14 [a]Job 33:25 [b]Luke 4:27

15 [a]Dan. 2:47; 3:29; 6:26, 27 [b]Gen. 33:11

16 [a]2Kgs. 3:14 [b]Gen. 14:23; Matt. 10:8; Acts 8:18, 20

18 [a]2Kgs. 7:2, 17

19 [I]Hebr. *a little piece of ground*

21 [I]Hebr. Is there *peace?*

[I]tower,[6076] he took *them* from their hand,
and bestowed *them* in the house: and he
let the men go, and they departed.

25 But he went in, and stood before
his master. And Elisha said unto him,
Whence *comest thou,* Gehazi? And he
said, Thy servant went [I]no whither.

26 And he said unto him, Went not
mine heart *with thee,* when the man
turned again[2015] from his chariot to meet
thee? *Is it* a time to receive money, and
to receive garments, and oliveyards,
and vineyards, and sheep, and oxen, and
menservants, and maidservants?

27 The leprosy therefore of Naaman
[a]shall cleave unto thee, and unto thy seed
for ever. And he went out from his presence [b]a leper *as white* as snow.

Elisha Makes an Axe Head Float

6 And [a]the sons of the prophets
said unto Elisha, Behold now, the
place where we dwell with thee is too
strait[6862] for us.

2 Let us go, we pray thee, unto
Jordan, and take thence every man a
beam, and let us make us a place there,
where we may dwell. And he
answered,[559] Go ye.

3 And one said, Be content,[2974] I
pray thee, and go with thy servants. And
he answered, I will go.

4 So he went with them. And when
they came to Jordan, they cut down
wood.

5 But as one was felling a beam, the
[I]axe head[1270] fell into the water: and he
cried, and said, Alas, master! for it was
borrowed.

6 And the man of God[430] said,
Where fell it? And he shewed him
the place. And [a]he cut down a stick, and
cast *it* in thither; and the iron did
swim.[6687]

7 Therefore said he, Take *it* up to
thee. And he put out his hand, and took
it.

Elisha and the Syrian Troops

8 Then the king[4428] of Syria warred
against Israel, and took counsel[3289] with
his servants, saying, In such and such a
place *shall be* my [I]camp.

9 And the man of God sent unto the
king of Israel, saying, Beware[8104] that
thou pass not such a place; for thither the
Syrians are come down.

10 And the king of Israel sent to the
place which the man of God told him
and warned[2094] him of, and saved[8104]
himself there, not once nor twice.

11 Therefore the heart of the king of
Syria was sore troubled[5590] for this thing;
and he called[7121] his servants, and said
unto them, Will ye not shew me which of
us *is* for the king of Israel?

12 And one of his servants said,
[I]None, my lord,[113] O king: but Elisha, the
prophet that *is* in Israel, telleth the king
of Israel the words[1697] that thou speakest in thy bedchamber.

13 And he said, Go and spy[7200]
where he *is,* that I may send and fetch
him. And it was told him, saying, Behold,
he is in [a]Dothan.

14 Therefore sent he thither horses,
and chariots, and a [I]great host: and they
came by night,[3915] and compassed the
city about.[5362]

15 And when the [I]servant of the
man of God was risen early, and gone
forth, behold, an host compassed the city
both with horses and chariots. And his
servant said unto him, Alas, my master!
how shall we do?[6213]

16 And he answered, Fear[3372] not: for
[a]they that *be* with us *are* more than they
that *be* with them.

17 And Elisha prayed,[6419] and said,
LORD, I pray thee, open his eyes, that
he may see. And the LORD opened
the eyes of the young man; and he saw:
and, behold, the mountain *was* full of
[a]horses and chariots of fire round about
Elisha.

24 [I]Or, *secret place*

25 [I]Hebr. *not hither or thither*

27 [a]1Tim. 6:10 [b]Ex. 4:6; Num. 12:10; 2Kgs. 15:5

1 [a]2Kgs. 4:38

5 [I]Hebr. *iron*

6 [a]2Kgs. 2:21

8 [I]Or, *encamping*

12 [I]Hebr. *No*

13 [a]Gen. 37:17

14 [I]Hebr. *heavy*

15 [I]Or, *minister*

16 [a]2Chr. 32:7; Ps. 55:18; Rom. 8:31

17 [a]2Kgs. 2:11; Ps. 34:7; 68:17; Zech. 1:8; 6:1-7

6:1 For a discussion of the "sons of the prophets" see note on 2 Kings 2:3, 5.

18 And when they came down to him, Elisha prayed unto the LORD, and said, Smite this people,[1471] I pray thee, with blindness. And [a]he smote them with blindness according to the word[1697] of Elisha.

19 And Elisha said unto them, This *is* not the way,[1870] neither *is* this the city: ‖follow me, and I will bring you to the man whom ye seek. But he led them to Samaria.

20 And it came to pass, when they were come into Samaria, that Elisha said, LORD, open the eyes of these *men,* that they may see. And the LORD opened their eyes, and they saw; and, behold, *they were* in the midst of Samaria.

21 And the king of Israel said unto Elisha, when he saw them, My father,[1] shall I smite[5221] *them?* shall I smite *them?*

22 And he answered, Thou shalt not smite *them:* wouldest thou smite those whom thou hast taken captive with thy sword and with thy bow? [a]set bread and water before them, that they may eat and drink, and go to their master.

23 And he prepared great provision for them: and when they had eaten and drunk, he sent them away, and they went to their master. So [a]the bands[1416] of Syria came no more into the land of Israel.

The Syrian Army Surrounds Samaria

24 And it came to pass after this, that Ben–hadad king of Syria gathered[6908] all his host, and went up, and besieged Samaria.

25 And there was a great famine in Samaria: and, behold, they besieged it, until an ass's head was *sold* for fourscore *pieces* of silver, and the fourth part of a cab[6894] of dove's dung for five *pieces* of silver.

26 And as the king of Israel was passing by[5674] upon the wall, there cried a woman[802] unto him, saying, Help,[3467] my lord, O king.

27 And he said, ‖If the LORD do not help thee, whence shall I help thee? out of the barnfloor, or out of the winepress?

28 And the king said unto her, What aileth thee? And she answered, This woman said unto me, Give thy son, that we may eat him to day, and we will eat my son to morrow.

29 So [a]we boiled my son, and did eat him: and I said unto her on the ‖next day, Give thy son, that we may eat him: and she hath hid her son.

30 And it came to pass, when the king heard the words of the woman, that he [a]rent his clothes; and he passed by[5674] upon the wall, and the people[5971] looked,[7200] and, behold, *he had* sackcloth within[1004] upon his flesh.[1320]

31 Then he said, [a]God do so and more also to me, if the head of Elisha the son of Shaphat shall stand on him this day.

32 But Elisha sat in his house, and [a]the elders[2205] sat with him; and *the king* sent a man from before him: but ere[2962] the messenger came to him, he said to the elders, [b]See ye how this son of [c]a murderer hath sent to take away mine head? look, when the messenger cometh, shut the door, and hold him fast[3905] at the door: *is* not the sound of his master's feet behind him?

33 And while he yet talked with them, behold, the messenger came down unto him: and he said, Behold, this evil[7451] *is* of the LORD; [a]what should I wait[3176] for the LORD any longer?

7 Then Elisha said, Hear ye the word[1697] of the LORD;[3068] Thus saith the LORD, [a]To morrow about this time *shall* a measure of fine flour *be sold* for a shekel, and two measures of barley for a shekel, in the gate of Samaria.

2 [a]Then ‖a lord[7991] on whose hand the king[4428] leaned[8172] answered the man of God,[430] and said, Behold, [b]*if* the LORD would make windows in heaven, might this thing be? And he said, Behold, thou shalt see *it* with thine eyes, but shalt not eat thereof.

---

18 [a]Gen. 19:11
19 ‖Hebr. *come ye after me*
22 [a]Rom. 12:20
23 [a]2Kgs. 5:2; 6:8, 9
27 ‖Or, *Let not the LORD save thee*
29 ‖Hebr. *other* [a]Lev. 26:29; Deut. 28:53, 57
30 [a]1Kgs. 21:27
31 [a]Ruth 1:17; 1Kgs. 19:2
32 [a]Ezek. 8:1; 20:1 [b]Luke 13:32 [c]1Kgs. 18:4
33 [a]Job 2:9
1 [a]2Kgs. 7:18, 19
2 ‖Hebr. *a lord which* belonged *to the king leaning upon his hand* [a]2Kgs. 7:17, 19, 20 [b]Mal. 3:10

The Syrians Retreat

3 And there were four leprous men [a]at the entering in of the gate: and they said one to another, Why sit we here until we die?[4191]

4 If we say, We will enter into the city, then the famine *is* in the city, and we shall die there: and if we sit still here, we die also. Now therefore come, and let us fall unto the host[4264] of the Syrians: if they save us alive, we shall live;[2421] and if they kill[4191] us, we shall but die.

5 And they rose up in the twilight, to go unto the camp[7121] of the Syrians: and when they were come to the uttermost part of the camp of Syria, behold, *there was* no man there.

6 For the Lord[136] had made the host of the Syrians [a]to hear a noise of chariots, and a noise of horses, *even* the noise of a great host:[2428] and they said one to another, Lo, the king of Israel hath hired against us [b]the kings of the Hittites, and the kings of the Egyptians, to come upon us.

7 Wherefore they [a]arose and fled in the twilight, and left[5800] their tents, and their horses, and their asses, even the camp as it *was,* and fled for their life.[5315]

8 And when these lepers came to the uttermost part of the camp, they went into one tent, and did eat and drink, and carried[5375] thence silver, and gold, and raiment, and went and hid *it;* and came again, and entered into another tent, and carried thence *also,* and went and hid *it.*

9 Then they said one to another, We do[6213] not well: this day[3117] *is* a day of good tidings,[2896] and we hold our peace: if we tarry till the morning light,[216] [I]some mischief will come upon us: now therefore come, that we may go and tell the king's[4428] household.

10 So they came and called[7121] unto the porter of the city: and they told them, saying, We came to the camp of the Syrians, and, behold, *there was* no man there, neither voice of man, but horses tied, and asses tied, and the tents as they *were.*

11 And he called the porters;[7778] and they told *it* to the king's house within.

12 And the king arose in the night,[3915] and said unto his servants, I will now shew you what the Syrians have done[6213] to us. They know[3045] that we *be* hungry; therefore are they gone out of the camp to hide themselves in the field,[7704] saying, When they come out of the city, we shall catch them alive,[2416] and get into the city.

13 And one of his servants answered and said, Let *some* take, I pray thee, five of the horses that remain, which are left[7604] [I]in the city, (behold, they *are* as all the multitude[1995] of Israel that are left in it: behold, *I say,* they *are* even as all the multitude of the Israelites that are consumed:[8552]) and let us send and see.

14 They took therefore two chariot horses; and the king sent after the host of the Syrians, saying, Go and see.

15 And they went after them unto Jordan: and, lo, all the way[1870] *was* full of garments and vessels, which the Syrians had cast away in their haste. And the messengers returned, and told the king.

16 And the people[5971] went out, and spoiled[962] the tents of the Syrians. So a measure of fine flour was *sold* for a shekel, and two measures of barley for a shekel, [a]according to the word of the LORD.

17 And the king appointed the lord on whose hand he leaned to have the charge of the gate: and the people trode upon him in the gate, and he died,[4191] [a]as the man of God had said, who spake when the king came down to him.

18 And it came to pass as the man of God had spoken to the king, saying, [a]Two measures of barley for a shekel, and a measure of fine flour for a shekel, shall be to morrow about this time in the gate of Samaria:

19 And that lord answered the man of God, and said, Now, behold, *if* the

---

3 [a]Lev. 13:46

6 [a]2Sam. 5:24; 2Kgs. 19:7; Job 15:21 [b]1Kgs. 10:29

7 [a]Ps. 48:4-6; Prov. 28:1

9 [I]Hebr. *we shall find punishment*

13 [I]Hebr. *in it*

16 [a]2Kgs. 7:1

17 [a]2Kgs. 6:32; 7:2

18 [a]2Kgs. 7:1

LORD should make windows in heaven, might such a thing be? And he said, Behold, thou shalt see it with thine eyes, but shalt not eat thereof.

20 And so it fell out[1961] unto him: for the people trode upon him in the gate, and he died.

The Woman Returns to Shunem

8 Then spake Elisha unto the woman,[802] [a]whose son he had restored to life, saying, Arise, and go thou and thine household, and sojourn wheresoever thou canst sojourn: for the LORD [b]hath called[7121] for a famine; and it shall also come upon the land seven years.

2 And the woman arose, and did[6213] after the saying of the man of God:[430] and she went with her household, and sojourned in the land of the Philistines seven years.

3 And it came to pass at the seven years' end, that the woman returned out of the land of the Philistines: and she went forth to cry unto the king for her house and for her land.

4 And the king talked with [a]Gehazi the servant of the man of God, saying, Tell me, I pray thee, all the great things that Elisha hath done.[6213]

5 And it came to pass, as he was telling the king how he had [a]restored a dead[4191] body to life, that, behold, the woman, whose son he had restored to life, cried to the king for her house and for her land. And Gehazi said, My lord,[113] O king, this *is* the woman, and this *is* her son, whom Elisha restored to life.

6 And when the king asked[7592] the woman, she told him. So the king appointed unto her a certain [I]officer,[5631] saying, Restore all that *was* hers, and all the fruits of the field[7704] since the day[3117] that she left[5800] the land, even until now.

Elisha Predicts Hazael's Rise to Power

7 And Elisha came to Damascus; and Ben–hadad the king of Syria was sick; and it was told him, saying, The man of God is come hither.

8 And the king said unto [a]Hazael, [b]Take a present[4503] in thine hand, and go, meet the man of God, and [c]enquire of the LORD by him, saying, Shall I recover of this disease?[2483]

9 So Hazael went to meet him, and took a present [I]with him, even of every good thing[2898] of Damascus, forty camels' burden,[4853] and came and stood before him, and said, Thy son Ben–hadad king of Syria hath sent me to thee, saying, Shall I recover of this disease?

🔑 10 And Elisha said unto him, Go, say unto him, Thou mayest certainly recover: howbeit the LORD hath shewed me that [a]he shall surely die.[4191]

11 And he settled his countenance [I]stedfastly, until he was ashamed:[954] and the man of God [a]wept.

12 And Hazael said, Why weepeth my lord? and he answered,[559] Because I know[3045] [a]the evil[7451] that thou wilt do[6213] unto the children[1121] of Israel: their strong holds wilt thou set on fire, and their young men wilt thou slay with the sword, and [b]wilt dash their children, and rip up their women with child.

13 And Hazael said, But what, [a]*is* thy servant a dog, that he should do this great thing? And Elisha answered, [b]The LORD hath shewed me that thou *shalt be* king over Syria.

14 So he departed from Elisha, and came to his master; who said to him, What said Elisha to thee? And he answered, He told me *that* thou shouldest surely recover.

15 And it came to pass on the morrow, that he took a thick cloth, and dipped[2881] *it* in water, and spread *it* on

1 [a]2Kgs. 4:35 [b]Ps. 105:16; Hag. 1:11
4 [a]2Kgs. 5:27
5 [a]2Kgs. 4:35
6 [I]Or, *eunuch*
8 [a]1Kgs. 19:15 [b]1Sam. 9:7; 1Kgs. 14:3; 2Kgs. 5:5 [c]2Kgs. 1:2
9 [I]Hebr. *in his hand*
10 [a]2Kgs. 8:15
11 [I]Hebr. *and set it* [a]Luke 19:41
12 [a]2Kgs. 10:32; 12:17; 13:3, 7; Amos 1:3 [b]2Kgs. 15:16; Hos. 13:16; Amos 1:13
13 [a]1Sam. 17:43 [b]1Kgs. 19:15

🔑 **8:10** In that Elisha knew of Hazael's plan to murder Ben-hadad and take over the throne, his words in this verse were spoken in sarcasm (cf. Micaiah's sarcasm in 1 Kgs. 22:15).

his face, so that he died:[4191] and Hazael
reigned in his stead.

Jehoram Rules Judah

16 And in the fifth year of Joram the
son of Ahab king of Israel, Jehoshaphat
being then king of Judah, [a]Jehoram the
son of Jehoshaphat king of Judah [I]began
to reign.
17 [a]Thirty and two years old was he
when he began to reign; and he reigned
eight years in Jerusalem.
18 And he walked in the way[1870] of
the kings[4428] of Israel, as did the house
of Ahab: for [a]the daughter of Ahab was
his wife:[802] and he did evil in the sight
of the LORD.[3068]
19 Yet the LORD would[14] not destroy[7843] Judah for David his servant's
sake, [a]as he promised him to give him
alway a [I]light,[5216] *and* to his children.
20 In his days [a]Edom revolted[6586]
from under the hand of Judah, [b]and made
a king over themselves.
21 So Joram went over to Zair, and
all the chariots with him: and he rose by
night,[3915] and smote the Edomites which
compassed him about, and the captains[8269] of the chariots: and the people[5971] fled into their tents.
22 [I][a]Yet Edom revolted from under
the hand of Judah unto this day. [b]Then
Libnah revolted at the same time.
23 And the rest of the acts[1697] of
Joram, and all that he did, *are* they not
written in the book[5612] of the chronicles
of the kings of Judah?
24 And Joram slept[7901] with his
fathers,[1] and was buried[6912] with his fathers in the city of David: and [a]Ahaziah
his son reigned in his stead.

Ahaziah Rules Judah

25 In the twelfth year of Joram the
son of Ahab king of Israel did Ahaziah
the son of Jehoram king of Judah begin
to reign.
26 [a]Two and twenty years old *was*
Ahaziah when he began to reign; and he
reigned one year in Jerusalem. And his
mother's name *was* Athaliah, the
[I][b]daughter of Omri king of Israel.
27 [a]And he walked in the way of the
house of Ahab, and did[6213] evil in
the sight of the LORD, as *did* the house
of Ahab: for he *was* the son in law of the
house of Ahab.
28 And he went [a]with Joram the son
of Ahab to the war against Hazael king
of Syria in Ramoth–gilead; and the
Syrians wounded[5221] Joram.
29 And [a]king[4428] Joram went back to
be healed in Jezreel of the [I]wounds[4347]
which the Syrians had given[5221] him at
[II][b]Ramah, when he fought against Hazael
king of Syria. [c]And Ahaziah the son of
Jehoram king of Judah went down to see
Joram the son of Ahab in Jezreel, because he was [III]sick.

Jehu Is Anointed King

9 And Elisha the prophet called[7121]
one of [a]the children[1121] of the
prophets, and said unto him, [b]Gird up
thy loins, and take this box of oil in thine
hand, [c]and go to Ramoth–gilead:
2 And when thou comest thither, look
out there Jehu the son of Jehoshaphat the
son of Nimshi, and go in, and make him
arise up from among [a]his brethren,[251] and
carry him to an [I]inner chamber;
3 Then [a]take the box of oil, and pour
it on his head, and say, Thus saith the
LORD, I have anointed[4886] thee king[4428]
over Israel. Then open the door, and flee,
and tarry not.
4 So the young man, *even* the young
man[5288] the prophet, went to Ramoth–
gilead.
5 And when he came, behold, the
captains[8269] of the host *were* sitting;
and he said, I have an errand to thee,
O captain. And Jehu said, Unto which
of all us? And he said, To thee, O captain.
6 And he arose, and went into the
house; and he poured the oil on his head,
and said unto him, [a]Thus saith the LORD
God[430] of Israel, I have anointed thee
king over the people[5971] of the LORD,
even over Israel.

16 [I]Hebr. *reigned.* Began to reign in consort with his father [a]2Chr. 21:3, 4

17 [a]2Chr. 21:5

18 [a]2Kgs. 8:26

19 [I]Hebr. *candle,* or, *lamp* [a]2Sam. 7:13; 1Kgs. 11:36; 15:4; 2Chr. 21:7

20 [a]Gen. 27:40; 2Kgs. 3:27; 2Chr. 21:8, 9, 10 [b]1Kgs. 22:47

22 [I]And so fulfilled [a]Gen. 27:40 [b]2Chr. 21:10

24 [a]2Chr. 21:17; 25:23, Jehoahaz; 2Chr. 22:1, 6, Azariah

26 [I]Or, *granddaughter* [a]2Chr. 22:2 [b]2Kgs. 8:18

27 [a]2Chr. 22:3, 4

28 [a]2Chr. 22:5

29 [I]Hebr. *wherewith the Syrians had wounded* [II]*Ramoth* [III]Hebr. *wounded* [a]2Kgs. 9:15 [b]2Kgs. 8:28 [c]2Kgs. 9:16; 2Chr. 22:6, 7

1 [a]1Kgs. 20:35 [b]2Kgs. 4:29; Jer. 1:17 [c]2Kgs. 8:28, 29

2 [I]Hebr. *chamber in a chamber* [a]2Kgs. 9:5, 11

3 [a]1Kgs. 19:16

6 [a]1Kgs. 19:16; 2Chr. 22:7

7 And thou shalt smite the house of Ahab thy master, that I may avenge[5358] the blood of my servants the prophets, and the blood[1818] of all the servants of the LORD, [a]at the hand of Jezebel.

8 For the whole house of Ahab shall perish:[6] and [a]I will cut off[3772] from Ahab [b]him that pisseth against the wall, and [c]him that is shut up[6113] and left[5800] in Israel:

9 And I will make the house of Ahab like the house of [a]Jeroboam the son of Nebat, and like the house of [b]Baasha the son of Ahijah:

10 [a]And the dogs shall eat Jezebel in the portion of Jezreel, and *there shall be* none to bury[6912] *her.* And he opened the door, and fled.

11 Then Jehu came forth to the servants of his lord:[113] and *one* said unto him, *Is* all well?[7965] wherefore came [a]this mad *fellow* to thee? And he said unto them, Ye know[3045] the man, and his communication.[7879]

12 And they said, *It is* false;[8267] tell us now. And he said, Thus and thus spake he to me, saying, Thus saith the LORD, I have anointed thee king over Israel.

13 Then they hasted, and [a]took every man his garment, and put *it* under him on the top of the stairs, and blew[8628] with trumpets, saying, Jehu [I]is king.[4427]

Jehu Assassinates Joram

14 So Jehu the son of Jehoshaphat the son[1121] of Nimshi conspired[7194] against Joram. (Now Joram had kept[8104] Ramoth–gilead, he and all Israel, because of Hazael king of Syria.

15 But [a]king [I]Joram was returned to be healed in Jezreel of the wounds[4347] which the Syrians [II]had given[5221] him, when he fought with Hazael king of Syria.) And Jehu said, If it be your minds,[5315] *then* [III]let none go forth *nor* escape out of the city to go to tell *it* in Jezreel.

16 So Jehu rode in a chariot, and went to Jezreel; for Joram lay there. [a]And Ahaziah king of Judah was come down to see Joram.

17 And there stood a watchman[6822] on the tower in Jezreel, and he spied the company of Jehu as he came, and said, I see a company. And Joram said, Take an horseman, and send to meet them, and let him say, *Is it* peace?[7965]

18 So there went one on horseback to meet him, and said, Thus saith the king, *Is it* peace? And Jehu said, What hast thou to do with peace? turn thee behind me. And the watchman told, saying, The messenger came to them, but he cometh not again.

19 Then he sent out a second on horseback, which came to them, and said, Thus saith the king, *Is it* peace? And Jehu answered,[559] What hast thou to do with peace? turn thee behind me.

20 And the watchman told, saying, He came even unto them, and cometh not again: and the [I]driving *is* like the driving of Jehu the son of Nimshi; for he driveth [II]furiously.[7697]

21 And Joram said, [I]Make ready.[631] And his chariot was made ready. And [a]Joram king of Israel and Ahaziah king of Judah went out, each[376] in his chariot, and they went out against Jehu, and [II]met him in the portion of Naboth the Jezreelite.

22 And it came to pass, when Joram saw Jehu, that he said, *Is it* peace, Jehu? And he answered, What peace, so long as the whoredoms[2183] of thy mother Jezebel and her witchcrafts[3785] *are so* many?

23 And Joram turned his hands, and fled, and said to Ahaziah, *There is* treachery,[4820] O Ahaziah.

24 And Jehu [I]drew a bow with his full strength, and smote Jehoram between his arms, and the arrow went out at his heart, and he [II]sunk down in his chariot.

25 Then said *Jehu* to Bidkar his captain, Take up, *and* cast him in the portion of the field[7704] of Naboth the Jezreelite: for remember how that, when I and thou rode together after Ahab his father,[1] [a]the LORD laid this burden[4853] upon him;

7 [a]1Kgs. 18:4; 21:15

8 [a]1Kgs. 14:10; 21:21 [b]1Sam. 25:22 [c]Deut. 32:36

9 [a]1Kgs. 14:10; 15:29; 21:22 [b]1Kgs. 16:3, 11

10 [a]1Kgs. 21:23; 2Kgs. 9:35, 36

11 [a]Jer. 29:26; John 10:20; Acts 26:24; 1Cor. 4:10

13 [I]Hebr. *reigneth* [a]Matt. 21:7

15 [I]Hebr. *Jehoram* [II]Hebr. *smote* [III]Hebr. *let no escaper go* [a]2Kgs. 8:29

16 [a]2Kgs. 8:25-29; 2Chr. 22:2-9

20 [I]Or, *marching* [II]Hebr. *in madness*

21 [I]Hebr. *Bind* [II]Hebr. *found* [a]2Chr. 22:7

24 [I]Hebr. *filled his hand with a bow* [II]Hebr. *bowed*

25 [a]1Kgs. 21:29

26 Surely, I have seen yesterday the [I]blood of Naboth, and the blood of his sons, saith the LORD; and [a]I will requite thee in this [II]plat, saith the LORD. Now therefore take *and* cast him into the plat *of ground,* according to the word[1697] of the LORD.

Jehu Assassinates Ahaziah

27 But when Ahaziah the king of Judah saw *this,* he fled by the way[1870] of the garden house. And Jehu followed after him, and said, Smite him also in the chariot. *And they did so* at the going up to Gur, which *is* by Ibleam. And he fled to [I][a]Megiddo, and died[4191] there.

28 And his servants carried him in a chariot to Jerusalem, and buried[6912] him in his sepulchre[6900] with his fathers[1] in the city of David.

29 And in the eleventh year of Joram the son of Ahab began Ahaziah to reign over Judah.

Jehu Assassinates Jezebel

30 And when Jehu was come to Jezreel, Jezebel heard *of it;* [a]and she [I]painted her face, and tired[3190] her head, and looked out at a window.

31 And as Jehu entered in at the gate, she said, [a]*Had* Zimri peace, who slew his master?

32 And he lifted up his face to the window, and said, Who *is* on my side? who? And there looked out to him two *or* three [I]eunuchs.[5631]

33 And he said, Throw her down. So they threw her down: and *some* of her blood was sprinkled on the wall, and on the horses: and he trode her under foot.[7429]

34 And when he was come in, he did eat and drink, and said, Go, see now this cursed[779] *woman,* and bury her: for [a]she *is* a king's[4428] daughter.

35 And they went to bury her: but they found no more of her than the skull, and the feet, and the palms[3709] of *her* hands.

36 Wherefore they came again, and told him. And he said, This *is* the word of the LORD, which he spake [I]by his servant Elijah the Tishbite, saying, [a]In the portion of Jezreel shall dogs eat the flesh[1320] of Jezebel:

37 And the carcase[5038] of Jezebel shall be [a]as dung upon the face of the field in the portion of Jezreel; *so* that they shall not say, This *is* Jezebel.

Ahab and Ahaziah's Family Members Are Assassinated

10 And Ahab had seventy sons in Samaria. And Jehu wrote letters,[5612] and sent to Samaria, unto the rulers of Jezreel, to the elders,[2205] and to [I]them that brought up[539] Ahab's *children,* saying,

2 Now as soon as this letter cometh to you, seeing your master's sons *are* with you, and *there are* with you chariots and horses, a fenced city also, and armour;[5402]

3 Look even out the best[2896] and meetest[3477] of your master's sons, and set *him* on his father's[1] throne, and fight for your master's house.

4 But they were exceedingly afraid,[3372] and said, Behold, two kings[4428] stood not before him: how then shall we stand?

5 And he that *was* over the house, and he that *was* over the city, the elders also, and the bringers up *of the children,* sent to Jehu, saying, We *are* thy servants, and will do[6213] all that thou shalt bid[559] us; we will not make any king:[4427] do thou *that which is* good[2896] in thine eyes.

6 Then he wrote a letter the second time to them, saying, If ye *be* [I]mine, and *if* ye will hearken unto my voice, take ye the heads of the men your master's sons, and come to me to Jezreel by to morrow this time. Now the king's sons, *being* seventy persons,[376] *were* with the great men of the city, which brought them up.

26 [I]Hebr. *bloods* [II]Or, *portion* [a]1Kgs. 21:19
27 [I]In the kingdom of *Samaria,* [a]2Chr. 22:9
30 [I]Hebr. *put her eyes in painting* [a]Ezek. 23:40
31 [a]1Kgs. 16:9-20
32 [I]Or, *chamberlains*
34 [a]1Kgs. 16:31
36 [I]Hebr. *by the hand of* [a]1Kgs. 21:23
37 [a]Ps. 83:10
1 [I]Hebr. *nourishers*
6 [I]Hebr. *for me*

7 And it came to pass, when the letter came to them, that they took the king's sons, and [a]slew seventy persons, and put their heads in baskets, and sent him *them* to Jezreel.

8 And there came a messenger, and told him, saying, They have brought the heads of the king's sons. And he said, Lay[7760] ye them in two heaps at the entering in of the gate until the morning.

9 And it came to pass in the morning, that he went out, and stood, and said to all the people,[5971] Ye *be* righteous: behold, [a]I conspired against my master, and slew him: but who slew all these?

10 Know[3045] now that there shall [a]fall unto the earth[776] nothing of the word[1697] of the LORD, which the LORD spake concerning the house of Ahab: for the LORD hath done[6213] *that* which he spake [I][b]by his servant Elijah.

11 So Jehu slew all that remained of the house of Ahab in Jezreel, and all his great men, and his [I]kinsfolks,[3045] and his priests, until he left[7604] him none remaining.[8300]

12 And he arose and departed, and came to Samaria. *And* as he *was* at the [I]shearing house in the way,[1870]

13 [a]Jehu [I]met with the brethren[251] of Ahaziah king[4428] of Judah, and said, Who *are* ye? And they answered,[559] We *are* the brethren of Ahaziah; and we go down [II]to salute the children of the king and the children of the queen.

14 And he said, Take them alive.[2416] And they took[8610] them alive, and slew them at the pit of the shearing house, *even* two and forty men; neither left he any of them.

15 And when he was departed thence, he [I]lighted on[4672] [a]Jehonadab the son of [b]Rechab *coming* to meet him: and he [II]saluted him, and said to him, Is thine heart right, as my heart *is* with thy heart? And Jehonadab answered, It is. If it be, [c]give *me* thine hand. And he gave *him* his hand; and he took him up to him into the chariot.

16 And he said, Come with me, and see my [a]zeal[7068] for the LORD. So they made him ride in his chariot.

17 And when he came to Samaria, [a]he slew all that remained unto Ahab in Samaria, till he had destroyed[8045] him, according to the saying of the LORD, [b]which he spake to Elijah.

Jehu Kills Baal Worshipers

18 And Jehu gathered all the people together,[6908] and said unto them, [a]Ahab served Baal a little; *but* Jehu shall serve him much.

19 Now therefore call[7121] unto me all the [a]prophets of Baal, all his servants, and all his priests; let none be wanting:[6485] for I have a great sacrifice *to do* to Baal; whosoever shall be wanting, he shall not live.[2421] But Jehu did *it* in subtilty,[6122] to the intent that he might destroy[6] the worshippers[5647] of Baal.

20 And Jehu said, [I]Proclaim a solemn assembly[6116] for Baal. And they proclaimed *it*.

21 And Jehu sent through all Israel: and all the worshippers of Baal came, so that there was not a man left that came not. And they came into the [a]house of Baal; and the house of Baal was [I]full from one end to another.

22 And he said unto him that *was* over the vestry,[4458] Bring forth vestments[3830] for all the worshippers of Baal. And he brought them forth vestments.[4403]

23 And Jehu went, and Jehonadab the son of Rechab, into the house of Baal, and said unto the worshippers of Baal, Search, and look that there be here with you none of the servants of the LORD, but the worshippers of Baal only.

24 And when they went in to offer sacrifices and burnt offerings, Jehu appointed[7760] fourscore men without, and said, *If* any of the men whom I have brought into your hands escape,[4422] *he*

7 [a]1Kgs. 21:21

9 [a]2Kgs. 9:14, 24

10 [I]Hebr. *by the hand of* [a]1Sam. 3:19 [b]1Kgs. 21:19, 21, 29

11 [I]Or, *acquaintance*

12 [I]Hebr. *house of shepherds binding* sheep

13 [I]Hebr. *found* [II]Hebr. *to the peace of* [a]2Kgs. 8:29; 2Chr. 22:8

15 [I]Hebr. *found* [II]Hebr. *blessed* [a]Jer. 35:6 [b]1Chr. 2:55 [c]Ezra 10:19

16 [a]1Kgs. 19:10

17 [a]2Kgs. 9:8; 2Chr. 22:8 [b]1Kgs. 21:21

18 [a]1Kgs. 16:31, 32

19 [a]1Kgs. 22:6

20 [I]Hebr. *Sanctify*

21 [I]Or, *so full, that they stood mouth to mouth* [a]1Kgs. 16:32

10:7 Jehu intended nothing less than complete extermination of the family of King Ahab of Israel.

that letteth him go, [a]his life[5315] *shall be*
for the life of him.
25 And it came to pass, as soon as
he had made an end[3615] of offering the
burnt offering, that Jehu said to the
guard7323 and to the captains,[7991] Go in,
and slay them; let none come forth. And
they smote them with [I]the edge[6310] of the
sword; and the guard and the captains
cast *them* out, and went to the city of the
house of Baal.
26 And they brought forth the
[I][a]images[4676] out of the house of Baal,
and burned[8313] them.
27 And they brake down the image
of Baal, and brake down the house of
Baal, [a]and made it a draught house4280
unto this day.[3117]
28 Thus Jehu destroyed[8045] Baal out
of Israel.
29 Howbeit *from* the sins of
Jeroboam the son of Nebat, who made
Israel to sin, Jehu departed[5493] not
from after them, *to wit,* [a]the golden
calves that *were* in Bethel, and that *were*
in Dan.
30 And the LORD said unto Jehu,
Because thou hast done well[2895] in
executing[6213] *that which is* right in mine
eyes, *and* hast done unto the house of
Ahab according to all that *was* in mine
heart, [a]thy children of the fourth *genera-*
tion shall sit on the throne of Israel.
31 But Jehu [I]took no heed to walk in
the law[8451] of the LORD God[430] of Israel
with all his heart: for he departed not
from [a]the sins of Jeroboam, which made
Israel to sin.

Jehu's Death

32 In those days[3117] the LORD began
[I]to cut Israel short:7096 and [a]Hazael smote
them in all the coasts of Israel;
33 From Jordan [I]eastward, all the
land of Gilead, the Gadites, and the
Reubenites, and the Manassites, from
Aroer, which *is* by the river Arnon, [II]even
[a]Gilead and Bashan.
34 Now the rest of the acts[1697] of
Jehu, and all that he did, and all his
might, *are* they not written in the
book[5612] of the chronicles of the kings of
Israel?
35 And Jehu slept with his fathers:[1]
and they buried[6912] him in Samaria.
And Jehoahaz his son reigned in his
stead.
36 And the [I]time that Jehu reigned
over Israel in Samaria *was* twenty and
eight years.

Athaliah Rules Judah

11 And when [a]Athaliah [b]the mother
of Ahaziah saw that her son was
dead,[4191] she arose and destroyed[6] all the
[I]seed royal.
2 But [a]Jehosheba, the daughter of
king Joram, sister of Ahaziah, took [I]Joash
the son of Ahaziah, and stole him from
among the king's[4428] sons *which were*
slain; and they hid him, *even* him and his
nurse, in the bedchamber from Athaliah,
so that he was not slain.
3 And he was with her hid in the
house of the LORD six years. And
Athaliah did reign over the land.
4 And [a]the seventh year Jehoiada
sent and fetched the rulers over hundreds, with the captains and the guard,
and brought them to him into the house
of the LORD, and made a covenant[1285]
with them, and took an oath of them in
the house of the LORD, and shewed them
the king's son.
5 And he commanded[6680] them, say-
ing, This *is* the thing that ye shall do;[6213]
A third part of you that enter in [a]on the
sabbath shall even be keepers[8104] of the
watch[4931] of the king's house;
6 And a third part *shall be* at the
gate of Sur; and a third part at the gate
behind the guard: so shall ye keep the
watch of the house, [I]that it be not broken down.
7 And two [I]parts[3027] of all you that
go forth on the sabbath, even they shall
keep the watch of the house of the LORD
about the king.
8 And ye shall compass[5362] the king
round about, every man with his
weapons in his hand: and he that cometh
within the ranges,7713 let him be slain:

24 [a]1Kgs. 20:39
25 [I]Hebr. *the mouth*
26 [I]Hebr. *statues* [a]1Kgs. 14:23
27 [a]Ezra 6:11; Dan. 2:5; 3:29
29 [a]1Kgs. 12:28, 29
30 [a]2Kgs. 10:35; 13:1, 10; 14:23; 15:8, 12
31 [I]Hebr. *observed not* [a]1Kgs. 14:16
32 [I]Hebr. *to cut off the ends* [a]2Kgs. 8:12
33 [I]Hebr. *toward the rising of the sun* [II]Or, *even to Gilead and Bashan* [a]Amos 1:3
36 [I]Hebr. *the days* were
1 [I]Hebr. *seed of the kingdom* [a]2Chr. 22:10 [b]2Kgs. 8:26
2 [I]Or, *Jehoash* [a]2Chr. 22:11, *Jehoshabeath*
4 [a]2Chr. 23:1
5 [a]1Chr. 9:25
6 [I]Or, *from breaking up*
7 [I]Or, *companies*

and be ye with the king as he goeth out and as he cometh in.

9 [a]And the captains over the hundreds did[6213] according to all *things* that Jehoiada the priest commanded: and they took every man his men that were to come in on the sabbath, with them that should go out on the sabbath, and came to Jehoiada the priest.

10 And to the captains over hundreds did the priest give king David's spears and shields, that *were* in the temple[1004] of the LORD.[3068]

11 And the guard stood, every man with his weapons in his hand, round about the king, from the right [I]corner of the temple to the left corner of the temple, *along* by the altar[4196] and the temple.

12 And he brought forth the king's son, and put the crown[5145] upon him, and *gave him* the testimony; and they made him king,[4427] and anointed[4886] him; and they clapped[5221] their hands, and said, [Ia]God save the king.

13 [a]And when Athaliah heard the noise of the guard *and* of the people,[5971] she came to the people into the temple of the LORD.

14 And when she looked,[7200] behold, the king stood by [a]a pillar, as the manner *was,* and the princes and the trumpeters by the king, and all the people of the land rejoiced, and blew[8628] with trumpets: and Athaliah rent her clothes, and cried,[7121] Treason, Treason.

15 But Jehoiada the priest commanded the captains of the hundreds, the officers of the host, and said unto them, Have her forth without the ranges: and him that followeth her kill[4191] with the sword. For the priest had said, Let her not be slain in the house of the LORD.

16 And they laid[7760] hands on her; and she went by the way[1870] by the which the horses came into the king's house: and there was she slain.

Jehoiada's Reforms

17 [a]And Jehoiada made[3772] a covenant between the LORD and the king and the people, that they should be the LORD's people; [b]between the king also and the people.

18 And all the people of the land went into the [a]house of Baal, and brake it down; his altars[4196] and his images[6754] [b]brake they in pieces[7665] thoroughly, and slew Mattan the priest of Baal before the altars. And the [c]priest appointed[7760] [I]officers over the house of the LORD.

19 And he took the rulers over hundreds, and the captains, and the guard, and all the people of the land; and they brought down the king from the house of the LORD, and came by the way of the gate of the guard[7323] to the king's house. And he sat on the throne of the kings.

20 And all the people of the land rejoiced, and the city was in quiet:[8252] and they slew Athaliah with the sword *beside* the king's house.

21 [a]Seven years old *was* Jehoash when he began to reign.

Jehoash Rules Judah

12 In the seventh year of Jehu [a]Jehoash began to reign; and forty years reigned he in Jerusalem. And his mother's name *was* Zibiah of Beer–sheba.

2 And Jehoash did[6213] *that which was* right in the sight of the LORD all his days[3117] wherein Jehoiada the priest instructed him.

3 But [a]the high places were not taken away: the people[5971] still sacrificed and burnt incense[6999] in the high places.

4 And Jehoash said to the priests, [a]All the money of the [I]dedicated things that is brought into the house of the LORD, *even* [b]the money of every one that passeth[5674] *the account,* [II]the money that every man is set at, *and* all the money that [IIIc]cometh into any man's heart to bring into the house of the LORD.

5 Let the priests take *it* to them, every man of his acquaintance:[4378] and let them repair the breaches of the house, wheresoever any breach shall be found.

6 But it was *so, that* [I]in the three and twentieth year of king Jehoash

9 [a]2Chr. 23:8

11 [I]Hebr. *shoulder*

12 [I]Hebr. *Let the king live* [a]1Sam. 10:24

13 [a]2Chr. 23:12

14 [a]2Kgs. 23:3; 2Chr. 34:31

17 [a]2Chr. 23:16 [b]2Sam. 5:3

18 [I]Hebr. *offices* [a]2Kgs. 10:26 [b]Deut. 12:3; 2Chr. 23:17 [c]2Chr. 23:18

21 [a]2Chr. 24:1

1 [a]2Chr. 24:1

3 [a]1Kgs. 15:14; 22:43; 2Kgs. 14:4

4 [I]Or, *holy things* [II]Hebr. *the money of the souls of his estimation* [III]Hebr. *ascendeth upon the heart of a man* [a]2Kgs. 22:4 [b]Ex. 30:13 [c]Ex. 35:5; 1Chr. 29:9

6 [I]Hebr. *in the twentieth year and third year*

[a]the priests had not repaired the breaches of the house.

🔑 7 [a]Then king Jehoash called[7121] for Jehoiada the priest, and the *other* priests, and said unto them, Why repair ye not the breaches of the house? now therefore receive no *more* money of your acquaintance, but deliver it for the breaches of the house.

8 And the priests consented to receive no *more* money of the people, neither to repair the breaches of the house.

9 But Jehoiada the priest took [a]a chest,[727] and bored[5344] a hole in the lid of it, and set it beside the altar,[4196] on the right side as one cometh into the house of the LORD: and the priests that kept[8104] the [I]door put therein all the money *that was* brought into the house of the LORD.[3068]

10 And it was *so,* when they saw that *there was* much money in the chest, that the king's [I]scribe and the high priest came up, and they [II]put up in bags, and told[4487] the money that was found in the house of the LORD.

11 And they gave the money, being told, into the hands of them that did the work,[4399] that had the oversight[6485] of the house of the LORD: and they [I]laid it out to the carpenters and builders,[1129] that wrought upon the house of the LORD,

12 And to masons, and hewers[2672] of stone, and to buy timber and hewed[4274] stone to repair the breaches of the house of the LORD, and for all that [I]was laid out for the house to repair *it.*

13 Howbeit [a]there were not made for the house of the LORD bowls of silver, snuffers, basons,[4219] trumpets, any vessels of gold, or vessels of silver, of the money *that was* brought into the house of the LORD:

14 But they gave that to the workmen, and repaired therewith the house of the LORD.

15 Moreover [a]they reckoned[2803] not with the men, into whose hand they delivered the money to be bestowed on workmen: for they dealt[6213] faithfully.[530]

16 [a]The trespass[816] money and sin[2403] money was not brought into the house of the LORD: [b]it was the priests'.

17 Then [a]Hazael king of Syria went up, and fought against Gath, and took it: and [b]Hazael set his face to go up to Jerusalem.

18 And Jehoash king of Judah [a]took all the hallowed things that Jehoshaphat, and Jehoram, and Ahaziah, his fathers, kings[4428] of Judah, had dedicated,[6942] and his own hallowed things, and all the gold *that was* found in the treasures of the house of the LORD, and in the king's house, and sent *it* to Hazael king of Syria: and he [I]went away from Jerusalem.

19 And the rest of the acts[1697] of Joash, and all that he did, *are* they not written in the book[5612] of the chronicles of the kings of Judah?

20 And [a]his servants arose, and made a conspiracy, and slew Joash in [I]the house of Millo, which goeth down to Silla.

21 For [a]Jozachar the son of Shimeath, and Jehozabad the son of [I]Shomer, his servants, smote him, and he died;[4191] and they buried[6912] him with his fathers in the city of David: and [b]Amaziah his son reigned in his stead.

Jehoahaz Rules Israel

13 In [I]the three and twentieth year of Joash the son of Ahaziah king of Judah Jehoahaz the son of Jehu began to reign over Israel in Samaria, *and reigned* seventeen years.

2 And he did *that which was* evil[7451] in the sight of the LORD, and [I]followed the sins of Jeroboam the son of Nebat, which made Israel to sin; he departed[5493] not therefrom.

6 [a]2Chr. 24:5
7 [a]2Chr. 24:6
9 [I]Hebr. *threshold* [a]2Chr. 24:8
10 [I]Or, *secretary* [II]Hebr. *bound up*
11 [I]Hebr. *brought it forth*
12 [I]Hebr. *went forth*
13 [a]2Chr. 24:14
15 [a]2Kgs. 22:7
16 [a]Lev. 5:15, 18 [b]Lev. 7:7; Num. 18:9
17 [a]2Kgs. 8:12 [b]2Chr. 24:23
18 [I]Hebr. *went up* [a]1Kgs. 15:18; 2Kgs. 18:15, 16
20 [I]Or, *Bethmillo* [a]2Kgs. 14:5; 2Chr. 24:25
21 [I]Or, *Shimrith* [a]2Chr. 24:26, *Zabad* [b]2Chr. 24:27
1 [I]Hebr. *the twentieth year and third year*
2 [I]Hebr. *walked after*

🔑 **12:7** It is inferred that donations that were made for repairs on the temple had to be used for the priest's own living expenses. The true priests were suffering because so many of the people were worshiping idols.

3 And [a]the anger[639] of the LORD was kindled[2734] against Israel, and he delivered them into the hand of [b]Hazael king of Syria, and into the hand of Ben–hadad the son of Hazael, all *their* days.[3117]

4 And Jehoahaz [a]besought2470 the LORD, and the LORD hearkened unto him: for [b]he saw the oppression of Israel, because the king of Syria oppressed them.

5 ([a]And the LORD gave Israel a saviour,[3467] so that they went out from under the hand of the Syrians: and the children[1121] of Israel dwelt in their tents, [I]as beforetime.

6 Nevertheless they departed not from the sins of the house of Jeroboam, who made Israel sin, *but* [I]walked therein: [a]and there [II]remained the grove[842] also in Samaria.)

7 Neither did he leave[7604] of the people[5971] to Jehoahaz but fifty horsemen, and ten chariots, and ten thousand footmen; for the king of Syria had destroyed[6] them, [a]and had made them like the dust[6083] by threshing.

8 Now the rest of the acts[1697] of Jehoahaz, and all that he did, and his might, *are* they not written in the book[5612] of the chronicles of the kings[4428] of Israel?

9 And Jehoahaz slept with his fathers;[1] and they buried[6912] him in Samaria: and [a]Joash his son reigned in his stead.

Jehoash Rules Israel

10 In the thirty and seventh year of Joash king of Judah began [I][a]Jehoash the son of Jehoahaz to reign over Israel in Samaria, *and reigned* sixteen years.

11 And he did *that which was* evil in the sight of the LORD; he departed not from all the sins of Jeroboam the son of Nebat, who made Israel sin: *but* he walked[1980] therein.

12 [a]And the rest of the acts of Joash, and [b]all that he did, and [c]his might wherewith he fought against Amaziah king of Judah, *are* they not written in the book of the chronicles of the kings of Israel?

13 And Joash slept with his fathers; and Jeroboam sat upon his throne: and Joash was buried in Samaria with the kings of Israel.

Elisha's Death

14 Now Elisha was fallen sick of his sickness whereof he died.[4191] And Joash the king of Israel came down unto him, and wept over his face, and said, O my father,[1] my father, [a]the chariot of Israel, and the horsemen thereof.

15 And Elisha said unto him, Take bow and arrows. And he took unto him bow and arrows.

16 And he said to the king of Israel, [I]Put thine hand upon the bow. And he put his hand *upon it:* and Elisha put his hands upon the king's hands.

17 And he said, Open the window eastward. And he opened *it.* Then Elisha said, Shoot. And he shot. And he said, The arrow of the LORD's deliverance,[8668] and the arrow of deliverance from Syria: for thou shalt smite the Syrians in [a]Aphek, till thou have consumed[3615] *them.*

18 And he said, Take the arrows. And he took *them.* And he said unto the king of Israel, Smite upon the ground.[776] And he smote thrice, and stayed.

19 And the man of God[430] was wroth[7107] with him, and said, Thou shouldest have smitten five or six times; then hadst thou smitten Syria till thou hadst consumed *it:* [a]whereas now thou shalt smite Syria *but* thrice.

20 And Elisha died, and they buried him. And the bands[1416] of the Moabites invaded the land at the coming in of the year.

21 And it came to pass, as they were burying[6912] a man, that, behold, they spied[7200] a band *of men;* and they cast the man into the sepulchre[6913] of Elisha: and when the man [I]was let down, and touched the bones[6106] of Elisha, he revived, and stood up on his feet.

---

3 [a]Judg. 2:14 [b]2Kgs. 8:12

4 [a]Ps. 78:34 [b]Ex. 3:7; 2Kgs. 14:26

5 [I]Hebr. *as yesterday,* and *third day* [a]2Kgs. 13:25; 14:25, 27

6 [I]Hebr. *he walked* [II]Hebr. *stood* [a]1Kgs. 16:33

7 [a]Amos 1:3

9 [a]2Kgs. 13:10, *Jehoash*

10 [I]Reigned in consort with his father [a]2Kgs. 14:1

12 [a]2Kgs. 14:15 [b]2Kgs. 13:14, 25 [c]2Kgs. 14:9; 2Chr. 25:17

14 [a]2Kgs. 2:12

16 [I]Hebr. *Make thine hand to ride*

17 [a]1Kgs. 20:26

19 [a]2Kgs. 13:25

21 [I]Hebr. *went down*

Wars With Syria

22 But [a]Hazael king of Syria oppressed Israel all the days of Jehoahaz.

23 [a]And the LORD was gracious[2603] unto them, and had compassion on them, and [b]had respect unto them, [c]because of his covenant[1285] with Abraham, Isaac, and Jacob, and would[14] not destroy[6] them, neither cast he them from his [I]presence as yet.

24 So Hazael king of Syria died; and Ben–hadad his son reigned in his stead.

25 And Jehoash the son of Jehoahaz [I]took again out of the hand of Ben–hadad the son of Hazael the cities, which he had taken out of the hand of Jehoahaz his father by war. [a]Three times did Joash beat[5221] him, and recovered the cities of Israel.

Amaziah Rules Judah

14 In [a]the second year of Joash son of Jehoahaz king[4428] of Israel reigned [b]Amaziah the son of Joash king of Judah.

2 He was twenty and five years old when he began to reign, and reigned twenty and nine years in Jerusalem. And his mother's name *was* Jehoaddan of Jerusalem.

3 And he did[6213] *that which was* right in the sight of the LORD, yet not like David his father:[1] he did according to all things as Joash his father did.

4 [a]Howbeit the high places were not taken away: as yet the people[5971] did sacrifice and burnt incense[6999] on the high places.

5 And it came to pass, as soon as the kingdom[4467] was confirmed[2388] in his hand, that he slew his servants [a]which had slain the king his father.

6 But the children[1121] of the murderers he slew not: according unto that which is written in the book[5612] of the law[8451] of Moses, wherein the LORD commanded,[6680] saying, [a]The fathers[1] shall not be put to death[4191] for the children, nor the children be put to death for the fathers; but every man shall be put to death for his own sin.

7 [a]He slew of Edom in [b]the valley of salt ten thousand, and took [I]Selah by war, [c]and called[7121] the name of it Joktheel unto this day.[3117]

8 [a]Then Amaziah sent messengers to Jehoash, the son of Jehoahaz son of Jehu, king of Israel, saying, Come, let us look one another in the face.

9 And Jehoash the king of Israel sent to Amaziah king of Judah, saying, [a]The thistle that *was* in Lebanon sent to the [b]cedar that *was* in Lebanon, saying, Give thy daughter to my son to wife: and there passed by[5674] a wild beast[2416] that *was* in Lebanon, and trode down the thistle.

10 Thou hast indeed smitten Edom, and [a]thine heart hath lifted thee up: glory[3513] *of this,* and tarry [I]at home: for why shouldest thou meddle to *thy* hurt, that thou shouldest fall, *even* thou, and Judah with thee?

11 But Amaziah would not hear. Therefore Jehoash king of Israel went up; and he and Amaziah king of Judah looked[7200] one another in the face at [a]Beth–shemesh, which *belongeth* to Judah.

12 And Judah [I]was put to the worse[5062] before Israel; and they fled every man to their tents.

13 And Jehoash king of Israel took Amaziah king of Judah, the son of Jehoash the son of Ahaziah, at Beth–shemesh, and came to Jerusalem, and brake down the wall of Jerusalem from [a]the gate of Ephraim unto [b]the corner gate, four hundred cubits.

14 And he took all [a]the gold and silver, and all the vessels that were found in the house of the LORD, and in the treasures of the king's[4428] house, and hostages, and returned to Samaria.

Jehoash's Death

15 [a]Now the rest of the acts[1697] of Jehoash which he did, and his might, and how he fought with Amaziah king of Judah, *are* they not written in the book of the chronicles of the kings of Israel?

---

22 [a]2Kgs. 8:12

23 [I]Hebr. *face* [a]2Kgs. 14:27 [b]Ex. 2:24, 25 [c]Ex. 32:13

25 [I]Hebr. *returned and took* [a]2Kgs. 13:18, 19

1 [a]2Kgs. 13:10 [b]2Chr. 25:1

4 [a]2Kgs. 12:3

5 [a]2Kgs. 12:20

6 [a]Deut. 24:16; Ezek. 18:4, 20

7 [I]Or, *The rock* [a]2Chr. 25:11 [b]2Sam. 8:13 [c]Josh. 15:38

8 [a]2Chr. 25:17, 18

9 [a]Judg. 9:8 [b]1Kgs. 4:33

10 [I]Hebr. *at thy house* [a]Deut. 8:14; 2Chr. 32:25; Ezek. 28:2-5, 17; Hab. 2:4

11 [a]Josh. 19:38; 21:16

12 [I]Hebr. *was smitten*

13 [a]Neh. 8:16; 12:39 [b]Jer. 31:38; Zech. 14:10

14 [a]1Kgs. 7:51

15 [a]2Kgs. 13:12

16 And Jehoash slept with his fathers, and was buried[6912] in Samaria with the kings of Israel; and Jeroboam his son reigned in his stead.

Amaziah's Death

17 [a]And Amaziah the son of Joash king of Judah lived[2421] after the death[4194] of Jehoash son of Jehoahaz king of Israel fifteen years.

18 And the rest of the acts of Amaziah, *are* they not written in the book of the chronicles of the kings of Judah?

19 Now [a]they made a conspiracy against him in Jerusalem: and he fled to Lachish; but they sent after him to [b]Lachish, and slew him there.

20 And they brought[5375] him on horses: and he was buried at Jerusalem with his fathers in the city of David.

21 And all the people of Judah took [a]Azariah, which *was* sixteen years old, and made him king[4427] instead of his father Amaziah.

22 He built [a]Elath, and restored it to Judah, after that the king slept with his fathers.

Jeroboam II Rules Israel

23 In the fifteenth year of Amaziah the son of Joash king of Judah Jeroboam the son of Joash king of Israel began to reign in Samaria, *and reigned* forty and one years.

24 And he did *that which was* evil[7451] in the sight of the LORD: he departed[5493] not from all the sins of Jeroboam the son of Nebat, who made Israel to sin.

25 He restored the coast of Israel [a]from the entering of Hamath unto [b]the sea of the plain,[6160] according to the word of the LORD God of Israel, which he spake by the hand of his servant [c]Jonah, the son of Amittai, the prophet, which *was* of [d]Gath–hepher.

26 For the LORD [a]saw the affliction of Israel, *that it was* very bitter:[4784] for [b]*there was* not any shut up,[6113] nor any left,[5800] nor any helper for Israel.

27 [a]And the LORD said not that he would blot out[4229] the name of Israel from under heaven: but he saved them by the hand of Jeroboam the son of Joash.

28 Now the rest of the acts of Jeroboam, and all that he did, and his might, how he warred, and how he recovered Damascus, and Hamath, [a]*which belonged* to Judah, for Israel, *are* they not written in the book of the chronicles of the kings of Israel?

29 And Jeroboam slept with his fathers, *even* with the kings of Israel; and [a]Zachariah his son reigned in his stead.

Azariah Rules Judah

15 In the twenty and seventh year of Jeroboam king[4428] of Israel [a]began [b]Azariah son of Amaziah king of Judah to reign.

2 Sixteen years old was he when he began to reign, and he reigned two and fifty years in Jerusalem. And his mother's name *was* Jecholiah of Jerusalem.

3 And he did[6213] *that which was* right[3477] in the sight of the LORD, according to all that his father[1] Amaziah had done;

4 [a]Save that the high places were not removed: the people[5971] sacrificed and burnt incense[6999] still on the high places.

5 And the LORD [a]smote the king, so that he was a leper unto the day[3117] of his death,[4194] and [b]dwelt in a several house. And Jotham the king's son *was* over the house, judging[8199] the people of the land.

6 And the rest of the acts[1697] of Azariah, and all that he did, *are* they not written in the book[5612] of the chronicles of the kings of Judah?

7 So Azariah slept with his fathers;[1] and [a]they buried[6912] him with his fathers in the city of David: and Jotham his son reigned in his stead.

Zachariah Rules Israel

8 In the thirty and eighth year of Azariah king of Judah did Zachariah the

17 [a]2Chr. 25:25
19 [a]2Chr. 25:27 [b]Josh. 10:31
21 [a]2Kgs. 15:13; 2Chr. 26:1, *Uzziah*
22 [a]2Kgs. 16:6; 2Chr. 26:2
25 [a]Num. 13:21; 34:8 [b]Deut. 3:17 [c]Jon. 1:1; Matt. 12:39, 40, called *Jonas* [d]Josh. 19:13
26 [a]2Kgs. 13:4 [b]Deut. 32:36
27 [a]2Kgs. 13:5
28 [a]2Sam. 8:6; 1Kgs. 11:24; 2Chr. 8:3
29 [a]2Kgs. 15:8
1 [a]2Kgs. 14:21; 2Chr. 26:1, 3, 4 [b]2Kgs. 15:13, 30; 2Chr. 26:1, *Uzziah*
4 [a]2Kgs. 12:3; 14:4; 15:35
5 [a]2Chr. 26:19-21 [b]Lev. 13:46
7 [a]2Chr. 26:23

son of Jeroboam reign over Israel in Samaria six months.

9 And he did *that which was* evil[7451] in the sight of the LORD, as his fathers had done: he departed[5493] not from the sins of Jeroboam the son of Nebat, who made Israel to sin.

10 And Shallum the son of Jabesh conspired against him, and [a]smote him before the people, and slew him, and reigned in his stead.

11 And the rest of the acts of Zachariah, behold, they *are* written in the book of the chronicles of the kings of Israel.

12 This *was* [a]the word[1697] of the LORD which he spake unto Jehu, saying, Thy sons shall sit on the throne of Israel unto the fourth *generation.* And so it came to pass.

Shallum Rules Israel

13 Shallum the son of Jabesh began to reign in the nine and thirtieth year of [a]Uzziah king of Judah; and he reigned [I]a full month in Samaria.

14 For Menahem the son of Gadi went up from [a]Tirzah, and came to Samaria, and smote Shallum the son of Jabesh in Samaria, and slew him, and reigned in his stead.

15 And the rest of the acts of Shallum, and his conspiracy which he made, behold, they *are* written in the book of the chronicles of the kings of Israel.

16 Then Menahem smote [a]Tiphsah, and all that *were* therein, and the coasts thereof from Tirzah: because they opened not *to him,* therefore he smote *it; and* all [b]the women therein that were with child he ripped up.[1234]

Menahem Rules Israel

17 In the nine and thirtieth year of Azariah king of Judah began Menahem the son of Gadi to reign over Israel, *and reigned* ten years in Samaria.

18 And he did *that which was* evil in the sight of the LORD: he departed

10 [a]Amos 7:9
12 [a]2Kgs. 10:30
13 [I]Hebr. *a month of days* [a]2Kgs. 15:1; Matt. 1:8, 9
14 [a]1Kgs. 14:17
16 [a]1Kgs. 4:24 [b]2Kgs. 8:12
19 [a]1Chr. 5:26; Isa. 9:1; Hos. 8:9 [b]2Kgs. 14:5
20 [I]Hebr. *caused to come forth*
27 [a]Isa. 7:1

not all his days[3117] from the sins of Jeroboam the son of Nebat, who made Israel to sin.

19 *And* [a]Pul the king of Assyria came against the land: and Menahem gave Pul a thousand talents of silver, that his hand might be with him to [b]confirm[2388] the kingdom[4467] in his hand.

20 And Menahem [I]exacted[2318] the money of Israel, *even* of all the mighty men of wealth,[2428] of each man fifty shekels of silver, to give to the king of Assyria. So the king of Assyria turned back, and stayed not there in the land.

21 And the rest of the acts[1697] of Menahem, and all that he did, *are* they not written in the book of the chronicles of the kings of Israel?

22 And Menahem slept with his fathers; and Pekahiah his son reigned in his stead.

Pekahiah Rules Israel

23 In the fiftieth year of Azariah king of Judah Pekahiah the son of Menahem began to reign over Israel in Samaria, *and reigned* two years.

24 And he did *that which was* evil in the sight of the LORD: he departed not from the sins of Jeroboam the son of Nebat, who made Israel to sin.

25 But Pekah the son of Remaliah, a captain[7791] of his, conspired against him, and smote him in Samaria, in the palace[759] of the king's house, with Argob and Arieh, and with him fifty men of the Gileadites: and he killed[4191] him, and reigned in his room.

26 And the rest of the acts of Pekahiah, and all that he did, behold, they *are* written in the book of the chronicles of the kings of Israel.

Pekah Rules Israel

27 In the two and fiftieth year of Azariah king of Judah [a]Pekah the son of Remaliah began to reign over Israel in Samaria, *and reigned* twenty years.

28 And he did *that which was* evil in the sight of the LORD: he departed not

from the sins of Jeroboam the son of Nebat, who made Israel to sin.

29 In the days of Pekah king of Israel [a]came Tiglath–pileser king of Assyria, and took [b]Ijon, and Abel–beth–maachah, and Janoah, and Kedesh, and Hazor, and Gilead, and Galilee, all the land of Naphtali, and carried them captive[1540] to Assyria.

30 And Hoshea the son of Elah made a conspiracy against Pekah the son of Remaliah, and smote him, and slew him, and [a]reigned in his stead, in the twentieth year of Jotham the son of Uzziah.

31 And the rest of the acts of Pekah, and all that he did, behold, they *are* written in the book of the chronicles of the kings of Israel.

Jotham Rules Judah

32 In the second year of Pekah the son of Remaliah king of Israel began [a]Jotham the son of Uzziah king of Judah to reign.

33 Five and twenty years old was he when he began to reign, and he reigned sixteen years in Jerusalem. And his mother's name *was* Jerusha, the daughter of Zadok.

34 And he did *that which was* right[3477] in the sight of the LORD: he did [a]according to all that his father Uzziah had done.

35 [a]Howbeit the high places were not removed: the people sacrificed and burned incense[6999] still in the high places. [b]He built the higher gate of the house of the LORD.[3068]

36 Now the rest of the acts of Jotham, and all that he did, *are* they not written in the book of the chronicles of the kings of Judah?

37 In those days the LORD began to send against Judah [a]Rezin the king of Syria, and [b]Pekah the son of Remaliah.

38 And Jotham slept with his fathers, and was buried with his fathers in the city of David his father: and Ahaz his son reigned in his stead.

Ahaz Rules Judah

16 In the seventeenth year of Pekah the son of Remaliah [a]Ahaz the son of Jotham king[4428] of Judah began to reign.

2 Twenty years old *was* Ahaz when he began to reign, and reigned sixteen years in Jerusalem, and did[6213] not *that which was* right in the sight of the LORD his God,[430] like David his father.[1]

3 But he walked in the way[1870] of the kings of Israel, yea, [a]and made his son to pass through the fire, according to the [b]abominations[8441] of the heathen, whom the LORD cast out[2423] from before the children[1121] of Israel.

4 And he sacrificed and burnt incense[6999] in the high places, and [a]on the hills, and under every green tree.

5 [a]Then Rezin king of Syria and Pekah son of Remaliah king of Israel came up to Jerusalem to war: and they besieged Ahaz, but could not overcome *him*.

6 At that time Rezin king of Syria [a]recovered Elath to Syria, and drave[5394] the Jews from [1]Elath: and the Syrians came to Elath, and dwelt there unto this day.[3117]

29 [a]1Chr. 5:26; Isa. 9:1 [b]1Kgs. 15:20
30 [a]2Kgs. 17:1; Hos. 10:3, 7, 15
32 [a]2Chr. 27:1
34 [a]2Kgs. 15:3
35 [a]2Kgs. 15:4 [b]2Chr. 27:3
37 [a]2Kgs. 16:5; Isa. 7:1 [b]2Kgs. 15:27
1 [a]2Chr. 28:1
3 [a]Lev. 18:21; 2Chr. 28:3; Ps. 106:37, 38 [b]Deut. 12:31
4 [a]Deut. 12:2; 1Kgs. 14:23
5 [a]Isa. 7:1, 4
6 [1]Hebr. *Eloth* [a]2Kgs. 14:22

15:29, 30 See notes on Isaiah 7:14 and Hosea 8:8, 9 concerning Assyria's conquests.

16:3 See note on Leviticus 18:21 concerning child sacrifice.

16:5–9 See notes on Isaiah 7:14 and Hosea 8:8, 9 concerning Assyria's conquests.

16:6 In the modern order of the Old Testament Scriptures, the word "Jews" appears for the first time here. The term is derived from the name "Judah" and applied to all members of the tribe bearing his name. It was also used for all subjects of the kingdom of Judah in contrast to the kingdom made up of the ten tribes who seceded. These ten tribes retained the name "Israelites." After the Babylonian Captivity, the name "Jew" seems to have been applied indiscriminately to the whole race of Israelites.

7 So Ahaz sent messengers [a]to Tiglath–pileser king of Assyria, saying, I *am* thy servant and thy son: come up, and save me out of the hand of the king of Syria, and out of the hand of the king of Israel, which rise up against me.

8 And Ahaz [a]took the silver and gold that was found in the house of the LORD, and in the treasures of the king's[4428] house, and sent *it for* a present to the king of Assyria.

9 And the king of Assyria hearkened unto him: for the king of Assyria went up against [I]Damascus, and [a]took it, and carried *the people of* it captive[1540] to Kir, and slew Rezin.

10 And king Ahaz went to Damascus to meet Tiglath–pileser king of Assyria, and saw an altar[4196] that *was* at Damascus: and king Ahaz sent to Urijah the priest the fashion[1823] of the altar, and the pattern[8403] of it, according to all the workmanship thereof.

11 And Urijah the priest built an altar according to all that king Ahaz had sent from Damascus: so Urijah the priest made *it* against king Ahaz came from Damascus.

12 And when the king was come from Damascus, the king saw the altar: and the [a]king approached[7126] to the altar, and offered thereon.

13 And he burnt his burnt offering and his meat offering, and poured[5258] his drink offering,[5262] and sprinkled the blood[1818] of [I]his peace offerings, upon the altar.

14 And he brought[7126] also [a]the brasen altar, which *was* before the LORD, from the forefront of the house, from between the altar and the house of the LORD, and put it on the north side of the altar.

15 And king Ahaz commanded[6680] Urijah the priest, saying, Upon the great altar burn[6999] [a]the morning burnt offering, and the evening meat offering,[4503] and the king's burnt sacrifice,[5930] and his meat offering, with the burnt offering of all the people[5971] of the land, and their meat offering, and their drink offerings; and sprinkle upon it all the blood of the burnt offering, and all the blood of the sacrifice: and the brasen altar shall be for me to enquire[1239] *by.*

16 Thus did Urijah the priest, according to all that king Ahaz commanded.

17 [a]And king Ahaz cut off [b]the borders of the bases, and removed the laver[3595] from off them; and took down [c]the sea from off the brasen oxen that *were* under it, and put it upon a pavement of stones.

18 And the covert[4329] for the sabbath that they had built in the house, and the king's entry without, turned he from the house of the LORD for the king of Assyria.

19 Now the rest of the acts[1697] of Ahaz which he did, *are* they not written in the book[5612] of the chronicles of the kings of Judah?

20 And Ahaz slept with his fathers,[1] and [a]was buried[6912] with his fathers in the city of David: and Hezekiah his son reigned in his stead.

Hoshea Rules Israel

17 In the twelfth year of Ahaz king[4428] of Judah began [a]Hoshea the son of Elah to reign in Samaria over Israel nine years.

2 And he did[6213] *that which was* evil[7451] in the sight of the LORD, but not as the kings of Israel that were before him.

3 Against him came up [a]Shalmaneser king of Assyria; and Hoshea became his servant, and [I]gave him [II]presents.[4503]

4 And the king of Assyria found conspiracy in Hoshea: for he had sent messengers to So king of Egypt, and brought[5927] no present to the king of Assyria, as *he had done* year by year: therefore the king of Assyria shut him up, and bound him in prison.

5 Then [a]the king of Assyria came up throughout all the land, and went up to Samaria, and besieged it three years.

---

7 [a]2Kgs. 15:29
8 [a]2Kgs. 12:18; 2Chr. 28:21
9 [I]Hebr. *Dammesek* [a]Amos 1:5
12 [a]2Chr. 26:16, 19
13 [I]Hebr. *which were his*
14 [a]2Chr. 4:1
15 [a]Ex. 29:39-41
17 [a]2Chr. 28:24 [b]1Kgs. 7:27, 28 [c]1Kgs. 7:23, 25
20 [a]2Chr. 28:27
1 [a]2Kgs. 15:30
3 [I]Hebr. *rendered* [II]Or, *tribute* [a]2Kgs. 18:9
5 [a]2Kgs. 18:9

🗝 6 [a]In the ninth year of Hoshea the
king of Assyria took Samaria, and
[b]carried Israel away into Assyria, [c]and
placed them in Halah and in Habor *by* the
river of Gozan, and in the cities of the
Medes.

The Reasons for Samaria's Fall and Exile

7 For *so* it was, that the children[1121]
of Israel had sinned against the LORD
their God,[430] which had brought them up
out of the land of Egypt, from under the
hand of Pharaoh king of Egypt, and had
feared[3372] other gods,[430]
8 And [a]walked in the statutes of the
heathen,[1471] whom the LORD cast out
from before the children of Israel, and of
the kings of Israel, which they had made.
9 And the children of Israel did
secretly[2644] *those* things that *were* not
right against the LORD their God, and
they built them high places in all their
cities, [a]from the tower of the watchmen[5341] to the fenced city.
10 [a]And they set them up [I]images[4676]
and [b]groves[842] [c]in every high hill, and
under every green tree:
11 And there they burnt incense[6999]
in all the high places, as *did* the heathen
whom the LORD carried away before
them; and wrought wicked[7451] things to
provoke the LORD to anger:[3707]
12 For they served idols,[1544] [a]whereof
the LORD had said unto them, [b]Ye shall
not do[6213] this thing.
13 Yet the LORD testified[5749] against
Israel, and against Judah, [I]by all the
prophets, *and by* all [a]the seers, saying,
[b]Turn ye from your evil ways,[1870] and
keep[8104] my commandments[4687] *and* my
statutes, according to all the law[8451]
which I commanded[4687] your fathers,[1]
and which I sent to you by my servants
the prophets.
14 Notwithstanding they would not
hear, but [a]hardened their necks, like to
the neck of their fathers, that did not
believe[539] in the LORD their God.
15 And they rejected[3988] his statutes,
[a]and his covenant[1285] that he made with
their fathers, and his testimonies which
he testified against them; and they followed [b]vanity, and [c]became vain,[1891] and
went after the heathen that *were* round
about them, *concerning* whom the LORD
had charged[6680] them, that they should
[d]not do like them.
16 And they left[5800] all the commandments of the LORD their God, and
[a]made them molten images, *even* two
calves, [b]and made a grove,[842] and
worshipped[7812] all the host of heaven,
[c]and served Baal.
17 [a]And they caused their sons and
their daughters to pass through the fire,
and [b]used[7080] divination[7081] and
enchantments,[5172] and [c]sold themselves
to do evil in the sight of the LORD, to provoke him to anger.
18 Therefore the LORD was very
angry[559] with Israel, and removed them
out of his sight: there was none left[7604]
[a]but the tribe of Judah only.
19 Also [a]Judah kept[8104] not the commandments of the LORD their God, but
walked in the statutes of Israel which
they made.
20 And the LORD rejected all the seed
of Israel, and afflicted them, and [a]deliv-
ered them into the hand of spoilers, until
he had cast them out of his sight.
21 For [a]he rent Israel from the house
of David; and [b]they made Jeroboam the
son of Nebat king:[4427] and Jeroboam

6 [a]2Kgs. 18:10, 11; Hos. 13:16 [b]Lev. 26:32, 33; Deut. 28:36, 64; 29:27, 28 [c]1Chr. 5:26
8 [a]Lev. 18:3; Deut. 18:9; 2Kgs. 16:3
9 [a]2Kgs. 18:8
10 [I]Hebr. *statues* [a]1Kgs. 14:23; Isa. 57:5 [b]Ex. 34:13; Deut. 16:21; Mic. 5:14 [c]Deut. 12:2; 2Kgs. 16:4
12 [a]Ex. 20:3, 4; Lev. 26:1; Deut. 5:7, 8 [b]Deut. 4:19
13 [I]Hebr. *by the hand of all* [a]1Sam. 9:9 [b]Jer. 18:11; 25:5; 35:15
14 [a]Deut. 31:27; Prov. 29:1
15 [a]Deut. 29:25 [b]Deut. 32:21; 1Kgs. 16:13; 1Cor. 8:4 [c]Ps. 115:8; Rom. 1:21 [d]Deut. 12:30, 31
16 [a]Ex. 32:8; 1Kgs. 12:28 [b]1Kgs. 14:15, 23; 15:13; 16:33 [c]1Kgs. 16:31; 22:53; 2Kgs. 11:18
17 [a]Lev. 18:21; 2Kgs. 16:3; Ezek. 23:37 [b]Deut. 18:10 [c]1Kgs. 21:20
18 [a]1Kgs. 11:13, 32
19 [a]Jer. 3:8
20 [a]2Kgs. 13:3; 15:29
21 [a]1Kgs. 11:11, 31 [b]1Kgs. 12:20, 28

🗝 **17:6–18** In 722 or 721 B.C., the Northern Kingdom of Israel fell to Assyria. Shalmaneser V began the attack but died before it was completed, so Israel fell to Sargon II who took the inhabitants captive. Verses seven through eighteen give a list of all the ways that Israel was unfaithful to the Lord. Hosea prophesied that, as a punishment from God for their breaking of His covenant, the northern tribes would not return to the land (Hos. 9:3). However, they were promised restoration to the land after God had finished punishing them (Zech. 10:6, 10). See Ezekiel 48:1–7, 25–28 for future allotments of land to the tribes of the Northern Kingdom.

drave[5077] Israel from following the LORD, and made them sin a great sin.

22 For the children of Israel walked in all the sins of Jeroboam which he did; they departed[5493] not from them;

23 Until the LORD removed Israel out of his sight, [a]as he had said by all his servants the prophets. [b]So was Israel carried away out of their own land[127] to Assyria unto this day.[3117]

Assyria Settles Foreigners In Israel

24 [a]And the king of Assyria brought *men* [b]from Babylon, and from Cuthah, and from [c]Ava, and from Hamath, and from Sepharvaim, and placed[3427] *them* in the cities of Samaria instead of the children of Israel: and they possessed[3423] Samaria, and dwelt in the cities thereof.

25 And *so* it was at the beginning of their dwelling there, *that* they feared not the LORD: therefore the LORD sent lions among them, which slew *some* of them.

26 Wherefore they spake to the king of Assyria, saying, The nations[1471] which thou hast removed, and placed in the cities of Samaria, know[3045] not the manner[4941] of the God of the land: therefore he hath sent lions among them, and, behold, they slay them, because they know not the manner of the God of the land.

27 Then the king of Assyria commanded, saying, Carry thither one of the priests whom ye brought from thence; and let them go and dwell there, and let him teach[3384] them the manner of the God of the land.

28 Then one of the priests whom they had carried away from Samaria came and dwelt in Bethel, and taught them how they should fear[3372] the LORD.[3068]

29 Howbeit every nation[1471] made gods of their own, and put *them* in the houses of the high places which the Samaritans had made, every nation in their cities wherein they dwelt.

30 And the men of [a]Babylon made Succoth–benoth, and the men of Cuth made Nergal, and the men of Hamath made Ashima,

31 [a]And the Avites made Nibhaz and Tartak, and the Sepharvites [b]burnt[8313] their children in fire to Adrammelech and Anammelech, the gods of Sepharvaim.

32 So they feared[3373] the LORD, [a]and made unto themselves of the lowest of them priests of the high places, which sacrificed for them in the houses of the high places.

33 [a]They feared the LORD, and served their own gods, after the manner of the nations [I]whom they carried away from thence.

34 Unto this day they do after the former[7223] manners: they fear[3373] not the LORD, neither do they after their statutes, or after their ordinances, or after the law and commandment[4687] which the LORD commanded the children of Jacob, [a]whom he named Israel;

35 With whom the LORD had made a covenant, and charged them, saying, [a]Ye shall not fear other gods, nor [b]bow yourselves[7812] to them, nor serve them, nor sacrifice to them:

36 But the LORD, who brought you up out of the land of Egypt with great power and [a]a stretched out arm, [b]him shall ye fear, and him shall ye worship,[7812] and to him shall ye do sacrifice.

37 And the statutes, and the ordinances,[4941] and the law, and the commandment, which he wrote for you, [a]ye shall observe to do for evermore; and ye shall not fear other gods.

38 And the covenant that I have made with you [a]ye shall not forget; neither shall ye fear other gods.

39 But the LORD your God ye shall fear; and he shall deliver[5337] you out of the hand of all your enemies.

40 Howbeit they did not hearken, but they did[6213] after their former manner.

41 [a]So these nations feared the LORD, and served their graven images,[6456] both their children, and their children's children: as did their fathers, so do they unto this day.

---

23 [a]1Kgs. 14:16 [b]2Kgs. 17:6
24 [a]Ezra 4:2, 10 [b]2Kgs. 17:30 [c]2Kgs. 18:34, *Ivah*
30 [a]2Kgs. 17:24
31 [a]Ezra 4:9 [b]Lev. 18:21; Deut. 12:31
32 [a]1Kgs. 12:31
33 [I]Or, *who carried them away from thence* [a]Zeph. 1:5
34 [a]Gen. 32:28; 35:10; 1Kgs. 11:31
35 [a]Judg. 6:10 [b]Ex. 20:5
36 [a]Ex. 6:6 [b]Deut. 10:20
37 [a]Deut. 5:32
38 [a]Deut. 4:23
41 [a]2Kgs. 17:32, 33

Hezekiah Rules Judah

18 Now it came to pass in the third year of Hoshea son of Elah king[4428] of Israel, *that* [a]Hezekiah the son of Ahaz king of Judah began to reign.

2 Twenty and five years old was he when he began to reign; and he reigned twenty and nine years in Jerusalem. His mother's name also *was* [a]Abi, the daughter of Zachariah.

3 And he did[6213] *that which was* right in the sight of the LORD, according to all that David his father[1] did.

4 [a]He removed the high places, and brake the [I]images,[4676] and cut down[3772] the groves,[842] and brake in pieces the [b]brasen serpent that Moses had made: for unto those days the children of Israel did burn incense[6999] to it: and he called[7121] it [II]Nehushtan.

5 He [a]trusted in the LORD God[430] of Israel; [b]so that after him was none like him among all the kings of Judah, nor *any* that were before him.

6 For he [a]clave to the LORD, *and* departed[5493] not [I]from following him, but kept[8104] his commandments,[4687] which the LORD commanded[6680] Moses.

7 And the LORD [a]was with him; *and* he [b]prospered[7919] whithersoever he went forth: and he [c]rebelled against the king of Assyria, and served him not.

8 [a]He smote the Philistines, *even* unto [I]Gaza, and the borders thereof, [b]from the tower of the watchmen[5341] to the fenced city.

9 And [a]it came to pass in the fourth year of king Hezekiah, which *was* the seventh year of Hoshea son of Elah king of Israel, *that* Shalmaneser king of Assyria came up against Samaria, and besieged it.

10 And at the end of three years they took[3920] it: *even* in the sixth year of Hezekiah, that *is* [a]the ninth year of Hoshea king of Israel, Samaria was taken.

11 [a]And the king of Assyria did carry away[1540] Israel unto Assyria, and put them [b]in Halah and in Habor *by* the river of Gozan, and in the cities of the Medes:

12 [a]Because they obeyed not the voice of the LORD their God, but transgressed his covenant,[1285] *and* all that Moses the servant of the LORD commanded, and would not hear *them,* nor do[6213] *them.*

Sennacherib Threatens Jerusalem

13 Now [a]in the fourteenth year of king Hezekiah did [I]Sennacherib king of Assyria come up against all the fenced[1219] cities of Judah, and took them.

14 And Hezekiah king of Judah sent to the king of Assyria to Lachish, saying, I have offended;[2398] return from me: that which thou puttest on me will I bear.[5375] And the king of Assyria appointed[7760] unto Hezekiah king of Judah three hundred talents of silver and thirty talents of gold.

15 And Hezekiah [a]gave *him* all the silver that was found in the house of the LORD, and in the treasures of the king's[4428] house.

16 At that time did Hezekiah cut off *the gold from* the doors of the temple of the LORD, and *from* the pillars which Hezekiah king of Judah had overlaid, and gave [I]it to the king of Assyria.

17 And the king of Assyria sent Tartan and Rab–saris and Rab–shakeh from Lachish to king Hezekiah with a [I]great host against Jerusalem. And they went up and came to Jerusalem. And when they were come up, they came and stood by the conduit of the upper[5945] pool, [a]which *is* in the highway of the fuller's[3526] field.[7704]

18 And when they had called to the king, there came out to them Eliakim the son of Hilkiah, which *was* over the household, and Shebna the [I]scribe, and Joah the son of Asaph the recorder.

19 And Rab–shakeh said unto them, Speak ye now to Hezekiah, Thus saith the great king, the king of Assyria, [a]What confidence[986] *is* this wherein thou trustest?

1 [a]2Chr. 28:27; 29:1

2 [a]2Chr. 29:1, *Abijah*

4 [I]Hebr. *statues* [II]That is, *A piece of brass* [a]2Chr. 31:1 [b]Num. 21:9

5 [a]2Kgs. 19:10; Job 13:15; Ps. 13:5 [b]2Kgs. 23:25

6 [I]Hebr. *from after him* [a]Deut. 10:20; Josh. 23:8

7 [a]2Chr. 15:2 [b]1Sam. 18:5, 14; Ps. 60:12 [c]2Kgs. 16:7

8 [I]Hebr. *Azzah* [a]1Chr. 4:41; Isa. 14:29 [b]2Kgs. 17:9

9 [a]2Kgs. 17:3

10 [a]2Kgs. 17:6

11 [a]2Kgs. 17:6 [b]1Chr. 5:26

12 [a]2Kgs. 17:7; Dan. 9:6, 10

13 [I]Hebr. *Sanherib* [a]2Chr. 32:1; Isa. 36:1

15 [a]2Kgs. 16:8

16 [I]Hebr. *them*

17 [I]Hebr. *heavy* [a]Isa. 7:3

18 [I]Or, *secretary*

19 [a]2Chr. 32:10

20 Thou [I]sayest, (but *they are but* [II]vain[8193] words,[1697]) [III]*I have* counsel[6098] and strength for the war. Now on whom dost thou trust, that thou rebellest against me?

21 [a]Now, behold, thou [I]trustest upon the staff of this bruised7533 reed, *even* upon Egypt, on which if a man lean, it will go into his hand, and pierce[5344] it: so *is* Pharaoh king of Egypt unto all that trust on him.

🗝 22 But if ye say unto me, We trust in the LORD[3068] our God: *is* not that he, [a]whose high places and whose altars[4196] Hezekiah hath taken away, and hath said to Judah and Jerusalem, Ye shall worship[7812] before this altar in Jerusalem?

23 Now therefore, I pray thee, give [I]pledges[6148] to my lord[113] the king of Assyria, and I will deliver thee two thousand horses, if thou be able on thy part to set riders upon them.

24 How then wilt thou turn away the face of one captain[6346] of the least of my master's servants, and put thy trust on Egypt for chariots and for horsemen?

25 Am I now come up without the LORD against this place to destroy[7843] it? The LORD said to me, Go up against this land, and destroy it.

26 Then said Eliakim the son of Hilkiah, and Shebna, and Joah, unto Rab–shakeh, Speak, I pray thee, to thy servants in the Syrian language; for we understand[8085] *it*: and talk not with us in the Jews' language in the ears[241] of the people[5971] that *are* on the wall.

27 But Rab–shakeh said unto them, Hath my master sent me to thy master, and to thee, to speak these words? *hath he* not *sent me* to the men which sit on the wall, that they may eat their own dung, and drink [I]their own piss with you?

28 Then Rab–shakeh stood and cried[7121] with a loud voice in the Jews' language, and spake, saying, Hear the word[1697] of the great king, the king of Assyria:

29 Thus saith the king, [a]Let not Hezekiah deceive you: for he shall not be able to deliver[5337] you out of his hand:

30 Neither let Hezekiah make you trust in the LORD, saying, The LORD will surely deliver us, and this city shall not be delivered into the hand of the king of Assyria.

31 Hearken not to Hezekiah: for thus saith the king of Assyria, [I]Make *an agreement* with me by a present,[1293] and come out to me, and *then* eat ye every man of his own vine, and every one of his fig tree, and drink ye every one the waters of his [II]cistern:[953]

32 Until I come and take you away to a land like your own land, a land of corn and wine, [a]a land of bread and vineyards, a land of oil olive and of honey, that ye may live,[2421] and not die:[4191] and hearken not unto Hezekiah, when he [I]persuadeth5496 you, saying, The LORD will deliver us.

33 [a]Hath any of the gods[430] of the nations[1471] delivered[5337] at all his land out of the hand of the king of Assyria?

34 [a]Where *are* the gods of Hamath, and of Arpad? where *are* the gods of Sepharvaim, Hena, and [b]Ivah? have they delivered Samaria out of mine hand?

35 Who *are* they among all the gods of the countries,[776] that have delivered their country out of mine hand, [a]that the LORD should deliver Jerusalem out of mine hand?

36 But the people held their peace,2790 and answered him not a word: for the king's commandment[4687] was, saying, Answer him not.

37 Then came Eliakim the son of Hilkiah, which *was* over the household, and Shebna the scribe, and Joah the son of Asaph the recorder, to Hezekiah [a]with *their* clothes rent, and told him the words of Rab–shakeh.

20 [I]Or, *talkest* [II]Hebr. *word of the lips* [III]Or, *But counsel and strength are for the war*

21 [I]Hebr. *trustest thee* [a]Ezek. 29:6, 7

22 [a]2Kgs. 18:4; 2Chr. 31:1; 32:12

23 [I]Or, *hostages*

27 [I]Hebr. *the water of their feet*

29 [a]2Chr. 32:15

31 [I]Or, *Seek my favor;* Hebr. *Make with me a blessing* [II]Or, *pit*

32 [I]Or, *deceiveth* [a]Deut. 8:7, 8

33 [a]2Kgs. 19:12; 2Chr. 32:14; Isa. 10:10, 11

34 [a]2Kgs. 19:13 [b]2Kgs. 17:24, *Ava*

35 [a]Dan. 3:15

37 [a]Isa. 33:7

🗝 **18:22** This was a false statement by Rabshakeh. Hezekiah had destroyed the Canaanite high places and altars in order to honor the true God.

Isaiah Reassures Hezekiah

19 ⚿ And [a]it came to pass, when king[4428] Hezekiah heard *it,* that he rent his clothes, and covered[3680] himself with sackcloth, and went into the house of the LORD.

2 And he sent Eliakim, which *was* over the household, and Shebna the scribe, and the elders[2205] of the priests, covered with sackcloth, to [a]Isaiah the prophet the son of Amoz.

3 And they said unto him, Thus saith Hezekiah, This day[3117] *is* a day of trouble, and of rebuke, and [I]blasphemy:[5007] for the children[1121] are come to the birth, and *there is* not strength to bring forth.

4 [a]It may be the LORD thy God[430] will hear all the words of Rab–shakeh, [b]whom the king of Assyria his master hath sent to reproach the living[2416] God; and will [c]reprove the words which the LORD thy God hath heard: wherefore lift up *thy* prayer[8605] for the remnant that are [I]left.

5 So the servants of king Hezekiah came to Isaiah.

6 [a]And Isaiah said unto them, Thus shall ye say to your master, Thus saith the LORD, Be not afraid[3372] of the words which thou hast heard, with which the [b]servants of the king of Assyria have blasphemed[1442] me.

7 Behold, I will send [a]a blast[7307] upon him, and he shall hear a rumour,[8052] and shall return to his own land; and I will cause him to fall by the sword in his own land.

Sennacherib Threatens Again

8 So Rab–shakeh returned, and found the king of Assyria warring against Libnah: for he had heard that he was departed [a]from Lachish.

9 And [a]when he heard say of Tirhakah king of Ethiopia, Behold, he is come out to fight against thee: he sent messengers again unto Hezekiah, saying,

10 Thus shall ye speak to Hezekiah king of Judah, saying, Let not thy God [a]in whom thou trustest deceive[5377] thee, saying, Jerusalem shall not be delivered into the hand of the king of Assyria.

11 Behold, thou hast heard what the kings of Assyria have done[6213] to all lands, by destroying them utterly:[2763] and shalt thou be delivered?[5337]

12 [a]Have the gods[430] of the nations[1471] delivered them which my fathers[1] have destroyed; *as* Gozan, and Haran, and Rezeph, and the children of [b]Eden which *were* in Thelasar?

13 [a]Where *is* the king of Hamath, and the king of Arpad, and the king of the city of Sepharvaim, of Hena, and Ivah?

14 [a]And Hezekiah received the letter[5612] of the hand of the messengers, and read it: and Hezekiah went up into the house of the LORD, and spread it before the LORD.

15 And Hezekiah prayed[6419] before the LORD, and said, O LORD God of Israel, [a]which dwellest *between* the cherubims,[3742] [b]thou art the God, *even* thou alone, of all the kingdoms[4467] of the earth; thou hast made heaven and earth.[776]

16 LORD, [a]bow down thine ear,[241] and hear: [b]open, LORD, thine eyes, and see: and hear the words of Sennacherib, [c]which hath sent him to reproach[2778] the living God.

17 Of a truth, LORD, the kings of Assyria have destroyed[2717] the nations and their lands,

18 And have [I]cast their gods into the fire: for they *were* no gods, but [a]the work

1 [a]Isa. 37:1
2 [a]Luke 3:4, *Ezaias*
3 [I]Or, *provocation*
4 [I]Hebr. *found* [a]2Sam. 16:12 [b]2Kgs. 18:35 [c]Ps. 50:21
6 [a]Isa. 37:6 [b]2Kgs. 18:17
7 [a]2Kgs. 19:35-37; Jer. 51:1
8 [a]2Kgs. 18:14
9 [a]1Sam. 23:27
10 [a]2Kgs. 18:5
12 [a]2Kgs. 18:33 [b]Ezek. 27:23
13 [a]2Kgs. 18:34
14 [a]Isa. 37:14
15 [a]1Sam. 4:4; Ps. 80:1 [b]1Kgs. 18:39; Isa. 44:6; Jer. 10:10-12
16 [a]Ps. 31:2 [b]2Chr. 6:40 [c]2Kgs. 19:16
18 [I]Hebr. *given* [a]Ps. 115:4; Jer. 10:3

⚿ **19:1–37** This passage is virtually identical to Isaiah 37:1–38. They are repeated to emphasize a different idea in each context. The passage in Isaiah marks the transition from Assyrian prominence (Is. 8:7; 20:1–6) to Babylonian supremacy (Is. 39:5–7). Here, the passage illustrates God's miraculous intervention on Judah's behalf (cf. 2 Kgs. 7:5–7).

of men's hands, wood and stone: therefore they have destroyed[6] them.
19 Now therefore, O LORD our God, I
beseech thee,[4994] save thou us out of his
hand, [a]that all the kingdoms of the earth
may know[3045] that thou *art* the LORD
God, *even* thou only.

Isaiah's Prophecy Against Assyria

20 Then Isaiah the son of Amoz sent
to Hezekiah, saying, Thus saith the LORD
God of Israel, [a]*That* which thou hast
prayed to me against Sennacherib king of
Assyria [b]I have heard.
21 This *is* the word[1697] that the LORD
hath spoken concerning him; The
virgin[1330] [a]the daughter of Zion hath despised thee, *and* laughed thee to
scorn;[3932] the daughter of Jerusalem
[b]hath shaken her head at thee.
22 Whom hast thou reproached and
blasphemed?[1442] and against whom hast
thou exalted *thy* voice, and lifted up thine
eyes on high? *even* against [a]the Holy[6918]
One of Israel.
23 [I][a]By thy messengers thou hast reproached the Lord, and hast said, [b]With
the multitude of my chariots I am come
up to the height of the mountains, to the
sides of Lebanon, and will cut down[3772]
[II]the tall cedar trees thereof, *and* the
choice fir trees thereof: and I will enter
into the lodgings of his borders, *and into*
[III][c]the forest of his Carmel.
24 I have digged and drunk strange
waters, and with the sole of my feet have
I dried up all the rivers of [I]besieged
places.
25 [I]Hast thou not heard long ago *how*
[a]I have done it, *and* of ancient[6924] times
that I have formed[3335] it? now have I
brought it to pass, that [b]thou shouldest
be to lay waste fenced cities *into* ruinous
heaps.
26 Therefore their inhabitants were
[I]of small[7116] power,[3027] they were
dismayed[2865] and confounded;[954] they
were *as* the grass of the field,[7704] and *as*
the green herb, *as* [a]the grass on the
house tops, and *as corn* blasted before it
be grown up.

27 But [a]I know thy [I]abode, and thy
going out, and thy coming in, and thy
rage against me.
28 Because thy rage against me and
thy tumult is come up into mine ears,[241]
therefore [a]I will put my hook in thy
nose,[639] and my bridle in thy lips,[8193] and
I will turn thee back [b]by the way[1870] by
which thou camest.
29 And this *shall be* [a]a sign[226] unto
thee, Ye shall eat this year such things as
grow of themselves, and in the second
year that which springeth of the same;
and in the third year sow ye, and reap,
and plant vineyards, and eat the fruits
thereof.
30 [a]And [I]the remnant that is
escaped[6413] of the house of Judah shall
yet again take root downward, and bear
fruit upward.
31 For out of Jerusalem shall go
forth a remnant,[7611] and [I]they that escape out of mount Zion: [a]the zeal[7068] of
the LORD *of hosts* shall do[6213] this.
32 Therefore thus saith the LORD concerning the king of Assyria, He shall not
come into this city, nor shoot an arrow
there, nor come before it with shield, nor
cast[8210] a bank against it.
33 By the way that he came, by the
same shall he return, and shall not come
into this city, saith the LORD.[3068]
34 For [a]I will defend this city, to save
it, for mine own sake, and [b]for my servant David's sake.
35 And [a]it came to pass that
night,[3915] that the angel[4397] of the LORD
went out, and smote in the camp[4264] of
the Assyrians an hundred fourscore and
five thousand: and when they arose early
in the morning, behold, they *were* all
dead[4191] corpses.[6297]
36 So Sennacherib king of Assyria
departed, and went and returned, and
dwelt at [a]Nineveh.
37 And it came to pass, as he was
worshipping[7812] in the house of Nisroch
his god, that [a]Adrammelech and Sharezer
his sons [b]smote him with the sword: and
they escaped[4422] into the land of
[I]Armenia. And [c]Esar–haddon his son
reigned in his stead.

---

19 [a]Ps. 83:18
20 [a]Isa. 37:21 [b]Ps. 65:2
21 [a]Lam. 2:13 [b]Job 16:4; Ps. 22:7, 8; Lam. 2:15
22 [a]Ps. 71:22; Isa. 5:24; Jer. 51:5
23 [I]Hebr. *By the hand of* [II]Hebr. *the tallness* [III]Or, *the forest* and *his fruitful field* [a]2Kgs. 18:17 [b]Ps. 20:7 [c]Isa. 10:18
24 [I]Or, *fenced*
25 [I]Or, *Hast thou not heard how I have made it long ago, and formed it of ancient times? should I now bring it to be laid waste,* and *fenced cities* to be *ruinous heaps?* [a]Isa. 45:7 [b]Isa. 10:5
26 [I]Hebr. *short of hand* [a]Ps. 129:6
27 [I]Or, *sitting* [a]Ps. 139:1
28 [a]Job 41:2; Ezek. 29:4; 38:4; Amos 4:2 [b]2Kgs. 19:33, 36, 37
29 [a]1Sam. 2:34; 2Kgs. 20:8, 9; Isa. 7:11, 14; Luke 2:12
30 [I]Hebr. *the escaping of the house of Judah that remaineth* [a]2Chr. 32:22, 23
31 [I]Hebr. *the escaping* [a]Isa. 9:7
34 [a]2Kgs. 20:6 [b]1Kgs. 11:12, 13
35 [a]2Chr. 32:21; Isa. 37:36
36 [a]Gen. 10:11
37 [a]2Chr. 32:21 [I]Hebr. *Ararat* [b]2Kgs. 19:7 [c]Ezra 4:2

Hezekiah Gets Sick

20 In [a]those days[3117] was Hezekiah sick unto death.[4191] And the prophet Isaiah the son of Amoz came to him, and said unto him, Thus saith the LORD, [I]Set thine house in order; for thou shalt die,[4191] and not live.[2421]

2 Then he turned his face to the wall, and prayed[6419] unto the LORD, saying,

3 I beseech[577] thee, O LORD,[3068] [a]remember now how I have [b]walked before thee in truth[571] and with a perfect[8003] heart, and have done[6213] *that which is* good[2896] in thy sight. And Hezekiah wept [I]sore.

4 And it came to pass, afore Isaiah was gone out into the middle [I]court, that the word[1697] of the LORD came to him, saying,

5 Turn again, and tell Hezekiah [a]the captain[5057] of my people,[5971] Thus saith the LORD, the God[430] of David thy father,[1] [b]I have heard thy prayer,[8605] I have seen [c]thy tears: behold, I will heal thee: on the third day thou shalt go up unto the house of the LORD.

6 And I will add unto thy days fifteen years; and I will deliver[5337] thee and this city out of the hand of the king[4428] of Assyria; and [a]I will defend this city for mine own sake, and for my servant David's sake.

7 And [a]Isaiah said, Take a lump of figs. And they took and laid[7760] *it* on the boil, and he recovered.

8 And Hezekiah said unto Isaiah, [a]What *shall be* the sign[226] that the LORD will heal me, and that I shall go up into the house of the LORD the third day?

9 And Isaiah said, [a]This sign shalt thou have of the LORD, that the LORD will do[6213] the thing that he hath spoken: shall the shadow go forward ten degrees, or go back ten degrees?

10 And Hezekiah answered,[559] It is a light thing for the shadow to go down ten degrees: nay, but let the shadow return backward ten degrees.

11 And Isaiah the prophet cried[7121] unto the LORD: and [a]he brought the shadow ten degrees backward, by which it had gone down in the [I]dial of Ahaz.

Hezekiah Boasts of His Wealth

12 [a]At that time [I]Berodach–baladan, the son of Baladan, king of Babylon, sent letters[5612] and a present unto Hezekiah: for he had heard that Hezekiah had been sick.

13 And [a]Hezekiah hearkened unto them, and shewed them all the house of his [I]precious things,[5238] the silver, and the gold, and the spices, and the precious ointment, and *all* the house of his armour,[3627] and all that was found in his treasures: there was nothing in his house, nor in all his dominion, that Hezekiah shewed them not.

14 Then came Isaiah the prophet unto king Hezekiah, and said unto him, What said these men? and from whence came they unto thee? And Hezekiah said, They are come from a far country,[776] *even* from Babylon.

15 And he said, What have they seen in thine house? And Hezekiah answered, [a]All *the things* that *are* in mine house have they seen: there is nothing among my treasures[214] that I have not shewed them.

16 And Isaiah said unto Hezekiah, Hear the word of the LORD.

17 Behold, the days come, that all that *is* in thine house, and that which thy fathers[1] have laid up in store unto this day, [a]shall be carried[5375] into Babylon: nothing shall be left,[3498] saith the LORD.

18 And of thy sons that shall issue from thee, which thou shalt beget, [a]shall they take away; [I]and they shall be eunuchs[5631] in the palace[1964] of the king of Babylon.

19 Then said Hezekiah unto Isaiah, [a]Good *is* the word of the LORD which thou hast spoken. And he said, [I]*Is it* not *good,* if peace[7965] and truth be in my days?

1 [I]Hebr. *Give charge concerning thine house* [a]2Chr. 32:24; Isa. 38:1-3

3 [I]Hebr. *with a great weeping* [a]Neh. 13:22 [b]Gen. 17:1; 1Kgs. 3:6

4 [I]Or, *city*

5 [a]1Sam. 9:16; 10:1 [b]2Kgs. 19:20; Ps. 65:2 [c]Ps. 39:12; 56:8

6 [a]2Kgs. 19:34

7 [a]Isa. 38:21

8 [a]Judg. 6:17, 37, 39; Isa. 7:11, 14; 38:22

9 [a]Isa. 38:7, 8

11 [I]Hebr. *degrees* [a]Josh. 10:12, 14; Isa. 38:8

12 [I]Or, *Merodach-baladan* [a]Isa. 39:1

13 [I]Or, *spicery* [a]2Chr. 32:27, 31

15 [a]2Kgs. 20:15

17 [a]2Kgs. 24:13; 25:13; Jer. 27:21, 22; 52:17

18 [I]Dan. 1:3 [a]2Kgs. 24:12; 2Chr. 33:11

19 [I]Or, *shall there not be peace and truth* [a]1Sam. 3:18; Job 1:21; Ps. 39:9

Hezekiah's Death

20 [a]And the rest of the acts[1697] of Hezekiah, and all his might, and how he [b]made a pool,[1295] and a conduit,[8585] and [c]brought water into the city, *are* they not written in the book[5612] of the chronicles of the kings[4428] of Judah?

21 And [a]Hezekiah slept with his fathers: and Manasseh his son reigned in his stead.

Manasseh Rules Judah

21 Manasseh [a]*was* twelve years old when he began to reign, and reigned fifty and five years in Jerusalem. And his mother's name *was* Hephzi–bah.

2 And he did[6213] *that which was* evil[7451] in the sight of the LORD, [a]after the abominations of the heathen, whom the LORD cast out[3423] before the children[1121] of Israel.

3 For he built up again the high places [a]which Hezekiah his father had destroyed;[6] and he reared up altars[4196] for Baal, and made a grove,[842] [b]as did Ahab king[4428] of Israel; and [c]worshipped[7812] all the host of heaven, and served them.

4 And [a]he built altars in the house of the LORD, of which the LORD said, [b]In Jerusalem will I put my name.

5 And he built altars for all the host of heaven in the two courts of the house of the LORD.

6 [a]And he made his son pass through the fire, and observed [b]times,[6049] and used enchantments,[5172] and dealt[6213] with familiar spirits and wizards:[3049] he wrought much wickedness[7451] in the sight of the LORD, to provoke *him* to anger.[3707]

7 And he set a graven image[6459] of the grove that he had made in the house, of which the LORD said to David, and to Solomon his son, [a]In this house, and in Jerusalem, which I have chosen[977] out of all tribes of Israel, will I put my name for ever:

8 [a]Neither will I make the feet of Israel move any more out of the land[127] which I gave their fathers;[1] only if they will observe to do[6213] according to all that I have commanded[6680] them, and according to all the law[8451] that my servant Moses commanded them.

9 But they hearkened not: and Manasseh [a]seduced them to do more evil than did the nations[1471] whom the LORD destroyed[8045] before the children of Israel.

10 And the LORD spake by his servants the prophets, saying,

11 [a]Because Manasseh king of Judah hath done[6213] these abominations, [b]*and* hath done wickedly above all that the Amorites did, which *were* before him, and [c]hath made Judah also to sin with his idols:[1544]

12 Therefore thus saith the LORD God[430] of Israel, Behold, I *am* bringing *such* evil upon Jerusalem and Judah, that whosoever heareth of it, both his [a]ears[241] shall tingle.

13 And I will stretch over Jerusalem [a]the line[6957] of Samaria, and the plummet[4949] of the house of Ahab: and I will wipe Jerusalem as *a man* wipeth[4229] a dish, [I]wiping *it,* and turning *it* upside down.

14 And I will forsake the remnant of mine inheritance,[5159] and deliver them into the hand of their enemies; and they shall become[1961] a prey and a spoil to all their enemies;

15 Because they have done *that which was* evil in my sight, and have provoked me to anger, since the day[3117] their fathers came forth out of Egypt, even unto this day.

20 [a]2Chr. 32:32 [b]Neh. 3:16 [c]2Chr. 32:30
21 [a]2Chr. 32:33
1 [a]2Chr. 33:1
2 [a]2Kgs. 16:3
3 [a]2Kgs. 18:4 [b]1Kgs. 16:32, 33 [c]Deut. 4:19; 17:3; 2Kgs. 17:16
4 [a]Jer. 32:34 [b]2Sam. 7:13; 1Kgs. 8:29; 9:3
6 [a]Lev. 18:21; 20:2; 2Kgs. 16:3; 17:17 [b]Lev. 19:26, 31; Deut. 18:10, 11; 2Kgs. 17:17
7 [a]2Sam. 7:13; 1Kgs. 8:29; 9:3; 2Kgs. 23:27; Ps. 132:13, 14; Jer. 32:34
8 [a]2Sam. 7:10
9 [a]Prov. 29:12
11 [a]2Kgs. 23:26, 27; 24:3, 4; Jer. 15:4 [b]1Kgs. 21:26 [c]2Kgs. 21:9
12 [a]1Sam. 3:11; Jer. 19:3
13 [I]Hebr. *he wipeth and turneth it upon the face thereof* [a]Isa. 34:11; Lam. 2:8; Amos 7:7, 8

20:20 The "pool" mentioned in this verse is a reference to the pool of Siloam, which was fed by a conduit from the spring of Gihon (2 Chr. 32:30). Hezekiah constructed the conduit to provide an ample water supply during any future attacks by Assyria. The 1750 foot long water tunnel survives today, and an inscription found in it (now in a museum) attributes the construction to Hezekiah.

16 [a]Moreover Manasseh shed innocent[5355] blood[1818] very much, till he had filled Jerusalem [I]from one end to another; beside his sin wherewith he made Judah to sin, in doing[6213] *that which was* evil in the sight of the LORD.

17 [a]Now the rest of the acts[1697] of Manasseh, and all that he did, and his sin that he sinned, *are* they not written in the book[5612] of the chronicles of the kings[4428] of Judah?

18 And [a]Manasseh slept with his fathers, and was buried[6912] in the garden of his own house, in the garden of Uzza: and Amon his son reigned in his stead.

Amon Rules Judah

19 [a]Amon *was* twenty and two years old when he began to reign, and he reigned two years in Jerusalem. And his mother's name *was* Meshullemeth, the daughter of Haruz of Jotbah.

20 And he did *that which was* evil in the sight of the LORD, [a]as his father Manasseh did.

21 And he walked in all the way[1870] that his father walked in, and served the idols that his father served, and worshipped them:

22 And he [a]forsook[5800] the LORD God of his fathers, and walked not in the way of the LORD.

23 [a]And the servants of Amon conspired against him, and slew the king in his own house.

24 And the people[5971] of the land slew all them that had conspired against king Amon; and the people of the land made Josiah his son king in his stead.

25 Now the rest of the acts of Amon which he did, *are* they not written in the book of the chronicles of the kings of Judah?

26 And he was buried in his sepulchre[6900] in the garden of Uzza: and [a]Josiah his son reigned in his stead.

Josiah Rules Judah

22 Josiah [a]*was* eight years old when he began to reign, and he reigned thirty and one years in Jerusalem. And his mother's name *was* Jedidah, the daughter of Adaiah of [b]Boscath.

2 And he did[6213] *that which was* right in the sight of the LORD, and walked in all the way[1870] of David his father,[1] and [a]turned not aside to the right hand or to the left.

A Copy of the Law Is Found

3 [a]And it came to pass in the eighteenth year of king[4428] Josiah, *that* the king sent Shaphan the son of Azaliah, the son of Meshullam, the scribe, to the house of the LORD, saying,

4 Go up to Hilkiah the high priest, that he may sum[8552] the silver which is [a]brought into the house of the LORD, which [b]the keepers[8104] of the [I]door have gathered[622] of the people:[5971]

5 And let them [a]deliver it into the hand of the doers of the work,[4399] that have the oversight of the house of the LORD: and let them give it to the doers of the work which *is* in the house of the LORD, to repair the breaches of the house,

6 Unto carpenters, and builders,[1129] and masons, and to buy timber and hewn[4274] stone to repair the house.

7 Howbeit [a]there was no reckoning made with them of the money that was delivered into their hand, because they dealt[6213] faithfully.[530]

8 And Hilkiah the high priest said unto Shaphan the scribe, [a]I have found the book[5612] of the law[8451] in the house of the LORD. And Hilkiah gave the book to Shaphan, and he read it.

9 And Shaphan the scribe came to the king, and brought the king word[1697] again, and said, Thy servants have [I]gathered the money that was found in the house, and have delivered it into the hand of them that do[6213] the work, that have the oversight of the house of the LORD.

10 And Shaphan the scribe shewed the king, saying, Hilkiah the priest hath delivered me a book. And Shaphan read it before the king.

11 And it came to pass, when the

16 [I]Hebr. *from mouth to mouth* [a]2Kgs. 24:4
17 [a]2Chr. 33:11-19
18 [a]2Chr. 33:20
19 [a]2Chr. 33:21-23
20 [a]2Kgs. 21:2-9
22 [a]1Kgs. 11:33
23 [a]2Chr. 33:24, 25
26 [a]Matt. 1:10, called *Josias*
1 [a]2Chr. 34:1 [b]Josh. 15:39
2 [a]Deut. 5:32
3 [a]2Chr. 34:8
4 [I]Hebr. *threshold* [a]2Kgs. 12:4 [b]2Kgs. 12:9; Ps. 84:10
5 [a]2Kgs. 12:11, 12, 14
7 [a]2Kgs. 12:15
8 [a]Deut. 31:24; 2Chr. 34:14
9 [I]Hebr. *melted*

king had heard the words[1697] of the book of the law, that he rent his clothes.

12 And the king commanded[6680] Hilkiah the priest, and Ahikam the son of Shaphan, and [a]Achbor the son of [I]Michaiah, and Shaphan the scribe, and Asahiah a servant of the king's,[4428] saying,

13 Go ye, enquire[1875] of the LORD for me, and for the people, and for all Judah, concerning the words of this book that is found: for great *is* [a]the wrath of the LORD that is kindled against us, because our fathers[1] have not hearkened unto the words of this book, to do according unto all that which is written concerning us.

14 So Hilkiah the priest, and Ahikam, and Achbor, and Shaphan, and Asahiah, went unto Huldah the prophetess, the wife[802] of Shallum the son of [a]Tikvah, the son of [I]Harhas, keeper[8104] of the [II]wardrobe; (now she dwelt in Jerusalem [III]in the college;) and they communed with her.

15 And she said unto them, Thus saith the LORD God[430] of Israel, Tell the man that sent you to me,

16 Thus saith the LORD, Behold, [a]I will bring evil[7451] upon this place, and upon the inhabitants thereof, *even* all the words of the book which the king of Judah hath read:

17 [a]Because they have forsaken[5800] me, and have burned incense[6999] unto other gods,[430] that they might provoke me to anger[3707] with all the works of their hands; therefore my wrath shall be kindled against this place, and shall not be quenched.

18 But to [a]the king of Judah which sent you to enquire of the LORD, thus shall ye say to him, Thus saith the LORD God of Israel, *As touching* the words which thou hast heard;

19 Because thine [a]heart was tender, and thou hast [b]humbled thyself before the LORD, when thou heardest what I spake against this place, and against the inhabitants thereof, that they should become[1961] [c]a desolation[8047] and [d]a curse,[7045] and hast rent thy clothes, and wept before me; I also have heard *thee,* saith the LORD.[3068]

20 Behold therefore, I will gather[622] thee unto thy fathers, and thou [a]shalt be gathered into thy grave in peace;[7965] and thine eyes shall not see all the evil which I will bring upon this place. And they brought the king word again.

Josiah's Reforms

23 And [a]the king[4428] sent, and they gathered[622] unto him all the elders[2205] of Judah and of Jerusalem.

2 And the king went up into the house of the LORD, and all the men of Judah and all the inhabitants of Jerusalem with him, and the priests, and the prophets, and all the people,[5971] [I]both small and great: and he read in their ears[241] all the words[1697] of the book[5612] of the covenant[1285] [a]which was found in the house of the LORD.

3 And the king [a]stood by a pillar, and made a covenant before the LORD, to walk after the LORD, and to keep[8104] his commandments[4587] and his testimonies and his statutes with all *their* heart and all *their* soul, to perform[6965] the words of this covenant that were written in this book. And all the people stood to the covenant.

4 And the king commanded[6680] Hilkiah the high priest, and the priests of the second order, and the keepers[8104] of the door, to bring forth out of the temple of the LORD all the vessels that were made for Baal, and for [a]the grove,[842] and for all the host of heaven: and he burned[8313] them without Jerusalem in the fields of Kidron, and carried the ashes[6083] of them unto Bethel.

5 And he [I]put down the [II]idolatrous priests,[3649] whom the kings of Judah had ordained to burn incense[6999] in the high places in the cities of Judah, and in the places round about Jerusalem; them also that burned incense unto Baal, to the sun, and to the moon, and to the [III]planets, and to [a]all the host of heaven.

6 And he brought out the [a]grove from the house of the LORD, without

12 [I]Or, *Micah* [a]2Chr. 34:20, Abdon
13 [a]Deut. 29:27
14 [I]Or, *Hasrah* [II]Hebr. *garments* [III]Or, *in the second part* [a]2Chr. 34:22, Tikvath
16 [a]Deut. 29:27; Dan. 9:11-14
17 [a]Deut. 29:25-27
18 [a]2Chr. 34:26
19 [a]Ps. 51:17; Isa. 57:15 [b]1Kgs. 21:29 [c]Lev. 26:31, 32 [d]Jer. 26:6; 44:22
20 [a]Ps. 37:37; Isa. 57:1, 2
1 [a]2Chr. 34:29, 30
2 [I]Hebr. *from small even unto great* [a]2Kgs. 22:8
3 [a]2Kgs. 11:14, 17
4 [a]2Kgs. 21:3-7
5 [I]Hebr. *caused to cease* [II]Hebr. *Chemarim* [III]Or, *twelve signs,* or, *constellations* [a]2Kgs. 21:3
6 [a]2Kgs. 21:7

Jerusalem, unto the brook Kidron, and
burned it at the brook Kidron, and
stamped *it* small to powder,[6083] and cast
the powder thereof upon [b]the graves[6913]
of the children[1121] of the people.
7 And he brake down the houses [a]of
the sodomites,[6945] that *were* by the house
of the LORD, [b]where the women[802] wove
[I]hangings[1004] for the grove.
8 And he brought all the priests out
of the cities of Judah, and defiled[2930] the
high places where the priests had burned
incense, from [a]Geba to Beer–sheba, and
brake down[5422] the high places of the
gates that *were* in the entering in of the
gate of Joshua the governor of the city,
which *were* on a man's left hand at the
gate of the city.
9 [a]Nevertheless the priests of the
high places came not up to the altar[4196]
of the LORD in Jerusalem, [b]but they did
eat of the unleavened bread[4682] among
their brethren.[251]
10 And he defiled [a]Topheth, which *is*
in [b]the valley of the children of Hinnom,
[c]that no man might make his son or his
daughter to pass through the fire to
Molech.
11 And he took away the horses that
the kings of Judah had given to the sun,
at the entering in of the house of the
LORD, by the chamber of Nathan–melech
the [I]chamberlain,[5631] which *was* in the
suburbs,[6503] and burned the chariots of
the sun with fire.
12 And the altars[4196] that *were* [a]on
the top of the upper chamber of Ahaz,
which the kings of Judah had made, and
the altars which [b]Manasseh had made in
the two courts of the house of the LORD,
did the king beat down, and [I]brake *them*
down from thence, and cast the dust[6083]
of them into the brook Kidron.
13 And the high places that *were* before Jerusalem, which *were* on the right
hand of [I]the mount of corruption,[4889]
which [a]Solomon the king of Israel had
builded for Ashtoreth[6252] the abomination[8251] of the Zidonians, and for Chemosh the abomination of the Moabites,
and for Milcom the abomination[8441] of
the children of Ammon, did the king
defile.[2930]
14 And he [a]brake in pieces[7665] the
images,[4676] and cut down[3772] the
groves,[842] and filled their places with
the bones[6106] of men.
15 Moreover the altar that *was* at
Bethel, *and* the high place [a]which
Jeroboam the son of Nebat, who made
Israel to sin, had made, both that altar
and the high place he brake down, and
burned the high place, *and* stamped *it*
small[1854] to powder, and burned the
grove.
16 And as Josiah turned himself, he
spied the sepulchres[6913] that *were* there in
the mount, and sent, and took the bones
out of the sepulchres, and burned *them*
upon the altar, and polluted[2930] it, according to the [a]word[1697] of the LORD
which the man of God[430] proclaimed,
who proclaimed these words.
17 Then he said, What title[6725] *is*
that that I see? And the men of the city
told him, *It is* [a]the sepulchre[6913] of the
man of God, which came from Judah,
and proclaimed these things that thou
hast done[6213] against the altar of Bethel.
18 And he said, Let him alone; let no
man move his bones. So they let his
bones [I]alone, with the bones of [a]the
prophet that came out of Samaria.
19 And all the houses also of the
high places that *were* [a]in the cities of
Samaria, which the kings of Israel had

6 [b]2Chr. 34:4
7 [I]Hebr. *houses* [a]1Kgs. 14:24; 15:12 [b]Ezek. 16:16
8 [a]1Kgs. 15:22
9 [a]Ezek. 44:10-14 [b]1Sam. 2:36
10 [a]Isa. 30:33; Jer. 7:31; 19:6, 11-13 [b]Josh. 15:8 [c]Lev. 18:21; Deut. 18:10; Ezek. 23:37, 39
11 [I]Or, *eunuch,* or, *officer*
12 [I]Or, *ran from thence* [a]Jer. 19:13; Zeph. 1:5 [b]2Kgs. 21:5
13 [I]That is, *the mount of Olives* [a]1Kgs. 11:7
14 [I]Hebr. *statues* [a]Ex. 23:24; Deut. 7:5, 25
15 [a]1Kgs. 12:28, 33
16 [a]1Kgs. 13:2
17 [a]1Kgs. 13:1, 30
18 [I]Hebr. *to escape* [a]1Kgs. 13:31
19 [a]2Chr. 34:6, 7

23:10 The reference in this verse is to Molech (this word has been transliterated into the Greek word "Moloch" [Amos 5:26; Acts 7:43]), a deity who was worshiped by pagans in Canaan and whose worship was introduced to the Israelites soon after they entered the Promised Land (Josh. 15:8). Their rituals included the casting of one's child or children into a fiery pit in order to appease the god. Jehovah condemned this practice on the part of His chosen people, Israel (Lev. 18:21; 20:2–5; 1 Kgs. 11:7; Jer. 32:35). Several kings in both Israel and Judah practiced the rituals of this religion (e.g., Manasseh in 2 Chr. 33:6).

made to provoke *the* LORD to anger,[3707] Josiah took away, and did to them according to all the acts that he had done in Bethel.

20 And [a]he [Ib]slew all the priests of the high places that *were* there upon the altars, and [c]burned men's bones upon them, and returned to Jerusalem.

21 And the king commanded all the people, saying, [a]Keep[6213] the passover[6453] unto the LORD your God, [b]as *it is* written in the book of this covenant.

22 Surely [a]there was not holden[6213] such a passover from the days[3117] of the judges[8199] that judged Israel, nor in all the days of the kings of Israel, nor of the kings of Judah;

23 But in the eighteenth year of king Josiah, *wherein* this passover was holden[6213] to the LORD in Jerusalem.

24 Moreover [a]the *workers with* familiar spirits, and the wizards,[3049] and the [Ib]images,[8655] and the idols,[1544] and all the abominations[8251] that were spied in the land of Judah and in Jerusalem, did Josiah put away, that he might perform the words of [c]the law[8451] which were written in the book that Hilkiah the priest found in the house of the LORD.

25 [a]And like unto him was there no king before him, that turned to the LORD with all his heart, and with all his soul, and with all his might, according to all the law of Moses; neither after him arose there *any* like him.

26 Notwithstanding the LORD[3068] turned not from the fierceness of his great wrath,[639] wherewith his anger[639] was kindled[2734] against Judah, [a]because of all the [I]provocations[3708] that Manasseh had provoked him withal.

27 And the LORD said, I will remove Judah also out of my sight, as [a]I have removed Israel, and will cast off this city Jerusalem which I have chosen,[977] and the house of which I said, [b]My name shall be there.

Josiah's Death

28 Now the rest of the acts[1697] of Josiah, and all that he did, *are* they not written in the book of the chronicles of the kings of Judah?

29 [a]In his days Pharaoh–nechoh king of Egypt went up against the king of Assyria to the river Euphrates: and king Josiah went against him; and he slew him at [b]Megiddo, when he [c]had seen him.

30 [a]And his servants carried him in a chariot dead[4191] from Megiddo, and brought him to Jerusalem, and buried[6912] him in his own sepulchre.[6900] And [b]the people of the land took Jehoahaz the son of Josiah, and anointed[4886] him, and made him king[4427] in his father's stead.

Jehohaz Rules Judah

31 [I]Jehoahaz *was* twenty and three years old when he began to reign; and he reigned three months in Jerusalem. And his mother's name *was* [a]Hamutal, the daughter of Jeremiah of Libnah.

32 And he did *that which was* evil[7451] in the sight of the LORD, according to all that his fathers[1] had done.

33 And Pharaoh–nechoh put him in bands[631] [a]at Riblah in the land of Hamath, [I]that he might not reign in Jerusalem; and [II]put the land to a tribute[6066] of an hundred talents of silver, and a talent of gold.

34 And [a]Pharaoh–nechoh made Eliakim the son of Josiah king in the room of Josiah his father, and [b]turned his name to [c]Jehoiakim, and took Jehoahaz away: [d]and he came to Egypt, and died[4191] there.

Jehoiakim Rules Judah

35 And Jehoiakim gave [a]the silver and the gold to Pharaoh; but he taxed the land to give the money according to the commandment of Pharaoh: he exacted the silver and the gold of the people of the land, of every one according to his taxation, to give *it* unto Pharaoh–nechoh.

36 [a]Jehoiakim *was* twenty and five years old when he began to reign; and he reigned eleven years in Jerusalem. And his mother's name *was* Zebudah, the daughter of Pedaiah of Rumah.

20 IOr, *sacrificed* [a]1Kgs. 13:2 [b]Ex. 22:20; 1Kgs. 18:40; 2Kgs. 11:18 [c]2Chr. 34:5

21 [a]2Chr. 35:1 [b]Ex. 12:3; Lev. 23:5; Num. 9:2; Deut. 16:2

22 [a]2Chr. 35:18, 19

24 IOr, *teraphim* [a]2Kgs. 21:6 [b]Gen. 31:19 [c]Lev. 19:31; 20:27; Deut. 18:11

25 [a]2Kgs. 18:5

26 IHebr. *angers* [a]2Kgs. 21:11, 12; 24:3, 4; Jer. 15:4

27 [a]2Kgs. 17:18, 20; 18:11; 21:13 [b]1Kgs. 8:29; 9:3; 2Kgs. 21:4, 7

29 [a]2Chr. 35:20 [b]Zech. 12:11 [c]2Kgs. 14:8

30 [a]2Chr. 35:24 [b]2Chr. 36:1

31 ICalled *Shallum* [a]1Chr. 3:15; Jer. 22:11 [b]2Kgs. 24:18

33 IOr, *because he reigned* IIHebr. *set a mulct upon the land* [a]2Kgs. 25:6; Jer. 52:27

34 [a]2Chr. 36:4 [b]2Kgs. 24:17; Dan. 1:7 [c]Matt. 1:11, called *Jakim* [d]Jer. 22:11, 12; Ezek. 19:3, 4

35 [a]2Kgs. 23:33

36 [a]2Chr. 36:5

37 And he did *that which was* evil in
the sight of the LORD, according to all
that his fathers had done.

24 🔑 In [a]his days[3117] Nebuchadnezzar king[4428] of Babylon came
up, and Jehoiakim became his servant
three years: then he turned and rebelled
against him.
2 [a]And the LORD sent against him
bands[1416] of the Chaldees, and bands of
the Syrians, and bands of the Moabites,
and bands of the children[1121] of Ammon,
and sent them against Judah to destroy[6]
it, [b]according to the word[1697] of the LORD,
which he spake [I]by his servants the
prophets.
🔑 3 Surely at the commandment of the
LORD came *this* upon Judah, to remove
them out of his sight, [a]for the sins of
Manasseh, according to all that he
did;[6213]
4 [a]And also for the innocent[5355]
blood[1818] that he shed: for he filled
Jerusalem with innocent blood; which the
LORD would[14] not pardon.[5545]
5 Now the rest of the acts[1697] of
Jehoiakim, and all that he did, *are* they
not written in the book[5612] of the chronicles of the kings[4428] of Judah?
6 [a]So Jehoiakim slept with his
fathers:[1] and Jehoiachin his son reigned
in his stead.
🔑 7 And [a]the king of Egypt came not
again any more out of his land: for [b]the
king of Babylon had taken from the river
of Egypt unto the river Euphrates all
that pertained to the king of Egypt.

Jehoiachin Rules Judah

8 [Ia]Jehoiachin *was* eighteen years old
when he began to reign, and he reigned
in Jerusalem three months. And his
mother's name *was* Nehushta, the daughter of Elnathan of Jerusalem.
9 And he did *that which was* evil[7451]
in the sight of the LORD, according to all
that his father[1] had done.[6213]
10 [a]At that time the servants of
Nebuchadnezzar king of Babylon came
up against Jerusalem, and the city [I]was
besieged.
11 And Nebuchadnezzar king of
Babylon came against the city, and his
servants did besiege it.
12 [a]And Jehoiachin the king of Judah
went out to the king of Babylon, he, and
his mother, and his servants, and his
princes,[8269] and his [I]officers:[5631] [b]and the
king of Babylon took him [c]in the eighth
year of his reign.
13 [a]And he carried out thence all the
treasures of the house of the LORD, and
the treasures of the king's house, and
[b]cut in pieces all the vessels of gold
which Solomon king of Israel had made
in the temple of the LORD, [c]as the LORD
had said.
14 And [a]he carried away all
Jerusalem, and all the princes, and all the
mighty men of valour,[2428] [b]*even* ten thousand captives,[1540] and [c]all the craftsmen
and smiths: none remained, save [d]the
poorest sort of the people[5971] of the land.
15 And [a]he carried away Jehoiachin
to Babylon, and the king's mother, and
the king's wives,[802] and his [I]officers, and
the mighty of the land, *those* carried he
into captivity[1473] from Jerusalem to
Babylon.
16 And [a]all the men of might, *even*
seven thousand, and craftsmen and
smiths a thousand, all *that were* strong
and apt[6213] for war, even them the
king of Babylon brought captive to
Babylon.
17 And [a]the king of Babylon made
Mattaniah [b]his father's brother[251] king in

1 [a]2Chr. 36:6; Jer. 25:1, 9; Dan. 1:1
2 [I]Hebr. *by the hand of* [a]Jer. 25:9; 32:28; Ezek. 19:8 [b]2Kgs. 20:17; 21:12-14; 23:27
3 [a]2Kgs. 21:2, 11; 23:26
4 [a]2Kgs. 21:16
6 [a]2Chr. 36:6, 8; Jer. 22:18, 19; 36:30
7 [a]Jer. 37:5, 7 [b]Jer. 46:2
8 [I]Called *Jeconiah* [a]2Chr. 36:9; Jer. 22:24, 28; 24:1
10 [I]Hebr. *came into siege* [a]Dan. 1:1
12 [I]Or, *eunuchs* [a]Jer. 24:1; 29:1, 2; Ezek. 17:12 [b]Jer. 25:1 [c]2Kgs. 25:27 [d]Jer. 52:28
13 [a]2Kgs. 20:17; Isa. 39:6 [b]Dan. 5:2, 3 [c]Jer. 20:5
14 [a]Jer. 24:1 [b]Jer. 52:28 [c]1Sam. 13:19, 22 [d]2Kgs. 25:12; Jer. 40:7
15 [I]Or, *eunuchs* [a]2Chr. 36:10; Esth. 2:6; Jer. 22:24
16 [a]Jer. 52:28
17 [a]Jer. 37:1 [b]1Chr. 3:15; 2Chr. 36:10

🔑 **24:1** From this verse it is clear that the army of the Babylonian Empire had conquered Assyria and had taken over its empire.
🔑 **24:3, 4** According to 2 Chronicles 33:12, 13, Manasseh repented and found mercy from God for the sins he committed. However, that did not remove the consequences of what he had done.
🔑 **24:7** As the Babylonian Empire grew stronger and stronger, the power of Egypt diminished.

his stead, and [c]changed his name to Zedekiah.

Zedekiah Rules Judah

18 [a]Zedekiah *was* twenty and one years old when he began to reign, and he reigned eleven years in Jerusalem. And his mother's name *was* [b]Hamutal, the daughter of Jeremiah of Libnah.

19 [a]And he did *that which was* evil in the sight of the LORD, according to all that Jehoiakim had done.

20 For through the anger[639] of the LORD it came to pass in Jerusalem and Judah, until he had cast them out from his presence, [a]that Zedekiah rebelled against the king of Babylon.

Jerusalem Falls

25 And it came to pass [a]in the ninth year of his reign, in the tenth month, in the tenth *day* of the month, *that* Nebuchadnezzar king[4428] of Babylon came, he, and all his host, against Jerusalem, and pitched against it; and they built forts[1785] against it round about.

2 And the city was besieged unto the eleventh year of king Zedekiah.

3 And on the ninth *day* of the [a]*fourth* month the famine prevailed[2388] in the city, and there was no bread for the people[5971] of the land.

4 And [a]the city was broken up,1234 and all the men of war *fled* by night[3915] by the way[1870] of the gate between two walls, which *is* by the king's[4428] garden: (now the Chaldees *were* against the city round about:) and [b]*the king* went the way toward the plain.[6160]

5 And the army[2428] of the Chaldees pursued after the king, and overtook him in the plains of Jericho: and all his army were scattered from him.

6 So they took the king, and brought him up[5927] to the king of Babylon [a]to Riblah; and they [I]gave judgment[4941] upon him.

7 And they slew the sons of Zedekiah before his eyes, and [Ia]put out the eyes of Zedekiah, and bound him with fetters of brass, and carried him to Babylon.

8 And in the fifth month, [a]on the seventh *day* of the month, which *is* [b]the nineteenth year of king Nebuchadnezzar king of Babylon, [c]came Nebuzar–adan, [I]captain of the guard,2876 a servant of the king of Babylon, unto Jerusalem:

9 [a]And he burnt[8313] the house of the LORD, [b]and the king's house, and all the houses of Jerusalem, and every great *man's* house burnt he with fire.

10 And all the army of the Chaldees, that *were with* the captain of the guard, [a]brake down the walls of Jerusalem round about.

11 [a]Now the rest of the people *that were* left[7604] in the city, and the [I]fugitives[5307] that fell away[5307] to the king of Babylon, with the remnant of the multitude, did Nebuzar–adan the captain of the guard carry away.

12 But the captain of the guard [a]left of the poor of the land *to be* vinedressers and husbandmen.1461

13 And [a]the [b]pillars of brass that *were* in the house of the LORD, and [c]the bases, and [d]the brasen sea that *was* in the house of the LORD, did the Chaldees break in pieces,[7665] and carried[5375] the brass of them to Babylon.

14 And [a]the pots, and the shovels, and the snuffers, and the spoons, and all the vessels of brass wherewith they ministered,[8334] took they away.

15 And the firepans, and the bowls, *and* such things as *were* of gold, *in* gold, and of silver, *in* silver, the captain of the guard took away.

16 The two pillars, [I]one sea, and the bases which Solomon had made for the house of the LORD; [a]the brass of all these vessels was without weight.

17 [a]The height of the one pillar *was* eighteen cubits, and the chapiter[3805] upon it *was* brass: and the height of the chapiter three cubits: and the wreathen work,7639 and pomegranates upon the chapiter round about, all of brass: and like unto these had the second pillar with wreathen work.

---

17 [c]2Kgs. 23:34; 2Chr. 36:4

18 [a]2Chr. 36:11; Jer. 37:1; 52:1 [b]2Kgs. 23:31

19 [a]2Chr. 36:12

20 [a]2Chr. 36:13; Ezek. 17:15

1 [a]2Chr. 36:17; Jer. 34:2; 39:1; 52:4, 5; Ezek. 24:1

3 [a]Jer. 39:2; 52:6

4 [a]Jer. 39:2; 52:7 [b]Jer. 39:4-7; 52:7; Ezek. 12:12

6 [I]Hebr. *spake judgment with him* [a]2Kgs. 23:33; Jer. 52:9

7 [I]Hebr. *made blind* [a]Jer. 39:7; Ezek. 12:13

8 [I]Or, *chief marshal* [a]Jer. 52:12-14 [b]2Kgs. 24:12; 25:27 [c]Jer. 39:9

9 [a]2Chr. 36:19; Ps. 79:1 [b]Jer. 39:8; Amos 2:5

10 [a]Neh. 1:3; Jer. 52:14

11 [I]Hebr. *fallen away* [a]Jer. 39:9; 52:15

12 [a]2Kgs. 24:14; Jer. 39:10; 40:7; 52:16

13 [a]2Kgs. 20:17; Jer. 27:19, 22; 52:17-23 [b]1Kgs. 7:15 [c]1Kgs. 7:27 [d]1Kgs. 7:23

14 [a]Ex. 27:3; 1Kgs. 7:45, 50

16 [I]Hebr. *the one sea* [a]1Kgs. 7:47

17 [a]1Kgs. 7:15; Jer. 52:21

18 [a]And the captain of the guard took [b]Seraiah the chief[7218] priest, and [c]Zephaniah the second priest, and the three keepers[8104] of the [I]door:

19 And out of the city he took an [I]officer that was set over the men of war, and [a]five men of them that [II]were in the king's presence, which were found in the city, and the [III]principal scribe of the host, which mustered[6633] the people of the land, and threescore men of the people of the land *that were* found in the city:

20 And Nebuzar–adan captain of the guard took these, and brought them to the king of Babylon to Riblah:

21 And the king of Babylon smote them, and slew them at Riblah in the land of Hamath. [a]So Judah was carried away out of their land.[127]

Gedaliah Becomes Governor of Judah

22 [a]And *as for* the people that remained in the land of Judah, whom Nebuchadnezzar king of Babylon had left, even over them he made Gedaliah the son of Ahikam, the son of Shaphan, ruler.

23 And when all the [a]captains[8269] of the armies,[2428] they and their men, heard that the king of Babylon had made Gedaliah governor,[6485] there came to Gedaliah to Mizpah, even Ishmael the son of Nethaniah, and Johanan the son of Careah, and Seraiah the son of Tanhumeth the Netophathite, and Jaazaniah the son of a Maachathite, they and their men.

18 [I]Hebr. *threshold* [a]Jer. 52:24 [b]1Chr. 6:14; Ezra 7:1 [c]Jer. 21:1; 29:25

19 [I]Or, *eunuch* [II]Hebr. *saw the king's face* [III]Or, *scribe of the captain of the host* [a]Jer. 52:25

21 [a]Lev. 26:33; Deut. 28:36, 64; 2Kgs. 23:27

22 [a]Jer. 40:5

23 [a]Jer. 40:7-9

25 [I]Hebr. *of the kingdom* [a]Jer. 41:1, 2

26 [a]Jer. 43:4, 7

27 [a]Jer. 52:31 [b]Gen. 40:13, 20

28 [I]Hebr. *good things with him*

29 [a]2Sam. 9:7

24 And Gedaliah sware to them, and to their men, and said unto them, Fear[3372] not to be the servants of the Chaldees: dwell in the land, and serve the king of Babylon; and it shall be well[3190] with you.

25 But [a]it came to pass in the seventh month, that Ishmael the son of Nethaniah, the son of Elishama, of the seed [I]royal, came, and ten men with him, and smote Gedaliah, that he died,[4191] and the Jews and the Chaldees that were with him at Mizpah.

26 And all the people, both small and great, and the captains of the armies, arose, [a]and came to Egypt: for they were afraid[3372] of the Chaldees.

Jehoiachin Is Restored to Honor

27 [a]And it came to pass in the seven and thirtieth year of the captivity[1546] of Jehoiachin king of Judah, in the twelfth month, on the seven and twentieth *day* of the month, *that* Evil–merodach king of Babylon in the year that he began to reign [b]did lift up the head of Jehoiachin king of Judah out of prison;

28 And he spake [I]kindly[2896] to him, and set his throne above the throne of the kings that *were* with him in Babylon;

29 And changed his prison garments: and he did [a]eat bread continually before him all the days[3117] of his life.[2416]

30 And his allowance[737] *was* a continual[8548] allowance given him of the king, a daily rate for every day, all the days of his life.

25:22 Shaphan had been King Josiah's secretary. The book which Josiah found in the temple was handed to him to read aloud to the people. After he read it, he took it to King Josiah (2 Kgs. 22:8–13).

25:27 The term "Evil-merodach" is an unflattering rendering (in Hebrew, the first word meant "fool") of the Babylonian ruler "Amel-marduk" (which means "Man of Marduk"). It is interesting that several Babylonian tablets have been recovered which verify that Jehoiachin and his five sons received special provisions while in exile, and that Jehoiachin was always regarded as the rightful king of Judah, not Zedekiah. Evil-merodach ruled for only two years. His brother-in-law assassinated him in 560 B.C.

The First Book of

CHRONICLES

The two books of Chronicles originally were only one volume. The title in the English Bible was derived from a Latin term used by Jerome, but the title in Hebrew (the first words of the Hebrew text) is translated "the words of the days." The latter reflects the content, which extends from the creation of man to the Babylonian Captivity. The Book of 1 Chronicles begins with extensive genealogies (chaps. 1—9) which trace the family lines all the way back to Adam. These records served to remind the returning exiles that the allotment of the land and religious duties were connected to tribal ancestry.

According to tradition, the books of 1 and 2 Chronicles were written by Ezra the scribe near the end of the period of Exile. This is supported by the fact that Ezra's purpose in coming to Jerusalem was to teach the people about God's laws (Ezra 7:10, 25) and by the emphasis of this book on the history of Jewish worship. Furthermore, the style of 1 and 2 Chronicles is very similar to the Book of Ezra.

Ezra, under the inspiration of the Holy Spirit, incorporated the writings of several prophets into the books of 1 and 2 Chronicles. Some of the prophets who wrote during this time are Nathan, Ahijah, and Iddo (2 Chr. 9:29), Shemaiah (2 Chr. 12:15), and Isaiah (2 Chr. 26:22; 32:32).

The intended lesson of these books is clear: obedience to God brings blessing (2 Chr. 15:12–15), disobedience brings disaster and defeat (1 Chr. 10:13, 14). God's people were responsible to fulfill the obligations inherent in their covenant relationship with Him. Although the books of 1 and 2 Chronicles contain much of the same information as the books of Samuel and Kings, they cover the material from a theological rather than a historical perspective.

Family Records From Adam to Abraham

1 Adam, [a]Sheth, Enosh,
2 Kenan, Mahalaleel, Jered,
3 Henoch, Methuselah, Lamech,
4 Noah, Shem, Ham, and Japheth.
5 [a]The sons of Japheth; Gomer, and
Magog, and Madai, and Javan, and Tubal,
and Meshech, and Tiras.
6 And the sons of Gomer; Ashchenaz, and [I]Riphath, and Togarmah.
7 And the sons of Javan; Elishah,
and Tarshish, Kittim, and [I]Dodanim.
8 [a]The sons of Ham; Cush, and
Mizraim, Put, and Canaan.
9 And the sons of Cush; Seba, and
Havilah, and Sabta, and Raamah, and
Sabtecha. And the sons of Raamah;
Sheba, and Dedan.
10 And Cush [a]begat Nimrod: he
began to be mighty upon the <u>earth</u>.[776]
11 And Mizraim begat Ludim, and
Anamim, and Lehabim, and Naphtuhim,
12 And Pathrusim, and Casluhim, (of
whom came the Philistines,) and
[a]Caphthorim.
13 And [a]Canaan begat Zidon his
firstborn, and Heth,
14 The Jebusite also, and the
Amorite, and the Girgashite,
15 And the Hivite, and the Arkite,
and the Sinite,
16 And the Arvadite, and the
Zemarite, and the Hamathite.
17 The sons of [a]Shem; Elam, and
Asshur, and Arphaxad, and Lud, and
Aram, and Uz, and Hul, and Gether,
and [Ib]Meshech.
18 And Arphaxad begat Shelah, and
Shelah begat Eber.
19 And unto Eber were born two
sons: the name of the one *was* [Ia]Peleg; because in his <u>days</u>[3117] the earth <u>was</u>
<u>divided</u>:[6385] and his <u>brother's</u>[251] name *was*
Joktan.
20 And [a]Joktan begat Almodad, and
Sheleph, and Hazar–maveth, and Jerah,

1 [a]Gen. 4:25, 26; 5:3, 9
5 [a]Gen. 10:2
6 [I]Some texts read, *Diphath*
7 [I]Some texts read, *Rodanim*
8 [a]Gen. 10:6
10 [a]Gen. 10:8, 13
12 [a]Deut. 2:23
13 [a]Gen. 10:15
17 [I]Or, *Mash* [a]Gen. 10:22; 11:10 [b]Gen. 10:23
19 [I]That is, *Division* [a]Gen. 10:25
20 [a]Gen. 10:26

21 Hadoram also, and Uzal, and Diklah,

22 And Ebal, and Abimael, and Sheba,

23 And Ophir, and Havilah, and Jobab. All these *were* the sons of Joktan.

24 [a]Shem, Arphaxad, Shelah,

25 [a]Eber, Peleg, Reu,

26 Serug, Nahor, Terah,

27 [a]Abram; the same *is* Abraham.

Ishmael's and Keturah's Family Records

28 The sons of Abraham; [a]Isaac, and [b]Ishmael.

29 These *are* their generations:[8535] The [a]firstborn of Ishmael, Nebaioth; then Kedar, and Adbeel, and Mibsam,

30 Mishma, and Dumah, Massa, [Ia]Hadad, and Tema,

31 Jetur, Naphish, and Kedemah. These are the sons of Ishmael.

32 Now [a]the sons of Keturah, Abraham's concubine: she bare Zimran, and Jokshan, and Medan, and Midian, and Ishbak, and Shuah. And the sons of Jokshan; Sheba, and Dedan.

33 And the sons of Midian; Ephah, and Epher, and Henoch, and Abida, and Eldaah. All these *are* the sons of Keturah.

Esau's Family Record

34 And [a]Abraham begat Isaac. [b]The sons of Isaac; Esau and Israel.

35 The sons of [a]Esau; Eliphaz, Reuel, and Jeush, and Jaalam, and Korah.

36 The sons of Eliphaz; Teman, and Omar, [Ia]Zephi, and Gatam, Kenaz, and Timna, and Amalek.

37 The sons of Reuel; Nahath, Zerah, Shammah, and Mizzah.

38 And [a]the sons of Seir; Lotan, and Shobal, and Zibeon, and Anah, and Dishon, and Ezar, and Dishan.

39 And the sons of Lotan; Hori, and [Ia]Homam: and Timna *was* Lotan's sister.[269]

40 The sons of Shobal; [Ia]Alian, and Manahath, and Ebal, [IIb]Shephi, and Onam. And the sons of Zibeon; Aiah, and Anah.

41 The sons of Anah; [a]Dishon. And the sons of Dishon; [Ib]Amram, and Eshban, and Ithran, and Cheran.

42 The sons of Ezer; Bilhan, and Zavan, *and* [Ia]Jakan. The sons of Dishan; Uz, and Aran.

43 Now these *are* the [a]kings[4428] that reigned in the land[776] of Edom before *any* king reigned over the children[1121] of Israel; Bela the son of Beor: and the name of his city *was* Dinhabah.

44 And when Bela was dead,[4191] Jobab the son of Zerah of Bozrah reigned in his stead.

45 And when Jobab was dead, Husham of the land of the Temanites reigned in his stead.

46 And when Husham was dead, Hadad the son of Bedad, which smote Midian in the field[7704] of Moab, reigned in his stead: and the name of his city *was* Avith.

47 And when Hadad was dead, Samlah of Masrekah reigned in his stead.

48 [a]And when Samlah was dead, Shaul of Rehoboth by the river reigned in his stead.

49 And when Shaul was dead, Baal–hanan the son of Achbor reigned in his stead.

50 And when Baal–hanan was dead, [Ia]Hadad reigned in his stead: and the name of his city *was* [IIb]Pai; and his wife's[802] name *was* Mehetabel, the daughter of Matred, the daughter of Mezahab.

51 Hadad died also. And the [a]dukes[441] of Edom were; duke Timnah, duke [I]Aliah, duke Jetheth,

52 Duke Aholibamah, duke Elah, duke Pinon,

53 Duke Kenaz, duke Teman, duke Mibzar,

24 [a]Gen. 11:10; Luke 3:34
25 [a]Gen. 11:15
27 [a]Gen. 17:5
28 [a]Gen. 21:2, 3 [b]Gen. 16:11, 15
29 [a]Gen. 25:13-16
30 [I]Or, *Hadar* [a]Gen. 25:15
32 [a]Gen. 25:1, 2
34 [a]Gen. 21:2, 3 [b]Gen. 25:25, 26
35 [a]Gen. 36:9, 10
36 [I]Or, *Zepho* [a]Gen. 36:11
38 [a]Gen. 36:20
39 [I]Or, *Hemam* [a]Gen. 36:22
40 [I]Or, *Alvan* [II]Or, *Shepho* [a]Gen. 36:23 [b]Gen. 36:23
41 [I]Or, *Hemdan* [a]Gen. 36:25 [b]Gen. 36:26
42 [I]Or, *Akan* [a]Gen. 36:27
43 [a]Gen. 36:31
48 [a]Gen. 36:37
50 [I]Or, *Hadar* [II]Or, *Pan* [a]Gen. 36:39 [b]Gen. 36:39
51 [I]Or, *Alvah* [a]Gen. 36:40

1:38 The rugged area of Seir was inhabited by a people called the Horites (Gen. 36:20). Some of them settled in Edom before the arrival of Esau (Deut. 2:12, 22).

54 Duke Magdiel, duke Iram. These *are* the dukes of Edom.

Israel's Sons

2 These *are* the sons of [I]Israel; [a]Reuben, Simeon, Levi, and Judah, Issachar, and Zebulun,

2 Dan, Joseph, and Benjamin, Naphtali, Gad, and Asher.

Judah's Family Record

3 The sons of [a]Judah; Er, and Onan, and Shelah: *which* three were born unto him of the daughter of [b]Shua the Canaanitess. And [c]Er, the firstborn of Judah, was evil[7451] in the sight of the LORD; and he slew him.

4 And [a]Tamar his daughter in law bare him Pharez and Zerah. All the sons of Judah *were* five.

5 The sons of [a]Pharez; Hezron, and Hamul.

6 And the sons of Zerah; [Ia]Zimri, [b]and Ethan, and Heman, and Calcol, and [II]Dara: five of them in all.

7 And the sons of [a]Carmi; [I]Achar, the troubler of Israel, who transgressed in the thing [b]accursed.[2764]

8 And the sons of Ethan; Azariah.

9 The sons also of Hezron, that were born unto him; Jerahmeel, and [Ia]Ram, and [IIb]Chelubai.

10 And Ram [a]begat Amminadab; and Amminadab begat Nahshon, [b]prince of the children[1121] of Judah;

11 And Nahshon begat [Ia]Salma, and Salma begat Boaz,

12 And Boaz begat Obed, and Obed begat Jesse,

13 [a]And Jesse begat his firstborn Eliab, and Abinadab the second, and [Ib]Shimma the third,

14 Nethaneel the fourth, Raddai the fifth,

🔑 15 Ozem the sixth, David the seventh:

🔑 16 Whose sisters *were* Zeruiah, and Abigail. [a]And the sons of Zeruiah; Abishai, and Joab, and Asahel, three.

17 And [a]Abigail bare Amasa: and the father of Amasa *was* [I]Jether the Ishmeelite.

18 And Caleb the son of Hezron begat *children* of Azubah *his* wife,[802] and of Jerioth: her sons *are* these; Jesher, and Shobab, and Ardon.

19 And when Azubah was dead, Caleb took unto him [a]Ephrath, which bare him Hur.

20 And Hur begat Uri, and Uri begat [a]Bezaleel.

21 And afterward Hezron went in to the daughter of [a]Machir the father of Gilead, whom he [I]married when he *was* threescore years old; and she bare him Segub.

22 And Segub begat Jair, who had three and twenty cities in the land[776] of Gilead.

23 [a]And he took Geshur, and Aram, with the towns of Jair, from them, with Kenath, and the towns thereof, *even* threescore cities. All these *belonged to* the sons of Machir the father of Gilead.

24 And after that Hezron was dead in Caleb–ephratah, then Abiah Hezron's wife bare him [a]Ashur the father of Tekoa.

25 And the sons of Jerahmeel the firstborn of Hezron were, Ram the firstborn, and Bunah, and Oren, and Ozem, *and* Ahijah.

26 Jerahmeel had also another wife, whose name *was* Atarah; she *was* the mother[517] of Onam.

27 And the sons of Ram the firstborn of Jerahmeel were, Maaz, and Jamin, and Eker.

28 And the sons of Onam were, Shammai, and Jada. And the sons of Shammai; Nadab, and Abishur.

1 [I]Or, *Jacob* [a]Gen. 29:32; 30:5; 35:18, 22; 46:8

3 [a]Gen. 38:3; 46:12; Num. 26:19 [b]Gen. 38:2 [c]Gen. 38:7

4 [a]Gen. 38:29, 30; Matt. 1:3

5 [a]Gen. 46:12; Ruth 4:18

6 [I]Or, *Zabdi* [II]Or, *Darda* [a]Josh. 7:1 [b]1Kgs. 4:31

7 [I]Or, *Achan* [a]2Chr. 4:1 [b]Josh. 6:18; 7:1

9 [I]Or, *Aram* [II]Or, *Caleb* [a]Matt. 1:3, 4 [b]1Chr. 2:18, 42

10 [a]Ruth 4:19, 20; Matt. 1:4 [b]Num. 1:7; 2:3

11 [I]Or, *Salmon* [a]Ruth 4:21; Matt. 1:4

13 [I]Or, *Shammah* [a]1Sam. 16:6 [b]1Sam. 16:9

16 [a]2Sam. 2:18

17 [I]2Sam. 17:25, *Ithra an Israelite* [a]2Sam. 17:25

19 [a]1Chr. 2:50

20 [a]Ex. 31:2

21 [I]Hebr. *took* [a]Num. 27:1

23 [a]Num. 32:41; Deut. 3:14; Josh. 13:30

24 [a]1Chr. 4:5

🔑 **2:15** Actually, David was the eighth son of Jesse (1 Sam. 16:10; 17:12). Apparently one son died without descendants, and so was omitted from the genealogy.

🔑 **2:16** Abigail and Zeruiah were half-sisters, having different fathers (2 Sam. 17:25).

29 And the name of the wife of Abishur *was* Abihail, and she bare him Ahban, and Molid.

30 And the sons of Nadab; Seled, and Appaim: but Seled died without children.

31 And the sons of Appaim; Ishi. And the sons of Ishi; Sheshan. And [a]the children of Sheshan; Ahlai.

32 And the sons of Jada the brother of Shammai; Jether, and Jonathan: and Jether died without children.

33 And the sons of Jonathan; Peleth, and Zaza. These were the sons of Jerahmeel.

34 Now Sheshan had no sons, but daughters. And Sheshan had a servant,[5650] an Egyptian, whose name *was* Jarha.

35 And Sheshan gave his daughter to Jarha his servant to wife; and she bare him Attai.

36 And Attai begat Nathan, and Nathan begat [a]Zabad,

37 And Zabad begat Ephlal, and Ephlal begat Obed,

38 And Obed begat Jehu, and Jehu begat Azariah,

39 And Azariah begat Helez, and Helez begat Eleasah,

40 And Eleasah begat Sisamai, and Sisamai begat Shallum,

41 And Shallum begat Jekamiah, and Jekamiah begat Elishama.

42 Now the sons of Caleb the brother of Jerahmeel *were,* Mesha his firstborn, which *was* the father of Ziph; and the sons of Mareshah the father of Hebron.

43 And the sons of Hebron; Korah, and Tappuah, and Rekem, and Shema.

44 And Shema begat Raham, the father of Jorkoam: and Rekem begat Shammai.

45 And the son of Shammai *was* Maon: and Maon *was* the father of Beth–zur.

46 And Ephah, Caleb's concubine, bare Haran, and Moza, and Gazez: and Haran begat Gazez.

47 And the sons of Jahdai; Regem, and Jotham, and Gesham, and Pelet, and Ephah, and Shaaph.

48 Maachah, Caleb's concubine, bare Sheber, and Tirhanah.

49 She bare also Shaaph the father of Madmannah, Sheva the father of Machbenah, and the father of Gibea: and the daughter of Caleb *was* [a]Achsa.

50 These were the sons of Caleb the son of Hur, the firstborn of [Ia]Ephratah; Shobal the father of Kirjath–jearim,

51 Salma the father of Bethlehem, Hareph the father of Beth–gader.

52 And Shobal the father of Kirjath–jearim had sons; [Ia]Haroeh, *and* [II]half of the Manahethites.

53 And the families[4940] of Kirjath–jearim; the Ithrites, and the Puhites, and the Shumathites, and the Mishraites; of them came the Zareathites, and the Eshtaulites.

54 The sons of Salma; Bethlehem, and the Netophathites, [I]Ataroth, the house of Joab, and half of the Manahethites, the Zorites.

55 And the families of the scribes[5608] which dwelt at Jabez; the Tirathites, the Shimeathites, *and* Suchathites. These *are* the [a]Kenites that came of Hemath, the father of the house of [b]Rechab.

David's Sons

3 Now these were the sons of David, which were born unto him in Hebron; the firstborn [a]Amnon, of Ahinoam the [b]Jezreelitess; the second [Ic]Daniel, of Abigail the Carmelitess:

31 [a]1Chr. 2:34, 35
36 [a]1Chr. 11:41
49 [a]Josh. 15:17
50 [I]Or, *Ephrath* [a]1Chr. 2:19
52 [I]Or, *Reaiah* [II]Or, *half of the Menuchites,* or, *Hatsihammenuchoth* [a]1Chr. 4:2
54 [I]Or, *Atarites,* or, *Crowns of the house of Joab*
55 [a]Judg. 1:16 [b]Jer. 35:2
1 [I]Or, *Chileab* [a]2Sam. 3:2 [b]Josh. 15:56 [c]2Sam. 3:3

2:49, 50 The Caleb (son of Hezron) mentioned in verse forty-nine is not the same Caleb (son of Jephunneh) that spied out the land of Canaan although he also had a daughter named Achsa (Josh. 15:16–19; Judg. 1:12–15). The Caleb (son of Hur) in verse fifty was the grandson of the Caleb referred to previously (2 Chr. 2:19).

2:55 The Kenites were from the family of Hobab, the brother-in-law of Moses. They became incorporated into the tribe of Judah (Judg. 1:16). Jehonadab (Jonadab), a later descendant of Rechab, was noted as a reformer who kept himself pure (2 Kgs. 10:15, 23–28; Jer. 35:1–19).

2 The third, Absalom the son of Maachah the daughter of Talmai king[4428] of Geshur: the fourth, Adonijah the son of Haggith:

3 The fifth, Shephatiah of Abital: the sixth, Ithream by [a]Eglah his wife.[802]

4 *These* six were born unto him in Hebron; and [a]there he reigned seven years and six months: and [b]in Jerusalem he reigned thirty and three years.

5 [a]And these were born unto him in Jerusalem; [Ib]Shimea, and Shobab, and Nathan, and [c]Solomon, four, of [IId]Bath–shua the daughter of [IIIe]Ammiel:

6 Ibhar also, and [Ia]Elishama, and Eliphelet,

7 And Nogah, and Nepheg, and Japhia,

8 And Elishama, and [Ia]Eliada, and Eliphelet, [b]nine.

9 *These were* all the sons of David, beside the sons of the concubines, and [a]Tamar their sister.[269]

Solomon's Family Record

10 And Solomon's son *was* [a]Rehoboam, [Ib]Abia his son, Asa his son, Jehoshaphat his son,

11 Joram his son, [a]Ahaziah his son, Joash his son,

12 Amaziah his son, [Ia]Azariah his son, Jotham his son,

13 Ahaz his son, Hezekiah his son, Manasseh his son,

14 Amon his son, Josiah his son.

15 And the sons of Josiah *were,* the firstborn [Ia]Johanan, the second [IIb]Jehoiakim, the third [IIIc]Zedekiah, the fourth Shallum.

16 And the sons of [a]Jehoiakim: [I]Jeconiah his son, Zedekiah [b]his son.

17 And the sons of Jeconiah; Assir, [I]Salathiel [a]his son,

18 Malchiram also, and Pedaiah, and Shenazar, Jecamiah, Hoshama, and Nedabiah.

19 And the sons of Pedaiah *were,* Zerubbabel, and Shimei: and the sons of Zerubbabel; Meshullam, and Hananiah, and Shelomith their sister:

20 And Hashubah, and Ohel, and Berechiah, and Hasadiah, Jushab–hesed, five.

21 And the sons of Hananiah; Pelatiah, and Jesaiah: the sons of Rephaiah, the sons of Arnan, the sons of Obadiah, the sons of Shechaniah.

22 And the sons of Shechaniah; Shemaiah: and the sons of Shemaiah; [a]Hattush, and Igeal, and Bariah, and Neariah, and Shaphat, six.

23 And the sons of Neariah; Elioenai, and [I]Hezekiah, and Azrikam, three.

24 And the sons of Elioenai *were,* Hodaiah, and Eliashib, and Pelaiah, and Akkub, and Johanan, and Dalaiah, and Anani, seven.

Judah's Family Record

4 The sons of Judah; [a]Pharez, Hezron, and [b]Carmi, and Hur, and Shobal.

2 And [Ia]Reaiah the son of Shobal begat Jahath; and Jahath begat Ahumai,

3 [a]2Sam. 3:5
4 [a]2Sam. 2:11 [b]2Sam. 5:5
5 [I]Or, *Shammua* [II]Or, *Bath-sheba* [III]Or, *Eliam* [a]2Sam. 5:14; 1Chr. 14:4 [b]2Sam. 5:14 [c]2Sam. 12:24 [d]2Sam. 11:3 [e]2Sam. 11:3
6 [I]Or, *Elishua* [a]2Sam. 5:15
8 [I]Or, *Beeliada* [a]1Chr. 14:7 [b]2Sam. 5:14-16
9 [a]2Sam. 13:1
10 [I]Or, *Abijam* [a]1Kgs. 11:43; 15:6 [b]1Kgs. 15:1
11 [a]2Chr. 21:17, Jehoahaz; 2Chr. 22:6, Azariah
12 [I]Or, *Uzziah* [a]2Kgs. 15:30
15 [I]Or, *Jehoahaz* [II]Or, *Eliakim* [III]Or, *Mattaniah* [a]2Kgs. 23:30 [b]2Kgs. 23:34 [c]2Kgs. 24:17
16 [I]Or, *Jehoiachin,* 2Kgs. 24:6; or, *Coniah,* Jer. 22:24 [a]Matt. 1:11 [b]2Kgs. 24:17, being his uncle
17 [I]Hebr. *Shealtiel* [a]Matt. 1:12
22 [a]Ezra 8:2
23 [I]Hebr. *Hiskijahu*

1 [a]Gen. 38:29; 46:12 [b]1Chr. 2:9, Chelubar; 1Chr. 2:18, Caleb
2 [I]Or, *Haroeh* [a]1Chr. 2:52

3:15 Shallum was also called Jehoahaz (2 Kgs. 23:31; 2 Chr. 36:2, cf. Jer. 22:11). Actually, he was older than Zedekiah (2 Kgs. 24:18), but he ruled for a shorter period of time.

3:17–19 Zerubbabel was considered the son of Pedaiah's brother, Shealtiel (Ezra 3:2; Hag. 1:12; 2:23; Matt. 1:12; Luke 3:27), perhaps as a result of a "levirate marriage" (Deut. 25:5–10; see note on Ruth 4:1–8). Another suggestion is that Zerubbabel was appointed as heir to the throne after Shealtiel, his uncle, died without any heirs. In any event, Zerubbabel was an heir to the throne of David, but he could not become king because of the curse that was placed on his grandfather, Jeconiah (Jer. 22:30). Zerubbabel was the leader of a group of Jews who returned to Palestine in 538 B.C. from exile in Babylon (Ezra 2:2; 3:2).

3:19–24 It is reasonable to say that Ezra could have written concerning these descendants of Zerubbabel since Ezra's writing took place near 400 B.C., roughly the time when the sixth descendant of Zerubbabel (who is dated approximately 520 B.C.) would have lived. This information is based on a minimum of twenty years for each generation.

and Lahad. These *are* the families[4940] of the Zorathites.

3 And these *were of* the father[1] of Etam; Jezreel, and Ishma, and Idbash: and the name of their sister[269] *was* Hazelelponi:

4 And Penuel the father of Gedor, and Ezer the father of Hushah. These *are* the sons of [a]Hur, the firstborn of Ephratah, the father of Bethlehem.

5 And [a]Ashur the father of Tekoa had two wives,[802] Helah and Naarah.

6 And Naarah bare him Ahuzam, and Hepher, and Temeni, and Haahashtari. These *were* the sons of Naarah.

7 And the sons of Helah *were,* Zereth, and Jezoar, and Ethnan.

8 And Coz begat Anub, and Zobebah, and the families of Aharhel the son of Harum.

9 And Jabez was [a]more honourable[3513] than his brethren:[251] and his mother[517] called[7121] his name [I]Jabez, saying, Because I bare him with sorrow.[6090]

10 And Jabez called on the God[430] of Israel, saying, [I]Oh that thou wouldest bless[1288] me indeed, and enlarge my coast, and that thine hand might be with me, and that thou wouldest [II]keep[6213] *me* from evil,[7451] that it may not grieve[6087] me! And God granted him that which he requested.

11 And Chelub the brother[251] of Shuah begat Mehir, which *was* the father of Eshton.

12 And Eshton begat Beth–rapha, and Paseah, and Tehinnah the father of [I]Ir–nahash. These *are* the men[582] of Rechah.

🗝 13 And the sons of Kenaz; [a]Othniel, and Seraiah: and the sons of Othniel; [I]Hathath.

14 And Meonothai begat Ophrah: and Seraiah begat Joab, the father of [a]the [I]valley of [II]Charashim; for they were craftsmen.[2796]

15 And the sons of Caleb the son of Jephunneh; Iru, Elah, and Naam: and the sons of Elah, [I]even Kenaz.

16 And the sons of Jehaleleel; Ziph, and Ziphah, Tiria, and Asareel.

17 And the sons of Ezra *were,* Jether, and Mered, and Epher, and Jalon: and she bare Miriam, and Shammai, and Ishbah the father of Eshtemoa.

18 And his wife[802] [I]Jehudijah bare Jered the father of Gedor, and Heber the father of Socho, and Jekuthiel the father of Zanoah. And these *are* the sons of Bithiah the daughter of Pharaoh, which Mered took.

19 And the sons of *his* wife [I]Hodiah the sister of Naham, the father of Keilah the Garmite, and Eshtemoa the Maachathite.

20 And the sons of Shimon *were,* Amnon, and Rinnah, Ben–hanan, and Tilon. And the sons of Ishi *were,* Zoheth, and Ben–zoheth.

21 The sons of Shelah [a]the son of Judah *were,* Er the father of Lecah, and Laadah the father of Mareshah, and the families of the house of them that wrought[5656] fine linen, of the house of Ashbea,

22 And Jokim, and the men of Chozeba, and Joash, and Saraph, who had the dominion[1166] in Moab, and Jashubi–lehem. And *these are* ancient things.

23 These *were* the potters, and those that dwelt among plants and hedges: there they dwelt with the king[4428] for his work.[4399]

Simeon's Family Record

24 The sons of Simeon *were,* [I][a]Nemuel, and Jamin, [II]Jarib, Zerah, *and* Shaul:

25 Shallum his son, Mibsam his son, Mishma his son.

26 And the sons of Mishma; Hamuel his son, Zacchur his son, Shimei his son.

27 And Shimei had sixteen sons and

4 [a]1Chr. 2:50
5 [a]1Chr. 2:24
9 [I]That is, *Sorrowful* [a]Gen. 34:19
10 [I]Hebr. *If thou wilt* [II]Hebr. *do me*
12 [I]Or, *The city of Nahash*
13 [I]Or, *Hathath, and Meonothai, who begat Joab* [a]Josh. 15:17
14 [I]Or, *inhabitants of the valley* [II]That is, *craftsmen* [a]Neh. 11:35
15 [I]Or, *Uknaz*
18 [I]Or, *The Jewess*
19 [I]Or, *Jehudijah*
21 [a]Gen. 38:1, 5; 46:12
24 [I]Or, *Jemuel* [II]Or, *Jachin, Zohar* [a]Gen. 46:10; Ex. 6:15; Num. 26:12

🗝 **4:13** Othniel was the son-in-law of Caleb. In 1381 B.C., he became the first of the judges (Judg. 3:9, 10).

six daughters; but his brethren had not many children,[1121] neither did all their family[4940] multiply, [I]like to the children of Judah.

28 And they dwelt at [a]Beer–sheba, and Moladah, and Hazar–shual,

29 And at [I][a]Bilhah, and at Ezem, and at [II][b]Tolad,

30 And at Bethuel, and at Hormah, and at Ziklag,

31 And at Beth–marcaboth, and [I][a]Hazar–susim, and at Beth–birei, and at Shaaraim. These *were* their cities unto the reign of David.

32 And their villages *were,* [I][a]Etam, and Ain, Rimmon, and Tochen, and Ashan, five cities:

33 And all their villages that *were* round about the same cities, unto [I][a]Baal. These *were* their habitations, and [II]their genealogy.

34 And Meshobab, and Jamlech, and Joshah the son of Amaziah,

35 And Joel, and Jehu the son of Josibiah, the son of Seraiah, the son of Asiel,

36 And Elioenai, and Jaakobah, and Jeshohaiah, and Asaiah, and Adiel, and Jesimiel, and Benaiah,

37 And Ziza the son of Shiphi, the son of Allon, the son of Jedaiah, the son of Shimri, the son of Shemaiah;

38 These [I]mentioned by *their* names *were* princes[5387] in their families: and the house of their fathers[1] increased greatly.

39 And they went to the entrance of Gedor, *even* unto the east side of the valley, to seek pasture for their flocks.

40 And they found fat8082 pasture and good,[2896] and the land[776] *was* wide, and quiet, and peaceable; for *they* of Ham had dwelt there of old.

41 And these written by name came in the days[3117] of Hezekiah king of Judah, and [a]smote[5221] their tents, and the habitations that were found there, and

27 [I]Hebr. *unto*
28 [a]Josh. 19:2
29 [I]Or, *Balah* [II]Or, *Eltolad* [a]Josh. 19:3 [b]Josh. 19:4
31 [I]Or, *Hazarsusah* [a]Josh. 19:5
32 [I]Or, *Ether* [a]Josh. 19:7
33 [I]Or, *Baalath-beer* [II]Or, *as they divided themselves by nations among them* [a]Josh. 19:8
38 [I]Hebr. *coming*
41 [a]2Kgs. 18:8
43 [a]1Sam. 15:8; 30:17; 2Sam. 8:12
1 [a]Gen. 29:32; 49:3 [b]Gen. 35:22; 49:4 [c]Gen. 48:15, 22
2 [I]Or, *prince* [a]Gen. 49:8, 10; Ps. 60:7; 108:8 [b]Mic. 5:2; Matt. 2:6
3 [a]Gen. 46:9; Ex. 6:14; Num. 26:5
6 [a]2Kgs. 15:29; 16:7
7 [a]1Chr. 5:17
8 [I]Or, *Shemaiah* [a]1Chr. 5:4 [b]Josh. 13:15, 16
9 [a]Josh. 22:9

destroyed them utterly[2763] unto this day,[3117] and dwelt in their rooms: because *there was* pasture there for their flocks.

42 And *some* of them, *even* of the sons of Simeon, five hundred men, went to mount Seir, having for their captains[7218] Pelatiah, and Neariah, and Rephaiah, and Uzziel, the sons of Ishi.

43 And they smote [a]the rest of the Amalekites that were escaped,[6413] and dwelt there unto this day.

Reuben's Family Record

5 Now the sons of Reuben the firstborn of Israel, (for [a]he *was* the firstborn; but, forasmuch as he [b]defiled[2490] his father's[1] bed, [c]his birthright[1062] was given unto the sons of Joseph the son of Israel: and the genealogy is not to be reckoned after the birthright.

2 For [a]Judah prevailed above his brethren,[251] and of him *came* the [b]chief [I]ruler; but the birthright1062 *was* Joseph's:)

3 The sons, *I say,* of [a]Reuben the firstborn of Israel *were,* Hanoch, and Pallu, Hezron, and Carmi.

4 The sons of Joel; Shemaiah his son, Gog his son, Shimei his son,

5 Micah his son, Reaia his son, Baal his son,

6 Beerah his son, whom [a]Tilgath–pilneser king[4428] of Assyria carried away[1540] *captive:* he *was* prince of the Reubenites.

7 And his brethren by their families,[4940] [a]when the genealogy of their generations[8435] was reckoned, *were* the chief,[7218] Jeiel, and Zechariah,

8 And Bela the son of Azaz, the son of [I][a]Shema, the son of Joel, who dwelt in [b]Aroer, even unto Nebo and Baal–meon:

9 And eastward he inhabited unto the entering in of the wilderness from the river Euphrates: because their cattle were multiplied [a]in the land[776] of Gilead.

4:43 Both Saul and David had won great victories over the Amalekites (1 Sam. 14:48; 15:7; 2 Sam. 8:12).

5:6 This verse is not describing the final fall of Samaria in 722 B.C., but probably the captivity of the two and one-half tribes (733 B.C.) which lived east of the Jordan River (2 Kgs. 15:29; 1 Chr. 5:26).

10 And in the days[3117] of Saul they
made[6213] war [a]with the Hagarites, who
fell[5307] by their hand: and they dwelt in
their tents [I]throughout all the east *land* of
Gilead.

Gad's Family Record

11 And the children[1121] of Gad dwelt
over against them, in the land of [a]Bashan
unto Salcah:
12 Joel the chief, and Shapham the
next, and Jaanai, and Shaphat in Bashan.
13 And their brethren of the house of
their fathers[1] *were,* Michael, and Meshullam, and Sheba, and Jorai, and Jachan,
and Zia, and Heber, seven.
14 These *are* the children of Abihail
the son of Huri, the son of Jaroah, the
son of Gilead, the son of Michael,
the son of Jeshishai, the son of Jahdo, the
son of Buz;
15 Ahi the son of Abdiel, the son of
Guni, chief of the house of their fathers.
16 And they dwelt in Gilead in
Bashan, and in her towns, and in all the
suburbs of [a]Sharon, upon [I]their borders.
17 All these were reckoned by genealogies[3187] in the days of [a]Jotham king
of Judah, and in the days of [b]Jeroboam
king of Israel.

The Eastern Tribes' Army

18 The sons of Reuben, and the
Gadites, and half the tribe of Manasseh,
[I]of valiant men, men[582] able to bear[5375]
buckler[4043] and sword, and to shoot with
bow, and skilful[3925] in war,[6635] *were* four
and forty thousand seven hundred and
threescore, that went out to the war.
19 And they made war with the
Hagarites, with [a]Jetur, and Nephish, and
Nodab.
20 And [a]they were helped against
them, and the Hagarites were delivered
into their hand, and all that *were* with
them: for they cried[2199] to God[430] in the
battle, and he was intreated[6279] of them;
because they [b]put their trust in him.
21 And they [I]took away their cattle;
of their camels fifty thousand, and of
sheep two hundred and fifty thousand,
and of asses two thousand, and of
[II]men[120] an hundred thousand.
22 For there fell down many
slain,[2491] because the war *was* of God.
And they dwelt in their steads until [a]the
captivity.[1473]

Sketch of Eastern Manasseh's History

23 And the children of the half tribe
of Manasseh dwelt in the land: they increased from Bashan unto Baal–hermon
and Senir, and unto mount Hermon.
24 And these *were* the heads of the
house of their fathers, even Epher, and
Ishi, and Eliel, and Azriel, and Jeremiah,
and Hodaviah, and Jahdiel, mighty men
of valour,[2428] [I]famous men, *and* heads of
the house of their fathers.
25 And they transgressed against the
God of their fathers, and went a [a]whoring
after the gods[430] of the people of the land,
whom God destroyed[8045] before them.
26 And the God of Israel stirred
up[5782] the spirit of [a]Pul king of Assyria,
and the spirit of [b]Tilgath–pilneser king
of Assyria, and he carried them away,
even the Reubenites, and the Gadites, and
the half tribe of Manasseh, and brought
them unto [c]Halah, and Habor, and Hara,
and to the river Gozan, unto this day.[3117]

Levi's Family Record

6 The sons of Levi; [I][a]Gershon, Kohath,
and Merari.
2 And the sons of Kohath; Amram,
[a]Izhar, and Hebron, and Uzziel.
🗝 3 And the children[1121] of Amram;
Aaron, and Moses, and Miriam. The sons

10 [I]Hebr. *upon all the face of the east* [a]Gen. 25:12

11 [a]Josh. 13:11, 24

16 [I]Hebr. *their goings forth* [a]1Chr. 27:29

17 [a]2Kgs. 15:5, 32 [b]2Kgs. 14:16, 28

18 [I]Hebr. *sons of valor*

19 [a]Gen. 25:15; 1Chr. 1:31

20 [a]1Chr. 5:22 [b]Ps. 22:4, 5

21 [I]Hebr. *led captive* [II]Hebr. *souls of men*

22 [a]2Kgs. 15:29; 17:6

24 [I]Hebr. *men of names*

25 [a]2Kgs. 17:7

26 [a]2Kgs. 15:19 [b]2Kgs. 15:29 [c]2Kgs. 17:6; 18:11

1 [I]Or, *Gershom* [a]Gen. 46:11; Ex. 6:16; Num. 26:57; 1Chr. 23:6

2 [a]1Chr. 6:22

🗝 **6:3–30** The list of high priests in verses four through thirty covers the 860 years between the exodus and the fall of Jerusalem. Not included in this list of descendants of Ithamar, who held the

(continued on next page)

also of Aaron; [a]Nadab, and Abihu, Eleazar, and Ithamar.

4 Eleazar begat Phinehas, Phinehas begat Abishua,

5 And Abishua begat Bukki, and Bukki begat Uzzi,

6 And Uzzi begat Zerahiah, and Zerahiah begat Meraioth,

7 Meraioth begat Amariah, and Amariah begat Ahitub,

8 And [a]Ahitub begat Zadok, and [b]Zadok begat Ahimaaz,

9 And Ahimaaz begat Azariah, and Azariah begat Johanan,

10 And Johanan begat Azariah, (he *it is* [a]that executed the priest's office[3547] [I]in the [b]temple that Solomon built in Jerusalem:)

11 And [a]Azariah begat Amariah, and Amariah begat Ahitub,

12 And Ahitub begat Zadok, and Zadok begat [Ia]Shallum,

13 And Shallum begat Hilkiah, and Hilkiah begat Azariah,

14 And Azariah begat [a]Seraiah, and Seraiah begat Jehozadak,

15 And Jehozadak went *into captivity,* [a]when the LORD carried away[1540] Judah and Jerusalem by the hand of Nebuchadnezzar.

16 The sons of Levi; [Ia]Gershom, Kohath, and Merari.

17 And these *be* the names of the sons of Gershom; Libni, and Shimei.

18 And the sons of Kohath *were,* Amram, and Izhar, and Hebron, and Uzziel.

19 The sons of Merari; Mahli, and Mushi. And these *are* the families[4940] of the Levites according to their fathers.[1]

3 [a]Lev. 10:1
8 [a]2Sam. 8:17 [b]2Sam. 15:27
10 [I]Hebr. *in the house* [a]2Chr. 26:17, 18 [b]1Kgs. 6; 2Chr. 3
11 [a]Ezra 7:3
12 [I]Or, *Meshullam* [a]1Chr. 9:11
14 [a]Neh. 11:11
15 [a]2Kgs. 25:18
16 [I]Or, *Gershon* [a]Ex. 6:16
20 [a]1Chr. 6:42
21 [a]1Chr. 6:42, Ethan [b]1Chr. 6:41, Adainah [c]1Chr. 6:4; Ethni
22 [a]1Chr. 6:2, 18, Izhar
24 [a]1Chr. 6:36; Zephaniah, Azariah, Joel
25 [a]1Chr. 6:35, 36
26 [I]Or, *Zuph* [a]1Sam. 1:1 [b]1Chr. 6:34, *Toah*
27 [a]1Chr. 6:34, *Eliel*
28 [I]Called also *Joel* [a]1Sam. 8:2; 1Chr. 6:33
31 [a]1Chr. 16:1
33 [I]Hebr. *stood*

20 Of Gershom; Libni his son, Jahath his son, [a]Zimmah his son,

21 [a]Joah his son, [b]Iddo his son, Zerah his son, [c]Jeaterai his son.

🔑 22 The sons of Kohath; [a]Amminadab his son, Korah his son, Assir his son,

23 Elkanah his son, and Ebiasaph his son, and Assir his son,

24 Tahath his son, [a]Uriel his son, Uzziah his son, and Shaul his son.

25 And the sons of Elkanah; [a]Amasai, and Ahimoth.

26 *As for* Elkanah: the sons of Elkanah; [Ia]Zophai his son, and [b]Nahath his son,

🔑 27 [a]Eliab his son, Jeroham his son, Elkanah his son.

28 And the sons of Samuel; the firstborn [Ia]Vashni, and Abiah.

29 The sons of Merari; Mahli, Libni his son, Shimei his son, Uzza his son,

30 Shimea his son, Haggiah his son, Asaiah his son.

The Temple Musicians

31 And these *are they* whom David set over the service of song in the house of the LORD, after that the [a]ark[727] had rest.

32 And they ministered[8334] before the dwelling place of the tabernacle of the congregation[4150] with singing, until Solomon had built the house of the LORD in Jerusalem: and *then* they waited on their office according to their order.[4941]

33 And these *are* they that [I]waited with their children. Of the sons of the Kohathites: Heman a singer, the son of Joel, the son of Shemuel,

34 The son of Elkanah, the son of

(continued from previous page)
office of the priest during the transition between the judges and the early kingdom of Israel, were the following: Eli, Phinehas II, Ahitub I, Ahimelech I (Ahiah), Abiathar, and Ahimelech II (1 Sam. 14:3; 22:20; 2 Sam. 8:17). Certain other high priests are not recorded here who are mentioned elsewhere—Amariah II (2 Chr. 19:11), Jehoiada (2 Kgs. 11:9), Zechariah (2 Chr. 24:20), Urijah (2 Kgs. 16:10), Azariah II (2 Chr. 31:10), and Meraioth (1 Chr. 9:11).

🔑 **6:3, 4** Notice that Nadab and Abihu had no descendants (vv.14, 15). They were killed in the wilderness for their irreverent behavior (Lev. 10:1, 2; Num. 3:4).

🔑 **6:22** Korah was swallowed by the earth for rebelling against Moses (see Num. 16).

🔑 **6:27, 28** Elkanah was the husband of Hannah and the father of Samuel (1 Sam. 1:1).

Jeroham, the son of Eliel, the son of [a]Toah,

35 The son of [I]Zuph, the son of Elkanah, the son of Mahath, the son of Amasai,

36 The son of Elkanah, the son of [a]Joel, the son of Azariah, the son of Zephaniah,

37 The son of Tahath, the son of Assir, the son of [a]Ebiasaph, the son of Korah,

38 The son of Izhar, the son of Kohath, the son of Levi, the son of Israel.

39 And his brother[251] Asaph, who stood on his right hand, *even* Asaph the son of Berachiah, the son of Shimea,

40 The son of Michael, the son of Baaseiah, the son of Malchiah,

41 The son of [a]Ethni, the son of Zerah, the son of Adaiah,

42 The son of Ethan, the son of Zimmah, the son of Shimei,

43 The son of Jahath, the son of Gershom, the son of Levi.

44 And their brethren[251] the sons of Merari *stood* on the left hand: [I]Ethan the son of [IIa]Kishi, the son of Abdi, the son of Malluch,

45 The son of Hashabiah, the son of Amaziah, the son of Hilkiah,

46 The son of Amzi, the son of Bani, the son of Shamer,

47 The son of Mahli, the son of Mushi, the son of Merari, the son of Levi.

48 Their brethren also the Levites *were* appointed unto all manner of service of the tabernacle[4908] of the house of God.[430]

Aaron's Family Record

49 But Aaron and his sons offered[6999] [a]upon the altar[4196] of the burnt offering,[5930] and [b]on the altar of incense,[7004] *and were appointed* for all the work[4399] of the *place* most holy, and

34 [a]1Chr. 6:26, *Nahath*
35 [I]Or, *Zophai*
36 [a]1Chr. 6:24, *Shaul, Uzziah, Uriel*
37 [a]Ex. 6:24
41 [a]1Chr. 6:21
44 [I]Called *Jeduthun* [II]Or, *Kushaiah* [a]1Chr. 9:16; 25:1, 3, 6 [b]1Chr. 15:17
49 [a]Lev. 1:9 [b]Ex. 30:7
54 [a]Josh. 21:7, 10
55 [a]Josh. 21:11, 12
56 [a]Josh. 14:13; 15:13
57 [a]Josh. 21:13
58 [I]Or, *Holon* [a]Josh. 21:15
59 [I]Or, *Ain* [a]Josh. 21:16
60 [I]Or, *Almon* [a]Josh. 21:18
61 [a]1Chr. 6:66 [b]Josh. 21:5

to make an atonement[3722] for Israel, according to all that Moses the servant of God had commanded.[6680]

50 And these *are* the sons of Aaron; Eleazar his son, Phinehas his son, Abishua his son,

51 Bukki his son, Uzzi his son, Zerahiah his son,

52 Meraioth his son, Amariah his son, Ahitub his son,

53 Zadok his son, Ahimaaz his son.

The Levites' Cities

54 [a]Now these *are* their dwelling places[4186] throughout their castles[2918] in their coasts, of the sons of Aaron, of the families of the Kohathites: for theirs was the lot.

55 [a]And they gave them Hebron in the land[776] of Judah, and the suburbs thereof round about it.

56 [a]But the fields[7704] of the city, and the villages thereof, they gave to Caleb the son of Jephunneh.

57 And [a]to the sons of Aaron they gave the cities of Judah, *namely,* Hebron, *the city* of refuge, and Libnah with her suburbs,[4054] and Jattir, and Eshtemoa, with their suburbs,

58 And [Ia]Hilen with her suburbs, Debir with her suburbs,

59 And [Ia]Ashan with her suburbs, and Beth–shemesh with her suburbs:

60 And out of the tribe of Benjamin; Geba with her suburbs, and [Ia]Alemeth with her suburbs, and Anathoth with her suburbs. All their cities throughout their families *were* thirteen cities.

61 And unto the sons of Kohath, [a]*which were* left[3498] of the family[4940] of that tribe, *were cities given* out of the half tribe, *namely, out of* the half *tribe* of Manasseh, [b]by lot, ten cities.

62 And to the sons of Gershom throughout their families out of the tribe of Issachar, and out of the tribe of

---

6:56 This grant of land was promised to Caleb by Moses and Joshua (Josh. 14:6–15).
6:57 See note on Deuteronomy 19:1–10 concerning the "cities of refuge."

Asher, and out of the tribe of Naphtali, and out of the tribe of Manasseh in Bashan, thirteen cities.

63 Unto the sons of Merari *were given* by lot, throughout their families, out of the tribe of Reuben, and out of the tribe of Gad, and out of the tribe of Zebulun, [a]twelve cities.

64 And the children of Israel gave to the Levites *these* cities with their suburbs.

65 And they gave by lot out of the tribe of the children of Judah, and out of the tribe of the children of Simeon, and out of the tribe of the children of Benjamin, these cities, which are called[7121] by *their* names.

66 And [a]*the residue* of the families of the sons of Kohath had cities of their coasts out of the tribe of Ephraim.

67 [a]And they gave unto them, *of* the cities of refuge, Shechem in mount Ephraim with her suburbs; *they gave* also Gezer with her suburbs,

68 And [a]Jokmeam with her suburbs, and Beth–horon with her suburbs,

69 And Aijalon with her suburbs, and Gath–rimmon with her suburbs:

70 And out of the half tribe of Manasseh; Aner with her suburbs, and Bileam with her suburbs, for the family of the remnant[3498] of the sons of Kohath.

71 Unto the sons of Gershom *were given* out of the family of the half tribe of Manasseh, Golan in Bashan with her suburbs, and Ashtaroth with her suburbs:

72 And out of the tribe of Issachar; Kedesh with her suburbs, Daberath with her suburbs,

73 And Ramoth with her suburbs, and Anem with her suburbs:

74 And out of the tribe of Asher; Mashal with her suburbs, and Abdon with her suburbs,

75 And Hukok with her suburbs, and Rehob with her suburbs:

76 And out of the tribe of Naphtali; Kedesh in Galilee with her suburbs, and Hammon with her suburbs, and Kirjathaim with her suburbs.

63 [a]Josh. 21:7, 34
66 [a]1Chr. 6:61
67 [a]Josh. 21:21
68 [a]Josh. 21:22-35, many of these cities have other names
1 [I]Phuvah, Job [a]Gen. 46:13; Num. 26:23
2 [a]2Sam. 24:1, 2; 1Chr. 27:1
6 [a]Gen. 46:21; Num. 26:38; 1Chr. 8:1

77 Unto the rest of the children of Merari *were given* out of the tribe of Zebulun, Rimmon with her suburbs, Tabor with her suburbs:

78 And on the other side Jordan by Jericho, on the east side of Jordan, *were given them* out of the tribe of Reuben, Bezer in the wilderness with her suburbs, and Jahzah with her suburbs,

79 Kedemoth also with her suburbs, and Mephaath with her suburbs:

80 And out of the tribe of Gad; Ramoth in Gilead with her suburbs, and Mahanaim with her suburbs,

81 And Heshbon with her suburbs, and Jazer with her suburbs.

Issachar's Family Record

7 Now the sons of Issachar *were,* [a]Tola, and [I]Puah, Jashub, and Shimrom, four.

2 And the sons of Tola; Uzzi, and Rephaiah, and Jeriel, and Jahmai, and Jibsam, and Shemuel, heads of their father's house, *to wit,* of Tola: *they were* valiant men1368 of might[2428] in their generations;[8435] [a]whose number *was* in the days[3117] of David two and twenty thousand and six hundred.

3 And the sons of Uzzi; Izrahiah: and the sons of Izrahiah; Michael, and Obadiah, and Joel, Ishiah, five: all of them chief[7218] men.

4 And with them, by their generations, after the house of their fathers,[1] *were* bands of soldiers for war, six and thirty thousand *men:* for they had many wives[802] and sons.

5 And their brethren[251] among all the families[4940] of Issachar *were* valiant men of might, reckoned in all by their genealogies fourscore and seven thousand.

Benjamin's Family Record

6 *The sons* of [a]Benjamin; Bela, and Becher, and Jediael, three.

7 And the sons of Bela; Ezbon, and Uzzi, Uzziel, and Jerimoth, and Iri, five; heads of the house of *their* fathers, mighty men1368 of valour;[2428] and were

reckoned by their genealogies twenty and two thousand and thirty and four.

8 And the sons of Becher; Zemira, and Joash, and Eliezer, and Elioenai, and Omri, and Jerimoth, and Abiah, and Anathoth, and Alameth. All these *are* the sons of Becher.

9 And the number of them, after their genealogy by their generations,[8435] heads of the house of their fathers, mighty men of valour, *was* twenty thousand and two hundred.

10 The sons also of Jediael; Bilhan: and the sons of Bilhan; Jeush, and Benjamin, and Ehud, and Chenaanah, and Zethan, and Tharshish, and Ahishahar.

11 All these the sons of Jediael, by the heads of their fathers, mighty men of valour, *were* seventeen thousand and two hundred *soldiers,* fit to go out for war[6635] *and* battle.

12 [a]Shuppim also, and Huppim, the children[1121] of [I][b]Ir, *and* Hushim, the sons of [II][c]Aher.

Naphtali's Sons

13 The sons of Naphtali; Jahziel, and Guni, and Jezer, and [a]Shallum, the sons of Bilhah.

Manasseh's Family Record

14 The sons of Manasseh; Ashriel, whom she bare: (*but* his concubine the Aramitess bare Machir the father of Gilead:

15 And Machir took to wife[802] *the sister* of Huppim and Shuppim, whose sister's name *was* Maachah;) and the name of the second *was* Zelophehad: and Zelophehad had daughters.

16 And Maachah the wife of Machir bare a son, and she called[7121] his name Peresh; and the name of his brother *was* Sheresh; and his sons *were* Ulam and Rakem.

17 And the sons of Ulam; [a]Bedan. These *were* the sons of Gilead, the son of Machir, the son of Manasseh.

18 And his sister Hammoleketh bare Ishod, and [a]Abiezer, and Mahalah.

12 [I]Or, *Iri* [II]Or, *Ahiram* [a]Num. 26:39, *Shupham,* and *Hupham* [b]1Chr. 7:7 [c]Num. 26:38

13 [a]Gen. 46:24, *Shillem*

17 [a]1Sam. 12:11

18 [a]Num. 26:30, *Jeezer*

20 [a]Num. 26:35

27 [a]Num. 13:8, 16

28 [I]Hebr. *daughters* [a]Josh. 16:7, *Naarath*

29 [a]Josh. 17:7 [b]Josh. 17:11

30 [a]Gen. 46:17; Num. 26:44

19 And the sons of Shemidah were, Ahian, and Shechem, and Likhi, and Aniam.

Ephraim's Family Record

20 And [a]the sons of Ephraim; Shuthelah, and Bered his son, and Tahath his son, and Eladah his son, and Tahath his son,

21 And Zabad his son, and Shuthelah his son, and Ezer, and Elead, whom the men[582] of Gath *that were* born in *that* land[776] slew, because they came down to take away their cattle.

22 And Ephraim their father mourned many days, and his brethren came to comfort[5162] him.

23 And when he went in to his wife, she conceived, and bare a son, and he called his name Beriah, because it went evil[7451] with his house.

24 (And his daughter *was* Sherah, who built Beth–horon the nether,[8481] and the upper,[5945] and Uzzen–sherah.)

25 And Rephah *was* his son, also Resheph, and Telah his son, and Tahan his son,

26 Laadan his son, Ammihud his son, Elishama his son,

27 [a]Non his son, Jehoshua his son.

28 And their possessions and habitations *were,* Bethel and the towns thereof, and eastward[4217] [a]Naaran, and westward[4628] Gezer, with the [I]towns[1323] thereof; Shechem also and the towns thereof, unto Gaza and the towns thereof:

29 And by the borders of the children of [a]Manasseh, Beth–shean and her towns, Taanach and her towns, [b]Megiddo and her towns, Dor and her towns. In these dwelt the children of Joseph the son of Israel.

Asher's Family Record

30 [a]The sons of Asher; Imnah, and Isuah, and Ishuai, and Beriah, and Serah their sister.

31 And the sons of Beriah; Heber, and Malchiel, who *is* the father of Birzavith.

32 And Heber begat Japhlet, and [a]Shomer, and Hotham, and Shua their sister.

33 And the sons of Japhlet; Pasach, and Bimhal, and Ashvath. These *are* the children of Japhlet.

34 And the sons of [a]Shamer; Ahi, and Rohgah, Jehubbah, and Aram.

35 And the sons of his brother Helem; Zophah, and Imna, and Shelesh, and Amal.

36 The sons of Zophah; Suah, and Harnepher, and Shual, and Beri, and Imrah,

37 Bezer, and Hod, and Shamma, and Shilshah, and Ithran, and Beera.

38 And the sons of Jether; Jephunneh, and Pispah, and Ara.

39 And the sons of Ulla; Arah, and Haniel, and Rezia.

40 All these *were* the children of Asher, heads of *their* father's house, choice[1305] *and* mighty men of valour, chief of the princes. And the number throughout the genealogy of them that were apt to the war *and* to battle *was* twenty and six thousand men.

Benjamin's Family Record

8 Now Benjamin begat [a]Bela his firstborn, Ashbel the second, and Aharah the third,

2 Nohah the fourth, and Rapha the fifth.

3 And the sons of Bela were, [1a]Addar, and Gera, and Abihud,

4 And Abishua, and Naaman, and Ahoah,

5 And Gera, and [1a]Shephuphan, and Huram.

6 And these *are* the sons of Ehud: these are the heads of the fathers[1] of the inhabitants of Geba, and they removed them to [a]Manahath:

7 And Naaman, and Ahiah, and Gera, he removed them, and begat Uzza, and Ahihud.

8 And Shaharaim begat *children* in the country[7704] of Moab, after he had sent them away; Hushim and Baara *were* his wives.

9 And he begat of Hodesh his wife,[802] Jobab, and Zibia, and Mesha, and Malcham,

10 And Jeuz, and Shachia, and Mirma. These *were* his sons, heads of the fathers.

11 And of Hushim he begat Abitub, and Elpaal.

12 The sons of Elpaal; Eber, and Misham, and Shamed, who built Ono, and Lod, with the towns thereof:

13 Beriah also, and [a]Shema, who *were* heads of the fathers of the inhabitants of Aijalon, who drove away[1272] the inhabitants of Gath:

14 And Ahio, Shashak, and Jeremoth,

15 And Zebadiah, and Arad, and Ader,

16 And Michael, and Ispah, and Joha, the sons of Beriah;

17 And Zebadiah, and Meshullam, and Hezeki, and Heber,

18 Ishmerai also, and Jezliah, and Jobab, the sons of Elpaal;

19 And Jakim, and Zichri, and Zabdi,

20 And Elienai, and Zilthai, and Eliel,

21 And Adaiah, and Beraiah, and Shimrath, the sons of [1a]Shimhi;

22 And Ishpan, and Heber, and Eliel,

23 And Abdon, and Zichri, and Hanan,

24 And Hananiah, and Elam, and Antothijah,

25 And Iphedeiah, and Penuel, the sons of Shashak;

26 And Shamsherai, and Shehariah, and Athaliah,

27 And Jaresiah, and Eliah, and Zichri, the sons of Jeroham.

28 These *were* heads of the fathers, by their generations,[8435] chief[7218] *men.* These dwelt in Jerusalem.

29 And at Gibeon dwelt the [1a]father of Gibeon; whose [b]wife's[802] name *was* Maachah:

30 And his firstborn son Abdon, and Zur, and Kish, and Baal, and Nadab,

31 And Gedor, and Ahio, and [1a]Zacher.

32 And Mikloth begat [1a]Shimeah. And these also dwelt with their brethren[251] in Jerusalem, over against them.

32 [a]1Chr. 7:34, *Shamer*

34 [a]1Chr. 7:32, *Shomer*

1 [a]Gen. 46:21; Num. 26:38; 1Chr. 7:6

3 [1]Or, *Ard* [a]Gen. 46:21

5 [1]Or, *Shupham* [a]Num. 26:39; 1Chr. 7:12

6 [a]1Chr. 2:52

13 [a]1Chr. 13:21, Shimhi

21 [1]Or, *Shema* [a]1Chr. 21:13

29 [1]Called *Jehiel* [a]1Chr. 9:35 [b]1Chr. 9:35

31 [1]Or, *Zechariah* [a]1Chr. 9:37

32 [1]Or, *Shimeam* [a]1Chr. 9:38

33 And [a]Ner begat Kish, and Kish begat Saul, and Saul begat Jonathan, and Malchi–shua, and [b]Abinadab, and [Ic]Esh–baal.

34 And the son of Jonathan *was* [Ia]Merib–baal; and Merib–baal begat [b]Micah.

35 And the sons of Micah *were,* Pithon, and Melech, and [I]Tarea, and Ahaz.

36 And Ahaz begat [a]Jehoadah; and Jehoadah begat Alemeth, and Azmaveth, and Zimri; and Zimri begat Moza,

37 And Moza begat Binea: [a]Rapha *was* his son, Eleasah his son, Azel his son:

38 And Azel had six sons, whose names *are* these, Azrikam, Bocheru, and Ishmael, and Sheariah, and Obadiah, and Hanan. All these *were* the sons of Azel.

39 And the sons of Eshek his brother *were,* Ulam his firstborn, Jehush the second, and Eliphelet the third.

40 And the sons of Ulam were mighty men[582] of valour,[2428] archers, and had many sons, and sons' sons, an hundred and fifty. All these *are* of the sons of Benjamin.

Jerusalem's Inhabitants After the Exile

9 So [a]all Israel were reckoned by genealogies;[3187] and, behold, they *were* written in the book[5612] of the kings[4428] of Israel and Judah, *who* were carried away to Babylon for their transgression.

2 [a]Now the first[7223] inhabitants that *dwelt* in their possessions in their cities *were,* the Israelites, the priests, Levites, and [b]the Nethinims.

3 And in [a]Jerusalem dwelt of the children[1121] of Judah, and of the children of Benjamin, and of the children of Ephraim, and Manasseh;

4 Uthai the son of Ammihud, the son of Omri, the son of Imri, the son of Bani, of the children of Pharez the son of Judah.

5 And of the Shilonites; Asaiah the firstborn, and his sons.

6 And of the sons of Zerah; Jeuel, and their brethren,[251] six hundred and ninety.

7 And of the sons of Benjamin; Sallu the son of Meshullam, the son of Hodaviah, the son of Hasenuah,

8 And Ibneiah the son of Jeroham, and Elah the son of Uzzi, the son of Michri, and Meshullam the son of Shephathiah, the son of Reuel, the son of Ibnijah;

9 And their brethren, according to their generations,[8435] nine hundred and fifty and six. All these men *were* chief[7218] of the fathers[1] in the house of their fathers.

10 [a]And of the priests; Jedaiah, and Jehoiarib, and Jachin,

11 And [a]Azariah the son of Hilkiah, the son of Meshullam, the son of Zadok, the son of Meraioth, the son[1121] of Ahitub, the ruler of the house of God;[430]

12 And Adaiah the son of Jeroham, the son of Pashur, the son of Malchijah, and Maasiai the son of Adiel, the son of Jahzerah, the son of Meshullam, the son of Meshillemith, the son of Immer;

13 And their brethren, heads of the house of their fathers, a thousand and seven hundred and threescore; [I]very able[2428] men for the work[4399] of the service of the house of God.

14 And of the Levites; Shemaiah the son of Hasshub, the son of Azrikam, the son of Hashabiah, of the sons of Merari;

15 And Bakbakkar, Heresh, and Galal, and Mattaniah the son of Micah, the son of Zichri, the son of Asaph;

16 And Obadiah the son of Shemaiah, the son of Galal, the son of Jeduthun, and Berechiah the son of Asa, the son of Elkanah, that dwelt in the villages of the Netophathites.

17 And the porters[7778] *were,* Shallum, and Akkub, and Talmon, and Ahiman, and their brethren: Shallum *was* the chief;

18 Who hitherto *waited* in the king's gate eastward: they *were* porters in the companies[4264] of the children of Levi.

33 IOr, *Ishbosheth* [a]1Sam. 14:51 [b]1Sam. 14:49, *Ishui* [c]2Sam. 2:8

34 IOr, *Mephibosheth* [a]2Sam. 4:4; 9:6, 10 [b]2Sam. 9:12

35 IOr, *Tahrea,* 1Chr. 9:41

36 [a]1Chr. 9:42, Jarah

37 [a]1Chr. 9:43, *Rephaiah*

1 [a]Ezra 2:59

2 [a]Ezra 2:70; Neh. 7:73 [b]Josh. 9:27; Ezra 2:43; 8:20

3 [a]Neh. 11:1

10 [a]Neh. 11:10 [b]Neh. 11:11, *Seraiah*

13 IHebr. *mighty men of valor*

🗝 19 And Shallum the son of Kore, the son of Ebiasaph, the son of Korah, and his brethren, of the house of his father, the Korahites, *were* over the work of the service, keepers[8104] of the [I]gates of the tabernacle: and their fathers, *being* over the host of the LORD, *were* keepers of the entry.

20 And [a]Phinehas the son of Eleazar was the ruler over them in time past, *and* the LORD *was* with him.

21 *And* Zechariah the son of Meshelemiah *was* porter of the door of the tabernacle of the congregation.[4150]

22 All these *which were* chosen[1305] to be porters in the gates *were* two hundred and twelve. These were reckoned by their genealogy in their villages, whom [a]David and Samuel [b]the seer [I]did ordain[3245] in their [II]set office.[530]

23 So they and their children *had* the oversight of the gates of the house of the LORD, *namely,* the house of the tabernacle, by wards.[4931]

24 In four quarters[7307] were the porters, toward the east, west, north, and south.

25 And their brethren, *which were* in their villages, *were* to come [a]after seven days from time to time with them.

26 For these Levites, the four chief porters, were in *their* [I]set office, and were over the [II]chambers and treasuries of the house of God.

27 And they lodged round about the house of God, because the charge[4931] *was* upon them, and the opening thereof every morning *pertained* to them.

28 And *certain* of them had the charge of the ministering[5656] vessels, that they should [I]bring them in and out by tale.

29 *Some* of them also *were* appointed to oversee the vessels, and all the [I]instruments of the sanctuary, and the fine flour, and the wine, and the oil,[8081] and the frankincense,[3828] and the spices.

30 And *some* of the sons of the priests made[7543] [a]the ointment of the spices.

31 And Mattithiah, *one* of the Levites, who *was* the firstborn of Shallum the Korahite, had the [I]set office [a]over the things that were made [II]in the pans.

32 And *other* of their brethren, of the sons of the Kohathites, [a]*were* over the [I]shewbread,[4635][3899] to prepare *it* every sabbath.[7676]

33 And these *are* [a]the singers, chief of the fathers of the Levites, *who remaining* in the chambers *were* free: for [I]they were employed in *that* work day[3119] and night.

34 These chief fathers of the Levites *were* chief throughout their generations; these dwelt at Jerusalem.

Saul's Family Record

35 And in Gibeon dwelt the father of Gibeon, Jehiel, whose wife's[802] name *was* [a]Maachah:

36 And his firstborn son Abdon, then Zur, and Kish, and Baal, and Ner, and Nadab,

37 And Gedor, and Ahio, and Zechariah, and Mikloth.

38 And Mikloth begat Shimeam. And they also dwelt with their brethren at Jerusalem, over against their brethren.

39 [a]And Ner begat Kish; and Kish begat Saul; and Saul begat Jonathan, and Malchi–shua, and Abinadab, and Esh–baal.

40 And the son of Jonathan *was* Merib–baal: and Merib–baal begat Micah.

41 And the sons of Micah *were,* Pithon, and Melech, and Tahrea, [a]*and Ahaz.*

42 And Ahaz begat Jarah; and Jarah begat Alemeth, and Azmaveth, and Zimri; and Zimri begat Moza;

19 [I]Hebr. *thresholds*
20 [a]Num. 31:6
22 [I]Hebr. *founded* [II]Or, *trust* [a]1Chr. 26:1, 2 [b]1Sam. 9:9
25 [a]2Kgs. 11:5
26 [I]Or, *trust* [II]Or, *storehouses*
28 [I]Hebr. *bring them in by tale, and carry them out by tale*
29 [I]Or, *vessels*
30 [a]Ex. 30:23
31 [I]Or, *trust* [II]Or, *on flat plates, or, slices* [a]Lev. 2:5; 6:21
32 [I]Hebr. *bread or ordering* [a]Lev. 24:8
33 [I]Hebr. *upon them* [a]1Chr. 6:31; 25:1
35 [a]1Chr. 8:29
39 [a]1Chr. 8:33
41 [a]1Chr. 8:35

🗝 **9:19** Though Korah and certain members of his family were destroyed (Num. 16), his descendants remained an important part of the Kohath clan of Levi, who was in charge of the care of the Tabernacle. Before the permanent temple was built by Solomon, the Tabernacle was a movable, flexible structure, and the tribes of Israel camped around it in areas assigned to them (Num. 2).

43 And Moza begat Binea; and Rephaiah his son, Eleasah his son, Azel his son.

44 And Azel had six sons, whose names *are* these, Azrikam, Bocheru, and Ishmael, and Sheariah, and Obadiah, and Hanan: these *were* the sons of Azel.

Saul's Death

10 Now [a]the Philistines fought against Israel; and the men[376] of Israel fled from before the Philistines, and fell down[5307] [I]slain in mount Gilboa.

2 And the Philistines followed hard[1692] after Saul, and after his sons; and the Philistines slew Jonathan, and [Ia]Abinadab, and Malchi–shua, the sons of Saul.

3 And the battle went sore against Saul, and the [I]archers[3384] [II]hit him, and he was wounded[2342] of the archers.

4 Then said Saul to his armourbearer, Draw thy sword, and thrust me through therewith; lest these uncircumcised[6189] come and [I]abuse me. But his armourbearer would[14] not; for he was sore afraid.[3372] So Saul took a sword, and fell upon it.

5 And when his armourbearer saw that Saul was dead,[4191] he fell likewise on the sword, and died.

6 So Saul died, and his three sons, and all his house died together.

7 And when all the men of Israel that *were* in the valley saw that they fled, and that Saul and his sons were dead, then they forsook[5800] their cities, and fled: and the Philistines came and dwelt in them.

8 And it came to pass on the morrow, when the Philistines came to strip the slain, that they found Saul and his sons fallen[5307] in mount Gilboa.

9 And when they had stripped him, they took his head, and his armour, and sent into the land[776] of the Philistines round about, to carry tidings unto their idols,[6091] and to the people.

10 [a]And they put his armour in the house of their gods,[430] and fastened[8628] his head in the temple of Dagon.

11 And when all Jabesh–gilead heard all that the Philistines had done[6213] to Saul,

12 They arose, all the valiant men, and took away the body[1480] of Saul, and the bodies of his sons, and brought them to Jabesh, and buried[6912] their bones[6106] under the oak in Jabesh, and fasted seven days.[3117]

13 So Saul died for his transgression which he [I]committed[4603] against the LORD,[3068] [a]*even* against the word[1697] of the LORD, which he kept[8104] not, and also for asking[7592] *counsel* of *one that had* a familiar spirit, [b]to enquire[1875] *of it;*

14 And enquired not of the LORD: therefore he slew him, and [a]turned the kingdom unto David the son of [I]Jesse.

David Becomes King Over All Israel

11 🗝 Then [a]all Israel gathered themselves[6908] to David unto Hebron, saying, Behold, we *are* thy bone and thy flesh.[1320]

2 And moreover [I]in time past, even when Saul was king,[4428] thou *wast* he that leddest out and broughtest in Israel: and the LORD thy God[430] said[559] unto thee, Thou shalt [IIa]feed my people Israel, and thou shalt be ruler over my people Israel.

3 Therefore came all the elders[2205] of Israel to the king to Hebron; and David made[3772] a covenant[1285] with them in Hebron before the LORD; and [a]they anointed[4886] David king over Israel, according to the word[1697] of the LORD [I]by [b]Samuel.

1 IOr, *wounded* [a]1Sam. 31:1, 2
2 IOr, *Ishui* [a]1Sam. 14:49
3 IHebr. *shooters with bows* IIHebr. *found him*
4 IOr, *mock me*
10 [a]1Sam. 31:10
13 IHebr. *transgressed* [a]1Sam. 13:13; 15:23 [b]1Sam. 28:7
14 IHebr. *Isai* [a]1Sam. 15:28; 2Sam. 3:9, 10; 5:3
1 [a]2Sam. 5:1
2 IHebr. *both yesterday and the third day* IIOr, *rule* [a]Ps. 78:71
3 [a]2Sam. 5:3 IHebr. *by the hand of* [b]1Sam. 16:1, 12, 13

🗝 **11:1** David ruled in Hebron over Judah for seven and a half years, from approximately 1010 B.C. to 1003 B.C. (2 Sam. 2—4). David's rule over all Israel began at this point (see 2 Sam. 5:1–10).

David Captures Zion

4 And David and all Israel [a]went to Jerusalem, which *is* Jebus; [b]where the Jebusites *were,* the inhabitants of the land.[776]

5 And the inhabitants of Jebus said to David, Thou shalt not come hither. Nevertheless David took the castle of Zion, which *is* the city of David.

6 And David said, Whosoever smiteth the Jebusites first[7223] shall be [I]chief[7218] and captain.[8269] So Joab the son of Zeruiah went first up, and was chief.

7 And David dwelt in the castle; therefore they called[7121] [Ia]it the city of David.

8 And he built the city round about, even from Millo round about: and Joab [I]repaired the rest of the city.

9 So David [I]waxed greater and greater: for the LORD of hosts *was* with him.

David's Mighty Men

10 [a]These also *are* the chief of the mighty men whom David had, who [I]strengthened themselves with him in his kingdom,[4438] *and* with all Israel, to make him king,[4427] according to [b]the word of the LORD concerning Israel.

11 And this *is* the number of the mighty men whom David had; Jashobeam, [I]an Hachmonite, the chief of the captains:[7991] he lifted up his spear against three hundred slain *by him* at one time.

12 And after him *was* Eleazar the son of Dodo, the Ahohite, who *was one* of the three mighties.

13 He was with David at [Ia]Pas-dammim, and there the Philistines were gathered together[622] to battle, where was a parcel of ground[7704] full of barley; and the people fled from before the Philistines.

14 And they [I]set themselves in the midst of *that* parcel, and delivered[5337] it, and slew the Philistines; and the LORD saved *them* by a great [II]deliverance.[8668]

15 Now [I]three of the thirty captains [a]went down to the rock to David, into the cave of Adullam; and the host of the Philistines, encamped [b]in the valley of Rephaim.

16 And David *was* then in the hold, and the Philistines' garrison *was* then at Bethlehem.

17 And David longed,[183] and said, Oh that one would give me drink of the water of the well[953] of Bethlehem, that *is* at the gate!

18 And the three brake through the host of the Philistines, and drew water out of the well of Bethlehem, that *was* by the gate, and took *it,* and brought *it* to David: but David would[14] not drink *of* it, but poured it out to the LORD,

19 And said, My God forbid it me, that I should do[6213] this thing: shall I drink the blood[1818] of these men[582] [I]that have put their lives[5315] in jeopardy? for with *the jeopardy of* their lives they brought it. Therefore he would not drink it. These things did these three mightiest.

20 [a]And Abishai the brother[251] of Joab, he was chief of the three: for lifting up his spear against three hundred, he slew *them,* and had a name among the three.

21 [a]Of the three, he was more honourable than the two; for he was their captain: howbeit he attained not to the *first* three.

22 Benaiah the son of Jehoiada, the son of a valiant man[376] of Kabzeel, [I]who had done many acts; [a]he slew two lionlike men of Moab: also he went down and slew a lion in a pit in a snowy day.[3117]

23 And he slew an Egyptian, [I]a man of *great* stature, five cubits high; and in the Egyptian's hand *was* a spear like a weaver's beam;[4500] and he went down to him with a staff, and plucked the spear out of the Egyptian's hand, and slew him with his own spear.

24 These *things* did Benaiah the son of Jehoiada, and had the name among the three mighties.[1368]

25 Behold, he was honourable among the thirty, but attained not to the *first* three: and David set him over his guard.[4928]

4 [a]2Sam. 5:6 [b]Judg. 1:21; 19:10

6 [I]Hebr. *head*

7 [I]That is, *Zion* [a]2Sam. 5:7

8 [I]Hebr. *revived*

9 [I]Hebr. *went in going and increasing*

10 [I]Or, *held strongly with him* [a]2Sam. 23:8 [b]1Sam. 16:1, 12

11 [I]Or, *son of Hachmoni*

13 [I]Or, *Ephesdammin* [a]1Sam. 17:1

14 [I]Or, *stood* [II]Or, *salvation*

15 [I]Or, *three captains over the thirty* [a]2Sam. 23:13 [b]1Chr. 14:9

19 [I]Hebr. *with their lives*

20 [a]2Sam. 23:18

21 [a]2Sam. 23:19

22 [I]Hebr. *great of deeds* [a]2Sam. 23:20

23 [I]Hebr. *man of measure*

26 Also the valiant men of the
armies[2428] *were,* [a]Asahel the brother of
Joab, Elhanan the son of Dodo of
Bethlehem,
27 [I]Shammoth the [IIa]Harorite, Helez
the [IIIb]Pelonite,
28 Ira the son of Ikkesh the Tekoite,
Abi–ezer the Antothite,
29 [I]Sibbecai the Hushathite, [II]Ilai the
Ahohite,
30 Maharai the Netophathite, [I]Heled
the son of Baanah the Netophathite,
31 Ithai the son of Ribai of Gibeah,
that pertained to the children[1121] of
Benjamin, Benaiah the Pirathonite,
32 [I]Hurai of the brooks of Gaash,
[II]Abiel the Arbathite,
33 Azmaveth the Baharumite,
Eliahba the Shaalbonite,
34 The sons of [Ia]Hashem the Gizonite,
Jonathan the son of Shage the Hararite,
35 Ahiam the son of [I]Sacar the
Hararite, [II]Eliphal the son of [III]Ur,
36 Hepher the Mecherathite, Ahijah
the Pelonite,
37 [I]Hezro the Carmelite, [II]Naarai the
son of Ezbai,
38 Joel the brother of Nathan,
Mibhar [I]the son of Haggeri,
39 Zelek the Ammonite, Naharai the
Berothite, the armourbearer[5375] 3627 of Joab
the son of Zeruiah,
40 Ira the Ithrite, Gareb the Ithrite,
41 Uriah the Hittite, Zabad the son of
Ahlai,
42 Adina the son of Shiza the
Reubenite, a captain[7218] of the
Reubenites, and thirty with him,
43 Hanan the son of Maachah, and
Joshaphat the Mithnite,
44 Uzzia the Ashterathite, Shama
and Jehiel the sons of Hothan the
Aroerite,
45 Jediael the [I]son of Shimri, and
Joha his brother, the Tizite,
46 Eliel the Mahavite, and Jeribai,
and Joshaviah, the sons of Elnaam, and
Ithmah the Moabite,

26 [a]2Sam. 23:24
27 [I]Or, *Shammah* [II]Or, *Harodite* [III]Or, *Paltite* [a]2Sam. 23:25 [b]2Sam. 23:26
29 [I]Or, *Mebunnai* [II]Or, *Zalmon*
30 [I]Or, *Heleb*
32 [I]Or, *Hiddai* [II]Or, *Abi-albon*
34 [I]Or, *Jashen* [a]2Sam. 23:32, 33
35 [I]Or, *Sharar* [II]Or, *Eliphelet* [III]Or, *Ahasbai*
37 [I]Or, *Hezrai* [II]Or, *Paarai the Arbite*
38 [I]Or, *the Haggerite*
45 [I]Or, *Shimrite*
1 [I]Hebr. *being yet shut up* [a]1Sam. 27:2 [b]1Sam. 27:6
2 [a]Judg. 20:16
3 [I]Or, *Hasmaah*
8 [I]Hebr. *of the host* [II]Hebr. *as the roes upon the mountains to make haste* [a]2Sam. 2:18

47 Eliel, and Obed, and Jasiel the Mesobaite.

David's Personal Army

12 Now [a]these *are* they that came to
David to [b]Ziklag, [I]while he yet
kept himself close6113 because of Saul
the son of Kish: and they *were* among
the mighty men, helpers of the war.
2 *They were* armed[5401] with bows,
and could use both the right hand and
[a]the left in *hurling* stones and *shooting* arrows out of a bow, *even* of Saul's
brethren[251] of Benjamin.
3 The chief[7218] *was* Ahiezer, then
Joash, the sons of [I]Shemaah the
Gibeathite; and Jeziel, and Pelet, the sons
of Azmaveth; and Berachah, and Jehu
the Antothite,
4 And Ismaiah the Gibeonite, a
mighty man among the thirty, and over
the thirty; and Jeremiah, and Jahaziel, and
Johanan, and Josabad the Gederathite,
5 Eluzai, and Jerimoth, and Bealiah,
and Shemariah, and Shephatiah the
Haruphite,
6 Elkanah, and Jesiah, and Azareel,
and Joezer, and Jashobeam, the Korhites,
7 And Joelah, and Zebadiah, the sons
of Jeroham of Gedor.
🗝 8 And of the Gadites there separated
themselves unto David into the hold to
the wilderness men[582] of might,[2428] *and*
men [I]of war[6635] *fit* for the battle, that
could handle shield and buckler,7420
whose faces *were like* the faces of lions,
and [IIa]*were* as swift as the roes[6643] upon
the mountains;
9 Ezer the first,[7218] Obadiah the second, Eliab the third,
10 Mishmannah the fourth, Jeremiah
the fifth,
11 Attai the sixth, Eliel the seventh,
12 Johanan the eighth, Elzabad the
ninth,
13 Jeremiah the tenth, Machbanai the
eleventh.

🗝 **12:8** This "hold" in the wilderness may refer to the cave of Adullam (cf. 1 Chr. 11:15 with 1 Sam. 22:1).

14 These *were* of the sons of Gad, captains of the host: [I]one of the least *was* over an hundred, and the greatest over a thousand,

15 These *are* they that went over Jordan in the first[7223] month, when it had [I]overflown all his [a]banks; and they put to flight all *them* of the valleys, *both* toward the east, and toward the west.

16 And there came of the children[1121] of Benjamin and Judah to the hold unto David.

17 And David went out [I]to meet them, and answered and said unto them, If ye be come peaceably unto me to help me, mine heart shall [II]be knit unto you: but if *ye be come* to betray me to mine enemies, seeing *there is* no [III]wrong[2555] in mine hands, the God[430] of our fathers[1] look *thereon,* and rebuke *it.*

18 Then [Ia]the spirit came upon [b]Amasai, *who was* chief of the captains,[7991] *and he said,* Thine *are we,* David, and on thy side, thou son of Jesse: peace, peace *be* unto thee, and peace *be* to thine helpers; for thy God helpeth thee. Then David received them and made them captains of the band.[1416]

19 And there fell[5307] *some* of Manasseh to David, [a]when he came with the Philistines against Saul to battle: but they helped them not: for the lords[5633] of the Philistines upon advisement[6098] sent him away, saying, [b]He will fall to his master[113] Saul [I]to *the jeopardy of* our heads.

20 As he went to Ziklag, there fell to him of Manasseh, Adnah, and Jozabad, and Jediael, and Michael, and Jozabad, and Elihu, and Zilthai, captains of the thousands that *were* of Manasseh.

21 And they helped David [I]against [a]the band *of the rovers:* for they *were* all mighty men of valour,[2428] and were captains[8269] in the host.

22 For at *that* time day[3117] by day there came to David to help him, until *it was* a great host, like the host of God.

23 And these *are* the numbers of the bands *that were* ready armed to the war, *and* [a]came to David to Hebron, to [b]turn the kingdom[4438] of Saul to him, [c]according to the word of the LORD.[3068]

24 The children of Judah that bare[5375] shield and spear *were* six thousand and eight hundred, ready [I]armed to the war.

25 Of the children of Simeon, mighty men of valour for the war, seven thousand and one hundred.

26 Of the children of Levi four thousand and six hundred.

27 And Jehoiada *was* the leader[5057] of the Aaronites, and with him *were* three thousand and seven hundred;

28 And [a]Zadok, a young man mighty of valour, and of his father's[1] house twenty and two captains.

29 And of the children of Benjamin, the [Ia]kindred of Saul, three thousand: for hitherto [IIb]the greatest part of them had kept[8104] the ward[4931] of the house of Saul.

30 And of the children of Ephraim twenty thousand and eight hundred, mighty men of valour, [I]famous[582,8034] throughout the house of their fathers.

31 And of the half tribe of Manasseh eighteen thousand, which were expressed[5344] by name, to come and make David king.[4427]

32 And of the children of Issachar, [a]*which were men* that had understanding[998] of the times, to know[3045] what Israel ought to do;[6213] the heads of them *were* two hundred; and all their brethren *were* at their commandment.[6310]

33 Of Zebulun, such as went forth to battle,[6635] [I]expert in war, with all instruments of war, fifty thousand, which could [II]keep rank: *they were* [IIIa]not of double heart.

34 And of Naphtali a thousand captains, and with them with shield and spear thirty and seven thousand.

35 And of the Danites expert in war twenty and eight thousand and six hundred.

36 And of Asher, such as went forth to battle, [I]expert in war, forty thousand.

37 And on the other side of Jordan, of the Reubenites, and the Gadites, and of the half tribe of Manasseh, with all

14 IOr, *one that was least* could *resist a hundred, and the greatest a thousand*

15 IHebr. *filled over* [a]Josh. 3:15

17 IHebr. *before them* IIHebr. *be one* IIIOr, *violence*

18 IHebr. *the spirit clothed Amasai* [a]Judg. 6:34 [b]2Sam. 17:25

19 IHebr. *on our heads* [a]1Sam. 29:2 [b]1Sam. 29:4

21 IOr, *with a band* [a]1Sam. 30:1, 9, 10

23 IOr, *captains,* or, *men;* Hebr. *heads* [a]2Sam. 2:3, 4; 5:1; 1Chr. 11:1 [b]1Chr. 10:14 [c]1Sam. 16:1, 3

24 IOr, *prepared*

28 [a]2Sam. 8:17

29 IHebr. *brethren* IIHebr. *multitude of them* [a]Gen. 31:23 [b]2Sam. 2:8, 9

30 IHebr. *men of names*

32 [a]Esth. 1:13

33 IOr, *rangers of battle,* or, *ranged in battle* IIOr, *set the battle in array* IIIHebr. *without a heart and a heart* [a]Ps. 12:2

36 IOr, *keeping their rank*

manner of instruments[3627] of war for the battle, an hundred and twenty thousand.

38 All these men of war, that could keep rank, came with a perfect heart to Hebron, to make David king over all Israel and all the rest also of Israel *were* of one heart to make David king.

39 And there they were with David three days,[3117] eating and drinking: for their brethren had prepared for them.

40 Moreover they that were nigh them, *even* unto Issachar and Zebulun and Naphtali, brought bread on asses, and on camels, and on mules, and on oxen, *and* [I]meat, meal, cakes of figs, and bunches of raisins, and wine, and oil,[8081] and oxen, and sheep abundantly: for *there was* joy in Israel.

David Moves the Ark of God

13 And David consulted[3289] with the captains[8269] of thousands and hundreds, *and* with every leader.[5057]

2 And David said[559] unto all the congregation[6951] of Israel, If *it seem* good[2895] unto you, and *that it be* of the LORD our God,[430] [I]let us send abroad unto our brethren[251] every where, *that are* [a]left[7604] in all the land[776] of Israel, and with them *also* to the priests and Levites *which are* [II]in their cities *and* suburbs, that they may gather themselves[6908] unto us:

3 And let us [I]bring again the ark[727] of our God to us: [a]for we enquired not at it in the days[3117] of Saul.

4 And all the congregation said that they would do so: for the thing was right in the eyes of all the people.

5 So [a]David gathered all Israel together,[6950] from [b]Shihor of Egypt even unto the entering of Hemath, to bring the ark of God [c]from Kirjath–jearim.

6 And David went up,[5927] and all Israel, to [a]Baalah, *that is,* to Kirjath–jearim, which *belonged* to Judah, to bring up thence the ark of God the LORD, [b]that dwelleth *between* the cherubims,[3742] whose name is called[7121] *on it.*

7 And they [I]carried the ark of God [a]in a new cart [b]out of the house of Abinadab: and Uzza and Ahio drave the cart.

8 [a]And David and all Israel played[7832] before God with all *their* might, and with [I]singing, and with harps, and with psalteries, and with timbrels,[8596] and with cymbals, and with trumpets.

🗝 9 And when they came unto the threshingfloor of [I][a]Chidon, Uzza put forth his hand to hold the ark; for the oxen [II]stumbled.

10 And the anger[639] of the LORD was kindled[2734] against Uzza, and he smote him, [a]because he put his hand to the ark: and there he [b]died before God.

11 And David was displeased,[2734] because the LORD had made a breach upon Uzza: wherefore that place is called [I]Perez–uzza to this day.[3117]

12 And David was afraid[3372] of God that day, saying, How shall I bring the ark of God *home* to me?

13 So David [I]brought not the ark *home* to himself to the city of David, but carried it aside into the house of Obed–edom the Gittite.

40 [I]Or, *victual of meal*

2 [I]Hebr. *let us break forth and send* [II]Hebr. *in the cities of their suburbs* [a]1Sam. 31:1; Isa. 37:4

3 [I]Hebr. *bring about* [a]1Sam. 7:1, 2

5 [a]1Sam. 7:1; 2Sam. 6:1 [b]Josh. 13:3 [c]1Sam. 6:21; 7:1

6 [a]Josh. 15:9, 60 [b]1Sam. 4:4; 2Sam. 6:2

7 [I]Hebr. *made the ark to ride* [a]Num. 4:15; 1Chr. 15:2, 13 [b]1Sam. 7:1

8 [I]Hebr. *songs* [a]2Sam. 6:5

9 [I]Called *Nachon* [II]Hebr. *shook it* [a]2Sam. 6:6

10 [a]Num. 4:15; 1Chr. 15:13, 15 [b]Lev. 10:2

11 [I]That is, *The breach of Uzza*

13 [I]Hebr. *removed*

🗝 **13:9, 10** Uzza was from the tribe of Levi, which had the responsibility for the Tabernacle and its contents, including the ark of the covenant. The ark rested for twenty years in the house of his father, Abinadab. The priests were responsible for covering the ark (as well as all the utensils and furniture of the sanctuary) for travel (Num. 4:5–14), and it would appear from the context that they were not to touch the ark while doing so. The family of Kohath was in charge of carrying the ark using the rings and poles provided (Ex. 25:14), but were promised death if they touched the ark when they were moving it (Num. 4:15). It was not to be carried on wagons, but on human shoulders (Num. 7:9). It appears that there was no priest in charge of its transportation (Num. 3:32). Uzza's death was in accordance with the warning given to the Kohathites. It certainly stood out as an example that effectively checked the evil spreading among the people (1 Chr. 15:2–13). See note on 2 Samuel 6:7.

⊶ 14 [a]And the ark of God remained with the family[4940] of Obed–edom in his house three months. And the LORD blessed[1288] [b]the house of Obed–edom, and all that he had.

David Prospers

14 Now [a]Hiram king of Tyre sent messengers[4397] to David, and timber of cedars, with masons and carpenters, to build him an house.

2 And David perceived[3045] that the LORD had confirmed[3559] him king over Israel, for his kingdom[4438] was lifted up on high, because of his people Israel.

3 And David took [I]more wives[802] at Jerusalem: and David begat more sons and daughters.

4 Now [a]these *are* the names of *his* children which he had in Jerusalem; Shammua, and Shobab, Nathan, and Solomon,

5 And Ibhar, and Elishua, and Elpalet,

6 And Nogah, and Nepheg, and Japhia,

7 And Elishama, and [I][a]Beeliada, and Eliphalet.

David Defeats the Philistines

8 And when the Philistines heard that [a]David was anointed[4886] king over all Israel, all the Philistines went up to seek David. And David heard *of it,* and went out against them.

9 And the Philistines came and spread themselves [a]in the valley of Rephaim.

10 And David enquired of God,[430] saying, Shall I go up against the Philistines? And wilt thou deliver them into mine hand? And the LORD said unto him, Go up; for I will deliver them into thine hand.

11 So they came up to Baal–perazim; and David smote them there. Then David said, God hath broken in upon mine enemies by mine hand like the breaking forth of waters: therefore they called[7121] the name of that place [I]Baal–perazim.

⊶ 12 And when they had left[5800] their gods[430] there, David gave a commandment,[559] and they were burned[8313] with fire.

13 [a]And the Philistines yet again spread themselves abroad in the valley.

14 Therefore David enquired again of God; and God said unto him, Go not up after them; turn away from them, [a]and come upon them over against the mulberry trees.

15 And it shall be, when thou shalt hear a sound of going[6807] in the tops of the mulberry trees, *that* then thou shalt go out to battle: for God is gone forth before thee to smite the host of the Philistines.

16 David therefore did[6213] as God commanded[6680] him: and they smote the host of the Philistines from [a]Gibeon even to Gazer.

17 And [a]the fame of David went out into all lands;[776] and the LORD [b]brought the fear[6343] of him upon all nations.

David Brings the Ark of God to Jerusalem

15 And *David* made[6213] him houses in the city of David, and prepared a place for the ark[727] of God,[430] [a]and pitched for it a tent.

⊶ 2 Then David said, [I]None ought to carry[5375] the [a]ark of God but the Levites: for them hath the LORD chosen[977] to carry the ark of God, and to minister[8334] unto him for ever.

3 And David [a]gathered all Israel together[6950] to Jerusalem, to bring up the

14 [a]2Sam. 6:11 [b]Gen. 30:27; 1Chr. 26:5
1 [a]2Sam. 5:11
3 [I]Hebr. *yet*
4 [a]1Chr. 3:5
7 [I]Or, *Eliada* [a]2Sam. 5:16
8 [a]2Sam. 5:17
9 [a]1Chr. 11:15
11 [I]That is, *A place of breaches*
13 [a]2Sam. 5:22
14 [a]2Sam. 5:23
16 [a]2Sam. 5:25, *Geba*
17 [a]Josh. 6:27; 2Chr. 26:8 [b]Deut. 2:25; 11:25
1 [a]1Chr. 16:1
2 [I]Hebr. *It is not to carry the ark of God, but for the Levites* [a]Num. 4:2, 15; Deut. 10:8; 31:9
3 [a]1Kgs. 8:1; 1Chr. 13:5

⊶ **13:14** Obed-edom was a Levite of the family of Korah in the clan of Kohath (1 Chr. 26:1, 4). Therefore, he was qualified to become the caretaker of the ark of the covenant.
⊶ **14:12** Burning the idols was required by the Law of Moses (Deut. 7:5, 25).
⊶ **15:2–13** See note on 1 Chronicles 13:9, 10 concerning Uzza.

ark of the LORD unto his place, which he had prepared for it.

4 And David assembled[622] the children[1121] of Aaron, and the Levites:

5 Of the sons of Kohath; Uriel the chief, and his [I]brethren[251] an hundred and twenty:

6 Of the sons of Merari; Asaiah the chief, and his brethren two hundred and twenty:

7 Of the sons of Gershom; Joel the chief, and his brethren an hundred and thirty:

8 Of the sons of [a]Elizaphan; Shemaiah the chief, and his brethren two hundred:

9 Of the sons of [a]Hebron; Eliel the chief, and his brethren fourscore:

10 Of the sons of Uzziel; Amminadab the chief, and his brethren an hundred and twelve.

11 And David called[7121] for Zadok and Abiathar the priests, and for the Levites, for Uriel, Asaiah, and Joel, Shemaiah, and Eliel, and Amminadab,

12 And said unto them, Ye *are* the chief[7218] of the fathers[1] of the Levites: sanctify yourselves, *both* ye and your brethren, that ye may bring up the ark of the LORD God of Israel unto *the place that* I have prepared for it.

13 For [a]because ye *did it* not at the first,[7223] [b]the LORD our God made a breach upon us, for that we sought him not after the due order.[4941]

14 So the priests and the Levites sanctified themselves to bring up the ark of the LORD God of Israel.

15 And the children of the Levites bare[5375] the ark of God upon their shoulders with the staves thereon, as [a]Moses commanded[6680] according to the word[1697] of the LORD.

16 And David spake to the chief of the Levites to appoint their brethren *to be* the singers with instruments of musick,[7892] psalteries and harps and cymbals, sounding, by lifting up the voice with joy.

5 [I]Or, *kinsmen*

8 [a]Ex. 6:22

9 [a]Ex. 6:18

13 [a]2Sam. 6:3; 1Chr. 13:7 [b]1Chr. 13:10, 11

15 [a]Ex. 25:14; Num. 4:15; 7:9

17 [a]1Chr. 6:33 [b]1Chr. 6:39 [c]1Chr. 6:44

20 [a]1Chr. 15:18, *Jaaziel*

21 [I]Or, *on the eighth to oversee*

22 [I]Or, was *for the carriage: he instructed about the carriage* [II]Hebr. *lifting up*

24 [a]Num. 10:8; Ps. 81:3

25 [a]2Sam. 6:12, 13; 1Kgs. 8:1

27 [I]Or, *carriage*

17 So the Levites appointed [a]Heman the son of Joel; and of his brethren, [b]Asaph the son of Berechiah; and of the sons of Merari their brethren, [c]Ethan the son of Kushaiah;

18 And with them their brethren of the second *degree,* Zechariah, Ben, and Jaaziel, and Shemiramoth, and Jehiel, and Unni, Eliab, and Benaiah, and Maaseiah, and Mattithiah, and Elipheleh, and Mikneiah, and Obed–edom, and Jeiel, the porters.[7778]

19 So the singers, Heman, Asaph, and Ethan, *were appointed* to sound with cymbals of brass;

20 And Zechariah, and [a]Aziel, and Shemiramoth, and Jehiel, and Unni, and Eliab, and Maaseiah, and Benaiah, with psalteries[5035] on Alamoth;

21 And Mattithiah, and Elipheleh, and Mikneiah, and Obed–edom, and Jeiel, and Azaziah, with harps [I]on the Sheminith to excel.

22 And Chenaniah, chief of the Levites, [I]*was* for [II]song: he instructed[3256] about the song because he *was* skilful.

23 And Berechiah and Elkanah *were* doorkeepers for the ark.

24 And Shebaniah, and Jehoshaphat, and Nethaneel, and Amasai, and Zechariah, and Benaiah, and Eliezer, the priests, [a]did blow with the trumpets before the ark of God: and Obed–edom and Jehiah *were* doorkeepers[7778] for the ark.

🔑 25 So [a]David, and the elders[2205] of Israel, and the captains[8269] over thousands, went to bring up the ark of the covenant[1285] of the LORD out of the house of Obed–edom with joy.

26 And it came to pass, when God helped the Levites that bare the ark of the covenant of the LORD, that they offered[2076] seven bullocks and seven rams.

27 And David *was* clothed with a robe of fine linen, and all the Levites that bare the ark, and the singers, and Chenaniah the master[8269] of the [I]song with the singers: David also *had* upon him an ephod of linen.

🔑 **15:25** Psalm 24 seems to have been written and set to music for this occasion.

28 [a]Thus all Israel brought up[5927] the ark of the covenant of the LORD with shouting, and with sound of the cornet, and with trumpets, and with cymbals, making a noise with psalteries and harps.

29 And it came to pass, [a]*as* the ark of the covenant of the LORD came to the city of David, that Michal the daughter of Saul looking out at a window saw king[4428] David dancing and playing: and she despised him in her heart.

16 So [a]they brought the ark[727] of God,[430] and set it in the midst of the tent that David had pitched for it: and they offered[7126] burnt sacrifices and peace offerings before God.

2 And when David had made an end[3615] of offering[5927] the burnt offerings and the peace offerings, he blessed[1288] the people in the name of the LORD.

3 And he dealt[2505] to every one of Israel, both man[376] and woman,[802] to every one[376] a loaf of bread, and a good piece of flesh, and a flagon[809] *of wine.*

4 And he appointed *certain* of the Levites to minister[8334] before the ark of the LORD, and to record,[2142] and to thank and praise the LORD God of Israel:

5 Asaph the chief,[7218] and next to him Zechariah, Jeiel, and Shemiramoth, and Jehiel, and Mattithiah, and Eliab, and Benaiah, and Obed–edom: and Jeiel [I]with psalteries and with harps; but Asaph made a sound with cymbals;

6 Benaiah also and Jahaziel the priests with trumpets continually[8548] before the ark of the covenant[1285] of God.

David's Psalm of Thanksgiving

⚿ 7 Then on that day[3117] David delivered [a]first[7218] *this psalm* to thank the LORD into the hand of Asaph and his brethren.[251]

8 [a]Give thanks unto the LORD, call[7121] upon his name, make known[3045] his deeds among the people.

9 Sing unto him, sing psalms unto him, talk ye of all his wondrous works.

10 Glory[1984] ye in his holy name: let the heart of them rejoice that seek the LORD.[3068]

11 Seek the LORD and his strength, seek his face continually.

12 Remember his marvellous[6381] works that he hath done,[6213] his wonders,[4159] and the judgments[4941] of his mouth;[6310]

13 O ye seed of Israel his servant, ye children[1121] of Jacob, his chosen ones.

14 He *is* the LORD our God; his judgments *are* in all the earth.[776]

15 Be ye mindful[2142] always[5769] of his covenant; the word[1697] *which* he commanded[6680] to a thousand generations;[1755]

16 *Even of the covenant* [a]which he made[3772] with Abraham, and of his oath[7621] unto Issac;

17 And hath confirmed the same to Jacob for a law,[2706] *and* to Israel *for* an everlasting[5769] covenant,

18 Saying, Unto thee will I give the land[776] of Canaan, [I]the lot of your inheritance;[5159]

19 When ye were but [I]few, [a]even a few, and strangers in it.

20 And *when* they went from nation to nation, and from *one* kingdom[4467] to another people;

21 He suffered[3240] no man to do them wrong; yea, he [a]reproved kings[4428] for their sakes,

22 *Saying,* [a]Touch not mine anointed,[4899] and do my prophets no harm.

23 [a]Sing unto the LORD, all the earth; shew forth from day to day his salvation.[3444]

24 Declare[5608] his glory[3519] among the heathen: his marvellous works among all nations.

25 For great *is* the LORD, and greatly

28 [a]1Chr. 13:8
29 [a]2Sam. 6:16
1 [a]2Sam. 6:17-19
5 [I]Hebr. *with instruments of psalteries and harps*
7 [a]2Sam. 23:1
8 [a]Ps. 105:1-15
16 [a]Gen. 17:2; 26:3; 28:13; 35:11
18 [I]Hebr. *the cord*
19 [I]Hebr. *men of number* [a]Gen. 34:30
21 [a]Gen. 12:17; 20:3; Ex. 7:15-18
22 [a]Ps. 105:15
23 [a]Ps. 96:1

⚿ **16:7–36** This psalm is an ideal song of praise, a general characterization of what should be sung in a worship service. It is composed of Psalm 105:1–15; 96:1–3, and 106:1, 47, 48.

to be praised: he also *is* to be feared[3372] above all gods.[430]

26 For all the gods [a]of the people *are* idols:[457] but the LORD made[6213] the heavens.

27 Glory and honour[1926] *are* in his presence; strength and gladness *are* in his place.

28 Give unto the LORD, ye kindreds of the people, give unto the LORD glory and strength.

29 Give unto the LORD the glory *due* unto his name: bring[5375] an offering,[4503] and come before him: worship[7812] the LORD in the beauty[1927] of holiness.

30 Fear[2342] before him, all the earth: the world[8398] also shall be stable, that it be not moved.

31 Let the heavens be glad, and let the earth rejoice: and let *men* say among the nations, The LORD reigneth.

32 Let the sea roar, and the fulness thereof: let the fields[7704] rejoice, and all that *is* therein.

33 Then shall the trees of the wood sing out at the presence of the LORD, because he cometh to judge[8199] the earth.

34 [a]O give thanks unto the LORD; for *he is* good;[2896] for his mercy[2617] *endureth* for ever.

35 [a]And say ye, Save us, O God of our salvation, and gather us together,[6908] and deliver[5337] us from the heathen, that we may give thanks to thy holy name, *and* glory[7623] in thy praise.

36 [a]Blessed *be* the LORD[3068] God of Israel for ever and ever. And all [b]the people said,[559] Amen,[543] and praised the LORD.

Those That Served in the Tabernacle

37 So he left[5800] there before the ark of the covenant of the LORD Asaph and his brethren, to minister before the ark continually, as every day's work required:

38 And Obed–edom with their brethren, threescore and eight; Obed–edom also the son of Jeduthun and Hosah *to be* porters:7778

39 And Zadok the priest, and his brethren the priests, [a]before the tabernacle of the LORD [b]in the high place that *was* at Gibeon,

40 To offer burnt offerings unto the LORD upon the altar[4196] of the burnt offering continually [1a]morning and evening, and *to do* according to all that is written in the law[8451] of the LORD, which he commanded Israel;

41 And with them Heman and Jeduthun, and the rest that were chosen,[1305] who were expressed[5344] by name, to give thanks to the LORD, [a]because his mercy *endureth* for ever;

42 And with them Heman and Jeduthun with trumpets and cymbals for those that should make a sound, and with musical[7892] instruments3627 of God. And the sons of Jeduthun *were* [1]porters.8179

43 [a]And all the people departed every man to his house: and David returned to bless[1288] his house.

God's Promise to David

17 Now [a]it came to pass, as David sat in his house, that David said to Nathan the prophet, Lo, I dwell in an house of cedars, but the ark[727] of the covenant[1285] of the LORD *remaineth* under curtains.

2 Then Nathan said unto David, Do all that *is* in thine heart; for God[430] *is* with thee.

3 And it came to pass the same night, that the word[1697] of God came to Nathan, saying,

🗝 4 Go and tell David my servant, Thus saith the LORD, Thou shalt not build me an house to dwell in:

5 For I have not dwelt in an house

26 [a]Lev. 19:4
34 [a]Ps. 106:1; 107:1; 118:1; 136:1
35 [a]Ps. 106:47, 48
36 [a]1Kgs. 8:15 [b]Deut. 27:15
39 [a]1Chr. 21:29; 2Chr. 1:3 [b]1Kgs. 3:4
40 [1]Hebr. *in the morning, and in the evening* [a]Ex. 29:38; Num. 28:3
41 [a]1Chr. 16:34; 2Chr. 5:13; 7:3; Ezra 3:11; Jer. 33:11
42 [1]Hebr. *for the gate*
43 [a]2Sam. 6:19, 20
1 [a]2Sam. 7:1

🗝 **17:4** God did not allow David to build the temple because he was a man of warfare (1 Chr. 22:8; 28:3), but he was allowed to accumulate a large part of the materials needed for its construction (1 Chr. 22:2–4, 14–16) in anticipation of his son Solomon being able to accomplish the task. Solomon was approved by God because he would be "a man of rest" (1 Chr. 22:9).

since the day[3117] that I brought up[5927] Israel unto this day; but [I]have gone from tent to tent, and from *one* tabernacle *to another.*

6 Wheresoever I have walked with all Israel, spake I a word to any of the judges[8199] of Israel, whom I commanded[6680] to feed my people, saying, Why have ye not built me an house of cedars?

7 Now therefore thus shalt thou say unto my servant David, Thus saith the LORD[3068] of hosts, I took thee from the sheepcote,[5116] *even* [I]from following the sheep, that thou shouldest be ruler over my people Israel:

8 And I have been with thee whithersoever thou hast walked, and have cut off[3772] all thine enemies from before thee, and have made[6213] thee a name like the name of the great men that *are* in the earth.[776]

🗝 9 Also I will ordain[7760] a place for my people Israel, and will plant them, and they shall dwell[7931] in their place, and shall be moved no more; neither shall the children[1121] of wickedness[5766] waste them any more, as at the beginning,[7223]

10 And since the time that I commanded judges *to be* over my people Israel. Moreover I will subdue all thine enemies. Furthermore I tell[5046] thee that the LORD will build thee an house.

11 And it shall come to pass, when thy days[3117] be expired that thou must go *to be* with thy fathers,[1] that I will raise up thy seed after thee, which shall be of thy sons; and I will establish his kingdom.[4438]

🗝 12 He shall build me an house, and I will stablish his throne for ever.

13 [a]I will be his father, and he shall be my son: and I will not take my mercy[2617] away from him, as I took *it* from *him* that was before thee:

14 But [a]I will settle[5975] him in mine house and in my kingdom for ever: and his throne shall be established[3559] for evermore.[5769]

15 According to all these words,[1697] and according to all this vision,[2377] so did Nathan speak unto David.

David's Prayer of Appreciation

16 [a]And David the king[4428] came and sat before the LORD, and said, Who *am* I, O LORD God, and what *is* mine house, that thou hast brought me hitherto?

17 And *yet* this was a small thing in thine eyes, O God; for thou hast *also* spoken of thy servant's house for a great while to come,[7350] and hast regarded me according to the estate[8448] of a man[120] of high degree, O LORD God.

18 What can David *speak* more to thee for the honour of thy servant? for thou knowest[3045] thy servant.

19 O LORD, for thy servant's sake, and according to thine own heart, hast thou done[6213] all this greatness, in making known all *these* [I]great things.

20 O LORD, *there is* none like thee, neither *is there any* God beside thee, according to all that we have heard with our ears.[241]

21 And what one nation in the earth *is* like thy people Israel, whom God went to redeem[6299] *to be* his own people, to make[7760] thee a name of greatness and terribleness,[3372] by driving out nations from before thy people, whom thou hast redeemed out of Egypt?

🗝 22 For thy people Israel didst thou make thine own people for ever; and thou, LORD, becamest their God.

23 Therefore now, LORD, let the thing that thou hast spoken concerning thy servant and concerning his house be established[539] for ever, and do as thou hast said.[1696]

5 [I]Hebr. *have been*
7 [I]Hebr. *from after*
13 [a]2Sam. 7:14, 15
14 [a]Luke 1:33
16 [a]2Sam. 7:18
19 [I]Hebr. *greatnesses*

🗝 **17:9** The Israelites were oppressed in Egypt and harassed by the Amalekites, Ammonites, Midianites, and Philistines.

🗝 **17:12** The building of God's house, the temple, was accomplished by Solomon (1 Kgs. 5:5).

🗝 **17:22** These last few words express a central promise of God's covenant (Gen. 17:7; Ex. 6:7; Rev. 21:3).

24 Let it even be established, that thy name may be magnified for ever, saying, The LORD of hosts *is* the God of Israel, *even* a God to Israel: and *let* the house of David thy servant *be* established before thee.

25 For thou, O my God, [I]hast told thy servant that thou wilt build him an house: therefore thy servant hath found *in his heart* to pray before thee.

26 And now, LORD, thou art God, and hast promised this goodness unto thy servant:

27 Now therefore [I]let it please thee to bless[1288] the house of thy servant, that it may be before thee for ever: for thou blessest, O LORD, and *it shall be* blessed for ever.

David's Military Success

18 Now after this [a]it came to pass, that David smote the Philistines, and subdued them, and took Gath and her towns out of the hand of the Philistines.

2 And he smote Moab; and the Moabites became David's servants, *and* brought[5375] gifts.

3 And David smote [Ia]Hadarezer king of Zobah unto Hamath, as he went to stablish his dominion by the river Euphrates.

4 And David took from him a thousand chariots, and [a]seven thousand horsemen, and twenty thousand footmen: David also houghed[6131] all the chariot *horses,* but reserved of them an hundred chariots.

5 And when the Syrians of [I]Damascus came to help Hadarezer king of Zobah, David slew of the Syrians two and twenty thousand men.[376]

6 Then David put *garrisons* in Syriadamascus; and the Syrians became David's servants, *and* brought gifts.[4503] Thus the LORD preserved David whithersoever he went.[1980]

7 And David took the shields of gold that were on the servants of Hadarezer, and brought them to Jerusalem.

🔑 8 Likewise from [I]Tibhath, and from Chun, cities of Hadarezer, brought David very much brass, wherewith [a]Solomon made[6213] the brasen sea, and the pillars, and the vessels of brass.

9 Now when [Ia]Tou king of Hamath heard how David had smitten all the host of Hadarezer king of Zobah;

10 He sent [Ia]Hadoram his son to king David, [II]to enquire[7592] of his welfare,[7965] and [III]to congratulate[1288] him, because he had fought against Hadarezer, and smitten him; (for Hadarezer [IV]had war with Tou;) and *with him* all manner of vessels of gold and silver and brass.

11 Them also king David dedicated[6942] unto the LORD, with the silver and the gold that he brought from all *these* nations; from Edom, and from Moab, and from the children[1121] of Ammon, and from the Philistines, and from Amalek.

12 Moreover [I]Abishai the son of Zeruiah slew of the Edomites in the valley of salt [a]eighteen thousand.

13 [a]And he put garrisons[5333] in Edom; and all the Edomites became David's servants. Thus the LORD preserved David whithersoever he went.

David's Officials

14 So David reigned over all Israel, and executed[6213] judgment[4941] and justice[6666] among all his people.

15 And Joab the son of Zeruiah *was* over the host; and Jehoshaphat the son of Ahilud, [I]recorder.

16 And Zadok the son of Ahitub, and [Ia]Abimelech the son of Abiathar, *were* the priests; and [b]Shavsha was scribe;

17 [a]And Benaiah the son of Jehoiada *was* over the Cherethites and the Pelethites; and the sons of David *were* chief[7223] about the king.

25 [I]Hebr. *hast revealed the ear of thy servant*
27 [I]Or, *it hath pleased thee*
1 [a]2Sam. 8:1
3 [I]Or, *Hadadezer* [a]2Sam. 8:3
4 [a]2Sam. 8:4, *seven hundred*
5 [I]Hebr. *Darmesek*
8 [I]Called in the book of Samuel *Betah, and Berothai* [a]1Kgs. 7:15, 23; 2Chr. 4:12, 15, 16
9 [I]Or, *Toi* [a]2Sam. 8:9
10 [I]Or, *Joram* [II]Or, *to salute* [III]Hebr. *to bless* [IV]Hebr. *was the man of wars* [a]2Sam. 8:10
12 [I]Hebr. *Abshai* [a]2Sam. 8:13
13 [a]2Sam. 8:14
15 [I]Or, *remembrancer*
16 [I]Called *Ahimelech* [a]2Sam. 8:17 [b]2Sam. 8:17, Seraiah; 1Kgs. 4:3, Shisha
17 [I]Hebr. *at the hand of the king* [a]2Sam. 8:18

🔑 **18:8** This was collected for the temple. The materials David had accumulated for Solomon's Temple are described in 1 Chronicles 22:2–5, 14–16.

Israel Defeats the Ammonites and Syrians

19 🔑 Now [a]it came to pass after this, that Nahash the king of the children[1121] of Ammon died, and his son reigned in his stead.

2 And David said, I will shew kindness[2617] unto Hanun the son of Nahash, because his father shewed kindness to me. And David sent messengers[4397] to comfort[5162] him concerning his father. So the servants of David came into the land[776] of the children of Ammon to Hanun, to comfort him.

3 But the princes of the children of Ammon said to Hanun, [I]Thinkest thou that David doth honour thy father, that he hath sent comforters unto thee? are not his servants come unto thee for to search, and to overthrow,[2015] and to spy out the land?

4 Wherefore Hanun took David's servants, and shaved them, and cut off[3772] their garments in the midst hard by their buttocks, and sent them away.

5 Then there went *certain,* and told David how the men[582] were served. And he sent to meet them: for the men were greatly ashamed. And the king said, Tarry at Jericho until your beards[2206] be grown, and *then* return.

6 And when the children of Ammon saw that they had made themselves [I]odious[887] to David, Hanun and the children of Ammon sent a thousand talents of silver to hire[7936] them chariots and horsemen out of Mesopotamia, and out of Syria–maachah, [a]and out of Zobah.

7 So they hired thirty and two thousand chariots, and the king of Maachah and his people; who came and pitched before Medeba. And the children of Ammon gathered themselves together[622] from their cities, and came to battle.

8 And when David heard *of it,* he sent Joab, and all the host of the mighty men.

9 And the children of Ammon came out, and put the battle in array before the gate of the city: and the kings[4428] that were come *were* by themselves in the field.[7704]

10 Now when Joab saw that [I]the battle was set against him before and behind, he chose out[977] of all the [II]choice of Israel, and put *them* in array against the Syrians.

11 And the rest of the people he delivered unto the hand of [I]Abishai his brother,[251] and they set *themselves* in array against the children of Ammon.

12 And he said, If the Syrians be too strong for me, then thou shalt help me: but if the children of Ammon be too strong for thee, then I will help thee.

13 Be of good courage,[2388] and let us behave ourselves valiantly for our people, and for the cities of our God:[430] and let the LORD do[6213] *that which is* good in his sight.

14 So Joab and the people that *were* with him drew nigh before the Syrians unto the battle; and they fled before him.

15 And when the children of Ammon saw that the Syrians were fled, they likewise fled before Abishai his brother, and entered into the city. Then Joab came to Jerusalem.

🔑 16 And when the Syrians saw that they were put to the worse[5062] before Israel, they sent messengers, and drew forth the Syrians that *were* beyond the [I]river: and [II][a]Shophach the captain[8269] of the host of Hadarezer *went* before them.

17 And it was told David; and he gathered all Israel, and passed over Jordan, and came upon them, and set *the battle* in array against them. So when David had put the battle in array against the Syrians, they fought with him.

1 [a]2Sam. 10:1
3 [I]Hebr. *In thine eyes doth David*
6 [I]Hebr. *to stink* [a]1Chr. 18:5, 9
10 [I]Hebr. *the face of the battle was* [II]Or, *young men*
11 [I]Hebr. *Abshai*
16 [I]That is, *Euphrates* [II]Or, *Shobach* [a]2Sam. 10:16

🔑 **19:1, 2** There is some question as to whether this Nahash was the same King Nahash of Ammon whom Saul fought some fifty-five years before (1 Sam. 11:1–15). It may have been a son who had the same name.

🔑 **19:16** See note on Deuteronomy 1:1 concerning the phrase "beyond the river."

18 But the Syrians fled[5127] before Israel; and David slew of the Syrians seven thousand *men which fought in* chariots, and forty thousand footmen, and killed[4191] Shophach the captain of the host.

19 And when the servants of Hadarezer saw that they were put to the worse before Israel, they made peace with David, and became his servants: neither would[14] the Syrians help the children of Ammon any more.

Another Victory Over the Ammonites

20 And [a]it came to pass, that [I]after the year was expired, at the time that kings go out *to battle,* Joab led forth the power of the army,[6635] and wasted[7843] the country[776] of the children[1121] of Ammon, and came and besieged Rabbah. But David tarried at Jerusalem. And [b]Joab smote Rabbah, and destroyed[2040] it.

2 And David [a]took the crown of their king[4428] from off his head, and found it [I]to weigh a talent of gold, and *there were* precious[3368] stones in it; and it was set upon David's head: and he brought also exceeding much spoil out of the city.

🔑 3 And he brought out the people that *were* in it, and cut *them* with saws, and with harrows[2757] of iron, and with axes. Even so dealt[6213] David with all the cities of the children of Ammon. And David and all the people returned to Jerusalem.

Philistine Giants Die in Battle

🔑 4 And it came to pass after this, [a]that there [I]arose war at [II]Gezer with the Philistines; at which time [b]Sibbechai the Hushathite slew [III][c]Sippai, *that was* of the children of [IV]the giant: and they were subdued.[3665]

5 And there was war again with the Philistines; and Elhanan the son of [I][a]Jair slew Lahmi the brother[251] of Goliath the Gittite, whose spear staff *was* like a weaver's beam.

6 And yet again [a]there was war at Gath, where was [I]a man[376] of *great* stature whose fingers and toes *were* four and twenty, six *on each hand,* and six *on each foot:* and he also was [II]the son of the giant.

7 But when he [I]defied[2778] Israel, Jonathan the son of [II][a]Shimea David's brother slew him.

8 These were born unto the giant in Gath; and they fell[5307] by the hand of David, and by the hand of his servants.

David Takes a Census

21 🔑 And [a]Satan stood up against Israel, and provoked David to number Israel.

2 And David said to Joab and to the rulers of the people, Go, number Israel from Beer–sheba even to Dan; [a]and bring the number of them to me, that I may know[3045] *it.*

3 And Joab answered,[559] The LORD make his people an hundred times so many more as they *be:* but, my lord,[113] the king,[4428] *are* they not all my lord's servants? why then doth my lord require this thing? why will he be a cause of trespass[819] to Israel?

4 Nevertheless the king's word[1697] prevailed against Joab. Wherefore Joab departed, and went throughout all Israel, and came to Jerusalem.

5 And Joab gave the sum of the

---

1 [I]Hebr. *at the return of the year* [a]2Sam. 11:1 [b]2Sam. 12:26

2 [I]Hebr. *the weight of* [a]2Sam. 12:30, 31

4 [I]Or, *continued;* Hebr. *stood* [II]Or, *Gob* [III]Or, *Saphr* [IV]Or, *Rapha* [a]2Sam. 21:18 [b]2Sam. 21:18 [c]1Chr. 11:29

5 [I]Called also *Jaare-oregim* [a]2Sam. 21:19

6 [I]Hebr. *a man of measure* [II]Hebr. *born to the giant,* or, *Rapha* [a]2Sam. 21:20

7 [I]Or, *reproached* [II]Called *Shammah* [a]1Sam. 16:9

1 [a]2Sam. 24:1

2 [a]1Chr. 27:23

🔑 **20:3** The proper understanding of the wording of this verse is that David did not mutilate the Ammonites, but forced them into slave labor in the fields and building projects (see 2 Samuel 12:31). The tools mentioned here were those that would be used on the buildings and the fields.

🔑 **20:4** See note on Numbers 13:32, 33 concerning the Hebrew words for "giant."

🔑 **21:1** There are no other instances in the Old Testament historical books where Satan is referred to by this specific title. The only other places where he is mentioned in the Old Testament are the books of Job, Psalms, and Zechariah.

number of the people unto David. And all *they of* Israel were a thousand thousand and an hundred thousand men[376] that drew sword: and Judah *was* four hundred threescore and ten thousand men that drew sword.

6 [a]But Levi and Benjamin counted he not among them: for the king's word was abominable[8581] to Joab.

David's Punishment

7 [I]And God[430] was displeased with this thing; therefore he smote Israel.

8 And David said unto God, [a]I have sinned greatly, because I have done[6213] this thing: [b]but now, I beseech thee,[4994] do away the iniquity[5771] of thy servant; for I have done very foolishly.

9 And the LORD spake unto Gad, David's [a]seer, saying,

10 Go and tell David, saying, Thus saith the LORD, I [I]offer thee three *things:* choose[977] thee one of them, that I may do[6213] *it* unto thee.

11 So Gad came to David, and said unto him, Thus saith the LORD, [I]Choose thee

12 [a]Either three years' famine; or three months to be destroyed[5595] before thy foes, while that the sword of thine enemies overtaketh *thee;* or else three days[3117] the sword of the LORD, even the pestilence, in the land,[776] and the angel[4397] of the LORD destroying[7843] throughout all the coasts of Israel. Now therefore advise thyself what word I shall bring again to him that sent me.

13 And David said unto Gad, I am in a great strait:[6887] let me fall now into the hand of the LORD; for very [I]great *are* his mercies: but let me not fall into the hand of man.[120]

14 So the LORD sent pestilence upon Israel: and there fell[5307] of Israel seventy thousand men.

15 And God sent an [a]angel unto Jerusalem to destroy[7843] it: and as he was destroying, the LORD beheld,[7200] and [b]he repented[5162] him of the evil,[7451] and said to the angel that destroyed,[7843] It is enough, stay now thine hand. And the angel of the LORD stood by the threshingfloor of [I]Ornan the Jebusite.

16 And David lifted up his eyes, and [a]saw the angel of the LORD stand between the earth[776] and the heaven, having a drawn sword in his hand stretched out over Jerusalem. Then David and the elders[2205] *of Israel, who were* clothed in sackcloth, fell upon their faces.

17 And David said unto God, *Is it* not I *that* commanded[559] the people to be numbered? even I it is that have sinned[2398] and done evil[7489] indeed; but *as for* these sheep, what have they done? let thine hand, I pray thee, O LORD[3068] my God, be on me, and on my father's[1] house; but not on thy people, that they should be plagued.

David Offers a Sacrifice

18 Then the [a]angel of the LORD commanded Gad to say to David, that David should go up, and set up an altar[4196] unto the LORD in the threshingfloor of Ornan the Jebusite.

19 And David went up at the saying of Gad, which he spake in the name of the LORD.

20 [I]And Ornan turned back, and saw the angel; and his four sons with him hid themselves. Now Ornan was threshing wheat.

21 And as David came to Ornan, Ornan looked and saw David, and went out of the threshingfloor, and bowed[7812] himself to David with *his* face[639] to the ground.[776]

22 Then David said to Ornan, [I]Grant me the place of *this* threshingfloor, that I may build an altar therein unto the LORD: thou shalt grant it me for the full price: that the plague may be stayed[6113] from the people.

23 And Ornan said unto David, Take *it* to thee, and let my lord the king do *that which is* good[2896] in his eyes: lo, I give *thee* the oxen *also* for burnt offerings, and the threshing instruments for wood, and the wheat for the meat offering;[4503] I give it all.

24 And king David said to Ornan,

6 [a]1Chr. 27:24
7 [I]Hebr. *And it was evil in the eyes of the LORD concerning this thing*
8 [a]2Sam. 24:10 [b]2Sam. 12:13
9 [a]1Sam. 9:9
10 [I]Hebr. *stretch out*
11 [I]Hebr. *Take to thee*
12 [a]2Sam. 24:13
13 [I]Or, *many*
15 [I]Or, *Araunah,* 2Sam. 24:18 [a]2Sam. 24:16 [b]Gen. 6:6
16 [a]2Chr. 3:1
18 [a]2Chr. 3:1
20 [I]Or, *When Ornan turned back and saw the angel, then he and his four sons with him hid themselves*
22 [I]Hebr. *Give*

Nay; but I will verily buy it for the full price: for I will not take *that* which *is* thine for the LORD, nor offer burnt offerings[5930] without cost.

25 So [a]David gave to Ornan for the place six hundred shekels of gold by weight.

26 And David built there an altar unto the LORD, and offered[5927] burnt offerings and peace offerings,[8002] and called[7121] upon the LORD;[3068] and [a]he answered him from heaven by fire upon the altar of burnt offering.

27 And the LORD commanded the angel; and he put up his sword again into the sheath thereof.

28 At that time when David saw that the LORD had answered him in the threshingfloor of Ornan the Jebusite, then he sacrificed[2076] there.

29 [a]For the tabernacle of the LORD, which Moses made in the wilderness, and the altar of the burnt offering, *were* at that season in the high place at [b]Gibeon.

30 But David could not go before it to enquire of God: for he was afraid[1204] because of the sword of the angel of the LORD.

22 Then David said,[559] [a]This *is* the house of the LORD God,[430] and this *is* the altar[4196] of the burnt offering for Israel.

David's Preparation for the Temple

2 And David commanded[559] to gather together[3664] [a]the strangers that *were* in the land[776] of Israel; and he set masons to hew[2672] wrought stones to build the house of God.

3 And David prepared iron in abundance for the nails for the doors of the gates, and for the joinings;[4226] and brass in abundance [a]without weight;

4 Also cedar trees in abundance: for the [a]Zidonians and they of Tyre brought much cedar wood to David.

5 And David said, [a]Solomon my son *is* young and tender,[7390] and the house *that is* to be builded for the LORD *must be* exceeding magnifical,[1431] of fame and of glory[8597] throughout all countries:[776] I will *therefore* now make preparation for it. So David prepared abundantly before his death.[4194]

6 Then he called[7121] for Solomon his son, and charged[6680] him to build an house for the LORD God of Israel.

7 And David said to Solomon, My son, as for me, [a]it was in my mind[3824] to build an house [b]unto the name of the LORD my God:

8 But the word[1697] of the LORD came to me, saying, [a]Thou hast shed blood[1818] abundantly, and hast made[6213] great wars: thou shalt not build an house unto my name, because thou hast shed much blood upon the earth[776] in my sight.

9 [a]Behold, a son shall be born to thee, who shall be a man[376] of rest; and I will give him [b]rest from all his enemies round about: for his name shall be [I]Solomon, and I will give peace and quietness unto Israel in his days.[3117]

10 [a]He shall build an house for my name; and [b]he shall be my son, and I *will be* his father; and I will establish the throne of his kingdom[4438] over Israel for ever.

11 Now, my son, [a]the LORD be with thee; and prosper thou, and build the house of the LORD thy God, as he hath said[1696] of thee.

12 Only the LORD [a]give thee wisdom[7922] and understanding,[998] and give thee charge[6680] concerning Israel,

25 [a]2Sam. 24:24
26 [a]Lev. 9:24; 2Chr. 3:1; 7:1
29 [a]1Chr. 16:39 [b]1Kgs. 3:4; 1Chr. 16:39; 2Chr. 1:3
1 [a]Deut. 12:5; 2Sam. 24:18; 1Chr. 21:18, 19, 26, 28; 2Chr. 3:1
2 [a]1Kgs. 9:21
3 [a]1Kgs. 7:47; 1Chr. 22:14
4 [a]1Kgs. 5:6
5 [a]1Chr. 19:1
7 [a]2Sam. 7:2; 1Kgs. 8:17; 1Chr. 17:1; 28:2 [b]Deut. 12:5, 11
8 [a]1Kgs. 5:3; 1Chr. 28:3
9 [I]That is, *Peaceable* [a]1Chr. 28:5 [b]1Kgs. 4:25; 5:4
10 [a]2Sam. 7:13; 1Kgs. 5:5; 1Chr. 17:12, 13; 28:6 [b]Heb. 1:5
11 [a]1Chr. 22:16
12 [a]1Kgs. 3:9, 12; Ps. 72:1

21:28 The threshing floor of Ornan was on Mount Moriah, where Abraham went to offer Isaac to God (Gen. 22:1–3). The temple would soon be built by Solomon on this mount (2 Chr. 3:1). It is believed that David wrote Psalm thirty in this place at this time.

22:5 Solomon was about twenty years old when he ascended to the throne of David.

22:8 See note on 2 Samuel 7:4–16 regarding David not being permitted to build the temple.

that thou mayest keep[8104] the law[8451] of the LORD thy God.

13 [a]Then shalt thou prosper, if thou takest heed to fulfil the statutes and judgments[4941] which the LORD charged Moses with concerning Israel: [b]be strong, and of good courage;[553] dread not, nor be dismayed.[2865]

14 Now, behold, [I]in my trouble[6040] I have prepared for the house of the LORD an hundred thousand talents of gold, and a thousand thousand talents of silver; and of brass and iron [a]without weight; for it is in abundance: timber also and stone have I prepared; and thou mayest add thereto.

15 Moreover *there are* workmen with thee in abundance, hewers[2672] and [I]workers of stone and timber, and all manner of cunning men[2450] for every manner of work.[4399]

16 Of the gold, the silver, and the brass, and the iron, *there is* no number. Arise *therefore,* and be doing, and [a]the LORD be with thee.

17 David also commanded[6680] all the princes of Israel to help Solomon his son, *saying,*

18 *Is* not the LORD your God with you? [a]and hath he *not* given you rest on every side? for he hath given the inhabitants of the land into mine hand; and the land is subdued before the LORD, and before his people.

19 Now [a]set[5414] your heart and your soul to seek the LORD your God; arise therefore, and build ye the sanctuary of the LORD God, to [b]bring the ark[727] of the covenant[1285] of the LORD, and the holy vessels of God, into the house that is to be built [c]to the name of the LORD.

23

So when David was old and full of days,[3117] he made [a]Solomon his son king[4427] over Israel.

The Levites and Their Duties

2 And he gathered together[622] all the princes of Israel, with the priests and the Levites.

3 Now the Levites were numbered from the age of [a]thirty years and upward: and their number by their polls, man[1397] by man, was thirty and eight thousand.

4 Of which, twenty and four thousand *were* [I]to set forward the work[4399] of the house of the LORD; and six thousand *were* [a]officers[7860] and judges:

5 Moreover four thousand *were* porters;[7778] and four thousand praised the LORD with the instruments [a]which I made, *said David,* to praise *therewith.*

6 And [a]David divided them into [I]courses[4256] among the sons of Levi, *namely,* Gershon, Kohath, and Merari.

7 Of the [a]Gershonites *were,* [I][b]Laadan, and Shimei.

8 The sons of Laadan; the chief[7218] *was* Jehiel, and Zetham, and Joel, three.

🗝 9 The sons of Shimei; Shelomith, and Haziel, and Haran, three. These *were* the chief of the fathers[1] of Laadan.

10 And the sons of Shimei *were,* Jahath, [I][a]Zina, and Jeush, and Beriah. These four *were* the sons of Shimei.

11 And Jahath was the chief, and Zizah the second: but Jeush and Beriah [I]had not many sons; therefore they were in one reckoning,[6486] according to *their* father's house.

12 [a]The sons of Kohath; Amram, Izhar, Hebron, and Uzziel, four.

13 The sons of [a]Amram; Aaron and Moses: and [b]Aaron was separated, that he should sanctify the most holy things,[6944] he and his sons for ever, [c]to burn incense[6999] before the LORD, [d]to minister[8334] unto him, and [e]to bless[1288] in his name for ever.

14 Now *concerning* Moses the man[376]

13 [a]Josh. 1:7, 8; 1Chr. 28:7 [b]Deut. 31:7, 8; Josh. 1:6, 7, 9; 1Chr. 28:20

14 [I]Or, *in my poverty* [a]1Chr. 22:3

15 [I]That is, *masons and carpenters*

16 [a]1Chr. 22:11

18 [a]Deut. 12:10; Josh. 22:4; 2Sam. 7:1; 1Chr. 23:25

19 [a]2Chr. 20:3 [b]1Kgs. 8:6, 21; 2Chr. 5:7; 6:11 [c]1Chr. 22:7; 1Kgs. 5:3

1 [a]1Kgs. 1:33-39; 1Chr. 28:5

3 [a]Num. 4:3, 47

4 [I]Or, *to oversee* [a]Deut. 16:18; 1Chr. 26:29; 2Chr. 19:8

5 [a]2Chr. 29:25, 26; Amos 6:5

6 [I]Hebr. *divisions* [a]Ex. 6:16; Num. 26:57; 1Chr. 6:1; 2Chr. 8:14; 29:25

7 [I]Or, *Libni* [a]1Chr. 26:21 [b]1Chr. 6:17

10 [I]Or, *Zizah* [a]1Chr. 23:11

11 [I]Hebr. *did not multiply sons*

12 [a]Ex. 6:18

13 [a]Ex. 6:20 [b]Ex. 28:1; Heb. 5:4 [c]Ex. 30:7; Num. 16:40; 1Sam. 2:28 [d]Deut. 21:5 [e]Num. 6:23

🗝 **23:9** The man named Shimei mentioned in verses seven and ten was the son of Gershon (Ex. 6:17; Num. 3:18) and the founder of a division of the Gershon family. Shimei mentioned in this verse was the head of a subdivision in the family of Laadan, which was a smaller part of the Gershon clan.

of God,[430] [a]his sons were named of the tribe of Levi.

15 [a]The sons of Moses *were,* Gershom, and Eliezer.

16 Of the sons of Gershom, [Ia]Shebuel *was* the chief.

17 And the sons of Eliezer *were,* [a]Rehabiah [I]the chief. And Eliezer had none other sons; but the sons of Rehabiah [II]were very many.

18 Of the sons of Izhar; [I]Shelomith the chief.

19 [a]Of the sons of Hebron; Jeriah the first, Amariah the second, Jahaziel the third, and Jekameam the fourth.

20 Of the sons of Uzziel; Micah the first, and Jesiah the second.

21 [a]The sons of Merari; Mahli, and Mushi. The sons of Mahli; Eleazar, and [b]Kish.

22 And Eleazar died,[4191] and [a]had no sons, but daughters: and their [I]brethren[251] the sons of Kish [b]took them.

23 [a]The sons of Mushi; Mahli, and Eder, and Jeremoth, three.

24 These *were* the sons of [a]Levi after the house of their fathers; *even* the chief of the fathers, as they were counted[6485] by number of names by their polls, that did[6213] the work for the service of the house of the LORD, from the age of [b]twenty years and upward.

25 For David said, The LORD God of Israel [a]hath given rest unto his people, [I]that they may dwell[7931] in Jerusalem for ever:

26 And also unto the Levites; they shall no *more* [a]carry[5375] the tabernacle, nor any vessels of it for the service thereof.

27 For by the last words[1697] of David the Levites *were* [I]numbered from twenty years old and above:

28 Because [Ia]their office[4612] *was* to wait on the sons of Aaron for the service of the house of the LORD, in the courts, and in the chambers, and in the purifying of all holy things, and the work of the service of the house of God;

29 Both for [a]the shewbread, and for [b]the fine flour for meat offering,[4503] and for [c]the unleavened[4682] cakes, and for [d]*that which is baked in* the [I]pan, and for that which is fried,[7246] and for all manner of [e]measure and size;

30 And to stand every morning to thank and praise the LORD, and likewise at even;

31 And to offer all burnt sacrifices unto the LORD [a]in the sabbaths,[7676] in the new moons, and on the [b]set feasts,[4150] by number, according to the order[4941] commanded unto them, continually[8548] before the LORD:

32 And that they should [a]keep[8104] the charge[4931] of the tabernacle of the congregation,[4150] and the charge of the holy *place,* and [b]the charge of the sons of Aaron their brethren, in the service of the house of the LORD.

The Organization of the Priests

24 Now *these are* the divisions[4256] of the sons of Aaron. [a]The sons of Aaron; Nadab, and Abihu, Eleazar, and Ithamar.

2 But [a]Nadab and Abihu died before their father, and had no children:[1121] therefore Eleazar and Ithamar executed the priest's office.

3 And David distributed them, both Zadok of the sons of Eleazar, and Ahimelech of the sons of Ithamar, according to their offices[6486] in their service.

🔑 4 And there were more chief[7218] men[1397] found of the sons of Eleazar than of the sons of Ithamar; and *thus* were they divided. Among the sons of

15 [a]Ex. 2:22; 18:3, 4
16 [I]*Shubael,* 1Chr. 24:20 [a]1Chr. 26:24
17 [I]Or, *the first* [II]Hebr. *were highly multiplied* [a]1Chr. 26:25
18 [I]*Shelomoth*
19 [a]1Chr. 24:23
21 [a]1Chr. 24:26 [b]1Chr. 24:29
22 [I]Or, *kinsmen* [a]1Chr. 24:28 [b]Num. 36:6, 8
23 [a]1Chr. 24:30
24 [a]Num. 10:17, 21 [b]Num. 1:3; 4:3; 8:24; 1Chr. 23:27; Ezra 3:8
25 [I]Or, *and he dwelleth in Jerusalem* [a]1Chr. 22:18
26 [a]Num. 4:5
27 [I]Hebr. *number*
28 [I]Hebr. *their station* was *at the hand of the sons of Aaron* [a]Neh. 11:24
29 [I]Or, *flat plate* [a]Ex. 25:30 [b]Lev. 6:20; 1Chr. 9:29 [c]Lev. 2:4 [d]Lev. 2:5, 7 [e]Lev. 19:35
31 [a]Num. 10:10; Ps. 81:3 [b]Lev. 23:4
32 [a]Num. 1:53 [b]Num. 3:6-9
1 [a]Lev. 10:1, 6; Num. 26:60
2 [a]Num. 3:4; 26:61

🔑 **24:4** The twenty-four classes continued in New Testament times as the basis for rotating the priestly duties. As some of these classes died out or had to be consolidated with others, new ones were formed to take their places. In the return from exile in 538 B.C., four registered classes were represented: David's second, third, and sixteenth, and a new class, Pashur (Ezra 2:36–39). By 520 B.C., twenty-two had been reinstated (Neh. 12:1–7, cf. Neh. 10:2–8; 12:12–21).

Eleazar *there were* sixteen chief men of
the house of *their* fathers,[1] and eight
among the sons of Ithamar according to
the house of their fathers.
5 Thus were they divided by lot, one
sort with another; for the governors[8269]
of the sanctuary, and governors *of the
house* of God,[430] were of the sons of
Eleazar, and of the sons of Ithamar.
6 And Shemaiah the son of Nethaneel
the scribe, *one* of the Levites, wrote them
before the king,[4428] and the princes, and
Zadok the priest, and Ahimelech the son
of Abiathar, and *before* the chief of the fathers of the priests and Levites: one
[I]principal[1] household being taken for
Eleazar, and *one* taken for Ithamar.
7 Now the first[7223] lot came forth to
Jehoiarib, the second to Jedaiah,
8 The third to Harim, the fourth to
Seorim,
9 The fifth to Malchijah, the sixth to
Mijamin,
10 The seventh to Hakkoz, the eighth
to [a]Abijah,
11 The ninth to Jeshuah, the tenth to
Shecaniah,
12 The eleventh to Eliashib, the
twelfth to Jakim,
13 The thirteenth to Huppah, the
fourteenth to Jeshebeab,
14 The fifteenth to Bilgah, the sixteenth to Immer,
15 The seventeenth to Hezir, the eighteenth to Aphses,
16 The nineteenth to Pethahiah, the
twentieth to Jehezekel,
17 The one and twentieth to Jachin,
the two and twentieth to Gamul,
18 The three and twentieth to Delaiah,
the four and twentieth to Maaziah.
19 These *were* the orderings[6486] of
them in their service [a]to come into the
house of the LORD, according to their
manner,[4941] under Aaron their father, as
the LORD God of Israel had commanded[6680] him.

The Levites Again

20 And the rest of the sons of Levi
were these: Of the sons of Amram;
[a]Shubael: of the sons of Shubael;
Jehdeiah.
21 Concerning [a]Rehabiah: of the sons
of Rehabiah, the first[7218] *was* Isshiah.
22 Of the Izharites; [a]Shelomoth: of
the sons of Shelomoth; Jahath.
23 And the [a]sons *of Hebron;* Jeriah
the first, Amariah the second, Jahaziel
the third, Jekameam the fourth.
24 *Of* the sons of Uzziel; Michah: of
the sons of Michah; Shamir.
25 The brother of Michah *was*
Isshiah: of the sons of Isshiah; Zechariah.
26 [a]The sons of Merari *were* Mahli
and Mushi: the sons of Jaaziah; Beno.
27 The sons of Merari by Jaaziah;
Beno, and Shoham, and Zaccur, and Ibri.
28 Of Mahli *came* Eleazar, [a]who had
no sons.
29 Concerning Kish: the son of Kish
was Jerahmeel.
30 [a]The sons also of Mushi; Mahli,
and Eder, and Jerimoth. These *were* the
sons of the Levites after the house of
their fathers.
31 These likewise cast[5307] lots over
against their brethren[251] the sons of
Aaron in the presence of David the king,
and Zadok, and Ahimelech, and the chief
of the fathers of the priests and Levites,
even the principal fathers over against
their younger brethren.

The Temple Musicians And Their Duties

25 Moreover David and the
captains[8269] of the host separated[914] to the service of the sons of
[a]Asaph, and of Heman, and of Jeduthun,
who should prophesy with harps, with
psalteries,[5035] and with cymbals: and the
number of the workmen according to
their service was:
2 Of the sons of Asaph; Zaccur, and
Joseph, and Nethaniah, and [I]Asarelah, the
sons of Asaph under the hands of
Asaph, which prophesied [II]according to
the order of the king.[4428]
3 Of Jeduthun: the sons of Jeduthun;
Gedaliah, and [I]Zeri, and Jeshaiah,
Hashabiah, and Mattithiah, [II]six, under

6 [I]Hebr. *house of the father*
10 [a]Neh. 12:4, 17; Luke 1:5
19 [a]1Chr. 9:25
20 [a]1Chr. 23:16, *Shebuel*
21 [a]1Chr. 23:17
22 [a]1Chr. 23:18, *Shelomith*
23 [a]1Chr. 23:19; 26:31
26 [a]Ex. 6:19; 1Chr. 23:21
28 [a]1Chr. 23:22
30 [a]1Chr. 23:23
1 [a]1Chr. 6:33, 39, 44
2 [I]Otherwise called *Jesharelah* [II]Hebr. *by the hands of the king*
3 [I]Or, *Izri* [II]With Shimei

the hands of their father Jeduthun, who prophesied with a harp, to give thanks and to praise the LORD.

4 Of Heman: the sons of Heman; Bukkiah, Mattaniah, [Ia]Uzziel, [IIb]Shebuel, and Jerimoth, Hananiah, Hanani, Eliathah, Giddalti, and Romamti–ezer, Joshbekashah, Mallothi, Hothir, *and* Mahazioth:

5 All these *were* the sons of Heman the king's seer in the [I]words[1697] of God,[430] to lift up the horn. And God gave to Heman fourteen sons and three daughters.

6 All these *were* under the hands of their father for song *in* the house of the LORD, with cymbals, psalteries, and harps, for the service of the house of God, [Ia]according to the king's order to Asaph, Jeduthun, and Heman.

7 So the number of them, with their brethren[251] that were instructed[3925] in the songs of the LORD, *even* all that were cunning,[995] was two hundred fourscore and eight.

8 And they cast[5307] lots, ward[4931] against *ward,* as well the small as the great, [a]the teacher as the scholar.[8527]

9 Now the first[7223] lot came forth for Asaph to Joseph: the second to Gedaliah, who with his brethren and sons *were* twelve:

10 The third to Zaccur, *he,* his sons, and his brethren, *were* twelve:

11 The fourth to Izri, *he,* his sons, and his brethren, *were* twelve:

12 The fifth to Nethaniah, *he,* his sons, and his brethren, *were* twelve:

13 The sixth to Bukkiah, *he,* his sons, and his brethren, *were* twelve:

14 The seventh to Jesharelah, *he,* his sons, and his brethren, *were* twelve:

15 The eighth to Jeshaiah, *he,* his sons, and his brethren, *were* twelve:

16 The ninth to Mattaniah, *he,* his sons, and his brethren, *were* twelve:

4 [I]Or, *Azareel* [II]Or, *Shubael* [a]1Chr. 25:18 [b]1Chr. 25:20

5 [I]Or, *matters*

6 [I]Hebr. *by the hands of the king* [a]1Chr. 25:2

8 [a]2Chr. 23:13

1 [I]Or, *Shelemiah* [II]Or, *Ebiasaph* [a]1Chr. 26:14 [b]1Chr. 6:37; 9:19

17 The tenth to Shimei, *he,* his sons, and his brethren, *were* twelve:

18 The eleventh to Azareel, *he,* his sons, and his brethren, *were* twelve:

19 The twelfth to Hashabiah, *he,* his sons, and his brethren, *were* twelve:

20 The thirteenth to Shubael, *he,* his sons, and his brethren, *were* twelve:

21 The fourteenth to Mattithiah, *he,* his sons, and his brethren, *were* twelve:

22 The fifteenth to Jeremoth, *he,* his sons, and his brethren, *were* twelve:

23 The sixteenth to Hananiah, *he,* his sons, and his brethren, *were* twelve:

24 The seventeenth to Joshbekashah, *he,* his sons, and his brethren, *were* twelve:

25 The eighteenth to Hanani, *he,* his sons, and his brethren, *were* twelve:

26 The nineteenth to Mallothi, *he,* his sons, and his brethren, *were* twelve:

27 The twentieth to Eliathah, *he,* his sons, and his brethren, *were* twelve:

28 The one and twentieth to Hothir, *he,* his sons, and his brethren, *were* twelve:

29 The two and twentieth to Giddalti, *he,* his sons, and his brethren, *were* twelve:

30 The three and twentieth to Mahazioth, *he,* his sons, and his brethren, *were* twelve:

31 The four and twentieth to Romamti–ezer, *he,* his sons, and his brethren, *were* twelve.

Other Temple Workers

26 🔑 Concerning the divisions[4256] of the porters: Of the Korhites *was* [Ia]Meshelemiah the son of Kore, of the sons of [IIb]Asaph.

2 And the sons of Meshelemiah *were,* Zechariah the firstborn, Jediael the second, Zebadiah the third, Jathniel the fourth,

🔑 **26:1** From 1 Chronicles 9:19 it appears that the full spelling of Kore's father's name was "Ebiasaph." The man named Asaph mentioned here should not to be confused with the psalmist who had the same name who was a member of the clan of Gershon because Korah and his descendants, who guarded the temple gates, belonged to the clan of Kohath.

3 Elam the fifth, Jehohanan the sixth, Elioenai the seventh.

4 Moreover the sons of Obed–edom *were,* Shemaiah the firstborn, Jehozabad the second, Joah the third, and Sacar the fourth, and Nethaneel the fifth,

5 Ammiel the sixth, Issachar the seventh, Peulthai the eighth: for God[430] blessed [Ia]him.

6 Also unto Shemaiah his son were sons born, that ruled throughout the house of their father: for they *were* mighty men of valour.[2428]

7 The sons of Shemaiah; Othni, and Rephael and Obed, Elzabad, whose brethren[251] *were* strong men, Elihu, and Semachiah.

8 All these of the sons of Obed–edom: they and their sons and their brethren, able[2428] men[376] for strength for the service, *were* threescore and two of Obed–edom.

9 And Meshelemiah had sons and brethren, strong men, eighteen.

10 Also [a]Hosah, of the children[1121] of Merari, had sons; Simri the chief,[7218] (for *though* he was not the firstborn, yet his father made[7760] him the chief;)

11 Hilkiah the second, Tebaliah the third, Zechariah the fourth: all the sons and brethren of Hosah *were* thirteen.

12 Among these *were* the divisions of the porters, *even* among the chief men,[1397] *having* wards[4931] one against another, to minister[8334] in the house of the LORD.

13 And they cast[5307] lots, [I]as well the small as the great, according to the house of their fathers,[1] for every gate.

14 And the lot eastward fell[5307] to [Ia]Shelemiah. Then for Zechariah his son, a wise[7922] counselor,[3289] they cast lots; and his lot came out northward.

15 To Obed–edom southward; and to his sons the house of [I]Asuppim.

16 To Shuppim and Hosah *the lot came forth* westward, with the gate Shallecheth, by the causeway[4546] of the going [a]up, ward against ward.

17 Eastward *were* six Levites, northward four a day,[3117] southward four a day, and toward Asuppim two *and* two.

18 At Parbar westward, four at the causeway, *and* two at Parbar.

19 These *are* the divisions of the porters among the sons of Kore, and among the sons of Merari.

20 And of the Levites, Ahijah *was* [a]over the treasures of the house of God, and over the treasures of the [I]dedicated things.[6944]

21 *As concerning* the sons of [Ia]Laadan; the sons of the Gershonite Laadan, chief fathers, *even* of Laadan the Gershonite, *were* [IIb]Jehieli.

22 The sons of Jehieli; Zetham, and Joel his brother,[251] *which were* over the treasures of the house of the LORD.

23 Of the Amramites, *and* the Izharites, the Hebronites, *and* the Uzzielites:

24 And [a]Shebuel the son of Gershom, the son of Moses, *was* ruler of the treasures.

25 And his brethren by Eliezer; Rehabiah his son, and Jeshaiah his son, and Joram his son, and Zichri his son, and [a]Shelomith his son.

26 Which Shelomith and his brethren *were* over all the treasures[214] of the dedicated things, which David the king,[4428] and the chief fathers, the captains[8269] over thousands and hundreds, and the captains of the host, had dedicated.

27 [I]Out of the spoils won in battles did they dedicate[6942] to maintain[2388] the house of the LORD.

28 And all that Samuel [a]the seer,[7200] and Saul the son of Kish, and Abner the son of Ner, and Joab the son of Zeruiah, had dedicated; *and* whosoever had dedicated *any thing, it was* under the hand of Shelomith, and of his brethren.

5 [I]That is, Obed-edom [a]1Chr. 13:14
10 [a]1Chr. 16:38
13 [I]*Or, as well for the small as for the great*
14 [I]Called *Meshelemiah* [a]1Chr. 26:1
15 [I]Hebr. *Gatherings*
16 [a]1Kgs. 10:5; 2Chr. 9:4
20 [I]Hebr. *holy things* [a]1Chr. 28:12; Mal. 3:10
21 [I]Or, *Libni* [II]Or, *Jehiel* [a]1Chr. 6:17 [b]1Chr. 23:8; 29:8
24 [a]1Chr. 23:16
25 [a]1Chr. 23:18
27 [I]Hebr. *Out of the battles and spoils*
28 [a]1Sam. 9:9

26:4 Obed-edom was the Levite who had received God's blessing when he maintained the ark of the covenant after the death of Uzza (1 Chr. 13:13, 14; 15:24, 25; 16:38).

Other Public Servants

29 Of the Izharites, Chenaniah and his sons *were* for the outward business[4399] over Israel, for [a]officers[7860] and judges.

30 *And* of the Hebronites, Hashabiah and his brethren, men of valour, a thousand and seven hundred, *were* [I]officers among them of Israel on this side Jordan westward in all the business of the LORD, and in the service of the king.

31 Among the Hebronites *was* [a]Jerijah the chief, *even* among the Hebronites, according to the generations[8435] of his fathers. In the fortieth year of the reign of David they were sought for, and there were found among them mighty men of valour [b]at Jazer of Gilead.

32 And his brethren, men of valour, *were* two thousand and seven hundred chief fathers, whom king David made rulers over the Reubenites, the Gadites, and the half tribe of Manasseh, for every matter[1697] pertaining to God, and [Ia]affairs[1697] of the king.

Monthly Organization of Public Service

27 Now the children of Israel after their number, *to wit,* the chief fathers and captains[8269] of thousands and hundreds, and their officers that served the king[4428] in any matter of the courses, which came in and went out month by month throughout all the months of the year, of every course *were* twenty and four thousand.

2 Over the first[7223] course for the first month *was* [a]Jashobeam the son of Zabdiel: and in his course *were* twenty and four thousand.

3 Of the children of Perez *was* the chief of all the captains of the host for the first month.

4 And over the course of the second month *was* [Ia]Dodai an Ahohite, and of his course *was* Mikloth also the ruler: in his course likewise *were* twenty and four thousand.

5 The third captain[8269] of the host for the third month *was* Benaiah the son of Jehoiada, a [Ia]chief priest: and in his course *were* twenty and four thousand.

6 This *is that* Benaiah, *who was* [a]mighty *among* the thirty, and above the thirty: and in his course *was* Ammizabad his son.

7 The fourth *captain* for the fourth month *was* [a]Asahel the brother[251] of Joab, and Zebadiah his son after him: and in his course *were* twenty and four thousand.

8 The fifth captain for the fifth month *was* Shamhuth the Izrahite: and in his course *were* twenty and four thousand.

9 The sixth *captain* for the sixth month *was* [a]Ira the son of Ikkesh the Tekoite: and in his course *were* twenty and four thousand.

10 The seventh *captain* for the seventh month *was* [a]Helez the Pelonite, of the children of Ephraim: and in his course[4256] *were* twenty and four thousand.

11 The eighth *captain* for the eighth month *was* [a]Sibbecai the Hushathite, of the Zarhites: and in his course *were* twenty and four thousand.

12 The ninth *captain* for the ninth month *was* [a]Abiezer the Anetothite, of the Benjamites: and in his course *were* twenty and four thousand.

13 The tenth *captain* for the tenth month *was* [a]Maharai the Netophathite, of the Zarhites: and in his course *were* twenty and four thousand.

14 The eleventh *captain* for the eleventh month *was* [a]Benaiah the Pirathonite, of the children of Ephraim: and in his course *were* twenty and four thousand.

15 The twelfth *captain* for the twelfth month *was* [Ia]Heldai the Netophathite, of Othniel: and in his course *were* twenty and four thousand.

Tribal Leaders

16 Furthermore over the tribes[7626] of Israel: the ruler of the Reubenites *was* Eliezer the son of Zichri: of the

29 [a]1Chr. 23:4
30 [I]Hebr. *over the charge*
31 [a]1Chr. 23:19 [b]Josh. 21:39
32 [I]Hebr. *thing* [a]2Chr. 19:11
2 [a]2Sam. 23:8; 1Chr. 11:11
4 [I]Or, *Dodo* [a]2Sam. 23:9
5 [I]Or, *principal officer* [a]1Kgs. 4:5
6 [a]2Sam. 23:20, 22, 23; 1Chr. 11:22
7 [a]2Sam. 23:24; 1Chr. 11:26
9 [a]1Chr. 11:28
10 [a]1Chr. 11:27
11 [a]2Sam. 21:18; 1Chr. 11:29
12 [a]1Chr. 11:28
13 [a]2Sam. 23:28; 1Chr. 11:30
14 [a]1Chr. 11:31
15 [I]Or, *Heled* [a]1Chr. 11:30

Simeonites, Shephatiah the son of Maachah:

17 Of the Levites, [a]Hashabiah the son of Kemuel: of the Aaronites, Zadok:

18 Of Judah, [a]Elihu, *one* of the brethren[251] of David: of Issachar, Omri the son of Michael:

19 Of Zebulun, Ishmaiah the son of Obadiah: of Naphtali, Jerimoth the son of Azriel:

20 Of the children of Ephraim, Hoshea the son of Azaziah: of the half[2677] tribe of Manasseh, Joel the son of Pedaiah:

21 Of the half *tribe* of Manasseh in Gilead, Iddo the son of Zechariah: of Benjamin, Jaasiel the son of Abner:

22 Of Dan, Azareel the son of Jeroham. These were the princes of the tribes of Israel.

23 But David took not the number of them from twenty years old and under: because [a]the LORD had said[559] he would increase Israel like to the stars of the heavens.

24 Joab the son of Zeruiah began to number, but he finished[3615] not, because [a]there fell[1961] wrath[7110] for it against Israel; neither [I]was the number put in the account of the chronicles of king David.

Administrators of David's Property

25 And over the king's treasures *was* Azmaveth the son of Adiel: and over the storehouses[214] in the fields,[7704] in the cities, and in the villages, and in the castles, *was* Jehonathan the son of Uzziah:

26 And over them that did[6213] the work of the field[7704] for tillage of the ground[127] *was* Ezri the son of Chelub:

27 And over the vineyards *was* Shimei the Ramathite: [I]over the increase of the vineyards for the wine cellars *was* Zabdi the Shiphmite:

28 And over the olive trees and the sycomore trees that *were* in the low plains *was* Baal–hanan the Gederite: and over the cellars of oil[8081] *was* Joash:

29 And over the herds that fed in Sharon *was* Shitrai the Sharonite: and over the herds *that were* in the valleys *was* Shaphat the son of Adlai:

30 Over the camels also *was* Obil the Ishmaelite: and over the asses *was* Jehdeiah the Meronothite:

31 And over the flocks *was* Jaziz the Hagerite. All these *were* the rulers of the substance[7399] which *was* king David's.

Those Close to David

32 Also Jonathan David's uncle was a counselor,[3289] a wise[995] man,[376] and a [I]scribe: and Jehiel the [II]son of Hachmoni *was* with the king's sons:

33 And [a]Ahithophel *was* the king's counselor: and [b]Hushai the Archite *was* the king's companion:[7453]

🗝 34 And after Ahithophel *was* Jehoiada the son of Benaiah, and [a]Abiathar: and the general[8269] of the king's army[6635] *was* [b]Joab.

God Has Chosen Solomon to Build the Temple

28 And David assembled[6950] all the princes of Israel, [a]the princes of the tribes, and [b]the captains[8269] of the companies that ministered[8334] to the king[4428] by course, and the captains over the thousands, and captains over the hundreds, and [c]the stewards over all the substance and [I]possession of the king, [II]and of his sons, with the [III]officers,[5631] and with [d]the mighty men, and with all the valiant men, unto Jerusalem.

2 Then David the king stood up upon his feet, and said, Hear me, my brethren,[251] and my people: *As for me,* [a]I *had* in mine heart to build an house of rest for the ark[727] of the covenant[1285] of the LORD, and for [b]the footstool of our God,[430] and had made ready for the building:

17 [a]1Chr. 26:30
18 [a]1Sam. 16:6, *Eliab*
23 [a]Gen. 15:5
24 [I]Hebr. *ascended* [a]2Sam. 24:15; 1Chr. 21:7
27 [I]Hebr. *over that which was of the vineyards*
32 [I]Or, *secretary* [II]Or, *Hachmonite*
33 [a]2Sam. 15:12 [b]2Sam. 15:37; 16:16
34 [a]1Kgs. 1:7 [b]1Chr. 11:6
1 [I]Or, *cattle* [II]Or, *and his sons* [III]Or, *eunuchs* [a]1Chr. 27:16 [b]1Chr. 27:1, 2 [c]1Chr. 27:25 [d]1Chr. 11:10
2 [a]2Sam. 7:2; Ps. 132:3-5 [b]Ps. 99:5; 132:7

🗝 **27:34** Ahithophel had deserted David in order to follow Absalom (2 Sam. 15:12, 31; 16:20–23), but when frustrated by Hushai (2 Sam. 15:32, 37; 17:1–16), he committed suicide (2 Sam. 17:23).

3 But God said unto me, [a]Thou shalt not build an house for my name, because thou *hast been* a man[376] of war, and hast shed [I]blood.[1818]

4 Howbeit the LORD God of Israel [a]chose[977] me before all the house of my father to be king over Israel for ever: for he hath chosen [b]Judah *to be* the ruler; and of the house of Judah, [c]the house of my father; and [d]among the sons of my father he liked[7521] me to make *me* king over all Israel:

5 [a]And of all my sons, (for the LORD hath given me many sons,) [b]he hath chosen Solomon my son to sit upon the throne of the kingdom[4438] of the LORD over Israel.

6 And he said unto me, [a]Solomon thy son, he shall build my house and my courts: for I have chosen him *to be* my son, and I will be his father.

7 Moreover I will establish his kingdom for ever, [a]if he be [I]constant[2388] to do[6213] my commandments[4687] and my judgments,[4941] as at this day.[3117]

8 Now therefore in the sight of all Israel the congregation[6951] of the LORD, and in the audience[241] of our God, keep[8104] and seek for all the commandments of the LORD your God: that ye may possess this good[2896] land,[776] and leave *it* for an inheritance[5157] for your children[1121] after you for ever.

9 And thou, Solomon my son, [a]know[3045] thou the God of thy father, and serve him [b]with a perfect heart and with a willing[2655] mind:[5315] for [c]the LORD searcheth[1875] all hearts, and understandeth[995] all the imaginations[3336] of the thoughts: [d]if thou seek him, he will be found of thee: but if thou forsake[5800] him, he will cast thee off for ever.

10 Take heed now; [a]for the LORD hath chosen thee to build an house for the sanctuary: be strong, and do *it.*

11 Then David gave to Solomon his son [a]the pattern[8403] of the porch, and of the houses thereof, and of the treasuries thereof, and of the upper chambers thereof, and of the inner parlours thereof, and of the place of the mercy seat,

12 And the pattern [I]of all that he had by the spirit, of the courts of the house of the LORD, and of all the chambers round about, [a]of the treasuries of the house of God, and of the treasuries of the dedicated things:[6944]

13 Also for the courses of the priests and the Levites, and for all the work[4399] of the service of the house of the LORD, and for all the vessels of service in the house of the LORD.

14 *He gave* of gold by weight for *things* of gold, for all instruments of all manner of service; *silver also* for all instruments of silver by weight, for all instruments of every kind of service:

15 Even the weight for the candlesticks of gold, and for their lamps[5216] of gold, by weight for every candlestick, and for the lamps thereof: and for the candlesticks of silver by weight, *both* for the candlestick, and *also* for the lamps thereof, according to the use[5656] of every candlestick.

16 And by weight *he gave* gold for the tables of shewbread,[4635] for every table; and *likewise* silver for the tables of silver:

17 Also pure gold for the fleshhooks, and the bowls, and the cups: and for the golden basons[3713] *he gave gold* by weight for every bason; and *likewise silver* by weight for every bason of silver:

18 And for the altar[4196] of incense[7004] refined gold by weight; and gold for the pattern of the chariot of the [a]cherubims,[3742] that spread out *their wings,* and covered the ark of the covenant of the LORD.

19 All *this, said David,* [a]the LORD made me understand[7919] in writing by *his* hand upon me, *even* all the works of this pattern.

20 And David said to Solomon his son, [a]Be strong and of good courage, and do *it:* fear[3372] not, nor be dismayed:[2865] for the LORD God, *even* my God, *will be* with thee; [b]he will not fail[7503] thee, nor forsake thee, until thou hast finished[3615] all the work for the service of the house of the LORD.

21 And, behold, the courses of the priests and the Levites, *even they shall be*

---

3 [I]Hebr. *bloods* [a]2Sam. 7:5, 13; 1Kgs. 5:3; 1Chr. 17:4; 22:8

4 [a]1Sam. 16:7-13 [b]Gen. 49:8; 1Chr. 5:2; Ps. 60:7; 78:68 [c]1Sam. 16:1 [d]1Sam. 16:12, 13

5 [a]1Chr. 3:1; 23:1 [b]1Chr. 22:9

6 [a]2Sam. 7:13, 14; 1Chr. 22:9, 10; 2Chr. 1:9

7 [I]Hebr. *strong* [a]1Chr. 22:13

9 [a]Jer. 9:24; Hos. 4:1; John 17:3 [b]2Kgs. 20:3; Ps. 101:2 [c]1Sam. 16:7; 1Kgs. 8:39; 1Chr. 29:17; Ps. 7:9; 139:2; Prov. 17:3; Jer. 11:20; 17:10; 20:12; Rev. 2:23 [d]2Chr. 15:2

10 [a]1Chr. 28:6

11 [a]Ex. 25:40; 1Chr. 28:19

12 [I]Hebr. *of all that was with him* [a]1Chr. 26:20

18 [a]Ex. 25:18-22; 1Sam. 4:4; 1Kgs. 6:23

19 [a]Ex. 25:40; 1Chr. 28:11, 12

20 [a]Deut. 31:7, 8; Josh. 1:6, 7, 9; 1Chr. 22:13 [b]Josh. 1:5

with thee for all the service of the house of God: and *there shall be* with thee for all manner of workmanship [a]every willing[5081] skilful man, for any manner of service: also the princes and all the people *will be* wholly at thy commandment.[1697]

An Offering for the Temple

29 Furthermore David the king said unto all the congregation,[6951] Solomon my son, whom alone God[430] hath chosen,[977] *is yet* [a]young and tender, and the work[4399] *is* great: for the palace *is* not for man,[120] but for the LORD God.

2 Now I have prepared with all my might for the house of my God the gold for *things to be made* of gold, and the silver for *things* of silver, and the brass for *things* of brass, the iron for *things* of iron, and wood for *things* of wood; [a]onyx stones, and *stones* to be set, glistering6320 stones, and of divers colours, and all manner of precious stones, and marble stones in abundance.

3 Moreover, because I have set my affection[7521] to the house of my God, I have of mine own proper good, of gold and silver, *which* I have given to the house of my God, over and above all that I have prepared for the holy house,

4 *Even* three thousand talents of gold, of the gold of [a]Ophir, and seven thousand talents of refined silver, to overlay the walls of the houses *withal:*

5 The gold for *things* of gold, and the silver for *things* of silver, and for all manner of work *to be made* by the hands of artificers.[2796] And who *then* is willing[5068] [I]to consecrate his service this day[3117] unto the LORD?

6 Then [a]the chief of the fathers[1] and princes of the tribes of Israel, and the captains[8269] of thousands and of hundreds, with [b]the rulers of the king's[4428] work, offered willingly,[5068]

7 And gave for the service of the house of God of gold five thousand talents and ten thousand drams,[150] and of silver ten thousand talents, and of brass eighteen thousand talents, and one hundred thousand talents of iron.

8 And they with whom *precious* stones were found gave *them* to the treasure of the house of the LORD, by the hand of [a]Jehiel the Gershonite.

9 Then the people rejoiced, for that they offered willingly, because with perfect heart they [a]offered willingly to the LORD: and David the king also rejoiced with great joy.

David Prays

10 Wherefore David blessed the LORD before all the congregation: and David said, Blessed *be* thou, LORD God of Israel our father, for ever and ever.

11 [a]Thine, O LORD, *is* the greatness,1420 and the power,1369 and the glory,[8597] and the victory,[5331] and the majesty:[1935] for all *that is* in the heaven and in the earth[776] *is thine;* thine *is* the kingdom,[4467] O LORD, and thou art exalted as head above all.

12 [a]Both riches and honour *come* of thee, and thou reignest over all; and in thine hand *is* power and might; and in thine hand *it is* to make great, and to give strength unto all.

13 Now therefore, our God, we thank thee, and praise thy glorious[8597] name.

14 But who *am* I, and what *is* my people, that we should [I]be able to offer so willingly after this sort? for all things *come* of thee, and [II]of thine own have we given thee.

15 For [a]we *are* strangers[1616] before thee, and sojourners,[8453] as *were* all our fathers: [b]our days on the earth *are* as a shadow, and *there is* none [I]abiding.

16 O LORD our God, all this store[1995] that we have prepared to build thee an house for thine holy name *cometh* of thine hand, and *is* all thine own.

17 I know[3045] also, my God, that thou [a]triest the heart, and [b]hast pleasure in uprightness.[4339] As for me, in the uprightness[3476] of mine heart I have willingly offered all these things: and now have I seen with joy thy people, which

21 [a]Ex. 35:25, 26; 36:1, 2

1 [a]1Kgs. 3:7; 1Chr. 22:5; Prov. 4:3

2 [a]Isa. 54:11, 12; Rev. 21:18

4 [a]1Kgs. 9:28

5 [I]Hebr. *to fill his hand*

6 [a]1Chr. 27:1

8 [a]1Chr. 26:21

9 [a]2Cor. 9:7

11 [a]Matt. 6:13; 1Tim. 1:17; Rev. 5:13

12 [a]Rom. 11:36

14 [I]Hebr. *retain, or, obtain strength* [II]Hebr. *of thine hand*

15 [I]Hebr. *expectation* [a]Ps. 30:12; Heb. 11:13; 1Pet. 2:11 [b]Job 14:2; Ps. 90:9; 102:11; 144:4

17 [a]1Sam. 16:7; 1Chr. 28:9 [b]Prov. 11:20

are [I]present here, to offer willingly unto thee.

18 O LORD God of Abraham, Isaac, and of Israel, our fathers, keep[8104] this for ever in the imagination[3336] of the thoughts of the heart of thy people, and [I][a]prepare their heart unto thee:

19 And [a]give unto Solomon my son a perfect heart, to keep thy commandments,[4687] thy testimonies, and thy statutes, and to do all *these things,* and to build the palace, *for* the which [b]I have made provision.

20 And David said to all the congregation, Now bless[1288] the LORD your God. And all the congregation blessed the LORD God of their fathers, and bowed down their heads, and worshipped[7812] the LORD, and the king.

Solomon Begins His Reign

21 And they sacrificed[2076] sacrifices[2077] unto the LORD, and offered[5927] burnt offerings unto the LORD, on the morrow after that day, *even* a thousand bullocks, a thousand rams, *and* a thousand lambs, with their drink offerings, and sacrifices in abundance for all Israel:

22 And did eat and drink before the LORD on that day with great gladness. And they made Solomon the son of David king[4427] the second time, and [a]anointed[4886] *him* unto the LORD *to be* the chief governor,[5057] and Zadok *to be* priest.

23 Then Solomon sat on the throne of the LORD as king instead of David his father, and prospered; and all Israel obeyed[8085] him.

24 And all the princes, and the mighty men, and all the sons likewise of king David, [I][a]submitted themselves unto Solomon the king.

25 And the LORD magnified Solomon exceedingly in the sight of all Israel, and [a]bestowed upon him *such* royal majesty as had not been on any king before him in Israel.

David's Death

26 Thus David the son of Jesse reigned over all Israel.

27 [a]And the time that he reigned over Israel *was* forty years; [b]seven years reigned he in Hebron, and thirty and three *years* reigned he in Jerusalem.

28 And he [a]died[4191] in a good old age, [b]full of days, riches, and honour: and Solomon his son reigned in his stead.

29 Now the acts[1697] of David the king, first[7223] and last, behold, they *are* written in the [I]book of Samuel the seer, and in the book of Nathan the prophet, and in the book of Gad the seer,

30 With all his reign and his might, [a]and the times that went over him, and over Israel, and over all the kingdoms[4467] of the countries.[776]

17 [I]Or, *found*
18 [I]Or, *establish* [a]Ps. 10:17
19 [a]Ps. 72:1 [b]1Chr. 22:14; 29:2
22 [a]1Kgs. 1:35, 39
24 [I]Hebr. *gave the hand under Solomon* [a]Eccl. 8:2
25 [a]1Kgs. 3:13; 2Chr. 1:12; Eccl. 2:9
27 [a]2Sam. 5:4; 1Kgs. 2:11 [b]2Sam. 5:5
28 [a]Gen. 25:8 [b]1Chr. 23:1
29 [I]Hebr. *words*
30 [a]Dan. 2:21

29:29 Most likely, these were ancient writings, perhaps similar to Jasher's works (Josh. 10:13; 2 Sam. 1:18), which were available to Ezra, but which have since been lost. It is assumed that many true prophets of God have written books which had parts incorporated into Scripture, but whose names are not given. Such incorporations are limited to the books of Samuel, Kings, and Chronicles. This reference illustrates what is called the "prophetic succession"; there were always prophets inspired of God recording the information that God intended to incorporate into His Scriptures. The Hebrew Scriptures allow for this by calling all the books from Joshua to 2 Kings the "former prophets."

The Second Book of
CHRONICLES

The Book of 2 Chronicles was originally included with 1 Chronicles. Ezra, the generally accepted author for the book (see introduction to 1 Chr.), restates the history of Israel and Judah as it related to their spiritual condition. The events recorded in this book parallel those of 1 and 2 Kings, but the attention is mainly focused on Solomon and the kings of Judah. The kings of Israel are mentioned only when they have some impact on the events or people in Judah. The major periods of revival in Judah are covered in greater detail. These revivals came under the reigns of Asa (chaps. 14—16), Jehoshaphat (chaps. 17—20), Joash (chaps. 23, 24), Hezekiah (chaps. 29—32), and Josiah (chaps. 34, 35).

It is important to remember that during those days many prophets were actively attacking the ritualistic approach to observing the Law. They called this formalism "idolatry in disguise." The revivals that did take place never lasted long because those kings who were right with God raised children who became evil idolators (e.g., Hezekiah and Manasseh).

Solomon Asks for Wisdom

1 And [a]Solomon the son of David was
strengthened in his kingdom,[4438] and
[b]the LORD his God[430] *was* with him, and
[c]magnified him exceedingly.
2 Then Solomon spake unto all
Israel, to [a]the captains[8269] of thousands
and of hundreds, and to the judges,[8199]
and to every governor in all Israel, the
chief[7218] of the fathers.[1]
3 So Solomon, and all the congregation[6951]
with him, went to the high place
that *was* at [a]Gibeon; for there was the
tabernacle[168] of the congregation[4150] of
God,[430] which Moses the servant of the
LORD had made in the wilderness.
4 [a]But the ark[727] of God had David
brought up[5927] from Kirjath–jearim to *the*
place which David had prepared for it:
for he had pitched a tent for it at
Jerusalem.
5 Moreover [a]the brasen altar,[4196] that
[b]Bezaleel the son of Uri, the son of Hur,
had made, [I]he put before the tabernacle[4908]
of the LORD: and Solomon and the
congregation sought unto it.
6 And Solomon went up thither to
the brasen altar before the LORD, which
was at the tabernacle of the congregation,
and [a]offered a thousand burnt offerings
upon it.
7 [a]In that night[3915] did God appear
unto Solomon, and said unto him,
Ask[7592] what I shall give thee.
8 And Solomon said unto God, Thou
hast shewed great mercy unto David my
father, and hast made me [a]to reign in his
stead.
9 Now, O LORD God, let thy promise
unto David my father be established:[539]
[a]for thou hast made me king[4427] over a
people[5971] [I]like the dust[6083] of the
earth[776] in multitude.
10 [a]Give me now wisdom[2451] and
knowledge, that I may [b]go out and come
in before this people: for who can
judge[8199] this thy people, *that is so* great?
11 [a]And God said to Solomon,
Because this was in thine heart, and thou
hast not asked[7592] riches, wealth, or honour,
nor the life[5315] of thine enemies,[8130]
neither yet hast asked long life; but hast
asked wisdom and knowledge for thyself,
that thou mayest judge my people, over
whom I have made thee king:

1 [a]1Kgs. 2:46 [b]Gen. 39:2 [c]1Chr. 29:25
2 [a]1Chr. 27:1
3 [a]1Kgs. 3:4; 1Chr. 16:39; 21:29
4 [a]2Sam. 6:2, 17; 1Chr. 15:1
5 [I]Or, was *there* [a]Ex. 27:1, 2; 38:1, 2 [b]Ex. 31:2
6 [a]1Kgs. 3:4
7 [a]1Kgs. 3:5, 6
8 [a]1Chr. 28:5
9 [I]Hebr. *much as the dust of the earth* [a]1Kgs. 3:7, 8
10 [a]1Kgs. 3:9 [b]Num. 27:17; Deut. 31:2
11 [a]1Kgs. 3:11-13

1:4 Although David had prepared a place in Jerusalem for the ark (1 Chr. 15:1, 2), the old Tabernacle and the bronze altar were still at Gibeon.

12 Wisdom and knowledge *is* granted unto thee; and I will give thee riches, and wealth, and honour, such as [a]none of the kings[4428] have had that *have been* before thee, neither shall there any after thee have the like.

13 Then Solomon came *from his journey* to the high place that *was* at Gibeon to Jerusalem, from before the tabernacle of the congregation, and reigned over Israel.

Solomon's Horses and Chariots

🔑 14 [a]And Solomon gathered[622] chariots and horsemen: and he had a thousand and four hundred chariots, and twelve thousand horsemen, which he placed in the chariot cities, and with the king at Jerusalem.

15 [a]And the king [I]made silver and gold at Jerusalem *as plenteous* as stones, and cedar trees made he as the sycomore trees that *are* in the vale[8219] for abundance.

16 [a]And [I]Solomon had horses brought out of Egypt, and linen yarn: the king's merchants received the linen yarn at a price.

17 And they fetched up, and brought forth out of Egypt a chariot for six hundred *shekels* of silver, and an horse for an hundred and fifty: and so brought they out *horses* for all the kings of the Hittites, and for the kings of Syria, [I]by their means.

Solomon Prepares to Build the Temple

2 And Solomon [a]determined[559] to build an house for the name of the LORD, and an house for his kingdom.[4438]

2 And [a]Solomon told out[5608] threescore and ten thousand men to bear burdens, and fourscore thousand to hew[2672] in the mountain, and three thousand and six hundred to oversee them.

🔑 3 And Solomon sent to [Ia]Huram the king[4428] of Tyre, saying, [b]As thou didst deal[6213] with David my father, and didst send him cedars to build him an house to dwell therein, *even so deal with me.*

4 Behold, [a]I build an house to the name of the LORD[3068] my God,[430] to dedicate[6942] *it* to him, *and* [b]to burn before him [I]sweet[5561] incense,[7004] and for [c]the continual[8548] shewbread, and for [d]the burnt offerings morning and evening, on the sabbaths, and on the new moons, and on the solemn feasts[4150] of the LORD our God. This *is an ordinance* for ever to Israel.

5 And the house which I build *is* great: for [a]great *is* our God above all gods.[430]

6 [a]But who [I]is able to build him an house, seeing the heaven and heaven of heavens cannot contain him? who *am* I then, that I should build him an house, save only to burn sacrifice before him?

7 Send me now therefore a man cunning[2450] to work[6213] in gold, and in silver, and in brass, and in iron, and in purple, and crimson, and blue, and that can skill[3045] [I]to grave with the cunning men that *are* with me in Judah and in Jerusalem, [a]whom David my father did provide.

8 [a]Send me also cedar trees, fir trees, and [Ib]algum[418] trees, out of Lebanon: for I know[3045] that thy servants can skill to cut[3772] timber in Lebanon; and, behold, my servants *shall be* with thy servants,

9 Even to prepare me timber in abundance: for the house which I am about to build *shall be* [I]wonderful[6381] great.

10 [a]And, behold, I will give to thy servants, the hewers[2404] that cut timber, twenty thousand measures of

---

12 [a]1Chr. 29:25; 2Chr. 9:22; Eccl. 2:9
14 [a]1Kgs. 4:26; 10:26; 2Chr. 9:25
15 [I]Hebr. *gave* [a]1Kgs. 10:27; 2Chr. 9:27; Job 22:24
16 [I]Hebr. *the going forth of the horses which was Solomon's* [a]1Kgs. 10:28, 29
17 [I]Hebr. *by their hand*
1 [a]1Kgs. 5:5
2 [a]1Kgs. 5:15; 2Chr. 2:18
3 [I]Or, *Hiram,* [a]1Kgs. 5:1 [b]1Chr. 14:1
4 [I]Hebr. *incense of spices* [a]2Chr. 2:1 [b]Ex. 30:7 [c]Ex. 25:30; Lev. 24:8 [d]Num. 28:3, 9, 11
5 [a]Ps. 135:5
6 [I]Hebr. *hath retained,* or, *obtained strength* [a]1Kgs. 8:27; 2Chr. 6:18; Isa. 66:1
7 [I]Hebr. *to grave gravings* [a]1Chr. 22:15
8 [I]Or, *almuggim* [a]1Kgs. 5:6 [b]1Kgs. 10:11
9 [I]Hebr. *great and wonderful*
10 [a]1Kgs. 5:11

🔑 **1:14** See note on Deuteronomy 17:16.
🔑 **2:3, 14** Huram, the king of Tyre, is called Hiram in 1 Kings 5:11 (see also 2 Sam. 5:11). He is to be distinguished from Huram, the master craftsman (1 Kgs. 7:13), who is also referred to as Hiram in the Book of 1 Kings.

beaten[4347] wheat, and twenty thousand measures of barley, and twenty thousand baths of wine, and twenty thousand baths of oil.

11 Then Huram the king of Tyre answered[559] in writing, which he sent to Solomon, [a]Because the LORD hath loved[160] his people,[5971] he hath made thee king over them.

12 Huram said moreover, [a]Blessed[1288] *be* the LORD God of Israel, [b]that made heaven and earth,[776] who hath given to David the king a wise[2450] son, [I]endued with prudence and understanding,[998] that might build an house for the LORD, and an house for his kingdom.

13 And now I have sent a cunning man, endued with understanding, of Huram my father's,[1]

🗝 14 [a]The son of a woman[802] of the daughters of Dan, and his father *was* a man of Tyre, skilful to work in gold, and in silver, in brass, in iron, in stone, and in timber, in purple, in blue, and in fine linen, and in crimson; also to grave any manner of graving,[6603] and to find out[2803] every device[4284] which shall be put to him, with thy cunning men, and with the cunning men of my lord[113] David thy father.

15 Now therefore the wheat, and the barley, the oil, and the wine, which [a]my lord hath spoken of, let him send unto his servants:

16 [a]And we will cut wood out of Lebanon, [I]as much as thou shalt need: and we will bring it to thee in floats[7513] by sea to [II][b]Joppa; and thou shalt carry it up to Jerusalem.

17 [a]And Solomon numbered[5608] all [I]the strangers that *were* in the land[776] of Israel, after the numbering wherewith [b]David his father had numbered them; and they were found an hundred and fifty thousand and three thousand and six hundred.

18 And he set [a]threescore and ten thousand of them *to be* bearers of burdens, and fourscore thousand *to be* hewers[2672] in the mountain, and three thousand and six hundred overseers to set the people a work.[5647]

Solomon Builds the Temple

3 🗝 Then [a]Solomon began to build the house of the LORD at [b]Jerusalem in mount Moriah, [I]where *the LORD* appeared[7200] unto David his father, in the place that David had prepared in the threshingfloor of [II][c]Ornan the Jebusite.

2 And he began to build in the second *day* of the second month, in the fourth year of his reign.

3 Now [a]these *are the things wherein* Solomon was [I]instructed[3245] for the building of the house of God.[430] The length[753] by cubits after the first[7223] measure *was* threescore cubits, and the breadth twenty cubits.

4 And the [a]porch that *was* in the front *of the house,* the length *of it was* according to the breadth of the house, twenty cubits, and the height *was* an hundred and twenty: and he overlaid it within with pure gold.

5 And [a]the greater house he cieled[2645] with fir tree, which he overlaid with fine gold, and set thereon palm trees and chains.

6 And he [I]garnished[6823] the house with precious stones for beauty:[8597] and the gold *was* gold of Parvaim.

7 He overlaid also the house, the beams, the posts, and the walls thereof, and the doors thereof, with gold; and graved[6605] cherubims[3742] on the walls.

8 And he made the most holy house, the length whereof *was* according to the breadth of the house, twenty cubits, and the breadth thereof twenty cubits: and he overlaid it with fine gold, *amounting* to six hundred talents.

9 And the weight of the nails *was* fifty shekels of gold. And he overlaid the upper chambers with gold.

10 [a]And in the most holy[6944] house

11 [a]1Kgs. 10:9; 2Chr. 9:8

12 [I]Hebr. *knowing prudence and understanding* [a]1Kgs. 5:7 [b]Gen. 1, 2; Ps. 33:6; 102:25; 124:8; 136:5, 6; Acts 4:24; 14:15; Rev. 10:6

14 [a]1Kgs. 7:13, 14

15 [a]2Chr. 2:10

16 [I]Hebr. *according to all thy need* [II]Hebr. *Japho* [a]1Kgs. 5:8, 9 [b]Josh. 19:46; Acts 9:36

17 [I]Hebr. *the men the strangers* [a]2Chr. 2:2; 1Kgs. 5:13, 15, 16; 9:20, 21; 2Chr. 8:7, 8 [b]1Chr. 22:2

18 [a]2Chr. 2:2

1 [I]Or, *which was seen of David his father* [II]Or, *Araunah* [a]1Kgs. 6:1 [b]Gen. 22:2, 14 [c]2Sam. 24:18; 1Chr. 21:18; 22:1

3 [I]Hebr. *founded* [a]1Kgs. 6:2

4 [a]1Kgs. 6:3

5 [a]1Kgs. 6:17

6 [I]Hebr. *covered*

10 [a]1Kgs. 6:23

🗝 **3:1** See note on 1 Chronicles 21:28 regarding Mount Moriah.

he made two cherubims [I]of image work, and overlaid them with gold.

11 And the wings of the cherubims *were* twenty cubits long:[753] one wing *of the one cherub was* five cubits, reaching to the wall of the house: and the other wing *was likewise* five cubits, reaching to the wing of the other cherub.

12 And *one* wing of the other cherub *was* five cubits, reaching to the wall of the house: and the other wing *was* five cubits *also,* joining to the wing of the other cherub.

13 The wings of these cherubims spread themselves forth twenty cubits: and they stood on their feet, and their faces *were* [I]inward.

14 And he made the [a]vail *of* blue, and purple, and crimson, and fine linen, and [I]wrought cherubims thereon.

15 Also he made before the house [a]two pillars of thirty and five cubits [I]high, and the chapiter that *was* on the top of each of them *was* five cubits.

16 And he made chains, *as* in the oracle,[1687] and put *them* on the heads of the pillars; and made [a]an hundred pomegranates, and put *them* on the chains.

17 And he [a]reared up the pillars before the temple, one on the right hand, and the other on the left; and called[7121] the name of that on the right hand [I]Jachin, and the name of that on the left [II]Boaz.

Furnishings for the Temple

4 Moreover he made [a]an altar[4196] of brass,[5178] twenty cubits[520] the length[753] thereof, and twenty cubits the breadth thereof, and ten cubits the height thereof.

2 [a]Also he made a molten sea of ten cubits [I]from brim[8193] to brim, round in compass, and five cubits the height thereof; and a line of thirty cubits did compass it round about.

3 [a]And under it *was* the similitude[1823] of oxen, which did compass it round about: ten in a cubit, compassing[5362] the sea round about. Two rows of oxen *were* cast, when it was cast.

4 It stood upon twelve oxen, three looking toward the north, and three looking toward the west, and three looking toward the south, and three looking toward the east: and the sea *was set* above upon them, and all their hinder parts *were* inward.

5 And the thickness of it *was* an handbreadth, and the brim of it like the work of the brim of a cup, [I]with flowers of lilies; *and* it received and held [a]three thousand baths.

6 He made also [a]ten lavers,[3595] and put five on the right hand, and five on the left, to wash[7364] in them: [I]such things as they offered for the burnt offering they washed[1740] in them; but the sea *was* for the priests to wash in.

7 [a]And he made ten candlesticks of gold [b]according to their form,[4941] and set *them* in the temple, five on the right hand, and five on the left.

8 [a]He made also ten tables, and placed *them* in the temple, five on the right side, and five on the left. And he made an hundred [I]basons[4219] of gold.

9 Furthermore [a]he made the court of the priests, and the great court, and doors for the court, and overlaid the doors of them with brass.

10 And [a]he set the sea on the right side of the east end, over against the south.

11 And [a]Huram made the pots, and the shovels, and the [I]basons. And Huram [II]finished[3615] the work[4399] that he was to make for king[4428] Solomon for the house of God;[430]

12 *To wit,* the two pillars, and [a]the pommels,[1543] and the chapiters *which were* on the top of the two pillars, and the two wreaths to cover[3680] the two pommels of the chapiters which *were* on the top of the pillars;

13 And [a]four hundred pomegranates on the two wreaths;[7639] two rows of pomegranates on each wreath, to cover the two pommels of the chapiters which *were* [I]upon the pillars.

10 [I]Or, (as some think) *of moveable work*

13 [I]Or, *toward the house*

14 [I]Hebr. *caused to ascend* [a]Ex. 26:31; Matt. 27:51; Heb. 9:3

15 [I]Hebr. *long* [a]1Kgs. 7:15-21; Jer. 52:21

16 [a]1Kgs. 7:20

17 [I]That is, *He shall establish* [II]That is, *In it is strength* [a]1Kgs. 7:21

1 [a]Ex. 27:1, 2; 2Kgs. 16:14; Ezek. 43:13, 16

2 [I]Hebr. *from his brim to his brim* [a]1Kgs. 7:23

3 [a]1Kgs. 7:24-26

5 [I]Or, *like a lily flower* [a]1Kgs. 7:26

6 [I]Hebr. *the work of burnt offering* [a]1Kgs. 7:38

7 [a]1Kgs. 7:49 [b]Ex. 25:31, 40; 1Chr. 28:12, 19

8 [I]Or, *bowls* [a]1Kgs. 7:48

9 [a]1Kgs. 6:36

10 [a]1Kgs. 7:39

11 [I]Or, *bowls* [II]Hebr. *finished to make* [a]1Kgs. 7:40

12 [a]1Kgs. 7:41

13 [I]Hebr. *upon the face* [a]1Kgs. 7:20

14 He made also [a]bases, and [I]lavers made he upon the bases;

15 One sea, and twelve oxen under it.

16 The pots[5518] also, and the shovels, and the fleshhooks, and all their instruments, did [a]Huram his father make to king Solomon for the house of the LORD of [I]bright brass.

17 [a]In the plain of Jordan did the king cast them, in the [I]clay ground[127] between Succoth and Zeredathah.

18 [a]Thus Solomon made all these vessels in great abundance: for the weight of the brass could not be found out.

19 And [a]Solomon made all the vessels that *were for* the house of God, the golden altar also, and the tables whereon [b]the shewbread *was set;*

20 Moreover the candlesticks with their lamps,[5216] that they should burn [a]after the manner before the oracle, of pure gold;

21 And [a]the flowers, and the lamps, and the tongs, *made he of* gold, *and* that [I]perfect gold;

22 And the snuffers, and the [I]basons, and the spoons, and the censers, *of* pure gold: and the entry of the house, the inner doors thereof for the most holy *place,* and the doors of the house of the temple, *were of* gold.

5 Thus [a]all the work[4399] that Solomon made for the house of the LORD was finished:[7999] and Solomon brought in *all* the things that David his father had dedicated;[6944] and the silver, and the gold, and all the instruments, put he among the treasures of the house of God.[430]

Solomon Brings the Ark of God Into the Temple

2 [a]Then Solomon assembled[6950] the elders[2205] of Israel, and all the heads of the tribes, the chief[5387] of the fathers[1] of the children[1121] of Israel, unto Jerusalem, to bring up the ark[727] of the covenant[1285] of the LORD [b]out of the city of David, which *is* Zion.

3 [a]Wherefore all the men of Israel assembled themselves unto the king[4428] [b]in the feast[2282] which *was* in the seventh month.

4 And all the elders of Israel came; and the Levites took up the ark.

🔑 5 And they brought up[5927] the ark, and the tabernacle of the congregation,[4150] and all the holy vessels that *were* in the tabernacle, these did the priests *and* the Levites bring up.

6 Also king Solomon, and all the congregation[5712] of Israel that were assembled[3259] unto him before the ark, sacrificed sheep and oxen, which could not be told nor numbered for multitude.

7 And the priests brought in the ark of the covenant of the LORD unto his place, to the oracle of the house, into the most holy *place, even* under the wings of the cherubims:[3742]

8 For the cherubims spread forth *their* wings over the place of the ark, and the cherubims covered[3680] the ark and the staves thereof above.

9 And they drew out the staves *of the ark,* that the ends of the staves were seen from the ark before the oracle; but they were not seen without. And [I][a]there it is unto this day.[3117]

🔑 10 *There was* nothing in the ark save the two tables which Moses [a]put *therein* at Horeb, [I]when the LORD made *a covenant* with the children of Israel, when they came out of Egypt.

11 And it came to pass, when the priests were come out of the holy *place:* (for all the priests *that were* [I]present were sanctified, *and* did not *then* wait[8104] by course:

12 [a]Also the Levites *which were* the singers, all of them of Asaph, of Heman,

14 [I]Or, *caldrons* [a]1Kgs. 7:27, 43
16 [I]Hebr. *made bright,* or, *scoured* [a]1Kgs. 7:14, 45
17 [I]Hebr. *thicknesses of the ground* [a]1Kgs. 7:46
18 [a]1Kgs. 7:47
19 [a]1Kgs. 7:48-50 [b]Ex. 25:30
20 [a]Ex. 27:20, 21
21 [I]Hebr. *perfections of gold* [a]Ex. 25:31
22 [I]Or, *bowls*
1 [a]1Kgs. 7:51
2 [a]1Kgs. 8:1 [b]2Sam. 6:12
3 [a]1Kgs. 8:2 [b]2Chr. 7:8-10
9 [I]Or, *they are there,* as [a]1Kgs. 8:8
10 [I]Or, *where* [a]Deut. 10:2, 5; 2Chr. 6:11
11 [I]Hebr. *found*
12 [a]1Chr. 25:1

🔑 **5:5** See note on 1 Chronicles 13:9, 10 regarding Uzza and the improper transporting of the ark of God.
🔑 **5:10** See note on Numbers 17:8 concerning the contents of the ark of the covenant.

of Jeduthun, with their sons and their brethren,[251] *being* arrayed in white linen, having cymbals and psalteries and harps, stood at the east end of the altar,[4196] [b]and with them an hundred and twenty priests sounding with trumpets:)

13 It came even to pass, as the trumpeters and singers *were* as one, to make one sound to be heard in praising[1984] and thanking[3034] the LORD; and when they lifted up *their* voice with the trumpets and cymbals and instruments of musick, and praised the LORD, *saying,* [a]For *he is* good;[2896] for his mercy *endureth* for ever: that *then* the house was filled with a cloud,[6051] *even* the house of the LORD;

14 So that the priests could not stand to minister by reason of the cloud: [a]for the glory[3519] of the LORD had filled the house of God.

Solomon Addresses the People

6 Then [a]said Solomon, The LORD hath said that he would dwell[7931] in the [b]thick darkness.[6205]

2 But I have built an house of habitation for thee, and a place for thy dwelling for ever.

3 And the king turned his face, and blessed[1288] the whole congregation[6951] of Israel: and all the congregation of Israel stood.

4 And he said, Blessed *be* the LORD God[430] of Israel, who hath with his hands fulfilled *that* which he spake with his mouth to my father David, saying,

5 Since the day[3117] that I brought forth my people[5971] out of the land[776] of Egypt I chose no city among all the tribes of Israel to build an house in, that my name might be there; neither chose I any man to be a ruler over my people Israel:

6 [a]But I have chosen[977] Jerusalem, that my name might be there; and [b]have chosen David to be over my people Israel.

7 Now [a]it was in the heart of David my father to build an house for the name of the LORD God of Israel.

8 But the LORD said to David my father, Forasmuch as it was in thine heart to build an house for my name, thou didst well[2895] in that it was in thine heart:

9 Notwithstanding thou shalt not build the house; but thy son which shall come forth out of thy loins, he shall build the house for my name.

10 The LORD therefore hath performed his word[1697] that he hath spoken: for I am risen up in the room of David my father, and am set on the throne of Israel, as the LORD promised, and have built the house for the name of the LORD God of Israel.

11 And in it have I put the ark,[727] [a]wherein *is* the covenant[1285] of the LORD, that he made with the children[1121] of Israel.

Solomon's Temple Prayer

12 [a]And he stood before the altar[4196] of the LORD in the presence of all the congregation of Israel, and spread forth his hands:

13 For Solomon had made a brasen scaffold, of five cubits [I]long,[753] and five cubits broad, and three cubits high, and had set it in the midst of the court: and upon it he stood, and kneeled down[1288] upon his knees before all the congregation of Israel, and spread forth his hands toward heaven.

14 And said, O LORD God of Israel, [a]*there is* no God like thee in the heaven, nor in the earth;[776] which keepest covenant, and *shewest* mercy unto thy servants, that walk before thee with all their hearts:

15 [a]Thou which hast kept[8104] with thy servant David my father that which thou hast promised him; and spakest

12 [b]1Chr. 15:24
13 [a]1Chr. 16:34, 41; Ps. 136
14 [a]Ex. 40:35; 2Chr. 7:2
1 [a]1Kgs. 8:12 [b]Lev. 16:2
6 [a]2Chr. 12:13 [b]1Chr. 28:4
7 [a]2Sam. 7:2; 1Chr. 17:1; 28:2
11 [a]2Chr. 5:10
12 [a]1Kgs. 8:22
13 [I]Hebr. *the length thereof*
14 [a]Ex. 15:11; Deut. 4:39; 7:9
15 [a]1Chr. 22:9

6:14–42 This prayer of Solomon is one of the most beautiful in all of Scripture. It revealed Solomon's great familiarity and reverence for the warnings of God that were given to all Israel through Moses (Lev. 26; Deut. 28).

with thy mouth, and hast fulfilled *it* with thine hand, as *it is* this day.

16 Now therefore, O LORD God of Israel, keep with thy servant David my father that which thou hast promised him, saying, [I][a]There shall not fail thee a man in my sight to sit upon the throne of Israel; [b]yet so that thy children take heed to their way[1870] to walk in my law,[8451] as thou hast walked before me.

17 Now then, O LORD God of Israel, let thy word be verified,[539] which thou hast spoken unto thy servant David.

18 But will God in very deed[552] dwell with men on the earth? [a]behold, heaven and the heaven of heavens cannot contain thee; how much less this house which I have built!

19 Have respect therefore to the prayer[8605] of thy servant, and to his supplication, O LORD my God, to hearken unto the cry and the prayer which thy servant prayeth before thee:

20 That thine eyes may be open upon this house day and night,[3915] upon the place whereof thou hast said that thou wouldest put thy name there; to hearken unto the prayer which thy servant prayeth [I]toward this place.

21 Hearken therefore unto the supplications[8469] of thy servant, and of thy people Israel, which they shall [I]make toward this place: hear thou from thy dwelling place, *even* from heaven; and when thou hearest, forgive.[5545]

22 If a man sin against his neighbour,[7453] [I]and an oath be laid upon him to make him swear, and the oath come before thine altar in this house;

23 Then hear thou from heaven, and do,[6213] and judge[8199] thy servants, by requiting the wicked,[7563] by recompensing his way upon his own head; and by justifying[6663] the righteous, by giving him according to his righteousness.

24 And if thy people Israel [I]be put to the worse[5062] before the enemy, because they have sinned against thee; and shall return and confess[3034] thy name, and pray[6419] and make supplication[2603] before thee [II]in this house;

25 Then hear thou from the heavens, and forgive the sin of thy people Israel, and bring them again unto the land[127] which thou gavest to them and to their fathers.[1]

26 When the [a]heaven is shut up,[6113] and there is no rain, because they have sinned against thee; *yet* if they pray toward this place, and confess thy name, and turn from their sin, when thou dost afflict them;

27 Then hear thou from heaven, and forgive the sin of thy servants, and of thy people Israel, when thou hast taught them the good[2896] way, wherein they should walk; and send rain upon thy land, which thou hast given unto thy people for an inheritance.[5159]

28 If there [a]be dearth in the land, if there be pestilence,[1698] if there be blasting, or mildew, locusts, or caterpillers; if their enemies besiege them [I]in the cities of their land; whatsoever sore[5061] or whatsoever sickness *there be:*

29 *Then* what prayer *or* what supplication soever shall be made of any man, or of all thy people Israel, when every one shall know[3045] his own sore and his own grief, and shall spread forth his hands [I]in this house:

30 Then hear thou from heaven thy dwelling place, and forgive, and render unto every man according unto all his ways,[1870] whose heart thou knowest; (for thou only [a]knowest the hearts of the children of men:)

31 That they may fear[3372] thee, to walk in thy ways, [I]so long as they live[2416] [II]in the land which thou gavest unto our fathers.

32 Moreover concerning the stranger, [a]which is not of thy people Israel, but is come from a far country for thy great

16 [I]Hebr. *There shall not a man be cut off* [a]2Sam. 7:12, 16; 1Kgs. 2:4; 6:12; 2Chr. 7:18 [b]Ps. 132:12
18 [a]2Chr. 2:6; Isa. 66:1; Acts 7:49
20 [I]Or, *in this place*
21 [I]Hebr. *pray*
22 [I]Hebr. *and he require an oath of him*
24 [I]Or, *be smitten* [II]Or, *toward*
26 [a]1Kgs. 17:1
28 [I]Hebr. *in the land of their gates* [a]2Chr. 20:9
29 [I]Or, *toward this house*
30 [a]1Chr. 28:9
31 [I]Hebr. *all the days which* [II]Hebr. *upon the face of the land*
32 [a]John 12:20; Acts 8:27

6:16 Solomon seemed to be conscious of God's condition in the promise that He gave to David (see 1 Kgs. 2:4; 6:12, 13, cf. Ex. 32:13; Num. 14:18; Neh. 1:8, 9; Dan. 9:13).
6:18 See note on 1 Kings 8:27.

name's sake, and thy mighty hand, and thy stretched out arm; if they come and pray in this house;

33 Then hear thou from the heavens, *even* from thy dwelling place, and do according to all that the stranger calleth[7121] to thee for; that all people of the earth may know thy name, and fear thee, as *doth* thy people Israel, and may know that [I]this house which I have built is called by thy name.

34 If thy people go out to war against their enemies by the way that thou shalt send them, and they pray unto thee toward this city which thou hast chosen, and the house which I have built for thy name;

35 Then hear thou from the heavens their prayer and their supplication, and maintain their [I]cause.[4941]

36 If they sin[2398] against thee, (for *there is* [a]no man which sinneth not,) and thou be angry[599] with them, and deliver them over before *their* enemies, and [I]they carry them away captives[7617] unto a land far off or near;

37 Yet *if* they [I]bethink[7725] themselves in the land whither they are carried captive, and turn and pray unto thee in the land of their captivity,[7628] saying, We have sinned, we have done amiss,[5753] and have dealt wickedly;[7561]

38 If they return[7725] to thee with all their heart and with all their soul in the land of their captivity, whither they have carried them captives, and pray toward their land, which thou gavest unto their fathers, and *toward* the city which thou hast chosen, and toward the house which I have built for thy name:

39 Then hear thou from the heavens, *even* from thy dwelling place, their prayer and their supplications, and maintain their [I]cause, and forgive thy people which have sinned against thee.

40 Now, my God, let, I beseech thee, thine eyes be open, and *let* thine ears[241] *be* attent[7183] [I]unto the prayer *that is made* in this place.

41 Now [a]therefore arise, O LORD God, into thy [b]resting place, thou, and the ark of thy strength: let thy priests, O LORD God, be clothed with salvation, and let thy saints [c]rejoice in goodness.

42 O LORD God, turn not away the face of thine anointed:[4899] [a]remember the mercies of David thy servant.

God's Glory Fills the Temple

7 Now [a]when Solomon had made an end[3615] of praying, the [b]fire came down from heaven, and consumed the burnt offering and the sacrifices; and [c]the glory[3519] of the LORD filled the house.

2 [a]And the priests could not enter into the house of the LORD, because the glory of the LORD had filled the LORD's house.

3 And when all the children[1121] of Israel saw how the fire came down, and the glory of the LORD upon the house, they bowed themselves[3766] with their faces to the ground[776] upon the pavement, and worshipped,[7812] and praised[3034] the LORD, [a]*saying,* For *he is* good;[2896] [b]for his mercy *endureth* for ever.

Sacrifice and Celebrations

4 [a]Then the king[4428] and all the people[5971] offered sacrifices before the LORD.

5 And king Solomon offered a sacrifice of twenty and two thousand oxen, and an hundred and twenty thousand sheep: so the king and all the people dedicated[2596] the house of God.[430]

6 [a]And the priests waited on their offices: the Levites also with instruments of musick of the LORD, which David the

33 [I]Hebr. *thy name is called upon this house*

35 [I]Or, *right*

36 [I]Hebr. *they that take them captives carry them away* [a]Prov. 20:9; Eccl. 7:20; James 3:2; 1John 1:8

37 [I]Hebr. *bring back to their heart*

39 [I]Or, *right*

40 [I]Hebr. *to the prayer of this place*

41 [a]Ps. 132:8-10, 16 [b]1Chr. 28:2 [c]Neh. 9:25

42 [a]Ps. 132:1; Isa. 55:3

1 [a]1Kgs. 8:54 [b]Lev. 9:24; Judg. 6:21; 1Kgs. 18:38; 1Chr. 21:26 [c]1Kgs. 8:10, 11; 2Chr. 5:13, 14; Ezek. 10:3, 4

2 [a]2Chr. 5:14

3 [a]2Chr. 5:13; Ps. 136:1 [b]1Chr. 16:41; 2Chr. 20:21

4 [a]1Kgs. 8:62, 63

6 [a]1Chr. 15:16

6:37–39 Daniel later acted according to the elements in Solomon's prayer (Daniel 9:5; see Ps. 106:6).

7:2 This occurrence of God's glory filling the temple is very similar to what happened at the dedication of the Tabernacle (Ex. 40:34, 35).

king had made to praise[3034] the LORD,
because his mercy *endureth* for ever,
when David praised[1984] [I]by their ministry; and [b]the priests sounded trumpets
before them, and all Israel stood.
7 Moreover [a]Solomon hallowed[6942]
the middle of the court that *was* before
the house of the LORD: for there he offered burnt offerings, and the fat of the
peace offerings, because the brasen
altar[4196] which Solomon had made was
not able to receive the burnt offerings,
and the meat offerings, and the fat.
8 [a]Also at the same time Solomon
kept[6213] the feast[2282] seven days, and all
Israel with him, a very great congregation, from the entering in of Hamath unto
[b]the river of Egypt.
9 And in the eighth day[3117] they
made [I]a solemn assembly:[6116] for they
kept the dedication[2598] of the altar seven
days, and the feast seven days.
10 And [a]on the three and twentieth
day of the seventh month he sent the
people away into their tents, glad and
merry[2896] in heart for the goodness that
the LORD had shewed unto David, and to
Solomon, and to Israel his people.

God Appears to Solomon

11 Thus [a]Solomon finished[3615] the
house of the LORD, and the king's[4428]
house: and all that came into Solomon's
heart to make in the house of the LORD,
and in his own house, he prosperously effected.
🗝 12 And the LORD appeared[7200] to
Solomon by night,[3915] and said unto him,
I have heard thy prayer,[8605] [a]and have
chosen[977] this place to myself for an
house of sacrifice.
13 [a]If I shut up6113 heaven that there
be no rain, or if I command[6680] the locusts to devour the land, or if I send
pestilence[1698] among my people;

6 [I]Hebr. *by their hand* [b]2Chr. 5:12

7 [a]1Kgs. 8:64

8 [a]1Kgs. 8:65 [b]Josh. 13:3

9 [I]Hebr. *a restraint*

10 [a]1Kgs. 8:66

11 [a]1Kgs. 9:1

12 [a]Deut. 12:5

13 [a]2Chr. 6:26, 28

14 [I]Hebr. *upon whom my name is called* [a]James 4:10 [b]2Chr. 6:27, 30

15 [I]Hebr. *to the prayer of this place* [a]2Chr. 6:40

16 [a]1Kgs. 9:3; 2Chr. 6:6

17 [a]1Kgs. 9:4

18 [I]Hebr. *There shall not be cut off to thee* [a]2Chr. 6:16

19 [a]Lev. 26:14, 33; Deut. 28:15, 36, 37

21 [a]Deut. 29:24; Jer. 22:8, 9

14 If my people, [I]which are called[7121]
by my name, shall [a]humble themselves,3665 and pray, and seek my face,
and turn from their wicked[7451] ways;[1870]
[b]then will I hear from heaven, and will
forgive[5545] their sin, and will heal their
land.
15 Now [a]mine eyes shall be open,
and mine ears[241] attent7183 [I]unto the
prayer *that is made* in this place.
16 For now have [a]I chosen and sanctified this house, that my name may be
there for ever: and mine eyes and mine
heart shall be there perpetually.
17 [a]And as for thee, if thou wilt
walk before me, as David thy father
walked, and do according to all that I
have commanded thee, and shalt observe
my statutes and my judgments;[4941]
18 Then will I stablish the throne of
thy kingdom,[4438] according as I have
covenanted[3772] with David thy father,
saying, [Ia]There shall not fail thee a man
to be ruler in Israel.
19 [a]But if ye turn away, and forsake[5800] my statutes and my commandments,[4687] which I have set before you,
and shall go and serve other gods,[430] and
worship[7812] them;
20 Then will I pluck them up by the
roots[5428] out of my land[127] which I have
given them; and this house, which I have
sanctified for my name, will I cast out of
my sight, and will make it *to be* a
proverb and a byword among all nations.[5971]
21 And this house, which is high,
shall be an astonishment[8074] to every
one that passeth[5674] by it; so that he
shall say, [a]Why hath the LORD done[6213]
thus unto this land, and unto this
house?
22 And it shall be answered,[559]
Because they forsook the LORD God of
their fathers,[1] which brought them forth
out of the land of Egypt, and laid hold
on other gods, and worshipped them, and

🗝 **7:12–14** Sacrifice was a central element in Old Testament worship (Lev. 17:11; Heb. 9:22). This is a key Old Testament passage which presents the conditions of true repentance: humbling oneself, praying, seeking God's face, and turning from evil.

served them: therefore hath he brought
all this evil[7451] upon them.

Solomon's Other Projects

8 And [a]it came to pass at the end
of twenty years, wherein Solomon
had built the house of the LORD, and his
own house,
2 That the cities which Huram had
restored to Solomon, Solomon built them,
and caused the children[1121] of Israel to
dwell there.
3 And Solomon went to Hamath–
zobah, and prevailed against it.
4 [a]And he built Tadmor in the
wilderness, and all the store cities, which
he built in Hamath.
5 Also he built Beth–horon the
upper,[5945] and Beth–horon the nether,8481
fenced cities, with walls, gates, and
bars;
6 And Baalath, and all the store4543
cities that Solomon had, and all the
chariot7393 cities, and the cities of the
horsemen, and [I]all that Solomon desired
to build in Jerusalem, and in Lebanon,
and throughout all the land of his
dominion.[4475]
7 [a]*As for* all the people[5971] *that
were* left[3498] of the Hittites, and the
Amorites, and the Perizzites, and the
Hivites, and the Jebusites, which *were* not
of Israel,
8 *But* of their children, who were left
after them in the land, whom the children
of Israel consumed[3615] not, them did
Solomon make to pay tribute until this
day.[3117]
9 But of the children of Israel did
Solomon make no servants for his
work;[4399] but they *were* men of war, and
chief of his captains,[7991] and captains[8269]
of his chariots and horsemen.
10 And these *were* the chief of
king[4428] Solomon's officers, *even* [a]two
hundred and fifty, that bare rule over the
people.
11 And Solomon [a]brought up[5927] the
daughter of Pharaoh out of the city of
David unto the house that he had built
for her: for he said, My wife[802] shall
not dwell in the house of David king
of Israel, because *the places are* [I]holy,
whereunto the ark[727] of the LORD hath
come.
12 Then Solomon offered burnt offerings unto the LORD on the altar[4196] of
the LORD, which he had built before the
porch,
13 Even after a certain rate [a]every
day, offering according to the commandment[4687] of Moses, on the sabbaths, and
on the new moons, and on the solemn
feasts,[4150] [b]three times in the year, *even*
in the feast of unleavened bread,[4682] and
in the feast of weeks,7620 and in the feast
of tabernacles.[5521]
14 And he appointed, according to
the order of David his father, the [a]courses
of the priests to their service, and [b]the
Levites to their charges, to praise[1984] and
minister before the priests, as the
duty[1697] of every day required: the
[c]porters7778 also by their courses at every
gate: for [I]so had David the man of
God[430] commanded.
15 And they departed[5493] not from
the commandment of the king unto the
priests and Levites concerning any matter, or concerning the treasures.
16 Now all the work of Solomon was
prepared unto the day of the foundation[4143] of the house of the LORD, and
until it was finished.[3615] *So* the house of
the LORD was perfected.[8003]
17 Then went Solomon to [a]Ezion–
geber, and to [I][b]Eloth, at the sea side in
the land of Edom.
18 [a]And Huram sent him by the
hands of his servants ships, and servants
that had knowledge[3045] of the sea; and
they went with the servants of Solomon
to Ophir, and took thence four hundred
and fifty talents of gold, and brought
them to king Solomon.

1 [a]1Kgs. 9:10
4 [a]1Kgs. 9:17
6 [I]Hebr. *all the desire of Solomon which he desired to build*
7 [a]1Kgs. 9:20
10 [a]1Kgs. 9:23
11 [I]Hebr. *holiness* [a]1Kgs. 3:1; 7:8; 9:24
13 [a]Ex. 29:38; Num. 28:3, 9, 11, 26; 20:1 [b]Ex. 23:14; Deut. 16:16
14 [I]Hebr. *so was the commandment of David the man of God* [a]1Chr. 24:1 [b]1Chr. 25:1 [c]1Chr. 9:17; 26:1
17 [I]Or, *Elath* [a]1Kgs. 9:26 [b]Deut. 2:8; 2Kgs. 14:22
18 [a]1Kgs. 9:27; 2Chr. 9:10, 13

8:1 Seven years were spent in building the temple (1 Kgs. 6:37, 38) while thirteen years were needed for Solomon's palace (1 Kgs. 7:1).

The Queen of Sheba Visits Solomon

9 And [a]when the queen[4436] of Sheba heard of the fame[8088] of Solomon, she came to prove Solomon with hard questions[2420] at Jerusalem, with a very great company,[2428] and camels that bare[5375] spices, and gold in abundance, and precious stones: and when she was come to Solomon, she communed with him of all that was in her heart.

2 And Solomon told her all her questions:[1697] and there was nothing[3808,1697] hid from Solomon which he told her not.

3 And when the queen of Sheba had seen the wisdom[2451] of Solomon, and the house that he had built,

4 And the meat of his table, and the sitting of his servants, and the attendance of his ministers, and their apparel; his [I]cupbearers also, and their apparel; and his ascent[5930] by which he went up into the house of the LORD; there was no more spirit in her.

5 And she said to the king,[4428] *It was* a true [I]report which I heard in mine own land[776] of thine [II]acts,[1697] and of thy wisdom:

6 Howbeit I believed[539] not their words,[1697] until I came, and mine eyes had seen *it:* and, behold, the one half of the greatness of thy wisdom was not told me: *for* thou exceedest the fame that I heard.

7 Happy *are* thy men, and happy *are* these thy servants, which stand continually[8548] before thee, and hear thy wisdom.

8 Blessed[1288] be the LORD thy God,[430] which delighted[2654] in thee to set thee on his throne, *to be* king for the LORD thy God: because thy God loved[160] Israel, to establish them for ever, therefore made he thee king over them, to do[6213] judgment[4941] and justice.[6666]

9 And she gave the king an hundred and twenty talents of gold, and of spices[1314] great abundance, and precious stones: neither was there any such spice as the queen of Sheba gave king Solomon.

10 And the servants also of Huram, and the servants of Solomon, [a]which brought gold from Ophir, brought [b]algum[418] trees and precious stones.

11 And the king made *of* the algum trees [I]terraces to the houses of the LORD, and to the king's palace, and harps and psalteries for singers: and there were none such seen before in the land of Judah.

12 And king Solomon gave to the queen of Sheba all her desire,[2656] whatsoever she asked, beside *that* which she had brought unto the king. So she turned, and went away to her own land, she and her servants.

Solomon's Wealth and Fame

13 Now the weight of gold that came to Solomon in one year was six hundred and threescore and six talents of gold;

14 Beside *that which* chapmen and merchants brought. And all the kings of Arabia and [I]governors[6346] of the country brought gold and silver to Solomon.

15 And king Solomon made two hundred targets *of* beaten[7820] gold: six hundred *shekels* of beaten gold went to one target.

16 And three hundred shields *made he of* beaten gold: three hundred *shekels* of gold went to one shield. And the king put them in the house of the forest of Lebanon.

17 Moreover the king made a great throne of ivory, and overlaid it with pure gold.

18 And *there were* six steps to the throne, with a footstool of gold, *which were* fastened to the throne, and [I]stays[3027] on each side of the sitting place, and two lions standing by the stays:

19 And twelve lions stood there on the one side and on the other upon the six steps. There was not the like made in any kingdom.[4467]

20 And all the drinking vessels of king Solomon *were of* gold, and all the

1 [a]1Kgs. 10:1; Matt. 12:42; Luke 11:31

4 [I]Or, *butlers*

5 [I]Hebr. *word* [II]Or, *sayings*

10 [a]2Chr. 8:18 [b]1Kgs. 10:11, *almug trees*

11 [I]Or, *stairs*

14 [I]Or, *captains*

18 [I]Hebr. *hands*

vessels of the house of the forest of Lebanon *were of* [I]pure gold: [II]none *were of* silver; it was *not* any thing accounted[2803] of in the days[3117] of Solomon.

21 For the king's ships went to Tarshish with the servants of Huram: every three years once came the ships of Tarshish bringing[5375] gold, and silver, [I]ivory, and apes, and peacocks.

22 And king Solomon passed all the kings of the earth[776] in riches and wisdom.

23 And all the kings of the earth sought the presence of Solomon, to hear his wisdom, that God had put in his heart.

24 And they brought every man his present, vessels of silver, and vessels of gold, and raiment, harness, and spices, horses, and mules, a rate[1697] year by year.

25 And Solomon [a]had four thousand stalls for horses and chariots, and twelve thousand horsemen; whom he bestowed in the chariot cities, and with the king at Jerusalem.

26 [a]And he reigned over all the kings [b]from the [I]river even unto the land of the Philistines, and to the border of Egypt.

27 [a]And the king [I]made silver in Jerusalem as stones, and cedar trees made he as the sycomore trees that *are* in the low plains[8219] in abundance.

28 [a]And they brought unto Solomon horses out of Egypt, and out of all lands.[776]

Solomon's Death

29 [a]Now the rest of the acts of Solomon, first[7223] and last, *are* they not written in the [I]book of Nathan the prophet, and in the prophecy of [b]Ahijah the Shilonite, and in the visions[2378] of [c]Iddo the seer against Jeroboam the son of Nebat?

30 [a]And Solomon reigned in Jerusalem over all Israel forty years.

31 And Solomon slept with his fathers,[1] and he was buried[6912] in the city of David his father: and Rehoboam his son reigned in his stead.

20 [I]Hebr. *shut up* [II]Or, there *was no silver* in them

21 [I]Or, *elephants' teeth*

25 [a]1Kgs. 4:26; 10:26; 2Chr. 1:14

26 [I]That is, *Euphrates* [a]1Kgs. 4:21 [b]Gen. 15:18; Ps. 72:8

27 [I]Hebr. *gave* [a]1Kgs. 10:27; 2Chr. 1:15

28 [a]1Kgs. 10:28; 2Chr. 1:16

29 [I]Hebr. *words* [a]1Kgs. 11:41 [b]1Kgs. 11:29 [c]2Chr. 12:15; 13:22

30 [a]1Kgs. 11:42, 43

1 [a]1Kgs. 12:1

2 [a]1Kgs. 11:40

11 [I]Hebr. *laded*

The Northern Tribes Revolt

10 And [a]Rehoboam went to Shechem: for to Shechem were all Israel come to make him king.[4427]

2 And it came to pass, when Jeroboam the son of Nebat, who *was* in Egypt, [a]whither he had fled from the presence of Solomon the king,[4428] heard *it,* that Jeroboam returned out of Egypt.

3 And they sent and called[7121] him. So Jeroboam and all Israel came and spake to Rehoboam, saying,

4 Thy father made our yoke grievous: now therefore ease thou somewhat the grievous[7186] servitude of thy father, and his heavy yoke that he put upon us, and we will serve thee.

5 And he said unto them, Come again unto me after three days.[3117] And the people[5971] departed.

6 And king Rehoboam took counsel[3289] with the old men that had stood before Solomon his father while he yet lived,[2416] saying, What counsel give ye *me* to return answer to this people?

7 And they spake unto him, saying, If thou be kind[2896] to this people, and please[7521] them, and speak good[2896] words to them, they will be thy servants for ever.

8 But he forsook[5800] the counsel[6098] which the old men gave him, and took counsel with the young men that were brought up with him, that stood before him.

9 And he said unto them, What advice give ye that we may return answer to this people, which have spoken to me, saying, Ease somewhat the yoke that thy father did put upon us?

10 And the young men that were brought up with him spake unto him, saying, Thus shalt thou answer[559] the people that spake unto thee, saying, Thy father made our yoke heavy, but make thou *it* somewhat lighter[7043] for us; thus shalt thou say unto them, My little *finger* shall be thicker than my father's[1] loins.

11 For whereas my father [I]put a heavy yoke upon you, I will put more to

your yoke: my father chastised[3256] you
with whips, but I *will chastise you* with
scorpions.
12 So Jeroboam and all the people
came to Rehoboam on the third day, as
the king bade, saying, Come again to me
on the third day.
13 And the king answered them
roughly; and king Rehoboam forsook the
counsel of the old men,
14 And answered them after the
advice[6098] of the young men, saying, My
father made your yoke heavy, but I will
add thereto: my father chastised you with
whips, but I *will chastise you* with scorpions.
15 So the king hearkened not unto
the people: [a]for the cause was of God,[430]
that the LORD might perform his word,
which he spake by the [b]hand of Ahijah
the Shilonite to Jeroboam the son of
Nebat.
16 And when all Israel *saw* that the
king would not hearken unto them, the
people answered the king, saying, What
portion have we in David? and *we have*
none inheritance[5159] in the son of Jesse:
every man to your tents, O Israel: *and*
now, David, see to thine own house. So
all Israel went to their tents.
17 But *as for* the children[1121] of
Israel that dwelt in the cities of Judah,
Rehoboam reigned over them.
18 Then king Rehoboam sent
Hadoram that *was* over the tribute; and
the children of Israel stoned him with
stones, that he died. But king Rehoboam
[l]made speed[553] to get him up to *his* chariot, to flee to Jerusalem.
19 [a]And Israel rebelled against the
house of David unto this day.

Civil War Is Averted

11 And [a]when Rehoboam was come
to Jerusalem, he gathered[6950] of
the house of Judah and Benjamin an hundred and fourscore thousand chosen *men,*
which were warriors, to fight against
Israel, that he might bring the kingdom[4467] again to Rehoboam.
2 But the word[1697] of the LORD came
[a]to Shemaiah the man of God,[430] saying,
3 Speak unto Rehoboam the son of
Solomon, king[4428] of Judah, and to all
Israel in Judah and Benjamin, saying,
4 Thus saith the LORD, Ye shall not
go up, nor fight against your brethren:[251]
return every man to his house: for this
thing is done of me. And they obeyed the
words of the LORD, and returned from
going against Jeroboam.

Rehoboam Prospers

5 And Rehoboam dwelt in Jerusalem,
and built cities for defence[4692] in Judah.
6 He built even Bethlehem, and
Etam, and Tekoa,
7 And Beth–zur, and Shoco, and
Adullam,
8 And Gath, and Mareshah, and
Ziph,
9 And Adoraim, and Lachish, and
Azekah,
10 And Zorah, and Aijalon, and
Hebron, which *are* in Judah and in
Benjamin fenced cities.
11 And he fortified[2388] the strong
holds, and put captains in them, and
store of victual,[3978] and of oil and wine.
12 And in every several city *he put*
shields and spears, and made them exceeding strong, having Judah and
Benjamin on his side.
13 And the priests and the Levites
that *were* in all Israel [l]resorted to him out
of all their coasts.
14 For the Levites left[5800] [a]their suburbs and their possession,[272] and came to
Judah and Jerusalem: for [b]Jeroboam and
his sons had cast them off from executing the priest's office[3547] unto the LORD:
15 [a]And he ordained him priests for

15 [a]1Sam. 2:25; 1Kgs. 12:15, 24 [b]1Kgs. 11:29

18 [l]Hebr. *strengthened himself*

19 [a]1Kgs. 12:19

1 [a]1Kgs. 12:21

2 [a]2Chr. 12:15

13 [l]Hebr. *presented themselves to him*

14 [a]Num. 35:2 [b]2Chr. 13:9

15 [a]1Kgs. 12:31; 13:33; 14:9; Hos. 13:2

10:16 The slogan, "What portion have we with David?" was used by Sheba in his rebellion against David (2 Sam. 20:1). The people used it here against Rehoboam to emphasize that they did not have to follow someone of David's lineage.

the high places, and for [b]the devils,[8163] and for [c]the calves which he had made.

16 [a]And after them out of all the tribes of Israel such as set their hearts to seek the LORD God of Israel came to Jerusalem, to sacrifice unto the LORD God of their fathers.[1]

17 So they [a]strengthened the kingdom[4438] of Judah, and made Rehoboam the son of Solomon strong, three years: for three years they walked in the way[1870] of David and Solomon.

18 And Rehoboam took him Mahalath the daughter of Jerimoth the son of David to wife,[802] *and* Abihail the daughter of Eliab the son of Jesse;

19 Which bare him children;[1121] Jeush, and Shamariah, and Zaham.

20 And after her he took [a]Maachah the daughter of Absalom; which bare him Abijah, and Attai, and Ziza, and Shelomith.

21 And Rehoboam loved[157] Maachah the daughter of Absalom above all his wives and his concubines: (for he took eighteen wives, and threescore concubines; and begat twenty and eight sons, and threescore daughters.)

22 And Rehoboam [a]made Abijah the son of Maachah the chief,[7218] *to be* ruler among his brethren: for *he thought* to make him king.[4427]

🗝 23 And he dealt wisely,[995] and dispersed of all his children throughout all the countries[776] of Judah and Benjamin, unto every fenced city: and he gave them victual[4202] in abundance. And he desired[7592] [I]many wives.

Rehoboam Sins and Is Punished

12 And [a]it came to pass, when Rehoboam had established[3559] the kingdom,[4438] and had strengthened himself, [b]he forsook the law[8451] of the LORD, and all Israel with him.

2 [a]And it came to pass, *that* in the fifth year of king[4428] Rehoboam Shishak king of Egypt came up[5927] against Jerusalem, because they had transgressed against the LORD,

3 With twelve hundred chariots, and threescore thousand horsemen: and the people[5971] *were* without number that came with him out of Egypt; [a]the Lubims, the Sukkiims, and the Ethiopians.

4 And he took the fenced cities which *pertained* to Judah, and came to Jerusalem.

5 Then came [a]Shemaiah the prophet to Rehoboam, and *to* the princes[8269] of Judah, that were gathered together[622] to Jerusalem because of Shishak, and said unto them, Thus saith the LORD,[3068] [b]Ye have forsaken[5800] me, and therefore have I also left[5800] you in the hand of Shishak.

6 Whereupon the princes of Israel and the king [a]humbled themselves; and they said, [b]The LORD *is* righteous.

7 And when the LORD saw that they humbled themselves, [a]the word[1697] of the LORD came to Shemaiah, saying, They have humbled themselves; *therefore* I will not destroy[7843] them, but I will grant them [I]some deliverance;[6413] and my wrath[2534] shall not be poured out upon Jerusalem by the hand of Shishak.

8 Nevertheless [a]they shall be his servants; that they may know[3045] [b]my service, and the service of the kingdoms[4467] of the countries.[776]

9 [a]So Shishak king of Egypt came up against Jerusalem, and took away the treasures of the house of the LORD, and the treasures of the king's house; he took all: he carried away also the shields of gold which Solomon had [b]made.

10 Instead of which king Rehoboam made shields of brass, and committed[6485] *them* [a]to the hands of the chief[5387] of the guard, that kept[8104] the entrance of the king's house.

11 And when the king entered into the house of the LORD, the guard came and fetched them, and brought them again into the guard chamber.

15 [b]Lev. 17:7; 1Cor. 10:20 [c]1Kgs. 12:28
16 [a]2Chr. 15:9; 30:11, 18
17 [a]2Chr. 12:1
20 [a]1Kgs. 15:2. She is called Michaiah the daughter of Uriel; 2Chr. 13:2
22 [a]Deut. 21:15-17
23 [I]Hebr. *a multitude of wives*
1 [a]2Chr. 11:17 [b]1Kgs. 14:22-24
2 [a]1Kgs. 14:24, 25
3 [a]2Chr. 16:8
5 [a]2Chr. 11:2 [b]2Chr. 15:2
6 [a]James 4:10 [b]Ex. 9:27
7 [I]Or, *a little while* [a]1Kgs. 21:28, 29
8 [a]Isa. 26:13 [b]Deut. 28:47, 48
9 [a]1Kgs. 14:25, 26 [b]1Kgs. 10:16, 17; 2Chr. 9:15, 16
10 [a]2Sam. 8:18

🗝 **11:23** Perhaps a lesson was learned from David's sad experience (2 Sam. 13:26, 27).

12 And when he humbled himself, the wrath of the LORD turned from him, that he would not destroy *him* altogether: [I][a]and also in Judah things went well.

Rehoboam's Death

13 So king Rehoboam strengthened himself in Jerusalem, and reigned: for [a]Rehoboam *was* one and forty years old when he began to reign, and he reigned seventeen years in Jerusalem, [b]the city which the LORD had chosen[977] out of all the tribes of Israel, to put his name there. And his mother's name *was* Naamah an Ammonitess.

14 And he did[6213] evil,[7451] because he [I]prepared not his heart to seek the LORD.

15 Now the acts[1697] of Rehoboam, first[7223] and last, *are* they not written in the [I]book of Shemaiah the prophet, [a]and of Iddo the seer concerning genealogies? [b]And *there were* wars between Rehoboam and Jeroboam continually.

16 And Rehoboam slept[7901] with his fathers,[1] and was buried[6912] in the city of David: and [a]Abijah his son reigned in his stead.

Abijah Rules Judah

13 Now [a]in the eighteenth year of king[4428] Jeroboam began Abijah to reign over Judah.

🗝 2 He reigned three years in Jerusalem. His mother's name also *was* [a]Michaiah the daughter of Uriel of Gibeah. And there was war between Abijah and Jeroboam.

3 And Abijah [I]set the battle in array with an army[2428] of valiant men of war, *even* four hundred thousand chosen men: Jeroboam also set the battle in array against him with eight hundred thousand chosen men, *being* mighty men of valour.[2428]

4 And Abijah stood up upon mount [a]Zemaraim, which *is* in mount Ephraim, and said, Hear me, thou Jeroboam, and all Israel;

🗝 5 Ought ye not to know[3045] that the LORD God[430] of Israel [a]gave the kingdom[4467] over Israel to David for ever, *even* to him and to his sons [b]by a covenant[1285] of salt?

6 Yet Jeroboam the son of Nebat, the servant of Solomon the son of David, is risen up, and hath [a]rebelled against his lord.[113]

7 And there are gathered[6908] unto him [a]vain[7386] men, the children[1121] of Belial,[1100] and have strengthened themselves against Rehoboam the son of Solomon, when Rehoboam was young and tenderhearted, and could not withstand[2388] them.

8 And now ye think to withstand the kingdom of the LORD in the hand of the sons of David; and ye *be* a great multitude, and *there are* with you golden calves, which Jeroboam [a]made you for gods.[430]

9 [a]Have ye not cast out the priests of the LORD, the sons of Aaron, and the Levites, and have made you priests after the manner of the nations[5971] of *other* lands?[776] [b]so that whosoever cometh [I][c]to consecrate himself with a young bullock and seven rams, *the same* may be a priest of *them that are* no gods.

10 But as for us, the LORD *is* our God, and we have not forsaken[5800] him; and the priests, which minister unto the LORD, *are* the sons of Aaron, and the Levites *wait* upon *their* business:[4399]

11 [a]And they burn[6999] unto the LORD every morning and every evening burnt sacrifices and sweet incense:[7004] the

12 [I]Or, *and yet in Judah there were good things* [a]Gen. 18:24; 1Kgs. 14:13; 2Chr. 19:3
13 [a]1Kgs. 14:21 [b]2Chr. 6:6
14 [I]Or, *fixed*
15 [I]Hebr. *words* [a]2Chr. 9:29; 13:22 [b]1Kgs. 14:30
16 [a]1Kgs. 14:31, *Abijam*
1 [a]1Kgs. 15:1
2 [a]2Chr. 11:20
3 [I]Hebr. *bound together*
4 [a]Josh. 18:22
5 [a]2Sam. 7:12, 13, 16 [b]Num. 18:19
6 [a]1Kgs. 11:26; 12:20
7 [a]Judg. 9:4
8 [a]1Kgs. 12:28; 14:9; Hos. 8:6
9 [I]Hebr. *to fill his hand* [a]2Chr. 11:14, 15 [b]Ex. 29:35 [c]Ex. 29:1; Lev. 8:2
11 [a]2Chr. 2:4

🗝 **13:2** Michaiah is called Maachah in 1 Kings 15:2 and 2 Chronicles 11:20; 15:16. She is called the daughter of Absalom though she was actually his granddaughter. It was a common practice among the Hebrews to call someone a son or daughter of a distant ancestor.

🗝 **13:5** Eating salt together signified an unbreakable friendship. Salt was used as a preservative. Therefore, it was an appropriate symbol for eternity. A covenant of salt could not be changed (see Num. 18:19).

[b]shewbread also *set they in order* upon
the pure table; and the candlestick of
gold with the lamps[5216] thereof, [c]to burn
every evening: for we keep[8104] the
charge[4931] of the LORD our God; but ye
have forsaken him.
12 And, behold, God himself *is* with
us for *our* captain,[7218] [a]and his priests
with sounding trumpets to cry alarm
against you. O children of Israel, [b]fight
ye not against the LORD God of your
fathers;[1] for ye shall not prosper.
13 But Jeroboam caused an ambushment to come about behind them: so they
were before Judah, and the ambushment
was behind them.
14 And when Judah looked back, behold, the battle *was* before and behind:
and they cried unto the LORD, and the
priests sounded with the trumpets.
15 Then the men of Judah gave a
shout: and as the men of Judah shouted,
it came to pass, that God [a]smote
Jeroboam and all Israel before Abijah and
Judah.
16 And the children of Israel fled before Judah: and God delivered them into
their hand.
17 And Abijah and his people[5971]
slew them with a great slaughter: so
there fell down[5307] slain of Israel five
hundred thousand chosen men.
18 Thus the children of Israel were
brought under[3665] at that time, and the
children of Judah prevailed, [a]because they
relied upon the LORD God of their fathers.
19 And Abijah pursued after Jeroboam, and took cities from him, Bethel
with the towns thereof, and Jeshanah with
the towns thereof, and [a]Ephrain with the
towns thereof.
20 Neither did Jeroboam recover
strength again in the days[3117] of Abijah:
and the LORD [a]struck him, and [b]he
died.
21 But Abijah waxed mighty, and
married fourteen wives,[802] and begat
twenty and two sons, and sixteen daughters.
22 And the rest of the acts[1697] of
Abijah, and his ways,[1870] and his say-

11 [b]Lev. 24:6 [c]Ex. 27:20, 21; Lev. 24:2, 3
12 [a]Num. 10:8 [b]Acts 5:39
15 [a]2Chr. 14:12
18 [a]1Chr. 5:20; Ps. 22:5
19 [a]Josh. 15:9
20 [a]1Sam. 25:38 [b]1Kgs. 14:20
22 [I]Or, *commentary* [a]2Chr. 12:15
1 [a]1Kgs. 15:8
3 [I]Hebr. *statues* [a]1Kgs. 15:14; 2Chr. 15:17 [b]Ex. 34:13 [c]1Kgs. 11:7
5 [I]Hebr. *sun images*
9 [a]2Chr. 16:8 [b]Josh. 15:44
11 [a]Ex. 14:10; 2Chr. 13:14; Ps. 22:5

ings, *are* written in the [I]story of the
prophet [a]Iddo.

Asa Rules Judah

14 So Abijah slept with his fathers,[1]
and they buried[6912] him in the
city of David: and [a]Asa his son reigned
in his stead. In his days[3117] the land[776]
was quiet[8252] ten years.
2 And Asa did[6213] *that which was*
good[2896] and right in the eyes of the
LORD his God:[430]
3 For he took away the altars[4196] of
the strange *gods,* and [a]the high places,
and [b]brake down[7665] the [I]images,[4676] [c]and
cut down the groves:[842]
4 And commanded[559] Judah to
seek the LORD God of their fathers, and
to do the law[8451] and the commandment.[4687]
5 Also he took away out of all the
cities of Judah the high places and the
[I]images:[2553] and the kingdom[4467] was
quiet before him.
6 And he built fenced cities in Judah:
for the land had rest, and he had no war
in those years; because the LORD had
given him rest.
7 Therefore he said unto Judah, Let
us build these cities, and make about
them walls, and towers, gates, and bars,
while the land *is* yet before us; because
we have sought the LORD our God, we
have sought[1875] *him,* and he hath given
us rest on every side. So they built and
prospered.
8 And Asa had an army[2428] *of men*
that bare[5375] targets and spears, out of
Judah three hundred thousand; and out of
Benjamin, that bare shields and drew
bows, two hundred and fourscore thousand: all these *were* mighty men of valour.[2428]
9 [a]And there came out against them
Zerah the Ethiopian with an host of a
thousand thousand, and three hundred
chariots; and came unto [b]Mareshah.
10 Then Asa went out against him,
and they set the battle in array in the valley of Zephathah at Mareshah.
11 And Asa [a]cried[7121] unto the LORD

his God, and said, LORD, *it is* [b]nothing with thee to help, whether with many, or with them that have no power: help us, O LORD our God; for we rest on thee, and [c]in thy name we go against this multitude. O LORD, thou *art* our God; let not [I]man prevail against thee.

12 So the LORD [a]smote the Ethiopians before Asa, and before Judah; and the Ethiopians fled.

13 And Asa and the people[5971] that *were* with him pursued[7291] them unto [a]Gerar: and the Ethiopians were overthrown, that they could not recover themselves; for they were [I]destroyed[7665] before the LORD, and before his host; and they carried away[5375] very much spoil.

14 And they smote all the cities round about Gerar; for [a]the fear[6343] of the LORD came upon them: and they spoiled all the cities; for there was exceeding much spoil in them.

15 They smote also the tents of cattle, and carried[5375] away sheep and camels in abundance, and returned to Jerusalem.

Asa's Reforms

15 And [a]the Spirit of God[430] came upon Azariah the son of Oded:

2 And he went out [I]to meet Asa, and said unto him, Hear ye me, Asa, and all Judah and Benjamin; [a]The LORD *is* with you, while ye be with him; and [b]if ye seek him, he will be found of you; but [c]if ye forsake[5800] him, he will forsake you.

3 Now [a]for a long season Israel *hath been* without the true God, and without [b]a teaching[3384] priest, and without law.[8451]

4 But [a]when they in their trouble did turn unto the LORD God of Israel, and sought him, he was found of them.

5 And [a]in those times *there was* no peace[7965] to him that went out, nor to him that came in, but great vexations[4103] *were* upon all the inhabitants of the countries.[776]

6 [a]And nation[1471] was [I]destroyed[3807] of nation, and city of city: for God did vex[2000] them with all adversity.

7 Be ye strong therefore, and let not your hands be weak:[7503] for your work shall be rewarded.

8 And when Asa heard these words,[1697] and the prophecy of Oded the prophet, he took courage,[2388] and put away the [I]abominable idols out of all the land[776] of Judah and Benjamin, and out of the cities [a]which he had taken from mount Ephraim, and renewed the altar[4196] of the LORD, that *was* before the porch of the LORD.

9 And he gathered[6908] all Judah and Benjamin, and [a]the strangers with them out of Ephraim and Manasseh, and out of Simeon: for they fell[5307] to him out of Israel in abundance, when they saw that the LORD his God *was* with him.

10 So they gathered themselves together at Jerusalem in the third month, in the fifteenth year of the reign of Asa.

11 [a]And they offered[2076] unto the LORD [I]the same time, of [b]the spoil *which* they had brought, seven hundred oxen and seven thousand sheep.

12 And they [a]entered into a covenant[1285] to seek the LORD God of their fathers[1] with all their heart and with all their soul;

13 [a]That whosoever would not seek the LORD God of Israel [b]should be put to death,[4191] whether small or great, whether man or woman.[802]

14 And they sware unto the LORD with a loud voice, and with shouting, and with trumpets, and with cornets.

15 And all Judah rejoiced at the oath: for they had sworn with all their heart, and [a]sought him with their whole desire;[7522] and he was found of them: and the LORD gave them rest round about.

🗝 16 And also *concerning* [a]Maachah the [I][b]mother of Asa the king,[4428] he removed

11 [I]Or, *mortal man* [b]1Sam. 14:6 [c]1Sam. 17:45; Prov. 18:10
12 [a]2Chr. 13:15
13 [I]Hebr. *broken* [a]Gen. 10:19; 20:1
14 [a]Gen. 35:5; 2Chr. 17:10
1 [a]Num. 24:2; Judg. 3:10; 2Chr. 20:14; 24:20
2 [I]Hebr. *before Asa* [a]James 4:8 [b]2Chr. 15:4, 15; 1Chr. 28:9; 2Chr. 33:12, 13; Jer. 29:13; Matt. 7:7 [c]2Chr. 24:20
3 [a]Hos. 3:4 [b]Lev. 10:11
4 [a]Deut. 4:29
5 [a]Judg. 5:6
6 [I]Hebr. *beaten in pieces* [a]Matt. 24:7
8 [I]Hebr. *abominations* [a]2Chr. 13:19
9 [a]2Chr. 11:16
11 [I]Hebr. *in that day* [a]2Chr. 14:15 [b]2Chr. 14:13
12 [a]2Kgs. 23:3; 2Chr. 34:31; Neh. 10:29
13 [a]Ex. 22:20 [b]Deut. 13:5, 9, 15
15 [a]2Chr. 15:2
16 [I]That is, *grandmother* [a]1Kgs. 15:13 [b]1Kgs. 15:2, 10

🗝 **15:16** Maachah was Absalom's granddaughter, as well as King Rehoboam's favorite wife (2 Chr. 11:21) and the grandmother of Asa (see notes on 1 Kgs. 15:10 and 2 Chr. 13:2).

her from *being* queen, because she had made an [II]idol,[4656] in a grove: and Asa cut down[3772] her idol, and stamped[1854] *it,* and burnt[8313] *it* at the brook Kidron.

17 But [a]the high places were not taken away out of Israel: nevertheless the heart of Asa was perfect[8003] all his days.[3117]

18 And he brought into the house of God the things that his father had dedicated,[6944] and that he himself had dedicated, silver, and gold, and vessels.

19 And there was no *more* war unto the five and thirtieth year of the reign of Asa.

Asa Seeks Syria's Help

16 In the six and thirtieth year of the reign of Asa [a]Baasha king of Israel came up against Judah, and built Ramah, [b]to the intent that he might let none go out or come in to Asa king[4428] of Judah.

2 Then Asa brought out silver and gold out of the treasures of the house of the LORD and of the king's house, and sent to Ben–hadad king of Syria, that dwelt at [I]Damascus, saying,

3 *There is* a league[1285] between me and thee, as *there was* between my father and thy father: behold, I have sent thee silver and gold; go, break[6565] thy league with Baasha king of Israel, that he may depart from me.

4 And Ben–hadad hearkened unto king Asa, and sent the captains[8269] of [I]his armies[2428] against the cities of Israel; and they smote Ijon, and Dan, and Abel–maim, and all the store cities of Naphtali.

5 And it came to pass, when Baasha heard *it,* that he left off building of Ramah, and let his work[4399] cease.[7673]

6 Then Asa the king took all Judah; and they carried away[5375] the stones of Ramah, and the timber thereof, wherewith Baasha was building; and he built therewith Geba and Mizpah.

7 And at that time [a]Hanani the seer came to Asa king of Judah, and said unto him, [b]Because thou hast relied on the king of Syria, and not relied on the LORD thy God,[430] therefore is the host of the king of Syria escaped[4422] out of thine hand.

8 Were not [a]the Ethiopians and [b]the Lubims [I]a huge host, with very many chariots and horsemen? yet, because thou didst rely on the LORD, he delivered them into thine hand.

9 [a]For the eyes of the LORD run to and fro throughout the whole earth,[776] [I]to shew himself strong in the behalf of *them* whose heart *is* perfect[8003] toward him. Herein [b]thou hast done foolishly: therefore from henceforth [c]thou shalt have wars.

10 Then Asa was wroth[3707] with the seer, and [a]put him in a prison house; for *he was* in a rage with him because of this *thing.* And Asa [I]oppressed[7533] *some* of the people[5971] the same time.

Asa's Death

11 [a]And, behold, the acts[1697] of Asa, first[7223] and last, lo, they *are* written in the book[5612] of the kings of Judah and Israel.

12 And Asa in the thirty and ninth year of his reign was diseased[2470] in his feet, until his disease[2483] *was* exceeding *great:* yet in his disease he [a]sought not to the LORD, but to the physicians.

13 [a]And Asa slept with his fathers,[1] and died in the one and fortieth year of his reign.

14 And they buried[6912] him in his own sepulchres,[6913] which he had [I]made for himself in the city of David, and laid him in the bed which was filled [a]with sweet odours and divers kinds *of spices* prepared by the apothecaries'[4842] art: and they made [b]a very great burning[8316] for him.

16 [II]Hebr. *horror*

17 [a]2Chr. 14:3, 5; 1Kgs. 15:14

1 [a]1Kgs. 15:17 [b]2Chr. 15:9

2 [I]Hebr. *Darmesek*

4 [I]Hebr. *which were his*

7 [a]1Kgs. 16:1; 2Chr. 19:2 [b]Isa. 31:1; Jer. 17:5

8 [I]Hebr. *in abundance* [a]2Chr. 14:9 [b]2Chr. 12:3

9 [I]Or, *strongly to hold with the* [a]Job 34:21; Prov. 5:21; 15:3; Jer. 16:17; 32:19; Zech. 4:10 [b]1Sam. 13:13 [c]1Kgs. 15:32

10 [I]Hebr. *crushed* [a]2Chr. 18:26; Jer. 20:2; Matt. 14:3

11 [a]1Kgs. 15:23

12 [a]Jer. 17:5

13 [a]1Kgs. 15:24

14 [I]Hebr. *digged* [a]Gen. 50:2; Mark 16:1; John 19:39, 40 [b]2Chr. 21:19; Jer. 34:5

15:19 The date is better understood as "the thirty-fifth year [of the kingdom of Judah], Asa then reigning." It was actually Asa's fifteenth year of rule.

Jehoshaphat Rules Judah

17 And [a]Jehoshaphat his son reigned in his stead, and strengthened himself against Israel.

2 And he placed forces in all the fenced[1219] cities of Judah, and set garrisons in the land[776] of Judah, and in the cities of Ephraim, [a]which Asa his father had taken.

3 And the LORD was with Jehoshaphat, because he walked in the first[7223] ways[1870] [I]of his father David, and sought not unto Baalim;

4 But sought to the *LORD* God[430] of his father, and walked in his commandments,[4687] and not after [a]the doings of Israel.

5 Therefore the LORD stablished[3559] the kingdom[4467] in his hand; and all Judah [I][a]brought to Jehoshaphat presents; [b]and he had riches and honour in abundance.

6 And his heart [I]was lifted up in the ways of the LORD: moreover [a]he took away the high places and groves[842] out of Judah.

7 Also in the third year of his reign he sent to his princes, *even* to Benhail, and to Obadiah, and to Zechariah, and to Nethaneel, and to Michaiah, [a]to teach[3925] in the cities of Judah.

8 And with them *he sent* Levites, *even* Shemaiah, and Nethaniah, and Zebadiah, and Asahel, and Shemiramoth, and Jehonathan, and Adonijah, and Tobijah, and Tob–adonijah, Levites; and with them Elishama and Jehoram, priests.

9 [a]And they taught in Judah, and *had* the book[5612] of the law[8451] of the LORD with them, and went about throughout all the cities of Judah, and taught the people.[5971]

10 And [a]the fear[6343] of the LORD [I]fell[1961] upon all the kingdoms of the lands that *were* round about Judah, so that they made no war against Jehoshaphat.

11 Also *some* of the Philistines [a]brought Jehoshaphat presents, and tribute[4853] silver; and the Arabians brought him flocks, seven thousand and seven hundred rams, and seven thousand and seven hundred he goats.

12 And Jehoshaphat waxed great exceedingly; and he built in Judah [I]castles, and cities of store.

13 And he had much business[4399] in the cities of Judah: and the men of war, mighty men of valour,[2428] *were* in Jerusalem.

14 And these *are* the numbers[6486] of them according to the house of their fathers:[1] Of Judah, the captains[8269] of thousands; Adnah the chief,[8269] and with him mighty men of valour three hundred thousand.

15 And [I]next to him *was* Jehohanan the captain, and with him two hundred and fourscore thousand.

16 And next to him *was* Amasiah the son of Zichri, [a]who willingly offered himself[5068] unto the LORD; and with him two hundred thousand mighty men of valour.

17 And of Benjamin; Eliada a mighty man of valour, and with him armed[5401] men with bow and shield two hundred thousand.

18 And next him *was* Jehozabad, and with him an hundred and fourscore thousand ready prepared for the war.[6635]

19 These waited on[8334] the king,[4428] beside [a]*those* whom the king put in the fenced cities throughout all Judah.

Micaiah Predicts Ahab and Jehoshaphat's Defeat

18 🗝 Now Jehoshaphat [a]had riches and honour in abundance, and [b]joined affinity[2859] with Ahab.

2 [a]And [I]after *certain* years he went down to Ahab to Samaria. And Ahab killed sheep and oxen[6629] for him in

---

17:1 [a]1Kgs. 15:24
2 [a]2Chr. 15:8
3 [I]Or, *of his father, and of David*
4 [a]1Kgs. 12:28
5 [I]Hebr. *gave* [a]1Sam. 10:27; 1Kgs. 10:25 [b]1Kgs. 10:27; 2Chr. 18:1
6 [I]That is, *was encouraged* [a]1Kgs. 22:43; 2Chr. 15:17; 19:3; 20:33
7 [a]2Chr. 15:3
9 [a]2Chr. 35:3; Neh. 8:7
10 [I]Hebr. *was* [a]Gen. 35:5
11 [a]2Sam. 8:2
12 [I]Or, *palaces*
15 [I]Hebr. *at his hand*
16 [a]Judg. 5:2, 9
19 [a]2Chr. 17:2
18:1 [a]2Chr. 17:5 [b]2Kgs. 8:18
2 [I]Hebr. *at the end of years* [a]1Kgs. 22:2

🗝 **18:1** Jehoshaphat's son, Jehoram, was given in marriage to Athaliah, the daughter of Ahab and Jezebel (2 Chr. 21:6). This alliance was condemned by God (2 Chr. 19:2; see also Amos 3:3; 1 Cor. 7:39; 2 Cor. 6:14).

abundance, and for the people[5971] that *he had* with him, and persuaded him to go up *with him* to Ramoth–gilead.

3 And Ahab king[4428] of Israel said unto Jehoshaphat king of Judah, Wilt thou go with me to Ramoth–gilead? And he answered[559] him, I *am* as thou *art,* and my people as thy people; and *we will be* with thee in the war.

4 And Jehoshaphat said unto the king of Israel, [a]Enquire, I pray thee, at the word[1697] of the LORD to day.[3117]

🗝 5 Therefore the king of Israel gathered together[6908] of prophets four hundred men, and said unto them, Shall we go to Ramoth–gilead to battle, or shall I forbear? And they said, Go up; for God[430] will deliver *it* into the king's hand.

6 But Jehoshaphat said, *Is there* not here a prophet of the LORD [I]besides, that we might enquire of him?

7 And the king of Israel said unto Jehoshaphat, *There is* yet one man, by whom we may enquire of the LORD: but I hate him; for he never prophesied good[2896] unto me, but always evil:[7451] the same *is* Micaiah the son of Imla. And Jehoshaphat said, Let not the king say so.

8 And the king of Israel called[7121] for one *of his* [I]officers, and said, [II]Fetch quickly Micaiah the son of Imla.

9 And the king of Israel and Jehoshaphat king of Judah sat either of them on his throne, clothed in *their* robes, and they sat in a [I]void place[1637] at the entering in of the gate of Samaria; and all the prophets prophesied before them.

10 And Zedekiah the son of Chenaanah had made him horns of iron, and said, Thus saith the LORD, With these thou shalt push Syria until [I]they be consumed.[3615]

11 And all the prophets prophesied so, saying, Go up to Ramoth–gilead, and prosper: for the LORD shall deliver *it* into the hand of the king.

12 And the messenger that went to call Micaiah spake to him, saying, Behold, the words[1697] of the prophets *declare* good to the king [I]with one assent;[6310] let thy word therefore, I pray thee, be like one of theirs, and speak thou good.

🗝 13 And Micaiah said, *As* the LORD liveth,[2416] [a]even what my God saith, that will I speak.

14 And when he was come to the king, the king said unto him, Micaiah, shall we go to Ramoth–gilead to battle, or shall I forbear? And he said, Go ye up, and prosper, and they shall be delivered into your hand.

15 And the king said to him, How many times shall I adjure[7650] thee that thou say nothing but the truth to me in the name of the LORD?[3068]

16 Then he said, I did see all Israel scattered upon the mountains, as sheep that have no shepherd: and the LORD said, These have no master; let them return *therefore* every man to his house in peace.[7965]

17 And the king of Israel said to Jehoshaphat, Did I not tell thee *that* he would not prophesy good unto me, [I]but evil?

18 Again he said, Therefore hear the word of the LORD; I saw the LORD sitting upon his throne, and all the host of heaven standing on his right hand and *on* his left.

19 And the LORD said, Who shall entice[6601] Ahab king of Israel, that he may go up and fall at Ramoth–gilead? And one spake saying after this manner, and another saying after that manner.

20 Then there came out a [a]spirit, and stood before the LORD, and said, I will entice him. And the LORD said unto him, Wherewith?

4 [a]1Sam. 23:2, 4, 9; 2Sam. 2:1
6 [I]Hebr. *yet, or, more*
8 [I]Or, *eunuchs* [II]Hebr. *Hasten*
9 [I]Or, *floor*
10 [I]Hebr. thou *consume them*
12 [I]Hebr. *with one mouth*
13 [a]Num. 22:18, 20, 35; 23:12, 26; 24:13; 1Kgs. 22:14
17 [I]Or, *but for evil*
20 [a]Job 1:6

🗝 **18:5, 6** The prophets mentioned here were probably those involved in the calf worship that was established by Jeroboam in Dan and Bethel. Although the religion of these prophets may have initially been presented as an alternate way to worship Jehovah, there can be no doubt that it was idolatry (1 Kgs. 12:28).

🗝 **18:13** This statement by Micaiah was similar to Baalam's resolve (Num. 22:18–20, 38; 24:13).

21 And he said, I will go out, and be a lying spirit in the mouth of all his prophets. And *the LORD* said, Thou shalt entice *him,* and thou shalt also prevail: go out, and do[6213] *even* so.

22 Now therefore, behold, [a]the LORD hath put a lying spirit in the mouth of these thy prophets, and the LORD hath spoken evil against thee.

23 Then Zedekiah the son of Chenaanah came near,[5066] and [a]smote Micaiah upon the cheek, and said, Which way[1870] went the Spirit of the LORD from me to speak unto thee?

24 And Micaiah said, Behold, thou shalt see on that day when thou shalt go [I]into [II]an inner chamber to hide thyself.

25 Then the king of Israel said, Take ye Micaiah, and carry him back to Amon the governor[8269] of the city, and to Joash the king's son;

26 And say, Thus saith the king, [a]Put this *fellow* in the prison, and feed him with bread of affliction[3906] and with water of affliction, until I return in peace.

27 And Micaiah said, If thou certainly return in peace, *then* hath not the LORD spoken by me. And he said, Hearken, all ye people.

Ahab Dies in Battle

28 So the king of Israel and Jehoshaphat the king of Judah went up to Ramoth–gilead.

29 And the king of Israel said unto Jehoshaphat, I will disguise myself, and will go to the battle; but put thou on thy robes. So the king of Israel disguised himself; and they went to the battle.

30 Now the king of Syria had commanded[6680] the captains[8269] of the chariots that *were* with him, saying, Fight ye not with small or great, save only with the king of Israel.

31 And it came to pass, when the captains of the chariots saw Jehoshaphat, that they said, It *is* the king of Israel. Therefore they compassed about him to fight: but Jehoshaphat cried out,[2199] and the LORD helped him; and God moved them *to depart* from him.

32 For it came to pass, that, when the captains of the chariots perceived[7200] that it was not the king of Israel, they turned back again [I]from pursuing him.

33 And a *certain* man drew a bow [I]at a venture,[8537] and smote the king of Israel [II]between the joints of the harness: therefore he said to his chariot man, Turn thine hand, that thou mayest carry me out of the host; for I am [III]wounded.

34 And the battle increased[5927] that day: howbeit the king of Israel stayed *himself* up in *his* chariot against the Syrians until the even: and about the time of the sun going down he died.

Jehu Confronts Jehoshaphat

19 And Jehoshaphat the king[4428] of Judah returned to his house in peace[7965] to Jerusalem.

2 And Jehu the son of Hanani [a]the seer went out to meet him, and said to king Jehoshaphat, Shouldest thou help the ungodly,[7563] and [b]love[157] them that hate the LORD? therefore *is* [c]wrath[7110] upon thee from before the LORD.

3 Nevertheless there are [a]good[2896] things found in thee, in that thou hast taken away the groves[842] out of the land,[776] and hast [b]prepared thine heart to seek God.[430]

Jehosphaphat Appoints Judges

4 And Jehoshaphat dwelt at Jerusalem: and [I]he went out again through the people[5971] from Beer–sheba to mount Ephraim, and brought them back unto the LORD God of their fathers.[1]

5 And he set judges[8199] in the land throughout all the fenced cities of Judah, city by city,

6 And said to the judges, Take heed what ye do:[6213] for [a]ye judge[8199] not for man, but for the LORD, [b]who *is* with you [I]in the judgment.[4941]

7 Wherefore now let the fear[6343] of the LORD be upon you; take heed and do *it:* for [a]*there is* no iniquity[5766] with the

22 [a]Job 12:16; Isa. 19:14; Ezek. 14:9

23 [a]Jer. 20:2; Mark 14:65; Acts 23:2

24 [I]Or, *from chamber to chamber* [II]Hebr. *a chamber in a chamber*

26 [a]2Chr. 16:10

32 [I]Hebr. *from after him*

33 [I]Hebr. *in his simplicity* [II]Hebr. *between the joints and between the breastplate* [III]Hebr. *made sick*

2 [a]1Sam. 9:9 [b]Ps. 139:21 [c]2Chr. 32:25

3 [a]2Chr. 17:4, 6; 2Chr. 12:12 [b]2Chr. 30:19; Ezra 7:10

4 [I]Hebr. *he returned and went out*

6 [I]Hebr. *in the matter of judgment* [a]Deut. 1:17 [b]Ps. 82:1; Eccl. 5:8

7 [a]Deut. 32:4; Rom. 9:14

LORD our God, nor [b]respect of persons, nor taking of gifts.[7810]

8 Moreover in Jerusalem did Jehoshaphat [a]set of the Levites, and *of* the priests, and of the chief[7218] of the fathers of Israel, for the judgment of the LORD, and for controversies,[7379] when they returned to Jerusalem.

9 And he charged[6680] them, saying, Thus shall ye do [a]in the fear[3374] of the LORD, faithfully[530], and with a perfect[8003] heart.

10 [a]And what cause[7379] soever shall come to you of your brethren[251] that dwell in their cities, between blood[1818] and blood, between law[8451] and commandment,[4687] statutes and judgments,[4941] ye shall even warn them that they trespass not against the LORD, and *so* [b]wrath come upon [c]you, and upon your brethren: this do, and ye shall not trespass.

11 And, behold, Amariah the chief priest *is* over you [a]in all matters of the LORD; and Zebadiah the son of Ishmael, the ruler of the house of Judah, for all the king's matters: also the Levites *shall be* officers before you. [I]Deal[6213] courageously,[2388] and the LORD shall be [b]with the good.

Moab and Ammon Are Defeated

20 It came to pass after this also, *that* the children[1121] of Moab, and the children of Ammon, and with them *other* beside the Ammonites, came against Jehoshaphat to battle.

🔑 2 Then there came some that told Jehoshaphat, saying, There cometh a great multitude against thee from beyond the sea on this side Syria; and, behold, they *be* [a]in Hazazon–tamar, which *is* [b]En–gedi.

3 And Jehoshaphat feared, and set [I]himself to [a]seek[1875] the LORD, and [b]proclaimed a fast throughout all Judah.

4 And Judah gathered themselves together,[6908] to ask[1245] *help* of the LORD: even out of all the cities of Judah they came to seek the LORD.

5 And Jehoshaphat stood in the congregation of Judah and Jerusalem, in the house of the LORD, before the new court,

6 And said, O LORD God[430] of our fathers,[1] *art* not thou [a]God in heaven? and [b]rulest *not* thou over all the kingdoms[4467] of the heathen? and [c]in thine hand *is there not* power and might, so that none is able to withstand thee?

7 *Art* not thou [a]our God, [I]*who* [b]didst drive out the inhabitants of this land[776] before thy people[5971] Israel, and gavest it to the seed of Abraham [c]thy friend[157] for ever?

8 And they dwelt therein, and have built thee a sanctuary[4720] therein for thy name, saying,

9 [a]If, *when* evil[7451] cometh upon us, *as* the sword, judgment, or pestilence,[1698] or famine, we stand before this house, and in thy presence, (for thy [b]name *is* in this house,) and cry[2199] unto thee in our affliction, then thou wilt hear and help.

10 And now, behold, the children of Ammon and Moab and mount Seir, whom thou [a]wouldest not let Israel invade, when they came out of the land of Egypt, but [b]they turned from them, and destroyed[8045] them not;

11 Behold, *I say, how* they reward us, [a]to come to cast us out of thy possession,[3425] which thou hast given us to inherit.[3423]

12 O our God, wilt thou not [a]judge[8199] them? for we have no might against this great company that cometh against us; neither know[3045] we what to do:[6213] but [b]our eyes *are* upon thee.

13 And all Judah stood before the LORD, with their little ones, their wives,[802] and their children.

14 Then upon Jahaziel the son of Zechariah, the son of Benaiah, the son of Jeiel, the son of Mattaniah, a Levite of

---

7 [b]Deut. 10:17; Job 34:19; Acts 10:34; Rom. 2:11; Gal. 2:6; Eph. 6:9; Col. 3:25; 1Pet. 1:17
8 [a]Deut. 16:18; 2Chr. 17:8
9 [a]2Sam. 23:3
10 [a]Deut. 17:8 [b]Num. 16:46 [c]Ezek. 3:18
11 [I]Hebr. *Take courage and do* [a]1Chr. 26:30 [b]2Chr. 15:2
2 [a]Gen. 14:7 [b]Josh. 15:62
3 [I]Hebr. *his face* [a]2Chr. 19:3 [b]Ezra 8:21; Jer. 36:9; Jon. 3:5
6 [a]Deut. 4:39; Josh. 2:11; 1Kgs. 8:23; Matt. 6:9 [b]Ps. 47:2, 8; Dan. 4:17, 25, 32 [c]1Chr. 29:12; Ps. 62:11; Matt. 6:13
7 [I]Hebr. *thou* [a]Gen. 17:7; Ex. 6:7 [b]Ps. 44:2 [c]Isa. 41:8; James 2:23
9 [a]1Kgs. 8:33, 37; 2Chr. 6:28-30 [b]2Chr. 6:20
10 [a]Deut. 2:4, 9, 19 [b]Num. 20:21
11 [a]Ps. 83:12
12 [a]1Sam. 3:13 [b]Ps. 25:15; 121:1, 2; 123:1, 2; 141:8

🔑 **20:2** The sea referred to here is the Dead Sea. For the proximity of En–gedi to the Dead Sea (Salt Sea) see map entitled "The Twelve Tribes."

the sons of Asaph, [a]came the Spirit[7307] of the LORD in the midst of the congregation;

15 And he said, Hearken ye, all Judah, and ye inhabitants of Jerusalem, and thou king[4428] Jehoshaphat, Thus saith the LORD unto you, [a]Be not afraid[3372] nor dismayed[2865] by reason of this great multitude; for the battle *is* not yours, but God's.

16 To morrow go ye down against them: behold, they come up by the [I]cliff of Ziz; and ye shall find them at the end of the [II]brook, before the wilderness of Jeruel.

17 [a]Ye shall not *need* to fight in this *battle:* set yourselves, stand ye *still,* and see the salvation of the LORD with you, O Judah and Jerusalem: fear not, nor be dismayed; to morrow go out against them: [b]for the LORD *will be* with you.

18 And Jehoshaphat [a]bowed his head with *his* face[639] to the ground:[776] and all Judah and the inhabitants of Jerusalem fell before the LORD, worshipping[7812] the LORD.

19 And the Levites, of the children of the Kohathites, and of the children of the Korhites, stood up to praise[1984] the LORD God of Israel with a loud voice on high.

20 And they rose early in the morning, and went forth into the wilderness of Tekoa: and as they went forth, Jehoshaphat stood and said, Hear me, O Judah, and ye inhabitants of Jerusalem; [a]Believe[539] in the LORD your God, so shall ye be established;[539] believe his prophets, so shall ye prosper.[6743]

21 And when he had consulted[3289] with the people, he appointed singers unto the LORD, [a]and [I]that should praise[3034] the beauty[1927] of holiness, as they went out before the army, and to say, [b]Praise the LORD; [c]for his mercy *endureth* for ever.

22 [I]And when they began [II]to sing[7440] and to praise,[8416] [a]the LORD set ambushments against the children of Ammon, Moab, and mount Seir, which were come against Judah; and [III]they were smitten.

23 For the children of Ammon and Moab stood up against the inhabitants of mount Seir, utterly to slay and destroy[8045] *them:* and when they had made an end[3615] of the inhabitants of Seir, every one helped [I]to destroy[4889] another.[7453]

24 And when Judah came toward the watch tower in the wilderness, they looked unto the multitude, and, behold, they *were* dead bodies fallen[5307] to the earth,[776] and [I]none escaped.[6413]

25 And when Jehoshaphat and his people came to take away the spoil of them, they found among them in abundance both riches with the dead bodies, and precious jewels, which they stripped off for themselves, more than they could carry away: and they were three days[3117] in gathering of the spoil, it was so much.

26 And on the fourth day they assembled themselves[6950] in the valley of [I]Berachah; for there they blessed[1288] the LORD: therefore the name of the same place was called,[7121] The valley of Berachah, unto this day.

27 Then they returned, every man of Judah and Jerusalem, and Jehoshaphat in the [I]forefront of them, to go again to Jerusalem with joy; for the LORD had [a]made them to rejoice over their enemies.

28 And they came to Jerusalem with psalteries and harps and trumpets unto the house of the LORD.[3068]

29 And [a]the fear[6343] of God was on all the kingdoms of *those* countries,[776] when they had heard that the LORD fought against the enemies of Israel.

30 So the realm of Jehoshaphat was quiet:[8252] for his [a]God gave him rest round about.

Summary of Jehoshaphat's Reign

31 [a]And Jehoshaphat reigned over Judah: *he was* thirty and five years old

14 [a]Num. 11:25, 26; 24:2; 2Chr. 15:1; 24:20
15 [a]Ex. 14:13, 14; Deut. 1:29, 30; 31:6, 8; 2Chr. 32:7
16 [I]Hebr. *ascent* [II]Or, *valley*
17 [a]Ex. 14:13, 14 [b]Num. 14:9; 2Chr. 15:2; 32:8
18 [a]Ex. 4:31
20 [a]Isa. 7:9
21 [I]Hebr. *praisers* [a]1Chr. 16:29 [b]1Chr. 16:34; Ps. 136:1 [c]1Chr. 16:41; 2Chr. 5:13; 7:3, 6
22 [I]Hebr. *And in the time that they* [II]Hebr. *in singing and praise* [III]Or, *they smote one another* [a]Judg. 7:22; 1Sam. 14:20
23 [I]Hebr. *for the destruction*
24 [I]Hebr. there was *not an escaping*
26 [I]That is, *Blessing*
27 [I]Hebr. *head* [a]Neh. 12:43
29 [a]2Chr. 17:10
30 [a]2Chr. 15:15; Job 34:29
31 [a]1Kgs. 22:41

20:15 The last clause is similar to what David said when he faced Goliath (1 Sam. 17:47).

when he began to reign, and he reigned twenty and five years in Jerusalem. And his mother's name *was* Azubah the daughter of Shilhi.

32 And he walked in the way[1870] of Asa his father, and departed[5493] not from it, doing[6213] *that which was* right in the sight of the LORD.

33 Howbeit [a]the high places were not taken away: for as yet the people had not [b]prepared their hearts unto the God of their fathers.

34 Now the rest of the acts[1697] of Jehoshaphat, first[7223] and last, behold, they *are* written in the [I]book of Jehu the son of Hanani, [a]who [II]*is* mentioned in the book[5612] of the kings of Israel.

35 And after this [a]did Jehoshaphat king of Judah join himself[6213] with Ahaziah king of Israel, who did very wickedly:

36 [a]And he joined himself with him to make ships to go to Tarshish: and they made the ships in Ezion–geber.

37 Then Eliezer the son of Dodavah of Mareshah prophesied against Jehoshaphat, saying, Because thou hast joined thyself with Ahaziah, the LORD hath broken thy works. [a]And the ships were broken,[7665] that they were not able to go [b]to Tarshish.

21 Now [a]Jehoshaphat slept with his fathers, and was buried[6912] with his fathers[1] in the city of David. And Jehoram his son [I]reigned in his stead.

Jehoram Rules Judah

2 And he had brethren[251] the sons of Jehoshaphat, Azariah, and Jehiel, and Zechariah, and Azariah, and Michael, and Shephatiah: all these *were* the sons of Jehoshaphat king[4428] of Israel.

3 And their father gave them great gifts of silver, and of gold, and of precious things, with fenced cities in Judah: but the kingdom[4467] gave he to [Ia]Jehoram; because he *was* the firstborn.

4 Now when Jehoram was risen up to the kingdom of his father, he strengthened himself, and slew all his brethren with the sword, and *divers* also of the princes of Israel.

5 [a]Jehoram *was* thirty and two years old when he began to reign, and he reigned eight years in Jerusalem.

6 And he walked in the way[1870] of the kings of Israel, like as did[6213] the house of Ahab: for he had the daughter of [a]Ahab to wife:[802] and he wrought that which was evil[7451] in the eyes of the LORD.

7 Howbeit the LORD would[14] not destroy[7843] the house of David, because of the covenant[1285] that he had made with David, and as he promised to give a [I]light[5216] to him and to his [a]sons for ever.

8 [a]In his days[3117] the Edomites revolted from under the [I]dominion[3027] of Judah, and made themselves a king.

9 Then Jehoram went forth with his princes, and all his chariots with him: and he rose up by night,[3915] and smote the Edomites which compassed him in, and the captains[8269] of the chariots.

10 So the Edomites revolted from under the hand of Judah unto this day. The same time *also* did Libnah revolt from under his hand; because he had forsaken[5800] the LORD God[430] of his fathers.

11 Moreover he made high places in the mountains of Judah, and caused the inhabitants of Jerusalem to [a]commit fornication,[2181] and compelled Judah *thereto.*

12 And there came a [Ia]writing[4385] to him from Elijah the prophet, saying, Thus saith the LORD God of David thy father, Because thou hast not walked in the ways of Jehoshaphat thy father, nor in the ways of Asa king of Judah,

13 But hast walked in the way of the kings of Israel, and hast [a]made Judah and the inhabitants of Jerusalem to [b]go a whoring, like to the [c]whoredoms of the house of Ahab, and also hast [d]slain thy brethren of thy father's house, *which were* better[2896] than thyself:

14 Behold, with [I]a great plague will the LORD smite thy people,[5971] and thy

33 [a]2Chr. 17:6 [b]2Chr. 12:14; 19:3

34 [I]Hebr. *words* [II]Hebr. *was made to ascend* [a]1Kgs. 16:1, 7

35 [a]1Kgs. 22:48, 49

36 [a]1Kgs. 22:49

37 [a]1Kgs. 22:48 [b]2Chr. 9:21

1 [I]Alone [a]1Kgs. 22:50

3 [I]Jehoramade partner of the kingdom with his father [a]2Kgs. 8:16

5 [a]2Kgs. 8:17

6 [a]2Chr. 22:2

7 [I]Hebr. *lamp,* or, *candle* [a]2Sam. 7:12, 13; 1Kgs. 11:36; 2Kgs. 8:19; Ps. 132:11

8 [I]Hebr. *hand* [a]2Kgs. 8:20

11 [a]Lev. 17:7; 20:5; 2Chr. 21:13

12 [I]Which was written before his death [a]2Kgs. 2:1

13 [a]2Chr. 21:11 [b]Ex. 34:15; Deut. 31:16 [c]1Kgs. 16:31-33; 2Kgs. 9:22 [d]2Chr. 21:4

14 [I]Hebr. *a great stroke*

children,[1121] and thy wives, and all thy
goods:
15 And thou *shalt have* great sickness by [a]disease[4245] of thy bowels,[4578]
until thy bowels fall out by reason of the
sickness day by day.
16 Moreover the LORD [a]stirred up
against Jehoram the spirit of the
Philistines, and of the Arabians, that
were near the Ethiopians:
17 And they came up into Judah,
and brake into it, and [I][a]carried away all
the substance that was found in the
king's house, and [b]his sons also, and his
wives; so that there was never a son
left[7604] him, save [II]Jehoahaz, the youngest
of his sons.
18 [I][a]And after all this the LORD smote
him [b]in his bowels with an incurable disease.
19 And it came to pass, that in
process of time, after the end of two
years, his bowels fell out by reason of his
sickness: so he died of sore diseases.[8463]
And his people made no burning[8316] for
him, like [a]the burning of his fathers.
20 Thirty and two years old was he
when he began to reign, and he reigned
in Jerusalem eight years, and departed
[I][a]without being desired. Howbeit they
buried him in the city of David, but not
in the sepulchres[6913] of the kings.

Ahaziah Rules Judah

22 And the inhabitants of Jerusalem
made [a]Ahaziah his youngest son
king[4427] in his stead: for the band[1416] of
men that came with the Arabians to the
camp had slain all the [b]eldest. So
Ahaziah the son of Jehoram king[4428] of
Judah reigned.
🔑 2 [a]Forty and two years old *was*
Ahaziah when he began to reign, and he
reigned one year in Jerusalem. His
mother's name also *was* [b]Athaliah the
daughter of Omri.
3 He also walked in the ways[1870] of
the house of Ahab: for his mother was
his counselor[3289] to do wickedly.[7561]
4 Wherefore he did[6213] evil[7451] in the
sight of the LORD like the house of Ahab:
for they were his counsellors after the
death[4194] of his father to his destruction.[4889]
🔑 5 He walked also after their counsel,[6098] and [a]went with Jehoram the son
of Ahab king of Israel to war against
Hazael king of Syria at Ramoth–gilead:
and the Syrians smote Joram.
6 [a]And he returned to be healed
in Jezreel because of the wounds[4347]
[I]which were given[5221] him at Ramah,
when he fought with Hazael king of
Syria. And [II]Azariah the son of Jehoram
king of Judah went down to see Jehoram
the son of Ahab at Jezreel, because he
was sick.

Jehu Assassinates Ahaziah

7 And the [I]destruction[8395] of
Ahaziah [a]was of God[430] by coming to
Joram: for when he was come, he [b]went
out with Jehoram against Jehu the son of
Nimshi, [c]whom the LORD had anointed[4886]
to cut off[3772] the house of Ahab.
8 And it came to pass, that when
Jehu was [a]executing[6213] judgment[8199]
upon the house of Ahab, and [b]found the

15 [a]2Chr. 21:18, 19
16 [a]1Kgs. 11:14, 23
17 [I]Hebr. *carried captive* [II]Or, *Ahaziah*, 2Chr. 22:1, or, *Azariah*, 2Chr. 22:6 [a]2Chr. 22:1 [b]2Chr. 24:7
18 [I]His son, *Ahaziah Prorex* [a]2Kgs. 9:29 [b]2Chr. 21:15
19 [a]2Chr. 16:14
20 [I]Hebr. *without desire* [a]Jer. 22:18
1 [a]2Kgs. 8:24; 2Chr. 21:17; 2Chr. 22:6 [b]2Chr. 21:17
2 [a]2Kgs. 8:26 [b]2Chr. 21:6
5 [a]2Kgs. 8:28
6 [I]Hebr. *wherewith they wounded him* [II]Otherwise called *Ahaziah*, 2Chr. 22:1, and Jehoahaz, 2Chr. 21:17 [a]2Kgs. 9:15
7 [I]Hebr. *treading down* [a]Judg. 14:4; 1Kgs. 12:15; 2Chr. 10:15 [b]2Kgs. 9:21 [c]2Kgs. 9:6, 7
8 [a]2Kgs. 10:10, 11 [b]2Kgs. 10:13, 14

🔑 **22:2** Athaliah was the daughter of Ahab and Jezebel who was given to Jehoram (the son of Jehoshaphat) to wife in an alliance with Jehoshaphat, king of Judah (see note on 2 Chr. 18:1).

🔑 **22:5** Jehoram, or the shorter spelling, Joram, is the name of two separate individuals, one of which ruled over the kingdom of Israel and the other over Judah. To make the matter even more confusing, these two men were in power during the same time. While the name Joram is almost always applied to the king of Israel (2 Kgs. 8:21, 23, 24, 28; 9:14–17, 21–23, 29; 2 Chr. 22:5, 7), he is referred to as Jehoram in 2 Kings 3:1, 6; 9:24, and in 2 Chronicles 22:5, 7 both spellings are used. The king of Judah is normally referred to as Jehoram (1 Kgs. 22:50; 2 Kgs. 12:18; 2 Chr. 21:1, 3–5, 9, 16; 22:1, 11) though on two occasions he is called Joram (2 Kgs. 11:2; 1 Chr. 3:11). In addition, there are a number of references in which both kings are mentioned (2 Kgs. 1:17 [both are called Jehoram]; 8:16, 25, 29; 2 Chr. 22:6 [Joram is king of Israel and Jehoram is king of Judah]).

princes of Judah, and the sons of the
brethren[251] of Ahaziah, that ministered to
Ahaziah, he slew them.
9 [a]And he sought Ahaziah: and they
caught him, (for he was hid in Samaria,)
and brought[935] him to Jehu: and when
they had slain him, they buried[6912] him:
Because, said they, he *is* the son of
Jehoshaphat, who [b]sought the LORD with
all his heart. So the house of Ahaziah
had no power to keep still the kingdom.[4467]

Athaliah Rules Judah

10 [a]But when Athaliah the mother of
Ahaziah saw that her son was dead,[4191]
she arose and destroyed all the seed royal
of the house of Judah.
11 But [a]Jehoshabeath, the daughter
of the king, took Joash the son of
Ahaziah, and stole[1589] him from among
the king's sons that were slain,[4191] and
put him and his nurse in a bedchamber.[2315,4296] So Jehoshabeath, the
daughter of king Jehoram, the wife[802] of
Jehoiada the priest, (for she was the sister of Ahaziah,) hid him from Athaliah,
so that she slew him not.
12 And he was with them hid in the
house of God six years: and Athaliah
reigned over the land.[776]

23 And [a]in the seventh year Jehoiada
strengthened himself, and took
the captains[8269] of hundreds, Azariah the
son of Jeroham, and Ishmael the son of
Jehohanan, and Azariah the son of Obed,
and Maaseiah the son of Adaiah, and
Elishaphat the son of Zichri, into
covenant[1285] with him.
2 And they went about in Judah, and
gathered[6908] the Levites out of all the
cities of Judah, and the chief[7218] of the
fathers[1] of Israel, and they came to
Jerusalem.

9 [a]2Kgs. 9:27, at *Megiddo* in the kingdom of *Samaria* [b]2Chr. 17:4

10 [a]2Kgs. 11:1

11 [a]2Kgs. 11:2, *Jehosheba*

1 [a]2Kgs. 11:4

3 [a]2Sam. 7:12; 1Kgs. 2:4; 9:5; 2Chr. 6:16; 7:18; 21:7

4 [I]Hebr. *thresholds* [a]1Chr. 9:25

6 [a]1Chr. 23:28, 29

10 [I]Hebr. *shoulder* [II]Hebr. *house*

3 And all the congregation made
a covenant with the king[4428] in the
house of God.[430] And he said unto
them, Behold, the king's son shall reign,
as the LORD hath [a]said of the sons of
David.
4 This *is* the thing that ye shall
do;[6213] A third part of you [a]entering on
the sabbath, of the priests and of the
Levites, *shall be* porters[7778] of the [I]doors;
5 And a third part *shall be* at the
king's house; and a third part at the gate
of the foundation:[3247] and all the
people[5971] *shall be* in the courts[2691] of
the house of the LORD.
6 But let none come into the house of
the LORD, save the priests, and [a]they that
minister of the Levites; they shall go in,
for they *are* holy: but all the people shall
keep[8104] the watch[4931] of the LORD.
7 And the Levites shall compass[5362]
the king round about, every man with
his weapons in his hand; and whosoever
else cometh into the house, he shall be
put to death:[4191] but be ye with the king
when he cometh in, and when he goeth
out.
8 So the Levites and all Judah did
according to all things that Jehoiada the
priest had commanded,[6680] and took
every man his men that were to come in
on the sabbath, with them that were to
go *out* on the sabbath: for Jehoiada the
priest dismissed not the courses.
9 Moreover Jehoiada the priest delivered to the captains of hundreds spears,
and bucklers,[4043] and shields, that *had
been* king David's, which *were* in the
house of God.
10 And he set all the people, every
man having his weapon in his hand,
from the right [I]side of the [II]temple to the
left side of the temple, along by the
altar[4196] and the temple, by the king
round about.
11 Then they brought out the king's
son, and put upon him the crown,[5145] and

23:11 The "testimony" referred to here was the Law of Moses (Ex. 25:21), which was meant to be the king's constant guide (Deut. 17:19, 20). He was supposed to write his own copy (Deut. 17:18), but it is not known whether Jehoiada ever did this.

[a]*gave him* the testimony, and made him king.[4427] And Jehoiada and his sons anointed[4886] him, and said, [I]God save[2421] the king.

12 Now when Athaliah heard the noise of the people running and praising[1984] the king, she came to the people into the house of the LORD:

13 And she looked,[7200] and, behold, the king stood at his pillar at the entering in, and the princes and the trumpets by the king: and all the people of the land[776] rejoiced, and sounded with trumpets, also the singers with instruments of musick, and [a]such as taught to sing praise.[1984] Then Athaliah rent her clothes, and said, [I]Treason,[7195] Treason.

14 Then Jehoiada the priest brought out the captains of hundreds that were set over the host, and said unto them, Have her forth[3318] of the ranges: and whoso followeth her, let him be slain with the sword. For the priest said, Slay her not in the house of the LORD.

15 So they laid[7760] hands on her; and when she was come to the entering [a]of the horse gate by the king's house, they slew her there.

Jehoiada's Reform

16 And Jehoiada made a covenant between him, and between all the people, and between the king, that they should be the LORD's people.

17 Then all the people went to the house of Baal, and brake it down,[5422] and brake[7665] his altars[4196] and his images[6754] in pieces, and [a]slew Mattan the priest of Baal before the altars.

18 Also Jehoiada appointed[7760] the offices of the house of the LORD by the hand of the priests the Levites, whom David had [a]distributed in the house of the LORD, to offer the burnt offerings of the LORD, as *it is* written in the [b]law[8451] of Moses, with rejoicing and with singing, *as it was ordained* [Ic]by David.

19 And he set the [a]porters at the gates of the house of the LORD, that none *which was* unclean[2931] in any thing should enter in.

20 [a]And he took the captains of hundreds, and the nobles,[117] and the governors[4910] of the people, and all the people of the land, and brought down the king from the house of the LORD: and they came through the high gate into the king's house, and set the king upon the throne of the kingdom.[4467]

21 And all the people of the land rejoiced: and the city was quiet,[8252] after that they had slain Athaliah with the sword.

Joash Rules Judah

24 Joash [a]*was* seven years old when he began to reign, and he reigned forty years in Jerusalem. His mother's name also *was* Zibiah of Beer–sheba.

2 And Joash [a]did *that which was* right in the sight of the LORD all the days[3117] of Jehoiada the priest.

3 And Jehoiada took for him two wives;[802] and he begat sons and daughters.

4 And it came to pass after this, *that* Joash was minded [I]to repair the house of the LORD.

5 And he gathered together[6908] the priests and the Levites, and said to them, Go out unto the cities of Judah, and [a]gather of all Israel money to repair the house of your God[430] from year to year, and see that ye hasten[4116] the matter. Howbeit the Levites hastened *it* not.

🗝 6 [a]And the king called for Jehoiada the chief,[7218] and said unto him, Why hast thou not required[1875] of the Levites to bring in out of Judah and out of Jerusalem the collection,[4864] *according to the commandment* of [b]Moses servant

11 [I]Hebr. *Let the king live* [a]Deut. 17:18

13 [I]Hebr. *Conspiracy* [a]1Chr. 25:8

15 [a]Neh. 3:28

17 [a]Deut. 13:9

18 [I]Hebr. *by the hands of David* [a]1Chr. 23:6, 30, 31; 24:1 [b]Num. 28:2 [c]1Chr. 25:2, 6

19 [a]1Chr. 26:1

20 [a]2Kgs. 11:19

1 [a]2Kgs. 11:21; 12:1

2 [a]2Chr. 26:5

4 [I]Hebr. *to renew*

5 [a]2Kgs. 12:4

6 [a]2Kgs. 12:7 [b]Ex. 30:12-14, 16

🗝 **24:6** The Tabernacle was called "the tent of the testimony" (Num. 9:15) because it housed the tables of the law or testimony (Ex. 25:16). "Temple" was also used as a name for the Tabernacle (1 Sam. 1:9; 3:3; 2 Sam. 22:7).

of the LORD, and of the congregation of Israel, for the [c]tabernacle of witness?[5715]

7 For [a]the sons of Athaliah, that wicked woman, had broken up the house of God; and also all the [b]dedicated things[6944] of the house of the LORD did they bestow upon Baalim.

8 And at the king's commandment[559] [a]they made a chest,[727] and set it without at the gate of the house of the LORD.

9 And they made [I]a proclamation[6963] through Judah and Jerusalem, to bring in to the LORD [a]the collection *that* Moses the servant of God *laid* upon Israel in the wilderness.

10 And all the princes and all the people[5971] rejoiced, and brought in, and cast into the chest, until they had made an end.[3615]

11 Now it came to pass, that at what time the chest was brought unto the king's office by the hand of the Levites, and [a]when they saw that *there was* much money, the king's scribe and the high priest's officer[6496] came and emptied the chest, and took it, and carried it to his place again. Thus they did day by day, and gathered[622] money in abundance.

12 And the king and Jehoiada gave it to such as did the work[4399] of the service of the house of the LORD, and hired masons and carpenters to repair the house of the LORD, and also such as wrought iron and brass to mend the house of the LORD.

13 So the workmen wrought, and [I]the work was perfected by them, and they set the house of God in his state,[4971] and strengthened it.

14 And when they had finished[3615] *it,* they brought the rest of the money before the king and Jehoiada, [a]whereof were made vessels for the house of the LORD, *even* vessels[3627] to minister, and [I]to offer *withal,* and spoons, and vessels of gold and silver. And they offered burnt offerings in the house of the LORD continually[8548] all the days of Jehoiada.

15 But Jehoiada waxed old, and was full of days when he died; an hundred and thirty years old *was he* when he died.

16 And they buried[6912] him in the city of David among the kings, because he had done[6213] good in Israel, both toward God,[430] and toward his house.

17 Now after the death[4194] of Jehoiada came the princes of Judah, and made obeisance[7812] to the king. Then the king hearkened unto them.

18 And they left[5800] the house of the LORD God of their fathers,[1] and served [a]groves[842] and idols:[6091] and [b]wrath[7110] came upon Judah and Jerusalem for this their trespass.

19 Yet he [a]sent prophets to them, to bring them again unto the LORD; and they testified against them: but they would not give ear.

🗝 20 And [a]the Spirit of God [I][b]came upon Zechariah the son of Jehoiada the priest, which stood above the people, and said unto them, Thus saith God, [c]Why transgress ye the commandments[4687] of the LORD, that ye cannot prosper? [d]because ye have forsaken[5800] the LORD, he hath also forsaken you.

21 And they conspired against him, and [a]stoned him with stones at the commandment of the king in the court of the house of the LORD.

22 Thus Joash the king remembered not the kindness[2617] which Jehoiada his father had done to him, but slew his son. And when he died, he said, The LORD look upon *it,* and require[1875] *it.*

23 And it came to pass [I]at the end of the year, *that* [a]the host of Syria came up against him: and they came to Judah and Jerusalem, and destroyed[7843] all the princes of the people from among the people, and sent all the spoil of them unto the king of [II]Damascus.

24 For the army[2428] of the Syrians

6 [c]Num. 1:50; Acts 7:44
7 [a]2Chr. 21:17 [b]2Kgs. 12:4
8 [a]2Kgs. 12:9
9 [I]Hebr. *a voice* [a]2Chr. 22:6
11 [a]2Kgs. 12:10
13 [I]Hebr. *the healing went up upon the work*
14 [I]Or, *pestils* [a]2Kgs. 12:13
18 [a]1Kgs. 14:23 [b]Judg. 5:8; 2Chr. 19:2; 28:13; 29:8; 32:25
19 [a]2Chr. 36:15; Jer. 7:25, 26; 25:4
20 [I]Hebr. *clothed* [a]2Chr. 15:1; 20:14 [b]Judg. 6:34 [c]Num. 14:41 [d]2Chr. 15:2
21 [a]Matt. 23:35; Acts 7:58, 59
23 [I]Hebr. *in the revolution of the year* [II]Hebr. *Darmesek* [a]2Kgs. 12:17

🗝 **24:20, 21** This passage was referred to by Jesus in Matthew 23:35 where Berechiah is another name for Jehoiada. This priest should not be confused with the prophet Zechariah, the son of Berechiah and author of the Book of Zechariah.

[a]came with a small company of men, and the LORD [b]delivered a very great host into their hand, because they had forsaken the LORD God of their fathers. So they [c]executed[6213] judgment[8201] against Joash.

25 And when they were departed from him, (for they left him in great diseases,[4251]) [a]his own servants conspired against him for the blood[1818] of the [b]sons of Jehoiada the priest, and slew him on his bed, and he died: and they buried him in the city of David, but they buried him not in the sepulchres[6913] of the kings.

26 And these are they that conspired against him; [I][a]Zabad the son of Shimeath an Ammonitess, and Jehozabad the son of [II]Shimrith a Moabitess.

27 Now *concerning* his sons, and the greatness of [a]the burdens[4853] *laid* upon him, and the [I]repairing of the house of God, behold, they *are* written in the [II]story of the book[5612] of the kings. [b]And Amaziah his son reigned in his stead.

Amaziah Rules Judah

25 Amaziah [a]*was* twenty and five years old *when* he began to reign, and he reigned twenty and nine years in Jerusalem. And his mother's name *was* Jehoaddan of Jerusalem.

2 And he did[6213] *that which was* right in the sight of the LORD, [a]but not with a perfect[8003] heart.

3 [a]Now it came to pass, when the kingdom[4467] was [I]established to him, that he slew his servants that had killed[5221] the king[4428] his father.

4 But he slew not their children,[1121] but *did* as *it is* written in the law[8451] in the book[5612] of Moses, where the LORD commanded,[6680] saying, [a]The fathers[1] shall not die[4191] for the children, neither shall the children die for the fathers, but every man shall die for his own sin.

5 Moreover Amaziah gathered Judah together,[6908] and made them captains[8269] over thousands, and captains over hundreds, according to the houses of *their* fathers, throughout all Judah and Benjamin: and he numbered[6485] them [a]from twenty years old and above, and found them three hundred thousand choice *men, able* to go forth to war,[6635] that could handle spear and shield.

6 He hired also an hundred thousand mighty men of valour[2428] out of Israel for an hundred talents of silver.

7 But there came a man of God[430] to him, saying, O king, let not the army[6635] of Israel go with thee; for the LORD *is* not with Israel, *to wit, with* all the children of Ephraim.

8 But if thou wilt go, do *it,* be strong for the battle: God shall make thee fall[3782] before the enemy: for God hath [a]power to help, and to cast down.

🔑 9 And Amaziah said to the man of God, But what shall we do for the hundred talents which I have given to the [I]army[1416] of Israel? And the man of God answered,[559] [a]The LORD is able to give thee much more than this.

10 Then Amaziah separated them, *to wit,* the army that was come to him out of Ephraim, to go [I]home again: wherefore their anger[639] was greatly kindled[2734] against Judah, and they returned home [II]in great[2750] anger.

11 And Amaziah strengthened himself, and led forth his people,[5971] and went to [a]the valley of salt, and smote of the children of Seir ten thousand.

12 And *other* ten thousand *left* alive[2416] did the children of Judah carry away captive,[7617] and brought them unto the top of the rock, and cast them down from the top of the rock, that they all were broken in pieces.

13 But [I]the soldiers of the army which Amaziah sent back, that they should not go with him to battle, fell upon the cities of Judah, from Samaria

24 [a]Lev. 26:8; Deut. 32:30; Isa. 30:17 [b]Lev. 26:25; Deut. 28:25 [c]2Chr. 22:8; Isa. 10:5
25 [a]2Kgs. 12:20 [b]2Chr. 24:21
26 [I]Or, *Jozachar* [II]Or, *Shomer* [a]2Kgs. 12:21
27 [I]Hebr. *founding* [II]Or, *commentary* [a]2Kgs. 12:18 [b]2Kgs. 12:21
1 [a]2Kgs. 14:1
2 [a]2Kgs. 14:4; 2Chr. 25:14
3 [I]Hebr. *confirmed upon him* [a]2Kgs. 14:5
4 [a]Deut. 24:16; 2Kgs. 14:6; Jer. 31:30; Ezek. 18:20
5 [a]Num. 1:3
8 [a]2Chr. 20:6
9 [I]Hebr. *band* [a]Prov. 10:22
10 [I]Hebr. *to their place* [II]Hebr. *in heat of anger*
11 [a]2Kgs. 14:7
13 [I]Hebr. *the sons of the band*

🔑 **25:9** The phrase "the LORD is able to give thee much more than this" asserts that which is promised in Matthew 6:33, Ephesians 3:20, and Philippians 4:19.

even unto Beth–horon, and smote three thousand of them, and took much spoil.

14 Now it came to pass, after that Amaziah was come from the slaughter of the Edomites, that [a]he brought the gods[430] of the children of Seir, and set them up *to be* [b]his gods, and bowed down himself[7812] before them, and burned incense[6999] unto them.

15 Wherefore the anger of the LORD was kindled against Amaziah, and he sent unto him a prophet, which said unto him, Why hast thou sought after [a]the gods of the people, which [b]could not deliver[5337] their own people out of thine hand?

16 And it came to pass, as he talked with him, that *the king* said unto him, Art thou made of the king's counsel?[3289] forbear; why shouldest thou be smitten? Then the prophet forbare, and said, I know[3045] that God hath [I][a]determined[3289] to destroy[7843] thee, because thou hast done this, and hast not hearkened unto my counsel.[6098]

17 Then [a]Amaziah king of Judah took advice, and sent to Joash, the son of Jehoahaz, the son of Jehu, king of Israel, saying, Come, let us see one another in the face.

18 And Joash king of Israel sent to Amaziah king of Judah, saying, The [I]thistle that *was* in Lebanon sent to the cedar that *was* in Lebanon, saying, Give thy daughter to my son to wife:[802] and there passed by[5674] [II]a wild beast[2416] that *was* in Lebanon, and trode down the thistle.

19 Thou sayest, Lo, thou hast smitten the Edomites; and thine heart lifteth thee up to boast:[3513] abide now at home; why shouldest thou meddle to *thine* hurt, that thou shouldest fall, *even* thou, and Judah with thee?

20 But Amaziah would not hear; for [a]it *came* of God, that he might deliver them into the hand *of their enemies,* because they [b]sought after the gods of Edom.

21 So Joash the king of Israel went up; and they saw one another in the face, *both* he and Amaziah king of Judah, at Beth–shemesh, which *belongeth* to Judah.

22 And Judah was [I]put to the worse[5062] before Israel, and they fled every man to his tent.

23 And Joash the king of Israel took Amaziah king of Judah, the son of Joash, the son of [a]Jehoahaz, at Beth–shemesh, and brought him to Jerusalem, and brake down the wall of Jerusalem from the gate of Ephraim to [I]the corner gate, four hundred cubits.

24 And *he took* all the gold and the silver, and all the vessels that were found in the house of God with Obed–edom, and the treasures of the king's house, the hostages also, and returned to Samaria.

25 [a]And Amaziah the son of Joash king of Judah lived[2421] after the death[4194] of Joash son of Jehoahaz king of Israel fifteen years.

26 Now the rest of the acts[1697] of Amaziah, first[7223] and last, behold, *are* they not written in the book of the kings of Judah and Israel?

27 Now after the time that Amaziah did turn away [I]from following the LORD they [II]made a conspiracy against him in Jerusalem; and he fled to Lachish: but they sent to Lachish after him, and slew him there.

28 And they brought[5375] him upon horses, and buried[6912] him with his fathers in the city of [I][a]Judah.

Uzziah Rules Judah

26 Then all the people[5971] of Judah took [I][a]Uzziah, who *was* sixteen years old, and made him king[4427] in the room of his father Amaziah.

2 He built Eloth, and restored it to Judah, after that the king[4428] slept with his fathers.[1]

3 Sixteen years old *was* Uzziah when he began to reign, and he reigned fifty and two years in Jerusalem. His mother's name also *was* Jecoliah of Jerusalem.

4 And he did[6213] *that which was*

14 [a]2Chr. 28:23 [b]Ex. 20:3, 5
15 [a]Ps. 96:5 [b]2Chr. 25:11
16 [I]Hebr. *counseled* [a]1Sam. 2:25
17 [a]2Kgs. 14:8, 9
18 [I]Or, *furze bush, or, thorn* [II]Hebr. *a beast of the field*
20 [a]1Kgs. 12:15; 2Chr. 22:7 [b]2Chr. 25:14
22 [I]Hebr. *smitten*
23 [I]Hebr. *the gate of it that looketh* [a]2Chr. 21:17; 22:1, 6
25 [a]2Kgs. 14:17
27 [I]Hebr. *from after* [II]Hebr. *conspired a conspiracy*
28 [I]That is, *The city of David* [a]2Kgs. 14:20
1 [I]Or, *Azariah* [a]2Kgs. 14:21, 22; 15:1

right in the sight of the LORD, according
to all that his father Amaziah did.
5 And [a]he sought God[430] in the days
of Zechariah, who [b]had understanding[995]
[I]in the visions[7200] of God: and as long as
he sought the LORD, God made him to
prosper.
6 And he went forth and [a]warred
against the Philistines, and brake down
the wall of Gath, and the wall of Jabneh, and the wall of Ashdod, and built
cities [I]about Ashdod, and among the
Philistines.
7 And God helped him against
[a]the Philistines, and against the Arabians
that dwelt in Gur–baal, and the Mehunims.
8 And the Ammonites [a]gave
gifts[4503] to Uzziah: and his name
[I]spread abroad *even* to the entering in of
Egypt; for he strengthened *himself* exceedingly.
9 Moreover Uzziah built towers in
Jerusalem at the [a]corner gate, and at the
valley gate, and at the turning *of the
wall,* and [I]fortified[2388] them.
10 Also he built towers in the desert,
and [I]digged many wells:[953] for he had
much cattle, both in the low country,
and in the plains: husbandmen[406]
also, and vine dressers in the mountains,
and in [II]Carmel: for he loved[157]
[III]husbandry.[127]
11 Moreover Uzziah had an host of
fighting men, that went out to war by
bands,[1416] according to the number of
their account[6486] by the hand of Jeiel the
scribe and Maaseiah the ruler, under the
hand of Hananiah, *one* of the king's
captains.[8269]
12 The whole number of the
chief[7218] of the fathers of the mighty
men of valour[2428] *were* two thousand and
six hundred.
13 And under their hand *was* [I]an
army,[6635] three hundred thousand and
seven thousand and five hundred, that
made war with mighty power, to help the
king against the enemy.
14 And Uzziah prepared[3559] for
them throughout all the host[6635] shields,
and spears, and helmets, and habergeons,[8302] and bows, and [I]slings *to cast*
stones.
15 And he made in Jerusalem
engines,[2810] invented by cunning men,[2803]
to be on the towers and upon the
bulwarks,[6438] to shoot arrows and great
stones withal. And his name [I]spread far
abroad; for he was marvellously helped,
till he was strong.
16 But [a]when he was strong, his
heart was [b]lifted up to *his* destruction:[7843]
for he transgressed[4603] against the LORD
his God, and [c]went into the temple of the
LORD[3068] to burn incense[6999] upon the
altar of incense.[7004]
17 And [a]Azariah the priest went in
after him, and with him fourscore priests
of the LORD, *that were* valiant men:
18 And they withstood Uzziah
the king, and said unto him, *It* [a]*appertaineth* not unto thee, Uzziah, to burn incense unto the LORD, but to the [b]priests
the sons of Aaron, that are consecrated[6942] to burn incense: go out of the
sanctuary; for thou hast trespassed; neither *shall it be* for thine honour from the
LORD God.
19 Then Uzziah was wroth,[2196]
and *had* a censer in his hand to burn incense: and while he was wroth with the
priests, [a]the leprosy even rose up in his
forehead before the priests in the house
of the LORD, from beside the incense
altar.
20 And Azariah the chief priest, and
all the priests, looked upon him, and, behold, he *was* leprous in his forehead, and
they thrust him out from thence; yea,
himself [a]hasted also to go out, because
the LORD had smitten him.
21 [a]And Uzziah the king was a leper
unto the day of his death,[4194] and dwelt
in a [I][b]several house, *being* a leper; for he
was cut off[1504] from the house of the
LORD: and Jotham his son *was* over the
king's house, judging[8199] the people of
the land.[776]
22 Now the rest of the acts[1697] of
Uzziah, first[7223] and last, did [a]Isaiah the
prophet, the son of Amoz, write.
23 [a]So Uzziah slept with his fathers,
and they buried[6912] him with his fathers

5 [I]Hebr. *in the seeing of God* [a]2Chr. 24:2 [b]Gen. 41:15; Dan. 1:17; 2:19; 10:1

6 [I]Or, *in the country of Ashdod* [a]Isa. 14:29

7 [a]2Chr. 21:16

8 [I]Hebr. *went* [a]2Sam. 8:2; 2Chr. 17:11

9 [I]Or, *repaired* [a]2Kgs. 14:13; Neh. 3:13, 19, 32; Zech. 14:10

10 [I]Or, *cut out many cisterns* [II]Or, *fruitful fields* [III]Hebr. *ground*

13 [I]Hebr. *the power of an army*

14 [I]Hebr. *stones of slings*

15 [I]Hebr. *went forth*

16 [a]Deut. 32:15 [b]Deut. 8:14; 2Chr. 25:19 [c]2Kgs. 16:12, 13

17 [a]1Chr. 6:10

18 [a]Num. 16:40; 18:7 [b]Ex. 30:7, 8

19 [a]Num. 12:10; 2Kgs. 5:27

20 [a]Esth. 6:12

21 [I]Hebr. *free* [a]2Kgs. 15:5 [b]Lev. 13:46; Num. 5:2

22 [a]Isa. 1:1

23 [a]2Kgs. 15:7; Isa. 6:1

in the field[7704] of the burial[6900] which *belonged* to the kings; for they said, He *is* a leper: and Jotham his son reigned in his stead.

Jotham Rules Judah

27 Jotham [a]*was* twenty and five years old when he began to reign, and he reigned sixteen years in Jerusalem. His mother's name also *was* Jerushah, the daughter of Zadok.

2 And he did[6213] *that which was* right in the sight of the LORD, according to all that his father Uzziah did: howbeit he entered not into the temple of the LORD. And [a]the people[5971] did yet corruptly.[7843]

3 He built the high gate of the house of the LORD, and on the wall of [I][a]Ophel he built much.

4 Moreover he built cities in the mountains of Judah, and in the forests he built castles and towers.

5 He fought also with the king[4428] of the Ammonites, and prevailed against them. And the children[1121] of Ammon gave him the same year an hundred talents of silver, and ten thousand measures of wheat, and ten thousand of barley. [I]So much did the children of Ammon pay unto him, both the second year, and the third.

6 So Jotham became mighty, because he [I]prepared his ways[1870] before the LORD his God.[430]

7 Now the rest of the acts[1697] of Jotham, and all his wars, and his ways, lo, they *are* written in the book[5612] of the kings of Israel and Judah.

8 He was five and twenty years old when he began to reign, and reigned sixteen years in Jerusalem.

9 [a]And Jotham slept[7901] with his fathers,[1] and they buried[6912] him in the city of David: and Ahaz his son reigned in his stead.

Ahaz Rules Judah

28 Ahaz [a]*was* twenty years old when he began to reign, and he reigned sixteen years in Jerusalem: but he did[6213] not *that which was* right in the sight of the LORD, like David his father:

2 For he walked in the ways[1870] of the kings[4428] of Israel, and made also [a]molten images for [b]Baalim.

🔑 3 Moreover he [I]burnt incense[6999] in [a]the valley of the son of Hinnom, and burnt [b]his children[1121] in the fire, after the abominations[8441] of the heathen whom the LORD had cast out[3423] before the children of Israel.

4 He sacrificed also and burnt incense in the high places, and on the hills, and under every green tree.

5 Wherefore [a]the LORD his God[430] delivered him into the hand of the king of Syria; and they [b]smote him, and carried away a great multitude of them captives,[7633] and brought *them* to [I]Damascus. And he was also delivered into the hand of the king of Israel, who smote him with a great slaughter.

6 For [a]Pekah the son of Remaliah slew in Judah an hundred and twenty thousand in one day,[3117] *which were* all [I]valiant men; because they had forsaken[5800] the LORD[3068] God of their fathers.[1]

7 And Zichri, a mighty man of Ephraim, slew Maaseiah the king's son, and Azrikam the governor of the house, and Elkanah *that was* [I]next to the king.

8 And the children of Israel carried away captive[7617] of their [a]brethren[251] two hundred thousand, women,[802] sons, and daughters, and took also away much spoil from them, and brought the spoil to Samaria.

9 But a prophet of the LORD was there, whose name *was* Oded: and he went out before the host that came to Samaria, and said unto them, Behold, [a]because the LORD God of your fathers was wroth[2534] with Judah, he hath deliv-

1 [a]2Kgs. 15:32
2 [a]2Kgs. 15:35
3 [I]Or, *The tower* [a]2Chr. 33:14; Neh. 3:26
5 [I]Hebr. *This*
6 [I]Or, *established*
9 [a]2Kgs. 15:38

1 [a]2Kgs. 16:2
2 [a]Ex. 34:17; Lev. 19:4 [b]Judg. 2:11
3 [I]Or, *offered sacrifice* [a]2Kgs. 23:10 [b]Lev. 18:21; 2Kgs. 16:3; 2Chr. 33:6
5 [I]Hebr. *Darmesek* [a]Isa. 7:1 [b]2Kgs. 16:5, 6
6 [I]Hebr. *sons of valor* [a]2Kgs. 15:27
7 [I]Hebr. *the second to the king*
8 [a]2Chr. 11:4
9 [a]Ps. 69:26; Isa. 10:5; 47:6; Ezek. 25:12, 15; 26:2; Obad. 1:10; Zech. 1:15

🔑 **28:3** See note on 2 Kings 23:10 concerning the sacrificing of humans to "Molech."

ered them into your hand, and ye have
slain them in a rage *that* [b]reacheth up
unto heaven.
10 And now ye purpose to keep
under the children of Judah and
Jerusalem for [a]bondmen[5650] and bondwomen unto you: *but are there* not with
you, even with you, sins against the LORD
your God?
11 Now hear me therefore, and
deliver the captives again,[7725] which ye
have taken captive of your brethren: [a]for
the fierce wrath of the LORD *is* upon you.
12 Then certain[582] of the heads of
the children of Ephraim, Azariah the son
of Johanan, Berechiah the son of
Meshillemoth, and Jehizkiah the son of
Shallum, and Amasa the son of Hadlai,
stood up against them that came from
the war,[6635]
13 And said unto them, Ye shall not
bring in the captives hither: for whereas
we have offended against the LORD *already,* ye intend[559] to add *more* to our
sins and to our trespass:[819] for our trespass is great, and *there is* fierce wrath
against Israel.
14 So the armed men left[5800] the captives and the spoil before the princes and
all the congregation.
🗝 15 And the men [a]which were
expressed[5344] by name rose up, and took
the captives, and with the spoil clothed all
that were naked among them, and arrayed
them, and shod[5274] them, and [b]gave them
to eat and to drink, and anointed[4886] them,
and carried all the feeble of them upon
asses, and brought them to Jericho, [c]the
city of palm trees, to their brethren: then
they returned to Samaria.
16 [a]At that time did king Ahaz send
unto the kings of Assyria to help him.
17 For again the Edomites had come
and smitten Judah, and carried away
[I]captives.[7628]
18 [a]The Philistines also had invaded
the cities of the low country,[8219] and of
the south of Judah, and had taken
Beth–shemesh, and Ajalon, and Gederoth,
and Shocho with the villages thereof, and
Timnah with the villages thereof, Gimzo
also and the villages thereof: and they
dwelt there.
19 For the LORD brought Judah low
because of Ahaz king of [a]Israel; for he
[b]made Judah naked,[6544] and transgressed
sore against the LORD.
20 And [a]Tilgath–pilneser king of Assyria came unto him, and distressed[6696]
him, but strengthened him not.
21 For Ahaz took away a portion *out*
of the house of the LORD, and *out* of the
house of the king, and of the princes,
and gave *it* unto the king of Assyria: but
he helped him not.
22 And in the time of his distress
did he trespass[4603] yet more against the
LORD: this *is that* king Ahaz.
23 For [a]he sacrificed unto the gods[430]
of [I]Damascus, which smote him: and he
said, Because the gods of the kings of
Syria help them, *therefore* will I sacrifice
to them, that [b]they may help me. But they
were the ruin of him, and of all Israel.
24 And Ahaz gathered together[622]
the vessels of the house of God, and cut
in pieces the vessels of the house of God,
[a]and shut up the doors of the house of
the LORD, and he made him altars[4196] in
every corner of Jerusalem.
25 And in every several city of
Judah he made high places [I]to burn incense unto other gods, and provoked to
anger[3707] the LORD God of his fathers.
26 [a]Now the rest of his acts[1697] and
of all his ways, first[7223] and last, behold,
they *are* written in the book[5612] of the
kings of Judah and Israel.
27 And Ahaz slept with his fathers,
and they buried[6912] him in the city, *even*
in Jerusalem: but they brought him not
into the sepulchres[6913] of the kings of
Israel: and Hezekiah his son reigned in
his stead.

9 [b]Ezra 9:6; Rev. 18:5
10 [a]Lev. 25:39, 42, 43, 46
11 [a]James 2:13
15 [a]2Chr. 28:12 [b]2Kgs. 6:22; Prov. 25:21, 22; Luke 6:27; Rom. 12:20 [c]Deut. 34:3; Judg. 1:16
16 [a]2Kgs. 16:7
17 [I]Hebr. *a captivity*
18 [a]Ezek. 16:27, 57
19 [a]2Chr. 21:2 [b]Ex. 32:25
20 [a]2Kgs. 15:29; 16:7-9
23 [I]Hebr. *Darmesek* [a]2Chr. 25:14 [b]Jer. 44:17, 18
24 [a]2Chr. 29:3, 7
25 [I]Or, *to offer*
26 [a]2Kgs. 16:19, 20

🗝 **28:15** Anointing was sometimes used for medicinal purposes. They could have used oil (Ex. 30:25; Is. 1:6), balm (Jer. 8:22; 46:11; 51:8), wine (Luke 10:34), or salve (Rev. 3:18). See note on James 5:14, 15.

Hezekiah Rules Judah

29 Hezekiah [a]began to reign *when he was* five and twenty years old, and he reigned nine and twenty years in Jerusalem. And his mother's name *was* Abijah, the daughter [b]of Zechariah.

2 And he did[6213] *that which was* right in the sight of the LORD, according to all that David his father had done.

Hezekiah's Temple Reforms

3 He in the first[7223] year of his reign, in the first month, [a]opened the doors of the house of the LORD, and repaired them.

4 And he brought in the priests and the Levites, and gathered them together[622] into the east street,[7339]

5 And said unto them, Hear me, ye Levites, [a]sanctify now yourselves, and sanctify the house of the LORD God[430] of your fathers,[1] and carry forth the filthiness out of the holy *place.*

6 For our fathers have trespassed, and done *that which was* evil[7451] in the eyes of the LORD our God, and have forsaken[5800] him, and have [a]turned away their faces from the habitation of the LORD, and [I]turned *their* backs.

7 [a]Also they have shut up the doors of the porch, and put out the lamps,[5216] and have not burned[6999] incense[7004] nor offered burnt offerings in the holy *place* unto the God of Israel.

8 Wherefore the [a]wrath[7110] of the LORD was upon Judah and Jerusalem, and he hath delivered them to [I][b]trouble, to astonishment,[8074] and to [c]hissing, as ye see with your eyes.

9 For, lo, [a]our fathers have fallen[5307] by the sword, and our sons and our daughters and our wives[802] *are* in captivity[7628] for this.

10 Now *it is* in mine heart to make [a]a covenant[1285] with the LORD God of Israel, that his fierce wrath may turn away from us.

11 My sons, [I]be not now negligent:[7952] for the LORD hath [a]chosen you to stand before him, to serve him, and that ye should minister unto him, and [II]burn incense.[6999]

12 Then the Levites arose, Mahath the son of Amasai, and Joel the son of Azariah, of the sons of the Kohathites: and of the sons of Merari, Kish the son of Abdi, and Azariah the son of Jehalelel: and of the Gershonites; Joah the son of Zimmah, and Eden the son of Joah:

13 And of the sons of Elizaphan; Shimri, and Jeiel: and of the sons of Asaph; Zechariah, and Mattaniah:

14 And of the sons of Heman; Jehiel, and Shimei: and of the sons of Jeduthun; Shemaiah, and Uzziel.

15 And they gathered their brethren,[251] and [a]sanctified themselves, and came, according to the commandment[4687] of the king,[4428] [I][b]by the words[1697] of the LORD, [c]to cleanse[2891] the house of the LORD.

16 And the priests went into the inner part of the house of the LORD, to cleanse *it,* and brought out all the uncleanness[2932] that they found in the temple of the LORD into the court of the house of the LORD. And the Levites took *it,* to carry *it* out abroad into the brook Kidron.

17 Now they began on the first *day* of the first month to sanctify, and on the eighth day[3117] of the month came they to the porch of the LORD: so they sanctified the house of the LORD in eight days; and in the sixteenth day of the first month they made an end.[3615]

18 Then they went in to Hezekiah the king, and said, We have cleansed all the house of the LORD, and the altar[4196] of burnt offering, with all the vessels thereof, and the shewbread table, with all the vessels thereof.

19 Moreover all the vessels, which king Ahaz in his reign did [a]cast away in his transgression,[4604] have we prepared and sanctified, and, behold, they *are* before the altar of the LORD.

20 Then Hezekiah the king rose early, and gathered the rulers of the city, and went up to the house of the LORD.

1 [a]2Kgs. 18:1 [b]2Chr. 26:5

3 [a]2Chr. 28:24; 2Chr. 29:7

5 [a]1Chr. 15:12; 2Chr. 35:6

6 [I]Hebr. *given the neck* [a]Jer. 2:27; Ezek. 8:16

7 [a]2Chr. 28:24

8 [I]Hebr. *commotion* [a]Deut. 28:25 [b]2Chr. 24:18 [c]1Kgs. 9:8; Jer. 18:16; 19:8; 25:9, 18; 29:18

9 [a]2Chr. 28:5, 6, 8, 17

10 [a]2Chr. 15:12

11 [I]Or, *be not now deceived* [II]Or, *offer sacrifice* [a]Num. 3:6; 8:14; 18:2, 6

15 [I]Or, *in the business of the LORD* [a]2Chr. 29:5 [b]2Chr. 30:12 [c]1Chr. 23:28

19 [a]2Chr. 28:24

🔑 21 And they brought seven bullocks,
and seven rams, and seven lambs, and
seven he goats, for a [a]sin offering for the
kingdom, and for the sanctuary, and for
Judah. And he commanded[559] the priests
the sons of Aaron to offer *them* on the
altar of the LORD.
22 So they killed[7819] the bullocks,
and the priests received the blood,[1818]
and [a]sprinkled *it* on the altar: likewise,
when they had killed the rams, they
sprinkled the blood upon the altar: they
killed also the lambs, and they sprinkled
the blood upon the altar.
23 And they brought [I]forth[5066] the
he goats *for* the sin offering before the
king and the congregation; and they laid
their [a]hands upon them:
24 And the priests killed them, and
they made reconciliation[2398] with their
blood upon the altar, [a]to make an atonement[3722] for all Israel: for the king commanded *that* the burnt offering and the
sin offering *should be made* for all Israel.
🔑 25 [a]And he set the Levites in the
house of the LORD with cymbals, with
psalteries, and with harps, [b]according to
the commandment of David, and of [c]Gad
the king's seer, and Nathan the prophet:
[d]for *so was* the commandment [I]of the
LORD [II]by his prophets.
26 And the Levites stood with the instruments [a]of David, and the priests with
[b]the trumpets.
27 And Hezekiah commanded to
offer the burnt offering upon the altar.
And [I]when the burnt offering[5930] began,
[a]the song of the LORD began *also* with
the trumpets, and with the [II]instruments
ordained by David king of Israel.
28 And all the congregation[6951]
worshipped,[7812] and the [I]singers sang,
and the trumpeters sounded: *and* all *this*
continued until the burnt offering was
finished.[3615]
29 And when they had made an end
of offering, [a]the king and all that were
[I]present with him bowed[3766] themselves,
and worshipped.
🔑 30 Moreover Hezekiah the king and
the princes commanded the Levites to
sing praise[1984] unto the LORD with the
words of David, and of Asaph the seer.
And they sang praises with gladness,
and they bowed their heads and worshipped.
31 Then Hezekiah answered and
said, Now ye have [I][a]consecrated yourselves unto the LORD, come near[5066] and
bring sacrifices and [b]thank offerings into
the house of the LORD. And the congregation brought in sacrifices and thank offerings; and as many as were of a free
heart burnt offerings.
32 And the number of the burnt offerings, which the congregation brought,
was threescore and ten bullocks, an hundred rams, *and* two hundred lambs: all
these *were* for a burnt offering to the
LORD.
33 And the consecrated things[6944]
were six hundred oxen and three thousand sheep.
🔑 34 But the priests were too few, so
that they could not flay[6584] all the burnt
offerings: wherefore [a]their brethren the
Levites [I]did help them, till the work[4399]
was ended,[3615] and until the *other* priests
had sanctified themselves: [b]for the Levites
were more [c]upright[3477] in heart to sanctify themselves than the priests.
35 And also the burnt offerings *were*

21 [a]Lev. 4:3, 14
22 [a]Lev. 8:14, 15, 19, 24; Heb. 9:21
23 [I]Hebr. *near* [a]Lev. 4:15, 24
24 [a]Lev. 14:20
25 [I]Hebr. *by the hand of the LORD* [II]Hebr. *by the hand of* [a]1Chr. 16:4; 25:6 [b]1Chr. 23:5; 25:1; 2Chr. 8:14 [c]2Sam. 24:11 [d]2Chr. 30:12
26 [a]1Chr. 23:5; Amos 6:5 [b]Num. 10:8, 10; 1Chr. 15:24; 16:6
27 [I]Hebr. *in the time* [II]Hebr. *hands of instruments* [a]2Chr. 23:18
28 [I]Hebr. *song*
29 [I]Hebr. *found* [a]2Chr. 20:18
31 [I]Or, *filled your hand* [a]2Chr. 13:9 [b]Lev. 7:12
34 [I]Hebr. *strengthened them* [a]2Chr. 35:11 [b]2Chr. 30:3 [c]Ps. 7:10

🔑 **29:21** Hezekiah did not want the priests to offer sacrifices on any of the false altars, like those of Ahaz (2 Chr. 28:24).

🔑 **29:25** This verse states a principle of inspiration: God is the true Source who speaks through an agent, such as a prophet, a writer, or a king (Jer. 1:2–9; Amos 3:7; Acts 1:16; Heb. 1:1; 2 Pet. 1:21). The use of a human agent does not reduce the authority of the statement.

🔑 **29:30** David and Asaph were the two principal authors of the Book of Psalms. David was the one who appointed Asaph to conduct regular praising of God with music (1 Chr. 16:5, 37).

🔑 **29:34** For long periods of time, neither the Levites nor the priests received enough support from tithes and offerings to sustain them and their families. Consequently, many had to find other work, and the number of active priests was decreasing.

in abundance, with [a]the fat of the peace offerings, and [b]the drink offerings for *every* burnt offering. So the service of the house of the LORD was set in order.

36 And Hezekiah rejoiced, and all the people,[5971] that God had prepared the people: for the thing was *done* suddenly.

Hezekiah Celebrates the Passover

30 And Hezekiah sent to all Israel and Judah, and wrote letters also to Ephraim and Manasseh, that they should come to the house of the LORD at Jerusalem, to keep[6213] the passover[6453] unto the LORD God[430] of Israel.

🗝 2 For the king[4428] had taken counsel,[3289] and his princes, and all the congregation in Jerusalem, to keep the passover in the second [a]month.

3 For they could not keep it [a]at that time, [b]because the priests had not sanctified themselves sufficiently, neither had the people[5971] gathered themselves together[622] to Jerusalem.

4 And the thing [I]pleased the king and all the congregation.

5 So they established a decree to make proclamation throughout all Israel, from Beer–sheba even to Dan, that they should come to keep the passover unto the LORD God of Israel at Jerusalem: for they had not done[6213] *it* of a long *time in such sort* as it was written.

6 So the posts went with the letters [I]from the king and his princes throughout all Israel and Judah, and according to the commandment[4687] of the king, saying, Ye children[1121] of Israel, [a]turn again unto the LORD God of Abraham, Isaac, and Israel, and he will return to the remnant of you, that are escaped[6413] out of the hand of [b]the kings of Assyria.

7 And be not ye [a]like your fathers,[1] and like your brethren,[251] which trespassed against the LORD God of their fathers, *who* therefore [b]gave them up to desolation, as ye see.

8 Now [I]be ye not [a]stiffnecked, as your fathers *were, but* [IIb]yield yourselves unto the LORD, and enter into his sanctuary, which he hath sanctified for ever: and serve the LORD your God, [c]that the fierceness[2740] of his wrath may turn away from you.

9 For if ye turn again unto the LORD, your brethren and your children *shall find* [a]compassion[7356] before them that lead them captive,[7617] so that they shall come again into this land:[776] for the LORD your God *is* [b]gracious[2587] and merciful, and will not turn away *his* face from you, if ye [c]return unto him.

10 So the posts passed[5674] from city to city through the country of Ephraim and Manasseh even unto Zebulun: but [a]they laughed them to scorn, and mocked them.

🗝 11 Nevertheless [a]divers[582] of Asher and Manasseh and of Zebulun humbled themselves, and came to Jerusalem.

12 Also in Judah [a]the hand of God was to give them one heart to do[6213] the commandment of the king and of the princes, [b]by the word[1697] of the LORD.

13 And there assembled[622] at Jerusalem much people to keep the feast[2282] of unleavened bread[4682] in the second month, a very great congregation.

14 And they arose and took away the [a]altars[4196] that *were* in Jerusalem, and all the altars for incense[6999] took they away, and cast *them* into the brook Kidron.

15 Then they killed[7819] the passover on the fourteenth *day* of the second month: and the priests and the Levites were [a]ashamed, and sanctified themselves, and brought in the burnt offerings into the house of the LORD.

16 And they stood in [I]their place

---

35 [a]Lev. 3:16 [b]Num. 15:5, 7, 10

2 [a]Num. 9:10, 11

3 [a]Ex. 12:6, 18 [b]2Chr. 29:34

4 [I]Hebr. *was right in the eyes of the king*

6 [I]Hebr. *from the hand* [a]Jer. 4:1; Joel 2:13 [b]2Kgs. 15:19, 29

7 [a]Ezek. 20:18 [b]2Chr. 29:8

8 [I]Hebr. *harden not your necks* [II]Hebr. *give the hand* [a]Deut. 10:16 [b]1Chr. 29:24; Ezra 10:19 [c]2Chr. 29:10

9 [a]Ps. 106:46 [b]Ex. 34:6 [c]Isa. 55:7

10 [a]2Chr. 36:16

11 [a]2Chr. 11:16; 2Chr. 30:18, 21

12 [a]Phil. 2:13 [b]2Chr. 29:25

14 [a]2Chr. 28:24

15 [a]2Chr. 29:34

16 [I]Hebr. *their standing*

🗝 **30:2** The Passover was not kept the first month, as prescribed in the Law of Moses (Ex. 12:18), because the temple was in the process of being cleansed (2 Chr. 29:17). However, this exception was allowed by Numbers 9:9–11.

🗝 **30:11** Humility must precede access to God (cf. Is. 57:15; Luke 18:13, 14).

after their manner, according to the law[8451] of Moses the man of God: the priests sprinkled the blood,[1818] *which they received* of the hand of the Levites.

17 For *there were* many in the congregation that were not sanctified: [a]therefore the Levites had the charge of the killing of the passovers[6453] for every one *that was* not clean,[2889] to sanctify *them* unto the LORD.

18 For a multitude of the people, *even* [a]many of Ephraim, and Manasseh, Issachar, and Zebulun, had not cleansed[2891] themselves, [b]yet did they eat the passover otherwise than it was written. But Hezekiah prayed[6419] for them, saying, the good[2896] LORD pardon[3722] every one

🗝 19 *That* [a]prepareth his heart to seek God, the LORD God of his fathers, though *he be* not *cleansed* according to the purification of the sanctuary.

20 And the LORD hearkened to Hezekiah, and healed the people.

21 And the children of Israel that were [I]present at Jerusalem kept[6213] [a]the feast of unleavened bread seven days[3117] with great gladness: and the Levites and the priests praised[1984] the LORD day by day, *singing* with [II]loud instruments unto the LORD.

🗝 22 And Hezekiah spake [I]comfortably[5921,3820] unto all the Levites [a]that taught the good knowledge of the LORD: and they did eat throughout the feast seven days, offering peace offerings, and [b]making confession[3034] to the LORD God of their fathers.

23 And the whole assembly[6951] took counsel to keep [a]other seven days: and they kept *other* seven days with gladness.

24 For Hezekiah king of Judah [Ia]did give to the congregation a thousand bullocks and seven thousand sheep; and the princes gave to the congregation a thousand bullocks and ten thousand sheep: and a great number of priests [b]sanctified themselves.

25 And all the congregation of Judah, with the priests and the Levites, and all the congregation [a]that came out of Israel, and the strangers[1616] that came out of the land of Israel, and that dwelt in Judah, rejoiced.

26 So there was great joy in Jerusalem: for since the time of Solomon the son of David king of Israel *there was* not the like in Jerusalem.

27 Then the priests the Levites arose and [a]blessed[1288] the people: and their voice was heard, and their prayer[8605] came *up* to [Ib]his holy dwelling place, *even* unto heaven.

Religious Reforms Continue

31 Now when all this was finished,[3615] all Israel that were [I]present went out to the cities of Judah, and [a]brake the [IIb]images[4676] in pieces, and cut down the groves,[842] and threw down the high places and the altars[4196] out of all Judah and Benjamin, in Ephraim also and Manasseh, [III]until they had utterly destroyed them all. Then all the children[1121] of Israel returned, every man to his possession,[272] into their own cities.

Hezekiah Provides for the Priests And Levites

2 And Hezekiah appointed [a]the courses of the priests and the Levites after their courses, every man according to his service, the priests and Levites [b]for burnt offerings and for peace offerings, to minister, and to give thanks, and to praise[1984] in the gates of the tents of the LORD.

3 *He appointed* also the king's[4428] portion of his substance for the burnt offerings, *to wit,* for the morning and

17 [a]2Chr. 29:34

18 [a]2Chr. 30:11 [b]Ex. 12:43

19 [a]2Chr. 19:3

21 [I]Hebr. *found* [II]Hebr. *instruments of strength* [a]Ex. 12:15; 13:6

22 [I]Hebr. *to the heart of all,* Isa. 40:2 [a]Deut. 33:10; 2Chr. 17:9; 35:3 [b]Ezra 10:11

23 [a]1Kgs. 8:65

24 [I]Hebr. *lifted up,* or, *offered* [a]2Chr. 35:7, 8 [b]2Chr. 29:34

25 [a]2Chr. 30:11, 18

27 [I]Hebr. *the habitation of his holiness* [a]Num. 6:23 [b]Ps. 68:5

1 [I]Hebr. *found* [II]Hebr. *statues* [III]Hebr. *until to make an end* [a]2Kgs. 13:4 [b]2Chr. 30:14

2 [a]1Chr. 23:6; 24:1 [b]1Chr. 23:30, 31

🗝 **30:19** This action by Hezekiah clearly stresses the spirit of the Law, not merely the letter of the Law (cf. Matt. 23:23; Luke 14:1–6).

🗝 **30:22** The feasts and offerings conducted at this time followed the instructions given in Exodus 12:16–18.

evening burnt offerings, and the burnt offerings for the sabbaths, and for the new moons, and for the set feasts,[4150] as *it is* written in the [a]law[8451] of the LORD.

⊶ 4 Moreover he commanded[559] the people[5971] that dwelt in Jerusalem to give the [a]portion of the priests and the Levites, that they might be encouraged[2388] in [b]the law of the LORD.

5 And as soon as the commandment[1697] [I]came abroad, the children of Israel brought in abundance [a]the firstfruits[7225] of corn, wine, and oil, and [II]honey, and of all the increase of the field;[7704] and the tithe of all *things* brought they in abundantly.

6 And *concerning* the children of Israel and Judah, that dwelt in the cities of Judah, they also brought in the tithe of oxen and sheep, and the [a]tithe of holy things which were consecrated unto the LORD their God,[430] and laid *them* [I]by heaps.

7 In the third month they began to lay the foundation[3245] of the heaps, and finished *them* in the seventh month.

8 And when Hezekiah and the princes came and saw the heaps, they blessed[1288] the LORD, and his people Israel.

9 Then Hezekiah questioned[1875] with the priests and the Levites concerning the heaps.

10 And Azariah the chief[7218] priest of the house of Zadok answered[559] him, and said, [a]Since *the people* began to bring the offerings into the house of the LORD, we have had enough to eat, and have left[3498] plenty: for the LORD hath blessed his people; and that which is left *is* this great store.

11 Then Hezekiah commanded to prepare [I]chambers in the house of the LORD; and they prepared *them,*

12 And brought in the offerings and the tithes and the dedicated[6944] *things* faithfully:[530] [a]over which Cononiah the Levite *was* ruler, and Shimei his brother[251] *was* the next.

13 And Jehiel, and Azaziah, and Nahath, and Asahel, and Jerimoth, and Jozabad, and Eliel, and Ismachiah, and Manath, and Benaiah, *were* overseers [I]under the hand of Cononiah and Shimei his brother, at the commandment[4662] of Hezekiah the king, and Azariah the ruler of the house of God.

14 And Kore the son of Imnah the Levite, the porter[7778] toward the east, *was* over the freewill offerings of God, to distribute the oblations[8641] of the LORD, and the most holy things.

15 And [I]next him *were* Eden, and Miniamin, and Jeshua, and Shemaiah, Amariah, and Shecaniah, in [a]the cities of the priests, in *their* [II][b]set office, to give to their brethren by courses, as well to the great as to the small:

16 Beside their genealogy of males, from three years old and upward, *even* unto every one that entereth into the house of the LORD, his daily[3117] portion[1697] for their service in their charges according to their courses;

17 Both to the genealogy[3187] of the priests by the house of their fathers,[1] and the Levites [a]from twenty years old and upward, in their charges by their courses;

18 And to the genealogy of all their little ones, their wives,[802] and their sons, and their daughters, through all the congregation: for in their [I]set office they sanctified themselves in holiness:

19 Also of the sons of Aaron the priests, *which were* in [a]the fields[7704] of the suburbs of their cities, in every several city, the men that were [b]expressed[5344] by name, to give portions to all the males among the priests, and to all that were reckoned by genealogies among the Levites.

20 And thus did[6213] Hezekiah

3 [a]Num. 28, 29
4 [a]Num. 18:8; Neh. 13:10 [b]Mal. 2:7
5 [I]Hebr. *broke forth* [II]Or, *dates* [a]Ex. 22:29; Neh. 13:12
6 [I]Hebr. *heaps, heaps* [a]Lev. 27:30; Deut. 14:28
10 [a]Mal. 3:10
11 [I]Or, *storehouses*
12 [a]Neh. 13:13
13 [I]Hebr. *at the hand*
15 [I]Hebr. *at his hand* [II]Or, *trust,* [a]Josh. 21:9 [b]1Chr. 9:22
17 [a]1Chr. 23:24, 27
18 [I]Or, *trust*
19 [a]Lev. 25:34; Num. 35:2 [b]2Chr. 31:12-15

⊶ **31:4** The priests and the Levites depended on the gifts of the people for their livelihood (Num. 18:12, 21, 24). Therefore, in times of backsliding, the priests and Levites were tempted to use other means to make a living (Judg. 17:10; 18:19). It was essential to restore proper tithing for a consecrated priesthood.

throughout all Judah, and [a]wrought *that which was* good[2896] and right and truth before the LORD his God.

21 And in every work that he began in the service of the house of God, and in the law, and in the commandments,[4687] to seek his God, he did *it* with all his heart, and prospered.

Sennacherib Threatens Jerusalem

32 After [a]these things, and the establishment[571] thereof, Sennacherib king[4428] of Assyria came, and entered into Judah, and encamped against the fenced cities, and thought [I]to win them for himself.

2 And when Hezekiah saw that Sennacherib was come, and that [I]he was purposed to fight against Jerusalem,

3 He took counsel[3289] with his princes and his mighty men to stop the waters of the fountains which *were* without the city: and they did help him.

4 So there was gathered[6908] much people[5971] together,[6908] who stopped all the fountains, and the brook that [I]ran through the midst of the land,[776] saying, Why should the kings of Assyria come, and find much water?

🗝 5 Also [a]he strengthened himself, [b]and built up all the wall that was broken, and raised *it* up to the towers, and another wall without, and repaired [c]Millo *in* the city of David, and made [I]darts[7973] and shields in abundance.

6 And he set captains[8269] of war over the people, and gathered them together to him in the street of the gate of the city, and [I][a]spake comfortably[3824,5921] to them, saying,

7 [a]Be strong and courageous, [b]be not afraid[3372] nor dismayed[2865] for the king of Assyria, nor for all the multitude that *is* with him: for [c]*there be* more with us than with him:

8 With him *is* an [a]arm of flesh;[1320] but [b]with us *is* the LORD our God[430] to help us, and to fight our battles. And the people [I]rested themselves[5564] upon the words[1697] of Hezekiah king of Judah.

9 [a]After this did Sennacherib king of Assyria send his servants to Jerusalem, (but he *himself laid siege* against Lachish, and all his [I]power[4475] with him,) unto Hezekiah king of Judah, and unto all Judah that *were* at Jerusalem, saying,

10 [a]Thus saith Sennacherib king of Assyria, Whereon do ye trust, that ye abide [I]in the siege in Jerusalem?

11 Doth not Hezekiah persuade you to give over yourselves to die[4191] by famine and by thirst, saying, [a]The LORD our God shall deliver[5337] us out of the hand of the king of Assyria?

12 [a]Hath not the same Hezekiah taken away his high places and his altars,[4196] and commanded[559] Judah and Jerusalem, saying, Ye shall worship[7812] before one altar,[4196] and burn incense[6999] upon it?

13 Know[3045] ye not what I and my fathers[1] have done[6213] unto all the people of *other* lands?[776] [a]were the gods[430] of the nations[1471] of those lands any ways[1870] able to deliver their lands out of mine hand?

14 Who *was there* among all the gods of those nations that my fathers utterly destroyed,[2763] that could deliver his people out of mine hand, that your God should be able to deliver you out of mine hand?

15 Now therefore [a]let not Hezekiah deceive you, nor persuade you on this manner, neither yet believe[539] him: for no god[433] of any nation[1471] or kingdom[4467] was able to deliver his people out of mine hand, and out of the hand of my fathers: how much less shall your God deliver you out of mine hand?

16 And his servants spake yet *more* against the LORD God, and against his servant Hezekiah.

17 [a]He wrote also letters[5612] to rail[2778] on the LORD God of Israel, and to speak against him, saying, [b]As the gods of the nations of *other* lands have not

20 [a]2Kgs. 20:3

1 [I]Hebr. *to break them up* [a]2Kgs. 18:13; Isa. 36:1

2 [I]Hebr. *his face was to war*

4 [I]Hebr. *overflowed*

5 [I]Or, *swords, or, weapons* [a]Isa. 22:9, 10 [b]2Chr. 25:23 [c]2Sam. 5:9; 1Kgs. 9:24

6 [I]Hebr. *spake to their heart* [a]2Chr. 30:22; Isa. 40:2

7 [a]Deut. 31:6 [b]2Chr. 20:15 [c]2Kgs. 6:16

8 [I]Hebr. *leaned* [a]Jer. 17:5; 1John 4:4 [b]2Chr. 13:12; Rom. 8:31

9 [I]Hebr. *dominion* [a]2Kgs. 18:17

10 [I]Or, *in the stronghold* [a]2Kgs. 18:19

11 [a]2Kgs. 18:30

12 [a]2Kgs. 18:22

13 [a]2Kgs. 18:33-35

15 [a]2Kgs. 18:29

17 [a]2Kgs. 19:9 [b]2Kgs. 19:12

🗝 **32:5** See note on 2 Samuel 5:6–10 concerning the "Millo."

delivered[5337] their people out of mine hand, so shall not the God of Hezekiah deliver his people out of mine hand.

18 [a]Then they cried[7121] with a loud voice in the Jews' speech unto the people of Jerusalem [b]that *were* on the wall, to affright[3372] them, and to trouble[926] them; that they might take the city.

19 And they spake against the God of Jerusalem, as against the gods of the people of the earth,[776] *which were* [a]the work of the hands of man.

God Rescues Jerusalem

🔑 20 [a]And for this *cause* Hezekiah the king, and [b]the prophet Isaiah the son of Amoz, prayed[6419] and cried[2199] to heaven.

21 [a]And the LORD sent an angel,[4397] which cut off[3582] all the mighty men of valour,[2428] and the leaders and captains in the camp of the king of Assyria. So he returned with shame of face to his own land. And when he was come into the house of his god, they that came forth of his own bowels[4578] [I]slew him there with the sword.

22 Thus the LORD saved Hezekiah and the inhabitants of Jerusalem from the hand of Sennacherib the king of Assyria, and from the hand of all *other,* and guided them on every side.

23 And many brought gifts[4503] unto the LORD to Jerusalem, and [Ia]presents to Hezekiah king of Judah: so that he was [b]magnified in the sight of all nations from thenceforth.

Hezekiah Gets Sick

🔑 24 [a]In those days[3117] Hezekiah was sick to the death,[4191] and prayed unto the LORD: and he spake unto him, and he [I]gave him a sign.

25 But Hezekiah [a]rendered not again according to the benefit *done* unto him; for [b]his heart was lifted up: [c]therefore there was wrath[7110] upon him, and upon Judah and Jerusalem.

26 [a]Notwithstanding Hezekiah humbled himself for [I]the pride[1363] of his heart, *both* he and the inhabitants of Jerusalem, so that the wrath of the LORD came not upon them [b]in the days of Hezekiah.

Hezekiah Prospers

27 And Hezekiah had exceeding much riches and honour: and he made himself treasuries for silver, and for gold, and for precious stones, and for spices, and for shields, and for all manner of [I]pleasant jewels;

28 Storehouses also for the increase of corn, and wine, and oil; and stalls for all manner of beasts, and cotes for flocks.

29 Moreover he provided him cities, and possessions of flocks and herds in abundance: for [a]God had given him substance very much.

🔑 30 [a]This same Hezekiah also stopped the upper[5945] watercourse of Gihon, and brought it straight down to the west side of the city of David. And Hezekiah prospered in all his works.

31 Howbeit in *the business of* the [I]ambassadors[3887] of the princes of Babylon, who [a]sent unto him to enquire of the wonder that was *done* in the land, God left[5800] him, to [b]try[5254] him, that he might know all *that was* in his heart.

Hezekiah's Death

🔑 32 Now the rest of the acts[1697] of Hezekiah, and his [I]goodness,[2617] behold, they *are* written in the vision[2377] of

18 [a]2Kgs. 18:28 [b]2Kgs. 18:26-28
19 [a]2Kgs. 19:18
20 [a]2Kgs. 19:15 [b]2Kgs. 19:2, 4
21 [I]Hebr. *made him fall* [a]2Kgs. 19:35
23 [I]Hebr. *precious things* [a]2Chr. 17:5 [b]2Chr. 1:1
24 [I]Or, *wrought a miracle for him* [a]2Kgs. 20:1 [b]Isa. 38:1
25 [a]Ps. 116:12; 2Chr. 26:16; Hab. 2:4 [b]2Chr. 24:18
26 [I]Hebr. *the lifting up* [a]Jer. 26:18, 19 [b]2Kgs. 20:19
27 [I]Hebr. *instruments of desire*
29 [a]1Chr. 29:12
30 [a]Isa. 22:9, 11
31 [I]Hebr. *interpreters* [a]2Kgs. 20:12; Isa. 39:1 [b]Deut. 8:2
32 [I]Hebr. *kindnesses*

🔑 **32:20–23** This is a practical example of how "righteousness exalteth a nation" (Prov. 14:34).
🔑 **32:24** The "sign" which was given to Hezekiah refers to the shadow on the sundial going backward ten degrees (see 2 Kgs. 20:8–11; Is. 38:7, 8).
🔑 **32:30** See note on 2 Kings 20:20 concerning the pool of Siloam.
🔑 **32:32, 33** This passage may suggest that Isaiah wrote portions of 2 Kings. Another possibility is that this refers to two different sources, Isaiah itself (chaps. 36–39) and the Book of 2 Kings. In

(continued on next page)

Isaiah the prophet, the son of Amoz, *and* in the [a]book[5612] of the kings of Judah and Israel.

33 [a]And Hezekiah slept with his fathers, and they buried[6912] him in the [I]chiefest of the sepulchres[6913] of the sons of David: and all Judah and the inhabitants of Jerusalem did him [b]honour at his death. And Manasseh his son reigned in his stead.

Manasseh Rules Judah

33 Manasseh [a]*was* twelve years old when he began to reign, and he reigned fifty and five years in Jerusalem:

2 But did[6213] *that which was* evil[7451] in the sight of the LORD, like unto the [a]abominations[8441] of the heathen, whom the LORD had cast out[3423] before the children[1121] of Israel.

3 For [I]he built again the high places which Hezekiah his father had [a]broken down, and he reared up altars[4196] for Baalim, and [b]made groves,[842] and worshipped[7812] [c]all the host of heaven, and served them.

4 Also he built altars in the house of the LORD, whereof the LORD had said, [a]In Jerusalem shall my name be for ever.

5 And he built altars for all the host of heaven [a]in the two courts of the house of the LORD.

6 [a]And he caused his children to pass through the fire in the valley of the son of Hinnom: [b]also he observed times, and used enchantments,[5172] and used witchcraft, and [c]dealt[6213] with a familiar spirit, and with wizards:[3049] he wrought much evil in the sight of the LORD, to provoke him to anger.[3707]

7 And [a]he set a carved image, the idol[5566] which he had made, in the house of God,[430] of which God had said to David and to Solomon his son, In [b]this house, and in Jerusalem, which I have chosen before all the tribes of Israel, will I put my name for ever:

8 [a]Neither will I any more remove the foot of Israel from out of the land[127] which I have appointed for your fathers; so that they will take heed[8104] to do all that I have commanded[6680] them, according to the whole law[8451] and the statutes and the ordinances by the hand of Moses.

9 So Manasseh made Judah and the inhabitants of Jerusalem to err,[8582] *and* to do worse[7451] than the heathen, whom the LORD had destroyed[8045] before the children of Israel.

10 And the LORD spake to Manasseh, and to his people:[5971] but they would not hearken.

11 [a]Wherefore the LORD brought upon them the captains[8269] of the host [I]of the king[4428] of Assyria, which took Manasseh among the thorns, and [b]bound him with [II]fetters, and carried him to Babylon.

12 And when he was in affliction, he besought the LORD his God, and [a]humbled himself greatly before the God of his fathers,

13 And prayed[6419] unto him: and he was [a]intreated[6279] of him, and heard his supplication, and brought him again to Jerusalem into his kingdom.[4438] Then Manasseh [b]knew[3045] that the LORD he *was* God.

14 Now after this he built a wall without the city of David, on the west side of [a]Gihon, in the valley, even to the entering in at the fish[1709] gate, and compassed [b]about [I]Ophel, and raised it up a very great height, and put captains of war in all the fenced cities of Judah.

15 And he took away [a]the strange[5236] gods,[430] and the idol out of the house of the LORD, and all the altars that he had built in the mount of the house of the LORD, and in Jerusalem, and cast *them* out of the city.

32 [a]2Kgs. 18:19, 20
33 [I]Or, *highest* [a]2Kgs. 20:21 [b]Prov. 10:7
1 [a]2Kgs. 21:1
2 [a]Deut. 18:9; 2Chr. 28:3
3 [I]Hebr. *he returned and built* [a]2Kgs. 18:4; 2Chr. 30:14; 31:1; 32:12 [b]Deut. 16:21 [c]Deut. 17:3
4 [a]Deut. 12:11; 1Kgs. 8:29; 9:3; 2Chr. 6:6; 7:16
5 [a]2Chr. 4:9
6 [a]Lev. 18:21; Deut. 18:10; 2Kgs. 23:10; 2Chr. 28:3; Ezek. 23:37, 39 [b]Deut. 18:10, 11 [c]2Kgs. 21:6
7 [a]2Kgs. 21:7 [b]Ps. 132:14
8 [a]2Sam. 7:10
11 [I]Hebr. *which were the king's* [II]Or, *chains* [a]Deut. 28:36 [b]Job 36:8; Ps. 107:10, 11
12 [a]1Pet. 5:6
13 [a]1Chr. 5:20; Ezra 8:23 [b]Ps. 9:16; Dan. 4:25
14 [I]Or, *The tower* [a]1Kgs. 1:33 [b]2Chr. 27:3
15 [a]2Chr. 33:3, 5, 7

(continued from previous page)
2 Kings 20:20, 21, there is a reference to the Book of Chronicles, which must have been added to the canon of Scripture later. The "book of the kings" may possibly refer to another chronicle which has been lost.

16 And he repaired the altar[4196] of
the LORD, and sacrificed thereon peace
offerings and [a]thank offerings, and
commanded[559] Judah to serve the LORD
God of Israel.
🗝 17 [a]Nevertheless the people did sacrifice still in the high places, *yet* unto the
LORD their God only.
18 Now the rest of the acts[1697] of
Manasseh, and his prayer[8605] unto his
God, and the words[1697] of [a]the seers that
spake to him in the name of the LORD
God of Israel, behold, they *are written* in
the book of the kings of Israel.
19 His prayer also, and *how God* was
intreated of him, and all his sins, and his
trespass, and the places wherein he built
high places, and set up groves and
graven images, before he was humbled:
behold, they *are* written among the sayings of the seers.
20 [a]So Manasseh slept[7901] with his
fathers, and they buried[6912] him in his
own house: and Amon his son reigned in
his stead.

Amon Rules Judah

21 [a]Amon *was* two and twenty years
old when he began to reign, and reigned
two years in Jerusalem.
22 But he did *that which was* evil
in the sight of the LORD, as did
Manasseh his father: for Amon sacrificed
unto all the carved images which
Manasseh his father[1] had made, and
served them;
23 And humbled not himself before
the LORD, [a]as Manasseh his father had
humbled himself; but Amon [I]trespassed
more and more.
24 [a]And his servants conspired
against him, and slew him in his own
house.
25 But the people of the land[776] slew
all them that had conspired against king
Amon; and the people of the land made
Josiah his son king[4427] in his stead.

16 [a]Lev. 7:12
17 [a]2Chr. 32:12
18 [a]1Sam. 9:9
20 [a]2Kgs. 21:18
21 [a]2Kgs. 21:19
23 [I]Hebr. *multiplied trespass* [a]2Chr. 33:12
24 [a]2Kgs. 21:23, 24
1 [a]2Kgs. 22:1
3 [a]2Chr. 15:2 [b]1Kgs. 13:2 [c]2Chr. 33:17, 22
4 [I]Or, *sun images* [II]Hebr. *face of the graves* [a]Lev. 26:30; 2Kgs. 23:4 [b]2Kgs. 23:6
5 [a]1Kgs. 13:2
7 [I]Hebr. *to make powder* [a]Deut. 9:21
8 [a]2Kgs. 22:3

Josiah Rules Judah

34 Josiah [a]*was* eight years old when
he began to reign, and he reigned
in Jerusalem one and thirty years.
2 And he did[6213] *that which was*
right in the sight of the LORD, and
walked in the ways[1870] of David his
father,[1] and declined[5493] *neither* to the
right hand, nor to the left.

Josiah Brings About Reforms

3 For in the eighth year of his reign,
while he was yet young, he began to
[a]seek[1875] after the God[430] of David his father: and in the twelfth year he began [b]to
purge Judah and Jerusalem [c]from the
high places, and the groves,[842] and the
carved images, and the molten images.
4 [a]And they brake down[5422] the
altars[4196] of Baalim in his presence; and
the [I]images,[2553] that *were* on high above
them, he cut down; and the groves, and
the carved images, and the molten images, he brake in pieces, and made dust
of them, [b]and strowed[2236] *it* upon the
[II]graves[6913] of them that had sacrificed
unto them.
5 And he [a]burnt[8313] the bones[6101] of
the priests upon their altars, and
cleansed[2891] Judah and Jerusalem.
6 And *so did he* in the cities of Manasseh, and Ephraim, and Simeon, even
unto Naphtali, with their mattocks[2719]
round about.
7 And when he had broken down the
altars and the groves, and had [a]beaten[3807]
the graven images [I]into powder, and cut
down all the idols[2553] throughout all the
land[776] of Israel, he returned to Jerusalem.

A Copy of the Law Is Found

8 Now [a]in the eighteenth year of his
reign, when he had purged the land, and
the house, he sent Shaphan the son of
Azaliah, and Maaseiah the governor[2587]

🗝 **33:17** This practice of sacrificing to the "high places" of the false gods was a pitfall for other kings: Asa (1 Kgs. 15:14) and even Solomon (1 Kgs. 3:3).

of the city, and Joah the son of Joahaz the recorder, to repair the house of the LORD his God.

9 And when they came to Hilkiah the high priest, they delivered [a]the money that was brought into the house of God, which the Levites that kept[8104] the doors had gathered[622] of the hand of Manasseh and Ephraim, and of all the remnant of Israel, and of all Judah and Benjamin; and they returned to Jerusalem.

10 And they put *it* in the hand of the workmen that had the oversight of the house of the LORD, and they gave it to the workmen that wrought in the house of the LORD, to repair and amend[2388] the house:

11 Even to the artificers[2796] and builders[1129] gave they *it,* to buy hewn[4274] stone, and timber for couplings, and [I]to floor the houses which the kings[4428] of Judah had destroyed.[7843]

12 And the men did the work[4399] faithfully:[530] and the overseers of them *were* Jahath and Obadiah, the Levites, of the sons of Merari; and Zechariah and Meshullam, of the sons of the Kohathites, to set *it* forward; and *other of* the Levites, all that could skill of instruments of musick.

13 Also *they were* over the bearers of burdens, and *were* overseers[5329] of all that wrought the work in any manner of service: [a]and of the Levites *there were* scribes, and officers, and porters.[7778]

14 And when they brought out the money that was brought into the house of the LORD, Hilkiah the priest [a]found a book[5612] of the law[8451] of the LORD *given* [I]by Moses.

15 And Hilkiah answered and said to Shaphan the scribe, I have found the book of the law in the house of the LORD. And Hilkiah delivered the book to Shaphan.

16 And Shaphan carried the book to the king, and brought the king word[1697] back again, saying, All that was committed [I]to thy servants, they do *it.*

17 And they have [I]gathered together the money that was found in the house of the LORD, and have delivered it into the hand of the overseers, and to the hand of the workmen.

18 Then Shaphan the scribe told the king, saying, Hilkiah the priest hath given me a book. And Shaphan read [I]it before the king.

🔑 19 And it came to pass, when the king had heard the words of the law, that he rent his clothes.

20 And the king commanded[6680] Hilkiah, and Ahikam the son of Shaphan, and [Ia]Abdon the son of Micah, and Shaphan the scribe, and Asaiah a servant of the king's, saying,

21 Go, enquire of the LORD for me, and for them that are left[7604] in Israel and in Judah, concerning the words of the book that is found: for great *is* the wrath[2534] of the LORD that is poured out upon us, because our fathers[1] have not kept the word of the LORD, to do after all that is written in this book.

22 And Hilkiah, and *they* that the king *had appointed,* went to Huldah the prophetess, the wife[802] of Shallum the son of [a]Tikvath, the son of [I]Hasrah, keeper[8104] of the [II]wardrobe; (now she dwelt in Jerusalem [III]in the college:) and they spake to her to that *effect.*

23 And she answered[559] them, Thus saith the LORD God of Israel, Tell ye the man that sent you to me,

24 Thus saith the LORD, Behold, I will bring evil[7451] upon this place, and upon the inhabitants thereof, *even* all the curses[423] that are written in the book which they have read before the king of Judah:

9 [a]2Kgs. 22:4

11 [I]Or, *to rafter*

13 [a]1Chr. 23:4, 5

14 [I]Hebr. *by the hand of* [a]2Kgs. 22:8

16 [I]Hebr. *to the hand of*

17 [I]Hebr. *poured out,* or, *melted*

18 [I]Hebr. *in it*

20 [I]Or, *Achbor* [a]2Kgs. 22:12

22 [I]Or, *Harhas* [II]Hebr. *garments* [III]Or, *in the school,* or, *in the second part* [a]2Kgs. 22:14

🔑 **34:19** Some suggest that this book given to Josiah was only the Book of Deuteronomy, but others contend that the text (v. 14) indicates that it was the whole Pentateuch (the first five books of the Old Testament). The latter is more accepted because the blessings and curses (Lev. 26 and Deut. 28), as well as the promises in Deuteronomy chapters twenty-nine and thirty, were instrumental in beginning Josiah's revival.

25 Because they have forsaken[5800] me, and have burned incense[6999] unto other gods,[430] that they might provoke me to anger[3707] with all the works of their hands; therefore my wrath shall be poured out upon this place, and shall not be quenched.

26 And as for the king of Judah, who sent you to enquire of the LORD, so shall ye say unto him, Thus saith the LORD God of Israel *concerning* the words which thou hast heard;

27 Because thine heart was tender, and thou didst humble thyself before God, when thou heardest his words against this place, and against the inhabitants thereof, and humbledst thyself before me, and didst rend[7167] thy clothes, and weep before me; I have even heard *thee* also, saith the LORD.

28 Behold, I will gather[622] thee to thy fathers, and thou shalt be gathered to thy grave[6913] in peace,[7965] neither shall thine eyes see all the evil that I will bring upon this place, and upon the inhabitants of the same. So they brought the king word again.

29 [a]Then the king sent and gathered together all the elders[2205] of Judah and Jerusalem.

30 And the king went up into the house of the LORD, and all the men of Judah, and the inhabitants of Jerusalem, and the priests, and the Levites, and all the people,[5971] [I]great and small: and he read in their ears[241] all the words of the book of the covenant[1285] that was found in the house of the LORD.

31 And the king stood in [a]his place, and made a covenant before the LORD, to walk after the LORD, and to keep[8104] his commandments,[4687] and his testimonies, and his statutes, with all his heart, and with all his soul, to perform[6213] the words of the covenant which are written in this book.

32 And he caused all that were [I]present in Jerusalem and Benjamin to stand *to it.* And the inhabitants of Jerusalem did according to the covenant of God, the God of their fathers.

33 And Josiah took away all the [a]abominations[8441] out of all the countries[776] that *pertained* to the children[1121] of Israel, and made all that were present in Israel to serve, *even* to serve the LORD their God. [b]*And* all his days[3117] they departed[5493] not [I]from following the LORD, the God of their fathers.

29 [a]2Kgs. 23:1

30 [I]Hebr. *from great even to small*

31 [a]2Kgs. 11:14; 23:3; 2Chr. 6:13

32 [I]Hebr. *found*

33 [I]Hebr. *from after* [a]1Kgs. 11:5 [b]Jer. 3:10

Josiah Celebrates the Passover

35 Moreover [a]Josiah kept[6213] a passover[6453] unto the LORD in Jerusalem: and they killed[7819] the passover on the [b]fourteenth *day* of the first[7223] month.

2 And he set the priests in their [a]charges, and [b]encouraged[2388] them to the service of the house of the LORD,

3 And said unto the Levites [a]that taught all Israel, which were holy unto the LORD, [b]Put the holy ark[727] [c]in the house which Solomon the son of David king[4428] of Israel did build; [d]*it shall* not *be* a burden[4853] upon *your* shoulders: serve now the LORD your God,[430] and his people[5971] Israel,

4 And prepare *yourselves* by the [a]houses of your fathers,[1] after your courses, according to the writing of

1 [a]2Kgs. 23:21, 22 [b]Ex. 12:6; Ezra 6:19

2 [a]2Chr. 23:18; Ezra 6:18 [b]2Chr. 29:5, 11

3 [a]Deut. 33:10; 2Chr. 30:22; Mal. 2:7 [b]2Chr. 34:14 [c]2Chr. 5:7 [d]1Chr. 23:26

4 [a]1Chr. 9:10

34:25 The phrase "works of their hands" is typical of language of contempt used to refer to idol making and worship (Deut. 4:28; 2 Chr. 32:19; Is. 40:18–21; 44:9–21; Dan. 5:23).

35:3 No mention is made of the ark after this order from Josiah that it be restored to the temple. It may have been carried away by King Nebuchadnezzar of Babylon along with the other sacred articles, when he plundered the temple in Jerusalem. Since no reference is made to the ark in the books of Ezra and Nehemiah, or even the writings of Josephus regarding the Babylonian Captivity, it is believed that there was no ark in the second temple and that the Holy of Holies stood empty. There is a Jewish tradition that, before Nebuchadnezzar plundered the temple, the priests hid the ark and its hiding place will be revealed by the Messiah at His coming. His knowledge of it will, they declare, be proof of His claims.

David king of Israel, and according to the [b]writing of Solomon his son.

5 And [a]stand in the holy *place* according to the divisions[6391] of [I]the families of the fathers of your brethren[251] [II]the people, and *after* the division of the families of the Levites.

6 So kill the passover, and [a]sanctify yourselves, and prepare your brethren, that *they* may do[6213] according to the word[1697] of the LORD by the hand of Moses.

7 And Josiah [I][a]gave to the people, of the flock, lambs and kids, all for the passover offerings, for all that were present, to the number of thirty thousand, and three thousand bullocks: these *were* of the king's substance.

8 And his princes [I]gave willingly[5071] unto the people, to the priests, and to the Levites: Hilkiah and Zechariah and Jehiel, rulers of the house of God, gave unto the priests for the passover offerings two thousand and six hundred *small cattle,* and three hundred oxen.

9 Conaniah also, and Shemaiah and Nethaneel, his brethren, and Hashabiah and Jeiel and Jozabad, chief[8269] of the Levites, [I]gave unto the Levites for passover offerings five thousand *small cattle,* and five hundred oxen.

10 So the service was prepared, and the priests [a]stood in their place, and the Levites in their courses, according to the king's commandment.[4687]

11 And they killed the passover, and the priests [a]sprinkled *the blood* from their hands, and the Levites [b]flayed[6584] *them.*

12 And they removed the burnt offerings, that they might give according to the divisions[4653] of the families of the people, to offer unto the LORD, as *it is* written [a]in the book[5612] of Moses. And so *did they* with the oxen.

13 And they [a]roasted the passover with fire according to the ordinance: but the *other* holy *offerings* [b]sod[1310] they in pots, and in caldrons, and in pans, and [I]divided *them* speedily among all the people.

14 And afterward they made ready for themselves, and for the priests: because the priests the sons of Aaron *were busied* in offering of burnt offerings and the fat until night;[3915] therefore the Levites prepared for themselves, and for the priests the sons of Aaron.

15 And the singers the sons of Asaph *were* in their [I]place, according to the [a]commandment of David, and Asaph, and Heman, and Jeduthun the king's seer; and the porters[7778] [b]*waited* at every gate; they might not depart[5493] from their service; for their brethren the Levites prepared for them.

16 So all the service of the LORD was prepared the same day,[3117] to keep[6213] the passover, and to offer burnt offerings upon the altar[4196] of the LORD, according to the commandment of king Josiah.

17 And the children[1121] of Israel that were [I]present kept the passover at that time, and the feast[2282] of [a]unleavened bread[4682] seven days.

18 And [a]there was no passover like to that kept in Israel from the days of Samuel the prophet; neither did all the kings of Israel keep such a passover as Josiah kept, and the priests, and the Levites, and all Judah and Israel that were present, and the inhabitants of Jerusalem.

19 In the eighteenth year of the reign of Josiah was this passover kept.

Josiah's Death

20 [a]After all this, when Josiah had prepared the [I]temple, Necho king of Egypt came up to fight against Carchemish by Euphrates: and Josiah went out against him.

21 But he sent ambassadors[4397] to

4 [b]2Chr. 8:14
5 [I]Hebr. *the house of the fathers* [II]Hebr. *the sons of the people* [a]Ps. 134:1
6 [a]2Chr. 29:5, 15; 30:3, 15; Ezra 6:20
7 [I]Hebr. *offered* [a]2Chr. 30:24
8 [I]Hebr. *offered*
9 [I]Hebr. *offered*
10 [a]Ezra 6:18
11 [a]2Chr. 29:22 [b]2Chr. 29:34
12 [a]Lev. 3:3
13 [I]Hebr. *made them run* [a]Ex. 12:8, 9; Deut. 16:7 [b]1Sam. 2:13-15
15 [I]Hebr. *station* [a]1Chr. 25:1 [b]1Chr. 9:17, 18; 26:14
17 [I]Hebr. *found* [a]Ex. 12:15; 13:6; 2Chr. 30:21
18 [a]2Kgs. 23:22, 23
20 [I]Hebr. *house* [a]2Kgs. 23:29; Jer. 46:2

35:12 Compare Hezekiah's Passover celebration (2 Chr. 30:15–18).

35:21 Babylon was fighting against and defeating Assyria. As a result, in 609 B.C. Assyria requested help from its ally Pharaoh Necho of Egypt. Josiah interfered, probably thinking that any

(continued on next page)

him, saying, What have I to do with thee, thou king of Judah? *I come* not against thee this day, but against [I]the house wherewith I have war: for God commanded[559] me to make haste: forbear thee from *meddling with* God, who *is* with me, that he destroy[7843] thee not.

22 Nevertheless Josiah would not turn his face from him, but [a]disguised himself, that he might fight with him, and hearkened not unto the words[1697] of Necho from the mouth of God, and came to fight in the valley of Megiddo.

23 And the archers[3384] shot at king Josiah; and the king said to his servants, Have me away; for I am sore [I][a]wounded.

24 [a]His servants therefore took him out of that chariot, and put him in the second chariot that he had; and they brought him to Jerusalem, and he died, and was buried[6912] [I]in *one of* the sepulchres[6913] of his fathers. And [b]all Judah and Jerusalem mourned for Josiah.

25 And Jeremiah [a]lamented for Josiah: and [b]all the singing men[7891] and the singing women spake of Josiah in their lamentations to this day, [c]and made them an ordinance in Israel: and, behold, they *are* written in the lamentations.

26 Now the rest of the acts[1697] of Josiah, and his [I]goodness,[2617] according to *that which was* written in the law[8451] of the LORD,

27 And his deeds,[1697] first and last, behold, they *are* written in the book of the kings of Israel and Judah.

Jehoahaz Rules Judah

36 Then [a]the people[5971] of the land[776] took Jehoahaz the son of Josiah, and made him king[4427] in his father's[1] stead in Jerusalem.

2 Jehoahaz *was* twenty and three years old when he began to reign, and he reigned three months in Jerusalem.

3 And the king[4428] of Egypt [I]put him down[5493] at Jerusalem, and [II]condemned[6064] the land in an hundred talents of silver and a talent of gold.

4 And the king of Egypt made Eliakim his brother[251] king over Judah and Jerusalem, and turned his name to Jehoiakim. And Necho took Jehoahaz his brother, and carried him to Egypt.

Jehoiakim Rules Judah

5 [a]Jehoiakim *was* twenty and five years old when he began to reign, and he reigned eleven years in Jerusalem: and he did *that which was* evil[7451] in the sight of the LORD his God.[430]

🗝 6 [a]Against him came up Nebuchadnezzar king of Babylon, and bound him in [I]fetters, to [b]carry him to Babylon.

7 [a]Nebuchadnezzar also carried of the vessels of the house of the LORD to Babylon, and put them in his temple at Babylon.

8 Now the rest of the acts[1697] of Jehoiakim, and his abominations[8441] which he did, and that which was found in him, behold, they *are* written in the book[5612] of the kings of Israel and Judah: and [a]Jehoiachin his son reigned in his stead.

Jehoiachin Is Taken to Babylon

9 [a]Jehoiachin *was* eight years old when he began to reign, and he reigned three months and ten days[3117] in Jerusa lem: and he did *that which was* evil in the sight of the LORD.

21 [I]Hebr. *the house of my war*
22 [a]1Kgs. 22:30
23 [I]Hebr. *made sick* [a]1Kgs. 22:34
24 [I]Or, *among the sepulchers* [a]2Kgs. 23:30 [b]Zech. 12:11
25 [a]Lam. 4:20 [b]Matt. 9:23 [c]Jer. 22:20
26 [I]Hebr. *kindnesses*
1 [a]2Kgs. 23:30
3 [I]Hebr. *removed him* [II]Hebr. *mulcted*
5 [a]2Kgs. 23:36, 37
6 [I]Or, *chains* [a]2Kgs. 24:1; Hab. 1:6 [b]2Kgs. 24:6; Jer. 22:18, 19; 36:30
7 [a]2Kgs. 24:13; Dan. 1:1, 2; 5:2
8 [a]1Chr. 3:16, Jeconiah; Jer. 22:24, Coniah
9 [a]2Kgs. 24:8

(continued from previous page)
friend of Assyria was his enemy. God chose to speak through a pagan king as He had done previously with regard to Abimelech and Abraham (Gen. 12:17–20; 20:3–7).

🗝 **36:6** Nebuchadnezzar defeated Pharaoh Necho at Carchemish (north of Judah) in 605 B.C. and subsequently conquered all of Syria and Palestine. Nebuchadnezzar bound King Jehoiakim in fetters, but for whatever reason, he was not carried back to Babylon (Dan. 1:2). Some suggest that when Nebuchadnezzar's father died suddenly, Nebuchadnezzar was in such a hurry to return to

(continued on next page)

10 And [I]when the year was expired, [a]king Nebuchadnezzar sent, and brought him to Babylon, [b]with the [II]goodly vessels of the house of the LORD, and made [III][c]Zedekiah his brother king over Judah and Jerusalem.

Zedekiah Rules Judah

11 [a]Zedekiah *was* one and twenty years old when he began to reign, and reigned eleven years in Jerusalem.

12 And he did *that which was* evil in the sight of the LORD his God, *and* humbled not himself before Jeremiah the prophet *speaking* from the mouth of the LORD.

13 And [a]he also rebelled against king Nebuchadnezzar, who had made him swear by God: but he [b]stiffened his neck, and hardened his heart from turning unto the LORD God of Israel.

14 Moreover all the chief[8267] of the priests, and the people, transgressed very much after all the abominations of the heathen; and polluted the house of the LORD which he had hallowed in Jerusalem.

15 [a]And the LORD God of their fathers sent to them [I]by his messengers, rising up [II]betimes,[7925] and sending; because he had compassion on his people, and on his dwelling place:

16 But [a]they mocked the messengers of God, and [b]despised his words,[1697] and [c]misused his prophets, until the [d]wrath[2534] of the LORD arose[5927] against his people, till *there was* no [I]remedy.[4832]

Judah Goes Into Exile

17 [a]Therefore he brought[5927] upon them the king of the Chaldees, who [b]slew their young men with the sword in the house of their sanctuary,[4720] and had no compassion upon young man or maiden, old man, or him that stooped for age: he gave *them* all into his hand.

18 [a]And all the vessels of the house of God, great and small, and the treasures of the house of the LORD, and the treasures of the king, and of his princes; all *these* he brought to Babylon.

19 [a]And they burnt[8313] the house of God, and brake down the wall of Jerusalem, and burnt all the palaces[759] thereof with fire, and destroyed[7843] all the goodly vessels thereof.

20 And [I][a]them that had escaped from the sword carried he away to Babylon; [b]where they were servants to him and his sons until the reign of the kingdom[4438] of Persia:

21 To fulfil the word of the LORD by the mouth of [a]Jeremiah, until the land [b]had enjoyed her sabbaths: *for* as long as she lay desolate[8074] [c]she kept sabbath, to fulfil threescore and ten years.

10 [I]Hebr. *at the return of the year* [II]Hebr. *vessels of desire* [III]Or, *Mattaniah, his father's brother* [a]2Kgs. 24:10-17 [b]Dan. 1:1, 2; 5:2 [c]2Kgs. 24:17; Jer. 37:1
11 [a]2Kgs. 24:18; Jer. 52:1
13 [a]Jer. 52:3; Ezek. 17:15, 18 [b]2Kgs. 17:14
15 [I]Hebr. *by the hand of his messengers* [II]That is, *continually and carefully* [a]Jer. 25:3, 4; 35:15; 44:4
16 [I]Hebr. *healing* [a]Jer. 5:12, 13 [b]Prov. 1:25, 30 [c]Jer. 32:3; 38:6; Matt. 23:34 [d]Ps. 74:1; 79:5
17 [a]Deut. 28:49; 2Kgs. 25:1; Ezra 9:7 [b]Ps. 74:20; 79:2, 3
18 [a]2Kgs. 25:13
19 [a]2Kgs. 25:9; Ps. 74:6, 7; 79:1, 7
20 [I]Hebr. *the remainder from the sword* [a]2Kgs. 25:11 [b]Jer. 27:7
21 [a]Jer. 25:9, 11, 12; 26:6, 7; 29:10 [b]Lev. 26:34, 35, 43; Dan. 9:2 [c]Lev. 25:4, 5

(continued from previous page)
Babylon and assume the throne of his father that he allowed Jehoiakim to remain king. Three years later, Jehoiakim rebelled against Nebuchadnezzar. Before Nebuchadnezzar could respond, God sent groups of the Chaldeans, Syrians, Moabites, and Ammonites to fight against Judah and Jehoiakim was killed (2 Kgs. 24:1–5; Jer. 36:30, 31).

36:10 Zedekiah was actually Jehoiachin's uncle (2 Kgs. 24:17). The word "brother" was used by the Hebrews to refer to any person of blood relation.

This was the second of three deportations to Babylon. At this time (597 B.C.) Ezekiel was led away into exile. Daniel had been taken in the first deportation which occurred in 605 B.C. The last of the exiles were carried away after the destruction of the city of Jerusalem in approximately 586 B.C..

36:21 Jeremiah stated that the reason for the Babylonian Captivity was the people's stubborn refusal to obey the word of the Lord (Jer. 25:1–11). The length of the period of punishment was chosen by God to highlight Israel's disobedience in not keeping the sabbatical years. This was only one of the many sins of the people, but the penalty was a tangible lesson from the Lord which was important for them to learn. The application for the believer is clear—if one refuses to do what God wants, He has ways of achieving His purposes anyway, though there may be suffering in the process.

Cyrus Frees the Exiles

22 [a]Now in the first year of Cyrus king of Persia, that the word of the LORD *spoken* by the mouth of [b]Jeremiah might be accomplished,[3615] the LORD stirred up the spirit of [c]Cyrus king of Persia, that he made a proclamation throughout all his kingdom, and *put it* also in writing, saying,

22 [a]Ezra 1:1 [b]Jer. 25:12, 13; 29:10; 33:10, 11, 14 [c]Isa. 44:28

23 [a]Ezra 1:2, 3

23 [a]Thus saith Cyrus king of Persia, All the kingdoms[4467] of the earth[776] hath the LORD God of heaven given me; and he hath charged[6485] me to build him an house in Jerusalem, which *is* in Judah. Who *is there* among you of all his people? The LORD his God *be* with him, and let him go up.

EZRA

The books of Ezra and Nehemiah were originally one volume. The Vulgate (a Latin translation of the Scripture) was the first edition of the Bible to separate them, but at that time they were designated as 1 and 2 Ezra (see introduction to Nehemiah). Like the Book of Daniel, portions of Ezra were written in Aramaic, the language of Babylon (Ezra 4:8—6:18).

The Book of Ezra recounts the efforts of the exiles who returned from Babylon to rebuild the temple. Under the leadership of Jeshua, the high priest, and Zerubbabel, the governor over the region, proper worship and the ceremonies associated with it were restored in Jerusalem. Many years later, Ezra arrived in Jerusalem with another group of exiles. Ezra was a very knowledgeable and adept scribe and was commissioned by King Artaxerxes to teach the statutes of the Mosaic Law to the people in Israel.

While there may have been many groups of exiles that returned to Jerusalem from Babylon, Scripture speaks only of three. The first group returned in 536 B.C. under the leadership of Zerubabbel, the second in 457 B.C. under Ezra, and the third in 444 B.C. under Nehemiah. The Book of Ezra tells of the first two groups of exiles. Long periods of time are not covered, however, because only those facts that are relevant to the religious life of Israel are given. Despite the fact that all those who desired to return to Jerusalem were free to do so, a great number of Jews chose to remain in Babylon. As a result, Babylon became an important center for Jewish learning until the city's decline near the end of the fourth century B.C.

The prophets Zechariah and Haggai were contemporary with Zerubbabel, and Esther lived not many years later. An excellent understanding of the life of the Jews after the Exile can be gained by collectively studying the books of these individuals along with Ezra and Nehemiah.

The Edict of Cyrus

1 🔑 Now in the first year of Cyrus king of Persia, that the word[1697] of the LORD [a]by the mouth[6310] of Jeremiah might be fulfilled,[3615] the LORD stirred up the spirit[7307] of Cyrus king[4428] of Persia, [b]that he [I]made[5674] a proclamation throughout all his kingdom,[4438] and *put it* also in writing, saying,

2 Thus saith[559] Cyrus king of Persia, The LORD God[430] of heaven[8064] hath given me all the kingdoms[4467] of the earth;[776] and he hath [a]charged[6485] me to build him an house[1004] at Jerusalem, which *is* in Judah.

3 Who *is there* among you of all his people?[5971] his God be with him, and let him go up to Jerusalem, which *is* in Judah, and build the house of the LORD God of Israel, ([a]he *is* the God,) which *is* in Jerusalem.

4 And whosoever remaineth[7604] in any place where he sojourneth,[1481] let the men[582] of his place [I]help him with silver, and with gold, and with goods, and with beasts, beside the freewill offering[5071] for the house of God that *is* in Jerusalem.

The Jewish Exiles Return to Jerusalem

5 Then rose up the chief[7218] of the fathers[1] of Judah and Benjamin, and the priests,[3548] and the Levites, with all *them* whose spirit [a]God had raised, to go up to build the house of the LORD which *is* in Jerusalem.

6 And all they that *were* about them [I]strengthened[2388] their hands[3027] with vessels of silver, with gold, with goods, and with beasts, and with precious

1 [I]Hebr. *caused a voice to pass* [a]2Chr. 36:22, 23; Jer. 25:12; 29:10 [b]Ezra 5:13, 14
2 [a]Isa. 44:28; 45:1, 13
3 [a]Dan. 6:26
4 [I]Hebr. *lift him up*
5 [a]Phil. 2:13
6 [I]That is, *helped them*

🔑 **1:1** "The first year of Cyrus" would have been 538 B.C. His reign in Persia began in 559 B.C., but he did not conquer Babylon until 539. His reign ended in 530 B.C.

things, beside all *that* was willingly offered.[5068]

7 [a]Also Cyrus the king brought forth the vessels of the house of the LORD, [b]which Nebuchadnezzar had brought forth out of Jerusalem, and had put them in the house of his gods;

8 Even those did Cyrus king of Persia bring forth by the hand[3027] of Mithredath the treasurer, and numbered[5608] them unto [a]Sheshbazzar, the prince[5387] of Judah.

9 And this *is* the number of them: thirty chargers[105] of gold, a thousand chargers of silver, nine and twenty knives,

10 Thirty basons[3713] of gold, silver basons of a second *sort* four hundred and ten, *and* other vessels a thousand.

11 All the vessels of gold and of silver *were* five thousand and four hundred. All *these* did Sheshbazzar bring up[5927] with *them of* [I]the captivity[1473] that were brought up from Babylon unto Jerusalem.

The Record of Those Who Returned

2 Now [a]these *are* the children[1121] of the province that went up[5927] out of the captivity,[7628] of those which had been carried away,[1540] [b]whom Nebuchadnezzar the king[4428] of Babylon had carried away unto Babylon, and came again unto Jerusalem and Judah, every one[376] unto his city;

2 Which came with Zerubbabel: Jeshua, Nehemiah, [Ia]Seraiah, [II]Reelaiah, Mordecai, Bilshan, [III]Mizpar, Bigvai, [IV]Rehum, Baanah. The number of the men[582] of the people[5971] of Israel:

3 The children of Parosh, two thousand an hundred seventy and two.

4 The children of Shephatiah, three hundred seventy and two.

5 The children of Arah, [a]seven hundred seventy and five.

6 The children of [a]Pahath–moab, of the children of Jeshua *and* Joab, two thousand eight hundred and twelve.

7 The children of Elam, a thousand two hundred fifty and four.

8 The children of Zattu, nine hundred forty and five.

9 The children of Zaccai, seven hundred and threescore.

10 The children of [Ia]Bani, six hundred forty and two.

11 The children of Bebai, six hundred twenty and three.

12 The children of Azgad, a thousand two hundred twenty and two.

13 The children of Adonikam, six hundred sixty and six.

14 The children of Bigvai, two thousand fifty and six.

15 The children of Adin, four hundred fifty and four.

16 The children of Ater of Hezekiah, ninety and eight.

17 The children of Bezai, three hundred twenty and three.

18 The children of [Ia]Jorah, an hundred and twelve.

19 The children of Hashum, two hundred twenty and three.

20 The children of [Ia]Gibbar, ninety and five.

21 The children of Bethlehem, an hundred twenty and three.

22 The men of Netophah, fifty and six.

23 The men of Anathoth, an hundred twenty and eight.

24 The children of [Ia]Azmaveth, forty and two.

7 [a]Ezra 5:14; 6:5 [b]2Kgs. 24:13; 2Chr. 36:7
8 [a]Ezra 5:14
11 [I]Hebr. *the transportation*
1 [a]Neh. 7:6 [b]2Kgs. 24:14-16; 25:11; 2Chr. 36:20
2 [I]Or, *Azariah* [II]Or, *Raamiah* [III]Or, *Mispereth* [IV]Or, *Nehum* [a]Neh. 7:7
5 [a]Neh. 7:10
6 [a]Neh. 7:11
10 [I]Or, *Binnui* [a]Neh. 7:15
18 [I]Or, *Hariph* [a]Neh. 7:24
20 [I]Or, *Gibeon* [a]Neh. 7:25
24 [I]Or, *Bethazmaveth* [a]Neh. 7:28

1:8 "Sheshbazzar" is thought to be the Chaldean name of Zerubbabel. Sheshbazzar means "joy in affliction," while Zerubbabel means "stranger in Babylon." Since Zerubbabel was the grandson of Jehoiachin (see 1 Chr. 3:17–19; Ezra 3:2), who was popular in Babylon, it is quite possible that he was the one to whom the treasures of the temple were entrusted. Other scholars speculate that Sheshbazzar was the officially appointed leader of the group returning to Jerusalem, and Zerubbabel was the unofficial, popular leader. Still others have identified Sheshbazzar with Shenazzar of 1 Chronicles 3:18.

25 The children of Kirjath–arim, Chephirah, and Beeroth, seven hundred and forty and three.

26 The children of Ramah and Gaba, six hundred twenty and one.

27 The men of Michmas, an hundred twenty and two.

28 The men of Bethel and Ai, two hundred twenty and three.

29 The children of Nebo, fifty and two.

30 The children of Magbish, an hundred fifty and six.

31 The children of the other [a]Elam, a thousand two hundred fifty and four.

32 The children of Harim, three hundred and twenty.

33 The children of Lod, [I]Hadid, and Ono, seven hundred twenty and five.

34 The children of Jericho, three hundred forty and five.

35 The children of Senaah, three thousand and six hundred and thirty.

36 The priests:[3548] the children of [a]Jedaiah, of the house[1004] of Jeshua, nine hundred seventy and three.

37 The children of [a]Immer, a thousand fifty and two.

38 The children of [a]Pashur, a thousand two hundred forty and seven.

39 The children of [a]Harim, a thousand and seventeen.

40 The Levites: the children of Jeshua and Kadmiel, of the children of [I][a]Hodaviah, seventy and four.

41 The singers:[7891] the children of Asaph, an hundred twenty and eight.

42 The children of the porters:[7778] the children of Shallum, the children of Ater, the children of Talmon, the children of Akkub, the children of Hatita, the children of Shobai, *in* all an hundred thirty and nine.

43 [a]The Nethinims: the children of Ziha, the children of Hasupha, the children of Tabbaoth,

44 The children of Keros, the children of [I]Siaha, the children of Padon.

45 The children of Lebanah, the children of Hagabah, the children of Akkub,

46 The children of Hagab, the children of [I]Shalmai, the children of Hanan,

47 The children of Giddel, the children of Gahar, the children of Reaiah,

48 The children of Rezin, the children of Nekoda, the children of Gazzam,

49 The children of Uzza, the children of Paseah, the children of Besai,

50 The children of Asnah, the children of Mehunim, the children of Nephusim,

51 The children of Bakbuk, the children of Hakupha, the children of Harhur,

52 The children of [I][a]Bazluth, the children of Mehida, the children of Harsha,

53 The children of Barkos, the children of Sisera, the children of Thamah,

54 The children of Neziah, the children of Hatipha.

55 The children of [a]Solomon's servants:[5650] the children[1121] of Sotai, the children of Sophereth, the children of [I][b]Pe ruda,

56 The children of Jaalah, the children of Darkon, the children of Giddel,

57 The children of Shephatiah, the children of Hattil, the children of Pochereth of Zebaim, the children of [I][a]Ami.

58 All the [a]Nethinims, and the children of [b]Solomon's servants, *were* three hundred ninety and two.

59 And these *were* they which went up from Tel–melah, Tel–harsa, Cherub, [I][a]Addan, *and* Immer: but they could not shew[5046] their father's[1] house, and their [II]seed,[2233] whether they *were* of Israel:

60 The children of Delaiah, the children of Tobiah, the children of Nekoda, six hundred fifty and two.

61 And of the children of the priests: the children of Habaiah, the children of Koz, the children of Barzillai; which took a wife[802] of the daughters of [a]Barzillai the Gileadite, and was called[7121] after their name:

62 These sought their register[3791] *among* those that were reckoned by genealogy, but they were not found: [a]therefore [I]were they, as polluted, put from the priesthood.[3550]

31 [a]Ezra 2:7

33 [I]Or, *Harid,* as it is in some texts

36 [a]1Chr. 24:7

37 [a]1Chr. 24:14

38 [a]1Chr. 9:12

39 [a]1Chr. 24:8

40 [I]Or, *Judah* [a]Neh. 7:43, Hodevah

43 [a]1Chr. 9:2

44 [I]Or, *Sia*

46 [I]Or, *Shamlai*

52 [I]Or, *Bazlith* [a]Neh. 7:54

55 [I]Or, *Perida* [a]1Kgs. 9:21 [b]Neh. 7:57

57 [I]Or, *Amon* [a]Neh. 7:59

58 [a]Josh. 9:21, 27; 1Chr. 9:2 [b]1Kgs. 9:21

59 [I]Or, *Addon* [II]Or, *pedigree* [a]Neh. 7:61

61 [a]2Sam. 17:27

62 [I]Hebr. *they were polluted from the priesthood* [a]Num. 3:10

🗝 63 And the [a]Tirshatha said[559] unto them, that they [b]should not eat of the most holy things,[6944] till there stood up a priest[3548] with [c]Urim[224] and with Thummim.[8537]

64 [a]The whole congregation[6951] together *was* forty and two thousand three hundred *and* threescore,

65 Beside their servants and their maids, of whom *there were* seven thousand three hundred thirty and seven: and *there were* among them two hundred singing men[7891] and singing women.

66 Their horses *were* seven hundred thirty and six; their mules, two hundred forty and five;

67 Their camels, four hundred thirty and five; *their* asses, six thousand seven hundred and twenty.

68 [a]And *some* of the chief[7218] of the fathers,[1] when they came to the house of the LORD[3068] which *is* at Jerusalem, offered freely[5068] for the house of God[430] to set it up in his place:

69 They gave after their ability unto the [a]treasure of the work[4399] threescore and one thousand drams[1871] of gold, and five thousand pound of silver, and one hundred priests' garments.

70 [a]So the priests, and the Levites, and *some* of the people, and the singers, and the porters, and the Nethinims, dwelt in their cities, and all Israel in their cities.

Worship Is Restored

3 And when the seventh month was come,[5060] and the children[1121] of Israel *were* in the cities, the people[5971] gathered themselves together as one man to Jerusalem.

2 Then stood up [I][a]Jeshua the son of Jozadak, and his brethren[251] the priests,[3548] and [II][b]Zerubbabel the son of [c]Shealtiel, and his brethren, and builded the altar[4196] of the God[430] of Israel, to offer burnt offerings[5930] thereon, as *it is* [d]written in the law[8451] of Moses the man of God.

3 And they set the altar upon his bases; for fear[367] *was* upon them because of the people of those countries:[776] and they offered[5927] burnt offerings thereon unto the Lord, *even* [a]burnt offerings morning and evening.

4 [a]They kept[6213] also the feast[2282] of tabernacles, [b]as *it is* written, and [c]*offered* the daily burnt offerings by number, according to the custom,[4941] [I]as the duty[1697] of every day required;

5 And afterward *offered* the [a]continual[8548] burnt offering, both of the new moons, and of all the set feasts[4150] of the LORD that were consecrated,[6942] and of every one that willingly offered[5068] a freewill offering[5071] unto the LORD.

6 From the first day of the seventh month began they to offer burnt offerings unto the LORD. But [I]the foundation of the temple[1964] of the LORD was not *yet* laid.

7 They gave money also unto the masons, and to the [I]carpenters; and [a]meat, and drink,[4960] and oil, unto them of Zidon, and to them of Tyre, to bring cedar trees from Lebanon to the sea of [b]Joppa, [c]according to the grant that they had of Cyrus king[4428] of Persia.

Rebuilding the Temple

8 Now in the second year of their coming unto the house[1004] of God at Jerusalem, in the second month, began Zerubbabel the son of Shealtiel, and Jeshua the son of Jozadak, and the remnant[7605] of their brethren the priests and the Levites, and all they that were come out of the captivity[7628] unto Jerusalem; [a]and appointed the Levites, from twenty years old and upward, to set forward the work[4399] of the house of the LORD.

9 Then stood [a]Jeshua *with* his

---

63 [a]Neh. 8:9 [b]Lev. 22:2, 10, 15, 16 [c]Ex. 28:30; Num. 27:21

64 [a]Neh. 7:66

68 [a]Or, *Neh. 7:70*

69 [a]1Chr. 26:20

70 [a]Ezra 6:16, 17; Neh. 7:73

2 [I]Or, *Joshua* [II]Called *Zorobabel* [a]Hag. 1:1; 2:2; Zech. 3:1 [b]Matt. 1:12; Luke 3:27 [c]Matt. 1:12; Luke 3:27 [d]Deut. 12:5

3 [a]Num. 28:3, 4

4 [I]Hebr. *the matter of the day in his day* [a]Neh. 8:14, 17; Zech. 14:16, 17 [b]Ex. 23:16 [c]Num. 29:12

5 [a]Ex. 29:38; Num. 28:3, 11, 19, 26; 29:2, 8, 13

6 [I]Hebr. *the temple of the LORD was not yet founded*

7 [I]Or, *workmen* [a]1Kgs. 5:6, 9; 2Chr. 2:10; Acts 12:20 [b]2Chr. 2:16; Acts 9:36 [c]Ezra 6:3

8 [a]1Chr. 23:24, 27

9 [a]Ezra 2:40

🗝 **2:63** "Tirshatha" means "governor" and is applied here to Zerubbabel. Concerning "Urim and Thummim," see note on Exodus 28:30.

sons[1121] and his brethren, Kadmiel and
his sons, the sons of [I][b]Judah, [II]together, to
set forward the workmen in the house of
God: the sons of Henadad, *with* their
sons and their brethren the Levites.
10 And when the builders[1129] laid
the foundation[3245] of the temple of the
LORD, [a]they set the priests in their apparel
with trumpets, and the Levites the sons
of Asaph with cymbals, to praise[1984] the
LORD, after the [b]ordinance of David king
of Israel.
11 [a]And they sang together by
course[6030] in praising[1984] and giving
thanks[3034] unto the LORD; [b]because *he is*
good,[2896] [c]for his mercy[2617] *endureth*
for ever[5769] toward Israel. And all the
people shouted[7321] with a great shout,
when they praised the LORD, because the
foundation of the house of the LORD was
laid.
12 [a]But many of the priests and
Levites and chief[7218] of the fathers,[1] *who
were* ancient men,[2204] that had seen[7200]
the first[7223] house, when the foundation
of this house was laid before their eyes,
wept with a loud voice; and many
shouted aloud for joy:
13 So that the people could not
discern[5234] the noise of the shout of joy
from the noise of the weeping of the people: for the people shouted with a loud
shout, and the noise was heard[8085] afar
off.

Enemies Oppose the Work

4 Now when [a]the adversaries of Judah
and Benjamin heard that [I]the children[1121] of the captivity[1473] builded the
temple[1964] unto the LORD God[430] of
Israel;
2 Then they came to Zerubbabel, and
to the chief[7218] of the fathers,[1] and
said[559] unto them, Let us build with you:
for we seek your God, as ye *do;* and we
do sacrifice[2076] unto him [a]since the

9 [I]Or, *Hodaviah* [II]Hebr. *as one* [b]Ezra 2:40

10 [a]1Chr. 16:5, 6, 42 [b]1Chr. 6:31; 16:4; 25:1

11 [a]Ex. 15:21; 2Chr. 7:3; Neh. 12:24 [b]1Chr. 16:34; Ps. 136:1 [c]1Chr. 16:41; Jer. 33:11

12 [a]Hag. 2:3

1 [I]Hebr. *the sons of the transportation* [a]Ezra 4:7-9

2 [a]2Kgs. 17:24, 32, 33; 19:37; Ezra 4:10

3 [a]Neh. 2:20 [b]Ezra 1:1-3

4 [a]Ezra 3:3

6 [I]Hebr. *Ahashverosh*

7 [I]Or, *in peace* [II]Hebr. *societies*

8 [I]Or, *secretary*

9 [I]Aram. *societies* [a]2Kgs. 17:30, 31

10 [I]Aram. *Cheeneth* [a]Ezra 4:10 [b]Ezra 4:11, 17; 7:12

days[3117] of Esar–haddon king[4428] of
Assur, which brought us up[5927] hither.
3 But Zerubbabel, and Jeshua, and
the rest[7605] of the chief of the fathers of
Israel, said unto them, [a]Ye have nothing
to do with us to build an house[1004] unto
our God; but we ourselves together will
build unto the LORD God of Israel, as
[b]king Cyrus the king of Persia hath
commanded[6680] us.
4 Then [a]the people[5971] of the land[776]
weakened[7503] the hands[3027] of the people
of Judah, and troubled them in building,
5 And hired counsellors[3289] against
them, to frustrate[6565] their purpose, all
the days of Cyrus king of Persia, even
until the reign[4438] of Darius king of
Persia.
🔑 6 And in the reign of [I]Ahasuerus, in
the beginning of his reign, wrote they
unto him an accusation[7855] against the
inhabitants of Judah and Jerusalem.
7 And in the days of Artaxerxes
wrote [I]Bishlam, Mithredath, Tabeel, and
the rest of their [II]companions, unto
Artaxerxes king of Persia; and the writing of the letter *was* written in the Syrian
tongue, and interpreted in the Syrian
tongue.
🔑 8 Rehum the chancellor[1169,2942] and
Shimshai the [I]scribe[5613] wrote a letter
against Jerusalem to Artaxerxes the
king[4430] in this sort:
9 Then *wrote* Rehum the chancellor,
and Shimshai the scribe, and the rest[7606]
of their [I]companions; [a]the Dinaites, the
Apharsathchites, the Tarpelites, the
Apharsites, the Archevites, the Babylonians, the Susanchites, the Dehavites, *and*
the Elamites,
10 [a]And the rest of the nations[524]
whom the great and noble Asnapper
brought over,[1541] and set in the cities of
Samaria, and the rest *that are* on this
side the river, [b]and [I]at such a time.
11 This *is* the copy of the letter that
they sent unto him, *even* unto Artaxerxes

🔑 **4:6** Ahasuerus, better known as Xerxes, reigned in Persia from 486 B.C. to 465 B.C. See note on Esther 1:1.

🔑 **4:8—6:18** This section of Ezra is written in Aramaic. See note on Daniel 2:4—7:28.

the king; Thy servants[5649] the men[606] on this side the river, and at such a time.

12 Be it known[3046] unto the king, that the Jews which came up from thee to us are come unto Jerusalem, building the rebellious[4779] and the bad[873] city, and have [I]set up[3635] the walls *thereof,* and [II]joined the foundations.

13 Be it known now unto the king, that, if this city be builded, and the walls set up *again, then* will they not [I]pay [a]toll, tribute, and custom, and *so* thou shalt endamage the [II]revenue of the kings.[4430]

14 Now because [I]we have maintenance[4415,4416] from *the king's* palace,[1964] and it was not meet for us to see[2370] the king's dishonour, therefore have we sent and certified the king;

15 That search may be made in the book[5609] of the records of thy fathers:[2] so shalt thou find in the book of the records, and know[3046] that this city *is* a rebellious city, and hurtful unto kings and provinces, and that they have [I]moved sedition [II]within the same of old[5957] time:[3118] for which cause was this city destroyed.[2718]

16 We certify[3046] the king that, if this city be builded *again,* and the walls thereof set up, by this means thou shalt have no portion on this side the river.

17 *Then* sent the king an answer[6600] unto Rehum the chancellor, and *to* Shimshai the scribe, and *to* the rest of their [I]companions that dwell in Samaria, and *unto* the rest beyond the river, Peace,[8001] and at such a time.

18 The letter which ye sent unto us hath been plainly read before me.

19 And [I]I commanded, and search hath been made, and it is found that this city of old time hath [II]made insurrection against kings, and *that* rebellion[4776] and sedition have been made therein.

20 There have been mighty kings also over Jerusalem, which have [a]ruled[7990] over all *countries* [b]beyond the river; and toll, tribute, and custom, was paid unto them.

21 [I]Give[7761] ye now commandment[2942] to cause these men[1400] to cease, and that this city be not builded, until *another* commandment shall be given from me.

22 Take heed[2095] now that ye fail not to do this: why should damage grow to the hurt of the kings?

23 Now when the copy of king Artaxerxes' letter *was* read before Rehum, and Shimshai the scribe, and their companions, they went up in haste to Jerusalem unto the Jews, and made them to cease [I]by force[153] and power.[2429]

🔑 24 Then ceased the work of the house of God[426] which *is* at Jerusalem. So it ceased unto the second year of the reign[4437] of Darius king of Persia.

The Temple Is Rebuilt

5 Then the prophets,[5029] [a]Haggai the prophet, and [b]Zechariah the son of Iddo, prophesied[5013] unto the Jews that *were* in Judah and Jerusalem in the name of the God[426] of Israel, *even* unto them.

2 Then rose up [a]Zerubbabel the son of Shealtiel, and Jeshua the son of Jozadak, and began to build the house of God which *is* at Jerusalem: and with them *were* the prophets of God helping them.

3 At the same time[2166] came to them [a]Tatnai, governor[6347] on this side the river, and Shethar-boznai, and their companions, and said[560] thus unto them, [b]Who hath commanded[7761,2942] you to build this house, and to make up[3635] this wall?

4 [a]Then said we unto them after this manner, What are the names of the men[1400] [I]that make this building?

5 But [a]the eye of their God was upon the elders[7868] of the Jews, that they could not cause them to cease, till the matter[2941] came to Darius: and then they

12 [I]Or, *finished* [II]Aram. *sown together*
13 [I]Aram. *give* [II]Or, *strength* [a]Ezra 7:24
14 [I]Aram. *we are salted with the salt of the palace*
15 [I]Aram. *made* [II]Aram. *in the midst thereof*
17 [I]Aram. *societies*
19 [I]Aram. *by me a decree is set* [II]Aram. *lifted up itself*
20 [a]1Kgs. 4:21; Ps. 72:8 [b]Gen. 15:18; Josh. 1:4
21 [I]Aram. *Make a decree*
23 [I]Aram. *by arm and power*
1 [a]Hag. 1:1 [b]Zech. 1:1
2 [a]Ezra 3:2
3 [a]Ezra 5:6; 6:6 [b]Ezra 5:9
4 [I]Aram. *that build this building* [a]Ezra 5:10
5 [a]Ezra 7:6, 28; Ps. 33:18

🔑 **4:24** Sixteen years passed between the laying of the foundation of the temple (chap. 3) and the second year of the reign of Darius (536–520 B.C.).

returned [b]answer by letter concerning this *matter.*

6 The copy of the letter[104] that Tatnai, governor on this side the river, and Shethar–boznai, [a]and his companions the Apharsachites, which *were* on this side the river, sent unto Darius the king:[4430]

7 They sent a letter[6600] unto him, [I]wherein was written thus; Unto Darius the king, all peace.[8001]

8 Be it known[3046] unto the king, that we went into the province of Judea, to the house of the great God, which is builded with [I]great stones, and timber is laid in the walls, and this work goeth fast on, and prospereth in their hands.[3028]

9 Then asked[7593] we those elders, *and* said unto them thus, [a]Who commanded you to build this house, and to make up these walls?

10 We asked their names also, to certify[3046] thee, that we might write the names of the men that *were* the chief[7217] of them.

11 And thus they returned us answer,[6600] saying, We are the servants[5649] of the God of heaven[8065] and earth, and build the house that was builded these many years ago,[6928] which a great king of Israel builded [a]and set up.[3635]

12 But [a]after that our fathers[2] had provoked the God of heaven unto wrath,[7265] he gave them into the hand[3038] of [b]Nebuchadnezzar the king of Babylon, the Chaldean, who destroyed[5642] this house, and carried the people[5972] away into Babylon.

13 But in the first year of [a]Cyrus the king of Babylon *the same* king Cyrus made a decree[2942] to build this house of God.

14 And [a]the vessels also of gold and silver of the house of God, which Nebuchadnezzar took out of the temple[1965] that *was* in Jerusalem, and brought them into the temple of Babylon, those did Cyrus the king take out of the temple of Babylon, and they were delivered unto *one,* [b]whose name *was* Sheshbazzar, whom he had made [I]governor;[6347]

15 And said unto him, Take these vessels, go, carry them into the temple that *is* in Jerusalem, and let the house of God be builded in his place.

16 Then came the same Sheshbazzar, *and* [a]laid the foundation of the house of God which *is* in Jerusalem: and since that time even until now hath it been in building, and [b]*yet* it is not finished.[8000]

17 Now therefore, if *it seem* good to the king, [a]let there be search made in the king's[4430] treasure house, which *is* there at Babylon, whether it be *so,* that a decree was made of Cyrus the king to build this house of God at Jerusalem, and let the king send his pleasure[7470] to us concerning this matter.

Cyrus' Edict Is Rediscovered

6 Then Darius the king[4430] made a decree,[2942] [a]and search was made in the house of the [I]rolls,[5609] where the treasures were [II]laid up in Babylon.

2 And there was found at [I]Achmetha, in the palace that *is* in the province of the Medes, a roll,[4040] and therein *was* a record thus written:

3 In the first year of Cyrus the king *the same* Cyrus the king made a decree *concerning* the house of God[426] at Jerusalem, Let the house be builded, the place where they offered[1684] sacrifices,[1685] and let the foundations thereof be strongly laid;[5446] the height thereof threescore cubits, *and* the breadth thereof threescore cubits;

4 [a]*With* three rows of great stones, and a row of new timber: and let the expenses be given out of the king's[4430] house:

5 And also let [a]the golden and silver vessels of the house of God, which Nebuchadnezzar took forth out of the temple[1965] which *is* at Jerusalem, and brought unto Babylon, be restored,[8421] and [I]brought again unto the temple which *is* at Jerusalem, *every one* to his place, and place *them* in the house of God.

6 [a]Now *therefore* Tatnai, governor[6347] beyond the river, Shethar–boznai, and [I]your companions the Apharsachites,

5 [b]Ezra 6:6
6 [a]Ezra 4:9
7 [I]Aram. *in the midst whereof*
8 [I]Aram. *stones of rolling*
9 [a]Ezra 5:3, 4
11 [a]1Kgs. 6:1
12 [a]2Chr. 36:16, 17 [b]2Kgs. 24:2; 25:8, 9, 11
13 [a]Ezra 1:1
14 [I]Or, *deputy* [a]Ezra 1:7, 8; 6:5 [b]Hag. 1:14; 2:2, 21
16 [a]Ezra 3:8, 10 [b]Ezra 6:15
17 [a]Ezra 6:1, 2
1 [I]Aram. *books* [II]Aram. *made to descend* [a]Ezra 5:17
2 [I]Or, *Echatana,* or, *in a coffer*
4 [a]1Kgs. 6:36
5 [I]Aram. *go* [a]Ezra 1:7, 8; 5:14
6 [I]Aram. *their societies* [a]Ezra 5:3

which *are* beyond the river, be ye far from thence:

7 Let the work of this house of God alone; let the governor of the Jews and the elders[7868] of the Jews build this house of God in his place.

8 Moreover [I]I make a decree what ye shall do to the elders of these Jews for the building of this house of God: that of the king's goods, *even* of the tribute beyond the river, forthwith[629] expenses be given unto these men,[1400] that they be not [II]hindered.

9 And that which they have need of, both young[1123] bullocks, and rams, and lambs, for the burnt offerings[5928] of the God of heaven,[8065] wheat, salt, wine, and oil,[4887] according to the appointment[3983] of the priests which *are* at Jerusalem, let it be given them day by day without fail:

10 [a]That they may offer sacrifices [I]of sweet savours unto the God of heaven, and [b]pray[6739] for the life[2417] of the king, and of his sons.[1123]

11 Also I have made a decree, that whosoever shall alter[8133] this word,[6600] let timber be pulled down[5256] from his house, and being set up, [I]let him be hanged thereon; [a]and let his house be made a dunghill for this.

12 And the God that hath caused his [a]name to dwell there destroy[4049] all kings[4430] and people,[5972] that shall put to their hand[3028] to alter *and* to destroy[2255] this house of God which is at Jerusalem. I Darius have made a decree; let it be done with speed.

The Temple Is Dedicated

13 Then Tatnai, governor on this side the river, Shethar–boznai, and their companions, according to that which Darius the king had sent, so they did speedily.

14 [a]And the elders of the Jews builded, and they prospered through the prophesying[5017] of Haggai the prophet[5029] and Zechariah the son of Iddo. And they builded, and finished[3635] *it,* according to the commandment[2941] of the God of Israel, and according to the [I]commandment[2942] of [b]Cyrus, and [c]Darius, and [d]Artaxerxes king of Persia.

15 And this house was finished on the third day of the month Adar, which was in the sixth year of the reign[4437] of Darius the king.

16 And the children[1121] of Israel, the priests, and the Levites, and the rest[7606] of [I]the children of the captivity,[1547] kept [a]the dedication of this house of God with joy,

17 And [a]offered at the dedication[2597] of this house of God an hundred bullocks, two hundred rams, four hundred lambs; and for a sin offering for all Israel, twelve he goats, according to the number of the tribes[7625] of Israel.

18 And they set the priests in their [a]divisions,[6392] and the Levites in their [b]courses, for the service of God, which *is* at Jerusalem; [Ic]as it is written in the book[5609] of Moses.

19 And the children of the captivity[1547] kept[6213] the passover[6453] [a]upon the fourteenth *day* of the first[7223] month.

20 For the priests[3548] and the Levites were [a]purified[2891] together, all of them *were* pure,[2889] and [b]killed[7819] the passover for all the children of the captivity, and for their brethren[251] the priests, and for themselves.

21 And the children of Israel, which were come again out of captivity, and all such as had separated themselves unto them from the [a]filthiness[2932] of the

8 [I]Aram. *by me a decree is made* [II]Aram. *made to cease*
10 [I]Aram. *of rest* [a]Ezra 7:23; Jer. 29:7 [b]1Tim. 2:1, 2
11 [I]Aram. *let him be destroyed* [a]Dan. 2:5; 3:29
12 [a]1Kgs. 9:3
14 [I]Aram. *decree* [a]Ezra 5:1, 2 [b]Ezra 1:1; 5:13; 6:3 [c]Ezra 4:24 [d]Ezra 7:1
16 [I]Aram. *the sons of the transportation* [a]1Kgs. 8:63; 2Chr. 7:5
17 [a]Ezra 8:35
18 [I]Aram. *according to the writing* [a]1Chr. 24:1 [b]1Chr. 23:6 [c]Num. 3:6; 8:9
19 [a]Ex. 12:6
20 [a]2Chr. 30:15 [b]2Chr. 35:11
21 [a]Ezra 9:11

6:15 The time between the destruction of the temple (586 B.C.) and the date that the rebuilding was finished (the early part of 515 B.C.), being rounded off to the nearest year (516 B.C.) gives a total of seventy years. This was the fulfillment of the prophecy of Jeremiah concerning how long Israel would be in captivity (Jer. 25:11).

6:16 Herod the Great (see Matt. 2:1–19) enlarged and beautified this temple, but it was destroyed by the Romans in A.D. 70. This temple was smaller and less ornate than Solomon's Temple, but God promised that the glory which would eventually fill it would be greater (Hag. 2:6–9).

heathen[1471] of the land,[776] to seek the LORD God[430] of Israel, did eat,

22 And kept the [a]feast[2282] of unleavened[4682] bread seven days[3117] with joy: for the LORD had made them joyful, and [b]turned the heart[3820] [c]of the king[4428] of Assyria unto them, to strengthen[2388] their hands[3027] in the work[4399] of the house[1004] of God, the God of Israel.

Ezra Arrives

7 Now after these things,[1697] in the reign[4438] of [a]Artaxerxes king[4428] of Persia, Ezra [b]the son of Seraiah, the son[1121] of Azariah, the son of Hilkiah,

2 The son of Shallum, the son of Zadok, the son of Ahitub,

3 The son of Amariah, the son of Azariah, the son of Meraioth,

4 The son of Zerahiah, the son of Uzzi, the son of Bukki,

5 The son of Abishua, the son of Phinehas, the son of Eleazar, the son of Aaron the chief[7218] priest:[3548]

6 This Ezra went up[5927] from Babylon; and he *was* [a]a ready scribe in the law[8451] of Moses, which the LORD God[430] of Israel had given: and the king granted him all his request, [b]according to the hand[3027] of the LORD his God upon him.

7 [a]And there went up *some* of the children[1121] of Israel, and of the priests,[3548] and [b]the Levites, and the singers,[7891] and the porters,[7778] and [c]the Nethinims, unto Jerusalem, in the seventh year of Artaxerxes the king.

🔑 8 And he came to Jerusalem in the fifth month, which *was* in the seventh year of the king.

9 For upon the first[7223] *day* of the first month [I]began he to go up from Babylon, and on the first *day* of the fifth month came he to Jerusalem, [a]according to the good[2896] hand of his God upon him.

10 For Ezra had prepared[3559] his heart[3824] to [a]seek the law of the LORD, and to do[6213] *it,* and to [b]teach[3925] in Israel statutes[2706] and judgments.[4941]

11 Now this *is* the copy of the letter that the king Artaxerxes gave unto Ezra the priest, the scribe, *even* a scribe of the words[1697] of the commandments[4687] of the LORD, and of his statutes to Israel.

🔑 12 Artaxerxes, [a]king[4430] of kings, [I]unto Ezra the priest, a scribe of the law[1882] of the God[426] of heaven,[8065] perfect[1585] *peace,* [b]and at such a time.

13 I make a decree,[2942] that all they of the people[5972] of Israel, and *of* his priests and Levites, in my realm,[4437] which are minded of their own freewill to go up to Jerusalem, go with thee.

14 Forasmuch as thou art sent [I]of the king, and of his [a]seven counsellors,[3272] to enquire concerning Judah and Jerusalem, according to the law of thy God which *is* in thine hand;[3028]

15 And to carry the silver and gold, which the king and his counsellors have freely offered unto the God of Israel, [a]whose habitation *is* in Jerusalem,

16 [a]And all the silver and gold that thou canst find in all the province of Babylon, with the freewill offering[5069] of the people, and of the priests, [b]offering willingly for the house of their God which *is* in Jerusalem:

17 That thou mayest buy speedily with this money bullocks, rams, lambs, with their [a]meat offerings[4504] and their drink offerings,[5261] and [b]offer them upon the altar of the house of your God which *is* in Jerusalem.

18 And whatsoever shall seem good to thee, and to thy brethren,[252] to do with the rest[7606] of the silver and the gold, that do after the will of your God.

19 The vessels also that are given thee for the service of the house of thy God, *those* deliver[8000] thou before the God of Jerusalem.

22 [a]Ex. 12:15; 13:6; 2Chr. 30:21; 35:17 [b]Prov. 21:1 [c]2Kgs. 23:29; 2Chr. 33:11; Ezra 1:1; 6:6

1 [a]Neh. 2:1 [b]1Chr. 6:14

6 [a]Ezra 7:11, 12, 21 [b]Ezra 7:9; 8:22, 31

7 [a]Ezra 8:1 [b]Ezra 8:15 [c]Ezra 2:43; 8:20

9 [I]Hebr. was *the foundation of the going up* [a]Ezra 7:6; Neh. 2:8, 18

10 [a]Ps. 119:45 [b]Ezra 6:25; Deut. 33:10; Neh. 8:1-8; Mal. 2:7

12 [I]Or, *to Ezra the priest, a perfect scribe of the law of the God of heaven,* peace [a]Ezek. 26:7; Dan. 2:37 [b]Ezra 4:10

14 [I]Aram. *from before the king* [a]Esth. 1:14

15 [a]2Chr. 6:2; Ps. 135:21

16 [a]Ezra 8:25 [b]1Chr. 29:6, 9

17 [a]Num. 15:4-13 [b]Deut. 12:5, 11

🔑 **7:8** A total of fifty-eight years elapsed between the dedication of the temple and Ezra's arrival in Jerusalem.

🔑 **7:12–26** This portion is written in Aramaic. See note on Daniel 2:4—7:28.

20 And whatsoever more shall be needful for the house of thy God, which thou shalt have occasion[5308] to bestow, bestow *it* out of the king's[4430] treasure house.

21 And I, *even* I Artaxerxes the king, do make a decree to all the treasurers which *are* beyond the river, that whatsoever Ezra the priest,[3548] the scribe of the law of the God of heaven, shall require[7593] of you, it be done speedily,

22 Unto an hundred talents of silver, and to an hundred [I]measures of wheat, and to an hundred baths of wine, and to an hundred baths of oil,[4887] and salt without prescribing *how much.*

23 [I]Whatsoever is commanded by the God of heaven, let it be diligently done for the house of the God of heaven: for why should there be wrath[7109] against the realm of the king and his sons?

24 Also we certify[3046] you, that touching any of the priests and Levites, singers, porters,[8652] Nethinims, or ministers[6399] of this house of God, it shall not be lawful to impose toll, tribute, or custom, upon them.

25 And thou, Ezra, after the wisdom[2452] of thy God, that *is* in thine hand, [a]set magistrates[8200] and judges,[1782] which may judge[1778] all the people that *are* beyond the river, all such as know[3046] the laws of thy God; and [b]teach ye them that know *them* not.

26 And whosoever will not do the law of thy God, and the law of the king, let judgment[1780] be executed speedily upon him, whether *it be* unto death,[4193] or [I]to banishment, or to confiscation[6065] of goods, or to imprisonment.

27 [a]Blessed[1288] *be* the LORD God of our fathers,[1] [b]which hath put *such a thing* as this in the king's[4428] heart, to beautify[6286] the house[1004] of the LORD which *is* in Jerusalem:

28 And [a]hath extended mercy[2617] unto me before the king, and his counsellors,[3289] and before all the king's mighty princes.[8269] And I was strengthened[2388] as [b]the hand of the LORD my God *was* upon me, and I gathered together[6908] out of Israel chief men to go up with me.

Those Who Returned with Ezra

8 These *are* now the chief[7218] of their fathers,[1] and *this is* the genealogy of them that went up[5927] with me from Babylon, in the reign[4438] of Artaxerxes the king.[4428]

2 Of the sons[1121] of Phinehas; Gershom: of the sons of Ithamar; Daniel: of the sons of David; [a]Hattush.

3 Of the sons of Shechaniah, of the sons of [a]Pharosh; Zechariah: and with him were reckoned by genealogy of the males[2145] an hundred and fifty.

4 Of the sons of Pahath–moab; Elihoenai the son of Zerahiah, and with him two hundred males.

5 Of the sons of Shechaniah; the son of Jahaziel, and with him three hundred males.

6 Of the sons also of Adin; Ebed the son of Jonathan, and with him fifty males.

7 And of the sons of Elam; Jeshaiah the son of Athaliah, and with him seventy males.

8 And of the sons of Shephatiah; Zebadiah the son of Michael, and with him fourscore males.

9 Of the sons of Joab; Obadiah the son of Jehiel, and with him two hundred and eighteen males.

10 And of the sons of Shelomith; the son of Josiphiah, and with him an hundred and threescore males.

11 And of the sons of Bebai; Zechariah the son of Bebai, and with him twenty and eight males.

12 And of the sons of Azgad; Johanan [I]the son of Hakkatan, and with him an hundred and ten males.

13 And of the last sons of Adonikam, whose names *are* these, Eliphelet, Jeiel, and Shemaiah, and with them threescore males.

14 Of the sons also of Bigvai; Uthai, and [I]Zabbud, and with them seventy males.

15 And I gathered them together[6908]

22 [I]Aram. *cords*

23 [I]Hebr. *Whatsoever is of the decree*

25 [a]Ex. 18:21, 22; Deut. 16:18 [b]Ezra 7:10; 2Chr. 17:7; Mal. 2:7; Matt. 23:2, 3

26 [I]Aram. *to rooting out*

27 [a]1Chr. 29:10 [b]Ezra 6:22

28 [a]Ezra 9:9 [b]Ezra 5:5; 7:6, 9; 8:18

2 [a]1Chr. 3:22

3 [a]Ezra 2:3

12 [I]Or, *the youngest son*

14 [I]Or, *Zaccur*

to the river that runneth to Ahava; and there [I]abode we in tents three days:[3117] and I viewed the people,[5971] and the priests,[3548] and found there none of the [a]sons of Levi.

16 Then sent I for Eliezer, for Ariel, for Shemaiah, and for Elnathan, and for Jarib, and for Elnathan, and for Nathan, and for Zechariah, and for Meshullam, chief men;[7218] also for Joiarib, and for Elnathan, men of understanding.[995]

17 And I sent them with commandment unto Iddo the chief at the place Casiphia, [I][a]and I told them what they should say[1696] unto Iddo, *and* to his brethren[251] the Nethinims, at the place Casiphia, that they should bring unto us ministers for the house[1004] of our God.[430]

18 And by the good[2896] hand[3027] of our God upon us they [a]brought us a man of understanding,[7922] of the sons of Mahli, the son of Levi, the son of Israel; and Sherebiah, with his sons and his brethren, eighteen;

19 And Hashabiah, and with him Jeshaiah of the sons of Merari, his brethren and their sons, twenty;

20 [a]Also of the Nethinims, whom David and the princes[8269] had appointed for the service[5656] of the Levites, two hundred and twenty Nethinims: all of them were expressed by name.

Ezra Leads the People

21 Then I [a]proclaimed a fast there, at the river of Ahava, that we might [b]afflict ourselves before our God, to seek of him a [c]right[3477] way[1870] for us, and for our little ones,[2945] and for all our substance.

22 For [a]I was ashamed[954] to require of the king a band of soldiers and horsemen to help us against the enemy in the way: because we had spoken[559] unto the king, saying, [b]The hand of our God *is* upon all them for [c]good that seek him; but his power and his wrath[639] *is* [d]against all them that [e]forsake[5800] him.

23 So we fasted and besought our God for this: and he was [a]intreated[6279] of us.

24 Then I separated[914] twelve of the chief of the priests, Sherebiah, Hashabiah, and ten of their brethren with them,

25 And weighed unto them [a]the silver, and the gold, and the vessels, *even* the offering[8641] of the house of our God, which the king, and his counsellors,[3289] and his lords, and all Israel *there* present, had offered:

26 I even weighed unto their hand six hundred and fifty talents of silver, and silver vessels an hundred talents, *and* of gold an hundred talents;

27 Also twenty basons[3713] of gold, of a thousand drams;[150] and two vessels of [I]fine copper, [II]precious as gold.

28 And I said[559] unto them, Ye *are* [a]holy[6944] unto the LORD; the vessels *are* [b]holy also; and the silver and the gold *are* a freewill offering[5071] unto the LORD God of your fathers.

29 Watch ye, and keep[8104] *them,* until ye weigh *them* before the chief of the priests and the Levites, and chief of the fathers of Israel, at Jerusalem, in the chambers of the house of the LORD.[3068]

30 So took the priests and the Levites the weight of the silver, and the gold, and the vessels, to bring *them* to Jerusalem unto the house of our God.

31 Then we departed from the river of Ahava on the twelfth *day* of the first[7223] month, to go unto Jerusalem: and [a]the hand of our God was upon us, and he delivered[5337] us from the hand[3709] of the enemy, and of such as lay in wait by the way.

32 And we [a]came to Jerusalem, and abode there three days.

33 Now on the fourth day was the silver and the gold and the vessels [a]weighed in the house of our God by the hand[3027] of Meremoth the son of Uriah the priest;[3548] and with him *was* Eleazar the son of Phinehas; and with them *was* Jozabad the son of Jeshua, and Noadiah the son of Binnui, Levites;

34 By number *and* by weight of every one: and all the weight was written at that time.[6256]

35 *Also* the children[1121] of those that had been carried away,[1473] which were

15 [I]Or, *pitched* [a]Ezra 7:7

17 [I]Hebr. *I put words in their mouth* [a]2Sam. 14:3, 19

18 [a]Neh. 8:7; 9:4, 5

20 [a]Ezra 2:43

21 [a]2Chr. 20:3 [b]Lev. 16:29; 23:29; Isa. 58:3, 5 [c]Ps. 5:8

22 [a]1Cor. 9:15 [b]Ezra 7:6, 9, 28 [c]Ps. 33:18, 19; 34:15, 22; Rom. 8:28 [d]Ps. 34:16 [e]2Chr. 15:2

23 [a]1Chr. 5:20; 2Chr. 33:13; Isa. 19:22

25 [a]Ezra 7:15, 16

27 [I]Hebr. *yellow,* or, *shining brass* [II]Hebr. *desirable*

28 [a]Lev. 21:6-8; Deut. 33:8 [b]Lev. 22:2, 3; Num. 4:4, 15, 19, 20

31 [a]Ezra 7:6, 9, 28

32 [a]Neh. 2:11

33 [a]Ezra 8:26, 30

come out of the captivity,[7628] [a]offered[7126] burnt offerings[5930] unto the God of Israel, twelve bullocks for all Israel, ninety and six rams, seventy and seven lambs, twelve he goats *for* a sin offering:[2403] all *this was* a burnt offering unto the LORD.

36 And they delivered the king's [a]commissions[1881] unto the king's lieutenants, and to the governors[6346] on this side the river: and they furthered[5375] the people, and the house of God.

Intermarriage With Pagans

9 Now when these things were done,[3615] the princes[8269] came to me, saying, The people of Israel, and the priests,[3548] and the Levites, have not [a]separated themselves[914] from the people[5971] of the lands,[776] [b]*doing* according to their abominations,[8441] *even* of the Canaanites, the Hittites, the Perizzites, the Jebusites, the Ammonites, the Moabites, the Egyptians, and the Amorites.

2 For they have [a]taken[5375] of their daughters for themselves, and for their sons:[1121] so that the [b]holy[6944] seed[2233] have [c]mingled themselves with the people of *those* lands: yea, the hand of the princes and rulers[5461] hath been chief[7223] in this trespass.[4604]

3 And when I heard[8085] this thing,[1697] [a]I rent my garment and my mantle,[4598] and plucked off the hair of my head[7218] and of my beard,[2206] and sat down [b]astonied.[8074]

4 Then were assembled[622] unto me every one that [a]trembled[2730] at the words[1697] of the God[430] of Israel, because of the transgression[4604] of those that had been carried away;[1473] and I sat astonied until the [b]evening sacrifice.[4503]

5 And at the evening sacrifice I arose up from my [I]heaviness;[8589] and having rent my garment and my mantle, I fell[3766] upon my knees, and [a]spread out my hands[3709] unto the LORD my God,

6 And said,[559] O my God, I am [a]ashamed[954] and blush[3637] to lift up my face to thee, my God: for [b]our iniquities[5771] are increased over *our* head, and our [I]trespass[819] is [c]grown up unto the heavens.[8064]

7 Since the days[3117] of our fathers[1] *have* [a]we *been* in a great trespass unto this day; and for our iniquities [b]have we, our kings, *and* our priests, been delivered into the hand of the kings of the lands, to the sword,[2719] to captivity,[7628] and to a spoil, and to [c]confusion[1322] of face, as *it is* this day.

8 And now for a [I]little space grace[8467] hath been *shewed* from the LORD our God, to leave us a remnant to escape,[6413] and to give us [II][a]a nail in his holy place, that our God may [b]lighten our eyes, and give us a little reviving[4241] in our bondage.[5659]

9 [a]For we *were* bondmen;[5650] [b]yet our God hath not forsaken[5800] us in our bondage, but [c]hath extended mercy[2617] unto us in the sight of the kings of Persia, to give us a reviving, to set up the house[1004] of our God, and [I]to repair the desolations[2723] thereof, and to give us [d]a wall in Judah and in Jerusalem.

10 And now, O our God, what shall we say[559] after this? for we have forsaken thy commandments,[4687]

11 Which thou hast commanded[6680] [I]by thy servants[5690] the prophets,[5030] saying, The land,[776] unto which ye go to possess[3423] it, is an unclean land with the [a]filthiness of the people of the lands, with their abominations, which have filled it [II][b]from one end to another with their uncleanness.[2932]

12 Now therefore [a]give not your daughters unto their sons, neither take[5375] their daughters unto your sons, [b]nor seek their peace or their wealth[2896] for ever:[5769] that ye may be strong,[2388] and eat the good of the land, and [c]leave *it* for an inheritance[3423] to your children[1121] for ever.

13 And after all that is come upon us for our evil[7451] deeds, and for our great trespass, seeing that thou our God [I][a]hast punished us less than our iniquities *deserve,* and hast given us *such* deliverance[6413] as this;

14 Should we [a]again break thy com-

---

35 [a]Ezra 6:17

36 [a]Ezra 7:21

1 [a]Ezra 6:21; Neh. 9:2 [b]Deut. 12:30, 31

2 [a]Ex. 34:16; Deut. 7:3; Neh. 13:23 [b]Ex. 19:6; 22:31; Deut. 7:6; 14:2 [c]2Cor. 6:14

3 [a]Job 1:20 [b]Ps. 143:4

4 [a]Ezra 10:3; Isa. 66:2 [b]Ex. 29:39

5 [I]Or, *affliction* [a]Ex. 9:29, 33

6 [I]Or, *guiltiness* [a]Dan. 9:7, 8 [b]Ps. 38:4 [c]2Chr. 28:9; Rev. 18:5

7 [a]Ps. 106:6; Dan. 9:5, 6, 8 [b]Deut. 28:36, 64; Neh. 9:30 [c]Dan. 9:7, 8

8 [I]Hebr. *moment* [II]Or, *a pin:* that is, *a constant and sure abode* [a]Isa. 22:23 [b]Ps. 13:3; 34:5

9 [I]Hebr. *to set up* [a]Neh. 9:36 [b]Ps. 136:23 [c]Ezra 7:28 [d]Isa. 5:2

11 [I]Hebr. *by the hand of thy servants* [II]Hebr. *from mouth to mouth* [a]Ezra 6:21 [b]2Kgs. 21:16

12 [a]Ex. 23:32; 34:16; Deut. 7:3 [b]Deut. 23:6 [c]Prov. 13:22; 20:7

13 [I]Hebr. *hast withheld beneath our iniquities* [a]Ps. 103:10

14 [a]John 5:14; 2Pet. 2:20, 21

mandments, and [b]join in affinity[2859] with
the people of these abominations?
wouldest not thou be [c]angry[599] with us
till thou hadst consumed[3615] *us,* so that
there should be no remnant[7611] nor
escaping?[6413]
15 O LORD God of Israel, [a]thou *art*
righteous:[6662] for we remain yet escaped,
as *it is* this day: behold, we *are* [b]before
thee [c]in our trespasses:[819] for we cannot
[d]stand before thee because of this.

Putting Away Foreign Wives And Children

10 Now [a]when Ezra had prayed,[6419]
and when he had confessed,[3034]
weeping and casting himself down [b]be-
fore the house[1004] of God,[430] there
assembled[6908] unto him out of Israel a
very great congregation[6951] of men[582]
and women[802] and children: for the
people[5971] [I]wept very sore.
2 And Shechaniah the son of Jehiel,
one of the sons of Elam, answered and
said unto Ezra, We have [a]trespassed[4603]
against our God, and have taken
strange[5237] wives[802] of the people of the
land:[776] yet now there is hope[4723] in
Israel concerning this thing.
3 Now therefore let us make [a]a
covenant[1285] with our God [I]to put away
all the wives, and such as are born of
them, according to the counsel[6098] of my
lord,[136] and of those that [b]tremble at [c]the
commandment[4687] of our God; and let it
be done[6213] according to the law.[8451]
4 Arise; for *this* matter[1697] *belongeth*
unto thee: we also *will be* with thee: [a]be
of good courage,[2388] and do[6213] *it.*
5 Then arose Ezra, and made the
chief priests,[3548] the Levites, and all
Israel, [a]to swear[7650] that they should do
according to this word.[1697] And they
sware.
6 Then Ezra rose up from before the
house of God, and went into the chamber of Johanan the son of Eliashib: and
when he came thither, he [a]did eat no
bread, nor drink water: for he mourned
because of the transgression[4604] of them
that had been carried away.[1473]
7 And they made proclamation
throughout Judah and Jerusalem unto
all the children[1121] of the captivity,[1473]
that they should gather themselves together unto Jerusalem;
8 And that whosoever would not
come within three days,[3117] according to
the counsel of the princes[8269] and the
elders,[2205] all his substance should be
[I]forfeited,[2763] and himself separated[914]
from the congregation of those that had
been carried away.
9 Then all the men of Judah and
Benjamin gathered themselves together[6908] unto Jerusalem within three
days. It *was* the ninth month, on the
twentieth *day* of the month; and [a]all the
people sat in the street of the house of
God, trembling[7460] because of *this* matter, and for [I]the great rain.
10 And Ezra the priest[3548] stood up,
and said unto them, Ye have transgressed,[4603] and have [I]taken strange
wives, to increase[3254] the trespass[819] of
Israel.
11 Now therefore [a]make confession[8426] unto the LORD God of your
fathers,[1] and do his pleasure:[7522] and
[b]separate yourselves[914] from the people of
the land, and from the strange wives.
12 Then all the congregation[6951] answered and said with a loud voice, As
thou hast said, so must we do.
13 But the people *are* many, and *it is*
a time[6256] of much rain, and we are not
able to stand without, neither *is this* a
work[4399] of one day or two: for [I]we are
many that have transgressed[6586] in this
thing.
14 Let now our rulers[8269] of all the
congregation stand, and let all them
which have taken strange wives in our
cities come at appointed[2163] times,[6256]
and with them the elders of every city,
and the judges[8199] thereof, until [a]the
fierce wrath[639] of our God [I]for this matter be turned from us.
15 Only Jonathan the son of Asahel
and Jahaziah the son of Tikvah [I]were
employed about this *matter:* and
Meshullam and Shabbethai the Levite
helped them.

14 [b]Ezra 9:2; Neh. 13:23, 27 [c]Deut. 9:8

15 [a]Neh. 9:33; Dan. 9:14 [b]Rom. 3:19 [c]1Cor. 15:17 [d]Ps. 130:3

1 [I]Hebr. *wept a great weeping* [a]Dan. 9:20 [b]2Chr. 20:9

2 [a]Neh. 13:27

3 [I]Hebr. *to bring forth* [a]2Chr. 34:31 [b]Ezra 9:4 [c]Deut. 7:2, 3

4 [a]1Chr. 28:10

5 [a]Neh. 5:12

6 [a]Deut. 9:18

8 [I]Hebr. *devoted*

9 [I]Hebr. *the showers* [a]1Sam. 12:18

10 [I]Hebr. *have caused to dwell,* or, *have brought back*

11 [a]Josh. 7:19; Prov. 28:13 [b]Ezra 10:3

13 [I]Or, *we have greatly offended in this thing*

14 [I]Or, *till this matter* be *dispatched* [a]2Chr. 30:8

15 [I]Hebr. *stood*

16 And the children of the captivity did[6213] so. And Ezra the priest, *with* certain chief of the fathers, after the house of their fathers, and all of them by *their* names, were separated, and sat down in the first day of the tenth month to examine the matter.

17 And they made an end[3615] with all the men that had taken strange wives by the first[7223] day of the first month.

The List of Men with Foreign Wives

18 And among the sons of the priests there were found that had taken strange wives: *namely,* of the sons of Jeshua the son of Jozadak, and his brethren;[251] Maaseiah, and Eliezer, and Jarib, and Gedaliah.

19 And they [a]gave their hands[3027] that they would put away their wives; and *being* [b]guilty,[816] *they offered* a ram of the flock for their trespass.

20 And of the sons of Immer; Hanani, and Zebadiah.

21 And of the sons of Harim; Maaseiah, and Elijah, and Shemaiah, and Jehiel, and Uzziah.

22 And of the sons of Pashur; Elioenai, Maaseiah, Ishmael, Nethaneel, Jozabad, and Elasah.

23 Also of the Levites; Jozabad, and Shimei, and Kelaiah, (the same *is* Kelita,) Pethahiah, Judah, and Eliezer.

24 Of the singers[7891] also; Eliashib: and of the porters;[7778] Shallum, and Telem, and Uri.

25 Moreover of Israel: of the sons of Parosh; Ramiah, and Jeziah, and Malchiah, and Miamin, and Eleazar, and Malchijah, and Benaiah.

26 And of the sons of Elam; Mattaniah, Zechariah, and Jehiel, and Abdi, and Jeremoth, and Eliah.

27 And of the sons of Zattu; Elioenai, Eliashib, Mattaniah, and Jeremoth, and Zabad, and Aziza.

28 Of the sons also of Bebai; Jehohanan, Hananiah, Zabbai, *and* Athlai.

29 And of the sons of Bani; Meshullam, Malluch, and Adaiah, Jashub, and Sheal, and Ramoth.

30 And of the sons of Pahath–moab; Adna, and Chelal, Benaiah, Maaseiah, Mattaniah, Bezaleel, and Binnui, and Manasseh.

31 And *of* the sons of Harim; Eliezer, Ishijah, Melchiah, Shemaiah, Shimeon,

32 Benjamin, Malluch, *and* Shemariah.

33 Of the sons of Hashum; Mattenai, Mattathah, Zabad, Eliphelet, Jeremai, Manasseh, *and* Shimei.

34 Of the sons of Bani; Maadai, Amram, and Uel,

35 Benaiah, Bedeiah, Chelluh,

36 Vaniah, Meremoth, Eliashib,

37 Mattaniah, Mattenai, and Jaasau,

38 And Bani, and Binnui, Shimei,

39 And Shelemiah, and Nathan, and Adaiah,

40 [I]Machnadebai, Shashai, Sharai,

41 Azareel, and Shelemiah, Shemariah,

42 Shallum, Amariah, *and* Joseph.

43 Of the sons of Nebo; Jeiel, Mattithiah, Zabad, Zebina, Jadau, and Joel, Benaiah.

44 All these had taken[5375] strange wives: and *some* of them had wives by whom they had children.

19 [a]2Kgs. 10:15; 1Chr. 29:24; 2Chr. 30:8 [b]Lev. 6:4, 6

40 [I]Or, *Mabnadebai,* according to some texts

NEHEMIAH

The books of Ezra and Nehemiah were originally one volume, but Jerome (ca. A.D. 342–420) split them into 1 and 2 Ezra in the Vulgate (a Latin translation of the Bible). Not long afterward, the second portion was named "Nehemiah" after its principal character. The name Nehemiah means "Jehovah comforts."

Nehemiah was concerned that the Lord's name was not being esteemed as it should have been because His city, Jerusalem, was in ruins. The people who had returned had no way to defend themselves (Neh. 1:3). As a result, Nehemiah desired to undertake the formidable task of reestablishing civil authority in Jerusalem. He let nothing distract him (Neh. 6:3) from his goal of making Jerusalem a strategic center of refuge for the remnant of the Israelites that lived in the region. Nehemiah was appointed governor of Judea by the Persian emperor and soon afterward came to Jerusalem (445 B.C.). In addition, he was given a military escort and government funding from Artaxerxes to aid him in repairing the city. With God's help, he planned and supervised the rebuilding of the wall around Jerusalem. Letters written on papyri (ancient paper) have been discovered in Egypt on the island of Elephantini in the Nile River which affirm that Sanballat, the man that led the opposition against Nehemiah, lived during Nehemiah's time. The description that is recorded in the Elephantine papyri of the overall political situation also coincides with the account here in Nehemiah.

This book beautifully demonstrates the fact that the Lord will sometimes use men who do not acknowledge Him as the one true God to accomplish His purpose. Nehemiah served under a heathen king, but God touched the heart of Artaxerxes so that he was willing to supply Nehemiah with the means to rebuild Jerusalem. This is true of other biblical characters such as Ezra, Esther, and Daniel who served under heathen kings.

Nehemiah Prays for Jerusalem

1 The words[1697] of [a]Nehemiah the son[1121] of Hachaliah. And it came to pass in the month Chisleu, in the twentieth year, as I was in Shushan the palace,

2 That Hanani, one of my brethren,[251] came, he and *certain* men[582] of Judah; and I asked[7592] them concerning the Jews that had escaped,[6413] which were left[7604] of the captivity,[7628] and concerning Jerusalem.

3 And they said unto me, The remnant that are left of the captivity there in the province *are* in great affliction[7451] and reproach:[2781] [a]the wall of Jerusalem also [b]*is* broken down, and the gates thereof are burned with fire.

4 And it came to pass, when I heard[8085] these words, that I sat down and wept, and mourned *certain* days,[3117] and fasted, and prayed[6419] before the God[430] of heaven,[8064]

5 And said, I beseech thee,[577] [a]O LORD God of heaven, the great and terrible[3372] God,[410] [b]that keepeth[8104] covenant[1285] and mercy[2617] for them that love[157] him and observe[8104] his commandments:[4687]

6 Let thine ear[241] now be attentive, and [a]thine eyes open, that thou mayest hear the prayer[8605] of thy servant,[5650] which I pray[6419] before thee now, day[3119] and night,[3915] for the children[1121] of Israel thy servants, and [b]confess[3034] the sins of the children of Israel, which we have sinned[2398] against thee: both I and my father's[1] house[1004] have sinned.

7 [a]We have dealt very corruptly[2254] against thee, and have [b]not kept the commandments, nor the statutes,[2706] nor the judgments,[4941] which thou commandedst[6680] thy servant Moses.

8 Remember, I beseech thee,[4994] the word[1697] that thou commandedst thy servant Moses, saying, [a]*If* ye trans-

1 [a]Neh. 10:1

3 [a]Neh. 2:17 [b]2Kgs. 25:10

5 [a]Dan. 9:4 [b]Ex. 20:6

6 [a]1Kgs. 8:28, 29; 2Chr. 6:40; Dan. 9:17, 18 [b]Dan. 9:20

7 [a]Ps. 106:6; Dan. 9:5 [b]Deut. 28:15

8 [a]Lev. 26:33; Deut. 4:25-27; 28:64

gress,[4603] I will scatter you abroad among the nations:[5971]

9 [a]But *if* ye turn[7725] unto me, and keep[8104] my commandments, and do[6213] them; [b]though there were of you cast out unto the uttermost part of the heaven, *yet* will I gather[6908] them from thence, and will bring them unto the place that I have chosen[977] to set my name there.

10 [a]Now these *are* thy servants and thy people,[5971] whom thou hast redeemed[6299] by thy great power, and by thy strong[2389] hand.[3027]

🔑 11 O LORD,[136] I beseech thee, [a]let now thine ear be attentive to the prayer of thy servant, and to the prayer of thy servants, who [b]desire[2655] to fear[3372] thy name: and prosper, I pray thee, thy servant this day,[3117] and grant him mercy[7356] in the sight of this man.[376] For I was the king's[4428] [c]cupbearer.

Nehemiah Goes to Jerusalem

2 And it came to pass in the month Nisan, in the twentieth year of [a]Artaxerxes the king, *that* wine *was* before him: and [b]I took up[5375] the wine, and gave *it* unto the king. Now I had not been *beforetime* sad[7451] in his presence.

2 Wherefore the king said unto me, Why *is* thy countenance sad, seeing thou *art* not sick? this *is* nothing *else* but [a]sorrow of heart.[3820] Then I was very sore afraid,

3 And said unto the king, [a]Let the king live[2421] for ever:[5769] why should not my countenance be sad, when [b]the city, the place of my fathers' sepulchres,[6913] *lieth* waste,[2720] and the gates thereof are consumed with fire?

4 Then the king said unto me, For what dost thou make request? So I prayed[6419] to the God[430] of heaven.[8064]

5 And I said unto the king, If it please[2895] the king, and if thy servant[5650] have found favour in thy sight, that thou wouldest send me unto Judah, unto the city of my fathers' sepulchres, that I may build it.

6 And the king said unto me, (the [1]queen[7694] also sitting by him,) For how long shall thy journey be? and when wilt thou return?[7725] So it pleased the king to send me; and I set him [a]a time.[2165]

7 Moreover I said unto the king, If it please the king, let letters be given me to the governors[6346] beyond the river, that they may convey me over[5674] till I come into Judah;

8 And a letter unto Asaph the keeper[8104] of the king's[4428] forest, that he may give me timber to make beams[7136] for the gates of the palace which *appertained* [a]to the house,[1004] and for the wall of the city, and for the house that I shall enter into. And the king granted me, [b]according to the good[2896] hand[3027] of my God upon me.

9 Then I came to the governors beyond the river, and gave them the king's letters. Now the king had sent captains[8269] of the army[2428] and horsemen with me.

🔑 10 When Sanballat the Horonite, and Tobiah the servant, the Ammonite, heard[8085] *of it,* it grieved them exceedingly that there was come a man[120] to seek the welfare of the children[1121] of Israel.

11 So I [a]came to Jerusalem, and was there three days.

9 [a]Lev. 26:39-45; Deut. 4:29-31; 30:2 [b]Deut. 30:4
10 [a]Deut. 9:29; Dan. 9:15
11 [a]Neh. 1:6 [b]Isa. 26:8; Heb. 13:18 [c]Neh. 2:1
1 [a]Ezra 7:1 [b]Neh. 1:11
2 [a]Prov. 15:13
3 [a]1Kgs. 1:31; Dan. 2:4; 5:10; 6:6, 21 [b]Neh. 1:3
6 [1]Hebr. *wife* [a]Neh. 5:14; 13:6
8 [a]Neh. 3:7 [b]Ezra 5:5; 7:6, 9, 28; Neh. 2:18
11 [a]Ezra 8:32

🔑 **1:11** The position of cupbearer was one of great trust. The cupbearer tasted the king's wine before the king drank it in order to guard against him being poisoned. Because of the sensitivity of the position, cupbearers were generally eunuchs. A eunuch was considered a low risk individual in regards to overthrowing the king because he had no children for whom he could plot.

🔑 **2:10** Sanballat was a Horonite, indicating he was either from Beth–horon in Ephraim or from Horonaim. The Elephantine papyri refer to him as governor of Samaria. His opposition to Nehemiah was therefore politically motivated—the rebuilding of Jerusalem would eliminate Samaria as the political center of Judea. Tobiah, called an Ammonite, probably governed the area east of Judea. He was either a subordinate of Sanballat or in close cooperation with him.

12 And I arose in the night,[3915] I and
some few men[582] with me; neither
told[5046] I *any* man what my God had put
in my heart to do at Jerusalem: neither
was there any beast with me, save the
beast that I rode upon.
13 And I went out by night [a]by the
gate of the valley, even before the
dragon[8577] well, and to the dung port,8179
and viewed the walls of Jerusalem, which
were [b]broken down, and the gates thereof
were consumed with fire.
14 Then I went on to the [a]gate of
the fountain, and to the king's pool: but
there was no place for the beast *that was*
under me to pass.
15 Then went I up in the night by
the [a]brook, and viewed[7665] the wall, and
turned back, and entered by the gate of
the valley, and *so* returned.[7725]
16 And the rulers[5461] knew[3045] not
whither I went, or what I did; neither had
I as yet told *it* to the Jews, nor to the
priests,[3548] nor to the nobles,[2715] nor to
the rulers, nor to the rest[3499] that did the
work.[4399]
17 Then said I unto them, Ye see the
distress[7451] that we *are* in, how Jerusalem
lieth waste, and the gates thereof are
burned with fire: come, and let us build
up the wall of Jerusalem, that we be no
more [a]a reproach.[2781]
18 Then I told them of [a]the hand
of my God which was good upon me;
as also the king's words[1697] that he had
spoken unto me. And they said, Let us
rise up and build. So they [b]strength-
ened[2388] their hands[3027] for *this* good
work.
19 But when Sanballat the Horonite,
and Tobiah the servant, the Ammonite,
and Geshem the Arabian, heard *it,* they
[a]laughed us to scorn, and despised us,
and said, What *is* this thing[1697] that
ye do? [b]will ye rebel[4775] against the
king?
20 Then answered I them, and said
unto them, The God of heaven, he will
prosper us; therefore we his servants[5650]
will arise and build: [a]but ye have no
portion,2506 nor right,[6666] nor me mor-
ial,[2146] in Jerusalem.

13 [a]2Chr. 26:9; Neh. 3:13 [b]Neh. 1:3; 2:17
14 [a]Neh. 3:15
15 [a]2Sam. 15:23; Jer. 31:40
17 [a]Neh. 1:3; Ps. 44:13; 79:4; Jer. 24:9; Ezek. 5:14, 15; 22:4
18 [a]Neh. 2:8 [b]2Sam. 2:7
19 [a]Ps. 44:13; 79:4; 80:6 [b]Neh. 6:6
20 [a]Ezra 4:3
1 [a]Neh. 12:10 [b]John 5:2 [c]Neh. 12:39 [d]Jer. 31:38; Zech. 14:10
2 [I]Hebr. *at his hand* [a]Ezra 2:34
3 [a]2Chr. 33:14; Neh. 12:39; Zeph. 1:10 [b]Neh. 6:1; 7:1
5 [a]Judg. 5:23
6 [a]Neh. 12:39
7 [a]Neh. 2:8
8 [I]Or, *left Jerusalem unto the broadwall* [a]Neh. 12:38

Rebuilding the Wall

3 Then [a]Eliashib the high priest[3548]
rose up with his brethren[251] the
priests, [b]and they builded the sheep gate;
they sanctified[6942] it, and set up the
doors of it; [c]even unto the tower of Meah
they sanctified it, unto the tower of
[d]Hananeel.
2 And [I]next unto him builded [a]the
men[582] of Jericho. And next to them
builded Zaccur the son[1121] of Imri.
3 [a]But the fish[1709] gate did the sons
of Hassenaah build, who *also* laid the
beams thereof, and [b]set up the doors
thereof, the locks thereof, and the bars
thereof.
4 And next unto them repaired[2388]
Meremoth the son of Urijah, the son of
Koz. And next unto them repaired
Meshullam the son of Berechiah, the son
of Meshezabeel. And next unto them repaired Zadok the son of Baana.
5 And next unto them the Tekoites
repaired; but their nobles[117] put not their
necks to [a]the work[5656] of their Lord.[113]
6 Moreover [a]the old3462 gate repaired
Jehoiada the son of Paseah, and
Meshullam the son of Besodeiah; they
laid the beams thereof, and set up the
doors thereof, and the locks thereof, and
the bars thereof.
7 And next unto them repaired
Melatiah the Gibeonite, and Jadon
the Meronothite, the men of Gibeon, and
of Mizpah, unto the [a]throne[3678] of the
governor[6346] on this side the river.
8 Next unto him repaired Uzziel the
son of Harhaiah, of the goldsmiths.[6884]
Next unto him also repaired Hananiah
the son of *one of* the apothecaries,7546
and they [I]fortified Jerusalem unto the
[a]broad wall.
9 And next unto them repaired Rephaiah the son of Hur, the ruler[8269] of
the half part of Jerusalem.
10 And next unto them repaired
Jedaiah the son of Harumaph, even over
against his house.[1004] And next unto him
repaired Hattush the son of Hashabniah.
11 Malchijah the son of Harim, and
Hashub the son of Pahath–moab, re-

paired the [I]other piece, [a]and the tower of the furnaces.

12 And next unto him repaired Shallum the son of Halohesh, the ruler of the half part of Jerusalem, he and his daughters.

13 [a]The valley[1516] gate repaired Hanun, and the inhabitants of Zanoah; they built it, and set up the doors thereof, the locks thereof, and the bars thereof, and a thousand cubits on the wall unto [b]the dung gate.

14 But the dung gate repaired Malchiah the son of Rechab, the ruler of part of Beth–haccerem; he built it, and set up the doors thereof, the locks thereof, and the bars thereof.

15 But [a]the gate of the fountain repaired Shallun the son of Colhozeh, the ruler of part of Mizpah; he built it, and covered it, and set up the doors thereof, the locks thereof, and the bars thereof, and the wall of the pool of [b]Siloah by the king's[4428] garden, and unto the stairs that go down from the city of David.

16 After him repaired Nehemiah the son of Azbuk, the ruler of the half part of Bethzur, unto *the place* over against the sepulchres[6913] of David, and to the [a]pool that was made,[6213] and unto the house of the mighty.

17 After him repaired the Levites, Rehum the son of Bani. Next unto him repaired Hashabiah, the ruler[8269] of the half part of Keilah, in his part.

18 After him repaired their brethren, Bavai the son of Henadad, the ruler of the half part of Keilah.

19 And next to him repaired Ezer the son of Jeshua, the ruler of Mizpah, another piece over against the going up to the armoury[5402] at the [a]turning *of the wall.*

20 After him Baruch the son of [I]Zabbai earnestly[2734] repaired the other piece, from the turning *of the wall* unto the door of the house of Eliashib the high priest.

21 After him repaired Meremoth the son of Urijah the son of Koz another piece, from the door of the house of Eliashib even to the end of the house of Eliashib.

11 [I]Hebr. *second measure* [a]Neh. 12:38

13 [a]Neh. 2:13 [b]Neh. 2:13

15 [a]Neh. 2:14 [b]John 9:7

16 [a]2Kgs. 20:20; Isa. 22:11

19 [a]2Chr. 26:9

20 [I]Or, *Zaccai*

24 [a]Neh. 3:19

25 [a]Jer. 32:2; 33:1; 37:21

26 [I]Or, which *dwelt in Ophel,* repaired *unto* [II]Or, *The tower* [a]Ezra 2:43; Neh. 11:21 [b]2Chr. 27:3 [c]Neh. 8:1, 3; 12:37

28 [a]2Kgs. 11:16; 2Chr. 23:15; Jer. 31:40

31 [I]Or, *corner chamber*

1 [a]Neh. 2:10, 19

22 And after him repaired the priests, the men of the plain.[3603]

23 After him repaired Benjamin and Hashub over against their house. After him repaired Azariah the son of Maaseiah the son of Ananiah by his house.

24 After him repaired Binnui the son of Henadad another piece, from the house of Azariah unto [a]the turning *of the wall,* even unto the corner.

25 Palal the son of Uzai, over against the turning *of the wall,* and the tower which lieth out from the king's high[5945] house, that *was* by the [a]court of the prison. After him Pedaiah the son of Parosh.

26 Moreover [a]the Nethinims [I]dwelt in [II][b]Ophel, unto *the place* over against [c]the water gate toward the east, and the tower that lieth out.

27 After them the Tekoites repaired another piece, over against the great tower that lieth out, even unto the wall of Ophel.

28 From above the [a]horse gate repaired the priests, every one[376] over against his house.

29 After them repaired Zadok the son of Immer over against his house. After him repaired also Shemaiah the son of Shechaniah, the keeper[8104] of the east gate.

30 After him repaired Hananiah the son of Shelemiah, and Hanun the sixth son of Zalaph, another piece. After him repaired Meshullam the son of Berechiah over against his chamber.

31 After him repaired Malchiah the goldsmith's son unto the place of the Nethinims, and of the merchants,[7402] over against the gate Miphkad, and to the [I]going up of the corner.

32 And between the going up[5944] of the corner unto the sheep gate repaired the goldsmiths and the merchants.

The Workers Guard the Wall

4 But it came to pass, [a]that when Sanballat heard[8085] that we builded the wall, he was wroth,[2734] and took

great indignation,[3707] and mocked the Jews.

2 And he spake before his brethren[251] and the army[2428] of Samaria, and said, What do these feeble Jews? will they [I]fortify themselves? will they sacrifice?[2076] will they make an end[3615] in a day?[3117] will they revive[2421] the stones out of the heaps of the rubbish[6083] which are burned?[8313]

3 Now [a]Tobiah the Ammonite *was* by him, and he said, Even that which they build, if a fox go up, he shall even break down their stone wall.

4 [a]Hear,[8085] O our God;[430] for we are [I]despised: and [b]turn[7725] their reproach[2781] upon their own head,[7218] and give them for a prey in the land[776] of captivity:[7633]

5 And [a]cover[3680] not their iniquity,[5771] and let not their sin be blotted out[4229] from before thee: for they have provoked *thee* to anger[3707] before the builders.[1129]

6 So built we the wall; and all the wall was joined together unto the half thereof: for the people[5971] had a mind[3820] to work.[6213]

7 But it came to pass, *that* [a]when Sanballat, and Tobiah, and the Arabians, and the Ammonites, and the Ashdodites, heard that the walls of Jerusalem [I]were made up,[5927,724] *and* that the breaches began to be stopped, then they were very wroth,

8 And [a]conspired all of them together to come *and* to fight against Jerusalem, and [I]to hinder[6213,8442] it.

9 Nevertheless [a]we made our prayer unto our God,[430] and set a watch against them day[3119] and night,[3915] because of them.

10 And Judah said, The strength of the bearers of burdens is decayed,[3782] and *there is* much rubbish; so that we are not able to build the wall.

11 And our adversaries said, They shall not know,[3045] neither see, till we come in the midst among them, and slay[2026] them, and cause[7673] the work[4399] to cease.[7673]

12 And it came to pass, that when the Jews which dwelt by them came, they said unto us ten times, [I]From all places whence ye shall return[7725] unto us *they will be upon you.*

13 Therefore set I [I]in the lower places behind the wall, *and* on the higher places, I even set the people after their families[4940] with their swords,[2719] their spears, and their bows.

14 And I looked, and rose up, and said unto the nobles,[2715] and to the rulers,[5461] and to the rest[3499] of the people, [a]Be not ye afraid of them: remember[2142] the Lord,[136] *which is* [b]great and terrible,[3372] and [c]fight for your brethren, your sons,[1121] and your daughters, your wives,[802] and your houses.[1004]

15 And it came to pass, when our enemies heard that it was known[3045] unto us, [a]and God had brought[6565] their counsel[6098] to nought,[6565] that we returned[7725] all of us to the wall, every one[376] unto his work.

16 And it came to pass from that time[3117] forth, *that* the half of my servants wrought in the work, and the other half of them held[2388] both the spears, the shields, and the bows, and the habergeons;[8302] and the rulers[8269] *were* behind all the house[1004] of Judah.

17 They which builded on the wall, and they that bare[5375] burdens, with those that laded, *every one* with one of his hands[3027] wrought in the work, and with the other *hand* held a weapon.

18 For the builders, every one had his sword[2719] girded [I]by his side, and *so* builded. And he that sounded[8628] the trumpet *was* by me.

19 And I said unto the nobles, and to the rulers, and to the rest of the people, The work *is* great and large, and we are separated[6504] upon the wall, one far from another.

20 In what place *therefore* ye hear the sound of the trumpet, resort[6908] ye thither unto us: [a]our God shall fight for us.

21 So we laboured in the work: and half of them held the spears from the rising[5927] of the morning till the stars appeared.

22 Likewise at the same time[6256] said

---

2 [I]Hebr. *leave to themselves*

3 [a]Neh. 2:10, 19

4 [I]Hebr. *despite* [a]Ps. 123:3, 4 [b]Ps. 79:12; Prov. 3:34

5 [a]Ps. 69:27, 28; 109:14, 15; Jer. 18:23

7 [I]Hebr. *ascended* [a]Neh. 4:1

8 [I]Hebr. *to make an error to it* [a]Ps. 83:3-5

9 [a]Ps. 50:15

12 [I]Or, *That from all places ye must return to us*

13 [I]Hebr. *from the lower parts of the place*

14 [a]Num. 14:9; Deut. 1:29 [b]Deut. 10:17 [c]2Sam. 10:12

15 [a]Job 5:12

18 [I]Hebr. *on his loins*

20 [a]Ex. 14:14, 25; Deut. 1:30; 3:22; 20:4; Josh. 23:10

I unto the people, Let every one with his
servant lodge within Jerusalem, that in
the night they may be a guard to us, and
labour[4399] on the day.
23 So neither I, nor my brethren, nor
my servants, nor the men[582] of the guard
which followed me, none of us put off
our clothes, [1][a]*saving that* every one put
them off for washing.

Abolishing Interest Payments

5 And there was a great [a]cry of the
people[5971] and of their wives against
their [b]brethren[251] the Jews.
2 For there were that said, We, our
sons, and our daughters, *are* many: therefore we take up corn *for them,* that we
may eat, and live.[2421]
3 *Some* also there were that said, We
have mortgaged[6148] our lands, vineyards,
and houses, that we might buy corn, because of the dearth.
4 There were also that said, We
have borrowed money for the king's tribute, *and that upon* our lands and vineyards.
5 Yet now [a]our flesh[1320] *is* as the
flesh of our brethren, our children as
their children: and, lo, we [b]bring into
bondage our sons and our daughters to
be servants,[5650] and *some* of our daughters are brought unto bondage[3533] *already:* neither *is it* in our power[3027] to *redeem them;* for other men[582] have our
lands and vineyards.
6 And I was very angry[2734] when I
heard[8085] their cry and these words.[1697]
7 Then [1]I consulted with myself, and
I rebuked the nobles,[2715] and the
rulers,[5461] and said unto them, [a]Ye exact
usury, every one of his brother. And I set
a great assembly[6952] against them.
8 And I said unto them, We after our
ability have [a]redeemed our brethren the
Jews, which were sold unto the heathen;[1471] and will ye even sell your
brethren? or shall they be sold unto us?
Then held they their peace, and found
nothing *to answer.*
9 Also I said, It *is* not good[2896] that
ye do: ought ye not to walk [a]in the
fear[3374] of our God [b]because of the
reproach[2781] of the heathen our enemies?
10 I likewise, *and* my brethren, and
my servants, might exact of them money
and corn: I pray you,[4994] let us leave
off[5800] this usury.
11 Restore,[7725] I pray you, to them,
even this day,[3117] their lands, their vineyards, their oliveyards, and their houses,
also the hundredth *part* of the money,
and of the corn, the wine, and the oil,[3323]
that ye exact of them.
12 Then said they, We will restore
them, and will require nothing of them;
so will we do as thou sayest.[559] Then I
called[7121] the priests,[3548] [a]and took an
oath[7650] of them, that they should do according to this promise.[1697]
13 Also [a]I shook my lap, and said, So
God shake out every man[376] from his
house,[1004] and from his labour, that performeth not this promise, even thus be he
shaken out, and [1]emptied. And all the
congregation[6951] said, Amen,[543] and
praised[1984] the LORD. [b]And the people did
according to this promise.
14 Moreover from the time[3117] that I
was appointed[6680] to be their governor[6346] in the land[776] of Judah, from the
twentieth year [a]even unto the two and
thirtieth year of Artaxerxes the king,[4428]
that is, twelve years, I and my brethren
have not [b]eaten the bread of the governor.
15 But the former[7723] governors that
had been before me were chargeable[3513]
unto the people, and had taken of them
bread and wine, beside forty shekels of
silver; yea, even their servants bare
rule[7980] over the people: but [a]so did not
I, because of the [b]fear of God.
16 Yea, also I continued[2388] in the
work[4399] of this wall, neither bought we
any land: and all my servants *were*
gathered[6908] thither unto the work.
17 Moreover *there were* [a]at my table
an hundred and fifty of the Jews and
rulers,[5461] beside those that came unto
us from among the heathen that *are*
about us.
18 Now *that* [a]which was prepared
for me daily[3117] *was* one ox *and* six

23 [1]Or, *every one went with his weapon for water* [a]Judg. 5:11
1 [a]Isa. 5:7 [b]Lev. 25:35-37; Deut. 15:7
5 [a]Isa. 58:7 [b]Ex. 21:7; Lev. 25:39
7 [1]Hebr. *my heart consulted in me* [a]Ex. 22:25; Lev. 25:36; Ezek. 22:12
8 [a]Lev. 25:48
9 [a]Lev. 25:36 [b]2Sam. 12:14; Rom. 2:24; 1Pet. 2:12
12 [a]Ezra 10:5; Jer. 34:8, 9
13 [1]Hebr. *empty, or, void* [a]Matt. 10:14; Acts 13:51; 18:6 [b]2Kgs. 23:3
14 [a]Neh. 13:6 [b]1Cor. 9:4, 15
15 [a]2Cor. 11:9; 12:13 [b]Neh. 5:9
17 [a]2Sam. 9:7; 1Kgs. 18:19
18 [a]1Kgs. 4:22

choice[1305] sheep; also fowls were prepared for me and once in ten days store of all sorts of wine: yet for all this [b]required not I the bread of the governor, because the bondage[5656] was heavy[3513] upon this people.

19 [a]Think[2142] upon me, my God, for good, *according* to all that I have done[6213] for this people.

Plots Against Nehemiah

6 Now it came to pass, [a]when Sanballat, and Tobiah, and [I][b]Geshem the Arabian, and the rest[3499] of our enemies, heard[8085] that I had builded the wall, and *that* there was no breach left[3498] therein; ([c]though at that time[6256] I had not set up the doors upon the gates;)

2 That Sanballat and Geshem [a]sent unto me, saying, Come, let us meet[3259] together in *some one of* the villages in the plain of [b]Ono. But they [c]thought[2803] to do me mischief.[7451]

3 And I sent messengers[4397] unto them, saying, I *am* doing a great work,[4399] so that I cannot come down: why should the work cease,[7673] whilst I leave it, and come down to you?

4 Yet they sent unto me four times after this sort; and I answered them after the same manner.

5 Then sent Sanballat his servant unto me in like manner the fifth time with an open letter in his hand;[3027]

6 Wherein *was* written, It is reported[8085] among the heathen,[1471] and [I][a]Gashmu saith *it,* [b]that thou and the Jews think[2803] to rebel:[4775] for which cause thou buildest1129 the wall, that thou mayest be their king, according to these words.[1697]

7 And thou hast also appointed prophets[5030] to preach of thee at Jerusalem, saying, *There is* a king in Judah: and now shall it be reported to the king according to these words. Come now therefore, and let us take counsel[3289] together.

8 Then I sent unto him, saying, There are no such things[1697] done as

18 [b]Neh. 5:14, 15

19 [a]Neh. 13:22

1 [I]Or, *Gashmu* [a]Neh. 2:10, 19; 4:1, 7 [b]Neh. 6:6 [c]Neh. 3:1, 3

2 [a]Prov. 26:24, 25 [b]1Chr. 8:12; Neh. 11:35 [c]Ps. 37:12, 32

6 [I]Or, *Geshem* [a]Neh. 6:1 [b]Neh. 2:19

12 [a]Ezek. 13:22

14 [a]Neh. 13:29 [b]Ezek. 13:17

16 [a]Neh. 2:10; 4:1, 7; 6:1 [b]Ps. 126:2

17 [I]Hebr. *multiplied their letters passing to Tobiah*

thou sayest,[559] but thou feignest[908] them out of thine own heart.[3820]

9 For they all made us afraid, saying, Their hands[3027] shall be weakened[7503] from the work, that it be not done. Now therefore, *O God,* strengthen[2388] my hands.

10 Afterward I came unto the house[1004] of Shemaiah the son[1121] of Delaiah the son of Mehetabeel, who *was* shut up; and he said, Let us meet together in the house of God, within the temple,[1964] and let us shut the doors of the temple: for they will come to slay[2026] thee; yea, in the night[3915] will they come to slay thee.

11 And I said, Should such a man[376] as I flee? and who *is there,* that, *being* as I *am,* would go into the temple to save his life?[2425] I will not go in.

12 And, lo, I perceived[5234] that God had not sent him; but that [a]he pronounced[1696] this prophecy[5016] against me: for Tobiah and Sanballat had hired him.

13 Therefore *was* he hired, that I should be afraid, and do so, and sin,[2398] and *that* they might have *matter* for an evil[7451] report, that they might reproach me.

14 [a]My God, think thou upon Tobiah and Sanballat according to these their works, and on the [b]prophetess[5031] Noadiah, and the rest of the prophets, that would have put me in fear.[3372]

15 So the wall was finished[7555] in the twenty and fifth *day* of *the month* Elul, in fifty and two days.[3117]

16 And it came to pass, that [a]when all our enemies heard *thereof,* and all the heathen that *were* about us saw[7200] *these things,* they were much cast down[5307] in their own eyes: for [b]they perceived[3045] that this work was wrought of our God.

17 Moreover in those days the nobles[2715] of Judah [I]sent[1980] many letters unto Tobiah, and *the letters* of Tobiah came unto them.

18 For *there were* many in Judah sworn unto him, because he *was* the son in law of Shechaniah the son of Arah; and his son Johanan had taken the

daughter of Meshullam the son of Berechiah.

19 Also they reported[559] his good deeds[2896] before me, and uttered my [I]words to him. *And* Tobiah sent letters to put me in fear.

Nehemiah Appoints Rulers

7 Now it came to pass, when the wall was built, and I had [a]set up the doors, and the porters[7778] and the singers[7891] and the Levites were appointed,

2 That I gave[6680] my brother[251] Hanani, and Hananiah the ruler[8269] [a]of the palace, charge[6680] over Jerusalem: for he *was* a faithful[571] man, and [b]feared God[430] above many.

3 And I said unto them, Let not the gates of Jerusalem be opened until the sun be hot; and while they stand by, let them shut the doors, and bar *them:* and appoint watches[4931] of the inhabitants of Jerusalem, every one in his watch, and every one *to be* over against his house.[1004]

4 Now the city *was* [I]large and great: but the people[5971] *were* few therein, and the houses *were* not builded.

The List of Returning Exiles

5 And my God put into mine heart[3820] to gather together[6908] the nobles,[2715] and the rulers,[5461] and the people, that they might be reckoned by genealogy. And I found a register[5612] of the genealogy of them which came up[5927] at the first[7223] and found written therein,

6 [a]These *are* the children[1121] of the province, that went up[5927] out of the captivity,[7628] of those that had been carried away,[1473] whom Nebuchadnezzar the king[4428] of Babylon had carried away,[1540] and came again to Jerusalem and to Judah, every one unto his city;

7 Who came with Zerubbabel, Jeshua, Nehemiah, [I][a]Azariah, Raamiah, Nahamani, Mordecai, Bilshan, Mispereth, Bigvai, Nehum, Baanah. The number, *I say,* of the men[582] of the people of Israel *was this;*

8 The children of Parosh, two thousand an hundred seventy and two.

9 The children of Shephatiah, three hundred seventy and two.

10 The children of Arah, six hundred fifty and two.

11 The children of Pahath–moab, of the children of Jeshua and Joab, two thousand and eight hundred *and* eighteen.

12 The children of Elam, a thousand two hundred fifty and four.

13 The children of Zattu, eight hundred forty and five.

14 The children of Zaccai, seven hundred and threescore.

15 The children of [I]Binnui, six hundred forty and eight.

16 The children of Bebai, six hundred twenty and eight.

17 The children of Azgad, two thousand three hundred twenty and two.

18 The children of Adonikam, six hundred threescore and seven.

19 The children of Bigvai, two thousand threescore and seven.

20 The children of Adin, six hundred fifty and five.

21 The children of Ater of Hezekiah, ninety and eight.

22 The children of Hashum, three hundred twenty and eight.

23 The children of Bezai, three hundred twenty and four.

24 The children of [I]Hariph, an hundred and twelve.

25 The children of [I]Gibeon, ninety and five.

26 The men of Bethlehem and Netophah, an hundred fourscore and eight.

27 The men of Anathoth, an hundred twenty and eight.

28 The men of [I]Beth–azmaveth, forty and two.

29 The men of [I]Kirjath–jearim, Chephirah, and Beeroth, seven hundred forty and three.

30 The men of Ramah and Gaba, six hundred twenty and one.

19 [I]Or, *matters*
1 [a]Neh. 6:1
2 [a]Neh. 2:8 [b]Ex. 18:21
4 [I]Hebr. *broad in spaces*
6 [a]Ezra 2:1
7 [I]Or, *Seraiah* [a]Ezra 2:2
15 [I]Or, *Bani*
24 [I]Or, *Jora*
25 [I]Or, *Gibbar*
28 [I]Or, *Azmaveth*
29 [I]Or, *Kirjath-arim*

31 The men of Michmas, an hundred and twenty and two.

32 The men of Bethel and Ai, an hundred twenty and three.

33 The men of the other Nebo, fifty and two.

34 The children of the other [a]Elam, a thousand two hundred fifty and four.

35 The children of Harim, three hundred and twenty.

36 The children of Jericho, three hundred forty and five.

37 The children of Lod, Hadid, and Ono, seven hundred twenty and one.

38 The children of Senaah, three thousand nine hundred and thirty.

39 The priests:[3548] the children of [a]Jedaiah, of the house of Jeshua, nine hundred seventy and three.

40 The children of [a]Immer, a thousand fifty and two.

41 The children of [a]Pashur, a thousand two hundred forty and seven.

42 The children of [a]Harim, a thousand and seventeen.

43 The Levites: the children of Jeshua, of Kadmiel, *and* of the children of [a]Hodevah, seventy and four.

44 The singers:[7891] the children of Asaph, an hundred forty and eight.

45 The porters:[7778] the children of Shallum, the children of Ater, the children of Talmon, the children of Akkub, the children of Hatita, the children of Shobai, an hundred thirty and eight.

46 The Nethinims:[5411] the children of Ziha, the children of Hashupha, the children of Tabbaoth,

47 The children of Keros, the children of [I]Sia, the children of Padon,

48 The children of Lebana, the children of Hagaba, the children of [I]Shalmai,

49 The children[1121] of Hanan, the children of Giddel, the children of Gahar,

50 The children of Reaiah, the children of Rezin, the children of Nekoda,

51 The children of Gazzam, the children of Uzza, the children of Phaseah,

52 The children of Besai, the children of Meunim, the children of [I]Nephishesim,

53 The children of Bakbuk, the children of Hakupha, the children of Harhur,

54 The children of [I]Bazlith, the children of Mehida, the children of Harsha,

55 The children of Barkos, the children of Sisera, the children of Tamah,

56 The children of Neziah, the children of Hatipha.

57 The children[1121] of Solomon's servants:[5650] the children of Sotai, the children of Sophereth, the children of [I]Perida,

58 The children of Jaala, the children of Darkon, the children of Giddel,

59 The children of Shephatiah, the children of Hattil, the children of Pochereth of Zebaim, the children of [I]Amon.

60 All the Nethinims, and the children of Solomon's servants, *were* three hundred ninety and two.

61 [a]And these *were* they which went up *also* from Tel–melah, Tel–haresha, Cherub, [I]Addon, and Immer: but they could not shew[5046] their father's house, nor their [II]seed,[2233] whether they *were* of Israel.

62 The children of Delaiah, the children of Tobiah, the children of Nekoda, six hundred forty and two.

63 And of the priests: the children of Habaiah, the children of Koz, the children of Barzillai, which took *one* of the daughters of Barzillai the Gileadite to wife, and was called[7121] after their name.

64 These sought their register[3791] *among* those that were reckoned by genealogy,[3187] but it was not found: therefore were they, as polluted, put from the priesthood.[3550]

🗝 65 And [I][a]the Tirshatha said unto them, that they should not eat of the most holy things,[6944] till there stood *up* a priest[3548] with Urim[224] and Thummim.[8537]

34 [a]Neh. 7:12
39 [a]1Chr. 24:7
40 [a]1Chr. 24:14
41 [a]1Chr. 9:12; 24:9
42 [a]1Chr. 24:8
43 [a]Ezra 2:40, *Hodaviah*; Ezra 3:9; *Judah*
47 [I]Or, *Siaha*
48 [I]Or, *Shamlai*
52 [I]Or, *Nephusim*
54 [I]Or, *Bazluth*
57 [I]Or, *Peruda*
59 [I]Or, *Ami*
61 [I]Or, *Addan* [II]Or, *pedigree* [a]Ezra 2:59
65 [I]Or, *the governor* [a]Neh. 8:9

🗝 **7:65** The Urim and the Thummim are mentioned here for the last time in the Old Testament. See note on Exodus 28:30.

66 The whole congregation[6951] together *was* forty and two thousand three hundred and threescore,

67 Beside their manservants and their maidservants, of whom *there were* seven thousand three hundred thirty and seven: and they had two hundred forty and five singing men[7891] and singing women.

68 Their horses, seven hundred thirty and six: their mules, two hundred forty and five:

69 *Their* camels, four hundred thirty and five: six thousand seven hundred and twenty asses.

70 And [I]some of the chief[7218] of the fathers[1] gave unto the work.[4399] [a]The Tirshatha gave to the treasure a thousand drams[1871] of gold, fifty basons,[4219] five hundred and thirty priests'[3548] garments.

71 And *some* of the chief of the fathers gave to the treasure of the work [a]twenty thousand drams of gold, and two thousand and two hundred pound of silver.

72 And *that* which the rest[7611] of the people gave *was* twenty thousand drams of gold, and two thousand pound of silver, and threescore and seven priests' garments.

73 So the priests, and the Levites, and the porters, and the singers, and *some* of the people, and the Nethinims, and all Israel, dwelt in their cities; [a]and when the seventh month came,[5060] the children of Israel *were* in their cities.

Ezra Reads the Law to the People

8 And all [a]the people[5971] gathered themselves together[622] as one man into the street that *was* [b]before the water gate; and they spake unto Ezra the [c]scribe[5608] to bring the book[5612] of the law[8451] of Moses, which the LORD had commanded[6680] to Israel.

2 And Ezra the priest[3548] brought [a]the law before the congregation[6951] both of men and women, and all [I]that could hear[8085] with understanding,[995] [b]upon the first day[3117] of the seventh month.

3 And he read[7121] therein before the street that *was* before the water gate [I]from the morning until midday, before the men[582] and the women, and those that could understand;[995] and the ears[241] of all the people *were attentive* unto the book of the law.

4 And Ezra the scribe stood upon a [I]pulpit of wood, which they had made[6213] for the purpose;[1697] and beside him stood Mattithiah, and Shema, and Anaiah, and Urijah, and Hilkiah, and Maaseiah, on his right hand; and on his left hand, Pedaiah, and Mishael, and Malchiah, and Hashum, and Hashbadana, Zechariah, *and* Meshullam.

5 And Ezra opened the book in the [I]sight of all the people; (for he was above all the people;) and when he opened it, all the people [a]stood up:

6 And Ezra blessed[1288] the LORD, the great God.[430] And all the people [a]answered, Amen,[543] Amen, with [b]lifting up their hands:[3027] and they [c]bowed their heads, and worshipped[7812] the LORD with *their* faces to the ground.[776]

7 Also Jeshua, and Bani, and Sherebiah, Jamin, Akkub, Shabbethai, Hodijah, Maaseiah, Kelita, Azariah, Jozabad, Hanan, Pelaiah, and the Levites, [a]caused the people to understand the law: and the people *stood* in their place.

🔑 8 So they read in the book in the law of God distinctly,[6567] and gave the sense,[7922] and caused *them* to understand the reading.[4744]

9 [a]And Nehemiah, which *is* [I]the Tirshatha, and Ezra the priest the scribe,

70 [I]Hebr. *part* [a]Neh. 8:9
71 [a]Ezra 2:69
73 [a]Ezra 3:1
1 [a]Ezra 3:1 [b]Neh. 3:26 [c]Ezra 7:6
2 [I]Hebr. *that understood in hearing* [a]Deut. 31:11, 12 [b]Lev. 23:24
3 [I]Hebr. *from the light*
4 [I]Hebr. *tower of wood*
5 [I]Hebr. *eyes* [a]Judg. 3:20
6 [a]1Cor. 14:16 [b]Lam. 3:41; 1Tim. 2:8 [c]Ex. 4:31; 12:27; 2Chr. 20:18
7 [a]Lev. 10:11; Deut. 33:10; 2Chr. 17:7-9; Mal. 2:7
9 [I]Or, *the governor* [a]Ezra 2:63; Neh. 7:65; 10:1

🔑 **8:8** Some of the people no longer understood Hebrew well because they had spoken only Aramaic in Babylon. This verse seems to refer to an extemporaneous translation of the book of the Law into Aramaic by Ezra, perhaps with additional comments so that the people could understand. Written translations into Aramaic were made later (which also included commentary) and were called Targums.

[b]and the Levites that taught the people, said unto all the people, [c]This day *is* holy[6918] unto the LORD your God; [d]mourn not, nor weep. For all the people wept, when they heard[8085] the words[1697] of the law.

10 Then he said unto them, Go your way, eat the fat, and drink the sweet, [a]and send portions unto them for whom nothing is prepared:[3559] for *this* day *is* holy unto our Lord:[113] neither be ye sorry;[6087] for the joy[2304] of the LORD is your strength.

11 So the Levites stilled all the people, saying, Hold your peace, for the day *is* holy; neither be ye grieved.

12 And all the people went their way to eat, and to drink, and to [a]send portions, and to make[6213] great mirth, because they had [b]understood[995] the words that were declared[3045] unto them.

The Feast of Tabernacles

13 And on the second day were gathered together the chief[7218] of the fathers[1] of all the people, the priests,[3548] and the Levites, unto Ezra the scribe, even [I]to understand[7919] the words of the law.

14 And they found written in the law which the LORD had commanded [I]by Moses, that the children[1121] of Israel should dwell in [a]booths[5521] in the feast[2282] of the seventh month:

15 And [a]that they should publish[8085] and proclaim in all their cities, and [b]in Jerusalem, saying, Go forth unto the mount, and [c]fetch olive branches, and pine[8081] branches, and myrtle branches, and palm branches, and branches of thick trees, to make booths, as *it is* written.

16 So the people went forth, and brought *them,* and made themselves booths, every one upon the [a]roof of his house, and in their courts,2691 and in the courts of the house of God, and in the street of the [b]water gate, [c]and in the street of the gate of Ephraim.

17 And all the congregation[6951] of them that were come again out of the captivity[7628] made booths, and sat under the booths: for since the days of Jeshua the son of Nun unto that day had not the children of Israel done so. And there was very [a]great gladness.

18 Also [a]day by day, from the first[7223] day unto the last day, he read in the book of the law of God. And they kept[6213] the feast seven days; and on the eighth day *was* [I]a solemn assembly,[6116] [b]according unto the manner.[4941]

The People Confess Their Sins

9 Now in the twenty and fourth day[3117] of [a]this month the children[1121] of Israel were assembled[622] with fasting, and with sackclothes,8242 [b]and earth[127] upon them.

2 And [a]the seed[2233] of Israel separated themselves[914] from all [I]strangers, and stood and confessed[3034] their sins, and the iniquities[5771] of their fathers.[1]

3 And they stood up in their place, and [a]read[7121] in the book[5612] of the law[8451] of the LORD their God[430] *one* fourth part of the day; and *another* fourth part they confessed, and worshipped[7812] the LORD their God.

4 Then stood up upon the [I]stairs, of the Levites, Jeshua, and Bani, Kadmiel, Shebaniah, Bunni, Sherebiah, Bani *and* Chenani, and cried[2199] with a loud voice unto the LORD their God.

5 Then the Levites, Jeshua, and Kadmiel, Bani, Hashabniah, Sherebiah, Hodijah, Shebaniah, *and* Pethahiah, said, Stand up *and* bless[1288] the LORD your God for ever[5769] and ever: and blessed be[1288] [a]thy glorious[3519] name, which is exalted above all blessing[1293] and praise.[8416]

6 [a]Thou, *even* thou, *art* LORD alone; [b]thou hast made[6213] heaven,8064 [c]the heaven of heavens, with [d]all their host,[6635] the earth,[776] and all *things* that *are* therein, the seas, and all that *is* therein, and thou [e]preservest[2421] them all; and the host of heaven worshippeth[7812] thee.

7 Thou *art* the LORD the God, who didst choose[977] [a]Abram, and broughtest

---

9 [b]2Chr. 35:3; Neh. 8:8 [c]Lev. 23:24; Num. 29:1 [d]Deut. 16:14, 15; Eccl. 3:4
10 [a]Esth. 9:19, 22; Rev. 11:10
12 [a]Neh. 8:10 [b]Neh. 8:7, 8
13 [I]Or, *that they might instruct in the words of the law*
14 [I]Hebr. *by the hand of* [a]Lev. 23:34, 42; Deut. 16:13
15 [a]Lev. 23:4 [b]Deut. 16:16 [c]Lev. 23:40
16 [a]Deut. 22:8 [b]Neh. 12:37 [c]2Kgs. 14:13; Neh. 12:39
17 *2Chr. 30:21*
18 [I]Hebr. *a restraint* [a]Deut. 31:10-13 [b]Lev. 23:36; Num. 29:35
1 [a]Neh. 8:2 [b]Josh. 7:6; 1Sam. 4:12; 2Sam. 1:2; Job 2:12
2 [I]Hebr. *strange children* [a]Ezra 10:11; Neh. 13:3, 30
3 [a]Neh. 8:7, 8
4 [I]Or, *scaffold*
5 [a]1Chr. 29:13
6 [a]2Kgs. 19:15, 19; Ps. 86:10; Isa. 37:16, 20 [b]Gen. 1:1; Ex. 20:11; Rev. 14:7 [c]Deut. 10:14; 1Kgs. 8:27 [d]Gen. 2:1 [e]Ps. 36:6
7 [a]Gen. 11:31; 12:1

him forth out of Ur of the Chaldees, and
gavest[7760] him the name of [b]Abraham;
8 And foundest his heart3824 [a]faith-
ful[539] before thee, and madest[3772] a
[b]covenant[1285] with him to give the land[776]
of the Canaanites, the Hittites, the
Amorites, and the Perizzites, and the
Jebusites, and the Girgashites, to give *it,*
I say, to his seed, and [c]hast performed
thy words;[1697] for thou *art* righteous:[6662]
9 [a]And didst see the affliction of our
fathers in Egypt, and [b]heardest[8085] their
cry by the Red sea;
10 And shewedst signs[226] and
wonders[4159] upon Pharaoh, and on all his
servants,[5650] and on all the people[5971] of
his land: for thou knewest[3045] that they
[a]dealt proudly[2102] against them. So didst
thou [b]get thee a name, as *it is* this day.
11 [a]And thou didst divide the sea before them, so that they went through the
midst of the sea on the dry land;[3004] and
their persecutors7291 thou threwest into
the deeps, [b]as a stone into the mighty
waters.
12 Moreover thou [a]leddest[5148] them
in the day[3119] by a cloudy pillar; and in
the night[3915] by a pillar of fire, to give
them light215 in the way[1870] wherein they
should go.
13 [a]Thou camest down also upon
mount Sinai, and spakest with them from
heaven, and gavest them [b]right[3477]
judgments,[4941] and [I]true[571] laws,[8451]
good[2896] statutes[2706] and commandments:[4687]
14 And madest known[3045] unto them
thy [a]holy[6944] sabbath,[7676] and commandedst[6680] them precepts,[4687] statutes, and
laws, by the hand[3027] of Moses thy
servant:[5650]
15 And [a]gavest them bread from
heaven for their hunger, and [b]broughtest
forth water for them out of the rock
for their thirst, and promisedst[559] them
that they should [c]go in to possess[3423] the
land [I]which thou hadst sworn to give
them.
16 [a]But they and our fathers dealt
proudly, and [b]hardened their necks, and
hearkened[8085] not to thy commandments,
17 And refused[3985] to obey, [a]neither
were mindful[2142] of thy wonders[6381] that
thou didst among them; but hardened
their necks, and in their rebellion[4805] appointed [b]a captain to return[7725] to their
bondage:[5659] but thou *art* [I]a God ready to
pardon,[5547] [c]gracious[2587] and merciful,
slow[750] to anger,[639] and of great kindness,[2617] and forsookest them not.
18 Yea, [a]when they had made them a
molten[4541] calf, and said, This *is* thy god
that brought thee up[5927] out of Egypt,
and had wrought great provocations;
19 Yet thou in thy [a]manifold mercies[7356] forsookest them not in the wilderness: the [b]pillar of the cloud[6051]
departed[5493] not from them by day,[3119] to
lead[5148] them in the way; neither the pillar of fire by night, to shew[5046] them
light, and the way wherein they should
go.
20 Thou gavest also thy [a]good
spirit[7307] to instruct[7919] them, and with-
heldest not thy [b]manna[4478] from their
mouth,[6310] and gavest them [c]water for
their thirst.
21 Yea, [a]forty years didst thou sustain them in the wilderness, *so that* they
lacked nothing; their [b]clothes waxed not
old, and their feet swelled not.
22 Moreover thou gavest them kingdoms[4467] and nations,[5971] and didst divide them into corners: so they possessed[3423] the land of [a]Sihon, and the
land of the king[4428] of Heshbon, and the
land of Og king of Bashan.
23 [a]Their children also multipliedst
thou as the stars of heaven, and broughtest them into the land, concerning which
thou hadst promised[559] to their fathers,
that they should go in to possess *it.*
24 So [a]the children went in and possessed the land, and [b]thou subduedst before them the inhabitants of the land, the
Canaanites, and gavest them into their
hands,[3027] with their kings, and the people of the land, that they might do with
them [I]as they would.[7522]
25 And they took strong cities, and a
[a]fat land, and possessed [b]houses[1004] full
of all goods,[2898] [I]wells[953] digged, vineyards, and oliveyards, and [II]fruit trees in
abundance: so they did eat, and were

7 [b]Gen. 17:5
8 [a]Gen. 15:6 [b]Gen. 12:7; 15:18; 17:7, 8 [c]Josh. 23:14
9 [a]Ex. 2:25; 3:7 [b]Ex. 14:10
10 [a]Ex. 18:11 [b]Ex. 9:16; Isa. 63:12, 14; Jer. 32:20; Dan. 9:15
11 [a]Ex. 14:21, 22, 27, 28; Ps. 78:13 [b]Ex. 15:5, 10
12 [a]Ex. 13:21
13 [I]Hebr. *laws of truth* [a]Ex. 19:20; 20:1 [b]Ps. 19:8, 9; Rom. 7:12
14 [a]Gen. 2:3; Ex. 20:8, 11
15 [I]Hebr. *which thou hadst lifted up thine hand to give them,* Num. 14:30 [a]Ex. 16:14, 15; John 6:31 [b]Ex. 17:6; Num. 20:9-13 [c]Deut. 1:8
16 [a]Neh. 9:29; Ps. 106:6 [b]Deut. 31:27; 2Kgs. 17:14; 2Chr. 30:8; Jer. 19:15
17 [I]Hebr. *a God of pardons* [a]Ps. 78:11, 42, 43 [b]Num. 14:4 [c]Ex. 34:6; Num. 14:18; Ps. 86:5, 15; Joel 2:13
18 [a]Ex. 32:4
19 [a]Neh. 9:27; Ps. 106:45 [b]Ex. 13:21, 22; Num. 14:14; 1Cor. 10:1
20 [a]Num. 11:17; Isa. 63:11 [b]Ex. 16:15; Josh. 5:12 [c]Ex. 17:6
21 [a]Deut. 2:7 [b]Deut. 8:4; 29:5
22 [a]Num. 21:21-26
23 [a]Gen. 22:17
24 [I]Hebr. *according to their will* [a]Josh. 1:2-6 [b]Ps. 44:2, 3
25 [I]Or, *cisterns* [II]Hebr. *tree of food* [a]Num. 13:27; Deut. 8:7, 8; Neh. 9:35; Ezek. 20:6 [b]Deut. 6:11

filled, and [c]became fat, and delighted themselves in thy great [d]goodness.

26 Nevertheless they [a]were disobedient,[4784] and rebelled[4775] against thee, and [b]cast thy law behind their backs, and slew[2026] thy [c]prophets[5030] which testified[5749] against them to turn[7725] them to thee, and they wrought great provocations.

27 [a]Therefore thou deliveredst[5414] them into the hand of their enemies, who vexed[6687] them: and in the time[6256] of their trouble, when they cried unto thee, thou [b]heardest *them* from heaven; and according to thy manifold mercies [c]thou gavest them saviours,[3467] who saved them out of the hand of their enemies.

28 But after they had rest, [Ia]they did evil[7451] again before thee: therefore leftest[5800] thou them in the hand of their enemies, so that they had the dominion[7287] over them: yet when they returned,[7725] and cried unto thee, thou heardest *them* from heaven; and [b]many times[6256] didst thou deliver[5337] them according to thy mercies;

29 And testifiedst against them, that thou mightest bring them again unto thy law: yet they [a]dealt proudly, and hearkened not unto thy commandments, but sinned[2398] against thy judgments, ([b]which if a man[120] do, he shall live[2421] in them;) and [I]withdrew[5637] the shoulder, and hardened their neck, and would not hear.[8085]

30 Yet many years didst thou [I]forbear them, and testifiedst [a]against them by thy spirit [IIb]in thy prophets: yet would they not give ear: [c]therefore gavest thou them into the hand of the people of the lands.[776]

31 Nevertheless for thy great mercies' sake [a]thou didst not utterly consume[3617] them, nor forsake[5800] them; for thou *art* [b]a gracious and merciful God.

32 Now therefore, our God, the great, the [a]mighty, and the terrible[3372] God, who keepest[8104] covenant and mercy,[2617] let not all the [I]trouble seem little before thee, [II]that hath come upon us, on our kings, on our princes,[8269] and on our priests,[3548] and on our prophets, and on our fathers, and on all thy people, [b]since the time[3117] of the kings of Assyria unto this day.

33 Howbeit [a]thou *art* just[6662] in all that is brought upon us; for thou hast done[6213] right,[571] but [b]we have done wickedly:[7561]

34 Neither have our kings, our princes, our priests, nor our fathers, kept[6213] thy law, nor hearkened[7181] unto thy commandments and thy testimonies,[5715] wherewith thou didst testify[5749] against them.

35 For they have [a]not served[5647] thee in their kingdom,[4438] and in [b]thy great goodness that thou gavest them, and in the large and [c]fat land which thou gavest before them, neither turned they from their wicked[7451] works.

36 Behold, [a]we *are* servants this day, and *for* the land that thou gavest unto our fathers to eat the fruit thereof and the good[2898] thereof, behold, we *are* servants in it:

37 And [a]it yieldeth much increase unto the kings whom thou hast set over us because of our sins: also they have [b]dominion[4910] over our bodies,[1472] and over our cattle, at their pleasure,[7522] and we *are* in great distress.

The People Make a Pledge

38 And because of all this we [a]make a sure[548] *covenant,* and write *it;* and our princes, Levites, *and* priests, [Ib]seal *unto it.*

10 Now [I]those that sealed *were,* [a]Nehemiah, [II]the Tirshatha, [b]the son of Hachaliah, and Zidkijah,

2 [a]Seraiah, Azariah, Jeremiah,

3 Pashur, Amariah, Malchijah,

4 Hattush, Shebaniah, Malluch,

5 Harim, Meremoth, Obadiah,

6 Daniel, Ginnethon, Baruch,

7 Meshullam, Abijah, Mijamin,

8 Maaziah, Bilgai, Shemaiah: these *were* the priests.[3548]

---

25 [c]Deut. 32:15 [d]Hos. 3:5
26 [a]Judg. 2:11, 12; Ezek. 20:21 [b]1Kgs. 14:9; Ps. 50:17 [c]1Kgs. 18:4; 19:10; 2Chr. 24:20, 21; Matt. 23:37; Acts 7:52
27 [a]Judg. 2:14; 3:8-11; Ps. 106:41, 42 [b]Ps. 106:44 [c]Judg. 2:18; 3:9
28 [I]Hebr. *they returned to do evil* [a]Judg. 3:11, 12, 30; 4:1; 5:31; 6:1 [b]Ps. 106:43
29 [I]Hebr. *they gave a withdrawing shoulder,* Zech. 7:11 [a]Neh. 9:16 [b]Lev. 18:5; Ezek. 20:11; Rom. 10:5; Gal. 3:12
30 [I]Hebr. *protract over them* [II]Hebr. *in the hand of thy prophets* [a]2Kgs. 17:13; 2Chr. 36:15; Jer. 7:25; 25:4 [b]Acts 7:51; 1Pet. 1:11; 2Pet. 1:21 [c]Isa. 5:5; 42:24
31 [a]Jer. 4:27; 5:10, 18 [b]Neh. 9:17
32 [I]Hebr. *weariness* [II]Hebr. *that hath found us* [a]Ex. 34:6, 7; 1:5 [b]2Kgs. 17:3
33 [a]Ps. 119:137; Dan. 9:14 [b]Ps. 106:6; Dan. 9:5, 6, 8
35 [a]Deut. 28:47 [b]Neh. 9:25 [c]Neh. 9:25
36 [a]Deut. 28:48; Ezra 9:9
37 [a]Deut. 28:33, 51 [b]Deut. 28:48
38 [I]Hebr. *are at the sealing,* or, *sealed* [a]2Kgs. 23:3; 2Chr. 29:10; 34:31; Ezra 10:3; Neh. 10:29 [b]Neh. 10:1

1 [I]Hebr. *at the sealings* [II]Or, *the governor* [a]Neh. 8:9 [b]Neh. 1:1
2 [a]Neh. 12:1-21

9 And the Levites: both Jeshua the son of Azaniah, Binnui of the sons[1121] of Henadad, Kadmiel;

10 And their brethren, Shebaniah, Hodijah, Kelita, Pelaiah, Hanan,

11 Micha, Rehob, Hashabiah,

12 Zaccur, Sherebiah, Shebaniah,

13 Hodijah, Bani, Beninu.

14 The chief[7218] of the people;[5971] [a]Parosh, Pahath–moab, Elam, Zatthu, Bani,

15 Bunni, Azgad, Bebai,

16 Adonijah, Bigvai, Adin,

17 Ater, Hizkijah, Azzur,

18 Hodijah, Hashum, Bezai,

19 Hariph, Anathoth, Nebai,

20 Magpiash, Meshullam, Hezir,

21 Meshezabeel, Zadok, Jaddua,

22 Pelatiah, Hanan, Anaiah,

23 Hoshea, Hananiah, Hashub,

24 Hallohesh, Pileha, Shobek,

25 Rehum, Hashabnah, Maaseiah,

26 And Ahijah, Hanan, Anan,

27 Malluch, Harim, Baanah.

28 [a]And the rest of the people, the priests, the Levites, the porters, the singers,[7891] the Nethinims,[5411] [b]and all they that had separated themselves[914] from the people of the lands[776] unto the law[8451] of God,[430] their wives, their sons, and their daughters, every one having knowledge,[3045] and having understanding;[995]

29 They clave to their brethren, their nobles,[117] [a]and entered into a curse,[423] and into an oath,[7621] [b]to walk in God's law, which was given [I]by Moses the servant of God, and to observe[8104] and do[6213] all the commandments[4687] of the LORD[3068] our Lord,[113] and his judgments[4941] and his statutes;[2706]

30 And that we would not give [a]our daughters unto the people of the land,[776] nor take their daughters for our sons:

31 [a]And *if* the people of the land bring ware[4728] or any victuals[7668] on the sabbath[7676] day[3117] to sell, *that* we would not buy it of them on the sabbath, or on the holy[6944] day: and *that* we would leave[5203] the [b]seventh year, and the [c]exaction of [I]every debt.

32 Also we made ordinances for us, to charge ourselves yearly with the third part of a shekel for the service[5656] of the house[1004] of our God;

33 For [a]the shewbread,[3899,4635] and for the [b]continual[8548] meat offering,[4503] and for the continual burnt offering,[5930] of the sabbaths, of the new moons, for the set feasts,[4150] and for the holy *things,* and for the sin offerings[2403] to make an atonement[3722] for Israel, and *for* all the work[4399] of the house of our God.

34 And we cast[5307] the lots among the priests, the Levites, and the people, [a]for the wood offering,[7133] to bring *it* into the house of our God, after the houses[1004] of our fathers,[1] at times[6256] appointed[2163] year by year, to burn upon the altar[4196] of the LORD our God, [b]as *it is* written in the law:

35 And [a]to bring the firstfruits of our ground,[127] and the firstfruits of all fruit of all trees, year by year, unto the house of the LORD:[3068]

36 Also the firstborn of our sons, and of our cattle, as *it is* written [a]in the law, and the firstlings of our herds and of our flocks, to bring to the house of our God, unto the priests that minister[8334] in the house of our God:

37 [a]And *that* we should bring the firstfruits[7225] of our dough, and our offerings,[8641] and the fruit of all manner of trees, of wine and of oil,[3323] unto the priests, to the chambers of the house of our God; and [b]the tithes of our ground unto the Levites, that the same Levites might have the tithes in all the cities of our tillage.[5656]

38 And the priest[3548] the son of Aaron shall be with the Levites, [a]when the Levites take tithes:[6237] and the Levites shall bring up[5927] the tithe[4643] of the tithes unto the house of our God, to [b]the chambers, into the treasure house.

39 For the children[1121] of Israel and the children of Levi [a]shall bring the offering[8641] of the corn, of the new wine, and the oil, into the chambers, where *are* the vessels of the sanctuary,[4720] and the priests that minister, and the porters, and the singers: [b]and we will not forsake[5800] the house of our God.

14 [a]Ezra 2:3-58; Neh. 7:8-63

28 [a]Ezra 2:36-43 [b]Ezra 9:1; 10:11, 12, 19; Neh. 13:3

29 [I]Hebr. *by the hand of* [a]Deut. 29:12, 14; Neh. 5:12, 13; Ps. 119:106 [b]2Kgs. 23:3; 2Chr. 34:31

30 [a]Ex. 34:16; Deut. 7:3; Ezra 9:12, 14

31 [I]Hebr. *every hand* [a]Ex. 20:10; Lev. 23:3; Deut. 5:12; Neh. 13:15-18 [b]Ex. 23:10, 11; Lev. 25:4 [c]Deut. 15:1, 2; Neh. 5:12

33 [a]Lev. 24:5-9; 2Chr. 2:4

34 [a]Neh. 13:31; Isa. 40:16 [b]Lev. 6:12

35 [a]Ex. 23:19; 34:26; Lev. 19:23; Num. 18:12; Deut. 26:2

36 [a]Ex. 13:2, 12, 13; Lev. 27:26, 27; Num. 18:15, 16

37 [a]Lev. 23:17; Num. 15:19; 18:12-19; Deut. 18:4; 26:2 [b]Lev. 27:30; Num. 18:21-24

38 [a]Num. 18:26 [b]1Chr. 9:26; 2Chr. 31:11

39 [a]Deut. 12:6, 11; 2Chr. 31:12; Neh. 13:12 [b]Neh. 13:10, 11

Those in Jerusalem

11 And the rulers[8269] of the people[5971] dwelt at Jerusalem: the rest[7605] of the people also cast[5307] lots, to bring one of ten to dwell in Jerusalem [a]the holy[6944] city, and nine parts[3027] to *dwell* in *other* cities.

2 And the people blessed[1288] all the men,[582] that [a]willingly offered themselves to dwell at Jerusalem.

3 [a]Now these *are* the chief[7218] of the province that dwelt in Jerusalem: but in the cities of Judah dwelt every one in his possession[272] in their cities, *to* wit, Israel, the priests,[3548] and the Levites, and [b]the Nethinims,[5411] and [c]the children of Solomon's servants.[5650]

4 And [a]at Jerusalem dwelt *certain* of the children of Judah, and of the children of Benjamin. Of the children of Judah; Athaiah the son of Uzziah, the son of Zechariah, the son of Amariah, the son of Shephatiah, the son of Mahalaleel, of the children of [b]Perez;

5 And Maaseiah the son of Baruch, the son of Colhozeh, the son of Hazaiah, the son of Adaiah, the son[1121] of Joiarib, the son of Zechariah, the son of Shiloni.

6 All the sons[1121] of Perez that dwelt at Jerusalem *were* four hundred threescore and eight valiant[2428] men.

7 And these *are* the sons of Benjamin; Sallu the son of Meshullam, the son of Joed, the son of Pedaiah, the son of Kolaiah, the son of Maaseiah, the son of Ithiel, the son of Jesaiah.

8 And after him Gabbai, Sallai, nine hundred twenty and eight.

9 And Joel the son of Zichri *was* their overseer:[6496] and Judah the son of Senuah *was* second over the city.

10 [a]Of the priests: Jedaiah the son of Joiarib, Jachin.

11 Seraiah the son of Hilkiah, the son of Meshullam, the son of Zadok, the son of Meraioth, the son of Ahitub, *was* the ruler[5057] of the house[1004] of God.[430]

12 And their brethren that did the work[4399] of the house *were* eight hundred twenty and two: and Adaiah the son of Jeroham, the son of Pelaliah, the son of Amzi, the son of Zechariah, the son of Pashur, the son of Malchiah,

13 And his brethren, chief of the fathers,[1] two hundred forty and two: and Amashai the son of Azareel, the son of Ahasai, the son of Meshillemoth, the son of Immer,

14 And their brethren, mighty men of valour,[2428] an hundred twenty and eight: and their overseer *was* Zabdiel, [I]the son of *one of* the great men.

15 Also of the Levites: Shemaiah the son of Hashub, the son of Azrikam, the son of Hashabiah, the son of Bunni;

16 And Shabbethai and Jozabad, of the chief of the Levites, [I]*had* the oversight of [a]the outward business[4399] of the house of God.

17 And Mattaniah the son of Micha, the son of Zabdi, the son of Asaph, *was* the principal[7218] to begin the thanksgiving[3034] in prayer:[8605] and Bakbukiah the second among his brethren, and Abda the son of Shammua, the son of Galal, the son of Jeduthun.

18 All the Levites in [a]the holy city *were* two hundred fourscore and four.

19 Moreover the porters,[7778] Akkub, Talmon, and their brethren that kept[8104] [I]the gates, *were* an hundred seventy and two.

20 And the residue[7605] of Israel, of the priests, *and* the Levites, *were* in all the cities of Judah, every one in his inheritance.[5159]

21 [a]But the Nethinims[5411] dwelt in [I]Ophel: and Ziha and Gispa *were* over the Nethinims.

22 The overseer also of the Levites at Jerusalem *was* Uzzi the son of Bani, the son of Hashabiah, the son of Mattaniah, the son of Micha. Of the sons of Asaph, the singers[7891] *were* over the business of the house of God.

23 For [a]*it was* the king's commandment[4687] concerning them, that [I]a certain portion[548] should be for the singers, due for every day.

24 And Pethahiah the son of Meshezabeel, of the children of [a]Zerah the son of Judah, *was* [b]at the king's

1 [a]Neh. 11:18; Matt. 4:5; 27:53
2 [a]Judg. 5:9
3 [a]1Chr. 9:2, 3 [b]Ezra 2:43 [c]Ezra 2:55
4 [a]1Chr. 9:3-9 [b]Gen. 38:29, *Pharez*
10 [a]1Chr. 9:10-13
14 [I]Or, *the son of Haggedolim*
16 [I]Hebr. were *over* [a]1Chr. 26:29
18 [a]Neh. 11:1
19 [I]Hebr. *at the gates*
21 [I]Or, *The tower* [a]Neh. 3:26
23 [I]Or, *a sure ordinance* [a]Ezra 6:8, 9; 7:20-23
24 [a]Gen. 38:30, *Zarah* [b]1Chr. 18:17; 23:28

hand[3027] in all matters concerning the
people.

Surrounding Towns and Villages

25 And for the villages, with their
fields,[7704] *some* of the children of Judah
dwelt at [a]Kirjath–arba, and *in* the villages thereof, and at Dibon, and *in* the
villages thereof, and at Jekabzeel, and *in*
the villages thereof,
26 And at Jeshua, and at Moladah,
and at Beth–phelet,
27 And at Hazar–shual, and at Beer–
sheba, and *in* the villages thereof,
28 And at Ziklag, and at Mekonah,
and in the villages thereof,
29 And at En–rimmon, and at
Zareah, and at Jarmuth,
30 Zanoah, Adullam, and *in* their
villages,2691 at Lachish, and the fields
thereof, at Azekah, and *in* the villages
thereof. And they dwelt from Beer–sheba
unto the valley of Hinnom.
31 The children also of Benjamin
[I]from Geba *dwelt* [II]at Michmash, and Aija,
and Bethel, and *in* their villages,
32 *And* at Anathoth, Nob, Ananiah,
33 Hazor, Ramah, Gittaim,
34 Hadid, Zeboim, Neballat,
35 Lod, and Ono, [a]the valley of
craftsmen.2796
36 And of the Levites *were* divisions
in Judah, *and* in Benjamin.

The List of Priests and Levites

12 Now these *are* the [a]priests[3548] and
the Levites that went up[5927] with
Zerubbabel the son of Shealtiel, and
Jeshua: [b]Seraiah, Jeremiah, Ezra,
2 Amariah, [Ia]Malluch, Hattush,
3 [Ia]Shechaniah, [IIb]Rehum, [IIIc]Mere-
moth,
4 Iddo, [Ia]Ginnetho, [b]Abijah,
5 [Ia]Miamin, [IIb]Maadiah, Bilgah,
6 Shemaiah, and Joiarib, Jedaiah,
7 [Ia]Sallu, Amok, Hilkiah, Jedaiah.
These *were* the chief[7218] of the priests
and of their brethren in the days[3117] of
[b]Jeshua.
8 Moreover the Levites: Jeshua,
Binnui, Kadmiel, Sherebiah, Judah, *and*
Mattaniah, [a]*which was* over [I]the thanksgiving, he and his brethren.
9 Also Bakbukiah and Unni, their
brethren, *were* over against them in the
watches.[4931]
10 And Jeshua begat Joiakim,
Joiakim also begat Eliashib, and Eliashib
begat Joiada,
11 And Joiada begat Jonathan, and
Jonathan begat Jaddua.
12 And in the days of Joiakim were
priests, the chief of the fathers:[1] of
Seraiah, Meraiah; of Jeremiah, Hananiah;
13 Of Ezra, Meshullam; of Amariah,
Jehohanan;
14 Of Melicu, Jonathan; of Shebaniah, Joseph;
15 Of Harim, Adna; of Meraioth,
Helkai;
16 Of Iddo, Zechariah; of Ginnethon,
Meshullam;
17 Of Abijah, Zichri; of Miniamin,
of Moadiah, Piltai;
18 Of Bilgah, Shammua; of Shemaiah, Jehonathan;
19 And of Joiarib, Mattenai; of
Jedaiah, Uzzi;
20 Of Sallai, Kallai; of Amok, Eber;
21 Of Hilkiah, Hashabiah; of Jedaiah,
Nethaneel.
22 The Levites in the days of
Eliashib, Joiada, and Johanan, and
Jaddua, *were* recorded chief of the fathers: also the priests, to the reign[4438] of
Darius the Persian.
23 The sons[1121] of Levi the chief of
the fathers, *were* written in the book[5612]
of the [a]chronicles, even until the days of
Johanan the son of Eliashib.
24 And the chief of the Levites:
Hashabiah, Sherebiah, and Jeshua the son
of Kadmiel, with their brethren over
against them, to praise[1984] *and* to give
thanks,[3034] [a]according to the commandment[4687] of David the man of God,[430]
[b]ward over against ward.4929
25 Mattaniah, and Bakbukiah,
Obadiah, Meshullam, Talmon, Akkub,
were porters7778 keeping[8104] the ward at
the [I]thresholds[624] of the gates.
26 These *were* in the days of Joiakim

25 [a]Josh. 14:15

31 [I]Or, *of Geba* [II]Or, *to Michmash*

35 [a]1Chr. 4:14

1 [a]Ezra 2:1, 2 [b]Neh. 10:2-8

2 [I]Or, *Melicu* [a]Neh. 12:14

3 [I]Or, *Shebaniah* [II]Or, *Harim* [III]Or, *Meraioth* [a]Neh. 12:14 [b]Neh. 12:15 [c]Neh. 12:15

4 [I]Or, *Ginnethon* [a]Neh. 12:16 [b]Luke 1:5

5 [I]Or, *Miniamin* [II]Or, *Moadiah* [a]Neh. 12:17 [b]Neh. 12:17

7 [I]Or, *Sallai* [a]Neh. 12:20 [b]Ezra 3:2; Hag. 1:1; Zech. 3:1

8 [I]That is, *the psalms of thanksgiving* [a]Neh. 11:17

23 [a]1Chr. 9:14-34

24 [a]1Chr. 23; 25; 26 [b]Ezra 3:11

25 [I]Or, *treasuries, or, assemblies*

the son of Jeshua, the son of Jozadak,
and in the days of Nehemiah [a]the governor,[6346] and of Ezra the priest,[3548] [b]the
scribe.[5608]

Nehemiah Dedicates the Wall

27 And at [a]the dedication[2598] of the
wall of Jerusalem they sought the Levites
out of all their places, to bring them to
Jerusalem, to keep[6213] the dedication with
gladness, [b]both with thanksgivings,[8426]
and with singing,[7892] *with* cymbals,
psalteries, and with harps.
28 And the sons of the singers[7891]
gathered themselves together,[622] both out
of the plain country[3603] round about
Jerusalem, and from the villages of
Netophathi;
29 Also from the house[1004] of Gilgal,
and out of the fields of Geba and
Azmaveth: for the singers had builded
them villages round about Jerusalem.
30 And the priests and the Levites
purified themselves, and purified the
people,[5971] and the gates, and the wall.
31 Then I brought up[5927] the
princes[8269] of Judah upon the wall, and
appointed two great *companies of them*
that gave thanks,[8426] *whereof* [a]*one* went
on the right hand upon the wall [b]toward
the dung gate:
32 And after them went Hoshaiah,
and half of the princes of Judah,
33 And Azariah, Ezra, and Meshullam,
34 Judah, and Benjamin, and
Shemaiah, and Jeremiah,
35 And *certain* of the priests'[3548]
sons [a]with trumpets; *namely,* Zechariah
the son of Jonathan, the son of Shemaiah, the son of Mattaniah, the son of
Michaiah, the son of Zaccur, the son of
Asaph:
36 And his brethren, Shemaiah, and
Azarael, Milalai, Gilalai, Maai, Nethaneel,
and Judah, Hanani, with [a]the musical[7892]
instruments of David the man of God,
and Ezra the scribe before them.
37 [a]And at the fountain gate, which
was over against them, they went up by
[b]the stairs[4609] of the city of David, at the

26 [a]Neh. 8:9 [b]Ezra 7:6, 11
27 [a]Deut. 20:5 [b]1Chr. 25:6; 2Chr. 5:13; 7:6
31 [a]Neh. 12:38 [b]Neh. 2:13; 3:13
35 [a]Num. 10:2, 8
36 [a]1Chr. 23:5
37 [a]Neh. 2:14; 3:15 [b]Neh. 3:15 [c]Neh. 3:26; 8:1, 3, 16
38 [a]Neh. 12:31 [b]Neh. 3:11 [c]Neh. 3:8
39 [a]2Kgs. 14:13; Neh. 8:16 [b]Neh. 3:6 [c]Neh. 3:3 [d]Neh. 3:1 [e]Neh. 3:32 [f]Jer. 32:2
42 [I]Hebr. *made their voice to be heard*
44 [a]Chr. 31:11, 12; Neh. 13:5, 12, 13 [I]That is, *appointed by the law* [II]Hebr. *for the joy of Judah* [III]Hebr. *that stood*
45 [a]1Chr. 25; 26
46 [a]1Chr. 25:1-7; 2Chr. 29:30

going up of the wall, above the house of
David, even unto [c]the water gate eastward.
38 [a]And the other *company of them*
that gave thanks went over against *them,*
and I after them, and the half of the people upon the wall, from beyond [b]the
tower of the furnaces even unto [c]the
broad wall;
39 [a]And from above the gate of
Ephraim, and above [b]the old gate, and
above [c]the fish[1709] gate, [d]and the tower of
Hananeel, and the tower of Meah, even
unto [e]the sheep gate: and they stood still
in [f]the prison gate.
40 So stood the two *companies of*
them that gave thanks in the house of
God, and I, and the half of the rulers[5461]
with me:
41 And the priests; Eliakim, Maaseiah, Miniamin, Michaiah, Elioenai,
Zechariah, *and* Hananiah, with trumpets;
42 And Maaseiah, and Shemaiah,
and Eleazar, and Uzzi, and Jehohanan,
and Malchijah, and Elam, and Ezer. And
the singers [I]sang loud,[8085] with Jezrahiah
their overseer.
43 Also that day[3117] they offered[2076]
great sacrifices,[2077] and rejoiced: for God
had made them rejoice with great joy:
the wives also and the children rejoiced:
so that the joy of Jerusalem was
heard[8085] even afar off.

Providing for Worship

44 [a]And at that time[3117] were some
appointed over the chambers for the
treasures, for the offerings,[8641] for the
firstfruits,[7225] and for the tithes, to
gather[3664] into them out of the fields of
the cities the portions [I]of the law[8451] for
the priests and Levites: [II]for Judah rejoiced for the priests and for the Levites
[III]that waited.
45 And both the singers and the
porters kept the ward[4931] of their God,
and the ward of the purification,[2893] [a] according to the commandment of David,
and of Solomon his son.
46 For in the days of David [a]and
Asaph of old[6924] *there were* chief of the

singers, and songs[7892] of praise[8416] and thanksgiving unto God.

47 And all Israel in the days of Zerubbabel, and in the days of Nehemiah, gave the portions of the singers and the porters, every day his portion:[1697] [a]and they [I]sanctified[6942] *holy things* unto the Levites; [b]and the Levites sanctified *them* unto the children of Aaron.

The Reforms of Nehemiah

13 On that day[3117] [I][a]they read[7121] in the book[5612] of Moses in the [II]audience[241] of the people;[5971] and therein was found written, [b]that the Ammonite and the Moabite should not come into the congregation[6951] of God[430] for ever;[5769]

2 Because they met not the children of Israel with bread and with water, but [a]hired Balaam against them, that he should curse[7043] them: [b]howbeit our God turned[2015] the curse[7045] into a blessing.[1293]

3 Now it came to pass, when they had heard[8085] the law,[8451] [a]that they separated[914] from Israel all the mixed multitude.[6154]

4 And before this, Eliashib the priest,[3548] [I]having the oversight of the chamber of the house[1004] of our God, *was* allied unto Tobiah:

5 And he had prepared for him a great chamber, [a]where aforetime they laid the meat offerings,[4503] the frankincense,3828 and the vessels, and the tithes of the corn, the new wine, and the oil,[3323] [I][b]which was commanded *to be given* to the Levites, and the singers,[7891] and the porters;7778 and the offerings of the priests.[3548]

6 But in all this *time* was not I at Jerusalem: [a]for in the two and thirtieth year of Artaxerxes king[4428] of Babylon came I unto the king, and [I]after certain days[3117] [II]obtained I leave[7592] of the king:

7 And I came to Jerusalem, and understood[995] of the evil[7451] that Eliashib did for Tobiah, in [a]preparing[6213] him a chamber in the courts of the house of God.

8 And it grieved me sore: therefore I cast forth all the household[1004] stuff of Tobiah out of the chamber.

9 Then I commanded,[559] and they [a]cleansed[2891] the chambers: and thither brought I again the vessels of the house of God, with the meat offering[4503] and the frankincense.

10 And I perceived[3045] that the portions of the Levites had [a]not been given *them:* for the Levites and the singers, that did the work,[4399] were fled every one to [b]his field.

11 Then [a]contended[7378] I with the rulers,[5461] and said, [b]Why *is* the house of God forsaken?[5800] And I gathered them together,[6908] and set them in their [I]place.

12 [a]Then brought all Judah the tithe[4643] of the corn and the new wine and the oil unto the [I]treasuries.

13 [a]And I made treasurers over the treasuries, Shelemiah the priest, and Zadok the scribe, and of the Levites, Pedaiah: and [I]next to them *was* Hanan the son of Zaccur, the son of Mattaniah: for they were counted[2803] [b]faithful,[539] and [II]their office *was* to distribute unto their brethren.

14 [a]Remember[2142] me, O my God, concerning this, and wipe not out my [I]good deeds[2617] that I have done[6213] for the house of my God, and for the [II]offices4249 thereof.

15 In those days saw[7200] I in Judah *some* treading wine presses [a]on the sabbath,[7676] and bringing in sheaves, and lading asses; as also wine, grapes, and figs, and all *manner of* burdens,[4853] [b]which they brought into Jerusalem on the sabbath day: and I testified[5749] *against them* in the day wherein they sold victuals.6718

16 There dwelt men of Tyre also therein, which brought fish,[1709] and all manner of ware,4377 and sold on the sabbath unto the children of Judah, and in Jerusalem.

17 [a]Then I contended with the nobles[2715] of Judah, and said unto them,

47 [I]That is, *set apart* [a]Num. 18:21, 24 [b]Num. 18:26

1 [I]Hebr. *there was read* [II]Hebr. *ears* [a]Deut. 31:11, 12; 2Kgs. 23:2; Neh. 8:3, 8; 9:3; Isa. 34:16 [b]Deut. 23:3, 4

2 [a]Num. 22:5; Josh. 24:9, 10 [b]Num. 23:11; 24:10; Deut. 23:5

3 [a]Neh. 9:2; 10:28

4 [I]Hebr. *being set over,* Neh. 12:44

5 [I]Hebr. *the commandment of the Levites* [a]Neh. 12:44 [b]Num. 18:21, 24

6 [I]Hebr. *at the end of days* [II]Or, *I earnestly requested* [a]Neh. 5:14

7 [a]Neh. 13:1, 5

9 [a]2Chr. 29:5, 15, 16, 18

10 [a]Mal. 3:8 [b]Num. 35:2

11 [I]Hebr. *standing* [a]Neh. 13:17, 25; Prov. 28:4 [b]Neh. 10:39

12 [I]Or, *storehouses* [a]Neh. 10:38, 39; 12:44

13 [I]Hebr. *at their hand* [II]Hebr. *it was upon them* [a]2Chr. 31:12; Neh. 12:44 [b]Neh. 7:2; 1Cor. 4:2

14 [I]Hebr. *kindnesses* [II]Or, *observations* [a]Neh. 5:19; 13:22, 31

15 [a]Ex. 20:10 [b]Neh. 10:31; Jer. 17:21, 22

17 [a]Neh. 13:11

What evil thing[1697] *is* this that ye do, and profane the sabbath day?

18 [a]Did not your fathers[1] thus, and did not our God bring all this evil upon us, and upon this city? yet ye bring more wrath upon Israel by profaning[2490] the sabbath.

19 And it came to pass, that when the gates of Jerusalem [a]began to be dark[6751] before the sabbath, I commanded that the gates should be shut, and charged that they should not be opened till after the sabbath: [b]and *some* of my servants[5650] set I at the gates, *that* there should no burden[4853] be brought in on the sabbath day.

20 So the merchants and sellers of all kind of ware[4465] lodged without Jerusalem once or twice.

21 Then I testified against them, and said unto them, Why lodge ye [I]about the wall? if ye do *so* again, I will lay hands[3027] on you. From that time[6256] forth came they no *more* on the sabbath.

22 And I commanded the Levites that [a]they should cleanse themselves,[2891] and *that* they should come *and* keep[8104] the gates, to sanctify[6942] the sabbath day. [b]Remember me, O my God, *concerning* this also, and spare me according to the [I]greatness of thy mercy.[2617]

23 In those days also saw I Jews *that* [Ia]had married wives[802] of Ashdod, of Ammon, *and* of Moab:

24 And their children spake[1696] half in the speech of Ashdod, and [I]could not speak in the Jews' language, but according to the language [II]of each people.

25 And I [a]contended with them, and [I]cursed[7043] them, and smote[5221] certain of them, and plucked off their hair, and made them [b]swear[7650] by God, *saying,* Ye shall not give your daughters unto their sons,[1121] nor take[5375] their daughters unto your sons, or for yourselves.

26 [a]Did not Solomon king of Israel sin[2398] by these things? yet [b]among many nations[1471] was there no king like him, [c]who was beloved of his God, and God made him king over all Israel: [d]nevertheless even him did[2398] outlandish[5237] women cause to sin.[2398]

27 Shall we then hearken[8085] unto you to do all this great evil, to [a]transgress[4603] against our God in marrying strange[5237] wives?

🗝 28 And *one* of the sons [a]of Joiada, the son of Eliashib the high priest, *was* son in law to Sanballat the Horonite; therefore I chased him from me.

29 [a]Remember them, O my God, [I]because they have defiled the priesthood,[3550] and [b]the covenant[1285] of the priesthood, and of the Levites.

30 [a]Thus cleansed I them from all strangers, and [b]appointed the wards[4931] of the priests and the Levites, every one in his business;[4399]

31 And for [a]the wood offering,[7133] at times[6256] appointed,[2163] and for the firstfruits. [b]Remember me, O my God, for good.[2896]

18 [a]Jer. 17:21-23
19 [a]Lev. 23:32 [b]Jer. 17:21, 22
21 [I]Hebr. *before the wall*
22 [I]Or, *multitude* [a]Neh. 12:30 [b]Neh. 13:14, 31
23 [I]Hebr. *had made to dwell with the* [a]Ezra 9:2
24 [I]Hebr. *they discerned not to speak* [II]Hebr. *of people and people*
25 [I]Or, *reviled them* [a]Neh. 13:11; Prov. 28:4 [b]Ezra 10:5; Neh. 10:29, 30
26 [a]1Kgs. 11:1-3 [b]1Kgs. 3:13; 2Chr. 1:12 [c]2Sam. 12:24 [d]1Kgs. 11:4-8
27 [a]Ezra 10:2
28 [a]Neh. 12:10, 22
29 [I]Hebr. *for the defilings* [a]Neh. 6:14 [b]Mal. 2:4, 11, 12
30 [a]Neh. 10:30 [b]Neh. 12:1-26
31 [a]Neh. 10:34 [b]Neh. 13:14, 22

🗝 **13:28** See note on Nehemiah 2:10.

The Book of ESTHER

The Book of Esther was the last of five books in a collection known as the Five Megilloth (scrolls). Each book was designated to be read publicly at one of the five major feasts of the Jews. For the sake of convenience, all the books were placed on one scroll. The other four books were the Song of Solomon, Ruth, Lamentations, and Ecclesiastes. Esther was read at the Feast of Purim, the commemoration of the great deliverance of the Jews that God brought about through Esther.

There are those that question whether the Book of Esther should be included in the canon of Scripture. They try to justify their position mainly by stressing that the name of God is never mentioned in the Book of Esther. This should not be a reason for concern, however, since the main theme of the book is clearly the providence of God and His care for His people. The mighty Ahasuerus (or Xerxes) was never beyond the control of God, and it was impossible for Haman to carry out his dreadful intentions while God was protecting His people.

The fact that Esther asked the Jews residing in the capital city to fast demonstrates that she was relying on the grace of God to resolve the desperate situation. The plan that Haman had set into action threatened to annihilate all of the Jewish people. The Persian Empire under Ahasuerus extended from India to Ethiopia, and virtually all of the Jews lived within this area.

The events of this book took place about thirty years prior to the efforts of Ezra and Nehemiah. Many have suggested that their successes would not have been possible had not Esther, Mordecai, and Daniel paved the way with their conduct and accomplishments.

Queen Vashti Defies King Ahasuerus

1 ⊶ Now it came to pass in the days[3117] of [a]Ahasuerus, (this *is* Ahasuerus which reigned,[4427] [b]from India even unto Ethiopia, [c]*over* an hundred and seven and twenty provinces:)

2 *That* in those days, when the king[4428] Ahasuerus [a]sat on the throne[3678] of his kingdom,[4438] which *was* in [b]Shushan the palace,

3 In the third year of his reign, he [a]made a feast[4960] unto all his princes[8269] and his servants;[5650] the power[2428] of Persia and Media, the nobles[6579] and princes of the provinces, *being* before him:

4 When he shewed[7200] the riches of his glorious kingdom and the honour of his excellent majesty many days, *even* an hundred and fourscore days.

5 And when these days were expired, the king made a feast unto all the people[5971] that were [I]present in Shushan the palace, both unto great and small, seven days, in the court of the garden of the king's palace;

6 *Where were* white, green, and [I]blue, *hangings,* fastened with cords of fine linen and purple to silver rings and pillars of marble: [a]the beds *were of* gold and silver, upon a pavement [II]of red, and blue, and white, and black, marble.

7 And they gave *them* drink in vessels of gold, (the vessels being diverse one from another,) and [I]royal[4438] wine in abundance, [II]according to the state[3027] of the king.

1 [a]Ezra 4:6; Dan. 9:1 [b]Esth. 8:9 [c]Dan. 6:1

2 [a]1Kgs. 1:46 [b]Neh. 1:1

3 [a]Gen. 40:20; Esth. 2:18; Mark 6:21

5 [I]Hebr. *found*

6 [I]Or, *violet* [II]Or, *of porphyry, and marble, and alabaster, and stone of blue color* [a]Esth. 7:8; Ezek. 23:41; Amos 2:8; 6:4

7 [I]Hebr. *wine of the kingdom* [II]Hebr. *according to the hand of the king*

⊶ **1:1** "Ahasuerus" is the Hebrew translation of the Persian name Khshayarsha. He is better known in history by his Greek name "Xerxes."

8 And the drinking *was* according to the law;[1881] none did compel:597 for so the king had appointed[3245] to all the officers of his house,[1004] that they should do[6213] according to every man's pleasure.[7522]

9 Also Vashti the queen[4436] made a feast for the women[802] *in* the royal house which *belonged* to king Ahasuerus.

10 On the seventh day, when [a]the heart[3820] of the king was merry[2896] with wine, he commanded[559] Mehuman, Biztha, [b]Harbona, Bigtha, and Abagtha, Zethar, and Carcas, the seven [I]chamberlains[5631] that served[8334] in the presence of Ahasuerus the king,

11 To bring Vashti the queen before the king with the crown royal, to shew[7200] the people and the princes her beauty: for she *was* [I]fair[2896] to look on.

12 But the queen Vashti refused[3985] to come at the king's commandment[1697] [I]by *his* chamberlains: therefore was the king very wroth,[7107] and his anger burned in him.

13 Then the king said to the [a]wise men,[2450] [b]which knew[3045] the times,[6256] (for so *was* the king's manner toward all that knew law and judgment:[1779]

14 And the next unto him *was* Carshena, Shethar, Admatha, Tarshish, Meres, Marsena, *and* Memucan, the [a]seven princes of Persia and Media, [b]which saw[7200] the king's face, *and* which sat the first[7223] in the kingdom;)

15 [I]What shall we do unto the queen Vashti according to law because she hath not performed the commandment[3982] of the king Ahasuerus by the chamberlains?

16 And Memucan answered[559] before the king and the princes, Vashti the queen hath not done wrong[5753] to the king only, but also to all the princes, and to all the people that *are* in all the provinces of the king Ahasuerus.

17 For *this* deed of the queen shall come abroad unto all women, so that they shall [a]despise959 their husbands in their eyes, when it shall be reported,[559] The king Ahasuerus commanded Vashti the queen to be brought in before him, but she came not.

18 *Likewise* shall the ladies[8282] of Persia and Media say[559] this day unto all the king's princes, which have heard[8085] of the deed of the queen. Thus *shall there arise* too much contempt and wrath.[7110]

19 [I]If it please[2895] the king, let there go a royal commandment [II]from him, and let it be written among the laws[1881] of the Persians and the Medes, [IIIa]that it be not altered, That Vashti come no more before king Ahasuerus; and let the king give her royal estate [IV]unto another[7468] that is better[2896] than she.

20 And when the king's decree[6599] which he shall make[6213] shall be published[8085] throughout all his empire,[4438] (for it is great,) all the wives[802] shall [a]give to their husbands honour, both to great and small.

21 And the saying[1697] [I]pleased the king and the princes; and the king did[6213] according to the word[1697] of Memucan:

22 For he sent letters[5612] into all the king's provinces, [a]into every province according to the writing thereof, and to every people after their language, that every man[376] should [b]bear rule[8323] in his own house, and [I]that *it* should be published[1696] according to the language of every people.

Esther Is Made Queen

2 After these things, when the wrath[2534] of king[4428] Ahasuerus was appeased, he remembered[2142] Vashti, and what she had done,[6213] and [a]what was decreed[1504] against her.

2 Then said the king's servants that ministered[8334] unto him, Let there be fair young virgins[1330] sought for the king:

3 And let the king appoint[6485] officers[6496] in all the provinces of his kingdom,[4438] that they may gather together[6908] all the fair young virgins unto Shushan the palace, to the house[1004] of the women,[802] [I]unto the custody[3027] of [IIa]Hege the king's chamberlain,[5631] keeper[8104] of the women; and let their things for purification[8562] be given *them:*

10 [I]Or, *eunuchs* [a]2Sam. 13:28 [b]Esth. 7:9

11 [I]Hebr. *good of countenance*

12 [I]Hebr. *which was by the hand of his eunuchs*

13 [a]Jer. 10:7; Dan. 2:12; Matt. 2:1 [b]1Chr. 12:32

14 [a]Ezra 7:14 [b]2Kgs. 25:19

15 [I]Hebr. *What to do*

17 [a]Eph. 5:33

19 [I]Hebr. *If it be good with the king* [II]Hebr. *from before him* [III]Hebr. *that it pass not away* [IV]Hebr. *unto her companion* [a]Esth. 8:8; Dan. 6:8, 12, 15

20 [a]Eph. 5:33; Col. 3:18; 1Pet. 3:1

21 [I]Hebr. *was good in the eyes of the king*

22 [I]Hebr. *that one should publish* it *according to the language of his people* [a]Esth. 8:9 [b]Eph. 5:22-24; 1Tim. 2:12

1 [a]Esth. 1:19, 20

3 [I]Hebr. *unto the hand* [II]Or, *Hegai* [a]Esth. 2:8

4 And let the maiden which pleaseth the king be queen[4427] instead of Vashti. And the thing[1697] pleased the king; and he did so.

5 *Now* in Shushan the palace there was a certain[376] Jew, whose name *was* Mordecai, the son[1121] of Jair, the son of Shimei, the son of Kish, a Benjamite;

6 [a]Who had been carried away[1540] from Jerusalem with the captivity[1473] which had been carried away with [I][b]Jeconiah king of Judah, whom Nebuchadnezzar the king of Babylon had carried away.

🗝 7 And he [I][a]brought up[539] Hadassah, that *is,* Esther, [b]his uncle's daughter: for she had neither father[1] nor mother,[517] and the maid *was* [II]fair and beautiful;[2896] 4758 whom Mordecai, when her father and mother were dead, took for his own daughter.

8 So it came to pass, when the king's commandment[1697] and his decree[1881] was heard,[8085] and when many maidens were [a]gathered together unto Shushan the palace, to the custody of Hegai, that Esther was brought also unto the king's house, to the custody of Hegai, keeper of the women.

9 And the maiden pleased him, and she obtained[5375] kindness[2617] of him; and he speedily gave her her [a]things for purification, with [I]such things as belonged to her, and seven maidens, *which were* meet to be given her, out of the king's house: and [II]he preferred 8138 her and her maids unto the best[2896] *place* of the house of the women.

10 [a]Esther had not shewed[5046] her people[5971] nor her kindred: for Mordecai had charged[6680] her that she should not shew *it.*

11 And Mordecai walked every day[3117] before the court of the women's house, [I]to know[3045] how Esther did, and what should become[6213] of her.

6 [I]Or, *Jehoiachin* [a]2Kgs. 24:14, 15; 2Chr. 36:10, 20; Jer. 24:1 [b]2Kgs. 24:6

7 [I]Hebr. *nourished* [II]Hebr. *fair of form, and good of countenance* [a]Eph. 6:4 [b]Esth. 2:15

8 [a]Esth. 2:3

9 [I]Hebr. *her portions* [II]Hebr. *he changed her* [a]Esth. 2:3, 12

10 [a]Esth. 2:20

11 [I]Hebr. *to know the peace*

15 [a]Esth. 2:7

17 [I]Or, *kindness* [II]Hebr. *before him*

18 [I]Hebr. *rest* [a]Esth. 1:3

12 Now when every maid's turn was come[5060] to go in to king Ahasuerus, after that she had been twelve months, according to the manner[1881] of the women, (for so were the days of their purifications[4795] accomplished, 4390 *to wit,* six months with oil[8081] of myrrh, 4753 and six months with sweet odours, and with *other* things for the purifying[8562] of the women;)

13 Then thus came *every* maiden unto the king; whatsoever she desired was given her to go with her out of the house of the women unto the king's house.

14 In the evening she went, and on the morrow she returned[7725] into the second house of the women, to the custody of Shaashgaz, the king's chamberlain, which kept[8104] the concubines: she came in unto the king no more, except the king delighted[2654] in her, and that she were called[7121] by name.

15 Now when the turn of Esther, [a]the daughter of Abihail the uncle of Mordecai, who had taken her for his daughter, was come to go in unto the king, she required 1245 nothing but what Hegai the king's chamberlain, the keeper of the women, appointed.[559] And Esther obtained favour[2580] in the sight of all them that looked upon her.

16 So Esther was taken unto king Ahasuerus into his house royal[4438] in the tenth month, which *is* the month Tebeth, in the seventh year of his reign.[4438]

17 And the king loved[157] Esther above all the women, and she obtained grace[2580] and [I]favour[2617] [II]in his sight more than all the virgins; so that he set[7760] the royal crown upon her head,[7218] and made her queen instead of Vashti.

18 Then the king [a]made[6213] a great feast[4960] unto all his princes[8269] and his servants,[5650] *even* Esther's feast; and he made a [I]release 2010 to the provinces, and

🗝 **2:7** Esther's Hebrew name was Hadassah, which means "myrtle." "Esther" probably comes form the Persian word for "star," though some scholars see a connection between it and the Babylonian goddess Ishtar. It appears that Esther had been orphaned and subsequently adopted by her cousin, Mordecai.

gave gifts,[4864] according to the state[3027] of the king.

Mordecai Saves the King's Life

19 And when the virgins were gathered together[6908] the second time, then Mordecai sat [a]in the king's gate.

20 [a]Esther had not *yet* shewed her kindred nor her people; as Mordecai had charged her: for Esther did the commandment[3982] of Mordecai, like as when she was brought up with him.

21 In those days, while Mordecai sat in the king's gate, two of the king's chamberlains,[5631] [I][a]Bigthan and Teresh, of those which kept [II]the door, were wroth,[7107] and sought to lay hand[3027] on the king Ahasuerus.

22 And the thing was known[3045] to Mordecai, [a]who told[5046] *it* unto Esther the queen;[4436] and Esther certified[559] the king *thereof* in Mordecai's name.

23 And when inquisition was made[1245] of the matter,[1697] it was found out; therefore they were both hanged on a tree: and it was written in [a]the book[5612] of the chronicles before the king.

Haman's Plot

3 🔑 After these things[1697] did king Ahasuerus promote Haman the son[1121] of Hammedatha the [a]Agagite, and advanced[5375] him, and set[7760] his seat[3678] above all the princes[8269] that *were* with him.

2 And all the king's[4428] servants, that *were* [a]in the king's gate, bowed,[3766] and reverenced[7812] Haman: for the king had so commanded[6680] concerning him. But Mordecai [b]bowed not, nor did *him* reverence.

3 Then the king's servants, which *were* in the king's gate, said unto Mordecai, Why transgressest thou the [a]king's commandment?[4687]

4 Now it came to pass, when they spake[559] daily unto him, and he hearkened[8085] not unto them, that they told[5046] Haman, to see whether Mordecai's matters would stand: for he had told them that he *was* a Jew.

5 And when Haman saw[7200] that Mordecai [a]bowed not, nor did him reverence, then was Haman [b]full of wrath.[2534]

6 And he thought scorn to lay hands[3027] on Mordecai alone; for they had shewed[5046] him the people[5971] of Mordecai: wherefore Haman [a]sought to destroy[8045] all the Jews that *were* throughout the whole kingdom[4438] of Ahasuerus, *even* the people of Mordecai.

🔑 7 In the first[7223] month, that *is,* the month Nisan, in the twelfth year of king Ahasuerus, [a]they cast Pur, that *is,* the lot, before Haman from day[3117] to day, and from month to month, *to* the twelfth *month,* that *is,* the month Adar.

8 And Haman said unto king Ahasuerus, There is a certain people scattered abroad[6340] and dispersed among the people in all the provinces of thy kingdom; and [a]their laws[1881] *are* diverse from all people; neither keep[6213] they the king's

19 [a]Esth. 2:21; 3:2
20 [a]Esth. 2:10
21 [I]Or, *Bigthana* [II]Hebr. *the threshold* [a]Esth. 6:2
22 [a]Esth. 6:2
23 [a]Esth. 6:1
1 [a]Num. 24:7; 1Sam. 15:8
2 [a]Esth. 2:19 [b]Esth. 3:5; Ps. 15:4
3 [a]Esth. 3:2
5 [a]Esth. 3:2; 5:9 [b]Dan. 3:19
6 [a]Ps. 83:4
7 [a]Esth. 9:24
8 [a]Ezra 4:13; Acts 16:20

🔑 **3:1** There are differing interpretations on the meaning of the term "Agagite." One view suggests that this was a descendant of Agag who was at one time king of the Amalekites (1 Sam. 15:8). Although the passage in 1 Samuel states that the Amalekites were annihilated, it is evident that this refers only to those who were in that vicinity (see 1 Sam. 30:1 and note on 1 Chr. 4:43). The Amalekites were a nomadic people who roamed in clans, and the slaughter accomplished by Saul probably was only concerned with one group of these people. Others believe that later in the book, "Agagite" is mentioned in close connection with the idea that this was an enemy of the Jews (Esth. 3:10; 9:24). In light of this, some deduce that "Agagite" (literally, "fiery one") was used to refer to a contemptible or hateful person.

🔑 **3:7** Here the lot was cast systematically by days and months in order to determine which date in particular would be best to destroy the Jews. In verse thirteen it is seen that specifically the thirteenth day of the twelfth month was chosen. The Feast of Purim, the Jewish feast commemorating the events of the Book of Esther, takes its name from this practice.

laws: therefore it *is* not [I]for the king's profit to suffer them.

9 If it please[2895] the king, let it be written [I]that they may be destroyed:[6] and I will [II]pay ten thousand talents of silver to the hands of those that have the charge of the business,[4399] to bring *it* into the king's treasuries.

10 And the king [a]took [b]his ring from his hand,[3027] and gave it unto Haman the son of Hammedatha the Agagite, the Jews' [I][c]enemy.

11 And the king said unto Haman, The silver *is* given to thee, the people also, to do[6213] with them as it seemeth good[2896] to thee.

12 [a]Then were the king's [I]scribes[5608] called[7121] on the thirteenth day of the first month, and there was written according to all that Haman had commanded unto the king's lieutenants, and to the governors[6346] that *were* over every province, and to the rulers[8269] of every people of every province [b]according to the writing thereof, and *to* every people after their language; [c]in the name of king Ahasuerus was it written, and sealed with the king's ring.

13 And the letters[5612] were [a]sent by posts 7323 into all the king's provinces, to destroy, to kill,[2026] and to cause to perish,[6] all Jews, both young and old,[2205] little children[2945] and women, [b]in one day, *even* upon the thirteenth *day* of the twelfth month, which *is* the month Adar, and [c]*to take* the spoil of them for a prey.

14 [a]The copy of the writing for a commandment to be given in every province was published[1540] unto all people, that they should be ready against that day.

15 The posts went out, being hastened by the king's commandment,[1697] and the decree[1881] was given in Shushan the palace. And the king and Haman sat down to drink; but [a]the city Shushan was perplexed. 943

Mordecai Asks for Esther's Help

4 When Mordecai perceived[3045] all that was done, Mordecai [a]rent his clothes, and put on sackcloth [b]with ashes, and went out into the midst of the city, and [c]cried[2199] with a loud and a bitter[4751] cry;

2 And came even before the king's gate: for none *might* enter into the king's gate clothed with sackcloth.

3 And in every province, whithersoever the king's commandment[1697] and his decree[1881] came,[5060] *there was* great mourning among the Jews, and fasting, and weeping, and wailing; and [I][a]many lay in sackcloth and ashes.

4 So Esther's maids and her [I]chamberlains[5631] came and told[5046] *it* her. Then was the queen exceedingly grieved;[2342] and she sent raiment to clothe Mordecai, and to take away his sackcloth from him: but he received 6901 *it* not.

5 Then called[7121] Esther for Hatach, *one* of the king's chamberlains, [I]whom he had appointed to attend upon her, and gave him a commandment to Mordecai, to know[3045] what it *was*, and why it *was*.

6 So Hatach went forth to Mordecai unto the street of the city, which *was* before the king's gate.

7 And Mordecai told him of all that had happened unto him, and of [a]the sum of the money that Haman had promised[559] to pay to the king's treasuries for the Jews, to destroy[6] them.

8 Also he gave him [a]the copy of the writing of the decree that was given at Shushan to destroy[8045] them, to shew[7200] *it* unto Esther, and to declare[5046] *it* unto her, and to charge[6680] her that she should go in unto the king,[4428] to make supplication[2603] unto him, and to make request before him for her people.[5971]

9 And Hatach came and told Esther the words[1697] of Mordecai.

10 Again Esther spake unto Hatach, and gave him commandment[6680] unto Mordecai;

11 All the king's servants,[5650] and the people of the king's provinces, do know, that whosoever, whether man or woman, shall come unto the king into [a]the inner court, who is not called, [b]*there is* one law[1881] of his to put *him* to death,[4191] except such [c]to whom the king

8 [I]Hebr. *meet, or, equal*

9 [I]Hebr. *to destroy them* [II]Hebr. *weigh*

10 [I]Or, *oppressor* [a]Gen. 41:42 [b]Esth. 8:2, 8 [c]Esth. 7:6

12 [I]Or, *secretaries* [a]Esth. 8:9 [b]Esth. 1:22; 8:9 [c]1Kgs. 21:8; Esth. 8:8, 10

13 [a]Esth. 8:10 [b]Esth. 8:12-17 [c]Esth. 8:11

14 [a]Esth. 8:13, 14

15 [a]Esth. 8:15; Prov. 29:2

1 [a]2Sam. 1:11 [b]Josh. 7:6; Ezek. 27:30 [c]Gen. 27:34

3 [I]Hebr. *sackcloth and ashes were laid under many* [a]Isa. 58:5; Dan. 9:3

4 [I]Hebr. *eunuchs*

5 [I]Hebr. *whom he had set before her*

7 [a]Esth. 3:9

8 [a]Esth. 3:14, 15

11 [a]Esth. 5:1 [b]Dan. 2:9 [c]Esth. 5:2; 8:4

shall hold out the golden sceptre,[8275] that he may live:[2421] but I have not been called to come in unto the king these thirty days.[3117]

12 And they told[5046] to Mordecai Esther's words.

13 Then Mordecai commanded[559] to answer[7725] Esther, Think[1819] not with thyself that thou shalt escape[4422] in the king's house,[1004] more than all the Jews.

14 For if thou altogether holdest thy peace at this time,[6256] *then* shall there [I][a]enlargement[7305] and deliverance arise to the Jews from another place; but thou and thy father's[1] house shall be destroyed:[6] and who knoweth whether thou art come[5060] to the kingdom[4438] for *such* a time as this?

15 Then Esther bade *them* return[7725] Mordecai *this answer,*

16 Go, gather together[3664] all the Jews that are [I]present in Shushan, and fast ye for me, and neither eat nor drink [a]three days,[3117] night[3915] or day: I also and my maidens will fast likewise; and so will I go in unto the king, which *is* not according to the law: [b]and if I perish,[6] I perish.

17 So Mordecai [I]went his way, and did according to all that Esther had commanded[6680] him.

The Banquet

5 Now it came to pass [a]on the third day,[3117] that Esther put on *her* royal[4438] *apparel,* and stood in [b]the inner court of the king's house,[1004] over against the king's house: and the king[4428] sat upon his royal throne[3678] in the royal house, over against the gate of the house.

2 And it was so, when the king saw[7200] Esther the queen[4436] standing in the court, *that* [a]she obtained[5375] favour[2580] in his sight: and [b]the king held out to Esther the golden sceptre[8275] that *was* in his hand.[3027] So Esther drew near, and touched[5060] the top of the sceptre.

3 Then said[559] the king unto her, What wilt thou, queen Esther? and what *is* thy request? [a]it shall be even given thee to the half of the kingdom.[4438]

4 And Esther answered,[559] If *it seem* good[2895] unto the king, let the king and Haman come this day unto the banquet[4960] that I have prepared[6213] for him.

5 Then the king said, Cause Haman to make haste, that he may do as Esther hath said. So the king and Haman came to the banquet that Esther had prepared.

6 [a]And the king said unto Esther at the banquet of wine, [b]What *is* thy petition?[7596] and it shall be granted thee: and what *is* thy request? even to the half of the kingdom it shall be performed.

7 Then answered Esther, and said, My petition and my request *is;*

8 If I have found favour in the sight of the king, and if it please[2895] the king to grant my petition, and [I]to perform[6213] my request, let the king and Haman come to the banquet that I shall prepare for them, and I will do to morrow as the king hath said.

9 Then went Haman forth that day joyful and with a glad[2896] heart:[3820] but when Haman saw Mordecai in the king's gate, [a]that he stood not up, nor moved[2111] for him, he was full of indignation[2534] against Mordecai.

10 Nevertheless Haman [a]refrained himself:[662] and when he came home,[1004] he sent and [I]called for his friends,[157] and Zeresh his wife.[802]

11 And Haman told[5608] them of the glory[3519] of his riches, and [a]the multitude of his children,[1121] and all *the things* wherein the king had promoted him, and how he had [b]advanced[5375] him above the princes[8269] and servants[5650] of the king.

12 Haman said moreover, Yea, Esther the queen did let no man come in with the king unto the banquet[4960] that she had prepared but myself; and to morrow am I invited[7121] unto her also with the king.

13 Yet all this availeth[7737] me nothing, so long as I see Mordecai the Jew sitting at the king's gate.

14 Then said Zeresh his wife and all his friends unto him, Let a [I][a]gallows be made[6213] of fifty cubits high, and to mor-

14 [I]Hebr. *respiration* [a]Job 9:18
16 [I]Hebr. *found* [a]Esth. 5:1 [b]Gen. 43:14
17 [I]Hebr. *passed*
1 [a]Esth. 4:16 [b]Esth. 4:11; 6:4
2 [a]Prov. 21:1 [b]Esth. 4:11; 8:4
3 [a]Mark 6:23
6 [a]Esth. 7:2 [b]Esth. 9:12
8 [I]Hebr. *to do*
9 [a]Esth. 3:5
10 [I]Hebr. *caused to come* [a]2Sam. 13:22
11 [a]Esth. 9:7-10 [b]Esth. 3:1
14 [I]Hebr. *tree* [a]Esth. 7:9

row [b]speak[559] thou unto the king that Mordecai may be hanged thereon: then go in merrily with the king unto the banquet. And the thing[1697] pleased Haman; and he caused [c]the gallows to be made.

The King Honors Mordecai

6 On that night[3915] [I]could not the king sleep, and he commanded[559] to bring [a]the book[5612] of records[2146] of the chronicles; and they were read[7121] before the king.

2 And it was found written, that Mordecai had told[5046] of [I][a]Bigthana and Teresh, two of the king's chamberlains,[5631] the keepers[8104] of the [II]door, who sought to lay hand[3027] on the king Ahasuerus.

3 And the king said, What honour and dignity[1420] hath been done[6213] to Mordecai for this? Then said[559] the king's servants[5650] that ministered[8334] unto him, There is nothing done for him.

4 And the king said, Who *is* in the court? Now Haman was come into [a]the outward court of the king's house,[1004] [b]to speak unto the king to hang Mordecai on the gallows that he had prepared[3559] for him.

5 And the king's servants said unto him, Behold, Haman standeth in the court. And the king said, Let him come in.

6 So Haman came in. And the king said unto him, What shall be done unto the man [I]whom the king delighteth[2654] to honour? Now Haman thought[559] in his heart,[3820] To whom would the king delight to do[6213] honour more than to myself?

7 And Haman answered[559] the king, For the man [I]whom the king delighteth to honour,

8 [I]Let the royal[4438] apparel be brought [II]which the king *useth* to wear, and [a]the horse that the king rideth upon, and the crown royal which is set upon his head:[7218]

9 And let this apparel and horse be delivered to the hand of one[376] of the king's most noble[6579] princes,[8269] that they may array the man *withal* whom the king delighteth to honour, and [I]bring him on horseback through the street of the city, [a]and proclaim[7121] before him, Thus shall it be done to the man whom the king delighteth to honour.

10 Then the king said to Haman, Make haste, *and* take the apparel and the horse, as thou hast said, and do even so to Mordecai the Jew, that sitteth at the king's gate: [I]let nothing fail of all that thou hast spoken.[1696]

11 Then took Haman the apparel and the horse, and arrayed Mordecai, and brought him on horseback through the street of the city, and proclaimed before him, Thus shall it be done unto the man whom the king delighteth to honour.

12 And Mordecai came again to the king's gate. But Haman [a]hasted to his house mourning, [b]and having his head covered.

13 And Haman told[5608] Zeresh his wife and all his friends[157] every *thing* that had befallen him. Then said his wise men[2450] and Zeresh his wife unto him, If Mordecai *be* of the seed[2233] of the Jews, before whom thou hast begun to fall, thou shalt not prevail against him, but shalt surely fall before him.

14 And while they *were* yet talking with him, came the king's chamberlains, and hasted[926] to bring Haman unto [a]the banquet[4960] that Esther had prepared.[6213]

Haman Is Hanged

7 So the king[4428] and Haman came [I]to banquet with Esther the queen.[4436]

2 And the king said again unto Esther on the second day [a]at the banquet[4960] of wine, What *is* thy petition,[7596] queen Esther? and it shall be granted thee: and what *is* thy request? and it shall be performed, *even* to the half of the kingdom.[4438]

3 Then Esther the queen answered and said, If I have found favour[2580] in thy sight, O king, and if it please[2895] the king, let my life[5315] be given me at my

14 [b]Esth. 6:4 [c]Esth. 7:10

1 [I]Hebr. *the king's sleep fled away* [a]Esth. 2:23

2 [I]Or, *Bigthan* [II]Hebr. *threshold* [a]Esth. 2:21

4 [a]Esth. 5:1 [b]Esth. 5:14

6 [I]Hebr. *in whose honor the king delighteth*

7 [I]Hebr. *in whose honor the king delighteth*

8 [I]Hebr. *Let them bring the royal apparel* [II]Hebr. *wherewith the king clotheth himself* [a]1Kgs. 1:33

9 [I]Hebr. *cause him to ride* [a]Gen. 41:43

10 [I]Hebr. *suffer not a whit to fall*

12 [a]2Chr. 26:20 [b]2Sam. 15:30; Jer. 14:3, 4

14 [a]Esth. 5:8

1 [I]Hebr. *to drink*

2 [a]Esth. 5:6

petition, and my people[5971] at my request:
4 For we are [a]sold, I and my people,
[I]to be destroyed,[8045] to be slain, and to
perish.[6] But if we had been sold for
bondmen[5650] and bondwomen, I had held
my tongue, although the enemy could not
countervail7737 the king's damage.
5 Then the king Ahasuerus answered[559] and said unto Esther the
queen, Who is he, and where is he,
[I]that durst presume in his heart[3820] to do
so?
6 And Esther said, [I]The adversary
and enemy *is* this wicked[7451] Haman.
Then Haman was afraid[1204] [II]before the
king and the queen.
7 And the king arising from the banquet of wine in his wrath[2534] *went* into
the palace garden: and Haman stood up
to make request for his life to Esther the
queen; for he saw[7200] that there was[3615]
evil[7451] determined[3615] against him by
the king.
8 Then the king returned[7725] out of
the palace garden into the place of the
banquet of wine; and Haman was
fallen[5307] upon [a]the bed whereon Esther
was. Then said the king, Will he force3533
the queen also [I]before me in the house?
As the word[1697] went out of the
king's[4428] mouth,[6310] they [b]covered
Haman's face.
9 And [a]Harbonah, one of the chamberlains,[5631] said before the king, Behold
also, [b]the [I]gallows fifty cubits high, which
Haman had made[6213] for Mordecai, who
had spoken[1696] good[2896] for the king,
standeth in the house of Haman. Then
the king said, Hang him thereon.
10 So [a]they hanged Haman on the
gallows that he had prepared[3559] for
Mordecai. Then was the king's wrath
pacified.7918

The Jews Are Authorized to Defend Themselves

8 On that day did the king Ahasuerus
give the house[1004] of Haman the
Jews' enemy unto Esther the queen.[4436]
And Mordecai came before the king; for
Esther had told[5046] [a]what he *was* unto
her.
2 And the king took off[5493] [a]his ring,
which he had taken from Haman, and
gave it unto Mordecai. And Esther set[7760]
Mordecai over the house of Haman.
3 And Esther spake yet again before
the king, and fell down[5307] at his feet,
[I]and besought[2603] him with tears to put
away[5674] the mischief[7451] of Haman the
Agagite, and his device[4284] that he had
devised[2803] against the Jews.
4 Then [a]the king held out the golden
sceptre[8275] toward Esther. So Esther
arose, and stood before the king,
5 And said,[559] If it please[2896] the
king, and if I have found favour[2580] in
his sight, and the thing[1697] *seem* right[3787]
before the king, and I *be* pleasing in his
eyes, let it be written to reverse[7725] [I]the
letters[5612] devised[4284] by Haman the son
of Hammedatha the Agagite, [II]which he
wrote to destroy[6] the Jews which *are* in
all the king's provinces:
6 For how can I [I]endure to see [a]the
evil[7451] that shall come unto my people?[5971] or how can I endure to see the
destruction[13] of my kindred?
7 Then the king Ahasuerus said unto
Esther the queen and to Mordecai the
Jew, Behold, [a]I have given Esther the
house of Haman, and him they have
hanged upon the gallows, because he laid
his hand[3027] upon the Jews.
8 Write ye also for the Jews, as it
liketh[2896] you, in the king's name, and
seal *it* with the king's ring: for the writing which is written in the king's name,
and sealed with the king's ring, [a]may no
man reverse.
9 [a]Then were the king's scribes[5608]
called[7121] at that time[6256] in the third
month, that *is,* the month Sivan, on the
three and twentieth *day* thereof; and it
was written according to all that
Mordecai commanded[6680] unto the Jews,
and to the lieutenants,323 and the
deputies[6346] and rulers[8269] of the
provinces which *are* [b]from India unto
Ethiopia, an hundred twenty and seven
provinces, unto every province [c]accord-
ing to the writing thereof, and unto every

---

4 [I]Hebr. *that they should destroy, and kill, and cause to perish* [a]Esth. 3:9; 4:7

5 [I]Hebr. *whose heart hath filled him*

6 [I]Hebr. *The man adversary* [II]Or, *at the presence of*

8 [I]Hebr. *with me* [a]Esth. 1:6 [b]Job 9:24

9 [I]Hebr. *tree* [a]Esth. 1:10 [b]Esth. 5:14; Ps. 7:16; Prov. 11:5, 6

10 [a]Ps. 37:35, 36; Dan. 6:24

1 [a]Esth. 2:7

2 [a]Esth. 3:10

3 [I]Hebr. *and she wept, and besought him*

4 [a]Esth. 4:11; 5:2

5 [I]Hebr. *the device* [II]Or, *who wrote*

6 [I]Hebr. *be able that I may see* [a]Neh. 2:3; Esth. 7:4

7 [a]Esth. 8:1; Prov. 13:22

8 [a]Esth. 1:19; Dan. 6:8, 12, 15

9 [a]Esth. 3:12 [b]Esth. 1:1 [c]Esth. 1:22; 3:12

people after their language, and to the Jews according to their writing, and according to their language.

10 [a]And he wrote in the king Ahasuerus' name, and sealed *it* with the king's ring, and sent letters by posts on horseback, *and* riders on mules, camels, *and* young dromedaries:7424

11 Wherein the king granted the Jews which *were* in every city to gather themselves together, and to stand for their life,[5315] to destroy,[8045] to slay,[2026] and to cause to perish,[6] all the power[2428] of the people and province that would assault them, *both* little ones[2945] and women, and [a]*to take* the spoil of them for a prey,

12 [a]Upon one day in all the provinces of king Ahasuerus, *namely,* upon the thirteenth *day* of the twelfth month, which *is* the month Adar.

13 [a]The copy of the writing for a commandment to be given in every province *was* [I]published[1540] unto all people, and that the Jews should be ready against that day to avenge themselves[5358] on their enemies.

14 *So* the posts that rode upon mules *and* camels went out, being hastened and pressed on by the king's commandment.[1697] And the decree[1881] was given at Shushan the palace.

15 And Mordecai went out from the presence of the king in royal[4438] apparel of [I]blue and white, and with a great crown of gold, and with a garment of fine linen and purple: and [a]the city of Shushan rejoiced and was glad.

16 The Jews had [a]light,[219] and gladness, and joy,8342 and honour.

17 And in every province, and in every city, whithersoever the king's commandment and his decree came,[5060] the Jews had joy8057 and gladness, a feast[4960] [a]and a good[2896] day. And many of the people of the land[776] [b]became Jews; for [c]the fear[6343] of the Jews fell upon them.

The Jews Destroy Their Enemies

9 Now [a]in the twelfth month, that *is,* the month Adar, on the thirteenth day of the same, [b]when the king's commandment[1697] and his decree[1881] drew near[5060] to be put in execution,[6213] in the day that the enemies of the Jews hoped to have power[7980] over them, (though it was turned to the contrary,[2015] that the Jews [c]had rule[7980] over them that hated[8130] them;)

2 The Jews [a]gathered themselves together[6950] in their cities throughout all the provinces of the king[4428] Ahasuerus, to lay hand[3027] on such as [b]sought their hurt:[7451] and no man could withstand them; for [c]the fear[6343] of them fell[5307] upon all people.[5971]

3 And all the rulers[8269] of the provinces, and the lieutenants, and the deputies,[6346] and [I]officers of the king, helped[5375] the Jews; because the fear of Mordecai fell upon them.

4 For Mordecai *was* great in the king's house,[1004] and his fame went out throughout all the provinces: for this man Mordecai [a]waxed greater and greater.

5 Thus the Jews smote[5221] all their enemies with the stroke[4347] of the sword, and slaughter,[2027] and destruction,[12] and did [I]what they would[7522] unto those that hated them.

6 And in Shushan the palace the Jews slew[2026] and destroyed[6] five hundred men.[376]

7 And Parshandatha, and Dalphon, and Aspatha,

8 And Poratha, and Adalia, and Aridatha,

9 And Parmashta, and Arisai, and Aridai, and Vajezatha,

10 [a]The ten sons of Haman the son[1121] of Hammedatha, the enemy of the Jews, slew they; [b]but on the spoil laid they not their hand.

11 On that day the number of those that were slain in Shushan the palace [I]was brought before the king.

12 And the king said unto Esther the queen,[4436] The Jews have slain and destroyed five hundred men in Shushan the palace, and the ten sons of Haman; what have they done[6213] in the rest[7605] of the king's provinces? now [a]what *is* thy petition?[7596] and it shall be granted thee: or

10 [a]1Kgs. 21:8; Esth. 3:12, 13
11 [a]Esth. 9:10, 15, 16
12 [a]Esth. 3:13-15; 9:1
13 [I]Hebr. *revealed* [a]Esth. 3:14, 15
15 [I]Or, *violet* [a]Esth. 3:15; Prov. 29:2
16 [a]Ps. 97:11
17 [a]1Sam. 25:8; Esth. 9:19, 22 [b]Ps. 18:43 [c]Gen. 35:5; Ex. 15:16; Deut. 2:25; 11:25; Esth. 9:2

1 [a]Esth. 8:12 [b]Esth. 3:13 [c]2Sam. 22:41
2 [a]Esth. 8:11; 9:16 [b]Ps. 71:13, 24 [c]Esth. 8:17
3 [I]Hebr. *those which did the business that belonged to the king*
4 [a]2Sam. 3:1; 1Chr. 11:9; Prov. 4:18
5 [I]Hebr. *according to their will*
10 [a]Esth. 5:11; Job 18:19; 27:13-15; Ps. 21:10 [b]Esth. 8:11
11 [I]Hebr. *came*
12 [a]Esth. 5:6; 7:2

what *is* thy request[1246] further? and it shall be done.

13 Then said Esther, If it please[2896] the king, let it be granted to the Jews which *are* in Shushan to do to morrow also [a]according unto this day's decree, and [I]let Haman's ten sons [b]be hanged upon the gallows.

14 And the king commanded[559] it so to be done: and the decree was given at Shushan; and they hanged Haman's ten sons.

15 For the Jews that *were* in Shushan [a]gathered themselves together on the fourteenth day also of the month Adar, and slew three hundred men at Shushan; [b]but on the prey they laid not their hand.

The Feast of Purim

16 But the other Jews that *were* in the king's provinces [a]gathered themselves together, and stood for their lives,[5315] and had rest from their enemies, and slew of their foes[8130] seventy and five thousand, [b]but they laid not their hands[3027] on the prey,

17 On the thirteenth day of the month Adar; and on the fourteenth day [I]of the same rested they, and made[6213] it a day of feasting[4960] and gladness.

18 But the Jews that *were* at Shushan assembled together[6950] [a]on the thirteenth *day* thereof, and on the fourteenth thereof; and on the fifteenth *day* of the same they rested, and made it a day of feasting and gladness.

19 Therefore the Jews of the villages, that dwelt in the unwalled towns, made the fourteenth day of the month Adar [a]*a day of* gladness and feasting, [b]and a good[2896] day, and of [c]sending portions[4490] one[376] to another.[7453]

20 And Mordecai wrote these things,[1697] and sent letters[5612] unto all the Jews that *were* in all the provinces of the king Ahasuerus, *both* nigh and far,

21 To stablish *this* among them, that they should keep[6213] the fourteenth day of the month Adar, and the fifteenth day of the same, yearly,

22 As the days[3117] wherein the Jews rested from their enemies, and the month which was [a]turned unto them from sorrow to joy, and from mourning into a good day: that they should make[6213] them days of feasting and joy, and of [b]sending portions one to another, and gifts to the poor.

23 And the Jews undertook[6901] to do as they had begun, and as Mordecai had written unto them;

24 Because Haman the son of Hammedatha, the Agagite, the enemy of all the Jews, [a]had devised[2803] against the Jews to destroy[6] them, and had cast Pur, that *is,* the lot, to [I]consume[2000] them, and to destroy them;

25 But [I][a]when *Esther* came before the king, he commanded by letters that his wicked[7451] device,[4284] which he devised against the Jews, should [b]return[7725] upon his own head,[7218] and that he and his sons should be hanged on the gallows.

🗝 26 Wherefore they called[7121] these days Purim after the name of [I]Pur. Therefore for all the words[1697] of [a]this letter, and *of that* which they had seen[7200] concerning this matter, and which had come[5060] unto them,

27 The Jews ordained,[6965] and took upon them, and upon their seed,[2233] and upon all such as [a]joined themselves unto them, so as it should not [I]fail,[5647] that they would keep these two days according to their writing, and according to their *appointed* time[2165] every year;

28 And *that* these days *should be* remembered[2142] and kept[6213] throughout every generation,[1755] every family,[4940] every province, and every city; and *that* these days of Purim should not [I]fail from among the Jews, nor the memorial[2143] of them [II]perish[5486] from their seed.

13 [I]Hebr. *let men hang* [a]Esth. 8:11 [b]2Sam. 21:6, 9

15 [a]Esth. 9:2; 8:11 [b]Esth. 9:10

16 [a]Esth. 9:2; 8:11 [b]Esth. 8:11

17 [I]Hebr. *in it*

18 [a]Esth. 9:11, 15

19 [a]Deut. 16:11, 14 [b]Esth. 8:17 [c]Neh. 8:10, 12; Esth. 9:22

22 [a]Ps. 30:11 [b]Neh. 8:10; Esth. 9:19

24 [I]Hebr. *crush* [a]Esth. 3:6, 7

25 [I]Hebr. *when she came* [a]Esth. 9:13, 14; Esth. 7:5-10; 8:3-8 [b]Esth. 7:10; Ps. 7:16

26 [I]That is, *Lot* [a]Esth. 9:20

27 [I]Hebr. *pass* [a]Esth. 8:17; Isa. 56:3, 6; Zech. 2:11

28 [I]Hebr. *pass* [II]Hebr. *be ended*

🗝 **9:26** This two day feast of rejoicing and sending of gifts is still kept by the Jews today on the fourteenth and fifteenth days of their twelfth month (our February or March).

29 Then Esther the queen, [a]the
daughter of Abihail, and Mordecai the
Jew, wrote with [I]all authority,[8633] to confirm this [b]second letter of Purim.
30 And he sent the letters unto all the
Jews, to [a]the hundred twenty and seven
provinces of the kingdom[4438] of Ahasuerus, *with* words of peace and truth,[571]
31 To confirm these days of Purim in
their times[2165] *appointed,* according as
Mordecai the Jew and Esther the queen
had enjoined[6965] them, and as they had decreed [I]for themselves and for their seed,
the matters of [a]the fastings and their cry.
32 And the decree[3982] of Esther confirmed these matters of Purim; and it
was written in the book.[5612]

29 [I]Hebr. *all strength* [a]Esth. 2:15 [b]Esth. 8:10; 9:20

30 [a]Esth. 1:1

31 [I]Hebr. *for their souls* [a]Esth. 4:3, 16

1 [a]Gen. 10:5; Ps. 72:10; Isa. 24:15

2 [I]Hebr. *made him great* [a]Esth. 8:15; 9:4

3 [a]Gen. 41:40; 2Chr. 28:7 [b]Neh. 2:10; Ps. 122:8, 9

Mordecai's Greatness

10 And the king[4428] Ahasuerus
laid[7760] a tribute upon the land,[776]
and *upon* [a]the isles of the sea.
2 And all the acts of his power and
of his might, and the declaration[6575] of
the greatness of Mordecai, [a]whereunto
the king [I]advanced him, *are* they not
written in the book[5612] of the chronicles
of the kings of Media and Persia?
3 For Mordecai the Jew *was* [a]next
unto king Ahasuerus, and great among
the Jews, and accepted[7521] of the multitude of his brethren,[251] [b]seeking the
wealth of his people,[5971] and speaking[1696] peace to all his seed.[2233]

The Book of

JOB

The Book of Job is one of the few books in the Hebrew Scriptures that does not derive its title from the first word in the text. The name is a transliteration of the Hebrew word *'Iyyôwb* (347), which means "the hated or persecuted one."

Although there is no mention of the author's name within the book, most scholars accept the Talmudic tradition that Moses is the author of the book. There are others who propose that Solomon was the author. They suggest that Solomon's vast knowledge of foreign countries and cultures would have provided him with the information to write the Book of Job. This fails to prove that only Solomon could have written the book, for would not Moses, having received the highest training in Egypt, have learned of numerous foreign nations? However, the main problem with the Solomonic view of authorship is the time span that separated the patriarchal period and Solomon's lifetime. On the other hand, Mosaic authorship is supported by the use of many words and phrases found in the Book of Job that are also used in the Pentateuch. Another argument in favor of this view is that the land of Uz was adjacent to Midian where Moses spent forty years prior to his return to Egypt. It seems entirely possible that he could have heard the story of Job there and been inspired by God to correctly relate the events and conversations that occurred. It is generally accepted that he dwelled in Midian between the years of 1485 and 1445 B.C.

Furthermore, there is good reason to believe that the events took place during the patriarchal period. No reference is made to the events of the Exodus, and the patriarchal name for God, "the Almighty," is used approximately thirty times in the book. The fact that Job acted as the priest for his family (Job 1:5) implies that the Mosaic Law had not yet been given. The length of Job's life (Job 42:16) is comparable to those living during the time of the patriarchs (Gen. 25:7; 35:28).

The Book of Job is the first of the so-called Poetical Books of the Bible. The truth is, however, that poetry is found throughout the Old Testament. For example, it is used in blessings and cursings (Gen. 49:2–27), in certain historical accounts (Ex. 15:1–18), and in dirges (2 Sam. 1:19–27). The poetry of the Old Testament is very different from modern poetry. It involves not the rhyming of sounds, but the "rhyming" of thoughts or ideas. This characteristic of Hebrew poetry is now called parallelism. For the most part, paralleism may either be antithetical (where the thoughts are opposite to one another, Prov. 10:12) or synonymous (where the thoughts are the same as or similar to one another, Ps. 24:1). Since rhymes of sound are difficult, if not impossible, to carry over in translation, the appreciation of English poetry is limited to those who know the language. On the other hand, the beauty of the "thought-rhythm" of Hebrew poetry may be carried over into any language.

The Book of Job is a beautiful example of Hebrew poetry, though in fact not all of the book is poetic in form. The prologue (Job 1, 2) and the epilogue (Job 42:7–16) are written in prose. The drama of Job's suffering, the majestic style, and the nature of the discussions have helped to make Job universally accepted as a literary masterpiece.

The purpose of the book is to show the unfathomable wisdom of God's providence, and the benevolence of God even in the trials brought upon His children. It also explains why God allows righteous people to suffer: to expose their frailty and sinfulness, to strengthen their faith, and to purify them. The spiritual perspective of the account and the fact that God exercised total control over Satan promotes complete trust in God.

Throughout the book, Job's friends relentlessly accused him of committing some great sin. Although he questioned God's actions in the midst of these onslaughts, it should not be assumed that his queries were motivated by a resentful, self-seeking attitude. On the contrary, they confirm his determination to hold on to his faith in God despite the circumstances that providence had brought upon him.

The Testing of Job

1 🔑 There was a man[376] [a]in the
land[776] of Uz, whose name *was* [b]Job;
and that man was [c]perfect[8535] and upright,[3477] and one that [d]feared[3373] God,[430]
and eschewed[5493] evil.[7451]
2 And there were born unto him
seven sons[1121] and three daughters.
3 His [I]substance[4735] also was seven
thousand sheep, and three thousand
camels, and five hundred yoke of oxen,
and five hundred she asses, and a very
great [II]household;[5657] so that this man was
the greatest of all the [III]men of the east.
4 And his sons went and feasted *in*
their houses,[1004] every one his day;[3117]
and sent and called[7121] for their three
sisters[269] to eat and to drink with them.
5 And it was so, when the days of
their feasting[4960] were gone about,[5362]
that Job sent and sanctified[6942] them, and
rose up early in the morning, [a]and offered[5927] burnt offerings[5930] *according* to
the number of them all: for Job said,[559]
It may be that my sons have sinned,[2398]
and [b]cursed God in their hearts.[3824] Thus
did[6213] Job [I]continually.
🔑 6 Now [a]there was a day [b]when the
sons of God[430] came to present[3320] themselves before the LORD,[3068] and [Ic]Satan[7854]
came also [II]among them.
7 And the LORD said unto Satan,
Whence comest thou? Then Satan answered the LORD, and said, From [a]going
to and fro in the earth,[776] and from walking up and down in it.
8 And the LORD said unto Satan,
[Ia]Hast thou considered my servant[5650]
Job, that *there is* none like him in the
earth, [b]a perfect and an upright man, one
that feareth God, and escheweth[5493] evil?
🔑 9 Then Satan answered the LORD, and
said, Doth Job fear[3372] God for nought?[2600]
10 [a]Hast not thou made an hedge[7753]
about him, and about his house,[1004] and
about all that he hath on every side?
[b]thou hast blessed[1288] the work of his
hands,[3027] and his [I]substance[4753] is increased in the land.
11 [a]But put forth thine hand[3027] now,
and touch[5060] all that he hath, [I]and he
will [b]curse thee to thy face.
12 And the LORD said unto Satan,
Behold, all that he hath *is* in thy
[Ia]power;[3027] only upon himself put not
forth thine hand. So Satan went forth
from the presence of the LORD.[3068]
🔑 13 And there was a day [a]when his

1 [a]Gen. 22:20, 21 [b]Ezek. 14:14; James 5:11 [c]Gen. 6:9; 17:1; Job 2:3 [d]Prov. 8:13; 16:6
3 [I]Or, *cattle* [II]Or, *husbandry* [III]Hebr. *sons of the east*
5 [I]Hebr. *all the days* [a]Gen. 8:20; Job 42:8 [b]1Kgs. 21:10, 13
6 [I]Hebr. *the Adversary* [II]Hebr. *in the midst of them* [a]Job 2:1 [b]1Kgs. 22:19 [c]1Chr. 21:1; Rev. 12:9, 10
7 [a]Job 2:2; Matt. 12:43; 1Pet. 5:8
8 [I]Hebr. *Hast thou set thy heart on* [a]Job 2:3 [b]Job 1:1
10 [I]Or, *cattle* [a]Ps. 34:7; Isa. 5:2 [b]Ps. 128:1, 2; Prov. 10:22
11 [I]Hebr. *if he curse thee not to thy face* [a]Job 2:5; 19:21 [b]Isa. 8:21; Mal. 3:13, 14
12 [I]Hebr. *hand* [a]Gen. 16:6
13 [a]Eccl. 9:12

🔑 **1:1** The land of Uz was located most likely between the city of Damascus and the Euphrates River. It most certainly was near the area occupied by the Sabeans and the Chaldeans. These were marauding bands of people who lived in close proximity to Job, at least close enough to wage an attack against him (Job 1:15, 17). This would place Uz near the modern day boundary between the countries of Iraq and Saudi Arabia.

🔑 **1:6–12** There is a controversy over this passage as to whether Satan was allowed to come before God's throne in heaven. It is clear in these verses that Satan came along with the "sons of God" to present himself before God. If these "sons of God" are in fact angelic beings, it is plausible to state that Satan appeared in heaven. The fact that Satan is not omnipresent is proven by the fact that he was said to have been "going to and fro in the earth." Another interesting truth that may be gleaned from this passage is that Satan is not free to act in the affairs of mankind. In verses ten through twelve Satan had to ask God to remove the protective "hedge" from around Job. If God does not remove His protection from His people, Satan can have no influence on them or their lives. Consequently, Satan cannot cause affliction nor can he cause a person to commit sin. Satan must submit himself to whatever God chooses to do.

🔑 **1:9–11** From the question, "Doth Job fear God for nought?" it is evident that Satan was challenging the motive behind Job's worship and service to God. Satan wanted to show that Job lived as he did because God had blessed him. This was not the case, for Job served the Lord from the heart. God's purpose in allowing these trials to come on Job was to purify and strengthen Job's faith in Him. God judges men on the motives behind their actions, not the actions themselves (Eph. 6:5, 6; Heb. 4:12).

🔑 **1:13** This verse marks the beginning of the sufferings of Job. Some would suggest that Scripture teaches that believers will suffer, even though they are living godly lives. However, this is not true

(continued on next page)

sons and his daughters *were* eating and
drinking wine in their eldest brother's[251]
house:
14 And there came a messenger[4397]
unto Job, and said, The oxen were plowing, and the asses feeding beside them:
15 And the Sabeans fell[5307] *upon*
them, and took them away; yea, they
have slain[5221] the servants with the
edge[6310] of the sword;[2719] and I only am
escaped[4422] alone to tell[5046] thee.
🔑 16 While he *was* yet speaking, there
came also another, and said, [I]The fire of
God is fallen[5307] from heaven,8064 and
hath burned up the sheep, and the servants, and consumed them; and I only am
escaped alone to tell thee.
17 While he *was* yet speaking, there
came also another, and said, The
Chaldeans made out[7760] three bands, and
[I]fell upon the camels, and have carried
them away, yea, and slain the servants
with the edge of the sword; and I only
am escaped alone to tell thee.
18 While he *was* yet speaking, there
came also another, and said, [a]Thy sons
and thy daughters *were* eating and drinking wine in their eldest brother's house:
19 And, behold, there came a great
wind[7307] [I]from the wilderness,4057 and
smote[5060] the four corners of the house,
and it fell upon the young men, and they
are dead;[4191] and I only am escaped alone
to tell thee.
20 Then Job arose, [a]and rent his
[I]mantle,4598 and shaved his head,[7218] and
[b]fell down[5307] upon the ground,[776] and
worshipped,[7812]
🔑 21 And said, [a]Naked[6174] came I out
of my mother's[517] womb,[990] and naked
shall I return[7725] thither: the LORD [b]gave,
and the LORD hath [c]taken away; [d]blessed
be the name of the LORD.
22 [a]In all this Job sinned[2398] not, nor
[I]charged[5414] God foolishly.8604

Job Is Tested Again

2 Again [a]there was a day[3117] when the
sons[1121] of God[430] came to present
themselves before the LORD, and
Satan[7854] came also among them to present himself3320 before the LORD.
2 And the LORD said[559] unto Satan,
From whence comest thou? And [a]Satan
answered the LORD, and said, From going

16 IOr, *A great fire*
17 IHebr. *rushed*
18 aJob 1:4, 13
19 IHebr. *from aside*
20 IOr, *robe* aGen. 37:29; Ezra 9:3 b1Pet. 5:6
21 aPs. 49:17; Eccl. 5:15; 1Tim. 6:7 bEccl. 5:19; James 1:17 cMatt. 20:15 dEph. 5:20; 1Thess. 5:18
22 IOr, *attributed folly to God* aJob 2:10
1 aJob 1:6
2 aJob 1:7

(continued from previous page)
of the Christian life, nor of Job's situation. The Scriptures explicitly state that the righteous will be blessed in both this life and in that which is to come (1 Tim. 4:8; 1 Pet. 3:10–12). This is the norm for believers who live uprightly. The thing that is often forgotten about Job's life is that he had been blessed abundantly before this time of testing, and that he was even more richly blessed as a result of his endurance of that suffering. There are times, however, that He sees fit to test the believer (as in the case of Job) for the purpose of strengthening and purifying his faith.

🔑 **1:16–18** The phrase, "while he was yet speaking," indicates that all the events took place one right after the other. This afforded Job no opportunity to prepare himself or regain his composure, making each one harder to bear. It is evident from the text that Job had realized there was a possibility of trouble coming into his life, and that his worst fears would become a reality. Thus, Job never took any of the blessings of God for granted (Job 3:25, 26).

🔑 **1:16** The question that arises from this verse is "did God actively participate in the temptation of Job?" It is obvious that God Himself does not have to satisfy any request that Satan makes, but He does allow Satan to afflict Job, knowing that Job's faith would in fact be strengthened (see note on Job 1:9–11). There are several scholars who interpret the phrase "the fire of God is fallen from heaven," as a suggestion that this was the action of Satan himself, and that God, who was not actively involved in tempting Job, only provided the means for Satan to act. Others suggest that this phrase simply meant a "fierce lightning from above." Satan has power over the forces of nature and could have caused something to happen that the people living at that time would have attributed to God (see Matt. 4:1–11).

🔑 **1:21, 22** Job's expression here was not a fatalistic submission to the inevitability of events, nor was it a mere yielding to God's sovereign hand. He was in fact acknowledging God's goodness. In all this, Job was able to keep a proper testimony before God by not accusing God falsely.

to and fro in the earth,[776] and from walking up and down in it.
3 And the LORD said unto Satan,
Hast thou considered my servant[5650] Job,
that *there is* none like him in the earth,
[a]a perfect[8535] and an upright[3477] man,[376]
one that feareth God, and escheweth[5493]
evil?[7451] and still he [b]holdeth fast[2388] his
integrity,[8538] although thou movedst[5496]
me against him, to [I][c]destroy[1104] him
without cause.[2600]
4 And Satan answered the LORD, and
said, Skin[5785] for skin, yea, all that a man
hath will he give for his life.[5315]
5 [a]But put forth thine hand[3027] now,
and touch[5060] his [b]bone[6106] and his
flesh,[1320] and he will curse thee to thy face.
6 [a]And the LORD said unto Satan,
Behold, he *is* in thine hand; [I]but save his
life.
7 So went Satan forth from the presence of the LORD, and smote[5221] Job with
sore[7451] boils[7822] [a]from the sole[3709] of his
foot unto his crown.
8 And he took him a potsherd[2789] to
scrape himself withal; [a]and he sat down
among the ashes.

9 Then said his wife[802] unto him,
[a]Dost thou still [b]retain thine integrity?
curse God, and die.[4191]
10 But he said unto her, Thou speakest as one of the foolish women speaketh.
What? [a]shall we receive good[2896] at the
hand of God, and shall we not receive
evil? [b]In all this did not Job [c]sin[2398] with
his lips.[8193]

Job's Three Friends

11 Now when Job's three [a]friends[7453]
heard[8085] of all this evil that was come
upon him, they came every one from his
own place; Eliphaz the [b]Temanite, and
Bildad the [c]Shuhite, and Zophar the
Naamathite: for they had made an
appointment[3259] together to come [d]to
mourn[5110] with him and to comfort[5162]
him.
12 And when they lifted up[5375] their
eyes afar off, and knew[5234] him not,
they lifted up their voice, and wept;
and they rent every one his mantle,[4598]
and [a]sprinkled[2236] dust[6083] upon their
heads[7218] toward heaven.[8064]

3 [I]Hebr. *to swallow him up* [a]Job 1:1, 8 [b]Job 27:5, 6 [c]Job 9:17
5 [a]Job 1:11 [b]Job 19:20
6 [I]Or, *only* [a]Job 1:12
7 [a]Isa. 1:6
8 [a]2Sam. 13:19; Job 42:6; Ezek. 27:30; Matt. 11:21
9 [a]Job 21:15 [b]Job 2:3
10 [a]Job 1:21; Rom. 12:12; James 5:10, 11 [b]Job 1:22 [c]Ps. 39:1
11 [a]Prov. 17:17 [b]Gen. 36:11; Jer. 49:7 [c]Gen. 25:2 [d]Job 42:11; Rom. 12:15
12 [a]Neh. 9:1; Lam. 2:10; Ezek. 27:30

2:9, 10 These verses reveal the discussion between Job and his wife. There is no basis for suggesting, as some do, that his wife was killed by God for her statements against Job and that Job later married someone else. The fact remains that she endured the earlier trials (e.g., the deaths of her children, the loss of wealth and possessions) just as he had; yet the sight of her husband's physical condition caused her to relinquish all hope. In fact, her greatest sin may have been that she was so dependent on him that she could not bear losing him. There is no hint that their marriage was bad or that she was not a "fit" help meet for such a righteous man. If she had been so, it is doubtful that Job, being a righteous man, would have married her. Job was obviously surprised at her words, indicating that he was not used to hearing this kind of thing from her. His rebuke of her statement seems to have been sufficient, and she once again retained a proper testimony before the Lord.

2:11–13 These men were true friends of Job. They were fitting company for an upright man, despite the fact that many people condemn them because they were reproved at the end of the book. Verse twelve states that "they lifted up their eyes afar off, and knew him not." Some believe that his disease had so disfigured him that Job could not even be recognized by his friends. Verse thirteen says that they were silent, concerned, and confused. In the discourses that followed, these three men missed the basic truth that affliction is not always punishment (see Ex. 4:12; John 9:3). Much of what they said was true but was misapplied to Job's situation. It may even be that they were taken into the service of Satan "unawares." It is highly possible that Satan used the words of these men in an attempt to cause Job to sin. Christians often attempt to relate one's physical condition to some great sin in his or her life. In seeking to comfort or reprove someone, people often misapply scriptural principles to another's life, because they do not fully understand the situation. Job's friends were convinced that God sent trouble on Job in proportion to the measure of his sins. Everything they said was based on this presupposition. By applying this to God's testing of Job, they made God appear arbitrary and pitiless.

13 So they sat down with him upon the ground[776] [a]seven days and seven nights,[3915] and none spake[1696] a word[1697] unto him: for they saw[7200] that *his* grief was very great.

Job Complains to God

3 🔑 After this opened Job his mouth,[6310] and cursed[7043] his day.[3117]

2 And Job [I]spake, and said,

3 [a]Let the day perish[6] wherein I was born, and the night[3915] *in which* it was said, There is a man child[1397] conceived.

4 Let that day be darkness;[2822] let not God[433] regard[1875] it from above, neither let the light shine upon it.

5 Let darkness and [a]the shadow of death[6757] [I]stain[1350] it; let a cloud dwell[7931] upon it; [II][b]let the blackness[3650] of the day terrify[1204] it.

6 *As for* that night, let darkness[652] seize[3947] upon it; [I]let it not be joined unto the days of the year, let it not come into the number of the months.

7 Lo, let that night be solitary,[1565] let no joyful[7445] voice come therein.

8 Let them curse[5344] it that curse[779] the day, [a]who are ready to raise up [I]their mourning.

9 Let the stars of the twilight[5399] thereof be dark;[2821] let it look for light,[216] but *have* none; neither let it see [I][a]the dawning[6079] of the day:

10 Because it shut not up the doors of my *mother's* womb,[990] nor hid[5641] sorrow[5999] from mine eyes.

11 [a]Why died[4191] I not from the womb? *why* did I *not* give up the ghost[1478] when I came out of the belly?[990]

12 [a]Why did the knees prevent[6923] me? or why the breasts that I should suck?

13 For now should I have lain still[7901] and been quiet,[8252] I should have slept: then had I been at rest,

14 With kings[4428] and counsellors[3289] of the earth,[776] which [a]built desolate places[2723] for themselves;

15 Or with princes[8267] that had gold, who filled their houses[1004] with silver:

16 Or [a]as an hidden untimely birth[5309] I had not been; as infants *which* never saw[7200] light.

17 There the wicked[7563] cease *from* troubling;[7267] and there the [I]weary[3019] be at rest.

18 *There* the prisoners[615] rest together; [a]they hear[8085] not the voice of the oppressor.

19 The small and great are there; and the servant[5650] *is* free from his master.[113]

20 [a]Wherefore is light given to him that is in misery,[6001] and life[2416] unto the [b]bitter[4751] *in* soul;[5315]

21 Which [I][a]long[2442] for death,[4194] but it *cometh* not; and dig[2658] for it more than [b]for hid[4301] treasures;

22 Which rejoice exceedingly, *and* are glad, when they can find the grave?[6913]

23 *Why is light given* to a man whose way[1870] is hid,[5641] [a]and whom God hath hedged in?[5526]

24 For my sighing[585] cometh [I]before I eat, and my roarings[7581] are poured out like the waters.

25 For [I]the thing which I greatly feared[6342] is come upon me, and that which I was afraid[3025] of is come unto me.

26 I was not in safety, neither had I rest,[8252] neither was I quiet; yet trouble[7267] came.

Eliphaz Rebukes Job

4 🔑 Then Eliphaz the Temanite answered and said,

2 *If* we assay[5254] [I]to commune[1697]

---

13 [a]Gen. 50:10
2 [I]Hebr. *answered*
3 [a]Job 10:18, 19; Jer. 15:10; 20:14
5 [I]Or, *challenge it* [II]Or, *let them terrify it, as those* who have *a bitter day* [a]Job 10:21, 22; 16:16; 28:3; Ps. 23:4; 44:19; 107:10, 14; Jer. 13:16; Amos 5:8 [b]Amos 8:10
6 [I]Or, *let it not rejoice among the days*
8 [I]Or, *a leviathan* [a]Jer. 9:17, 18
9 [I]Hebr. *the eyelids of the morning* [a]Job 41:18
11 [a]Job 10:18
12 [a]Gen. 30:3; Isa. 66:12
14 [a]Job 15:28
16 [a]Ps. 58:8
17 [I]Hebr. *wearied* in *strength*
18 [a]Job 39:7
20 [a]Jer. 20:18 [b]1Sam. 1:10; 2Kgs. 4:27; Prov. 31:6
21 [I]Hebr. *wait* [a]Rev. 9:6 [b]Prov. 2:4
23 [a]Job 19:8; Lam. 3:7
24 [I]Hebr. *before my meat*
25 [I]Hebr. *I feared a fear, and it came upon me*
2 [I]Hebr. *a word*

🔑 **3:1** Job's conflict really begins in this passage. He had been struggling to determine the cause of his affliction. The only reasonable conclusion seemed to be that either Job was guilty of some sin worthy of this punishment or that God was unjust. None of them recognized that God was testing Job. In all this, however, Job never abandoned his faith in God.

🔑 **4:1** The name "Eliphaz" means "God is strong" or "God is dispenser." He was the oldest of Job's three friends (Job 15:10). Teman, the land from which he came, was known for its men of

(continued on next page)

with thee, wilt thou be grieved? but
[II]who can withhold himself from speaking?[4405]
3 Behold, thou hast instructed[3256]
many, and thou [a]hast strengthened[2388] the
weak hands.
4 Thy words[4405] have upholden[6965]
him that was falling, and thou [a]hast
strengthened [I][b]the feeble[3766] knees.
5 But now it is come upon thee, and
thou faintest;[3811] it toucheth[5060] thee, and
thou art troubled.[926]
6 *Is* not *this* [a]thy fear,[3374] [b]thy confidence,[3690] thy hope,[8615] and the uprightness[8537] of thy ways?[1870]
7 Remember,[2142] I pray thee, [a]who
ever perished,[6] being innocent?[5355] or
where were the righteous[6662] cut off?
8 Even as I have seen,[7200] [a]they that
plow iniquity,[205] and sow wickedness,[5999]
reap the same.
9 By the blast[5397] of God[433] they
perish,[6] and [I][a]by the breath[7307] of his
nostrils[639] are they consumed.[3615]
10 The roaring of the lion, and the
voice of the fierce[7826] lion, and [a]the teeth
of the young lions, are broken.
11 [a]The old lion perisheth[6] for lack
of prey, and the stout lion's whelps[1121]
are scattered abroad.
12 Now a thing[1697] was [I]secretly[1589]
brought[1589] to me, and mine ear[241] received a little thereof.
13 [a]In thoughts from the visions[2384]
of the night,[3915] when deep sleep falleth[5307] on men,[582]
14 Fear[6343] [I]came upon me, and
[a]trembling,[7461] which made[6342] [II]all my
bones[6106] to shake.[6342]
15 Then a spirit[7307] passed before
my face; the hair of my flesh[1320] stood
up:
16 It stood still, but I could not
discern[5234] the form thereof: an image[8544]
was before mine eyes, [I]*there was* silence,
and I heard[8085] a voice, *saying,*
17 [a]Shall mortal man[582] be more
just[6663] than God? shall a man be more
pure than his maker?[6213]
18 Behold, he [a]put no trust[539] in his
servants;[5650] [I]and his angels he charged
with folly:
19 [a]How much less *in* them that
dwell[7931] in [b]houses of clay, whose
foundation[3247] *is* in the dust,[6083] *which*
are crushed[1792] before the moth?
20 [a]They are [I]destroyed[3807] from
morning to evening: they perish for
ever[5331] without any regarding[7760] *it.*
21 [a]Doth not their excellency[3499]
which is in them go away? [b]they die,[4191]
even without wisdom.[2451]

5 Call[7121] now, if there be any that will
answer thee; and to which of the
saints[6918] wilt thou [I]turn?
2 For wrath[3708] killeth the foolish
man, and [I]envy[7068] slayeth[4191] the silly
one.
3 [a]I have seen[7200] the foolish taking
root: but suddenly I cursed[5344] his habitation.
4 [a]His children[1121] are far from
safety,[3468] and they are crushed[1792] in
the gate, [b]neither *is there* any to deliver[5337] *them.*
5 Whose harvest the hungry eateth
up, and taketh it even out of the thorns,
and [a]the robber swalloweth up[7602] their
substance.[2428]
🔑 6 Although [I]affliction[205] cometh not
forth of the dust,[6083] neither doth trouble[5999] spring out of the ground;[127]

2 [II]Hebr. *who can refrain from words*
3 [a]Isa. 35:3
4 [I]Hebr. *the bowing knees* [a]Isa. 35:3 [b]Heb. 12:12
6 [a]Job 1:1 [b]Prov. 3:26
7 [a]Ps. 37:25
8 [a]Ps. 7:14; Prov. 22:8; Hos. 10:13; Gal. 6:7, 8
9 [I]That is, *by his anger* [a]Ex. 15:8; Job 1:19; 15:30; Isa. 11:4; 30:33; 2Thess. 2:8
10 [a]Ps. 58:6
11 [a]Ps. 34:10
12 [I]Hebr. *by stealth*
13 [a]Job 33:15
14 [I]Hebr. *met me* [II]Hebr. *the multitude of my bones* [a]Hab. 3:16
16 [I]Or, *I heard a still voice*
17 [a]Job 9:2
18 [I]Or, *nor in his angels,* in whom *he put light* [a]Job 15:15; 25:5; 2Pet. 2:4
19 [a]Job 15:16 [b]2Cor. 4:7; 5:1
20 [I]Hebr. *beaten in pieces* [a]Ps. 90:5, 6
21 [a]Ps. 39:11; 49:14 [b]Job 36:12

1 [I]Or, *look*
2 [I]Or, *indignation*
3 [a]Ps. 37:35, 36; Jer. 12:2, 3
4 [a]Ps. 119:155; 127:5 [b]Ps. 109:12
5 [a]Job 18:9
6 [I]Or, *iniquity*

(continued from previous page)
wisdom (Jer. 49:7). Eliphaz became convinced that Job had committed some great sin for which he was being punished. He based this idea on his experiences, which had taught him that man is wicked, and that he is punished according to his wickedness.

🔑 **5:6, 7** These verses are a vivid illustration of man's depravity. Eliphaz is wrong, however, in his assumption that this explained Job's suffering. The sinfulness of mankind (original sin) explains only the existence of sorrow and suffering. What Eliphaz was unaware of was that God was permitting this affliction to come on Job for a purpose other than his mere sinful nature, namely the purifying and strengthening of Job's faith.

7 Yet man[120] is [a]born unto [I]trouble, as [II]the sparks fly upward.

8 I would seek unto God,[410] and unto God[430] would I commit[7760] my cause:[1700]

9 [a]Which doeth[6213] great things [I]and unsearchable; marvellous things[6381] [II]without number:

10 [a]Who giveth rain upon the earth,[776] and sendeth waters upon the [I]fields:

11 [a]To set up[7760] on high those that be low; that those which mourn[6937] may be exalted[7682] to safety.

12 [a]He disappointeth[6565] the devices[4284] of the crafty,[6175] so that their hands[3027] [I]cannot perform *their* enterprise.[8454]

13 [a]He taketh the wise[2450] in their own craftiness:[6193] and the counsel[6098] of the froward[6617] is carried headlong.[4116]

14 [a]They [I]meet with darkness[2822] in the daytime,[3119] and grope[4959] in the noonday as in the night.[3915]

15 But [a]he saveth[3467] the poor from the sword,[2719] from their mouth,[6310] and from the hand[3027] of the mighty.[2389]

16 [a]So the poor hath hope, and iniquity[5766] stoppeth her mouth.

17 [a]Behold, happy[835] *is* the man[582] whom God[433] correcteth:[3198] therefore despise[3988] not thou the chastening[4148] of the Almighty:[7706]

18 [a]For he maketh sore, and bindeth up:[2280] he woundeth,[4272] and his hands make whole.

19 [a]He shall deliver thee in six troubles: yea, in seven [b]there shall[5060] no evil[7451] touch[5060] thee.

20 [a]In famine he shall redeem[6299] thee from death:[4194] and in war [I]from the power[3027] of the sword.

21 [a]Thou shalt be hid [I]from the scourge[7752] of the tongue: neither shalt thou be afraid[3372] of destruction[7701] when it cometh.

22 At destruction and famine thou shalt laugh: [a]neither shalt thou be afraid of the beasts[2416] of the earth.

23 [a]For thou shalt be in league[1285] with the stones of the field:[7704] and the beasts of the field shall be at peace[7999] with thee.

7 [I]Or, *labor* [II]Hebr. *the sons of the burning coal lift up to fly* [a]Gen. 3:17-19; 1Cor. 10:13
9 [I]Hebr. *and there is no search* [II]Hebr. *till* there be *no number* [a]Job 9:10; 37:5; Ps. 40:5; 72:18; 145:3; Rom. 11:33
10 [I]Hebr. *outplaces* [a]Job 28:26; Ps. 65:9, 10; 147:8; Jer. 5:24; 10:13; 51:16; Acts 14:17
11 [a]1Sam. 2:7; Ps. 113:7
12 [I]Or, *cannot perform anything* [a]Neh. 4:15; Ps. 33:10; Isa. 8:10
13 [a]Ps. 9:15; 1Cor. 3:19
14 [I]Or, *run into* [a]Deut. 28:29; Isa. 59:10; Amos 8:9
15 [a]Ps. 35:10
16 [a]1Sam. 2:9; Ps. 107:42
17 [a]Ps. 94:12; Prov. 3:11, 12; Heb. 12:5; James 1:12; Rev. 3:19
18 [a]Deut. 32:39; 1Sam. 2:6; Isa. 30:26; Hos. 6:1
19 [a]Ps. 34:19; 91:3; Prov. 24:16; 1Cor. 10:13 [b]Ps. 91:10
20 [I]Hebr. *from the hands* [a]Ps. 33:19; 37:19
21 [I]Or, *when the tongue scourgeth* [a]Ps. 31:20
22 [a]Isa. 11:9; 35:9; 65:25; Ezek. 34:25
23 [a]Ps. 91:12; Hos. 2:18
24 [I]Or, *that peace is thy tabernacle* [II]Or, *err*
25 [I]Or, *much* [a]Ps. 112:2 [b]Ps. 72:16
26 [I]Hebr. *ascendeth* [a]Prov. 9:11; 10:27
27 [I]Hebr. *for thyself,* Prov. 9:12 [a]Ps. 111:2

24 And thou shalt know[3045] [I]that thy tabernacle[168] *shall be* in peace; and thou shalt visit[6485] thy habitation, and shalt not [II]sin.[2398]

25 Thou shalt know also that [a]thy seed[2233] *shall be* [I]great, and thine offspring [b]as the grass of the earth.

26 [a]Thou shalt come to *thy* grave[6913] in a full age, like as a shock of corn [I]cometh in[5927] in his season.[6256]

27 Lo this, we have [a]searched[2713] it, so it *is;* hear[8085] it, and know thou *it* [I]for thy good.[2896]

Job Answers Eliphaz

6 But Job answered and said,

2 Oh that my grief[3708] were thoroughly weighed,[8254] and my calamity[1942] [I]laid in the balances together!

3 For now it would be heavier[3513] [a]than the sand of the sea: therefore [I][b]my words[1697] are swallowed up.[3886]

4 [a]For the arrows of the Almighty[7706] *are* within me, the poison[2534] whereof drinketh up my spirit:[7307] [b]the terrors[1161] of God[433] do set themselves in array against me.

5 Doth the wild ass bray [I]when he hath grass? or loweth[1600] the ox over his fodder?

6 Can that which is unsavoury be eaten without salt? or is there *any* taste[2940] in the white[7388] of an egg?[2495]

7 The things *that* my soul[5315] refused[3985] to touch[5060] *are* as my sorrowful[1741] meat.

8 Oh that I might have my request;[7596] and that God would grant *me* [I]the thing that I long for!

9 Even [a]that it would please[2974] God to destroy[1792] me; that he would let loose his hand,[3027] and cut me off![1214]

10 Then should I yet have comfort;[5165] yea, I would harden myself in sorrow:[2427] let him not spare; for [a]I have not concealed the words[561] of [b]the Holy One.[6918]

1 [I]Hebr. *lifted up*
3 [I]That is, *I want* *words to express my grief* [a]Prov. 27:3 [b]Ps. 77:4
4 [a]Ps. 38:2 [b]Ps. 88:15, 16 **5** [I]Hebr. *at grass*
8 [I]Hebr. *my expectation* **9** [a]1Kgs. 19:4
10 [a]Acts 20:20 [b]Lev. 19:2; Isa. 57:15; Hos. 11:9

11 What *is* my strength, that I should hope?[3176] and what *is* mine end, that I should prolong[748] my life?[5315]

12 *Is* my strength the strength of stones? or *is* my flesh[1320] [I]of brass?

13 *Is* not my help in me? and is wisdom[8454] driven quite from me?

14 [I][a]To him that is afflicted[4523] pity[2617] *should be shewed* from his friend;[7453] but he forsaketh[5800] the fear[3374] of the Almighty.

15 [a]My brethren[251] have dealt deceitfully[898] as a brook, *and* [b]as the stream of brooks they pass away;[5674]

16 Which are blackish[6937] by reason of the ice, *and* wherein the snow is hid:[5956]

17 What time[6256] they wax warm, [I]they vanish:[6789] [II]when it is hot, they are [III]consumed out of their place.

18 The paths[734] of their way[1870] are turned aside; they go to nothing,[8414] and perish.[6]

19 The troops[734] of [a]Tema looked, the companies of [b]Sheba waited[6960] for them.

20 They were [a]confounded[954] because they had hoped;[682] they came thither, and were ashamed.[2659]

⊶ 21 [I]For now [a]ye are [II]nothing; ye see *my* casting down,[2866] and [b]are afraid.[3372]

22 Did I say, Bring unto me? or, Give a reward for me of your substance?

23 Or, Deliver me from the enemy's hand? or, Redeem[6299] me from the hand of the mighty?[6184]

24 Teach[3384] me, and I will hold my tongue: and cause me to understand[995] wherein I have erred.[7683]

25 How forcible[4834] are right[3476] words! but what doth your arguing[3198] reprove?[3198]

26 Do ye imagine[2803] to reprove words,[4405] and the speeches[561] of one that is desperate,[2976] *which are* as wind?[7307]

27 Yea, [I]ye overwhelm[5307] the fatherless, and ye [a]dig[3738] *a pit* for your friend.

28 Now therefore be content,[2974] look upon me; for *it is* [I]evident unto you if I lie.[3576]

29 [a]Return,[7725] I pray you,[4994] let it not be iniquity;[5766] yea, return again, my righteousness[6664] *is* [I]in it.

30 Is there iniquity in my tongue? cannot [I]my taste discern perverse things?[1942]

7 *Is there* not [I][a]an appointed time[6635] to man[582] upon earth?[776] *are not* his days also like the days of an hireling?

2 As a servant[5650] [I]earnestly desireth the shadow,[6738] and as an hireling looketh for[6960] *the reward of* his work:

3 So am I made to possess[5157] [a]months of vanity,[7723] and wearisome nights[3915] are appointed to me.

4 [a]When I lie down, I say, When shall I arise, and [I]the night[6153] be gone? and I am full of tossings to and fro unto the dawning[5399] of the day.

5 My flesh[1320] is [a]clothed[3847] with worms[7415] and clods of dust;[6083] my skin[5785] is broken, and become loathsome.

6 [a]My days are swifter[7043] than a weaver's shuttle, and are spent[3615] without hope.

7 O remember[2142] that [a]my life[2416] *is* wind:[7307] mine eye [I]shall no more [II]see good.[2896]

8 [a]The eye of him that hath seen[7210] me shall see me no *more:* thine eyes *are* upon me, and [I]I *am not.*

9 *As* the cloud[6051] is consumed[3615] and vanisheth away:[3212] so [a]he that goeth down to the grave[7585] shall come up[5927] no *more.*

10 He shall return[7725] no more to his house,[1004] [a]neither shall his place know[5234] him any more.

11 Therefore I will [a]not refrain my

12 [I]Hebr. *brazen*
14 [I]Hebr. *To him that melteth* [a]Prov. 17:17
15 [a]Ps. 38:11; 41:9 [b]Jer. 15:18
17 [I]Hebr. *they are cut off* [II]Hebr. *in the heat thereof* [III]Hebr. *extinguished*
19 [a]Gen. 25:15 [b]1Kgs. 10:1; Ps. 72:10; Ezek. 27:22, 23
20 [a]Jer. 14:3
21 [I]Or, *For now ye are like to them* [II]Hebr. *not* [a]Job 13:4 [b]Ps. 38:11
27 [I]Hebr. *ye cause to fall upon* [a]Ps. 57:6
28 [I]Hebr. *before your face*
29 [I]That is, *in this matter* [a]Job 17:10
30 [I]Hebr. *my palate,* Job 12:11; 34:3

1 [I]Or, *a warfare* [a]Job 14:5, 13, 14; Ps. 39:4
2 [I]Hebr. *gapeth after*
3 [a]Job 29:2
4 [I]Hebr. *the evening be measured* [a]Deut. 28:67; Job 17:12
5 [a]Isa. 14:11
6 [a]Job 9:25; 16:22; 17:11; Ps. 90:6; 102:11; 103:15; 144:4; Isa. 38:12; 40:6; James 4:14
7 [I]Hebr. *shall not return* [II]*to see,* that is, *to enjoy* [a]Ps. 78:39; 89:47
8 [I]That is, *I can live no longer* [a]Job 20:9
9 [a]2Sam. 12:23
10 [a]Job 8:18; 20:9; Ps. 103:16
11 [a]Ps. 39:1, 9; 40:9

⊶ **6:21–23** Job's statement reveals the possibility that his friends feared God would do to them what He had done to Job, especially if they helped or sympathized with him. They strongly believed that Job had sinned greatly and was being punished for it.

mouth;[6310] I will speak[1696] in the
anguish[6862] of my spirit;[7307] I will
[b]complain[7878] in the bitterness[4751] of my
soul.[5315]
12 *Am* I a sea, or a whale,[8577] that
thou settest[7760] a watch over me?
13 [a]When I say, My bed shall
comfort[5162] me, my couch shall ease[5375]
my complaint;[7878]
14 Then thou scarest[2865] me with
dreams, and terrifiest[1204] me through
visions:[2384]
15 So that my soul chooseth[977] strangling, *and* death[4194] rather [I]than my
life.[6106]
16 [a]I loathe[3988] *it;* I would not live[2421]
alway: [b]let me alone; for [c]my days *are*
vanity.[1892]
17 [a]What *is* man, that thou shouldest
magnify[1431] him? and that thou shouldest
set thine heart[3820] upon him?
18 And *that* thou shouldest visit[6485]
him every morning, *and* try[974] him every
moment?
19 How long wilt thou not depart
from me, nor let me alone[7503] till I
swallow down[1104] my spittle?
20 I have sinned;[2398] what shall I do
unto thee, [a]O thou preserver[5341] of
men?[120] why [b]hast thou set[7760] me as a
mark against thee, so that I am a
burden[4853] to myself?
21 And why dost thou not par-
don[5375] my transgression,[6588] and take
away[5674] mine iniquity?[5771] for now
shall I sleep in the dust; and thou shalt
seek me in the morning, but I *shall*
not *be.*

Bildad Speaks for God

8 🔑 Then answered Bildad the
Shuhite, and said,
2 How long wilt thou speak[4448] these
things? and *how long shall* the words[561]
of thy mouth[6310] *be like* a strong
wind?[7307]
3 [a]Doth[5791] God[410] pervert[5791] judgment?[4941] or doth the Almighty[7706] pervert justice?[6664]
4 If [a]thy children[1121] have sinned[2398]
against him, and he have cast them
away[7971] [I]for their transgression;[6588]
5 [a]If thou wouldest seek unto God
betimes,[7836] and make thy supplication[2603] to the Almighty;
🔑 6 If thou *wert* pure[2134] and upright;[3477] surely now he would awake for
thee, and make[7999] the habitation[5116] of
thy righteousness[6664] prosperous.[7999]
7 Though thy beginning[7225] was
small, yet thy latter[319] end should greatly
increase.
8 [a]For enquire,[7592] I pray thee,[4994] of
the former[7223] age,[1755] and prepare[3559]
thyself to the search of their fathers:[1]
9 (For [a]we *are but of* yesterday, and
know[3045] [I]nothing, because our days
upon earth[776] *are* a shadow:[6738])
10 Shall not they teach[3384] thee, *and*
tell[559] thee, and utter words[4405] out of
their heart?[3820]
11 Can[1342] the rush[1573] grow up[1342]
without mire? can the flag[260] grow without water?
12 [a]Whilst it *is* yet in his greenness,
and not cut down, it withereth[3001] before
any *other* herb.
13 So *are* the paths[734] of all that forget God; and the [a]hypocrite's[2611] hope
shall perish:[6]
14 Whose hope[3689] shall be cut off,
and whose trust *shall be* [Ia]a spider's
web.[1004]
15 [a]He shall lean[8172] upon his
house,[1004] but it shall not stand: he shall
hold it fast, but it shall not endure.
16 He *is* green before the sun,
and his branch shooteth forth in his garden.

11 [b]1Sam. 1:10; Job 10:1
13 [a]Job 9:27
15 [I]Hebr. *than my bones*
16 [a]Job 10:1 [b]Job 10:20; 14:6; Ps. 39:13 [c]Ps. 62:9
17 [a]Ps. 8:4; 144:3; Heb. 2:6
20 [a]Ps. 36:6 [b]Job 16:12; Ps. 21:12; Lam. 3:12
3 [a]Gen. 18:25; Deut. 32:4; 2Chr. 19:7; Job 34:12, 17; Dan. 9:14; Rom. 3:5
4 [I]Hebr. *in the hand of their transgression* [a]Job 1:5, 18
5 [a]Job 5:8; 11:13; 22:23-30
8 [a]Deut. 4:32; 32:7; Job 15:18
9 [I]Hebr. *not* [a]Gen. 47:9; 1Chr. 29:15; Job 7:6; Ps. 39:5; 102:11; 144:4
12 [a]Ps. 129:6; Jer. 17:6
13 [a]Job 11:20; 18:14; 27:8; Ps. 112:10; Prov. 10:28
14 [I]Hebr. *a spider's house* [a]Isa. 59:5, 6
15 [a]Job 27:18

🔑 **8:1, 6** "Bildad" means "son of contention." He was from the east, namely of Shuah or Sukhu in the Euphrates area (as was Zophar; see 1 Kgs. 4:30). As Job's other two friends had suggested, Bildad feels that Job is being punished for his sin; while before, he had been blessed with wealth and prosperity for his righteousness. He arrived at this conclusion based on tradition, namely, that was the way it had always been.

17 His roots are wrapped about the heap, *and* seeth[2372] the place of stones.

18 [a]If he destroy[1104] him from his place, then *it* shall deny him, *saying,* I have not seen[7200] thee.

19 Behold, this *is* the joy of his way,[1870] and [a]out of the earth[6083] shall others grow.

20 Behold, God will not cast away[3988] a perfect[8535] *man,* neither will he [I]help[2388] the evil doers:[7489]

21 Till he fill thy mouth with laughing, and thy lips[8193] with [I]rejoicing.

22 They that hate[8130] thee shall be [a]clothed with shame; and the dwelling place[168] of the wicked[7563] [I]shall come to nought.369

Job Replies to Bildad

9 Then Job answered and said,

🔑 2 I know[3045] *it is* so of a truth:[551] but how should[6663] [a]man[582] be just[6663] [I]with God?[410]

3 If he will contend[7378] with him, he cannot answer him one of a thousand.

4 [a]He is wise[2450] in heart,3824 and mighty in strength: who hath hardened7185 *himself* against him, and hath prospered?[7999]

5 Which removeth6275 the mountains, and they know not: which overturneth[2015] them in his anger.[639]

6 Which [a]shaketh[7264] the earth[776] out of her place, and [b]the pillars thereof tremble.

7 Which commandeth[559] the sun, and it riseth not; and sealeth up the stars.

8 [a]Which alone spreadeth out the heavens,8064 and treadeth upon the [I]waves[1116] of the sea.

9 [a]Which maketh[6213] [I]Arcturus, Orion, and Pleiades, and the chambers of the south.

10 [a]Which doeth[6213] great things past finding out;369,2714 yea, and wonders[6381] without number.

11 [a]Lo, he goeth by me, and I see *him* not: he passeth on also, but I perceive[995] him not.

12 [a]Behold, he taketh away, [I][b]who can hinder[7725] him? who will say unto him, What doest[6213] thou?

13 *If* God[433] will not withdraw[7725] his anger, [a]the [I]proud helpers do stoop under him.

14 How much less shall I answer him, *and* choose out[977] my words[1697] *to reason* with him?

15 [a]Whom, though I were righteous,[6663] *yet* would I not answer, *but* I would make supplication[2603] to my judge.[8199]

16 If I had called,[7121] and he had answered me; *yet* would I not believe[539] that he had hearkened[238] unto my voice.

17 For he breaketh me with a tempest,8183 and multiplieth my wounds [a]without cause.[2600]

18 He will not suffer me to take[7725] my breath,[7307] but filleth me with bitterness.[4472]

19 If *I speak* of strength, lo, *he is* strong: and if of judgment,[4941] who shall set[3259] me a time *to plead?*

20 If I justify[6663] myself, mine own mouth[6310] shall condemn[7561] me: *if I say,* I *am* perfect,[8535] it shall also prove me perverse.6140

21 *Though* I *were* perfect, *yet* would I not know my soul:[5315] I would despise[3988] my life.[2416]

22 This *is* one *thing,* therefore I said *it,* [a]He destroyeth[3615] the perfect and the wicked.[7563]

23 If the scourge7752 slay[4191] suddenly, he will laugh3932 at the trial[4531] of the innocent.[5355]

24 The earth is given into the hand[3027] of the wicked: [a]he covereth the faces of the judges[8199] thereof; if not, where, *and* who *is* he?

25 Now [a]my days are swifter[7043] than a post:7323 they flee away, they see no good.[2896]

18 [a]Job 7:10; 20:9; Ps. 37:36
19 [a]Ps. 113:7
20 [I]Hebr. *take the ungodly by the hand*
21 [I]Hebr. *shouting for joy*
22 [I]Hebr. *shall not be* [a]Ps. 35:26; 109:29

2 [I]Or, *before God* [a]Ps. 143:2; Rom. 3:20
4 [a]Job 36:5
6 [a]Isa. 2:19, 21; Hag. 2:6, 21; Heb. 12:26 [b]Job 26:11
8 [I]Hebr. *heights* [a]Gen. 1:6; Ps. 104:2, 3
9 [I]Hebr. *Ash, Cesil, and Cimah* [a]Gen. 1:16; Job 38:31, 32; Amos 5:8
10 [a]Job 5:9; Ps. 71:15
11 [a]Job 23:8, 9; 35:14
12 [I]Hebr. *who can turn him away* [a]Isa. 45:9; Jer. 18:6; Rom. 9:20 [b]Job 11:10
13 [I]Hebr. *helpers of pride,* or, *strength* [a]Job 26:12; Isa. 30:7
15 [a]Job 10:15
17 [a]Job 2:3; 34:6
22 [a]Eccl. 9:2, 3; Ezek. 21:3
24 [a]2Sam. 15:30; 19:4; Jer. 14:4
25 [a]Job 7:6, 7

🔑 **9:2** The Hebrew word translated "man" in this verse is *'enōsh* (582), and it refers to the depravity that is evident in all of mankind.

26 They are passed away as the [I]swift16 ships: [a]as the eagle *that* hasteth2907 to the prey.

27 [a]If I say, I will forget my complaint,[7878] I will leave off my heaviness,[6440] and comfort *myself:*

28 [a]I am afraid[3025] of all my sorrows,[6094] I know that thou [b]wilt not hold me innocent.[5352]

29 *If* I be wicked,[7561] why then labour I in vain?

30 [a]If I wash myself[7364] with snow water, and make[2141] my hands[3709] never so clean;[2141]

31 Yet shalt thou plunge[2881] me in the ditch,[7845] and mine own clothes shall [I]abhor[8581] me.

32 For [a]*he is* not a man,[376] as I *am, that* I should answer him, *and* we should come together in judgment.[4941]

33 [a]Neither is there [I]any [II]daysman[3198] betwixt us, *that* might lay his hand upon us both.

34 [a]Let him take his rod away[5493] from me, and let not his fear[367] terrify[1204] me:

35 *Then* would I speak, and not fear[3372] him; [I]but *it is* not so with me.

10

My [a]soul[5315] is [I]weary5354 of my life;[2416] I will leave[5800] my complaint[7878] upon myself; [b]I will speak[1696] in the bitterness[4751] of my soul.

2 I will say unto God,[433] Do not condemn[7561] me; shew[3045] me wherefore thou contendest[7378] with me.

3 *Is it* good[2896] unto thee that thou shouldest oppress, that thou shouldest despise[3988] [I][a]the work of thine hands,[3709] and shine3313 upon the counsel[6098] of the wicked?[7563]

4 Hast thou eyes of flesh?[1320] or [a]seest thou as man[582] seeth?[7200]

5 *Are* thy days as the days of man? *are* thy years as man's[1397] days,

6 That thou enquirest1245 after mine iniquity,[5771] and searchest after my sin?[2403]

7 [I][a]Thou knowest[1847] that I am not wicked;[7561] and *there is* none that can deliver[5337] out of thine hand.[3027]

26 [I]Hebr. *ships of desire* [a]Hab. 1:8
27 [a]Job 7:13
28 [a]Ps. 119:120 [b]Ex. 20:7
30 [a]Jer. 2:22
31 [I]Or, *make me to be abhorred*
32 [a]Eccl. 6:10; Isa. 45:9; Jer. 49:19; Rom. 9:20
33 [I]Hebr. *one that should argue* [II]Or, *umpire* [a]Job 9:19; 1Sam. 2:25
34 [a]Job 13:20-22; 33:7; Ps. 39:10
35 [I]Hebr. *but I am not so with myself*

1 [I]Or, *cut off while I live* [a]1Kgs. 19:4; Job 7:16; Jon. 4:3, 8 [b]Job 7:11
3 [I]Hebr. *the labor of thine hands* [a]Ps. 138:8; Isa. 64:8
4 [a]1Sam. 16:7
7 [I]Hebr. It is *upon thy knowledge* [a]Ps. 139:12
8 [I]Hebr. *took pains about me* [a]Ps. 119:73
9 [a]Gen. 2:7; 3:19; Isa. 64:8
10 [a]Ps. 139:14-16
11 [I]Hebr. *hedged*
14 [a]Ps. 139:1
15 [a]Isa. 3:11 [b]Job 9:12, 15, 20, 21 [c]Ps. 25:18
16 [a]Isa. 38:13; Lam. 3:10
17 [I]That is, *thy plagues* [a]Ruth 1:21
18 [a]Job 3:11
20 [a]Job 7:6, 16; 8:9; Ps. 39:5 [b]Ps. 39:13 [c]Job 7:16, 19
21 [a]Ps. 88:12 [b]Ps. 23:4

8 [a]Thine hands [I]have made[6087] me and fashioned[6213] me together round about; yet thou dost destroy[1104] me.

9 Remember I beseech thee,[4994] that [a]thou hast made[6213] me as the clay; and wilt thou bring me into dust[6083] again?

10 [a]Hast thou not poured me out as milk, and curdled me like cheese?

11 Thou hast clothed me with skin[5785] and flesh,[1320] and hast [I]fenced me with bones[6106] and sinews.

12 Thou hast granted[6213] me life and favour,[2617] and thy visitation[6486] hath preserved[8104] my spirit.[7307]

13 And these *things* hast thou hid6845 in thine heart:3824 I know[3045] that this *is* with thee.

14 If I sin,[2398] then [a]thou markest[8104] me, and thou wilt not acquit[5352] me from mine iniquity.

15 If I be wicked,[7561] [a]woe unto me; [b]and *if* I be righteous,[6663] *yet* will I not lift up[5375] my head.[7218] *I am* full of confusion;7036 therefore [c]see thou mine affliction;

16 For it increaseth.[1342] [a]Thou huntest me as a fierce lion: and again thou shewest thyself marvellous[6381] upon me.

17 Thou renewest [I][a]thy witnesses against me, and increasest thine indignation[3708] upon me; changes2487 and war[6635] *are* against me.

18 [a]Wherefore then hast thou brought me forth out of the womb? Oh that I had given up the ghost,[1478] and no eye had seen[7200] me!

19 I should have been as though I had not been; I should have been carried from the womb[990] to the grave.[6913]

20 [a]*Are* not my days few? [b]cease *then, and* [c]let me alone, that I may take comfort1082 a little,

21 Before I go *whence* I shall not return,[7725] [a]*even* to the land[776] of darkness[2822] [b]and the shadow of death;[6757]

22 A land of darkness,[5890] as darkness[652] *itself; and* of the shadow of death, without any order, and *where* the light *is* as darkness.[652]

Zophar Accuses Job of Sin

11 Then answered Zophar the Naamathite, and said,

2 Should not the multitude of words[1697] be answered? and should[6663] [I][a] man[376] full of talk be justified?[6663]

3 Should thy [I]lies[907] make men hold their peace? and when thou mockest, shall no man make thee ashamed?[3637]

4 For [a]thou hast said, My doctrine[3948] *is* pure,[2134] and I am clean[1249] in thine eyes.

5 But oh that God[433] would speak,[1696] and open his lips[8193] against thee;

6 And that he would shew[5046] thee the secrets of wisdom,[2451] that *they are* double to that which is! Know[3045] therefore that [a]God exacteth[5382] of thee *less* than thine iniquity[5771] *deserveth.*

7 [a]Canst thou by searching[2714] find out God? canst thou find out the Almighty[7706] unto perfection?[8503]

8 *It is* [I]as high as heaven;[8064] what canst thou do? deeper than hell;[7585] what canst thou know?

9 The measure thereof *is* longer[752] than the earth,[776] and broader than the sea.

10 [a]If he [I]cut off,[2498] and shut up,[5462] or gather together,[6950] then [II][b]who can hinder him?

11 For [a]he knoweth vain[7723] men: he seeth[7200] wickedness[205] also; will he not then consider[995] *it?*

12 For [I][a]vain man would be wise,[3823] though man[120] be born *like* a wild ass's colt.

13 [a]If thou [b]prepare[3559] thine heart,[3820] and [c]stretch out thine hands[3709] toward him;

14 If iniquity[205] *be* in thine hand,[3027] put it far away, and [a]let not wickedness[5766] dwell[7931] in thy tabernacles.[168]

15 [a]For then shalt thou lift up[5375] thy face without spot;[3971] yea, thou shalt be stedfast, and shalt not fear:[3372]

16 Because thou shalt [a]forget *thy* misery,[5991] *and* remember[2142] *it* as waters *that* pass away:[5674]

17 And *thine* age[2465] [I][a]shall be clearer[6965] than the noonday; thou shalt shine forth, thou shalt be as the morning.

18 And thou shalt be secure,[982] because there is hope;[8615] yea, thou shalt dig[2658] *about thee, and* [a]thou shalt take thy rest[7901] in safety.[983]

19 Also thou shalt lie down, and none shall make *thee* afraid;[2729] yea, many shall [I]make suit[2470] unto thee.

20 But [a]the eyes of the wicked[7563] shall fail,[3615] and [I]they shall not escape,[6] and [b]their hope *shall be as* [II]the giving up[4646] of the ghost.[5313]

2 [I]Hebr. *a man of lips*
3 [I]Or, *devices*
4 [a]Job 6:10; 10:7
6 [a]Ezra 9:13
7 [a]Eccl. 3:11; Rom. 11:33
8 [I]Hebr. *the heights of heaven*
10 [I]Or, *make a change* [II]Hebr. *who can turn him away* [a]Job 9:12; 12:14; Rev. 3:7 [b]Job 9:12
11 [a]Ps. 10:11, 14; 35:22; 94:11
12 [I]Hebr. *empty* [a]Ps. 73:22; 92:6; Eccl. 3:18; Rom. 1:22
13 [a]Job 5:8; 22:21 [b]1Sam. 7:3; Ps. 78:8 [c]Ps. 88:9; 143:6
14 [a]Ps. 101:3
15 [a]Gen. 4:5, 6; Job 22:26; Ps. 119:6; 1John 3:21
16 [a]Isa. 65:16
17 [I]Hebr. *shall arise above the noonday* [a]Ps. 37:6; 112:4; Isa. 58:8, 10
18 [a]Lev. 26:5, 6; Ps. 3:5; 4:8; Prov. 3:24
19 [I]Hebr. *entreat thy face*
20 [I]Hebr. *flight shall perish from them* [II]Or, *a puff of breath* [a]Lev. 26:16; Deut. 28:65 [b]Job 8:14; 18:14; Prov. 11:7

Job Responds to Zophar

12 And Job answered and said,
2 No doubt[551] but ye *are* the people,[5971] and wisdom[2451] shall die[4191] with you.

3 But [a]I have [I]understanding[3824] as well as you; [II]I *am* not inferior[5307] to you: yea, [III]who knoweth not such things as these?

4 [a]I am *as* one mocked of his neighbour,[7453] who [b]calleth[7121] upon God,[433] and he answereth him: the just upright[8549] *man is* laughed to scorn.

5 [a]He that is ready to slip with *his* feet *is as* a lamp despised in the thought of him that is at ease.

3 [I]Hebr. *a heart* [II]Hebr. *I fall not lower than you* [III]Hebr. *with who are not such as these* [a]Job 13:2
4 [a]Job 16:10; 17:2, 6; 21:3; 30:1 [b]Ps. 91:15
5 [a]Prov. 14:2

11:1 Zophar's home was in the land of Naamah, which may have been located in Northern Arabia. His name means "chatterer" or "rough." Like Bildad, he was from the East (1 Kgs. 4:30). He also believed that Job had committed some horrible sin, but he reached this conclusion from a legalistic interpretation of the circumstances. It is not known whether this truth had been written, revealed, or was the outworking of the conscience at this time. It certainly could not have been the Law of Moses, for that had not yet been given (see introduction to Job). Zophar suggests that in some way Job had broken this law and was being judged for this sin. His reasoning is that if the punishment for sin is suffering, then all who suffer must have sinned. He, like Job's other two friends, emphasized that man was rewarded for good (obeying God) and punished for evil (disobedience).

6 [a]The tabernacles[168] of robbers[7703] prosper, and they that provoke God[410] are secure;[987] into whose hand[3072] God bringeth *abundantly.*

7 But ask[7592] now the beasts, and they shall teach[3384] thee; and the fowls of the air,[8064] and they shall tell[5046] thee:

8 Or speak[7878] to the earth,[776] and it shall teach thee: and the fishes[1709] of the sea shall declare[5608] unto thee.

9 Who knoweth not in all these that the hand of the LORD hath wrought this?

10 [a]In whose hand *is* the [I]soul[5315] of every living thing,[2416] and the breath[7307] of [II]all mankind.

11 [a]Doth[974] not the ear[241] try[974] words?[4405] and the [Ib]mouth taste his meat?

12 [a]With the ancient[3453] *is* wisdom;[2451] and in length[753] of days understanding.[8394]

13 [Ia]With him *is* wisdom and strength,[1369] he hath counsel[6098] and understanding.

14 Behold, [a]he breaketh down,[2040] and it cannot be built again: he [b]shutteth [I]up a man,[376] and there can be no opening.

15 Behold, he [a]withholdeth the waters, and they dry up:[3001] also he [b]sendeth them out, and they overturn[2015] the earth.

16 [a]With him *is* strength[5797] and wisdom:[8454] the deceived[7683] and the deceiver[7686] *are* his.

17 He leadeth counsellors[3289] away spoiled,[7758] and [a]maketh[1984] the judges[8199] fools.[1984]

18 He looseth the bond[4148] of kings,[4428] and girdeth their loins with a girdle.[232]

19 He leadeth princes[3548] away spoiled, and overthroweth the mighty.

20 [a]He removeth away[5493] [I]the speech[8193] of the trusty,[539] and taketh away the understanding[2940] of the aged.[2205]

21 [a]He poureth[8210] contempt upon princes,[5081] and [I]weakeneth[7503] the strength[4206] of the mighty.

22 [a]He discovereth deep things out of darkness,[2822] and bringeth out to light[216] the shadow of death.[6757]

23 [a]He increaseth the nations,[1471] and destroyeth[6] them: he enlargeth the nations, and [I]straiteneth[5148] them *again.*

24 He taketh away the heart[3820] of the chief[7218] of the people of the earth, and [a]causeth them to wander[8582] in a wilderness[8414] *where there is* no way.[1870]

25 [a]They grope in the dark[2822] without light, and he maketh them to [Ib]stagger[8582] like *a* drunken *man.*

13 Lo, mine eye hath seen[7200] all *this,* mine ear[241] hath heard[8085] and understood[995] it.

2 [a]What ye know,[1847] *the same* do I know[3045] also: I *am* not inferior[5307] unto you.

3 [a]Surely I would speak[1696] to the Almighty,[7706] and I desire[2654] to reason[3198] with God.[410]

🗝 4 But ye *are* forgers[2950] of lies,[8267] [a]ye *are* all physicians of no value.[457]

5 O that ye would altogether hold your peace! and [a]it should be your wisdom.[2451]

6 Hear[8085] now my reasoning,[8433] and hearken[7181] to the pleadings of my lips.[8193]

7 [a]Will ye speak wickedly[5766] for God? and talk[1696] deceitfully[7423] for him?

8 Will ye accept[5375] his person? will ye contend[7378] for God?

9 Is it good[2896] that he should search you out? or as one man[582] mocketh another, do ye *so* mock him?

10 He will surely reprove[3198] you, if ye do secretly accept persons.

11 Shall not his excellency make you afraid?[1204] and his dread[6343] fall upon you?

12 Your remembrances[2146] *are* like unto ashes, your bodies to bodies of clay.

6 [a]Job 21:7; Ps. 37:1, 35; 73:11, 12; 92:7; Jer. 12:1; Mal. 3:15
10 [I]Or, *life* [II]Hebr. *all flesh of man* [a]Num. 16:22; Dan. 5:23; Acts 17:28
11 [I]Hebr. *palate,* [a]Job 34:3 [b]Job 6:30
12 [a]Job 32:7
13 [I]That is, *With God* [a]Job 9:4; 36:5
14 [I]Hebr. *upon* [a]Job 11:10 [b]Isa. 22:22; Rev. 3:7
15 [a]1Kgs. 8:35; 17:1 [b]Gen. 7:11
16 [a]Job 12:13
17 [a]2Sam. 15:31; 17:14, 23; Isa. 19:12; 29:14; 1Cor. 1:19
20 [I]Hebr. *the lip of the faithful* [a]Job 32:9; Isa. 3:1-3
21 [I]Or, *looseth the girdle of the strong* [a]Ps. 107:40; Dan. 2:21
22 [a]Dan. 2:22; Matt. 10:26; 1Cor. 4:5
23 [I]Hebr. *leadeth in* [a]Ps. 107:38; Isa. 9:3; 26:15
24 [a]Ps. 107:4, 40
25 [I]Hebr. *wander* [a]Deut. 28:29; Job 5:14 [b]Ps. 107:27

2 [a]Job 12:3
3 [a]Job 23:3; 31:35
4 [a]Job 6:21; 16:2
5 [a]Prov. 17:28
7 [a]Job 17:5; 32:21; 36:4

🗝 **13:4** Job reflects on the fact that his friends were providing no comfort at all, and he now realizes that there is no hope of obtaining pity from them (see note on Job 6:21–23).

13 [I]Hold your peace,2790 let me alone, that I may speak, and let come on me what *will*.

14 Wherefore [a]do I take[5375] my flesh[1320] in my teeth, and [b]put my life[5315] in mine hand?[3709]

15 [a]Though he slay me, yet will I trust[3176] in him: [b]but I will [I]maintain[3198] mine own ways[1870] before him.

16 He also *shall be* my salvation:[3444] for an hypocrite[2611] shall not come before him.

17 Hear diligently my speech,[4405] and my declaration[262] with your ears.[241]

18 Behold now, I have ordered *my* cause;[4941] I know that I shall be justified.[6663]

19 [a]Who *is* he *that* will plead[7378] with me? for now, if I hold my tongue, I shall give up the ghost.[1478]

20 [a]Only do not two *things* unto me: then will I not hide myself from thee.

21 [a]Withdraw7368 thine hand far from me: and let not thy dread[367] make me afraid.

22 Then call[7121] thou, and I will answer: or let me speak, and answer[7725] thou me.

23 How many *are* mine iniquities[5771] and sins? make me to know my transgression[6588] and my sin.[2403]

24 [a]Wherefore hidest thou thy face, and [b]holdest[2803] me for thine enemy?

25 [a]Wilt thou break[6206] a leaf driven to and fro? and wilt thou pursue the dry[3002] stubble?7179

26 For thou writest bitter things4846 against me, and [a]makest me to possess[3423] the iniquities of my youth.

27 [a]Thou puttest[7760] my feet also in the stocks, and [I]lookest narrowly[8104] unto all my paths;[734] thou settest a print2707 upon the [II]heels of my feet.

13 [I]Hebr. *Be silent from me*
14 [a]Job 18:4 [b]1Sam. 28:21; Ps. 119:109
15 [I]Hebr. *prove,* or, *argue* [a]Ps. 23:4; Prov. 14:32 [b]Job 27:5
19 [a]Job 33:6; Isa. 50:8
20 [a]Job 9:34; 33:7
21 [a]Ps. 39:10
24 [a]Deut. 32:20; Ps. 13:1; 44:24; 88:14; Isa. 8:17 [b]Deut. 32:42; Ruth 1:21; Job 16:9; 19:11; 33:10; Lam. 2:5
25 [a]Isa. 42:3
26 [a]Job 20:11; Ps. 25:7
27 [I]Hebr. *observest* [II]Hebr. *roots* [a]Job 33:11

1 [I]Hebr. *short of days* [a]Job 5:7; Eccl. 2:23
2 [a]Job 8:9; Ps. 90:5, 6, 9; 102:11; 103:15; 144:4; Isa. 40:6; James 1:10, 11; 4:14; 1Pet. 1:24
3 [a]Ps. 144:3 [b]Ps. 143:2
4 [I]Hebr. *Who will give* [a]Gen. 5:3; Ps. 51:5; John 3:6; Rom. 5:12; Eph. 2:3
5 [a]Job 7:1
6 [I]Hebr. *cease* [a]Job 7:16, 19; 10:20; Ps. 39:13 [b]Job 7:1
7 [a]Job 14:14
10 [I]Hebr. *is weakened,* or, *cut off*
12 [a]Ps. 102:26; Isa. 51:6; 65:17; 66:22; Acts 3:21; Rom. 8:20; 2Pet. 3:7, 10, 11; Rev. 20:11; 21:1

28 And he, as a rotten thing,7538 consumeth, as a garment that is moth eaten.

14

Man[120] *that is* born of a woman[802] *is* [I]of few days, and [a]full of trouble.[7267]

2 [a]He cometh forth like a flower, and is cut down:[5243] he fleeth also as a shadow, and continueth not.

3 And [a]dost thou open thine eyes upon such an one, and [b]bringest me into judgment[4941] with thee?

4 [I]Who [a]can bring a clean[2889] *thing* out of an unclean?[2931] not one.

5 [a]Seeing his days *are* determined, the number of his months *are* with thee, thou hast appointed his bounds[2706] that he cannot pass;

6 [a]Turn from him, that he may [I]rest, till he shall accomplish,[7521] [b]as an hireling, his day.[3117]

7 For there is hope of a tree, if it be cut down,[3772] [a]that it will sprout again, and that the tender branch thereof will not cease.

8 Though the root thereof wax old[2204] in the earth,[776] and the stock thereof die[4191] in the ground;[6083]

9 *Yet* through the scent7381 of water it will bud, and bring forth[6213] boughs like a plant.

10 But man[1397] dieth,[4191] and [I]wasteth away:2522 yea, man giveth up the ghost,[1478] and where *is* he?

11 *As* the waters fail235 from the sea, and the flood decayeth[2717] and drieth up:[3001]

12 So man[376] lieth down, and riseth not: [a]till the heavens8064 *be* no more, they shall not awake, nor be raised out of their sleep.

🔑 13 O that thou wouldest hide me in the grave,[7585] that thou wouldest keep

---

🔑 **14:13–15** Job thinks that his life is coming to an end and desires some hope with which to sustain himself. It is important to remember that at this time no portions of Scripture had been written down, so there was no way that Job could have known all that has been revealed to us about heaven. At the time of the patriarchs, very little had been revealed about the resurrection of the body, so that they rested in the hope that their disembodied spirit would remain. Job's usage of

(continued on next page)

me secret,5641 until thy wrath[639] be past,
that thou wouldest appoint me a set
time,[2706] and remember[2142] me!
14 If a man die, shall he live[2421]
again? all the days of my appointed
time[6635] [a]will I wait,[3176] [b]till my change
come.
15 [a]Thou shalt call,[7121] and I will answer thee: thou wilt have a desire to the
work of thine hands.[3027]
16 [a]For now thou numberest my
steps: dost thou not watch[8104] over my
sin?[2403]
17 [a]My transgression[6588] *is* sealed up
in a bag, and thou sewest up2950 mine
iniquity.[5771]
18 And surely the mountain falling
[I]cometh to nought,5034 and the rock is removed out of his place.
19 The waters wear[7833] the stones:
thou [I]washest away[7857] the things which
grow *out* of the dust[6083] of the earth;
and thou destroyest[6] the hope of man.[582]
20 Thou prevailest for ever[5331]
against him, and he passeth: thou
changest his countenance, and sendest
him away.
21 His sons[1121] come to honour,[3513]
and [a]he knoweth[3045] *it* not; and they are
brought low, but he perceiveth[995] *it* not of
them.
22 But his flesh[1320] upon him shall
have pain,3510 and his soul[5315] within him
shall mourn.[56]

Eliphaz Reprimands Job

15 Then answered Eliphaz the
Temanite, and said,
2 Should a wise man[2450] utter
[I]vain[7307] knowledge,[1847] and fill his
belly[990] with the east wind?[7307]
3 Should he reason[3198] with unprofitable talk? or with speeches[4405] wherewith he can do no good?

14 [a]Job 13:15 [b]Job 14:7
15 [a]Job 13:22
16 [a]Job 10:6, 14; 13:27; 31:4; 34:21; Ps. 56:8; 139:1–3; Prov. 5:21; Jer. 32:19
17 [a]Deut. 32:34; Hos. 13:12
18 [I]Hebr. *fadeth*
19 [I]Hebr. *overflowest*
21 [a]Eccl. 9:5; Isa. 63:16
2 [I]Hebr. *knowledge of wind*
4 [I]Hebr. *thou makest void* [II]Or, *speech*
5 [I]Hebr. *teacheth*
6 [a]Luke 19:22
7 [a]Ps. 90:2; Prov. 8:25
8 [a]Rom. 11:34; 1Cor. 2:11
9 [a]Job 13:2
10 [a]Job 32:6, 7
14 [a]1Kgs. 8:46; 2Chr. 6:36; Job 14:4; Ps. 14:3; Prov. 20:9; Eccl. 7:20; 1John 1:8, 10
15 [a]Job 4:18; 25:5
16 [a]Job 4:19; Ps. 14:3; 53:3 [b]Job 34:7; Prov. 19:28
18 [a]Job 8:8

4 Yea, [I]thou castest off[6565] fear,[3374]
and restrainest [II]prayer[7881] before God.[410]
5 For thy mouth[6310] [I]uttereth[502] thine
iniquity,[5771] and thou choosest[977] the
tongue of the crafty.[6175]
6 [a]Thine own mouth condemneth[7561]
thee, and not I: yea, thine own lips[8193]
testify against thee.
7 *Art* thou the first[7223] man[120] *that*
was born? [a]or wast thou made[2342] before
the hills?
8 [a]Hast thou heard[8085] the secret[5475]
of God?[433] and dost thou restrain
wisdom[2451] to thyself?
9 [a]What knowest[3045] thou, that we
know not? *what* understandest[995] thou,
which *is* not in us?
10 [a]With us *are* both the gray
headed[7867] and very aged men,[3453] much
elder than thy father.[1]
11 *Are* the consolations8575 of God
small with thee? is there any secret[328]
thing[1697] with thee?
12 Why doth thine heart[3820] carry
thee away? and what do thy eyes wink
at,7335
13 That thou turnest[7725] thy
spirit[7307] against God, and lettest *such*
words go out of thy mouth?
14 [a]What *is* man,[582] that he should
be clean?[2135] and *he which is* born of a
woman,[802] that he should be righteous?[6663]
15 [a]Behold, he putteth no trust[539] in
his saints;[6918] yea, the heavens8064 are
not clean[2141] in his sight.
16 [a]How much more abominable[8581]
and filthy *is* man,[376] [b]which drinketh
iniquity[5766] like water?
17 I will shew thee, hear[8085] me; and
that *which* I have seen[2372] I will
declare;[5608]
18 Which wise men have told[5046]
[a]from their fathers,[1] and have not hid3582
it:

(continued from previous page)
phrases like "the grave" and "keep me secret" reflect his desire for the time when his soul would be separated from his present affliction and would be vindicated by God from the accusations his friends were making. At this time, Job begins to trust in a physical resurrection of his body (see note on Job 19:25).

19 Unto whom alone the earth[776] was given, and [a]no stranger[2114] passed[5674] among them.

20 The wicked man[7563] travaileth with pain[2342] all *his* days, [a]and the number of years is hidden to the oppressor.

21 [I]A dreadful[6343] sound *is* in his ears:[241] [a]in prosperity[7965] the destroyer[7703] shall come upon him.

22 He believeth[539] not that he shall return[7725] out of darkness,[2822] and he is waited for of the sword.[2719]

23 He [a]wandereth abroad5074 for bread, *saying,* Where *is it*? he knoweth that [b]the day[3117] of darkness is ready[3559] at his hand.[3027]

24 Trouble6862 and anguish4691 shall make him afraid;[1204] they shall prevail against him, as a king ready to the battle.

25 For he stretcheth out his hand against God, and strengtheneth himself against the Almighty.[7706]

26 He runneth upon him, *even* on *his* neck, upon the thick bosses1354 of his bucklers:4043

27 [a]Because he covereth[3680] his face with his fatness, and maketh[6213] collops6371 of fat on *his* flanks.

28 And he dwelleth[7931] in desolate cities, *and* in houses which no man inhabiteth, which are ready to become heaps.1530

29 He shall not be rich, neither shall his substance[2428] continue, neither shall he prolong5186 the perfection4512 thereof upon the earth.

30 He shall not depart[5493] out of darkness; the flame shall dry up[3001] his branches, and [a]by the breath[7307] of his mouth shall he go away.

31 Let not him that is deceived[8582] [a]trust in vanity:[7723] for vanity shall be his recompence.[8545]

32 It shall be [I]accomplished[4390] [a]before his time,[3117] and his branch shall not be green.

33 He shall shake off[2554] his unripe grape as the vine, and shall cast off his flower as the olive.

34 For the congregation[5712] of hypocrites[2611] *shall be* desolate, and fire

19 [a]Joel 3:17
20 [a]Ps. 90:12
21 [I]Hebr. *A sound of fears* [a]1Thess. 5:3
23 [a]Ps. 59:15; 109:10 [b]Job 18:12
27 [a]Ps. 17:10
30 [a]Job 4:9
31 [a]Isa. 59:4
32 [I]Or, *cut off* [a]Job 22:16; Ps. 55:23
35 [I]Or, *iniquity* [a]Ps. 7:14; Isa. 59:4; Hos. 10:13
2 [I]Or, *troublesome* [a]Job 13:4
3 [I]Hebr. *words of wind*
4 [a]Ps. 22:7; 109:25; Lam. 2:15
6 [I]Hebr. *what goeth from me?*
9 [a]Job 10:16, 17 [b]Job 13:24
10 [a]Ps. 22:13 [b]Lam. 3:30; Mic. 5:1 [c]Ps. 35:15
11 [I]Hebr. *hath shut me up* [a]Job 1:15, 17
12 [a]Job 7:20

shall consume398 the tabernacles[168] of bribery.

35 [a]They conceive mischief,[5999] and bring forth [I]vanity,[205] and their belly prepareth deceit.[4820]

Job Complains Again

16 Then Job answered and said,

2 I have heard[8085] many such things: [I][a]miserable[5999] comforters[5162] *are* ye all.

3 Shall [I]vain[7307] words[1697] have an end? or what emboldeneth thee that thou answerest?

4 I also could speak[1696] as ye *do:* if your soul[5315] were in my soul's stead, I could heap up2266 words[4405] against you, and [a]shake5128 mine head[7218] at you.

5 *But* I would strengthen[553] you with my mouth,[6310] and the moving of my lips[8193] should asswage[2820] *your grief.*

6 Though I speak, my grief is not asswaged:[2820] and *though* I forbear,2308 [I]what am I eased?

7 But now he hath made me weary:[3811] thou hast made desolate[8074] all my company.[5712]

8 And thou hast filled me with wrinkles, *which* is a witness *against me:* and my leanness3585 rising up in me beareth witness to my face.

9 [a]He teareth[2963] *me* in his wrath,[639] who hateth7852 me: he gnasheth2786 upon me with his teeth; [b]mine enemy sharpeneth his eyes upon me.

10 They have [a]gaped upon me with their mouth; they [b]have smitten[5221] me upon the cheek reproachfully;[2781] they have [c]gathered themselves[4390] together against me.

11 God[410] [I][a]hath delivered me to the ungodly,[5760] and turned me over3399 into the hands[3027] of the wicked.[7563]

12 I was at ease, but he hath broken me asunder:[6565] he hath also taken *me* by my neck, and shaken me to pieces,6327 and [a]set me up for his mark.

13 His archers compass me round about, he cleaveth6398 my reins3629 asunder,6398 and doth not spare; he

poureth out[8210] my gall[4845] upon the ground.[776]

14 He breaketh[6555] me with breach upon breach, he runneth upon me like a giant.

15 I have sewed sackcloth upon my skin,[1539] and [a]defiled[5953] my horn[7161] in the dust.[6083]

16 My face is foul[2560] with weeping, and on my eyelids *is* the shadow of death;[6757]

17 Not for *any* injustice[2555] in mine hands:[3709] also my prayer[8605] *is* pure.[2134]

18 O earth,[776] cover[3680] not thou my blood,[1818] and [a]let my cry have no place.

19 Also now, behold, [a]my witness *is* in heaven,[8064] and my record *is* [I]on high.

20 My friends[7453] [I]scorn[3887] me: *but* mine eye poureth out *tears* unto God.[433]

21 [a]O that one might plead[3198] for a man[1397] with God, as a man[120] *pleadeth* for his [I]neighbour![7453]

22 When [I]a few years are come, then I shall [a]go the way[734] *whence* I shall not return.[7725]

17 My [I]breath[7307] is corrupt,[2254] my days are extinct, [a]the graves[6913] *are ready* for me.

2 *Are there* not mockers with me? and doth not mine eye [I]continue[3885] in their [a]provocation?[4784]

3 Lay down[7760] now, put me in a surety[6148] with thee; who *is* he *that* [a]will strike[8628] hands[3027] with me?

4 For thou hast hid[6845] their heart[3820] from understanding:[7922] therefore shalt thou not exalt *them*.

5 He that speaketh[5046] flattery[2506] to *his* friends,[7453] even the eyes of his children[1121] shall fail.[3615]

6 He hath made me also [a]a byword[4914] of the people;[5971] and [I]aforetime I was as a tabret.[8611]

7 [a]Mine eye also is dim by reason of sorrow,[3708] and all [I]my members *are* as a shadow.

8 Upright *men* shall be astonied[8074] at this, and the innocent[5355] shall stir up himself against the hypocrite.[2611]

9 The righteous[6662] also shall hold on his way,[1870] and he that hath [a]clean hands [I]shall be stronger and stronger.

10 But as for you all, [a]do ye return,[7725] and come now: for I cannot find *one* wise[2450] *man* among you.

11 [a]My days are past,[5674] my purposes[2154] are broken off, *even* [I]the thoughts[4180] of my heart.[3824]

12 They change the night[3915] into day:[3117] the light[216] *is* [I]short because of darkness.[2822]

13 If I wait,[6960] the grave[7585] *is* mine house:[1004] I have made my bed in the darkness.

14 I have [I]said to corruption,[7845] Thou *art* my father:[1] to the worm, *Thou art* my mother,[517] and my sister.[269]

15 And where *is* now my hope? as for my hope, who shall see it?

16 They shall go down [a]to the bars[905] of the pit,[7585] when *our* [b]rest together *is* in the dust.[6083]

Bildad's Sermon

18 Then answered Bildad the Shuhite, and said,

2 How long *will it be ere* ye make[7760] an end of words?[4405] mark,[995] and afterwards we will speak.[1696]

3 Wherefore are we counted[2803] [a]as beasts, *and* reputed vile[2933] in your sight?

4 [a]He teareth [I]himself in his anger:[639] shall[5800] the earth[776] be forsaken[5800] for thee? and shall the rock be removed out of his place?

5 Yea, [a]the light[216] of the wicked[7563] shall be put out, and the spark of his fire shall not shine.

6 The light shall be dark[2821] in his tabernacle,[168] [a]and his [I]candle[5216] shall be put out with him.

7 The steps of his strength[202] shall be straitened,[3334] and [a]his own counsel[6098] shall cast him down.

8 For [a]he is cast into a net by his own feet, and he walketh upon a snare.[7639]

15 [a]Job 30:19; Ps. 7:5

18 [a]Job 27:9; Ps. 66:18, 19

19 [I]Hebr. *in the high places* [a]Rom. 1:9

20 [I]Hebr. are *my scorners*

21 [I]Or, *friend* [a]Job 31:35; Eccl. 6:10; Isa. 45:9; Rom. 9:20

22 [I]Hebr. *years of number* [a]Eccl. 12:5

1 [I]Or, *spirit is spent* [a]Ps. 88:3, 4

2 [I]Hebr. *lodge* [a]1Sam. 1:6, 7

3 [a]Prov. 6:1; 17:18; 22:26

6 [I]Or, *before them* [a]Job 30:9

7 [I]Or, *my thoughts* [a]Ps. 6:7; 31:9

9 [I]Hebr. *shall add strength* [a]Ps. 24:4

10 [a]Job 6:29

11 [I]Hebr. *the possessions* [a]Job 7:6; 9:25

12 [I]Hebr. *near*

14 [I]Hebr. *cried,* or, *called*

16 [a]Job 18:13 [b]Job 3:17–19

3 [a]Ps. 73:22

4 [I]Hebr. *his soul* [a]Job 13:14

5 [a]Prov. 13:9; 20:20; 24:20

6 [I]Or, *lamp* [a]Job 21:17; Ps. 18:28

7 [a]Job 5:13

8 [a]Job 22:10; Ps. 9:15; 35:8

9 The gin[6341] shall take[270] *him* by
the heel,[6119] *and* [a]the robber[6782] shall
prevail[2388] against him.
10 The snare[2256] *is* [I]laid for him in
the ground,[776] and a trap[4434] for him in
the way.
11 [a]Terrors[1091] shall make him
afraid[1204] on every side, and shall
[I]drive[6327] him to his feet.
12 His strength shall be hungerbit-
ten,[7457] and [a]destruction[343] *shall be*
ready[3559] at his side.
13 It shall devour the [I]strength of his
skin:[5785] *even* the firstborn of death[4194]
shall devour his strength.[905]
14 [a]His confidence shall be rooted out
of his tabernacle, and it shall bring him
to the king[4428] of terrors.
15 It shall dwell[7931] in his tabernacle,[168] because *it is* none of his:
brimstone[1614] shall be scattered upon his
habitation.[5116]
16 [a]His roots shall be dried up[3001] beneath, and above shall his branch be cut
off.
17 [a]His remembrance[2143] shall perish[6] from the earth, and he shall have no
name in the street.
18 [I]He shall be driven[1920] from light
into darkness,[2822] and chased out of the
world.[8398]
19 [a]He shall neither have son nor
nephew among his people,[5971] nor any
remaining[8300] in his dwellings.[4033]
20 They that come after *him* shall be
astonied[8074] at [a]his day,[3117] as they that
[I]went before [II]were affrighted.[8178]
21 Surely such *are* the dwellings[4908]
of the wicked,[5767] and this *is* the place *of*
him that [a]knoweth not God.[410]

Job Is Confident

19 Then Job answered and said,
2 How long will ye vex[3013] my

9 [a]Job 5:5

10 [I]Hebr. *hidden*

11 [I]Hebr. *scatter him* [a]Job 15:21; 20:25; Jer. 6:25; 20:3; 46:5; 49:29

12 [a]Job 15:23

13 [I]Hebr. *bars*

14 [a]Job 8:14; 11:20; Ps. 112:10; Prov. 10:28

16 [a]Job 29:19; Isa. 5:24; Amos 2:9; Mal. 4:1

17 [a]Ps. 34:16; 109:13; Prov. 2:22; 10:7

18 [I]Hebr. *They shall drive him*

19 [a]Isa. 14:22; Jer. 22:30

20 [I]Or, *lived with him* [II]Hebr. *laid hold on horror* [a]Ps. 37:13

21 [a]Jer. 9:3; 10:25; 1Thess. 4:5; 2Thess. 1:8; Titus 1:16

3 [I]Or, *harden yourselves against me* [a]Gen. 31:7; Lev. 26:26

5 [a]Ps. 38:16

7 [I]Or, *violence*

8 [a]Job 3:23; Ps. 88:8

9 [a]Ps. 89:44

11 [a]Job 13:24; Lam. 2:5

12 [a]Job 30:12

13 [a]Ps. 31:11; 38:11; 69:8; 88:8, 18

soul,[5315] and break me in pieces[1792] with
words?[4405]
3 These [a]ten times have ye reproached me: ye are not ashamed[954] *that*
ye [I]make yourselves strange to me.
4 And be it indeed[551] *that* I have
erred,[7683] mine error[4879] remaineth with
myself.
5 If indeed ye will [a]magnify[1431] *your-*
selves against me, and plead[3198] against
me my reproach:[2781]
6 Know[3045] now that God[433] hath
overthrown[5791] me, and hath compassed[5362] me with his net.[4685]
7 Behold, I cry out[6817] of [I]wrong,[2555]
but I am not heard: I cry aloud,[7768] but
there is no judgment.[4941]
🔑 8 [a]He hath fenced up[1443] my way[734]
that I cannot pass, and he hath set[7760]
darkness[2822] in my paths.
9 [a]He hath stripped[6584] me of my
glory,[3519] and taken the crown *from* my
head.[7218]
10 He hath destroyed[5422] me on every
side, and I am gone: and mine hope hath
he removed[5265] like a tree.
11 He hath also kindled[2374] his
wrath[639] against me, and [a]he counteth[2803]
me unto him as *one of* his enemies.
12 His troops[1416] come together,
and [a]raise up their way[1870] against me,
and encamp round about my tabernacle.[168]
13 [a]He hath put my brethren[251] far
from me, and mine acquaintance[3045] are
verily estranged[2114] from me.
14 My kinsfolk have failed, and my
familiar friends[3045] have forgotten me.
15 They that dwell[1481] in mine
house,[1004] and my maids, count me for a
stranger:[2114] I am an alien[5237] in their
sight.
16 I called[7121] my servant,[5650] and he
gave *me* no answer; I intreated[2603] him
with my mouth.[6310]

🔑 **19:8–12, 20, 21** Job's statements in these verses reveal his confusion, for it seems that God has turned against him. Job's internal conflict is at its highest point. The arguments of the three friends follow a logical pattern, but Job knew that their conclusions were being misapplied to his situation. Nevertheless, if Job had rejected their conclusions as general truths, he too would have been conceding that God was arbitrary and unjust.

17 My breath[7307] is strange[2114] to my wife,[802] though I intreated for the children's *sake* of [I]mine own body.[990]

18 Yea, [Ia]young children[1121] despised[3988] me; I arose, and they spake[1696] against me.

19 [a]All [I]my inward[5475] friends abhorred[8581] me: and they whom I loved[157] are turned[2015] against me.

🔑 20 [a]My bone[6106] cleaveth to my skin[5785] [I]and to my flesh,[1320] and I am escaped[4422] with the skin of my teeth.

21 Have pity3603 upon me, have pity upon me, O ye my friends;[7453] [a]for the hand[3027] of God hath touched[5060] me.

22 Why do ye [a]persecute me as God,[410] and are not satisfied with my flesh?

23 [I]Oh that my words were now written! oh that they were printed[2710] in a book![5612]

24 That they were graven with an iron pen and lead in the rock for ever![5703]

🔑 25 For I know *that* my Redeemer[1350] liveth,[2416] and *that* he shall stand at the latter[314] *day* upon the earth:[6083]

26 [I]And *though* after my skin *worms* destroy[5362] this *body,* yet [a]in my flesh[1320] shall I see[2372] God:

27 Whom I shall see for myself, and mine eyes shall behold,[7200] and not [I]another;[2114] [II]*though* my reins3629 be consumed[3615] [III]within me.

28 But ye should say, [a]Why persecute7291 we him, [I]seeing the root8328 of the matter[1697] is found in me?

29 Be ye afraid[1481] of the sword:[2719] for wrath[2534] *bringeth* the punishments[5771] of the sword, [a]that ye may know *there is* a judgment.[1779]

17 [I]Hebr. *my belly* **18** [I]Or, *the wicked* [a]2Kgs. 2:23 **19** [I]Hebr. *the men of my secret* [a]Ps. 41:9; 55:13, 14, 20 **20** [I]Or, *as* [a]Job 30:30; Ps. 102:5; Lam. 4:8 **21** [a]Job 1:11; Ps. 38:2 **22** [a]Ps. 69:26 **23** [I]Hebr. *Who will give* **26** [I]Or, *After I shall awake, though this body be destroyed, yet out of my flesh shall I see God* [a]Ps. 17:15; 1Cor. 13:12; 1John 3:2 **27** [I]Hebr. *a stranger* [II]Or, *my reins within me are consumed with earnest desire* [for that day] [III]Hebr. *in my bosom* **28** [I]Or, *and what root of matter is found in me* [a]Job 19:22 **29** [a]Ps. 58:10, 11

2 [I]Hebr. *my haste is in me* **5** [I]Hebr. *from near* [a]Ps. 37:35, 36 **6** [I]Hebr. *cloud* [a]Isa. 14:13, 14; Obad. 1:3, 4 **7** [a]Ps. 83:10 **8** [a]Ps. 73:20; 90:5 **9** [a]Job 7:8, 10; 8:18; Ps. 37:36; 103:16 **10** [I]Or, *the poor shall oppress his children* [a]Job 20:18 **11** [a]Job 13:26; Ps. 25:7 [b]Job 21:26 **13** [I]Hebr. *in the midst of his palate*

Zophar's Sermon

20 Then answered Zophar the Naamathite, and said,

2 Therefore do[7725] my thoughts[5587] cause me to answer,[7725] and for *this* [I]I make haste.

3 I have heard[8085] the check[4148] of my reproach,[3639] and the spirit[7307] of my understanding[998] causeth me to answer.

4 Knowest[3045] thou *not* this of old, since man[120] was placed[7760] upon earth,[776]

5 [a]That the triumphing7445 of the wicked[7563] *is* [I]short, and the joy8057 of the hypocrite[2611] *but* for a moment?

6 [a]Though his excellency mount up[5927] to the heavens,8064 and his head[7218] reach[5060] unto the [I]clouds;

7 *Yet* he shall perish[6] for ever[5331] [a]like his own dung: they which have seen[7200] him shall say, Where *is* he?

8 He shall fly away [a]as a dream, and shall not be found: yea, he shall be chased away5074 as a vision[2384] of the night.[3915]

9 [a]The eye also *which* saw him shall *see him* no more; neither shall his place any more behold him.

10 [I]His children[1121] shall seek to please[7521] the poor, and his hands[3027] [a]shall restore[7725] their goods.

11 His bones[6106] are [a]full *of the sin* of his youth, [b]which shall lie down with him in the dust.[6083]

12 Though wickedness[7451] be sweet in his mouth,[6310] *though* he hide it under his tongue;

13 *Though* he spare it, and forsake[5800] it not; but keep it still [I]within his mouth:

🔑 **19:25** This verse mentions several important words and phrases. The word "Redeemer" pertains to the concept of the kinsman-redeemer (Job 16:19; see note on Ruth 4:1–8). Job sought for one who would redress his wrong and avenge his injuries. In this verse, he acknowledges that God alone can be this "Redeemer." In admitting this fact, Job recognized more fully that he was serving the living God. By this, Job did not mean that God merely existed, or that God may have been realized on a conscious level; but Job believed that God was alive and concerned with his individual life, unlike the pagan idols who never answered the worship they were given. Knowing that his Redeemer was living and could vindicate him, Job uses the phrase "at the latter day" to refer to the time when his name would be cleared. It is debated whether Job hoped for vindication in his lifetime (at the conclusion of this time of suffering) or at some time after his death, when God would clear him of any wrong.

14 *Yet* his meat in his bowels[4578] is turned,[2015] *it is* the gall[4846] of asps[6620] within[7130] him.

15 He hath swallowed down[1104] riches,[2428] and he shall vomit them up again: God[410] shall cast[3423] them out of his belly.[990]

16 He shall suck the poison of asps: the viper's tongue shall slay[2026] him.

17 He shall not see [a]the rivers,[6390] [I]the floods,[5104] the brooks[5158] of honey and butter.

18 That which he laboured for [a]shall restore, and shall not swallow *it* down: [I]according to *his* substance[2428] *shall* the restitution[8545] *be,* and he shall not rejoice[5965] *therein.*

19 Because he hath [I]oppressed[7533] *and* hath forsaken[5800] the poor; *because* he hath violently taken away[1497] an house[1004] which he builded not;

20 [a]Surely he shall not [I]feel quietness[7961] in his belly, he shall not save[4422] of that which he desired.

21 [I]There shall none of his meat be left;[8300] therefore shall no man look[2342] for his goods.[2898]

22 In the fulness of his sufficiency[5607] he shall be in straits:[3334] every hand[3027] of the [I]wicked shall come upon him.

23 *When* he is about to fill his belly, *God* shall cast[7971] the fury of his wrath[639] upon him, and shall rain *it* upon him [a]while he is eating.[3894]

24 [a]He shall flee from the iron weapon,[5402] *and* the bow of steel shall strike him through.

25 It is drawn, and cometh out of the body; yea, [a]the glittering[1300] sword cometh out of his gall: [b]terrors[367] *are* upon him.

26 All darkness[2822] *shall be* hid[2244] in his secret places:[6485] [a]a fire not blown shall consume him; it shall go ill[3415] with him that is left in his tabernacle.[168]

27 The heaven[8064] shall reveal[1540] his iniquity;[5771] and the earth shall rise up against him.

28 The increase of his house shall depart,[1540] *and his goods* shall flow away[5064] in the day[3117] of his wrath.

29 [a]This *is* the portion[2506] of a wicked man from God,[430] and the heritage[5159] [I]appointed[561] unto him by God.[410]

Job Describes the Wicked

21 But Job answered and said,

2 Hear diligently my speech, and let this be your consolations.[8575]

3 Suffer[5375] me that I may speak;[1696] and after that I have spoken,[1696] [a]mock on.

4 As for me, *is* my complaint[7878] to man?[120] and if *it were so,* why should[7114] not my spirit[7307] be [I]troubled?[7114]

5 [I]Mark me, and be astonished,[8074] [a]and lay[7760] *your* hand[3027] upon *your* mouth.[6310]

6 Even when I remember[2142] I am afraid,[926] and trembling[6427] taketh hold on my flesh.[1320]

7 [a]Wherefore do[2421] the wicked[7563] live,[2421] become old, yea, are mighty[1396] in power?[2428]

8 Their seed[2233] is established[3559] in their sight with them, and their offspring before their eyes.

9 Their houses[1004] [I]*are* safe[7965] from fear,[6343] [a]neither *is* the rod of God[433] upon them.

10 Their bull gendereth,[5674] and faileth not; their cow calveth, and [a]casteth[7921] not her calf,

11 They send forth their little ones like a flock, and their children dance.

12 They take the timbrel[8596] and harp, and rejoice at the sound of the organ.[5748]

13 They [a]spend[3615] their days [I]in wealth,[2896] and in a moment go down[2865] to the grave.[7585]

14 [a]Therefore they say unto God,[410] Depart[5493] from us; for we desire[2654] not the knowledge[1847] of thy ways.[1870]

15 [a]What *is* the Almighty,[7706] that we should serve[5647] him? and [b]what profit should we have, if we pray unto him?

16 Lo, their good[2898] *is* not in their hand: [a]the counsel[6098] of the wicked is far from me.

---

17 [I]Or, *streaming brooks* [a]Ps. 36:9; Jer. 17:6

18 [I]Hebr. *according to the substance of his exchange* [a]Job 20:10, 15

19 [I]Hebr. *crushed*

20 [I]Hebr. *know* [a]Eccl. 5:13, 14

21 [I]Or, *There shall be none left for his meat*

22 [I]Or, *troublesome*

23 [a]Num. 11:33; Ps. 78:30, 31

24 [a]Isa. 24:18; Jer. 48:43; Amos 5:19

25 [a]Job 16:13 [b]Job 18:11

26 [a]Ps. 21:9

29 [I]Hebr. *of his decree from God* [a]Job 27:13; 31:2, 3

3 [a]Job 16:10; 17:2

4 [I]Hebr. *shortened*

5 [I]Hebr. *Look unto me* [a]Judg. 18:19; Job 29:9; 40:4; Ps. 39:9

7 [a]Job 12:6; Ps. 17:10, 14; 73:3, 12; Jer. 12:1; Hab. 1:16

9 [I]Hebr. *are peace from fear* [a]Ps. 73:5

10 [a]Ex. 23:26

13 [I]Or, *in mirth* [a]Job 36:11

14 [a]Job 22:17

15 [a]Ex. 5:2; Job 34:9 [b]Job 35:3; Mal. 3:14

16 [a]Job 22:18; Ps. 1:1; Prov. 1:10

17 [a]How oft is the [I]candle[5216] of the wicked put out! and *how oft* cometh their destruction[343] upon them! *God* [b]distributeth sorrows[2256] in his anger.[639]

18 [a]They are as stubble8401 before the wind,[7307] and as chaff4671 that the storm [I]carrieth away.

19 God layeth up6845 [I]his iniquity[205] [a]for his children:[1121] he rewardeth[7999] him, and he shall know[3045] *it.*

20 His eyes shall see his destruction,[3589] and [a]he shall drink of the wrath[2534] of the Almighty.

21 For what pleasure[2656] *hath* he in his house after him, when the number of his months is cut off in the midst?

22 [a]Shall *any* teach[3925] God knowledge? seeing he judgeth[8199] those that are high.

🗝 23 One dieth[4191] [I]in his full[8537] strength,[6106] being wholly at ease and quiet.7961

24 His [I]breasts5845 are full of milk, and his bones[6106] are moistened with marrow.

25 And another dieth in the bitterness[4751] of his soul,[5315] and never eateth with pleasure.[2896]

26 They shall [a]lie down alike in the dust,[6083] and the worms shall cover[3680] them.

27 Behold, I know your thoughts,[4284] and the devices[4209] *which* ye wrongfully imagine[2554] against me.

28 For ye say, [a]Where *is* the house of the prince?[5081] and where *are* [I]the dwelling places of the wicked?

29 Have ye not asked[7592] them that go by the way?[1870] and do ye not know[5234] their tokens,[226]

30 [a]That the wicked[7451] is reserved[2820] to the day[3117] of destruction?[343] they shall be brought forth to [I]the day of wrath.[5678]

31 Who shall declare[5046] his way [a]to his face? and who shall repay[7999] him *what* he hath done?[6213]

32 Yet shall he be brought to the [I]grave,[6913] and shall [II]remain8245 in the tomb.

33 The clods7263 of the valley shall be sweet unto him, and [a]every man shall draw after him, as *there are* innumerable before him.

34 How then comfort[5162] ye me in vain, seeing in your answers there remaineth[7604] [I]falsehood?[4604]

17 [I]Or, *lamp* [a]Job 18:6 [b]Luke 12:46
18 [I]Hebr. *stealeth away* [a]Ps. 1:4; 35:5; Isa. 17:13; 29:5; Hos. 13:3
19 [I]That is, *the punishment of his iniquity* [a]Ex. 20:5
20 [a]Ps. 75:8; Isa. 51:17; Jer. 25:15; Rev. 14:10; 19:15
22 [a]Isa. 40:13; 45:9; Rom. 11:34; 1Cor. 2:16
23 [I]Hebr. *in his very perfection,* or, *in the strength of his perfection*
24 [I]Or, *milk pails*
26 [a]Job 20:11; Eccl. 9:2
28 [I]Hebr. *the tent of the tabernacles of the wicked* [a]Job 20:7
30 [I]Hebr. *the day of wraths* [a]Prov. 16:4; 2Pet. 2:9
31 [a]Gal. 2:11
32 [I]Hebr. *graves* [II]Hebr. *watch in the heap*
33 [a]Heb. 9:27
34 [I]Hebr. *transgression*

2 [I]Or, *if he may be profitable,* doth his *good success* depend *thereon* [a]Job 35:7; Ps. 16:2; Luke 17:10
6 [I]Hebr. *stripped the clothes of the naked* [a]Ex. 22:26, 27; Deut. 24:10-13; Job 24:3, 9; Ezek. 18:12
7 [a]Job 31:17; Deut. 15:7-11; Isa. 58:7; Ezek. 18:7, 16; Matt. 25:42
8 [I]Hebr. *the man of arm* [II]Hebr. *eminent,* or, *accepted for countenance*
9 [a]Job 31:21; Isa. 10:2; Ezek. 22:7

Eliphaz Accuses Job

22 Then Eliphaz the Temanite answered and said,

2 [a]Can[5532] a man[1397] be profitable[5532] unto God,[410] [I]as he that is wise[7919] may be profitable unto himself?

3 *Is it* any pleasure[2656] to the Almighty,[7706] that thou art righteous?[6663] or *is it* gain *to him,* that thou makest[8552] thy ways[1870] perfect?[8552]

4 Will he reprove[3198] thee for fear[3374] of thee? will he enter with thee into judgment?[4941]

🗝 5 *Is* not thy wickedness[7451] great? and thine iniquities[5771] infinite?369,7093

6 For thou hast [a]taken a pledge[2254] from thy brother[251] for nought,[2600] and [I]stripped the naked[6174] of their clothing.

7 Thou hast not given water to the weary5889 to drink, and thou [a]hast withholden4513 bread from the hungry.

8 But *as for* [I]the mighty[2220] man,[376] he had the earth;[776] and the [II]honourable[5375,6440] man dwelt in it.

9 Thou hast sent widows away empty,7387 and the arms of [a]the fatherless have been broken.[1792]

🗝 **21:23–26** Due to their false presuppositions about Job's suffering, Job's friends were unable to determine why some people never have trouble while some never have anything else. Job acknowledges that even though some are prosperous and some are not, they both have the same end—death.

🗝 **22:5–10** Although there is no evidence nor witnesses to support it, Job is now accused of great iniquity. Eliphaz claims that even if the principles about the punishment of sin do not hold true in a general manner (see note on Job 21:23–26), they do apply to Job's case.

10 Therefore [a]snares[6341] *are* round about thee, and sudden fear[6343] troubleth[926] thee;

11 Or darkness,[2822] *that* thou canst not see; and abundance of [a]waters cover[3680] thee.

12 *Is* not God[433] in the height1363 of heaven?8064 and behold[7200] [I]the height[7218] of the stars, how high they are!

13 And thou sayest, [Ia]How doth God know?[3045] can he judge[8199] through the dark cloud?[6205]

14 [a]Thick clouds *are* a covering to him, that he seeth[7200] not; and he walketh in the circuit2329 of heaven.

15 Hast thou marked[8104] the old[5769] way[734] which wicked[205] men have trodden?

16 Which [a]were cut down7059 out of time,[6256] [I]whose foundation[3247] was overflown3332 with a flood:

17 [a]Which said unto God, Depart[5493] from us: and [b]what can the Almighty do [I]for them?

18 Yet he filled their houses[1004] with good[2896] *things:* but [a]the counsel[6098] of the wicked[7563] is far from me.

19 [a]The righteous[6662] see *it,* and are glad: and the innocent[5355] laugh them to scorn.

20 Whereas our [I]substance is not cut down,3582 but [II]the remnant[3499] of them the fire consumeth.

21 Acquaint[5532] now thyself [I]with him, and [a]be at peace:[7999] thereby good shall come unto thee.

22 Receive, I pray thee,[4994] the law[8451] from his mouth,[6310] and [a]lay up[7760] his words[561] in thine heart.3824

23 [a]If thou return[7725] to the Almighty, thou shalt be built up, thou shalt put away iniquity[5766] far from thy tabernacles.[168]

24 Then shalt thou [a]lay up gold1220 [I]as dust,[6083] and the *gold* of Ophir as the stones of the brooks.

25 Yea, the Almighty shall be thy [I]defence, and thou shalt have [II]plenty8443 of silver.

10 [a]Job 18:8-10; 19:6
11 [a]Ps. 69:1, 2; 124:4; Lam. 3:54
12 [I]Hebr. *the head of the stars*
13 [I]Or, *What* [a]Ps. 10:11; 59:7; 73:11; 94:7
14 [a]Ps. 139:11, 12
16 [I]Hebr. *a flood was poured upon their foundation,* Gen. 7:11; 2Pet. 2:5 [a]Job 15:32; Ps. 55:23; 102:24; Eccl. 7:17
17 [I]Or, *to them* [a]Job 21:14 [b]Ps. 4:6
18 [a]Job 21:16
19 [a]Ps. 58:10; 107:42
20 [I]Or, *estate* [II]Or, *their excellency*
21 [I]That is, *with God* [a]Isa. 27:5
22 [a]Ps. 119:11
23 [a]Job 8:5, 6; 11:13, 14
24 [I]Or, *on the dust* [a]2Chr. 1:15
25 [I]Or, *gold* [II]Hebr. *silver of strength*
26 [a]Job 27:10; Isa. 58:14 [b]Job 11:15
27 [a]Ps. 50:14, 15; Isa. 58:9
29 [I]Hebr. *him that hath low eyes* [a]Prov. 29:23; James 4:6; 1Pet. 5:5
30 [I]Or, *The innocent shall deliver the island* [a]Gen. 18:26-33

2 [I]Hebr. *my hand*
3 [a]Job 13:3; 16:21
6 [a]Isa. 27:4, 8; 57:16
8 [a]Job 9:11
10 [I]Hebr. *the way that is with me* [a]Ps. 139:1-3 [b]Ps. 17:3; 66:10; James 1:12

26 For then shalt thou have thy [a]delight6026 in the Almighty, and [b]shalt lift up[5375] thy face unto God.

27 [a]Thou shalt make thy prayer[6279] unto him, and he shall hear[8085] thee, and thou shalt pay thy vows.[5088]

28 Thou shalt also decree a thing,562 and it shall be established unto thee: and the light[216] shall shine upon thy ways.

29 When *men* are cast down,8213 then thou shalt say,[559] *There is* lifting up;1467 and [a]he shall save[3467] [I]the humble person.

30 [a]He shall deliver[4422] the island336 of the innocent: and it is delivered by the pureness of thine hands.[3709]

Job Wants Access to God

23 Then Job answered and said,
2 Even to day *is* my complaint[7878] bitter:[4805] [I]my stroke[3027] is heavier[3513] than my groaning.

3 [a]Oh that I knew[3045] where I might find him! *that* I might come *even* to his seat!

4 I would order6186 *my* cause[4941] before him, and fill my mouth[6310] with arguments.[8433]

5 I would know the words[4405] *which* he would answer me, and understand[995] what he would say unto me.

6 [a]Will he plead[7379] against me with *his* great power? No; but he would put[7760] *strength* in me.

7 There the righteous[3477] might dispute[3198] with him; so should I be delivered for ever[5331] from my judge.[8199]

8 [a]Behold, I go forward, but he *is* not *there;* and backward, but I cannot perceive him:

9 On the left hand, where he doth work,[6213] but I cannot behold *him:* he hideth himself on the right hand, that I cannot see *him:*

⊶ 10 But he [a]knoweth [I]the way[1870] that I take:5978 *when* [b]he hath tried[974] me, I shall come forth as gold.

⊶ **23:10** Job may have known he was being tested by God, but he did not meditate on the possibility long enough to see its validity.

11 [a]My foot hath held[270] his steps, his way have I kept,[8104] and not declined.[5186]

12 Neither have I gone back[4185] from the commandment[4687] of his lips;[8193] [I][a]I have esteemed[6845] the words[561] of his mouth more than [II]my necessary[2706] *food.*

13 But he *is* in one *mind,* and [a]who can turn[7725] him? and *what* [b]his soul[5315] desireth,[183] even *that* he doeth.[6213]

14 For he performeth[7999] *the thing that is* [a]appointed[2706] for me: and many such *things are* with him.

15 Therefore am I troubled[926] at his presence: when I consider,[995] I am afraid[6342] of him.

16 For God[410] [a]maketh my heart soft,[7401] and the Almighty[7706] troubleth[926] me:

17 Because I was not cut off[6789] before the darkness,[2822] *neither* hath he covered[3680] the darkness[652] from my face.

24 🔑 Why, seeing [a]times[6256] are not hidden[6845] from the Almighty,[7706] do[2372] they that know[3045] him not see[2372] his days?

2 *Some* remove the [a]landmarks;[7367] they violently take away[1497] flocks, and [I]feed *thereof.*

3 They drive away[5090] the ass of the fatherless, they [a]take the widow's ox for a pledge.

4 They turn the needy[34] out of the way: [a]the poor[6035] of the earth[776] hide themselves together.

5 Behold, *as* wild asses in the desert, go they forth to their work; rising betimes[7836] for a prey: the wilderness[6160] *yieldeth* food for them *and* for *their* children.

6 They reap *every one* his [I]corn in the field:[7704] and [II]they gather[3953] the vintage of the wicked.[7563]

7 They [a]cause[3885] the naked[6174] to lodge[3885] without clothing, that *they have* no covering in the cold.

8 They are wet with the showers of the mountains, and [a]embrace the rock for want of a shelter.

9 They pluck the fatherless from the breast, and take a pledge[2254] of the poor.[6041]

10 They cause *him* to go naked without clothing, and they take away[5375] the sheaf *from* the hungry;

11 *Which* make oil within their walls, *and* tread *their* winepresses, and suffer thirst.

12 Men[4962] groan from out of the city, and the soul[5315] of the wounded[2491] crieth out: yet God[433] layeth[7760] not folly *to them.*

13 They are of those that rebel[4775] against the light;[216] they know[5234] not the ways[1870] thereof, nor abide[3427] in the paths[5410] thereof.

14 [a]The murderer[7523] rising with the light killeth the poor[6041] and needy, and in the night[3915] is as a thief.

15 [a]The eye also of the adulterer[5003] waiteth for[8104] the twilight, [b]saying, No eye shall see me: and [I]disguiseth[7760][5643] *his* face.

16 In the dark[2822] they dig through[2864] houses, *which* they had marked for themselves in the daytime:[3119] [a]they know[3045] not the light.

17 For the morning *is* to them even as the shadow of death:[6757] if *one* know[5234] *them, they are in* the terrors[1091] of the shadow of death.

18 He *is* swift as the waters; their portion is cursed[7043] in the earth: he beholdeth not the way of the vineyards.

19 Drought and heat [I]consume the snow waters: *so doth* the grave[7585] *those which* have sinned.[2398]

20 The womb shall forget him; the worm shall feed sweetly on him; [a]he shall be no more remembered;[2142] and wickedness[5766] shall be broken[7665] as a tree.

11 [a]Ps. 44:18
12 [I]Hebr. *I have hid,* or, *laid up* [II]Or, *my appointed portion* [a]John 4:32, 34
13 [a]Job 12:12-14; Rom. 9:19 [b]Ps. 115:3
14 [a]1 Thess. 3:3
16 [a]Ps. 22:14
1 [a]Acts 1:7
2 [I]Or, *feed the* [a]Deut. 19:14; 27:17; Prov. 22:28; 23:10; Hos. 5:10
3 [a]Deut. 24:6, 10, 12, 17; Job 22:6
4 [a]Prov. 28:28
6 [I]Hebr. *mingled corn,* or, *dredge* [II]Hebr. *the wicked gather the vintage*
7 [a]Ex. 22:26, 27; Deut. 24:12, 13; Job 22:6
8 [a]Lam. 4:5
14 [a]Ps. 10:8
15 [I]Hebr. *setteth his face in secret* [a]Prov. 7:9 [b]Ps. 10:11
16 [a]John 3:20
19 [I]Hebr. *violently take*
20 [a]Prov. 10:7

🔑 **24:1–16** Job's argument concerning the evil that the wicked get away with is so convincing that his three friends have only one feeble speech left (see chap. 25).

21 He evil entreateth the barren[6135] *that* beareth not: and doeth not good[3190] to the widow.

22 He draweth also the mighty[47] with his power: he riseth up, [I]and no *man* is sure[539] of life.[2416]

23 *Though* it be given him *to be* in safety, whereon he resteth;[8172] yet [a]his eyes *are* upon their ways.

24 They are exalted[7426] for a little while, but [I]are gone and brought low; they are [II]taken out of the way as all *other,* and cut off[5243] as the tops[7218] of the ears of corn.

25 And if *it be* not *so* now, who will make[7760] me a liar,[3576] and make my speech nothing worth?

Bildad Protests

25 Then answered Bildad the Shuhite, and said,[559]

2 Dominion and fear[6343] *are* with him, he maketh[6213] peace in his high places.

3 Is there any number of his armies?[1416] and upon whom doth not [a]his light[216] arise?

4 [a]How then can[6663] man[582] be justified[6663] with God?[410] or how can he be clean[2135] *that is* born of a woman?[802]

5 Behold even to the moon, and it shineth[166] not; yea, the stars are not pure[2141] in his sight.

6 How much less man, *that is* [a]a worm?[7415] and the son[1121] of man,[120] *which is* a worm?[8438]

Job's Rebuttal

26 But Job answered and said,

2 How hast thou helped *him that is* without power?[3581] *how* savest[3467] thou the arm *that hath* no strength?[5797]

3 How hast thou counselled[3289] *him that hath* no wisdom?[2451] and *how* hast thou plentifully declared[3045] the thing as it is?[8454]

4 To whom hast thou uttered[5046] words?[4405] and whose spirit came from thee?

5 Dead[7496] *things* are formed[2342] from under the waters, [I]and the inhabitants[7931] thereof.

6 [a]Hell[7585] *is* naked[6174] before him, and destruction[11] hath no covering.

🔑 7 [a]He stretcheth out the north over the empty place,[8414] *and* hangeth[8518] the earth[776] upon nothing.

8 [a]He bindeth up[6887] the waters in his thick clouds; and the cloud[6051] is not rent under them.

9 He holdeth back the face of his throne,[3678] *and* spreadeth his cloud upon it.

10 [a]He hath compassed[2328] the waters with bounds, [I]until the day[215] and night[2822] come to an end.[8503]

11 The pillars of heaven[8064] tremble[7322] and are astonished at his reproof.[1606]

12 [a]He divideth[7280] the sea with his power,[3581] and by his understanding[8394] he smiteth through[4272] [I]the proud.

13 [a]By his spirit[7307] he hath garnished[8231] the heavens; his hand[3027] hath formed [b]the crooked[1281] serpent.[5175]

14 Lo, these *are* parts[7098] of his ways:[1870] but how little a portion[1697] is heard[8085] of him? but the thunder of his power[1369] who can understand?[995]

Job Describes the Fate of the Wicked

27 🔑 Moreover Job [I]continued his parable, and said,

2 *As* God[410] liveth,[2416] [a]*who* hath

22 [I]Or, *he trusteth not his own life*

23 [a]Ps. 11:4; Prov. 15:3

24 [I]Hebr. *are not* [II]Hebr. *closed up*

3 [a]James 1:17

4 [a]Job 4:17-21; 15:14-16

6 [a]Ps. 22:6

5 [I]Or, *with the inhabitants*

6 [a]Ps. 139:8, 11; Prov. 15:11; Heb. 4:13

7 [a]Job 9:8; Ps. 24:2; 104:2-5

8 [a]Prov. 30:4

10 [I]Hebr. *until the end of light with darkness* [a]Job 38:8; Ps. 33:7; 104:9; Prov. 8:29; Jer. 5:22

12 [I]Hebr. *pride* [a]Ex. 14:21; Ps. 74:13; Isa. 51:15; Jer. 31:35

13 [a]Ps. 33:6 [b]Isa. 27:1

1 [I]Hebr. *added to take up*

2 [a]Job 34:5,

🔑 **26:7** Many believe that the "empty place" is representative of heaven. The word "stretcheth" is a present participle in the Hebrew, and conveys the idea of continuous action. This fact could very well explain the scientific phenomena of an "expanding universe." Those who support an evolutionary explanation to the origin of the universe have suggested that the universe is expanding as the result of a large explosion. In this verse, however, the expanding universe is a result of God's creative design.
🔑 **27:1–6** Though some contend that Job's words in this passage are self-righteous, it seems that they are more likely intended to balance the accusations against him.

taken away[5493] my judgment;[4941] and the
Almighty,[7706] *who* hath [I][b]vexed[4843] my
soul;[5315]
3 All the while my breath[5397] *is* in
me, and [I][a]the spirit[7307] of God[433] *is* in my
nostrils;[639]
4 My lips[8193] shall not speak[1696]
wickedness,[5766] nor my tongue utter deceit.
5 God forbid that I should justify[6663]
you: till I die[1478] [a]I will not remove[5493]
mine integrity[8538] from me.
6 My righteousness[6666] I [a]hold
fast,[2388] and will not let it go: [b]my
heart[3824] shall not reproach[2778] *me* [I]so
long as I live.
7 Let mine enemy[341] be as the
wicked,[7563] and he that riseth up against
me as the unrighteous.[5767]
8 [a]For what *is* the hope of the
hypocrite,[2611] though he hath gained,[1214]
when God taketh away[7953] his soul?
9 [a]Will God hear[8085] his cry when
trouble[6869] cometh upon him?
10 [a]Will he delight himself in the
Almighty? will[7121] he always[6256] call
upon[7121] God?
11 I will teach[3384] you [I]by the
hand[3027] of God: *that* which *is* with the
Almighty will I not conceal.
12 Behold, all ye yourselves have
seen[2372] *it;* why then are ye thus altogether vain?[1891]
13 [a]This *is* the portion[2506] of a
wicked man[120] with God, and the
heritage[5159] of oppressors,[6184] *which* they
shall receive of the Almighty.
14 [a]If his children[1121] be multiplied,
it is for the sword:[2719] and his offspring
shall not be satisfied[7646] with bread.
15 Those that remain[8300] of him
shall be buried[6912] in death:[4194] and [a]his
widows shall not weep.
16 Though he heap up[6651] silver as
the dust,[6083] and prepare[3559] raiment as
the clay;[2563]
17 He may prepare *it,* but [a]the just
shall put *it* on, and the innocent[5355] shall
divide the silver.
18 He buildeth his house[1004] as a
moth, and [a]as a booth[5521] *that* the keeper
maketh.[6213]

2 [I]Hebr. *made my soul bitter* [b]Ruth 1:20; 2Kgs. 4:27
3 [I]That is, *the breath which God gave him,* [a]Gen. 2:7
5 [a]Job 2:9; 13:15
6 [I]Hebr. *from my days* [a]Job 2:3 [b]Acts 24:16
8 [a]Matt. 16:26; Luke 12:20
9 [a]Job 35:12; Ps. 18:41; 109:7; Prov. 1:28; 28:9; Isa. 1:15; Jer. 14:12; Ezek. 8:18; Mic. 3:4; John 9:31; James 4:3
10 [a]Job 22:26, 27
11 [I]Or, being *in the hand*
13 [a]Job 20:29
14 [a]Deut. 28:41; Esth. 9:10; Hos. 9:13
15 [a]Ps. 78:64
17 [a]Prov. 28:8; Eccl. 2:26
18 [a]Isa. 1:8; Lam. 2:6
20 [a]Job 18:11
22 [I]Hebr. *in fleeing he would flee*
1 [I]Or, *a mine*
2 [I]Or, *dust*
6 [I]Or, *gold ore*
9 [I]Or, *flint*
11 [I]Hebr. *from weeping*

19 The rich man shall lie down, but
he shall not be gathered:[622] he openeth
his eyes, and he *is* not.
20 [a]Terrors[1091] take hold on[5381] him
as waters, a tempest stealeth him away
in the night.[3915]
21 The east wind carrieth him away,
and he departeth: and as a storm
hurleth[8175] him out of his place.
22 For *God* shall cast[7993] upon him,
and not spare: [I]he would fain[1272] flee out
of his hand.
23 *Men* shall clap[5606] their hands[3709]
at him, and shall hiss him out of his
place.

In Praise of Wisdom

28 Surely there is [I]a vein[4161] for the
silver, and a place for gold *where*
they fine[2212] *it.*
2 Iron is taken out of the [I]earth,[6083]
and brass *is* molten *out of* the stone.
3 He setteth[7760] an end to darkness,[2822] and searcheth out[2713] all perfection: the stones of darkness,[652] and
the shadow of death.[6757]
4 The flood breaketh out from the
inhabitant;[1481] *even the waters* forgotten
of the foot: they are dried up, they are
gone away from men.[582]
5 *As for* the earth,[776] out of it
cometh bread: and under it is turned
up[2015] as it were fire.
6 The stones of it *are* the place
of sapphires: and it hath [I]dust[6083] of
gold.
7 *There is* a path which no fowl
knoweth, and which the vulture's eye
hath not seen:
8 The lion's whelps[1121] have not
trodden it, nor the fierce lion passed
by it.
9 He putteth forth his hand[3027] upon
the [I]rock; he overturneth[2015] the mountains by the roots.
10 He cutteth out rivers among the
rocks; and his eye seeth[7200] every precious thing.[3366]
11 He bindeth[2280] the floods [I]from
overflowing; and *the thing that is* hid[8587]
bringeth he forth to light.[216]

12 [a]But where shall wisdom[2451] be
found? and where *is* the place of understanding?[998]
13 Man[582] knoweth not the [a]price[6187]
thereof; neither is it found in the land[776]
of the living.[2416]
14 [a]The depth[8415] saith, It *is* not
in me: and the sea saith, *It is* not
with me.
15 [I]It [a]cannot be gotten for gold, neither shall silver be weighed[8254] *for* the
price[4242] thereof.
16 It cannot be valued with the gold
of Ophir, with the precious[3368] onyx, or
the sapphire.
17 The gold and the crystal cannot
equal it: and the exchange of it *shall not
be for* [I]jewels of fine gold.
18 No mention shall be made of
[I]coral, or of pearls: for the price[4901] of
wisdom *is* above rubies.
19 The topaz of Ethiopia shall not
equal it, neither shall it be valued with
pure gold.
20 [a]Whence then cometh wisdom?
and where *is* the place of understanding?
21 Seeing it is hid[5956] from the eyes
of all living, and kept close[5641] from the
fowls of the [I]air.
22 [a]Destruction[11] and death[4194] say,
We have heard[8085] the fame[8088] thereof
with our ears.[241]
23 God[430] understandeth[995] the
way[1870] thereof, and he knoweth the
place thereof.
24 For he looketh to the ends of the
earth, *and* [a]seeth under the whole
heaven;[8064]
25 [a]To make[6213] the weight[4948] for
the winds;[7307] and he weigheth[8505] the
waters by measure.
26 When he [a]made a decree[2706] for
the rain, and a way for the lightning of
the thunder:
27 Then did he see[7200] it, and
[I]declare it; he prepared[3559] it, yea, and
searched it out.[2713]

12 [a]Job 28:20; Eccl. 7:24

13 [a]Prov. 3:15

14 [a]Job 28:22; Rom. 11:33, 34

15 [I]Hebr. *Fine gold shall not be given for it* [a]Prov. 3:13-15; 8:10, 11, 19; 16:16

17 [I]Or, *vessels of fine gold*

18 [I]Or, *Ramoth*

20 [a]Job 28:12

21 [I]Or, *heaven*

22 [a]Job 28:14

24 [a]Prov. 15:3

25 [a]Ps. 135:7

26 [a]Job 38:25

27 [I]Or, *number it*

28 [a]Deut. 4:6; Ps. 111:10; Prov. 1:7; 9:10; Eccl. 12:13

1 [I]Hebr. *added to take up*

2 [a]Job 7:3

3 [I]Or, *lamp* [a]Job 18:6 [b]Ps. 18:28

4 [a]Ps. 25:14

6 [I]Hebr. *with me* [a]Gen. 49:11; Deut. 32:13; 33:24; Job 20:17 [b]Ps. 81:16

9 [a]Job 21:5

10 [I]Hebr. *The voice of the nobles was hid* [a]Ps. 137:6

12 [a]Ps. 72:12; Prov. 21:13; 24:11

28 And unto man[120] he said, Behold,
[a]the fear[3374] of the LORD,[136] that *is* wisdom; and to depart[5493] from evil[7451] *is*
understanding.

Job Remembers

29 Moreover Job [I]continued his parable, and said,
2 Oh that I were [a]as *in* months past,
as *in* the days *when* God[433] preserved[8104]
me;
3 [a]When his [I][b]candle[5216] shined[1984]
upon my head,[7218] *and when* by his
light[216] I walked *through* darkness;[2822]
4 As I was in the days of my youth,
when [a]the secret[5475] of God *was* upon
my tabernacle;[168]
5 When the Almighty[7706] *was* yet
with me, *when* my children *were* about
me;
6 When [a]I washed[7364] my steps with
butter, and [b]the rock poured [I]me out
rivers of oil;[8081]
7 When I went out to the gate
through the city, *when* I prepared[3559] my
seat[4186] in the street!
8 The young men saw[7200] me, and
hid themselves: and the aged[3453] arose,
and stood up.
9 The princes[8269] refrained talk-
ing,[4405] and [a]laid[7760] *their* hand[3709] on
their mouth.[6310]
10 [I]The nobles held their peace, and
their [a]tongue cleaved to the roof of their
mouth.
⊶ 11 When the ear[241] heard[8085] *me,*
then it blessed[833] me; and when the eye
saw *me,* it gave witness[5749] to me:
12 Because [a]I delivered[4422] the
poor[6041] that cried, and the fatherless,
and *him that had* none to help him.
13 The blessing[1293] of him that was
ready to perish[6] came upon me: and I
caused the widow's heart[3820] to sing for
joy.

⊶ **29:11–14** Job has now become so adamant in his own defense that some feel he gives the impression of trust in salvation by works, when in fact he is merely expressing his own righteousness (see note on Job 31:35–40).

14 [a]I put on righteousness,[6664] and it
clothed me: my judgment[4941] *was* as a
robe and a diadem.6797
15 I was [a]eyes to the blind, and feet
was I to the lame.
16 I *was* a father[1] to the poor: and
[a]the cause[7379] *which* I knew[3045] not I
searched out.
17 And I brake[7665] [I][a]the jaws of the
wicked,[5767] and [II]plucked the spoil2964 out
of his teeth.
18 Then I said, [a]I shall die[1478] in my
nest, and I shall multiply *my* days as the
sand.
19 [a]My root *was* [I]spread out6605 [b]by
the waters, and the dew lay all night
upon my branch.
20 My glory[3519] *was* [I]fresh in me, and
[a]my bow was [II]renewed in my hand.[3027]
21 Unto me *men* gave ear, and
waited,[3176] and kept silence at my counsel.[6098]
22 After my words[1697] they spake
not again; and my speech dropped[5197]
upon them.
23 And they waited for me as for the
rain; and they opened their mouth wide
as for [a]the latter rain.[4456]
24 *If* I laughed7832 on them, they
believed[539] *it* not; and the light of my
countenance they cast not down.[5307]
25 I chose out[977] their way,[1870] and
sat chief,[7218] and dwelt[7931] as a king[4428]
in the army,[1416] as one *that* comforteth[5162] the mourners.

30 🗝 But now *they that are*
[I]younger than I have me in derision, whose fathers[1] I would have
disdained[3988] to have set with the dogs of
my flock.
2 Yea, whereto *might* the strength of
their hands[3027] *profit* me, in whom old
age was perished?[6]
3 For want and famine *they were*
[I]solitary;1565 fleeing into the wilder-
ness6723 [II]in former time desolate[7722] and
waste.

14 [a]Deut. 24:13; Ps. 132:9; Isa. 59:17; 61:10; Eph. 6:14; 1Thess. 5:8

15 [a]Num. 10:31

16 [a]Prov. 29:7

17 [I]Hebr. *the jaw teeth, or, the grinders* [II]Hebr. *cast* [a]Ps. 58:6; Prov. 30:14

18 [a]Ps. 30:6

19 [I]Hebr. *opened* [a]Job 18:16 [b]Ps. 1:3; Jer. 17:8

20 [I]Hebr. *new* [II]Hebr. *changed* [a]Gen. 49:24

23 [a]Zech. 10:1

1 [I]Hebr. *of fewer days than I*

3 [I]Or, *dark as the night* [II]Hebr. *last night*

6 [I]Hebr. *holes*

8 [I]Hebr. *men of no name*

9 [a]Job 17:6; Ps. 35:15; 69:12; Lam. 3:14, 63

10 [I]Hebr. *and withhold not spittle from my face* [a]Num. 12:14; Deut. 25:9; Isa. 50:6; Matt. 26:67; 27:30

11 [a]Job 12:18

12 [a]Job 19:12

15 [I]Hebr. *my principal one*

16 [a]Ps. 42:4

4 Who cut up6998 mallows4408 by the
bushes,[7880] and juniper roots *for* their
meat.
5 They were driven forth from
among *men,* (they cried[7321] after them as
after a thief;)
6 To dwell[7931] in the clifts of the valleys, *in* [I]caves of the earth,[6083] and *in*
the rocks.
7 Among the bushes they brayed;
under the nettles they were gathered together.
8 *They were* children[1121] of fools,
yea, children of [I]base men: they were
viler5217 than the earth.[776]
9 [a]And now am I their song, yea, I
am their byword.[4405]
10 They abhor[8581] me, they flee far
from me, [I]and spare not [a]to spit in my
face.
11 Because he [a]hath loosed6605 my
cord, and afflicted6031 me, they have also
let loose7971 the bridle before me.
12 Upon *my* right *hand* rise the
youth; they push away7971 my feet, and
[a]they raise up against me the ways[734] of
their destruction.[343]
13 They mar5420 my path, they set
forward my calamity,[1942] they have no
helper.
14 They came *upon me* as a wide
breaking in *of waters:* in the desolation[7722] they rolled themselves[1556] *upon
me.*
15 Terrors1091 are turned[2015] upon
me: they pursue [I]my soul as the wind:[7307]
and my welfare[3444] passeth away[5674] as
a cloud.
16 [a]And now my soul[5315] is poured
out[8210] upon me; the days of affliction
have taken hold270 upon me.
17 My bones[6106] are pierced in me in
the night[3915] season: and my sinews take
no rest.
18 By the great force3581 *of my disease* is my garment changed:[2664] it
bindeth me about as the collar[6310] of my
coat.
19 He hath cast[3384] me into the

🗝 **30:1–10** Job bemoans the fact that the very lowest class of people now look down upon him.

mire, and I am become like dust[6083] and ashes.

20 I cry unto thee, and thou dost not hear me: I stand up, and thou regardest[995] me *not.*

21 Thou art [I]become cruel[393] to me: with [II]thy strong hand[3027] thou opposest thyself[7852] against me.

22 Thou liftest me up to the wind; thou causest me to ride *upon it,* and dissolvest[4127] my [I]substance.[8454]

23 For I know[3045] *that* thou wilt bring me *to* death,[4194] and *to* the house[1004] [a]appointed[4150] for all living.[2416]

24 Howbeit he will not stretch out *his* hand to the [I]grave,[1164] though they cry in his destruction.[6365]

25 [a]Did not I weep [I]for him that was in trouble? was *not* my soul grieved for the poor?[34]

26 [a]When I looked[6960] for good,[2896] then evil[7451] came *unto me:* and when I waited[3176] for light,[216] there came darkness.[652]

27 My bowels[4578] boiled, and rested not: the days of affliction prevented me.

28 [a]I went mourning[6937] without the sun: I stood up, *and* I cried in the congregation.[6951]

29 [a]I am a brother[251] to dragons,[8577] and a companion to [I]owls.

30 [a]My skin[5785] is black[7835] upon me, and [b]my bones are burned[2787] with heat.

31 My harp also is *turned* to mourning,[60] and my organ into the voice of them that weep.

31

I made[3772] a covenant[1285] with mine [a]eyes: why then should I think upon a maid?[1330]

2 For what [a]portion of God[433] *is there* from above? and *what* inheritance[5159] of the Almighty[7706] from on high?

3 *Is* not destruction[343] to the wicked?[5767] and a strange[5235] *punishment* to the workers of iniquity?[205]

4 [a]Doth not he see my ways,[1870] and count[5608] all my steps?

5 If I have walked with vanity,[7723] or if my foot hath hasted to deceit;[4820]

6 [I]Let me be weighed in an even balance that God may know[3045] mine integrity.[3887]

7 If my step hath turned out of the way, and [a]mine heart[3820] walked after mine eyes, and if any blot[3971] hath cleaved to mine hands;[3709]

8 *Then* [a]let me sow, and let another eat; yea, let my offspring be rooted out.

9 If mine heart have been deceived[6601] by a woman,[802] or *if* I have laid wait at my neighbour's[7453] door;

10 *Then* let my wife[802] grind[2912] unto [a]another, and let others bow down[3766] upon her.

11 For this *is* an heinous crime;[2154] yea, [a]it *is* an iniquity[5771] *to be punished by* the judges.[6414]

12 For it *is* a fire *that* consumeth to destruction,[11] and would root out all mine increase.

13 If I did despise[3988] the cause[4941] of my manservant[5650] or of my maidservant, when they contended[7379] with me;

14 What then shall I do when [a]God[410] riseth up? and when he visiteth, what shall I answer[7725] him?

15 [a]Did not he that made[6213] me in the womb[990] make him? and [I]did not one fashion[3559] us in the womb?

16 If I have withheld the poor[1800] from *their* desire,[2656] or have caused the eyes of the widow to fail;[3615]

17 Or have eaten my morsel myself alone, and the fatherless hath not eaten thereof;

18 (For from my youth he was brought up with me, as *with* a father,[1] and I have guided[5148] [I]her from my mother's[517] womb;)

19 If I have seen[7200] any perish[6] for want of clothing, or any poor[34] without covering;

20 If his loins have not [a]blessed[1288] me, and *if* he were *not* warmed with the fleece of my sheep;

21 If I have lifted up[5130] my hand[3027] [a]against the fatherless, when I saw[7200] my help in the gate:

---

21 [I]Hebr. *turned to be cruel* [II]Hebr. *the strength of thy hand*

22 [I]Or, *wisdom*

23 [I]Hebr. *heap* [a]Heb. 9:27

25 [I]Hebr. *for him that was hard of day* [a]Ps. 35:13, 14; Rom. 12:15

26 [a]Jer. 8:15

28 [a]Ps. 38:6; 42:9; 43:2

29 [I]Or, *ostriches* [a]Ps. 102:6; Mic. 1:8

30 [a]Ps. 119:83; Lam. 4:8; 5:10 [b]Ps. 102:3

1 [a]Matt. 5:28

2 [a]Job 20:29; 27:13

4 [a]2Chr. 16:9; Job 34:21; Prov. 5:21; 15:3; Jer. 32:19

6 [I]Hebr. *Let him weigh me in balances of justice*

7 [a]Num. 15:39; Eccl. 11:9; Ezek. 6:9; Matt. 5:29

8 [a]Lev. 26:16; Deut. 28:30, 38-48

10 [a]2Sam. 12:11; Jer. 8:10

11 [a]Gen. 38:24; Lev. 20:10; Deut. 22:22; Job 31:28

14 [a]Ps. 44:21

15 [I]Or, *did he not fashion us in one womb* [a]Job 34:19; Prov. 14:31; 22:2; Mal. 2:10

18 [I]That is, *the widow*

20 [a]Deut. 24:13

21 [a]Job 22:9

22 *Then* let mine arm3802 fall from
my shoulder blade, and mine arm248 be
broken[7665] from the bone.
23 For [a]destruction *from* God *was* a
terror[6343] to me, and by reason of his
highness I could not endure.
24 [a]If I have made gold my hope,[3689]
or have said to the fine gold, *Thou art*
my confidence;
25 [a]If I rejoiced because my
wealth[2428] *was* great, and because mine
hand had [I]gotten much;
26 [a]If I beheld[7200] [I]the sun when it
shined,[1984] or the moon walking [II]*in*
brightness;
27 And my heart hath been secretly
enticed,6601 or [I]my mouth[6310] hath
kissed[5401] my hand:
28 This also *were* [a]an iniquity *to be*
punished by the judge: for I should have
denied3584 the God *that is* above.
29 [a]If I rejoiced at the destruction[6365]
of him that hated[8130] me, or lifted up
myself when evil[7451] found him:
30 [a]Neither have I suffered [I]my
mouth to sin[2398] by wishing[7592] a
curse[423] to his soul.[5315]
31 If the men of my tabernacle[168]
said not, Oh that we had of his flesh[1320]
we cannot be satisfied.
32 [a]The stranger[1616] did not lodge in
the street: *but* I opened my doors [I]to the
traveller.[734]
33 If I covered[3680] my transgressions[6588] [Ia]as Adam, by hiding2934 mine
iniquity in my bosom:
34 Did I fear[6206] a great [a]multitude,
or did the contempt of families[4940]
terrify[2865] me, that I kept silence, *and*
went not out of the door?
🗝 35 [a]Oh that one would hear[8085] me!
[I]behold, my desire *is, that* [b]the Almighty
would answer me, and *that* mine adversary[7379] had written a book.[5612]
36 Surely I would take it upon my
shoulder, *and* bind it *as* a crown to me.
37 I would declare[5046] unto him the
number of my steps; as a prince[5057]
would I go near[7126] unto him.
38 If my land[127] cry[2199] against me,
or that the furrows8525 likewise thereof
[I]complain;1058
39 If [a]I have eaten [I]the fruits thereof
without money,3701 or [b]have [II]caused
the owners[1167] thereof to lose their
life:[5315]
40 Let [a]thistles grow instead of
wheat, and [I]cockle[890] instead of barley.
The words[1697] of Job are ended.[8552]

Elihu Speaks

32 So these three men[582] ceased[7673]
[I]to answer Job, because he *was*
[a]righteous[6662] in his own eyes.
🗝 2 Then was kindled[2734] the wrath of
Elihu the son[1121] of Barachel [a]the Buzite,
of the kindred4950 of Ram: against Job
was his wrath[639] kindled, because he
justified[6663] [I]himself rather than God.[430]
3 Also against his three friends[7453]
was his wrath kindled, because they had
found no answer, and *yet* had condemned
Job.

23 [a]Isa. 13:6; Joel 1:15
24 [a]Mark 10:24; 1Tim. 6:17
25 [I]Hebr. *found much* [a]Ps. 62:10; Prov. 11:28
26 [I]Hebr. *the light* [II]Hebr. *bright* [a]Deut. 4:19; 11:16; 17:3; Ezek. 8:16
27 [I]Hebr. *my hand hath kissed my mouth*
28 [a]Job 31:11
29 [a]Prov. 17:5
30 [I]Hebr. *my palate* [a]Matt. 5:44; Rom. 12:14
32 [I]Or, *to the way* [a]Gen. 19:2, 3; Judg. 19:20, 21; Rom. 12:13; Heb. 13:2; 1Pet. 4:9
33 [I]Or, *after the manner of men* [a]Gen. 3:8, 12; Prov. 28:13; Hos. 6:7
34 [a]Ex. 23:2
35 [I]Or, *behold, my sign* is that *the Almighty will answer me* [a]Job 33:6 [b]Job 13:22
38 [I]Hebr. *weep*
39 [I]Hebr. *the strength thereof* [II]Hebr. *caused the soul of the owners thereof to expire,* or, *breathe out* [a]James 5:4 [b]1Kgs. 21:19
40 [I]Or, *noisome weeds* [a]Gen. 3:18

1 [I]Hebr. *from answering* [a]Job 33:9
2 [I]Hebr. *his soul* [a]Gen. 22:21

🗝 **31:35–40** Job has reached the height of emotional self-righteousness and has determined that no one can justly accuse him of any wrong.

🗝 **32:2** Elihu is said to have been of the "kindred of Ram." The word "Ram" may be a shortened form of the word "Aram," which was an area located close to the border of the modern day countries of Syria and Turkey. Balak sent for Baalam who lived in Aram (Num. 23:17; 24:16), because it was an area known for its prophets. In contrast, Job's other three friends were from the East, an area known for the wisdom of man. The other three friends relied solely on their reasoning and presuppositions to explain the works of God. It seems evident that Elihu, and perhaps others, had been there throughout the ordeal, especially during the discussions between Job and his friends (Job 32:8, 9). Elihu's speeches introduce God as a teacher and Job's suffering as didactic (Job 35:10, 11). It is interesting that Elihu's words are never condemned by God, while the three friends of Job were severely reprimanded for their false presuppositions about God.

4 Now Elihu had [I]waited till Job had spoken, because they *were* [II]elder than he.

5 When Elihu saw[7200] that *there was* no answer in the mouth[6310] of *these* three men, then his wrath was kindled.

6 And Elihu the son of Barachel the Buzite answered and said, I *am* [I]young, [a]and ye *are* very old;[3453] wherefore I was afraid,[2119] and [II]durst not shew you mine opinion.[1843]

7 I said, Days should speak,[1696] and multitude of years should teach[3045] wisdom.[2451]

8 But *there is* a spirit[7307] in man: and [a]the inspiration[5397] of the Almighty[7706] giveth them understanding.[995]

9 [a]Great men are not *always* wise:[2449] neither do the aged[2205] understand judgment.[4941]

10 Therefore I said, Hearken[8085] to me; I also will shew mine opinion.[1843]

11 Behold, I waited[3176] for your words;[1697] I gave ear[238] to your [I]reasons,[8394] whilst ye searched out[2713] [II]what to say.

12 Yea, I attended[995] unto you, and, behold, *there was* none of you that convinced[3198] Job, *or* that answered[6030] his words:[561]

13 [a]Lest ye should say,[559] We have found out wisdom: God[410] thrusteth him down,[5086] not man.[376]

14 Now he hath not [I]directed[6186] *his* words[4405] against me: neither will I answer[7725] him with your speeches.[561]

15 They were amazed,[2865] they answered[6030] no more: [I]they left off speaking.[4405]

16 When I had waited, (for they spake[1696] not, but stood still, *and* answered no more;)

17 *I said,* I will answer also my part, I also will shew mine opinion.

18 For I am full of [I]matter,[4405] [II]the spirit within me constraineth[6693] me.

19 Behold, my belly[990] *is* as wine *which* [I]hath no vent; it is ready to burst like new bottles.

20 I will speak, [I]that I may be refreshed:[7304] I will open my lips[8193] and answer.

21 Let me not, I pray you,[4994] [a]accept[5375] any man's person, neither let me give flattering titles unto man.[120]

22 For I know[3045] not to give flattering titles; *in so doing* my maker[6213] would soon take me away.

33

Wherefore, Job, I pray thee, hear[8085] my speeches,[4405] and hearken[238] to all my words.[1697]

2 Behold, now I have opened my mouth,[6310] my tongue hath spoken[1696] [I]in my mouth.

3 My words[561] *shall be of* the uprightness[3476] of my heart:[3820] and my lips[8193] shall utter[4448] knowledge[1847] clearly.[1305]

4 [a]The Spirit[7307] of God[410] hath made[6213] me, and the breath[5397] of the Almighty[7706] hath given me life.[2421]

5 If thou canst answer[7725] me, set *thy words* in order[6186] before me, stand up.

🗝 6 [a]Behold, I *am* [I]according to thy wish[6310] in God's stead: I also am [II]formed out of the clay.

7 [a]Behold, my terror[367] shall not make thee afraid,[1204] neither shall my hand be heavy[3513] upon thee.

8 Surely thou hast spoken[559] [I]in mine hearing,[241] and I have heard[8085] the voice of *thy* words,[4405] *saying,*

9 [a]I am clean[2134] without transgression,[6588] I *am* innocent;[2643] neither *is there* iniquity[5771] in me.

10 Behold, he findeth occasions[8569]

4 [I]Hebr. *expected Job in words* [II]Hebr. *elder for days*
6 [I]Hebr. *few of days* [II]Hebr. *feared* [a]Job 15:10
8 [a]1Kgs. 3:12; 4:29; Job 35:11; 38:36; Prov. 2:6; Eccl. 2:26; Dan. 1:17; 2:21; Matt. 11:25; James 1:5
9 [a]1Cor. 1:26
11 [I]Hebr. *understandings* [II]Hebr. *words*
13 [a]Jer. 9:23; 1Cor. 1:29
14 [I]Or, *ordered his words*
15 [I]Hebr. *they removed speeches from themselves*
18 [I]Hebr. *words* [II]Hebr. *the spirit of my belly*
19 [I]Hebr. *is not opened*
20 [I]Hebr. *that I may breathe*
21 [a]Lev. 19:15; Deut. 1:17; 16:19; Prov. 24:23; Matt. 22:16
2 [I]Hebr. *in my palate*
4 [a]Gen. 2:7
6 [I]Hebr. *according to thy mouth* [II]Hebr. *cut out of the clay* [a]Job 9:34, 35; 13:20, 21; 31:35
7 [a]Job 9:34; 13:21
8 [I]Hebr. *in mine ears*
9 [a]Job 9:17; 10:7; 11:4; 16:17; 23:10, 11; 27:5; 29:14; 31:1

🗝 **33:6–8** When Elihu made the statement, "my terror shall not make thee afraid," he was emphasizing that although he was the representative of God (Job 32:8–10), there was no aura about him nor any supernatural force at work. He was a man who was on equal footing with Job (v. 6) and was the answer to Job's request for someone to go between them (Job 31:35). It is possible that Elihu is a type of Christ in that he was the mediator between God and Job, just as Christ is between God and man.

against me, [a]he counteth[2803] me for his enemy,

11 [a]He putteth[7760] my feet in the stocks, he marketh[8104] all my paths.[734]

12 Behold, *in* this thou art not just:[6663] I will answer thee, that God[433] is greater than man.[582]

13 Why dost thou [a]strive[7378] against him? for [I]he giveth not account6030 of any of his matters.

14 [a]For God speaketh[1696] once, yea twice, *yet man* perceiveth7789 it not.

15 [a]In a dream, in a vision[2384] of the night,[3915] when deep sleep falleth[5307] upon men,[582] in slumberings upon the bed;

16 [a]Then [I]he openeth[1540] the ears[241] of men, and sealeth2856 their instruction,

17 That he may withdraw[5493] man[120] *from his* [I]purpose, and hide[3680] pride from man.[1397]

18 He keepeth back his soul[5315] from the pit,[7845] and his life[2416] [I]from perishing[5674] by the sword.

19 He is chastened[3198] also with pain upon his bed, and the multitude[7379] of his bones[6106] with strong *pain:*

20 [a]So that his life abhorreth2092 bread, and his soul [I]dainty8378 meat.

🔑 21 His flesh[1320] is consumed away,[3615] that it cannot be seen; and his bones *that* were not seen[7200] stick out.[8205]

22 Yea, his soul draweth near[7126] unto the grave,[7845] and his life to the destroyers.[4191]

23 If there be a messenger[4397] with him, an interpreter,[3887] one among a thousand, to shew[5046] unto man his uprightness:

24 Then he is gracious[2603] unto him, and saith, Deliver[6308] him from going down to the pit: I have found [I]a ransom.[3724]

25 His flesh shall be fresher [I]than a child's: he shall return[7725] to the days of his youth:

26 He shall pray[6279] unto God, and he will be favourable[7521] unto him: and he shall see his face with joy: for he will render[7725] unto man his righteousness.[6666]

27 [I]He looketh upon men, and *if any* [a]say, I have sinned,[2398] and perverted[5753] *that which was* right,[3477] and it [b]profited7737 me not;

28 [I]He will [a]deliver[6299] his soul from going into the pit, and his life shall see the light.[216]

29 Lo, all these *things* worketh God [I]oftentimes6471,7969 with man,

30 [a]To bring back his soul from the pit, to be enlightened with the light of the living.[2416]

31 Mark well, O Job, hearken[8085] unto me: hold thy peace, and I will speak.[1696]

32 If thou hast any thing to say,[4405] answer me: speak, for I desire[2654] to justify[6663] thee.

33 If not, [a]hearken unto me: hold thy peace, and I shall teach[502] thee wisdom.[2451]

34

Furthermore Elihu answered and said,

2 Hear[8085] my words,[4405] O ye wise[2450] *men;* and give ear[238] unto me, ye that have knowledge.[3045]

3 [a]For the ear trieth[974] words, as the [I]mouth tasteth meat.

4 Let us choose[977] to us judgment:[4941] let us know[3045] among ourselves what *is* good.[2896]

5 For Job hath said, [a]I am righteous:[6663] and [b]God[410] hath taken away[5493] my judgment.

6 [a]Should I lie[3576] against my right?[4941] [I][b]my wound[2671] *is* incurable without transgression.[6588]

7 What man[1397] *is* like Job, [a]*who* drinketh up scorning3933 like water?

8 Which goeth in company with the workers of iniquity,[205] and walketh with wicked[7562] men.

10 [a]Job 13:24; 16:9; 19:11
11 [a]Job 13:27; 14:16; 31:4
13 [I]Hebr. *he answereth not* [a]Isa. 45:9
14 [a]Job 40:5; Ps. 62:11
15 [a]Num. 12:6; Job 4:13
16 [I]Hebr. *he revealeth,* or, *uncovereth* [a]Job 36:10, 15
17 [I]Hebr. *work*
18 [I]Hebr. *from passing by the sword*
20 [I]Hebr. *meat of desire* [a]Ps. 107:18
24 [I]Or, *an atonement*
25 [I]Hebr. *than childhood*
27 [I]Or, *He shall look upon men, and say, I have sinned* [a]2Sam. 12:13; Prov. 28:13; Luke 15:21; 1John 1:9 [b]Rom. 6:21
28 [I]Or, *He hath delivered my soul and my life* [a]Isa. 38:17
29 [I]Hebr. *twice and thrice*
30 [a]Job 33:28; Ps. 56:13
33 [a]Ps. 34:11

3 [I]Hebr. *palate* [a]Job 6:30; 12:11
5 [a]Job 33:9 [b]Job 27:2
6 [I]Hebr. *mine arrow* [a]Job 9:17 [b]Job 6:4; 16:13
7 [a]Job 15:16

🔑 **33:21** Some suggest that the disease with which Job was afflicted may have been a form of elephantiasis, which causes parts of the body to be swollen and other parts to be bony.

9 For [a]he hath said, It profiteth a man nothing that he should delight[7521] himself with God.[430]

10 Therefore hearken[8085] unto me ye [a]men of understanding: [b]far be it from God, *that he should do* wickedness;[7562] and *from* the Almighty,[7706] *that he should commit* iniquity.[5766]

11 [a]For the work of a man[120] shall he render[7999] unto him, and cause every man[376] to find according to *his* ways.[734]

12 Yea, surely[551] God will not do wickedly,[7561] neither will the Almighty [a]pervert[5791] judgment.

13 Who hath given him a charge[6485] over the earth? or who hath disposed[7760] [I]the whole world?[8398]

14 If he set[7760] his heart[3820] [I]upon man, *if* he [a]gather[622] unto himself his spirit[7307] and his breath;[5397]

15 [a]All flesh shall perish[1478] together, and man shall turn again[7725] unto dust.[6083]

16 If now *thou hast* understanding,[998] hear this: hearken[238] to the voice of my words.

17 [a]Shall[2280] even he that hateth[8130] right [I]govern?[2280] and wilt thou condemn[7561] him that is most just?

18 [a]*Is it fit* to say to a king,[4428] *Thou art* wicked?[1100] *and* to princes,[5081] *Ye are* ungodly?[7563]

19 *How much less to him* that [a]accepteth[5375] not the persons of princes,[8269] nor regardeth the rich more than the poor? for [b]they all *are* the work of his hands.[3027]

20 In a moment shall they die,[4191] and the people shall be troubled1607 [a]at midnight, and pass away:[5674] and [I]the mighty[47] shall be taken away[5493] without hand.

21 [a]For his eyes *are* upon the ways[1870] of man, and he seeth[7200] all his goings.

22 [a]*There is* no darkness,[2822] nor shadow of death,[6757] where the workers of iniquity may hide themselves.

23 For he will not lay[7760] upon man more *than right;* that he should [I]enter[1980] into judgment with God.

24 [a]He shall break in pieces[7489] mighty men [I]without number, and set others in their stead.

25 Therefore he knoweth their works, and he overturneth[2015] *them* in the night,[3915] so that they are [I]destroyed.[1792]

26 He striketh[5606] them as wicked[7563] men [I]in the open4725 sight of others;

27 Because they [a]turned back [I]from him, and [b]would not consider[7919] any of his ways:

28 So that they [a]cause the cry of the poor1800 to come unto him, and he [b]heareth[8085] the cry of the afflicted.6041

🗝 29 When he giveth quietness,[8252] who then can make trouble?[7561] and when he hideth *his* face, who then can behold him? whether *it be done* against a nation,[1471] or against a man only:

30 That the hypocrite[2611] reign[4427] not, lest [a]the people be ensnared.[4170]

31 Surely it is meet to be said unto God, [a]I have borne[5375] *chastisement,* I will not offend[2254] *any more:*

32 *That which* I see not teach[3384] thou me: if I have done iniquity, I will do no more.

33 [I]*Should it be* according to thy mind? he will recompense[7999] it, whether thou refuse, or whether thou choose; and not I: therefore speak[1696] what thou knowest.[3045]

34 Let men [I]of understanding tell[559] me, and let a wise man hearken unto me.

35 [a]Job hath spoken without knowledge,[1847] and his words[1697] *were* without wisdom.[7919]

9 [a]Job 9:22, 23, 30; 35:3; Mal. 3:14
10 [I]Hebr. *men of heart* [a]Gen. 18:25; Deut. 32:4; 2Chr. 19:7; Job 8:3; 36:23; Ps. 92:15; Rom. 9:14
11 [a]Ps. 62:12; Prov. 24:12; Jer. 32:19; Ezek. 33:20; Matt. 16:27; Rom. 2:6; 2Cor. 5:10; 1Pet. 1:17; Rev. 22:12
12 [a]Job 8:3
13 [I]Hebr. *all of it*
14 [I]Hebr. *upon him* [a]Ps. 104:29
15 [a]Gen. 3:19; Eccl. 12:7
17 [I]Hebr. *bind* [a]Gen. 18:25; 2Sam. 23:3
18 [a]Ex. 22:28
19 [a]Deut. 10:17; 2Chr. 19:7; Acts 10:34; Rom. 2:11; Gal. 2:6; Eph. 6:9; Col. 3:25; 1Pet. 1:17 [b]Job 31:15
20 [I]Hebr. *they shall take away the mighty* [a]Ex. 12:29, 30
21 [a]2Chr. 16:9; Job 31:4; Ps. 34:15; Prov. 5:21; 15:3; Jer. 16:17; 32:19
22 [a]Ps. 139:12; Amos 9:2, 3; Heb. 4:13
23 [I]Hebr. *go*
24 [I]Hebr. *without searching out* [a]Dan. 2:21
25 [I]Hebr. *crushed*
26 [I]Hebr. *in the place of beholders*
27 [I]Hebr. *from after him* [a]1Sam. 15:11 [b]Ps. 28:5; Isa. 5:12
28 [a]Job 35:9; James 5:4 [b]Ex. 22:23
30 [a]1Kgs. 12:28, 30; 2Kgs. 21:9
31 [a]Dan. 9:7-14
33 [I]Hebr. Should it be *from with thee?*
34 [I]Hebr. *of heart*
35 [a]Job 35:16

🗝 **34:29–33** God's purposes will be accomplished regardless of man's desires. Since God's people are not in any position to choose their own chastisement from the Lord, they should humbly receive that which is given.

🔑 36 [I]My desire *is that* Job may be tried[974] unto the end[5331] because of *his* answers for wicked[205] men.

37 For he addeth rebellion unto his sin,[2403] he clappeth[5606] *his hands* among us, and multiplieth[7235] his words[561] against God.

35

Elihu spake moreover, and said,

2 Thinkest[2803] thou this to be right,[4941] *that* thou saidst, My righteousness[6664] *is* more than God's?

3 For [a]thou saidst, What advantage[5532] will it be unto thee? *and,* What profit[3276] shall I have, [I]*if I be cleansed* from my sin?[2403]

4 [I]I will answer[7725] thee, and [a]thy companions with thee.

5 [a]Look unto the heavens,[8064] and see; and behold the clouds[7834] *which* are higher than thou.

6 If thou sinnest, what doest[6213] thou [a]against him? or *if* thy transgressions[6588] be multiplied,[7231] what doest thou unto him?

7 [a]If thou be righteous,[6663] what givest thou him? or what receiveth he of thine hand?[3027]

8 Thy wickedness[7562] *may hurt* a man[376] as thou *art;* and thy righteousness[6666] *may profit* the son[1121] of man.[120]

🔑 9 [a]By reason of the multitude of oppressions they make *the oppressed* to cry:[2199] they cry out by reason of the arm of the mighty.

10 But none saith, [a]Where *is* God[433] my maker,[6213] [b]who giveth songs in the night;[3915]

11 Who [a]teacheth[502] us more than the beasts of the earth,[776] and maketh us wiser[2449] than the fowls of heaven?[8064]

12 [a]There they cry, but none giveth answer, because of the pride of evil[7451] men.

13 [a]Surely God[410] will not hear[8085] vanity,[7723] neither will[7789] the Almighty[7706] regard[7789] it.

14 [a]Although thou sayest thou shalt not see him, *yet* judgment[1779] *is* before him; therefore [b]trust[2342] thou in him.

15 But now, because *it is* not *so,* [I]he hath [a]visited[6485] in his anger;[639] yet [II]he knoweth *it* not in great extremity:[6580]

🔑 16 [a]Therefore doth Job open his mouth[6310] in vain; he multiplieth words[4405] without knowledge.[1847]

36

🔑 Elihu also proceeded, and said,

2 Suffer[3803] me a little, and I will shew thee [I]that *I have* yet to speak on God's behalf.

3 I will fetch[5375] my knowledge[1843] from afar, and will ascribe righteousness[6664] to my Maker.

4 For truly[551] my words[4405] *shall* not *be* false:[8267] he that is perfect[8549] in knowledge[1844] *is* with thee.

5 Behold, God[410] *is* mighty, and despiseth[3988] not *any: he is* [a]mighty in strength *and* [I]wisdom.[3820]

6 He preserveth[2421] not the life of the wicked:[7563] but giveth right[4941] to the [I]poor.[6041]

7 [a]He withdraweth[1639] not his eyes from the righteous:[6662] but [b]with kings *are they* on the throne;[3678] yea, he doth

36 [I]Or, *My father, let Job be tried*
3 [I]Or, *by it more than by my sin* [a]Job 21:15; 34:9
4 [I]Hebr. *I will return to thee words* [a]Job 34:8
5 [a]Job 22:12
6 [a]Prov. 8:36; Jer. 7:19
7 [a]Job 22:2, 3; Ps. 16:2; Prov. 9:12; Rom. 11:35
9 [a]Ex. 2:23; Job 34:28
10 [a]Isa. 51:13 [b]Ps. 42:8; 77:6; 149:5; Acts 16:25
11 [a]Ps. 94:12
12 [a]Prov. 1:28
13 [a]Job 27:9; Prov. 15:29; Isa. 1:15; Jer. 11:11
14 [a]Job 9:11 [b]Ps. 37:5, 6
15 [I]That is, *God* [II]That is, *Job* [a]Ps. 89:32
16 [a]Job 34:35, 37; 38:2
2 [I]Hebr. *that there are yet words for God*
5 [I]Hebr. *heart* [a]Job 9:4; 12:13, 16; 37:23; Ps. 99:4
6 [I]Or, *afflicted*
7 [a]Ps. 33:18; 34:15 [b]Ps. 113:8

🔑 **34:36** Elihu is not wishing for Job's death, nor that he should continue to be tested to the very end of his life, but that his trial would soon be completed.

🔑 **35:9–14** In this passage, Elihu makes the point that Job was thinking himself to be more righteous than God. In truth, Job's own opinion about his goodness does not affect God in any way. It seems that Job has never bothered to come to God during this entire ordeal. Job's reasoning was condemned by Elihu saying that Job had no excuse for wondering at God's existence or His care.

🔑 **35:16** There are two possible interpretations for this verse. Some suggest that what Job said in his previous discussions was vain. Others contend that Job thought that God did not take sin seriously (Job 14, 15); therefore, Job's words will not matter (Nah. 1:1–3).

🔑 **36:1–33** This chapter marks the proper application of scriptural principles to Job's situation.

establish them for ever,[5331] and they are exalted.1361

8 And [a]if *they be* bound in fetters, *and* be holden3920 in cords of affliction;

9 Then he sheweth them their work, and their transgressions[6588] that they have exceeded.[1396]

10 [a]He openeth[1540] also their ear to discipline,[4148] and commandeth[559] that they return[7725] from iniquity.[205]

11 If they obey and serve[5647] *him,* they shall [a]spend[3615] their days in prosperity,[2896] and their years in pleasures.[5273]

12 But if they obey not, [I]they shall perish by the sword, and they shall die[1478] without knowledge.[1847]

13 But the hypocrites[2611] in heart[3820] [a]heap up wrath:[639] they cry not when he bindeth them.

14 [I][a]They die[4191] in youth, and their life *is* among the [II][b]unclean.[6945]

15 He delivereth[2502] the [I]poor in his affliction, and openeth their ears[241] in oppression.

16 Even so would he have removed5496 thee out of the strait6862 [a]*into* a broad place, where *there is* no straitness: and [I][b]that which should be set on thy table *should be* full of [c]fatness.

17 But thou hast fulfilled the judgment of the wicked: [I]judgment[1779] and justice take hold *on thee.*

18 Because *there is* wrath,[2534] *beware* lest he take thee away with *his* stroke:5607 then [a]a great ransom[3724] cannot [I]deliver thee.

19 [a]Will he esteem6186 thy riches? *no,* not gold, nor all the forces3581 of strength.

20 Desire not the night,[3915] when people[5971] are cut off[5927] in their place.

21 Take heed,[8104] [a]regard6437 not iniquity: for [b]this hast thou chosen[977] rather than affliction.

22 Behold, God exalteth7682 by his power: [a]who teacheth[3384] like him?

23 [a]Who hath enjoined[6485] him his way?[1870] or [b]who can say, Thou hast wrought iniquity?[5766]

24 Remember[2142] that thou [a]magnify his work, which men behold.[7891]

25 Every man[120] may see it; man[582] may behold *it* afar off.

26 Behold, God *is* great, and we [a]know[3045] *him* not, [b]neither can the number of his years be searched out.

27 For he [a]maketh small1639 the drops of water: they pour down[2212] rain according to the vapour thereof:

28 [a]Which the clouds do drop *and* distil7491 upon man abundantly.

29 Also can *any* understand[995] the spreadings4666 of the clouds, *or* the noise of his tabernacle?[5521]

30 Behold, he [a]spreadeth6566 his light[216] upon it, and covereth[3680] [I]the bottom of the sea.

31 For [a]by them judgeth[1777] he the people; he [b]giveth meat in abundance.

32 [a]With clouds[3709] he covereth the light; and commandeth[6680] it *not to shine* by *the cloud* that cometh betwixt.[6293]

33 [a]The noise thereof sheweth[5046] concerning it, the cattle also concerning [I]the vapour.

37

At this also my heart[3820] trembleth,[2729] and is moved5425 out of his place.

2 [I]Hear[8085] attentively the noise[7267] of his voice, and the sound[1899] *that* goeth out of his mouth.[6310]

3 He directeth[3474] it under the whole heaven,8064 and his [II]lightning unto the [II]ends of the earth.[776]

4 After it [a]a voice roareth: he thundereth7481 with the voice of his excellency; and he will not stay[6117] them when his voice is heard.[8085]

5 God[410] thundereth marvellously[6381] with his voice; [a]great things doeth he, which we cannot comprehend.[3045]

6 For [a]he saith to the snow, Be thou *on* the earth; [I]likewise to the small rain, and to the great rain of his strength.

7 He sealeth up the hand of every man;[120] [a]that all men[582] may know his work.

8 Then the beasts[2416] [a]go into dens, and remain in their places.

9 [I]Out of the south cometh the

8 [a]Ps. 107:10
10 [a]Job 33:16, 23
11 [a]Job 21:13; Isa. 1:19, 20
12 [I]Hebr. *they shall pass away by the sword*
13 [a]Rom. 2:5
14 [I]Hebr. *Their soul dieth* [II]Or, *sodomites* [a]Job 15:32; 22:16; Ps. 55:23; [b]Deut. 23:17
15 [I]Or, *afflicted*
16 [I]Hebr. *the rest of thy table* [a]Ps. 18:19; 31:8; 118:5 [b]Ps. 23:5 [c]Ps. 36:8
17 [I]Or, *judgment and justice should uphold thee*
18 [I]Hebr. *turn thee aside* [a]Ps. 49:7
19 [a]Prov. 11:4
21 [a]Ps. 66:18 [b]Heb. 11:25
22 [a]Isa. 40:13, 14; Rom. 11:34; 1Cor. 2:16
23 [a]Job 34:13 [b]Job 34:10
24 [a]Ps. 92:5; Rev. 15:3
26 [a]1Cor. 13:12 [b]Ps. 90:2; 102:24, 27; Heb. 1:12
27 [a]Ps. 147:8
28 [a]Prov. 3:20
30 [I]Hebr. *the roots* [a]Job 37:3
31 [a]Job 37:13; 38:23 [b]Ps. 136:25; Acts 14:17
32 [a]Ps. 147:8
33 [I]Hebr. *that which goeth up* [a]1Kgs. 18:41, 45

2 [I]Hebr. *Hear in hearing*
3 [I]Hebr. *light* [II]Hebr. *wings of the earth*
4 [a]Ps. 29:3; 68:33
5 [a]Job 5:9; 9:10; 36:26; Rev. 15:3
6 [I]Hebr. *and to the shower of rain, and to the showers of rain of his strength* [a]Ps. 147:16, 17
7 [a]Ps. 109:27
8 [a]Ps. 104:22
9 [I]Hebr. *Out of the chamber*

whirlwind:[5591] and cold out of the [II]north.

10 [a]By the breath[5397] of God frost[7140] is given: and the breadth of the waters is straitened.[4164]

11 Also by watering[7377] he wearieth the thick cloud:[5645] he scattereth [I]his bright[216] cloud:[6051]

12 And it is turned[2015] round about by his counsels: that they may [a]do whatsoever he commandeth[6680] them upon the face of the world[8398] in the earth.

13 [a]He causeth it to come, whether for [I]correction,[7626] or [b]for his land,[776] or [c]for mercy.[2617]

14 Hearken[238] unto this, O Job: stand still, and [a]consider[995] the wondrous works[6381] of God.

15 Dost thou know when God[433] disposed[7760] them, and caused the light of his cloud to shine?

16 [a]Dost thou know the balancings of the clouds, the wondrous works[4652] of [b]him which is perfect[8549] in knowledge?[1843]

17 How thy garments *are* warm, when he quieteth[8252] the earth by the south *wind*?

18 Hast thou with him [a]spread out[7554] the sky,[7834] *which is* strong,[2389] *and* as a molten looking glass?[7209]

19 Teach[3045] us what we shall say unto him; *for* we cannot order[6186] *our speech* by reason of darkness.[2822]

20 Shall it be told[5608] him that I speak?[1696] if a man speak,[559] surely he shall be swallowed up.[1104]

21 And now *men* see not the bright light which *is* in the clouds:[7834] but the wind passeth,[5674] and cleanseth[2891] them.

22 [I]Fair weather[2091] cometh out of the north: with God *is* terrible[3372] majesty.[1935]

23 *Touching* the Almighty,[7706] [a]we cannot find him out: [b]*he is* excellent in power, and in judgment,[4941] and in plenty of justice:[6666] he will not afflict.[6031]

24 Men do therefore [a]fear[3372] him: he respecteth[7200] not any *that are* [b]wise[2450] of heart.

God Speaks

38 ⊶ Then the LORD answered Job [a]out of the whirlwind, and said,[559]

2 [a]Who *is* this that darkeneth[2821] counsel[6098] by [b]words[4405] without knowledge?[1847]

⊶ 3 [a]Gird up now thy loins like a man: for I will demand[7592] of thee, and [I]answer thou me.

4 [a]Where wast thou when I laid the foundations[3245] of the earth?[776] declare,[5046] [I]if thou hast understanding.[998]

5 Who hath laid[7760] the measures thereof, if thou knowest?[3045] or who hath stretched the line[6957] upon it?

6 Whereupon are the [I]foundations thereof [II]fastened?[2883] or who laid[3384] the corner stone thereof;

7 When the morning stars sang together, and all [a]the sons[1121] of God[430] shouted for joy?[7321]

8 [a]Or *who* shut up the sea with doors, when it brake forth, *as if* it had issued out of the womb?

9 When I made[7760] the cloud[6051] the garment thereof, and thick darkness[6205] a swaddlingband[2854] for it,

10 And [I][a]brake up[7665] for it my

---

9 [II]Hebr. *scattering winds*
10 [a]Job 38:29, 30; Ps. 147:17, 18
11 [I]Hebr. *the cloud of his light*
12 [a]Ps. 148:8
13 [I]Hebr. *a rod* [a]Ex. 9:18, 23; 1Sam. 12:18, 19; Ezra 10:9; Job 36:31 [b]Job 38:26, 27 [c]2Sam. 21:10; 1Kgs. 18:45
14 [a]Ps. 111:2
16 [a]Job 36:29 [b]Job 36:4
18 [a]Gen. 1:6; Isa. 44:24
22 [I]Hebr. *Gold*
23 [a]1Tim. 6:16 [b]Job 36:5
24 [a]Matt. 10:28 [b]Matt. 11:25; 1Cor. 1:26

1 [a]Ex. 19:16, 18; 1Kgs. 19:11; Ezek. 1:4; Nah. 1:3
2 [a]Job 34:35; 42:3 [b]1Tim. 1:7
3 [I]Hebr. *make me know* [a]Job 40:7
4 [I]Hebr. *if thou knowest understanding* [a]Ps. 104:5; Prov. 8:29; 30:4
6 [I]Hebr. *sockets* [II]Hebr. *made to sink*
7 [a]Job 1:6
8 [a]Gen. 1:9; Ps. 33:7; 104:9; Prov. 8:29; Jer. 5:22
10 [I]Or, *established my decree upon it* [a]Job 26:10

⊶ **38:1—42:6** These chapters record the seventy-four questions that God asked of Job. They are given not to answer the mystery of Job's suffering nor to vindicate God Himself, for in doing so, it would allow men to judge Him. Also, these questions are not designed to reveal God's omnipotence, for Job's submission in this manner would have been fatalism, not scriptural resignation. In addition to this, these challenges to Job were not given to reveal God's infinite wisdom. (There are many marvelous things about God and his works which are never answered.) God's purpose was to rescue Job. It is important to remember that faith does not have to look forward to vindication at the resurrection in order to survive.

⊶ **38:3** The word translated "man" in the Hebrew is *gever* (1397), which pictures man at his best and proudest moments.

decreed[2706] *place,* and set[7760] bars and doors,

11 And said, Hitherto shalt thou come, but no further: and here shall [I]thy proud[1347] waves [a]be stayed?

12 Hast thou [a]commanded[6680] the morning since thy days; *and* caused[3045] the dayspring[7837] to know[3045] his place;

13 That it might take hold of the [I]ends of the earth, that [a]the wicked[7563] might be shaken[5287] out of it?

14 It is turned[2015] as clay *to* the seal;[2368] and they stand as a garment.

15 And from the wicked their [a]light[216] is withholden,[4513] and [b]the high arm shall be broken.[7665]

16 Hast thou [a]entered into the springs of the sea? or hast thou walked in the search[2714] of the depth?

17 Have [a]the gates of death[4194] been opened[1540] unto thee? or hast thou seen the doors of the shadow of death?[6757]

18 Hast thou perceived[995] the breadth of the earth? declare if thou knowest it all.

19 Where *is* the way[1870] *where* light dwelleth?[7931] and *as for* darkness,[2822] where *is* the place thereof,

20 That thou shouldest take it [I]to the bound thereof, and that thou shouldest know[995] the paths *to* the house[1004] thereof?

21 Knowest thou *it,* because thou wast then born? or *because* the number of thy days *is* great?

22 Hast thou entered into [a]the treasures[214] of the snow? or hast thou seen the treasures of the hail,

23 [a]Which I have reserved against the time[6256] of trouble,[6862] against the day[3117] of battle and war?

24 By what way is the light parted,[2505] *which* scattereth the east wind upon the earth?

25 Who [a]hath divided[6385] a watercourse for the overflowing of waters,[7858] or a way for the lightning of thunder;

26 To cause it to rain on the earth, *where* no man[376] *is; on* the wilderness,[4057] wherein *there is* no man;[120]

27 [a]To satisfy the desolate[7722] and waste[4875] *ground;* and to cause the bud of the tender herb to spring forth?

28 [a]Hath the rain a father?[1] or who hath begotten[3205] the drops of dew?

29 Out of whose womb[990] came the ice? and the [a]hoary frost[3713] of heaven,[8064] who hath gendered it?

30 The waters are hid as *with* a stone, and the face of the deep [I]is [a]frozen.[3920]

31 Canst thou bind the sweet influences[4575] of [I][a]Pleiades,[3598] or loose the bands of [II]Orion?[3685]

32 Canst thou bring forth [I]Mazzaroth[4216] in his season?[6256] or canst thou [II]guide[5148] Arcturus[5906] with his sons?

33 Knowest thou [a]the ordinances[2708] of heaven? canst thou set the dominion thereof in the earth?

34 Canst thou lift up thy voice to the clouds,[5645] that abundance of waters may cover[3680] thee?

35 Canst thou send lightnings, that they may go, and say[559] unto thee, [I]Here we *are?*

36 [a]Who hath put wisdom[2451] in the inward parts?[2910] or who hath given understanding to the heart?[7907]

37 Who can number[5608] the clouds[7834] in wisdom? or [I]who can stay the bottles[5305] of heaven,

38 [I]When the dust[6083] [II]groweth into hardness,[4165] and the clods cleave fast together?

39 [a]Wilt thou hunt the prey for the lion? or fill [I]the appetite of the young lions,

40 When they couch in *their* dens, *and* abide in the covert[5521] to lie in wait?

41 [a]Who provideth for the raven his food? when his young ones cry[7768] unto God, they wander[8582] for lack of meat.

39

Knowest[3045] thou the time[6256] when the wild goats of the rock bring forth? *or* canst thou mark[8104] when [a]the hinds[355] do calve?[2342]

2 Canst thou number[5608] the months *that* they fulfil? or knowest thou the time when they bring forth?

3 They bow[3766] themselves, they

---

11 [I]Hebr. *the pride of thy waves* [a]Ps. 89:9; 93:4

12 [a]Ps. 74:16; 148:5

13 [I]Hebr. *wings* [a]Ps. 104:35

15 [a]Job 18:5 [b]Ps. 10:15

16 [a]Ps. 77:19

17 [a]Ps. 9:13

20 [I]Or, *at*

22 [a]Ps. 135:7

23 [a]Ex. 9:18; Josh. 10:11; Isa. 30:30; Ezek. 13:11, 13; Rev. 16:21

25 [a]Job 28:26

27 [a]Ps. 107:35

28 [a]Ps. 147:8; Jer. 14:22

29 [a]Ps. 147:16

30 [I]Hebr. *is taken* [a]Job 37:10

31 [I]Or, *The seven stars;* [II]Hebr. *Cesil* [a]Job 9:9; Amos 5:8

32 [I]Or, *The twelve signs* [II]Hebr. *guide them*

33 [a]Jer. 31:35

35 [I]Hebr. *Behold us*

36 [a]Job 32:8; Ps. 51:6; Eccl. 2:26

37 [I]Hebr. *who can cause to lie down*

38 [I]Or, *When the dust is turned into mire* [II]Hebr. *is poured*

39 [I]Hebr. *the life* [a]Ps. 104:21; 145:15

41 [a]Ps. 147:9; Matt. 6:26

1 [a]Ps. 29:9

bring forth their young ones, they cast out their sorrows.[2256]

4 Their young ones[1121] are in good liking, they grow up with corn; they go forth, and return[7725] not unto them.

5 Who hath sent out the wild ass free? or who hath loosed the bands of the wild ass?

6 [a]Whose house[1004] I have made[7760] the wilderness,[6160] and the [I]barren[4420] land his dwellings.[4908]

7 He scorneth the multitude of the city, neither regardeth[8085] he the crying [I][a]of the driver.

8 The range of the mountains *is* his pasture, and he searcheth after every green thing.

9 Will the [a]unicorn be willing[14] to serve[5647] thee, or abide by thy crib?[18]

10 Canst thou bind the unicorn with his band in the furrow?[8525] or will he harrow[7702] the valleys after thee?

11 Wilt thou trust[982] him, because his strength[3581] *is* great? or wilt thou leave[5800] thy labour to him?

12 Wilt thou believe[539] him, that he will bring home thy seed,[2233] and gather[622] *it into* thy barn?

13 *Gavest thou* the goodly wings unto the peacocks? or [I]wings and feathers unto the ostrich?

14 Which leaveth her eggs in the earth,[776] and warmeth them in dust,[6083]

15 And forgetteth that the foot may crush them, or that the wild beast[2416] may break them.

16 She is [a]hardened[7188] against her young ones, as though *they were* not hers: her labour is in vain without fear;[6343]

17 Because God[433] hath deprived her of wisdom,[2451] neither hath he [a]imparted[2505] to her understanding.[998]

18 What time she lifteth up[4754] herself on high, she scorneth the horse and his rider.

19 Hast thou given the horse strength?[1369] hast thou clothed his neck with thunder?

20 Canst thou make him afraid[7493] as a grasshopper? the glory[1935] of his nostrils *is* [I]terrible.[367]

21 [I]He paweth[2658] in the valley, and rejoiceth in *his* strength: [a]he goeth on to meet [II]the armed men.

22 He mocketh at fear, and is not affrighted;[2865] neither turneth he back from the sword.[2719]

23 The quiver rattleth against him, the glittering spear and the shield.

24 He swalloweth[1572] the ground[776] with fierceness and rage:[7267] neither believeth[539] he that *it is* the sound of the trumpet.

25 He saith[559] among the trumpets, Ha, ha; and he smelleth[7306] the battle afar off, the thunder of the captains,[8269] and the shouting.

26 Doth the hawk fly by thy wisdom,[998] *and* stretch her wings toward the south?

27 Doth the eagle mount up [I]at thy command, and [a]make her nest on high?

28 She dwelleth[7931] and abideth[3885] on the rock, upon the crag of the rock, and the strong place.

29 From thence she seeketh the prey, *and* her eyes behold afar off.

30 Her young ones also suck up blood:[1818] and [a]where the slain[2491] *are,* there *is* she.

40 Moreover the LORD answered Job, and said,[559]

2 Shall[3250] he that [a]contendeth[7378] with the Almighty[7706] instruct[3250] *him?* he that reproveth[3198] God,[433] let him answer it.

Job Answers God

3 Then Job answered the LORD, and said,

4 [a]Behold, I am vile;[7043] what shall I answer[7725] thee? [b]I will lay[7760] mine hand[3027] upon my mouth.[6310]

5 Once have I spoken;[1696] but I will not answer: yea, twice; but I will proceed no further.

God Speaks Again

6 [a]Then answered the LORD unto Job out of the whirlwind, and said,

---

6 [I]Hebr. *salt places* [a]Job 24:5; Jer. 2:24; Hos. 8:9

7 [I]Hebr. *of the exactor* [a]Job 3:18

9 [a]Num. 23:22; Deut. 33:17

13 [I]Or, *the feathers of the stork and ostrich*

16 [a]Lam. 4:3

17 [a]Job 35:11

20 [I]Hebr. *terror*

21 [I]Or, His feet *dig* [II]Hebr. *the armor* [a]Jer. 8:6

27 [I]Hebr. *by thy mouth* [a]Jer. 49:16; Obad. 1:4

30 [a]Matt. 24:28; Luke 17:37

2 [a]Job 33:13

4 [a]Ezra 9:6; Job 42:6; Ps. 51:4 [b]Job 29:9; Ps. 39:9

6 [a]Job 38:1

7 [a]Gird up thy loins now like a
man:[1397] [b]I will demand[7592] of thee, and
declare thou unto me.
🔑 8 [a]Wilt thou also disannul[6565] my
judgment?[4941] wilt thou condemn[7561] me,
that thou mayest be righteous?[6663]
9 Hast thou an arm like God?[410] or
canst thou thunder with [a]a voice like
him?
10 [a]Deck thyself now *with*
majesty[1347] and excellency;[1363] and array
thyself with glory[1935] and beauty.[1926]
11 Cast abroad the rage[5678] of thy
wrath:[639] and behold[7200] every one *that is*
proud, and abase[8213] him.
12 Look on every one *that is* [a]proud,
and bring him low; and tread down the
wicked[7563] in their place.
13 Hide[2934] them in the dust together; *and* bind[2280] their faces in
secret.[2934]
14 Then will I also confess[3034] unto
thee that thine own right hand can
save[3467] thee.
15 Behold now [I]behemoth,[930] which I
made[6213] with thee; he eateth grass as an
ox.
16 Lo now, his strength *is* in his
loins, and his force[202] *is* in the navel of
his belly.[990]
17 [I]He moveth[2654] his tail like a
cedar: the sinews of his stones are
wrapped together.
18 His bones[6106] *are as* strong pieces
of brass; his bones[1634] *are* like bars of
iron.
19 He *is* the chief of the ways[1870] of
God: he that made him can make his
sword[2719] to approach[5066] *unto him.*
20 Surely the mountains [a]bring him
forth[5375] food, where all the beasts[2416] of
the field[7704] play.
21 He lieth under the shady trees, in
the covert[5643] of the reed, and fens.[1207]
22 The shady trees cover him *with*
their shadow;[6752] the willows of the
brook compass him about.
23 Behold, [I]he drinketh up a river,
and hasteth[2648] not: he trusteth[982] that he
can draw up Jordan into his mouth.
24 [I][a]He taketh it with his eyes: *his*
nose pierceth[5344] through snares.[4170]

41

Canst thou draw out [a]leviathan[3882]
with an hook?[100] or his tongue
with a cord[2256] [I]*which* thou lettest down?
2 Canst thou [a]put an hook[2443] into
his nose? or bore[5344] his jaw through
with a thorn?
3 Will he make many supplica-
tions[8469] unto thee? will he speak[1696] soft
words unto thee?
4 Will he make a covenant[1285] with
thee? wilt thou take him for a servant[5650]
for ever?[5769]
5 Wilt thou play with him as *with* a
bird? or wilt thou bind him for thy maidens?
6 Shall the companions make a
banquet[3738] of him? shall they part him
among the merchants?
7 Canst thou fill his skin[5785] with
barbed irons?[7905] or his head with fish
spears?[6767]
8 Lay[7760] thine hand[3709] upon him,
remember[2142] the battle, do no more.
9 Behold, the hope[8431] of him is in
vain:[3576] shall not *one* be cast down even
at the sight of him?
10 None *is so* fierce[393] that dare stir
him up: who then is able to stand before
me?
11 [a]Who hath prevented[6923] me, that
I should repay[7999] *him?* [b]*whatsoever is*
under the whole heaven[8064] is mine.
12 I will not conceal[2790] his parts,
nor his power, nor his comely[2433] proportion.
13 Who can discover[1540] the face of
his garment? *or* who can come *to him*
[I]with his double bridle?
14 Who can open the doors of his
face? his teeth are terrible[367] round about.
15 *His* [I]scales *are his* pride,[1346] shut
up together *as with* a close seal.[2368]

7 [a]Job 38:3 [b]Job 42:4
8 [a]Ps. 51:4; Rom. 3:4
9 [a]Job 37:4; Ps. 29:3, 4
10 [a]Ps. 93:1; 104:1
12 [a]Isa. 2:12; Dan. 4:37
15 [I]Or, *the elephant*
17 [I]Or, *He setteth up*
20 [a]Ps. 104:14
23 [I]Hebr. *he oppresseth*
24 [I]Or, *Will any take him in his sight, or, bore his nose with a gin* [a]Job 41:1, 2
1 [I]Hebr. *which thou drownest* [a]Ps. 104:26; Isa. 27:1
2 [a]Isa. 37:29
11 [a]Rom. 11:35 [b]Ex. 19:5; Deut. 10:14; Ps. 24:1; 50:12; 1Cor. 10:26, 28
13 [I]Or, *within*
15 [I]Hebr. *strong pieces of shields*

🔑 **40:8, 9** God sees the heart and knows when there is a need for correction that man cannot see. Job had no authority to judge God.

16 One is so near[5066] to another, that no air can come between them.

17 They are joined one[376] to another, they stick together, that they cannot be sundered.6504

18 By his [I]neesings a light[216] doth shine,[1984] and his eyes *are* like the eyelids of the morning.

19 Out of his mouth go burning lamps,3940 *and* sparks of fire leap out.4922

20 Out of his nostrils goeth smoke, as *out* of a seething5301 pot or caldron.

21 His breath[5315] kindleth coals, and a flame goeth out of his mouth.

22 In his neck remaineth strength, and [I]sorrow[1670] is turned into joy before him.

23 [I]The flakes4651 of his flesh[1320] are joined together: they are firm in themselves; they cannot be moved.

24 His heart[3820] is as firm as a stone; yea, as hard as a piece of the nether8482 *millstone.*

25 When he raiseth up himself, the mighty[410] are afraid:[1481] by reason of breakings[7667] they purify themselves.[2398]

26 The sword[2719] of him that layeth at him cannot hold: the spear, the dart, nor the [I]habergeon.8302

27 He esteemeth[2803] iron as straw, *and* brass as rotten wood.

28 The arrow cannot make him flee: slingstones are turned[2015] with him into stubble.

29 Darts are counted[2803] as stubble: he laugheth at the shaking7494 of a spear.

30 [I]Sharp stones[2789] *are* under him: he spreadeth sharp pointed things upon the mire.

31 He maketh the deep to boil like a pot: he maketh[7760] the sea like a pot of ointment.

32 He maketh a path to shine after him; *one* would think[2803] the deep *to be* hoary.[7872]

33 Upon earth[6083] there is not his like, [I]who is made[6213] without fear.[2844]

34 He beholdeth[7200] all high *things:* he *is* a king over all the children[1121] of pride.7830

Job's Humility

42 Then Job answered the LORD, and said,[559]

2 I know[3045] that thou [a]canst do every *thing,* and *that* [I]no thought[4209] can be withholden1219 from thee.

3 [a]Who *is* he that hideth counsel[6098] without knowledge?[3045] therefore have I uttered[5046] that I understood[995] not; [b]things too wonderful[6381] for me, which I knew not.

4 Hear, I beseech thee,[4994] and I will speak: [a]I will demand[7592] of thee, and declare thou unto me.

5 I have heard[8085] of thee by the hearing[8088] of the ear: but now mine eye seeth[7200] thee.

6 Wherefore I [a]abhor *myself,* and repent[5162] in dust[6083] and ashes.

God Rebukes Job's Friends

7 And it was *so,* that after the LORD had spoken[1696] these words[1697] unto Job, the LORD said to Eliphaz the Temanite, My wrath[639] is kindled[2734] against thee, and against thy two friends:[7453] for ye have not spoken of me *the thing that is* right, as my servant[5650] Job *hath.*

8 Therefore take unto you now [a]seven bullocks and seven rams, and [b]go to my servant Job, and offer up for yourselves a burnt offering;[5930] and my servant Job shall [c]pray[6419] for you: for [I][d]him will I accept:[5375] lest I deal[6213] with you *after your* folly,5039 in that ye have not spoken of me *the thing which is* right, like my servant Job.

9 So Eliphaz the Temanite and Bildad the Shuhite *and* Zophar the Naamathite went, and did[6213] according as the LORD commanded[1696] them: the LORD also accepted[5375] [I]Job.

Restoration of Job's Prosperity

10 [a]And the LORD turned the captivity[7622] of Job, when he prayed[6419] for his friends: also the LORD [I]gave Job [b]twice as much as he had before.

18 [I]Or, *sneezes*

22 [I]Hebr. *sorrow rejoiceth*

23 [I]Hebr. *The fallings*

26 [I]Or, *breastplate*

30 [I]Hebr. *Sharp pieces of potsherd*

33 [I]Or, *who behave themselves without fear*

2 [I]Or, *no thought of thine can be hindered* [a]Gen. 18:14; Matt. 19:26; Mark 10:27; 14:37; Luke 18:27

3 [a]Job 38:2 [b]Ps. 40:5; 131:1; 139:6

4 [a]Job 38:3; 40:7

6 [a]Ezra 9:6; Job 40:4

8 [I]Hebr. *his face,* or, *person* [a]Num. 23:1 [b]Matt. 5:24 [c]Gen. 20:17; James 5:15, 16; 1John 5:16; [d]1Sam. 25:35; Mal. 1:8

9 [I]Hebr. *the face of Job*

10 [I]Hebr. *added all that had been to Job unto the double* [a]Ps. 14:7; 126:1 [b]Isa. 40:2

11 Then came there unto him [a]all his brethren,[251] and all his sisters,[269] and all they that had been of his acquaintance[3045] before, and did eat bread with him in his house:[1004] and they bemoaned him, and comforted[5162] him over all the evil[7451] that the LORD had brought upon him: every man[376] also gave him a piece of money, and every one an earring of gold.

12 So the LORD blessed[1288] [a]the latter end[319] of Job more than his beginning:[7225] for he had [b]fourteen thousand sheep, and six thousand camels, and a thousand yoke of oxen, and a thousand she asses.

13 [a]He had also seven sons[1121] and three daughters.

14 And he called[7121] the name of the first, Jemima; and the name of the second, Kezia; and the name of the third, Kerenhappuch.

15 And in all the land were no women[802] found *so* fair as the daughters of Job: and their father gave them inheritance[5159] among their brethren.

16 After this [a]lived[2421] Job an hundred and forty years, and saw[7200] his sons, and his sons' sons, *even* four generations.[1755]

17 So Job died,[4191] *being* old[2205] and [a]full of days.

11 [a]Job 19:13

12 [a]Job 8:7; James 5:11 [b]Job 1:3

13 [a]Job 1:2

16 [a]Job 5:26; Prov. 3:16

17 [a]Gen. 25:8

THE PSALMS

The Hebrew title for this book is "Book of Praises." The English title, however, was derived from the Greek word *psalmoí* (5568), which means "pious songs" or "music of stringed instruments."

The Book of Psalms is a collection of the works of at least six authors. The titles of the psalms credit David with writing seventy-three psalms, and two others are assigned to him in the New Testament (Ps. 2, see Acts 4:25; Ps. 95, see Heb. 4:7). Asaph was the author of twelve psalms (Ps. 50; 73—83), or at least he is responsible for their preservation. The sons of Korah wrote eleven psalms (Ps. 42; 44—49; 84; 85; 87; 88); Solomon composed two (Ps. 72; 127); Psalm 89 is attributed to Ethan; and Moses is the author of Psalm 90 (and possibly Ps. 91).

The Book of Psalms was originally five separate books (Ps. 1—41; 42—72; 73—89; 90—106; 107—150). Each of the first four books conclude with a doxology and the fifth is a fitting finale for the book as a whole. Consequently, it is believed that the psalms were used for liturgical purposes. This is supported by Jewish tradition and the fact that the five books of Psalms correspond to the five books of the Pentateuch. The individual psalms are often classified according to their content: Didactic Psalms are those which give instruction (e.g., Ps. 119); the Messianic Psalms contain prophecy relating to the Messiah (see note on Ps. 22:1–31); the Imprecatory Psalms involve pleas to God for the punishment of the wicked (see note on Ps. 109:1–29); Penitential Psalms express not only the feelings of a repentant heart, but also an appeal for divine cleansing (Ps. 6; 32; 38; 51; 102; 130; 143).

Other psalms are classified according to their titles: psalms of degrees or ascent were sung at the beginning of the worship services at the temple and by those who were traveling up to Jerusalem (Ps. 120—134); *miktām* psalms deal with atonement or the covering over of sin (Ps. 16; 56—60).

The Psalms powerfully convey the feelings common to believers of all ages. The nature of Hebrew poetry (see introduction to Job) is especially well suited to express strong feelings. The psalms are intimately personal in that they explore the whole realm of human emotion: from deep despair to ecstatic delight; from a yearning for vengeance to a spirit of humility and forgiveness; from earnest pleading with God for protection to jubilant praise for His deliverance. The general principle that can be seen in all of the psalms is that the writers have a serene confidence in God's guidance and provision.

BOOK I

The Righteous Are Blessed

1 Blessed[835] [a]*is* the man[376] that walketh not in the counsel of the [I]ungodly,[7563] nor standeth in the way[1870] of sinners,[2400] [b]nor sitteth in the seat[4186] of the scornful.[3887]

2 But [a]his delight[2656] *is* in the law[8451] of the LORD; [b]and in his law doth he meditate[1897] day[3119] and night.[3915]

3 And he shall be like a tree [a]planted by the rivers of water, that bringeth forth his fruit in his season;[6256] his leaf also shall not [I]wither; and whatsoever he doeth[6213] shall [b]prosper.

1 [I]Or, *wicked* [a]Prov. 4:14, 15 [b]Ps. 26:4; Jer. 15:17
2 [a]Ps. 119:35, 47, 92 [b]Josh. 1:8; Ps. 119:1, 97
3 [I]Hebr. *fade* [a]Jer. 17:8; Ezek. 47:12 [b]Gen. 39:3, 23; Ps. 128:2; Isa. 3:10

1:1 The reasons for being "blessed" are not the same here as in Psalm 32:1. Here blessings are a result of right conduct, while Psalm 32 speaks of blessings that come from God's forgiveness. The forgiveness of God in Psalm 32 makes it possible to accomplish the practical righteousness of Psalm 1. However, both situations result in the spiritual and emotional joy and contentment which the word "blessedness" expresses.

4 The ungodly *are* not so: but *are*
[a]like the chaff which the wind[7307] driveth away.
5 Therefore the ungodly shall not
stand in the judgment,[4941] nor sinners in
the congregation[5712] of the righteous.[6662]
6 For [a]the LORD knoweth the way of
the righteous: but the way of the ungodly shall perish.[6]

The Anointed One

2 🔑 Why [a]do[7283] the heathen[1471]
[I]rage,[7283] and the people[3816]
[II]imagine[1897] a vain thing?
2 The kings[4428] of the earth[776] set
themselves,[3320] and the rulers[7336] take
counsel[3245] together, against the LORD,
and against his [a]anointed,[4899] *saying,*
3 [a]Let us break their bands asunder,[5423] and cast away their cords from
us.
4 [a]He that sitteth in the heavens[8064]
[b]shall laugh: the Lord[136] shall have them
in derision.
5 Then shall he speak[1696] unto them
in his wrath,[639] and [I]vex[926] them in his
sore displeasure.
6 Yet have I [I]set[5258] my king[4428]
[IIa]upon my holy[6944] hill of Zion.
7 I will declare[5608] [I]the decree: the
LORD hath said unto me, [a]Thou *art* my
Son;[1121] this day[3117] have I begotten[3205]
thee.
8 [a]Ask[7592] of me, and I shall give
thee the heathen *for* thine inheritance,[5159]
and the uttermost parts of the earth *for*
thy possession.[272]
🔑 9 [a]Thou shalt break[7489] them with a
rod[7626] of iron; thou shalt dash them in
pieces like a potter's[3335] vessel.
10 Be wise[7919] now therefore, O ye
kings: be instructed,[3256] ye judges[8199] of
the earth.
11 [a]Serve[5647] the LORD with fear,[3374]
and rejoice [b]with trembling.[7460]
12 [a]Kiss[5401] the Son, lest he be
angry,[599] and ye perish[6] *from* the
way,[1870] when [b]his wrath is kindled but
a little. [c]Blessed[835] *are* all they that put
their trust[2620] in him.

A Morning Prayer

A Psalm of David, when he fled from Absalom his son.

3 LORD, [a]how are they increased that
trouble me! many *are* they that rise
up against me.
🔑 2 Many *there be* which say[559] of my
soul,[5315] [a]*There is* no help[3444] for him in
God.[430] Selah.
3 But thou, O LORD, *art* [a]a shield [I]for
me; my glory,[3519] and [b]the lifter up of
mine head.
4 I cried[7121] unto the LORD with my
voice, and [a]he heard me out of his
[b]holy[6944] hill. Selah.
5 [a]I laid me down and slept; I
awaked; for the LORD sustained[5564] me.
6 [a]I will not be afraid[3372] of ten thousands of people,[5971] that have set *themselves* against me round about.

4 [a]Job 21:18; Ps. 35:5; Isa. 17:13; 29:5; Hos. 13:3 **6** [a]Ps. 37:18; Nah. 1:7; John 10:14; 2Tim. 2:19

1 [I]Or, *tumultuously assemble* [II]Hebr. *meditate* [a]Ps. 46:6; Acts 4:25, 26 **2** [a]Ps. 45:7; John 1:41 **3** [a]Jer. 5:5; Luke 19:14 **4** [a]Ps. 11:4 [b]Ps. 37:13; 59:8; Prov. 1:26 **5** [I]Or, *trouble* **6** [I]Hebr. *anointed* [II]Hebr. *upon Zion, the hill of my holiness* [a]2Sam. 5:7 **7** [I]Or, *for a decree* [a]Acts 13:33; Heb. 1:5; 5:5 **8** [a]Ps. 22:27; 72:8; 89:27; Dan. 7:13, 14; John 17:4, 5; 19:15 **9** [a]Ps. 89:23; Rev. 2:27; 12:5 **11** [a]Heb. 12:28 [b]Phil. 2:12 **12** [a]Gen. 41:40; 1Sam. 10:1; John 5:23 [b]Rev. 6:16, 17 [c]Ps. 34:8; 84:12; Prov. 16:20; Isa. 30:18; Jer. 17:7; Rom. 9:33; 10:11; 1Pet. 2:6

1 [a]2Sam. 15:12; 16:15 **2** [a]2Sam. 16:8; Ps. 71:11 **3** [I]Or, *about* [a]Gen. 15:1; Ps. 28:7; 119:114 [b]Ps. 27:6 **4** [a]Ps. 34:4 [b]Ps. 2:6; 43:3; 99:9 **5** [a]Lev. 26:6; Ps. 4:8; Prov. 3:24 **6** [a]Ps. 27:3

🔑 **2:1–9** See the note on Psalm 22:1–31 for a discussion of the Messianic Psalms.

🔑 **2:9** The "rod" that Christ has is not a scepter, an emblem of his royal office, but is in actuality a rod of correction. The fact that the rod is made of iron indicates the severity and harshness of the judgment that will be meted out by Him at his return (Rev. 19:15). This harsh judgment is consistent with the meekness and gentleness of Christ. Meekness does not exclude anger, but simply means that one is angry for the right reasons, at the right person, and at the right time (John 2:13–17). Jesus could truthfully claim to be gentle without contradicting His claim to be the Judge (Matt. 11:28–30; 23:2–39).

🔑 **3:2** The word "Selah" occurs frequently in the Psalms, indicating a transition. It is probably a musical or liturgical note that is not part of the text of the psalm. Other musical or liturgical terms occur in the Psalms, and are easily identified because they are left untranslated (*higāyōn, shigāyōn, miktām*, etc.). These terms are so old that even the ancient rabbis were unsure of their precise meanings.

7 Arise, O LORD; save[3467] me, O my
God: [a]for thou hast smitten[5221] all mine
enemies *upon* the cheek bone; thou hast
broken[7665] the teeth of the ungodly.[7563]
8 [a]Salvation[3444] *belongeth* unto the
LORD: thy blessing[1293] *is* upon thy people.
Selah.

An Evening Prayer

To the chief Musician on Neginoth, A Psalm of David.

4 🔑 Hear6030 me when I call,[7121] O
God[430] of my righteousness:[6664] thou
hast enlarged me *when I was* in distress;
[I]have mercy[2603] upon me, and hear[8085]
my prayer.[8605]
2 O ye sons of men,[376] how long *will*
ye turn my glory[3519] into shame? *how*
long will ye love[157] vanity, *and* seek after
leasing?[3577] Selah.
3 But know that [a]the LORD hath set
apart6395 him that is godly[2623] for himself: the LORD will hear when I call unto
him.
4 [a]Stand in awe,[7264] and sin[2398] not:
[b]commune with your own heart3824 upon
your bed, and be still. Selah.
5 Offer[2076] [a]the sacrifices[2077] of righteousness, and [b]put your trust[982] in the
LORD.
6 *There be* many that say,[559] Who
will shew[7200] us *any* good?[2896] [a]LORD, lift
thou up the light[216] of thy countenance
upon us.
7 Thou hast put [a]gladness in my
heart,[3820] more than in the time[6256] *that*
their corn and their wine increased.

7 [a]Job 16:10; 29:17; Ps. 58:6; Lam. 3:30
8 [a]Prov. 21:31; Isa. 43:11; Jer. 3:23; Hos. 13:4; Jon. 2:9; Rev. 7:10; 19:1

1 [I]Or, *be gracious unto me*
3 [a]2Tim. 2:19; 2Pet. 2:9
4 [a]Eph. 4:26; Ps. 77:6; 2Cor. 13:5
5 [a]Deut. 33:19; Ps. 50:14; 51:19; 2Sam. 15:12 [b]Ps. 37:3; 62:8
6 [a]Num. 6:26; Ps. 80:3, 7, 19; 119:135
7 [a]Isa. 9:3
8 [a]Job 11:18, 19; Ps. 3:5 [b]Lev. 25:18, 19; 26:5; Deut. 12:10

2 [a]Ps. 3:4 [b]Ps. 65:2
3 [a]Ps. 30:5; 88:13; 130:6
5 [I]Hebr. *before thine eyes* [a]Hab. 1:13
6 [I]Hebr. *the man of bloods and deceit* [a]Rev. 21:8 [b]Ps. 55:23
7 [I]Hebr. *the temple of thy holiness* [a]1Kgs. 8:29, 30, 35, 38; Ps. 28:2; 132:7; 138:2
8 [I]Hebr. *those which observe me* [a]Ps. 25:5 [b]Ps. 25:4; 27:11 [c]Ps. 27:11
9 [I]Or, *steadfastness* [II]Hebr. *in his mouth,* that is, *in the mouth of any of them*

8 [a]I will both lay me down in peace,
and sleep: [b]for thou, LORD, only makest
me dwell in safety.

A Prayer for Protection

To the chief Musician upon Nehiloth, A Psalm of David.

5 Give ear[238] to my words,[561] O LORD,
consider[995] my meditation.
2 Hearken[7181] unto the [a]voice of my
cry, my King,[4428] and my God:[430] for
[b]unto thee will I pray.[6419]
3 [a]My voice shalt thou hear[8085] in the
morning, O LORD; in the morning will I
direct *my prayer* unto thee, and will look
up.
4 For thou *art* not a God[410] that hath
pleasure[2655] in wickedness:[7562] neither
shall[1481] evil[7451] dwell[1481] with thee.
🔑 5 [a]The foolish[1984] shall not stand [I]in
thy sight: thou hatest[8130] all workers of
iniquity.[205]
6 [a]Thou shalt destroy[6] them that
speak[1696] leasing:[3577] [b]the LORD will
abhor[8581] [I]the bloody[1818] and deceitful[4820]
man.[376]
7 But as for me, I will come *into*
thy house[1004] in the multitude of thy
mercy:[2617] *and* in thy fear[3374] will I
worship[7812] [a]toward [I]thy holy[6944] temple.[1964]
8 [a]Lead[5148] me, O LORD, in thy righteousness[6666] because of [I][b]mine enemies;
[c]make[3474] thy way[1870] straight[3474] before
my face.
9 For *there is* no [I]faithfulness[3559] [II]in
their mouth;[6310] their inward part[7130] *is*

🔑 **4:1** This psalm was written while David was fleeing from Absalom (2 Sam. 15—18).

🔑 **5:5** There are differing views as to what is meant when it says that God hates those who sin (Ps. 11:5). The first view suggests that God hates only the sin that the wicked do and not the people who commit the sins. They propose that if God hates sinners for their sin, then there is no hope for those who are believers, for they still have a sin nature and still commit sin (Rom. 7:14–20; 1 John 3:6–9). The problem with this view is that there is nothing in the context or grammar of the passage to support this understanding of the verse. Simply stated, "God hates all those who do iniquity."

Others believe that the Scriptures teach that God has in fact chosen to love some and hate others (2 Chr. 19:2; Mal. 1:2, 3). Of those who hold to this theory, some propose that God chooses to hate only those who remain in their sins, and to love those who come to Him in repentance. Others who hold this view say that God chooses to love some and not others based solely on His sovereign purpose.

[II]very wickedness;[1942] [a]their throat *is* an open sepulchre;[6913] [b]they flatter with their tongue.

10 [I]Destroy[816] thou them, O God; [a]let them fall [II]by their own counsels; cast them out in the multitude of their transgressions;[6588] for they have rebelled[4784] against thee.

11 But let all those that put their trust[2620] in thee [a]rejoice: let them ever shout for joy, because [I]thou defendest[5526] them: let them also that love[157] thy name be joyful in thee.

12 For thou, LORD, [a]wilt bless[1288] the righteous;[6662] with favour[7522] wilt thou [I]compass him as *with* a shield.

A Prayer for Mercy in Time of Trouble

To the chief Musician on Neginoth upon Sheminith, A Psalm of David.

6 O [a]LORD, rebuke[3198] me not in thine anger,[639] neither chasten me in thy hot displeasure.[2534]

2 [a]Have mercy[2603] upon me, O LORD; for I *am* weak: O LORD, [b]heal me; for my bones[6106] are vexed.[926]

3 My soul[5315] is also sore vexed: but thou, O LORD, [a]how long?

4 Return,[7725] O LORD, deliver[2502] my soul: oh save[3467] me for thy mercies' sake.

🔑 5 [a]For in death[4194] *there is* no remembrance[2143] of thee: in the grave[7585] who shall give thee thanks?

6 I am weary with my groaning; [I]all the night[3915] make I my bed to swim; I water my couch with my tears.

7 [a]Mine eye is consumed because of grief;[3708] it waxeth old because of all mine enemies.

8 [a]Depart[5493] from me, all ye workers

9 [II]wickednesses [a]Luke 11:44; Rom. 3:13 [b]Ps. 62:4

10 [I]Or, *Make them guilty* [II]Or, *from their counsels* [a]2Sam. 15:31; 17:14, 23

11 [I]Hebr. *thou coverest over,* or, *protectest them* [a]Isa. 65:13

12 [I]Hebr. *crown him* [a]Ps. 115:13

1 [a]Ps. 38:1; Jer. 10:24; 46:28

2 [a]Ps. 41:4 [b]Hos. 6:1

3 [a]Ps. 90:13

5 [a]Ps. 30:9; 88:11; 115:17; 118:17; Isa. 38:18

6 [I]Or, *every night*

7 [a]Job 17:7; Ps. 31:9; 38:10; 88:9; Lam. 5:17

8 [a]Ps. 119:115; Matt. 7:23; 25:41; Luke 13:27 [b]Ps. 3:4

1 [a]Ps. 31:15

2 [I]Hebr. *not a deliverer* [a]Isa. 38:13 [b]Ps. 50:22

3 [a]2Sam. 16:7, 8 [b]1Sam. 24:11

4 [a]1Sam. 24:7; 26:9

6 [a]Ps. 94:2 [b]Ps. 44:23

8 [a]Ps. 18:20; 35:24

of iniquity;[205] for the LORD hath [b]heard[8005] the voice of my weeping.

9 The LORD[3068] hath heard my supplication;[8467] the LORD will receive my prayer.[8605]

10 Let all mine enemies be ashamed and sore vexed: let them return *and* be ashamed[954] suddenly.

A Prayer for Justice

Shiggaion of David, which he sang unto the LORD, concerning the words of Cush the Benjamite.

7 🔑 O LORD my God,[430] in thee do I put my trust:[2620] [a]save[3467] me from all them that persecute me, and deliver[5337] me:

2 [a]Lest he tear my soul[5315] like a lion, [b]rending *it* in pieces,[6561] while *there is* [I]none to deliver.

3 O LORD my God, [a]if I have done[6213] this; if there be [b]iniquity[5766] in my hands;[3709]

4 If I have rewarded[1580] evil[7451] unto him that was at peace[7999] with me; (yea, [a]I have delivered[2502] him that without cause is mine enemy:)

5 Let the enemy persecute my soul, and take *it;* yea, let him tread down my life[2416] upon the earth,[776] and lay mine honour[3519] in the dust.[6083] Selah.

6 Arise, O LORD, in thine anger,[639] [a]lift up thyself[5375] because of the rage[5678] of mine enemies: and [b]awake for me *to* the judgment[4941] *that* thou hast commanded.[6680]

7 So shall the congregation[5712] of the people[3816] compass thee about: for their sakes therefore return[7725] thou on high.

8 The LORD shall judge[1777] the people:[5971] judge[8199] me, O LORD, [a]according

🔑 **6:5** This highly poetic and figurative passage represents the dead as entirely separated from earthly scenes, employments, and society. It is not by any means intimating that there is no existence past the grave, but merely that existence thereafter has no similarity to the affairs of this life. This passage, along with Ecclesiastes 9:5, 6 and Isaiah 38:18, speaks of death as viewed from an earthly aspect, understanding it only in relation to this present life (cf. Gen. 37:35; 1 Sam. 28:15, 19; 2 Sam. 12:23; Luke 16:27, 28, 30; 1 Pet. 4:6).

🔑 **7:1** David penned this psalm when he was defending himself from the accusations of the man named Cush, and while he was being hunted by Saul (1 Sam. 24:9; 26:19).

to my righteousness,[6664] and according
to mine integrity[8537] *that is* in me.
9 Oh let the wickedness[7451] of the
wicked[7563] come to an end;[1584] but establish the just: [a]for the righteous[6662] God
trieth[974] the hearts[3026] and reins.[3629]
10 [I]My defence *is* of God, which
saveth[3467] the [a]upright[3477] in heart.[3820]
🔑 11 [I]God[410] judgeth[8199] the righteous,
and God is angry[2194] *with the wicked*
every day.
12 If he turn[7725] not, he will [a]whet
his sword;[2719] he hath bent his bow, and
made it ready.[3559]
13 He hath also prepared[3559] for him
the instruments of death;[4194] [a]he or-
daineth his arrows against the persecutors.
14 [a]Behold, he travaileth[2254] with iniquity,[205] and hast conceived mischief,[5999]
and brought forth falsehood.
15 [I]He made a pit,[953] and digged it,
[a]and is fallen[5307] into the ditch[7845] *which*
he made.
16 [a]His mischief shall return upon
his own head,[7218] and his violent dealing[2555] shall come down upon his own
pate.[6936]
17 I will praise[3034] the LORD according to his righteousness: and will sing
praise to the name of the LORD most
high.[5945]

God's Glory and Man's Honor

To the chief Musician upon Gittith, A Psalm of David.

8 O LORD our Lord,[113] how [a]excel-
lent[117] *is* thy name in all the
earth![776] who [b]hast set thy glory[1935]
above the heavens.[8064]
2 [a]Out of the mouth[6310] of babes[5768]
and sucklings hast thou [I]ordained[3245]
strength because of thine enemies, that
thou mightest still [b]the enemy and the
avenger.[5358]
3 When I [a]consider[7200] thy heavens,
the work of thy fingers, the moon and
the stars, which thou hast ordained;
4 [a]What is man,[582] that thou art
mindful[2142] of him? and the son[1121] of
man,[120] that thou visitest[6485] him?
5 For thou hast made him a little
lower than the angels, and hast crowned
him with glory[3519] and honour.
6 [a]Thou madest him to have dominion[4910] over the works of thy hands;[3027]
[b]thou hast put all *things* under his feet:
7 [I]All sheep and oxen, yea, and the
beasts of the field;[7704]
8 The fowl of the air,[8064] and the
fish[1709] of the sea, *and whatsoever* passeth through[5674] the paths[734] of the seas.
9 [a]O LORD our Lord, how excellent *is*
thy name in all the earth!

Thanksgiving for God's Justice

To the chief Musician upon Muthlabben, A Psalm of David.

9 I will praise[3034] *thee,* O LORD, with
my whole heart;[3820] I will shew
forth[5608] all thy marvellous works.[6381]
2 I will be glad and [a]rejoice in thee:
I will sing praise to thy name, O [b]thou
most High.[5945]
3 When mine enemies are turned
back, they shall fall[3782] and perish[6] at
thy presence.
4 For [I]thou hast maintained[6213] my
right[4941] and my cause;[1779] thou satest
in the throne[3678] judging[8199] [II]right.[6664]
5 Thou hast rebuked[1605] the hea-
then,[1471] thou hast destroyed[6] the
wicked,[7563] thou hast [a]put out[4229] their
name for ever and ever.[5703]
6 [I]O thou enemy, destructions[2723] are
come to a perpetual[5331] end:[8552] and thou
hast destroyed cities; their memorial[2143] is
perished[6] with them.
7 [a]But the LORD shall endure for ever:
he hath prepared[3559] his throne for judgment.[4941]
8 And [a]he shall judge[8199] the
world[8398] in righteousness,[6664] he shall
minister judgment[1777] to the people[3816]
in uprightness.[4334]
9 [a]The LORD also will be [I]a refuge

9 [a]1Sam. 16:7; 1Chr. 28:9; Ps. 139:1; Jer. 11:20; 17:10; 20:12; Rev. 2:23
10 [I]Hebr. *My buckler is upon God* [a]Ps. 125:4
11 [I]Or, *God is a righteous judge*
12 [a]Deut. 32:41
13 [a]Deut. 32:23, 42; Ps. 64:7
14 [a]Job 15:35; Isa. 33:11; 59:4; James 1:15
15 [I]Hebr. *He hath digged a pit* [a]Esth. 7:10; Job 4:8; Ps. 9:15; 10:2; 35:8; 94:23; 141:10; Prov. 5:22; 26:27; Eccl. 10:8
16 [a]1Kgs. 2:32; Esth. 9:25

1 [a]Ps. 148:13 [b]Ps. 113:4
2 [I]Hebr. *founded* [a]Matt. 11:25; 21:16; 1Cor. 1:27 [b]Ps. 44:16
3 [a]Ps. 111:2
4 [a]Job 7:17; Ps. 144:3; Heb. 2:6
6 [a]Gen. 1:26, 28 [b]1Cor. 15:27; Heb. 2:8
7 [I]Hebr. *Flocks and oxen all of them*
9 [a]Ps. 8:1

2 [a]Ps. 5:11 [b]Ps. 56:2; 83:18
4 [I]Hebr. *thou hast made my judgment* [II]Hebr. *in righteousness*
5 [a]Deut. 9:14; Prov. 10:7
6 [I]Or, *The destructions of the enemy are come to a perpetual end: and their cities hast thou destroyed.*
7 [a]Ps. 102:12, 26; Heb. 1:11
8 [a]Ps. 96:13; 98:9
9 [I]Hebr. *a highplace* [a]Ps. 32:7; 37:39; 46:1; 91:2

🔑 **7:11–17** See the note on Psalm 109:1–29 for a discussion of the Imprecatory Psalms.

for the oppressed, a refuge in times[6256] of trouble.

10 And they that [a]know thy name will put their trust[982] in thee: for thou, LORD, hast not forsaken[5800] them that seek thee.

11 Sing praises to the LORD, which dwelleth in Zion: [a]declare[5046] among the people[5971] his doings.

12 [a]When he maketh inquisition[1875] for blood,[1818] he remembereth[2142] them: he forgetteth not the cry of the [I]humble.

13 Have mercy[2603] upon me, O LORD; consider[7200] my trouble *which I suffer* of them that hate[8130] me, thou that liftest me up from the gates of death:[4194]

14 That I may shew forth all thy praise[8416] in the gates of the daughter of Zion: I will [a]rejoice in thy salvation.[3444]

15 [a]The heathen are sunk down in the pit[7845] *that* they made:[6213] in the net which they hid is their own foot taken.

16 The LORD is [a]known[3045] *by* the judgment *which* he executeth:[6213] the wicked is snared in the work of his own hands.[3709] [I][b]Higgaion. Selah.

17 The wicked shall be turned into hell,[7585] *and* all the nations[1471] [a]that forget God.[430]

18 [a]For the needy shall not alway[5331] be forgotten: [b]the expectation of the poor shall *not* perish for ever.

19 Arise, O LORD; let not man[582] prevail: let the heathen be judged[8199] in thy sight.

20 Put them in fear,[4172] O LORD: *that* the nations may know themselves *to be but* men. Selah.

A Prayer for Justice

10 Why standest thou afar off, O LORD? *why* hidest thou *thyself* in times[6256] of trouble?

2 [I]The wicked[7563] in *his* pride doth persecute the poor: [a]let them be taken in the devices[4209] that they have imagined.[2803]

3 For the wicked [a]boasteth[1984] of his [I]heart's desire, and [II][b]blesseth[1288] the covetous,[1214] *whom* the LORD abhorreth.[5006]

4 The wicked, through the pride of his countenance,[639] [a]will not seek *after God:* [I]God *is* not in all his [b]thoughts.[4209]

5 His ways[1870] are always grievous;[2342] [a]thy judgments[4941] *are* far above out of his sight: *as for* all his enemies, [b]he puffeth[6315] at them.

6 [a]He hath said in his heart,[3820] I shall not be moved: [b]for *I shall* [I]never *be* in adversity.[7451]

7 [a]His mouth[6310] is full of cursing[423] and [I]deceit[4820] and fraud: [b]under his tongue *is* mischief[5999] [c]and [II]vanity.[205]

8 He sitteth in the lurking places of the villages: [a]in the secret places doth he murder[2026] the innocent:[5355] [b]his eyes [I]are privily set[6845] against the poor.

9 [a]He lieth in wait [I]secretly as a lion in his den: he lieth in wait to catch the poor: he doth catch the poor, when he draweth him into his net.

10 [I]He croucheth, *and* humbleth himself, that the poor may fall [II]by his strong ones.

11 He hath said in his heart, God[410] hath forgotten: [a]he hideth his face; he will never see *it.*

12 Arise, O LORD; O God, [a]lift up[5375] thine hand:[3027] forget not the [I]humble.

13 Wherefore doth the wicked contemn[5006] God? he hath said in his heart, Thou wilt not require *it.*

14 Thou hast seen[7200] *it;* for thou beholdest mischief and spite,[3708] to requite *it* with thy hand: the poor [I][a]committeth[5800] himself unto thee; [b]thou art the helper of the fatherless.

15 [a]Break[7665] thou the arm of the wicked and the evil[7451] *man:* seek out his wickedness[7562] *till* thou find none.

16 [a]The LORD *is* King[4428] for ever[5769] and ever:[5703] the heathen[1471] are perished[6] out of his land.[776]

10 [a]Ps. 91:14
11 [a]Ps. 107:22
12 [I]Or, *afflicted* [a]Gen. 9:5
14 [a]Ps. 13:5; 20:5; 35:9
15 [a]Ps. 7:15, 16; 35:8; 57:6; 94:23; Prov. 5:22; 22:8; 26:27
16 [I]That is, *Meditation* [a]Ex. 7:5; 14:4, 10, 31 [b]Ps. 19:14; 92:3
17 [a]Job 8:13; Ps. 50:22
18 [a]Ps. 9:12; 12:5 [b]Prov. 23:18; 24:14

2 [I]Hebr. *In the pride of the wicked he doth persecute* [a]Ps. 7:16; 9:15, 16; Prov. 5:22
3 [I]Hebr. *soul's* [II]Or, *the covetous blesseth* himself, *he abhorreth the LORD* [a]Ps. 94:4 [b]Prov. 28:4; Rom. 1:32
4 [I]Or, *all his thoughts* are, There is *no God* [a]Ps. 14:2 [b]Ps. 14:1; 53:1
5 [a]Prov. 24:7; Isa. 26:11 [b]Ps. 12:5
6 [I]Hebr. *unto generation and generation* [a]Ps. 30:6; Eccl. 8:11; Isa. 56:12 [b]Rev. 18:7
7 [I]Hebr. *deceits* [II]Or, *iniquity* [a]Rom. 3:14 [b]Job 20:12 [c]Ps. 12:2
8 [I]Hebr. *hide themselves* [a]Hab. 3:14 [b]Ps. 17:11
9 [I]Hebr. *in the secret places* [a]Ps. 17:12; Mic. 7:2
10 [I]He breaketh himself [II]Or, *into his strong parts*
11 [a]Job 22:13; Ps. 73:11; 94:7; Ezek. 8:12; 9:9
12 [I]Or, *afflicted* [a]Mic. 5:9
14 [I]Hebr. *leaveth* [a]2Tim. 1:12; 1Pet. 4:19 [b]Ps. 68:5; Hos. 14:3
15 [a]Ps. 37:17 **16** [a]Ps. 29:10; 145:13; 146:10; Jer. 10:10; Lam. 5:19; Dan. 4:34; 6:26; 1Tim. 1:17

10:1 See note on Psalm 46:1.

17 LORD, thou hast heard[8085] the desire of the humble: thou wilt [I][a]prepare[3559] their heart, thou wilt cause thine ear[241] to hear:

18 To [a]judge[8199] the fatherless and the oppressed, that the man[582] of the earth[776] may no more [I]oppress.[6206]

Trusting God

To the chief Musician, *A Psalm* of David.

11 🔑 [a]In the LORD put I my trust:[2620] [b]how say[559] ye to my soul,[5315] Flee *as* a bird to your mountain?

2 For, lo, [a]the wicked[7563] bend *their* bow, [b]they make ready[3559] their arrow upon the string, that they may[3384] [I]privily[652] shoot[3384] at the upright[3477] in heart.[3820]

3 [a]If the foundations be destroyed,[2040] what can the righteous[6662] do?

4 [a]The LORD *is* in his holy[6944] temple,[1964] the LORD's [b]throne[3678] *is* in heaven:[8064] [c]his eyes behold,[2372] his eyelids try,[974] the children of men.[120]

5 The LORD [a]trieth the righteous: but the wicked and him that loveth[157] violence[2555] his soul hateth.[8130]

6 [a]Upon the wicked he shall rain [I]snares, fire and brimstone,[1614] and [II]an horrible[2152] tempest:[7307] [b]*this shall be* the portion of their cup.

7 For the righteous[6666] LORD [a]loveth righteousness; [b]his countenance doth behold the upright.

A Plea for Help

To the chief Musician upon Sheminith, A Psalm of David.

12 [I]Help,[3467] LORD; for [a]the godly man[2623] ceaseth;[1584] for the faithful fail from among the children[1121] of men.[120]

2 [a]They speak vanity[7723] every one[376] with his neighbour:[7453] [b]*with* flattering lips[8193] *and* with [I][c]a double heart[3820] do they speak.

3 The LORD shall cut off[3772] all flattering lips, *and* the tongue that speaketh [I][a]proud things:

4 Who have said, With our tongue will we prevail; our lips [I]*are* our own: who *is* lord[113] over us?

5 For the oppression[7701] of the poor, for the sighing of the needy, [a]now will I arise, saith the LORD; I will set *him* in safety[3468] *from him that* [I][b]puffeth[6315] at him.

6 The words[565] of the LORD *are* [a]pure words: *as* silver tried[6884] in a furnace of earth,[776] purified[2212] seven times.

7 Thou shalt keep[8104] them, O LORD, thou shalt preserve[5341] [I]them from this generation[1755] for ever.[5769]

8 The wicked[7563] walk on every side, when [I]the vilest[2149] men are exalted.

A Prayer for Help

To the chief Musician, A Psalm of David.

13 How long wilt thou forget me, O LORD? for ever?[5331] [a]how long wilt thou hide thy face from me?

2 How long shall I take counsel[6098] in my soul,[5315] *having* sorrow in my heart[3824] daily? how long shall mine enemy be exalted over me?

3 Consider *and* hear me, O LORD my God:[430] [a]lighten mine eyes, [b]lest I sleep the *sleep of* death;[4194]

4 [a]Lest mine enemy say,[559] I have prevailed against him; *and* those that trouble me rejoice when I am moved.

5 But I have [a]trusted[982] in thy mercy;[2617] my heart[3820] shall rejoice in thy salvation.[3444]

6 I will sing[7891] unto the LORD, because he hath [a]dealt bountifully[1580] with me.

17 [I]Or, *establish* [a]1Chr. 29:18
18 [I]Or, *terrify* [a]Ps. 82:3; Isa. 11:4

1 [a]Ps. 56:11 [b]1Sam. 26:19, 20
2 [I]Hebr. *in darkness* [a]Ps. 64:3, 4 [b]Ps. 21:12
3 [a]Ps. 82:5
4 [a]Hab. 2:20 [b]Ps. 2:4; Isa. 66:1; Matt. 5:34; 23:22; Acts 7:49; Rev. 4:2 [c]Ps. 33:13; 34:15, 16; 66:7
5 [a]Gen. 22:1; James 1:12
6 [I]Or, *quick burning coals* [II]Or, *a burning tempest* [a]Gen. 10:24; Ezek. 38:22 [b]Gen. 43:34; 1Sam. 1:4; 9:23; Ps. 75:8
7 [a]Ps. 45:7; 146:8 [b]Job 36:7; Ps. 33:18; 34:15; 1Pet. 3:12

1 [I]Or, *Save* [a]Isa. 57:1; Mic. 7:2
2 [I]Hebr. *a heart and a heart* [a]Ps. 10:7 [b]Ps. 28:3; 62:4; Jer. 9:8; Rom. 16:18 [c]1Chr. 12:33
3 [I]Hebr. *great things* [a]1Sam. 2:3; Ps. 17:10; Dan. 7:8, 25
4 [I]Hebr. are *with us*
5 [I]Or, *would ensnare him* [a]Ex. 3:7, 8; Isa. 33:10 [b]Ps. 10:5
6 [a]2Sam. 22:31; Ps. 18:30; 19:8; 119:140; Prov. 30:5
7 [I]Hebr. *him,* that is, *every one of the*
8 [I]Hebr. *the vilest of the sons of men are exalted*

1 [a]Deut. 31:17; Job 13:24; Ps. 44:24; 88:14; 89:46; Isa. 59:2
3 [a]Ezra 9:8 [b]Jer. 51:39
4 [a]Ps. 25:2; 35:19; 38:16
5 [a]Ps. 33:21
6 [a]Ps. 116:7; 119:17

🔑 **11:1** This psalm was written after David was advised to flee Saul's presence by Jonathan (1 Sam. 18; 19).

The Sinfulness of Men

To the chief Musician, *A Psalm* of David

14 🔑 The [a]fool hath said in his
heart,[3820] *There is* no God.[430]
[b]They are corrupt,[7843] they have done
abominable[8581] works, *there is* none that
doeth[6213] good.[2896]
2 [a]The LORD looked down from
heaven[8064] upon the children of men, to
see if there were any that did understand,[7919] *and* seek God.
3 [a]They are all gone aside,[5493] they
are *all* together become [I]filthy: *there is*
none that doeth good, no, not one.
4 Have all the workers of iniquity[205]
no knowledge?[3045] who [a]eat up my people[5971] *as* they eat bread, and [b]call not
upon[7121] the LORD.[3068]
5 There [Ia]were they in great fear:[6342]
for God *is* in the generation[1755] of the
righteous.[6662]
6 Ye have shamed the counsel[6098] of
the poor, because the LORD *is* his [a]refuge.
7 [Ia]Oh that the salvation[3444] of Israel
were come out of Zion! [b]when the LORD
bringeth back[7725] the captivity[7622] of his
people, Jacob shall rejoice, *and* Israel
shall be glad.

True Worshipers

A Psalm of David.

15 🔑 LORD, [a]who shall [I]abide[1481] in
thy tabernacle?[168] who shall
dwell[7931] in [b]thy holy[6944] hill?
2 [a]He that walketh uprightly, and
worketh righteousness,[6664] and [b]speaketh
the truth[571] in his heart.[3824]
3 [a]*He that* backbiteth[7270] not with his
tongue, nor doeth[6213] evil[7451] to his
neighbour,[7453] [b]nor [I]taketh up[5375] a reproach[2781] against his neighbour.
4 [a]In whose eyes a vile person[3988]
is contemned;[959] but he honoureth[3513]
them that fear[3373] the LORD. *He that*
[b]sweareth[7650] to *his own* hurt,[7489] and
changeth not.
5 [a]*He that* putteth not out his money
to usury, [b]nor taketh reward against the
innocent.[5355] He that doeth these *things*
[c]shall never be moved.

A Prayer of Confidence

Michtam of David.

16 Preserve[8104] me, O God:[410] [a]for in
thee do I put my trust.[2620]
2 *O my soul,* thou hast said unto the
LORD, Thou *art* my Lord:[136] [a]my goodness[2896] *extendeth* not to thee;
3 *But* to the saints[6918] that *are* in the
earth,[776] and *to* the excellent,[117] in whom
is all my delight.[2656]
4 Their sorrows[6094] shall be multiplied *that* [I]hasten *after* another *god:* their
drink offerings[5262] of blood[1818] will I not
offer,[5258] [a]nor take up[5375] their names into
my lips.[8193]
5 [a]The LORD *is* the portion [I]of mine
inheritance and [b]of my cup: thou maintainest my lot.
6 The lines[2256] are fallen[5307] unto me
in pleasant *places;* yea, I have a goodly
heritage.[5159]
7 I will bless[1288] the LORD, who hath
given me counsel:[3289] [a]my reins[3629] also
instruct[3256] me in the night seasons.[3915]

1 [a]Ps. 10:4; 53:1 [b]Gen. 6:11, 12; Rom. 3:10
2 [a]Ps. 33:13; 102:19
3 [I]Hebr. *stinking* [a]Rom. 3:10-12
4 [a]Jer. 10:25; Amos 8:4; Mic. 3:3 [b]Ps. 79:6; Isa. 64:7
5 [I]Hebr. *they feared a fear* [a]Ps. 53:5
6 [a]Ps. 9:9; 142:5
7 [I]Hebr. *Who will give* [a]Ps. 53:6; Rom. 11:26 [b]Job 42:10; Ps. 126:1

1 [I]Hebr. *sojourn* [a]Ps. 24:3 [b]Ps. 2:6; 3:4
2 [a]Isa. 33:15 [b]Zech. 8:16; Eph. 4:25
3 [I]Or, *receiveth,* or, *endureth* [a]Lev. 19:16; Ps. 34:13 [b]Ex. 23:1
4 [a]Esth. 3:2 [b]Judg. 11:35
5 [a]Ex. 22:25; Lev. 25:36; Deut. 23:19; Ezek. 18:8; 22:12 [b]Ex. 23:8; Deut. 16:19 [c]Ps. 16:8; 2Pet. 1:10

1 [a]Ps. 25:20
2 [a]Job 22:2, 3; 35:7, 8; Ps. 50:9; Rom. 11:35
4 [I]Or, *give gifts to another* [a]Ex. 23:13; Josh. 23:7; Hos. 2:16, 17
5 [I]Hebr. *of my part* [a]Deut. 32:9; Ps. 73:26; 119:57; 142:5; Jer. 10:16; Lam. 3:24 [b]Ps. 11:6
7 [a]Ps. 17:3

🔑 **14:1–3** This passage is cited in Romans 3:10–12 to emphasize the universality of sin (cf. 1 Kgs. 8:46; Prov. 20:9; Eccl. 7:20; Mark 10:18; Rom. 3:18, 23; 1 John 1:8). Some people see a contradiction between this clear doctrine of Scripture (that all have sinned) and passages like Genesis 6:9; Job. 1:1; Psalm 24:3, 4; 86:2; Luke 6:45; and 1 John 2:1; 3:6, 9, which describe men as "perfect," "pure," and "holy." It must be realized that terms like "good" have a comparative meaning as well as an absolute one. All the goodness, holiness, or purity of any person is so only in relation to the unholiness or impurity of other people. Only God possesses these attributes in their absolute state. Every person stands in need of the forgiveness and pardon of God, which can only be obtained by appropriating the merit of Christ's work on the cross. For a thorough discussion of sinfulness, see the note on 1 John 1:5–10.

🔑 **15:1** David wrote this psalm on the occasion of moving the ark of the covenant to Mount Zion (2 Sam. 6:12–19).

8 [a]I have set the LORD always[8548] before me: because [b]*he is* at my right hand, [c]I shall not be moved.

9 Therefore my heart[3820] is glad, [a]and my glory[3519] rejoiceth: my flesh[1320] also shall [I]rest in hope.[983]

10 [a]For thou wilt not leave[5800] [b]my soul in hell;[7585] neither wilt thou suffer thine Holy One[2623] to see corruption.[7845]

11 Thou wilt shew[3045] me the [a]path[734] of life:[2416] [b]in thy presence *is* fulness of joy; [c]at thy right hand *there are* pleasures for evermore.

An Innocent Man's Prayer

A Prayer of David.

17 Hear[8085] [I]the right,[6664] O LORD, attend unto my cry, give ear[238] unto my prayer,[8605] *that goeth* [II]not out of feigned[4820] lips.[8193]

2 Let my sentence come forth from thy presence; let thine eyes behold[2372] the things that are equal.

3 Thou hast proved[974] mine heart;[3820] [a]thou hast visited[6485] *me* in the night;[3915] [b]thou hast tried[6884] me, *and* shalt find nothing; I am purposed[2161] *that* my mouth[6310] shall not transgress.[5674]

4 Concerning the works of men,[120] by the word[1697] of thy lips I have kept[8104] *me from* the paths[734] of the destroyer.[6530]

5 [a]Hold up my goings in thy paths, *that* my footsteps [I]slip not.

6 [a]I have called upon[7121] thee, for thou wilt hear me, O God:[410] incline thine ear[241] unto me, *and hear* my speech.[565]

7 [a]Shew thy marvellous lovingkindness, O thou that savest[3467] by thy right hand them which put their trust[2620] *in thee* from those that rise up *against them.*

8 [a]Keep[8104] me as the apple of the eye, [b]hide me under the shadow of thy wings,

9 From the wicked[7563] [I]that oppress[7703] me, *from* [II]my deadly[5315] enemies, *who* compass me about.[5362]

10 [a]They are inclosed in their own fat: with their mouth they [b]speak[1696] proudly.

11 They have now [a]compassed us in our steps: [b]they have set their eyes bowing down to the earth;[776]

12 [I]Like as a lion *that* is greedy of his prey, and as it were a young lion [II]lurking in secret places.

13 Arise, O LORD, [I]disappoint him, cast him down: deliver my soul[5315] from the wicked, [II][a]*which is* thy sword:[2719]

14 From men *which are* thy hand,[3027] O LORD, from men of the world,[2465] [a]*which have* their portion in *this* life,[2416] and whose belly[990] thou fillest with thy hid *treasure:* [I]they are full of children,[1121] and leave the rest[3499] of their *substance* to their babes.[5768]

15 As for me, [a]I will behold thy face in righteousness:[6664] [b]I shall be satisfied, when I awake, with thy likeness.[8544]

8 [a]Acts 2:25 [b]Ps. 73:23; 110:5; 121:5 [c]Ps. 15:5 **9** [I]Hebr. *dwell confidently* [a]Ps. 30:12; 57:8 **10** [a]Ps. 49:15; Acts 2:27, 31; 13:35 [b]Lev. 19:28; Num. 6:6 **11** [a]Matt. 7:14 [b]Ps. 17:15; 21:6; Matt. 5:8; 1Cor. 13:12; 1John 3:2 [c]Ps. 36:8

1 [I]Hebr. *justice* [II]Hebr. *without lips of deceit* **3** [a]Ps. 16:7 [b]Job 23:10; Ps. 26:2; 66:10; 139:2; Zech. 13:9; Mal. 3:2, 3; 1Pet. 1:7 **5** [I]Hebr. *be not moved* [a]Ps. 119:133 **6** [a]Ps. 116:2 **7** [a]Ps. 31:21 **8** [a]Deut. 32:10; Zech. 2:8 [b]Ruth 2:12; Ps. 36:7; 57:1; 61:4; 63:7; 91:1, 4; Matt. 23:37 **9** [I]Hebr. *that waste me* [II]Hebr. *my enemies against the soul* **11** [a]1Sam. 23:26 [b]Ps. 10:8, 9, 10 **12** [I]Hebr. *The likeness of him* (that is, *of every one of them*) is *as a lion* that *desireth to raven* [II]Hebr. *sitting* **13** [I]Hebr. *prevent his face* [II]Or, by *thy sword* [a]Isa. 10:5 **14** [I]Or, their *children are full* [a]Ps. 73:12; Luke 16:25; James 5:5 **15** [a]1John 3:2 [b]Ps. 4:6, 7; 16:11; 65:4

16:8–11 See the note on Psalm 109:1–29 for a discussion of the Imprecatory Psalms.

17:15 In this verse the reward of God's people is summed up as enjoying His presence (cf. Ps. 16:11; 1 John 3:2; Rev. 21:3; 22:3, 4). This reward is a result of God's grace, apart from any merit of man (Matt. 20:14; John 14:2; Rom. 2:7; Col. 3:24; Heb. 11:16). All those whose names are written in the Lamb's Book of Life will experience this bliss. In Scripture this is called "being with Christ" (John 12:26), "beholding His glory" (John 17:24), and "being glorified with Him" (Rom. 8:17, 18; Col. 3:4). All saints (cf. Ps. 16:3) will reign with Christ, and sit in judgment even over angels (Dan. 7:22; Matt. 19:28; 1 Cor. 6:3; 2 Tim. 2:12; Rev. 22:5). This expectation of believers is called "an inheritance" and is already secure for us in heaven (Matt. 25:34; Acts 20:32; Rom. 8:17; Heb. 9:15; 1 Pet. 1:4). Christ will reward those who have performed distinguished service with incorruptible crowns of righteousness, life, and glory (1 Cor. 9:25; 2 Tim. 4:8; James 1:12; 1 Pet. 5:4). This secure hope, which is an "anchor of the soul" (Heb. 6:19), ought not lead one to complacency, but rather challenge one to press forward and endure hardships for Christ's sake (2 Cor. 4:16–18; Phil. 3:14; 2 Tim. 2:1–5; Rev. 2:10).

A Song of Victory

To the chief Musician, *A Psalm* of David, the servant of the LORD, who spake unto the LORD the words of this song in the day *that* the LORD delivered him from the hand of all his enemies, and from the hand of Saul: And he said,

18 I [a]will love[7355] thee, O LORD, my strength.[2391]

2 The LORD *is* my rock, and my fortress, and my deliverer; my God,[410] [I]my strength, [a]in whom I will trust;[2620] my buckler,4043 and the horn of my salvation,[3468] *and* my high tower.

3 I will call[7121] upon the LORD, [a]*who is worthy* to be praised:[1984] so shall I be saved[3467] from mine enemies.

4 [a]The sorrows[2256] of death[4194] compassed me, and the floods of [I]ungodly men made me afraid.[1204]

5 The [I]sorrows of hell[7585] compassed me about: the snares[4170] of death prevented6923 me.

6 In my distress I called upon[7121] the LORD, and cried unto my God:[430] he heard[8085] my voice out of his temple,[1964] and my cry came before him, *even* into his ears.[241]

7 [a]Then the earth[776] shook1607 and trembled;[7493] the foundations[4146] also of the hills moved and were shaken, because he was wroth.[2734]

8 There went up[5927] a smoke [I]out of his nostrils,[639] and fire out of his mouth[6310] devoured: coals were kindled by it.

9 [a]He bowed the heavens8064 also, and came down: and darkness[6205] *was* under his feet.

10 [a]And he rode upon a cherub,[3742] and did fly: yea, [b]he did fly upon the wings of the wind.[7307]

11 He made darkness[2822] his secret place; [a]his pavilion round about him *were* dark[2824] waters *and* thick clouds of the skies.[7834]

12 [a]At the brightness *that was* before him his thick clouds passed,[5674] hail *stones* and coals of fire.

13 The LORD also thundered in the heavens, and the Highest[5945] gave [a]his voice; hail *stones* and coals of fire.

1 [a]Ps. 144:1
2 [I]Hebr. *my rock* [a]Heb. 2:13
3 [a]Ps. 76:4
4 [I]Hebr. *Belial* [a]Ps. 116:3
5 [I]Or, *cords*
7 [a]Acts 4:31
8 [I]Hebr. *by his*
9 [a]Ps. 144:5
10 [a]Ps. 99:1 [b]Ps. 104:3
11 [a]Ps. 97:2
12 [a]Ps. 97:3
13 [a]Ps. 29:3
14 [a]Josh. 10:10; Ps. 144:6; Isa. 30:30
15 [a]Ex. 15:8; Ps. 106:9
16 [I]Or, *great waters* [a]Ps. 144:7
19 [a]Ps. 31:8; 118:5
20 [a]1Sam. 24:19
23 [I]Hebr. *with*
24 [a]1Sam. 26:23
25 [a]1Kgs. 8:32
26 [I]Or, *wrestle* [a]Lev. 26:23, 24, 27, 28; Prov. 3:34
27 [a]Ps. 101:5; Prov. 6:17
28 [I]Or, *lamp* [a]Job 18:6; 29:3
29 [I]Or, *broken*

14 [a]Yea, he sent out his arrows, and scattered them; and he shot out lightnings, and discomfited[2000] them.

15 [a]Then the channels of waters were seen,[7200] and the foundations of the world[8398] were discovered at thy rebuke,[1606] O LORD, at the blast of the breath[7307] of thy nostrils.

16 [a]He sent from above, he took me, he drew me out of [I]many waters.

17 He delivered[5337] me from my strong enemy, and from them which hated[8130] me: for they were too strong for me.

18 They prevented me in the day[3117] of my calamity:[343] but the LORD was my stay.

19 [a]He brought me forth also into a large place; he delivered[2502] me, because he delighted[2654] in me.

20 [a]The LORD rewarded[1580] me according to my righteousness;[6664] according to the cleanness[1252] of my hands[3027] hath he recompensed[7725] me.

21 For I have kept[8104] the ways[1870] of the LORD, and have not wickedly departed[7561] from my God.

22 For all his judgments[4941] *were* before me, and I did not put away[5493] his statutes[2708] from me.

23 I was also upright[8549] [I]before him, and I kept myself from mine iniquity.[5771]

24 [a]Therefore hath the LORD recompensed me according to my righteousness, according to the cleanness of my hands in his eyesight.

25 [a]With the merciful[2623] thou wilt shew thyself merciful; with an upright[8549] man[1397] thou wilt shew thyself upright;[8552]

26 With the pure[1305] thou wilt shew thyself pure; and [a]with the froward6141 thou wilt [I]shew thyself froward.6617

27 For thou wilt save[3467] the afflicted people;[5971] but wilt bring down [a]high looks.

28 [a]For thou wilt light my [I]candle:[5216] the LORD my God will enlighten my darkness.

29 For by thee I have [I]run

through[7323] a troop;[1416] and by my God have I leaped over a wall.

30 *As for* God, [a]his way *is* perfect:[8549] [b]the word[565] of the LORD *is* [I]tried:[6884] he *is* a buckler [c]to all those that trust in him.

31 [a]For who *is* God[433] save the LORD? or who *is* a rock save our God?

32 *It is* God that [a]girdeth me with strength,[2428] and maketh my way perfect.

33 [a]He maketh my feet like hinds'[355] *feet,* and [b]setteth me upon my high places.[1116]

34 [a]He teacheth[3925] my hands to war, so that a bow of steel is broken by mine arms.

35 Thou hast also given me the shield of thy salvation: and thy right hand hath holden me up,[5582] and [I]thy gentleness hath made me great.

36 Thou hast enlarged my steps under me, [a]that [I]my feet did not slip.

37 I have pursued mine enemies, and overtaken them: neither did I turn again[7725] till they were consumed.[3615]

38 I have wounded[4272] them that they were not able to rise: they are fallen[5307] under my feet.

39 For thou hast girded me with strength unto the battle: thou hast [I]subdued[3766] under me those that rose up against me.

40 Thou hast also given me the necks of mine enemies; that I might destroy[6789] them that hate[8130] me.

41 They cried, *but there was* none to save *them:* [a]even unto the LORD, but he answered them not.

42 Then did I beat[7833] them small as the dust[6083] before the wind: I did [a]cast them out as the dirt in the streets.

43 [a]Thou hast delivered me from the strivings[7379] of the people; *and* [b]thou hast made[7760] me the head[7218] of the heathen:[1471] [c]a people *whom* I have not known[3045] shall serve[5647] me.

44 [I]As soon as they hear[8085] of me, they shall obey me: [II]the strangers [a]shall [III]submit themselves unto me.

45 [a]The strangers shall fade away, and be afraid[2727] out of their close places.

46 The LORD liveth;[2416] and blessed[1288] *be* my rock; and let the God of my salvation be exalted.

47 *It is* God that [I]avengeth[5414,5360] me, [a]and [II]subdueth[1696] the people under me.

48 He delivereth me from mine enemies: yea, [a]thou liftest me up above those that rise up against me: thou hast delivered me from the [I]violent[2555] man.[376]

49 [a]Therefore will I [I]give thanks[3034] unto thee, O LORD, among the heathen, and sing praises unto thy name.

50 [a]Great deliverance[3444] giveth he to his king;[4428] and sheweth[6213] mercy[2617] to his anointed,[4899] to David, and to his seed[2233] [b]for evermore.[5769]

God's Creation

To the chief Musician, A Psalm of David.

19 The [a]heavens[8064] declare[5608] the glory[3519] of God;[410] and the firmament[7549] sheweth[5046] his handywork.

2 Day[3117] unto day uttereth speech,[562] and night[3915] unto night sheweth knowledge.[1847]

3 *There is* no speech nor language, [I]*where* their voice is not heard.

4 [I][a]Their line is gone out through all the earth,[776] and their words[4405] to the end of the world.[8398] In them hath he set[7760] a tabernacle[168] for the sun,

5 Which *is* as a bridegroom coming out of his chamber, [a]*and* rejoiceth as a strong man to run a race.[734]

6 His going forth *is* from the end of the heaven, and his circuit unto the ends of it: and there is nothing hid from the heat thereof.

God's Law

7 [a]The [I]law[8451] of the LORD *is* perfect,[8549] [II]converting[7725] the soul:[5315] the testimony[5715] of the LORD *is* sure,[539] making wise[2449] the simple.

8 The statutes[6490] of the LORD *are* right,[3477] rejoicing the heart:[3820] [a]the commandment[4687] of the LORD *is* pure, [b]enlightening the eyes.

---

30 [I]Or, *refined* [a]Deut. 32:4; Dan. 4:37; Rev. 15:3 [b]Ps. 12:6; 119:140; Prov. 30:5; Ps. 17:7
31 [a]Deut. 32:31, 39; 1Sam. 2:2; Ps. 86:8; Isa. 45:5
32 [a]Ps. 91:2
33 [a]2Sam. 2:18; Hab. 3:19 [b]Deut. 32:13; 33:29
34 [a]Ps. 144:4
35 [I]Or, *with thy meekness thou hast multiplied me*
36 [I]Hebr. *mine ankles* [a]Prov. 4:12
39 [I]Hebr. *caused to bow*
41 [a]Job 27:9; 35:12; Prov. 1:28; Isa. 1:15; Jer. 11:11; 14:12; Ezek. 8:18; Mic. 3:4; Zech. 7:13
42 [a]Zech. 10:5
43 [a]2Sam. 2:9, 10; 3:1 [b]2Sam. 8 [c]Isa. 52:15; 55:5
44 [I]Hebr. *At the hearing of the ear* [II]Hebr. *the sons of the stranger* [III]Or, *yield feigned obedience* [a]Deut. 33:29; Ps. 66:3; 81:15
45 [a]Mic. 7:17
47 [I]Hebr. *giveth avengements for me* [II]Or, *destroyeth* [a]Ps. 47:3
48 [I]Hebr. *man of violence* [a]Ps. 59:1
49 [I]Or, *confess* [a]Rom. 15:9
50 [a]Ps. 144:10 [b]2Sam. 7:13

1 [a]Gen. 1:6; Isa. 40:22; Rom. 1:19, 20
3 [I]Or, *without these their voice is heard*
4 [I]Or, *Their rule, or, direction* [a]Rom. 10:18
5 [a]Eccl. 1:5
7 [I]Or, *doctrine* [II]Or, *restoring* [a]Ps. 111:7
8 [a]Ps. 12:6 [b]Ps. 13:3

9 The fear[3374] of the LORD *is* clean,[2889] enduring[5975] for ever:[5703] the judgments[4941] of the LORD *are* [I]true[571] *and* righteous[6663] altogether.

10 More to be desired *are they* than gold, [a]yea, than much fine gold: [b]sweeter also than honey and [I]the honeycomb.

11 Moreover by them is[2094] thy servant[5650] warned:[2094] *and* [a]in keeping[8104] of them *there is* great reward.

12 [a]Who can understand[995] *his* errors?[7691] [b]cleanse[5352] thou me from [c]secret *faults*.

🔑 13 [a]Keep back thy servant also from presumptuous[2086] *sins*; [b]let them not have dominion[4910] over me: then shall I be upright,[8552] and I shall be innocent[5352] from [I]the great transgression.[6588]

14 [a]Let the words[561] of my mouth,[6310] and the meditation of my heart, be acceptable[7522] in thy sight, O LORD, [I][b]my strength, and my [c]redeemer.[1350]

9 [I]Hebr. *truth* **10** [I]Hebr. *the dropping of honeycombs* [a]Ps. 119:72, 127; Prov. 8:10, 11, 19 [b]Ps. 119:103 **11** [a]Prov. 29:18 **12** [a]Ps. 40:12 [b]Lev. 4:2 [c]Ps. 90:8 **13** [I]Or, *much* [a]Gen. 20:6; 1Sam. 25:32, 33, 34, 39 [b]Ps. 119:133; Rom. 6:12, 14 **14** [I]Hebr. *my rock* [a]Ps. 51:15 [b]Ps. 18:1 [c]Isa. 43:14; 44:6; 47:4; 1Thess. 1:10

A Prayer for Victory

To the chief Musician, A Psalm of David.

20 The LORD hear thee in the day[3117] of trouble; [a]the name of the God[430] of Jacob [I]defend thee;

2 Send [I]thee help from [a]the sanctuary,[6944] and [II]strengthen thee out of Zion;

3 Remember[2142] all thy offerings,[4503] and [I]accept[1878] thy burnt sacrifice;[5930] Selah.

4 [a]Grant thee according to thine own heart,[3824] and fulfil all thy counsel.[6098]

5 We will [a]rejoice in thy salvation,[3444] and [b]in the name of our God we will set up *our* banners:[1713] the LORD fulfil all thy petitions.

6 Now know I that the LORD saveth[3467] [a]his anointed;[4899] he will hear him [I]from his holy[6944] heaven[8064] [II]with the saving[3468] strength of his right hand.

7 [a]Some *trust* in chariots, and some in horses: [b]but we will remember the name of the LORD our God.

8 They are brought down[3766] and fallen:[5307] but we are risen, and stand upright.

9 Save,[3467] LORD: let the king hear us when we call.[7121]

1 [I]Hebr. *set thee on a high place* [a]Prov. 18:10 **2** [I]Hebr. *thy help* [II]Hebr. *support thee* [a]1Kgs. 6:16; 2Chr. 20:8; Ps. 73:17 **3** [I]Hebr. *turn to ashes*: or, *make fat* **4** [a]Ps. 21:2 **5** [a]Ps. 9:14 [b]Ex. 17:15; Ps. 60:4 **6** [I]Hebr. *from the heaven of his holiness* [II]Hebr. *by the strength of the salvation of his right hand* [a]Ps. 2:2 **7** [a]Ps. 33:16, 17; Prov. 21:31; Isa. 31:1 [b]2Chr. 32:8

Praise for Victory

To the chief Musician, A Psalm of David.

21 🔑 The king[4428] shall joy in thy strength, O LORD; and [a]in thy salvation[3444] how greatly shall he rejoice!

2 [a]Thou hast given him his heart's[3820] desire, and hast not withholden[4513] the request of his lips.[8193] Selah.

3 For thou preventest[6923] him with the blessings[1293] of goodness:[2896] thou [a]settest a crown of pure gold on his head.[7218]

4 [a]He asked[7592] life[2416] of thee, *and* thou gavest *it* him, [b]*even* length[753] of days for ever[5769] and ever.[5703]

5 His glory[3519] *is* great in thy salvation: honour[1935] and majesty[1926] hast thou laid upon him.

6 For thou hast [I][a]made him most blessed for ever: [b]thou hast made him exceeding glad with thy countenance.

7 For the king trusteth[982] in the LORD, and through the mercy[2617] of the most High[5945] he [a]shall not be moved.

1 [a]Ps. 20:5, 6 **2** [a]Ps. 20:4, 5 **3** [a]2Sam. 12:30; 1Chr. 20:2 **4** [a]Ps. 61:5, 6 [b]2Sam. 7:19; Ps. 91:16 **6** [I]Hebr. *set him to be blessings* [a]Gen. 12:2; Ps. 72:17 [b]Ps. 16:11; 45:7; Acts 2:28 **7** [a]Ps. 16:8

🔑 **19:13** Inadvertent sins are compared here with "presumptuous sins," which are offenses against God carried out with a conscious knowledge that they are wrong. It is possible for believers to commit such sins. Because they continually receive grace from God, they may be tempted to use that grace as a license to sin. However, individuals who sin proudly, knowing the wrongness of their actions, all too often have never really been born again. It is for this reason that Scripture challenges believers to be sure of their salvation (Rom. 6:1, 2; 2 Cor. 13:5; 2 Pet. 1:10).

🔑 **21:1** Some believe that the words of this psalm, in combination with 2 Samuel 7, are pointing toward Christ.

8 Thine hand[3027] shall [a]find out all thine enemies: thy right hand shall find out those that hate[8130] thee.

9 [a]Thou shalt make them as a fiery oven in the time[6256] of thine anger: the LORD shall [b]swallow them up[1104] in his wrath,[639] [c]and the fire shall devour them.

10 [a]Their fruit shalt thou destroy[6] from the earth,[776] and their seed[2233] from among the children[1121] of men.[120]

11 For they intended evil[7451] against thee: they [a]imagined[2803] a mischievous device,[4209] *which* they are not able *to perform.*

12 Therefore [a]shalt thou make them turn their [I]back, *when* thou shalt make ready[3559] *thine arrows* upon thy strings against the face of them.

13 Be thou exalted, LORD, in thine own strength: *so* will we sing[7891] and praise thy power.

Anguish and Praise

To the chief Musician upon Aijeleth Shahar, A Psalm of David.

22 🔑 My [a]God,[410] my God, why hast thou forsaken[5800] me? *why art thou so* far [I]from helping me, *and from* [b]the words[1697] of my roaring?

2 O my God,[430] I cry[7121] in the daytime,[3119] but thou hearest not; and in the night season,[3915] and [I]am not silent.

3 But thou *art* holy,[6918] *O thou* that inhabitest the [a]praises[8416] of Israel.

4 Our fathers[1] trusted[982] in thee: they trusted, and thou didst deliver them.

5 They cried[2199] unto thee, and were delivered:[4422] [a]they trusted in thee, and were not confounded.[954]

6 But I *am* [a]a worm, and no man;[376] [b]a reproach[2781] of men,[120] and despised of the people.[5971]

7 [a]All they that see me laugh me to scorn: they [I]shoot out the lip, [b]they shake the head,[7218] *saying,*

8 [I][a]He trusted[1556] on the LORD *that* he would deliver him: [b]let him deliver[5337] him, [II]seeing he delighted[2654] in him.

9 [a]But thou *art* he that took me out of the womb:[990] thou [I]didst make me hope[982] *when I was* upon my mother's[517] breasts.

10 I was cast upon thee from the womb: [a]thou *art* my God from my mother's belly.[990]

11 Be not far from me; for trouble *is* near; for *there is* none to help.

12 [a]Many bulls have compassed me:

8 [a]1Sam. 31:3
9 [a]Mal. 4:1 [b]Ps. 56:1, 2 [c]Ps. 18:8; Isa. 26:11
10 [a]1Kgs. 13:34; Job 18:16, 17, 19; Ps. 37:28; 109:13; Isa. 14:20
11 [a]Ps. 2:1
12 [I]Hebr. *shoulder* [a]Job 7:20; 16:12; Lam. 3:12

1 [I]Hebr. *from my salvation* [a]Matt. 27:46; Mark 15:34 [b]Heb. 5:7
2 [I]Hebr. *there is no silence to me*
3 [a]Deut. 10:21
5 [a]Ps. 25:2, 3; 31:1; 71:1; Isa. 49:23; Rom. 9:33
6 [a]Job 25:6; Isa. 41:14 [b]Isa. 53:3
7 [I]Hebr. *open* [a]Matt. 27:39; Mark 15:29; Luke 23:35 [b]Job 16:4; Ps. 109:25
8 [I]Hebr. *He rolled* himself *on the LORD* [II]Or, *if he delight in him* [a]Matt. 27:43 [b]Ps. 91:14
9 [I]Or, *keptest me in safety* [a]Ps. 71:6
10 [a]Isa. 46:3; 49:1
12 [a]Deut. 32:14; Ps. 68:30; Ezek. 39:18; Amos 4:1

🔑 **22:1–31** This psalm is one of the so-called Messianic Psalms. There has been, however, much division among theologians as to which psalms are actually Messianic. There are three methods that are used to determine which psalms are "Messianic." The first way is by the testimony of the writers of the Old Testament. There are a few occurrences of these particular psalms found in other books, which attribute them to a discussion on the Messiah. Second, there are the references in the New Testament to these psalms, either by Christ Himself or by writers who made note of them as pertaining to Christ. Third, there is testimony by the Jews and the Church itself denoting that these psalms refer to the Messiah.

Along with these methods, there are several views as to the proper application of these "Messianic Psalms." One view suggests that these writings of David were describing him as well as the Messiah. By this, it is meant to say that they are to be applied directly to David and indirectly to Christ. Another opinion proposes that David's trials are spoken of only, not those of the coming Messiah. The key problem with this method of application is that there are some things mentioned as having been suffered by Christ that were in fact never experienced by David. For example, David could not very well say that he had been forsaken (v. 1) when he later acknowledges (vv. 26–31) that he did indeed have One that he could depend on for help. The last view suggests that these are in fact prophecies of Christ, and David merely looked at them for comfort in his times of trial. This application is based on the fact that all these so-called "Messianic Psalms" can refer to Christ, and there are portions that do apply to Christ exclusively (Ps. 22:16–18). In regards to the latter view, Christians can also look back to these particular psalms in order to find comfort in times of suffering (2 Cor. 1:5).

strong[47] *bulls* of Bashan have beset me round.

13 [a]They [I]gaped upon me *with* their mouths,[6310] *as* a ravening and a roaring lion.

14 I am poured out[8210] like water, [a]and all my bones[6106] are [I]out of joint:[6504] [b]my heart[3820] is like wax; it is melted in the midst of my bowels.[4578]

15 [a]My strength is dried up[3001] like a potsherd;[2789] and [b]my tongue cleaveth to my jaws; and thou hast brought me into the dust[6083] of death.[4194]

16 For [a]dogs have compassed me: the assembly[5712] of the wicked[7489] have inclosed[5362] me: [b]they pierced my hands[3027] and my feet.

17 I may tell[5608] all my bones: [a]they look *and* stare upon me.

18 [a]They part my garments among them, and cast[5307] lots upon my vesture.

19 But [a]be not thou far from me, O LORD: O my strength, haste thee to help me.

20 Deliver my soul[5315] from the sword;[2719] [I][a]my darling[3173] [II]from the power[3027] of the [b]dog.

21 [a]Save[3467] me from the lion's mouth:[6310] [b]for thou hast heard me from the horns of the unicorns.

22 [a]I will declare[5608] thy name unto [b]my brethren:[251] in the midst of the congregation[6951] will I praise[1984] thee.

23 [a]Ye that fear[3373] the LORD, praise him; all ye the seed[2233] of Jacob, glorify[3513] him; and fear[1481] him, all ye the seed of Israel.

24 For he hath not despised nor abhorred[8262] the affliction of the afflicted; neither hath he hid his face from him; but [a]when he cried unto him, he heard.[8085]

25 [a]My praise[8416] *shall be* of thee in the great congregation: [b]I will pay my vows[5088] before them that fear him.

26 [a]The meek shall eat and be satisfied: they shall praise the LORD that seek him: your heart[3824] [b]shall live[2421] for ever.[5703]

27 [a]All the ends of the world shall remember[2142] and turn[7725] unto the LORD: [b]and all the kindreds of the nations[1471] shall worship[7812] before thee.

28 [a]For the kingdom *is* the LORD's: and he *is* the governor[4910] among the nations.

29 [a]All *they that be* fat upon earth[776] shall eat and worship: [b]all they that go down to the dust shall bow[3766] before him: and none can keep alive[2421] his own soul.

30 A seed shall serve[5647] him; [a]it shall be accounted[5608] to the Lord[136] for a generation.[1755]

31 [a]They shall come, and shall declare[5046] his righteousness[6666] unto a people that shall be born, that he hath done[6213] *this.*

"The Lord Is My Shepherd"

A Psalm of David.

23 🔑 The LORD *is* [a]my shepherd; [b]I shall not want.[2637]

13 [I]Hebr. *opened their mouths against me* [a]Job 16:10; Ps. 35:21; Lam. 2:16; 3:46
14 [I]Or, *sundered* [a]Dan. 5:6 [b]Josh. 7:5; Job 23:16
15 [a]Prov. 17:22 [b]Job 29:10; Lam. 4:4; John 19:28
16 [a]Rev. 22:15 [b]Matt. 27:35; Mark 15:24; Luke 23:33; John 19:23, 37; 20:25
17 [a]Luke 23:27, 35
18 [a]Luke 23:34; John 19:23, 24
19 [a]Ps. 10:1; 22:11
20 [I]Hebr. *my only one* [II]Hebr. *from the hand* [a]Ps. 35:17 [b]Ps. 22:16
21 [a]2Tim. 4:17 [b]Isa. 34:7; Acts 4:27
22 [a]Ps. 40:9; Heb. 2:12 [b]John 20:17; Rom. 8:29
23 [a]Ps. 135:19, 20
24 [a]Heb. 5:7
25 [a]Ps. 35:18; 40:9, 10; 111:1 [b]Ps. 66:13; 116:14; Eccl. 5:4
26 [a]Lev. 7:11, 12, 15, 16; Ps. 69:32; Isa. 65:13 [b]John 6:51
27 [a]Ps. 2:8; 72:11; 86:9; 98:3; Isa. 49:6 [b]Ps. 96:7
28 [a]Ps. 47:8; Obad. 21; Zech. 14:9; Matt. 6:13
29 [a]Ps. 45:12 [b]Isa. 26:19; Phil. 2:10
30 [a]Ps. 87:6
31 [a]Ps. 78:6; 86:9; 102:18; Isa. 60:3; Rom. 3:21, 22
1 [a]Isa. 40:11; Jer. 23:4; Ezek. 34:11, 12, 23; John 10:11; 1Pet. 2:25; Rev. 7:17 [b]Phil. 4:19

🔑 **23:1–6** This is doubtless the best-loved passage in the Old Testament. The setting is not given, but it is clearly the song of one who has lost worldly comfort and security. It may have been composed during David's years of flight from Saul, or while he tended his father's sheep. The image of Christ as the Shepherd is an intimate and personal one. He is not set forth as the distant King or Lord, nor as the impersonal Rock or Shield, but as the Shepherd who takes care of all the needs of His sheep. David's own faithful care for his father's sheep may have led him to consider how fully he could trust in the Lord, his heavenly Shepherd. The Shepherd's ability to provide is never doubted, for David said, "I shall not want" (v. 1). However, God is described not only as One who meets the needs of the sheep, but also as a Friend who desires to generously bestow His blessings upon them. David realizes that his situation is not just one of the absence of want, but one where his "cup overflows" (v. 5). This psalm is picturing the peaceful relationship one may have with God as a deep reservoir of comfort for many.

2 [a]He maketh me to lie down in [I]green pastures:[4999] [b]he leadeth[5095] me beside the [II]still waters.

3 He restoreth[7725] my soul:[5315] [a]he leadeth[5148] me in the paths of righteousness[6664] for his name's sake.

4 Yea, though I walk through the valley of [a]the shadow of death,[6757] [b]I will fear[3372] no evil:[7451] [c]for thou *art* with me; thy rod[7626] and thy staff they comfort[5162] me.

5 [a]Thou preparest a table before me in the presence of mine enemies: thou [I][b]anointest[1878] my head[7218] with oil;[8081] my cup runneth over.

6 Surely goodness[2896] and mercy[2617] shall follow me all the days[3117] of my life:[2416] and I will dwell in the house[1004] of the LORD [I]for ever.

The "King of Glory"

A Psalm of David.

24 The [a]earth[776] *is* the LORD's, and the fulness thereof; the world,[8398] and they that dwell therein.

2 [a]For he hath founded[3245] it upon the seas, and established[3559] it upon the floods.

3 [a]Who shall ascend[5927] into the hill of the LORD? or who shall stand in his holy[6944] place?

4 [I][a]He that hath [b]clean hands,[3709] and [c]a pure[1249] heart;[3824] who hath not lifted up[5375] his soul[5315] unto vanity,[7723] nor [d]sworn deceitfully.[4820]

5 He shall receive[5375] the blessing[1293] from the LORD, and righteousness[6666] from the God[430] of his salvation.[3468]

6 This *is* the generation[1755] of them that seek him, that [a]seek thy face, [I]O Jacob. Selah.

7 [a]Lift up your heads,[7218] O ye gates; and be ye lift up, ye everlasting[5769] doors; [b]and the King[4428] of glory[3519] shall come in.

8 Who *is* this King of glory? The LORD strong and mighty, the LORD mighty in battle.

9 Lift up your heads, O ye gates; even lift *them* up, ye everlasting doors; and the King of glory shall come in.

10 Who is this King of glory? The LORD of hosts,[6635] he *is* the King of glory. Selah.

A Prayer for Guidance and Protection

A Psalm of David.

25 Unto [a]thee, O LORD, do I lift up[5375] my soul.[5315]

2 O my God,[430] I [a]trust[982] in thee: let me not be ashamed,[954] [b]let not mine enemies triumph over me.

3 Yea, let none that wait on[6960] thee be ashamed: let them be ashamed which transgress without cause.

4 [a]Shew[3045] me thy ways,[1870] O LORD; teach[3925] me thy paths.[734]

5 Lead me in thy truth,[571] and teach me: for thou *art* the God of my salvation;[3468] on thee do I wait all the day.[3117]

6 Remember,[2142] O LORD, [I][a]thy tender mercies[7356] and thy lovingkindnesses; for they *have been* ever of old.

7 Remember not [a]the sins of my youth, nor my transgressions:[6588] [b]according to thy mercy[2617] remember thou me for thy goodness' sake, O LORD.

8 Good[2896] and upright[3477] *is* the LORD: therefore will he teach[3384] sinners[2400] in the way.[1870]

9 The meek will he guide in judgment:[4941] and the meek will he teach his way.

10 All the paths of the LORD *are* mercy and truth unto such as keep[5341] his covenant[1285] and his testimonies.[5713]

11 [a]For thy name's sake, O LORD, pardon[5545] mine iniquity;[5771] [b]for it *is* great.

12 What man[376] *is* he that feareth

23: 2 [I]Hebr. *pastures of tender grass* [II]Hebr. *waters of quietness* [a]Ezek. 34:14 [b]Rev. 7:17
3 [a]Ps. 5:8; 31:3; Prov. 8:20
4 [a]Job 3:5; 10:21, 22; 24:17; Ps. 44:19 [b]Ps. 3:6; 27:1; 118:6 [c]Isa. 43:2
5 [I]Hebr. *makest fat* [a]Ps. 104:15 [b]Ps. 92:10
6 [I]Hebr. *to length of days*

24: 1 [a]Ex. 9:29; 19:5; Deut. 10:14; Job 41:11; Ps. 50:12; 1Cor. 10:26, 28
2 [a]Gen. 1:9; Job 38:6; Ps. 104:5; 136:6; 2Pet. 3:5
3 [a]Ps. 15:1
4 [I]Hebr. *The clean of hands* [a]Isa. 33:15, 16 [b]Job 17:9; 1Tim. 2:8 [c]Matt. 5:8 [d]Ps. 15:4
6 [I]Or, O God of *Jacob* [a]Ps. 27:8; 105:4
7 [a]Isa. 26:2 [b]Ps. 97:6; Hag. 2:7; Mal. 3:1; 1Cor. 2:8

25: 1 [a]Ps. 86:4; 143:8; Lam. 3:41
2 [a]Ps. 22:5; 31:1; 34:8; Isa. 28:16; 49:23; Rom. 10:11 [b]Ps. 13:4
4 [a]Ex. 33:13; Ps. 5:8; 27:11; 86:11; 119; 143:8, 10
6 [I]Hebr. *thy bowels* [a]Ps. 103:17; 106:1; 107:1; Isa. 63:15; Jer. 33:11
7 [a]Job 13:26; 20:11; Jer. 3:25 [b]Ps. 51:1
11 [a]Ps. 31:3; 79:9; 109:21; 143:11 [b]Rom. 5:20

24:1 This psalm reflects David's jubilant attitude as a result of the capture of the "city of Zion" and the moving of the ark of the covenant to Jerusalem (2 Sam. 6:1–23).

the LORD? [a]him shall he teach[3384] in the way *that* he shall choose.[977]

13 [a]His soul [I]shall dwell at ease;[2896] and [b]his seed[2233] shall inherit[3423] the earth.[776]

14 [a]The secret[5475] of the LORD *is* with them that fear[3373] him; [I]and he will shew them his covenant.

15 [a]Mine eyes *are* ever[8548] toward the LORD; for he shall [I]pluck my feet out of the net.

16 [a]Turn thee unto me, and have mercy[2603] upon me; for I *am* desolate[3173] and afflicted.

17 The troubles of my heart[3824] are enlarged: *O* bring thou me out of my distresses.[4691]

18 [a]Look upon[7200] mine affliction and my pain;[5999] and forgive[5375] all my sins.

19 Consider[7200] mine enemies; for they are many; and they hate[8130] me with [I]cruel hatred.[8135]

20 O keep[8104] my soul, and deliver[5337] me: [a]let me not be ashamed; for I put my trust[2620] in thee.

21 Let integrity[8537] and uprightness[3476] preserve[5341] me; for I wait on thee.

22 [a]Redeem[6299] Israel, O God, out of all his troubles.

A Prayer for Protection

A Psalm of David.

26 Judge[8199] [a]me, O LORD; for I have [b]walked in mine integrity:[8537] [c]I have trusted[982] also in the LORD; *therefore* I shall not slide.

2 [a]Examine[974] me, O LORD, and prove[5254] me; try[6884] my reins[3629] and my heart.[3820]

3 For thy lovingkindness *is* before mine eyes: and [a]I have walked in thy truth.[571]

4 [a]I have not sat with vain[7723] persons, neither will I go in with dissemblers.[5956]

5 I have [a]hated the congregation[6951] of evil doers; [b]and will not sit with the wicked.[7563]

6 [a]I will wash[7364] mine hands[3709] in innocency:[5356] so will I compass thine altar,[4196] O LORD:[3068]

7 That I may publish[8085] with the voice of thanksgiving,[8425] and tell[5608] of all thy wondrous works.[6381]

8 LORD, [a]I have loved[157] the habitation of thy house,[1004] and the place [I]where thine honour[3519] dwelleth.[4908]

9 [I][a]Gather[622] not my soul[5315] with sinners,[2400] nor my life[2416] with bloody[1818] men:[582]

10 In whose hands[3027] *is* mischief, and their right hand is [I]full of [a]bribes.

11 But as for me, I will [a]walk in mine integrity: redeem[6299] me, and be merciful[2603] unto me.

12 [a]My foot standeth in an [b]even place: [c]in the congregations will I bless[1288] the LORD.

A Prayer of Praise

A Psalm of David.

27 The LORD *is* [a]my light[216] and [b]my salvation;[3468] whom shall I fear?[3372] [c]the LORD *is* the strength of my life;[2416] of whom shall I be afraid?[6342]

2 When the wicked,[7489] *even* mine enemies and my foes, [I]came upon me to [a]eat up my flesh,[1320] they stumbled[3782] and fell.[5307]

3 [a]Though an host[4264] should encamp against me, my heart[3820] shall not fear: though war should rise against me, in this *will* I *be* confident.[982]

4 [a]One *thing* have I desired[7592] of the LORD, that will I seek after; that I may [b]dwell in the house[1004] of the LORD all the days[3117] of my life, to behold[2372] [I][c]the beauty of the LORD, and to enquire in his temple.[1964]

5 For [a]in the time[3117] of trouble[7451] he shall hide me in his pavilion: in the secret of his tabernacle[168] shall he hide me; he shall [b]set me up upon a rock.

6 And now shall [a]mine head[7218] be lifted up above mine enemies round about me: therefore will I offer[2076] in his tabernacle sacrifices[2077] [I]of joy; I will sing,[7891] yea, I will sing praises[2167] unto the LORD.

---

12 [a]Ps. 37:23
13 [I]Hebr. *shall lodge in goodness* [a]Prov. 19:23 [b]Ps. 37:11, 22, 29
14 [I]Or, *and his covenant to make them know it* [a]Prov. 3:32; John 7:17; 15:15
15 [I]Hebr. *bring forth* [a]Ps. 141:8
16 [a]Ps. 69:16; 86:16
18 [a]2Sam. 16:12
19 [I]Hebr. *hatred of violence*
20 [a]Ps. 25:2
22 [a]Ps. 130:8

1 [a]Ps. 7:8 [b]2Kgs. 20:3; Ps. 26:11; Prov. 20:7 [c]Ps. 28:7; 31:14; Prov. 29:25
2 [a]Ps. 7:9; 17:3; 66:10; 139:23; Zech. 13:9
3 [a]2Kgs. 20:3
4 [a]Ps. 1:1; Jer. 15:17
5 [a]Ps. 31:6; 139:21, 22 [b]Ps. 1:1
6 [a]Ex. 30:19, 20; Ps. 73:13; 1Tim. 2:8
8 [I]Hebr. *of the tabernacle of thy honor* [a]Ps. 27:4
9 [I]Or, *Take not away* [a]1Sam. 25:29; Ps. 28:3
10 [I]Hebr. *filled with* [a]Ex. 23:8; Deut. 16:19; 1Sam. 8:3; Isa. 33:15
11 [a]Ps. 26:1
12 [a]Ps. 40:2 [b]Ps. 27:11 [c]Ps. 22:22; 107:32; 111:1

1 [a]Ps. 84:11; Isa. 60:19, 20; Mic. 7:8 [b]Ex. 15:2 [c]Ps. 62:2, 6; 118:14, 21; Isa. 12:2
2 [I]Hebr. *approached against me* [a]Ps. 14:4
3 [a]Ps. 3:6
4 [I]Or, *the delight* [a]Ps. 26:8 [b]Ps. 65:4; Luke 2:37 [c]Ps. 90:17
5 [a]Ps. 31:20; 83:3; 91:1; Isa. 4:6 [b]Ps. 40:2
6 [I]Hebr. *of shouting* [a]Ps. 3:3

7 Hear,[8085] O LORD, *when* I cry[7121] with my voice: have mercy[2603] also upon me, and answer me.

8 [I]*When thou saidst,* [a]Seek ye my face; my heart said unto thee, Thy face, LORD, will I seek.

9 [a]Hide not thy face *far* from me; put not thy servant[5650] away in anger:[639] thou hast been my help; leave[5203] me not, neither forsake[5800] me, O God[430] of my salvation.

10 [a]When my father[1] and my mother[517] forsake me, then the LORD [I]will take me up.

11 [a]Teach[3384] me thy way,[1870] O LORD, and lead[5148] me in [I][b]a plain path,[734] because of [II][c]mine enemies.

12 [a]Deliver me not over unto the will of mine enemies: for [b]false[8267] witnesses are risen up against me, and such as [c]breathe out cruelty.[2555]

13 *I had fainted,* unless I had believed[539] to see the goodness of the LORD [a]in the land[776] of the living.[2416]

14 [a]Wait on[6960] the LORD: be of good courage,[2388] and he shall strengthen thine heart: wait, I say, on the LORD.

A Prayer for Help

A Psalm of David.

28 Unto thee will I cry,[7121] O LORD my rock; [a]be not silent[2790] [I]to me: [b]lest, *if* thou be silent[2814] to me, I become like them that go down into the pit.[953]

2 Hear[8085] the voice of my supplications,[8469] when I cry unto thee, [a]when I lift up[5375] my hands[3027] [I][b]toward thy holy[6944] oracle.[1687]

3 [a]Draw me not away with the wicked,[7563] and with the workers of iniquity,[205] [b]which speak peace to their neighbours,[7453] but mischief[7451] *is* in their hearts.[3824]

4 [a]Give them according to their deeds, and according to the wickedness[7455] of their endeavours: give them after the work of their hands; render[7725] to them their desert.

5 Because [a]they regard[995] not the works of the LORD, nor the operation of his hands, he shall destroy[2040] them, and not build them up.

6 Blessed[1288] *be* the LORD, because he hath heard[8085] the voice of my supplications.

7 The LORD *is* [a]my strength and my shield; my heart[3820] [b]trusted[982] in him, and I am helped: therefore my heart greatly rejoiceth; and with my song[7892] will I praise[3034] him.

8 The LORD *is* [I]their strength, and he *is* the [II][a]saving[3444] strength of his anointed.[4899]

9 Save[3467] thy people,[5971] and bless [a]thine inheritance:[5159] [I]feed them also, [b]and lift them up for ever.[5769]

"The Voice of the Lord"

A Psalm of David.

29 [a]Give unto the Lord, O [I]ye mighty,[410] give unto the Lord glory[3519] and strength.

2 Give unto the LORD [I]the glory due unto his name; worship[7812] the LORD [II]in [a]the beauty[1927] of holiness.[6944]

3 The voice of the LORD *is* upon the waters: [a]the God[410] of glory thundereth: the LORD *is* upon [I]many waters.

4 The voice of the LORD *is* [I]powerful; the voice of the LORD *is* [II]full of majesty.[1926]

5 The voice of the LORD breaketh[7665] the cedars; yea, the LORD breaketh [a]the cedars of Lebanon.

6 [a]He maketh them also to skip[7540] like a calf; Lebanon and [b]Sirion like a young unicorn.

7 The voice of the LORD [I]divideth the flames of fire.

8 The voice of the LORD shaketh[2342] the wilderness; the LORD shaketh the wilderness of [a]Kadesh.

9 The voice of the LORD maketh[2342] [a]the hinds[355] [I]to calve,[2342] and discovereth[2834] the forests: and in his temple[1964] [II]doth every one speak[559] of *his* glory.

8 [I]Or, *My heart said unto thee, Let my face seek thy face* [a]Ps. 24:6; 105:4
9 [a]Ps. 69:17; 143:7
10 [I]Hebr. *will gather me,* Isa. 40:11 [a]Isa. 49:15
11 [I]Hebr. *away of plainness* [II]Hebr. *those which observe me* [a]Ps. 26:12 [b]Ps. 5:8; 54:5 [c]Ps. 25:4; 86:11; 119
12 [a]Ps. 35:25 [b]1Sam. 22:9; 2Sam. 16:7, 8; Ps. 35:11 [c]Acts 9:1
13 [a]Ps. 56:13; 116:9; 142:5; Jer. 11:19; Ezek. 26:20
14 [a]Ps. 31:24; 62:1, 5; 130:5; Isa. 25:9; Hab. 2:3

1 [I]Hebr. *from me* [a]Ps. 83:1 [b]Ps. 88:4; 143:7
2 [I]Or, *toward the oracle of thy sanctuary* [a]1Kgs. 6:22, 23; 8:28, 29; Ps. 5:7 [b]Ps. 138:2
3 [a]Ps. 26:9 [b]Ps. 12:2; 55:21; 62:4; Jer. 9:8
4 [a]2Tim. 4:14; Rev. 18:6
5 [a]Job 34:27; Isa. 5:12
7 [a]Ps. 18:2 [b]Ps. 13:5; 22:4
8 [I]Or, *his strength* [II]Hebr. *strength of salvations* [a]Ps. 20:6
9 [I]Or, *rule,* [a]Deut. 9:29; 1Kgs. 8:51, 53 [b]Ps. 78:71

1 [I]Hebr. *ye sons of the mighty* [a]1Chr. 16:28, 29; Ps. 96:7, 8, 9
2 [I]Hebr. *the honor of his name* [II]Or, *in his glorious sanctuary* [a]2Chr. 20:21
3 [I]Or, *great waters* [a]Job 37:4, 5
4 [I]Hebr. *in power* [II]Hebr. *in majesty*
5 [a]Isa. 2:13
6 [a]Ps. 114:4 [b]Deut. 3:9 **7** [I]Hebr. *cutteth out*
8 [a]Num. 13:26 **9** [I]Or, *to be in pain* [II]Or, *every whit of it uttereth* [a]Job 39:1-3

10 The LORD [a]sitteth upon the flood; yea, [b]the LORD sitteth King[4428] for ever.[5769]

11 [a]The LORD will give strength unto his people;[5971] the LORD will bless[1288] his people with peace.

A Prayer of Thanksgiving

A Psalm *and* Song *at* the dedication of the house of David.

30 🔑 I will extol thee, O LORD; for thou hast [a]lifted me up, and hast not made my foes to [b]rejoice over me.

2 O LORD my God,[430] I cried unto thee, and thou hast [a]healed me.

3 O LORD, [a]thou hast brought up[5927] my soul[5315] from the grave:[7585] thou hast kept me alive, that I should not [b]go down to the pit.[953]

4 [a]Sing[2167] unto the LORD, O ye saints[2623] of his, and give thanks[3034] [I]at the remembrance[2143] of his holiness.[6944]

5 For [I][a]his anger[639] *endureth but* a moment; [b]in his favour[7522] *is* life:[2416] weeping may endure [II]for a night, [c]but [III]joy *cometh* in the morning.

6 And [a]in my prosperity I said, I shall never be moved.

7 LORD, by thy favour thou hast [I]made my mountain to stand strong: [a]thou didst hide thy face, *and* I was troubled.[926]

8 I cried[7121] to thee, O LORD; and unto the LORD I made supplication.[2603]

9 What profit *is there* in my blood,[1818] when I go down to the pit?[7845] [a]Shall[3034] the dust[6083] praise[3034] thee? shall it declare[5046] thy truth?[571]

10 Hear,[8085] O LORD, and have mercy[2603] upon me: LORD, be thou my helper.

11 [a]Thou hast turned[2015] for me my mourning into dancing: thou hast put off my sackcloth, and girded me with gladness;

12 To the end that [I][a]*my* glory[3519] may sing praise[2167] to thee, and not be silent. O LORD my God, I will give thanks unto thee for ever.[5769]

Commitment to God

To the chief Musician, A Psalm of David.

31 In [a]thee, O LORD, do I put my trust;[2620] let me never be ashamed:[954] [b]deliver me in thy righteousness.[6666]

2 [a]Bow down thine ear[241] to me; deliver[5337] me speedily: be thou [I]my strong rock, for an house of defence to save[3467] me.

3 [a]For thou *art* my rock and my fortress; therefore [b]for thy name's sake lead[5148] me, and guide me.

4 Pull me out of the net that they have laid privily[2934] for me: for thou *art* my strength.

5 [a]Into thine hand[3027] I commit my spirit:[7307] thou hast redeemed[6299] me, O LORD God[410] of truth.[571]

6 I have hated them [a]that regard[8104] lying[7723] vanities: but I trust[982] in the LORD.

7 I will be glad and rejoice in thy mercy:[2617] for thou hast considered[7200] my trouble; thou hast [a]known[3045] my soul[5315] in adversities;

8 And hast not [a]shut me up into the hand of the enemy: [b]thou hast set my feet in a large room.

9 Have mercy[2603] upon me, O LORD, for I am in trouble: [a]mine eye is consumed with grief,[3708] *yea,* my soul and my belly.[990]

10 For my life[2416] is spent[3615] with grief, and my years with sighing: my strength faileth[3782] because of mine iniquity,[5771] and [a]my bones[6106] are consumed.

11 [a]I was a reproach[2781] among all mine enemies, but [b]especially among my neighbours,[7934] and a fear[6343] to mine acquaintance:[3045] [c]they that did see me without fled from me.

---

10 [a]Gen. 6:17; Job 38:8, 25 [b]Ps. 10:16
11 [a]Ps. 28:8

1 [a]Ps. 28:9 [b]Ps. 25:2; 35:19, 24
2 [a]Ps. 6:2; 103:3
3 [a]Ps. 86:13 [b]Ps. 28:1
4 [I]Or, *to the memorial* [a]1Chr. 16:4; Ps. 97:12
5 [I]Hebr. there is but *a moment in his anger* [II]Hebr. *in the evening* [III]Hebr. *singing* [a]Ps. 103:9; Isa. 26:20; 54:7, 8; 2Cor. 4:17 [b]Ps. 63:3 [c]Ps. 126:5
6 [a]Job 29:18
7 [I]Hebr. *settled strength for my mountain* [a]Ps. 104:29
9 [a]Ps. 6:5; 88:11; 115:17; 118:17; Isa. 38:18
11 [a]2Sam. 6:14; Isa. 61:3; Jer. 31:4
12 [I]That is, my *tongue,* or, my *soul* [a]Gen. 49:6; Ps. 16:9; 57:8

1 [a]Ps. 22:5; 25:2; 71:1; Isa. 49:23 [b]Ps. 143:1
2 [I]Hebr. *to me for a rock of strength* [a]Ps. 71:2
3 [a]Ps. 18:2 [b]Ps. 23:3; 25:11
5 [a]Luke 23:46; Acts 7:59
6 [a]Jon. 2:8
7 [a]John 10:27
8 [a]Deut. 32:30; 1Sam. 17:46; 24:18 [b]Ps. 4:1; 18:19
9 [a]Ps. 6:7
10 [a]Ps. 32:3; 102:3
11 [a]Ps. 41:8; Isa. 53:4 [b]Job 19:13; Ps. 38:11; 88:8, 18 [c]Ps. 64:8

🔑 **30:1** David wrote this psalm to celebrate the dedication of his house and the beginning of his reign in Jerusalem (2 Sam. 5:11; 7:2).

12 [a]I am forgotten as a dead man[4191] out of mind:[3820] I am like [I]a broken vessel.

13 [a]For I have heard[8085] the slander of many: [b]fear[4032] *was* on every side: while they [c]took counsel[3245] together against me, they devised[2161] to take away my life.[5315]

14 But I trusted[982] in thee, O LORD: I said, Thou *art* my God.[430]

15 My times[6256] *are* in thy hand: deliver me from the hand of mine enemies, and from them that persecute me.

16 [a]Make thy face to shine upon thy servant:[5650] save me for thy mercies' sake.

17 [a]Let me not be ashamed, O LORD; for I have called upon[7121] thee: let the wicked[7563] be ashamed, *and* [I][b]let them be silent in the grave.[7585]

18 [a]Let the lying lips[8193] be put to silence; which [b]speak[1696] [I]grievous things proudly and contemptuously against the righteous.[6662]

19 [a]*Oh* how great *is* thy goodness, which thou hast laid up for them that fear[3373] thee; *which* thou hast wrought for them that trust in thee before the sons[1121] of men![120]

20 [a]Thou shalt hide them in the secret of thy presence from the pride of man:[376] [b]thou shalt keep them secretly in a pavilion from the strife[7379] of tongues.

21 Blessed[1288] *be* the LORD: for [a]he hath shewed me his marvellous[6381] kindness[2617] [b]in a [I]strong city.

22 For [a]I said in my haste, [b]I am cut off from before thine eyes: nevertheless thou heardest[8085] the voice of my supplications[8469] when I cried unto thee.

23 [a]O love[157] the LORD, all ye his saints:[2623] *for* the LORD preserveth[5341] the faithful,[539] and plentifully rewardeth[7999] the proud doer.[6213]

24 [a]Be of good courage,[2388] and he shall strengthen your heart,[3824] all ye that hope[3176] in the LORD.

12 [I]Hebr. *a vessel that perisheth* [a]Ps. 88:4, 5
13 [a]Jer. 20:10 [b]Jer. 6:25; 20:3; Lam. 2:22 [c]Matt. 27:1
16 [a]Num. 6:25, 26; Ps. 4:6; 67:1
17 [I]Or, *let them be cut off for the grave* [a]Ps. 25:2 [b]1Sam. 2:9; Ps. 115:17
18 [I]Hebr. *a hard thing* [a]Ps. 12:3 [b]1Sam. 2:3; Ps. 94:4; Jude 1:15
19 [a]Isa. 64:4; 1Cor. 2:9
20 [a]Ps. 27:5; 32:7 [b]Job 5:21
21 [I]Or, *fenced city* [a]Ps. 17:7 [b]1Sam. 23:7
22 [a]1Sam. 23:26; Ps. 116:11 [b]Isa. 38:11, 12; Lam. 3:54; Jon. 2:4
23 [a]Ps. 34:9
24 [a]Ps. 27:14

1 [a]Ps. 85:2; Rom. 4:6, 7, 8
2 [a]2Cor. 5:19 [b]John 1:47
4 [a]1Sam. 5:6, 11; Job 33:7; Ps. 38:2
5 [a]Prov. 28:13; Isa. 65:24; Luke 15:18, 21; 1John 1:9
6 [I]Hebr. *in a time of finding* [a]1Tim. 1:16 [b]Isa. 55:6; John 7:34
7 [a]Ps. 9:9; 27:5; 31:20; 119:114 [b]Ex. 15:1; Judg. 5:1; 2Sam. 22:1
8 [I]Hebr. *I will counsel* thee, *mine eye* shall be *upon thee*
9 [a]Prov. 26:3; James 3:3 [b]Job 35:11
10 [a]Prov. 13:21; Rom. 2:9 [b]Ps. 34:8; 84:12; Prov. 16:20; Jer. 17:7
11 [a]Ps. 64:10; 68:3

Confession and Forgiveness

A Psalm of David, Maschil.

32 🔑 Blessed[835] *is he whose* [a]transgression[6588] *is* forgiven,[5375] *whose* sin[2401] *is* covered.[3680]

2 Blessed *is* the man[120] unto whom the LORD [a]imputeth[2803] not iniquity,[5771] and [b]in whose spirit[7307] *there is* no guile.

3 When I kept silence, my bones[6106] waxed old through my roaring all the day[3117] long.

4 For day[3119] and night[3915] thy [a]hand[3027] was heavy[3513] upon me: my moisture is turned[2015] into the drought of summer. Selah.

5 I acknowledged[3045] my sin unto thee, and mine iniquity have I not hid. [a]I said, I will confess[3034] my transgressions[6588] unto the LORD; and thou forgavest[5375] the iniquity of my sin.[2403] Selah.

6 [a]For this shall every one that is godly[2623] [b]pray[6419] unto thee [I]in a time[6256] when thou mayest be found: surely in the floods[7858] of great waters they shall not come nigh[5060] unto him.

7 [a]Thou *art* my hiding place; thou shalt preserve[5341] me from trouble; thou shalt compass me about with [b]songs of deliverance. Selah.

8 I will instruct thee and teach[3384] thee in the way[1870] which thou shalt go: [I]I will guide[3289] thee with mine eye.

9 [a]Be ye not as the horse, *or* as the mule, *which* have [b]no understanding:[995] whose mouth must be held in with bit and bridle, lest they come near[7126] unto thee.

10 [a]Many sorrows *shall be* to the wicked:[7563] but [b]he that trusteth[982] in the LORD, mercy[2617] shall compass him about.

11 [a]Be glad in the LORD, and rejoice, ye righteous:[6662] and shout for joy, all *ye that are* upright[3477] in heart.[3820]

🔑 **32:1** Written about the same time as Psalm 51, David expresses in this psalm his desire for blessing and forgiveness from God. Psalm 32 is the first in the group of psalms known as the "Penitential Psalms" (Ps. 35; 51; 102; 130; 143).

Praising God

33 Rejoice [a]in the LORD, O ye righteous:[6662] *for* [b]praise[8416] is comely[5000] for the upright.[3477]

2 Praise[3034] the LORD with harp: sing[2167] unto him with the psaltery [a]*and* an instrument of ten strings.

3 [a]Sing[7891] unto him a new song;[7892] play skilfully[3190] with a loud noise.

4 For the word[1697] of the LORD *is* right;[3477] and all his works *are done* in truth.[530]

5 [a]He loveth[157] righteousness[6666] and judgment:[4941] [b]the earth[776] is full of the [I]goodness[2617] of the LORD.

6 [a]By the word of the LORD were[6213] the heavens[8064] made;[6213] and [b]all the host[6635] of them [c]by the breath[7307] of his mouth.[6310]

7 [a]He gathereth the waters of the sea together[3664] as an heap: he layeth up the depth in storehouses.

8 Let all the earth fear[3372] the LORD: let all the inhabitants of the world[8398] stand in awe of him.

9 For [a]he spake,[559] and it was *done;* he commanded,[6680] and it stood fast.

10 [a]The LORD [I]bringeth[6331] the counsel[6098] of the heathen[1471] to nought:[6331] he maketh the devices[4284] of the people[5971] of none effect.

11 [a]The counsel of the LORD standeth for ever,[5769] the thoughts[4284] of his heart[3820] [I]to all generations.[1755]

12 [a]Blessed[835] *is* the nation[1471] whose God[430] *is* the LORD; *and* the people *whom* he hath [b]chosen for his own inheritance.[5159]

13 [a]The LORD looketh from heaven; he beholdeth[7200] all the sons[1121] of men.[120]

14 From the place of his habitation he looketh upon all the inhabitants of the earth.

15 He fashioneth[3335] their hearts[3820] alike; [a]he considereth[995] all their works.

16 [a]There is[3467] no king[4428] saved[3467] by the multitude of an host:[2428] a mighty man is not delivered[5337] by much strength.

17 [a]An horse *is* a vain thing[8267] for safety:[8668] neither shall he deliver *any* by his great strength.[2428]

18 [a]Behold, the eye of the LORD *is* [b]upon them that fear[3373] him, upon them that hope[3176] in his mercy;[2617]

19 To deliver[5337] their soul[5315] from death,[4194] and [a]to keep them alive in famine.

20 [a]Our soul waiteth for the LORD: [b]he *is* our help and our shield.

21 For our [a]heart shall rejoice in him, because we have trusted[982] in his holy[6944] name.

22 Let thy mercy, O LORD, be upon us, according as we hope in thee.

Praising God for Deliverance

A Psalm of David, when he changed his behaviour before Abimelech; who drove him away, and he departed.

34 I will [a]bless[1288] the LORD at all times:[6256] his praise[8416] *shall* continually[8548] *be* in my mouth.[6310]

2 My soul[5315] shall make her [a]boast[1984] in the LORD: [b]the humble shall hear[8085] *thereof,* and be glad.

3 O [a]magnify the LORD with me, and let us exalt his name together.

4 I [a]sought the LORD, and he heard me, and delivered[5337] me from all my fears.[4035]

5 [I]They looked unto him, and were lightened: and their faces were not ashamed.

6 [a]This poor man cried,[7121] and the LORD heard[8085] *him,* and [b]saved[3467] him out of all his troubles.

7 [a]The angel[4397] of the LORD [b]encampeth round about them that fear[3373] him, and delivereth[2502] them.

8 O [a]taste and see that the LORD *is* good:[2896] [b]blessed[835] *is* the man[1397] *that* trusteth[2620] in him.

9 [a]O fear[3372] the LORD, ye his saints:[6918] for *there is* no want to them that fear[3373] him.

10 [a]The young lions do lack, and suffer hunger: [b]but they that seek the LORD shall not want any good *thing.*

1 [a]Ps. 32:11; 97:12 [b]Ps. 147:1
2 [a]Ps. 92:3; 144:9
3 [a]Ps. 96:1; 98:1; 144:9; 149:1; Isa. 42:10; Rev. 5:9
5 [I]Or, *mercy* [a]Ps. 11:7; 45:7 [b]Ps. 119:64
6 [a]Gen. 1:6, 7; Heb. 11:3; 2Pet. 3:5 [b]Gen. 2:1 [c]Job 26:13
7 [a]Gen. 1:9; Job 26:10; 38:8
9 [a]Gen. 1:3; Ps. 148:5
10 [I]Hebr. *maketh frustrate* [a]Isa. 8:10; 19:3
11 [I]Hebr. *to generation and generation* [a]Job 23:13; Prov. 19:21; Isa. 46:10
12 [a]Ps. 65:4; 144:15 [b]Ex. 19:5; Deut. 7:6
13 [a]2Chr. 16:9; Job 28:24; Ps. 11:4; 14:2; Prov. 15:3
15 [a]Job 34:21; Jer. 32:19
16 [a]Ps. 44:6
17 [a]Ps. 20:7; 147:10; Prov. 21:31
18 [a]Job 36:7; Ps. 34:15; 1Pet. 3:12 [b]Ps. 147:11
19 [a]Job 5:20; Ps. 37:19
20 [a]Ps. 62:1, 5; 130:6 [b]Ps. 115:9, 10, 11
21 [a]Ps. 13:5; Zech. 10:7; John 16:22

1 [a]Eph. 5:20; 1Thess. 5:18; 2Thess. 1:3; 2:13
2 [a]Jer. 9:24; 1Cor. 1:31; 2Cor. 10:17 [b]Ps. 119:74; 142:7
3 [a]Ps. 69:30; Luke 1:46
4 [a]Matt. 7:7; Luke 11:9
5 [I]Or, *They flowed* unto him
6 [a]Ps. 3:4 [b]2Sam. 22:1; Ps. 34:17, 19
7 [a]Dan. 6:22; Heb. 1:14 [b]Gen. 32:1, 2; 2Kgs. 6:17; Zech. 9:8
8 [a]1Pet. 2:3 [b]Ps. 2:12
9 [a]Ps. 31:23
10 [a]Job 4:10, 11 [b]Ps. 84:11

11 Come, ye children,[1121] hearken[8085] unto me: [a]I will teach[3925] you the fear[3374] of the LORD.

12 [a]What man[376] *is he that* desireth[2655] life,[2416] *and* loveth[157] *many* days,[3117] that he may see good?

13 Keep[5341] thy tongue from evil,[7451] and thy lips[8193] from [a]speaking[1696] guile.[4820]

14 [a]Depart[5493] from evil, and do[6213] good; [b]seek peace, and pursue it.

15 [a]The eyes of the LORD *are* upon the righteous,[6662] and his ears[241] *are open* unto their [b]cry.

16 [a]The face of the LORD *is* against them that do evil, [b]to cut off[3772] the remembrance[2143] of them from the earth.[776]

17 *The righteous* cry, and [a]the LORD heareth,[8085] and delivereth[5337] them out of all their troubles.

18 [a]The LORD *is* nigh [b]unto them that are of a broken[7665] heart;[3820] and saveth[3467] such as be of a contrite[1793] spirit.[7307]

19 [a]Many *are* the afflictions[7451] of the righteous: [b]but the LORD delivereth him out of them all.

🔑 20 He keepeth[8104] all his bones:[6106] [a]not one of them is broken.

21 [a]Evil shall slay[4191] the wicked:[7563] and they that hate[8130] the righteous [I]shall be desolate.

22 The LORD [a]redeemeth[6299] the soul of his servants:[5650] and none of them that trust[2620] in him shall be desolate.[816]

A Prayer for Rescue

A Psalm of David.

35 🔑 Plead[7378] [a]*my cause,* O LORD, with them that strive with me: [b]fight against them that fight against me.

2 [a]Take hold of shield and buckler,[6793] and stand up for mine help.

3 Draw out also the spear, and stop *the way* against them that persecute me: say[559] unto my soul,[5315] I *am* thy salvation.[3444]

4 [a]Let them be confounded[954] and put to shame that seek after my soul: let them be [b]turned back and brought to confusion that devise[2803] my hurt.[7451]

5 [a]Let them be as chaff before the wind:[7307] and let the angel[4397] of the LORD chase *them.*

6 Let their way be [Ia]dark[2822] and slippery: and let the angel of the LORD persecute them.

7 For without cause have they [a]hid for me their net *in* a pit,[7845] *which* without cause they have digged for my soul.

8 Let [a]destruction come upon him [I]at unawares;[3808,3045] and [b]let his net that he hath hid catch himself: into that very destruction let him fall.

9 And my soul shall be joyful in the LORD: [a]it shall rejoice in his salvation.

10 [a]All my bones[6106] shall say, LORD, [b]who *is* like unto thee, which deliverest[5337] the poor from him that is too strong[2389] for him, yea, the poor and the needy from him that spoileth him?

11 [Ia]False[2555] witnesses did rise up; [II]they laid to my charge *things* that I knew[3045] not.

12 [a]They rewarded[7999] me evil[7451] for good[2896] *to* the [I]spoiling[7908] of my soul.

13 But as for me, [a]when they were sick, my clothing *was* sackcloth: I [I]humbled my soul with fasting; [b]and my prayer[8605] returned[7725] into mine own bosom.

14 I [I]behaved myself [II]as though *he had been* my friend[7453] *or* brother:[251] I bowed down heavily,[6937] as one that mourneth *for his* mother.[517]

15 But in mine [Ia]adversity[6761] they

11 [a]Ps. 32:8 **12** [a]1Pet. 3:10, 11 **13** [a]1Pet. 2:22 **14** [a]Ps. 37:27; Isa. 1:16, 17 [b]Rom. 12:18; Heb. 12:14 **15** [a]Job 36:7; Ps. 33:18; 1Pet. 3:12 [b]Ps. 34:6, 17 **16** [a]Lev. 17:10; Jer. 44:11; Amos 9:4 [b]Prov. 10:7 **17** [a]Ps. 34:6, 15, 19; 145:19, 20 **18** [a]Ps. 145:18 [b]Ps. 51:17; Isa. 57:15; 61:1; 66:2 **19** [a]Prov. 24:16; 2Tim. 3:11, 12 [b]Ps. 34:6, 17 **20** [a]John 19:36 **21** [I]Or, *shall be guilty* [a]Ps. 94:23 **22** [a]2Sam. 4:9; 1Kgs. 1:29; Ps. 71:23; 103:4; Lam. 3:58

1 [a]Ps. 43:1; 119:154; Lam. 3:58 [b]Ex. 14:25 **2** [a]Isa. 42:13 **4** [a]Ps. 34:26; 40:14, 15; 70:2, 3 [b]Ps. 129:5 **5** [a]Job 21:18; Ps. 1:4; 83:13; Isa. 29:5; Hos. 13:3 **6** [I]Hebr. *darkness and slipperiness* [a]Ps. 73:18; Jer. 23:12 **7** [a]Ps. 9:15 **8** [I]Hebr. which *he knoweth not of* [a]1Thess. 5:3 [b]Ps. 7:15, 16; 57:6; 141:9, 10; Prov. 5:22 **9** [a]Ps. 13:5 **10** [a]Ps. 51:8 [b]Ex. 15:11; Ps. 71:19 **11** [I]Hebr. *Witnesses of wrong* [II]Hebr. *they asked me* [a]Ps. 27:12 **12** [I]Hebr. *depriving* [a]Ps. 38:20; 109:3-5; Jer. 18:20; John 10:32 **13** [I]Or, *afflicted* [a]Job 30:25; Ps. 69:10, 11 [b]Matt. 10:13; Luke 10:6 **14** [I]Hebr. *walked* [II]Hebr. *as a friend, as a brother to me* **15** [I]Hebr. *halting* [a]Ps. 38:17

🔑 **34:20** See the note on Psalm 22:1–31 for a discussion of the Messianic Psalms.

🔑 **35:1–28** This psalm reflects David's cry for help while he was being pursued by Saul and other enemies. See the note on Psalm 109:1–29 for a discussion of the Imprecatory Psalms.

rejoiced, and gathered themselves together:[622] *yea,* [b]the abjects[5222] gathered themselves together against me, and I knew *it* not; they did [c]tear *me,* and ceased not:

16 With hypocritical[2611] mockers in feasts, [a]they gnashed[2786] upon me with their teeth.

17 Lord,[136] how long wilt thou [a]look on? rescue[7725] my soul from their destructions,[7722] [I][b]my darling[3173] from the lions.

18 [a]I will give thee thanks in the great congregation:[6951] I will praise[1984] thee among [I]much people.[5971]

19 [a]Let not them that are mine enemies [I]wrongfully[8267] rejoice over me: *neither* [b]let them wink[7169] with the eye [c]that hate[8130] me without a cause.

20 For they speak[1696] not peace: but they devise deceitful[4820] matters against *them that are* quiet in the land.[776]

21 Yea, they [a]opened their mouth[6310] wide against me, *and* said, [b]Aha, aha, our eye hath seen[7200] *it.*

22 *This* thou hast [a]seen, O LORD: [b]keep not silence: O Lord, be not [c]far from me.

23 [a]Stir up thyself, and awake to my judgment,[4941] *even* unto my cause,[7379] my God[430] and my Lord.

24 [a]Judge[8199] me, O LORD my God, [b]according to thy righteousness;[6664] and [c]let them not rejoice over me.

25 [a]Let them not say in their hearts, [I]Ah, so would we have it: let them not say, [b]We have swallowed him up.[1104]

26 [a]Let them be ashamed[954] and brought to confusion[2659] together that rejoice at mine hurt: let them be [b]clothed with shame and dishonour that [c]magnify *themselves* against me.

27 [a]Let them shout for joy, and be glad, that favour[2655] [I]my righteous[6664] cause: yea, let them [b]say continually,[8548] Let the LORD be magnified, [c]which hath pleasure[2655] in the prosperity[7965] of his servant.[5650]

28 [a]And my tongue shall speak[1897] of thy righteousness *and* of thy praise[8416] all the day[3117] long.

15 [b]Job 30:1, 8, 12 [c]Job 16:9
16 [a]Job 16:9; Ps. 37:12; Lam. 2:16
17 [I]Hebr. *my only one* [a]Hab. 1:13 [b]Ps. 22:20
18 [I]Hebr. *strong* [a]Ps. 22:25, 31; 40:9, 10; 111:1
19 [I]Hebr. *falsely,* Ps. 38:19 [a]Ps. 13:4; 25:2; 38:16 [b]Job 15:12; Prov. 6:13; 10:10 [c]Ps. 69:4; 109:3; 119:161; Lam. 3:52; John 15:25
21 [a]Ps. 22:13 [b]Ps. 40:15; 54:7; 70:3
22 [a]Ex. 3:7; Acts 7:34 [b]Ps. 28:1; 83:1 [c]Ps. 10:1; 22:11, 19; 38:21; 71:12
23 [a]Ps. 44:23; 80:2
24 [a]Ps. 26:1 [b]2Thess. 1:6 [c]Ps. 35:19
25 [I]Hebr. *Ah, ah, our soul* [a]Ps. 27:12; 70:3; 140:8 [b]Lam. 2:16
26 [a]Ps. 35:4; Ps. 40:14 [b]Ps. 109:29; 132:18 [c]Ps. 38:16
27 [I]Hebr. *my righteousness,* Prov. 8:18 [a]Rom. 12:15; 1Cor. 12:26 [b]Ps. 70:4 [c]Ps. 149:4
28 [a]Ps. 50:15; 51:14; 71:24

1 [a]Rom. 3:18
2 [I]Hebr. *to find his iniquity to hate* [a]Deut. 29:19; Ps. 10:3; 49:18
3 [a]Ps. 12:2 [b]Jer. 4:22
4 [I]Or, *vanity* [a]Prov. 4:16; Mic. 2:1 [b]Isa. 65:2
5 [a]Ps. 57:10; 108:4
6 [I]Hebr. *the mountains of God* [a]Job 11:8; Ps. 77:19; Rom. 11:33 [b]Job 7:20; Ps. 145:9; 1Tim. 4:10
7 [I]Hebr. *precious* [a]Ps. 31:19 [b]Ruth 2:12; Ps. 17:8; 91:4

The Wickedness of Man

To the chief Musician, *A Psalm* of David the servant of the LORD.

36 The transgression[6588] of the wicked[7563] saith[5002] within[7130] my heart,[3820] *that* [a]there is no fear[6343] of God[430] before his eyes.

2 For [a]he flattereth himself in his own eyes, [I]until his iniquity[5771] be found to be hateful.

3 The words[1697] of his mouth[6310] *are* iniquity[205] and [a]deceit:[4820] [b]he hath left off to be wise,[7919] *and* to do good.[3190]

4 [a]He deviseth[2803] [I]mischief upon his bed; he setteth himself [b]in a way[1870] *that is* not good;[2896] he abhorreth[3988] not evil.[7451]

The Goodness of God

5 [a]Thy mercy,[2617] O LORD, *is* in the heavens;[8064] *and* thy faithfulness[530] *reacheth* unto the clouds.[7834]

6 Thy righteousness[6666] *is* like [I]the great mountains; [a]thy judgments[4941] *are* a great deep: O LORD, [b]thou preservest[3467] man[120] and beast.

7 [a]How [I]excellent *is* thy lovingkindness, O God! therefore the children[1121] of men[120] [b]put their trust[2620] under the shadow of thy wings.

8 [a]They shall be [I]abundantly satisfied with the fatness of thy house;[1004] and thou shalt make them drink of [b]the river [c]of thy pleasures.

9 [a]For with thee *is* the fountain of life:[2416] [b]in thy light shall we see light.[216]

10 O [I]continue thy lovingkindness [a]unto them that know thee; and thy righteousness to the [b]upright[3477] in heart.

11 Let not the foot of pride come against me, and let not the hand[3027] of the wicked remove me.

12 There are the workers of iniquity fallen:[5307] they are cast down, [a]and shall not be able to rise.

8 [I]Hebr. *watered* [a]Ps. 65:4 [b]Job 20:17; Rev. 22:1 [c]Ps. 16:11 **9** [a]Jer. 2:13; John 4:10, 14 [b]1Pet. 2:9
10 [I]Hebr. *draw out at length* [a]Jer. 22:16 [b]Ps. 7:10; 94:15; 97:11 **12** [a]Ps. 1:5

God Takes Care of His Own

A Psalm of David.

37 Fret [a]not thyself[2734] because of evildoers,[7489] neither be thou envious[7065] against the workers of iniquity.[5766]

2 For they shall soon be cut down [a]like the grass, and wither as the green herb.

3 Trust[982] in the LORD, and do[6213] good;[2896] *so* shalt thou dwell[7931] in the land,[776] and [I]verily[530] thou shalt be fed.

4 [a]Delight thyself[6026] also in the LORD; and he shall give thee the desires[4862] of thine heart.[3820]

5 [I][a]Commit[1556] thy way[1870] unto the LORD; trust also in him; and he shall bring *it* to pass.

6 [a]And he shall bring forth thy righteousness[6664] as the light,[216] and thy judgment[4941] as the noonday.

7 [I][a]Rest in the LORD, [b]and wait patiently[2342] for him: [c]fret not thyself because of him who prospereth in his way, because of the man[376] who bringeth wicked devices[4209] to pass.

8 Cease[7503] from anger,[639] and forsake[5800] wrath:[2534] [a]fret not thyself in any wise to do evil.[7489]

9 [a]For evildoers shall be cut off:[3772] but those that wait upon[6960] the LORD, they shall [b]inherit[3423] the earth.[776]

10 For [a]yet a little while, and the wicked[7563] *shall* not *be:* yea, [b]thou shalt diligently consider[995] his place, and it *shall* not *be.*

11 [a]But the meek shall inherit the earth; and shall delight themselves in the abundance of peace.

12 The wicked [I]plotteth[2161] against the just, [a]and gnasheth[2786] upon him with his teeth.

13 [a]The Lord[136] shall laugh at him: for he seeth[7200] that [b]his day[3117] is coming.

14 The wicked have drawn out the sword,[2719] and have bent their bow, to cast down[5307] the poor and needy, *and* to slay[2873] [I]such as be of upright[8549] conversation.[1870]

15 [a]Their sword shall enter into their own heart, and their bows shall be broken.[7665]

16 [a]A little that a righteous man[6662] hath *is* better[2896] than the riches of many wicked.

17 For [a]the arms of the wicked shall be broken: but the LORD upholdeth[5564] the righteous.

18 The LORD [a]knoweth the days of the upright:[8549] and their inheritance[5159] shall be [b]for ever.[5769]

19 They shall not be ashamed[954] in the evil[7451] time:[6256] and [a]in the days of famine they shall be satisfied.

20 But the wicked shall perish,[6] and the enemies of the LORD *shall be* as [I]the fat of lambs:[3733] they shall consume; [a]into smoke shall they consume away.

21 The wicked borroweth, and payeth not again:[7999] but [a]the righteous sheweth mercy,[2603] and giveth.

22 [a]For *such as be* blessed[1288] of him shall inherit the earth; and *they that be* cursed[7043] of him [b]shall be cut off.

23 [a]The steps of a *good* man[1397] are [I]ordered[3559] by the LORD: and he delighteth[2654] in his way.

24 [a]Though he fall, he shall not be utterly cast down: for the LORD upholdeth *him with* his hand.[3027]

🔑 25 I have been young, and *now* am old;[2204] yet have I not seen[7200] the righteous forsaken,[5800] nor his seed[2233] [a]begging[1245] bread.

1 [a]Ps. 73:3; Ps. 37:7; Prov. 23:17; 24:1, 19
2 [a]Ps. 90:5, 6
3 [I]Hebr. *in truth,* or, *stableness*
4 [a]Isa. 58:14
5 [I]Hebr. *Roll thy way upon the LORD* [a]Ps. 55:22; Prov. 16:3; Matt. 6:25; Luke 12:22; 1Pet. 5:7
6 [a]Job 11:17; Mic. 7:9
7 [I]Hebr. *Be silent to the LORD* [a]Ps. 62:1 [b]Isa. 30:15; Lam. 3:26 [c]Ps. 37:1, 8; Jer. 12:1
8 [a]Ps. 73:3; Eph. 4:26
9 [a]Job 27:13, 14 [b]Ps. 37:11, 22, 29; Isa. 57:13
10 [a]Heb. 10:36, 37 [b]Job 7:10; 20:9
11 [a]Matt. 5:5
12 [I]Or, *practiseth* [a]Ps. 35:16
13 [a]Ps. 2:4 [b]1Sam. 26:10
14 [I]Hebr. *the upright of way*
15 [a]Mic. 5:6
16 [a]Prov. 15:16; 16:8; 1Tim. 6:6
17 [a]Job 38:15; Ps. 10:15; Ezek. 30:21
18 [a]Ps. 1:6 [b]Isa. 60:21
19 [a]Job 5:20; Ps. 33:19
20 [I]Hebr. *the preciousness of lambs* [a]Ps. 102:3
21 [a]Ps. 112:5, 9
22 [a]Prov. 3:33 [b]Ps. 37:9
23 [I]Or, *established* [a]1Sam. 2:9; Prov. 16:9
24 [a]Ps. 34:19, 20; 40:2; 91:12; Prov. 24:16; Mic. 7:8; 2Cor. 4:9
25 [a]Job 15:23; Ps. 59:15; 109:10

🔑 **37:25** The psalmist here merely described his own experience. He personally had never seen "the righteous forsaken nor his seed begging bread." This does not mean that this never occurs. God does take care of His people. There is enough wealth in the world to provide food, clothing, and shelter for all. However, some do get more than their share, and others suffer. If a good man is wasteful, acts unwisely, or speculates unduly, then God will not necessarily intervene to keep him from ruin.

26 [a]*He is* [I]ever merciful,[2603] and lendeth; and his seed *is* blessed.[1293]

27 [a]Depart[5493] from evil, and do good; and dwell for evermore.[5769]

28 For the LORD [a]loveth[157] judgment, and forsaketh[5800] not his saints;[2623] they are preserved[8104] for ever: [b]but the seed of the wicked shall be cut off.

29 [a]The righteous shall inherit the land, and dwell therein for ever.[5703]

30 [a]The mouth[6310] of the righteous speaketh[1897] wisdom,[2451] and his tongue talketh of judgment.

31 [a]The law[8451] of his God[430] *is* in his heart; none of his [I]steps shall slide.

32 The wicked [a]watcheth the righteous, and seeketh to slay[4191] him.

33 The LORD [a]will not leave[5800] him in his hand, nor [b]condemn[7561] him when he is judged.[8199]

34 [a]Wait on[6960] the LORD, and keep[8104] his way, and he shall exalt thee to inherit the land: [b]when the wicked are cut off, thou shall see *it.*

35 [a]I have seen the wicked in great power, and spreading himself like [I]a green bay tree.

36 Yet he [a]passed away,[5674] and, lo, he *was* not: yea, I sought him, but he could not be found.

37 Mark[8104] the perfect[8535] *man,* and behold[7200] the upright: for [a]the end[319] of *that* man *is* peace.

38 [a]But the transgressors[6586] shall be destroyed[8045] together: the end of the wicked shall be cut off.

39 But [a]the salvation[8668] of the righteous *is* of the LORD: *he is* their strength [b]in the time of trouble.

40 And [a]the LORD shall help them, and deliver them: he shall deliver[6403] them from the wicked, and save[3467] them, [b]because they trust[2620] in him.

A Prayer of Penitence

A Psalm of David, to bring to remembrance.

38 O [a]LORD, rebuke[3198] me not in thy wrath:[7110] neither chasten me in thy hot displeasure.[2534]

2 For [a]thine arrows stick fast in me, and [b]thy hand[3027] presseth me sore.

3 *There is* no soundness in my flesh[1320] because of thine anger;[2195] [a]neither *is there any* [I]rest in my bones[6106] because of my sin.[2403]

4 For [a]mine iniquities[5771] are gone over mine head:[7218] as an heavy burden[4853] they are too [b]heavy[3513] for me.

5 My wounds stink[887] *and* are corrupt because of my foolishness.

6 I am troubled;[5753] [a]I am bowed down greatly; [b]I go mourning[6937] all the day[3117] long.

7 For my loins are filled with a [a]loathsome[7033] *disease:* and *there is* [b]no soundness in my flesh.

8 I am feeble[6313] and sore broken: [a]I have roared by reason of the disquietness of my heart.[3820]

9 Lord,[136] all my desire *is* before thee; and my groaning is not hid from thee.

10 My heart panteth, my strength faileth[5800] me: as for [a]the light[216] of mine eyes, it also [I]is gone from me.

11 [a]My lovers[157] and my friends[7453] [b]stand aloof from my [I]sore;[5061] and [II]my kinsmen [c]stand afar off.

12 They also that seek after my life[5315] [a]lay snares[5367] *for me:* and they that seek my hurt[7451] [b]speak[1696] mischievous things,[1942] and [c]imagine[1897] deceits all the day long.

13 But [a]I, as a deaf *man,* heard[8085] not; [b]and *I was* as a dumb man *that* openeth not his mouth.[6310]

14 Thus I was as a man[376] that heareth not, and in whose mouth *are* no reproofs.[8433]

15 For [I]in thee, O LORD, [a]do I hope:[3176] thou wilt [II]hear, O Lord my God.[430]

16 For I said, *Hear me,* [a]lest *otherwise* they should rejoice over me: when my [b]foot slippeth, they [c]magnify *themselves* against me.

17 For I *am* ready[3559] [I][a]to halt, and my sorrow *is* continually[8548] before me.

18 For I will [a]declare[5046] mine iniquity;[5771] I will be [b]sorry for my sin.

26 [I]Hebr. *all the day* [a]Deut. 15:8, 10; Ps. 112:5, 9
27 [a]Ps. 34:14; Isa. 1:16, 17
28 [a]Ps. 11:7 [b]Ps. 21:10; Prov. 2:22; Isa. 14:20
29 [a]Prov. 2:21
30 [a]Matt. 12:35
31 [I]Or, *goings* [a]Deut. 6:6; Ps. 40:8; 119:98; Isa. 51:7
32 [a]Ps. 10:8
33 [a]2Pet. 2:9 [b]Ps. 109:31
34 [a]Ps. 27:14; 37:9; Prov. 20:22 [b]Ps. 52:5, 6; 91:8
35 [I]Or, *a green tree that groweth in his own soil* [a]Job 5:3
36 [a]Job 20:5
37 [a]Isa. 32:17; 57:2
38 [a]Ps. 1:4; 52:5
39 [a]Ps. 3:8 [b]Ps. 9:9
40 [a]Isa. 31:5 [b]1Chr. 5:20; Dan. 3:17, 28; 6:23

1 [a]Ps. 6:1
2 [a]Job 6:4 [b]Ps. 32:4
3 [I]Hebr. *peace, or, health* [a]Ps. 6:2
4 [a]Ezra 9:6; Ps. 40:12 [b]Matt. 11:28
6 [a]Ps. 35:14 [b]Job 30:28; Ps. 42:9; 43:2
7 [a]Job 7:5 [b]Ps. 38:3
8 [a]Job 3:24; Ps. 22:1; Isa. 59:11
10 [I]Hebr. *is not with me* [a]Ps. 6:7; 88:9
11 [I]Hebr. *stroke* [II]Or, *my neighbors* [a]Ps. 31:11 [b]Luke 10:31, 32 [c]Luke 23:49
12 [a]2Sam. 17:1-3 [b]2Sam. 16:7, 8 [c]Ps. 35:20
13 [a]2Sam. 16:10 [b]Ps. 39:2, 9
15 [I]Or, *thee do I wait for* [II]Or, *answer* [a]2Sam. 16:12; Ps. 39:7
16 [a]Ps. 13:4 [b]Deut. 32:35 [c]Ps. 35:26
17 [I]Hebr. *for halting* [a]Ps. 35:15
18 [a]Ps. 32:5; Prov. 28:13 [b]2Cor. 7:9, 10

19 But mine enemies [I]*are* lively, *and* they are strong: and they that [a]hate[8130] me wrongfully[8267] are multiplied.

20 They also [a]that render[7999] evil[7451] for good[2896] are mine adversaries;[7853] [b]because I follow *the thing that* good *is.*

21 Forsake[5800] me not, O LORD: O my God, [a]be not far from me.

22 Make haste [I]to help me, O Lord [a]my salvation.[8668]

Vanity of Life

To the chief Musician, *even* to Jeduthun, A Psalm of David.

39 I said, I will [a]take heed[8104] to my ways,[1870] that I sin[2398] not with my tongue: I will keep[8104] [Ib]my mouth[6310] with a bridle, [c]while the wicked[7563] is before me.

2 [a]I was dumb with silence, I held my peace, *even* from good;[2896] and my sorrow was [I]stirred.

3 My heart[3820] was hot within[7130] me, while I was musing[1901] [a]the fire burned: *then* spake[1696] I with my tongue,

4 LORD, [a]make me to know mine end, and the measure of my days,[3117] what it *is: that* I may know [I]how frail I *am.*

5 Behold, thou hast made my days *as* an handbreadth; and [a]mine age[2465] *is* as nothing before thee: [b]verily every man[120] [I]at his best state[5324] *is* altogether vanity. Selah.

6 Surely every man[376] walketh in [Ia]a vain shew: surely they are disquieted in vain: [b]he heapeth up *riches,* and knoweth not who shall gather[622] them.

7 And now, Lord,[136] what wait I for?[6960] [a]my hope[8431] *is* in thee.

8 Deliver[5337] me from all my transgressions:[6588] make[7760] me not [a]the reproach[2781] of the foolish.

9 [a]I was dumb, I opened not my mouth; because [b]thou didst[6213] *it.*

10 [a]Remove thy stroke[5061] away from me: I am consumed[3615] by the [I]blow of thine hand.[3027]

11 When thou with rebukes[8433] dost correct[3256] man for iniquity,[5771] thou makest [I]his beauty[2530] [a]to consume away like a moth: [b]surely every man *is* vanity. Selah.

12 Hear[8085] my prayer,[8605] O LORD, and give ear[238] unto my cry; hold not thy peace at my tears: [a]for I *am* a stranger with thee, *and* a sojourner,[8453] [b]as all my fathers[1] *were.*

13 [a]O spare me, that I may recover strength, before I go hence, and [b]be no more.

A Song of Deliverance

To the chief Musician, A Psalm of David.

40 [I]I [a]waited patiently[6960] for the LORD; and he inclined unto me, and heard[8085] my cry.

2 He brought me up[5927] also out of [I]an horrible[7588] pit,[953] out of [a]the miry[3121] clay, and [b]set my feet upon a rock, *and* [c]established[3559] my goings.

3 [a]And he hath put a new song[7892] in my mouth,[6310] *even* praise[8416] unto our God:[430] [b]many shall see *it,* and fear,[3372] and shall trust[982] in the LORD.

4 [a]Blessed[835] *is* that man[1397] that maketh[7760] the LORD his trust, and [b]respecteth not the proud, nor such as [c]turn aside to lies.[3577]

5 [a]Many, O LORD my God, *are* thy wonderful works[6381] *which* thou hast done,[6213] [b]and thy thoughts[4284] *which are* to us-ward: [I]they cannot be reckoned up in order unto thee: *if* I would declare[5046] and speak[1696] *of them,* they are more than can be numbered.[5608]

🔑 6 [a]Sacrifice[2077] and offering[4503] thou didst not desire;[2654] mine ears[241] hast thou [Ib]opened: burnt offering[5930] and sin offering[2401] hast thou not required.[7592]

7 Then said I, Lo, I come: in the

19 [I]Hebr. being *living, are strong* [a]Ps. 35:19
20 [a]Ps. 35:12 [b]1Pet. 3:13; 1John 3:12
21 [a]Ps. 35:22
22 [I]Hebr. *for my help* [a]Ps. 27:1; 62:2, 6; Isa. 12:2

1 [I]Hebr. *a bridle,* or, *muzzle for my mouth* [a]1Kgs. 2:4; 2Kgs. 10:31 [b]Ps. 141:3; James 3:2 [c]Col. 4:5
2 [I]Hebr. *troubled* [a]Ps. 38:13
3 [a]Jer. 20:9
4 [I]Or, *what time I have here* [a]Ps. 90:12; 119:84
5 [I]Hebr. *settled* [a]Ps. 90:4 [b]Ps. 39:11; 62:9; 144:4
6 [I]Hebr. *an image* [a]1Cor. 7:31; James 4:14 [b]Job 27:17; Eccl. 2:18, 21, 26; 5:14; Luke 12:20, 21
7 [a]Ps. 38:15
8 [a]Ps. 44:13; 79:4
9 [a]Lev. 10:3; Job 40:4, 5; Ps. 38:13 [b]2Sam. 16:10; Job 2:10
10 [I]Hebr. *conflict* [a]Job 9:34; 13:21
11 [I]Hebr. *that which is to be desired in him to melt away* [a]Job 4:19; 13:28; Isa. 50:9; Hos. 5:12 [b]Ps. 39:5
12 [a]Lev. 25:23; 1Chr. 29:15; Ps. 119:19; 2Cor. 5:6; Heb. 11:13; 1Pet. 1:17; 2:11 [b]Gen. 47:9
13 [a]Job 10:20, 21; 14:5, 6 [b]Job 14:10-12

1 [I]Hebr. *In waiting I waited* [a]Ps. 27:14; 37:7
2 [I]Hebr. *a pit of noise* [a]Ps. 69:2, 14 [b]Ps. 27:5 [c]Ps. 37:23
3 [a]Ps. 33:3 [b]Ps. 52:6
4 [a]Ps. 34:8; Jer. 17:7 [b]Ps. 101:3, 7 [c]Ps. 125:5
5 [I]Or, *none can order them unto thee* [a]Ex. 15:11; Job 5:9; 9:10; Ps. 71:15; 92:5; 139:6, 17 [b]Isa. 55:8
6 [I]Hebr. *digged* [a]1Sam. 15:22; Ps. 50:8; 51:16; Isa. 1:11; 66:3; Hos. 6:6; Matt. 9:13; 12:7; Heb. 10:5 [b]Ex. 21:6

🔑 **40:6–8** See the note on Psalm 22:1–31 for a discussion of the Messianic Psalms.

volume[4039] of the book[5612] *it is* [a]written of me,

8 [a]I delight[2654] to do thy will,[7522] O my God: yea, thy law[8451] *is* [I][b]within my heart.[4578]

9 [a]I have preached[1319] righteousness[6664] in the great congregation:[6951] lo, [b]I have not refrained my lips,[8193] O LORD, [c]thou knowest.[3045]

10 [a]I have not hid thy righteousness[6666] within my heart;[3820] I have declared[559] thy faithfulness[530] and thy salvation:[8668] I have not concealed thy lovingkindness[2617] and thy truth[571] from the great congregation.

11 Withhold not thou thy tender mercies[7356] from me, O LORD: [a]let thy lovingkindness and thy truth continually[8548] preserve[5341] me.

A Prayer for Help

12 For innumerable evils have compassed me about: [a]mine iniquities[5771] have taken hold upon me, so that I am not able to look up;[7200] they are more than the hairs of mine head:[7218] therefore [b]my heart [I]faileth[5800] me.

13 [a]Be pleased, O LORD, to deliver[5337] me: O LORD, make haste to help me.

14 [a]Let them be ashamed[954] and confounded together that seek after my soul[5315] to destroy[5595] it; let them be driven backward and put to shame that wish[2655] me evil.[7451]

15 [a]Let them be [b]desolate[8074] for a reward of their shame that say[559] unto me, Aha, aha.

16 [a]Let all those that seek thee rejoice and be glad in thee: let such as love[157] thy salvation [b]say continually, The LORD be magnified.

17 [a]But I *am* poor and needy; *yet* [b]the Lord[136] thinketh[2803] upon me: thou *art* my help and my deliverer; make no tarrying, O my God.

7 [a]Luke 24:44
8 [I]Hebr. *in the midst of my bowels* [a]Ps. 119:16, 24, 47, 92; John 4:34; Rom. 7:22 [b]Ps. 37:31; Jer. 31:33; 2Cor. 3:3
9 [a]Ps. 22:22, 25; 35:18 [b]Ps. 119:13 [c]Ps. 139:2
10 [a]Acts 20:20, 27
11 [a]Ps. 43:3; 57:3; 61:7
12 [I]Hebr. *forsaketh* [a]Ps. 38:4 [b]Ps. 73:26
13 [a]Ps. 70:1
14 [a]Ps. 35:4, 26; 70:2, 3; 71:13
15 [a]Ps. 70:3 [b]Ps. 73:19
16 [a]Ps. 70:4 [b]Ps. 35:27
17 [a]Ps. 70:5 [b]1Pet. 5:7

1 [I]Or, *the weak, or, sick* [II]Hebr. *in the day of evil* [a]Prov. 14:21
2 [I]Or, *do not thou deliver* [a]Ps. 27:12
3 [I]Hebr. *turn*
4 [a]2Chr. 30:20; Ps. 6:2; 147:3
6 [a]Ps. 12:2; Prov. 26:24-26
7 [I]Hebr. *evil to me*
8 [I]Hebr. *A thing of Belial*
9 [I]Hebr. *the man of my peace* [II]Hebr. *magnified* [a]2Sam. 15:12; Job 19:19; Ps. 55:12, 13, 20; Jer. 20:10 [b]Obad. 1:7; John 13:18
12 [a]Job 36:7; Ps. 34:15
13 [a]Ps. 106:48

David's Prayer in Sickness

To the chief Musician, A Psalm of David.

41 Blessed[835] [a]*is* he that considereth[7919] [I]the poor: the LORD will deliver him [II]in time[3117] of trouble.[7451]

2 The LORD will preserve[8104] him, and keep him alive; *and* he shall be blessed[833] upon the earth:[776] [a]and [I]thou wilt not deliver him unto the will of his enemies.

3 The LORD will strengthen him upon the bed of languishing: thou wilt [I]make all his bed in his sickness.

4 I said, LORD, be merciful[2603] unto me: [a]heal my soul;[5315] for I have sinned[2398] against thee.

5 Mine enemies speak[559] evil[7451] of me, When shall he die,[4191] and his name perish?[6]

6 And if he come to see *me,* he [a]speaketh vanity:[7723] his heart[3820] gathereth[6908] iniquity[205] to itself; *when* he goeth abroad, he telleth[1696] *it.*

7 All that hate[8130] me whisper[3907] together against me: against me do they devise[2803] [I]my hurt.[7451]

8 [I]An evil[1100] disease,[1697] *say they,* cleaveth fast unto him: and *now* that he lieth he shall rise up no more.

9 [a]Yea, [I]mine own familiar friend,[376,7965] in whom I trusted,[982] [b]which did eat of my bread, hath [II]lifted up *his* heel[6119] against me.

10 But thou, O LORD, be merciful unto me, and raise me up, that I may requite them.

11 By this I know that thou favourest[2654] me, because mine enemy doth not triumph[7321] over me.

12 And as for me, thou upholdest[8551] me in mine integrity,[8537] and [a]settest[5324] me before thy face for ever.[5769]

13 [a]Blessed[1288] *be* the LORD[3068] God[430] of Israel from everlasting,[5769] and to everlasting. Amen,[543] and Amen.

41:1 This psalm of David recounts his great sorrow over losing his first son born to Bath-sheba (2 Sam. 11—16).

41:9 See the note on Psalm 22:1–31 for a discussion of the Messianic Psalms.

BOOK II

Thirsting for God

To the chief Musician, Maschil, for the sons of
Korah.

42 As the hart [I]panteth after the
water brooks, so panteth my
soul[5315] after thee, O God.[430]
2 [a]My soul thirsteth for God, for [b]the
living[2416] God:[410] when shall I come and
appear[7200] before God?
3 [a]My tears have been my meat
day[3119] and night,[3915] while [b]they continually say unto me, Where *is* thy
God?
4 When I remember[2142] these *things*,
[a]I pour out[8210] my soul in me: for I had
gone with the multitude, [b]I went with
them to the house[1004] of God, with the
voice of joy and praise,[8426] with a multitude that kept holyday.[2287]
5 [a]Why art thou [I]cast down, O my
soul? and *why* art thou disquieted in me?
[b]hope[3176] thou in God: for I shall yet
[II]praise[3034] him [III]*for* the help[3444] of his
countenance.
6 O my God, my soul is cast down
within me: therefore will I remember thee
from the land[776] of Jordan, and of the
Hermonites, from [I]the hill Mizar.
7 [a]Deep calleth[7121] unto deep at
the noise of thy waterspouts: [b]all thy
waves and thy billows are gone over[5674]
me.
8 *Yet* the LORD will [a]command[6680] his
lovingkindness in the daytime,[3119] and
[b]in the night his song[7892] *shall be* with
me, *and* my prayer[8605] unto the God of
my life.[2416]
9 I will say unto God my rock, Why
hast thou forgotten me? [a]why go I mourning[6937] because of the oppression of the
enemy?
10 *As* with a [I]sword in my bones,[6106]
mine enemies reproach me; [a]while they
say daily unto me, Where *is* thy God?
11 [a]Why art thou cast down, O my
soul? and why art thou disquieted within
me? hope thou in God: for I shall yet
praise him, *who is* the health of my countenance, and my God.

1 [I]Hebr. *brayeth*
2 [a]Ps. 63:1; 84:2; John 7:37 [b]1Thess. 1:9
3 [a]Ps. 80:5; 102:9 [b]Ps. 42:10; 79:10; 115:2
4 [a]Job 30:16; Ps. 62:8 [b]Isa. 30:29
5 [I]Hebr. *bowed down* [II]Or, *give thanks* [III]Or, *his presence* is *salvation* [a]Ps. 42:11; 43:5 [b]Lam. 3:24
6 [I]Or, *the little hill*, Ps. 133:3
7 [a]Jer. 4:20; Ezek. 7:26 [b]Ps. 88:7; Jon. 2:3
8 [a]Lev. 25:21; Deut. 28:8; Ps. 133:3 [b]Job 35:10; Ps. 32:7; 63:6; 149:5
9 [a]Ps. 38:6; 43:2
10 [I]Or, *killing* [a]Ps. 42:3; Joel 2:17; Mic. 7:10
11 [a]Ps. 42:5; 43:5

A Man in Exile

43 [a]Judge[8199] me, O God,[430] and
[b]plead my cause[7379] against
an [I]ungodly nation:[1471] O deliver me
[II]from the deceitful[4820] and unjust[5766]
man.[376]
2 For thou *art* the God of [a]my
strength: why dost thou cast me off?
[b]why go I mourning[6937] because of the
oppression of the enemy?
3 [a]O send out thy light[216] and thy
truth:[571] let them lead[5148] me; let them
bring me unto [b]thy holy[6944] hill, and to
thy tabernacles.[4908]
4 Then will I go unto the altar[4196] of
God, unto God[410] [I]my exceeding joy: yea,
upon the harp will I praise[3034] thee, O
God, my God.
5 [a]Why art thou cast down, O my
soul?[5315] and why art thou disquieted
within me? hope[3176] in God: for I shall
yet praise him, *who is* the health of my
countenance, and my God.

1 [I]Or, *unmerciful* [II]Hebr. *from a man of deceit and iniquity* [a]Ps. 26:1; 35:24 [b]Ps. 35:1
2 [a]Ps. 28:7 [b]Ps. 42:9
3 [a]Ps. 40:11; 57:3 [b]Ps. 3:4
4 [I]Hebr. *the gladness of my joy*
5 [a]Ps. 42:5, 11

A Prayer for Protection

To the chief Musician for the sons of Korah,
Maschil.

44 We have heard[8085] with our
ears,[241] O God,[430] [a]our fathers[1]
have told[5608] us, *what* work thou didst in
their days,[3117] in the times of old.[6924]
2 *How* [a]thou didst drive out[3423] the
heathen[1471] with thy hand,[3027] and plantedst them; *how* thou didst afflict the people,[3816] and cast them out.
3 For [a]they got not the land[776] in
possession by their own sword,[2719] neither did their own arm save[3467] them: but
thy right hand, and thine arm, and the
light[216] of thy countenance, [b]because
thou hadst a favour unto them.
4 [a]Thou art my King,[4428] O God:
command[6680] deliverances[3444] for Jacob.
5 Through thee [a]will we push down
our enemies: through thy name will
we tread them under[947] that rise up
against us.
6 For [a]I will not trust[982] in my bow,
neither shall my sword save me.

1 [a]Ex. 12:26, 27; Ps. 78:3
2 [a]Ex. 15:17; Deut. 7:1; Ps. 78:55; 80:8
3 [a]Deut. 8:17; Josh. 24:12 [b]Deut. 4:37; 7:7, 8
4 [a]Ps. 74:12
5 [a]Dan. 8:4
6 [a]Ps. 33:16; Hos. 1:7

7 But thou hast saved[3467] us from our enemies, and hast [a]put them to shame[954] that hated us.

8 [a]In God we boast[1984] all the day[3117] long, and praise[3034] thy name for ever.[5769] Selah.

9 But [a]thou hast cast off, and put us to shame; and goest not forth with our armies.[6635]

10 Thou makest us to [a]turn[7725] back from the enemy: and they which hate[8130] us spoil[8154] for themselves.

11 [a]Thou hast given us [I]like sheep *appointed* for meat; and hast [b]scattered us among the heathen.

12 [a]Thou sellest thy people[5971] [I]for nought,[3808] 1952 and dost not increase *thy wealth* by their price.

13 [a]Thou makest[7760] us a reproach[2781] to our neighbours, 7935 a scorn and a derision to them that are round about us.

14 [a]Thou makest us a byword among the heathen, [b]a shaking of the head[7218] among the people.

15 My confusion *is* continually before me, and the shame of my face hath covered[3680] me,

16 For the voice of him that reproacheth and blasphemeth; 1442 [a]by reason of the enemy and avenger.[5358]

17 [a]All this is come upon us; yet have we not forgotten thee, neither have we dealt falsely in thy covenant.[1285]

18 Our heart[3820] is not turned back, [a]neither have our [I]steps declined from thy way;[734]

19 Though thou hast sore broken us in [a]the place of dragons,[8577] and covered us [b]with the shadow of death.[6757]

20 If we have forgotten the name of our God, or [a]stretched out our hands[3709] to a strange[2114] god;[410]

21 [a]Shall not God search this out? for he knoweth the secrets of the heart.

22 [a]Yea, for thy sake are we killed[2026] all the day long; we are counted[2803] as sheep for the slaughter.[2878]

23 [a]Awake, why sleepest thou, O Lord?[136] arise, [b]cast *us* not off for ever.[5331]

24 [a]Wherefore hidest thou thy face, *and* forgettest our affliction and our oppression?

25 For [a]our soul[5315] is bowed down to the dust:[6083] our belly[990] cleaveth unto the earth.[776]

26 Arise [I]for our help, and redeem[6299] us for thy mercies' sake.

A Royal Wedding Song

To the chief Musician upon Shoshannim, for the sons of Korah, Maschil, A Song of loves.

45 My heart[3820] [I]is inditing[7370] a good[2896] matter:[1697] I speak[559] of the things which I have made touching the king:[4428] my tongue *is* the pen of a ready writer.[5608]

2 Thou art fairer than the children[1121] of men:[120] [a]grace[2580] is poured into thy lips:[8193] therefore God[430] hath blessed[1288] thee for ever.

3 Gird thy [a]sword[2719] upon *thy* thigh,[3409] [b]O *most* mighty, with thy glory[1935] and thy majesty.[1926]

4 [a]And in thy majesty [I]ride prosperously because of truth[571] and meekness *and* righteousness;[6664] and thy right hand shall teach[3384] thee terrible things.[3372]

5 Thine arrows *are* sharp[8150] in the heart of the king's enemies; *whereby* the people[5971] fall under thee.

6 [a]Thy throne,[3678] O God, *is* for ever[5769] and ever:[5703] the sceptre[7626] of thy kingdom[4438] *is* a right sceptre.

7 [a]Thou lovest[157] righteousness, and hatest wickedness:[7562] therefore [I][b]God, thy God, [c]hath anointed[4886] thee with the oil[8081] [d]of gladness above thy fellows.

8 [a]All thy garments *smell* of myrrh, 4753 and aloes, 174 *and* cassia, 7102 out of the ivory palaces,[1964] whereby they have made thee glad.

9 [a]Kings' daughters *were* among thy honourable women: [b]upon thy right hand

7 [a]Ps. 40:14
8 [a]Ps. 34:2; Jer. 9:24; Rom. 2:17
9 [a]Ps. 60:1, 10; 74:1; 88:14; 89:38; 108:11
10 [a]Lev. 26:17; Deut. 28:25; Josh. 7:8, 12
11 [I]Hebr. *as sheep of meat* [a]Rom. 8:36 [b]Deut. 4:27; 28:64; Ps. 60:1
12 [I]Hebr. *without riches* [a]Isa. 52:3, 4; Jer. 15:13
13 [a]Deut. 28:37; Ps. 79:4; 80:6
14 [a]Jer. 24:9 [b]2Kgs. 19:21; Job 16:4; Ps. 22:7
16 [a]Ps. 8:2
17 [a]Dan. 9:13
18 [I]Or, *goings* [a]Job 23:11; Ps. 119:51, 157
19 [a]Isa. 34:13; 35:7 [b]Ps. 23:4
20 [a]Job 11:13; Ps. 68:31
21 [a]Job 31:14; Ps. 139:1; Jer. 17:10
22 [a]Rom. 8:36
23 [a]Ps. 7:6; 35:23; 59:4, 5; 78:65 [b]Ps. 44:9
24 [a]Job 13:24; Ps. 13:1; 88:14
25 [a]Ps. 119:25
26 [I]Hebr. *a help for us*

1 [I]Hebr. *boileth, or, bubbleth up*
2 [a]Luke 4:22
3 [a]Isa. 49:2; Heb. 4:12; Rev. 1:16; 19:15 [b]Isa. 9:6
4 [I]Hebr. *prosper thou, ride thou* [a]Rev. 6:2
6 [a]Ps. 93:2; Heb. 1:8
7 [I]Or, *O God* [a]Ps. 33:5 [b]Isa. 61:1 [c]1Kgs. 1:39, 40 [d]Ps. 21:6
8 [a]Song 1:3
9 [a]Song 6:8 [b]1Kgs. 2:19

45:1–9 See the note on Psalm 22:1–31 for a discussion of the Messianic Psalms.

did stand[5324] the queen[7694] in gold of Ophir.

10 Hearken,[8085] O daughter, and consider,[7200] and incline thine ear;[241] [a]forget also thine own people, and thy father's house;[1004]

11 So shall the king greatly desire[183] thy beauty: [a]for he *is* thy Lord;[113] and worship[7812] thou him.

12 And the daughter of Tyre *shall be there* with a gift; *even* [a]the rich among the people shall intreat [I]thy favour.

13 [a]The king's daughter *is* all glorious within: her clothing *is* of wrought gold.

14 [a]She shall be brought unto the king in raiment of needlework: the virgins[1330] her companions that follow her shall be brought unto thee.

15 With gladness and rejoicing shall they be brought: they shall enter into the king's palace.

16 Instead of thy fathers[1] shall be thy children, [a]whom thou mayest make princes[8269] in all the earth.[776]

17 [a]I will make thy name to be remembered[2142] in all generations:[1755] therefore shall the people praise[3034] thee for ever and ever.

"God Is Our Refuge and Strength"

To the chief Musician for the sons of Korah, A Song upon Alamoth.

46 God[430] *is* our [a]refuge and strength, [b]a very present help in trouble.

2 Therefore will not we fear,[3372] though the earth[776] be removed, and though the mountains be carried into [I]the midst of the sea;

3 [a]*Though* the waters thereof roar *and* be troubled, *though* the mountains shake[7493] with the swelling thereof. Selah.

4 *There is* [a]a river, the streams whereof shall make glad [b]the city of God, the holy[6918] *place* of the tabernacles[4908] of the most High.[5945]

5 God *is* [a]in the midst[7130] of her; she shall not be moved: God shall help her, [I][b]*and that* right early.

6 [a]The heathen[1471] raged, the kingdoms[4467] were moved: he uttered his voice, [b]the earth melted.

7 [a]The LORD of hosts[6635] *is* with us; the God of Jacob *is* [I][b]our refuge. Selah.

8 [a]Come, behold[2372] the works of the LORD, what desolations[8047] he hath made[7760] in the earth.

9 [a]He maketh wars to cease[7673] unto the end of the earth; [b]he breaketh[7665] the bow, and cutteth the spear in sunder; [c]he burneth[8313] the chariot in the fire.

10 Be still,[7503] and know that I *am* God: [a]I will be exalted among the heathen, I will be exalted in the earth.

11 [a]The LORD of hosts *is* with us; the God of Jacob *is* our refuge. Selah.

God Is King

To the chief Musician, A Psalm for the sons of Korah.

47 O [a]clap[8628] your hands,[3709] all ye people;[5971] shout[7321] unto God[430] with the voice of triumph.

2 For the LORD most high[5945] *is* [a]terrible;[3372] [b]*he is* a great King[4428] over all the earth.[776]

3 [a]He shall subdue[1696] the people under us, and the nations[3816] under our feet.

4 He shall choose[977] our [a]inheritance[5159] for us, the excellency of Jacob whom he loved.[157] Selah.

5 [a]God is gone up[5927] with a shout, the LORD with the sound of a trumpet.

6 Sing praises[2167] to God, sing

45:10 [a]Deut. 21:13
11 [a]Ps. 95:6; Isa. 54:5
12 [I]Hebr. *thy face* [a]Ps. 22:29; 72:10; Isa. 49:23; 60:3
13 [a]Rev. 19:7, 8
14 [a]Song 1:4
16 [a]1Pet. 2:9; Rev. 1:6; 5:10; 20:6
17 [a]Mal. 1:11

46:1 [a]Ps. 62:7, 8; 91:2; 142:5 [b]Deut. 4:7; Ps. 145:18
2 [I]Hebr. *the heart of the seas*
3 [a]Ps. 93:3, 4; Jer. 5:22; Matt. 7:25
4 [a]Isa. 8:7 [b]Ps. 48:1, 8; Isa. 60:14
5 [I]Hebr. *when the morning appeareth* [a]Deut. 23:14; Isa. 12:6; Ezek. 43:7, 9; Hos. 11:9; Joel 2:27; Zeph. 3:15; Zech. 2:5, 10, 11; 8:3 [b]Ex. 14:24, 27; 2Chr. 20:20; Ps. 30:5; 143:8
6 [a]Ps. 2:1 [b]Josh. 2:9, 24
7 [I]Hebr. *a high place for us* [a]Ps. 9:9 [b]Num. 14:9; 2Chr. 13:12; Ps. 46:11
8 [a]Ps. 66:5
9 [a]Isa. 2:4 [b]Ps. 76:3 [c]Ezek. 39:9
10 [a]Isa. 2:11, 17
11 [a]Ps. 46:7

47:1 [a]Isa. 55:12
2 [a]Deut. 7:21; Neh. 1:5; Ps. 76:12 [b]Mal. 1:4
3 [a]Ps. 18:47
4 [a]1Pet. 1:4
5 [a]Ps. 68:24, 25

46:1 God is a "present help" for those who depend upon Him, but the unregenerate have no access to Him (Ps. 10:1; Lam. 3:44; Ezek. 20:3). Even His children do not have access to the fullness of His glory (Ex. 33:20; 1 Tim. 6:16). The phrase "very present" in the Hebrew is from *matsa'* (4672) and *me'ōd* (3966). These words emphasize the speed, completeness, and might of the Lord's help.

praises: sing praises unto our King, sing praises.

7 [a]For God *is* the King of all the earth: [b]sing ye praises [I]with understanding.

8 [a]God reigneth[4427] over the heathen:[1471] God sitteth upon the throne[3678] of his holiness.[6944]

9 [I]The princes[5081] of the people are gathered together,[622] [a]*even* the people of the God of Abraham: [b]for the shields of the earth *belong* unto God: he is greatly exalted.[5927]

The Glory of Zion

A Song and Psalm for the sons of Korah.

48 Great *is* the LORD, and greatly to be praised[1984] [a]in the city of our God,[430] *in* the [b]mountain of his holiness.[6944]

2 [a]Beautiful for situation,[5131] [b]the joy of the whole earth,[776] *is* mount Zion, [c]*on* the sides of the north, [d]the city of the great King.[4428]

3 God is known[3045] in her palaces[759] for a refuge.

4 For, lo, [a]the kings[4428] were assembled,[3259] they passed by[5674] together.

5 They saw[7200] *it, and* so they marvelled; they were troubled,[926] *and* hasted away.

6 Fear[7461] [a]took hold upon them there, [b]*and* pain, as of a woman in travail.

7 Thou [a]breakest the ships of Tarshish [b]with an east wind.[7307]

8 As we have heard,[8085] so have we seen in [a]the city of the LORD of hosts,[6635] in the city of our God: God will [b]establish it for ever. Selah.

9 We have thought of [a]thy lovingkindness, O God, in the midst[7130] of thy temple.[1964]

10 According to [a]thy name, O God, so *is* thy praise[8416] unto the ends of the earth: thy right hand is full of righteousness.[6664]

11 Let mount Zion rejoice, let the daughters of Judah be glad, because of thy judgments.[4941]

12 Walk about Zion, and go round about[5362] her: tell[5608] the towers thereof.

13 [I]Mark ye well her bulwarks, [II]consider her palaces; that ye may tell *it* to the generation[1755] following.

14 For this God *is* our God for ever[5769] and ever:[5703] he will [a]be our guide *even* unto death.[4192]

Trusting Riches Is Foolish

To the chief Musician, A Psalm for the sons of Korah.

49 Hear[8085] this, all *ye* people;[5971] give ear,[238] all *ye* inhabitants of the world:[2465]

2 Both [a]low and high,[376] rich and poor, together.

3 My mouth[6310] shall speak[1696] of wisdom;[2454] and the meditation[1900] of my heart[3820] *shall be* of understanding.[8394]

4 [a]I will incline mine ear[241] to a parable: I will open my dark saying[2420] upon the harp.

5 Wherefore should I fear[3372] in the days[3117] of evil, *when* [a]the iniquity of my heels shall compass me about?

6 They that [a]trust[982] in their wealth,[2428] and boast themselves[1984] in the multitude of their riches;

7 None *of them* can by any means redeem[6299] his brother,[251] nor [a]give to God[430] a ransom[3724] for him:

8 (For [a]the redemption of their soul[5315] *is* precious, and it ceaseth for ever:[5769])

9 That he should still live[2421] for ever,[5703] *and* [a]not see corruption.[7845]

10 For he seeth[7200] [a]*that* wise men[2450] die,[4191] likewise the fool and the brutish person perish,[6] [b]and leave[5800] their wealth to others.

11 Their inward thought[7130] *is, that* their houses *shall continue* for ever, *and* their dwelling places[4908] [I]to all generations;[1755] they [a]call[7121] *their* lands after their own names.

12 Nevertheless man[120] *being* in honour abideth not: he is like the beasts *that* perish.[1820]

13 This their way[1870] *is* their

---

7 [I]Or, *every one that hath understanding* [a]Zech. 14:9 [b]1Cor. 14:15, 16

8 [a]1Chr. 16:31; Ps. 93:1; 96:10; 97:1; 99:1; Rev. 19:6

9 [I]Or, *The voluntary of the people are gathered* unto *the people of the God of Abraham* [a]Rom. 4:11, 12 [b]Ps. 80:18

1 [a]Ps. 46:4; 87:3 [b]Isa. 2:2, 3; Mic. 4:1; Zech. 8:3

2 [a]Ps. 50:2; Jer. 3:19; Lam. 2:15; Dan. 8:9; 11:16 [b]Ezek. 20:6 [c]Isa. 14:13 [d]Matt. 5:35

4 [a]2Sam. 10:6, 14, 16, 18, 19

6 [a]Ex. 15:15 [b]Hos. 13:13

7 [a]Ezek. 27:26 [b]Jer. 18:17

8 [a]Ps. 48:1, 2 [b]Isa. 2:2; Mic. 4:1

9 [a]Ps. 26:3; 40:10

10 [a]Deut. 28:58; Josh. 7:9; Ps. 113:3; Mal. 1:11, 14

13 [I]Hebr. *Set your heart to her bulwarks* [II]Or, *raise up*

14 [a]Isa. 58:11

2 [a]Ps. 62:9

4 [a]Ps. 78:2; Matt. 13:35

5 [a]Ps. 38:4

6 [a]Job 31:24, 25; Ps. 52:7; 62:10; Mark 10:24; 1Tim. 6:17

7 [a]Matt. 16:26

8 [a]Job 36:18, 19

9 [a]Ps. 89:48

10 [a]Eccl. 2:16 [b]Prov. 11:4; Eccl. 2:18, 21

11 [I]Hebr. *to generation and generation* [a]Gen. 4:17

[a]folly:[3689] yet their posterity [I]approve[7521] their sayings.[6310] Selah.

14 Like sheep they are laid in the grave;[7585] death[4194] shall feed on them; and [a]the upright shall have dominion[7287] over them in the morning; [b]and their [I]beauty[6736] shall consume [II]in the grave from their dwelling.

15 But God [a]will redeem my soul [I]from the power[3027] of [II]the grave: for he shall receive me. Selah.

16 Be not thou afraid[3372] when one[376] is made rich, when the glory[3519] of his house[1004] is increased;

17 [a]For when he dieth[4194] he shall carry nothing away: his glory shall not descend after him.

18 Though [I]while he lived[2416] [a]he blessed[1288] his soul: and *men* will praise[3034] thee, when thou doest well[3190] to thyself.

19 [I]He shall [a]go to the generation[1755] of his fathers;[1] they shall never see [b]light.[216]

20 [a]Man *that is* in honour, and understandeth[995] not, [b]is like the beasts *that* perish.

God Is the Judge

A Psalm of Asaph.

50 The [a]mighty[410] God, *even* the LORD, hath spoken,[1696] and called[7121] the earth[776] from the rising of the sun unto the going down thereof.

2 Out of Zion, [a]the perfection of beauty, [b]God hath shined.

3 Our God shall come, and shall not keep silence: [a]a fire shall devour before him, and it shall be very tempestuous[8175] round about him.

4 [a]He shall call to the heavens[8064] from above, and to the earth, that he may judge[1777] his people.[5971]

5 Gather[622] [a]my saints[2623] together[622] unto me; [b]those that have made[3772] a covenant[1285] with me by sacrifice.[2077]

6 And [a]the heavens shall declare[5046] his righteousness:[6664] for [b]God *is* judge[8199] himself. Selah.

7 [a]Hear,[8085] O my people, and I will speak; O Israel, and I will testify[5749] against thee: [b]I *am* God, *even* thy God.

8 [a]I will not reprove[3198] thee [b]for thy sacrifices[2077] or thy burnt offerings,[5930] *to have been* continually[8548] before me.

9 [a]I will take no bullock out of thy house,[1004] *nor* he goats out of thy folds.

10 For every beast[2416] of the forest *is* mine, *and* the cattle upon a thousand hills.

11 I know all the fowls of the mountains: and the wild beasts of the field[7704] *are* [I]mine.

12 If I were hungry, I would not tell[559] thee: [a]for the world[8398] *is* mine, and the fulness thereof.

13 Will I eat the flesh[1320] of bulls,[47] or drink the blood[1818] of goats?

14 [a]Offer[2076] unto God thanksgiving;[8426] and [b]pay thy vows[5088] unto the most High:[5945]

15 And [a]call upon me in the day[3117] of trouble: I will deliver[2502] thee, and thou shalt [b]glorify[3513] me.

16 But unto the wicked[7563] God saith,[559] What hast thou to do to declare[5608] my statutes,[2706] or *that* thou shouldest take[5375] my covenant in thy mouth?[6310]

17 [a]Seeing thou hatest instruction,[4148] and [b]casteth my words[1697] behind thee.

18 When thou sawest[7200] a thief, then thou [a]consentedst[7521] with him, and [I]hast been [b]partaker with adulterers.[5003]

19 [I]Thou givest thy mouth to evil,[7451] and [a]thy tongue frameth deceit.[4820]

20 Thou sittest *and* speakest against thy brother;[251] thou slanderest thine own mother's[517] son.[1121]

21 These *things* hast thou done,[6213] [a]and I kept silence; [b]thou thoughtest that I was altogether *such an one* as thyself: *but* [c]I will reprove thee, and set *them* in order before thine eyes.

22 Now consider[995] this, ye that [a]forget God,[433] lest I tear *you* in pieces, and *there be* none to deliver.[5337]

13 [I]Hebr. *delight in their mouth* [a]Luke 12:20 **14** [I]Or, *strength* [II]Or, *the grave being a habitation to every one of them* [a]Ps. 47:3; Dan. 7:22; Mal. 4:3; Luke 22:30; 1Cor. 6:2; Rev. 2:26; 20:4 [b]Job 4:21; Ps. 39:11 **15** [I]Hebr. *from the hand of the grave* [II]Or, *hell* [a]Ps. 56:13; Hos. 13:14 **17** [a]Job 27:19 **18** [I]Hebr. *in his life* [a]Deut. 29:19; Luke 12:19 **19** [I]Hebr. The soul *shall go* [a]Gen. 15:15 [b]Job 33:30; Ps. 56:13 **20** [a]Ps. 49:12 [b]Eccl. 3:19

1 [a]Neh. 9:32; Isa. 9:6; Jer. 32:18 **2** [a]Ps. 48:2 [b]Deut. 33:2; Ps. 80:1 **3** [a]Lev. 10:2; Num. 16:35; Ps. 97:3; Dan. 7:10 **4** [a]Deut. 4:26; 31:28; 32:1; Isa. 1:2; Mic. 6:1, 2 **5** [a]Deut. 33:3; Isa. 13:3 [b]Ex. 24:7 **6** [a]Ps. 97:6 [b]Ps. 75:7 **7** [a]Ps. 81:8 [b]Ex. 20:2 **8** [a]Isa. 1:11; Jer. 7:22 [b]Hos. 6:6 **9** [a]Mic. 6:6; Acts 17:25 **11** [I]Heb. *with me* **12** [a]Ex. 19:5; Deut. 10:14; Job 41:11; Ps. 24:1; 1Cor. 10:26, 28 **14** [a]Hos. 14:2; Heb. 13:15 [b]Deut. 23:21; Job 22:27; Ps. 76:11; Eccl. 5:4, 5 **15** [a]Job 22:27; Ps. 91:15; 107:6, 13, 19, 28; Zech. 13:9 [b]Ps. 22:23; 50:23 **17** [a]Rom. 2:21, 22 [b]Neh. 9:26 **18** [I]Hebr. *thy portion was with adulterers* [a]Rom. 1:32 [b]1Tim. 5:22 **19** [I]Hebr. *Thou sendest* [a]Ps. 52:2 **21** [a]Eccl. 8:11, 12; Isa. 26:10; 57:11 [b]Rom. 2:4 [c]Ps. 90:8 **22** [a]Job 8:13; Ps. 9:17; Isa. 51:13

23 [a]Whoso offereth praise[8426] glorifieth[3513] me: and [b]to him [I]that ordereth *his* conversation[1870] *aright* will I shew[7200] the salvation[3468] of God.

A Prayer for Spiritual Cleansing

To the chief Musician, A Psalm of David, when Nathan the prophet came unto him, after he had gone in to Bath–sheba.

51 🔑 Have mercy[2603] upon me, O God,[430] according to thy lovingkindness: according unto the multitude of thy tender mercies[7356] [a]blot out[4229] my transgressions.[6588]

🔑 2 [a]Wash[3526] me throughly from mine iniquity, and cleanse[5352] me from my sin.[2403]

3 For [a]I acknowledge[3045] my transgressions: and my sin *is* ever[8548] before me.

4 [a]Against thee, thee only, have I sinned,[2398] and done[6213] *this* evil[7451] [b]in thy sight: [c]that thou mightest be justified[6663] when thou speakest,[1696] *and* be clear when thou judgest.[8199]

5 [a]Behold, I was shapen[2342] in iniquity; [b]and in sin[2399] did my mother[517] [I]conceive me.

6 Behold, thou desirest[2654] truth[571] [a]in the inward parts: and in the hidden *part* thou shalt make me to know wisdom.[2451]

7 [a]Purge[2398] me with hyssop,[231] and I shall be clean:[2891] wash me, and I shall be [b]whiter than snow.

8 Make me to hear[8085] joy and gladness; *that* the bones[6106] *which* thou hast broken [a]may rejoice.

9 [a]Hide thy face from my sins,[2399] and [b]blot out all mine iniquities.[5771]

10 [a]Create[1254] in me a clean[2889] heart,[3820] O God; and renew [I]a right spirit[7307] within[7130] me.

11 Cast me not away [a]from thy presence; and take not thy [b]holy[6944] spirit from me.

12 Restore[7725] unto me the joy of thy salvation;[3468] and uphold me *with thy* [a]free spirit.

13 *Then* will I teach[3925] transgressors[6586] thy ways;[1870] and sinners[2400] shall be converted[7725] unto thee.

14 Deliver[5337] me from [I][a]bloodguiltiness,[1818] O God, thou God of my salvation:[8668] *and* [b]my tongue shall sing aloud of thy righteousness.[6666]

15 O Lord, open thou my lips;[8193] and my mouth shall shew forth[5046] thy praise.

16 For [a]thou desirest not sacrifice;[2077] [I]else would I give *it:* thou delightest[7521] not in burnt offering.[5930]

17 [a]The sacrifices of God *are* a broken[7665] spirit: a broken and a contrite[1794] heart, O God, thou wilt not despise.

18 Do good[3190] in thy good pleasure[7522] unto Zion: build thou the walls[2426] of Jerusalem.

19 Then shalt thou be pleased[2654] with [a]the sacrifices of righteousness,[6664] with burnt offering and whole burnt of-

23 [I]Hebr. *that disposeth his way* [a]Ps. 27:6; Rom. 12:1 [b]Gal. 6:16

1 [a]Ps. 51:9; Isa. 43:25; 44:22; Col. 2:14
2 [a]Heb. 9:14; 1John 1:7, 9; Rev. 1:5
3 [a]Ps. 32:5; 38:18
4 [a]Gen. 20:6; 39:9; Lev. 5:19; 6:2; 2Sam. 12:13 [b]Luke 15:21 [c]Rom. 3:4
5 [I]Hebr. *warm me* [a]Job 14:4; Ps. 58:3; John 3:6; Rom. 5:12; Eph. 2:3 [b]Job 14:4
6 [a]Job 38:36
7 [a]Lev. 14:4, 6, 49; Num. 19:18; Heb. 9:19 [b]Isa. 1:18
8 [a]Matt. 5:4
9 [a]Jer. 16:17 [b]Ps. 51:1
10 [I]Or, *a constant spirit* [a]Acts 15:9; Eph. 2:10
11 [a]Gen. 4:14; 2Kgs. 13:23 [b]Rom. 8:9; Eph. 4:30
12 [a]2Cor. 3:17
14 [I]Hebr. *bloods* [a]2Sam. 11:17; 12:9 [b]Ps. 35:28
16 [I]Or, *that I should give it* [a]Num. 15:27, 30; Ps. 40:6; 50:8; Isa. 1:11; Jer. 7:22; Hos. 6:6
17 [a]Ps. 34:18; Isa. 57:15; 66:2
19 [a]Ps. 4:5; Mal. 3:3

🔑 **51:1–19** This is one of the greatest passages in the entire Bible concerning confession and forgiveness. It was written after David had committed adultery with Bath–sheba and subsequently had her husband Uriah killed in battle (see 2 Sam. 11:2–17). David's repentance included: 1) a godly sorrow for his sin (cf. 2 Cor. 7:10); 2) a verbal confession; 3) a turning away from sin and denouncement of it; 4) forgiveness; 5) restoration to God's favor; 6) rejoicing in salvation; and 7) a willingness to testify to others about the grace of God.

🔑 **51:2** In this verse, David is picturing how God cleansed him of his sin. The idea David expresses is that God alone can forgive his sin and remove it (cf. 1 John 1:9). It is not something that David can provide for himself. People often interpret this verse to mean that an individual must constantly receive cleansing from his sin for salvation. However, this passage is speaking of David confessing the specific sin that he committed with Bath–sheba in order to receive forgiveness for that sin only. In the Old Testament, a person was required to go before a priest and have a sacrifice offered to receive a "covering" for his or her sin. Under the New Testament system of grace, however, a believer can go directly to the great High Priest, Jesus Christ, boldly approaching God's throne and receiving forgiveness for sin, which was covered by Christ's shed blood (Heb. 4:16).

fering:[3632] then shall they offer bullocks
upon thine altar.[4196]

God's Judgment and Grace

To the chief Musician, Maschil, *A Psalm* of David, [†]when Doeg the Edomite came and [•]told Saul, and said unto him, David is come to the house of Ahimelech.

52 Why boastest thou thyself[1984] in
mischief,[7451] O [a]mighty man? the
goodness[2617] of God[410] *endureth* continually.
2 [a]Thy tongue deviseth[2803] mischiefs;[1942] [b]like a sharp razor, working
deceitfully.
3 Thou lovest[157] evil[7451] more than
good;[2896] *and* [a]lying rather than to speak
righteousness.[6664] Selah.
4 Thou lovest all devouring[1105]
words, [I]O *thou* deceitful[4820] tongue.
5 God shall likewise [I]destroy[5422] thee
for ever,[5331] he shall take thee away, and
pluck[5255] thee out of *thy* dwelling
place,[168] and [a]root thee out of the land[776]
of the living.[2416] Selah.
6 [a]The righteous[6662] also shall see,
and fear,[3372] [b]and shall laugh at him:
7 Lo, *this is* the man[1397] *that*
made[7760] not God[430] his strength; but
[a]trusted[982] in the abundance of his
riches, *and* strengthened himself in his
[I]wickedness.[1942]
8 But I *am* [a]like a green olive tree in
the house[1004] of God: I trust in the
mercy[2617] of God for ever[5769] and
ever.[5703]
9 I will praise[3034] thee for ever, because thou hast done[6213] *it:* and I will
wait on[6960] thy name; [a]for *it is* good before thy saints.[2623]

People Are Evil

To the chief Musician upon Mahalath, Maschil, *A Psalm* of David.

53 The [a]fool hath said in his
heart,[3820] *There is* no God.[430]
Corrupt are they, and have done abominable[8581] iniquity:[5766] [b]*there is* none that
doeth[6213] good.[2896]
2 God [a]looked down from heaven[8064]
upon the children[1121] of men,[120] to see if
there were *any* that did understand,[7919]
that did [b]seek God.
3 Every one of them is gone
back:[5472] they are altogether become
filthy; *there is* none that doeth good, no,
not one.
4 Have the workers of iniquity[205] [a]no
knowledge?[3045] who eat up my people[5971]
as they eat bread: they have not called
upon[7121] God.
5 [a]There [I]were they in great fear,[6343]
where no fear was: for God hath [b]scat-
tered the bones[6106] of him that encampeth *against* thee: thou hast put *them* to
shame,[954] because God hath despised[3988]
them.
6 [I][a]Oh that the salvation[3444] of Israel
were come out of Zion! When God
bringeth back[7725] the captivity[7622] of his
people, Jacob shall rejoice, *and* Israel
shall be glad.

A Prayer for Relief

To the chief Musician on Neginoth, Maschil, *A Psalm* of David, when the Ziphims came and said to Saul, Doth not David hide himself with us?

54 Save[3467] me, O God,[430] by thy
name, and judge[1777] me by thy
strength.
2 Hear[8085] my prayer,[8605] O God;
give ear[238] to the words[561] of my
mouth.[6310]
3 For [a]strangers[2114] are risen up
against me, and oppressors seek after my
soul:[5315] they have not set[7760] God before
them. Selah.
4 Behold, God *is* mine helper: [a]the
Lord *is* with them that uphold my soul.
5 He shall reward[7725] evil[7451] unto
[I]mine enemies: cut them off [a]in thy
truth.[571]

† +1Sam. 22:9 •Ezek. 22:9
1 a1Sam. 21:7
2 aPs. 50:19 bPs. 57:4; 59:7; 64:3
3 aJer. 9:4, 5
4 IOr, *and the deceitful tongue*
5 IHebr. *beat thee down* aProv. 2:22
6 aJob 22:19; Ps. 37:34; 40:3; 64:9; Mal. 1:5 bPs. 58:10
7 IOr, *substance* aPs. 49:6
8 aJer. 11:16; Hos. 14:6
9 aPs. 54:6
1 aPs. 10:4; 14:1-7 bRom. 3:10
2 aPs. 33:13 b2Chr. 15:2; 19:3
4 aJer. 4:22
5 IHebr. *they feared a fear,* Ps. 14:5 aLev. 26:17, 36; Prov. 28:1 bEzek. 6:5
6 IHebr. *Who will give salvations* aPs. 14:7
3 aPs. 86:14
4 aPs. 118:7
5 IHebr. *those that observe me,* Ps. 5:8 aPs. 89:49

54:1 David's occasion for writing this psalm was the oppression he received from the Ziphites who were from the tribe of Judah (1 Sam. 23:19–23; 26:1–3).

6 I will[2076] freely[5071] sacrifice[2076] unto thee: I will praise[3034] thy name, O LORD; [a]for *it is* good.[2896]

7 For he hath delivered[5337] me out of all trouble: [a]and mine eye hath seen[7200] *his desire* upon mine enemies.

Betrayed

To the chief Musician on Neginoth, Maschil, *A Psalm* of David.

55 Give ear[238] to my prayer,[8605] O God;[430] and hide not thyself from my supplication.[8467]

2 Attend unto me, and hear me: I [a]mourn in my complaint,[7878] and make a noise;[1949]

3 Because of the voice of the enemy, because of the oppression of the wicked:[7563] [a]for they cast iniquity[205] upon me, and in wrath[639] they hate me.

4 [a]My heart[3820] is sore pained[2342] within[7130] me: and the terrors[367] of death[4194] are fallen[5307] upon me.

5 Fearfulness[3374] and trembling[7460] are come upon me, and horror[6427] hath [I]overwhelmed[3680] me.

6 And I said, Oh that I had wings like a dove! *for then* would I fly away, and be at rest.

7 Lo, *then* would I wander[5074] far off, *and* remain in the wilderness. Selah.

8 I would hasten my escape from the windy storm *and* tempest.

9 Destroy,[1104] O Lord,[136] *and* divide[6385] their tongues: for I have seen[7200] [a]violence[2555] and strife in the city.

10 Day[3119] and night[3915] they go about it upon the walls[2426] thereof: mischief also and sorrow *are* in the midst[7130] of it.

11 Wickedness *is* in the midst thereof: deceit and guile[4820] depart not from her streets.

12 [a]For *it was* not an enemy *that* reproached me; then I could have borne[5375] *it:* neither *was it* he that hated me *that* did [b]magnify *himself* against me; then I would have hid myself from him:

13 But *it was* thou, [I]a man[582] mine equal,[6187] [a]my guide,[441] and mine acquaintance.[3045]

14 [I]We took sweet counsel[5475] together, *and* [a]walked unto the house[1004] of God in company.[7285]

15 Let death seize upon them, *and* let them [a]go down quick[2416] into [I]hell:[7585] for wickedness[7451] *is* in their dwellings,[4033] *and* among[7130] them.

16 As for me, I will call[7121] upon God; and the LORD shall save[3467] me.

17 [a]Evening, and morning, and at noon, will I pray,[7878] and cry aloud: and he shall hear[8085] my voice.

18 He hath delivered[6299] my soul[5315] in peace from the battle *that was* against me: for [a]there were many with me.

19 God[410] shall hear, and afflict them, [a]even he that abideth of old.[6924] Selah. [I]Because they have no changes, therefore they fear[3372] not God.

20 He hath [a]put forth his hands[3027] against such as [b]be at peace[7965] with him: [I]he hath broken[2490] his covenant.[1285]

21 [a]*The words* of his mouth[6310] were smoother than butter, but war *was* in his heart: his words[1697] were softer than oil,[8081] yet *were* they drawn swords.

22 [a]Cast thy [I]burden upon the LORD, and he shall sustain thee: [b]he shall never suffer the righteous[6662] to be moved.

23 But thou, O God, shalt bring them down into the pit of destruction:[7845] [a]bloody[1818] and deceitful[4820] men[582] [b]shall not live out half their days;[3117] but I will trust[982] in thee.

A Prayer of Trust

To the chief Musician upon Jonath–elem–rechokim, Michtam of David, when the Philistines took him in Gath.

56 Be [a]merciful[2603] unto me, O God:[430] for man[582] would swallow me up; he fighting daily oppresseth me.

2 [I][a]Mine enemies would daily [b]swallow *me* up: for *they be* many that fight against me, O thou most High.

3 What time I am afraid,[3372] I will trust[982] in thee.

---

6 [a]Ps. 52:9
7 [a]Ps. 59:10; 92:11
2 [a]Isa. 38:14
3 [a]2Sam. 16:7, 8; 19:19
4 [a]Ps. 116:3
5 [I]Hebr. *covered me*
9 [a]Jer. 6:7
12 [a]Ps. 41:9 [b]Ps. 35:26; 38:16
13 [I]Hebr. *a man according to my rank* [a]2Sam. 15:12; 16:23; Ps. 41:9; Jer. 9:4
14 [I]Hebr. *Who sweetened counsel* [a]Ps. 42:4
15 [I]Or, *the grave* [a]Num. 16:30
17 [a]Dan. 6:10; Luke 18:1; Acts 3:1; 10:3, 9, 30; 1Thess. 5:17
18 [a]2Chr. 32:7, 8
19 [I]Or, *With whom* also there be *no changes, yet they fear not God* [a]Deut. 33:27
20 [I]Hebr. *he hath profaned* [a]Acts 12:1 [b]Ps. 7:4
21 [a]Ps. 28:3; 57:4; 62:4; 64:3; Prov. 5:3, 4; 12:18
22 [I]Or, *gift* [a]Ps. 37:5; Matt. 6:25; Luke 12:22; 1Pet. 5:7 [b]Ps. 37:24
23 [a]Ps. 5:6 [b]Job 15:32; Prov. 10:27; Eccl. 7:17
1 [a]Ps. 57:1
2 [I]Hebr. *Mine observers* [a]Ps. 54:5 [b]Ps. 57:3

4 [a]In God I will praise[1984] his word,[1697] in God I have put my trust; [b]I will not fear[3372] what flesh[1320] can do[6213] unto me.

5 Every day they wrest[6087] my words: all their thoughts[4284] *are* against me for evil.[7451]

6 [a]They gather themselves together,[1481] they hide themselves, they mark[8104] my steps,[6119] [b]when they wait for[6960] my soul.[5315]

7 Shall they escape by iniquity?[205] in *thine* anger[639] cast down the people,[5971] O God.

8 Thou tellest[5608] my wanderings: put thou my tears into thy bottle: [a]*are they* not in thy book?[5612]

9 When I cry[7121] *unto thee,* then shall mine enemies turn[7725] back: this I know; for [a]God *is* for me.

10 [a]In God will I praise *his* word: in the LORD will I praise *his* word.

11 In God have I put my trust: I will not be afraid what man[120] can do unto me.

12 Thy vows[5088] *are* upon me, O God: I will render[7999] praises[8426] unto thee.

13 For [a]thou hast delivered[5337] my soul from death:[4194] *wilt* not *thou deliver* my feet from falling, that I may walk before God in [b]the light[216] of the living?[2416]

Pleading for God's Help

To the chief Musician, Al–taschith, Michtam of David, when he fled from Saul in the cave.

57 🔑 Be [a]merciful[2603] unto me, O God,[430] be merciful unto me: for my soul[5315] trusteth[2620] in thee: [b]yea, in the shadow of thy wings will I make my refuge,[2620] [c]until *these* calamities be overpast.[5674]

2 I will cry[7121] unto God most high;[5945] unto God[410] [a]that performeth[1584] *all things* for me.

3 [a]He shall send from heaven,8064 and save[3467] me [I]*from* the reproach of him that would [b]swallow me up. Selah. God [c]shall send forth his mercy[2617] and his truth.[571]

4 My soul *is* among lions: *and* I lie *even among* them that are set on fire, *even* the sons[1121] of men,[120] [a]whose teeth *are* spears and arrows, and [b]their tongue a sharp sword.[2719]

5 [a]Be thou exalted,7311 O God, above the heavens;8064 *let* thy glory[3519] *be* above all the earth.[776]

6 [a]They have prepared[3559] a net for my steps; my soul is bowed down: they have digged a pit before me, into the midst whereof they are fallen[5307] *themselves.* Selah.

7 [a]My heart[3820] is [I]fixed,[3559] O God, my heart is fixed: I will sing[7891] and give praise.

8 Awake up, [a]my glory; awake, psaltery and harp: I *myself* will awake early.

9 [a]I will praise[3034] thee, O Lord,[136] among the people:[5971] I will sing[2167] unto thee among the nations.[3816]

10 [a]For thy mercy *is* great unto the heavens, and thy truth unto the clouds.[7834]

11 [a]Be thou exalted, O God, above the heavens: *let* thy glory *be* above all the earth.

A Prayer for the Punishment of The Wicked

To the chief Musician, Al–taschith, Michtam of David.

58 🔑 Do ye indeed[552] speak righteousness,[6664] O congregation? do ye judge[8199] uprightly,[4339] O ye sons of men?

2 Yea, in heart[3820] ye work wickedness;[5766] [a]ye weigh the violence[2555] of your hands[3027] in the earth.[776]

3 [a]The wicked[7563] are estranged[2114] from the womb: they go astray[8582] [I]as soon as they be born,[990] speaking lies.[3577]

4 [a]Ps. 56:10, 11 [b]Ps. 118:6; Isa. 31:3; Heb. 13:6
6 [a]Ps. 59:3; 140:2 [b]Ps. 71:10
8 [a]Mal. 3:16
9 [a]Rom. 8:31
10 [a]Ps. 56:4
13 [a]Ps. 116:8 [b]Job 33:30
1 [a]Ps. 56:1 [b]Ps. 17:8; 63:7 [c]Isa. 26:20
2 [a]Ps. 138:8
3 [I]*Or, he reproacheth him that would swallow me up* [a]Ps. 144:5, 7 [b]Ps. 56:1 [c]Ps. 40:11; 43:3; 61:7
4 [a]Prov. 30:14 [b]Ps. 55:21; 64:3
5 [a]Ps. 57:11; 108:5
6 [a]Ps. 7:15, 16; 9:15
7 [I]*Or, prepared* [a]Ps. 108:1-5
8 [a]Ps. 16:9; 30:12; 108:1, 2
9 [a]Ps. 108:3
10 [a]Ps. 36:5; 71:19; 103:11; 108:4
11 [a]Ps. 57:5
2 [a]Ps. 94:20; Isa. 10:1
3 [I]Hebr. *from the belly* [a]Ps. 51:5; Isa. 48:8

🔑 **57:1** David wrote this psalm while running for his life from Saul (1 Sam. 24:1–22).
🔑 **58:1–11** See the note on Psalm 109:1–29 for a discussion of the Imprecatory Psalms.

4 [a]Their poison *is* [I]like the poison[2534] of a serpent:[5175] *they are* like [b]the deaf [II]adder[6620] *that* stoppeth her ear;[241]

5 Which will not hearken[8085] to the voice of charmers,[3907] [I]charming never so wisely.[2449]

6 [a]Break[2040] their teeth, O God,[430] in their mouth:[6310] break out[5422] the great teeth of the young lions, O LORD.

7 [a]Let them melt away as waters *which* run continually: *when* he bendeth *his bow to shoot* his arrows, let them be as cut in pieces.[4135]

8 As a snail *which* melteth, let *every one of them* pass away: [a]*like* the untimely birth[5309] of a woman, *that* they may not see[2372] the sun.

9 Before your pots can feel[995] the thorns, he shall take them away [a]as with a whirlwind,[8175] [I]both living,[2416] and in *his* wrath.

10 [a]The righteous[6662] shall rejoice when he seeth the vengeance:[5359] [b]he shall wash[7364] his feet in the blood[1818] of the wicked.

11 [a]So that a man[120] shall say, Verily *there is* [I][b]a reward for the righteous; verily he is a God that [c]judgeth[8199] in the earth.

A Prayer for Deliverance

To the chief Musician, Al–taschith, Michtam of David; when Saul sent, and they watched the house to kill him.

59 🔑 Deliver[5337] [a]me from mine enemies, O my God:[430] [I]defend me from them that rise up against me.

2 Deliver me from the workers of iniquity,[205] and save[3467] me from bloody[1818] men.[582]

3 For, lo, they lie in wait for my soul:[5315] [a]the mighty are gathered against me; [b]not *for* my transgression, nor *for* my sin,[2403] O LORD.

4 They run and prepare themselves[3559] without *my* fault: [a]awake [I]to help me, and behold.[7200]

5 Thou therefore, O LORD God of hosts,[6635] the God of Israel, awake to visit[6485] all the heathen:[1471] be not merciful[2603] to any wicked[205] transgressors.[898] Selah.

6 [a]They return[7725] at evening: they make a noise like a dog, and go round about the city.

7 Behold, they belch out[5042] with their mouth:[6310] [a]swords[2719] *are* in their lips:[8193] for [b]who, *say they,* doth hear?[8085]

8 But [a]thou, O LORD, shalt laugh[7832] at them; thou shalt have all the heathen in derision.

9 *Because of* his strength will I wait upon thee: [a]for God *is* [I]my defence.

10 The God of my mercy[2617] shall [a]prevent[6923] me: God shall let [b]me see *my desire* upon [I][c]mine enemies.

11 [a]Slay[2026] them not, lest my people[5971] forget: scatter them by thy power;[2428] and bring them down, O Lord[136] our shield.

12 [a]*For* the sin of their mouth *and* the words[1697] of their lips let them even be taken in their pride: and for cursing[423] and lying *which* they speak.

13 [a]Consume *them* in wrath,[2534] consume *them,* that they *may* not *be:* and [b]let them know that God ruleth[4910] in Jacob unto the ends of the earth.[776] Selah.

14 And [a]at evening let them return; *and* let them make a noise like a dog, and go round about the city.

15 Let them [a]wander up and down [I]for meat, [II]and grudge if they be not satisfied.

16 But I will sing[7891] of thy power; yea, I will sing aloud[7442] of thy mercy in the morning: for thou hast been my defence and refuge in the day[3117] of my trouble.

17 Unto thee, [a]O my strength, will I sing:[2167] [b]for God *is* my defence, *and* the God of my mercy.

4 [I]Hebr. *according to the likeness* [II]Or, *asp* [a]Ps. 140:3; Eccl. 10:11 [b]Jer. 8:17
5 [I]Or, be *the charmer never so cunning*
6 [a]Job 4:10; Ps. 3:7
7 [a]Josh. 7:5; Ps. 112:10
8 [a]Job 3:16; Eccl. 6:3
9 [I]Hebr. *as living as wrath* [a]Prov. 10:25
10 [a]Ps. 52:6; 64:10; 107:42 [b]Ps. 68:23
11 [I]Hebr. *fruit of the* [a]Ps. 92:15 [b]Isa. 3:10 [c]Ps. 67:4; 96:13; 98:9

1 [I]Hebr. *set me on high* [a]Ps. 18:48
3 [a]Ps. 56:6 [b]1Sam. 24:11
4 [I]Hebr. *to meet me* [a]Ps. 35:23; 44:23
6 [a]Ps. 59:14
7 [a]Ps. 57:4; Prov. 12:18 [b]Ps. 10:11, 13; 64:5; 73:11; 94:7
8 [a]1Sam. 19:16; Ps. 2:4
9 [I]Hebr. *my highplace* [a]Ps. 59:17; 62:2
10 [I]Hebr. *mine observers* [a]Ps. 21:3 [b]Ps. 54:7; 92:11; 112:8 [c]Ps. 56:2
11 [a]Gen. 4:12, 15
12 [a]Prov. 12:13; 18:7
13 [a]Ps. 7:9 [b]Ps. 83:18
14 [a]Ps. 59:6
15 [I]Hebr. *to eat* [II]Or, *if they be not satisfied, then they will stay all night* [a]Job 15:23; Ps. 109:10
17 [a]Ps. 18:1 [b]Ps. 59:9, 10

🔑 **59:1** David wrote these words while Saul placed guards at David's house with orders to kill David (1 Sam. 19:11–18).

A Prayer After Defeat

To the chief Musician upon Shushan–eduth, Michtam of David, to teach; when he strove with Aram–naharaim and with Aram–zobah, when Joab returned, and smote of Edom in the valley of salt twelve thousand.

60 🔑 O God,[430] [a]thou hast cast us
off, thou hast [I]scattered us, thou
hast been displeased;[599] O turn thyself to
us again.[7725]
2 Thou hast made the earth to
tremble;[7493] thou hast broken it:
[a]heal the breaches[7667] thereof; for it
shaketh.
3 [a]Thou hast shewed thy people[5971]
hard things:[7186] [b]thou hast made us to
drink the wine of astonishment.
4 [a]Thou hast given a banner to
them that fear[3373] thee, that it may
be displayed because of the truth.[7189]
Selah.
5 [a]That thy beloved[3039] may be delivered;[2502] save[3467] *with* thy right hand,
and hear me.
6 God hath [a]spoken[1696] in his holiness;[6944] I will rejoice, I will [b]divide
[c]Shechem, and mete out[4058] [d]the valley
of Succoth.
7 Gilead *is* mine, and Manasseh
is mine; [a]Ephraim also *is* the strength
of mine head;[7218] [b]Judah *is* my lawgiver;[2710]
8 [a]Moab *is* my washpot;[7366] [b]over
Edom will I cast out my shoe: [c]Philistia,
[I][d]triumph[7321] thou because of me.
9 Who will bring me *into* the
[I][a]strong city? who will lead[5148] me into
Edom?
10 *Wilt* not thou, O God, *which* [a]hadst
cast us off? and *thou,* O God, *which* didst
[b]not go out with our armies?[6635]
11 Give us help[8668] from trouble: for
[a]vain[7723] *is* the [I]help of man.
12 Through God [a]we shall do[6213]
valiantly:[2428] for he *it is that* shall [b]tread
down[947] our enemies.

1 [I]Hebr. *broken* [a]Ps. 44:9
2 [a]2Chr. 7:14
3 [a]Ps. 71:20 [b]Isa. 51:17, 22; Jer. 25:15
4 [a]Ps. 20:5
5 [a]Ps. 108:6
6 [a]Ps. 89:35 [b]Josh. 1:6 [c]Gen. 12:6 [d]Josh. 13:27
7 [a]Deut. 33:17 [b]Gen. 49:10
8 [I]Or, *triumph thou over me* [a]2Sam. 8:2 [b]2Sam. 8:14; Ps. 108:9 [c]2Sam. 8:1 [d]Ps. 108:9
9 [I]Hebr. *city of strength* [a]2Sam. 11:1; 12:26
10 [a]Ps. 44:9; 61:1; 108:11 [b]Josh. 7:12
11 [I]Hebr. *salvation* [a]Ps. 118:8; 146:3
12 [a]Num. 24:18; 1Chr. 19:13 [b]Isa. 63:3

3 [a]Prov. 18:10
4 [I]Or, *make my refuge* [a]Ps. 27:4 [b]Ps. 17:8; 57:1; 91:4
6 [I]Hebr. *Thou shalt add days to the days of the king* [II]Hebr. *as generation and generation* [a]Ps. 21:4
7 [a]Ps. 40:11; Prov. 20:28

1 [I]Or, *Only* [II]Hebr. *is silent* [a]Ps. 65:1 [b]Ps. 33:20
2 [I]Hebr. *high place* [a]Ps. 59:9, 17 [b]Ps. 62:6 [c]Ps. 37:24
3 [a]Isa. 30:13
4 [a]Ps. 28:3

Confidence in God's Protection

To the chief Musician upon Neginah, *A Psalm* of David.

61 Hear[8085] my cry, O God;[430] attend
unto my prayer.[8605]
2 From the end of the earth[776] will I
cry[7121] unto thee, when my heart[3820] is
overwhelmed: lead[5148] me to the rock *that*
is higher than I.
3 For thou hast been a shelter
for me, *and* [a]a strong tower from the
enemy.
4 [a]I will abide[1481] in thy tabernacle[168]
for ever:[5769] [b]I will [I]trust[2620] in the
covert[5643] of thy wings. Selah.
5 For thou, O God, hast heard my
vows:[5088] thou hast given *me* the heritage[3425] of those that fear[3373] thy name.
6 [I][a]Thou wilt prolong the king's[4428]
life: *and* his years [II]as many generations.[1755]
7 He shall abide before God for ever:
O prepare mercy[2617] [a]and truth,[571] *which*
may preserve[5341] him.
8 So will I sing praise[2167] unto thy
name for ever,[5703] that I may daily perform[7999] my vows.

Depending on God

To the chief Musician, to Jeduthun, A Psalm of David.

62 [I]Truly [a]my [b]soul[5315] [II]waiteth
upon God:[430] from him *cometh*
my salvation.[3444]
2 [a]He only *is* my rock and my salvation; *he is* my [I][b]defence; [c]I shall not be
greatly moved.[4131]
3 How long will ye imagine mischief
against a man? ye shall be slain[7523] all of
you: [a]as a bowing wall *shall ye be, and*
as a tottering fence.
4 They only consult[3289] to cast *him*
down from his excellency: they de-
light[7521] in lies:[3577] [a]they bless[1288] with

🔑 **60:1** In this psalm, David is meditating on the battles that he fought against Edom and Syria (2 Sam. 8:13, 14; 10:6, 16; 1 Chr. 18:12, 13; 2 Chr. 18:12, 25).

their mouth,[6310] but they curse[7043] [I]inwardly. Selah.

5 [a]My soul, wait[1826] thou only upon God; for my expectation *is* from him.

6 He only *is* my rock and my salvation: *he is* my defence; I shall not be moved.

7 [a]In God *is* my salvation[3468] and my glory:[3519] the rock of my strength, *and* my refuge, *is* in God.

8 Trust[982] in him at all times;[6256] ye people,[5971] [a]pour out[8210] your heart[3824] before him: God *is* [b]a refuge for us. Selah.

9 [a]Surely men of low degree[1121,120] *are* vanity, *and* men of high degree[1121,376] *are* a lie:[3576] to be laid in the balance, they *are* [I]altogether *lighter* than vanity.

10 Trust not in oppression, and become not vain in robbery: [a]if riches[2428] increase, set not your heart[3820] *upon them.*

11 God hath spoken[1696] [a]once; twice have I heard[8085] this; that [I][b]power *belongeth* unto God.

12 Also unto thee, O Lord, *belongeth* [a]mercy:[2617] for [b]thou renderest[7999] to every man according to his work.

Yearning for God

A Psalm of David, [+]when he was in the wilderness of Judah.

63 O God,[430] thou *art* my God;[410] early will I seek thee: [a]my soul[5315] thirsteth for thee, my flesh[1320] longeth for thee in a dry and [I]thirsty land,[776] where no water is;

2 To see[7200] [a]thy power and thy glory,[3519] so *as* I have seen[2372] thee in the sanctuary.[6944]

3 [a]Because thy lovingkindness *is* better[2896] than life,[2416] my lips[8193] shall praise[7623] thee.

4 Thus will I bless[1288] thee [a]while I live:[2416] I will lift up[5375] my hands[3709] in thy name.

5 My soul shall be [a]satisfied as *with* [I]marrow and fatness; and my mouth[6310] shall praise[1984] *thee* with joyful lips:

6 When [a]I remember[2142] thee upon my bed, *and* meditate[1897] on thee in the *night* watches.

7 Because thou hast been my help, therefore [a]in the shadow of thy wings will I rejoice.

8 My soul followeth hard[1692] after thee: thy right hand upholdeth[8551] me.

9 But those *that* seek my soul, to destroy[7722] *it,* shall go into the lower parts of the earth.[776]

10 [I][a]They shall fall by the sword:[2719] they shall be a portion for foxes.

11 But the king[4428] shall rejoice in God; [a]every one that sweareth[7650] by him shall glory:[1984] but the mouth of them that speak[1696] lies[8267] shall be stopped.

A Prayer for Deliverance

To the chief Musician, A Psalm of David.

64 🔑 Hear[8085] my voice, O God,[430] in my prayer:[7879] preserve[5341] my life[2416] from fear[6343] of the enemy.

2 Hide me from the secret counsel[5475] of the wicked;[7489] from the insurrection[7285] of the workers of iniquity:[205]

3 [a]Who whet[8150] their tongue like a sword,[2719] [b]*and* bend *their bows to shoot* their arrows, *even* bitter[4751] words:[1697]

4 That they may shoot[3384] in secret at the perfect:[8535] suddenly do they shoot at him, and fear[3372] not.

5 [a]They encourage[2388] themselves *in* an evil[7451] [I]matter:[1697] they commune [II]of laying snares[4170] privily;[2934] [b]they say, Who shall see them?

6 They search out iniquities; [I]they accomplish[8552] [II]a diligent search: both the inward[7130] *thought* of every one *of them,* and the heart,[3820] *is* deep.

4 [I]Hebr. *in their inward parts*
5 [a]Ps. 62:1, 2
7 [a]Jer. 3:23
8 [a]1Sam. 1:15; Ps. 42:4; Lam. 2:19 [b]Ps. 18:2
9 [I]Or, *alike* [a]Ps. 39:5, 11; Isa. 40:15, 17; Rom. 3:4
10 [a]Job 31:25; Ps. 52:7; Luke 12:15; 1Tim. 6:17
11 [I]Or, *strength* [a]Job 33:14 [b]Rev. 19:1
12 [a]Ps. 86:15; 103:8; Dan. 9:9 [b]Job 34:11; Prov. 24:12; Jer. 32:19; Ezek. 7:27; 33:20; Matt. 16:27; Rom. 2:6; 1Cor. 3:8; 2Cor. 5:10; Eph. 6:8; Col. 3:25; 1Pet. 1:17; Rev. 22:12

† +1Sam. 22:5; 23:14, 15, 16
1 [I]Hebr. *weary* [a]Ps. 42:2; 84:2; 143:6
2 [a]1Sam. 4:21; 1Chr. 16:11; Ps. 27:4; 78:61
3 [a]Ps. 30:5
4 [a]Ps. 104:33; 146:2
5 [I]Hebr. *fatness* [a]Ps. 36:8
6 [a]Ps. 42:8; 119:55; 149:5
7 [a]Ps. 61:4
10 [I]Hebr. *They shall make him run out like water by the hands of the sword* [a]Ezek. 35:5
11 [a]Deut. 6:13; Isa. 45:23; 65:16; Zeph. 1:5

3 [a]Ps. 11:2; 57:4 [b]Ps. 58:7; Jer. 9:3
5 [I]Or, *speech* [II]Hebr. *to hide snares* [a]Prov. 1:11 [b]Ps. 10:11; 59:7
6 [I]Or, *we are consumed by that which they have thoroughly searched* [II]Hebr. *a search searched*

🔑 **64:1** This psalm may be related to either of two accounts in the life of David: when David was betrayed by Doeg (1 Sam. 21:7—22:23) or when Ahithophel joined Absalom's rebellion against David (2 Sam. 15—17).

7 [a]But God shall shoot at them *with* an arrow; suddenly [I]shall they be wounded.[4347]

8 So they shall make [a]their own tongue to fall upon themselves: [b]all that see them shall flee away.

9 [a]And all men[120] shall fear, and shall [b]declare[5046] the work of God; for they shall wisely consider[7919] of his doing.

10 [a]The righteous[6662] shall be glad in the LORD, and shall trust[2620] in him; and all the upright in heart shall glory.[1984]

Thanking God for Nature

To the chief Musician, A Psalm *and* Song of David.

65 Praise[8416] [Ia]waiteth for thee, O God,[430] in Sion: and unto thee shall the vow be performed.[7999]

2 O thou that hearest[8085] prayer,[8605] [a]unto thee shall all flesh[1320] come.

3 [Ia]Iniquities[5771] prevail against me: *as for* our transgressions,[6588] thou shalt [b]purge them away.

4 [a]Blessed[835] *is the man whom* thou [b]choosest,[977] and causest to approach[7126] *unto thee, that* he may dwell in thy courts: [c]we shall be satisfied with the goodness of thy house, *even* of thy holy[6918] temple.[1964]

5 *By* terrible things[3372] in righteousness[6664] wilt thou answer us, O God of our salvation; *who art* the confidence of [a]all the ends of the earth,[776] and of them that are afar off *upon* the sea:

6 Which by his strength setteth fast[3559] the mountains; [a]*being* girded with power:

7 [a]Which stilleth[7623] the noise[7588] of the seas, the noise of their waves, [b]and the tumult of the people.[3816]

8 They also that dwell in the uttermost parts are afraid[3372] at thy tokens:[226] thou makest the outgoings of the morning and evening [I]to rejoice.

9 Thou [a]visitest[6485] the earth, and [Ib]waterest it: thou greatly enrichest it [c]with the river of God, *which* is full of water: thou preparest[3559] them corn, when thou hast so provided for it.

10 Thou waterest the ridges thereof abundantly: [I]thou settlest the furrows[1417] thereof: [II]thou makest it soft with showers: thou blessest the springing thereof.

11 Thou crownest the year with thy goodness;[2896] and thy paths drop fatness.

12 They drop *upon* the pastures[4999] of the wilderness: and the little hills [I]rejoice on every side.

13 The pastures[3733] are clothed with flocks; [a]the valleys also are covered over with corn; they shout for joy,[7321] they also sing.[7891]

Praise and Thanksgiving

To the chief Musician, A Song *or* Psalm.

66 [a]Make a joyful noise[7321] unto God,[430] [I]all ye lands:[776]

2 Sing forth[2167] the honour[3519] of his name: make[7760] his praise[8416] glorious.[3519]

3 Say[559] unto God, How [a]terrible[3372] *art thou in* thy works! [b]through the greatness of thy power shall thine enemies [Ic]submit themselves unto thee.

4 [a]All the earth[776] shall worship[7812] thee, and [b]shall sing unto thee; they shall sing *to* thy name. Selah.

5 [a]Come and see the works of God: *he is* terrible *in his* doing toward the children[1121] of men.[120]

6 [a]He turned[2015] the sea into dry[3004] *land:* [b]they went through the flood on foot: there did we rejoice in him.

7 He ruleth[4910] by his power for ever;[5769] [a]his eyes behold the nations:[1471] let not the rebellious[5637] exalt themselves. Selah.

8 O bless[1288] our God, ye people,[5971] and make the voice of his praise to be heard:[8085]

9 Which [I]holdeth[7760] our soul[5315] in life,[2416] and [a]suffereth[5414] not our feet to be moved.

10 For [a]thou, O God, hast proved[974]

---

7 [I]Hebr. *their wound shall be* [a]Ps. 7:12, 13
8 [a]Prov. 12:13; 18:7 [b]Ps. 31:11; 52:6
9 [a]Ps. 40:3 [b]Jer. 50:28; 51:10
10 [a]Ps. 32:11; 58:10; 68:3

1 [I]Hebr. *is silent* [a]Ps. 62:1
2 [a]Isa. 66:23
3 [I]Hebr. *Words,* or, *Matters of iniquities* [a]Ps. 38:4; 40:12 [b]Ps. 51:2; 79:9; Isa. 6:7; Heb. 9:14; 1John 1:7, 9
4 [a]Ps. 33:12; 84:4 [b]Ps. 4:3 [c]Ps. 36:8
5 [a]Ps. 22:27
6 [a]Ps. 93:1
7 [a]Ps. 89:9; 107:29; Matt. 8:26 [b]Ps. 76:10; Isa. 17:12, 13
8 [I]Or, *to sing*
9 [I]Or, *after thou hadst made it to desire* rain [a]Deut. 11:12 [b]Ps. 68:9, 10; 104:13; Jer. 5:24 [c]Ps. 46:4
10 [I]Hebr. *thou causest rain to descend* into *the furrows thereof* [II]Hebr. *thou dissolvest it*
12 [I]Hebr. *are girded with joy*
13 [a]Isa. 55:12

1 [I]Hebr. *all the earth* [a]Ps. 100:1
3 [I]Or, *yield feigned obedience* [a]Ps. 65:5 [b]Ps. 18:44 [c]Ps. 18:44; 81:15
4 [a]Ps. 22:27; 67:3; 117:1 [b]Ps. 96:1, 2
5 [a]Ps. 46:8
6 [a]Ex. 14:21 [b]Josh. 3:14, 16
7 [a]Ps. 11:4
9 [I]Hebr. *putteth* [a]Ps. 121:3
10 [a]Ps. 17:3; Isa. 48:10

us: [b]thou hast tried us, as silver *is* tried.[6884]

11 [a]Thou broughtest us into the net;[4685] thou laidst[7760] affliction upon our loins.

12 [a]Thou hast caused men[582] to ride over our heads;[7218] [b]we went through fire and through water: but thou broughtest us out into a [I]wealthy *place.*

13 [a]I will go into thy house[1004] with burnt offerings:[5930] [b]I will pay thee my vows,[5088]

14 Which my lips[8193] have [I]uttered, and my mouth[6310] hath spoken,[1696] when I was in trouble.

15 I will offer unto thee burnt sacrifices[5930] of [I]fatlings, with the incense[7004] of rams; I will offer[6213] bullocks with goats. Selah.

16 [a]Come *and* hear,[8085] all ye that fear[3373] God, and I will declare[5608] what he hath done[6213] for my soul.

17 I cried[7121] unto him with my mouth, and he was extolled with my tongue.

18 [a]If I regard[7200] iniquity[205] in my heart,[3820] the Lord[136] will not hear *me:*

19 *But* verily God [a]hath heard *me;* he hath attended[7181] to the voice of my prayer.[8605]

20 Blessed *be* God, which hath not turned away my prayer, nor his mercy[2617] from me.

Let All Nations Praise God!

To the chief Musician on Neginoth, A Psalm *or* Song.

67 God[430] be merciful[2603] unto us, and bless[1288] us; *and* [a]cause his face to shine [I]upon us; Selah.

2 That [a]thy way[1870] may be known[3045] upon earth,[776] [b]thy saving health[3444] among all nations.[1471]

3 [a]Let the people[5971] praise[3034] thee, O God; let all the people praise thee.

4 O let the nations[3816] be glad and sing for joy: [a]for thou shalt judge[8199] the people righteously,[4334] and [I]govern[5148] the nations upon earth. Selah.

5 Let the people praise thee, O God; let all the people praise thee.

6 [a]*Then* shall the earth yield her increase; *and* God, *even* our own God, shall bless us.

7 God shall bless us; and [a]all the ends of the earth shall fear[3372] him.

The True God

To the chief Musician, A Psalm *or* Song of David.

68 Let [a]God[430] arise, let his enemies be scattered: let them also that hate[8130] him flee [I]before him.

2 [a]As smoke is driven away, *so* drive *them* away: [b]as wax melteth before the fire, *so* let the wicked[7563] perish[6] at the presence of God.

3 But [a]let the righteous[6662] be glad; let them rejoice[5970] before God: yea, let them [I]exceedingly rejoice.[7797]

4 [a]Sing[7891] unto God, sing praises[2167] to his name: [b]extol him that rideth upon the heavens[6160] [c]by his name JAH,[3050] and rejoice[5937] before him.

5 [a]A father[1] of the fatherless, and a judge[1781] of the widows, *is* God in his holy[6944] habitation.

6 [a]God setteth the solitary[3173] [I]in families:[1004] [b]he bringeth out those which are bound with chains: but [c]the rebellious[5637] dwell[7931] in a dry *land.*

7 O God, [a]when thou wentest forth before thy people,[5971] when thou didst march through the wilderness; Selah:

8 [a]The earth[776] shook,[7493] the heavens[8064] also dropped[5197] at the presence of God: *even* Sinai itself *was moved* at the presence of God, the God of Israel.

9 [a]Thou, O God, didst [I]send[5130] a plentiful rain, whereby thou didst confirm thine inheritance,[5159] when it was weary.

10 Thy congregation[2416] hath dwelt therein: [a]thou, O God, hast prepared[3559] of thy goodness[2896] for the poor.

11 The Lord gave the word:[562] great *was* the [I]company[6635] of those that published[1319] *it.*

12 [a]Kings of armies[6635] did flee

10 [b]Zech. 13:9; 1Pet. 1:6, 7
11 [a]Lam. 1:13
12 [I]Hebr. *moist* [a]Isa. 51:23 [b]Isa. 43:2
13 [a]Ps. 100:4; 116:14, 17, 18, 19 [b]Eccl. 5:4
14 [I]Hebr. *opened*
15 [I]Hebr. *marrow*
16 [a]Ps. 34:11
18 [a]Job 27:9; Prov. 15:29; 28:9; Isa. 1:15; John 9:31; James 4:3
19 [a]Ps. 116:1, 2

1 [I]Hebr. *with us* [a]Num. 6:25; Ps. 4:6; 31:16; 80:3, 7, 19; 119:135
2 [a]Acts 18:25 [b]Luke 2:30, 31; Titus 2:11
3 [a]Ps. 66:4
4 [I]Hebr. *lead* [a]Ps. 96:10, 13; 98:9
6 [a]Lev. 26:4; Ps. 85:12; Ezek. 34:27
7 [a]Ps. 22:27

1 [I]Hebr. *from his face* [a]Num. 10:35; Isa. 33:3
2 [a]Isa. 9:18; Hos. 13:3 [b]Ps. 97:5; Mic. 1:4
3 [I]Hebr. *rejoice with gladness* [a]Ps. 32:11; 58:10; 64:10
4 [a]Ps. 66:4 [b]Deut. 33:26; [c]Ex. 6:3
5 [a]Ps. 10:14, 18; 146:9
6 [I]Hebr. *in a house* [a]1Sam. 2:5; Ps. 113:9 [b]Ps. 107:10, 14; 146:7; Acts 12:6 [c]Ps. 107:34, 40
7 [a]Ex. 13:21; Judg. 4:14; Hab. 3:13
8 [a]Ex. 19:16, 18; Judg. 5:4; Isa. 64:1, 3
9 [I]Hebr. *shake out* [a]Deut. 11:11, 12; Ezek. 34:26
10 [a]Deut. 26:5, 9; Ps. 74:19
11 [I]Hebr. *army*
12 [a]Num. 31:8, 9, 54; Josh. 10:16; 12:8

apace: and she that tarried at home[1004]
divided the spoil.
13 [a]Though ye have lien among the
pots, [b]*yet shall ye be as* the wings of a
dove covered with silver, and her feathers with yellow gold.
14 [a]When the Almighty[7706] scattered
kings [I]in it, it was *white* as snow in
Salmon.
15 The hill of God *is as* the hill of
Bashan; an high hill *as* the hill of
Bashan.
16 [a]Why leap ye, ye high hills? [b]*this*
is the hill *which* God desireth[2530] to dwell
in; yea, the LORD will dwell *in it* for
ever.[5331]
17 [a]The chariots of God *are* twenty
thousand,[505] [I]*even* thousands of angels:[8136] the Lord[136] *is* among them, *as in*
Sinai, in the holy *place*.
18 [a]Thou hast ascended on high,
[b]thou hast led[7617] captivity[7628] captive:[7617] [c]thou hast received gifts [I]for
men;[120] yea, *for* [d]the rebellious also, [e]that
the LORD God might dwell *among them*.
19 Blessed[1288] *be* the Lord, *who* daily
loadeth us *with benefits, even* the God[410]
of our salvation.[3444] Selah.
20 *He that is* our God *is* the God of
salvation;[4190] and [a]unto GOD the Lord *be-*
long the issues from death.[4194]
21 But [a]God shall wound[4272] the
head[7218] of his enemies, [b]*and* the hairy
scalp of such an one as goeth on still in
his trespasses.
22 The Lord said, I will bring
[a]again[7725] from Bashan, I will bring *my*
people again [b]from the depths of the sea:
23 [a]That thy foot may be [I]dipped[4272]
in the blood[1818] of *thine* enemies, [b]*and*
the tongue of thy dogs in the same.
24 They have seen[7200] thy goings, O
God; *even* the goings of my God, my
King,[4428] in the sanctuary.[6944]
25 [a]The singers[7891] went before, the
players on instruments *followed* after;
among *them were* the damsels[5959] playing
with timbrels.[8608]
26 Bless ye God in the congregations,
even the Lord, [I]from [a]the fountain of
Israel.
27 There *is* [a]little Benjamin *with* their
ruler,[7287] the princes of Judah [I]*and* their
council, the princes of Zebulun, *and* the
princes[8269] of Naphtali.
28 Thy God hath [a]commanded[6680]
thy strength: strengthen, O God, that
which thou hast wrought for us.
29 Because of thy temple[1964] at
Jerusalem [a]shall kings bring presents
unto thee.
30 Rebuke[1605] [Ia]the company[2416] of
spearmen, [b]the multitude[5712] of the
bulls,[47] with the calves of the people, *till*
every one [c]submit himself with pieces of
silver: [II]scatter thou the people *that* delight[2654] in war.
31 [a]Princes[2831] shall come out of
Egypt; [b]Ethiopia shall soon [c]stretch out
her hands[3027] unto God.
32 Sing unto God, ye kingdoms[4467] of
the earth; O sing praises unto the Lord;
Selah:
33 To him [a]that rideth upon the heavens of heavens, *which were* of old;[6924] lo,
[b]he doth [I]send out his voice, *and that* a
mighty voice.
34 [a]Ascribe ye strength unto God: his
excellency *is* over Israel, and his strength
is in the [I]clouds.[7834]
35 O God, [a]*thou art* terrible[3372] out of
thy holy places: the God of Israel *is* he
that giveth strength and power unto *his*
people. Blessed *be* God.

A Cry of Distress

To the chief Musician upon Shoshannim, *A Psalm* of David.

69 Save[3467] me, O God;[430] for [a]the
waters are come in unto *my*
soul.[5315]
2 [a]I sink in deep mire, where *there is*
no standing: I am come into deep waters,
where the floods overflow[7857] me.
3 [a]I am weary of my crying:[7121] my
throat is dried:[2787] [b]mine eyes fail[3615]
while I wait[3176] for my God.
4 They that [a]hate[8130] me without a
cause[2600] are more than the hairs of mine
head:[7218] they that would destroy[6789]

13 [a]Ps. 81:6 [b]Ps. 105:37
14 [I]Or, *for her, she was* [a]Num. 21:3; Josh. 10:10; 12:1
16 [a]Ps. 114:4, 6 [b]Deut. 12:5, 11; 1Kgs. 9:3; Ps. 87:1, 2; 132:13, 14
17 [I]Or, *even many thousands* [a]Deut. 33:2; 2Kgs. 6:16, 17; Dan. 7:10; Heb. 12:22; Rev. 9:16
18 [I]Hebr. *in the man* [a]Acts 1:9; Eph. 4:8 [b]Judg. 5:12 [c]Acts 2:4, 33 [d]1Tim. 1:13 [e]Ps. 78:60
20 [a]Deut. 32:39; Prov. 4:23; Rev. 1:18; 20:1
21 [a]Ps. 110:6; Hab. 3:13 [b]Ps. 55:23
22 [a]Num. 21:33 [b]Ex. 14:22
23 [I]Or, *red* [a]Ps. 58:10 [b]1Kgs. 21:19
25 [a]1Chr. 13:8; 15:16; Ps. 47:5
26 [I]Or, *ye that are of the fountain of Israel* [a]Deut. 33:28; Isa. 48:1
27 [I]Or, with *their company* [a]1Sam. 9:21
28 [a]Ps. 42:8
29 [a]1Kgs. 10:10, 24, 25; 2Chr. 32:23; Ps. 72:10; 76:11; Isa. 60:16, 17
30 [I]Or, *the beasts of the reeds* [II]Or, *he scattereth* [a]Jer. 51:32, 33 [b]Ps. 22:12 [c]2Sam. 8:2, 6
31 [a]Isa. 19:19, 21 [b]Ps. 72:9; Isa. 45:14; Zeph. 3:10; Acts 8:27 [c]Ps. 44:20
33 [I]Hebr. *give* [a]Ps. 18:10; 68:9; 104:3 [b]Ps. 29:3
34 [I]Or, *heavens* [a]Ps. 29:1
35 [a]Ps. 45:4; 65:5; 66:5; 76:12

1 [a]Ps. 69:2, 14, 15; Jon. 2:5
2 [a]Ps. 40:2
3 [a]Ps. 6:6 [b]Ps. 119:82, 123 [c]Isa. 38:14
4 [a]Ps. 35:19; John 15:25

me, *being* mine enemies wrongfully,[8267] are mighty: then I restored[7725] *that* which I took not away.

5 O God, thou knowest[3045] my foolishness; and my [I]sins[819] are not hid from thee.

6 Let not them that wait on[6960] thee, O Lord[136] GOD of hosts,[6635] be ashamed[954] for my sake: let not those that seek thee be confounded for my sake, O God of Israel.

7 Because for thy sake I have borne[5375] reproach;[2781] shame hath covered[3680] my face.

8 [a]I am become[1961] a stranger[2114] unto my brethren,[251] and an alien[5237] unto my mother's[517] children.[1121]

9 [a]For the zeal[7068] of thine house hath eaten me up; [b]and the reproaches[2781] of them that reproached thee are fallen[5307] upon me.

10 [a]When I wept, *and chastened* my soul with fasting, that was to my reproach.

11 I made sackcloth also my garment; [a]and I became a proverb to them.

12 They that sit in the gate speak[7878] against me; and [a]I *was* the song of the [I]drunkards.

13 But as for me, my prayer[8605] *is* unto thee, O LORD, [a]*in* an acceptable[7522] time:[6256] O God, in the multitude of thy mercy[2617] hear me, in the truth[571] of thy salvation.[3468]

14 Deliver[5337] me out of the mire, and let me not sink: [a]let me be delivered from them that hate me, and out of [b]the deep waters.

15 Let not the waterflood overflow me, neither let the deep swallow me up,[1104] and let not the pit [a]shut her mouth[6310] upon me.

16 Hear me, O LORD; [a]for thy lovingkindness *is* good:[2896] [b]turn unto me according to the multitude of thy tender mercies.[7356]

17 And [a]hide not thy face from thy servant;[5650] for I am in trouble: [I]hear me speedily.

18 Draw nigh unto my soul, *and* redeem[1350] it: deliver[6299] me because of mine enemies.

19 Thou hast known[3045] [a]my reproach, and my shame, and my dishonour: mine adversaries *are* all before thee.

20 Reproach hath broken[7665] my heart;[3820] and I am full of heaviness: and [a]I looked[6960] *for some* [I]to take pity, but *there was* none; and for [b]comforters,[5162] but I found none.

🔑 21 They gave me also gall[7219] for my meat; [a]and in my thirst they gave me vinegar to drink.

🔑 22 [a]Let their table become a snare[6341] before them: and *that which should have been* for *their* welfare,[7965] *let it become* a trap.[4170]

23 [a]Let their eyes be darkened,[2821] that they see not; and make their loins continually[8548] to shake.

24 [a]Pour out[8210] thine indignation[2195] upon them, and let thy wrathful anger[639] take hold of them.

25 [a]Let [I]their habitation be desolate;[8074] *and* [II]let none dwell in their tents.[168]

26 For [I]they persecute [a]*him* whom thou hast smitten;[5221] and they talk[5608] to the grief of [I]those whom thou hast wounded.[2491]

27 [a]Add [I]iniquity[5771] unto their iniquity: [b]and let them not come into thy righteousness.[6666]

28 Let them [a]be blotted out[4229] of the book[5612] of the living,[2416] [b]and not be written with the righteous.[6662]

29 But I *am* poor and sorrowful: let thy salvation,[3444] O God, set me up on high.

30 [a]I will praise[1984] the name of God with a song, and will magnify him with thanksgiving.[8426]

31 [a]*This* also shall please the LORD better[3190] than an ox *or* bullock that hath horns and hoofs.

5 IHebr. *guiltiness*
8 [a]Ps. 31:11; Isa. 53:3; John 1:11; 7:5
9 [a]Ps. 119:139; John 2:17 [b]Ps. 89:50, 51; Rom. 15:3
10 [a]Ps. 35:13, 14
11 [a]1Kgs. 9:7; Jer. 24:9
12 IHebr. *drinkers of strong drink* [a]Job 30:9; Ps. 35:15, 16
13 [a]Isa. 49:8; 55:6; 2Cor. 6:2
14 [a]Ps. 144:7 [b]Ps. 69:1, 2, 15
15 [a]Num. 16:33
16 [a]Ps. 63:3 [b]Ps. 25:16; 86:16
17 IHebr. *make haste to hear me* [a]Ps. 27:9; 102:2
19 [a]Ps. 22:6, 7; Isa. 53:3; Heb. 12:2
20 IHebr. *to lament* with me [a]Ps. 142:4; Isa. 63:5 [b]Job 16:2
21 [a]Matt. 27:34, 48; Mark 15:23; John 19:29
22 [a]Rom. 11:9, 10
23 [a]Isa. 6:9, 10; John 12:39, 40; Rom. 11:10; 2Cor. 3:14
24 [a]1Thess. 2:16
25 IHebr. *their palace* IIHebr. *let there not be a dweller* [a]Matt. 23:38; Acts 1:20
26 IHebr. *thy wounded* [a]2Chr. 28:9; Zech. 1:15 [b]Isa. 53:4
27 IOr, *punishment of iniquity* [a]Rom. 1:28 [b]Isa. 26:10; Rom. 9:31
28 [a]Ex. 32:32; Phil. 4:3; Rev. 3:5; 13:8 [b]Ezek. 13:9; Luke 10:20; Heb. 12:23
30 [a]Ps. 28:7
31 [a]Ps. 50:13, 14, 23

🔑 **69:21** See the note on Psalm 22:1–31 for a discussion of the Messianic Psalms.
🔑 **69:22–28** See the note on Psalm 109:1–29 for a discussion of the Imprecatory Psalms.

32 [a]The [I]humble shall see *this, and* be glad: and [b]your heart[3824] shall live[2421] that seek God.

33 For the LORD heareth[8085] the poor, and despiseth not [a]his prisoners.

34 [a]Let the heaven[8064] and earth[776] praise him, the seas, [b]and every thing that [I]moveth therein.

35 [a]For God will save Zion, and will build the cities of Judah: that they may dwell there, and have it in possession.

36 [a]The seed[2233] also of his servants[5650] shall inherit[5157] it: and they that love[157] his name shall dwell[7931] therein.

A Prayer for Deliverance

To the chief Musician, *A Psalm* of David, to bring to remembrance.

70 *Make* haste, [a]O God,[430] to deliver[5337] me; make haste to help me, O LORD.

2 [a]Let them be ashamed[954] and confounded that seek after my soul:[5315] let them be turned backward, and put to confusion, that desire[2655] my hurt.[7451]

3 [a]Let them be turned back for a reward of their shame that say,[559] Aha, aha.

4 Let all those that seek thee rejoice and be glad in thee: and let such as love[157] thy salvation say continually,[8548] Let God be magnified.

5 [a]But I *am* poor and needy: [b]make haste unto me, O God: thou *art* my help and my deliverer; O LORD, make no tarrying.

The Prayer of an Old Man

71 🔑 In [a]thee, O LORD, do I put my trust:[2620] let me never be put to confusion.[954]

2 [a]Deliver[5337] me in thy righteousness,[6666] and cause me to escape: [b]incline thine ear[241] unto me, and save[3467] me.

3 [I][a]Be thou my strong habitation, whereunto I may continually[8548] resort: thou hast given [b]commandment to save me; for thou *art* my rock and my fortress.

4 [a]Deliver me, O my God,[430] out of the hand[3027] of the wicked,[7563] out of the hand of the unrighteous[5765] and cruel[2556] man.

5 For thou *art* [a]my hope, O Lord[136] GOD: *thou art* my trust from my youth.

6 [a]By thee have I been holden up[5564] from the womb:[990] thou art he that took me out of my mother's[517] bowels:[4578] my praise[8416] *shall be* continually of thee.

7 [a]I am as a wonder[4159] unto many; but thou *art* my strong refuge.

8 Let [a]my mouth[6310] be filled *with* thy praise *and with* thy honour[8597] all the day.[3117]

9 [a]Cast me not off in the time[6256] of old age;[2209] forsake[5800] me not when my strength faileth.[3615]

10 For mine enemies speak[559] against me; and they that [I]lay wait[8104] for my soul[5315] [a]take counsel[3289] together,

11 Saying, God hath forsaken[5800] him: persecute and take him; for *there is* none to deliver *him*.

12 [a]O God, be not far from me: O my God, [b]make haste for my help.

13 [a]Let them be confounded[954] *and* consumed[3615] that are adversaries[7853] to my soul; let them be covered *with* reproach[2781] and dishonour that seek my hurt.[7451]

14 But I will hope[3176] continually, and will yet praise thee more and more.

15 [a]My mouth shall shew forth[5608] thy righteousness *and* thy salvation[8668] all the day; for [b]I know not the numbers *thereof*.

16 I will go in the strength[1369] of the Lord GOD: I will make mention of thy righteousness, *even* of thine only.

17 O God, thou hast taught[3925] me from my youth: and hitherto have I declared[5046] thy wondrous works.[6381]

18 [a]Now also [I]when I am old and grayheaded, O God, forsake me not; until I have shewed[5046] [II]thy strength unto *this* generation,[1755] *and* thy power to every one *that* is to come.

32 [I]Or, *meek* [a]Ps. 34:2 [b]Ps. 22:26
33 [a]Eph. 3:1
34 [I]Hebr. *creepeth* [a]Ps. 96:11; 148:1; Isa. 44:23; 49:13 [b]Isa. 55:12
35 [a]Ps. 51:18; Isa. 44:26
36 [a]Ps. 102:28

1 [a]Ps. 40:13; 71:12
2 [a]Ps. 35:4, 26; 71:13
3 [a]Ps. 40:15
5 [a]Ps. 40:17 [b]Ps. 141:1

1 [a]Ps. 25:2, 3; 31:1
2 [a]Ps. 31:1 [b]Ps. 17:6
3 [I]Hebr. *Be thou to me for a rock of habitation* [a]Ps. 31:2, 3 [b]Ps. 44:4
4 [a]Ps. 140:1, 4
5 [a]Jer. 17:7, 17
6 [a]Ps. 22:9, 10; Isa. 46:3
7 [a]Isa. 8:18; Zech. 3:8; 1Cor. 4:9
8 [a]Ps. 35:28
9 [a]Ps. 71:18
10 [I]Hebr. *watch, or, observe* [a]2Sam. 17:1; Matt. 27:1
12 [a]Ps. 22:11, 19; 35:22; 38:21, 22 [b]Ps. 70:1
13 [a]Ps. 35:4, 26; 40:14; 70:2; 71:24
15 [a]Ps. 35:28; 71:8, 24 [b]Ps. 40:5; 139:17, 18
18 [I]Hebr. *unto old age and gray hairs* [II]Hebr. *thine arm* [a]Ps. 71:9

🔑 **71:1–20** See the note on Psalm 22:1–31 for a discussion of the Messianic Psalms.

19 [a]Thy righteousness also, O God, *is* very high, who hast done[6213] great things: [b]O God, who *is* like unto thee!

20 [a]*Thou,* which hast shewed[7200] me great and sore[7451] troubles, [b]shalt quicken[2421] me again, and shalt bring me up again from the depths of the earth.[776]

21 Thou shalt increase my greatness, and comfort[5162] me on every side.

22 I will also praise[3034] thee [I][a]with the psaltery, *even* thy truth,[571] O my God: unto thee will I sing[2167] with the harp, O thou [b]Holy One[6918] of Israel.

23 My lips[8193] shall greatly rejoice when I sing unto thee; and [a]my soul, which thou hast redeemed.[6299]

24 [a]My tongue also shall talk[1897] of thy righteousness all the day long: for [b]they are confounded, for they are brought unto shame, that seek my hurt.

A Prayer for the King

A Psalm for Solomon.

72 Give the king[4428] thy judgments,[4941] O God,[430] and thy righteousness[6666] unto the king's son.[1121]

2 [a]He shall judge[177] thy people[5971] with righteousness,[6664] and thy poor with judgment.[4941]

3 [a]The mountains shall bring[5375] peace to the people, and the little hills, by righteousness.

4 [a]He shall judge[8199] the poor of the people, he shall save[3467] the children[1121] of the needy, and shall break in pieces[1792] the oppressor.

5 They shall fear[3372] thee [a]as long as the sun and moon endure, throughout all generations.[1755]

6 [a]He shall come down like rain upon the mown grass: as showers *that* water the earth.[776]

7 In his days[3117] shall the righteous[6662] flourish; [a]and abundance of peace [I]so long as the moon endureth.

8 [a]He shall have dominion[7287] also from sea to sea, and from the river unto the ends of the earth.

9 [a]They that dwell in the wilderness shall bow[3766] before him; [b]and his enemies shall lick the dust.[6083]

10 [a]The kings of Tarshish and of the isles shall bring presents:[4503] the kings of Sheba and Seba shall offer[7126] gifts.

11 [a]Yea, all kings shall fall down[7812] before him: all nations[1471] shall serve[5647] him.

12 For he [a]shall deliver[5337] the needy when he crieth; the poor also, and *him* that hath no helper.

13 He shall spare the poor and needy, and shall save the souls[5315] of the needy.

14 He shall redeem[1350] their soul from deceit and violence:[2555] and [a]precious shall their blood[1818] be in his sight.

15 And he shall live,[2421] and to him shall be given of the gold of Sheba: prayer also shall be made for him continually;[8548] *and* daily shall he be praised.[1288]

16 There shall be an handful of corn in the earth upon the top of the mountains; the fruit thereof shall shake[7493] like Lebanon: [a]and *they* of the city shall flourish like grass of the earth.

17 [a]His name [I]shall endure for ever:[5769] [II]his name shall be continued as long as the sun: and [b]*men* shall be blessed[1288] in him: [c]all nations shall call him blessed.[833]

18 [a]Blessed *be* the LORD God, the God of Israel, [b]who only doeth[6213] wondrous things.[6381]

19 And [a]blessed *be* his glorious[3519] name for ever: [b]and let the whole earth be filled *with* his glory; Amen,[543] and Amen.

20 The prayers[8605] of David the son of Jesse are ended.[3615]

BOOK III

The Fate of the Wicked

A Psalm of Asaph.

73 [I]Truly God[430] *is* good[2896] to Israel, *even* to such as are [II]of a clean[1249] heart.[3824]

---

19 [a]Ps. 57:10 [b]Ps. 35:10; 86:8; 89:6, 8
20 [a]Ps. 60:3 [b]Hos. 6:1, 2
22 [I]Hebr. *with the instrument of psaltery* [a]Ps. 92:1, 2, 3; 150:3 [b]2Kgs. 19:22; Isa. 60:9
23 [a]Ps. 103:4
24 [a]Ps. 71:8, 15 [b]Ps. 71:13

2 [a]Isa. 11:2-4; 32:1
3 [a]Ps. 85:10; Isa. 32:17; 52:7
4 [a]Isa. 11:4
5 [a]Ps. 72:7, 17; 89:36, 37
6 [a]2Sam. 23:4; Hos. 6:3
7 [I]Hebr. *till* there be *no moon* [a]Isa. 2:4; Dan. 2:44; Luke 1:33
8 [a]Ex. 23:31; 1Kgs. 4:21, 24; Ps. 2:8; 80:11; 89:25; Zech. 9:10
9 [a]Ps. 74:14 [b]Isa. 49:23; Mic. 7:17
10 [a]2Chr. 9:21; Ps. 45:12; 68:29; Isa. 49:7; 60:6, 9
11 [a]Isa. 49:22, 23
12 [a]Job 29:12
14 [a]Ps. 116:15
16 [a]1Kgs. 4:20
17 [I]Hebr. *shall be* [II]Hebr. *shall be as a son to continue his father's name for ever* [a]Ps. 89:36 [b]Gen. 12:3; 22:18; Jer. 4:2 [c]Luke 1:48
18 [a]1Chr. 29:10; Ps. 41:13; 106:48 [b]Ex. 15:11; Ps. 77:14; 136:4
19 [a]Neh. 9:5 [b]Num. 14:21; Zech. 14:9

1 [I]Or, *Yet* [II]Hebr. *clean of heart*

2 But as for me, my feet were almost
gone; my steps had well nigh slipped.[8210]
3 [a]For I was envious at the fool-
ish,[1984] *when* I saw[7200] the prosperity[7965]
of the wicked.[7563]
4 For *there are* no bands in their
death:[4194] but their strength *is* [I]firm.
5 [a]They *are* not [I]in trouble[5999] *as*
other men;[582] neither are they plagued[5060]
[II]like *other* men.[120]
6 Therefore pride compasseth them
about as a chain; violence[2555] covereth
them [a]*as* a garment.
7 [a]Their eyes stand out with fatness:
[I]they have more than heart could
wish.[4906]
8 [a]They are corrupt,[4167] and
[b]speak[1696] wickedly[7451] *concerning* oppression: they [c]speak loftily.
9 They set their mouth[6310] [a]against
the heavens,8064 and their tongue walketh
through the earth.[776]
10 Therefore his people[5971] return[7725]
hither: [a]and waters of a full *cup* are
wrung out to them.
11 And they say,[559] [a]How doth
God[410] know? and is there knowledge[1844]
in the most High?[5945]
12 Behold, these *are* the ungodly,[7563]
who [a]prosper in the world;[5769] they increase *in* riches.[2428]
13 [a]Verily I have cleansed[2135] my
heart *in* vain, and [b]washed[7364] my
hands[3709] in innocency.[5356]
14 For all the day[3117] long have I
been plagued, and [I]chastened[8433] every
morning.
15 If I say, I will speak thus; behold,
I should offend[898] *against* the generation[1755] of thy children.[1121]
16 [a]When I thought[2803] to know this,
[I]it *was* too painful[5999] for me;
17 Until [a]I went into the sanctuary[4720] of God; *then* understood[995] I
[b]their end.[319]
18 Surely [a]thou didst set them in
slippery places: thou castedst them down
into destruction.[4876]
19 How are they *brought* into desolation,[8047] as in a moment! they are utterly consumed[8552] with terrors.
🔑 20 [a]As a dream when *one* awaketh;
so, O Lord,[136] [b]when thou awakest, thou
shalt despise their image.[6754]
21 Thus my heart was [a]grieved,[2556]
and I was pricked[8150] in my reins.3627
22 [a]So foolish1198 *was* I, and
[I]ignorant: I was *as* a beast [II]before thee.
23 Nevertheless I *am* continually[8548]
with thee: thou hast holden270 *me* by my
right hand.[3027]
24 [a]Thou shalt guide[5148] me with thy
counsel,[6098] and afterward receive me *to*
glory.[3519]
25 [a]Whom have I in heaven8064 *but*
thee? and *there is* none upon earth *that* I
desire[2654] beside thee.
26 [a]My flesh and my heart
faileth:[3615] *but* God *is* the [I]strength of my
heart, and [b]my portion for ever.[5769]
27 For, lo, [a]they that are far from
thee shall perish:[6] thou hast destroyed[6789]
all them that [b]go a whoring[2181] from
thee.
28 But *it is* good for me to [a]draw
near to God: I have put my trust in the

3 [a]Job 21:7; Ps. 37:1; Jer. 12:1
4 [I]Hebr. *fat*
5 [I]Hebr. *in the trouble of* other *men* [II]Hebr. *with* [a]Job 21:9
6 [a]Ps. 109:18
7 [I]Hebr. *they pass the thoughts of the heart* [a]Job 15:27; Ps. 17:10; 119:70; Jer. 5:28
8 [a]Ps. 53:1 [b]Hos. 7:16 [c]2Pet. 2:18; Jude 1:16
9 [a]Rev. 13:6
10 [a]Ps. 75:8
11 [a]Job 22:13; Ps. 10:11; 94:7
12 [a]Ps. 73:3
13 [a]Job 21:15; 34:9; 35:3; Mal. 3:14 [b]Ps. 26:6
14 [I]Hebr. *my chastisement* was
16 [I]Hebr. *it was labor in mine eyes* [a]Eccl. 8:17
17 [a]Ps. 77:13 [b]Ps. 37:38
18 [a]Ps. 35:6
20 [a]Job 20:8; Ps. 90:5; Isa. 29:7, 8 [b]Ps. 78:65
21 [a]Ps. 73:3
22 [I]Hebr. *I knew not* [II]Hebr. *with thee* [a]Ps. 92:6; Prov. 30:2
24 [a]Ps. 32:8; Isa. 58:8
25 [a]Phil. 3:8
26 [I]Hebr. *rock* [a]Ps. 84:2; 119:81 [b]Ps. 16:5; 119:57
27 [a]Ps. 119:155 [b]Ex. 34:15; Num. 15:39; James 4:4
28 [a]Heb. 10:22

🔑 **73:20** How can it be that God would need to awake if He never sleeps (cf. Ps. 121:3, 4)? The answer to this dilemma is seen in the proper understanding of the meanings of the original Hebrew words. The word found in Psalm 73:20, translated "awakest," is the Hebrew word *ūr* (5782), which should be understood figuratively of awakening in the sense of beginning to act. This verse begins with a simile: "As a dream when one awaketh." The psalmist was relating how God acts in response to the wicked to how one acts upon awakening from a deep sleep (Judg. 5:12). Paul says of this time that God "winked at" their ignorance (Acts 17:30). In Psalm 121:3, 4, the writer makes it clear that God never sleeps as men do, losing consciousness. He makes it clear that since he does not slumber (*nūm* [5123], "become drowsy"), how could it be that he should sleep (*yāshēn* [3462], "sleep")? The psalmist is using this form of literature, which his readers could relate to, in order to show that while God may seem to be "sleeping" and allowing them to continue in their wickedness, He will not fail to punish the ungodly.

Lord GOD, that I may [b]declare[5608] all thy works.

An Appeal to God

Maschil of Asaph.

74 O God,[430] why hast thou [a]cast *us* off for ever?[5331] *why* doth[6225] thine anger[639] [b]smoke[6225] against [c]the sheep of thy pasture?

2 Remember[2142] thy congregation,[5712] [a]*which* thou hast purchased of old;[6924] the [I][b]rod[7626] of thine inheritance,[5159] *which* thou hast redeemed;[1350] this mount Zion, wherein thou hast dwelt.[7931]

3 Lift up thy feet unto the perpetual desolations: *even* all *that* the enemy hath done wickedly[7489] in the sanctuary.[6944]

4 [a]Thine enemies roar in the midst[7130] of thy congregations; [b]they set up[7760] their ensigns *for* signs.[226]

5 *A man* was famous[3045] according as he had lifted up axes upon the thick trees.

6 But now they break down [a]the carved work thereof at once with axes and hammers.

7 [I][a]They have cast fire into thy sanctuary,[4720] they have defiled[2490] [b]*by casting down* the dwelling place of thy name to the ground.[776]

8 [a]They said in their hearts,[3820] Let us [I]destroy[3238] them together: they have burned up[8313] all the synagogues of God[410] in the land.[776]

9 We see not our signs: [a]*there is* no more any prophet:[5030] neither *is there* among us any that knoweth how long.

10 O God, how long shall the adversary reproach? shall the enemy blaspheme[5006] thy name for ever?

11 [a]Why withdrawest[7725] thou thy hand,[3027] even thy right hand? pluck *it* out of thy bosom.

12 For [a]God *is* my King[4428] of old, working[6466] salvation[3444] in the midst of the earth.[776]

13 [a]Thou didst [I]divide[6565] the sea by thy strength: [b]thou brakest[7665] the heads[7218] of the [II]dragons[8577] in the waters.

14 Thou brakest the heads of leviathan in pieces, *and* gavest him [a]*to be* meat [b]to the people[5971] inhabiting the wilderness.

15 [a]Thou didst cleave the fountain and the flood: [b]thou driedst up [I]mighty rivers.

16 The day[3117] *is* thine, the night[3915] also *is* thine: [a]thou hast prepared[3559] the light[3974] and the sun.

17 Thou hast [a]set all the borders of the earth: [b]thou hast [I]made[3335] summer and winter.

18 [a]Remember this, *that* the enemy hath reproached, O LORD, and *that* [b]the foolish people have blasphemed[5006] thy name.

19 O deliver not the soul[5315] [a]of thy turtledove unto the multitude[2416] *of the wicked:* [b]forget not the congregation[2416] of thy poor for ever.

20 [a]Have respect unto the covenant:[1285] for the dark places[4285] of the earth are full of the habitations[4999] of cruelty.[2555]

21 O let not the oppressed return[7725] ashamed: let the poor and needy praise[1984] thy name.

22 Arise, O God, plead thine own cause:[7379] [a]remember how the foolish man reproacheth thee daily.

23 Forget not the voice of thine enemies: the tumult[7588] of those that rise up against thee [I][a]increaseth continually.[8548]

God Will Judge Fairly

To the chief Musician, Al–taschith, A Psalm *or* Song of Asaph.

75 Unto thee, O God,[430] do we give thanks,[3034] *unto thee* do we give thanks: for *that* thy name is near thy wondrous works[6381] declare.[5608]

2 [I]When I shall receive the congregation[4150] I will judge[8199] uprightly.[4334]

3 The earth and all the inhabitants thereof are dissolved:[4127] I bear up the pillars of it. Selah.

---

28 [b]Ps. 107:22; 118:17

1 [a]Ps. 44:9, 23; 60:1, 10; 77:7; Jer. 31:37; 33:24 [b]Deut. 29:20 [c]Ps. 95:7; 100:3

2 [I]Or, *tribe* [a]Ex. 15:16; Deut. 9:29 [b]Deut. 32:9; Jer. 10:16

4 [a]Lam. 2:7 [b]Dan. 6:27

6 [a]1Kgs. 6:18, 29, 32, 35

7 [I]Hebr. *They have sent thy sanctuary into the fire* [a]2Kgs. 25:9 [b]Ps. 89:39

8 [I]Hebr. *break* [a]Ps. 83:4

9 [a]1Sam. 3:1; Amos 8:11

11 [a]Lam. 2:3

12 [a]Ps. 44:4

13 [I]Hebr. *break* [II]Or, *whales* [a]Ex. 14:21 [b]Isa. 51:9, 10; Ezek. 29:3; 32:2

14 [a]Num. 14:9 [b]Ps. 72:9

15 [I]Hebr. *rivers of strength* [a]Ex. 17:5, 6; Num. 20:11; Ps. 105:41; Isa. 48:21 [b]Josh. 3:13

16 [a]Gen. 1:14

17 [I]Hebr. *made them* [a]Acts 17:26 [b]Gen. 8:22

18 [a]Ps. 74:22; Rev. 16:19 [b]Ps. 39:8

19 [a]Song 2:14 [b]Ps. 68:10

20 [a]Gen. 17:7, 8; Lev. 26:44, 45; Ps. 106:45; Jer. 33:21

22 [a]Ps. 74:18; 89:51

23 [I]Hebr. *ascendeth* [a]Jon. 1:2

2 [I]Or, *When I shall take a set time*

4 I said unto the fools,[1984] Deal not foolishly:[1984] and to the wicked,[7563] [a]Lift not up the horn:

5 Lift not up your horn on high: speak *not with* a stiff neck.

6 For promotion[7311] *cometh* neither from the east, nor from the west, nor from the [I]south.

7 But [a]God *is* the judge: [b]he putteth down one, and setteth up another.

8 For [a]in the hand[3027] of the LORD *there is* a cup, and the wine is red; it is [b]full of mixture; and he poureth out of the same: [c]but the dregs[8105] thereof, all the wicked of the earth shall wring *them* out, *and* drink *them.*

9 But I will declare[5046] for ever;[5769] I will sing praises to the God of Jacob.

10 [a]All the horns of the wicked also will I cut off; *but* [b]the horns of the righteous[6662] shall be exalted.

4 [a]Zech. 1:21
6 [I]Hebr. *desert*
7 [a]Ps. 50:6; 58:11 [b]1Sam. 2:7; Dan. 2:21
8 [a]Job 21:20; Ps. 60:3; Jer. 25:15; Rev. 14:10; 16:19 [b]Prov. 23:30 [c]Ps. 73:10
10 [a]Ps. 101:8; Jer. 48:25 [b]Ps. 89:17; 148:14

The God of Victory and Judgment

To the chief Musician on Neginoth, A Psalm *or* Song of Asaph.

76 In [a]Judah *is* God[430] known:[3045] his name *is* great in Israel.

2 In Salem also is his tabernacle, and his dwelling place in Zion.

3 [a]There brake[7665] he the arrows of the bow, the shield, and the sword,[2719] and the battle. Selah.

4 Thou *art* more glorious *and* excellent[117] [a]than the mountains of prey.

5 [a]The stouthearted are spoiled, [b]they have slept their sleep: and none of the men[582] of might[2428] have found their hands.[3027]

6 [a]At thy rebuke,[1606] O God of Jacob, both the chariot and horse are cast into a dead sleep.

7 Thou, *even* thou, *art* to be feared:[3372] and [a]who may stand in thy sight when once[227] thou art angry?[639]

8 [a]Thou didst cause judgment[1779] to be heard from heaven;[8064] [b]the earth[776] feared, and was still,[8252]

9 When God [a]arose to judgment,[4941] to save[3467] all the meek of the earth. Selah.

10 [a]Surely the wrath[2534] of man[120] shall praise[3034] thee: the remainder[7611] of wrath shalt thou restrain.

11 [a]Vow,[5087] and pay unto the LORD your God: [b]let all that be round about him bring presents [I]unto him that ought to be feared.[4172]

12 He shall cut off the spirit[7307] of princes:[5057] [a]*he is* terrible[3372] to the kings[4428] of the earth.

1 [a]Ps. 48:1
3 [a]Ps. 46:9; Ezek. 39:9
4 [a]Ezek. 38:12, 13; 39:4
5 [a]Isa. 46:12 [b]Ps. 13:3; Jer. 51:39
6 [a]Ex. 15:1, 21; Ezek. 39:20; Nah. 2:13; Zech. 12:4
7 [a]Nah. 1:6
8 [a]Ezek. 38:20 [b]2Chr. 20:29, 30
9 [a]Ps. 9:7-9; 72:4
10 [a]Ex. 9:16; 18:11; Ps. 65:7
11 [I]Hebr. *to fear* [a]Eccl. 5:4-6 [b]2Chr. 32:22, 23; Ps. 68:29; 89:7
12 [a]Ps. 68:35

Comfort Comes from God

To the chief Musician, to Jeduthun, A Psalm of Asaph.

77 [a]I cried unto God with my voice, *even* unto God[430] with my voice; and he gave ear[238] unto me.

2 [a]In the day[3117] of my trouble I [b]sought the Lord:[136] [I]my sore ran in the night,[3915] and ceased not: my soul[5315] refused[3985] to be comforted.[5162]

3 I remembered[2142] God, and was troubled: I complained,[7878] and [a]my spirit[7307] was overwhelmed. Selah.

4 Thou holdest mine eyes waking: I am so troubled that I cannot speak.

5 [a]I have considered[2803] the days of old,[6924] the years of ancient times.[5769]

6 I call to remembrance[2142] [a]my song in the night: [b]I commune[7878] with mine own heart:[3824] and my spirit made diligent search.

7 [a]Will the Lord cast off for ever?[5769] and will he [b]be favourable[7521][3254] no more?

8 Is[656] his mercy[2617] clean gone[656] for ever?[5331] [a]doth[1584] *his* promise[562] fail[1584] [I]for evermore?

9 Hath God[410] [a]forgotten to be gracious? hath he in anger[639] shut up his tender mercies?[7356] Selah.

10 And I said, This *is* [a]my infirmity: *but I will remember* the years of the right hand of the most High.[5945]

11 [a]I will remember[2142] the works of the LORD: surely I will remember thy wonders[6382] of old.

12 I will meditate[1897] also of all thy work, and talk[7878] of thy doings.

13 [a]Thy way,[1870] O God, *is* in the

1 [a]Ps. 3:4
2 [I]Hebr. *my hand* [a]Ps. 50:15 [b]Isa. 26:9, 16
3 [a]Ps. 142:3; 143:4
5 [a]Deut. 32:7; Ps. 143:5; Isa. 51:9
6 [a]Ps. 42:8 [b]Ps. 4:4
7 [a]Ps. 74:1 [b]Ps. 85:1
8 [I]Hebr. *to generation and generation* [a]Rom. 9:6
9 [a]Isa. 49:15
10 [a]Ps. 31:22
11 [a]Ps. 143:5
13 [a]Ps. 73:17

sanctuary:[6944] [b]who *is so* great a God[410] as *our* God?

14 Thou *art* the God that doest[6213] wonders: thou hast declared[3045] thy strength among the people.[5971]

15 [a]Thou hast with *thine* arm redeemed[1350] thy people, the sons[1121] of Jacob and Joseph. Selah.

16 [a]The waters saw[7200] thee, O God, the waters saw thee; they were afraid:[2342] the depths also were troubled.

17 [I]The clouds poured out water: the skies[7834] sent out a sound: [a]thine arrows also went abroad.

18 The voice of thy thunder *was* in the heaven:[1534] [a]the lightnings lightened the world:[8398] [b]the earth[776] trembled and shook.

19 [a]Thy way *is* in the sea, and thy path in the great waters, [b]and thy footsteps[6119] are not known.[3045]

20 [a]Thou leddest[5148] thy people like a flock by the hand[3027] of Moses and Aaron.

God Loves His People

Maschil of [†]Asaph.

78 [a]Give ear,[238] O my people,[5971] *to* my law:[8451] incline your ears to the words[561] of my mouth.[6310]

2 [a]I will open my mouth in a parable: I will utter dark sayings[2420] of old:[6924]

3 [a]Which we have heard[8085] and known,[3045] and our fathers[1] have told[5608] us.

4 [a]We will not hide *them* from their children,[1121] [b]shewing to the generation[1755] to come the praises[8416] of the LORD, and his strength, and his wonderful works[6381] that he hath done.[6213]

5 For [a]he established a testimony[5715] in Jacob, and appointed[7760] a law in Israel, which he commanded[6680] our fathers, [b]that they should make them known to their children:

6 [a]That the generation to come might know *them, even* the children *which* should be born; *who* should arise and declare[5608] *them* to their children:

7 That they might set[7760] their hope[3689] in God,[430] and not forget the works of God,[410] but keep[5341] his commandments:[4687]

8 And [a]might not be as their fathers, [b]a stubborn[5637] and rebellious generation; a generation [Ic]*that* set not their heart[3820] aright, and whose spirit[7307] was not stedfast[539] with God.

9 The children of Ephraim, *being* armed,[5401] *and* [I]carrying bows, turned back[2015] in the day of battle.

10 [a]They kept[8104] not the covenant[1285] of God, and refused[3985] to walk in his law;

11 And [a]forgat his works, and his wonders[6381] that he had shewed[7200] them.

12 [a]Marvellous things did he in the sight of their fathers, in the land[776] of Egypt, [b]*in* the field[7704] of Zoan.

13 [a]He divided the sea, and caused them to pass through;[5674] and [b]he made the waters to stand[5324] as an heap.

14 [a]In the daytime[3119] also he led[5148] them with a cloud,[6051] and all the night[3915] with a light[216] of fire.

15 [a]He clave the rocks in the wilderness, and gave *them* drink as *out of* the great depths.

16 He brought [a]streams also out of the rock, and caused waters to run down like rivers.

17 And they sinned[2398] yet more against him by [a]provoking[4784] the most High[5945] in the wilderness.

18 And [a]they tempted[5254] God in their heart[3824] by asking[7592] meat for their lust.[5315]

19 [a]Yea, they spake[1696] against God; they said,[559] Can God [I]furnish a table in the wilderness?

20 [a]Behold, he smote[5221] the rock, that the waters gushed out, and the streams overflowed;[7857] can he give bread also? can he provide flesh for his people?

21 Therefore the LORD heard *this,* and [a]was wroth;[5674] so a fire was kindled against Jacob, and anger[639] also came up[5927] against Israel;

22 Because they [a]believed[539] not in

13 [b]Ex. 15:11
15 [a]Ex. 6:6; Deut. 9:29
16 [a]Ex. 14:21; Josh. 3:15, 16; Ps. 114:3; Hab. 3:8
17 [I]Hebr. *The clouds were poured forth with water* [a]2Sam. 22:15; Hab. 3:11
18 [a]Ps. 97:4 [b]2Sam. 22:8
19 [a]Hab. 3:15 [b]Ex. 14:28
20 [a]Ex. 13:21; 14:19; Ps. 78:52; 80:1; Isa. 63:11, 12; Hos. 12:13

† +Or, A Psalm *for Asaph to give instruction*
1 [a]Isa. 51:4
2 [a]Ps. 49:4; Matt. 13:35
3 [a]Ps. 44:1
4 [a]Deut. 4:9; 6:7; Joel 1:3 [b]Ex. 12:26, 27; 13:8, 14; Josh. 4:6, 7
5 [a]Ps. 147:19 [b]Deut. 4:9; 6:7; 11:19
6 [a]Ps. 102:18
8 [I]Hebr. that *prepared not their heart* [a]2Kgs. 17:14; Ezek. 20:18 [b]Ex. 32:9; 33:3; 34:9; Deut. 9:6, 13; 31:27; Ps. 68:6 [c]2Chr. 20:33; Ps. 78:37
9 [I]Hebr. *throwing forth*
10 [a]2Kgs. 17:15
11 [a]Ps. 106:13
12 [a]Ex. 7—12 [b]Gen. 32:3; Num. 13:22; Ps. 78:43; Isa. 19:11, 13; Ezek. 30:14
13 [a]Ex. 14:21 [b]Ex. 15:8; Ps. 33:7
14 [a]Ex. 13:21; 14:24; Ps. 105:39
15 [a]Ex. 17:6; Num. 20:11; Ps. 105:41; 1Cor. 10:4
16 [a]Deut. 9:21; Ps. 105:41
17 [a]Deut. 9:22; Ps. 95:8; Heb. 3:16
18 [a]Ex. 16:2
19 [I]Hebr. *order* [a]Num. 11:4
20 [a]Ex. 17:6; Num. 20:11

21 [a]Num. 11:1, 10 **22** [a]Heb. 3:18; Jude 1:5

God, and trusted[982] not in his salvation:[3444]

23 Though he had commanded the clouds[7834] from above, [a]and opened the doors of heaven,[8064]

24 [a]And had rained down manna[4478] upon them to eat, and had given them of the corn of heaven.

25 [Ia]Man[376] did eat angels'[47] food: he sent them meat to the full.

26 [a]He caused an east wind [I]to blow in the heaven: and by his power he brought in the south wind.

27 He rained flesh also upon them as dust,[6083] and [I]feathered fowls like as the sand of the sea:

28 And he let *it* fall in the midst[7130] of their camp, round about their habitations.[4908]

29 [a]So they did eat, and were well filled: for he gave them their own desire;[8378]

30 They were not estranged[2114] from their lust. But [a]while their meat *was* yet in their mouths,[6310]

31 The wrath[639] of God came upon them, and slew[2026] the fattest of them, and [Ia]smote down[3766] the [II]chosen *men* of Israel.

32 For all this they sinned still, and [a]believed not for his wondrous works.[6381]

33 [a]Therefore their days did he consume in vanity, and their years in trouble.

34 [a]When he slew them, then they sought him: and they returned[7725] and enquired early after God.

35 And they remembered[2142] that [a]God *was* their rock, and the high God [b]their Redeemer.[1350]

36 Nevertheless they did [a]flatter him with their mouth, and they lied[3576] unto him with their tongues.

37 For [a]their heart was not right with him, neither were they stedfast[3559] in his covenant.

38 [a]But he, *being* full of compassion, forgave *their* iniquity,[5771] and destroyed[7843] *them* not: yea, many a time [b]turned he his anger away, [c]and did not stir up all his wrath.[2534]

39 For [a]he remembered [b]that they *were but* flesh;[1320] [c]a wind[7307] that passeth away, and cometh not again.

40 How oft did they [Ia]provoke[4784] him in the wilderness, *and* grieve[6087] him in the desert!

41 Yea, [a]they turned back and tempted God, and [b]limited[8428] the Holy One[6918] of Israel.

42 They remembered not his hand,[3027] *nor* the day when he delivered[6299] them [I]from the enemy.

43 How [a]he had [I]wrought his signs[226] in Egypt, and his wonders[4159] in the field of Zoan:

44 [a]And had turned their rivers into blood;[1818] and their floods, that they could not drink.

45 [a]He sent divers sorts of flies among them, which devoured them; and [b]frogs, which destroyed them.

46 [a]He gave also their increase unto the caterpiller, and their labour unto the locust.

47 [a]He [I]destroyed[2026] their vines with hail, and their sycomore trees with [II]frost.

48 [Ia]He gave up their cattle also to the hail, and their flocks to [II]hot thunderbolts.

49 He cast upon them the fierceness of his anger, wrath,[5678] and indignation,[2195] and trouble, by sending evil[7451] angels[4397] *among them.*

50 [I]He made a way to his anger; he spared not their soul[5315] from death,[4194] but gave [IIa]their life[2416] over to the pestilence;[1698]

51 [a]And smote all the firstborn in Egypt; the chief[7225] of *their* strength in [b]the tabernacles[168] of Ham:

52 But [a]made his own people to go forth like sheep, and guided them in the wilderness like a flock.

53 And he [a]led them on safely,[983] so that they feared[6342] not: but the sea [Ib]overwhelmed[3680] their enemies.

54 And he brought them to the border of his [a]sanctuary,[6944] *even to* this mountain, [b]*which* his right hand had purchased.

23 [a]Gen. 7:11; Mal. 3:10
24 [a]Ex. 16:4, 14; Ps. 105:40; John 6:31; 1Cor. 10:3
25 [I]Or, *Every one did eat the bread of the mighty* [a]Ps. 103:20
26 [I]Hebr. *to go* [a]Num. 11:31
27 [I]Hebr. *fowl of wing*
29 [a]Num. 11:20
30 [a]Num. 11:33
31 [I]Hebr. *made to bow* [II]Or, *young men*
32 [a]Ps. 78:22
33 [a]Num. 14:29, 35; 26:64, 65
34 [a]Hos. 5:15
35 [a]Deut. 32:4, 15, 31 [b]Ex. 15:13; Deut. 7:8; Isa. 41:14; 44:6; 63:9
36 [a]Ezek. 33:31
37 [a]Ps. 78:8
38 [a]Num. 14:18, 20 [b]Isa. 48:9 [c]1Kgs. 21:29
39 [a]Ps. 103:14, 16 [b]Gen. 6:3; John 3:6 [c]Job 7:7, 16; James 4:14
40 [I]Or, *rebel against him* [a]Ps. 78:17; 95:9, 10; Isa. 7:13; 63:10; Eph. 4:30; Heb. 3:16, 17
41 [a]Num. 14:22; Deut. 6:16 [b]Ps. 78:20
42 [I]Or, *from affliction*
43 [I]Hebr. *set* [a]Ps. 78:12; 105:27
44 [a]Ex. 7:20; Ps. 105:29
45 [a]Ex. 8:24; Ps. 105:31 [b]Ex. 8:6; Ps. 105:30
46 [a]Ex. 10:13, 15; Ps. 105:34, 35
47 [I]Hebr. *killed* [II]Or, *great hailstones* [a]Ex. 9:23, 25; Ps. 105:33
48 [I]Hebr. *He shut up* [II]Or, *lightnings* [a]Ex. 9:23, 24, 25; Ps. 105:32
50 [I]Hebr. *He weighed a path* [II]Or, *their beasts to the murrain* [a]Ex. 9:3, 6
51 [a]Ex. 12:29; Ps. 105:36; 136:10 [b]Ps. 106:22
52 [a]Ps. 77:20
53 [I]Hebr. *covered* [a]Ex. 14:19, 20 [b]Ex. 14:27, 28; 15:10
54 [a]Ex. 15:17 [b]Ps. 44:3

55 [a]He cast out the heathen[1471] also before them, and [b]divided them an inheritance[5159] by line,[2256] and made[7931] the tribes[7626] of Israel to dwell[7931] in their tents.[168]

56 [a]Yet they tempted and provoked[4784] the most high God, and kept not his testimonies:[5713]

57 But [a]turned back, and dealt unfaithfully[898] like their fathers: they were turned aside [b]like a deceitful bow.

58 [a]For they provoked him to anger[3707] with their [b]high places,[1116] and moved him to jealousy with their graven images.

59 When God heard *this,* he was wroth, and greatly abhorred[3988] Israel:

60 [a]So that he forsook the tabernacle[4908] of Shiloh, the tent[168] *which* he placed[7931] among men;[120]

61 [a]And delivered his strength into captivity,[7628] and his glory[8597] into the enemy's hand.

62 [a]He gave his people over also unto the sword;[2719] and was wroth with his inheritance.

63 The fire consumed their young men; and [a]their maidens[1330] were not [I]given to marriage.

64 [a]Their priests[3548] fell[5307] by the sword; and [b]their widows made no lamentation.

65 Then the LORD[136] [a]awaked as one out of sleep, *and* [b]like a mighty man that shouteth by reason of wine.

66 And [a]he smote his enemies in the hinder parts: he put them to a perpetual[5769] reproach.[2781]

67 Moreover he refused the tabernacle[168] of Joseph, and chose[977] not the tribe[7626] of Ephraim:

68 But chose the tribe of Judah, the mount Zion [a]which he loved.[157]

69 And he [a]built his sanctuary[4720] like high *palaces,* like the earth[776] which he hath [I]established[3245] for ever.[5769]

70 [a]He chose David also his servant,[5650] and took him from the sheepfolds:

71 [I]From following [a]the ewes[5763] great with young he brought him [b]to feed

55 [a]Ps. 44:2 [b]Josh. 13:7; 19:51; Ps. 136:21, 22
56 [a]Judg. 2:11, 12
57 [a]Ps. 78:41; Ezek. 20:27, 28 [b]Hos. 7:16
58 [a]Deut. 32:16, 21; Judg. 2:12, 20; Ezek. 20:28 [b]Deut. 12:2, 4; 1Kgs. 11:7; 12:31
60 [a]1Sam. 4:11; Jer. 7:12, 14; 26:6, 9
61 [a]Judg. 18:30
62 [a]1Sam. 4:10
63 [I]Hebr. *praised* [a]Jer. 7:34; 16:9; 25:10
64 [a]1Sam. 4:11; 22:18 [b]Job 27:15; Ezek. 24:23
65 [a]Ps. 44:23 [b]Isa. 42:13
66 [a]1Sam. 5:6, 12; 6:4
68 [a]Ps. 87:2
69 [I]Hebr. *founded* [a]1Kgs. 6:1
70 [a]1Sam. 16:11, 12; 2Sam. 7:8
71 [I]Hebr. *From after* [a]Gen. 33:13; Isa. 40:11 [b]2Sam. 5:2; 1Chr. 11:2
72 [a]1Kgs. 9:4

1 [a]Ex. 15:17; Ps. 74:2 [b]Ps. 74:7 [c]2Kgs. 25:9, 10; 2Chr. 36:19; Mic. 3:12
2 [a]Jer. 7:33; 16:4; 34:20
3 [a]Ps. 141:7; Jer. 14:16; 16:4; Rev. 11:9
4 [a]Ps. 44:13; 80:6
5 [a]Ps. 74:1, 9, 10; 85:5; 89:46 [b]Zeph. 1:18; 3:8
6 [a]Jer. 10:25; Rev. 16:1 [b]Isa. 45:4, 5; 2Thess. 1:8 [c]Ps. 53:4
8 [I]Or, *the iniquities of them that were before us* [a]Isa. 64:9 [b]Deut. 28:43; Ps. 142:6
9 [a]2Chr. 14:11 [b]Jer. 14:7, 21
10 [I]Hebr. *vengeance* [a]Ps. 42:10; 115:2
11 [a]Ps. 102:20

Jacob his people, and Israel his inheritance.

72 So he fed them according to the [a]integrity[8537] of his heart; and guided[5148] them by the skilfulness[8394] of his hands.[3709]

Sorrow Over Jerusalem

A Psalm of Asaph.

79 O God,[430] the heathen[1471] are come into [a]thine inheritance;[5159] [b]thy holy[6944] temple[1964] have they defiled;[2930] [c]they have laid[7760] Jerusalem on heaps.

2 [a]The dead bodies[5038] of thy servants[5650] have they given *to be* meat unto the fowls of the heaven,[8064] the flesh[1320] of thy saints[2623] unto the beasts[2416] of the earth.[776]

3 Their blood[1818] have they shed[8210] like water round about Jerusalem; [a]and *there was* none to bury[6912] *them.*

4 [a]We are become[1961] a reproach[2781] to our neighbours,[7934] a scorn and derision to them that are round about us.

5 [a]How long, LORD? wilt thou be angry[599] for ever?[5331] shall thy [b]jealousy[7068] burn like fire?

6 [a]Pour out[8210] thy wrath[2534] upon the heathen that have [b]not known[3045] thee, and upon the kingdoms[4467] that have [c]not called upon[7121] thy name.

7 For they have devoured Jacob, and laid waste[8074] his dwelling place.

8 [a]O remember[2142] not against us [I]former[7223] iniquities:[5771] let thy tender mercies[7356] speedily prevent[6923] us: for we are [b]brought very low.

9 [a]Help us, O God of our salvation,[3468] for the glory[3519] of thy name: and deliver[5337] us, and purge away[3722] our sins, [b]for thy name's sake.

10 [a]Wherefore should the heathen say, Where *is* their God? let him be known[3045] among the heathen in our sight *by* the [I]revenging[5360] of the blood of thy servants *which is* shed.

11 Let [a]the sighing of the prisoner come before thee; according to the great-

ness of [I]thy power [II]preserve[3498] thou those that are appointed to die;

12 And render[7725] unto our neighbours [a]sevenfold into their bosom [b]their reproach, wherewith they have reproached thee, O Lord.[136]

13 So [a]we thy people[5971] and sheep of thy pasture will give thee thanks for ever:[5769] [b]we will shew forth[5608] thy praise[8416] [I]to all generations.[1755]

A Prayer for Restoration

To the chief Musician upon Shoshannim–Eduth, A Psalm of Asaph.

80 Give ear,[238] O Shepherd of Israel, thou that leadest Joseph [a]like a flock; [b]thou that dwellest *between* the cherubims,[3742] [c]shine forth.

2 [a]Before Ephraim and Benjamin and Manasseh stir up thy strength, and [I]come *and* save us.

3 [a]Turn us again,[7725] O God,[430] [b]and cause thy face to shine; and we shall be saved.[3467]

4 O LORD God of hosts,[6635] how long [I][a]wilt thou be angry[6225] against the prayer[8605] of thy people?[5971]

5 [a]Thou feedest them with the bread of tears; and givest them tears to drink in great measure.[7991]

6 [a]Thou makest us a strife unto our neighbours:[7934] and our enemies laugh among themselves.

7 [a]Turn us again, O God of hosts, and cause thy face to shine; and we shall be saved.

8 Thou hast brought [a]a vine out of Egypt: [b]thou hast cast out the heathen,[1471] and planted it.

9 Thou [a]preparedst *room* before it, and didst cause it to take deep root, and it filled the land.[776]

10 The hills were covered[3680] with the shadow of it, and the boughs thereof *were like* [I]the goodly[410] cedars.

11 She sent out her boughs unto the sea, and her branches [a]unto the river.

12 Why hast thou *then* [a]broken down her hedges, so that all they which pass by the way[1870] do pluck her?

13 The boar out of the wood doth waste it, and the wild beast of the field[7704] doth devour it.

14 Return,[7725] we beseech thee,[4994] O God of hosts: [a]look down from heaven,[8064] and behold,[7200] and visit[6485] this vine;

15 And the vineyard which thy right hand hath planted, and the branch *that* thou madest strong [a]for thyself.

16 *It is* burned[8313] with fire, *it is* cut down: [a]they perish[6] at the rebuke[1606] of thy countenance.

17 [a]Let thy hand be upon the man[376] of thy right hand,[3027] upon the son[1121] of man[120] *whom* thou madest strong for thyself.

18 So will not we go back from thee: quicken[2421] us, and we will call[7121] upon thy name.

19 [a]Turn us again, O LORD God of hosts, cause thy face to shine; and we shall be saved.

A Song for a Feast

To the chief Musician upon Gittith, A Psalm of Asaph.

81 Sing aloud unto God[430] our strength: make a joyful noise[7321] unto the God of Jacob.

2 Take[5375] a psalm, and bring hither the timbrel,[8596] the pleasant harp with the psaltery.

3 Blow up[8628] the trumpet in the new moon, in the time appointed, on our solemn feast[2282] day.[3117]

4 For [a]this *was* a statute[2706] for Israel, *and* a law[4941] of the God of Jacob.

5 This he ordained[7760] in Joseph *for* a testimony,[5715] when he went out [I]through the land[776] of Egypt: [a]*where* I heard[8085] a language[8193] *that* I understood[3045] not.

6 [a]I removed[5493] his shoulder from the burden: his hands[3709] [I]were delivered from [b]the pots.

7 [a]Thou calledst[7121] in trouble, and I delivered[2502] thee; [b]I answered thee in the secret place of thunder: I [c]proved[974] thee at the waters of [I]Meribah. Selah.

11 IHebr. *thine arm* IIHebr. *reserve the children of death*
12 aGen. 4:15; Isa. 65:6, 7; Jer. 32:18; Luke 6:38 bPs. 74:18, 22
13 IHebr. *to generation and generation* aPs. 74:1; 95:7; 100:3 bIsa. 43:21

1 aPs. 77:20 bEx. 25:20, 22; 1Sam. 4:4; 2Sam. 6:2; Ps. 99:1 cDeut. 33:2; Ps. 50:2; 94:1
2 IHebr. *come for salvation to us* aNum. 2:18-23
3 aPs. 80:7, 19; Lam. 5:21 bNum. 6:25; Ps. 4:6; 67:1
4 IHebr. *wilt thou smoke* aPs. 74:1
5 aPs. 42:3; 102:9; Isa. 30:20
6 aPs. 44:13; 79:4
7 aPs. 80:3, 19
8 aIsa. 5:1, 7; Jer. 2:21; Ezek. 15:6; 17:6; 19:10 bPs. 44:2; 78:55
9 aEx. 23:28; Josh. 24:12
10 IHebr. *the cedars of God*
11 aPs. 72:8
12 aPs. 89:40, 41; Isa. 5:5; Nah. 2:2
14 aIsa. 63:15
15 aIsa. 49:5
16 aPs. 39:11; 76:7
17 aPs. 89:21
19 aPs. 80:3, 7

4 aLev. 23:24; Num. 10:10
5 IOr, *against* aPs. 114:1
6 IHebr. *passed away* aIsa. 9:4; 10:27 bEx. 1:14
7 IOr, *Strife* aEx. 2:23; 14:10; Ps. 50:15 bEx. 19:19 cEx. 17:6, 7; Num. 20:13

8 [a]Hear,[8085] O my people,[5971] and I
will testify[5749] unto thee: O Israel, if thou
wilt hearken[8085] unto me;
9 [a]There shall no [b]strange[2114] god[410]
be in thee; neither shalt thou worship[7812]
any strange[5236] god.
10 [a]I *am* the LORD thy God, which
brought[5937] thee out of the land of
Egypt: [b]open thy mouth[6310] wide, and I
will fill it.
11 But my people would not hearken
to my voice; and Israel would[14] [a]none of
me.
12 [a]So I gave them up [I]unto their
own hearts' lust:[8307] *and* they walked in
their own counsels.
13 [a]Oh that my people had hearkened[8085] unto me, *and* Israel had walked
in my ways![1870]
14 I should soon have subdued their
enemies, and turned my hand[3027] against
their adversaries.
15 [a]The haters of the LORD should
have [I][b]submitted themselves unto him:
but their time[6256] should have endured
for ever.[5769]
16 He should [a]have fed them also
[I]with the finest of the wheat: and with
honey [b]out of the rock should I have satisfied[7646] thee.

8 [a]Ps. 50:7
9 [a]Ex. 20:3, 5 [b]Deut. 32:12; Isa. 43:12
10 [a]Ex. 20:2 [b]Ps. 37:3, 4; John 15:7; Eph. 3:20
11 [a]Ex. 32:1; Deut. 32:15, 18
12 [I]Or, *to the hardness of their hearts,* or, *imaginations* [a]Acts 7:42; 14:16; Rom. 1:24, 26
13 [a]Deut. 5:29; 10:12, 13; 32:29; Isa. 48:18
15 [I]Or, *yielded feigned obedience* [a]Ps. 18; 45; Rom. 1:3 [b]Ps. 18:44; 66:3
16 [I]Hebr. *with the fat of wheat* [a]Deut. 32:13, 14; Ps. 147:14 [b]Job 29:6

God Is in Control

A Psalm of Asaph.

82 God[430] [a]standeth[5324] in the congregation[5712] of the mighty;[410] he
judgeth[8199] among [b]the gods.[430]
2 How long will ye judge[8199] unjustly,[5766] and [a]accept[5375] the persons of
the wicked?[7563] Selah.
3 [I]Defend[8199] the poor and fatherless:
[a]do justice[6663] to the afflicted and needy.
4 [a]Deliver the poor and needy: rid[5337]
them out of the hand[3027] of the wicked.
5 They [a]know not, neither will they
understand;[995] they walk on in darkness:[2825] [b]all the foundations[4146] of the
earth[776] are [I]out of course.[4131]
6 [a]I have said,[559] Ye *are* gods; and all
of you *are* children[1121] of the most
High.[5945]
7 But [a]ye shall die[4191] like men,[8947]
and fall like one of the princes.[8269]

1 [a]2Chr. 19:6; Eccl. 5:8 [b]Ex. 21:6; 22:28
2 [a]Deut. 1:17; 2Chr. 19:7; Prov. 18:5
3 [I]Hebr. *Judge* [a]Jer. 22:3
4 [a]Job 29:12; Prov. 24:11
5 [I]Hebr. *moved* [a]Mic. 3:1 [b]Ps. 11:3; 75:3
6 [a]Ex. 22:9, 28; Ps. 82:1; John 10:34
7 [a]Job 21:32; Ps. 49:12; Ezek. 31:14

82:6 Some people attempt to explain the phrase "ye are gods" to mean that human beings can be gods as equal to God in His essence. The answer to this misinterpretation is found in the proper understanding of the word for "god" in Hebrew. It is the word *elohim* (430), which is used of God in reference to His office as a Judge and Diviner of justice. In the establishment of the office of judge in the Old Testament, men were given the responsibility of representing this office of God. Thus, the usage of the term *elohim* would not be confusing to one who understands that the human judge merely represents Jehovah. In this psalm, however, God is condemning those who had perverted justice and had abused their God-given privilege to hold the office of a judge. The warning given in verse seven is that though they be "gods," though they hold this honorable office among humankind to rule over them as God's representative, yet they are but human beings and will die like all other men or women.

The distinction of the other names for God in Scripture can also help to understand this passage better. No other names of God, and in particular such names as *Jehovah* (3068 [Ex. 3:14]), *El Shaddai* (410, 7706 [Gen. 17:1]), or *Yah* (3050 [Ps. 68:4]), are ever used of human beings. These names speak of or represent God's essence and attributes, of which man shall never partake. This fact is seen in the conclusion to verse six where it is stated that "all of you are children of the most High," meaning that though they represent God, they are held accountable and are responsible to Him for their actions. This psalm is a cry to God for retribution for the injustices that these wicked judges have carried out and mentions God's response as well. The lesson that can also be learned from this psalm is that God was condemning these judges for their sin, not the office to which they were called. There is an application for today in this: pastors and other church leaders often disobey God and fall into sin; however, the office of the pastor or deacon should continue to be respected as one that is God-ordained. It was the person who sinned.

8 [a]Arise, O God, judge the earth: [b]for thou shalt inherit[5157] all nations.[1471]

A Prayer for Enemies to Be Defeated

A Song *or* Psalm of Asaph.

83 🔑 Keep [a]not thou silence, O God:[430] hold not thy peace, and be not still,[8252] O God.[410]

2 For, lo, [a]thine enemies make a tumult: and they that [b]hate[8130] thee have lifted up[5375] the head.[7218]

3 They have taken crafty[6191] counsel[5475] against thy people,[5971] and consulted[3289] [a]against thy hidden ones.

4 They have said, Come, and [a]let us cut them off from *being* a nation;[1471] that the name of Israel may be no more in remembrance.[2142]

5 For they have consulted together with one [I]consent: they are confederate against thee:

6 [a]The tabernacles[168] of Edom, and the Ishmaelites; of Moab, and the Hagarenes;

7 Gebal, and Ammon, and Amalek; the Philistines with the inhabitants of Tyre;

8 Assur also is joined with them: [I]they have holpen[2220] the children of Lot. Selah.

9 Do[6213] unto them as *unto* the [a]Midianites; as *to* [b]Sisera, as *to* Jabin, at the brook of Kison:

10 *Which* perished[8045] at Endor: [a]they became *as* dung for the earth.[127]

11 Make their nobles[5081] like [a]Oreb, and like Zeeb: yea, all their princes[5257] as [b]Zebah, and as Zalmunna:

12 Who said, Let us take to ourselves the houses[4999] of God in possession.

13 [a]O my God, make them like a wheel;[1534] [b]as the stubble before the wind.[7307]

14 As the fire burneth a wood, and as the flame [a]setteth the mountains on fire;

15 So persecute them [a]with thy tempest, and make them afraid[926] with thy storm.

16 [a]Fill their faces with shame; that they may seek thy name, O LORD.

17 Let them be confounded[954] and troubled[926] for ever;[5703] yea, let them be put to shame, and perish:[6]

18 [a]That *men* may know that thou, whose [b]name alone *is* JEHOVAH, *art* [c]the most High[5945] over all the earth.[776]

Yearning for God's House

To the chief Musician upon Gittith, A Psalm for the sons of Korah.

84 How [a]amiable[3039] *are* thy tabernacles,[4908] O LORD of hosts![6635]

2 [a]My soul[5315] longeth, yea, even fainteth[3615] for the courts of the LORD: my heart[3820] and my flesh[1320] crieth out for the living[2416] God.[410]

3 Yea, the sparrow hath found an house,[1004] and the swallow a nest for herself, where she may lay her young, *even* thine altars,[4196] O LORD of hosts, my King,[4428] and my God.[430]

4 [a]Blessed[835] *are* they that dwell in thy house: they will be still praising[1984] thee. Selah.

5 Blessed *is* the man[120] whose strength *is* in thee; in whose heart[3824] *are* the ways *of them.*

6 *Who* passing through[5674] the valley [I][a]of Baca[1056] make it a well; the rain also [II]filleth the pools.

7 They go [I][a]from strength[2428] to strength, *every one of them* in Zion [b]appeareth[7200] before God.

8 O LORD God of hosts, hear[8085] my prayer:[8605] give ear,[238] O God of Jacob. Selah.

9 Behold,[7200] [a]O God our shield, and look upon the face of thine anointed.[4899]

10 For a day[3117] in thy courts *is* better[2896] than a thousand. [I]I had rather be a doorkeeper in the house of my God, than to dwell in the tents[168] of wickedness.[7562]

8 [a]Mic. 7:2, 7 [b]Ps. 2:8; Rev. 11:15

1 [a]Ps. 28:1; 35:22; 109:1

2 [a]Ps. 2:1; Acts 4:25 [b]Ps. 81:15

3 [a]Ps. 27:5; 31:20

4 [a]Esth. 3:6, 9; Jer. 11:19; 31:36

5 [I]Hebr. *heart*

6 [a]2Chr. 20:1, 10, 11

8 [I]Hebr. *they have been an arm to the children of Lot*

9 [a]Num. 31:7; Judg. 7:22 [b]Judg. 4:15, 24; 5:21

10 [a]2Kgs. 9:37; Zeph. 1:17

11 [a]Judg. 7:25 [b]Judg. 8:12, 21

13 [a]Isa. 17:13, 14 [b]Ps. 35:5

14 [a]Deut. 32:22

15 [a]Job 9:17

16 [a]Ps. 35:4, 26

18 [a]Ps. 59:13 [b]Ex. 6:3 [c]Ps. 92:8

1 [a]Ps. 27:4

2 [a]Ps. 42:1, 2; 63:1; 73:26; 119:20

4 [a]Ps. 65:4

6 [I]Or, *of mulberry trees make him a well* [II]Hebr. *covereth* [a]2Sam. 5:22, 23

7 [I]Or, *from company to company* [a]Prov. 4:18; 2Cor. 3:18 [b]Deut. 16:16; Zech. 14:16

9 [a]Gen. 15:1; Ps. 84:11

10 [I]Hebr. *I would choose rather to sit at the threshold*

🔑 **83:1–18** See the note on Psalm 109:1–29 for a discussion of the Imprecatory Psalms.

11 For the LORD God *is* [a]a sun and [b]shield: the LORD will give grace[2580] and glory:[3519] [c]no good[2896] *thing* will he withhold from them that walk uprightly.[8549]

12 O LORD of hosts, [a]blessed *is* the man that trusteth[982] in thee.

Invoking God's Mercy

To the chief Musician, A Psalm for the sons of Korah.

85 LORD, thou hast been [I][a]favourable unto thy land:[776] thou hast [b]brought back the captivity[7622] of Jacob.

2 [a]Thou hast forgiven[5375] the iniquity[5771] of thy people,[5971] thou hast covered[3680] all their sin.[2403] Selah.

3 Thou hast taken away[622] all thy wrath:[5678] [I][a]thou hast turned *thyself* from the fierceness of thine anger.[639]

4 [a]Turn[7725] us, O God[430] of our salvation,[3468] and cause thine anger toward us to cease.

5 [a]Wilt thou be angry[599] with us for ever?[5769] wilt thou draw out thine anger to all generations?[1755]

6 Wilt thou not [a]revive[2421] us again: that thy people may rejoice in thee?

7 Shew[7200] us thy mercy,[2617] O LORD, and grant us thy salvation.

8 [a]I will hear[8085] what God[410] the LORD will speak:[1696] for [b]he will speak peace unto his people, and to his saints:[2623] but let them not [c]turn again to folly.[3690]

9 Surely [a]his salvation *is* nigh them that fear[3373] him; [b]that glory[3519] may dwell[7931] in our land.

10 Mercy and truth[571] are met together;[6298] [a]righteousness[6664] and peace have kissed[5401] *each other.*

11 [a]Truth shall spring out of the earth;[776] and righteousness shall look down from heaven.[8064]

12 [a]Yea, the LORD shall give *that which is* good;[2896] and [b]our land shall yield her increase.

13 [a]Righteousness shall go before him; and shall set[7760] *us* in the way[1870] of his steps.

A Cry for Help

A Prayer of David.

86 Bow down thine ear,[241] O LORD, hear me: for I *am* poor and needy.

2 Preserve[8104] my soul;[5315] for I *am* [I]holy:[2623] O thou my God,[430] save[3467] thy servant[5650] [a]that trusteth[982] in thee.

3 [a]Be merciful[2603] unto me, O Lord:[136] for I cry[7121] unto thee [I]daily.

4 Rejoice the soul of thy servant: [a]for unto thee, O Lord, do I lift up[5375] my soul.

5 [a]For thou, Lord, *art* good,[2896] and ready to forgive;[5546] and plenteous in mercy[2617] unto all them that call[7121] upon thee.

6 Give ear,[238] O LORD, unto my prayer;[8605] and attend to the voice of my supplications.[8469]

7 [a]In the day[3117] of my trouble I will call upon thee: for thou wilt answer me.

8 [a]Among the gods[430] *there is* none like unto thee, O Lord; [b]neither *are there any works* like unto thy works.

9 [a]All nations[1471] whom thou hast made[6213] shall come and worship[7812] before thee, O Lord; and shall glorify[3513] thy name.

10 For thou *art* great, and [a]doest[6213] wondrous things:[6381] [b]thou *art* God alone.

11 [a]Teach[3384] me thy way,[1870] O LORD; I will walk in thy truth:[571] unite my heart[3824] to fear[3372] thy name.

12 I will praise[3034] thee, O Lord my God, with all my heart: and I will glorify thy name for evermore.[5769]

13 For great *is* thy mercy toward me: and thou hast [a]delivered[5337] my soul from the lowest [I]hell.[7585]

14 O God, [a]the proud[2086] are risen against me, and the assemblies of [I]violent *men* have sought after my soul; and have not set[7760] thee before them.

15 [a]But thou, O Lord, *art* a God[410] full of compassion, and gracious,[2587] longsuffering, and plenteous in mercy and truth.

16 O [a]turn unto me, and have mercy[2603] upon me; give thy strength

11 [a]Isa. 60:19 [b]Gen. 15:1; Ps. 84:9; 115:9, 10, 11; 119:114; Prov. 2:7 [c]Ps. 34:9, 10
12 [a]Ps. 2:12

1 [I]Or, *well pleased* [a]Ps. 77:7 [b]Ezra 1:11; 2:1; Ps. 14:7; Jer. 30:18; 31:23; Ezek. 39:25; Joel 3:1
2 [a]Ps. 32:1
3 [I]Or, *thou hast turned thine anger from waxing hot* [a]Deut. 13:17
4 [a]Ps. 80:7
5 [a]Ps. 74:1; 79:5; 80:4
6 [a]Hab. 3:2
8 [a]Hab. 2:1 [b]Zech. 9:10 [c]2Pet. 2:20, 21
9 [a]Isa. 46:13 [b]Zech. 2:5; John 1:14
10 [a]Ps. 72:3; Isa. 32:17; Luke 2:14
11 [a]Isa. 45:8
12 [a]Ps. 84:11; James 1:17 [b]Ps. 67:6
13 [a]Ps. 89:14

2 [I]Or, *one whom thou favorest* [a]Isa. 26:3
3 [I]Or, *all the day* [a]Ps. 56:1; 57:1
4 [a]Ps. 25:1; 143:8
5 [a]Ps. 86:15; 130:7; 145:9; Joel 2:13
7 [a]Ps. 50:15
8 [a]Ex. 15:11; Ps. 89:6 [b]Deut. 3:24
9 [a]Ps. 22:31; 102:18; Isa. 43:7; Rev. 15:4
10 [a]Ex. 15:11; Ps. 72:18; 77:14 [b]Deut. 6:4; 32:39; Isa. 37:16; 44:6; Mark 12:29; 1Cor. 8:4; Eph. 4:6
11 [a]Ps. 25:4; 27:11; 119:33; 143:8
13 [I]Or, *grave* [a]Ps. 56:13; 116:8
14 [I]Hebr. *terrible* [a]Ps. 54:3
15 [a]Ex. 34:6; Num. 14:18; Neh. 9:17; Ps. 86:5; 103:8; 111:4; 130:4, 7; 145:8; Joel 2:13
16 [a]Ps. 25:16; 69:16

unto thy servant, and save [b]the son[1121] of
thine handmaid.
17 Shew[6213] me a token[226] for good;
that they which hate[8130] me may see *it,*
and be ashamed:[954] because thou, LORD,
hast holpen5826 me, and comforted[5162]
me.

Zion

A Psalm *or* Song for the sons of Korah.

87 His foundation[3248] *is* [a]in the
holy[6944] mountains.
2 [a]The LORD loveth[157] the gates of
Zion more than all the dwellings[4908] of
Jacob.
3 Glorious things[3513] are spoken[1696]
of thee, O city of God.[430] Selah.
4 I will make mention of [a]Rahab and
Babylon to them that know me: behold
Philistia, and Tyre, with Ethiopia; this
man was born there.
5 And of Zion it shall be said,[559]
This and that man[376] was born in her:
and the highest[5945] himself shall establish her.
6 [a]The LORD shall count,[5608] when he
[b]writeth up the people,[5971] *that* this *man*
was born there. Selah.
7 As well the singers[7891] as the players on instruments *shall be there:* all my
springs *are* in thee.

A Prayer for Deliverance From Death

A Song *or* Psalm for the sons of Korah, to the chief Musician upon Mahalath Leannoth, Maschil of Heman the Ezrahite.

88 O Lord [a]God[430] of my salvation,[3444] I have [b]cried day[3117] *and*
night[3915] before thee:
2 Let my prayer[8605] come before thee:
incline thine ear[241] unto my cry;
3 For my soul[5315] is full of trou-
bles:[7451] and my life[2416] [a]draweth nigh[5060]
unto the grave.[7585]
4 [a]I am counted[2803] with them that
go down into the pit:[953] [b]I am as a
man[1397] *that hath* no strength:
5 Free among the dead,[4191] like the

16 [b]Ps. 116:16

1 [a]Ps. 48:1

2 [a]Ps. 78:67, 68

4 [a]Ps. 89:10; Isa. 51:9

6 [a]Ps. 22:30 [b]Ezek. 13:9

1 [a]Ps. 27:9; 51:14 [b]Luke 18:7

3 [a]Ps. 107:18

4 [a]Ps. 28:1 [b]Ps. 31:12

5 [I]Or, *by thy hand* [a]Isa. 53:8

7 [a]Ps. 42:7

8 [a]Job 19:13, 19; Ps. 31:11; 142:4 [b]Lam. 3:7

9 [a]Ps. 38:10 [b]Ps. 86:3 [c]Job 11:13; Ps. 143:6

10 [a]Ps. 6:5; 30:9; 115:17; 118:17; Isa. 38:18

12 [a]Job 10:21; Ps. 143:3 [b]Ps. 31:12; 88:5; Eccl. 8:10; 9:5

13 [a]Ps. 5:3; 119:147

14 [a]Ps. 43:2 [b]Job 13:24; Ps. 13:1

15 [a]Job 6:4

17 [I]Or, *all the day* [a]Ps. 22:16

18 [a]Job 19:13; Ps. 31:11; 38:11

1 [I]Hebr. *to generation and generation* [a]Ps. 101:1 [b]Ps. 89:4; 119:90

slain2491 that lie in the grave,[6913] whom
thou rememberest[2142] no more: and they
are [a]cut off [I]from thy hand.[3027]
6 Thou hast laid me in the lowest
pit, in darkness,[4285] in the deeps.
7 Thy wrath[2534] lieth hard5564 upon
me, and [a]thou hast afflicted *me* with all
thy waves. Selah.
8 [a]Thou hast put away mine
acquaintance[3045] far from me; thou hast
made me an abomination[8441] unto
them: [b]*I am* shut up, and I cannot come
forth.
9 [a]Mine eye mourneth by reason of
affliction: LORD, [b]I have called[7121] daily
upon thee, [c]I have stretched out my
hands[3709] unto thee.
10 [a]Wilt thou shew[6213] wonders[6382]
to the dead? shall the dead[7496] arise *and*
praise[3034] thee? Selah.
11 Shall thy lovingkindness be declared[5608] in the grave? *or* thy faithfulness[530] in destruction?[11]
12 [a]Shall thy wonders be known[3045]
in the dark?[2822] [b]and thy righteousness[6666] in the land[776] of forgetfulness?
13 But unto thee have I cried, O
LORD; and [a]in the morning shall my
prayer prevent6923 thee.
14 LORD, [a]why castest thou off my
soul? *why* [b]hidest thou thy face from
me?
15 I *am* afflicted and ready to die[1478]
from *my* youth up: *while* [a]I suffer[5375] thy
terrors[367] I am distracted.
16 Thy fierce wrath goeth over me;
thy terrors have cut me off.
17 They came round about me [I]daily
like water; they [a]compassed me about[5362]
together.
18 [a]Lover and friend[7453] hast thou
put far from me, *and* mine acquaintance
into darkness.

God's Agreement With David

Maschil of Ethan the Ezrahite.

89 [a]I will sing of the mercies[2617] of
the LORD for ever:[5769] with my
mouth[6310] will I make known[3045] thy
faithfulness[530] [I][b]to all generations.[1755]

2 For I have said, Mercy[2617] shall be built up for ever: [a]thy faithfulness shalt thou establish in the very heavens.[8064]

3 [a]I have made[3772] a covenant[1285] with my chosen, I have [b]sworn unto David my servant,[5650]

4 [a]Thy seed[2233] will I establish for ever, and build up thy throne[3678] [b]to all generations. Selah.

5 And [a]the heavens shall praise[3034] thy wonders, O LORD: thy faithfulness also in the congregation[6951] [b]of the saints.[6918]

6 For [a]who in the heaven[7834] can be compared unto the LORD? *who* among the sons[1121] of the mighty[410] can be likened unto the LORD?

7 [a]God[410] *is* greatly to be feared[6206] in the assembly[5475] of the saints, and to be had in reverence[3372] of all *them that are* about him.

8 O LORD God[430] of hosts,[6635] who *is* a strong LORD [a]like unto thee? or to thy faithfulness round about thee?

9 [a]Thou rulest[4910] the raging of the sea: when the waves thereof arise, thou stillest[7623] them.

10 [a]Thou hast broken[1792] [I]Rahab in pieces, as one that is slain;[2491] thou hast scattered thine enemies with thy strong arm.

11 [a]The heavens *are* thine, the earth[776] also *is* thine: *as for* the world[8398] and the fulness thereof, thou hast founded[3245] them.

12 [a]The north and the south thou hast created[1254] them: [b]Tabor and [c]Hermon shall rejoice in thy name.

13 Thou hast [I]a mighty arm: strong is thy hand,[3027] *and* high is thy right hand.

14 [a]Justice[6664] and judgment[4941] *are* the [I]habitation of thy throne: [b]mercy and truth[571] shall go before thy face.

15 Blessed[835] *is* the people[5971] that know the [a]joyful sound: they shall walk, O LORD, in the [b]light[216] of thy countenance.

16 In thy name shall they rejoice all the day:[3117] and in thy righteousness[6666] shall they be exalted.

17 For thou *art* the glory[8597] of their strength: [a]and in thy favour[7522] our horn shall be exalted.

18 For [Ia]the LORD *is* our defence; and the Holy One[6918] of Israel *is* our king.[4428]

19 Then thou spakest[1696] in vision[2377] to thy holy one,[2623] and saidst,[559] I have laid help upon *one that is* mighty; I have exalted *one* [a]chosen out of the people.

20 [a]I have found David my servant; with my holy[6944] oil have I anointed[4886] him:

21 [a]With whom my hand shall be established:[3559] mine arm also shall strengthen him.

22 [a]The enemy shall not exact upon him; nor the son of wickedness[5766] afflict him.

23 [a]And I will beat down[3807] his foes before his face, and plague[5063] them that hate[8130] him.

24 But [a]my faithfulness and my mercy *shall be* with him: and [b]in my name shall his horn be exalted.

25 [a]I will set[7760] his hand also in the sea, and his right hand in the rivers.

26 He shall cry[7121] unto me, Thou *art* [a]my father,[1] my God, and [b]the rock of my salvation.[3444]

27 Also I will make him [a]*my* firstborn, [b]higher[5945] than the kings[4428] of the earth.

28 [a]My mercy will I keep[8104] for him for evermore,[5769] and [b]my covenant shall stand fast with him.

29 [a]His seed also will I make[7760] *to endure* for ever,[5703] [b]and his throne [c]as the days of heaven.[8064]

30 [a]If his children[1121] [b]forsake[5800] my law,[8451] and walk not in my judgments;[4941]

31 If they [I]break[2490] my statutes,[2708] and keep not my commandments;[4687]

32 Then [a]will I visit[6485] their transgression[6588] with the rod,[7626] and their iniquity[5771] with stripes.

33 [a]Nevertheless my lovingkindness [I]will I not utterly take[6331] from him, nor suffer my faithfulness [II]to fail.[8266]

2 [a]Ps. 119:89
3 [a]1Kgs. 8:16; Isa. 42:1 [b]2Sam. 7:11; 1Chr. 17:10; Jer. 30:9; Ezek. 34:23; Hos. 3:5
4 [a]Ps. 89:29, 36 [b]Ps. 89:1; Luke 1:32, 33
5 [a]Ps. 19:1; 97:6; Rev. 7:10, 11, 12 [b]Ps. 89:7
6 [a]Ps. 40:5; 71:19; 86:8; 113:5
7 [a]Ps. 76:7, 11
8 [a]Ex. 15:11; 1Sam. 2:2; Ps. 35:10; 71:19
9 [a]Ps. 65:7; 93:3, 4; 107:29
10 [I]Or, *Egypt* [a]Ex. 14:26, 27, 28; Ps. 87:4; Isa. 30:7; 51:9
11 [a]Gen. 1:1; 1Chr. 29:11; Ps. 24:1, 2; 50:12
12 [a]Job 26:7 [b]Josh. 19:22 [c]Josh. 12:1
13 [I]Hebr. *an arm with might*
14 [I]Or, *establishment* [a]Ps. 97:2 [b]Ps. 85:13
15 [a]Num. 10:10; 23:21; Ps. 98:6 [b]Ps. 4:6; 44:3
17 [a]Ps. 75:10; 89:24; 92:10; 132:17
18 [I]Or, *our shield is of the LORD, and our king is of the Holy One of Israel* [a]Ps. 47:9
19 [a]1Kgs. 11:34; Ps. 89:3
20 [a]1Sam. 16:1, 12
21 [a]Ps. 80:17
22 [a]2Sam. 7:13
23 [a]2Sam. 7:9
24 [a]Ps. 61:7 [b]Ps. 89:17
25 [a]Ps. 72:8; 80:11
26 [a]2Sam. 7:14; 1Chr. 22:10 [b]2Sam. 22:47
27 [a]Ps. 2:7; Col. 1:15, 18 [b]Num. 24:7
28 [a]Isa. 55:3 [b]Ps. 89:34
29 [a]Ps. 89:4, 36 [b]Ps. 89:4; Isa. 9:7; Jer. 33:17 [c]Deut. 11:21
30 [a]2Sam. 7:14 [b]Ps. 119:53; Jer. 9:13
31 [I]Hebr. *profane my statutes*
32 [a]2Sam. 7:14; 1Kgs. 11:31 **33** [I]Hebr. *I will not make void from him* [II]Hebr. *to lie* [a]2Sam. 7:13

34 My covenant will I not break, nor alter[8138] the thing that is gone out of my lips.

35 Once have I sworn [a]by my holiness[6944] [I]that I will not lie[3576] unto David.

36 [a]His seed shall endure for ever, and his throne [b]as the sun before me.

37 It shall be established for ever as the moon, and *as* a faithful[539] witness in heaven. Selah.

38 But thou hast [a]cast off and [b]abhorred,[3988] thou hast been wroth[5674] with thine anointed.[4899]

39 Thou hast made void the covenant of thy servant: [a]thou hast profaned[2490] his crown[5145] *by casting it* to the ground.[776]

40 [a]Thou hast broken down all his hedges; thou hast brought[7760] his strong holds to ruin.[4288]

41 All that pass by the way[1870] spoil him: he is [a]a reproach[2781] to his neighbours.[7934]

42 Thou hast set up the right hand of his adversaries; thou hast made all his enemies to rejoice.

43 Thou hast also turned the edge of his sword,[2719] and hast not made him to stand in the battle.

44 Thou hast made[7673] his [I]glory[2892] to cease,[7673] and [a]cast his throne down to the ground.

45 The days of his youth hast thou shortened: thou hast covered him with shame.[955] Selah.

46 [a]How long, LORD? wilt thou hide thyself for ever?[5331] [b]shall thy wrath[2534] burn like fire?

47 [a]Remember[2142] how short my time[2465] is: wherefore hast thou made all men[120] in vain?[7723]

48 [a]What man[1397] *is he that* liveth, and shall not [b]see death?[4194] shall he deliver his soul[5315] from the hand of the grave?[7585] Selah.

49 Lord,[136] where *are* thy former[7223] lovingkindnesses, *which* thou [a]swarest[7650] unto David [b]in thy truth?[530]

50 Remember, Lord, the reproach of thy servants;[5650] [a]*how* I do bear[5375] in my bosom *the reproach of* all the mighty people;

51 [a]Wherewith thine enemies have reproached, O LORD; wherewith they have reproached the footsteps[6119] of thine anointed.

52 [a]Blessed[1288] *be* the LORD for evermore. Amen,[543] and Amen.

BOOK IV

God Is Eternal

A Prayer of Moses the man of God.

90 Lord,[136] [a]thou hast been our dwelling place [I]in all generations.[1755]

2 [a]Before the mountains were brought forth, or ever thou hadst formed[2342] the earth[776] and the world,[8398] even from everlasting[5769] to everlasting, thou *art* God.[410]

3 Thou turnest man[582] to destruction;[1793] and sayest,[559] [a]Return,[7725] ye children[1121] of men.[120]

4 [a]For a thousand years in thy sight *are but* as yesterday [I]when it is past,[5674] and *as* a watch in the night.[3915]

5 Thou carriest them away as with a flood; [a]they are *as* a sleep: in the morning [b]*they are* like grass *which* [I]groweth up.

6 [a]In the morning it flourisheth, and groweth up; in the evening it is cut down,[4135] and withereth.[3001]

7 For we are consumed[3615] by thine anger,[639] and by thy wrath[2534] are we troubled.[926]

8 [a]Thou hast set our iniquities[5771] before thee, our [b]secret *sins* in the light[3974] of thy countenance.

9 For all our days[3117] are [I]passed away in thy wrath:[5678] we spend[3615] our years [II]as a tale[1899] *that is told.*

10 [I]The days of our years *are* threescore years and ten; and if by reason of strength *they be* fourscore years, yet *is* their strength labour[5999] and sorrow;[205] for it is soon cut off,[1504] and we fly away.

11 Who knoweth the power of thine anger? even according to thy fear,[3374] *so is* thy wrath.

---

35 [I]Hebr. *if I lie* [a]Amos 4:2

36 [a]2Sam. 7:16; Ps. 89:4, 29; Luke 1:33; John 12:34 [b]Ps. 72:5, 17; Jer. 33:20

38 [a]1Chr. 28:9; Ps. 44:9; 60:1, 10 [b]Deut. 32:19; Ps. 78:59

39 [a]Ps. 74:7; Lam. 5:16

40 [a]Ps. 80:12

41 [a]Ps. 44:13; 79:4

44 [I]Hebr. *brightness* [a]Ps. 89:39

46 [a]Ps. 79:5 [b]Ps. 78:63

47 [a]Job 7:7; 10:9; 14:1; Ps. 39:5; 119:84

48 [a]Ps. 49:9 [b]Heb. 11:5

49 [a]2Sam. 7:15; Isa. 55:3 [b]Ps. 54:5

50 [a]Ps. 69:9, 19

51 [a]Ps. 74:22

52 [a]Ps. 41:13

1 [I]Hebr. *in generation and generation* [a]Deut. 33:27; Ez. 11:16

2 [a]Prov. 8:25, 26

3 [a]Gen. 3:19; Eccl. 12:7

4 [I]Or, *when he hath passed* the [a]2Pet. 3:8

5 [I]Or, *is changed* [a]Ps. 73:20 [b]Ps. 103:15; Isa. 40:6

6 [a]Job 14:2; Ps. 92:7

8 [a]Ps. 50:21; Jer. 16:17 [b]Ps. 19:12

9 [I]Hebr. *turned away* [II]Or, *as a meditation*

10 [I]Hebr. As for *the days of our years, in them are seventy years*

12 [a]So teach[3045] *us* to number our days, that we may [I]apply *our* hearts[3824] unto wisdom.[2451]

13 Return, O LORD, how long? and let it [a]repent[5162] thee concerning thy servants.[5650]

14 O satisfy us early with thy mercy;[2617] [a]that we may rejoice and be glad all our days.

15 Make us glad according to the days *wherein* thou hast afflicted us, *and* the years *wherein* we have seen[7200] evil.[7451]

16 Let [a]thy work appear[7200] unto thy servants, and thy glory[1926] unto their children.

17 [a]And let the beauty of the LORD our God[430] be upon us: and [b]establish thou the work of our hands[3027] upon us; yea, the work of our hands establish thou it.

Abiding In God's Care

91 He [a]that dwelleth in the secret place of the most High[5945] shall [I]abide [b]under the shadow of the Almighty.[7706]

2 [a]I will say[559] of the LORD, *He is* my refuge and my fortress: my God;[430] in him will I trust.[982]

3 Surely [a]he shall deliver[5337] thee from the snare[6341] of the fowler, *and* from the noisome[1942] pestilence.[1698]

4 [a]He shall cover thee with his feathers, and under his wings shalt thou trust:[2620] his truth[571] *shall be thy* shield and buckler.[5507]

5 [a]Thou shalt not be afraid[3372] for the terror[6343] by night;[3915] *nor* for the arrow *that* flieth by day;[3119]

6 *Nor* for the pestilence *that* walketh in darkness;[652] *nor* for the destruction[6986] *that* wasteth at noonday.

7 A thousand shall fall at thy side, and ten thousand at thy right hand; *but* it shall not come nigh[5066] thee.

8 Only [a]with thine eyes shalt thou behold and see the reward[8011] of the wicked.[7563]

9 Because thou hast made[7760] the LORD, *which is* [a]my refuge, *even* the most High, [b]thy habitation;[4583]

10 [a]There shall no evil[7451] befall thee, neither shall any plague[5061] come nigh thy dwelling.

11 [a]For he shall give[6680] his angels[4397] charge[6680] over thee, to keep[8104] thee in all thy ways.[1870]

12 They shall bear thee up[5375] in *their* hands,[3709] [a]lest thou dash[5062] thy foot against a stone.

13 Thou shalt tread upon the lion and [I]adder:[6620] the young lion and the dragon[8577] shalt thou trample under feet.

14 Because he hath set his love[2836] upon me, therefore will I deliver him: I will set him on high, because he hath [a]known[3045] my name.

15 [a]He shall call[7121] upon me, and I will answer him: [b]I *will be* with him in trouble; I will deliver[2502] him, and [c]honour[3513] him.

16 With [I][a]long[753] life will I satisfy him, and shew[7200] him my salvation.[3444]

God's Goodness

A Psalm *or* Song for the sabbath day.

92 *It is* a [a]good[2896] *thing* to give thanks[3034] unto the LORD, and to sing praises[2167] unto thy name, O most High:[5945]

2 To [a]shew forth[5046] thy lovingkindness in the morning, and thy faithfulness[530] [I]every night,[3915]

3 [a]Upon an instrument of ten strings, and upon the psaltery; upon the harp with [b]a solemn sound.[1902]

4 For thou, LORD, hast made me glad through thy work: I will triumph in the works of thy hands.[3027]

5 [a]O LORD, how great are thy works! *and* [b]thy thoughts[4284] are very deep.

6 [a]A brutish man[376] knoweth not; neither doth a fool understand[995] this.

7 When [a]the wicked[7563] spring as the grass, and when all the workers of iniquity[205] do flourish; *it is* that they shall be destroyed[8045] for ever:[5703]

12 IHebr. *cause to come* [a]Ps. 39:4
13 [a]Deut. 32:36; Ps. 135:14
14 [a]Ps. 85:6; 149:2
16 [a]Hab. 3:2
17 [a]Ps. 27:4 [b]Isa. 26:12

1 IHebr. *lodge* [a]Ps. 27:5; 31:20; 32:7 [b]Ps. 17:8
2 [a]Ps. 142:5
3 [a]Ps. 124:7
4 [a]Ps. 17:8; 57:1; 61:4
5 [a]Job 5:19; Ps. 112:7; 121:6; Prov. 3:23, 24; Isa. 43:2
8 [a]Ps. 37:34; Mal. 1:5
9 [a]Ps. 91:2 [b]Ps. 71:3; 90:1
10 [a]Prov. 12:21
11 [a]Ps. 34:7; 71:3; Matt. 4:6; Luke 4:10, 11; Heb. 1:14
12 [a]Job 5:23; Ps. 37:24
13 IOr, *asp*
14 [a]Ps. 9:10
15 [a]Ps. 50:15 [b]Isa. 43:2 [c]1Sam. 2:30
16 IHebr. *length of days* [a]Prov. 3:2

1 [a]Ps. 147:1
2 IHebr. *in the nights* [a]Ps. 89:1
3 [a]1Chr. 23:5; Ps, 33:2 [b]Ps. 9:16
5 [a]Ps. 40:5; 139:17 [b]Isa. 28:29; Rom. 11:33, 34
6 [a]Ps. 73:22; 94:8
7 [a]Job 12:6; 21:7; Ps. 37:1, 2, 35, 38; Jer. 12:1, 2; Mal. 3:15

8 [a]But thou, LORD, *art most* high for evermore.[5769]

9 For, lo, thine enemies, O LORD, for, lo, thine enemies shall perish;[6] all the workers of iniquity shall [a]be scattered.

10 But [a]my horn shalt thou exalt like *the horn of* an unicorn: I shall be [b]anointed[1101] with fresh oil.[8081]

11 [a]Mine eye also shall see *my desire* on mine enemies, *and* mine ears[241] shall hear[8085] *my desire* of the wicked[7489] that rise up against me.

12 [a]The righteous[6662] shall flourish like the palm tree: he shall grow like a cedar in Lebanon.

13 Those that be planted in the house[1004] of the LORD shall flourish [a]in the courts of our God.[430]

14 They shall still bring forth fruit in old age;[7872] they shall be fat and [I]flourishing;

15 To shew that the LORD *is* upright: [a]*he is* my rock, and [b]*there is* no unrighteousness[5766] in him.

God's Majesty

93 The [a]LORD reigneth,[4427] [b]he is clothed with majesty; the LORD is clothed with strength, [c]*wherewith* he hath girded himself: [d]the world[8398] also is stablished,[3559] that it cannot be moved.

2 [a]Thy throne[3678] *is* established [I]of old:[227] thou *art* from everlasting.[5769]

3 The floods have lifted up,[5375] O LORD, the floods have lifted up their voice; the floods lift up their waves.

4 [a]The LORD on high *is* mightier[117] than the noise of many waters, *yea, than* the mighty waves of the sea.

5 Thy testimonies[5713] are very sure:[539] holiness[6944] becometh thine house,[1004] O LORD, [I]for ever.

God Is the Judge

94 O Lord [I]God,[410] [a]to whom vengeance[5360] belongeth; O God, to whom vengeance belongeth, [II]shew thyself.

2 [a]Lift up thyself,[5375] thou [b]judge[8199] of the earth:[776] render[7725] a reward to the proud.

3 LORD, [a]how long shall the wicked,[7563] how long shall the wicked triumph?

4 *How long* shall they [a]utter *and* speak[1696] hard things? *and* all the workers of iniquity[205] boast themselves?[559]

5 They break in pieces[1792] thy people,[5971] O LORD, and afflict thine heritage.[5159]

6 They slay[2026] the widow and the stranger,[1616] and murder[7523] the fatherless.

7 [a]Yet they say,[559] the LORD shall not see, neither shall[995] the God[430] of Jacob regard[995] *it.*

8 [a]Understand,[995] ye brutish among the people: and *ye* fools, when will ye be wise?[7919]

9 [a]He that planted the ear,[241] shall he not hear?[8085] he that formed[3335] the eye, shall he not see?

10 He that chastiseth[3256] the heathen,[1471] shall not he correct?[3198] he that [a]teacheth[3925] man[120] knowledge,[1847] *shall not he know*?

11 [a]The LORD knoweth[3045] the thoughts[4284] of man, that they *are* vanity.

12 [a]Blessed[835] *is* the man[1397] whom thou chastenest,[3256] O LORD, and teachest him out of thy law;[8451]

13 That thou mayest give him rest[8252] from the days[3117] of adversity,[7451] until the pit[7845] be digged for the wicked.

14 [a]For the LORD will not cast off[5203] his people, neither will he forsake[5800] his inheritance.[5159]

15 But judgment[4941] shall return[7725] unto righteousness: and all the upright in heart[3820] [I]shall follow it.

16 Who will rise up for me against the evildoers?[7489] *or* who will stand up for me against the workers of iniquity?

17 [a]Unless the LORD *had been* my help, my soul[5315] had [I]almost dwelt[7931] in silence.

18 When I said, [a]My foot slippeth; thy mercy,[2617] O LORD, held me up.

19 In the multitude[7230] of my

---

8 [a]Ps. 56:2; 83:18
9 [a]Ps. 68:1; 89:10
10 [a]Ps. 89:17, 24 [b]Ps. 23:5
11 [a]Ps. 54:7; 59:10; 112:8
12 [a]Ps. 52:8; Isa. 65:22; Hos. 14:5, 6
13 [a]Ps. 100:4; 135:2
14 [I]Hebr. *green*
15 [a]Deut. 32:4 [b]Rom. 9:14
1 [a]Ps. 96:10; 97:1; 99:1; Isa. 52:7; Rev. 19:6 [b]Ps. 104:1 [c]Ps. 65:6 [d]Ps. 96:10
2 [I]Hebr. *from then* [a]Ps. 45:6; Prov. 8:22
4 [a]Ps. 65:7; 89:9
5 [I]Hebr. *to length of days*
1 [I]Hebr. *God of revenges* [II]Hebr. *shine forth* [a]Deut. 32:35; Nah. 1:2; Ps. 80:1
2 [a]Ps. 7:6 [b]Gen. 18:25
3 [a]Job 20:5
4 [a]Ps. 31:18; Jude 1:5
7 [a]Ps. 10:11, 13; 59:7
8 [a]Ps. 73:22; 92:6
9 [a]Ex. 4:11; Prov. 20:12
10 [a]Job 35:11; Isa. 28:26
11 [a]1Cor. 3:20
12 [a]Job 5:17; Prov. 3:11; 1Cor. 11:32; Heb. 12:5
14 [a]1Sam. 12:22; Rom. 11:1, 2
15 [I]Hebr. shall be *after it*
17 [I]Or, *quickly* [a]Ps. 124:1, 2
18 [a]Ps. 38:16

thoughts[8312] within[7130] me thy comforts[8375] delight my soul.

20 Shall [a]the throne[3678] of iniquity[1942] have fellowship with thee, which [b]frameth[3335] mischief[5999] by a law?[2706]

21 [a]They gather themselves together[1413] against the soul of the righteous,[6662] and [b]condemn[7561] the innocent[5355] blood.[1818]

22 But the LORD is [a]my defence; and my God *is* the rock of my refuge.

23 And [a]he shall bring upon them their own iniquity, and shall cut them off in their own wickedness;[7451] *yea,* the LORD our God shall cut them off.

Praise and Worship

95 O Come, let us sing unto the LORD: [a]let us make a joyful noise[7321] to [b]the rock of our salvation.[3468]

2 Let us [I]come before his presence with thanksgiving,[8426] and make a joyful noise unto him with psalms.

3 For [a]the LORD *is* a great God,[410] and a great King[4428] above all gods.[430]

4 [I]In his hand[3027] *are* the deep places of the earth:[776] [II]the strength of the hills *is* his also.

5 [Ia]The sea *is* his, and he made it: and his hands[3027] formed[3335] the dry[3006] *land.*

6 O come, let us worship[7812] and bow down:[3766] let [a]us kneel[1288] before the LORD our maker.[6213]

🔑 7 For he *is* our God;[430] and [a]we *are* the people[5971] of his pasture, and the sheep of his hand. [b]To day if ye will hear[8085] his voice,

8 Harden not your heart,[3824] [a]as in the [I]provocation,[4808] *and* as *in* the day of temptation[4531] in the wilderness:

9 When [a]your fathers[1] tempted[5254] me, proved[974] me, and [b]saw[7200] my work.

10 [a]Forty years long was I grieved with *this* generation,[1755] and said, It *is* a people that do err[8582] in their heart, and they have not known[3045] my ways:[1870]

11 Unto whom [a]I sware[7650] in my wrath[639] [I]that they should not enter into my rest.

God Is the True King

96 O [a]sing[7891] unto the LORD a new song: sing unto the LORD, all the earth.[776]

2 Sing unto the LORD, bless[1288] his name; shew forth his salvation[3444] from day[3117] to day.

3 Declare[5608] his glory[3519] among the heathen,[1471] his wonders[6381] among all people.[5971]

4 For [a]the LORD *is* great, and [b]greatly to be praised:[1984] [c]he *is* to be feared[3372] above all gods.[430]

5 For [a]all the gods of the nations[5971] *are* idols:[457] [b]but the LORD made[6213] the heavens.[8064]

6 Honour[1935] and majesty[1926] *are* before him: strength and [a]beauty[8597] *are* in his sanctuary.[4720]

7 [a]Give unto the LORD, O ye kindreds of the people, give unto the LORD glory and strength.

8 Give unto the LORD the glory [I]*due unto* his name: bring[5375] an offering,[4503] and come into his courts.

9 O worship[7812] the LORD [Ia]in the beauty[1927] of holiness:[6944] fear before him, all the earth.

10 Say among the heathen *that* [a]the LORD reigneth:[4427] the world[8398] also shall be established[3559] that it shall not be moved: [b]he shall judge[1777] the people righteously.

11 [a]Let the heavens rejoice, and let the earth be glad; [b]let the sea roar, and the fulness thereof.

12 Let the field[7704] be joyful, and all that *is* therein: then shall all the trees of the wood rejoice

13 Before the LORD:[3068] for he cometh, for he cometh[935] to judge the

20 [a]Amos 6:3 [b]Ps. 58:2; Isa. 10:1
21 [a]Matt. 27:1 [b]Ex. 23:7; Prov. 17:15
22 [a]Ps. 59:9; 62:2, 6
23 [a]Ps. 7:16; Prov. 2:22; 5:22

1 [a]Ps. 100:1 [b]Deut. 32:15; 2Sam. 22:47
2 [I]Hebr. *prevent his face*
3 [a]Ps. 96:4; 97:9; 135:5
4 [I]Hebr. *In whose* [II]Or, *the heights of the hills are his*
5 [I]Hebr. *Whose the sea is* [a]Gen. 1:9, 10
6 [a]1Cor. 6:20
7 [a]Ps. 79:13; 80:1; 100:3 [b]Heb. 3:7, 15; 4:7
8 [I]Hebr. *contention* [a]Ex. 17:2, 7; Num. 14:22; 20:13; Deut. 6:16
9 [a]Ps. 78:18, 40, 56; 1Cor. 10:9 [b]Num. 14:22
10 [a]Heb. 3:10, 17
11 [I]Hebr. *if they enter into my rest* [a]Num. 14:23, 28, 30; Heb. 3:11, 18; 4:3, 5

1 [a]1Chr. 16:23-33; Ps. 33:3
4 [a]Ps. 145:3 [b]Ps. 18:3 [c]Ps. 95:3
5 [a]Jer. 10:11, 12 [b]Ps. 115:15; Isa. 42:5
6 [a]Ps. 29:2
7 [a]Ps. 29:1, 2
8 [I]Hebr. *of his name*
9 [I]Or, *in the glorious sanctuary* [a]Ps. 29:2; 110:3
10 [a]Ps. 93:1; 97:1; Rev. 11:15; 19:6 [b]Ps. 67:4; 96:13; 98:9
11 [a]Ps. 69:34 [b]Ps. 98:7

🔑 **95:7–11** See note on Numbers 13:26.

earth: [a]he shall judge[8199] the world[8398] with righteousness,[6664] and the people with his truth.[530]

The Power of God

97 The [a]LORD reigneth;[4427] let the earth[776] rejoice; let the [I]multitude of [b]isles be glad *thereof.*

2 [a]Clouds[6051] and darkness[6205] *are* round about him: [b]righteousness[6664] and judgment[4941] *are* the [I]habitation of his throne.[3678]

3 [a]A fire goeth before him, and burneth up his enemies round about.

4 [a]His lightnings enlightened the world:[8398] the earth saw,[7200] and trembled.

5 [a]The hills melted like wax at the presence of the LORD, at the presence of the LORD[113] of the whole earth.

6 [a]The heavens[8064] declare[5046] his righteousness, and all the people[5971] see his glory.[3519]

7 [a]Confounded be[954] all they that serve[5647] graven images, that boast[1984] themselves of idols:[457] [b]worship[7812] him, all *ye* gods.[430]

8 Zion heard,[8085] and was glad; and the daughters of Judah rejoiced because of thy judgments,[4941] O LORD.

9 For thou, LORD, *art* [a]high[5945] above all the earth: [b]thou art exalted[5927] far above all gods.

10 Ye that love[157] the LORD, [a]hate[8130] evil:[7451] [b]he preserveth[8104] the souls[5315] of his saints;[2623] [c]he delivereth[5337] them out of the hand[3027] of the wicked.[7563]

11 [a]Light[216] is sown for the righteous,[6662] and gladness for the upright in heart.[3820]

12 [a]Rejoice in the LORD, ye righteous; [b]and give thanks[3034] [I]at the remembrance[2143] of his holiness.[6944]

God Rules the World

A Psalm.

98 O [a]sing[7891] unto the LORD a new song; for [b]he hath done[6213] marvellous things:[6381] [c]his right hand, and his holy[6944] arm, hath gotten him the victory.

2 [a]The LORD hath made known[3045] his salvation:[3444] [b]his righteousness[6666] hath he [I]openly shewed in the sight of the heathen.[1471]

3 He hath [a]remembered[2142] his mercy[2617] and his truth[530] toward the house[1004] of Israel: [b]all the ends of the earth[776] have seen[7200] the salvation of our God.[430]

4 [a]Make a joyful noise[7321] unto the LORD, all the earth: make a loud noise, and rejoice, and sing praise.[2167]

5 Sing unto the LORD with the harp; with the harp, and the voice of a psalm.

6 [a]With trumpets and sound of cornet make a joyful noise before the LORD, the King.[4428]

7 [a]Let the sea roar, and the fulness thereof; the world,[8398] and they that dwell therein.

8 Let the floods [a]clap *their* hands:[3709] let the hills be joyful together

9 Before the LORD; [a]for he cometh to judge the earth: with righteousness[6664] shall he judge[8199] the world, and the people[5971] with equity.[4339]

God Is Faithful

99 The [a]LORD reigneth;[4427] let the people[5971] tremble: [b]he sitteth *between* the cherubims;[3742] let the earth[776] [I]be moved.

2 The LORD *is* great in Zion; and he *is* [a]high above all the people.

3 Let them praise[3034] [a]thy great and terrible[3372] name; *for* it *is* holy.[6918]

4 [a]The king's strength[5797] also loveth[157] judgment;[4941] thou dost establish equity,[4339] thou executest[6213] judgment and righteousness[6666] in Jacob.

5 [a]Exalt ye the LORD our God,[430] and worship[7812] at [b]his footstool; *for* [I][c]he *is* holy.

6 [a]Moses and Aaron among his priests,[3548] and Samuel among them that call upon[7121] his name; they [b]called upon the LORD, and he answered them.

13 [a]Ps. 67:4; Rev. 19:11

1 [I]Hebr. *many, or, great isles* [a]Ps. 96:10 [b]Isa. 60:9
2 [I]Or, *establishment* [a]1Kgs. 8:12; Ps. 18:11 [b]Ps. 89:14
3 [a]Ps. 18:8; 50:3; Dan. 7:10; Hab. 3:5
4 [a]Ex. 19:18; Ps. 77:18; 104:32
5 [a]Judg. 5:5; Mic. 1:4; Nah. 1:5
6 [a]Ps. 19:1; 50:6
7 [a]Ex. 20:4; Lev. 26:1; Deut. 5:8; 27:15 [b]Heb. 1:6
9 [a]Ps. 83:18 [b]Ex. 18:11; Ps. 95:3; 96:4
10 [a]Ps. 34:14; 37:27; 101:3; Amos 5:15; Rom. 12:9 [b]Ps. 31:23; 37:28; 145:20; Prov. 2:8 [c]Ps. 37:39, 40; Dan. 3:28; 6:22, 27
11 [a]Job 22:28; Ps. 112:4; Prov. 4:18
12 [I]Or, *to the memorial* [a]Ps. 33:1 [b]Ps. 30:4

1 [a]Ps. 33:3; 96:1; Isa. 42:10 [b]Ex. 15:11; Ps. 77:14; 86:10; 105:5; 136:4; 139:14 [c]Ex. 15:6; Isa. 59:16; 63:5
2 [I]Or, *revealed* [a]Isa. 52:10; Luke 2:30, 31 [b]Isa. 62:2; Rom. 3:25, 26
3 [a]Luke 1:54, 55, 72 [b]Isa. 49:6; 52:10; Luke 2:30, 31; 3:6; Acts 13:47; 28:28
4 [a]Ps. 95:1; 100:1
6 [a]Num. 10:10; 1Chr. 15:28; 2Chr. 29:27
7 [a]Ps. 96:11
8 [a]Isa. 55:12
9 [a]Ps. 96:10, 13

1 [I]Hebr. *stagger* [a]Ps. 93:1 [b]Ex. 25:22; Ps. 18:10; 80:1
2 [a]Ps. 97:9
3 [a]Deut. 28:58; Rev. 15:4
4 [a]Job 36:5-7
5 [I]Or, *it is holy* [a]Ps. 99:9 [b]1Chr. 28:2; Ps. 132:7 [c]Lev. 19:2
6 [a]Jer. 15:1 [b]Ex. 14:15; 15:25; 1Sam. 7:9; 12:18

7 [a]He spake unto them in the cloudy pillar: they kept[8104] his testimonies,[5713] and the ordinance[2706] *that* he gave them.

8 Thou answeredst them, O LORD our God:[410] [a]thou wast a God that forgavest[5375] them, though [b]thou tookest vengeance[5358] of their inventions.

9 [a]Exalt the LORD our God, and worship at his holy[6944] hill; for the LORD our God *is* holy.

A Hymn of Praise

A Psalm of praise.

100 Make [a]a joyful noise[7321] unto the LORD, [I]all ye lands.[776]

2 Serve[5647] the LORD with gladness: come before his presence with singing.

3 Know ye that the LORD he *is* God:[430] [a]*it is* he *that* hath made[6213] us, [I]and not we ourselves; [b]*we are* his people,[5971] and the sheep of his pasture.

4 [a]Enter into his gates with thanksgiving,[8426] *and* into his courts with praise:[8416] be thankful unto him, *and* bless[1288] his name.

5 For the LORD *is* good;[2896] [a]his mercy[2617] *is* everlasting;[5769] and his truth[530] *endureth* [I][b]to all generations.[1755]

David's Promise

A Psalm of David.

101 🔑 [a]I will sing[7891] of mercy[2617] and judgment:[4941] unto thee, O LORD, will I sing.[2167]

2 I will [a]behave myself wisely[7919] in a perfect[8549] way.[1870] O when wilt thou come unto me? I will [b]walk within[7130] my house[1004] with a perfect[8537] heart.[3824]

3 I will set no [I]wicked[1100] thing[1697] before mine eyes: [a]I hate the work[6213] of them [b]that turn aside; *it* shall not cleave to me.

4 A froward[6141] heart[3824] shall depart[5493] from me: I will not [a]know a wicked[7451] *person.*

5 Whoso privily[5643] slandereth his neighbour,[7453] him will I cut off:[6789] [a]him that hath an high look and a proud heart will not I suffer.[3201]

6 Mine eyes *shall be* upon the faithful[539] of the land,[776] that they may dwell with me: he that walketh [I][a]in a perfect way, he shall serve[8334] me.

7 He that worketh[6213] deceit shall not dwell within my house: he that telleth[1696] lies[8267] [I]shall not tarry in my sight.

8 I will[6789] [a]early[1242] destroy[6789] all the wicked[7563] of the land; that I may cut off[3772] all wicked[205] doers [b]from the city of the LORD.

An Afflicted Man's Prayer for Help

A Prayer of the afflicted, when he is overwhelmed, and poureth out his complaint before the LORD.

102 Hear[8085] my prayer,[8605] O LORD, and let my cry [a]come unto thee.

2 [a]Hide not thy face from me in the day[3117] *when* I am in trouble; [b]incline thine ear[241] unto me: in the day *when* I call[7121] answer me speedily.

3 [a]For my days are consumed[3615] [I]like smoke, and [b]my bones[6106] are burned[2787] as an hearth.

4 My heart[3824] is smitten,[5221] and [a]withered[3001] like grass; so that I forget to eat my bread.

5 By reason of the voice of my groaning [a]my bones cleave to my [I]skin.

6 [a]I am like [b]a pelican of the wilderness: I am like an owl of the desert.[2723]

7 I [a]watch, and am as a sparrow [b]alone upon the house top.

8 Mine enemies reproach me all the day; *and* they that are [a]mad[1984] against me are [b]sworn against me.

9 For I have eaten ashes like bread, and [a]mingled my drink with weeping,

7 [a]Ex. 33:9
8 [a]Num. 14:20; Jer. 46:28; Zeph. 3:7 [b]Ex. 32:2; Num. 20:12, 24; Deut. 9:20
9 [a]Ex. 15:2; Ps. 34:3; 99:5; 118:28

1 [I]Hebr. *all the earth* [a]Ps. 95:1; 98:4
3 [I]Or, *and his we are* [a]Ps. 119:73; 139:13; 149:2; Eph. 2:10 [b]Ps. 95:7; Ezek. 34:30, 31
4 [a]Ps. 66:13; 116:17-19
5 [I]Hebr. *to generation and generation* [a]Ps. 136:1 [b]Ps. 89:1

1 [a]Ps. 89:1
2 [a]1Sam. 18:14 [b]1Kgs. 9:4; 11:4
3 [I]Hebr. *thing of Belial* [a]Ps. 97:10 [b]Josh. 23:6; 1Sam. 12:20, 21; Ps. 40:4; 125:5
4 [a]Matt. 7:23; 2Tim. 2:19
5 [a]Ps. 18:27; Prov. 6:17
6 [I]Or, *perfect in the way* [a]Ps. 119:1
7 [I]Hebr. *shall not be established*
8 [a]Ps. 75:10; Jer. 21:12 [b]Ps. 48:2, 8

1 [a]Ex. 2:23; 1Sam. 9:16; Ps. 18:6
2 [a]Ps. 27:9; 69:17 [b]Ps. 71:2; 88:2
3 [I]Or, *into smoke* [a]Ps. 119:83; James 4:14 [b]Job 30:30; Ps. 31:10; Lam. 1:13
4 [a]Ps. 37:2; 102:11
5 [I]Or, *flesh* [a]Job 19:20; Lam. 4:8
6 [a]Job 30:29 [b]Isa. 34:11; Zeph. 2:14
7 [a]Ps. 77:4 [b]Ps. 38:11
8 [a]Acts 26:11 [b]Acts 23:12
9 [a]Ps. 42:3; 80:5

🔑 **101:1** This psalm was written when David moved the ark of God to Jerusalem (2 Sam. 6:1–15).

10 Because of thine indignation[2195] and thy wrath:[7110] for [a]thou hast lifted me up, and cast me down.

11 [a]My days *are* like a shadow that declineth; and [b]I am withered like grass.

12 But [a]thou, O LORD, shalt endure for ever;[5769] and [b]thy remembrance[2143] unto all generations.[1755]

13 Thou shalt arise, *and* [a]have mercy[7355] upon Zion: for the time[6256] to favour[2603] her, yea, the [b]set time, is come.

14 For thy servants[5650] take pleasure[7521] in [a]her stones, and favour the dust[6083] thereof.

15 So the heathen[1471] shall [a]fear[3372] the name of the LORD, and all the kings[4428] of the earth[776] thy glory.[3519]

16 When the LORD shall build up Zion, [a]he shall appear[7200] in his glory.

17 [a]He will regard the prayer of the destitute, and not despise their prayer.

18 This shall be [a]written for the generation to come: and [b]the people[5971] which shall be created[1254] shall praise[1984] the LORD.

19 For he hath [a]looked down from the height of his sanctuary;[6944] from heaven[8064] did the LORD behold the earth;

20 [a]To hear the groaning of the prisoner; to loose [l]those that are appointed to death;

21 To [a]declare[5608] the name of the LORD in Zion, and his praise[8416] in Jerusalem;

22 When the people are gathered[6908] together, and the kingdoms,[4467] to serve[5647] the LORD.

23 He [l]weakened my strength in the way;[1870] he [a]shortened my days.

24 [a]I said, O my God,[410] take me not away in the midst of my days: [b]thy years *are* throughout all generations.

🔑 25 [a]Of old hast thou laid the foundation[3245] of the earth: and the heavens[8064] *are* the work of thy hands.[3027]

26 [a]They shall perish,[6] but [b]thou shalt [l]endure: yea, all of them shall wax old like a garment; as a vesture shalt thou change them, and they shall be changed:

27 But [a]thou *art* the same, and thy years shall have no end.[8552]

28 [a]The children of thy servants shall continue,[7931] and their seed[2233] shall be established[3559] before thee.

God's Love

A Psalm of David.

103 Bless[1288] [a]the LORD, O my soul:[5315] and all that is within[7130] me, *bless* his holy[6944] name.

2 Bless the LORD, O my soul, and forget not all his benefits:[1576]

3 [a]Who forgiveth[5545] all thine iniquities;[5771] who [b]healeth all thy diseases;[8463]

4 Who [a]redeemeth[1350] thy life[2416] from destruction;[7845] [b]who crowneth thee with lovingkindness and tender mercies;[7356]

5 Who satisfieth thy mouth with good[2896] *things; so that* [a]thy youth is renewed like the eagle's.

6 [a]The LORD executeth[6213] righteousness[6666] and judgment[4941] for all that are oppressed.

7 [a]He made known[3045] his ways[1870] unto Moses, his acts unto the children[1121] of Israel.

8 [a]The LORD *is* merciful and gracious,[2587] slow[750] to anger,[639] and [l]plenteous in mercy.[2617]

9 [a]He will[7378] not always[5331] chide:[7378] neither will he keep *his anger* for ever.[5769]

10 [a]He hath not dealt[6213] with us after our sins;[2399] nor rewarded[1580] us according to our iniquities.

11 [a]For [l]as the heaven[8064] is high above the earth,[776] *so* great is his mercy toward them that fear[3373] him.

12 As far as the east is from the

10 [a]Ps. 30:7
11 [a]Job 14:2; Ps. 109:23; 144:4; Eccl. 6:12 [b]Ps. 102:4; Isa. 40:6-8; James 1:10
12 [a]Ps. 9:7; 102:26; Lam. 5:19 [b]Ps. 135:13
13 [a]Isa. 60:10; Zech. 1:12 [b]Isa. 40:2
14 [a]Ps. 79:1
15 [a]1Kgs. 8:43; Ps. 138:4; Isa. 60:3
16 [a]Isa. 60:1, 2
17 [a]Neh. 1:6, 11; 2:8
18 [a]Rom. 15:4; 1Cor. 10:11 [b]Ps. 22:31; Isa. 43:21
19 [a]Deut. 26:15; Ps. 14:2; 33:13, 14
20 [l]Hebr. *the children of death* [a]Ps. 79:11
21 [a]Ps. 22:22
23 [l]Hebr. *afflicted* [a]Job 21:21
24 [a]Isa. 38:10 [b]Ps. 90:2; Hab. 1:12
25 [a]Gen. 1:1; 2:1; Heb. 1:10
26 [l]Hebr. *stand* [a]Isa. 34:4; 51:6; 65:17; 66:22; Rom. 8:20; 2Pet. 3:7, 10-12 [b]Ps. 102:12
27 [a]Mal. 3:6; Heb. 13:8; James 1:17
28 [a]Ps. 69:36

1 [a]Ps. 103:1; 104:1; 146:1
3 [a]Ps. 130:8; Isa. 33:24; Matt. 9:2, 6; Mark 2:5, 10, 11; Luke 7:47 [b]Ex. 15:26; Ps. 147:3; Jer. 17:14
4 [a]Ps. 34:22; 56:13 [b]Ps. 5:12
5 [a]Isa. 40:31
6 [a]Ps. 146:7
7 [a]Ps. 147:19
8 [l]Hebr. *great of mercy* [a]Ex. 34:6, 7; Num. 14:18; Deut. 5:10; Neh. 9:17; Ps. 86:15; Jer. 32:18
9 [a]Ps. 30:5; Isa. 57:16; Jer. 3:5; Mic. 7:18
10 [a]Ezra 9:13
11 [l]Hebr. *according to the height of the heaven* [a]Ps. 57:10; Eph. 3:18

🔑 **102:25–27** See note on Genesis 8:21, 22. Also, compare Hebrews 1:10–12.

west, *so* far hath he [a]removed our transgressions[6588] from us.

13 [a]Like as a father[1] pitieth *his* children, *so* the LORD pitieth[7355] them that fear him.

14 For he knoweth our frame;[3336] [a]he remembereth[2142] that we *are* [b]dust.[6083]

15 *As for* man,[582] [a]his days[3117] *are* as grass: [b]as a flower of the field,[7704] so he flourisheth.

16 For the wind[7307] passeth over[5674] it, and [I]it is gone; and [a]the place thereof shall know it no more.

17 But the mercy of the LORD *is* from everlasting[5769] to everlasting upon them that fear him, and his righteousness [a]unto children's children;

18 [a]To such as keep[8104] his covenant,[1285] and to those that remember[2142] his commandments[6490] to do them.

19 The LORD hath prepared[3559] his [a]throne[3678] in the heavens;[8064] and [b]his kingdom[4438] ruleth[4910] over all.

20 [a]Bless the LORD, ye his angels,[4397] [I][b]that excel in strength, that [c]do his commandments,[1697] hearkening unto the voice of his word.[1697]

21 Bless ye the LORD, all *ye* [a]his hosts;[6635] [b]*ye* ministers[8334] of his, that do his pleasure.[7522]

22 [a]Bless the LORD, all his works in all places of his dominion:[4475] [b]bless the LORD, O my soul.

God Is the Creator

104 Bless[1288] [a]the LORD, O my soul.[5315] O LORD my God,[430] thou art very great; [b]thou art clothed with honour[1935] and majesty.[1926]

2 [a]Who coverest *thyself* with light[216] as *with* a garment: [b]who stretchest out the heavens[8064] like a curtain:

3 [a]Who layeth the beams[7136] of his chambers in the waters: [b]who maketh[7760] the clouds his chariot: [c]who walketh upon the wings of the wind:[7307]

4 [a]Who maketh[6213] his angels[4397] spirits;[7307] [b]his ministers[8334] a flaming fire:

12 [a]Isa. 43:25; Mic. 7:18
13 [a]Mal. 3:17
14 [a]Ps. 78:39 [b]Gen. 3:19; Eccl. 12:7
15 [a]Ps. 90:5, 6; 1Pet. 1:24 [b]Job 14:1, 2; James 1:10, 11
16 [I]Hebr. *it is not* [a]Job 7:10; 20:9
17 [a]Ex. 20:6
18 [a]Deut. 7:9
19 [a]Ps. 11:4 [b]Ps. 47:2; Dan. 4:25, 34, 35
20 [I]Hebr. *mighty in strength* [a]Ps. 148:2 [b]Ps. 78:25 [c]Matt. 6:10; Heb. 1:14
21 [a]Gen. 32:2; Josh. 5:14; Ps. 68:17 [b]Dan. 7:9, 10; Heb. 1:14
22 [a]Ps. 145:10 [b]Ps. 103:1

1 [a]Ps. 103:1; 104:35 [b]Ps. 93:1
2 [a]Dan. 7:9 [b]Isa. 40:22; 45:12
3 [a]Amos 9:6 [b]Isa. 19:1 [c]Ps. 18:10
4 [a]Heb. 1:7 [b]2Kgs. 2:11; 6:17
5 [I]Hebr. *He hath founded the earth upon her bases* [a]Job 26:7; 38:4, 6; Ps. 24:2; 136:6; Eccl. 1:4
6 [a]Gen. 7:19
7 [a]Gen. 8:1
8 [I]Or, *The mountains ascend, the valleys descend* [a]Gen. 8:5 [b]Job 38:10, 11
9 [a]Job 26:10; Ps. 33:7; Jer. 5:22 [b]Gen. 9:11, 15
10 [I]Hebr. *Who sendeth* [II]Hebr. *walk*
11 [I]Hebr. *break*
12 [I]Hebr. *give a voice*
13 [a]Ps. 147:8 [b]Ps. 65:9, 10 [c]Jer. 10:13; 14:22
14 [a]Gen. 1:29, 30; 3:18; 9:3; Ps. 147:8 [b]Job 28:5; Ps. 136:25; 147:9
15 [I]Hebr. *to make his face shine with oil, or, more than oil* [a]Judg. 9:13; Ps. 23:5; Prov. 31:6, 7
16 [a]Num. 24:6
18 [a]Prov. 30:26
19 [a]Gen. 1:14 [b]Job 38:12
20 [a]Isa. 45:7

5 [I][a]*Who* laid the foundations of the earth,[776] *that* it should not be removed for ever.[5703,5769]

6 [a]Thou coveredst[3680] it with the deep as *with* a garment: the waters stood above the mountains.

7 [a]At thy rebuke[1606] they fled; at the voice of thy thunder they hasted away.

8 [I][a]They go up by the mountains; they go down by the valleys unto [b]the place which thou hast founded[3245] for them.

9 [a]Thou hast set[7760] a bound that they may not pass over;[5674] [b]that they turn not again[7725] to cover[3680] the earth.

10 [I]He sendeth the springs into the valleys, *which* [II]run among the hills.

11 They give drink to every beast[2416] of the field:[7704] the wild asses [I]quench[7665] their thirst.

12 By them shall the fowls of the heaven[8064] have their habitation,[7931] *which* [I]sing among the branches.

13 [a]He watereth the hills from his chambers: [b]the earth is satisfied with [c]the fruit of thy works.

14 [a]He causeth the grass to grow for the cattle, and herb for the service[5656] of man:[120] that he may bring forth [b]food out of the earth;

15 And [a]wine *that* maketh glad the heart[3824] of man,[582] *and* [I]oil[8081] to make *his* face to shine, and bread *which* strengtheneth man's heart.

16 The trees of the LORD are full *of sap;* the cedars of Lebanon, [a]which he hath planted;

17 Where the birds make their nests: *as for* the stork, the fir trees *are* her house.[1004]

18 The high hills *are* a refuge for the wild goats; *and* the rocks for [a]the conies.[8227]

19 [a]He appointed[6213] the moon for seasons:[4150] the sun [b]knoweth his going down.

20 [a]Thou makest darkness,[2822] and it

is night:[3915] wherein [I]all the beasts[2416] of the forest do creep *forth.*

21 [a]The young lions roar after their prey, and seek their meat from God.[410]

22 The sun ariseth, they gather themselves together,[622] and lay them down in their dens.

23 Man goeth forth unto [a]his work and to his labour until the evening.

24 [a]O LORD, how manifold are thy works! in wisdom[2451] hast thou made[6213] them all: the earth is full of thy riches.

25 *So is* this great and wide sea, wherein *are* things creeping innumerable, both small and great beasts.

26 There go the ships: *there is* that [a]leviathan, *whom* thou hast [I]made[3335] to play therein.

27 [a]These wait all upon thee; that thou mayest give *them* their meat in due season.[6256]

28 *That* thou givest them they gather:[3950] thou openest thine hand,[3027] they are filled with good.[2896]

29 Thou hidest thy face, they are troubled:[926] [a]thou takest away their breath,[7307] they die,[1478] and return[7725] to their dust.[6083]

30 [a]Thou sendest forth thy spirit,[7307] they are created:[1254] and thou renewest the face of the earth.[127]

31 The glory[3519] of the LORD [I]shall endure for ever: the LORD [a]shall rejoice in his works.

32 He looketh on the earth, and it [a]trembleth:[7460] [b]he toucheth[5060] the hills, and they smoke.[6225]

33 [a]I will sing[7891] unto the LORD as long as I live:[2416] I will sing praise[2167] to my God while I have my being.

34 My meditation[7879] of him shall be sweet:[6148] I will be glad in the LORD.

35 Let [a]the sinners[2400] be consumed[8552] out of the earth, and let the wicked[7563] be no more. [b]Bless thou the LORD, O my soul. Praise[1984] ye the LORD.

God Takes Care of His People

105 O [a]give thanks[3034] unto the LORD; call[7121] upon his name: [b]make known[3045] his deeds among the people.[5971]

2 Sing[7891] unto him, sing[2167] psalms unto him: [a]talk[7878] ye of all his wondrous works.[6381]

3 Glory[1984] ye in his holy[6944] name: let the heart[3820] of them rejoice that seek the LORD.

4 Seek the LORD, and his strength: [a]seek his face evermore.[8548]

5 [a]Remember[2142] his marvellous works[6381] that he hath done;[6213] his wonders,[4159] and the judgments[4941] of his mouth;[6310]

6 O ye seed[2233] of Abraham his servant,[5650] ye children[1121] of Jacob his chosen.

7 He *is* the LORD our God:[430] [a]his judgments *are* in all the earth.[776]

8 He hath [a]remembered[2142] his covenant[1285] for ever,[5769] the word[1697] *which* he commanded to a thousand generations.[1755]

9 [a]Which *covenant* he made[3772] with Abraham, and his oath[7621] unto Isaac;

10 And confirmed the same unto Jacob for a law,[2706] *and* to Israel *for* an everlasting[5769] covenant:

11 Saying, [a]Unto thee will I give the land[776] of Canaan, [I]the lot of your inheritance:[5159]

12 [a]When they were *but* a few men in number; yea, very few, [b]and strangers[1481] in it.

13 When they went from one nation[1471] to another, from *one* kingdom[4467] to another people;

14 [a]He suffered no man[120] to do them wrong:[6231] yea, [b]he reproved[3198] kings[4428] for their sakes;

15 *Saying,* Touch[5060] not mine anointed,[4899] and do[7489] my prophets[5030] no harm.[7489]

16 Moreover [a]he called[7121] for a famine upon the land: he brake the whole [b]staff[4294] of bread.

17 [a]He sent a man[376] before them, *even* Joseph, *who* [b]was sold for a servant:

18 [a]Whose feet they hurt with fetters: [I]he was laid in iron:

19 Until the time[6256] that his word

20 [I]Hebr. *all the beasts thereof do trample on the forest*
21 [a]Job 38:39; Joel 1:20
23 [a]Gen. 3:10
24 [a]Prov. 3:19
26 [I]Hebr. *formed* [a]Job 41:1
27 [a]Ps. 136:25; 145:15; 147:9
29 [a]Job 34:14, 15; Ps. 146:4; Eccl. 12:7
30 [a]Isa. 32:15; Ezek. 37:9
31 [I]Hebr. *shall be* [a]Gen. 1:31
32 [a]Hab. 3:10 [b]Ps. 144:5
33 [a]Ps. 63:4; 146:2
35 [a]Ps. 37:38; Prov. 2:22 [b]Ps. 104:1

1 [a]1Chr. 16:8-22; Isa. 12:4 [b]Ps. 145:4, 5, 11
2 [a]Ps. 77:12; 119:27
4 [a]Ps. 27:8
5 [a]Ps. 77:11
7 [a]Isa. 26:9
8 [a]Luke 1:72
9 [a]Gen. 17:2; 22:16; 26:3; 28:13; 35:11; Luke 1:73; Heb. 6:17
11 [I]Hebr. *the cord* [a]Gen. 13:15; 15:18
12 [a]Gen. 34:30; Deut. 7:7; 26:5 [b]Heb. 11:9
14 [a]Gen. 35:5 [b]Gen. 12:17; 20:3, 7
16 [a]Gen. 41:54 [b]Lev. 26:26; Isa. 3:1; Ezek. 4:16
17 [a]Gen. 45:5; 50:20 [b]Gen. 37:28, 36
18 [I]Hebr. *his soul came into iron* [a]Gen. 39:20; 40:15

came: [a]the word[565] of the LORD tried[6884] him.

20 [a]The king sent and loosed him; *even* the ruler[4910] of the people, and let him go free.

21 [a]He made[7760] him lord[113] of his house,[1004] and ruler of all his [I]substance:

22 To bind his princes[8269] at his pleasure;[5315] and teach his senators[2205] wisdom.[2449]

23 [a]Israel also came into Egypt; and Jacob sojourned[1481] [b]in the land of Ham.

24 And [a]he increased his people greatly; and made them stronger than their enemies.

25 [a]He turned[2015] their heart to hate[8130] his people, to deal subtilly with his servants.[5650]

26 [a]He sent Moses his servant; *and* Aaron [b]whom he had chosen.[977]

27 [a]They shewed[7760] [I]his signs among them, [b]and wonders in the land of Ham.

28 [a]He sent darkness,[2822] and made it dark;[2821] and [b]they rebelled[4784] not against his word.

29 [a]He turned their waters into blood,[1818] and slew[4191] their fish.[1710]

30 [a]Their land brought forth frogs in abundance, in the chambers of their kings.

31 [a]He spake,[559] and there came divers sorts of flies, *and* lice in all their coasts.

32 [I][a]He gave them hail for rain, *and* flaming fire in their land.

33 [a]He smote[5221] their vines also and their fig trees; and brake the trees of their coasts.

34 [a]He spake, and the locusts came, and caterpillers, and that without number,

35 And did eat up all the herbs in their land, and devoured the fruit of their ground.[127]

36 [a]He smote also all the firstborn in their land, [b]the chief[7225] of all their strength.

37 [a]He brought them forth also with silver and gold: and *there was* not one feeble[3782] *person* among their tribes.[7626]

38 [a]Egypt was glad[8056] when they departed: for the fear[6343] of them fell[5307] upon them.

39 [a]He spread a cloud[6051] for a covering; and fire to give light[215] in the night.[3915]

40 [a]*The people* asked,[7592] and he brought quails, and [b]satisfied them with the bread of heaven.[8064]

41 [a]He opened the rock, and the waters gushed out; they ran in the dry places *like* a river.

42 For he remembered [a]his holy promise,[1697] *and* Abraham his servant.

43 And he brought forth his people with joy, *and* his chosen with [I]gladness:

44 [a]And gave them the lands of the heathen:[1471] and they inherited[3423] the labour[5999] of the people;[3816]

45 [a]That they might observe[8104] his statutes,[2706] and keep[5341] his laws.[8451] [I]Praise[1984] ye the LORD.[3050]

Israel Prone to Rebellion

106 [I]Praise[1984] ye the LORD. [a]O [b]give thanks[3034] unto the LORD; for *he is* good:[2896] for his mercy[2617] *endureth* for ever.[5769]

2 [a]Who can utter[4448] the mighty acts of the LORD? *who* can shew forth[8085] all his praise?[8416]

3 Blessed[835] *are* they that keep[8104] judgment,[4941] *and* he that [a]doeth[6213] righteousness[6666] at [b]all times.[6256]

4 [a]Remember[2142] me, O LORD, with the favour[7522] *that thou bearest unto* thy people:[5971] O visit[6485] me with thy salvation;[3444]

5 That I may see the good of thy chosen, that I may rejoice in the gladness of thy nation,[1471] that I may glory[1984] with thine inheritance.

6 [a]We have sinned[2398] with our fathers,[1] we have committed iniquity,[5753] we have done wickedly.[7561]

7 Our fathers understood[7919] not thy wonders[6381] in Egypt; they remembered[2142] not the multitude of thy mercies;[2617] [a]but provoked[4784] *him* at the sea, *even* at the Red sea.

8 Nevertheless he saved[3467] them

19 [a]Gen. 41:25
20 [a]Gen. 41:14
21 [I]Hebr. *possession* [a]Gen. 41:40
23 [a]Gen. 46:6 [b]Ps. 78:51; 106:22
24 [a]Ex. 1:7
25 [a]Ex. 1:8
26 [a]Ex. 3:10; 4:12, 14; Num. 16:5; 17:5
27 [I]Hebr. *words of his signs* [a]Ps. 78:43 [b]Ps. 106:22
28 [a]Ex. 10:22 [b]Ps. 99:7
29 [a]Ex. 7:20; Ps. 78:44
30 [a]Ex. 8:6; Ps. 78:45
31 [a]Ex. 8:17, 24; Ps. 78:45
32 [I]Hebr. *He gave their rain hail* [a]Ex. 9:23, 25; Ps. 78:48
33 [a]Ps. 78:47
34 [a]Ex. 10:4, 13, 14; Ps. 78:46
36 [a]Ex. 12:29; Ps. 78:51 [b]Gen. 49:3
37 [a]Ex. 12:35
38 [a]Ex. 12:33
39 [a]Ex. 13:21; Neh. 9:12
40 [a]Ex. 16:12; Ps. 78:18, 27 [b]Ps. 78:24, 25
41 [a]Ex. 17:6; Num. 20:11; Ps. 78:15, 16; 1Cor. 10:4
42 [a]Gen. 15:14
43 [I]Hebr. *singing*
44 [a]Deut. 6:10, 11; Josh. 13:7; Ps. 78:55
45 [I]Hebr. *Hallelujah* [a]Deut. 4:1, 40; 6:21-25

1 [I]Hebr. *Hallelujah* [a]1Chr. 16:34 [b]Ps. 107:1; 118:1; 136:1
2 [a]Ps. 40:5
3 [a]Ps. 15:2 [b]Acts 24:16; Gal. 6:9
4 [a]Ps. 119:132
6 [a]Lev. 26:40; 1Kgs. 8:47; Dan. 9:5
7 [a]Ex. 14:11,12

[a]for his name's sake, [b]that he might make his mighty power to be known.[3045]

9 [a]He rebuked[1605] the Red sea also, and it was dried up:[2717] so [b]he led them through the depths, as through the wilderness.

10 And he [a]saved them from the hand[3027] of him that hated *them,* and redeemed[1350] them from the hand of the enemy.

11 [a]And the waters covered[3680] their enemies: there was not one of them left.[3498]

12 [a]Then believed[539] they his words;[1697] they sang his praise.

13 [I][a]They soon forgat his works; they waited not for his counsel:[6098]

14 [a]But [I]lusted[183] exceedingly in the wilderness, and tempted[5254] God[410] in the desert.

15 [a]And he gave them their request;[7596] but [b]sent leanness into their soul.

16 [a]They envied[7065] Moses also in the camp, *and* Aaron the saint[6918] of the LORD.

17 [a]The earth[776] opened and swallowed up[1104] Dathan, and covered the company[5712] of Abiram.

18 [a]And a fire was kindled in their company; the flame burned up the wicked.[7563]

19 [a]They made[6213] a calf in Horeb, and worshipped[7812] the molten[4541] image.[6754]

20 Thus [a]they changed their glory[3519] into the similitude[8403] of an ox that eateth grass.

21 They [a]forgat God their saviour,[3467] which had done great things in Egypt;

22 Wondrous works[6381] in [a]the land[776] of Ham, *and* terrible things[3372] by the Red sea.

23 [a]Therefore he said that he would destroy[8045] them, had not Moses his chosen [b]stood before him in the breach, to turn away[7725] his wrath,[2534] lest he should destroy[7843] *them.*

24 Yea, they despised[3988] [I][a]the pleasant land, they [b]believed not his word:[1697]

25 [a]But murmured in their tents,[168] *and* hearkened[8085] not unto the voice of the LORD.[3068]

26 [a]Therefore he [b]lifted up[5375] his hand against them, to overthrow[5307] them in the wilderness:

27 [I][a]To overthrow their seed[2233] also among the nations,[1471] and to scatter them in the lands.

28 [a]They joined themselves also unto Baal–peor, and ate the sacrifices[2077] of the dead.[4191]

29 Thus they provoked *him* to anger[3707] with their inventions: and the plague brake in upon them.

30 [a]Then stood up Phinehas, and executed judgment:[6419] and *so* the plague was stayed.

31 And that was counted[2803] unto him [a]for righteousness unto all generations[1755] for evermore.[5769]

32 [a]They angered[7107] *him* also at the waters of strife, [b]so that it went ill[3415] with Moses for their sakes:

33 [a]Because they provoked his spirit,[7307] so that he spake unadvisedly[981] with his lips.[8413]

34 [a]They did not destroy the nations,[5971] [b]concerning whom the LORD commanded[559] them:

35 [a]But were mingled[6148] among the heathen,[1471] and learned[3925] their works.

36 And [a]they served their idols:[6091] [b]which were a snare[4170] unto them.

🔑 37 Yea, [a]they sacrificed[2076] their

8 [a]Ezek. 20:14 [b]Ex. 9:16
9 [a]Ex. 14:21; Ps. 18:15; Nah. 1:4 [b]Isa. 63:11-14
10 [a]Ex. 14:30
11 [a]Ex. 14:27, 28; 15:5
12 [a]Ex. 14:31; 15:1
13 [I]Hebr. *They made haste, they forgat* [a]Ex. 15:24; 16:2; 17:2; Ps. 78:11
14 [I]Hebr. *lusted a lust* [a]Num. 11:4, 33; Ps. 78:18; 1Cor. 10:6
15 [a]Num. 11:31; Ps. 78:29 [b]Isa. 10:16
16 [a]Num. 16:1
17 [a]Num. 16:31, 32; Deut. 11:6
18 [a]Num. 16:35, 46
19 [a]Ex. 32:4
20 [a]Jer. 2:11; Rom. 1:23
21 [a]Ps. 78:11, 12
22 [a]Ps. 78:51; 105:23, 27
23 [a]Ex. 32:10, 11, 32; Deut. 9:19, 25; 10:10; Ezek. 20:13 [b]Ezek. 13:5; 22:30
24 [I]Hebr. *a land of desire* [a]Deut. 8:7; Jer. 3:19; Ezek. 20:6 [b]Heb. 3:18
25 [a]Num. 14:2, 27
26 [a]Num. 14:28, ff; Ps. 95:11; Ezek. 20:15; Heb. 3:11, 18 [b]Ex. 6:8; Deut. 32:40
27 [I]Hebr. *To make them fall* [a]Lev. 26:33; Ps. 44:11; Ezek. 20:23
28 [a]Num. 25:2, 3; 31:16; Deut. 4:3; 32:17; Hos. 9:10; Rev. 2:14
30 [a]Num. 25:7, 8
31 [a]Num. 25:11-13
32 [a]Num. 20:3, 13; Ps. 81:7 [b]Num. 20:12; Deut. 1:37; 3:26
33 [a]Num. 20:10
34 [a]Judg. 1:21, 27-29 [b]Deut. 7:2, 16; Judg. 2:2
35 [a]Judg. 2:2; 3:5, 6; Isa. 2:6; 1Cor. 5:6
36 [a]Judg. 2:12, 13, 17, 19; 3:6, 7 [b]Ex. 23:33; Deut. 7:16; Judg. 2:3, 14, 15
37 [a]2Kgs. 16:3; Isa. 57:5; Ezek. 16:20; 20:26

🔑 **106:37, 38** These verses state that children were actually burned alive as offerings to Canaanite gods (Molech, Milcom, Chemosh, and others; see note on 2 Kgs. 23:10). It is hard to understand how brutal the grip of such pagan superstitions must have been on people that they would burn their own children (see Jer. 7:31). Those who engaged in such practices assumed that the victims were purged of their dross (i.e., their physical body) so that they might attain union with the deity.

sons[1121] and their daughters unto [b]devils,[7700]

38 And shed[8210] innocent[5355] blood,[1818] *even* the blood of their sons and of their daughters, whom they sacrificed unto the idols of Canaan: and [a]the land was polluted[2610] with blood.

39 Thus were they [a]defiled[2930] with their own works, and [b]went a whoring[2181] with their own inventions.

40 Therefore [a]was[2734] the wrath[639] of the LORD kindled[2734] against his people, insomuch that he abhorred[8581] [b]his own inheritance.

41 And [a]he gave them into the hand of the heathen; and they that hated them ruled[4910] over them.

42 Their enemies also oppressed them, and they were brought into subjection under their hand.

43 [a]Many times did he deliver[5337] them; but they provoked *him* with their counsel, and were [I]brought low for their iniquity.[5771]

44 Nevertheless he regarded[7200] their affliction, when [a]he heard[8085] their cry:

45 [a]And he remembered[5162] for them his covenant,[1285] and [b]repented [c]according to the multitude of his mercies.

46 [a]He made them also to be pitied[7356] of all those that carried them captives.[7617]

47 [a]Save[3467] us, O LORD our God,[430] and gather[6908] us from among the heathen, to give thanks[3034] unto thy holy[6944] name, *and* to triumph[7623] in thy praise.

48 [a]Blessed[1288] *be* the LORD God of Israel from everlasting[5769] to everlasting: and let all the people say, Amen.[543] [I]Praise ye the LORD.

BOOK V

God Rescues Us

107 O [a]give thanks[3034] unto the LORD, for [b]*he is* good:[2896] for his mercy[2617] *endureth* for ever.[5769]

2 Let the redeemed[1350] of the LORD say[559] *so,* [a]whom he hath redeemed from the hand[3027] of the enemy;

3 And [a]gathered[6908] them out of the lands, from the east, and from the west, from the north, and [I]from the south.

4 They [a]wandered[8582] in [b]the wilderness in a solitary way;[1870] they found no city to dwell in.

5 Hungry and thirsty, their soul fainted in them.

6 [a]Then they cried unto the LORD in their trouble,[7451] *and* he delivered[5337] them out of their distresses.[4691]

7 And he led them forth by the [a]right[3477] way, that they might go to a city of habitation.

8 [a]Oh that *men* would praise[3034] the LORD *for* his goodness,[2617] and *for* his wonderful works[6381] to the children[1121] of men![120]

9 For [a]he satisfieth the longing soul, and filleth the hungry soul with goodness.[2896]

10 Such as [a]sit in darkness[2822] and in the shadow of death,[6757] *being* [b]bound in affliction and iron;

11 Because they [a]rebelled[4784] against the words[561] of God,[410] and contemned[5006] [b]the counsel[6098] of the most High:[5945]

12 Therefore he brought down their heart[3820] with labour;[5999] they fell down,[3782] and *there was* [a]none to help.

13 [a]Then they cried[2199] unto the LORD in their trouble, *and* he saved[3467] them out of their distresses.

14 [a]He brought them out of darkness and the shadow of death, and brake their bands in sunder.

15 [a]Oh that *men* would praise the LORD *for* his goodness, and *for* his wonderful works to the children of men!

16 For he hath [a]broken[7665] the gates of brass, and cut the bars of iron in sunder.

17 Fools [a]because of their transgression,[6588] and because of their iniquities,[5771] are afflicted.

18 [a]Their soul abhorreth[8581] all manner of meat; and they [b]draw near unto the gates of death.[4194]

37 [b]Lev. 17:7; Deut. 32:17; 2Chr. 11:15; 1Cor. 10:20
38 [a]Num. 35:33
39 [a]Ezek. 20:18, 30, 31 [b]Lev. 17:7; Num. 15:39; Ezek. 20:30
40 [a]Judg. 2:14; Ps. 78:59, 62 [b]Deut. 9:29
41 [a]Judg. 2:14; Neh. 9:27
43 [I]Or, *impoverished,* or, *weakened* [a]Judg. 2:16; Neh. 9:27
44 [a]Judg. 3:9; 4:3; 6:7; 10:10; Neh. 9:27
45 [a]Lev. 26:41, 42 [b]Judg. 2:18 [c]Ps. 51:1; 69:16; Isa. 63:7; Lam. 3:32
46 [a]Ezra 9:9; Jer. 42:12
47 [a]1Chr. 16:35, 36
48 [I]Hebr. *Hallelujah* [a]Ps. 41:13

1 [a]Ps. 106:1; 118:1; 136:1 [b]Ps. 119:68; Matt. 19:17
2 [a]Ps. 106:10
3 [I]Hebr. *from the sea* [a]Ps. 106:47; Isa. 43:5, 6; Jer. 29:14; 31:8, 10; Ezek. 39:27, 28
4 [a]Ps. 107:40 [b]Deut. 32:10
6 [a]Ps. 50:15; 107:13, 19, 28; Hos. 5:15
7 [a]Ezra 8:21
8 [a]Ps. 107:15, 21, 31
9 [a]Ps. 34:10; Luke 1:53
10 [a]Luke 1:79 [b]Job 36:8
11 [a]Lam. 3:42 [b]Ps. 73:24; 119:24; Luke 7:30; Acts 20:27
12 [a]Ps. 22:11; Isa. 63:5
13 [a]Ps. 107:6, 19, 28
14 [a]Ps. 68:6; 146:7; Acts 12:7; 16:26
15 [a]Ps. 107:8, 21, 31
16 [a]Isa. 45:2
17 [a]Lam. 3:39
18 [a]Job 33:20 [b]Job 33:22; Ps. 9:13; 88:3

19 [a]Then they cry[2199] unto the LORD in their trouble, *and* he saveth[3467] them out of their distresses.

20 [a]He sent his word,[1697] and [b]healed them, and [c]delivered[4422] *them* from their destructions.[7825]

21 [a]Oh that *men* would praise the LORD *for* his goodness, and *for* his wonderful works to the children of men!

22 And [a]let them sacrifice[2076] the sacrifices[2077] of thanksgiving,[8426] and [b]declare[5608] his works with [I]rejoicing.

23 They that go down to the sea in ships, that do[6213] business[4399] in great waters;

24 These see the works of the LORD, and his wonders in the deep.

25 For he commandeth,[559] and [I][a]raiseth the stormy wind,[7307] which lifteth up the waves thereof.

26 They mount up[5927] to the heaven,8064 they go down again to the depths: [a]their soul is melted because of trouble.

27 They reel to and fro, and stagger like a drunken man, and [I]are at their wit's end.

28 [a]Then they cry unto the LORD in their trouble, and he bringeth them out of their distresses.

29 [a]He maketh[6965] the storm a calm, so that the waves thereof are still.

30 Then are they glad because they be quiet; so he bringeth[5148] them unto their desired haven.

31 [a]Oh that *men* would praise the LORD *for* his goodness, and *for* his wonderful works to the children of men!

32 Let them exalt him also [a]in the congregation[6951] of the people,[5971] and praise[1984] him in the assembly[4186] of the elders.[2205]

33 He [a]turneth[7760] rivers into a wilderness, and the watersprings into dry ground;6774

34 A [a]fruitful land[776] into [I]barrenness, for the wickedness[7451] of them that dwell therein.

35 [a]He turneth the wilderness into a standing water, and dry ground into watersprings.

36 And there he maketh the hungry to dwell, that they may prepare[3559] a city for habitation;

37 And sow the fields,[7704] and plant vineyards, which may yield[6213] fruits of increase.

38 [a]He blesseth[1288] them also, so that they [b]are multiplied greatly; and suffereth not their cattle to decrease.

39 Again, they are [a]minished and brought low through oppression, affliction,[7451] and sorrow.

40 [a]He poureth[8210] contempt upon princes,[5081] and causeth them to wander[8582] in the [I]wilderness,[8414] *where there is* no way.

41 [a]Yet setteth he the poor on high [I]from affliction, and [b]maketh[7760] *him* families[4940] like a flock.

42 [a]The righteous[3477] shall see *it,* and rejoice: and all [b]iniquity[5766] shall stop her mouth.[6310]

43 [a]Whoso *is* wise,[2450] and will observe[8104] these *things,* even they shall understand[995] the lovingkindness of the LORD.

A Cry for Help

A Song *or* Psalm of David.

108 O [a]God,[430] my heart[3820] is fixed;[3559] I will sing[7891] and give praise, even with my glory.[3519]

2 [a]Awake, psaltery and harp: I *myself* will awake early.

3 I will praise[3034] thee, O LORD, among the people:[5971] and I will sing praises[2167] unto thee among the nations.[3816]

4 For thy mercy[2617] *is* great above the heavens:8064 and thy truth[571] *reacheth* unto the [I]clouds.[7834]

5 [a]Be thou exalted, O God, above the heavens: and thy glory above all the earth;

6 [a]That thy beloved[3039] may be delivered:[2502] save[3467] *with* thy right hand, and answer me.

7 God hath spoken[1696] in his holiness;[6944] I will rejoice, I will divide Shechem, and mete out4058 the valley of Succoth.

---

19 [a]Ps. 107:6; 132:8
20 [a]2Kgs. 20:4, 5; Ps. 147:15, 18; Matt. 8:8 [b]Ps. 30:2; 103:3 [c]Job 33:28, 30; Ps. 30:3; 49:15; 56:13; 103:4
21 [a]Ps. 107:8, 15, 31
22 [I]Hebr. *singing* [a]Lev. 7:12; Ps. 50:14; 116:17; Heb. 13:15 [b]Ps. 9:11; 73:28; 118:17
25 [I]Hebr. *maketh to stand* [a]Jon. 1:4
26 [a]Ps. 22:14; 119:28; Nah. 2:10
27 [I]Hebr. *all their wisdom is swallowed up*
28 [a]Ps. 107:8, 13, 19
29 [a]Ps. 89:9; Matt. 8:26
31 [a]Ps. 107:8, 15, 21
32 [a]Ps. 22:22, 25; 111:1
33 [a]1Kgs. 17:1, 7
34 [I]Hebr. *saltness* [a]Gen. 13:10; 14:3; 19:25
35 [a]Ps. 114:8; Isa. 41:18
38 [a]Gen. 12:2; 17:16, 20 [b]Ex. 1:7
39 [a]2Kgs. 10:32
40 [I]Or, *void place* [a]Job 12:21, 24
41 [I]Or, *after* [a]1Sam. 2:8; Ps. 113:7, 8 [b]Ps. 78:52
42 [a]Job 22:19; Ps. 52:6; 58:10 [b]Job 5:16; Ps. 63:11; Prov. 10:11; Rom. 3:19
43 [a]Ps. 64:9; Jer. 9:12; Hos. 14:9

1 [a]Ps. 57:7
2 [a]Ps. 57:8-11
4 [I]Or, *skies*
5 [a]Ps. 57:5, 11
6 [a]Ps. 60:5

8 Gilead *is* mine; Manasseh *is* mine;
Ephraim also *is* the strength of mine
head;[7218] [a]Judah *is* my lawgiver;[2710]
9 Moab *is* my washpot;[7366] [5518] over
Edom will I cast out my shoe; over
Philistia will I triumph.[7321]
10 [a]Who will bring me into the
strong city? who will lead[5148] me into
Edom?
11 *Wilt* not *thou,* O God, *who* hast
cast us off? and wilt not thou, O God, go
forth with our hosts?[6635]
12 Give us help[8668] from trouble: for
vain[7723] *is* the help of man.[120]
13 [a]Through God we shall do[6213]
valiantly:[2428] for he *it is that* shall tread
down[947] our enemies.

A Cry for Retribution

To the chief Musician, A Psalm of David.

109 Hold [a]not thy peace, O
God[430] of my praise;[8416]
2 For the mouth of the wicked[7563]
and the [I]mouth of the deceitful[4820] [II]are
opened against me: they have spoken[1696]
against me with a lying tongue.
3 They compassed me about also
with words[1697] of hatred;[8135] and fought
against me [a]without *a* cause.
4 For my love[160] they are my
adversaries:[7853] but I *give myself unto*
prayer.[8605]
5 And [a]they have rewarded me
evil[7451] for good,[2896] and hatred for my
love.
6 Set thou a wicked man over him:
and let [I][a]Satan[7854] stand at his right
hand.
7 When he shall be judged,[8199] let
him [I]be condemned:[7563] and [a]let his
prayer become[1961] sin.[2401]
8 Let his days[3117] be few; *and* [a]let
another take his [I]office.[6486]
9 [a]Let his children[1121] be fatherless,
and his wife[802] a widow.

8 [a]Gen. 49:10
10 [a]Ps. 60:9
13 [a]Ps. 60:12
1 [a]Ps. 83:1
2 [I]Hebr. *mouth of deceit* [II]Hebr. *have opened themselves*
3 [a]Ps. 35:7; 69:4; John 15:25
5 [a]Ps. 35:7, 12; 38:20
6 [I]Or, *an adversary* [a]Zech. 3:1
7 [I]Hebr. *go out guilty,* or, *wicked* [a]Prov. 28:9
8 [I]Or, *charge* [a]Acts 1:20
9 [a]Ex. 22:24

109:1–29 This is one of the psalms that are known as the "Imprecatory Psalms" (see Ps. 7:11–17; 35; 58; 69; 83; and 137). Imprecation is the giving of prayers to invoke God's wrath upon the wicked. Down through the centuries there have been two extremes of thought on the proper use of imprecation. In the first instance, there are those who claim not only that imprecation is proper, but also that the punishment should be meted out by God's children. Others feel that imprecation was only proper in Old Testament times. They insist that New Testament "grace" demands that believers are never to pray in this manner. However, is not the command to love one's neighbor also found in the Old Testament (Ex. 23:4, 5; Prov. 20:22; 24:17)? Did not the Lord even then proclaim that vengeance is His (Deut. 32:35, cf. Rom. 12:19)? In the same manner note that David, the author of most of the imprecatory prayers of the Old Testament, was unwilling to hurt Saul, one of his worst enemies, even when he was delivered into his hand. Even more convincing is the fact that there are instances of such imprecation in the New Testament (Acts 1:20; 5; 8:20–23; 13:10, 11; Rom. 11:9, 10 [cf. Ps. 69:22, 23]; 2 Tim. 4:14).

In contrast to these two extremes the historic Christian view approves of imprecation, but points out a number of stipulations that apply. First, though it is impossible to remove entirely the personal aspect of these requests, the vengeance that is prayed for is actually more of a vindication. The wicked have not been provoked, nor do they commit acts of which the psalmist himself is guilty. Instead, the psalmist is concerned about God's reputation and cause. The imprecatory psalms exhibit only a righteous indignation for sin in which it is impossible to separate the sin from the sinner. The issue is given over to God (Ps. 35:1, 2; 69:7; 2 Tim. 4:14). Those who hate God and commit heinous sin will some day be judged for their wickedness. Believers should groan in agony that even one soul shall endure eternal punishment, yet they must accept the righteousness of God in so doing.

It is helpful to remember that these psalms are not hastily worded expressions of anger, but carefully written works of literature. Moreover, they are not the result of human hands, but inspired by the Holy Spirit. Like all Scriptural warnings, these psalms have been instrumental in the conversion of sinners.

Four elements that should accompany imprecation are noted in this psalm: love (v. 4); prayer (v. 4); doing good (v. 21); and blessing (v. 28).

10 Let his children be continually[8548] vagabonds, and beg:[7592] let them seek *their bread* also out of their desolate places.[2723]

11 [a]Let the extortioner catch[5367] all that he hath; and let the strangers[2114] spoil his labour.

12 Let there be none to extend mercy[2617] unto him: neither let there be any to favour[2603] his fatherless children.

13 [a]Let his posterity[319] be cut off;[3772] *and* in the generation[1755] following let their [b]name be blotted out.[4229]

14 [a]Let the iniquity[5771] of his fathers[1] be remembered[2142] with the LORD; and let not the sin[2403] of his mother[517] [b]be blotted out.

15 Let them be before the LORD continually, that he may [a]cut off the memory[2143] of them from the earth.[776]

16 Because that he remembered not to shew[6213] mercy, but persecuted the poor and needy man,[376] that he might even slay[4191] the [a]broken in heart.[3824]

17 [a]As he loved[157] cursing,[7045] so let it come unto him: as he delighted[2654] not in blessing,[1293] so let it be far from him.

18 As he clothed himself with cursing like as with his garment, so let it [a]come [I]into his bowels[7130] like water, and like oil[8081] into his bones.[6106]

19 Let it be unto him as the garment *which* covereth him, and for a girdle[4206] wherewith he is girded continually.

20 *Let* this *be* the reward of mine adversaries from the LORD, and of them that speak evil against my soul.

21 But do thou for me, O GOD the Lord,[136] for thy name's sake: because thy mercy *is* good, deliver[5337] thou me.

22 For I *am* poor and needy, and my heart[3820] is wounded[2490] within[7130] me.

23 I am gone [a]like the shadow when it declineth: I am tossed up and down as the locust.

24 My [a]knees are weak[3782] through fasting; and my flesh[1320] faileth of fatness.[8081]

25 I became also [a]a reproach[2781] unto them: *when* they looked[7200] upon me [b]they shaked their heads.[7218]

26 Help me, O LORD my God: O save[3467] me according to thy mercy:

27 [a]That they may know that this *is* thy hand;[3027] *that* thou, LORD, hast done[6213] it.

28 [a]Let them curse,[7043] but bless[1288] thou: when they arise, let them be ashamed;[954] but let [b]thy servant[5650] rejoice.

29 [a]Let mine adversaries be clothed with shame, and let them cover themselves with their own confusion, as with a mantle.[4598]

30 I will greatly praise[3034] the LORD with my mouth; yea, [a]I will praise[1984] him among the multitude.

31 For [a]he shall stand at the right hand of the poor, to save *him* [I]from those that condemn[8199] his soul.

The Chosen King of the Lord

A Psalm of David.

110 🔑 The [a]LORD said[5002] unto my Lord,[113] Sit thou at my right hand, until I make thine enemies thy footstool.

2 The LORD shall send the rod[4294] of thy strength out of Zion: rule[7287] thou in the midst[7130] of thine enemies.

3 [a]Thy people[5971] *shall be* willing in the day[3117] of thy power,[2428] [b]in the beauties[1926] of holiness[6944] [I]from the womb of the morning: thou hast the dew of thy youth.

4 The LORD hath sworn, and [a]will not repent,[5162] [b]Thou *art* a priest[3548] for ever[5769] after the order[1700] of Melchizedek.

5 The LORD[136] [a]at thy right hand shall strike through[4272] kings[4428] [b]in the day of his wrath.[639]

6 He shall judge[1777] among the heathen,[1471] he shall fill *the places* with the dead bodies;[1472] [a]he shall wound[4272] the heads[7218] over [I]many countries.[776]

11 [a]Job 5:5; 18:9
13 [a]Job 18:19; Ps. 37:28 [b]Prov. 10:7
14 [a]Ex. 20:5 [b]Neh. 4:5; Jer. 18:23
15 [a]Job 18:17; Ps. 34:16
16 [a]Ps. 34:18
17 [a]Prov. 14:14; Ezek. 35:6
18 [I]Hebr. *within him* [a]Num. 5:22
23 [a]Ps. 102:11; 144:4
24 [a]Heb. 12:12
25 [a]Ps. 22:6, 7 [b]Matt. 27:39
27 [a]Job 37:7
28 [a]2Sam. 16:11, 12 [b]Isa. 65:14
29 [a]Ps. 35:26; 132:18
30 [a]Ps. 35:18; 111:1
31 [I]Hebr. *from the judges of his soul* [a]Ps. 16:8; 73:23; 110:5; 121:5

1 [a]Ps. 45:6, 7; Matt. 22:44; Mark 12:36; Luke 20:42; Acts 2:34; 1Cor. 15:25; Heb. 1:13; 1Pet. 3:22
3 [I]Or, *more than the womb of the morning: thou shalt have* [a]Judg. 5:2 [b]Ps. 96:9
4 [a]Num. 23:19 [b]Zech. 6:13; Heb. 5:6; 6:20; 7:17, 21
5 [a]Ps. 16:8 [b]Ps. 2:5, 12; Rom. 2:5; Rev. 11:18
6 [I]Or, *great* [a]Ps. 68:21

🔑 **110:1–7** See the note on Psalm 22:1–31 for a discussion of the Messianic Psalms.

7 [a]He shall drink of the brook in the
way:[1870] [b]therefore shall he lift up the
head.[7218]

Praising God

111 [I]Praise[1984] ye the LORD. [a]I will
praise[3034] the LORD with *my*
whole heart,3824 in the assembly[5475] of
the upright, and *in* the congregation.[5712]
2 [a]The works of the LORD *are* great,
[b]sought out of all them that have pleasure[2656] therein.
3 His work *is* [a]honourable and glorious: and his righteousness[6666] endureth
for ever.[5703]
4 He hath made[6213] his wonderful
works[6381] to be remembered: [a]the LORD *is*
gracious[2587] and full of compassion.
5 He hath given [Ia]meat unto them
that fear[3373] him: he will ever be mindful[2143] of his covenant.[1285]
6 He hath shewed[5046] his people[5971]
the power of his works, that he may give
them the heritage[5159] of the heathen.[1471]
7 The works of his hands[3027] *are*
[a]verity[571] and judgment;[4941] [b]all his commandments[6490] *are* sure.[539]
8 [a]They [I]stand fast for ever[5703] and
ever,[5769] *and are* [b]done in truth[571] and
uprightness.[3477]
9 [a]He sent redemption[6304] unto his
people: he hath commanded[6680] his
covenant for ever: [b]holy[6918] and reverend[3372] *is* his name.
10 [a]The fear[3374] of the LORD *is* the
beginning[7225] of wisdom:[2451] [b][I]a good[2896]
understanding792 have all they [II]that do
his commandments: his praise[8416] endureth for ever.

A Godly Person Is Prosperous

112 [I]Praise[1984] ye the LORD.
[a]Blessed[835] *is* the man *that*
feareth the LORD, *that* [b]delighteth[2654]
greatly in his commandments.[4687]

7 [a]Judg. 7:5, 6 [b]Isa. 53:12

1 [I]Hebr. *Hallelujah* [a]Ps. 35:18; 89:5; 107:32; 109:30; 149:1
2 [a]Job 38; 39; 40; 41; Ps. 92:5; 139:14; Rev. 15:3 [b]Ps. 143:5
3 [a]Ps. 145:4, 5, 10
4 [a]Ps. 86:5; 103:8
5 [I]Hebr. *prey* [a]Matt. 6:26, 33
7 [a]Rev. 15:3 [b]Ps. 19:7
8 [I]Hebr. are *established* [a]Isa. 40:8; Matt. 5:18 [b]Ps. 19:9; Rev. 15:3
9 [a]Matt. 1:21; Luke 1:68 [b]Luke 1:49
10 [I]Or, *good success* [II]Hebr. *that do them* [a]Deut. 4:6; Job 28:28; Prov. 1:7; 9:10; Eccl. 12:13 [b]Prov. 3:4

1 [I]Hebr. *Hallelujah* [a]Ps. 128:1 [b]Ps. 119:16, 35, 47, 70, 143
2 [a]Ps. 25:13; 37:26; 102:28
3 [a]Matt. 6:33
4 [a]Job 11:17; Ps. 97:11
5 [I]Hebr. *judgment* [a]Ps. 37:26; Luke 6:35 [b]Eph. 5:15; Col. 4:5
6 [a]Ps. 15:5 [b]Prov. 10:7
7 [a]Prov. 1:33 [b]Ps. 57:7 [c]Ps. 64:10
8 [a]Prov. 1:33 [b]Ps. 59:10; 118:7
9 [a]2Cor. 9:9 [b]Deut. 24:13; ver. 3 [c]Ps. 75:10
10 [a]Luke 13:28 [b]Ps. 37:12 [c]Ps. 58:7, 8 [d]Prov. 10:28; 11:7

1 [I]Hebr. *Hallelujah* [a]Ps. 135:1
2 [a]Dan. 2:20

🗝 2 [a]His seed[2233] shall be mighty upon
earth: the generation[1755] of the upright
shall be blessed.[1288]
3 [a]Wealth and riches *shall be* in his
house: and his righteousness[6666] endureth
for ever.[5703]
4 [a]Unto the upright there ariseth
light[216] in the darkness:[2822] *he is* gracious,[2587] and full of compassion, and
righteous.[6662]
5 [a]A good[2896] man sheweth
favour,[2603] and lendeth: he will guide his
affairs[1697] [b]with [I]discretion.[4941]
6 Surely [a]he shall not be moved for
ever:[5769] [b]the righteous shall be in everlasting[5769] remembrance.[2143]
7 [a]He shall not be afraid[3372] of
evil[7451] tidings: his [b]heart[3820] is fixed,[3559]
[c]trusting[982] in the LORD.
8 His heart *is* established,5564 [a]he
shall not be afraid, until he [b]see *his desire* upon his enemies.
9 [a]He hath dispersed, he hath given
to the poor; [b]his righteousness endureth
for ever; [c]his horn shall be exalted with
honour.[3519]
10 [a]The wicked[7563] shall see *it*, and
be grieved;[3707] [b]he shall gnash2786 with
his teeth, and [c]melt away: [d]the desire of
the wicked shall perish.[6]

God Raises up the Humble

113 [I]Praise[1984] ye the LORD. [a]Praise,
O ye servants[5650] of the LORD,
praise the name of the LORD.
2 [a]Blessed[1288] be the name of the
LORD from this time forth and for evermore.[5769]
3 [a]From the rising of the sun unto
the going down of the same the LORD's
name *is* to be praised.[1984]
4 The LORD *is* [a]high above all
nations,[1471] *and* [b]his glory[3519] above the
heavens.8064

3 [a]Isa. 59:19; Mal. 1:11 4 [a]Ps. 97:9; 99:2 [b]Ps. 8:1

🗝 **112:2, 3** Neither the acquisition nor the possession of earthly riches is forbidden, but the worshiping of wealth is prohibited (cf. Job 22:23, 24; Prov. 15:6; see also Matt. 6:19, 21; Luke 6:20, 24; 12:21; James 5:1–3).

5 [a]Who *is* like unto the LORD our God,[430] who [I]dwelleth on high,

6 [a]Who humbleth *himself* to behold[7200] *the things that are* in heaven,8064 and in the earth![776]

7 [a]He raiseth up the poor out of the dust,[6083] *and* lifteth the needy out of the dunghill;

8 That he may [a]set *him* with princes,[5081] *even* with the princes of his people.[5971]

9 [a]He maketh the barren woman6135 [I]to keep house, *and to be* a joyful mother of children. Praise ye the LORD.

A Song for the Passover Feast

114 When [a]Israel went out of Egypt, the house[1004] of Jacob [b]from a people[5971] of strange language;[3937]

2 [a]Judah was his sanctuary,[6944] *and* Israel his dominion.[4475]

3 [a]The sea saw[7200] *it,* and fled: [b]Jordan was driven back.

4 [a]The mountains skipped7540 like rams, *and* the little hills like lambs.

5 [a]What *ailed* thee, O thou sea, that thou fleddest? thou Jordan, *that* thou wast driven back?

6 Ye mountains, *that* ye skipped like rams; *and* ye little hills, like lambs?

7 Tremble,[2342] thou earth,[776] at the presence of the LORD,[113] at the presence of the God[433] of Jacob;

8 [a]Which turned[2015] the rock *into* a standing water, the flint into a fountain of waters.

The One True God

115 Not [a]unto us, O LORD, not unto us, but unto thy name give glory,[3519] for thy mercy,[2617] *and* for thy truth's sake.

2 Wherefore should the heathen[1471] say, [a]Where *is* now their God?[430]

3 [a]But our God *is* in the heavens: he hath done[6213] whatsoever he hath pleased.[2654]

4 [a]Their idols[6091] *are* silver and gold, the work of men's[120] hands.[3027]

5 They have mouths,[6310] but they speak[1696] not: eyes have they, but they see not:

6 They have ears,[241] but they hear[8085] not: noses have they, but they smell[7306] not:

7 They have hands, but they handle not: feet have they, but they walk not: neither speak[1897] they through their throat.

8 [a]They that make them are like unto them; *so is* every one that trusteth in them.

9 [a]O Israel, trust[982] thou in the LORD: [b]he *is* their help and their shield.

10 O house[1004] of Aaron, trust in the LORD: he *is* their help and their shield.

11 Ye that fear[3373] the LORD, trust in the LORD: he *is* their help and their shield.

12 The LORD hath been mindful[2142] of us: he will bless *us;* he will bless[1288] the house of Israel; he will bless the house of Aaron.

13 [a]He will bless them that fear the LORD, *both* small [I]and great.

14 The LORD shall increase you more and more, you and your children.[1121]

15 Ye *are* [a]blessed of the LORD [b]which made[6213] heaven8064 and earth.[776]

16 The heaven, *even* the heavens, *are* the LORD's: but the earth hath he given to the children of men.[120]

17 [a]The dead[4191] praise[1984] not the LORD, neither any that go down into silence.

18 [a]But we will bless the LORD from this time forth and for evermore.[5769] Praise the LORD.

Rescued From Death

116 I [a]love[157] the LORD, because he hath heard[8085] my voice *and* my supplications.[8469]

2 Because he hath inclined his ear[241] unto me, therefore will I call upon *him* [I]as long as I live.

3 [a]The sorrows[2256] of death[4194] compassed me, and the pains of hell[7585] [I]gat hold upon4672 me: I found trouble and sorrow.

4 Then called[7121] I upon the name of

113:5 [I]Hebr. *exalteth himself to dwell* [a]Ps. 89:6
6 [a]Ps. 11:4; 138:6; Isa. 57:15
7 [a]1Sam. 2:8; Ps. 107:41
8 [a]Job 36:7
9 [I]Hebr. *to dwell in a house* [a]1Sam. 2:5; Ps. 68:6; Isa. 54:1; Gal. 4:27

114:1 [a]Ex. 13:3 [b]Ps. 81:5
2 [a]Ex. 6:7; 19:6; 25:8; 29:45, 46; Deut. 27:9
3 [a]Ex. 14:21; Ps. 77:16 [b]Josh. 3:13, 16
4 [a]Ps. 29:6; 68:16; Hab. 3:6
5 [a]Hab. 3:8
8 [a]Ex. 17:6; Num. 20:11; Ps. 107:35

115:1 [a]Isa. 48:11; Ezek. 36:32
2 [a]Ps. 42:3, 10; 79:10; Joel 2:17
3 [a]1Chr. 16:26; Ps. 135:6; Dan. 4:35
4 [a]Deut. 4:28; Ps. 135:15-17; Jer. 10:3
8 [a]Ps. 135:18; Isa. 44:9, 10, 11; Jon. 2:8; Hab. 2:18, 19
9 [a]Ps. 118:2-4; 135:19, 20 [b]Ps. 33:20; Prov. 30:5
13 [I]Hebr. *with* [a]Ps. 128:1, 4
15 [a]Gen. 14:19 [b]Gen. 1:1; Ps. 96:5
17 [a]Ps. 6:5; 88:10, 11, 12; Isa. 38:18
18 [a]Ps. 113:2; Dan. 2:20

116:1 [a]Ps. 18:1
2 [I]Hebr. *in my days*
3 [I]Hebr. *found me* [a]Ps. 18:4-6

the LORD; O LORD, I beseech[577] thee, deliver my soul.[5315]
5 [a]Gracious[2587] *is* the LORD, and
[b]righteous;[6662] yea, our God[430] *is* merciful.
6 The LORD preserveth[8104] the simple:
I was brought low, and he helped[3467] me.
7 Return[7725] unto thy [a]rest, O my
soul; for [b]the LORD hath dealt bountifully[1580] with thee.
8 [a]For thou hast delivered[2502] my
soul from death, mine eyes from tears,
and my feet from falling.
9 I will walk before the LORD [a]in the
land of the living.[2416]
10 [a]I believed,[539] therefore have I spoken:[1696] I was greatly afflicted:
11 [a]I said[559] in my haste, [b]All men[120]
are liars.[3576]
12 What shall I render[7725] unto the
LORD *for* all his benefits toward me?
13 I will take[5375] the cup of salvation,[3444] and call[7121] upon the name of
the LORD.
14 [a]I will pay my vows[5088] unto the
LORD now in the presence of all his people.[5971]
15 [a]Precious in the sight of the LORD
is the death of his saints.[2623]
16 O LORD, truly [a]I *am* thy servant;[5650] I *am* thy servant, *and* [b]the
son[1121] of thine handmaid: thou hast
loosed my bonds.
17 I will offer[2076] to thee [a]the sacrifice[2077] of thanksgiving,[8426] and will call
upon the name of the LORD.
18 [a]I will pay my vows unto the
LORD now in the presence of all his people,
19 In the [a]courts of the LORD's house,
in the midst of thee, O Jerusalem.
Praise[1984] ye the LORD.

Praise the Lord

117 O [a]praise[1984] the LORD, all ye
nations:[1471] praise[7623] him, all
ye people.[523]
2 For his merciful kindness[2617] is
great toward us: and [a]the truth[571] of the
LORD *endureth* for ever.[5769] Praise ye the
LORD.

Thanksgiving

118 O [a]give thanks[3034] unto the
LORD; for *he is* good:[2896] be-
cause his mercy[2617] *endureth* for ever.[5769]
2 [a]Let Israel now say, that his mercy
endureth for ever.
3 Let the house[1004] of Aaron now
say, that his mercy *endureth* for ever.
4 Let them now that fear[3373] the
LORD say, that his mercy *endureth* for
ever.
5 [a]I called upon[7121] the LORD[3050] [I]in
distress: the LORD answered me, *and set*
me in a [b]large place.
6 [a]The LORD *is* [I]on my side; I will
not fear:[3372] what can man[120] do unto
me?
7 [a]The LORD taketh my part with
them that help me: therefore shall [b]I see
my desire upon them that hate[8130] me.
8 [a]*It is* better[2896] to trust[2620] in the
LORD than to put confidence[982] in man.
9 [a]*It is* better to trust in the LORD
than to put confidence in princes.[5081]
10 All nations[1471] compassed me
about: but in the name of the LORD will
I [I]destroy[4135] them.
11 They [a]compassed me about;
yea, they compassed me about: but in
the name of the LORD I will destroy
them.
12 They compassed me about [a]like
bees; they are quenched [b]as the fire of
thorns: for in the name of the LORD I will
[I]destroy them.
13 Thou hast thrust sore at me that
I might fall: but the LORD helped me.
14 [a]The LORD *is* my strength and
song, and is become[1961] my salvation.[3444]
15 The voice of rejoicing and salvation *is* in the tabernacles[168] of the righteous:[6662] the right hand of the LORD
doeth[6213] valiantly.[2428]
16 [a]The right hand of the LORD is exalted: the right hand of the LORD doeth
valiantly.
17 [a]I shall not die,[4191] but live,[2421]
and [b]declare[5608] the works of the LORD.
18 The LORD hath [a]chastened[3256] me
sore: but he hath not given me over unto
death.[4194]

5 [a]Ps. 103:8 [b]Ezra 9:15; Neh. 9:8; Ps. 119:137; 145:17
7 [a]Jer. 6:16; Matt. 11:29 [b]Ps. 13:6; 119:17
8 [a]Ps. 56:13
9 [a]Ps. 27:13
10 [a]2Cor. 4:13
11 [a]Ps. 31:22 [b]Rom. 3:4
14 [a]Ps. 22:25; 116:18; Jon. 2:9
15 [a]Ps. 72:14
16 [a]Ps. 119:125; 143:12 [b]Ps. 86:16
17 [a]Lev. 7:12; Ps. 50:14; 107:22
18 [a]Ps. 116:14
19 [a]Ps. 96:8; 100:4; 135:2

1 [a]Rom. 15:11
2 [a]Ps. 100:5

1 [a]1Chr. 16:8, 34; Ps. 106:1; 107:1; 136:1
2 [a]See Ps. 115:9-11
5 [I]Hebr. *out of distress* [a]Ps. 120:1 [b]Ps. 18:19
6 [I]Hebr. *for me* [a]Ps. 27:1; 56:4, 11; 146:5; Isa. 51:12; Heb. 13:6
7 [a]Ps. 54:4 [b]Ps. 59:10
8 [a]Ps. 40:4; 62:8, 9; Jer. 17:5, 7
9 [a]Ps. 146:3
10 [I]Hebr. *cut them off*
11 [a]Ps. 88:17
12 [I]Hebr. *cut down* [a]Deut. 1:44 [b]Eccl. 7:6; Nah. 1:10
14 [a]Ex. 15:2; Isa. 12:2
16 [a]Ex. 15:6
17 [a]Ps. 6:5; Hab. 1:12 [b]Ps. 73:28
18 [a]2Cor. 6:9

19 [a]Open to me the gates of righteousness:[6664] I will go into them, *and* I will praise[3034] the LORD:

20 [a]This gate of the LORD, [b]into which the righteous shall enter.

21 I will praise thee: for thou hast [a]heard me, and [b]art become my salvation.[3444]

🔑 22 [a]The stone *which* the builders[1129] refused is become the head[7218] *stone* of the corner.

23 [I]This is the LORD's doing; it *is* marvellous[6381] in our eyes.

24 This *is* the day[3117] *which* the LORD hath made;[6213] we will rejoice and be glad in it.

25 Save[3467] now, I beseech[577] thee, O LORD: O LORD, I beseech thee, send now prosperity.

26 [a]Blessed[1288] *be* he that cometh in the name of the LORD: we have blessed you out of the house of the LORD.

27 God[410] *is* the LORD, which hath shewed us [a]light:[215] bind the sacrifice with cords, *even* unto the horns of the altar.[4196]

28 Thou *art* my God, and I will praise thee: [a]*thou art* my God,[430] I will exalt thee.

29 [a]O give thanks unto the LORD; for *he is* good: for his mercy *endureth* for ever.

The Law of the Lord

Aleph

119 Blessed[835] *are* the [I]undefiled[8549] in the way,[1870] [a]who walk in the law[8451] of the LORD.

2 Blessed *are* they that keep[5341] his testimonies,[5713] *and that* seek him with the whole heart.[3820]

3 [a]They also do no iniquity:[5766] they walk in his ways.

4 Thou hast commanded[6680] *us* to keep[8104] thy precepts[6490] diligently.

19 [a]Isa. 26:2
20 [a]Ps. 24:7 [b]Isa. 35:8; Rev. 21:27; 22:14, 15
21 [a]Ps. 116:1 [b]Ps. 118:14
22 [a]Matt. 21:42; Mark 12:10; Luke 20:17; Acts 4:11; Eph. 2:20; 1Pet. 2:4, 7
23 [I]Hebr. *This is from the LORD*
26 [a]Zech. 4:7; Matt. 21:9; 23:39; Mark 11:9; Luke 19:38
27 [a]Esth. 8:16; 1Pet. 2:9
28 [a]Ex. 15:2; Isa. 25:1
29 [a]Ps. 118:1

1 [I]Or, *perfect,* or, *sincere* [a]Ps. 128:1
3 [a]1John 3:9; 5:18
6 [a]Job 22:26; 1John 2:28
7 [I]Hebr. *judgments of thy righteousness* [a]Ps. 119:171
10 [a]2Chr. 15:15 [b]Ps. 119:21, 118
11 [a]Ps. 37:31; Luke 2:19, 51
12 [a]Ps. 25:4; 119:26, 33, 64, 68, 108, 124
13 [a]Ps. 34:11
15 [a]Ps. 1:2; 119:23, 48, 78
16 [a]Ps. 1:2; 119:35, 47, 70, 77
17 [a]Ps. 116:7
18 [I]Hebr. *Reveal*
19 [a]Gen. 47:9; 1Chr. 29:15; Ps. 39:12; 2Cor. 5:6; Heb. 11:13
20 [a]Ps. 42:1, 2; 63:1; 84:2; 119:40, 131

5 O that my ways were directed to keep thy statutes![2706]

6 [a]Then shall I not be ashamed,[954] when I have respect[5027] unto all thy commandments.[4687]

7 [a]I will praise[3034] thee with uprightness[3476] of heart,[3824] when I shall have learned[3925] [I]thy righteous[6664] judgments.[4941]

8 I will keep thy statutes: O forsake[5800] me not utterly.

Beth

9 Wherewithal shall a young man cleanse his way?[734] by taking heed *thereto* according to thy word.[1697]

10 With my whole heart have I [a]sought thee: O let me not [b]wander[7686] from thy commandments.

11 [a]Thy word[565] have I hid in mine heart, that I might not sin[2398] against thee.

12 Blessed[1288] *art* thou, O LORD: [a]teach[3925] me thy statutes.

13 With my lips[8193] have I [a]declared[5608] all the judgments of thy mouth.[6310]

14 I have rejoiced in the way of thy testimonies,[5715] as *much as* in all riches.

15 I will [a]meditate[7878] in thy precepts, and have respect unto thy ways.[734]

16 I will [a]delight myself in thy statutes:[2708] I will not forget thy word.

Gimel

17 [a]Deal bountifully[1580] with thy servant,[5650] *that* I may live,[2421] and keep thy word.

18 [I]Open[1540] thou mine eyes, that I may behold wondrous things[6381] out of thy law.

19 [a]I am a stranger in the earth:[776] hide not thy commandments from me.

20 [a]My soul[5315] breaketh for the

🔑 **118:22** See note on Isaiah 8:14 regarding the imagery of a stone and the note on Psalm 22:1–31 for a discussion of the Messianic Psalms.

longing *that it hath* unto thy judgments at all times.[6256]

21 Thou hast rebuked[1605] the proud[2086] *that are* cursed,[779] which do [a]err[7686] from thy commandments.

22 [a]Remove[1556] from me reproach[2781] and contempt; for I have kept[5341] thy testimonies.

23 Princes[8269] also did sit *and* speak[1696] against me: *but* thy servant did [a]meditate in thy statutes.

24 [a]Thy testimonies also *are* my delight[8191] *and* [I]my counsellors.

Daleth

25 [a]My soul cleaveth unto the dust:[6083] [b]quicken[2421] thou me according to thy word.

26 I have declared my ways, and thou heardest me: [a]teach me thy statutes.

27 Make me to understand[995] the way of thy precepts: so [a]shall I talk[7878] of thy wondrous works.[6381]

28 [a]My soul [I]melteth for heaviness:[8424] strengthen thou me according unto thy word.

29 Remove from me the way of lying: and grant me thy law graciously.

30 I have chosen[977] the way of truth:[530] thy judgments have I laid *before me.*

31 I have stuck unto thy testimonies: O LORD, put me not to shame.[954]

32 I will run the way of thy commandments, when thou shalt [a]enlarge my heart.

He

33 [a]Teach[3384] me, O LORD, the way of thy statutes; and I shall keep it [b]*unto* the end.

34 [a]Give me understanding,[995] and I shall keep thy law; yea, I shall observe[8104] it with *my* whole heart.

35 Make me to go in the path of thy commandments; for therein do I [a]delight.[2654]

36 Incline my heart unto thy testimonies, and not to [a]covetousness.[1215]

37 [Ia]Turn away[5674] mine eyes from [b]beholding[7200] vanity;[7723] *and* [c]quicken thou me in thy way.

38 [a]Stablish thy word unto thy servant, who *is devoted* to thy fear.[3374]

39 Turn away my reproach which I fear:[3025] for thy judgments *are* good.[2896]

40 Behold, I have [a]longed after thy precepts: [b]quicken me in thy righteousness.[6666]

Waw

41 [a]Let thy mercies[2617] come also unto me, O LORD, *even* thy salvation,[8668] according to thy word.

42 [I]So shall I have wherewith to answer him that reproacheth me: for I trust[982] in thy word.

43 And take not the word of truth[571] utterly out of my mouth; for I have hoped[3176] in thy judgments.

44 So shall I keep thy law continually[8548] for ever[5769] and ever.[5703]

45 And I will walk [I]at liberty:[7342] for I seek thy precepts.

46 [a]I will speak of thy testimonies also before kings,[4428] and will not be ashamed.

47 And I will [a]delight myself in thy commandments, which I have loved.[157]

48 My hands[3709] also will I lift up[5375] unto thy commandments, which I have loved; and I will [a]meditate in thy statutes.

Zayin

49 Remember[2142] the word unto thy servant, upon which thou hast caused me to [a]hope.[3176]

50 This *is* my [a]comfort[5162] in my affliction: for thy word hath quickened[2421] me.

51 The proud have had me greatly [a]in derision:[3887] *yet* have I not [b]declined from thy law.

---

21 [a]Ps. 119:10, 110, 118
22 [a]Ps. 39:8
23 [a]Ps. 119:15
24 [I]Hebr. *men of my counsel* [a]Ps. 119:77, 92
25 [a]Ps. 44:25 [b]Ps. 119:40; 143:11
26 [a]Ps. 25:4; 27:11; 86:11
27 [a]Ps. 145:5, 6
28 [I]Hebr. *droppeth* [a]Ps. 107:26
32 [a]1Kgs. 4:29; Isa. 60:5; 2Cor. 6:11
33 [a]Ps. 119:12 [b]Ps. 119:112; Matt. 10:22; Rev. 2:26
34 [a]Ps. 119:73; Prov. 2:6; James 1:5
35 [a]Ps. 119:16
36 [a]Ezek. 33:31; Mark 7:21, 22; Luke 12:15; 1Tim. 6:10; Heb. 13:5
37 [I]Hebr. *Make to pass* [a]Isa. 33:15 [b]Prov. 23:5 [c]Ps. 119:40
38 [a]2Sam. 7:25
40 [a]Ps. 119:20 [b]Ps. 119:25, 37, 88, 107, 149, 156, 159
41 [a]Ps. 106:4; 119:77
42 [I]Or, *So shall I answer him that reproacheth me in a thing*
45 [I]Hebr. *at large*
46 [a]Ps. 138:1; Matt. 10:18, 19; Acts 26:1, 2
47 [a]Ps. 119:16
48 [a]Ps. 119:15
49 [a]Ps. 119:74, 81, 147
50 [a]Rom. 15:4
51 [a]Jer. 20:7 [b]Job 23:11; Ps. 44:18; 119:157

52 I remembered[2142] thy judgments of old,[5769] O LORD; and have comforted[5162] myself.

53 [a]Horror[2152] hath taken hold upon me because of the wicked[7563] that forsake thy law.

54 Thy statutes have been my songs in the house[1004] of my pilgrimage.[4033]

55 [a]I have remembered thy name, O LORD, in the night,[3915] and have kept[8104] thy law.

56 This I had, because I kept thy precepts.

Cheth

57 [a]*Thou art* my portion, O LORD: I have said[559] that I would keep thy words.[1697]

58 I intreated thy [I]favour with *my* whole heart: be merciful[2603] unto me [a]according to thy word.

59 I [a]thought on[2803] my ways, and turned my feet unto thy testimonies.

60 I made haste, and delayed not to keep thy commandments.

61 The [I]bands[2256] of the wicked have robbed[5749] me: *but* I have not forgotten thy law.

62 [a]At midnight I will rise to give thanks[3034] unto thee because of thy righteous judgments.

63 I *am* a companion of all *them* that fear[3372] thee, and of them that keep thy precepts.

64 [a]The earth, O LORD, is full of thy mercy:[2617] [b]teach me thy statutes.

Teth

65 Thou hast dealt[6213] well with thy servant, O LORD, according unto thy word.

66 Teach me good[2898] judgment[2940] and knowledge:[1847] for I have believed[539] thy commandments.

67 [a]Before I was afflicted I went astray:[7683] but now have I kept thy word.

68 Thou *art* [a]good,[2895] and doest good; [b]teach me thy statutes.

69 The proud have [a]forged[2950] a lie against me: *but* I will keep thy precepts with *my* whole heart.

70 [a]Their heart is as fat as grease; *but* I [b]delight in thy law.

71 [a]*It is* good for me that I have been afflicted; that I might learn[3925] thy statutes.

72 [a]The law of thy mouth *is* better[2896] unto me than thousands[505] of gold and silver.

Yodh

73 [a]Thy hands have made[6213] me and fashioned[3559] me: [b]give me understanding, that I may learn thy commandments.

74 [a]They that fear[3373] thee will be glad when they see me; because [b]I have hoped in thy word.

75 I know, O LORD, that thy judgments *are* [I]right,[6664] and [a]*that* thou in faithfulness[530] hast afflicted me.

76 Let, I pray thee, thy merciful kindness[2617] be [I]for my comfort, according to thy word unto thy servant.

77 [a]Let thy tender mercies[7356] come unto me, that I may live: for [b]thy law *is* my delight.

78 Let the proud [a]be ashamed; [b]for they dealt perversely[5791] with me without a cause:[8267] *but* I will [c]meditate in thy precepts.

79 Let those that fear thee turn[7725] unto me, and those that have known[3045] thy testimonies.

80 Let my heart be sound[8549] in thy statutes; that I be not ashamed.

Kaph

81 [a]My soul fainteth[3615] for thy salvation: *but* [b]I hope in thy word.

82 [a]Mine eyes fail[3615] for thy word, saying, When wilt thou comfort me?

83 For [a]I am become[1961] like a bottle in the smoke; *yet* do I not forget thy statutes.

84 [a]How many *are* the days[3117] of thy servant? [b]when wilt thou execute judgment[4941] on them that persecute me?

---

53 [a]Ezra 9:3
55 [a]Ps. 63:6
57 [a]Ps. 16:5; Jer. 10:16; Lam. 3:24
58 [I]Hebr. *face,* Job 11:19 [a]Ps. 119:41
59 [a]Luke 15:17, 18
61 [I]Or, *companies*
62 [a]Acts 16:25
64 [a]Ps. 33:5 [b]Ps. 119:12, 26
67 [a]Ps. 119:71; Jer. 31:18, 19; Heb. 12:11
68 [a]Ps. 106:1; 107:1; Matt. 19:17 [b]Ps. 119:12, 26
69 [a]Job 13:4; Ps. 109:2
70 [a]Ps. 17:10; Isa. 6:10; Acts 28:27 [b]Ps. 119:35
71 [a]Ps. 119:67; Heb. 12:10, 11
72 [a]Ps. 19:10; 119:127; Prov. 8:10, 11, 19
73 [a]Job 10:8; Ps. 100:3; 138:8; 139:14 [b]Ps. 119:34, 144
74 [a]Ps. 34:2 [b]Ps. 119:49, 147
75 [I]Hebr. *righteousness* [a]Heb. 12:10
76 [I]Hebr. *to comfort me*
77 [a]Ps. 119:41 [b]Ps. 119:24, 47, 174
78 [a]Ps. 25:3 [b]Ps. 119:86 [c]Ps. 119:23
81 [a]Ps. 73:26; 84:2 [b]Ps. 119:74, 114
82 [a]Ps. 69:3; 119:123
83 [a]Job 30:30
84 [a]Ps. 39:4 [b]Rev. 6:10

85 [a]The proud have digged pits[7882] for me, which *are* not after thy law.

86 All thy commandments *are* [I]faithful:[530] [a]they persecute me [b]wrongfully;[8267] help thou me.

87 They had almost consumed[3615] me upon earth; but I forsook[5800] not thy precepts.

88 [a]Quicken me after thy lovingkindness; so shall I keep the testimony[5715] of thy mouth.

Lamedh

89 [a]For ever,[5769] O LORD, thy word is settled[5324] in heaven.[8064]

90 Thy faithfulness *is* [I][a]unto all generations:[1755] thou hast established[3559] the earth, and it [II]abideth.

91 They continue this day[3117] according to [a]thine ordinances:[4941] for all *are* thy servants.[5650]

92 Unless [a]thy law *had been* my delights, I should then have perished[6] in mine affliction.

93 I will never forget thy precepts: for with them thou hast quickened me.

94 I *am* thine, save[3467] me; for I have sought thy precepts.

95 The wicked have waited[6960] for me to destroy[6] me: *but* I will consider[995] thy testimonies.

96 [a]I have seen[7200] an end of all perfection: *but* thy commandment[4687] *is* exceeding broad.

Mem

97 O how love[157] I thy law! [a]it *is* my meditation[7881] all the day.

98 Thou through thy commandments hast made me [a]wiser[2449] than mine enemies: for [I]they *are* ever with me.

99 I have more understanding than all my teachers:[3925] [a]for thy testimonies *are* my meditation.

100 [a]I understand more than the ancients,[2205] because I keep thy precepts.

101 I have [a]refrained my feet from every evil[7451] way, that I might keep thy word.

102 I have not departed[5493] from thy judgments: for thou hast taught[3384] me.

103 [a]How sweet are thy words[565] unto my [I]taste! *yea, sweeter* than honey to my mouth!

104 Through thy precepts I get understanding: therefore [a]I hate[8130] every false[8267] way.

Nun

105 [a]Thy word *is* a [I]lamp[5216] unto my feet, and a light[216] unto my path.

106 [a]I have sworn, and I will perform *it,* that I will keep thy righteous judgments.

107 I am afflicted very much: [a]quicken me, O LORD, according unto thy word.

108 Accept,[7521] I beseech thee,[4994] [a]the freewill offerings[5071] of my mouth, O LORD, and [b]teach me thy judgments.

109 [a]My soul *is* continually in my hand: yet do I not forget thy law.

110 [a]The wicked have laid a snare[6341] for me: yet I [b]erred[8582] not from thy precepts.

111 [a]Thy testimonies have I taken as an heritage[5157] for ever: for [b]they *are* the rejoicing of my heart.

112 I have inclined mine heart [I]to perform[6213] thy statutes alway, [a]*even unto* the end.

Samekh

113 I hate vain thoughts:[5588] but thy law do I love.

114 [a]Thou *art* my hiding place and my shield: [b]I hope in thy word.

115 [a]Depart[5493] from me, ye evildoers:[7489] for I will keep the commandments of my God.[430]

116 Uphold me according unto thy word, that I may live: and let me not [a]be ashamed of my hope.

117 Hold thou me up, and I shall be safe:[3467] and I will have respect[8159] unto thy statutes continually.

118 Thou hast trodden down all them that [a]err from thy statutes: for their deceit *is* falsehood.

85 [a]Ps. 35:7; Prov. 16:27
86 [I]Hebr. *faithfulness* [a]Ps. 119:78 [b]Ps. 35:19; 38:19
88 [a]Ps. 119:40
89 [a]Ps. 89:2; Matt. 24:34, 35; 1Pet. 1:25
90 [I]Hebr. *to generation and generation* [II]Hebr. *standeth* [a]Ps. 89:1
91 [a]Jer. 33:25
92 [a]Ps. 119:24
96 [a]Matt. 5:18; 24:35
97 [a]Ps. 1:2
98 [I]Hebr. *it is ever with me* [a]Deut. 4:6, 8
99 [a]2Tim. 3:15
100 [a]Job 32:7-9
101 [a]Prov. 1:15
103 [I]Hebr. *palate* [a]Ps. 19:10; Prov. 8:11
104 [a]Ps. 119:128
105 [I]Or, *candle* [a]Prov. 6:23
106 [a]Neh. 10:29
107 [a]Ps. 119:88
108 [a]Hos. 14:2; Heb. 13:15 [b]Ps. 119:12, 26
109 [a]Job 13:14
110 [a]Ps. 140:5; 141:9 [b]Ps. 119:10, 21
111 [a]Deut. 33:4 [b]Ps. 119:77, 92, 174
112 [I]Hebr. *to do* [a]Ps. 119:33
114 [a]Ps. 32:7; 91:1 [b]Ps. 119:81
115 [a]Ps. 6:8; 139:19; Matt. 7:23
116 [a]Ps. 25:2; Rom. 5:5; 9:33; 10:11
118 [a]Ps. 119:21

119 Thou [I]puttest away[7673] all the wicked of the earth [a]*like* dross:[5509] therefore I love thy testimonies.

120 [a]My flesh[1320] trembleth for fear of thee; and I am afraid[3372] of thy judgments.

Ayin

121 I have done[6213] judgment and justice:[6664] leave me not to mine oppressors.

122 Be [a]surety[6148] for thy servant for good: let not the proud oppress me.

123 [a]Mine eyes fail for thy salvation,[3444] and for the word of thy righteousness.[6664]

124 Deal[6213] with thy servant according unto thy mercy, and [a]teach me thy statutes.

125 [a]I *am* thy servant; give me understanding, that I may know thy testimonies.

126 *It is* time[6256] for *thee,* LORD, to work:[6213] *for* they have made void[6565] thy law.

127 [a]Therefore I love thy commandments above gold; yea, above fine gold.

128 Therefore I esteem all *thy* precepts *concerning* all *things to be* right;[3474] *and* I [a]hate every false way.

Pe

129 Thy testimonies *are* wonderful:[6382] therefore doth my soul keep them.

130 The entrance of thy words giveth light; [a]it giveth understanding[995] unto the simple.

131 I opened my mouth, and panted: for I [a]longed for thy commandments.

132 [a]Look thou upon me, and be merciful unto me, [I][b]as thou usest to do[4941] unto those that love thy name.

133 [a]Order[3559] my steps in thy word: and [b]let not any iniquity[205] have dominion[7980] over me.

134 [a]Deliver[6299] me from the oppression of man:[120] so will I keep thy precepts.

135 [a]Make thy face to shine upon thy servant; and [b]teach me thy statutes.

136 [a]Rivers of waters run down mine eyes, because they keep not thy law.

Tsadde

137 [a]Righteous[6662] *art* thou, O LORD, and upright *are* thy judgments.

138 [a]Thy testimonies *that* thou hast commanded *are* [I]righteous and very [II]faithful.

139 [a]My zeal[7068] hath [I]consumed[6789] me, because mine enemies have forgotten thy words.

140 [a]Thy word *is* very [I]pure:[6884] therefore thy servant loveth[157] it.

141 I *am* small and despised: *yet* do not I forget thy precepts.

142 Thy righteousness *is* an everlasting[5769] righteousness, and thy law *is* [a]the truth.

143 Trouble and anguish[4689] have [I]taken hold on me: *yet* thy commandments *are* [a]my delights.

144 The righteousness of thy testimonies *is* everlasting: [a]give me understanding, and I shall live.

Qoph

145 I cried[7121] with *my* whole heart; hear[6030] me, O LORD: I will keep thy statutes.

146 I cried unto thee; save me, [I]and I shall keep thy testimonies.

147 [a]I prevented[6923] the dawning of the morning, and cried: [b]I hoped in thy word.

148 [a]Mine eyes prevent the *night* watches, that I might meditate in thy word.

149 Hear my voice according unto thy lovingkindness: O LORD, [a]quicken me according to thy judgment.

150 They draw nigh that follow after mischief: they are far from thy law.

151 Thou *art* [a]near, O LORD; [b]and all thy commandments *are* truth.

152 Concerning thy testimonies, I have known of old[6924] that thou hast founded[3245] them [a]for ever.

---

119 IHebr. *causest to cease* aEzek. 22:18
120 aHab. 3:16
122 aHeb. 7:22
123 aPs. 119:81, 82
124 aPs. 119:12
125 aPs. 116:16
127 aPs. 119:10; 119:72; Prov. 8:11
128 aPs. 119:104
130 aPs. 19:7; Prov. 1:4
131 aPs. 119:20
132 IHebr. *according to the custom towards those* aPs. 106:4 b2Thess. 1:6, 7
133 aPs. 17:5 bPs. 19:13; Rom. 6:12
134 aLuke 1:74
135 aPs. 4:6 bPs. 119:12, 26
136 aJer. 9:1; 14:17; Ezek. 9:4
137 aEzra 9:15; Neh. 9:33; Jer. 12:1; Dan. 9:7
138 IHebr. *righteousness* IIHebr. *faithfulness* aPs. 19:7-9
139 IHebr. *cut me off* aPs. 69:9; John 2:17
140 IHebr. *tried, or, refined* aPs. 12:6; 18:30; 19:8; Prov. 30:5
142 aPs. 19:9; 119:151; John 17:17
143 IHebr. *found me* aPs. 119:77
144 aPs. 119:34, 73, 169
146 Ior, *that I may keep*
147 aPs. 5:3; 88:13; 130:6 bPs. 119:74
148 aPs. 63:1, 6
149 aPs. 119:40, 154
151 aPs. 145:18 bPs. 119:142
152 aLuke 21:33

Resh

153 [a]Consider[7200] mine affliction, and deliver[2502] me: for I do not forget thy law.

154 [a]Plead my cause,[7379] and deliver me: [b]quicken me according to thy word.

155 [a]Salvation *is* far from the wicked: for they seek not thy statutes.

156 [I]Great *are* thy tender mercies,[7356] O LORD: [a]quicken me according to thy judgments.

157 Many *are* my persecutors and mine enemies; *yet* do I not [a]decline from thy testimonies.

158 I beheld the transgressors,[898] and [a]was grieved; because they kept not thy word.

159 Consider how I love thy precepts: [a]quicken me, O LORD, according to thy lovingkindness.

160 [I]Thy word *is* true[571] *from* the beginning:[7218] and every one of thy righteous judgments *endureth* for ever.

Shin

161 [a]Princes have persecuted me without a cause: but my heart standeth in awe[6342] of thy word.

162 I rejoice at thy word, as one that findeth great spoil.

163 I hate and abhor[8581] lying: *but* thy law do I love.

164 Seven times a day do I praise[1984] thee because of thy righteous judgments.

165 [a]Great peace have they which love thy law: and [I]nothing shall offend[4383] them.

166 [a]LORD, I have hoped for thy salvation, and done thy commandments.

167 My soul hath kept thy testimonies; and I love them exceedingly.

168 I have kept thy precepts and thy testimonies: [a]for all my ways *are* before thee.

Taw

169 Let my cry come near[7126] before thee, O LORD: [a]give me understanding according to thy word.

170 Let my supplication come before thee: deliver[5337] me according to thy word.

171 [a]My lips shall utter praise,[8416] when thou hast taught[3925] me thy statutes.

172 My tongue shall speak of thy word: for all thy commandments *are* righteousness.

173 Let thine hand[3027] help me; for [a]I have chosen thy precepts.

174 [a]I have longed for thy salvation, O LORD; and [b]thy law *is* my delight.

175 Let my soul live, and it shall praise thee; and let thy judgments help me.

176 [a]I have gone astray[8582] like a lost[6] sheep; seek thy servant; for I do not forget thy commandments.

A Prayer for Deliverance

A Song of degrees.

120 In [a]my distress I cried[7121] unto the LORD, and he heard me.

2 Deliver[5337] my soul,[5315] O LORD, from lying lips,[8193] *and* from a deceitful tongue.

3 [I]What shall be given unto thee? or what shall be [II]done unto thee, thou false tongue?

4 [I]Sharp arrows of the mighty, with coals of juniper.

5 Woe is me, that I sojourn[1481] in [a]Mesech, [b]*that* I dwell[7931] in the tents[168] of Kedar!

6 My soul hath long dwelt[7931] with him that hateth peace.

7 I *am* [I]*for* peace: but when I speak,[1696] they *are* for war.

Help Comes From the Lord

A Song of degrees.

121 [I][a]I will lift up[5375] mine eyes unto the hills, from whence cometh my help.

2 [a]My help *cometh* from the LORD, which made[6213] heaven8064 and earth.[776]

3 [a]He will not suffer thy foot to be

119:153 [a]Lam. 5:1
154 [a]1Sam. 24:15; Ps. 35:1; Mic. 7:9 [b]Ps. 119:40
155 [a]Job 5:4
156 [I]Or, *Many* [a]Ps. 119:149
157 [a]Ps. 44:18; 119:51
158 [a]Ps. 119:136; Ezek. 9:4
159 [a]Ps. 119:88
160 [I]Hebr. *The beginning of thy word is true*
161 [a]1Sam. 24:11, 14; 26:18; Ps. 119:23
165 [I]Hebr. *they shall have no stumbling block* [a]Prov. 3:2; Isa. 32:17
166 [a]Gen. 49:18; Ps. 119:174
168 [a]Prov. 5:21
169 [a]Ps. 119:144
171 [a]Ps. 119:17
173 [a]Josh. 24:22; Prov. 1:29; Luke 10:42
174 [a]Ps. 119:166 [b]Ps. 119:16, 24, 47, 77, 111
176 [a]Isa. 53:6; Luke 15:4; 1Pet. 2:25

120:1 [a]Ps. 118:5; Jon. 2:2
3 [I]Or, *What shall the deceitful tongue give unto thee? or, What shall it profit thee?* [II]Hebr. *added*
4 [I]Or, It is as *the sharp arrows of the mighty man, with coals of juniper*
5 [a]Gen. 10:2; Ezek. 27:13 [b]Gen. 25:13; 1Sam. 25:1; Jer. 49:28, 29
7 [I]Or, a man *of peace*

121:1 [I]Or, *Shall I lift up mine eyes to the hills? whence should my help come?* [a]Jer. 3:23
2 [a]Ps. 124:8
3 [a]1Sam. 2:9; Prov. 3:23, 26

moved: [b]he that keepeth[8104] thee will not
slumber.
4 Behold, he that keepeth Israel shall
neither slumber nor sleep.
5 The LORD *is* thy keeper:[8104] the
LORD *is* [a]thy shade [b]upon thy right
hand.[3027]
6 [a]The sun shall not smite[5221] thee
by day,[3119] nor the moon by night.[3915]
7 The LORD shall preserve[8104] thee
from all evil:[7451] he shall [a]preserve thy
soul.[5315]
8 The LORD shall [a]preserve thy going
out and thy coming in from this time
forth, and even for evermore.[5769]

Jerusalem

A Song of degrees of David.

122 I was glad when they said[559]
unto me, [a]Let us go into the
house[1004] of the LORD.
2 Our feet shall stand within thy
gates, O Jerusalem.
3 Jerusalem is builded as a city that
is [a]compact[2266] together:
4 [a]Whither the tribes[7626] go up, the
tribes of the LORD, unto [b]the testimony[5715] of Israel, to give thanks[3034]
unto the name of the LORD.
5 [a]For there [1]are set thrones[3678] of
judgment,[4941] the thrones of the house
of David.
6 [a]Pray for the peace of Jerusalem:
they shall prosper that love[157] thee.
7 Peace be within thy walls, *and*
prosperity within thy palaces.[759]
8 For my brethren[251] and companions' sakes, I will now say,[1696] Peace *be*
within thee.
9 Because of the house of the LORD
our God[430] I will [a]seek thy good.[2896]

A Prayer for Mercy

A Song of degrees.

123 Unto thee [a]lift I up mine eyes,
O thou [b]that dwellest in the
heavens.[8064]
2 Behold, as the eyes of servants[5650]
look unto the hand[3027] of their masters,[113] *and* as the eyes of a maiden unto
the hand of her mistress;[1404] so our eyes
wait upon the LORD our God,[430] until that
he have mercy[2603] upon us.
3 Have mercy upon us, O LORD, have
mercy upon us: for we are exceedingly
filled with contempt.
4 Our soul[5315] is exceedingly filled
with the scorning of those that are at
ease, *and* with the contempt of the
proud.[3238]

God Protects His People

A Song of degrees of David.

124 If *it had not been* the LORD
who was on our side, [a]now
may Israel say;[559]
2 If *it had not been* the LORD who
was on our side, when men[120] rose up
against us:
3 Then they had [a]swallowed us
up[1104] quick,[2416] when their wrath[639] was
kindled[2734] against us:
4 Then the waters had overwhelmed[7857] us, the stream had gone
over our soul:[5315]
5 Then the proud waters had gone
over our soul.
6 Blessed[1288] *be* the LORD, who
hath not given us *as* a prey to their
teeth.
7 Our soul is escaped[4422] [a]as a bird
out of the snare of the fowlers:[3369] the
snare[6341] is broken,[7665] and we are escaped.
8 [a]Our help *is* in the name of the
LORD, [b]who made[6213] heaven[8064] and
earth.[776]

God Surrounds His People

A Song of degrees.

125 They that trust[982] in the LORD
shall be as mount Zion, *which*
cannot be removed, *but* abideth for
ever.[5769]
2 As the mountains *are* round about
Jerusalem, so the LORD *is* [a]round about
his people[5971] from henceforth even for
ever.

3 [b]Ps. 127:1; Isa. 27:3
5 [a]Isa. 25:4 [b]Ps. 16:8; 109:31
6 [a]Ps. 91:5; Isa. 49:10; Rev. 7:16
7 [a]Ps. 41:2; 97:10; 145:20
8 [a]Deut. 28:6; Prov. 2:8; 3:6
1 [a]Isa. 2:3; Zech. 8:21
3 [a]2Sam. 5:9
4 [a]Ex. 23:17; Deut. 16:16 [b]Ex. 16:34
5 [1]Hebr. *do sit* [a]Deut. 17:8; 2Chr. 19:8
6 [a]Ps. 51:18
9 [a]Neh. 2:10
1 [a]Ps. 121:1; 141:8 [b]Ps. 2:4; 11:4; 115:3
1 [a]Ps. 129:1
3 [a]Ps. 56:1, 2; 57:3; Prov. 1:12
7 [a]Ps. 91:3; Prov. 6:5
8 [a]Ps. 121:2 [b]Gen. 1:1; Ps. 134:3
2 [a]Ps. 34:7; 89:8

3 For [a]the rod of [I]the wicked[7562] shall not rest upon the lot of the righteous;[6662] lest the righteous put forth their hands[3027] unto iniquity.[5766]

4 Do good,[2895] O LORD, unto *those that be* good,[2896] and to *them that are* upright in their hearts.[3826]

5 As for such as turn aside unto their [a]crooked ways, the LORD shall lead them forth with the workers of iniquity:[205] *but* [b]peace *shall be* upon Israel.

Thanksgiving for Restoration

A Song of degrees.

126 When the LORD [I][a]turned again[7725] the captivity[7622] of Zion, [b]we were like them that dream.

2 Then [a]was our mouth[6310] filled with laughter, and our tongue with singing: then said[559] they among the heathen,[1471] The LORD [I]hath done[6213] great things for them.

3 The LORD hath done great things for us; *whereof* we are glad.

4 Turn again our captivity, O LORD, as the streams in the south.

5 [a]They that sow in tears shall reap in [I]joy.[7440]

6 He that goeth forth and weepeth, bearing[5375] [I]precious seed,[2233] shall doubtless come again with rejoicing, bringing[5375] his sheaves *with him.*

Prosperity Is From the LORD

A Song of degrees for Solomon.

127 Except the LORD build the house,[1004] they labour in vain[7723] [I]that build it: except [a]the LORD keep[8104] the city, the watchman[8104] waketh *but* in vain.

2 *It is* vain for you to rise up early, to sit up late, to [a]eat the bread of sorrows:[6089] *for* so he giveth his beloved[3039] sleep.

3 Lo, [a]children[1121] *are* an heritage[5159] of the LORD: *and* [b]the fruit of the womb[990] *is his* reward.

4 As arrows *are* in the hand[3027] of a mighty man; so *are* children of the youth.

5 Happy[835] *is* the man[1397] that [I]hath his quiver full of them: [a]they shall not be ashamed,[954] but they [II]shall speak[1696] with the enemies in the gate.

One Who Reveres God Is Blessed

A Song of degrees.

128 Blessed[835] [a]*is* every one that feareth[3373] the LORD; that walketh in his ways.[1870]

2 [a]For thou shalt eat the labour of thine hands:[3709] happy[835] *shalt* thou *be,* and *it shall be* well with thee.

3 Thy wife[802] *shall be* [a]as a fruitful vine by the sides of thine house:[1004] thy children[1121] [b]like olive plants round about thy table.

4 Behold, that thus shall the man[1397] be blessed that feareth the LORD.[3068]

5 [a]The LORD shall bless[1288] thee out of Zion: and thou shalt see the good[2898] of Jerusalem all the days[3117] of thy life.[3576]

6 Yea, thou shalt [a]see thy children's children, *and* [b]peace upon Israel.

A Prayer Against the Enemies Of Israel

A Song of degrees.

129 [I]Many a time have they afflicted me from [a]my youth, [b]may Israel now say:

2 Many a time have they afflicted me from my youth: yet they have not prevailed against me.

3 The plowers plowed upon my back: they made long[748] their furrows.[4618]

4 The LORD *is* righteous:[6662] he hath cut asunder the cords of the wicked.[7563]

5 Let them all be confounded[954] and turned back that hate[8130] Zion.

6 Let them be as [a]the grass *upon* the housetops, which withereth[3001] afore[6924] it groweth up:

7 Wherewith the mower filleth not his hand; nor he that bindeth sheaves his bosom.

---

3 [I]Hebr. *wickedness* [a]Prov. 22:8; Isa. 14:5

5 [a]Prov. 2:15 [b]Ps. 128:6; Gal. 6:16

1 [I]Hebr. *returned the returning of Zion* [a]Ps. 53:6; 85:1; Hos. 6:11; Joel 3:1 [b]Acts 12:9

2 [I]Hebr. *hath magnified to do with them* [a]Job 8:21

5 [I]Or, *singing* [a]Jer. 31:9

6 [I]Or, *seed basket*

1 [I]Hebr. that are *builders of it in it* [a]Ps. 121:3, 4, 5

2 [a]Gen. 3:17, 19

3 [a]Gen. 33:5; 48:4; Josh. 24:3, 4 [b]Deut. 28:4

5 [I]Hebr. *hath filled his quiver with them* [II]Or, *shall subdue,* [a]Job 5:4; Prov. 27:11 [b]Ps. 18:47, *destroy*

1 [a]Ps. 112:1; 115:13; 119:1

2 [a]Isa. 3:10

3 [a]Ezek. 19:10 [b]Ps. 52:8; 144:12

5 [a]Ps. 134:3

6 [a]Gen. 50:23; Job 42:16 [b]Ps. 125:5

1 [I]Or, *Much* [a]Ezek. 23:3; Hos. 2:15; 11:1 [b]Ps. 124:1

6 [a]Ps. 37:2

8 Neither do they which go by say,
[a]The blessing[1293] of the LORD *be* upon
you: we bless[1288] you in the name of the
LORD.

Hoping for Redemption

A Song of degrees.

130 Out [a]of the depths have I
cried[7121] unto thee, O LORD.
2 Lord,[136] hear[8085] my voice: let thine
ears[241] be attentive to the voice of my
supplications.[8469]
3 [a]If thou, LORD, shouldest mark[8104]
iniquities,[5771] O Lord, who shall
stand?
4 But *there is* [a]forgiveness[5547] with
thee, that [b]thou mayest be feared.[3372]
5 [a]I wait[6960] for the LORD, my
soul[5315] doth wait, and [b]in his word[1697]
do I hope.[3176]
6 [a]My soul *waiteth* for the Lord more
than they that watch[8104] for the morning:
[I]*I say, more than* they that watch for the
morning.
7 [a]Let Israel hope in the LORD: for
[b]with the LORD *there is* mercy,[2617] and
with him *is* plenteous redemption.[6304]
8 And [a]he shall redeem[6299] Israel
from all his iniquities.

Childlike Trust

A Song of degrees of David.

131 🗝 LORD, my heart[3820] is
not haughty, nor mine eyes
lofty: [a]neither do I [I]exercise[1980] myself in
great matters, or in things too [II]high
for me.
2 Surely I have behaved[7737] and quieted [I]myself, [a]as a child that is weaned
of his mother:[517] my soul[5315] *is* even as
a weaned child.
3 [a]Let Israel hope[3176] in the LORD
[I]from henceforth and for ever.[5769]

God's Temple

A Song of degrees.

132 LORD, remember[2142] David,
and all his afflictions:
2 How he sware[7650] unto the LORD,
[a]*and* vowed[5087] unto [b]the mighty *God* of
Jacob;
3 Surely I will not come into the tabernacle[168] of my house,[1004] nor go up
into my bed;
4 I will [a]not give sleep to mine eyes,
or slumber to mine eyelids,
5 Until I [a]find out a place for the
LORD, [I]an habitation[4908] for the mighty
God of Jacob.
6 Lo, we heard[8085] of it [a]at Ephratah:
[b]we found it [c]in the fields[7704] of the wood.
7 We will go into his tabernacles:[4908]
[a]we will worship[7812] at his footstool.
8 [a]Arise, O LORD, into thy rest; thou,
and [b]the ark[727] of thy strength.
9 Let thy priests[3548] [a]be clothed with
righteousness;[6664] and let thy saints[2623]
shout for joy.
10 For thy servant[5650] David's sake
turn not away[7725] the face of thine
anointed.[4899]
11 [a]The LORD hath sworn *in* truth[571]
unto David; he will not turn from it; [b]Of
the fruit of [I]thy body[990] will I set upon
thy throne.[3678]
12 If thy children[1121] will keep[8104]
my covenant[1285] and my testimony[5713]
that I shall teach[3925] them, their children
shall also sit upon thy throne for evermore.[5703]
13 [a]For the LORD hath chosen[977] Zion;
he hath desired *it* for his habitation.
14 [a]This *is* my rest for ever:[5703] here
will I dwell; for I have desired it.
15 [a]I will [I]abundantly bless[1288] her
provision: I will satisfy her poor with
bread.
16 [a]I will also clothe her priests with
salvation:[3468] [b]and her saints shall shout
aloud for joy.

129:8 [a]Ruth 2:4; Ps. 118:26

130:1 [a]Lam. 3:55; Jon. 2:2
3 [a]Ps. 143:2; Rom. 3:20, 23, 24
4 [a]Ex. 34:7 [b]1Kgs. 8:40; Ps. 2:11; Jer. 33:8, 9
5 [a]Ps. 27:14; 33:20; 40:1; Isa. 8:17; 26:8; 30:18 [b]Ps. 119:81
6 [I]Or, *which watch unto the morning* [a]Ps. 63:6; 119:147
7 [a]Ps. 131:3 [b]Ps. 86:5, 15; Isa. 55:7
8 [a]Ps. 103:3, 4; Matt. 1:21

131:1 [I]Hebr. *walk* [II]Hebr. *wonderful* [a]Rom. 12:16
2 [I]Hebr. *my soul* [a]Matt. 18:3; 1Cor. 14:20
3 [I]Hebr. *from now* [a]Ps. 130:7

132:2 [a]Ps. 65:1 [b]Gen. 49:24
4 [a]Prov. 6:4
5 [I]Hebr. *habitations* [a]Acts 7:46
6 [a]1Sam. 17:12 [b]1Sam. 7:1 [c]1Chr. 13:5
7 [a]Ps. 5:7; 99:5
8 [a]Num. 10:35; 2Chr. 6:41, 42 [b]Ps. 78:61
9 [a]Job 29:14; Ps. 132:16; Isa. 61:10
11 [I]Hebr. *thy belly* [a]Ps. 89:3, 4, 33; 110:4 [b]2Sam. 7:12; 1Kgs. 8:25; 2Chr. 6:16; Luke 1:69; Acts 2:30
13 [a]Ps. 48:1, 2
14 [a]Ps. 68:16
15 [I]Or, *surely* [a]Ps. 147:14
16 [a]2Chr. 6:41; Ps. 132:9; Ps. 149:4 [b]Hos. 11:12

🗝 **131:1** This verse reflects the attitude of David at his ascension to the throne (2 Sam. 5:1–5; 1 Chr. 11:1–3).

17 [a]There will I make the horn of David to bud: [b]I have ordained a [I]lamp[5216] for mine anointed.

18 His enemies will I [a]clothe with shame: but upon himself shall his crown[5145] flourish.

Brotherhood

A Song of degrees of David.

133 🔑 Behold, how good[2896] and how pleasant *it is* for [a]brethren[251] to dwell [I]together in unity!

2 *It is* like [a]the precious[2896] ointment[8081] upon the head,[7218] that ran down upon the beard,[2206] *even* Aaron's beard: that went down to the skirts of his garments;

3 As the dew of [a]Hermon, *and as the dew* that descended upon the mountains of Zion: for [b]there the LORD commanded[6680] the blessing,[1293] *even* life[2416] for evermore.[5769]

Night-Watchers

A Song of degrees.

134 Behold, bless[1288] ye the LORD, [a]all *ye* servants[5650] of the LORD, [b]which by night[3915] stand in the house[1004] of the LORD.

2 [a]Lift up[5375] your hands[3027] [I]*in* the sanctuary,[6944] and bless the LORD.

3 [a]The LORD that made[6213] heaven[8064] and earth[776] [b]bless thee out of Zion.

The True God and Idols

135 Praise[1984] ye the LORD. Praise ye the name of the LORD; [a]praise *him,* O ye servants[5650] of the LORD.

2 [a]Ye that stand in the house[1004] of the LORD, in [b]the courts of the house of our God,[430]

3 Praise the LORD; for [a]the LORD *is* good:[2896] sing praises[2167] unto his name; [b]for *it is* pleasant.

4 For [a]the LORD hath chosen[977] Jacob unto himself, *and* Israel for his peculiar treasure.[5459]

5 For I know that [a]the LORD *is* great, and *that* our Lord[113] *is* above all gods.[430]

6 [a]Whatsoever the LORD pleased,[2654] *that* did[6213] he in heaven,[8064] and in earth,[776] in the seas, and all deep places.

7 [a]He causeth the vapours to ascend[5927] from the ends of the earth; [b]he maketh[6213] lightnings for the rain; he bringeth the wind[7307] out of his [c]treasuries.

8 [a]Who smote[5221] the firstborn of Egypt, [I]both of man[120] and beast.

9 *Who* sent tokens[226] and wonders[4159] into the midst of thee, O Egypt, [a]upon Pharaoh, and upon all his servants.

10 [a]Who smote great nations,[1471] and slew[2026] mighty kings;[4428]

11 Sihon king[4428] of the Amorites, and Og king of Bashan, and [a]all the kingdoms[4467] of Canaan:

12 [a]And gave their land[776] *for* an heritage,[5159] an heritage unto Israel his people.[5971]

13 [a]Thy name, O LORD, *endureth* for ever,[5769] *and* thy memorial,[2143] O LORD, [I]throughout all generations.[1755]

14 [a]For the LORD will judge[1777] his people, and he will repent himself[5162] concerning his servants.

15 [a]The idols[6091] of the heathen[1471] *are* silver and gold, the work of men's[120] hands.[3027]

16 They have mouths,[6310] but they speak[1696] not; eyes have they, but they see not;

17 They have ears,[241] but they hear[238] not; neither is there *any* breath[7307] in their mouths.

18 They that make[6213] them are like unto them: *so is* every one that trusteth[982] in them.

132:17 [I]Or, *candle* [a]Ezek. 29:21; Luke 1:69 [b]1Kgs. 11:36; 15:4; 2Chr. 21:7
18 [a]Ps. 35:26; 109:29

133:1 [I]Hebr. *even together* [a]Gen. 13:8; Heb. 13:1
2 [a]Ex. 30:25, 30
3 [a]Deut. 4:48 [b]Lev. 25:21; Deut. 28:8; Ps. 42:8

134:1 [a]Ps. 135:1, 2 [b]1Chr. 9:33
2 [I]Or, in *holiness* [a]1Tim. 2:8
3 [a]Ps. 124:8 [b]Ps. 128:5; 135:21

135:1 [a]Ps. 113:1; 134:1
2 [a]Luke 2:37 [b]Ps. 92:13; 96:8; 116:19
3 [a]Ps. 119:68 [b]Ps. 147:1
4 [a]Ex. 19:5; Deut. 7:6, 7; 10:15
5 [a]Ps. 95:3; 97:9
6 [a]Ps. 115:3
7 [a]Jer. 10:13; 51:16 [b]Job 28:25, 26; 38:24; Zech. 10:1 [c]Job 38:22
8 [I]Hebr. *from an unto beast* [a]Ex. 12:12, 29; Ps. 78:51; 136:10
9 [a]Ps. 136:15
10 [a]Num. 21:24-26, 34, 35; Ps. 136:17
11 [a]Josh. 12:7
12 [a]Ps. 78:55; 136:21, 22
13 [I]Hebr. *to generation and generation* [a]Ex. 3:15; Ps. 102:12
14 [a]Deut. 32:36
15 [a]Ps. 115:4-8

🔑 **133:1** This psalm reveals David's feelings when he regained his throne after Absalom's rebellion (2 Sam. 5:1; 19:14; 1 Chr. 12:38–40).

19 [a]Bless[1288] the LORD, O house of Israel: bless the LORD, O house of Aaron:

20 Bless the LORD, O house of Levi: ye that fear[3373] the LORD, bless the LORD.

21 Blessed[1288] be the LORD [a]out of Zion, which dwelleth[7931] at Jerusalem. Praise ye the LORD.

His Mercy Endureth Forever

136 O [a]give thanks[3034] unto the LORD; for *he is* good:[2896] [b]for his mercy *endureth* for ever.[5769]

2 O give thanks unto [a]the God[430] of gods: for his mercy *endureth* for ever.

3 O give thanks to the Lord[113] of lords: for his mercy *endureth* for ever.

4 To him [a]who alone doeth[6213] great wonders:[6381] for his mercy *endureth* for ever.

5 [a]To him that by wisdom[8394] made the heavens:[8064] for his mercy *endureth* for ever.

6 [a]To him that stretched out[7554] the earth[776] above the waters: for his mercy *endureth* for ever.

7 [a]To him that made great lights: for his mercy *endureth* for ever:

8 [a]The sun [I]to rule[4475] by day:[3117] for his mercy *endureth* for ever:

9 The moon and stars to rule by night:[3915] for his mercy *endureth* for ever.

10 [a]To him that smote[5221] Egypt in their firstborn: for his mercy *endureth* for ever:

11 [a]And brought out Israel from among them: for his mercy *endureth* for ever:

12 [a]With a strong[2389] hand,[3027] and with a stretched out arm: for his mercy *endureth* for ever.

13 [a]To him which divided[1504] the Red sea into parts:[1506] for his mercy[2617] *endureth* for ever:

14 And made Israel to pass through[5674] the midst of it: for his mercy *endureth* for ever:

15 [a]But [I]overthrew Pharaoh and his host in the Red sea: for his mercy *endureth* for ever.

16 [a]To him which led his people[5971] through the wilderness: for his mercy *endureth* for ever.

17 [a]To him which smote great kings:[4428] for his mercy *endureth* for ever:

18 [a]And slew[2026] famous[117] kings: for his mercy *endureth* for ever:

19 [a]Sihon king of the Amorites: for his mercy *endureth* for ever:

20 [a]And Og the king of Bashan: for his mercy *endureth* for ever:

21 [a]And gave their land[776] for an heritage:[5159] for his mercy *endureth* for ever:

22 *Even* an heritage unto Israel his servant:[5650] for his mercy *endureth* for ever.

23 Who [a]remembered[2142] us in our low estate: for his mercy *endureth* for ever:

24 And hath redeemed us from our enemies: for his mercy *endureth* for ever.

25 [a]Who giveth food to all flesh: for his mercy *endureth* for ever.

26 O give thanks unto the God[410] of heaven:[8064] for his mercy *endureth* for ever.

The Mourning of the Exiles In Babylon

137 🔑 By the rivers of Babylon, there we sat down, yea, we wept, when we remembered[2142] Zion.

2 We hanged our [a]harps upon the willows in the midst thereof.

3 For there they that carried us away captive[7617] required[7592] of us [I]a song;[7892] and they that [II][a]wasted us *required of us* mirth, *saying,* Sing[7891] us *one* of the songs of Zion.

---

19 [a]Ps. 115:9
21 [a]Ps. 134:3
1 [a]Ps. 106:1; 107:1; 118:1 [b]1Chr. 16:34, 41; 2Chr. 20:21
2 [a]Deut. 10:17
4 [a]Ps. 72:18
5 [a]Gen. 1:1; Prov. 3:19; Jer. 51:15
6 [a]Gen. 1:9; Ps. 24:2; Jer. 10:12
7 [a]Gen. 1:14
8 [I]Hebr. *for the rulings by day* [a]Gen. 1:16
10 [a]Ex. 12:29; Ps. 135:8
11 [a]Ex. 12:51; 13:3, 17
12 [a]Ex. 6:6
13 [a]Ex. 14:21, 22; Ps. 78:13
15 [I]Hebr. *shaked off* [a]Ex. 14:27; Ps. 135:9
16 [a]Ex. 13:18; 15:22; Deut. 8:15
17 [a]Ps. 135:10, 11
18 [a]Deut. 29:7
19 [a]Num. 21:21
20 [a]Num. 21:33
21 [a]Josh. 12:1; Ps. 135:12
23 [a]Gen. 8:1; Deut. 32:36; Ps. 113:7
25 [a]Ps. 104:27; 145:15; 147:9
2 [a]Neh. 12:27
3 [I]Hebr. *the words of a song* [II]Hebr. *laid us on heaps* [a]Ps. 79:1

🔑 **137:1–9** See the note on Psalm 109:1–29 for a discussion of the Imprecatory Psalms.

4 How shall we sing the LORD's song in a [I]strange[5236] land?[127]

5 If I forget thee, O Jerusalem, let my right hand forget *her cunning.*

6 If I do not remember[2142] thee, let my [a]tongue cleave to the roof of my mouth; if I prefer[5927] not Jerusalem above [I]my chief[7218] joy.

7 Remember, O LORD, [a]the children[1121] of Edom in the day[3117] of Jerusalem; who said,[559] [I]Rase[6168] *it,* raze *it, even* to the foundation[3247] thereof.

8 O daughter of Babylon, [a]who art to be [I]destroyed; happy[835] *shall he be,* [II][b]that rewardeth[7999] thee as thou hast served us.

9 Happy *shall he be,* that taketh and [a]dasheth thy little ones against [I]the stones.

A Prayer of Thanksgiving

A Psalm of David.

138 I will praise[3034] thee with my whole heart:[3820] [a]before the gods[430] will I sing praise[2167] unto thee.

2 [a]I will worship[7812] [b]toward thy holy[6944] temple,[1964] and praise thy name for thy lovingkindness and for thy truth:[571] for thou hast [c]magnified thy word[565] above all thy name.

3 In the day[3117] when I cried[7121] thou answeredst me, *and* strengthenedst me *with* strength in my soul.[5315]

4 [a]All the kings[4428] of the earth[776] shall praise thee, O LORD, when they hear[8085] the words[561] of thy mouth.[6310]

5 Yea, they shall sing[7891] in the ways[1870] of the LORD: for great *is* the glory[3519] of the LORD.

6 [a]Though the LORD *be* high, yet [b]hath he respect unto[7200] the lowly: but the proud he knoweth afar off.

7 [a]Though I walk in the midst[7130] of trouble, thou wilt revive[2421] me: thou shalt stretch forth thine hand against the wrath[639] of mine enemies, and thy right hand[3027] shall save[3467] me.

8 [a]The LORD will perfect[1584] *that which* concerneth me: thy mercy,[2617] O LORD, *endureth* for ever:[5769] [b]forsake[7503] not the works of thine own hands.

4 [I]Hebr. *land of a stranger*
6 [I]Hebr. *the head of my joy* [a]Ezek. 3:26
7 [I]Hebr. *Make bare* [a]Jer. 49:7; Lam. 4:22; Ezek. 25:12; Obad. 1:10
8 [I]Hebr. *wasted* [II]Hebr. *that recompenseth unto thee thy deed which thou didst to us* [a]Isa. 13:1, 6; 47:1; Jer. 25:12; 50:2 [b]Jer. 50:15, 29; Rev. 18:6
9 [I]Hebr. *the rock* [a]Isa. 13:16

1 [a]Ps. 119:46
2 [a]Ps. 28:2 [b]1Kgs. 8:29, 30; Ps. 5:7 [c]Isa. 42:21
4 [a]Ps. 102:15, 22
6 [a]Ps. 113:5, 6; Isa. 57:15 [b]Prov. 3:34; James 4:6; 1Pet. 5:5
7 [a]Ps. 23:3, 4
8 [a]Ps. 57:2; Phil. 1:6 [b]Job 10:3, 8; 14:15

1 [a]Ps. 17:3; Jer. 12:3
2 [a]2Kgs. 19:27 [b]Matt. 9:4; John 2:24, 25
3 [a]Job 31:4
4 [a]Heb. 4:13
6 [a]Job 42:3; Ps. 40:5; 131:1
7 [a]Jer. 23:24; Jon. 1:3
8 [a]Amos 9:2-4 [b]Job 26:6; Prov. 15:11
12 [I]Hebr. *darkeneth not* [II]Hebr. *as is the darkness, so is the light* [a]Job 26:6; 34:22; Dan. 2:22; Heb. 4:13
14 [I]Hebr. *greatly*
15 [I]Or, *strength, or, body* [a]Job 10:8, 9; Eccl. 11:5

God Is Omnipresent and Omniscient

To the chief Musician, A Psalm of David.

139 O LORD, [a]thou hast searched me, and known[3045] *me.*

2 [a]Thou knowest my downsitting and mine uprising,[6965] thou [b]understandest[995] my thought afar off.

3 [a]Thou compassest my path[734] and my lying down, and art acquainted[5532] *with* all my ways.[1870]

4 For *there is* not a word[4405] in my tongue, *but,* lo, O LORD, [a]thou knowest it altogether.

5 Thou hast beset me behind and before, and laid thine hand upon me.

6 [a]*Such* knowledge[1847] *is* too wonderful[6383] for me; it is high, I cannot *attain* unto it.

7 [a]Whither shall I go from thy spirit?[7307] or whither shall I flee from thy presence?

8 [a]If I ascend up[5927] into heaven,[8064] thou *art* there: [b]if I make my bed in hell,[7585] behold, thou *art there.*

9 *If* I take[5375] the wings of the morning, *and* dwell[7931] in the uttermost parts[319] of the sea;

10 Even there shall[5148] thy hand[3027] lead[5148] me, and thy right hand shall hold me.

11 If I say,[559] Surely the darkness[2822] shall cover me; even the night[3915] shall be light[216] about me.

12 Yea, [a]the darkness [I]hideth[2821] not from thee; but the night shineth as the day:[3117] [II]the darkness[2825] and the light[219] *are* both alike *to thee.*

13 For thou hast possessed my reins:[3629] thou hast covered me in my mother's[517] womb.[990]

14 I will praise[3034] thee; for I am fearfully[3372] *and* wonderfully made: marvellous[6381] *are* thy works; and *that* my soul[5315] knoweth [I]right well.

15 [a]My [I]substance was not hid from thee, when I was made[6213] in secret, *and* curiously wrought in the lowest parts of the earth.[776]

16 Thine eyes did see my substance, yet being unperfect; and in thy book[5612]

[I]all *my members* were written, [II]*which* in continuance were fashioned,[3335] when *as yet there was* none of them.

17 [a]How precious also are thy thoughts unto me, O God![410] how great is the sum[7218] of them!

18 *If* I should count[5608] them, they are more in number than the sand: when I awake, I am still with thee.

19 Surely thou wilt [a]slay the wicked,[7563] O God:[433] [b]depart[5493] from me therefore, ye bloody[1818] men.[582]

20 For they [a]speak[559] against thee wickedly,[4209] *and* thine enemies take *thy name* in vain.

21 [a]Do not I hate them, O LORD, that hate[8130] thee? and am not I grieved with those that rise up against thee?

22 I hate them with perfect hatred:[8135] I count them mine enemies.

23 [a]Search me, O God, and know[3045] my heart:3824 try[974] me, and know my thoughts:[8312]

24 And see if *there be any* [I]wicked[6090] way[1870] in me, and [a]lead me in the way everlasting.[5769]

Relief From Religious Persecution

To the chief Musician, A Psalm of David.

140 🗝 Deliver[2502] me, O LORD, from the evil[7451] man:[120] [a]preserve[5341] me from the violent[2555] man;[376]

2 Which imagine[2803] mischiefs[7451] in *their* heart;[3820] [a]continually are they gathered together *for* war.

3 They have sharpened[8150] their tongues like a serpent;[5175] [a]adders'5919 poison[2534] *is* under their lips.[8193] Selah.

4 [a]Keep[8104] me, O LORD, from the hands[3027] of the wicked;[7563] [b]preserve me from the violent man; who have purposed[2803] to overthrow my goings.

5 [a]The proud have hid a snare[6341] for me, and cords; they have spread a net by the wayside; they have set gins[4170] for me. Selah.

6 I said[559] unto the LORD, Thou *art* my God:[410] hear[238] the voice of my supplications, O LORD.

7 O GOD the Lord,[136] the strength of my salvation,[3444] thou hast covered my head[7218] in the day[3117] of battle.[5402]

8 Grant not, O LORD, the desires3970 of the wicked: further not his wicked device;[2162] [Ia]*lest* they exalt themselves. Selah.

9 *As for* the head of those that compass me about, [a]let the mischief[5999] of their own lips cover[3680] them.

10 [a]Let burning coals fall upon them: let them be cast[5307] into the fire; into deep pits, that they rise not up again.

11 Let not [I]an evil speaker be established[3559] in the earth:[776] evil shall hunt the violent man to overthrow *him.*

12 I know[3045] that the LORD will [a]maintain[6213] the cause[1779] of the afflicted, *and* the right[4941] of the poor.

13 Surely the righteous[6662] shall give thanks[3034] unto thy name: the upright shall dwell in thy presence.

A Prayer for Preservation From Evil

A Psalm of David.

141 LORD, I cry[7121] unto thee: [a]make haste unto me; give ear[238] unto my voice, when I cry unto thee.

2 Let [a]my prayer[8605] be [I]set forth[3559] before thee [b]*as* incense;[7004] *and* [c]the lifting up of my hands[3709] *as* [d]the evening sacrifice.[4503]

3 Set a watch, O LORD, before my mouth;[6310] keep[5341] the door of my lips.[8193]

4 Incline not my heart[3820] to *any* evil[7451] thing, to practise wicked[7562] works with men[376] that work iniquity:[205] [a]and let me not eat of their dainties.

5 [Ia]Let the righteous[6662] smite[1986] me;

---

16 [I]Hebr. *all of them* [II]Or, what *days they should be fashioned*
17 [a]Ps. 40:5
19 [a]Isa. 11:4 [b]Ps. 119:115
20 [a]Jude 1:15
21 [a]2Chr. 19:2; Ps. 119:158
23 [a]Job 31:6; Ps. 26:2
24 [I]Hebr. *way of pain, or, grief* [a]Ps. 5:8; 143:10

1 [a]Ps. 140:4
2 [a]Ps. 56:6
3 [a]Ps. 58:4; Rom. 3:13
4 [a]Ps. 71:4; Ps. 140:1
5 [a]Ps. 35:7; 57:6; 119:110; 141:9; Jer. 18:22
8 [I]Or, *let them not be exalted* [a]Deut. 32:27
9 [a]Ps. 7:16; 94:23; Prov. 12:13; 18:7
10 [a]Ps. 11:6
11 [I]Hebr. *a man of tongue;*
12 [a]1Kgs. 8:45; Ps. 9:4

1 [a]Ps. 70:5
2 [I]Hebr. *directed* [a]Rev. 5:8; 8:3, 4 [b]Rev. 8:3 [c]Ps. 134:2; 1Tim. 2:8 [d]Ex. 29:39
4 [a]Prov. 23:6
5 [I]Or, *Let the righteous smite me kindly, and reprove me; let not* their *precious oil break my head* [a]Prov. 9:8; 19:25; 25:12

🗝 **140:1** David cried for deliverance from his enemies, namely those who sought to destroy him by betrayal (2 Sam. 22, 23).

it shall be a kindness:[2617] and let him
reprove[3198] me; *it shall be* an excellent
oil,[8081] *which* shall not break[5106] my
head:[7218] for yet my prayer also *shall be*
in their calamities.
6 When their judges[8199] are overthrown in stony places, they shall
hear[8085] my words;[561] for they are sweet.
7 Our bones[6106] are scattered [a]at the
grave's[7585] mouth, as when one cutteth
and cleaveth *wood* upon the earth.[776]
8 But [a]mine eyes *are* unto thee, O
GOD the Lord:[136] in thee is my trust;[2620]
[I]leave not my soul[5315] destitute.
9 Keep[8104] me from [a]the snares[6341]
which they have laid[3369] for me, and the
gins[4170] of the workers of iniquity.
10 [a]Let the wicked[7563] fall into their
own nets, whilst that I withal [I]escape.

In Time of Trouble

Maschil of David; A Prayer when he was in the cave.

142 🔑 I cried[2199] unto the LORD
with my voice; with my voice
unto the LORD did I make my supplication.[2603]
2 [a]I poured out[8210] my complaint[7878]
before him; I shewed[5046] before him my
trouble.
3 [a]When my spirit[7307] was overwhelmed within me, then thou
knewest[3045] my path. [b]In the way[734]
wherein I walked have they privily[2934]
laid a snare[6341] for me.
4 [I][a]I looked on *my* right hand, and
beheld, but [b]*there was* no man that would
know[5234] me: refuge [II]failed[6] me; [III]no
man cared for my soul.[5315]
5 I cried unto thee, O LORD: I said,
[a]Thou *art* my refuge *and* [b]my portion [c]in
the land[776] of the living.[2416]
6 Attend unto my cry; for I am
[a]brought very low: deliver[5337] me from
my persecutors; for they are stronger
than I.
🔑 7 Bring my soul out of prison, that
I may praise[3034] thy name: [a]the righteous[6662] shall compass me about; [b]for
thou shalt deal bountifully[1580] with me.

Hear My Prayer!

A Psalm of David.

143 🔑 Hear[8085] my prayer,[8605] O
LORD, give ear[238] to my suppli-
cations:[8469] [a]in thy faithfulness[530] answer
me, *and* in thy righteousness.[6666]
2 And [a]enter not into judgment[4941]
with thy servant:[5650] for [b]in thy sight
shall[6663] no man living[2416] be justified.[6663]
3 For the enemy hath persecuted my
soul;[5315] he hath smitten[1792] my life[2416]
down to the ground;[776] he hath made me
to dwell in darkness,[4285] as those that
have been long[5769] dead.
4 [a]Therefore is my spirit[7307] overwhelmed within me; my heart[3820] within
me is desolate.[8074]
5 [a]I remember[2142] the days[3117] of
old;[6924] I meditate[1897] on all thy works; I
muse[7878] on the work of thy hands.[3027]
6 [a]I stretch forth my hands unto thee:
[b]my soul *thirsteth* after thee, as a thirsty
land.[776] Selah.
7 Hear me speedily, O LORD: my
spirit faileth:[3615] hide not thy face from
me, [I][a]lest I be like unto them that go
down into the pit.[953]
8 Cause me to hear thy lovingkindness [a]in the morning; for in thee do I
trust:[982] [b]cause me to know[3045] the
way[1870] wherein I should walk; for [c]I lift
up[5375] my soul unto thee.

7 [a]2Cor. 1:9
8 [I]Hebr. *make not my soul bare* [a]2Chr. 20:12; Ps. 25:15; 123:1, 2
9 [a]Ps. 119:110; 140:5; 142:3
10 [I]Hebr. *pass over* [a]Ps. 35:8

2 [a]Isa. 26:16
3 [a]Ps. 143:4 [b]Ps. 140:5
4 [I]Or, *Look on the right hand, and see* [II]Hebr. *perished from me* [III]Hebr. *no man sought after my soul* [a]Ps. 69:20 [b]Ps. 31:11; 88:8, 18
5 [a]Ps. 46:1; 91:2 [b]Ps. 16:5; 73:26; 119:57; Lam. 3:24 [c]Ps. 27:13
6 [a]Ps. 116:6
7 [a]Ps. 34:2 [b]Ps. 13:6; 119:17

1 [a]Ps. 31:1
2 [a]Job 14:3 [b]Ex. 34:7; Job 4:17; 9:2; 15:14; 25:4; Ps. 130:3; Eccl. 7:20; Rom. 3:20; Gal. 2:16
4 [a]Ps. 77:3; 142:3
5 [a]Ps. 77:5, 10, 11
6 [a]Ps. 88:9; Ps. 63:1
7 [I]Or, *for I am become like* [a]Ps. 28:1; 88:4
8 [a]Ps. 46:5 [b]Ps. 5:8 [c]Ps. 25:1

🔑 **142:1** David wrote this psalm upon the disparity of his soul in the cave of Adullam at En–gedi (1 Sam. 22; 24).

🔑 **142:7** The "prison" mentioned here probably refers to David's current situation—he was hemmed in by enemies and opposition (see Ps. 143:11). This is a companion psalm to Psalm 57 (see the titles of each). David's mood in these Psalms indicates that he was affected by the stress of being a fugitive.

🔑 **143:1** The occasion for this psalm was David's fleeing from Absalom (2 Sam. 15—18).

9 Deliver[5337] me, O LORD, from mine enemies: I [I]flee unto thee to hide[3680] me.

10 [a]Teach[3925] me to do[6213] thy will;[7522] for thou *art* my God:[430] [b]thy spirit *is* good;[2896] lead[5148] me into [c]the land of uprightness.

11 [a]Quicken[2421] me, O LORD, for thy name's sake: for thy righteousness' sake bring my soul out of trouble.

12 And of thy mercy[2617] [a]cut off[6789] mine enemies, and destroy[6] all them that afflict my soul: for [b]I *am* thy servant.

David Thanks God

A Psalm of David.

144 Blessed[1288] *be* the LORD [I][a]my strength, [b]which teacheth[3925] my hands[3027] to war, *and* my fingers to fight:

2 [I][a]My goodness,[2617] and my fortress; my high tower, and my deliverer; my shield, and *he* in whom I trust;[2620] who subdueth my people[5971] under me.

3 [a]LORD, what *is* man,[120] that thou takest knowledge[3045] of him! *or* the son[1121] of man,[582] that thou makest account of him!

4 [a]Man is like to vanity: [b]his days[3117] *are* as a shadow that passeth away.[5674]

5 [a]Bow thy heavens,[8064] O LORD, and come down: [b]touch[5060] the mountains, and they shall smoke.[6225]

6 [a]Cast forth lightning, and scatter them: shoot out thine arrows, and destroy[1949] them.

7 [a]Send thine [I]hand[3027] from above; [b]rid me, and deliver[5337] me out of great waters, from the hand of [c]strange children;[1121]

8 Whose mouth[6310] [a]speaketh vanity,[7723] and their right hand *is* a right hand of falsehood.

9 I will [a]sing[2167] a new song[7892] unto thee, O God:[430] upon a psaltery *and* an instrument of ten strings will I sing praises[2167] unto thee.

10 [a]*It is he* that giveth [I]salvation[8668] unto kings:[4428] who delivereth David his servant[5650] from the hurtful[7451] sword.[2719]

9 [I]Hebr. *hide me with thee*

10 [a]Ps. 25:4, 5; 139:24 [b]Neh. 9:20 [c]Isa. 26:10

11 [a]Ps. 119:25, 37, 40

12 [a]Ps. 54:5 [b]Ps. 116:16

1 [I]Hebr. *my rock* [a]Ps. 18:2, 31 [b]2Sam. 22:35; Ps. 18:34

2 [I]Or, *My mercy* [a]2Sam. 22:2, 3, 40, 48

3 [a]Job 7:17; Ps. 8:4; Heb. 2:6

4 [a]Job 4:19; 14:2; Ps. 39:5; 62:9 [b]Ps. 102:11

5 [a]Ps. 18:9; Isa. 64:1 [b]Ps. 104:32

6 [a]Ps. 18:13, 14

7 [I]Hebr. *hands* [a]Ps. 18:16 [b]Ps. 69:1, 2, 14; 144:11 [c]Ps. 54:3; Mal. 2:11

8 [a]Ps. 12:2

9 [a]Ps. 33:2, 3; 40:3

10 [I]Or, *victory* [a]Ps. 18:50

11 [a]Ps. 144:7, 8

12 [I]Hebr. *cut* [a]Ps. 128:3

13 [I]Hebr. *from kind to kind*

14 [I]Hebr. *able to bear burdens,* or, *laden* with flesh

15 [a]Deut. 33:29; Ps. 33:12; 65:4; 146:5

3 [I]Hebr. *and of his greatness* there is *no search* [a]Ps. 96:4; 147:5 [b]Job 5:9; 9:10; Rom. 11:33

4 [a]Isa. 33:19

5 [I]Hebr. *things,* or, *words*

6 [I]Hebr. *declare it*

8 [I]Hebr. *great in mercy* [a]Ex. 34:6, 7; Num. 14:18; Ps. 86:5, 15; 103:8

9 [a]Ps. 100:5; Nah. 1:7

11 [a]Rid me, and deliver me from the hand of strange[5236] children, whose mouth speaketh vanity, and their right hand *is* a right hand of falsehood:

12 That our sons[1121] *may be* [a]as plants grown up in their youth; *that* our daughters *may be* as corner stones, [I]polished *after* the similitude[8403] of a palace:[1964]

13 *That* our garners[4200] *may be* full, affording [I]all manner of store: *that* our sheep may bring forth thousands and ten thousands in our streets:

14 *That* our oxen *may be* [I]strong to labour; *that there be* no breaking in, nor going out; that *there be* no complaining in our streets.

15 [a]Happy[835] *is that* people, that is in such a case: *yea,* happy *is that* people, whose God *is* the LORD.

David's Psalm of Praise

David's *Psalm* of Praise.

145 I will extol thee, my God,[430] O king;[4428] and I will bless[1288] thy name for ever[5769] and ever.[5703]

2 Every day will I bless thee; and I will praise[1984] thy name for ever and ever.

3 [a]Great *is* the LORD, and greatly to be praised;[1984] [I]and [b]his greatness *is* unsearchable.

4 [a]One generation[1755] shall praise[7623] thy works to another, and shall declare[5046] thy mighty acts.

5 I will speak[7878] of the glorious[3519] honour[1926] of thy majesty,[1935] and of thy wondrous [I]works.[6381]

6 And *men* shall speak[559] of the might of thy terrible acts:[3372] and I will [I]declare[5608] thy greatness.

7 They shall abundantly utter the memory[2143] of thy great goodness, and shall sing of thy righteousness.[6666]

8 [a]The LORD *is* gracious,[2587] and full of compassion; slow to anger,[639] and [I]of great mercy.[2617]

9 [a]The LORD *is* good[2896] to all: and his tender mercies[7356] *are* over all his works.

10 [a]All thy works shall praise[3034] thee, O LORD; and thy saints[2623] shall bless thee.

11 They shall speak of the glory[3519] of thy kingdom,[4438] and talk[1696] of thy power;

12 To make known[3045] to the sons[1121] of men[120] his mighty acts, and the glorious majesty[1926] of his kingdom.

13 [a]Thy kingdom *is* [I]an everlasting[5769] kingdom, and thy dominion[4475] *endureth* throughout all generations.[1755]

14 The LORD upholdeth5564 all that fall, and [a]raiseth up all *those that be* bowed down.

15 [a]The eyes of all [I]wait upon thee; and [b]thou givest them their meat in due season.[6256]

16 Thou openest thine hand,[3027] [a]and satisfiest the desire[7522] of every living thing.[2416]

17 The LORD *is* righteous[6662] in all his ways,[1870] and [I]holy[2623] in all his works.

18 [a]The LORD *is* nigh unto all them that call[7121] upon him, to all that call upon him [b]in truth.[571]

19 He will fulfil the desire of them that fear[3373] him: he also will hear[8085] their cry, and will save[3467] them.

20 [a]The LORD preserveth[8104] all them that love[157] him: but all the wicked[7563] will he destroy.[8045]

21 My mouth[6310] shall speak[1696] the praise[8416] of the LORD: and let all flesh[1320] bless his holy[6944] name for ever[5769] and ever.[5703]

God Is an Abundant Help

146 [I]Praise[1984] ye the LORD. [a]Praise the LORD, O my soul.[5315]

2 [a]While I live[2416] will I praise the LORD: I will sing praises[2167] unto my God[430] while I have any being.

3 [a]Put not your trust[982] in princes,[5081] *nor* in the son[1121] of man,[120] in whom *there is* no [I]help.[8668]

4 [a]His breath[7307] goeth forth, he returneth[7725] to his earth;[127] in that very day[3117] [b]his thoughts perish.[6]

5 [a]Happy[835] *is he* that *hath* the God[410] of Jacob for his help, whose hope *is* in the LORD his God:

6 [a]Which made[6213] heaven,8064 and earth,[776] the sea, and all that therein *is:* which keepeth[8104] truth[571] for ever:[5769]

7 [a]Which executeth[6213] judgment[4941] for the oppressed: [b]which giveth food to the hungry. [c]The LORD looseth the prisoners:

8 [a]The LORD openeth *the eyes of* the blind: [b]the LORD raiseth them that are bowed down: the LORD loveth[157] the righteous:[6662]

9 [a]The LORD preserveth[8104] the strangers;[1616] he relieveth the fatherless and widow: [b]but the way[1870] of the wicked[7563] he turneth upside down.[5791]

10 [a]The LORD shall reign[4427] for ever, *even* thy God, O Zion, unto all generations.[1755] Praise ye the LORD.

Praising the Almighty

147 Praise[1984] ye the LORD: for [a]*it is* good[2896] to sing praises[2167] unto our God;[430] [b]for *it is* pleasant; *and* [c]praise[8416] is comely.5000

2 The LORD doth [a]build up Jerusalem: [b]he gathereth together[3664] the outcasts of Israel.

3 [a]He healeth the broken[7665] in heart,[3820] and bindeth up[2280] their [I]wounds.[6093]

4 [a]He telleth the number of the stars; he calleth[7121] them all by *their* names.

5 [a]Great *is* our Lord,[113] and of [b]great power: [I][c]his understanding[8394] *is* infinite.

6 [a]The LORD lifteth up the meek: he casteth the wicked[7563] down to the ground.[776]

7 Sing unto the LORD with thanksgiving;[8426] sing praise[2167] upon the harp unto our God:

8 [a]Who covereth[3680] the heaven8064 with clouds, who prepareth rain for the earth,[776] who maketh grass to grow upon the mountains.

9 [a]He giveth to the beast his food, *and* [b]to the young[1121] ravens which cry.[7121]

---

10 [a]Ps. 19:1
13 [I]Hebr. *a kingdom of all ages* [a]Ps. 146:10; 1Tim. 1:17
14 [a]Ps. 146:8
15 [I]Or, *look unto thee* [a]Ps. 104:27 [b]Ps. 136:25
16 [a]Ps. 104:21; 147:9
17 [I]Or, *merciful,* or, *bountiful*
18 [a]Deut. 4:7 [b]John 4:24
20 [a]Ps. 31:23; 97:10

1 [I]Hebr. *Hallelujah* [a]Ps. 103:1
2 [a]Ps. 104:33
3 [I]Or, *salvation* [a]Ps. 118:8, 9; Isa. 2:22
4 [a]Ps. 104:29; Eccl. 12:7; Isa. 2:22 [b]1Cor. 2:6
5 [a]Ps. 144:15; Jer. 17:7
6 [a]Gen. 1:1; Rev. 14:7
7 [a]Ps. 103:6 [b]Ps. 107:9 [c]Ps. 68:6; 107:10, 14
8 [a]Matt. 9:30; John 9:7-32 [b]Ps. 145:14; 147:6; Luke 13:13
9 [a]Deut. 10:18; Ps. 68:5 [b]Ps. 147:6
10 [a]Ex. 15:18; Ps. 10:16; 145:13; Rev. 11:15

1 [a]Ps. 92:1 [b]Ps. 135:3 [c]Ps. 33:1
2 [a]Ps. 102:16 [b]Deut. 30:3
3 [I]Hebr. *griefs* [a]Ps. 51:17; Isa. 57:15; 61:1; Luke 4:18
4 [a]Gen. 15:5; Isa. 40:26
5 [I]Hebr. *of his understanding there is no number* [a]1Chr. 16:25; Ps. 48:1; 96:4; 145:3 [b]Nah. 1:3 [c]Isa. 40:28
6 [a]Ps. 146:8, 9
8 [a]Job 38:26, 27; Ps. 104:13, 14
9 [a]Job 38:41; Ps. 104:27, 28; 136:25; 145:15 [b]Job 38:41; Matt. 6:26

10 [a]He delighteth[2654] not in the strength of the horse: he taketh not pleasure in the legs of a man.[376]

11 The LORD taketh pleasure in them that fear[3373] him, in those that hope[3176] in his mercy.[2617]

12 Praise[7623] the LORD, O Jerusalem; praise thy God, O Zion.

13 For he hath strengthened[2388] the bars of thy gates; he hath blessed[1288] thy children[1121] within[7130] thee.

14 [I][a]He maketh[7760] peace *in* thy borders, *and* [b]filleth thee with the [II][c]finest of the wheat.

15 [a]He sendeth forth his commandment[565] *upon* earth: his word[1697] runneth very swiftly.

16 [a]He giveth snow like wool: he scattereth the hoarfrost3713 like ashes.

17 He casteth forth his ice like morsels: who can stand before his cold?

18 [a]He sendeth out his word, and melteth them: he causeth his wind[7307] to blow, *and* the waters flow.

19 [a]He sheweth[5046] [I]his word unto Jacob, [b]his statutes[2706] and his judgments[4941] unto Israel.

20 [a]He hath not dealt[6213] so with any nation:[1471] and *as for his* judgments, they have not known[3045] them. Praise ye the LORD.

Praise the Lord!

148 [I]Praise[1984] ye the LORD. Praise ye the LORD from the heavens:8064 praise him in the heights.

2 [a]Praise ye him, all his angels:[4397] praise ye him, all his hosts.[6635]

3 Praise ye him, sun and moon: praise him, all ye stars of light.[216]

4 Praise him, [a]ye heavens of heavens, and [b]ye waters that *be* above the heavens.

5 Let them praise the name of the LORD: for [a]he commanded,[6680] and they were created.[1254]

6 [a]He hath also stablished5975 them for ever[5703] and ever:[5769] he hath made a decree which shall not pass.

10 [a]Ps. 33:16, 17, 18; Hos. 1:7
14 [I]Hebr. *Who maketh thy border peace* [II]Hebr. *fat of wheat* [a]Isa. 60:17, 18 [b]Ps. 132:15 [c]Deut. 32:14; Ps. 81:16
15 [a]Job 37:12; Ps. 107:20
16 [a]Job 37:6
18 [a]Job 37:10; Ps. 147:15
19 [I]Hebr. *his words* [a]Deut. 33:2-4; Ps. 76:1; 78:5; 103:7 [b]Mal. 4:4
20 [a]Deut. 4:32-34; Rom. 3:1, 2

1 [I]Hebr. *Hallelujah*
2 [a]Ps. 103:20, 21
4 [a]1Kgs. 8:27; 2Cor. 12:2 [b]Gen. 1:7
5 [a]Gen. 1:1, 6, 7; Ps. 33:6, 9
6 [a]Ps. 89:37; 119:90, 91; Jer. 31:35, 36; 33:25
7 [a]Isa. 43:20
8 [a]Ps. 147:15-18
9 [a]Isa. 44:23; 49:13; 55:12
10 [I]Hebr. *birds of wing*
13 [I]Hebr. *exalted* [a]Ps. 8:1; Isa. 12:4 [b]Ps. 113:4
14 [a]Ps. 75:10 [b]Ps. 149:9 [c]Eph. 2:17

1 [I]Hebr. *Hallelujah* [a]Ps. 33:3; Isa. 42:10
2 [a]Job 35:10; Ps. 100:3; Isa. 54:5 [b]Zech. 9:9; Matt. 21:5
3 [I]Or, *with the pipe* [a]Ps. 81:2; 150:4
4 [a]Ps. 35:27 [b]Ps. 132:16
5 [a]Job 35:10
6 [I]Hebr. *in their throat* [a]Heb. 4:12; Rev. 1:16
9 [a]Deut. 7:1, 2

7 Praise the LORD from the earth,[776] [a]ye dragons,[8577] and all deeps:

8 Fire, and hail; snow, and vapours; stormy wind[7307] [a]fulfilling his word:[1697]

9 [a]Mountains, and all hills; fruitful trees, and all cedars:

10 Beasts,[2416] and all cattle; creeping things, and [I]flying fowl:

11 Kings[4428] of the earth, and all people;[3816] princes, and all judges[8199] of the earth:

12 Both young men, and maidens;[1330] old men,[2205] and children:

13 Let them praise the name of the LORD: for [a]his name alone is [I]excellent; [b]his glory[1935] *is* above the earth and heaven.8064

14 [a]He also exalteth7311 the horn of his people,[5971] [b]the praise[8416] of all his saints;[2623] *even* of the children[1121] of Israel, [c]a people near unto him. Praise ye the LORD.

A Hymn of Praise

149 [I]Praise[1984] ye the LORD. [a]Sing[7891] unto the LORD a new song,[7892] *and* his praise[8416] in the congregation[6951] of saints.[2623]

2 Let Israel rejoice in [a]him that made[6213] him: let the children[1121] of Zion be joyful in their [b]King.[4428]

3 [a]Let them praise his name [I]in the dance: let them sing praises[2167] unto him with the timbrel8596 and harp.

4 For [a]the LORD taketh pleasure in his people:[5971] [b]he will beautify the meek with salvation.[3444]

5 Let the saints be joyful in glory:[3519] let them [a]sing aloud upon their beds.

6 *Let* the high *praises* of God[410] *be* [I]in their mouth, and [a]a twoedged sword[2719] in their hand;[3027]

7 To execute vengeance[5360] upon the heathen,[1471] *and* punishments[8433] upon the people;[3816]

8 To bind their kings with chains, and their nobles with fetters of iron;

9 [a]To execute[6213] upon them the

judgment[4941] written: [b]this honour have all his saints. Praise ye the LORD.

"Praise God"

150 [I]Praise[1984] ye the LORD. Praise God[410] in his sanctuary:[6944] praise him in the firmament[7549] of his power.

2 [a]Praise him for his mighty acts; praise him according to his excellent [b]greatness.

3 Praise him with the sound of the [Ia]trumpet: [b]praise him with the psaltery and harp.

4 Praise him [a]with the timbrel[8596] and [Ib]dance: praise him with [c]stringed instruments and organs.

5 Praise him upon the loud[8088] [a]cymbals: praise him upon the high sounding cymbals.

6 Let every thing that hath breath[5397] praise the LORD. Praise ye the LORD.

9 [b]Ps. 148:14
1 [I]Hebr. *Hallelujah*
2 [a]Ps. 145:5, 6 [b]Deut. 3:24
3 [I]Or, *cornet* [a]Ps. 98:6 [b]Ps. 81:2; 149:3
4 [I]Or, *pipe* [a]Ex. 15:20 [b]Ps. 149:3 [c]Ps. 33:2; 92:3; 144:9; Isa. 38:20
5 [a]1Chr. 15:16, 19, 28; 16:5; 25:1, 6

THE PROVERBS

The Hebrew title comes from the word *māshāl* (4912 [Prov. 1:1]), which means "to be like." This word challenges readers to understand these analogies between spiritual and material things. The actual term "Proverbs" was derived from the Latin title that the book was given, "Proverbium." The theme of the book is found in Proverbs 1:7, where the means by which wisdom comes is revealed—fearing the Lord. The results of the proper application of wisdom include the ability to use God-given talents wisely, the realization of one's moral obligations, and one's own intellectual maturity.

Though numerous authors contributed to the Book of Proverbs, the book is often attributed to Solomon because he wrote the largest portion. Solomon's proverbs are divided into three sections: the longer, connected poems (chaps. 1—9); short, unrelated verses (chaps. 10—22:16); and longer, didactic poems (chaps. 25—29). Some would suggest that because the first and last section are similar, they were collected by the men of Hezekiah (Prov. 25:1). Another group of proverbs is referred to as "the sayings of the wise" (chaps. 22:17—24:34). Agar, the son of Jakeh wrote as well (chap. 30). The last collection of proverbs was written by King Lemuel (chap. 31). These were lessons that he was taught by his mother (v. 1).

Several portions of the Book of Proverbs can be grouped together based on their content. The first is commonly referred to as "wisdom" proverbs (chaps. 1; 8; 9). These chapters are grouped together because of their personification of wisdom (Prov. 8:4, 12). Another section contains the proverbs of advice to the young (chaps. 1—9). These are basically long, explanatory poems usually employing second person pronouns for direct address. Other phrases that note direct address are "my son" or "ye children." Solomon also addresses a number of proverbs to those who have a more mature mind (Prov. 10—22:16). Here, third person pronouns are used in a form of indirect address. Some concepts included in this portion are God's sovereignty (chaps. 16; 21) and child training (chap. 22). The fourth division is found in chapters twenty-two through thirty-one. These are a collection of universal admonitions, directed at both the young and old alike. Some of the topics mentioned in the book are: benevolence (Prov. 11:24–26), the contrast between the "right way" and the "wrong way" (Prov. 14:12; 16:25), separation (Prov. 18:2–5), and abstinence from alcohol (Prov. 20:1; 23:29–32).

The Value of Proverbs

1 ⊶ The [a]proverbs of Solomon the
son[1121] of David, king[4428] of Israel;
2 To know[3045] wisdom[2451] and
instruction;[4148] to perceive the words[561]
of understanding;[998]
3 To [a]receive the instruction of wisdom,[7919] justice,[6664] and judgment,[4941]
and [I]equity;[4339]
4 To give subtilty[6195] to the [a]simple,6612 to the young man knowledge[1847]
and [I]discretion.[4209]

5 [a]A wise[2450] *man* will hear,[8085] and
will increase learning;[3948] and a man of
understanding[995] shall attain unto wise
counsels:
6 To understand[995] a proverb, and
[I]the interpretation; the words[1697] of the
wise, and their [a]dark sayings.[2420]

Advice to Young Men

7 [a]The fear[3374] of the LORD *is* [I]the
beginning[7225] of knowledge: *but* fools despise wisdom and instruction.

1 [a]1Kgs. 4:32; Prov. 10:1; 25:1; Eccl. 12:9
3 [I]Hebr. *equities* [a]Prov. 2:1, 9
4 [I]Or, *advisement* [a]Prov. 9:4
5 [a]Prov. 9:9
6 [I]Or, *an eloquent speech* [a]Ps. 78:2
7 [I]Or, *the principal part* [a]Job 28:28; Ps. 111:10; Prov. 9:10; Eccl. 12:13

⊶ **1:1–7** The first seven verses provide the title (v. 1), the purpose (vv. 2–6), and the theme (v. 7) of the book as a whole. The procurement of wisdom is presented as the paramount concern throughout the book.

8 [a]My son, hear the instruction of thy father,[1] and forsake[5203] not the law[4851] of thy mother:[517]

9 For [a]they *shall be* [I]an ornament of grace[2580] unto thy head,[7218] and chains about thy neck.

10 My son, if sinners[2400] entice6601 thee, [a]consent[14] thou not.

11 If they say,[559] Come with us, let us [a]lay wait for blood,[1818] let us lurk privily for the innocent[5355] without cause:

12 Let us swallow them up[1104] alive[2416] as the grave;[7585] and whole,[8549] [a]as those that go down into the pit:[953]

13 We shall find all precious substance, we shall fill our houses[1004] with spoil:

14 Cast in[5307] thy lot among us; let us all have one purse:

15 My son, [a]walk not thou in the way[1870] with them; [b]refrain thy foot from their path:

16 [a]For their feet run to evil,[7451] and make haste to shed[8210] blood.

17 Surely in vain the net is spread [I]in the sight of any bird.

18 And they lay wait for their *own* blood; they lurk privily for their *own* lives.[5315]

19 [a]So *are* the ways[734] of every one that is greedy[1214] of gain; *which* taketh away the life[5315] of the owners[1167] thereof.

20 [I][a]Wisdom[2454] crieth without; she uttereth her voice in the streets:

21 She crieth in the chief place[7218] of concourse,1993 in the openings of the gates: in the city she uttereth her words, *saying,*

22 How long, ye simple ones, will ye love[157] simplicity? and the scorners[3887] delight in their scorning, and fools3684 hate[8130] knowledge?

23 Turn[7725] you at my reproof:[8433] behold, [a]I will pour out my spirit[7307] unto you, I will make known[3045] my words unto you.

24 [a]Because I have called,[7121] and ye refused;[3985] I have stretched out my hand,[3027] and no man regarded;

25 But ye [a]have set at nought[6544] all my counsel,[6098] and would[14] none of my reproof:

26 [a]I also will laugh at your calamity;[343] I will mock when your fear[6343] cometh;

27 When [a]your fear cometh as desolation,[7584] and your destruction[343] cometh as a whirlwind; when distress and anguish6695 cometh upon you.

28 [a]Then shall they call upon me, but I will not answer; they shall seek me early, but they shall not find me:

29 For that they [a]hated knowledge, and did not [b]choose[977] the fear of the LORD:

30 [a]They would none of my counsel: they despised[5006] all my reproof.

31 Therefore [a]shall they eat of the fruit of their own way, and be filled with their own devices.

32 For the [I]turning away of the simple shall slay[2026] them, and the prosperity of fools shall destroy[6] them.

33 But [a]whoso hearkeneth unto me shall dwell[7931] safely,[983] and [b]shall be quiet from fear of evil.

The Rewards of Wisdom

2 My son,[1121] if thou wilt receive my words,[561] and [a]hide my commandments[4687] with thee;

2 So that thou incline[7181] thine ear[241] unto wisdom,[2451] *and* apply thine heart[3820] to understanding;[8394]

3 Yea, if thou criest[7121] after knowledge, *and* [I]liftest up thy voice for understanding;

4 [a]If thou seekest her as silver, and searchest for her as *for* hid treasures;

5 Then shalt thou understand[995] the fear[3374] of the LORD, and find the knowledge[1847] of God.[430]

6 [a]For the LORD giveth wisdom: out of his mouth[6310] *cometh* knowledge and understanding.

7 He layeth up sound wisdom[8454] for the righteous:[3477] [a]*he is* a buckler4043 to them that walk uprightly.[8537]

8 He keepeth[5341] the paths[734] of judgment,[4941] and [a]preserveth[8104] the way[1870] of his saints.[2623]

1:8 [a]Prov. 4:1; 6:20
9 [I]Hebr. *an adding* [a]Prov. 3:22
10 [a]Gen. 39:7-12; Ps. 1:1; Eph. 5:11
11 [a]Jer. 5:26
12 [a]Ps. 28:1; 143:7
15 [a]Ps. 1:1; Prov. 4:14 [b]Ps. 119:101
16 [a]Isa. 59:7; Rom. 3:15
17 [I]Hebr. *in the eyes of every thing that hath a wing*
19 [a]Prov. 15:27; 1Tim. 6:10
20 [I]Hebr. *Wisdoms, Excellent wisdom* [a]Prov. 8:1-4; 9:3; John 7:37
23 [a]Joel 2:28
24 [a]Isa. 65:12; 66:4; Jer. 7:13; Zech. 7:11
25 [a]Ps. 107:11; Prov. 1:30; Luke 7:30
26 [a]Ps. 2:4
27 [a]Prov. 10:24
28 [a]Job 27:9; 35:12; Isa. 1:15; Jer. 11:11; 14:12; Ezek. 8:18; Mic. 3:4; Zech. 7:13; James 4:3
29 [a]Job 21:14; Prov. 1:22 [b]Ps. 119:173
30 [a]Ps. 81:11; Prov. 1:25
31 [a]Job 4:8; Prov. 14:14; 22:8; Isa. 3:11; Jer. 6:19
32 [I]Or, *ease of the simple*
33 [a]Ps. 25:12, 13 [b]Ps. 112:7

2:1 [a]Prov. 4:21; 7:1
3 [I]Hebr. *givest thy voice*
4 [a]Prov. 3:14; Matt. 13:44
6 [I]1Kgs. 3:9, 12; James 1:5
7 [a]Ps. 84:11; Prov. 30:5
8 [a]1Sam. 2:9; Ps. 66:9

9 Then shalt thou understand righteousness,[6664] and judgment, and equity;[4339] *yea,* every good[2896] path.

10 When wisdom entereth into thine heart, and knowledge is pleasant unto thy soul;[5315]

11 Discretion[4209] shall preserve thee, [a]understanding shall keep[5341] thee:

12 To deliver[5337] thee from the way of the evil[7451] *man,* from the man[376] that speaketh froward things;[8419]

13 Who leave[5800] the paths of uprightness,[3476] to [a]walk in the ways[1870] of darkness;[2822]

14 Who [a]rejoice to do[6213] evil, *and* [b]delight in the frowardness[8419] of the wicked;[7451]

15 [a]Whose ways[734] *are* crooked, and *they* froward[3868] in their paths:

16 To deliver thee from the strange woman,[2114] [a]*even* from the stranger *which* flattereth with her words;

17 [a]Which forsaketh[5800] the guide of her youth, and forgetteth the covenant[1285] of her God.

18 For [a]her house[1004] inclineth unto death,[4194] and her paths unto the dead.[7496]

19 None that go unto her return again,[7725] neither take they hold of the paths of life.[2416]

20 That thou mayest walk in the way of good *men,* and keep[8104] the paths of the righteous.[6662]

21 [a]For the upright[3477] shall dwell[7931] in the land,[776] and the perfect[8549] shall remain[3498] in it.

22 [a]But the wicked[7563] shall be cut off[3772] from the earth,[776] and the transgressors shall be [I]rooted[5255] out of it.

More Advice

3 My son,[1121] forget not my law;[8451] [a]but let thine heart[3820] keep[5341] my commandments:[4687]

2 For length[753] of days,[3117] and [I]long[753] life,[2416] and [a]peace, shall they add to thee.

3 Let not mercy[2617] and truth[571] forsake[5800] thee: [a]bind them about thy neck; [b]write them upon the table of thine heart:

4 [a]So shalt thou find favour[2580] and [I]good[2896] understanding[7922] in the sight of God[430] and man.[120]

5 [a]Trust[982] in the LORD with all thine heart; [b]and lean[8172] not unto thine own understanding.[998]

6 [a]In all thy ways[1870] acknowledge[3045] him, and he shall [b]direct[3474] thy paths.[734]

7 [a]Be not wise[2450] in thine own eyes: [b]fear[3372] the LORD, and depart[5493] from evil.[7451]

8 It shall be [I]health to thy navel, and [II][a]marrow to thy bones.[6106]

9 [a]Honour[3513] the LORD with thy substance, and with the firstfruits[7225] of all thine increase:

10 [a]So shall thy barns be filled with plenty, and thy presses[3342] shall burst out with new wine.

11 [a]My son, despise[3988] not the chastening[4148] of the LORD; neither be weary[6973] of his correction:[8433]

12 For whom the LORD loveth[157] he correcteth;[3198] [a]even as a father[1] the son *in whom* he delighteth.[7521]

🔑 13 [a]Happy[835] *is* the man *that* findeth wisdom,[2451] and [I]the man *that* getteth understanding.[8394]

14 [a]For the merchandise of it *is* better[2896] than the merchandise of silver, and the gain thereof than fine gold.

15 She *is* more precious than rubies: and [a]all the things thou canst desire[2656] are not to be compared unto her.

16 [a]Length of days *is* in her right hand; *and* in her left hand riches and honour.[3519]

17 [a]Her ways *are* ways of pleasantness,[5278] and all her paths *are* peace.

18 She *is* [a]a tree of life to them that lay hold[2388] upon her: and happy[833] *is* *every one* that retaineth her.

11 [a]Prov. 6:22
13 [a]John 3:19, 20
14 [a]Prov. 10:23; Jer. 11:15 [b]Rom. 1:32
15 [a]Ps. 125:5
16 [a]Prov. 5:20 [b]Prov. 5:3; 6:24; 7:5
17 [a]Mal. 2:14, 15
18 [a]Prov. 7:27
21 [a]Ps. 37:29
22 [I]Or, *plucked up* [a]Job 18:17; Ps. 37:28; 104:35

1 [a]Deut. 8:1; 30:16, 20
2 [I]Hebr. *years of life* [a]Ps. 119:165
3 [a]Ex. 13:9; Deut. 6:8; Prov. 6:21; 7:3 [b]Jer. 17:1; 2Cor. 3:3
4 [I]Or, *good success* [a]1Sam. 2:26; Ps. 111:10; Luke 2:52; Acts 2:47; Rom. 14:18
5 [a]Ps. 37:3, 5 [b]Jer. 9:23
6 [a]1Chr. 28:9 [b]Jer. 10:23
7 [a]Rom. 12:16 [b]Job 1:1; Prov. 16:6
8 [I]Hebr. *medicine* [II]Hebr. *watering,* or, *moistening* [a]Job 21:24
9 [a]Ex. 22:29; 23:19; 34:26; Deut. 26:2; Mal. 3:10; Luke 14:13
10 [a]Deut. 28:8
11 [a]Job 5:17; Ps. 94:12; Heb. 12:5, 6; Rev. 3:19
12 [a]Deut. 8:5
13 [I]Hebr. *the man* that *draweth out understanding* [a]Prov. 8:34, 35
14 [a]Job 28:13-19; Ps. 19:10; Prov. 2:4; 8:11, 19; 16:16
15 [a]Matt. 13:44
16 [a]Prov. 8:18; 1Tim. 4:8
17 [a]Matt. 11:29, 30
18 [a]Gen. 2:9; 3:22

🔑 **3:13–18** True wisdom yields better and more enduring benefits than mere material things. The result of having wisdom is a quality of life full of tranquility and confidence.

19 [a]The LORD by wisdom hath founded[3245] the earth;[776] by understanding hath he [I]established[3559] the heavens.[8064]

20 [a]By his knowledge[1847] the depths are broken up, and [b]the clouds[7834] drop down the dew.

21 My son, let not them depart from thine eyes: keep sound wisdom[8454] and discretion:[4209]

22 So shall they be life unto thy soul,[5315] and [a]grace[2580] to thy neck.

23 [a]Then shalt thou walk in thy way[1870] safely,[983] and thy foot shall not stumble.[5062]

24 [a]When thou liest down, thou shalt not be afraid:[6342] yea, thou shalt lie down, and thy sleep shall be sweet.[6148]

25 [a]Be not afraid[3372] of sudden fear,[6343] neither of the desolation[7722] of the wicked,[7563] when it cometh.

26 For the LORD shall be thy confidence,[3689] and shall keep[8104] thy foot from being taken.

27 [a]Withhold not good from [I]them to whom it is due, when it is in the power[410] of thine hand[3027] to do[6213] *it*.

28 [a]Say[559] not unto thy neighbour,[7453] Go, and come again, and to morrow I will give; when thou hast it by thee.

29 [I]Devise not evil against thy neighbour, seeing he dwelleth securely[983] by thee.

30 [a]Strive[7378] not with a man without cause,[2600] if he have done thee no harm.[7451]

31 [a]Envy[7065] thou not [I]the oppressor, and choose[977] none of his ways.

32 For the froward[3868] *is* abomination[8441] to the LORD: [a]but his secret[5475] *is* with the righteous.[3477]

33 [a]The curse of the LORD *is* in the house[1004] of the wicked: but [b]he blesseth[1288] the habitation of the just.

34 [a]Surely he scorneth[3887] the scorners: but he giveth grace unto the lowly.

35 The wise shall inherit[5157] glory:[3519] but shame [I]shall be the promotion[7311] of fools.

The Benefits of Wisdom

4 Hear,[8085] [a]ye children, the instruction[4148] of a father, and attend to know[3045] understanding.[998]

2 For I give you good[2896] doctrine,[3948] forsake[5800] ye not my law.[8451]

3 For I was my father's son, [a]tender and only[3173] *beloved* in the sight of my mother.

4 [a]He taught[3384] me also, and said unto me, Let thine heart[3820] retain my words:[1697] [b]keep[8104] my commandments,[4687] and live.[2421]

5 [a]Get wisdom,[2451] get understanding: forget *it* not; neither decline from the words[561] of my mouth.[6310]

6 Forsake her not, and she shall preserve[8104] thee: [a]love[157] her, and she shall keep[5341] thee.

7 [a]Wisdom *is* the principal thing;[7225] *therefore* get wisdom: and with all thy getting get understanding.

8 [a]Exalt her, and she shall promote thee: she shall bring thee to honour,[3513] when thou dost embrace her.

9 She shall give to thine head[7218] [a]an ornament of grace:[2580] [I]a crown of glory[8597] shall she deliver to thee.

10 Hear, O my son, and receive my sayings;[561] [a]and the years of thy life[2416] shall be many.

11 I have taught thee in the way[1870] of wisdom; I have led thee in right[3476] paths.

12 When thou goest, [a]thy steps shall not be straitened;[3334] [b]and when thou runnest, thou shalt not stumble.[3782]

13 Take fast hold[2388] of instruction; let *her* not go: keep[5341] her; for she *is* thy life.

14 [a]Enter not into the path[734] of the wicked,[7563] and go not in the way of evil[7451] *men*.

15 Avoid[6544] it, pass not by it, turn from it, and pass away.

16 [a]For they sleep not, except they have done mischief;[7489] and their sleep is taken away, unless they cause *some* to fall.[3782]

17 For they eat the bread of wicked-

19 IOr, *prepared* [a]Ps. 104:24; 136:5; Prov. 8:27; Jer. 10:12; 51:15
20 [a]Gen. 1:9 [b]Deut. 33:28; Job 36:28
22 [a]Prov. 1:9
23 [a]Ps. 37:24; 91:11, 12; Prov. 10:9
24 [a]Lev. 26:6; Ps. 3:5; 4:8
25 [a]Ps. 91:5; 112:7
27 IHebr. *the owners thereof* [a]Rom. 13:7; Gal. 6:10
28 [a]Lev. 19:13; Deut. 24:15
29 IOr, *Practice no evil*
30 [a]Rom. 12:18
31 IHebr. *a man of violence* [a]Ps. 37:1; 73:3; Prov. 24:1
32 [a]Ps. 25:14
33 [a]Lev. 26:14-17; Ps. 37:22; Zech. 5:4; Mal. 2:2 [b]Ps. 1:3
34 [a]James 4:6; 1Pet. 5:5
35 IHebr. *exalteth the fools*

1 [a]Ps. 34:11; Prov. 1:8
3 [a]1Chr. 29:1
4 [a]1Chr. 28:9; Eph. 6:4 [b]Prov. 7:2
5 IProv. 2:2, 3
6 [a]2Thess. 2:10
7 [a]Matt. 13:44; Luke 10:42
8 [a]1Sam. 2:30
9 IOr, *she shall compass thee with a crown of glory* [a]Prov. 1:9; 3:22
10 [a]Prov. 3:2
12 [a]Ps. 18:36 [b]Ps. 91:11, 12
14 [a]Ps. 1:1; Prov. 1:10, 15
16 [a]Ps. 36:4; Isa. 57:20

ness,[7562] and drink the wine of violence.[2555]

18 [a]But the path of the just [b]*is* as the shining light,[216] that shineth more and more unto the perfect day.[3117]

19 [a]The way of the wicked *is* as darkness:[653] they know not at what they stumble.

20 My son, attend to my words; incline thine ear[241] unto my sayings.

21 [a]Let them not depart from thine eyes; [b]keep[8104] them in the midst of thine heart.[3824]

22 For they *are* life unto those that find them, and [I][a]health to all their flesh.[1320]

23 Keep[5341] thy heart [I]with all diligence;[4929] for out of it *are* the issues of life.

24 Put away[5493] from thee [I]a froward[6143] mouth, and perverse lips[8193] put far from thee.

25 Let thine eyes look right on, and let thine eyelids look straight[3474] before thee.

26 Ponder[6424] the path[4570] of thy feet, and [I]let all thy ways be established.[3559]

27 [a]Turn not to the right hand nor to the left: [b]remove[5493] thy foot from evil.

Warning Against Sexual Sin

5 My son,[1121] attend unto my wisdom,[2451] *and* bow thine ear[241] to my understanding:[8394]

2 That thou mayest regard[8104] discretion,[4209] and *that* thy lips[8193] may [a]keep[5341] knowledge.[1847]

3 [a]For the lips of a strange woman[2114] drop[5197] *as* an honeycomb, and her [I]mouth *is* [b]smoother than oil:[8081]

4 But her end[319] is [a]bitter[4751] as wormwood,[3939] [b]sharp as a twoedged[6310] sword.[2719]

5 [a]Her feet go down to death;[4194] her steps take hold on hell.[7585]

6 Lest thou shouldest ponder the path[734] of life,[2416] her ways are moveable, *that* thou canst not know[3045] *them.*

7 Hear[8085] me now therefore, O ye children,[1121] and depart[5493] not from the words[561] of my mouth.[6310]

8 Remove thy way[1870] far from her, and come not nigh the door of her house:[1004]

9 Lest thou give thine honour[1935] unto others, and thy years unto the cruel:

10 Lest strangers[2114] be filled with [I]thy wealth; and thy labours[6089] *be* in the house of a stranger;

11 And thou mourn at the last, when thy flesh[1320] and thy body[7607] are consumed,[3615]

12 And say,[559] How have I [a]hated[8130] instruction,[4148] and my heart[3820] [b]despised[5006] reproof;

13 And have not obeyed[8085] the voice of my teachers, nor inclined mine ear to them that instructed[3925] me!

14 I was almost in all evil[7451] in the midst of the congregation[6951] and assembly.[5712]

15 Drink waters out of thine own cistern,[953] and running waters out of thine own well.

16 Let thy fountains be dispersed abroad, *and* rivers of waters in the streets.

17 Let them be only thine own, and not strangers' with thee.

18 Let thy fountain be blessed:[1288] and rejoice with [a]the wife[802] of thy youth.

19 [a]*Let her be as* the loving[158] hind[365] and pleasant[2580] roe; let her breasts [I]satisfy thee at all times;[6256] and [II]be thou ravished[7686] always[8548] with her love.[160]

20 And why wilt thou, my son, be ravished with [a]a strange woman, and embrace the bosom of a stranger?[5237]

21 [a]For the ways of man[376] *are* before the eyes of the LORD, and he pondereth all his goings.

22 [a]His own iniquities[5771] shall take the wicked[7563] himself, and he shall be holden[8551] with the cords of his [I]sins.

23 [a]He shall die without instruction;[4148] and in the greatness of his folly he shall go astray.[7686]

---

18 [a]Matt. 5:14, 45; Phil. 2:15 [b]2Sam. 23:4

19 [a]1Sam. 2:9; Job 18:5, 6; Isa. 59:9, 10; Jer. 23:12; John 12:35

21 [a]Prov. 3:3, 21 [b]Prov. 2:1

22 [I]Hebr. *medicine* [a]Prov. 3:8; 12:18

23 [I]Hebr. *above all keeping*

24 [I]Hebr. *from wardness of mouth, and perverseness of lips*

26 [I]Or, *all thy ways shall be ordered aright*

27 [a]Deut. 5:32; 28:14; Josh. 1:7 [b]Isa. 1:16; Rom. 12:9

2 [a]Mal. 2:7

3 [I]Hebr. *palate* [a]Prov. 2:16; 6:24 [b]Ps. 55:21

4 [a]Eccl. 7:26 [b]Heb. 4:12

5 [a]Prov. 7:27

10 [I]Hebr. *thy strength*

12 [a]Prov. 1:29 [b]Prov. 1:25; 12:1

18 [a]Mal. 2:14

19 [I]Hebr. *water thee* [II]Hebr. *err thou always in her love* [a]Song 2:9; 4:5; 7:3

20 [a]Prov. 2:16; 7:5

21 [a]2Chr. 16:9; Job 31:4; 34:21; Prov. 15:3; Jer. 16:17; 32:19; Hos. 7:2; Heb. 4:13

22 [I]Hebr. *sin* [a]Ps. 9:15

23 [a]Job 4:21; 36:12

Warnings Against Idleness and Deceit

6 My son, [a]if thou be surety[6148] for thy friend,[7453] *if* thou hast stricken[8628] thy hand[3709] with a stranger,[2114]

2 Thou art snared[3369] with the words[561] of thy mouth,[6310] thou art taken with the words of thy mouth.

3 Do[6213] this now, my son, and deliver[5337] thyself, when thou art come into the hand of thy friend; go, humble thyself, [I]and make sure[7292] thy friend.

4 [a]Give not sleep to thine eyes, nor slumber to thine eyelids.

5 Deliver thyself as a roe from the hand[3027] *of the hunter,* and as a bird from the hand of the fowler.

6 [a]Go to the ant, thou sluggard;[6102] consider[7200] her ways,[1870] and be wise:[2449]

7 Which having no guide,[7101] overseer,[7860] or ruler,

8 Provideth her meat in the summer, *and* gathereth her food in the harvest.

9 [a]How long wilt thou sleep,[7901] O sluggard? when wilt thou arise out of thy sleep?

10 *Yet* a little sleep, a little slumber, a little folding of the hands[3027] to sleep:

11 [a]So shall thy poverty come as one that travelleth, and thy want as an armed man.[376]

12 A naughty[1100] person, a wicked[205] man, walketh with a froward[6143] mouth.

13 [a]He winketh[7169] with his eyes, he speaketh[4468] with his feet, he teacheth[3384] with his fingers;

14 Frowardness[8419] *is* in his heart,[3820] [a]he deviseth mischief[7451] continually; [b]he [I]soweth discord.

15 Therefore shall his calamity[343] come suddenly; suddenly shall he [a]be broken[7665] [b]without remedy.

16 These six *things* doth the LORD hate:[8130] yea, seven *are* an abomination[8441] [I]unto him:

17 [I][a]A proud look, [b]a lying tongue, and [c]hands that shed[8210] innocent[5355] blood,[1818]

18 [a]An heart that deviseth wicked imaginations,[4284] [b]feet that be swift in running to mischief,

19 [a]A false[8267] witness *that* speaketh[6315] lies,[3577] and he [b]that soweth discord among brethren.[251]

Warning Against Adultery

20 [a]My son, keep[5341] thy father's[1] commandment,[4687] and forsake[5203] not the law[8451] of thy mother:[517]

21 [a]Bind them continually[8548] upon thine heart, *and* tie them about thy neck.

22 [a]When thou goest, it shall lead[5148] thee; when thou sleepest, [b]it shall keep thee; and *when* thou awakest, it shall talk[7878] with thee.

23 [a]For the commandment *is* a [I]lamp;[5216] and the law *is* light;[216] and reproofs[8433] of instruction[4148] *are* the way[1870] of life:[2416]

24 [a]To keep thee from the evil[7451] woman,[802] from the flattery [I]of the tongue of a strange woman.[5237]

25 [a]Lust[2530] not after her beauty in thine heart;[3824] neither let her take thee with her eyelids.

26 For [a]by means of a whorish[2181] woman *a man is brought* to a piece of bread: [b]and [I]the adulteress will [c]hunt for the precious life.[5315]

27 Can a man take fire in his bosom, and his clothes not be burned?[8313]

28 Can one[376] go upon hot coals, and his feet not be burned?

29 So he that goeth in to his neighbour's[7453] wife;[802] whosoever toucheth[5060] her shall not be innocent.[5352]

30 *Men* do not despise a thief, if he steal to satisfy his soul[5315] when he is hungry;

31 But *if* he be found, [a]he shall restore[7999] sevenfold; he shall give all the substance of his house.[1004]

32 *But* whoso committeth adultery[5003] with a woman [a]lacketh [I]understanding:[3820] he *that* doeth[6213] it destroyeth[7843] his own soul.

33 A wound[5061] and dishonour shall he get; and his reproach[2781] shall not be wiped away.[4229]

34 For jealousy[7068] *is* the rage of a

1 [a]Prov. 11:15; 17:18; 20:16; 22:26; 27:13
3 [I]Or, *so shalt thou prevail with thy friend*
4 [a]Ps. 132:4
6 [a]Job 12:7
9 [a]Prov. 24:33, 34
11 [a]Prov. 10:4; 13:4; 20:4
13 [a]Job 15:12; Ps. 35:19; Prov. 10:10
14 [I]Hebr. *casteth forth* [a]Mic. 2:1 [b]Prov. 6:19
15 [a]Jer. 19:11 [b]2Chr. 36:16
16 [I]Hebr. *of his soul*
17 [I]Hebr. *Haughty eyes* [a]Ps. 18:27; 101:5 [b]Ps. 120:2, 3 [c]Isa. 1:15
18 [a]Gen. 6:5 [b]Isa. 59:7; Rom. 3:15
19 [a]Ps. 27:12; Prov. 19:5, 9 [b]Prov. 6:14
20 [a]Prov. 1:8; Eph. 6:1
21 [a]Prov. 3:3; 7:3
22 [a]Prov. 3:23, 24 [b]Prov. 2:11
23 [I]Or, *candle* [a]Ps. 19:8; 119:105
24 [I]Or, *of the strange tongue* [a]Prov. 2:16; 5:3; 7:5
25 [a]Matt. 5:28
26 [I]Hebr. *the woman of a man,* or, *a man's wife* [a]Prov. 29:3 [b]Gen. 39:14 [c]Ezek. 13:18
31 [a]Ex. 22:1, 4
32 [I]Hebr. *heart* [a]Prov. 7:7

man:[1397] therefore he will not spare in the day[3117] of vengeance.[5359]

35 [I]He will not regard any ransom;[3724] neither will he rest content,[14] though thou givest many gifts.[7810]

A Prostitute's Trap

7 My son, keep[8104] my words,[561] and [a]lay up my commandments[4687] with thee.

2 [a]Keep my commandments, and live;[2421] [b]and my law[8451] as the apple of thine eye.

3 [a]Bind them upon thy fingers, write them upon the table of thine heart.[3820]

4 Say unto wisdom,[2451] Thou *art* my sister;[269] and call[7121] understanding[998] *thy* kinswoman:

5 [a]That they may keep thee from the strange woman,[2114] from the stranger *which* flattereth with her words.

6 For at the window of my house[1004] I looked through my casement,[822]

7 And beheld[7200] among the simple ones,[6612] I discerned[995] among [I]the youths, a young man [a]void of understanding,[3820]

8 Passing[5674] through the street near her corner; and he went the way[1870] to her house,

9 [a]In the twilight, [I]in the evening, in the black and dark[653] night:[3915]

10 And, behold, there met him a woman *with* the attire of an harlot,[2181] and subtil of heart.

11 ([a]She *is* loud and stubborn;[5637] [b]her feet abide not in her house:

12 Now *is she* without, now in the streets, and lieth in wait at every corner.)

13 So she caught[2388] him, and kissed[5401] him, *and* [I]with an impudent[5810] face said unto him,

14 [I]*I have* peace offerings[8002] with me; this day[3117] have I payed[7999] my vows.[5088]

15 Therefore came I forth to meet thee, diligently to seek thy face, and I have found thee.

16 I have decked my bed with coverings of tapestry, with carved *works,* with [a]fine linen of Egypt.

17 I have perfumed[5130] my bed with myrrh,[4753] aloes,[174] and cinnamon.

18 Come, let us take our fill[7301] of love[1730] until the morning: let us solace ourselves[5965] with loves.[159]

19 For the goodman[376] *is* not at home,[1004] he is gone a long journey:[1870]

20 He hath taken a bag of money [I]with him, *and* will come home at [II]the day appointed.

21 With [a]her much fair speech[3948] she caused him to yield, [b]with the flattering of her lips[8193] she forced[5080] him.

22 He goeth after her [I]straightway,[6597] as an ox goeth to the slaughter,[2874] or as a fool to the correction[4148] of the stocks;

23 Till a dart strike through his liver; [a]as a bird hasteth to the snare, and knoweth not that it *is* for his life.[5315]

24 Hearken[8085] unto me now therefore, O ye children, and attend to the words of my mouth.[6310]

25 Let not thine heart decline to her ways, go not astray[8582] in her paths.

26 For she hath cast down[5307] many wounded:[2491] yea, [a]many strong *men* have been slain[2026] by her.

27 [a]Her house *is* the way to hell,[7585] going down to the chambers of death.[4194]

Wisdom

8 🗝 Doth[7121] not [a]wisdom[2451] cry?[7121] and understanding[8394] put forth her voice?

2 She standeth[5324] in the top[7218] of high places, by the way in the places[1004] of the paths.

3 She crieth at the gates, at the entry of the city, at the coming in at the doors.

35 [I]Hebr. *He will not accept the face of any ransom*

7:1 [a]Prov. 2:1

2 [a]Lev. 18:5; Prov. 4:4; Isa. 55:3 [b]Deut. 32:10

3 [a]Deut. 6:8; 11:18; Prov. 3:3; 6:21

5 [a]Prov. 2:16; 5:3; 6:24

7 [I]Hebr. *the sons* [a]Prov. 6:32; 9:4, 16

9 [I]Hebr. *in the evening of the day* [a]Job 24:15

11 [a]Prov. 9:13 [b]1Tim. 5:13; Titus 2:5

13 [I]Hebr. *she strengthened her face, and said*

14 [I]Hebr. *Peace offerings are upon me*

16 [a]Isa. 19:9

20 [I]Hebr. *in his hand* [II]Or, *the new moon*

21 [a]Prov. 5:3 [b]Ps. 12:2

22 [I]Hebr. *suddenly*

23 [a]Eccl. 9:12

26 [a]Neh. 13:26

27 [a]Prov. 2:18; 5:5; 9:18

8:1 [a]Prov. 1:20; 9:3

🗝 **8:1—9:6** "Wisdom" is the key term of Proverbs. In chapters eight and nine, wisdom is personified. It is available to the simplest (Prov. 8:2, 5), but it is also profound—if God Himself did nothing without Wisdom (8:22–31), who are we to attempt to guide our own lives without it?

4 Unto you, O men,[376] I call;[7121] and my voice *is* to the sons[1121] of man.[120]

5 O ye simple, understand[995] wisdom:[6195] and, ye fools, be ye of an understanding[995] heart.[3820]

6 Hear;[8085] for I will speak[1696] of [a]excellent things;[5057] and the opening of my lips[8193] *shall be* right things.[4334]

7 For my mouth shall speak[1897] truth;[571] and wickedness[7562] *is* [I]an abomination[8441] to my lips.

8 All the words[561] of my mouth[6310] *are* in righteousness;[6664] *there is* nothing [I]froward[6617] or perverse in them.

9 They *are* all plain[5228] to him that understandeth,[995] and right[3477] to them that find knowledge.[1847]

10 Receive my instruction,[4148] and not silver; and knowledge rather than choice[977] gold.

11 [a]For wisdom *is* better[2896] than rubies; and all the things that may be desired are not to be compared to it.

12 I wisdom dwell[7931] with [I]prudence,[6195] and find out knowledge of witty inventions.[4209]

13 [a]The fear[3374] of the LORD *is* to hate[8130] evil:[7451] [b]pride, and arrogancy, and the evil way, and [c]the froward[8419] mouth, do I hate.

14 Counsel[6098] *is* mine, and sound wisdom:[8454] I *am* understanding;[998] [a]I have strength.

15 [a]By me kings[4428] reign,[4427] and princes[7336] decree[2710] justice.[6664]

16 By me princes[8269] rule,[8323] and nobles,[5081] *even* all the judges[8199] of the earth.[776]

17 [a]I love[157] them that love me; and [b]those that seek me early shall find me.

18 [a]Riches and honour[3519] *are* with me: *yea,* durable riches and righteousness.[6666]

19 [a]My fruit *is* better than gold, yea, than fine gold; and my revenue than choice silver.

20 I [I]lead in the way[734] of righteousness, in the midst[8432] of the paths of judgment:[4941]

21 That I may cause those that love me to inherit[5157] substance; and I will fill their treasures.

🔑 22 [a]The LORD possessed me in the beginning[7225] of his way, before his works of old.[227]

23 [a]I was set up[5258] from everlasting,[5769] from the beginning,[7218] or ever the earth was.

24 When *there were* no depths, I was brought forth;[2342] when *there were* no fountains abounding[3513] with water.

25 [a]Before the mountains were settled, before the hills was I brought forth:

26 While as yet he had not made[6213] the earth, nor the [I]fields, nor [II]the highest part of the dust[6083] of the world.[8398]

27 When he prepared[3559] the heavens,[8064] I *was* there: when he set[2710] [I]a compass[2329] upon the face of the depth:

28 When he established[553] the clouds[7834] above: when he strengthened[5810] the fountains of the deep:

29 [a]When he gave to the sea his decree,[2706] that the waters should not pass his commandment:[6310] when [b]he appointed[2710] the foundations[4146] of the earth:

6 [a]Prov. 22:20
7 [I]Hebr. *the abomination of my lips*
8 [I]Hebr. wreathed
11 [a]Job 28:15-19; Ps. 19:10; 119:127; Prov. 3:14, 15; 4:5, 7; 16:16
12 [I]Or, *subtlety*
13 [a]Prov. 16:6 [b]Prov. 6:17 [c]Prov. 4:24
14 [a]Eccl. 7:19
15 [a]Dan. 2:21; Rom. 13:1
17 [a]1Sam. 2:30; Ps. 91:14; John 14:21 [b]James 1:5
18 [a]Prov. 3:16; Matt. 6:33
19 [a]Prov. 3:14; Prov. 8:10
20 [I]Or, *walk*
22 [a]Prov. 3:19; John 1:1
23 [a]Ps. 2:6
25 [a]Job 15:7, 8
26 [I]Or, *open places* [II]Or, *the chief part*
27 [I]Or, *a circle*
29 [a]Gen. 1:9, 10; Job 38:10, 11; Ps. 33:7; 104:9; Jer. 5:22 [b]Job 38:4

🔑 **8:22–31** This passage has been understood by many scholars to be referring directly to Christ because of similar passages in the New Testament. The characteristics which belong to this personality called "Wisdom" do coincide with those of Christ: He existed before creation (Col. 1:16; Rev. 3:14, cf. vv. 23–30), He was with the Lord at creation (John 1:1, cf. v. 30), and His "delights were with the sons of men" (John 1:14; 13:1, cf. v. 31). Another factor which suggests that Deity is being spoken of is that the preposition "by" in the phrase "I was by him" (v. 30) has been found in every other case where it is used in the Old Testament (more than 60) to indicate the close spatial relationship between two specific persons or substances. Another view expresses the simple explanation that this is figurative poetic language which personifies the concept of wisdom. This interpretation does not necessarily demand, however, that pointing out similarities to the person of Christ is improper. A third view proposes that while it is wisdom that is being discussed, it can be regarded as typical of Christ.

30 [a]Then I was by him, *as* one brought up *with him:* [b]and I was daily *his* delight, rejoicing always[6256] before him;

31 Rejoicing in the habitable part[8398] of his earth; and [a]my delights *were* with the sons of men.[120]

32 Now therefore hearken[8085] unto me, O ye children:[1121] for [a]blessed[835] *are they that* keep[8104] my ways.[1870]

33 Hear instruction, and be wise,[2449] and refuse it not.

34 [a]Blessed *is* the man that heareth me, watching daily at my gates, waiting at the posts of my doors.

35 For whoso findeth me findeth life,[2416] and shall [I][a]obtain favour[7522] of the LORD.

36 But he that sinneth[2398] against me [a]wrongeth[2554] his own soul:[5315] all they that hate me love death.[4194]

Wisdom and the Foolish Woman

9 Wisdom[2454] hath [a]builded her house, she hath hewn out[2672] her seven pillars:

2 [a]She hath killed[2873] [I]her beasts;[2874] [b]she hath mingled her wine; she hath also furnished her table.

3 She hath [a]sent forth her maidens: [b]she crieth [c]upon the highest places of the city,

4 [a]Whoso *is* simple,6612 let him turn in hither: *as for* him that wanteth understanding,[3820] she saith to him,

5 [a]Come, eat of my bread, and drink of the wine *which* I have mingled.

6 Forsake[5800] the foolish, and live;[2421] and go in the way[1870] of understanding.[998]

7 He that reproveth[3256] a scorner[3887] getteth to himself shame: and he that rebuketh[3198] a wicked[7563] *man getteth* himself a blot.[3971]

8 [a]Reprove[3198] not a scorner, lest he hate[8130] thee: [b]rebuke a wise man,[2450] and he will love[157] thee.

9 Give *instruction* to a wise *man,* and he will be yet wiser:[2449] teach[3045] a just *man,* [a]and he will increase in learning.[3948]

10 [a]The fear[3374] of the LORD *is* the beginning of wisdom:[2451] and the knowledge[1847] of the holy[6918] *is* understanding.

11 [a]For by me thy days[3117] shall be multiplied, and the years of thy life[2416] shall be increased.

12 [a]If thou be wise, thou shalt be wise for thyself: but *if* thou scornest,[3887] thou alone shalt bear[5375] *it.*

🔑 13 [a]A foolish[3687] woman[802] *is* clamorous: *she is* simple, and knoweth nothing.

14 For she sitteth at the door of her house, on a seat[3678] [a]in the high places of the city,

15 To call[7121] passengers who go right[3474] on their ways:[734]

16 [a]Whoso *is* simple, let him turn in hither: and *as for* him that wanteth understanding, she saith to him,

17 [a]Stolen waters are sweet, and bread [I]*eaten* in secret is pleasant.

18 But he knoweth not that [a]the dead[7496] *are* there; *and that* her guests[7121] *are* in the depths of hell.[7585]

Some Proverbs of Solomon

10 The proverbs of Solomon. [a]A wise[2450] son[1121] maketh a glad father:[1] but a foolish son *is* the heaviness8424 of his mother.[517]

2 [a]Treasures of wickedness[7562] profit

30 [a]John 1:1, 2, 18 [b]Matt. 3:17; Col. 1:13
31 [a]Ps. 16:3
32 [a]Ps. 119:1, 2; 128:1, 2; Luke 11:28
34 [a]Prov. 3:13, 18
35 [I]Hebr. *bring forth* [a]Prov. 12:2
36 [a]Prov. 20:2

1 [a]Matt. 16:18; Eph. 2:20, 21, 22; 1Pet. 2:5
2 [I]Hebr. *her killing* [a]Matt. 22:3, 4 [b]Prov. 9:5; 23:30
3 [a]Rom. 10:15 [b]Prov. 8:1, 2 [c]Prov. 9:14
4 [a]Prov. 6:32; 9:16; Matt. 11:25
5 [a]Prov. 9:2; Song 5:1; Isa. 55:1; John 6:27
8 [a]Matt. 7:6 [b]Ps. 141:5
9 [a]Matt. 13:12
10 [a]Job 28:28; Ps. 111:10; Prov. 1:7
11 [a]Prov. 3:2, 16; 10:27
12 [a]Job 35:6, 7; Prov. 16:26
13 [a]Prov. 7:11
14 [a]Prov. 9:3
16 [a]Prov. 9:4
17 [I]Hebr. *of secresies* [a]Prov. 20:17
18 [a]Prov. 2:18; 7:27

1 [a]Prov. 15:20; 17:21, 25; 19:13; 29:3, 15
2 [a]Ps. 49:6-9; Prov. 11:4; Luke 12:19, 20

🔑 **9:13–18** Wisdom, which is personified as a woman in the first portion of this chapter, is contrasted here with the woman of folly. They have similar methods in that they both sit in the most noticeable places of the city (Prov. 8:2, 3; 9:3, cf. v. 14) and appeal to the simple (Prov. 8:6; 9:5, cf. v. 16). Wisdom offers rewards that are more valuable than any kind of riches (Prov. 8:10, 11, 18, 19), while the woman of foolishness recommends the sweetness of "stolen waters" and the pleasantness of "bread eaten in secret" (v. 17). The consequences connected with these choices are altogether opposite. The guests of Wisdom receive many blessings (Prov. 8:34, 35), but those who turn to foolishness perish and pass into the depths of hell (v. 18).

nothing: [b]but righteousness[6666] delivereth[5337] from death.[4194]

3 [a]The LORD will not suffer the soul[5315] of the righteous[6662] to famish: but he casteth away [I]the substance of the wicked.[7563]

4 [a]He becometh poor that dealeth *with* a slack7423 hand:[3709] but [b]the hand[3027] of the diligent maketh rich.

5 He that gathereth in summer *is* a wise[7919] son: *but* he that sleepeth in harvest *is* [a]a son that causeth shame.[954]

6 Blessings[1293] *are* upon the head[7218] of the just: but [a]violence[2555] covereth[3680] the mouth[6310] of the wicked.

7 [a]The memory[2143] of the just *is* blessed: but the name of the wicked shall rot.

8 The wise in heart[3820] will receive commandments:[4687] [a]but [I]a prating[8193] fool [II]shall fall.

9 [a]He that walketh uprightly[8537] walketh surely: but he that perverteth his ways[1870] shall be known.[3045]

10 [a]He that winketh7169 with the eye causeth sorrow: [b]but a prating fool [I]shall fall.

11 [a]The mouth of a righteous *man is* a well of life:[2416] but [b]violence covereth the mouth of the wicked.

12 Hatred[8135] stirreth up strifes: but [a]love[160] covereth all sins.[6588]

13 In the lips[8193] of him that hath understanding[995] wisdom[2451] is found: but [a]a rod[7626] *is* for the back[1460] of him that is void of [I]understanding.[3820]

14 Wise *men* lay up knowledge:[1847] but [a]the mouth of the foolish *is* near destruction.[4288]

15 [a]The rich man's wealth *is* his strong city: the destruction of the poor *is* their poverty.

16 The labour of the righteous *tendeth* to life: the fruit of the wicked to sin.[2403]

17 He *is in* the way[734] of life that keepeth[8104] instruction:[4148] but he that refuseth reproof [I]erreth.[8582]

18 He that hideth hatred *with* lying lips, and [a]he that uttereth a slander, *is* a fool.3684

19 [a]In the multitude of words[1697] there wanteth2308 not sin: but [b]he that refraineth his lips *is* wise.

20 The tongue of the just *is as* choice[977] silver: the heart of the wicked *is* little worth.

21 The lips of the righteous feed many: but fools die for want [I]of wisdom.[3820]

22 [a]The blessing[1293] of the LORD, it maketh rich, and he addeth no sorrow[6089] with it.

23 [a]*It is* as sport to a fool to do[6213] mischief: but a man[376] of understanding[8394] hath wisdom.

24 [a]The fear[4034] of the wicked, it shall come upon him: but [b]the desire of the righteous shall be granted.

25 As the whirlwind passeth,[5674] [a]so *is* the wicked no *more:* but [b]the righteous *is* an everlasting[5769] foundation.

26 As vinegar to the teeth, and as smoke to the eyes, so *is* the sluggard6102 to them that send him.

27 [a]The fear[3374] of the LORD [I]prolongeth days:[3117] but [b]the years of the wicked shall be shortened.

28 The hope[8431] of the righteous *shall be* gladness: but the [a]expectation8615 of the wicked shall perish.[6]

29 The way[1870] of the LORD *is* strength to the upright:[8537] [a]but destruction *shall be* to the workers of iniquity.[205]

30 [a]The righteous shall never be removed: but the wicked shall not inhabit[7931] the earth.[776]

31 [a]The mouth of the just bringeth forth wisdom: but the froward8419 tongue shall be cut out.[3772]

32 The lips of the righteous know[3045] what is acceptable:[7522] but the mouth of the wicked *speaketh* [I]frowardness.8419

11 A [I][a]false[4820] balance *is* abomination[8441] to the LORD: but [II]a just[8003] weight *is* his delight.[7522]

2 [a]*When* pride[2087] cometh, then

2 [b]Dan. 4:27
3 [I]Or, *the wicked for* their *wickedness* [a]Ps. 10:14; 34:9, 10; 37:25
4 [a]Prov. 12:24; 19:15 [b]Prov. 13:4; 21:5
5 [a]Prov. 12:4; 17:2; 19:26
6 [a]Prov. 10:11; Esth. 7:8
7 [a]Ps. 9:5, 6; 112:6; Eccl. 8:10
8 [I]Hebr. *a fool of lips* [II]Or, *shall be beaten* [a]Prov. 10:10
9 [a]Ps. 23:4; Prov. 28:18; Isa. 33:15, 16
10 [I]Or, *shall be beaten* [a]Prov. 6:13 [b]Prov. 10:8
11 [a]Ps. 37:30; Prov. 13:14; 18:4 [b]Ps. 107:42; Prov. 10:6
12 [a]Prov. 17:9; 1Cor. 13:4; 1Pet. 4:8
13 [I]Hebr. *heart* [a]Prov. 26:3
14 [a]Prov. 18:7; 21:23
15 [a]Job 31:24; Ps. 52:7; Prov. 18:11; 1Tim. 6:17
17 [I]Or, *causeth to err*
18 [a]Ps. 15:3
19 [a]Eccl. 5:3 [b]James 3:2
21 [I]Hebr. *of heart*
22 [a]Gen. 24:35; 26:12; Ps. 37:22
23 [a]Prov. 14:9; 15:21
24 [a]Job 15:21 [b]Ps. 145:19; Matt. 5:6; 1John 5:14, 15
25 [a]Ps. 37:9, 10 [b]Prov. 10:30; Ps. 15:5; Matt. 7:24, 25; 16:18
27 [I]Hebr. *addeth* [a]Prov. 9:11 [b]Job 15:32, 33; 22:16; Ps. 55:23; Eccl. 7:17
28 [a]Job 8:13; 11:20; Ps. 112:10; Prov. 11:7
29 [a]Ps. 1:6; 37:20
30 [a]Ps. 37:22, 29; 125:1; Prov. 10:25
31 [a]Ps. 37:30

32 [I]Hebr. *from wardnesses* 1 [I]Hebr. *Balances of deceit* [II]Hebr. *a perfect stone* [a]Lev. 19:35; 36; Deut. 25:13-16; Prov. 16:11; 20:10, 23 2 [a]Prov. 15:33; 16:18; 18:12; Dan. 4:30, 31

cometh shame: but with the lowly *is* wisdom.[2451]

3 [a]The integrity[8538] of the upright[3477] shall guide[5148] them: but the perverseness of transgressors shall destroy[7703] them.

4 [a]Riches profit not in the day[3117] of wrath:[5678] but [b]righteousness[6666] delivereth[5337] from death.[4194]

5 The righteousness of the perfect[8549] shall [I]direct[3474] his way:[1870] but the wicked[7563] shall fall by his own wickedness.[7564]

6 The righteousness of the upright shall deliver[5337] them: but [a]transgressors shall be taken in *their own* naughtiness.[1942]

7 [a]When a wicked man[120] dieth, *his* expectation shall perish:[6] and the hope[8431] of unjust[205] *men* perisheth.

8 [a]The righteous[6662] is delivered[2502] out of trouble, and the wicked cometh in his stead.

9 An [a]hypocrite[2611] with *his* mouth[6310] destroyeth[7843] his neighbour:[7453] but through knowledge[1847] shall the just be delivered.

10 [a]When it goeth well[2898] with the righteous, the city rejoiceth: and when the wicked perish, *there is* shouting.7440

11 [a]By the blessing[1293] of the upright the city is exalted: but it is overthrown by the mouth of the wicked.

12 He that is [I]void of wisdom[3820] despiseth his neighbour: but a man[376] of understanding holdeth his peace.

13 [I][a]A talebearer revealeth[1540] secrets:[5475] but he that is of a faithful[539] spirit[7307] concealeth[3680] the matter.[1697]

14 [a]Where no counsel *is,* the people[5971] fall: but in the multitude of counsellors[3289] *there is* safety.[8668]

15 [a]He that is surety[6148] for a stranger[2114] [I]shall smart *for it:* and he that hateth[8130] [II]suretiship[8628] is sure.

16 [a]A gracious woman[802] retaineth honour:[3519] and strong *men* retain riches.

17 [a]The merciful[2617] man doeth good to his own soul:[5315] but *he that is* cruel troubleth his own flesh.[7607]

18 The wicked worketh[6213] a deceitful[8267] work: but [a]to him that soweth righteousness *shall be* a sure[571] reward.

19 As righteousness *tendeth* to life:[2416] so he that pursueth evil[7451] *pursueth it* to his own death.

20 They that are of a froward6141 heart[3820] *are* abomination to the LORD: but *such as are* upright[8549] in *their* way *are* his delight.

21 [a]*Though* hand[3027] *join* in hand, the wicked[7451] shall not be unpunished:[5352] but [b]the seed[2233] of the righteous shall be delivered.[4422]

22 *As* a jewel of gold in a swine's snout, *so is* a fair woman which [I]is without discretion.[2940]

23 The desire of the righteous *is* only good:[2896] *but* the expectation of the wicked [a]*is* wrath.

24 There is that [a]scattereth, and yet increaseth; and *there is* that withholdeth more than is meet,[3476] but *it tendeth* to poverty.

25 [I][a]The liberal[1293] soul shall be made fat:[1878] [b]and he that watereth7301 shall be watered[3384] also himself.

26 [a]He that withholdeth corn, the people[3816] shall curse[5344] him: but [b]blessing *shall be* upon the head[7218] of him that selleth *it.*

27 He that diligently seeketh good procureth favour:[7522] [a]but he that seeketh mischief,[7451] it shall come unto him.

28 [a]He that trusteth[982] in his riches shall fall; but [b]the righteous shall flourish as a branch.

29 He that troubleth his own house[1004] [a]shall inherit[5157] the wind:[7307] and the fool[191] *shall be* servant[5650] to the wise[2450] of heart.

30 The fruit of the righteous *is* a tree of life; and [a]he that [I]winneth souls[5315] *is* wise.

31 [a]Behold, the righteous shall be recompensed[7999] in the earth:[776] much more the wicked and the sinner.[2398]

12 Whoso loveth[157] instruction[4148] loveth knowledge:[1847] but he that hateth[8130] reproof *is* brutish.

2 [a]A good[2896] *man* obtaineth6329 fa-

3 [a]Prov. 13:6
4 [a]Prov. 10:2; Ezek. 7:19; Zeph. 1:18 [b]Gen. 7:1
5 [I]Hebr. *rectify*
6 [a]Prov. 5:22; Eccl. 10:8
7 [a]Prov. 10:28
8 [a]Prov. 21:18
9 [a]Job 8:13
10 [a]Esth. 8:15; Prov. 28:12, 28
11 [a]Prov. 29:8
12 [I]Hebr. *destitute of heart*
13 [I]Hebr. *He that walketh, being a talebearer* [a]Lev. 19:16; Prov. 20:19
14 [a]1Kgs. 12:1-11; Prov. 15:22; 24:6
15 [I]Hebr. *shall be sore broken* [II]Hebr. *those that strike hands* [a]Prov. 6:1
16 [a]Prov. 31:30
17 [a]Matt. 5:7; 25:34-46
18 [a]Hos. 10:12; Gal. 6:8, 9; James 3:18
21 [a]Prov. 16:5 [b]Ps. 112:2
22 [I]Hebr. *departeth from*
23 [a]Rom. 2:8, 9
24 [a]Ps. 112:9
25 [I]Hebr. *The soul of blessing* [a]2Cor. 9:6-10 [b]Matt. 5:7
26 [a]Amos 8:5, 6 [b]Job 29:13
27 [a]Esth. 7:10; Ps. 7:15, 16; 9:15, 16; 10:2; 57:6
28 [a]Job 31:24; Ps. 52:7; Mark 10:24; Luke 12:21; 1Tim. 6:17 [b]Ps. 1:3; 52:8; 92:12-15; Jer. 17:8
29 [a]Eccl. 5:16
30 [I]Hebr. *taketh* [a]Dan. 12:3; 1Cor. 9:19-22; James 5:20
31 [a]Jer. 25:29; 1Pet. 4:17, 18

2 [a]Prov. 8:35

vour[7522] of the LORD: but a man[376] of wicked devices[4209] will he condemn.[7561]

3 A man[120] shall not be established[3559] by wickedness:[7562] but the [a]root of the righteous[6662] shall not be moved.

4 [a]A virtuous[2428] woman[802] *is* a crown to her husband:[1167] but she that maketh ashamed[954] *is* [b]as rottenness in his bones.[6106]

5 The thoughts[4284] of the righteous *are* right:[4941] *but* the counsels of the wicked[7563] *are* deceit.[4820]

6 [a]The words[1697] of the wicked *are* to lie in wait for blood:[1818] [b]but the mouth[6310] of the upright[3477] shall deliver[5337] them.

7 [a]The wicked are overthrown,2013 and *are* not: but the house[1004] of the righteous shall stand.

8 A man shall be commended[6310] according to his wisdom:[7922] [a]but he that is [I]of a perverse[5753] heart[3820] shall be despised.[937]

9 [a]*He that is* despised,7034 and hath a servant,[5650] *is* better[2896] than he that honoureth himself,[3513] and lacketh bread.

10 [a]A righteous *man* regardeth[3045] the life[5315] of his beast: but the [I]tender mercies[7356] of the wicked *are* cruel.

11 [a]He that tilleth[5647] his land[127] shall be satisfied with bread: but he that followeth vain *persons is* [b]void of understanding.[3820]

12 The wicked desireth[2530] [I]the net of evil[7451] *men:* but the root of the righteous yieldeth *fruit.*

13 [I][a]The wicked[7451] is snared[4170] by the transgression[6588] of *his* lips:[8193] [b]but the just shall come out of trouble.

14 [a]A man shall be satisfied with good by the fruit of *his* mouth: [b]and the recompence of a man's[120] hands[3027] shall be rendered[7725] unto him.

15 [a]The way[1870] of a fool *is* right[3477] in his own eyes: but he that hearkeneth unto counsel[6098] *is* wise.[2450]

16 [a]A fool's wrath[3708] is [I]presently known:[3045] but a prudent[6175] *man* covereth[3680] shame.

17 [a]*He that* speaketh[6315] truth[530] sheweth forth[5046] righteousness:[6664] but a false[8267] witness deceit.

18 [a]There is that speaketh[981] like the piercings of a sword:[2719] but the tongue of the wise *is* health.

19 The lip of truth[571] shall be established for ever:[5703] [a]but a lying tongue *is* but for a moment.7280

20 Deceit *is* in the heart of them that imagine evil: but to the counsellors[3289] of peace *is* joy.

21 There shall no evil happen to the just: but the wicked shall be filled with mischief.[7451]

22 [a]Lying lips *are* abomination[8441] to the LORD: but they that deal[6213] truly *are* his delight.[7522]

23 [a]A prudent man concealeth[3680] knowledge: but the heart of fools proclaimeth[7121] foolishness.

24 [a]The hand[3027] of the diligent shall bear rule:[4910] but the [I]slothful shall be under tribute.

25 [a]Heaviness[1674] in the heart of man maketh it stoop:[7812] but [b]a good word[1697] maketh it glad.

26 The righteous *is* more [I]excellent than his neighbour:[7453] but the way of the wicked seduceth[8582] them.

27 The slothful7423 *man* roasteth not that which he took in hunting: but the substance of a diligent2742 man *is* precious.

28 In the way[734] of righteousness[6666] *is* life:[2416] and *in* the pathway *thereof there is* no death.[4194]

13 A wise[2450] son *heareth* his father's[1] instruction:[4148] [a]but a scorner[3887] heareth not rebuke.[1606]

2 [a]A man[376] shall eat good[2896] by the fruit of *his* mouth:[6310] but the soul[5315] of the transgressors *shall eat* violence.[2555]

3 [a]He that keepeth[5341] his mouth keepeth[8104] his life:[5315] *but* he that openeth wide his lips[8193] shall have destruction.[4288]

4 [a]The soul of the sluggard6102 desireth,[183] and *hath* nothing: but the soul of the diligent shall be made fat.[1878]

---

3 [a]Prov. 10:25
4 [a]Prov. 31:23; 1Cor. 11:7 [b]Prov. 14:30
6 [a]Prov. 1:11, 18 [b]Prov. 14:3
7 [a]Ps. 37:36, 37; Prov. 11:21; Matt. 7:24-27
8 [I]Hebr. *perverse of heart* [a]1Sam. 25:17
9 [a]Prov. 13:7
10 [I]Or, *bowels* [a]Deut. 25:4
11 [a]Gen. 3:19; Prov. 28:19 [b]Prov. 6:32
12 [I]Or, *the fortress*
13 [I]Hebr. *The snare of the wicked* is *in the transgression of lips* [a]Prov. 18:7 [b]2Pet. 2:9
14 [a]Prov. 13:2; 18:20 [b]Isa. 3:10, 11
15 [a]Prov. 3:7; Luke 18:11
16 [I]Hebr. *in that day* [a]Prov. 29:11
17 [a]Prov. 14:5
18 [a]Ps. 57:4; 59:7; 64:3
19 [a]Ps. 52:5; Prov. 19:9
22 [a]Prov. 6:17; 11:20; Rev. 22:15
23 [a]Prov. 13:16; 15:2
24 [I]Or, *deceitful* [a]Prov. 10:4
25 [a]Prov. 15:13 [b]Isa. 50:4
26 [I]Or, *abundant*

1 [a]1Sam. 2:25
2 [a]Prov. 12:14
3 [a]Ps. 39:1; Prov. 21:23; James 3:2
4 [a]Prov. 10:4

5 A righteous[6662] *man* hateth[8130] lying: but a wicked[7563] *man* is loathsome,[887] and cometh to shame.

6 [a]Righteousness[6666] keepeth *him that is* upright[8537] in the way:[1870] but wickedness[7564] overthroweth [I]the sinner.

7 [a]There is that maketh himself rich, yet *hath* nothing: *there is* that maketh himself poor, yet *hath* great riches.

8 The ransom[3724] of a man's life *are* his riches: but the poor heareth not rebuke.

9 The light[216] of the righteous rejoiceth: [a]but the [I]lamp[5216] of the wicked shall be put out.

10 Only by pride[2087] cometh contention: but with the well advised[3289] *is* wisdom.[2451]

11 [a]Wealth *gotten* by vanity shall be diminished: but he that gathereth[6908] [I]by labour shall increase.

12 Hope[8431] deferred maketh the heart[3820] sick: but [a]*when* the desire cometh, *it is* a tree of life.[2416]

13 Whoso [a]despiseth the word[1697] shall be destroyed:[2254] but he that feareth the commandment[4687] [I]shall be rewarded.[7999]

14 [a]The law[8451] of the wise *is* a fountain of life, to depart[5493] from [b]the snares of death.[4194]

15 Good understanding[7922] giveth favour:[2580] but the way of transgressors[898] *is* hard.[386]

16 [a]Every prudent[6175] *man* dealeth with knowledge:[1847] but a fool[3684] [I]layeth open *his* folly.

17 A wicked messenger[4397] falleth[5307] into mischief:[7451] but [I][a]a faithful[529] ambassador[6735] *is* health.

18 Poverty and shame *shall be to* him that refuseth[6544] instruction: but [a]he that regardeth[8104] reproof shall be honoured.

19 [a]The desire accomplished[1961] is sweet[6148] to the soul: but *it is* abomination[8441] to fools to depart from evil.[7451]

20 He that walketh with wise *men* shall be wise: but a companion of fools [I]shall be destroyed.[7321]

6 [I]Hebr. *sin* [a]Prov. 11:3, 5, 6
7 [a]Prov. 12:9
9 [I]Or, *candle* [a]Job 18:5, 6; 21:17; Prov. 24:20
11 [I]Hebr. *with the hand* [a]Prov. 10:2; 20:21
12 [a]Prov. 13:19
13 [I]Or, *shall be in peace* [a]2Chr. 36:16
14 [a]Prov. 10:11; 14:27; 16:22 [b]2Sam. 22:6
16 [I]Hebr. *spreadeth* [a]Prov. 12:23; 15:2
17 [I]Hebr. *an ambassador of faithfulness* [a]Prov. 25:13
18 [a]Prov. 15:5, 31
19 [a]Prov. 13:12
20 [I]Hebr. *shall be broken*
21 [a]Ps. 32:10
22 [a]Job 27:16, 17; Prov. 28:8; Eccl. 2:26
23 [a]Prov. 12:11
24 [a]Prov. 19:18; 22:15; 23:13; 29:15, 17
25 [a]Ps. 34:10; 37:3

1 [a]Prov. 24:3 [b]Ruth 4:11
2 [a]Job 12:4
3 [a]Prov. 12:6
5 [a]Ex. 20:16; 23:1; Prov. 6:19; 12:17; 14:25
6 [a]Prov. 8:9; 17:24
9 [a]Prov. 10:23
10 [I]Hebr. *the bitterness of his soul*
11 [a]Job 8:15

21 [a]Evil pursueth sinners:[2400] but to the righteous good shall be repayed.

22 A good *man* leaveth an inheritance[5157] to his children's children: and [a]the wealth[2428] of the sinner[2398] *is* laid up for the just.

23 [a]Much food *is in* the tillage[5215] of the poor: but there is *that is* destroyed[5595] for want of judgment.[4941]

24 [a]He that spareth his rod[7626] hateth his son: but he that loveth[157] him chasteneth him betimes.[7836]

25 [a]The righteous eateth to the satisfying of his soul: but the belly[990] of the wicked shall want.

14

Every [a]wise woman[802] [b]buildeth her house:[1004] but the foolish plucketh it down[2040] with her hands.[3027]

2 He that walketh in his uprightness[3476] feareth the LORD: [a]but *he that is* perverse in his ways[1870] despiseth him.

3 In the mouth[6310] of the foolish *is* a rod of pride: [a]but the lips[8193] of the wise[2450] shall preserve[8104] them.

4 Where no oxen *are,* the crib[18] *is* clean:[1249] but much increase *is* by the strength of the ox.

5 [a]A faithful[529] witness will not lie:[3576] but a false[8267] witness will utter lies.[3577]

6 A scorner[3887] seeketh wisdom,[2451] and *findeth it* not: but [a]knowledge[1847] *is* easy[7043] unto him that understandeth.[995]

7 Go from the presence of a foolish[3684] man,[376] when thou perceivest[3045] not *in him* the lips of knowledge.

8 The wisdom of the prudent[6175] *is* to understand his way:[1870] but the folly of fools *is* deceit.[4820]

9 [a]Fools make a mock[3887] at sin:[817] but among the righteous[3477] *there is* favour.[7522]

10 The heart[3820] knoweth [I]his own bitterness;[4751] and a stranger[2114] doth not intermeddle[6148] with his joy.

11 [a]The house of the wicked[7563] shall be overthrown:[8045] but the tabernacle[168] of the upright[3477] shall flourish.

12 [a]There is a way which seemeth right[3477] unto a man, but [b]the end[319] thereof *are* the ways of death.[4194]

13 Even in laughter the heart is sorrowful;3510 and [a]the end of that mirth *is* heaviness.

14 The backslider5472 in heart shall be [a]filled with his own ways: and a good[2896] man *shall be satisfied* from himself.

15 The simple believeth[539] every word:[1697] but the prudent *man* looketh well[995] to his going.

16 [a]A wise *man* feareth, and departeth from evil:[7451] but the fool rageth,[5674] and is confident.

17 *He that is* soon angry[639] dealeth foolishly: and a man of wicked devices[4209] is hated.[8130]

18 The simple inherit[5157] folly: but the prudent are crowned with knowledge.

19 The evil bow before the good; and the wicked at the gates of the righteous.[6662]

20 [a]The poor is hated even of his own neighbour:[7453] but [I]the rich *hath* many friends.[157]

21 He that despiseth his neighbour sinneth:[2398] [a]but he that hath mercy[2603] on the poor, happy[835] *is* he.

22 Do they not err[8582] that devise evil? but mercy[2617] and truth[571] *shall be* to them that devise good.

23 In all labour[6089] there is profit: but the talk of the lips *tendeth* only to penury.4270

24 The crown of the wise *is* their riches: *but* the foolishness200 of fools *is* folly.

25 [a]A true[571] witness delivereth[5337] souls:[5315] but a deceitful[4820] *witness* speaketh[6315] lies.

26 In the fear[3374] of the LORD *is* strong confidence: and his children[1121] shall have a place of refuge.

27 [a]The fear of the LORD *is* a fountain of life,[2416] to depart[5493] from the snares of death.

28 In the multitude of people[5971] *is* the king's[4428] honour:[1927] but in the want of people[3816] *is* the destruction[4288] of the prince.[7333]

29 [a]*He that is* slow[750] to wrath[639] *is* of great understanding:[8394] but *he that is* [I]hasty7116 of spirit[7307] exalteth7311 folly.

30 A sound heart *is* the life of the flesh:[1320] but [a]envy[7068] [b]the rottenness of the bones.[6106]

31 [a]He that oppresseth the poor reproacheth [b]his Maker:[6213] but he that honoureth[3513] him hath mercy on the poor.

32 The wicked is driven away in his wickedness:[7561] but [a]the righteous hath hope[2620] in his death.

33 Wisdom resteth in the heart of him that hath understanding:[995] but [a]*that which is* in the midst[7130] of fools is made known.[3045]

34 Righteousness[6666] exalteth a nation:[1471] but sin[2403] *is* a reproach[2617] [I]to any people.

35 [a]The king's favour *is* toward a wise[7919] servant:[5650] but his wrath[5678] is *against* him that causeth shame.[954]

15 A [a]soft answer4617 turneth away[7725] wrath:[2534] but [b]grievous[6089] words[1697] stir up anger.

2 The tongue of the wise[2450] useth knowledge[1847] aright: [a]but the mouth[6310] of fools [I]poureth out foolishness.

3 [a]The eyes of the LORD *are* in every place, beholding6822 the evil[7451] and the good.[2896]

4 [I]A wholesome[4832] tongue *is* a tree of life:[2416] but perverseness5558 therein *is* a breach[7667] in the spirit.[7307]

5 [a]A fool despiseth[5006] his father's[1] instruction:[4148] [b]but he that regardeth[8104] reproof is prudent.[6191]

6 In the house[1004] of the righteous[6662] *is* much treasure: but in the revenues of the wicked[7563] is trouble.

7 The lips[8193] of the wise disperse knowledge: but the heart[3820] of the foolish *doeth* not so.

8 [a]The sacrifice[2077] of the wicked *is* an abomination[8441] to the LORD: but the prayer[8605] of the upright[3477] *is* his delight.[7522]

9 The way[1870] of the wicked *is* an

12 [a]Prov. 16:25 [b]Rom. 6:21

13 [a]Prov. 5:4; Eccl. 2:2

14 [a]Prov. 1:31; 12:14

16 [a]Prov. 22:3

20 [I]Hebr. *many are the lovers of the rich* [a]Prov. 19:7

21 [a]Ps. 41:1; 112:9

25 [a]Prov. 14:5

27 [a]Prov. 13:14

29 [I]Hebr. *short of spirit* [a]Prov. 16:32; James 1:19

30 [a]Ps. 112:10 [b]Prov. 12:4

31 [a]Prov. 17:5; Matt. 25:40, 45 [b]Job 31:15, 16; Prov. 22:2

32 [a]Job 13:15; 19:26; Ps. 23:4; 37:37; 2Cor. 1:9; 5:8; 2Tim. 4:18

33 [a]Prov. 12:16; 29:11

34 [I]Hebr. *to nations*

35 [a]Matt. 24:45, 47

1 [a]Judg. 8:1-3; 25:15 [b]1Sam. 25:10; 1Kgs. 12:13, 14, 16

2 [I]Hebr. *belches or bubbles* [a]Prov. 12:28; 13:16; 15:28

3 [a]Job 34:21; Prov. 5:21; Jer. 16:17; 32:19; Heb. 4:13

4 [I]Hebr. *The healing of the tongue*

5 [a]Prov. 10:1 [b]Prov. 13:8; 15:31; 32

8 [a]Prov. 21:27; 28:9; Isa. 1:11; 61:8; 66:3; Jer. 6:20; 7:22; Amos 5:22

abomination unto the LORD: but he loveth[157] him that [a]followeth after righteousness.[6666]

10 [I]Correction[4148] *is* [a]grievous[7451] unto him that forsaketh[5800] the way:[734] *and* [b]he that hateth[8130] reproof shall die.

11 [a]Hell[7585] and destruction[11] *are* before the LORD: how much more then [b]the hearts[3826] of the children[1121] of men?[120]

12 [a]A scorner[3887] loveth not one that reproveth[3198] him: neither will he go unto the wise.

13 [a]A merry heart maketh a cheerful[3190] countenance: but [b]by sorrow of the heart the spirit is broken.

14 The heart of him that hath understanding[995] seeketh knowledge: but the mouth of fools feedeth on foolishness.

15 All the days[3117] of the afflicted *are* evil: [a]but he that is of a merry[2896] heart *hath* a continual[8548] feast.

16 [a]Better[2896] *is* little with the fear[3374] of the LORD than great treasure and trouble[4103] therewith.

17 [a]Better *is* a dinner of herbs where love[160] is, than a stalled ox and hatred[8135] therewith.

18 [a]A wrathful[2534] man[376] stirreth up strife: but *he that is* slow[750] to anger appeaseth[8252] strife.[7379]

19 [a]The way of the slothful *man is* as an hedge of thorns: but the way of the righteous[3477] [I]*is* made plain.[5549]

20 [a]A wise son[1121] maketh a glad father:[1] but a foolish man[120] despiseth his mother.[517]

21 [a]Folly *is* joy to *him that is* [I]destitute of wisdom:[3820] [b]but a man of understanding[8394] walketh uprightly.[3474]

22 [a]Without counsel[5475] purposes[4284] are disappointed:[6565] but in the multitude of counsellors[3289] they are established.

23 A man hath joy by the answer of his mouth: and [a]a word *spoken* [I]in due season,[6256] how good *is it!*

24 [a]The way of life *is* above to the wise,[7919] that he may depart[5493] from hell beneath.

25 [a]The LORD will destroy[5255] the house of the proud: but [b]he will establish[5324] the border of the widow.

26 [a]The thoughts[4284] of the wicked[7451] *are* an abomination to the LORD: [b]but *the words* of the pure[2889] *are* [I]pleasant words.

27 [a]He that is greedy[1214] of gain troubleth his own house; but he that hateth gifts shall live.[2421]

28 The heart of the righteous [a]studieth[1897] to answer: but the mouth of the wicked poureth out evil things.

29 [a]The LORD *is* far from the wicked: but [b]he heareth[8085] the prayer of the righteous.

30 The light[3974] of the eyes rejoiceth the heart: *and* a good report maketh[1878] the bones[6106] fat.[1878]

31 [a]The ear[241] that heareth the reproof of life abideth among[7130] the wise.

32 He that refuseth[6544] [I]instruction despiseth[3988] his own soul:[5315] but he that [II]heareth reproof [III]getteth understanding.[3820]

33 [a]The fear of the LORD *is* the instruction of wisdom;[2451] and [b]before honour[3519] *is* humility.

16

The [I][a]preparations of the heart[3820] in man,[120] [b]and the answer of the tongue, *is* from the LORD.

2 [a]All the ways[1870] of a man[376] *are* clean[2134] in his own eyes; but [b]the LORD weigheth the spirits.

3 [I][a]Commit[1556] thy works unto the LORD, and thy thoughts[4284] shall be established.[3559]

4 [a]The LORD hath made all *things* for himself: [b]yea, even the wicked[7563] for the day[3117] of evil.[7451]

5 [a]Every one *that is* proud in heart *is* an abomination[8441] to the LORD: [b]*though* hand[3027] *join* in hand, he shall not be [I]unpunished.[5352]

6 [a]By mercy[2617] and truth[571] iniq-

9 [a]Prov. 21:21; 1Tim. 6:11
10 [I]Or, *Instruction* [a]1Kgs. 22:8 [b]Prov. 5:12; 10:17
11 [a]1Job 26:6; Ps. 139:8 [b]2Chr. 6:30; Ps. 7:9; 44:21; John 2:24, 25; 21:17; Acts 1:24
12 [a]Amos 5:10; 2Tim. 4:3
13 [a]Prov. 17:22 [b]Prov. 12:25
15 [a]Prov. 17:22
16 [a]Ps. 37:16; Prov. 16:8; 1Tim. 6:6
17 [a]Prov. 17:1
18 [a]Prov. 26:21; 29:22
19 [I]Hebr. is *raised up as a causeway* [a]Prov. 22:5
20 [a]Prov. 10:1; 29:3
21 [I]Hebr. *void of heart* [a]Prov. 10:23 [b]Eph. 5:15
22 [a]Prov. 11:14; 20:18
23 [I]Hebr. *in his season* [a]Prov. 25:11
24 [a]Phil. 3:20; Col. 3:1, 2
25 [a]Prov. 12:7; 14:11 [b]Ps. 68:5, 6; 146:9
26 [I]Hebr. *words of pleasantness* [a]Prov. 6:16, 18 [b]Prov. 37:30
27 [a]Prov. 11:19; Isa. 5:8; Jer. 17:11
28 [a]1Pet. 3:15
29 [a]Ps. 10:1; 34:16 [b]Ps. 145:18, 19
31 [a]Prov. 15:5
32 [I]Or, *correction* [II]Or, *obeyeth* [III]Hebr. *possesseth a heart*
33 [a]Prov. 1:7 [b]Prov. 18:12

1 [I]Or, *disposings* [a]Ps. 16:9; Prov. 19:21; 20:24; Jer. 10:23 [b]Matt. 10:19, 20
2 [a]Prov. 21:2 [b]2Sam. 16:7
3 [I]Hebr. *Roll* [a]Ps. 37:5; 55:22; Matt. 6:25; Luke 12:22; Phil. 4:6; 1Pet. 5:7
4 [a]Isa. 43:7; Rom. 11:36 [b]Job 21:30; Rom. 9:22
5 [I]Hebr. *held innocent* [a]Prov. 6:17; 8:13 [b]Prov. 11:21
6 [a]Dan. 4:27; Luke 11:41

uity[5771] is purged:[3722] and [b]by the fear[3374] of the LORD *men* depart[5493] from evil.

7 When a man's ways please[7521] the LORD, he maketh even his enemies to be at peace[7999] with him.

8 [a]Better[2896] *is* a little with righteousness[6666] than great revenues without right.[4941]

9 [a]A man's[120] heart deviseth[2803] his way:[1870] [b]but the LORD directeth[3559] his steps.

10 [I]A divine[7081] sentence *is* in the lips[8193] of the king:[4428] his mouth[6310] transgresseth[4603] not in judgment.[4941]

11 [a]A just[4941] weight and balance *are* the LORD's: [I]all the weights of the bag *are* his work.

12 *It is* an abomination to kings[4428] to commit[6213] wickedness:[7562] for [a]the throne[3678] is established by righteousness.

13 [a]Righteous[6664] lips *are* the delight[7522] of kings; and they love[157] him that speaketh right.[3477]

14 [a]The wrath[2534] of a king *is as* messengers[4397] of death:[4194] but a wise[2450] man will pacify[3722] it.

15 In the light[216] of the king's countenance *is* life;[2416] and [a]his favour[7522] *is* [b]as a cloud of the latter rain.

16 [a]How much better *is it* to get wisdom[2451] than gold! and to get understanding[998] rather to be chosen[977] than silver!

17 The highway of the upright[3477] *is* to depart[5493] from evil: he that keepeth[5341] his way preserveth[8104] his soul.[5315]

18 [a]Pride *goeth* before destruction,[7667] and an haughty spirit[7307] before a fall.

19 Better *it is to be* of an humble spirit with the lowly, than to divide the spoil with the proud.

20 [I]He that handleth a matter wisely[7919] shall find good:[2896] and whoso [a]trusteth[982] in the LORD, happy[835] *is* he.

21 The wise in heart shall be called[7121] prudent:[995] and the sweetness of the lips increaseth learning.[3948]

22 [a]Understanding[7922] *is* a well spring of life unto him that hath it: but the instruction[4148] of fools *is* folly.

23 [a]The heart of the wise [I]teacheth[7919] his mouth, and addeth learning to his lips.

24 Pleasant words *are as* an honeycomb, sweet to the soul, and health to the bones.[6106]

25 [a]There is a way that seemeth right unto a man, but the end[319] thereof *are* the ways of death.

26 [I][a]He that laboureth[6001] laboureth for himself; for his mouth [II]craveth it of him.

27 [I]An ungodly[1100] man diggeth up evil: and in his lips *there is* as a burning fire.

28 [a]A froward[8419] man [I]soweth strife: and [b]a whisperer separateth chief friends.

29 A violent[2555] man [a]enticeth[6601] his neighbour,[7453] and leadeth him into the way *that is* not good.

30 He shutteth his eyes to devise[2803] froward things: moving his lips he bringeth evil to pass.

31 [a]The hoary head[7872] *is* a crown of glory,[8597] *if* it be found in the way of righteousness.

32 [a]*He that is* slow[750] to anger[639] *is* better than the mighty; and he that ruleth[4910] his spirit than he that taketh a city.

33 The lot is cast into the lap; but the whole disposing[4941] thereof *is* of the LORD.

17 Better[2896] *is* [a]a dry[2720] morsel, and quietness therewith, than an house[1004] full of [I]sacrifices[2077] *with* strife.[7379]

2 A wise[7919] servant[5650] shall have rule[4910] over [a]a son[1121] that causeth shame,[954] and shall have part of the inheritance[5159] among the brethren.[251]

3 [a]The fining pot *is* for silver, and the furnace for gold: but the LORD trieth[974] the hearts.[3826]

4 A wicked doer[7489] giveth heed[7181] to false[205] lips;[8193] *and* a liar[8267] giveth ear[238] to a naughty[1942] tongue.

6 [b]Prov. 14:16
8 [a]Ps. 37:16; Prov. 15:16
9 [a]Prov. 16:5; 19:21 [b]Ps. 37:23; Prov. 20:24; Jer. 10:23
10 [I]Hebr. *Divination*
11 [I]Hebr. *all the stones* [a]Lev. 19:36; Prov. 11:1
12 [a]Prov. 25:5; 29:14
13 [a]Prov. 14:35; 22:11
14 [a]Prov. 19:12; 20:2
15 [a]Prov. 19:12 [b]Job 29:33; Zech. 10:1
16 [a]Prov. 8:11, 19
18 [a]Prov. 11:2; 17:19; 18:12
20 [I]Or, *He that understandeth a matter* [a]Ps. 2:12; 34:8; 125:1; Isa. 30:18; Jer. 17:7
22 [a]Prov. 13:14; 14:27
23 [I]Hebr. *maketh wise* [a]Ps. 37:30; Matt. 12:34
25 [a]Prov. 14:12
26 [I]Hebr. *The soul of him that laboureth* [II]Hebr. *boweth unto him* [a]Prov. 9:12; Eccl. 6:7
27 [I]Hebr. *A man of Belial*
28 [I]Hebr. *sendeth forth* [a]Prov. 6:14, 19; 15:18; 26:21; 29:22 [b]Prov. 17:9
29 [a]Prov. 1:10
31 [a]Prov. 20:29
32 [a]Prov. 19:11
1 [I]Or, *good cheer* [a]Prov. 15:17
2 [a]Prov. 10:5; 19:26
3 [a]Ps. 26:2; Prov. 27:21; Jer. 17:10; Mal. 3:3

5 [a]Whoso mocketh the poor reproacheth his Maker:[6213] *and* [b]he that is glad at calamities shall not be [I]unpunished.[5352]

6 [a]Children's children[1121] *are* the crown of old men;[2205] and the glory[8597] of children *are* their fathers.[1]

7 [I]Excellent[3499] speech[8193] becometh not a fool: much less do [II]lying lips a prince.[5081]

8 [a]A gift7810 *is as* [I]a precious[2580] stone in the eyes of him that hath it: whithersoever it turneth, it prospereth.[7919]

9 [a]He that covereth[3680] a transgression[6588] [I]seeketh love;[160] but [b]he that repeateth a matter[1697] separateth *very* friends.

10 A reproof[1606] entereth more into a wise[995] man than an hundred stripes[5221] into a fool.

11 An evil[7451] *man* seeketh only rebellion:[4805] therefore a cruel messenger[4397] shall be sent against him.

12 Let [a]a bear robbed of her whelps[7909] meet a man,[376] rather than a fool3684 in his folly.

13 Whoso [a]rewardeth[7725] evil for good,[2896] evil shall not depart from his house.

14 The beginning[7225] of strife *is as* when one letteth out water: therefore [a]leave off[5203] contention,[7379] before it be meddled with.

15 [a]He that justifieth[6663] the wicked,[7563] and he that condemneth[7561] the just, even they both *are* abomination[8441] to the LORD.

16 Wherefore *is there* a price in the hand[3027] of a fool to get wisdom,[2451] [a]seeing *he hath* no heart[3820] to *it?*

17 [a]A friend[7453] loveth[157] at all times,[6256] and a brother[251] is born for adversity.

18 [a]A man[120] void of [I]understanding[3820] striketh[8628] hands,[3709] *and* becometh[6148] surety[6161] in the presence of his friend.

19 He loveth transgression that loveth strife: *and* [a]he that exalteth his gate seeketh destruction.[7667]

20 [I]He that hath a froward6141 heart findeth no good: and he that hath [a]a perverse tongue falleth[5307] into mischief.[7451]

21 [a]He that begetteth a fool *doeth it* to his sorrow: and the father of a fool hath no joy.

22 [a]A merry heart doeth good[3190] [I]*like* a medicine: [b]but a broken spirit[7307] drieth[3001] the bones.

23 A wicked *man* taketh a gift out of the bosom [a]to pervert the ways[734] of judgment.[4941]

24 [a]Wisdom *is* before him that hath understanding;[995] but the eyes of a fool *are* in the ends of the earth.[776]

25 [a]A foolish son *is* a grief[3708] to his father, and bitterness to her that bare him.

26 Also [a]to punish[6064] the just *is* not good, *nor* to strike[5221] princes for equity.[3476]

27 [a]He that hath knowledge[1847] spareth his words:[561] *and* a man of understanding[8394] is of [I]an excellent7119 spirit.

28 [a]Even a fool,[191] when he holdeth his peace, is counted[2803] wise:[2450] *and* he that shutteth his lips *is esteemed* a man of understanding.

18

[I][a]Through desire8378 a man, having separated himself, seeketh *and* intermeddleth with all wisdom.[8454]

2 A fool hath no delight[2654] in understanding,[8394] but that his heart[3820] may discover[1540] itself.

3 When the wicked[7563] cometh, *then* cometh also contempt, and with ignominy reproach.[2781]

4 [a]The words[1697] of a man's mouth[6310] *are as* deep waters, [b]*and* the wellspring of wisdom[2451] *as* a flowing brook.

5 [a]*It is* not good[2896] to accept[5375] the person of the wicked, to overthrow the righteous[6662] in judgment.[4941]

6 A fool's lips[8193] enter into contention,[7379] and his mouth calleth[7121] for strokes.

7 [a]A fool's mouth[6310] *is* his destruc-

---

5 [I]Hebr. *held innocent* [a]Prov. 14:31 [b]Job 31:29
6 [a]Ps. 127:3; 128:3
7 [I]Hebr. *A lip of excellency* [II]Hebr. *a lip of lying*
8 [I]Hebr. *a stone of grace* [a]Prov. 18:16; 19:6
9 [I]Or, *procureth* [a]Prov. 10:12 [b]Prov. 16:28
12 [a]Hos. 13:8
13 [a]Ps. 109:4, 5; Jer. 18:20; Rom. 12:17; 1Thess. 5:15; 1Pet. 3:9
14 [a]Prov. 20:3; 1Thess. 4:11
15 [a]Ex. 23:7; Prov. 24:24; Isa. 5:23
16 [a]Prov. 21:25, 26
17 [a]Ruth 1:16; Prov. 18:24
18 [I]Hebr. *heart* [a]Prov. 6:1; 11:15
19 [a]Prov. 16:18
20 [I]Hebr. *The from ward of heart* [a]James 3:8
21 [a]Prov. 10:1; 17:25; 19:13
22 [I]Or, *to a medicine* [a]Prov. 12:25; 15:13, 15 [b]Ps. 22:15
23 [a]Ex. 23:8
24 [a]Prov. 14:6; Eccl. 2:14; 8:1
25 [a]Prov. 10:1; 15:20; 17:21; 19:13
26 [a]Prov. 17:15; 18:5
27 [I]Or, *a cool spirit* [a]James 1:19
28 [a]Job 13:5

1 [I]Or, *He that separateth himself seeketh according to his desire, and intermeddleth in every business* [a]Jude 1:19
4 [a]Prov. 10:11; 20:5 [b]Ps. 78:2
5 [a]Lev. 19:15; Deut. 1:17; 16:19; Prov. 24:23; 28:21
7 [a]Prov. 10:14; 12:13; 13:3; Eccl. 10:12

tion,[4288] and his lips *are* the snare[4170] of his soul.[5315]

8 [a]The words of a [I]talebearer *are* [II]as wounds, and they go down into the [III]innermost parts of the belly.[990]

9 He also that is slothful[7503] in his work[4399] is [a]brother[251] to him that is a great waster.

10 [a]The name of the LORD *is* a strong tower: the righteous runneth into it, and [I]is safe.[7682]

11 [a]The rich man's wealth *is* his strong city, and as an high wall in his own conceit.[4906]

12 [a]Before destruction[7667] the heart of man is haughty, and before honour[3519] *is* humility.

13 He that [I]answereth[7725] a matter[1697] [a]before he heareth[8085] *it,* it *is* folly and shame unto him.

14 The spirit[7307] of a man will sustain his infirmity; but a wounded spirit who can bear?[5375]

15 The heart of the prudent[995] getteth knowledge;[1847] and the ear[241] of the wise[2450] seeketh knowledge.

16 [a]A man's[120] gift maketh room for him, and bringeth[5148] him before great men.

17 *He that is* first[7223] in his own cause[7379] *seemeth* just; but his neighbour[7453] cometh and searcheth[2713] him.

18 The lot causeth contentions to cease,[7673] and parteth between the mighty.

19 A brother offended[6586] *is harder to be won* than a strong city: and *their* contentions *are* like the bars of a castle.[759]

20 [a]A man's belly shall be satisfied with the fruit of his mouth; *and* with the increase of his lips shall he be filled.

21 [a]Death[4194] and life[2416] *are* in the power[3027] of the tongue: and they that love[157] it shall eat the fruit thereof.

22 [a]*Whoso* findeth a wife[802] findeth a good *thing,* and obtaineth favour[7522] of the LORD.

23 The poor useth intreaties;[8469] but the rich answereth [a]roughly.

24 A man *that hath* friends[7453] must shew himself friendly:[7489] [a]and there is a friend[157] *that* sticketh closer[1695] than a brother.

8 IOr, *whisperer* IIOr, *like as when men are wounded* IIIHebr. *chambers* [a]Prov. 12:18; 26:22
9 [a]Prov. 28:24
10 IHebr. *is set aloft* [a]2Sam. 22:3, 51; Ps. 18:2; 27:1; 61:3, 4; 91:2; 144:2
11 [a]Prov. 10:15
12 [a]Prov. 11:2; 15:33; 16:18
13 IHebr. *returneth a word* [a]John 7:51
16 [a]Gen. 32:20; 1Sam. 25:27; Prov. 17:8; 21:14
20 [a]Prov. 12:14; 13:2
21 [a]Matt. 12:37
22 [a]Prov. 19:14; 31:10
23 [a]James 2:3
24 [a]Prov. 17:17

1 [a]Prov. 28:6
3 [a]Ps. 37:7
4 [a]Prov. 14:20
5 IHebr. *held innocent* [a]Ex. 23:1; Deut. 19:16, 19; Prov. 6:19; 19:9; 21:28
6 IHebr. *a man of gifts* [a]Prov. 20:26 [b]Prov. 17:8; 18:16; 21:14
7 [a]Prov. 14:20 [b]Ps. 38:11
8 IHebr. *a heart* [a]Prov. 16:20
9 [a]Prov. 19:5
10 [a]Prov. 30:22; Eccl. 10:6, 7
11 IOr, *prudence* [a]Prov. 14:29 [b]Prov. 16:32
12 [a]Prov. 16:14, 15; 20:2; 28:15 [b]Hos. 14:5
13 [a]Prov. 10:1; 15:20; 17:21, 25 [b]Prov. 21:9, 19; 27:15
14 [a]2Cor. 12:14 [b]Prov. 18:22

19

Better[2896] [a]*is* the poor that walketh in his integrity,[8537] than *he that is* perverse in his lips,[8193] and is a fool.

2 Also, *that* the soul[5315] *be* without knowledge,[1847] *it is* not good;[2896] and he that hasteth with *his* feet sinneth.[2398]

3 The foolishness of man[120] perverteth his way:[1870] [a]and his heart[3820] fretteth[2196] against the LORD.

4 [a]Wealth maketh many friends;[7453] but the poor is separated from his neighbour.[7453]

5 [a]A false[8267] witness shall not be [I]unpunished,[5352] and *he that* speaketh[6315] lies[3577] shall not escape.[4422]

6 [a]Many will intreat the favour of the prince:[5081] and [b]every man *is* a friend to [I]him that giveth gifts.

7 [a]All the brethren[251] of the poor do hate[8130] him: how much more do his friends go [b]far from him? he pursueth *them with* words,[561] *yet* they *are* wanting *to him.*

8 He that getteth [I]wisdom[3820] loveth[157] his own soul: he that keepeth[8104] understanding[8394] [a]shall find good.

9 [a]A false witness shall not be unpunished, and *he that* speaketh lies shall perish.[6]

10 Delight[8588] is not seemly for a fool; much less [a]for a servant[5650] to have rule[4910] over princes.[8269]

11 [a]The [I]discretion[7922] of a man deferreth[748] his anger;[639] [b]and *it is* his glory[8597] to pass over a transgression.[6588]

12 [a]The king's[4428] wrath[2197] *is* as the roaring of a lion; but his favour[7522] *is* [b]as dew upon the grass.

13 [a]A foolish son *is* the calamity[1942] of his father:[1] [b]and the contentions[4079] of a wife[802] *are* a continual dropping.

14 [a]House[1004] and riches *are* the inheritance[5159] of fathers: and [b]a prudent[7919] wife *is* from the LORD.

15 [a]Slothfulness casteth into a deep sleep; and an idle[7423] soul shall [b]suffer hunger.

16 [a]He that keepeth the commandment[4687] keepeth his own soul; *but* he that despiseth his ways shall die.

17 [a]He that hath pity[2603] upon the poor lendeth unto the LORD; and [I]that which he hath given will he pay him again.

18 [a]Chasten thy son while there is hope, and let not thy soul spare[5375] [I]for his crying.[4191]

19 A man of great wrath[2534] shall suffer[5375] punishment:[6066] for if thou deliver[5337] *him,* yet thou must [I]do it again.

20 Hear[8085] counsel,[6098] and receive instruction,[4148] that thou mayest be wise[2449] [a]in thy latter end.[319]

21 [a]*There are* many devices[4284] in a man's heart; nevertheless the counsel of the LORD, that shall stand.

22 The desire of a man *is* his kindness:[2617] and a poor man *is* better than a liar.[3576]

23 [a]The fear[3374] of the LORD *tendeth* to life:[2416] and *he that hath it* shall abide satisfied; he shall not be visited[6485] with evil.[7451]

24 [a]A slothful *man* hideth his hand[3027] in *his* bosom, and will not so much as bring it to his mouth[6310] again.

25 [a]Smite[5221] a scorner,[3887] and the simple [I][b]will beware:[6191] and [c]reprove[3198] one that hath understanding,[995] *and* he will understand knowledge.

26 He that wasteth[7703] *his* father, *and* chaseth away *his* mother,[517] *is* [a]a son that causeth shame,[954] and bringeth reproach.

27 Cease, my son, to hear the instruction *that causeth* to err[7686] from the words of knowledge.

28 [I]An ungodly[1100] witness scorneth[3887] judgment:[4941] and [a]the mouth of the wicked[7563] devoureth[1104] iniquity.[205]

29 Judgments[8201] are prepared[3559] for scorners,[3887] [a]and stripes for the back[1460] of fools.

20

Wine [a]*is* a mocker,[3887] strong drink *is* raging:[1993] and whosoever is deceived[7686] thereby is not wise.

2 [a]The fear[367] of a king[4428] *is* as the roaring of a lion: *whoso* provoketh him to anger[5674] [b]sinneth[2398] *against* his own soul.[5315]

3 [a]*It is* an honour[3519] for a man[376] to cease from strife:[7379] but every fool will be meddling.

4 [a]The sluggard[6102] will not plow by reason of the [I]cold; [b]*therefore* shall he beg[7592] in harvest, and *have* nothing.

5 [a]Counsel[6098] in the heart[3820] of man *is like* deep water; but a man of understanding[8394] will draw it out.

6 [a]Most men will proclaim[7121] every one[376] his own [I]goodness:[2617] but [b]a faithful[529] man who can find?

7 [a]The just *man* walketh in his integrity:[8537] [b]his children[1121] *are* blessed[835] after him.

8 [a]A king that sitteth in the throne[3678] of judgment[1779] scattereth away all evil[7451] with his eyes.

9 [a]Who can say, I have made my heart clean,[2135] I am pure from my sin?[2403]

10 [I][a]Divers weights, *and* [II]divers measures, both of them *are* alike abomination[8441] to the LORD.

11 Even a child is [a]known[5234] by his doings, whether his work *be* pure,[2134] and whether *it be* right.[3477]

12 [a]The hearing[8085] ear,[241] and the seeing[7200] eye, the LORD hath made[6213] even both of them.

13 [a]Love[157] not sleep, lest thou come to poverty;[3423] open thine eyes, *and* thou shalt be satisfied with bread.

14 *It is* naught,[7451] *it is* naught, saith the buyer: but when he is gone his way, then he boasteth.[1984]

15 There is gold, and a multitude of rubies: but the lips[8193] of knowledge[1847] *are* a precious jewel.

16 [a]Take his garment that is surety[6148] *for* a stranger:[2114] and take

15 [a]Prov. 6:9 [b]Prov. 10:4; 20:13; 23:21
16 [a]Luke 10:28; 11:28
17 [I]Or, *his deed* [a]Prov. 28:27; Eccl. 11:1; Matt. 10:42; 25:40; 2Cor. 9:6-8; Heb. 6:10
18 [I]Or, *to his destruction:* or, *to cause him to die* [a]Prov. 13:24; 23:13; 29:17
19 [I]Hebr. *add*
20 [a]Ps. 37:37
21 [a]Job 23:13; Ps. 33:10, 11; Prov. 16:1, 9; Isa. 14:26, 27; 46:10; Acts 5:39; Heb. 6:17
23 [a]1Tim. 4:8
24 [a]Prov. 15:19; 26:13, 15
25 [I]Hebr. *will be cunning* [a]Prov. 21:11 [b]Deut. 13:11 [c]Prov. 9:8
26 [a]Prov. 17:2
28 [I]Hebr. *A witness of Belial* [a]Job 15:16; 20:12, 13; 34:7
29 [a]Prov. 10:13; 26:3

1 [a]Gen. 9:21; Prov. 23:29, 30; Isa. 28:7; Hos. 4:11
2 [a]Prov. 16:14; 19:12 [b]Prov. 8:36
3 [a]Prov. 17:14
4 [I]Or, *winter* [a]Prov. 10:4; 19:24 [b]Prov. 19:15
5 [a]Prov. 18:4
6 [I]Or, *bounty* [a]Prov. 25:14; Matt. 6:2; Luke 18:11 [b]Ps. 12:1; Luke 18:8
7 [a]2Cor. 1:12 [b]Ps. 37:26; 112:2
8 [a]Prov. 20:26
9 [a]1Kgs. 8:46; 2Chr. 6:36; Job 14:4; Ps. 51:5; Eccl. 7:20; 1Cor. 4:4; 1John 1:8
10 [I]Hebr. *A stone and a stone* [II]Hebr. *an ephah and an ephah* [a]Deut. 25:13; Prov. 11:1; 16:11; 20:23; Mic. 6:10, 11
11 [a]Matt. 7:16
12 [a]Ex. 4:11; Ps. 94:9
13 [a]Prov. 6:9; 12:11; 19:15; Rom. 12:11
15 [a]Job 28:12, 16-19; Prov. 3:15; 8:11
16 [a]Prov. 22:26, 27; 27:13

a pledge[2254] of him for a strange
woman.[5237]
17 [I][a]Bread of deceit *is* sweet to a
man; but afterwards his mouth[6310] shall
be filled with gravel.
18 [a]*Every* purpose[4284] is established[3559] by counsel: [b]and with good[2896]
advice make[6213] war.
19 [a]He that goeth about *as* a talebearer revealeth[1540] secrets:[5475] therefore
meddle[2019] not with him [b]that [I]flattereth
with his lips.
20 [a]Whoso curseth[7043] his father[1] or
his mother,[517] [b]his [I]lamp[5216] shall be put
out in obscure darkness.[2822]
21 [a]An inheritance[5159] *may be* gotten
hastily[973] at the beginning;[7223] [b]but the
end[319] thereof shall not be blessed.[1288]
22 [a]Say not thou, I will recom-
pense[7999] evil; *but* [b]wait on[6960] the LORD,
and he shall save[3467] thee.
23 [a]Divers weights *are* an abomination unto the LORD; and [I]a false[4820] balance *is* not good.
24 [a]Man's[1397] goings *are* of the LORD;
how can a man[120] then understand[995] his
own way?[1870]
25 *It is* a snare[4190] to the man *who*
devoureth *that which is* holy,[6944] and
[a]after vows[5088] to make enquiry.
26 [a]A wise[2450] king scattereth the
wicked,[7563] and bringeth the wheel[212]
over them.
🔑 27 [a]The spirit[5397] of man *is* the
[I]candle[5216] of the LORD, searching all the
inward parts of the belly.[990]
28 [a]Mercy[2617] and truth[571] preserve[5341] the king: and his throne is upholden[5582] by mercy.
29 The glory[8597] of young men *is*
their strength: and [a]the beauty[1926] of old
men[2205] *is* the gray head.[7872]
30 The blueness of a wound
[I]cleanseth away[8562] evil: so *do* stripes[4347]
the inward parts of the belly.

21 The king's[4428] heart[3820] *is* in the
hand[3027] of the LORD, *as* the
rivers of water: he turneth it whithersoever he will.[2654]
2 [a]Every way[1870] of a man[376] *is*
right[3477] in his own eyes: [b]but the LORD
pondereth[8505] the hearts.[3826]
3 [a]To do[6213] justice[6666] and judgment[4941] *is* more acceptable[977] to the
LORD than sacrifice.[2077]
🔑 4 [I][a]An high look, and a proud heart,
and [I]the plowing[5215] of the wicked,[7563] *is*
sin.[2403]
5 [a]The thoughts[4284] of the diligent
tend only to plenteousness; but of every
one *that is* hasty only to want.
6 [a]The getting of treasures by a
lying tongue *is* a vanity tossed to and fro
of them that seek death.[4194]
7 The robbery[7701] of the wicked
shall [I]destroy[1641] them; because they
refuse[3985] to do judgment.
8 The way of man *is* froward[2019]
and strange:[2054] but *as for* the pure,[2134]
his work *is* right.
9 [a]*It is* better[2896] to dwell in a corner
of the housetop, than with [I]a brawling[4066] woman in [II]a wide[2267] house.
10 [a]The soul[5315] of the wicked de-

17 [I]Hebr. *Bread of lying,* or, *falsehood* [a]Prov. 9:17
18 [a]Prov. 15:22; 24:6 [b]Luke 14:31
19 [I]Or, *enticeth* [a]Prov. 11:13 [b]Rom. 16:18
20 [I]Or, *candle* [a]Ex. 21:17; Lev. 20:9; Matt. 15:4 [b]Job 18:5, 6; Prov. 24:20
21 [a]Prov. 28:20 [b]Hab. 2:6
22 [a]Deut. 32:35; Prov. 17:13; 24:29; Rom. 12:17, 19; 1Thess. 5:15; 1Pet. 3:9 [b]2Sam. 16:12
23 [I]Hebr. *balances of deceit* [a]Prov. 20:10
24 [a]Ps. 37:23; Prov. 16:9; Jer. 10:23
25 [a]Eccl. 5:4, 5
26 [a]Ps. 101:5; Prov. 20:18
27 [I]Or, *lamp* [a]1Cor. 2:11
28 [a]Ps. 101:1; Prov. 29:14
29 [a]Prov. 16:31
30 [I]Hebr. is *a purging medicine against evil*

2 [a]Prov. 16:2 [b]Prov. 24:12; Luke 16:15
3 [a]1Sam. 15:22; Ps. 50:8; Prov. 15:8; Isa. 1:11; Hos. 6:6; Mic. 6:7, 8
4 [I]Hebr. *Haughtiness of eyes* [II]Or, *the light of the wicked* [a]Prov. 6:17
5 [a]Prov. 10:4; 13:4
6 [a]Prov. 10:2; 13:11; 20:21; 2Pet. 2:3
7 [I]Hebr. *dwell with the woman of contentions* [II]Hebr. *a house of society* [a]Prov. 19:13; 21:19; 25:24; 27:15
9 [I]Hebr. *a*
10 [a]James 4:5

🔑 **20:27** The word for "spirit" in Hebrew literally means "breath," as we find it translated in Genesis 2:7. Many feel that this verse refers to the conscience that man is given by God to aid in self-examination and self-control. It is an internal control just as chastening blows are external controls (Prov. 20:30). Note how the use of both can affect the entire person—"the inward parts."

🔑 **21:4** Since the vowel sounds of the words were not written in the original Hebrew manuscripts, there are two possible translations for the Hebrew word which is rendered "plowing" in this verse. By inserting other vowel sounds, this could also be translated "lamp." Both readings are supported by a number of later Hebrew manuscripts in which the vowel sounds have been inserted. If "plowing" is used, then the verse affirms that even the activities of the wicked, which would otherwise be constructive, are sin. If "lamp" is correct, the most logical interpretation would be that such actions are a figurative representation of the person's entire spirit.

sireth[183] evil:[7451] his neighbour[7453]
[I]findeth no favour[2603] in his eyes.
11 [a]When the scorner[3887] is punished, the simple is made wise:[2449] and
when the wise[2450] is instructed,[7191] he receiveth knowledge.[1847]
12 The righteous[6662] *man* wisely considereth[7919] the house of the wicked: *but*
God overthroweth the wicked for *their*
wickedness.[7451]
13 [a]Whoso stoppeth his ears[241] at the
cry[2201] of the poor, he also shall cry himself, but shall not be heard.
14 [a]A gift in secret pacifieth anger:[639]
and a reward[7810] in the bosom strong
wrath.[2534]
15 *It is* joy to the just to do judgment: [a]but destruction[4288] *shall be* to the
workers of iniquity.[205]
16 The man[120] that wandereth[8582]
out of the way of understanding shall
remain in the congregation[6951] of the
dead.[7496]
17 He that loveth[157] [I]pleasure *shall be*
a poor man: he that loveth wine and
oil[8081] shall not be rich.
18 [a]The wicked *shall be* a ransom[3724]
for the righteous, and the transgressor[898]
for the upright.[3477]
19 [a]*It is* better to dwell [I]in the wilderness, than with a contentious and an
angry[3708] woman.
20 [a]*There is* treasure to be desired
and oil in the dwelling of the wise; but
a foolish man spendeth it up.
21 [a]He that followeth after righteousness[6666] and mercy[2617] findeth life,[2416]
righteousness, and honour.[3519]
22 [a]A wise *man* scaleth[5927] the city
of the mighty, and casteth down the
strength of the confidence thereof.
23 [a]Whoso keepeth[8104] his mouth
and his tongue keepeth his soul from
troubles.

10 [I]Hebr. *is not favored*
11 [a]Prov. 19:25
13 [a]Matt. 7:2; 18:30; James 2:13
14 [a]Prov. 17:8, 23; 18:16
15 [a]Prov. 10:29
17 [I]Or, *sport*
18 [a]Prov. 11:8; Isa. 43:3, 4
19 [I]Hebr. *in the land of the desert* [a]Prov. 21:9
20 [a]Ps. 112:3; Matt. 25:3, 4
21 [a]Prov. 15:9; Matt. 5:6
22 [a]Eccl. 9:14
23 [a]Prov. 12:13; 13:3; 18:21; James 3:2
24 [I]Hebr. *in the wrath of pride*
25 [a]Prov. 13:4
26 [a]Ps. 37:26; 112:9
27 [I]Hebr. *in wickedness* [a]Ps. 50:9; Prov. 15:8; Isa. 66:3; Jer. 6:20; Amos 5:22
28 [I]Hebr. *A witness of lies* [a]Prov. 19:5, 9
29 [I]Or, *considereth*
30 [a]Isa. 8:9, 10; Jer. 9:23; Acts 5:39
31 [I]Or, *victory* [a]Ps. 20:7; 33:17; Isa. 31:1 [b]Ps. 3:8

1 [I]Or, *favor is better than* [a]Eccl. 7:1
2 [a]Prov. 29:13; 1Cor. 12:21 [b]Job 31:15; Prov. 14:31
3 [a]Prov. 14:16; 27:12
4 [I]Or, *The reward of humility* [a]Ps. 112:3; Matt. 6:33
5 [a]Prov. 15:19 [b]1John 5:18
6 [I]Or, *Catechise* [II]Hebr. *in his way* [a]Eph. 6:4; 2Tim. 3:15

24 Proud[2086] *and* haughty scorner
is his name, who dealeth [I]in proud
wrath.[5678]
25 [a]The desire of the slothful killeth[4191] him; for his hands refuse to
labour.
26 He coveteth[183] greedily all the
day[3117] long: but the [a]righteous giveth
and spareth not.
27 [a]The sacrifice of the wicked
is abomination:[8441] how much more,
when he bringeth it [I]with a wicked
mind?[2154]
28 [I][a]A false witness shall perish:[6] but
the man that heareth[8085] speaketh constantly.[5331]
29 A wicked man hardeneth his face:
but *as for* the upright, he [I]directeth[3559]
his way.
30 [a]*There is* no wisdom[2451] nor understanding[8394] nor counsel[6098] against
the LORD.
31 [a]The horse *is* prepared[3559] against
the day of battle: but [I][b]safety[8668] *is* of
the LORD.

22 A [a]*good* name *is* rather to be chosen[977] than great riches, *and*
[I]loving favour[2580] rather than silver and
gold.
2 [a]The rich and poor meet together:
[b]the LORD *is* the maker[6213] of them all.
3 [a]A prudent[6175] *man* foreseeth the
evil,[7451] and hideth himself: but the simple[6612] pass on,[5674] and are punished.[6064]
4 [I][a]By humility *and* the fear[3374] of
the LORD *are* riches, and honour,[3519] and
life.[2416]
5 [a]Thorns *and* snares[6341] *are* in the
way[1870] of the froward:[6141] [b]he that doth
keep[8104] his soul[5315] shall be far from
them.
6 [I][a]Train up[2596] a child [II]in the way

22:6 The Hebrew word translated "train up" is usually translated "dedicate." Thus, it may indicate that the child is to be devoted to God (though not as Hannah did; 1 Sam. 1:11), or it may simply indicate that the child is to be prepared for the responsibility he or she will know as an adult. The phrase translated "in the way he should go" literally means "according to the mouth of the way." It might best be rendered "according to the way he acts," indicating that the instruction given should

(continued on next page)

he should go: and when he is old,[2204] he will not depart[5493] from it.

7 [a]The rich ruleth[4910] over the poor, and the borrower *is* servant[5650] [I]to the lender.

8 [a]He that soweth iniquity[5766] shall reap vanity:[205] [I]and the rod[7626] of his anger[5678] shall fail.[3615]

9 [Ia]He that hath a bountiful[2896] eye shall be blessed;[1288] for he giveth of his bread to the poor.

10 [a]Cast out the scorner,[3887] and contention shall go out; yea, strife[1779] and reproach shall cease.[7673]

11 [a]He that loveth[157] pureness[2889] of heart,[3820] [I]*for* the grace[2580] of his lips[8193] the king[4428] *shall be* his friend.[7453]

12 The eyes of the LORD preserve[5341] knowledge,[1847] and he overthroweth [I]the words[1697] of the transgressor.[898]

13 [a]The slothful *man* saith, *There is* a lion without, I shall be slain[7523] in the streets.

14 [a]The mouth[6310] of strange women[2114] *is* a deep pit:[7745] [b]he that is abhorred[2194] of the LORD shall fall therein.

15 Foolishness *is* bound in the heart of a child; *but* [a]the rod of correction[4148] shall drive it far from him.

16 He that oppresseth the poor to increase his *riches, and* he that giveth to the rich, *shall* surely *come* to want.

17 Bow down thine ear,[241] and hear[8085] the words of the wise,[2450] and apply thine heart unto my knowledge.

18 For *it is* a pleasant thing if thou keep them [I]within thee; they shall withal be fitted[3559] in thy lips.

19 That thy trust may be in the LORD, I have made known[3045] to thee this day,[3117] [I]even to thee.

20 Have not I written to thee [a]excellent things[8032] in counsels and knowledge,

21 [a]That I might make thee know[3045] the certainty of the words[561] of truth;[7189] [b]that thou mightest answer[7725] the words of truth[571] [I]to them that send unto thee?

22 [a]Rob not the poor, because he *is* poor: [b]neither oppress[1792] the afflicted in the gate:

23 [a]For the LORD will plead[7378] their cause,[7379] and spoil the soul of those that spoiled them.

24 Make no friendship with an angry man;[1167,639] and with a furious[2534] man thou shalt not go:

25 Lest thou learn[502] his ways,[734] and get a snare[4170] to thy soul.

26 [a]Be not thou *one* of them that strike[8628] hands,[3709] *or* of them that are sureties[6148] for debts.

27 If thou hast nothing to pay, why should he [a]take away thy bed from under thee?

28 [a]Remove not the ancient[5769] [I]landmark, which thy fathers[1] have set.

7 [I]Hebr. *to the man that lendeth* [a]James 2:6
8 [I]Or, *and with the rod of his anger he shall be consumed* [a]Job 4:8; Hos. 10:13
9 [I]Hebr. *Good of eye* [a]2Cor. 9:6
10 [a]Gen. 21:9, 10; Ps. 101:5
11 [I]Or, and hath *grace in his lips* [a]Ps. 101:6; Prov. 16:13
12 [I]Or, *the matters*
13 [a]Prov. 26:13
14 [a]Prov. 2:16; 5:3; 7:5; 23:27 [b]Eccl. 7:26
15 [a]Prov. 13:24; 19:18; 23:13, 14; 29:15, 17
18 [I]Hebr. *in thy belly*
19 [I]Or, trust *thou also*
20 [a]Prov. 8:6
21 [I]Or, *to those that send thee* [a]Luke 1:3, 4 [b]1Pet. 3:15
22 [a]Ex. 23:6; Job 31:16, 21 [b]Zech. 7:10; Mal. 3:5
23 [a]1Sam. 24:12; 25:39; Ps. 12:5; 35:1, 10; 68:5; 140:12; Prov. 23:11; Jer. 51:36
26 [a]Prov. 6:1; 11:15
27 [a]Prov. 20:16
28 [I]Or, *bound* [a]Deut. 19:14; 27:17; Prov. 23:10

(continued from previous page)
be in accordance with that which is proper for that specific child. This may mean that it is only the stage of intellectual and spiritual development that is referred to, or it may mean that this instruction should include the customs and traditions of the child's native land.

While such training may provide fertile ground for the Holy Spirit to work, it does not necessarily mean that the child will be saved. In addition, it does not mean that all the children who have turned to a life of sin will someday return (as did the prodigal son to his father [Luke 15:11–32]) just because they have been given a good upbringing.

The quality of training which the child receives is a critical concern. Parents should not assume that simply bringing their children up in a moral atmosphere is all that is needed. The primary goal in training up a child is that they be educated in the knowledge of God (Eph. 6:4), but they should also be provided with a thorough preparation for life in general. When a child does choose to rebel and lead a corrupt life, it may be that the parents have failed in some way as teachers or in being the proper examples. It must be recognized, however, that there will be instances when the parents have done their best to correctly train a child, yet he or she will choose to reject the instruction they have received and go their own way.

29 Seest[2372] thou a man diligent4106 in his business?[4399] he shall stand before kings;[4428] he shall not stand before [l]mean *men.*

23

When thou sittest to eat with a ruler, consider[995] diligently what *is* before thee:

2 And put a knife to thy throat, if thou *be* a man given to appetite.[1167,5315]

3 Be not desirous[183] of his dainties: for they *are* deceitful[3577] meat.

4 [a]Labour not to be rich: [b]cease from thine own wisdom.[998]

5 [l]Wilt thou set thine eyes upon that which is not? for *riches* certainly make[6213] themselves wings; they fly away as an eagle toward heaven.8064

6 [a]Eat thou not the bread of *him that hath* [b]an evil[7451] eye, neither desire[183] thou his dainty meats:

7 For as he thinketh[8176] in his heart,[5315] so *is* he: Eat and drink, [a]saith[559] he to thee; but his heart[3820] *is* not with thee.

8 The morsel *which* thou hast eaten shalt thou vomit up, and lose[7843] thy sweet words.[1697]

9 [a]Speak[1696] not in the ears[241] of a fool: for he will despise the wisdom[7922] of thy words.[4405]

10 [a]Remove not the old[5769] [l]landmark; and enter not into the fields[7704] of the fatherless:

11 [a]For their redeemer[1350] *is* mighty;[2389] he shall plead[7378] their cause[7379] with thee.

12 Apply thine heart unto instruction,[4148] and thine ears to the words[561] of knowledge.[1847]

13 [a]Withhold not correction[4148] from the child: for *if* thou beatest[5221] him with the rod,[7626] he shall not die.

14 Thou shalt beat him with the rod, and [a]shalt deliver[5337] his soul[5315] from hell.[7585]

15 My son,[1121] [a]if thine heart be wise,[2449] my heart shall rejoice, [l]even mine.

16 Yea, my reins3629 shall rejoice, when thy lips[8193] speak right things.[4339]

17 [a]Let not thine heart envy[7065] sinners:[2400] but [b]*be thou* in the fear[3374] of the LORD all the day[3117] long.

18 [a]For surely there is an [l]end;[319] and thine expectation8615 shall not be cut off.[3772]

19 Hear[8085] thou, my son, and be wise, and [a]guide thine heart in the way.[1870]

20 [a]Be not among winebibbers;5433,3196 among riotous eaters [l]of flesh:[1320]

21 For the drunkard and the glutton shall come to poverty:[3423] and [a]drowsiness shall clothe *a man* with rags.

22 [a]Hearken[8085] unto thy father[1] that begat thee, and despise not thy mother[517] when she is old.[2204]

23 [a]Buy7069 the truth,[571] and sell *it* not; *also* wisdom,[2451] and instruction, and understanding.[998]

24 [a]The father of the righteous[6662] shall greatly rejoice: and he that begetteth a wise[2450] *child* shall have joy of him.

25 Thy father and thy mother shall be glad, and she that bare thee shall rejoice.

26 My son, give me thine heart, and let thine eyes observe[7521] my ways.[1870]

27 [a]For a whore[2181] *is* a deep ditch;[7745] and a strange woman[5237] *is* a narrow pit.

28 [a]She also lieth in wait [l]as *for* a prey, and increaseth the transgressors among men.[120]

29 [a]Who hath woe? who hath sor-

29 [l]Hebr. *obscure en*
4 [a]Prov. 28:20; 1Tim. 6:9, 10 [b]Prov. 3:5; Rom. 12:16
5 [l]Hebr. *Wilt thou cause thine eyes to fly upon*
6 [a]Ps. 141:4 [b]Deut. 15:9
7 [a]Ps. 12:2
9 [a]Prov. 9:8; Matt. 7:6
10 [l]Or, *bound* [a]Deut. 19:14; 27:17; Prov. 22:28
11 [a]Job 31:21; Prov. 22:23
13 [a]Prov. 13:24; 19:18; 22:15; 29:15, 17
14 [a]1Cor. 5:5
15 [l]Or, *even I* will rejoice [a]Prov. 23:24, 25; 29:3
17 [a]Ps. 37:1; 73:3; Prov. 3:31; 24:1 [b]Prov. 28:14
18 [l]Or, *reward* [a]Ps. 37:37; Prov. 24:14; Luke 16:25
19 [a]Prov. 4:23
20 [l]Hebr. *of their flesh* [a]Isa. 5:22; Matt. 24:49; Luke 21:34; Rom. 13:13; Eph. 5:18
21 [a]Prov. 19:15
22 [a]Prov. 1:8; 30:17; Eph. 6:1, 2
23 [a]Prov. 4:5, 7; Matt. 13:44
24 [a]Prov. 10:1; 15:20; 23:15
27 [a]Prov. 22:14
28 [l]Or, *as a robber* [a]Prov. 7:12; Eccl. 7:26
29 [a]Isa. 5:11, 22

23:11 God was the true owner of all the Promised Land, even though He had permanently allotted it to the families of Israel (see Dan. 12:13). A redeemer, according to the Old Testament Law, was someone who bought the land and possessions of one of his relatives when that kinsman could not retain possession of it (see note on Ruth 4:1–8). This was done so that the land would still be owned by someone in the same family. However, the Redeemer mentioned here directly refers to the God of Israel.

row?17 who hath contentions? who hath babbling?[7879] who hath wounds without cause? who [b]hath redness of eyes?

30 [a]They that tarry long at the wine; they that go to seek [b]mixed wine.

31 Look not thou upon the wine when it is red,[119] when it giveth his colour in the cup, *when* it moveth itself aright.

32 At the last it biteth like a serpent,[5175] and stingeth like [I]an adder.6848

33 Thine eyes shall behold[7200] strange women,[2114] and thine heart shall utter perverse things.

34 Yea, thou shalt be as he that lieth down [I]in the midst[3820] of the sea, or as he that lieth upon the top[7218] of a mast.

35 [a]They have stricken me, *shalt thou say, and* I was not sick; they have beaten[1986] me, *and* [Ib]I felt *it* not: [c]when shall I awake? I will seek it yet again.

24

Be not thou [a]envious against evil[7451] men,[582] [b]neither desire[183] to be with them.

2 [a]For their heart[3820] studieth[1897] destruction,[7701] and their lips[8193] talk[1696] of mischief.[5999]

3 Through wisdom[2451] is an house builded; and by understanding[8394] it is established:[3559]

4 And by knowledge[1847] shall the chambers be filled with all precious and pleasant riches.

5 [a]A wise[2450] man[1397] [I]*is* strong;5797 yea, a man[376] of knowledge [II]increaseth strength.3581

6 [a]For by wise counsel thou shalt make thy war: and in multitude of counsellors[3289] *there is* safety.[8668]

7 [a]Wisdom[2454] *is* too high for a fool: he openeth not his mouth[6310] in the gate.

8 He that [a]deviseth[2803] to do evil[7489] shall be called[7121] a mischievous person.[1167,4209]

9 The thought[2154] of foolishness *is* sin:[2403] and the scorner[3887] *is* an abomination[8441] to men.[120]

10 *If* thou faint[7503] in the day[3117] of adversity, thy strength *is* [I]small.

11 [a]If thou forbear to deliver[5337] *them that are* drawn unto death,[4194] and *those that are* ready to be slain;[2027]

12 If thou sayest,[559] Behold, we knew[3045] it not; doth[995] not [a]he that pondereth the heart[3826] consider[995] *it*? and he that keepeth[5341] thy soul,[5315] doth *not* he know *it*? and shall *not* he render[7725] to *every* man[120] [b]according to his works?

13 My son, [a]eat thou honey, because *it is* good;[2896] and the honeycomb, *which is* sweet [I]to thy taste:

14 [a]So *shall* the knowledge[3045] of wisdom *be* unto thy soul: when thou hast found *it*, [b]then there shall be a reward,[319] and thy expectation shall not be cut off.[3772]

15 [a]Lay not wait, O wicked[7563] *man*, against the dwelling of the righteous;[6662] spoil[7703] not his resting place:

16 [a]For a just *man* falleth[5307] seven times, and riseth up again: [b]but the wicked shall fall[3782] into mischief.[7451]

17 [a]Rejoice not when thine enemy falleth, and let not thine heart be glad when he stumbleth:

18 Lest the LORD see *it*, and [I]it displease him, and he turn away[7725] his wrath[639] from him.

19 [Ia]Fret[2734] not thyself because of evil *men*, neither be thou envious at the wicked;

20 For [a]there shall be no reward to the evil *man*; [b]the [I]candle[5216] of the wicked shall be put out.

🔑 21 My son, [a]fear[3372] thou the LORD

29 [b]Gen. 49:12
30 [a]Prov. 20:1; Eph. 5:18 [b]Ps. 75:8; Prov. 9:2
32 [I]Or, *a cockatrice*
34 [I]Hebr. *in the heart of the sea*
35 [I]Hebr. *I knew it not* [a]Prov. 27:22; Jer. 5:3 [b]Eph. 4:19 [c]Deut. 29:19; Isa. 56:12

1 [a]Ps. 37:1; 73:3; Prov. 3:31; 23:17; 24:19 [b]Prov. 1:15
2 [a]Ps. 10:7
5 [I]Hebr. *is in strength* [II]Hebr. *strengtheneth might* [a]Prov. 21:22; Eccl. 9:16
6 [a]Prov. 11:14; 15:22; 20:18; Luke 14:31
7 [a]Ps. 10:5; Prov. 14:6
8 [a]Rom. 1:30
10 [I]Hebr. *narrow*
11 [a]Ps. 82:4; Isa. 58:6, 7; 1John 3:16
12 [a]Prov. 21:2 [b]Job 34:11; Ps. 62:12; Jer. 32:19; Rom. 2:6; Rev. 2:23; 22:12
13 [I]Hebr. *upon thy palate* [a]Song 5:1
14 [a]Ps. 19:10; 119:103 [b]Prov. 23:18
15 [a]Ps. 10:9, 10
16 [a]Job 5:19; Ps. 34:19; 37:24; Mic. 7:8 [b]Esth. 7:10; Amos 5:2; 8:14; Rev. 18:21
17 [a]Job 31:29; Ps. 35:15, 19; Prov. 17:5; Obad. 1:12
18 [I]Hebr. *it be evil in his eyes*
19 [I]Or, *Keep not company with the wicked* [a]Ps. 37:1; 73:3; Prov. 23:17; 24:1
20 [I]Or, *lamp* [a]Ps. 11:6 [b]Job 18:5, 6; 21:17; Prov. 13:9; 20:20
21 [a]Rom. 13:7; 1Pet. 2:17

🔑 **24:21** The men that are referred to here as being "given to change" are not necessarily those who merely attempt to bring about change or improvements, because change is beneficial in many cases. The emphasis of this warning is that one should avoid people that delight in making changes just for the sake of making changes. It is directed at individuals who are prone to follow men that

(continued on next page)

and the king:[4428] *and* meddle[6148] not with [I]them that are given to change:

22 For their calamity[343] shall rise suddenly; and who knoweth the ruin[6365] of them both?

23 These *things* also *belong* to the wise. [a]*It is* not good to have respect[5234] of persons in judgment.[4941]

24 [a]He that saith[559] unto the wicked, Thou *art* righteous; him shall[5344] the people[5971] curse,[5344] nations[3816] shall abhor[2194] him:

25 But to them that rebuke[3198] *him* shall be delight, and [I]a good blessing[1293] shall come upon them.

26 *Every man* shall kiss[5401] *his* lips [I]that giveth a right[5228] answer.[1697]

27 [a]Prepare[3559] thy work[4399] without, and make it fit for thyself in the field;[7704] and afterwards build thine house.

28 [a]Be not a witness against thy neighbour[7453] without cause; and deceive *not* with thy lips.

29 [a]Say not, I will do[6213] so to him as he hath done to me: I will render to the man according to his work.

30 I went by the field of the slothful, and by the vineyard of the man void of understanding;[3820]

31 And, lo, [a]it was all grown over with thorns, *and* nettles had covered[3680] the face thereof, and the stone wall thereof was broken down.

32 Then I saw,[2372] *and* [I]considered *it* well: I looked upon[7200] *it, and* received instruction.[4148]

33 [a]*Yet* a little sleep, a little slumber, a little folding of the hands[3027] to sleep:

34 So shall thy poverty come *as* one that travelleth; and thy want as [I]an armed man.

More Proverbs From Solomon

25 [a]These *are* also proverbs of Solomon, which the men[582] of Hezekiah king[4428] of Judah copied out.

2 [a]*It is* the glory[3519] of God[430] to conceal a thing:[1697] but the honour[3519] of kings *is* [b]to search out a matter.[1697]

3 The heaven[8064] for height, and the earth[776] for depth, and the heart[3820] of kings [I]*is* unsearchable.

4 [a]Take away the dross[5509] from the silver, and there shall come forth a vessel for the finer.[6884]

5 [a]Take away the wicked[7563] *from* before the king, and [b]his throne[3678] shall be established[3559] in righteousness.[6664]

6 [I]Put not forth thyself in the presence of the king, and stand not in the place of great *men:*

7 [a]For better[2896] *it is* that it be said unto thee, Come up[5927] hither; than that thou shouldest be put lower in the presence of the prince[5081] whom thine eyes have seen.[7200]

8 [a]Go not forth hastily to strive,[7378] lest *thou know not* what to do in the end[319] thereof, when thy neighbour[7453] hath put thee to shame.

9 [a]Debate[7378] thy cause[7379] with thy neighbour *himself;* and [I]discover[1540] not a secret[5475] to another:

10 Lest he that heareth[8085] *it* put thee to shame,[2616] and thine infamy turn not away.[7725]

11 [a]A word[1697] [I]fitly spoken[1696] *is like* apples of gold in pictures[4906] of silver.

12 As an earring of gold, and an ornament of fine gold, *so is* a wise[2450] reprover[3198] upon an obedient[8085] ear.[241]

13 [a]As the cold of snow in the time of harvest, *so is* a faithful[539] messenger to them that send him: for he refresheth the soul[5315] of his masters.[113]

14 [a]Whoso boasteth himself[1984] [I]of a false[8267] gift *is like* [b]clouds[5387] and wind[7307] without rain.

15 [a]By long[753] forbearing is a prince[7101] persuaded, and a soft tongue breaketh[7665] the bone.

21 [I]Hebr. *changers*
23 [a]Lev. 19:15; Deut. 1:17; 16:19; Prov. 18:5; 28:21; John 7:24
24 [a]Prov. 17:15; Isa. 5:23
25 [I]Hebr. *a blessing of good*
26 [I]Hebr. *that answereth right words*
27 [a]1Kgs. 5:17, 18; Luke 14:28
28 [a]Eph. 4:25
29 [a]Prov. 20:22; Matt. 5:39, 44; Rom. 12:17, 19
31 [a]Gen. 3:18
32 [I]Hebr. *set my heart*
33 [a]Prov. 6:9
34 [I]Hebr. *a man of shield*

1 [a]1Kgs. 4:32
2 [a]Deut. 29:29; Rom. 11:33 [b]Job 29:16
3 [I]Hebr. *there is no searching*
4 [a]2Tim. 2:21
5 [a]Prov. 20:8 [b]Prov. 16:12; 29:14
6 [I]Hebr. *Set not out thy glory*
7 [a]Luke 14:8-10
8 [a]Prov. 17:14; Matt. 5:25
9 [I]Or, *discover not the secret of another* [a]Matt. 5:25; 18:15
11 [I]Hebr. *spoken upon his wheels* [a]Prov. 15:23; Isa. 50:4
13 [a]Prov. 13:17
14 [I]Hebr. *in a gift of falsehood* [a]Prov. 20:6 [b]Jude 1:12
15 [a]Gen. 32:4; 1Sam. 25:24; Prov. 15:1; 16:14

(continued from previous page)
recklessly challenge authority without any worthy purpose or objective in mind (cf. Prov. 1:10–19). Although the primary focus seems to be upon those who desire to irresponsibly introduce changes in the governmental system or its workings, it may also be applied to agitators of any kind.

16 [a]Hast thou found honey? eat so much as is sufficient for thee, lest thou be filled therewith, and vomit it.

17 [I]Withdraw thy foot from thy neighbour's[7453] house;[1004] lest he be [II]weary of thee, and *so* hate[8130] thee.

18 [a]A man that beareth false witness against his neighbour *is* a maul, and a sword,[2719] and a sharp[8150] arrow.

19 Confidence in an unfaithful man in[898] time of trouble *is like* a broken tooth, and a foot out of joint.

20 As he that taketh away a garment in cold weather, *and as* vinegar upon nitre,[5427] so *is* he that [a]singeth[7891] songs[7892] to an heavy heart.

21 [a]If thine enemy[8130] be hungry, give him bread to eat; and if he be thirsty, give him water to drink:

22 For thou shalt heap coals of fire upon his head,[7218] [a]and the LORD shall reward[7999] thee.

23 [Ia]The north wind driveth away[2342] rain: so *doth* an angry[2194] countenance [b]a backbiting[5643] tongue.

24 [a]*It is* better to dwell in the corner of the housetop, than with a brawling[4066] woman[802] and in a wide house.

25 *As* cold waters to a thirsty soul, so *is* good[2896] news from a far country.[776]

26 A righteous man[6662] falling down before the wicked *is as* a troubled fountain, and a corrupt[7843] spring.

27 [a]*It is* not good to eat much honey: so *for men* [b]to search their own glory *is not* glory.

28 [a]He that *hath* no rule[4623] over his own spirit[7307] *is like a* city *that is* broken down, *and* without walls.

26

As snow in summer, [a]and as rain in harvest, so honour[3519] is not seemly[5000] for a fool.

2 As the bird by wandering, as the swallow by flying, so [a]the curse[7045] causeless shall not come.

3 [a]A whip for the horse, a bridle for the ass, and a rod[7626] for the fool's back.[1460]

4 Answer not a fool according to his folly, lest thou also be like unto him.

5 [a]Answer a fool according to his folly, lest he be wise[2450] in [I]his own conceit.

6 He that sendeth a message by the hand[3027] of a fool cutteth off the feet, *and* drinketh [I]damage.[2555]

7 The legs of the lame [I]are not equal: so *is* a parable in the mouth[6310] of fools.

8 [I]As he that bindeth a stone in a sling, so *is* he that giveth honour to a fool.

9 *As* the thorn goeth up into the hand of a drunkard, so *is* a parable[4912] in the mouth of fools.

10 [I]The great *God* that formed[2342] all *things* both rewardeth the fool, and rewardeth transgressors.[5674]

11 [a]As a dog returneth[7725] to his vomit, [b]*so* a fool [I]returneth[8138] to his folly.

12 [a]Seest thou a man[376] wise in his own conceit? *there is* more hope of a fool than of him.

13 [a]The slothful[6102] *man* saith, *There is* a lion in the way;[1870] a lion *is* in the streets.

14 *As* the door turneth upon his hinges, so *doth* the slothful upon his bed.

15 [a]The slothful hideth his hand in *his* bosom; [I]it grieveth[3811] him to bring it again to his mouth.

16 The sluggard[6102] *is* wiser[2450] in his own conceit than seven men that can render[7725] a reason.[2940]

17 He that passeth by,[5674] *and* [I]meddleth[5674] with strife[7379] *belonging* not to him, *is like* one that taketh[2388] a dog by the ears.[241]

18 As a mad *man* who casteth[3384] [I]firebrands, arrows, and death,[4194]

19 So *is* the man *that* deceiveth his neighbour,[7453] and saith, [a]Am not I in sport?

20 [I]Where no wood is, *there* the fire goeth out: so [a]where *there is* no [II]talebearer, the strife [III]ceaseth.

21 [a]*As* coals *are* to burning coals, and wood to fire; so *is* a contentious man to kindle[2787] strife.

22 [a]The words[1697] of a talebearer *are* as wounds, and they go down into the [I]innermost parts of the belly.[990]

16 [a]Prov. 25:27
17 [I]Or, *Let thy foot be seldom in thy neighbor's house* [II]Hebr. *full of thee*
18 [a]Ps. 57:4; 120:3, 4; Prov. 12:18
20 [a]Dan. 6:18; Rom. 12:15
21 [a]Ex. 23:4, 5; Matt. 5:44; Rom. 12:20
22 [a]2Sam. 16:12
23 [I]Or, *The north wind bringeth forth rain; so doth a backbiting tongue an angry countenance* [a]Job 37:22 [b]Ps. 101:5
24 [a]Prov. 19:13; 21:9, 19
27 [a]Prov. 25:16 [b]Prov. 27:2
28 [a]Prov. 16:32

1 [a]1Sam. 12:17
2 [a]Num. 23:8; Deut. 23:5
3 [a]Ps. 32:9; Prov. 10:13
5 [I]Hebr. *his own eyes* [a]Matt. 16:1-4; 21:24-27
6 [I]Or, *violence*
7 [I]Hebr. *are lifted up*
8 [I]Or, *As he that putteth a precious stone in a heap of stones*
10 [I]Or, *A great man grieveth all, and he hireth the fool, he hireth also transgressors*
11 [I]Hebr. *repeats his folly* [a]2Pet. 2:22 [b]Ex. 8:15
12 [a]Prov. 29:20; Luke 18:11; Rom. 12:16; Rev. 3:17
13 [a]Prov. 22:13
15 [I]Or, *he is weary* [a]Prov. 19:24
17 [I]Or, *is enraged*
18 [I]Hebr. *flames, or, sparks*
19 [a]Eph. 5:4
20 [I]Hebr. *Without wood* [II]Or, *whisperer* [III]Hebr. *is silent* [a]Prov. 22:10
21 [a]Prov. 15:18; 29:22
22 [I]Hebr. *chambers* [a]Prov. 18:8

23 Burning lips[8193] and a wicked[7451] heart[3820] *are like* a potsherd[2789] covered with silver dross.[5509]

24 He that hateth[8130] [I]dissembleth[5234] with his lips, and layeth up deceit[4820] within[7130] him;

25 [a]When he [I]speaketh fair,[2603] believe[539] him not: for *there are* seven abominations[8441] in his heart.

26 *Whose* [I]hatred[8135] is covered[3680] by deceit, his wickedness shall be shewed before the *whole* congregation.[6951]

27 [a]Whoso diggeth a pit[7845] shall fall therein: and he that rolleth[1556] a stone, it will return[7725] upon him.

28 A lying tongue hateth *those that are* afflicted by it; and a flattering mouth worketh[6213] ruin.

27 Boast [a]not thyself[1984] of [I]to morrow; for thou knowest[3045] not what a day[3117] may bring forth.

2 [a]Let another man[2114] praise[1984] thee, and not thine own mouth;[6310] a stranger,[5237] and not thine own lips.[8193]

3 A stone *is* [I]heavy, and the sand weighty; but a fool's wrath[3708] *is* heavier[8513] than them both.

4 [I]Wrath[2534] *is* cruel, and anger[639] *is* outrageous;[7858] but [a]who *is* able to stand before [II]envy?[7068]

5 [a]Open[1540] rebuke[8433] *is* better[2896] than secret love.[160]

6 [a]Faithful[539] *are* the wounds of a friend;[157] but the kisses of an enemy[8130] *are* [I]deceitful.

7 The full soul[5315] [I]loatheth[947] an honeycomb; but [a]to the hungry[7456] soul every bitter thing[4751] is sweet.

8 As a bird that wandereth from her nest, so *is* a man[376] that wandereth from his place.

9 Ointment[8081] and perfume[7004] rejoice the heart:[3820] so *doth* the sweetness of a man's friend[7453] [I]by hearty[5315] counsel.[6098]

10 Thine own friend, and thy father's[1] friend, forsake[5800] not; neither go into thy brother's house[1004] in the day of thy calamity:[343] *for* [a]better *is* a neighbour[7934] *that is* near than a brother[251] far off.

11 [a]My son,[1121] be wise,[2449] and make my heart glad, [b]that I may answer[7725,1697] him that reproacheth me.

12 [a]A prudent[6175] *man* foreseeth the evil,[7451] *and* hideth himself; *but* the simple pass on,[5674] *and* are punished.[6064]

13 [a]Take his garment that is surety[6148] for a stranger,[2114] and take a pledge[2254] of him for a strange woman.[5237]

14 He that blesseth[1288] his friend with a loud voice, rising early in the morning, it shall be counted[2803] a curse[7045] to him.

15 [a]A continual dropping in a very rainy day and a contentious woman[802] are alike.

16 Whosoever hideth her hideth the wind,[7307] and the ointment of his right hand, *which* bewrayeth[7121] *itself.*

17 Iron sharpeneth iron; so a man sharpeneth the countenance of his friend.

18 [a]Whoso keepeth[5341] the fig tree shall eat the fruit thereof: so he that waiteth on his master[113] shall be honoured.

19 As in water face *answereth* to face, so the heart of man[120] to man.

20 [a]Hell[7585] and destruction[10] are [I]never full; so [b]the eyes of man are never satisfied.

21 [a]*As* the fining pot for silver, and the furnace for gold; so *is* a man to his praise.

22 [a]Though thou shouldest bray[3806] a fool in a mortar among wheat with a pestle,[5940] *yet* will not his foolishness depart[5493] from him.

23 Be thou diligent to know the state[6440] of thy flocks, *and* [I]look well to thy herds.

24 For [I]riches *are* not for ever:[5769] and doth the crown[5145] *endure* [II]to every generation?[1755]

25 [a]The hay appeareth, and the tender grass sheweth itself,[7200] and herbs of the mountains are gathered.[622]

26 The lambs *are* for thy clothing, and the goats *are* the price of the field.[7704]

24 [I]Or, *is known*

25 [I]Hebr. *maketh his voice gracious* [a]Ps. 28:3; Jer. 9:8

26 [I]Or, *hatred is covered in secret*

27 [a]Ps. 7:15, 16; 9:15; 10:2; 57:6; Prov. 28:10; Eccl. 10:8

1 [I]Hebr. *tomorrow day* [a]Luke 12:19, 20; James 4:13, 14

2 [a]Prov. 25:27

3 [I]Hebr. *heaviness*

4 [I]Hebr. *Wrath* is *cruelty, and anger an overflowing* [II]Or, *jealousy* [a]1John 3:12 [b]Prov. 6:34

5 [a]Prov. 28:23; Gal. 2:14

6 [I]Or, *earnest,* or, *frequent* [a]Ps. 141:5

7 [I]Hebr. *treadeth under foot* [a]Job 6:7

9 [I]Hebr. *from the counsel of the soul*

10 [a]Prov. 17:17; 18:24; 19:7

11 [a]Prov. 10:1; 23:15, 24 [b]Ps. 127:5

12 [a]Prov. 22:3

13 [a]Ex. 22:26; Prov. 20:16

15 [a]Prov. 19:13

18 [a]1Cor. 9:7, 13

20 [I]Hebr. *not* [a]Prov. 30:16; Hab. 2:5 [b]Eccl. 1:8; 6:7

21 [a]Prov. 17:3

22 [a]Prov. 23:35; Isa. 1:5; Jer. 5:3

23 [I]Hebr. *set thy heart*

24 [I]Hebr. *strength* [II]Hebr. *to generation and generation*

25 [a]Ps. 104:14

27 And *thou shalt have* goats' milk enough for thy food, for the food of thy household,[1004] and *for* the [I]maintenance for thy maidens.

28

The [a]wicked[7563] flee when no man pursueth: but the righteous[6662] are bold[982] as a lion.

2 For the transgression[6588] of a land[776] many *are* the princes[8269] thereof: but [I]by a man[120] of understanding[995] *and* knowledge[3045] the state[3651] *thereof* shall be prolonged.[748]

3 [a]A poor man[1397] that oppresseth the poor *is like* a sweeping rain [I]which leaveth no food.

4 [a]They that forsake[5800] the law[8451] praise[1984] the wicked: [b]but such as keep[8104] the law contend with them.

5 [a]Evil[7451] men[582] understand[995] not judgment:[4941] but [b]they that seek the LORD understand all *things*.

6 [a]Better[2896] *is* the poor that walketh in his uprightness,[8537] than *he that is* perverse *in his* ways,[1870] though he *be* rich.

7 [a]Whoso keepeth[5341] the law *is* a wise[995] son:[1121] but he that [I]is a companion of riotous *men* shameth his father.[1]

8 [a]He that by usury and [I]unjust gain increaseth his substance, he shall gather it for him that will pity the poor.

9 [a]He that turneth away his ear[241] from hearing[8085] the law, [b]even his prayer[8605] *shall be* abomination.[8441]

10 [a]Whoso causeth[7686] the righteous[3477] to go astray[7686] in an evil way, he shall fall himself into his own pit:[7816] [b]but the upright shall have good *things* in possession.

11 The rich man[376] *is* wise[2450] [I]in his own conceit; but the poor that hath understanding searcheth him out.

12 [a]When righteous *men* do rejoice, *there is* great glory:[8597] but when the wicked rise, a man is [I]hidden.

13 [a]He that covereth[3680] his sins[6588] shall not prosper:[6743] but whoso confesseth[3034] and forsaketh[5800] *them* shall have mercy.[7355]

14 Happy[835] *is* the man [a]that feareth[6342] alway:[8548] [b]but he that hardeneth his heart[3820] shall fall into mischief.[7451]

15 [a]As a roaring lion, and a ranging bear; [b]*so is* a wicked ruler over the poor people.[5971]

16 The prince[5057] that wanteth understanding[8394] *is* also a great oppressor: *but* he that hateth[8130] covetousness[1215] shall prolong[748] *his* days.[3117]

17 [a]A man that doeth violence[6231] to the blood[1818] of *any* person[5315] shall flee to the pit;[953] let no man stay him.

18 [a]Whoso walketh uprightly[8549] shall be saved:[3467] but [b]*he that is* perverse *in his* ways shall fall at once.

19 [a]He that tilleth[5647] his land[127] shall have plenty of bread: but he that followeth after vain *persons* shall have poverty enough.

20 A faithful[530] man shall abound[7227] with blessings:[1293] [a]but he that maketh haste to be rich shall not be [I]innocent.[5352]

21 [a]To have respect[5234] of persons *is* not good:[2896] for [b]for a piece of bread *that* man will transgress.[6586]

22 [Ia]He that hasteth[926] to be rich *hath* an evil eye, and considereth[3045] not that poverty shall come upon him.

23 [a]He that rebuketh[3198] a man afterwards shall find more favour[2580] than he that flattereth with the tongue.

24 Whoso robbeth his father or his mother,[517] and saith,[559] *It is* no transgression; the same [a]*is* the companion of [I]a destroyer.[376,7843]

25 [a]He that is of a proud heart[5315] stirreth up strife: [b]but he that putteth his trust[982] in the LORD shall be made fat.[1878]

26 He that trusteth[982] in his own heart is a fool: but whoso walketh wisely, he shall be delivered.[4422]

27 [a]He that giveth unto the poor shall not lack: but he that hideth his eyes shall have many a curse.

28 [a]When the wicked rise, [b]men[120]

27 [I]Hebr. *life*

1 [a]Lev. 26:17, 36; Ps. 53:5
2 [I]Or, *by men of understanding* and *wisdom shall they likewise be prolonged*
3 [I]Hebr. *without food* [a]Matt. 18:28
4 [a]Ps. 10:3; 49:18; Rom. 1:32 [b]1Kgs. 18:18, 21; Matt. 3:7; 14:4; Eph. 5:11
5 [a]Ps. 92:6 [b]John 7:17; 1Cor. 2:15; 1John 2:20, 27
6 [a]Prov. 19:1; 28:18
7 [I]Or, *feedeth gluttons* [a]Prov. 29:3
8 [I]Hebr. *by increase* [a]Job 27:16, 17; Prov. 13:22; Eccl. 2:26
9 [a]Zech. 7:11 [b]Ps. 66:18; 109:7; Prov. 15:8
10 [a]Prov. 26:27 [b]Matt. 6:33
11 [I]Hebr. *in his eyes*
12 [I]Or, *sought for* [a]Prov. 11:10; 28:28; 29:2; Eccl. 10:6
13 [a]Ps. 32:3, 5; 1John 1:8-10
14 [a]Ps. 16:8; Prov. 23:17 [b]Rom. 2:5; 11:20
15 [a]1Pet. 5:8 [b]Ex. 1:14, 16, 22; Matt. 2:16
17 [a]Gen. 9:6; Ex. 21:14
18 [a]Prov. 10:9, 25 [b]Prov. 28:6
19 [a]Prov. 12:11
20 [I]Or, *unpunished* [a]Prov. 13:11; 20:21; 23:4; 28:22; 1Tim. 6:9
21 [a]Prov. 18:5; 24:23 [b]Ezek. 13:19
22 [I]Or, *He that hath an evil eye hasteth to be rich* [a]Prov. 28:20
23 [a]Prov. 27:5, 6
24 [I]Hebr. *a man destroying* [a]Prov. 18:9
25 [a]Prov. 13:10 [b]1Tim. 6:6
27 [a]Deut. 15:7; Prov. 19:17; 22:9
28 [a]Prov. 28:12; 29:2 [b]Job 24:4

hide themselves: but when they perish,[6] the righteous increase.

29

29 [I][a]He, that being often reproved[8433] hardeneth *his* neck, shall suddenly be destroyed,[7665] and that without remedy.

2 [a]When the righteous[6662] are [I]in authority,[7235] the people[5971] rejoice: but when the wicked[7563] beareth rule,[4910] [b]the people mourn.

3 [a]Whoso loveth[157] wisdom[2451] rejoiceth his father:[1] [b]but he that keepeth company with harlots spendeth *his* substance.

4 The king[4428] by judgment[4941] establisheth[5975] the land:[776] but [I]he that receiveth gifts overthroweth it.

5 A man[1397] that flattereth his neighbour[7453] spreadeth a net for his feet.

6 In the transgression[6588] of an evil[7451] man[376] *there is* a snare:[4170] but the righteous doth sing and rejoice.

7 [a]The righteous considereth[3045] the cause[1779] of the poor: *but* the wicked regardeth not to know[1847] *it.*

8 [a]Scornful men [I]bring a city into a snare:[6315] but wise[2450] *men* [b]turn away[7725] wrath.[639]

9 *If* a wise man contendeth[8199] with a foolish man, [a]whether he rage or laugh, *there is* no rest.

10 [I][a]The bloodthirsty[582, 1818] hate[8130] the upright:[8535] but the just[3477] seek his soul.[5315]

11 A [a]fool uttereth all his mind:[7307] but a wise *man* keepeth it in[7623] till afterwards.

12 If a ruler hearken[7181] to lies,[8267] all his servants *are* wicked.

13 The poor and [I]the deceitful man [a]meet together: [b]the LORD lighteneth both their eyes.

14 [a]The king that [b]faithfully[571] judgeth[8199] the poor, his throne[3678] shall be established[3559] for ever.[5703]

15 [a]The rod[7626] and reproof[8433] give wisdom: but [b]a child left *to himself* bringeth his mother to shame.[954]

16 When the wicked are multiplied, transgression increaseth: [a]but the righteous shall see their fall.[4658]

17 [a]Correct[3256] thy son,[1121] and he shall give thee rest; yea, he shall give delight unto thy soul.

18 [a]Where *there is* no vision,[2377] the people [I]perish:[6544] but [b]he that keepeth[8104] the law,[8451] happy[835] *is* he.

19 A servant[5650] will not be corrected[3256] by words:[1697] for though he understand[995] he will not answer.

20 Seest[2372] thou a man *that is* hasty [I]in his words? [a]*there is* more hope of a fool[3684] than of him.

21 He that delicately bringeth up his servant from a child shall have him become *his* son[4497] at the length.

22 [a]An angry[639] man stirreth up strife, and a furious[2534] man aboundeth[7227] in transgression.

23 [a]A man's[120] pride shall bring him low: but honour[3519] shall uphold the humble in spirit.[7307]

24 Whoso is partner with a thief hateth[8130] his own soul: [a]he heareth[8085] cursing,[423] and bewrayeth[5046] *it* not.

25 [a]The fear[2731] of man bringeth a snare: but whoso putteth his trust in the LORD [I]shall be safe.[7682]

26 [a]Many seek [I]the ruler's favour; but *every* man's judgment *cometh* from the LORD.

27 An unjust[5766] man *is* an abomination[8441] to the just: and *he that is* upright[3477] in the way[1870] *is* abomination to the wicked.

The Observations of Agur

30

30 The words[1697] of Agur the son[1121] of Jakeh, *even* [a]the prophecy:[4853] the man[1397] spake[5002] unto Ithiel, even unto Ithiel and Ucal,

2 [a]Surely I *am* more brutish than *any* man,[376] and have not the understanding[998] of a man.[120]

3 I neither learned[3925] wisdom,[2451] nor [I]have the knowledge[1847] of the holy.[6918]

4 [a]Who hath ascended up[5927] into heaven,[8064] or descended? [b]who hath

1 [I]Hebr. *A man of reproofs* [a]1Sam. 2:25; 2Chr. 36:16; Prov. 1:24-27
2 [I]Or, *increased* [a]Esth. 8:15; Prov. 11:10; 28:12, 28 [b]Esth. 3:15
3 [a]Prov. 10:1; 15:20; 27:11 [b]Prov. 5:9, 10; 6:26; 28:7; Luke 15:13, 30
4 [I]Hebr. *a man of oblations*
7 [a]Job 29:16; 31:13; Ps. 41:1
8 [I]Or, *set a city on fire* [a]Prov. 11:11 [b]Ezek. 22:30
9 [a]Matt. 11:17
10 [I]Hebr. *Men of blood* [a]Gen. 4:5, 8; 1John 3:12
11 [a]Judg. 16:17; Prov. 12:16; 14:33
13 [I]Or, *the usurer* [a]Prov. 22:2 [b]Matt. 5:45
14 [a]Prov. 20:28; 25:5 [b]Ps. 72:2, 4, 13, 14
15 [a]Prov. 29:17 [b]Prov. 10:1; 17:21, 25
16 [a]Ps. 37:36; 58:10; 91:8; 92:11
17 [a]Prov. 13:24; 19:18; 22:15; 23:13-15
18 [I]Or, *is made naked* [a]1Sam. 3:1; Amos 8:11, 12 [b]John 13:17; James 1:25
20 [I]Or, *in his matters* [a]Prov. 26:12
22 [a]Prov. 15:18; 26:21
23 [a]Job 22:29; Prov. 15:33; 18:12; Isa. 66:2; Dan. 4:30, 31; Matt. 23:12; Luke 14:11; 18:14; Acts 12:23; James 4:6, 10; 1Pet. 5:5
24 [a]Lev. 5:1
25 [I]Hebr. *shall be set on high* [a]Gen. 12:12; 20:2, 11
26 [I]Hebr. *the face of a ruler* [a]Ps. 20:9; Prov. 19:6

1 [a]Prov. 31:1
2 [a]Ps. 73:22
3 [I]Hebr. *know*

4 [a]John 3:13 [b]Job 38:4; Ps. 104:3; Isa. 40:12

gathered[622] the wind in his fists? who hath bound the waters in a garment? who hath established all the ends of the earth?[776] what *is* his name, and what *is* his son's name, if thou canst tell?[3045]

🔑 5 [a]Every word[565] of God[430] *is* [I]pure:[6884] [b]he *is* a shield unto them that put their trust[2620] in him.

6 [a]Add thou not unto his words, lest he reprove[3198] thee, and thou be found a liar.[3576]

7 Two *things* have I required[7592] of thee; [I]deny me *them* not before I die:

8 Remove far from me vanity[7723] and lies:[3577] give me neither poverty nor riches; [a]feed[2963] me with food [I]convenient[2706] for me:

9 [a]Lest I be full, and [I]deny *thee,* and say,[559] Who *is* the LORD? or lest I be poor, and steal, and take[8610] the name of my God[430] *in vain.*

10 [I]Accuse[3960] not a servant[5650] unto his master,[113] lest he curse[7043] thee, and thou be found guilty.[816]

11 *There is* a generation[1755] *that* curseth their father,[1] and doth not bless[1288] their mother.[517]

12 *There is* a generation [a]*that are* pure[2889] in their own eyes, and *yet* is not washed[7364] from their filthiness.

13 *There is* a generation, O how [a]lofty are their eyes! and their eyelids are lifted up.[5375]

14 [a]*There is* a generation, whose teeth *are as* swords,[2719] and their jaw teeth *as* knives, [b]to devour the poor from off the earth, and the needy from *among* men.[120]

15 The horseleach hath two daughters, *crying,* Give, give. There are three *things that* are never satisfied, *yea,* four *things* say not, [I]*It is* enough:

16 [a]The grave;[7585] and the barren[6115] womb; the earth *that is* not filled with water; and the fire *that* saith not, *It is* enough.

17 [a]The eye *that* mocketh at *his* father, and despiseth to obey[3349] *his* mother, the ravens of [I]the valley shall pick it out, and the young eagles shall eat it.

🔑 18 There be three *things which* are too wonderful[6381] for me, yea, four which I know[3045] not:

19 The way[1870] of an eagle in the air;[8064] the way of a serpent[5175] upon a rock; the way of a ship in the [I]midst of the sea; and the way of a man with a maid.[5959]

20 Such *is* the way of an adulterous[5003] woman;[802] she eateth, and wipeth[4229] her mouth,[6310] and saith, I have done[6466] no wickedness.[205]

21 For three *things* the earth is disquieted, and for four *which* it cannot bear:[5375]

22 [a]For a servant when he reigneth;[4427] and a fool when he is filled with meat;

23 For an odious[8130] *woman* when she is married;[1166] and a handmaid that is heir[3423] to her mistress.[1404]

24 There be four *things which are* little upon the earth, but they *are* [I]exceeding wise:[2450]

25 [a]The ants *are* a people[5971] not strong, yet they prepare[3559] their meat in the summer;

26 [a]The conies[8227] *are but* a feeble folk, yet make[7760] they their houses in the rocks;

5 [I]Hebr. *purified* [a]Ps. 12:6; 18:30; 19:8; 119:140 [b]Ps. 18:30; 84:11; 115:9-11
6 [a]Deut. 4:2; 12:32; Rev. 22:18, 19
7 [I]Hebr. *withhold not from me*
8 [I]Hebr. *of my allowance* [a]Matt. 6:11
9 [I]Hebr. *believe thee* [a]Deut. 8:12; 14:17; 31:20; 32:15; Neh. 9:25, 26; Job 31:24, 25, 28; Hos. 13:6
10 [I]Hebr. *Hurt not with thy tongue*
12 [a]Luke 18:11
13 [a]Ps. 131:1; Prov. 6:17
14 [a]Job 29:17; Ps. 52:2; 57:4; Prov. 12:18 [b]Ps. 14:4; Amos 8:4
15 [I]Hebr. *Wealth*
16 [a]Prov. 27:20; Hab. 2:5
17 [I]Or, *the brook* [a]Gen. 9:22; Lev. 20:9; Prov. 20:20; 23:22
19 [I]Hebr. *heart*
22 [a]Prov. 19:10; Eccl. 10:7
24 [I]Hebr. *wise, made wise*
25 [a]Prov. 6:6
26 [a]Ps. 104:18

🔑 **30:5, 6** Verse five declares that every word of God is completely free of imperfections. This fact demands that the words of Scripture not be slighted or considered to be in error in any way. Furthermore, no part of it should ever be neglected or regarded as less important (2 Tim. 3:16). Church history is full of those who concentrated so heavily upon certain biblical concepts in favorite passages that they became blind to other important truths. Sound preaching and balanced devotions will not be restricted to the same portions of Scripture over and over again. It is crucial to remember that the Bible should be interpreted with the whole of its doctrines and principles in mind.

🔑 **30:18–20** The common factor in these comparisons is that each one describes something that does not leave any lasting indication of where they have been; they leave no trace behind them. This describes the behavior of an adulterous woman who feels no shame (v. 20).

27 The locusts have no king,[4428] yet go they forth all of them [I]by bands;

28 The spider taketh hold[8610] with her hands,[3027] and is in kings' palaces.[1964]

29 There be three *things* which go[6806] well,[3190] yea, four are comely[3190] in going:

30 A lion *which is* strongest among beasts, and turneth not away[7725] for any;

31 A [I]greyhound; an he goat also; and a king, against whom *there is* no rising up.

32 If thou hast done foolishly in lifting up thyself,[5375] or if thou hast thought evil,[2161] [a]*lay* thine hand[3027] upon thy mouth.

33 Surely the churning[4330] of milk bringeth forth butter, and the wringing[4330] of the nose[639] bringeth forth blood:[1818] so the forcing[4330] of wrath[639] bringeth forth strife.[7379]

Advice to a King

31 The words[1697] of king[4428] Lemuel, [a]the prophecy[4853] that his mother[517] taught[3256] him.

2 What, my son? and what, [a]the son of my womb?[990] and what, the son of my vows?[5088]

3 [a]Give not thy strength[2428] unto women,[802] nor thy ways[1870] [b]to that which destroyeth[4229] kings.

4 [a]*It is* not for kings, O Lemuel, *it is* not for kings to drink wine; nor for princes[7336] strong drink:

5 [a]Lest they drink, and forget the law,[2710] and [I]pervert the judgment[1779] [II]of any of the afflicted.

6 [a]Give strong drink unto him that is ready to perish,[6] and wine unto those that be [Ib]of heavy[4751] hearts.

7 Let him drink, and forget his poverty, and remember[2142] his misery[5999] no more.

8 [a]Open thy mouth[6310] for the dumb [b]in the cause[1779] of all [I]such as are appointed to destruction.

9 Open thy mouth, [a]judge[8199] righteously,[6664] and [b]plead the cause[1777] of the poor and needy.

A Good Woman

🗝 10 [a]Who can find a virtuous[2428] woman?[802] for her price *is* far above rubies.

11 The heart[3820] of her husband[1167] doth safely trust[982] in her, so that he shall have no need of spoil.

12 She will do[1580] him good[2896] and not evil[7451] all the days[3117] of her life.[2416]

13 She seeketh wool, and flax, and worketh[6213] willingly[2656] with her hands.[3709]

14 She is like the merchants' ships; she bringeth her food from afar.

15 [a]She riseth also while it is yet night,[3915] and [b]giveth meat to her household,[1004] and a portion[2706] to her maidens.

16 She considereth[2161] a field,[7704] and [I]buyeth it: with the fruit of her hands she planteth a vineyard.

17 She girdeth her loins with strength, and strengtheneth her arms.

18 [I]She perceiveth that her merchandise *is* good: her candle[5216] goeth not out by night.

19 She layeth her hands[3027] to the spindle, and her hands hold the distaff.[6418]

20 [Ia]She stretcheth out her hand[3709] to the poor; yea, she reacheth forth her hands to the needy.

27 [I]Hebr. *gathered together*

31 [I]Or, *horse;* Hebr. *girt in the loins*

32 [a]Job 21:5; 40:4; Eccl. 8:3; Mic. 7:16

1 [a]Prov. 30:1

2 [a]Isa. 49:15

3 [a]Prov. 5:9 [b]Deut. 17:17; Neh. 13:26; Prov. 7:26; Hos. 4:11

4 [a]Eccl. 10:17

5 [I]Hebr. *alter* [II]Hebr. *of all the sons of affliction* [a]Hos. 4:11

6 [I]Hebr. *bitter of soul* [a]Ps. 104:15 [b]1Sam. 1:10

8 [I]Hebr. *the sons of destruction* [a]Job 29:15, 16 [b]1Sam. 19:4; Esth. 4:16

9 [a]Lev. 19:15; Deut. 1:16 [b]Job 29:12; Isa. 1:17; Jer. 22:16

10 [a]Prov. 12:4; 18:22; 19:14

15 [a]Rom. 12:11 [b]Luke 12:42

16 [I]Hebr. *taketh*

18 [I]Hebr. *She tasteth*

20 [I]Hebr. *She spreadeth* [a]Eph. 4:28; Heb. 13:16

🗝 **31:10–31** This passage is an acrostic poem. Each letter of the Hebrew alphabet is used in sequence to begin the first word of each verse (another acrostic poem is Ps. 119). This poem sings the praises of a good wife. It extols the honor and dignity of women, and emphasizes the importance of the mother in the home. The secret of her dignity and honor is that she "fears the Lord" (v. 30). As a result, her husband trusts in her, and she becomes a source of honor to her whole family. The poem does not criticize physical beauty as some claim (v. 30); it merely asserts that being physically attractive is a temporary condition, while virtue has eternal worth.

21 She is not afraid[3372] of the snow for her household: for all her household *are* clothed with [1]scarlet.

22 She maketh[6213] herself coverings of tapestry; her clothing *is* silk and purple.

23 [a]Her husband is known[3045] in the gates, when he sitteth among the elders[2205] of the land.[776]

24 She maketh fine linen, and selleth *it;* and delivereth girdles[2289] unto the merchant.

25 Strength and honour[1926] *are* her clothing; and she shall rejoice in time to come.

26 She openeth her mouth with wisdom;[2451] and in her tongue *is* the law[8451] of kindness.[2617]

27 She looketh well[6822] to the ways of her household, and eateth not the bread of idleness.

28 Her children[1121] arise up, and call her blessed;[833] her husband *also,* and he praiseth[1984] her.

29 Many daughters [1]have done virtuously, but thou excellest them all.

30 Favour[2580] *is* deceitful,[8267] and beauty *is* vain: *but* a woman *that* feareth the LORD, she shall be praised.

31 Give her of the fruit of her hands; and let her own works praise her in the gates.

21 [1]Or, *double garments*
23 [a]Prov. 12:4
29 [1]Or, *have gotten riches*

The Book of

ECCLESIASTES

The title of this book in Hebrew, *Qōheleth* (6953), is the word translated "Preacher" in chapter one, verse one. The English title is a transliteration of the title in the Septuagint, the Greek translation of the Old Testament. The Greek word *Ekklesiastes*, which means "speaker of a called out assembly," is derived from the word *ekklēsia* (1577), which is the New Testament word for "church."

Solomon's name does not explicitly appear in the text, but tradition has uniformly ascribed the book to him. In verse one, the author describes himself as the "son of David, king in Jerusalem." Though other "sons" of David did become king in Jerusalem, the contents of the book and the facts about the author make it clear that it was Solomon. No one could claim to be over Jerusalem and as wise as Solomon (Eccl. 1:16). Furthermore, who else had the wherewithal to build and acquire goods that Solomon had (Eccl. 2:3–8)? Likewise, are any so well known for the setting forth of many proverbs (Eccl. 12:9)? It seems that Solomon, near the end of a life spent seeking after the things of this world, was brought to repentance by the rebuke of the Lord (1 Kgs. 11:9–13). Most likely, he sat down at this time and wrote, under the inspiration of the Holy Spirit, about the vanity of his worldly pursuits and attempts to find peace and joy in temporal things. The application of this book to the Christian life is seen in that Solomon is cautioning those believers who have been lured away by the values, riches, and philosophies of this world to return from their prodigal ways. Those who are not believers are warned by Solomon's own example that life at its best is but vanity without Christ.

The perspective of Solomon at the time he wrote is the key to the proper understanding the Book of Ecclesiastes and to explaining its general pessimism. Solomon writes from the same perspective by which he had lived most of his life, that of one "under the sun" (Eccl. 1:3 and 30 other occurrences). It is from the earthly, secular perspective that life becomes futile. Yet even so, there are times when Solomon's faith in God is made known (Eccl. 12:13–14 is usually referred to, but this is only the climax of thoughts like 2:25; 3:11, 17; 8:12–13; 11:9).

Solomon's consideration of life without God led him to the assessment that life is unjust. Oppression goes on, the wicked prosper, and the fruits of man's labor pass from his control (Eccl. 1:15; 2:21; 4:1, 8; 6:2; 7:15). Not only this, but the Preacher ended up like the pleasure-seekers of today; "You may as well enjoy yourself, because life will soon be over" (see Eccl. 2:24; 3:12; 5:18; 8:15; 9:7–10).

Countless lives throughout history have confirmed the Preacher's findings; wisdom, pleasure, alchohol, human achievement, great riches, sex—all lead to emptiness, "vanity," if there is not a proper relationship to God (Eccl. 1:13; 2:1, 3, 8, 10, 12).

All Is Vanity

1 The words [a]of the Preacher,[6953] the son of David, king in Jerusalem.

2 [a]Vanity[1892] of vanities, saith the Preacher, vanity of vanities; [b]all *is* vanity.

3 [a]What profit hath a man[120] of all his labour[5999] which he taketh under the sun?

4 *One* generation[1755] passeth away, and *another* generation cometh: [a]but the earth[776] abideth for ever.[5769]

1 [a]Eccl. 1:12; 7:27; 12:8-10
2 [a]Ps. 39:5, 6; 62:9; 144:4; Eccl. 12:8 [b]Rom. 8:20
3 [a]Eccl. 2:22; 3:9
4 [a]Ps. 104:5; 119:90

1:2 The theme of the Book of Ecclesiastes is that "under the sun [i.e., "without God in the picture"], all is vanity." The key word in the book is "vanity," occurring thirty-eight times. It is used to

(continued on next page)

5 [a]The sun also ariseth, and the sun goeth down, and [I]hasteth to his place where he arose.

6 [a]The wind[7307] goeth toward the south, and turneth about unto the north; it whirleth about continually, and the wind returneth again[7725] according to his circuits.

7 [a]All the rivers run into the sea; yet the sea *is* not full; unto the place from whence the rivers come, thither they [I]return again.

8 All things *are* full of labour; man[376] cannot utter *it:* [a]the eye is not satisfied with seeing,[7200] nor the ear[241] filled with hearing.[8085]

9 [a]The thing that hath been, it *is that* which shall be; and that which is done *is* that which shall be done: and *there is* no new *thing* under the sun.

10 Is there *any* thing whereof it may be said, See, this *is* new? it hath been already of old time,[5769] which was before us.

11 *There is* no remembrance[2146] of former[7223] *things;* neither shall there be *any* remembrance of *things* that are to come with *those* that shall come after.

Solomon's Own Experience

12 [a]I the Preacher was king over Israel in Jerusalem.

13 And I gave my heart[3820] to seek and search out by wisdom[2451] concerning all *things* that are done under heaven:[8064] [a]this sore[7451] travail hath God[430] given to the sons[1121] of man [I]to be exercised therewith.

14 I have seen[7200] all the works that are done under the sun; and, behold, all *is* vanity and vexation[7469] of spirit.[7307]

15 [a]*That which is* crooked[5791] cannot be made straight: and [I]that which is wanting cannot be numbered.

16 I communed[1696] with mine own heart, saying, Lo, I am come to great estate,[1431] and have gotten[3254] [a]more wisdom than all *they* that have been before me in Jerusalem: yea, my heart [I]had great experience[7200] of wisdom and knowledge.[1847]

17 [a]And I gave my heart to know[3045] wisdom, and to know madness and folly: I perceived[3045] that this also is vexation[7475] of spirit.

18 For [a]in much wisdom *is* much grief:[3708] and he that increaseth knowledge increaseth sorrow.

2 [a]I said[559] in mine heart,[3820] Go to now, I will prove[5254] thee with mirth, therefore enjoy[7200] pleasure:[2896] and, behold, this also *is* vanity.

2 [a]I said of laughter, *It is* mad:[1984] and of mirth, What doeth it?

3 [a]I sought[8446] in mine heart [I]to give myself unto wine, yet acquainting[5090] mine heart with wisdom;[2451] and to lay hold on folly,[5531] till I might see what *was* that good[2896] for the sons[1121] of men,[120] which they should do under the heaven[8064] [II]all the days[3117] of their life.[2416]

4 I made me great works; I builded me houses;[1004] I planted me vineyards:

5 I made[6213] me gardens and orchards, and I planted trees in them of all *kind of* fruits:

6 I made me pools of water, to water therewith the wood that bringeth forth trees:

7 I got *me* [I]servants and maidens, and had servants born in my house;[1004] also I had great possessions of great and

5 [I]Hebr. *panteth* [a]Ps. 19:5, 6

6 [a]John 3:8

7 [I]Hebr. *return to go* [a]Job 38:10; Ps. 104:8, 9

8 [a]Prov. 27:20

9 [a]Eccl. 3:15

12 [a]Eccl. 1:1

13 [I]Or, *to afflict them* [a]Gen. 3:19; 3:10

15 [I]Hebr. *defect* [a]Eccl. 7:13

16 [I]Hebr. *had seen much* [a]1Kgs. 3:12, 13; 4:30; 10:7, 23

17 [a]Eccl. 2:3, 12; 7:23, 25; 1Thess. 5:21

18 [a]Eccl. 12:12

1 [a]Luke 12:19 [b]Isa. 50:11

2 [a]Prov. 14:13; Eccl. 7:6

3 [I]Hebr. *to draw my flesh with wine* [II]Hebr. *the number of the days of their life* [a]Eccl. 1:17

7 [I]Hebr. *sons of my house*

(continued from previous page)
describe outward and tangible things (Eccl. 2:15, 19; 8:10, 14) as well as inward thoughts (Eccl. 1:14; 2:11). The word "vanity" is from the Hebrew *hevel* (1892), which emphasizes that which is empty and passing. The phrase "vanity of vanities" denotes the Hebrew way of expressing a superlative (it could be translated "most futile"). This method is also seen in the phrase "most holy place" (Ex. 26:34), of which the literal meaning in the Hebrew is "holy of Holies."

small cattle above all that were in Jerusalem before me:

8 [a]I gathered[3664] me also silver and gold, and the peculiar treasure[5459] of kings[4428] and of the provinces: I gat me men singers[7891] and women singers, and the delights[8588] of the sons of men, *as* [I]musical instruments, and that of all sorts.

9 So [a]I was great, and increased more than all that were before me in Jerusalem: also my wisdom remained with me.

10 And whatsoever mine eyes desired I kept not from them, I withheld not my heart from any joy; for my heart rejoiced in all my labour: and [a]this was my portion of all my labour.[5999]

🔑 11 Then I looked on all the works that my hands[3027] had wrought, and on the labour that I had laboured to do: and, behold, all *was* [a]vanity[1892] and vexation[7469] of spirit,[7307] and *there was* no profit under the sun.

12 And I turned myself to behold[7200] wisdom, [a]and madness, and folly: for what *can* the man[120] *do* that cometh after the king? [I]*even* that which hath been already done.

13 Then I saw[7200] [I]that wisdom excelleth folly, as far as light[216] excelleth darkness.[2822]

14 [a]The wise man's[2450] eyes *are* in his head;[7218] but the fool walketh in darkness: and I myself perceived[3045] also that [b]one event happeneth to them all.

15 Then said I in my heart, As it happeneth to the fool,[3684] so it [I]happeneth even to me; and why was I then more wise?[2449] Then I said[1696] in my heart, that this also *is* vanity.

16 For *there is* no remembrance[2146] of the wise[2450] more than of the fool for ever;[5769] seeing that which now *is* in the days to come shall all be forgotten. And how dieth[4191] the wise *man?* as the fool.

17 Therefore I hated[8130] life; because the work that is wrought under the sun *is* grievous[7451] unto me: for all *is* vanity and vexation of spirit.

18 Yea, I hated all my labour which I had [I]taken[6001] under the sun: because [a]I should leave it unto the man that shall be after me.

19 And who knoweth whether he shall be a wise *man* or a fool? yet shall he have rule[7980] over all my labour wherein I have laboured, and wherein I have shewed myself wise under the sun. This *is* also vanity.

20 Therefore I went about to cause my heart to despair[2976] of all the labour which I took under the sun.

21 For there is a man whose labour *is* in wisdom, and in knowledge,[1847] and in equity;[3788] yet to a man that hath not laboured therein shall he [I]leave it *for* his portion. This also *is* vanity and a great evil.[7451]

22 [a]For what hath man of all his labour, and of the vexation[7475] of his heart, wherein he hath laboured[6001] under the sun?

23 For all his days *are* [a]sorrows, and his travail grief;[3708] yea, his heart taketh not rest in the night.[3915] This is also vanity.

🔑 24 [a]*There is* nothing better[2896] for a

8 [I]Hebr. *musical instrument and instruments* [a]1Kgs. 9:28; 10:10, 14, 21
9 [a]Eccl. 1:16
10 [a]Eccl. 3:22; 5:18; 9:9
11 [a]Eccl. 1:3, 14
12 [I]Or, *in those things which have been already done* [a]Eccl. 1:17; 7:25
13 [I]Hebr. *that there is an excellency in wisdom more than in folly*
14 [a]Prov. 17:24; Eccl. 8:1 [b]Ps. 49:10; Eccl. 9:2, 3, 11
15 [I]Hebr. *happeneth to me, even to me*
18 [I]Hebr. *labored* [a]Ps. 49:10
21 [I]Hebr. *give*
22 [a]Eccl. 1:3; 3:9
23 [a]Job 5:7; 14:1
24 [a]Eccl. 3:12, 13, 22; 5:18; 8:15

🔑 **2:11** This verse is Solomon's reflection on all that he had accomplished. The result of it all was emptiness, and it had become unprofitable. The words that best describe Solomon's feelings at this point are "vanity and vexation of spirit." In all of the supposed pleasures of life, he found no satisfaction (Heb. 11:25). The cause of all this "vanity and vexation" was that Solomon had not learned how to restrain his desires. There are many believers (even preachers and church leaders) that have not learned this lesson well enough. In the end, however, they will see that the fulfillment of fleshly desires will be unprofitable. Their accomplishments for God are a testimony of Him to the world, but the times when the flesh is not restrained will result in a reproach on the cause of Christ.

🔑 **2:24** This verse shows that life should be lived to its fullest. Solomon was not expressing the hedonistic view seen in the phrase, "take thine ease, eat, drink, and be merry" (Luke 12:19). Rather, he is suggesting that people should keep the pleasures that they enjoy in this life in perspective

(continued on next page)

man, *than* that he should eat and drink, and *that* he [I]should make his soul[5315] enjoy good in his labour. This also I saw, that it *was* from the hand[3027] of God.[430]

25 For who can eat, or who else can hasten *hereunto,* more than I?

26 For *God* giveth to a man that *is* good [I][a]in his sight wisdom, and knowledge, and joy: but to the sinner[2398] he giveth travail, to gather[622] and to heap up,[3664] that [b]he may give to *him that is* good before God. This also *is* vanity and vexation[7469] of spirit.

A Time for Everything

3 🔑 To every *thing there is* a season,[2165] and a [a]time[6256] to every purpose[2656] under the heaven:[8064]

2 A time [I]to be born, and a [a]time to die;[4191] a time to plant, and a time to pluck up *that which is* planted;

3 A time to kill,[2026] and a time to heal; a time to break down, and a time to build up;

4 A time to weep, and a time to laugh; a time to mourn, and a time to dance;

5 A time to cast away stones, and a time to gather stones together;[3664] a time to embrace, and [a]a time [I]to refrain from embracing;

6 A time to [I]get, and a time to lose; a time to keep,[8104] and a time to cast away;

7 A time to rend,[7167] and a time to sew; [a]a time to keep silence, and a time to speak;[1696]

8 A time to love,[157] and a time to [a]hate;[8130] a time of war, and a time of peace.

9 [a]What profit hath he that worketh[6213] in that wherein he laboureth?[6001]

10 [a]I have seen[7200] the travail, which God[430] hath given to the sons[1121] of men[120] to be exercised[6031] in it.

🔑 11 He hath made every *thing* beautiful in his time: also he hath set the world[5769] in their heart,[3820] so that [a]no man[120] can find out the work that God

24 [I]Or, *delight his senses*
26 [I]Hebr. *before him* [a]Gen. 7:1; Luke 1:6 [b]Job 27:16, 17; Prov. 28:8
1 [a]Eccl. 3:17; 8:6
2 [I]Hebr. *to bear* [a]Heb. 9:27
5 [I]Hebr. *to be far from* [a]Joel 2:16; 1Cor. 7:5
6 [I]Or, *seek*
7 [a]Amos 5:13
8 [a]Luke 14:26
9 [a]Eccl. 1:3
10 [a]Eccl. 1:13
11 [a]Eccl. 8:17; Rom. 11:33

(continued from previous page)

to their responsibility to God (1 Tim. 4:4, 5; 6:17). Also, in light of the theme of the Book of Ecclesiastes, it should be understood that all good things that come about as a result of the fulfillment of fleshly desires are "vanity." However, if a person works diligently, acknowledging that God's hand is on his or her life, that person will be blessed. They must exhibit pure hearts in all their actions (see note on Eccl. 7:16, 17). Hence, the key is to "do all to the glory of God" (1 Cor. 10:31).

🔑 **3:1** Solomon continues his defense of his labors in the flesh by suggesting that there must be some profit in seeking to establish stability in one's life. There is much in the world that is changing, and Solomon is trusting in things that he thinks have provided him with security. What he discovers is that there is One who keeps the world in order—that is God. He is the One who causes all things to happen in their "seasons" and gives everything a "purpose." It is evident from the examination of God's character that He is all-knowing. He knows the end of everything, and all that is done is controlled by His providential hand. All the events of history have been fitted into God's timetable. For instance, the deliverance of His chosen people, the Israelites, out of bondage in Egypt was done because of God's promise made to Abraham (see note on Gen. 15:13–16). The fulfillment of this promise is seen in the usage of the phrase "the selfsame day" (Ex. 12:41), noting that God was bringing the children of Israel out of Egypt at the precise time that He had said. The prophecies about the coming of Christ were fulfilled "when the fullness of time was come" (Gal. 4:4). Christ came and accomplished all the Father's will just as it had been planned. God's purpose had been carried out specifically in regard to the time of Christ's incarnation. The fact that God is immutable and unaffected by the circumstances of this world is incomprehensible to the human mind. The only way that Solomon could find true happiness was in knowing that in God's providence all events would be worked out according to His purpose (Rom. 8:28).

🔑 **3:11** God is able to use anything and anyone for the fulfillment of His purposes. Furthermore, He knows the events that have transpired in the past as well as those things that will be in the future. God has made all things which are by their nature good and pleasing to Him, and which things

(continued on next page)

maketh[6213] from the beginning[7218] to the end.

12 [a]I know[3045] that *there is* no good[2896] in them, but for *a man* to rejoice, and to do[6213] good in his life.[2416]

13 And also [a]that every man should eat and drink, and enjoy[7200] the good of all his labour,[5999] it *is* the gift of God.

14 I know that, whatsoever God doeth, it shall be for ever:[5769] [a]nothing can be put to it, nor any thing taken from it: and God doeth *it,* that *men* should fear[3372] before him.

15 [a]That which hath been is now; and that which is to be hath already been; and God requireth[1245] [I]that which is past.

Injustice

16 And moreover [a]I saw[7200] under the sun the place of judgment,[4941] *that* wickedness[7562] *was* there; and the place of righteousness,[6664] *that* iniquity[7562] *was* there.

17 I said[559] in mine heart, [a]God shall judge[8199] the righteous[6662] and the wicked:[7563] for *there is* [b]a time there for every purpose and for every work.

18 I said in mine heart concerning the estate[1700] of the sons of men, [I]that God might manifest[1305] them, and that they might see that they themselves are beasts.

19 [a]For that which befalleth the sons of men befalleth beasts; even one thing befalleth them: as the one dieth,[4194] so dieth the other; yea, they have all one breath;[7307] so that a man hath no preeminence[4195] above a beast: for all *is* vanity.

20 All go unto one place; [a]all are of the dust,[6083] and all turn to dust again.[7725]

21 [a]Who knoweth the spirit[7307] [I]of man that [II]goeth upward, and the spirit of the beast that goeth downward to the earth?[776]

22 [a]Wherefore I perceive[7200] that *there is* nothing better,[2896] than that a man should rejoice in his own works; for [b]that *is* his portion: [c]for who shall bring him to see what shall be after him?

4 So I returned,[7725] and considered[7200] all the [a]oppressions that are done under the sun: and behold the tears of *such as were* oppressed, and they had no comforter;[5162] and on the [I]side[3027] of their oppressors *there was* power; but they had no comforter.

2 [a]Wherefore I praised[7623] the dead[4191] which are already dead more than the living[2416] which are yet alive.[2416]

3 [a]Yea, better[2896] *is he* than both they, which hath not yet been, who hath not seen[7200] the evil[7451] work that is done under the sun.

4 Again, I considered all travail,[5999] and [I]every right[3788] work, that [II]for this a man[376] is envied[7068] of his neighbour.[7453] This *is* also vanity and vexation[7469] of spirit.[7307]

5 [a]The fool foldeth his hands[3027] together, and eateth his own flesh.[1320]

6 [a]Better *is* an handful *with* quietness, than both the hands full *with* travail and vexation of spirit.

7 Then I returned, and I saw[7200] vanity under the sun.

8 There is one *alone,* and *there is* not a second; yea, he hath neither child[1121] nor brother:[251] yet *is there* no end of all

12 [a]Eccl. 3:22
13 [a]Eccl. 2:24
14 [a]James 1:17
15 [I]Hebr. *that which is driven away* [a]Eccl. 1:9
16 [a]Eccl. 5:8
17 [a]Rom. 2:6, 7, 8; 2Cor. 5:10; 2Thess. 1:6, 7 [b]Eccl. 3:1
18 [I]Or, *that they might clear God and see*
19 [a]Ps. 49:12, 20; 73:22; Eccl. 2:16
20 [a]Gen. 3:19
21 [I]Hebr. *of the sons of man* [II]Hebr. *is ascending* [a]Eccl. 12:7
22 [a]Eccl. 2:24; 3:12; 5:18; 11:9 [b]Eccl. 2:10 [c]Eccl. 6:12; 8:7; 10:14

1 [I]Hebr. *hand* [a]Eccl. 3:16; 5:8
2 [a]Job 3:17
3 [a]Job 3:11, 16, 21; Eccl. 6:3
4 [I]Hebr. *all the rightness of work* [II]Hebr. *this is the envy of a man from his neighbor*
5 [a]Prov. 6:10; 24:33
6 [a]Prov. 15:16, 17; 16:8

(continued from previous page)
will please Him at the appointed time that He has established (see note on Eccl. 3:1). In His omniscience, God knows how the events of time will unfold to fulfill His eternal plan. The capacity of man to understand these factors is limited by the fact that he is a finite creature, not an eternal one. He is also limited in that he can only amass a certain amount of knowledge about God in his lifetime. Therefore, man is incapable of finding "out the work that God maketh from the beginning to the end." In other words, God knows the end as well as the beginning. Since He knows the outcome, God can see how each piece fits into His plan. The only alternative for man, since he cannot see the end from the beginning, is to trust completely in God.

his labour;[5999] neither is his [a]eye satisfied
with riches; [b]neither *saith he,* For whom
do I labour,[6001] and bereave my soul[5315]
of good?[2896] This *is* also vanity,[1892] yea,
it *is* a sore[7451] travail.
9 Two *are* better than one; because
they have a good reward for their labour.
10 For if they fall, the one will lift up
his fellow:[2270] but woe to him *that is*
alone when he falleth;[5307] for *he hath* not
another to help him up.
11 Again, if two lie together, then
they have heat: but how can one be
warm *alone?*
🔑 12 And if one prevail against him,
two shall withstand him; and a threefold
cord[2256] is not quickly broken.
13 Better *is* a poor and a wise[2450]
child than an old[2205] and foolish king,[4428]
[I]who will no more be admonished.
14 For out of prison he cometh to
reign;[4427] whereas also *he that is* born in
his kingdom[4438] becometh poor.
15 I considered all the living which
walk under the sun, with the second child
that shall stand up in his stead.
16 *There is* no end of all the
people,[5971] *even* of all that have been before them: they also that come after shall
not rejoice in him. Surely this also *is* vanity and vexation[7475] of spirit.

Rash Promises

5 Keep[8104] [a]thy foot when thou goest
to the house[1004] of God,[430] and be
more ready to hear,[8085] [b]than to give the
sacrifice[2077] of fools: for they consider[3045]
not that they do evil.[7451]
2 Be not rash[926] with thy mouth,[6310]
and let not thine heart[3820] be hasty to
utter *any* [I]thing before God: for God *is* in
heaven,[8064] and thou upon earth:[776] therefore let thy words[1697] [a]be few.
3 For a dream cometh through the
multitude of business; and [a]a fool's voice
is known by multitude of words.
4 [a]When thou vowest[5087] a vow unto
God, defer not to pay it; for *he hath* no
pleasure[2656] in fools: [b]pay that which
thou hast vowed.
5 [a]Better[2896] *is it* that thou shouldest
not vow,[5087] than that thou shouldest
vow and not pay.
6 Suffer not thy mouth to cause[2398]
thy flesh[1320] to sin;[2398] [a]neither say[559]
thou before the angel,[4397] that it *was* an
error:[7684] wherefore should God be
angry[7107] at thy voice, and destroy[2254]
the work of thine hands?[3027]
7 For in the multitude of dreams and
many words *there are* also *divers* vanities: but [a]fear[3372] thou God.

The Vanity of Life

8 If thou [a]seest the oppression of the
poor, and violent perverting of judgment[4941] and justice[6664] in a province,
marvel not [I]at the matter: for [b]*he that is*
higher than the highest regardeth;[8104] and
there be higher than they.

8 [a]Prov. 27:20; 1John 2:16 [b]Ps. 39:6

13 [I]Hebr. *who knoweth not to be admonished*

1 [a]Ex. 3:5; Isa. 1:12 [b]1Sam. 15:22; Ps. 50:8; Prov. 15:8; 21:27; Hos. 6:6

2 [I]Or, *word* [a]Prov. 10:19; Matt. 6:7

3 [a]Prov. 10:19

4 [a]Num. 30:2; Deut. 23:21, 22, 23; Ps. 50:14; 76:11 [b]Ps. 66:13, 14

5 [a]Prov. 20:25; Acts 5:4

6 [a]1Cor. 11:10

7 [a]Eccl. 12:13

8 [I]Hebr. *at the will, or, purpose* [a]Eccl. 3:16 [b]Ps. 12:5; 58:11; 82:1

🔑 **4:12** In the phrase "a threefold cord is not quickly broken," it is clear that Solomon is pointing out the advantages of companionship. Moreover, he presents this illustration to show how God in mercy provides help to those who will depend on Him. In Ecclesiastes 4:9–11, Solomon explains further by examples how this concept of companionship is beneficial. He shows that there are definite advantages to working together (vv. 9, 10). He also reveals how terrible the circumstances would be if one had to face adversity alone.

This concept of unity and working together is one that is seen throughout Scripture. From the time of creation, God provided companionship by making a help meet for Adam (Gen. 2:18). Even Christ, in the commissioning of his disciples, sent them "two and two" (Luke 10:1–3). He knew that they would face adversity and persecution from the world. In providing companionship, they would be able to lift one another up and continue their ministry even when they were persecuted. The concept of the "unity of the body of believers" is seen in the books of the New Testament. Phrases like "the whole body, fitly joined together" (Eph. 4:15) and "have the same care one for another" (1 Cor. 12:25) adequately explain the idea that God desires unity among the believers in the Church (John 17:21).

9 Moreover the profit of the earth is for all: the king[4428] *himself* is served[5647] by the field.[7704]

10 He that loveth[157] silver shall not be satisfied with silver; nor he that loveth abundance with increase: this *is* also vanity.1892

11 When goods increase, they are increased that eat them: and what good[3788] *is there* to the owners[1167] thereof, saving the beholding[7200] *of them* with their eyes?

12 The sleep of a labouring[5647] man *is* sweet, whether he eat little or much: but the abundance of the rich will not suffer him to sleep.

13 [a]There is a sore evil *which* I have seen[7200] under the sun, *namely,* riches kept[8104] for the owners thereof to their hurt.[7451]

14 But those riches perish[6] by evil travail: and he begetteth a son,[1121] and *there is* nothing in his hand.[3027]

15 [a]As he came forth of his mother's[517] womb,[990] naked[6174] shall he return[7725] to go as he came, and shall take[5375] nothing of his labour,[5999] which he may carry away in his hand.

16 And this also *is* a sore evil, *that* in all points as he came, so shall he go: and [a]what profit hath he [b]that hath laboured for the wind?[7307]

17 All his days[3117] also [a]he eateth in darkness,[2822] and *he hath* much sorrow[3707] and wrath[7110] with his sickness.

18 Behold *that* which I have seen: [I][a]*it is* good[2896] and comely3303 *for one* to eat and to drink, and to enjoy[7200] the good of all his labour that he taketh under the sun [II]all the days of his life,[2416] which God giveth him: [b]for it *is* his portion.

19 [a]Every man[120] also to whom God hath given riches and wealth, and hath given him power[7980] to eat thereof, and to take his portion, and to rejoice in his labour; this *is* the gift of God.

20 [I]For he shall not much remember[2142] the days of his life; because God answereth *him* in the joy of his heart.

6 [a]There is an evil[7451] which I have seen[7200] under the sun, and it *is* common among men:[120]

2 A man[376] to whom God[430] hath given riches, wealth, and honour,[3519] [a]so that he wanteth nothing for his soul[5315] of all that he desireth,[183] [b]yet God giveth him not power[7980] to eat thereof, but a stranger eateth it: this *is* vanity, and it *is* an evil disease.2483

3 If a man beget an hundred *children,* and live[2421] many years, so that the days[3117] of his years be many, and his soul be not filled with good,[2896] and [a]also *that* he have no burial;[6900] I say, *that* [b]an untimely birth[5309] *is* better[2896] than he.

4 For he cometh in with vanity, and departeth in darkness,[2822] and his name shall be covered[3680] with darkness.

5 Moreover he hath not seen the sun, nor known[3045] *any thing:* this hath more rest than the other.

6 Yea, though he live a thousand years twice *told,* yet hath he seen no good: do not all go to one place?

7 [a]All the labour[5999] of man[120] *is* for his mouth,[6310] and yet the [I]appetite[5315] is not filled.

8 For what hath the wise[2450] more than the fool? what hath the poor, that knoweth to walk before the living?[2416]

9 Better *is* the sight of the eyes [I]than the wandering of the desire:[5315] this *is* also vanity and vexation7469 of spirit.[7307]

10 That which hath been is named[7121] already, and it is known that it *is* man: [a]neither may he contend[1777] with him that is mightier than he.

11 Seeing there be many things that increase vanity, what *is* man the better?

12 For who knoweth what *is* good for man in *this* life,[2416] [I]all the days of his vain life which he spendeth[6213] as [a]a shadow? for [b]who can tell[5046] a man what shall be after him under the sun?

Comparing Wisdom and Folly

7 A [a]good name *is* better[2896] than precious[2896] ointment;[8081] and the day[3117] of death[4194] than the day of one's birth.

---

13 [a]Eccl. 6:1

15 [a]Job 1:21; Ps. 49:17; 1Tim. 6:7

16 [a]Eccl. 1:3 [b]Prov. 11:29

17 [a]Ps. 127:2

18 [I]Hebr. *there is a good that is comely* [II]Hebr. *the number of the days* [a]Eccl. 2:24; 3:12, 13, 22; 9:7; 11:9; 1Tim. 6:17 [b]Eccl. 2:10; 3:22

19 [a]Eccl. 2:24; 3:13; 6:2

20 [I]Or, *Though he give not much, yet he remembereth*

1 [a]Eccl. 5:13

2 [a]Job 21:10; Ps. 17:14; 73:7 [b]Luke 12:20

3 [a]2Kgs. 9:35; Isa. 14:19, 20; Jer. 22:19 [b]Job 3:16; Ps. 58:8; Eccl. 4:3

7 [I]Hebr. *soul* [a]Prov. 16:26

9 [I]Hebr. *than the walking of the soul*

10 [a]Job 9:32; Isa. 45:9; Jer. 49:19

12 [I]Hebr. *the number of the days of the life of his vanity* [a]Ps. 102:11; 109:23; 144:4; James 4:14 [b]Ps. 39:6; Eccl. 8:7

1 [a]Prov. 15:30; 22:1

2 *It is* better to go to the house[1004] of mourning, than to go to the house of feasting:[4960] for that *is* the end of all men;[120] and the living[2416] will lay *it* to his heart.[3820]

3 [I]Sorrow[3708] *is* better[2896] than laughter: [a]for by the sadness[7455] of the countenance the heart is made better.[3190]

4 The heart of the wise[2450] *is* in the house of mourning; but the heart of fools *is* in the house of mirth.

5 [a]*It is* better to hear[8085] the rebuke[1606] of the wise, than for a man[376] to hear the song[7892] of fools.

6 [a]For as the [I]crackling of thorns under a pot, so *is* the laughter of the fool: this also *is* vanity.[1892]

7 Surely oppression maketh a wise man mad;[1984] [a]and a gift destroyeth[6] the heart.

8 Better *is* the end[319] of a thing[1697] than the beginning[7225] thereof: *and* [a]the patient[750] in spirit[7307] *is* better than the proud in spirit.

9 [a]Be not hasty[926] in thy spirit to be angry:[3707] for anger resteth in the bosom of fools.

10 Say[559] not thou, What is *the cause* that the former[7223] days[3117] were better than these? for thou dost not enquire[7592] [I]wisely concerning this.

11 Wisdom[2451] *is* [I]good with an inheritance:[5159] and *by it there is* profit [a]to them that see the sun.

12 For wisdom *is* a [I]defence,[6738] *and* money *is* a defence: but the excellency of knowledge[1847] *is, that* wisdom giveth life[2421] to them that have it.

13 Consider[7200] the work of God:[430] for [a]who can make *that* straight, which he hath made crooked?[5791]

14 [a]In the day of prosperity[2896] be joyful,[2896] but in the day of adversity[7451] consider: God also hath [I]set the one over against the other, to the end[1700] that man[120] should find nothing after him.

15 All *things* have I seen[7200] in the days of my vanity: [a]there is a just *man* that perisheth[6] in his righteousness,[6664] and there is a wicked[7563] *man* that prolongeth[748] *his life* in his wickedness.[7451]

16 [a]Be not righteous[6662] over much; [b]neither make thyself over wise:[2449] why shouldest thou [I]destroy thyself?[8074]

17 Be not over much wicked, neither be thou foolish: [a]why shouldest thou die[4191] [I]before thy time?[6256]

18 *It is* good that thou shouldest take hold of this; yea, also from this withdraw not thine hand:[3027] for he that feareth God shall come forth of them all.

19 [a]Wisdom strengtheneth the wise more than ten mighty[7989] *men* which are in the city.

20 [a]For *there is* not a just[6662] man upon earth,[776] that doeth[6213] good, and sinneth[2398] not.

3 [I]Or, *Anger* [a]2Cor. 7:10
5 [a]Ps. 141:5; Prov. 13:18; 15:31, 32
6 [I]Hebr. *sound* [a]Ps. 118:12; Eccl. 2:2
7 [a]Ex. 23:8; Deut. 16:19
8 [a]Prov. 14:29
9 [a]Prov. 14:17; 16:32; James 1:19
10 [I]Hebr. *out of wisdom*
11 [I]Or, *as good as an inheritance, yea, better too* [a]Eccl. 11:7
12 [I]Hebr. *shadow*
13 [a]Job 12:14; Eccl. 1:15; Isa. 14:27
14 [I]Hebr. *made* [a]Deut. 28:47; Eccl. 3:4
15 [a]Eccl. 8:14
16 [I]Hebr. *be desolate* [a]Prov. 25:16 [b]Rom. 12:3
17 [I]Hebr. *not in thy time* [a]Job 15:32; Ps. 55:23; Prov. 10:27
19 [a]Prov. 21:22; 24:5; Eccl. 9:16, 18
20 [a]1Kgs. 8:46; 2Chr. 6:36; Prov. 20:9; Rom. 3:23; 1John 1:8

7:16, 17 There are two unique concepts explained in this passage. First, there is the possibility that in doing righteous things, one may become ritualistic, merely going through the formality of religion. In doing so, he or she never takes the truth to heart. In contrast, the wicked find security in their ways, but to continue in them will only result in death and destruction (see note on Job 21:23–26). They see themselves as being able to escape God's wrath, when in reality, they are acting foolishly (Prov. 15:3).

Some interpret this passage as giving them the right to establish their own standards and rules in their own minds for living life. They do this based on the notion that these verses are teaching that there is danger in having too much substance to one's religious practices. In reality, however, God examines the heart of the individual and knows the motives behind one's actions (Heb. 4:12; see note on Job 35:9–14). God alone knows whether a person is practicing religion in form only, or if he or she is sincere. Jesus addressed the Pharisees on this issue. He condemned them for their wrong motives in serving God. He referred to them as "whited sepulchres" (Matt. 23:27). In knowing their thoughts, Christ saw that they sought prestige from their religious positions. The phrase that Solomon used in verse sixteen, "righteous over much," adequately describes the Pharisees' vain approach to service to God. Solomon did not write concerning the excessive nature of righteousness, but against the development of a wrong attitude about service to God.

21 Also [I]take no heed unto all words[1697] that are spoken;[1696] lest thou hear thy servant[5650] curse thee:

22 For oftentimes also thine own heart knoweth that thou thyself likewise hast cursed others.

23 All this have I proved[5254] by wisdom: [a]I said,[559] I will be wise; but it *was* far from me.

24 [a]That which is far off, and [b]exceeding deep, who can find it out?

25 [I][a]I applied mine heart to know[3045] and to search, and to seek out wisdom, and the reason *of things,* and to know the wickedness[7562] of folly,[3689] even of foolishness *and* madness:

26 [a]And I find more bitter[4751] than death the woman,[802] whose heart *is* snares[4685] and nets,[2764] *and* her hands[3027] *as* bands: [I]whoso pleaseth God shall escape[4422] from her; but the sinner[2398] shall be taken by her.

27 Behold,[7200] this have I found, saith[559] [a]the preacher,[6953] [I]*counting* one by one, to find out the account.

28 Which yet my soul[5315] seeketh, but I find not: [a]one man among a thousand have I found; but a woman among all those have I not found.

29 Lo, this only have I found, [a]that God hath made[6213] man upright;[3476] but [b]they have sought out many inventions.[2810]

8 Who *is* as the wise[2450] *man?* and who knoweth the interpretation of a thing?[1697] [a]a man's[120] wisdom[2451] maketh his face to shine, [I][b]and the boldness of his face shall be changed.

Obey the King

2 I *counsel thee* to keep[8104] the king's[4428] commandment,[6310] [a]and *that* in regard[1700] of the oath[7621] of God.[430]

3 [a]Be not hasty[926] to go out of his sight: stand not in an evil[7451] thing; for he doeth whatsoever pleaseth him.

4 Where the word[1697] of a king *is, there is* power:[7983] and [a]who may say[559] unto him, What doest thou?

5 Whoso keepeth[8104] the commandment[4687] [I]shall feel no evil thing: and a wise man's heart[3820] discerneth[3045] both time[6256] and judgment.[4941]

6 Because [a]to every purpose[2656] there is time and judgment, therefore the misery of man[120] *is* great upon him.

7 [a]For he knoweth not that which shall be: for who can tell[5046] him [I]when it shall be?

🔑 8 [a]*There is* no man that hath power[7989] [b]over the spirit[7307] to retain the spirit; neither *hath he* power[7983] in the day[3117] of death:[4194] and *there is* no [I]discharge in *that* war; neither shall wickedness[7562] deliver those that are given to it.

Life Seems Unfair

9 All this have I seen,[7200] and applied my heart unto every work that is done under the sun: *there is* a time wherein one man ruleth[7980] over another to his own hurt.[7451]

10 And so I saw[7200] the wicked[7563] buried,[6912] who had come and gone from the place of the holy,[6918] and they were

21 [I]Hebr. *give not thine heart*
23 [a]Rom. 1:22
24 [a]Job 28:12, 20; 1Tim. 6:16 [b]Rom. 11:33
25 [I]Hebr. *I and my heart compassed* [a]Eccl. 1:17; 2:12
26 [I]Hebr. he that is *good before God* [a]Prov. 5:3, 4; 22:14
27 [I]Or, *weighing one thing after another, to find out the reason* [a]Eccl. 1:1, 2
28 [a]Job 33:23; Ps. 12:1
29 [a]Gen. 1:27 [b]Gen. 3:6, 7

1 [I]Hebr. *the strength* [a]Prov. 4:8, 9; 17:24; Acts 6:15 [b]Deut. 28:50
2 [a]1Chr. 29:24; Ezek. 17:18; Rom. 13:5
3 [a]Eccl. 10:4
4 [a]Job 34:18
5 [I]Hebr. *shall know*
6 [a]Eccl. 3:1
7 [I]Or, *how it shall be* [a]Prov. 24:22; Eccl. 6:12; 9:12; 10:14
8 [I]Or, *casting off weapons* [a]Ps. 49:6, 7 [b]Job 14:5

🔑 **8:8** Solomon is simply stating that no person can control the time of his or her death. When the time comes for a person to die, there is no power within that person to stop or even delay it from happening. The attitude of uncertainty concerning death and its inescapability has plagued humankind throughout their existence. If they knew the specific time that the end was coming, they would certainly seek to delay it. The truth is that God is in control of man's destiny. Only Christ was able to say that He had "power to lay [His life] down" and the "power to take it again" (John 10:18). In humanity's view, the only solution for death is to attempt to prolong life. Medical methods have improved over the centuries, but it is still by God's grace and power that He allows people to continue living. The truth is every person has been appointed a time to die (Heb. 9:27). Even in the Christian's life, he or she must acknowledge that becoming a believer does not exempt one from death. For the believer, there is the promise of eternal life following death, which should be a source of hope to continue living for God.

forgotten in the city where they had so done: this *is* also vanity.

11 [a]Because sentence[6599] against an evil work is not executed[6213] speedily, therefore the heart of the sons of men is fully set in them to do[6213] evil.

12 [a]Though a sinner[2398] do evil an hundred times, and his *days* be prolonged,[748] yet surely I know[3045] that [b]it shall be well with them that fear God, which fear[3372] before him:

13 But it shall not be well with the wicked, neither shall he prolong *his* days,[3117] *which are* as a shadow; because he feareth not before God.

14 There is a vanity which is done upon the earth;[776] that there be just *men,* unto whom it [a]happeneth[5060] according to the work of the wicked; again, there be wicked *men,* to whom it happeneth according to the work of the righteous:[6662] I said[559] that this also *is* vanity.

15 [a]Then I commended[7623] mirth, because a man hath no better thing[2896] under the sun, than to eat, and to drink, and to be merry: for that shall abide with him of his labour[5999] the days of his life, which God giveth him under the sun.

16 When I applied mine heart to know wisdom, and to see the business that is done upon the earth: (for also *there is that* neither day nor night[3915] seeth[7200] sleep with his eyes:)

17 Then I beheld[7200] all the work of God, that [a]a man cannot find out the work that is done under the sun: because though a man labour to seek *it* out, yet he shall not find *it;* yea further; though a wise *man* think[559] to know *it,* [b]yet shall he not be able to find *it.*

9 For all this [I]I considered in my heart[3820] even to declare all this, [a]that the righteous,[6662] and the wise,[2450] and their works, *are* in the hand[3027] of God:[430] no man[120] knoweth either love[160] or hatred[8135] *by* all *that is* before them.

2 [a]All *things come* alike to all: *there is* one event to the righteous, and to the wicked;[7563] to the good[2896] and to the clean,[2889] and to the unclean;[2931] to him that sacrificeth,[2076] and to him that sacrificeth not: as *is* the good, so *is* the sinner;[2398] *and* he that sweareth,[7650] as *he* that feareth an oath.[7621]

3 This *is* an evil[7451] among all *things* that are done under the sun, that *there is* one event unto all: yea, also the heart of the sons[1121] of men[120] is full of evil, and madness *is* in their heart[3824] while they live,[2416] and after that *they go* to the dead.[4191]

4 For to him that is joined to all the living[2416] there is hope:[986] for a living dog is better[2896] than a dead lion.

5 For the living know[3045] that they shall die:[4191] but [a]the dead know not any thing, neither have they any more a reward; for [b]the memory[2143] of them is forgotten.

6 Also their love, and their hatred, and their envy,[7068] is now perished;[6] neither have they any more a portion for ever[5769] in any *thing* that is done under the sun.

7 Go thy way, [a]eat thy bread with joy, and drink thy wine with a merry[2896] heart; for God now accepteth[7521] thy works.

8 Let thy garments be always white; and let thy head[7218] lack no ointment.[8081]

9 [I]Live joyfully with the wife[802] whom thou lovest[157] all the days[3117] of the life of thy vanity,[1892] which he hath given thee under the sun, all the days of thy vanity: [a]for that *is* thy portion in *this* life, and in thy labour[5999] which thou takest[6001] under the sun.

10 Whatsoever thy hand findeth to do, do *it* with thy might; for *there is* no work, nor device, nor knowledge,[1847] nor

11 [a]Ps. 10:6; 50:21; Isa. 26:10

12 [a]Isa. 65:20; Rom. 2:5 [b]Ps. 37:11, 18, 19; Prov. 1:32, 33; Isa. 3:10, 11; Matt. 25:34, 41

14 [a]Ps. 73:14; Eccl. 2:14; 7:15; 9:1-3

15 [a]Eccl. 2:24; 3:12, 22; 5:18; 9:7

17 [a]Job 5:9; Eccl. 3:11; Rom. 11:33 [b]Ps. 73:16

1 [I]Hebr. *I gave,* or, *set to my heart* [a]Eccl. 8:14

2 [a]Job 21:7; Ps. 73:3, 12, 13; Mal. 3:15

5 [a]Job 14:21; Isa. 63:16 [b]Job 7:8-10; Isa. 26:14

7 [a]Eccl. 8:15

9 [I]Hebr. *See,* or, *Enjoy life* [a]Eccl. 2:10, 24; 3:13, 22; 5:18

8:11 See note on Genesis 6:1–4 concerning the "sons of men."

9:10 Solomon, in writing these words, provides a ruling principle which should govern one's accomplishments in this life. Goals should be set and they should be reached with all the fervor and

(continued on next page)

wisdom,[2451] in the grave,[7585] whither
thou goest.
🗝 11 I returned,[7725] [a]and saw[7200] under
the sun, that the race *is* not to the swift,
nor the battle to the strong, neither yet
bread to the wise, nor yet riches to men
of understanding,[995] nor yet favour[2580]
to men of skill;[3045] but time[6256] and
chance happeneth to them all.
12 For [a]man also knoweth not his
time: as the fishes[1709] that are taken in an
evil net, and as the birds that are caught
in the snare;[6341] so *are* the sons of men
[b]snared[3369] in an evil time, when it
falleth[5307] suddenly upon them.

Wisdom and Foolishness

13 This wisdom have I seen[7200] also
under the sun, and it *seemed* great unto
me:
14 [a]*There was* a little city, and few
men[582] within it; and there came a great
king[4428] against it, and besieged it, and
built great bulwarks[4685] against it:
15 Now there was found in it a poor
wise man,[376] and he by his wisdom delivered the city; yet no man remembered[2142] that same poor man.
16 [a]Then said[559] I, Wisdom *is* better
than strength: nevertheless [b]the poor
man's wisdom *is* despised, and his
words[1697] are not heard.[8085]
17 The words of wise *men are* heard
in quiet more than the cry of him that
ruleth[4910] among fools.
18 [a]Wisdom *is* better than weapons
of war: but [b]one sinner destroyeth[6] much
good.

10 [I]Dead[4194] flies cause the ointment[8081] of the apothecary[7543] to
send forth a stinking savour: *so doth* a
little folly him that is in reputation for
wisdom[2451] *and* honour.[3519]
2 A wise[2450] man's heart[3820] *is* at his
right hand;[3027] but a fool's[3684] heart at
his left.
3 Yea also, when he that is a fool[5530]
walketh by the way,[1870] [I]his wisdom[3820]
faileth *him,* [a]and he saith to every one
that he *is* a fool.
4 If the spirit[7307] of the ruler rise
up[5927] against thee, [a]leave not thy place;
for [b]yielding pacifieth great offences.
5 There is an evil[7451] *which* I have
seen[7200] under the sun, as an error[7684]
which proceedeth [I]from the ruler:[7989]
6 [a]Folly is set [I]in great dignity, and
the rich sit in low place.
7 I have seen servants [a]upon horses,
and princes[8269] walking as servants upon
the earth.[776]
8 [a]He that diggeth a pit[1475] shall fall
into it; and whoso breaketh an hedge, a
serpent[5175] shall bite him.
9 Whoso removeth stones shall be

11 [a]Jer. 9:23; Amos 2:14, 15
12 [a]Eccl. 8:7 [b]Prov. 29:6; Luke 12:20, 39; 17:26; 1Thess. 5:3
14 [a]2Sam. 20:16-22
16 [a]Prov. 21:22; 24:5; Eccl. 7:19; 9:18 [b]Mark 6:2, 3
18 [a]Eccl. 9:16 [b]Josh. 7:1, 11, 12

1 [I]Hebr. *Flies of death*
3 [I]Hebr. *his heart* [a]Prov. 13:16; 18:2
4 [a]Eccl. 8:3 [b]1Sam. 25:24-35; Prov. 25:15
5 [I]Hebr. *from before*
6 [I]Hebr. *in great heights* [a]Esth. 3:1
7 [a]Prov. 19:10; 30:22
8 [a]Ps. 7:15; Prov. 26:27

(continued from previous page)
energy that one can display. In doing so, it should be understood that there are limits to what is meant by the phrase "whatever thy hand findeth to do." People need to use wisdom in determining which goals are within their capabilities and to set their priorities in agreement with God's commands. Furthermore, there is the need to realize that some things should not be done at all, specifically those things which bring reproach to Christ's name. The guiding principle for fulfilling one's goals should be to follow God's direction and will with a pure heart. Paul encouraged believers to "not [be] slothful in business" but "fervent in spirit, serving the Lord" (Rom. 12:11). The focus of this verse in Ecclesiastes is on the attitude of the heart, or better the motives behind the actions. Solomon wrote "do it with thy might." This word "might" is also used to describe how one's worship for God should be conducted: "love the LORD thy God . . . with all thy might" (Deut. 6:5). God's desire is for obedience, but He also requires that it be done from a pure heart.

In the last portion of this verse it is stated that certain things that people see as important in this life will not be taken with them into eternity. Wealth, prestige, and position will all be left behind. Indeed, believers should continue to "work out [their] own salvation with fear and trembling" (Phil 2:12). They must, however, keep in mind the motives behind what is done here on earth (see note on Eccl. 8:8).

🗝 **9:11** See note on Ecclesiastes 3:1 concerning the providence of God.

hurt[6087] therewith; *and* he that cleaveth wood shall be endangered thereby.

10 If the iron be blunt, and he do not whet[7043] the edge, then must he put to more strength:[2428] but wisdom *is* profitable to direct.[3787]

11 Surely the serpent will bite [a]without enchantment;[3908] and [I]a babbler[3956] is no better.

12 [a]The words[1697] of a wise man's mouth[6310] *are* [I]gracious; but [b]the lips[8193] of a fool will swallow up[1104] himself.

13 The beginning of the words of his mouth *is* foolishness and the end[319] of [I]his talk *is* mischievous[7451] madness.

14 [a]A fool also [I]is full of words: a man[120] cannot tell[5046] what shall be; and [b]what shall be after him, who can tell him?

15 The labour[5999] of the foolish wearieth every one of them, because he knoweth not how to go to the city.

16 [a]Woe to thee, O land,[776] when thy king[4428] *is* a child, and thy princes eat in the morning!

17 Blessed[835] *art* thou, O land, when thy king *is* the son[1121] of nobles,[2715] and [a]thy princes eat in due season,[6256] for strength,[1369] and not for drunkenness[8358]

18 By much slothfulness the building decayeth; and through idleness of the hands[3027] the house[1004] droppeth through.

19 A feast is made[6213] for laughter, and [a]wine [I]maketh merry: but money answereth all *things.*

20 [a]Curse[7043] not the king, no not in thy [I][b]thought;[4093] and curse not the rich in thy bedchamber: for a bird of the air[8064] shall carry the voice, and that which hath wings shall tell the matter.[1697]

11 [I]Hebr. *the master of the tongue* [a]Ps. 58:4, 5; Jer. 8:17

12 [I]Hebr. *grace* [a]Prov. 10:32; 12:13 [b]Prov. 10:14; 18:7

13 [I]Hebr. *his mouth*

14 [I]Hebr. *multiplieth words* [a]Prov. 15:2 [b]Eccl. 3:22; 6:12; 8:7

16 [a]Isa. 3:4, 5, 12; 5:11

17 [a]Prov. 31:4

19 [I]Hebr. *maketh glad the life* [a]Ps. 104:15

20 [I]Or, *conscience* [a]Ex. 22:28; Acts 23:5 [b]Luke 19:40

1 [I]Hebr. *upon the face of the waters* [a]Isa. 32:20 [b]Deut. 15:10; Prov. 19:17; Matt. 10:42; 2Cor. 9:8; Gal. 6:9, 10; Heb. 6:10

2 [a]Ps. 112:9; Luke 6:30; 1Tim. 6:18, 19 [b]Mic. 5:5 [c]Eph. 5:16

5 [a]John 3:8 [b]Ps. 139:14, 15

6 [I]Hebr. *shall be right*

7 [a]Eccl. 7:11

9 [a]Num. 15:39

A Wise Man

11 Cast thy bread [I][a]upon the waters: [b]for thou shalt find it after many days.[3117]

2 [a]Give a portion [b]to seven, and also to eight; [c]for thou knowest[3045] not what evil[7451] shall be upon the earth.[776]

3 If the clouds be full of rain, they empty *themselves* upon the earth: and if the tree fall toward the south, or toward the north, in the place where the tree falleth,[5307] there it shall be.

4 He that observeth[8104] the wind[7307] shall not sow; and he that regardeth[7200] the clouds shall not reap.

5 As [a]thou knowest not what *is* the way[1870] of the spirit,[7307] [b]*nor* how the bones[6106] *do grow* in the womb[990] of her that is with child: even so thou knowest not the works of God[430] who maketh[6213] all.

6 In the morning sow thy seed,[2233] and in the evening withhold not thine hand:[3027] for thou knowest not whether [a]shall prosper,[3787] either this or that, or whether they both *shall be* alike good.[2896]

7 Truly the light[216] *is* sweet, and a pleasant[2896] *thing it is* for the eyes [a]to behold[7200] the sun:

8 But if a man[120] live[2421] many years, *and* rejoice in them all; yet let him remember[2142] the days of darkness;[2822] for they shall be many. All that cometh *is* vanity.

Advice to Young People

9 Rejoice, O young man, in thy youth; and let thy heart[3820] cheer[2895] thee in the days of thy youth, [a]and walk in the ways[1870] of thine heart, and in the sight of thine eyes: but know[3045] thou,

10:20 This verse is an injunction concerning speaking against those who have been placed in positions of authority. Though the person may have mishandled his or her position, it must be understood that God has established their office. Therefore, the office must continue to be respected, even though the person occupying that office may fail in their duty (see note on Ps. 82:6).

11:1 God is giving the promise that though it may seem that effort is being wasted in service to Him, there will be rewards in heaven (2 Tim. 4:8). It may seem that believers go through their lives without recognition or glory, but the governing principle of their service should be to please and glorify the Heavenly Father, which is far greater than the satisfaction of the flesh.

that for all these *things* [b]God will bring
thee into judgment.[4941]
10 Therefore remove [I]sorrow[3708] from
thy heart, and [a]put away[5674] evil from
thy flesh:[1320] [b]for childhood and youth
are vanity.[1892]

12 🔑 Remember[2142] [a]now thy
Creator[1254] in the days[3117] of thy
youth, while the evil[7451] days come not,
nor the years draw nigh,[5060] [b]when thou
shalt say,[559] I have no pleasure in them;
2 While the sun, or the light,[216] or
the moon, or the stars, be not darkened,[2821] nor the clouds return[7725] after
the rain:
3 In the day[3117] when the keepers[8104]
of the house[1004] shall tremble,[2111] and
the strong men[582] shall bow themselves,[5791] and [I]the grinders cease because they are few, and those that look
out[7200] of the windows be darkened,

9 [b]Eccl. 12:14; Rom. 2:6-11

10 [I]Or, *anger* [a]2Cor. 7:1; 2Tim. 2:22 [b]Ps. 39:5

1 [a]Prov. 22:6; Lam. 3:27 [b]2Sam. 19:35

3 [I]Or, *the grinders fail, because they grind little*

4 [a]2Sam. 19:35

5 [a]Job 17:13 [b]Jer. 9:17

7 [a]Gen. 3:19; Job 34:15; Ps. 90:3 [b]Eccl. 3:21 [c]Num. 16:22; 27:16; Job 34:14; Isa. 57:16; Zech. 12:1

8 [a]Ps. 62:9; Eccl. 1:2

4 And the doors shall be shut in the
streets, when the sound of the grinding
is low, and he shall rise up at the voice
of the bird, and all [a]the daughters of
musick[7892] shall be brought low;
5 Also *when* they shall be afraid[3372]
of *that which is* high, and fears[2849] *shall*
be in the way,[1870] and the almond tree
shall flourish,[5006] and the grasshopper
shall be a burden, and desire shall
fail:[6565] because man[120] goeth to [a]his
long[5769] home,[1004] and [b]the mourners go
about the streets:
6 Or ever the silver cord be loosed, or
the golden bowl be broken,[7665] or the
pitcher be broken at the fountain, or the
wheel[1534] broken at the cistern.[953]
🔑 7 [a]Then shall the dust[6083] return
to the earth[776] as it was: [b]and the
spirit[7307] shall return unto God[430] [c]who
gave it.
8 [a]Vanity of vanities, saith[559] the
preacher;[6953] all *is* vanity.

🔑 **12:1** Solomon is admonishing young men and women, warning them about the dangers of not restraining their fleshly desires. Solomon had failed miserably in this area. He had many wives and much riches, all of which turned his heart away from serving God (1 Kgs. 11:1–8). The use of the term "Creator" reveals that every person owes a great debt to the One who has formed him. How can anyone do less than devote his or her life to God? When this fact is realized, then one can reflect on his or her life with peace. The result of this reflection is the acknowledgment that the pleasures of this life cannot compare to the joy that comes from living for God. Solomon had lived foolishly, yielding to those fleshly desires and being held captive by them. However, he writes at the end of his life to encourage young people to follow God while they are still in their youth; so that in their old age, they will look back on a fruitful life, having been blessed of God.

🔑 **12:7** The belief in an afterlife has always been a part of God's revealed faith. This is seen in that Enoch "was not [on earth] for God took him" (Gen. 5:24). There are some who deny that there is such a thing as an "immortal soul" that is separate from the body. They teach that all those who have died are now in a state of unconsciousness and will remain so until the resurrection of the dead by God. Numerous passages of Scripture clearly teach that the soul exists even after death (Luke 16:19–31; 2 Cor. 5:8). Examples of those who expressed a knowledge of an existence after death are seen throughout the Old Testament: David expected to be reunited with his dead child (2 Sam. 12:23); Job spoke of a bodily resurrection and communion with God (see note on Job 19:25); and even Isaiah made reference to a life after death (Is. 26:19). A number of passages in the Psalms reflect expectations of reward and punishment after death (Ps. 17:15; 49:15; 73:24, 26). This verse in Ecclesiastes chapter twelve provides the basis for the concept that every human being has both material and immaterial substance. The two results of death are seen here: the "dust," which is the material part, returns to its place of origin; while the "spirit," the immaterial part, returns to God who gave it to man at his creation "[God] breathed into his nostrils the breath of life, and man became a living soul" (Gen. 2:7). In fact, in 2 Timothy 1:10, the Apostle Paul states that in Christ's resurrection from the dead, "He abolished death, and hath brought life and immortality to light through the gospel." He is referring to the day when there will be a reuniting of the bodies and souls of those who have trusted in Christ for salvation. See note on Ecclesiastes 8:8.

The Conclusion

9 And [I]moreover, because the preacher was wise,2450 he still taught3925 the people5971 knowledge;1847 yea, he gave good heed,238 and sought out, *and* [a]set in order many proverbs.

10 The preacher sought to find out [I]acceptable2656 words:1697 and *that which was* written *was* upright, *even* words of truth.571

11 The words of the wise *are* as goads,1861 and as nails fastened *by* the masters1167 of assemblies,627 *which* are given from one shepherd.

12 And further, by these, my son,1121 be admonished:2094 of making many books *there is* no end; and [a]much [I]study *is* a weariness of the flesh.1320

🗝 13 [I]Let us hear8085 the conclusion of the whole matter:1697 [a]Fear3372 God, and keep8104 his commandments:4687 for this is the whole *duty* of man.

14 For [a]God shall bring every work into judgment,4941 with every secret thing, whether *it be* good, or whether *it be* evil.

9 [I]Or, *the more wise the Preacher was* [a]1Kgs. 4:32
10 [I]Hebr. *words of delight*
12 [I]Or, *reading* [a]Eccl. 1:18
13 [I]Or, *The end of the matter, even all that hath been heard, is* [a]Deut. 6:2; 10:12
14 [a]Eccl. 11:9; Matt. 12:36; Acts 17:30, 31; Rom. 2:16; 1Cor. 4:5; 2Cor. 5:10

🗝 **12:13, 14** Solomon had been on a long journey "under the sun," (see note on Eccl. 1:2). This journey was a life of futility and emptiness. Now, at the conclusion, the Preacher puts all his works into proper perspective. All the things done for selfish gain are unimportant, pointless, and futile because they are secondary. The primary focus of man should be to "fear God and keep His commandments." This is the only proper course for the believer to follow. God will evaluate all the deeds that are done in order to reveal the motives behind them. All will be brought before Him, even the things done in secret. This evaluation will be conducted based on obedience to the commandments that He has given as a guide for the believer's life (2 Cor. 5:10).

THE SONG OF SOLOMON

The Hebrew name of this book, "Song of Songs," remained the same in the Septuagint and the Latin Vulgate. The Song of Solomon is part of a collection of Old Testament books known as the "Megilloth" (scrolls). The other books that are included in this group are Ruth, Esther, Ecclesiastes, and Lamentations. The Song of Solomon is important in Jewish tradition because portions of it were sung at the annual Feast of Passover.

This book of songs was written by King Solomon of Israel (Song 1:1). One factor which substantiates this fact is that ancient Jewish tradition has held that he was the author. Furthermore, the style and vocabulary are very similar to the Book of Ecclesiastes, which was also written by Solomon. All the cities mentioned in the book point to an undivided kingdom, which continued only until just after Solomon's death (Song 6:4). There are also references to horses, royal luxury, an abundance of wealth, and numerous plants and animals from the area of Palestine, all of which seem to identify Solomon as the author of the book (1 Kgs. 4:27–33). The references to Solomon's harem, which housed his wives and concubines (Song 6:8), would place the writing of the book at approximately 950 B.C.

The Song of Solomon has been the most misunderstood book in all of Scripture. Perhaps this is because it is the only book of Scripture in which the main plot is about "human love." Some view the book as a literal, historical depiction of pure human love and marriage. They suggest that no figurative or allegorical meaning was ever intended. Within this group are those who say that Solomon was only writing a book of profane love and wedding songs that have little or no spiritual value. Another interpretation of the book is that its meaning is allegorical and that all that is said is figurative. Supporters of this view say that Solomon wrote under the inspiration of the Holy Spirit to show the Lord's love for Israel and His love for the Church and each believer. As the "bride" of Christ, believers are required to return that love as if bound by wedding vows. The typical interpretation acknowledges the historical setting, but believes that the characters and relationships are typical of Christ and the Church.

Some suggest that the speakers are only Solomon and the Shulamite woman, a view rarely held. In contrast, most believe that there are three people involved in the narrative: Solomon, the Shulamite, and the shepherd lover (Song 1:7; 4:7–15). The historical perspective is of importance in that Solomon and the Shulamite woman are describing the ramifications of pure love, while the shepherd is trying to turn the woman's heart away from Solomon. It is the emphasis of the shepherd to show that the woman has been taken from her homeland to the palace of King Solomon as his bride, yet she would rather be at home with the shepherd, close to all that she holds dear. The typical aspect of the characters revolves around the relationship of God with His people. Solomon represents God and Christ, and the Shulamite woman (as the bride) represents His chosen people (Is. 54:5, 6; Jer. 2:2; Eph. 5:23–25). Finally, the shepherd lover is a picture of the world and its entrapments, which seek to destroy the bond that is formed between God and His people.

1 The [a]song[7892] of songs, which *is* Solomon's.

The First Song

2 Let him kiss[5401] me with the kisses of his mouth:[6310] [a]for [I]thy love[1730] *is* better[2896] than wine.

3 Because of the savour of thy good[2896] ointments[8081] thy name *is as* ointment poured forth, therefore do[157] the virgins[5959] love[157] thee.

4 [a]Draw me, [b]we will run after thee: the king[4428] [c]hath brought me into his chambers: we will be glad and rejoice in thee, we will remember[2142] thy love

1 [a]1Kgs. 4:32

2 [I]Hebr. *thy loves* [a]Song 4:10

4 [a]Hos. 11:4; John 6:44; 12:32 [b]Phil. 3:12-14 [c]Ps. 45:14, 15; John 14:2; Eph. 2:6

more than wine: [I]the upright[4334] love thee.

5 I *am* black, but comely,5000 O ye daughters of Jerusalem, as the tents[168] of Kedar, as the curtains of Solomon.

6 Look[7200] not upon me, because I *am* black, because the sun hath looked7805 upon me: my mother's[517] children[1121] were angry[2734] with me; they made[7760] me the keeper5201 of the vineyards; *but* mine own vineyard have I not kept.

7 Tell[5046] me, O thou whom my soul[5315] loveth, where thou feedest, where thou makest *thy flock* to rest at noon: for why should I be [I]as one that turneth aside5844 by the flocks of thy companions?

8 If thou know[3045] not, [a]O thou fairest3303 among women,[802] go thy way forth by the footsteps of the flock, and feed thy kids beside the shepherds' tents.

9 I have compared1819 thee, [a]O my love,7474 [b]to a company of horses in Pharaoh's chariots.

10 [a]Thy cheeks are comely4998 with rows2737 *of jewels,* thy neck with chains *of gold.*

11 We will make[6213] thee borders of gold with studs of silver.

12 While the king *sitteth* at his table, my spikenard5373 sendeth forth the smell thereof.

13 A bundle of myrrh4753 *is* my wellbeloved unto me; he shall lie all night betwixt my breasts.

14 My beloved[1730] *is* unto me *as* a cluster of [Ia]camphire[3724] in the vineyards of En–gedi.

15 [a]Behold, thou *art* fair,3302 [I]my love; behold, thou *art* fair; thou *hast* doves' eyes.

16 Behold, thou *art* fair, my beloved, yea, pleasant:5273 also our bed *is* green.

17 The beams of our house[1004] *are* cedar, *and* our [I]rafters of fir.

4 [I]Or, *they love thee uprightly*

7 [I]Or, *as one that is vailed*

8 [a]Song 5:9; 6:1

9 [a]Song 2:2, 10, 13; 4:1, 7; 5:2; 6:4; John 15:14, 15 [b]2Chr. 1:16, 17

10 [a]Ezek. 16:11-13

14 [I]Or, *cypress* [a]Song 4:13

15 [I]Or, *my companion* [a]Song 4:1; 5:12

17 [I]Or, *galleries*

2 I am the rose of Sharon, *and* the lily of the valleys.

2 As the lily among thorns, so *is* my love among the daughters.

3 As the apple tree among the trees of the wood, so *is* my beloved among the sons.[1121] [I]I sat down under his shadow with great delight,[2530] [a]and his fruit *was* sweet to my [II]taste.

4 He brought me to the [I]banqueting3196 house, and his banner1714 over me *was* love.[160]

5 Stay5564 me with flagons,809 [I]comfort7502 me with apples: for I *am* sick of love.

6 [a]His left hand *is* under my head,[7218] and his right hand doth embrace me.

7 [Ia]I charge you, O ye daughters of Jerusalem, by the roes,[6643] and by the hinds355 of the field,[7704] that ye stir not up,5782 nor awake *my* love,[160] till he please.[2654]

The Second Song

8 The voice of my beloved! behold, he cometh leaping upon the mountains, skipping7072 upon the hills.

9 [a]My beloved is like a roe or a young hart: behold, he standeth behind our wall, he looketh forth at the windows, [I]shewing6692 himself through the lattice.2762

10 My beloved spake, and said unto me, [a]Rise up, my love,7474 my fair one, and come away.

11 For, lo, the winter is past,[5674] the rain is over *and* gone;

12 The flowers appear[7200] on the earth;[776] the time[6256] of the singing *of birds* is come,[5060] and the voice of the turtle is heard[8085] in our land;[776]

13 The fig tree putteth forth her green figs, and the vines *with* the tender grape give a *good* smell. [a]Arise, my love, my fair one, and come away.

14 O my dove, *that art* in the clefts of the rock, in the secret *places* of the stairs,4095 let me see thy countenance, [a]let me hear thy voice; for sweet *is* thy voice, and thy countenance *is* comely.5000

3 [I]Hebr. *I delighted and sat down* [II]Hebr. *palate* [a]Rev. 22:1, 2

4 [I]Hebr. *house of wine*

5 [I]Hebr. *strew me with apples*

6 [a]Song 8:3

7 [I]Hebr. *I adjure you* [a]Song 3:5; 8:4

9 [I]Hebr. *flourishing* [a]Song 2:17

10 [a]Song 2:13

13 [a]Song 2:10

14 [a]Song 8:13

🔑 15 Take us [a]the foxes, the little foxes, that spoil[2254] the vines: for our vines *have* tender grapes.

16 [a]My beloved *is* mine, and I *am* his: he feedeth among the lilies.

🔑 17 [a]Until the day[3117] break,[6315] and the shadows6752 flee away, turn, my beloved, and be thou [b]like a roe or a young hart upon the mountains [I]of Bether.

3 By [a]night[3915] on my bed I sought him whom my soul[5315] loveth:[157] I sought him, but I found him not.

2 I will rise now, and go about the city in the streets, and in the broad ways I will seek him whom my soul loveth: I sought him, but I found him not.

3 [a]The watchmen[8104] that go about the city found me: *to whom I said,* Saw[7200] ye him whom my soul loveth?

4 *It was* but a little that I passed[5674] from them, but I found him whom my soul loveth: I held him, and would not let him go, until I had brought him into my mother's house, and into the chamber of her that conceived me.

5 [a]I charge you, O ye daughters of Jerusalem, by the roes,[6643] and by the hinds355 of the field,[7704] that ye stir not up, nor awake *my* love, till he please.[2654]

2:15 [a]Ps. 80:13; Ezek. 13:4; Luke 13:32
2:16 [a]Song 6:3; 7:10
2:17 [I]Or, *of division* [a]Song 4:6 [b]Song 2:9; 8:14
3:1 [a]Isa. 26:9
3:3 [a]Song 5:7
3:5 [a]Song 2:7; 8:4

The Third Song

6 [a]Who *is* this that cometh out of the wilderness like pillars of smoke, perfumed[6999] with myrrh4753 and frankincense,3828 with all powders of the merchant?

7 Behold his bed, which is Solomon's; threescore valiant men *are* about it, of the valiant of Israel.

8 They all hold swords,7219 *being* expert in war: every man[376] *hath* his sword upon his thigh[3409] because of fear[6343] in the night.

9 King Solomon made[6213] himself [I]a chariot of the wood of Lebanon.

10 He made the pillars thereof *of* silver, the bottom thereof *of* gold, the covering of it *of* purple, the midst[8432] thereof being paved7528 *with* love, for the daughters of Jerusalem.

11 Go forth, O ye daughters of Zion, and behold[7200] king Solomon with the crown wherewith his mother crowned him in the day of his espousals,2861 and in the day of the gladness of his heart.[3820]

4 Behold, [a]thou *art* fair, my love; behold, thou *art* fair; thou *hast* doves' eyes within thy locks:6777 thy hair *is* as a [b]flock of goats, [I]that appear from mount Gilead.

3:6 [a]Song 8:5
3:9 [I]Or, *a bed*
4:1 [I]Or, *that eat of* [a]Song 1:15; 5:12 [b]Song 6:5

🔑 **2:15** This verse is a warning not to allow little and seemingly insignificant sins to overtake one's life, robbing him or her of the joys of a pure relationship with the Lord. The "little foxes" are characteristic of those things that oftentimes come unawares and go unnoticed, and ultimately ruin a person's life. Christians need to learn from this passage not to be so proud in their own spirituality. Otherwise, they fail to guard against the attack of Satan on their lives. The term "tender grapes" suggests that these sins may become a problem while a person is still young and not yet able to determine the consequences of being overtaken by them.

🔑 **2:17** The phrase "turn . . . upon the mountains of Bether" is a reference to the situation in which the believer has placed himself, and the prayer of that believer that Christ would come and remove the "mountains" or barriers that separate him from God. The word "Bether" is found only here as a proper name. It generally refers to a place of division, and the mention of mountains may suggest that it is a place of rough terrain and danger. God's hand of protection is there to guide the believer through the times of trial and danger. The "roe" (or gazelle) and the "young hart" (a young deer) are animals known for their quickness and agility. However, they tend to remain in places of danger, waiting for their rescue, which may, in fact, never come. These animals illustrate the need of believers to patiently walk in the mystery of providence within the world. They should anticipate the coming of the "dawn," that is, Christ's return. Christ desires to come to His own for fellowship, so that the blessings that He bestows will be shared with the ones He loves. These times of fellowship with the Lord should be the longing of the believer's heart.

2 [a]Thy teeth *are* like a flock *of sheep that are even* shorn, which came up[5927] from the washing;[7367] whereof every one bear twins, and none *is* barren[7909] among them.

3 Thy lips[8193] *are* like a thread of scarlet, and thy speech *is* comely:[5000] [a]thy temples *are* like a piece of a pomegranate within thy locks.

4 [a]Thy neck *is* like the tower of David builded [b]for an armoury, whereon there hang a thousand bucklers,[4043] all shields[7982] of mighty men.

5 [a]Thy two breasts *are* like two young roes[6646] that are twins, which feed among the lilies.

6 [a]Until the day [I]break,[6315] and the shadows[6752] flee away, I will get me to the mountain of myrrh,[4753] and to the hill of frankincense.[3828]

7 [a]Thou *art* all fair, my love; *there is* no spot[3971] in thee.

8 Come with me from Lebanon, *my* spouse, with me from Lebanon: look from the top[7218] of Amana, from the top of Shenir [a]and Hermon, from the lions' dens, from the mountains of the leopards.

9 Thou hast [I]ravished my heart,[3823] my sister,[269] *my* spouse; thou hast ravished my heart with one of thine eyes, with one chain of thy neck.

10 How fair is thy love,[1730] my sister, *my* spouse! [a]how much better is[2895] thy love than wine! and the smell of thine ointments[8081] than all spices!

11 Thy lips, O *my* spouse, drop *as* the honeycomb: [a]honey and milk *are* under thy tongue; and the smell of thy garments *is* [b]like the smell of Lebanon.

12 A garden [I]inclosed *is* my sister, *my* spouse; a spring shut up, a fountain sealed.

13 Thy plants *are* an orchard of pomegranates, with pleasant fruits; [I][a]camphire, with spikenard,[5373]

14 Spikenard and saffron;[3750] calamus[7070] and cinnamon, with all trees of frankincense; myrrh and aloes,[174] with all the chief[7218] spices:

15 A fountain of gardens, a well of [a]living[2416] waters, and streams from Lebanon.

16 Awake, O north wind; and come, thou south; blow[6315] upon my garden, *that* the spices thereof may flow out. [a]Let my beloved come into his garden, and eat his pleasant[4022] fruits.

5 I [a]am come into my garden, my sister,[269] *my* spouse: I have gathered my myrrh[4753] with my spice; [b]I have eaten my honeycomb with my honey; I have drunk my wine with my milk: eat, O [c]friends;[7453] drink, [I]yea, drink abundantly, O beloved.

The Fourth Song

2 I sleep, but my heart[3820] waketh: *it is* the voice of my beloved [a]that knocketh, *saying,* Open to me, my sister, my love, my dove, my undefiled:[8535] for my head[7218] is filled with dew, *and* my locks with the drops of the night.[3915]

3 I have put off my coat; how shall I put it on? I have washed[7364] my feet; how shall I defile them?

4 My beloved put in his hand[3027] by the hole *of the door,* and my bowels[4578] were moved[1993] [I]for him.

5 I rose up to open to my beloved; and my hands dropped[5197] *with* myrrh, and my fingers *with* [I]sweet smelling[5674] myrrh, upon the handles[3709] of the lock.

6 I opened to my beloved; but my beloved had withdrawn[2559] himself, *and* was gone: my soul[5315] failed when he spake:[1696] [a]I sought him, but I could not find him; I called[7121] him, but he gave me no answer.

7 [a]The watchmen[8104] that went about the city found me, they smote[5221] me, they wounded me; the keepers[8104] of the walls took away[5375] my veil from me.

8 I charge you, O daughters of Jerusalem, if ye find my beloved, [I]that ye tell[5046] him, that I *am* sick of love.[160]

9 What *is* thy beloved more than *another* beloved, [a]O thou fairest among women?[802] what *is* thy beloved more than *another* beloved, that thou dost so charge us?

2 [a]Song 6:6
3 [a]Song 6:7
4 [a]Song 7:4 [b]Neh. 3:19
5 [a]Prov. 5:19; Song 7:3
6 [I]Hebr. *breathe* [a]Song 2:17
7 [a]Eph. 5:27
8 [a]Deut. 3:9
9 [I]Or, *taken away my heart*
10 [a]Song 1:2
11 [a]Prov. 24:13, 14; Song 5:1 [b]Gen. 27:27; Hos. 14:6, 7
12 [I]Hebr. *barred*
13 [I]Or, *cypress* [a]Song 1:14
15 [a]John 4:10; 7:38
16 [a]Song 5:1
1 [I]Or, *and be drunken with loves* [a]Song 4:16 [b]Song 4:11 [c]Luke 15:7, 10; John 3:29; 15:14
2 [a]Rev. 3:20
4 [I]Or, (as some texts read) *in me*
5 [I]Hebr. *passing,* or, *running about*
6 [a]Song 3:1
7 [a]Song 3:3
8 [I]Hebr. *what*
9 [a]Song 1:8

🗝 10 My beloved *is* white and ruddy,[122]
[I]the chiefest[1713] among ten thousand.
11 His head *is as* the most fine gold,
his locks *are* [I]bushy, *and* black as a
raven.
12 [a]His eyes *are* as *the eyes* of doves
by the rivers of waters, washed with
milk, *and* [I]fitly set.
13 His cheeks *are* as a bed of spices,
as [I]sweet flowers: his lips[8193] *like* lilies,
dropping[5197] sweet smelling myrrh.
14 His hands *are as* gold rings set
with the beryl: his belly[4578] *is as* bright
ivory overlaid *with* sapphires.
15 His legs *are as* pillars of marble,
set upon sockets of fine gold: his countenance *is* as Lebanon, excellent[977] as the
cedars.
16 [I]His mouth *is* most sweet: yea, he
is altogether lovely.[4261] This *is* my
beloved, and this *is* my friend,[7453] O
daughters of Jerusalem.

6 Whither is thy beloved[1730] gone, [a]O
thou fairest among women?[7802]
whither is thy beloved turned aside? that
we may seek him with thee.
2 My beloved is gone down into his
garden, to the beds of spices, to feed in
the gardens, and to gather[3950] lilies.
3 [a]I *am* my beloved's, and my
beloved *is* mine: he feedeth among the
lilies.

10 [I]Hebr. *a standardbearer*
11 [I]Or, *curled*
12 [I]Hebr. *sitting in fullness,* that is, *fitly placed, and set as a precious stone in the foil of a ring* [a]Song 1:15; 4:1
13 [I]Or, *towers of perfumes*
16 [I]Hebr. *His palate*
1 [a]Song 1:8
3 [a]Song 2:16; 7:10
4 [a]Song 6:10
5 [I]Or, *they have puffed me up* [a]Song 4:1
6 [a]Song 4:2
7 [a]Song 4:3
10 [a]Song 6:4
11 [a]Song 7:12
12 [I]Hebr. *I knew not* [II]Or, *set me on the chariots of my willing people*

The Fifth Song

🗝 4 Thou *art* beautiful,[3303] O my love,
as Tirzah, comely[5000] as Jerusalem,
[a]terrible[366] as *an army* with banners.
5 Turn away thine eyes from me, for
[I]they have overcome me: thy hair *is* [a]as a
flock of goats that appear from Gilead.
6 [a]Thy teeth *are* as a flock of sheep
which go up from the washing,[7367]
whereof every one beareth twins, and
there is not one barren[7909] among them.
7 [a]As a piece of a pomegranate *are*
thy temples within thy locks.
8 There are threescore queens,[4436]
and fourscore concubines, and virgins[5959]
without number.
9 My dove, my undefiled[8535] is *but*
one; she *is* the *only* one of her mother,[517]
she *is* the choice[1249] *one* of her that bare
her. The daughters saw[7200] her, and
blessed[833] her; *yea,* the queens and the
concubines, and they praised[1984] her.
10 Who *is* she *that* looketh forth as
the morning, fair[3303] as the moon,
clear[1249] as the sun, [a]*and* terrible as *an*
army with banners?
11 I went down into the garden of
nuts to see the fruits of the valley, *and*
[a]to see whether the vine flourished, *and*
the pomegranates budded.
12 [I]Or ever I was aware,[3045] my
soul[5315] [II]made[7760] me *like* the chariots of
Ammi–nadib.
13 Return,[7725] return, O Shulamite;

🗝 **5:10** The picture given in this verse is of one adorned with all the splendor and graces that exhibit one's physical beauty. The phrase "the chiefest among ten thousand" illustrates that none can be compared to her beloved's beauty. The expression "white and ruddy" notes the perfect nature of a person's complexion, one of healthiness and beauty. These terms are used in the description of David in his youth (1 Sam. 16:12). It is a fitting description of how Christ's Church will be presented as "glorious . . . not having spot, or wrinkle . . . and without blemish" (Eph. 5:27).

🗝 **6:4** The name "Tirzah" means "true beauty and delight." This city was mentioned as one that was conquered by Joshua in the conquest of the Promised Land (Josh. 12:24). It was also the capital of the Northern Kingdom until the time of Omri (1 Kgs. 14:17; 15:21; 16:6), when the capital was moved to Samaria. The city of Tirzah represented all that was beautiful in royal splendor. Apparently, Solomon had erected magnificent structures there to display the majesty of his kingdom. For this reason also, Jerusalem is compared to the beauty of Solomon's beloved. As the center of politics and religion in Israel, Jerusalem was the epitome of all the splendor that Solomon could display. The Lord compares His beloved to "a city that is set on an hill [which] cannot be hid" (Matt. 5:14). In the further description of the beloved one, he is depicted as "terrible as an army with banners." This denotes the idea that when one appears in radiant beauty, the beholder becomes awe-struck.

return, return, that we may look[2372] upon thee. What will ye see[2372] in the Shulamite? As it were the company [Ia]of two armies.[4264]

7 How beautiful are thy feet with shoes, [a]O prince's daughter! the joints of thy thighs *are* like jewels, the work of the hands[3027] of a cunning542 workman.

2 Thy navel *is like* a round goblet, *which* wanteth not [I]liquor: thy belly[990] *is like* an heap of wheat set about with lilies.

3 [a]Thy two breasts *are* like two young roes6646 *that are* twins.

4 [a]Thy neck *is* as a tower of ivory; thine eyes *like* the fishpools in Heshbon, by the gate of Bath–rabbim: thy nose[639] *is* as the tower of Lebanon which looketh toward Damascus.

5 Thine head[7218] upon thee *is* like [I]Carmel, and the hair of thine head like purple; the king *is* [II]held in the galleries.7298

6 How fair and how pleasant art thou, O love,[160] for delights!

7 This thy stature is like to a palm tree, and thy breasts to clusters *of grapes.*

8 I said,[559] I will go up to the palm tree, I will take hold of the boughs thereof: now also thy breasts shall be as clusters of the vine, and the smell of thy nose like apples;

9 And the roof of thy mouth like the best[2896] wine for my beloved,[1730] that goeth *down* [I]sweetly,[4334] causing the lips[8193] [II]of those that are asleep to speak.[1680]

10 [a]I *am* my beloved's, and [b]his desire[8669] *is* toward me.

11 Come, my beloved, let us go forth into the field;[7704] let us lodge in the villages.

12 Let us get up early to the vineyards; let us [a]see if the vine flourish, *whether* the tender grape [I]appear, *and* the pomegranates bud forth: there will I give thee my loves.

13 The [a]mandrakes[1736] give a smell, and at our gates [b]*are* all manner of pleasant *fruits,* new and old, *which* I have laid up for thee, O my beloved.

8 O that thou *wert* as my brother,[251] that sucked the breasts of my mother[517] *when* I should find thee without, I would kiss[5401] thee; yea, [I]I should not be despised.

2 I would lead thee, *and* bring thee into my mother's house, *who* would instruct me: I would cause thee to drink of [a]spiced wine of the juice of my pomegranate.

3 [a]His left hand *should be* under my head,[7218] and his right hand should embrace me.

4 [a]I charge you, O daughters of Jerusalem, [I]that ye stir not up, nor awake *my* love,[160] until he please.[2654]

The Sixth Song

5 [a]Who *is* this that cometh up[5927] from the wilderness, leaning upon her beloved?[1730] I raised thee up under the apple tree: there thy mother brought thee forth: there she brought thee forth *that* bare thee.

6 [a]Set[7760] me as a seal upon thine heart,[3820] as a seal upon thine arm: for

6:13 [I]Or, *of Mahanaim* [a]Gen. 32:2
7:1 [a]Ps. 45:13
2 [I]Hebr. *mixture*
3 [a]Song 4:5
4 [a]Song 4:4
5 [I]Or, *crimson* [II]Hebr. *bound*
9 [I]Hebr. *straightly* [II]Or, *of the ancient*
10 [a]Song 2:16; 6:3 [b]Ps. 45:11
12 [I]Hebr. *open* [a]Song 6:11
13 [a]Gen. 30:14 [b]Matt. 13:52
8:1 [I]Hebr. *they should not despise me*
2 [a]Prov. 9:2
3 [a]Song 2:6
4 [I]Hebr. *why should ye stir up,* or, *why* [a]Song 2:7; 3:5
5 [a]Song 3:6
6 [a]Isa. 49:16; Jer. 22:24; Hag. 2:23

8:6, 7 The "seal" mentioned in verse six is referring to the Jewish practice of wearing jewelry next to the heart with the name or portrait of a loved one or family member engraved on it. This represented the close relationship that existed between Solomon and his beloved. The phrase "seal upon thine arm" denotes the closeness when the beloved is embraced in the arms of Solomon. His statements that follow (i.e., "love is strong as death; jealousy is cruel as the grave") reveal the desire that his beloved would remain faithful to him. The feelings expressed here are similar to the one's that prompted the revenge of Levi and Simeon in regard to the rape of their sister, Dinah (Gen. 49:5–7, cf. Gen. 34:1–31). This is applied to Solomon's situation to illustrate that there is nothing that can suppress his love. The last portion of the verse states that this love is an ignited flame

(continued on next page)

love *is* strong as death;[4194] jealousy[7068] *is* [I]cruel as the grave:[7585] the coals thereof *are* coals of fire, *which hath* a most vehement[3050] flame.

7 Many waters cannot quench love, neither can the floods drown[7857] it: [a]if a man[376] would give all the substance of his house for love, it would utterly be contemned.936

8 [a]We have a little sister,[269] and she hath no breasts: what shall we do for our sister in the day[3117] when she shall be spoken[1696] for?

9 If she *be* a wall, we will build upon her a palace of silver: and if she *be* a door, we will inclose her with boards of cedar.

10 I *am* a wall, and my breasts like towers: then was I in his eyes as one that found [I]favour.[7965]

11 Solomon had a vineyard at Baal–hamon; [a]he let out the vineyard unto keepers; every one[376] for the fruit thereof was to bring a thousand *pieces* of silver.

12 My vineyard, which *is* mine, *is* before me: thou, O Solomon, *must have* a thousand, and those that keep the fruit thereof two hundred.

13 Thou that dwellest in the gardens, the companions hearken[7181] to thy voice: [a]cause me to hear[8085] *it*.

🗝 14 [I][a]Make haste, my beloved, and [b]be thou like to a roe or to a young hart upon the mountains of spices.

6 [I]Hebr. *hard*
7 [a]Prov. 6:35
8 [a]Ezek. 23:33
10 [I]Hebr. *peace*
11 [a]Matt. 21:33
13 [a]Song 2:14
14 [I]Hebr. *Flee away* [a]Rev. 22:17, 20 [b]Song 2:17

(continued from previous page)
of Jehovah. This is the only time the name of God is used in the Song of Solomon. The KJV uses the phrase "a most vehement flame" to describe the power of God when it is unleashed to its fullest extent (1 Kgs. 18:38). Verse seven states that the fires of pure love cannot be easily extinguished. The end of this verse reveals the futility of building one's love on material things.

🗝 **8:14** See note on Song of Solomon 2:17 concerning the "roe and the young hart."

The Book of

ISAIAH

The theme of this book is expressed in the meaning of the name Isaiah, "the LORD saves" or "the LORD is Savior." The Book of Isaiah contains more prophecies about the Messiah than any other book in the Old Testament. In fact, the plan of salvation is so comprehensively revealed in Isaiah's work that Augustine called it the fifth Gospel, and others have referred to it as "the Bible in miniature." Some have attempted to discredit the authenticity of the prophecies of Isaiah by suggesting that Isaiah was not the author of them all. The historical view as to the authorship of this book, however, has consistently held that Isaiah composed the entire book. This view is supported by the fact that each time a portion which the liberals dispute is quoted in the New Testament, Isaiah is named as the author.

Traditionally, Isaiah is thought to have been the son of a prince of Judah. He certainly did not feel uncomfortable in the presence of kings (Is. 7:3–12; 37:21), and the richness of his vocabulary suggests that he was a man of culture and education. He ministered for over forty years (740–697 B.C.) during the reigns of four Judean kings (Is. 1:1): Uzziah, Jotham, Ahaz, and Hezekiah. While Uzziah and Jotham were in power there was relative peace and prosperity, but Isaiah's writings, as well as those of the contemporary prophets Hosea, Amos, and Micah, reveal that the people were spiritually destitute (Hos. 4:1, 2, 6–8; Amos 2:6–8; Mic. 1:5; 3:1–11). When King Ahaz came to power, Syria besieged Jerusalem (2 Kgs. 16:5). Isaiah was given the task of urging him to trust the Lord for a favorable outcome, but Ahaz called on Assyria for help instead (2 Kgs. 16:7). Hezekiah made great strides in bringing about religious reform in the nation and was well acquainted with Isaiah (2 Kgs. 18:1–7; 19:1, 2; 20:1–11). It is not known precisely when Isaiah died, but according to tradition, he was sawed in half with a timber saw during the reign of King Manasseh (cf. Heb. 11:37).

1 The [a]vision[2377] of Isaiah the son[1121]
of Amoz, which he saw[2372] concerning Judah and Jerusalem in the days[3117]
of Uzziah, Jotham, Ahaz, *and* Hezekiah,
kings[4428] of Judah.

A Sinful Nation

2 [a]Hear,[8085] O heavens,8064 and give
ear,[238] O earth:[776] for the LORD hath
spoken,[1696] [b]I have nourished and
brought up children,[1121] and they have
rebelled[6586] against me.
3 [a]The ox knoweth his owner, and
the ass his master's crib:18 *but* Israel
[b]doth not know,[3045] my people[5971] [c]doth
not consider.[995]
4 Ah sinful nation,[1471] a people
[I]laden with iniquity,[5771] [a]a seed[2233] of
evildoers,[7489] children that are cor-
rupters:7843 they have forsaken[5800] the
LORD, they have provoked[5006] the Holy
One[6918] of Israel unto anger, they are
[II][b]gone away[2114] backward.
5 [a]Why should ye be stricken any
more? ye will [I]revolt[5627] more and more:
the whole head[7218] is sick, and the whole
heart3824 faint.
6 From the sole[3709] of the foot even
unto the head *there is* no soundness4974
in it; *but* wounds, and bruises, and putrifying sores: [a]they have not been closed,
neither bound up, neither mollified with
[I]ointment.[8081]
7 [a]Your country[776] *is* desolate,[8077]
your cities *are* burned[8313] with fire: your
land,[127] strangers[2114] devour it in your
presence, and *it is* desolate, [I]as overthrown by strangers.
8 And the daughter of Zion is left[3498]
[a]as a cottage[5521] in a vineyard, as a lodge
in a garden of cucumbers, [b]as a besieged[5341] city.
9 [a]Except the LORD of hosts[6635] had

1 [a]Num. 12:6
2 [a]Deut. 32:1; Jer. 2:12; 6:19; 22:29; Ezek. 36:4; Mic. 1:2; 6:1, 2 [b]Isa. 5:1, 2
3 [a]Jer. 8:7 [b]Jer. 9:3, 6 [c]Isa. 5:12
4 [I]Hebr. of heaviness [II]Hebr. *alienated,* or, *separated* [a]Isa. 57:3, 4; Matt. 3:7 [b]Ps. 58:3
5 [I]Hebr. *increase revolt* [a]Isa. 9:13; Jer. 2:30; 5:3
6 [I]Or, *oil* [a]Jer. 8:22
7 [I]Hebr. *as the overthrow of strangers* [a]Deut. 28:51, 52
8 [a]Job 27:18; Lam. 2:6 [b]Jer. 4:17
9 [a]Lam. 3:22; Rom. 9:29

left unto us a very small remnant,[8300] we should have been as [b]Sodom, *and* we should have been like unto Gomorrah.

10 Hear the word[1697] of the LORD, ye rulers[7101] [a]of Sodom; give ear unto the law[8451] of our God, ye people of Gomorrah.

11 To what purpose *is* the multitude of your [a]sacrifices[2077] unto me? saith[559] the LORD: I am full of the burnt offerings[5930] of rams, and the fat of fed beasts; and I delight not in the blood[1818] of bullocks, or of lambs, or of [I]he goats.

12 When ye come [I][a]to appear[7200] before me, who hath required this at your hand,[3027] to tread my courts?

13 Bring no more [a]vain[7723] oblations;[4503] incense[7004] is an abomination unto me; the new moons and sabbaths,[7676] [b]the calling of assemblies, I cannot away with; *it is* [I]iniquity,[205] even the solemn meeting.[6116]

14 Your [a]new moons and your [b]appointed feasts[4150] my soul[5315] hateth:[8130] they are a trouble unto me; [c]I am weary to bear[5375] *them.*

15 And [a]when ye spread forth your hands,[3709] I will hide mine eyes from you: [b]yea, when ye [I]make many prayers,[8605] I will not hear: your hands are full of [II][c]blood.

16 [a]Wash[7364] you, make you clean;[2135] put away[5493] the evil[7455] of your doings from before mine eyes; [b]cease to do evil;[7489]

17 Learn[3925] to do well;[3190] [a]seek judgment,[4941] [I]relieve[833] the oppressed, judge[8199] the fatherless, plead[7378] for the widow.

🗝 18 Come now, and [a]let us reason together,[3198] saith the LORD: though your sins[2399] be as scarlet, [b]they shall be as white as snow; though they be red[119] like crimson, they shall be as wool.

19 If ye be willing[14] and obedient,[8085] ye shall eat the good[2898] of the land:[776]

9 [b]Gen. 19:24
10 [a]Deut. 32:32; Ezek. 16:46
11 [I]Hebr. *great he goats* [a]1Sam. 15:22; Ps. 50:8, 9; 51:16; Prov. 15:8; 21:27; Isa. 66:3; Jer. 6:20; 7:21; Amos 5:21, 22; Mic. 6:7
12 [I]Hebr. *to be seen* [a]Ex. 23:17; 34:23
13 [I]Or, *grief* [a]Matt. 15:9 [b]Joel 1:14; 2:15
14 [a]Num. 28:11 [b]Lev. 23:2; Lam. 2:6 [c]Isa. 43:24
15 [I]Hebr. *multiply prayer* [II]Hebr. *bloods* [a]Job 27:9; Ps. 134:2; Prov. 1:28; Isa. 59:2; Jer. 14:12; Mic. 3:4 [b]Ps. 66:18; 1Tim. 2:8 [c]Isa. 59:3
16 [a]Jer. 4:14 [b]Ps. 34:14; 37:27; Amos 5:15; Rom. 12:9; 1Pet. 3:11
17 [I]Or, *righten* [a]Jer. 22:3, 16; Mic. 6:8; Zech. 7:9; 8:16
18 [a]Isa. 43:26; Mic. 6:2 [b]Ps. 51:7; Rev. 7:14
20 [a]Num. 23:19; Titus 1:2
21 [a]Jer. 2:20, 21
22 [a]Jer. 6:28, 30; Ezek. 22:18, 19
23 [a]Hos. 9:15 [b]Prov. 29:24 [c]Jer. 22:17; Ezek. 22:12; Hos. 4:18; Mic. 3:11; 7:3 [d]Jer. 5:28; Zech. 7:10
24 [a]Deut. 28:63; Ezek. 5:13
25 [I]Hebr. *according to pureness* [a]Jer. 6:29; 9:7; Mal. 3:3
26 [a]Jer. 33:7 [b]Zech. 8:3
27 [I]Or, *they that return of her*

20 But if ye refuse[3985] and rebel,[4784] ye shall be devoured with the sword:[2719] [a]for the mouth[6310] of the LORD hath spoken *it.*

Zion, the Sinful City

21 [a]How is[1961] the faithful[539] city become[1961] an harlot[2181] it was full of judgment; righteousness[6664] lodged in it; but now murderers.[7523]

22 [a]Thy silver is become dross,5509 thy wine mixed with water:

23 [a]Thy princes[8269] *are* rebellious,[5637] and [b]companions of thieves: [c]every one loveth[157] gifts, and followeth after rewards:[8021] they [d]judge not the fatherless, neither doth the cause[7379] of the widow come unto them.

24 Therefore saith5002 the LORD,[113] the LORD of hosts, the mighty One[47] of Israel, Ah, [a]I will ease me of mine adversaries, and avenge[5358] me of mine enemies:

25 And I will turn[7725] my hand upon thee, and [I][a]purely[1252] purge away[6884] thy dross, and take away all thy tin:

26 And I will restore[7725] thy judges[8199] [a]as at the first,[7223] and thy counsellors[3289] as at the beginning: afterward [b]thou shalt be called,[7121] The city of righteousness, the faithful city.

27 Zion shall be redeemed[6299] with judgment, and [I]her converts[7725] with righteousness.[6666]

28 And the [I][a]destruction[7667] of the transgressors[6586] and of the sinners[2400] *shall be* together, and they that forsake[5800] the LORD shall be consumed.[3615]

29 For they shall be ashamed[954] of [a]the oaks which ye have desired, [b]and ye shall be confounded for the gardens that ye have chosen.[977]

30 For ye shall be as an oak whose

28 [I]Hebr. *breaking* [a]Job 31:3; Ps. 1:6; 5:6; 73:27; 92:9; 104:35 29 [a]Isa. 57:5 [b]Isa. 65:3; 66:17

🗝 **1:18** This is a statement of God's intent—Israel will be righteous. The context preceding and following this verse reveals that Israel will either become righteous through repentance (Is. 1:16, 17, 19), or God will achieve their purification through judgment (Is. 1:20).

leaf fadeth, and as a garden that hath no
water.
31 [a]And the strong shall be [b]as tow,
[I]and the maker of it as a spark, and they
shall both burn together, and none shall
quench *them.*

True Peace

2 The word[1697] that Isaiah the son of
Amoz saw[2372] concerning Judah and
Jerusalem.
🔑 2 And [a]it shall come to pass [b]in the
last days,[3117] [c]*that* the mountain of the
LORD's house[1004] shall be [I]established[3559]
in the top[7218] of the mountains, and shall
be exalted above the hills; [d]and all
nations[1471] shall flow unto it.
3 And many people[5971] shall go and
say,[559] [a]Come ye, and let us go up to the
mountain of the LORD, to the house of
the God of Jacob; and he will teach[3384]
us of his ways,[1870] and we will walk in
his paths:[734] [b]for out of Zion shall go
forth the law,[8451] and the word of the
LORD from Jerusalem.
4 And he shall judge[8199] among the
nations, and shall rebuke[3198] many people: and [a]they shall beat[3807] their
swords[2719] into plowshares, and their
spears into [I]pruninghooks: nation[1471]
shall not lift up[5375] sword[2719] against nation, [b]neither shall they learn[3925] war any
more.

The Proud Will Be Destroyed

5 O house of Jacob, come ye, and let
us [a]walk in the light[216] of the LORD.
6 Therefore thou hast forsaken[5203]
thy people the house of Jacob, because
they be replenished [I][a]from the east, and
[b]*are* soothsayers[6049] like the Philistines,
[c]and they [II]please themselves[5606] in the
children of strangers.[5237]
7 [a]Their land[776] also is full of silver
and gold, neither *is there any* end of their
treasures; their land is also full of horses,
neither *is there any* end of their chariots:
8 [a]Their land also is full of idols;[457]
they worship[7812] the work of their own
hands,[3027] that which their own fingers
have made:[6213]
9 And the mean man[120] boweth
down, and the great man[376] humbleth[8213]
himself: therefore forgive[5375] them not.
10 [a]Enter into the rock, and hide thee
in the dust,[6083] for fear[6343] of the LORD,
and for the glory[1926] of his majesty.
11 The [a]lofty looks of man[120] shall
be humbled, and the haughtiness of
men[582] shall be bowed down, and the
LORD alone shall be exalted [b]in that
day.[3117]
12 For the day of the LORD of
hosts[6635] *shall be* upon every *one that is*
proud and lofty, and upon every *one that*
is lifted up;[5375] and he shall be brought
low:
13 And upon all [a]the cedars of
Lebanon, *that are* high and lifted up, and
upon all the oaks of Bashan,
14 And [a]upon all the high mountains,
and upon all the hills *that are* lifted up,
15 And upon every high tower, and
upon every fenced[1219] wall,
16 [a]And upon all the ships of Tarshish, and upon all [I]pleasant pictures.
17 [a]And the loftiness of man shall
be bowed down, and the haughtiness of
men shall be made low: and the LORD
alone shall be exalted [b]in that day.
18 And [I]the idols he shall[2498] utterly[3632] abolish.[2498]
19 And they shall go into the [a]holes
of the rocks, and into the caves of [I]the
earth,[6083] [b]for fear of the LORD, and for
the glory of his majesty, when he ariseth
[c]to shake terribly[6206] the earth.[776]
20 [a]In that day a man shall cast [I]his
idols of silver, and his idols of gold,
[II]which they made *each one* for himself
to worship, to the moles and to the bats;
21 [a]To go into the clefts of the rocks,
and into the tops of the ragged rocks,

31 [I]Or, *and his work* [a]Ezek. 32:21 [b]Isa. 43:17

2 [I]Or, *prepared* [a]Mic. 4:1 [b]Gen. 49:1; Jer. 23:20 [c]Ps. 68:15, 16 [d]Ps. 72:8; Isa. 27:13
3 [a]Jer. 31:6; 50:5; Zech. 8:21, 23; Luke 24:47
4 [I]Or, *scythes* [a]Ps. 46:9; Hos. 2:18; Zech. 9:10 [b]Ps. 72:3, 7
5 [a]Eph. 5:8
6 [I]Or, *more than the east* [II]Or, *abound with the children* [a]Num. 23:7 [b]Deut. 18:14 [c]Ps. 106:35; Jer. 10:2
7 [a]Deut. 17:16; 17
8 [a]Jer. 2:28
10 [a]Isa. 2:19, 21; Rev. 6:15
11 [a]Isa. 2:17; 5:15, 16; 13:11 [b]Isa. 4:1; 11:10, 11; 12:1, 4; 24:21; 25:9; 26:1; 27:1, 2, 12, 13; 28:5; 29:18; 30:23; 52:6; Jer. 30:7, 8; Ezek. 38:14, 19; 39:11, 22; Hos. 2:16, 18, 21; Joel 3:18; Amos 9:11; Obad. 1:8; Mic. 4:6; 5:10; 7:11, 12; Zeph. 3:11, 16; Zech. 9:16
13 [a]Isa. 14:8; 37:24; Ezek. 31:3; Zech. 11:1, 2
14 [a]Isa. 30:25
16 [I]Hebr. *pictures of desire* [a]1Kgs. 10:22
17 [a]Isa. 2:1 [b]Isa. 2:11
18 [I]Or, *the idols shall utterly pass away*
19 [I]Hebr. *the dust* [a]Isa. 2:10; Hos. 10:8; Luke 23:30; Rev. 6:16; 9:6 [b]2Thess. 1:9 [c]Isa. 30:32; Hag. 2:6, 21; Heb. 12:26

20 [I]Hebr. *the idols of his silver* [II]Or, *which they made for him* [a]Isa. 30:22; 31:7 **21** [a]Isa. 2:19

🔑 **2:2–4** See note on Micah 4:3.

[b]for fear[6343] of the LORD, and for the
glory of his majesty, when he ariseth to
shake terribly the earth.
22 [a]Cease ye from man, whose
[b]breath[5397] *is* in his nostrils:[639] for
wherein is he to be accounted of?[2803]

God Judges Judah and Jerusalem

3 For, behold, the Lord,[113] the LORD[3068]
of hosts,[6635] [a]doth take away from
Jerusalem and from Judah [b]the stay and
the staff, the whole stay[4937] of bread, and
the whole stay of water,
2 [a]The mighty man, and the man[376]
of war, the judge,[8199] and the prophet,[5030]
and the prudent,[7080] and the ancient,[2204]
3 The captain[8269] of fifty, and [I]the
honourable man, and the counselor,[3289]
and the cunning[2450] artificer,[2796] and the
[II]eloquent[995] orator.[3908]
4 And I will give [a]children *to be* their
princes,[8269] and babes[8586] shall rule[4910]
over them.
5 And the people[5971] shall be oppressed, every one[376] by another, and
every one by his neighbour:[7453] the child
shall behave himself proudly against the
ancient, and the base against the honourable.
6 When a man shall take hold of his
brother[251] of the house[1004] of his father,[1]
saying, Thou hast clothing, be thou our
ruler,[7101] and *let* this ruin[4384] *be* under
thy hand:[3027]
7 In that day[3117] shall he [I][a]swear,
saying, I will not be an [II]healer;[2280] for in
my house *is* neither bread nor clothing:
make[7760] me not a ruler of the people.
8 For [a]Jerusalem is ruined,[3782] and
Judah is fallen:[5307] because their tongue
and their doings *are* against the LORD, to
provoke[4784] the eyes of his glory.[3519]
9 The shew[1971] of their countenance
doth witness against them; and they
declare[5046] their sin as [a]Sodom, they hide
it not. Woe unto their soul[5315] for they
have rewarded[1580] evil[7451] unto themselves.
10 Say[559] ye to the righteous,[6662]
[a]that *it shall be* well *with him:* [b]for they
shall eat the fruit of their doings.
11 Woe unto the wicked[7563] [a]*it shall*
be ill *with him:* for the reward of his
hands[3027] shall be [I]given him.
12 *As for* my people, [a]children *are*
their oppressors, and women[802] rule
over them. O my people, [I][b]they which
lead[833] thee cause *thee* to err,[8582] and
[II]destroy[1104] the way[1870] of thy paths.[734]
13 The LORD standeth up[5324] [a]to
plead,[7378] and standeth to judge[1777] the
people.
14 The LORD will enter into judg-
ment[4941] with the ancients[2204] of his people, and the princes thereof: for ye have
[I]eaten up [a]the vineyard; the spoil of the
poor *is* in your houses.
15 What mean ye *that* ye [a]beat my
people to pieces, and grind the faces of
the poor? saith[5002] the Lord[136] GOD of
hosts.

The Women of Jerusalem

16 Moreover the LORD saith,[559]
Because the daughters of Zion are
haughty, and walk with stretched forth
necks and [I]wanton[8265] eyes, walking and
[II]mincing[2952] *as* they go, and making a
tinkling with their feet:
17 Therefore the Lord will smite with
[a]a scab the crown of the head of the
daughters of Zion, and the LORD will
[I][b]discover[6168] their secret parts.
18 In that day the Lord will take
away the bravery[8597] of *their* tinkling ornaments *about their feet,* and *their*
[I]cauls,[7636] and *their* [a]round tires like the
moon,[7720]
19 The [I]chains, and the bracelets, and
the [II]mufflers,[7479]
20 The bonnets, and the ornaments
of the legs, and the headbands, and the
[I]tablets,[5315] and the earrings,
21 The rings, and nose[639] jewels,
22 The changeable suits of apparel,
and the mantles,[4595] and the wimples,[4304]
and the crisping pins,[2754]
23 The glasses,[1549] and the fine linen,
and the hoods, and the vails.
24 And it shall come to pass, *that* instead of sweet smell there shall be stink;
and instead of a girdle[2290] a rent; and in-

21 [b]Isa. 2:10, 19
22 [a]Ps. 146:3; Jer. 17:5 [b]Job 27:3
1 [a]Jer. 37:21; 38:9 [b]Lev. 26:26
2 [a]2Kgs. 24:14
3 [I]Hebr. *a man eminent in countenance* [II]Or, *skillful of speech*
4 [a]Eccl. 10:16
7 [I]Hebr. *lift up the hand* [II]Hebr. *binder up* [a]Gen. 14:22
8 [a]Mic. 3:12
9 [a]Gen. 13:13; 18:20, 21; 19:5
10 [a]Eccl. 8:12 [b]Ps. 128:2
11 [I]Hebr. *done to him* [a]Ps. 11:6; Eccl. 8:13
12 [I]Or, *they which call thee blessed* [II]Hebr. *swallow up* [a]Isa. 3:4 [b]Isa. 9:16
13 [a]Mic. 6:2
14 [I]Or, *burnt* [a]Isa. 5:7; Matt. 21:33
15 [a]Isa. 58:4; Mic. 3:2, 3
16 [I]Hebr. *deceiving with their eyes* [II]Or, *tripping nicely*
17 [I]Hebr. *make naked* [a]Deut. 28:27 [b]Isa. 47:2, 3; Jer. 13:22; Nah. 3:5
18 [I]Or, *networks* [a]Judg. 8:21
19 [I]Or, *sweet balls* [II]Or, *spangled ornaments*
20 [I]Hebr. *houses of the soul*

stead of well set hair [a]baldness; and instead of a stomacher[6614] a girding of
sackcloth; *and* burning instead of beauty.
25 Thy men shall fall by the
sword,[2719] and thy [I]mighty in the war.
26 [a]And her gates shall lament and
mourn; and she *being* [I]desolate[5352] [b]shall
sit upon the ground.[776]

4 And [a]in that day[3117] seven women[802]
shall take hold of one man,[376] saying, We will [b]eat our own bread, and
wear our own apparel: only [I]let us be
called[7121] by thy name, [II]to take away
[c]our reproach.[2781]

The Future of Jerusalem

2 In that day shall [a]the branch[6780] of
the LORD be [I]beautiful[6643] and glorious,[3519] and the fruit of the earth[776] *shall*
be excellent and comely[8597] [II]for them
that are escaped[6413] of Israel.
3 And it shall come to pass, *that he*
that is left[7604] in Zion, and *he that*
remaineth[3498] in Jerusalem, [a]shall be
called holy,[6918] *even* every one that is
[b]written [I]among the living[2416] in Jerusalem:
4 When [a]the Lord[136] shall have
washed away[7346] the filth of the daughters of Zion, and shall have purged[1740]
the blood[1818] of Jerusalem from the
midst[7130] thereof by the spirit[7307] of
judgment,[4941] and by the spirit of burning.
5 And the LORD will create[1254] upon
every dwelling place of mount Zion, and
upon her assemblies,[4744] [a]a cloud[6051] and
smoke by day,[3119] and [b]the shining of a
flaming fire by night:[3915] for [I]upon all
the glory[3519] *shall be* [II][c]a defence.
6 And there shall be a tabernacle[5521]
for a shadow in the daytime[3119] from the
heat, and [a]for a place of refuge, and for
a covert[4563] from storm and from rain.

The Parable of the Vineyard

5 🗝Now will I sing to my wellbeloved[3039] a song[7892] of my beloved[1730] touching [a]his vineyard. My wellbeloved hath a vineyard in [I]a very fruitful
hill:
2 And he [I]fenced it, and gathered out
the stones thereof, and planted it with
the choicest vine, and built a tower in the
midst of it, and also [II]made a winepress
therein: [a]and he looked[6960] that it should
bring forth[6213] grapes, and it brought
forth wild grapes.
3 And now, O inhabitants of Jerusalem, and men[376] of Judah, [a]judge,[8199]
I pray you,[4994] betwixt me and my
vineyard.
4 What could have been done more
to my vineyard, that I have not done in
it? wherefore, when I looked that it
should bring forth grapes, brought it
forth wild grapes?
5 And now go to; I will tell[3045] you
what I will do[6213] to my vineyard: [a]I
will take away the hedge thereof, and it
shall be eaten up; *and* break down the
wall thereof, and it shall be [I]trodden
down:
6 And I will lay it waste: it shall not
be pruned, nor digged; but there shall
come up[5927] briers and thorns: I will also
command[6680] the clouds that they rain
no rain upon it.
7 For the vineyard of the LORD of
hosts[6635] *is* the house of Israel, and the
men of Judah [I]his pleasant plant: and he
looked for judgment,[4941] but behold
[II]oppression; for righteousness,[6666] but behold a cry.

The Fate of the Wicked

8 Woe unto them that join [a]house to
house, *that* lay field[7704] to field, till *there*
be no place, that [I]they may be placed
alone in the midst[7130] of the earth[776]

24 [a]Isa. 22:12; Mic. 1:16
25 [I]Hebr. *might*
26 [I]Hebr. *cleansed* [a]Jer. 14:2; Lam. 1:4 [b]Lam. 2:10
1 [I]Hebr. *let thy name be called upon us* [II]Or, *take thou away* [a]Isa. 2:11, 17 [b]2Thess. 3:12 [c]Luke 1:25
2 [I]Hebr. *beauty and glory* [II]Hebr. *for the escaping of Israel* [a]Jer. 23:5; Zech. 3:8; 6:12
3 [I]Or, *to life* [a]Isa. 60:21 [b]Phil. 4:3; Rev. 3:5
4 [a]Mal. 3:2, 3
5 [I]Or, *above* [II]Hebr. *a covering* [a]Ex. 13:21 [b]Zech. 2:5 [c]Isa. 8:14
6 [a]Isa. 25:4
1 [I]Hebr. *the horn of the son of oil* [a]Ps. 80:8; Song 8:12; Isa. 27:2; Jer. 2:21; Matt. 21:33; Mark 12:1; Luke 20:9
2 [I]Or, *made a wall about it* [II]Hebr. *hewed* [a]Deut. 32:6; Isa. 1:2, 3
3 [a]Rom. 3:4
5 [I]Hebr. *for a treading* [a]Ps. 80:12
7 [I]Hebr. *plant of his pleasures* [II]Hebr. *a scab*
8 [I]Hebr. *ye* [a]Mic. 2:2

🗝 **5:1–7** This passage is called "The Parable of the Vineyard." The imagery used here to describe Israel as God's vineyard was used by Jesus in His "Parable of the Wicked Tenants" (Matt. 21:33–41; Mark 12:1–9; Luke 20:9–16).

9 [I][a]In mine ears[241] *said* the LORD of hosts, [II]Of a truth many houses shall be desolate,[8047] *even* great and fair,[2896] without inhabitant.

10 Yea, ten acres of vineyard shall yield one [a]bath, and the seed[2233] of an homer[2563] shall yield[6213] an ephah.

11 [a]Woe unto them that rise up early in the morning, *that* they may follow strong drink; that continue until night, *till* wine [I]inflame them!

12 And [a]the harp, and the viol, the tabret,[8596] and pipe, and wine, are in their feasts:[4960] but [b]they regard[5027] not the work of the LORD, neither consider[7200] the operation of his hands.[3027]

13 [a]Therefore my people[5971] are gone into captivity,[1540] [b]because *they have* no knowledge: and [I]their honourable men *are* famished, and their multitude dried up with thirst.

14 Therefore hell[7585] hath enlarged herself, and opened her mouth[6310] without measure: and their glory,[1926] and their multitude, and their pomp,[7588] and he that rejoiceth, shall descend into it.

15 And [a]the mean man[120] shall be brought down, and the mighty man[376] shall be humbled, and the eyes of the lofty shall be humbled:

16 But the LORD of hosts shall be exalted in judgment, and [I]God[410] that is holy[6918] shall be sanctified[6942] in righteousness.

17 Then shall the lambs feed after their manner, and the waste places[2723] of [a]the fat ones shall strangers[1481] eat.

18 Woe unto them that draw iniquity[5771] with cords of vanity,[7723] and sin as it were with a cart rope:

19 [a]That say,[559] Let him make speed, *and* hasten his work, that we may see *it:* and let the counsel[6098] of the Holy One of Israel draw nigh and come, that we may know[3045] *it!*

20 Woe unto them [I]that call[559] evil[7451] good,[2896] and good evil; that put darkness[2822] for light,[216] and light for darkness; that put bitter[4751] for sweet, and sweet for bitter!

21 Woe unto *them that are* [a]wise[2450] in their own eyes, and prudent[995] [I]in their own sight!

22 [a]Woe unto *them that are* mighty to drink wine, and men[582] of strength[2428] to mingle strong drink:

23 Which [a]justify[6663] the wicked[7563] for reward, and take away the righteousness of the righteous[6662] from him!

24 Therefore [a]as [I]the fire devoureth the stubble, and the flame consumeth[7503] the chaff, *so* [b]their root shall be as rottenness, and their blossom shall go up as dust:[80] because they have cast away[3988] the law[8451] of the LORD of hosts, and despised[5006] the word[565] of the Holy One of Israel.

25 [a]Therefore is[2734] the anger[639] of the LORD kindled[2734] against his people, and he hath stretched forth his hand[3027] against them, and hath smitten[5221] them: and [b]the hills did tremble, and their carcases[5038] *were* [I]torn in the midst of the streets. [c]For all this his anger is not turned away, but his hand *is* stretched out still.

26 [a]And he will lift up[5375] an ensign to the nations[1471] from far, and will [b]hiss unto them from [c]the end of the earth: and, behold, [d]they shall come with speed swiftly:

27 None shall be weary nor stumble[3782] among them; none shall slumber nor sleep; neither [a]shall the girdle[232] of their loins be loosed, nor the latchet[8288] of their shoes be broken:

28 [a]Whose arrows *are* sharp,[8150] and all their bows bent, their horses' hoofs shall be counted[2803] like flint, and their wheels[1534] like a whirlwind:

29 Their roaring *shall be* like a lion, they shall roar like young lions: yea, they shall roar, and lay hold of the prey, and shall carry *it* away safe, and none shall deliver[5337] *it.*

30 And in that day[3117] they shall roar against them like the roaring of the sea: and if *one* [a]look unto the land,[776] behold darkness *and* [I]sorrow, [II]and the light is darkened[2821] in the heavens[6183] thereof.

9 [I]Or, *This is in mine ears, saith the LORD* [II]Hebr. *If not* [a]Isa. 22:14

10 [a]Ezek. 45:11

11 [I]Or, *pursue them* [a]Prov. 23:29, 30; Eccl. 10:16; Isa. 5:22

12 [a]Amos 6:5, 6 [b]Job 34:27; Ps. 28:5

13 [I]Hebr. *their glory are men of famine* [a]Hos. 4:6 [b]Isa. 1:3; Luke 19:44

15 [a]Isa. 2:9, 11, 17

16 [I]Or, *the holy God;* Hebr. *the God the holy*

17 [a]Isa. 10:16

19 [a]Isa. 66:5; Jer. 17:15; Amos 5:18; 2Pet. 3:3, 4

20 [I]Hebr. *that say concerning evil,* It is *good*

21 [I]Hebr. *before their face* [a]Prov. 3:7; Rom. 1:22; 12:16

22 [a]Isa. 5:11

23 [a]Prov. 17:15; 24:24

24 [I]Hebr. *the tongue of fire* [a]Ex. 15:7 [b]Job 18:16; Hos. 9:16; Amos 2:9

25 [I]Or, *as dung* [a]2Kgs. 22:13, 17 [b]Jer. 4:24 [c]Lev. 26:14; Isa. 9:12, 17, 21; 10:4

26 [a]Isa. 11:12 [b]Isa. 7:18 [c]Deut. 28:49; Ps. 72:8; Mal. 1:11 [d]Joel 2:7

27 [a]Dan. 5:6

28 [a]Jer. 5:16

30 [I]Or, *distress* [II]Or, *when it is light, it shall be dark in the destructions thereof* [a]Isa. 8:22; Jer. 4:23; Lam. 3:2

God Calls Isaiah

6 🔑In the year that [a]king[4428] Uzziah died[4194] I [b]saw[7200] also the Lord[136] sitting upon a throne,[3678] high and lifted up,[5375] and [I]his train[7757] filled the temple.[1964]

2 Above it stood the seraphims:[8314] each one had six wings; [a]with twain he covered[3680] his face, and with [b]twain[8147] he covered his feet, and with twain he did fly.

3 And [I]one cried[7121] unto another, and said,[559] [a]Holy,[6918] holy, holy, *is* the LORD of hosts:[6635] [IIb]the whole earth[776] *is* full of his glory.[3519]

4 And the posts of the [I]door moved at the voice of him that cried, and [a]the house[1004] was filled with smoke.

5 [a]Then said I, Woe *is* me! for I am [I]undone;[1820] because I *am* a man[376] of unclean[2931] lips,[8193] and I dwell in the midst of a people[5971] of unclean lips: for mine eyes have seen[7200] the King, the LORD of hosts.

6 Then flew one of the seraphims unto me, [I]having a live coal in his hand,[3027] *which* he had taken with the tongs from off [a]the altar:[4196]

7 And he [Ia]laid *it* upon my mouth,[6310] and said, Lo, this hath touched[5060] thy lips; and thine iniquity[5771] is taken away,[5493] and thy sin[2403] purged.[3722]

8 Also I heard[8085] the voice of the Lord, saying, Whom shall I send, and who will go for [a]us? Then said I, [I]Here *am* I; send me.

9 And he said, Go, and tell[559] this people, [a]Hear[8085] ye [I]indeed, but understand[995] not; and see ye [II]indeed, but perceive[3045] not.

10 Make [a]the heart[3820] of this people fat, and make their ears heavy,[3513] and shut their eyes; [b]lest they see with their eyes, and hear with their ears, and understand with their heart,[3824] and convert,[7725] and be healed.

11 Then said I, Lord, how long? And he answered,[559] [a]Until the cities be wasted without inhabitant, and the houses[1004] without man,[120] and the land[127] be[7582] [I]utterly[8077] desolate,[7582]

12 [a]And the LORD have removed men[120] far away, and *there be* a great forsaking in the midst[7130] of the land.[776]

13 But yet in it *shall be* a tenth, [I]and *it* shall return,[7725] and shall be eaten: as a teil tree, and as an oak, whose [II]substance[4678] *is* in them, when they cast *their leaves: so* [a]the holy[6944] seed[2233] *shall be* the substance thereof.

1 [I]Or, *the skirts thereof* [a]2Kgs. 15:7 [b]1Kgs. 22:19; John 12:41; Rev. 4:2 **2** [a]Ezek. 1:11 **3** [I]Hebr. *this cried to this* [II]Hebr. *his glory is the fullness of the whole earth* [a]Rev. 4:8 [b]Ps. 72:19 **4** [I]Hebr. *thresholds* [a]Ex. 40:34; 1Kgs. 8:10 **5** [I]Hebr. *cut off* [a]Ex. 4:10; 6:30; Judg. 6:22; 13:22; Jer. 1:6 **6** [I]Hebr. *and in his hand a live coal* [a]Rev. 8:3 **7** [I]Hebr. *caused it to touch* [a]Jer. 1:9; Dan. 10:16 **8** [I]Hebr. *Behold me* [a]Gen. 1:26; 3:22; 11:7 **9** [I]Hebr. *hear ye in hearing* [II]Hebr. *in seeing* [a]Isa. 43:8; Matt. 13:14; Mark 4:12; Luke 8:10; John 12:40; Acts 28:26; Rom. 11:8 **10** [a]Ps. 119:70; Isa. 63:17 [b]Jer. 5:21 **11** [I]Hebr. *desolate with desolation* [a]Mic. 3:12 **12** [a]2Kgs. 25:21 **13** [I]Or, *when it is returned, and hath been browsed* [II]Or, *it stock*, or, *stem* [a]Ezra 9:2; Mal. 2:15; Rom. 11:5

A Message for King Ahaz

7 And it came to pass in the days of [a]Ahaz the son of Jotham, the son of Uzziah, king of Judah, *that* Rezin the king of Syria, and Pekah the son of Remaliah, king of Israel, went up[5927] toward Jerusalem to war against it, but could not prevail against it.

2 And it was told[5046] the house[1004] of David, saying, Syria [I]is confederate[5117]

1 [a]2Kgs. 16:5; 2Chr. 28:5, 6 **2** [I]Hebr. *resteth on Ephrai*

🔑 **6:1–13** This chapter presents God's calling of Isaiah. Some see this as Isaiah's initial call to his prophetic ministry. Others, who note that the book is generally arranged chronologically, suggest that it was a special call after he had already begun his ministry.

Isaiah's call began with a vision of God's holiness (vv. 1–4). This vision terrified Isaiah and made him feel totally inadequate and unclean (v. 5; see also Job 42:5, 6; Ezek. 1:28; 4:23 and Dan. 10:8, 11). When the angel touched Isaiah's lips with the hot coal from the altar and said that his sins were forgiven (vv. 6, 7), Isaiah was fit for service to God. Later, when God asked for a representative, Isaiah responded with an answer that has been an example to believers ever since—"Here am I; send me" (v. 8). Like Jeremiah (Jer. 1:17–19) and Ezekiel (Ezek. 2:3–7), Isaiah was commissioned to speak to obstinate people who rejected God. The words of Isaiah's commission (Is. 6:9, 10) were used repeatedly by Jesus in the New Testament to explain why He taught in parables (Matt. 13:14, 15; Mark 4:12; Luke 8:10). John also referred to them when he explained why so few Jews had responded to Jesus' message (John 12:40), and Paul used them to explain why he had switched the emphasis of his ministry from the Jews to the Gentiles (Acts 28:26, 27).

with Ephraim. And his heart[3824] was
moved, and the heart of his people,[5971] as
the trees of the wood are moved with
the wind.[7307]
🔑 3 Then said the LORD unto Isaiah, Go
forth now to meet Ahaz, thou, [a]and
[I][b]Shear–jashub thy son, at the end of the
[c]conduit of the upper[5945] pool in the
[II]highway of the fuller's[3526] field;[7704]
4 And say unto him, Take heed,[8104]
and be quiet;[8252] fear[3372] not, [I]neither be
fainthearted for the two tails of these
smoking firebrands, for the fierce[2750]
anger[639] of Rezin with Syria, and of the
son of Remaliah.
5 Because Syria, Ephraim, and the
son of Remaliah, have taken evil counsel[3289] against thee, saying,
6 Let us go up against Judah, and
[I]vex[6973] it, and let us make a breach
therein for us, and set a king in the midst
of it, *even* the son of Tabeal:
7 Thus saith[559] the Lord[136] GOD, [a]It
shall not stand, neither shall it come to
pass.
8 [a]For the head[7218] of Syria *is*
Damascus, and the head of Damascus *is*
Rezin; and within threescore and five
years shall Ephraim be broken, [I]that it be
not a people.
9 And the head of Ephraim *is* Samaria, and the head of Samaria *is* Remaliah's son. [I][a]If ye will not believe,[539]
surely ye shall not be established.[539]

A Virgin

10 [I]Moreover the LORD spake[1696]
again unto Ahaz, saying,
11 [a]Ask[7592] thee a sign[226] of the
LORD thy God;[430] [I]ask it either in the
depth, or in the height above.
12 But Ahaz said, I will not ask, neither will I tempt[5254] the LORD.
13 And he said, Hear[8085] ye now, O
house of David; *Is it* a small thing for
you to weary men,[582] but will ye weary
my God also?
🔑 14 Therefore the Lord himself shall
give you a sign; [a]Behold, a virgin[5959]

3 [I]That is, *The remnant shall return* [II]Or, *causeway* [a]Isa. 10:21 [b]Isa. 6:13; 10:21 [c]2Kgs. 18:17; Isa. 36:2

4 [I]Hebr. *let not thy heart be tender*

6 [I]Or, *waken*

7 [a]Prov. 21:30; Isa. 8:10

8 [I]Hebr. *from a people* [a]2Sam. 8:6

9 [I]Or, *Do ye not believe?* it is *because ye are not stable* [a]2Chr. 20:20

10 [I]Hebr. *And the LORD added to speak*

11 [I]Or, *make thy petition deep* [a]Judg. 6:36; Matt. 12:38

14 [a]Matt. 1:23; Luke 1:31, 34

🔑 **7:3** See note on Isaiah 8:1–4 regarding Isaiah's sons.

🔑 **7:14** The famous prophecy of Christ's virgin birth is contained in this verse. The events of chapter seven occurred about 734 B.C. Isaiah was sent to King Ahaz with a reassuring word (Is. 7:4–9), but Isaiah's word also challenged him to exercise faith in God during this crisis (cf. Hezekiah's response in Is. 36—38). The Lord generously offered to grant a sign to Ahaz to bolster his faith (Is. 7:11). However in this crisis, Ahaz was not trusting in God, but in his alliance with Assyria (2 Kgs. 16:7–9). His reply, "I will not ask, neither will tempt the LORD" was pure hypocrisy (v. 14).

Few passages have provoked such controversy as this verse, even among those who hold to a conservative viewpoint. Recent studies have a uniform tendency to downplay the miraculous aspects, and rationalize that this verse is a prophecy that some young woman would shortly bear a child in the normal way, and the brief time of his youth would see the downfall of those countries now threatening Judah and King Ahaz. Some of the reasons that these approaches do not do justice to the text are summarized below.

(1) The meaning of the Hebrew word *'almāh* (5959). It has become commonplace to suggest that *'almāh* does not mean virgin, and that in fact, had Isaiah meant "virgin," he would have used the Hebrew word *b[e]thūlāh* (1330). The facts of language are otherwise. *'Almāh* is the clearest word Isaiah could have chosen to convey the idea of virginity. There is no appearance of *'almāh* in the Old Testament where the meaning "virgin" cannot be used. *B[e]thūlāh*, on the other hand, often needs qualification to clarify whether or not "virgin" is intended (e.g., Gen. 24:16, where Rebekah is described as a "virgin [*b[e]thūlāh*], neither had any man known her." Note that *'almāh,* which occurs later in the same context [Gen. 24:43], needs no such qualification. The qualification is doubtless needed because *b[e]thūlāh*, unlike *'almāh,* can sometimes refer to a married woman [Deut. 22:24; Joel 1:8].)

On the basis of Hebrew usage alone, it is evident that *'almāh* ought to be translated "virgin." But this is not the extent of the argument. The Greeks, who translated the Old Testament into their language hundreds of years before Christ, had no question; they translated Isaiah 7:14, in the

(continued on next page)

shall conceive, and bear [b]a son, [I][c]and
shall call[7121] his name [d]Immanuel.
15 Butter and honey shall he eat, that
he may know[3045] to refuse the evil, and
choose[977] the good.[2896]
16 [a]For before the child shall know to
refuse the evil, and choose the good, the
land[127] that thou abhorrest[6973] shall be
forsaken[5800] of [b]both her kings.[4428]
17 [a]The LORD shall bring upon thee,
and upon thy people, and upon thy
father's[1] house, days that have not come,
from the day[3117] that [b]Ephraim departed
from Judah; *even* the king of Assyria.
18 And it shall come to pass in that
day, *that* the LORD [a]shall hiss for the fly
that *is* in the uttermost part of the rivers
of Egypt, and for the bee that *is* in the
land[776] of Assyria.
19 And they shall come, and shall
rest all of them in the desolate valleys,
and in [a]the holes of the rocks, and upon
all thorns, and upon all [I]bushes.
20 In the same day shall the Lord
shave with a [a]razor that is hired, *namely,*
by them beyond the river, by the king of
Assyria, the head, and the hair of the
feet: and it shall also consume[5595] the
beard.[2206]
21 And it shall come to pass in that

14 [I]Or, *thou,* O virgin, *shalt call* [b]Isa. 9:6 [c]Gen. 4:1, 25; 16:11; 29:32; 30:6, 8; 1Sam. 4:21 [d]Isa. 8:8
16 [a]Isa. 8:4 [b]2Kgs. 15:30; 16:9
17 [a]2Chr. 28:19 [b]1Kgs. 12:16
18 [a]Isa. 5:26
19 [I]Or, *commendable trees* [a]Isa. 2:19; Jer. 16:16
20 [a]2Kgs. 16:7, 8; 2Chr. 28:20, 21; Ezek. 5:1

(continued from previous page)

Septuagint, with the Greek word *parthēnós*, the word for "virgin." Finally, the Holy Spirit affirmed this as the meaning when He guided Matthew to use *parthēnós* when quoting Isaiah 7:14 in Matthew 1:23.

(2) The meaning of the word *'ōth* (224), "sign." Those who suggest that the birth mentioned in Isaiah 7:14 would be a normal birth contradict the significance of *'ōth*. This word never refers to ordinary events, but always to special or distinctive actions or things. With reference to God, it is commonly translated as or understood to refer to a "miracle." This is particularly true of its uses in Isaiah, which, aside from this context, are concentrated with reference to God's miraculous sign of the sundial (chaps. 37; 38), and with God's miraculous millennial dealings with Israel (chaps. 55; 56). Therefore, the "sign" would need to be something extraordinary, not merely the normal birth of a male child who would live to see the downfall of Syria. It certainly would not be the defeat of Syria and Israel by Assyria! That was the very thing Ahaz was scheming to do without God's involvement!

(3) The specific reference of the prophecy. One must note that after Ahaz refuses a sign, God does not address him again. Verse fourteen is addressed to the whole "house of David." This immediately takes us beyond a rigid focus on the current scene. Moreover, the language of the announcement "Behold, a virgin shall conceive, and bring forth . . ." is reminiscent of pagan phraseology used to announce the birth of "gods." It is not suggested that Isaiah is likening Christ's birth to that of some pagan idol, merely that the idol-worshiping Ahaz would recognize the significance of the prophecy. Note also that both "virgin" in verse fourteen and "child" in verse sixteen have the definite article. It is agreed that these are articles of general reference, and that "a virgin" is the proper translation in verse fourteen. But note what happens if we translate "a child" in verse sixteen. That prophetic verse makes excellent sense on its own as a statement about the length of the crisis, with no reference to verse fourteen. One must also observe that the Hebrew word *ben* (1121), which means "son," is used in verse fourteen, while a completely different Hebrew word, *na'ar* (5288), meaning "young man," appears in verse sixteen.

(4) The child born. The name is "Immanuel," or "God with us." He cannot be just any child for in Isaiah 8:8 (and probably 8:10), "Immanuel" is presented as the true owner of the land (cf. the implications of Lev. 25:23), and the one who will vanquish Assyria. Further, the "son" to be born is mentioned again in Isaiah 9:6 and 11:1–5, and is clearly seen there to be a divine Person. No child of normal parentage could fulfill these prophecies; certainly not the child of Isaiah or Ahaz, as some commentators have suggested.

(5) The nature of messianic prophecy. Throughout the Old Testament, passages of messianic importance are presented without chronological separation or distinction. Peter explicitly states that the prophets were ignorant regarding when the messianic prophecies would be fulfilled (1 Pet. 1:10–12). It was indeed this prophecy of Isaiah 7:14 itself which was to be a sign. Its mysterious reference to a virgin birth would remain (as it did) to challenge students of God's word until the proper time came for it to be fulfilled.

day, *that* a man[376] shall nourish a young cow, and two sheep;

22 And it shall come to pass, for the abundance of milk *that* they shall give he shall eat butter: for butter and honey shall every one eat that is left [I]in the land.

23 And it shall come to pass in that day, *that* every place shall be, where there were a thousand vines at a thousand silverlings, [a]it shall *even* be for briers and thorns.

24 With arrows and with bows shall *men* come thither; because all the land shall become[1961] briers and thorns.

25 And *on* all hills that shall be digged with the mattock,4576 there shall not come thither the fear[3374] of briers and thorns: but it shall be for the sending forth of oxen, and for the treading of lesser cattle.

The Sign of Isaiah's Son

8 Moreover the LORD said unto me, Take thee a great roll,1549 and [a]write in it with a man's pen[2747] concerning [I]Maher–shalal–hash–baz.

2 And I took unto me faithful[539] witnesses to record, [a]Uriah the priest,[3548] and Zechariah the son of Jeberechiah.

3 And [I]I went unto the prophetess;[5031] and she conceived, and bare a son. Then said the LORD to me, Call[7121] his name Maher–shalal–hash–baz.

4 [a]For before the child shall have knowledge[3045] to cry,[7121] My father,[1] and my mother,[517] [I][b]the riches[2428] of Damascus and the spoil of Samaria shall be taken away[5375] before the king of Assyria.

The Assyrians Are Coming!

5 The LORD spake also unto me again, saying,

6 Forasmuch as this people[5971] refuseth[3988] the waters of [a]Shiloah that go softly, and rejoice [b]in Rezin and Remaliah's son;

7 Now therefore, behold, the Lord[136] bringeth up[5927] upon them the waters of the river, strong and many, *even* [a]the king of Assyria, and all his glory:[3519] and he shall come up[5927] over all his channels, and go over[5674] all his banks:

8 And he shall pass through Judah; he shall overflow[7857] and go over, [a]he shall reach[5060] *even* to the neck; and [I]the stretching out of his wings shall fill the breadth of thy land,[776] O [b]Immanuel.

9 [a]Associate yourselves, O ye people, [I]and ye shall be broken in pieces; and give ear,[238] all ye of far countries:[776] gird yourselves, and ye shall be broken in pieces; gird yourselves, and ye shall be broken in pieces.

10 [a]Take counsel together,[6098] 5779 and it shall come to nought;[6565] speak[1696] the word,[1697] [b]and it shall not stand: [c]for God[410] *is* with us.

11 For the LORD spake[559] thus to me [I]with a strong[2393] hand,[3027] and instructed[3256] me that I should not walk in the way[1870] of this people, saying,

12 Say[559] ye not, A confederacy, to all *them to* whom [a]this people shall say, A confederacy; [b]neither fear[3372] ye their fear,[4172] nor be afraid.[6206]

13 [a]Sanctify[6942] the LORD of hosts[6635] himself; and [b]let him *be* your fear, and *let* him *be* your dread.[6206]

22 [I]Hebr. *in the midst of the land*

23 [a]Isa. 5:6

1 [I]Hebr. *In making speed to the spoil he hasteneth the prey,* or, *Make speed* [a]Isa. 30:8; Hab. 2:2

2 [a]2Kgs. 16:10

3 [I]Hebr. *approached unto*

4 [I]Or, *he that is before the king of Assyria shall take away the riches* [a]Isa. 7:16 [b]2Kgs. 15:29; 16:9; Isa. 17:3

6 [a]Neh. 3:15; John 9:7 [b]Isa. 7:1, 2, 6

7 [a]Isa. 10:12

8 [I]Hebr. *the fullness of the breadth of thy land shall be the stretching out of his wings* [a]Isa. 30:28 [b]Isa. 7:14

9 [I]Or, *yet* [a]Joel 3:9, 11

10 [a]Job 5:12 [b]Isa. 7:7 [c]Isa. 7:14; Acts 5:38, 39; Rom. 8:31

11 [I]Hebr. *in strength of hand*

12 [a]Isa. 7:2 [b]1Pet. 3:14, 15

13 [a]Num. 20:12 [b]Ps. 76:7; Luke 12:5

8:1–4 This is the second child of Isaiah whose name was given for a "sign" to God's people (Is. 8:18). Before the child was born, God told Isaiah to write "Maher–shalal–hash–baz" (v. 1), which means "the spoil hastens, the prey speeds." This is a warning of the imminent destruction that was to come on Damascus and Samaria. Isaiah's other son's name, "Shear-jashub" (Is. 7:3) means "a remnant will return" (Is. 10:20–22). The significance of the latter name extends far beyond the current crisis, to the return from exile in Babylon. See note on Ezekiel 24:15–24.

8:8 Ahaz refused to heed Isaiah's two signs, so this oracle spelled out the consequences for Judah. The words "even to the neck" probably refer to the fact that when Sennacherib devastated Judah in 701 B.C, Jerusalem herself did not fall. See note on Micah 1:9.

🔑 14 And [a]he shall be for a sanctuary;[4720] but for [b]a stone[68] of stumbling[5063] and for a rock[6697] of offence[4383] to both the houses[1004] of Israel, for a gin[6341] and for a snare[4170] to the inhabitants of Jerusalem.

15 And many among them shall [a]stumble,[3782] and fall, and be broken,[7665] and be snared,[3369] and be taken.

A Warning

16 Bind up the testimony,[8584] seal the law[8451] among my disciples.[3928]

17 And I will wait upon the LORD, that [a]hideth his face from the house of Jacob, and I [b]will look for him.

18 [a]Behold, I and the children whom the LORD hath given me [b]*are* for signs and for wonders[4159] in Israel from the LORD of hosts, which dwelleth[7931] in mount Zion.

19 And when they shall say unto you, [a]Seek unto them that have familiar spirits,[178] and unto wizards[3049] [b]that peep, and that mutter: should not a people seek unto their God?[430] for the living[2416] [c]to the dead?[4191]

20 [a]To the law and to the testimony: if they speak not according to this word, *it is* because [b]*there is* [I]no light in them.

21 And they shall pass through[5674] it, hardly bestead[7185] and hungry: and it shall come to pass, that when they shall be hungry, they shall fret themselves,[7107] and [a]curse their king and their God, and look upward.

22 And [a]they shall look unto the earth;[776] and behold trouble and darkness,[2825] [b]dimness[4588] of anguish;[6695] and *they shall be* driven to darkness.[653]

14 [a]Ezek. 11:16 [b]Isa. 28:16; Luke 2:34; Rom. 9:33; 1Pet. 2:8
15 [a]Matt. 21:44; Luke 20:18; Rom. 9:32; 11:25
17 [a]Isa. 54:8 [b]Hab. 2:3; Luke 2:25, 38
18 [a]Heb. 2:13 [b]Ps. 71:7; Zech. 3:8
19 [a]1Sam. 28:8; Isa. 19:3 [b]Isa. 29:4 [c]Ps. 106:28
20 [I]Hebr. *no morning* [a]Luke 16:29 [b]Mic. 3:6
21 [a]Rev. 16:11
22 [a]Isa. 5:30 [b]Isa. 9:1

1 [I]Or, *populous* [a]Isa. 8:22 [b]2Kgs. 15:29; 2Chr. 16:4 [c]Lev. 26:24; 2Kgs. 17:5, 6; 1Chr. 5:26
2 [a]Matt. 4:16; Eph. 5:8, 14
3 [I]Or, *to him* [a]Judg. 5:30
4 [I]Or, *When thou brakest* [a]Isa. 10:5; 14:5 [b]Judg. 7:22; Ps. 83:9; Isa. 10:26
5 [I]Or, *When the whole battle of the warrior was* [II]Or, *and it was* [III]Hebr. *meat* [a]Isa. 66:15, 16
6 [a]Isa. 7:14; Luke 2:11 [b]John 3:16 [c]Matt. 28:18; 1Cor. 15:25 [d]Judg. 13:18 [e]Titus 2:13 [f]Eph. 2:14
7 [a]Dan. 2:44; Luke 1:32, 33 [b]2Kgs. 19:31; Isa. 37:32

The Prince of Peace

9 Nevertheless [a]the dimness[4155] *shall* not *be* such as *was* in her vexation,[4164] when at the [b]first[7223] he lightly afflicted[7043] the land[776] of Zebulun and the land of Naphtali, and [c]afterward did more grievously afflict[3513] *her by* the way[1870] of the sea, beyond Jordan, in Galilee [I]of the nations.[1471]

2 [a]The people[5971] that walked in darkness[2822] have seen[7200] a great light:[216] they that dwell in the land of the shadow of death,[6757] upon them hath the light shined.

3 Thou hast multiplied the nation,[1471] *and* [I]not increased the joy: they joy before thee according to the joy in harvest, *and* as *men* rejoice [a]when they divide the spoil.

4 [I]For thou hast broken[2865] the yoke of his burden, and [a]the staff[4294] of his shoulder, the rod[7626] of his oppressor, as in the day[3117] of [b]Midian.

5 [I]For every battle of the warrior *is* with confused noise,[7494] and garments rolled[1556] in blood;[1818] [II][a]but *this* shall be with burning[8316] *and* [III]fuel of fire.

6 [a]For unto us a child is born, unto us a [b]son[1121] is given: and the [c]government shall be upon his shoulder: and his name shall be called[7121] [d]Wonderful,[6382] Counselor,[3289] [e]The mighty God,[410] The everlasting[5703] Father,[1] [f]The Prince[8269] of Peace.

7 Of the increase of *his* government and peace [a]*there shall be* no end, upon the throne[3678] of David, and upon his kingdom,[4467] to order[3559] it, and to establish it with judgment[4941] and with justice[6666] from henceforth even for ever.[5769] The [b]zeal[7068] of the LORD of hosts[6625] will perform[6213] this.

🔑 **8:14** This verse is one of three passages in the Old Testament that describe the coming of the Messiah using the imagery of a stone (see also Ps. 118:22 and Is. 28:16). Several other uses of the word "stone" are not clear references to Christ, but may be understood in this way (Dan. 2:34, 35, 45; Zech. 3:9). Jesus used Psalm 118:22 to explain why the Jewish leaders had rejected Him (Matt. 21:42; Mark 12:10, 11; Luke 20:17). Peter explained that Jesus Christ was the "head of the corner" or "cornerstone" (Acts 4:11) and that believers were "stones" in a spiritual house (1 Pet. 2:6–8). Paul used the rejection of the "stone" to show why the Jews misunderstood the Messiah and the Gentiles did not (Rom. 9:32, 33).

God's Anger

8 The Lord[136] sent a word[1697] into Jacob, and it hath lighted[5307] upon Israel.

9 And all the people shall know,[3045] *even* Ephraim and the inhabitant of Samaria, that say in the pride and stoutness of heart,3824

10 The bricks are fallen down,[5307] but we will build with hewn stones:1496 the sycomores are cut down, but we will change *them into* cedars.

11 Therefore the LORD shall set up the adversaries of Rezin against him, and [I]join his enemies together;

12 The Syrians before, and the Philistines behind; and they shall devour Israel [I]with open mouth.[6310] [a]For all this his anger[639] is not turned away, but his hand[3027] *is* stretched out still.

13 For [a]the people turneth[7725] not unto him that smiteth them, neither do they seek the LORD of hosts.

14 Therefore the LORD will cut off[3772] from Israel head[7218] and tail, branch and rush, [a]in one day.

15 The ancient[2204] and honourable, he *is* the head; and the prophet[5030] that teacheth[3384] lies,[8267] he *is* the tail.

16 For [I][a]the leaders[833] of this people cause *them* to err;[8582] and [II]*they that are* led[833] of them *are* [III]destroyed.[1104]

17 Therefore the LORD [a]shall have no joy in their young men, neither shall have mercy[7355] on their fatherless and widows: [b]for every one *is* an hypocrite[2611] and an evildoer,[7489] and every mouth speaketh [I]folly.5039 [c]For all this his anger is not turned away, but his hand *is* stretched out still.

18 For wickedness[7564] [a]burneth as the fire: it shall devour the briers and thorns, and shall kindle in the thickets of the forest, and they shall mount up *like* the lifting up of smoke.

19 Through the wrath[5678] of the LORD of hosts is [a]the land darkened, and the people shall be as the [I]fuel of the fire: [b]no man[376] shall spare his brother.[251]

20 And he shall [I]snatch[1504] on the right hand, and be hungry; and he shall eat on the left hand, [a]and they shall not be satisfied: [b]they shall eat every man[376] the flesh[1320] of his own arm:

21 Manasseh, Ephraim; and Ephraim, Manasseh: *and* they together *shall be* against Judah. [a]For all this his anger is not turned away, but his hand *is* stretched out still.

10 Woe unto them that [a]decree[2710] unrighteous decrees,[2711] and [I]that write grievousness[5999] *which* they have prescribed;

2 To turn aside the needy from judgment,[1779] and to take away the right[4941] from the poor of my people,[5971] that widows may be their prey, and *that* they may rob the fatherless!

3 And [a]what will ye do[6213] in [b]the day[3117] of visitation,[6486] and in the desolation[7722] *which* shall come from far? to whom will ye flee for help? and where will ye leave[5800] your glory?[3519]

4 Without me they shall bow down[3766] under the prisoners, and they shall fall under the slain.[2026] [a]For all this his anger[639] is not turned away, but his hand[3027] *is* stretched out still.

Assyria, the Instrument of God

5 [I]O [II]Assyrian, [a]the rod[7626] of mine anger, [III]and the staff[4294] in their hand is mine indignation.[2195]

6 I will send him against [a]an hypocritical[2611] nation,[1471] and against the people of my wrath[5678] will I [b]give him a charge,[6680] to take the spoil, and to take the prey, and [I]to tread them down like the mire of the streets.

7 [a]Howbeit he meaneth not so, neither doth his heart think[2803] so; but *it is* in his heart3824 to destroy[8045] and cut off[3772] nations[1471] not a few.

8 [a]For he saith, *Are* not my princes[8269] altogether kings?[4428]

9 *Is* not [a]Calno [b]as Carchemish? *is* not Hamath as Arpad? *is* not Samaria [c]as Damascus?

10 As my hand hath found the kingdoms[4467] of the idols,[457] and whose

11 [I]Hebr. *mingle*
12 [I]Hebr. *with whole mouth* [a]Isa. 5:25; 10:4; Jer. 4:8
13 [a]Jer. 5:3; Hos. 7:10
14 [a]Isa. 10:17; Rev. 18:8
16 [I]Or, *they that call the blessed* [II]Or, *they that are called blessed of them* [III]Hebr. *swallowed up* [a]Isa. 3:12
17 [I]Or, *villany* [a]Ps. 147:10, 11 [b]Mic. 7:2 [c]Isa. 5:25; 9:12, 21; 10:4
18 [a]Isa. 10:17; Mal. 4:1
19 [I]Hebr. *meat* [a]Isa. 8:22 [b]Mic. 7:2, 6
20 [I]Hebr. *cut* [a]Lev. 26:26 [b]Isa. 49:26; Jer. 19:9
21 [a]Isa. 5:25; 9:12, 17; 10:4

1 [I]Or, *to the writers that write grievousness* [a]Ps. 58:2; 94:20
3 [a]Job 31:14 [b]Hos. 9:7; Luke 19:44
4 [a]Isa. 5:25; 9:12, 17, 21
5 [I]Or, *Woe to the Assyrian* [II]Hebr. *Asshur* [III]Or, *though* [a]Jer. 51:20
6 [I]Hebr. *to lay them a treading* [a]Isa. 9:17 [b]Jer. 34:22
7 [a]Gen. 50:20; Mic. 4:12
8 [a]2Kgs. 18:24, 33; 19:10
9 [a]Amos 6:2 [b]2Chr. 35:20 [c]2Kgs. 16:9

graven images did excel them of Jerusalem and of Samaria;

11 Shall I not, as I have done unto Samaria and her idols,[6091] so do to Jerusalem and her idols?

12 Wherefore it shall come to pass, *that* when the Lord[136] hath performed[1214] his whole work [a]upon mount Zion and on Jerusalem, [b]I will [I]punish[6485] the fruit [II]of the stout heart of the king of Assyria, and the glory of his high looks.

13 [a]For he saith, By the strength of my hand I have done *it,* and by my wisdom;[2451] for I am prudent:[995] and I have removed[5493] the bounds of the people, and have robbed[8154] their treasures, and I have put down the inhabitants [I]like a valiant *man:*

14 And [a]my hand hath found as a nest the riches[2428] of the people: and as one gathereth[622] eggs *that are* left,[5800] have I gathered all the earth;[776] and there was none that moved the wing, or opened the mouth,[6310] or peeped.

15 Shall [a]the axe boast itself[6286] against him that heweth[2672] therewith? *or* shall the saw magnify itself against him that shaketh[5130] it? [I]as if the rod should shake[5130] *itself* against them that lift it up, *or* as if the staff should lift up [II]*itself, as if it were* no wood.

16 Therefore shall the Lord,[136] the Lord of hosts,[6625] send among his [a]fat ones leanness; and under his glory he shall kindle a burning like the burning of a fire.

17 And the light[216] of Israel shall be for a fire, and his Holy One[6918] for a flame: [a]and it shall burn and devour his thorns and his briers in one day;

18 And shall consume[3615] the glory of his forest, and of [a]his fruitful field, [I]both soul[5315] and body: and they shall be as when a standardbearer fainteth.

19 And the rest[7605] of the trees of his forest shall be [I]few, that a child may write them.

A Remnant Will Return

20 And it shall come to pass in that day, *that* the remnant[7605] of Israel, and such as are escaped[6413] of the house[1004] of Jacob, [a]shall no more again stay upon him that smote[5221] them; but shall stay[8172] upon the LORD, the Holy One of Israel, in truth.[571]

21 [a]The remnant shall return,[7725] *even* the remnant of Jacob, unto the mighty God.

22 [a]For though thy people Israel be as the sand of the sea, [b]*yet* a remnant [I]of them shall return: [c]the consumption decreed shall overflow[7857] [II]with righteousness.[6666]

23 [a]For the Lord GOD of hosts shall make[6213] a consumption,[3617] even determined, in the midst[7130] of all the land.[776]

24 Therefore thus saith the Lord GOD of hosts, O my people that dwellest in Zion, [a]be not afraid[3372] of the Assyrian: he shall smite[5221] thee with a rod, [I]and shall lift up[5375] his staff against thee, after the manner[1870] of [b]Egypt.

25 [a]For yet a very little while, [b]and the indignation shall cease, and mine anger in their destruction.[8399]

26 And the LORD of hosts shall stir up [a]a scourge[7752] for him according to the slaughter[4347] of [b]Midian at the rock of Oreb: and [c]*as* his rod[4294] *was* upon the sea, so shall he lift it up after the manner of Egypt.

27 And it shall come to pass in that day, *that* [a]his burden [I]shall be taken away[5493] from off thy shoulder, and his yoke from off thy neck, and the yoke shall be destroyed[2254] because of [b]the anointing.[8081]

The Attack

28 He is come to Aiath, he is passed[5674] to Migron; at Michmash he hath laid up his carriages:

29 They are gone over[5674] [a]the passage: they have taken up their lodging at Geba; Ramah is afraid;[2729] [b]Gibeah of Saul is fled.

30 [I]Lift up thy voice, O daughter [a]of Gallim: cause it to be heard unto [b]Laish, [c]O poor Anathoth.

31 [a]Madmenah is removed; the in-

12 [I]Hebr. *visit upon* [II]Hebr. *of the greatness of the heart* [a]2Kgs. 19:31 [b]Jer. 50:18

13 [I]Or, *like many people* [a]Isa. 37:24; Ezek. 28:4; Dan. 4:30

14 [a]Job 31:25

15 [I]Or, *as if a rod should shake them that lift it up* [II]Or, that which is *not wood* [a]Jer. 51:20

16 [a]Isa. 5:17

17 [a]Isa. 9:18; 27:4

18 [I]Hebr. *from the soul, and even to the flesh* [a]2Kgs. 19:23

19 [I]Hebr. *number*

20 [a]2Kgs. 16:7; 2Chr. 28:20

21 [a]Isa. 7:3

22 [I]Hebr. *in,* or, *among* [II]Or, *in* [a]Rom. 9:27 [b]Isa. 6:13 [c]Isa. 28:22

23 [a]Isa. 28:22; Dan. 9:27; Rom. 9:28

24 [I]Or, *but he shall lift up his staff for thee* [a]Isa. 37:6 [b]Ex. 14

25 [a]Isa. 54:7 [b]Dan. 11:36

26 [a]2Kgs. 19:35 [b]Judg. 7:25; Isa. 9:4 [c]Ex. 14:26, 27

27 [I]Hebr. *shall remove* [a]Isa. 14:25 [b]Ps. 105:15; Dan. 9:24; 1John 2:20

29 [a]1Sam. 13:23 [b]1Sam. 11:4

30 [I]Hebr. *Cry shrill with thy voice* [a]1Sam. 25:44 [b]Judg. 18:7 [c]Josh. 21:18

31 [a]Josh. 15:31

habitants of Gebim gather themselves to flee.

32 As yet shall he remain [a]at Nob that day: he shall [b]shake[5130] his hand *against* the mount of [c]the daughter of Zion, the hill of Jerusalem.

33 Behold, the Lord, the LORD of hosts, shall lop the bough with terror: and [a]the high ones of stature *shall be* hewn down,[1438] and the haughty shall be humbled.

34 And he shall cut down[5362] the thickets of the forest with iron, and Lebanon shall fall [I]by a mighty one.[117]

A Kingdom of Peace

11 And [a]there shall come forth a rod[2415] out of the stem of [b]Jesse, and [c]a Branch[5342] shall grow out of his roots:

2 [a]And the spirit[7307] of the LORD shall rest upon him, the spirit of wisdom[2451] and understanding,[998] the spirit of counsel[6098] and might, the spirit of knowledge[1847] and of the fear[3374] of the LORD;

3 And shall make him of [I]quick understanding[7306] in the fear of the LORD: and he shall not judge[8199] after the sight of his eyes, neither reprove[3198] after the hearing of his ears:[241]

4 But [a]with righteousness[6664] shall he judge the poor, and [I]reprove with equity[4334] for the meek of the earth:[776] and he shall [b]smite[5221] the earth with the rod[7626] of his mouth,[6310] and with the breath[7307] of his lips[8193] shall he slay[4191] the wicked.[7563]

5 And [a]righteousness shall be the girdle[232] of his loins, and faithfulness[530] the girdle of his reins.[2504]

6 [a]The wolf also shall dwell[1481] with the lamb, and the leopard shall lie down with the kid; and the calf and the young lion and the fatling together; and a little child shall lead[5090] them.

7 And the cow and the bear shall feed; their young ones shall lie down together: and the lion shall eat straw like the ox.

8 And the sucking child shall play on the hole of the asp,[6620] and the weaned child shall put his hand[3027] on the [I]cockatrice'[6848] den.

9 [a]They shall not hurt[7489] nor destroy[7843] in all my holy[6944] mountain: for [b]the earth shall be full of the knowledge[1844] of the LORD, as the waters cover[3680] the sea.

Coming Home

10 [a]And in that day[3117] [b]there shall be a root[8328] of Jesse, which shall stand for an ensign[5251] of the people;[5971] to it shall the [c]Gentiles[1471] seek: and [d]his rest shall be [I]glorious.[3519]

11 And it shall come to pass [a]in that day, *that* the Lord[136] shall set his hand again the second time to recover the remnant[7605] of his people, which shall be left,[7604] [b]from Assyria, and from Egypt, and from Pathros, and from Cush, and from Elam, and from Shinar, and from Hamath, and from the islands of the sea.

12 And he shall set up[5375] an ensign for the nations,[1471] and shall assemble[622] the outcasts of Israel, and gather together[6908] [a]the dispersed of Judah from the four [I]corners of the earth.

13 [a]The envy[7068] also of Ephraim shall depart,[5493] and the adversaries of Judah shall be cut off:[3772] Ephraim shall not envy[7065] Judah, and Judah shall not vex[6887] Ephraim.

14 But they shall fly upon the shoulders of the Philistines toward the west; they shall spoil [I]them of the east together: [II][a]they shall lay their hand upon Edom and Moab; [III]and the children[1121] of Ammon [b]shall obey[4928] them.

15 And the LORD [a]shall utterly destroy[2763] the tongue of the Egyptian sea; and with his mighty wind[7307] shall he shake[5130] his hand over the river, and shall smite it in the seven streams, [b]and make *men* go over [I]dryshod.

16 And [a]there shall be an highway for the remnant of his people, which shall be left, from Assyria; [b]like as it was to Israel in the day that he came up[5927] out of the land[776] of Egypt.

32 [a]1Sam. 21:1; 22:19; Neh. 11:32 [b]Isa. 13:2 [c]Isa. 37:22
33 [a]Amos 2:9
34 [I]Or, *mightily*
1 [a]Isa. 53:2; Zech. 6:12; Rev. 5:5 [b]Isa. 11:2; Acts 13:23 [c]Isa. 4:2; Jer. 23:5
2 [a]Isa. 61:1; Matt. 3:16; John 1:32, 33; 3:34
3 [I]Hebr. *scent, or, smell*
4 [I]Or, *argue* [a]Ps. 72:2, 4; Rev. 19:11 [b]Job 4:9; Mal. 4:6; 2Thess. 2:8; Rev. 1:16; 2:16; 19:15
5 [a]Eph. 6:14
6 [a]Isa. 65:25; Ezek. 34:25; Hos. 2:18
8 [I]Or, *adder's*
9 [a]Job 5:23; Isa. 2:4; 35:9 [b]Hab. 2:14
10 [I]Hebr. *glory* [a]Isa. 2:11 [b]Isa. 11:1; Rom. 15:12 [c]Rom. 15:10 [d]Heb. 4:1
11 [a]Isa. 2:11 [b]Zech. 10:10
12 [I]Hebr. *wings* [a]John 7:35; James 1:1
13 [a]Jer. 3:18; Ezek. 37:16, 17, 22; Hos. 1:11
14 [I]Hebr. *the children of the east* [II]Hebr. *Edom and Moab* shall be *the laying on of their hand* [III]Hebr. *the children of Ammon their obedience* [a]Dan. 11:41 [b]Isa. 60:14
15 [I]Hebr. *in shoes* [a]Zech. 10:11 [b]Rev. 16:12
16 [a]Isa. 19:23 [b]Ex. 14:29; Isa. 51:10; 63:12, 13 [c]Isa. 2:11

A Hymn of Thanksgiving

12 And [a]in that day[3117] thou shalt say,[559] O LORD, I will praise[3034] thee: though thou wast angry[599] with me, thine anger[639] is turned away, and thou comfortedst[5162] me.

2 Behold, God[410] *is* my salvation;[3444] I will trust,[982] and not be afraid:[6342] for the LORD[3050] [a]JEHOVAH[3068] *is* my [b]strength and *my* song; he also is become[1961] my salvation.

3 Therefore with joy shall ye draw [a]water out of the wells of salvation.

4 And in that day shall ye say, [a]Praise the LORD, [I]call[7121] upon his name, [b]declare his doings among the people,[5971] make mention that his [c]name is exalted.

5 [a]Sing unto the LORD; for he hath done excellent things: this *is* known[3045] in all the earth.[776]

6 [a]Cry out and shout, thou [I]inhabitant of Zion: for great *is* [b]the Holy One[6918] of Israel in the midst[7130] of thee.

Babylon

13 The [a]burden[4853] of Babylon, which Isaiah the son[1121] of Amoz did see.[2372]

2 [a]Lift ye up a banner [b]upon the high mountain, exalt the voice unto them, [c]shake[5130] the hand,[3027] that they may go into the gates of the nobles.[5081]

3 I have commanded[6680] my sanctified ones,[6942] I have also called[7121] [a]my mighty ones for mine anger,[639] *even* them that [b]rejoice in my highness.

4 The noise of a multitude in the mountains, [I]like as of a great people;[5971] a tumultuous[7588] noise of the kingdoms[4467] of nations[1471] gathered together: the LORD of hosts[6635] mustereth[6485] the host of the battle.

5 They come from a far country,[776] from the end of heaven,8064 *even* the LORD, and the weapons of his indignation,[2195] to destroy[2254] the whole land.[776]

6 Howl ye; [a]for the day[3117] of the LORD *is* at hand; [b]it shall come as a destruction[7701] from the Almighty.[7706]

7 Therefore shall all hands [I]be faint,[7503] and every man's heart3824 shall melt:

8 And they shall be afraid:[926] [a]pangs and sorrows[2256] shall take hold of them; they shall be in pain[2342] as a woman that travaileth:3205 they shall [I]be amazed [II]one[376] at another;[7453] their faces *shall be as* [III]flames.

9 Behold, [a]the day of the LORD cometh, cruel both with wrath[5678] and fierce anger, to lay[7760] the land desolate:[8047] and he shall destroy[8045] [b]the sinners[2400] thereof out of it.

10 For the stars of heaven and the constellations thereof shall not give their light:[216] the sun shall be [a]darkened[2821] in his going forth, and the moon shall not cause her light to shine.

11 And I will punish[6485] the world[8398] for *their* evil,[7451] and the wicked[7563] for their iniquity;[5771] [a]and I will cause[7673] the arrogancy of the proud[2086] to cease,[7673] and will lay low the haughtiness of the terrible.

12 I will make a man[582] more precious than fine gold; even a man[120] than the golden wedge of Ophir.

13 [a]Therefore I will shake the heavens,8064 and the earth[776] shall remove[7493] out of her place, in the wrath of the LORD of hosts, and in [b]the day of his fierce anger.

14 And it shall be as the chased roe, and as a sheep that no man taketh up: [a]they shall every man[376] turn to his own people, and flee every one into his own land.

15 Every one that is found shall be thrust through; and every one that is joined *unto them* shall fall by the sword.[2719]

16 Their children also shall be [a]dashed to pieces before their eyes; their houses[1004] shall be spoiled, and their wives[802] ravished.

17 [a]Behold, I will stir up the Medes against them, which shall not regard[2803] silver; and *as for* gold, they shall not delight in it.

18 *Their* bows also shall dash the young men to pieces; and they shall have

---

2 [a]Ps. 83:18 [b]Ex. 15:2; Ps. 118:14
3 [a]John 4:10, 14; 7:37, 38
4 [I]Or, *proclaim his name* [a]1Chr. 16:8; Ps. 105:1 [b]Ps. 145:4-6 [c]Ps. 34:3
5 [a]Ex. 15:1, 21; Ps. 68:32; 98:1
6 [I]Hebr. *inhabitress* [a]Isa. 54:1; Zeph. 3:14 [b]Ps. 71:22; 89:18; Isa. 41:14, 16

1 [a]Isa. 21:1; 47:1; Jer. 50; 51
2 [a]Isa. 5:26; 18:3; Jer. 50:2 [b]Jer. 51:25 [c]Isa. 10:32
3 [a]Joel 3:11 [b]Ps. 149:2, 5, 6
4 [I]Hebr. *the likeness of*
6 [a]Zeph. 1:7; Rev. 6:17 [b]Job 31:23; Joel 1:15
7 [I]Or, *fall down*
8 [I]Hebr. *wonder* [II]Hebr. *every man at his neighbor* [III]Hebr. *faces of the flames* [a]Ps. 48:6; Isa. 21:3
9 [a]Mal. 4:1 [b]Ps. 104:35; Prov. 2:22
10 [a]Isa. 24:21, 23; Ezek. 32:7; Joel 2:31; 3:15; Matt. 24:29; Mark 13:24; Luke 21:25
11 [a]Isa. 2:17
13 [a]Hag. 2:6 [b]Ps. 110:5; Lam. 1:12
14 [a]Jer. 50:16; 51:9
16 [a]Ps. 137:9; Nah. 3:10; Zech. 14:2
17 [a]Isa. 21:2; Jer. 51:11, 28; Dan. 5:28, 31

no pity[7355] on the fruit of the womb;[990] their eye shall not spare children.[1121]

19 [a]And Babylon, the glory[6643] of kingdoms, the beauty[8597] of the Chaldees' excellency, shall be [I]as when God[430] overthrew [b]Sodom and Gomorrah.

20 [a]It shall never be inhabited, neither shall it be dwelt in from generation[1755] to generation: neither shall the Arabian pitch tent there; neither shall the shepherds make their fold there.

21 [a]But wild beasts of the desert shall lie there; and their houses shall be full of doleful creatures;255 and [I]owls shall dwell[7931] there, and satyrs[8163] shall dance there.

22 And the wild beasts of the islands shall cry in their [I]desolate houses,[490] and dragons[8577] in *their* pleasant palaces:[1964] [a]and her time[6256] *is* near to come, and her days shall not be prolonged.

The King of Babylon

14 For the LORD [a]will have mercy[7355] on Jacob, and [b]will yet choose[977] Israel, and set them in their own land:[127] [c]and the strangers[1616] shall be joined with them, and they shall cleave to the house[1004] of Jacob.

2 And the people[5971] shall take them, [a]and bring them to their place: and the house of Israel shall possess[5157] them in the land of the LORD for servants[5650] and handmaids: and they shall take them captives,[7617] [I]whose captives they were; [b]and they shall rule[7287] over their oppressors.

3 And it shall come to pass in the day that the LORD shall give thee rest from thy sorrow,[6090] and from thy fear,[7267] and from the hard[7186] bondage[5656] wherein thou wast made to serve,[5647]

🔑 4 That thou [a]shalt take up[5375] this [I]proverb against the king[4428] of Babylon, and say, How hath the oppressor ceased[7673] the [II][b]golden city ceased!

5 The LORD hath broken[7665] [a]the staff[4294] of the wicked,[7563] *and* the sceptre[7626] of the rulers.[4910]

6 He who smote[5221] the people in wrath[5678] with [I]a continual stroke,[4347] he that ruled the nations[1471] in anger,[639] is persecuted, *and* none hindereth.

7 The whole earth[776] is at rest, *and* is quiet:[8252] they break forth into singing.

8 [a]Yea, the fir trees rejoice at thee, *and* the cedars of Lebanon, *saying,* Since thou art laid down, no feller[3772] is come up[5927] against us.

9 [I][a]Hell[7585] from beneath is moved[7264] for thee to meet *thee* at thy coming: it stirreth up the dead[7496] for thee, *even* all the [II]chief ones of the earth; it hath raised up from their thrones[3678] all the kings of the nations.

10 All they shall speak and say unto thee, Art thou also become weak as we? art thou become like4911 unto us?

11 Thy pomp1347 is brought down to the grave,[7585] *and* the noise of thy viols:5035 the worm is spread under thee, and the worms cover thee.

12 [a]How art thou fallen[5307] from heaven,8064 [I]O Lucifer,1966 son[1121] of the morning! *how* art thou cut down to the ground,[776] which didst weaken the nations!

13 For thou hast said[559] in thine heart,3824 [a]I will ascend[5927] into heaven, [b]I will exalt my throne[3678] above the stars of God:[410] I will sit also upon the mount of the congregation,[4150] [c]in the sides of the north:

14 I will ascend above the heights of the clouds; [a]I will be like1819 the most High.[5945]

15 Yet thou [a]shalt be brought down to hell, to the sides of the pit.[953]

16 They that see thee shall narrowly look7688 upon thee, *and* consider[995] thee, *saying, Is* this the man[376] that made the earth to tremble, that did shake[7493] kingdoms;[4467]

17 *That* made[7760] the world[8398] as a wilderness, and destroyed[2040] the cities

19 [I]Hebr. *as the overthrowing* [a]Isa. 14:4, 22 [b]Gen. 19:24, 25; Deut. 29:23; Jer. 49:18; 50:40

20 [a]Jer. 50:3, 39; 51:29, 62

21 [I]Hebr. *daughters of the owl* [a]Isa. 34:11-15; Rev. 18:2

22 [I]Or, *palaces* [a]Jer. 51:33

1 [a]Ps. 102:13 [b]Zech. 1:17; 2:12 [c]Isa. 60:4, 5, 10; Eph. 2:12, 13

2 [I]Hebr. *that had taken the captives* [a]Isa. 49:22; 60:9; 66:20 [b]Isa. 60:14

4 [I]Or, *taunting speech* [II]Or, *exactress of gold* [a]Isa. 13:19; Hab. 2:6 [b]Rev. 18:16

5 [a]Ps. 125:3

6 [I]Hebr. *a stroke without removing*

8 [a]Isa. 55:12; Ezek. 31:16

9 [I]Or, *The grave* [II]Hebr. *leaders* [a]Ezek. 32:21

12 [I]Or, *O daystar* [a]Isa. 34:4

13 [a]Matt. 11:23 [b]Dan. 8:10 [c]Ps. 48:2

14 [a]Isa. 47:8; 2Thess. 2:4

15 [a]Matt. 11:23

🔑 **14:4–23** See note on Ezekiel 28:12–19.

thereof; *that* [I]opened not the house of his prisoners?

18 All the kings of the nations, *even* all of them, lie in glory,[3519] every one[376] in his own house.

19 But thou art cast out of thy grave[6913] like an abominable[8581] branch, *and as* the raiment of those that are slain,[2026] thrust through with a sword,[2719] that go down to the stones of the pit; as a carcase[6297] trodden under feet.

20 Thou shalt not be joined with them in burial,[6900] because thou hast destroyed[7843] thy land, *and* slain thy people: [a]the seed[2233] of evildoers[7489] shall never be renowned.[7121]

21 Prepare[3559] slaughter for his children[1121] [a]for the iniquity[5771] of their fathers;[1] that they do not rise, nor possess[3423] the land, nor fill the face of the world with cities.

22 For I will rise up against them, saith[5002] the LORD of hosts,[6635] and cut off[3772] from Babylon [a]the name, and [b]remnant,[7605] [c]and son, and nephew, saith the LORD.

23 [a]I will also make[7760] it a possession for the bittern, and pools of water: and I will sweep it with the besom[4292] of destruction,[8045] saith the LORD of hosts.

The Assyrians

24 The LORD of hosts hath sworn, saying, Surely as I have thought, so shall it come to pass; and as I have purposed,[3289] *so* shall it stand:

25 That I will break[7665] the Assyrian in my land, and upon my mountains tread him under foot:[947] then shall [a]his yoke depart[5493] from off them, and his burden depart from off their shoulders.

26 This *is* the purpose[6098] that is purposed upon the whole earth: and this *is* the hand[3027] that is stretched out upon all the nations.

27 For the LORD of hosts hath [a]purposed, and who shall disannul[6565] *it?* and his hand *is* stretched out, and who shall turn it back?[7725]

The Philistines

28 In the year that [a]king Ahaz died[4194] was this burden.[4853]

29 Rejoice not thou, whole Palestina, [a]because the rod[7626] of him that smote thee is broken: for out of the serpent's[5175] root shall come forth a [I]cockatrice,[6848] [b]and his fruit *shall be* a fiery[8314] flying serpent.

30 And the firstborn of the poor shall feed, and the needy shall lie down in safety: and I will kill[4191] thy root with famine, and he shall slay[2026] thy remnant.[7611]

31 Howl, O gate; cry,[2199] O city; thou, whole Palestina, *art* dissolved:[4127] for there shall come from the north a smoke, and [I]none *shall be* alone in his [II]appointed times.[4151]

32 What shall *one* then answer the messengers[4397] of the nation?[1471] That [a]the LORD hath founded[3245] Zion, and [b]the poor of his people shall [I]trust[2620] in it.

Moab

15 The [a]burden[4853] of Moab. Because in the night[3915] [b]Ar of Moab is laid waste,[7703] *and* [I]brought to silence;[1820] because in the night Kir of Moab is laid waste, *and* brought to silence;

2 [a]He is gone up[5927] to Bajith, and to Dibon, the high places,[1116] to weep: Moab shall howl over Nebo, and over Medeba: [b]on all their heads[7218] *shall be* baldness, *and* every beard[2206] cut off.

3 In their streets they shall gird themselves with sackcloth: [a]on the tops of their houses, and in their streets, every one shall howl, [I]weeping abundantly.

4 And Heshbon shall cry,[2199] [a]and Elealeh: their voice shall be heard[8085] *even* unto Jahaz: therefore the armed soldiers of Moab shall cry out;[7321] his life[5315] shall be grievous[3415] unto him.

5 [a]My heart[3820] shall cry out for Moab; [I]his fugitives *shall flee* unto Zoar, an [b]heifer of three years old: for [c]by the mounting up of Luhith with weeping shall they go it up; for in the way[1870] of

17 [I]Or, *did not let his prisoners loose homeward*

20 [a]Job 18:19; Ps. 21:10; 37:28; 109:13

21 [a]Ex. 20:5; Matt. 23:35

22 [a]Prov. 10:7; Jer. 51:62 [b]1Kgs. 14:10 [c]Job 18:19

23 [a]Isa. 34:11; Zeph. 2:14

25 [a]Isa. 10:27

27 [a]2Chr. 20:6; Job 9:12; 23:13; Ps. 33:11; Prov. 19:21; 21:30; Isa. 43:13; Dan. 4:31, 35

28 [a]2Kgs. 16:20

29 [I]Or, *adder* [a]2Chr. 26:6 [b]2Kgs. 18:8

31 [I]Or, he shall *not be alone* [II]Or, *assemblies*

32 [I]Or, *betake themselves unto it* [a]Ps. 87:1, 5; 102:16 [b]Zeph. 3:12; Zech. 11:11

1 [I]Or, *cut off* [a]Jer. 48:1; Ezek; 25:8-11; Amos 2:1 [b]Num. 21:28

2 [a]Isa. 16:12 [b]Lev. 21:5; Isa. 3:24; 22:12; Jer. 47:5; 48:1, 37, 38; Ezek. 7:18

3 [I]Hebr. *descending into weeping,* or, *coming down with weeping* [a]Jer. 48:38

4 [a]Isa. 16:9

5 [I]Or, *to the borders thereof, even to Zoar,* as *a heifer* [a]Isa. 16:11; Jer. 48:31 [b]Isa. 16:14; Jer. 48:34 [c]Jer. 48:5

Horonaim they shall raise up a cry of
[II]destruction.[7667]
6 For the waters [a]of Nimrim shall
be [I]desolate: for the hay is withered
away,[3001] the grass faileth, there is no
green thing.
7 Therefore the abundance they have
gotten,[6213] and that which they have laid
up,[6486] shall they carry away[5375] to the
[I]brook of the willows.
8 For the cry is gone round about[5362]
the borders of Moab; the howling thereof
unto Eglaim, and the howling thereof
unto Beer–elim.
9 For the waters of Dimon shall be
full of blood:[1818] for I will bring [I]more
upon Dimon, [a]lions upon him that
escapeth[6413] of Moab, and upon the
remnant[7611] of the land.[127]

16 [a]Send ye the lamb[3733] to the
ruler[4910] of the land[776] [b]from
[I]Sela to the wilderness, unto the mount of
the daughter of Zion.
2 For it shall be, *that,* as a wandering bird [I]cast out of the nest, so the
daughters of Moab shall be at the fords
of [a]Arnon.
3 [I]Take counsel,[6098] execute judgment;[6415] make thy shadow as the
night[3915] in the midst of the noonday;
hide the outcasts;[5080] bewray[1540] not him
that wandereth.
4 Let mine outcasts dwell[1481] with
thee, Moab; be thou a covert[5643] to them
from the face of the spoiler:[7703] for the
[I]extortioner is at an end, the spoiler[7701]
ceaseth, [II]the oppressors are consumed[8552]
out of the land.
5 And in mercy[2617] [a]shall[3559] the
throne[3678] be [I]established:[3559] and he
shall sit upon it in truth[571] in the tabernacle[168] of David, [b]judging,[8199] and
seeking judgment,[4941] and hasting righteousness.[6664]
6 We have heard[8085] of the [a]pride of
Moab; *he is* very proud: *even* of his
haughtiness, and his pride, and his
wrath:[5678] [b]*but* his lies *shall* not *be* so.
7 Therefore shall Moab [a]howl for
Moab, every one shall howl: for the
foundations [b]of Kir–hareseth shall ye
[I]mourn;[1897] surely *they are* stricken.
8 For [a]the fields of Heshbon languish, *and* [b]the vine of Sibmah: the
lords[1167] of the heathen[1471] have broken
down[1986] the principal plants thereof,
they are come[5060] *even* unto Jazer, they
wandered[8582] *through* the wilderness: her
branches are [I]stretched out,[5203] they are
gone over[5674] the sea.
9 Therefore [a]I will bewail[1058] with
the weeping of Jazer the vine of Sibmah:
I will water thee with my tears, [b]O
Heshbon, and Elealeh: for [I]the shouting
for thy summer fruits and for thy harvest
is fallen.[5307]
10 And [a]gladness is taken away,[622]
and joy out of the plentiful field; and in
the vineyards there shall be no singing,
neither shall there be shouting:[7321] the
treaders shall tread out no wine in *their*
presses; I have made *their vintage* shouting to cease.[7673]
11 Wherefore [a]my bowels[4578] shall
sound like an harp for Moab, and mine
inward parts[7130] for Kir–haresh.
12 And it shall come to pass, when
it is seen[7200] that Moab is weary on [a]the
high place,[1116] that he shall come to his
sanctuary[4720] to pray;[6419] but he shall not
prevail.
13 This *is* the word[1697] that the LORD
hath spoken[1696] concerning Moab since
that time.[227]
14 But now the LORD hath spoken,
saying, Within three years, [a]as the years
of an hireling, and the glory[3519] of Moab
shall be contemned,[7034] with all that
great multitude; and the remnant[7605] *shall
be* very small *and* [I]feeble.

Damascus

17 The [a]burden[4853] of Damascus.
Behold, Damascus is taken
away[5493] from *being* a city, and it shall
be a ruinous heap.
2 The cities of Aroer *are* forsaken:[5800] they shall be for flocks, which
shall lie down, and [a]none shall make
them afraid.[2729]
3 [a]The fortress also shall cease[7673]

5 [II]Hebr. *breaking*
6 [I]Hebr. *desolations* [a]Num. 32:36
7 [I]Or, *valley of the Arabians*
9 [I]Hebr. *additions* [a]2Kgs. 17:25
1 [I]Or, *Petra;* Hebr. *A rock* [a]2Kgs. 3:4 [b]2Kgs. 14:7
2 [I]Or, *a nest forsaken* [a]Num. 21:13
3 [I]Hebr. *Bring*
4 [I]Hebr. *wringer* [II]Hebr. *the treaders down*
5 [I]Or, *prepared* [a]Dan. 7:14, 27; Mic. 4:7; Luke 1:33 [b]Ps. 72:2; 96:13; 98:9
6 [a]Jer. 48:29; Zeph. 2:10 [b]Isa. 28:15
7 [I]Or, *mutter* [a]Jer. 48:20 [b]2Kgs. 3:25
8 [I]Or, *plucked up* [a]Isa. 24:7 [b]Isa. 16:9
9 [I]Or, *the alarm is fallen upon* [a]Jer. 48:32 [b]Isa. 15:4
10 [a]Isa. 24:8; Jer. 48:33
11 [a]Isa. 15:5; 63:15; Jer. 48:36
12 [a]Isa. 15:2
14 [I]Or, *not many* [a]Isa. 21:16
1 [a]2Kgs. 16:9; Jer. 49:23; Amos 1:3; Zech. 9:1
2 [a]Jer. 7:33
3 [a]Isa. 7:16; 8:4

from Ephraim, and the kingdom[4467] from Damascus, and the remnant[7605] of Syria: they shall be as the glory[3519] of the children of Israel, saith[5002] the LORD of hosts.[6635]

4 And in that day[3117] it shall come to pass, *that* the glory of Jacob shall be made thin, and [a]the fatness of his flesh[1320] shall wax lean.

5 [a]And it shall be as when the harvestman gathereth[622] the corn, and reapeth the ears with his arm; and it shall be as he that gathereth[3950] ears in the valley of Rephaim.[7497]

6 [a]Yet gleaning grapes shall be left[7604] in it, as the shaking of an olive tree, two *or* three berries in the top[7218] of the uppermost bough, four *or* five in the outmost fruitful branches thereof, saith the LORD God[430] of Israel.

7 At that day shall[8159] a man[120] [a]look[8159] to his Maker,[6213] and his eyes shall have respect[7200] to the Holy One[6918] of Israel.

8 And he shall not look to the altars,[4196] the work of his hands,[3027] neither shall respect *that* which his fingers have made,[6213] either the groves,[842] or the [I]images.[2553]

9 In that day shall his strong cities be as a forsaken bough, and an uppermost branch, which they left[5800] because of the children of Israel: and there shall be desolation.[8077]

10 Because thou hast forgotten [a]the God of thy salvation,[3468] and hast not been mindful[2142] of the rock of thy strength, therefore shalt thou plant pleasant plants, and shalt set it with strange[2114] slips:[2156]

11 In the day shalt thou make thy plant to grow, and in the morning shalt thou make thy seed[2233] to flourish: *but* the harvest *shall be* [I]a heap in the day of grief and of desperate[605] sorrow.

12 Woe to the [I]multitude of many people,[5971] *which* make a noise [a]like the noise of the seas; and to the rushing[3816] of nations, *that* make a rushing like the rushing of [II]mighty waters!

13 The nations shall rush like the rushing of many waters: but *God* shall [a]rebuke[1605] them, and they shall flee far off, and [b]shall be chased as the chaff of the mountains before the wind,[7307] and like [I]a rolling thing[1534] before the whirlwind.

14 And behold at eveningtide trouble; *and* before the morning he *is* not. This *is* the portion[2506] of them that spoil[8154] us, and the lot of them that rob us.

Ethiopia

18 Woe [a]to the land[776] shadowing with wings, which *is* beyond the rivers of Ethiopia:

2 That sendeth ambassadors[6735] by the sea, even in vessels of bulrushes upon the waters, *saying,* Go, ye swift messengers,[4397] to [a]a nation [I]scattered and peeled,[4178] to a people[5971] terrible[3372] from their beginning hitherto; [II]a nation[1471] meted out[6978] and trodden down, [III]whose land the rivers have spoiled!

3 All ye inhabitants of the world,[8398] and dwellers[7931] on the earth,[776] see ye, [a]when he lifteth up an ensign on the mountains; and when he bloweth[8628] a trumpet, hear[8085] ye.

4 For so the LORD said[559] unto me, I will take my rest,[8252] and I will [I]consider[5027] in my dwelling place like a clear heat [II]upon herbs, *and* like a cloud of dew in the heat of harvest.

5 For afore the harvest, when the bud is perfect,[8552] and the sour grape is ripening in the flower, he shall both cut off[3772] the sprigs with pruning hooks, and take away *and* cut down the branches.

6 They shall be left[5800] together unto the fowls of the mountains, and to the beasts of the earth: and the fowls shall summer upon them, and all the beasts of the earth shall winter upon them.

7 In that time[6256] [a]shall the present be brought unto the LORD of hosts[6635] of a people [I][b]scattered and peeled, and from a people terrible from their beginning hitherto; a nation meted out and trodden under foot, whose land the rivers have

4 [a]Isa. 10:16

5 [a]Jer. 51:33

6 [a]Isa. 24:13

7 [a]Mic. 7:7

8 [I]Or, *sun images*

10 [a]Ps. 68:19

11 [I]Or, *removed in the day of inheritance, and there shall be deadly sorrow*

12 [I]Or, *noise* [II]Or, *many* [a]Jer. 6:23

13 [I]Or, *thistle down* [a]Ps. 9:5 [b]Ps. 83:13; Hos. 13:3

1 [a]Isa. 20:4, 5; Ezek. 30:4, 5, 9; Zeph. 2:12; 3:10

2 [I]Or, *outspread and polished* [II]Hebr. *a nation of line, line, and treading underfoot* [III]Or, *whose land the rivers despise* [a]Isa. 13:7

3 [a]Isa. 5:26

4 [I]Or, *regard my set dwelling* [II]Or, *after rain*

7 [I]Or, *outspread and polished* [a]Ps. 68:31; 72:10; Isa. 16:1; Zeph. 3:10; Mal. 1:11 [b]Isa. 13:2

spoiled, to the place of the name of the
LORD of hosts, the mount Zion.

Egypt

19 The [a]burden[4853] of Egypt.
Behold, the LORD [b]rideth upon a
swift cloud, and shall come into Egypt:
and [c]the idols[457] of Egypt shall be moved
at his presence, and the heart[3824] of
Egypt shall melt in the midst[7130] of it.
2 And I will [I][a]set the Egyptians
against the Egyptians: and they shall
fight every one against his brother,[251]
and every one against his neighbour;[7453]
city against city, *and* kingdom[4467] against
kingdom.
3 And the spirit[7307] of Egypt [I]shall
fail in the midst thereof; and I will
[II]destroy[1104] the counsel[6098] thereof: and
they shall [a]seek to the idols, and to the
charmers,[328] and to them that have
familiar spirits,[178] and to the wizards.[3049]
4 And the Egyptians will I [I]give over
[a]into the hand[3027] of a cruel[7186] lord;[113]
and a fierce king[4428] shall rule[4910] over
them, saith[5002] the Lord, the LORD of
hosts.[6635]
5 [a]And the waters shall fail from the
sea, and the river shall be wasted[2717] and
dried up.[3001]
6 And they shall turn the rivers far
away; *and* the brooks [a]of defence shall be
emptied and dried up:[2717] the reeds and
flags[5488] shall wither.
7 The paper reeds by the brooks, by
the mouth[6310] of the brooks, and every
thing sown by the brooks, shall
wither,[3001] be driven away, [I]and be no
more.
8 The fishers also shall mourn, and
all they that cast angle into the brooks
shall lament, and they that spread nets
upon the waters shall languish.
9 Moreover they that work[5647] in
[a]fine flax, and they that weave [I]networks,
shall be confounded.[954]
10 And they shall be broken[1792] in
the [I]purposes[8356] thereof, all that
make[6213] sluices *and* ponds [II]for fish.[5315]
11 Surely the princes[8269] of [a]Zoan
are fools, the counsel of the wise[2450]
counsellors[3289] of Pharaoh is become
brutish: how say[559] ye unto Pharaoh, I
am the son[1121] of the wise, the son of
ancient[6924] kings?
12 [a]Where *are* they? where *are* thy
wise *men?* and let them tell[5046] thee now,
and let them know[3045] what the LORD of
hosts hath purposed[3289] upon Egypt.
13 The princes of Zoan are become
fools, [a]the princes of Noph are deceived;
they have also seduced[8582] Egypt, *even*
[I]*they that are* the stay of the tribes[7626]
thereof.
14 The LORD hath mingled [I][a]a perverse spirit in the midst thereof: and they
have caused Egypt to err[8582] in every
work thereof, as a drunken *man* staggereth[8582] in his vomit.
15 Neither shall there be *any* work
for Egypt, which [a]the head[7218] or tail,
branch or rush, may do.[6213]
16 In that day[3117] shall Egypt [a]be
like unto women:[802] and it shall be
afraid[2729] and fear[6342] because of the
shaking[8573] of the hand of the LORD of
hosts, [b]which he shaketh[5130] over it.
17 And the land[127] of Judah shall be
a terror[2283] unto Egypt, every one that
maketh mention thereof shall be
afraid[6342] in himself, because of the counsel of the LORD of hosts, which he hath
determined[3289] against it.
18 In that day shall five cities in the
land[776] of Egypt [a]speak[1696] [I]the language[8193] of Canaan, and swear[7650] to
the LORD of hosts; one shall be called,
The city [II]of destruction.
19 In that day [a]shall there be an
altar[4196] to the LORD in the midst of the
land of Egypt, and a pillar[4676] at the border thereof to the LORD.
20 And [a]it shall be for a sign[226]
and for a witness unto the LORD of hosts
in the land of Egypt: for they shall
cry unto the LORD because of the oppressors, and he shall send them a saviour,[3467] and a great one, and he shall
deliver[5337] them.
21 And the LORD shall be known[3045]
to Egypt, and the Egyptians shall know
the LORD in that day, and [a]shall do[5647]
sacrifice[2077] and oblation;[4503] yea, they

1 [a]Jer. 46:13; Ezek. 29; 30 [b]Ps. 18:10; 104:3 [c]Ex. 12:12; Jer. 43:12

2 [I]Or, *mingle* [a]Judg. 7:22; 1Sam. 14:16, 20; 2Chr. 20:23

3 [I]Hebr. *shall be emptied* [II]Hebr. *swallow up* [a]Isa. 8:19; 47:12

4 [I]Or, *shut up* [a]Isa. 20:4; Jer. 46:26; Ezek. 29:19

5 [a]Jer. 51:36; Ezek. 30:12

6 [a]2Kgs. 19:24

7 [I]Hebr. *and shall not be*

9 [I]Or, *white works* [a]1Kgs. 10:28; Prov. 7:16

10 [I]Hebr. *foundations* [II]Hebr. *of living things*

11 [a]Num. 13:22

12 [a]1Cor. 1:20

13 [I]Or, *governors* [a]Jer. 2:16

14 [I]Hebr. *a spirit of perverseness* [a]1Kgs. 22:22; Isa. 29:10

15 [a]Isa. 9:14

16 [a]Jer. 51:30; Nah. 3:13 [b]Isa. 11:15

18 [I]Hebr. *the lip* [II]Or, *of Heres,* or, *of the sun* [a]Zeph. 3:9

19 [a]Gen. 28:18; Ex. 24:4; Josh. 22:10, 26, 27

20 [a]Josh. 4:20; 22:27

21 [a]Mal. 1:11

shall vow[5087] a vow unto the LORD, and perform *it.*

22 And the LORD shall smite[5062] Egypt: he shall smite and heal *it:* and they shall return[7725] *even* to the LORD, and he shall be intreated of them, and shall heal them.

23 In that day [a]shall there be a highway out of Egypt to Assyria, and the Assyrian shall come into Egypt, and the Egyptian into Assyria, and the Egyptians shall serve[5647] with the Assyrians.

24 In that day shall Israel be the third with Egypt and with Assyria, *even* a blessing[1293] in the midst of the land:

25 Whom the LORD of hosts shall bless,[1288] saying, Blessed *be* Egypt my people,[5971] and Assyria [a]the work of my hands, and Israel mine inheritance.[5159]

The Captivity of Egypt and Ethiopia

20 In the year that [a]Tartan came unto Ashdod, (when Sargon the king[4428] of Assyria sent him,) and fought against Ashdod, and took it;

🔑 2 At the same time[6256] spake[1696] the LORD [I]by Isaiah the son[1121] of Amoz, saying, Go and loose [a]the sackcloth from off thy loins, and put off thy shoe from thy foot. And he did[6213] so, [b]walking naked[6174] and barefoot.

3 And the LORD said,[559] Like as my servant[5650] Isaiah hath walked naked and barefoot three years [a]*for* a sign and wonder upon Egypt and upon Ethiopia;

4 So shall the king of Assyria lead away [I]the Egyptians prisoners,[7628] and the Ethiopians captives,[1546] young and old,[2205] naked and barefoot, [a]even with *their* buttocks uncovered, to the [II]shame[6172] of Egypt.

5 [a]And they shall be afraid[2865] and ashamed[954] of Ethiopia their expectation, and of Egypt their glory.[8597]

6 And the inhabitant of this [Ia]isle shall say in that day,[3117] Behold, such *is* our expectation, whither we flee for help to be delivered[5337] from the king of Assyria: and how shall we escape?[4422]

The Fall of Babylon

21 The burden[4853] of the desert of the sea. As [a]whirlwinds in the south pass through; *so* it cometh from the desert, from a terrible[3372] land.[776]

2 A [I]grievous[7186] vision[2380] is declared[5046] unto me; [a]the treacherous[898] dealer dealeth treacherously, and the spoiler spoileth.[7703] [b]Go up, O Elam: besiege, O Media; all the sighing thereof have I made to cease.[7673]

3 Therefore [a]are my loins filled with pain: [b]pangs have taken hold upon me, as the pangs of a woman that travaileth:[3205] I was bowed down[5791] at the hearing[8085] *of it;* I was dismayed at the seeing[7200] *of it.*

4 [I]My heart[3824] panted,[8582] fearfulness[6427] affrighted[1204] me: [a]the night of my pleasure[2837] hath he [II]turned into fear unto me.

5 [a]Prepare the table, watch in the watchtower,[6844] eat, drink: arise, ye princes,[8269] *and* anoint[4886] the shield.

6 For thus hath the LORD[136] said unto me, Go, set a watchman, let him declare[5046] what he seeth.

7 [a]And he saw a chariot *with* a couple of horsemen, a chariot of asses, *and* a chariot of camels; and he hearkened[7181] diligently with much heed:

8 And [I]he cried,[7121] A lion: My lord, I stand continually[8548] upon the [a]watchtower[4707] in the daytime,[3119] and I am set[5324] in my ward[4931] [II]whole nights:[3915]

9 And, behold, here cometh a chariot of men,[376] *with* a couple of horsemen. And he answered and said, [a]Babylon is fallen,[5307] is fallen; and [b]all the graven images of her gods[430] he hath broken[7665] unto the ground.[776]

10 [a]O my threshing, and the [I]corn of my floor: that which I have heard[8085] of the LORD of hosts,[6635] the God[430] of Israel, have I declared unto you.

23 [a]Isa. 11:16
25 [a]Ps. 100:3; Isa. 29:23; Hos. 2:23; Eph. 2:10

1 [a]2Kgs. 18:17
2 [I]Hebr. *by the hand of Isaiah* [a]Zech. 13:4 [b]1Sam. 19:24; Mic. 1:8, 11
3 [a]Isa. 8:18
4 [I]Hebr. *the captivity of Egypt* [II]Hebr. *nakedness* [a]2Sam. 10:4; Isa. 3:17; Jer. 13:22, 26; Mic. 1:11
5 [a]2Kgs. 18:21; Isa. 30:3, 5, 7; 36:6
6 [I]Or, *country* [a]Jer. 47:4

1 [a]Zech. 9:14
2 [I]Hebr. *hard* [a]Isa. 33:1 [b]Isa. 13:17; Jer. 49:34
3 [a]Isa. 15:5; 16:11 [b]Isa. 13:8
4 [I]Or, *My mind wandered* [II]Hebr. *put* [a]Deut. 28:67
5 [a]Dan. 5:5
7 [a]Isa. 21:9
8 [I]Or, *cried as a lion* [II]Or, *every night* [a]Hab. 2:1
9 [a]Jer. 51:8; Rev. 14:8; 18:2 [b]Isa. 46:1; Jer. 50:2; 51:44
10 [I]Hebr. *son* [a]Jer. 51:33

🔑 **20:2, 3** See note on Micah 1:8.

Edom

11 [a]The burden of Dumah. He calleth[7121] to me out of Seir, Watchman,[8104] what of the night?[3915] Watchman, what of the night?

12 The watchman said, The morning cometh, and also the night: if ye will enquire,[1158] enquire ye: return,[7725] come.

Arabia

13 [a]The burden upon Arabia. In the forest in Arabia shall ye lodge, O ye travelling companies736 [b]of Dedanim.

14 The inhabitants of the land of Tema [I]brought water to him that was thirsty, they prevented6923 with their bread him that fled.

15 For they fled [I]from the swords,[2719] from the drawn[5203] sword, and from the bent bow, and from the grievousness of war.

16 For thus hath the Lord said unto me, Within a year, [a]according to the years of an hireling, and all the glory[3519] of [b]Kedar shall fail:[3615]

17 And the residue[7605] of the number of [I]archers, the mighty men of the children of Kedar, shall be diminished: for the LORD God of Israel hath spoken[1696] *it.*

Jerusalem

22 The burden[4853] of the valley of vision.[2384] What aileth thee now, that thou art wholly gone up[5927] to the housetops?

2 Thou that art full of stirs,8663 a tumultuous city, [a]a joyous city: thy slain2491 *men are* not slain with the sword,[2719] nor dead[4191] in battle.

3 All thy rulers[7101] are fled together, they are bound [I]by the archers: all that are found in thee are bound together, *which* have fled from far.

4 Therefore said I, Look away from me; [I][a]I will weep bitterly, labour not to comfort[5162] me, because of the spoiling[7701] of the daughter of my people.[5971]

5 [a]For *it is* a day[3117] of trouble,[4103] and of treading down, and of perplexity [b]by the Lord[136] GOD of hosts[6635] in the valley of vision, breaking down the walls, and of crying to the mountains.

6 [a]And Elam bare[5375] the quiver with chariots of men[120] *and* horsemen, and [b]Kir [I]uncovered the shield.

7 And it shall come to pass, *that* [I]thy choicest valleys shall be full of chariots, and the horsemen shall set themselves in array [II]at the gate.

8 And he discovered[1540] the covering of Judah, and thou didst look in that day to the armour[5402] [a]of the house[1004] of the forest.

9 [a]Ye have seen[7200] also the breaches of the city of David, that they are many: and ye gathered together[6908] the waters of the lower pool.

10 And ye have numbered[5608] the houses of Jerusalem, and the houses have ye broken down[5422] to fortify the wall.

11 [a]Ye made[6213] also a ditch between the two walls for the water of the old pool: but ye have not looked unto [b]the maker[6213] thereof, neither had respect[7200] unto him that fashioned[3335] it long ago.

12 And in that day did the Lord GOD of hosts [a]call[7121] to weeping, and to mourning, and [b]to baldness, and to girding with sackcloth:

13 And behold joy and gladness, slaying oxen, and killing[7819] sheep, eating flesh,[1320] and drinking wine: [a]let us eat and drink; for to morrow we shall die.[4191]

14 [a]And it was revealed[1540] in mine ears[241] by the LORD of hosts, Surely this iniquity[5771] [b]shall not be purged[3722] from you till ye die, saith[559] the Lord GOD of hosts.

Shebna

15 Thus saith the Lord GOD of hosts, Go, get thee unto this treasurer, *even* unto [a]Shebna, [b]which *is* over the house, *and say,*

16 What hast thou here? and whom hast thou here, that thou hast hewed thee out2672 a sepulchre here, [I]*as* he [a]that heweth him out a sepulchre[6913] on high,

11 [a]1Chr. 1:30; Jer. 49:7, 8; Ezek. 35:2; Obad. 1:1

13 [a]Jer. 49:28 [b]1Chr. 1:9, 32

14 [I]Or, *bring ye*

15 [I]Or, *for fear* [II]Hebr. *from the face*

16 [a]Isa. 16:14 [b]Ps. 120:5; Isa. 60:7

17 [I]Hebr. *bows*

2 [a]Isa. 32:13

3 [I]Hebr. *of the bow*

4 [I]Hebr. *I will be bitter in weeping* [a]Jer. 4:19; 9:1

5 [a]Isa. 37:3 [b]Lam. 1:5; 2:2

6 [I]Hebr. *made naked* [a]Jer. 49:35 [b]Isa. 15:1

7 [I]Hebr. *the choice of thy valleys* [II]Or, *toward*

8 [a]1Kgs. 7:2; 10:17

9 [a]2Kgs. 20:20; 2Chr. 32:4, 5, 30

11 [a]Neh. 3:16 [b]Isa. 37:26

12 [a]Joel 1:13 [b]Ezra 9:3; Isa. 15:2; Mic. 1:16

13 [a]Isa. 56:12; 1Cor. 15:32

14 [a]Isa. 5:9 [b]1Sam. 3:14; Ezek. 24:13

15 [a]2Kgs. 18:37; Isa. 36:3 [b]1Kgs. 4:6

16 [I]Or, *O he* [a]2Sam. 18:18; Matt. 27:60

and that graveth[2710] an habitation[4908] for himself in a rock?

17 Behold, [I]the LORD will carry thee away2904 with [II]a mighty[1397] captivity, [a]and will surely cover thee.

18 He will surely violently turn and toss thee *like* a ball into a [I]large country:[776] there shalt thou die, and there the chariots of thy glory[3519] *shall be* the shame of thy lord's house.

19 And I will drive thee from thy station, and from thy state4612 shall he pull thee down.[2040]

20 And it shall come to pass in that day, that I will call my servant[5650] [a]Eliakim the son[1121] of Hilkiah:

21 And I will clothe him with thy robe, and strengthen[2388] him with thy girdle,73 and I will commit thy government[4475] into his hand:[3027] and he shall be a father to the inhabitants of Jerusalem, and to the house of Judah.

22 And the key of the house of David will I lay upon his shoulder; so he shall [a]open, and none shall shut; and he shall shut, and none shall open.

23 And I will fasten[8628] him *as* [a]a nail in a sure[539] place; and he shall be for a glorious[3519] throne[3678] to his father's[1] house.

24 And they shall hang upon him all the glory of his father's house, the offspring and the issue, all vessels of small quantity, from the vessels of cups, even to all the [I]vessels of flagons.5035

25 In that day, saith5002 the LORD of hosts, shall the nail that is fastened[8628] in the sure[539] place be removed, and be cut down, and fall; and the burden that *was* upon it shall be cut off:[3772] for the LORD hath spoken[1696] *it*.

Phoenicia

23 The [a]burden[4853] of Tyre. Howl, ye ships of Tarshish; for it is laid waste,[7703] so that there is no house,[1004] no entering in: [b]from the land[776] of Chittim it is revealed[1540] to them.

2 Be [I]still, ye inhabitants of the isle; thou whom the merchants of Zidon, that pass over[5674] the sea, have replenished.

3 And by great waters the seed[2233] of Sihor, the harvest of the river, *is* her revenue; and [a]she is a mart of nations.71

4 Be thou ashamed,[954] O Zidon: for the sea hath spoken,[559] *even* the strength of the sea, saying, I travail[2342] not, nor bring forth children, neither do I nourish up young men, *nor* bring up virgins.[1330]

5 [a]As at the report[8088] concerning Egypt, *so* shall they be sorely pained[2342] at the report of Tyre.

6 Pass ye over to Tarshish; howl, ye inhabitants of the isle.

7 *Is* this your [a]joyous *city*, whose antiquity[6927] *is* of ancient[6924] days?[3117] her own feet shall carry her [I]afar off to sojourn.[1481]

8 Who hath taken this counsel[3289] against Tyre, [a]the crowning *city*, whose merchants *are* princes,[8269] whose trafficker3669 *are* the honourable[3513] of the earth?[776]

9 The LORD of hosts[6635] hath purposed[3289] it, [I]to stain the pride of all glory,[6643] *and* to bring into contempt all the honourable of the earth.

10 Pass through thy land as a river, O daughter of Tarshish: *there is* no more [I]strength.

11 He stretched out his hand[3027] over the sea, he shook the kingdoms:[4467] the LORD hath given a commandment[4687] [I]against [II]the merchant *city*, to destroy[8045] the [III]strong holds thereof.

12 And he said, [a]Thou shalt no more rejoice, O thou oppressed virgin,[1330] daughter of Zidon: arise, [b]pass over to Chittim; there also shalt thou have no rest.

13 Behold the land of the Chaldeans; this people[5971] was not, *till* the Assyrian founded[3245] it for [a]them that dwell in the wilderness: they set up the towers thereof, they raised up the palaces[759] thereof; *and* he brought[7760] it to ruin.

14 [a]Howl, ye ships of Tarshish: for your strength is laid waste.

15 And it shall come to pass in that day, that Tyre shall be forgotten seventy years, according to the days of one king: after the end of seventy years [I]shall Tyre sing as an harlot.[2181]

---

17 [I]Or, *the LORD who covered thee with an excellent covering, and clothed thee gorgeously, shall surely* [II]Hebr. *the captivity of a man* [a]Esth. 7:8

18 [I]Hebr. *large of spaces*

20 [a]2Kgs. 18:18

22 [a]Job 12:14; Rev. 3:7

23 [a]Ezra 9:8

24 [I]Or, *instruments of viols*

1 [a]Jer. 25:22; 47:4; Ezek. 26–28; Amos 1:9; Zech. 9:2, 4 [b]Isa. 23:12

2 [I]Hebr. *silent*

3 [a]Ezek. 27:3

5 [a]Isa. 19:16

7 [I]Hebr. *from afar off* [a]Isa. 22:2

8 [a]Ezek. 28:2, 12

9 [I]Hebr. *to pollute*

10 [I]Hebr. *girdle*

11 [I]Or, *concerning a merchantman* [II]Hebr. *Canaan* [III]Or, *strengths*

12 [a]Rev. 18:22 [b]Isa. 23:1

13 [a]Ps. 72:9

14 [a]Isa. 23:11; Ezek. 27:25, 30

15 [I]Hebr. *it shall be unto Tyre as the song of a harlot*

16 Take an harp, go about the city, thou harlot that hast been forgotten; make sweet[3190] melody, sing many songs,[7892] that thou mayest be remembered.[2142]

17 And it shall come to pass after the end of seventy years, that the LORD will visit[6485] Tyre, and she shall turn[7725] to her hire, and [a]shall commit fornication[2181] with all the kingdoms of the world upon the face of the earth.[127]

18 And her merchandise and her hire [a]shall be holiness[6944] to the LORD: it shall not be treasured nor laid up; for her merchandise shall be for them that dwell before the LORD, to eat sufficiently, and for [I]durable clothing.

God's Judgment on the Whole Earth

24 Behold, the LORD maketh the earth empty, and maketh it waste, and [I]turneth[5753] it upside down,[6440] and scattereth abroad the inhabitants thereof.

2 And it shall be, as with the people,[5971] so with the [I][a]priest;[3548] as with the servant,[5650] so with his master;[113] as with the maid, so with her mistress;[1404] [b]as with the buyer, so with the seller; as with the lender, so with the borrower; as with the taker of usury, so with the giver of usury to him.

3 The land[776] shall be utterly[3632] emptied, and utterly spoiled: for the LORD hath spoken[1696] this word.[1697]

4 The earth[776] mourneth *and* fadeth away, the world[8398] languisheth *and* fadeth away, [I]the haughty people of the earth do languish.

5 [a]The earth also is defiled[2610] under the inhabitants thereof; because they have transgressed[5674] the laws, changed the ordinance,[2706] broken[6565] the everlasting[5769] covenant.[1285]

6 Therefore hath [a]the curse[423] devoured the earth, and they that dwell therein are desolate:[816] therefore the inhabitants of the earth are burned,[2787] and few men[582] left.[7604]

7 [a]The new wine mourneth, the vine languisheth, all the merry-hearted do sigh.

8 The mirth [a]of tabrets[8596] ceaseth,[7673] the noise[7588] of them that rejoice endeth, the joy of the harp ceaseth.

9 They shall not drink wine with a song;[7892] strong drink shall be bitter to them that drink it.

10 The city of confusion[8414] is broken down:[7665] every house[1004] is shut up, that no man may come in.

11 *There is* a crying for wine in the streets; all joy is darkened, the mirth of the land is gone.

12 In the city is left desolation,[8047] and the gate is smitten[3807] with destruction.[7591]

13 When thus it shall be in the midst[7130] of the land among the people, [a]*there shall be* as the shaking of an olive tree, *and* as the gleaning grapes when the vintage is done.[3615]

14 They shall lift up[5375] their voice, they shall sing for the majesty of the LORD, they shall cry aloud from the sea.

15 Wherefore glorify[3513] ye the LORD in the [I]fires,[217] *even* [a]the name of the LORD God[430] of Israel in the isles of the sea.

16 From the [I]uttermost part of the earth have we heard[8085] songs, *even* glory to the righteous.[6662] But I said,[559] [II]My leanness, my leanness, woe unto me! [a]the treacherous dealers have dealt treacherously;[898] yea, the treacherous dealers have dealt very treacherously.

17 [a]Fear,[6343] and the pit,[6354] and the snare,[6341] *are* upon thee, O inhabitant of the earth.

18 And it shall come to pass, *that* he who fleeth from the noise of the fear shall fall into the pit; and he that cometh up[5927] out of the midst of the pit shall be taken in the snare: for [a]the windows from on high are open, and [b]the foundations[4146] of the earth do shake.[7493]

19 [a]The earth is utterly broken down,[7489] the earth is clean dissolved,[6565] the earth is moved exceedingly.

20 The earth shall [a]reel to and fro like a drunkard, and shall be removed like a cottage; and the transgression[6588]

17 [a]Rev. 17:2
18 [I]Hebr. *old* [a]Zech. 14:20, 21
1 [I]Hebr. *perverteth the face thereof*
2 [I]Or, *prince* [a]Hos. 4:9 [b]Ezek. 7:12, 13
4 [I]Hebr. *the height of the people*
5 [a]Gen. 3:17; Num. 35:33
6 [a]Mal. 4:6
7 [a]Isa. 16:8, 9; Joel 1:10, 12
8 [a]Jer. 7:34; 16:9; 25:10; Ezek. 26:13; Hos. 2:11; Rev. 18:22
13 [a]Isa. 17:5, 6
15 [I]Or, valleys [a]Mal. 1:11
16 [I]Hebr. *wing* [II]Hebr. *Leanness to me,* or, *My secret to me* [a]Jer. 5:11
17 [a]1Kgs. 19:17; Jer. 48:43, 44; Amos 5:19
18 [a]Gen. 7:11; [b]Ps. 18:7
19 [a]Jer. 4:23
20 [a]Isa. 10:14

thereof shall be heavy[3513] upon it; and it shall fall, and not rise again.

21 And it shall come to pass in that day,[3117] *that* the LORD shall [I]punish[6485] the host[6635] of the high ones *that are* on high, [a]and the kings[4428] of the earth[127] upon the earth.

22 And they shall be gathered[622] together,[626] [I]*as* prisoners are gathered in the [II]pit,[953] and shall be shut up in the prison, and after many days shall they be [III]visited.[6485]

23 Then the [a]moon shall be confounded, and the sun ashamed,[954] when the LORD of hosts[6635] shall [b]reign[4427] in [c]mount Zion, and in Jerusalem, and [I]before his ancients[2204] gloriously.

Praise God!

25 O LORD, thou *art* my God;[430] [a]I will exalt thee, I will praise[3034] thy name; [b]for thou hast done[6213] wonderful[6382] *things*; [c]thy counsels of old *are* faithfulness[530] *and* truth.

2 For thou hast made[7760] [a]of a city an heap; *of* a defenced city a ruin: a palace[759] of strangers[2114] to be no city; it shall never be built.

3 Therefore shall[3513] the strong people[5971] [a]glorify[3513] thee, the city of the terrible nations[1471] shall fear[3372] thee.

4 For thou hast been a strength[4581] to the poor, a strength to the needy in his distress, [a]a refuge from the storm, a shadow from the heat, when the blast[7307] of the terrible ones *is* as a storm *against* the wall.

5 Thou shalt bring down the noise[7588] of strangers, as the heat in a dry place; *even* the heat with the shadow of a cloud: the branch of the terrible ones shall be brought low.

6 And in [a]this mountain shall[6213] [b]the LORD of hosts[6635] make[6213] unto [c]all people a feast[4960] of fat things,[8081] a feast of wines on the lees, of fat things full of marrow, of wines on the lees[8105] well refined.[2212]

7 And he will [I]destroy[1104] in this mountain the face of the covering [II]cast over all people, and [a]the vail that is spread over all nations.

8 He will [a]swallow up death[4194] in victory;[5331] and the Lord[136] GOD[3068] will [b]wipe away tears from off all faces; and the rebuke[2781] of his people shall he take away from off all the earth:[776] for the LORD hath spoken[1696] *it*.

9 And it shall be said[559] in that day, Lo, this *is* our God; [a]we have waited[6960] for him, and he will save[3467] us: this *is* the LORD; we have waited for him, [b]we will be glad and rejoice in his salvation.[3444]

10 For in this mountain shall the hand[3027] of the LORD rest, and Moab shall be [I]trodden down under him, even as straw is [II]trodden down for the dunghill.

11 And he shall spread forth his hands in the midst[7130] of them, as he that swimmeth spreadeth forth *his hands* to swim: and he shall bring down their pride together with the spoils of their hands.

12 And the [a]fortress of the high fort of thy walls shall he bring down, lay low, *and* bring to the ground,[776] *even* to the dust.[6083]

God's People Will Be Victorious

26 In [a]that day[3117] shall[7891] this song[7892] be sung[7891] in the land[776] of Judah; We have a strong city; [b]salvation[3444] will *God* appoint *for* walls and bulwarks.

2 [a]Open ye the gates, that the righteous[6662] nation[1471] which keepeth[8104] the [I]truth[529] may enter in.

3 Thou wilt keep[5341] *him* in [I][a]perfect peace, *whose* [II]mind[3336] *is* stayed *on thee:* because he trusteth[982] in thee.

4 Trust ye in the LORD for ever:[5957] [a]for in the LORD[3050] JEHOVAH[3068] *is* [I][b]everlasting[5769] strength:

5 For he bringeth down them that dwell on high; [a]the lofty city, he layeth it low; he layeth it low, *even* to the ground;[776] he bringeth it *even* to the dust.[6083]

---

21 [I]Hebr. *visit upon* [a]Ps. 76:12

22 [I]Hebr. *with the gathering of prisoners* [II]Or, *dungeon* [III]Or, *found wanting*

23 [I]Or, there shall be *glory before his ancients* [a]Isa. 13:10; 60:19; Ezek. 32:7; Joel 2:31; 3:15 [b]Rev. 10:4, 6 [c]Heb. 12:22

1 [a]Ex. 15:2; Ps. 118:28 [b]Ps. 98:1 [c]Num. 23:19

2 [a]Isa. 21:9; 23:13; Jer. 51:37

3 [a]Rev. 11:13

4 [a]Isa. 4:6

6 [a]Isa. 2:2, 3 [b]Prov. 9:2; Matt. 22:4 [c]Dan. 7:14; Matt. 8:11

7 [I]Hebr. *swallow up* [II]Hebr. *covered* [a]2Cor. 3:15; Eph. 4:18

8 [a]Hos. 13:14; 1Cor. 15:54; Rev. 20:14; 21:4 [b]Rev. 7:17; 21:4

9 [a]Gen. 49:18; Titus 2:13 [b]Ps. 20:5

10 [I]Or, *threshed* [II]Or, *threshed in Madmenah*

12 [a]Isa. 26:5

1 [a]Isa. 2:11 [b]Isa. 60:18

2 [I]Hebr. *truths* [a]Ps. 118:19, 20

3 [I]Hebr. *peace, peace* [II]Or, *thought,* or, *imagination* [a]Isa. 57:19

4 [I]Hebr. *the rock of ages* [a]Isa. 45:17 [b]Deut. 32:4

5 [a]Isa. 25:12; 32:19

6 The foot shall tread it down, *even* the feet of the poor, *and* the steps of the needy.

7 The way[734] of the just *is* uprightness:4339 [a]thou, most upright,[3477] dost weigh the path of the just.

8 Yea, [a]in the way of thy judgments,[4941] O LORD, have we waited[6960] for thee; the desire of *our* soul[5315] *is* to thy name, and to the remembrance[2143] of thee.

9 [a]With my soul have I desired thee in the night;[3915] yea, with my spirit[7307] within[7130] me will I seek thee early: for when thy judgments *are* in the earth,[776] the inhabitants of the world[8398] will learn[3925] righteousness.[6664]

10 [a]Let favour be shewed[2603] to the wicked,[7563] *yet* will he not learn righteousness; in [b]the land of uprightness will he deal unjustly,[5765] and will not behold[7200] the majesty of the LORD.

11 LORD, *when* thy hand[3027] is lifted up, [a]they will not see:[2372] *but* they shall see, and be ashamed[954] for *their* envy[7068] [I]at the people;[5971] yea, the fire of thine enemies shall devour them.

12 LORD, thou wilt ordain peace for us: for thou also hast wrought all our works [I]in us.

13 O LORD our God, [a]*other* lords beside thee have had dominion[1166] over us: *but* by thee only will we make mention of thy name.

14 *They are* dead,[4191] they shall not live;[2421] *they are* deceased,[7496] they shall not rise: therefore hast thou visited[6485] and destroyed[8045] them, and made[6] all their memory[2143] to perish.[6]

15 Thou hast increased the nation, O LORD, thou hast increased the nation: thou art glorified:[3513] thou hadst removed *it* far *unto* all the ends of the earth.

16 LORD, [a]in trouble have they visited thee, they poured out a [I]prayer[3908] *when* thy chastening[4148] *was* upon them.

17 Like as [a]a woman with child, *that* draweth near the time[6256] of her delivery, is in pain,[2342] *and* crieth out in her pangs;[2256] so have we been in thy sight, O LORD.

18 We have been with child, we have been in pain, we have as it were brought forth wind;[7307] we have not wrought any deliverance[3444] in the earth; neither have [a]the inhabitants of the world fallen.[5307]

🔑 19 [a]Thy dead[7496] *men* shall live, *together with* my dead body[5038] shall they arise. [b]Awake and sing, ye that dwell[7931] in dust: for thy dew *is as* the dew of herbs, and the earth shall cast out[5307] the dead.

20 Come, my people, [a]enter thou into thy chambers, and shut thy doors about thee: hide thyself as it were [b]for a little moment, until the indignation[2195] be overpast.[5674]

21 For, behold, the LORD [a]cometh out of his place to punish[6485] the inhabitants of the earth for their iniquity:[5771] the earth also shall disclose[1540] her [I]blood,[1818] and shall no more cover[3680] her slain.[2026]

The Deliverance of Israel

27 In that day[3117] the LORD with his sore[7186] and great and strong[2389] sword[2719] shall punish[6485] leviathan the [I]piercing serpent,[5175] [a]even leviathan that crooked serpent; and he shall slay[2026] [b]the dragon[8577] that *is* in the sea.

2 In that day [a]sing ye unto her, [b]A vineyard of red wine.

3 [a]I the LORD do keep[5341] it; I will water it every moment: lest *any* hurt it, I will keep it night[3915] and day.

4 Fury *is* not in me: who would set [a]the briers *and* thorns against me in battle? I would [I]go through them, I would burn them together.

5 Or let him take hold [a]of my strength, *that* he may [b]make[6213] peace with me; *and* he shall make peace with me.

6 He shall cause them that come of Jacob [a]to take root: Israel shall blossom and bud, and fill the face of the world[8398] with fruit.

---

7 [a]Ps. 37:23
8 [a]Isa. 64:5
9 [a]Ps. 63:6; Song 3:1
10 [a]Eccl. 8:12; Rom. 2:4 [b]Ps. 143:10
11 [I]Or, *toward thy people* [a]Job 34:27; Ps. 28:5; Isa. 5:12
12 [I]Or, *for us*
13 [a]2Chr. 12:8
16 [I]Hebr. *secret speech* [a]Hos. 5:15
17 [a]Isa. 13:8; John 16:21
18 [a]Ps. 17:14
19 [a]Ezek. 37:1 [b]Dan. 12:2
20 [a]Ex. 12:22, 23 [b]Ps. 30:5; Isa. 54:7, 8; 2Cor. 4:17
21 [I]Hebr. *bloods* [a]Mic. 1:3; Jude 1:14
1 [I]Or, *crossing like a bar* [a]Ps. 74:13, 14 [b]Isa. 51:9; Ezek. 29:3; 32:2
2 [a]Isa. 5:1 [b]Ps. 80:8; Jer. 2:21
3 [a]Ps. 121:4, 5
4 [I]Or, *march against* [a]2Sam. 23:6; Isa. 9:18
5 [a]Isa. 25:4 [b]Job 22:21
6 [a]Isa. 37:31; Hos. 14:5, 6

🔑 **26:19** See note on Daniel 12:1–4.

7 Hath he smitten[5221] him, [I]as he
smote[4347] those that smote[5221] him? *or* is
he slain[2026] according to the slaughter[2027]
of them that are slain by him?
8 [a]In measure, [I]when it shooteth
forth, thou wilt debate[7378] with it: [IIb]he
stayeth his rough[7186] wind[7307] in the day
of the east wind.
9 By this therefore shall[3722] the
iniquity[5771] of Jacob be purged;[3722] and
this *is* all the fruit to take away his
sin;[2403] when he maketh[7760] all the stones
of the altar[4196] as chalkstones that are
beaten in sunder, the groves[842] and
[I]images[2553] shall not stand up.
10 Yet the defenced city *shall be* desolate, *and* the habitation forsaken, and
left[5800] like a wilderness: [a]there shall the
calf feed, and there shall he lie down,
and consume[3615] the branches thereof.
11 When the boughs thereof are
withered,[3001] they shall be broken off:[7665]
the women[802] come, *and* set them on fire:
for [a]it *is* a people[5971] of no understanding: therefore he that made[6213] them will
not have mercy[7355] on them, and [b]he that
formed[3335] them will shew them no
favour.[2603]
12 And it shall come to pass in that
day, *that* the LORD shall beat off from
the channel of the river unto the stream
of Egypt, and ye shall be gathered[3950]
one by one, O ye children[1121] of Israel.
13 [a]And it shall come to pass in that
day, [b]*that* the great trumpet shall be
blown,[8628] and they shall come which
were ready to perish[6] in the land[776] of
Assyria, and the outcasts in the land of
Egypt, and shall worship[7812] the LORD in
the holy[6944] mount at Jerusalem.

The Judgment of Ephraim

28 Woe to [a]the crown of pride, to
the drunkards of Ephraim, whose
[b]glorious[6643] beauty[8597] *is* a fading flower,
which *are* on the head[7218] of the fat[8081]
valleys of them that are [I]overcome[1986]
with wine!
2 Behold, the LORD[136] hath a
mighty[2389] and strong one, [a]which as a
tempest of hail *and* a destroying[6986]
storm,[8178] as a flood of mighty waters
overflowing,[7857] shall cast down to the
earth[776] with the hand.[3027]
3 [a]The crown of pride, the drunkards of Ephraim, shall be trodden [I]under
feet:
4 And [a]the glorious beauty, which *is*
on the head of the fat valley, shall be a
fading flower, *and* as the hasty fruit before the summer; which *when* he that
looketh upon it seeth,[7200] while it is yet
in his hand[3709] he [I]eateth it up.
5 In that day[3117] shall the LORD of
hosts[6635] be for a crown of glory, and
for a diadem 6843 of beauty, unto the
residue[7605] of his people,[5971]
6 And for a spirit[7307] of judgment[4941] to him that sitteth in judgment,
and for strength 1369 to them that turn[7725]
the battle to the gate.

A Warning to Jerusalem

7 But they also [a]have erred[7686]
through wine, and through strong drink
are out of the way;[8582] [b]the priest[3548] and
the prophet[5030] have erred[7686] through
strong drink, they are swallowed up[1104]
of wine, they are out of the way through
strong drink; they err[7686] in vision,[7203]
they stumble *in* judgment.
8 For all tables are full of vomit *and*
filthiness, *so that there is* no place *clean.*
9 [a]Whom shall he teach[3384] knowledge? and whom shall he make to
understand[995] [I]doctrine? 8052 *them that are*
weaned from the milk, *and* drawn from
the breasts.
10 For precept 6673 [I]*must be* upon precept, precept upon precept; line 6957 upon
line, line upon line; here a little, *and* there
a little:
11 For with [Ia]stammering 3934 lips[8193]
and another tongue [II]will he speak[1696] to
this people.
12 To whom he said,[559] This *is* the
rest *wherewith* ye may cause the weary to
rest; and this *is* the refreshing: yet they
would[14] not hear.[8085]
13 But the word[1697] of the LORD was
unto them precept upon precept, precept
upon precept; line upon line, line upon

7 IHebr. *according to the stroke of those*
8 IOr, *when thou sendest it forth* IIOr, *when he removeth it* [a]Job 23:6; Ps. 6:1; Jer. 10:24; 30:11; 46:28; 1Cor. 10:13 [b]Ps. 78:38
9 IOr, *sun images*
10 [a]Isa. 17:2; 32:14
11 [a]Deut. 32:28; Isa. 1:3; Jer. 8:7 [b]Deut. 32:18; Isa. 43:1, 7; 44:2, 21, 24
13 [a]Isa. 2:11 [b]Matt. 24:31; Rev. 11:15
1 IHebr. *broken* [a]Isa. 28:3 [b]Isa. 28:4
2 [a]Isa. 30:30; Ezek. 13:11
3 IHebr. *with feet* [a]Isa. 28:1
4 IHebr. *swalloweth* [a]Isa. 28:1
7 [a]Prov. 20:1; Hos. 4:11 [b]Isa. 56:10, 12
9 IHebr. *the hearing* [a]Jer. 6:10
10 IOr, hath been
11 IHebr. *stammerings of lips* IIOr, *he hath spoken* [a]1Cor. 14:21

line; here a little, *and* there a little; that they might go, and fall[3782] backward, and be broken,[7665] and snared,[3369] and taken.

The Cornerstone

14 Wherefore hear the word of the LORD, ye scornful men,[582] that rule[4910] this people which *is* in Jerusalem.

15 Because ye have said, We have made[3772] a covenant[1285] with death,[4194] and with hell[7585] are we at agreement;[2374] when the overflowing scourge7885 shall pass through, it shall not come unto us: [a]for we have made[7760] lies[3577] our refuge, and under falsehood have we hid ourselves:

🔑 16 Therefore thus saith the LORD GOD, Behold, I lay in Zion for a foundation[3248] [a]a stone, a tried[976] stone, a precious corner *stone,* a sure[3245] foundation;[4143] he that believeth[539] shall not make haste.

17 Judgment also will I lay[7760] to the line, and righteousness[6666] to the plummet:4949 and the hail shall sweep away [a]the refuge of lies, and the waters shall overflow[7857] the hiding place.

18 And your covenant with death shall be disannulled,[3722] and your agreement[2380] with hell shall not stand; when the overflowing scourge7752 shall pass through, then ye shall be [I]trodden down by it.

19 From the time that it goeth forth[5674] it shall take you: for morning by morning shall it pass over,[5674] by day and by night:[3915] and it shall be a vexation2113 only [I]*to* understand the report.

20 For the bed is shorter than that *a man* can stretch himself *on it:* and the covering[4541] narrower than that he can wrap himself[3664] *in it.*

21 For the LORD shall rise up as *in* mount [a]Perazim, he shall be wroth as *in* the valley of [b]Gibeon, that he may do[6213] his work, [c]his strange[2114] work; and bring to pass[5647] his act,[5656] his strange[5237] act.

22 Now therefore be ye not mockers,[3887] lest your bands be made strong:[2388] for I have heard[8085] from the Lord GOD of hosts [a]a consumption,[3617] even determined upon the whole earth.

23 Give ye ear, and hear my voice; hearken,[7181] and hear my speech.[565]

24 Doth the plowman plow all day to sow? doth he open and break the clods of his ground?[127]

25 When he hath made plain the face thereof, doth he not cast abroad the fitches,7100 and scatter the cummin,3646 and cast in [I]the principal wheat and the appointed barley and the [II]rie in their [III]place?

26 [I]For his God[430] doth instruct[3256] him to discretion,[4941] *and* doth teach him.

27 For the fitches are not threshed with a threshing instrument, neither is a cart wheel[212] turned about upon the cummin; but the fitches are beaten out with a staff,[4294] and the cummin with a rod.[7626]

28 Bread *corn* is bruised; because he will not ever be threshing it, nor break *it with* the wheel[1536] of his cart, nor bruise it *with* his horsemen.

29 This also cometh forth from the LORD of hosts, [a]*which* is wonderful[6381] in counsel,[6098] *and* excellent in working.[8454]

The Fate of Jerusalem

29 [I]Woe [a]to Ariel, to Ariel, [II]the city [b]*where* David dwelt2583 add ye year to year; let them [III]kill[5362] sacrifices.

2 Yet I will distress6693 Ariel, and there shall be heaviness and sorrow: and it shall be unto me as Ariel.

3 And I will camp2583 against thee round about, and will lay siege against thee with a mount, and I will raise forts against thee.

4 And thou shalt be brought down, *and* shalt speak[1696] out of the ground,[776]

---

15 [a]Amos 2:4
16 [a]Gen. 49:24; Ps. 118:22; Matt. 21:42; Acts 4:11; Rom. 9:33; 10:11; Eph. 2:20; 1Pet. 2:6-8
17 [a]Isa. 28:15
18 [I]Hebr. *a treading down to it*
19 [I]Or, *where he shall make* you *to understand doctrine*
21 [a]2Sam. 5:20; 1Chr. 14:11 [b]Josh. 10:10, 12; 2Sam. 5:25; 1Chr. 14:16 [c]Lam. 3:33
22 [a]Isa. 10:22, 23; Dan. 9:27
25 [I]Or, *the wheat in the principal* place, *and barley in the appointed* place [II]Or, *spelt* [III]Hebr. *border*
26 [I]Or, *And he bindeth it in such sort as his God doth teach him*
29 [a]Ps. 92:5; Jer. 32:19
1 [I]Or, *O Ariel,* that is, *the lion of God* [II]Or, *of the city* [III]Hebr. *cut off the heads* [a]Ezek. 43:15, 16 [b]2Sam. 5:9

🔑 **28:16** See note on Isaiah 8:14.

and thy speech[565] shall be low out of the dust,[6083] and thy voice shall be, as of one that hath a familiar spirit,[178] [a]out of the ground, and thy speech shall [I]whisper out of the dust.

5 Moreover the multitude of thy [a]strangers[2114] shall be like small[1851] dust, and the multitude of the terrible ones *shall be* [b]as chaff that passeth away:[5674] yea, it shall be [c]at an instant suddenly.

6 [a]Thou shalt be visited[6485] of the LORD of hosts[6635] with thunder, and with earthquake,[7494] and great noise, with storm and tempest, and the flame of devouring fire.

7 [a]And the multitude of all the nations[1471] that fight[6633] against Ariel, even all that fight against her and her munition, and that distress her, shall be [b]as a dream of a night[3915] vision.[2377]

8 [a]It shall even be as when an hungry *man* dreameth, and, behold, he eateth; but he awaketh, and his soul[5315] is empty: or as when a thirsty man dreameth, and, behold, he drinketh; but he awaketh, and, behold, *he is* faint,[5889] and his soul hath appetite: so shall the multi tude of all the nations be, that fight against mount Zion.

The Blindness and Hypocrisy of Israel

9 Stay yourselves,[4102] and wonder; [I]cry ye out,[8173] and cry: [a]they are drunken, [b]but not with wine; they stagger, but not with strong drink.

10 For [a]the LORD hath poured out[5258] upon you the spirit[7307] of deep sleep, and hath [b]closed your eyes: the prophets[5030] and your [I]rulers,[7218] [c]the seers[2374] hath he covered.[3680]

11 And the vision[2380] of all is become[1961] unto you as the words of a [I]book[5612] [a]that is sealed, which *men* deliver to one that is learned,[3045] saying, Read[7121] this, I pray thee:[4994] [b]and he saith, I cannot; for it *is* sealed:

12 And the book is delivered to him that is not learned, saying, Read this, I pray thee: and he saith, I am not learned.

13 Wherefore the LORD[136] said, [a]Forasmuch as this people[5971] draw near[5066] *me* with their mouth,[6310] and with their lips[8193] do honour[3513] me, but have removed their heart[3820] far from me, and their fear[3374] toward me is taught[3925] by [b]the precept[4687] of men:[582]

14 [a]Therefore, behold, [I]I will proceed to do a marvellous work among this people, *even* a marvellous work[6381] and a wonder: [b]for the wisdom[2451] of their wise[2450] *men* shall perish,[6] and the understanding[998] of their prudent[995] *men* shall be hid.

Hope

15 [a]Woe unto them that seek deep to hide their counsel[6098] from the LORD, and their works are in the dark,[4285] and [b]they say, Who seeth[7200] us? and who knoweth us?

16 Surely your turning of things upside down[2017] shall be esteemed[2803] as the potter's[3335] clay: for shall the [a]work say of him that made[6213] it, He made me not? or shall the thing framed[3336] say of him that framed it, He had no understanding?[995]

17 *Is* it not yet a very little while, and [a]Lebanon shall be turned into a fruitful field, and the fruitful field shall be esteemed as a forest?

18 And [a]in that day[3117] shall the deaf hear[8085] the words of the book, and the eyes of the blind shall see out of obscurity,[652] and out of darkness.[2822]

19 [a]The meek also [I]shall increase *their* joy in the LORD, and [b]the poor among men[120] shall rejoice in the Holy One[6918] of Israel.

20 For the terrible one is brought to nought,[656] and [a]the scorner[3887] is consumed,[3615] and all that [b]watch for iniquity[205] are cut off:[3772]

21 That make a man an offender[2398] for a word,[1697] and [a]lay a snare[6983] for him that reproveth[3198] in the gate, and turn aside the just [b]for a thing of nought.[8414]

22 Therefore thus saith the LORD, [a]who redeemed[6299] Abraham, concerning the house of Jacob, Jacob shall not now

4 [I]Hebr. *peep, or, chirp* [a]Isa. 8:19
5 [a]Isa. 25:5 [b]Job 21:18; Isa. 17:13 [c]Isa. 30:13
6 [a]Isa. 28:2; 30:30
7 [a]Isa. 37:36 [b]Job 20:8
8 [a]Ps. 73:20
9 [I]Or, *take your pleasure, and riot* [a]Isa. 28:7, 8 [b]Isa. 51:21
10 [I]Hebr. *heads* Isa. 3:2; Jer. 26:8 [a]Rom. 11:8 [b]Ps. 69:23; Isa. 6:10 [c]1Sam. 9:9
11 [I]Or, *letter* [a]Isa. 8:16 [b]Dan. 12:4, 9; Rev. 5:1-5, 9; 6:1
13 [a]Ezek. 33:31; Matt. 15:8, 9; Mark 7:6, 7
14 [I]Hebr. *I will add* [a]Hab. 1:5 [b]Jer. 49:7; Obad. 1:8; 1Cor. 1:19
15 [a]Isa. 30:1 [b]Ps. 94:7
16 [a]Isa. 45:9; Rom. 9:20
17 [a]Isa. 32:15
18 [a]Isa. 35:5
19 [I]Hebr. *shall add* [a]Isa. 61:1 [b]James 2:5
20 [a]Isa. 28:14, 22 [b]Mic. 2:1
21 [a]Amos 5:10, 12 [b]Prov. 28:21
22 [a]Josh. 24:3

be ashamed,[954] neither shall his face now wax pale.

23 But when he seeth his children, [a]the work of mine hands,[3027] in the midst[7130] of him, they shall sanctify[6942] my name, and sanctify the Holy One of Jacob, and shall fear[6206] the God[430] of Israel.

24 They also [a]that erred[8582] in spirit [I]shall come to understanding, and they that murmured shall learn[3925] doctrine.[3948]

Reliance Upon Egypt Is Vain

30 Woe to the rebellious[5637] children, saith[5002] the LORD, [a]that take counsel,[6098] but not of me; and that cover[5258] with a covering,[4541] but not of my spirit,[7307] [b]that they may add sin[2403] to sin:

2 [a]That walk to go down into Egypt, and [b]have not asked[7592] at my mouth;[6310] to strengthen themselves in the strength of Pharaoh, and to trust[2620] in the shadow of Egypt!

3 [a]Therefore shall the strength of Pharaoh be your shame, and the trust[2622] in the shadow of Egypt *your* confusion.

4 For his princes[8269] were at [a]Zoan, and his ambassadors[4397] came[5060] to Hanes.

5 [a]They were all ashamed[954] of a people[5971] *that* could not profit them, nor be an help nor profit, but a shame, and also a reproach.[2781]

6 [a]The burden[4853] of the beasts of the south: into the land[776] of trouble and anguish,[6695] from whence *come* the young and old lion, [b]the viper and fiery[8314] flying serpent, they will carry[5375] their riches[2428] upon the shoulders of young asses, and their treasures upon the bunches of camels, to a people *that* shall not profit *them.*

7 [a]For the Egyptians shall help in vain, and to no purpose: therefore have I cried[7121] [I]concerning this, [b]Their strength *is* to sit still.[767]

8 Now go, [a]write it before them in a table, and note[2710] it in a book,[5612] that it may be for [I]the time to come for ever[5703] and ever:

9 That [a]this *is* a rebellious[4805] people, lying[3586] children, children *that* will not hear[8085] the law[8451] of the LORD:

10 [a]Which say to the seers, See not; and to the prophets,[2374] Prophesy[5012] not unto us right things,[5228] [b]speak unto us smooth things, prophesy deceits:

11 Get you out of the way,[1870] turn aside out of the path,[734] cause[7673] the Holy One[6918] of Israel to cease[7673] from before us.

12 Wherefore thus saith[559] the Holy One of Israel, Because ye despise[3988] this word, and trust[982] in [I]oppression and perverseness, and stay[8172] thereon:

13 Therefore this iniquity[5771] shall be to you [a]as a breach ready to fall,[5307] swelling out in a high wall, whose breaking [b]cometh suddenly at an instant.

14 And [a]he shall break[7665] it as the breaking of [I]the potters' vessel that *is* broken in pieces;[3807] he shall not spare: so that there shall not be found in the bursting of it a sherd[2789] to take fire from the hearth, or to take water *withal* out of the pit.

15 For thus saith the Lord[136] GOD, the Holy One of Israel; [a]In returning and rest shall ye be saved;[3467] in quietness[8252] and in confidence[985] shall be your strength: [b]and ye would[14] not.

16 But ye said, No; for we will flee upon horses; therefore shall ye flee: and, We will ride upon the swift; therefore shall they that pursue you be swift.

17 [a]One thousand *shall flee* at the rebuke[1606] of one; at the rebuke of five shall ye flee: till ye be left[3498] as [I]a beacon upon the top[7218] of a mountain, and as an ensign on an hill.

18 And therefore will the LORD wait, that he may be gracious[2603] unto you, and therefore will he be exalted, that he may have mercy[7355] upon you: for the LORD *is* a God[430] of judgment:[4941] [a]blessed[835] *are* all they that wait for him.

God Will Bless His People

19 For the people [a]shall dwell in Zion at Jerusalem: thou shalt weep no more: he will be very gracious unto thee at the

---

23 [a]Isa. 19:25; 45:11; 60:21; Eph. 2:10
24 [I]Hebr. *shall know understanding* [a]Isa. 28:7
1 [a]Isa. 29:15 [b]Deut. 29:19
2 [a]Isa. 31:1 [b]Num. 27:21; Josh. 9:14; 1Kgs. 22:7; Jer. 21:2; 42:2, 20
3 [a]Isa. 20:5; Jer. 37:5, 7
4 [a]Isa. 19:11
5 [a]Jer. 2:36
6 [a]Isa. 57:9; Hos. 8:9; 12:1 [b]Deut. 8:15
7 [I]Or, *to her* [a]Jer. 37:7 [b]Isa. 7:4; 30:15
8 [I]Hebr. *the latter day* [a]Hab. 2:2
9 [a]Deut. 32:20; Isa. 1:4; 30:1
10 [a]Jer. 11:21; Amos 2:12; 7:13; Mic. 2:6 [b]1Kgs. 22:13; Mic. 2:11
12 [I]Or, *fraud*
13 [a]Ps. 62:3 [b]Isa. 29:5
14 [I]Hebr. *the bottle of potters* [a]Ps. 2:9; Jer. 19:11
15 [a]Isa. 7:4; 30:7 [b]Matt. 23:37
17 [I]Or, *a tree bereft of branches,* or, *boughs:* or, *a mast* [a]Lev. 26:8; Deut. 28:25; 32:30; Josh. 23:10
18 [a]Ps. 2:12; 34:8; Prov. 16:20; Jer. 17:7
19 [a]Isa. 65:9

voice of thy cry; when he shall hear it, he will answer thee.

20 And *though* the Lord give you [a]the bread of adversity,6862 and the water of [I]affliction,3906 yet shall not [b]thy teachers be removed into a corner any more, but thine eyes shall see thy teachers:

21 And thine ears[241] shall hear a word behind thee, saying, This *is* the way, walk ye in it, when ye [a]turn to the right hand,[541] and when ye turn to the left.

22 [a]Ye shall defile[2930] also the covering of [I]thy graven images of silver, and the ornament of thy molten images[4541] of gold: thou shalt [II]cast them away as a menstruous cloth; [b]thou shalt say unto it, Get thee hence.

23 [a]Then shall he give the rain of thy seed,[2233] that thou shalt sow the ground[127] withal; and bread of the increase of the earth,[127] and it shall be fat and plenteous: in that day[3117] shall thy cattle feed in large pastures.[3733]

24 The oxen likewise and the young asses that ear[5647] the ground shall eat [I]clean provender,1098 which hath been winnowed2219 with the shovel and with the fan.

25 And there shall be [a]upon every high mountain, and upon every [I]high[5375] hill, rivers *and* streams of waters in the day of the great slaughter,[2027] when the towers fall.

26 Moreover [a]the light[216] of the moon shall be as the light of the sun, and the light of the sun shall be sevenfold, as the light of seven days, in the day that the LORD bindeth up[2280] the breach[7667] of his people, and healeth the stroke[4273] of their wound.[4347]

Assyria's Punishment

27 Behold, the name of the LORD cometh from far, burning *with* his anger,[639] [I]and the burden *thereof is* [II]heavy: his lips[8193] are full of indignation,[2195] and his tongue as a devouring fire:

28 And [a]his breath,[7307] as an overflowing[7857] stream, [b]shall reach to the midst of the neck, to sift the nations[1471] with the sieve of vanity:[7723] and *there shall be* [c]a bridle in the jaws of the people, causing *them* to err.[8582]

29 Ye shall have a song,[7892] as in the night[3915] [a]*when* a holy solemnity is kept; and gladness of heart,3824 as when one goeth with a pipe to come into [b]the mountain of the LORD, to the [I][c]mighty One of Israel.

30 [a]And the LORD shall cause [I]his glorious voice to be heard,[8085] and shall shew[7200] the lighting down of his arm, with the indignation[2197] of *his* anger, and *with* the flame of a devouring fire, *with* scattering, and tempest, [b]and hailstones.

31 For [a]through the voice of the LORD shall the Assyrian be beaten down,[2865] [b]*which* smote[5221] with a rod.[7626]

32 And [I]*in* every place where the grounded[4145] staff[4294] shall pass, which the LORD shall [II]lay upon him, *it* shall be with tabrets8596 and harps: and in battles of [a]shaking[8573] will he fight [III]with it.

33 [a]For Tophet *is* ordained [I]of old; yea, for the king it is prepared;[3559] he hath made *it* deep *and* large: the pile thereof *is* fire and much wood; the breath[5397] of the LORD, like a stream of brimstone,1614 doth kindle it.

Egypt Is Frail

31 Woe to them [a]that go down to Egypt for help; and [b]stay[8172] on horses, and trust[982] in chariots, because *they are* many; and in horsemen, because they are very strong; but they look not unto the Holy One[6918] of Israel, [c]neither seek the LORD!

2 Yet he also *is* wise,[2450] and will bring evil,[7451] and [a]will not [I]call back his words: but will arise against the house of the evildoers,[7489] and against the help of them that work6466 iniquity.[205]

3 Now the Egyptians *are* [a]men, and not God;[410] and their horses flesh,[1320] and not spirit.[7307] When the LORD shall stretch out his hand,[3027] both he that helpeth shall fall,[3782] and he that is holpen5826 shall fall down, and they all shall fail[3615] together.

20 [I]Or, *oppression* [a]1Kgs. 22:27; Ps. 127:2 [b]Ps. 74:9; Amos 8:11

21 [a]Josh. 1:7

22 [I]Hebr. *the graven images of thy silver* [II]Hebr. *scatter* [a]2Chr. 31:1; Isa. 2:20; 31:7 [b]Hos. 14:8

23 [a]Matt. 6:33; 1Tim. 4:8

24 [I]Or, *savory;* Hebr. *leavened*

25 [I]Hebr. *lifted up* [a]Isa. 2:14, 15; 44:3

26 [a]Isa. 60:19, 20

27 [I]Or, *and the grievousness of flame* [II]Hebr. *heaviness*

28 [a]Isa. 11:4; 2Thess. 2:8 [b]Isa. 8:8 [c]Isa. 37:20

29 [I]Hebr. *Rock* [a]Ps. 42:4 [b]Isa. 2:3 [c]Deut. 32:4

30 [I]Hebr. *the glory of his voice* [a]Isa. 29:6 [b]Isa. 28:2; 32:19

31 [a]Isa. 37:36 [b]Isa. 10:5, 24

32 [I]Hebr. *every passing of the rod founded* [II]Hebr. *cause to rest upon him* [III]Or, *against them* [a]Isa. 11:15; 19:16

33 [I]Hebr. *from yesterday* [a]Jer. 7:31; 19:6

1 [a]Isa. 30:2; 36:6; Ezek. 17:15 [b]Ps. 20:7; Isa. 36:9 [c]Dan. 9:13; Hos. 7:7

2 [I]Hebr. *remove* [a]Num. 23:19

3 [a]Ps. 146:3, 5

4 For thus hath the LORD spoken unto me, [a]Like as the lion and the young lion roaring[1897] on his prey, when a multitude of shepherds is called forth[7121] against him, *he* will not be afraid[2865] of their voice, nor abase himself6031 for the [I]noise of them: [b]so shall the LORD of hosts[6635] come down to fight[6633] for mount Zion, and for the hill thereof.

5 [a]As birds flying, so will the LORD of hosts defend Jerusalem; [b]defending also he will deliver[5337] *it; and* passing over[5674] he will preserve[4422] *it.*

6 Turn[7725] ye unto *him from* whom the children of Israel have [a]deeply revolted.

7 For in that day[3117] every man shall [a]cast away[3988] his idols[457] of silver, and [I]his idols of gold, which your own hands have made[6213] unto you *for* [b]a sin.[2399]

8 Then shall the Assyrian [a]fall with the sword,[2719] not of a mighty man;[376] and the sword, not of a mean man,[120] shall devour him: but he shall flee [I]from the sword, and his young men shall be [II]discomfited.

9 And [I][a]he shall pass over[5674] to [II]his strong hold for fear,[4032] and his princes[8269] shall be afraid of the ensign, saith the LORD, whose fire217 *is* in Zion, and his furnace in Jerusalem.

The Righteous King

32 Behold, [a]a king shall reign[4427] in righteousness,[6664] and princes[8269] shall rule[8323] in judgment.[4941]

2 And a man shall be as an hiding place from the wind, and [a]a covert5643 from the tempest; as rivers of water in a dry place, as the shadow of a [I]great rock in a weary land.[776]

3 And [a]the eyes of them that see shall not be dim, and the ears[241] of them that hear[8085] shall hearken.[7181]

4 The heart3824 also of the [I]rash shall understand[995] knowledge,[1847] and the tongue of the stammerers shall be ready to speak [II]plainly.

5 The vile person5036 shall be no more called[7121] liberal,[5081] nor the churl3596 said *to be* bountiful.

6 For the vile person will speak villany,5039 and his heart[3820] will work iniquity,[205] to practise hypocrisy,[2612] and to utter error8442 against the LORD, to make empty the soul[5315] of the hungry, and he will cause the drink of the thirsty to fail.

7 The instruments also of the churl *are* evil:[7451] he deviseth[3289] wicked devices to destroy[2254] the poor with lying words,[561] even [I]when the needy speaketh right.[4941]

8 But the liberal deviseth liberal things; and by liberal things shall he [I]stand.

Judgment and Restoration

9 Rise up, ye women[802] [a]that are at ease; hear my voice, ye careless[982] daughters; give ear[238] unto my speech.[565]

10 [I]Many days and years shall ye be troubled, ye careless women: for the vintage shall fail,[3615] the gathering[625] shall not come.

11 Tremble,[2729] ye women that are at ease; be troubled, ye careless ones: strip you, and make you bare, and gird *sackcloth* upon *your* loins.

12 They shall lament for the teats, for [I]the pleasant fields,[7704] for the fruitful vine.

13 [a]Upon the land[127] of my people[5971] shall come up[5927] thorns *and* briers; [I]yea, upon all the houses of joy *in* [b]the joyous city:

14 [a]Because the palaces[759] shall be forsaken;[5203] the multitude of the city shall be left;[5800] the [I]forts and towers shall be for dens for ever,[5769] a joy of wild asses, a pasture of flocks;

15 Until [a]the spirit[7307] be poured upon us from on high, and [b]the wilderness be a fruitful field, and the fruitful field be counted[2803] for a forest.

16 Then judgment shall dwell[7931] in the wilderness, and righteousness[6666] remain in the fruitful field.

17 [a]And the work of righteousness shall be peace; and the effect[5656] of righteousness quietness[8252] and assurance[983] for ever.

18 And my people shall dwell in a

---

4 [I]Or, *multitude* [a]Hos. 11:10; Amos 3:8 [b]Isa. 42:13
5 [a]Deut. 32:11; Ps. 91:4 [b]Ps. 37:40
6 [a]Hos. 9:9
7 [I]Hebr. *the idols of this gold* [a]Isa. 2:20; 30:22 [b]1Kgs. 12:30
8 [I]Or, *for the fear of the sword* [II]Or, *tributary;* Hebr. *for melting,* or, *tribute* [a]2Kgs. 19:35, 36; Isa. 37:36
9 [I]Hebr. *his rock shall pass away for fear* [II]Or, *his strength* [a]Isa. 37:37

1 [a]Ps. 45:1; Jer. 23:5; Hos. 3:5; Zech. 9:9
2 [I]Hebr. *heavy* [a]Isa. 4:6; 25:4
3 [a]Isa. 29:18; 35:5, 6
4 [I]Hebr. *hasty* [II]Or, *elegantly*
7 [I]Or, *when he speaketh against the poor in judgment*
8 [I]Or, *be established*
9 [a]Amos 6:1
10 [I]Hebr. *Days above a year*
12 [I]Hebr. *the fields of desire*
13 [I]Or, *burning upon* [a]Isa. 34:13; Hos. 9:6 [b]Isa. 22:2
14 [I]Or, *cliffs and watchtowers* [a]Isa. 27:10
15 [a]Ps. 104:30; Joel 2:28 [b]Isa. 29:17; 35:2
17 [a]James 3:18

peaceable habitation, and in sure dwellings,[4908] and in quiet resting places;

19 [a]When it shall hail, coming down [b]on the forest; [I]and the city shall be low in a low place.

20 Blessed[835] *are* ye that sow beside all waters, that send forth *thither* the feet of [a]the ox and the ass.

Salvation

33 Woe to thee [a]that spoilest, and thou *wast* not spoiled;[7703] and dealest treacherously,[898] and they dealt not treacherously with thee! [b]when thou shalt cease[8552] to spoil, thou shalt be spoiled; *and* when thou shalt make an end to deal treacherously, they shall deal treacherously with thee.

2 O LORD, be gracious unto us; [a]we have waited[6960] for thee: be thou their arm every morning, our salvation[3444] also in the time[6256] of trouble.

3 At the noise of the tumult the people[5971] fled; at the lifting up of thyself the nations[1471] were scattered.

4 And your spoil shall be gathered *like* the gathering[625] of the caterpiller: as the running to and fro of locusts shall he run upon them.

5 [a]The LORD is exalted; for he dwelleth[7931] on high: he hath filled Zion with judgment[4941] and righteousness.[6666]

6 And wisdom[2451] and knowledge shall be the stability[530] of thy times, *and* strength of [I]salvation: the fear[3374] of the LORD *is* his treasure.

7 Behold, their [I]valiant ones shall cry without: [a]the ambassadors[4397] of peace shall weep bitterly.[4751]

8 [a]The highways lie waste,[8074] the wayfaring man ceaseth:[7673] [b]he hath broken[6565] the covenant,[1285] [c]he hath despised[3988] the cities, he regardeth[2803] no man.[582]

9 [a]The earth[776] mourneth *and* languisheth: Lebanon is ashamed *and* [I]hewn down:[7060] Sharon is like a wilderness;[6160] and Bashan and Carmel shake off *their fruits.*

10 [a]Now will I rise, saith the LORD; now will I be exalted; now will I lift up myself.[5375]

11 [a]Ye shall conceive chaff, ye shall bring forth stubble: your breath,[7307] *as* fire, shall devour you.

12 And the people shall be *as* the burnings of lime: [a]*as* thorns cut up shall they be burned in the fire.

13 Hear,[8085] [a]ye *that are* far off, what I have done; and, ye *that are* near, acknowledge[3045] my might.

14 The sinners[2400] in Zion are afraid;[6342] fearfulness[7461] hath surprised the hypocrites.[2611] Who among us shall dwell[1481] with the devouring fire? who among us shall dwell with everlasting[5769] burnings?

15 He that [a]walketh [I]righteously, and speaketh [II]uprightly;[4334] he that despiseth[3988] the gain of [III]oppressions, that shaketh his hands[3709] from holding of bribes, that stoppeth his ears[241] from hearing[8085] of [IV]blood,[1818] and [b]shutteth his eyes from seeing[7200] evil;[7451]

16 He shall dwell[7931] on [I]high: his place of defence *shall be* the munitions[4679] of rocks: bread shall be given him; his waters *shall be* sure.[539]

The Glorious Future

17 Thine eyes shall see[2372] the king in his beauty: they shall behold[7200] [I]the land[776] that is very far off.

18 Thine heart[3820] shall meditate[1897] terror.[367] [a]Where *is* the scribe?[5608] where *is* the [I]receiver?[8254] where *is* he that counted the towers?

19 [a]Thou shalt not see a fierce people, [b]a people of a deeper[6012] speech[8193] than thou canst perceive; of a [I]stammering tongue, *that thou canst* not understand.[998]

20 [a]Look upon[2372] Zion, the city of our solemnities:[4150] thine eyes shall see [b]Jerusalem a quiet habitation, a tabernacle[168] *that* shall not be taken down; [c]not one of [d]the stakes thereof shall ever be removed, neither shall any of the cords thereof be broken.

21 But there the glorious[117] LORD *will*

---

19 [I]Or, *and the city shall be utterly abased* [a]Isa. 30:30 [b]Zech. 11:2

20 [a]Isa. 30:24

1 [a]Isa. 21:2; Hab. 2:8 [b]Rev. 13:10

2 [a]Isa. 25:9

5 [a]Ps. 97:9

6 [I]Hebr. *salvations*

7 [I]Or, *messengers* [a]2Kgs. 18:18, 37

8 [a]Judg. 5:6 [b]2Kgs. 18:14-17

9 [I]Or, *withered away* [a]Isa. 24:4

10 [a]Ps. 12:5

11 [a]Ps. 7:14; Isa. 59:4

12 [a]Isa. 9:18

13 [a]Isa. 49:1

15 [I]Hebr. *in righteousnesses* [II]Hebr. *uprightnesses* [III]Or, *deceits* [IV]Hebr. *bloods* [a]Ps. 15:2; 24:4 [b]Ps. 119:37

16 [I]Hebr. *heights,* or, *high places*

17 [I]Hebr. *the land of far distances*

18 [I]Hebr. *weigher* [a]1Cor. 1:20

19 [I]Or, *ridiculous* [a]2Kgs. 19:32 [b]Deut. 28:49, 50; Jer. 5:15

20 [a]Ps. 48:12 [b]Ps. 46:5; 125:1, 2 [c]Isa. 37:33 [d]Isa. 54:2

be unto us a place [I]of broad rivers *and* streams; wherein shall go no galley with oars, neither shall[5674] gallant[117] ship pass thereby.[5674]

22 For the LORD *is* our judge,[8199] the LORD *is* our [Ia]lawgiver,[2710] [b]the LORD *is* our king; he will save[3467] us.

23 [I]Thy tacklings[2256] are loosed;[5203] they could not well strengthen[2388] their mast, they could not spread the sail: then is the prey of a great spoil divided; the lame take the prey.

24 And the inhabitant[7934] shall not say, I am sick: [a]the people that dwell therein *shall be* forgiven[5375] *their* iniquity.[5771]

God's Vengeance

34 [a]Come near,[7126] ye nations,[1471] to hear;[8085] and hearken,[7181] ye people:[3816] [b]let the earth[776] hear, and [I]all that is therein; the world,[8398] and all things that come forth of it.

2 For the indignation[7110] of the LORD *is* upon all nations, and *his* fury upon all their armies:[6635] he hath utterly destroyed[2763] them, he hath delivered them to the slaughter.[2874]

3 Their slain[2491] also shall be cast out, and [a]their stink shall come up[5927] out of their carcases,[6297] and the mountains shall be melted with their blood.[1818]

4 And [a]all the host[6635] of heaven[8064] shall be dissolved,[4743] and the heavens shall be [b]rolled together[1556] as a scroll: [c]and all their host shall fall down, as the leaf falleth off from the vine, and as a [d]falling *fig* from the fig tree.

5 For [a]my sword[2719] shall be bathed[7301] in heaven: behold, it [b]shall come down upon Idumea, and upon the people[5971] of my curse,[2764] to judgment.[4941]

6 The sword of the LORD is filled with blood, it is made fat[1878] with fatness, *and* with the blood of lambs[3733] and goats, with the fat of the kidneys of rams: for [a]the LORD hath a sacrifice[2077] in Bozrah, and a great slaughter in the land[776] of Idumea.

7 And the [I]unicorns[7214] shall come down with them, and the bullocks with the bulls;[47] and their land shall be [II]soaked with blood, and their dust[6083] made fat with fatness.

8 For *it is* the day[3117] of the LORD's [a]vengeance,[5359] *and* the year of recompences[7966] for the controversy[7379] of Zion.

9 [a]And the streams thereof shall be turned[2015] into pitch, and the dust thereof into brimstone,[1614] and the land thereof shall become[1961] burning pitch.

10 It shall not be quenched night[3915] nor day;[3119] [a]the smoke thereof shall go up for ever:[5769] [b]from generation[1755] to generation it shall lie waste;[2717] none shall pass[5674] through it for ever[5331] and ever.

11 [a]But the [I]cormorant and the bittern shall possess[3423] it; the owl also and the raven shall dwell[7931] in it: and [b]he shall stretch out upon it the line of confusion,[8414] and the stones of emptiness.

12 They shall call[7121] the nobles[2715] thereof to the kingdom, but none *shall be* there, and all her princes[8269] shall be nothing.

13 And [a]thorns shall come up in her palaces,[759] nettles and brambles in the fortresses thereof: and [b]it shall be an habitation of dragons,[8577] *and* a court for [I]owls.

14 The wild beasts of the desert shall also meet with the wild beasts of the island, and the satyr[8163] shall cry[7121] to his fellow;[7453] the [I]screech owl also shall rest there, and find for herself a place of rest.

15 There shall the great owl make her nest, and lay, and hatch, and gather under her shadow: there shall the vultures also be gathered,[6908] every one[802] with her mate.[7468]

16 Seek ye out of [a]the book[5612] of the LORD, and read:[7121] no one of these shall fail, none[802,3808] shall want her mate: for my mouth[6310] it hath commanded,[6680] and his spirit[7307] it hath gathered them.

17 And he hath cast[5307] the lot for them, and his hand[3027] hath divided it

21 [I]Hebr. *broad of spaces, or, hands*

22 [I]Hebr. *statute maker* [a]James 4:12 [b]Ps. 89:18

23 [I]Or, *They have forsaken thy tacklings*

24 [a]Jer. 50:20

1 [I]Hebr. *the fullness thereof* [a]Ps. 49:1 [b]Deut. 32:1

3 [a]Joel 2:20

4 [a]Ps. 102:26; Ezek. 32:7, 8; Joel 12:31; 3:15; Matt. 24:29; 2Pet. 3:10 [b]Rev. 6:14 [c]Isa. 14:12 [d]Rev. 6:13

5 [a]Jer. 46:10 [b]Jer. 49:7; Mal. 1:4

6 [a]Isa. 63:1; Jer. 49:13; Zeph. 1:7

7 [I]Or, *rhinoceroses* [II]Or, *drunken*

8 [a]Isa. 63:4

9 [a]Deut. 29:23

10 [a]Rev. 14:11; 18:18; 19:3 [b]Mal. 1:4

11 [I]Or, *pelican* [a]Isa. 14:23; Zeph. 2:14; Rev. 18:2 [b]2Kgs. 21:13; Lam. 2:8

13 [I]Hebr. *daughters of the owl* [a]Isa. 32:13; Hos. 9:6 [b]Isa. 13:21

14 [I]Or, *night monster*

16 [a]Mal. 3:16

unto them by line: they shall possess it for ever, from generation[1755] to generation shall they dwell therein.

The Path of Holiness

35 The [a]wilderness and the solitary place[6723] shall be glad for them; and the desert[6160] shall rejoice, and blossom as the rose.

2 [a]It shall blossom abundantly, and rejoice even with joy and singing: the glory[3519] of Lebanon shall be given unto it, the excellency[1926] of Carmel and Sharon, they shall see the glory of the LORD, *and* the excellency of our God.[430]

3 [a]Strengthen[2388] ye the weak[7504] hands, and confirm[553] the feeble[3782] knees.

4 Say to them *that are* of a [I]fearful heart,[3820] Be strong, fear[3372] not: behold, your God will come *with* vengeance,[5359] *even* God *with* a recompence; he will come and save[3467] you.

5 Then the [a]eyes of the blind shall be opened, and [b]the ears[241] of the deaf shall be unstopped.

6 Then shall the [a]lame *man* leap as an hart, and the [b]tongue of the dumb sing: for in the wilderness shall [c]waters break out, and streams in the desert.

7 And the parched ground shall become[1961] a pool, and the thirsty land springs of water: in [a]the habitation of dragons,[8577] where each lay, *shall be* [I]grass with reeds and rushes.

8 And an highway shall be there, and a way,[1870] and it shall be called[7121] The way of holiness;[6944] [a]the unclean[2931] shall not pass over[5674] it; [I]but it *shall be* for those: the wayfaring men, though fools, shall not err[8582] *therein.*

9 [a]No lion shall be there, nor *any* ravenous[6530] beast[2416] shall go up thereon, it shall not be found there; but the redeemed[1350] shall walk *there:*

10 And the [a]ransomed[6299] of the LORD shall return,[7725] and come to Zion with songs and everlasting[5769] joy upon their heads:[7218] they shall obtain joy and gladness, and [b]sorrow and sighing shall flee away.

The Invasion of Sennacherib

36 Now [a]it came to pass in the fourteenth year of king Hezekiah, *that* Sennacherib king of Assyria came up[5927] against all the defenced cities of Judah, and took them.

2 And the king of Assyria sent Rabshakeh from Lachish to Jerusalem unto king Hezekiah with a great army.[2426] And he stood by the conduit of the upper[5945] pool in the highway of the fuller's[3526] field.[7704]

3 Then came forth unto him Eliakim, Hilkiah's son, which was over the house, and Shebna the [I]scribe,[5608] and Joah, Asaph's son, the recorder.[2142]

4 [a]And Rabshakeh said unto them, Say ye now to Hezekiah, Thus saith the great king, the king of Assyria, What confidence[986] *is* this wherein thou trustest?[982]

5 I say, *sayest thou,* (but *they are but* [I]vain[8193] words) [II]*I* have counsel[6098] and strength for war: now on whom dost thou trust, that thou rebellest[4775] against me?

6 Lo, thou trustest in the [a]staff of this broken reed, on Egypt; whereon if a man[376] lean, it will go into his hand,[3709] and pierce[5344] it: so *is* Pharaoh king of Egypt to all that trust in him.

7 But if thou say to me, We trust in the LORD our God:[430] *is it* not he, whose high places and whose altars[4196] Hezekiah hath taken away,[5493] and said to Judah and to Jerusalem, Ye shall worship[7812] before this altar?[4196]

8 Now therefore give [I]pledges,[6148] I pray thee,[4994] to my master[113] the king of Assyria, and I will give thee two thousand horses, if thou be able on thy part to set riders upon them.

9 How then wilt thou turn away[7725] the face of one captain[6346] of the least of my master's[113] servants,[5650] and put thy trust on Egypt for chariots and for horsemen?

10 And am I now come up[5927] without the LORD against this land[776] to destroy[7843] it? the LORD said unto me, Go up against this land, and destroy it.

11 Then said Eliakim and Shebna

---

1 [a]Isa. 55:12
2 [a]Isa. 32:15
3 [a]Job 4:3, 4; Heb. 12:12
4 [I]Hebr. *hasty*
5 [a]Isa. 29:18; 32:3, 4; 42:7; Matt. 9:27; 11:5; 12:22; 20:30; 21:14; John 9:6, 7 [b]Matt. 11:5; Mark 7:32
6 [a]Matt. 11:5; 15:30; 21:14; John 5:8, 9; Acts 3:2; 8:7; 14:8 [b]Isa. 32:4; Matt. 9:32, 33; 12:22; 15:30 [c]Isa. 41:18; 43:19; John 7:38, 39
7 [I]Or, *a court for reeds* [a]Isa. 34:13
8 [I]Or, *for he shall be with them* [a]Isa. 52:1; Joel 3:17; Rev. 21:27
9 [a]Lev. 26:6; Isa. 11:9; Ezek. 34:25
10 [a]Isa. 51:11 [b]Isa. 25:8; 65:19; Rev. 7:17; 21:4

1 [a]2Kgs. 18:13, 17; 2Chr. 32:1
3 [I]Or, *secretary*
4 [a]2Kgs. 18:19
5 [I]Hebr. *a word of lips* [II]Or, *but counsel and strength are for the war*
6 [a]Ezek. 29:6, 7
8 [I]Or, *hostages*

and Joah unto Rabshakeh, Speak, I pray thee, unto thy servants in the Syrian language; for we understand[8085] *it:* and speak not to us in the Jews' language,[8193] in the ears[241] of the people[5971] that *are* on the wall.

12 But Rabshakeh said, Hath my master sent me to thy master and to thee to speak these words? *hath he* not *sent me* to the men[582] that sit upon the wall, that they may eat their own dung, and drink their own piss with you?

13 Then Rabshakeh stood, and cried[7121] with a loud voice in the Jews' language, and said, Hear[8085] ye the words of the great king, the king of Assyria.

14 Thus saith the king, Let not Hezekiah deceive you: for he shall not be able to deliver[5337] you.

15 Neither let Hezekiah make you trust in the LORD, saying, The LORD will surely deliver us: this city shall not be delivered into the hand[3027] of the king of Assyria.

16 Hearken[8085] not to Hezekiah: for thus saith the king of Assyria, [I]Make[6213] *an agreement* with me *by* a present,[1293] and come out to me: [a]and eat ye every one[376] of his vine, and every one of his fig tree, and drink ye every one the waters of his own cistern;[953]

17 Until I come and take you away to a land like your own land, a land of corn and wine, a land of bread and vineyards.

18 *Beware* lest Hezekiah persuade you, saying, The LORD will deliver[5337] us. Hath any of the gods[430] of the nations[1471] delivered his land out of the hand of the king of Assyria?

19 Where *are* the gods of Hamath and Arphad? where *are* the gods of Sepharvaim? and have they delivered Samaria out of my hand?

20 Who *are they* among all the gods of these lands, that have delivered their land out of my hand, that the LORD should deliver Jerusalem out of my hand?

21 But they held their peace, and answered him not a word: for the king's commandment was, saying, Answer him not.

22 Then came Eliakim, the son of Hilkiah, that *was* over the household, and Shebna the scribe, and Joah, the son of Asaph, the recorder, to Hezekiah with their clothes rent, and told[5046] him the words of Rabshakeh.

Hezekiah's Fear and Isaiah's Encouragement

37 And [a]it came to pass, when king[4428] Hezekiah heard[8085] *it,* that he rent his clothes, and covered himself[3680] with sackcloth, and went into the house[1004] of the LORD.

2 And he sent Eliakim, who *was* over the household,[1004] and Shebna the scribe,[5608] and the elders[2205] of the priests[3548] covered with sackcloth, unto Isaiah the prophet[5030] the son[1121] of Amoz.

3 And they said[559] unto him, Thus saith Hezekiah, This day[3117] *is* a day of trouble, and of rebuke,[8433] and of [I]blasphemy:5007 for the children[1121] are come to the birth, and *there is* not strength to bring forth.

4 It may be the LORD thy God[430] will hear[8085] the words[1697] of Rabshakeh, whom the king of Assyria his master[113] hath sent to reproach the living[2416] God, and will reprove[3198] the words which the LORD thy God hath heard: wherefore lift up[5375] *thy* prayer[8605] for the remnant[7611] that is [I]left.

5 So the servants[5650] of king Hezekiah came to Isaiah.

6 And Isaiah said unto them, Thus shall ye say unto your master, Thus saith the LORD, Be not afraid[3372] of the words that thou hast heard, wherewith the servants of the king of Assyria have blasphemed1442 me.

7 Behold, I will [I]send a blast[7307] upon him, and he shall hear a rumour,8052 and return to his own land; and I will cause him to fall by the sword[2719] in his own land.[776]

8 So Rabshakeh returned,[7725] and found the king of Assyria warring against Libnah: for he had heard that he was departed from Lachish.

16 [I]Or, *Seek my favor by a present;* Hebr. *Make with me a blessing* [a]Zech. 3:10

1 [a]2Kgs. 10:1

3 [I]Or, *provocation*

4 [I]Hebr. *found*

7 [I]Or, *put a spirit into him*

9 And he heard say concerning Tirhakah king of Ethiopia, He is come forth to make war with thee. And when he heard *it,* he sent messengers[4397] to Hezekiah, saying,

10 Thus shall ye speak to Hezekiah king of Judah, saying, Let not thy God, in whom thou trustest,[982] deceive thee, saying, Jerusalem shall not be given into the hand[3027] of the king of Assyria.

11 Behold, thou hast heard what the kings of Assyria have done[6213] to all lands by destroying them utterly;[2763] and shalt thou be delivered?[5337]

12 Have the gods[430] of the nations[1471] delivered them which my fathers[1] have destroyed,[7843] *as* Gozan, and Haran, and Rezeph, and the children of Eden which *were* in Telassar?

13 Where *is* the king of [a]Hamath, and the king of Arphad, and the king of the city of Sepharvaim, Hena, and Ivah?

14 And Hezekiah received the letter[5612] from the hand of the messengers, and read[7121] it: and Hezekiah went up[5927] unto the house of the LORD, and spread it before the LORD.

15 And Hezekiah prayed[6419] unto the LORD, saying,

16 O LORD of hosts,[6635] God of Israel, that dwellest *between* the cherubims,[3742] that *art* the God, *even* thou alone, of all the kingdoms[4467] of the earth: thou hast made[6213] heaven[8064] and earth.[776]

17 [a]Incline thine ear,[241] O LORD, and hear; open thine eyes, O LORD, and see: and hear all the words of Sennacherib, which hath sent to reproach[2778] the living God.

18 Of a truth,[551] LORD, the kings of Assyria have laid waste[2717] all the [I]nations, and their countries,[776]

19 And have [I]cast their gods into the fire: for they *were* no gods, but the work of men's[120] hands,[3027] wood and stone: therefore they have destroyed[6] them.

20 Now therefore, O LORD our God, save[3467] us from his hand, that all the kingdoms of the earth may know[3045] that thou *art* the LORD, *even* thou only.

13 [a]Jer. 49:23

17 [a]Dan. 9:18

18 [I]Hebr. *lands*

19 [I]Hebr. *given*

24 [I]Hebr. *By the hand of thy servants* [II]Hebr. *the tallness of the cedars thereof,* and *the choice of the fir trees thereof* [III]Or, *the forest* and *his fruitful field*

25 [I]Or, *fenced and closed*

26 [I]Or, *Hast thou not heard* how I have made it long ago, and *formed it of ancient times? should I now bring it to be laid waste,* and *defenced cities* to be *ruinous heaps?* [a]2Kgs. 19:25

27 [I]Hebr. *short of hand*

28 [I]Or, *sitting*

29 [a]Isa. 30:28; Ezek. 38:4

Isaiah's Message to the King

21 Then Isaiah the son of Amoz sent unto Hezekiah, saying, Thus saith the LORD God of Israel, Whereas thou hast prayed to me against Sennacherib king of Assyria:

22 This *is* the word[1697] which the LORD hath spoken[1696] concerning him; The virgin,[1330] the daughter of Zion, hath despised thee, *and* laughed thee to scorn; the daughter of Jerusalem hath shaken her head[7218] at thee.

23 Whom hast thou reproached and blasphemed? and against whom hast thou exalted *thy* voice, and lifted up[5375] thine eyes on high? *even* against the Holy One[6918] of Israel.

24 [I]By thy servants hast thou reproached the Lord,[136] and hast said, By the multitude of my chariots am I come up to the height of the mountains, to the sides of Lebanon; and I will cut down[3772] [II]the tall cedars thereof, *and* the choice fir trees thereof: and I will enter into the height of his border, *and* [III]the forest of his Carmel.

25 I have digged, and drunk water; and with the sole[3709] of my feet have I dried up all the rivers of the [I]besieged places.

26 [I][a]Hast thou not heard long ago, *how* I have done it; *and* of ancient[6924] times, that I have formed[3335] it? now have I brought it to pass, that thou shouldest be to lay waste defenced cities *into* ruinous heaps.

27 Therefore their inhabitants *were* [I]of small power,[3027] they were dismayed[2865] and confounded:[954] they were *as* the grass of the field,[7704] and *as* the green herb, *as* the grass on the housetops, and *as corn* blasted before it be grown up.

28 But I know thy [I]abode, and thy going out, and thy coming in, and thy rage against me.

29 Because thy rage against me, and thy tumult, is come up[5927] into mine ears,[241] therefore [a]will I put my hook in thy nose,[639] and my bridle in thy lips,[8193] and I will turn thee back[7725] by the way[1870] by which thou camest.

30 And this *shall be* a sign[226] unto
thee, Ye shall eat *this* year such as
growth of itself; and the second year
that which springeth of the same: and in
the third year sow ye, and reap, and plant
vineyards, and eat the fruit thereof.
31 And [I]the remnant that is escaped[6413] of the house of Judah shall
again take root downward, and bear fruit
upward:
32 For out of Jerusalem shall go
forth a remnant, and [I]they that escape
out of mount Zion: the [a]zeal[7068] of the
LORD of hosts shall do[6213] this.
33 Therefore thus saith the LORD concerning the king of Assyria, He shall not
come into this city, nor shoot an arrow
there, nor come before it with [I]shields,
nor cast[8210] a bank against it.
34 By the way that he came, by the
same shall he return, and shall not come
into this city, saith[5002] the LORD.
35 For I will [a]defend this city to save
it for mine own sake, and for my servant[5650] David's sake.
36 Then the [a]angel[4397] of the LORD
went forth, and smote[5221] in the camp[4264]
of the Assyrians a hundred and
fourscore and five thousand: and when
they arose early in the morning, behold,
they *were* all dead[4191] corpses.[6297]
37 So Sennacherib king of Assyria
departed, and went and returned, and
dwelt at Nineveh.
38 And it came to pass, as he was
worshipping[7812] in the house of Nisroch
his god, that Adrammelech and Sharezer
his sons smote him with the sword; and
they escaped[4422] into the land of
[I]Armenia: and Esar–haddon his son
reigned[4427] in his stead.

The Sickness of Hezekiah

38 In [a]those days was Hezekiah sick
unto death.[4191] And Isaiah the
prophet[5030] the son of Amoz came unto
him, and said unto him, Thus saith the
LORD, [I][b]Set thine house[1004] in order: for
thou shalt die, and not live.[2421]
2 Then Hezekiah turned his face toward the wall, and prayed[6419] unto the
LORD,
3 And said, [a]Remember[2142] now, O
LORD, I beseech thee,[577] how I have
walked before thee in truth[571] and with
a perfect[8003] heart,[3820] and have done[6213]
that which is good[2896] in thy sight. And
Hezekiah wept [I]sore.
4 Then came the word[1697] of the
LORD to Isaiah, saying,
5 Go, and say to Hezekiah, Thus
saith the LORD, the God[430] of David thy
father,[1] I have heard[8085] thy prayer,[8605] I
have seen[7200] thy tears: behold, I will add
unto thy days fifteen years.
6 And I will deliver[5337] thee and this
city out of the hand of the king of Assyria: and [a]I will defend this city.
🔑 7 And this *shall be* [a]a sign unto thee
from the LORD, that the LORD will do[6213]
this thing[1697] that he hath spoken;
8 Behold, I will bring again[7725] the
shadow of the degrees, which is gone
down in the [I]sun dial of Ahaz, ten degrees backward. So the sun returned[7725]
ten degrees, by which degrees it was
gone down.
9 The writing of Hezekiah king of
Judah, when he had been sick, and was
recovered of his sickness:
10 I said in the cutting off of my
days, I shall go to the gates of the
grave:[7585] I am deprived[6485] of the
residue[3499] of my years.
11 I said, I shall not see the LORD,
even the LORD, [a]in the land[776] of the
living:[2416] I shall behold[7200] man[120] no
more with the inhabitants of the
world.[2309]
12 [a]Mine age is departed,[5265] and is
removed from me as a shepherd's tent:[168]
I have cut off[7088] like a weaver my
life:[2416] he will cut me off[1214] [I]with pining
sickness:[1803] from day[3117] *even* to
night[3915] wilt thou make an end of me.

31 [I]Hebr. *the escaping of the house of Judah that remaineth*
32 [I]Hebr. *the escaping* [a]2Kgs. 19:31; Isa. 9:7
33 [I]Hebr. *shield*
35 [a]2Kgs. 20:6; Isa. 38:6
36 [a]2Kgs. 19:35
38 [I]Hebr. *Ararat*
1 [I]Hebr. *Give charge concerning thy house* [a]2Kgs. 20:1; 2Chr. 32:24 [b]2Sam. 17:23
3 [I]Hebr. *with great weeping* [a]Neh. 13:14
6 [a]Isa. 37:35
7 [a]2Kgs. 20:8; Isa. 7:11
8 [I]Hebr. *degrees by, or, with the sun*
11 [a]Ps. 27:13; 116:9
12 [I]Or, *from the thrum* [a]Job 7:6

🔑 **38:7, 8** See note on Joshua 10:12–14 regarding Hezekiah's sundial as compared to God causing the sun to "stand still" for Joshua.

13 I reckoned till morning, *that,* as a lion, so will he break[7665] all my bones:[6106] from day *even* to night wilt thou make an end of me.

14 Like a crane *or* a swallow, so did I chatter: [a]I did mourn[1897] as a dove: mine eyes fail *with looking* upward: O LORD, I am oppressed; [I]undertake[6148] for me.

15 What shall I say?[1696] he hath both spoken[559] unto me, and himself hath done *it:* I shall go softly all my years [a]in the bitterness[4751] of my soul.[5315]

16 O Lord,[136] by these *things men* live, and in all these *things is* the life of my spirit:[7307] so wilt thou recover me, and make me to live.

17 Behold, [I]for peace I had great bitterness: but [II]thou hast in love[2836] to my soul *delivered it* from the pit[7845] of corruption: for thou hast cast all my sins[2399] behind thy back.[1460]

18 For [a]the grave can not praise[3034] thee, death[4194] can *not* celebrate[1984] thee: they that go down into the pit[953] cannot hope for thy truth.

19 The living, the living, he shall praise thee, as I *do* this day: [a]the father to the children shall make known[3045] thy truth.

20 The LORD *was ready* to save[3467] me: therefore we will sing my songs to the stringed instruments all the days of our life in the house of the LORD.

21 For [a]Isaiah had said, Let them take[5375] a lump of figs, and lay *it* for a plaister upon the boil, and he shall recover.[2421]

22 [a]Hezekiah also had said, What *is* the sign that I shall go up to the house of the LORD?

Ambassadors From Babylon

39 At [a]that time[6256] Merodach–baladan, the son of Baladan, king of Babylon, sent letters[5612] and a present[4503] to Hezekiah: for he had heard[8085] that he had been sick, and was recovered.[2388]

2 [a]And Hezekiah was glad of them, and shewed[7200] them the house of his [I]precious things,[5238] the silver, and the gold, and the spices, and the precious[2896] ointment,[8081] and all the house of his [II]armour,[3627] and all that was found in his treasures:[214] there was nothing in his house, nor in all his dominion,[4475] that Hezekiah shewed them not.

3 Then came Isaiah the prophet[5030] unto king Hezekiah, and said unto him, What said these men?[582] and from whence came they unto thee? And Hezekiah said, They are come from a far country[776] unto me, *even* from Babylon.

4 Then said he, What have they seen[7200] in thine house? And Hezekiah answered, All that *is* in mine house have they seen: there is nothing among my treasures that I have not shewed them.

5 Then said Isaiah to Hezekiah, Hear[8085] the word[1697] of the LORD of hosts:[6635]

6 Behold, the days[3117] come, [a]that all that *is* in thine house, and *that* which thy fathers[1] have laid up in store until this day, shall be carried[5375] to Babylon: nothing shall be left,[3498] saith the LORD.

7 And of thy sons that shall issue from thee, which thou shalt beget, shall they take away; and [a]they shall be eunuchs[5631] in the palace[1964] of the king of Babylon.

8 Then said Hezekiah to Isaiah, [a]Good[2896] *is* the word of the LORD which thou hast spoken. He said moreover, For there shall be peace and truth[571] in my days.

Words of Comfort

40 Comfort[5162] ye, comfort ye my people,[5971] saith[559] your God.[430]

2 Speak[1696] ye [I]comfortably[3820] [5921] to Jerusalem, and cry[7121] unto her, that her [II]warfare[6635] is accomplished,[4390] that her iniquity[5771] is pardoned: [a]for she hath received of the LORD's hand[3027] double for all her sins.

---

14 [I]Or, *ease me* [a]Isa. 59:11

15 [a]Job 7:11; 10:1

17 [I]Or, *on my peace* came *great bitterness* [II]Hebr. *thou hast loved my soul from the pit*

18 [a]Ps. 6:5; 30:9; 88:11; 115:17; Eccl. 9:10

19 [a]Deut. 4:9; 6:7; Ps. 78:3, 4

21 [a]2Kgs. 20:7

22 [a]2Kgs. 20:8

1 [a]2Kgs. 20:12

2 [I]Or, *spicery* [II]Hebr. *vessels,* or, *instruments* [a]2Chr. 32:31

6 [a]Jer. 20:5

7 [a]Dan. 1:2, 3, 7

8 [a]1Sam. 3:18

2 [I]Hebr. *to the heart* [II]Or, *appointed time* [a]Job 42:10; Isa. 61:7

3 [a]The voice of him that crieth in the
wilderness, [b]Prepare ye the way[1870] of
the LORD, [c]make straight[3474] in the
desert[6160] a highway for our God.
4 Every valley shall be exalted, and
every mountain and hill shall be made
low: [a]and the crooked[6121] shall be
made [I]straight, and the rough places
[II]plain:
5 And the glory[3519] of the LORD shall
be revealed,[1540] and all flesh[1320] shall see
it together: for the mouth[6310] of the LORD
hath spoken *it*.
6 The voice said, Cry. And he said,
What shall I cry? [a]All flesh *is* grass, and
all the goodliness[2617] thereof *is* as the
flower of the field:[7704]
7 The grass withereth,[3001] the flower
fadeth: because [a]the spirit[7307] of the LORD
bloweth5380 upon it: surely the people *is*
grass.
8 The grass withereth, the flower
fadeth: but [a]the word[1697] of our God
shall stand for ever.[5769]
9 [Ia]O Zion, that bringest good
tidings,[1319] get thee up into the high
mountain; [II]O Jerusalem, that bringest
good tidings, lift up thy voice with
strength; lift *it* up, be not afraid;[3372] say
unto the cities of Judah, Behold your
God!
10 Behold, the Lord[136] GOD will come
[I]with strong[2389] *hand,* and [a]his arm shall
rule[4910] for him: behold, [b]his reward *is*
with him, and [IIc]his work before him.
11 He shall [a]feed his flock like a
shepherd: he shall gather[6908] the lambs
with his arm, and carry[5375] *them* in his
bosom, *and* shall gently lead5095 those
[I]that are with young.

Israel's Incomparable God

12 [a]Who hath measured the waters
in the hollow of his hand, and meted
out8505 heaven8064 with the span, and
comprehended3557 the dust[6083] of the
earth[776] in [I]a measure,[7991] and weighed
the mountains in scales, and the hills in
a balance?
13 [a]Who hath directed8505 the Spirit
of the LORD, or *being* [I]his counselor hath
taught[3045] him?
14 With whom took he counsel,[3289]
and *who* [I]instructed[995] him, and
taught[3925] him in the path[734] of judgment,[4941] and taught him knowledge, and
shewed[3045] to him the way of [II]under-
standing?[8394]
15 Behold, the nations[1471] *are* as a
drop of a bucket, and are counted[2803] as
the small dust[7834] of the balance: behold,
he taketh up the isles as a very little
thing.
16 And Lebanon *is* not sufficient to
burn, nor the beasts[2416] thereof sufficient
for a burnt offering.[5930]
17 All nations before him *are* as
[a]nothing; and [b]they are counted to him
less than nothing,657 and vanity.[8414]
18 To whom then will ye [a]liken
God?[410] or what likeness[1823] will ye
compare6186 unto him?
19 [a]The workman melteth[5258] a
graven image, and the goldsmith[6884]
spreadeth it over with gold, and casteth
silver chains.
20 He that [I]*is* so impoverished that
he hath no oblation[8641] chooseth[977] a
tree *that* will not rot; he seeketh unto
him a cunning[2450] workman [a]to prepare[3559] a graven image, *that* shall not be
moved.
21 [a]Have ye not known?[3045] have ye
not heard?[8085] hath it not been told[5046]
you from the beginning?[7218] have ye not
understood[995] from the foundations[4146] of
the earth?
22 [I]*It is* he that sitteth upon the circle of the earth, and the inhabitants
thereof *are* as grasshoppers; that
[a]stretcheth out the heavens8064 as a curtain, and spreadeth them out as a tent[168]
to dwell in:

3 [a]Matt. 3:3; Mark 1:3; Luke 3:4; John 1:23 [b]Mal. 3:1 [c]Ps. 68:4; Isa. 49:11
4 [I]Or, *a straight place* [II]Or, *a plain place* [a]Isa. 45:2
6 [a]Job 14:2; Ps. 90:5; 102:11; 103:15; James 1:10; 1Pet. 1:24
7 [a]Ps. 103:16
8 [a]John 12:34; 1Pet. 1:25
9 [I]Or, *O thou that tellest good tidings to Zion* [II]Or, *O thou that tellest good tidings to Jerusalem* [a]Isa. 41:27; 52:7
10 [I]Or, *against the strong* [II]Or, *recompense for his work* [a]Isa. 59:16 [b]Isa. 62:11; Rev. 22:12 [c]Isa. 49:4
11 [I]Or, *that give suck* [a]Isa. 49:10; Ezek. 34:23; 37:24; John 10:11; Heb. 13:20; 1Pet. 2:25; 5:4; Rev. 7:17
12 [I]Hebr. *a tierce* [a]Prov. 30:4
13 [I]Hebr. *man of his counsel* [a]Job 21:22; 36:22, 23; Rom. 11:34; 1Cor. 2:16
14 [I]Hebr. *made him understand* [II]Hebr. *understandings*
17 [a]Dan. 4:35 [b]Ps. 62:9
18 [a]Isa. 40:25; 46:5; Acts 17:29
19 [a]Isa. 41:6, 7; 44:12; Jer. 10:3
20 [I]Hebr. *is poor of oblation* [a]Isa. 41:7; Jer. 10:4
21 [a]Ps. 19:1; Acts 14:17; Rom. 1:19, 20
22 [I]Or, *Him that sitteth* [a]Job 9:8; Ps. 104:2; Isa. 42:5; 44:24; 51:13; Jer. 10:12

40:3 The prophecy found in this verse gives a fascinating insight into the ministry of John the Baptist, the forerunner of Jesus Christ. John himself and the writers of the Gospels realized that his ministry was the fulfillment of this verse (Matt. 3:3; Mark 1:3; Luke 1:76; 3:4; John 1:23).

23 That bringeth the [a]princes[7336] to nothing; he maketh[6213] the judges[8199] of the earth as vanity.[8414]

24 Yea, they shall not be planted; yea, they shall not be sown: yea, their stock shall not take root in the earth: and he shall also blow upon them, and they shall wither,[3001] and the whirlwind shall take them away[5375] as stubble.

25 [a]To whom then will ye liken me, or shall I be equal? saith the Holy One.[6918]

26 Lift up[5375] your eyes on high, and behold[7200] who hath created[1254] these *things,* that bringeth out their host[6635] by number: [a]he calleth[7121] them all by names by the greatness of his might, for that *he is* strong in power; not one[376] faileth.

27 Why sayest[559] thou, O Jacob, and speakest,[1696] O Israel, My way is hid from the LORD, and my judgment is passed over[5674] from my God?

28 Hast thou not known? hast thou not heard, *that* the everlasting[5769] God, the LORD, the Creator[1254] of the ends of the earth, fainteth not, neither is weary? [a]*there is* no searching[2714] of his understanding.

29 He giveth power[3581] to the faint; and to *them that have* no might[202] he increaseth strength.

30 Even the youths shall faint and be weary, and the young men shall utterly fall:[3782]

31 But they that wait upon[6960] the LORD [a]shall [I]renew their strength; they shall mount up[5927] with wings as eagles; they shall run, and not be weary; *and* they shall walk, and not faint.

God's Assurance to Israel

41 [a]Keep silence before me, O islands; and let the people[3816] renew *their* strength: let them come near;[5066] then let them speak:[1696] let us come near[7126] together to judgment.[4941]

2 Who raised up [I]the righteous[6664] *man* [a]from the east, called[7121] him to his foot, [b]gave the nations[1471] before him, and made *him* rule[7287] over kings?[4428] he gave *them* as the dust[6083] to his sword,[2719] *and* as driven stubble to his bow.

3 He pursued them, *and* passed[5674] [I]safely;[7965] *even* by the way[734] *that* he had not gone with his feet.

4 [a]Who hath wrought and done[6213] *it,* calling[7121] the generations[1755] from the beginning?[7218] I the LORD, the [b]first,[7223] and with the last; I *am* he.

5 The isles saw[7200] *it,* and feared;[3372] the ends of the earth[776] were afraid,[2729] drew near, and came.

6 [a]They helped every one[376] his neighbour;[7453] and *every one* said to his brother,[251] [I]Be of good courage.[2388]

7 [a]So the carpenter encouraged[2388] the [I]goldsmith,[6884] *and* he that smootheth *with* the hammer [II]him that smote[1986] the anvil, [III]saying, It *is* ready for the sodering:[1694] and he fastened[2388] it with nails, [b]*that* it should not be moved.

8 But thou, Israel, *art* my servant,[5650] Jacob whom I have [a]chosen,[977] the seed[2233] of Abraham my [b]friend.[157]

9 *Thou* whom I have taken[2388] from the ends of the earth, and called thee from the chief men[678] thereof, and said unto thee, Thou *art* my servant; I have chosen thee, and not cast thee away.

10 [a]Fear[3372] thou not; [b]for I *am* with thee: be not dismayed;[8159] for I *am* thy God:[430] I will strengthen thee; yea, I will help thee; yea, I will uphold thee with the right hand of my righteousness.[6664]

11 Behold, all they that were incensed[2734] against thee shall be [a]ashamed[954] and confounded: they shall be as nothing; and [I]they that strive with thee shall perish.[6]

12 Thou shalt seek them, and shalt not find them, *even* [I]them that contended with thee: [II]they that war against thee shall be as nothing, and as a thing of nought.[657]

13 For I the LORD thy God will hold thy right hand, saying unto thee, [a]Fear not; I will help thee.

14 Fear not, thou worm[8438] Jacob, *and* ye [I]men of Israel; I will help thee, saith[5002] the LORD,[3068] and thy Redeemer,[1350] the Holy One[6918] of Israel.

---

23 [a]Job 12:21; Ps. 107:40
25 [a]Isa. 40:18; Deut. 4:15
26 [a]Ps. 147:4
28 [a]Ps. 147:5; Rom. 11:33
31 [I]Hebr. *change* [a]Ps. 103:5

1 [a]Zech. 2:13
2 [I]Hebr. *righteousness* [a]Isa. 46:11 [b]Gen. 14:14; Isa. 41:25; 45:1
3 [I]Hebr. *in peace*
4 [a]Isa. 41:26; 44:7; 46:10 [b]Isa. 43:10; 44:6; 48:12; Rev. 1:17; 22:13
6 [I]Hebr. *Be strong* [a]Isa. 40:19; 44:12
7 [I]Or, *founder* [II]Or, *the smiting* [III]Or, *saying of the solder, It is good* [a]Isa. 40:19 [b]Isa. 40:20
8 [a]Deut. 7:6; 10:15; 14:2; Ps. 135:4; Isa. 43:1; 44:1 [b]2Chr. 20:7; James 2:23
10 [a]Isa. 41:13, 14; 43:5 [b]Deut. 31:6, 8
11 [I]Hebr. *the men of thy strife* [a]Ex. 23:22; Isa. 45:24; 60:12; Zech. 12:3
12 [I]Hebr. *the men of thy contention* [II]Hebr. *the men of thy war*
13 [a]Isa. 41:10
14 [I]Or, *few men*

15 Behold, [a]I will make[7760] thee a
new sharp threshing instrument having
[I]teeth: thou shalt thresh the mountains,
and beat *them* small, and shalt make the
hills as chaff.
16 Thou shalt [a]fan them, and the
wind[7307] shall carry them away,[5375] and
the whirlwind[5591] shall scatter them: and
thou shalt rejoice in the LORD, *and* [b]shalt
glory[1984] in the Holy One of Israel.
17 *When* the poor and needy seek
water, and *there is* none, *and* their tongue
faileth for thirst, I the LORD will hear
them, *I* the God of Israel will not
forsake[5800] them.
18 I will open [a]rivers in high places,
and fountains in the midst of the valleys:
I will make the [b]wilderness a pool of
water, and the dry land[776] springs of
water.
19 I will plant in the wilderness the
cedar, the shittah tree, and the myrtle,
and the oil[8081] tree; I will set[7760] in the
desert[6160] the fir tree, *and* the pine,[8410]
and the box tree together:
20 [a]That they may see,[7200] and
know,[3045] and consider,[7760] and understand[7919] together, that the hand[3027] of
the LORD hath done this, and the Holy
One of Israel hath created[1254] it.

A Challenge

21 [I]Produce[7126] your cause,[7379]
saith[559] the LORD; bring forth[5066] your
strong *reasons,* saith the King of Jacob.
22 [a]Let them bring *them* forth, and
shew[5046] us what shall happen: let them
shew the former things,[7223] what they *be,*
that we may [I]consider them, and know
the latter end[319] of them; or declare[8085]
us things for to come.

15 [I]Hebr. *mouths* [a]Mic. 4:13; 2Cor. 10:4, 5
16 [a]Jer. 51:2 [b]Isa. 45:25
18 [a]Isa. 35:6, 7; 43:19; 44:3 [b]Ps. 107:35
20 [a]Job 12:9
21 [I]Hebr. *Cause to come near*
22 [I]Hebr. *set our heart* upon the [a]Isa. 45:21
23 [a]Isa. 42:9; 44:7, 8; 45:3; John 13:19 [b]Jer. 10:5
24 [I]Or, worse *than nothing* [II]Or, worse *than of a viper* [a]Ps. 115:8; Isa. 44:9; 1Cor. 8:4
25 [a]Ezra 1:2 [b]Isa. 41:2
26 [a]Isa. 43:9
27 [a]Isa. 41:4 [b]Isa. 40:9
28 [I]Hebr. *return* [a]Isa. 63:5
29 [a]Isa. 41:24
1 [a]Isa. 43:10; 49:3, 6; 52:13; 53:11; Matt. 12:18-20; Phil. 2:7 [b]Matt. 3:17; 17:5; Eph. 1:6 [c]Isa. 11:2; John 3:34

23 [a]Shew the things that are to come
hereafter, that we may know that ye *are*
gods:[430] yea, [b]do good, or do evil,[7489] that
we may be dismayed, and behold *it* together.
24 Behold, [a]ye *are* [I]of nothing, and
your work [II]of nought:[659] an abomination
is he that chooseth you.
25 I have raised up *one* from the
north, and he shall come: from the rising
of the sun [a]shall he call[7121] upon my
name: [b]and he shall come upon
princes[5461] as *upon* morter, and as the
potter treadeth clay.
26 [a]Who hath declared[5046] from the
beginning, that we may know? and beforetime, that we may say, *He is* righteous?[6662] yea, *there is* none that
sheweth,[5046] yea, *there is* none that declareth,[8085] yea, *there is* none that
heareth[8085] your words.[561]
27 [a]The first [b]*shall say* to Zion,
Behold, behold them: and I will give to
Jerusalem one that bringeth good tidings.[1319]
28 [a]For I beheld,[7200] and *there was*
no man;[376] even among them, and *there*
was no counselor,[3289] that, when I
asked[7592] of them, could [I]answer[7725] a
word.[1697]
29 [a]Behold, they *are* all vanity;[205]
their works *are* nothing: their molten
images[5262] *are* wind and confusion.[8414]

God's Special Servant

42 Behold [a]my servant,[5650] whom
I uphold; mine elect,[972] *in whom*
my soul[5315] [b]delighteth;[7521] [c]I have put
my spirit[7307] upon him: he shall bring
forth judgment[4941] to the Gentiles.[1471]
2 He shall not cry, nor lift up,[5375] nor

42:1–9 This is the first of four "Servant Songs" in Isaiah (see also Is. 49:1–9; 50:4–11; 52:13—53:12 [some would add 61:1–3 although the term "servant" does not appear there]). Some Jewish theologians tend to identify the "servant" in these passages as the people of Israel. This is primarily a reaction to the Christian view that these songs are prophecies of Christ. However, there are several problems with this Jewish interpretation, which include Israel being presented as the beneficiary of the servant's action (Is. 49:6). A similar difficulty arises from the statement that the servant suffers vicariously for the sins of others (Is. 53:5, 6). There were no righteous people in Israel who could suffer for others (Jer. 5:1), especially since Israel was suffering for their own sins (Jer.

(continued on next page)

cause his voice to be heard[8085] in the street.

3 A bruised reed shall he not break,[7665] and the [I]smoking3544 flax shall he not [II]quench: he shall bring forth judgment unto truth.[571]

4 He shall not fail3543 nor be [I]discouraged,7533 till he have set[7760] judgment in the earth:[776] [a]and the isles shall wait[3176] for his law.[8451]

5 Thus saith God[410] the LORD, [a]he that created[1254] the heavens,8064 and stretched them out; [b]he that spread forth[7554] the earth, and that which cometh out of it; [c]he that giveth breath[5397] unto the people[5971] upon it, and spirit to them that walk therein:

6 [a]I the LORD have called[7121] thee in righteousness,[6664] and will hold thine hand,[3027] and will keep[5341] thee, [b]and give thee for a covenant[1285] of the people, for [c]a light[216] of the Gentiles;

7 [a]To open the blind eyes, to [b]bring out the prisoners from the prison, *and* them that sit in [c]darkness[2822] out of the prison house.

8 I am the LORD: that *is* my name: and my [a]glory[3519] will I not give to another, neither my praise[8416] to graven images.

9 Behold, the former things[7223] are come to pass, and new things do I declare:[5046] before they spring forth I tell you of them.

A Song of Praise

10 [a]Sing unto the LORD a new song,[7892] *and* his praise from the end of the earth, [b]ye that go down to the sea, and [I]all that is therein; the isles, and the inhabitants thereof.

11 Let the wilderness and the cities thereof lift up *their voice,* the villages *that* Kedar doth inhabit: let the inhabitants of the rock sing, let them shout from the top[7218] of the mountains.

12 Let them give[7760] glory unto the LORD, and declare his praise in the islands.

13 The LORD shall go forth as a mighty man,[376] he shall stir up jealousy[7068] like a man of war: he shall cry, [a]yea, roar; he shall [I]prevail against his enemies.

14 I have[2814] long time[5769] holden my peace;2814 I have been still, *and* refrained myself: *now* will I cry like a travailing woman; I will destroy[5359] and [I]devour at once.

15 I will make waste[2717] mountains and hills, and dry up[3001] all their herbs; and I will make the rivers islands, and I will dry up the pools.

16 And I will bring the blind by a way[1870] *that* they knew[3045] not; I will lead them in paths *that* they have not known: I will make darkness[4285] light before them, and crooked things [I]straight. These things will I do[6213] unto them, and not forsake[5800] them.

17 They shall be [a]turned back, they shall be greatly ashamed,[954] that trust[982] in graven images, that say to the molten images,[4541] Ye *are* our gods.[430]

Israel Is Stubborn

18 Hear,[8085] ye deaf; and look, ye blind, that ye may see.

19 [a]Who *is* blind, but my servant? or deaf, as my messenger[4397] *that* I sent? who *is* blind as *he that is* perfect,[7999] and blind as the LORD's servant?

3 [I]Or, *dimly burning* [II]Hebr. *quench it*
4 [I]Hebr. *broken* [a]Gen. 49:10
5 [a]Isa. 44:24; Zech. 12:1 [b]Ps. 136:6 [c]Acts 17:25
6 [a]Isa. 43:1 [b]Isa. 49:8 [c]Isa. 49:6; Luke 2:32; Acts 13:47
7 [a]Isa. 35:5 [b]Isa. 61:1; Luke 4:18; 2Tim. 2:26; Heb. 2:14, 15 [c]Isa. 9:2
8 [a]Isa. 48:11
10 [I]Hebr. *the fullness thereof* [a]Ps. 33:3; 40:3; 98:1 [b]Ps. 107:23
13 [I]Or, *behave himself mightily* [a]Isa. 31:4
14 [I]Hebr. *swallow, or, eat up*
16 [I]Hebr. *into straightness*
17 [a]Ps. 97:7; Isa. 1:29; 44:11; 45:16
19 [a]Isa. 43:8; Ezek. 12:2; John 9:39, 41

(continued from previous page)
25:1–10). The servant is clearly said to be an individual (Is. 52:13—53:12), but the language of the passage in chapter forty-two shows an objective point of view which means that Isaiah cannot be referring to himself. Furthermore, there are references to future events that exclude historical characters (Is. 52:13, 15; 53:11). The servant's sinless character, resurrection, and work go infinitely beyond man's capabilities (Is. 42:4; 49:5; 53:4–6, 11). These passages can only refer to Christ. In fact, the New Testament explicitly identifies the servant as Jesus (Matt. 12:18–21; Luke 2:32; Acts 13:47; 26:23), especially in relation to Isaiah 52:13—53:11.

20 Seeing[7200] many things, [a]but thou observest[8104] not; opening the ears,[241] but he heareth not.

21 The LORD is well pleased[2654] for his righteousness' sake; he will magnify the law, and make [I]*it* honourable.[142]

22 But this *is* a people robbed and spoiled;[8154] [I]*they are* all of them snared in holes, and they are hid in prison houses: they are for a prey, and none delivereth;[5337] for [II]a spoil, and none saith, Restore.[7725]

23 Who among you will give ear[238] to this? *who* will hearken[7181] and hear [I]for the time to come?

24 Who gave Jacob for a spoil, and Israel to the robbers? did not the LORD, he against whom we have sinned?[2398] for they would[14] not walk in his ways, neither were they obedient[8085] unto his law.

25 Therefore he hath poured[8210] upon him the fury of his anger,[639] and the strength of battle: [a]and it hath set him on fire round about, [b]yet he knew not; and it burned him, yet he laid[7760] *it* not to heart.[3820]

43 But now thus saith the LORD [a]that created[1254] thee, O Jacob, [b]and he that formed[3335] thee, O Israel, Fear[3372] not: [c]for I have redeemed[1350] thee, [d]I have called[7121] *thee* by thy name; thou *art* mine.

2 [a]When thou passest[5674] through the waters, [b]I *will be* with thee; and through the rivers, they shall not overflow[7857] thee: when thou [c]walkest through the fire, thou shalt not be burned; neither shall the flame kindle upon thee.

3 For I *am* the LORD thy God,[430] the Holy One[6918] of Israel, thy Saviour:[3467] [a]I gave Egypt *for* thy ransom,[3724] Ethiopia and Seba for thee.

4 Since thou wast precious in my sight, thou hast been honourable,[3513] and I have loved[157] thee: therefore will I give men[120] for thee, and people[3816] for thy [I]life.[5315]

5 [a]Fear not: for I *am* with thee: I will bring thy seed[2233] from the east, and gather[6908] thee from the west;

6 I will say to the north, Give up; and to the south, Keep not back: bring my sons from far, and my daughters from the ends of the earth;[776]

7 *Even* every one that is [a]called by my name: for [b]I have created him for my glory,[3519] [c]I have formed him; yea, I have made[6213] him.

8 [a]Bring forth the blind people[5971] that have eyes, and the deaf that have ears.[241]

9 Let all the nations[1471] be gathered together,[6908] and let the people be assembled:[622] [a]who among them can declare[5046] this, and shew us former things?[7223] let them bring forth their witnesses, that they may be justified:[6663] or let them hear,[8085] and say, *It is* truth.[571]

10 [a]Ye *are* my witnesses, saith[5002] the LORD, [b]and my servant[5650] whom I have chosen;[977] that ye may know[3045] and believe[539] me, and understand[995] that I *am* he: [c]before me there was [I]no God[410] formed, neither shall there be after me.

11 I, *even* I, [a]*am* the LORD;[3068] and beside me *there is* no saviour.

12 I have declared,[5046] and have saved,[3467] and I have shewed,[8085] when *there was* no [a]strange[2114] *god* among you: [b]therefore ye *are* my witnesses, saith the LORD, that I *am* God.

13 [a]Yea, before the day[3117] *was* I *am* he; and *there is* none that can deliver[5337] out of my hand:[3027] I will work, and who shall [I][b]let it?

14 Thus saith the LORD, your Redeemer,[1350] the Holy One[6918] of Israel; For your sake I have sent to Babylon, and have brought down all their [I]nobles, and the Chaldeans, whose cry *is* in the ships.

15 I *am* the LORD, your Holy One, the creator[1254] of Israel, your King.[4428]

16 Thus saith the LORD, which [a]maketh a way[1870] in the sea, and a [b]path in the mighty waters;

17 Which [a]bringeth forth the chariot and horse, the army[2428] and the power; they shall lie down together, they shall not rise: they are extinct, they are quenched as tow.

20 [a]Rom. 2:21

21 [I]Or, him

22 [I]Or, *in snaring all the young men of them* [II]Hebr. *a treading*

23 [I]Hebr. *for the after time?*

25 [a]2Kgs. 25:9 [b]Hos. 7:9

1 [a]Isa. 43:7 [b]Isa. 43:21; 44:2, 21, 24 [c]Isa. 44:6 [d]Isa. 42:6; 45:4

2 [a]Ps. 66:12; 91:3 [b]Deut. 31:6, 8 [c]Dan. 3:25, 27

3 [a]Prov. 11:8; 21:18

4 [I]Or, *person*

5 [a]Isa. 41:10, 14; 44:2; Jer. 30:10, 11; 46:27, 28

7 [a]Isa. 63:19; James 2:7 [b]Ps. 100:3; Isa. 29:23; John 3:3, 5; 2Cor. 5:17; Eph. 2:10 [c]Isa. 43:1

8 [a]Isa. 6:9; 42:19; Ezek. 12:2

9 [a]Isa. 41:21, 22, 26

10 [I]Or, *nothing formed of God* [a]Isa. 44:8 [b]Isa. 42:1; 55:4 [c]Isa. 41:4; 44:6

11 [a]Isa. 45:21; Hos. 13:4

12 [a]Deut. 32:16; Ps. 81:9 [b]Isa. 43:10; 44:8

13 [I]Hebr. *turn it back* [a]Ps. 90:2; John 8:58 [b]Job 9:12; Isa. 14:27

14 [I]Hebr. *bars*

16 [a]Ex. 14:16, 22; Ps. 77:19; Isa. 51:10 [b]Josh. 3:13, 16

17 [a]Ex. 14:4-9, 25

18 [a]Remember[2142] ye not the former things, neither consider[995] the things of old.

19 Behold, I will do[6213] a [a]new thing; now it shall spring forth; shall ye not know it? [b]I will even make[7760] a way in the wilderness, *and* rivers in the desert.

20 The beast[2416] of the field[7704] shall honour[3513] me, the dragons[8577] and the [I]owls: because [a]I give waters in the wilderness, *and* rivers in the desert, to give drink to my people, my chosen.

21 [a]This people have I formed for myself; they shall shew forth[5608] my praise.[8416]

22 But thou hast not called upon[7121] me, O Jacob; but thou [a]hast been weary of me, O Israel.

23 [a]Thou hast not brought me the [I]small cattle of thy burnt offerings;[5930] neither hast thou honoured me with thy sacrifices.[2077] I have not caused thee to serve[5647] with an offering,[4503] nor wearied thee with incense.

24 Thou hast bought me no sweet cane with money, neither hast thou [I]filled me with the fat of thy sacrifices: but thou hast made me to serve with thy sins, thou hast [a]wearied me with thine iniquities.[5771]

25 I, *even* I, *am* he that [a]blotteth out[4229] thy transgressions[6588] [b]for mine own sake, [c]and will not remember thy sins.

26 Put me in remembrance:[2142] let us plead together: declare[5608] thou, that thou mayest be justified.

27 Thy first[7223] father[1] hath sinned,[2398] and thy [I][a]teachers[3887] have transgressed[6586] against me.

28 Therefore [a]I have profaned[2490] the [I]princes[8269] of the sanctuary,[6944] [b]and have given Jacob to the curse,[2764] and Israel to reproaches.

The LORD Is the Only God

44 Yet now hear,[8085] [a]O Jacob my servant;[5650] and Israel, whom I have chosen:[977]

2 Thus saith the LORD that made[6213] thee, [a]and formed[3335] thee from the womb,[990] *which* will help thee; Fear[3372] not, O Jacob, my servant; and thou, [b]Jeshurun, whom I have chosen.

3 For I will [a]pour water upon him that is thirsty, and floods upon the dry ground:[3004] I will pour my spirit upon thy seed,[2233] and my blessing[1293] upon thine offspring:

4 And they shall spring up *as* among the grass, as willows by the water courses.

5 One shall say, I *am* the LORD's; and another shall call[7121] *himself* by the name of Jacob; and another shall subscribe *with* his hand[3027] unto the LORD, and surname *himself* by the name of Israel.

6 Thus saith the LORD the King[4428] of Israel, [a]and his redeemer[1350] the LORD of hosts;[6635] [b]I *am* the first,[7223] and I *am* the last; and beside me *there is* no God.[430]

7 And [a]who, as I, shall call, and shall declare[5046] it, and set it in order for me, since I appointed[7760] the ancient[5769] people?[5971] and the things that are coming, and shall come, let them shew[5046] unto them.

8 Fear[6342] ye not, neither be afraid:[7297] [a]have not I told[8085] thee from that time,[227] and have declared[5046] *it?* [b]ye *are* even my witnesses. Is there a God[433] beside me? yea, [c]*there is* [I][d]no God; I know[3045] not *any.*

9 [a]They that make[3335] a graven image *are* all of them vanity;[8414] and their [I]delectable things[2530] shall not profit; and they *are* their own witnesses; [b]they see not, nor know; that they may be ashamed.[954]

10 Who hath formed a god,[410] or molten[5258] a graven image [a]*that* is profitable for nothing?

11 Behold, all his fellows shall be [a]ashamed: and the workmen, they *are* of men:[120] let them all be gathered together,[6908] let them stand up; *yet* they shall fear, *and* they shall be ashamed together.

12 [a]The smith [I]with the tongs both worketh in the coals, and fashioneth[3335] it with hammers, and worketh it with the

18 [a]Jer. 16:14; 23:7
19 [a]2Cor. 5:17; Rev. 21:5 [b]Ex. 17:6; Num. 20:11; Deut. 8:15; Ps. 78:16; Isa. 35:6; 41:18
20 [I]Hebr. *daughters of the owl* [a]Isa. 48:21
21 [a]Ps. 102:18; Isa. 43:1, 7; Luke 1:74, 75; Eph. 1:5, 6
22 [a]Mal. 1:13
23 [I]Hebr. *lambs,* or, *kids* [a]Amos 5:25
24 [I]Hebr. *made me drunk,* or, *abundantly moistened* [a]Isa. 1:14; Mal. 2:17
25 [a]Isa. 44:22; 48:9; Jer. 50:20; Acts 3:19 [b]Ezek. 36:22 [c]Isa. 1:18; Jer. 31:34
27 [I]Hebr. *interpreters* [a]Mal. 2:7, 8
28 [I]Or, *holy princes* [a]Isa. 47:6; Lam. 2:2, 6, 7 [b]Ps. 79:4; Jer. 24:9; Dan. 9:11; Zech. 8:13

1 [a]Isa. 41:8; 43:1; 44:21; Jer. 30:10; 46:27, 28
2 [a]Isa. 43:1, 7 [b]Deut. 32:15
3 [a]Isa. 35:7; Joel 2:28; John 7:38; Acts 2:18
6 [a]Isa. 43:1, 14; 44:24 [b]Isa. 41:4; 48:12; Rev. 1:8, 17; 22:13
7 [a]Isa. 41:4, 22; 45:21
8 [I]Hebr. *rock* [a]Isa. 41:22 [b]Isa. 43:10, 12 [c]Deut. 4:35, 39; 32:39; 1Sam. 2:2; 2Sam. 22:32; Isa. 45:5 [d]Deut. 32:4
9 [I]Hebr. *desirable* [a]Isa. 41:24, 29 [b]Ps. 115:4
10 [a]Jer. 10:5; Hab. 2:18
11 [a]Ps. 97:7; Isa. 1:29; 42:17; 45:16
12 [I]Or, *with an axe* [a]Isa. 40:19; 41:6; Jer. 10:3

strength of his arms: yea, he is hungry, and his strength faileth: he drinketh no water, and is faint.

13 The carpenter stretcheth out *his* rule;[6957] he marketh it out with a line;[8279] he fitteth it with planes,[4741] and he marketh it out with the compass, and maketh[6213] it after the figure[8403] of a man, according to the beauty[8597] of a man; that it may remain in the house.

14 He heweth him down[3772] cedars, and taketh the cypress and the oak, which he [I]strengtheneth for himself among the trees of the forest: he planteth an ash, and the rain doth nourish *it.*

15 Then shall it be for a man to burn: for he will take thereof, and warm himself; yea, he kindleth *it,* and baketh bread; yea, he maketh a god, and worshippeth[7812] *it;* he maketh it a graven image, and falleth down thereto.

16 He burneth[8313] part thereof in the fire; with part thereof he eateth flesh;[1320] he roasteth roast, and is satisfied: yea, he warmeth *himself,* and saith, Aha, I am warm, I have seen[7200] the fire:[217]

17 And the residue[7611] thereof he maketh a god, *even* his graven image: he falleth down unto it, and worshippeth *it,* and prayeth[6419] unto it, and saith, Deliver[5337] me; for thou *art* my god.

18 [a]They have not known[3045] nor understood:[995] for [b]he hath [I]shut[2902] their eyes, that they cannot see; *and* their hearts,[3826] that they cannot understand.[7919]

19 And none [I][a]considereth[7725] in his heart,[3820] neither *is there* knowledge nor understanding[8394] to say, I have burned part of it in the fire; yea, also I have baked bread upon the coals thereof; I have roasted flesh, and eaten *it:* and shall I make the residue[3499] thereof an abomination? shall I fall down[5456] to [II]the stock of a tree?

20 He feedeth on ashes: [a]a deceived heart hath turned him aside, that he cannot deliver his soul,[5315] nor say, *Is there* not a lie in my right hand?

21 Remember[2142] these, O Jacob and Israel; for [a]thou *art* my servant: I have formed thee; thou *art* my servant: O Israel, thou shalt not be forgotten of me.

22 [a]I have blotted out,[4229] as a thick cloud, thy transgressions,[6588] and, as a cloud,[6051] thy sins: return[7725] unto me; for [b]I have redeemed[1350] thee.

23 [a]Sing, O ye heavens;[8064] for the LORD hath done[6213] *it:* shout,[7321] ye lower parts of the earth:[776] break forth into singing, ye mountains, O forest, and every tree therein: for the LORD hath redeemed Jacob, and glorified himself[6286] in Israel.

24 Thus saith the LORD, [a]thy redeemer, and [b]he that formed thee from the womb, I *am* the LORD that maketh all *things;* [c]that stretcheth forth the heavens alone; that spreadeth abroad the earth by myself;

25 That [a]frustrateth[6565] the tokens[226] [b]of the liars, and maketh diviners[7080] mad; that turneth[7725] wise[2450] *men* backward, [c]and maketh their knowledge foolish;

26 [a]That confirmeth the word[1697] of his servant, and performeth[7999] the counsel[6098] of his messengers;[4426] that saith to Jerusalem, Thou shalt be inhabited; and to the cities of Judah, Ye shall be built, and I will raise up the [I]decayed places[2723] thereof:

27 [a]That saith to the deep, Be dry,[2717] and I will dry up[3001] thy rivers:

🔑 28 That saith of Cyrus, *He is* my shepherd, and shall perform all my

14 [I]Or, *taketh courage*

18 [I]Hebr. *daubed* [a]Isa. 45:20 [b]2Thess. 2:11

19 [I]Hebr. *setteth to his heart* [II]Hebr. *that which comes of a tree?* [a]Isa. 46:8

20 [a]Hos. 4:12; Rom. 1:21; 2Thess. 2:11

21 [a]Isa. 44:1, 2

22 [a]Isa. 43:25 [b]Isa. 43:1; 48:20; 1Cor. 6:20; 1Pet. 1:18, 19

23 [a]Ps. 69:34; 96:11, 12; Isa. 42:10; 49:13; Jer. 51:48; Rev. 18:20

24 [a]Isa. 43:14; 44:6 [b]Isa. 43:1 [c]Job 9:8; Ps. 104:2; Isa. 40:22; 42:5; 45:12; 51:13

25 [a]Isa. 47:13 [b]Jer. 50:36 [c]1Cor. 1:20

26 [I]Hebr. *wastes* [a]Zech. 1:6

27 [a]Jer. 50:38; 51:32, 36

🔑 **44:28** In 539 B.C. Cyrus the Medo-Persian king conquered Babylon, where the Jews had been exiled. He also allowed the exiles to return to Jerusalem. Isaiah predicted his name and actions 150 years before his birth. Note that God calls Cyrus "my shepherd" and "my anointed" (Is. 45:1), terms which are also used of Jesus. The Hebrew word for "anointed" is the root from which the term "Messiah" is derived. Consequently, there were some Jews who lived during the time of Christ that thought these words about Cyrus actually meant that the Messiah would come as a mighty conqueror.

pleasure:[2656] even saying to Jerusalem, [a]Thou shalt be built; and to the temple,[1964] Thy foundation[3245] shall be laid.

God Commissions Cyrus

45 Thus saith the LORD to his anointed,[4899] to Cyrus, whose [a]right hand I [I]have holden,[2388] [b]to subdue nations[1471] before him; and I will loose the loins of kings,[4428] to open before him the two leaved gates; and the gates shall not be shut;

2 I will go before thee, [a]and make the crooked places straight:[3474] [b]I will break in pieces[7665] the gates of brass, and cut in sunder the bars of iron:

3 And I will give thee the treasures of darkness,[2822] and hidden riches of secret places, [a]that thou mayest know that I, the LORD, which [b]call[7121] *thee* by thy name, *am* the God[430] of Israel.

4 For [a]Jacob my servant's sake, and Israel mine elect,[972] I have even called thee by thy name: I have surnamed thee, though thou hast [b]not known[3045] me.

5 I [a]*am* the LORD, and [b]*there is* none else, *there is* no God beside me: [c]I girded thee, though thou hast not known me:

6 [a]That they may know from the rising of the sun, and from the west, that *there is* none beside me. I *am* the LORD, and *there is* none else.

7 I form the light,[216] and create darkness: I make peace,[7965] and [a]create[1254] evil:[7451] I the LORD do[6213] all these *things*.

8 [a]Drop down, ye heavens,[8064] from above, and let the skies[7834] pour down righteousness:[6664] let the earth[776] open, and let them bring forth salvation,[3468] and let righteousness spring up together; I the LORD have created[1254] it.

The Lord of Creation and History

9 Woe unto him that striveth[7378] with [a]his Maker[3335] *Let* the potsherd[2789] *strive* with the potsherds of the earth.[127] [b]Shall the clay say to him that fashioneth[3335] it, What makest[6213] thou? or thy work, He hath no hands?[3027]

10 Woe unto him that saith unto *his* father,[1] What begettest thou? or to the woman,[802] What hast thou brought forth?[2342]

11 Thus saith the LORD, the Holy One[6918] of Israel, and his Maker, Ask[7592] me of things to come concerning [a]my sons, and concerning [b]the work of my hands command[6680] ye me.

12 [a]I have made[6213] the earth, and [b]created man upon it: I, *even* my hands, have stretched out the heavens, and [c]all their host[6635] have I commanded.[6680]

13 [a]I have raised him up in righteousness, and I will [I]direct[3474] all his ways:[1870] he shall [b]build my city, and he shall let go my captives,[1546] [c]not for price nor reward, saith the LORD of hosts.[6635]

14 Thus saith the LORD, [a]The labour of Egypt, and merchandise of Ethiopia and of the Sabeans, men[582] of stature,[4060] shall come over unto thee, and they shall be thine: they shall come after thee; [b]in chains they shall come over, and they shall fall down[7812] unto thee, they shall make supplication[6419] unto thee, *saying,* [c]Surely God *is* in thee; and [d]*there is* none else, *there is* no God.

15 Verily thou *art* a God[410] [a]that hidest thyself, O God of Israel, the Saviour.[3467]

16 They shall be ashamed,[954] and also confounded, all of them: they shall go to confusion[3639] together *that are* [a]makers of idols.[6736]

17 [a]*But* Israel shall be saved[3467] in the LORD with an everlasting[5769] salvation:[8668] ye shall not be ashamed nor confounded world without end.[5769]

18 For thus saith the LORD [a]that created the heavens; God himself that formed[3335] the earth and made it; he hath established[3559] it, he created it not in vain,[8414] he formed it to be inhabited: [b]I *am* the LORD; and *there is* none else.

19 I have not spoken[1696] in [a]secret, in a dark[2822] place of the earth: I said[559] not unto the seed[2233] of Jacob, Seek ye me in vain: [b]I the LORD speak righteousness, I declare[5046] things that are right.[4339]

28 [a]2Chr. 36:22, 23; Ezra 1:1; Isa. 45:13

1 [I]Or, *strengthened* [a]Isa. 41:13 [b]Isa. 41:2; Dan. 5:30

2 [a]Isa. 40:4 [b]Ps. 107:16

3 [a]Isa. 41:23 [b]Ex. 33:12, 17; Isa. 43:1; 49:1

4 [a]Isa. 44:1 [b]1Thess. 4:5

5 [a]Deut. 4:35, 39; 32:39; Isa. 44:8; 46:9 [b]Isa. 45:14, 18, 21, 22 [c]Ps. 18:32, 39

6 [a]Ps. 102:15; Isa. 37:20; Mal. 1:11

7 [a]Amos 3:6

8 [a]Ps. 72:3; 85:11

9 [a]Isa. 64:8 [b]Isa. 29:16; Jer. 18:6; Rom. 9:20

11 [a]Jer. 31:9 [b]Isa. 29:23

12 [a]Isa. 42:5; Jer. 27:5 [b]Gen. 1:26, 27 [c]Gen. 2:1

13 [I]Or, *make straight* [a]Isa. 41:2 [b]2Chr. 36:22, 23; Ezra 1:1; Isa. 44:28 [c]Isa. 52:3; Rom. 3:24

14 [a]Ps. 68:31; 72:10, 11; Isa. 49:23; 60:9, 10, 14, 16; Zech. 8:22, 23 [b]Ps. 149:8 [c]1Cor. 14:25 [d]Isa. 45:5

15 [a]Ps. 44:24; Isa. 8:17; 57:17

16 [a]Isa. 44:11

17 [a]Isa. 26:4; 45:25; Rom. 11:26

18 [a]Isa. 42:5 [b]Isa. 45:5

19 [a]Deut. 30:11; Isa. 48:16 [b]Ps. 19:8; 119:137, 138

The False Gods of Babylon

20 Assemble yourselves[6908] and come; draw near[5066] together, ye *that are* escaped of the nations: [a]they have no knowledge[3045] that set up[5375] the wood of their graven image, and pray[6419] unto a god *that* cannot save.[3467]

21 Tell[3045] ye, and bring *them* near;[5066] yea, let them take counsel[3289] together: [a]who hath declared[8085] this from ancient time?[6924] *who* hath told[5046] it from that time?[227] *have* not I the LORD? [b]and *there is* no God else beside me; a just God and a Saviour; *there is* none beside me.

22 [a]Look[6437] unto me, and be ye saved, all the ends of the earth: for I *am* God, and *there is* none else.

23 [a]I have sworn by myself, the word[1697] is gone out of my mouth[6310] *in* righteousness, and shall not return,[7725] That unto me every [b]knee shall bow,[3766] [c]every tongue shall swear.[7650]

24 [I]Surely, shall *one* say, in the LORD have I [II][a]righteousness and strength: *even* to him shall *men* come; and [b]all that are incensed[2734] against him shall be ashamed.

25 [a]In the LORD shall all the seed of Israel be justified,[6663] and [b]shall glory.[1984]

46 Bel [a]boweth down,[3766] Nebo stoopeth, their idols were upon the beasts,[2416] and upon the cattle: your carriages *were* heavy loaden; [b]*they are* a burden[4853] to the weary *beast.*

2 They stoop, they bow down together; they could not deliver the burden, [a]but [I]themselves are gone into captivity.[7628]

3 Hearken[8085] unto me, O house of Jacob, and all the remnant[7611] of the house of Israel, [a]which are borne *by me* from the belly, which are carried[5375] from the womb:

4 And *even* to *your* old age[2209] [a]I *am* he; and *even* to hoar hairs[7872] [b]will I carry *you:* I have made,[6213] and I will bear; even I will carry, and will deliver *you.*

5 [a]To whom will ye liken me, and make *me* equal,[7737] and compare[4911] me, that we may be like?

6 [a]They lavish gold out of the bag, and weigh silver in the balance, *and* hire a goldsmith;[6884] and he maketh it a god: they fall down,[5456] yea, they worship.[7812]

7 [a]They bear him upon the shoulder, they carry him, and set him in his place, and he standeth; from his place shall he not remove: yea, [b]*one* shall cry[6817] unto him, yet can he not answer, nor save[3467] him out of his trouble.

8 Remember[2142] this, and shew yourselves men:[377] [a]bring *it* again to mind,[3820] O ye transgressors.[6586]

9 [a]Remember the former things[7223] of old:[5769] for I *am* God,[410] and [b]*there is* none else; I *am* God,[430] and *there is* none like me,

10 [a]Declaring[5046] the end[319] from the beginning,[7225] and from ancient times[6924] *the things* that are not *yet* done,[6213] saying, [b]My counsel[6098] shall stand, and I will do all my pleasure:[2656]

11 Calling[7121] a ravenous bird [a]from the east, [I]the man[376] [b]that executeth my counsel from a far country:[776] yea, [c]I have spoken[1696] *it,* I will also bring it to pass; I have purposed[3335] *it,* I will also do it.

12 Hearken unto me, ye [a]stouthearted,[47,3820] [b]that *are* far from righteousness:[6666]

13 [a]I bring near[7126] my righteousness: it shall not be far off, and my salvation[8668] [b]shall not tarry: and I will place [c]salvation in Zion for Israel my glory.

Judgment on Babylon

47 Come [a]down, and [b]sit in the dust,[6083] O virgin[1330] daughter of Babylon, sit on the ground:[776] *there is* no throne,[3678] O daughter of the Chaldeans: for thou shalt no more be called[7121] tender and delicate.

2 [a]Take the millstones, and grind meal; uncover[1540] thy locks, make bare the leg, uncover the thigh, pass over[5674] the rivers.

---

20 [a]Isa. 44:17-19; 46:7; 48:7; Rom. 1:22, 23
21 [a]Isa. 41:22; 43:9; 44:7; 46:10; 48:14 [b]Isa. 44:8; 45:5, 14, 18; 46:9; 48:3
22 [a]Ps. 22:27; 65:5
23 [a]Gen. 22:16; Heb. 6:13 [b]Rom. 14:11; Phil. 2:10 [c]Gen. 31:53; Deut. 6:13; Ps. 63:11; Isa. 65:16
24 [I]Or, *Surely, he shall say of me, In the* LORD *is all righteousness and strength* [II]Hebr. *righteousnesses* [a]Jer. 23:5; 1Cor. 1:30 [b]Isa. 41:11
25 [a]Isa. 45:17 [b]1Cor. 1:31

1 [a]Isa. 21:9; Jer. 50:2; 51:44 [b]Jer. 10:5
2 [I]Hebr. *their soul* [a]Jer. 48:7
3 [a]Ex. 19:4; Deut. 1:31; 32:11; Ps. 71:6; Isa. 63:9
4 [a]Ps. 102:27; Mal. 3:6 [b]Ps. 48:14; 71:18
5 [a]Isa. 40:18, 25
6 [a]Isa. 40:19; 41:6; 44:12, 19; Jer. 10:3
7 [a]Jer. 10:5 [b]Isa. 45:20
8 [a]Isa. 44:19; 47:7
9 [a]Deut. 32:7 [b]Isa. 45:5, 21
10 [a]Isa. 45:21 [b]Ps. 33:11; Prov. 19:21; 21:30; Acts 5:39; Heb. 6:17
11 [I]Hebr. *the man of my counsel* [a]Isa. 41:2, 25 [b]Isa. 44:28; 45:13 [c]Num. 23:19
12 [a]Ps. 76:5 [b]Rom. 10:3
13 [a]Isa. 51:5; Rom. 1:17; 3:21 [b]Hab. 2:3 [c]Isa. 62:11

1 [a]Jer. 48:18 [b]Isa. 3:26
2 [a]Ex. 11:5; Judg. 16:21; Matt. 24:41

3 [a]Thy nakedness[6172] shall be uncovered, yea, thy shame shall be seen:[7200] [b]I will take vengeance,[5359] and I will not meet *thee as* a man.[120]

4 *As for* [a]our redeemer,[1350] the LORD of hosts[6635] *is* his name, the Holy One[6918] of Israel.

5 Sit thou [a]silent, and get thee into darkness,[2822] O daughter of the Chaldeans: [b]for thou shalt no more be called, The lady[1404] of kingdoms.[4467]

6 [a]I was wroth[7107] with my people, [b]I have polluted[2490] mine inheritance, and given them into thine hand:[3027] thou didst shew[7760] them no mercy;[7356] [c]upon the ancient[2204] hast thou very heavily laid thy yoke.

7 And thou saidst, I shall be [a]a lady for ever:[5769] so that thou didst not [b]lay[7760] these *things* to thy heart,[3820] [c]neither didst remember[2142] the latter end[319] of it.

8 Therefore hear[8085] now this, *thou that art* given to pleasures,5719 that dwellest carelessly,[983] that sayest in thine heart,3824 [a]I *am,* and none else beside me; [b]I shall not sit *as* a widow, neither shall I know[3045] the loss of children:

9 But [a]these two *things* shall come to thee [b]in a moment in one day, the loss of children,[7908] and widowhood: they shall come upon thee in their perfection[8537] [c]for the multitude of thy sorceries, *and* for the great abundance of thine enchantments.[2267]

10 For thou [a]hast trusted[982] in thy wickedness:[7451] [b]thou hast said,[559] None seeth[7200] me. Thy wisdom[2451] and thy knowledge,[1847] it hath [I]perverted[7725] thee; [c]and thou hast said in thine heart, I *am,* and none else beside me.

11 Therefore shall evil[7451] come upon thee; thou shalt not know [I]from whence it riseth: and mischief[1943] shall fall upon thee; thou shalt not be able to [II]put it off:[3722] and [a]desolation[7722] shall come upon thee suddenly, *which* thou shalt not know.

12 Stand now with thine enchantments, and with the multitude of thy sorceries,[3785] wherein thou hast laboured3021 from thy youth; if so be thou shalt be able to profit, if so be thou mayest prevail.[6206]

13 [a]Thou art wearied in the multitude of thy counsels. Let now [b]the [I]astrologers,8064 the stargazers,[2374] [II]the monthly prognosticators,[3045] stand up, and save[3467] thee from *these things* that shall come upon thee.

14 Behold, they shall be [a]as stubble; the fire shall burn[8313] them; they shall not deliver[5337] [I]themselves from the power[3027] of the flame: *there shall* not *be* a coal to warm at, *nor* fire217 to sit before it.

15 Thus shall they be unto thee with whom thou hast laboured, *even* [a]thy merchants, from thy youth: they shall wander[8582] every one[376] to his quarter; none shall save thee.

God Holds the Future

48 Hear[8085] ye this, O house[1004] of Jacob, which are called[7121] by the name of Israel, and [a]are come forth out of the waters of Judah, [b]which swear[7650] by the name of the LORD, and make mention of the God[430] of Israel, [c]*but* not in truth,[571] nor in righteousness.[6666]

2 For they call themselves[7121] [a]of the holy[6944] city, and [b]stay themselves upon the God of Israel; The LORD of hosts[6635] *is* his name.

3 [a]I have declared[5046] the former things[7223] from the beginning;[227] and they went forth out of my mouth,[6310] and I shewed[8085] them; I did[6213] *them* suddenly, [b]and they came to pass.

4 Because I knew that thou *art* [I]obstinate,[7186] and [a]thy neck *is* an iron sinew, and thy brow brass;

5 [a]I have even from the beginning[227] declared *it* to thee; before it came to pass I shewed *it* thee: lest thou shouldest say, Mine idol[6090] hath done[6213] them, and my graven image, and my molten image,[5262] hath commanded[6680] them.

6 Thou hast heard, see[2372] all this; and will not ye declare[5046] *it?* I have shewed thee new things from this time, even hidden things, and thou didst not know[3045] them.

---

3 [a]Isa. 3:17; 20:4; Jer. 13:22, 26; Nah. 3:5 [b]Rom. 12:19

4 [a]Isa. 43:3, 14; Jer. 50:34

5 [a]1Sam. 2:9 [b]Isa. 13:19; Isa. 47:7; Dan. 2:37

6 [a]2Sam. 24:14; 2Chr. 28:9; Zech. 1:15 [b]Isa. 43:28 [c]Deut. 28:50

7 [a]Isa. 47:5; Rev. 18:7 [b]Isa. 46:8 [c]Deut. 32:29

8 [a]Isa. 47:10; Zeph. 2:15 [b]Rev. 18:7

9 [a]Isa. 51:19 [b]1Thess. 5:3 [c]Nah. 3:4

10 [I]Or, *caused thee to turn away* [a]Ps. 52:7 [b]Isa. 29:15; Ezek. 8:12; 9:9 [c]Isa. 47:8

11 [I]Hebr. *the morning thereof* [II]Hebr. *expiate* [a]1Thess. 5:3

13 [I]Hebr. *viewers of the heavens* [II]Hebr. *that give knowledge concerning the months* [a]Isa. 57:10 [b]Isa. 44:25; Dan. 2:2

14 [I]Hebr. *their souls* [a]Nah. 1:10; Mal. 4:1

15 [a]Rev. 18:11

1 [a]Ps. 68:26 [b]Deut. 6:13; Isa. 65:16; Zeph. 1:5 [c]Jer. 4:2; 5:2

2 [a]Isa. 52:1 [b]Mic. 3:11; Rom. 2:17

3 [a]Isa. 41:22; 42:9; 43:9; 44:7, 8; 45:21; 46:9, 10 [b]Josh. 21:45

4 [I]Hebr. *hard* [a]Ex. 32:9; Deut. 31:27

5 [a]Isa. 48:3

7 They are created[1254] now, and not from the beginning; even before the day[3117] when thou heardest[8085] them not; lest thou shouldest say, Behold, I knew them.

8 Yea, thou heardest not; yea, thou knewest not; yea, from that time[227] *that* thine ear[241] was not opened: for I knew that thou wouldest deal very treacherously,[898] and wast called [a]a transgressor from the womb.[990]

9 [a]For my name's sake [b]will I defer[748] mine anger,[639] and for my praise[8416] will I refrain for thee, that I cut thee not off.[3772]

10 Behold, [a]I have refined[6884] thee, but not [1b]with silver; I have chosen[977] thee in the furnace of affliction.

11 [a]For mine own sake, *even* for mine own sake, will I do *it:* for [b]how should *my name* be polluted?[2490] and [c]I will not give my glory[3519] unto another.

12 Hearken[8085] unto me, O Jacob and Israel, my called; [a]I *am* he; I *am* the [b]first,[7223] I also *am* the last.

13 [a]Mine hand[3027] also hath laid the foundation[3245] of the earth,[776] and [1]my right hand hath spanned the heavens:[8064] *when* [b]I call unto them, they stand up together.

14 [a]All ye, assemble yourselves,[6908] and hear; which among them hath declared these *things?* [b]The LORD hath loved[157] him: [c]he will do his pleasure[2656] on Babylon, and his arm *shall be on* the Chaldeans.

15 I, *even* I, have spoken;[1696] yea, [a]I have called him: I have brought him, and he shall make his way[1870] prosperous.

16 Come ye near unto me, hear ye this; [a]I have not spoken in secret from the beginning;[7218] from the time[6256] that it was, there *am* I: and now [b]the Lord[136] GOD, and his Spirit,[7307] hath sent me.

17 Thus saith[559] [a]the LORD, thy Redeemer,[1350] the Holy One[6918] of Israel; I *am* the LORD thy God which teacheth[3925] thee to profit, [b]which leadeth thee by the way *that* thou shouldest go.

18 [a]O that thou hadst hearkened[7181] to my commandments![4687] [b]then had thy peace been as a river, and thy righteousness as the waves of the sea:

19 [a]Thy seed[2233] also had been as the sand, and the offspring of thy bowels[4578] like the gravel thereof; his name should not have been cut off[3772] nor destroyed[8045] from before me.

20 [a]Go ye forth of Babylon, flee ye from the Chaldeans, with a voice of singing declare ye, tell this, utter it *even* to the end of the earth; say ye, The LORD hath [b]redeemed[1350] his servant[5650] Jacob.

21 And they thirsted not *when* he led them through the deserts:[2723] he [a]caused the waters to flow out of the rock for them: he clave the rock also, and the waters gushed out.

22 [a]There is no peace, saith the LORD, unto the wicked.[7563]

Israel, God's Servant

49 Listen,[8085] [a]O isles, unto me; and hearken,[7181] ye people,[3816] from far; [b]The LORD hath called[7121] me from the womb;[990] from the bowels[4578] of my mother[517] hath he made mention of my name.

2 And he hath made[7760] [a]my mouth[6310] like a sharp sword;[2719] [b]in the shadow of his hand[3027] hath he hid me, and made me [c]a polished shaft; in his quiver hath he hid me;

3 And said unto me, [a]Thou *art* my servant,[5650] O Israel, [b]in whom I will be glorified.[6286]

4 [a]Then I said, I have laboured in vain, I have spent[3615] my strength for nought,[8414] and in vain:[1892] *yet* surely my judgment[4941] *is* with the LORD, and [1b]my work with my God.[430]

8 [a]Ps. 58:3
9 [a]Ps. 79:9; 106:8; Isa. 43:25; 48:11; Ezek. 20:9, 14, 22, 44 [b]Ps. 78:38
10 [1]Or, *for silver* [a]Ps. 66:10 [b]Ezek. 22:20-22
11 [a]Isa. 48:9 [b]Deut. 32:26, 27; Ezek. 20:9 [c]Isa. 42:8
12 [a]Deut. 32:39 [b]Isa. 41:4; 44:6; Rev. 1:17; 22:13
13 [1]Or, *the palm of my right hand hath spread out* [a]Ps. 102:25 [b]Isa. 40:26
14 [a]Isa. 41:22; 43:9; 44:7; 45:20, 21 [b]Isa. 45:1 [c]Isa. 44:28
15 [a]Isa. 45:1, 2
16 [a]Isa. 45:19 [b]Isa. 61:1; Zech. 2:8, 9, 11
17 [a]Isa. 43:14; 44:6, 24; 48:20 [b]Ps. 32:8
18 [a]Deut. 32:29; Ps. 81:13 [b]Ps. 119:165
19 [a]Gen. 22:17; Hos. 1:10
20 [a]Isa. 52:11; Jer. 50:8; 51:6, 45; Zech. 2:6, 7; Rev. 18:4 [b]Ex. 19:4-6; Isa. 44:22, 23
21 [a]Ex. 17:6; Num. 20:11; Ps. 105:41
22 [a]Isa. 57:21

1 [a]Isa. 41:1 [b]Isa. 49:5; Jer. 1:5; Matt. 1:20, 21; Luke 1:15, 31; John 10:36; Gal. 1:15
2 [a]Isa. 11:4; 51:16; Hos. 6:5; Heb. 4:12; Rev. 1:16 [b]Isa. 51:16 [c]Ps. 45:5
3 [a]Isa. 42:1; Zech. 3:8 [b]Isa. 44:23; John 13:31; 15:8; Eph. 1:6
4 [1]Or, *my reward* [a]Ezek. 3:19 [b]Isa. 40:10; 62:11

49:1–6 See note on Isaiah 42:1–4 regarding the "Servant Songs."

5 And now, saith the LORD [a]that formed[3335] me from the womb *to be* his servant, to bring Jacob again to him, [I]Though Israel [b]be not gathered, yet shall I be glorious in the eyes of the LORD, and my God shall be my strength.

6 And he said, [I]It is a light thing[7043] that thou shouldest be my servant to raise up the tribes[7626] of Jacob, and to restore[7725] the [II]preserved of Israel: I will also give thee for a [a]light[216] to the Gentiles,[1471] that thou mayest be my salvation[3444] unto the end of the earth.[776]

7 Thus saith the LORD,[3068] the Redeemer[1350] of Israel, *and* his Holy One,[6918] [I][a]to him whom man despiseth, to him whom the nation abhorreth,[8581] to a servant of rulers,[4910] [b]Kings[4428] shall see and arise, princes[8269] also shall worship,[7812] because of the LORD that is faithful,[539] *and* the Holy One of Israel, and he shall choose[977] thee.

Zion Will Be Restored

8 Thus saith the LORD, [a]In an acceptable[7522] time[6256] have I heard thee, and in a day of salvation have I helped thee: and I will preserve[5341] thee, [b]and give thee for a covenant[1285] of the people,[5971] to [I]establish the earth, to cause to inherit[5157] the desolate[8076] heritages;

9 That thou mayest say [a]to the prisoners, Go forth; to them that *are* in darkness,[2822] Shew yourselves.[1540] They shall feed in the ways, and their pastures *shall be* in all high places.

10 They shall not [a]hunger nor thirst; [b]neither shall the heat nor sun smite[5221] them: for he that hath mercy on them [c]shall lead them, even by the springs of water shall he guide them.

11 [a]And I will make[7760] all my mountains a way,[1870] and my highways shall be exalted.

12 Behold, [a]these shall come from far: and, lo, these from the north and from the west; and these from the land[776] of Sinim.

13 [a]Sing, O heavens;[8064] and be joyful, O earth; and break forth into singing, O mountains: for the LORD hath comforted[5162] his people, and will have mercy[7355] upon his afflicted.

14 [a]But Zion said, The LORD hath forsaken[5800] me, and my Lord[136] hath forgotten me.

15 [a]Can a woman[802] forget her sucking child, [I]that she should not have compassion[7355] on the son[1121] of her womb? yea, they may forget, [b]yet will I not forget thee.

16 Behold, [a]I have graven[2710] thee upon the palms of *my* hands;[3709] thy walls *are* continually[8548] before me.

17 Thy children[1121] shall make haste; [a]thy destroyers[2040] and they that made thee waste[2717] shall go forth of thee.

18 [a]Lift up[5375] thine eyes round about, and behold:[7200] all these gather themselves together,[6908] *and* come to thee. As I live,[2416] saith the LORD, thou shalt surely clothe thee with them all, [b]as with an ornament, and bind them *on thee,* as a bride *doeth.*

19 For thy waste[2723] and thy desolate places,[8074] and the land of thy destruction, [a]shall even now be too narrow by reason of the inhabitants, and they that swallowed thee up[1104] shall be far away.

20 [a]The children which thou shalt have, [b]after thou hast lost the other, shall say again in thine ears,[241] The place *is* too strait[6862] for me: give place[5066] to me that I may dwell.

21 Then shalt thou say in thine heart,[3824] Who hath begotten[3205] me these, seeing I have lost my children, and am desolate, a captive, and removing to and fro?[5493] and who hath brought up these? Behold, I was left[7604] alone; these, where *had* they *been?*

22 [a]Thus saith the Lord GOD, Behold, I will lift up mine hand to the Gentiles, and set up my standard to the people: and they shall bring thy sons in *their* [I]arms, and thy daughters shall be carried[5375] upon *their* shoulders.

23 [a]And kings shall be thy [I]nursing fathers, and their [II]queens[8282] thy nursing mothers: they shall bow down to thee with *their* face[639] toward the earth, and [b]lick up the dust[6083] of thy feet; and thou

5 [I]Or, *That Israel may be gathered to him, and I may* [a]Isa. 49:1 [b]Matt. 23:37

6 [I]Or, *Art thou lighter than that thou shouldest* [II]Or, *desolations* [a]Isa. 42:6; 60:3; Luke 2:32; Acts 13:47; 26:18

7 [I]Or, *to him that is despised in soul* [a]Isa. 53:3; Matt. 26:67 [b]Ps. 72:10, 11; Isa. 49:23

8 [I]Or, *raise up* [a]Ps. 69:13; 2Cor. 6:2 [b]Isa. 42:6

9 [a]Isa. 42:7; Zech. 9:12

10 [a]Rev. 7:16 [b]Ps. 121:6 [c]Ps. 23:2

11 [a]Isa. 40:4

12 [a]Isa. 43:5, 6

13 [a]Isa. 44:23

14 [a]Isa. 40:27

15 [I]Hebr. *from having compassion* [a]Ps. 103:13; Mal. 3:17; Matt. 7:11 [b]Rom. 11:29

16 [a]Ex. 13:9; Song 8:6

17 [a]Isa. 49:19

18 [a]Isa. 60:4 [b]Prov. 17:6

19 [a]Isa. 54:1, 2; Zech. 2:4; 10:10

20 [a]Isa. 60:4 [b]Matt. 3:9; Rom. 11:11, 12

22 [I]Hebr. *bosom* [a]Isa. 60:4; 66:20

23 [I]Hebr. *nourishers* [II]Hebr. *princesses* [a]Ps. 72:11; Isa. 49:7; 52:15; 60:16 [b]Ps. 72:9; Mic. 7:17

shalt know[3045] that I *am* the LORD: for [c]they shall not be ashamed[954] that wait for[6960] me.

24 [a]Shall the prey be taken from the mighty, or [I]the lawful[6662] captive delivered?[4422]

25 But thus saith the LORD, Even the [I]captives[7628] of the mighty shall be taken away, and the prey of the terrible shall be delivered: for I will contend[7378] with him that contendeth with thee, and I will save[3467] thy children.

26 And I will [a]feed them that oppress[3238] thee with their own flesh;[1320] and they shall be drunken with their own [b]blood,[1818] as with [I]sweet wine: and all flesh [c]shall know that I the LORD *am* thy Saviour[3467] and thy Redeemer, the mighty One of Jacob.

God Helps Those Who Trust Him

50 Thus saith[559] the LORD, Where *is* [a]the bill[5612] of your mother's divorcement,[3748] whom I have put away? or which of my [b]creditors *is it* to whom I have sold you? Behold, for your iniquities[5771] [c]have ye sold yourselves, and for your transgressions[6588] is your mother[517] put away.

2 Wherefore, when I came, *was there* no man?[376] [a]when I called,[7121] *was there* none to answer? [b]Is my hand[3027] shortened at all, that it cannot redeem?[6304] or have I no power to deliver?[5337] behold, [c]at my rebuke[1606] I [d]dry up[2717] the sea, I make[7760] the [e]rivers a wilderness: [f]their fish stinketh,[887] because *there is* no water, and dieth[4191] for thirst.

3 [a]I clothe the heavens[8064] with blackness,[6940] [b]and I make sackcloth their covering.

🔑 4 [a]The Lord[136] GOD hath given me the tongue of the learned,[3928] that I should know[3045] how to speak a word in season[5790] to *him that is* [b]weary: he wakeneth morning by morning, he wakeneth mine ear[241] to hear[8085] as the learned.

23 [c]Ps. 34:22; Rom. 5:5; 9:33; 10:11
24 [I]Hebr. *the captivity of the just* [a]Matt. 12:29; Luke 11:21, 22
25 [I]Hebr. *captivity*
26 [I]Or, *new wine* [a]Isa. 9:20 [b]Rev. 14:20; 16:6 [c]Ps. 9:16; Isa. 60:16
1 [a]Deut. 24:1; Jer. 3:8; Hos. 2:2 [b]2Kgs. 4:1; Matt. 18:25 [c]Isa. 52:3
2 [a]Prov. 1:24; Isa. 65:12; 66:4; Jer. 7:13; 35:15 [b]Num. 11:23; Isa. 59:1 [c]Ps. 106:9; Nah. 1:4 [d]Ex. 14:21 [e]Josh. 3:16 [f]Ex. 7:18, 21
3 [a]Ex. 10:21 [b]Rev. 6:12
4 [a]Ex. 4:11 [b]Matt. 11:28
5 [a]Ps. 40:6-8 [b]Matt. 26:39; John 14:31; Phil. 2:8; Heb. 10:5
6 [a]Matt. 26:67; 27:26; John 18:22 [b]Lam. 3:30
7 [a]Ezek. 3:8, 9
8 [I]Hebr. *the master of my cause* [a]Rom. 8:32-34
9 [a]Job 13:28; Ps. 102:26; Isa. 51:6 [b]Isa. 51:8
10 [a]Ps. 23:4 [b]2Chr. 20:20; Ps. 20:7
11 [a]John 9:39 [b]Ps. 16:4
1 [a]Isa. 51:7 [b]Rom. 9:30-32
2 [a]Rom. 4:1, 16; Heb. 11:11, 12 [b]Gen. 12:1, 2 [c]Gen. 24:1, 35
3 [a]Ps. 102:13; Isa. 40:1; 51:12; 52:9

5 The Lord GOD [a]hath opened mine ear, and I was not [b]rebellious, neither turned away back.

6 [a]I gave my back[1460] to the smiters,[5221] and [b]my cheeks to them that plucked off the hair: I hid not my face from shame and spitting.

7 For the Lord GOD will help me; therefore shall I not be confounded:[3637] therefore have [a]I set[7760] my face like a flint, and I know that I shall not be ashamed.[954]

8 [a]*He is* near that justifieth[6663] me; who will contend[7378] with me? let us stand together: who *is* [I]mine adversary? let him come near[5066] to me.

9 Behold, the Lord GOD will help me; who *is* he *that* shall condemn[7561] me? [a]lo, they all shall wax old as a garment; [b]the moth shall eat them up.

10 Who *is* among you that feareth the LORD, that obeyeth[8085] the voice of his servant,[5650] that [a]walketh *in* darkness,[2825] and hath no light? [b]let him trust[982] in the name of the LORD, and stay[8172] upon his God.[430]

11 Behold, all ye that kindle a fire, that compass *yourselves* about with sparks: walk in the light[217] of your fire, and in the sparks *that* ye have kindled. [a]This shall ye have of mine hand; ye shall lie down [b]in sorrow.[4620]

Comforting Words for Jerusalem

51 [a]Hearken[8085] to me, [b]ye that follow after righteousness,[6664] ye that seek the LORD: look unto the rock *whence* ye are hewn,[2672] and to the hole of the pit[953] *whence* ye are digged.

2 [a]Look unto Abraham your father,[1] and unto Sarah *that* bare you: [b]for I called[7121] him alone, and [c]blessed[1288] him, and increased him.

3 For the LORD [a]shall comfort[5162] Zion: he will comfort all her waste places;[2723] and he will make[7760] her wilderness like Eden, and her desert[6160]

🔑 **50:4–11** See note on Isaiah 42:1–4 concerning the "Servant Songs."

[b]like the garden of the LORD; joy and gladness shall be found therein, thanksgiving,[8426] and the voice of melody.

4 Hearken[7181] unto me, my people;[5971] and give ear[238] unto me, O my nation: [a]for a law[8451] shall proceed from me, and I will make my judgment[4941] to rest [b]for a light[216] of the people.

5 [a]My righteousness *is* near; my salvation[3468] is gone forth, [b]and mine arms shall judge[8199] the people; [c]the isles shall wait[6960] upon me, and [d]on mine arm shall they trust.[3176]

6 [a]Lift up[5375] your eyes to the heavens,[8064] and look upon the earth[776] beneath: for [b]the heavens shall vanish away like smoke, [c]and the earth shall wax old like a garment, and they that dwell therein shall die[4191] in like manner: but my salvation[3444] shall be for ever,[5769] and my righteousness[6666] shall not be abolished.[2865]

7 [a]Hearken unto me, ye that know[3045] righteousness, the people [b]in whose heart[3820] *is* my law; [c]fear[3372] ye not the reproach[2781] of men,[582] neither be ye afraid[2865] of their revilings.

8 For [a]the moth shall eat them up like a garment, and the worm shall eat them like wool: but my righteousness shall be for ever, and my salvation from generation[1755] to generation.

9 [a]Awake, awake, [b]put on strength,[5797] O arm of the LORD; awake, [c]as in the ancient[6924] days,[3117] in the generations[1755] of old.[5769] [d]*Art* thou not it that hath cut[2672] [e]Rahab, *and* wounded[2490] the [f]dragon?[8577]

10 *Art* thou not it which hath [a]dried the sea, the waters of the great deep; that hath made[7760] the depths of the sea a way[1870] for the ransomed[1350] to pass over?[5674]

11 Therefore [a]the redeemed[6299] of the LORD shall return,[7725] and come with singing unto Zion; and everlasting[5769] joy *shall be* upon their head:[7218] they shall obtain gladness and joy; *and* sorrow and mourning shall flee away.

12 I, *even* I, *am* he [a]that comforteth[5162] you: who *art* thou, that thou shouldest be afraid[3372] [b]of a man[582] *that* shall die, and of the son[1121] of man[120] *which* shall be made [c]*as* grass;

13 And forgettest the LORD thy maker,[6213] [a]that hath stretched forth the heavens, and laid the foundations[3245] of the earth; and hast feared[6342] continually[8548] every day because of the fury of the oppressor, as if he [I]were ready[3559] to destroy?[7843] [b]and where *is* the fury of the oppressor?

14 The captive exile hasteneth that he may be loosed, [a]and that he should not die in the pit,[7845] nor that his bread should fail.

15 But I *am* the LORD thy God,[430] that [a]divided the sea, whose waves roared: The LORD of hosts[6635] *is* his name.

16 And [a]I have put my words[1697] in thy mouth,[6310] and [b]I have covered[3680] thee in the shadow of mine hand,[3027] [c]that I may plant the heavens, and lay the foundations of the earth, and say unto Zion, Thou *art* my people.

17 [a]Awake, awake, stand up, O Jerusalem, which [b]hast drunk at the hand of the LORD the cup of his fury; [c]thou hast drunken the dregs[6907] of the cup of trembling, *and* wrung *them* out.

18 *There is* none to guide her among all the sons *whom* she hath brought forth; neither *is there any* that taketh[2388] her by the hand of all the sons *that* she hath brought up.

19 [a]These two *things* [I]are come unto thee; who shall be sorry for thee? desolation,[7701] and [II]destruction,[7667] and the famine, and the sword:[2719] [b]by whom shall I comfort thee?

20 [a]Thy sons have fainted, they lie at the head of all the streets, as a wild bull in a net: they are full of the fury of the LORD, the rebuke[1606] of thy God.

21 Therefore hear[8085] now this, thou afflicted, and drunken, [a]but not with wine:

22 Thus saith[559] thy Lord[113] the LORD, and thy God [a]*that* pleadeth[7378] the cause of his people, Behold, I have taken out of thine hand the cup of trembling,[8653] *even* the dregs of the cup of

3 [b]Gen. 13:10; Joel 2:3
4 [a]Isa. 2:3; 42:4 [b]Isa. 42:6
5 [a]Isa. 46:13; 56:1; Rom. 1:16, 17 [b]Ps. 67:4; 98:9 [c]Isa. 60:9 [d]Rom. 1:16
6 [a]Isa. 40:26 [b]Ps. 102:26; Matt. 24:35; 2Pet. 3:10, 12 [c]Isa. 50:9
7 [a]Isa. 51:1 [b]Ps. 37:31 [c]Matt. 10:28; Acts 5:41
8 [a]Isa. 50:9
9 [a]Ps. 44:23; Isa. 52:1 [b]Ps. 93:1; Rev. 11:17 [c]Ps. 44:1 [d]Job 26:12 [e]Ps. 87:4; 89:10 [f]Ps. 74:13, 14; Isa. 27:1; Ezek. 29:3
10 [a]Ex. 14:21; Isa. 43:16
11 [a]Isa. 35:10
12 [a]Isa. 51:3; 2Cor. 1:3 [b]Ps. 118:6 [c]Isa. 40:6; 1Pet. 1:24
13 [I]Or, *made himself ready* [a]Job 9:8; Ps. 104:2; Isa. 40:22; 42:5; 44:24 [b]Job 20:7
14 [a]Zech. 9:11
15 [a]Job 26:12; Ps. 74:13; Jer. 31:35
16 [a]Deut. 18:18; Isa. 59:21; John 3:34 [b]Isa. 49:2 [c]Isa. 65:17; 66:22
17 [a]Isa. 52:1 [b]Job 21:20; Jer. 25:15, 16 [c]Deut. 28:28, 34; Ps. 60:3; 75:8; Ezek. 23:32-34; Zech. 12:2; Rev. 14:10
19 [I]Hebr. *happened* [II]Hebr. *breaking* [a]Isa. 47:9 [b]Amos 7:2
20 [a]Lam. 2:11, 12
21 [a]Isa. 51:17; Lam. 3:15
22 [a]Jer. 50:34

my fury; thou shalt no more drink it again:

23 But [a]I will put it into the hand of them that afflict[3013] thee; [b]which have said to thy soul,[5315] Bow down, that we may go over:[5674] and thou hast laid[7760] thy body[1460] as the ground,[776] and as the street, to them that went over.

Zion Will Escape

52 Awake, [a]awake; put on thy strength, O Zion; put on thy beautiful[8597] garments, O Jerusalem, [b]the holy[6944] city: for [c]henceforth there shall no more come into thee the uncircumcised[6189] [d]and the unclean.[2931]

2 [a]Shake thyself from the dust;[6083] arise, *and* sit down, O Jerusalem: [b]loose thyself from the bands of thy neck, O captive[7628] daughter of Zion.

3 For thus saith[559] the LORD, [a]Ye have sold yourselves for nought;[2600] and ye shall be redeemed[1350] without money.

4 For thus saith the Lord[136] GOD, My people[5971] went down aforetime into [a]Egypt to sojourn there; and the Assyrian oppressed them without cause.

5 Now therefore, what have I here, saith[5002] the LORD, that my people is taken away for nought? they that rule[4910] over them make them to howl, saith the LORD; and my name continually[8548] every day[3117] *is* [a]blasphemed.[5006]

6 Therefore my people shall know my name: therefore *they shall know* in that day that I *am* he that doth speak:[1696] behold, *it is* I.

7 [a]How beautiful upon the mountains are the feet of him that bringeth good tidings,[1319] that publisheth[8085] peace; that bringeth good tidings of good, that publisheth salvation;[3444] that saith unto Zion, [b]Thy God[430] reigneth![4427]

8 Thy watchmen shall lift up the voice; with the voice together shall they sing: for they shall see eye to eye, when the LORD shall bring again[7725] Zion.

9 Break forth into joy, sing[7442] together, ye waste places[2723] of Jerusalem: [a]for the LORD[3068] hath comforted[5162] his people, [b]he hath redeemed Jerusalem.

10 [a]The LORD hath made bare his holy arm in the eyes of all the nations;[1471] and [b]all the ends of the earth[776] shall see the salvation of our God.

11 [a]Depart[5493] ye, depart ye, go ye out from thence, touch[5060] no unclean *thing;* go ye out of the midst[8432] of her; [b]be ye clean,[1305] that bear[5375] the vessels of the LORD.

12 For [a]ye shall not go out with haste, nor go by flight: [b]for the LORD will go before you; [c]and the God of Israel *will* [I]be your rereward.[622]

The Suffering Servant

🗝 13 Behold, [a]my servant[5650] shall [I]deal prudently,[7919] [b]he shall be exalted and extolled, and be very high.

14 As many were astonied[8074] at thee; his [a]visage[4758] was so marred[4893] more than any man,[376] and his form[8389] more than the sons[1121] of men:[120]

15 [a]So shall he sprinkle[5137] many nations; [b]the kings[4428] shall shut their mouths[6310] at him: for *that* [c]which had not been told[5608] them shall they see; and *that* which they had not heard[8085] shall they consider.[995]

53 Who [a]hath believed[539] our [I]report? and to whom is [b]the arm of the LORD revealed?[1540]

23 [a]Jer. 25:17, 26, 28; Zech. 12:2 [b]Ps. 66:11, 12

1 [a]Isa. 51:9, 17 [b]Neh. 11:1; Isa. 48:2; Matt. 4:5; Rev. 21:2 [c]Isa. 35:8; 60:21; Nah. 1:15 [d]Rev. 21:27

2 [a]Isa. 3:26; 51:23 [b]Zech. 2:7

3 [a]Ps. 44:12; Isa. 45:13; Jer. 15:13

4 [a]Gen. 46:6; Acts 7:14

5 [a]Ezek. 36:20, 23; Rom. 2:24

7 [a]Nah. 1:15; Rom. 10:15 [b]Ps. 93:1; 96:10; 97:1

9 [a]Isa. 51:3 [b]Isa. 48:20

10 [a]Ps. 98:2, 3 [b]Luke 3:6

11 [a]Isa. 48:20; Jer. 50:8; 51:6, 45; Zech. 2:6, 7; 2Cor. 6:17; Rev. 18:4 [b]Lev. 22:2

12 [I]Hebr. *gather you up* [a]Ex. 12:33, 39 [b]Mic. 2:13 [c]Num. 10:25; Isa. 58:8; Ex. 14:19

13 [I]Or, *prosper,* Isa. 53:10; Jer. 23:5 [a]Isa. 42:1 [b]Phil. 2:9

14 [a]Ps. 22:6, 7; Isa. 53:2, 3

15 [a]Ezek. 36:25; Acts 2:33; Heb. 9:13, 14 [b]Isa. 49:7, 23 [c]Isa. 55:5; Rom. 15:21; 16:25, 26; Eph. 3:5, 9

1 [I]Hebr. *hearing* [a]John 12:38; Rom. 10:16 [b]Isa. 51:9; Rom. 1:16; 1Cor. 1:18

🗝 **52:13—53:12** This "Servant Song" is one of the most explicit prophecies of Christ's atoning work on Calvary. It caused a great struggle within Judaism because it clearly connected the Messiah with suffering and death. As a result, some Jewish scholars even suggested two messiahs: one who would suffer, and another who would reign. They could not see ahead of time how Jesus could fulfill both sets of prophecies. Jesus applied this prophecy to Himself (Luke 22:37), as did His disciples (Matt. 8:17; John 12:38; Heb. 9:28; Rev. 5:6, 12; 13:8).

2 For [a]he shall grow up before him as a tender plant,3126 and as a root out of a dry ground:776 [b]he hath no form nor comeliness;1926 and when we shall see him, *there is* no beauty that we should desire2530 him.

3 [a]He is despised and rejected2310 of men;376 a man of sorrows,4341 and [b]acquainted3045 with grief:2483 and [I]we hid as it were *our* faces from him; he was despised, and [c]we esteemed2803 him not.

4 Surely [a]he hath borne5375 our griefs, and carried our sorrows: yet we did esteem him stricken,5060 smitten5221 of God,430 and afflicted.

5 But he *was* [I][a]wounded2490 for our transgressions,6588 *he was* bruised1792 for our iniquities:5771 the chastisement4148 of our peace *was* upon him; and with his [II][b]stripes2250 we are healed.7495

6 [a]All we like sheep have gone astray;8582 we have turned every one to his own way;1870 and the LORD [I]hath laid on him the iniquity5771 of us all.

7 He was oppressed, and he was afflicted, yet [a]he opened not his mouth:6310 [b]he is brought as a lamb to the slaughter,2874 and as a sheep before her shearers is dumb, so he openeth not his mouth.

8 [I]He was taken from prison and from judgment:4941 and who shall declare7878 his generation?1755 for [a]he was cut off1504 out of the land776 of the living:2416 for the transgression6588 of my people5971 [II]was he stricken.5061

9 [a]And he made his grave6913 with the wicked,7563 and with the rich in his [I]death;4194 because he had done6213 no violence,2555 neither *was any* [b]deceit4820 in his mouth.

10 Yet it pleased2654 the LORD to bruise him; he hath put *him* to grief: [I]when thou shalt make7760 his soul5315 [a]an offering for sin,817 he shall see *his* seed,2233 [b]he shall prolong748 *his* days,3117 and [c]the pleasure2656 of the LORD shall prosper6743 in his hand.3027

11 He shall see of the travail5999 of his soul, *and* shall be satisfied: [a]by his knowledge shall6663 [b]my righteous6662 [c]servant5650 [d]justify6663 many; [e]for he shall bear their iniquities.

12 [a]Therefore will I divide him *a portion* with the great, [b]and he shall divide the spoil with the strong; because he hath poured out6168 his soul unto death: and he was [c]numbered with the transgressors;6586 and he bare5375 the sin2399 of many, and [d]made intercession for the transgressors.

God Loves Israel

54 [a]Sing, O barren,6135 thou *that* didst not bear; break forth into singing, and cry aloud, thou *that* didst not travail with child:2342 for [b]more *are* the children1121 of the desolate8074 than the children of the married wife,1166 saith559 the LORD.

2 [a]Enlarge the place of thy tent,168 and let them stretch forth the curtains of thine habitations:4908 spare not, lengthen748 thy cords, and strengthen2388 thy stakes;

3 For thou shalt break forth on the right hand and on the left; [a]and thy seed2233 shall inherit3423 the Gentiles,1471 and make the desolate8077 cities to be inhabited.

4 Fear3372 not; for thou shalt not be ashamed:954 neither be thou confounded;3637 for thou shalt not be put to shame: for thou shalt forget the shame of thy youth, and shalt not remember2142 the reproach2781 of thy widowhood any more.

5 [a]For thy Maker *is* thine husband;1166 the [b]LORD of hosts6635 *is* his name; and thy Redeemer1350 the Holy One6918 of Israel; [c]The God430 of the whole earth776 shall he be called.7121

6 For the LORD [a]hath called thee as a woman802 forsaken5800 and grieved in spirit,7307 and a wife802 of youth, when thou wast refused, saith thy God.

7 [a]For a small moment have I forsaken thee; but with great mercies7356 will I gather6908 thee.

8 In a little wrath7110 I hid my face from thee for a moment; [a]but with ever-

2 [a]Isa. 11:1 [b]Isa. 52:14; Mark 9:12
3 [I]Or, *he hid as it were his face from us;* Hebr. *as a hiding of faces from him,* or, *from us* [a]Ps. 22:6; Isa. 49:7 [b]Heb. 4:15 [c]John 1:10, 11
4 [a]Matt. 8:17; Heb. 9:28; 1Pet. 2:24
5 [I]Or, *tormented* [II]Hebr. *bruise* [a]Rom. 4:25; 1Cor. 15:3; 1Pet. 3:18 [b]1Pet. 2:24
6 [I]Hebr. *hath made the iniquity of us all to meet on him* [a]Ps. 119:176; 1Pet. 2:25
7 [a]Matt. 26:63; 27:12, 14; Mark 14:61; 15:5; 1Pet. 2:23 [b]Acts 8:32
8 [I]Or, *He was taken away by distress and judgment: but* [II]Hebr. was *the stroke upon him* [a]Dan. 9:26
9 [I]Hebr. *deaths* [a]Matt. 27:57, 58, 60 [b]1Pet. 2:22; 1John 3:5
10 [I]Or, *when his soul shall make an offering* [a]2Cor. 5:21; 1Pet. 2:24 [b]Rom. 6:9 [c]Eph. 1:5, 9; 2Thess. 1:11
11 [a]John 17:3; 2Pet. 1:3 [b]1John 2:1 [c]Isa. 42:1; 49:3 [d]Rom. 5:18, 19 [e]Isa. 53:4, 5
12 [a]Ps. 2:8; Phil. 2:9 [b]Col. 2:15 [c]Mark 15:28; Luke 22:37 [d]Luke 23:34; Rom. 8:34; Heb. 7:25; 9:24; 1John 2:1

1 [a]Zeph. 3:14; Gal. 4:27 [b]1Sam. 2:5
2 [a]Isa. 49:19, 20
3 [a]Isa. 55:5; 61:9
5 [a]Jer. 3:14 [b]Luke 1:32 [c]Zech. 14:9; Rom. 3:29
6 [a]Isa. 62:4
7 [a]Ps. 30:5; Isa. 26:20; 60:10; 2Cor. 4:17
8 [a]Isa. 55:3; Jer. 31:3

lasting[5769] kindness[2617] will I have mercy[7355] on thee, saith the LORD thy Redeemer.

9 For this *is as* the waters of [a]Noah unto me: for *as* I have sworn that the waters of Noah should no more go over[5674] the earth; so have I sworn that I would not be wroth[7107] with thee, nor rebuke[1605] thee.

10 For [a]the mountains shall depart, and the hills be removed; [b]but my kindness shall not depart from thee, neither shall the covenant[1285] of my peace be removed, saith the LORD that hath mercy on thee.

Jerusalem in the Future

11 O thou afflicted, tossed with tempest, *and* not comforted,[5162] behold, I will lay thy stones with [a]fair colours,[6320] and lay thy foundations[3245] with sapphires.

12 And I will make[7760] thy windows of agates, and thy gates of carbuncles, and all thy borders of pleasant[2656] stones.

13 And all thy children *shall be* [a]taught[3928] of the LORD; and [b]great *shall be* the peace of thy children.

14 In righteousness[6666] shalt thou be established:[3559] thou shalt be far from oppression; for thou shalt not fear: and from terror;[4288] for it shall not come near[7126] thee.

15 Behold, they shall surely gather together,[1481] *but* not by me: whosoever shall gather together against thee shall fall for thy sake.

16 Behold, I have created[1254] the smith that bloweth[5301] the coals in the fire, and that bringeth forth an instrument for his work; and I have created the waster[7843] to destroy.[2254]

17 No weapon that is formed[3335] against thee shall prosper; and every tongue *that* shall rise against thee in judgment[4941] thou shalt condemn.[7561] This *is* the heritage[5159] of the servants[5650] of the LORD, [a]and their righteousness *is* of me, saith[5002] the LORD.

9 [a]Gen. 8:21; 9:11; Isa. 55:11; Jer. 31:35, 36
10 [a]Ps. 46:2; Isa. 51:6; Matt. 5:18 [b]Ps. 89:33, 34
11 [a]1Chr. 29:2; Rev. 21:18
13 [a]Isa. 11:9; Jer. 31:34; John 6:45; 1Cor. 2:10; 1Thess. 4:9; 1John 2:20 [b]Ps. 119:165
17 [a]Isa. 45:24, 25
1 [a]John 4:14; 7:37; Rev. 21:6; 22:17 [b]Matt. 13:44, 46; Rev. 3:18
2 [I]Hebr. *weigh*
3 [a]Matt. 11:28 [b]Isa. 54:8; 61:8; Jer. 32:40 [c]2Sam. 7:8; Ps. 89:28; Acts 13:34
4 [a]John 18:37; Rev. 1:5 [b]Jer. 30:9; Ezek. 34:23; Dan. 9:25; Hos. 3:5
5 [a]Isa. 52:15; Eph. 2:11, 12 [b]Isa. 60:5 [c]Isa. 60:9; Acts 3:13
6 [a]Ps. 32:6; Matt. 5:25; 25:11; John 7:34; 8:21; 2Cor. 6:1, 2; Heb. 3:13
7 [I]Hebr. *the man of iniquity* [II]Hebr. *he will multiply to pardon* [a]Isa. 1:16 [b]Zech. 8:17 [c]Ps. 130:7; Jer. 3:12
8 [a]2Sam. 7:19
9 [a]Ps. 103:11
10 [a]Deut. 32:2
11 [a]Isa. 54:9

God Offers Mercy

55 Ho, [a]every one that thirsteth, come ye to the waters, and he that hath no money; [b]come ye, buy, and eat; yea, come, buy wine and milk without money and without price.

2 Wherefore do ye [I]spend money for *that which is* not bread? and your labour for *that which* satisfieth not? hearken[8085] diligently unto me, and eat ye *that which is* good,[2896] and let your soul[5315] delight itself in fatness.

3 Incline your ear,[241] and [a]come unto me: hear,[8085] and your soul shall live;[2421] [b]and I will make an everlasting[5769] covenant[1285] with you, *even* the [c]sure[539] mercies[2617] of David.

4 Behold, I have given him *for* [a]a witness to the people,[3816] [b]a leader and commander[6680] to the people.

5 [a]Behold, thou shalt call[7121] a nation[1471] *that* thou knowest not, [b]and nations *that* knew[3045] not thee shall run unto thee because of the LORD[3068] thy God,[430] and for the Holy One[6918] of Israel; [c]for he hath glorified[6286] thee.

6 [a]Seek[1875] ye the LORD while he may be found, call ye upon him while he is near:

7 [a]Let the wicked[7563] forsake[5800] his way, and [I]the unrighteous[205] man[376] [b]his thoughts:[4284] and let him return[7725] unto the LORD, [c]and he will have mercy[7355] upon him; and to our God, for [II]he will abundantly pardon.[5545]

8 [a]For my thoughts[4284] *are* not your thoughts, neither *are* your ways[1870] my ways, saith the LORD.

9 [a]For *as* the heavens[8064] are higher than the earth,[776] so are my ways higher than your ways, and my thoughts than your thoughts.

10 For [a]as the rain cometh down, and the snow from heaven, and returneth[7725] not thither, but watereth the earth, and maketh it bring forth and bud, that it may give seed[2233] to the sower, and bread to the eater:

11 [a]So shall my word[1697] be that goeth forth out of my mouth:[6310] it shall not return unto me void, but it shall

accomplish[6213] that which I please,[2654] and it shall prosper *in the thing* whereto I sent it.

12 [a]For ye shall go out with joy, and be led forth[2986] with peace: the mountains and the hills shall [b]break forth before you into singing, and [c]all the trees of the field[7704] shall clap *their* hands.[3709]

13 [a]Instead of [b]the thorn shall come up[5927] the fir tree, and instead of the brier shall come up the myrtle tree: and it shall be to the LORD [c]for a name, for an everlasting sign *that* shall not be cut off.[3772]

Keeping the Sabbath

56 Thus saith[559] the LORD, Keep ye [I]judgment,[4941] and do justice:[6666] [a]for my salvation[3444] *is* near to come, and my righteousness[6666] to be revealed.[1540]

2 Blessed[835] *is* the man[582] *that* doeth[6213] this, and the son[1121] of man[120] *that* layeth hold on it; [a]that keepeth[8104] the sabbath[7676] from polluting[2490] it, and keepeth his hand[3027] from doing any evil.[7451]

3 Neither let [a]the son of the stranger,[5236] that hath joined himself to the LORD, speak, saying, The LORD hath utterly separated[914] me from his people:[5971] neither let the eunuch[5631] say, Behold, I *am* a dry tree.

4 For thus saith the LORD unto the eunuchs that keep my sabbaths,[7676] and choose[977] *the things* that please[2654] me, and take hold of my covenant;[1285]

5 Even unto them will I give in [a]mine house[1004] and within my walls a place [b]and a name better[2896] than of sons[1121] and of daughters: I will give them an everlasting[5769] name, that shall not be cut off.[3772]

6 Also the sons of the stranger, that join themselves to the LORD, to serve[8334] him, and to love[157] the name of the LORD, to be his servants,[5650] every one that keepeth the sabbath from polluting it, and taketh hold[2388] of my covenant;

7 Even them will I [a]bring to my holy[6944] mountain, and make them joyful in my house of prayer:[8605] [b]their burnt offerings[5930] and their sacrifices[2077] *shall be* accepted[7522] upon mine altar;[4196] for [c]mine house shall be called[7121] an house of prayer [d]for all people.

8 The Lord[136] GOD [a]which gathereth[6908] the outcasts of Israel saith,[5002] [b]Yet will I gather *others* to him, [I]beside those that are gathered unto him.

Israel's Leaders Are Condemned

9 [a]All ye beasts[2416] of the field,[7704] come to devour, *yea,* all ye beasts in the forest.

10 His watchmen *are* [a]blind: they are all ignorant, [b]they *are* all dumb dogs, they cannot bark; [I]sleeping, lying down, loving to slumber.

11 Yea, *they are* [Ia]greedy[5315][5794] dogs *which* [IIb]can never have enough, and they *are* shepherds *that* cannot understand:[995] they all look to their own way,[1870] every one for his gain, from his quarter.

12 Come ye, *say they,* I will fetch wine, and we will fill ourselves with strong drink; [a]and to morrow shall be as this day,[3117] *and* much more abundant.[3499]

Condemnation of Israel's Idolatry

57 The righteous[6662] perisheth,[6] and no man[376] layeth[7760] *it* to heart:[3820] and [Ia]merciful[2617] men[582] *are* taken away, [b]none considering[995] that the righteous is taken away[622] [II]from the evil[7451] *to come.*

2 He shall [Ia]enter into peace: they shall rest in [b]their beds, *each one* walking [II]*in* his uprightness.[5228]

3 But draw near[7126] hither, [a]ye sons[1121] of the sorceress,[6049] the seed[2233] of the adulterer[5003] and the whore.[2181]

4 Against whom do ye sport yourselves?[6026] against whom make ye a wide mouth,[6310] *and* draw out[748] the tongue? *are* ye not children of transgression,[6588] a seed of falsehood,

5 Enflaming yourselves [Ia]with idols[410] [b]under every green tree, [c]slaying

12 [a]Isa. 35:10; 65:13, 14 [b]Ps. 96:12; 98:8; Isa. 14:8; 35:1, 2; 42:11 [c]1Chr. 16:33
13 [a]Isa. 41:10 [b]Mic. 7:4 [c]Jer. 13:11

1 [I]Or, *equity* [a]Isa. 46:13; Matt. 3:2; 4:17; Rom. 13:11, 12
2 [a]Isa. 58:13
3 [a]Deut. 23:1-3; Acts 8:27; 10:1, 2, 34; 17:4; 18:7; 1Pet. 1:1
5 [a]1Tim. 3:15 [b]John 1:12; 1John 3:1
7 [a]Isa. 2:2; 1Pet. 1:1, 2 [b]Rom. 12:1; Heb. 13:15; 1Pet. 2:5 [c]Matt. 21:13; Mark 11:17; Luke 19:46 [d]Mal. 1:11
8 [I]Hebr. *to his gathered* [a]Ps. 147:2; Isa. 11:12 [b]John 10:16; Eph. 1:10; 2:14-16
9 [a]Jer. 12:9
10 [I]Or, *dreaming,* or, *talking in their sleep* [a]Matt. 15:14; 23:16 [b]Phil. 3:2
11 [I]Hebr. *strong of appetite* [II]Hebr. *know not to be satisfied* [a]Mic. 3:11 [b]Ezek. 34:2, 3
12 [a]Ps. 10:6; Prov. 23:35; Isa. 22:13; Luke 12:19; 1Cor. 15:32

1 [I]Hebr. *men of kindness,* or, *godliness* [II]Or, *from that which is evil* [a]Ps. 12:1; Mic. 7:2 [b]1Kgs. 14:13; 2Kgs. 22:20
2 [I]Or, *go in peace* [II]Or, *before him* [a]Luke 2:29 [b]2Chr. 16:14
3 [a]Matt. 16:4
5 [I]Or, *among the oaks* [a]Isa. 1:29 [b]2Kgs. 16:4; 17:10; Jer. 2:20 [c]Lev. 18:21; 20:2; 2Kgs. 16:3; 23:10; Jer. 7:31; Ezek. 16:20; 20:26

the children in the valleys under the clifts of the rocks?

6 Among the smooth *stones* of the stream *is* thy portion; they, they *are* thy lot: even to them hast thou poured[8210] a drink offering,[5262] thou hast offered[5927] a meat offering.[4503] Should I receive comfort[5162] in these?

7 [a]Upon a lofty and high[5375] mountain hast thou set[7760] [b]thy bed: even thither wentest thou up to offer[2076] sacrifice.[2077]

8 Behind the doors also and the posts hast thou set up thy remembrance:[2146] for thou hast discovered *thyself to another* than me, and art gone up;[5927] thou hast enlarged thy bed, and [I]made[3772] thee *a covenant* with them; [a]thou lovedst[157] their bed [II]where thou sawest *it.*

9 And [I][a]thou wentest to the king[4428] with ointment,[8081] and didst increase thy perfumes, and didst send thy messengers far off, and didst debase *thyself even* unto hell.[7585]

10 Thou art wearied in the greatness of thy way;[1870] [a]*yet* saidst thou not, There is no hope: thou hast found the [I]life[2416] of thine hand;[3027] therefore thou wast not grieved.

11 And [a]of whom hast thou been afraid[1672] or feared,[3372] that thou hast lied,[3576] and hast not remembered[2142] me, nor laid[7760] *it* to thy heart? [b]have not I held my peace even of old,[5769] and thou fearest me not?

12 I will declare[5046] thy righteousness,[6666] and thy works; for they shall not profit thee.

13 When thou criest, let thy companies deliver[5337] thee; but the wind shall carry them all away;[5375] vanity shall take *them:* but he that putteth his trust[2620] in me shall possess[5157] the land,[776] and shall inherit[3423] my holy[6944] mountain.

Return to God!

14 And shall say, [a]Cast ye up, cast ye up, prepare the way, take up the stumblingblock[4383] out of the way of my people.[5971]

15 For thus saith the high and lofty[5375] One that inhabiteth eternity,[5703] [a]whose name *is* Holy;[6918] [b]I dwell[7931] in the high and holy *place,* [c]with him also *that is* of a contrite[1793] and humble8217 spirit,[7307] [d]to revive[2421] the spirit of the humble, and to revive the heart of the contrite ones.

16 [a]For I will not contend[7378] for ever,[5769] neither will I be always[5331] wroth: for the spirit should fail before me, and the souls[5397] [b]*which* I have made.[6213]

17 For the iniquity of [a]his covetousness was I wroth,[7107] and smote[5221] him: [b]I hid me, and was wroth, [c]and he went on [I]frowardly7726 in the way of his heart.

18 I have seen[7200] his ways, and [a]will heal him: I will lead[5148] him also, and restore[7999] comforts5150 unto him and to [b]his mourners.

19 I create[1254] [a]the fruit of the lips;[8193] Peace, peace [b]to *him that is* far off, and to *him that is* near, saith the LORD; and I will heal him.

20 [a]But the wicked[7563] *are* like the troubled sea, when it cannot rest,[8252] whose waters cast up mire and dirt.

21 [a]*There is* no peace, saith my God,[430] to the wicked.

Genuine Fasting

58 Cry[7121] [I]aloud,1627 spare not, lift up thy voice like a trumpet, and shew[5046] my people[5971] their transgression,[6588] and the house[1004] of Jacob their sins.

2 Yet they seek me daily, and delight to know[1847] my ways,[1870] as a nation[1471] that did[6213] righteousness,[6666] and forsook[5800] not the ordinance[4941] of their God:[430] they ask[7592] of me the ordinances of justice;[6664] they take delight[2654] in approaching to God.

3 [a]Wherefore have we fasted, *say they,* and thou seest not? *wherefore* have we [b]afflicted our soul,[5315] and thou takest no knowledge?[3045] Behold, in the day of your fast ye find pleasure,[2656] and exact5065 all your [I]labours.[6092]

7 [a]Ezek. 16:16, 25 [b]Ezek. 23:41

8 [I]Or, *hewed it for thyself* larger *than theirs* [II]Or, *thou providedst room* [a]Ezek. 16:26, 28; 23:2-20

9 [I]Or, *thou respectedst the king* [a]Isa. 30:6; Ezek. 16:33; 23:16; Hos. 7:11; 12:1

10 [I]Or, *living* [a]Jer. 2:25

11 [a]Isa. 51:12, 13 [b]Ps. 50:21

14 [a]Isa. 40:3; 62:10

15 [a]Job 6:10; Luke 1:49 [b]Ps. 68:4; Zech. 2:13 [c]Ps. 34:18; 51:17; 138:6; Isa. 66:2 [d]Ps. 147:3; Isa. 61:1

16 [a]Ps. 85:5; 103:9; Mic. 7:18 [b]Num. 16:22; Job 34:14; Heb. 12:9

17 [I]Hebr. *turning away* [a]Jer. 6:13 [b]Isa. 8:17; 45:15 [c]Isa. 9:13

18 [a]Jer. 3:22 [b]Isa. 61:2

19 [a]Heb. 13:15 [b]Acts 2:39; Eph. 2:17

20 [a]Job 15:20; Prov. 4:16

21 [a]Isa. 48:22

1 [I]Hebr. *with the throat*

3 [I]Or, *things wherewith ye grieve others* [a]Mal. 3:14 [b]Lev. 16:29, 31; 23:27

4 [a]Behold, ye fast for strife[7379] and debate, and to smite[5221] with the fist of wickedness:[7562] ye shall not fast as *ye do this* day, to make your voice to be heard[8085] on high.

5 Is it [a]such a fast that I have chosen?[977] [I][b]a day for a man[120] to afflict his soul? *is it* to bow down his head[7218] as a bulrush, and [c]to spread sackcloth and ashes *under him?* wilt thou call[7121] this a fast, and an acceptable[7522] day to the LORD?

6 *Is* not this the fast that I have chosen? to loose the bands of wickedness, [a]to undo [I]the heavy[4133] burdens, and [b]to let the [II]oppressed go free, and that ye break every yoke?[4133]

7 *Is it* not [a]to deal[6536] thy bread to the hungry, and that thou bring the poor that are [I]cast out to thy house? [b]when thou seest the naked,[6174] that thou cover[3680] him; and that thou hide not thyself from [c]thine own flesh?[1320]

8 [a]Then shall thy light[216] break forth as the morning, and thine health[724] shall spring forth speedily: and thy righteousness[6664] shall go before thee; [b]the glory[3519] of the LORD [I]shall be thy rereward.[622]

9 Then shalt thou call, and the LORD shall answer; thou shalt cry, and he shall say,[559] Here I *am.* If thou take away from the midst of thee the yoke, the putting forth[7971] of the finger, and [a]speaking[1696] vanity;[205]

10 And *if* thou draw out[6329] thy soul to the hungry, and satisfy the afflicted soul; then shall thy light rise in obscurity,[2822] and thy darkness[653] *be* as the noon day:

11 And the LORD shall guide[5148] thee continually,[8548] and satisfy thy soul in [I]drought, and make fat thy bones:[6106] and thou shalt be like a watered garden, and like a spring of water, whose waters [II]fail[3576] not.

12 And *they that shall be* of thee [a]shall build the old[5769] waste places:[2723] thou shalt raise up the foundations[4146] of many generations;[1755] and thou shalt be called, The repairer of the breach, The restorer[7725] of paths to dwell in.

Keeping the Sabbath

13 If [a]thou turn away[7725] thy foot from the sabbath,[7676] *from* doing thy pleasure on my holy[6944] day; and call the sabbath a delight, the holy[6918] of the LORD, honourable; and shalt honour[3513] him, not doing thine own ways, nor finding thine own pleasure, nor speaking *thine own* words:[1697]

14 [a]Then shalt thou delight thyself in the LORD; and I will cause thee to [b]ride upon the high places[1116] of the earth,[776] and feed thee with the heritage[5159] of Jacob thy father:[1] [c]for the mouth[6310] of the LORD hath spoken *it.*

Isaiah Reproves Israel

59 Behold, the LORD's hand[3027] is not [a]shortened, that it cannot save;[3467] neither his ear[241] heavy,[3513] that it cannot hear:[8085]

2 But your iniquities[5771] have separated[914] between you and your God,[430] and your sins [I]have hid *his* face from you, that he will not hear.

3 For [a]your hands[3709] are defiled with blood,[1818] and your fingers with iniquity;[5771] your lips[8193] have spoken[1696] lies,[8267] your tongue hath muttered[1897] perverseness.[5766]

4 None calleth[7121] for justice,[6664] nor *any* pleadeth[8199] for truth:[530] they trust[982] in vanity,[8414] and speak lies;[7723] [a]they conceive mischief,[5999] and bring forth iniquity.[205]

5 They hatch [I]cockatrice'[6848] eggs, and weave the spider's web: he that eateth of their eggs dieth,[4191] and [II]that which is crushed breaketh out into a viper.

6 [a]Their webs shall not become[1961] garments, neither shall they cover themselves[3680] with their works: their works *are* works of iniquity, and the act of violence[2555] *is* in their hands.

7 [a]Their feet run to evil,[7451] and they make haste to shed[8210] innocent[5355] blood: their thoughts[4284] *are* thoughts of iniquity; wasting[7701] and [I]destruction[7667] *are* in their paths.

---

4 [a]1Kgs. 21:9, 12, 13

5 [I]Or, *to afflict his soul* for a *day* [a]Zech. 7:5 [b]Lev. 16:29 [c]Esth. 4:3; Job 2:8; Dan. 9:3; Jon. 3:6

6 [I]Hebr. *the bundles of the yoke* [II]Hebr. *broken* [a]Neh. 5:10-12 [b]Jer. 34:9

7 [I]Or, *afflicted* [a]Ezek. 18:7, 16; Matt. 25:35 [b]Job 31:19 [c]Gen. 29:14; Neh. 5:5

8 [I]Hebr. *shall gather thee up* [a]Job 11:17 [b]Ex. 14:19; Isa. 52:12

9 [a]Ps. 12:2

11 [I]Hebr. *droughts* [II]Hebr. *lie, or, deceive*

12 [a]Isa. 61:4

13 [a]Isa. 56:2

14 [a]Job 22:26 [b]Deut. 32:13; 33:29 [c]Isa. 1:20; 40:5; Mic. 4:4

1 [a]Num. 11:23; Isa. 50:2

2 [I]Or, *have made* him *hide*

3 [a]Isa. 1:15

4 [a]Job 15:35; Ps. 7:14

5 [I]Or, *adder's* [II]Or, *that which is sprinkled* is as if *there brake out a viper*

6 [a]Job 8:14, 15

7 [I]Hebr. *breaking* [a]Prov. 1:16; Rom. 3:15

8 The way[1870] of peace they know[3045] not; and *there is* no [I]judgment[4941] in their goings: [a]they have made them crooked paths: whosoever goeth therein shall not know peace.

9 Therefore is judgment far from us, neither doth justice[6666] overtake us: [a]we wait[6960] for light,[216] but behold obscurity;[2822] for brightness, *but* we walk in darkness.[653]

10 [a]We grope for the wall like the blind, and we grope as if *we had* no eyes: we stumble[3782] at noon day as in the night; *we are* in desolate places as dead[4191] *men.*

11 We roar all like bears, and [a]mourn[1897] sore like doves: we look for judgment, but *there is* none; for salvation,[3444] *but* it is far off from us.

12 For our transgressions[6588] are multiplied before thee, and our sins testify against us: for our transgressions *are* with us; and *as for* our iniquities, we know them;

13 In transgressing[6586] and lying[3584] against the LORD, and departing away from our God, speaking oppression and revolt,[5627] conceiving and uttering[1897] [a]from the heart[3820] words of falsehood.

14 And judgment is turned away backward, and justice standeth afar off: for truth[571] is fallen[3782] in the street, and equity[5229] cannot enter.

15 Yea, truth faileth;[5737] and he *that* departeth from evil [I]maketh himself a prey: and the LORD saw[7200] *it,* and [II]it displeased[5869] [7849] him that *there was* no judgment.

16 [a]And he saw that *there was* no man,[376] and [b]wondered[8074] that *there was* no intercessor: [c]therefore his arm brought salvation unto him; and his righteousness,[6666] it sustained him.

17 [a]For he put on righteousness as a breastplate, and an helmet of salvation upon his head;[7218] and he put on the garments of vengeance[5359] *for* clothing, and was clad with zeal[7068] as a cloke.

18 [a]According to *their* [I]deeds, accordingly he will repay,[7999] fury to his adversaries, recompence to his enemies; to the islands he will repay recompence.

19 [a]So shall they fear[3372] the name of the LORD from the west, and his glory[3519] from the rising of the sun. When the enemy shall come in [b]like a flood, the Spirit of the LORD shall [I]lift up a standard[5127] against him.

20 And [a]the Redeemer[1350] shall come to Zion, and unto them that turn[7725] from transgression[6588] in Jacob, saith[5002] the LORD.

21 [a]As for me, this *is* my covenant[1285] with them, saith[559] the LORD; My spirit that *is* upon thee, and my words which I have put in thy mouth,[6310] shall not depart out of thy mouth, nor out of the mouth of thy seed,[2233] nor out of the mouth of thy seed's seed, saith the LORD, from henceforth[6258] and for ever.[5769]

The Future Glory of Zion

60 Arise, [Ia]shine; for thy light[216] is come, and [b]the glory[3519] of the LORD is risen upon thee.

2 For, behold, the darkness[2822] shall cover[3680] the earth,[776] and gross darkness[6205] the people:[3816] but the LORD shall arise[2224] upon thee, and his glory shall be seen[7200] upon thee.

3 And the [a]Gentiles[1471] shall come to thy light, and kings[4428] to the brightness of thy rising.

4 [a]Lift up[5375] thine eyes round about, and see: all they gather themselves together,[6908] [b]they come to thee: thy sons[1121] shall come from far, and thy daughters shall be nursed[539] at *thy* side.

5 Then thou shalt see, and flow together, and thine heart[3824] shall fear,[6342] and be enlarged; because [a]the [I]abundance of the sea shall be converted[2015] unto thee, the [IIb]forces[2428] of the Gentiles shall come unto thee.

6 The multitude of camels shall cover thee, the dromedaries of Midian and [a]Ephah; all they from [b]Sheba shall come: they shall bring[5375] [c]gold and incense; and they shall shew forth[1319] the praises[8416] of the LORD.

7 All the flocks of [a]Kedar shall be

8 [I]Or, *right* [a]Ps. 125:5; Prov. 2:15
9 [a]Jer. 8:15
10 [a]Deut. 28:29; Job 5:14; Amos 8:9
11 [a]Isa. 38:14; Ezek. 7:16
13 [a]Matt. 12:34
15 [I]Or, *is accounted mad* [II]Hebr. *it was evil in his eyes* [a]Ezek. 22:30 [b]Mark 6:6 [c]Ps. 98:1; Isa. 63:5
17 [a]Eph. 6:14, 17; 1Thess. 5:8
18 [I]Hebr. *recompenses* [a]Isa. 63:6
19 [I]Or, *put him to flight* [a]Ps. 113:3; Mal. 1:11 [b]Rev. 12:15
20 [a]Rom. 11:26
21 [a]Heb. 8:10; 10:16
1 [I]Or, *be enlightened; for thy light cometh* [a]Eph. 5:14 [b]Mal. 4:2
3 [a]Isa. 49:6, 23; Rev. 21:24
4 [a]Isa. 49:18 [b]Isa. 49:20-22; 66:12
5 [I]Or, *noise of the sea shall be turned toward thee* [II]Or, *wealth* [a]Rom. 11:25 [b]Isa. 60:11; 61:6
6 [a]Gen. 25:4 [b]Ps. 72:10 [c]Isa. 61:6; Matt. 2:11
7 [a]Gen. 25:13

gathered together unto thee, the rams of Nebaioth shall minister[8334] unto thee: they shall come up[5927] with acceptance[7522] on mine altar,[4196] and [b]I will glorify[6286] the house[1004] of my glory.[8597]

8 Who *are* these *that* fly as a cloud, and as the doves to their windows?

9 [a]Surely the isles shall wait[6960] for me, and the ships of Tarshish first,[7223] [b]to bring thy sons from far, [c]their silver and their gold with them, [d]unto the name of the LORD thy God,[430] and to the Holy One[6918] of Israel, [e]because *he* hath glorified[6286] thee.

10 And [a]the sons of strangers shall build up thy walls, [b]and their kings shall minister unto thee: for [c]in my wrath[7110] I smote[5221] thee, [d]but in my favour[7522] have I had mercy on thee.

11 Therefore thy gates [a]shall be open continually:[8548] they shall not be shut day[3119] nor night;[3915] that *men* may bring unto thee the [1][b]forces of the Gentiles, and *that* their kings *may be* brought.

12 [a]For the nation and kingdom[4467] that will not serve[5647] thee shall perish;[6] yea, *those* nations[1471] shall be utterly wasted.[2717]

13 [a]The glory of Lebanon shall come unto thee, the fir tree, the pine tree,[8410] and the box together, to beautify[6286] the place of my sanctuary;[4720] and I will make[7760] [b]the place of my feet glorious.[3513]

14 The sons also of them that afflicted thee shall come bending unto thee; and all they that despised[5006] thee shall [a]bow themselves down at the soles[3709] of thy feet; and they shall call[7121] thee, The city of the LORD, [b]The Zion of the Holy One of Israel.

15 Whereas thou hast been forsaken[5800] and hated,[8130] so that no man went through *thee,* I will make thee an eternal[5769] excellency, a joy of many generations.[1755]

16 Thou shalt also suck the milk of the Gentiles, [a]and shalt suck the breast of kings: and thou shalt know[3045] that [b]I the LORD[3068] *am* thy Saviour[3467] and thy Redeemer,[1350] the mighty One[46] of Jacob.

17 For brass I will bring gold, and for iron I will bring silver, and for wood brass, and for stones iron: I will also make thy officers peace, and thine exactors righteousness.[6666]

18 Violence[2555] shall no more be heard[8085] in thy land,[776] wasting[7701] nor destruction[7667] within thy borders; but thou shalt call [a]thy walls Salvation,[3468] and thy gates Praise.[8416]

19 The [a]sun shall be no more thy light by day; neither for brightness shall the moon give light unto thee: but the LORD shall be unto thee an everlasting[5769] light, and [b]thy God thy glory.

20 [a]Thy sun shall no more go down; neither shall thy moon withdraw[622] itself: for the LORD shall be thine everlasting light, and the days[3117] of thy mourning shall be ended.[7999]

21 [a]Thy people[5971] also *shall be* all righteous:[6662] [b]they shall inherit[3423] the land for ever,[5769] [c]the branch[5342] of my planting, [d]the work of my hands,[3027] that I may be glorified.

22 [a]A little one shall become[1961] a thousand, and a small one a strong nation: I the LORD will hasten it in his time.[6256]

Those Who Endure Affliction Will Be Exalted

61 The [a]Spirit[7307] of the Lord[136] GOD *is* upon me; because the LORD [b]hath anointed[4886] me to preach good tidings[1319] unto the meek; he hath sent me [c]to bind up[2280] the brokenhearted, to proclaim[7121] [d]liberty to the captives,[7628] and the opening of the prison to *them that are* bound;

2 [a]To proclaim the acceptable[7522] year of the LORD, and [b]the day[3117] of vengeance[5359] of our God;[430] [c]to comfort[5162] all that mourn;

3 To appoint[7760] unto them that mourn in Zion, [a]to give unto them beauty for ashes, the oil[8081] of joy for mourning, the garment of praise[8416] for the spirit of heaviness;[3544] that they might be called[7121] trees of righteousness,[6664] [b]the

7 [b]Hag. 2:7, 9

9 [a]Ps. 72:10; Isa. 42:4; 51:5 [b]Gal. 4:26 [c]Ps. 68:30; Zech. 14:14 [d]Jer. 3:17 [e]Isa. 55:5

10 [a]Zech. 6:15 [b]Isa. 49:23; Rev. 21:24 [c]Isa. 57:17 [d]Isa. 54:7, 8

11 [1]Or, *wealth* [a]Rev. 21:25 [b]Isa. 60:5

12 [a]Zech. 14:17, 19; Matt. 21:44

13 [a]Isa. 35:2; 41:19 [b]1Chr. 28:2; Ps. 132:7

14 [a]Isa. 49:23; Rev. 3:9 [b]Heb. 12:22; Rev. 14:1

16 [a]Isa. 49:23; 61:6; 66:11, 12 [b]Isa. 43:3

18 [a]Isa. 26:1

19 [a]Rev. 21:23; 22:5 [b]Zech. 2:5

20 [a]Amos 8:9

21 [a]Isa. 52:1; Rev. 21:27 [b]Ps. 37:11, 22; Matt. 5:5 [c]Isa. 61:3; Matt. 15:13; John 15:2 [d]Isa. 29:23; 45:11; Eph. 2:10

22 [a]Matt. 13:31, 32

1 [a]Isa. 11:2; Luke 4:18; John 1:32; 3:34 [b]Ps. 45:7 [c]Ps. 147:3; Isa. 57:15 [d]Isa. 42:7; Jer. 34:8

2 [a]Lev. 25:9 [b]Isa. 34:8; 63:4; 66:14; Mal. 4:1, 3; 2Thess. 1:7-9 [c]Isa. 57:18; Matt. 5:4

3 [a]Ps. 30:11 [b]Isa. 60:21

planting of the LORD, [c]that he might be glorified.[6286]

4 And they shall [a]build the old[5769] wastes,[2723] they shall raise up the former[7223] desolations,[8074] and they shall repair the waste cities, the desolations of many generations.[1755]

5 And [a]strangers[2114] shall stand and feed your flocks, and the sons[1121] of the alien[5236] *shall be* your plowmen and your vinedressers.

6 [a]But ye shall be named[7121] the Priests[3548] of the LORD: *men* shall call[7121] you the Ministers[8334] of our God: [b]ye shall eat the riches of the Gentiles,[1471] and in their glory[3519] shall ye boast yourselves.[3235]

7 [a]For your shame *ye shall have* double; and *for* confusion[3639] they shall rejoice in their portion: therefore in their land[776] they shall possess[3423] the double: everlasting[5769] joy shall be unto them.

8 For [a]I the LORD love[157] judgment,[4941] [b]I hate[8130] robbery for burnt offering;[5930] and I will direct their work in truth,[571] [c]and I will make an everlasting covenant[1285] with them.

9 And their seed[2233] shall be known[3045] among the Gentiles, and their offspring among the people:[5971] all that see them shall acknowledge[5234] them, [a]that they *are* the seed *which* the LORD hath blessed.[1288]

10 [a]I will greatly rejoice in the LORD, my soul[5315] shall be joyful in my God; for [b]he hath clothed me with the garments of salvation,[3468] he hath covered me with the robe of righteousness,[6666] [c]as a bridegroom [I]decketh[3547] *himself* with ornaments, and as a bride adorneth *herself* with her jewels.

11 For as the earth[776] bringeth forth her bud, and as the garden causeth the things that are sown in it to spring forth; so the Lord GOD will cause [a]righteousness and [b]praise to spring forth before all the nations.[1471]

62 For Zion's sake will I not hold my peace, and for Jerusalem's sake I will not rest,[8252] until the righteousness[6664] thereof go forth as brightness, and the salvation[3444] thereof as a lamp *that* burneth.

2 [a]And the Gentiles[1471] shall see thy righteousness, and all kings[4428] thy glory:[3519] [b]and thou shalt be called[7121] by a new name, which the mouth of the LORD shall name.

3 Thou shalt also be [a]a crown of glory[8597] in the hand[3027] of the LORD, and a royal diadem[6797] in the hand[3709] of thy God.[430]

4 [a]Thou shalt no more be termed[559] [b]Forsaken;[5800] neither shall thy land[776] any more be termed [c]Desolate:[8077] but thou shalt be called [I]Hephzi-bah,[2657] and thy land [II]Beulah:[1166] for the LORD delighteth[2654] in thee, and thy land shall be married.

5 For *as* a young man marrieth[1166] a virgin,[1330] *so* shall thy sons marry thee: and [I]*as* the bridegroom rejoiceth over the bride, *so* [a]shall thy God rejoice over thee.

6 [a]I have set watchmen[8104] upon thy walls, O Jerusalem, *which* shall never hold their peace day[3117] nor night:[3915] [I]ye that make mention of the LORD, keep not silence,

7 And give him no [I]rest, till he establish, and till he make[7760] Jerusalem [a]a praise[8416] in the earth.[776]

8 The LORD hath sworn by his right hand, and by the arm of his strength,[5797] [I]Surely I will no more [a]give thy corn *to be* meat for thine enemies; and the sons of the stranger[5236] shall not drink thy wine, for the which thou hast laboured:

9 But they that have gathered it shall eat it, and praise[1984] the LORD; and they that have brought it together shall drink it [a]in the courts of my holiness.[6944]

10 Go through, go through the gates; [a]prepare ye the way[1870] of the people;[5971] cast up, cast up the highway; gather out the stones; [b]lift up a standard for the people.

11 Behold, the LORD hath proclaimed unto the end of the world, [a]Say ye to the daughter of Zion, Behold, thy salva-

3 [c]John 15:8
4 [a]Isa. 49:8; 58:12; Ezek. 36:33-36
5 [a]Eph. 2:12
6 [a]Ex. 19:6; Isa. 60:17; 66:21; 1Pet. 2:5, 9; Rev. 1:6; 5:10 [b]Isa. 60:5, 11, 16
7 [a]Isa. 40:2; Zech. 9:12
8 [a]Ps. 11:7 [b]Isa. 1:11, 13 [c]Isa. 55:3
9 [a]Isa. 65:23
10 [I]Hebr. *decketh as a priest* [a]Hab. 3:18 [b]Ps. 132:9, 16 [c]Isa. 49:18; Rev. 21:2
11 [a]Ps. 72:3; 85:11 [b]Isa. 60:18; 62:7
2 [a]Isa. 60:3 [b]Isa. 62:4, 12; Isa. 65:15
3 [a]Zech. 9:16
4 [I]That is, *My delight is in her* [II]That is, *Married* [a]Hos. 1:10; 1Pet. 2:10 [b]Isa. 49:14; 54:6, 7 [c]Isa. 54:1
5 [I]Hebr. *with the joy of the bridegroom* [a]Isa. 65:19
6 [I]Or, *ye that are the LORD's remembrancers* [a]Ezek. 3:17; 33:7
7 [I]Hebr. *silence* [a]Isa. 61:11; Zeph. 3:20
8 [I]Hebr. *If I give* [a]Deut. 28:31; Jer. 5:17
9 [a]Deut. 12:12; 14:23, 26; 16:11, 14
10 [a]Isa. 40:3; 57:14 [b]Isa. 11:12
11 [a]Zech. 9:9; Matt. 21:5; John 12:15

tion[3468] cometh; behold, his [b]reward *is*
with him, and his [I]work before him.
12 And they shall call them, The
holy[6944] people, The redeemed[1350] of the
LORD: and thou shalt be called, Sought
out,[1875] A city [a]not forsaken.

Victory

63 Who *is* this that cometh from
Edom, with dyed[2556] garments
from Bozrah? this *that is* [I]glorious[1921] in
his apparel, travelling[6808] in the greatness of his strength? I that speak in
righteousness,[6666] mighty to save.[3467]
2 Wherefore [a]*art thou* red[122] in thine
apparel, and thy garments like him that
treadeth in the winefat?
3 I have [a]trodden the winepress
alone; and of the people[5971] *there was*
none with me: for I will tread them in
mine anger,[639] and trample them in my
fury; and their blood[5332] shall be sprinkled[5137] upon my garments, and I will
stain all my raiment.
4 For the [a]day[3117] of vengeance[5359] *is*
in mine heart,[3820] and the year of my
redeemed[1350] is come.
5 [a]And I looked, and [b]*there was* none
to help; and I wondered[8074] that *there*
was none to uphold: therefore mine own
[c]arm brought salvation unto me; and my
fury,[2534] it upheld me.
6 And I will tread down[947] the people in mine anger, and [a]make them drunk
in my fury, and I will bring down their
strength[5332] to the earth.[776]

The Lord Is Good to Israel

7 I will mention the lovingkindnesses[2617] of the LORD, *and* the
praises[8416] of the LORD, according to all
that the LORD hath bestowed[1580] on us,
and the great goodness toward the house
of Israel, which he hath bestowed on
them according to his mercies,[7356] and
according to the multitude of his lovingkindnesses.
8 For he said, Surely they *are* my
people, children *that* will not lie:[8266] so he
was their Saviour.[3467]
9 [a]In all their affliction he was afflicted, [b]and the angel[4397] of his presence
saved[3467] them: [c]in his love[160] and in his
pity[2551] he redeemed them; and [d]he
bare[5190] them, and carried[5375] them all
the days of old.[5769]
10 But they [a]rebelled,[4784] and
[b]vexed[6087] his holy[6944] Spirit:[7307] [c]there-
fore he was turned[2015] to be their enemy,
and he fought against them.
11 Then he remembered[2142] the days
of old, Moses, *and* his people, *saying,*
Where *is* he that [a]brought them up[5927]
out of the sea with the [I]shepherd of his
flock? [b]where *is* he that put his holy
Spirit within[7130] him?
12 That led *them* by the right hand
of Moses [a]with his glorious[8597] arm, [b]di-
viding the water before them, to make[6213]
himself an everlasting[5769] name?
13 [a]That led them through the deep,
as an horse in the wilderness, *that* they
should not stumble?[3782]
14 As a beast goeth down into the
valley, the Spirit of the LORD caused him
to rest: so didst thou lead thy people, [a]to
make thyself a glorious name.

A Prayer for Vengeance

15 [a]Look down from heaven,[8064] and
behold[7200] [b]from the habitation of thy
holiness[6944] and of thy glory:[8597] where
is thy zeal[7068] and thy strength, [I]the
sounding[1995] [c]of thy bowels[4578] and of
thy mercies toward me? are they restrained?
16 [a]Doubtless thou *art* our father,[1]
though Abraham [b]be ignorant of us, and
Israel acknowledge[5234] us not: thou, O
LORD, *art* our father, [I]our Redeemer:[1350]
thy name *is* from everlasting.
17 O LORD, why hast thou [a]made us
to err[8582] from thy ways,[1870] *and* [b]hard-
ened[7188] our heart from thy fear?[3374]
[c]Return[7725] for thy servants' sake, the
tribes[7626] of thine inheritance.[5159]
18 [a]The people of thy holiness have
possessed[3423] *it* but a little while: [b]our ad-

11 [I]Or, *recompense* [b]Isa. 40:10; Rev. 22:12
12 [a]Isa. 62:4

1 [I]Hebr. *decked*
2 [a]Rev. 19:13
3 [a]Lam. 1:15; Rev. 14:19, 20; 19:15
4 [a]Isa. 34:8; 61:2
5 [a]Isa. 41:28; 59:16 [b]John 16:32 [c]Ps. 98:1; Isa. 59:16
6 [a]Rev. 16:6
9 [a]Judg. 10:16; Zech. 2:8; Acts 9:4 [b]Ex. 14:19; 23:20, 21; 33:14; Mal. 3:1; Acts 12:11 [c]Deut. 7:7, 8 [d]Ex. 19:4; Deut. 1:31; 32:11, 12; Isa. 46:3, 4
10 [a]Ex. 15:24; Num. 14:11; Ps. 78:56; 95:9 [b]Ps. 78:40; Acts 7:51; Eph. 4:30 [c]Ex. 23:21
11 [I]Or, *shepherds* [a]Ex. 14:30; 32:11, 12; Num. 14:13, 14; Jer. 2:6 [b]Ps. 77:20 [c]Num. 11:17, 25; Neh. 9:20; Dan. 4:8; Hag. 2:5
12 [a]Ex. 15:6 [b]Ex. 14:21; Josh. 3:16
13 [a]Ps. 106:9
14 [a]2Sam. 7:23
15 [I]Or, *the multitude* [a]Deut. 26:15; Ps. 80:14 [b]Ps. 33:14 [c]Jer. 31:20; Hos. 11:8
16 [I]Or, *our Redeemer from everlasting* is *thy name* [a]Deut. 32:6; 1Chr. 29:10; Isa. 64:8 [b]Job 14:21; Eccl. 9:5
17 [a]Ps. 119:10 [b]Isa. 6:10; John 12:40; Rom. 9:18 [c]Num. 10:36; Ps. 90:13
18 [a]Deut. 7:6; 26:19; Isa. 62:12; Dan. 8:24 [b]Ps. 74:7

versaries have trodden down[947] thy sanctuary.[4720]

19 We are *thine:* thou never barest rule[4910] over them; [I][a]they were not called[7121] by thy name.

64 Oh that thou wouldest [a]rend[7167] the heavens,[8064] that thou wouldest come down, that [b]the mountains might flow down at thy presence,

2 As *when* [I]the melting fire burneth, the fire causeth the waters to boil,[1158] to make thy name known[3045] to thine adversaries, *that* the nations[1471] may tremble at thy presence!

3 When [a]thou didst[6213] terrible things[3372] *which* we looked[6960] not for, thou camest down, the mountains flowed down at thy presence.

4 For since the beginning of the world[5769] [a]*men* have not heard, nor perceived by the ear,[238] neither hath the eye [I]seen,[7200] O God,[430] beside thee, *what* he hath prepared for him that waiteth for him.

5 Thou meetest[6293] him that rejoiceth [a]and worketh[6213] righteousness,[6664] [b]*those that* remember[2142] thee in thy ways:[1870] behold, thou art wroth;[7107] for we have sinned:[2398] [c]in those is continuance,[5769] and we shall be saved.[3467]

6 But we are all as an unclean[2931] *thing,* and all [a]our righteousnesses *are* as filthy rags; and we all do [b]fade as a leaf; and our iniquities,[5771] like the wind, have taken us away.[5375]

7 And [a]*there is* none that calleth[7121] upon thy name, that stirreth up himself[5782] to take hold of thee: for thou hast hid thy face from us, and hast [I]consumed us, [II][b]because of our iniquities.

8 [a]But now, O LORD, thou *art* our father;[1] we *are* the clay, [b]and thou our potter; and we all *are* [c]the work of thy hand.[3027]

9 Be not [a]wroth very sore, O LORD, neither remember[2142] iniquity[5771] for ever:[5957] behold, see, we beseech thee,[4994] [b]we *are* all thy people.[5971]

10 Thy holy[6944] cities are a wilderness, Zion is a wilderness, [a]Jerusalem a desolation.[8077]

11 [a]Our holy and our beautiful[8597] house,[1004] where our fathers praised[1984] thee, is burned up with fire: and all [b]our pleasant things are laid waste.[2723]

12 [a]Wilt thou refrain thyself for these *things,* O LORD? [b]wilt thou hold thy peace, and afflict us very sore?

The Rebellious Will Be Punished

65 I [a]am sought of *them that* asked[7592] not *for me;* I am found of *them that* sought me not: I said,[559] Behold me, behold me, unto a nation[1471] *that* [b]was not called[7121] by my name.

2 [a]I have spread out my hands all the day unto a rebellious[5637] people,[5971] which walketh in a way[1870] *that was* not good,[2896] after their own thoughts;[4284]

3 A people [a]that provoketh me to anger[3707] continually[8548] to my face; [b]that sacrificeth[2076] in gardens, and burneth incense[6999] [I]upon altars of brick;

4 [a]Which remain among the graves,[6913] and lodge in the monuments,[5341] [b]which eat swine's flesh,[1320] and [I]broth of abominable[6292] *things is* in their vessels;

5 [a]Which say, Stand[7126] by thyself, come not near[5066] to me; for I am holier[6942] than thou. These *are* a smoke in my [I]nose,[639] a fire that burneth all the day.

6 Behold, [a]*it is* written before me: [b]I will not keep silence, [c]but will recompense,[7999] even recompense into their bosom,

7 Your iniquities,[5771] and [a]the iniquities of your fathers[1] together, saith the LORD, [b]which have burned incense[6999] upon the mountains, [c]and blasphemed[2778] me upon the hills: therefore will I measure their former[7223] work into their bosom.

8 Thus saith the LORD, As the new wine is found in the cluster, and *one* saith, Destroy[7843] it not; for [a]a blessing[1293] *is* in it: so will I do[6213] for my servants' sakes, that I may not destroy them all.

---

19 [I]Or, *thy name was not called upon them* [a]Isa. 65:1

1 [a]Ps. 144:5 [b]Judg. 5:5; Mic. 1:4

2 [I]Hebr. *the fire of meltings*

3 [a]Ex. 34:10; Judg. 5:4, 5; Ps. 68:8; Hab. 3:3, 6

4 [I]Or, *seen a God besides thee,* which *doeth so for him* [a]Ps. 31:19; 1Cor. 2:9

5 [a]Acts 10:35 [b]Isa. 26:8 [c]Mal. 3:6

6 [a]Phil. 3:9 [b]Ps. 90:5, 6

7 [I]Hebr. *melted* [II]Hebr. *by the hand* [a]Hos. 7:7 [b]Job 8:4

8 [a]Isa. 63:16 [b]Isa. 29:16; 45:9; Jer. 18:6; Rom. 9:20, 21 [c]Eph. 2:10

9 [a]Ps. 74:1, 2; 79:8 [b]Ps. 79:13

10 [a]Ps. 79:1

11 [a]2Kgs. 25:9; 2Chr. 36:19; Ps. 74:7 [b]Ezek. 24:21, 25

12 [a]Isa. 42:14 [b]Ps. 83:1

1 [a]Rom. 9:24-26, 30; 10:20; Eph. 2:12, 13 [b]Isa. 63:19

2 [a]Rom. 10:21

3 [I]Hebr. *upon bricks* [a]Deut. 32:21 [b]Isa. 1:29; 66:17; Lev. 17:5

4 [I]Or, *pieces* [a]Deut. 18:11 [b]Isa. 66:17; Lev. 11:7

5 [I]Or, *anger* [a]Matt. 9:11; Luke 5:30; 18:11; Jude 1:19

6 [a]Deut. 32:34; Mal. 3:16 [b]Ps. 50:3 [c]Ps. 79:12; Jer. 16:18; Ezek. 11:21

7 [a]Ex. 20:5 [b]Ezek. 18:6 [c]Ezek. 20:27, 28

8 [a]Joel 2:14

9 And I will bring forth a seed[2233] out of Jacob, and out of Judah an inheritor of my mountains: and mine [a]elect972 shall inherit[3423] it, and my servants[5650] shall dwell[7931] there.

10 And [a]Sharon shall be a fold of flocks, and [b]the valley of Achor a place for the herds to lie down in, for my people that have sought me.

11 But ye *are* they that forsake[5800] the LORD, that forget [a]my holy[6944] mountain, that prepare [b]a table for that [I]troop,1409 and that furnish the drink offering unto that [II]number.4507

12 Therefore will I number you to the sword,[2719] and ye shall all bow down[3766] to the slaughter:[2874] [a]because when I called, ye did not answer; when I spake,[1696] ye did not hear;[8085] but did evil[7451] before mine eyes, and did choose[977] *that* wherein I delighted[2654] not.

13 Therefore thus saith the Lord[136] GOD, Behold, my servants shall eat, but ye shall be hungry: behold, my servants shall drink, but ye shall be thirsty: behold, my servants shall rejoice, but ye shall be ashamed:[954]

14 Behold, my servants shall sing for joy[2898] of heart, but ye shall cry for sorrow of heart,[3820] and [a]shall howl for [I]vexation[7667] of spirit.[7307]

15 And ye shall leave your name [a]for a curse[7621] unto [b]my chosen: for the Lord GOD shall slay[4191] thee, and [c]call his servants by another name:

16 [a]That he who blesseth himself[1288] in the earth[776] shall bless himself in the God[430] of truth;[543] and [b]he that sweareth[7650] in the earth shall swear by the God of truth; because the former troubles are forgotten, and because they are hid from mine eyes.

New Heavens and a New Earth

🗝 17 For, behold, I create[1254] [a]new heavens8064 and a new earth: and the former shall not be remembered,[2142] nor [I]come into mind.[3820]

18 But be ye glad and rejoice for ever[5957] *in that* which I create: for, behold, I create Jerusalem a rejoicing, and her people a joy.

19 And [a]I will rejoice in Jerusalem, and joy in my people: and the [b]voice of weeping shall be no more heard[8085] in her, nor the voice of crying.

20 There shall be no more thence an infant of days,[3117] nor an old man[2205] that hath not filled his days: for the child shall die[4191] an hundred years old; [a]but the sinner[2398] *being* an hundred years old shall be accursed.[7043]

21 And [a]they shall build houses,[1004] and inhabit *them;* and they shall plant vineyards, and eat the fruit of them.

22 They shall not build, and another inhabit; they shall not plant, and another eat: for [a]as the days of a tree *are* the days of my people, and [b]mine elect972 [I]shall long enjoy the work of their hands.

23 They shall not labour in vain, [a]nor bring forth for trouble;[928] for [b]they *are* the seed of the blessed of the LORD, and their offspring with them.

24 And it shall come to pass, that [a]before they call, I will answer; and while they are yet speaking, I will hear.

25 The [a]wolf and the lamb shall feed together, and the lion shall eat straw like the bullock: [b]and dust[6083] *shall be* the serpent's[5175] meat. They shall not hurt[7489] nor destroy in all my holy mountain, saith the LORD.

God Judges the Nations

66 Thus saith[559] the LORD, [a]The heaven8064 *is* my throne,[3678] and the earth[776] *is* my footstool: where *is* the house[1004] that ye build unto me? and where *is* the place of my rest?

2 For all those *things* hath mine hand[3027] made,[6213] and all those *things*

9 [a]Isa. 65:15, 22; Matt. 24:22; Rom. 11:5, 7
10 [a]Isa. 33:9; 35:2 [b]Josh. 7:24, 26; Hos. 2:15
11 [I]Or, *Gad* [II]Or, *Meni* [a]Isa. 56:7; 57:13; 65:25 [b]Ezek. 23:41; 1Cor. 10:21
12 [a]2Chr. 36:15, 16; Prov. 1:24; Isa. 66:4; Jer. 7:13; Zech. 7:7; Matt. 21:34-43
14 [I]Hebr. *breaking* [a]Matt. 8:12; Luke 13:28
15 [a]Jer. 29:22; Zech. 8:13 [b]Isa. 65:9, 22 [c]Isa. 62:2; Acts 11:26
16 [a]Ps. 72:17; Jer. 4:2 [b]Deut. 6:13; Ps. 63:11; Isa. 19:18; 45:23; Zeph. 1:5
17 [I]Hebr. *come upon the heart* [a]Isa. 51:16; 66:22; 2Pet. 3:13; Rev. 21:1
19 [a]Isa. 62:5 [b]Isa. 35:10; 51:11; Rev. 7:17; 21:4
20 [a]Eccl. 8:12
21 [a]Lev. 26:16; Deut. 28:30; Isa. 62:8; Amos 9:14
22 [I]Hebr. *shall make them continue long,* or, *shall wear out* [a]Ps. 92:12 [b]Isa. 65:9, 15
23 [a]Deut. 28:41; Hos. 9:12 [b]Isa. 61:9
24 [a]Ps. 32:5; Dan. 9:21
25 [a]Isa. 11:6, 7, 9 [b]Gen. 3:14
1 [a]1Kgs. 8:27; 2Chr. 6:18; Matt. 5:34, 35; Acts 7:48, 49; 17:24

🗝 **65:17** God reveals that the universe will ultimately be transformed into a place that is free from the curse of the Fall (Rom. 8:21, 22). Peter and John further explained God's revelation to Jeremiah when they described the new world that God will fashion after the Millennium (2 Pet. 3:13; Rev. 21:1–4).

have been, saith[5002] the LORD: [a]but to this *man* will I look, [b]*even* to *him that is* poor[6041] and of a contrite[5223] spirit,[7307] and [c]trembleth[2730] at my word.

3 [a]He that killeth[7819] an ox *is as if* he slew[5221] a man;[376] he that sacrificeth[2076] a [I]lamb, *as if* he [b]cut off a dog's neck; he that offereth[5927] an oblation,[4503] *as if he offered* swine's blood;[1818] he that [II][c]burneth[2142] incense, *as if* he blessed[1288] an idol. Yea, they have chosen[977] their own ways,[1870] and their soul[5315] delighteth[2654] in their abominations.[8251]

4 I also will choose their [I]delusions,[8586] and will bring their fears[4035] upon them; [a]because when I called,[7121] none did answer; when I spake,[1696] they did not hear:[8085] but they did[6213] evil[7451] before mine eyes, and chose *that* in which I delighted not.

5 Hear the word of the LORD, [a]ye that tremble at his word; Your brethren[251] that hated[8130] you, that cast you out for my name's sake, said, [b]Let the LORD be glorified:[3513] but [c]he shall appear[7200] to your joy, and they shall be ashamed.[954]

6 A voice of noise[7588] from the city, a voice from the temple,[1964] a voice of the LORD that rendereth recompence to his enemies.

7 Before she travailed, she brought forth; before her pain came, she was delivered of a man child.

8 Who hath heard[8085] such a thing? who hath seen[7200] such things? Shall the earth be made to bring forth in one day?[3117] *or* shall a nation[1471] be born at once? for as soon as Zion travailed,[2342] she brought forth her children.

9 Shall I bring to the birth, and not [I]cause to bring forth? saith the LORD: shall I cause to bring forth, and shut *the womb*? saith thy God.[430]

10 Rejoice ye with Jerusalem, and be glad with her, all ye that love[157] her: rejoice for joy with her, all ye that mourn for her:

11 That ye may suck, and be satisfied with the breasts of her consolations;[8575] that ye may milk out, and be delighted with the [I]abundance of her glory.[3519]

12 For thus saith the LORD, Behold, [a]I will extend peace to her like a river, and the glory of the Gentiles[1471] like a flowing[7857] stream: then shall ye [b]suck, ye shall be [c]borne[5375] upon *her* sides, and be dandled upon *her* knees.

13 As one whom his mother[5172] comforteth, so will I comfort[5162] you; and ye shall be comforted in Jerusalem.

14 And when ye see *this,* your heart[3820] shall rejoice, and [a]your bones[6106] shall flourish like an herb: and the hand of the LORD shall be known[3045] toward his servants,[5650] and *his* indignation[2194] toward his enemies.

15 [a]For, behold, the LORD will come with fire, and with his chariots like a whirlwind, to render[7725] his anger[639] with fury, and his rebuke[1606] with flames of fire.

16 For by fire and by [a]his sword[2719] will the LORD plead[8199] with all flesh:[1320] and the slain[2491] of the LORD shall be many.

17 [a]They that sanctify themselves,[6942] and purify themselves[2891] in the gardens [I]behind one *tree* in the midst, eating swine's flesh, and the abomination,[8263] and the mouse, shall be consumed[5486] together, saith the LORD.

18 For I *know* their works and their thoughts:[4284] it shall come, that I will gather[6908] all nations[1471] and tongues; and they shall come, and see my glory.

19 [a]And I will set[7760] a sign among them, and I will send those that escape of them unto the nations, *to* Tarshish, Pul, and Lud, that draw the bow, *to* Tubal, and Javan, *to* the isles afar off, that have not heard my fame, neither have seen my glory: [b]and they shall declare[5046] my glory among the Gentiles.

20 And they shall bring all your brethren [a]*for* an offering[4503] unto the LORD out of all nations upon horses, and in chariots, and in [I]litters, and upon mules, and upon swift beasts, to my holy[6944] mountain Jerusalem, saith the LORD, as the children of Israel bring an

2 [a]Isa. 57:15; 61:1 [b]Ps. 34:18; 51:17 [c]Ezra 9:4; 10:3; Prov. 28:14; Isa. 66:5

3 [I]Or, *kid* [II]Hebr. *maketh a memorial of* [a]Isa. 1:11 [b]Deut. 23:18 [c]Lev. 2:2

4 [I]Or, *devices* [a]Prov. 1:24; Isa. 65:12; Jer. 7:13

5 [a]Isa. 66:2 [b]Isa. 5:19 [c]2Thess. 1:10; Titus 2:13

9 [I]Or, *beget*

11 [I]Or, *brightness*

12 [a]Isa. 48:18; 60:5 [b]Isa. 60:16 [c]Isa. 49:22; 60:4

14 [a]Ezek. 37:1

15 [a]Isa. 9:5; 2Thess. 1:8

16 [a]Isa. 27:1

17 [I]Or, *one after another* [a]Isa. 65:3, 4

19 [a]Luke 2:34 [b]Mal. 1:11

20 [I]Or, *coaches* [a]Rom. 15:16

offering in a clean[2889] vessel into the house of the LORD.

21 And I will also take of them for [a]priests[3548] *and* for Levites, saith the LORD.

22 For as [a]the new heavens[8064] and the new earth, which I will make,[6213] shall remain before me, saith the LORD, so shall your seed[2233] and your name remain.

23 And [a]it shall come to pass, *that* [I]from one new moon to another, and from one sabbath[7676] to another, [b]shall all flesh come to worship[7812] before me, saith the LORD.

24 And they shall go forth, and look[7200] upon [a]the carcases[6297] of the men[582] that have transgressed[6586] against me: for their [b]worm shall not die,[4191] neither shall their fire be quenched; and they shall be an abhorring[1860] unto all flesh.

21 [a]Ex. 19:6; Isa. 61:6; 1Pet. 2:9; Rev. 1:6
22 [a]Isa. 65:17; 2Pet. 3:13; Rev. 21:1
23 [I]Hebr. *from new moon to his new moon, and from sabbath to his sabbath* [a]Zech. 14:16 [b]Ps. 65:2
24 [a]Isa. 66:16 [b]Mark 9:44, 46, 48

The Book of

JEREMIAH

The name Jeremiah means "whom Jehovah has appointed." He was appointed a prophet before his birth (Jer. 1:5, cf. Paul's statement about his own call in Gal. 1:15, 16). In God's touching Jeremiah's mouth and giving His message to him (Jer. 1:9), one is reminded of Isaiah's call (Is. 6:6, 7). His complaint of lack of ability (Jer. 1:6) is similar to Moses' words (Ex. 4:10).

Jeremiah's ministry extended from 627 B.C. until after the fall of Jerusalem in 586 B.C., a period of roughly fifty years (Jer. 1:2; 25:3). He stated that his message was primarily one of judgment upon Judah for its shameful and persistent sins (Jer. 1:10). Moreover, Jeremiah encouraged the people to submit to Babylon to avoid further bloodshed (Is. 27:1–17). This message was hardly popular with the inhabitants or their rulers, and often Jeremiah's life was in jeopardy (Is. 26:1–24; 37:1—38:13).

There is archaeological confirmation of the people's opinion concerning Jeremiah's message in the "Lachish Letters." These are pottery fragments used as "scratch paper" by the defenders of Lachish against Babylon. The people of Lachish criticized the defeatism induced by "the prophet" in Jerusalem, who can hardly be any but Jeremiah. These external circumstances and the sadness of his message, coupled with Jeremiah's own periodic depression, contributed to the style with which Jeremiah wrote (Is. 4:19–22; 20:7–18). For this reason he is called the "weeping prophet."

Nonetheless, Jeremiah also received some great visions of promise: the return from captivity (chaps. 25, 29); the New Covenant (chap. 31); and the ultimate return of the Messiah to Jerusalem (chap. 23). The Book of Jeremiah is not arranged in chronological order, but is grouped according to subjects: God's dealings with His people (chaps. 1—45); God's dealings with foreign nations (chaps. 46—51); and the destruction of Jerusalem and the temple (chap. 52).

Some would suggest that Jeremiah is a type of Christ. He was accused of political treason, as was Christ, and was tried, persecuted, and imprisoned for the words he had spoken (Jer. 11:18–23; 20:1–6, cf. Mark 14:53–65). In addition to this, Jeremiah and Christ both foretold and wept over the destruction of the temple in Jerusalem (Jer. 22:5–7, cf. Matt. 23:37–39). Furthermore, each was rejected by his own people (Jer. 20:1–3; 36:32, cf. John 1:11).

Jeremiah's Call

1 🔑 The words of Jeremiah the son
of Hilkiah, of the priests[3548] that
[a]*were* in Anathoth in the land[776] of
Benjamin:
2 To whom the word[1697] of the LORD
came in the days[3117] of Josiah the son of
Amon king[4428] of Judah, [a]in the thirteenth year of his reign.[4427]
3 It came also in the days of
Jehoiakim the son of Josiah king of
Judah, [a]unto the end of the eleventh year
of Zedekiah the son of Josiah king of
Judah, [b]unto the carrying away of
Jerusalem captive[1540] [c]in the fifth month.
4 Then the word of the LORD came
unto me, saying,
5 Before I [a]formed[3335] thee in the
belly [b]I knew[3045] thee; and before thou
camest forth out of the womb I [c]sanctified[6942] thee, *and* I [I]ordained thee a
prophet[5030] unto the nations.[1471]

1 [a]Josh. 21:18; 1Chr. 6:60; Jer. 32:7-9

2 [a]Jer. 25:3

3 [a]Jer. 39:2 [b]Jer. 52:12, 15 [c]2Kgs. 25:8

5 [I]Hebr. *gave* [a]Isa. 49:1, 5 [b]Ex. 33:12, 17 [c]Luke 1:15, 41; Gal. 1:15, 16

🔑 **1:1** Anathoth was about three miles northeast of Jerusalem and was one of the cities originally given to the priests after the conquest of Canaan (Josh. 21:18). Abiathar, a priest and close associate of King David, was banished there by Solomon because he had backed the unsuccessful attempt by Adonijah to succeed David (1 Kgs. 2:26).

6 Then said[559] I, [a]Ah, Lord[136] GOD! behold, I cannot speak:[1696] for I *am* a child.

7 But the LORD said unto me, Say not, I *am* a child: for thou shalt go to all that I shall send thee, and [a]whatsoever I command[6680] thee thou shalt speak.

8 [a]Be not afraid[3372] of their faces: for [b]I *am* with thee to deliver[5337] thee, saith[5002] the LORD.

9 Then the LORD put forth his hand,[3027] and [a]touched[5060] my mouth.[6310] And the LORD said unto me, Behold, I have [b]put my words in thy mouth.

10 [a]See, I have this day[3117] set thee over the nations and over the kingdoms, to [b]root out, and to pull down,[5422] and to destroy,[6] and to throw down,[2040] to build, and to plant.

11 Moreover the word of the LORD came unto me, saying, Jeremiah, what seest thou? And I said, I see a rod of an almond tree.

12 Then said the LORD unto me, Thou hast well[3190] seen:[7200] for I will hasten[8245] my word to perform[6213] it.

13 And the word of the LORD came unto me the second time, saying, What seest thou? And I said, I see [a]a seething pot; and the face thereof *is* [I]toward the north.

14 Then the LORD said unto me, Out of the [a]north an evil[7451] [I]shall break forth upon all the inhabitants of the land.

15 For, lo, I will [a]call[7121] all the families[4940] of the kingdoms of the north, saith the LORD; and they shall come, and they shall [b]set every one[376] his throne[3678] at the entering of the gates of Jerusalem, and against all the walls thereof round about, and against all the cities of Judah.

16 And I will utter my judgments[4941] against them touching all their wickedness,[7451] [a]who have forsaken[5800] me, and have burned incense[6999] unto other gods,[430] and worshipped[7812] the works of their own hands.[3027]

17 Thou therefore [a]gird up thy loins, and arise, and speak unto them all that I command thee: [b]be not dismayed[2865] at their faces, lest I [I]confound[2865] thee before them.

18 For, behold, I have made thee this day [a]a defenced city, and an iron pillar, and brasen walls against the whole land, against the kings[4428] of Judah, against the princes[8269] thereof, against the priests thereof, and against the people[5971] of the land.

19 And they shall fight against thee; but they shall not prevail against thee; [a]for I *am* with thee, saith the LORD, to deliver[5337] thee.

Israel Must Repent

2 Moreover the word[1697] of the LORD came to me, saying,

🔑 2 Go and cry[2199] in the ears[241] of Jerusalem, saying, Thus saith[559] the LORD; I remember[2142] [I]thee, the kindness[2617] of thy [a]youth, the love[160] of thine espousals,[3623] [b]when thou wentest after me in the wilderness, in a land[776] *that was* not sown.

3 [a]Israel *was* holiness unto the LORD, *and* [b]the firstfruits[7235] of his increase: [c]all that devour him shall offend;[816] evil[7451] shall come upon them, saith[5002] the LORD.

4 Hear[8085] ye the word of the LORD, O house[1004] of Jacob, and all the families[4940] of the house of Israel:

5 Thus saith the LORD, [a]What iniquity[5766] have your fathers[1] found in me, that they are gone far from me, [b]and have walked after vanity, and are become vain?

6 Neither said they, Where *is* the LORD that [a]brought us up[5927] out of the

---

6 [a]Ex. 4:10; 6:12, 30; Isa. 6:5
7 [a]Num. 22:20, 38; Matt. 28:20
8 [a]Ezek. 2:6; 3:9; Jer. 1:17 [b]Ex. 3:12; Deut. 31:6, 8; Josh. 1:5; Jer. 15:20; Acts 26:17; Heb. 13:6
9 [a]Isa. 6:7 [b]Isa. 51:16; Jer. 5:14
10 [a]1Kgs. 19:17 [b]Jer. 18:7; 2Cor. 10:4, 5
13 [I]Hebr. *from the face of the north* [a]Ezek. 11:3, 7; 24:3
14 [I]Hebr. *shall be opened* [a]Jer. 4:6; 6:1
15 [a]Jer. 5:15; 6:22; 10:22; 25:9 [b]Jer. 39:3; 43:10
16 [a]Deut. 28:20; Jer. 17:13
17 [I]Or, *break to pieces* [a]1Kgs. 18:46; 2Kgs. 4:29; 9:1; Job 38:3; Luke 12:35; 1Pet. 1:13 [b]Ex. 3:12; Jer. 1:8; Ezek. 2:6
18 [a]Isa. 50:7; Jer. 6:27; 15:20
19 [a]Jer. 1:8

2 [I]Or, *for thy sake* [a]Ezek. 16:8, 22, 60; 23:3, 8, 19; Hos. 2:15 [b]Deut. 2:7
3 [a]Ex. 19:5, 6 [b]James 1:18; Rev. 14:4 [c]Jer. 12:14; 50:7
5 [a]Isa. 5:4; Mic. 6:3 [b]2Kgs. 17:15; Jon. 2:8
6 [a]Isa. 63:9, 11, 13; Hos. 13:4

🔑 **2:2–37** Though chapter one discusses the signs that authenticated Jeremiah's calling, this chapter marks the beginning of Jeremiah's ministry and reveals the sinful condition of the people of Judah. It begins with a reflection back on the wilderness experience of Israel (cf. Num. 14:32, 33). This passage also echoes God's earlier description of faithless Israel as His "bride" (Hos. 2:15). In relation to this analogy, chapter three characterizes both Israel and Judah as unfaithful wives.

land of Egypt, that led us through [b]the wilderness, through a land of deserts and of pits,[7745] through a land of drought, and of the shadow of death,[6757] through a land that no man[376] passed[5674] through, and where no man[120] dwelt?

7 And I brought you into [I][a]a plentiful country,[776] to eat the fruit thereof and the goodness thereof; but when ye entered, ye [b]defiled[2930] my land, and made[7760] mine heritage[5159] an abomination.[8441]

8 The priests[3548] said not, Where *is* the LORD? and they that handle[8610] the [a]law[8451] knew[3045] me not: the pastors also transgressed[6586] against me, [b]and the prophets[5030] prophesied[5012] by Baal, and walked after *things that* [c]do not profit.

9 Wherefore [a]I will yet plead[7378] with you, saith the LORD, and [b]with your children's children[1121] will I plead.

10 For pass [I]over[5674] the isles of Chittim, and see; and send unto Kedar, and consider[995] diligently, and see if there be such a thing.

11 [a]Hath a nation[1471] changed *their* gods,[430] which *are* [b]yet no gods? [c]but my people[5971] have changed their glory[3519] for [d]*that which* doth not profit.

12 [a]Be astonished,[8074] O ye heavens,[8064] at this, and be horribly afraid,[8175] be ye very desolate,[2717] saith the LORD.

13 For my people have committed[6213] two evils; they have forsaken[5800] me the [a]fountain of living[2416] waters, *and* hewed them out[2672] cisterns, broken[7665] cisterns, that can hold no water.

14 *Is* Israel [a]a servant?[5650] *is* he a homeborn *slave?* why is he [I]spoiled?

15 [a]The young lions roared upon him, *and* [I]yelled, and they made his land waste:[8047] his cities are burned without inhabitant.

16 Also the children of Noph and [a]Tahapanes [I][b]have broken the crown of thy head.

17 [a]Hast thou not procured[6213] this unto thyself, in that thou hast forsaken the LORD thy God,[430] when [b]he led thee by the way?[1870]

18 And now what hast thou to do [a]in the way of Egypt, to drink the waters of [b]Sihor? or what hast thou to do in the way of Assyria, to drink the waters of the river?

19 Thine own [a]wickedness[7451] shall correct[3256] thee, and thy backslidings[4878] shall reprove[3198] thee: know[3045] therefore and see that *it is* an evil *thing* and bitter,[4751] that thou hast forsaken the LORD thy God, and that my fear[6345] *is* not in thee, saith the Lord[136] GOD of hosts.[6635]

20 For of old time[5769] I have broken thy yoke, *and* burst thy bands; and [a]thou saidst, I will not [I]transgress;[5647] when [b]upon every high hill and under every green tree thou wanderest, [c]playing the harlot.[2181]

21 Yet I had [a]planted thee a noble vine, wholly a right[571] seed:[2233] how then art thou turned into [b]the degenerate plant of a strange vine unto me?

22 For though thou [a]wash thee[3526] with nitre,[5427] and take thee much soap, *yet* [b]thine iniquity[5771] is marked before me, saith the Lord GOD.

23 [a]How canst thou say, I am not polluted,[2930] I have not gone after Baalim? see thy way [b]in the valley, know what thou hast done: *thou art* a swift dromedary traversing her ways;[1870]

24 [a]A wild ass used to the wilderness, *that* snuffeth up the wind[7307] at [I]her pleasure;[5315] in her occasion who can [II]turn her away?[7725] all they that seek her will not weary themselves; in her month they shall find her.

25 Withhold thy foot from being unshod,[3182] and thy throat from thirst: but [a]thou saidst, [I]There is no hope: no; for I have loved[157] [b]strangers,[2114] and after them will I go.

26 As the thief is ashamed when he is found, so is the house of Israel ashamed;[954] they, their kings,[4428] their princes,[8269] and their priests, and their prophets,

27 Saying to a stock, Thou *art* my father;[1] and to a stone, Thou hast [I]brought me forth: for they have turned

---

6 [b]Deut. 8:15; 32:10
7 [I]Or, *the land of Carmel* [a]Num. 13:27; 14:7, 8; Deut. 8:7-9 [b]Lev. 18:25, 27, 28; Num. 35:33, 34; Ps. 78:58, 59; 106:38; Jer. 3:1; 16:18
8 [a]Mal. 2:6, 7; Rom. 2:20 [b]Jer. 23:13 [c]Jer. 2:11; Hab. 2:18
9 [a]Ezek. 20:35, 36; Mic. 6:2 [b]Ex. 20:5; Lev. 20:5
10 [I]Or, *over to*
11 [a]Mic. 4:5 [b]Ps. 115:4; Isa. 37:19; Jer. 16:20 [c]Ps. 106:20; Rom. 1:23 [d]Jer. 2:8
12 [a]Isa. 1:2; Jer. 6:19
13 [a]Ps. 36:9; Jer. 17:13; 18:14; John 4:14
14 [I]Hebr. *become a spoil* [a]Ex. 4:22
15 [I]Hebr. *gave out their voice* [a]Isa. 1:7; Jer. 4:7
16 [I]Or, *feed on thy crown* [a]Deut. 33:20; Isa. 8:8 [b]Jer. 43:7-9
17 [a]Jer. 4:18 [b]Deut. 32:10
18 [a]Isa. 30:1, 2 [b]Josh. 13:3
19 [a]Isa. 3:9; Hos. 5:5
20 [I]Or, *serve* [a]Ex. 19:8; Josh. 24:18; Judg. 10:16; 1Sam. 12:10 [b]Deut. 12:2; Isa. 57:5, 7; Jer. 3:6 [c]Ex. 34:15, 16
21 [a]Ex. 15:17; Ps. 44:2; 80:8; Isa. 5:1; 60:21; Matt. 21:33; Mark 12:1; Luke 20:9 [b]Deut. 32:32; Isa. 1:21; 5:4
22 [a]Job 9:30 [b]Deut. 32:34; Job 14:17; Hos. 13:12
23 [a]Prov. 30:12; [b]Jer. 7:31
24 [I]Hebr. *the desire of her heart* [II]Or, *reverse it* [a]Job 39:5; Jer. 14:6
25 [I]Or, *Is the case desperate?*

[a]Jer. 18:12 [b]Deut. 32:16; Jer. 3:13 **27** [I]Or, *begotten me*

[II]*their* back unto me, and not *their* face: but in the time[6256] of their [a]trouble[7451] they will say, Arise, and save[3467] us.

28 But [a]where *are* thy gods that thou hast made[6213] thee? let them arise, if they [b]can save thee in the time of thy [I]trouble: for [c]*according to* the number of thy cities are thy gods, O Judah.

29 [a]Wherefore will ye plead with me? ye all have transgressed against me, saith the LORD.

30 In vain[7723] have I [a]smitten[5221] your children; they received no correction:[4148] your own sword[2719] hath [b]devoured your prophets, like a destroying[7843] lion.

31 O generation,[1755] see ye the word of the LORD. [a]Have I been a wilderness unto Israel? a land of darkness? wherefore say my people, [Ib]We are lords;[7300] [c]we will come no more unto thee?

32 Can a maid[1330] forget her ornaments, *or* a bride her attire? yet my people [a]have forgotten me days[3117] without number.

33 Why trimmest[3190] thou thy way to seek love? therefore hast thou also taught[3925] the wicked[7451] ones thy ways.

34 Also in thy skirts is found [a]the blood[1818] of the souls[5315] of the poor innocents: I have not found it by [I]secret search, but upon all these.

35 [a]Yet thou sayest, Because I am innocent,[5352] surely his anger[639] shall turn from me. Behold, [b]I will plead[8199] with thee, [c]because thou sayest, I have not sinned.[2398]

36 [a]Why gaddest thou about[235] so much to change thy way? [b]thou also shalt be ashamed of Egypt, [c]as thou wast ashamed of Assyria.

37 Yea, thou shalt go forth from him, and [a]thine hands[3027] upon thine head:[7218] for the LORD hath rejected[3988] thy confidences, and thou shalt not prosper in them.

Unfaithfulness

3 [I]They say,[559] If a man[376] put away his wife,[802] and she go from him, and become another man's, [a]shall he return unto her again? shall not that [b]land[776] be greatly polluted?[2610] but thou hast [c]played the harlot[2181] with many lovers; [d]yet return again to me, saith[5002] the LORD.

2 Lift up[5375] thine eyes unto [a]the high places,[8205] and see where thou hast not been lien with. [b]In the ways[1870] hast thou sat for them, as the Arabian in the wilderness; [c]and thou hast polluted the land with thy whoredoms[2184] and with thy wickedness.[7451]

3 Therefore the [a]showers have been withholden,[4513] and there hath been no latter rain; and thou hadst a [b]whore's[2181] forehead, thou refusedst[3985] to be ashamed.

4 Wilt thou not from this time cry[2199] unto me, My father,[1] thou *art* [a]the guide[441] of [b]my youth?

5 [a]Will he reserve[5201] *his anger* for ever? will he keep[8104] *it* to the end?[5531] Behold, thou hast spoken[1696] and done evil things[7451] as thou couldest.

6 The LORD said also unto me in the days[3117] of Josiah the king,[4428] Hast thou seen[7200] *that* which [a]backsliding[4878] Israel hath done? she is [b]gone up upon every high mountain and under every green tree, and there hath played the harlot.

7 [a]And I said after she had done all these *things,* Turn[7725] thou unto me. But she returned not. And her treacherous [b]sister[269] Judah saw[7200] *it.*

8 And I saw, when [a]for all the causes whereby backsliding Israel committed adultery[5003] I had [b]put her away, and given her a bill[5612] of divorce;[3748] [c]yet her treacherous[898] sister Judah feared[3372] not, but went and played the harlot also.

9 And it came to pass through the [I]lightness of her whoredom,[2184] that she [a]defiled[2610] the land, and committed adultery with [b]stones and with stocks.

10 And yet for all this her treacherous sister Judah hath not turned unto me [a]with her whole heart,[3820] but [I]feignedly,[8267] saith the LORD.

11 And the LORD[3068] said unto me,

27 IIHebr. *the hinder part of the neck* aJudg. 10:10; Ps. 78:34; Isa. 26:16
28 IHebr. *evil* aDeut. 32:37; Judg. 10:14 bIsa. 45:20 cJer. 11:13
29 aJer. 2:23, 35
30 aIsa. 1:5; 9:13; Jer. 5:3 b2Chr. 36:16; Neh. 9:26; Matt. 23:29; Acts 7:52; 1Thess. 2:15
31 IHebr. *We have dominion* aJer. 2:5 bPs. 12:4 cDeut. 32:15
32 aPs. 106:21; Jer. 13:25; Hos. 8:14
34 IHebr. *digging* aPs. 106:38; Jer. 19:4
35 aJer. 2:23, 29 bJer. 2:9 cProv. 28:13; 1John 1:8, 10
36 aJer. 2:18; 31:22; Hos. 5:13; 12:1 bIsa. 30:3; Jer. 37:7 c2Chr. 28:16, 20, 21
37 a2Sam. 13:19

1 IHebr. *Saying* aDeut. 24:4 bJer. 2:7 cJer. 2:20; Ezek. 16:26, 28, 29 dJer. 4:1; Zech. 1:3
2 aDeut. 12:2; Jer. 2:20 bGen. 38:14; Prov. 23:28; Ezek. 16:24, 25 cJer. 2:7; 3:9
3 aLev. 26:19; Deut. 28:23, 24; Jer. 9:12; 14:4 bJer. 5:3; 6:15; 8:12; Ezek. 3:7; Zeph. 3:5
4 aProv. 2:17 bJer. 2:2; Hos. 2:15
5 aPs. 77:7; 103:9; Isa. 57:16; Jer. 3:12
6 aJer. 3:11, 14; 7:24 bJer. 2:20
7 a2Kgs. 17:13 bEzek. 16:46; 23:2, 4
8 aEzek. 23:9 b2Kgs. 17:6, 18 cEzek. 23:11
9 IOr, *fame* aJer. 2:7; 3:2 bJer. 2:27
10 IHebr. *in falsehood* a2Chr. 34:33; Hos. 7:14

[a]The backsliding Israel hath justified[6663] herself more than treacherous Judah.

12 Go and proclaim[7121] these words[1697] toward the [a]north, and say, Return, thou backsliding Israel, saith the LORD; *and* I will not cause mine anger to fall upon you: for I *am* [b]merciful,[2623] saith the LORD, *and* I will not keep *anger* for ever.[5769]

13 [a]Only acknowledge[3045] thine iniquity,[5771] that thou hast transgressed[6586] against the LORD thy God,[430] and hast [b]scattered thy ways to the [c]strangers[2114] [d]under every green tree, and ye have not obeyed[8085] my voice, saith the LORD.

14 Turn, O backsliding7726 children,[1121] saith the LORD; [a]for I am married[1166] unto you: and I will take you [b]one of a city, and two of a family,[4940] and I will bring you to Zion:

15 And I will give you [a]pastors according to mine heart, which shall [b]feed you with knowledge[1844] and understanding.[7919]

16 And it shall come to pass, when ye be multiplied and increased in the land, in those days, saith the LORD, they shall say no more, The ark[727] of the covenant[1285] of the LORD: [a]neither shall it [I]come to mind:[3820] neither shall they remember[2142] it; neither shall they visit[6485] *it;* neither shall [II]*that* be done any more.

17 At that time[6256] they shall call[7121] Jerusalem the throne[3678] of the LORD; and all the nations[1471] shall be gathered unto it, [a]to the name of the LORD, to Jerusalem: neither shall they [b]walk any more after the [I]imagination[8307] of their evil heart.

18 In those days [a]the house[1004] of Judah shall walk [I]with the house of Israel, and they shall come together out of the land of [b]the north to [c]the land that I have [II]given for an inheritance[5157] unto your fathers.[1]

19 But I said, How shall I put thee among the children, and give thee [a]a [I]pleasant land, [II]a goodly heritage[5159] of the hosts[6635] of nations? and I said, Thou shalt call me, [b]My father; and shalt not turn away[7725] [III]from me.

20 Surely *as* a wife treacherously departeth[898] from her [I]husband,[7453] so [a]have ye dealt treacherously[898] with me, O house of Israel, saith the LORD.

21 A voice was heard[8085] upon [a]the high places, weeping *and* supplications[8469] of the children of Israel: for they have perverted[5753] their way, *and* they have forgotten the LORD their God.

22 [a]Return, ye backsliding children, *and* [b]I will heal your backslidings.4878 Behold, we come unto thee; for thou *art* the LORD our God.

23 [a]Truly in vain[8267] *is salvation hoped for* from the hills, *and from* the multitude of mountains: [b]truly in the LORD our God *is* the salvation[8668] of Israel.

24 [a]For shame hath devoured the labour of our fathers from our youth; their flocks and their herds, their sons[1121] and their daughters.

25 We lie down in our shame, and our confusion[3639] covereth[3680] us: [a]for we have sinned[2398] against the LORD our God, we and our fathers, from our youth even unto this day,[3117] and [b]have not obeyed the voice of the LORD our God.

Return to God!

4 If thou wilt return,[7725] O Israel, saith the LORD, [a]return unto me: and if thou wilt put away[5493] thine abominations[8251] out of my sight, then shalt thou not remove.

2 [a]And thou shalt swear,[7650] The LORD liveth,[2416] [b]in truth,[571] in judgment,[4941] and in righteousness;[6666] [c]and the nations[1471] shall bless themselves[1288] in him, and in him shall they [d]glory.[1984]

3 For thus saith the LORD to the men[376] of Judah and Jerusalem, [a]Break up your fallow ground,5215 and [b]sow not among thorns.

4 [a]Circumcise yourselves[4135] to the LORD, and take away the foreskins[6190] of your heart,3824 ye men of Judah and inhabitants of Jerusalem: lest my fury

11 [a]Ezek. 16:51; 23:11
12 [a]2Kgs. 17:6 [b]Ps. 86:15; 103:8, 9; Jer. 3:5
13 [a]Lev. 26:40; Deut. 30:1, 2; Prov. 28:13 [b]Jer. 3:2; Ezek. 16:15, 24, 25 [c]Jer. 2:25 [d]Deut. 12:2
14 [a]Jer. 31:22; Hos. 2:19, 20 [b]Rom. 11:5
15 [a]Jer. 23:4; Ezek. 34:23; Eph. 4:11 [b]Acts 20:28
16 [I]Hebr. *come upon the heart* [II]Or, *it be magnified* [a]Isa. 65:17
17 [I]Or, *stubbornness* [a]Isa. 60:9 [b]Jer. 11:8
18 [I]Or, *to* [II]Or, *caused your fathers to possess* [a]Isa. 11:13; Ezek. 37:16-22; Hos. 1:11 [b]Jer. 3:12; 31:8 [c]Amos 9:15
19 [I]Hebr. *land of desire* [II]Hebr. *heritage of glory, or, beauty* [III]Hebr. *from after me* [a]Ps. 106:24; Ezek. 20:6; Dan. 8:9; 11:16, 41, 45 [b]Isa. 63:16
20 [I]Hebr. *friend* [a]Isa. 48:8; Jer. 5:11
21 [a]Isa. 15:2
22 [a]Jer. 3:14; Hos. 14:1 [b]Hos. 6:1; 14:4
23 [a]Ps. 121:1, 2 [b]Ps. 3:8
24 [a]Jer. 11:13; Hos. 9:10
25 [a]Ezra 9:7 [b]Jer. 22:21

1 [a]Jer. 3:1, 22; Joel 2:12
2 [a]Deut. 10:20; Isa. 45:23; 65:16; Jer. 5:2 [b]Isa. 48:1; Zech. 8:8 [c]Gen. 22:18; Ps. 72:17; Gal. 3:8 [d]Isa. 45:25; 1Cor. 1:31
3 [a]Hos. 10:12 [b]Matt. 13:7, 22
4 [a]Deut. 10:16; 30:6; Jer. 9:26; Rom. 2:28, 29; Col. 2:11

come forth like fire, and burn that none can quench *it,* because of the evil[7455] of your doings.

5 Declare[5046] ye in Judah, and publish[8085] in Jerusalem; and say, Blow[8628] ye the trumpet in the land:[776] cry,[2199] gather together, and say, [a]Assemble[622] yourselves, and let us go into the defenced cities.

6 Set up[5375] the standard toward Zion: [I]retire, stay not: for I will bring evil[7451] from the [a]north, and a great [II]destruction.[7667]

7 [a]The lion is come up[5927] from his thicket, and [b]the destroyer[7843] of the Gentiles[1471] is on his way; he is gone forth from his place [c]to make[7760] thy land desolate;[8047] *and* thy cities shall be laid waste, without an inhabitant.

8 For this [a]gird you with sackcloth, lament and howl: for the fierce anger[639] of the LORD is not turned back from us.

9 And it shall come to pass at that day,[3117] saith5002 the LORD, *that* the heart[3820] of the king[4428] shall perish,[6] and the heart of the princes;[8269] and the priests[3548] shall be astonished,[8074] and the prophets[5030] shall wonder.

10 Then said[559] I, Ah, Lord GOD! [a]surely thou hast greatly deceived this people[5971] and Jerusalem, [b]saying, Ye shall have peace; whereas the sword[2719] reacheth[5060] unto the soul.[5315]

11 At that time[6256] shall it be said to this people and to Jerusalem, [a]A dry wind[7307] of the high places[8205] in the wilderness toward the daughter of my people, not to fan, nor to cleanse,[1305]

12 *Even* [I]a full wind from those *places* shall come unto me: now also [a]will I [II]give sentence against them.

13 Behold, he shall come up as clouds, and [a]his chariots *shall be* as a whirlwind: [b]his horses are swifter[7043] than eagles. Woe unto us! for we are spoiled.[7703]

14 O Jerusalem, [a]wash[3526] thine heart from wickedness,[7451] that thou mayest be saved.[3467] How long shall thy vain thoughts[4284] lodge within[7130] thee?

15 For a voice declareth[5046] [a]from Dan, and publisheth[8085] affliction[205] from mount Ephraim.

16 Make ye mention to the nations; behold, publish against Jerusalem, *that* watchers[5341] come [a]from a far country,[776] and give out their voice against the cities of Judah.

17 [a]As keepers[8104] of a field,[7704] are they against her round about; because she hath been rebellious against me, saith the LORD.

18 [a]Thy way[1870] and thy doings have procured[6213] these *things* unto thee; this *is* thy wickedness, because it is bitter,[4751] because it reacheth unto thine heart.

19 My [a]bowels,[4578] my bowels! I am pained[3176] at [I]my very[7023] heart; my heart maketh a noise1993 in me; I cannot hold my peace, because thou hast heard,[8085] O my soul, the sound of the trumpet, the alarm of war.

20 [a]Destruction upon destruction is cried;[7121] for the whole land is spoiled: suddenly are [b]my tents[168] spoiled, *and* my curtains in a moment.

21 How long shall I see the standard, *and* hear[8085] the sound of the trumpet?

22 For my people *is* foolish,191 they have not known[3045] me; they *are* sottish5530 children,[1121] and they have none understanding:[995] [a]they *are* wise[2450] to do evil,[7489] but to do good[3190] they have no knowledge.[3045]

🔑 23 [a]I beheld[7200] the earth,[776] and, lo, *it was* [b]without form,[8414] and void;922

5 [a]Jer. 8:14

6 [I]Or, *strengthen* [II]Hebr. *breaking* [a]Jer. 1:13-15; 6:1, 22

7 [a]2Kgs. 24:1; Jer. 5:6; Dan. 7:4 [b]Jer. 25:9 [c]Isa. 1:7; Jer. 2:15

8 [a]Isa. 22:12; Jer. 6:26

10 [a]Ezek. 14:9; 2Thess. 2:11 [b]Jer. 5:12; 14:13

11 [a]Jer. 51:1; Ezek. 17:10; Hos. 13:15

12 [I]Or, *a fuller wind than those* [II]Hebr. *utter judgments* [a]Jer. 1:16

13 [a]Isa. 5:28 [b]Deut. 28:49; Lam. 4:19; Hos. 8:1; Hab. 1:8

14 [a]Isa. 1:16; James 4:8

15 [a]Jer. 8:16

16 [a]Jer. 5:15

17 [a]2Kgs. 25:1, 4

18 [a]Ps. 107:17; Isa. 50:1; Jer. 2:17, 19

19 [I]Hebr. *the walls of my heart* [a]Isa. 15:5; 16:11; 21:3; 22:4; Jer. 9:1, 10; Luke 19:42

20 [a]Ps. 42:7; Ezek. 7:26 [b]Jer. 10:20

22 [a]Rom. 16:19

23 [a]Isa. 24:19 [b]Gen. 1:2

🔑 **4:23–29** These verses are used to support the "gap theory," which suggests that a large span of time and a divine judgment occurred between the events of Genesis 1:1 and 1:2. The phrase in verse twenty-three, "formless and void," is the same as the one used in Genesis 1:2. However, the context here (especially Jer. 4:27) makes explicit that this is not a total destruction wherein nothing remains. It is also clear that poetic imagery is being used (cf. 4:23 with 4:28 and 4:25 with 4:29). Therefore, this passage gives no support to those advocating a "gap."

and the heavens,8064 and they *had* no
light.[216]
24 [a]I beheld the mountains, and, lo,
they trembled,[7493] and all the hills moved
lightly.[7043]
25 I beheld, and, lo, *there was* no
man,[120] and [a]all the birds of the heavens
were fled.
26 I beheld, and, lo, the fruitful place
was a wilderness, and all the cities
thereof were broken down[5422] at the
presence of the LORD, *and* by his fierce
anger.
27 For thus hath the LORD said, The
whole land shall be desolate;[8077] [a]yet will
I not make[6213] a full end.[3617]
28 For this [a]shall the earth mourn,
and [b]the heavens above be black:[6937] because I have spoken[1696] *it,* I have
purposed[2161] *it,* and [c]will not repent,[5162]
neither will I turn back[7725] from it.
29 The whole city shall flee for the
noise of the horsemen and bowmen; they
shall go into thickets, and climb up upon
the rocks: every city *shall be* forsaken,[5800]
and not a man[376] dwell therein.
30 And *when* thou *art* spoiled, what
wilt thou do? Though thou clothest thyself with crimson, though thou deckest
thee with ornaments of gold, [a]though
thou rentest7167 thy [I]face with painting, in
vain[7723] shalt thou make thyself fair; [b]*thy*
lovers[5689] will despise[3988] thee, they will
seek thy life.[5315]
31 For I have heard a voice as of
a woman in travail, *and* the anguish6869
as of her that bringeth forth her first
child, the voice of the daughter of Zion,
that bewaileth herself, *that* [a]spreadeth
her hands,[3709] *saying,* Woe *is* me now!
for my soul is wearied because of murderers.[2026]

The Sins of Jerusalem And Judah

5 Run ye to and fro through the streets
of Jerusalem, and see now, and
know,[3045] and seek in the broad places
thereof, [a]if ye can find1245 a man,[376] [b]if
there be *any* that executeth[6213] judgment,[4941] that seeketh the truth;[530] [c]and
I will pardon[5545] it.
2 And [a]though they say, [b]The LORD
liveth;[2416] surely they [c]swear[7650]
falsely.[8267]
3 O LORD, *are* not [a]thine eyes upon
the truth? thou hast [b]stricken them,
but they have not grieved;[2342] thou
hast consumed[3615] them, *but* [c]they have
refused[3985] to receive correction:[4148] they
have made their faces harder than a rock;
they have refused to return.[7725]
4 Therefore I said, Surely these *are*
poor; they are foolish: for [a]they know not
the way[1870] of the LORD, *nor* the judgment of their God.[430]
5 I will get me unto the great men,
and will speak unto them; for [a]they have
known[3045] the way of the LORD, *and* the
judgment of their God: but these have altogether [b]broken[7665] the yoke, *and* burst
the bonds.
6 Wherefore [a]a lion out of the forest
shall slay[5221] them, [b]*and* a wolf of the
[I]evenings[6160] shall spoil[7703] them, [c]a leopard shall watch over their cities: every
one that goeth out thence shall be torn in
pieces: because their transgressions[6588]
are many, *and* their backslidings4878 [II]are
increased.
7 How shall I pardon thee for this?
thy children[1121] have forsaken[5800] me,
and [a]sworn by *them that* [b]*are* no gods:[430]
[c]when I had fed them to the full, they
then committed adultery,5003 and assembled themselves by troops[1413] in the harlots' houses.[1004]
8 [a]They were *as* fed horses in the
morning: every one[376] [b]neighed after his
neighbour's[7453] wife.[802]
9 [a]Shall I not visit[6485] for these
things? saith5002 the LORD: [b]and shall[5358]
not my soul[5315] be avenged[5358] on such
a nation[1471] as this?
10 [a]Go ye up upon her walls, and destroy; [b]but make[6213] not a full end:[3617]
take away her battlements;5189 for they
are not the LORD'S.
11 For [a]the house[1004] of Israel and
the house of Judah have dealt very
treacherously[898] against me, saith the
LORD.

24 [a]Isa. 5:25; Ezek. 38:20
25 [a]Zeph. 1:3
27 [a]Jer. 5:10, 18; 30:11; 46:28
28 [a]Hos. 4:3 [b]Isa. 5:30; 50:3 [c]Num. 23:19; Jer. 7:16
30 [I]Hebr. *eyes* [a]2Kgs. 9:30; Ezek. 23:40 [b]Jer. 22:20, 22; Lam. 1:2, 19
31 [a]Isa. 1:15; Lam. 1:17
1 [a]Ezek. 22:30 [b]Gen. 18:23; Ps. 12:1 [c]Gen. 18:26
2 [a]Titus 1:16 [b]Jer. 4:2 [c]Jer. 7:9
3 [a]2Chr. 16:9 [b]Isa. 1:5; 9:13; Jer. 2:30 [c]Jer. 7:28; Zeph. 3:2
4 [a]Jer. 8:7
5 [a]Mic. 3:1 [b]Ps. 2:3
6 [I]Or, *deserts* [II]Hebr. *are strong* [a]Jer. 4:7 [b]Ps. 104:20; Hab. 1:8; Zeph. 3:3 [c]Hos. 13:7
7 [a]Josh. 23:7; Zeph. 1:5 [b]Deut. 32:21; Gal. 4:8 [c]Deut. 32:15
8 [a]Ezek. 22:11 [b]Jer. 13:27
9 [a]Jer. 5:29; 9:9 [b]Jer. 44:22
10 [a]Jer. 39:8 [b]Jer. 4:27; 5:18
11 [a]Jer. 3:20

12 [a]They have belied the LORD, and said, [b]*It is* not he; neither shall evil[7451] come upon us; [c]neither shall we see sword[2719] nor famine:

13 And the prophets[5030] shall become[1961] wind,[7307] and the word *is* not in them: thus shall it be done unto them.

14 Wherefore thus saith the LORD God of hosts,[6635] Because ye speak this word, [a]behold, I will make my words in thy mouth[6310] fire, and this people[5971] wood, and it shall devour them.

15 Lo, I will bring a [a]nation upon you [b]from far, O house of Israel, saith the LORD; it *is* a mighty nation, it *is* an ancient[5769] nation, a nation whose language thou knowest[3045] not, neither understandest what they say.

16 Their quiver *is* as an open sepulchre,[6913] they *are* all mighty men.

17 And they shall eat up thine [a]harvest, and thy bread, *which* thy sons[1121] and thy daughters should eat: they shall eat up thy flocks and thine herds: they shall eat up thy vines and thy fig trees: they shall impoverish thy fenced cities, wherein thou trustedst,[982] with the sword.

18 Nevertheless in those days,[3117] saith the LORD, I [a]will not make a full end with you.

19 And it shall come to pass, when ye shall say, [a]Wherefore doeth the LORD our God all these *things* unto us? then shalt thou answer them, Like as ye have [b]forsaken me, and served[5647] strange[5236] gods in your land,[776] so [c]shall ye serve strangers[2114] in a land *that is* not yours.

20 Declare[5046] this in the house of Jacob, and publish[8085] it in Judah, saying,

21 Hear[8085] now this, O [a]foolish people, and without [I][b]understanding;[3820] which have eyes, and see not; which have ears,[241] and hear not:

22 [a]Fear[3372] ye not me? saith the LORD: will ye not tremble[2342] at my presence, which have placed the sand *for* the [b]bound of the sea by a perpetual[5769] decree,[2706] that it cannot pass it: and though the waves thereof toss themselves, yet can they not prevail; though they roar, yet can they not pass over[5674] it?

23 But this people hath a revolting[5637] and a rebellious heart;[3820] they are revolted and gone.

24 Neither say they in their heart,[3824] Let us now fear the LORD our God, [a]that giveth rain, both the [b]former and the latter, in his season:[6256] [c]he reserveth[8104] unto us the appointed weeks of the harvest.

25 [a]Your iniquities[5771] have turned away these *things,* and your sins have withholden[4513] good[2896] *things* from you.

26 For among my people are found wicked[7563] *men:* [I]they [a]lay wait, as he that setteth snares; they set[5324] a trap,[4889] they catch men.[582]

27 As a [I]cage is full of birds, so *are* their houses full of deceit:[4820] therefore they are become great, and waxen rich.

28 They are waxen [a]fat, they shine: yea, they overpass[5674] the deeds[1697] of the wicked:[7451] they judge[1777] not [b]the cause,[1779] the cause of the fatherless, [c]yet they prosper; and the right[4941] of the needy do they not judge.[8199]

29 [a]Shall I not visit for these *things?* saith the LORD: shall not my soul be avenged on such a nation as this?

30 [I]A wonderful[8047] and [a]horrible thing[8186] is committed[1961] in the land;

31 The prophets prophesy[5012] [a]falsely, and the priests[3548] [I]bear rule[7287] by their means;[3027] and my people [b]love[157] *to have it* so: and what will ye do in the end[319] thereof?

The Siege of Jerusalem

6 O ye children[1121] of Benjamin, gather yourselves to flee out of the midst[7130] of Jerusalem, and blow[8628] the trumpet in Tekoa, and set up[5375] a sign of fire in [a]Beth–haccerem: [b]for evil[7451] appeareth out of the north, and great destruction.[7667]

2 I have likened the daughter of Zion to a [I]comely[5000] and delicate *woman.*

3 The shepherds with their flocks shall come unto her; [a]they shall pitch[8628]

---

12 [a]2Chr. 36:16; Jer. 4:10 [b]Isa. 28:15 [c]Jer. 14:13

14 [a]Jer. 1:9

15 [a]Deut. 28:49; Isa. 5:26; Jer. 1:15; 6:22 [b]Isa. 39:3; Jer. 4:16

17 [a]Lev. 26:16; Deut. 28:31, 33

18 [a]Jer. 4:27

19 [a]Deut. 29:24; 1Kgs. 9:8, 9; Jer. 13:22; 16:10 [b]Jer. 2:13 [c]Deut. 28:48

21 [I]Hebr. *heart* [a]Isa. 6:9; Ezek. 12:2; Matt. 13:14; John 12:40; Acts 28:26; Rom. 11:8 [b]Hos. 7:11

22 [a]Rev. 15:4 [b]Job 26:10; 38:10, 11; Ps. 104:9; Prov. 8:29

24 [a]Ps. 147:8; Jer. 14:22; Matt. 5:45; Acts 14:17 [b]Deut. 11:14; Joel 2:23 [c]Gen. 8:22

25 [a]Jer. 3:3

26 [I]Or, *they pry as fowlers lie in wait* [a]Prov. 1:11, 17, 18; Hab. 1:15

27 [I]Or, *coop*

28 [a]Deut. 32:15 [b]Isa. 1:23; Zech. 7:10 [c]Job 12:6; Ps. 73:12; Jer. 12:1

29 [a]Jer. 5:9; Mal. 3:5

30 [I]Or, *Astonishment and filthiness* [a]Jer. 23:14; Hos. 6:10

31 [I]Or, *take into their hands* [a]Jer. 14:14; 23:25, 26; Ezek. 13:6 [b]Mic. 2:11

1 [a]Neh. 3:14 [b]Jer. 1:14; 4:6

2 [I]Or, *dwelling at home*

3 [a]2Kgs. 25:1, 4; Jer. 4:17

their tents[168] against her round about; they shall feed every one in his place.

4 [a]Prepare[6942] ye war against her; arise, and let us go up at [b]noon. Woe unto us! for the day[3117] goeth away, for the shadows[6752] of the evening are stretched out.

5 Arise, and let us go by night,[3915] and let us destroy her palaces.[759]

6 For thus hath the LORD of hosts[6635] said, Hew ye down[3772] trees, and [I]cast[8210] a mount against Jerusalem: this *is* the city to be visited;[6485] she *is* wholly oppression in the midst of her.

7 [a]As a fountain[953] casteth out her waters, so she casteth out her wickedness:[7451] [b]violence[2555] and spoil[7701] is heard in her; before me continually[8548] *is* grief and wounds.[4347]

8 Be thou instructed,[3256] O Jerusalem, lest [a]my soul[5315] [I]depart from thee; lest I make[7760] thee desolate,[8077] a land[776] not inhabited.

9 Thus saith the LORD of hosts, They shall throughly glean the remnant[7611] of Israel as a vine: turn back[7725] thine hand[3027] as a grapegatherer into the baskets.

10 To whom shall I speak, and give warning, that they may hear? behold, their [a]ear[241] *is* uncircumcised,[6189] and they cannot hearken:[7181] behold, [b]the word[1697] of the LORD is unto them a reproach;[2781] they have no delight[2654] in it.

11 Therefore I am full of the fury of the LORD; [a]I am weary with holding in: I will pour it out[8210] [b]upon the children abroad, and upon the assembly[5475] of young men together: for even the husband[376] with the wife[802] shall be taken, the aged with *him that is* full of days.[3117]

12 And [a]their houses[1004] shall be turned unto others, *with their* fields[7704] and wives together: for I will stretch out my hand upon the inhabitants of the land, saith[5002] the LORD.

13 For from the least of them even unto the greatest of them every one *is* given to [a]covetousness;[1215] and from the prophet[5030] even unto the priest[3548] every one dealeth falsely.[8267]

14 They have [a]healed also the [I]hurt[7667] *of the daughter* of my people[5971] slightly, [b]saying, Peace, peace; when *there is* no peace.

15 Were they [a]ashamed[954] when they had committed[6213] abomination?[8441] nay, they were not at all ashamed, neither could they blush: therefore they shall fall among them that fall: at the time[6256] *that* I visit[6485] them they shall be cast down,[3782] saith the LORD.

16 Thus saith the LORD, Stand ye in the ways,[1870] and see, and ask[7592] for the [a]old[5769] paths, where *is* the good[2896] way,[1870] and walk therein, and ye shall find [b]rest for your souls.[5315] But they said, We will not walk *therein.*

17 Also I set [a]watchmen over you, *saying,* Hearken to the sound of the trumpet. But they said, We will not hearken.

18 Therefore hear, ye nations,[1471] and know,[3045] O congregation,[5712] what *is* among them.

19 [a]Hear, O earth:[776] behold, I will bring evil upon this people, *even* [b]the fruit of their thoughts,[4284] because they have not hearkened[7181] unto my words,[1697] nor to my law,[8451] but rejected[3988] it.

20 [a]To what purpose cometh there to me incense [b]from Sheba, and the sweet cane from a far country?[776] [c]your burnt offerings[5930] *are* not acceptable,[7522] nor your sacrifices[2077] sweet[6148] unto me.

21 Therefore thus saith the LORD, Behold, I will lay stumblingblocks[4383] before this people, and the fathers and the sons together shall fall[3782] upon them; the neighbour[7934] and his friend shall perish.[6]

22 Thus saith the LORD, Behold, a people cometh from the [a]north country, and a great nation[1471] shall be raised from the sides of the earth.

23 They shall lay hold on[2388] bow and spear; they *are* cruel, and have no mercy; their voice [a]roareth like the sea; and they ride upon horses, set in array as men for war against thee, O daughter of Zion.

4 [a]Jer. 51:27; Joel 3:9 [b]Jer. 15:8

6 [I]Or, *pour out the engine of shot*

7 [a]Isa. 57:20 [b]Ps. 55:9-11; Jer. 20:8; Ezek. 7:11, 23

8 [I]Hebr. *be loosed,* or, *disjointed* [a]Ezek. 23:18; Hos. 9:12

10 [a]Ex. 6:12; Jer. 7:26; Acts 7:51 [b]Jer. 20:8

11 [a]Jer. 20:9 [b]Jer. 9:21

12 [a]Deut. 28:30; Jer. 8:10

13 [a]Isa. 56:11; Jer. 8:10; 14:18; 23:11; Mic. 3:5, 11

14 [I]Hebr. *bruise,* or, *breach* [a]Jer. 8:11; Ezek. 13:10 [b]Jer. 4:10; 14:13; 23:17

15 [a]Jer. 3:3; 8:12

16 [a]Isa. 8:20; Jer. 18:15; Mal. 4:4; Luke 16:29 [b]Matt. 11:29

17 [a]Isa. 21:11; 58:1; Jer. 25:4; Ezek. 3:17; Hab. 2:1

19 [a]Isa. 1:2 [b]Prov. 1:31

20 [a]Ps. 40:6; 50:7-9; Isa. 1:11; 66:3; Amos 5:21; Mic. 6:6 [b]Isa. 60:6 [c]Jer. 7:21

22 [a]Jer. 1:15; 5:15; 10:22; 50:41-43

23 [a]Isa. 5:30

24 We have heard the fame thereof: our hands[3027] wax feeble:[7503] [a]anguish[6869] hath taken hold[2388] of us, *and* pain, as of a woman in travail.

25 Go not forth into the field,[7704] nor walk by the way; for the sword[2719] of the enemy *and* fear[4032] *is* on every side.

26 O daughter of my people, [a]gird *thee* with sackcloth, [b]and wallow thyself in ashes: [c]make[6213] thee mourning, *as for* an only[3173] son, most bitter lamentation: for the spoiler[7703] shall suddenly come upon us.

27 I have set thee *for* a tower[969] *and* [a]a fortress[4013] among my people, that thou mayest know and try[974] their way.

28 [a]They *are* all grievous[5493] revolters,[5637] [b]walking with slanders: *they are* [c]brass and iron; they *are* all corrupters.[7843]

29 The bellows are burned,[2787] the lead is consumed[8552] of the fire; the founder melteth[6884] in vain: for the wicked[7451] are not plucked away.

30 [I][a]Reprobate[3988] silver shall *men* call[7121] them, because the LORD hath rejected them.

Jeremiah Preaches

7 The word that came to Jeremiah from the LORD, saying,

🔑 2 [a]Stand in the gate of the LORD's house,[1004] and proclaim[7121] there this word, and say,[559] Hear[8085] the word of the LORD, all *ye of* Judah, that enter in at these gates to worship[7812] the LORD.

3 Thus saith the LORD of hosts,[6635] the God[430] of Israel, [a]Amend[3190] your ways[1870] and your doings, and I will cause you to dwell[7931] in this place.

4 [a]Trust[982] ye not in lying words, saying, The temple[1964] of the LORD, The temple of the LORD, The temple of the LORD, *are* these.

5 For if ye throughly amend your ways and your doings; if ye throughly [a]execute judgment[4941] between a man[376] and his neighbour;[7453]

6 *If* ye oppress not the stranger,[1616] the fatherless, and the widow, and shed[I][8210] not innocent[5355] blood[1818] in this place, [a]neither walk after other gods[430] to your hurt:[7451]

7 [a]Then will I cause you to dwell in this place, in [b]the land[776] that I gave to your fathers,[1] for ever and ever.

8 Behold, [a]ye trust in [b]lying words, that cannot profit.

9 [a]Will ye steal, murder,[7523] and commit adultery,[5003] and swear[7650] falsely,[8267] and burn incense[6999] unto Baal, and [b]walk after other gods whom ye know[3045] not;

10 [a]And come and stand before me in this house, [I][b]which is called[7121] by my name, and say, We are delivered to do[6213] all these abominations?[8441]

11 Is [a]this house, which is called by my name, become a [b]den of robbers[6530] in your eyes? Behold, even I have seen[7200] *it,* saith[5002] the LORD.

12 But go ye now unto [a]my place which *was* in Shiloh, [b]where I set[7931] my name at the first,[7223] and see [c]what I did to it for the wickedness[7451] of my people[5971] Israel.

13 And now, because ye have done all these works, saith the LORD, and I

24 [a]Jer. 4:31; 13:21; 49:24; 50:43
26 [a]Jer. 4:8 [b]Jer. 25:34; Mic. 1:10 [c]Zech. 12:10
27 [a]Jer. 1:18; 15:20
28 [a]Jer. 5:23 [b]Jer. 9:4 [c]Ezek. 22:18
30 [I]Or, *Refuse silver* [a]Isa. 1:22
2 [a]Jer. 26:2
3 [a]Jer. 18:11; 26:13
4 [a]Mic. 3:11
5 [a]Jer. 22:3
6 [a]Deut. 6:14, 15; 8:19; 11:28; Jer. 13:10
7 [a]Deut. 4:40 [b]Jer. 3:18
8 [a]Jer. 7:4 [b]Jer. 5:31; 14:13, 14
9 [a]1Kgs. 18:21; Hos. 4:1, 2; Zeph. 1:5 [b]Ex. 20:3; Jer. 7:6
10 [I]Hebr. *whereupon my name is called* [a]Ezek. 23:39 [b]Jer. 7:11, 14, 30; 32:34; 34:15
11 [a]Isa. 56:7 [b]Matt. 21:13; Mark 11:17; Luke 19:46
12 [a]Josh. 18:1; Judg. 18:31 [b]Deut. 12:11 [c]1Sam. 4:10, 11; Ps. 78:60; Jer. 26:6

🔑 **7:2–15** Jeremiah is showing the folly of trusting in inanimate objects. Even more pertinently, he condemns those who somehow feel they have special favor from God. The Jews felt that they were safe because God was obligated to protect His temple. Isaiah had already warned them that this was not true (Is. 66:1, 2), yet they refused to listen (Jer. 7:4). God now makes it clear that He will destroy the temple, just as He allowed the Tabernacle at Shiloh to be destroyed (v. 14, cf. Jer. 12:7; 26:6). The situation was similar in Jesus' day; the Jews felt they had a right to God's miraculous intervention. Jesus reminded them of two instances in the Old Testament where God intervened for non-Jews while leaving Jews to suffer (2 Kgs. 5, Naaman the Syrian; 1 Kgs. 17, the widow of Zarephath). Even though Jesus was quoting the Scripture, the Jews were so incensed that they sought to kill Him (Luke 4:24–29).

spake[1696] unto you, [a]rising up early and
speaking, but ye heard[8085] not; and I
[b]called you, but ye answered not;
14 Therefore will I do unto *this*
house, which is called by my name,
wherein ye trust, and unto the place
which I gave to you and to your fathers,
as I have done to [a]Shiloh.
15 And I will cast you out of my
sight, [a]as I have cast out all your
brethren,[251] [b]*even* the whole seed[2233] of
Ephraim.
16 Therefore [a]pray[6419] not thou for
this people, neither lift up[5375] cry nor
prayer[8605] for them, neither make
intercession to me: [b]for I will not hear
thee.
17 Seest thou not what they do in
the cities of Judah and in the streets of
Jerusalem?
18 [a]The children[1121] gather[3950] wood,
and the fathers kindle the fire, and the
women[802] knead *their* dough, to make[6213]
cakes to the [I]queen[4446] of heaven,[8064] and
to [b]pour out[5258] drink offerings[5262] unto
other gods, that they may provoke me to
anger.[3707]
19 [a]Do they provoke me to anger?
saith the LORD: *do they* not *provoke* themselves to the confusion[1322] of their own
faces?
20 Therefore thus saith the Lord
GOD; Behold, mine anger[639] and my fury
shall be poured out upon this place, upon
man,[120] and upon beast, and upon the
trees of the field,[7704] and upon the fruit
of the ground,[127] and it shall burn, and
shall not be quenched.
21 Thus saith the LORD of hosts, the
God of Israel; [a]Put your burnt offerings[5930] unto your sacrifices[2077] and eat
flesh.[1320]
22 [a]For I spake not unto your fathers,
nor commanded[6680] them in the day[3117]
that I brought them out of the land of
Egypt, [I]concerning burnt offerings or sacrifices:
23 But this thing commanded I them,
saying, [a]Obey[8085] my voice, and [b]I will be
your God, and ye shall be my people:
and walk ye in all the ways that I have
commanded you, that it may be well[3190]
unto you.
24 [a]But they hearkened[8085] not, nor
inclined their ear,[241] but [b]walked in the
counsels *and* in the [I]imagination[8307] of
their evil[7451] heart,[3820] and [II][c]went backward, and not forward.
25 Since the day that your fathers
came forth out of the land of Egypt unto
this day I have even [a]sent unto you all
my servants[5650] the prophets,[5030] [b]daily
rising up early and sending *them:*
26 [a]Yet they hearkened not unto me,
nor inclined their ear, but [b]hardened their
neck: [c]they did worse[7489] than their fathers.
27 Therefore [a]thou shalt speak[1696] all
these words unto them; but they will not
hearken[8085] to thee: thou shalt also
call[7121] unto them; but they will not answer thee.
28 But thou shalt say unto them,
This *is* a nation[1471] that obeyeth[8085]
not the voice of the LORD their God,
[a]nor receiveth [I]correction: [b]truth[530] is
perished,[6] and is cut off[3772] from their
mouth.[6310]
29 [a]Cut off thine hair, *O Jerusalem,*
and cast *it* away, and take up[5375] a
lamentation on high places;[8205] for the
LORD hath rejected[3988] and forsaken[5203]
the generation[1755] of his wrath.[5678]
30 For the children of Judah have
done evil in my sight, saith the LORD:
[a]they have set[7760] their abominations[8251]
in the house which is called by my name,
to pollute it.
31 And they have built the [a]high
places[1116] of Tophet, which *is* in the valley of the son[1121] of Hinnom, to
[b]burn[8313] their sons and their daughters
in the fire; [c]which I commanded *them* not,
neither [I]came it into my heart.
32 Therefore, behold, [a]the days[3117]
come, saith the LORD, that it shall no

13 [a]2Chr. 36:15; Jer. 7:25; 11:7 [b]Prov. 1:24; Isa. 65:12; 66:4
14 [a]1Sam. 4:10, 11; Ps. 78:60; Jer. 26:6
15 [a]2Kgs. 17:23 [b]Ps. 78:67, 68
16 [a]Ex. 32:10; Jer. 11:14; 14:11 [b]Jer. 15:1
18 [I]Or, *frame,* or, *workmanship of heaven* [a]Jer. 44:17, 19 [b]Jer. 19:13
19 [a]Deut. 32:16, 21
21 [a]Isa. 1:11; Jer. 6:20; Amos 5:21; Hos. 8:13
22 [I]Hebr. *concerning the matter of* [a]1Sam. 15:22; Ps. 51:16, 17; Hos. 6:6
23 [a]Ex. 15:26; Deut. 6:3; Jer. 11:4, 7 [b]Ex. 19:5; Lev. 26:12
24 [I]Or, *stubbornness* [II]Hebr. *were* [a]Ps. 81:11; Jer. 11:8 [b]Deut. 29:19; Ps. 81:12 [c]Jer. 2:27; 32:33; Hos. 4:16
25 [a]2Chr. 36:15; Jer. 25:4; 29:19 [b]Jer. 7:13
26 [a]Jer. 7:24; 11:8; 17:23; 25:3, 4 [b]Neh. 9:17, 29; Jer. 19:15 [c]Jer. 16:12
27 [a]Ezek. 2:7
28 [I]Or, *instruction* [a]Jer. 5:3; 32:33 [b]Jer. 9:3
29 [a]Job 1:20; Isa. 15:2; Jer. 16:6; 48:37; Mic. 1:16
30 [a]2Kgs. 21:4, 7; 2Chr. 33:4, 5, 7; Jer. 23:11; 32:34; Ezek. 7:20; 8:5, 6; Dan. 9:27
31 [I]Hebr. *came it upon my heart* [a]2Kgs. 23:10; Jer. 19:5; 32:35 [b]Ps. 106:38 [c]Deut. 17:3
32 [a]Jer. 19:6

7:31 See note on Leviticus 18:21 concerning the worship of the false god Molech.

more be called Tophet, nor the valley of the son of Hinnom, but the valley of slaughter:[2028] [b]for they shall bury[6912] in Tophet, till there be no place.

33 And the [a]carcases[5038] of this people shall be meat for the fowls of the heaven, and for the beasts of the earth;[776] and none shall fray *them* away.[2729]

34 Then will I cause to [a]cease[7673] from the cities of Judah, and from the streets of Jerusalem, the voice of mirth, and the voice of gladness, the voice of the bridegroom, and the voice of the bride: for [b]the land shall be desolate.

8 At that time,[6256] saith the LORD, they shall bring out the bones[6106] of the kings[4428] of Judah, and the bones of his princes,[8269] and the bones of the priests,[3548] and the bones of the prophets,[5030] and the bones of the inhabitants of Jerusalem, out of their graves:[6913]

2 And they shall spread them before the sun, and the moon, and all the host of heaven,8064 whom they have loved,[157] and whom they have served,[5647] and after whom they have walked, and whom they have sought, and [a]whom they have worshipped:[7812] they shall not be gathered, [b]nor be buried;[6912] they shall be for [c]dung upon the face of the earth.[127]

3 And [a]death[4194] shall be chosen[977] rather than life[2416] by all the residue[7611] of them that remain of this evil[7451] family,[4940] which remain in all the places whither I have driven them, saith the LORD of hosts.[6635]

4 Moreover thou shalt say unto them, Thus saith[559] the LORD; Shall they fall, and not arise? shall he turn away,[7725] and not return?[7725]

5 Why *then* is this people[5971] of Jerusalem [a]slidden back by a perpetual[5331] backsliding?4878 [b]they hold fast[2388] deceit, [c]they refuse[3985] to return.

6 [a]I hearkened[7181] and heard,[8085] *but* they spake[1696] not aright: no man[376] repented[5162] him of his wickedness,[7451] saying, What have I done? every one

32 [b]2Kgs. 23:10; Jer. 19:11; Ezek. 6:5

33 [a]Deut. 28:26; Ps. 79:2; Jer. 12:9; 16:4; 34:20

34 [a]Isa. 24:7, 8; Jer. 16:9; 25:10; 33:11; Ezek. 26:13; Hos. 2:11; Rev. 18:23 [b]Lev. 26:33; Isa. 1:7; 3:26

2 [a]2Kgs. 23:5; Ezek. 8:16 [b]Jer. 22:19 [c]2Kgs. 9:36; Ps. 83:10; Jer. 9:22; 16:4

3 [a]Job 3:21, 22; 7:15, 16; Rev. 9:6

5 [a]Jer. 7:24 [b]Jer. 9:6 [c]Jer. 5:3

6 [a]2Pet. 3:9

7 [a]Isa. 1:3 [b]Song 2:12 [c]Jer. 5:4, 5

8 IOr, *the false pen of the scribes worketh for falsehood* [a]Rom. 2:17 [b]Isa. 10:1

9 IOr, *Have they been ashamed* IIHebr. *the wisdom of what thing* [a]Jer. 6:15

10 [a]Deut. 28:30; Jer. 6:12; Amos 5:11; Zeph. 1:13 [b]Isa. 56:11; Jer. 6:13

11 [a]Jer. 6:14 [b]Ezek. 13:10

12 [a]Jer. 3:3; 6:15

13 IOr, *In gathering I will consume* [a]Isa. 5:1; Joel 1:7 [b]Matt. 21:19; Luke 13:6

14 IOr, *poison* [a]Jer. 4:5 [b]Jer. 9:15; 23:15

15 [a]Jer. 14:19

16 [a]Jer. 4:15

turned to his course, as the horse rusheth[7857] into the battle.

7 Yea, [a]the stork in the heaven knoweth her appointed[4150] times;[6256] and [b]the turtle and the crane and the swallow observe[8104] the time of their coming; but [c]my people know[3045] not the judgment[4941] of the LORD.

8 How do ye say, We *are* wise,[2450] [a]and the law[8451] of the LORD *is* with us? Lo, certainly [I][b]in vain[8267] made he *it;* the pen of the scribes[5608] *is* in vain.

9 [I][a]The wise *men* are ashamed,[954] they are dismayed[2865] and taken: lo, they have rejected[3988] the word of the LORD; and [II]what wisdom[2451] *is* in them?

10 Therefore [a]will I give their wives[802] unto others, *and* their fields[7704] to them that shall inherit[3423] *them:* for every one from the least even unto the greatest is given to [b]covetousness,1215 from the prophet[5030] even unto the priest[3548] every one dealeth falsely.[8267]

11 For they have [a]healed the hurt[7667] of the daughter of my people slightly, saying, [b]Peace, peace; when *there is* no peace.

12 Were they [a]ashamed when they had committed[6213] abomination?[8441] nay, they were not at all ashamed, neither could they blush: therefore shall they fall among them that fall: in the time of their visitation[6486] they shall be cast down,[3782] saith the LORD.

13 [I]I will surely consume[622] them, saith5002 the LORD: *there shall be* no grapes [a]on the vine, nor figs on the [b]fig tree, and the leaf shall fade; and *the things that* I have given them shall pass away from them.

14 Why do we sit still? [a]assemble[622] yourselves, and let us enter into the defenced cities, and let us be silent there: for the LORD our God[430] hath put us to silence, and given us [b]water of [I]gall7219 to drink, because we have sinned[2398] against the LORD.

15 We [a]looked for peace, but no good[2896] *came; and* for a time of health, and behold trouble!

16 The snorting of his horses was heard from [a]Dan: the whole land[776]

trembled[7493] at the sound of the neighing of his [b]strong ones;[47] for they are come, and have devoured the land, and [I]all that is in it; the city, and those that dwell therein.

17 For, behold, I will send serpents,[5175] cockatrices,[6848] among you, which *will* not *be* [a]charmed,[3908] and they shall bite you, saith the LORD.

Jeremiah's Sorrow

18 *When* I would comfort myself against sorrow, my heart[3820] *is* faint [I]in me.

19 Behold the voice of the cry of the daughter of my people [I]because of them that dwell in [a]a far country:[776] *Is* not the LORD in Zion? *is* not her king[4428] in her? Why have they [b]provoked me to anger[3707] with their graven images, *and* with strange[5236] vanities?

20 The harvest is past,[5674] the summer is ended,[3615] and we are not saved.[3467]

21 [a]For the hurt of the daughter of my people am I hurt;[7665] I am [b]black;[6937] astonishment[8047] hath taken hold[2388] on me.

22 *Is there* no [a]balm in Gilead; *is there* no physician there? why then is[5927] not the health[724] of the daughter of my people [I]recovered?[5927]

9 [I]Oh [a]that my head[7218] were waters, and mine eyes a fountain of tears, that I might weep day[3119] and night[3915] for the slain[2491] of the daughter of my people[5971]

2 Oh that I had in the wilderness a lodging place of wayfaring men;[732] that I might leave[5800] my people, and go from them! for [a]they *be* all adulterers,[5003] an assembly[6116] of treacherous[898] men.

3 And [a]they bend their tongues *like* their bow *for* lies:[8267] but they are not valiant for the truth[530] upon the earth;[776] for they proceed from evil[7451] to evil, and they [b]know[3045] not me, saith the LORD.

4 [a]Take ye heed every one of his [I]neighbour,[7453] and trust[982] ye not in any brother:[251] for every brother will utterly supplant,[6117] and every neighbour will [b]walk with slanders.

5 And they will [I]deceive every one his neighbour, and will not speak[1696] the truth:[571] they have taught[3925] their tongue to speak lies, *and* weary themselves to commit iniquity.[5753]

6 Thine habitation *is* in the midst of deceit;[4820] through deceit they refuse[3985] to know me, saith the LORD.

7 Therefore thus saith[559] the LORD of hosts,[6635] Behold, [a]I will melt[6884] them, and try[974] them; [b]for how shall I do[6213] for the daughter of my people?

8 Their tongue *is as* an arrow shot out;[7819] it speaketh [a]deceit: *one* speaketh [b]peaceably[7965] to his neighbour with his mouth,[6310] but [I]in heart he layeth[7760] [II]his wait.

9 [a]Shall I not visit[6485] them for these *things?* saith[5002] the LORD: shall[5358] not my soul[5315] be avenged[5358] on such a nation[1471] as this?

10 For the mountains will I take up[5375] a weeping and wailing, and [a]for the [I]habitations of the wilderness a lamentation, because they are [II]burned up, so that none can pass through[5674] *them;* neither can *men* hear[8085] the voice of the cattle; [III][b]both the fowl of the heavens[8064] and the beast are fled; they are gone.

11 And I will make Jerusalem [a]heaps, *and* [b]a den of dragons;[8577] and I will make the cities of Judah [I]desolate,[8077] without an inhabitant.

12 [a]Who *is* the wise[2450] man, that may understand[995] this? and *who is he* to whom the mouth of the LORD hath spoken,[1696] that he may declare[5046] it, for what the land[776] perisheth[6] *and* is burned up like a wilderness, that none passeth through?[5674]

13 And the LORD saith, Because they have forsaken[5800] my law[8451] which I set before them, and have not obeyed[8085] my voice, neither walked therein;

14 But have [a]walked after the [I]imagination[8307] of their own heart,[3820] and after Baalim, [b]which their fathers taught them:

16 [I]Hebr. *the fullness thereof* [b]Judg. 5:22; Jer. 47:3

17 [a]Ps. 58:4, 5; Eccl. 10:11

18 [I]Hebr. *upon*

19 [I]Hebr. *because of the country of them that are far off* [a]Isa. 39:3 [b]Deut. 32:21; Isa. 1:4

21 [a]Jer. 4:19; 9:1; 14:17 [b]Joel 2:6; Nah. 2:10

22 [I]Hebr. *gone up* [a]Gen. 37:25; 43:11; Jer. 46:11; 51:8

1 [I]Hebr. *Who will give my head* [a]Isa. 22:4; Jer. 4:19; 13:17; 14:17; Lam. 2:11; 3:48

2 [a]Jer. 5:7, 8

3 [a]Ps. 64:3; Isa. 59:4, 13, 15 [b]1Sam. 2:12; Hos. 4:1

4 [I]Or, *friend* [a]Jer. 12:6; Mic. 7:5, 6 [b]Jer. 6:28

5 [I]Or, *mock*

7 [a]Isa. 1:25; Mal. 3:3 [b]Hos. 11:8

8 [I]Hebr. *in the midst of him* [II]Or, *wait for him* [a]Ps. 12:2; 120:3; Jer. 9:3 [b]Ps. 28:3; 55:21

9 [a]Jer. 5:9, 29

10 [I]Or, *pastures* [II]Or, *desolate* [III]Hebr. *from the fowl even to* [a]Jer. 12:4; 23:10; Hos. 4:3 [b]Jer. 4:25

11 [I]Hebr. *desolation* [a]Isa. 25:2 [b]Isa. 13:22; 34:13; Jer. 10:22

12 [a]Ps. 107:43; Hos. 14:9

14 [I]Or, *stubbornness* [a]Jer. 3:17; 7:24 [b]Gal. 1:14

15 Therefore thus saith the LORD of hosts, the God[430] of Israel; Behold, I will [a]feed them, *even* this people, [b]with wormwood,3939 and give them water of gall7219 to drink.

16 I will [a]scatter them also among the heathen,[1471] whom neither they nor their fathers have known:[3045] [b]and I will send a sword[2719] after them, till I have consumed[3615] them.

Jerusalem Cries Out for Help

17 Thus saith the LORD of hosts, Consider[995] ye, and call[7121] for [a]the mourning women, that they may come; and send for cunning[2450] *women,* that they may come:

18 And let them make haste, and take up a wailing for us, that [a]our eyes may run down with tears, and our eyelids gush out with waters.

19 For a voice of wailing is heard[8085] out of Zion, How are we spoiled[7703] we are greatly confounded,[954] because we have forsaken the land, because [a]our dwellings[4908] have cast *us* out.

20 Yet hear the word of the LORD, O ye women,[802] and let your ear[241] receive the word of his mouth, and teach[3925] your daughters wailing, and every one[802] her neighbour[7468] lamentation.

21 For death[4194] is come up[5927] into our windows, *and* is entered into our palaces,[759] to cut off[3772] [a]the children from without, *and* the young men from the streets.

22 Speak, Thus saith the LORD, Even the carcases[5038] of men[120] shall fall [a]as dung upon the open field,[7704] and as the handful after the harvestman, and none shall gather[622] *them.*

23 Thus saith the LORD, [a]Let not the wise *man* glory in his wisdom,[2451] neither let the mighty *man* glory[1984] in his might, let not the rich *man* glory in his riches:

24 But [a]let him that glorieth glory in this, that he understandeth[7919] and knoweth me, that I *am* the LORD which exercise[6213] lovingkindness,[2617] judgment,[4941] and righteousness,[6666] in the earth: [b]for in these *things* I delight,[2654] saith the LORD.

25 Behold, the days[3117] come, saith the LORD, that [a]I will [I]punish[6485] all *them which are* circumcised[4135] with the uncircumcised;[6190]

26 Egypt, and Judah, and Edom, and the children[1121] of Ammon, and Moab, and all *that are* [I]in the [a]utmost corners, that dwell in the wilderness: for all *these* nations[1471] *are* uncircumcised,[6189] and all the house[1004] of Israel *are* [b]uncircumcised in the heart.

The True God and Idolatry

10 Hear[8085] ye the word which the LORD speaketh unto you, O house[1004] of Israel:

2 Thus saith the LORD, [a]Learn[3925] not the way[1870] of the heathen,[1471] and be not dismayed[2865] at the signs[226] of heaven;8064 for the heathen are dismayed at them.

3 For the [I]customs of the people[5971] *are* vain: for [a]*one* cutteth[3772] a tree out of the forest, the work of the hands[3027] of the workman, with the axe.

4 They deck it with silver and with gold; they [a]fasten[2388] it with nails and with hammers, that it move not.

5 They *are* upright as the palm tree, [a]but speak not: they must needs be [b]borne,[5375] because they cannot go. Be not afraid[3372] of them; for [c]they cannot do evil,[7489] neither also *is it* in them to do good.[3190]

6 Forasmuch as *there is* none [a]like unto thee, O LORD; thou *art* great, and thy name *is* great in might.

7 [a]Who would not fear[3372] thee, O King[4428] of nations?[1471] for [I]to thee doth it appertain: forasmuch as [b]among all the wise[2450] *men* of the nations, and in all their kingdoms,[4467] *there is* none like unto thee.

8 But they are [I]altogether [a]brutish and foolish:[3688] the stock *is* a doctrine[4148] of vanities.

9 Silver spread[7554] into plates is brought from Tarshish, and [a]gold from Uphaz, the work of the workman, and of

15 [a]Ps. 80:5 [b]Jer. 8:14; 23:15; Lam. 3:15, 19
16 [a]Lev. 26:33; Deut. 28:64 [b]Lev. 26:33; Jer. 44:27; Ezek. 5:2, 12
17 [a]2Chr. 35:25; Job 3:8; Eccl. 12:5; Amos 5:16; Matt. 9:23
18 [a]Jer. 14:17
19 [a]Lev. 18:28; 20:22
21 [a]Jer. 6:11
22 [a]Jer. 8:2; 16:4
23 [a]Eccl. 9:11
24 [a]1Cor. 1:31; 2Cor. 10:17 [b]Mic. 6:8; 7:18
25 [I]Hebr. *visit upon* [a]Rom. 2:8, 9
26 [I]Hebr. *cut off into corners,* or, *having the corners* of their hair *polled* [a]Jer. 25:23; 49:32 [b]Lev. 26:41; Ezek. 44:7; Rom. 2:28, 29

2 [a]Lev. 18:3; 20:23
3 [I]Hebr. *statutes,* or, *ordinances are vanity* [a]Isa. 40:19, 20; 44:9, 10; 45:20
4 [a]Isa. 41:7; 46:7
5 [a]Ps. 115:5; 135:16; Hab. 2:19; 1Cor. 12:2 [b]Ps. 115:7; Isa. 46:1, 7 [c]Isa. 41:23
6 [a]Ex. 15:11; Ps. 86:8, 10
7 [I]Or, *it liketh thee* [a]Rev. 15:4 [b]Ps. 89:6
8 [I]Hebr. *in one,* or, *at once* [a]Ps. 115:8; Isa. 41:29; Hab. 2:18; Zech. 10:2; Rom. 1:21, 22
9 [a]Dan. 10:5

the hands of the founder:[6884] blue and purple *is* their clothing: they *are* all [b]the work of cunning[2450] *men.*

10 But the LORD *is* the [I][a]true[571] God,[430] he *is* [b]the living[2416] God, and an [II][c]everlasting[5769] king: at his wrath[7110] the earth[776] shall tremble,[7493] and the nations shall not be able to abide his indignation.[2195]

11 Thus shall ye say[560] unto them, [a]The gods[426] that have not made the heavens[8065] and the earth,[778] *even* [b]they shall perish[7] from the earth, and from under these heavens.

12 He [a]hath made the earth by his power, he hath [b]established[3559] the world[8398] by his wisdom,[2451] and [c]hath stretched out the heavens[8064] by his discretion.[8394]

13 [a]When he uttereth his voice, *there is* a [I]multitude of waters in the heavens, and [b]he causeth the vapours to ascend[5927] from the ends of the earth; he maketh lightnings [II]with rain, and bringeth forth the wind[7307] out of his treasures.

14 [a]Every man[120] [I]is [b]brutish[1197] in *his* knowledge:[1847] [c]every founder is confounded by the graven image:[6459] [d]for his molten image[5262] *is* falsehood, and *there is* no breath[7307] in them.

15 They *are* vanity, *and* the work of errors:[8595] in the time[6256] of their visitation[6486] [a]they shall perish.[6]

16 [a]The portion of Jacob *is* not like them: for he *is* the former[3335] of all *things;* and [b]Israel *is* the rod[7626] of his inheritance:[5159] [c]The LORD of hosts[6635] *is* his name.

The Desolation of Judah

17 [a]Gather up[622] thy wares[3666] out of the land,[776] O [I]inhabitant of the fortress.

18 For thus saith the LORD, Behold, I will [a]sling out the inhabitants of the land at this once, and will distress them, [b]that they may find *it so.*

19 [a]Woe is me for my hurt[7667] my wound[4347] is grievous: but I said,[559] [b]Truly this *is* a grief, and [c]I must bear[5375] it.

20 [a]My tabernacle[168] is spoiled,[7703] and all my cords are broken: my children[1121] are gone forth of me, and they *are* not: *there is* none to stretch forth my tent[168] any more, and to set up my curtains.

21 For the pastors are become brutish, and have not sought the LORD: therefore they shall not prosper,[7919] and all their flocks shall be scattered.

22 Behold, the noise of the bruit is come, and a great commotion out of the [a]north country,[776] to make[7760] the cities of Judah desolate,[8077] *and* a [b]den of dragons.[8577]

23 O LORD, I know[3045] that the [a]way of man *is* not in himself: *it is* not in man that walketh to direct[3559] his steps.

24 O LORD, [a]correct[3256] me, but with judgment;[4941] not in thine anger,[639] lest thou [I]bring me to nothing.

25 [a]Pour out[8210] thy fury upon the heathen [b]that know thee not, and upon the families[4940] that call[7121] not on thy name: for they have eaten up Jacob, and [c]devoured him, and consumed[3615] him, and have made his habitation desolate.[8074]

The Broken Covenant

11 The word that came to Jeremiah from the LORD, saying,

2 Hear[8085] ye the words of this covenant,[1285] and speak[1696] unto the men of Judah, and to the inhabitants of Jerusalem;

3 And say thou unto them, Thus saith the LORD God[430] of Israel; [a]Cursed[779] *be* the man that obeyeth[8085] not the words of this covenant,

4 Which I commanded[6680] your fathers in the day[3117] *that* I brought them forth out of the land[776] of Egypt, [a]from the iron furnace, saying, [b]Obey my voice, and do them, according to all which I command you: so shall ye be my people,[5971] and I will be your God:

5 That I may perform[6965] the [a]oath[7621] which I have sworn[7650] unto your fathers, to give them a land flowing with milk and honey, as *it is* this day.

---

9 [b]Ps. 115:4
10 [I]Hebr. *God of truth* [II]Hebr. *King of eternity* [a]1Tim. 6:17 [b]Ps. 31:5 [c]Ps. 10:16
11 [a]Ps. 96:5 [b]Jer. 10:15; Isa. 2:18; Zech. 13:2
12 [a]Gen. 1:1, 6, 9; Ps. 136:5, 6; Jer. 51:15 [b]Ps. 93:1 [c]Job 9:8; Ps. 104:2; Isa. 40:22
13 [I]Or, *noise* [II]Or, *for rain* [a]Job 38:34 [b]Ps. 135:7
14 [I]Or, *is more brutish than to know* [a]Jer. 51:17, 18 [b]Prov. 30:2 [c]Isa. 42:17; 44:11; 45:16 [d]Hab. 2:18
15 [a]Jer. 10:11
16 [a]Ps. 16:5; 73:26; 119:57; Jer. 51:19; Lam. 3:24 [b]Deut. 32:9; Ps. 74:2 [c]Isa. 47:4; 51:15; 54:5; Jer. 31:35; 32:18; 50:34
17 [I]Hebr. *inhabitress* [a]Jer. 6:1; Ezek. 12:3
18 [a]1Sam. 25:29; Jer. 16:13 [b]Ezek. 6:10
19 [a]Jer. 4:19; 8:21; 9:1 [b]Ps. 77:10 [c]Mic. 7:9
20 [a]Jer. 4:20
22 [a]Jer. 1:15; 4:6; 5:15; 6:22 [b]Jer. 9:11
23 [a]Prov. 16:1; 20:24
24 [I]Hebr. *diminish me* [a]Ps. 6:1; 38:1; Jer. 30:11
25 [a]Ps. 79:6 [b]Job 18:21; 1Thess. 4:5; 2Thess. 1:8 [c]Jer. 8:16

3 [a]Deut. 27:26; Gal. 3:10
4 [a]Deut. 4:20; 1Kgs. 8:51 [b]Lev. 26:3, 12; Jer. 7:23
5 [a]Deut. 7:12, 13; Ps. 105:9, 10

Then answered I, and said, [Ib]So be it, O LORD.

6 Then the LORD said unto me, Proclaim[7121] all these words in the cities of Judah, and in the streets of Jerusalem, saying, Hear ye the words of this covenant, [a]and do them.

7 For I earnestly protested[5749] unto your fathers in the day *that* I brought them up[5927] out of the land of Egypt, *even* unto this day, [a]rising early and protesting, saying, Obey my voice.

8 [a]Yet they obeyed[8085] not, nor inclined their ear,[241] but [b]walked every one in the [I]imagination[8307] of their evil[7451] heart:[3820] therefore I will bring upon them all the words of this covenant, which I commanded[6680] *them* to do; but they did *them* not.

9 And the LORD said unto me, [a]A conspiracy[7195] is found among the men of Judah, and among the inhabitants of Jerusalem.

10 They are turned back to [a]the iniquities[5771] of their forefathers, which refused[3985] to hear my words; and they went after other gods[430] to serve[5647] them: the house[1004] of Israel and the house of Judah have broken[6565] my covenant which I made[3772] with their fathers.

11 Therefore thus saith the LORD, Behold, I will bring evil upon them, which they shall not be able [I]to escape; and [a]though they shall cry[2199] unto me, I will not hearken[8085] unto them.

12 Then shall the cities of Judah and inhabitants of Jerusalem go, and [a]cry unto the gods unto whom they offer incense:[6999] but they shall not save[3467] them at all in the time[6256] of their [I]trouble.[7451]

13 For *according to* the number of thy [a]cities were thy gods, O Judah; and *according to* the number of the streets of Jerusalem have ye set up[7760] altars[4196] to *that* [Ib]shameful thing, *even* altars to burn incense[6999] unto Baal.

14 Therefore [a]pray[6419] not thou for this people, neither lift up[5375] a cry[7121] or prayer[8605] for them: for I will not hear *them* in the time that they cry unto me for their [I]trouble.

15 [Ia]What hath my beloved[3039] to do in mine house, *seeing* she hath [b]wrought lewdness[4209] with many, and [c]the holy[6944] flesh[1320] is passed[5674] from thee? [II]when thou doest evil, then thou [d]rejoicest.

16 The LORD called[7121] thy name, [a]A green olive tree, fair, *and* of goodly fruit: with the noise of a great tumult[1999] he hath kindled fire upon it, and the branches of it are broken.[7489]

17 For the LORD of hosts,[6635] [a]that planted thee, hath pronounced evil against thee, for the evil of the house of Israel and of the house of Judah, which they have done against themselves to provoke me to anger[3707] in offering incense unto Baal.

The Plot to Kill Jeremiah

18 And the LORD hath given me knowledge[3045] *of it,* and I know[3045] *it:* then thou shewedst[7200] me their doings.

19 But I *was* like a lamb *or* an ox *that* is brought to the slaughter;[2873] and I knew not that [a]they had devised[2803] devices[4284] against me, *saying,* Let us destroy [I]the tree with the fruit thereof, [b]and let us cut him off[3772] from [c]the land of the living,[2416] that his name may be no more remembered.[2142]

20 But, O LORD of hosts, that judgest[8199] righteously,[6664] that [a]triest the reins[3629] and the heart, let me see thy vengeance[5360] on them: for unto thee have I revealed[1540] my cause.[7379]

21 Therefore thus saith the LORD of the men[582] of Anathoth, [a]that seek thy life,[5315] saying, [b]Prophesy[5012] not in the name of the LORD, that thou die[4191] not by our hand:[3027]

22 Therefore thus saith the LORD of hosts, Behold, I will [I]punish[6485] them: the young men shall die by the sword;[2719] their sons[1121] and their daughters shall die by famine:

23 And there shall be no remnant[7611] of them: for I will bring evil upon the men of Anathoth, *even* [a]the year of their visitation.[6489]

---

5 [I]Hebr. *Amen* [b]Deut. 27:15-26

6 [a]Rom. 2:13; James 1:22

7 [a]Jer. 7:13, 25; 35:15

8 [I]Or, *stubbornness* [a]Jer. 7:26 [b]Jer. 3:17; 7:24; 9:14

9 [a]Ezek. 22:25; Hos. 6:9

10 [a]Ezek. 20:18

11 [I]Hebr. *to go forth of* [a]Ps. 18:41; Prov. 1:28; Isa. 1:15; Jer. 14:12; Ezek. 8:18; Mic. 3:4; Zech. 7:13

12 [I]Hebr. *evil* [a]Deut. 32:37, 38

13 [I]Hebr. *shame* [a]Jer. 2:28 [b]Jer. 3:24; Hos. 9:10

14 [I]Hebr. *evil* [a]Ex. 32:10; Jer. 7:16; 14:11; 1John 5:16

15 [I]Hebr. *What is to my beloved in my house?* [II]Or, *when thy evil is* [a]Ps. 50:16; Isa. 1:11 [b]Ezek. 16:25 [c]Hag. 2:12, 13, 14; Titus 1:15 [d]Prov. 2:14

16 [a]Ps. 52:8; Rom. 11:17

17 [a]Isa. 5:2; Jer. 2:21

19 [I]Hebr. *the stalk with his bread* [a]Jer. 18:18 [b]Ps. 83:4 [c]Ps. 27:13; 116:9; 142:5

20 [a]1Sam. 16:7; 1Chr. 28:9; Ps. 7:9; Jer. 17:10; 20:12; Rev. 2:23

21 [a]Jer. 12:5, 6 [b]Isa. 30:10; Amos 2:12; 7:13, 16; Mic. 2:6

22 [I]Hebr. *visit upon*

23 [a]Jer. 23:12; 46:21; 48:44; 50:27; Luke 19:44

Jeremiah's Complaint and God's Answer

12 Righteous[6662] [a]*art* thou, O LORD, when I plead[7378] with thee: yet [I]let me talk[1696] with thee of *thy* judgments:[4941] [b]Wherefore doth the way[1870] of the wicked[7563] prosper? *wherefore* are all they happy that deal very treacherously?[898]

2 Thou hast planted them, yea, they have taken root: [I]they grow, yea, they bring forth[6213] fruit: [a]thou *art* near in their mouth,[6310] and far from their reins.3629

3 But thou, O LORD, [a]knowest me: thou hast seen[7200] me, and [b]tried[974] mine heart[3820] [I]toward thee: pull them out like sheep for the slaughter,[2873] and prepare[6942] them for [c]the day[3117] of slaughter.[2028]

4 How long shall [a]the land[776] mourn, and the herbs of every field[7704] wither,[3001] [b]for the wickedness[7451] of them that dwell therein? [c]the beasts are consumed,[5595] and the birds; because they said, He shall not see our last end.[319]

5 If thou hast run with the footmen, and they have wearied thee, then how canst thou contend[2734] with horses? and *if* in the land of peace, *wherein* thou trustedst,[982] *they wearied thee,* then how wilt thou do in [a]the swelling1347 of Jordan?

6 For even [a]thy brethren,[251] and the house[1004] of thy father,[1] even they have dealt treacherously[898] with thee; yea, [I]they have called[7121] a multitude after thee: [b]believe[539] them not, though they speak [II]fair[2896] words unto thee.

7 I have forsaken[5800] mine house, I have left[5203] mine heritage;[5159] I have given [I]the dearly beloved[3033] of my soul[5315] into the hand[3709] of her enemies.

8 Mine heritage is unto me as a lion in the forest; it [I]crieth out against me: therefore have I hated it.

9 Mine heritage *is* unto me *as* a [I]speckled bird, the birds round about *are* against her; come ye, assemble[622] all the beasts4216 of the field, [II][a]come to devour.

10 Many [a]pastors have destroyed[7843] [b]my vineyard, they have [c]trodden my portion under foot, they have made my [I]pleasant portion a desolate[8077] wilderness.

11 They have made[7760] it desolate, *and being* desolate [a]it mourneth unto me; the whole land is made desolate, because [b]no man layeth[7760] *it* to heart.

12 The spoilers[7703] are come upon all high places[8205] through the wilderness: for the sword[2719] of the LORD shall devour from the *one* end of the land even to the *other* end of the land: no flesh[1320] shall have peace.

13 [a]They have sown wheat, but shall reap thorns: they have put themselves to pain, *but* shall not profit: and [I]they shall be ashamed[954] of your revenues because of the fierce anger[639] of the LORD.

14 Thus saith the LORD against all mine evil[7451] neighbours,[7934] that [a]touch[5060] the inheritance[5159] which I have caused[5157] my people[5971] Israel to inherit;[5157] Behold, I will [b]pluck them out of their land,[127] and pluck out the house of Judah from among them.

15 [a]And it shall come to pass, after that I have plucked them out I will return,[7725] and have compassion[7355] on them, [b]and will bring them again, every man to his heritage, and every man to his land.

16 And it shall come to pass, if they will diligently learn[3925] the ways[1870] of my people, [a]to swear[7650] by my name, The LORD liveth;[2416] as they taught[3925] my people to swear by Baal; then shall they be [b]built in the midst of my people.

17 But if they will not [a]obey,[8085] I will utterly pluck up and destroy[6] that nation,[1471] saith5002 the LORD.

The Sign of the Marked Undergarment

13 Thus saith[559] the LORD unto me, Go and get thee a linen girdle,232 and put it upon thy loins, and put it not in water.

---

1 [I]Or, *let me reason the case with thee* [a]Ps. 51:4 [b]Job 12:6; 21:7; Ps. 37:1, 35; 73:3; Jer. 5:28; Hab. 1:4; Mal. 3:15
2 [I]Hebr. *they go on* [a]Isa. 29:13; Matt. 15:8; Mark 7:6
3 [I]Hebr. *with thee* [a]Ps. 17:3; 139:1 [b]Jer. 11:20 [c]James 5:5
4 [a]Jer. 23:10; Hos. 4:3 [b]Ps. 107:34 [c]Jer. 4:25; 7:20; 9:10; Hos. 4:3
5 [a]Josh. 3:15; 1Chr. 12:15; Jer. 49:19; 50:44
6 [I]Or, *they cried after thee fully* [II]Hebr. *good things* [a]Jer. 9:4; 11:19, 21 [b]Prov. 26:25
7 [I]Hebr. *the love*
8 [I]Hebr. *giveth out his voice*
9 [I]Or, *bird having talons* [II]Or, *cause them to come* [a]Isa. 56:9; Jer. 7:33
10 [I]Hebr. *portion of desire* [a]Jer. 6:3 [b]Isa. 5:1, 5; Isa. 63:18
11 [a]Jer. 12:4 [b]Isa. 42:25
13 [I]Or, *ye* [a]Lev. 26:16; Deut. 28:38; Mic. 6:15; Hag. 1:6
14 [a]Zech. 2:8 [b]Deut. 30:3; Jer. 32:37
15 [a]Ezek. 28:25 [b]Amos 9:14
16 [a]Jer. 4:2 [b]Eph. 2:20, 21; 1Pet. 2:5
17 [a]Isa. 60:12

2 So I got a girdle according to the word[1697] of the LORD, and put *it* on my loins.

3 And the word of the LORD came unto me the second time, saying,

4 Take the girdle that thou hast got, which *is* upon thy loins, and arise, go to Euphrates, and hide it there in a hole of the rock.

5 So I went, and hid it by Euphrates, as the LORD commanded me.

6 And it came to pass after many days, that the LORD said unto me, Arise, go to Euphrates, and take the girdle from thence, which I commanded thee to hide there.

7 Then I went to Euphrates, and digged, and took the girdle from the place where I had hid it: and, behold, the girdle was marred,[7843] it was profitable for nothing.

8 Then the word of the LORD came unto me, saying,

9 Thus saith the LORD, After this manner [a]will I mar the pride of Judah, and the great pride of Jerusalem.

10 This evil[7451] people,[5971] which refuse[3987] to hear[8085] my words, which [a]walk in the [I]imagination[8307] of their heart,[3820] and walk after other gods,[430] to serve[5647] them, and to worship[7812] them, shall even be as this girdle, which is good for nothing.

11 For as the girdle cleaveth to the loins of a man, so have I caused to cleave unto me the whole house[1004] of Israel and the whole house of Judah, saith the LORD; that [a]they might be unto me for a people, and [b]for a name, and for a praise,[8416] and for a glory:[8597] but they would not hear.

The Bottles of Wine

12 Therefore thou shalt speak unto them this word; Thus saith the LORD God[430] of Israel, Every bottle shall be filled with wine: and they shall say unto thee, Do we not certainly know that every bottle shall be filled with wine?

13 Then shalt thou say unto them, Thus saith the LORD, Behold, I will fill all the inhabitants of this land,[776] even the kings[4428] that sit upon David's throne,[3678] and the priests,[3548] and the prophets,[5030] and all the inhabitants of Jerusalem, [a]with drunkenness.[7943]

14 And [a]I will dash them [I]one against another, even the fathers and the sons together, saith the LORD: I will not pity, nor spare, nor have mercy,[7355] [II]but destroy them.

Jeremiah Warns Against Pride

15 Hear ye, and give ear;[238] be not proud: for the LORD hath spoken.

16 [a]Give glory[3511] to the LORD your God, before he cause [b]darkness, and before your feet stumble[5062] upon the dark mountains, and, while ye [c]look for light,[216] he turn it into [d]the shadow of death,[6757] *and* make *it* gross darkness.[6205]

17 But if ye will not hear it, my soul[5315] shall weep in secret places for *your* pride; and [a]mine eye shall weep sore, and run down with tears, because the LORD's flock is carried away captive.[7617]

18 Say unto [a]the king[4428] and to the queen, Humble yourselves, sit down: for your [I]principalities[4761] shall come down, *even* the crown of your glory.

19 The cities of the south shall be shut up, and none shall open *them:* Judah shall be carried away captive[1540] all of it, it shall be wholly[7965] carried away captive.

20 Lift up[5375] your eyes, and behold[7200] them [a]that come from the north: where *is* the flock *that* was given thee, thy beautiful[8597] flock?

21 What wilt thou say when he shall [I]punish[6485] thee? for thou hast taught[3925] them *to be* captains, *and* as chief[7218] over thee: shall not [a]sorrows[2256] take thee, as a woman[802] in travail?

22 And if thou say in thine heart,[3824] [a]Wherefore come these things upon me? For the greatness of thine iniquity[5771] are [b]thy skirts discovered, *and* thy heels[6119] [I]made bare.[2554]

23 Can the Ethiopian change his skin,[5785] or the leopard his spots? *then*

9 [a]Lev. 26:19

10 [I]Or, *stubbornness* [a]Jer. 9:14; 11:8; 16:12

11 [a]Ex. 19:5 [b]Jer. 33:9

13 [a]Isa. 51:17, 21; 63:6; Jer. 25:27; 51:7

14 [I]Hebr. *a man against his brother* [II]Hebr. *from destroying them* [a]Ps. 2:9

16 [a]Josh. 7:19 [b]Isa. 5:30; 8:22; Amos 8:9 [c]Isa. 59:9 [d]Ps. 44:19

17 [a]Jer. 9:1; 14:17; Lam. 1:2, 16; 2:18

18 [I]Or, *head tires* [a]2Kgs. 24:12; Jer. 22:26

20 [a]Jer. 6:22

21 [I]Hebr. *visit upon* [a]Jer. 6:24

22 [I]Or, *shall be violently taken away* [a]Jer. 5:19; 16:10 [b]Isa. 3:17; 47:2, 3; Jer. 13:26; Ezek. 16:37-39; Nah. 3:5

may ye also do good,[3190] that are [I]accustomed[3928] to do evil.[7489]

24 Therefore will I scatter them [a]as the stubble that passeth away[5674] by the wind[7307] of the wilderness.

25 [a]This *is* thy lot, the portion of thy measures from me, saith the LORD; because thou hast forgotten me, and trusted[982] in [b]falsehood.

26 Therefore [a]will I discover thy skirts upon thy face, that thy shame may appear.[7200]

27 I have seen[7200] thine adulteries5004 and thy [a]neighings, the lewdness[2154] of thy whoredom,[2184] *and* thine abominations[8251] [b]on the hills in the fields.[7704] Woe unto thee, O Jerusalem! wilt thou not be made clean?[2891] [I]when *shall it* once *be?*

The Drought

14 The word of the LORD that came to Jeremiah concerning [I]the dearth.

2 Judah mourneth, and [a]the gates thereof languish; they are [b]black[6937] unto the ground;[776] and [c]the cry of Jerusalem is gone up.[5927]

3 And their nobles[117] have sent their little ones to the waters: they came to the pits, *and* found no water; they returned[7725] with their vessels empty; they were [a]ashamed[954] and confounded, [b]and covered their heads.[7218]

4 Because the ground[127] is chapt, for there was no rain in the earth,[776] the plowmen were ashamed, they covered their heads.

5 Yea, the hind365 also calved in the field,[7704] and forsook[5800] *it,* because there was no grass.

6 And [a]the wild asses did stand in the high places,[8205] they snuffed up the wind[7307] like dragons;[8577] their eyes did fail,[3615] because *there was* no grass.

7 O LORD, though our iniquities[5771] testify against us, do thou *it* [a]for thy name's sake: for our backslidings4878 are many; we have sinned[2398] against thee.

8 [a]O the hope[4723] of Israel, the saviour[3467] thereof in time[6256] of trouble, why shouldest thou be as a stranger[1616] in the land,[776] and as a wayfaring man732 *that* turneth aside to tarry for a night?

9 Why shouldest thou be as a man astonied,1724 as a mighty man [a]*that* cannot save?[3467] yet thou, O LORD, [b]*art* in the midst[7130] of us, and [Ic]we are called[7121] by thy name; leave us not.

10 Thus saith the LORD unto this people,[5971] [a]Thus have they loved[157] to wander, they have not refrained their feet, therefore the LORD doth not accept[7521] them; [b]he will now remember[2142] their iniquity,[5771] and visit[6485] their sins.

11 Then said the LORD unto me, [a]Pray[6419] not for this people for *their* good.[2896]

12 [a]When they fast, I will not hear[8085] their cry; and [b]when they offer burnt offering[5930] and an oblation,[4503] I will not accept them: but [c]I will consume them by the sword,[2719] and by the famine, and by the pestilence.[1698]

13 [a]Then said I, Ah, Lord[136] GOD! behold, the prophets say unto them, Ye shall not see the sword, neither shall ye have famine; but I will give you [I]assured[571] peace in this place.

14 Then the LORD said unto me, [a]The prophets prophesy[5012] lies[8267] in my name: [b]I sent them not, neither have I commanded[6680] them, neither spake unto them: they prophesy unto you a false[8267] vision[2377] and divination,[7081] and a thing of nought,[457] and the deceit of their heart.[3820]

15 Therefore thus saith the LORD concerning the prophets that prophesy in my name, and I sent them not, [a]yet they say, Sword and famine shall not be in this land; By sword and famine shall those prophets be consumed.[8552]

16 And the people to whom they prophesy shall be cast out in the streets of Jerusalem because of the famine and the sword; [a]and they shall have none to bury[6912] them, them, their wives,[802] nor their sons,[1121] nor their daughters: for I will pour[8210] their wickedness[7451] upon them.

23 [I]Hebr. *taught*

24 [a]Ps. 1:4; Hos. 13:3

25 [a]Job 20:29; Ps. 11:6 [b]Jer. 10:14

26 [a]Jer. 13:2; Lam. 1:8; Ezek. 16:37; 23:29; Hos. 2:10

27 [I]Hebr. *after when yet?* [a]Jer. 5:8 [b]Isa. 65:7; Jer. 2:20; 3:2, 6; Ezek. 6:13

1 [I]Hebr. *the words of the dearths,* or, *restraints*

2 [a]Isa. 3:26 [b]Jer. 8:21 [c]1Sam. 5:12

3 [a]Ps. 40:14 [b]2Sam. 15:30

6 [a]Jer. 2:24

7 [a]Ps. 25:11

8 [a]Jer. 17:13

9 [I]Hebr. *thy name is called upon us* [a]Isa. 59:1 [b]Ex. 29:45, 46; Lev. 26:11, 12 [c]Dan. 9:18, 19

10 [a]Jer. 2:23-25 [b]Hos. 8:13; 9:9

11 [a]Ex. 32:10; Jer. 7:16; 11:14

12 [a]Prov. 1:28; Isa. 1:15; 58:3; Jer. 11:11; Ezek. 8:18; Mic. 3:4; Zech. 7:13 [b]Jer. 6:20; 7:21, 22 [c]Jer. 9:16

13 [I]Hebr. *peace of truth* [a]Jer. 4:10

14 [a]Jer. 27:10 [b]Jer. 23:21; 27:15; 29:8, 9

15 [a]Jer. 5:12, 13

16 [a]Ps. 79:3

17 Therefore thou shalt say this
word unto them; [a]Let mine eyes run
down with tears night[3915] and day,[3119]
and let them not cease:[1820] [b]for the
virgin[1330] daughter of my people is
broken[7665] with a great breach,[7667] with
a very grievous blow.
18 If I go forth into [a]the field, then
behold the slain[2491] with the sword! and
if I enter into the city, then behold them
that are sick with famine! yea, both the
prophet[5030] and the priest[3548] [I][b]go about
into a land that they know[3045] not.

The People Plead With God

19 [a]Hast thou utterly rejected[3988]
Judah? hath thy soul lothed Zion? why
hast thou smitten[5221] us, and [b]*there is* no
healing for us? [c]we looked for peace, and
there is no good; and for the time of healing, and behold trouble!
20 We acknowledge,[3045] O LORD, our
wickedness,[7562] *and* the iniquity of our
fathers:[1] for [a]we have sinned against thee.
21 Do not abhor[5006] *us,* for thy
name's sake, do not disgrace[5034] the
throne[3678] of thy glory:[3519] [a]remember,
break[6565] not thy covenant[1285] with us.
22 [a]Are there *any* among [b]the vanities of the Gentiles[1471] that can cause
rain? or can the heavens[8064] give showers? [c]*art* not thou he, O LORD our God?[430]
therefore we will wait[6960] upon thee: for
thou hast made[6213] all these *things.*

The LORD's Fury

15 Then said the LORD unto me,
[a]Though [b]Moses and [c]Samuel
stood before me, *yet* my mind[5315] *could*
not *be* toward this people:[5971] cast
them out of my sight, and let them go
forth.
2 And it shall come to pass, if they
say unto thee, Whither shall we go forth?
then thou shalt tell them, Thus saith the
LORD; [a]Such as *are* for death,[4194] to death;
and such as *are* for the sword, to the
sword;[2719] and such as *are* for the
famine, to the famine; and such as *are* for
the captivity,[7628] to the captivity.

17 [a]Jer. 9:1; 13:17; Lam. 1:16; 2:18; [b]Jer. 8:21
18 [I]Or, make merchandise against a land, and en acknowledge it not [a]Ezek. 7:15 [b]Jer. 5:31
19 [a]Lam. 5:22 [b]Jer. 15:18 [c]Jer. 8:15
20 [a]Ps. 106:6; Dan. 9:8
21 [a]Ps. 74:2, 20; 106:45
22 [a]Zech. 10:1; 2 [b]Deut. 32:21 [c]Ps. 135:7; 147:8; Isa. 30:23; Jer. 5:24; 10:13

1 [a]Ezek. 14:14 [b]Ex. 32:11, 12; Ps. 99:6 [c]1Sam. 7:9
2 [a]Jer. 43:11; Ezek. 5:2, 12; Zech. 11:9
3 [I]Hebr. *families* [a]Lev. 26:16 [b]Deut. 28:26; Jer. 7:33
4 [I]Hebr. *I will give them for a removing* [a]Deut. 28:25; Jer. 24:9; Ezek. 23:46 [b]2Kgs. 21:11; 23:26; 24:3, 4
5 [I]Hebr. *to ask of thy peace* [a]Isa. 51:19
6 [a]Jer. 2:13 [b]Jer. 7:24 [c]Hos. 13:14
7 [I]Or, *whatsoever is dear* [a]Isa. 9:13; Jer. 5:3; Amos 4:10, 11
8 [I]Or, *against the mother city a young man spoiling,* or, *against the mother* and *the young men*
9 [a]1Sam. 2:5 [b]Amos 8:9
10 [a]Job 3:1; Jer. 20:14
11 [I]Or, *I will entreat the enemy for thee* [a]Jer. 39:11, 12; 40:4, 5

3 And I will [a]appoint[6485] over them
four [I]kinds,[4940] saith[5002] the LORD: the
sword to slay,[2026] and the dogs to tear,
and [b]the fowls of the heaven,[8064] and the
beasts of the earth,[776] to devour and destroy.
4 And [I]I will cause them to be [a]re-
moved into all kingdoms[4467] of the earth,
because of [b]Manasseh the son of
Hezekiah king[4428] of Judah, for *that*
which he did in Jerusalem.
5 For [a]who shall have pity upon thee,
O Jerusalem? or who shall bemoan thee?
or who shall go aside [I]to ask[7592] how
thou doest?
6 [a]Thou hast forsaken[5203] me, saith
the LORD, thou art [b]gone backward: therefore will I stretch out my hand[3027]
against thee, and destroy thee; [c]I am
weary with repenting.
7 And I will fan[2219] them with a fan
in the gates of the land;[776] I will bereave
them of [I]children,[1121] I will destroy[6] my
people, *since* [a]they return[7725] not from
their ways.[1870]
8 Their widows are increased to
me above the sand of the seas: I
have brought upon them [I]against the
mother[517] of the young men a spoiler[7703]
at noonday: I have caused *him* to fall
upon it suddenly, and terrors[928] upon the
city.
9 [a]She that hath borne seven languisheth: she hath given up the
ghost;[5315] [5301] [b]her sun is gone down while
it was yet day:[3119] she hath been
ashamed[954] and confounded: and the
residue[7611] of them will I deliver to
the sword before their enemies, saith the
LORD.

Jeremiah's Complaints

10 [a]Woe is me, my mother, that thou
hast borne me a man of strife[7379] and a
man of contention to the whole earth! I
have neither lent on usury, nor men have
lent to me on usury; *yet* every one of
them doth curse[7043] me.
11 The LORD said, Verily it shall be
well with thy remnant;[8293] verily [I]I will
cause [a]the enemy to entreat thee *well* in

the time[6256] of evil[7451] and in the time of affliction.

12 Shall iron break[7489] the northern iron and the steel?

13 Thy substance[2428] and thy treasures will I give to the [a]spoil without price, and *that* for all thy sins, even in all thy borders.

14 And I will make *thee* to pass with thine enemies [a]into a land *which* thou knowest[3045] not: for a [b]fire is kindled in mine anger,[639] *which* shall burn upon you.

15 O LORD, [a]thou knowest: remember[2142] me, and visit[6485] me, and [b]revenge me of my persecutors; take me not away in thy longsuffering: know[3045] that [c]for thy sake I have suffered rebuke.[2781]

16 Thy words[1697] were found, and I did [a]eat them; and [b]thy word was unto me the joy and rejoicing of mine heart:3824 for [I]I am called[7121] by thy name, O LORD God[430] of hosts.[6635]

17 [a]I sat not in the assembly[5475] of the mockers, nor rejoiced; I sat alone because of thy hand: for thou hast filled me with indignation.[2195]

18 Why is my [a]pain perpetual,[5331] and my wound[4347] incurable, *which* refuseth[3985] to be healed? wilt thou be altogether unto me [b]as a liar, *and* [c]*as* waters *that* [I]fail?[3808,539]

19 Therefore thus saith the LORD, [a]If thou return, then will I bring thee again, *and* thou shalt [b]stand before me: and if thou [c]take forth the precious from the vile,2151 thou shalt be as my mouth:[6310] let them return unto thee; but return not thou unto them.

20 And I will make thee unto this people a fenced brasen [a]wall: and they shall fight against thee, but [b]they shall not prevail against thee: for I *am* with thee to save[3467] thee and to deliver[5337] thee, saith the LORD.

21 And I will deliver thee out of the hand[3709] of the wicked,[7451] and I will redeem[6299] thee out of the hand of the terrible.6184

Judgment Upon the People

16 The word of the LORD came also unto me, saying,

🔑 2 Thou shalt not take thee a wife,[802] neither shalt thou have sons or daughters in this place.

3 For thus saith the LORD concerning the sons and concerning the daughters that are born in this place, and concerning their mothers that bare them, and concerning their fathers that begat them in this land;[776]

4 They shall die of [a]grievous deaths; they shall not [b]be lamented; neither shall they be buried;[6912] *but* they shall be [c]as dung upon the face of the earth:[127] and they shall be consumed[3615] by the sword,[2719] and by famine; and their [d]carcases[5038] shall be meat for the fowls of heaven,8064 and for the beasts of the earth.[776]

5 For thus saith the LORD, [a]Enter not into the house[1004] of [I]mourning, neither go to lament nor bemoan them: for I have taken away[622] my peace from this people,[5971] saith the LORD,[3068] *even* lovingkindness and mercies.[7356]

6 Both the great and the small shall die in this land: they shall not be buried, [a]neither shall *men* lament for them, nor [b]cut themselves,[1413] nor [c]make themselves bald for them:

7 Neither shall *men* [Ia]tear *themselves* for them in mourning, to comfort[5162] them for the dead;[4191] neither shall *men*

13 [a]Ps. 44:12; Jer. 17:3

14 [a]Jer. 16:13; 17:4 [b]Deut. 32:22

15 [a]Jer. 12:3 [b]Jer. 11:20; 20:12 [c]Ps. 69:7

16 [I]Hebr. *thy name is called upon me* [a]Ezek. 3:1, 3; Rev. 10:9, 10 [b]Job 23:12; Ps. 119:72, 111

17 [a]Ps. 1:1; 26:4, 5

18 [I]Hebr. *be not sure* [a]Jer. 30:15 [b]Jer. 1:18, 19 [c]Job 6:15

19 [a]Zech. 3:7 [b]Jer. 15:1 [c]Ezek. 22:26; 44:23

20 [a]Jer. 1:18; 6:27 [b]Jer. 20:11, 12

4 [a]Jer. 15:2 [b]Jer. 22:18, 19; 25:33 [c]Ps. 83:10; Jer. 8:2; 9:22 [d]Ps. 79:2; Jer. 7:33; 34:20

5 [I]Or, *mourning feast* [a]Ezek. 24:17, 22, 23

6 [a]Jer. 22:18 [b]Lev. 19:28; Deut. 14:1; Jer. 41:5; 47:5 [c]Isa. 22:12; Jer. 7:29

7 [I]Or, *break bread for them* [a]Ezek. 24:17; Hos. 9:4; Deut. 26:14; Job 42:11

🔑 **16:2–5** In contrast to Isaiah (Is. 8:1–3) and Ezekiel (Ezek. 24:18), Jeremiah was told not to marry because of the horrors that families with children would endure, particularly during the final siege of Jerusalem (see note on Ezek. 24:15–24). This passage reiterates a prominent theme of Jeremiah: there can be no peace outside of obedience to God. Jeremiah's message opposed that of the false prophets who were continually crying "peace" (Jer. 6:14; 8:11; 14:13; 28:9, cf. Ezek. 13:10, 16), even when there was no peace to be found (Jer. 8:15; 14:19). The only peace the Jews could pray for was the "peace of Babylon," for they were about to spend seventy years there (Jer. 29:7).

give them the cup of consolation[8575] to [b]drink for their father or for their mother.

8 Thou shalt not also go into the house of feasting,[4960] to sit with them to eat and to drink.

9 For thus saith the LORD of hosts,[6635] the God[430] of Israel; Behold, [a]I will cause to cease[7673] out of this place in your eyes, and in your days,[3117] the voice of mirth, and the voice of gladness, the voice of the bridegroom, and the voice of the bride.

10 And it shall come to pass, when thou shalt shew[5046] this people all these words,[1697] and they shall say[559] unto thee, [a]Wherefore hath the LORD pronounced all this great evil[7451] against us? or what *is* our iniquity?[5771] or what *is* our sin[2403] that we have committed[2398] against the LORD our God?

11 Then shalt thou say unto them, [a]Because your fathers have forsaken[5800] me, saith the LORD, and have walked after other gods,[430] and have served[5647] them, and have worshipped[7812] them, and have forsaken me, and have not kept[8104] my law;[8451]

12 And ye have done [a]worse[7489] than your fathers; for, behold, [b]ye walk every one after the [I]imagination[8307] of his evil heart,[3820] that they may not hearken[8085] unto me:

13 [a]Therefore will I cast you out of this land [b]into a land that ye know[3045] not, *neither* ye nor your fathers; and there shall ye serve[5647] other gods day[3119] and night;[3915] where I will not shew you favour.

A Return Predicted

14 Therefore, behold, the [a]days come, saith the LORD, that it shall no more be said, The LORD liveth,[2416] that brought up[5927] the children[1121] of Israel out of the land of Egypt;

15 But, The LORD liveth, that brought up the children of Israel from the land of the north, and from all the lands[776] whither he had driven them: and [a]I will bring them again into their land that I gave unto their fathers.

16 Behold, I will send for many [a]fishers, saith the LORD, and they shall fish them; and after will I send for many hunters, and they shall hunt them from every mountain, and from every hill, and out of the holes of the rocks.

17 For mine [a]eyes *are* upon all their ways:[1870] they are not hid from my face, neither is their iniquity hid from mine eyes.

18 And first[7223] I will recompense[7999] their iniquity and their sin [a]double; because [b]they have defiled[2490] my land, they have filled mine inheritance[5159] with the carcases of their detestable[8251] and abominable things.[8441]

19 O LORD, [a]my strength, and my fortress, and [b]my refuge in the day[3117] of affliction, the Gentiles[1471] shall come unto thee from the ends of the earth, and shall say, Surely our fathers have inherited lies,[8267] vanity, and *things* [c]wherein *there is* no profit.

20 Shall a man[120] make gods unto himself, and [a]they *are* no gods?

21 Therefore, behold, I will this once cause them to know, I will cause them to know mine hand[3027] and my might;[1369] and they shall know that [a]my name *is* [I]The LORD.

The Sin of Judah

17 The sin[2403] of Judah *is* written with a [a]pen of iron, *and* with the [I]point of a diamond: *it is* [b]graven upon the table of their heart,[3820] and upon the horns of your altars;[4196]

2 Whilst their children[1121] remember[2142] their altars and their [a]groves[842] by the green trees upon the high hills.

3 O my mountain in the field,[7704] [a]I will give thy substance[2428] *and* all thy treasures to the spoil, *and* thy high places[1116] for sin, throughout all thy borders.

4 And thou, even [I]thyself, shalt discontinue from thine heritage[5159] that I gave thee; and I will cause thee to

7 [b]Prov. 31:6, 7

9 [a]Isa. 24:7, 8; Jer. 7:34; 25:10; Ezek. 26:13; Hos. 2:11; Rev. 18:23

10 [a]Deut. 29:24; Jer. 5:19; 13:22; 22:8

11 [a]Deut. 29:25; Jer. 22:9

12 [I]Or, *stubbornness* [a]Jer. 7:26 [b]Jer. 13:10

13 [a]Deut. 4:26-28; 28:36, 64, 65 [b]Jer. 15:14

14 [a]Isa. 43:18; Jer. 23:7, 8

15 [a]Jer. 24:6; 30:3; 32:37

16 [a]Amos 4:2; Hab. 1:15

17 [a]Job 34:21; Prov. 5:21; 15:3; Jer. 32:19

18 [a]Isa. 40:2; Jer. 17:18 [b]Ezra 43:7, 9

19 [a]Ps. 18:2 [b]Jer. 17:17 [c]Isa. 44:10; Jer. 2:11; 10:5

20 [a]Isa. 37:19; Jer. 2:11; Gal. 4:8

21 [I]Or, *JEHOVAH* [a]Ex. 15:3; Jer. 33:2; Amos 5:8 [b]Ps. 83:18

1 [I]Hebr. *nail* [a]Job 19:24 [b]Prov. 3:3; 2Cor. 3:3

2 [a]Judg. 3:7; 2Chr. 24:18; 33:3, 19; Isa. 1:29; 17:8; Jer. 2:20

3 [a]Jer. 15:13

4 [I]Hebr. *in thyself*

serve[5647] thine enemies in [a]the land[776] which thou knowest[3045] not: for [b]ye have kindled a fire in mine anger,[639] *which* shall burn for ever.[5769]

Trust in the LORD

5 Thus saith the LORD; [a]Cursed[779] *be* the man[1397] that trusteth[982] in man,[120] and maketh [b]flesh[1320] his arm, and whose heart departeth from the LORD.

6 For he shall be [a]like the heath6176 in the desert,[6160] and [b]shall not see when good[2896] cometh; but shall inhabit[7931] the parched places[2788] in the wilderness, [c]*in* a salt land and not inhabited.

7 [a]Blessed[1288] *is* the man that trusteth in the LORD, and whose hope the LORD is.

8 For he shall be [a]as a tree planted by the waters, and *that* spreadeth out her roots by the river, and shall not see when heat cometh, but her leaf shall be green; and shall not be careful in the year of [I]drought, neither shall cease from yielding[6213] fruit.

9 The heart *is* deceitful[6121] above all *things,* and desperately wicked:605 who can know[3045] it?

10 I the LORD [a]search2713 the heart, *I* try[974] the reins,3629 [b]even to give every man according to his ways,[1870] *and* according to the fruit of his doings.

11 *As* the partridge [I]sitteth *on eggs,* and hatcheth *them* not; *so* he that getteth[6213] riches, and not by right,[4941] [a]shall leave[5800] them in the midst of his days, and at his end[319] shall be [b]a fool.

12 A glorious[3519] high throne[3678] from the beginning[7223] *is* the place of our sanctuary.[4720]

13 O LORD, [a]the hope[4723] of Israel, [b]all that forsake[5800] thee shall be ashamed,[954] *and* they that depart from me shall be [c]written in the earth,[776] because they have forsaken[5800] the LORD, the [d]fountain of living[2416] waters.

Jeremiah Pleads With God

14 Heal me, O LORD, and I shall be healed; save[3467] me, and I shall be saved: for [a]thou *art* my praise.[8416]

15 Behold, they say[559] unto me, [a]Where *is* the word[1697] of the LORD? let it come now.

16 As for me, [a]I have not hastened from *being* a pastor [I]to follow thee: neither have I desired the woeful day;[3117] thou knowest: that which came out of my lips[8193] was *right* before thee.

17 Be not a terror[4288] unto me: [a]thou *art* my hope in the day of evil.[7451]

18 [a]Let them be confounded[954] that persecute me, but [b]let not me be confounded: let them be dismayed,[2865] but let not me be dismayed: bring upon them the day of evil, and [I][c]destroy[7665] them with double destruction.[7670]

The Sabbath Must Be Observed

19 Thus said the LORD unto me; Go and stand in the gate of the children of the people,[5971] whereby the kings[4428] of Judah come in, and by the which they go out, and in all the gates of Jerusalem;

20 And say unto them, [a]Hear[8085] ye the word of the LORD, ye kings of Judah, and all Judah, and all the inhabitants of Jerusalem, that enter in by these gates:

21 Thus saith the LORD; [a]Take heed[8104] to yourselves, and bear[5375] no burden[4853] on the sabbath[7676] day, nor bring *it* in by the gates of Jerusalem;

22 Neither carry forth a burden out of your houses[1004] on the sabbath day, neither do[6213] ye any work,[4399] but hallow[6942] ye the sabbath day, as I [a]commanded[6680] your fathers.[1]

23 [a]But they obeyed[8085] not, neither inclined their ear,[241] but made their neck stiff, that they might not hear, nor receive instruction.[4148]

24 And it shall come to pass, if ye diligently hearken[8085] unto me, saith5002 the LORD, to bring in no burden through the gates of this city on the sabbath day, but hallow the sabbath day, to do no work therein;

25 [a]Then shall there enter into the gates of this city kings and princes[8269] sitting upon the throne of David, riding in chariots and on horses, they, and their princes, the men[376] of Judah, and the in-

4 [a]Jer. 16:13 [b]Jer. 15:14

5 [a]Isa. 30:1, 2; 31:1

6 [a]Jer. 48:6 [b]Job 20:17 [c]Deut. 29:23

7 [a]Ps. 2:12; 34:8; 125:1; 146:5; Prov. 16:20; Isa. 30:18

8 [I]Or, *restraint* [a]Job 8:16; Ps. 1:3

10 [a]1Sam. 16:7; 1Chr. 28:9; Ps. 7:9; 139:23, 24; Prov. 17:3; Jer. 11:20; 20:12; Rom. 8:27; Rev. 2:23 [b]Ps. 62:12; Jer. 32:19; Rom. 2:6

11 [I]Or, *gathereth young which she hath not brought forth* [a]Ps. 55:23 [b]Luke 12:20

13 [a]Jer. 14:8 [b]Ps. 73:27; Isa. 1:28 [c]Luke 10:20 [d]Jer. 2:13

14 [a]Deut. 10:21; Ps. 109:1; 148:14

15 [a]Isa. 5:19; Ezek. 12:22; Amos 5:18; 2Pet. 3:4

16 [I]Hebr. *after thee* [a]Jer. 1:4

17 [a]Jer. 16:19

18 [I]Hebr. *break them with a double breach* [a]Ps. 35:4; 40:14; 70:2 [b]Ps. 25:2 [c]Jer. 11:20

20 [a]Jer. 19:3; 22:2

21 [a]Num. 15:32; Neh. 13:19

22 [a]Ex. 20:8; 23:12; 31:13; Ezek. 20:12

23 [a]Jer. 7:24, 26; 11:10

25 [a]Jer. 22:4

habitants of Jerusalem: and this city shall remain for ever.

26 And they shall come from the cities of Judah, and from [a]the places about Jerusalem, and from the land of Benjamin, and from [b]the plain, and from the mountains, and from [c]the south, bringing burnt offerings,[5930] and sacrifices,[2077] and meat offerings,[4503] and incense, and bringing [d]sacrifices of praise,[8426] unto the house[1004] of the LORD.

27 But if ye will not hearken unto me to hallow the sabbath day, and not to bear a burden, even entering in at the gates of Jerusalem on the sabbath day; then [a]will I kindle a fire in the gates thereof, [b]and it shall devour the palaces[759] of Jerusalem, and it shall not be quenched.

The Potter and the Clay

18 The word[1697] which came to Jeremiah from the LORD, saying,

2 Arise, and go down to the potter's[3335] house,[1004] and there I will cause thee to hear[8085] my words.

3 Then I went down to the potter's house, and, behold, he wrought a work[4399] on the [I]wheels.

4 And the vessel [I]that he made of clay was marred[7843] in the hand[3027] of the potter: so he [II]made it again another vessel, as seemed good[3474] to the potter to make *it.*

5 Then the word of the LORD came to me, saying,

6 O house of Israel, [a]cannot I do with you as this potter? saith the LORD. Behold, [b]as the clay *is* in the potter's hand, so *are* ye in mine hand, O house of Israel.

🗝 7 *At what* instant I shall speak[1696] concerning a nation,[1471] and concerning a kingdom,[4467] to [a]pluck up, and to pull down,[5422] and to destroy[6] *it;*

8 [a]If that nation, against whom I have pronounced, turn[7725] from their evil,[7451] [b]I will repent[5162] of the evil that I thought[2803] to do unto them.

9 And *at what* instant I shall speak concerning a nation, and concerning a kingdom, to build and to plant *it;*

10 If it do evil in my sight, that it obey[8085] not my voice, then I will repent of the good,[2896] wherewith I said I would benefit[3190] them.

11 Now therefore go to,[4994] speak[559] to the men[376] of Judah, and to the inhabitants of Jerusalem, saying, Thus saith the LORD; Behold, I frame[3335] evil against you, and devise[4284] a device[2803] against you: [a]return ye now every one from his evil way,[1870] and make your ways and your doings good.[3190]

12 And they said, [a]There is no hope:[2976] but we will walk after our own devices,[4284] and we will every one do the imagination[8307] of his evil heart.[3820]

13 Therefore thus saith the LORD; [a]Ask[7592] ye now among the heathen,[1471] who hath heard[8085] such things: the virgin[1330] of Israel hath done[6213] [b]a very horrible thing.[8186]

14 Will *a man* leave[5800] [I]the snow of Lebanon *which cometh* from the rock of the field?[7704] *or* shall the cold flowing waters that come from another[2114] place be forsaken?

26 [a]Jer. 32:44; 33:13 [b]Zech. 7:7 [c]Zech. 7:7 [d]Ps. 107:22; 116:17
27 [a]Jer. 21:14; 49:27; Lam. 4:11; Amos 1:4, 7, 10, 12; 2:2, 5 [b]2Kgs. 25:9; Jer. 52:13
3 [I]Or, *frames,* or, *seats*
4 [I]Or, *that he made was marred, as clay in the hand of the potter* [II]Hebr. *returned and made*
6 [a]Isa. 45:9; Rom. 9:20, 21 [b]Isa. 64:8
7 [a]Jer. 1:10
8 [a]Ezek. 18:21; 33:11 [b]Jer. 26:3; Jon. 3:10
11 [a]2Kgs. 17:13; Jer. 7:3; 25:5; 26:13; 35:15
12 [a]Jer. 2:25
13 [a]Jer. 2:10; 1Cor. 5:1 [b]Jer. 5:30
14 [I]Or, *my fields for a rock,* or *for the snow of Lebanon? shall the running waters be forsaken for the strange cold waters?*

🗝 **18:7–10** God chooses to consider man's conduct, and respond accordingly. Perhaps this is best illustrated in the case of Nineveh. Jonah came to Nineveh with a word of judgment which offered no opportunity for repentance (Jon. 3:4). Yet because the people put their faith in God and repented, God stayed His judgment (Jon. 3:5–10). Jonah already knew that God was merciful, and would respond in this way (Jon. 4:1–3). Later, the people of Nineveh returned to their wickedness; then God did judge Nineveh as He had said, and the city is a ruin to this day. It is important to recognize when God makes an unconditional affirmation of what He will do. This kind of promise will not change regardless of what man does. Notice the promises in Jeremiah chapters thirty-three and thirty-four where God affirms that the coming judgment is temporal and does not nullify His former promises to Israel (Deut. 7:6, 7; 2 Sam. 7:8–17). God compares the security of those promises with the constancy of day and night (Jer. 33:20, 21, 25, 26; see also 31:35–37).

15 Because my people[5971] hath forgotten [a]me, they have burned incense[6999] to [b]vanity,[7723] and they have caused them to stumble[3784] in their ways *from* the [c]ancient[5769] paths, to walk in paths, *in* a way not cast up;

16 To make[7760] their land[776] [a]desolate,[8047] *and* a perpetual[5769] [b]hissing; every one that passeth[5674] thereby shall be astonished,[8074] and wag5110 his head.[7218]

17 [a]I will scatter them [b]as with an east wind[7307] before the enemy; [c]I will shew[7200] them the back, and not the face, in the day[3117] of their calamity.[343]

Another Plot Against Jeremiah

18 Then said they, [a]Come, and let us devise devices against Jeremiah; [b]for the law[8451] shall not perish[6] from the priest,[3548] nor counsel[6098] from the wise,[2450] nor the word from the prophet.[5030] Come, and let us smite[5221] him [I]with the tongue, and let us not give heed[7181] to any of his words.

19 Give heed to me, O LORD, and hearken[8085] to the voice of them that contend with me.

20 [a]Shall evil be recompensed[7999] for good? for [b]they have digged a pit[7745] for my soul.[5315] Remember[2142] that I stood before thee to speak good for them, *and* to turn away[7725] thy wrath[2534] from them.

21 Therefore [a]deliver up their children[1121] to the famine, and [I]pour out their *blood* by the force of the sword;[2719] and let their wives[802] be bereaved of their children,[7909] and *be* widows; and let their men[582] be put to death;[4194] *let* their young men *be* slain[5221] by the sword in battle.

22 Let a cry be heard from their houses,[1004] when thou shalt bring a troop[1416] suddenly upon them: for [a]they have digged a pit[7882] to take me, and hid snares[6341] for my feet.

23 Yet, LORD, thou knowest[3045] all their counsel against me [I]to slay *me:* [a]forgive[3722] not their iniquity,[5771] neither blot out[4229] their sin[2403] from thy sight, but let them be overthrown[3782] before thee; deal[6213] *thus* with them in the time[6256] of thine anger.[639]

The Broken Pot

19 Thus saith the LORD, Go and get a potter's[3335] earthen[2789] bottle, and *take* of the ancients[2204] of the people,[5971] and of the ancients of the priests;[3548]

2 And go forth unto [a]the valley of the son[1121] of Hinnom, which *is* by the entry of [I]the east gate, and proclaim[7121] there the words[1697] that I shall tell[1696] thee,

3 [a]And say, Hear[8085] ye the word[1697] of the LORD, O kings[4428] of Judah, and inhabitants of Jerusalem; Thus saith the LORD of hosts,[6635] the God[430] of Israel; Behold, I will bring evil[7451] upon this place, the which whosoever heareth, his ears[241] shall [b]tingle.

4 Because they [a]have forsaken[5800] me, and have estranged[5234] this place, and have burned incense[6999] in it unto other gods,[430] whom neither they nor their fathers[1] have known,[3045] nor the kings of Judah, and have filled this place with [b]the blood[1818] of innocents;

5 [a]They have built also the high places[1116] of Baal, to burn[8313] their sons with fire *for* burnt offerings unto Baal, [b]which I commanded[6680] not, nor spake[1696] *it,* neither came *it* into my mind:[3820]

6 Therefore, behold, the days[3117] come, saith5002 the LORD, that this place shall no more be called[7121] Tophet, nor [a]The valley of the son of Hinnom, but The valley of slaughter.[2028]

7 And I will make void the counsel[6098] of Judah and Jerusalem in this place; [a]and I will cause them to fall by the sword[2719] before their enemies, and by the hands[3027] of them that seek their lives:[5315] and their [b]carcases[5038] will I give to be meat for the fowls of the heaven,8064 and for the beasts of the earth.[776]

8 And I will make[7760] this city [a]desolate,[8047] and an hissing; every one

15 [a]Jer. 2:13, 32; 3:21; 13:25; 17:13 [b]Jer. 10:15; 16:19 [c]Jer. 6:16

16 [a]Jer. 19:8; 49:13; 50:13 [b]1Kgs. 9:8; Lam. 2:15; Mic. 6:16

17 [a]Jer. 13:24 [b]Ps. 48:7 [c]Jer. 2:27

18 [I]Or, *for the tongue* [a]Jer. 11:19 [b]Lev. 10:11; Mal. 2:7; John 7:48, 49

20 [a]Ps. 109:4, 5 [b]Ps. 35:7; 57:6; Jer. 18:22

21 [I]Hebr. *pour them out* [a]Ps. 109:9, 10

22 [a]Jer. 18:20

23 [I]Hebr. *for death* [a]Ps. 35:4; 109:14; Jer. 11:20; 15:15

2 [I]Hebr. *the sun gate* [a]Josh. 15:8; 2Kgs. 23:10; Jer. 7:31

3 [a]Jer. 17:20 [b]1Sam. 3:11; 2Kgs. 21:12

4 [a]Deut. 28:20; Isa. 65:11; Jer. 2:13, 17, 19; 15:6; 17:13 [b]2Kgs. 21:16; Jer. 2:34

5 [a]Jer. 7:31, 32; 32:35 [b]Lev. 18:21

6 [a]Josh. 15:8

7 [a]Lev. 26:17; Deut. 28:25 [b]Ps. 79:2; Jer. 7:33; 16:4; 34:20

8 [a]Jer. 18:16; 49:13; 50:13

that passeth[5674] thereby shall be astonished[8074] and hiss because of all the plagues[4347] thereof.

9 And I will cause them to eat the [a]flesh[1320] of their sons and the flesh of their daughters, and they shall eat every one[376] the flesh of his friend in the siege and straitness, wherewith their enemies, and they that seek their lives, shall straiten6693 them.

10 [a]Then shalt thou break[7665] the bottle in the sight of the men[582] that go with thee,

11 And shalt say unto them, Thus saith the LORD of hosts; [a]Even so will I break this people and this city, as *one* breaketh a potter's vessel, that cannot [I]be made whole again: and they shall [b]bury[6912] *them* in Tophet, till *there be* no place to bury.

12 Thus will I do unto this place, saith the LORD, and to the inhabitants thereof, and *even* make this city as Tophet:

13 And the houses[1004] of Jerusalem, and the houses of the kings of Judah, shall be defiled[2931] [a]as the place of Tophet, because of all the houses upon whose [b]roofs they have burned incense unto all the host[6635] of heaven, and [c]have poured out[5258] drink offerings[5262] unto other gods.

14 Then came Jeremiah from Tophet, whither the LORD had sent him to prophesy;[5012] and he stood in [a]the court of the LORD's house;[1004] and said to all the people,

15 Thus saith the LORD of hosts, the God of Israel; Behold, I will bring upon this city and upon all her towns all the evil that I have pronounced against it, because [a]they have hardened their necks, that they might not hear my words.

The Curse Upon Pashur

20 Now Pashur the son of [a]Immer the priest,[3548] who *was* also chief governor[5057] in the house[1004] of the LORD, heard[8085] that Jeremiah prophesied[5012] these things.[1697]

2 Then Pashur smote[5221] Jeremiah the prophet,[5030] and put him in the stocks that *were* in the high[5945] gate of Benjamin, which *was* by the house of the LORD.

3 And it came to pass on the morrow, that Pashur brought forth Jeremiah out of the stocks. Then said Jeremiah unto him, The LORD hath not called[7121] thy name Pashur, but [I][a]Magor–missabib.

4 For thus saith the LORD, Behold,[7200] I will make thee a terror[4032] to thyself, and to all thy friends:[157] and they shall fall by the sword[2719] of their enemies, and thine eyes shall behold *it:* and I will give all Judah into the hand[3027] of the king[4428] of Babylon, and he shall carry them captive[1540] into Babylon, and shall slay[5221] them with the sword.

5 Moreover I [a]will deliver all the strength2633 of this city, and all the labours3018 thereof, and all the precious things thereof, and all the treasures of the kings[4428] of Judah will I give into the hand of their enemies, which shall spoil them, and take them, and carry them to Babylon.

6 And thou, Pashur, and all that dwell in thine house shall go into captivity:[7628] and thou shalt come to Babylon, and there thou shalt die,[4191] and shalt be buried[6912] there, thou, and all thy friends, to whom thou hast [a]prophesied lies.[8267]

Jeremiah's Lamentation

🗝 7 O LORD, thou hast deceived6601 me, and I was [I]deceived: [a]thou art stronger[2388] than I, and hast prevailed: [b]I am in derision daily, every one mocketh me.

8 For since I spake,[1696] [a]I cried out,[2199] I cried[7121] violence[2555] and spoil;[7701] because the word[1697] of the

---

9 [a]Lev. 26:29; Deut. 28:53; Isa. 9:20; Lam. 4:10

10 [a]Jer. 51:63, 64

11 [I]Hebr. *be healed* [a]Ps. 2:9; Isa. 30:14; Lam. 4:2 [b]Jer. 7:32

13 [a]2Kgs. 23:10 [b]2Kgs. 23:12; Jer. 32:29; Zeph. 1:5 [c]Jer. 7:18

14 [a]2Chr. 20:5

15 [a]Jer. 7:26; 17:23

1 [a]1Chr. 24:14

3 [I]That is, *Fear round about* [a]Ps. 31:13; Jer. 6:25; 20:10; 46:5; 49:29

5 [a]2Kgs. 20:17; 24:12-16; 25:13; Jer. 3:24

6 [a]Jer. 14:13, 14; 28:15; 29:21

7 [I]Or, *enticed* [a]Jer. 1:6, 7 [b]Lam. 3:14

8 [a]Jer. 6:7

🗝 **20:7–18** This passage clearly reveals why Jeremiah is called "the weeping prophet." He is shown to be a human being, but one who was chosen to carry out God's work. Jeremiah was subject to

(continued on next page)

LORD was made a reproach[2781] unto me, and a derision, daily.

9 Then I said, I will not make mention of him, nor speak any more in his name. But *his word* was in mine heart[3820] as a [a]burning fire shut up in my bones,[6106] and I was weary with forbearing, and [b]I could not *stay.*

10 [a]For I heard the defaming of many, fear[4032] on every side. Report,[5046] *say they,* and we will report it. [1][b]All my familiars watched for my halting, *saying,* Peradventure[194] he will be enticed,[6601] and we shall prevail against him, and we shall take our revenge[5360] on him.

11 But [a]the LORD *is* with me as a mighty terrible one:[6184] therefore my persecutors shall stumble,[3782] and they shall not [b]prevail: they shall be greatly ashamed;[954] for they shall not prosper:[7919] *their* [c]everlasting[5769] confusion shall never be forgotten.

12 But, O LORD of hosts,[6635] that [a]triest the righteous,[6662] *and* seest the reins[3629] and the heart, [b]let me see thy vengeance[5360] on them: for unto thee have I opened my cause.[7379]

13 Sing[7891] unto the LORD, praise[1984] ye the LORD: for [a]he hath delivered the soul[5315] of the poor from the hand of evildoers.[7489]

14 [a]Cursed[779] *be* the day[3117] wherein I was born: let not the day wherein my mother[517] bare me be blessed.[1288]

15 Cursed *be* the man who brought tidings[1319] to my father, saying, A man[2145] child[1121] is born unto thee; making him very glad.

16 And let that man be as the cities which the LORD [a]overthrew,[2015] and repented[5162] not: and let him [b]hear[8085] the cry in the morning, and the shouting at noontide;

17 [a]Because he slew me not from the womb; or that my mother might have been my grave, and her womb *to be* always[5769] great *with me.*

18 [a]Wherefore came I forth out of the womb to [b]see labour[5999] and sorrow,[3015] that my days[3117] should be consumed[3615] with shame?

Jerusalem Will Be Destroyed

21 The word which came unto Jeremiah from the LORD, when king[4428] Zedekiah sent him [a]Pashur the son of Melchiah, and [b]Zephaniah the son of Maaseiah the priest,[3548] saying,

2 [a]Enquire, I pray thee,[4994] of the LORD for us; for Nebuchadrezzar king of Babylon maketh war against us; if so be that the LORD will deal[6213] with us according to all his wondrous works,[6381] that he may go up from us.

3 Then said Jeremiah unto them, Thus shall ye say to Zedekiah:

4 Thus saith the LORD[3068] God[430] of Israel; Behold, I will turn back the weapons of war that *are* in your hands,[3027] wherewith ye fight against the king of Babylon, and *against* the Chaldeans, which besiege you without the walls, and [a]I will assemble[622] them into the midst of this city.

5 And I myself will fight against you with an [a]outstretched hand[3027] and with a strong[2389] arm, even in anger,[639] and in fury, and in great wrath.[7110]

6 And I will smite[5221] the inhabitants of this city, both man[120] and beast: they shall die[4191] of a great pestilence.[1698]

7 And afterward, saith[5002] the LORD, [a]I will deliver Zedekiah king of Judah, and his servants,[5650] and the people,[5971] and such as are left[7604] in this city from the pestilence, from the sword,[2719] and from the famine, into the hand of Nebuchadrezzar king of Babylon, and into the hand of their enemies, and into the hand

9 [a]Job 32:18, 19; Ps. 39:3 [b]Job 32:18; Acts 18:5

10 [1]Hebr. *Every man of my peace* [a]Ps. 31:13 [b]Job 19:19; Ps. 41:9; 55:13, 14; Luke 11:53, 54

11 [a]Jer. 1:8, 19 [b]Jer. 15:20; 17:18 [c]Jer. 23:40

12 [a]Jer. 11:20; 17:10 [b]Ps. 54:7; 50:10

13 [a]Ps. 35:9, 10; 109:30, 31

14 [a]Job 3:3; Jer. 15:10

16 [a]Gen. 19:25 [b]Jer. 18:22

17 [a]Job 3:10, 11 [b]Job 3:20 [c]Lam. 3:1

1 [a]Jer. 38:1 [b]2Kgs. 25:18; Jer. 29:25; 37:3

2 [a]Jer. 37:3, 7

4 [a]Isa. 13:4

5 [a]Ex. 6:6

7 [a]Jer. 37:17; 39:5; 52:9

(continued from previous page)

the same emotions that are common to all people. Yet through it all, Jeremiah continued to preach God's message (v. 8) because he was compelled by God's call (v. 9, cf. Paul's experience in 1 Cor. 9:16). In verse one he complained that God has deceived him, but in verse thirteen he is singing praises to God. Then in the very next verse he begins to wish he had never been born (v. 14).

of those that seek their life:[5315] and he
shall smite them with the edge[6310] of the
sword; [b]he shall not spare them, neither
have pity, nor have mercy.[7355]
8 And unto this people thou shalt
say, Thus saith the LORD; Behold, [a]I set
before you the way[1870] of life,[2416] and
the way of death.[4194]
9 He that [a]abideth in this city shall
die by the sword, and by the famine, and
by the pestilence: but he that goeth out,
and falleth[5307] to the Chaldeans that besiege you, he shall live,[2421] and [b]his life
shall be unto him for a prey.
10 For I have [a]set[7760] my face against
this city for evil,[7451] and not for good,[2896]
saith the LORD: [b]it shall be given into the
hand of the king of Babylon, and he
shall [c]burn[8313] it with fire.
11 And touching the house[1004] of the
king of Judah, *say,* Hear[8085] ye the word
of the LORD;
12 O house of David, thus saith the
LORD; [I][a]Execute[1777] judgment[4941] [b]in the
morning, and deliver[5337] *him that is*
spoiled out of the hand of the oppressor,
lest my fury go out like fire, and burn
that none can quench *it,* because of the
evil[7455] of your doings.
13 Behold, [a]I *am* against thee, O inhabitant of the valley, *and* rock of the
plain, saith the LORD; which say, [b]Who
shall come down against us? or who shall
enter into our habitations?
14 But I will [I]punish[6485] you according to the [a]fruit of your doings, saith the
LORD: and I will kindle a fire in the forest thereof, and [b]it shall devour all things
round about it.

Prophecies Against the Kings of Judah

22 Thus saith[559] the LORD; Go down
to the house[1004] of the king[4428]
of Judah, and speak[1696] there this
word,[1697]
2 And say, [a]Hear[8085] the word of the
LORD, O king of Judah, that sittest upon
the throne[3678] of David, thou, and thy
servants,[5650] and thy people[5971] that enter
in by these gates:
3 Thus saith the LORD; [a]Execute
ye judgment[4941] and righteousness,[6666]
and deliver[5337] the spoiled out of the
hand[3027] of the oppressor: and [b]do no
wrong,[3238] do no violence[2554] to the
stranger,[1616] the fatherless, nor the
widow, neither shed[8210] innocent[5355]
blood[1818] in this place.
4 For if ye do this thing[1697] indeed,
[a]then shall there enter in by the gates of
this house kings[4428] sitting [I]upon the
throne of David, riding in chariots and
on horses, he, and his servants, and his
people.
5 But if ye will not hear these words,
[a]I swear[7650] by myself, saith[5002] the LORD,
that this house shall become[1961] a desolation.[2723]
6 For thus saith the LORD unto the
king's house of Judah; Thou *art* Gilead
unto me, *and* the head[7218] of Lebanon:
yet surely I will make thee a wilderness,
and cities *which* are not inhabited.
7 And I will prepare[6942] destroyers
against thee, every one[376] with his
weapons: and they shall cut down[3772]
[a]thy choice cedars, [b]and cast *them* into
the fire.
8 And many nations[1471] shall pass
by this city, and they shall say every man
to his neighbour,[7453] [a]Wherefore hath the
LORD done thus unto this great city?
9 Then they shall answer,[559] [a]Be-
cause they have forsaken[5800] the covenant[1285] of the LORD their God,[430] and
worshipped[7812] other gods,[430] and
served[5647] them.
10 Weep ye not for [a]the dead, neither
bemoan him: *but* weep sore for him [b]that
goeth away: for he shall return[7725] no
more, nor see his native country.[776]
11 For thus saith the LORD touching
[a]Shallum the son of Josiah king of Judah,
which reigned[4427] instead of Josiah his
father, [b]which went forth out of this
place; He shall not return thither any
more:
12 But he shall die[4191] in the place
whither they have led him captive,[1540]
and shall see this land[776] no more.
13 [a]Woe unto him that buildeth his
house by unrighteousness, and his cham-

7 [b]Deut. 28:50; 2Chr. 36:17
8 [a]Deut. 30:19
9 [a]Jer. 38:2, 17, 18 [b]Jer. 39:18; 45:5
10 [a]Lev. 17:10; Jer. 44:11; Amos 9:4 [b]Jer. 38:3 [c]Jer. 34:2, 22; 37:10; 38:18, 23; 52:13
12 [I]Hebr. *Judge* [a]Jer. 22:3; Zech. 7:9 [b]Ps. 101:8
13 [a]Ezek. 13:8 [b]Jer. 49:4
14 [I]Hebr. *visit upon* [a]Prov. 1:31; Isa. 3:10, 11 [b]2Chr. 36:19; Jer. 52:13
2 [a]Jer. 17:20
3 [a]Jer. 21:12 [b]Jer. 22:17
4 [I]Hebr. *for David upon his throne* [a]Jer. 17:25
5 [a]Heb. 6:13, 17
7 [a]Isa. 37:24 [b]Jer. 21:14
8 [a]Deut. 29:24, 25; 1Kgs. 9:8, 9
9 [a]2Kgs. 22:17; 2Chr. 34:25
10 [a]2Kgs. 22:20 [b]Jer. 22:11
11 [a]2Kgs. 23:30; 1Chr. 3:15 [b]2Kgs. 23:34
13 [a]2Kgs. 23:35; Jer. 22:18

bers by wrong; [b]*that* useth his neighbour's[7453] service[5647] without wages, and
giveth him not for his work;
14 That saith, I will build me a wide
house and [I]large[7304] chambers, and cutteth him out [II]windows; and *it is*
cieled5603 with cedar, and painted[4886]
with vermilion.8350
15 Shalt thou reign,[4427] because thou
closest *thyself* in cedar? [a]did not thy father eat and drink, and do judgment and
justice,[6666] *and* then [b]*it was* well with
him?
16 He judged[1777] the cause[1779] of the
poor and needy; then *it was* well *with*
him: was not this to know[1847] me? saith
the LORD.
17 [a]But thine eyes and thine heart[3820]
are not but for thy covetousness,1215 and
for to shed innocent blood, and for oppression, and for [I]violence, to do *it.*
18 Therefore thus saith the LORD concerning Jehoiakim the son of Josiah king
of Judah; [a]They shall not lament for him,
saying, [b]Ah my brother[251] or, Ah sister[269]
they shall not lament for him, *saying,* Ah
lord[113] or, Ah his glory!
19 [a]He shall be buried[6912] with the
burial[6900] of an ass, drawn and cast forth
beyond the gates of Jerusalem.
20 Go up to Lebanon, and cry; and
lift up thy voice in Bashan, and cry from
the passages: for all thy lovers[157] are
destroyed.[7665]
21 I spake[1696] unto thee in thy
[I]prosperity; *but* thou saidst,[559] I will not
hear. [a]This *hath been* thy manner[1870]
from thy youth, that thou obeyedst[8085]
not my voice.
22 The wind[7307] shall eat up all [a]thy

13 [b]Lev. 19:13; Deut. 24:14, 15; Mic. 3:10; Hab. 2:9; James 5:4
14 [I]Hebr. *through aired* [II]Or, *my windows*
15 [a]2Kgs. 23:25 [b]Ps. 128:2; Isa. 3:10
17 [I]Or, *incursion* [a]Ezek. 19:6
18 [a]Jer. 16:4, 6 [b]1Kgs. 13:30
19 [a]2Chr. 36:6; Jer. 36:30
21 [I]Hebr. *prosperities* [a]Jer. 3:25; 7:23
22 [a]Jer. 23:1 [b]Jer. 22:20
23 [a]Jer. 6:24
24 [a]2Kgs. 24:6, 8; 1Chr. 3:16; 37:1 [b]Song 8:6; Hag. 2:23
25 [a]Jer. 34:20
26 [a]2Kgs. 24:15; 2Chr. 36:10
27 [I]Hebr. *lift up their mind* [a]Jer. 44:14
28 [a]Ps. 31:12; Jer. 48:38; Hos. 8:8
29 [a]Deut. 32:1; Isa. 1:2; 34:1; Mic. 1:2
30 [a]1Chr. 3:16, 17; Matt. 1:12 [b]Jer. 36:30

pastors, and [b]thy lovers shall go into
captivity:[7628] surely then shalt thou be
ashamed[954] and confounded for all thy
wickedness.[7451]
23 O [a]inhabitant of Lebanon, that
makest thy nest in the cedars, how
gracious[2603] shalt thou be when
pangs[2256] come upon thee, the pain as of
a woman in travail!
🔑 24 *As* I live,[2416] saith the LORD,
[a]though Coniah the son of Jehoiakim
king of Judah [b]were the signet upon
my right hand, yet would I pluck thee
thence;
25 [a]And I will give thee into the
hand of them that seek thy life,[5315] and
into the hand *of them* whose face thou
fearest, even into the hand of Nebuchadrezzar king of Babylon, and into the
hand of the Chaldeans.
26 [a]And I will cast thee out, and thy
mother[517] that bare thee, into another
country, where ye were not born; and
there shall ye die.
27 But to the land whereunto they
[I][a]desire to return, thither shall they not
return.
28 *Is* this man Coniah a despised broken idol?[6089] *is he* [a]a vessel wherein *is* no
pleasure?[2656] wherefore are they cast out,
he and his seed,[2233] and are cast into a
land which they know[3045] not?
29 [a]O earth,[776] earth, earth, hear the
word of the LORD.
30 Thus saith the LORD, Write ye this
man [a]childless, a man[1397] *that* shall not
prosper in his days:[3117] for no man of his
seed shall prosper, [b]sitting upon the
throne of David, and ruling any more in
Judah.

🔑 **22:24–30** Jeremiah proclaims the Lord's rejection of the line of Coniah from the kingship of his people. The fact that he was "written childless" does not mean that he had no children, but that none of his children (mentioned in 1 Chr. 3:17, 18) would sit on the throne. Coniah was succeeded by his uncle Zedekiah, the last king of Judah. The curse regarding God's replacement of Coniah in the promises of the Davidic Covenant seems to have been expiated according to Haggai 2:23 where Zerubbabel (said to be the son of Shealtiel) is chosen by God (Hag. 2:23). This did not abrogate the Davidic Covenant given in 2 Samuel 7:11–13 (see Ps. 132:11; Is. 9:6, 7; 16:5; Jer. 33:15–17; Ezek. 34:23, 24; Luke 1:32). Jeremiah 23:5, 6 again makes this clear. Although this has not yet taken place, it will upon Christ's return (Luke 1:32; Rev. 4:10, 11; 5:13; 12:5). See note on 1 Chronicles 3:17–19 for a discussion of the relationship of Zerubbabel to Pedaiah.

The Promised Return of the Remnant

23 Woe [a]be unto the pastors that destroy[6] and scatter the sheep of my pasture! saith[5002] the LORD.

2 Therefore thus saith[559] the LORD God[430] of Israel against the pastors that feed my people;[5971] Ye have scattered my flock, and driven them away, and have not visited[6485] them: [a]behold, I will visit upon you the evil[7455] of your doings, saith the LORD.

3 And [a]I will gather[6908] the remnant[7611] of my flock out of all countries[776] whither I have driven them, and will bring them again to their folds; and they shall be fruitful and increase.

4 And I will set up [a]shepherds over them which shall feed them: and they shall fear[3372] no more, nor be dismayed,[2865] neither shall they be lacking,[6485] saith the LORD.

🗝 5 Behold, [a]the days[3117] come, saith the LORD, that I will raise unto David a righteous[6662] Branch, and a King[4428] shall reign[4427] and prosper,[7919] [b]and shall execute judgment[4941] and justice[6666] in the earth.[776]

6 [a]In his days Judah shall be saved,[3467] and Israel [b]shall dwell[7931] safely:[983] and [c]this *is* his name whereby he shall be called,[7121] [I]THE LORD OUR RIGHTEOUSNESS.[6664]

7 Therefore, behold, [a]the days come, saith the LORD, that they shall no more say, The LORD liveth,[2416] which brought up[5927] the children[1121] of Israel out of the land[776] of Egypt;

8 But, The LORD liveth, which brought up and which led the seed[2233] of the house[1004] of Israel out of the north country, [a]and from all countries whither I had driven them; and they shall dwell in their own land.[127]

Jeremiah Preaches Against Lying Prophets

🗝 9 Mine heart[3820] within[7130] me is broken[7665] because of the prophets;[5030] [a]all my bones[6106] shake; I am like a drunken man,[376] and like a man[1397] whom wine hath overcome, because of the LORD, and because of the words[1697] of his holiness.

10 For [a]the land is full of adulterers;[5003] for [b]because of [I]swearing[423] the land mourneth; [c]the pleasant places[4999] of the wilderness are dried up,[3001] and their [II]course is evil,[7451] and their force *is* not right.

11 For [a]both prophet[5030] and priest[3548] are profane;[2610] yea, [b]in my house have I found their wickedness,[7451] saith the LORD.

12 [a]Wherefore their way[1870] shall be unto them as slippery *ways* in the darkness:[653] they shall be driven on, and fall therein: for I [b]will bring evil upon them, *even* the year of their visitation,[6486] saith the LORD.

13 And I have seen[7200] [I]folly in the prophets of Samaria; [a]they prophesied[5012] in Baal, and [b]caused my people Israel to err.[8582]

14 I have seen also in the prophets of

1 [a]Jer. 10:21; 22:22; Ezek. 34:2
2 [a]Ex. 32:34
3 [a]Jer. 32:37; Ezek. 34:13
4 [a]Jer. 3:15; Ezek. 34:23
5 [a]Isa. 4:2; 11:1; 40:10, 11; Jer. 33:14-16; Dan. 9:24; Zech. 3:8; 6:12; John 1:45 [b]Ps. 72:2; Isa. 9:7; 32:1, 18
6 [I]Hebr. *Jehovah-tsidkenu* [a]Deut. 33:28; Zech. 14:11 [b]Jer. 32:37 [c]Jer. 33:16; 1Cor. 1:30
7 [a]Jer. 16:14, 15
8 [a]Isa. 43:5, 6; Jer. 23:3
9 [a]Hab. 3:16
10 [I]Or, *cursing* [II]Or, *violence* [a]Jer. 5:7, 8; 9:2 [b]Hos. 4:2, 3 [c]Jer. 9:10; 12:4
11 [a]Jer. 6:13; 8:10; Zeph. 3:4 [b]Jer. 7:30; 11:15; 32:34; Ezek. 8:11; 23:39
12 [a]Ps. 35:6; Prov. 4:19; Jer. 13:16 [b]Jer. 11:23
13 [I]Hebr. *unsavory* [a]Jer. 2:8 [b]Isa. 9:16

🗝 **23:5–8** This is one of several passages that refer to the Messiah. He is described by four terms which parallel the four Gospels. The first is found in this passage, "unto David a righteous Branch, and a King," signifying His rulership as seen in the Gospel of Matthew (see also Is. 11:1; Jer. 33:15). The other three phrases and their passages are as follows: "my servant the BRANCH," in Zechariah 3:8, referring to the Messiah's service to God, which is seen in the Gospel of Mark; "the man whose name is the BRANCH," in Zechariah 6:12, depicting His humanity seen also in the Gospel of Luke; and "the branch of the LORD," from Isaiah 4:2 referring to the Messiah's deity as seen in the Gospel of John. Since He is identified as a "servant," He is connected as well with the messianic "Servant Songs" in Isaiah (see note on Is. 42:1–9).

This passage also contains a key unfulfilled prophecy concerning God's future dealings with Israel (23:7, 8). There is coming a day when Israel will no longer identify themselves with the exodus from Egypt, but with the return of all Jews from worldwide captivity. This has clearly not happened yet.

🗝 **23:9–32** See note on Deuteronomy 18:20–22.

Jerusalem [I]an horrible thing:[8186] [a]they commit adultery,[5003] and [b]walk in lies:[8267] they [c]strengthen[2388] also the hands[3027] of evildoers,[7489] that none doth return[7725] from his wickedness: they are all of them unto me as [d]Sodom, and the inhabitants thereof as Gomorrah.

15 Therefore thus saith the LORD of hosts[6635] concerning the prophets; Behold, I will feed them with [a]wormwood,[3939] and make them drink the water of gall:[7219] for from the prophets of Jerusalem is [I]profaneness[2613] gone forth into all the land.

16 Thus saith the LORD of hosts, Hearken[8085] not unto the words of the prophets that prophesy[5012] unto you: they make you vain: [a]they speak a vision[2377] of their own heart, *and* not out of the mouth[6310] of the LORD.

17 They say still unto them that despise me, The LORD hath said, [a]Ye shall have peace; and they say unto every one that walketh after the [I][b]imagination[8307] of his own heart, [c]No evil shall come upon you.

18 For [a]who hath stood in the [I]counsel[5475] of the LORD, and hath perceived[7200] and heard[8085] his word?[1697] who hath marked his word, and heard *it?*

19 Behold, a [a]whirlwind of the LORD is gone forth in fury, even a grievous whirlwind: it shall fall grievously[2342] upon the head[7218] of the wicked.

20 The [a]anger[639] of the LORD shall not return, until he have executed,[6213] and till he have performed the thoughts[4209] of his heart: [b]in the latter[319] days ye shall consider[995] it perfectly.[998]

21 [a]I have not sent these prophets, yet they ran: I have not spoken to them, yet they prophesied.

22 But if they had [a]stood in my counsel, and had caused my people to hear my words, then they should have [b]turned them from their evil way, and from the evil of their doings.

23 *Am* I a God at hand, saith the LORD, and not a God afar off?

24 Can any [a]hide himself in secret places that I shall not see him? saith the LORD. [b]Do not I fill heaven[8064] and earth? saith the LORD.

25 I have heard what the prophets said, that prophesy lies in my name, saying, I have dreamed, I have dreamed.

26 How long shall *this* be in the heart of the prophets that prophesy lies? yea, *they are* prophets of the deceit of their own heart;

27 Which think[2803] to cause my people to forget my name by their dreams which they tell[5608] every man to his neighbour,[7453] [a]as their fathers[1] have forgotten my name for Baal.

28 The prophet [I]that hath a dream, let him tell a dream; and he that hath my word, let him speak my word faithfully.[571] What *is* the chaff to the wheat? saith the LORD.

29 *Is* not my word like as a fire? saith the LORD; and like a hammer *that* breaketh the rock in pieces?

30 Therefore, behold, [a]I *am* against the prophets, saith the LORD, that steal my words every one from his neighbour.

31 Behold, I *am* against the prophets, saith the LORD, [I]that use their tongues, and say, He saith.

32 Behold, I *am* against them that prophesy false[8267] dreams, saith the LORD, and do tell them, and cause my people to err by their lies, and by [a]their lightness; yet I sent them not, nor commanded[6680] them: therefore they shall not profit this people at all, saith the LORD.

The Burden of the LORD

33 And when this people, or the prophet, or a priest, shall ask[7592] thee, saying, What *is* [a]the burden[4853] of the LORD? thou shalt then say unto them, What burden? [b]I will even forsake[5203] you, saith the LORD.

34 And *as for* the prophet, and the priest, and the people, that shall say, The burden of the LORD, I will even [I]punish[6485] that man and his house.

35 Thus shall ye say every one to his neighbour, and every one to his brother,[251] What hath the LORD an-

---

14 IOr, *filthiness* [a]Jer. 29:23 [b]Jer. 23:26 [c]Ezek. 13:22 [d]Deut. 32:32; Isa. 1:9, 10

15 IOr, *hypocrisy* [a]Jer. 8:14; 9:15

16 [a]Jer. 14:14; 23:21

17 IOr, *stubbornness* [a]Jer. 6:14; 8:11; Ezek. 13:10; Zech. 10:2 [b]Jer. 13:10 [c]Mic. 3:11

18 IOr, *secret* [a]Job 15:8; 1Cor. 2:16

19 [a]Jer. 25:32; 30:23

20 [a]Jer. 30:24 [b]Gen. 49:1

21 [a]Jer. 14:14; 27:15; 29:9 [b]Jer. 23:18 [c]Jer. 25:5

24 [a]Ps. 139:7; Amos 9:2, 3 [b]1Kgs. 8:27; Ps. 139:7

27 [a]Judg. 3:7; 8:33, 34

28 IHebr. *with whom is*

30 [a]Deut. 18:20; Jer. 14:14, 15

31 IOr, *that smooth their tongues*

32 [a]Zeph. 3:4

33 [a]Mal. 1:1 [b]Jer. 23:39

34 IHebr. *visit upon*

swered? and, What hath the LORD spoken?

36 And the burden of the LORD shall ye mention no more: for every man's word shall be his burden; for ye have perverted the words of the living[2416] God, of the LORD of hosts our God.

37 Thus shalt thou say to the prophet, What hath the LORD answered thee? and, What hath the LORD spoken?

38 But since ye say, The burden of the LORD; therefore thus saith the LORD; Because ye say this word, The burden of the LORD, and I have sent unto you, saying, Ye shall not say, The burden of the LORD;

39 Therefore, behold, I, even I, [a]will utterly forget you, and [b]I will forsake you, and the city that I gave you and your fathers, *and cast you* out of my presence:

40 And I will bring [a]an everlasting[5769] reproach[2781] upon you, and a perpetual[5769] shame, which shall not be forgotten.

The Good Figs and the Bad Figs

24 The [a]LORD shewed[7200] me, and, behold, two baskets of figs *were* set[3259] before the temple[1964] of the LORD, after that Nebuchadrezzar [b]king of Babylon had carried away captive[1540] [c]Jeconiah the son of Jehoiakim king[4428] of Judah, and the princes[8269] of Judah, with the carpenters and smiths, from Jerusalem, and had brought them to Babylon.

2 One basket *had* very good[2896] figs, *even* like the figs *that are* first ripe: and the other basket *had* very naughty[7451] figs, which could not be eaten, [I]they were so bad.[7455]

3 Then said the LORD unto me, What seest thou, Jeremiah? And I said, Figs; the good figs, very good; and the evil,[7451] very evil, that cannot be eaten, they are so evil.[7455]

4 Again the word[1697] of the LORD came unto me, saying,

5 Thus saith the LORD, the God[430] of Israel; Like these good figs, so will I acknowledge[5234] [I]them that are carried away captive[1546] of Judah, whom I have sent out of this place into the land[776] of the Chaldeans for *their* good.

6 For I will set[7760] mine eyes upon them for good, and [a]I will bring them again to this land: and [b]I will build them, and not pull *them* down,[2040] and I will plant them, and not pluck *them* up.

7 And I will give them [a]an heart[3820] to know[3045] me, that I *am* the LORD: and they shall be [b]my people,[5971] and I will be their God: for they shall return[7725] unto me [c]with their whole heart.

8 And as the evil [a]figs, which cannot be eaten, they are so evil; surely thus saith the LORD, So will I give Zedekiah the king of Judah, and his princes, and the residue[7611] of Jerusalem, that remain in this land, and them that dwell in the land of Egypt:

9 And I will deliver them [I]to [a]be removed into all the kingdoms[4467] of the earth for *their* hurt,[7451] [b]*to be* a reproach[2781] and a proverb, a taunt [c]and a curse,[7045] in all places whither I shall drive them.

10 And I will send the sword,[2719] the famine, and the pestilence,[1698] among them, till they be consumed[8552] from off the land[127] that I gave unto them and to their fathers.[1]

Seventy Years of Desolation

25 The word[1697] that came to Jeremiah concerning all the people[5971] of Judah [a]in the fourth year of Jehoiakim the son of Josiah king[4428] of Judah, that *was* the first[7224] year of Nebuchadrezzar king of Babylon;

2 The which Jeremiah the prophet[5030] spake[1696] unto all the people of Judah, and to all the inhabitants of Jerusalem, saying,

3 [a]From the thirteenth year of Josiah the son of Amon king of Judah, even unto this day,[3117] that *is* the three and twentieth year, the word of the LORD hath come unto me, and I have spoken unto you, rising early and speaking; [b]but ye have not hearkened.[8085]

---

39 [a]Hos. 4:6 [b]Jer. 23:33

40 [a]Jer. 20:11

1 [a]Amos 7:1, 4; 8:1 [b]2Kgs. 24:12; 2Chr. 36:10 [c]Jer. 22:24; 29:2

2 [I]Hebr. *for badness*

5 [I]Hebr. *the captivity*

6 [a]Jer. 12:15; 29:10 [b]Jer. 32:41; 33:7; 42:10

7 [a]Deut. 30:6; Jer. 32:39; Ezek. 11:19; 36:26, 27 [b]Jer. 30:22; 31:33; 32:38 [c]Jer. 29:13

8 [a]Jer. 29:17

9 [I]Hebr. *for removing,* or, *vexation* [a]Deut. 28:25, 37; 1Kgs. 9:7; 2Chr. 7:20; Jer. 15:4; 29:18; 34:17 [b]Ps. 44:13, 14 [c]Jer. 29:18, 22

1 [a]Jer. 36:1

3 [a]Jer. 1:2 [b]Jer. 7:13; 11:7, 8, 10; 13:10, 11; 16:12; 17:23; 18:12; 19:15; 22:21

4 And the LORD hath sent unto you
all his servants[5650] the prophets,[5030] [a]ris-
ing early and sending *them;* but ye have
not hearkened, nor inclined your ear[241] to
hear.[8085]
5 They said, [a]Turn ye again[7725] now
everyone from his evil[7451] way,[1870] and
from the evil[7455] of your doings, and
dwell in the land[127] that the LORD hath
given unto you and to your fathers[1] for
ever[5769] and ever:
6 And go not after other gods[430] to
serve[5647] them, and to worship[7812] them,
and provoke me not to anger[3707] with the
works of your hands;[3027] and I will do
you no hurt.[7489]
7 Yet ye have not hearkened unto me,
saith the LORD; that ye might [a]provoke
me to anger with the works of your
hands to your own hurt.[7451]
8 Therefore thus saith[559] the LORD of
hosts;[6635] Because ye have not heard[8085]
my words,[1697]
9 Behold, I will send and take [a]all
the families[4940] of the north, saith the
LORD, and Nebuchadrezzar the king of
Babylon, [b]my servant,[5650] and will bring
them against this land,[776] and against the
inhabitants thereof, and against all these
nations[1471] round about, and will utterly
destroy[2763] them, and [c]make[7760] them an
astonishment,[8047] and an hissing, and
perpetual[5769] desolations.
10 Moreover [I]I will take from them
the [a]voice of mirth, and the voice of gladness, the voice of the bridegroom, and
the voice of the bride, [b]the sound of the
millstones, and the light[216] of the
candle.[5216]
11 And this whole land shall be a
desolation,[2723] *and* an astonishment; and
these nations shall serve the king of
Babylon seventy years.
12 And it shall come to pass, [a]when
seventy years are accomplished,[4390] *that*
I will [I]punish[6485] the king of Babylon,
and that nation,[1471] saith the LORD, for
their iniquity,[5771] and the land of the
Chaldeans, [b]and will make it perpetual
desolations.[8077]
13 And I will bring upon that land
all my words which I have pronounced
against it, *even* all that is written in this
book,[5612] which Jeremiah hath prophesied[5012] against all the nations.
14 [a]For many nations [b]and great
kings[4428] shall [c]serve themselves of them
also: [d]and I will recompense[7999] them according to their deeds, and according to
the works of their own hands.

The Cup of Wrath for the Nations

15 For thus saith the LORD God[430] of
Israel unto me; Take the [a]wine cup of
this fury at my hand,[3027] and cause
all the nations, to whom I send thee, to
drink it.
16 And [a]they shall drink, and be
moved, and be mad,[1984] because of the
sword[2719] that I will send among them.
17 Then took I the cup at the LORD's
hand, and made all the nations to drink,
unto whom the LORD had sent me:
18 *To wit,* Jerusalem, and the cities of
Judah, and the kings thereof, and the
princes[8269] thereof, to make them [a]a desolation, an astonishment, an hissing, and
[b]a curse;[7045] as *it is* this day;
19 [a]Pharaoh king of Egypt, and his
servants, and his princes, and all his people;
20 And all [a]the mingled people,[6154]
and all the kings of [b]the land of Uz, [c]and
all the kings of the land of the
Philistines, and Ashkelon, and Azzah,
and Ekron, and [d]the remnant[7611] of
Ashdod,
21 [a]Edom, and [b]Moab, and the children[1121] of [c]Ammon,
22 And all the kings of [a]Tyrus, and
all the kings of Zidon, and the kings of
the [I]isles which *are* beyond the [b]sea,
23 [a]Dedan, and Tema, and Buz, and
all [I][b]*that are* in the utmost corners,
24 And [a]all the kings of Arabia, and
all the kings of the [b]mingled people that
dwell[7931] in the desert,
25 And all the kings of Zimri, and
all the kings of [a]Elam, and all the kings
of the Medes,
26 [a]And all the kings of the north,
far and near, one with another, and all the
kingdoms[4467] of the world, which *are*

4 [a]Jer. 7:13, 25; 26:5; 29:19
5 [a]2Kgs. 17:13; Jer. 18:11; 35:15; Jon. 3:8
7 [a]Deut. 32:21; Jer. 7:19; 32:30
9 [a]Jer. 1:15 [b]Jer. 27:6; 40:2; 43:10; Isa. 44:28; 45:1 [c]Jer. 18:16
10 [I]Hebr. *I will cause to perish from them* [a]Isa. 24:7; Jer. 7:34; 16:9; Ezek. 26:13; Hos. 2:11; Rev. 18:23 [b]Eccl. 12:4
12 [I]Hebr. *visit upon* [a]2Chr. 36:21, 22; Ezra 1:1; Jer. 29:10; Dan. 9:2 [b]Isa. 13:19; 14:23; 21:1; 47:1 [c]Jer. 50:3, 13, 23, 39, 40, 45; 51:25, 26
14 [a]Jer. 50:9; 51:27, 28 [b]Jer. 50:41; 51:27 [c]Jer. 27:7 [d]Jer. 50:29; 51:6, 24
15 [a]Job 21:20; Ps. 75:8; Isa. 51:17; Rev. 14:10
16 [a]Jer. 51:7; Ezek. 23:34; Nah. 3:11
18 [a]Jer. 25:9, 11 [b]Jer. 24:9
19 [a]Jer. 46:2, 25
20 [a]Jer. 25:24 [b]Job 1:1 [c]Jer. 47:1, 5, 7 [d]Isa. 20:1
21 [a]Jer. 49:7 [b]Jer. 48:1 [c]Jer. 49:1
22 [I]Or, *region by the sea side* [a]Jer. 47:4 [b]Jer. 49:23
23 [I]Hebr. *cut off into corners,* or, *having the corners of the hair polled* [a]Jer. 49:8 [b]Jer. 9:26; 49:32
24 [a]2Chr. 9:14 [b]Jer. 25:20; 49:31; 50:37; Ezek. 30:5
25 [a]Jer. 49:34
26 [a]Jer. 50:9

upon the face of the earth:[127] [b]and the king of Sheshach shall drink after them.

27 Therefore thou shalt say unto them, Thus saith the LORD of hosts, the God of Israel; [a]Drink ye, and [b]be drunken, and spue, and fall, and rise no more, because of the sword which I will send among you.

28 And it shall be, if they refuse[3985] to take the cup at thine hand to drink, then shalt thou say unto them, Thus saith the LORD of hosts; Ye shall certainly drink.

29 For, lo, [a]I begin to bring evil[7489] on the city [I][b]which is called[7121] by my name, and should ye be utterly unpunished?[5352] Ye shall not be unpunished: for [c]I will call[7121] for a sword upon all the inhabitants of the earth, saith the LORD of hosts.

30 Therefore prophesy[5012] thou against them all these words, and say unto them, The LORD shall [a]roar from on high, and utter his voice from [b]his holy[6944] habitation; he shall mightily roar upon [c]his habitation; he shall give [d]a shout, as they that tread *the grapes,* against all the inhabitants of the earth.

31 A noise[7588] shall come *even* to the ends of the earth; for the LORD hath [a]a controversy[7379] with the nations, [b]he will plead[8199] with all flesh;[1320] he will give them *that are* wicked[7563] to the sword, saith the LORD.

32 Thus saith the LORD of hosts, Behold, evil shall go forth from nation to nation, and [a]a great whirlwind shall be raised up from the coasts of the earth.

33 [a]And the slain[2491] of the LORD shall be at that day from *one* end of the earth even unto the *other* end of the earth: they shall not be [b]lamented, [c]neither gathered, nor buried;[6912] they shall be dung upon the ground.[127]

34 [a]Howl, ye shepherds, and cry;[2199] and wallow yourselves *in the ashes,* ye principal[117] of the flock: for [I]the days[3117] of your slaughter[2873] and of your dispersions are accomplished; and ye shall fall like [II][a]a pleasant vessel.

35 And [I][a]the shepherds shall have no way to flee, nor the principal of the flock to escape.[6413]

36 A voice of the cry of the shepherds, and an howling of the principal of the flock, *shall be heard:* for the LORD hath spoiled[7703] their pasture.

37 And the peaceable habitations are cut down because of the fierce anger[639] of the LORD.

38 He hath forsaken[5800] [a]his covert,[5520] as the lion: for their land is [I]desolate[8047] because of the fierceness of the oppressor,[3238] and because of his fierce anger.

Jeremiah on Trial

26 In the beginning[7225] of the reign[4468] of Jehoiakim the son of Josiah king[4428] of Judah came this word[1697] from the LORD, saying,

2 Thus saith[559] the LORD; Stand in [a]the court of the LORD's house, and speak[1696] unto all the cities of Judah, which come to worship[7812] in the LORD's house,[1004] [b]all the words[1697] that I command[6680] thee to speak unto them; [c]diminish not a word:

3 [a]If so be they will hearken,[8085] and turn[7725] every man from his evil[7451] way,[1870] that I may [b]repent[5162] me of the evil, which I purpose[2803] to do unto them because of the evil[7455] of their doings.

🔑 4 And thou shalt say unto them, Thus saith the LORD; [a]If ye will not hearken to me, to walk in my law,[8451] which I have set before you,

5 To hearken to the words of my servants[5650] the prophets,[5030] [a]whom I sent unto you, both rising up early, and sending *them,* but ye have not hearkened;[8085]

6 Then will I make this house like [a]Shiloh, and will make this city

26 [b]Jer. 51:41
27 [a]Hab. 2:16 [b]Isa. 51:21; 63:6
29 [I]Hebr. *upon which my name is called* [a]Prov. 11:31; Jer. 49:12; Ezek. 9:6; Obad. 1:16; Luke 23:31; 1Pet. 4:17 [b]Dan. 9:18, 19 [c]Ezek. 38:21
30 [a]Isa. 42:13; Joel 3:16; Amos 1:2 [b]Ps. 11:4; Jer. 17:12 [c]1Kgs. 9:3; Ps. 132:14 [d]Isa. 16:9; Jer. 48:33
31 [a]Hos. 4:1; Mic. 6:2 [b]Isa. 66:16; Joel 3:2
32 [a]Jer. 23:19; 30:23
33 [a]Isa. 66:16 [b]Jer. 16:4, 6 [c]Ps. 79:3; Jer. 8:2; Rev. 11:9
34 [I]Hebr. *your days for slaughter* [II]Hebr. *a vessel of desire* [a]Jer. 4:8; 6:26
35 [I]Hebr. *flight shall perish from the shepherds, and escaping from* [a]Amos 2:14
38 [I]Hebr. *a desolation* [a]Ps. 76:2
2 [a]Jer. 19:14 [b]Ezek. 3:10; Matt. 28:20 [c]Acts 20:27
3 [a]Jer. 36:3 [b]Jer. 18:8; Jon. 3:8, 9
4 [a]Lev. 26:14; Deut. 28:15
5 [a]Jer. 7:13, 25; 11:7; 25:3, 4
6 [a]1Sam. 4:10, 11; Ps. 78:60; Jer. 7:12, 14

🔑 **26:4–9** See note on Jeremiah 7:2–15.

[b]a curse[7045] to all the nations[1471] of the earth.[776]

7 So the priests[3548] and the prophets and all the people[5971] heard[8085] Jeremiah speaking these words in the house of the LORD.

8 Now it came to pass, when Jeremiah had made an end[3615] of speaking all that the LORD had commanded[6680] *him* to speak unto all the people, that the priests and the prophets and all the people took him, saying, Thou shalt surely die.[4191]

9 Why hast thou prophesied[5012] in the name of the LORD, saying, This house shall be like Shiloh, and this city shall be desolate[2717] without an inhabitant? And all the people were gathered[6950] against Jeremiah in the house of the LORD.

10 When the princes[8269] of Judah heard these things,[1697] then they came up[5927] from the king's[4428] house unto the house of the LORD, and sat down [I]in the entry of the new gate of the LORD'S *house*.

11 Then spake the priests and the prophets unto the princes and to all the people, saying, [I]This man *is* worthy to die;[4194] [a]for he hath prophesied against this city, as ye have heard with your ears.[241]

12 Then spake Jeremiah unto all the princes and to all the people, saying, The LORD sent me to prophesy[5012] against this house and against this city all the words that ye have heard.

13 Therefore now [a]amend[3190] your ways[1870] and your doings, and obey[8085] the voice of the LORD your God;[430] and the LORD will [b]repent him of the evil that he hath pronounced against you.

14 As for me, behold, [a]I *am* in your hand:[3027] do with me [I]as seemeth good[2896] and meet unto you.

15 But know[3045] ye for certain, that if ye put me to death,[4191] ye shall surely bring innocent[5355] blood[1818] upon yourselves, and upon this city, and upon the inhabitants thereof: for of a truth[571] the LORD hath sent me unto you to speak all these words in your ears.

16 Then said the princes and all the people unto the priests and to the prophets; This man *is* not worthy to die: for he hath spoken to us in the name of the LORD our God.

17 [a]Then rose up certain[582] of the elders[2205] of the land,[776] and spake to all the assembly[6951] of the people, saying,

18 [a]Micah the Morasthite prophesied in the days[3117] of Hezekiah king of Judah, and spake to all the people of Judah, saying, Thus saith the LORD of hosts;[6635] [b]Zion shall be plowed *like* a field,[7704] and Jerusalem shall become[1961] heaps, and the mountain of the house as the high places[1116] of a forest.

19 Did Hezekiah king of Judah and all Judah put him at all to death? [a]did he not fear the LORD, and besought [I]the LORD, and the LORD [b]repented[5162] him of the evil which he had pronounced against them? [c]Thus might we procure[6213] great evil against our souls.[5315]

20 And there was also a man that prophesied in the name of the LORD, Urijah the son of Shemaiah of Kirjath–jearim, who prophesied against this city and against this land according to all the words of Jeremiah:

21 And when Jehoiakim the king, with all his mighty men, and all the princes, heard his words, the king sought to put him to death: but when Urijah heard it, he was afraid,[3372] and fled, and went into Egypt;

22 And Jehoiakim the king sent men[582] into Egypt, *namely,* Elnathan the son of Achbor, and *certain* men with him into Egypt.

23 And they fetched forth Urijah out of Egypt, and brought him unto Jehoiakim the king; who slew[5221] him with the sword,[2719] and cast his dead body[5038] into the graves[6913] of the [I]common people.

24 Nevertheless [a]the hand of Ahikam the son of Shaphan was with Jeremiah, that they should not give him into the hand of the people to put him to death.

6 [b]Isa. 65:15; Jer. 24:9

10 [I]Or, *at the door*

11 [I]Hebr. *The judgment of death is for this man* [a]Jer. 38:4

13 [a]Jer. 7:3 [b]Jer. 26:3, 19

14 [I]Hebr. *as it is good and right in your eyes* [a]Jer. 38:5

17 [a]Acts 5:34

18 [a]Mic. 1:1 [b]Mic. 3:12

19 [I]Hebr. *the face of the LORD* [a]2Chr. 32:26 [b]Ex. 32:14; 2Sam. 24:16 [c]Acts 5:39

23 [I]Hebr. *sons of the people*

24 [a]2Kgs. 22:12, 14; Jer. 39:14

The Command to Serve Nebuchadnezzar

27 In the beginning[7225] of the reign of Jehoiakim the son of Josiah [a]king[4428] of Judah came this word unto Jeremiah from the LORD, saying,

2 Thus [I]saith the LORD to me; Make thee bonds and yokes, [a]and put them upon thy neck,

3 And send them to the king of Edom, and to the king of Moab, and to the king of the Ammonites, and to the king of Tyrus, and to the king of Zidon, by the hand[3027] of the messengers which come to Jerusalem unto Zedekiah king of Judah;

4 And command[6680] them [I]to say unto their masters,[113] Thus saith the LORD of hosts,[6635] the God[430] of Israel; Thus shall ye say unto your masters;

5 [a]I have made the earth,[776] the man[120] and the beast that *are* upon the ground,[776] by my great power and by my outstretched arm, and [b]have given it unto whom it seemed meet unto me.

6 [a]And now have I given all these lands[776] into the hand of Nebuchadnezzar the king of Babylon, [b]my servant;[5650] and [c]the beasts[2416] of the field[7704] have I given him also to serve[5647] him.

7 [a]And all nations[1471] shall serve him, and his son, and his son's son, [b]until the very time[6256] of his land come: [c]and then many nations and great kings[4428] shall serve themselves of him.

8 And it shall come to pass, *that* the nation[1471] and kingdom[4467] which will not serve the same Nebuchadnezzar the king of Babylon, and that will not put their neck under the yoke of the king of Babylon, that nation will I punish,[6485] saith[5002] the LORD, with the sword,[2719] and with the famine, and with the pestilence,[1698] until I have consumed[8552] them by his hand.

9 Therefore hearken[8085] not ye to your prophets,[5030] nor to your diviners,[7080] nor to your [I]dreamers, nor to your enchanters,[6049] nor to your sorcerers,[3786] which speak[559] unto you, saying, Ye shall not serve the king of Babylon:

10 [a]For they prophesy[5012] a lie unto you, to remove you far from your land;[127] and that I should drive you out, and ye should perish.[6]

11 But the nations that bring their neck under the yoke of the king of Babylon, and serve him, those will I let remain still in their own land, saith the LORD; and they shall till it, and dwell therein.

12 I spake[1696] also to [a]Zedekiah king of Judah according to all these words,[1697] saying, Bring your necks under the yoke of the king of Babylon, and serve him and his people,[5971] and live.[2421]

13 [a]Why will ye die,[4191] thou and thy people, by the sword, by the famine, and by the pestilence, as the LORD hath spoken against the nation that will not serve the king of Babylon?

14 Therefore hearken not unto the words of the prophets that speak unto you, saying, Ye shall not serve the king of Babylon: for they prophesy [a]a lie unto you.

15 For I have not sent them, saith the LORD, yet they prophesy [I]a lie in my name; that I might drive you out, and that ye might perish, ye, and the prophets that prophesy unto you.

16 Also I spake to the priests[3548] and to all this people, saying, Thus saith the LORD; Hearken not to the words of your prophets that prophesy unto you, saying, Behold, [a]the vessels of the LORD's house[1004] shall now shortly be brought again[7725] from Babylon: for they prophesy a lie unto you.

17 Hearken not unto them; serve the king of Babylon, and live: wherefore should this city be laid waste?[2723]

18 But if they *be* prophets, and if the word of the LORD be with them, let them now make intercession to the LORD of hosts, that the vessels which are left[3498] in the house of the LORD, and *in* the house of the king of Judah, and at Jerusalem, go not to Babylon.

19 For thus saith the LORD of hosts [a]concerning the pillars, and concerning

1 [a]Jer. 27:3, 12, 20; 28:1

2 [I]Or, *hath the LORD said* [a]Jer. 28:10, 12; Ezek. 4:1; 12:3; 24:3

4 [I]Or, *concerning their masters, saying*

5 [a]Ps. 115:15; 146:6; Isa. 45:12 [b]Ps. 115:16; Dan. 4:17, 25, 32

6 [a]Jer. 28:14 [b]Jer. 25:9; 43:10; Ezek. 29:18, 20 [c]Jer. 28:14; Dan. 2:38

7 [a]2Chr. 36:20 [b]Ezek. 25:12; 50:27; Dan. 5:26 [c]Ezek. 25:14

9 [I]Hebr. *dreams*

10 [a]Jer. 27:14

12 [a]Jer. 28:1; 38:17

13 [a]Ezek. 18:31

14 [a]Jer. 14:14; 23:21; 29:8, 9

15 [I]Hebr. *in a lie,* or, *lyingly*

16 [a]2Chr. 36:7, 10; Jer. 28:3; Dan. 1:2

19 [a]2Kgs. 25:13; Jer. 52:17, 20, 21

the sea, and concerning the bases, and concerning the residue[3499] of the vessels that remain[3498] in this city,

20 Which Nebuchadnezzar king of Babylon took not, when he carried away [a]captive[1540] Jeconiah the son of Jehoiakim king of Judah from Jerusalem to Babylon, and all the nobles[2715] of Judah and Jerusalem;

21 Yea, thus saith the LORD of hosts, the God of Israel, concerning the vessels that remain *in* the house of the LORD, and *in* the house of the king of Judah and of Jerusalem;

22 They shall be [a]carried to Babylon, and there shall they be until the day[3117] that I [b]visit[6485] them, saith the LORD; then [c]will I bring them up, and restore[7725] them to this place.

Hananiah's False Prophecy

28 And [a]it came to pass the same year, in the beginning[7225] of the reign of Zedekiah king[4428] of Judah, in the fourth year, *and* in the fifth month, *that* Hananiah the son of Azur the prophet,[5030] which *was* of Gibeon, spake unto me in the house[1004] of the LORD, in the presence of the priests[3548] and of all the people,[5971] saying,

2 Thus speaketh the LORD of hosts,[6635] the God[430] of Israel, saying, I have broken[7665] [a]the yoke of the king of Babylon.

3 [a]Within [I]two full years will I bring again[7725] into this place all the vessels of the LORD's house, that Nebuchadnezzar king of Babylon took away from this place, and carried them to Babylon:

4 And I will bring again to this place Jeconiah the son of Jehoiakim king of Judah, with all the [I]captives[1546] of Judah, that went into Babylon, saith[5002] the LORD: for I will break[7665] the yoke of the king of Babylon.

5 Then the prophet Jeremiah said[559] unto the prophet Hananiah in the presence of the priests, and in the presence of all the people that stood in the house of the LORD,

6 Even the prophet Jeremiah said, [a]Amen:[543] the LORD do so: the LORD perform thy words which thou hast prophesied,[5012] to bring again the vessels of the LORD's house, and all that is carried away captive, from Babylon into this place.

7 Nevertheless hear[8085] thou now this word[1697] that I speak[1696] in thine ears,[241] and in the ears of all the people;

🔑 8 The prophets[5030] that have been before me and before thee of old[5769] prophesied both against many countries,[776] and against great kingdoms,[4467] of war, and of evil,[7451] and of pestilence.[1698]

9 [a]The prophet which prophesieth[5012] of peace, when the word of the prophet shall come to pass, *then* shall the prophet be known,[3045] that the LORD hath truly[571] sent him.

10 Then Hananiah the prophet took the [a]yoke from off the prophet Jeremiah's neck, and brake[7665] it.

11 And Hananiah spake in the presence of all the people, saying, Thus saith the LORD; Even so will I break the yoke of Nebuchadnezzar king of Babylon [a]from the neck of all nations[1471] within the space of two full years. And the prophet Jeremiah went his way.[1870]

12 Then the word of the LORD came unto Jeremiah *the prophet,* after that Hananiah the prophet had broken the yoke from off the neck of the prophet Jeremiah, saying,

13 Go and tell Hananiah, saying, Thus saith the LORD; Thou hast broken the yokes of wood; but thou shalt make for them yokes of iron.

14 For thus saith the LORD of hosts, the God of Israel; [a]I have put a yoke of iron upon the neck of all these nations, that they may serve[5647] Nebuchadnezzar king of Babylon; and they shall serve him: and [b]I have given him the beasts[2416] of the field[7704] also.

20 [a]2Kgs. 24:14, 15; Jer. 24:1
22 [a]2Kgs. 25:13; 2Chr. 36:18 [b]2Chr. 36:21; Jer. 29:10; 32:5 [c]Ezra 1:7; 7:19
1 [a]Jer. 27:1
2 [a]Jer. 27:12
3 [I]Hebr. *two years of days* [a]Jer. 27:16
4 [I]Hebr. *captivity*
6 [a]1Kgs. 1:36
9 [a]Deut. 18:22
10 [a]Jer. 27:2
11 [a]Jer. 27:7
14 [a]Deut. 28:48; Jer. 27:7 [b]Jer. 27:6

🔑 **28:8, 9, 16** See note on Deuteronomy 18:20–22.

15 Then said the prophet Jeremiah
unto Hananiah the prophet, Hear now,
Hananiah; The LORD hath not sent thee;
but [a]thou makest this people to trust[982]
in a lie.
🔑 16 Therefore thus saith the LORD;
Behold, I will cast thee from off the face
of the earth:[127] this year thou shalt die,
because thou hast taught [I][a]rebellion[5627]
against the LORD.
17 So Hananiah the prophet died the
same year in the seventh month.

Jeremiah's Letter to The Captives

29 🔑Now these *are* the words[1697]
of the letter[5612] that Jeremiah the
prophet[5030] sent from Jerusalem unto the
residue[3499] of the elders[2205] which were
carried away captives,[1473] and to the
priests,[3548] and to the prophets,[5030] and to
all the people[5971] whom Nebuchadnezzar
had carried away captive[1540] from Jerusalem to Babylon;
2 (After that [a]Jeconiah the king,[4428]
and the queen, and the [I]eunuchs,[5631] the
princes[8269] of Judah and Jerusalem, and
the carpenters, and the smiths, were departed from Jerusalem;)
3 By the hand[3027] of Elasah the son
of Shaphan, and Gemariah the son of
Hilkiah, (whom Zedekiah king of Judah
sent unto Babylon to Nebuchadnezzar
king of Babylon) saying,
4 Thus saith the LORD of hosts,[6635]
the God[430] of Israel, unto all that are carried away captives, whom I have caused
to be carried away[1540] from Jerusalem
unto Babylon;
5 [a]Build ye houses,[1004] and dwell *in
them;* and plant gardens, and eat the fruit
of them;
6 Take ye wives,[802] and beget sons
and daughters; and take wives for your
sons, and give your daughters to husbands,[582] that they may bear sons and
daughters; that ye may be increased
there, and not diminished.
7 And seek the peace of the city
whither I have caused you to be carried
away captives, [a]and pray[6419] unto the
LORD for it: for in the peace thereof shall
ye have peace.
8 For thus saith the LORD of hosts,
the God of Israel; Let not your prophets
and your diviners,[7080] that *be* in the
midst[7130] of you, [a]deceive you, neither
hearken[8085] to your dreams which ye
cause to be dreamed.
9 [a]For they prophesy[5012] [I]falsely[8267]
unto you in my name: I have not sent
them, saith the LORD.
10 For thus saith the LORD, That
after [a]seventy years be accomplished[4390]
at Babylon I will visit[6485] you, and perform[6965] my good[2896] word[1697] toward
you, in causing you to return[7725] to this
place.
11 For I know[3045] the thoughts[4284]
that I think[2803] toward you, saith the LORD,
thoughts of peace, and not of evil,[7451] to
give you an [I]expected[8615] end.[319]
12 Then shall ye [a]call[7121] upon me,
and ye shall go and pray unto me, and I
will hearken unto you.

15 [a]Jer. 29:31; Ezek. 13:22
16 [I]Hebr. *revolt* [a]Deut. 13:5; Jer. 29:32
2 [I]Or, *chamberlains* [a]2Kgs. 24:12; Jer. 22:26; 28:4
5 [a]Jer. 29:28
7 [a]Ezra 6:10; 1Tim. 2:2
8 [a]Jer. 14:14; 23:21; 27:14, 15; Eph. 5:6
9 [I]Hebr. *in a lie* [a]Jer. 29:31
10 [a]2Chr. 36:21, 22; Ezra 1:1; Jer. 25:12; 27:22; Dan. 9:2
11 [I]Hebr. *end and expectation*
12 [a]Dan. 9:3

🔑 **29:1–32** This chapter records an ongoing correspondence between Jeremiah in Jerusalem and the exiles in Babylon. It reveals that the ones who were exiled were encouraged by false prophets (Jer. 28:2–4, 10, 11; 29:21, 25–31) and had refused to accept Jeremiah's earlier word (Jer. 25:11). They were living as if they were not going be in Babylon the full seventy years. Consequently, Jeremiah reaffirmed that the Exile would last seventy years and challenged the people to accept it and live accordingly. The Lord even told them to pray for His blessing to be upon Babylon (v. 7). This did not mean that they would lose their identity. In fact, over one hundred years later, the Jews were still a distinct element in the Persian Empire (Esth. 3:8).

There are two possibilities presented for the beginning and end of the Seventy Year Exile: either from the first deportation of exiles in 605 B.C. to the return under Zerubbabel in 536 B.C., or from the destruction of the temple in 586 B.C. to its rebuilding in 516 B.C. The time is accounted for in either case. Not only was the seventy years a measure of God's judgment on Israel, it was also the basis for the prophecy of the "seventy weeks of Daniel" (see note on Dan. 9:24–27).

13 And [a]ye shall seek me, and find *me,* when ye shall search for me [b]with all your heart.[3824]

14 And [a]I will be found of you, saith the LORD: and I will turn away[7725] your captivity,[7622] and [b]I will gather[6908] you from all the nations,[1471] and from all the places whither I have driven you, saith the LORD; and I will bring you again into the place whence I caused you to be carried away captive.

15 Because ye have said, The LORD hath raised us up prophets in Babylon;

16 *Know* that thus saith the LORD of the king that sitteth upon the throne[3678] of David, and of all the people that dwelleth in this city, *and* of your brethren[251] that are not gone forth with you into captivity;[1473]

17 Thus saith the LORD of hosts; Behold, I will send upon them the [a]sword,[2719] the famine, and the pestilence,[1698] and will make them like [b]vile[8182] figs, that cannot be eaten, they are so evil.[7455]

18 And I will persecute them with the sword, with the famine, and with the pestilence, and [a]will deliver them to be removed to all the kingdoms[4467] of the earth,[776] [I]to be [b]a curse,[423] and an astonishment,[8047] and an hissing, and a reproach,[2781] among all the nations whither I have driven them:

19 Because they have not hearkened to my words, saith the LORD, which [a]I sent unto them by my servants[5650] the prophets, rising up early and sending *them;* but ye would not hear,[8085] saith the LORD.

20 Hear ye therefore the word of the LORD, all ye of the captivity, whom I have sent from Jerusalem to Babylon:

21 Thus saith the LORD of hosts, the God of Israel, of Ahab the son of Kolaiah, and of Zedekiah the son of Maaseiah, which prophesy a lie unto you in my name; Behold, I will deliver them into the hand of Nebuchadrezzar king of Babylon; and he shall slay[5221] them before your eyes;

22 [a]And of them shall be taken up a curse[7045] by all the captivity[1546] of Judah which *are* in Babylon, saying, The LORD make[7760] thee like Zedekiah and like Ahab, [b]whom the king of Babylon roasted in the fire;

23 Because [a]they have committed[6213] villany[5039] in Israel, and have committed adultery[5003] with their neighbours'[7453] wives, and have spoken lying words in my name, which I have not commanded[6680] them; even I know, and *am* a witness, saith the LORD.

24 *Thus* shalt thou also speak to Shemaiah the [I]Nehelamite, saying,

25 Thus speaketh the LORD of hosts, the God of Israel, saying, Because thou hast sent letters[5612] in thy name unto all the people that *are* at Jerusalem, [a]and to Zephaniah the son of Maaseiah the priest,[3548] and to all the priests, saying,

26 The LORD hath made thee priest in the stead of Jehoiada the priest, that ye should be [a]officers[6496] in the house[1004] of the LORD, for every man *that is* [b]mad,[7696] and maketh himself a prophet,[5012] that thou shouldest [c]put him in prison, and in the stocks.

27 Now therefore why hast thou not reproved Jeremiah of Anathoth, which maketh himself a prophet to you?

28 For therefore he sent unto us *in* Babylon, saying, This *captivity is* long:[752] [a]build ye houses, and dwell *in them;* and plant gardens, and eat the fruit of them.

29 And Zephaniah the priest read[7121] this letter in the ears[241] of Jeremiah the prophet.

30 Then came the word of the LORD unto Jeremiah, saying,

31 Send to all them of the captivity, saying, Thus saith the LORD concerning Shemaiah the Nehelamite; Because that Shemaiah hath prophesied[5012] unto you, [a]and I sent him not, and he caused you to trust[982] in a lie:

32 Therefore thus saith the LORD; Behold,[7200] I will punish[6485] Shemaiah the Nehelamite, and his seed:[2233] he shall not have a man to dwell among this people; neither shall he behold the good that I will do for my people, saith the LORD; [a]because he hath taught [I]rebellion[5627] against the LORD.

13 [a]Lev. 26:39, 40; Deut. 30:1 [b]Jer. 24:7

14 [a]Deut. 4:7; Ps. 32:6; 46:1; Isa. 55:6 [b]Jer. 23:3, 8; 30:3; 32:37

17 [a]Jer. 24:10 [b]Jer. 24:8

18 [I]Hebr. *for a curse* [a]Deut. 28:25; 2Chr. 29:8; 15:4; 24:9; 34:17 [b]Jer. 26:6; Jer. 42:18

19 [a]Jer. 25:4; 32:33

22 [a]Gen. 48:20; Isa. 65:15 [b]Dan. 3:6

23 [a]Jer. 23:14

24 [I]Or, *dreamer*

25 [a]2Kgs. 25:18; Jer. 21:1

26 [a]Jer. 20:1 [b]2Kgs. 9:11; Acts 26:24 [c]Jer. 20:2

28 [a]Jer. 29:5

31 [a]Jer. 28:15

32 [I]Hebr. *revolt* [a]Jer. 28:16

Israel Will Return to the Land

30 The word that came to Jeremiah from the LORD, saying,

2 Thus speaketh the LORD God[430] of Israel, saying, Write thee all the words[1697] that I have spoken[1696] unto thee in a book.[5612]

🔑 3 For, lo, the days[3117] come, saith[5002] the LORD, that [a]I will bring again[7725] the captivity[7622] of my people[5971] Israel and Judah, saith[559] the LORD: [b]and I will cause them to return[7725] to the land[776] that I gave to their fathers,[1] and they shall possess[3423] it.

4 And these *are* the words that the LORD spake concerning Israel and concerning Judah.

5 For thus saith the LORD; We have heard[8085] a voice of trembling,[2731] [1]of fear, and not of peace.

6 Ask[7592] ye now, and see whether [1]a man[2145] doth travail with child? wherefore do I see every man[1397] with his hands[3027] on his loins, [a]as a woman in travail, and all faces are turned[2015] into paleness?

7 [a]Alas! for that day[3117] *is* great, [b]so that none *is* like it: it *is* even the time[6256] of Jacob's trouble; but he shall be saved[3467] out of it.

8 For it shall come to pass in that day, saith the LORD of hosts,[6635] *that* I will break[7665] his yoke from off thy neck, and will burst[5423] thy bonds,[4147] and strangers[2114] shall no more serve[5647] themselves of him:

9 But they shall serve the LORD their God, and [a]David their king,[4428] whom I will [b]raise up unto them.

10 Therefore [a]fear[3372] thou not, O my servant[5650] Jacob, saith the LORD; neither be dismayed,[2865] O Israel: for, lo, I will save[3467] thee from afar, and thy seed[2233] [b]from the land of their captivity; and Jacob shall return, and shall be in rest,[8252] and be quiet, and none shall make *him* afraid.[2729]

11 For I *am* with thee, saith the LORD, to save thee: [a]though I make a full end[3617] of all nations[1471] whither I have scattered thee, [b]yet will I not make a full end of thee: but I will correct[3256] thee [c]in measure,[4941] and will not leave thee altogether unpunished.[5352]

12 For thus saith the LORD, [a]Thy bruise[7667] *is* incurable, *and* thy wound[4347] *is* grievous.

13 *There is* none to plead[1777] thy cause,[1779] [1]that thou mayest be bound up: [a]thou hast no healing medicines.

14 [a]All thy lovers[157] have forgotten thee; they seek thee not; for I have wounded[5221] thee with the wound [b]of an enemy, with the chastisement[4148] [c]of a cruel one, for the multitude of thine iniquity;[5771] [d]*because* thy sins were increased.

15 Why [a]criest thou for thine affliction?[7667] thy sorrow *is* incurable for the multitude of thine iniquity: *because* thy sins were increased, I have done these things unto thee.

16 Therefore all they that devour thee [a]shall be devoured; and all thine adversaries, every one of them, shall go into captivity;[7628] and they that spoil[7701] thee shall be a spoil, and all that prey upon thee will I give for a prey.

17 [a]For I will restore[5927] health[724] unto thee, and I will heal thee of thy wounds,[4347] saith the LORD; because they

3 [a]Jer. 29:18; 32:44; Ezek. 39:25; Amos 9:14, 15 [b]Jer. 16:15
5 [1]Or, there is *fear, and not peace*
6 [1]Hebr. *a male* [a]Jer. 4:31; 6:24
7 [a]Joel 2:11, 31; Amos 5:18; Zeph. 1:14 [b]Dan. 12:1
9 [a]Isa. 55:3, 4; Ezek. 34:23; 37:24; Hos. 3:5 [b]Luke 1:69; Acts 2:30; 13:23
10 [a]Isa. 41:13; 43:5; 44:2; Jer. 46:27, 28 [b]Jer. 3:18
11 [a]Amos 9:8 [b]Jer. 4:27 [c]Ps. 6:1; Isa. 27:8; Jer. 10:24; 46:28
12 [a]2Chr. 36:16; Jer. 15:18
13 [1]Hebr. *for binding up*, or, *pressing* [a]Jer. 8:22
14 [a]Lam. 1:2 [b]Job 13:24; 16:9; 19:11 [c]Job 30:21 [d]Jer. 5:6
15 [a]Jer. 15:18
16 [a]Ex. 23:22; Isa. 33:1; 41:11; Jer. 10:25
17 [a]Jer. 33:6

🔑 **30:3—31:26** This passage is a promise not only of the Israelites' return from exile, but of their ultimate restoration (31:12). However, before the time of this blessing will come the Great Tribulation, described here as "the time of Jacob's trouble" (30:7). This will be brought about because of Israel's sin (30:11–15), but ultimately "he shall be saved out of it" (30:7). Following this trouble will be the reign of the Messiah (30:9, 21), The manifestation of God's "everlasting love" (31:3) will be seen in His rebuilding of the nation (30:17–20; 31:4–7, 28, cf. Jer. 1:10b). Within this interaction of judgment and blessing is the prophecy of the mourning of Jerusalem's fall, as well as Herod's slaughter of the infants (31:15, cf. Matt. 2:18). There is a note of comfort, nevertheless (30:16, 17), because the whole scene is eschatological, forming the setting for the announcement of the New Covenant (see note on Jer. 31:31–34).

called[7121] thee an Outcast,5080 *saying,* This *is* Zion, whom no man seeketh after.

18 Thus saith the LORD; Behold, [a]I will bring again the captivity of Jacob's tents,[168] and [b]have mercy[7355] on his dwellingplaces; and the city shall be builded upon her own [I]heap, and the palace[759] shall remain after the manner[4941] thereof.

19 And [a]out of them shall proceed thanksgiving[8426] and the voice of them that make merry: [b]and I will multiply them, and they shall not be few; I will also glorify[3513] them, and they shall not be small.

20 Their children[1121] also shall be [a]as aforetime,[6924] and their congregation[5712] shall be established[3559] before me, and I will punish[6485] all that oppress them.

21 And their nobles[117] shall be of themselves, [a]and their governor shall proceed from the midst[7130] of them; and I will [b]cause him to draw near,[7126] and he shall approach[5066] unto me: for who *is* this that engaged his heart[3820] to approach unto me? saith the LORD.

22 And ye shall be [a]my people, and I will be your God.

23 Behold, the [a]whirlwind of the LORD[3068] goeth forth with fury,[2534] a [I]continuing[1641] whirlwind: it shall [II]fall with pain[2342] upon the head[7218] of the wicked.[7563]

24 The fierce anger[639] of the LORD shall not return, until he have done *it,* and until he have performed the intents[4209] of his heart: [a]in the latter[319] days ye shall consider[995] it.

A Happy Return

31 At [a]the same time,[6256] saith5002 the LORD, [b]will I be the God[430] of all the families[4940] of Israel, and they shall be my people.[5971]

2 Thus saith[559] the LORD, The people *which were* left[8300] of the sword[2719] found grace[2580] in the wilderness; *even* Israel, when [a]I went to cause him to rest.

3 The LORD hath appeared[7200] [I]of old unto me, *saying,* Yea, [a]I have loved[157] thee with [b]an everlasting[5769] love:[160] therefore [II]with lovingkindness[2617] have I [c]drawn thee.

4 Again [a]I will build thee, and thou shalt be built, O virgin[1330] of Israel: thou shalt again be adorned5710 with thy [I][b]tabrets,8596 and shalt go forth in the dances of them that make merry.

5 [a]Thou shalt yet plant vines upon the mountains of Samaria: the planters shall plant, and shall [I][b]eat *them* as common things.

6 For there shall be a day,[3117] *that* the watchman[5341] upon the mount Ephraim shall cry,[7121] [a]Arise ye, and let us go up to Zion unto the LORD our God.

7 For thus saith the LORD; [a]Sing with gladness for Jacob, and shout among the chief[7218] of the nations:[1471] publish[8085] ye, praise[1984] ye, and say,[559] O LORD, save[3467] thy people, the remnant[7611] of Israel.

8 Behold, I will bring them [a]from the north country,[776] and [b]gather[6908] them from the coasts of the earth,[776] *and* with them the blind and the lame, the woman with child and her that travaileth with child3205 together: a great company[6951] shall return[7725] thither.

9 [a]They shall come with weeping, and with [I][b]supplications[8469] will I lead them: I will cause them to walk [c]by the rivers of waters in a straight[3477] way,[1870] wherein they shall not stumble:[3782] for I am a father[1] to Israel, and Ephraim *is* my [d]firstborn.

10 Hear[8085] the word[1697] of the LORD, O ye nations, and declare[5046] *it* in the isles afar off, and say, He that scattered Israel [a]will gather him, and keep[8104] him, as a shepherd *doth* his flock.

11 For [a]the LORD hath redeemed[6299] Jacob, and ransomed[1350] him [b]from the hand[3027] of *him that was* stronger than he.

12 Therefore they shall come and sing in [a]the height of Zion, and shall flow together to [b]the goodness of the LORD, for wheat, and for wine, and for oil,[3323] and for the young[1121] of the flock and of the herd: and their soul[5315] shall be as a

18 [I]Or, *little hill* [a]Jer. 30:3; 33:7, 11 [b]Ps. 102:13
19 [a]Isa. 35:10; 51:11; Jer. 31:4, 12, 13; 33:10, 11 [b]Zech. 10:8
20 [a]Isa. 1:26
21 [a]Gen. 49:10 [b]Num. 16:5
22 [a]Jer. 24:7; 31:1, 33; 32:38; Ezek. 11:20; 36:28; 37:27
23 [I]Hebr. *cutting* [II]Or, *remain* [a]Jer. 23:19, 20; 25:32
24 [a]Gen. 49:1

1 [a]Jer. 30:24 [b]Jer. 30:22
2 [a]Num. 10:33; Deut. 1:33; Ps. 95:11; Isa. 63:14
3 [I]Hebr. *from afar* [II]Or, *have I extended lovingkindness unto thee* [a]Mal. 1:2 [b]Rom. 11:28, 29 [c]Hos. 11:4
4 [I]Or, *timbrels* [a]Jer. 33:7 [b]Ex. 15:20; Judg. 11:34; Ps. 149:3
5 [I]Hebr. *profane* [a]Isa. 65:21; Amos 9:14 [b]Deut. 20:6; 28:30
6 [a]Isa. 2:3; Mic. 4:2
7 [a]Isa. 12:5, 6
8 [a]Jer. 3:12, 18; 23:8 [b]Ezek. 20:34, 41; 34:13
9 [I]Or, *favors* [a]Ps. 126:5, 6; Jer. 50:4 [b]Zech. 12:10 [c]Isa. 35:8; 43:19; 49:10, 11 [d]Ex. 4:22
10 [a]Isa. 40:11; Ezek. 34:12-14
11 [a]Isa. 44:23; 48:20 [b]Isa. 49:24, 25
12 [a]Ezek. 17:23; 20:40 [b]Hos. 3:5

[c]watered garden; [d]and they shall not sorrow any more at all.

13 Then shall the virgin rejoice in the dance, both young men and old[2205] together: for I will turn[7725] their mourning into joy, and will comfort[5162] them, and make them rejoice from their sorrow.

14 And I will satiate[7301] the soul of the priests[3548] with fatness, and my people shall be satisfied with my goodness, saith the LORD.

God's Mercy

15 Thus saith the LORD; [a]A voice was heard[8085] in [b]Ramah, lamentation, *and* bitter weeping; Rachel weeping for her children[1121] refused[3985] to be comforted[5162] for her children, because [c]they *were* not.

16 Thus saith the LORD; Refrain thy voice from weeping, and thine eyes from tears: for thy work shall be rewarded, saith the LORD; and [a]they shall come again from the land[776] of the enemy.

17 And there is hope in thine end,[319] saith the LORD, that thy children shall come again to their own border.

18 I have surely heard Ephraim bemoaning himself *thus;* Thou hast chastised[3256] me, and I was chastised, as a bullock unaccustomed *to the yoke:* [a]turn[7725] thou me, and I shall be turned; for thou *art* the LORD my God.

19 Surely [a]after that I was turned, I repented;[5162] and after that I was instructed, I smote[5606] upon *my* thigh:[3409] I was ashamed,[954] yea, even confounded, because I did bear[5375] the reproach[2781] of my youth.

20 *Is* Ephraim my dear son?[1121] *is he* a pleasant child? for since I spake against him, I do earnestly remember[2142] him still: [a]therefore my bowels[4578] [I]are troubled for him; [b]I will surely have mercy[7355] upon him, saith the LORD.

21 Set thee up[5324] waymarks,[6725] make[7760] thee high heaps: [a]set thine heart[3820] toward the highway, *even* the way *which* thou wentest: turn again, O virgin of Israel, turn again[7725] to these thy cities.

22 How long wilt thou [a]go about, O thou [b]backsliding[7728] daughter? for the LORD hath created[1254] a new thing in the earth, A woman[5347] shall compass[5437] a man.[1397]

23 Thus saith the LORD of hosts,[6635] the God of Israel; As yet they shall use this speech[1697] in the land of Judah and in the cities thereof, when I shall bring again[7725] their captivity;[7622] [a]The LORD bless[1288] thee, O habitation of justice,[6664] *and* [b]mountain of holiness.

24 And there shall dwell in Judah itself, and [a]in all the cities thereof together, husbandmen,[406] and they *that* go forth with flocks.

25 For I have satiated the weary soul, and I have replenished every sorrowful soul.

26 Upon this I awaked, and beheld;[7200] and my sleep was sweet[6148] unto me.

The New Covenant

27 Behold, the days[3117] come, saith the LORD, that [a]I will sow the house of Israel and the house[1004] of Judah with the seed[2233] of man,[120] and with the seed of beast.

28 And it shall come to pass, *that* like as I have [a]watched over them, [b]to pluck up, and to break down, and to throw down,[2040] and to destroy,[6] and to afflict; so will I watch over them, [c]to build, and to plant, saith the LORD.

🔑 29 [a]In those days they shall say no more, The fathers[1] have eaten a sour grape, and the children's teeth are set on edge.

30 [a]But every one shall die[4191] for his own iniquity:[5771] every man that eateth the sour grape, his teeth shall be set on edge.

12 [c]Isa. 58:11 [d]Isa. 35:10; 65:19; Rev. 21:4
15 [a]Matt. 2:17, 18 [b]Josh. 18:25 [c]Gen. 42:13
16 [a]Jer. 31:4, 5; Ezra 1:5; Hos. 1:11
18 [a]Lam. 5:21
19 [a]Deut. 30:2
20 [I]Hebr. *sound* [a]Deut. 32:36; Isa. 63:15; Hos. 11:8 [b]Isa. 57:18; Hos. 14:4
21 [a]Jer. 50:5
22 [a]Jer. 2:18, 23, 36 [b]Jer. 3:6, 8, 11, 12, 14, 22
23 [a]Ps. 122:5-8; Isa. 1:26 [b]Zech. 8:3
24 [a]Jer. 33:12, 13
27 [a]Ezek. 36:9-11; Hos. 2:23; Zech. 10:9
28 [a]Jer. 44:27 [b]Jer. 1:10; 18:7 [c]Jer. 24:6
29 [a]Ezek. 18:2, 3
30 [a]Gal. 6:5, 7

🔑 **31:29, 30** See note on Ezekiel 18:1–32.

31 Behold, the [a]days come, saith the
LORD, that I will make a new covenant[1285]
with the house of Israel, and with the
house of Judah:
32 Not according to the covenant that
I made[3772] with their fathers in the day
that [a]I took[2388] them by the hand to bring
them out of the land of Egypt; which my
covenant they brake,[6565] [l]although I was
an husband[1166] unto them, saith the
LORD:
33 [a]But this *shall be* the covenant
that I will make with the house of Israel;
After those days, saith the LORD, [b]I will
put my law[8451] in their inward parts,[7130]
and write it in their hearts;[3820] [c]and will
be their God, and they shall be my people.
34 And they shall teach[3925] no more
every man his neighbour,[7453] and every
man his brother,[251] saying, Know[3045] the
LORD: for [a]they shall all know me, from
the least of them unto the greatest of
them, saith the LORD: for [b]I will forgive[5545] their iniquity, and I will remember their sin[2403] no more.
35 Thus saith the LORD, [a]which
giveth the sun for a light[216] by day,[3119]
and the ordinances[2708] of the moon and
of the stars for a light by night,[3915]
which divideth [b]the sea when the waves
thereof roar; [c]The LORD of hosts *is* his
name:
36 [a]If those ordinances depart from
before me, saith the LORD, *then* the seed
of Israel also shall cease[7673] from being
a nation[1471] before me for ever.
37 Thus saith the LORD; [a]If
heaven[8064] above can be measured, and
the foundations[4146] of the earth searched
out beneath, I will also cast off[3988] all the
seed of Israel for all that they have done,
saith the LORD.
38 Behold, the days come, saith the
LORD, that the city shall be built to the
LORD [a]from the tower of Hananeel unto
the gate of the corner.
39 And [a]the measuring line shall
yet go forth over against it upon the
hill Gareb, and shall compass about to
Goath.
40 And the whole valley of the dead
bodies,[6297] and of the ashes, and all the
fields unto the brook of Kidron, [a]unto the
corner of the horse gate toward the east,
[b]*shall be* holy[6944] unto the LORD; it shall
not be plucked up, nor thrown down[2040]
any more for ever.[5769]

31 [a]Jer. 32:40; 33:14; Ezek. 37:26; Heb. 8:8-12; 10:16, 17
32 [l]Or, *should I have continued a husband unto them?* [a]Deut. 1:31
33 [a]Jer. 32:40 [b]Ps. 40:8; Ezek. 11:19, 20; 36:26, 27; 2Cor. 3:3 [c]Jer. 24:7; 30:22; 32:38
34 [a]Isa. 54:13; John 6:45; 1Cor. 2:10; 1John 2:20 [b]Jer. 33:8; 50:20; Mic. 7:18; Acts 10:43; 13:39; Rom. 11:27
35 [a]Gen. 1:16; Ps. 72:5, 17; 89:2, 36, 37; 119:91 [b]Isa. 51:15 [c]Jer. 10:16
36 [a]Ps. 148:6; Isa. 54:9, 10 [b]Jer. 33:20
37 [a]Jer. 33:22
38 [a]Neh. 3:1; Zech. 14:10
39 [a]Ezek. 40:8; Zech. 2:1
40 [a]2Chr. 23:15; Neh. 3:28 [b]Joel 3:17

1 [a]2Kgs. 25:1, 2; Jer. 39:1
2 [a]Neh. 3:25; Jer. 33:1; 37:21; 38:6; 39:14
3 [a]Jer. 34:2
4 [a]Jer. 34:3; 38:18, 23; 39:5; 52:9

Jeremiah Buys a Field

32 The word[1697] that came to
Jeremiah from the LORD [a]in the
tenth year of Zedekiah king[4428] of Judah,
which *was* the eighteenth year of
Nebuchadrezzar.
2 For then the king of Babylon's
army[2428] besieged Jerusalem: and
Jeremiah the prophet[5030] was shut up[3607]
[a]in the court of the prison, which *was* in
the king of Judah's house.[1004]
3 For Zedekiah king of Judah had
shut him up, saying, Wherefore dost thou
prophesy,[5012] and say, Thus saith the
LORD, [a]Behold, I will give this city into
the hand[3027] of the king of Babylon, and
he shall take it;
4 And Zedekiah king of Judah [a]shall
not escape[4422] out of the hand of the
Chaldeans, but shall surely be delivered

31:31–34 This is one of the most important passages in the Old Testament. Here are several specifics concerning this New Covenant: 1) It is a covenant with the whole, reunited nation of Israel, not the Church, which is "grafted in" to Israel's promised covenant (Rom. 11:16–27). 2) The realization of it for the nation of Israel is reserved for the "last days" (cf. 31:27, 31, 38; 32:42; 33:14; Ezek. 37:26; Heb. 8:8). 3) It is based upon the full and eternal atonement secured by Christ's death (31:34b, cf. Matt. 26:26, 27; 1 Cor. 11:25; Heb. 9:15), by which sins are not only forgiven, but God remembers them no more (31:34b). 4) It will be based on an individual, personal knowledge of God and His Law (31:33, 34), which can only be acquired by the indwelling of God's Spirit (Ezek. 36:26, 27; 37:14). 5) It will be an everlasting, eternal covenant of peace, administered by God's Leader, the Son of David, the Prince of Peace (Is. 9:6; 55:3; Ezek. 34:23–25; 37:24–26). More details of the fulfillment of the New Covenant are found in the note on Daniel 9:24–27.

into the hand of the king of Babylon, and shall speak with him mouth[6310] to mouth, and his eyes shall behold[7200] his eyes;

5 And he shall lead Zedekiah to Babylon, and there shall he be [a]until I visit[6485] him, saith[5002] the LORD: [b]though ye fight with the Chaldeans, ye shall not prosper.

6 And Jeremiah said,[559] The word of the LORD came unto me, saying,

7 Behold, Hanameel the son of Shallum thine uncle shall come unto thee, saying, Buy thee my field[7704] that *is* in Anathoth: for the [a]right[4941] of redemption[1353] *is* thine to buy *it.*

8 So Hanameel mine uncle's son came to me in the court of the prison according to the word of the LORD, and said unto me, Buy my field, I pray thee,[4994] that *is* in Anathoth, which *is* in the country[776] of Benjamin: for the right of inheritance[3425] *is* thine, and the redemption *is* thine; buy *it* for thyself. Then I knew[3045] that this *was* the word of the LORD.

9 And I bought the field of Hanameel my uncle's son, that *was* in Anathoth, and [a]weighed him the money, *even* [I]seventeen shekels of silver.

10 And I [I]subscribed[3789] the evidence,[5612] and sealed *it,* and took witnesses, and weighed *him* the money in the balances.

11 So I took the evidence of the purchase, *both* that which was sealed *according* to the law and custom,[2706] and that which was open:[1540]

12 And I gave the evidence of the purchase unto [a]Baruch the son of Neriah, the son of Maaseiah, in the sight of Hanameel mine uncle's *son,* and in the presence of the [b]witnesses that subscribed the book[5612] of the purchase, before all the Jews that sat in the court of the prison.

13 And I charged[6680] Baruch before them, saying,

14 Thus saith the LORD of hosts,[6635] the God[430] of Israel; Take these evidences, this evidence of the purchase, both which is sealed, and this evidence which is open; and put them in an earthen[2789] vessel, that they may continue many days.[3117]

15 For thus saith the LORD of hosts, the God of Israel; Houses[1004] and fields[7704] and vineyards [a]shall be possessed again in this land.[776]

Jeremiah Prays

16 Now when I had delivered the evidence of the purchase unto Baruch the son of Neriah, I prayed[6419] unto the LORD, saying,

17 Ah Lord[136] GOD[3068] behold, [a]thou hast made[6213] the heaven and the earth[776] by thy great power and stretched out arm, *and* [b]there is nothing [I]too hard[6381] for thee:

18 Thou shewest [a]lovingkindness unto thousands,[505] and recompensest[7999] the iniquity[5771] of the fathers[1] into the bosom of their children after them: the Great, [b]the Mighty God,[410] [c]the LORD of hosts, *is* his name,

19 [a]Great in counsel,[6098] and mighty in [I]work: for thine [b]eyes *are* open upon all the ways[1870] of the sons of men:[120] [c]to give every one according to his ways, and according to the fruit of his doings:

20 Which hast set[7760] signs[226] and wonders[4159] in the land of Egypt, *even* unto this day,[3117] and in Israel, and among *other* men; and hast made thee [a]a name, as at this day;

21 And [a]hast brought forth thy people[5971] Israel out of the land of Egypt with signs, and with wonders, and with a strong[2389] hand, and with a stretched out arm, and with great terror;[4172]

22 And hast given them this land, which thou didst swear[7650] to their fathers to give them, [a]a land flowing with milk and honey;

23 And they came in,[935] and possessed[3423] it; but [a]they obeyed[8085] not thy voice, neither walked in thy law;[8451] they have done nothing of all that thou commandedst[6680] them to do: therefore thou hast caused all this evil[7451] to come upon them:

---

5 [a]Jer. 27:22 [b]Jer. 21:4; 33:5

7 [a]Lev. 25:24, 25, 32; Ruth 4:4

9 [I]Or, *seven shekels and ten* pieces *of silver* [a]Gen. 23:16; Zech. 11:12

10 [I]Hebr. *wrote in the book*

12 [a]Jer. 36:4 [b]Isa. 8:2

15 [a]Jer. 32:37, 43

17 [I]Or, *hid from thee* [a]2Kgs. 19:15 [b]Gen. 18:14; Jer. 32:27; Luke 1:37

18 [a]Ex. 20:6; 34:7; Deut. 5:9, 10 [b]Isa. 9:6 [c]Jer. 10:16

19 [I]Hebr. *doing* [a]Isa. 28:29 [b]Job 34:21; Ps. 33:13; Prov. 5:21; Jer. 16:17 [c]Jer. 17:10

20 [a]Ex. 9:16; 1Chr. 17:21; Isa. 63:12; Dan. 9:15

21 [a]Ex. 6:6; 2Sam. 7:23; 1Chr. 17:21; Ps. 136:11, 12

22 [a]Ex. 3:8, 17; Jer. 11:5

23 [a]Neh. 9:26; Jer. 11:8; Dan. 9:10-14

24 Behold the [I][a]mounts, they are come unto the city to take it; and the city [b]is given into the hand of the Chaldeans, that fight against it, because of [c]the sword,[2719] and of the famine, and of the pestilence:[1698] and what thou hast spoken[1696] is come to pass; and, behold, thou seest *it.*

25 And thou hast said unto me, O Lord GOD, Buy thee the field for money, and take witnesses; [I]for [a]the city is given into the hand of the Chaldeans.

26 Then came the word of the LORD unto Jeremiah, saying,

27 Behold, I *am* the LORD, the [a]God of all flesh:[1320] [b]is there any thing too hard for me?

28 Therefore thus saith the LORD; Behold, [a]I will give this city into the hand of the Chaldeans, and into the hand of Nebuchadrezzar king of Babylon, and he shall take it:

29 And the Chaldeans, that fight against this city, shall come and [a]set fire on this city, and burn[8313] it with the houses, [b]upon whose roofs they have offered incense[6999] unto Baal, and poured out[5258] drink offerings[5262] unto other gods,[430] to provoke me to anger.[3707]

30 For the children of Israel and the children of Judah [a]have only done evil before me from their youth: for the children of Israel have only provoked me to anger with the work of their hands,[3027] saith the LORD.

31 For this city hath been to me *as* [I][a] provocation of mine anger[639] and of my fury from the day that they built it even unto this day; [a]that I should remove it from before my face,

32 Because of all the evil of the children of Israel and of the children of Judah, which they have done to provoke me to anger, [a]they, their kings,[4428] their princes,[8269] their priests,[3548] and their prophets,[5030] and the men of Judah, and the inhabitants of Jerusalem.

33 And they have turned unto me the [I][a]back, and not the face: though I taught[3925] them, [b]rising up early and teaching *them,* yet they have not hearkened[8085] to receive instruction.[4148]

34 But they [a]set[7760] their abominations[8251] in the house, which is called[7121] by my name, to defile it.

35 And they built the high places[1116] of Baal, which *are* in the valley of the son of Hinnom, to [a]cause their sons and their daughters to pass through[5674] *the fire* unto [b]Molech; [c]which I commanded[6680] them not, neither came it into my mind,[3820] that they should do this abomination,[8441] to cause Judah to sin.[2398]

Hope of Restoration

36 And now therefore thus saith the LORD, the God of Israel, concerning this city, whereof ye say, [a]It shall be delivered into the hand of the king of Babylon by the sword, and by the famine, and by the pestilence;

37 Behold, I will [a]gather[6908] them out of all countries,[776] whither I have driven them in mine anger, and in my fury, and in great wrath;[7110] and I will bring them again unto this place, and I will cause them [b]to dwell safely:[983]

38 And they shall be [a]my people, and I will be their God:

39 And I will [a]give them one heart,[3820] and one way,[1870] that they may fear[3372] me [I]for ever, for the good[2896] of them, and of their children after them:

40 And [a]I will make an everlasting[5769] covenant[1285] with them, that I will not turn away[7725] [I]from them, to do them good;[3190] but [b]I will put my fear[3374] in their hearts,[3824] that they shall not depart[5493] from me.

41 Yea, [a]I will rejoice over them to do them good,[2895] and [b]I will plant them in this land [I]assuredly[571] with my whole heart and with my whole soul.[5315]

42 For thus saith the LORD; [a]Like as I have brought all this great evil upon this people, so will I bring upon them all the good that I have promised[1696] them.

43 And [a]fields shall be bought in this land, [b]whereof ye say, *It is* desolate[8077] without man[120] or beast; it is given into the hand of the Chaldeans.

24 IOr, *engines of shot* [a]Jer. 33:4 [b]Jer. 32:25, 36 [c]Jer. 14:12
25 IOr, *though* [a]Jer. 32:24
27 [a]Num. 16:22 [b]Jer. 32:17
28 [a]Jer. 32:3 [b]Jer. 21:10; 37:8, 10; 52:13 [c]Jer. 19:13
30 [a]Jer. 2:7; 3:25; 7:22-26; 22:21; Ezek. 20:28
31 IHebr. *for my anger* [a]2Kgs. 23:27; 24:3
32 [a]Isa. 1:4, 6; Dan. 9:8
33 IHebr. *neck* [a]Jer. 2:27; 7:24 [b]Jer. 7:13
34 [a]Jer. 7:30, 31; 23:11; Ezek. 8:5, 6
35 [a]Jer. 7:31; 19:5 [b]Lev. 18:21; 1Kgs. 11:33 [c]Jer. 7:31
36 [a]Jer. 32:24
37 [a]Deut. 30:3; Jer. 23:3; 29:14; 31:10; Ezek. 37:21 [b]Jer. 23:6; 33:16
38 [a]Jer. 24:7; 30:22; 31:33
39 IHebr. *all days* [a]Jer. 24:7; Ezek. 11:19, 20
40 IHebr. *from after them* [a]Isa. 55:3; Jer. 31:31 [b]Jer. 31:33
41 IHebr. *in truth,* or, *stability* [a]Deut. 30:9; Zeph. 3:17 [b]Jer. 24:6; 31:28; Amos 9:15
42 [a]Jer. 31:28
43 [a]Jer. 32:15 [b]Jer. 33:10

44 Men shall buy fields for money,
and subscribe evidences, and seal *them,*
and take witnesses in [a]the land of
Benjamin, and in the places about
Jerusalem, and in the cities of Judah, and
in the cities of the mountains, and in the
cities of the valley, and in the cities of
the south: for [b]I will cause their captivity[7622] to return, saith the LORD.

Prosperity Will Return to Jerusalem

33 Moreover the word of the LORD
came unto Jeremiah the second
time, while he was yet [a]shut up in the
court of the prison, saying,
2 Thus saith the LORD the [a]maker
thereof, the LORD that formed it, to establish it; [I][b]the LORD *is* his name;
3 [a]Call[7121] unto me, and I will answer thee, and shew[5046] thee great and
[I][b]mighty things,[1219] which thou knowest[3045] not.
4 For thus saith the LORD, the God[430]
of Israel, concerning the houses[1004] of
this city, and concerning the houses of
the kings[4428] of Judah, which are thrown
down[5422] by [a]the mounts, and by the
sword;[2719]
5 [a]They come to fight with the
Chaldeans, but *it is* to fill them with the
dead bodies[6297] of men,[120] whom I have
slain[5221] in mine anger[639] and in my fury,
and for all whose wickedness[7451] I have
hid my face from this city.
6 Behold, [a]I will bring it health[724]
and cure,[4832] and I will cure[7495] them,
and will reveal unto them the abundance
of peace and truth.[571]
7 And [a]I will cause[7725] the captivity[7622] of Judah and the captivity of
Israel to return,[7725] and will build them,
[b]as at the first.[7223]
8 And I will [a]cleanse[2891] them from
all their iniquity,[5771] whereby they have
sinned[2398] against me; and I will [b]par-
don[5545] all their iniquities,[5771] whereby
they have sinned, and whereby they have
transgressed[6586] against me.
9 [a]And it shall be to me a name of
joy, a praise[8416] and an honour[8597] before
all the nations[1471] of the earth,[776] which
shall hear[8085] all the good[2896] that I
do unto them: and they shall [b]fear and
tremble for all the goodness and for
all the prosperity[7965] that I procure[6213]
unto it.
10 Thus saith the LORD; Again there
shall be heard[8085] in this place, [a]which
ye say *shall be* desolate[2717] without
man[120] and without beast, *even* in the
cities of Judah, and in the streets of
Jerusalem, that are desolate,[8074] without
man, and without inhabitant, and without
beast,
11 The [a]voice of joy, and the voice of
gladness, the voice of the bridegroom,
and the voice of the bride, the voice of
them that shall say, [b]Praise[3034] the LORD
of hosts:[6635] for the LORD *is* good; for his
mercy[2617] *endureth* for ever:[5769] *and* of
them that shall bring [c]the sacrifice of
praise[8426] into the house[1004] of the LORD.
For [d]I will cause to return the captivity
of the land,[776] as at the first, saith the
LORD.
12 Thus saith the LORD of hosts;
[a]Again in this place, which is desolate
without man and without beast, and in
all the cities thereof, shall be an habitation of shepherds causing *their* flocks to
lie down.
13 [a]In the cities of the mountains, in
the cities of the vale,[8219] and in the cities
of the south, and in the land of
Benjamin, and in the places about
Jerusalem, and in the cities of Judah,
shall the flocks [b]pass again under the
hands[3027] of him that telleth *them,* saith
the LORD.
14 [a]Behold, the days[3117] come,
saith[5002] the LORD, that [b]I will perform
that good thing which I have promised[1696] unto the house of Israel and to
the house of Judah.
15 In those days, and at that
time,[6256] will I cause the [a]Branch[6780] of
righteousness[6666] to grow up unto David;
and he shall execute judgment[4941] and
righteousness in the land.
16 [a]In those days shall Judah be
saved,[3467] and Jerusalem shall dwell[7931]
safely:[983] and this *is the name* wherewith

44 [a]Jer. 17:26 [b]Jer. 33:7, 11, 26
1 [a]Jer. 32:2, 3
2 [I]Or, *JEHOVAH* [a]Isa. 37:26 [b]Ex. 15:3; Amos 5:8; 9:6
3 [I]Or, *hidden* [a]Ps. 91:15; Jer. 29:12 [b]Isa. 48:6
4 [a]Jer. 32:24
5 [a]Jer. 32:5
6 [a]Jer. 30:17
7 [a]Jer. 30:3; 32:44; 33:11 [b]Isa. 1:26; Jer. 24:6; 30:20; 31:4, 28; 42:10
8 [a]Ezek. 36:25; Zech. 13:1; Heb. 9:13, 14 [b]Jer. 31:34; Mic. 7:18
9 [a]Isa. 62:7; Jer. 13:11 [b]Isa. 60:5
10 [a]Jer. 32:43
11 [a]Jer. 7:34; 16:9; 25:10; Rev. 18:23 [b]1Chr. 16:8, 34; 2Chr. 5:13; 7:3; Ezra 3:11; Ps. 136:1; Isa. 12:4 [c]Lev. 7:12; Ps. 107:22; 116:17 [d]Jer. 33:7
12 [a]Isa. 65:10; Jer. 31:24; 50:19
13 [a]Jer. 17:26; 32:44 [b]Lev. 27:32
14 [a]Jer. 23:5; 31:27, 31 [b]Jer. 29:10
15 [a]Isa. 4:2; 11:1; Jer. 23:5
16 [a]Jer. 23:6

she shall be called,[7121] [I]The LORD our righteousness.[6664]

17 For thus saith the LORD; [I]David shall never [a]want a man[376] to sit upon the throne[3678] of the house of Israel;

18 Neither shall the priests[3548] the Levites want a man before me to [a]offer burnt offerings,[5930] and to kindle[6999] meat offerings,[4503] and to do sacrifice[2077] continually.

19 And the word of the LORD came unto Jeremiah, saying,

20 Thus saith the LORD; [a]If ye can break[6565] my covenant of the day,[3117] and my covenant[1285] of the night,[3915] and that there should not be day[3119] and night in their season;[6256]

21 *Then* may also [a]my covenant be broken[6565] with David my servant,[5650] that he should not have a son[1121] to reign[4427] upon his throne; and with the Levites the priests, my ministers.[8334]

22 As [a]the host[6635] of heaven[8064] cannot be numbered,[5608] neither the sand of the sea measured: so will I multiply the seed[2233] of David my servant, and the Levites that minister[8334] unto me.

23 Moreover the word of the LORD came to Jeremiah, saying,

24 Considerest[7200] thou not what this people[5971] have spoken, saying, [a]The two families[4940] which the LORD hath chosen,[977] he hath even cast them off? thus they have despised my people, that they should be no more a nation[1471] before them.

25 Thus saith the LORD; If [a]my covenant *be* not with day and night, *and if* I have not [b]appointed[7760] the ordinances[2708] of heaven and earth;

26 [a]Then will I cast away[3988] the seed of Jacob, and David my servant, *so* that I will not take *any* of his seed *to be* rulers[4910] over the seed of Abraham, Isaac, and Jacob: for [b]I will cause their captivity to return, and have mercy[7355] on them.

Jeremiah's Warning to Zedekiah

34 The word which came unto Jeremiah from the LORD, [a]when

16 [I]Hebr. *Jehovah-tsidkenu*

17 [I]Hebr. *There shall not be cut off from David* [a]2Sam. 7:16; 1Kgs. 2:4; Ps. 89:29, 36; Luke 1:32, 33

18 [a]Rom. 12:1; 15:16; 1Pet. 2:5, 9; Rev. 1:6

20 [a]Ps. 89:37; Isa. 54:9; Jer. 31:36; 33:25

21 [a]Ps. 89:34

22 [a]Gen. 13:16; 15:5; 22:17; Jer. 31:37

24 [a]Jer. 33:21, 22

25 [a]Jer. 33:20; Gen. 8:22 [b]Ps. 74:16, 17; 104:19; Jer. 31:35, 36

26 [a]Jer. 31:37 [b]Jer. 33:7, 11; Ezra 2:1

1 [I]Hebr. *the dominion of his hand* [a]2Kgs. 25:1; Jer. 39:1; 52:4 [b]Jer. 1:15

2 [a]Jer. 21:10; 32:3, 28 [b]Jer. 32:29; 34:22

3 [I]Hebr. *his mouth shall speak to thy mouth* [a]Jer. 32:4

5 [a]2Chr. 16:14; 21:19 [b]Dan. 2:46 [c]Jer. 22:18

7 [a]2Kgs. 18:13; 19:8; 2Chr. 11:5, 9

8 [a]Ex. 21:2; Lev. 25:10; Jer. 34:14

9 [a]Neh. 5:11 [b]Lev. 25:39-46

Nebuchadnezzar king[4428] of Babylon, and all his army,[2428] and [b]all the kingdoms[4467] of the earth[776] [I]of his dominion, and all the people,[5971] fought against Jerusalem, and against all the cities thereof, saying,

2 Thus saith the LORD, the God[430] of Israel; Go and speak to Zedekiah king of Judah, and tell him, Thus saith the LORD; Behold, [a]I will give this city into the hand[3027] of the king of Babylon, and [b]he shall burn[8313] it with fire:

3 And [a]thou shalt not escape[4422] out of his hand, but shalt surely be taken, and delivered into his hand; and thine eyes shall behold[7200] the eyes of the king of Babylon, and [I]he shall speak with thee mouth[6310] to mouth, and thou shalt go to Babylon.

4 Yet hear[8085] the word of the LORD, O Zedekiah king of Judah; Thus saith the LORD of thee, Thou shalt not die by the sword:[2719]

5 *But* thou shalt die in peace: and with [a]the burnings of thy fathers,[1] the former[7223] kings[4428] which were before thee, [b]so shall they burn *odours* for thee; and [c]they will lament thee, *saying,* Ah lord[113] for I have pronounced the word, saith the LORD.

6 Then Jeremiah the prophet[5030] spake all these words unto Zedekiah king of Judah in Jerusalem,

7 When the king of Babylon's army fought against Jerusalem, and against all the cities of Judah that were left,[3498] against Lachish, and against Azekah: for [a]these defenced cities remained[7604] of the cities of Judah.

The Broken Covenant

8 *This is* the word that came unto Jeremiah from the LORD, after that the king Zedekiah had made[3772] a covenant[1285] with all the people which *were* at Jerusalem, to proclaim[7121] [a]liberty unto them;

9 [a]That every man[376] should let his manservant,[5650] and every man his maidservant, *being* an Hebrew or an Hebrewess, go free; [b]that none should

serve[5647] himself of them, *to wit,* of a Jew his brother.[251]

10 Now when all the princes,[8269] and all the people, which had entered into the covenant, heard[8085] that every one should let his manservant, and every one his maidservant, go free, that none should serve themselves of them any more, then they obeyed,[8085] and let *them* go.

11 But [a]afterward they turned, and caused[7725] the servants[5650] and the handmaids, whom they had let go free, to return,[7725] and brought them into subjection for servants and for handmaids.

12 Therefore the word of the LORD came to Jeremiah from the LORD, saying,

13 Thus saith the LORD, the God of Israel; I made a covenant with your fathers in the day[3117] that I brought them forth out of the land[776] of Egypt, out of the house[1004] of bondmen,[5650] saying,

14 At the end of [a]seven years let ye go every man his brother an Hebrew, which [I]hath been sold unto thee; and when he hath served[5647] thee six years, thou shalt let him go free from thee: but your fathers hearkened[8085] not unto me, neither inclined their ear.[241]

15 And ye were [I]now turned, and had done[6213] right[3477] in my sight, in proclaiming liberty every man to his neighbour;[7453] and ye had [a]made a covenant before me [b]in the house [II]which is called[7121] by my name:

16 But ye turned and [a]polluted[2490] my name, and caused every man his servant,[5650] and every man his handmaid, whom he had set at liberty at their pleasure,[5315] to return, and brought them into subjection, to be unto you for servants and for handmaids.

17 Therefore thus saith the LORD; Ye have not hearkened unto me, in proclaiming liberty, every one to his brother, and every man to his neighbour: [a]behold, I proclaim a liberty for you, saith the LORD, [b]to the sword, to the pestilence,[1698] and to the famine; and I will make you [I]to be [c]removed into all the kingdoms of the earth.

11 [a]Jer. 34:21; 37:5

14 [I]Or, *hath sold himself* [a]Ex. 21:2; 23:10; Deut. 15:12

15 [I]Hebr. *today* [II]Hebr. *whereupon my name is called* [a]2Kgs. 23:3; Neh. 10:29

16 [a]Ex. 20:7; Lev. 19:12

17 [I]Hebr. *for a removing* [a]Matt. 7:2; Gal. 6:7; James 2:13 [b]Jer. 32:24, 36 [c]Deut. 28:25, 64; Jer. 29:18

18 [a]Gen. 15:10, 17

20 [a]Jer. 7:33; 16:4; 19:7

21 [a]Jer. 37:5, 11

22 [a]Jer. 37:8, 10 [b]Jer. 38:3; 39:1, 2, 8; 52:7, 13 [c]Jer. 9:11; 44:2, 6

2 [a]2Kgs. 10:15; 1Chr. 2:55 [b]1Kgs. 6:5

18 And I will give the men[582] that have transgressed[5674] my covenant, which have not performed the words of the covenant which they had made before me, when [a]they cut[3772] the calf in twain,[8147] and passed[5674] between the parts thereof,

19 The princes of Judah, and the princes of Jerusalem, the eunuchs,[5631] and the priests,[3548] and all the people of the land, which passed between the parts of the calf;

20 I will even give them into the hand of their enemies, and into the hand of them that seek their life:[5315] and their [a]dead bodies[5038] shall be for meat unto the fowls of the heaven,[8064] and to the beasts of the earth.

21 And Zedekiah king of Judah and his princes will I give into the hand of their enemies, and into the hand of them that seek their life, and into the hand of the king of Babylon's army, [a]which are gone up[5674] from you.

22 [a]Behold, I will command,[6680] saith the LORD, and cause them to return to this city; and they shall fight against it, [b]and take it, and burn it with fire: and [c]I will make the cities of Judah a desolation[8077] without an inhabitant.

The Rechabites

35 The word which came unto Jeremiah from the LORD in the days[3117] of Jehoiakim the son of Josiah king[4428] of Judah, saying,

2 Go unto the house[1004] of the [a]Rechabites, and speak unto them, and bring them into the house of the LORD, into one of [b]the chambers, and give them wine to drink.

3 Then I took Jaazaniah the son of Jeremiah, the son of Habaziniah, and his brethren,[251] and all his sons, and the whole house of the Rechabites;

4 And I brought them into the house of the LORD, into the chamber of the sons of Hanan, the son of Igdaliah, a man of God,[430] which *was* by the chamber of the princes,[8269] which *was* above the chamber

of Maaseiah the son of Shallum, [a]the keeper[8104] of the [I]door:

5 And I set before the sons of the house of the Rechabites pots full of wine, and cups, and I said unto them, Drink ye wine.

6 But they said, We will drink no wine: for [a]Jonadab the son of Rechab our father[1] commanded[6680] us, saying, Ye shall drink no wine, *neither* ye, nor your sons for ever:[5769]

7 Neither shall ye build house, nor sow seed,[2233] nor plant vineyard, nor have *any:* but all your days ye shall dwell in tents;[168] [a]that ye may live[2421] many days in the land[127] where ye *be* strangers.[1481]

8 Thus have we obeyed[8085] the voice of Jonadab the son of Rechab our father in all that he hath charged[6680] us, to drink no wine all our days, we, our wives,[802] our sons, nor our daughters;

9 Nor to build houses[1004] for us to dwell in: neither have we vineyard, nor field,[7704] nor seed:

10 But we have dwelt in tents, and have obeyed, and done[6213] according to all that Jonadab our father commanded us.

11 But it came to pass, when Nebuchadrezzar king of Babylon came up[5927] into the land,[776] that we said, Come, and let us go to Jerusalem for fear of the army[2428] of the Chaldeans, and for fear of the army of the Syrians: so we dwell at Jerusalem.

12 Then came the word of the LORD unto Jeremiah, saying,

13 Thus saith the LORD of hosts,[6635] the God of Israel; Go and tell the men of Judah and the inhabitants of Jerusalem, Will ye not [a]receive instruction[4148] to hearken[8085] to my words?[1697] saith the LORD.

14 The words of Jonadab the son of Rechab, that he commanded his sons not to drink wine, are performed; for unto this day[3117] they drink none, but obey[8085] their father's[1] commandment:[4687] [a]notwithstanding I have spoken unto you, [b]rising early and speaking; but ye hearkened[8085] not unto me.

15 [a]I have sent also unto you all my servants[5650] the prophets,[5030] rising up early and sending *them,* saying, [b]Return[7725] ye now every man from his evil[7451] way,[1870] and amend[3190] your doings, and go not after other gods[430] to serve[5647] them, and ye shall dwell in the land which I have given to you and to your fathers:[1] but ye have not inclined your ear,[241] nor hearkened unto me.

16 Because the sons of Jonadab the son of Rechab have performed the commandment of their father, which he commanded them; but this people[5971] hath not hearkened unto me:

17 Therefore thus saith the LORD God of hosts, the God of Israel; Behold, I will bring upon Judah and upon all the inhabitants of Jerusalem all the evil that I have pronounced against them: [a]because I have spoken unto them, but they have not heard;[8085] and I have called[7121] unto them, but they have not answered.

18 And Jeremiah said unto the house of the Rechabites, Thus saith the LORD of hosts, the God of Israel; Because ye have obeyed the commandment of Jonadab your father, and kept[8104] all his precepts,[4687] and done according unto all that he hath commanded you:

19 Therefore thus saith the LORD of hosts, the God of Israel; [I]Jonadab the son of Rechab shall not want a man to [a]stand before me for ever.

4 [I]Hebr. *threshold,* or, *vessel* [a]2Kgs. 12:9; 25:18; 1Chr. 9:18, 19
6 [a]2Kgs. 10:15
7 [a]Ex. 20:12; Eph. 6:2, 3
13 [a]Jer. 32:33
14 [a]2Chr. 36:15 [b]Jer. 7:13; 25:3
15 [a]Jer. 7:25; 25:4 [b]Jer. 18:11; 25:5, 6
17 [a]Prov. 1:24; Isa. 65:12; 66:4; Jer. 7:13
19 [I]Hebr. *There shall not a man be cut off from Jonadab the son of Rechab to stand* [a]Jer. 15:19
2 [a]Isa. 8:1; Ezek. 2:9; Zech. 5:1

The Burning of the Scroll

36 And it came to pass in the fourth year of Jehoiakim the son of Josiah king[4428] of Judah, *that* this word came unto Jeremiah from the LORD, saying,

🗝 2 Take thee a [a]roll[4039] of a book,[5612]

🗝 **36:2** In order to encourage Judah to repent, God wanted Jeremiah to write down all the words that He had given him since Jeremiah began to prophesy more than twenty years before. Jeremiah

(continued on next page)

and [b]write therein all the words that I have spoken unto thee against Israel, and against Judah, and against [c]all the nations,[1471] from the day[3117] I spake unto thee, from the days of [d]Josiah, even unto this day.

3 [a]It may be that the house[1004] of Judah will hear[8085] all the evil[7451] which I purpose[2803] to do[6213] unto them; that they may [b]return[7725] every man from his evil way;[1870] that I may forgive[5545] their iniquity[5771] and their sin.[2403]

4 Then Jeremiah [a]called[7121] Baruch the son of Neriah: and [b]Baruch wrote from the mouth[6310] of Jeremiah all the words of the LORD, which he had spoken unto him, upon a roll of a book.

5 And Jeremiah commanded[6680] Baruch, saying, I *am* shut up;[6113] I cannot go into the house of the LORD:

6 Therefore go thou, and read[7121] in the roll, which thou hast written from my mouth, the words of the LORD in the ears[241] of the people[5971] in the LORD's house upon [a]the fasting day: and also thou shalt read them in the ears of all Judah that come out of their cities.

7 [a]It may be [I]they will present[5307] their supplication[8467] before the LORD, and will return every one from his evil way: for great *is* the anger[639] and the fury that the LORD hath pronounced against this people.

8 And Baruch the son of Neriah did according to all that Jeremiah the prophet[5030] commanded him, reading in the book the words of the LORD in the LORD's house.

9 And it came to pass in the fifth year of Jehoiakim the son of Josiah king of Judah, in the ninth month, *that* they proclaimed[7121] a fast before the LORD to all the people in Jerusalem, and to all the people that came from the cities of Judah unto Jerusalem.

10 Then read Baruch in the book the words of Jeremiah in the house of the LORD, in the chamber of Gemariah the son of Shaphan the scribe, in the higher court, at the [I][a]entry of the new gate of the LORD's house, in the ears of all the people.

11 When Michaiah the son of Gemariah, the son of Shaphan, had heard[8085] out of the book all the words of the LORD,

12 Then he went down into the king's[4428] house, into the scribe's chamber: and, lo, all the princes[8269] sat there, *even* Elishama the scribe, and Delaiah the son of Shemaiah, and Elnathan the son of Achbor, and Gemariah the son of Shaphan, and Zedekiah the son of Hananiah, and all the princes.

13 Then Michaiah declared unto them all the words that he had heard, when Baruch read the book in the ears of the people.

14 Therefore all the princes sent Jehudi the son of Nethaniah, the son of Shelemiah, the son of Cushi, unto Baruch, saying, Take in thine hand[3027] the roll wherein thou hast read in the ears of the people, and come. So Baruch the son of Neriah took the roll in his hand, and came unto them.

15 And they said unto him, Sit down now, and read it in our ears. So Baruch read *it* in their ears.

16 Now it came to pass, when they had heard all the words, they were afraid[6342] both one and other, and said unto Baruch, We will surely tell[5046] the king of all these words.

17 And they asked[7592] Baruch, saying, Tell us now, How didst thou write all these words at his mouth?

2 [b]Jer. 30:2 [c]Jer. 25:15 [d]Jer. 25:3

3 [a]Jer. 26:3; 36:7 [b]Jer. 18:8; Jon. 3:8

4 [a]Jer. 32:12 [b]Jer. 45:1

6 [a]Lev. 16:29; 23:27-32; Acts 27:9

7 [I]Hebr. *their supplication shall fall* [a]Jer. 36:3

10 [I]Or, *door* [a]Jer. 26:10

(continued from previous page)

dictated the words to Baruch, his scribe (Jer. 36:4). The scroll was eventually read by King Jehoiakim, and he destroyed it piece by piece (Jer. 36:23). God simply directed Jeremiah to write it again, giving him additional words, and Jeremiah and Baruch repeated the process (Jer. 36:27, 32). Earlier, Isaiah had written and sealed up an oracle at God's command (Is. 8:1, 16), and Habakkuk was told to write down a vision as well (Hab. 2:2).

18 Then Baruch answered[559] them, He pronounced all these words unto me with his mouth, and I wrote *them* with ink in the book.

19 Then said the princes unto Baruch, Go, hide thee, thou and Jeremiah; and let no man know[3045] where ye be.

20 And they went in to the king into the court, but they laid up the roll in the chamber of Elishama the scribe, and told all the words in the ears of the king.

21 So the king sent Jehudi to fetch the roll: and he took it out of Elishama the scribe's chamber. And Jehudi read it in the ears of the king, and in the ears of all the princes which stood beside the king.

22 Now the king sat in [a]the winterhouse in the ninth month: and *there was a fire* on the hearth burning before him.

23 And it came to pass, *that* when Jehudi had read three or four leaves, he cut it with the penknife, and cast *it* into the fire that *was* on the hearth, until all the roll was consumed[8552] in the fire that *was* on the hearth.

24 Yet they were not afraid, nor [a]rent their garments, *neither* the king, nor any of his servants[5650] that heard all these words.

25 Nevertheless Elnathan and Delaiah and Gemariah had made intercession[6293] to the king that he would not burn[8313] the roll: but he would not hear them.

26 But the king commanded Jerahmeel the son [I]of Hammelech, and Seraiah the son of Azriel, and Shelemiah the son of Abdeel, to take Baruch the scribe and Jeremiah the prophet: but the LORD hid them.

The Second Scroll

27 Then the word of the LORD came to Jeremiah, after that the king had burned[8313] the roll, and the words which Baruch wrote at the mouth of Jeremiah, saying,

28 Take thee again another roll, and write in it all the former[7223] words that were in the first roll, which Jehoiakim the king of Judah hath burned.

29 And thou shalt say to Jehoiakim king of Judah, Thus saith the LORD; Thou hast burned this roll, saying, Why hast thou written therein, saying, The king of Babylon shall certainly come and destroy this land,[776] and shall cause to cease[7673] from thence man[120] and beast?

30 Therefore thus saith the LORD of Jehoiakim king of Judah; [a]He shall have none to sit upon the throne[3678] of David: and his dead body[5038] shall be [b]cast out in the day to the heat, and in the night[3915] to the frost.

31 And I will [I][a]punish[6485] him and his seed[2233] and his servants for their iniquity; and I will bring upon them, and upon the inhabitants of Jerusalem, and upon the men of Judah, all the evil that I have pronounced against them; but they hearkened[8085] not.

32 Then took Jeremiah another roll, and gave it to Baruch the scribe, the son of Neriah; who wrote therein from the mouth of Jeremiah all the words of the book which Jehoiakim king of Judah had burned in the fire: and there were added besides unto them many [I]like words.

Jeremiah Is Put in Prison

37 And king[4428] [a]Zedekiah the son of Josiah reigned[4427] instead of Coniah the son of Jehoiakim, whom Nebuchadrezzar king of Babylon made king in the land[776] of Judah.

2 [a]But neither he, nor his servants,[5650] nor the people[5971] of the land, did hearken[8085] unto the words of the LORD, which he spake [I]by the prophet[5030] Jeremiah.

3 And Zedekiah the king sent Jehucal the son of Shelemiah and [a]Zephaniah the son of Maaseiah the priest[3548] to the prophet Jeremiah, saying, Pray[6419] now unto the LORD our God[430] for us.

4 Now Jeremiah came in and went out among the people: for they had not put him into prison.

22 [a]Amos 3:15
24 [a]2Kgs. 22:11; Isa. 36:22; 37:1
26 [I]Or, *of the king*
30 [a]Jer. 22:30 [b]Jer. 22:19
31 [I]Hebr. *visit upon* [a]Jer. 23:34
32 [I]Hebr. *as they*
1 [a]2Kgs. 24:17; 2Chr. 36:10; Jer. 22:24
2 [I]Hebr. *by the hand of the prophet* [a]2Chr. 36:12, 14
3 [a]Jer. 21:1, 2; 29:25; 52:24

5 Then [a]Pharaoh's army[2428] was
come forth out of Egypt: [b]and when the
Chaldeans that besieged Jerusalem
heard[8085] tidings[8088] of them, they departed from Jerusalem.
6 Then came the word of the LORD
unto the prophet Jeremiah, saying,
7 Thus saith the LORD, the God of
Israel; Thus shall ye say to the king of
Judah, [a]that sent you unto me to enquire
of me; Behold, Pharaoh's army, which is
come forth to help you, shall return[7725] to
Egypt into their own land.
8 [a]And the Chaldeans shall come
again, and fight against this city, and
take it, and burn[8313] it with fire.
9 Thus saith the LORD; Deceive not
[I]yourselves, saying, The Chaldeans shall
surely depart from us: for they shall not
depart.
10 [a]For though ye had smitten[5221] the
whole army of the Chaldeans that fight
against you, and there remained[7604] *but*
[I]wounded men[582] among them, *yet* should
they rise up every man[376] in his tent,[168]
and burn this city with fire.
11 [a]And it came to pass, that when
the army of the Chaldeans was [I]broken
up[5927] from Jerusalem for fear of Pharaoh's army,
12 Then Jeremiah went forth out of
Jerusalem to go into the land of
Benjamin, [I]to separate himself[2505] thence
in the midst of the people.
13 And when he was in the gate of
Benjamin, a captain[1167] of the ward[6488]
was there, whose name *was* Irijah, the
son of Shelemiah, the son of Hananiah;
and he took Jeremiah the prophet, saying, Thou fallest away[5307] to the Chaldeans.
14 Then said Jeremiah, *It is* [I]false,[8267]
I fall not away to the Chaldeans. But he
hearkened[8085] not to him: so Irijah took
Jeremiah, and brought him to the
princes.[8269]
15 Wherefore the princes were
wroth[7107] with Jeremiah, and smote[5221]
him, [a]and put him in prison in the
house[1004] of Jonathan the scribe:[5608] for
they had made that the prison.
16 When Jeremiah was entered into

5 [a]2Kgs. 24:7; Ezek. 17:15 [b]Jer. 34:21; 37:11
7 [a]Jer. 21:2
8 [a]Jer. 34:22
9 [I]Hebr. *souls*
10 [I]Hebr. *thrust through* [a]Jer. 21:4, 5
11 [I]Hebr. *made to ascend* [a]Jer. 37:5
12 [I]Or, *to slip away from thence in the midst of the people*
14 [I]Hebr. *falsehood*, or, *a lie*
15 [a]Jer. 38:26
16 [I]Or, *cells* [a]Jer. 38:6
20 [I]Hebr. *let my supplication fall*
21 [a]Jer. 32:2; 38:13, 28 [b]Jer. 38:9; 52:6
1 [a]Jer. 37:3 [b]Jer. 21:1 [c]Jer. 21:8
2 [a]Jer. 21:9
3 [a]Jer. 21:10; 32:3

[a]the dungeon, and into the [I]cabins, and
Jeremiah had remained there many
days;[3117]
17 Then Zedekiah the king sent, and
took him out: and the king asked[7592] him
secretly in his house, and said, Is there
any word from the LORD? And Jeremiah
said, There is: for, said he, thou shalt be
delivered into the hand[3027] of the king of
Babylon.
18 Moreover Jeremiah said unto king
Zedekiah, What have I offended[2398]
against thee, or against thy servants, or
against this people, that ye have put me
in prison?
19 Where *are* now your prophets[5030]
which prophesied[5012] unto you, saying,
The king of Babylon shall not come
against you, nor against this land?
20 Therefore hear[8085] now, I pray
thee,[4994] O my lord[113] the king: [I]let my
supplication,[8467] I pray thee, be accepted[5307] before thee; that thou cause
me not to return to the house of Jonathan
the scribe, lest I die there.
21 Then Zedekiah the king commanded[6680] that they should commit
Jeremiah [a]into the court of the prison,
and that they should give him daily a
piece of bread out of the bakers' street,
[b]until all the bread in the city were
spent.[8552] Thus Jeremiah remained in the
court of the prison.

Jeremiah Rescued From the Dry Well

38 Then Shephatiah the son of
Mattan, and Gedaliah the son of
Pashur, and [a]Jucal the son of Shelemiah,
and [b]Pashur the son of Malchiah,
[c]heard[8085] the words that Jeremiah had
spoken unto all the people,[5971] saying,
2 Thus saith the LORD, [a]He that remaineth in this city shall die[4191] by the
sword,[2719] by the famine, and by the
pestilence:[1698] but he that goeth forth to
the Chaldeans shall live;[2421] for he shall
have his life[5315] for a prey, and shall
live.[2425]
3 Thus saith the LORD, [a]This city
shall surely be given into the hand[3027] of

the king[4428] of Babylon's army,[2428] which shall take it.

4 Therefore the princes[8269] said unto the king, We beseech thee, [a]let this man[376] be put to death:[4191] for thus he weakeneth[7503] the hands[3027] of the men[582] of war that remain in this city, and the hands of all the people, in speaking such words unto them: for this man seeketh not the [I]welfare[7965] of this people, but the hurt.[7451]

5 Then Zedekiah the king said, Behold, he *is* in your hand: for the king *is* not *he that* can do *any* thing against you.

6 [a]Then took they Jeremiah, and cast him into the dungeon[953] of Malchiah the son [I]of Hammelech, that *was* in the court of the prison: and they let down Jeremiah with cords. And in the dungeon *there was* no water, but mire: so Jeremiah sunk in the mire.

7 [a]Now when Ebed–melech the Ethiopian, one of the eunuchs[5631] which was in the king's[4428] house,[1004] heard that they had put Jeremiah in the dungeon; the king then sitting in the gate of Benjamin;

8 Ebed–melech went forth out of the king's house, and spake to the king, saying,

9 My lord[113] the king, these men have done evil[7489] in all that they have done[6213] to Jeremiah the prophet,[5030] whom they have cast into the dungeon; and [I]he is like to die for hunger in the place where he is: for *there is* no more bread in the city.

10 Then the king commanded[6680] Ebed–melech the Ethiopian, saying, Take from hence thirty men [I]with thee, and take up Jeremiah the prophet out of the dungeon, before he die.

11 So Ebed–melech took the men with him, and went into the house of the king under the treasury, and took thence old cast clouts[5499] and old rotten rags, and let them down by cords into the dungeon to Jeremiah.

12 And Ebed–melech the Ethiopian said unto Jeremiah, Put now *these* old cast clouts and rotten rags under thine armholes under the cords. And Jeremiah did so.

13 [a]So they drew up Jeremiah with cords, and took him up out of the dungeon: and Jeremiah remained [b]in the court of the prison.

Zedekiah Seeks Counsel From Jeremiah

14 Then Zedekiah the king sent, and took Jeremiah the prophet unto him into the [I]third entry that *is* in the house of the LORD: and the king said unto Jeremiah, I will ask[7592] thee a thing; hide nothing from me.

15 Then Jeremiah said unto Zedekiah, If I declare[5046] *it* unto thee, wilt thou not surely put me to death? and if I give thee counsel,[3289] wilt thou not hearken[8085] unto me?

16 So Zedekiah the king sware[7650] secretly unto Jeremiah, saying, *As* the LORD liveth,[2416] [a]that made us this soul,[5315] I will not put thee to death, neither will I give thee into the hand of these men that seek thy life.

17 Then said Jeremiah unto Zedekiah, Thus saith the LORD, the God[430] of hosts,[6635] the God of Israel; If thou wilt assuredly [a]go forth [b]unto the king of Babylon's princes, then thy soul shall live, and this city shall not be burned[8313] with fire; and thou shalt live, and thine house:

18 But if thou wilt not go forth to the king of Babylon's princes, then shall this city be given into the hand of the Chaldeans, and they shall burn[8313] it with fire, and [a]thou shalt not escape[4422] out of their hand.

19 And Zedekiah the king said unto Jeremiah, I am afraid[1672] of the Jews that are fallen[5307] to the Chaldeans, lest they deliver me into their hand, and they [a]mock me.

20 But Jeremiah said, They shall not deliver *thee*. Obey,[8085] I beseech thee, the voice of the LORD, which I speak[1696] unto thee: so it shall be well[3190] unto thee, and thy soul shall live.

21 But if thou refuse[3986] to go forth,

4 [I]Hebr. *peace* [a]Jer. 26:11
6 [I]Or, *of the king* [a]Jer. 37:21
7 [a]Jer. 39:16
9 [I]Hebr. *he will die*
10 [I]Hebr. *in thine hand*
13 [a]Jer. 38:6 [b]Jer. 37:21
14 [I]Or, *principal*
16 [a]Isa. 57:16
17 [a]2Kgs. 24:12 [b]Jer. 39:3
18 [a]Jer. 32:4; 34:3; 38:23
19 [a]1Sam. 31:4

this *is* the word[1697] that the LORD hath shewed[7200] me:

22 And, behold, all the women[802] that are left[7604] in the king of Judah's house *shall be* brought forth to the king of Babylon's princes, and those *women* shall say,[559] [I]Thy friends[7965] have set thee on, and have prevailed against thee: thy feet are sunk in the mire, *and* they are turned away back.

23 So they shall bring out all thy wives[802] and [a]thy children[1121] to the Chaldeans: and [b]thou shalt not escape out of their hand, but shalt be taken by the hand of the king of Babylon: and [I]thou shalt cause this city to be burned with fire.

24 Then said Zedekiah unto Jeremiah, Let no man know[3045] of these words, and thou shalt not die.

25 But if the princes hear[8085] that I have talked[1696] with thee, and they come unto thee, and say unto thee, Declare unto us now what thou hast said unto the king, hide it not from us, and we will not put thee to death; also what the king said unto thee:

26 Then thou shalt say unto them, [a]I presented[5307] my supplication[8467] before the king, that he would not cause me to return[7725] [b]to Jonathan's house, to die there.

27 Then came all the princes unto Jeremiah, and asked[7592] him: and he told[5046] them according to all these words that the king had commanded. So [I]they left off speaking with him; for the matter[1697] was not perceived.[8085]

28 So [a]Jeremiah abode in the court of the prison until the day[3117] that Jerusalem was taken: and he was *there* when Jerusalem was taken.

Jerusalem Falls

39 🗝In the [a]ninth year of Zedekiah king[4428] of Judah, in the tenth month, came Nebuchadrezzar king of Babylon and all his army[2428] against Jerusalem, and they besieged it.

2 *And* in the eleventh year of Zedekiah, in the fourth month, the ninth *day* of the month, the city was broken up.

3 [a]And all the princes[8269] of the king of Babylon came in, and sat in the middle gate, *even* Nergal–sharezer, Samgar–nebo, Sarsechim, Rab–saris, Nergal–sharezer, Rab–mag, with all the residue[7611] of the princes of the king of Babylon.

4 [a]And it came to pass, *that* when Zedekiah the king of Judah saw[7200] them, and all the men[582] of war, then they fled, and went forth out of the city by night,[3915] by the way[1870] of the king's[4428] garden, by the gate betwixt the two walls: and he went out the way of the plain.[6160]

5 But the Chaldeans' army pursued after them, and [a]overtook Zedekiah in the plains of Jericho: and when they had taken him, they brought him up[5927] to Nebuchadnezzar king of Babylon to [b]Riblah in the land[776] of Hamath, where he [Ic]gave judgment[4941] upon him.

6 Then the king of Babylon slew[7819] the sons[1121] of Zedekiah in Riblah before his eyes: also the king of Babylon slew all the nobles[2715] of Judah.

7 Moreover [a]he put out Zedekiah's eyes, and bound him [I]with chains, to carry him to Babylon.

8 [a]And the Chaldeans burned[8313] the king's house,[1004] and the houses of the people,[5971] with fire, and brake down[5422] the walls of Jerusalem.

9 [a]Then Nebuzar–adan the [Ib]captain of the guard carried away captive[1540] into Babylon the remnant[3499] of the people that remained[7604] in the city, and those that fell away,[5307] that fell to him, with the rest[3499] of the people that remained.

10 But Nebuzar–adan the captain of the guard left[7604] of the poor of the people, which had nothing, in the land of

22 [I]Hebr. *Men of thy peace*

23 [I]Hebr. *thou shalt burn* [a]Jer. 39:6; 41:10 [b]Jer. 38:18

26 [a]Jer. 37:20 [b]Jer. 37:15

27 [I]Hebr. *they were silent from him*

28 [a]Jer. 37:21; 39:14

1 [a]2Kgs. 25:1-4; Jer. 52:4-7

3 [a]Jer. 38:17

4 [a]2Kgs. 25:4; Jer. 52:7

5 [I]Hebr. *spake with him judgments* [a]Jer. 32:4; 38:18, 23 [b]2Kgs. 23:33 [c]Jer. 4:12

7 [I]Hebr. *with two brazen chains,* or, *fetters* [a]Jer. 32:9; Ezek. 12:13

8 [a]2Kgs. 25:9; Jer. 38:18; 52:13

9 [I]Or, *chief marshal* [a]2Kgs. 25:11; Jer. 52:15 [b]Gen. 37:36; Jer. 39:10, 11

🗝 **39:1–10** Ezekiel prophesied all of this from Babylon before it actually happened (Ezek. 12:8–16).

Judah, and gave them vineyards and
fields [I]at the same time.[3117]
11 Now Nebuchadrezzar king of
Babylon gave charge[6680] concerning
Jeremiah [I]to Nebuzar–adan the captain of
the guard, saying,
12 Take him, and [I]look well to him,
and do[6213] him no harm;[7451] but do unto
him even as he shall say[1696] unto thee.
13 So Nebuzar–adan the captain of
the guard sent, and Nebushasban,
Rab–saris, and Nergal–sharezer, Rab–
mag, and all the king of Babylon's
princes;
14 Even they sent, [a]and took
Jeremiah out of the court of the prison,
and committed him [b]unto Gedaliah the
son of [c]Ahikam the son of Shaphan, that
he should carry him home:[1004] so he
dwelt among the people.
15 Now the word of the LORD came
unto Jeremiah, while he was shut up in
the court of the prison, saying,
16 Go and speak to [a]Ebed–melech
the Ethiopian, saying, Thus saith the
LORD of hosts,[6635] the God[430] of Israel;
Behold, [b]I will bring my words upon this
city for evil,[7451] and not for good;[2896] and
they shall be *accomplished* in that day[3117]
before thee.
17 But I will deliver[5337] thee in that
day, saith the LORD: and thou shalt not be
given into the hand[3027] of the men of
whom thou *art* afraid.[3025]
18 For I will surely deliver thee, and
thou shalt not fall by the sword,[2719] but
[a]thy life[5315] shall be for a prey unto thee:
[b]because thou hast put thy trust[982] in me,
saith the LORD.

Jeremiah and Gedaliah

40 The word that came to Jeremiah
from the LORD,[3068] [a]after that
Nebuzar–adan the captain of the guard
had let him go from Ramah, when he
had taken him being bound in [I]chains
among all that were carried away
captive[1546] of Jerusalem and Judah,
which were carried away captive[1540] unto
Babylon.
2 And the captain of the guard took
Jeremiah, and [a]said unto him, The LORD
thy God[430] hath pronounced this evil[7451]
upon this place.
3 Now the LORD hath brought *it,* and
done according as he hath said: [a]because
ye have sinned[2398] against the LORD, and
have not obeyed[8085] his voice, therefore
this thing is come upon you.
4 And now, behold,[7200] I loose thee
this day[3117] from the chains which [I]*were*
upon thine hand.[3027] [a]If it seem good[2896]
unto thee to come with me into Babylon,
come; and [II]I will look well unto thee: but
if it seem ill[7489] unto thee to come with
me into Babylon, forbear: behold, [b]all the
land[776] *is* before thee: whither it seemeth
good and convenient[3477] for thee to go,
thither go.
5 Now while he was not yet gone
back,[7725] *he said,* Go back also to
Gedaliah the son of Ahikam the son of
Shaphan, [a]whom the king[4428] of Babylon
hath made governor[6485] over the cities of
Judah, and dwell with him among the
people:[5971] or go wheresoever it seemeth
convenient unto thee to go. So the captain
of the guard gave him victuals[737] and a
reward,[4864] and let him go.
6 [a]Then went Jeremiah unto Gedaliah
the son of Ahikam to [b]Mizpah; and dwelt
with him among the people that were
left[7604] in the land.
7 [a]Now when all the captains[8269] of
the forces[2428] which *were* in the fields,[7704]
even they and their men,[582] heard[8085] that
the king of Babylon had made Gedaliah
the son of Ahikam governor in the land,
and had committed[6485] unto him men,
and women,[802] and children,[2945] and of
[b]the poor of the land, of them that were
not carried away captive to Babylon;
8 Then they came to Gedaliah to
Mizpah, [a]even Ishmael the son of
Nethaniah, and Johanan and Jonathan the
sons of Kareah, and Seraiah the son of
Tanhumeth, and the sons of Ephai the
Netophathite, and Jezaniah the son of
Maachathite, they and their men.
9 And Gedaliah the son of Ahikam
the son of Shaphan sware[7650] unto them
and to their men, saying, Fear[3372] not to
serve[5647] the Chaldeans: dwell in the land,

10 [I]Hebr. *in that day*
11 [I]Hebr. *by the hand of*
12 [I]Hebr. *set thine eyes upon him*
14 [a]Jer. 38:28 [b]Jer. 40:5 [c]Jer. 26:24
16 [a]Jer. 38:7, 12 [b]Dan. 9:12
18 [a]Jer. 21:9; 45:5 [b]1Chr. 5:20; Ps. 37:40
1 [I]Or, *manacles* [a]Jer. 39:14
2 [a]Jer. 50:7
3 [a]Deut. 29:24, 25; Dan. 9:11
4 [I]Or, are *upon thine hand* [II]Hebr. *I will set mine eye upon thee* [a]Jer. 39:12 [b]Gen. 20:15
5 [a]2Kgs. 25:22
6 [a]Jer. 39:14 [b]Judg. 20:1
7 [a]2Kgs. 25:23 [b]Jer. 39:10
8 [a]Jer. 41:1

and serve the king of Babylon, and it shall be well[3190] with you.

10 As for me, behold, I will dwell at Mizpah, [I][a]to serve the Chaldeans, which will come unto us: but ye, gather[622] ye wine, and summer fruits, and oil,[8081] and put *them* in your vessels, and dwell in your cities that ye have taken.

11 Likewise when all the Jews that *were* in Moab, and among the Ammonites, and in Edom, and that *were* in all the countries,[776] heard that the king of Babylon had left a remnant[7611] of Judah, and that he had set[6485] over them Gedaliah the son of Ahikam the son of Shaphan;

12 Even all the Jews returned[7725] out of all places whither they were driven, and came to the land of Judah, to Gedaliah, unto Mizpah, and gathered[622] wine and summer fruits very much.

Gedaliah Is Murdered

13 Moreover Johanan the son of Kareah, and all the captains of the forces that *were* in the fields, came to Gedaliah to Mizpah,

14 And said unto him, Dost thou certainly know[3045] that [a]Baalis the king of the Ammonites hath sent Ishmael the son of Nethaniah [I]to slay thee? But Gedaliah the son of Ahikam believed[539] them not.

15 Then Johanan the son of Kareah spake to Gedaliah in Mizpah secretly, saying, Let me go, I pray thee, and I will slay[5221] Ishmael the son of Nethaniah, and no man shall know *it:* wherefore should he slay thee, that all the Jews which are gathered[6908] unto thee should be scattered, and the remnant in Judah perish?[6]

16 But Gedaliah the son of Ahikam said unto Johanan the son of Kareah, Thou shalt not do this thing: for thou speakest falsely[8267] of Ishmael.

41 Now it came to pass in the seventh month, [a]that Ishmael the son of Nethaniah the son of Elishama, of the seed[2233] royal, and the princes of the king,[4428] even ten men[582] with him, came unto Gedaliah the son of Ahikam to Mizpah; and there they did eat bread together in Mizpah.

2 Then arose Ishmael the son of Nethaniah, and the ten men that were with him, and [a]smote[5221] Gedaliah the son of Ahikam the son of Shaphan with the sword,[2719] and slew him, whom the king of Babylon had made governor[6485] over the land.[776]

3 Ishmael also slew[5221] all the Jews that were with him, *even* with Gedaliah, at Mizpah, and the Chaldeans that were found there, *and* the men of war.

4 And it came to pass the second day[3117] after he had slain[4191] Gedaliah, and no man[376] knew[3045] *it,*

5 That there came certain[582] from Shechem, from Shiloh, and from Samaria, *even* fourscore men,[376] [a]having their beards[2206] shaven, and their clothes rent, and having cut themselves,[1413] with offerings[4503] and incense in their hand,[3027] to bring *them* to [b]the house[1004] of the LORD.

6 And Ishmael the son of Nethaniah went forth from Mizpah to meet them, [I]weeping all along as he went: and it came to pass, as he met them, he said unto them, Come to Gedaliah the son of Ahikam.

7 And it was *so,* when they came into the midst of the city, that Ishmael the son of Nethaniah slew[7819] them, *and cast them* into the midst of the pit,[953] he, and the men that *were* with him.

8 But ten men were found among them that said unto Ishmael, Slay[4191] us not: for we have treasures in the field,[7704] of wheat, and of barley, and of oil,[8081] and of honey. So he forbare, and slew them not among their brethren.[251]

9 Now the pit wherein Ishmael had cast all the dead bodies[6297] of the men, whom he had slain[5221] [I]because of Gedaliah, *was* it [a]which Asa the king had made for fear of Baasha king of Israel:

10 [I]Hebr. *to stand before* [a]Deut. 1:38
14 [I]Hebr. *to strike thee in soul* [a]Jer. 41:10
1 [a]2Kgs. 25:25; Jer. 40:6, 8
2 [a]2Kgs. 25:25
5 [a]Lev. 19:27, 28; Deut. 14:1; Isa. 15:2 [b]1Sam. 1:7; 2Kgs. 25:9
6 [I]Hebr. *in going and weeping*
9 [I]Hebr. *by the hand,* or, *by the side of Gedaliah* [a]1Kgs. 15:22; 2Chr. 16:6

and Ishmael the son of Nethaniah filled it with *them that were* slain.[2491]

10 Then Ishmael carried away captive[7617] all the residue[7611] of the people[5971] that *were* in Mizpah, [a]*even* the king's[4428] daughters, and all the people that remained[7604] in Mizpah, [b]whom Nebuzar–adan the captain of the guard had committed[6485] to Gedaliah the son of Ahikam: and Ishmael the son of Nethaniah carried them away captive, and departed to go over[5674] to [c]the Ammonites.

11 But when Johanan the son of Kareah, and all [a]the captains[8269] of the forces[2428] that *were* with him, heard[8085] of all the evil[7451] that Ishmael the son of Nethaniah had done,

12 Then they took all the men, and went to fight with Ishmael the son of Nethaniah, and found him by [a]the great waters that *are* in Gibeon.

13 Now it came to pass, *that* when all the people which *were* with Ishmael saw[7200] Johanan the son of Kareah, and all the captains of the forces that *were* with him, then they were glad.

14 So all the people that Ishmael had carried away captive from Mizpah cast about and returned,[7725] and went unto Johanan the son of Kareah.

15 But Ishmael the son of Nethaniah escaped[4422] from Johanan with eight men, and went to the Ammonites.

16 Then took Johanan the son of Kareah, and all the captains of the forces that *were* with him, all the remnant[7611] of the people whom he had recovered[7725] from Ishmael the son of Nethaniah, from Mizpah, after *that* he had slain Gedaliah the son of Ahikam, *even* mighty[1397] men of war, and the women,[802] and the children,[2945] and the eunuchs,[5631] whom he had brought again[7725] from Gibeon:

17 And they departed, and dwelt in the habitation of [a]Chimham, which is by Bethlehem, to go to enter into Egypt,

18 Because of the Chaldeans: for they were afraid[3372] of them, because Ishmael the son of Nethaniah had slain Gedaliah the son of Ahikam, [a]whom the king of Babylon made governor in the land.

Jeremiah's Message to Johanan

42 Then all the captains[8269] of the forces,[2428] [a]and Johanan the son of Kareah, and Jezaniah the son of Hoshaiah, and all the people[5971] from the least even unto the greatest, came near,[5066]

2 And said unto Jeremiah the prophet,[5030] [1]Let, we beseech thee,[4994] our supplication[8467] be accepted[5307] before thee, and [a]pray[6419] for us unto the LORD thy God,[430] *even* for all this remnant;[7611] (for we are left[7604] *but* [b]a few of many, as thine eyes do behold[7200] us:)

3 That the LORD thy God may shew[5046] us [a]the way[1870] wherein we may walk, and the thing that we may do.

4 Then Jeremiah the prophet said unto them, I have heard[8085] *you;* behold, I will pray unto the LORD your God according to your words; and it shall come to pass, *that* [a]whatsoever thing the LORD shall answer you, I will declare[5046] *it* unto you; I will [b]keep nothing back from you.

5 Then they said to Jeremiah, [a]The LORD be a true[571] and faithful[539] witness between us, if we do not even according to all things for the which the LORD thy God shall send thee to us.

6 Whether *it be* good,[2896] or whether *it be* evil,[7451] we will obey[8085] the voice of the LORD our God, to whom we send thee; [a]that it may be well with us, when we obey the voice of the LORD our God.

7 And it came to pass after ten days, that the word of the LORD came unto Jeremiah.

8 Then called[7121] he Johanan the son of Kareah, and all the captains of the forces which *were* with him, and all the people from the least even to the greatest,

9 And said unto them, Thus saith the LORD, the God of Israel, unto whom ye sent me to present[5307] your supplication before him;

10 [a]Jer. 43:6 [b]Jer. 40:7 [c]Jer. 40:14
11 [a]Jer. 40:7, 8, 13
12 [a]2Sam. 2:13
17 [a]2Sam. 19:37, 38
18 [a]Jer. 40:5
1 [a]Jer. 40:8, 13; 41:11
2 [1]Or, *Let our supplication fall before thee* [a]1Sam. 7:8; 12:19; Isa. 37:4; James 5:16 [b]Lev. 26:22
3 [a]Ezra 8:21
4 [a]1Kgs. 22:14 [b]1Sam. 3:18; Acts 20:20
5 [a]Gen. 31:50
6 [a]Deut. 6:3; Jer. 7:23

10 If ye will still abide in this land,[776] then [a]will I build you, and not pull *you* down,[2040] and I will plant you, and not pluck *you* up: for I [b]repent[5162] me of the evil that I have done unto you.

11 Be not afraid[3372] of the king[4428] of Babylon, of whom ye are afraid;[3373] be not afraid of him, saith[5002] the LORD: [a]for I *am* with you to save[3467] you, and to deliver[5337] you from his hand.[3027]

12 And [a]I will shew mercies[7356] unto you, that he may have mercy[7355] upon you, and cause you to return[7725] to your own land.[127]

13 But if [a]ye say,[559] We will not dwell in this land, neither obey the voice of the LORD your God,

14 Saying, No; but we will go into the land of Egypt, where we shall see no war, nor hear[8085] the sound of the trumpet, nor have hunger of bread; and there will we dwell:

15 And now therefore hear the word of the LORD, ye remnant of Judah; Thus saith the LORD of hosts,[6635] the God of Israel; If ye [a]wholly set[7760] [b]your faces to enter into Egypt, and go to sojourn[1481] there;

16 Then it shall come to pass, *that* the sword,[2719] [a]which ye feared,[3373] shall overtake you there in the land of Egypt, and the famine, whereof ye were afraid,[1672] [I]shall follow close after you there in Egypt; and there ye shall die.[4191]

17 [I]So shall it be with all the men[582] that set their faces to go into Egypt to sojourn there; they shall die [a]by the sword, by the famine, and by the pestilence:[1698] and [b]none of them shall remain[8300] or escape from the evil that I will bring upon them.

18 For thus saith the LORD of hosts, the God of Israel; As mine anger[639] and my fury[2534] hath been [a]poured forth upon the inhabitants of Jerusalem; so shall my fury be poured forth[5413] upon you, when ye shall enter into Egypt: and [b]ye shall be an execration,[423] and an astonishment,[8047] and a curse,[7045] and a reproach;[2781] and ye shall see this place no more.

19 The LORD hath said concerning you, O ye remnant of Judah; [a]Go ye not into Egypt: know[3045] certainly that I have [I]admonished[5749] you this day.

20 For [I]ye dissembled[8582] in your hearts, when ye sent me unto the LORD your God, saying, [a]Pray for us unto the LORD our God; and according unto all that the LORD our God shall say, so declare unto us, and we will do *it.*

21 And *now* I have this day declared *it* to you; but ye have not obeyed[8085] the voice of the LORD your God, nor any *thing* for the which he hath sent me unto you.

22 Now therefore know[3045] certainly that [a]ye shall die by the sword, by the famine, and by the pestilence, in the place whither ye desire [I]to go *and* to sojourn.

Jeremiah Taken to Egypt

43 And it came to pass, *that* when Jeremiah had made an end[3615] of speaking[1696] unto all the people[5971] all the words[1697] of the LORD their God,[430] for which the LORD their God had sent him to them, *even* all these words,

2 [a]Then spake[559] Azariah the son of Hoshaiah, and Johanan the son of Kareah, and all the proud[2086] men,[582] saying unto Jeremiah, Thou speakest falsely:[8267] the LORD our God hath not sent thee to say, Go not into Egypt to sojourn[1481] there:

3 But Baruch the son of Neriah setteth thee on[5496] against us, for to deliver us into the hand[3027] of the Chaldeans, that they might put us to death,[4191] and carry us away captives[1540] into Babylon.

4 So Johanan the son of Kareah, and all the captains[8269] of the forces,[2428] and all the people, obeyed[8085] not the voice of the LORD, to dwell in the land[776] of Judah.

5 But Johanan the son of Kareah, and all the captains of the forces, took [a]all the remnant[7611] of Judah, that were returned[7725] from all nations,[1471] whither they had been driven, to dwell[1481] in the land of Judah;

6 *Even* men,[1397] and women,[802] and

---

10 [a]Jer. 24:6; 31:28; 33:7 [b]Deut. 32:36; Jer. 18:8

11 [a]Isa. 43:5; Rom. 8:31

12 [a]Ps. 106:45, 46

13 [a]Jer. 44:16

15 [a]Deut. 17:16; Jer. 44:12-14 [b]Luke 9:51

16 [I]Hebr. *shall cleave after you* [a]Ezek. 11:8

17 [I]Hebr. *So shall all the men be* [a]Jer. 24:10; 42:22 [b]Jer. 44:14, 28

18 [a]Jer. 7:20 [b]Jer. 18:16; 24:9; 26:6; 29:18, 22; 44:12; Zech. 8:13

19 [I]Hebr. *testified against you* [a]Deut. 17:16

20 [I]Or, *ye have used deceit against your souls* [a]Jer. 42:2

22 [I]Or, *to go to sojourn* [a]Jer. 42:17; Ezek. 6:11

2 [a]Jer. 42:1

5 [a]Jer. 40:11, 12

children,[2945] [a]and the king's[4428] daughters, [b]and every person that
Nebuzar–adan the captain of the guard
had left with Gedaliah the son of
Ahikam the son of Shaphan, and
Jeremiah the prophet,[5030] and Baruch the
son of Neriah.
7 So they came into the land of
Egypt: for they obeyed not the voice of
the LORD: thus came they *even* to
[a]Tahpanhes.
8 Then came the word of the LORD
unto Jeremiah in Tahpanhes, saying,
9 Take great stones in thine hand
and hide them in the clay in the brick-
kiln, which *is* at the entry of Pharaoh's
house[1004] in Tahpanhes, in the sight of
the men of Judah;
10 And say unto them, Thus saith
the LORD of hosts,[6635] the God of Israel;
Behold, I will send and take Nebuchadrezzar the king[4428] of Babylon,
[a]my servant,[5650] and will set[7760] his
throne[3678] upon these stones that I have
hid; and he shall spread his royal pavilion over them.
11 [a]And when he cometh, he shall
smite[5221] the land of Egypt, *and deliver*
[b]such *as are* for death[4194] to death; and
such *as are* for captivity[7628] to captivity;
and such *as are* for the sword[2719] to the
sword.
12 And I will kindle a fire in the
houses[1004] of [a]the gods[430] of Egypt; and
he shall burn[8313] them, and carry them
away captives:[7617] and he shall array
himself with the land of Egypt, as a
shepherd putteth on his garment; and he
shall go forth from thence in peace.
13 He shall break[7665] also the
[I]images[4676] of [II]Beth–shemesh, that *is* in
the land of Egypt; and the houses of the
gods of the Egyptians shall he burn with
fire.

6 [a]Jer. 41:10 [b]Jer. 39:10; 40:7
7 [a]Isa. 30:4; Jer. 2:16; 44:1
10 [a]Jer. 25:9; 27:6; Ezek. 29:18, 20
11 [a]Jer. 44:13; 46:13 [b]Jer. 15:2; Zech. 11:9
12 [a]Jer. 46:25
13 [I]Hebr. *statues, or, standing images* [II]Or, *The house of the sun*
1 [a]Ex. 14:2; Jer. 46:14 [b]Jer. 43:7 [c]Isa. 19:13
2 [a]Jer. 9:11; 34:22
3 [a]Jer. 19:4 [b]Deut. 13:6; 32:17
4 [a]2Chr. 36:15; Jer. 7:25; 25:4; 26:5; 29:19
6 [a]Jer. 42:18
7 [I]Hebr. *out of the midst of Judah* [a]Num. 16:38; Jer. 7:19
8 [a]Jer. 25:6, 7

Jeremiah Preaches in Egypt

44 The word that came to Jeremiah
concerning all the Jews which
dwell in the land[776] of Egypt, which
dwell at [a]Migdol, and at [b]Tahpanhes, and
at [c]Noph, and in the country[776] of
Pathros, saying,
2 Thus saith the LORD of hosts,[6635]
the God[430] of Israel; Ye have seen[7200] all
the evil[7451] that I have brought upon
Jerusalem, and upon all the cities of
Judah; and, behold, this day[3117] they *are*
[a]a desolation,[2723] and no man dwelleth
therein,
3 Because of their wickedness[7451]
which they have committed[6213] to
provoke me to anger,[3707] in that they
went [a]to burn incense,[6999] *and* to
[b]serve[5647] other gods,[430] whom they
knew[3045] not, *neither* they, ye, nor your
fathers.[1]
4 Howbeit [a]I sent unto you all my
servants[5650] the prophets,[5030] rising
early and sending *them,* saying, Oh, do
not this abominable[8441] thing that I
hate.[8130]
5 But they hearkened[8085] not, nor inclined their ear[241] to turn[7725] from their
wickedness, to burn no incense unto
other gods.
6 Wherefore [a]my fury and mine
anger[639] was poured forth, and was kindled in the cities of Judah and in the
streets of Jerusalem; and they are
wasted[2723] *and* desolate,[8077] as at this
day.
7 Therefore now thus saith the LORD,
the God of hosts, the God of Israel;
Wherefore commit[6213] ye *this* great evil
[a]against your souls,[5315] to cut off[3772] from
you man[376] and woman,[802] child and
suckling, [I]out of Judah, to leave[3498] you
none to remain;[7611]
🔑8 In that ye [a]provoke me unto

🔑 **44:8** Apparently, the group of Jews who had fled to Egypt were still involved in idolatry. These people somehow thought that their well-being depended upon their worship of "the queen of heaven" (44:17, 18, cf. Amos 4:4–11). Only the reality of seventy years in exile finally cured Israel of idolatry. Israel had problems with legalism and pharisaism after the Exile, but never again did idolatry become prevalent.

wrath[3707] with the works of your hands,[3027] burning incense unto other gods in the land of Egypt, whither ye be gone to dwell,[1481] that ye might cut yourselves off, and that ye might be [b]a curse[7045] and a reproach[2781] among all the nations[1471] of the earth?[776]

9 Have ye forgotten the [I]wickedness of your fathers, and the wickedness of the kings[4428] of Judah, and the wickedness of their wives,[802] and your own wickedness, and the wickedness of your wives, which they have committed in the land of Judah, and in the streets of Jerusalem?

10 They are not [I][a]humbled[1792] *even* unto this day, neither have they [b]feared,[3372] nor walked in my law,[8451] nor in my statutes,[2708] that I set before you and before your fathers.

11 Therefore thus saith the LORD of hosts, the God of Israel; Behold, [a]I will set[7760] my face against you for evil, and to cut off all Judah.

12 And I will take the remnant[7611] of Judah, that have set their faces to go into the land of Egypt to sojourn[1481] there, and [a]they shall all be consumed,[8552] *and* fall in the land of Egypt; they shall *even* be consumed by the sword *and* by the famine: they shall die,[4191] from the least even unto the greatest, by the sword[2719] and by the famine: and [b]they shall be an execration,[423] *and* an astonishment,[8047] and a curse, and a reproach.

13 [a]For I will punish[6485] them that dwell in the land of Egypt, as I have punished Jerusalem, by the sword, by the famine, and by the pestilence:[1698]

14 So that none of the remnant of Judah, which are gone into the land of Egypt to sojourn there, shall escape or remain,[8300] that they should return[7725] into the land of Judah, to the which they [I]have a desire to return to dwell there: for [a]none shall return but such as shall escape.

15 Then all the men[582] which knew that their wives had burned incense[6999] unto other gods, and all the women that stood by, a great multitude,[6951] even all the people[5971] that dwelt in the land of Egypt, in Pathros, answered Jeremiah, saying,

16 *As for* the word that thou hast spoken unto us in the name of the LORD, [a]we will not hearken[8085] unto thee.

17 But we will certainly do [a]whatsoever thing goeth forth out of our own mouth,[6310] to burn incense unto the [I][b]queen[4446] of heaven,[8064] and to pour out[5258] drink offerings[5262] unto her, as we have done, we, and our fathers, our kings, and our princes,[8269] in the cities of Judah, and in the streets of Jerusalem: for *then* had we plenty of [II]victuals,[3899] and were well, and saw[7200] no evil.

18 But since we left off to burn incense to the queen of heaven, and to pour out drink offerings unto her, we have wanted[2637] all *things,* and have been consumed by the sword and by the famine.

19 [a]And when we burned incense to the queen of heaven, and poured out[5258] drink offerings[5262] unto her, did we make her cakes to worship[6087] her, and pour out drink offerings unto her, without our [I]men?

20 Then Jeremiah said unto all the people, to the men,[1397] and to the women, and to all the people which had given him *that* answer, saying,

21 The incense that ye burned in the cities of Judah, and in the streets of Jerusalem, ye, and your fathers, your kings, and your princes, and the people of the land, did not the LORD remember[2142] them, came it *not* into his mind?[3820]

22 So that the LORD could no longer bear,[5375] because of the evil[7455] of your doings, *and* because of the abominations[8441] which ye have committed; therefore is your land [a]a desolation, and an astonishment, and a curse, without an inhabitant, [b]as at this day.

23 Because ye have burned incense, and because ye have sinned[2398] against the LORD, and have not obeyed[8085] the voice of the LORD, nor walked in his law, nor in his statutes, nor in his testimonies;[5715] [a]therefore this evil is happened unto you, as at this day.

8 [b]Jer. 42:18; 44:12

9 [I]Hebr. *wickednesses,* or, *punishments*

10 [I]Hebr. *contrite,* [a]Ps. 51:17 [b]Prov. 28:14

11 [a]Lev. 17:10; 20:5, 6; Jer. 21:10; Amos 9:4

12 [a]Jer. 42:15-17, 22 [b]Jer. 42:18

13 [a]Jer. 43:11

14 [I]Hebr. *lift up their soul* [a]Jer. 44:28

16 [a]Jer. 6:16

17 [I]Or, *frame of heaven* [II]Hebr. *bread* [a]Num. 30:12; Deut. 23:23; Judg. 11:36; Jer. 44:25 [b]Jer. 7:18

19 [I]Or, *husbands* [a]Jer. 7:18

22 [a]Jer. 25:11, 18, 38 [b]Jer. 44:6

23 [a]Dan. 9:11, 12

24 Moreover Jeremiah said unto all the people, and to all the women, Hear[8085] the word of the LORD, all Judah [a]that *are* in the land of Egypt:

25 Thus saith the LORD of hosts, the God of Israel, saying; [a]Ye and your wives have both spoken[1696] with your mouths,[6310] and fulfilled with your hand,[3027] saying, We will surely perform[6213] our vows[5088] that we have vowed,[5087] to burn incense to the queen of heaven, and to pour out drink offerings unto her: ye will surely accomplish[6965] your vows, and surely perform your vows.

26 Therefore hear ye the word of the LORD, all Judah that dwell in the land of Egypt; Behold, [a]I have sworn by my great name, saith the LORD, that [b]my name shall no more be named[7121] in the mouth of any man of Judah in all the land of Egypt, saying, The Lord[136] GOD liveth.[2416]

27 [a]Behold, I will watch over them for evil, and not for good:[2896] and all the men[376] of Judah that *are* in the land of Egypt [b]shall be consumed by the sword and by the famine, until there be an end[3615] of them.

28 Yet [a]a small number that escape the sword shall return out of the land of Egypt into the land of Judah, and all the remnant of Judah, that are gone into the land of Egypt to sojourn there, shall know[3045] whose [b]words[1697] shall stand, Imine, or theirs.

29 And this *shall be* a sign[226] unto you, saith5002 the LORD, that I will punish you in this place, that ye may know that my words shall [a]surely stand against you for evil:

30 Thus saith the LORD; Behold, [a]I will give Pharaoh-hophra king[4428] of Egypt into the hand of his enemies, and into the hand of them that seek his life;[5315] as I gave [b]Zedekiah king of Judah into the hand of Nebuchadrezzar king of Babylon, his enemy, and that sought his life.

Jeremiah's Message to Baruch

45 The [a]word[1697] that Jeremiah the prophet[5030] spake[1696] unto Baruch the son of Neriah, when he had written these words in a book[5612] at the mouth[6310] of Jeremiah, in the fourth year of Jehoiakim the son of Josiah king[4428] of Judah, saying,

2 Thus saith[559] the LORD, the God[430] of Israel, unto thee, O Baruch;

3 Thou didst say, Woe is me now! for the LORD hath added grief to my sorrow; I fainted in my sighing, and I find no rest.

4 Thus shalt thou say unto him, The LORD saith thus; Behold, [a]*that* which I have built will I break down,[2040] and that which I have planted I will pluck up, even this whole land.[776]

5 And seekest thou great things for thyself? seek *them* not; for, behold, [a]I will bring evil[7451] upon all flesh,[1320] saith the LORD: but thy life[5315] will I give unto thee [b]for a prey in all places whither thou goest.

The Battle of Carchemish

46 The word[1697] of the LORD which came to Jeremiah the prophet[5030] against [a]the Gentiles;[1471]

2 Against Egypt, [a]against the army[2428] of Pharaoh-necho king[4428] of Egypt, which was by the river Euphrates in Carchemish, which Nebuchadrezzar king of Babylon smote[5221] in the fourth year of Jehoiakim the son of Josiah king of Judah.

3 [a]Order6186 ye the buckler4043 and shield, and draw near[5066] to battle.

4 Harness the horses; and get up, ye horsemen, and stand forth with *your* helmets; furbish4838 the spears, *and* put on the brigandines.5630

5 Wherefore have I seen[7200] them dismayed *and* turned away back? and their mighty ones are Ibeaten down,[3807] and are IIfled apace, and look not back: *for* [a]fear[4032] *was* round about, saith the LORD.

6 Let not the swift flee away, nor the mighty man escape;[4422] they shall [a]stumble,[3782] and fall toward the north by the river Euphrates.

7 Who *is* this *that* cometh up[5927]

---

24 [a]Jer. 43:7; 44:15

25 [a]Jer. 44:15

26 [a]Gen. 22:16 [b]Ezek. 20:39

27 [a]Jer. 1:10; 31:28; Ezek. 7:6 [b]Jer. 44:12

28 IHebr. *from me, or them* [a]Jer. 44:14; Isa. 27:13 [b]Jer. 44:17, 25, 26

29 [a]Ps. 33:11

30 [a]Jer. 46:25, 26; Ezek. 29:3; 30:21 [b]Jer. 39:5

1 [a]Jer. 36:1, 4, 32

4 [a]Isa. 5:5

5 [a]Jer. 25:26 [b]Jer. 21:9; 38:2; 39:18

1 [a]Jer. 25:15

2 [a]2Kgs. 23:29; 2Chr. 35:20

3 [a]Jer. 51:11, 12; Nah. 2:1; 3:14

5 IHebr. *broken in pieces* IIHebr. *fled a flight* [a]Jer. 6:25; 49:29

6 [a]Dan. 11:19

[a]as a flood, whose waters are moved as the rivers?

8 Egypt riseth up like a flood, and *his* waters are moved like the rivers; and he saith, I will go up, *and* will cover[3680] the earth;[776] I will destroy[6] the city and the inhabitants thereof.

9 Come up, ye horses; and rage,[1984] ye chariots; and let the mighty men come forth; [I]the Ethiopians and [II]the Libyans, that handle the shield; and the Lydians, [a]that handle *and* bend the bow.

10 For this *is* [a]the day[3117] of the Lord[136] GOD of hosts,[6635] a day of vengeance,[5360] that he may avenge[5358] him of his adversaries: and [b]the sword[2719] shall devour, and it shall be satiate and made drunk with their blood:[1818] for the Lord GOD of hosts [c]hath a sacrifice[2077] in the north country[776] by the river Euphrates.

11 [a]Go up into Gilead, and take balm, [b]O virgin,[1330] the daughter of Egypt: in vain[7723] shalt thou use many medicines; *for* [I][c]thou shalt not be cured.[8585]

12 The nations[1471] have heard[8085] of thy shame, and thy cry hath filled the land:[776] for the mighty man hath stumbled[3782] against the mighty, *and* they are fallen[5307] both together.

Nebuchadrezzar's Coming

13 The word that the LORD spake[1696] to Jeremiah the prophet, how Nebuchadrezzar king of Babylon should come *and* [a]smite[5221] the land of Egypt.

14 Declare[5046] ye in Egypt, and publish[8085] in Migdol, and publish in Noph and in Tahpanhes: say[559] ye, [a]Stand fast, and prepare[3559] thee; for [b]the sword shall devour round about thee.

15 Why are thy valiant[47] *men* swept away? they stood not, because the LORD did drive them.

16 He [I]made many to fall,[3782] yea, [a]one[376] fell[5307] upon another:[7453] and they said, Arise, and let us go again[7725] to our own people,[5971] and to the land of our nativity, from the oppressing[3238] sword.

17 They did cry[7121] there, Pharaoh king of Egypt *is but* a noise;[7588] he hath passed[5674] the time appointed.[4150]

18 *As* I live,[2416] saith[5002] the King, [a]whose name *is* the LORD of hosts, Surely as Tabor *is* among the mountains, and as Carmel by the sea, *so* shall he come.

19 O [a]thou daughter dwelling in Egypt, [I]furnish thyself [b]to go into captivity:[1473] for Noph shall be waste[8047] and desolate without an inhabitant.

20 Egypt *is like* a very fair [a]heifer, *but* destruction[7171] cometh; it cometh [b]out of the north.

21 Also her hired men *are* in the midst[7130] of her like [I]fatted bullocks; for they also are turned back, *and* are fled away together: they did not stand, because [a]the day of their calamity[343] was come upon them, *and* the time[6256] of their visitation.[6489]

22 [a]The voice thereof shall go like a serpent;[5175] for they shall march with an army, and come against her with axes, as hewers[2404] of wood.

23 They shall [a]cut down[3772] her forest, saith the LORD, though it cannot be searched; because they are more than [b]the grasshoppers, and *are* innumerable.

24 The daughter of Egypt shall be confounded; she shall be delivered into the hand[3027] of [a]the people of the north.

25 The LORD of hosts, the God[430] of Israel, saith; Behold, I will punish[6485] the [I]multitude of [a]No, and Pharaoh, and Egypt, [b]with their gods,[430] and their kings;[4428] even Pharaoh, and *all* them that trust[982] in him:

26 [a]And I will deliver them into the hand of those that seek their lives,[5315] and into the hand of Nebuchadrezzar king of Babylon, and into the hand of his servants: and [b]afterward it shall be inhabited,[7931] as in the days[3117] of old,[6924] saith the LORD.

27 [a]But fear[3372] not thou, O my servant[5650] Jacob, and be not dismayed,[2865] O Israel: for, behold, I will save[3467] thee from afar off, and thy seed[2233] from the land of their captivity;[7628] and Jacob shall return,[7725] and be in rest[8252] and at ease, and none shall make *him* afraid.[2729]

7 [a]Isa. 8:7, 8; Jer. 47:2; Dan. 11:22

9 [I]Hebr. *Cush* [II]Hebr. *Put* [a]Isa. 66:19

10 [a]Isa. 13:6; Joel 1:15; 2:1 [b]Deut. 32:42; Isa. 34:6 [c]Isa. 34:6; Zeph. 1:7; Ezek. 39:17

11 [I]Hebr. *no cure* shall be *unto thee* [a]Jer. 8:22; 51:8 [b]Isa. 47:1 [c]Ezek. 30:21

13 [a]Isa. 19:1; Jer. 43:10, 11

14 [a]Jer. 46:3, 4 [b]Jer. 46:10

16 [I]Hebr. *multiplied the faller* [a]Lev. 26:37

18 [a]Isa. 47:4; 48:2; Jer. 48:15

19 [I]Hebr. *make thee instruments of captivity* [a]Jer. 48:18 [b]Isa. 20:4

20 [a]Hos. 10:11 [b]Jer. 1:14; 46:6, 10; 47:2

21 [I]Hebr. *bullocks of the stall* [a]Ps. 37:13; Jer. 50:27

22 [a]Isa. 29:4

23 [a]Isa. 10:34 [b]Judg. 6:5

24 [a]Jer. 1:15

25 [I]Or, *nourisher* [a]Ezek. 30:14-16; Nah. 3:8 [b]Jer. 43:12, 13; Ezek. 30:13

26 [a]Jer. 44:30; Ezek. 32:11 [b]Ezek. 29:11, 13, 14

27 [a]Isa. 41:13, 14; 43:5; 44:2; Jer. 30:10, 11

28 Fear thou not, O Jacob my servant, saith the LORD: for I *am* with thee; for I will make a full end[3617] of all the nations whither I have driven thee: but I will not make [a]a full end of thee, but correct[3256] thee in measure;[4941] yet will I [I]not leave thee wholly unpunished.[5352]

The Philistines

47 The word of the LORD that came to Jeremiah the prophet[5030] [a]against the Philistines, [b]before that Pharaoh smote[5221] [I]Gaza.

2 Thus saith the LORD; Behold, [a]waters rise up[5927] [b]out of the north, and shall be an overflowing[7857] flood, and shall overflow the land,[776] and [I]all that is therein; the city, and them that dwell therein: then the men[120] shall cry,[2199] and all the inhabitants of the land shall howl.

3 At the [a]noise of the stamping of the hoofs of his strong[47] *horses,* at the rushing of his chariots, *and at* the rumbling of his wheels,[1534] the fathers[1] shall not look back to *their* children[1121] for feebleness of hands;[3027]

4 Because of the day[3117] that cometh to spoil[7703] all the Philistines, *and* to cut off[3772] from [a]Tyrus and Zidon every helper that remaineth:[8300] for the LORD will spoil the Philistines, [b]the remnant[7611] of [I]the country of [c]Caphtor.

5 [a]Baldness is come upon Gaza; [b]Ashkelon is cut off[1820] *with* the remnant of their valley: how long wilt thou [c]cut thyself?

6 O thou [a]sword[2719] of the LORD, how long *will it be* ere thou be quiet?[8252] [I]put up thyself into thy scabbard, rest, and be still.

7 [I]How can it be quiet, seeing the LORD hath [a]given it a charge[6680] against Ashkelon, and against the sea shore? there hath he [b]appointed[3259] it.

Moab

48 Against [a]Moab thus saith[559] the LORD of hosts,[6635] the God[430] of Israel; Woe unto [b]Nebo! for it is spoiled:[7703] [c]Kiriathaim is confounded *and* taken: [I]Misgab is confounded and dismayed.[2865]

2 [a]*There shall be* no more praise[8416] of Moab: in [b]Heshbon they have devised[2803] evil[7451] against it; come, and let us cut it off[3772] from *being* a nation.[1471] Also thou shalt [Ic]be cut down, O Madmen; the sword[2719] shall [II]pursue thee.

3 [a]A voice of crying *shall be* from Horonaim, spoiling[7701] and great destruction.[7667]

4 Moab is destroyed;[7665] her little ones have caused a cry to be heard.[8085]

5 [a]For in the going up of Luhith [I]continual weeping shall go up; for in the going down of Horonaim the enemies have heard a cry of destruction.

6 [a]Flee, save[3467] your lives,[5315] and be like [I]the [b]heath[6176] in the wilderness.

7 For because thou hast trusted[982] in thy works and in thy treasures, thou shalt also be taken: and [a]Chemosh shall go forth into captivity[1473] *with* his [b]priests[3548] and his princes[8269] together.

8 And [a]the spoiler[7703] shall come upon every city, and no city shall escape:[4422] the valley also shall perish,[6] and the plain shall be destroyed,[8045] as the LORD hath spoken.

9 [a]Give wings unto Moab, that it may flee and get away: for the cities thereof shall be desolate,[8047] without any to dwell therein.

10 [a]Cursed[779] *be* he that doeth[6213] the work[4399] of the LORD [I]deceitfully,[7423] and cursed *be* he that keepeth back his sword from blood.[1818]

11 Moab hath been at ease from his youth, and he [a]hath settled[8252] on his lees,[8105] and hath not been emptied from vessel to vessel, neither hath he gone into captivity: therefore his taste[2940] [I]remained in him, and his scent is not changed.

12 Therefore, behold, the days[3117] come, saith[5002] the LORD, that I will send unto him wanderers, that shall cause him to wander, and shall empty his vessels, and break their bottles.

---

28 IOr, *not utterly cut thee off* aJer. 10:24; 30:11

1 IHebr. *Azzah* aJer. 25:20; Ezek. 25:15, 16; Zeph. 2:4, 5 bAmos 1:6-8

2 IHebr. *the fullness thereof* aIsa. 8:7; Jer. 46:7, 8 bJer. 1:14; 46:20

3 aJer. 8:16; Nah. 3:2

4 IHebr. *the isle* aJer. 25:22 bEzek. 25:16; Amos 1:8; 9:7 cGen. 10:14

5 aAmos 1:7; Mic. 1:16; Zeph. 2:4, 7; Zech. 9:5 bJer. 25:20 cJer. 16:6; 41:5; 48:37

6 IHebr. *gather thyself* aDeut. 32:41; Ezek. 21:3-5

7 IHebr. *How canst thou* aEzek. 14:17 bMic. 6:9

1 IOr, *The high place* aJer. 25:21; 27:3; Ezek. 25:9; Amos 2:1, 2 bNum. 32:38; 33:47; Isa. 15:2 cNum. 32:37

2 IOr, *be brought to silence* IIHebr. *go after thee* aIsa. 16:14 bIsa. 15:4 cIsa. 15:1

3 aJer. 48:5

5 IHebr. *weeping with weeping* aIsa. 15:5

6 IOr, *a naked tree* aJer. 51:6 bJer. 17:6

7 aNum. 21:29; Judg. 11:24; Isa. 46:1, 2; Jer. 43:12 bJer. 49:3

8 aJer. 6:26; 48:18

9 aPs. 55:6; Jer. 48:28

10 IOr, *negligently* aJudg. 5:23; 1Sam. 15:3, 9; 1Kgs. 20:42

11 IHebr. *stood* aZeph. 1:12

13 And Moab shall be ashamed[954] of [a]Chemosh, as the house[1004] of Israel [b]was ashamed of [c]Bethel their confidence.

14 How say[559] ye, [a]We *are* mighty and strong men[582] for the war?

15 [a]Moab is spoiled, and gone up *out of* her cities, and [I]his chosen young men are [b]gone down to the slaughter,[2874] saith [c]the King,[4428] whose name *is* the LORD of hosts.

16 The calamity[343] of Moab *is* near to come, and his affliction[7451] hasteth fast.

17 All ye that are about him, bemoan him; and all ye that know[3045] his name, say, [a]How is[7665] the strong staff[4294] broken,[7665] *and* the beautiful[8597] rod!

18 [a]Thou daughter that dost inhabit [b]Dibon, come down from *thy* glory,[3519] and sit in thirst; for [c]the spoiler of Moab shall come upon thee, *and* he shall destroy thy strong holds.

19 O inhabitant of [a]Aroer, [b]stand by the way,[1870] and espy;[6822] ask[7592] him that fleeth, and her that escapeth,[4422] *and* say, What is done?

20 Moab is confounded; for it is broken down:[2865] [a]howl and cry;[2199] tell[5046] ye it in [b]Arnon, that Moab is spoiled,

21 And judgment[4941] is come upon [a]the plain[4334] country;[776] upon Holon, and upon Jahazah, and upon Mephaath,

22 And upon Dibon, and upon Nebo, and upon Beth–diblathaim,

23 And upon Kiriathaim, and upon Beth–gamul, and upon Beth–meon,

24 And upon [a]Kerioth, and upon Bozrah, and upon all the cities of the land[776] of Moab, far or near.

25 [a]The horn of Moab is cut off, and his [b]arm is broken, saith the LORD.

26 [a]Make ye him drunken: for he magnified *himself* against the LORD: Moab also shall wallow[5606] in his vomit, and he also shall be in derision.

27 For [a]was not Israel a derision unto thee? [b]was he found among thieves? for since thou spakest of him, thou skippedst for joy.[5110]

28 O ye that dwell in Moab, leave[5800] the cities, and [a]dwell[7931] in the rock, and be like [b]the dove *that* maketh her nest in the sides of the hole's[6354] mouth.[6310]

29 We have heard the [a]pride[1347] of Moab, (he is exceeding proud) his loftiness, and his arrogancy, and his pride, and the haughtiness of his heart.[3820]

30 I know his wrath,[5678] saith the LORD; but *it shall* not *be* so; [a]his lies shall not so effect *it.*

31 Therefore [a]will I howl for Moab, and I will cry out for all Moab; *mine heart* shall mourn[1897] for the men of Kir–heres.

32 [a]O vine of Sibmah, I will weep for thee with the weeping of Jazer: thy plants are gone over[5674] the sea, they reach[5060] *even* to the sea of Jazer: the spoiler is fallen[5307] upon thy summer fruits and upon thy vintage.

33 And [a]joy and gladness is taken from the plentiful field, and from the land of Moab; and I have caused wine to fail from the winepresses: none shall tread with shouting; *their* shouting *shall be* no shouting.

34 [a]From the cry of Heshbon *even* unto Elealeh, *and even* unto Jahaz, have they uttered their voice, [b]from Zoar *even* unto Horonaim, *as* an heifer of three years old: for the waters also of Nimrim shall be [I]desolate.

35 Moreover I will cause to cease[7673] in Moab, saith the LORD, [a]him that offereth[5927] in the high places,[1116] and him that burneth incense[6999] to his gods.[430]

36 Therefore [a]mine heart shall sound for Moab like pipes,[2485] and mine heart shall sound like pipes for the men of Kir–heres: because [b]the riches *that* he hath gotten[6213] are perished.[6]

37 For [a]every head[7218] *shall be* bald, and every beard[2206] [I]clipped: upon all the hands[3027] *shall be* cuttings, and [b]upon the loins sackcloth.

38 *There shall be* lamentation generally upon all the housetops of Moab, and in the streets thereof: for I have broken Moab like [a]a vessel wherein *is* no pleasure,[2656] saith the LORD.

39 They shall howl, *saying,* How is it broken down! how hath Moab turned the

13 [a]Judg. 11:24; 1Kgs. 11:7 [b]Hos. 10:6 [c]1Kgs. 12:29
14 [a]Isa. 16:6
15 [I]Hebr. *the choice of* [a]Jer. 48:8, 9, 18 [b]Jer. 50:27 [c]Jer. 46:18; 51:57
17 [a]Isa. 9:4; 14:4, 5
18 [a]Isa. 47:1; Jer. 46:19 [b]Num. 21:30; Isa. 15:2 [c]Jer. 48:8
19 [a]Deut. 2:36 [b]1Sam. 4:13, 16
20 [a]Isa. 16:7 [b]Num. 21:13
21 [a]Jer. 48:8
24 [a]Jer. 48:41; Amos 2:2
25 [a]Ps. 75:10 [b]Ezek. 30:21
26 [a]Jer. 25:15, 27
27 [a]Zeph. 2:8 [b]Jer. 2:26
28 [a]Ps. 55:6, 7; Jer. 48:9 [b]Song 2:14
29 [a]Isa. 16:6
30 [a]Isa. 16:6; Jer. 50:36
31 [a]Isa. 15:5; 16:7, 11
32 [a]Isa. 16:8, 9
33 [a]Isa. 16:10; Joel 1:12
34 [I]Hebr. *desolations* [a]Isa. 15:4-6 [b]Isa. 15:5, 6; Jer. 48:5
35 [a]Isa. 15:2; 16:12
36 [a]Isa. 15:5; 16:11 [b]Isa. 15:7
37 [I]Hebr. *diminished* [a]Isa. 15:2, 3; Jer. 47:5 [b]Gen. 37:34
38 [a]Jer. 22:28

[I]back with shame[954] so shall Moab be a derision and a dismaying[4288] to all them about him.

40 For thus saith the LORD; Behold, [a]he shall fly as an eagle, and shall [b]spread his wings over Moab.

41 [I][a]Kerioth is taken, and the strong holds are surprised, and [b]the mighty men's hearts[3821] in Moab at that day[3117] shall be as the heart of a woman[802] in her pangs.

42 And Moab shall be destroyed [a]from *being* a people,[5971] because he hath magnified *himself* against the LORD.

43 [a]Fear, and the pit,[6354] and the snare,[6341] *shall be* upon thee, O inhabitant of Moab, saith the LORD.

44 He that fleeth from the fear shall fall into the pit; and he that getteth up[5927] out of the pit shall be taken in the snare: for [a]I will bring upon it, *even* upon Moab, the year of their visitation,[6486] saith the LORD.

45 They that fled stood under the shadow of Heshbon because of the force: but [a]a fire shall come forth out of Heshbon, and a flame from the midst of Sihon, and [b]shall devour the corner of Moab, and the crown of the head of the [I]tumultuous ones.

46 [a]Woe be unto thee, O Moab! the people of Chemosh perisheth:[6] for thy sons are taken [I]captives,[7628] and thy daughters captives.[7633]

47 Yet will I bring again[7725] the captivity[7622] of Moab [a]in the latter[319] days, saith the LORD. Thus far *is* the judgment of Moab.

The Ammonites

49 [I]Concerning [a]the Ammonites, thus saith the LORD; Hath Israel no sons?[1121] hath he no heir?[3423] why *then* doth [II]their king[4428] inherit [b]Gad, and his people[5971] dwell in his cities?

2 Therefore, behold, the days[3117] come, saith the LORD, that I will cause an alarm of war to be heard[8085] in [a]Rabbah of the Ammonites; and it shall be a desolate[8077] heap, and her daughters shall be burned with fire: then shall Israel be heir unto them that were his heirs, saith the LORD.

3 Howl, O Heshbon, for Ai is spoiled:[7703] cry, ye daughters of Rabbah, [a]gird you with sackcloth; lament, and run to and fro by the hedges; for [I][b]their king shall go into captivity,[1473] *and* his [c]priests[3548] and his princes[8269] together.

4 Wherefore gloriest[1984] thou in the valleys, [I]thy flowing valley, O [a]backsliding[7728] daughter? that trusted[982] in her treasures, [b]*saying,* Who shall come unto me?

5 Behold, I will bring a fear upon thee, saith the Lord[136] GOD of hosts,[6635] from all those that be about thee; and ye shall be driven out every man right forth; and none shall gather up[6908] him that wandereth.

6 And [a]afterward I will bring again[7725] the captivity[7622] of the children[1121] of Ammon, saith the LORD.

Edom

7 [a]Concerning Edom, thus saith the LORD of hosts; [b]*Is* wisdom[2451] no more in Teman? [c]is[6] counsel[6098] perished[6] from the prudent?[995] is their wisdom vanished?

8 [a]Flee ye, [I]turn back, dwell deep, O inhabitants of [b]Dedan; for I will bring the calamity[343] of Esau upon him, the time[6256] *that* I will visit[6485] him.

9 If [a]grapegatherers come to thee, would they not leave[7604] *some* gleaning grapes? if thieves by night,[3915] they will destroy [I]till they have enough.

10 [a]But I have made Esau bare, I have uncovered[1540] his secret places, and he shall not be able to hide himself: his seed[2233] is spoiled, and his brethren,[251] and his neighbours,[7934] and [b]he *is* not.

11 Leave[5800] thy fatherless children, I will preserve *them* alive;[2421] and let thy widows trust[982] in me.

12 For thus saith the LORD; Behold, [a]they whose judgment[4941] *was* not to drink of the cup have assuredly drunken; and *art* thou he *that* shall altogether go unpunished?[5352] thou shalt not go

39 [I]Hebr. *neck*

40 [a]Deut. 28:49; Jer. 49:22; Dan. 7:4; Hos. 8:1; Hab. 1:8 [b]Isa. 8:8

41 [I]Or, *The cities* [a]Jer. 41:24 [b]Isa. 13:8; 21:3; Jer. 30:6; 49:22, 24; 50:43; 51:30; Mic. 4:9

42 [a]Ps. 83:4; Isa. 7:8

43 [a]Isa. 24:17, 18

44 [a]Jer. 11:23

45 [I]Hebr. *children of noise* [a]Num. 21:28 [b]Num. 24:17

46 [I]Hebr. *in captivity* [a]Num. 21:29

47 [a]Jer. 49:6, 39

1 [I]Or, *Against* [II]Or, *Melcom* [a]Ezek. 21:28; 25:2; Amos 1:13; Zeph. 2:8, 9 [b]Amos 1:13

2 [a]Ezek. 25:5; Amos 1:14

3 [I]Or, *Melcom* [a]Isa. 32:11; Jer. 4:8; 6:26 [b]1Kgs. 11:5, 33 [c]Jer. 48:7; Amos 1:15

4 [I]Or, *thy valley floweth away* [a]Jer. 3:14; 7:24 [b]Jer. 21:13

6 [a]Jer. 48:47; 49:39

7 [a]Ezek. 25:12; Amos 1:11 [b]Obad. 1:8 [c]Isa. 19:11

8 [I]Or, *they are turned back* [a]Jer. 49:30 [b]Jer. 25:23

9 [I]Hebr. *their sufficiency* [a]Obad. 1:5

10 [a]Mal. 1:3 [b]Isa. 17:14

12 [a]Jer. 25:29; Obad. 1:16

unpunished, but thou shalt surely drink *of it.*

13 For [a]I have sworn by myself, saith the LORD, that [b]Bozrah shall become[1961] a desolation,[8047] a reproach,[2781] a waste, and a curse;[7045] and all the cities thereof shall be perpetual[5769] wastes.[2723]

14 I have heard a [a]rumour[8052] from the LORD, and an ambassador[6735] is sent unto the heathen,[1471] *saying,* Gather ye together, and come against her, and rise up to the battle.

15 For, lo, I will make thee small among the heathen, *and* despised among men.[120]

16 Thy terribleness hath deceived thee, *and* the pride[2087] of thine heart,[3820] O thou that dwellest[7931] in the clefts of the rock, that holdest the height of the hill: [a]though thou shouldest make thy [b]nest as high as the eagle, [c]I will bring thee down from thence, saith the LORD.

17 Also Edom shall be a desolation: [a]every one that goeth by it shall be astonished,[8074] and shall hiss at all the plagues[4347] thereof.

18 [a]As in the overthrow of Sodom and Gomorrah and the neighbour[7934] *cities* thereof, saith the LORD, no man shall abide there, neither shall[1481] a son[1121] of man[120] dwell[1481] in it.

19 [a]Behold, he shall come up[5927] like a lion from [b]the swelling of Jordan against the habitation of the strong: but I will suddenly make him run away from her: and who *is* a chosen *man, that* I may appoint[6485] over her? for [c]who *is* like me? and who will appoint me the time?[3259] and [d]who *is* that shepherd that will stand before me?

20 [a]Therefore hear[8085] the counsel of the LORD, that he hath taken against Edom; and his purposes,[4284] that he hath purposed[2803] against the inhabitants of Teman: Surely the least of the flock shall draw them out: surely he shall make their habitations desolate[8074] with them.

21 [a]The earth[776] is moved[7493] at the noise of their fall, at the cry the noise thereof was heard in the [I]Red sea.

22 Behold, [a]he shall come up and fly as the eagle, and spread his wings over Bozrah: and at that day[3117] shall the heart of the mighty men of Edom be as the heart of a woman[802] in her pangs.

Damascus

23 [a]Concerning Damascus. Hamath is confounded,[954] and Arpad: for they have heard evil[7451] tidings: they are [I]fainthearted; [b]*there is* sorrow[1674] [II]on the sea; it cannot be quiet.[8252]

24 Damascus is waxed feeble,[7503] *and* turneth herself to flee, and fear[7374] hath seized on *her:* [a]anguish[6869] and sorrows[2256] have taken her, as a woman in travail.

25 How is[5800] [a]the city of praise[8416] not left,[5800] the city of my joy!

26 [a]Therefore her young men shall fall in her streets, and all the men[582] of war shall be cut off in that day, saith the LORD of hosts.

27 And I will kindle a [a]fire in the wall of Damascus, and it shall consume the palaces[759] of Ben–hadad.

The Tribe of Kedar And the City of Hazor

28 [a]Concerning Kedar, and concerning the kingdoms[4467] of Hazor, which Nebuchadrezzar king of Babylon shall smite,[5221] thus saith the LORD; Arise ye, go up to Kedar, and spoil[7703] [b]the men of the east.

29 Their [a]tents[168] and their flocks shall they take away:[5375] they shall take to themselves their curtains, and all their vessels, and their camels; and they shall cry[7121] unto them, [b]Fear[4032] *is* on every side.

30 [a]Flee, [I]get you far off, dwell deep, O ye inhabitants of Hazor, saith the LORD; for Nebuchadrezzar king of Babylon hath taken counsel against you, and hath conceived a purpose[4284] against you.

31 Arise, get you up unto [a]the [I]wealthy nation,[1471] that dwelleth without care,[983] saith the LORD, which have

13 [a]Gen. 22:16; Isa. 45:23; Amos 6:8 [b]Isa. 34:6; 63:1
14 [a]Obad. 1:1-3
16 [a]Obad. 1:4 [b]Job 39:27 [c]Amos 9:2
17 [a]Jer. 18:16; 50:13
18 [a]Gen. 19:25; Deut. 29:23; Jer. 50:40; Amos 4:11
19 [a]Jer. 50:44 [b]Jer. 12:5 [c]Ex. 15:11 [d]Job 41:10
20 [a]Jer. 50:45
21 [I]Hebr. *Weedy sea* [a]Jer. 50:46
22 [a]Jer. 4:13; 48:40, 41
23 [I]Hebr. *melted* [II]Or, *as on the sea* [a]Isa. 17:1; 37:13; Amos 1:3; Zech. 9:1, 2 [b]Isa. 57:20
24 [a]Isa. 13:8; Jer. 4:31; 6:24; 30:6; 48:41; 49:22
25 [a]Jer. 33:9; 51:41
26 [a]Jer. 50:30; 51:4
27 [a]Amos 1:4
28 [a]Isa. 21:13 [b]Judg. 6:3; Job 1:3
29 [a]Ps. 120:5 [b]Jer. 6:25; 46:5
30 [I]Hebr. *flit greatly* [a]Jer. 49:8
31 [I]Or, *that is at ease* [a]Ezek. 38:11

neither gates nor bars, *which* [b]dwell[7931] alone.

32 And their camels[1581] shall be a booty,[957] and the multitude[527] of their cattle a spoil: and I will [a]scatter into all winds[7307] [b]them *that are* [I]in the utmost corners; and I will bring their calamity from all sides thereof, saith the LORD.

33 And Hazor [a]shall be a dwelling for dragons,[8577] *and* a desolation[8077] for ever:[5769] [b]there shall no man abide there, nor *any* son of man dwell in it.

Elam

34 The word of the LORD that came to Jeremiah the prophet[5030] against [a]Elam in the beginning of the reign[4438] of Zedekiah king of Judah, saying,

35 Thus saith the LORD of hosts; Behold, I will break[7665] [a]the bow of Elam, the chief[7225] of their might.

36 And upon Elam will I bring the four winds from the four quarters of heaven,[8064] and [a]will scatter them toward all those winds; and there shall be no nation whither the outcasts of Elam shall not come.

37 For I will cause Elam to be dismayed[2865] before their enemies, and before them that seek their life:[5315] and I will bring evil upon them, *even* my fierce anger,[639] saith the LORD; [a]and I will send the sword[2719] after them, till I have consumed[3615] them:

38 And I will [a]set[7760] my throne[3678] in Elam, and will destroy[6] from thence the king and the princes, saith the LORD.

39 But it shall come to pass [a]in the latter[319] days, *that* I will bring again the captivity of Elam, saith the LORD.

Babylon

50 The word[1697] that the LORD spake[1696] [a]against Babylon *and* against the land[776] of the Chaldeans [I]by Jeremiah the prophet.[5030]

2 Declare[5046] ye among the nations,[1471] and publish,[8085] and [I]set up[5375]

31 [b]Num. 23:9; Deut. 33:28; Mic. 7:14

32 [I]Hebr. *cut off into corners,* or, *that have the corners* of their hair *polled* [a]Jer. 49:36; Ezek. 5:10 [b]Jer. 9:26; 25:23

33 [a]Jer. 9:11; 10:22; Mal. 1:3 [b]Jer. 49:18 [c]Jer. 25:25

35 [a]Isa. 22:6

36 [a]Jer. 49:32

37 [a]Jer. 9:16; 48:2

38 [a]Jer. 43:10

39 [a]Jer. 48:47; 49:6

1 [I]Hebr. *by the hand of Jeremiah* [a]Isa. 13:1; 21:1; 47:1

2 [I]Hebr. *lift up* [a]Isa. 46:1; Jer. 51:44 [b]Jer. 43:12, 13

3 [a]Jer. 51:48 [b]Isa. 13:17, 18, 20; Jer. 50:39, 40

4 [a]Hos. 1:11 [b]Ezra 3:12, 13; Ps. 126:5, 6; Jer. 31:9; Zech. 12:10 [c]Hos. 3:5

5 [a]Jer. 31:31; 32:40

6 [I]Hebr. *place to lie down in* [a]Isa. 53:6; Jer. 50:17; 1Pet. 2:25 [b]Jer. 2:20; 3:6, 23

7 [a]Ps. 79:7 [b]Jer. 40:2, 3; Zech. 11:5 [c]Jer. 2:3; Dan. 9:16 [d]Ps. 90:1; 91:1 [e]Ps. 22:4

8 [a]Isa. 48:20 [b]Jer. 51:6, 45; Zech. 2:6, 7; Rev. 18:4

9 [I]Or, *destroyer* [a]Jer. 15:14; 50:3, 41; 51:27 [b]Jer. 50:14, 29 [c]2Sam. 1:22

10 [a]Rev. 17:16

11 [I]Hebr. *big,* or, *corpulent* [a]Isa. 47:6

a standard; publish, *and* conceal not: say,[559] Babylon is taken, [a]Bel is confounded, Merodach is broken in pieces; [b]her idols[6091] are confounded, her images[1544] are broken in pieces.[2865]

3 [a]For out of the north there cometh up[5927] [b]a nation[1471] against her, which shall make her land desolate,[8047] and none shall dwell therein: they shall remove, they shall depart, both man[120] and beast.

4 In those days,[3117] and in that time,[6256] saith[5002] the LORD, the children[1121] of Israel shall come, [a]they and the children of Judah together, [b]going and weeping: they shall go, [c]and seek the LORD their God.[430]

5 They shall ask[7592] the way[1870] to Zion with their faces thitherward, *saying,* Come, and let us join ourselves to the LORD in [a]a perpetual[5769] covenant[1285] *that* shall not be forgotten.

6 My people[5971] hath been [a]lost[6] sheep: their shepherds have caused them to go astray,[8582] they have turned them away *on* [b]the mountains: they have gone from mountain to hill, they have forgotten their [I]restingplace.

7 All that found them have [a]devoured them: and [b]their adversaries said, [c]We offend[816] not, because they have sinned[2398] against the LORD, [d]the habitation of justice,[6664] even the LORD, [e]the hope[4723] of their fathers.[1]

8 [a]Remove out of the midst of Babylon, and go forth out of the land of the Chaldeans, and be as the he goats before the flocks.

9 [a]For, lo, I will raise and cause to come up[5927] against Babylon an assembly[6951] of great nations from the north country:[776] and they shall [b]set themselves in array against her; from thence she shall be taken: their arrows *shall be* as of a mighty [I]expert man; [c]none shall return[7725] in vain.

10 And Chaldea shall be a spoil: [a]all that spoil her shall be satisfied, saith the LORD.

11 [a]Because ye were glad, because ye rejoiced, O ye destroyers[8154] of mine heritage,[5159] because ye are grown [I]fat

[b]as the heifer at grass, and [II]bellow as bulls;[47]

12 Your mother[517] shall be sore confounded;[954] she that bare you shall be ashamed: behold, the hindermost[319] of the nations *shall be* a wilderness, a dry land, and a desert.[6160]

13 Because of the wrath[7110] of the LORD it shall not be inhabited, [a]but it shall be wholly desolate:[8077] [b]every one that goeth by Babylon shall be astonished,[8074] and hiss at all her plagues.[4347]

14 [a]Put yourselves in array against Babylon round about: all ye [b]that bend the bow, shoot at her, spare no arrows: for she hath sinned against the LORD.

15 Shout[7321] against her round about: she hath [a]given her hand:[3027] her foundations are fallen,[5307] [b]her walls are thrown down:[2040] for [c]it *is* the vengeance[5360] of the LORD: take vengeance[5358] upon her; [d]as she hath done, do unto her.

16 Cut off[3772] the sower from Babylon, and him that handleth the [I]sickle in the time of harvest: for fear of the oppressing[3238] sword[2719] [a]they shall turn every one to his people, and they shall flee every one to his own land.

Israel Will Return

17 Israel *is* [a]a scattered sheep; [b]the lions have driven *him* away: first[7223] [c]the king[4428] of Assyria hath devoured him; and last this [d]Nebuchadrezzar king of Babylon hath broken his bones.[6106]

18 Therefore thus saith the LORD of hosts,[6635] the God of Israel; Behold, I will punish[6485] the king of Babylon and his land, as I have punished the king of Assyria.

19 [a]And I will bring Israel again to his habitation, and he shall feed on Carmel and Bashan, and his soul[5315] shall be satisfied upon mount Ephraim and Gilead.

20 In those days, and in that time, saith the LORD, [a]the iniquity[5771] of Israel shall be sought for, and *there shall be* none; and the sins of Judah, and they shall not be found: for I will pardon[5545] them [b]whom I reserve.[7604]

The People of Babylon

21 Go up against the land [I]of Merathaim, *even* against it, and against the inhabitants of [II][a]Pekod: waste[2717] and utterly destroy[2763] after them, saith the LORD, and do [b]according to all that I have commanded[6680] thee.

22 [a]A sound of battle *is* in the land, and of great destruction.[7667]

23 How is [a]the hammer of the whole earth[776] cut asunder and broken! how is Babylon become[1961] a desolation[8047] among the nations!

24 I have laid a snare for thee, and thou art also taken, O Babylon, [a]and thou wast not aware:[3045] thou art found, and also caught, because thou hast striven against the LORD.

25 The LORD hath opened his armoury, and hath brought forth [a]the weapons of his indignation:[2195] for this *is* the work[4399] of the Lord[136] GOD of hosts in the land of the Chaldeans.

26 Come against her [I]from the utmost border, open her storehouses: [II]cast her up as heaps, and destroy her utterly: let nothing of her be left.

27 Slay[2717] all her [a]bullocks; let them go down to the slaughter:[2874] woe unto them! for their day[3117] is come, the time of [b]their visitation.[6486]

28 The voice of them that flee and escape out of the land of Babylon, [a]to declare in Zion the vengeance of the LORD our God, the vengeance of his temple.[1964]

29 Call together[8085] the archers against Babylon: [a]all ye that bend the bow, camp against it round about; let none thereof escape:[6413] [b]recompense[7999] her according to her work; according to all that she hath done, do unto her: [c]for she hath been proud against the LORD, against the Holy One[6918] of Israel.

30 [a]Therefore shall her young men fall in the streets, and all her men[582] of war shall be cut off in that day, saith the LORD.

---

11 [II]Or, *neigh as steeds* [b]Hos. 10:11

13 [a]Jer. 25:12 [b]Jer. 49:17

14 [a]Jer. 50:9; 51:2 [b]Jer. 49:35; 50:29

15 [a]1Chr. 29:24; 2Chr. 30:8; Lam. 5:6; Ezek. 17:18 [b]Jer. 51:58 [c]Jer. 51:6, 11 [d]Ps. 137:8; Jer. 50:29; Rev. 18:6

16 [I]Or, *scythe* [a]Isa. 13:14; Jer. 51:9

17 [a]Jer. 50:6 [b]Jer. 2:15 [c]2Kgs. 17:6 [d]2Kgs. 24:10, 14

19 [a]Isa. 65:10; Jer. 33:12; Ezek. 34:13, 14

20 [a]Jer. 31:34 [b]Isa. 1:9

21 [I]Or, *of the rebels* [II]Or, *Visitation* [a]Ezek. 23:23 [b]2Sam. 16:11; 2Kgs. 18:25; 2Chr. 36:23; Isa. 10:6; 44:28; 48:14; Jer. 34:22

22 [a]Jer. 51:54

23 [a]Isa. 14:6; Jer. 51:20

24 [a]Jer. 51:8, 31, 39, 57; Dan. 5:30, 31

25 [a]Isa. 13:5

26 [I]Hebr. *from the end* [II]Or, *tread her*

27 [a]Ps. 22:12; Isa. 34:7; Jer. 46:21 [b]Jer. 48:44; 50:31

28 [a]Jer. 51:10, 11

29 [a]Jer. 50:14 [b]Jer. 50:15; 51:56; Rev. 18:6 [c]Isa. 47:10

30 [a]Jer. 49:26; 51:4

31 Behold, I *am* against thee, *O thou* [I]most proud,[2087] saith the Lord GOD of hosts: for [a]thy day is come, the time *that* I will visit[6485] thee.

32 And [I]the most proud shall stumble[3782] and fall, and none shall raise him up: and [a]I will kindle a fire in his cities, and it shall devour all round about him.

33 Thus saith the LORD of hosts; The children of Israel and the children of Judah *were* oppressed together: and all that took them captives[7617] held them fast;[2388] they refused[3985] to let them go.

34 [a]Their Redeemer[1350] *is* strong; [b]the LORD of hosts *is* his name: he shall throughly plead[7378] their cause,[7379] that he may give rest to the land, and disquiet the inhabitants of Babylon.

35 A sword *is* upon the Chaldeans, saith the LORD, and upon the inhabitants of Babylon, and [a]upon her princes,[8269] and upon [b]her wise[2450] *men.*

36 A sword *is* [a]upon the liars; and they shall dote:[2973] a sword *is* upon her mighty men; and they shall be dismayed.[2865]

37 A sword *is* upon their horses, and upon their chariots, and upon all [a]the mingled people[6154] that *are* in the midst of her; and [b]they shall become as women: a sword *is* upon her treasures; and they shall be robbed.

38 [a]A drought *is* upon her waters; and they shall be dried up:[3001] for it *is* the land of [b]graven images, and they are mad[1984] upon *their* idols.[367]

39 [a]Therefore the wild beasts of the desert with the wild beasts of the islands shall dwell[3427] *there,* and the owls shall dwell therein: [b]and it shall be no more inhabited for ever;[5331] neither shall it be dwelt in from generation[1755] to generation.

40 [a]As God overthrew Sodom and Gomorrah and the neighbour[7934] *cities* thereof, saith the LORD; *so* shall no man abide there, neither shall[1481] any son[1121] of man dwell[1481] therein.

41 [a]Behold, a people shall come from the north, and a great nation, and many kings[4428] shall be raised up from the coasts of the earth.

31 [I]Hebr. *pride* [a]Jer. 50:27

32 [I]Hebr. *pride* [a]Jer. 21:14

34 [a]Rev. 18:8 [b]Isa. 47:4

35 [a]Dan. 5:30 [b]Isa. 47:13

36 [a]Isa. 44:25; Jer. 48:30

37 [a]Jer. 25:20, 24; Ezek. 30:5; Jer. 51:30; Nah. 3:13

38 [a]Isa. 44:27; Jer. 51:32, 36; Rev. 16:12 [b]Jer. 50:2; 51:44, 47, 52

39 [a]Isa. 13:21, 22; 34:14; Jer. 51:37; Rev. 18:2 [b]Isa. 13:20; Jer. 25:12

40 [a]Gen. 19:25; Isa. 13:19; Jer. 49:18; 51:26

41 [a]Jer. 6:22; 25:14; 50:9; 51:27; Rev. 17:16

42 [a]Jer. 6:23 [b]Isa. 13:18 [c]Isa. 5:30

43 [a]Jer. 49:24

44 [a]Jer. 49:19 [b]Job 41:10; Jer. 49:19

45 [a]Isa. 14:24; Jer. 51:11

46 [a]Rev. 18:9

1 [I]Hebr. *heart* [a]2Kgs. 19:7; Jer. 4:11

2 [a]Jer. 15:7 [b]Jer. 50:14

3 [a]Jer. 50:14 [b]Jer. 50:21

42 [a]They shall hold the bow and the lance: [b]they *are* cruel, and will not shew mercy:[7355] [c]their voice shall roar like the sea, and they shall ride upon horses, *every one* put in array, like a man to the battle, against thee, O daughter of Babylon.

43 The king of Babylon hath heard[8085] the report[8088] of them, and his hands[3027] waxed feeble:[7503] [a]anguish[6869] took hold[2388] of him, *and* pangs as of a woman in travail.

44 [a]Behold, he shall come up like a lion from the swelling of Jordan unto the habitation of the strong: but I will make them suddenly run away from her: and who *is* a chosen *man, that* I may appoint[6485] over her? for who *is* like me? and who will appoint me the time?[3259] and [b]who *is* that shepherd that will stand before me?

45 Therefore hear[8085] ye [a]the counsel[6098] of the LORD, that he hath taken against Babylon; and his purposes,[4284] that he hath purposed[2803] against the land of the Chaldeans: Surely the least of the flock shall draw them out: surely he shall make *their* habitation desolate[8074] with them.

46 [a]At the noise of the taking of Babylon the earth is moved, and the cry is heard among the nations.

God's Judgment Upon Babylon

51 Thus saith the LORD; Behold, I will raise up against Babylon, and against them that dwell in the [I]midst[3820] of them that rise up against me, [a]a destroying[7843] wind;[7307]

2 And will send unto Babylon [a]fanners,[2114] that shall fan her, and shall empty her land:[776] [b]for in the day[3117] of trouble[7451] they shall be against her round about.

3 Against *him that* bendeth [a]let the archer bend his bow, and against *him that* lifteth himself up in his brigandine:[5630] and spare ye not her young men; [b]destroy ye utterly all her host.[6635]

4 Thus the slain[2491] shall fall in the

land of the Chaldeans, [a]and *they that are* thrust through in her streets.

5 For Israel *hath* not *been* forsaken,[488] nor Judah of his God,[430] of the LORD of hosts;[6635] though their land was filled with sin[817] against the Holy One[6918] of Israel.

6 [a]Flee out of the midst of Babylon, and deliver every man his soul:[5315] be not cut off[1826] in her iniquity;[5771] for [b]this *is* the time[6256] of the LORD's vengeance;[5360] [c]he will render[7999] unto her a recompence.

7 [a]Babylon *hath been* a golden cup in the LORD's hand,[3027] that made all the earth[776] drunken: [b]the nations[1471] have drunken of her wine; therefore the nations [c]are mad.[1984]

8 Babylon is suddenly [a]fallen[5307] and destroyed:[7665] [b]howl for her; [c]take balm for her pain, if so be she may be healed.

9 We would have healed Babylon, but she is not healed: forsake[5800] her, and [a]let us go every one into his own country:[776] [b]for her judgment[4941] reacheth[5060] unto heaven,[8064] and is lifted up[5375] *even* to the skies.[7834]

10 The LORD hath [a]brought forth our righteousness:[6666] come, and let us [b]declare[5608] in Zion the work of the LORD our God.

11 [a]Make [I]bright the arrows; gather the shields:[7982] [b]the LORD hath raised up the spirit[7307] of the kings[4428] of the Medes: [c]for his device[4209] *is* against Babylon, to destroy it; because it *is* [d]the vengeance of the LORD, the vengeance of his temple.[1964]

12 [a]Set up[5375] the standard upon the walls of Babylon, make the watch strong,[2388] set up the watchmen,[8104] prepare[3559] the [I]ambushes: for the LORD hath both devised[2161] and done[6213] that which he spake[1696] against the inhabitants of Babylon.

13 [a]O thou that dwellest[7931] upon many waters, abundant[7227] in treasures, thine end is come, *and* the measure of thy covetousness.[1215]

14 [a]The LORD of hosts hath sworn [I]by himself, *saying,* Surely I will fill thee with men,[120] [b]as with caterpillers; and they shall [II]lift [c]up a shout against thee.

A Hymn of Praise to God

15 [a]He hath made the earth by his power, he hath established[3559] the world[8398] by his wisdom,[2451] and [b]hath stretched out the heaven by his understanding.[8394]

16 [a]When he uttereth *his* voice, *there is* a [I]multitude[527] of waters in the heavens;[8064] and [b]he causeth the vapours to ascend[5927] from the ends of the earth: he maketh lightnings with rain, and bringeth forth the wind out of his treasures.

17 [a]Every man[120] [I]is brutish[1197] by *his* knowledge;[1847] every founder[6884] is confounded by the graven image:[6459] [b]for his molten image[5262] *is* falsehood, and *there is* no breath[7307] in them.

18 [a]They *are* vanity, the work of errors:[8595] in the time of their visitation[6486] they shall perish.[6]

19 [a]The portion of Jacob *is* not like them; for he *is* the former[3335] of all things: and *Israel is* the rod[7626] of his inheritance:[5159] the LORD of hosts *is* his name.

God's Tool

20 [a]Thou *art* my battle axe *and* weapons of war: for [I]with thee will I break in pieces the nations, and with thee will I destroy kingdoms;[4467]

21 And with thee will I break in pieces the horse and his rider; and with thee will I break in pieces the chariot and his rider;

22 With thee also will I break in pieces man[376] and woman;[802] and with thee will I break in pieces [a]old[2205] and young; and with thee will I break in pieces the young man and the maid;[1330]

23 I will also break in pieces with thee the shepherd and his flock; and with thee will I break in pieces the husbandman[406] and his yoke of oxen; and with thee will I break in pieces captains[6346] and rulers.[5461]

4 [a]Jer. 49:26; 50:30, 37

6 [a]Jer. 50:8; Rev. 18:4 [b]Jer. 50:15, 28 [c]Jer. 25:14

7 [a]Rev. 17:4 [b]Rev. 14:8 [c]Jer. 25:16

8 [a]Isa. 21:9; Rev. 14:8; 18:2 [b]Jer. 48:20; Rev. 18:9, 11, 19 [c]Jer. 46:11

9 [a]Isa. 13:14; Jer. 50:16 [b]Rev. 18:5

10 [a]Ps. 37:6 [b]Jer. 50:28

11 IHebr. *pure* [a]Jer. 46:4 [b]Isa. 13:17; Jer. 51:28 [c]Jer. 50:45 [d]Jer. 50:28

12 IHebr. *liers in wait* [a]Nah. 2:1; 3:14

13 [a]Rev. 17:1, 15

14 IHebr. *by his soul* IIHebr. *utter* [a]Jer. 49:13; Amos 6:8 [b]Nah. 3:15 [c]Jer. 50:15

15 [a]Gen. 1:1, 6; Jer. 10:12 [b]Job 9:8; Ps. 104:2; Isa. 40:22

16 IOr, *noise* [a]Jer. 10:13 [b]Ps. 135:7

17 IOr, *is more brutish than to know* [a]Jer. 10:14 [b]Jer. 50:2

18 [a]Jer. 10:15

19 [a]Jer. 10:16

20 IOr, *in thee,* or, *by thee* [a]Isa. 10:5, 15; Jer. 50:23

22 [a]2Chr. 36:17

24 [a]And I will render unto Babylon and to all the inhabitants of Chaldea all their evil[7451] that they have done in Zion in your sight, saith[5002] the LORD.

25 Behold, I *am* against thee, [a]O destroying[4889] mountain, saith the LORD, which destroyest[7843] all the earth: and I will stretch out mine hand upon thee, and roll thee down[1556] from the rocks, [b]and will make thee a burnt[8316] mountain.

26 And they shall not take of thee a stone for a corner, nor a stone for foundations;[4146] [a]but thou shalt be [I]desolate[8077] for ever,[5769] saith the LORD.

27 [a]Set ye up a standard in the land, blow[8628] the trumpet among the nations, [b]prepare[6942] the nations against her, call together against her [c]the kingdoms of Ararat, Minni, and Ashchenaz; appoint[6485] a captain[2951] against her; cause the horses to come up[5927] as the rough caterpillers.

28 Prepare against her the nations with [a]the kings of the Medes, the captains thereof, and all the rulers thereof, and all the land of his dominion.

29 And the land shall tremble[7493] and sorrow: for every purpose[4284] of the LORD shall be performed against Babylon, [a]to make[7760] the land of Babylon a desolation[8047] without an inhabitant.

30 The mighty men of Babylon have forborn[2308] to fight, they have remained in *their* holds: their might hath failed; [a]they became as women:[802] they have burned her dwellingplaces; [b]her bars are broken.

31 [a]One post[7323] shall run to meet another, and one messenger[5046] to meet another, to shew[5046] the king[4428] of Babylon that his city is taken at *one* end,

32 And that [a]the passages are stopped, and the reeds they have burned[8313] with fire, and the men[582] of war are affrighted.[926]

33 For thus saith the LORD of hosts, the God[430] of Israel; The daughter of Babylon *is* [a]like a threshingfloor, [I][b]*it is* time to thresh her: yet a little while, [c]and the time of her harvest shall come.

34 Nebuchadrezzar the king of Babylon hath [a]devoured me, he hath crushed[2000] me, he hath made me an empty vessel, he hath swallowed me up[1104] like a dragon,[8577] he hath filled his belly with my delicates, he hath cast me out.[1740]

35 [I]The violence[2555] done to me and to my [II]flesh[7607] *be* upon Babylon, shall the inhabitant of Zion say;[559] and my blood[1818] upon the inhabitants of Chaldea, shall Jerusalem say.

God Will Rescue Israel

36 Therefore thus saith the LORD; Behold, [a]I will plead[7378] thy cause,[7379] and take vengeance for thee; [b]and I will dry up[2717] her sea, and make her springs dry.[3001]

37 [a]And Babylon shall become[1961] heaps, a dwellingplace for dragons,[8577] [b]an astonishment,[8047] and an hissing, without an inhabitant.

38 They shall roar together like lions: they shall [I]yell as lions' whelps.[1484]

39 In their heat I will make their feasts, and [a]I will make them drunken, that they may rejoice, and sleep a perpetual[5769] sleep, and not wake, saith the LORD.

40 I will bring them down like lambs[3733] to the slaughter,[2873] like rams with he goats.

41 How is [a]Sheshach taken! and how is [b]the praise[8416] of the whole earth surprised! how is Babylon become an astonishment among the nations!

42 [a]The sea is come up[5927] upon Babylon: she is covered[3680] with the multitude of the waves thereof.

43 [a]Her cities are a desolation, a dry land, and a wilderness,[6160] a land wherein no man dwelleth, neither doth *any* son[1121] of man pass thereby.

44 [a]And I will punish[6485] Bel in Babylon, and I will bring forth out of his mouth[6310] that which he hath swallowed up:[1105] and the nations shall not flow together any more unto him: yea, [b]the wall of Babylon shall fall.

45 [a]My people,[5971] go ye out of the midst of her, and deliver ye every man

24 [a]Jer. 50:15, 29
25 [a]Isa. 13:2; Zech. 4:7 [b]Rev. 8:8
26 [I]Hebr. *everlasting desolations* [a]Jer. 50:40
27 [a]Isa. 13:2 [b]Jer. 25:14 [c]Jer. 50:41
28 [a]Jer. 51:11
29 [a]Jer. 50:13, 39, 40; 51:43
30 [a]Isa. 19:16; Jer. 48:41; 50:37 [b]Lam. 2:9; Amos 1:5; Nah. 3:13
31 [a]Jer. 50:24
32 [a]Jer. 50:38
33 [I]Or, *in the time that he thresheth her* [a]Isa. 21:10; Amos 1:3; Mic. 4:13 [b]Isa. 41:15; Hab. 3:12 [c]Isa. 17:5; Hos. 6:11; Joel 3:13; Rev. 14:15, 18
34 [a]Jer. 50:17
35 [I]Hebr. *My violence* [II]Or, *remainder*
36 [a]Jer. 50:34 [b]Jer. 50:38
37 [a]Isa. 13:22; Jer. 50:39; Rev. 18:2 [b]Jer. 25:9, 18
38 [I]Or, *shake themselves*
39 [a]Jer. 51:57
41 [a]Jer. 25:26 [b]Isa. 13:19; Jer. 49:25; Dan. 4:30
42 [a]Isa. 8:7, 8
43 [a]Jer. 50:39, 40; 51:29
44 [a]Isa. 46:1; Jer. 50:2 [b]Jer. 51:58
45 [a]Jer. 50:8; 51:6; Rev. 18:4

his soul from the fierce anger[639] of the LORD.

46 And [I]lest your heart faint, and ye fear[3372] [a]for the rumour that shall be heard[8085] in the land; a rumour shall both come *one* year, and after that in *another* year *shall come* a rumour, and violence in the land, ruler against ruler.

47 Therefore, behold, the days[3117] come, that [a]I will [I]do judgment[6485] upon the graven images of Babylon: and her whole land shall be confounded,[954] and all her slain shall fall in the midst of her.

48 Then [a]the heaven and the earth, and all that *is* therein, shall sing for Babylon: [b]for the spoilers[7703] shall come unto her from the north, saith the LORD.

49 [I]As Babylon *hath caused* the slain of Israel to fall, so at Babylon shall fall the slain of all [II]the earth.

God Speaks to Jews in Babylon

50 [a]Ye that have escaped the sword,[2719] go away, stand not still: remember[2142] the LORD afar off, and let Jerusalem come into your mind.[3824]

51 [a]We are confounded, because we have heard reproach:[2781] shame hath covered our faces: for strangers[2114] are come into the sanctuaries[4720] of the LORD'S house.[1004]

52 Wherefore, behold, the days come, saith the LORD, [a]that I will do judgment upon her graven images: and through all her land the wounded[2491] shall groan.

53 [a]Though Babylon should mount up[5927] to heaven, and though she should fortify the height of her strength, *yet* from me shall spoilers come unto her, saith the LORD.

54 [a]A sound of a cry *cometh* from Babylon, and great destruction[7667] from the land of the Chaldeans:

55 Because the LORD hath spoiled[7703] Babylon, and destroyed[6] out of her the great voice; when her waves do roar like great waters, a noise[7588] of their voice is uttered:

56 Because the spoiler is come upon her, *even* upon Babylon, and her mighty men are taken, every one of their bows is broken:[2865] [a]for the LORD God[410] of recompences shall surely requite.[7999]

57 [a]And I will make drunk her princes,[8269] and her wise[2450] *men,* her captains,[6346] and her rulers,[5461] and her mighty men: and they shall sleep a perpetual sleep, and not wake, saith [b]the King, whose name *is* the LORD of hosts.

58 Thus saith the LORD of hosts; [I][a]The broad walls of Babylon shall be utterly [II]broken, and her high gates shall be burned with fire; and [b]the people shall labour in vain, and the folk[3816] in the fire, and they shall be weary.

59 The word[1697] which Jeremiah the prophet[5030] commanded[6680] Seraiah the son of Neriah, the son of Maaseiah, when he went [I]with Zedekiah the king of Judah into Babylon in the fourth year of his reign.[4427] And *this* Seraiah *was* a [II]quiet[4496] prince.[8269]

60 So Jeremiah wrote in a book[5612] all the evil[7451] that should come upon Babylon, *even* all these words that are written against Babylon.

61 And Jeremiah said to Seraiah, When thou comest to Babylon, and shalt see, and shalt read[7121] all these words;

62 Then shalt thou say, O LORD, thou hast spoken[1696] against this place, to cut it off, that [a]none shall remain in it, neither man nor beast, but that it shall be [I]desolate for ever.

63 And it shall be, when thou hast made an end[3615] of reading this book, [a]*that* thou shalt bind a stone to it, and cast it into the midst of Euphrates:

64 And thou shalt say, Thus shall Babylon sink, and shall not rise from the evil that I will bring upon her: [a]and they shall be weary. Thus far *are* the words of Jeremiah.

The Reign of Zedekiah

52 Zedekiah *was* [a]one and twenty years old when he [I]began to reign,[4427] and he reigned eleven years in Jerusalem. And his mother's[517] name *was* Hamutal the daughter of Jeremiah of Libnah.

2 And he did *that which was* evil[7451]

46 [I]Or, *let not* [a]2Kgs. 19:7

47 [I]Hebr. *visit upon* [a]Jer. 50:2; 51:52

48 [a]Isa. 44:23; 49:13; Rev. 18:20 [b]Jer. 50:3, 41

49 [I]Or, *Both Babylon is to fall, O ye slain of Israel, and with Babylon* [II]Or, *the country*

50 [a]Jer. 44:28

51 [a]Ps. 44:15, 16; 79:4

52 [a]Jer. 51:47

53 [a]Jer. 49:16; Amos 9:2; Obad. 1:4

54 [a]Jer. 50:22

56 [a]Ps. 94:1; Jer. 50:29; 51:24

57 [a]Jer. 51:39 [b]Jer. 46:18; 48:15

58 [I]Or, *The walls of broad Babylon* [II]Or, *made naked* [a]Jer. 51:44 [b]Hab. 2:13

59 [I]Or, *on the behalf of* [II]Or, *prince of Menucha,* or, *chief chamberlain*

62 [I]Hebr. *desolations* [a]Jer. 50:3, 39; 51:29

63 [a]Rev. 18:21

64 [a]Jer. 51:58

1 [I]Hebr. *reigned* [a]2Kgs. 24:18

in the eyes of the LORD, according to all that Jehoiakim had done.

3 For through the anger[639] of the LORD it came to pass in Jerusalem and Judah, till he had cast them out from his presence, that Zedekiah rebelled[4775] against the king[4428] of Babylon.

The Fall of Jerusalem

4 And it came to pass in the [a]ninth year of his reign, in the tenth month, in the tenth *day* of the month, *that* Nebuchadrezzar king of Babylon came, he and all his army,[2428] against Jerusalem, and pitched against it, and built forts against it round about.

5 So the city was besieged unto the eleventh year of king Zedekiah.

6 And in the fourth month, in the ninth *day* of the month, the famine was sore[2388] in the city, so that there was no bread for the people[5971] of the land.[776]

7 Then the city was broken up, and all the men[582] of war fled, and went forth out of the city by night[3915] by the way[1870] of the gate between the two walls, which *was* by the king's[4428] garden; (now the Chaldeans *were* by the city round about:) and they went by the way of the plain.

8 But the army of the Chaldeans pursued after the king, and overtook Zedekiah in the plains[6160] of Jericho; and all his army was scattered from him.

9 [a]Then they took8610 the king, and carried him up unto the king of Babylon to Riblah in the land of Hamath; where he gave judgment[4941] upon him.

10 [a]And the king of Babylon slew[7819] the sons[1121] of Zedekiah before his eyes: he slew also all the princes[8269] of Judah in Riblah.

11 Then he [I]put out the eyes of Zedekiah; and the king of Babylon bound him in [II]chains, and carried him to Babylon, and put him in [III]prison till the day of his death.[4194]

The Destruction of the Temple

12 [a]Now in the fifth month, in the tenth *day* of the month, [b]which *was* the nineteenth year of Nebuchadrezzar king of Babylon, [c]came Nebuzar–adan, [I]captain of the guard, *which* [II]served the king of Babylon, into Jerusalem,

13 And burned[8313] the house[1004] of the LORD, and the king's house; and all the houses of Jerusalem, and all the houses of the great *men,* burned he with fire:

14 And all the army of the Chaldeans, that *were* with the captain of the guard, brake down[5422] all the walls of Jerusalem round about.

15 [a]Then Nebuzar–adan the captain of the guard carried away captive[1540] *certain* of the poor of the people, and the residue[3499] of the people that remained[7604] in the city, and those that fell away,[5307] that fell to the king of Babylon, and the rest[3499] of the multitude.[527]

16 But Nebuzar–adan the captain of the guard left[7604] *certain* of the poor of the land for vinedressers and for husbandmen.3009

17 [a]Also the [b]pillars of brass that *were* in the house of the LORD, and the bases, and the brasen sea that *was* in the house of the LORD, the Chaldeans brake,[7665] and carried[5375] all the brass of them to Babylon.

18 [a]The caldrons also, and the [I]shovels,3257 and the snuffers,4212 and the [II]bowls, and the spoons,[3709] and all the vessels of brass wherewith they ministered,[8334] took they away.

19 And the basons,5592 and the [I]firepans, and the bowls, and the caldrons, and the candlesticks, and the spoons, and the cups; *that* which *was* of gold *in* gold, and *that* which *was* of silver *in* silver, took the captain of the guard away.

20 The two pillars, one sea, and twelve brasen bulls that *were* under the bases, which king Solomon had made[6213] in the house of the LORD: [I][a]the brass of all these vessels was without weight.

21 And *concerning* the [a]pillars, the height of one pillar *was* eighteen cubits; and a [I]fillet2339 of twelve cubits did compass it; and the thickness thereof *was* four fingers: *it was* hollow.

4 [a]2Kgs. 25:1-27; Jer. 39:1; Zech. 8:19

9 [a]Jer. 32:4

10 [a]Ezek. 12:13

11 [I]Hebr. *blinded* [II]Or, *fetters* [III]Hebr. *house of the wards*

12 [I]Or, *chief marshal* [II]Hebr. *stood before* [a]Zech. 7:5; 8:19 [b]Jer. 52:29 [c]Jer. 39:9

15 [a]Jer. 39:9

17 [a]Jer. 27:19 [b]1Kgs. 7:15, 23, 27, 50

18 [I]Or, *instruments to remove the ashes* [II]Or, *basins* [a]Ex. 27:3; 2Kgs. 25:14-16

19 [I]Or, *censers*

20 [I]Hebr. *their brass* [a]1Kgs. 7:47

21 [I]Hebr. *thread* [a]1Kgs. 7:15; 2Kgs. 25:17; 2Chr. 3:15

22 And a chapiter3805 of brass *was* upon it; and the height of one chapiter *was* five cubits, with network and pomegranates upon the chapiters round about, all *of* brass. The second pillar also and the pomegranates *were* like unto these.

23 And there were ninety and six pomegranates on a side; *and* [a]all the pomegranates upon the network *were* an hundred round about.

The Deportation

24 And [a]the captain of the guard took Seraiah the chief7218 priest,3548 [b]and Zephaniah the second priest, and the three keepers8104 of the [I]door:

25 He took also out of the city an eunuch,5631 which had the charge6496 of the men of war; and seven men of them that [I]were near the king's person, which were found in the city; and the [II]principal8269 scribe5608 of the host,6635 who mustered6633 the people of the land; and threescore men376 of the people of the land, that were found in the midst of the city.

26 So Nebuzar–adan the captain of the guard took them, and brought them to the king of Babylon to Riblah.

27 And the king of Babylon smote5221 them, and put them to death4191 in Riblah in the land127 of Hamath. Thus Judah was carried away captive out of his own land.

28 [a]This *is* the people whom Nebuchadrezzar carried away captive:1540 in the [b]seventh year [c]three thousand Jews and three and twenty:

29 [a]In the eighteenth year of Nebuchadrezzar he carried away captive from Jerusalem eight hundred thirty and two [I]persons:5315

30 In the three and twentieth year of Nebuchadrezzar Nebuzar–adan the captain of the guard2876 carried away captive of the Jews seven hundred forty and five persons: all the persons *were* four thousand and six hundred.

31 [a]And it came to pass in the seven and thirtieth year of the captivity1546 of Jehoiachin king of Judah, in the twelfth month, in the five and twentieth *day* of the month, *that* Evil–merodach king of Babylon in the *first* year of his reign4438 [b]lifted up5375 the head7218 of Jehoiachin king of Judah, and brought him forth out of prison,

32 And spake [I]kindly unto him, and set his throne3678 above the throne of the kings4428 that *were* with him in Babylon,

33 And changed his prison garments: [a]and he did continually8548 eat bread before him all the days3117 of his life.2416

34 And *for* his diet,737 there was a continual8548 diet given him of the king of Babylon, [I]every day a portion1697 until the day of his death, all the days of his life.

23 [a]1Kgs. 7:20

24 [I]Hebr. *threshold* [a]2Kgs. 25:18 [b]Jer. 21:1; 29:25

25 [I]Hebr. *saw the face of the king* [II]Or, *scribe of the captain of the host*

28 [a]2Kgs. 24:2 [b]2Kgs. 24:12 [c]2Kgs. 24:14

29 [I]Hebr. *souls* [a]Jer. 39:9; 52:12

31 [a]2Kgs. 25:27-30 [b]Gen. 40:13, 20

32 [I]Hebr. good things with him

33 [a]2Sam. 9:13

34 [I]Hebr. *the matter of the day in his day*

THE LAMENTATIONS

of Jeremiah

Lamentations was originally part of the Book of Jeremiah. It was later isolated because it was included in the Five Megilloth (or scrolls; see introduction to the Book of Ruth). Lamentations is read publicly each year at Tisha B'av, a fast commemorating the destruction of the temple in Jerusalem (2 Kgs. 25:8, 9) in both 586 B.C. and A.D. 70. The style and content leave no doubt that Jeremiah, the "weeping prophet," is the author. The book focuses on the destruction of Jerusalem as observed by an eyewitness (cf. Jer. 37—39). Jeremiah alternates between accounts of the horrible aftermath of the destruction of the city and the confessions of the people's deep sins, and then to his appeals to God for mercy.

Each of the five chapters of the book is a separate poem of mourning. The first four are acrostics (each of the 22 letters of the Hebrew alphabet are used to begin each stanza of the poem). The acrostic is a literary device that makes it easier to remember and abstractly suggests that the author has covered his subject from beginning to end. It may also be that Jeremiah, under the inspiration of the Holy Spirit, made himself conform to this method to keep his grief from overwhelming him. Lamentations is a valuable commentary on sin and its consequences, and about returning to God for mercy (Lam. 3:22–24).

The Sorrows of Jerusalem

1 How doth the city sit solitary, *that*
was full of people[5971] [a]*how* is she
become[1961] as a widow! she *that was*
great among the nations,[1471] *and* [b]prin-
cess[8282] among the provinces, *how* is
she become tributary!
2 She [a]weepeth sore in the [b]night,[3915]
and her tears *are* on her cheeks: [c]among
all her lovers[157] [d]she hath none to
comfort[5162] *her:* all her friends[7453] have
dealt treacherously[898] with her, they are
become her enemies.
3 [a]Judah is gone into captivity[1540] because of affliction, and [I]because of great
servitude:[5656] [b]she dwelleth among the
heathen,[1471] she findeth no rest: all her
persecutors overtook her between the
straits.
4 The ways[1870] of Zion do mourn,
because none come to the solemn
feasts:[4150] all her gates are desolate:[8074]
her priests[3548] sigh, her virgins[1330] are
afflicted, and she *is* in bitterness.
5 Her adversaries [a]are the chief,[7218]
her enemies prosper; for the LORD hath
afflicted her [b]for the multitude of her
transgressions:[6588] her [c]children are gone
into captivity[7628] before the enemy.
6 And from the daughter of Zion all
her beauty[1926] is departed: her princes[8269]
are become like harts *that* find no pasture, and they are gone without strength
before the pursuer.
7 Jerusalem remembered[2142] in the
days[3117] of her affliction and of her miseries all her [I][a]pleasant things that she
had in the days of old,[6924] when her people fell[5307] into the hand[3027] of the
enemy, and none did help her: the adversaries saw[7200] her, *and* did mock at her
sabbaths.
8 [a]Jerusalem hath grievously[2399]
sinned;[2398] therefore she [I]is removed: all
that honoured her despise her, because
[b]they have seen her nakedness:[6172] yea,
she sigheth, and turneth backward.[7725]
9 Her filthiness[2932] *is* in her skirts;
she [a]remembereth not her last end; therefore she came down wonderfully:[6382] [b]she
had no comforter.[5162] O LORD, behold[7200]
my affliction: for the enemy hath magnified *himself.*
10 The adversary hath spread out his
hand upon [a]all her [I]pleasant things: for

1 [a]Isa. 47:7, 8 [b]Ezra 4:20

2 [a]Jer. 13:17 [b]Job 7:3; Ps. 6:6 [c]Jer. 4:30; 30:14; Lam. 1:19 [d]Lam. 1:9, 16, 17, 21

3 [I]Hebr. *for the greatness of servitude* [a]Jer. 52:27 [b]Deut. 28:64, 65; Lam. 2:9

5 [a]Deut. 28:43, 44 [b]Jer. 30:14, 15; Dan. 9:7, 16 [c]Jer. 52:28

7 [I]Or, *desirable* [a]Lam. 1:10

8 [I]Hebr. *is become a removing,* or, *wandering* [a]1Kgs. 8:46 [b]Jer. 13:22, 26; Ezek. 16:37; 23:29; Hos. 2:10

9 [a]Deut. 32:29; Isa. 47:7 [b]Lam. 1:2, 17, 21

10 [I]Or, *desirable* [a]Lam. 1:7

she hath seen *that* [b]the heathen[1471] entered into her sanctuary,[4720] whom thou didst command[6680] *that* [c]they should not enter into thy congregation.[6951]

11 All her people sigh, [a]they seek bread; they have given their pleasant things for meat [I]to relieve[7725] the soul:[5315] see, O LORD, and consider; for I am become vile.[2151]

🔑 12 [I]*Is it* nothing to you, all ye that [II]pass by? behold, and see [a]if there be any sorrow like unto my sorrow, which is done unto me, wherewith the LORD hath afflicted *me* in the day of his fierce anger.[639]

13 From above hath he sent fire into my bones,[6106] and it prevaileth against them: he hath [a]spread a net for my feet, he hath turned me back: he hath made me desolate *and* faint all the day.

14 [a]The yoke of my transgressions is bound by his hand: they are wreathed, *and* come up[5927] upon my neck: he hath made my strength to fall,[3782] the Lord[136] hath delivered me into *their* hands,[3027] *from whom* I am not able to rise up.

15 The Lord hath trodden under foot all my mighty[47] *men* in the midst[7130] of me: he hath called[7121] an assembly against me to crush[7665] my young men: [a]the Lord hath trodden [I]the virgin,[1330] the daughter of Judah, *as* in a winepress.

16 For these *things* I weep; [a]mine eye, mine eye runneth down with water, because [b]the comforter that should [I]relieve my soul is far from me: my children[1121] are desolate, because the enemy prevailed.

17 [a]Zion spreadeth forth her hands, *and* [b]*there is* none to comfort her: the LORD hath commanded[6680] concerning Jacob, *that* his adversaries *should be* round about him: Jerusalem is as a menstruous woman among them.

18 The LORD is [a]righteous;[6662] for I have rebelled[4784] against his [I]commandment:[6310] hear, I pray you,[4994] all people, and behold my sorrow: my virgins and my young men are gone into captivity.

🔑 19 I called for my lovers, *but* [a]they deceived me: my priests and mine elders[2205] gave up the ghost[1478] in the city, [b]while they sought their meat to relieve their souls.[5315]

20 Behold, O LORD; for I *am* in distress: my [a]bowels[4578] are troubled; mine heart[3820] is turned[2015] within[7130] me; for I have grievously rebelled: [b]abroad the sword[2719] bereaveth, at home *there is* as death.[4194]

21 They have heard[8085] that I sigh: [a]*there is* none to comfort me: all mine enemies have heard of my trouble;[7451] they are glad that thou hast done[6213] *it:* thou wilt bring the day *that* thou hast [I]called, and they shall be like unto me.

22 [a]Let all their wickedness[7451] come before thee; and do unto them, as thou hast done unto me for all my transgressions: for my sighs *are* many, and [b]my heart *is* faint.

God Punished Zion

2 How hath[5743] the Lord[136] covered the daughter of Zion with a cloud[5743] in his anger,[639] [a]*and* cast down from heaven[8064] unto the earth[776] [b]the beauty[8597] of Israel, and remembered[2142] not [c]his footstool in the day of his anger!

10 [b]Jer. 51:51 [c]Deut. 23:3; Neh. 13:1

11 [I]Or, *to make the soul to come again* [a]Jer. 38:9; 52:6; Lam. 2:12; 4:4

12 [I]Or, It is *nothing* [II]Hebr. *pass by the way* [a]Dan. 9:12

13 [a]Ezek. 12:13; 17:20

14 [a]Deut. 28:48

15 [I]Or, *the winepress of the virgin* [a]Isa. 63:3; Rev. 14:19, 20; 19:15

16 [I]Hebr. *bring back* [a]Jer. 13:17; 14:17; Lam. 2:18 [b]Lam. 1:2, 9

17 [a]Jer. 4:31 [b]Lam. 1:2, 9

18 [I]Hebr. *mouth* [a]Neh. 9:33; Dan. 9:7, 14 [b]1Sam. 12:14, 15

19 [a]Lam. 1:2; Jer. 30:14 [b]Lam. 1:11

20 [a]Job 30:27; Isa. 16:11; Jer. 4:19; 48:36; Lam. 2:11; Hos. 11:8 [b]Deut. 32:25; Ezek. 7:15

21 [I]Or, *proclaimed* [a]Lam. 1:2

22 [a]Ps. 109:15 [b]Lam. 5:17

1 [a]Matt. 11:23 [b]2Sam. 1:19 [c]1Chr. 28:2; Ps. 99:5; 132:7

🔑 **1:12** Some have compared this verse to Jesus' sorrow when he looked at Jerusalem and saw the impending destruction of the city, even as Jeremiah had seen in his day (see Matt. 23:37–39; Luke 13:34, 35). Others suggest that this verse refers to Christ's agony on the cross of Calvary, as he cried for those who are separated from God as a result of sin. The true sorrow of Christ's suffering, as in this verse, is that it was inflicted by the Father Himself (Luke 23:26–38).

🔑 **1:19** The term "lovers," found also in verse two, refers to the allies that Judah had joined with in hopes that they would protect them from Assyria. These "lovers" soon betrayed them and joined with Judah's enemies to fight against her and destroy Jerusalem. The Babylonians, Syrians, and Egyptians were close allies with Judah during Jeremiah's day (Jer. 2:18, 19; 22:20–25). These alliances of Judah are mentioned in Ezekiel's prophecy concerning Egypt (Ezek. 29:6–16).

2 The Lord hath swallowed up[1104] all the habitations[4999] of Jacob, [a]and hath not pitied: he hath thrown down[2040] in his wrath[5678] the strong holds of the daughter of Judah; he hath [I]brought *them* down to the ground:[776] [b]he hath polluted the kingdom[4467] and the princes[8269] thereof.

3 He hath cut off in *his* fierce[2750] anger all the horn of Israel: [a]he hath drawn back[7725] his right hand from before the enemy, [b]and he burned against Jacob like a flaming fire, *which* devoureth round about.

4 [a]He hath bent his bow like an enemy: he stood[5324] with his right hand as an adversary, and slew[2026] [I][b]all *that were* pleasant to the eye in the tabernacle[168] of the daughter of Zion: he poured out[8210] his fury like fire.

5 [a]The Lord was as an enemy: he hath swallowed up Israel, [b]he hath swallowed up all her palaces:[759] he hath destroyed[7843] his strong holds, and hath increased in the daughter of Judah mourning and lamentation.

6 And he hath violently [a]taken away[2554] his [I]tabernacle, [b]as *if it were of* a garden: he hath destroyed his places of the assembly: [c]the LORD hath caused the solemn feasts[4150] and sabbaths[7676] to be forgotten in Zion, and hath despised[5006] in the indignation[2195] of his anger the king[4428] and the priest.[3548]

7 The Lord hath cast off his altar,[4196] he hath abhorred his sanctuary,[4720] he hath [I]given up into the hand[3027] of the enemy the walls of her palaces; [a]they have made a noise in the house of the LORD, as in the day of a solemn feast.

8 The LORD hath purposed[2803] to destroy[7843] the wall of the daughter of Zion: [a]he hath stretched out a line, he hath not withdrawn[7725] his hand from [I]destroying:[1104] therefore he made the rampart[2426] and the wall to lament; they languished together.

9 Her gates are sunk into the ground; he hath destroyed[6] and [a]broken[7665] her bars: [b]her king and her princes *are* among the Gentiles:[1471] [c]the law[8451] *is* no *more;* her [d]prophets also find no vision[2377] from the LORD.

10 The elders[2205] of the daughter of Zion [a]sit upon the ground, *and* keep silence: they have [b]cast up[5927] dust[6083] upon their heads;[7218] they have [c]girded themselves with sackcloth: the virgins[1330] of Jerusalem hang down their heads to the ground.

11 [a]Mine eyes do fail[3615] with tears, [b]my bowels[4578] are troubled, [c]my liver is poured upon the earth, for the destruction of the daughter of my people;[5971] because [d]the children and the sucklings [I]swoon in the streets of the city.

12 They say[559] to their mothers,[517] Where *is* corn and wine? when they swooned as the wounded[2491] in the streets of the city, when their soul[5315] was poured out into their mothers' bosom.

13 What thing shall I take to witness[5749] for thee? [a]what thing shall I liken to thee, O daughter of Jerusalem? what shall I equal to thee, that I may comfort[5162] thee, O virgin daughter of Zion? for thy breach[7667] *is* great like the sea: who can heal thee?

14 Thy [a]prophets have seen[2372] vain[7723] and foolish things for thee: and they have not [b]discovered thine iniquity,[5771] to turn away[7725] thy captivity;[7622] but have seen for thee

2 [I]Hebr. *made to touch* [a]Lam. 2:17; 21; 3:43 [b]Ps. 89:39

3 [a]Ps. 74:11 [b]Ps. 89:46

4 [I]Hebr. *all the desirable of the eye* [a]Isa. 63:10; Lam. 2:5 [b]Ezek. 24:25

5 [a]Lam. 2:4; Jer. 30:14 [b]2Kgs. 25:9; Jer. 52:13

6 [I]Or, *hedge* [a]Ps. 80:12; 89:40; Isa. 5:5 [b]Isa. 1:8 [c]Lam. 1:4; Zeph. 3:18

7 [I]Hebr. *shut up* [a]Ps. 74:4

8 [I]Hebr. *swallowing up* [a]2Kgs. 21:13; Isa. 34:11

9 [a]Jer. 51:30 [b]Deut. 28:36; 2Kgs. 24:15; 25:7; Lam. 1:3; 4:20 [c]2Chr. 15:3 [d]Ps. 74:9; Ezek. 7:26

10 [a]Job 2:13; Isa. 3:26; Lam. 3:28 [b]Job 2:12 [c]Isa. 15:3; Ezek. 7:18; 27:31

11 [I]Or, *faint* [a]Ps. 6:7; Lam. 3:48 [b]Lam. 1:20 [c]Job 16:13; Ps. 22:14 [d]Lam. 2:19; 4:4

13 [a]Lam. 1:12; Dan. 9:12

14 [a]Jer. 2:8; 5:31; 14:14; 23:16; 27:14; 29:8, 9; Ezek. 13:2 [b]Isa. 58:1

2:4, 6 The word "tabernacle" is found in both these verses, but is a translation of two different Hebrew words. In verse four the Hebrew word is *ōhel* (168), which simply means one's "dwelling place" or "house." The second usage of "tabernacle" (v. 6) comes from the word *sōk* (7900), meaning a "pavilion" or "protective hedge." This second usage is a reference to God's house, the temple in Jerusalem, the place of God's presence and glory. God, in His providence, used foreign invaders to destroy His temple so that the people could no longer offer their vain sacrifices and worship false gods there. The analogy of the "garden" is a depiction of a person who protects what is his own possession. In the same way, the temple was God's sacred possession.

false[7723] burdens[4864] and causes of banishment.

15 [a]All that pass [I]by [b]clap[5606] *their* hands[3709] at thee; they hiss [c]and wag5128 their head[7218] at the daughter of Jerusalem, *saying, Is* this the city that *men* call[559] [d]The perfection[3632] of beauty, The joy of the whole earth?

16 [a]All thine enemies have opened their mouth[6310] against thee: they hiss and gnash2786 the teeth: they say, [b]We have swallowed *her* up: certainly this *is* the day that we looked for; we have found, [c]we have seen[7200] *it.*

17 The LORD hath done[6213] *that* which he had [a]devised;[2161] he hath fulfilled[1214] his word[565] that he had commanded[6680] in the days[3117] of old:[6924] [b]he hath thrown down, and hath not pitied: and he hath caused *thine* enemy to [c]rejoice over thee, he hath set up the horn of thine adversaries.

18 Their heart[3820] cried unto the Lord, O [a]wall of the daughter of Zion, [b]let tears run down like a river day[3119] and night:[3915] give thyself no rest; let not the apple of thine eye cease.

19 Arise, [a]cry out in the night: in the beginning[7218] of the watches [b]pour out[8210] thine heart like water before the face of the Lord: lift up[5375] thy hands toward him for the life[5315] of thy young children, [c]that faint for hunger [d]in the top[7218] of every street.

20 Behold,[7200] O LORD, and consider to whom thou hast done this. [a]Shall the women[802] eat their fruit, *and* children [I]of a span long? [b]shall[2026] the priest and the prophet[5030] be slain[2026] in the sanctuary of the Lord?

21 [a]The young and the old[2205] lie on the ground in the streets: my virgins and my young men are fallen[5307] by the sword;[2719] thou hast slain *them* in the day of thine anger; [b]thou hast killed, *and* not pitied.

22 Thou hast called[7121] as in a solemn day [a]my terrors[4032] round about, so that in the day of the LORD's anger none escaped nor remained:[8300] [b]those that I have swaddled2946 and brought up7235 hath mine enemy consumed.[3615]

15 [I]Hebr. *by the way* [a]1Kgs. 9:8; Jer. 18:16; Nah. 3:19 [b]Ezek. 25:6 [c]2Kgs. 19:21; Ps. 44:14 [d]Ps. 48:2; 50:2
16 [a]Job 16:9, 10; Ps. 22:13; Lam. 3:46 [b]Ps. 56:2 [c]Ps. 35:21
17 [a]Lev. 26:16; Deut. 28:15 [b]Lam. 2:2 [c]Ps. 38:16; 89:42
18 [a]Lam. 2:8 [b]Jer. 14:17; Lam. 1:16
19 [a]Ps. 119:147 [b]Ps. 62:8 [c]Lam. 2:11 [d]Isa. 51:20; Lam. 4:1; Nah. 3:10
20 [I]Or, *swaddled with their hands* [a]Lev. 26:29; Deut. 28:52; Jer. 19:9; Lam. 4:10; Ezek. 5:10 [b]Lam. 4:13, 16
21 [a]2Chr. 36:17 [b]Lam. 3:43
22 [a]Ps. 31:13; Jer. 6:25; 46:5 [b]Hos. 9:12, 13
4 [a]Job 16:8 [b]Ps. 51:8; Isa. 38:13; Jer. 50:17
6 [a]Ps. 88:5, 6; 143:3
7 [a]Job 3:23; 19:8; Hos. 2:6
8 [a]Job 30:20; Ps. 22:2
10 [a]Job 10:16; Isa. 38:13; Hos. 5:14; 13:7, 8
11 [a]Hos. 6:1
12 [a]Job 7:20; 16:12; Ps. 38:2
13 [I]Hebr. *sons* [a]Job 6:4
14 [a]Jer. 20:7 [b]Job 30:9; Ps. 69:12; Lam. 3:63
15 [I]Hebr. *bitternesses* [a]Jer. 9:15
16 [I]Or, *rolled me in the ashes* [a]Prov. 20:17
17 [I]Hebr. *good*
18 [a]Ps. 31:22
19 [I]Or, *Remember* [a]Jer. 9:15

Repentance and Hope

3 I am the man[1397] *that* hath seen[7200] affliction by the rod[7626] of his wrath.[5678]

2 He hath led me, and brought *me into* darkness,[2822] but not *into* light.[216]

3 Surely against me is he turned; he turneth[7725] his hand[3027] *against me* all the day.[3117]

4 [a]My flesh[1320] and my skin[5785] hath he made old; he hath [b]broken[7665] my bones.[6106]

5 He hath builded against me, and compassed[5362] *me* with gall7219 and travail.

6 [a]He hath set me in dark places,[4285] as *they that be* dead[4191] of old.[5769]

7 [a]He hath hedged me about, that I cannot get out: he hath made my chain heavy.[3513]

8 Also [a]when I cry[2199] and shout, he shutteth out my prayer.[8605]

9 He hath inclosed my ways[1870] with hewn stone,[1496] he hath made my paths crooked.[5753]

10 [a]He *was* unto me *as* a bear lying in wait, *and as* a lion in secret places.

11 He hath turned aside my ways, and [a]pulled me in pieces: he hath made[7760] me desolate.[8076]

12 He hath bent his bow, and [a]set[5324] me as a mark for the arrow.

13 He hath caused [a]the [I]arrows of his quiver to enter into my reins.3629

14 I was a [a]derision to all my people;[5971] *and* [b]their song all the day.

15 [a]He hath filled me with [I]bitterness, he hath made me drunken with wormwood.3939

16 He hath also broken my teeth [a]with gravel stones, he hath [I]covered[3728] me with ashes.

17 And thou hast removed my soul[5315] far off from peace: I forgat [I]prosperity.[2896]

18 [a]And I said, My strength[5331] and my hope[8431] is perished[6] from the LORD:

19 [I]Remembering mine affliction and my misery,4788 [a]the wormwood and the gall.

20 My soul hath *them* still in remembrance,[2142] and is [I]humbled in me.

21 This I [I]recall to my mind,[3820] therefore have I hope.[3176]

🔑 22 [a]*It is of* the LORD's mercies[2617] that we are not consumed,[8552] because his compassions fail[3615] not.

23 *They are* new [a]every morning: great *is* thy faithfulness.[530]

24 The LORD *is* my [a]portion, saith my soul; therefore will I hope in him.

25 The LORD *is* good[2896] unto them that [a]wait[6960] for him, to the soul *that* seeketh him.

26 *It is* good that *a man* should both hope[2342] [a]and quietly wait[1748] for the salvation of the LORD.

27 [a]*It is* good for a man that he bear[5375] the yoke in his youth.

28 [a]He sitteth alone and keepeth silence, because he hath borne *it* upon him.

29 [a]He putteth his mouth[6310] in the dust;[6083] if so be there may be hope.

30 [a]He giveth *his* cheek to him that smiteth him: he is filled full with reproach.[2781]

31 [a]For the Lord[136] will not cast off for ever:[5769]

32 But though he cause grief, yet will he have compassion[7355] according to the multitude of his mercies.[2617]

🔑 33 For [a]he doth not afflict [I]willingly[3820] nor grieve the children[1121] of men.[376]

34 To crush[1792] under his feet all the prisoners of the earth,[776]

35 To turn aside the right[4941] of a man before the face of [I]the most High,[5945]

36 To subvert[5719] a man[120] in his cause,[7379] [a]the Lord [I]approveth[7200] not.

🔑 37 Who *is* he [a]*that* saith, and it cometh to pass, *when* the Lord commandeth[6680] *it* not?

38 Out of the mouth of the most High proceedeth not [a]evil[7451] and good?

39 [a]Wherefore doth a living[2416] man[120] [I]complain, [b]a man[1397] for the punishment of his sins?[2399]

40 Let us search[2664] and try[2713] our ways, and turn again[7725] to the LORD.

41 [a]Let us lift up[5375] our heart with *our* hands[3709] unto God[410] in the heavens.[8064]

42 [a]We have transgressed[5060] and have rebelled:[4784] thou hast not pardoned.[5545]

43 Thou hast covered with anger,[639] and persecuted us: [a]thou hast slain,[2026] thou hast not pitied.

44 Thou hast covered thyself with a cloud,[6051] [a]that *our* prayer should not pass through.[5674]

45 Thou hast made us *as* the [a]offscouring and refuse in the midst[7130] of the people.

46 [a]All our enemies have opened their mouths[6310] against us.

20 [I]Hebr. *bowed*
21 [I]Hebr. *make to return to my heart*
22 [a]Mal. 3:6
23 [a]Isa. 33:2
24 [a]Ps. 16:5; 73:26; 119:57; Jer. 10:16
25 [a]Ps. 130:6; Isa. 30:18; Mic. 7:7
26 [a]Ps. 37:7
27 [a]Ps. 94:12; 119:71
28 [a]Jer. 15:17; Lam. 2:10
29 [a]Job 42:6
30 [a]Isa. 50:6; Matt. 5:39
31 [a]Ps. 94:14
33 [I]Hebr. *from his heart* [a]Ezek. 33:11; Heb. 12:10
35 [I]Or, *a superior*
36 [I]Or, *seeth not* [a]Hab. 1:13
37 [a]Ps. 33:9
38 [a]Job 2:10; Isa. 45:7; Amos 3:6
39 [I]Or, *murmur* [a]Prov. 19:3 [b]Mic. 7:9
41 [a]Ps. 86:4
42 [a]Dan. 9:5
43 [a]Lam. 2:2, 17, 21
44 [a]Lam. 3:8
45 [a]1Cor. 4:13
46 [a]Lam. 2:16

🔑 **3:22–24** Jeremiah is so overwhelmed by the destruction of Jerusalem, by the sin that brought it about, and by the suffering that resulted from it, that he finds it difficult to be diverted from his somber frame of mind. Although Jeremiah did acknowledge God's sovereignty over these events, he also expressed his confusion over the fact that God had allowed such suffering. The message of Jeremiah in these verses is a statement of God's mercy to His people on a daily basis, despite the Israelites' constant unfaithfulness to Him. He was reminded that all the blessings in life come from God (see James 5:11), and that his trust should be in God alone.

🔑 **3:33** The term "willingly" that is used in this verse comes from a phrase using the Hebrew word *lēb* (3820, heart), which means "from his heart." God does not want to have to bring hardships into people's lives, but He may do so in order to teach, convict, and bring them into a right relationship with Him. Even though the children of Israel were having their cities destroyed and were being carried away into captivity, the message of this verse is that the people had, by their sin, brought this judgment upon themselves.

🔑 **3:37–39** Jeremiah uses a series of rhetorical questions here to point out that God is just in all that He does. In verse thirty-eight, the word translated "evil" is actually from the Hebrew word *ra'* (7451), which means "judgment." The justice of God, when applied to man's sinful state, requires that there be a swift and immediate judgment (v. 39).

47 [a]Fear[6343] and a snare[6354] is come upon us, [b]desolation and destruction.

48 [a]Mine eye runneth down with rivers of water for the destruction of the daughter of my people.

49 [a]Mine eye trickleth down, and ceaseth[1820] not, without any intermission,

50 Till the LORD [a]look down, and behold[7200] from heaven.8064

51 Mine eye affecteth [I]mine heart[5315] [II]because of all the daughters of my city.

52 Mine enemies chased me sore, like a bird, [a]without cause.[2600]

53 They have cut off my life[2416] [a]in the dungeon,[953] and [b]cast a stone upon me.

54 [a]Waters flowed over mine head;[7218] *then* [b]I said, I am cut off.[1504]

55 [a]I called upon[7121] thy name, O LORD, out of the low dungeon.

56 [a]Thou hast heard[8085] my voice: hide not thine ear[241] at my breathing,[7309] at my cry.

57 Thou [a]drewest near in the day *that* I called upon thee: thou saidst, Fear[3372] not.

58 O Lord, thou hast [a]pleaded[7378] the causes of my soul; [b]thou hast redeemed[1350] my life.

59 O LORD, thou hast seen my wrong:[5792] [a]judge[8199] thou my cause.[4941]

60 Thou hast seen all their vengeance[5360] *and* all their [a]imaginations[4284] against me.

61 Thou hast heard their reproach, O LORD, *and* all their imaginations against me;

62 The lips[8193] of those that rose up against me, and their device against me all the day.

63 Behold their [a]sitting down, and their rising up; [b]I *am* their musick.4485

64 [a]Render[7725] unto them a recompence, O LORD, according to the work of their hands.[3027]

65 Give them [I]sorrow of heart,[3820] thy curse unto them.

66 Persecute and destroy[8045] them in anger [a]from under the [b]heavens of the LORD.

47 [a]Isa. 24:17; Jer. 48:43 [b]Isa. 51:19
48 [a]Jer. 4:19; 9:1; 14:17; Lam. 2:11
49 [a]Ps. 77:2; Lam. 1:16
50 [a]Isa. 63:15
51 [I]Hebr. *my soul* [II]Or, *more than all*
52 [a]Ps. 35:7, 19; 69:4; 109:3; 119:161
53 [a]Jer. 37:16; 38:6, 9, 10 [b]Dan. 6:17
54 [a]Ps. 69:2; 124:4, 5 [b]Ps. 31:22; Isa. 38:10, 11; Lam. 3:18
55 [a]Ps. 130:1; Jon. 2:2
56 [a]Ps. 3:4; 6:8; 18:6; 66:19; 116:1
57 [a]James 4:8
58 [a]Ps. 35:1; Jer. 51:36 [b]Ps. 71:23
59 [a]Ps. 9:4; 35:23
60 [a]Jer. 11:19
63 [a]Ps. 139:2 [b]Lam. 3:14
64 [a]Ps. 28:4; Jer. 11:20; 2Tim. 4:14
65 [I]Or, *obstinacy of heart*
66 [a]Deut. 25:19; Jer. 10:11 [b]Ps. 8:3

The Results of the Siege

4 How is the gold become dim! *how* is the most fine gold changed! the stones of the sanctuary[6944] are poured out[8210] [a]in the top[7218] of every street.

2 The precious sons[1121] of Zion, comparable to fine gold, how are they esteemed[2803] [a]as earthen[2789] pitchers, the work of the hands[3027] of the potter!

3 Even the [I]sea monsters[8577] draw out the breast, they give suck to their young ones: the daughter of my people[5971] *is become* cruel, [a]like the ostriches in the wilderness.

4 [a]The tongue of the sucking child cleaveth to the roof of his mouth for thirst: [b]the young children ask[7592] bread, *and* no man breaketh *it* unto them.

5 They that did feed delicately are desolate[8074] in the streets: they that were brought up in scarlet [a]embrace dunghills.

6 For the [I]punishment of the iniquity[5771] of the daughter of my people is greater than the punishment of the sin[2403] of Sodom, that was [a]overthrown[2015] as in a moment, and no hands stayed[2342] on her.

7 Her Nazarites[5139] were purer[2141] than snow, they were whiter than milk, they were more ruddy[119] in body[6106] than rubies, their polishing *was* of sapphire:

8 Their visage8389 is [I][a]blacker[2821] than a coal;[7815] they are not known in the streets: [b]their skin[5785] cleaveth to their bones;[6106] it is withered,[3001] it is become[1961] like a stick.

9 *They that be* slain2491 with the sword[2719] are better[2896] than *they that be* slain with hunger: for these [I]pine away,2100 stricken through for *want of* the fruits of the field.[7704]

1 [a]Lam. 2:19
2 [a]Isa. 30:14; Jer. 19:11; 2Cor. 4:7
3 [I]Or, *sea calves* [a]Job 39:14, 16
4 [a]Ps. 22:15 [b]Lam. 2:11, 12
5 [a]Job 24:8
6 [I]Or, *iniquity* [a]Gen. 19:25
8 [I]Hebr. *darker than blackness* [a]Lam. 5:10; Joel 2:6; Nah. 2:10 [b]Ps. 102:5
9 [I]Hebr. *flow out*

4:6 See note on Genesis 14:2 concerning the destruction of Sodom.

10 [a]The hands of the [b]pitiful women[802] have sodden1310 their own children: they were their [c]meat in the destruction of the daughter of my people.

11 The LORD hath accomplished[3615] his fury; [a]he hath poured out his fierce anger,[639] and [b]hath kindled a fire in Zion, and it hath devoured the foundations[3247] thereof.

12 The kings[4428] of the earth,[776] and all the inhabitants of the world,[8398] would not have believed[539] that the adversary and the enemy should have entered into the gates of Jerusalem.

13 [a]For the sins[2399] of her prophets,[5030] *and* the iniquities[5771] of her priests,[3548] [b]that have shed[8210] the blood[1818] of the just in the midst[7130] of her,

14 They have wandered *as* blind *men* in the streets, [a]they have polluted themselves with blood, [I][b]so that men could not touch[5060] their garments.

15 They cried[7121] unto them, Depart[5493] ye; [I]*it is* [a]unclean;[2931] depart, depart, touch not: when they fled away and wandered, they said among the heathen,[1471] They shall no more sojourn[1481] *there.*

16 The [I]anger[6440] of the LORD hath divided them; he will no more regard them: [a]they respected[5375] not the persons[6440] of the priests, they favoured[2603] not the elders.[2205]

17 As for us, [a]our eyes as yet failed for our vain help: in our watching we have watched for a nation[1471] *that* could not save[3467] *us.*

18 [a]They hunt our steps, that we cannot go in our streets: our end is near, our days[3117] are fulfilled; for [b]our end is come.

19 Our persecutors are [a]swifter than the eagles of the heaven:8064 they pursued us upon the mountains, they laid wait for us in the wilderness.

20 The [a]breath[7307] of our nostrils,[639] the anointed[4899] of the LORD, [b]was taken in their pits,[7825] of whom we said, Under his shadow we shall live[2421] among the heathen.

21 [a]Rejoice and be glad, O daughter of Edom, that dwellest in the land[776] of Uz; [b]the cup also shall pass through[5674] unto thee: thou shalt be drunken, and shalt make thyself naked.

22 [I][a]The punishment of thine iniquity is accomplished,[8552] O daughter of Zion; he will no more carry thee away into captivity:[1540] [b]he will visit[6485] thine iniquity, O daughter of Edom; he will [II]discover[1540] thy sins.

A Plea for Mercy

5 [a]Remember,[2142] O LORD, what is come upon us: consider, and behold[7200] [b]our reproach.[2781]

2 [a]Our inheritance[5159] is turned[2015] to strangers,[2114] our houses[1004] to aliens.[5237]

3 We are orphans and fatherless, our mothers[517] *are* as widows.

4 We have drunken our water for money; our wood [I]is sold unto us.

5 [I][a]Our necks *are* under persecution:7291 we labour, *and* have no rest.

6 [a]We have given the hand[3027] [b]*to* the Egyptians, *and to* the Assyrians, to be satisfied with bread.

7 [a]Our fathers[1] have sinned,[2398] *and* [b]are not; and we have borne their iniquities.[5771]

8 [a]Servants[5650] have ruled[4910] over us: *there is* none that doth deliver *us* out of their hand.

9 We gat our bread with *the peril of* our lives[5315] because of the sword[2719] of the wilderness.

10 Our [a]skin[5785] was black like an oven because of the [I]terrible[2152] famine.

11 [a]They ravished the women[802] in

10 [a]Lam. 2:20 [b]Isa. 49:15 [c]Deut. 28:57; 2Kgs. 6:29
11 [a]Jer. 7:20 [b]Deut. 32:22; Jer. 21:14
13 [a]Jer. 5:31; 6:13; 14:14; 23:11, 21; Ezek. 22:26, 28; Zeph. 3:4 [b]Matt. 23:31, 37
14 [I]Or, *in that they could not but touch* [a]Jer. 2:34 [b]Num. 19:16
15 [I]Or, *ye polluted* [a]Lev. 13:45
16 [I]Or, *face* [a]Lam. 5:12
17 [a]2Kgs. 24:7; Isa. 20:5; 30:6, 7; Jer. 37:7; Ezek. 29:16
18 [a]2Kgs. 25:4, 5 [b]Ezek. 7:2, 3, 6; Amos 8:2
19 [a]Deut. 28:49; Jer. 4:13
20 [a]Gen. 2:7; Lam. 2:9 [b]Jer. 52:9; Ezek. 12:13; 19:4, 8
21 [a]Eccl. 11:9 [b]Jer. 25:15, 16, 21; Obad. 1:10
22 [I]Or, *Thine iniquity* [II]Or, *carry* thee *captive for thy sins* [a]Isa. 40:2 [b]Ps. 137:7

1 [a]Ps. 89:50, 51 [b]Ps. 79:4; Lam. 2:15
2 [a]Ps. 79:1
4 [I]Hebr. *cometh for price*
5 [I]Hebr. *On our necks are we persecuted* [a]Deut. 28:48; Jer. 28:14
6 [a]Gen. 24:2; Jer. 50:15 [b]Hos. 12:1
7 [a]Jer. 31:29; Ezek. 18:2 [b]Gen. 42:13; Zech. 1:5
8 [a]Neh. 5:15
10 [I]Or, *terrors, or, storms* [a]Job 30:30; Ps. 119:83; Lam. 4:8
11 [a]Isa. 13:16; Zech. 14:2

4:10 This verse reveals that the famine in the land was so severe that the people resorted to eating their own children. Another occurrence of this action was at the siege of Samaria by the Assyrians (2 Kgs. 9:25–29).

5:10 The phrase "our skin was black like an oven" is a figure of speech that describes the condition of people who become feverish as a result of starvation.

Zion, *and* the maids[1330] in the cities of Judah.

12 Princes[8269] are hanged up by their hand: [a]the faces of elders[2205] were not honoured.[1921]

13 They took[5375] the young men [a]to grind, and the children fell under the wood.

14 The elders have ceased[7673] from the gate, the young men from their musick.

15 The joy of our heart[3820] is ceased; our dance is turned into mourning.

16 [I][a]The crown is fallen[5307] *from* our head:[7218] woe unto us, that we have sinned!

17 For this [a]our heart is faint; [b]for these *things* our eyes are dim.[2821]

18 Because of the mountain of Zion, which is desolate,[8074] the foxes walk upon it.

19 Thou, O LORD, [a]remainest for ever;[5769] [b]thy throne[3678] from generation[1755] to generation.

20 [a]Wherefore dost thou forget us for ever,[5331] *and* forsake[5800] us [I]so long[753] time?

🔑 21 [a]Turn[7725] thou us unto thee, O LORD, and we shall be turned; renew our days as of old.[6924]

22 [I]But thou hast utterly rejected us; thou art very wroth[7107] against us.

12 [a]Isa. 47:6; Lam. 4:16
13 [a]Judg. 16:21
16 [I]Hebr. *The crown of our head is fallen* [a]Job 19:9; Ps. 89:39
17 [a]Lam. 1:22 [b]Ps. 6:7; Lam. 2:11
19 [a]Ps. 9:7; 10:16; 29:10; 90:2; 102:12, 26, 27; 145:13; Hab. 1:12 [b]Ps. 45:6
20 [I]Hebr. *for length of days* [a]Ps. 13:1
21 [a]Ps. 80:3, 7, 19; Jer. 31:18
22 [I]Or, *For wilt thou utterly reject us?*

🔑 **5:21** This prayer by Jeremiah reflects the hope that the people of Jerusalem would return to a proper relationship with God. Compare the days when His glory filled the temple at its consecration by Solomon (1 Kgs. 8:10, 11).

The Book of

EZEKIEL

The name Ezekiel means "God strengthens" and is appropriate in light of the difficulties Ezekiel would endure. Ezekiel was, along with Jeremiah and Zechariah, one of three prophets who were also priests. He was taken to Babylon from Jerusalem in the second deportation (597 B.C.) along with King Jehoiachin (2 Kgs. 24:8–17; Jer. 22:24–30). At the age of thirty (Ezek. 1:1), when a priest would normally begin his ministry, Ezekiel received his prophetic call from the Lord (593 B.C.). He spent the rest of his life in Babylon, but he received visions of both contemporary and future events relating to Jerusalem. As might be expected from a priest, Ezekiel was concerned about the pollution of the temple that existed in his time and the glory of the millennial temple in the future. The last date that Ezekiel records (Ezek. 29:17) is twenty-two years after his call.

The main topics discussed in the book fall into three basic sections: those prophecies that stress the impending disaster of Jerusalem's fall (chaps. 1—24); the judgments pronounced on surrounding nations (chaps. 25—32); and the future hopes and trials of God's people (chaps. 33—48). The purpose of Ezekiel's book can be described as threefold: 1) to show that Judah and Jerusalem were being judged for their sin; 2) to encourage the exiles with prophecies of God's future blessing on Israel; and 3) to emphasize God's glory and His character as that which should be most important to His people. This third reason is expressed over seventy-five times in the phrases "for mine holy name's sake" (Ezek. 36:22) and "they shall know that I am the LORD" (Ezek. 36:38).

The key phrase in the book, "the son of man" (Ezek. 2:1), is used about forty-five times. It stresses the idea that one possesses the qualities and characteristics of his father. Consequently, when Jesus used the terms "Son of man" and "Son of God" to refer to Himself, He was showing that He had the characteristics of both deity and humanity. "The glory of the LORD" is also a prominent theme, being mentioned many times in the book (Ezek. 3:12, 23; 8:4; 9:3; 10:4, 18, 19; 11:22, 23; 39:21; 43:2 [twice], 4, 5; 44:4).

The First Vision

1 Now it came to pass in the thirtieth
year, in the fourth *month,* in the fifth
day of the month, as I *was* among the
[I]captives[1473] [a]by the river of Chebar, *that*
[b]the heavens[8064] were opened, and I
saw[7200] [c]visions[4759] of God.[430]

2 In the fifth *day* of the month,
which *was* the fifth year of [a]king[4428]
Jehoiachin's captivity,[1546]

3 The word[1697] of the LORD came expressly unto [I]Ezekiel the priest,[3548] the son[1121] of Buzi, in the land[127] of the Chaldeans by the river Chebar; and [a]the hand[3027] of the LORD was there upon him.

4 And I looked,[7200] and, behold, [a]a
whirlwind came [b]out of the north, a great

1 [I]Hebr. *captivity* [a]Ezek. 1:3; 3:15, 23; 10:15, 20, 22; 43:3 [b]Matt. 3:16; Acts 7:56; 10:11; Rev. 19:11 [c]Ezek. 8:3 **2** [a]2Kgs. 24:12, 15 **3** [I]Hebr. *Jehezkel* [a]1Kgs. 18:46; 2Kgs. 3:15; Ezek. 3:14, 22; 8:1; 40:1 **4** [a]Jer. 23:19; 25:32 [b]Jer. 1:14; 4:6; 6:1

1:4–28 Ezekiel received his calling to be a prophet through a visionary experience. There are four main elements in this vision: 1) The four living creatures (Ezek. 1:4–14) are called cherubim (Ezek. 10:15, 20), which is a group of angels (Gen. 3:24), possibly related to the seraphim (Is. 6:1–6), and the living creatures of Revelation chapters four and five. Some suggest that the four faces of these cherubs are indicative of God's character, while others believe they are simply four examples of God's creative work. 2) The wheels and the "wheel in the middle of a wheel" (Ezek. 1:15–21)

(continued on next page)

cloud,[6051] and a fire [I]infolding itself, and
a brightness5051 *was* about it, and out of
the midst thereof as the colour of amber,
out of the midst of the fire.
5 [a]Also out of the midst thereof
came the likeness[1823] of four living
creatures.[2416] And [b]this *was* their appearance; they had [c]the likeness of a
man.[120]
6 And every one had four faces, and
every one had four wings.
7 And their feet *were* [I]straight[3474]
feet; and the sole of their feet *was* like
the sole[3709] of a calf's foot: and they
sparkled [a]like the colour of burnished
brass.
8 [a]And *they had* the hands[3027] of a
man under their wings on their four
sides; and they four had their faces and
their wings.
9 [a]Their wings *were* joined one[802] to
another;[269] [b]they turned not when they
went; they went every one[376] straight forward.
10 As for [a]the likeness of their faces,
they four [b]had the face of a man, [c]and
the face of a lion, on the right side: [d]and
they four had the face of an ox on the
left side; [e]they four also had the face of
an eagle.
11 Thus *were* their faces: and their
wings *were* [I]stretched upward; two *wings*
of every one *were* joined one to
another,[376] and [a]two covered[3680] their
bodies.[1472]
12 And [a]they went every one straight
forward: [b]whither the spirit[7307] was to
go, they went; *and* [c]they turned not when
they went.
13 As for the likeness of the living
creatures,[2416] their appearance[4758] *was*
like burning coals of fire, [a]*and* like the
appearance of lamps: it went up and
down[1980] among the living creatures; and
the fire was bright, and out of the fire
went forth lightning.
14 And the living creatures [a]ran and
returned[7725] [b]as the appearance of a
flash of lightning.
15 Now as I beheld[7200] the living
creatures, behold [a]one wheel[212] upon the
earth[776] by the living creatures, with his
four faces.
16 [a]The appearance of the wheels
and their work *was* [b]like unto the colour
of a beryl: and they four had one likeness: and their appearance and their
work4639 *was* as it were a wheel in the
middle of a wheel.
17 When they went, they went upon
their four sides: [a]*and* they turned not
when they went.
18 As for their rings,1354 they were
so high that they were dreadful;[3374] and
their [I]rings *were* [a]full of eyes round about
them four.
19 And [a]when the living creatures
went, the wheels went by them: and
when the living creatures were lifted
up[5375] from the earth, the wheels were
lifted up.
20 [a]Whithersoever the spirit was to
go, they went, thither *was their* spirit to
go; and the wheels were lifted up over
against them: [b]for the spirit [I]of the living
creature[2416] *was* in the wheels.
21 [a]When those went, *these* went;
and when those stood, *these* stood; and
when those were lifted up from the earth,
the wheels were lifted up over against
them: for the spirit [I]of the living creature
was in the wheels.
22 [a]And the likeness of the firmament[7549] upon the heads[7218] of the living creature *was* as the colour of the
terrible[3372] crystal, stretched forth over
their heads above.
23 And under the firmament *were*

4 IHebr. *catching itself*
5 aRev. 4:6 bEzek. 10:8 cEzek. 1:10; 10:14, 21
7 IHebr. *a straight foot* aDan. 10:6; Rev. 1:15
8 aEzek. 10:8, 21
9 aEzek. 1:11 bEzek. 1:12; 10:11
10 aRev. 4:7 bNum. 2:10 cNum. 2:3 dNum. 2:18 eNum. 2:25
11 IOr, *divided above* aIsa. 6:2
12 aEzek. 1:9; 10:22 bEzek. 1:20 cEzek. 1:9, 17
13 aRev. 4:5
14 aZech. 4:10 bMatt. 24:27
15 aEzek. 10:9
16 aEzek. 10:9, 10 bDan. 10:6
17 aEzek. 1:12
18 IOr, *strakes* aEzek. 10:12; Zech. 4:10
19 aEzek. 10:16, 17
20 IOr, *of life* aEzek. 1:12 bEzek. 10:17
21 IOr, *of life* aEzek. 1:19, 20; 10:17
22 aEzek. 10:1

(continued from previous page)
were thought by teachers of Judaism to be God's chariot. As a result of this interpretation, mystical interpretations were commonly incorporated into the meaning of this portion of Ezekiel's vision. The simplest explanation of the image is that it speaks of God's omnipotence and sovereignty over the universe. 3) The brilliance of the firmament (Ezek. 1:22–24) is representative of God's holiness and majesty (see Rev. 4:6). 4) The throne, which is occupied by the "appearance of a man" (Ezek. 1:25–28), affirms that God is in control of the affairs of man and active in judgment.

their wings straight, the one toward the other: every one had two, which covered on this side, and every one had two, which covered on that side, their bodies.

24 [a]And when they went, I heard[8085] the noise of their wings, [b]like the noise of great waters, as [c]the voice of the Almighty,[7706] the voice of speech,[1999] as the noise of an host:[4264] when they stood, they let down[7503] their wings.

25 And there was a voice from the firmament that *was* over their heads, when they stood, *and* had let down their wings.

26 [a]And above the firmament that *was* over their heads *was* the likeness of a throne, [b]as the appearance of a sapphire stone: and upon the likeness of the throne[3678] *was* the likeness as the appearance of a man above upon it.

27 [a]And I saw as the colour of amber, as the appearance of fire round about within[1004] it, from the appearance of his loins even upward, and from the appearance of his loins even downward, I saw as it were the appearance of fire, and it had brightness[5051] round about.

28 [a]As the appearance of the bow that is in the cloud in the day[3117] of rain, so *was* the appearance of the brightness round about. [b]This *was* the appearance of the likeness of the glory[3519] of the LORD. And when I saw *it,* [c]I fell[5307] upon my face, and I heard a voice of one that spake.[1696]

God Calls Ezekiel

2 And he said[559] unto me, Son[1121] of man,[120] [a]stand upon thy feet, and I will speak[1696] unto thee.

2 And [a]the spirit[7307] entered into me when he spake unto me, and set me upon my feet, that I heard[8085] him that spake unto me.

3 And he said unto me, Son of man, I send thee to the children[1121] of Israel, to a rebellious [I]nation[1471] that hath rebelled[4775] against me: [a]they and their fathers[1] have transgressed[6586] against me, *even* unto this very day.[3117]

4 [a]For *they are* [I]impudent children and stiffhearted. I do send thee unto them; and thou shalt say[559] unto them, Thus saith the Lord[136] GOD.

5 [a]And they, whether they will hear, or whether they will forbear, (for they *are* a rebellious[4805] house,[1004]) yet [b]shall know[3045] that there hath been a prophet[5030] among them.

6 And thou, son of man, [a]be not afraid[3372] of them, neither be afraid of their words, though [I][b]briers and thorns *be* with thee, and thou dost dwell among scorpions: [c]be not afraid of their words,[1697] nor be dismayed[2865] at their looks, [d]though they *be* a rebellious house.

7 [a]And thou shalt speak my words unto them, [b]whether they will hear, or whether they will forbear:[2308] for they *are* [I]most rebellious.

🗝 8 But thou, son of man, hear what I say[1696] unto thee; Be not thou rebellious like that rebellious house: open thy mouth,[6310] and [a]eat that I give thee.

9 And when I looked,[7200] behold, [a]an hand[3027] *was* sent unto me; and, lo, [b]a roll[4039] of a book[5612] *was* therein;

10 And he spread it before me; and it *was* written within and without: and *there was* written therein lamentations, and mourning,[1899] and woe.

24 [a]Ezek. 10:5 [b]Ezek. 43:2; Dan. 10:6; Rev. 1:15 [c]Job 37:4, 5; Ps. 29:3, 4; 68:33

26 [a]Ezek. 10:1 [b]Ex. 24:10

27 [a]Ezek. 8:2

28 [a]Rev. 4:3; 10:1 [b]Ezek. 3:23; 8:4 [c]Ezek. 3:23; Dan. 8:17; Acts 9:4; Rev. 1:17

1 [a]Dan. 10:11

2 [a]Ezek. 3:24

3 [I]Hebr. *nations* [a]Jer. 3:25; Ezek. 20:18, 21, 30

4 [I]Hebr. *hard of face* [a]Ezek. 3:7

5 [a]Ezek. 3:11, 26, 27 [b]Ezek. 33:33

6 [I]Or, *rebels* [a]Jer. 1:8, 17; Luke 12:4 [b]Isa. 9:18; Jer. 6:28; Mic. 7:4 [c]Ezek. 3:9; 1Pet. 3:14 [d]Ezek. 3:9, 26, 27

7 [I]Hebr. *rebellion* [a]Jer. 1:7, 17 [b]Ezek. 2:5

8 [a]Rev. 10:9

9 [a]Ezek. 8:3; Jer. 1:9 [b]Ezek. 3:1

🗝 **2:8—3:3** Ezekiel was directed by God to perform many unusual acts in connection with the message that he had received from God. In this vision he ate a scroll, presumably because it had on it the words he was to utter (cf. Rev. 10:8–10). Another time, Ezekiel acted out an escape through the city wall by some of his fellow countrymen back in Jerusalem (Ezek. 12:3–7). He used a type of shadowboxing to depict the Babylonian slaughter that was coming (Ezek. 21:14–17). At times during his preaching he would clap his hands, stamp his feet and cry, "Alas" (Ezek. 6:11), or as he cried and wailed, he would slap his thighs (Ezek. 21:12). As a sign to the people, he used a brick to represent Jerusalem and built a model depicting its siege (Ezek. 4:1–3). To represent the length of punishment of Israel and Judah, respectively, he was bound with cords and lay on his left side

(continued on next page)

3 Moreover he said[559] unto me, Son[1121] of man,[120] eat that thou findest; [a]eat this roll, and go speak[1696] unto the house[1004] of Israel.

2 So I opened my mouth,[6310] and he caused me to eat that roll.

3 And he said unto me, Son of man, cause thy belly to eat, and fill thy bowels[4578] with this roll that I give thee. Then did I [a]eat *it;* and it was in my mouth [b]as honey for sweetness.

4 And he said unto me, Son of man, go, get thee unto the house of Israel, and speak with my words[1697] unto them.

5 For thou *art* not sent to a people[5971] [I][a]of a strange[6012] speech[8193] and of an hard language,[3956] *but* to the house of Israel;

6 Not to many people [I]of a strange speech and of an hard[3515] language, whose words thou canst not understand.[8085] [II]Surely, [a]had I sent thee to them, they would have hearkened[8085] unto thee.

7 But the house of Israel will not hearken unto thee; [a]for they will not hearken unto me: [b]for all the house of Israel *are* [I]impudent and hardhearted.

8 Behold, I have made thy face strong against their faces, and thy forehead strong[2389] against their foreheads.

9 [a]As an adamant[8068] harder than flint have I made thy forehead: [b]fear[3372] them not, neither be dismayed[2865] at their looks, though they *be* a rebellious[4809] house.

10 Moreover he said unto me, Son of man, all my words that I shall speak unto thee receive in thine heart,[3824] and hear[8085] with thine ears.[241]

11 And go, get thee to them of the captivity,[1473] unto the children[1121] of thy people, and speak unto them, and tell[559] them, [a]Thus saith[559] the Lord GOD; whether they will hear, or whether they will forbear.

12 Then [a]the spirit[7307] took me up,[5375] and I heard[8085] behind me a voice of a great rushing, *saying,* Blessed[1288] *be* the glory[3519] of the LORD from his place.

13 *I heard* also the noise of the wings of the living creatures[2416] that [I]touched[5401] one[802] another,[269] and the noise of the wheels[212] over against them, and a noise of a great rushing.

14 So [a]the spirit lifted me up, and took me away, and I went [I]in bitterness,[4751] in the [II]heat[2534] of my spirit; but [b]the hand[3027] of the LORD was strong[2388] upon me.

15 Then I came to them of the captivity at Tel–abib, that dwelt by the river of Chebar, and [a]I sat where they sat, and remained there astonished[8074] among them seven days.[3117]

Ezekiel, a Watchman

16 And it came to pass at the end of seven days, that the word[1697] of the LORD came unto me, saying,

17 [a]Son of man, I have made thee [b]a watchman unto the house of Israel: therefore hear the word at my mouth, and give them warning[2094] from me.

18 When I say[559] unto the wicked, Thou shalt surely die;[4191] and thou givest him not warning, nor speakest[1696] to warn the wicked[7563] from his wicked way,[1870] to save his life;[2421] the same wicked *man* [a]shall die in his iniquity;[5771] but his blood[1818] will I require at thine hand.

19 Yet if thou warn the wicked, and he turn[7725] not from his wickedness,[7562]

1 [a]Ezek. 2:8, 9

3 [a]Jer. 15:6; Rev. 10:9 [b]Ps. 19:10; 119:103

5 [I]Hebr. *deep of lip, and heavy of tongue* [a]Ezek. 2:6

6 [I]Hebr. *deep of lip, and heavy of language* [II]Or, *If I had sent thee, would they not have hearkened unto thee?* [a]Matt. 11:21, 23

7 [I]Hebr. *stiff of forehead, and hard of heart* [a]John 15:20 [b]Ezek. 2:4

9 [a]Isa. 50:7; Jer. 1:18; 15:20; Mic. 3:8 [b]Jer. 1:8, 17; Ezek. 2:6

11 [a]Ezek. 2:5, 7; 3:27

12 [a]1Kgs. 18:12; 2Kgs. 2:16; Ezek. 3:14; 8:3; Acts 8:30

13 [I]Hebr. *kissed*

14 [I]Hebr. *bitter* [II]Hebr. *hot anger* [a]Ezek. 3:12; 8:3 [b]2Kgs. 3:15; Ezek. 1:3; 8:1; 37:1

15 [a]Job 2:13; Ps. 137:1

17 [a]Ezek. 33:7-9 [b]Isa. 52:8; 56:10; 62:6; Jer. 6:17

18 [a]Ezek. 33:6; John 8:21, 24

(continued from previous page)

for 390 days and on his right side for forty days (Ezek. 4:4–8). During that first period, he consumed only rationed food and water to symbolize the plight of those left in Jerusalem (Ezek. 4:9–17). He also cut his hair, divided it into thirds, and disposed of it in three different manners, to indicate the ways in which the inhabitants of Jerusalem would perish (Ezek. 5:1–12). Ezekiel did this to reinforce the message he had been given from God.

nor from his wicked way, he shall die in his iniquity; [a]but thou hast delivered[5337] thy soul.[5315]

20 Again, When a [a]righteous[6662] *man* doth turn from his [I]righteousness,[6664] and commit[6213] iniquity,[5766] and I lay a stumblingblock[4383] before him, he shall die: because thou hast not given him warning, he shall die in his sin,[2403] and his righteousness[6666] which he hath done[6213] shall not be remembered;[2142] but his blood will I require at thine hand.

21 Nevertheless if thou warn the righteous *man,* that the righteous sin[2398] not, and he doth not sin, he shall surely live,[2421] because he is warned;[2094] also thou hast delivered thy soul.

The Prophet Made Speechless

22 [a]And the hand of the LORD was there upon me; and he said unto me, Arise, go forth [b]into the plain,[1237] and I will there talk[1696] with thee.

23 Then I arose, and went forth into the plain: and, behold, [a]the glory of the LORD stood there, as the glory which I [b]saw[7200] by the river of Chebar: [c]and I fell[5307] on my face.

24 Then [a]the spirit entered into me, and set me upon my feet, and spake[1696] with me, and said unto me, Go, shut thyself within thine house.

25 But thou, O son of man, behold, [a]they shall put bands[5688] upon thee, and shall bind thee with them, and thou shalt not go out among them:

26 And [a]I will make thy tongue cleave to the roof of thy mouth, that thou shalt be dumb, and shalt not be to them [I]a reprover:[3198] [b]for they *are* a rebellious house.

27 [a]But when I speak with thee, I will open thy mouth, and thou shalt say unto them, [b]Thus saith the Lord[136] GOD; He that heareth,[8085] let him hear; and he that forbeareth, let him forbear: [c]for they *are* a rebellious house.

Siege of Jerusalem Pourtrayed

4 Thou also, son[1121] of man,[120] take thee a tile, and lay it before thee, and pourtray[2710] upon it the city, *even* Jerusalem:

2 And lay siege against it, and build a fort against it, and cast[8210] a mount against it; set the camp[4264] also against it, and set[7760] [a]*battering* rams[3733] against it round about.

3 Moreover take thou unto thee [I]an iron pan, and set it *for* a wall of iron between thee and the city: and set thy face against it, and it shall be besieged, and thou shalt lay siege against it. [a]This *shall be* a sign[226] to the house[1004] of Israel.

4 Lie thou also upon thy left side, and lay[7760] the iniquity[5771] of the house of Israel upon it: *according* to the number of the days[3117] that thou shalt lie upon it thou shalt bear[5375] their iniquity.

5 For I have laid upon thee the years of their iniquity,[5771] according to the number of the days, three hundred and ninety days: [a]so shalt thou bear the iniquity of the house of Israel.

6 And when thou hast accomplished[3615] them, lie again on thy right side, and thou shalt bear the iniquity of the house of Judah forty days: I have appointed thee [I]each day[3117] for a year.

7 Therefore thou shalt set thy face toward the siege of Jerusalem, and thine arm *shall be* uncovered, and thou shalt prophesy[5012] against it.

8 [a]And, behold, I will lay bands upon thee, and thou shalt not turn[2015] thee [I]from one side to another, till thou hast ended[3615] the days of thy siege.

9 Take thou also unto thee wheat, and barley, and beans, and lentiles, and millet, and [I]fitches,[3698] and put them in one vessel, and make[6213] thee bread thereof, *according* to the number of the days that thou shalt lie upon thy side, three hundred and ninety days shalt thou eat thereof.

10 And thy meat which thou shalt eat *shall be* by weight, twenty shekels a day: from time[6256] to time shalt thou eat it.

11 Thou shalt drink also water by measure, the sixth part of an hin: from time to time shalt thou drink.

19 [a]Isa. 49:4, 5; Acts 20:26
20 [I]Hebr. *righteousnesses* [a]Ezek. 18:24; 33:12, 13
22 [a]Ezek. 1:3; 3:14 [b]Ezek. 8:4
23 [a]Ezek. 1:28 [b]Ezek. 1:1 [c]Ezek. 1:28
24 [a]Ezek. 2:2
25 [a]Ezek. 4:8
26 [I]Hebr. *a man reproving* [a]Ezek. 24:27; Luke 1:20, 22 [b]Ezek. 2:5-7
27 [a]Ezek. 24:27; 33:22 [b]Ezek. 3:11 [c]Ezek. 3:9, 26; 12:2, 3
2 [a]Ezek. 21:22
3 [I]Or, *a flat plate, or, slice* [a]Ezek. 12:6, 11; 24:24, 27
5 [a]Num. 14:34
6 [I]Hebr. *a day for a year, a day for a year*
8 [I]Hebr. *from thy side to thy side* [a]Ezek. 3:25
9 [I]Or, *spelt*

12 And thou shalt eat it *as* barley cakes, and thou shalt bake it with dung that cometh out of man, in their sight.

13 And the LORD said,[559] Even thus [a]shall the children[1121] of Israel eat their defiled bread among the Gentiles,[1471] whither I will drive them.

14 Then said I, [a]Ah Lord[136] GOD! behold, my soul[5315] hath not been polluted:[2930] for from my youth up even till now have I not eaten of [b]that which dieth of itself,[5038] or is torn in pieces; neither came there [c]abominable[6292] flesh into my mouth.[6310]

15 Then he said unto me, Lo, I have given thee cow's dung for man's[120] dung, and thou shalt prepare thy bread therewith.

16 Moreover he said unto me, Son of man, behold, I will break[7665] the [a]staff[4294] of bread in Jerusalem: and they shall [b]eat bread by weight, and with care;[1674] and they shall [c]drink water by measure, and with astonishment:

17 That they may want bread and water, and be astonied[8074] one[376] with another, and [a]consume away[4743] for their iniquity.

Ezekiel Cuts His Hair as a Sign

5 And thou, son[1121] of man,[120] take thee a sharp knife,[2719] take thee a barber's razor, [a]and cause *it* to pass upon thine head[7218] and upon thy beard:[2206] then take thee balances to weigh, and divide the *hair.*

2 [a]Thou shalt burn with fire a third part in the midst of [b]the city, when [c]the days[3117] of the siege are fulfilled: and thou shalt take a third part, *and* smite[5221] about it with a knife: and a third part thou shalt scatter in the wind;[7307] and I will draw out a sword[2719] after them.

3 [a]Thou shalt also take thereof a few in number, and bind them in thy [1]skirts.

4 Then take of them again, and [a]cast them into the midst of the fire, and burn them in the fire; *for* thereof shall a fire come forth into all the house[1004] of Israel.

5 Thus saith[559] the Lord[136] GOD; This *is* Jerusalem: I have set[7760] it in the midst of the nations[1471] and countries[776] *that are* round about her.

6 And she hath changed[4784] my judgments[4941] into wickedness[7564] more than the nations, and my statutes[2708] more than the countries that *are* round about her: for they have refused my judgments and my statutes, they have not walked in them.

7 Therefore thus saith the Lord GOD; Because ye multiplied[1995] more than the nations that *are* round about you, *and* have not walked in my statutes, neither have kept[6213] my judgments, [a]neither have done according to the judgments of the nations that *are* round about you;

8 Therefore thus saith the Lord GOD; Behold, I, even I, *am* against thee, and will execute judgments in the midst of thee in the sight of the nations.

9 [a]And I will do[6213] in thee that which I have not done, and whereunto I will not do any more the like, because of all thine abominations.[8441]

10 Therefore the fathers[1] [a]shall eat the sons[1121] in the midst of thee, and the sons shall eat their fathers; and I will execute judgments[8201] in thee, and the whole remnant[7611] of thee will I [b]scatter into all the winds.[7307]

11 Wherefore, *as* I live,[2416] saith[5002] the Lord GOD; surely, because thou hast [a]defiled[2930] my sanctuary[4720] with all thy [b]detestable things,[8251] and with all thine abominations, therefore will I also diminish *thee;* [c]neither shall mine eye spare, neither will I have any pity.

12 [a]A third part of thee shall die[4191] with the pestilence,[1698] and with famine shall they be consumed[3615] in the midst of thee: and a third part shall fall by the sword round about thee; and [b]I will scatter a third part into all the winds, and [c]I will draw out a sword after them.

13 Thus shall[3615] mine anger[639] [a]be accomplished,[3615] and I will [b]cause my fury to rest upon them, [c]and I will be comforted:[5162] [d]and they shall know[3045]

13 [a]Hos. 9:3

14 [a]Acts 10:14 [b]Ex. 22:31; Lev. 11:40; 17:15 [c]Deut. 14:3; Isa. 65:4

16 [a]Lev. 26:26; Ps. 105:16; Isa. 3:1; Ezek. 5:16; 14:13 [b]Ezek. 4:10; 12:19 [c]Ezek. 4:11

17 [a]Lev. 26:39; Ezek. 24:23

1 [a]Lev. 21:5; Isa. 7:20; Ezek. 44:20

2 [a]Ezek. 5:12 [b]Ezek. 4:1 [c]Ezek. 4:8, 9

3 [1]Hebr. *wings* [a]Jer. 40:6; 52:16

4 [a]Jer. 41:1, 2; 44:14

7 [a]Jer. 2:10, 11; Ezek. 16:47

9 [a]Lam. 4:6; Dan. 9:12; Amos 3:2

10 [a]Lev. 26:29; Deut. 28:53; 2Kgs. 6:29; Jer. 19:9; Lam. 2:20; 4:10 [b]Lev. 26:33; Deut. 28:64; Zech. 2:6

11 [a]2Chr. 36:14; Ezek. 7:20; 8:5; 23:38 [b]Ezek. 11:21 [c]Ezek. 7:4, 9; 8:18; 9:10

12 [a]Jer. 15:2; 21:9; Ezek. 5:2; 6:12 [b]Jer. 9:16; Ezek. 5:2, 10; 6:8 [c]Lev. 26:33; Ezek. 5:2; 12:14

13 [a]Lam. 4:11; Ezek. 6:12; 7:8 [b]Ezek. 21:17 [c]Deut. 32:36; Isa. 1:24 [d]Ezek. 36:6; 38:19

that I the LORD have spoken[1696] *it* in my
zeal,[7068] when I have accomplished my
fury in them.
14 Moreover [a]I will make thee
waste,[2723] and a reproach[2781] among the
nations that *are* round about thee, in the
sight of all that pass by.
15 So it shall be a [a]reproach and a
taunt, an instruction[4148] and an astonishment[8047] unto the nations that *are*
round about thee, when I shall execute
judgments in thee in anger and in fury
and in [b]furious[2534] rebukes.[8433] I the
LORD have spoken *it*.
16 When I shall [a]send upon them the
evil[7451] arrows of famine, which shall be
for *their* destruction,[4889] *and* which I will
send to destroy[7843] you: and I will increase the famine upon you, and will
break[7665] your [b]staff[4294] of bread:
17 So will I send upon you famine
and [a]evil beasts,[2416] and they shall bereave thee; and [b]pestilence and blood[1818]
shall pass[5674] through thee; and I will
bring the sword upon thee. I the LORD
have spoken *it*.

Idolatry Condemned

6 And the word[1697] of the LORD came
unto me, saying,
2 Son[1121] of man,[120] [a]set[7760] thy face
toward the [b]mountains of Israel, and
prophesy[5012] against them,
3 And say,[559] Ye mountains of Israel,
hear[8085] the word of the Lord[136] GOD;
Thus saith the Lord GOD to the mountains, and to the hills, to the rivers, and
to the valleys; Behold, I, *even* I, will bring
a sword[2719] upon you, and [a]I will
destroy[6] your high places.[1116]
4 And your altars[4196] shall be
desolate,[8074] and your [I][a]images[2553] shall
be broken:[7665] and [b]I will cast down[5307]
your slain[2491] *men* before your idols.[1544]
5 And I will [I]lay the dead car-
cases[6297] of the children[1121] of Israel before their idols; and I will scatter your
bones[6106] round about your altars.
6 In all your dwellingplaces the cities
shall be laid waste,[2717] and the high
places shall be desolate;[3456] that your
altars may be laid waste and made
desolate,[816] and your idols may be broken
and cease,[7673] and your images may be
cut down, and your works may be
abolished.[4229]
7 And the slain shall fall in the midst
of you, and [a]ye shall know[3045] that I *am*
the LORD.
🔑 8 [a]Yet will I leave a remnant,[3498] that
ye may have *some* that shall escape the
sword among the nations,[1471] when ye
shall be scattered through the countries.[776]
9 And they that escape of you shall
remember[2142] me among the nations
whither they shall be carried captives,[7617]
because [a]I am broken with their whorish
heart,[3820] which hath departed[5493] from
me, and [b]with their eyes, which go a
whoring[2181] after their idols: and [c]they
shall lothe themselves[6962] for the evils
which they have committed[6213] in all
their abominations.[8441]
10 And they shall know that I *am*
the LORD, *and that* I have not said[1696] in
vain that I would do[6213] this evil[7451] unto
them.
11 Thus saith the Lord GOD;
Smite[5221] [a]with thine hand,[3709] and
stamp[7554] with thy foot, and say, Alas
for all the evil abominations of the
house[1004] of Israel! [b]for they shall fall by
the sword, by the famine, and by the
pestilence.[1698]
12 He that is far off shall die[4191] of
the pestilence; and he that is near shall
fall by the sword; and he that remaineth[7604] and is besieged[5341] shall die
by the famine: [a]thus will I accomplish[3615]
my fury upon them.
13 Then [a]shall ye know that I *am*
the LORD, when their slain *men* shall be

14 [a]Lev. 26:31, 32; Neh. 2:17

15 [a]Deut. 28:37; 1Kgs. 9:7; Ps. 79:4; Jer. 24:9; Lam. 2:15 [b]Ezek. 25:17

16 [a]Deut. 32:23, 24 [b]Lev. 26:26; Ezek. 4:16; 14:13

17 [a]Lev. 26:22; Deut. 32:24; Ezek. 14:21; 33:27; 34:25 [b]Ezek. 38:22

2 [a]Ezek. 20:46; 21:2; 25:2 [b]Ezek. 36:1

3 [a]Lev. 26:30

4 [I]Or, *sun images,* and so [a]Ezek. 6:6 [b]Lev. 26:30

5 [I]Hebr. *give*

7 [a]Ezek. 6:6; 7:4, 9; 11:10, 12; 12:15

8 [a]Jer. 44:28; Ezek. 5:2, 12; 12:16; 14:22

9 [a]Ps. 78:40; Isa. 7:13; 43:24; 63:10 [b]Num. 15:39; Ezek. 20:7, 24 [c]Lev. 26:39; Job 42:6; Ezek. 20:43; 36:31

11 [a]Ezek. 21:14 [b]Ezek. 5:12

12 [a]Ezek. 5:13

13 [a]Ezek. 6:7

🔑 **6:8–10** There are several other instances where Ezekiel mentions the "remnant" that would escape the destruction of Jerusalem and be scattered from the Promised Land (Ezek. 5:10; 11:13; 14:22).

among their idols round about their altars, [b]upon every high hill, [c]in all the tops[7218] of the mountains, and [d]under every green tree, and under every thick oak, the place where they did offer sweet savour to all their idols.

14 So will I [a]stretch out my hand[3027] upon them, and make the land[127] desolate,[8077] yea, [I]more desolate[8047] than the wilderness toward [b]Diblath, in all their habitations:[4186] and they shall know that I *am* the LORD.

Prophecy of Pending Judgment

7 Moreover the word[1697] of the LORD came unto me, saying,

2 Also, thou son[1121] of man,[120] thus saith[559] the Lord[136] GOD unto the land[776] of Israel; [a]An end,7093 the end is come upon the four corners of the land.

3 Now *is* the end *come* upon thee, and I will send mine anger[639] upon thee, and [a]will judge[8199] thee according to thy ways,[1870] and will [I]recompense upon thee all thine abominations.[8441]

4 And [a]mine eye shall not spare thee, neither will I have pity:2550 but I will recompense thy ways upon thee, and thine abominations shall be in the midst of thee: [b]and ye shall know[3045] that I *am* the LORD.

5 Thus saith the Lord GOD; An evil,[7451] an only evil, behold, is come.

6 An end is come, the end is come: it [I]watcheth for thee; behold, it is come.

7 [a]The morning is come unto thee, O thou that dwellest in the land: [b]the time[6256] is come, the day[3117] of trouble[4103] *is* near, and not the [I]sounding again of the mountains.

8 Now will I shortly [a]pour out[8210] my fury upon thee, and accomplish[3615] mine anger upon thee: [b]and I will judge thee according to thy ways, and will recompense thee for all thine abominations.

9 And [a]mine eye shall not spare, neither will I have pity: I will recompense [I]thee according to thy ways and thine abominations *that* are in the midst of thee; [b]and ye shall know that I *am* the LORD that smiteth.

10 Behold the day, behold, it is come: [a]the morning is gone forth; the rod[4294] hath blossomed, pride[2087] hath budded.

11 [a]Violence[2555] is risen up into a rod of wickedness:[7562] none of them *shall remain,* nor of their [I]multitude, nor of any of [II]theirs: [b]neither *shall there be* wailing for them.

12 [a]The time is come, the day draweth near: let not the buyer rejoice, nor the seller mourn: for wrath *is* upon all the multitude thereof.

13 For the seller shall not return[7725] to that which is sold, [I]although they were yet alive:[2416] for the vision[2377] *is* touching the whole multitude thereof, *which* shall not return; neither shall any strengthen himself[2388] [II]in [III]the iniquity[5771] of his life.[2416]

14 They have blown[8628] the trumpet, even to make all ready;[3559] but none goeth to the battle: for my wrath *is* upon all the multitude thereof.

15 [a]The sword[2719] *is* without, and the pestilence[1698] and the famine within:[1004] he that *is* in the field[7704] shall die[4191] with the sword; and he that *is* in the city, famine and pestilence shall devour him.

16 But [a]they that escape of them shall escape, and shall be on the mountains like doves of the valleys, all of them mourning, every one[376] for his iniquity.

17 All [a]hands[3027] shall be feeble,[7503] and all knees shall [I]be weak[1980] *as* water.

18 They shall also [a]gird *themselves* with sackcloth, and [b]horror[6427] shall cover[3680] them; and shame *shall be* upon all faces, and baldness upon all their heads.[7218]

19 They shall cast their silver in the streets, and their gold shall be [I]removed: their [a]silver and their gold shall not be able to deliver[5337] them in the day of the wrath[5678] of the LORD: they shall not satisfy their souls,[5315] neither fill their bowels:[4578] [II]because it is [b]the stumblingblock[4383] of their iniquity.

20 As for the beauty[6643] of his ornament,5716 he set[7760] it in majesty:

13 [b]Jer. 2:20 [c]Hos. 4:13 [d]Isa. 57:5
14 [I]Or, *desolate from the wilderness* [a]Isa. 5:25 [b]Num. 33:46; Jer. 48:22
2 [a]Ezek. 7:3, 6; Amos 8:2; Matt. 24:6, 13, 14
3 [I]Hebr. *give* [a]Ezek. 7:8, 9
4 [a]Ezek. 5:11; 7:9; 8:18; 9:10 [b]Ezek. 6:7; 7:27; 12:20
6 [I]Hebr. *awaketh against thee*
7 [I]Or, *echo* [a]Ezek. 7:10 [b]Ezek. 7:12; Zeph. 1:14, 15
8 [a]Ezek. 20:8, 21 [b]Ezek. 7:3
9 [I]Hebr. *upon thee* [a]Ezek. 7:4 [b]Ezek. 7:4
10 [a]Ezek. 7:7
11 [I]Or, *tumult* [II]Or, *their tumultuous persons* [a]Jer. 6:7 [b]Jer. 16:5, 6; Ezek. 24:16, 22
12 [a]Ezek. 7:7
13 [I]Hebr. *though their life* were *yet among the living* [II]Or, *whose life* is *in his iniquity* [III]Hebr. *his iniquity*
15 [a]Deut. 32:25; Lam. 1:20; Ezek. 5:12
16 [a]Ezek. 6:8
17 [I]Hebr. *go into water* [a]Isa. 13:7; Jer. 6:24; Ezek. 21:7
18 [a]Isa. 3:24; 15:2, 3; Jer. 48:37; Amos 8:10 [b]Ps. 55:5
19 [I]Hebr. *for a separation,* or, *uncleanness* [II]Or, *because their iniquity is* their *stumblingblock* [a]Prov. 11:4; Zeph. 1:18 [b]Ezek. 14:3, 4; 44:12

[a]but they made[6213] the images[6754] of their abominations *and* of their detestable things[8251] therein: therefore have I [I]set it far from them.

21 And I will give it into the hands of the strangers for a prey, and to the wicked[7562] of the earth[776] for a spoil; and they shall pollute[2490] it.

22 My face will I turn also from them, and they shall pollute my secret *place:* for the [I]robbers[6530] shall enter into it, and defile[2490] it.

23 Make[6213] a chain: for [a]the land is full of bloody[1818] crimes,[4941] and the city is full of violence.

24 Wherefore I will bring the worst[7451] of the heathen,[1471] and they shall possess[3423] their houses:[1004] I will also make the pomp of the strong to cease;[7673] and [I]their holy places[6942] shall be defiled.

25 [I]Destruction[7089] cometh; and they shall seek peace, and *there shall be* none.

26 [a]Mischief[1943] shall come upon mischief, and rumour shall be upon rumour; [b]then shall they seek a vision of the prophet;[5030] but the law[8451] shall perish[6] from the priest,[3548] and counsel[6098] from the ancients.[2204]

27 The king[4428] shall mourn, and the prince[5387] shall be clothed with desolation,[8077] and the hands of the people[5971] of the land shall be troubled:[926] I will do[6213] unto them after their way,[1870] and [I]according to their deserts[4941] will I judge them; [a]and they shall know that I *am* the LORD.

The Second Vision

8 And it came to pass in the sixth year, in the sixth *month,* in the fifth *day* of the month, *as* I sat in mine house,[1004] and [a]the elders[2205] of Judah sat before me, that [b]the hand[3027] of the Lord[136] GOD fell[5307] there upon me.

2 [a]Then I beheld,[7200] and lo a likeness[1823] as the appearance[4758] of fire: from the appearance of his loins even downward, fire; and from his loins even upward, as the appearance of brightness, [b]as the colour of amber.

3 And he [a]put forth the form[8403] of an hand, and took me by a lock of mine head;[7218] and [b]the spirit[7307] lifted me up between the earth[776] and the heaven,[8064] and [c]brought me in the visions[4759] of God[430] to Jerusalem, to the door of the inner gate that looketh toward the north; [d]where *was* the seat[4186] of the image[5566] of jealousy,[7068] which [e]provoketh to jealousy.

4 And, behold, the glory[3519] of the God of Israel *was* there, according to the vision that I [a]saw[7200] in the plain.

5 Then said[559] he unto me, Son[1121] of man,[120] lift up[5375] thine eyes now the way[1870] toward the north. So I lifted up mine eyes the way toward the north, and behold northward at the gate of the altar[4196] this image of jealousy in the entry.

6 He said furthermore unto me, Son of man, seest thou what they do?[6213] *even* the great abominations[8441] that the house of Israel committeth[6213] here, that I should go far off from my sanctuary?[4720] but turn thee yet again,[7725] *and* thou shalt see greater abominations.

🔑 7 And he brought me to the door of the court; and when I looked,[7200] behold a hole in the wall.

8 Then said he unto me, Son of man, dig now in the wall: and when I had digged in the wall, behold a door.

20 [I]Or, *made it unto them an unclean thing* [a]Jer. 7:30
22 [I]Or, *burglars*
23 [a]2Kgs. 21:16; Ezek. 9:9; 11:6
24 [I]Or, *they shall inherit their holy places*
25 [I]Hebr. *Cutting off*
26 [a]Deut. 32:23; Jer. 4:20 [b]Ps. 74:9; Lam. 2:9; Ezek. 20:1, 3
27 [I]Hebr. *with their judgments* [a]Ezek. 7:4
1 [a]Ezek. 14:1; 20:1; 33:31 [b]Ezek. 1:3; 3:22
2 [a]Ezek. 1:26, 27 [b]Ezek. 1:4
3 [a]Dan. 5:5 [b]Ezek. 3:14 [c]Ezek. 11:1, 24; 40:2 [d]Jer. 7:30; 32:34; Ezek. 5:11 [e]Deut. 32:16, 21
4 [a]Ezek. 1:28; 3:22, 23

🔑 **8:7–18** Here God reveals to Ezekiel the incredible depths of idolatry being practiced even within His temple. The animal worship (Ezek. 8:10–12) may have been Egyptian in origin. "Tammuz" (Ezek. 8:14) was an Assyrian fertility god, and weeping for him was supposed to bring him back from the dead. The sun was worshiped (Ezek. 8:16) in both Egypt (as *Ra* or *Amon-Ra*) and in the Semitic nations (as *Shamash*). The "branch to their nose" (Ezek. 8:17) may refer to obscene rituals associated with the worship of Asherah or Ishtar. The ignorance of the elders of Israel is shown in that

(continued on next page)

9 And he said unto me, Go in, and behold[7200] the wicked[7451] abominations that they do here.

10 So I went in and saw; and behold every form of creeping things, and abominable[8263] beasts, and all the idols[1544] of the house of Israel, pourtrayed[2707] upon the wall round about.

11 And there stood before them seventy men[376] of the ancients[2204] of the house of Israel, and in the midst of them stood Jaazaniah the son of Shaphan, with every man[376] his censer in his hand; and a thick cloud[6051] of incense[7044] went up.[5927]

12 Then said he unto me, Son of man, hast thou seen what the ancients of the house of Israel do in the dark,[2822] every man in the chambers of his imagery?[4906] for they say,[559] [a]The LORD seeth[7200] us not; the LORD hath forsaken[5800] the earth.

13 He said also unto me, Turn thee yet again, *and* thou shalt see greater abominations that they do.

14 Then he brought me to the door of the gate of the LORD's house which *was* toward the north; and, behold, there sat women[802] weeping for Tammuz.

15 Then said he unto me, Hast thou seen *this,* O son of man? turn thee yet again, *and* thou shalt see greater abominations than these.

16 And he brought me into the inner court of the LORD's house, and, behold, at the door of the temple[1964] of the LORD, [a]between the porch and the altar, [b]*were* about five and twenty men, [c]with their backs toward the temple of the LORD, and their faces toward the east; and they worshipped[7812] [d]the sun toward the east.

17 Then he said unto me, Hast thou seen *this,* O son of man? [I]Is it a light thing[7043] to the house of Judah that they commit[6213] the abominations which they commit here? for they have [a]filled the land[776] with violence,[2555] and have returned[7725] to provoke me to anger:[3707] and, lo, they put the branch to their nose.[639]

18 [a]Therefore will I also deal[6213] in fury: mine [b]eye shall not spare,[2347] neither will I have pity: and though they [c]cry[7121] in mine ears[241] with a loud voice, *yet* will I not hear[8085] them.

Jerusalem's Punishment

9 He cried also in mine ears[241] with a loud voice, saying, Cause[7126] them that have charge[6486] over the city to draw near,[7126] even every man[376] *with* his destroying weapon in his hand.[3027]

2 And, behold, six men[582] came from the way[1870] of the higher[5945] gate, [I]which lieth toward the north, and every man [II]a slaughter[4460] weapon in his hand; [a]and one man among them *was* clothed with linen, with a writer's[5608] inkhorn [III]by his side: and they went in, and stood beside the brasen altar.[4196]

3 And [a]the glory[3519] of the God[430] of Israel was gone up from the cherub,[3742] whereupon he was, to the threshold of the house.[1004] And he called to the man clothed with linen, which *had* the writer's inkhorn by his side;

4 And the LORD said[559] unto him, Go through the midst of the city, through the midst of Jerusalem, and [I]set [a]a mark[8420] upon the foreheads of the men [b]that sigh and that cry for all the abominations[8441] that be done[6213] in the midst thereof.

5 And to the others he said in [I]mine hearing,[241] Go ye after him through the city, and smite:[5221] [a]let not your eye spare, neither have ye pity:

6 [a]Slay[2026] [I]utterly old[2205] *and* young, both maids, and little children, and

---

12 [a]Ezek. 9:9

16 [a]Joel 2:17 [b]Ezek. 11:1 [c]Jer. 2:27; 32:33 [d]Deut. 4:19; 2Kgs. 23:5, 11; Job 31:26; Jer. 44:17

17 [I]Or, *Is there any thing lighter than to commit* [a]Ezek. 9:9

18 [a]Ezek. 5:13; 16:42; 24:13 [b]Ezek. 5:11; 7:4, 9; 9:5, 10 [c]Prov. 1:28; Isa. 1:15; Jer. 11:11; 14:12; Mic. 3:4; Zech. 7:13

2 [I]Hebr. *which is turned* [II]Hebr. *a weapon of his breaking in pieces* [III]Hebr. *upon his loins* [a]Lev. 16:4; Ezek. 10:2, 6, 7; Rev. 15:6

3 [a]Ezek. 3:23; 8:4; 10:4, 18; 11:22, 23

4 [I]Hebr. *mark a mark* [a]Ex. 12:7; Rev. 7:3; 9:4; 13:16, 17; 20:4 [b]Ps. 119:53, 136; Jer. 13:17; 2Cor. 12:21; 2Pet. 2:8

5 [I]Hebr. *mine ears* [a]Ezek. 5:11; 9:10

6 [I]Hebr. *to destruction* [a]2Chr. 36:17

(continued from previous page)

they thought they could hide their idolatry from God's sight as if they were in a dark room (Ezek. 8:12). A corresponding prophecy can be found in Zephaniah 1:12, "it shall come to pass at that time, that I will search Jerusalem with candles."

women:[802] but [b]come not near any man
upon whom *is* the mark; and [c]begin at
my sanctuary.[4720] [d]Then they began at
the ancient[2204] men which *were* before
the house.
7 And he said unto them, Defile[2930]
the house, and fill the courts with the
slain:[2491] go ye forth. And they went
forth, and slew[5221] in the city.
8 And it came to pass, while they
were slaying them, and I was left,[7604]
that I [a]fell[5307] upon my face, and cried,
and said, [b]Ah Lord[136] GOD! wilt thou
destroy[7843] all the residue[7611] of Israel in
thy pouring out[8210] of thy fury upon
Jerusalem?
9 Then said he unto me, The iniquity[5771] of the house of Israel and Judah
is exceeding great, and [a]the land[776] is
[I]full of blood,[1818] and the city full of
[II]perverseness:[4297] for they say,[559] [b]The
LORD hath forsaken[5800] the earth,[776] and
[c]the LORD seeth[7200] not.
10 And as for me also, mine [a]eye
shall not spare, neither will I have pity,
but [b]I will recompense[5414] their way upon
their head.[7218]
11 And, behold, the man clothed
with linen, which *had* the inkhorn by
his side, [I]reported the matter,[1697] saying, I have done as thou hast commanded[6680] me.

God's Glory Departs From the Temple

10 🔑Then I looked,[7200] and, behold,
in the [a]firmament[7549] that was
above the head[7218] of the cherubims[3742]
there appeared[7200] over them as it were
a sapphire stone, as the appearance of
the likeness[1823] of a throne.[3678]
2 [a]And he spake[559] unto the man[376]
clothed with linen, and said,[559] Go in between the wheels,[1534] *even* under the
cherub,[3742] and fill [I]thine hand with
[b]coals of fire from between the cherubims, and [c]scatter *them* over the city. And
he went in in my sight.
3 Now the cherubims stood on the
right side of the house,[1004] when the man
went in; and the cloud[6051] filled the inner
court.
4 [a]Then the glory[3519] of the LORD
[I]went up from the cherub, *and stood* over
the threshold of the house; and [b]the
house was filled with the cloud, and
the court was full of the brightness of
the LORD's glory.
5 And the [a]sound of the cherubims'
wings was heard[8085] *even* to the outer
court, as [b]the voice of the Almighty[7706]
God[410] when he speaketh.
6 And it came to pass, *that* when he
had commanded[6680] the man clothed with
linen, saying, Take fire from between the
wheels, from between the cherubims;
then he went in, and stood beside the
wheels.[212]
7 And *one* cherub [I]stretched forth his
hand[3027] from between the cherubims
unto the fire that *was* between the cherubims, and took[5375] *thereof,* and put *it* into
the hands of *him that was* clothed with
linen: who took *it,* and went out.
8 [a]And there appeared in the cherubims the form of a man's[120] hand under
their wings.
9 [a]And when I looked, behold the
four wheels by the cherubims, one wheel
by one cherub, and another wheel[212] by
another cherub: and the appearance of
the wheels *was* as the colour of a [b]beryl
stone.
10 And *as for* their appearances,[4758]
they four had one likeness, as if a wheel
had been in the midst of a wheel.
11 [a]When they went, they went upon
their four sides; they turned not as they
went, but to the place whither the head

6 [b]Rev. 9:4 [c]Jer. 25:29; 1Pet. 4:17 [d]Ezek. 8:11, 12, 16

8 [a]Num. 14:5; 16:4, 22, 45; Josh. 7:6 [b]Ezek. 11:13

9 [I]Hebr. *filled with* [II]Or, *wresting of judgment* [a]2Kgs. 21:16; Ezek. 8:17 [b]Ezek. 8:12 [c]Ps. 10:11; Isa. 29:15

10 [a]Ezek. 5:11; 7:4; 8:18 [b]Ezek. 11:21

11 [I]Hebr. *returned the word*

1 [a]Ezek. 1:22, 26

2 [I]Hebr. *the hollow of thine hand* [a]Ezek. 9:2, 3 [b]Ezek. 1:13 [c]Rev. 8:5

4 [I]Hebr. *was lifted up* [a]Ezek. 1:28; 9:3; 10:18 [b]1Kgs. 8:10, 11; Ezek. 43:5

5 [a]Ezek. 1:24 [b]Ps. 29:3

7 [I]Hebr. *sent forth*

8 [a]Ezek. 1:8; 10:21

9 [a]Ezek. 1:15 [b]Ezek. 1:16

11 [a]Ezek. 1:17

🔑 **10:1—11:23** The glory of the Lord is pictured as departing in stages. First, it went up from the cherubim over the ark to the threshold of the temple (Ezek. 10:4). Then, it stood over the cherubim (Ezek. 10:18) as they went to the east gate of the temple (Ezek. 10:19), and then to the Mount of Olives (Ezek. 11:23). The glory will not return until the millennial temple is prepared (see note on Ezek. 43:1–5).

looked they followed it; they turned not as they went.

12 And their whole [I]body, and their backs, and their hands,[3027] and their wings, and [a]the wheels, *were* full of eyes round about, *even* the wheels that they four had.

13 As for the wheels, [I]it was cried unto them in my hearing,[241] O wheel.[1534]

14 [a]And every one had four faces: the first face *was* the face of a cherub, and the second face *was* the face of a man,[120] and the third the face of a lion, and the fourth the face of an eagle.

15 And the cherubims were lifted up. This *is* [a]the living creature[2416] that I saw[7200] by the river of Chebar.

16 [a]And when the cherubims went, the wheels went by them: and when the cherubims lifted up[5375] their wings to mount up from the earth,[776] the same wheels also turned not from beside them.

17 [a]When they stood, *these* stood; and when they were lifted up, *these* lifted up themselves *also:* for the spirit[7307] [I]of the living creature *was* in them.

18 Then [a]the glory of the LORD [b]departed from off the threshold of the house, and stood over the cherubims.

19 And [a]the cherubims lifted up their wings, and mounted up from the earth in my sight: when they went out, the wheels also *were* beside them, and *every one* stood at the door of the east gate of the LORD's house; and the glory of the God[430] of Israel *was* over them above.

20 [a]This *is* the living creature that I saw under the God of Israel [b]by the river of Chebar; and I knew[3045] that they *were* the cherubims.

21 [a]Every one had four faces apiece, and every one four wings; [b]and the likeness of the hands of a man *was* under their wings.

22 And [a]the likeness of their faces *was* the same faces which I saw by the river of Chebar, their appearances and themselves: [b]they went every one[376] straight forward.

12 [I]Hebr. *flesh* [a]Ezek. 1:18
13 [I]Or, *they were called in my hearing, wheel*
14 [a]Ezek. 1:6, 10
15 [a]Ezek. 1:5
16 [a]Ezek. 1:19
17 [I]Or, *of life* [a]Ezek. 1:12, 20, 21
18 [a]Ezek. 10:4 [b]Hos. 9:12
19 [a]Ezek. 11:22
20 [a]Ezek. 1:22; 10:15 [b]Ezek. 1:1
21 [a]Ezek. 1:6; 10:14 [b]Ezek. 1:8; 10:8
22 [a]Ezek. 1:10 [b]Ezek. 1:12

1 [a]Ezek. 3:12, 14; 8:3; 11:24 [b]Ezek. 10:19 [c]Ezek. 8:16
3 [I]Or, It is *not* for us *to build houses near* [a]Ezek. 12:22, 27; 2Pet. 3:4 [b]Jer. 1:13; Ezek. 24:3
5 [a]Ezek. 2:2; 3:24
6 [a]Ezek. 7:23; 22:3, 4
7 [a]Ezek. 24:3, 6, 10, 11; Mic. 3:3 [b]Ezek. 11:9
9 [a]Ezek. 5:8
10 [a]2Kgs. 25:19-21; Jer. 39:6; 52:10 [b]1Kgs. 8:65; 2Kgs. 14:25 [c]Ps. 9:16; Ezek. 6:7; 13:9, 14, 21, 23
11 [a]Ezek. 11:3
12 [I]Or, *which have not walked* [a]Ezek. 11:10 [b]Lev. 18:3, 24; Deut. 12:30, 31; Ezek. 8:10, 14, 16

God Condemns Jerusalem

11 Moreover [a]the spirit[7307] lifted me up, and brought me unto [b]the east gate of the LORD's house,[1004] which looketh eastward: and behold [c]at the door of the gate five and twenty men;[376] among whom I saw[7200] Jaazaniah the son[1121] of Azur, and Pelatiah the son of Benaiah, princes[8269] of the people.[5971]

2 Then said[559] he unto me, Son of man,[120] these *are* the men[582] that devise[2803] mischief, and give wicked[7451] counsel[6098] in this city:

3 Which say, [I]*It is* not [a]near; let us build houses:[1004] [b]this *city is* the caldron, and we *be* the flesh.

4 Therefore prophesy[5012] against them, prophesy, O son of man.

5 And [a]the Spirit of the LORD fell[5307] upon me, and said unto me, Speak; Thus saith the LORD; Thus have ye said, O house of Israel: for I know[3045] the things that come into your mind,[7307] *every one of* them.

6 [a]Ye have multiplied your slain[2491] in this city, and ye have filled the streets thereof with the slain.

7 Therefore thus saith the Lord[136] GOD; [a]Your slain whom ye have laid in the midst of it, they *are* the flesh, and this *city is* the caldron: [b]but I will bring you forth out of the midst of it.

8 Ye have feared[3372] the sword;[2719] and I will bring a sword upon you, saith[5002] the Lord GOD.

9 And I will bring you out of the midst thereof, and deliver you into the hands[3027] of strangers, and [a]will execute judgments[8201] among you.

10 [a]Ye shall fall by the sword; I will judge you in [b]the border of Israel; [c]and ye shall know that I *am* the LORD.

11 [a]This *city* shall not be your caldron, neither shall ye be the flesh in the midst thereof; *but* I will judge[8199] you in the border of Israel:

12 And [a]ye shall know that I *am* the LORD: [I]for ye have not walked in my statutes,[2706] neither executed[6213] my judgments,[4941] but [b]have done after the

manners[4941] of the heathen[1471] that *are* round about you.

13 And it came to pass, when I prophesied,[5012] that [a]Pelatiah the son of Benaiah died.[4191] Then [b]fell I down[5307] upon my face, and cried with a loud voice, and said, Ah Lord GOD! wilt thou make[6213] a full end[3617] of the remnant[7611] of Israel?

God Promises Restoration

14 Again the word[1697] of the LORD came unto me, saying,

15 Son of man, thy brethren,[251] *even* thy brethren, the men of thy kindred,[1353] and all the house of Israel wholly, *are* they unto whom the inhabitants of Jerusalem have said, Get you far from the LORD: unto us is this land[776] given in possession.[4181]

16 Therefore say, Thus saith the Lord GOD; Although I have cast them far off among the heathen, and although I have scattered them among the countries,[776] [a]yet will I be to them as a little sanctuary[4720] in the countries where they shall come.

17 Therefore say, Thus saith the Lord GOD; [a]I will even gather[6908] you from the people, and assemble[622] you out of the countries where ye have been scattered, and I will give you the land[127] of Israel.

18 And they shall come thither, and [a]they shall take away all the detestable things[8251] thereof and all the abominations[8441] thereof from thence.

19 And [a]I will give them one heart,[3820] and I will put [b]a new spirit within[7130] you; and I will take [c]the stony heart out of their flesh, and will give them an heart of flesh:

20 [a]That they may walk in my statutes,[2708] and keep[8104] mine ordinances,[4941] and do[6213] them: [b]and they shall be my people, and I will be their God.[430]

21 But *as for them* whose heart walketh after the heart of their detestable things and their abominations, [a]I will recompense their way[1870] upon their own heads,[7218] saith the Lord GOD.

22 Then did the cherubims[3742] [a]lift up their wings, and the wheels[212] beside them; and the glory[3519] of the God of Israel *was* over them above.

23 And [a]the glory of the LORD went up[5927] from the midst of the city, and stood [b]upon the mountain [c]which *is* on the east side of the city.

24 Afterwards [a]the spirit took me up,[5375] and brought me in a vision by the Spirit of God into Chaldea, to them of the captivity.[1473] So the vision that I had seen[7200] went up from me.

25 Then I spake[1696] unto them of the captivity all the things that the LORD had shewed me.

Ezekiel Pourtrays the Deportation

12 The word[1697] of the LORD also came unto me, saying,

2 Son[1121] of man,[120] thou dwellest in the midst of [a]a rebellious[4805] house,[1004] which [b]have eyes to see, and see not; they have ears[241] to hear,[8085] and hear not: [c]for they *are* a rebellious house.

🔑 3 Therefore, thou son of man, prepare thee [I]stuff[3627] for removing,[1473] and remove[1540] by day[3119] in their sight; and thou shalt remove from thy place to another place in their sight: it may be they will consider,[7200] though they *be* a rebellious house.

4 Then shalt thou bring forth thy stuff by day in their sight, as stuff for removing: and thou shalt go forth at even in their sight, [I]as they that go forth into captivity.[1473]

5 [I]Dig thou through the wall in their sight, and carry out thereby.

6 In their sight shalt thou bear[5375] *it* upon *thy* shoulders, *and* carry *it* forth in the twilight: thou shalt cover[3680] thy face, that thou see not the ground:[776]

13 [a]Ezek. 11:1; Acts 5:5 [b]Ezek. 9:8
16 [a]Ps. 90:1; 91:9; Isa. 8:14
17 [a]Jer. 24:5; Ezek. 28:25; 34:13; 36:24
18 [a]Ezek. 37:23
19 [a]Jer. 32:39; Ezek. 36:26, 27; Zeph. 3:9 [b]Ps. 51:10; Jer. 31:33; 32:39; Ezek. 18:31 [c]Zech. 7:12
20 [a]Ps. 105:45 [b]Jer. 24:7; Ezek. 14:11; 36:28; 37:27
21 [a]Ezek. 9:10; 22:31
22 [a]Ezek. 1:19; 10:19
23 [a]Ezek. 8:4; 9:3; 10:4, 18; 43:4 [b]Zech. 14:4 [c]Ezek. 43:2
24 [a]Ezek. 8:3
2 [a]Ezek. 2:3, 6-8; 3:26, 27 [b]Isa. 6:9; 42:20; Jer. 5:21; Matt. 13:13, 14 [c]Ezek. 2:5
3 [I]Or, *instruments*
4 [I]Hebr. *as the goings forth of captivity*
5 [I]Hebr. *Dig for thee*

🔑 **12:3–7** See note on Ezekiel 2:8—3:3.

[a]for I have set thee *for* a sign[4159] unto the house of Israel.

7 And I did[6213] so as I was commanded:[6680] I brought forth my stuff by day, as stuff for captivity, and in the even I [I]digged through the wall with mine hand;[3027] I brought *it* forth in the twilight, *and* I bare[5375] *it* upon *my* shoulder in their sight.

8 And in the morning came the word of the LORD unto me, saying,

9 Son of man, hath not the house of Israel, [a]the rebellious house, said unto thee, [b]What doest thou?

10 Say thou unto them, Thus saith the Lord[136] GOD; This [a]burden[4853] *concerneth* the prince[5387] in Jerusalem, and all the house of Israel that *are* among them.

11 Say, [a]I *am* your sign: like as I have done,[6213] so shall it be done unto them: [I][b]they shall remove[1743] *and* go into captivity.[7628]

12 And [a]the prince that *is* among them shall bear upon *his* shoulder in the twilight, and shall go forth: they shall dig through the wall to carry out thereby: he shall cover his face, that he see not the ground with *his* eyes.

🔑 13 My [a]net also will I spread upon him, and he shall be taken in my snare: and [b]I will bring him to Babylon *to* the land[776] of the Chaldeans; yet shall he not see it, though he shall die[4191] there.

14 And [a]I will scatter toward every wind[7307] all that *are* about him to help him, and all his bands; and [b]I will draw out the sword[2719] after them.

15 [a]And they shall know[3045] that I *am* the LORD, when I shall scatter them among the nations,[1471] and disperse them in the countries.[776]

16 [a]But I will leave[3498] [I]a few men[582] of them from the sword, from the famine, and from the pestilence;[1698] that they may declare[5608] all their abominations[8441] among the heathen[1471] whither they come; and they shall know that I *am* the LORD.

17 Moreover the word of the LORD came to me, saying,

18 Son of man, [a]eat thy bread with quaking, and drink thy water with trembling[7269] and with carefulness;[1674]

19 And say unto the people[5971] of the land,[127] Thus saith the Lord GOD of the inhabitants of Jerusalem, *and* of the land of Israel; They shall eat their bread with carefulness, and drink their water with astonishment, that her land may [a]be desolate[3456] from [I]all that is therein, [b]because of the violence[2555] of all them that dwell therein.

20 And the cities that are inhabited shall be laid waste,[2717] and the land shall be desolate;[8077] and ye shall know that I *am* the LORD.

🔑 21 And the word of the LORD came unto me, saying,

22 Son of man, what *is* that proverb *that* ye have in the land of Israel, saying, [a]The days[3117] are prolonged,[748] and every vision[2377] faileth?[6]

23 Tell[559] them therefore, Thus saith the Lord GOD; I will make this proverb to cease,[7673] and they shall no more use it as a proverb in Israel; but say[1696] unto them, [a]The days are at hand,[7126] and the effect[1697] of every vision.

24 For [a]there shall be no more any [b]vain[7723] vision nor flattering divination[4738] within the house of Israel.

25 For I *am* the LORD: I will speak,[1696] and [a]the word that I shall speak shall come to pass;[6213] it shall be no more prolonged: for in your days, O

6 [a]Isa. 8:18; Ezek. 4:3; 12:11; 24:24
7 [I]Hebr. *digged for me*
9 [a]Ezek. 2:5 [b]Ezek. 17:12; 24:19
10 [a]Mal. 1:1
11 [I]Hebr. *by removing go into captivity* [a]Ezek. 12:6 [b]2Kgs. 25:4, 5, 7
12 [a]Jer. 39:4
13 [a]Job 19:6; Jer. 52:9; Lam. 1:13; Ezek. 17:20 [b]2Kgs. 25:7; Jer. 52:11; Ezek. 17:16
14 [a]2Kgs. 25:4, 5; Ezek. 5:10 [b]Ezek. 5:2, 12
15 [a]Ps. 9:16; Ezek. 6:7, 14; 11:10; 12:16, 20
16 [I]Hebr. *men of number* [a]Ezek. 6:8-10
18 [a]Ezek. 4:16
19 [I]Hebr. *the fullness thereof* [a]Zech. 7:14 [b]Ps. 107:34
22 [a]Ezek. 11:3; 12:27; Amos 6:3; 2Pet. 3:4
23 [a]Joel 2:1; Zeph. 1:14
24 [a]Ezek. 13:23 [b]Lam. 2:14
25 [a]Isa. 55:11; Ezek. 12:28; Dan. 9:12; Luke 21:33

🔑 **12:13** See note on Jeremiah 39:1–10.

🔑 **12:21–25** This proverb spoken by God revealed the lack of faith in God among the people of Israel. The problem was not that the visions were failing, but that the Jews were given prophecies about destruction they did not want to hear. The only visions that they accepted were those that promised peace and were proclaimed by the false prophets (cf. 13:2–10, 16). In the New Testament, Peter warned that there would also be scoffers in the last days who would deny Jesus' Second Coming (2 Pet. 3:3, 4).

rebellious house, will I say the word, and
will perform[6213] it, saith[5002] the Lord
GOD.
26 Again the word of the LORD came
to me, saying,
27 [a]Son of man, behold, *they of* the
house of Israel say, The vision that he
seeth[2372] *is* [b]for many days *to come,* and
he prophesieth[5012] of the times[6256] *that*
are far off.
28 [a]Therefore say unto them, Thus
saith the Lord GOD; There shall none of
my words be prolonged any more, but
the word[1697] which I have spoken[1696]
shall be done, saith the Lord GOD.

False Prophets

13 🔑And the word[1697] of the LORD
came unto me, saying,
2 Son[1121] of man,[120] prophesy[5012]
against the prophets[5030] of Israel that
prophesy, and say[559] thou unto [I][a]them
that prophesy out of their own
[b]hearts,[3820] Hear[8085] ye the word of the
LORD;
3 Thus saith[559] the Lord[136] GOD; Woe
unto the foolish prophets, that [I]follow
their own spirit,[7307] [II]and have seen[7200]
nothing!
4 O Israel, thy prophets are [a]like the
foxes in the deserts.[2723]
5 Ye [a]have not gone up[5927] into the
[I]gaps, neither [II]made up[1443] the hedge for
the house[1004] of Israel to stand in the
battle in the day[3117] of the LORD.
6 [a]They have seen[2372] vanity[7723] and
lying[3577] divination,[7081] saying, The LORD
saith:[5002] and the LORD hath not sent
them: and they have made *others* to
hope[3176] that they would confirm the
word.
7 Have ye not seen a vain[7723]
vision,[4236] and have ye not spoken[1696] a
lying divination,[4738] whereas ye say, The
LORD saith *it;* albeit I have not spoken?[559]
8 Therefore thus saith the Lord GOD;
Because ye have spoken vanity, and seen
lies,[3577] therefore, behold, I *am* against
you, saith the Lord GOD.
9 And mine hand[3027] shall be upon
the prophets that see vanity, and that
divine[7080] lies: they shall not be in the
[I]assembly[5475] of my people,[5971] [a]neither
shall they be written in the writing of the
house of Israel, [b]neither shall they enter
into the land[127] of Israel; [c]and ye shall
know[3045] that I *am* the Lord GOD.
10 Because, even because they have
seduced my people, saying, [a]Peace; and
there was no peace; and one built up [I]a
wall, and, lo, others [b]daubed it with
untempered[8602] *morter:*
11 Say unto them which daub *it* with
untempered *morter,* that it shall fall:
[a]there shall be an overflowing[7857] shower;
and ye, O great hailstones, shall fall; and
a stormy wind[7307] shall rend[1234] *it.*
12 Lo, when the wall is fallen,[5307]
shall it not be said[559] unto you, Where *is*
the daubing wherewith ye have daubed
it?
13 Therefore thus saith the Lord
GOD; I will even rend *it* with a stormy
wind in my fury; and there shall be an
overflowing shower in mine anger,[639] and
great hailstones in *my* fury to consume[3615] *it.*
14 So will I break down[2040] the wall
that ye have daubed with untempered
morter, and bring it down to the
ground,[776] so that the foundation[3247]
thereof shall be discovered, and it shall
fall, and ye shall be consumed[3615] in the
midst thereof: [a]and ye shall know that I
am the LORD.
15 Thus will I accomplish[3615] my
wrath[2534] upon the wall, and upon them
that have daubed it with untempered
morter, and will say unto you, The wall
is no *more,* neither they that daubed it;
16 *To wit,* the prophets of Israel
which prophesy concerning Jerusalem,
and which [a]see visions[2377] of peace for
her, and *there is* no peace, saith the Lord
GOD.

27 [a]Ezek. 12:22 [b]2Pet. 3:4
28 [a]Ezek. 12:23, 25
2 [I]Hebr. *them that are prophets out of their own hearts* [a]Ezek. 12:17 [b]Jer. 14:14; 23:16, 26
3 [I]Hebr. *walk after* [II]Or, *and things which they have not seen*
4 [a]Song 2:15
5 [I]Or, *breaches* [II]Hebr. *hedged the hedge* [a]Ps. 106:23, 30; Ezek. 22:30
6 [a]Ezek. 12:24; 13:23; 22:28
9 [I]Or, *secret,* or, *council* [a]Ezra 2:59, 62; Neh. 7:5; Ps. 69:28 [b]Ezek. 20:38 [c]Ezek. 11:10, 12
10 [I]Or, *a slight wall* [a]Jer. 6:14; 8:11 [b]Ezek. 22:28
11 [a]Ezek. 38:22
14 [a]Ezek. 13:9, 21, 23; 14:8
16 [a]Jer. 6:14; 28:9

🔑 **13:1–16** See note on Deuteronomy 18:20–22.

17 Likewise, thou son of man, [a]set[7760] thy face against the daughters of thy people, [b]which prophesy out of their own heart;[3820] and prophesy thou against them,

18 And say, Thus saith the Lord GOD; Woe to the *women* that sew pillows[3704] to all [1]armholes, and make[6213] kerchiefs upon the head[7218] of every stature to hunt souls[5315] Will ye [a]hunt[6679] the souls of my people, and will ye save[2421] the souls alive *that come* unto you?

19 And will ye pollute[2490] me among my people [a]for handfuls of barley and for pieces of bread, to slay[4191] the souls that should not die, and to save the souls alive that should not live,[2421] by your lying[3576] to my people that hear *your* lies?

20 Wherefore thus saith the Lord GOD; Behold, I *am* against your pillows, wherewith ye there hunt the souls [1]to make *them* fly, and I will tear them from your arms, and will let the souls go, *even* the souls that ye hunt to make *them* fly.

21 Your kerchiefs also will I tear, and deliver[5337] my people out of your hand, and they shall be no more in your hand to be hunted; [a]and ye shall know that I *am* the LORD.

22 Because with lies ye have made the heart of the righteous[6662] sad, whom I have not made sad;[3510] and [a]strengthened[2388] the hands[3027] of the wicked,[7451] that he should not return[7725] from his wicked[7563] way,[1870] [1]by promising him life:[2421]

23 Therefore [a]ye shall see[2372] no more vanity, nor divine[7080] divinations:[7081] for I will deliver my people out of your hand: [b]and ye shall know that I *am* the LORD.

Idolaters

14 Then [a]came certain[582] of the elders[2205] of Israel unto me, and sat before me.

2 And the word[1697] of the LORD came unto me, saying,

3 Son[1121] of man,[120] these men[582] have set up their idols[1544] in their heart,[3820] and put [a]the stumblingblock[4383] of their iniquity[5771] before their face: [b]should I be enquired of at all by them?

4 Therefore speak[1696] unto them, and say[559] unto them, Thus saith the Lord[136] GOD; Every man[376] of the house[1004] of Israel that setteth up[5927] his idols in his heart, and putteth[7760] the stumblingblock of his iniquity before his face, and cometh to the prophet;[5030] I the LORD will answer him that cometh according to the multitude of his idols;

5 That I may take the house of Israel in their own heart, because they are all estranged[2114] from me through their idols.

6 Therefore say unto the house of Israel, Thus saith the Lord GOD; Repent,[7725] and turn [1]*yourselves* from your idols; and turn away your faces from all your abominations.[8441]

7 For every one of the house of Israel, or of the stranger[1616] that sojourneth[1481] in Israel, which separateth himself[5144] from me, and setteth up his idols in his heart, and putteth the stumblingblock of his iniquity before his face, and cometh to a prophet to enquire of him concerning me: I the LORD will answer him by myself:

8 And [a]I will set my face against that man, and will make him a [b]sign[226] and a proverb, and I will cut him off[3772] from the midst of my people;[5971] [c]and ye shall know[3045] that I *am* the LORD.

9 And if the prophet be deceived when he hath spoken[1696] a thing,[1697] I the LORD [a]have deceived that prophet, and I will stretch out my hand[3027] upon him, and will destroy[8045] him from the midst of my people Israel.

10 And they shall bear[5375] the punishment[5771] of their iniquity: the punishment of the prophet shall be even as the punishment of him that seeketh *unto him;*

11 That the house of Israel may [a]go no more astray[8582] from me, neither be polluted[2930] any more with all their transgressions;[6588] [b]but that they may be

---

17 [a]Ezek. 20:46; 21:2 [b]Ezek. 13:2

18 [1]Or, *elbows* [a]2Pet. 2:14

19 [a]Prov. 28:21; Mic. 3:5

20 [1]Or, *into gardens*

21 [a]Ezek. 13:9

22 [1]Or, *that I should save his life;* Hebr. *by quickening him* [a]Jer. 23:14

23 [a]Ezek. 12:24; 13:6; Mic. 3:6 [b]Ezek. 13:9; 14:8; 15:7

1 [a]Ezek. 8:1; 20:1; 33:31

3 [a]Ezek. 7:19; 14:4, 7 [b]2Kgs. 3:13

6 [1]Or, others

8 [a]Lev. 17:10; 20:3, 5, 6; Jer. 44:11; Ezek. 15:7 [b]Num. 26:10; Deut. 28:37 [c]Ezek. 5:15 [d]Ezek. 6:7

9 [a]1Kgs. 22:23; Job 12:16; Jer. 4:10; 2Thess. 2:11

11 [a]2Pet. 2:15 [b]Ezek. 11:20; 37:27

my people, and I may be their God,[430] saith the Lord GOD.

The Surety of Judgment

12 The word of the LORD came again to me, saying,

13 Son of man, when the land[776] sinneth[2398] against me by trespassing grievously, then will I stretch out mine hand upon it, and will break[7665] the [a]staff[4294] of the bread thereof, and will send famine upon it, and will cut off[3772] man and beast from it:

14 [a]Though these three men, Noah, Daniel, and Job, were in it, they should deliver[5337] *but* their own souls[5315] [b]by their righteousness,[6666] saith the Lord GOD.

15 If I cause[5674] [a]noisome[7451] beasts[2416] to pass[5674] through the land, and they [1]spoil it, so that it be desolate,[8077] that no man may pass through because of the beasts:

16 [a]*Though* these three men *were* [1]in it, *as* I live,[2416] saith the Lord GOD, they shall deliver neither sons[1121] nor daughters; they only shall be delivered,[5337] but the land shall be desolate.

17 Or *if* [a]I bring a sword[2719] upon that land, and say, Sword, go through the land; so that I [b]cut off man and beast from it:

18 [a]Though these three men *were* in it, *as* I live, saith the Lord GOD, they shall deliver neither sons nor daughters, but they only shall be delivered themselves.

19 Or *if* I send [a]a pestilence[1698] into that land, and pour out[8210] my fury upon it in blood,[1818] to cut off from it man and beast:

20 [a]Though Noah, Daniel, and Job, *were* in it, *as* I live, saith the Lord GOD, they shall deliver neither son nor daughter; they shall *but* deliver their own souls by their righteousness.

21 For thus saith the Lord GOD; [1]How much more when [a]I send my four sore[7451] judgments[8201] upon Jerusalem, the sword, and the famine, and the noisome beast,[2416] and the pestilence, to cut off from it man and beast?

22 [a]Yet, behold, therein shall be left[3498] a remnant[6413] that shall be brought forth, *both* sons and daughters: behold, they shall come forth unto you, and [b]ye shall see their way[1870] and their doings: and ye shall be comforted[5162] concerning the evil[7451] that I have brought upon Jerusalem, *even* concerning all that I have brought upon it.

23 And they shall comfort you, when ye see their ways[1870] and their doings: and ye shall know that I have not done[6213] [a]without cause all that I have done in it, saith the Lord GOD.

A Useless Vine

15 And the word[1697] of the LORD came unto me, saying,

2 Son[1121] of man,[120] What is the vine tree more than any tree, *or than* a branch which is among the trees of the forest?

3 Shall wood be taken thereof to do[6213] any work?[4399] or will *men* take a pin of it to hang any vessel thereon?

4 Behold, [a]it is cast into the fire for fuel; the fire devoureth both the ends of it, and the midst of it is burned.[2787] [1]Is it meet for *any* work?

5 Behold, when it was whole,[8549] it was [1]meet[6213] for no work: how much less shall it be meet yet for *any* work, when the fire hath devoured it, and it is burned?

6 Therefore thus saith[559] the Lord[136] GOD; As the vine tree among the trees of the forest, which I have given to the fire for fuel, so will I give the inhabitants of Jerusalem.

7 And [a]I will set[7760] my face against them; [b]they shall go out from *one* fire, and *another* fire shall devour them;

13 [a]Lev. 26:26; Isa. 3:1; Ezek. 4:16; 5:16
14 [a]Jer. 7:16; 11:14; 14:11; 15:1; Ezek. 14:16, 18, 20 [b]Prov. 11:4
15 [1]Or, *bereave* [a]Lev. 26:22; Ezek. 5:17
16 [1]Hebr. *in the midst of it* [a]Ezek. 14:14, 18, 20
17 [a]Lev. 26:25; Ezek. 5:12; 21:3, 4; 29:8; 38:21 [b]Ezek. 25:13; Zeph. 1:3
18 [a]Ezek. 14:14
19 [a]2Sam. 24:15; Ezek. 38:22 [b]Ezek. 7:8
20 [a]Ezek. 14:14
21 [1]Or, *Also when* [a]Ezek. 5:17; 33:27
22 [a]Ezek. 6:8 [b]Ezek. 20:43
23 [a]Jer. 22:8, 9
4 [1]Hebr. *Will it prosper* [a]John 15:6
5 [1]Hebr. *made* fit
7 [a]Lev. 17:10; Ezek. 14:8 [b]Isa. 24:18

14:12–20 See note on Ezekiel 18:1–32.

[c]and ye shall know[3045] that I *am* the
LORD, when I set my face against them.
8 And I will make the land[776] desolate,[8077] because they have [I]committed[4603]
a trespass,[4604] saith[5002] the Lord GOD.

The Unfaithfulness of Jerusalem

16 Again the word[1697] of the LORD
came unto me, saying,
2 Son[1121] of man,[120] [a]cause Jerusalem to know[3045] her abominations,[8441]
3 And say, Thus saith[559] the Lord[136]
GOD unto Jerusalem; Thy [I]birth [a]and thy
nativity *is* of the land[776] of Canaan;
[b]thy father[1] *was* an Amorite, and thy
mother[517] an Hittite.
4 And *as for* thy nativity, [a]in the
day[3117] thou wast born thy navel was
not cut,[3772] neither wast thou washed[7364]
in water [I]to supple[4935] *thee;* thou wast
not salted at all, nor swaddled[2853] at
all.
5 None eye pitied thee, to do[6213] any
of these unto thee, to have compassion
upon thee; but thou wast cast out in the
open field,[7704] to the lothing of thy
person,[5315] in the day that thou wast
born.
6 And when I passed[5674] by thee,
and saw[7200] thee [I]polluted[947] in thine own
blood,[1818] I said unto thee *when thou
wast* in thy blood, Live;[2421] yea, I said
unto thee *when thou wast* in thy blood,
Live.
7 [a]I have [I]caused thee to multiply as
the bud of the field, and thou hast increased and waxen great, and thou art
come to [II]excellent ornaments: *thy* breasts
are fashioned,[3559] and thine hair is
grown, whereas thou *wast* naked and
bare.[6181]
8 Now when I passed by thee, and
looked[7200] upon thee, behold, thy time[6256]
was the time of love;[1730] [a]and I spread
my skirt over thee, and covered[3680] thy
nakedness:[6172] yea, I sware[7650] unto thee,
and entered into a covenant[1285] with thee,
saith[5002] the Lord GOD, and [b]thou becamest mine.
9 Then washed[7364] I thee with water;
yea, I throughly washed away[7857] thy
[I]blood from thee, and I anointed[5480] thee
with oil.[8081]
10 I clothed thee also with broidered
work, and shod[5274] thee with badgers'
skin, and I girded thee about[2280] with
fine linen, and I covered thee with
silk.
11 I decked thee also with ornaments, and I [a]put bracelets upon thy
hands,[3027] [b]and a chain on thy neck.
12 And I put a jewel on thy
[I][a]forehead,[639] and earrings in thine
ears,[241] and a beautiful[8597] crown upon
thine head.[7218]
13 Thus wast thou decked with gold
and silver; and thy raiment *was of* fine
linen, and silk, and broidered work;
[a]thou didst eat fine flour, and honey, and
oil: and thou wast exceeding [b]beautiful,
and thou didst prosper[6743] into a kingdom.
14 And [a]thy renown went forth
among the heathen[1471] for thy beauty:
for it *was* perfect[3632] through my comeliness,[1926] which I had put upon thee, saith
the Lord GOD.
15 [a]But thou didst trust[982] in thine
own beauty, [b]and playedst the harlot[2181]
because of thy renown, and pouredst out
thy fornications[8457] on every one that
passed by; his it was.
16 [a]And of thy garments thou didst
take, and deckedst[6213] thy high places[1116]
with divers colours, and playedst the harlot thereupon: *the like things* shall not
come, neither shall it be so.
17 Thou hast also taken thy fair[8597]
jewels of my gold and of my silver,
which I had given thee, and madest to
thyself images[6754] [I]of men, and didst
commit whoredom[2181] with them,
18 And tookest thy broidered garments, and coveredst them: and thou hast
set mine oil and mine incense[7004] before
them.
19 [a]My meat also which I gave thee,
fine flour, and oil, and honey, *wherewith*
I fed thee, thou hast even set it before
them for [I]a sweet savour: and *thus* it was,
saith the Lord GOD.
20 [a]Moreover thou hast taken thy
sons[1121] and thy daughters, whom thou

7 [c]Ezek. 6:7; 7:4; 11:10; 20:38, 42, 44

8 [I]Hebr. *trespassed a trespass*

2 [a]Ezek. 20:4; 22:2; 33:7-9

3 [I]Hebr. *cutting out,* or, *habitation* [a]Ezek. 21:30 [b]Ezek. 16:45 [II]Or, *when I looked* upon thee [c]Hos. 2:3

6 [I]Or, *trodden under foot*

7 [I]Hebr. *made thee a million* [II]Hebr. *ornament of ornaments* [a]Ex. 1:7

8 [a]Ruth 3:9 [b]Ex. 19:5; Jer. 2:2

9 [I]Hebr. *bloods*

11 [a]Gen. 24:22, 47 [b]Prov. 1:9

12 [I]Hebr. *nose* [a]Isa. 3:21

13 [a]Deut. 32:13, 14 [b]Ps. 48:2

14 [a]Lam. 2:15

15 [a]Deut. 32:15; Jer. 7:4; Mic. 3:11 [b]Isa. 1:21; 57:8; Jer. 2:20; 3:2, 6, 20; Ezek. 23:3, 8, 11, 12; Hos. 1:2

16 [a]2Kgs. 23:7; Ezek. 7:20; Hos. 2:8

17 [I]Hebr. *of a male*

19 [I]Hebr. *a savour of rest* [a]Hos. 2:8

20 [a]2Kgs. 16:3; Ps. 106:37, 38; Isa. 57:5; Jer. 7:31; 32:35; Ezek. 20:26; 23:37

hast borne unto me, and these hast thou sacrificed[2076] unto them [I]to be devoured. *Is this* of thy whoredoms[8457] a small matter,

21 That thou hast slain[7891] my children,[1121] and delivered them to cause them to pass through[5674] *the fire* for them?

22 And in all thine abominations and thy whoredoms thou hast not remembered[2142] the days[3117] of thy [a]youth, [b]when thou wast naked and bare, *and* wast polluted in thy blood.

23 And it came to pass after all thy wickedness,[7451] (woe, woe unto thee! saith the Lord GOD;)

24 *That* [a]thou hast also built unto thee an [I]eminent place, and [b]hast made[6213] thee an high place in every street.

25 Thou hast built thy high place [a]at every head of the way,[1870] and hast made thy beauty to be abhorred,[8581] and hast opened thy feet to every one that passed by, and multiplied thy whoredoms.

26 Thou hast also committed fornication[2181] with [a]the Egyptians thy neighbours,[7934] great of flesh; and hast increased thy whoredoms, to provoke me to anger.[3707]

27 Behold, therefore I have stretched out my hand[3027] over thee, and have diminished thine ordinary[2706] *food,* and delivered thee unto the will of them that hate[8130] thee, [a]the [I]daughters of the Philistines, which are ashamed of thy lewd[2154] way.

28 [a]Thou hast played the whore[2181] also with the Assyrians, because thou wast unsatiable; yea, thou hast played the harlot with them, and yet couldest not be satisfied.

29 Thou hast moreover multiplied thy fornication[8457] in the land of Canaan [a]unto Chaldea; and yet thou wast not satisfied herewith.

30 How weak is thine heart,[3826] saith the Lord GOD, seeing thou doest[6213] all these *things,* the work of an imperious whorish[2181] woman;[802]

31 [I]In that [a]thou buildest[1129] thine eminent place[1354] in the head of every way, and makest[6213] thine high place in every street; and hast not been as an harlot, in that thou scornest hire;

32 *But as* a wife[802] that committeth adultery,[5003] *which* taketh strangers instead of her husband[376]

33 They give gifts to all whores:[2181] but [a]thou givest thy gifts to all thy lovers,[157] and [I]hirest them, that they may come unto thee on every side for thy whoredom.[8457]

34 And the contrary is in thee from *other* women in thy whoredoms, whereas none followeth thee to commit whoredoms: and in that thou givest a reward,[868] and no reward is given unto thee, therefore thou art contrary.

The Judgment of God

35 Wherefore, O harlot, hear[8085] the word of the LORD:

36 Thus saith the LORD GOD; Because thy filthiness was poured out,[8210] and thy nakedness discovered through thy whoredoms with thy lovers, and with all the idols[1544] of thy abominations, and by [a]the blood of thy children, which thou didst give unto them;

37 Behold, therefore [a]I will gather[6908] all thy lovers, with whom thou hast taken pleasure,[6148] and all *them* that thou hast loved,[157] with all *them* that thou hast hated; I will even gather them round about against thee, and will discover[1540] thy nakedness unto them, that they may see all thy nakedness.

38 And I will judge[8199] thee, [I]as [a]women that break wedlock and [b]shed[8210] blood are judged; and I will give thee blood in fury and jealousy.

39 And I will also give thee into their hand, and they shall throw down[2040] [a]thine eminent place, and shall break down thy high places: [b]they shall strip thee also of thy clothes, and shall take [I]thy fair jewels, and leave thee naked and bare.

40 [a]They shall also bring up[5927] a company[6951] against thee, [b]and they shall

20 [I]Hebr. *to devour*

22 [a]Jer. 2:2; Ezek. 16:43, 60; Hos. 11:1 [b]Ezek. 16:4-6

24 [I]Or, *brothel house* [a]Ezek. 16:31 [b]Isa. 57:5, 7; Jer. 2:20; 3:2

25 [a]Prov. 9:14

26 [a]Ezek. 8:10, 14; 20:7, 8; 23:19-21

27 [I]Or, *cities* [a]2Chr. 28:18, 19; Ezek. 16:57

28 [a]2Kgs. 16:7, 10; 2Chr. 28:23; Jer. 2:18, 36; Ezek. 23:12

29 [a]Ezek. 23:14

31 [I]Or, *In thy daughters* is *thine* [a]Ezek. 16:24, 39

33 [I]Hebr. *bribest* [a]Isa. 30:6; Hos. 8:9

36 [a]Ezek. 16:20; Jer. 2:34

37 [a]Jer. 13:22, 26; Lam. 1:8; Ezek. 23:9, 10, 22, 29; Hos. 2:10; 8:10; Nah. 3:5

38 [I]Hebr. *with judgments of* [a]Lev. 20:10; Deut. 22:22; Ezek. 23:45 [b]Gen. 9:6; Ex. 21:12; Ezek. 16:20, 36

39 [I]Hebr. *instruments of thine ornament* [a]Ezek. 16:24, 31 [b]Ezek. 23:26; Hos. 2:3

40 [a]Ezek. 23:46, 47 [b]John 8:5, 7

stone thee with stones, and thrust thee through with their swords.[2719]

41 And they shall [a]burn thine houses[1004] with fire, and [b]execute judgments[8201] upon thee in the sight of many women: and I will cause thee to [c]cease[7673] from playing the harlot, and thou also shalt give no hire any more.

42 So [a]will I make my fury toward thee to rest, and my jealousy shall depart[5493] from thee, and I will be quiet,[8252] and will be no more angry.[3707]

43 Because [a]thou hast not remembered the days of thy youth, but hast fretted[7264] me in all these *things;* behold, therefore [b]I also will recompense thy way upon *thine* head, saith the Lord GOD: and thou shalt not commit[6213] this lewdness[2154] above all thine abominations.

44 Behold, every one that useth proverbs shall use *this* proverb against thee, saying, As *is* the mother, *so is* her daughter.

45 Thou *art* thy mother's[517] daughter, that lotheth her husband and her children; and thou *art* the sister[269] of thy sisters, which lothed their husbands[582] and their children: [a]your mother *was* an Hittite, and your father an Amorite.

46 And thine elder sister *is* Samaria, she and her daughters that dwell at thy left hand: and [I][a]thy younger sister, that dwelleth at thy right hand, *is* Sodom and her daughters.

47 Yet hast thou not walked after their ways,[1870] nor done[6213] after their abominations: but, as *if* [I]*that were* a very little *thing,* [a]thou wast corrupted[7843] more than they in all thy ways.

48 As I live,[2416] saith the Lord GOD, [a]Sodom thy sister hath not done, she nor her daughters, as thou hast done, thou and thy daughters.

49 Behold, this was the iniquity[5771] of thy sister Sodom, pride, [a]fulness of bread, and abundance of idleness[8252] was in her and in her daughters, neither did she strengthen[2388] the hand of the poor and needy.

50 And they were haughty, and [a]committed[6213] abomination[8441] before me: therefore [b]I took them away as I saw *good.*

51 Neither hath Samaria committed[2398] half of thy sins; but thou hast multiplied thine abominations more than they, and [a]hast justified[6663] thy sisters in all thine abominations which thou hast done.

52 Thou also, which hast judged thy sisters, bear[5375] thine own shame for thy sins that thou hast committed more abominable[8581] than they: they are more righteous[6663] than thou: yea, be thou confounded[954] also, and bear thy shame, in that thou hast justified thy sisters.

Sodom and Samaria

53 [a]When I shall bring again[7725] their captivity,[7622] [b]the captivity of Sodom and her daughters, and the captivity of Samaria and her daughters, then *will I bring again* the captivity of thy captives[7628] in the midst of them:

54 That thou mayest bear thine own shame,[3637] and mayest be confounded in all that thou hast done, in that thou art [a]a comfort[5162] unto them.

55 When thy sisters, Sodom and her daughters, shall return[7725] to their former estate,[6927] and Samaria and her daughters shall return to their former estate, then thou and thy daughters shall return to your former estate.

56 For thy sister Sodom was not [I]mentioned by thy mouth[6310] in the day of thy [II]pride,

57 Before thy wickedness was discovered, as at the time of *thy* [a]reproach[2781] of the daughters of [I]Syria, and all *that are* round about her, [b]the daughters of the Philistines, which [II]despise thee round about.

58 [a]Thou hast [I]borne[5375] thy lewdness and thine abominations, saith the LORD.

59 For thus saith the Lord GOD; I will even deal[6213] with thee as thou hast done, which hast [a]despised [b]the oath[423] in breaking[6565] the covenant.

60 Nevertheless I will [a]remember my

41 [a]Deut. 13:16; 2Kgs. 25:9; Jer. 39:8; 52:13 [b]Ezek. 5:8; 23:10, 48 [c]Ezek. 23:27
42 [a]Ezek. 5:13
43 [a]Ps. 78:42; Ezek. 16:22 [b]Ezek. 9:10; 11:21; 22:31
45 [a]Ezek. 16:3
46 [I]Hebr. *lesser than thou* [a]Deut. 32:32; Isa. 1:10
47 [I]Or, *that was loathed as a small* thing [a]2Kgs. 21:9; Ezek. 5:6, 7; 16:48, 51
48 [a]Matt. 10:15; 11:24
49 [a]Gen. 13:10
50 [a]Gen. 13:13; 18:20; 19:5 [b]Gen. 19:24
51 [a]Jer. 3:11; Matt. 12:41, 42
53 [a]Isa. 1:9; Ezek. 16:60, 61 [b]Jer. 20:16
54 [a]Ezek. 14:22, 23
56 [I]Hebr. *for a report,* or, *hearing* [II]Hebr. *prides,* or, *excellencies*
57 [I]Hebr. *Aram* [II]Or, *spoil* [a]2Kgs. 16:5; 2Chr. 28:18; Isa. 7:1; 14:28 [b]Ezek. 16:27
58 [I]Hebr. *borne them* [a]Ezek. 23:49
59 [a]Ezek. 17:13, 16 [b]Deut. 29:12, 14
60 [a]Ps. 106:45

covenant with thee in the days of thy
youth, and I will establish unto thee [b]an
everlasting[5769] covenant.
61 Then [a]thou shalt remember thy
ways, and be ashamed, when thou shalt
receive thy sisters, thine elder and thy
younger: and I will give them unto thee
for [b]daughters, [c]but not by thy covenant.
62 [a]And I will establish my covenant
with thee; and thou shalt know that I *am*
the LORD:
63 That thou mayest [a]remember, and
be confounded, [b]and never open thy
mouth any more because of thy shame,
when I am pacified[3722] toward thee for
all that thou hast done, saith the Lord
GOD.

The Eagles and the Vine

17 And the word[1697] of the LORD
came unto me, saying,
2 Son[1121] of man,[120] put forth a
riddle,[2420] and speak a parable unto the
house[1004] of Israel;
3 And say,[559] Thus saith the Lord[136]
GOD; [a]A great eagle with great wings,
longwinged, full of feathers, which had
[I]divers colours, came unto Lebanon,
and [b]took the highest branch of the
cedar:
4 He cropped off the top[7218] of his
young twigs, and carried it into a land[776]
of traffick;3667 he set[7760] it in a city of
merchants.
5 He took also of the seed[2233] of the
land, and [I]planted it in [a]a fruitful
field;[7704] he placed *it* by great waters,
and set it [b]*as* a willow tree.
6 And it grew, and became a spreading vine [a]of low stature, whose branches
turned toward him, and the roots thereof
were under him: so it became a vine, and
brought forth[5375] branches, and shot
forth sprigs.
7 There was also another great eagle
with great wings and many feathers: and,
behold, [a]this vine did bend her roots toward him, and shot forth her branches toward him, that he might water it by the
furrows6170 of her plantation.

8 It was planted in a good[2896] [I]soil
by great waters, that it might bring
forth[6213] branches, and that it might
bear[5375] fruit, that it might be a goodly
vine.
9 Say thou, Thus saith the Lord GOD;
Shall it prosper? [a]shall he not pull up the
roots thereof, and cut off the fruit thereof,
that it wither?[3001] it shall wither in all the
leaves of her spring, even without great
power or many people[5971] to pluck it up
by the roots thereof.
10 Yea, behold, *being* planted, shall it
prosper? [a]shall it not utterly wither, when
the east wind[7307] toucheth[5060] it? it shall
wither in the furrows where it grew.
11 Moreover the word of the LORD
came unto me, saying,
12 Say now to [a]the rebellious[4805]
house, Know[3045] ye not what these *things*
mean? tell[559] *them,* Behold, [b]the king[4428]
of Babylon is come to Jerusalem, and
hath taken the king thereof, and the
princes[8269] thereof, and led them with
him to Babylon;
13 [a]And hath taken of the king's
seed, and made[3772] a covenant[1285] with
him, [b]and hath [I]taken an oath[423] of him:
he hath also taken the mighty of the
land:
14 That the kingdom[4467] might be
[a]base,8217 that it might not lift itself up,
[I]*but* that by keeping[8104] of his covenant
it might stand.
15 But [a]he rebelled[4775] against him
in sending his ambassadors[4397] into
Egypt, [b]that they might give him horses
and much people. [c]Shall he prosper? shall
he escape[4422] that doeth[6213] such *things?*
or shall he break the covenant, and be
delivered?[4422]
16 *As* I live,[2416] saith5002 the Lord
GOD, surely [a]in the place *where* the
king[4428] *dwelleth* that made him king,
whose oath he despised, and whose
covenant he brake,[6565] *even* with him in
the midst of Babylon he shall die.[4191]
17 [a]Neither shall Pharaoh with *his*
mighty army[2428] and great company[6951]
make[6213] for him in the war, [b]by casting
up[8210] mounts, and building forts, to cut
off[3772] many persons:[5315]

60 [b]Jer. 32:40; 50:5

61 [a]Ezek. 20:43; 36:31 [b]Isa. 54:1; 60:4; Gal. 4:26 [c]Jer. 31:31

62 [a]Hos. 2:19, 20

63 [a]Ezek. 16:61 [b]Rom. 3:19

3 [I]Hebr. *embroidering* [a]Ezek. 17:12 [b]2Kgs. 24:12

5 [I]Hebr. *put it in a field of seed* [a]Deut. 8:7-9 [b]Isa. 44:4

6 [a]Ezek. 17:14

7 [a]Ezek. 17:15

8 [I]Hebr. *field*

9 [a]2Kgs. 25:7

10 [a]Ezek. 19:12; Hos. 13:15

12 [a]Ezek. 2:5; 12:9 [b]Ezek. 17:3; 2Kgs. 24:11-16

13 [I]Hebr. *brought him to an oath* [a]2Kgs. 24:17 [b]2Chr. 36:13

14 [I]Hebr. *to keep his covenant, to stand to it* [a]Ezek. 17:6; 29:14

15 [a]2Kgs. 24:20; 2Chr. 36:13 [b]Deut. 17:16; Isa. 31:1, 3; 36:6, 9 [c]Ezek. 17:9

16 [a]Jer. 32:5; 34:3; 52:11; Ezek. 12:13

17 [a]Jer. 37:7 [b]Jer. 52:4; Ezek. 4:2

18 Seeing he despised the oath by breaking[6565] the covenant, when, lo, he had [a]given his hand,[3027] and hath done[6213] all these *things,* he shall not escape.

19 Therefore thus saith the Lord GOD; *As* I live, surely mine oath that he hath despised, and my covenant that he hath broken, even it will I recompense upon his own head.[7218]

20 And I will [a]spread my net upon him, and he shall be taken in my snare, and I will bring him to Babylon, and [b]will plead[8199] with him there for his trespass[4604] that he hath trespassed against me.

21 And [a]all his fugitives with all his bands shall fall by the sword,[2719] and they that remain shall be scattered toward all winds:[7307] and ye shall know that I the LORD have spoken[1696] *it.*

22 Thus saith the Lord GOD; I will also take of the highest [a]branch of the high cedar, and will set *it;* I will crop off[6998] from the top of his young twigs [b]a tender one, and will [c]plant *it* upon an high mountain and eminent:

23 [a]In the mountain of the height of Israel will I plant it: and it shall bring forth[5375] boughs, and bear fruit, and be a goodly cedar: and [b]under it shall dwell[7931] all fowl of every wing; in the shadow of the branches thereof shall they dwell.

24 And all the trees of the field shall know that I the LORD [a]have brought down the high tree, have exalted the low tree, have dried up[3001] the green tree, and have made the dry[3002] tree to flourish: [b]I the LORD have spoken and have done *it.*

"The Soul That Sinneth, It Shall Die"

18 The word[1697] of the LORD came unto me again, saying,

2 What mean ye, that ye use this proverb concerning the land[127] of Israel, saying, The [a]fathers have eaten sour grapes, and the children's teeth are set on edge?[6949]

3 As I live,[2416] saith[5002] the Lord[136] GOD, ye shall not have *occasion* any more to use this proverb in Israel.

4 Behold, all souls[5315] are mine; as the soul of the father,[1] so also the soul of the son[1121] is mine: [a]the soul that sinneth,[2398] it shall die.[4191]

5 But if a man[376] be just, and do[6213] [I]that which is lawful[4941] and right,[6666]

6 [a]*And* hath not eaten upon the mountains, neither hath lifted up[5375] his eyes to the idols[1544] of the house[1004] of Israel, neither hath [b]defiled[2930] his neighbour's[7453] wife,[802] neither hath come near[7126] to [c]a menstruous woman,

7 And hath not [a]oppressed[3238] any, *but* hath restored[7725] to the debtor his [b]pledge,[2258] hath spoiled none by violence,[1500] hath [c]given his bread to the hungry, and hath covered[3680] the naked with a garment;

8 He *that* hath not given forth upon [a]usury, neither hath taken any increase, *that* hath withdrawn[7725] his hand[3027] from iniquity,[5766] [b]hath executed[6213]

---

18 [a]1Chr. 29:24; Lam. 5:6
20 [a]Ezek. 12:13; 32:3 [b]Ezek. 20:36
21 [a]Ezek. 12:14
22 [a]Isa. 11:1; Jer. 23:5; Zech. 3:8 [b]Isa. 53:2 [c]Ps. 2:6
23 [a]Isa. 2:2, 3; Ezek. 20:40; Mic. 4:1 [b]Ezek. 31:6; Dan. 4:12
24 [a]Luke 1:52 [b]Ezek. 22:14; 24:14
2 [a]Jer. 31:29; Lam. 5:7
4 [a]Ezek. 18:20; Rom. 6:23
5 [I]Hebr. *judgment and justice*
6 [a]Ezek. 22:9 [b]Lev. 18:20; 20:10 [c]Lev. 18:19; 20:18
7 [a]Ex. 22:21; Lev. 19:15; 25:14 [b]Ex. 22:26; Deut. 24:12, 13 [c]Deut. 15:7, 8; Isa. 58:7; Matt. 25:35, 36
8 [a]Ex. 22:25; Lev. 25:36, 37; Deut. 23:19; Neh. 5:7; Ps. 15:5 [b]Deut. 1:16; Zech. 8:16

18:1–32 One of the distinctive features of the Book of Ezekiel is the presentation of individual responsibility (Ezek. 3:16–21; 14:12–20; 18:1–32; 33:1–20). In this passage the Lord was setting aside an old proverb in Israel (Ezek. 18:2, cf. Jer. 31:29, 30; Lam. 5:7) and replacing it with one of His own: "The soul that sinneth, it shall die" (Ezek. 18:4, 20). In the Old Testament, God's people were treated as a national unit, and their material existence and prosperity was often affected by the sins of the minority (cf. Josh. 7:1, 4–11, 18–26). Consequently, God was just when He spoke of "visiting the iniquity of the fathers upon the children" (Ex. 20:5). This passage, however, looks beyond material ramifications, and considers the eternal results of sin. This is implied by the use of the term "soul" and the command to "make you a new heart and a new spirit" (Ezek. 18:31). Many righteous people were going to die in the siege, and many would be carried to Babylon (as Ezekiel and Daniel were). God wanted His people to understand that the eternal destiny of each person was determined by his or her individual relationship with Him.

true[571] judgment[4941] between man and man,

9 Hath walked in my statutes,[2708] and hath kept[8104] my judgments, to deal[6213] truly;[571] he *is* just, he shall surely [a]live,[2421] saith the Lord GOD.

10 If he beget a son *that is* a [I]robber,[6530] [a]a shedder of blood,[1818] and [II]*that* doeth the like to *any* one of these *things,*

11 And that doeth not any of those *duties,* but even hath eaten upon the mountains, and defiled his neighbour's wife,

12 Hath oppressed the poor and needy, hath spoiled[1497] by violence, hath not restored the pledge, and hath lifted up his eyes to the idols, hath [a]committed[6213] abomination,[8441]

13 Hath given forth upon usury, and hath taken increase: shall he then live?[2425] he shall not live; he hath done[6213] all these abominations;[8441] he shall surely die;[4191] [a]his blood shall be upon him.

14 Now, lo, *if* he beget a son, that seeth[7200] all his father's[1] sins which he hath done, and considereth,[7200] and doeth not such like,

15 [a]*That* hath not eaten upon the mountains, neither hath lifted up his eyes to the idols of the house of Israel, hath not defiled his neighbour's wife,

16 Neither hath oppressed any, [I]hath not withholden[2254] the pledge, neither hath spoiled by violence, *but* hath given his bread to the hungry, and hath covered the naked with a garment,

17 *That* hath taken off[7725] his hand from the poor, *that* hath not received usury nor increase, hath executed my judgments, hath walked in my statutes; he shall not die for the iniquity[5771] of his father, he shall surely live.

18 As *for* his father, because he cruelly oppressed, spoiled his brother[251] by violence, and did[6213] *that* which *is* not good[2896] among his people,[5971] lo, even [a]he shall die in his iniquity.

19 Yet say[559] ye, Why? [a]doth not the son bear[5375] the iniquity of the father? When the son hath done that which is lawful and right, *and* hath kept all my

9 [a]Ezek. 20:11; Amos 5:4

10 [I]Or, *breaker up of a house* [II]Or, *that doeth to his brother besides any of these* [a]Gen. 9:6; Ex. 21:12; Num. 35:31

12 [a]Ezek. 8:6, 17

13 [a]Lev. 20:9, 11-13, 16, 27; Ezek. 3:18; 33:4; Acts 18:6

15 [a]Ezek. 18:6

16 [I]Hebr. *hath not pledged the pledge,* or, *taken to pledge*

18 [a]Ezek. 3:18

19 [a]Ex. 20:5; Deut. 5:9; 2Kgs. 23:26; 24:3, 4

20 [a]Ezek. 18:4 [b]Deut. 24:16; 2Kgs. 14:6; 2Chr. 25:4; Jer. 31:29, 30 [c]Isa. 3:10, 11 [d]Rom. 2:9

21 [a]Ezek. 18:27; 33:12, 19

22 [a]Ezek. 33:16

23 [a]Ezek. 18:32; 33:11; 1Tim. 2:4; 2Pet. 3:9

24 [a]Ezek. 3:20; 33:12, 13, 18 [b]2Pet. 2:20

25 [a]Ezek. 18:29; 33:17, 20

26 [a]Ezek. 18:24

27 [a]Ezek. 18:21

28 [a]Ezek. 18:14

statutes, and hath done them, he shall surely live.

20 [a]The soul that sinneth, it shall die. [b]The son shall not bear the iniquity of the father, neither shall the father bear the iniquity of the son: [c]the righteousness[6666] of the righteous[6662] shall be upon him, [d]and the wickedness[7564] of the wicked shall be upon him.

God's Way Is Just

21 But [a]if the wicked will turn[7725] from all his sins that he hath committed, and keep[8104] all my statutes, and do that which is lawful and right, he shall surely live, he shall not die.

22 [a]All his transgressions[6588] that he hath committed, they shall not be mentioned[2142] unto him: in his righteousness that he hath done he shall live.

23 [a]Have I any pleasure at all that the wicked should die? saith the Lord GOD: *and* not that he should return from his ways,[1870] and live?

24 But [a]when the righteous turneth away from his righteousness, and committeth[6213] iniquity, *and* doeth according to all the abominations that the wicked *man* doeth, shall he live? [b]All his righteousness that he hath done shall not be mentioned: in his trespass[4604] that he hath trespassed, and in his sin[2403] that he hath sinned,[2398] in them shall he die.

25 Yet ye say, [a]The way[1870] of the Lord is not equal.[8505] Hear[8085] now, O house of Israel; Is not my way equal? are not your ways unequal?

26 [a]When a righteous *man* turneth away from his righteousness, and committeth iniquity, and dieth[4191] in them; for his iniquity that he hath done shall he die.

27 Again, [a]when the wicked *man* turneth away from his wickedness that he hath committed, and doeth that which is lawful and right, he shall save his soul alive.[2421]

28 Because he [a]considereth, and turneth away from all his transgressions that he hath committed, he shall surely live, he shall not die.

29 [a]Yet saith the house of Israel, The
way of the Lord is not equal. O house of
Israel, are not my ways equal? are not
your ways unequal?
30 [a]Therefore I will judge[8199] you, O
house of Israel, every one[376] according to
his ways, saith the Lord GOD. [b]Repent,[7725]
and turn *yourselves* from all your transgressions; so iniquity shall not be your
ruin.[4383]
31 [a]Cast away from you all your
transgressions, whereby ye have transgressed;[6586] and make[6213] you a [b]new
heart[3820] and a new spirit:[7307] for why
will ye die, O house of Israel?
32 For [a]I have no pleasure in the
death[4194] of him that dieth, saith the
Lord GOD: wherefore turn *yourselves,* and
live ye.

A Lamentation

19 Moreover [a]take thou up[5375] a
lamentation for the princes[5387] of
Israel,
2 And say,[559] What *is* thy mother?[517]
A lioness: she lay down among lions, she
nourished her whelps[1482] among young
lions.
3 And she brought up[5927] one of her
whelps: [a]it became a young lion, and it
learned[3925] to catch the prey; it devoured
men.[120]
4 The nations[1471] also heard[8085] of
him; he was taken in their pit,[7845] and
they brought him with chains unto the
land[776] of [a]Egypt.
5 Now when she saw[7200] that she
had waited,[3176] *and* her hope was lost,[6]
then she took [a]another of her whelps,
and made[7760] him a young lion.
6 [a]And he went up and down among
the lions, [b]he became a young lion, and
learned to catch the prey, *and* devoured
men.
7 And he knew[3045] [I]their desolate
palaces,[490] and he laid waste[2717] their
cities; and the land was desolate,[3456] and
the fulness thereof, by the noise of his
roaring.
8 [a]Then the nations set against him
on every side from the provinces, and
spread their net over him: [b]he was taken
in their pit.
9 [a]And they put him in ward[5474] [I]in
chains, and brought him to the king[4428]
of Babylon: they brought him into holds,
that his voice should no more be heard
upon [b]the mountains of Israel.
10 Thy mother *is* [a]like a vine [I]in thy
blood,[1818] planted by the waters: she was
[b]fruitful and full of branches by reason
of many waters.
11 And she had strong[5794] rods for
the sceptres[7626] of them that bare
rule,[4910] and her [a]stature was exalted
among the thick branches, and she
appeared[7200] in her height with the multitude of her branches.
12 But she was plucked up in fury,
she was cast down to the ground,[776] and
the [a]east wind[7307] dried up[3001] her fruit:
her strong rods were broken and
withered;[3001] the fire consumed them.
13 And now she *is* planted in the
wilderness, in a dry and thirsty ground.
14 [a]And fire is gone out of a rod[4294]
of her branches, *which* hath devoured her
fruit, so that she hath no strong rod *to
be* a sceptre[7626] to rule. [b]This *is* a lamentation, and shall be for a lamentation.

Israel Defies God

20 And it came to pass in the seventh year, in the fifth *month,* the
tenth *day* of the month, *that* [a]certain[582]
of the elders[2205] of Israel came to enquire
of the LORD, and sat before me.
2 Then came the word[1697] of the
LORD unto me, saying,
3 Son[1121] of man,[120] speak[1696] unto
the elders of Israel, and say[559] unto them,
Thus saith the Lord GOD; Are ye come to
enquire of me? *As* I live,[2416] saith[5002] the
Lord[136] GOD, [a]I will not be enquired of
by you.
4 Wilt thou [Ia]judge[8199] them, son of
man, wilt thou judge *them?* [b]cause them
to know[3045] the abominations[8441] of their
fathers:[1]
5 And say unto them, Thus saith the
Lord GOD; In the day[3117] when [a]I chose[977]
Israel, and [Ib]lifted up[5375] mine hand[3027]

29 [a]Ezek. 18:25
30 [a]Ezek. 7:3; 33:20 [b]Matt. 3:2; Rev. 2:5
31 [a]Eph. 4:22, 23 [b]Jer. 32:39; Ezek. 11:19; 36:26
32 [a]Lam. 3:33; Ezek. 18:23; 33:11; 2Pet. 3:9
1 [a]Ezek. 26:17; 27:2
3 [a]2Kgs. 23:31, 32; Ezek. 19:6
4 [a]2Kgs. 23:33; 2Chr. 36:4; Jer. 22:11, 12
5 [a]2Kgs. 23:34
6 [a]Jer. 22:13-17 [b]Ezek. 19:3
7 [I]Or, *their widows*
8 [a]2Kgs. 24:2 [b]Ezek. 19:4
9 [I]Or, *in hooks* [a]2Chr. 36:6; Jer. 22:18 [b]Ezek. 6:2
10 [I]Or, *in thy quietness,* or, *in thy likeness* [a]Ezek. 17:6 [b]Deut. 8:7-9
11 [a]Ezek. 31:3; Dan. 4:11
12 [a]Ezek. 17:10; Hos. 13:15
14 [a]Judg. 9:15; 2Kgs. 24:20; Ezek. 17:18 [b]Lam. 4:20
1 [a]Ezek. 8:1; 14:1 [b]Ezek. 14:3; 20:31
4 [I]Or, *plead for them* [a]Ezek. 22:2; 23:36 [b]Ezek. 16:2
5 [I]Or, *sware* [a]Ex. 6:7; Deut. 7:6 [b]Ex. 6:8

unto the seed[2233] of the house[1004] of Jacob, and made myself [c]known unto them in the land[776] of Egypt, when I lifted up mine hand unto them, saying, [d]I *am* the LORD[3068] your God;[430]

6 In the day *that* I lifted up mine hand unto them, [a]to bring them forth of the land of Egypt into a land that I had espied for them, flowing with milk and honey, [b]which *is* the glory[6643] of all lands:[776]

7 Then said I unto them, [a]Cast ye away every man[376] [b]the abominations[8251] of his eyes, and defile[2930] not yourselves with [c]the idols[1544] of Egypt: I *am* the LORD your God.

8 But they rebelled[4784] against me, and would[14] not hearken[8085] unto me: they did not every man cast away the abominations of their eyes, neither did they forsake[5800] the idols of Egypt: then I said, I will [a]pour out[8210] my fury upon them, to accomplish[3615] my anger[639] against them in the midst of the land of Egypt.

9 [a]But I wrought for my name's sake, that it should not be polluted[2490] before the heathen,[1471] among whom they *were,* in whose sight I made myself known unto them, in bringing them forth out of the land of Egypt.

10 Wherefore I [a]caused them to go forth out of the land of Egypt, and brought them into the wilderness.

11 [a]And I gave them my statutes,[2708] and [I]shewed[3045] them my judgments,[4941] [b]which *if* a man do,[6213] he shall even live[2425] in them.

12 Moreover also I gave them my [a]sabbaths,[7676] to be a sign[226] between me and them, that they might know that I *am* the LORD that sanctify[6942] them.

13 But the house of Israel [a]rebelled against me in the wilderness: they walked not in my statutes, and they [b]despised[3988] my judgments, which *if* a man do, he shall even live in them; and my sabbaths they greatly [c]polluted: then I said, I would pour out my fury upon them in the [d]wilderness, to consume[3615] them.

14 [a]But I wrought for my name's sake, that it should not be polluted before the heathen, in whose sight I brought them out.

15 Yet also [a]I lifted up my hand unto them in the wilderness, that I would not bring them into the land which I had given *them,* flowing with milk and honey, [b]which *is* the glory of all lands;

16 [a]Because they despised my judgments, and walked not in my statutes, but polluted my sabbaths: for [b]their heart[3820] went after their idols.

17 [a]Nevertheless mine eye spared them from destroying[7843] them, neither did I make[6213] an end[3617] of them in the wilderness.

18 But I said unto their children[1121] in the wilderness, Walk ye not in the statutes[2706] of your fathers, neither observe[8104] their judgments, nor defile yourselves with their idols:

19 I *am* the LORD your God; [a]walk in my statutes, and keep[8104] my judgments, and do them;

20 [a]And hallow[6942] my sabbaths; and they shall be a sign between me and you, that ye may know that I *am* the LORD your God.

21 Notwithstanding [a]the children rebelled against me: they walked not in my statutes, neither kept my judgments to do them, [b]which *if* a man do, he shall even live in them; they polluted my sabbaths: then I said, [c]I would pour out my fury[2534] upon them, to accomplish my anger against them in the wilderness.

22 [a]Nevertheless I withdrew mine hand, and [b]wrought for my name's sake, that it should not be polluted in the sight of the heathen, in whose sight I brought them forth.

23 I lifted up mine hand unto them also in the wilderness, that [a]I would scatter them among the heathen, and disperse them through the countries;[776]

24 [a]Because they had not executed[6213] my judgments, but had despised my statutes, and had polluted my sabbaths, and [b]their eyes were after their fathers'[1] idols.

25 Wherefore [a]I gave them also

5 [c]Ex. 3:8; 4:31; Deut. 4:34 [d]Ex. 20:2
6 [a]Ex. 3:8, 17; Deut. 8:7-9; Jer. 32:22 [b]Ps. 48:2; Ezek. 20:15; Dan. 8:9; 11:16, 41; Zech. 7:14
7 [a]Ezek. 18:31 [b]2Chr. 15:8 [c]Lev. 17:7; 18:3; Deut. 29:16-18; Josh. 24:14
8 [a]Ezek. 7:8; 20:13, 21
9 [a]Ex. 32:12; Num. 14:13; Deut. 9:28; Ezek. 20:14, 22; 36:21, 22
10 [a]Ex. 13:18
11 [I]Hebr. *made them to know* [a]Deut. 4:8; Neh. 9:13, 14; Ps. 147:19, 20 [b]Lev. 18:5; Ezek. 20:13, 21; Rom. 10:5; Gal. 3:12
12 [a]Ex. 20:8; 31:13; 35:2; Deut. 5:12; Neh. 9:14
13 [a]Num. 14:22; Ps. 78:40; 95:8-10 [b]Prov. 1:25; Ezek. 20:16, 24 [c]Ex. 16:27 [d]Num. 14:29; 26:65; Ps. 106:23
14 [a]Ezek. 20:9, 22
15 [a]Num. 14:28; Ps. 95:11; 106:26 [b]Ezek. 20:6
16 [a]Ezek. 20:13, 24 [b]Num. 15:39; Ps. 78:37; Amos 5:25, 26; Acts 7:42, 43
17 [a]Ps. 78:38
19 [a]Deut. 5:32, 33
20 [a]Jer. 17:22; Ezek. 20:12
21 [a]Num. 25:1, 2; Deut. 9:23, 24; 31:27 [b]Ezek. 20:11, 13 [c]Ezek. 20:8, 13
22 [a]Ps. 78:38; Ezek. 20:17; Ezek. 20:9, 14
23 [a]Lev. 26:33; Deut. 28:64; Ps. 106:27; Jer. 15:4
24 [a]Ezek. 20:13, 16 [b]Ezek. 6:9
25 [a]Ps. 81:12; Ezek. 20:39; Rom. 1:24; 2Thess. 2:11

statutes *that were* not good,[2896] and judgments whereby they should not live;[2421]

26 And I polluted[2930] them in their own gifts, in that they caused to pass [a]through[5674] *the fire* all that openeth the womb, that I might make them desolate,[8074] to the end that they [b]might know that I *am* the LORD.

27 Therefore, son of man, speak unto the house of Israel, and say unto them, Thus saith the Lord GOD; Yet in this your fathers have [a]blasphemed[1442] me, in that they have [I]committed a trespass[4604] against me.

28 *For* when I had brought them into the land, *for* the which I lifted up mine hand to give it to them, then [a]they saw[7200] every high hill, and all the thick trees, and they offered[2076] there their sacrifices,[2077] and there they presented the provocation[3708] of their offering:[7133] there also they made[7760] their [b]sweet savour, and poured out[5258] there their drink offerings.[5262]

29 Then [I]I said unto them, What *is* the high place[1116] whereunto ye go? And the name thereof is called[7121] Bamah[1117] unto this day.

30 Wherefore say unto the house of Israel, Thus saith the Lord GOD; Are ye polluted after the manner of your fathers? and commit[2181] ye whoredom after their abominations?

31 For when ye offer[5375] [a]your gifts, when ye make your sons[1121] to pass through the fire, ye pollute yourselves with all your idols, even unto this day: and [b]shall I be enquired of by you, O house of Israel? *As* I live, saith the Lord GOD, I will not be enquired of by you.

32 And that [a]which cometh into your mind[7307] shall not be at all, that ye say, We will be as the heathen, as the families[4940] of the countries, to serve[8334] wood and stone.

God Punishes but Forgives

33 *As* I live, saith the Lord GOD, surely with a mighty[2389] hand, and [a]with a stretched out arm, and with fury poured out,[8210] will I rule[4427] over you:

34 And I will bring you out from the people,[5971] and will gather[6908] you out of the countries wherein ye are scattered, with a mighty hand, and with a stretched out arm, and with fury poured out.

35 And I will bring you into the wilderness of the people, and there [a]will I plead[8199] with you face to face.

36 [a]Like as I pleaded[8199] with your fathers in the wilderness of the land of Egypt, so will I plead with you, saith the Lord GOD.

37 And I will cause you to [a]pass under the rod,[7626] and I will bring you into [I]the bond of the covenant:[1285]

38 And [a]I will purge out[1305] from among you the rebels,[4775] and them that transgress[6586] against me: I will bring them forth out of the country[776] where they sojourn,[4033] and [b]they shall not enter into the land[127] of Israel: [c]and ye shall know that I *am* the LORD.

39 As for you, O house of Israel, thus saith the Lord GOD; [a]Go ye, serve[5647] ye every one[376] his idols, and hereafter *also,* if ye will not hearken unto me: [b]but pollute[2490] ye my holy[6944] name no more with your gifts, and with your idols.

40 For [a]in mine holy mountain, in the mountain of the height of Israel, saith the Lord GOD, there shall all the house of Israel, all of them in the land, serve me: there [b]will I accept[7521] them, and there will I require your offerings,[8641] and the [I]firstfruits[7225] of your oblations,[4864] with all your holy things.

41 I will accept you with your [Ia]sweet savour, when I bring you out from the people, and gather you out of the countries wherein ye have been scattered; and I will be sanctified[6942] in you before the heathen.

42 [a]And ye shall know that I *am* the LORD, [b]when I shall bring you into the land of Israel, into the country *for* the which I lifted up mine hand to give it to your fathers.

43 And [a]there shall ye remember[2142] your ways,[1870] and all your doings,

26 [a]2Kgs. 17:17; 21:6; 2Chr. 28:3; 33:6; Jer. 32:35; Ezek. 16:20, 21; Ezek. 20:6, 7

27 [I]Hebr. *trespassed a trespass* [a]Rom. 2:24

28 [a]Isa. 57:5; Ezek. 6:13 [b]Ezek. 16:19

29 [I]Or, *I told them what the high place was,* or, *Bamah*

31 [a]Ezek. 20:26 [b]Ezek. 20:3

32 [a]Ezek. 11:5

33 [a]Jer. 21:5

35 [a]Jer. 2:9, 35; Ezek. 17:20

36 [a]Num. 14:21-23, 28, 29

37 [I]Or, *a delivering* [a]Lev. 27:32; Jer. 33:13

38 [a]Ezek. 34:17, 20; Matt. 25:32, 33 [b]Jer. 44:14 [c]Ezek. 6:7; 15:7; 23:49

39 [a]Judg. 10:14; Ps. 81:12; Amos 4:4 [b]Isa. 1:13; Ezek. 23:38, 39

40 [I]Or, *chief* [a]Isa. 2:2, 3; Ezek. 17:23; Mic. 4:1 [b]Isa. 56:7; 60:7; Zech. 8:20; Mal. 3:4; Rom. 12:1

41 [I]Hebr. *savor of rest* [a]Eph. 5:2; Phil. 4:18

42 [a]Ezek. 20:38, 44; 36:23; 38:23 [b]Ezek. 11:17; 34:13; 36:24

43 [a]Ezek. 16:61

wherein ye have been defiled,[2930] and [b]ye
shall lothe yourselves[6962] in your own
sight for all your evils that ye have
committed.[6213]
44 [a]And ye shall know that I *am* the
LORD, when I have wrought with you [b]for
my name's sake, not according to your
wicked[7451] ways, nor according to your
corrupt[7843] doings, O ye house of Israel,
saith the Lord GOD.

The Prophecy Against the Forest of the South

45 Moreover the word of the LORD
came unto me, saying,
46 [a]Son of man, set[7760] thy face
toward[1870] the south, and drop[5197] *thy
word* toward the south, and prophesy[5012]
against the forest of the south field;[7704]
47 And say to the forest of the
south, Hear[8085] the word of the LORD;
Thus saith the Lord GOD; Behold, [a]I will
kindle a fire in thee, and it shall devour
[b]every green tree in thee, and every
dry[3002] tree: the flaming flame shall not
be quenched, and all faces [c]from the
south to the north shall be burned
therein.
48 And all flesh shall see that I the
LORD have kindled it: it shall not be
quenched.
49 Then said I, Ah Lord GOD! they
say of me, Doth he not speak parables?

The Sword of the LORD

21 And the word[1697] of the LORD
came unto me, saying,
2 [a]Son[1121] of man,[120] set[7760] thy face
toward Jerusalem, and [b]drop[5197] *thy word*
toward the holy places, and prophesy[5012]
against the land[127] of Israel,
3 And say[559] to the land of Israel,
Thus saith the LORD; Behold, I *am*
against thee, and will draw forth my
sword[2719] out of his sheath, and will cut
off[3772] from thee [a]the righteous[6662] and
the wicked.[7563]

43 [b]Lev. 26:39; Ezek. 6:9; Hos. 5:15
44 [a]Ezek. 20:38; 24:24 [b]Ezek. 36:22
46 [a]Ezek. 6:2; 21:2
47 [a]Jer. 21:14 [b]Luke 23:31
2 [a]Ezek. 21:4 [b]Ezek. 20:46 [c]Deut. 32:2; Amos 7:16; Mic. 2:6, 11
3 [a]Job 9:22
4 [a]Ezek. 20:47
5 [a]Isa. 45:23; 55:11
6 [a]Isa. 22:4
7 [I]Hebr. *shall go into water* [a]Ezek. 7:17
9 [a]Deut. 32:41; Ezek. 21:15, 28
10 [I]Or, *it is the rod of my son, it despiseth every tree*
11 [a]Ezek. 21:19
12 [I]Or, *they are thrust down to the sword with my people* [a]Jer. 31:19
13 [I]Or, *When the trial* hath been, *what then? shall they not also belong to the despising rod* [a]Job 9:23; 2Cor. 8:2 [b]Ezek. 21:27
14 [I]Hebr. *hand to hand* [a]Num. 24:10; Ezek. 6:11; 21:1, 7

4 Seeing then that I will cut off from
thee the righteous and the wicked, therefore shall my sword go forth out of his
sheath against all flesh [a]from the south
to the north:
5 That all flesh may know[3045] that I
the LORD have drawn forth my sword out
of his sheath: it [a]shall not return[7725] any
more.
6 [a]Sigh[584] therefore, thou son of man,
with the breaking[7670] of *thy* loins; and
with bitterness sigh before their eyes.
7 And it shall be, when they say
unto thee, Wherefore sighest thou? that
thou shalt answer,[559] For the tidings;
because it cometh: and every heart[3820]
shall melt, and [a]all hands[3027] shall be
feeble,[7503] and every spirit[7307] shall faint,
and all knees [I]shall be weak *as* water: behold, it cometh, and shall be brought to
pass, saith[5002] the Lord[136] GOD.
8 Again the word of the LORD came
unto me, saying,
9 Son of man, prophesy, and say,
Thus saith the LORD; Say, [a]A sword, a
sword is sharpened, and also furbished:[4803]
10 It is sharpened to make a sore
slaughter; it is furbished that it may glitter: should we then make mirth? [I]it
contemneth[3988] the rod[7626] of my son, *as*
every tree.
11 And he hath given it to be furbished, that it may be handled: this
sword is sharpened, and it is furbished,
to give it into the hand[3027] of [a]the slayer.
🗝 12 Cry[2199] and howl, son of man: for
it shall be upon my people,[5971] it *shall
be* upon all the princes[5387] of Israel:
[I]terrors[4048] by reason of the sword shall
be upon my people: [a]smite[5606] therefore
upon *thy* thigh.[3409]
13 [I]Because *it is* [a]a trial,[974] and what
if *the sword* contemn even the rod? [b]it
shall be no *more,* saith the Lord GOD.
14 Thou therefore, son of man,
prophesy, and [a]smite[5221] *thine* [I]hands[3709]
together, and let the sword be doubled[3717]
the third time,[6256] the sword of the

🗝 **21:12–17** See note on Ezekiel 2:8—3:3.

slain:[2491] it *is* the sword of the great *men that are* slain, which entereth into their [b]privy chambers.[2314]

15 I have set the [I]point of the sword against all their gates, that *their* heart may faint, and *their* ruins[4383] be multiplied: ah! [a]*it is* made bright,[1300] *it is* [II]wrapped up for the slaughter.[2874]

16 [a]Go thee one way or other, *either* on the right hand, [I]*or* on the left, whithersoever thy face *is* set.[3259]

17 I will also [a]smite mine hands together, and [b]I will cause my fury to rest: I the LORD have said[1696] *it.*

The King of Babylon

18 The word of the LORD came unto me again, saying,

19 Also, thou son of man, appoint[7760] thee two ways,[1870] that the sword of the king[4428] of Babylon may come: both twain[8147] shall come forth out of one land:[776] and choose thou a place, choose *it* at the head[7218] of the way[1870] to the city.

20 Appoint a way, that the sword may come to [a]Rabbath of the Ammonites, and to Judah in Jerusalem the defenced.

21 For the king of Babylon stood at the [I]parting of the way, at the head of the two ways, to use[7080] divination:[7081] he made *his* [II]arrows bright,[7043] he consulted[7592] with [III]images,[8655] he looked in the liver.

22 At his right hand was the divination for Jerusalem, to appoint [Ia]captains,[3733] to open the mouth[6310] in the slaughter, to [b]lift up the voice with shouting, [c]to appoint *battering* rams[3733] against the gates, to cast[8210] a mount, *and* to build a fort.

23 And it shall be unto them as a false[7723] divination[7080] in their sight, [I]to them that [a]have sworn oaths: but he will call to remembrance[2142] the iniquity,[5771] that they may be taken.

24 Therefore thus saith the Lord GOD; Because ye have made your iniquity to be remembered, in that your transgressions[6588] are discovered, so that in all your doings your sins do appear;[7200] because, I *say,* that ye are come to remembrance, ye shall be taken with the hand.

25 And thou, [a]profane[2491] wicked prince[5387] of Israel, [b]whose day[3117] is come, when iniquity *shall have* an end,

26 Thus saith the Lord GOD; Remove the diadem,[4701] and take off the crown: this *shall* not *be* the same: [a]exalt *him that is* low, and abase[8213] *him that is* high.

27 [I]I will overturn, overturn, overturn, it: [a]and it shall be no *more,* until he come whose right[4941] it is; and I will give it *him.*

Judgment Upon the Ammonites

28 And thou, son of man, prophesy and say, Thus saith the Lord GOD [a]concerning the Ammonites, and concerning their reproach;[2781] even say thou, [b]The sword, the sword *is* drawn: for the slaughter *it is* furbished, to consume because of the glittering:

29 Whiles they [a]see[2372] vanity[7723] unto thee, whiles they divine[7080] a lie[3576] unto thee, to bring thee upon the necks of *them that are* slain, of the wicked, [b]whose day is come, when their iniquity *shall have* an end.

30 [Ia]Shall I cause *it* to return into his sheath? [b]I will judge[8199] thee in the place where thou wast created,[1254] [c]in the land of thy nativity.

31 And I will [a]pour out[8210] mine indignation[2195] upon thee, I will [b]blow[6315] against thee in the fire of my wrath,[5678] and deliver thee into the hand of [I]brutish men,[582] *and* skilful to destroy.[4889]

32 Thou shalt be for fuel to the fire; thy blood[1818] shall be in the midst of the land; [a]thou shalt be no *more* remembered: for I the LORD have spoken[1696] *it.*

The Sins of Jerusalem

22 Moreover the word[1697] of the LORD came unto me, saying,

---

14 [b]1Kgs. 20:30; 22:25

15 [I]Or, *glittering, or, fear* [II]Or, *sharpened* [a]Ezek. 21:10, 28

16 [I]Hebr. *set thyself, take the left hand* [a]Ezek. 14:17

17 [a]Ezek. 21:14, 22:13 [b]Ezek. 5:13

20 [a]Jer. 49:2; Ezek. 25:5; Amos 1:14

21 [I]Hebr. *mother of the way* [II]Or, *knives* [III]Hebr. *teraphim*

22 [I]Or, battering *rams* [a]Jer. 51:14 [b]Ezek. 4:2

23 [I]Or, *for the oaths made unto them* [a]Ezek. 17:13, 15, 16, 18

25 [a]2Chr. 36:13; Jer. 52:2; Ezek. 17:19 [b]Ezek. 21:29; 35:5

26 [a]Ezek. 17:24; Luke 1:52

27 [I]Hebr. *Perverted, perverted, perverted, will I make it* [a]Gen. 49:10; Ezek. 21:13; Luke 1:32, 33; John 1:49

28 [a]Jer. 49:1; Ezek. 25:2, 3, 6; Zeph. 2:8, 9, 10 [b]Ezek. 21:9, 10

29 [a]Ezek. 12:24; 22:28 [b]Job 18:20; Ps. 37:13; Ezek. 21:25

30 [I]Or, *Cause it to return* [a]Jer. 47:6, 7 [b]Gen. 15:14; Ezek. 16:38 [c]Ezek. 16:3

31 [I]Or, *burning* [a]Ezek. 7:8; 14:19; 22:22 [b]Ezek. 22:20, 21

32 [a]Ezek. 25:10

2 Now, thou son[1121] of man,[120] [a]wilt
thou [I]judge,[8199] wilt thou judge [b]the
[II]bloody[1818] city? yea, thou shalt [III][c]shew
her all her abominations.[8441]
3 Then say[559] thou, Thus saith the
Lord[136] GOD, The city sheddeth[8210] blood
in the midst of it, that her time[6256] may
come, and maketh[6213] idols[1544] against
herself to defile[2930] herself.
4 Thou art become guilty[816] in thy
blood that thou hast [a]shed; and hast defiled thyself in thine idols which thou
hast made; and thou hast caused thy
days[3117] to draw near,[7126] and art come
even unto thy years: [b]therefore have I
made thee a reproach[2781] unto the
heathen,[1471] and a mocking to all countries.[776]
5 *Those that be* near, and *those that
be* far from thee, shall mock thee, *which
art* [I]infamous *and* much vexed.[4103]
6 Behold, [a]the princes[5387] of Israel,
every one[376] were in thee to their [I]power
to shed blood.
7 In thee have they [a]set light by
father[1] and mother:[517] in the midst of
thee have they [b]dealt[6213] by [I]oppression
with the stranger:[1616] in thee have they
vexed[3238] the fatherless and the widow.
8 Thou hast [a]despised mine holy
things,[6944] and hast [b]profaned[2490] my
sabbaths.[7676]
9 In thee are [I][a]men[582] that carry tales
to shed blood: [b]and in thee they eat upon
the mountains: in the midst of thee they
commit[6213] lewdness.[2154]
10 In thee have they [a]discovered their
fathers'[1] nakedness:[6172] in thee have they
humbled her that was [b]set apart for
pollution.[2931]
11 And [I]one hath committed
abomination[8441] [a]with his neighbour's[7453]
wife;[802] and another[376] [b]hath [II]lewdly defiled his daughter in law; and another in
thee hath humbled his [c]sister,[269] his father's daughter.
12 In thee [a]have they taken gifts to
shed blood; [b]thou hast taken usury and
increase, and thou hast greedily
gained[1214] of thy neighbours[7453] by extortion, and [c]hast forgotten me, saith[5002]
the Lord GOD.

13 Behold, therefore I have [a]smit-
ten[5221] mine hand at thy dishonest gain
which thou hast made, and at thy blood
which hath been in the midst of thee.
14 [a]Can thine heart[3820] endure, or
can[2388] thine hands[3027] be strong,[2388] in
the days that I shall deal[6213] with thee?
[b]I the LORD have spoken[1696] *it,* and will
do[6213] *it.*
15 And [a]I will scatter thee among the
heathen, and disperse thee in the countries, and [b]will consume thy filthiness[2932]
out of thee.
16 And thou [I]shalt take thine inheritance in thyself in the sight of the heathen, and [a]thou shalt know[3045] that I *am*
the LORD.
17 And the word of the LORD came
unto me, saying,
18 Son of man,[120] [a]the house[1004] of
Israel is to me become[1961] dross:[5509] all
they *are* brass, and tin, and iron, and
lead, in the midst of the furnace; they are
even the [I]dross of silver.
19 Therefore thus saith the Lord
GOD; Because ye are all become dross,
behold, therefore I will gather[6908] you
into the midst of Jerusalem.
20 [I]As they gather[6910] silver, and
brass, and iron, and lead, and tin, into the
midst of the furnace, to blow the fire
upon it, to melt *it;* so will I gather *you* in
mine anger[639] and in my fury, and I will
leave *you there,* and melt you.
21 Yea, I will gather[3664] you, and
[a]blow upon you in the fire of my wrath,
and ye shall be melted in the midst
thereof.
22 As silver is melted in the midst of
the furnace, so shall ye be melted in the
midst thereof; and ye shall know that I
the LORD have [a]poured out[8210] my fury
upon you.
23 And the word of the LORD came
unto me, saying,
24 Son of man, say unto her, Thou
art the land[776] that is not cleansed,[2891]
nor rained upon in the day[3117] of indignation.[2195]
25 [a]*There is* a conspiracy of her
prophets[5030] in the midst thereof, like
a roaring lion ravening the prey; they

2 IOr, *plead for* IIHebr. *city of bloods* IIIHebr. *make her know* [a]Ezek. 20:4; 23:36 [b]Ezek. 24:6, 9; Nah. 3:1 [c]Ezek. 16:2
4 [a]2Kgs. 21:16 [b]Deut. 28:37; 1Kgs. 9:7; Ezek. 5:14; Dan. 9:16
5 IHebr. *polluted of name, much in vexation*
6 IHebr. *arm* [a]Isa. 1:23; Mic. 3:1-3; Zeph. 3:3
7 IOr, *deceit* [a]Deut. 27:16 [b]Ex. 22:21, 22
8 [a]Ezek. 22:26 [b]Lev. 19:30; Ezek. 23:38
9 IHebr. *men of slanders* [a]Ex. 23:1; Lev. 19:16 [b]Ezek. 18:6, 11
10 [a]Lev. 18:7, 8; 20:11; 1Cor. 5:1 [b]Lev. 18:19; 20:18; Ezek. 18:6
11 IOr, *every one* IIOr, *by lewdness* [a]Lev. 18:20; 20:10; Deut. 22:22; Jer. 5:8; Ezek. 18:11 [b]Lev. 18:15; 20:12 [c]Lev. 18:9; 20:17
12 [a]Ex. 23:8; Deut. 16:19; 27:25 [b]Ex. 22:25; Lev. 25:36; Deut. 23:19; Ezek. 18:13 [c]Deut. 32:18; Jer. 3:21; Ezek. 23:35
13 [a]Ezek. 21:17
14 [a]Ezek. 21:7 [b]Ezek. 17:24
15 [a]Deut. 4:27; 28:25, 64; Ezek. 12, 14, 15 [b]Ezek. 23:27, 48
16 IOr, *shalt be profaned* [a]Ps. 9:16; Ezek. 6:7
18 IHebr. *drosses* [a]Isa. 1:22; Jer. 6:28; Ps. 119:119
20 IHebr. *According to the gathering*
21 [a]Ezek. 22:20-22
22 [a]Ezek. 20:8, 33; 22:31
25 [a]Hos. 6:9

[b]have devoured souls; [c]they have taken
the treasure and precious things; they
have made her many widows in the midst
thereof.
26 [a]Her priests[3548] have [I]violated[2554]
my law,[8451] and have [b]profaned mine
holy things: they have put no [c]differ-
ence[914] between the holy and profane,[2455]
neither have they shewed[3045] *difference*
between the unclean[2931] and the
clean,[2889] and have hid their eyes from
my sabbaths, and I am profaned among
them.
27 Her [a]princes[8269] in the midst[7130]
thereof *are* like wolves ravening the prey,
to shed blood, *and* to destroy[6] souls, to
get dishonest gain.
28 And [a]her prophets have daubed
them with untempered[8602] *morter,*
[b]seeing vanity,[7723] and divining[7080]
lies[3577] unto them, saying, Thus saith
the Lord GOD, when the LORD hath not
spoken.
29 [a]The people[5971] of the land have
used [I]oppression, and exercised robbery,
and have vexed the poor and needy: yea,
they have [b]oppressed the stranger
[II]wrongfully.
30 [a]And I sought for a man[376]
among them, that should [b]make up the
hedge, and [c]stand in the gap before me
for the land, that I should not destroy[7843]
it: but I found none.
31 Therefore have I [a]poured out mine
indignation upon them; I have consumed[3615] them with the fire of my
wrath: [b]their own way[1870] have I recompensed upon their heads,[7218] saith the
Lord GOD.

The Sin of Aholah and Aholibah

23 The word[1697] of the LORD came
again unto me, saying,
2 Son[1121] of man,[120] there were
[a]two women,[802] the daughters of one
mother:[517]
3 And [a]they committed whoredoms[2181] in Egypt; they committed
whoredoms in [b]their youth: there
were their breasts pressed, and there
they bruised[6213] the teats of their virginity.[1331]
4 And the names of them *were*
Aholah the elder, and Aholibah her
sister:[269] and [a]they were mine, and they
bare sons and daughters. Thus *were* their
names; Samaria *is* Aholah, and Jerusalem
[b]Aholibah.
5 And Aholah played the harlot
when she was mine; and she doted[5689] on
her lovers,[157] on [a]the Assyrians *her*
neighbours,
6 Which *were* clothed with blue,
captains[6346] and rulers,[5461] all of them
desirable young men, horsemen riding
upon horses.
7 Thus she [I]committed her whoredoms[8457] with them, with all them *that*
were [II]the chosen men of Assyria, and
with all on whom she doted: with all their
idols[1544] she defiled herself.[2930]
8 Neither left[5800] she her whoredoms
brought [a]from Egypt: for in her youth
they lay with her, and they bruised the
breasts of her virginity, and poured[8210]
their whoredom upon her.
9 Wherefore I have delivered her into
the hand[3027] of her lovers, into the hand
of the [a]Assyrians, upon whom she doted.
10 These [a]discovered her nakedness:[6172] they took her sons and her
daughters, and slew her with the
sword:[2719] and she became [I]famous
among women; for they had executed[6213]
judgment upon her.
11 And [a]when her sister Aholibah
saw[7200] *this,* [Ib]she was more corrupt[7843]
in her inordinate love than she, and in
her whoredoms[2183] [II]more than her sister
in *her* whoredoms.
12 She doted upon the [a]Assyrians
her neighbours, [b]captains and rulers
clothed most gorgeously,[4358] horsemen
riding upon horses, all of them desirable
young men.
13 Then I saw that she was defiled,
that they *took* both one way,[1870]
14 And *that* she increased[3254] her
whoredoms:[8457] for when she saw men[582]
pourtrayed[2707] upon the wall, the images[6754] of the Chaldeans pourtrayed[2710]
with vermilion,[8350]

25 [b]Matt. 23:14 [c]Mic. 3:11; Zeph. 3:3, 4
26 [I]Hebr. *offered violence to* [a]Mal. 2:8 [b]Lev. 22:2; 1Sam. 2:29 [c]Lev. 10:10; Jer. 15:19; Ezek. 44:23
27 [a]Isa. 1:23; Ezek. 22:6; Mic. 3:2, 3, 9-11; Zeph. 3:3
28 [a]Ezek. 13:10 [b]Ezek. 13:6, 7; 21:29
29 [I]Or, *deceit* [II]Hebr. *without right* [a]Jer. 5:26-28; Ezek. 18:12 [b]Ex. 22:21; 23:9; Lev. 19:33; Ezek. 22:7
30 [a]Jer. 5:1 [b]Ezek. 13:5 [c]Ps. 106:23
31 [a]Ezek. 22:22 [b]Ezek. 9:10; 11:21; 16:43
2 [a]Jer. 3:7, 8, 10; Ezek. 16:46
3 [a]Lev. 17:7; Josh. 24:14; Ezek. 20:8 [b]Ezek. 16:22
4 [a]Ezek. 16:8, 20 [b]1Kgs. 8:29
5 [a]2Kgs. 15:19; 16:7; 17:3; Hos. 8:9
7 [I]Hebr. *bestowed her whoredoms upon them* [II]Hebr. *the choice of the children of Asshur*
8 [a]Ezek. 23:3
9 [a]2Kgs. 17:3-6, 23; 18:9-11
10 [I]Hebr. *a name* [a]Ezek. 16:37, 41
11 [I]Hebr. *she corrupted her inordinate love more than* [II]Hebr. *more than the whoredoms of her sister* [a]Jer. 3:8 [b]Jer. 3:11; Ezek. 16:47, 51
12 [a]2Kgs. 16:7, 10; 2Chr. 28:16-23; Ezek. 16:28 [b]Ezek. 23:6, 23

15 Girded with girdles[232] upon their loins, exceeding in dyed attire upon their heads,[7218] all of them princes[7991] to look to, after the manner of the Babylonians of Chaldea, the land[776] of their nativity:

16 [a]And [I]as soon as she saw them with her eyes, she doted upon them, and sent messengers unto them into Chaldea.

17 And the [I]Babylonians came to her into the bed of love,[1730] and they defiled her with their whoredom, and she was polluted[2930] with them, and [a]her mind[5315] was [II]alienated[3363] from them.

18 So she discovered her whoredoms, and discovered her nakedness: then [a]my mind was alienated from her, like as my mind was alienated from her sister.

19 Yet she multiplied her whoredoms, in calling to remembrance[2142] the days[3117] of her youth, [a]wherein she had played the harlot in the land of Egypt.

20 For she doted upon their paramours,[6370] [a]whose flesh *is as* the flesh of asses, and whose issue *is like* the issue of horses.

21 Thus thou calledst to remembrance[6485] the lewdness[2154] of thy youth, in bruising thy teats by the Egyptians for the paps[7699] of thy youth.

The Younger Sister

22 Therefore, O Aholibah, thus saith[559] the Lord[136] GOD; [a]Behold, I will raise up thy lovers against thee, from whom thy mind is alienated, and I will bring them against thee on every side;

23 The Babylonians, and all the Chaldeans, [a]Pekod, and Shoa, and Koa, *and* all the Assyrians with them: [b]all of them desirable young men, captains and rulers, great lords[7991] and renowned,[7121] all of them riding upon horses.

24 And they shall come against thee with chariots, wagons, and wheels,[1534] and with an assembly[6951] of people,[5971] *which* shall set against thee buckler[6793] and shield and helmet round about: and I will set[5414] judgment[4941] before them, and they shall judge[8199] thee according to their judgments.

25 And I will set my jealousy against thee, and they shall deal[6213] furiously with thee: they shall take away thy nose[639] and thine ears;[241] and thy remnant[319] shall fall by the sword: they shall take thy sons and thy daughters; and thy residue[319] shall be devoured by the fire.

26 [a]They shall also strip thee out of thy clothes, and take away thy [I]fair[8597] jewels.

27 Thus [a]will I make thy lewdness to cease[7673] from thee, and [b]thy whoredom[2184] *brought* from the land of Egypt: so that thou shalt not lift up[5375] thine eyes unto them, nor remember[2142] Egypt any more.

28 For thus saith the Lord GOD; Behold, I will deliver thee into the hand *of them* [a]whom thou hatest,[8130] into the hand *of them* [b]from whom thy mind is alienated:

29 And they shall deal with thee hatefully,[8135] and shall take away all thy labour, and [a]shall leave[5800] thee naked and bare:[6181] and the nakedness of thy whoredoms shall be discovered, both thy lewdness and thy whoredoms.

30 I will do these *things* unto thee, because thou hast [a]gone a whoring[2181] after the heathen,[1471] *and* because thou art polluted with their idols.

31 Thou hast walked in the way of thy sister; therefore will I give her [a]cup into thine hand.

32 Thus saith the Lord GOD; Thou shalt drink of thy sister's[269] cup deep and large: [a]thou shalt be laughed to scorn and had in derision; it containeth much.

33 Thou shalt be filled with drunkenness[7943] and sorrow, with the cup of astonishment[8047] and desolation,[8077] with the cup of thy sister Samaria.

34 Thou shalt [a]even drink it and suck *it* out, and thou shalt break[1633] the sherds[2789] thereof, and pluck off thine

16 [I]Hebr. *at the sight of her eyes* [a]2Kgs. 24:1; Ezek. 16:29
17 [I]Hebr. *children of Babel* [II]Hebr. *loosed,* or, *disjointed* [a]Ezek. 23:22, 28
18 [a]Jer. 6:8
19 [a]Ezek. 23:3
20 [a]Ezek. 16:26
22 [a]Ezek. 16:37; 23:28
23 [a]Jer. 50:21 [b]Ezek. 23:12
26 [I]Hebr. *instruments of thy decking* [a]Ezek. 16:39
27 [a]Ezek. 16:41; 22:15 [b]Ezek. 23:3, 19
28 [a]Ezek. 16:37 [b]Ezek. 23:17
29 [a]Ezek. 16:39; 23:26
30 [a]Ezek. 6:9
31 [a]Jer. 25:15
32 [a]Ezek. 22:4, 5
34 [a]Ps. 75:8; Isa. 51:17

own breasts: for I have spoken[1696] *it,* saith the Lord GOD.

35 Therefore thus saith the Lord GOD; Because thou [a]hast forgotten me, and [b]cast me behind thy back,[1458] therefore bear[5375] thou also thy lewdness and thy whoredoms.

Judgment Upon Aholah and Aholibah

36 The LORD said moreover unto me; Son of man, wilt thou [I][a]judge Aholah and Aholibah? yea, [b]declare[5046] unto them their abominations;[8441]

37 That they have committed adultery,[5003] and [a]blood[1818] *is* in their hands,[3027] and with their idols have they committed adultery, and have also caused their sons, [b]whom they bare unto me, to pass for them through *the fire,* to devour *them.*

38 Moreover this they have done[6213] unto me: they have defiled my sanctuary in the same day,[3117] and [a]have profaned[2490] my sabbaths.[7676]

39 For when they had slain[7819] their children[1121] to their idols, then they came the same day into my sanctuary[4720] to profane it; and, lo, [a]thus have they done in the midst of mine house.[1004]

40 And furthermore, that ye have sent for men [I]to come from far, [a]unto whom a messenger[4397] *was* sent; and, lo, they came: for whom thou didst [b]wash thyself,[7364] [c]paintedst thy eyes, and deckedst thyself with ornaments,

41 And satest upon a [I]stately [a]bed, and a table prepared before it, [b]whereupon thou hast set mine incense[7004] and mine oil.[8081]

42 And a voice of a multitude being at ease[7961] *was* with her: and with the men [I]of the common sort[7230] *were* brought [II]Sabeans from the wilderness, which put bracelets upon their hands, and beautiful[8597] crowns upon their heads.

43 Then said I unto *her that was* old in adulteries,[5004] Will they now commit [I]whoredoms[2181] with her, and she *with them?*

44 Yet they went in unto her, as they go in unto a woman[802] that playeth the harlot: so went they in unto Aholah and unto Aholibah, the lewd[2154] women.

45 And the righteous[6662] men, they shall [a]judge them after the manner[4941] of adulteresses,[5003] and after the manner of women that shed[8210] blood; because they *are* adulteresses, and [b]blood *is* in their hands.

46 For thus saith the Lord GOD; [a]I will bring up[5927] a company[6951] upon them, and will give them [I]to be removed and spoiled.

47 [a]And the company shall stone them with stones, and [I]dispatch them with their swords;[2719] [b]they shall slay[4191] their sons and their daughters, and burn up their houses[1004] with fire.

48 Thus [a]will I cause lewdness to cease out of the land, [b]that all women may be taught[3256] not to do[6213] after your lewdness.

49 And they shall recompense your lewdness upon you, and ye shall [a]bear the sins[2398] of your idols: [b]and ye shall know[3045] that I *am* the Lord GOD.

The Boiling Pot

24 Again in the ninth year, in the tenth month, in the tenth *day* of the month, the word[1697] of the LORD came unto me, saying,

2 Son[1121] of man,[120] write thee the name of the day,[3117] *even* of this same day: the king[4428] of Babylon set himself against Jerusalem [a]this same day.

3 [a]And utter a parable unto the rebellious[4805] house,[1004] and say unto them, Thus saith the Lord[136] GOD; [b]Set on a pot, set *it* on, and also pour water into it:

4 Gather[622] the pieces thereof into it, *even* every good[2896] piece, the thigh,[3409] and the shoulder; fill *it* with the choice bones.[6106]

5 Take the choice of the flock, and [I]burn also the bones under it, *and* make it boil well, and let them seethe the bones of it therein.

6 Wherefore thus saith the Lord GOD;

35 [a]Jer. 2:32; 3:21; 13:25; Ezek. 22:12 [b]1Kgs. 14:9; Neh. 9:26

36 [I]Or, *plead for* [a]Ezek. 20:4; 22:2 [b]Isa. 58:1

37 [a]Ezek. 16:38; 23:45 [b]Ezek. 16:20, 21, 36, 45; 20:26, 31

38 [a]Ezek. 22:8

39 [a]2Kgs. 21:4

40 [I]Hebr. *coming* [a]Isa. 57:9 [b]Ruth 3:3 [c]2Kgs. 9:30; Jer. 4:30 [d]Esth. 1:6; Isa. 57:7; Amos 2:8; 6:4

41 [I]Hebr. *honorable* [a]Prov. 7:17; Ezek. 16:18, 19; Hos. 2:8

42 [I]Hebr. *of the multitude of men* [II]Or, *drunkards*

43 [I]Hebr. *her whoredoms*

45 [a]Ezek. 16:38 [b]Ezek. 23:37

46 [I]Hebr. *for a removing and spoil* [II]Or, *single them out* [a]Ezek. 16:40

47 [a]Ezek. 16:40 [b]2Chr. 36:17, 19; Ezek. 24:21

48 [a]Ezek. 22:15; 23:27 [b]Deut. 13:11; 2Pet. 2:6

49 [a]Ezek. 23:35 [b]Ezek. 20:38, 42, 44; 25:5

2 [a]2Kgs. 25:1; Jer. 39:1; 52:4

3 [a]Ezek. 17:12 [b]Jer. 1:13; Ezek. 11:3

5 [I]Or, *heap*

Woe to [a]the bloody[1818] city, to the pot
whose scum *is* therein, and whose scum
is not gone out of it! bring it out piece
by piece; let no [b]lot fall upon it.
7 For her blood is in the midst of
her; she set[7760] it upon the top of a rock;
[a]she poured[8210] it not upon the ground,[776]
to cover[3680] it with dust;[6083]
8 That it might cause fury to come
up[5927] to take vengeance;[5359] [a]I have set
her blood upon the top of a rock, that it
should not be covered.
9 Therefore thus saith the Lord GOD;
[a]Woe to the bloody city! I will even make
the pile for fire great.
10 Heap on wood, kindle the fire,
consume the flesh, and spice it well, and
let the bones be burned.[2787]
11 Then set it empty upon the coals
thereof, that the brass of it may be hot,
and may burn, and *that* [a]the filthiness[2932]
of it may be molten in it, *that* the scum
of it may be consumed.[8552]
12 She hath wearied[3811] *herself* with
lies, and her great scum went not forth
out of her: her scum[2457] *shall be* in the
fire.
13 In thy filthiness *is* lewdness:[2154]
because I have purged thee, and thou
wast not purged, thou shalt not be
purged from thy filthiness any more,
[a]till I have caused my fury to rest upon
thee.
14 [a]I the LORD have spoken[1696] *it:* it
shall come to pass, and I will do[6213] *it;* I
will not go back,[6544] [b]neither will I spare,
neither will I repent;[5162] according to thy
ways,[1870] and according to thy doings,
shall they judge[8199] thee, saith[5002] the
LORD GOD.

6 [a]Ezek. 22:3; 23:37; 24:9 [b]2Sam. 8:2; Joel 3:3; Obad. 1:11; Nah. 3:10

7 [a]Lev. 17:13; Deut. 12:16, 24

8 [a]Matt. 7:2

9 [a]Ezek. 24:6; Nah. 3:1; Hab. 2:12

11 [a]Ezek. 22:15

13 [a]Ezek. 5:13; 8:18; 16:42

14 [a]1Sam. 15:29 [b]Ezek. 5:11

16 [I]Hebr. *go*

17 [I]Hebr. *Be silent* [II]Hebr. *upper lip* [a]Jer. 16:5-7 [b]Lev. 10:6; 21:10 [c]Ezek. 24:22 [d]2Sam. 15:30 [e]Mic. 3:7

19 [a]Ezek. 12:9; 37:18

21 [I]Hebr. *the pity of your soul* [a]Jer. 7:14; Ezek. 7:20-22 [b]Ps. 27:4 [c]Ezek. 23:47

22 [a]Jer. 16:6, 7; Ezek. 24:17

23 [a]Job 27:15; Ps. 78:64 [b]Lev. 26:39; Ezek. 33:10

The Death of Ezekiel's Wife

🔑 15 Also the word of the LORD came
unto me, saying,
16 Son of man, behold, I take away
from thee the desire[4261] of thine eyes with
a stroke: yet neither shalt thou mourn nor
weep, neither shall thy tears [I]run down.
17 [I]Forbear to cry, [a]make[6213] no
mourning for the dead,[4191] [b]bind[2280] the
tire[6287] of thine head upon thee, and [c]put
on thy shoes upon thy feet, and [d]cover
not *thy* [II][e]lips,[8222] and eat not the bread
of men.[582]
18 So I spake[1696] unto the people[5971]
in the morning: and at even my wife[802]
died; and I did in the morning as I was
commanded.[6680]
19 And the people said[559] unto me,
[a]Wilt thou not tell[5046] us what these
things are to us, that thou doest *so?*
20 Then I answered[559] them, The
word of the LORD came unto me, saying,
21 Speak unto the house of Israel,
Thus saith the LORD GOD; Behold, [a]I will
profane my sanctuary,[4720] the excellency[1347] of your strength, [b]the desire of
your eyes, and [I]that which[4263] your
soul[5315] pitieth;[4263] [c]and your sons[1121]
and your daughters whom ye have
left[5800] shall fall by the sword.[2719]
22 And ye shall do as I have
done:[6213] [a]ye shall not cover *your* lips,
nor eat the bread of men.
23 And your tires[6287] *shall be* upon
your heads,[7218] and your shoes upon
your feet: [a]ye shall not mourn nor weep;
but [b]ye shall pine away[4743] for your
iniquities,[5771] and mourn one[376] toward
another.

🔑 **24:15–24** This is a clear example of the costs involved in serving God. The names of Isaiah's and Hosea's children were signs to all Israel (Is. 7:3; 8:3, 4; Hos. 1:4, 6, 9). Hosea was told to take a wife who would be unfaithful (Hos. 1:2; 3:1). Jeremiah was told not to marry at all (Jer. 16:2). Ezekiel, however, faced a test that was even more severe. God took his wife whom he dearly loved ("the desire of [his] eyes," Ezek. 24:16), and commanded him not to mourn (Ezek. 24:16, 17). This biblical custom is often difficult for people in western cultures to understand. "Professional mourners" were hired and all who were in mourning wore sackcloth and ashes. They helped the people to externalize and cope with their grief. These actions were also regarded as a demonstration of respect for the deceased. In other words, Ezekiel's failure to mourn the death of his wife gave to the people the impression that he had no true affection for his wife, when in fact Ezekiel was obeying God's command.

24 Thus [a]Ezekiel is unto you a sign:[4159] according to all that he hath done shall ye do: [b]and when this cometh, [c]ye shall know[3045] that I *am* the Lord GOD.

25 Also, thou son of man, *shall it* not *be* in the day when I take from them [a]their strength, the joy of their glory,[8597] the desire of their eyes, and [I]that whereupon they set their minds,[5315] their sons and their daughters,

26 *That* [a]he that escapeth in that day shall come unto thee, to cause *thee* to hear *it* with *thine* ears?[241]

27 [a]In that day shall thy mouth[6310] be opened to him which is escaped, and thou shalt speak,[1696] and be no more dumb: and [b]thou shalt be a sign unto them; and they shall know that I *am* the LORD.

The Ammonites

25 The word[1697] of the LORD came again unto me, saying,

2 Son[1121] of man,[120] [a]set[7760] thy face [b]against the Ammonites, and prophesy[5012] against them;

3 And say unto the Ammonites, Hear[8085] the word of the Lord[136] GOD; Thus saith the Lord GOD; [a]Because thou saidst, Aha, against my sanctuary,[4720] when it was profaned;[2490] and against the land[127] of Israel, when it was desolate;[8074] and against the house[1004] of Judah, when they went into captivity;[1473]

4 Behold, therefore I will deliver thee to the [I]men of the east for a possession,[4181] and they shall set their palaces in thee, and make their dwellings[4908] in thee: they shall eat thy fruit, and they shall drink thy milk.

5 And I will make [a]Rabbah [b]a stable for camels, and the Ammonites a couchingplace[4769] for flocks: [c]and ye shall know[3045] that I *am* the LORD.

6 For thus saith the Lord GOD; Because thou [a]hast clapped *thine* [I]hands,[3027] and stamped[7554] with the [II]feet, and [b]rejoiced in [III]heart[5315] with all thy despite against the land of Israel;

7 Behold, therefore I will [a]stretch out mine hand[3027] upon thee, and will deliver thee for [I]a spoil to the heathen;[1471] and I will cut thee off[3772] from the people,[5971] and I will cause thee to perish[6] out of the countries:[776] I will destroy[8045] thee; and thou shalt know that I *am* the LORD.

Moab

8 Thus saith the Lord GOD; Because that [a]Moab and [b]Seir do say, Behold, the house of Judah *is* like unto all the heathen;

9 Therefore, behold, I will open the [I]side of Moab from the cities, from his cities *which are* on his frontiers,[7097] the glory[6643] of the country,[776] Beth–jeshimoth, Baal–meon and Kiriathaim,

10 [a]Unto the men of the east [I]with the Ammonites, and will give them in possession, that the Ammonites [b]may not be remembered[2142] among the nations.[1471]

11 And I will execute judgments[8201] upon Moab; and they shall know that I *am* the LORD.

Edom

12 Thus saith the Lord GOD; [a]Because that Edom hath dealt[6213] against the house of Judah [I]by taking vengeance,[5359] and hath greatly offended,[816] and revenged himself upon them;

13 Therefore thus saith the Lord GOD; I will also stretch out mine hand upon Edom, and will cut off[3772] man and beast from it; and I will make it desolate from Teman; and [I]they of Dedan shall fall by the sword.[2719]

14 And [a]I will lay my vengeance[5360] upon Edom by the hand of my people Israel: and they shall do[6213] in Edom according to mine anger[639] and according to my fury; and they shall know my vengeance, saith[5002] the Lord GOD.

---

24 [a]Isa. 20:3; Ezek. 4:3; 12:6, 11 [b]Jer. 17:15; John 13:19; 14:29 [c]Ezek. 6:7; 25:5

25 [I]Hebr. *the lifting up of their soul* [a]Ezek. 24:21

26 [a]Ezek. 33:21, 22

27 [a]Ezek. 3:26, 27; 29:21; 33:22 [b]Ezek. 24:24

2 [a]Ezek. 6:2; 35:2 [b]Jer. 49:1; Ezek. 21:28; Amos 1:13; Zeph. 2:9

3 [a]Prov. 17:5; Ezek. 26:2

4 [I]Hebr. *children* [a]Ezek. 21:20 [b]Isa. 17:2; 32:14; Zeph. 2:14, 15 [c]Ezek. 24:24, 26:6, 35:9

6 [I]Hebr. *hand* [II]Hebr. *foot* [III]Hebr. *soul* [a]Job 27:23; Lam. 2:15; Zeph. 2:15 [b]Ezek. 36:5; Zeph. 2:8, 10

7 [I]Or, *meat* [a]Ezek. 35:3

8 [a]Jer. 48:1; Amos 2:1 [b]Ezek. 35:2, 5, 12

9 [I]Hebr. *shoulder of Moab*

10 [I]Or, *against the children of Ammon* [a]Ezek. 25:4 [b]Ezek. 21:32

12 [I]Hebr. *by revenging revengement* [a]2Chr. 28:17; Ps. 137:7; Jer. 49:7, 8; Ezek. 35:2; Amos 1:11; Obad. 1:10

13 [I]Or, *they shall fall by the sword unto Dedan*

14 [a]Isa. 11:14; Jer. 49:2

The Philistines

15 Thus saith the Lord GOD; [a]Because [b]the Philistines have dealt by revenge,[5360] and have taken vengeance with a despiteful[7589] heart,[5315] to destroy[4889] *it* [I]for the old[5769] hatred;[342]

16 Therefore thus saith the Lord GOD; Behold, [a]I will stretch out mine hand upon the Philistines, and I will cut off the [b]Cherethims [c]and destroy the remnant[7611] of the [I]sea coast.

17 And I will [a]execute great [I]vengeance upon them with furious[2534] rebukes;[8433] [b]and they shall know that I *am* the LORD, when I shall lay my vengeance upon them.

Tyre

26 And it came to pass in the eleventh year, in the first *day* of the month, *that* the word[1697] of the LORD came unto me, saying,

2 Son[1121] of man,[120] [a]because that Tyrus hath said[559] against Jerusalem, [b]Aha, she is broken[7665] *that was* the gates of the people:[5971] she is turned unto me: I shall be replenished,[4390] *now* she is laid waste:[2717]

🗝 3 Therefore thus saith[559] the Lord[136] GOD; Behold, I *am* against thee, O Tyrus, and will cause[5927] many nations[1471] to come up[5927] against thee, as the sea causeth his waves to come up.

4 And they shall destroy[7843] the walls of Tyrus, and break down[2040] her towers: I will also scrape her dust[6083] from her, and [a]make her like the top of a rock.

5 It shall be *a place for* the spreading of nets[2764] [a]in the midst of the sea: for I have spoken *it,* saith the Lord GOD: and it shall become[1961] a spoil to the nations.

6 And her daughters which *are* in the field[7704] shall be slain[2026] by the sword;[2719] [a]and they shall know[3045] that I *am* the LORD.

7 For thus saith the Lord GOD; Behold, I will bring upon Tyrus Nebuchadrezzar king[4428] of Babylon, [a]a king of kings, from the north, with horses, and with chariots, and with horsemen, and companies, and much people.

8 He shall slay[4191] with the sword thy daughters in the field: and he shall [a]make a fort against thee, and [I]cast[8210] a mount against thee, and lift up the buckler[6793] against thee.

9 And he shall set engines[4239] of war against thy walls, and with his axes he shall break down thy towers.

10 By reason of the abundance of his horses their dust[80] shall cover[3680] thee: thy walls shall shake[7493] at the noise of the horsemen, and of the wheels,[1534] and of the chariots, when he shall enter into thy gates, [I]as men enter into a city wherein is made a breach.

11 With the hoofs of his horses shall he tread down all thy streets: he shall slay thy people by the sword, and thy strong garrisons[4676] shall go down to the ground.[776]

12 And they shall make a spoil of thy riches,[2428] and make a prey of thy merchandise: and they shall break down thy walls, and destroy[5422] [I]thy pleasant houses:[1004] and they shall lay[7760] thy

15 [I]Or, *with perpetual hatred* [a]Jer. 25:20; 47:1; Joel 3:4; Amos 1:6 [b]2Chr. 28:18

16 [I]Or, *haven of the sea* [a]Zeph. 2:4 [b]1Sam. 30:14 [c]Jer. 47:4

17 [I]Hebr. *vengeances* [a]Ezek. 5:15 [b]Ps. 9:16

2 [a]Jer. 25:22; 47:4; Amos 1:9; Zech. 9:2 [b]Ezek. 25:3; 36:2

4 [a]Ezek. 26:14

5 [a]Ezek. 27:32

6 [a]Ezek. 25:5

7 [a]Ezra 7:12; Dan. 2:37

8 [I]Or, *pour out the engine of shot* [a]Ezek. 21:22

10 [I]Hebr. *according to the enterings of a city broken up*

12 [I]Hebr. *houses of thy desire*

🗝 **26:3–14** This prophecy of the destruction of the city of Tyre is an illustration of the "gaps" that are evident in many prophetic chronologies (see note on Dan. 9:24–27). God announces a program of judgment against Tyre (Ezek. 26:2) in which Tyre will end up being "a place for the spreading of nets" (Ezek. 26:5). God begins with the attacks of Nebuchadnezzar, who destroyed the city on the mainland in approximately 573 B.C. after a thirteen year siege. The city was rebuilt on an island, but it was destroyed in 332 B.C. by Alexander the Great. Between the prophecies given in verses eleven and twelve there is an interval of 240 years, for it was Alexander, not Nebuchadnezzar, who laid the stones and timber in the water (Ezek. 26:12) in order to build a causeway to conquer the island city. The causeway Alexander built trapped the sand carried by the tides, and to this day fishermen do indeed spread their nets on the beaches where this great city once stood.

stones and thy timber and thy dust in the midst of the water.

13 [a]And I will cause[7673] the noise of [b]thy songs[7892] to cease;[7673] and the sound of thy harps shall be no more heard.[8085]

14 And [a]I will make thee like the top of a rock: thou shalt be *a place* to spread nets upon; thou shalt be built no more: for I the LORD have spoken *it,* saith the Lord GOD.

15 Thus saith the Lord GOD to Tyrus; Shall not the isles [a]shake at the sound of thy fall,[4658] when the wounded2491 cry, when the slaughter[2027] is made in the midst of thee?

16 Then all the [a]princes[5387] of the sea shall [b]come down from their thrones, and lay away[5493] their robes, and put off their broidered garments: they shall clothe themselves with [I]trembling;[2731] [c]they shall sit upon the ground, and [d]shall tremble[2729] at *every* moment, and [e]be astonished[8074] at thee.

17 And they shall take up[5375] a [a]lamentation for thee, and say[559] to thee, How art thou destroyed, *that wast* inhabited [I]of seafaring men, the renowned city, which wast [b]strong[2389] in the sea, she and her inhabitants, which cause their terror[2851] *to be* on all that haunt it!

18 Now shall [a]the isles tremble in the day[3117] of thy fall; yea, the isles that *are* in the sea shall be troubled[926] at thy departure.

19 For thus saith the Lord GOD; When I shall make thee a desolate[2717] city, like the cities that are not inhabited; when I shall bring up[5927] the deep upon thee, and great waters shall cover thee;

20 When I shall bring thee down [a]with them that descend into the pit,[953] with the people of old time,[5769] and shall set thee in the low parts of the earth,[776] in places desolate of old, with them that go down to the pit, that thou be not inhabited; and I shall set glory[6643] [b]in the land[776] of the living;[2416]

21 [a]I will make[5414] thee [I]a terror, and thou *shall be* no *more:* [b]though thou be sought for, yet shalt thou never be found again, saith the Lord GOD.

A Funeral Dirge for Tyre

27 The word[1697] of the LORD came again unto me, saying,

2 Now, thou son[1121] of man,[120] [a]take up[5375] a lamentation for Tyrus;

3 And say unto Tyrus, [a]O thou that art situate[3427] at the entry of the sea, *which art* [b]a merchant of the people[5971] for many isles, Thus saith[559] the Lord[136] GOD; O Tyrus, thou hast said,[559] [c]I *am* [I]of perfect[3632] beauty.

4 Thy borders *are* in the [I]midst[3820] of the seas, thy builders1129 have perfected[3634] thy beauty.

5 They have [I]made all thy *ship* boards of fir trees of [a]Senir: they have taken cedars from Lebanon to make masts for thee.

6 *Of* the oaks of Bashan have they made thine oars; [I]the company of the Ashurites have made thy benches7175 *of* ivory, *brought* out of [a]the isles of Chittim.

7 Fine linen with broidered work from Egypt was that which thou spreadest forth to be thy sail; [I]blue and purple from the isles of Elishah was that which covered4374 thee.

8 The inhabitants of Zidon and Arvad were thy mariners: thy wise[2450] *men,* O Tyrus, *that* were in thee, were thy pilots.

9 The ancients[2204] of [a]Gebal and the wise *men* thereof were in thee thy [I]calkers: and all the ships of the sea with their mariners were in thee to occupy[6148] thy merchandise.

10 They of Persia and of Lud and of [a]Phut were in thine army,[2428] thy men[582] of war: they hanged the shield and helmet in thee; they set forth thy comeliness.[1926]

11 The men of Arvad with thine army *were* upon thy walls round about, and the Gammadims were in thy towers: they hanged their shields[7982] upon thy walls round about; they have made [a]thy beauty perfect.[3634]

13 [a]Isa. 14:11; 24:8; Jer. 7:34; 16:9; 25:10 [b]Isa. 23:16; Ezek. 28:13; Rev. 18:22

14 [a]Ezek. 26:4, 5

15 [a]Jer. 49:21; Ezek. 26:18; 27:28; 31:16

16 [I]Hebr. *tremblings* [a]Isa. 23:8 [b]Jon. 3:6 [c]Job 2:13 [d]Ezek. 32:10; Ezek. 27:35

17 [I]Hebr. *of the seas* [a]Ezek. 27:32; Rev. 18:9 [b]Isa. 23:4

18 [a]Ezek. 26:15

20 [a]Ezek. 32:18, 24 [b]Ezek. 32:23, 26, 27, 32

21 [I]Hebr. *terrors* [a]Ezek. 27:36; 28:19 [b]Ps. 37:36

2 [a]Ezek. 19:1; 26:17; 28:12; 32:2

3 [I]Hebr. *perfect of beauty* [a]Ezek. 28:2 [b]Isa. 23:3 [c]Ezek. 28:12

4 [I]Hebr. *heart*

5 [I]Hebr. *built* [a]Deut. 3:9

6 [I]Or, *they have made thy hatches of ivory well trodden* [a]Jer. 2:10

7 [I]Or, *purple and scarlet*

9 [I]Hebr. *strengtheners* [a]1Kgs. 5:18; Ps. 83:7

10 [a]Jer. 46:9; Ezek. 30:5; 38:5

11 [a]Ezek. 27:3

12 [a]Tarshish *was* thy merchant[5503] by reason of the multitude of all *kind of* riches; with silver, iron, tin, and lead, they traded in thy fairs.[5801]

13 [a]Javan, Tubal, and Meshech, they *were* thy merchants: they traded [b]the persons[5315] of men[120] and vessels of brass in thy [I]market.

14 They of the house[1004] of [a]Togarmah traded in thy fairs with horses and horsemen and mules.

15 The men of [a]Dedan *were* thy merchants; many isles *were* the merchandise of thine hand:[3027] they brought thee *for* a present horns of ivory and ebony.

16 Syria *was* thy merchant by reason of the multitude of [I]the wares[4639] of thy making: they occupied in thy fairs with emeralds, purple, and broidered work, and fine linen, and coral, and [II]agate.

17 Judah, and the land[776] of Israel, they *were* thy merchants: they traded in thy market [a]wheat of [b]Minnith, and Pannag, and honey, and oil,[8081] and [I][c]balm.

18 Damascus *was* thy merchant in the multitude of the wares of thy making, for the multitude of all riches; in the wine of Helbon, and white wool.

19 Dan also and Javan going to and fro[235] occupied in thy fairs: bright iron, cassia,[6916] and calamus,[7070] were in thy market.

20 [a]Dedan *was* thy merchant in [I]precious clothes for chariots.

21 Arabia, and all the princes[5387] of [a]Kedar, [I]they occupied with[3027][5503] thee in lambs,[3733] and rams, and goats: in these *were they* thy merchants.

22 The merchants of [a]Sheba and Raamah, they *were* thy merchants: they occupied in thy fairs with chief[7218] of all spices, and with all precious stones, and gold.

23 [a]Haran, and Canneh, and Eden, the merchants of [b]Sheba, Asshur, *and* Chilmad, *were* thy merchants.

24 These *were* thy merchants in [I]all sorts *of things,* in blue [II]clothes, and broidered work, and in chests of rich apparel, bound with cords, and made of cedar, among thy merchandise.

25 [a]The ships of Tarshish did sing of thee in thy market: and thou wast replenished, and made very glorious[3513] [b]in the midst of the seas.

26 Thy rowers have brought thee into great waters: [a]the east wind[7307] hath broken[7665] thee in the [I]midst of the seas.

27 Thy [a]riches, and thy fairs, thy merchandise, thy mariners, and thy pilots, thy calkers, and the occupiers[6148] of thy merchandise, and all thy men of war, that *are* in thee, [I]and in all thy company[6951] which *is* in the midst of thee, shall fall into the [II]midst of the seas in the day[3117] of thy ruin.[4658]

28 The [I]suburbs [a]shall shake[7493] at the sound of the cry of thy pilots.

29 And [a]all that handle the oar, the mariners, *and* all the pilots of the sea, shall come down from their ships, they shall stand upon the land;

30 And shall cause their voice to be heard[8085] against thee, and shall cry[2199] bitterly, and shall [a]cast up[5927] dust[6083] upon their heads,[7218] they [b]shall wallow themselves in the ashes:

31 And they shall [a]make themselves utterly bald for thee, and gird them with sackcloth, and they shall weep for thee with bitterness[4751] of heart[5315] *and* bitter wailing.

32 And in their wailing they shall [a]take up a lamentation for thee, and lament over thee, *saying,* [b]What *city is* like Tyrus, like the destroyed[1822] in the midst of the sea?

33 [a]When thy wares[5801] went forth out of the seas, thou filledst many people; thou didst enrich the kings[4428] of the earth[776] with the multitude of thy riches and of thy merchandise.

34 In the time[6256] *when* [a]thou shalt be broken by the seas in the depths of the waters [b]thy merchandise and all thy company in the midst of thee shall fall.

35 [a]All the inhabitants of the isles shall be astonished[8074] at thee, and their kings shall be[8175] sore[8178] afraid,[8175] they shall be troubled in *their* countenance.

36 The merchants among the people

12 [a]Gen. 10:4; 2Chr. 20:36
13 [I]Or, *merchandise* [a]Gen. 10:2 [b]Rev. 18:13
14 [a]Gen. 10:3; Ezek. 38:6
15 [a]Gen. 10:7
16 [I]Hebr. *thy works* [II]Hebr. *chrysoprase*
17 [I]Or, *rosin* [a]1Kgs. 5:9, 11; Ezra 3:7; Acts 12:20 [b]Judg. 11:33 [c]Jer. 8:22
20 [I]Hebr. *clothes of freedom* [a]Gen. 25:3
21 [I]Hebr. *they were the merchants of thy hand* [a]Gen. 25:13; Isa. 60:7
22 [a]Gen. 10:7; 1Kgs. 10:1, 2; Ps. 72:10, 15; Isa. 60:6
23 [a]Gen. 11:31; 2Kgs. 19:12 [b]Gen. 25:3
24 [I]Or, *excellent things* [II]Hebr. *foldings*
25 [a]Ps. 48:7; Isa. 2:16; 23:14 [b]Ezek. 27:4
26 [I]Hebr. *heart* [a]Ps. 48:7
27 [I]Or, *even with all* [II]Hebr. *heart* [a]Prov. 11:4; Ezek. 27:34; Rev. 18:9
28 [I]Or, *waves* [a]Ezek. 26:15, 18
29 [a]Rev. 18:17
30 [a]Job 2:12; Rev. 18:19 [b]Esth. 4:1, 3; Jer. 6:26
31 [a]Jer. 16:6; 47:5; Mic. 1:16
32 [a]Ezek. 26:17; 27:2 [b]Rev. 18:18
33 [a]Rev. 18:19
34 [a]Ezek. 26:19 [b]Ezek. 27:27
35 [a]Ezek. 26:15, 16

[a]shall hiss at thee; [b]thou shalt be [I]a terror,[1091] and [II]never *shalt be* any more.

The King of Tyre

28 The word[1697] of the LORD came again unto me, saying,

2 Son[1121] of man,[120] say unto the prince[5057] of Tyrus, Thus saith the Lord[136] GOD; Because thine heart[3820] *is* lifted up, and [a]thou hast said, I *am* a God,[410] I sit *in* the seat[4186] of God,[430] [b]in the [I]midst[3820] of the seas; [c]yet thou *art* a man, and not God, though thou set thine heart as the heart of God:

3 Behold, [a]thou *art* wiser[2450] than Daniel; there is no secret that they can hide from thee:

4 With thy wisdom[2451] and with thine understanding thou hast gotten[6213] thee riches,[2428] and hast gotten gold and silver into thy treasures:

5 [I][a]By thy great wisdom *and* by thy traffick[7404] hast thou increased thy riches, and thine heart[3824] is lifted up because of thy riches:

6 Therefore thus saith the Lord GOD; Because thou hast set thine heart as the heart of God;

7 Behold, therefore I will bring strangers upon thee, [a]the terrible[6184] of the nations:[1471] and they shall draw their swords[2719] against the beauty of thy wisdom, and they shall defile[2490] thy brightness.

8 They shall bring thee down to the pit,[7845] and thou shalt die[4191] the deaths of *them that are* slain[2491] in the midst of the seas.

9 Wilt thou yet [a]say before him that slayeth[2026] thee, I *am* God? but thou *shalt be* a man, and no God, in the hand[3027] of him that [I]slayeth thee.

10 Thou shalt die the deaths[4194] of [a]the uncircumcised[6189] by the hand of strangers: for I have spoken[1696] *it,* saith the Lord GOD.

11 Moreover the word of the LORD came unto me, saying,

🗝 12 Son of man, [a]take up[5375] a lamentation upon the king[4428] of Tyrus, and say unto him, Thus saith the Lord GOD; [b]Thou sealest up the sum, full of wisdom, and perfect[3632] in beauty.

13 Thou hast been in [a]Eden the garden of God; every precious stone *was* thy covering, the [I]sardius, topaz, and the diamond, the [II]beryl, the onyx, and the jasper, the sapphire, the [III]emerald, and the carbuncle, and gold: the workmanship of [b]thy tabrets[8596] and of thy pipes was prepared[3559] in thee in the day[3117] that thou wast created.[1254]

14 Thou *art* the anointed[4473] [a]cherub[3742] that covereth; and I have set thee *so:* thou wast upon [b]the holy[6944] mountain of God; thou hast walked up and down in the midst of the stones of fire.

15 Thou *wast* perfect[8549] in thy ways[1870] from the day that thou wast created, till iniquity[5766] was found in thee.

16 By the multitude of thy merchandise they have filled the midst of thee with violence,[2555] and thou hast sinned:[2398] therefore I will cast thee as profane[2490] out of the mountain of God: and I will destroy[6] thee, [a]O covering cherub, from the midst of the stones of fire.

17 [a]Thine heart was lifted up[1361] because of thy beauty,[3308] thou hast

36 [I]Hebr. *terrors* [II]Hebr. shalt *not* be *forever* [a]Jer. 18:16 [b]Ezek. 26:21

2 [I]Hebr. *heart* [a]Ezek. 28:9 [b]Ezek. 27:3, 4 [c]Isa. 31:3

3 [a]Zech. 9:2

5 [I]Hebr. *By the greatness of thy wisdom* [a]Ps. 62:10; Zech. 9:3

7 [a]Ezek. 30:11; 31:12; 32:12

9 [I]Or, *woundeth* [a]Ezek. 28:2

10 [a]Ezek. 31:18; 32:19, 21, 25, 27

12 [a]Ezek. 27:2 [b]Ezek. 27:3; 28:3

13 [I]Or, *ruby* [II]Or, *chrysolite* [III]Or, *chrysoprase* [a]Ezek. 31:8, 9 [b]Ezek. 26:13

14 [a]Ex. 25:20; Ezek. 28:16 [b]Ezek. 20:40

16 [a]Ezek. 28:14

17 [a]Ezek. 28:2, 5

🗝 **28:12–19** This oracle is similar to the one found in Isaiah chapter fourteen, in that each begins as a prophecy against an earthly ruler, but leads into an oracle against Satan, the real power behind the pagan king. In Isaiah, the ruler of Babylon is the initial subject, while in this passage Ezekiel begins with the ruler of Tyre. Here the change in the person spoken to is made plain by the use of the term "prince" (Ezek. 28:2) instead of "king" (Ezek. 28:12). Some scholars claim that this passage refers to an earthly king, but the word "cherub" (Ezek. 28:14, 16) is used in Scripture only of angelic beings (Gen. 3:24; Ex. 25:18–20; Ezek. 9:3; 10:1–22). Moreover, this individual was "in Eden the garden of God" (Ezek. 28:13), "upon the holy mountain of God" (cf. Is. 14:13), "walked . . . in the midst of the stones of fire" (v. 14), and was "created" (v. 15).

corrupted[7843] thy wisdom by reason of thy brightness: I will cast thee to the ground,[776] I will lay thee before kings,[4428] that they may behold[7200] thee.

18 Thou hast defiled thy sanctuaries[4720] by the multitude of thine iniquities,[5771] by the iniquity of thy traffick; therefore will I bring forth a fire from the midst of thee, it shall devour thee, and I will bring thee to ashes upon the earth[776] in the sight of all them that behold thee.

19 All they that know[3045] thee among the people[5971] shall be astonished[8074] at thee: [a]thou shalt be [I]a terror, and never *shalt* thou *be* any more.

Zidon

20 Again the word of the LORD came unto me, saying,

21 Son of man, [a]set[7760] thy face [b]against Zidon, and prophesy[5012] against it,

22 And say, Thus saith the Lord GOD: [a]Behold, I *am* against thee, O Zidon; and I will be glorified in the midst of thee: and [b]they shall know that I *am* the LORD, when I shall have executed[6213] judgments[8201] in her, and shall be [c]sanctified[6942] in her.

23 [a]For I will send into her pestilence,[1698] and blood[1818] into her streets; and the wounded[2491] shall be judged[5307] in the midst of her by the sword[2719] upon her on every side; and they shall know that I *am* the LORD.

Israel

24 And there shall be no more a [a]pricking brier unto the house[1004] of Israel, nor *any* grieving thorn of all *that are* round about them, that despised them; and they shall know that I *am* the Lord GOD.

25 Thus saith the Lord GOD; When I shall have [a]gathered[6908] the house of Israel from the people among whom they are scattered, and shall be [b]sanctified in them in the sight of the heathen,[1471] then shall they dwell in their land[127] that I have given to my servant[5650] Jacob.

26 And they shall [a]dwell [I]safely[983] therein, and shall [b]build houses,[1004] and [c]plant vineyards; yea, they shall dwell with confidence,[983] when I have executed judgments upon all those that [II]despise them round about them; and they shall know that I *am* the LORD their God.

19 [I]Hebr. *terrors* [a]Ezek. 26:21; 27:36

21 [a]Ezek. 6:2; 25:2; 29:2 [b]Isa. 23:4, 12; Jer. 25:22; 27:3; Ezek. 32:30

22 [a]Ex. 14:4, 17; Ezek. 39:13 [b]Ps. 9:16 [c]Ezek. 20:41; 28:25; 36:23

23 [a]Ezek. 38:22

24 [a]Num. 33:55; Josh. 23:13

25 [a]Isa. 11:12; Ezek. 11:17; 20:41; 34:13; 37:21 [b]Ezek. 28:22

26 [I]Or, *with confidence* [II]Or, *spoil* [a]Jer. 23:6; Ezek. 36:28 [b]Isa. 65:21; Amos 9:14 [c]Jer. 31:5

2 [a]Ezek. 28:21 [b]Isa. 19:1; Jer. 25:19; 46:2, 25

3 [a]Jer. 44:30; Ezek. 28:22; 29:10 [b]Ps. 74:13, 14; Isa. 27:1; 51:9; Ezek. 32:2 [c]Ezek. 28:2

4 [a]Isa. 37:29; Ezek. 38:4

5 [I]Hebr. *face of the field* [a]Jer. 8:2; 16:4; 25:33 [b]Jer. 7:33; 34:20

6 [a]2Kgs. 18:21; Isa. 36:6

7 [a]Jer. 37:5, 7, 11; Ezek. 17:17

Egypt

29 In the tenth year, in the tenth *month,* in the twelfth *day* of the month, the word[1697] of the LORD came unto me, saying,

2 Son[1121] of man,[120] [a]set[7760] thy face against Pharaoh king[4428] of Egypt, and prophesy[5012] against him, and [b]against all Egypt:

3 Speak,[1696] and say, Thus saith the Lord[136] GOD; [a]Behold, I *am* against thee, Pharaoh king of Egypt, the great [b]dragon[8577] that lieth in the midst of his rivers, [c]which hath said, My river *is* mine own, and I have made *it* for myself.

4 But [a]I will put hooks in thy jaws, and I will cause the fish[1710] of thy rivers to stick unto thy scales, and I will bring thee up out of the midst of thy rivers, and all the fish of thy rivers shall stick unto thy scales.

5 And I will leave[5203] thee *thrown* into the wilderness, thee and all the fish of thy rivers: thou shalt fall upon the [I]open fields;[7704] [a]thou shalt not be brought together, nor gathered:[6908] [b]I have given thee for meat to the beasts[2416] of the field and to the fowls of the heaven.[8064]

6 And all the inhabitants of Egypt shall know[3045] that I *am* the LORD, because they have been a [a]staff of reed to the house[1004] of Israel.

7 [a]When they took hold of thee by thy hand,[3709] thou didst break, and rend all their shoulder: and when they leaned[8172] upon thee, thou brakest,[7665] and madest all their loins to be at a stand.[5975]

8 Therefore thus saith the Lord GOD;

Behold, I will bring [a]a sword[2719] upon thee, and cut off[3772] man and beast out of thee.

9 And the land[776] of Egypt shall be desolate[8077] and waste;[2723] and they shall know that I *am* the LORD: because he hath said, The river *is* mine, and I have made[6213] *it.*

10 Behold, therefore I *am* against thee, and against thy rivers, [a]and I will make the land of Egypt [I]utterly waste *and* desolate, [IIb]from the tower of [III]Syene even unto the border of Ethiopia.

11 [a]No foot of man shall pass[5674] through it, nor foot of beast shall pass through it, neither shall it be inhabited forty years.

12 [a]And I will make the land of Egypt desolate in the midst of the countries[776] *that are* desolate,[8074] and her cities among the cities *that are* laid waste[2717] shall be desolate forty years: and I will scatter the Egyptians among the nations,[1471] and will disperse them through the countries.

13 Yet thus saith the Lord GOD; At the [a]end of forty years will I gather[6908] the Egyptians from the people[5971] whither they were scattered:

14 And I will bring again[7725] the captivity[7622] of Egypt, and will cause them to return[7725] *into* the land of Pathros, into the land of their [I]habitation; and they shall be there a [IIa]base[8217] kingdom.[4467]

15 It shall be the basest of the kingdoms;[4467] neither shall it exalt itself[5375] any more above the nations: for I will diminish them, that they shall no more rule[7287] over the nations.

16 And it shall be no more [a]the confidence[4009] of the house of Israel, which bringeth[2142] *their* iniquity[5771] to remembrance,[2142] when they shall look after them: but they shall know that I *am* the Lord GOD.

Nebuchadrezzar's Conquests

17 And it came to pass in the seven and twentieth year, in the first[7223] *month,* in the first *day* of the month, the word of the LORD came unto me, saying,

18 Son of man, [a]Nebuchadrezzar king of Babylon caused his army[2428] to serve[5647] a great service[5656] against Tyrus: every head[7218] *was* made bald, and every shoulder *was* peeled:[4803] yet had he no wages, nor his army, for Tyrus, for the service that he had served against it:

19 Therefore thus saith the Lord GOD; Behold, I will give the land of Egypt unto Nebuchadrezzar king of Babylon; and he shall take[5375] her multitude, and [I]take her spoil, and take her prey; and it shall be the wages for his army.

20 I have given him the land of Egypt [I]*for* his labour wherewith he [a]served against it, because they wrought for me, saith[5002] the Lord GOD.

21 In that day[3117] [a]will I cause the horn of the house of Israel to bud forth, and I will give thee [b]the opening of the mouth[6310] in the midst of them; and they shall know that I *am* the LORD.

God Will Punish Egypt

30 The word[1697] of the LORD came again unto me, saying,

2 Son[1121] of man,[120] prophesy[5012] and say,[559] Thus saith the Lord[136] GOD; [a]Howl ye, Woe worth the day![3117]

3 For [a]the day *is* near, even the day of the LORD *is* near, a cloudy day; it shall be the time[6256] of the heathen.[1471]

4 And the sword[2719] shall come upon Egypt, and great [I]pain shall be in Ethiopia, when the slain[2491] shall fall in Egypt, and they [a]shall take away her multitude, and [b]her foundations[3247] shall be broken down.

5 Ethiopia, and [Ia]Libya, and Lydia, and [b]all the mingled people,[6154] and Chub, and the [II]men of the land[776] that is in league,[1285] shall fall with them by the sword.

6 Thus saith the LORD; They also that uphold Egypt shall fall; and the pride of her power shall come down:

---

8 [a]Ezek. 14:17; 32:11-13

10 [I]Hebr. *wastes of waste* [II]Or, *from Migdol to Syene* [III]Hebr. *Seveneh* [a]Ezek. 30:12 [b]Ex. 14:2; Jer. 44:1; Ezek. 30:6

12 [a]Ezek. 32:13 [b]Ezek. 30:7, 26

13 [a]Isa. 19:23; Jer. 46:26

14 [I]Or, *birth* [II]Hebr. *low* [a]Ezek. 17:6, 14

16 [a]Isa. 30:2, 3; 36:4, 6

18 [a]Jer. 27:6; Ezek. 26:7, 8

19 [I]Hebr. *spoil her spoil, and prey her prey*

20 [I]Or, *for his hire* [a]Jer. 25:9

21 [a]Ps. 132:17 [b]Ezek. 24:27

2 [a]Isa. 13:6

3 [a]Ezek. 7:7, 12; Joel 2:1; Zeph. 1:7

4 [I]Or, *fear* [a]Ezek. 29:19 [b]Jer. 50:15 [c]Jer. 25:20, 24

5 [I]Hebr. *Phut* [II]Hebr. *children* [a]Ezek. 27:10

[I][a]from the tower of Syene shall they fall
in it by the sword, saith the Lord GOD.
7 [a]And they shall be desolate[8074] in
the midst of the countries[776] *that are* desolate, and her cities shall be in the midst
of the cities *that are* wasted.[2717]
8 And they shall know[3045] that I *am*
the LORD, when I have set a fire in Egypt,
and *when* all her helpers shall be
[I]destroyed.[7665]
9 In that day [a]shall messengers go
forth from me in ships to make[2729] the
careless[983] Ethiopians afraid,[2729] and
great pain[2479] shall come upon them, as
in the day of Egypt: for, lo, it cometh.
10 Thus saith the Lord GOD; [a]I will
also make the multitude of Egypt to
cease[7673] by the hand[3027] of Nebuchadrezzar king[4428] of Babylon.
11 He and his people with him, [a]the
terrible of the nations,[1471] shall be
brought to destroy[7843] the land: and they
shall draw their swords[2719] against
Egypt, and fill the land with the slain.
12 And [a]I will make the rivers
[I]dry,[2724] and [b]sell the land into the hand
of the wicked:[7451] and I will make the
land waste,[8074] and [II]all that is therein, by
the hand of strangers: I the LORD have
spoken[1696] *it.*
13 Thus saith the Lord GOD; I will
also [a]destroy[6] the idols,[1544] and I will
cause *their* images[457] to cease out of
Noph; [b]and there shall be no more a
prince[5387] of the land of Egypt: [c]and I
will put a fear[3374] in the land of Egypt.
14 And I will make [a]Pathros deso-
late, and will set fire in [I][b]Zoan, [c]and will
execute judgments[8201] in No.
15 And I will pour[8210] my fury upon
[I]Sin, the strength of Egypt; and [a]I will
cut off[3772] the multitude of No.
16 And I will [a]set fire in Egypt: Sin
shall have great pain, and No shall be
rent asunder, and Noph *shall have*
distresses[6862] daily.
17 The young men of [I]Aven[206] and
of [II]Pi–beseth shall fall by the sword: and
these *cities* shall go into captivity.[7628]
18 [a]At Tehaphnehes also the day
shall be [I]darkened,[2821] when I shall
break[7665] there the yokes of Egypt: and
the pomp of her strength shall cease in
her: as for her, a cloud[6051] shall cover[3680]
her, and her daughters shall go into captivity.
19 Thus will I execute judgments in
Egypt: and they shall know that I *am* the
LORD.
20 And it came to pass in the
eleventh year, in the first[7223] *month,* in
the seventh *day* of the month, *that* the
word of the LORD came unto me, saying,
21 Son of man, I have [a]broken[7665]
the arm of Pharaoh king of Egypt; and,
lo, [b]it shall not be bound up to be healed,
to put a roller to bind[2280] it, to make it
strong[2388] to hold the sword.
22 Therefore thus saith the Lord
GOD; Behold, I *am* against Pharaoh king
of Egypt, and will [a]break his arms, the
strong,[2389] and that which was broken;
and I will cause the sword to fall out of
his hand.
23 [a]And I will scatter the Egyptians
among the nations, and will disperse
them through the countries.
24 And I will strengthen the arms of
the king of Babylon, and put my sword
in his hand: but I will break Pharaoh's
arms, and he shall groan before him with
the groanings of a deadly wounded[2491]
man.
25 But I will strengthen the arms of
the king of Babylon, and the arms of
Pharaoh shall fall down; and [a]they shall
know that I *am* the LORD, when I shall
put my sword into the hand of the king
of Babylon, and he shall stretch it out
upon the land of Egypt.
26 [a]And I will scatter the Egyptians
among the nations, and disperse[2219] them
among the countries; and they shall know
that I *am* the LORD.

A Warning to Pharaoh

31 And it came to pass in the
eleventh year, in the third *month,*
in the first *day* of the month, *that* the
word[1697] of the LORD came unto me, saying,
2 Son[1121] of man,[120] speak[559] unto
Pharaoh king[4428] of Egypt, and to his

6 [I]Or, *from Migdol to Syene* [a]Ezek. 29:10
7 [a]Ezek. 29:12
8 [I]Hebr. *broken*
9 [a]Isa. 18:1, 2
10 [a]Ezek. 29:19
11 [a]Ezek. 28:7
12 [I]Hebr. *drought* [II]Hebr. *the fullness thereof* [a]Isa. 19:5, 6 [b]Isa. 19:4
13 [a]Isa. 19:1; Jer. 43:12; 46:25; Zech. 13:2 [b]Zech. 10:11 [c]Isa. 19:16
14 [I]Or, *Tanis* [a]Ezek. 29:14 [b]Ps. 78:12, 43 [c]Nah. 3:8-10
15 [I]Or, *Pelusium* [a]Jer. 46:24
16 [a]Ezek. 30:8
17 [I]Or, *Heliopolis* [II]Or, *Pubastum*
18 [I]Or, *restrained* [a]Jer. 2:16
21 [a]Jer. 48:25 [b]Jer. 46:11
22 [a]Ps. 37:17
23 [a]Ezek. 29:12; 30:26
25 [a]Ps. 9:16
26 [a]Ezek. 29:12; 30:23

multitude; [a]Whom art thou like in thy greatness?

3 [a]Behold, the Assyrian *was* a cedar in Lebanon [I]with fair branches, and with a shadowing[6751] shroud,[2793] and of an high stature; and his top was among the thick boughs.

4 [a]The waters [I]made him great, the deep [II]set him up on high with her rivers running round about his plants, and sent out her [III]little rivers unto all the trees of the field.[7704]

5 Therefore [a]his height was exalted above all the trees of the field, and his boughs were multiplied, and his branches became long[748] because of the multitude of waters, [I]when he shot forth.

6 All the [a]fowls of heaven made their nests in his boughs, and under his branches did all the beasts[2416] of the field bring forth their young, and under his shadow dwelt all great nations.[1471]

7 Thus was he fair in his greatness, in the length[753] of his branches: for his root was by great waters.

8 The cedars in the [a]garden of God[430] could not hide him: the fir trees were not like his boughs, and the chesnut trees were not like his branches; nor any tree in the garden of God was like unto him in his beauty.

9 I have made him fair by the multitude of his branches: so that all the trees of Eden, that *were* in the garden of God, envied[7065] him.

10 Therefore thus saith the Lord[136] GOD; Because thou hast lifted up thyself in height, and he hath shot up his top among the thick boughs, and [a]his heart[3824] is lifted up in his height;

11 I have therefore delivered him into the hand[3027] of the mighty one[410] of the heathen;[1471] [I]he shall surely deal[6213] with him: I have driven him out for his wickedness.[7562]

12 And strangers, [a]the terrible of the nations, have cut him off,[3772] and have left[5203] him: [b]upon the mountains and in all the valleys his branches are fallen,[5307] and his boughs are broken[7665] by all the rivers of the land;[776] and all the people[5971] of the earth[776] are gone down from his shadow, and have left him.

13 [a]Upon his ruin[4658] shall all the fowls of the heaven remain, and all the beasts of the field shall be upon his branches:

14 To the end that none of all the trees by the waters exalt themselves for their height, neither shoot up their top among the thick boughs, neither their trees [I]stand up in their height, all that drink water: for [a]they are all delivered unto death,[4194] [b]to the nether parts[8482] of the earth, in the midst of the children[1121] of men,[120] with them that go down to the pit.[953]

15 Thus saith the Lord GOD; In the day[3117] when he went down to the grave[7585] I caused a mourning: I covered[3680] the deep for him, and I restrained the floods thereof, and the great waters were stayed: and I caused Lebanon [I]to mourn[6937] for him, and all the trees of the field fainted for him.

16 I made the nations to [a]shake[7493] at the sound of his fall,[4658] when I [b]cast him down to hell[7585] with them that descend into the pit: and [c]all the trees of Eden, the choice and best[2896] of Lebanon, all that drink water, [d]shall be comforted[5162] in the nether parts of the earth.

17 They also went down into hell with him unto *them that be* slain[2491] with the sword;[2719] and *they that were* his arm, *that* [a]dwelt under his shadow in the midst of the heathen.

18 [a]To whom art thou thus like in glory[3519] and in greatness among the trees of Eden? yet shalt thou be brought down with the trees of Eden unto the nether parts of the earth: [b]thou shalt lie in the midst of the uncircumcised[6189] with *them that be* slain by the sword. This *is* Pharaoh and all his multitude, saith[5002] the Lord GOD.

Lamentation for Pharaoh

32 And it came to pass in the twelfth year, in the twelfth month, in the first *day* of the month, *that* the

---

2 [a]Ezek. 31:18
3 [I]Hebr. *fair of branches* [a]Dan. 4:10
4 [I]Or, *nourished* [II]Or, *brought him up* [III]Or, *conduits* [a]Jer. 51:36
5 [I]Or, *when it sent them forth* [a]Dan. 4:11
6 [a]Ezek. 17:23; Dan. 4:12
8 [a]Gen. 2:8; 13:10; Ezek. 28:13
10 [a]Dan. 5:20
11 [I]Hebr. *in doing he shall do unto him*
12 [a]Ezek. 28:7 [b]Ezek. 32:5; 35:8
13 [a]Isa. 18:6; Ezek. 32:4
14 [I]Or, *stand upon themselves for their height* [a]Ps. 82:7 [b]Ezek. 32:18
15 [I]Hebr. *to be black*
16 [a]Ezek. 26:15 [b]Isa. 14:15 [c]Isa. 14:8 [d]Ezek. 32:31
17 [a]Lam. 4:20
18 [a]Ezek. 31:2; 32:19 [b]Ezek. 23:10; 32:19, 21, 24

word[1697] of the LORD came unto me, saying,

2 Son[1121] of man,[120] [a]take up[5375] a lamentation for Pharaoh king[4428] of Egypt, and say[559] unto him, [b]Thou art like a young lion of the nations,[1471] [c]and thou *art* as a [I]whale[8577] in the seas: and thou camest forth with thy rivers, and troubledst the waters with thy feet, and [d]fouledst their rivers.

3 Thus saith[559] the Lord[136] GOD; I will therefore [a]spread out my net[2764] over thee with a company[6951] of many people;[5971] and they shall bring thee up in my net.

4 Then [a]will I leave[5203] thee upon the land,[776] I will cast thee forth upon the open field,[7704] and [b]will cause all the fowls of the heaven[8064] to remain upon thee, and I will fill the beasts[2416] of the whole earth[776] with thee.

5 And I will lay thy flesh [a]upon the mountains, and fill the valleys with thy height.

6 I will also water with thy blood[1818] [I]the land wherein thou swimmest, *even* to the mountains; and the rivers shall be full of thee.

7 And when I shall [I]put thee out, [a]I will cover the heaven, and make the stars thereof dark;[6937] I will cover[3680] the sun with a cloud,[6051] and the moon shall not give her light.[216]

8 All the [I]bright lights[3974] of heaven will I make [II]dark over thee, and set darkness[2822] upon thy land, saith the Lord GOD.

9 I will also [I]vex[3707] the hearts[3820] of many people, when I shall bring thy destruction[7667] among the nations, into the countries[776] which thou hast not known.[3045]

10 Yea, I will make many people [a]amazed at thee, and their kings[4428] shall be horribly afraid[8175] for thee, when I shall brandish my sword[2719] before them; and [b]they shall tremble[2729] at *every* moment, every man[376] for his own life,[5315] in the day[3117] of thy fall.[4658]

11 [a]For thus saith the Lord GOD; The sword of the king of Babylon shall come upon thee.

2 [I]Or, *dragon* [a]Ezek. 27:2; 32:16 [b]Ezek. 19:3, 6; 38:13 [c]Ezek. 29:3 [d]Ezek. 34:18

3 [a]Ezek. 12:13; 17:20; Hos. 7:12

4 [a]Ezek. 29:5 [b]Ezek. 31:13

5 [a]Ezek. 31:12

6 [I]Or, *the land of thy swimming*

7 [I]Or, *extinguish* [a]Isa. 13:10; Joel 2:31; 3:15; Amos 8:9; Matt. 24:29; Rev. 6:12, 13

8 [I]Hebr. *lights of the light in heaven* [II]Hebr. *them dark*

9 [I]Hebr. *provoke to anger,* or, *grief*

10 [a]Ezek. 27:35 [b]Ezek. 26:16

11 [a]Jer. 46:26; Ezek. 30:4

12 [a]Ezek. 28:7 [b]Ezek. 29:19

13 [a]Ezek. 29:11

15 [I]Hebr. *desolate from the fullness thereof* [a]Ex. 7:5; 14:4, 18; Ps. 9:16; Ezek. 6:7

16 [a]2Sam. 1:17; 2Chr. 35:25; Ezek. 26:17; 32:2

18 [a]Ezek. 26:20; 31:14

19 [a]Ezek. 31:2, 18 [b]Ezek. 28:10; 32:21, 24

20 [I]Or, *the sword is laid*

21 [a]Isa. 1:31; 14:9, 10; Ezek. 32:27 [b]Ezek. 32:19, 25

22 [a]Ezek. 32:24, 26, 29, 30

12 By the swords[2719] of the mighty will I cause thy multitude to fall, [a]the terrible of the nations, all of them: and [b]they shall spoil[7703] the pomp of Egypt, and all the multitude thereof shall be destroyed.

13 I will destroy[6] also all the beasts thereof from beside the great waters; [a]neither shall the foot of man trouble[1804] them any more, nor the hoofs of beasts trouble them.

14 Then will I make their waters deep, and cause their rivers to run like oil,[8081] saith the Lord GOD.

15 When I shall make the land of Egypt desolate,[8077] and the country[776] shall be [I]destitute of that whereof it was full, when I shall smite[5221] all them that dwell therein, [a]then shall they know[3045] that I *am* the LORD.

16 This *is* the [a]lamentation wherewith they shall lament her: the daughters of the nations shall lament her: they shall lament for her, *even* for Egypt, and for all her multitude, saith the Lord GOD.

The Egyptians in Sheol

17 It came to pass also in the twelfth year, in the fifteenth *day* of the month, *that* the word of the LORD came unto me, saying,

18 Son of man, wail for the multitude of Egypt, and [a]cast them down, *even* her, and the daughters of the famous[117] nations, unto the nether parts[8482] of the earth, with them that go down into the pit.[953]

19 [a]Whom dost thou pass in beauty? [b]go down, and be thou laid with the uncircumcised.[6189]

20 They shall fall in the midst of *them that are* slain[2491] by the sword: [I]she is delivered to the sword: draw her and all her multitudes.

21 [a]The strong[410] among the mighty shall speak[1696] to him out of the midst of hell[7585] with them that help him: they are [b]gone down, they lie uncircumcised, slain by the sword.

22 [a]Asshur *is* there and all her com-

pany: his graves[6913] *are* about him: all of them slain, fallen[5307] by the sword:

23 [a]Whose graves are set in the sides of the pit,[953] and her company is round about her grave:[6900] all of them slain, fallen by the sword, which [b]caused [I]terror[2851] in the land of the living.[2416]

24 There *is* [a]Elam and all her multitude round about her grave, all of them slain, fallen by the sword, which are [b]gone down uncircumcised into the nether parts of the earth, [c]which caused their terror in the land of the living; yet have they borne[5375] their shame with them that go down to the pit.

25 They have set her a bed in the midst of the slain with all her multitude: her graves *are* round about him: all of them uncircumcised, slain by the sword: though their terror was caused in the land of the living, yet have they borne their shame3639 with them that go down to the pit: he is put in the midst of *them that be* slain.

26 There *is* [a]Meshech, Tubal, and all her multitude: her graves *are* round about him: all of them [b]uncircumcised, slain by the sword, though they caused their terror in the land of the living.

27 [a]And they shall not lie with the mighty *that are* fallen of the uncircumcised, which are gone down to hell [I]with their weapons of war: and they have laid their swords under their heads,[7218] but their iniquities[5771] shall be upon their bones,[6106] though *they were* the terror of the mighty in the land of the living.

28 Yea, thou shalt be broken[7665] in the midst of the uncircumcised, and shalt lie with *them that are* slain with the sword.

29 There *is* [a]Edom, her kings, and all her princes,[5387] which with their might are [I]laid by *them that were* slain by the sword: they shall lie with the uncircumcised, and with them that go down to the pit.

30 [a]There *be* the princes[5257] of the north, all of them, and all the [b]Zidonians, which are gone down with the slain; with their terror they are ashamed[954] of their might; and they lie uncircumcised with *them that be* slain by the sword, and bear[5375] their shame with them that go down to the pit.

31 Pharaoh shall see them, and shall be [a]comforted[5162] over all his multitude, *even* Pharaoh and all his army[2428] slain by the sword, saith the Lord GOD.

32 For I have caused my terror in the land of the living: and he shall be laid in the midst of the uncircumcised with *them that are* slain with the sword, *even* Pharaoh and all his multitude, saith the Lord GOD.

The Watchman's Duty

33 Again the word[1697] of the LORD came unto me, saying,

2 Son of man,[120] speak[1696] to [a]the children[1121] of thy people, and say[559] unto them, [I][b]When I bring the sword[2719] upon a land,[776] if the people[5971] of the land take a man[376] of their coasts, and set him for their [c]watchman:

3 If when he seeth[7200] the sword come upon the land, he blow[8628] the trumpet, and warn the people;

4 Then [I]whosoever heareth the sound of the trumpet, and taketh not warning;[2094] if the sword come, and take him away, [a]his blood[1818] shall be upon his own head.[7218]

5 He heard[8085] the sound of the trumpet, and took not warning; his blood shall be upon him. But he that taketh warning shall deliver his soul.[5315]

6 But if the watchman see the sword come, and blow not the trumpet, and the people be not warned; if the sword come, and take *any* person[5315] from among

23 [I]Or, *dismaying* [a]Isa. 14:15 [b]Ezek. 26:17, 20; 32:24-27, 32
24 [a]Jer. 49:34 [b]Ezek. 32:21 [c]Ezek. 32:23
26 [a]Gen. 10:2; Ezek. 27:13; 38:2 [b]Ezek. 32:19, 20
27 [I]Hebr. *with weapons of their war* [a]Ezek. 32:21; Isa. 14:18, 19
29 [I]Hebr. *given,* or, *put* [a]Ezek. 25:12
30 [a]Ezek. 38:6, 15; 39:2 [b]Ezek. 28:21
31 [a]Ezek. 31:16
1 [a]Ezek. 3:11
2 [I]Hebr. *A land when I bring a sword upon her* [a]Ezek. 14:17 [b]2Sam. 18:24, 25; 2Kgs. 9:17; Ezek. 33:7; Hos. 9:8
4 [I]Hebr. *he that hearing heareth* [a]Ezek. 18:13

33:1–20 Ezekiel had already been commissioned as a "watchman" (see Ezek. 3:17), but God renewed this commission because Ezekiel's message was being changed to one of future cleansing of the people and hope for their return to Jerusalem.

them, [a]he is taken away in his iniquity;[5771] but his blood will I require at the watchman's hand.[3027]

7 [a]So thou, O son of man, I have set thee a watchman unto the house[1004] of Israel; therefore thou shalt hear the word at my mouth,[6310] and warn them from me.

8 When I say unto the wicked,[7563] O wicked *man,* thou shalt surely die;[4191] if thou dost not speak to warn the wicked from his way,[1870] that wicked *man* shall die in his iniquity; but his blood will I require at thine hand.

9 Nevertheless, if thou warn the wicked of his way to turn[7725] from it; if he do not turn from his way, he shall die in his iniquity; but thou hast delivered[5337] thy soul.

Personal Accountability

10 Therefore, O thou son of man, speak[559] unto the house of Israel; Thus ye speak, saying, If our transgressions[6588] and our sins *be* upon us, and we [a]pine away[4743] in them, [b]how should we then live?[2421]

11 Say unto them, *As* I live, saith the Lord[136] GOD, [a]I have no pleasure in the death[4194] of the wicked; but that the wicked turn from his way and live:[2416] turn ye, turn ye from your evil[7451] ways;[1870] for [b]why will ye die, O house of Israel?

12 Therefore, thou son of man, say unto the children of thy people, The [a]righteousness[6666] of the righteous[6662] shall not deliver[5337] him in the day[3117] of his transgression:[6588] as for the wickedness[7564] of the wicked, [b]he shall not fall[3782] thereby in the day that he turneth[7725] from his wickedness;[7562] neither shall the righteous be able to live for his *righteousness* in the day that he sinneth.[2398]

13 When I shall say to the righteous, *that* he shall surely live; [a]if he trust[982] to his own righteousness, and commit iniquity,[5766] all his righteousnesses shall not be remembered;[2142] but for his iniquity that he hath committed,[6213] he shall die for it.

14 Again, [a]when I say unto the wicked, Thou shalt surely die; if he turn from his sin,[2403] and do [I]that which is lawful[4941] and right;[6666]

15 *If* the wicked [a]restore[7725] the pledge,[2258] [b]give again that he had robbed, walk in [c]the statutes[2708] of life,[2416] without committing iniquity; he shall surely live, he shall not die.

16 [a]None of his sins that he hath committed[2398] shall be mentioned[2142] unto him: he hath done[6213] that which is lawful and right; he shall surely live.

17 [a]Yet the children of thy people say, The way of the Lord is not equal:[8505] but as for them, their way is not equal.

18 [a]When the righteous turneth from his righteousness, and committeth[6213] iniquity, he shall even die thereby.

19 But if the wicked turn from his wickedness, and do that which is lawful and right, he shall live thereby.

20 Yet ye say, [a]The way of the Lord is not equal. O ye house of Israel, I will judge[8199] you every one[376] after his ways.

The News of Jerusalem's Fall

21 And it came to pass in the twelfth year [a]of our captivity,[1546] in the tenth *month,* in the fifth *day* of the month, [b]*that* one that had escaped out of Jerusalem came unto me, saying, [c]The city is smitten.[5221]

22 Now [a]the hand of the LORD was upon me in the evening, afore he that was escaped came; and had opened my mouth, until he came to me in the morning; [b]and my mouth was opened, and I was no more dumb.

23 Then the word of the LORD came unto me, saying,

24 Son of man, [a]they that inhabit those [b]wastes[2723] of the land[127] of Israel speak, saying, [c]Abraham was one, and he inherited[3423] the land: [d]but we *are* many; the land is given us for inheritance.[4181]

6 [a]Ezek. 33:8
7 [a]Ezek. 3:17
10 [a]Ezek. 24:23 [b]Isa. 49:14; Ezek. 37:11
11 [a]2Sam. 14:14; Ezek. 18:23, 32; 2Pet. 3:9 [b]Ezek. 18:31
12 [a]Ezek. 3:20; 18:24, 26, 27 [b]2Chr. 7:14
13 [a]Ezek. 3:20; 18:24
14 [I]Hebr. *judgment and justice* [a]Ezek. 3:18, 19; 18:27
15 [a]Ezek. 18:7 [b]Ex. 22:1, 4; Lev. 6:2, 4, 5; Num. 5:6, 7; Luke 19:8 [c]Lev. 18:5; Ezek. 20:11, 13, 21
16 [a]Ezek. 18:22
17 [a]Ezek. 18:25, 29; 33:20
18 [a]Ezek. 18:26, 27
20 [a]Ezek. 18:25, 29; 33:17
21 [a]Ezek. 1:2 [b]Ezek. 24:26 [c]2Kgs. 25:4
22 [a]Ezek. 1:3 [b]Ezek. 24:27
24 [a]Ezek. 34:2 [b]Ezek. 33:27; 36:4 [c]Isa. 51:2; Acts 7:5 [d]Mic. 3:11; Matt. 3:9; John 8:39

25 Wherefore say unto them, Thus saith[559] the Lord GOD; [a]Ye eat with the blood, and [b]lift up[5375] your eyes toward your idols,[1544] and [c]shed[8210] blood: and shall ye possess[3423] the land?

26 Ye stand upon your sword, ye work[6213] abomination,[8441] and ye [a]defile[2930] every one his neighbour's[7453] wife:[802] and shall ye possess the land?

27 Say thou thus unto them, Thus saith the Lord GOD; *As* I live, surely [a]they that *are* in the wastes shall fall by the sword, and him that *is* in the open field[7704] [b]will I give to the beasts[2416] [I]to be devoured, and they that *be* in the forts and [c]in the caves shall die of the pestilence.[1698]

28 [a]For I will lay the land [I]most desolate,[8077] and the [b]pomp of her strength shall cease;[7673] and [c]the mountains of Israel shall be desolate,[8074] that none shall pass through.[5674]

29 Then shall they know[3045] that I *am* the LORD, when I have laid the land most desolate because of all their abominations[8441] which they have committed.

30 Also, thou son of man, the children of thy people still are talking [I]against thee by the walls and in the doors of the houses,[1004] and [a]speak one to another, every one to his brother,[251] saying, Come, I pray you,[4994] and hear what is the word that cometh forth from the LORD.

31 And [a]they come unto thee [I]as the people cometh, and [II]they [b]sit before thee *as* my people, and they hear thy words,[1697] but they will not do them: [c]for with their mouth [III]they shew[6213] much love, *but* [d]their heart[3820] goeth after their covetousness.[1215]

32 And, lo, thou *art* unto them as [I]a very lovely song[7892] of one that hath a pleasant voice, and can play well[2895] on an instrument: for they hear thy words, but they do them not.

33 [a]And when this cometh to pass, (lo, it will come,) then [b]shall they know that a prophet[5030] hath been among them.

The Shepherds of Israel

34 And the word[1697] of the LORD came unto me, saying,

2 Son[1121] of man,[120] prophesy[5012] against the [a]shepherds of Israel, prophesy, and say[559] unto them, Thus saith the Lord[136] GOD unto the shepherds; [b]Woe *be* to the shepherds of Israel that do feed themselves! should not the shepherds feed the flocks?

3 [a]Ye eat the fat, and ye clothe you with the wool, [b]ye kill[2076] them that are fed: *but* ye feed not the flock.

4 [a]The diseased[2456] have ye not strengthened,[2388] neither have ye healed that which was sick, neither have ye bound up *that which was* broken,[7665] neither have ye brought again[7725] that which was driven away, neither have ye [b]sought that which was lost;[6] but with [c]force[2394] and with cruelty have ye ruled[7287] them.

5 [a]And they were [b]scattered, [I]because *there is* no shepherd: [c]and they became meat to all the beasts[2416] of the field,[7704] when they were scattered.

6 My sheep wandered[7686] through all the mountains, and upon every high hill: yea, my flock was scattered upon all the face of the earth,[776] and none did search or seek *after them*.

7 Therefore, ye shepherds, hear[8085] the word of the LORD;

8 *As* I live,[2416] saith[5002] the Lord GOD, surely because my flock became a prey, and my flock [a]became meat to every beast[2416] of the field, because *there was* no shepherd, neither did my shepherds search for my flock, [b]but the shepherds fed themselves, and fed not my flock;

9 Therefore, O ye shepherds, hear the word of the LORD;

25 [a]Gen. 9:4; Lev. 3:17; 7:26; 17:10; 19:26; Deut. 12:16 [b]Ezek. 18:6 [c]Ezek. 22:6, 9

26 [a]Ezek. 18:6; 22:11

27 [I]Hebr. *to devour him* [a]Ezek. 33:24 [b]Ezek. 39:4 [c]Judg. 6:2; 1Sam. 13:6

28 [I]Hebr. *desolation and desolation* [a]Jer. 44:2, 6, 22; Ezek. 36:34, 35 [b]Ezek. 7:24; 24:21; 30:6, 7 [c]Ezek. 6:2, 3, 6

30 [I]Or, *of thee* [a]Isa. 29:13

31 [I]Hebr. *according to the coming of the people* [II]Or, *my people sit before thee* [III]Hebr. *they make loves,* or, *jests* [a]Ezek. 14:1; 20:1 [b]Ezek. 8:1 [c]Ps. 78:36, 37; Isa. 29:13 [d]Matt. 13:22

32 [I]Hebr. *a song of loves*

33 [a]1Sam. 3:20 [b]Ezek. 2:5

2 [a]Ezek. 33:24 [b]Jer. 23:1; Zech. 11:17

3 [a]Isa. 56:11; Zech. 11:16 [b]Ezek. 33:25, 26; Mic. 3:1-3; Zech. 11:5

4 [a]Ezek. 34:16; Zech. 11:16 [b]Luke 15:4 [c]1Pet. 5:3

5 [I]Or, *without a shepherd* [a]Ezek. 33:21, 28 [b]1Kgs. 22:17; Matt. 9:36 [c]Isa. 56:9; Jer. 12:9; Ezek. 34:8

8 [a]Ezek. 34:5, 6 [b]Ezek. 34:2, 10

33:25, 26 The sins mentioned here almost exactly parallel those that the Jewish brethren in Jerusalem asked the Gentile Christians to avoid (Acts 15:20, 29).

10 Thus saith the Lord GOD; Behold, I *am* against the shepherds; and [a]I will require[1875] my flock at their hand,[3027] and cause them to cease[7673] from feeding the flock; neither shall the shepherds [b]feed themselves any more; for I will deliver[5337] my flock from their mouth,[6310] that they may not be meat for them.

The True Shepherd

11 For thus saith the Lord GOD; Behold, I, *even* I, will both search my sheep, and seek them out.

12 [I]As a shepherd seeketh out his flock in the day[3117] that he is among his sheep *that are* scattered; so will I seek out my sheep, and will deliver them out of all places where they have been scattered in [a]the cloudy and dark[6205] day.

13 And [a]I will bring them out from the people,[5971] and gather[6908] them from the countries,[776] and will bring them to their own land,[127] and feed them upon the mountains of Israel by the rivers,[650] and in all the inhabited places[4186] of the country.[776]

14 [a]I will feed them in a good[2896] pasture, and upon the high mountains of Israel shall their fold be: [b]there shall they lie in a good fold, and *in* a fat pasture shall they feed upon the mountains of Israel.

15 I will feed my flock, and I will cause them to lie down, saith the Lord GOD.

16 [a]I will seek that which was lost, and bring again[7725] that which was driven away, and will bind up[2280] *that which was* broken, and will strengthen[2388] that which was sick: but I will destroy[8045] [b]the fat and the strong;[2389] I will feed them [c]with judgment.[4941]

17 And *as for* you, O my flock, thus saith the Lord GOD; [a]Behold, I judge[8199] between [I]cattle and cattle, between the rams and the [II]he goats.

18 *Seemeth it* a small thing unto you to have eaten up the good pasture, but ye must tread down with your feet the residue[3499] of your pastures? and to have drunk of the deep waters, but ye must foul[7515] the residue[3498] with your feet?

19 And *as for* my flock, they eat that which ye have trodden with your feet; and they drink that which ye have fouled with your feet.

20 Therefore thus saith the Lord GOD unto them; [a]Behold, I, *even* I, will judge between the fat cattle[7716] and between the lean cattle.

21 Because ye have thrust with side and with shoulder, and pushed all the diseased with your horns, till ye have scattered them abroad;

22 Therefore will I save[3467] my flock, and they shall no more be a prey; and [a]I will judge between cattle and cattle.

23 And I will set up one [a]shepherd over them, and he shall feed them, [b]*even* my servant[5650] David; he shall feed them, and he shall be their shepherd.

24 And [a]I the LORD will be their God,[430] and my servant David [b]a prince[5387] among them; I the LORD have spoken[1696] *it*.

25 And [a]I will make with them a covenant[1285] of peace, and [b]will cause the evil[7451] beasts to cease out of the land:[776] and they [c]shall dwell safely[983] in the wilderness, and sleep in the woods.

26 And I will make them and the places round about [a]my hill [b]a blessing;[1293] and I will [c]cause the shower to come down in his season;[6256] there shall be [d]showers of blessing.

27 And [a]the tree of the field shall yield her fruit, and the earth shall yield her increase, and they shall be safe in their land, and shall know[3045] that I *am* the LORD, when I have [b]broken the bands of their yoke, and delivered[5337] them out of the hand of those that [c]served[5647] themselves of them.

28 And they shall no more [a]be a prey to the heathen,[1471] neither shall the beast of the land devour them; but [b]they shall dwell safely, and none shall make *them* afraid.[2729]

29 And I will raise up for them a [a]plant [I]of renown, and they shall be no

10 [a]Ezek. 3:18; Heb. 13:17 [b]Ezek. 34:2, 8

12 [I]Hebr. *According to the seeking* [a]Ezek. 30:3; Joel 2:2

13 [a]Isa. 65:9, 10; Jer. 23:3; Ezek. 28:25; 36:24; 37:21, 22

14 [a]Ps. 23:2 [b]Jer. 33:12

16 [a]Ezek. 34:4; Isa. 40:11; Mic. 4:6; Matt. 18:11; Mark 2:17; Luke 5:32 [b]Isa. 10:16; Amos 4:1 [c]Jer. 10:24

17 [I]Hebr. *small cattle of lambs and kids* [II]Hebr. *great he goats* [a]Ezek. 20:37, 38; 34:20, 22; Zech. 10:3; Matt. 25:32, 33

20 [a]Ezek. 34:17

22 [a]Ezek. 34:17

23 [a]Isa. 40:11; Jer. 23:4, 5; John 10:11; Heb. 13:20; 1Pet. 2:25; 5:4 [b]Jer. 30:9; Ezek. 37:24, 25; Hos. 3:5

24 [a]Ex. 29:45; Ezek. 34:30; 37:27 [b]Ezek. 37:22; Luke 1:32, 33

25 [a]Ezek. 37:26 [b]Lev. 26:6; Isa. 11:6-9; Hos. 2:18 [c]Jer. 23:6; Ezek. 34:28

26 [a]Isa. 56:7; Ezek. 20:40 [b]Gen. 12:2; Isa. 19:24; Zech. 8:13 [c]Lev. 26:4 [d]Ps. 68:9; Mal. 3:10

27 [a]Lev. 26:4; Ps. 85:12; Isa. 4:2 [b]Lev. 26:13; Jer. 2:20 [c]Jer. 25:14

28 [a]Ezek. 34:8; 36:4 [b]Jer. 30:10; 46:27; Ezek. 34:25

29 [I]Or, *for renown* [a]Isa. 11:1; Jer. 23:5

more [II]consumed[622] with hunger in the land, [b]neither bear[5375] the shame of the heathen any more.

30 Thus shall they know that [a]I the LORD their God *am* with them, and *that* they, *even* the house[1004] of Israel, *are* my people, saith the Lord GOD.

31 And ye my [a]flock, the flock of my pasture, *are* men,[120] *and* I *am* your God, saith the Lord GOD.

Edom

35 Moreover the word[1697] of the LORD came unto me, saying,

2 Son[1121] of man,[120] [a]set[7760] thy face against [b]mount Seir, and [c]prophesy[5012] against it,

3 And say[559] unto it, Thus saith the Lord[136] GOD; Behold, O mount Seir, I *am* against thee, and [a]I will stretch out mine hand against thee, and I will make thee [Ib]most desolate.

4 [a]I will lay[7760] thy cities waste,[2723] and thou shalt be desolate, and thou shalt know[3045] that I *am* the LORD.

5 [a]Because thou hast had a [Ib]perpetual[5769] hatred,[342] and hast [II]shed *the blood of* the children[1121] of Israel by the [III]force of the sword in the time[6256] of their calamity,[343] [c]in the time *that their* iniquity[5771] *had* an end:

6 Therefore, as I live,[2416] saith[5002] the Lord GOD, I will prepare thee unto blood,[1818] and blood shall pursue thee: [a]sith thou hast not hated blood, even blood shall pursue thee.

7 Thus will I make mount Seir [Ia]most desolate, and cut off[3772] from it [b]him that passeth out[5674] and him that returneth.[7725]

8 [a]And I will fill his mountains with his slain[2491] *men*: in thy hills, and in thy valleys, and in all thy rivers, shall they fall that are slain with the sword.

9 [a]I will make thee perpetual desolation, and thy cities shall not return: [b]and ye shall know that I *am* the LORD.

10 Because thou hast said, These two nations[1471] and these two countries[776] shall be mine, and we will [a]possess[3423] it; [I]whereas [b]the LORD was there:

11 Therefore, *as* I live, saith the Lord GOD, I will even do[6213] [a]according to thine anger,[639] and according to thine envy[7068] which thou hast used out of thy hatred[8135] against them; and I will make myself known[3045] among them, when I have judged[8199] thee.

12 [a]And thou shalt know that I *am* the LORD, *and that* I have heard[8085] all thy blasphemies[5007] which thou hast spoken[559] against the mountains of Israel, saying, They are laid desolate,[8074] they are given us [I]to consume.

13 Thus [a]with your mouth[6310] ye have [I]boasted against me, and have multiplied your words[1697] against me: I have heard *them*.

14 Thus saith the Lord GOD; [a]When the whole earth[776] rejoiceth, I will make[6213] thee desolate.

15 [a]As thou didst rejoice at the inheritance[5159] of the house[1004] of Israel, because it was desolate, so will I do unto thee: [b]thou shalt be desolate,[8077] O mount Seir, and all Idumea, *even* all of it: and they shall know that I *am* the LORD.

The Future Restoration of Israel

36 Also, thou son[1121] of man,[120] prophesy[5012] unto the [a]mountains of Israel, and say,[559] Ye mountains of Israel, hear[8085] the word[1697] of the LORD:

2 Thus saith the Lord[136] GOD; Because [a]the enemy hath said against you, Aha, [b]even the ancient[5769] high places[1116] [c]are ours in possession:[4181]

3 Therefore prophesy and say, Thus saith the Lord GOD; Because they have made *you* desolate,[8074] and swallowed you up on every side, that ye might be a possession unto the residue[7611] of the heathen,[1471] [a]and [I]ye are taken up[5927] in the lips[8193] of talkers, and *are* an infamy[1681] of the people:[5971]

4 Therefore, ye mountains of Israel, hear the word of the Lord GOD; Thus saith the Lord GOD to the mountains, and to the hills, to the [I]rivers, and to the val-

29 [II]Hebr. *taken away* [b]Ezek. 36:3, 6, 15
30 [a]Ezek. 34:24; 37:27
31 [a]Ps. 100:3; John 10:11

2 [a]Ezek. 6:2 [b]Deut. 2:5 [c]Jer. 49:7, 8; Ezek. 25:12; Amos 1:11; Obad. 1:10
3 [I]Hebr. *desolation and desolation* [a]Ezek. 6:14 [b]Ezek. 35:7
4 [a]Ezek. 35:9
5 [I]Or, *hatred of old* [II]Hebr. *poured out the children* [III]Hebr. *hands* [a]Ezek. 25:12; Obad. 1:10 [b]Ezek. 25:15 [c]Ps. 137:7; Ezek. 21:25, 29; Dan. 9:24; Obad. 1:11
6 [a]Ps. 109:17
7 [I]Hebr. *desolation and desolation* [a]Ezek. 35:3 [b]Judg. 5:6; Ezek. 29:11
8 [a]Ezek. 31:12; 32:5
9 [a]Jer. 49:17, 18; Ezek. 25:13; 35:4; Mal. 1:3, 4 [b]Ezek. 6:7; 7:4, 9; 36:11
10 [I]Or, *though the LORD was there* [a]Ps. 83:4, 12; Ezek. 36:5; Obad. 1:13 [b]Ps. 48:1, 3; 132:13, 14; Ezek. 48:35
11 [a]Matt. 7:2; James 2:13
12 [I]Hebr. *to devour* [a]Ps. 9:16; Ezek. 6:7
13 [I]Hebr. *magnified* [a]1Sam. 2:3; Rev. 13:6
14 [a]Isa. 65:13, 14
15 [a]Obad. 1:12, 15 [b]Ezek. 35:3, 4

1 [a]Ezek. 6:2, 3
2 [a]Ezek. 25:3; 26:2 [b]Deut. 32:13 [c]Ezek. 35:10
3 [I]Or, *ye are made to come upon the lip of the tongue* [a]Deut. 28:37; 1Kgs. 9:7; Lam. 2:15; Dan. 9:16
4 [I]Or, *bottoms, or, dales*

leys, to the desolate[8076] wastes,[2723] and to the cities that are forsaken,[5800] which [a]became a prey and [b]derision to the residue of the heathen that *are* round about;

5 Therefore thus saith the Lord GOD; [a]Surely in the fire of my jealousy have I spoken[1696] against the residue of the heathen, and against all Idumea, [b]which have appointed my land[776] into their possession with the joy of all *their* heart,[3824] with despiteful[7589] minds,[5315] to cast it out for a prey.

6 Prophesy therefore concerning the land[127] of Israel, and say unto the mountains, and to the hills, to the rivers, and to the valleys, Thus saith the Lord GOD; Behold, I have spoken in my jealousy and in my fury, because ye have [a]borne[5375] the shame of the heathen:

7 Therefore thus saith the Lord GOD; I have [a]lifted up[5375] mine hand,[3027] Surely the heathen that *are* about you, they shall bear their shame.

8 But ye, O mountains of Israel, ye shall shoot forth your branches, and yield your fruit to my people of Israel; for they are at hand[7126] to come.

9 For, behold, I *am* for you, and I will turn[6437] unto you, and ye shall be tilled and sown:

10 And I will multiply men[120] upon you, all the house[1004] of Israel, *even* all of it: and the cities shall be inhabited, and [a]the wastes shall be builded:

11 And [a]I will multiply upon you man and beast; and they shall increase and bring fruit: and I will settle you after your old estates,[6927] and will do better[2896] *unto you* than at your beginnings:[7221] [b]and ye shall know[3045] that I *am* the LORD.

12 Yea, I will cause men to walk upon you, *even* my people Israel; [a]and they shall possess[3423] thee, and thou shalt be their inheritance,[5159] and thou shalt no more henceforth [b]bereave them *of men.*

13 Thus saith the Lord GOD; Because they say unto you, [a]Thou *land* devourest up men, and hast bereaved thy nations;[1471]

14 Therefore thou shalt devour men no more, neither [1]bereave thy nations any more, saith the Lord GOD.

15 [a]Neither will I cause *men* to hear in thee the shame of the heathen any more, neither shalt thou bear the reproach[2781] of the people any more, neither shalt thou cause thy nations to fall[3782] any more, saith the Lord GOD.

16 Moreover the word of the LORD came unto me, saying,

17 Son of man, when the house of Israel dwelt in their own land, [a]they defiled[2930] it by their own way[1870] and by their doings: their way was before me as [b]the uncleanness[2932] of a removed woman.[5079]

18 Wherefore I poured[8210] my fury upon them [a]for the blood[1818] that they had shed[8210] upon the land, and for their idols[1544] *wherewith* they had polluted[2930] it:

19 And I [a]scattered them among the heathen, and they were dispersed through the countries:[776] [b]according to their way and according to their doings I judged[8199] them.

20 And when they entered unto the heathen, whither they went, they [a]profaned[2490] my holy[6944] name, when they said to them, These *are* the people of the LORD, and are gone forth out of his land.

21 But I had pity[2550] [a]for mine holy name, which the house of Israel had profaned among the heathen, whither they went.

🗝 22 Therefore say unto the house of

4 [a]Ezek. 34:28 [b]Ps. 79:4
5 [a]Deut. 4:24; Ezek. 38:19 [b]Ezek. 35:10, 12
6 [a]Ps. 123:3, 4; Ezek. 34:29; 36:15
7 [a]Ezek. 20:5
10 [a]Isa. 58:12; 61:4; Ezek. 36:33; Amos 9:14
11 [a]Jer. 31:27; 33:12 [b]Ezek. 35:9; 37:6, 13
12 [a]Obad. 1:17 [b]Jer. 15:7
13 [a]Num. 13:32
14 [1]Or, *cause to fall*
15 [a]Ezek. 34:29
17 [a]Lev. 18:25, 27, 28; Jer. 2:7 [b]Lev. 15:19
18 [a]Ezek. 16:36, 38; 23:37
19 [a]Ezek. 22:15 [b]Ezek. 7:3; 18:30; 39:24
20 [a]Isa. 52:5; Rom. 2:24
21 [a]Ezek. 20:9, 14

🗝 **36:22–38** This is a key prophecy of the regathering of Israel at the end of the Great Tribulation (see Ezek. 34:1–31), as well as a description of the New Covenant and its spiritual implications. This passage clarifies the order of events: the regathering from the nations (v. 24) will precede God's national cleansing of Israel (v. 25, cf. Zech. 13:1) and the placing of His "Spirit" within His people (Ezek. 36:26, 27; 37:14, cf. Zech. 12:10). Thus, the judgment spoken of in chapters twenty and thirty-four will take place between the gathering and the actual settling of God's people in the Promised Land.

Israel, Thus saith the Lord GOD; I do[6213] not *this* for your sakes, O house of Israel, [a]but for mine holy name's sake, which ye have profaned among the heathen, whither ye went.

23 And I will sanctify[6942] my great name, which was profaned among the heathen, which ye have profaned in the midst of them; and the heathen shall know that I *am* the LORD, saith the Lord GOD, when I shall be [a]sanctified in you before [I]their eyes.

24 For [a]I will take you from among the heathen, and gather[6908] you out of all countries, and will bring you into your own land.

25 [a]Then will I sprinkle[2236] clean[2889] water upon you, and ye shall be clean:[2891] [b]from all your filthiness,[2932] and from all your idols, will I cleanse you.

26 A [a]new heart[3820] also will I give you, and a new spirit[7307] will I put within[7130] you: and I will take away the stony heart out of your flesh, and I will give you an heart of flesh.

27 And I will put my [a]spirit within you, and cause you to walk in my statutes,[2706] and ye shall keep[8104] my judgments,[4941] and do *them.*

28 [a]And ye shall dwell in the land that I gave to your fathers;[1] [b]and ye shall be my people, and I will be your God.[430]

29 I will also [a]save[3467] you from all your uncleannesses: and [b]I will call[7121] for the corn, and will increase it, and [c]lay no famine upon you.

30 [a]And I will multiply the fruit of the tree, and the increase of the field,[7704] that ye shall receive no more reproach of famine among the heathen.

31 Then [a]shall ye remember[2142] your own evil[7451] ways,[1870] and your doings that *were* not good,[2896] and [b]shall lothe yourselves in your own sight for your iniquities[5771] and for your abominations.[8441]

32 [a]Not for your sakes do I *this,* saith the Lord GOD, be it known[3045] unto you: be ashamed[954] and confounded for your own ways, O house of Israel.

33 Thus saith the Lord GOD; In the day[3117] that I shall have cleansed[2891] you from all your iniquities I will also cause *you* to dwell in the cities, [a]and the wastes shall be builded.

34 And the desolate[8077] land shall be tilled, whereas it lay desolate in the sight of all that passed by.[5674]

35 And they shall say, This land that was desolate is become[1961] like the garden of [a]Eden; and the waste[2720] and desolate and ruined[2040] cities *are become* fenced, *and* are inhabited.

36 Then the heathen that are left[7604] round about you shall know that I the LORD build the ruined *places, and* plant that that was desolate: [a]I the LORD have spoken *it,* and I will do *it.*

37 Thus saith the Lord GOD; [a]I will yet *for* this be enquired of by the house of Israel, to do *it* for them; I will [b]increase them with men like a flock.

38 As the [I]holy flock, as the flock of Jerusalem in her solemn feasts;[4150] so shall the waste cities be filled with flocks of men: and they shall know that I *am* the LORD.

The Valley of Dry Bones

37 The [a]hand[3027] of the LORD was upon me, and carried me out

22 [a]Ps. 106:8
23 [I]Or, *your* [a]Ezek. 20:41; 28:22
24 [a]Ezek. 34:13; 37:21
25 [a]Isa. 52:15; Heb. 10:22 [b]Jer. 33:8
26 [a]Jer. 32:39; Ezek. 11:19
27 [a]Ezek. 11:19; 37:14
28 [a]Ezek. 28:25; 37:25 [b]Jer. 30:22; Ezek. 11:20; 37:27
29 [a]Matt. 1:21; Rom. 11:26 [b]Ps. 105:16 [c]Ezek. 34:29
30 [a]Ezek. 34:27
31 [a]Ezek. 16:61, 63 [b]Lev. 26:39; Ezek. 6:9; 20:43
32 [a]Deut. 9:5; Ezek. 36:22
33 [a]Ezek. 36:10
35 [a]Isa. 51:3; Ezek. 28:13; Joel 2:3
36 [a]Ezek. 17:24; 22:14; 37:14
37 [a]Ezek. 14:3; 20:3, 31 [b]Ezek. 36:10
38 [I]Hebr. *flock of holy things*
1 [a]Ezek. 1:3

37:1–38 This famous vision of the "Valley of Dry Bones" was given to Ezekiel to reassure the exiles that the promises of God are secure. After being away from their homeland for so long, they felt like dry bones; all their hope was gone. Nevertheless, God affirmed that He would bring them back to their homeland from wherever they were (vv. 12–14). Some suggest that the word "graves" (v. 12) should be understood in a dual sense. They primarily represent the foreign nations where they were exiled, but they may also be the literal graves of the righteous dead of Israel (cf. God's statement to Daniel in Dan. 12:13). This vision is explicitly concerned with God's renewal of His promises to Israel. God's Spirit is placed within Israel (Ezek. 37:14, cf. note on 36:22–38), the reign of the Messiah begins (Ezek. 37:24, 25), the confirmation of the New Covenant is given (Ezek. 37:26;

(continued on next page)

[b]in the spirit[7307] of the LORD, and set me
down in the midst of the valley which
was full of bones,[6106]
2 And caused me to pass by them
round about: and, behold, *there were* very
many in the open valley; and, lo, *they*
were very dry.[3002]
3 And he said unto me, Son[1121] of
man,[120] can these bones live?[2421] And I
answered,[559] O Lord[136] GOD, [a]thou knowest.[3045]
4 Again he said unto me, Prophesy[5012] upon these bones, and say unto
them, O ye dry bones, hear[8085] the
word[1697] of the LORD.
5 Thus saith the Lord GOD unto these
bones; Behold, I will [a]cause breath[7307] to
enter into you, and ye shall live:
6 And I will lay sinews upon you,
and will bring up[5927] flesh upon you, and
cover you with skin,[5785] and put breath
in you, and ye shall live; [a]and ye shall
know that I *am* the LORD.
7 So I prophesied as I was commanded:[6680] and as I prophesied, there
was a noise, and behold a shaking, and
the bones came together,[7126] bone[6106] to
his bone.
8 And when I beheld,[7200] lo, the
sinews and the flesh came up upon them,
and the skin covered them above: but
there was no breath in them.
9 Then said he unto me, Prophesy
unto the [1]wind,[7307] prophesy, son of man,
and say to the wind, Thus saith the Lord
GOD; [a]Come from the four winds, O
breath, and breathe upon these slain,[2027]
that they may live.
10 So I prophesied as he commanded
me, [a]and the breath came into them, and
they lived,[2421] and stood up upon their
feet, an exceeding great army.[2428]
11 Then he said unto me, Son of
man, these bones are the whole house[1004]
of Israel: behold, they say, [a]Our bones
are dried,[3001] and our hope is lost:[6] we
are cut off[1504] for our parts.

1 [b]Ezek. 3:14; 8:3; 11:24; Luke 4:1
3 [a]Deut. 32:39; 1Sam. 2:6; John 5:21; Rom. 4:17; 2Cor. 1:9
5 [a]Ps. 104:30; Ezek. 37:9
6 [a]Ezek. 6:7; 35:12; Joel 2:27; 3:17
9 [1]Or, *breath* [a]Ps. 104:30; Ezek. 37:5
10 [a]Rev. 11:11
11 [a]Ps. 141:7; Isa. 49:14
12 [a]Isa. 26:19; Hos. 13:14 [b]Ezek. 36:24; 37:25
14 [a]Ezek. 36:27
16 [a]Num. 17:2 [b]2Chr. 11:12, 13, 16; 15:9; 30:11, 18
17 [a]Ezek. 37:22, 24
18 [a]Ezek. 12:9; 24:19
19 [a]Zech. 10:6; Ezek. 37:16, 17
20 [a]Ezek. 12:3
21 [a]Ezek. 36:24

12 Therefore prophesy and say unto
them, Thus saith the Lord GOD; Behold,
[a]O my people,[5971] I will open your
graves,[6913] and cause you to come up[5927]
out of your graves, and [b]bring you into
the land[127] of Israel.
13 And ye shall know that I *am* the
LORD, when I have opened your graves,
O my people, and brought you up[5927] out
of your graves,
14 And [a]shall put my spirit in you,
and ye shall live, and I shall place you in
your own land: then shall ye know that
I the LORD have spoken[1696] *it,* and performed *it,* saith[5002] the LORD.

The Reunion of Judah and Israel

15 The word of the LORD came again
unto me, saying,
16 Moreover, thou son of man, [a]take
thee one stick, and write upon it, For
Judah, and for [b]the children[1121] of Israel
his companions: then take another stick,
and write upon it, For Joseph, the stick
of Ephraim, and *for* all the house of
Israel his companions:[2270]
17 And [a]join[7126] them one to another
into one stick; and they shall become[1961]
one in thine hand.
18 And when the children of thy
people shall speak[559] unto thee, saying,
[a]Wilt thou not shew[5046] us what thou
meanest by these?
19 [a]Say[1696] unto them, Thus saith the
Lord GOD; Behold, I will take [b]the stick
of Joseph, which *is* in the hand of
Ephraim, and the tribes[7626] of Israel his
fellows, and will put them with him, *even*
with the stick of Judah, and make[6213]
them one stick, and they shall be one in
mine hand.
20 And the sticks whereon thou
writest shall be in thine hand [a]before
their eyes.
21 And say unto them, Thus saith
the Lord GOD; Behold, [a]I will take the

(continued from previous page)
see note on Jer. 31:31–34), and God's presence and identification with His redeemed people are evident (Ezek. 37:27; see Hos. 1:10; 2:23; Rev. 21:3–7).

children of Israel from among the heathen,[1471] whither they be gone, and will gather[6908] them on every side, and bring them into their own land:

22 And [a]I will make them one nation[1471] in the land[776] upon the mountains of Israel; and [b]one king[4428] shall be king to them all: and they shall be no more two nations, neither shall they be divided into two kingdoms[4467] any more at all:

23 [a]Neither shall they defile themselves[2930] any more with their idols,[1544] nor with their detestable things,[8251] nor with any of their transgressions:[6588] but [b]I will save[3467] them out of all their dwellingplaces, wherein they have sinned,[2398] and will cleanse[2891] them: so shall they be my people, and I will be their God.[430]

24 And [a]David my servant[5650] *shall be* king over them; and [b]they all shall have one shepherd: [c]they shall also walk in my judgments,[4941] and observe[8104] my statutes,[2708] and do[6213] them.

25 [a]And they shall dwell in the land that I have given unto Jacob my servant, wherein your fathers[1] have dwelt; and they shall dwell therein, *even* they, and their children, and their children's children [b]for ever:[5769] and [c]my servant David *shall be* their prince[5387] for ever.

26 Moreover I will make a [a]covenant[1285] of peace with them; it shall be an everlasting[5769] covenant with them: and I will place them, and [b]multiply them, and will set my [c]sanctuary[4720] in the midst of them for evermore.[5769]

27 [a]My tabernacle[4908] also shall be with them: yea, I will be [b]their God, and they shall be my people.

28 [a]And the heathen shall know that I the LORD do [b]sanctify[6942] Israel, when my sanctuary[4720] shall be in the midst of them for evermore.

Gog

38 🗝And the word[1697] of the LORD came unto me, saying,

2 [a]Son[1121] of man,[120] [b]set[7760] thy face against [c]Gog, the land[776] of Magog, [1]the chief[7218] prince[5387] of [d]Meshech and Tubal, and prophesy[5012] against him,

3 And say,[559] Thus saith the Lord[136] GOD: Behold, I *am* against thee, O Gog, the chief prince of Meshech and Tubal:

4 And [a]I will turn thee back,[7725] and put hooks into thy jaws, and I will bring thee forth, and all thine army,[2428] horses and horsemen, [b]all of them clothed with all sorts of *armour, even* a great company[6951] *with* bucklers[6793] and shields, all of them handling swords:[2719]

5 Persia, Ethiopia, and [1][a]Libya with them; all of them with shield and helmet:

6 [a]Gomer, and all his bands; the house[1004] of [b]Togarmah of the north quarters, and all his bands: *and* many people[5971] with thee.

22 [a]Isa. 11:13; Jer. 3:18; 50:4; Hos. 1:11 [b]Ezek. 34:23, 24; John 10:16
23 [a]Ezek. 36:25 [b]Ezek. 36:28, 29
24 [a]Isa. 40:11; Jer. 23:5; 30:9; Ezek. 34:23, 24; Hos. 3:5; Luke 1:32 [b]Ezek. 37:22; John 10:16 [c]Ezek. 36:27
25 [a]Ezek. 36:28 [b]Isa. 60:21; Joel 3:20; Amos 9:15 [c]Ezek. 37:24; John 12:34
26 [a]Ps. 89:3; Isa. 55:3; Jer. 32:40; Ezek. 34:25 [b]Ezek. 36:10, 37 [c]2Cor. 6:16
27 [a]Lev. 26:11, 12; Ezek. 43:7; John 1:14 [b]Ezek. 11:20; 14:11; 36:28
28 [a]Ezek. 36:23 [b]Ezek. 20:12

2 [1]Or, *prince of the chief* [a]Ezek. 39:1 [b]Ezek. 35:2, 3 [c]Rev. 20:8 [d]Ezek. 32:26
4 [a]2Kgs. 19:28; Ezek. 29:4; 39:2 [b]Ezek. 23:12
5 [1]Or, *Phut* [a]Ezek. 27:10; 30:5
6 [a]Gen. 10:2 [b]Ezek. 27:14

🗝 **38:1—39:29** This prophecy of Gog and Magog is subject to considerable dispute among conservative scholars. The prophecy has two main sections: the description of the invasion of Gog and Magog (38:1–16), and the judgment that falls on them (38:17—39:29). There are several points of controversy that have arisen from this passage. One is the identity of the nations mentioned. Rosh, Meshech, Tubal, Gog, and Magog cannot be identified with any certainty, though a number of scholars attempt to identify Rosh as modern Russia. There is general agreement that these nations lie to the north of the Promised Land, since this coincides with the general prophetic descriptions of an end–time attack from the north. The second difficulty is the specific time of the attack. Suggestions include: 1) near the end of the present age; 2) during the Tribulation; 3) after Christ's return but before the Millennium; and 4) after the Millennium, or more specifically, the battle with Gog and Magog mentioned in Revelation 20:7–9. Regarding the third theory, it must be noted that the events preceding and following the battles are quite different. What must be remembered is that God is going to fulfill all of His promises to Israel, especially their restoration (Ezek. 39:25). Involved in this restoration is a renewed reverence of God and the forsaking of idolatry (Ezek. 39:22), the regathering of God's chosen people into the Promised Land (Ezek. 39:27, 28), and the outpouring of God's Spirit (Ezek. 39:29).

7 [a]Be thou prepared,[3559] and prepare
for thyself, thou, and all thy company
that are assembled[6950] unto thee, and be
thou a guard unto them.
8 [a]After many days[3117] [b]thou shalt
be visited:[6485] in the latter[319] years thou
shalt come into the land *that is* brought
back from the sword,[2719] [c]*and is*
gathered[6908] out of many people, against
[d]the mountains of Israel, which have
been always[8548] waste:[2723] but it is
brought forth out of the nations,[1471] and
they shall [e]dwell safely[983] all of them.
9 Thou shalt ascend[5927] and come
[a]like a storm,[7722] thou shalt be [b]like a
cloud[6051] to cover[3680] the land, thou, and
all thy bands, and many people with
thee.
10 Thus saith the Lord GOD; It shall
also come to pass, *that* at the same
time[3117] shall things[1697] come into thy
mind,[3824] and thou shalt [I]think[2803] an
evil[7451] thought:
11 And thou shalt say, I will go up
to the land of unwalled villages; I will
[a]go to them that are at rest,[8252] [b]that
dwell [I]safely, all of them dwelling without walls, and having neither bars nor
gates,
12 [I][a]To take a spoil, and to take a
prey; to turn thine hand[3027] upon [b]the
desolate places[2723] *that are now* inhabited, [c]and upon the people *that are*
gathered[622] out of the nations, which
have gotten[6213] cattle and goods, that
dwell in the midst of the land.
13 [a]Sheba, and [b]Dedan, and the merchants [c]of Tarshish, with all [d]the young
lions thereof, shall say unto thee, Art
thou come to take a spoil? hast thou
gathered[6950] thy company to take a prey?
to carry away[5375] silver and gold, to take
away cattle and goods, to take a great
spoil?
14 Therefore, son of man, prophesy
and say unto Gog, Thus saith the Lord
GOD; [a]In that day[3117] when my people of
Israel [b]dwelleth safely, shalt thou not
know[3045] *it?*
15 [a]And thou shalt come from thy
place out of the north parts, thou, [b]and
many people with thee, all of them riding upon horses, a great company, and a
mighty army:
16 [a]And thou shalt come up[5927]
against my people of Israel, as a cloud
to cover the land; [b]it shall be in the latter days, and I will bring thee against my
land, [c]that the heathen[1471] may know me,
when I shall be sanctified[4720] in thee, O
Gog, before their eyes.
17 Thus saith the Lord GOD; *Art*
thou he of whom I have spoken[1696] in old
time [I]by my servants[5650] the prophets[5030]
of Israel, which prophesied[5012] in those
days *many* years that I would bring thee
against them?
18 And it shall come to pass at the
same time when Gog shall come against
the land[127] of Israel, saith[5002] the Lord
GOD, *that* my fury shall come up[5927] in
my face.[639]
19 For [a]in my jealousy [b]*and* in the
fire of my wrath[5678] have I spoken,[1696]
[c]Surely in that day there shall be a great
shaking[7494] in the land of Israel;
20 So that [a]the fishes[1709] of the sea,
and the fowls of the heaven,[8064] and the
beasts[2416] of the field,[7704] and all creeping things that creep upon the earth,[127]
and all the men[120] that *are* upon the face
of the earth, shall shake[7493] at my presence, [b]and the mountains shall be thrown
down,[2040] and the [I]steep places shall fall,
and every wall shall fall to the ground.[776]
21 And I will [a]call[7121] for [b]a sword
against him throughout all my mountains, saith the Lord GOD: [c]every man's
sword shall be against his brother.[251]
22 And I will [a]plead[8199] against him
with [b]pestilence[1698] and with blood;[1818]
and [c]I will rain upon him, and upon his
bands, and upon the many people that
are with him, an overflowing[7857] rain,
and [d]great hailstones, fire, and brimstone.[1614]
23 Thus will I magnify myself, and
[a]sanctify myself;[6942] [b]and I will be
known[3045] in the eyes of many nations,
and they shall know that I *am* the LORD.

39 Therefore, [a]thou son[1121] of
man,[120] prophesy[5012] against Gog,

7 [a]Isa. 8:9, 10; Jer. 46:3, 4, 14; 51:12
8 [a]Gen. 49:1; Deut. 4:30; Ezek. 38:16 [b]Isa. 29:6 [c]Ezek. 34:13; 38:12 [d]Ezek. 36:1, 4, 8 [e]Jer. 23:6; Ezek. 28:26; 34:25, 28; 38:11
9 [a]Isa. 28:2 [b]Jer. 4:13; Ezek. 38:16
10 [I]Or, *conceive a mischievous purpose*
11 [I]Or, *confidently* [a]Jer. 49:31 [b]Ezek. 38:8
12 [I]Hebr. *To spoil the spoil, and to prey the prey* [a]Ezek. 29:19 [b]Ezek. 36:34, 35 [c]Ezek. 38:8
13 [a]Ezek. 27:22, 23 [b]Ezek. 27:15, 20 [c]Ezek. 27:12 [d]Ezek. 19:3, 5
14 [a]Isa. 4:1 [b]Ezek. 38:8
15 [a]Ezek. 39:2 [b]Ezek. 38:6
16 [a]Ezek. 38:9 [b]Ezek. 38:8 [c]Ex. 14:4; Ezek. 36:23; 39:21
17 [I]Hebr. *by the hands*
19 [a]Ezek. 36:5, 6; 39:25 [b]Ps. 89:46 [c]Hag. 2:6, 7; Rev. 16:18
20 [I]Or, *towers, or, stairs* [a]Hos. 4:3 [b]Jer. 4:24; Nah. 1:5, 6
21 [a]Ps. 105:16 [b]Ezek. 14:17 [c]Judg. 7:22; 1Sam. 14:20; 2Chr. 20:23
22 [a]Isa. 66:16; Jer. 25:31 [b]Ezek. 5:17 [c]Ps. 11:6; Isa. 29:6; 30:30 [d]Ezek. 13:11; Rev. 16:21
23 [a]Ezek. 36:23 [b]Ps. 9:16; Ezek. 37:28; 38:16; 39:7
1 [a]Ezek. 38:2, 3

and say,[559] Thus saith the Lord[136] GOD; Behold, I *am* against thee, O Gog, the chief[7218] prince[5387] of Meshech and Tubal:

2 And I will turn[7725] thee back, and [I][a]leave but the sixth part of thee, [b]and will cause thee to come up[5927] from [II]the north parts, and will bring thee upon the mountains of Israel:

3 And I will smite[5221] thy bow out of thy left hand,[3027] and will cause thine arrows to fall out of thy right hand.

4 [a]Thou shalt fall upon the mountains of Israel, thou, and all thy bands, and the people[5971] that *is* with thee: [b]I will give thee unto the ravenous birds of every [I]sort, and *to* the beasts[2416] of the field[7704] [II]to be devoured.

5 Thou shalt fall upon [I]the open field: for I have spoken[1696] *it,* saith5002 the Lord GOD.

6 [a]And I will send a fire on Magog, and among them that dwell [I]carelessly[983] in [b]the isles: and they shall know[3045] that I *am* the LORD.

7 [a]So will I make my holy[6944] name known in the midst of my people Israel; and I will not *let them* [b]pollute[2490] my holy name any more: [c]and the heathen[1471] shall know that I *am* the LORD, the Holy One[6918] in Israel.

8 [a]Behold, it is come, and it is done, saith the Lord GOD; this *is* the day[3117] [b]whereof I have spoken.

9 And they that dwell in the cities of Israel shall go forth, and shall set on fire and burn the weapons,[5402] both the shields and the bucklers,6793 the bows and the arrows, and the [I]handstaves,4731 and the spears, and they shall [II]burn them with fire seven years:

10 So that they shall take[5375] no wood out of the field, neither cut down *any* out of the forests; for they shall burn the weapons with fire: [a]and they shall spoil those that spoiled them, and rob those that robbed them, saith the Lord GOD.

11 And it shall come to pass in that day, *that* I will give unto Gog a place there of graves[6913] in Israel, the valley of the passengers[5674] on the east of the sea: and it shall stop the [I]*noses* of the passengers: and there shall they bury[6912] Gog and all his multitude: and they shall call[7121] *it* The valley of [II]Hamon–gog.

12 And seven months shall the house[1004] of Israel be burying of them, [a]that they may cleanse[2891] the land.[776]

13 Yea, all the people of the land shall bury *them;* and it shall be to them a renown the day that [a]I shall be glorified, saith the Lord GOD.

14 And they shall sever out[914] [I]men[582] of continual employment,[8548] passing through the land to bury with the passengers those that remain[3498] upon the face of the earth,[776] [a]to cleanse it: after the end of seven months shall they search.

15 And the passengers *that* pass through[5674] the land, when *any* seeth[7200] a man's[120] bone,[6106] then shall he [I]set up a sign by it, till the buriers have buried it in the valley of Hamon–gog.

16 And also the name of the city *shall be* [I]Hamonah. Thus shall they [a]cleanse the land.

17 And, thou son of man, thus saith the Lord GOD; [a]Speak[559] [I]unto every feathered fowl, and to every beast[2416] of the field, [b]Assemble[6908] yourselves, and come; gather[622] yourselves on every side to my [II]sacrifice that I do sacrifice[2076] for you, *even* a great sacrifice[2077] [c]upon the mountains of Israel, that ye may eat flesh, and drink blood.[1818]

18 [a]Ye shall eat the flesh of the mighty, and drink the blood of the princes[5387] of the earth, of rams, of lambs,[3733] and of [I]goats, of bullocks, all of them [b]fatlings of Bashan.

19 And ye shall eat fat till ye be full, and drink blood till ye be drunken, of my sacrifice[2076] which I have sacrificed for you.

20 [a]Thus ye shall be filled at my table with horses and chariots, [b]with mighty men, and with all men[376] of war, saith the Lord GOD.

---

2 [I]Or, *strike thee with six plagues;* or, *draw thee back with a hook of six teeth* [II]Hebr. *the sides of the north* [a]Ezek. 38:4 [b]Ezek. 38:15

4 [I]Hebr. *wing* [II]Hebr. *to devour* [a]Ezek. 38:21; 39:17 [b]Ezek. 33:27

5 [I]Hebr. *the face of the field*

6 [I]Or, *confidently* [a]Ezek. 38:22; Amos 1:4 [b]Ps. 72:10

7 [a]Ezek. 39:22 [b]Lev. 18:21; Ezek. 20:39 [c]Ezek. 38:16, 23

8 [a]Rev. 16:17; 21:6 [b]Ezek. 38:17

9 [I]Or, *javelins* [II]Or, *make a fire of them*

10 [a]Isa. 14:2

11 [I]Or, *mouths* [II]Or, *The multitude of Gog*

12 [a]Deut. 21:23; Ezek. 39:14, 16

13 [a]Ezek. 28:22

14 [I]Hebr. *men of continuance* [a]Ezek. 39:12

15 [I]Hebr. *build*

16 [I]Or, *The multitude* [a]Ezek. 39:12

17 [I]Hebr. *to the fowl of every wing* [II]Or, *slaughter* [a]Rev. 19:17 [b]Isa. 18:6; 34:6; Jer. 12:9; Zeph. 1:7 [c]Ezek. 39:4

18 [I]Hebr. *great goats* [a]Rev. 19:18 [b]Deut. 32:14; Ps. 22:12

20 [a]Ps. 76:6; Ezek. 38:4 [b]Rev. 19:18

Israel Restored

21 [a]And I will set my glory[3519] among the heathen, and all the heathen shall see my judgment[4941] that I have executed,[6213] and [b]my hand that I have laid[7760] upon them.

22 [a]So the house of Israel shall know that I *am* the LORD their God[430] from that day and forward.

23 [a]And the heathen shall know that the house of Israel went into captivity[1540] for their iniquity:[5771] because they trespassed[4603] against me, therefore [b]hid I my face from them, and [c]gave them into the hand of their enemies: so fell[5307] they all by the sword.[2719]

24 [a]According to their uncleanness[2932] and according to their transgressions[6588] have I done[6213] unto them, and hid my face from them.

25 Therefore thus saith the Lord GOD; [a]Now will I bring again[7725] the captivity[7622] of Jacob, and have mercy[7355] upon the [b]whole house of Israel, and will be jealous[7065] for my holy[6944] name;

26 [a]After that they have borne[5375] their shame, and all their trespasses[4604] whereby they have trespassed against me, when they [b]dwelt safely[983] in their land,[127] and none made *them* afraid.[2729]

27 [a]When I have brought them again from the people, and gathered[6908] them out of their enemies' lands,[776] and [b]am sanctified[6942] in them in the sight of many nations;[1471]

28 [a]Then shall they know that I *am* the LORD their God, [I]which caused them to be led into captivity[1473] among the heathen: but I have gathered[3664] them unto their own land, and have left[3498] none of them any more there.

29 [a]Neither will I hide my face any more from them: for I have [b]poured out[8210] my spirit[7307] upon the house of Israel, saith the Lord GOD.

The Prophet's Vision of the Temple

40 In the five and twentieth year of our captivity,[1546] in the beginning[7218] of the year, in the tenth *day* of the month, in the fourteenth year after that [a]the city was smitten,[5221] in the selfsame day[3117] [b]the hand[3027] of the LORD was upon me, and brought me thither.

2 [a]In the visions[4759] of God[430] brought he me into the land[776] of Israel, [b]and set me upon a very high mountain, [I]by which *was* as the frame of a city on the south.

3 And he brought me thither, and, behold, *there was* a man,[376] whose appearance *was* [a]like the appearance of brass, [b]with a line of flax in his hand, [c]and a measuring reed; and he stood in the gate.

4 And the man said[1696] unto me, [a]Son[1121] of man,[120] behold[7200] with thine eyes, and hear[8085] with thine ears,[241] and set[7760] thine heart[3820] upon all that I shall shew thee; for to the intent that I might shew *them* unto thee *art* thou brought hither: [b]declare[5046] all that thou seest to the house[1004] of Israel.

5 And behold [a]a wall on the outside of the house round about, and in the man's hand a measuring reed of six cubits *long* by the cubit and an hand breadth: so he measured the breadth of the building, one reed; and the height, one reed.

6 Then came he unto the gate [I]which looketh toward[1870] the east, and went up[5927] the stairs thereof, and measured the threshold[5592] of the gate, *which was* one reed broad; and the other threshold *of the gate, which was* one reed broad.

7 And *every* little chamber *was* one reed long,[753] and one reed broad; and between the little chambers *were* five cubits; and the threshold of the gate by the porch of the gate within[1004] *was* one reed.

8 He measured also the porch of the gate within, one reed.

9 Then measured he the porch of the gate, eight cubits; and the posts thereof, two cubits; and the porch of the gate *was* inward.[1004]

10 And the little chambers of the gate eastward *were* three on this side,

21 [a]Ezek. 38:16, 23 [b]Ex. 7:4

22 [a]Ezek. 39:7, 28

23 [a]Ezek. 36:18-20, 23 [b]Deut. 31:17; Isa. 59:2 [c]Lev. 26:25

24 [a]Ezek. 36:19

25 [a]Jer. 30:3, 18; Ezek. 34:13; 36:24 [b]Ezek. 20:40; Hos. 1:11

26 [a]Dan. 9:16 [b]Lev. 26:5, 6

27 [a]Ezek. 28:25, 26 [b]Ezek. 36:23, 24; 38:16

28 [I]Hebr. *by my causing of them* [a]Ezek. 34:30; 39:22

29 [a]Isa. 54:8 [b]Joel 2:28; Zech. 12:10; Acts 2:17

1 [a]Ezek. 33:21 [b]Ezek. 1:3

2 [I]Or, *upon which* [a]Ezek. 8:3 [b]Rev. 21:10

3 [a]Ezek. 1:7; Dan. 10:6 [b]Ezek. 47:3 [c]Rev. 11:1; 21:15

4 [a]Ezek. 44:5 [b]Ezek. 43:10

5 [a]Ezek. 42:20

6 [I]Hebr. *whose face was the way toward the east*

and three on that side; they three *were* of one measure: and the posts had one measure on this side and on that side.

11 And he measured the breadth of the entry of the gate, ten cubits; *and* the length[753] of the gate, thirteen cubits.

12 The [I]space also before the little chambers *was* one cubit *on this side,* and the space *was* one cubit on that side: and the little chambers *were* six cubits on this side, and six cubits on that side.

13 He measured then the gate from the roof of *one* little chamber to the roof of another: the breadth *was* five and twenty cubits, door against door.

14 He made[6213] also posts of threescore cubits, even unto the post of the court round about the gate.

15 And from the face of the gate of the entrance unto the face of the porch of the inner gate *were* fifty cubits.

16 And *there were* [I][a]narrow[331] windows to the little chambers, and to their posts within the gate round about, and likewise to the [II]arches: and windows *were* round about [III]inward: and upon *each* post *were* palm trees.

17 Then brought he me into [a]the outward court, and, lo, *there were* [b]chambers, and a pavement made for the court round about: [c]thirty chambers *were* upon the pavement.

18 And the pavement by the side of the gates over against the length of the gates *was* the lower pavement.

19 Then he measured the breadth from the forefront[6440] of the lower gate unto the forefront of the inner court [I]without, an hundred cubits eastward and northward.

20 And the gate of the outward court [I]that looked toward the north, he measured the length thereof, and the breadth thereof.

21 And the little chambers thereof *were* three on this side and three on that side; and the posts thereof and the [I]arches thereof were after the measure of the first[7223] gate: the length thereof *was* fifty cubits, and the breadth five and twenty cubits.

22 And their windows, and their arches, and their palm trees, *were* after the measure of the gate that looketh toward the east; and they went up unto it by seven steps; and the arches thereof *were* before them.

23 And the gate of the inner court *was* over against the gate toward the north, and toward the east; and he measured from gate to gate an hundred cubits.

24 After that he brought me toward the south, and behold a gate toward the south: and he measured the posts[352] thereof and the arches thereof according to these measures.

25 And *there were* windows in it and in the arches thereof round about, like those windows: the length *was* fifty cubits, and the breadth five and twenty cubits.

26 And *there were* seven steps to go up to it, and the arches thereof *were* before them: and it had palm trees, one on this side, and another on that side, upon the posts thereof.

27 And *there was* a gate in the inner court toward the south: and he measured from gate to gate toward the south an hundred cubits.

28 And he brought me to the inner court by the south gate: and he measured the south gate according to these measures;

29 And the little chambers thereof, and the posts thereof, and the arches thereof, according to these measures: and *there were* windows in it and in the arches thereof round about: *it was* fifty cubits long, and five and twenty cubits broad.

30 And the arches round about *were* [a]five and twenty cubits long, and five cubits [I]broad.

31 And the arches thereof *were* toward the utter court; and palm trees *were* upon the posts thereof: and the going up to it *had* eight steps.

32 And he brought me into the inner court toward the east: and he measured the gate according to these measures.

12 [I]Hebr. *limit,* or, *bound*

16 [I]Hebr. *closed* [II]Or, *galleries,* or, *porches* [III]Or, *within* [a]1Kgs. 6:4

17 [a]Rev. 11:2 [b]1Kgs. 6:5 [c]Ezek. 45:5

19 [I]Or, *from without*

20 [I]Hebr. *whose face* was

21 [I]Or, *galleries,* or, *porches*

30 [I]Hebr. *breadth* [a]Ezek. 40:21, 25, 33, 36

33 And the little chambers thereof, and the posts thereof, and the arches thereof, *were* according to these measures: and *there were* windows therein and in the arches thereof round about: *it was* fifty cubits long, and five and twenty cubits broad.

34 And the arches thereof *were* toward the outward court; and palm trees *were* upon the posts352 thereof, on this side, and on that side: and the going up to it *had* eight steps.

35 And he brought me to the north gate, and measured *it* according to these measures;

36 The little chambers thereof, the posts thereof, and the arches thereof, and the windows to it round about: the length *was* fifty cubits, and the breadth five and twenty cubits.

37 And the posts thereof *were* toward the utter court; and palm trees *were* upon the posts thereof, on this side, and on that side: and the going up to it *had* eight steps.

38 And the chambers and the entries thereof *were* by the posts of the gates, where they washed1740 the burnt offering.5930

39 And in the porch of the gate *were* two tables on this side, and two tables on that side, to slay7819 thereon the burnt offering and [a]the sin offering and [b]the trespass offering.817

40 And at the side without [I]as one goeth up to the entry of the north gate, *were* two tables; and on the other side, which *was* at the porch of the gate, *were* two tables.

41 Four tables *were* on this side, and four tables on that side, by the side of the gate; eight tables, whereupon they slew7819 *their sacrifices.*

42 And the four tables *were* of hewn1496 stone for the burnt offering,5930 of a cubit and an half long, and a cubit and an half broad, and one cubit high: whereupon also they laid the instruments wherewith they slew the burnt offering and the sacrifice.

43 And within *were* [I]hooks, an hand broad, fastened round about: and upon the tables *was* the flesh of the offering.7133

44 And without the inner gate *were* the chambers of [a]the singers7891 in the inner court, which *was* at the side of the north gate; and their prospect6440 *was* toward the south: one at the side of the east gate *having* the prospect toward the north.

45 And he said unto me, This chamber,3957 whose prospect *is* toward the south, *is* for the priests,3548 [a]the keepers8104 of the [I]charge4931 of the house.

46 And the chamber whose prospect *is* toward the north *is* for the priests, [a]the keepers of the charge of the altar:4196 these *are* the sons1121 of [b]Zadok among the sons of Levi, which come near to the LORD to minister8334 unto him.

47 So he measured the court, an hundred cubits long, and an hundred cubits broad, foursquare; and the altar *that was* before the house.

48 And he brought me to the porch of the house, and measured *each* post of the porch, five cubits on this side, and five cubits on that side: and the breadth of the gate *was* three cubits on this side, and three cubits on that side.

49 [a]The length of the porch *was* twenty cubits, and the breadth eleven cubits; and *he brought me* by the steps whereby they went up to it: and *there were* [b]pillars by the posts, one on this side, and another on that side.

41 Afterward he brought me to the temple,1964 and measured the posts, six cubits broad on the one side, and six cubits broad on the other side, *which* was the breadth of the tabernacle.

2 And the breadth of the [I]door *was* ten cubits; and the sides of the door *were* five cubits on the one side, and five cubits on the other side: and he measured the length753 thereof, forty cubits: and the breadth, twenty cubits.

3 Then went he inward,6441 and measured the post of the door, two cu-

39 [a]Lev. 4:2, 3 [b]Lev. 5:6; 6:6; 7:1

40 [I]Or, *at the step*

43 [I]Or, *andirons,* or, *the two hearthstones*

44 [a]1Chr. 6:31

45 [I]Or, *ward,* or, *ordinance* [a]Lev. 8:35; Num. 3:27, 28, 32, 38; 18:5; 1Chr. 9:23; 2Chr. 13:11; Ps. 134:1

46 [a]Num. 18:5; Ezek. 44:15 [b]1Kgs. 2:35; Ezek. 43:19; 44:15, 16

49 [a]1Kgs. 6:3 [b]1Kgs. 7:21

2 [I]Or, *entrance*

bits; and the door, six cubits; and the breadth of the door, seven cubits.

4 So [a]he measured the length thereof, twenty cubits; and the breadth, twenty cubits, before the temple: and he said[559] unto me, This *is* the most holy[6944] *place.*

5 After he measured the wall of the house,[1004] six cubits; and the breadth of *every* side chamber, four cubits, round about the house on every side.

6 [a]And the side chambers *were* three, [I]one over another, and thirty in order; and they entered into the wall which *was* of the house for the side chambers round about, that they might [II]have hold, but they had not hold in the wall of the house.

7 And [I][a]*there was* an enlarging,[7337] and a winding about still upward to the side chambers: for the winding about of the house went still upward round about the house: therefore the breadth of the house *was still* upward, and so increased[5927] *from* the lowest *chamber* to the highest[5945] by the midst.

8 I saw[7200] also the height of the house round about: the foundations of the side chambers *were* [a]a full reed of six great cubits.

9 The thickness of the wall, which *was* for the side chamber without, *was* five cubits: and *that* which *was* left *was* the place of the side chambers that *were* within.[1004]

10 And between the chambers *was* the wideness of twenty cubits round about the house on every side.

11 And the doors of the side chambers *were* toward *the place that was* left, one door toward[1870] the north, and another door toward the south: and the breadth of the place that was left *was* five cubits round about.

12 Now the building that *was* before the separate place[1508] at the end toward the west *was* seventy cubits broad; and the wall of the building *was* five cubits thick round about, and the length thereof ninety cubits.

13 So he measured the house, an hundred cubits long; and the separate place, and the building, with the walls thereof, an hundred cubits long;[753]

14 Also the breadth of the face of the house, and of the separate place toward the east, an hundred cubits.

15 And he measured the length of the building over against the separate place which *was* behind it, and the [I]galleries[862] thereof on the one side and on the other side, an hundred cubits, with the inner temple, and the porches of the court;

16 The door posts, and [a]the narrow windows, and the galleries[862] round about on their three stories, over against the door, [I]cieled[7824] with wood round about, [II]and from the ground[776] up to the windows, and the windows *were* covered;[3680]

17 To that above the door, even unto the inner house, and without, and by all the wall round about within and without, by [I]measure.

18 And *it was* made[6213] [a]with cherubims[3742] and palm trees, so that a palm tree *was* between a cherub and a cherub; and *every* cherub had two faces;

19 [a]So that the face of a man[120] *was* toward the palm tree on the one side, and the face of a young lion toward the palm tree on the other side: *it was* made through all the house round about.

20 From the ground unto above the door *were* cherubims and palm trees made, and *on* the wall of the temple.

21 The [I]posts of the temple *were* squared, *and* the face of the sanctuary;[6944] the appearance *of the one* as the appearance *of the other.*

22 [a]The altar[4196] of wood *was* three cubits high, and the length thereof two cubits; and the corners thereof, and the length thereof, and the walls thereof, *were* of wood: and he said[1696] unto me, This *is* [b]the table that *is* [c]before the LORD.

23 [a]And the temple and the sanctuary had two doors.

24 And the doors[1817] had two leaves[1817] *apiece,* two turning leaves; two

4 [a]1Kgs. 6:20; 2Chr. 3:8

6 [I]Hebr. *side chamber over side chamber* [II]Hebr. *beholden* [a]1Kgs. 6:5, 6

7 [I]Hebr. it was *made broader, and went round* [a]1Kgs. 6:8

8 [a]Ezek. 40:5

15 [I]Or, *several walks, or, walks with pillars*

16 [I]Hebr. *ceiling of wood* [II]Or, *and the ground unto the windows* [a]Ezek. 40:16; 41:26

17 [I]Hebr. *measures*

18 [a]1Kgs. 6:29

19 [a]Ezek. 1:10

21 [I]Hebr. *post*

22 [a]Ex. 30:1 [b]Ezek. 44:16; Mal. 1:7, 12 [c]Ex. 30:8

23 [a]1Kgs. 6:31-35

leaves for the one door, and two leaves for the other *door.*

25 And *there were* made on them, on the doors of the temple, cherubims and palm trees, like as *were* made upon the walls; and *there were* thick planks upon the face of the porch without.

26 And *there were* [a]narrow windows and palm trees on the one side and on the other side, on the sides of the porch, and *upon* the side chambers of the house, and thick planks.

42 Then he brought me forth into the utter[2435] court, the way[1870] toward[1870] the north: and he brought me into [a]the chamber that *was* over against the separate place, and which *was* before the building toward the north.

2 Before the length[753] of an hundred cubits *was* the north door, and the breadth *was* fifty cubits.

3 Over against the twenty *cubits* which *were* for the inner court, and over against the pavement which *was* for the utter court, *was* [a]gallery against gallery in three *stories.*

4 And before the chambers *was* a walk of ten cubits breadth inward, a way of one cubit; and their doors toward the north.

5 Now the upper[5945] chambers *were* shorter: for the galleries[862] [I]were higher than these, than the lower, and than the middlemost of the building.

6 For they *were* in three *stories,* but had not pillars as the pillars of the courts: therefore *the building* was straitened[680] more than the lowest and the middlemost from the ground.[776]

7 And the wall that *was* without over against the chambers, toward the utter court on the forepart[6440] of the chambers, the length thereof *was* fifty cubits.

8 For the length of the chambers that *were* in the outer court *was* fifty cubits: and, lo, before the temple[1964] *were* an hundred cubits.

9 And [I]from under these chambers *was* [II]the entry on the east side, [III]as one goeth into them from the outer court.

10 The chambers *were* in the thickness of the wall of the court toward the east, over against the separate place,[1508] and over against the building.

11 And [a]the way before them *was* like the appearance of the chambers which *were* toward the north, as long[753] as they, *and* as broad as they: and all their goings out *were* both according to their fashions,[4941] and according to their doors.

12 And according to the doors of the chambers that *were* toward the south *was* a door in the head[7218] of the way, *even* the way directly before the wall toward the east, as one entereth into them.

13 Then said[559] he unto me, The north chambers *and* the south chambers, which *are* before the separate place, they *be* holy[6944] chambers, where the priests[3548] that approach unto the LORD [a]shall eat the most holy things:[6944] there shall they lay the most holy things, and [b]the meat offering,[4503] and the sin offering,[2403] and the trespass offering;[817] for the place *is* holy.[6918]

14 [a]When the priests enter therein, then shall they not go out of the holy *place* into the utter court, but there they shall lay their garments wherein they minister;[8334] for they *are* holy; and shall put on other garments, and shall approach[7126] to *those things* which *are* for the people.[5971]

15 Now when he had made an end[3615] of measuring the inner house,[1004] he brought me forth toward the gate whose prospect *is* toward the east, and measured it round about.

16 He measured the east [I]side with the measuring reed, five hundred reeds, with the measuring reed round about.

17 He measured the north side, five hundred reeds, with the measuring reed round about.

18 He measured the south side, five hundred reeds, with the measuring reed.

19 He turned about[5437] to the west

26 [a]Ezek. 40:16; 41:16

1 [a]Ezek. 41:12, 15

3 [a]Ezek. 41:16

5 [I]Or, *did eat of these*

9 [I]Or, *from the place* [II]Or, *he that brought me* [III]Or, *as he came*

11 [a]Ezek. 42:4

13 [a]Lev. 6:16, 26; 24:9 [b]Lev. 2:3, 10; 6:14, 17, 25, 29; 7:1; 10:13, 14; Num. 18:9, 10

14 [a]Ezek. 44:19

16 [I]Hebr. *wind*

side, *and* measured five hundred reeds
with the measuring reed.
20 He measured it by the four sides:
[a]it had a wall round about, [b]five hundred
reeds long, and five hundred broad, to
make a separation[914] between the
sanctuary[6944] and the profane place.[2455]

God's Glory Fills the Temple Again

43 Afterward he brought me to
the gate, *even* the gate [a]that
looketh toward[1870] the east:
2 [a]And, behold, the glory[3519] of the
God[430] of Israel came from the way[1870]
of the east: and [b]his voice *was* like a
noise of many waters: [c]and the earth[776]
shined with his glory.
3 And *it was* [a]according to the appearance of the vision which I saw,[7200]
even according to the vision that I saw
[I][b]when I came [c]to destroy[7843] the city:
and the visions4759 *were* like the vision
that I saw [d]by the river Chebar; and I
fell[5307] upon my face.
4 [a]And the glory of the LORD came
into the house[1004] by the way of the gate
whose prospect *is* toward the east.
5 [a]So the spirit took me up,[5375] and
brought me into the inner court; and, behold, [b]the glory of the LORD filled the
house.
6 And I heard[8085] *him* speaking[1696]
unto me out of the house; and [a]the
man[376] stood by me.
7 And he said[559] unto me, Son[1121] of
man,[120] [a]the place of my throne, and [b]the
place of the soles[3709] of my feet, [c]where
I will dwell[7931] in the midst of the
children[1121] of Israel for ever,[5769] and my
holy[6944] name, shall the house of Israel
[d]no more defile,[2930] *neither* they, nor their
kings,[4428] by their whoredom,[2184] nor by
[e]the carcases of their kings in their high
places.[1116]
8 [a]In their setting of their threshold
by my thresholds, and their post by my
posts, [I]and the wall between me and
them, they have even defiled my holy
name by their abominations[8441] that they
have committed:[6213] wherefore I have consumed them in mine anger.[639]
9 Now let them put away their
whoredom, and [a]the carcases of their
kings, far from me, [b]and I will dwell[7931]
in the midst of them for ever.
10 Thou son of man, [a]shew[5046] the
house to the house of Israel, that they
may be ashamed of their iniquities:[5771]
and let them measure the [I]pattern.
11 And if they be ashamed of all
that they have done,[6213] shew[3045] them
the form of the house, and the fashion thereof, and the goings out thereof,
and the comings in thereof, and all the
forms thereof, and all the ordinances
thereof, and all the forms thereof, and all
the laws thereof: and write *it* in their
sight, that they may keep[8104] the whole
form thereof, and all the ordinances[2708]
thereof, and do them.
12 This *is* the law[8451] of the house;
Upon [a]the top[7218] of the mountain the
whole limit thereof round about *shall be*
most holy.[6944] Behold, this *is* the law of
the house.
13 And these *are* the measures of
the altar[4196] after the cubits: [a]The cubit

20 [a]Ezek. 40:5 [b]Ezek. 45:2
1 [a]Ezek. 10:19; 44:1; 46:1
2 [a]Ezek. 11:23 [b]Ezek. 1:24; Rev. 1:15; 14:2; 19:1, 6 [c]Ezek. 10:4; Rev. 18:1
3 IOr, *when I came to* prophesy *that the city should be destroyed* [a]Ezek. 1:4, 28; 8:4 [b]Ezek. 9:1, 5 [c]Jer. 1:10 [d]Ezek. 1:3; 3:23
4 [a]Ezek. 10:19; 44:2
5 [a]Ezek. 3:12, 14; 8:3 [b]1Kgs. 8:10, 11; Ezek. 44:4
6 [a]Ezek. 40:3
7 [a]Ps. 99:1 [b]1Chr. 28:2; Ps. 99:5 [c]Ex. 29:45; Ps. 68:16; 132:14; Joel 3:17; John 1:14; 2Cor. 6:16 [d]Ezek. 39:7 [e]Lev. 26:30; Jer. 16:18
8 IOr, *for* there was but *a wall between me and them* [a]2Kgs. 16:14; 21:4, 5, 7; Ezek. 8:3; 23:39; 44:7
9 [a]Ezek. 43:7 [b]Ezek. 43:7
10 IOr, *sum,* or, *number* [a]Ezek. 40:4
12 [a]Ezek. 40:2
13 [a]Ezek. 40:5; 41:8

43:1–7 In this passage, the glory of the Lord, which departed before Jerusalem's fall (see note on Ezek. 10:1—11:23), returns from the same place to which it departed. Note that now the glory coming from the Mount of Olives is personified ("and His voice," v. 2; "soles of my feet," v. 7, cf. Zech 14:4). This may also be a reference to the presence of Christ in His full glory at His Second Coming (Matt. 17:1–8; John 17:5, cf. Rev. 21:23).

43:13–27 These verses (along with Ezek. 40:38) have given many biblical scholars difficulty. If this is a description of the temple that will be in the millennial kingdom, and if Christ "offered one sacrifice for sins forever" (Heb. 10:12), why will there be the offering of sacrifices? The simple answer to this question is that the sacrifices described here picture the purification that God will impose upon the people after they return from exile. The dimensions and descriptions that are given merely denote the reconstructed temple and the altar that will be built following the return of the

(continued on next page)

is a cubit and an hand breadth; even the [I]bottom *shall be* a cubit, and the breadth a cubit, and the border thereof by the [II]edge thereof round about *shall be* a span: and this *shall be* the higher place of the altar.

14 And from the bottom *upon* the ground[776] *even* to the lower settle *shall be* two cubits, and the breadth one cubit; and from the lesser settle *even* to the greater settle *shall be* four cubits, and the breadth *one* cubit.

15 So [I]the altar *shall be* four cubits; and from [IIa]the altar and upward *shall be* four horns.

16 And the altar *shall be* twelve *cubits* long,[753] twelve broad, square in the four squares thereof.

17 And the settle[5835] *shall be* fourteen *cubits* long and fourteen broad in the four squares thereof; and the border about it *shall be* half a cubit; and the bottom thereof *shall be* a cubit about; and [a]his stairs shall look toward the east.

18 And he said unto me, Son of man, thus saith[559] the Lord[136] GOD; These *are* the ordinances of the altar in the day[3117] when they shall make it, to offer burnt offerings[5930] thereon, and to [a]sprinkle[2236] blood[1818] thereon.

19 And thou shalt give to [a]the priests[3548] the Levites that be of the seed[2233] of Zadok, which approach unto me, to minister[8334] unto me, saith the Lord GOD, [b]a young bullock for a sin offering.[2403]

20 And thou shalt take of the blood thereof, and put *it* on the four horns of it, and on the four corners of the settle, and upon the border round about: thus shalt thou cleanse[2398] and purge[3722] it.

21 Thou shalt take the bullock also of the sin offering, and he [a]shall burn it in the appointed place of the house, [b]without the sanctuary.[4720]

22 And on the second day thou shalt offer[7126] a kid[8163] of the goats without blemish[8549] for a sin offering; and they shall cleanse the altar, as they did cleanse *it* with the bullock.

23 When thou hast made an end[3615] of cleansing[2398] *it,* thou shalt offer a young bullock without blemish, and a ram out of the flock without blemish.

24 And thou shalt offer them before the LORD, [a]and the priests shall cast salt upon them, and they shall offer them up *for* a burnt offering[5930] unto the LORD.

25 [a]Seven days[3117] shalt thou prepare every day a goat[8163] *for* a sin offering: they shall also prepare[3559] a young bullock, and a ram out of the flock, without blemish.

26 Seven days shall they purge the altar and purify[2891] it; and they shall [Ia]consecrate themselves.

27 [a]And when these days are expired,[3615] it shall be, *that* upon the eighth day, and *so* forward, the priests shall make your burnt offerings upon the altar, and your [I]peace offerings;[8002] and I will [b]accept[7521] you, saith the Lord GOD.

44

Then he brought me back the way[1870] of the gate of the outward sanctuary[4720] [a]which looketh toward the east; and it *was* shut.

2 Then said[559] the LORD unto me;

13 [I]Hebr. *bosom* [II]Hebr. *lip*

15 [I]Hebr. *Harel,* that is, *the mountain of God* [II]Hebr. *Ariel,* that is, *the lion of God* [a]Isa. 29:1

17 [a]Ex. 20:26

18 [a]Lev. 1:5

19 [a]Ezek. 44:15 [b]Ex. 29:10, 12; Lev. 8:14, 15; Ezek. 45:18, 19

21 [a]Ex. 29:14 [b]Heb. 13:11

24 [a]Lev. 2:13

25 [a]Ex. 29:35, 36; Lev. 8:33

26 [I]Hebr. *fill their hands* [a]Ex. 29:24

27 [I]Or, *thank offerings* [a]Lev. 9:1 [b]Job 42:8; Ezek. 20:40, 41; Rom. 12:1; 1Pet. 2:5

1 [a]Ezek. 43:1

(continued from previous page)
people, which, in fact, occurred in the time of the prophet Haggai. Ezekiel is also previewing the reinstitution of the levitical system of sacrifices. The need for cleansing mentioned in this passage (vv. 26, 27) may be Ezekiel's prediction of the desecration of the temple by Antiochus IV Epiphanes when he offered a pig on the altar of the temple. After he was driven out of the temple, this process of cleansing was conducted.

Another view of this passage is that the temple is referring to one that will be constructed during the Millennium. Just as the levitical sacrifices looked forward to Christ's atoning work on the cross, the millennial sacrifices will look back to that time. The eschatological view of a millennial temple and the need for a cleansing of the altar within it are indicative of the desecration of the temple in Jerusalem during the Great Tribulation.

This gate shall be shut, it shall not be opened, and no man[376] shall enter in by it; [a]because the LORD, the God[430] of Israel, hath entered in by it, therefore it shall be shut.

3 *It is* for the prince;[5387] the prince, he shall sit in it to [a]eat bread before the LORD; [b]he shall enter by the way of the porch of *that* gate, and shall go out by the way of the same.

4 Then brought he me the way of the north gate before the house:[1004] and I looked,[7200] and, [a]behold, the glory[3519] of the LORD filled the house of the LORD: [b]and I fell[5307] upon my face.

5 And the LORD said unto me, [a]Son[1121] of man,[120] [I]mark well, and behold[7200] with thine eyes, and hear[8085] with thine ears[241] all that I say[1696] unto thee concerning all the ordinances[2708] of the house of the LORD, and all the laws thereof; and mark well the entering in of the house, with every going forth of the sanctuary.

6 And thou shalt say[559] to the [a]rebellious,[4805] *even* to the house of Israel, Thus saith the Lord[136] GOD; O ye house of Israel, [b]let it suffice you of all your abominations,[8441]

7 [a]In that ye have brought *into my sanctuary* [Ib]strangers, [c]uncircumcised[6189] in heart,[3820] and uncircumcised in flesh, to be in my sanctuary, to pollute[2490] it, *even* my house, when ye offer[7126] [d]my bread, [e]the fat and the blood,[1818] and they have broken[6565] my covenant[1285] because of all your abominations.

8 And ye have not [a]kept[8104] the charge[4931] of mine holy things:[6944] but ye have set[7760] keepers[8104] of my [Ib]charge in my sanctuary for yourselves.

9 Thus saith the Lord GOD; [a]No stranger, uncircumcised in heart, nor uncircumcised in flesh, shall enter into my sanctuary, of any stranger that *is* among the children[1121] of Israel.

10 [a]And the Levites that are gone away far from me, when Israel went astray, which went astray away from me after their idols;[1544] they shall even bear[5375] their iniquity.[5771]

11 Yet they shall be ministers[8334] in my sanctuary, [a]*having* charge at the gates of the house, and ministering to the house: [b]they shall slay[7819] the burnt offering[5930] and the sacrifice for the people,[5971] and [c]they shall stand before them to minister unto them.

12 Because they ministered unto them before their idols, and [Ia]caused the house of Israel to fall[4383] into iniquity; therefore have I [b]lifted up[5375] mine hand[3027] against them, saith[5002] the Lord GOD, and they shall bear their iniquity.

13 [a]And they shall not come near unto me, to do the office of a priest[3547] unto me, nor to come near[5066] to any of my holy things, in the most holy[6944] *place:* but they shall [b]bear their shame, and their abominations which they have committed.[6213]

14 But I will make them [a]keepers of the charge of the house, for all the service[5656] thereof, and for all that shall be done[6213] therein.

15 [a]But the priests[3548] the Levites, [b]the sons[1121] of Zadok, that kept the charge of my sanctuary [c]when the children of Israel went astray from me, they shall come near[7126] to me to minister unto me, and they [d]shall stand before me to offer unto me [e]the fat and the blood, saith the Lord GOD:

16 They shall enter into my sanctuary, and they shall come near to [a]my table, to minister unto me, and they shall keep[8104] my charge.

17 And it shall come to pass, *that* when they enter in at the gates of the inner court, [a]they shall be clothed with linen garments; and no wool shall come upon them, whiles they minister in the gates of the inner court, and within.[1004]

18 [a]They shall have linen bonnets[6287] upon their heads,[7218] and shall have linen breeches upon their loins; they shall not gird *themselves* with any thing that causeth sweat.

19 And when they go forth into the utter court, *even* into the utter court to the people, [a]they shall put off their garments wherein they ministered, and lay them in the holy chambers, and they shall put on other garments; and they

2 [a]Ezek. 43:4

3 [a]Gen. 31:54; 1Cor. 10:18 [b]Ezek. 46:2, 8

4 [a]Ezek. 3:23; 43:5 [b]Ezek. 1:28

5 [I]Hebr. *set thine heart* [a]Ezek. 40:4

6 [a]Ezek. 2:5 [b]Ezek. 45:9; 1Pet. 4:3

7 [I]Hebr. *children of a stranger* [a]Ezek. 43:8; Acts 21:28 [b]Lev. 22:25 [c]Lev. 26:41; Deut. 10:16; Acts 7:51 [d]Lev. 21:6, 8, 17, 21 [e]Lev. 3:16; 17:11

8 [I]Or, *ward,* or, *ordinance* [a]Lev. 22:2 [b]Ezek. 40:45; 44:14, 16

9 [a]Ezek. 44:7

10 [a]2Kgs. 23:8; 2Chr. 29:4, 5; Ezek. 48:11

11 [a]1Chr. 26:1 [b]2Chr. 29:34 [c]Num. 16:9

12 [I]Hebr. *were for a stumblingblock of iniquity unto* [a]Isa. 9:16; Ezek. 14:3, 4; Mal. 2:8 [b]Ps. 106:26

13 [a]Num. 18:3; 2Kgs. 23:9 [b]Ezek. 32:30; 36:7

14 [a]Num. 18:4; 1Chr. 23:28, 32

15 [a]Ezek. 40:46; 43:19 [b]1Sam. 2:35 [c]Ezek. 44:10 [d]Deut. 10:8 [e]Ezek. 44:7

16 [a]Ezek. 41:22

17 [a]Ex. 28:39, 40, 43; 39:27, 28

18 [a]Ex. 28:40, 42; 39:28

19 [a]Ezek. 42:14

shall [b]not sanctify[6942] the people with their garments.

20 [a]Neither shall they shave their heads, nor suffer their locks to grow long; they shall only poll[3697] their heads.

21 [a]Neither shall any priest[3548] drink wine, when they enter into the inner court.

22 Neither shall they take for their wives[802] a [a]widow, nor her that is [I]put away: but they shall take maidens[1330] of the seed[2233] of the house of Israel, or a widow [II]that had a priest before.

23 And [a]they shall teach[3384] my people *the difference* between the holy and profane,[2455] and cause them to discern[3045] between the unclean[2931] and the clean.

24 And [a]in controversy[7379] they shall stand in judgment; *and* they shall judge[8199] it according to my judgments: and they shall keep my laws and my statutes[2708] in all mine assemblies;[4150] [b]and they shall hallow[6942] my sabbaths.[7676]

25 And they shall come at no [a]dead[4191] person to defile[2930] themselves: but for father,[1] or for mother,[517] or for son, or for daughter, for brother,[251] or for sister[269] that hath had no husband,[376] they may defile themselves.

26 And [a]after he is cleansed,[2893] they shall reckon[5608] unto him seven days.[3117]

27 And in the day that he goeth into the sanctuary,[6944] [a]unto the inner court, to minister in the sanctuary, [b]he shall offer his sin offering,[2403] saith the Lord GOD.

28 And it shall be unto them for an inheritance:[5159] I [a]*am* their inheritance: and ye shall give them no possession[272] in Israel: I *am* their possession.

29 [a]They shall eat the meat offering,[4503] and the sin offering, and the trespass offering;[817] and [b]every [I]dedicated thing[2764] in Israel shall be theirs.

30 And the [I][a]first[7225] of all the firstfruits of all *things,* and every oblation[8641] of all, of every *sort* of your oblations, shall be the priest's:[3548] ye [b]shall also give unto the priest the first of your dough, [c]that he may cause the blessing[1293] to rest in thine house.

31 The priests shall not eat of any thing that is [a]dead of itself,[5038] or torn, whether it be fowl or beast.

God's Portion of the Land

45 Moreover, [I]when ye shall [a]divide by lot[5307] the land[776] for inheritance,[5159] ye shall [b]offer an oblation unto the LORD, [II]an holy portion[6944] of the land: the length *shall be* the length of five and twenty thousand *reeds,* and the breadth *shall be* ten thousand. This *shall be* holy in all the borders thereof round about.

2 Of this there shall be for the sanctuary[6944] [a]five hundred *in length,* with five hundred *in breadth,* square round about; and fifty cubits round about for the [I]suburbs thereof.

3 And of this measure shalt thou measure the length[753] of five and twenty thousand, and the breadth of ten thousand: [a]and in it shall be the sanctuary[4720] *and* the most holy *place.*

4 [a]The holy *portion* of the land shall be for the priests[3548] the ministers of the sanctuary, which shall come near to minister[8334] unto the LORD: and it shall be a place for their houses,[1004] and an holy place for the sanctuary.

5 [a]And the five and twenty thousand of length, and the ten thousand of breadth, shall also the Levites, the ministers of the house, have for themselves, for a possession[272] for [b]twenty chambers.

6 [a]And ye shall appoint the possession of the city five thousand broad, and five and twenty thousand long,[753] over against the oblation of the holy *portion:* it shall be for the whole house of Israel.

7 [a]And *a portion shall be* for the prince[5387] on the one side and on the other side of the oblation of the holy[6944] *portion,* and of the possession of the city, before the oblation of the holy *portion,* and before the possession of the city, from the west side westward, and from the east side eastward: and the length

19 [b]Ezek. 46:20; Ex. 29:37; 30:29; Lev. 6:27; Matt. 23:17, 19
20 [a]Lev. 21:5
21 [a]Lev. 10:9
22 [I]Hebr. *thrust forth* [II]Hebr. *from a priest* [a]Lev. 21:7, 13, 14
23 [a]Lev. 10:10, 11; Ezek. 22:26; Mal. 2:7
24 [a]Deut. 17:8; 2Chr. 19:8, 10 [b]Ezek. 22:26
25 [a]Lev. 21:1
26 [a]Num. 6:10; 19:11
27 [a]Ezek. 44:17 [b]Lev. 4:3
28 [a]Num. 18:20; Deut. 10:9; 18:1, 2; Josh. 13:14, 33
29 [I]Or, *devoted* [a]Lev. 6:18, 29; 7:6 [b]Lev. 27:21, 28; Num. 18:14
30 [I]Or, *chief* [a]Ex. 13:2; 22:29, 30; 23:19; Num. 3:13; 18:12, 13 [b]Num. 15:20; Neh. 10:37 [c]Prov. 3:9, 10; Mal. 3:10
31 [a]Ex. 22:31; Lev. 22:8
1 [I]Hebr. *when ye cause the land to fall* [II]Hebr. *holiness* [a]Ezek. 47:22 [b]Ezek. 48:8
2 [I]Or, *void places* [a]Ezek. 42:20
3 [a]Ezek. 48:10
4 [a]Ezek. 45:1; 48:10
5 [a]Ezek. 48:13 [b]Ezek. 40:17
6 [a]Ezek. 48:15
7 [a]Ezek. 48:21

shall be over against one of the portions, from the west border unto the east border.

8 In the land shall be his possession in Israel: and [a]my princes[5387] shall no more oppress[3238] my people;[5971] and *the rest of* the land shall they give to the house of Israel according to their tribes.[7626]

9 Thus saith[559] the Lord[136] GOD; [a]Let it suffice you, O princes of Israel: [b]remove violence[2555] and spoil,[7701] and execute judgment[4941] and justice,[6666] take away your [I]exactions from my people, saith[5002] the Lord GOD.

10 Ye shall have just[6664] [a]balances, and a just ephah, and a just bath.

11 The ephah and the bath shall be of one measure, that the bath may contain the tenth part[4643] of an homer,[2563] and the ephah the tenth part of an homer: the measure thereof shall be after the homer.

12 And the [a]shekel *shall be* twenty gerahs:[1626] twenty shekels, five and twenty shekels, fifteen shekels, shall be your maneh.[4488]

13 This *is* the oblation that ye shall offer; the sixth part of an ephah[374] of an homer of wheat, and ye shall give the sixth part of an ephah of an homer of barley:

14 Concerning the ordinance[2706] of oil,[8081] the bath[1324] of oil, *ye shall offer* the tenth part of a bath out of the cor, *which is* an homer of ten baths; for ten baths *are* an homer:

15 And one [I]lamb out of the flock, out of two hundred, out of the fat pastures of Israel; for a meat offering,[4503] and for a burnt offering, and for [II]peace offerings,[8002] [a]to make reconciliation[3722] for them, saith the Lord GOD.

16 All the people of the land [I]shall give this oblation [II]for the prince in Israel.

17 And it shall be the prince's part *to give* burnt offerings,[5930] and meat offerings, and drink offerings,[5262] in the feasts,[2282] and in the new moons, and in the sabbaths,[7676] in all solemnities[4150] of the house of Israel: he shall prepare[3559] the sin offering,[2403] and the meat offering, and the burnt offering, and the [I]peace offerings, to make reconciliation for the house of Israel.

The Feast Days

18 Thus saith the Lord GOD; In the first[7223] *month,* in the first *day* of the month, thou shalt take a young bullock without blemish,[8549] and [a]cleanse[2398] the sanctuary:

19 [a]And the priest[3548] shall take of the blood[1818] of the sin offering, and put *it* upon the posts of the house, and upon the four corners of the settle of the altar,[4196] and upon the posts of the gate of the inner court.

20 And so thou shalt do[6213] the seventh *day* of the month [a]for every one[376] that erreth,[7686] and for *him that is* simple:[6612] so shall ye reconcile[3722] the house.

21 [a]In the first *month,* in the fourteenth day[3117] of the month, ye shall have the passover,[6453] a feast[2282] of seven days; unleavened bread[4682] shall be eaten.

22 And upon that day shall the prince prepare for himself and for all the people of the land [a]a bullock *for* a sin offering.

23 And [a]seven days of the feast he shall prepare a burnt offering to the LORD, seven bullocks and seven rams without blemish daily the seven days; [b]and a kid[8163] of the goats daily *for* a sin offering.

24 [a]And he shall prepare a meat offering of an ephah for a bullock, and an ephah for a ram, and an hin of oil for an ephah.

25 In the seventh *month,* in the fifteenth day of the month, shall he do the like in the [a]feast of the seven days, according to the sin offering, according to the burnt offering, and according to the meat offering, and according to the oil.

The Prince and the Festivals

46 Thus saith[559] the Lord[136] GOD; The gate of the inner court that

---

8 [a]Jer. 22:17; Ezek. 22:27; 46:18
9 [I]Hebr. *expulsions* [a]Ezek. 44:6 [b]Jer. 22:3
10 [a]Lev. 19:35, 36; Prov. 11:1
12 [a]Ex. 30:13; Lev. 27:25; Num. 3:47
15 [I]Or, *kid* [II]Or, *thank offerings* [a]Lev. 1:4
16 [I]Hebr. *shall be for* [II]Or, *with*
17 [I]Or, *thank offerings*
18 [a]Lev. 16:16
19 [a]Ezek. 43:20
20 [a]Lev. 4:27
21 [a]Ex. 12:18; Lev. 23:5, 6; Num. 9:2, 3; 28:16, 17; Deut. 16:1
22 [a]Lev. 4:14
23 [a]Lev. 23:8 [b]Num. 28:15, 22, 30; 29:5, 11, 16, 19
24 [a]Ezek. 46:5, 7
25 [a]Lev. 23:34; Num. 29:12; Deut. 16:13

looketh toward[1870] the east shall be shut the six working days;[3117] but on the sabbath[7676] it shall be opened, and in the day of the new moon it shall be opened.

2 [a]And the prince[5387] shall enter by the way[1870] of the porch of *that* gate without, and shall stand by the post of the gate, and the priests[3548] shall prepare[3559] his burnt offering[5930] and his peace offerings,[8002] and he shall worship[7812] at the threshold of the gate: then he shall go forth; but the gate shall not be shut until the evening.

3 Likewise the people[5971] of the land[776] shall worship at the door of this gate before the LORD in the sabbaths and in the new moons.

4 And the burnt offering that [a]the prince shall offer[7126] unto the LORD in the sabbath day *shall be* six lambs without blemish,[8549] and a ram without blemish.

5 [a]And the meat offering[4503] *shall be* an ephah for a ram, and the meat offering for the lambs [I][b]as he shall be able to give, and an hin of oil[8081] to an ephah.

6 And in the day of the new moon *it shall be* a young bullock without blemish, and six lambs,[3532] and a ram: they shall be without blemish.

7 And he shall prepare a meat offering, an ephah for a bullock, and an ephah for a ram, and for the lambs according as his hand[3027] shall attain unto, and an hin of oil to an ephah.

8 [a]And when the prince shall enter, he shall go in by the way of the porch of *that* gate, and he shall go forth by the way thereof.

9 But when the people of the land [a]shall come before the LORD in the solemn feasts,[4150] he that entereth in by the way of the north gate to worship shall go out by the way of the south gate; and he that entereth by the way of the south gate shall go forth by the way of the north gate: he shall not return[7725] by the way of the gate whereby he came in, but shall go forth over against it.

10 And the prince in the midst of them, when they go in, shall go in; and when they go forth, shall go forth.

11 And in the feasts[2282] and in the solemnities[4150] [a]the meat offering shall be an ephah to a bullock, and an ephah to a ram, and to the lambs as he is able to give, and an hin of oil to an ephah.

12 Now when the prince shall prepare a voluntary[5071] burnt offering or peace offerings[8002] voluntarily unto the LORD, [a]*one* shall then open him the gate that looketh toward the east, and he shall prepare his burnt offering and his peace offerings, as he did[6213] on the sabbath day: then he shall go forth; and after his going forth *one* shall shut the gate.

13 [a]Thou shalt daily[3117] prepare a burnt offering unto the LORD *of* a lamb [I]of the first year without blemish: thou shalt prepare it [II]every morning.

14 And thou shalt prepare a meat offering[4503] for it every morning, the sixth part of an ephah, and the third part of an hin of oil, to temper with the fine flour; a meat offering continually[8548] by a perpetual[5769] ordinance[2708] unto the LORD.

15 Thus shall they prepare the lamb, and the meat offering, and the oil, every morning *for* a continual burnt offering.

16 Thus saith the Lord GOD; If the prince give a gift unto any of his sons,[1121] the inheritance[5159] thereof shall be his sons'; it *shall be* their possession[272] by inheritance.

17 But if he give a gift of his inheritance to one of his servants,[5650] then it shall be his to [a]the year of liberty;[1865] after it shall return to the prince: but his inheritance shall be his sons' for them.

18 Moreover [a]the prince shall not take of the people's[5971] inheritance[5159] by oppression,[3238] to thrust them out of their possession; *but* he shall give his sons inheritance out of his own possession: that my people be not scattered every man[376] from his possession.

19 After he brought me through the entry, which *was* at the side of the gate,

2 [a]Ezek. 44:3; 46:8
4 [a]Ezek. 45:17
5 [I]Hebr. *the gift of his hand* [a]Ezek. 45:24; 46:7, 11 [b]Deut. 16:17
8 [a]Ezek. 46:2
9 [a]Ex. 23:14-17; Deut. 16:16
11 [a]Ezek. 46:5
12 [a]Ezek. 44:3; 46:2
13 [I]Hebr. *a son of his year* [II]Hebr. *morning by morning* [a]Ex. 29:38; Num. 28:3
17 [a]Lev. 25:10
18 [a]Ezek. 45:8

into the holy[6944] chambers of the priests, which looked toward the north: and, behold, there *was* a place on the two sides westward.

20 Then said[559] he unto me, This *is* the place where the priests shall [a]boil the trespass offering[817] and the sin offering,[2403] where they shall [b]bake the meat offering; that they bear *them* not out into the utter court, [c]to sanctify[6942] the people.

21 Then he brought me forth into the utter court, and caused me to pass by the four corners of the court; and, behold, [I]in every corner of the court *there was* a court.

22 In the four corners of the court *there were* courts [I]joined of forty *cubits* long[753] and thirty broad: these four [II]corners *were* of one measure.

23 And *there was* a row *of building* round about in them, round about them four, and *it was* made[6213] with boiling places[4018] under the rows round about.

24 Then said he unto me, These *are* the places[1004] of them that boil, where the ministers[8334] of the house[1004] shall [a]boil the sacrifice of the people.

The Healing Waters From the Temple

47 Afterward he brought me again unto the door of the house; and, behold, [a]waters issued out from under the threshold of the house eastward: for the forefront[6440] of the house *stood toward* the east, and the waters came down from under from the right side of the house, at the south *side* of the altar.[4196]

2 Then brought he me out of the way[1870] of the gate northward, and led me about the way without unto the utter gate by the way that looketh eastward; and, behold, there ran out waters on the right side.

3 And when [a]the man that had the line in his hand[3027] went forth eastward, he measured a thousand cubits, and he brought me through the waters; the [I]waters *were* to the ankles.

20 [a]2Chr. 35:13 [b]Lev. 2:4, 5, 7 [c]Ezek. 44:19

21 [I]Hebr. *a court in a corner of a court, and a court in a corner of a court*

22 [I]Or, *made with chimneys* [II]Hebr. *cornered*

24 [a]Ezek. 24:20

1 [a]Joel 3:18; Zech. 13:1; 14:8; Rev. 22:1

3 [I]Hebr. *waters of the ankles* [a]Ezek. 40:3

5 [I]Hebr. *waters of swimming*

7 [I]Hebr. *lip* [a]Ezek. 47:12; Rev. 22:2

8 [I]Or, *plain:* Deut. 3:17; 4:49; Josh. 3:16

9 [I]Hebr. *two rivers*

10 [a]Num. 34:6; Josh. 23:4; Ezek. 48:28

11 [I]Or, *and that* which *shall not be healed*

12 [I]Hebr. *shall come up* [II]Or, *principal* [III]Or, *for bruises and sores* [a]Ezek. 47:7 [b]Job 8:16; Ps. 1:3; Jer. 17:8 [c]Rev. 22:2

4 Again he measured a thousand, and brought me through the waters; the waters *were* to the knees. Again he measured a thousand, and brought me through; the waters *were* to the loins.

5 Afterward he measured a thousand; *and it was* a river that I could not pass over:[5674] for the waters were risen,[1342] [I]waters to swim in, a river that could not be passed over.

6 And he said[559] unto me, Son[1121] of man,[120] hast thou seen[7200] *this*? Then he brought me, and caused me to return[7725] to the brink[8193] of the river.

7 Now when I had returned,[7725] behold, at the [I]bank[8193] of the river *were* very many [a]trees on the one side and on the other.

8 Then said he unto me, These waters issue out toward the east country,[1552] and go down into the [I]desert,[6160] and go into the sea: *which being* brought forth into the sea, the waters shall be healed.

9 And it shall come to pass, *that* every thing that liveth,[2416] which moveth, whithersoever the [I]rivers shall come, shall live[2421] and there shall be a very great multitude of fish,[1710] because these waters shall come thither: for they shall be healed; and every thing shall live[2425] whither the river cometh.

10 And it shall come to pass, *that* the fishers shall stand upon it from En–gedi even unto En–eglaim; they shall be a *place* to spread forth nets;[2764] their fish shall be according to their kinds, as the fish [a]of the great sea, exceeding many.

11 But the miry places[1207] thereof and the marishes thereof [I]shall not be healed; they shall be given to salt.

12 And [a]by the river upon the bank thereof, on this side and on that side, [I]shall grow all trees for meat, [b]whose leaf shall not fade, neither shall the fruit thereof be consumed:[8552] it shall bring forth [II]new fruit according to his months, because their waters they issued out of the sanctuary:[4720] and the fruit thereof shall be for meat, and the leaf thereof [III]for [c]medicine.

The Boundaries of the Land

13 Thus saith the Lord[136] GOD; This *shall be* the border, whereby ye shall inherit[5157] the land[776] according to the twelve tribes[7626] of Israel: [a]Joseph *shall have two* portions.[2256]

14 And ye shall inherit[3423] it, one[376] as well as another: *concerning* the which I [I][a]lifted up[5375] mine hand to give it unto your fathers:[1] and this land shall [b]fall unto you for inheritance.[5159]

15 And this *shall be* the border of the land toward the north side, from the great sea, [a]the way of Hethlon, as men go to [b]Zedad;

16 [a]Hamath, [b]Berothah, Sibraim, which *is* between the border of Damascus and the border of Hamath; [I]Hazar–hatticon, which *is* by the coast of Hauran.

17 And the border[1366] from the sea shall be [a]Hazar–enan, the border of Damascus, and the north northward, and the border of Hamath. And *this is* the north side.

18 And the east side ye shall measure [I]from Hauran, and from Damascus, and from Gilead, and from the land of Israel *by* Jordan, from the border unto the east sea. And *this is* the east side.

19 And the south side southward, from Tamar *even* to [a]the waters of [I]strife *in* Kadesh, the [II]river to the great sea. And *this is* [III]the south side southward.

20 The west side also *shall be* the great sea from the border, till a man come over against Hamath. This *is* the west side.

21 So shall ye divide[5307] this land unto you according to the tribes of Israel.

22 And it shall come to pass, *that* ye shall divide it by lot for an inheritance unto you, [a]and to the strangers[1616] that sojourn among you, which shall beget children[1121] among you: [b]and they shall be unto you as born in the country among the children of Israel; they shall have inheritance with you among the tribes of Israel.

13 [a]Gen. 48:5; 1Chr. 5:1; Ezek. 48:4, 5
14 [I]Or, *swore* [a]Gen. 12:7; 13:15; 15:7; 17:8; 26:3; 28:13; Ezek. 20:5, 6, 28, 42 [b]Ezek. 48:29
15 [a]Ezek. 48:1 [b]Num. 34:8
16 [I]Or, *The middle village* [a]Num. 34:8 [b]2Sam. 8:8
17 [a]Num. 34:9; Ezek. 48:1
18 [I]Hebr. *from between*
19 [I]Or, *Meribah* [II]Or, *valley* [III]Or, *toward Teman* [a]Num. 20:13; Deut. 32:51; Ps. 81:7
22 [a]Eph. 3:6; Rev. 7:9, 10 [b]Rom. 10:12; Gal. 3:28; Col. 3:11
1 [a]Ezek. 47:15
8 [a]Ezek. 45:1-6

23 And it shall come to pass, *that* in what tribe the stranger sojourneth,[1481] there shall ye give *him* his inheritance, saith[5002] the Lord GOD.

Apportionment

48 Now these *are* the names of the tribes.[7626] [a]From the north end to the coast of the way[1870] of Hethlon, as one goeth to Hamath, Hazar–enan, the border of Damascus northward, to the coast of Hamath; for these are his sides east *and* west; a *portion for* Dan.

2 And by the border of Dan, from the east side unto the west side, a *portion for* Asher.

3 And by the border of Asher, from the east side even unto the west side, a *portion for* Naphtali.

4 And by the border of Naphtali, from the east side unto the west side, a *portion for* Manasseh.

5 And by the border of Manasseh, from the east side unto the west side, a *portion for* Ephraim.

6 And by the border of Ephraim, from the east side even unto the west side, a *portion for* Reuben.

7 And by the border of Reuben, from the east side unto the west side, a *portion for* Judah.

8 And by the border of Judah, from the east side unto the west side, shall be [a]the offering[8641] which ye shall offer of five and twenty thousand *reeds in* breadth, and *in* length as one of the *other* parts, from the east side unto the west side: and the sanctuary[4720] shall be in the midst of it.

9 The oblation[8641] that ye shall offer unto the LORD *shall be* of five and twenty thousand in length, and of ten thousand in breadth.

10 And for them, *even* for the priests,[3548] shall be *this* holy[6944] oblation; toward the north five and twenty thousand *in length,* and toward the west ten thousand in breadth, and toward the east ten thousand in breadth, and toward the south five and twenty thousand in length:

and the sanctuary of the LORD shall be in the midst thereof.

11 [I][a]*It shall be* for the priests that are sanctified[6942] of the sons[1121] of Zadok; which have kept[8104] my [II]charge,[4931] which went not astray when the children[1121] of Israel went astray, [b]as the Levites went astray.

12 And *this* oblation[8642] of the land[776] that is offered shall be unto them a thing most holy by the border of the Levites.

13 And over against the border of the priests the Levites *shall have* five and twenty thousand in length, and ten thousand in breadth: all the length *shall be* five and twenty thousand, and the breadth ten thousand.

14 [a]And they shall not sell of it, neither exchange, nor alienate[5674] the firstfruits[7225] of the land: for *it is* holy unto the LORD.

15 [a]And the five thousand, that are left[3498] in the breadth over against the five and twenty thousand, shall be [b]a profane[2455] *place* for the city, for dwelling,[4186] and for suburbs: and the city shall be in the midst thereof.

16 And these *shall be* the measures thereof; the north side four thousand and five hundred, and the south side four thousand and five hundred, and on the east side four thousand and five hundred, and the west side four thousand and five hundred.

17 And the suburbs[4054] of the city shall be toward the north two hundred and fifty, and toward the south two hundred and fifty, and toward the east two hundred and fifty, and toward the west two hundred and fifty.

18 And the residue[3498] in length over against the oblation[8641] of the holy[6944] *portion shall be* ten thousand eastward, and ten thousand westward: and it shall be over against the oblation of the holy *portion;* and the increase thereof shall be for food unto them that serve[5647] the city.

19 [a]And they that serve the city shall serve it out of all the tribes of Israel.

20 All the oblation *shall be* five and twenty thousand by five and twenty thousand: ye shall offer the holy oblation foursquare, with the possession[272] of the city.

21 [a]And the residue *shall be* for the prince,[5387] on the one side and on the other of the holy oblation, and of the possession of the city, over against the five and twenty thousand of the oblation toward the east border, and westward over against the five and twenty thousand toward the west border, over against the portions for the prince: and it shall be the holy oblation; [b]and the sanctuary of the house[1004] *shall be* in the midst thereof.

22 Moreover from the possession of the Levites, and from the possession of the city, *being* in the midst *of that* which is the prince's, between the border of Judah and the border of Benjamin, shall be for the prince.

23 As for the rest[3499] of the tribes, from the east side unto the west side, Benjamin *shall have* a *portion.*

24 And by the border of Benjamin, from the east side unto the west side, Simeon *shall have* a *portion.*

25 And by the border of Simeon, from the east side unto the west side, Issachar a *portion.*

26 And by the border of Issachar, from the east side unto the west side, Zebulun a *portion.*

27 And by the border of Zebulun, from the east side unto the west side, Gad a *portion.*

28 And by the border of Gad, at the south side southward, the border shall be even from Tamar *unto* [a]the waters of [I]strife *in* Kadesh, *and* to the river toward the great sea.

29 [a]This *is* the land which ye shall divide by lot[5307] unto the tribes of Israel for inheritance,[5159] and these *are* their portions, saith[5002] the Lord[136] GOD.

30 And these *are* the goings out of the city on the north side, four thousand and five hundred measures.

31 [a]And the gates of the city *shall be* after the names of the tribes of Israel: three gates northward; one gate of Reuben, one gate of Judah, one gate of Levi.

11 [I]Or, *The sanctified portion shall be for the priests* [II]Or, *ward,* or, *ordinance* [a]Ezek. 44:15 [b]Ezek. 44:10

14 [a]Ex. 22:29; Lev. 27:10, 28, 33

15 [a]Ezek. 45:6 [b]Ezek. 42:20

19 [a]Ezek. 45:6

21 [a]Ezek. 45:7; [b]Ezek. 48:8, 10

28 [I]Hebr. *Meribah-kadesh* [a]Ezek. 47:19

29 [a]Ezek. 47:14, 21, 22

31 [a]Rev. 21:12

32 And at the east side four thousand and five hundred: and three gates; and one gate of Joseph, one gate of Benjamin, one gate of Dan.

33 And at the south side four thousand and five hundred measures: and three gates; one gate of Simeon, one gate of Issachar, one gate of Zebulun.

34 At the west side four thousand and five hundred, *with* their three gates; one gate of Gad, one gate of Asher, one gate of Naphtali.

35 *It was* round about eighteen thousand *measures:* [a]and the name of the city from *that* day[3117] *shall be,* [I][b]The LORD *is* there.

35 [I]Hebr. *Jehovah-shammah* [a]Jer. 33:16 [a]Ex. 17:15; Judg. 6:24; Jer. 3:17; Joel 3:21; Zech. 2:10; Rev. 21:3; 22:3

The Book of

DANIEL

Daniel was a nobleman of Israel (possibly a prince) who was taken to Babylon in the first deportation (605 B.C.), probably while in his early teens (Dan. 1:3, 4). His ministry lasted the entire length of the Babylonian Exile, his last dated prophecy being made in 536 B.C. when he was in his eighties. The meaning of Daniel's name, "my God is Judge," is certainly in harmony with the overall theme of the book—the sovereignty of God. This book describes current and future world conflicts, but God's control over all events is clearly demonstrated.

Daniel is probably the most highly organized book in Scripture. Some attribute this to the fact that near the end of his life, Daniel rewrote and organized the whole book into one consolidated message. The intricate arrangement of the ideas in the book demonstrates the extraordinary wisdom of Daniel (Dan. 1:17, 19, 20; 4:9; 5:11).

The things that appear in Daniel's visions, such as the great statue, the beasts, the angelic messengers, and the description of God's glory are very similar to the things that are portrayed in the Book of Revelation. The Book of Revelation cannot be properly interpreted without a general knowledge of the Book of Daniel. Material from every chapter of Daniel is either quoted or alluded to in Revelation, and only two chapters in Revelation do not have some background in Daniel.

Dare to Stand

1 In the third year of the reign[4438]
of Jehoiakim king[4428] of Judah [a]came
Nebuchadnezzar king of Babylon unto
Jerusalem, and besieged it.
2 And the Lord[136] gave Jehoiakim
king of Judah into his hand,[3027] with
[a]part of the vessels of the house[1004] of
God:[430] which he carried [b]into the land[776]
of Shinar to the house of his god; [c]and
he brought the vessels into the treasure
house of his god.
3 And the king spake unto Ashpenaz
the master of his eunuchs,[5631] that he
should bring [a]*certain* of the children[1121]
of Israel, and of the king's seed,[2233] and
of the princes;[6579]
4 Children [a]in whom *was* no
blemish,[3971] but well favoured, and skilful[7919] in all wisdom,[2451] and cunning in
knowledge,[1847] and understanding[995]
science,[4093] and such as *had* ability in
them to stand in the king's palace,[1964]
and [b]whom they might teach[3925] the
learning[5612] and the tongue of the Chaldeans.
5 And the king appointed them a
daily provision of the king's meat,[6598]

1 [a]2Kgs. 24:1; 2Chr. 36:6
2 [a]Jer. 27:19, 20 [b]Gen. 10:10; 11:2; Isa. 11:11; Zech. 5:11 [c]2Chr. 36:7
3 [a]2Kgs. 20:17, 18; Isa. 39:7
4 [a]Lev. 24:19, 20 [b]Acts 7:22

1:1 The "third year of Jehoiakim" is the same year as "the fourth year of Jehoiakim" in Jeremiah 25:1. Both dates are correct but were written from different perspectives for counting years. Daniel used the Chaldean method that did not count the accession year of a king as part of the actual reign. Jeremiah was writing according to the Judean method, which did include the accession year of King Jehoiakim's reign.

1:3 Oriental kings customarily had eunuchs for their high officials. Since these men would have no sons to carry on a kingly line, the motivation for intrigue and assassination attempts were minimized. See note on Nehemiah 1:11.

1:4, 5 Scholars suggest three possible reasons for taking the youths of the nobility and royal family into captivity: 1) to hold them as hostages, thereby ensuring the loyalty of their families; 2) to develop men who already had some education to serve in Nebuchadnezzar's rapidly expanding bureaucracy; 3) to indoctrinate them with Babylonian ideals in the hope of employing them as liaisons between Babylon and the province of Judea.

and of [I]the wine which he drank:[4960] so nourishing them three years, that at the end thereof they might [a]stand before the king.

6 Now among these were of the children of Judah, Daniel, Hananiah, Mishael, and Azariah:

7 [a]Unto whom the prince[8269] of the eunuchs gave names: [b]for he gave unto Daniel *the name* of Belteshazzar; and to Hananiah, of Shadrach; and to Mishael, of Meshach; and to Azariah, of Abed–nego.

8 But Daniel purposed[7760] in his heart[3820] that he would not defile himself[1351] [a]with the portion of the king's meat, nor with the wine which he drank: therefore he requested of the prince of the eunuchs that he might not defile himself.

9 Now [a]God had brought Daniel into favour[2617] and tender love[7356] with the prince of the eunuchs.

10 And the prince of the eunuchs said[559] unto Daniel, I fear[3373] my lord[113] the king, who hath appointed your meat and your drink:[4960] for why should he see your faces [I]worse liking[2196] than the children which *are* of your [II]sort? then shall ye make *me* endanger my head[7218] to the king.

11 Then said Daniel to [I]Melzar, whom the prince of the eunuchs had set over Daniel, Hananiah, Mishael, and Azariah,

12 Prove[5254] thy servants,[5650] I beseech thee,[4994] ten days;[3117] and let them give us [I]pulse[2235] [II]to eat, and water to drink.

13 Then let our countenances[4758] be looked upon[7200] before thee, and the countenance of the children that eat of the portion of the king's meat: and as thou seest, deal[6213] with thy servants.

14 So he consented[8085] to them in this matter,[1697] and proved them ten days.

15 And at the end of ten days their countenances appeared[7200] fairer[2896] and fatter in flesh[1320] than all the children which did eat the portion of the king's meat.

16 Thus Melzar took away[5375] the portion of their meat, and the wine that they should drink; and gave them pulse.

17 As for these four children, [a]God gave them [b]knowledge and skill[7919] in all learning and wisdom: and [I]Daniel had [c]understanding in all visions[2377] and dreams.

18 Now at the end of the days that the king had said he should bring them in, then the prince of the eunuchs brought them in before Nebuchadnezzar.

19 And the king communed[1696] with them; and among them all was found none like Daniel, Hananiah, Mishael, and Azariah: therefore [a]stood they before the king.

20 [a]And in all matters of [I]wisdom *and* understanding,[998] that the king enquired of them, he found them ten times better than all the magicians[2748] *and* astrologers[825] that *were* in all his realm.

21 [a]And Daniel continued *even* unto the first year of king Cyrus.

The Dream of Nebuchadnezzar

2 And in the second year of the reign[4438] of Nebuchadnezzar, Nebuchadnezzar dreamed dreams, [a]wherewith his spirit was troubled, and [b]his sleep brake[1961] from him.

2 [a]Then the king[4428] commanded[559] to call[7121] the magicians, and the astrologers, and the sorcerers,[3784] and the Chaldeans, for to shew[5046] the king his

5 [I]Hebr. *the wine of his drink* [a]Gen. 41:46; 1Kgs. 10:8; Dan. 1:19

7 [a]Gen. 41:45; 2Kgs. 24:17 [b]Dan. 4:8; 5:12

8 [a]Deut. 32:38; Ezek. 4:13; Hos. 9:3

9 [a]Gen. 39:21; Ps. 106:46; Prov. 16:7

10 [I]Hebr. *sadder* [II]Or, *term,* or, *continuance*

11 [I]Or, *The steward*

12 [I]Hebr. *of pulse* [II]Hebr. *that we may eat*

17 [I]Or, *he made Daniel understand* [a]1Kgs. 3:12; James 1:5, 17 [b]Acts 7:22 [c]Num. 12:6; 2Chr. 26:5; Dan. 5:11, 12, 14; 10:1

19 [a]Gen. 41:46; Dan. 1:5

20 [I]Hebr. *wisdom of understanding* [a]1Kgs. 10:1

21 [a]Dan. 6:28; 10:1

1 [a]Gen. 41:8; Dan. 4:5 [b]Esth. 6:1; Dan. 6:18

2 [a]Gen. 41:8; Ex. 7:11; Dan. 5:7

1:7 The meanings of these four Hebrew names affirm God's sovereignty and mercy. Daniel means "God is Judge"; Hananiah means "God is gracious"; Azariah means "God is my Help"; and Mishael means "Who is like God?" The meanings of their new names contradict the truth of their original names. Daniel becomes Belteshazzar, "Bel will protect"; Hananiah becomes Shadrach, "inspired of Aku"; Mishael becomes Meshach, "belonging to Aku"; and Azariah becomes Abed-nego, "servant of Nego."

dreams. So they came and stood before
the king.
3 And the king said[559] unto them, I
have dreamed a dream, and my spirit
was troubled to know[3045] the dream.
🔑 4 Then spake[1696] the Chaldeans to
the king[4430] in Syriack, [a]O king, live[2418]
for ever:[5957] tell[560] thy servants[5649] the
dream, and we will shew the interpretation.
5 The king answered and said[560] to
the Chaldeans, The thing[4406] is gone from
me: if ye will not make known[3046] unto
me the dream, with the interpretation
thereof, ye shall be [Ia]cut in pieces, and
your houses shall be made a dunghill.
6 [a]But if ye shew the dream, and the
interpretation thereof, ye shall receive of
me gifts and [Ib]rewards and great honour:
therefore shew me the dream, and the interpretation thereof.
7 They answered again and said, Let
the king tell his servants the dream, and
we will shew the interpretation of it.
8 The king answered and said, I
know[3046] of certainty[3330] that ye would
[Ia]gain the time, because ye see[2370] the
thing is gone from me.
9 But if ye will not make known
unto me the dream, [a]*there is but* one decree[1882] for you: for ye have prepared[2164]
lying and corrupt[7844] words[4406] to
speak[560] before me, till the time be
changed:[8133] therefore tell me the dream,
and I shall know that ye can shew me the
interpretation thereof.
10 The Chaldeans answered before
the king, and said, There is not a man[606]
upon the earth[3007] that can shew the
king's[4430] matter:[4406] therefore *there is* no
king, lord, nor ruler,[7990] *that* asked[7593]
such things at any magician,[2749] or
astrologer,[826] or Chaldean.
11 And *it is* a rare thing that the
king requireth,[7593] and there is none other
that can shew it before the king, [a]except
the gods,[426] whose dwelling is not with
flesh.[1321]
12 For this cause the king was angry[1149] and very furious,[7108] and commanded[560] to destroy[7] all the wise *men*
of Babylon.
13 And the decree went forth that
the wise *men* should be slain; and they
sought Daniel and his fellows to be slain.
🔑 14 Then Daniel [I]answered with
counsel[5843] and wisdom[2942] to Arioch the
[IIa]captain of the king's guard, which was
gone forth to slay the wise *men* of Babylon:
15 He answered and said to Arioch
the king's captain,[7990] Why *is* the decree
so hasty from the king? Then Arioch
made the thing known to Daniel.
16 Then Daniel went in, and desired[1156] of the king that he would give
him time,[2166] and that he would shew the
king the interpretation.

4 [a]1Kgs. 1:31; Dan. 3:9; 5:10; 6:6, 21
5 [I]Aram. *made pieces* [a]2Kgs. 10:27; Ezra 6:11; Dan. 3:29
6 [I]Or, *fee* [a]Dan. 5:16 [b]Dan. 2:48; 5:17
8 [I]Aram. *buy* [a]Eph. 5:16
9 [a]Esth. 4:11
11 [a]Dan. 2:28; 5:11
14 [I]Aram. *returned* [II]Or, *chief marshal;* Aram. *chief of the executioners,* or, *slaughter men* [a]Gen. 37:36

🔑 **2:4—7:28** This section of Daniel is in Aramaic, a language related to Hebrew but distinct from it. Aside from Daniel chapters two through seven, only Ezra 4:8—6:18; 7:12–26, and Jeremiah 10:11 are in Aramaic. Other words and phrases in the older books of the Old Testament are said to be Aramaic, but are more likely an early form of the Canaanite language, a common ancestor to both Hebrew and Aramaic. It is interesting that "LORD" ("YAHWEH" or "Jehovah") does not appear in the Aramaic section. Instead, expressions like the "King of heaven" (Dan. 4:37) or "high God" (Dan. 4:2, 24) are used in order to distinguish Him from the gods of the pagans. Since Aramaic was the international language of Daniel's day (cf. 2 Kgs. 18:26), it is appropriate for chapters two through seven, where the subject matter is God's sovereignty over the gentile world. On the other hand, the remainder of the book focuses on God's program for Israel (chaps. 1, 8—12). The change is probably made within a chapter (and even in the middle of 2:4) to draw attention to it. By New Testament times, Aramaic had become the common language of Palestine, and even in Ezra's day many of the returned exiles understood Aramaic better than Hebrew (Neh. 8:7, 8, 12).

🔑 **2:14–18** In this passage, Daniel provides an excellent example of how one should relate to authority. Note that he acted respectfully, went through the proper channels, and did not challenge anyone's position (Dan. 1:10; 2:14–16). See the note on Psalm 82:6 about respecting the office a person holds, even if that person is contemptible.

17 Then Daniel went to his house, and made the thing known to Hananiah, Mishael, and Azariah, his companions:

18 [a]That they would desire mercies [I]of the God[426] of heaven[8065] concerning this secret; [II]that Daniel and his fellows should not perish[7] with the rest[7606] of the wise *men* of Babylon.

19 Then was the secret revealed unto Daniel [a]in a night[3916] vision.[2376] Then Daniel blessed the God of heaven.

20 Daniel answered and said, [a]Blessed be the name of God for ever and ever: [b]for wisdom[2452] and might are his:

21 And he changeth [a]the times and the seasons:[2166] [b]he removeth kings,4430 and setteth up kings: [c]he giveth wisdom unto the wise, and knowledge[4486] to them that know understanding:999

22 [a]He revealeth1541 the deep and secret things:[5642] [b]he knoweth what *is* in the darkness, and [c]the light[5094] dwelleth with him.

23 I thank[3029] thee, and praise[7624] thee, O thou God of my fathers,[2] who hast given me wisdom and might, and hast made known3046 unto me now what we [a]desired of thee: for thou hast *now* made known unto us the king's matter.

24 Therefore Daniel went in unto Arioch, whom the king had ordained4483 to destroy the wise *men* of Babylon: he went and said thus unto him; Destroy not the wise *men* of Babylon: bring me in before the king, and I will shew unto the king the interpretation.

25 Then Arioch brought in Daniel before the king in haste,927 and said thus unto him, [I]I have found a man[1400] of the [II]captives of Judah, that will make known unto the king the interpretation.

26 The king answered and said to Daniel, whose name *was* Belteshazzar, Art thou able to make known unto me the dream which I have seen,[2370] and the interpretation thereof?

27 Daniel answered in the presence of the king, and said, The secret which the king hath demanded[7593] cannot the wise *men,* the astrologers,[826] the magicians,[2749] the soothsayers,[1505] shew unto the king;

28 [a]But there is a God in heaven that revealeth secrets, and [I]maketh known to the king Nebuchadnezzar [b]what shall be in the latter days.[3118] Thy dream, and the visions[2376] of thy head[7217] upon thy bed, are these;

29 As for thee, O king, thy thoughts [I]came *into thy mind* upon thy bed, what should come to pass hereafter: [a]and he that revealeth secrets maketh known to thee what shall come to pass.1934

30 [a]But as for me, this secret is not revealed to me for *any* wisdom that I have more than any living,[2417] [I]but for *their* sakes that shall make known the interpretation to the king, [b]and that thou mightest know the thoughts of thy heart.[3825]

31 Thou, O king, [I]sawest,[2370] and be-

18 [I]Aram. *from before God* [a]Matt. 18:19 [II]Or, *that they should not destroy Daniel*
19 [a]Num. 12:6; Job 33:15, 16
20 [a]Ps. 113:2; 115:18 [b]Jer. 32:19
21 [a]1Chr. 29:30; Esth. 1:13; Dan. 7:25; 11:6 [b]Job 12:18; Ps. 75:6, 7; Jer. 27:5; Dan. 4:17 [c]James 1:5
22 [a]Job 12:22; Ps. 25:14; Dan. 2:28, 29 [b]Ps. 139:11, 12; Heb. 4:13 [c]Dan. 5:11, 14; James 1:17
23 [a]Dan. 2:18
25 [I]Aram. *That I have found* [II]Aram. *children of the captivity of Judah*
28 [I]Aram. *hath made known* [a]Gen. 40:8; 41:16; Dan. 2:18, 47; Amos 4:13 [b]Gen. 49:1
29 [I]Aram. *came up* [a]Dan. 2:22, 28
30 [I]Or, *but for the intent that the interpretation may be made known to the king* [a]Gen. 41:16; Acts 3:12 [b]Dan. 2:47
31 [I]Aram. *wast seeing*

2:31–45 This vision deals with four world empires and is crucial to a proper understanding of world history. It is important to remember that it is one image that is divided into individual kingdoms. The most consistent interpretation of the vision asserts that Jesus Christ will establish a world rule in the "last days." Scholars of all eschatological opinions accept that the four kingdoms described in the interpretation (vv. 38–40) are Babylon, Medo-Persia, Greece, and Rome. The value of the materials in each section of the image decreases from head to foot, but increases in military strength. The decreased value of the elements in each successive section seems to relate to a decrease in the absolute rule by the kings in each portion. Following the kingdom of Nebuchadnezzar, every empire had a ruler who exhibited external controls, and Rome was technically a republic even though the emperors exercised dictatorial powers.

All of the kingdoms were physical, earthly empires that are called "world empires" (because of the language in v. 39, "over all the earth" or "all the land"), but none of them actually ruled the whole planet. They did not even rule over the same areas. However, the one area ruled outright by all the kingdoms is the Promised Land.

(continued on next page)

hold a great image.[6755] This great image, whose brightness *was* excellent,[3493] stood before thee; and the form thereof *was* terrible.[1763]

32 [a]This image's[6755] head *was* of fine[2869] gold, his breast and his arms of silver, his belly and his [I]thighs of brass,

33 His legs of iron, his feet part of iron and part of clay.

34 Thou sawest till that a stone was cut out[1505] [I][a][b]without hands,[3028] which smote[4223] the image upon his feet *that were* of iron and clay, and brake them to pieces.

35 Then was the iron, the clay, the brass, the silver, and the gold, broken to pieces[1855] together, and became [a]like the chaff of the summer threshingfloors; and the wind[7308] carried them away, that [b]no place was found for them: and the stone that smote the image [c]became a great mountain, [d]and filled the whole earth.[772]

36 This *is* the dream; and we will tell the interpretation thereof before the king.

37 [a]Thou, O king, *art* a king of kings: [b]for the God of heaven hath given thee a kingdom,[4437] power, and strength, and glory.

38 [a]And wheresoever the children[1123] of men[606] dwell, the beasts of the field and the fowls of the heaven hath he given into thine hand,[3028] and hath made thee ruler[7981] over them all. [b]Thou *art* this head of gold.

39 And after thee shall arise [a]another kingdom [b]inferior[772] to thee, and another third kingdom of brass, which shall bear rule[7981] over all the earth.

40 And [a]the fourth kingdom shall be strong as iron: forasmuch as iron breaketh in pieces and subdueth[2827] all *things:* and as iron that breaketh[7940] all these, shall it break in pieces and bruise.[7490]

41 And whereas thou sawest [a]the feet and toes, part of potters' clay, and part of iron, the kingdom shall be divided;[6386] but there shall be in it of the strength[5326] of the iron, forasmuch as thou sawest the iron mixed[6151] with miry[2917] clay.

42 And *as* the toes of the feet *were* part of iron, and part of clay, *so* the kingdom shall be partly strong, and partly [I]broken.

43 And whereas thou sawest iron mixed with miry clay, they shall mingle themselves[6151] with the seed[2234] of men: but they shall not cleave [I]one to another, even as iron is not mixed with clay.

44 And in [I]the days of these kings [a]shall the God of heaven set up a kingdom, [b]which shall never be destroyed:[2255] and the [II]kingdom shall not be left to

32 [I]Or, *sides* [a]Dan. 2:38, 39
34 [I]Or, *which was not in hands* [a]Dan. 8:25; Zech. 4:6; 2Cor. 5:1; Heb. 9:24 [b]Dan. 2:45
35 [a]Ps. 1:4; Hos. 13:3 [b]Ps. 37:10, 36 [c]Isa. 2:2, 3 [d]Ps. 80:9
37 [a]Ezra 7:12; Isa. 47:5; Jer. 27:6, 7; Ezek. 26:7; Hos. 8:10 [b]Ezra 1:2
38 [a]Dan. 4:21, 22; Jer. 27:6 [b]Dan. 2:32
39 [a]Dan. 5:28, 31 [b]Dan. 2:32
40 [a]Dan. 7:7, 23
41 [a]Dan. 2:33
42 [I]Or, *brittle*
43 [I]Aram. *this with this*
44 [I]Aram. *their days* [II]Aram. *kingdom thereof* [a]Dan. 2:28 [b]Dan. 4:3, 34; 6:26; 7:14, 27; Mic. 4:7; Luke 1:32, 33

(continued from previous page)

The image is divided into five sections. The feet are distinguished in the vision (v. 33), but the interpretation explains the toes of the feet (v. 42). The stone (vv. 34, 45), which most agree represents Christ and His rule, does not strike the legs (Rome), but the feet. This last section of the image causes the most controversy as to the identity of the "feet." Many proponents of the premillennial view of eschatology believe that this refers to a "revived Roman Empire."

The way the stone destroys the image (vv. 34, 35, 45) is a key factor in being able to interpret the vision correctly. It strikes only the feet, but the whole image is crushed. The striking of the feet shows the timing of Christ in exercising His divine right to rule, while the crushing of the whole image teaches that Christ's reign will put an end to all forms of human government (cf. the relation of the stone to Israel and the world [Is. 8:14, 15, cf. Matt. 21:44]).

There is a prophetic "gap" in the chronology of this passage. The four empires take us up to the time of Christ, but there His clock for human government stopped. It will begin again for Daniel's "seventieth week" (see note on Dan. 9:24–27). The feet and toes represent the governments in existence at that time, which will be overwhelmed by the return of Christ.

Some argue that a kingdom cannot endure forever (v. 44) because God promised to make a "new heaven and a new earth" (Is. 65:17; 66:22; Rev. 21:1). This argument involves a common misunderstanding of the term "kingdom." The prophetic use of this word in both the Old Testament and the New Testament refers not to Christ's rule over a specific piece of territory, but to Christ's sovereignty, which will continue unbroken even after the new heavens and new earth are inhabited.

other people,[5972] [c]*but* it shall break in pieces and consume[5487] all these kingdoms,[4437] and it shall stand for ever.

45 [a]Forasmuch as thou sawest that the stone was cut out of the mountain [I]without hands, and that it brake in pieces the iron, the brass, the clay, the silver, and the gold; the great God hath made known to the king what shall come to pass [II]hereafter: and the dream *is* certain,3330 and the interpretation thereof sure.[540]

The King Rewards Daniel

🔑 46 [a]Then the king Nebuchadnezzar fell[5308] upon his face, and worshipped[5457] Daniel, and commanded that they should offer an oblation[4504] [b]and sweet odours unto him.

47 The king answered unto Daniel, and said, Of a truth[7187] *it is,* that your God *is* a God of gods, and a Lord[4756] of kings, [a]and a revealer1541 of secrets, seeing thou couldest reveal this secret.

48 Then the king made Daniel a great man, [a]and gave him many great gifts, and made him ruler over the whole province of Babylon, and [b]chief of the governors[5460] over all the wise *men* of Babylon.

49 Then Daniel requested[1156] of the king, [a]and he set Shadrach, Meshach, and Abed–nego, over the affairs of the province of Babylon: but Daniel [b]*sat* in the gate of the king.

The Fiery Furnace

3 Nebuchadnezzar the king4430 made an image[6755] of gold, whose height *was* threescore cubits, *and* the breadth thereof six cubits: he set it up in the plain of Dura, in the province of Babylon.

2 Then Nebuchadnezzar the king sent to gather together the princes,[324] the governors, and the captains,[6347] the judges,[148] the treasurers, the counsellors,1884 the sheriffs, and all the rulers[7984] of the provinces, to come to the dedication[2597] of the image which Nebuchadnezzar the king had set up.

3 Then the princes, the governors, and captains, the judges, the treasurers, the counsellors, the sheriffs, and all the rulers of the provinces, were gathered together[3673] unto the dedication of the image that Nebuchadnezzar the king had set up; and they stood before the image that Nebuchadnezzar had set up.

4 Then an herald cried [I]aloud,[2429] To you [II]it is commanded,[560] [a]O people,[5972] nations,[524] and languages,

5 *That* at what time ye hear[8086] the sound of the cornet, flute, harp, sackbut,5443 psaltery, [I]dulcimer, and all kinds of musick, ye fall down[5308] and worship the golden image that Nebuchadnezzar the king hath set up:

6 And whoso falleth not down and worshippeth[5457] shall the same hour [a]be cast into the midst of a burning fiery furnace.

7 Therefore at that time,[2166] when all the people heard[8086] the sound of the cornet, flute, harp, sackbut, psaltery,6460 and all kinds of musick, all the people, the nations, and the languages, fell down[5308] *and* worshipped[5457] the golden image that Nebuchadnezzar the king had set up.

🔑 8 Wherefore at that time certain[1400] Chaldeans [a]came near, and accused the Jews.

9 They spake and said[560] to the king Nebuchadnezzar, [a]O king, live[2418] for ever.[5957]

10 Thou, O king, hast made a decree,[2942] that every man[606] that shall hear the sound of the cornet, flute, harp,

44 [c]Ps. 2:9; Isa. 60:12; 1Cor. 15:24

45 [I]Or, *which was not in hands* [II]Aram. *after this* [a]Isa. 28:16; Dan. 2:24-35

46 [a]Acts 10:25; 14:13; 28:6 [b]Ezra 6:10

47 [a]Dan. 2:28

48 [a]Dan. 2:6 [b]Dan. 4:9; 5:11

49 [a]Dan. 3:12 [b]Esth. 2:19, 21; 3:2

4 [I]Aram. *with might* [II]Aram. *they command* [a]Dan. 4:1; 6:25

5 [I]Or, *singing;* Aram. *symphony*

6 [a]Jer. 29:22; Rev. 13:15

8 [a]Dan. 6:12

9 [a]Dan. 2:4; 5:10; 6:6, 21

🔑 **2:46, 47** These verses do not mean that the king actually bowed down and worshiped Daniel, but that he worshiped Daniel's God. This is the first time Nebuchadnezzar recognized that God was more powerful than the gods whom he worshiped in Babylon (see notes on Daniel 3:28, 29 and 4:1–37).

🔑 **3:8–18** The persecution faced by the three young men is viewed by many to be typical of the final persecution of Israel that will be led by the Antichrist.

sackbut, psaltery, and dulcimer,5481 and all kinds of musick, shall fall down and worship the golden image:

11 And whoso falleth not down and worshippeth, *that* he should be cast into the midst of a burning fiery furnace.

12 [a]There are certain Jews whom thou hast set over the affairs of the province of Babylon, Shadrach, Meshach, and Abed–nego; these men,[1400] O king, [I]have not regarded thee: they serve[6399] not thy gods,[426] nor worship the golden image which thou hast set up.

13 Then Nebuchadnezzar in *his* rage[7266] and fury commanded to bring Shadrach, Meshach, and Abed–nego. Then they brought these men before the king.

14 Nebuchadnezzar spake and said unto them, *Is it* [Ia]true,[6656] O Shadrach, Meshach, and Abed–nego, do not ye serve my gods, nor worship the golden image which I have set up?

15 Now if ye be ready that at what time ye hear the sound of the cornet, flute, harp, sackbut, psaltery, and dulcimer, and all kinds of musick, ye fall down and worship the image which I have made; [a]*well*: but if ye worship not, ye shall be cast the same hour into the midst of a burning fiery furnace; [b]and who *is* that God[426] that shall deliver you out of my hands?

16 Shadrach, Meshach, and Abed–nego, answered and said to the king, O Nebuchadnezzar, [a]we *are* not careful2818 to answer thee in this matter.[6600]

17 If it be *so,* our God whom we serve is able to deliver us from the burning fiery furnace, and he will deliver *us* out of thine hand,[3028] O king.

18 But if not, be it known3046 unto thee, O king, that we will not serve thy gods, nor worship the golden image which thou hast set up.

19 Then was Nebuchadnezzar [I]full of fury, and the form[6755] of his visage600 was changed against Shadrach, Meshach, and Abed–nego: *therefore* he spake, and commanded that they should heat the furnace one seven times more than it was wont[2370] to be heated.

20 And he commanded the [I]most[2429] mighty[1401] men that *were* in his army[2429] to bind Shadrach, Meshach, and Abed–nego, *and* to cast *them* into the burning fiery furnace.

21 Then these men were bound in their [I]coats, their hosen,6361 and their [II]hats, and their *other* garments, and were cast into the midst of the burning fiery furnace.

22 Therefore because the king's4430 [I]commandment[4406] was urgent,2685 and the furnace exceeding hot, the [II]flame of the fire slew those men that took up Shadrach, Meshach, and Abed–nego.

23 And these three men, Shadrach, Meshach, and Abed–nego, fell down bound into the midst of the burning fiery furnace.

24 Then Nebuchadnezzar the king was astonied,8429 and rose up in haste,927 *and* spake, and said unto his [I]counsellors, Did not we cast three men bound into the midst of the fire? They answered and said unto the king, True, O king.

🗝 25 He answered and said, Lo, I see[2370] four men loose, [a]walking in the midst of the fire, and [I]they have no hurt; and the form of the fourth is like [b]the Son1247 of God.[426]

26 Then Nebuchadnezzar came near to the [I]mouth of the burning fiery fur-

12 [a]Dan. 2:49 [I]Aram. *have set no regard upon thee*

14 [I]Or, *of purpose* [a]Ex. 21:13

15 [a]Ex. 32:32; Luke 13:9 [b]Ex. 5:2; 2Kgs. 18:35

16 [a]Matt. 10:19

19 [I]Aram. *filled*

20 [I]Aram. *mighty of strength*

21 [I]Or, *mantles* [II]Or, *turbans*

22 [I]Aram. *word* [II]Or, *spark*

24 [I]Or, *governors*

25 [I]Aram. *there is no hurt in them* [a]Isa. 43:2 [b]Job 1:6; 38:7; Ps. 34:7; Dan. 3:28

26 [I]Aram. *door*

🗝 **3:25** The identity of the fourth figure has been a subject of dispute. Since the earliest days, Christians have held that it was a preincarnate appearance of Jesus Christ. This is supported by the fact that Daniel uses "Son of man" in Daniel 7:13 in connection with divine glory. This gives the use of "Son of God" a similar weight by implication. The Jews, on the other hand, suggest that this was simply an angel. In examining the word for "God" that was used by Nebuchadnezzar, one can note the similarity to the Hebrew word *'Elohim* (430). He used the Chaldean word *'Elahin* (426) to refer to the God of the three Hebrew children. Some suggest that Nebuchadnezzar merely used an accurate quote of a word that he had heard the Hebrews use. Others support the idea that Nebuchadnezzar actually believed in the true God of the Hebrews.

nace, *and* spake, and said, Shadrach, Meshach, and Abed–nego, ye servants[5649] of the most high[5943] God, come forth,5312 and come858 *hither.* Then Shadrach, Meshach, and Abed–nego, came forth of the midst of the fire.

27 And the princes, governors, and captains, and the king's counsellors, being gathered together, saw these men, [a]upon whose bodies[1655] the fire had no power,[7981] nor was an hair of their head[7217] singed, neither were their coats changed, nor the smell of fire had passed5709 on them.

28 *Then* Nebuchadnezzar spake, and said, Blessed *be* the God of Shadrach, Meshach, and Abed–nego, who hath sent his angel,[4398] and delivered his servants that [a]trusted in him, and have changed the king's word,[4406] and yielded their bodies, that they might not serve nor worship any god, except their own God.

29 [a]Therefore [I]I make a decree, That every people, nation,[524] and language, which speak[560] [II]any thing amiss7955 against the God of Shadrach, Meshach, and Abed–nego, shall be [III][b]cut in pieces, and their houses shall be made a dunghill: [c]because there is no other God that can deliver[5338] after this sort.

30 Then the king [I]promoted Shadrach, Meshach, and Abed–nego, in the province of Babylon.

A Second Dream

4 Nebuchadnezzar the king,4430 [a]unto all people,[5972] nations,[524] and languages, that dwell in all the earth;[772] Peace[8001] be multiplied unto you.

2 [I]I thought it good to shew the signs and wonders[8540] [a]that the high[5943] God[426] hath wrought toward me.

3 [a]How great *are* his signs! and how mighty *are* his wonders! his kingdom[4437] *is* [b]an everlasting kingdom, and his dominion[7985] *is* from generation[1859] to generation.

4 I Nebuchadnezzar was at rest in mine house, and flourishing in my palace:[1965]

5 I saw a dream which made me afraid,[1763] [a]and the thoughts upon my bed and the visions[2376] of my head[7217] [b]troubled927 me.

6 Therefore made I a decree[2942] to bring in all the wise *men* of Babylon before me, that they might make known3046 unto me the interpretation of the dream.

7 [a]Then came in the magicians,[2749] the astrologers,[826] the Chaldeans, and the soothsayers:[1505] and I told[560] the dream before them; but they did not make known unto me the interpretation thereof.

8 But at the last Daniel came in before me, [a]whose name *was* Belteshazzar, according to the name of my god, [b]and in whom *is* the spirit[7308] of the holy[6922] gods:[426] and before him I told the dream, *saying,*

9 O Belteshazzar, [a]master of the magicians, because I know3046 that the spirit of the holy gods *is* in thee, and no secret troubleth thee, tell[560] me the visions[2376] of my dream that I have seen,[2370] and the interpretation6591 thereof.

10 Thus *were* the visions of mine head in my bed; [I]I saw, and behold [a]a tree in the midst of the earth, and the height thereof *was* great.

11 The tree grew, and was strong,[8631] and the height thereof reached unto

27 [a]Heb. 11:34
28 [a]Ps. 34:7, 8; Jer. 17:7; Dan. 6:22, 23
29 [I]Aram. *a decree is made by me* [II]Aram. *error* [III]Aram. *made pieces* [a]Dan. 6:26 [b]Dan. 2:5 [c]Dan. 6:27
30 [I]Aram. *made to prosper*
1 [a]Dan. 3:4; 6:25
2 [I]Aram. *It was seemly before me* [a]Dan. 3:26
3 [a]Dan. 6:27 [b]Dan. 4:34; Dan. 2:44; 6:26
5 [a]Dan. 2:28, 29 [b]Dan. 2:1
7 [a]Dan. 2:2
8 [a]Dan. 1:7 [b]Isa. 63:11; Dan. 4:18; Dan. 2:11; 5:11, 14
9 [a]Dan. 2:48; 5:11
10 [I]Aram. *I was seeing* [a]Ezek. 31:3-9; Dan. 4:20

3:28, 29 This is the second step in Nebuchadnezzar's acknowledgment of the Lord. Although he still describes God as "the God of Shadrach, Meshach, and Abed-nego," he now acknowledges His uniqueness and recognizes that He is worthy of receiving worship from all people.

4:1–37 Nebuchadnezzar's precise relationship to God at the end of this chapter is a matter of dispute, but several factors suggest that he was truly converted to the worship of the God of Israel. Nebuchadnezzar speaks of his being driven insane as something God did "toward" him (v. 2). Moreover, he no longer calls God "the God of Shadrach, Meshach, and Abed-nego" (cf. Dan. 3:28), but "the most High" (v. 34) and "King of heaven" (v. 37). He understood that God was able to humble anyone who has a proud heart.

heaven,[8065] and the sight[2379] thereof to
the end of all the earth:
12 The leaves thereof *were* fair, and
the fruit thereof much, and in it *was*
meat for all: [a]the beasts of the field had
shadow under it, and the fowls of the
heaven dwelt in the boughs thereof, and
all flesh[1321] was fed of it.
13 I saw in the visions of my head
upon my bed, and, behold, [a]a watcher[5894]
and [b]an holy one[6922] came down from
heaven;
14 He cried [l]aloud,[2429] and said[560]
thus, [a]Hew down[1414] the tree, and cut off
his branches, shake off his leaves, and
scatter his fruit: [b]let the beasts get away
from under it, and the fowls from his
branches:
15 Nevertheless leave the stump of
his roots in the earth, even with a band
of iron and brass, in the tender grass of
the field; and let it be wet with the dew
of heaven, and *let* his portion *be* with the
beasts in the grass of the earth:
16 Let his heart[3825] be changed from
man's,[606] and let a beast's heart be given
unto him: and let seven [a]times[5732] pass
over him.
17 This matter[6600] *is* by the decree of
the watchers, and the demand[7595] by the
word[3983] of the holy ones:[6922] to the intent [a]that the living[2417] may know [b]that
the most High[5943] ruleth[7990] in the kingdom of men,[606] and giveth it to whomsoever he will, and setteth up over it the
basest of men.
18 This dream I king Nebuchadnezzar have seen. Now thou, O Belteshazzar, declare[560] the interpretation
thereof, [a]forasmuch as all the wise *men*
of my kingdom are not able to make
known[3046] unto me the interpretation: but
thou *art* able; [b]for the spirit of the holy
gods *is* in thee.

12 [a]Ezek. 17:23; 31:6; Lam. 4:20
13 [a]Ps. 103:20; Dan. 4:17, 23 [b]Deut. 33:2; Dan. 8:13; Zech. 14:5; Jude 1:14
14 [l]Aram. *with might* [a]Matt. 3:10 [b]Ezek. 31:12
16 [a]Dan. 11:13; 12:7
17 [a]Ps. 9:16 [b]Dan. 2:21; 4:25, 32; 5:21
18 [a]Gen. 41:8, 15; Dan. 5:8, 15 [b]Dan. 4:8
19 [a]Dan. 4:8 [b]2Sam. 18:32; Jer. 29:7
20 [a]Dan. 4:10-12
22 [a]Dan. 2:38 [b]Jer. 27:6-8
23 [a]Dan. 4:13 [b]Dan. 5:21
25 [a]Dan. 4:32; Dan. 5:21-31 [b]Ps. 106:20

Daniel Explains the Dream

19 Then Daniel, [a]whose name *was*
Belteshazzar, was astonied for one hour,
and his thoughts troubled[927] him. The
king spake, and said, Belteshazzar, let not
the dream, or the interpretation thereof,
trouble thee. Belteshazzar answered and
said, My lord,[4756] [b]the dream *be* to them
that hate[8131] thee, and the interpretation
thereof to thine enemies.
20 [a]The tree that thou sawest,[2370]
which grew, and was strong, whose
height reached unto the heaven, and the
sight thereof to all the earth;
21 Whose leaves *were* fair, and the
fruit thereof much, and in it *was* meat
for all; under which the beasts of the
field dwelt, and upon whose branches
the fowls of the heaven had their habitation:
22 [a]It *is* thou, O king, that art
grown[7236] and become strong: for thy
greatness is grown, and reacheth unto
heaven, [b]and thy dominion to the end of
the earth.
23 [a]And whereas the king saw a
watcher and an holy one coming down
from heaven, and saying, Hew the tree
down, and destroy[2255] it; yet leave the
stump of the roots thereof in the earth,
even with a band of iron and brass, in
the tender grass of the field; and let it be
wet with the dew of heaven, [b]and *let* his
portion *be* with the beasts of the field, till
seven times pass over him;
24 This *is* the interpretation, O king,
and this *is* the decree of the most High,
which is come upon my lord the king:
25 That they shall [a]drive thee from
men, and thy dwelling shall be with the
beasts of the field, and they shall make
thee [b]to eat grass as oxen, and they
shall wet thee with the dew of heaven,
and seven times[5732] shall pass over thee,

4:19 Here is a true picture of the kind of service that Paul describes in Ephesians 6:5–8. Nebuchadnezzar was the man who had destroyed Jerusalem and carried Daniel away in his service. However, when Daniel received a message from God of judgment upon Nebuchadnezzar, he urged Nebuchadnezzar to repent (4:27), in hopes that the consequences could be avoided. It could also be inferred that Daniel watched over the Empire during the time when these consequences took place (4:28–37).

[c]till thou know that the most High ruleth in the kingdom of men, and [d]giveth it to whomsoever he will.

26 And whereas they commanded[560] to leave the stump of the tree roots; thy kingdom shall be sure[7011] unto thee, after that thou shalt have known that the [a]heavens[8065] do rule.

27 Wherefore, O king, let my counsel be acceptable[8232] unto thee, and [a]break off thy sins[2408] by righteousness,[6665] and thine iniquities[5758] by shewing mercy[2604] to the poor; [b]if it may be [I][c]a lengthening[754] of thy tranquillity.[7963]

28 All this came upon the king Nebuchadnezzar.

29 At the end of twelve months he walked [I]in the palace of the kingdom of Babylon.

30 The king [a]spake, and said, Is not this great Babylon, that I have built for the house of the kingdom by the might of my power, and for the honour of my majesty?[1923]

31 [a]While the word *was* in the king's[4430] mouth, there fell[5308] [b]a voice from heaven, *saying,* O king Nebuchadnezzar, to thee it is spoken; The kingdom is departed from thee.

32 And [a]they shall drive thee from men, and thy dwelling *shall be* with the beasts of the field: they shall make thee to eat grass as oxen, and seven times shall pass over thee, until thou know that the most High ruleth in the kingdom of men, and giveth it to whomsoever he will.

33 The same hour was[5487] the thing[4406] fulfilled[5487] upon Nebuchadnezzar: and he was driven from men, and did eat grass as oxen, and his body[1655] was wet with the dew of heaven, till his hairs were grown like eagles' *feathers,* and his nails like birds' *claws.*

34 And [a]at the end of the days[3118] I Nebuchadnezzar lifted up mine eyes unto heaven, and mine understanding[4486] returned[7725] unto me, and I blessed the most High, and I praised[7624] and honoured[1922] him [b]that liveth[2416] for ever,[5957] whose dominion *is* [c]an everlasting dominion, and his kingdom is from generation to generation:

35 And [a]all the inhabitants of the earth *are* reputed as nothing: and [b]he doeth according to his will in the army[2429] of heaven, and *among* the inhabitants of the earth: and [c]none can stay[4223] his hand,[3028] or say[560] unto him, [d]What doest thou?

36 At the same time[2166] my reason[4486] returned unto me; [a]and for the glory[3367] of my kingdom, mine honour[1923] and brightness returned unto me; and my counsellors and my lords[7261] sought unto me; and I was established in my kingdom, and excellent majesty was [b]added unto me.

37 Now I Nebuchadnezzar praise and extol and honour[1922] the King of heaven, [a]all whose works *are* truth,[7187] and his ways judgment:[1780] [b]and those that walk in pride he is able to abase.[8214]

The Handwriting on the Wall

5 Belshazzar the king[4430] [a]made a great feast to a thousand of his lords,[7261] and drank wine before the thousand.

2 Belshazzar, whiles he tasted the wine, commanded[560] to bring the golden and silver vessels [a]which his [I][b]father[2] Nebuchadnezzar had [II]taken out of the

25 [c]Ps. 83:18; Dan. 4:17, 32 [d]Jer. 27:5
26 [a]Matt. 21:25; Luke 15:18, 21
27 [I]Or, *a healing of thine error* [a]1Pet. 4:8 [b]Ps. 41:1-3 [c]1Kgs. 21:29
29 [I]Or, *upon*
30 [a]Prov. 16:18; Dan. 5:20
31 [a]Dan. 5:5; Luke 12:20 [b]Dan. 4:24
32 [a]Dan. 4:25
34 [a]Dan. 4:26 [b]Dan. 12:7; Rev. 4:10 [c]Ps. 10:16; Dan. 2:44; 7:14; Mic. 4:7; Luke 1:33
35 [a]Isa. 40:15, 17 [b]Ps. 115:3; 135:6 [c]Job 34:29 [d]Job 9:12; Isa. 45:9; Ro 9:20
36 [a]Dan. 4:26 [b]Job 42:12; Prov. 22:4; Matt. 6:33
37 [a]Ps. 33:4; Rev. 15:3; 16:7 [b]Ex. 18:11; Dan. 5:20
1 [a]Esth. 1:3
2 [I]Or, *grandfather* [II]Aram. *brought forth* [a]Jer. 52:19; Dan. 1:2 [b]Jer. 27:7; 2Sam. 9:7; 2Chr. 15:16; Dan. 5:11, 13

5:1, 2 For many years liberal scholars considered Belshazzar to be a character of "historical fiction." However, he is now known to have reigned as co-regent in Babylon while his father, Nabonidus, was conducting archaeological expeditions in Arabia. For this reason he could offer Daniel only the third rulership in the kingdom (Dan. 5:16). Nebuchadnezzar is called Belshazzar's "father" (Dan. 5:18) though he was in fact his grandfather (cf. Jer. 27:7). It was a common Semitic practice to refer to one's grandfather as his father (see note 1 Kgs. 15:10). Notice that until this time, the vessels from the temple in Jerusalem, which had been taken almost seventy years before, had been kept as sacred in the temple treasury of Marduk. Some people have suggested that Belshazzar, probably in a drunken stupor, ordered them to be brought out for profane use.

temple[1965] which *was* in Jerusalem; that the king, and his princes,[7261] his wives, and his concubines, might drink therein.

3 Then they brought the golden vessels3984 that were taken out of the temple of the house of God[426] which *was* at Jerusalem; and the king, and his princes, his wives, and his concubines, drank in them.

4 They drank wine, [a]and praised[7624] the gods[426] of gold, and of silver, of brass, of iron, of wood, and of stone.

5 [a]In the same hour came forth fingers of a man's[606] hand,[3028] and wrote over against the candlestick upon the plaister of the wall of the king's4430 palace:[1965] and the king saw the part of the hand that wrote.

6 Then the king's [Ia]countenance2122 [II]was changed, and his thoughts troubled927 him, so that the [IIIb]joints of his loins were loosed,8271 and his [c]knees smote[5368] one against another.

7 [a]The king cried [I]aloud[2429] to bring in [b]the astrologers,[826] the Chaldeans, and the soothsayers.[1505] *And* the king spake, and said[560] to the wise *men* of Babylon, Whosoever shall read this writing, and shew me the interpretation thereof, shall be clothed with [II]scarlet, and *have* a chain of gold about his neck, [c]and shall be the third ruler[7981] in the kingdom.[4437]

8 Then came in all the king's wise *men*: [a]but they could not read the writing, nor make known3046 to the king the interpretation thereof.

9 Then was king Belshazzar greatly [a]troubled, and his [Ib]countenance was changed in him, and his lords were astonied.7672

10 *Now* the queen[4433] by reason of the words[4406] of the king and his lords came into the banquet house: *and* the queen spake and said, [a]O king, live for ever:[5957] let not thy thoughts trouble927 thee, nor let thy countenance be changed:

11 [a]There is a man[1400] in thy kingdom, in whom *is* the spirit[7308] of the holy[6922] gods; and in the days[3118] of thy [Ib]father light[5094] and understanding[7924] and wisdom,[2452] like the wisdom of the gods, was found in him; whom the king Nebuchadnezzar thy [IIc]father, the king, *I say,* thy father, made [d]master of the magicians,[2749] astrologers, Chaldeans, *and* soothsayers;[1505]

12 [a]Forasmuch as an excellent spirit, and knowledge,[4486] and understanding, [I]interpreting of dreams, and shewing of hard sentences, and [II]dissolving of [III]doubts, were found in the same Daniel, [b]whom the king named Belteshazzar: now let Daniel be called, and he will shew the interpretation.

13 Then was Daniel brought in before the king. *And* the king spake and said unto Daniel, *Art* thou that Daniel, which *art* of the children1123 of the captivity[1547] of Judah, whom the king my [I]father brought out of Jewry?

14 I have even heard[8086] of thee, that [a]the spirit of the gods *is* in thee, and *that* light and understanding and excellent wisdom is found in thee.

15 And now [a]the wise *men,* the astrologers, have been brought in before me, that they should read this writing, and make known unto me the interpretation thereof: but they could not shew the interpretation of the thing:[4406]

16 And I have heard of thee, that thou canst [I]make interpretations, and dissolve doubts:7001 [a]now if thou canst read the writing, and make known to me the interpretation thereof, thou shalt be clothed with scarlet, and *have* a chain of gold about thy neck, and shalt be the third ruler in the kingdom.

17 Then Daniel answered and said before the king, Let thy gifts be to thyself, and give thy [Ia]rewards to another; yet I will read the writing unto the king, and make known to him the interpretation.

18 O thou king, [a]the most high[5943] God gave Nebuchadnezzar thy father a kingdom, and majesty, and glory, and honour:[1923]

19 And for the majesty7328 that he gave him, [a]all people,[5972] nations,[524] and languages, trembled and feared[1763] before him: whom he would he slew; and whom he would he kept alive;2148 and whom he

---

4 [a]Rev. 9:20

5 [a]Dan. 4:31

6 [I]Aram. *brightnesses* [II]Aram. *changed it* [III]Or, *girdles* Aram. *bindings,* or, *knots* [a]Dan. 5:9 [b]Isa. 5:27 [c]Nah. 2:10

7 [I]Aram. *with might* [II]Or, *purple* [a]Dan. 2:2; 4:6 [b]Isa. 47:13 [c]Dan. 6:2

8 [a]Dan. 2:27; 4:7

9 [I]Aram. *brightnesses* [a]Dan. 2:1 [b]Dan. 5:6

10 [a]Dan. 2:4; 3:9

11 [I]Or, *grandfather* [II]Or, *grandfather* [a]Dan. 2:48; 4:8, 9, 18 [b]Dan. 5:2 [c]Dan. 5:2 [d]Dan. 4:9

12 [I]Or, *of an interpreter* [II]Or, *of a dissolver* [III]Aram. *knots* [a]Dan. 6:3 [b]Dan. 1:7

13 [I]Or, *grandfather*

14 [a]Dan. 5:11, 12

15 [a]Dan. 5:7, 8

16 [I]Aram. *interpret* [a]Dan. 5:7

17 [I]Or, *fee* [a]Dan. 2:6

18 [a]Dan. 2:37, 38; 4:17, 22, 25

19 [a]Jer. 27:7; Dan. 3:4

would he set up; and whom he would he put down.

20 [a]But when his heart[3825] was lifted up, and his mind[7308] hardened[8631] [I][b]in pride, he was [II]deposed from his kingly[4437] throne,[3764] and they took his glory from him:

21 And he was [a]driven from the sons[1123] of men;[606] and [I]his heart was made like the beasts, and his dwelling *was* with the wild asses: they fed him with grass like oxen, and his body[1655] was wet with the dew of heaven;[8065] [b]till he knew that the most high God ruled[7990] in the kingdom of men, and *that* he appointeth over it whomsoever he will.

22 And thou his son, O Belshazzar, [a]hast not humbled thine heart, though thou knewest[3046] all this;

23 [a]But hast lifted up thyself against the Lord[4756] of heaven; and they have brought the vessels of his house before thee, and thou, and thy lords, thy wives, and thy concubines, have drunk wine in them; and thou hast praised the gods of silver, and gold, of brass, iron, wood, and stone, [b]which see[2370] not, nor hear,[8086] nor know: and the God in whose hand thy breath *is,* [c]and whose *are* all thy ways, hast thou not glorified:[1922]

24 Then was the part of the hand sent from him; and this writing was written.

25 And this *is* the writing that was written, MENE, MENE, TEKEL, UPHARSIN.

26 This *is* the interpretation of the thing: MENE; God hath numbered[4483] thy kingdom, and finished[8000] it.

27 TEKEL; [a]Thou art weighed[8625] in the balances, and art found wanting.

28 PERES; Thy kingdom is divided,[6537] and given to the [a]Medes and [b]Persians.

29 Then commanded Belshazzar, and they clothed Daniel with scarlet, and *put* a chain of gold about his neck, and made a proclamation concerning him, [a]that he should be the third ruler[7990] in the kingdom.

30 [a]In that night[3916] was Belshazzar the king of the Chaldeans slain.

31 [a]And Darius the Median took the kingdom, *being* [I]about threescore and two years old.

Daniel in the Lions' Den

6 It pleased Darius to set [a]over the kingdom[4437] an hundred and twenty princes,[324] which should be over the whole kingdom;

2 And over these three presidents;[5632] of whom Daniel *was* first: that the princes might give accounts[2941] unto them, and the king[4430] should have no damage.[5142]

3 Then this Daniel was preferred[5330] above the presidents and princes, [a]because an excellent spirit[7308] *was* in him; and the king thought to set him over the whole realm.[4437]

4 [a]Then the presidents and princes sought to find occasion against Daniel concerning the kingdom; but they could find none occasion nor fault;[7844] forasmuch as he *was* faithful,[540] neither was there any error[7960] or fault found in him.

5 Then said[560] these men,[1400] We shall not find any occasion against this Daniel, except we find *it* against him concerning the law[1882] of his God.[426]

6 Then these presidents and princes [I]assembled together[7284] to the king, and

20 [I]Or, *to deal proudly* [II]Aram. *made to come down* [a]Dan. 4:30, 37 [b]Ex. 18:11
21 [I]Or, *he made his heart equal* [a]Dan. 4:32-37 [b]Dan. 4:17, 25
22 [a]2Chr. 33:23; 36:12
23 [a]Dan. 5:3, 4 [b]Ps. 115:5, 6 [c]Jer. 10:23
27 [a]Job 31:6; Ps. 62:9; Jer. 6:30
28 [a]Isa. 21:2; Dan. 5:31; 9:1 [b]Dan. 6:28
29 [a]Dan. 5:7
30 [a]Jer. 51:31, 39, 57
31 [I]Or, *now* [a]Dan. 9:1
1 [a]Esth. 1:1
3 [a]Dan. 5:12
4 [a]Eccl. 4:4
6 [I]Or, *came tumultuously*

5:29–31 The Babylonians supposed that their huge walls were impregnable, but the Persians diverted the Euphrates River, which flowed through the city, and crept under the wall at night by means of the riverbed. The capture of the city is well attested by both Babylonian and Persian historical records.

6:1 A dispute has developed regarding the identity of Darius, because the name in Scripture is apparently not the one used in the official records that have been found. There are two possibilities that coincide with the available data: Darius is either another name for the Persian emperor Cyrus the Great, or it is another name for Gubaru, the governor Cyrus appointed over Babylonia and Syria–Palestine.

said thus unto him, [a]King Darius, live for ever.[5957]

7 All the presidents of the kingdom, the governors, and the princes, the counsellors, and the captains,[6347] have consulted together to establish a royal statute,[7010] and to make a firm [I]decree, that whosoever shall ask[1156] a petition[1159] of any God or man[606] for thirty days,[3118] save of thee, O king, he shall be cast into the den of lions.

8 Now, O king, establish the decree, and sign the writing, that it be not changed, according to the [a]law of the Medes and Persians, which [I]altereth[5709] not.

9 Wherefore king Darius signed the writing and the decree.

10 Now when Daniel knew[3046] that the writing was signed, he went into his house; and his windows being open in his chamber [a]toward Jerusalem, he kneeled upon his knees [b]three times[2166] a day,[3118] and prayed,[6739] and gave thanks[3029] before his God, as he did aforetime.

11 Then these men assembled, and found Daniel praying[1156] and making supplication[2604] before his God.

12 [a]Then they came near, and spake[560] before the king concerning the king's[4430] decree; Hast thou not signed a decree, that every man that shall ask *a petition* of any God or man within thirty days, save of thee, O king, shall be cast into the den of lions? The king answered and said, The thing *is* true,[3330] [b]according to the law of the Medes and Persians, which altereth not.

13 Then answered they and said before the king, That Daniel, [a]which *is* of the children[1123] of the captivity[1547] of Judah, [b]regardeth[7761,2942] not thee, O king, nor the decree that thou hast signed, but maketh his petition three times a day.

14 Then the king, when he heard[8086] *these* words,[4406] [a]was sore displeased with himself, and set *his* heart[1079] on Daniel to deliver him: and he laboured till the going down of the sun to deliver[5338] him.

15 Then these men assembled unto the king, and said unto the king, Know,[3046] O king, that [a]the law of the Medes and Persians *is,* That no decree nor statute which the king establisheth[6966] may be changed.

16 Then the king commanded,[560] and they brought Daniel, and cast *him* into the den of lions. *Now* the king spake and said unto Daniel, Thy God whom thou servest[6399] continually, he will deliver thee.

17 [a]And a stone was brought, and laid[7760] upon the mouth of the den; [b]and the king sealed it with his own signet, and with the signet of his lords;[7261] that the purpose might not be changed concerning Daniel.

18 Then the king went to his palace,[1965] and passed the night fasting: neither were [I]instruments of musick brought before him: [a]and his sleep went from him.

19 Then the king arose very early in the morning, and went in haste[927] unto the den of lions.

20 And when he came to the den, he cried with a lamentable[6088] voice unto Daniel: *and* the king spake and said to Daniel, O Daniel, servant[5649] of the living[2417] God, [a]is thy God, whom thou servest continually, able to deliver thee from the lions?

21 Then said Daniel unto the king, [a]O king, live for ever.

22 [a]My God hath sent his angel,[4398] and hath [b]shut the lions' mouths, that they have not hurt[2255] me: forasmuch as before him innocency[2136] was found in me; and also before thee, O king, have I done no hurt.

23 Then was the king exceeding glad for him, and commanded that they should take Daniel up out of the den. So Daniel was taken up out of the den, and no manner of hurt was found upon him, [a]because he believed[540] in his God.

24 And the king commanded, [a]and they brought those men which had accused Daniel, and they cast *them* into the den of lions, them, [b]their children, and their wives; and the lions had the mastery[7981] of them, and brake all their

---

6 [a]Neh. 2:3; Dan. 6:21; Dan. 2:4
7 [I]Or, *interdict*
8 [I]Aram. *passeth not* [a]Esth. 1:19; 8:8
10 [a]1Kgs. 8:44, 48; Ps. 5:7; Jon. 2:4 [b]Ps. 55:17; Acts 2:1, 2, 15; 3:1; 10:9
12 [a]Dan. 3:8 [b]Dan. 6:8
13 [a]Dan. 1:6; 5:13 [b]Dan. 3:12
14 [a]Mark 6:26
15 [a]Dan. 6:8
17 [a]Lam. 3:53 [b]Matt. 27:66
18 [I]Or, *table* [a]Dan. 2:1
20 [a]Dan. 3:15
21 [a]Dan. 2:4
22 [a]Dan. 3:28 [b]Heb. 11:33
23 [a]Heb. 11:33
24 [a]Deut. 19:19 [b]Esth. 9:10; Deut. 24:16; 2Kgs. 14:6

bones in pieces or ever they came at the
bottom of the den.
25 [a]Then king Darius wrote unto all
people,[5972] nations,[524] and languages, that
dwell in all the earth;[772] Peace[8001] be
multiplied unto you.
26 [a]I make a decree,[2942] That in
every dominion[7985] of my kingdom men
[b]tremble and fear[1763] before the God of
Daniel: [c]for he *is* the living God, and stedfast for ever, and his kingdom *that* which
shall not be [d]destroyed,[2255] and his dominion *shall be even* unto the end.
27 He delivereth and rescueth,[5338]
[a]and he worketh signs and wonders[8540] in
heaven[8065] and in earth, who hath delivered Daniel from the [I]power[3028] of the
lions.
28 So this Daniel prospered in the
reign[4437] of Darius, [a]and in the reign of
[b]Cyrus the Persian.

The Four Beasts

7 In the first year of Belshazzar
king[4430] of Babylon [a]Daniel [I]had[2370]
a dream and [b]visions[2376] of his head[7217]
upon his bed: then he wrote the dream,
and told[560] the sum[7217] of the [II]matters.
2 Daniel spake and said, I saw in my
vision[2376] by night,[3916] and, behold, the
four winds[7308] of the heaven[8065] strove
upon the great sea.
3 And four great beasts [a]came up
from the sea, diverse one from another.
4 The first *was* [a]like a lion, and had
eagle's wings: I beheld[2370] till the wings
thereof were plucked, [I]and it was lifted
up from the earth,[772] and made stand
upon the feet as a man,[606] and a man's
heart[3825] was given to it.
5 [a]And behold another beast, a second, like to a bear, and [I]it raised up itself on one side, and *it had* three ribs in
the mouth of it between the teeth of it:
and they said thus unto it, Arise, devour
much flesh.[1321]
6 After this I beheld, and lo another,
like a leopard, which had upon the back
of it four wings of a fowl; the beast had
also [a]four heads;[7217] and dominion[7985]
was given to it.
7 After this I saw in the night visions, and behold [a]a fourth beast,

25 [a]Dan. 4:1
26 [a]Dan. 3:29 [b]Ps. 99:1 [c]Dan. 4:34 [d]Dan. 2:44; 4:3, 34; 7:14, 27; Luke 1:33
27 IHebr. *hand* [a]Dan. 4:3
28 [a]Dan. 1:21 [b]Ezra 1:1, 2
1 IAram. *saw* IIOr, *words* [a]Num. 12:6; Amos 3:7 [b]Dan. 2:28
3 [a]Rev. 13:1
4 IOr, *wherewith* [a]Deut. 28:49; 2Sam. 1:23; Jer. 4:7, 13; 48:40; Ezek. 17:3; Hab. 1:8
5 IOr, *it raised up one dominion* [a]Dan. 2:39
6 [a]Dan. 8:8, 22
7 [a]Dan. 2:40; 7:19, 23

7:1–28 Chapter seven precedes chapter five chronologically (v. 1; cf. Dan. 5:30). This vision of four beasts parallels the vision of Nebuchadnezzar in chapter two. The image of chapter two represents the overall concept of human government while the four beasts individually represent types of human government. However, here in chapter seven there is a greater emphasis on the eschatological events. *The lion* represents *Nebuchadnezzar* (as in chapter two, his empire is personalized in him). The plucking of the wings refers to his insanity, and the granting of a "human mind" (literally "heart of a man") refers to his conversion (see note one Dan. 4:1–37). *The bear* typifies *the Medo-Persian Empire.* Being "raised up on one side" (Dan. 7:5) refers to the two unequal partners in the empire: the Persians gradually gained the supremacy over the Medes. The three ribs probably refer to the three empires absorbed by Persia: Babylon, Egypt, and Lydia. The *leopard* refers *to Greece* and its four wings and heads speak of the division of the Greek empire into four sections following the death of Alexander the Great (cf. Dan. 8:8, 21, 22). *The unnamed beast* represents *Rome*. The iron teeth (Dan. 7:7) speak of Rome's unequalled military strength (7:19; as does the iron present in the feet of the image in chap. 2). The trampling and crushing illustrates the imposition of Rome's culture and laws on conquered peoples (7:7, 19).

The ten horns (corresponding to the ten toes of the image) take us across the prophetic "gap" to the end times. They are not separately identified, as the toes were in chapter two, because they are continuations of the Roman system of government, which has all but taken over the civilized world. The eyes of the "little horn" denote supernatural intelligence and ability (Dan. 7:8). The mouth that speaks blasphemies against God correlates to the description of the beast in Revelation 13:5–7. It campaigns against the saints for three and a half "times" (forty-two months, Rev. 13:5–7), but is finally destroyed and cast into the lake of fire (Dan. 7:11, cf. Rev. 19:20).

7:7, 8 The ten horns are ten kings (dictators) who will be ruling in the area of the old Roman Empire in the last days. The coming Antichrist is represented as a "little horn," who eliminates three

(continued on next page)

dreadful[1763] and terrible, and strong exceedingly; and it had great iron teeth: it
devoured and brake in pieces,[1855] and
stamped the residue[7606] with the feet of
it: and it *was* diverse from all the beasts
that *were* before it; [b]and it had ten horns.
8 I considered[7920] the horns, and, behold, [a]there came up among them another
little horn, before whom there were three
of the first horns plucked up by the
roots: and, behold, in this horn *were* eyes
like the eyes [b]of man, [c]and a mouth
speaking[4449] great things.
9 [a]I beheld till the thrones[3764] were
cast down, and [b]the Ancient of days[3118]
did sit, [c]whose garment *was* white as
snow, and the hair of his head like the
pure wool: his throne *was like* the fiery
flame, [d]*and* his wheels[1535] *as* burning
fire.
10 [a]A fiery stream issued and came
forth from before him: [b]thousand thousands ministered[8120] unto him, and ten
thousand times ten thousand stood before him: [c]the judgment[1780] was set, and
the books were opened.
11 I beheld then because of the voice
of the great words[4406] which the horn
spake:[4449] [a]I beheld *even* till the beast
was slain, and his body[1655] destroyed,[7]
and given to the burning flame.
12 As concerning the rest[7606] of the
beasts, they had their dominion taken
away: yet [I]their lives were prolonged for
a season[2166] and time.
🔑 13 I saw in the night visions, and, behold, [a]*one* like the Son of man came with
the clouds[6050] of heaven, and came to
[b]the Ancient of days, and they brought
him near before him.
14 [a]And there was given him dominion, and glory, and a kingdom,[4437] that all
[b]people,[5972] nations,[524] and languages,
should serve[6399] him: his dominion *is* [c]an
everlasting dominion, which shall not
pass away, and his kingdom *that* which
shall not be destroyed.
15 I Daniel [a]was grieved in my
spirit[7308] in the midst of *my* [I]body,[5085]
and the visions of my head troubled[927]
me.
16 I came near unto one of them that
stood by, and asked him the truth of all
this. So he told me, and made me
know[3046] the interpretation of the things.
17 [a]These great beasts, which are
four, *are* four kings,[4430] *which* shall arise
out of the earth.
18 But [a]the saints[6922] of the most
[I]High[5746] shall take the kingdom, and
possess the kingdom for ever,[5957] even
for ever and ever.
19 Then I would know the truth[3321]
of [a]the fourth beast, which was diverse
[I]from all the others, exceeding dreadful,[1763] whose teeth *were of* iron, and his
nails *of* brass; *which* devoured, brake in
pieces, and stamped the residue with his
feet;
20 And of the ten horns that *were* in
his head, and *of* the other which came
up, and before whom three fell;[5308] even
of that horn that had eyes, and a mouth
that spake very great things, whose
look[2376] *was* more stout[7229] than his fellows.
21 I beheld, [a]and the same horn
made war with the saints, and prevailed
against them;
22 [a]Until the Ancient of days came,
[b]and judgment was given to the saints
of the most High; and the time[2166]
came that the saints possessed the kingdom.
23 Thus he said, The fourth beast
shall be [a]the fourth kingdom upon earth,
which shall be diverse from all kingdoms,[4437] and shall devour the whole
earth, and shall tread it down, and break
it in pieces.

7 [b]Dan. 2:41; Rev. 13:1
8 [a]Dan. 7:20, 21, 24; 8:9 [b]Rev. 9:7 [c]Ps. 12:3; Dan. 7:25; Rev. 13:5
9 [a]Rev. 20:4 [b]Ps. 90:2; Dan. 7:13, 22 [c]Ps. 104:2; Rev. 1:14 [d]Ezek. 1:15, 16
10 [a]Ps. 50:3; 97:3; Isa. 30:33; 66:15 [b]1Kgs. 22:19; Ps. 68:17; Heb. 12:22; Rev. 5:11 [c]Rev. 20:4, 12
11 [a]Rev. 19:20
12 [I]Aram. *a prolonging in life was given them*
13 [a]Ezek. 1:26; Matt. 24:30; 26:64; Rev. 1:7, 13; 14:14 [b]Dan. 7:9
14 [a]Ps. 2:6-8; 8:6; 110:1, 2; Matt. 11:27; 28:18; John 3:35; 1Cor. 15:27; Eph. 1:22 [b]Dan. 3:4 [c]Ps. 145:13; Dan. 2:44; 7:27; Mic. 4:7; Luke 1:33; John 12:34; Heb. 12:28
15 [I]Aram. *sheath* [a]Dan. 7:28
17 [a]Dan. 7:3
18 [I]Aram. *high ones,* that is, *things,* or, *places* [a]Isa. 60:12-14; Dan. 7:22, 27; 2Tim. 2:11, 12; Rev. 2:26, 27; 3:21; 20:4
19 [I]Aram. *from all those* [a]Dan. 7:7
21 [a]Dan. 8:12, 24; 11:31; Rev. 11:7; 13:7; 17:14; 19:19
22 [a]Dan. 7:9 [b]Dan. 7:18; 1Cor. 6:2; Rev. 1:6; 5:10; 20:4
23 [a]Dan. 2:40

(continued from previous page)
of the original ten horns. He is later called "a king of fierce countenance, and understanding dark sentences" (Dan. 8:23). See notes on Daniel 9:24–27 and Revelation 13:1–18.

🔑 **7:13, 14** This passage speaks of the "Son of man" receiving the glory and power that belongs only to God. Christ quoted portions of these two verses in answer to the chief priest when asked if He was the Christ, the Son of God (Mark 14:62).

24 [a]And the ten horns out of this kingdom *are* ten kings *that* shall arise: and another shall rise after them; and he shall be diverse from the first, and he shall subdue three kings.

25 [a]And he shall speak[4449] *great* words against the most High,[5943] and shall [b]wear out[1080] the saints of the most High,[5946] and [c]think to change times and laws:[1882] and [d]they shall be given into his hand[3028] [e]until a time and times and the dividing[6387] of time.

26 [a]But the judgment shall sit, and they shall take away his dominion, to consume[8046] and to destroy[7] *it* unto the end.

27 And the [a]kingdom and dominion, and the greatness of the kingdom under the whole heaven, shall be given to the people of the saints of the most High,[5945] [b]whose kingdom *is* an everlasting kingdom, [c]and all [I]dominions[7985] shall serve and obey[8086] him.

28 Hitherto *is* the end of the matter.[4406] As for me Daniel, [a]my cogitations much troubled me, and my countenance changed in me: but I [b]kept the matter in my heart.[3821]

The Ram and the Goat

8 🔑In the third year of the reign[4438] of king[4428] Belshazzar a vision[2377] appeared[7200] unto me, *even unto* me Daniel, after that which appeared unto me [a]at the first.

2 And I saw[7200] in a vision; and it came to pass, when I saw, that I *was* at [a]Shushan *in* the palace, which *is* in the province of Elam; and I saw in a vision, and I was by the river of Ulai.

3 Then I lifted up[5375] mine eyes, and saw, and, behold, there stood before the river a ram which had *two* horns: and the *two* horns *were* high; but one *was* higher than [I]the other, and the higher came up[5927] last.

4 I saw the ram pushing westward, and northward, and southward; so that no beasts[2416] might stand before him, neither *was there any* that could deliver[5337] out of his hand;[3027] [a]but he did[6213] according to his will,[7522] and became great.

5 And as I was considering,[995] behold, an he goat came from the west on the face of the whole earth,[776] and [I]touched[5060] not the ground:[776] and the goat *had* [II][a]a notable[2380] horn between his eyes.

6 And he came to the ram that had *two* horns, which I had seen standing before the river, and ran unto him in the fury of his power.

7 And I saw him come close[5060] unto the ram, and he was moved with choler[4843] against him, and smote[5221] the ram, and brake[7665] his two horns: and there was no power in the ram to stand before him, but he cast him down to the ground, and stamped upon him: and there was none that could deliver the ram out of his hand.

8 Therefore the he goat waxed very great: and when he was strong, the great horn was broken;[7665] and for it came up [a]four notable ones toward the four winds[7307] of heaven.

9 [a]And out of one of them came forth a little horn, which waxed exceeding great, [b]toward the south, and toward the east, and toward the [c]pleasant[6643] *land.*

10 [a]And it waxed great, *even* [I]to [b]the host[6635] of heaven; and [c]it cast down[5307] *some* of the host and of the stars to the ground, and stamped upon them.

11 Yea, [a]he magnified *himself* even [I]to [b]the prince[8269] of the host, [c]and [II]by him [d]the daily[8548] *sacrifice* was taken away,[7311] and the place of his sanctuary[4720] was cast down.[7999]

12 And [I][a]an host was given *him* against the daily *sacrifice* by reason of

24 [a]Dan. 7:7, 8, 20; Rev. 17:12
25 [a]Isa. 37:23; Dan. 8:24, 25; 11:28, 30, 31, 36; Rev. 13:5, 6 [b]Rev. 17:6; 18:24 [c]Dan. 2:21 [d]Rev. 13:7 [e]Dan. 12:7; Rev. 12:14
26 [a]Dan. 7:10, 22
27 [I]Or, *rulers* [a]Dan. 7:14, 18, 22 [b]Dan. 2:44; Luke 1:33; John 12:34; Rev. 11:15 [c]Isa. 60:12
28 [a]Dan. 7:15; 8:27; 10:8, 16 [b]Luke 2:19, 51

1 [a]Dan. 7:1
2 [a]Esth. 1:2
3 [I]Hebr. *the second*
4 [a]Dan. 5:19; 11:3, 16
5 [I]Or, *none touched* him *in the earth* [II]Hebr. *a horn of sight* [a]Dan. 8:21
8 [a]Dan. 7:6; 11:4; 8:22
9 [a]Dan. 7:8; 11:21 [b]Dan. 11:25 [c]Ps. 48:2; Ezek. 20:6, 15; Dan. 11:16, 41, 45
10 [I]Or, *against the host* [a]Dan. 11:28 [b]Isa. 14:13 [c]Rev. 12:4
11 [I]Or, *against* [II]Or, *from him* [a]Jer. 48:26, 42; Dan. 11:36; Dan. 8:25 [b]Josh. 5:14 [c]Dan. 11:31; 12:11 [d]Ex. 29:38; Num. 28:3; Ezek. 46:13
12 [I]Or, *the host was given over for the transgression against the daily* sacrifice [a]Dan. 11:31

🔑 **8:1–27** This vision deals with the Medo-Persian Empire and Greece, two of the four empires represented in the visions of chapters two and seven. It closely parallels the vision of chapters eleven and twelve.

transgression,[6588] and it cast down [b]the
truth[571] to the ground; and it [c]prac-
tised,[6213] and prospered.
13 Then I heard[8085] [a]one saint
speaking,[1696] and another saint said[559]
unto [I]that certain *saint* which spake, How
long *shall be* the vision *concerning* the
daily *sacrifice,* and the transgression [IIb]of
desolation,[8074] to give both the sanctuary[6944] and the host to be trodden under
foot?
14 And he said unto me, Unto two
thousand and three hundred [I]days; then
shall the sanctuary be [II]cleansed.[6663]
15 And it came to pass, when I, *even*
I Daniel, had seen the vision, and [a]sought
for the meaning,[998] then, behold, there
stood before me [b]as the appearance of a
man.[1397]
🔑 16 And I heard a man's[120] voice [a]be-
tween *the banks of* Ulai, which called,[7121]
and said, [b]Gabriel, make this *man* to
understand[995] the vision.
17 So he came near where I stood:
and when he came, I was afraid,[1204] and
[a]fell[5307] upon my face: but he said unto
me, Understand, O son[1121] of man:[120] for
at the time[6256] of the end *shall be* the vision.
18 [a]Now as he was speaking with
me, I was in a deep sleep[7290] on my face
toward the ground: [b]but he touched me,
and [I]set me upright.
19 And he said, Behold, I will
make thee know[3045] what shall be in
the last end of the indignation:[2195] [a]for
at the time appointed[4150] the end *shall
be.*
20 [a]The ram which thou sawest having *two* horns *are* the kings of Media
and Persia.
21 [a]And the rough[8163] goat *is* the
king of Grecia: and the great horn that
is between his eyes [b]*is* the first[7223] king.
22 [a]Now that being broken, whereas
four stood up for it, four kingdoms shall
stand up out of the nation,[1471] but not in
his power.3581
23 And in the latter[319] time of their
kingdom,[4438] when the transgressors [I]are
come to the full,[8552] a king [a]of fierce
countenance, and understanding[995] dark
sentences,[2420] [b]shall stand up.
24 And his power shall be mighty,
[a]but not by his own power: and he shall
destroy[7843] wonderfully,[6381] [b]and shall
prosper, and practice, [c]and shall destroy
the mighty and the [I]holy[6918] people.[5971]
25 And [a]through his policy[7922] also
he shall cause craft[4820] to prosper in his
hand; [b]and he shall magnify *himself* in
his heart,3824 and by [I]peace7962 shall destroy many: [c]he shall also stand up
against the Prince of princes;[8269] but he
shall be [d]broken without hand.
🔑 26 [a]And the vision of the evening
and the morning which was told[559] *is*
true: [b]wherefore shut thou up the vision;
for it *shall be* for many days.[3117]
🔑 27 [a]And I Daniel fainted,[1961] and was
sick *certain* days; afterward I rose up,
[b]and did the king's business;[4399] and I
was astonished[8074] at the vision, [c]but
none understood *it.*

12 [b]Ps. 119:43, 142; Isa. 59:14 [c]Dan. 8:4; 11:28, 36
13 IOr, *the numberer of secrets,* or, *the wonderful numberer;* Hebr. *Palmoni* IIOr, *making desolate* [a]Dan. 4:13; 12:6; 1Pet. 1:12 [b]Dan. 11:31; 12:11
14 IHebr. *evening morning* IIHebr. *justified*
15 [a]Dan. 12:8; 1Pet. 1:10, 11 [b]Ezek. 1:26
16 [a]Dan. 12:6, 7 [b]Dan. 9:21; Luke 1:19, 26
17 [a]Ezek. 1:28; Rev. 1:17
18 IHebr. *made me stand upon my standing* [a]Dan. 10:9, 10; Luke 9:32 [b]Ezek. 2:2
19 [a]Dan. 9:27; 11:27, 35, 36; 12:7; Hab. 2:3
20 [a]Dan. 8:3
21 [a]Dan. 8:5 [b]Dan. 11:3
22 [a]Dan. 8:8; 11:4
23 IHebr. *are accomplished* [a]Deut. 28:50 [b]Dan. 8:6
24 IHebr. *people of the holy ones* [a]Rev. 17:13, 17 [b]Dan. 8:12; 11:36 [c]Dan. 8:10; Dan. 7:25
25 IOr, *prosperity* [a]Dan. 11:21, 23, 24 [b]Dan. 8:11; 11:36 [c]Dan. 8:11; 11:36 [d]Job 34:20; Lam. 4:6; Dan. 2:34, 45
26 [a]Dan. 10:1 [b]Ezek. 12:27; Dan. 10:14; 12:4, 9; Rev. 22:10 **27** [a]Dan. 7:28; 10:8, 16 [b]Dan. 6:2, 3 [c]Dan. 8:16

🔑 **8:16** Only two holy angels are named in Scripture, and Daniel names both. Gabriel, mentioned in this verse, seems to be God's special messenger (see also Dan. 9:21; cf. Luke 1:19, 26). The other is Michael, who is described as "one of the chief princes" (Dan. 10:13), "your prince" (Dan. 10:21), "the great prince" (Dan. 12:1), and "the archangel" (Jude 1:9). He is also a leader of God's armies (Rev. 12:7) and the guardian of Israel (Dan. 12:1).

🔑 **8:26** The "shutting up of the vision" referred to in this verse is speaking about the sealing up of the prophecy for the purpose of later validation (cf. Is. 8:16).

🔑 **8:27** This verse graphically shows the physical and emotional drain that Daniel felt after these overwhelming visionary experiences (cf. Dan. 7:15, 28; 10:8). It also reveals that the prophets did not always fully understand the things that they recorded. This is why Peter said, "We have also a more sure word of prophecy" (2 Pet. 1:19) in reference to the revelation of the completed word of God.

Daniel Prays for His People

9 In the first year [a]of Darius the son[1121] of Ahasuerus, of the seed[2233] of the Medes, [1]which was made king[4427] over the realm of the Chaldeans;

2 In the first year of his reign[4427] I Daniel understood[995] by books[5612] the number of the years, whereof the word[1697] of the LORD came to [a]Jeremiah the prophet,[5030] that he would accomplish[4390] seventy years in the desolations[2723] of Jersualem.

🔑 3 [a]And I set my face unto the Lord[136] God,[430] to seek by prayer[8605] and supplications,[8469] with fasting, and sackcloth, and ashes:

4 And I prayed[6419] unto the LORD my God, and made my confession,[3034] and said, O [a]Lord, the great and dreadful[3372] God,[410] keeping[8104] the covenant[1285] and mercy[2617] to them that love[157] him, and to them that keep his commandments;[1697]

5 [a]We have sinned,[2398] and have committed iniquity,[5753] and have done wickedly,[7561] and have rebelled,[4775] even by departing from thy precepts[4687] and from thy judgments:[4941]

6 [a]Neither have we hearkened[8085] unto thy servants[5650] the prophets,[5030] which spake in thy name to our kings,[4428] our princes,[8269] and our fathers,[1] and to all the people[5971] of the land.[776]

7 O Lord, [a]righteousness[6666] [1]*belongeth* unto thee, but unto us confusion[1322] of faces, as at this day;[3117] to the men[376] of Judah, and to the inhabitants of Jerusalem, and unto all Israel, *that are* near, and *that are* far off, through all the countries[776] whither thou hast driven them, because of their trespass[4604] that they have trespassed[4603] against thee.

8 O Lord, to us *belongeth* [a]confusion of face, to our kings, to our princes, and to our fathers, because we have sinned against thee.

9 [a]To the Lord our God *belong* mercies[7356] and forgiveness,[5547] though we have rebelled against him;

10 [a]Neither have we obeyed[8085] the voice of the LORD our God, to walk in his laws,[8451] which he set before us by his servants the prophets.

11 Yea, [a]all Israel have transgressed[5674] thy law,[8451] even by departing, that they might not obey thy voice; therefore the curse[423] is poured upon us, and the oath[7621] that *is* written in the [b]law of Moses the servant[5650] of God, because we have sinned against him.

12 And he hath [a]confirmed his words,[1697] which he spake against us, and against our judges that judged[8199] us, by bringing upon us a great evil:[7451] [b]for under the whole heaven hath not been done[6213] as hath been done upon Jerusalem.

13 [a]As *it is* written in the law of Moses, all this evil is come upon us: [b]yet [1]made we not our prayer before the LORD our God, that we might turn[7725] from our iniquities,[5771] and understand[7919] thy truth.[571]

14 Therefore hath the LORD [a]watched upon the evil, and brought it upon us: for [b]the LORD our God *is* righteous[6662] in all his works which he doeth: [c]for we obeyed not his voice.

15 And now, O Lord our God, [a]that hast brought thy people forth out of the land of Egypt with a mighty[2389] hand,[3027] and hast [1]gotten[6213] thee [b]renown, as at this day; [c]we have sinned, we have done wickedly.

16 O Lord, [a]according to all thy righteousness, I beseech thee,[4994] let thine anger[639] and thy fury be turned away from thy city Jerusalem, [b]thy holy[6944] mountain: because for our sins,[2399] [c]and for the iniquities of our fathers, [d]Jerusalem and thy people [e]*are become* a reproach[2781] to all *that are* about us.

17 Now therefore, O our God,

1 [1]Or, *in which he* [a]Dan. 1:21; 5:31; 6:28
2 [a]2Chr. 36:21; Jer. 25:11, 12; 29:10
3 [a]Neh. 1:4; Jer. 29:12, 13; Dan. 6:10; James 4:8-10
4 [a]Ex. 20:6; Deut. 7:9; Neh. 1:5; 9:32
5 [a]1Kgs. 8:47, 48; Neh. 1:6, 7; 9:33, 34; Ps. 106:6; Isa. 64:5, 6, 7; Jer. 14:7; Dan. 9:15
6 [a]2Chr. 36:15, 16; Dan. 9:10
7 [1]Or, *thou hast* [a]Neh. 9:33
8 [a]Dan. 9:7
9 [a]Neh. 9:17; Ps. 130:4, 7
10 [a]Dan. 9:6
11 [a]Isa. 1:4-6; Jer. 8:5, 10 [b]Lev. 26:14-46; Deut. 27:15-26; 28:15-68; 29:20-28; 30:17, 18; 31:17-21; 32:19-28; Lam. 2:17
12 [a]Zech. 1:6 [b]Lam. 1:12; 2:13; Ezek. 5:9; Amos 3:2
13 [1]Hebr. *entreated we not the face of the* [a]Lev. 26:14-46; Deut. 28:15; Lam. 2:17 [b]Isa. 9:13; Jer. 2:30; 5:3; Hos. 7:7, 10
14 [a]Jer. 31:28; 44:27 [b]Neh. 9:33; Dan. 9:7 [c]Dan. 9:10
15 [1]Hebr. *made thee a name* [a]Ex. 6:1, 6; 32:11; 1Kgs. 8:51; Neh. 1:10; Jer. 32:21 [b]Ex. 14:18; Neh. 9:10; Jer. 32:20 [c]Dan. 9:5
16 [a]1Sam. 12:7; Ps. 31:1; 71:2; Mic. 6:4, 5 [b]Dan. 9:20; Zech. 8:3 [c]Ex. 20:5 [d]Lam. 2:15, 16 [e]Ps. 44:13, 14; 79:4

🔑 **9:3–19** This prayer of Daniel's is the longest prayer in the Old Testament and was used as a model for other prayers in the Bible (cf. Neh. 1:4–11). It is based on promises he had found in Scripture (Jer. 29:10, 11).

hear[8085] the prayer of thy servant, and
his supplications, [a]and cause thy face to
shine upon thy sanctuary[4720] [b]that is
desolate,[8074] [c]for the Lord's sake.
18 [a]O my God, incline thine ear,[241]
and hear; open thine eyes, [b]and
behold[7200] our desolations,[8074] and the
city [I][c]which is called[7121] by thy name:
for we do not [II][d]present[5307] our supplications before thee for our righteousnesses,
but for thy great mercies.
19 O Lord, hear; O Lord, forgive;[5545]
O Lord, hearken[7181] and do; defer not,
[a]for thine own sake, O my God: for thy
city and thy people are called by thy
name.

The Seventy Weeks

20 [a]And whiles I *was* speaking,[1696]
and praying, and confessing[3034] my
sin[2403] and the sin of my people Israel,
and presenting[5307] my supplication[8467]
before the LORD my God for the holy
mountain of my God;
21 Yea, whiles I *was* speaking in
prayer, even the man[376] [a]Gabriel, whom I
had seen[7200] in the vision[2377] at the beginning, being caused to fly [I]swiftly,
[b]touched[5060] me [c]about the time[6256] of
the evening oblation.[4503]
22 And he informed[995] *me,* and
talked[1696] with me, and said, O Daniel, I
am now come forth [I]to give thee skill[7919]
and understanding.[998]
23 At the beginning of thy supplications the [I]commandment[1697] came forth,
and [a]I am come to shew[5046] *thee;* [b]for
thou *art* [II]greatly beloved: therefore
[c]understand[995] the matter,[1697] and consider[995] the vision.[4758]
🔑 24 Seventy weeks are determined
upon thy people and upon thy holy city,
[I]to finish[3607] the transgression,[6588] and
[II]to make an end[2856] of sins, [a]and to
make reconciliation[3722] for iniquity,[5771]
[b]and to bring in everlasting[5769] righteousness,[6664] and to seal up the vision
and prophecy, [c]and to anoint[4886] the most
Holy.
25 [a]Know[3045] therefore and understand, *that* [b]from the going forth[4161] of
the commandment [c]to restore[7725] and to
build Jerusalem unto [d]the Messiah[4899]
[e]the Prince[5057] *shall be* seven weeks, and
threescore and two weeks: the street[7339]
[I]shall be built again, and the wall,[2742]
[f]even in troublous[6695] times.[6256]
26 And after threescore and two
weeks [a]shall Messiah be cut off,[3772] [b]but
not for himself: [I][c]and [d]the people of the

17 [a]Num. 6:25; Ps. 67:1; 80:3, 7, 19 [b]Lam. 5:18 [c]Dan. 9:19; John 16:24
18 [I]Hebr. *whereupon thy name is called* [II]Hebr. *cause to fall* [a]Isa. 37:17 [b]Ex. 3:7; Ps. 80:14-19 [c]Jer. 25:29 [d]Jer. 36:7
19 [a]Ps. 79:9, 10; 102:15, 16
20 [a]Ps. 32:5; Isa. 65:24
21 [I]Hebr. *with weariness,* or, *flight* [a]Dan. 8:16 [b]Dan. 8:18; 10:10, 16 [c]1Kgs. 18:36
22 [I]Hebr. *to make thee skillful of understanding*
23 [I]Hebr. *word* [II]Hebr. a man of *desires* [a]Dan. 10:12 [b]Dan. 10:11, 19 [c]Matt. 24:15
24 [I]Or, *to restrain* [II]Or, *to seal up,* Lam. 4:22 [a]Num. 14:34; Ezek. 4:6 [b]Isa. 53:10 [c]Isa. 53:11; Jer. 23:5, 6; Heb. 9:12; Rev. 14:6 [d]Ps. 45:7; Luke 1:35; John 1:41; Heb. 9:11
25 [I]Hebr. *shall return and be built* [a]Dan. 9:23; Matt. 24:15 [b]Ezra 4:24; 6:1, 15; 7:1-28; Neh. 2:1, 3, 5, 6, 8 [c]2Sam. 15:25; Ps. 71:20 [d]John 1:41; 4:25 [e]Isa. 55:4 [f]Neh. 4:8, 16-18; 6:15 **26** [I]Or, *and* [*the Jews*] *they shall be no more his people,* or, *the prince's future people* [a]Isa. 53:8; Mark 9:12; Luke 24:26, 46 [b]1Pet. 2:21; 3:18 [c]Dan. 11:17 [d]Matt. 22:7

🔑 **9:24–27** This is one of the most important and controversial prophecies in Scripture. Daniel had been praying about the rebuilding of Jerusalem and the return of his people. God gave Daniel a time frame for all His dealings with Israel. Verse twenty-four is the key to understanding the prophecy. It speaks of Daniel's people and the holy city (i.e., Jerusalem). Atonement for iniquity would be made for all sin at Calvary; it applies to individuals, not to the nation of Israel (cf. Zech. 12:10—13:1; 14:4–9). They are still a sinful people, but they will be purged (cf. Ezek. 20:34–43). The "most holy place" is now destroyed, but it will be reestablished (cf. Ezek. 40—48). The beginning of the time is the decree to rebuild Jerusalem. The "seventy weeks" can only refer to years, since Daniel specifies "three full weeks" in Daniel 10:2, when he refers to seven day periods. Also, the prophecy is an expansion of God's earlier revelation of the seventy years' captivity. Some biblical scholars suggest that in all probability, the sixty-nine weeks began with the decree that was issued to Nehemiah in 445—444 B.C. and ended 483 years later (based on 360–day years, Rev. 11:3; 12:6; 13:5) on Palm Sunday. Then there is a gap in Daniel's prophecy, a feature that is characteristic of Daniel's writings. This occurs because over thirty years elapsed between the crucifixion of Christ ("shall Messiah be cut off, but not for Himself," v. 26) and the destruction of Jerusalem ("destroy the city and the sanctuary," v. 26). However, all this follows the first sixty-nine weeks. As long as God is gathering the Church out of the world, this seventieth week remains future. Once the "times of the Gentiles" (Luke 21:24) are complete, the clock of God's judgment will count off the last remaining week in the seven-year tribulation.

prince that shall come [e]shall destroy[7843] the city [f]and the sanctuary;[6944] [g]and the end thereof *shall be* [h]with a flood,[7858] and unto the end of the war [II]desolations are determined.

27 And he shall confirm[1396] [I][a]the covenant with [b]many for one week: and in the midst of the week he shall cause[7673] the sacrifice[2077] and the oblation to cease,[7673] [II]and for the overspreading[3671] of [c]abominations[8251] he shall make *it* desolate,[8074] [d]even until the consummation,[3617] and that determined[2782] shall be poured upon the desolate.

Daniel's Terrifying Vision

10 In the third year of Cyrus king[4428] of Persia a thing was revealed[1540] unto Daniel, [a]whose name was called[7121] Belteshazzar; [b]and the thing *was* true,[571] [c]but the time appointed[6635] *was* [I]long:[1419] and [d]he understood[995] the thing, and had understanding[998] of the vision.

2 In those days[3117] I Daniel was mourning three [I]full weeks.

3 I ate no [I]pleasant[2530] bread, neither came flesh[1320] nor wine in my mouth,[6310] [a]neither did I anoint[5480] myself at all, till three whole[3117] weeks were fulfilled.

4 And in the four and twentieth day of the first[7223] month, as I was by the side[3027] of the great river, which *is* [a]Hiddekel;

🔑 5 Then [a]I lifted up[5375] mine eyes, and looked,[7200] and [b]behold [I]a certain man[376] clothed in linen, whose loins *were* [c]girded with [d]fine gold of Uphaz:

6 His body[1472] also *was* [a]like the beryl, and his face [b]as the appearance of lightning, [c]and his eyes as lamps of fire, and his arms [d]and his feet like in colour to polished brass, [e]and the voice of his words[1697] like the voice of a multitude.

7 And I Daniel [a]alone saw[7200] the vision:[4759] for the men[582] that were with me saw not the vision; but a great quaking[2731] fell[5307] upon them, so that they fled to hide themselves.

8 Therefore I was left[7604] alone, and saw this great vision, [a]and there remained[7604] no strength in me: for my [I][b]comeliness[1935] was turned[2015] in me into corruption,[4889] and I retained no strength.

9 Yet heard[8085] I the voice of his words: [a]and when I heard the voice of his words, then was I in a deep sleep on my face, and my face toward the ground.[776]

10 [a]And, behold, an hand[3027] touched[5060] me, which [I]set me upon my knees and *upon* the palms[3709] of my hands.[3027]

11 And he said[559] unto me, O Daniel, [I][a]a man greatly beloved, understand[995] the words that I speak[1696] unto thee, and [II]stand upright: for unto thee am I now sent. And when he had spoken this word[1697] unto me, I stood trembling.[7460]

12 Then said he unto me, [a]Fear[3372] not, Daniel: for from the first day that thou didst set thine heart[3820] to understand, and to chasten thyself[6031] before thy God,[430] [b]thy words were heard, and I am come for thy words.

13 [a]But the prince[8269] of the kingdom[4438] of Persia withstood me one and twenty days: but, lo, [b]Michael, [I]one of the chief[7223] princes, came to help me; and I remained[3498] there with the kings of Persia.

14 Now I am come to make thee understand what shall befall thy people[5971] [a]in the latter[319] days: [b]for yet the vision[2377] *is* for *many* days.

15 And when he had spoken such words unto me, [a]I set my face toward the ground, and I became dumb.[481]

16 And, behold, [a]*one* like the similitude[1823] of the sons[1121] of men[120] [b]touched my lips:[8193] then I opened my mouth, and spake, and said unto him that stood before me, O my lord,[113] by the

26 [II]Or, *it shall be cut off by desolations* [e]Luke 19:44 [f]Matt. 24:2 [g]Matt. 24:6, 14 [h]Isa. 8:7, 8; Dan. 11:10, 22; Nah. 1:8
27 [I]Or, *a* [II]Or, *and upon the battlements shall be the idols of the desolator* [a]Isa. 42:6; 55:3; Jer. 31:31; Ezek. 16:60-62 [b]Isa. 53:11; Matt. 26:28; Rom. 5:15, 19; Heb. 9:28 [c]Matt. 24:15; Mark 13:14; Luke 21:20 [d]Isa. 10:22, 23; 28:22; Dan. 11:36; Luke 21:24; Rom. 11:26

1 [I]Hebr. *great* [a]Dan. 1:7 [b]Dan. 8:26; Rev. 19:9 [c]Dan. 10:14 [d]Dan. 1:17; 8:16
2 [I]Hebr. *weeks of days*
3 [I]Hebr. *bread of desires* [a]Matt. 6:17
4 [a]Gen. 2:14
5 [I]Hebr. *one man* [a]Josh. 5:13 [b]Dan. 12:6, 7 [c]Rev. 1:13-15; 15:6 [d]Jer. 10:9
6 [a]Ezek. 1:16 [b]Ezek. 1:14 [c]Rev. 1:14; 19:12 [d]Ezek. 1:7; Rev. 1:15 [e]Ezek. 1:24; Rev. 1:15
7 [a]2Kgs. 6:17; Acts 9:7
8 [I]Or, *vigor* [a]Dan. 8:27 [b]Dan. 7:28
9 [a]Dan. 8:18
10 [I]Hebr. *moved* [a]Jer. 1:9; Dan. 9:21; Rev. 1:17
11 [I]Hebr. *a man of desires* [II]Hebr. *stand upon thy standing* [a]Dan. 9:23
12 [a]Rev. 1:17 [b]Dan. 9:3, 4, 22, 23; Acts 10:4
13 [I]Or, *the first* [a]Dan. 10:20 [b]Dan. 10:21; Jude 1:9; Rev. 12:7
14 [a]Gen. 49:1; Dan. 2:28 [b]Dan. 8:26; 10:1; Hab. 2:3
15 [a]Dan. 8:18, 10:9
16 [a]Dan. 8:15 [b]Dan. 10:10; Jer. 1:9

🔑 **10:5–9** This is a vision of the Lord Jesus in a preincarnate appearance (cf. Rev. 1:12–17).

vision [c]my sorrows[6735] are turned upon me, and I have retained no strength.

17 For how can [I]the servant[5650] of this my lord talk[1696] with this my lord? for as for me, straightway[6258] there remained no strength in me, neither is there breath[5397] left in me,

18 Then there came again and touched me *one* like the appearance of a man,[120] and he strengthened[2388] me.

19 [a]And said, O man greatly beloved, [b]fear not: peace *be* unto thee, be strong,[2388] yea, be strong. And when he had spoken unto me, I was strengthened, and said, Let my lord speak; for thou hast strengthened me.

20 Then said he, Knowest[3045] thou wherefore I come unto thee? and now will I return[7725] to fight [a]with the prince of Persia: and when I am gone forth, lo, the prince of Grecia shall come.

21 But I will shew[5046] thee that which is noted in the scripture[3791] of truth:[571] and *there is* none that [I]holdeth[2388] with me in these things, [a]but Michael your prince.

11

Also I [a]in the first year of [b]Darius the Mede, *even* I, stood to confirm[2388] and to strengthen him.

The Kingdoms of Egypt and Syria

2 And now will I shew[5046] thee the truth.[571] Behold, there shall stand up yet three kings[4428] in Persia; and the fourth shall be far richer than *they* all: and by his strength[2393] through his riches he shall stir up all against the realm of Grecia.

3 And [a]a mighty king shall stand up, that shall rule[4910] with great dominion,[4474] and [b]do[6213] according to his will.[7522]

4 And when he shall stand up, [a]his kingdom[4438] shall be broken,[7665] and shall be divided toward the four winds[7307] of heaven; and not to his posterity,[319] [b]nor according to his dominion[4915] which he ruled: for his kingdom shall be plucked up, even for others beside those.

5 And the king of the south shall be strong,[2388] and *one* of his princes;[8269] and he shall be strong above him, and have dominion;[4910] his dominion *shall be* a great dominion.[4474]

6 And in the end of years they [I]shall join themselves together; for the king's daughter of the south shall come to the king of the north to make[6213] [II]an agreement:[4339] but she shall not retain the power of the arm; neither shall he stand, nor his arm: but she shall be given up, and they that brought her, and [III]he that begat her, and he that strengthened[2388] her in *these* times.[6256]

7 But out of a branch of her roots shall *one* stand up [I][a]in his estate,[3653] which shall come with an army,[2428] and shall enter into the fortress of the king of the north, and shall deal[6213] against them, and shall prevail:[2388]

8 And shall also carry captives[7628] into Egypt their gods,[430] with their princes,[5257] *and* with [I]their precious vessels of silver and of gold; and he shall continue *more* years than the king of the north.

9 So the king of the south shall come into *his* kingdom, and shall return[7725] into his own land.[127]

10 But his sons[1121] [I]shall be stirred up, and shall assemble[622] a multitude of great forces:[2428] and *one* shall certainly come, [a]and overflow,[7857] and pass through:[5674] [II]then shall he return, and be stirred up, [b]*even* to his fortress.

11 And the king of the south shall be moved with choler,[4843] and shall come forth and fight with him, *even* with the

16 [c]Dan. 10:8
17 [I]Or, *this servant of my lord*
19 [a]Dan. 10:11 [b]Judg. 6:23
20 [a]Dan. 10:13
21 [I]Hebr. *strengtheneth himself* [a]Dan. 10:13; Jude 1:9; Rev. 12:7
1 [a]Dan. 9:1 [b]Dan. 5:31
3 [a]Dan. 7:6; 8:5 [b]Dan. 8:4; 11:16, 36
4 [a]Dan. 8:8 [b]Dan. 8:22
6 [I]Hebr. *shall associate themselves* [II]Hebr. *rights* [III]Or, *whom she brought forth*
7 [I]Or, *in his place,* or, *office* [a]Dan. 11:20
8 [I]Hebr. *vessels of their desire*
10 [I]Or, *shall war* [a]Isa. 8:8; Dan. 9:26 [II]Or, *then shall he be stirred up again* [b]Dan. 11:7

10:21 See note on Daniel 8:16.

11:1–20 These verses give the prediction of the events of world history from approximately 500–175 B.C. The kings of the North and the South (v. 5, 13) refer to the succeeding rulers of the Ptolemaic and Seleucid dynasties, founded by two of Alexander the Great's sons.

king of the north: and he shall set forth
a great multitude; but the multitude shall
be given into his hand.[3027]
12 *And* when he hath taken away[5375]
the multitude, his heart[3824] shall be lifted
up; and he shall cast down[5307] *many*
ten thousands:[506] but he shall not be
strengthened *by it.*
13 For the king of the north shall return, and shall set forth a multitude
greater than the former,[7223] and shall certainly come [Ia]after certain years with a
great army and with much riches.
14 And in those times there shall
many stand up against the king of the
south: also [I]the robbers[6530] of thy people[5971] shall exalt themselves to establish
the vision;[2377] but they shall fall.[3782]
15 So the king of the north shall
come, and cast up[8210] a mount, and take
[I]the most fenced[4013] cities: and the arms
of the south shall not withstand, neither
[II]his chosen people, neither *shall there be*
any strength to withstand.
16 But he that cometh against him
[a]shall do according to his own will, and
[b]none shall stand before him: and he shall
stand in the [Ic]glorious[6643] land,[776] which
by his hand shall be consumed.[3615]
17 He shall also [a]set[7760] his face to
enter with the strength of his whole kingdom, and [I]upright ones[3477] with him; thus
shall he do: and he shall give him the
daughter of women, [II]corrupting[7843] her:
but she shall not stand *on his side,* [b]nei-
ther be for him.
18 After this shall he turn[7725] his
face unto the isles, and shall take many:
but a prince[7101] [I]for his own behalf shall
cause [II]the reproach offered by him to
cease;[7673] without his own reproach[2781]
he shall cause *it* to turn upon him.
19 Then he shall turn his face toward
the fort of his own land: but he shall
stumble[3782] and fall, [a]and not be found.
20 Then shall stand up [Ia]in his estate
a [II]raiser of taxes[5065] *in* the glory[1925] of
the kingdom: but within few days[3117] he
shall be destroyed,[7665] neither in anger,[639]
nor in battle.
🔑 21 And [I]in his estate [a]shall stand up
a vile person,[959] to whom they shall not
give the honour[1935] of the kingdom: but
he shall come in peaceably, and obtain[2388]
the kingdom by flatteries.[2519]
22 [a]And with the arms of a flood[7858]
shall they be overflown[7857] from before
him, and shall be broken; [b]yea, also the
prince[5057] of the covenant.[1285]
23 And after the league *made* with
him [a]he shall work[6213] deceitfully:[4820] for
he shall come up,[5927] and shall become
strong with a small people.[1471]
24 He shall enter [I]peaceably even
upon the fattest places of the province;
and he shall do *that* which his fathers[1]
have not done,[6213] nor his fathers' fathers;
he shall scatter among them the prey, and
spoil, and riches: *yea,* and he shall
[II]forecast[2803] his devices against the
strong holds, even for a time.[6256]
25 And he shall stir up his power
and his courage[3824] against the king of
the south with a great army; and the
king of the south shall be stirred up to
battle with a very great and mighty
army; but he shall not stand: for they
shall forecast devices against him.
26 Yea, they that feed of the portion
of his meat shall destroy[7665] him, and
his army shall [a]overflow: and many shall
fall down slain.[2491]
27 And both these kings' [I]hearts[3824]
shall be to do mischief, and they shall
speak[1696] lies[3577] at one table; but it shall
not prosper: for [a]yet the end *shall be* at
the time appointed.[4150]
28 Then shall he return into his land
with great riches; and [a]his heart *shall be*
against the holy[6944] covenant; and he
shall do *exploits,* and return to his own
land.

13 [I]Hebr. *at the end of times, even years,* [a]Dan. 4:16; 12:7
14 [I]Hebr. *the children of robbers*
15 [I]Hebr. *the city of munitions* [II]Hebr. *the people of his choices*
16 [I]Or, *goodly land;* Hebr. *the land of ornament* [a]Dan. 8:4, 7; 11:3, 36 [b]Josh. 1:5 [c]Dan. 8:9; 11:41, 45
17 [I]Or, *much uprightness;* or, *equal conditions* [II]Hebr. *to corrupt* [a]2Chr. 20:3 [b]Dan. 9:26
18 [I]Hebr. *for him* [II]Hebr. *his reproach*
19 [a]Job 20:8; Ps. 37:36; Ezek. 26:21
20 [I]Or, *in his place* [II]Hebr. *one that causeth an exactor to pass over* [a]Dan. 11:7
21 [I]Or, *in his place* [a]Dan. 7:8; 8:9, 23, 25
22 [a]Dan. 11:10 [b]Dan. 8:10, 11, 25
23 [a]Dan. 8:25
24 [I]Or, *into the peaceable and fat* [II]Hebr. *think his thoughts*
26 [a]Dan. 11:10, 22
27 [I]Hebr. *their hearts* [a]Dan. 11:29, 35, 40; Dan. 8:19
28 [a]Dan. 11:22

🔑 **11:21–35** These verses describe an event in the life of Antiochus IV Epiphanes, whom some believe is the "small horn" of Daniel 8:9. He is a precursor of the Antichrist, and both his persecution of the Jews, and his desecration of the temple (Dan. 11:31) foreshadow the offences that the Antichrist will commit against the Jewish nation. See note on Ezekiel 43:13–27.

29 At the time appointed he shall return, and come toward the south; [a]but it shall not be as the former,[7223] [b]or as the latter.[314]

30 [a]For the ships of Chittim shall come against him: therefore he shall be grieved, and return, and have indignation[2194] [b]against the holy covenant: so shall he do; he shall even return, and have intelligence[995] with them that forsake[5800] the holy covenant.

31 And arms shall stand on his part, [a]and they shall pollute the sanctuary[4720] of strength, and shall take away the daily[8548] *sacrifice,* and they shall place the abomination[8251] that [I]maketh desolate.[8074]

32 And such as do wickedly[7561] against the covenant shall he [I]corrupt[2610] by flatteries:[2514] but the people that do know[3045] their God[430] shall be strong, and do *exploits.*

33 [a]And they that understand[7919] among the people shall instruct[995] many: [b]yet they shall fall by the sword,[2719] and by flame, by captivity,[7628] and by spoil, *many* days.

34 Now when they shall fall, they shall be holpen[5826] with a little help: but many shall cleave to them with flatteries.[2519]

35 And *some* of them of understanding shall fall, [a]to try[6884] [I]them, and to purge,[1305] and to make *them* white, [b]*even* to the time of the end: [c]because *it is* yet for a time appointed.

🗝 36 And the king [a]shall do according to his will; and he shall [b]exalt himself, and magnify himself above every god,[410] and shall speak marvellous things[6381] [c]against the God of gods, and shall prosper [d]till the indignation[2195] be accomplished:[3615] for that that is determined shall be done.

37 Neither shall he regard[995] the God of his fathers, [a]nor the desire[2532] of women,[802] [b]nor regard any god: for he shall magnify himself above all.

38 [I]But [II]in his estate shall he honour[3513] the God[433] of [III]forces:[4581] and a god whom his fathers knew[3045] not shall he honour with gold, and silver, and with precious stones, and [IV][a]pleasant things.[2532]

39 Thus shall he do in the [I]most strong holds with a strange[5236] god, whom he shall acknowledge[5234] *and* increase with glory:[3519] and he shall cause them to rule over many, and shall divide[2505] the land for [II]gain.

40 [a]And at the time of the end shall the king of the south push[5055] at him: and the king of the north shall come against him [b]like a whirlwind,[8175] with chariots, [c]and with horsemen, and with many ships; and he shall enter into the countries,[776] [d]and shall overflow and pass over.[5674]

41 He shall enter also into the [I]glorious[6643] land, and many *countries* shall be overthrown:[3782] but these shall escape[4422] out of his hand, [a]*even* Edom, and Moab, and the chief[7225] of the children[1121] of Ammon.

42 He shall [I]stretch forth his hand also upon the countries: and the land of Egypt shall not escape.[6413]

43 But he shall have power[4910] over the treasures of gold and of silver, and over all the precious things of Egypt: and the Libyans and the Ethiopians *shall be* [a]at his steps.

44 But tidings out of the east and out of the north shall trouble[926] him: therefore he shall go forth with great fury to destroy,[8045] and utterly to make away many.

45 And he shall plant the taber-

29 [a]Dan. 11:23 [b]Dan. 11:25
30 [a]Num. 24:24; Jer. 2:10 [b]Dan. 11:28
31 [I]Or, *astonisheth* [a]Dan. 8:11; 12:11
32 [I]Or, *cause to dissemble*
33 [a]Mal. 2:7 [b]Heb. 11:35-40
35 [I]Or, *by them* [a]Dan. 12:10; 1Pet. 1:7 [b]Dan. 8:17, 19; 11:40 [c]Dan. 11:29
36 [a]Dan. 11:16 [b]Dan. 7:8, 25; 8:25; 2Thess. 2:4; Rev. 13:5, 6 [c]Dan. 8:11, 24, 25 [d]Dan. 9:27
37 [a]1Tim. 4:3 [b]Isa. 14:13; 2Thess. 2:4
38 [I]Or, *But in his stead* [II]Hebr. *as for the Almighty God, in his seat he shall honor, yea, he shall honor a god, whom* [III]Or, *munitions;* Hebr. *Manzzim,* or, *God's protectors* [IV]Hebr. *things desired* [a]Isa. 44:9
39 [I]Hebr. *fortresses of munitions* [II]Hebr. *a price*
40 [a]Dan. 11:35 [b]Isa. 21:1; Zech. 9:14 [c]Ezek. 38:4, 15; Rev. 9:16 [d]Dan. 11:10, 22
41 [I]Or, *goodly land;* Hebr. *land of delight,* or, *ornament* [a]Dan. 11:16 [b]Isa. 11:14
42 [I]Hebr. *send forth*
43 [a]Ex. 11:8; Judg. 4:10

🗝 **11:36** There is a gap here in the prophetic revelation, as in chapter eight, which moves from the type (Antiochus IV) to the antitype (the Antichrist). The shift is made obvious by the fact that Antiochus was one of the "kings of the North" (a Seleucid), while the Antichrist is attacked by the kings of the North and the South (Dan. 11:40). Furthermore, his voicing of blasphemies against God is also a characteristic of the Antichrist (Dan. 11:36, cf. 7:8, 20, 25). Finally, Daniel 12:1 (which continues the narrative from chap. 11) identifies the time of his activity as the "time of distress" known as the Great Tribulation (cf. Is. 26:20; Jer. 30:7; Matt. 24:21; Mark 13:19).

nacles[168] of his palace between the seas in [a]the [I]glorious holy mountain; [b]yet he shall come to his end, and none shall help him.

The Time of the End

12 🗝And at that time shall [a]Michael stand up, the great prince[8269] which standeth for the children[1121] of thy people:[5971] [b]and there shall be a time of trouble,6869 such as never was since there was a nation[1471] *even* to that same time: and at that time thy people [c]shall be delivered,[4422] every one that shall be found [d]written in the book.[5612]

2 And many of them that sleep in the dust[6083] of the earth[127] shall awake, [a]some to everlasting[5769] life, and some to shame[2781] [b]*and* everlasting contempt.[1860]

3 And [a]they that be [I]wise[7919] shall [b]shine[2094] as the brightness of the firmament;[7549] [c]and they that turn many to righteousness[6663] [d]as the stars for ever[5769] and ever.[5703]

4 [a]But thou, O Daniel, [b]shut up the words,[1697] and seal the book, *even* to [c]the time of the end: many shall run to and fro,7751 and knowledge shall be increased.

5 Then I Daniel looked,[7200] and, behold, there stood other two, the one on this side of the [I]bank[8193] of the river, and the other on that side of the bank [a]of the river.

6 And *one* said[559] to [a]the man[376] clothed in linen, which *was* [I]upon the waters of the river, [b]How long *shall it be to* the end of these wonders?[6382]

7 And I heard[8085] the man clothed in linen, which *was* upon the waters of the river, when he [a]held up his right hand and his left hand unto heaven, and sware[7650] by him [b]that liveth[2416] for ever [c]that *it shall be* for a time,[4150] times, and [I]an half; [d]and when he shall have accomplished[3615] to scatter5310 the power[3027] of [e]the holy[6944] people, all these *things* shall be finished.[3615]

8 And I heard, but I understood[995] not: then said I, O my Lord, what *shall be* the end[319] of these *things?*

9 And he said, Go thy way, Daniel: for the words *are* closed up and sealed [a]till the time of the end.

10 [a]Many shall be purified,[1305] and made white, and tried;[6884] [b]but the wicked[7563] shall do wickedly:[7561] and none of the wicked shall understand;[995] but [c]the wise shall understand.

11 And from the time [a]*that* the daily[8548] *sacrifice* shall be taken away,[5493] and [I]the abomination[8251] that [II]maketh desolate[8074] set up, *there shall be* a thousand two hundred and ninety days.[3117]

12 Blessed[835] *is* he that waiteth, and cometh[5060] to the thousand three hundred and five and thirty days.

🗝13 But [a]go thou thy way till the end *be:* [I][b]for thou shalt rest, [c]and stand in thy lot1486 at the end of the days.

45 [I]Or, *goodly* [II]Hebr. *mountain of delight of holiness* [a]Ps. 48:2; Dan. 11:16, 41; 2Thess. 2:4 [b]2Thess. 2:8; Rev. 19:20
1 [a]Dan. 10:13, 21 [b]Isa. 26:20, 21; Jer. 30:7; Matt. 24:21; Rev. 16:18 [c]Rom. 11:26 [d]Ex. 32:32; Ps. 56:8; 69:28; Ezek. 13:9; Luke 10:20; Phil. 4:3; Rev. 3:5; 13:8
2 [a]Matt. 25:46; John 5:28, 29; Acts 24:15 [b]Isa. 66:24; Rom. 9:21
3 [I]Or, *teachers* [a]Dan. 11:33, 35 [b]Prov. 4:18; Matt. 13:43 [c]James 5:20 [d]1Cor. 15:41, 42
4 [a]Dan. 8:26; 12:9 [b]Rev. 10:4; 22:10 [c]Dan. 10:1; 12:9
5 [I]Hebr. *lip* [a]Dan. 10:4
6 [I]Or, *from above* [a]Dan. 10:5 [b]Dan. 8:13
7 [I]Or, *part* [a]Deut. 32:40; Rev. 10:5, 6 [b]Dan. 4:34 [c]Dan. 7:25; 11:13; Rev. 12:14 [d]Luke 21:24; Rev. 10:7 [e]Dan. 8:24
9 [a]Dan. 12:4
10 [a]Dan. 11:35; Zech. 13:9 [b]Hos. 14:9; Rev. 9:20; 22:11 [c]Dan. 11:33, 35; John 7:17; 8:47; 18:37
11 [I]Hebr. *to set up the abomination* [II]Or, *astonisheth* [a]Dan. 8:11; 11:31
13 [I]Or, *and thou* [a]Dan. 12:9 [b]Isa. 57:2; Rev. 14:13 [c]Ps. 1:5

🗝 **12:1–4** This passage is the clearest Old Testament reference to the resurrection of the dead (see note on Eccl. 12:7). As in Isaiah, the setting is the Great Tribulation. Here there are two resurrections being noted, though the time period between them is not mentioned (contrast Rev. 20:4). The implication of this passage is that the understanding of these visions would be made clear at "the time of the end" (v. 4). See note on Daniel 8:16 regarding Daniel and Michael.

🗝 **12:13** The Book of Daniel ends on a note of great promise that is often overlooked. Daniel, who had lived almost his whole life in Babylon and was now in his late eighties, is promised that he will receive his "lot." This refers to that portion of the Promised Land allocated to Daniel's family.

The Book of HOSEA

Hosea is the first book of what the Hebrews call "The Twelve," or what are otherwise known as the Minor Prophets. The name Hosea means "Salvation." There is very little known about him other than what is contained in his prophecy. Judging by the time period of the kings during whose reigns he prophesied (Hos. 1:1), Hosea's ministry extended from about 770–725 B.C. The prophecies of Amos, a younger contemporary, are closely related to those of Hosea. Their ministries were different, however, in that Hosea was a native of the Northern Kingdom, and Amos was a Judean who journeyed to Israel to prophesy. Hosea was called to exemplify the relationship between God and Israel through his marriage to a harlot, while Amos was sent by the Lord to pronounce judgment upon the rebellious people of Israel.

Hosea began prophesying at the end of a period of great material prosperity under King Jeroboam II of Israel (2 Kgs. 14:23–27). Unfortunately, however, during most of Hosea's lifetime, the people were spiritually bankrupt. Their leaders permitted them to practice idolatry (2 Chr. 27:2; 2 Kgs. 15:35) and commit spiritual "harlotry" against the Lord (Hos. 1:2; 2:8; 4:12–15). They refused to recognize that God had provided them with the wealth that they possessed (Hos. 2:8). In fact, they attributed their prosperity to the idols (Hos. 2:5; 10:1). The people had become covetous and greedy, oppressing those who were least able to defend themselves (Hos. 4:2; 10:13; 12:6–8).

Despite the punishment that God promises to bring upon them (Hos. 5; 9; 10), there is a strong attitude of hope that is evident throughout the book. Just as Hosea bought back his unfaithful wife, Israel will be redeemed by God in the last days (Hos. 1:10, 11; 2:14–23; 3:4, 5; 11:10, 11; 14:4–7).

Hosea Marries

1 The word[1697] of the LORD that came
unto Hosea, the son of Beeri, in the
days[3117] of Uzziah, Jotham, Ahaz, *and*
Hezekiah, kings of Judah, and in the
days of Jeroboam the son of Joash, king
of Israel.
🔑 2 The beginning of the word of the
LORD by Hosea. And the LORD said[559] to
Hosea, [a]Go, take unto thee a wife[802] of
whoredoms[2183] and children of whoredoms: for [b]the land[776] hath committed
great whoredom,[2181] *departing* from the
LORD.
3 So he went and took Gomer the
daughter of Diblaim; which conceived,
and bare him a son.[1121]
4 And the LORD said unto him,
Call[7121] his name Jezreel; for yet a little
while, [a]and I will [I]avenge[6485] the blood[1818]
of Jezreel upon the house[1004] of Jehu,
[b]and will cause to cease[7673] the kingdom[4468] of the house of Israel.
5 [a]And it shall come to pass at that
day, that I will break[7665] the bow of
Israel in the valley of Jezreel.
6 And she conceived again, and bare
a daughter. And *God* said unto him, Call
her name [I]Lo–ruhamah: [a]for [II]I will no
more have mercy[7355] upon the house of

2 [a]Hos. 3:1 [b]Deut. 31:16; Ps. 73:27; Jer. 2:13; Ezek. 23:3-21

4 [I]Hebr. *visit* [a]2Kgs. 10:11 [b]2Kgs. 15:10, 12

5 [a]2Kgs. 15:29

6 [I]That is, *Not having obtained mercy* [II]Hebr. *I will not add any more to* [a]2Kgs. 17:6, 23

🔑 **1:2–4** Many have questioned why God would tell Hosea to marry a harlot, but it must be understood that God intended to use this marriage as an illustration of His dealings with Israel. God used it to expose Israel's sin in this way because it vividly reflected Israel's unfaithfulness to Him. Jezreel, Hosea's first son, was legitimate because it is stated that Gomer (Hosea's wife) "bare him [Hosea] a son" (1:3). The other two children, however, are identified as "children of harlotry" (Hos. 2:1, 4) and are pictures of Israel's illegitimate children (Hos. 5:7).

Israel; [III]but I will utterly take them away.[5375]

7 [a]But I will have mercy upon the house of Judah, and will save[3467] them by the LORD their God,[430] and [b]will not save them by bow, nor by sword,[2719] nor by battle, by horses, nor by horsemen.

8 Now when she had weaned Lo–ruhamah, she conceived, and bare a son.

9 Then said *God,* Call his name [I]Lo–ammi: for ye *are* not my people,[5971] and I will not be your *God.*

Israel Comes Back

🔑10 Yet [a]the number of the children of Israel shall be as the sand of the sea, which cannot be measured nor numbered;[5608] [b]and it shall come to pass, *that* [I]in the place where it was said unto them, [c]Ye *are* not my people, *there* it shall be said unto them, *Ye are* [d]the sons of the living[2416] God.[410]

11 [a]Then shall the children of Judah and the children of Israel be gathered together,[6908] and appoint themselves one head,[7218] and they shall come up[5927] out of the land: for great *shall be* the day of Jezreel.

2

Say[559] ye unto your brethren,[251] [I]Ammi;[5971] and to your sisters,[269] [II]Ruhamah.[7355]

2 Plead[7378] with your mother,[517] plead: for [a]she *is* not my wife,[802] neither *am* I her husband:[376] let her therefore put away[5493] her [b]whoredoms[2183] out of her sight, and her adulteries[5005] from between her breasts;

3 Lest [a]I strip her naked,[6174] and set her as in the day[3117] that she was [b]born, and make her [c]as a wilderness, and set her like a dry land,[776] and slay[4191] her with [d]thirst.

4 And I will not have mercy[7355] upon her children;[1121] for they *be* the [a]children of whoredoms.

🔑5 [a]For their mother hath played the harlot:[2181] she that conceived them hath done shamefully: for she said, I will go after my lovers,[157] [b]that give *me* my bread and my water, my wool and my flax, mine oil[8081] and my [I]drink.

6 Therefore, behold, [a]I will hedge up[7753] thy way[1870] with thorns, and [I]make a wall, that she shall not find her paths.

7 And she shall follow after her lovers, but she shall not overtake them; and she shall seek them, but shall not find *them:* then shall she say, [a]I will go and return[7725] to my [b]first husband; for then *was it* better[2896] with me than now.

8 For she did not [a]know that [b]I gave her corn, and [I]wine, and oil,[3323] and multiplied her silver and gold, [II][c]*which* they prepared[6213] for Baal.

9 Therefore will I return, and [a]take away my corn in the time[6256] thereof, and my wine in the season[4150] thereof, and

6 [III]Or, *that I should altogether pardon the*
7 [a]2Kgs. 19:35 [b]Zech. 4:6; 9:10
9 [I]That is, *Not my people*
10 [I]Or, *instead of that* [a]Gen. 32:12; Rom. 9:27, 28 [b]Rom. 9:25, 26; 1Pet. 2:10 [c]Hos. 2:23 [d]John 1:12; 1John 3:1
11 [a]Isa. 11:12, 13; Jer. 3:18; Ezek. 34:23; 37:16-24

1 [I]That is, *My people* [II]That is, *Having obtained mercy*
2 [a]Isa. 50:1 [b]Ezek. 16:25
3 [a]Jer. 13:22, 26; Ezek. 16:37, 39 [b]Ezek. 16:4 [c]Ezek. 19:13 [d]Amos 8:11, 13
4 [a]John 8:41
5 [I]Hebr. *drinks* [a]Isa. 1:21; Jer. 3:1, 6, 8, 9; Ezek. 16:15, 16 [b]Jer. 44:17; Hos. 2:8, 12
6 [I]Hebr. *wall a wall* [a]Job 3:23; 19:8; Lam. 3:7, 9
7 [a]Hos. 5:15; Luke 15:18 [b]Ezek. 16:8
8 [I]Hebr. *new wine* [II]Or, *wherewith they made Baal* [a]Isa. 1:3 [b]Ezek. 16:17-19 [c]Hos. 8:4
9 [a]Hos. 2:3

🔑 **1:10—2:1** This brief prophecy of the millennial reign of Christ gives several significant details. First, it clearly affirms that the restoration of God's people to the land of Israel will be a physical one. They will be called "sons of the living God" in the same place where Hosea called them "not my people" (v. 10; the northern section of the Promised Land, possibly Samaria, cf. Ezek. 37:14, 21–25). Second, they will be reunited under one leader, and will be called God's children (v. 11, cf. Ezek. 36:10, 11, 28) when they return from the lands in which they have been captives. Third, the meanings of the names of Hosea's two youngest children will not apply to Israel anymore, because their situation will be reversed.

🔑 **2:5–13** The term "lovers" used in this passage refers to the pagan idols that Israel worshiped. Israel trusted in these idols for prosperity. The Baals were weather gods that supposedly controlled agricultural prosperity. Thus when Elijah called for the drought, it just as effectively demonstrated their powerlessness as their inability to send fire from heaven in the showdown at Mount Carmel (1 Kgs. 17:1—18:46). Fertility was thought to be affected by many idolatrous practices, such as "weeping for Tammuz" (see note on Ezek. 8:7–18) and engaging in cult prostitution (Hos. 4:14). These kind of practices had even crept into the temple observances (cf. Is. 1:11–15; Hos. 8:13).

will [I]recover[5337] my wool and my flax
given to cover[3680] her nakedness.[6172]
10 And now [a]will I discover[1540] her
[I]lewdness in the sight of her lovers, and
none shall deliver[5337] her out of mine
hand.[3027]
11 [a]I will also cause all her mirth to
cease,[7673] her [b]feast days,[2282] her new
moons, and her sabbaths,[7676] and all her
solemn feasts.[4150]
12 And I will [I]destroy[8074] her vines
and her fig trees, [a]whereof she hath said,
These *are* my rewards that my lovers
have given me: and [b]I will make[7760] them
a forest, and the beasts[2416] of the
field[7704] shall eat them.
13 And I will visit[6485] upon her the
days of Baalim, wherein she burned
incense[6999] to them, and she [a]decked herself with her earrings and her jewels,
and she went after her lovers, and forgat
me, saith[5002] the LORD.

God Loves His Unfaithful People

🔑 14 Therefore, behold, I will allure[6601]
her, and [a]bring her into the wilder-
ness, and speak[1696] [I]comfortably[3820][5921] unto
her.
15 And I will give her her vineyards
from thence, and [a]the valley of Achor for
a door of hope: and she shall sing there,
as in [b]the days of her youth, and [c]as in
the day when she came up[5927] out of the
land of Egypt.
16 And it shall be at that day, saith
the LORD, *that* thou shalt call me [I]Ishi;
and shalt call me no more [II]Baali.
17 For [a]I will take away[5493] the
names of Baalim out of her mouth, and
they shall no more be remembered[2142] by
their name.
18 And in that day will I make[3772]
a [a]covenant[1285] for them with the beasts
of the field, and with the fowls of
heaven,[8064] and *with* the creeping things
of the ground:[127] and [b]I will break[7665]
the bow and the sword and the battle
out of the earth,[776] and will make them
to [c]lie down safely.[983]
19 And I will betroth[781] thee unto me
for ever;[5769] yea, I will betroth thee unto
me in righteousness, and in judgment,[4941]
and in lovingkindness,[2617] and in mercies.[7356]
20 I will even betroth thee unto me
in faithfulness:[530] and [a]thou shalt
know[3045] the LORD.
21 And it shall come to pass in that
day, [a]I will hear, saith the LORD, I will
hear the heavens,[8064] and they shall hear
the earth;
22 And the earth shall hear the corn,
and the wine, and the oil; [a]and they shall
hear Jezreel.
23 And [a]I will sow her unto me in
the earth; [b]and I will have mercy[7355]
upon her that had not obtained
mercy;[7355] and I [c]will say to *them which*
were not my people, Thou *art* my people;
and they shall say, *Thou art* my God.[430]

Hosea Takes Back His Unfaithful Wife

3 🔑Then said[559] the LORD unto me,
[a]Go yet, love[157] a woman[802]
beloved[157] of *her* [b]friend,[7453] yet an
adulteress,[5003] according to the love[160]
of the LORD toward the children[1121] of

9 [I]Or, *take away*
10 [I]Hebr. *folly,* or, *villainy* [a]Ezek. 16:37; 23:29
11 [a]Amos 8:10 [b]1Kgs. 12:32; Amos 8:5
12 [I]Hebr. *make desolate* [a]Hos. 2:5 [b]Ps. 80:12, 13; Isa. 5:5
13 [a]Ezek. 23:40, 42
14 [I]Or, *friendly* [II]Hebr. *to her heart* [a]Ezek. 20:35
15 [a]Josh. 7:26; Isa. 65:10 [b]Jer. 2:2; Ezek. 16:8, 22, 60 [c]Ex. 15:1
16 [I]That is, *My husband* [II]That is, *My lord*
17 [a]Ex. 23:13; Josh. 23:7; Ps. 16:4; Zech. 13:2
18 [a]Job 5:23; Isa. 11:6-9; Ezek. 34:25 [b]Ps. 46:9; Isa. 2:4; Ezek. 39:9, 10; Zech. 9:10 [c]Lev. 26:5; Jer. 23:6
20 [a]Jer. 31:33, 34; John 17:3
21 [a]Zech. 8:12
22 [a]Hos. 1:4
23 [a]Jer. 31:27; Zech. 10:9 [b]Hos. 1:6 [c]Hos. 1:10; Zech. 13:9; Rom. 9:26; 1Pet. 2:10
1 [a]Hos. 1:2 [b]Jer. 3:20

🔑 **2:14–23** This passage speaks of Israel's eventual restoration as a new, permanent betrothal to God (Hos. 2:19–20). Jeremiah likened it to Israel's relationship to God in the wilderness (see note on Jer. 2:2–37). God had been removing the material aspects of their prosperity, but when He regathers Israel, He will grant a great new prosperity and reverse the significance of the name of Jezreel, Hosea's first child. While the name Jezreel had previously connoted judgment (Hos. 1:5), the new meaning of the name, "God sows," points to God's millennial blessings (Hos. 2:22).

🔑 **3:1–5** Hosea acts out God's buying back His strayed people. It is not coincidence that the value of the items that Hosea paid to regain his own wife added up to thirty shekels (cf. Zech. 11:12, 13; Matt. 26:15). The prophetic aspects of verse four are even now being fulfilled: Israel has no king, and no temple at which to offer sacrifices, yet they are free from idolatry. However, the fulfillment of verse five is still future.

Israel, who look to other gods,[430] and love[157] flagons809 [I]of wine.

2 So I bought3739 her to me for fifteen *pieces* of silver, and *for* an homer2563 of barley, and an half homer of barley:

3 And I said unto her, Thou shalt [a]abide for me many days; thou shalt not play the harlot, and thou shalt not be[1961] for *another* man:[376] so *will* I also *be* for thee.

4 For the children of Israel shall abide many days [a]without a king, and without a prince,[8269] and without a sacrifice,[2077] and without [I][b]an image,[4676] and without an [c]ephod, and *without* [d]teraphim:[8655]

5 Afterward shall the children of Israel return,[7725] and [a]seek the LORD their God,[430] and [b]David their king; and shall fear[6342] the LORD and his goodness[2898] in the [c]latter[319] days.

God Blames Israel

4 🗝Hear the word[1697] of the LORD, ye children[1121] of Israel: for the LORD hath a [a]controversy[7379] with the inhabitants of the land,[776] because *there is* no truth,[571] nor mercy,[2617] nor [b]knowledge[1847] of God[430] in the land.

2 By swearing,[422] and lying, and killing, and stealing, and committing adultery, they break out, and [I]blood[1818] toucheth[5060] blood.

3 Therefore [a]shall the land mourn,535 and [b]every one that dwelleth therein shall languish, with the beasts[2416] of the field,[7704] and with the fowls of heaven;8064 yea, the fishes of the sea also shall be taken away.[622]

4 Yet let no man[376] strive,[7378] nor reprove[3198] another:[376] for thy people[5971] *are* as they [a]that strive with the priest.[3548]

5 Therefore shalt thou fall[3782] [a]in the day,[3117] and the prophet[5030] also shall fall with thee in the night,[3915] and I will [I]destroy[1820] thy mother.[517]

6 [a]My people are [I]destroyed for lack of knowledge:[1847] because thou hast rejected[3988] knowledge, I will also reject thee, that thou shalt be no priest[3547] to me: seeing thou hast forgotten the law[8451] of thy God, I will also forget thy children.

7 [a]As they were increased, so they sinned[2398] against me: [b]*therefore* will I change their glory[3519] into shame.

8 They eat up the sin[2403] of my people, and they [I]set[5375] their heart[5315] on their iniquity.[5771]

9 And there shall be, [a]like people, like priest: and I will [I]punish[6485] them for their ways,[1870] and [II]reward[7725] them their doings.

10 For [a]they shall eat, and not have enough: they shall commit whoredom,[2181] and shall not increase: because they have left off[5800] to take heed[8104] to the LORD.

11 Whoredom[2184] and wine and new wine8492 [a]take away the heart.[3820]

12 My people ask counsel[7592] at their [a]stocks, and their staff declareth[5046] unto them: for [b]the spirit[7307] of whoredoms[2183] hath caused *them* to err,[8582] and they have gone a whoring from under their God.[430]

13 [a]They sacrifice upon the tops[7218] of the mountains, and burn incense[6999] upon the hills, under oaks and poplars and elms, because the shadow thereof *is* good:[2896] [b]therefore your daughters shall commit whoredom, and your spouses shall commit adultery.

14 [I]I will not punish[6485] your daughters when they commit whoredom, nor

1 [I]Hebr. *of grapes*
3 [a]Deut. 21:13
4 [I]Hebr. *a standing,* or, *statue,* or, *pillar* [a]Hos. 10:3 [b]Isa. 19:19 [c]Ex. 28:6 [d]Judg. 17:5
5 [a]Jer. 50:4, 5; Hos. 5:6 [b]Jer. 30:9; Ezek. 34:23, 24; 37:22, 24 [c]Isa. 2:2; Jer. 30:24; Ezek. 38:8, 16; Dan. 2:28; Mic. 4:1

1 [a]Isa. 1:18; 3:13, 14; Jer. 25:31; Hos. 12:2; Mic. 6:2 [b]Jer. 4:22; 5:4
2 [I]Hebr. *bloods*
3 [a]Jer. 4:28; 12:4; Amos 5:16; 8:8 [b]Zeph. 1:3
4 [a]Deut. 17:12
5 [I]Hebr. *cut off* [a]Jer. 6:4, 5; 15:8
6 [I]Hebr. *cut off* [a]Isa. 5:13
7 [a]Hos. 13:6 [b]1Sam. 2:30; Mal. 2:9; Phil. 3:19
8 [I]Hebr. *lift up their soul to their iniquity*
9 [I]Hebr. *visit upon* [II]Hebr. *cause to return* [a]Isa. 24:2; Jer. 5:31
10 [a]Lev. 26:26; Mic. 6:14; Hag. 1:6
11 [a]Isa. 28:7; Eccl. 7:7
12 [a]Jer. 2:27; Hab. 2:19 [b]Isa. 44:20; Hos. 5:4
13 [a]Isa. 1:29; 57:5, 7; Ezek. 6:13; 20:28 [b]Amos 7:17; Rom. 1:28
14 [I]Or, *Shall I not*

🗝 **4:1–6** God is "stating His case" against Israel. Their idolatry caused them to violate God's Law in its moral, social, and religious aspects (Hos. 4:1–2). This led to poverty and famine (Hos. 4:3). However, since the whole nation was guilty, the leaders as well as the people, no one was in a position to blame anyone else (Hos. 4:4–6, cf. 4:14). God summarized the problem as a lack of knowledge of God (Hos. 4:1, 6, 10, 11, 14). He valued a relationship with His people more than their offerings (see note on Hos. 6:6). It was not that God would not make Himself available to them, rather because they had rejected Him (Hos. 4:6). God was aware that they could not fulfill their responsibility to love Him without diligent instruction (see note on Deut. 6:4–9).

your spouses when they commit adultery: for themselves are separated with whores,[2181] and they sacrifice with harlots:[6948] therefore the people *that* [a]doth not understand[995] shall [II]fall.

15 Though thou, Israel, play the harlot,[2181] *yet* let not Judah offend; [a]and come not ye unto Gilgal, neither go ye up[5927] to [b]Beth–aven, [c]nor swear,[7650] The LORD liveth.[2416]

16 For Israel [a]slideth back as a backsliding[5637] heifer: now the LORD will feed them as a lamb in a large place.

17 Ephraim *is* joined to idols:[6091] [a]let him alone.[3240]

18 Their drink [I]is sour:[5493] they have committed whoredom continually: [a]her [II]rulers[4043] *with* shame do love,[157] Give[3051] ye.

🔑19 [a]The wind[7307] hath bound her up in her wings, and [b]they shall be ashamed[954] because of their sacrifices.[2077]

God Punishes Israel

5 🔑Hear ye this, O priests;[3548] and hearken,[7181] ye house[1004] of Israel; and give ye ear,[238] O house of the king; for judgment[4941] *is* toward you, because [a]ye have been a snare[6341] on Mizpah, and a net spread upon Tabor.

2 And the revolters are [a]profound[6009] to make slaughter,[7819] [I]though I *have been* [II]a rebuker[4148] of them all.

3 [a]I know Ephraim, and Israel is not hid from me: for now, O Ephraim, [b]thou committest whoredom,[2181] *and* Israel is defiled.[2930]

4 [I]They will not frame their doings to turn[7725] unto their God:[430] for [a]the spirit[7307] of whoredoms[2183] *is* in the midst of them, and they have not known[3045] the LORD.

5 And [a]the pride of Israel doth testify to his face: therefore shall Israel and Ephraim fall[3782] in their iniquity;[5771] Judah also shall fall with them.

6 [a]They shall go with their flocks and with their herds to seek the LORD; but they shall not find *him;* he hath withdrawn[2502] himself from them.

7 They have [a]dealt treacherously[898] against the LORD: for they have begotten[3205] strange[2114] children:[1121] now shall [b]a month devour them with their portions.

8 [a]Blow[8628] ye the cornet in Gibeah, *and* the trumpet in Ramah: [b]cry aloud[7321] *at* [c]Beth–aven, [d]after thee, O Benjamin.

9 Ephraim shall be desolate[8047] in the day[3117] of rebuke:[8433] among the tribes[7626] of Israel have I made known[3045] that which shall surely be.[539]

10 The princes[8269] of Judah were like them that [a]remove the bound:[1366] *therefore* I will pour out[8210] my wrath[5678] upon them like water.

11 Ephraim *is* [a]oppressed[6231] *and* broken in judgment, because he willingly[2974] walked after [b]the commandment.

12 Therefore *will* I *be* unto Ephraim as a moth, and to the house of Judah [a]as [I]rottenness.

13 When Ephraim saw[7200] his sickness, and Judah *saw* his [a]wound, then went Ephraim [b]to the Assyrian, [c]and sent [I]to king Jareb: yet could he not heal you, nor cure[1455] you of your wound.

14 For [a]I *will be* unto Ephraim as a lion, and as a young lion to the house of Judah: [b]I, *even* I, will tear and go away; I will take away, and none shall rescue[5337] *him.*

15 I will go *and* return to my place, [I]till [a]they acknowledge their offence,[816] and seek my face: [b]in their affliction they will seek me early.[7836]

Israel Isn't Sincere

6 Come, and let us return[7725] unto the LORD: for [a]he hath torn, and [b]he will

14 [II]Or, *be punished* [a]Hos. 4:1, 6
15 [a]Hos. 9:15; 12:11; Amos 4:4; 5:5 [b]1Kgs. 12:29; Hos. 10:5; [c]Amos 8:14; Zeph. 1:5
16 [a]Jer. 3:6; 7:24; 8:5; Zech. 7:11
17 [a]Matt. 15:14
18 [I]Hebr. *is gone* [II]Hebr. *shields* [a]Ps. 47:9; Mic. 3:11; 7:3
19 [a]Jer. 4:11, 12; 51:1 [b]Isa. 1:29; Jer. 2:26

1 [a]Hos. 6:9
2 [I]Or, *and* [II]Hebr. *a correction* [a]Isa. 29:15
3 [a]Amos 3:2 [b]Ezek. 23:5; Hos. 4:17
4 [I]Hebr. *They will not give* [II]Or, *Their doings will not suffer* them [a]Hos. 4:12
5 [a]Hos. 7:10
6 [a]Prov. 1:28; Isa. 1:15; Jer. 11:11; Ezek. 8:18; Mic. 3:4; John 7:34
7 [a]Isa. 48:8; Jer. 3:20; 5:11; Hos. 6:7; Mal. 2:11 [b]Zech. 11:8
8 [a]Hos. 8:1; Joel 2:1 [b]Isa. 10:30 [c]Josh. 7:2; Hos. 4:15 [d]Judg. 5:14
10 [a]Deut. 19:14; 27:17
11 [a]Deut. 28:33 [b]1Kgs. 12:28; Mic. 6:16
12 [I]Or, *a worm* [a]Prov. 12:4
13 [I]Or, *to the king of Jareb:* or, *to the king* that *should plead* [a]Jer. 30:12 [b]2Kgs. 15:19; Hos. 7:11; 12:1 [c]Hos. 10:6
14 [a]Lam. 3:10; Hos. 13:7, 8 [b]Ps. 50:22
15 [I]Hebr. *till they be guilty* [a]Lev. 26:40, 41; Jer. 29:12, 13; Ezek. 6:9; 20:43; 36:31 [b]Ps. 78:34

1 [a]Deut. 32:39; 1Sam. 2:6; Job 5:18; Hos. 5:14 [b]Jer. 30:17

🔑 **4:19** The impending Assyrian invasion is pictured here as a wind. Elsewhere, God depicts the attacks of Assyria by using the images of a razor (Is. 7:20), a river (Is. 8:7), and a rod (Is. 10:5).

🔑 **5:1–15** See note on Lamentations 1:19 concerning Judah's alliances with Egypt and Syria.

heal us; he hath smitten,[5221] and he will
bind us up.[2280]
2 [a]After two days will he revive[2421]
us: in the third day he will raise us up,
and we shall live[2421] in his sight.
3 [a]Then shall we know, *if* we follow
on to know[3045] the LORD: his going forth
is prepared[3559] [b]as the morning; and
[c]he shall come unto us [d]as the rain, as
the latter *and* former rain unto the
earth.[776]
4 [a]O Ephraim, what shall I do[6213]
unto thee? O Judah, what shall I do unto
thee? for your [I]goodness[2617] *is* [b]as a
morning cloud,[6051] and as the early dew
it goeth away.
5 Therefore have I hewed2672 *them*
[a]by the prophets;[5030] I have slain[2026] them
by [b]the words of my mouth:[6310] [I]and thy
judgments[4941] *are as* the light[216] *that*
goeth forth.
6 For I desired[2654] [a]mercy,[2617] and
[b]not sacrifice;[2077] and the [c]knowledge[1847]
of God[430] more than burnt offerings.[5930]
7 But they [Ia]like men[120] [b]have transgressed[5674] the covenant:[1285] there [c]have
they dealt treacherously[898] against me.
8 [a]Gilead *is* a city of them that work
iniquity,[205] *and is* [I]polluted[6121] with
blood.[1818]
9 And as troops of robbers[1416] wait
for a man,[376] *so* [a]the company of
priests[3548] murder[7523] in the way[1870]
[I]by consent:7926 for they commit[6213]
[II]lewdness.[2154]
10 I have seen[7200] [a]an horrible
thing[8186] in the house[1004] of Israel: there
is [b]the whoredom[2184] of Ephraim, Israel
is defiled.[2930]
11 Also, O Judah, [a]he hath set an
harvest for thee, [b]when I returned[7725] the
captivity[7622] of my people.[5971]

2 [a]1Cor. 15:4
3 [a]Isa. 54:13 [b]2Sam. 23:4 [c]Ps. 72:6; [d]Job 29:23
4 [I]Or, *mercy*, or, *kindness* [a]Hos. 11:8 [b]Hos. 13:3
5 [I]Or, *that thy judgments might be* [a]Jer. 1:10; 5:14 [b]Jer. 23:29; Heb. 4:12
6 [a]1Sam. 15:22; Eccl. 5:1; Mic. 6:8; Matt. 9:13; 12:7 [b]Ps. 50:8, 9; Prov. 21:3; Isa. 1:11 [c]Jer. 22:16; John 17:3
7 [I]Or, *like Adam* [a]Job 31:33 [b]Hos. 8:1 [c]Hos. 5:7
8 [I]Or, *cunning for blood* [a]Hos. 12:11
9 [I]Hebr. *with one shoulder*, or, *to Shechem* [II]Or, *enormity* [a]Jer. 11:9; Ezek. 22:25; Hos. 5:1, 2
10 [a]Jer. 5:30 [b]Hos. 4:12, 13, 17
11 [a]Jer. 51:33; Joel 3:13; Rev. 14:15 [b]Ps. 126:1

Israel Rebels

7 When I would have healed Israel,
then the iniquity[5771] of Ephraim was
discovered,[1540] and the [I]wickedness[7451] of
Samaria: for [a]they commit6466 falsehood;[8267] and the thief cometh in, *and* the
troop of robbers[1416] [II]spoileth without.
2 And they [I]consider[559] not in their
hearts3824 *that* I [a]remember[2142] all their
wickedness: now [b]their own doings have
beset them about; they are [c]before my
face.
3 They make the king glad with their
wickedness, and the princes[8269] [a]with
their lies.
4 [a]They *are* all adulterers,5003 as an
oven heated by the baker, [I]*who*
ceaseth[7673] [II]from raising after he hath
kneaded the dough, until it be leavened.
5 In the day[3117] of our king the
princes have made *him* sick [I]with
bottles[2534] of wine; he stretched out his
hand[3027] with scorners.
6 For they have [I]made ready[7126] their
heart[3820] like an oven, whiles they lie in
wait: their baker sleepeth all the night; in
the morning it burneth as a flaming fire.
7 They are all hot as an oven, and
have devoured their judges;[8199] [a]all their
kings [b]are fallen:[5307] [c]*there is* none among
them that calleth[7121] unto me.
8 Ephraim, he [a]hath mixed him-
self[1101] among the people;[5971] Ephraim is
a cake not turned.[2015]

1 [I]Hebr. *evils* [II]Hebr. *strippeth* [a]Hos. 5:1; 6:10
2 [I]Hebr. *say not to* [a]Jer. 17:1 [b]Ps. 9:16; Prov. 5:22 [c]Ps. 90:8
3 [a]Rom. 1:32
4 [I]Or, *the raiser will cease* [II]Or, *from waking* [a]Jer. 9:2
5 [I]Or, *with heat through wine*
6 [I]Or, *applied*
7 [a]Hos. 8:4 [b]2Kgs. 15:10, 25, 30 [c]Isa. 64:7
8 [a]Ps. 106:35

6:6 This verse is the climax of Hosea's theology, emphasizing man's most important responsibility: no matter what outward or physical accomplishments are achieved, God is concerned with the attitude of the heart. He desires that an individual's total being be involved in the pursuit of the knowledge of God. Jesus quoted this verse to explain His disciples' harvesting on the Sabbath (see Matt. 12:7).

7:1–9 Hosea used analogies from baking to describe the errors and plight of Israel. The phrase "an oven heated by the baker" (Hos. 7:4, 6, 7) refers to the schemes of the wicked to carry out their plans without God. The particular focus seems to be on the numerous plots against the kings (Hos. 7:5, 7); in fact, four of Israel's last six kings were assassinated. "A cake not turned" (Hos. 7:8) is burnt on the bottom, but that side is not visible. This illustration was intended to show how the children of Israel were being consumed in their sin and were unaware of it (Hos. 7:9).

9 [a]Strangers[2114] have devoured his strength, and he knoweth *it* not: yea, gray hairs are [I]here and there[2236] upon him, yet he knoweth not.

10 And the [a]pride of Israel testifieth to his face: and [b]they do not return[7725] to the LORD their God,[430] nor seek him for all this.

🗝 11 [a]Ephraim also is like a silly6601 dove without heart: [b]they call[7121] to Egypt, they go to Assyria.

12 When they shall go, [a]I will spread my net upon them; I will bring them down as the fowls of the heaven;8064 I will chastise[3256] them, [b]as their congregation[5712] hath heard.

13 Woe unto them! for they have fled from me: [I]destruction[7701] unto them! because they have transgressed[6586] against me: though [a]I have redeemed[6299] them, yet they have spoken[1696] lies[3577] against me.

14 [a]And they have not cried[2199] unto me with their heart, when they howled upon their beds: they assemble themselves[1481] for corn and wine, *and* they rebel[5493] against me.

15 Though I [I]have bound[3256] *and* strengthened[2388] their arms, yet do they imagine[2803] mischief[7451] against me.

16 [a]They return,[7725] *but* not to the most High: [b]they are like a deceitful7423 bow: their princes shall fall by the sword[2719] for the [c]rage[2195] of their tongue: this *shall be* their derision [d]in the land of Egypt.

Israel Continues to Worship Idols

8 *Set* [a]the trumpet to [I]thy mouth. *He shall come* [b]as an eagle against the house of the LORD, because [c]they have transgressed[5674] my covenant,[1285] and trespassed[6586] against my law.[8451]

2 [a]Israel shall cry unto me, My God,[430] [b]we know[3045] thee.

3 Israel hath cast off *the thing that is* good:[2896] the enemy shall pursue him.

🗝 4 [a]They have set up kings,[4427] but not by me: they have made[6213] princes,[7786] and I knew *it* not: [b]of their silver and their gold have they made them idols,[6091] that they may be cut off.[3772]

5 Thy calf, O Samaria, hath cast *thee* off; mine anger[639] is kindled[2734] against them: [a]how long *will it be* ere they attain to innocency?[5356]

6 For from Israel *was* it also: the workman made it; therefore it *is* not God: but the calf of Samaria shall be broken in pieces.

7 For [a]they have sown the wind,[7307] and they shall reap the whirlwind: it hath no [I]stalk: the bud shall yield[6213] no meal: if so be it yield, [b]the strangers[2114] shall swallow it up.[1104]

🗝 8 [a]Israel is swallowed up: now shall they be among the Gentiles[1471] [b]as a vessel wherein *is* no pleasure.[2656]

9 For [a]they are gone up[5927] to Assyria, [b]a wild ass alone by himself: Ephraim [c]hath hired [I]lovers.[158]

10 Yea, though they have hired among the nations,[1471] now [a]will I gather[6908] them, and they shall [I]sorrow[2490] [II][b]a little for the burden[4853] of [c]the king of princes.[8269]

11 Because Ephraim hath made [a]many altars[4196] to sin,[2398] altars shall be unto him to sin.

12 I have written to him [a]the great things of my law, *but* they were counted[2803] as a strange thing.[2114]

9 [I]Hebr. *sprinkled* [a]Hos. 8:7
10 [a]Hos. 5:5 [b]Isa. 9:13
11 [a]Hos. 11:11 [b]2Kgs. 15:19; 17:4; Hos. 5:13; 9:3; 12:1
12 [a]Ezek. 12:13 [b]Lev. 26:14; Deut. 28:15; 2Kgs. 17:13, 18
13 [I]Hebr. *spoil* [a]Mic. 6:4
14 [a]Job 35:9, 10; Ps. 78:36; Jer. 3:10; Zech. 7:5
15 [I]Or, *chastened*
16 [a]Hos. 11:7 [b]Ps. 78:57 [c]Ps. 73:9 [d]Hos. 9:3, 6

1 [I]Hebr. *the roof of thy mouth* [a]Hos. 5:8 [b]Deut. 28:49; Jer. 4:13; Hab. 1:8 [c]Hos. 6:7
2 [a]Ps. 78:34; Hos. 5:15 [b]Titus 1:16
4 [a]2Kgs. 15:13, 17, 25, Shallum, Menahem, Pekahiah [b]Hos. 2:8; 13:2
5 [a]Jer. 13:27
7 [I]Or, *standing corn* [a]Prov. 22:8; 10:12, 13 [b]Hos. 7:9
8 [a]2Kgs. 17:6 [b]Jer. 22:28; 48:38
9 [I]Hebr. *loves* [a]2Kgs. 15:19 [b]Jer. 2:24 [c]Isa. 30:6; Ezek. 16:33, 34
10 [I]Or, *begin* [II]Or, *in a little while* Ezek. 16:37; Hos. 10:10 [a]Hag. 2:6 [b]Isa. 10:8; Ezek. 26:7; Dan. 2:37
11 [a]Hos. 12:11
12 [a]Deut. 4:6, 8; Ps. 119:18; 147:19, 20

🗝 **7:11** See note on Lamentations 1:19 concerning Judah's alliances with Egypt and Syria.

🗝 **8:4–6** God was mocking the worship of idols in Israel: "the workman made it, therefore it is not God" (cf. Is. 44:15–17; 46:6, 7; Jer. 10:2–6; Hos. 13:2; 14:3). Israel would reap more than they sowed, but the harvest would yield only punishment for their sin (Hos. 8:7). Israel found no allies that could avert God's judgment.

🗝 **8:8, 9** Although the destruction and full exile of Israel did not take place until 722 B.C., some of the northern part of the nation was captured and deported by the Assyrian emperor Tiglath-pileser III in 732 B.C. (2 Kgs. 15:29).

13 [I][a]They sacrifice[2076] flesh[1319] *for* the sacrifices[2077] of mine offerings,[1890] and eat *it;* [b]but the LORD accepteth[7521] them not; [c]now will he remember[2142] their iniquity,[5771] and visit[6485] their sins:[2403] [d]they shall return[7725] to Egypt.

14 [a]For Israel hath forgotten [b]his Maker,[6213] and [c]buildeth temples;[1964] and Judah hath multiplied fenced cities: but [d]I will send a fire upon his cities, and it shall devour the palaces[759] thereof.

God Keeps on Punishing Israel

9 Rejoice not, O Israel, for joy, as *other* people:[5971] for thou [a]hast gone a whoring[2181] from thy God,[430] thou hast loved[157] a [b]reward 868 [I]upon every cornfloor.

2 [a]The floor and the [I]winepress shall not feed them, and the new wine 8492 shall fail in her.

3 They shall not dwell in [a]the LORD's land;[776] [b]but Ephraim shall return[7725] to Egypt, and [c]they shall eat unclean[2931] *things* [d]in Assyria.

4 [a]They shall not offer[5258] wine *offerings* to the LORD, [b]neither shall they be pleasing[6148] unto him: [c]their sacrifices[2077] *shall be* unto them as the bread of mourners;[205] all that eat thereof shall be polluted:[2930] for their bread [d]for their soul[5315] shall not come into the house[1004] of the LORD.

5 What will ye do[6213] in [a]the solemn[4150] day, and in the day of the feast[2282] of the LORD?

6 For, lo, they are gone because of [I]destruction:[7701] [a]Egypt shall gather them up,[6908] Memphis shall bury[6912] them: [II]the pleasant *places* for their silver, [b]nettles shall possess[3423] them: thorns *shall be* in their tabernacles.[168]

7 The days[3117] of visitation[6486] are come, the days of recompence[7966] are come; Israel shall know[3045] *it:* the prophet[5030] *is* a fool, [a]the [I]spiritual[7307] man[376] *is* mad, 7696 for the multitude of thine iniquity,[5771] and the great hatred.

8 The [a]watchman of Ephraim *was* with my God: *but* the prophet *is* a snare[6341] of a fowler in all his ways,[1870] *and* hatred [I]in the house of his God.

9 [a]They have deeply corrupted *themselves,* as in the days of [b]Gibeah: [c]*therefore* he will remember[2142] their iniquity, he will visit[6485] their sins.[2403]

10 I found Israel like grapes in the wilderness; I saw[7200] your fathers[1] as [a]the firstripe in the fig tree [b]at her first time:[7225] *but* they went to [c]Baal–peor, and [d]separated themselves[5144] [e]unto *that* shame; [f]and *their* abominations[8251] were according as they loved.[157]

🗝 11 *As for* Ephraim, their glory[3519] shall fly away like a bird, from the birth, and from the womb,[990] and from the conception.

12 [a]Though they bring up their children,[1121] yet [b]will I bereave them, *that there shall* not *be* a man[120] *left:* yea, [c]woe also to them when I [d]depart from them!

13 Ephraim, [a]as I saw Tyrus, *is* planted in a pleasant place: [b]but Ephraim shall bring forth his children to the murderer.[2026]

14 Give them, O LORD: what wilt thou give? give them [a]a [I]miscarrying womb and dry breasts.

15 All their wickedness[7451] [a]*is* in Gilgal: for there I hated[8130] them: [b]for the wickedness[7455] of their doings I will drive them out of mine house, I will love[160] them no more: [c]all their princes[8269] *are* revolters.[5637]

16 Ephraim is smitten,[5221] their root is dried up,[3001] they shall bear[6213] no fruit: yea, [a]though they bring forth, yet

13 [I]Or, *In the sacrifices of mine offerings they* [a]Jer. 7:21; Zech. 7:6 [b]Jer. 14:10, 12; Hos. 5:6; 9:4; Amos 5:22 [c]Hos. 9:9; Amos 8:7 [d]Deut. 28:68; Hos. 9:3, 6; 11:5
14 [a]Deut. 32:18 [b]Isa. 29:23; Eph. 2:10 [c]1Kgs. 12:31 [d]Jer. 17:27; Amos 2:5

1 [I]Or, *in* [a]Hos. 4:12; 5:4, 7 [b]Jer. 44:17; Hos. 2:12
2 [I]Or, *wine vat* [a]Hos. 2:9, 12
3 [a]Lev. 25:23; Jer. 2:7; 16:18 [b]Hos. 8:13; 11:5 [c]Ezek. 4:13; Dan. 1:8 [d]2Kgs. 17:6; Hos. 11:11
4 [a]Hos. 3:4 [b]Jer. 6:20; Hos. 8:13 [c]Deut. 26:14 [d]Lev. 17:11
5 [a]Hos. 2:11
6 [I]Hebr. *spoil* [II]Or, *their silver shall be desired, the nettle;* Hebr. *the desire* [a]Hos. 7:16; Hos. 9:3 [b]Isa. 5:6; 32:13; 34:13; Hos. 10:8
7 [I]Hebr. *man of the spirit* [a]Ezek. 13:3-16; Mic. 2:11; Zeph. 3:4
8 [I]Or, *against* [a]Jer. 6:17; 31:6; Ezek. 3:17; 33:7
9 [a]Isa. 31:6; Hos. 10:9 [b]Judg. 19:22 [c]Hos. 8:13
10 [a]Isa. 28:4; Mic. 7:1 [b]Hos. 2:15 [c]Num. 25:3; Ps. 106:28 [d]Hos. 4:14 [e]Jer. 11:13; Judg. 6:32 [f]Ps. 81:12; Ezek. 20:8; Amos 4:5
12 [a]Job 27:14 [b]Deut. 28:41, 62 [c]Deut. 31:17; 2Kgs. 17:18; Hos. 5:6 [d]1Sam. 28:15, 16
13 [a]Hos. 9:16 [b]Hos. 13:16
14 [I]Hebr. *that casteth the fruit* [a]Luke 23:29
15 [a]Hos. 4:15; 12:11 [b]Hos. 1:6 [c]Isa. 1:23
16 [a]Hos. 9:13

🗝 **9:11–17** In ancient times, when women were unable to have children, it was considered a great tragedy (cf. 1 Sam. 1; Luke 1:24, 25, 58). However, the judgment mentioned in this passage would be worse than a lack of conception, for even the children that were born would be killed (Hos. 9:13, 16).

will I slay[4191] *even* [I]the beloved *fruit* of
their womb.
17 My God[430] will cast them
away,[3988] because they did not hearken[8085] unto him: and they shall be [a]wan-
derers among the nations.[1471]

10 Israel *is* [I][a]an empty[1238] vine, he
bringeth forth fruit unto himself:
according to the multitude of his fruit [b]he
hath increased the altars;[4196] according
to the goodness[2896] of his land[776] [c]they
have made goodly[2895] [II]images.[4676]
2 [I]Their heart[3820] is [a]divided; now
shall they be found faulty:[816] he shall
[II]break down their altars, he shall
spoil[7703] their images.
🔑 3 [a]For now they shall say,[559] We
have no king, because we feared[3372] not
the LORD; what then should a king do[6213]
to us?
4 They have spoken[1696] words,[1697]
swearing[422] falsely[7723] in making[3772] a
covenant:[1285] thus judgment[4941] springeth up [a]as hemlock in the furrows[8525] of
the field.[7704]
5 The inhabitants[7934] of Samaria
shall fear[1481] because of [a]the calves of
[b]Beth–aven: for the people[5971] thereof
shall mourn over it, and [I]the priests[3649]
thereof *that* rejoiced on it, [c]for the
glory[3519] thereof, because it is departed[1540] from it.
6 It shall be also carried unto
Assyria *for* a present[4503] to [a]king Jareb:
Ephraim shall receive shame,[1322] and
Israel shall be ashamed[954] [b]of his own
counsel.[6098]
7 [a]*As for* Samaria, her king is
cut off[1820] as the foam[7110] upon [I]the
water.
8 [a]The high places[1116] also of Aven,
[b]the sin[2403] of Israel, shall be destroyed:[8045] [c]the thorn and the thistle
shall come up[5927] on their altars; [d]and
they shall say to the mountains, Cover[3680]
us; and to the hills, Fall[5307] on us.
9 [a]O Israel, thou hast sinned[2398]
from the days of Gibeah: there they
stood: [b]the battle in Gibeah against the
children[1121] of iniquity[5932] did not overtake them.
10 [a]*It is* in my desire that I should
chastise[3256] them; and [b]the people shall
be gathered[622] against them, [I]when they
shall bind themselves in their two furrows.[5869]
11 And Ephraim *is as* [a]an heifer *that
is* taught,[3925] *and* loveth[157] to tread out
the corn; but I passed over[5674] upon [I]her
fair[2898] neck: I will make Ephraim to ride;
Judah shall plow, *and* Jacob shall break
his clods.
12 [a]Sow to yourselves in righteousness,[6666] reap in mercy;[2617] [b]break
up your fallow ground:[5215] for *it is*
time[6256] to seek the LORD, till he come
and rain[3384] righteousness[6664] upon
you.
13 [a]Ye have plowed wickedness,[7562]
ye have reaped iniquity;[5771] ye have eaten
the fruit of lies: because thou didst
trust[982] in thy way,[1870] in the multitude
of thy mighty men.
14 [a]Therefore shall a tumult[7588] arise
among thy people, and all thy fortresses
shall be spoiled, as Shalman spoiled[7701]
[b]Beth–arbel in the day[3117] of battle: [c]the
mother[517] was dashed in pieces upon *her*
children.
15 So shall Bethel do unto you because of [I]your great wickedness:[7451] in a
morning [a]shall the king of Israel utterly
be cut off.[1820]

16 [I]Hebr. *the desires,* Ezek. 24:21
17 [a]Deut. 28:64, 65

1 [I]Or, *a vine emptying the fruit which it giveth* [II]Hebr. *statues,* or, *standing images* [a]Nah. 2:2 [b]Hos. 8:11; 12:11 [c]Hos. 8:4
2 [I]Or, *He hath divided their heart* [II]Hebr. *behead* [a]1Kgs. 18:21; Matt. 6:24
3 [a]Hos. 3:4; 11:5; Mic. 4:9; Hos. 10:7
4 [a]Deut. 29:18; Amos 5:7; 6:12; Acts 8:23; Heb. 12:15
5 [I]Or, *Chemarim,* 2Kgs. 23:5; Zeph. 1:4 [a]1Kgs. 12:28, 29; Hos. 8:5, 6 [b]Hos. 4:15 [c]1Sam. 4:21, 22; Hos. 9:11
6 [a]Hos. 5:13 [b]Hos. 11:6
7 [I]Hebr. *the face of the water* [a]Hos. 10:3, 15
8 [a]Hos. 4:15 [b]Deut. 9:21; 1Kgs. 12:30 [c]Hos. 9:6 [d]Isa. 2:19; Luke 23:30; Rev. 6:16; 9:6
9 [a]Hos. 9:9
10 [I]Or, *when I shall bind them for their two transgressions,* or, *in their two habitations* [a]Deut. 28:63 [b]Jer. 16:16; Ezek. 23:46, 47; Hos. 8:10
11 [I]Hebr. *the beauty of her neck* [a]Jer. 50:11; Mic. 4:13
12 [a]Prov. 11:18 [b]Jer. 4:3
13 [a]Job 4:8; Prov. 22:8; Hos. 8:7; Gal. 6:7, 8 [c]Hos. 13:16 10:7
14 [a]Hos. 13:16 [b]2Kgs. 18:34; 19:13
15 [I]Hebr. *the evil of your evil* [a]Hos.

🔑 **10:3, 4** Israel rejected all authority, and refused to trust anyone outside of themselves (cf. Hos. 10:1). Since they did not respect God's leading, why would they accept the authority of a king? These self-centered people had "no fear of God before their eyes" (Ps. 36:1). As a result, their oaths and covenants were worthless, and they kept them only as long as it was advantageous for them to do so (v. 4).

God Still Loves His Sinful Children

11 🔑When [a]Israel *was* a child, then
I loved[157] him, and [b]called[7121] my
[c]son[1121] out of Egypt.
2 *As* they called them, so they went
from them: [a]they sacrificed[2076] unto
Baalim, and burned incense[6999] to graven
images.[6456]
3 [a]I taught Ephraim also to go,[7270]
taking them by their arms; but they
knew[3045] not that [b]I healed them.
4 I drew[4900] them with cords[2256] of a
man,[120] with bands of love:[160] and [a]I
was to them as they that [I]take off the
yoke on their jaws, and [b]I laid meat unto
them.
5 [a]He shall not return[7725] into the
land[776] of Egypt, but the Assyrian shall
be his king, [b]because they refused[3985] to
return.
6 And the sword[2719] shall abide[2342]
on his cities, and shall consume[3615] his
branches, and devour *them,* [a]because of
their own counsels.
7 And my people[5971] are bent[8511] to
[a]backsliding[4878] from me: [b]though they
called them to the most High, [I]none at all
would exalt *him.*
8 [a]How shall I give thee up,[5414]
Ephraim? *how* shall I deliver thee, Israel?
how shall I make thee as [b]Admah? *how*
shall I set[7760] thee as Zeboim? [c]mine
heart[3820] is turned[2015] within me, my
repentings[5150] are kindled together.
9 I will not execute[6213] the fierceness
of mine anger,[639] I will not return to
destroy[7843] Ephraim: [a]for I *am* God,[410]
and not man;[376] the Holy One[6918] in the
midst[7130] of thee: and I will not enter
into the city.
10 They shall walk after the LORD:
[a]he shall roar like a lion: when he shall
roar, then the children shall tremble[2729]
[b]from the west.
11 They shall tremble as a bird out
of Egypt, [a]and as a dove out of the land
of Assyria: [b]and I will place them in their
houses,[1004] saith the LORD.
12 [a]Ephraim compasseth me about
with lies,[3585] and the house of Israel with
deceit:[4820] but Judah yet ruleth[7300] with
God,[410] and is faithful[539] [I]with the saints.

Ephraim Is a Liar

12 🔑Ephraim [a]feedeth on[7462]
wind,[7307] and followeth after the
east wind: he daily increaseth lies[3577] and
desolation;[7701] [b]and they do make[3772] a
covenant[1285] with the Assyrians, and
[c]oil[8081] is carried into Egypt.
2 [a]The LORD hath also a contro-
versy[7379] with Judah, and will [I]punish[6485]
Jacob according to his ways;[1870] according to his doings will he recompense[7725] him.
3 He took[6117] his brother[251] [a]by the
heel[6117] in the womb,[990] and by his
strength[202] he [I][b]had power[8280] with
God:[430]
4 Yea, he had power[7786] over the
angel,[4397] and prevailed: he wept, and
made supplication[2603] unto him: he found
him *in* [a]Bethel, and there he spake[1696]
with us;

1 [a]Hos. 2:15 [b]Matt. 2:15 [c]Ex. 4:22, 23
2 [a]2Kgs. 17:16; Hos. 2:13; 13:2
3 [a]Deut. 1:31; 32:10-12; Isa. 46:3 [b]Ex. 15:26
4 [I]Hebr. *lift up* [a]Lev. 26:13 [b]Ps. 78:25; Hos. 2:8
5 [a]Hos. 8:13; 9:3 [b]2Kgs. 17:13, 14
6 [a]Hos. 10:6
7 [I]Hebr. *together they exalted not* [a]Jer. 3:6-18; 8:5; Hos. 4:16 [b]Hos. 7:16
8 [a]Jer. 9:7; Hos. 6:4 [b]Gen. 14:8; 19:24, 25; Deut. 29:23; Amos 4:11 [c]Deut. 32:36; Isa. 63:15; Jer. 31:20
9 [a]Num. 23:19; Isa. 55:8, 9; Mal. 3:6
10 [a]Isa. 31:4; Joel 3:16; Amos 1:2 [b]Zech. 8:7
11 [a]Isa. 60:8; Hos. 7:11 [b]Ezek. 28:25, 26; 37:21, 25
12 [I]Or, *with the most holy* [a]Hos. 12:1

1 [a]Hos. 8:7 [b]2Kgs. 17:4; Hos. 5:13; 7:11 [c]Isa. 30:6; 57:9
2 [I]Hebr. *visit upon* [a]Hos. 4:1; Mic. 6:2
3 [a]Gen. 25:26 [I]Hebr. *was a prince,* or, *behaved himself princely* [b]Gen. 32:24-26
4 [a]Gen. 28:12, 19; 35:9, 10, 15

🔑 **11:1** Here is an application of the Old Testament concept of "corporate personality," or the practice of speaking of a group of people as if they were an individual (see note on Is. 42:1–9). Israel as a nation was called God's "son" and "firstborn" when they left Egypt (Ex. 4:22). The Lord Jesus Christ, who is above all God's "Son" and "Firstborn," was "called out of Egypt" centuries later (Matt. 2:15).

🔑 **12:1–14** God calls Israel to examine the life of Jacob. The phrase "and by his strength he had power with God" refers to Jacob's attempt to use his physical strength to obtain blessing from God. This was evident when he wrestled with God's angel at Peniel (Gen. 32:30; cf. Hos. 12:4, 5). Jacob ultimately submitted to God's leading in his life and returned to the place where he first had fellowship with God, Bethel (Gen. 28:16–22, cf. Hos. 12:4, 5). Jacob's tenaciousness in desiring God's blessing was what God wanted Israel to learn from his example. If they would only turn back to God from their sin, and earnestly desire His mercy and forgiveness, the blessings of God would be their's as well (Hos. 12:6).

5 Even the LORD God of hosts;[6635]
the LORD *is* his [a]memorial.[2143]
6 [a]Therefore turn[7725] thou to thy
God: keep[8104] mercy[2617] and judgment,[4941] and [b]wait[6960] on thy God
continually.[8548]
7 *He is* [I][a]a merchant, [b]the balances of
deceit[4820] *are* in his hand:[3027] he loveth[157]
to [II]oppress.
8 And Ephraim said,[559] [a]Yet I am become rich, I have found me out substance: [I]*in* all my labours they shall find
none iniquity[5771] in me [II]that *were* sin.[2399]
9 And [a]I *that am* the LORD thy God
from the land[776] of Egypt [b]will yet make
thee to dwell in tabernacles,[168] as in the
days of the solemn feast.[4150]
10 [a]I have also spoken by the
prophets,[5030] and I have multiplied
visions,[2377] and used similitudes,[1819] [I]by
the ministry[3027] of the prophets.
11 [a]*Is there* iniquity *in* Gilead? surely
they are vanity:[7723] they sacrifice[2076] bullocks in [b]Gilgal; yea, [c]their altars[4196] *are*
as heaps in the furrows[8525] of the
fields.[7704]
12 And Jacob [a]fled into the country[7704] of Syria, and Israel [b]served[5647]
for a wife,[802] and for a wife he kept[8104]
sheep.
13 [a]And by a prophet the LORD
brought[5927] Israel out of Egypt, and by
a prophet was he preserved.[8104]
14 [a]Ephraim provoked *him* to anger[3707] [I]most bitterly: therefore shall he
leave[5203] his [II][b]blood[1818] upon him, and
his [c]reproach[2781] shall his Lord[113] return
unto him.

The LORD Is Angry With Israel

13 When Ephraim spake trembling,
he exalted[5375] himself in Israel;
but [a]when he offended[816] in Baal, he
died.[4191]
2 And now [I]they sin[2398] more and
more, and [a]have made[6213] them molten
images[4541] of their silver, *and* idols[6091]
according to their own understanding,[8394]
all of it the work of the craftsmen: they
say of them, Let [II]the men[120] that sacrifice [b]kiss[5401] the calves.

5 [a]Ex. 3:15
6 [a]Hos. 14:1; Mic. 6:8 [b]Ps. 37:7
7 [I]Or, *Canaan:* [II]Or, *deceive* [a]Ezek. 16:3 [b]Prov. 11:1; Amos 8:5, 8
8 [I]Or, *all my labors suffice me not:* he shall have *punishment of iniquity in whom is sin* [II]Hebr. *which* [a]Zech. 11:5; Rev. 3:17
9 [a]Hos. 13:4 [b]Lev. 23:42, 43; Neh. 8:17; Zech. 14:16
10 [I]Hebr. *by the hand* [a]2Kgs. 17:13
11 [a]Hos. 5:1; 6:8 [b]Hos. 4:15; 9:15; Amos 4:4; 5:5 [c]Hos. 8:11; 10:1
12 [a]Gen. 28:5; Deut. 26:5 [b]Gen. 29:20, 28
13 [a]Ex. 12:50, 51; 13:3; Ps. 77:20; Isa. 63:11; Mic. 6:4
14 [I]Hebr. *with bitternesses* [II]Hebr. *bloods* [a]2Kgs. 17:11-18 [b]Ezek. 18:13; 24:7, 8 [c]Deut. 28:37; Dan. 11:18

1 [a]2Kgs. 17:16, 18; Hos. 11:2
2 [I]Hebr. *they add to sin* [II]Or, *the sacrificers of men* [a]Hos. 2:8; 8:4 [b]1Kgs. 19:18
3 [a]Hos. 6:4 [b]Dan. 2:35
4 [a]Isa. 43:11; Hos. 12:9 [b]Isa. 43:11; 45:21
5 [I]Hebr. *droughts* [a]Deut. 2:7; 32:10 [b]Deut. 8:15; 32:10
6 [a]Deut. 8:12, 14; 32:15 [b]Hos. 8:14
7 [a]Lam. 3:10; Hos. 5:14 [b]Jer. 5:6
8 [I]Hebr. *the beast of the field* [a]2Sam. 17:8; Prov. 17:12
9 [I]Hebr. *in thy help* [a]Prov. 6:32; Hos. 14:1; Mal. 1:9 [b]Hos. 13:4

3 Therefore they shall be [a]as the
morning cloud,[6051] and as the early dew
that passeth away, [b]as the chaff *that is*
driven with the whirlwind[5590] out of the
floor, and as the smoke out of the
chimney.[699]
4 Yet [a]I *am* the LORD thy God from
the land of Egypt, and thou shalt know
no god[430] but me: for [b]*there is* no
saviour[3467] beside me.
5 [a]I did know[3045] thee in the wilderness, [b]in the land of [I]great drought.
6 [a]According to their pasture, so
were they filled; they were filled, and
their heart[3820] was exalted; therefore
[b]have they forgotten me.
7 Therefore [a]I will be unto them as a
lion: as [b]a leopard by the way[1870] will I
observe[7789] *them:*
8 I will meet them [a]as a bear *that is*
bereaved[7909] *of her whelps,* and will
rend[7167] the caul[5458] of their heart, and
there will I devour them like a lion: [I]the
wild[7704] beast shall tear them.
9 O Israel, [a]thou hast destroyed
thyself,[7843] [b]but in me [I]*is* thine help.
10 [I][a]I will be thy king: [b]where *is any*
other that may save[3467] thee in all thy
cities? and thy judges[8199] of whom [c]thou
saidst, Give me a king and princes?[8269]
11 [a]I gave thee a king in mine
anger,[639] and took *him* away in my
wrath.[5678]
12 [a]The iniquity[5771] of Ephraim *is*
bound up; his sin[2403] *is* hid.
13 [a]The sorrows[2256] of a travailing
woman shall come upon him: he *is* [b]an
unwise son;[1121] for he should not [c]stay
[I]long[6256] in *the place of* the breaking
forth of children.[1121]
14 [a]I will ransom[6299] them from [I]the
power[3027] of the grave;[7585] I will
redeem[1350] them from death: [b]O death, I
will be thy plagues;[1698] O grave, I will be
thy destruction:[6987] [c]repentance[5164] shall
be hid from mine eyes.

10 [I]Rather, *Where is thy King* [a]2Kgs. 17:4 [b]Deut. 32:38; Hos. 10:3; Hos. 13:4 [c]1Sam. 8:5, 19
11 [a]1Sam. 8:7; 10:19; 15:22, 23; 16:1; Hos. 10:3
12 [a]Deut. 32:34; Job 14:17
13 [a]Isa. 13:8; Jer. 30:6 [b]Prov. 22:3 [I]Hebr. *a time* [c]2Kgs. 19:3
14 [I]Hebr. *the hand* [a]Isa. 25:8; Ezek. 37:12 [b]1Cor. 15:54, 55 [c]Jer. 15:6; Rom. 11:29

15 Though [a]he be fruitful among *his* brethren,[251] [b]an east wind[7307] shall come, the wind of the LORD shall come up[5927] from the wilderness, and his spring shall become dry,[954] and his fountain shall be dried up:[2717] he shall spoil[8154] the treasure of all [I][c]pleasant vessels.

16 [a]Samaria shall become desolate;[816] [b]for she hath rebelled[4784] against her God:[430] [c]they shall fall[5307] by the sword:[2719] their infants shall be dashed in pieces, and their women with child shall be ripped up.

Hosea Begs Israel to Come Back

14 O Israel, [a]return[7725] unto the LORD thy God;[430] [b]for thou hast fallen[3782] by thine iniquity.[5771]

2 Take with you words,[1697] and turn[7725] to the LORD: say unto him, Take away all iniquity, and [I]receive *us* graciously:[2896] so will we render the [a]calves of our lips.[8193]

3 [a]Asshur shall not save[3467] us; [b]we will not ride upon horses: [c]neither will we say any more to the work of our hands,[3027] *Ye are* our gods:[430] [d]for in thee the fatherless findeth mercy.[7355]

4 I will heal [a]their backsliding,[4878] I will love[157] them [b]freely:[5071] for mine anger[639] is turned away[7725] from him.

5 I will be as [a]the dew unto Israel: he shall [I]grow as the lily, and [II]cast forth his roots as Lebanon.

6 His branches [I]shall spread, and [a]his beauty[1935] shall be as the olive tree, and [b]his smell as Lebanon.

7 [a]They that dwell under his shadow shall return; they shall revive[2421] *as* the corn, and [I]grow as the vine: the [II]scent[2143] thereof *shall be* as the wine of Lebanon.

8 Ephraim *shall say,* [a]What have I to do any more with idols?[6091] [b]I have heard[6030] *him,* and observed him: I *am* like a green fir tree. [c]From me is thy fruit found.

9 [a]Who *is* wise,[2450] and he shall understand[995] these *things?* prudent,[995] and he shall know[3045] them? for [b]the ways[1870] of the LORD *are* right,[3477] and the just[6662] shall walk in them: but the transgressors[6586] shall fall[3782] therein.

15 [I]Hebr. *vessels of desire* [a]Gen. 41:52; 48:19 [b]Jer. 4:11; Ezek. 17:10; 19:12; Hos. 4:19 [c]Nah. 2:9
16 [a]2Kgs. 17:6 [b]2Kgs. 18:12 [c]2Kgs. 8:12; 15:16; Isa. 13:16; Hos. 10:14, 15; Amos 1:13; Nah. 3:10

1 [a]Hos. 12:6; Joel 2:13 [b]Hos. 13:9
2 [I]Or, *give good* [a]Heb. 13:15
3 [a]Jer. 31:18; Hos. 5:13; 12:1 [b]Deut. 17:16; Ps. 33:17; Isa. 30:2, 16; 31:1 [c]Hos. 2:17; Hos. 14:8 [d]Ps. 10:14; 68:5
4 [a]Jer. 5:6; 14:7; Hos. 11:7 [b]Eph. 1:6
5 [I]Or, *blossom* [II]Hebr. *strike* [a]Job 29:19; Prov. 19:12
6 [I]Hebr. *shall go* [a]Ps. 52:8; 128:3 [b]Gen. 27:27; Song 4:11
7 [I]Hebr. Or, *blossom* [II]Or, *memorial* [a]Ps. 91:1
8 [a]Hos. 14:3 [b]Jer. 31:18 [c]James 1:17
9 [a]Ps. 107:43; Jer. 9:12; Dan. 12:10; John 8:47; 18:37 [b]Prov. 10:29; Luke 2:34; 2Cor. 2:16; 1Pet. 2:7, 8

14:1–9 Hosea ends his book on a note of blessing. This passage looks far beyond the upcoming captivity, to the time when God will again bless His people. Before He can do this, He must first purge them of their apostasy (Hos. 14:4).

The Book of

JOEL

The contents of the book indicate that it was written fairly early in the reign of Joash (835–796 B.C.). Three factors that substantiate this date are: 1) The enemies named are the Phoenicians, Philistines, Egyptians, and Edomites (Joel 3:4, 19). These are early enemies of Judah; later opponents would have included Assyria and Babylon. 2) The position of the book in the collection of the works of the prophets indicates that the Jews considered it the oldest book addressed to Judah. 3) There is no mention of a reigning king, and an emphasis on elders and priests (Joel 1:1, 9, 13, 14; 2:16) would be appropriate for Joash, since he was crowned while still a very young boy and was under the guardianship of the high priest, Jehoiada (see 2 Kgs. 11:1–21; 2 Chr. 22:10–23:15).

Joel prophesied against the Southern Kingdom (Judah). The prophecies in this book can be divided into four sections: 1) A prophetic type of the Day of the Lord (Joel 1:1–20; see note on Zeph. 1:7); 2) the direct prophecy of the Day of the Lord itself (Joel 2:1–32); 3) the prophecy of the judgment of the nations (Joel 3:1–17); and 4) a prophecy of the full kingdom blessing of Israel (Joel 3:18–21).

Joel means "Jehovah is God." An important theme addressed within the Book of Joel is that Jehovah is the "Lord of life." God was in control over the people's economic situation (Joel 1:4–12) and their armies (Joel 2:1–11). He alone could grant mercy to them (Joel 2:12–17).

Locusts Destroy the Crops

1 The word[1697] of the LORD that came
to Joel the son[1121] of Pethuel.
2 Hear this, ye old men,[2205] and give
ear,[238] all ye inhabitants of the land.[776]
[a]Hath this been in your days,[3117] or even
in the days of your fathers?[1]
3 [a]Tell[5608] ye your children[1121] of it,
and *let* your children *tell* their children,
and their children another generation.[1755]
4 [I][a]That which the palmerworm[1501]
hath left[3499] hath the locust[697] eaten; and
that which the locust hath left hath the
cankerworm[3218] eaten; and that which
the cankerworm hath left hath the
caterpillar[2625] eaten.
5 Awake, ye drunkards, and weep;
and howl, all ye drinkers of wine, because of the new wine; [a]for it is cut
off[3772] from your mouth.[6310]
6 For [a]a nation[1471] is come up[5927]
upon my land, strong, and without number, [b]whose teeth *are* the teeth of a lion,
and he hath the cheek teeth of a great
lion.
7 He hath [a]laid[7760] my vine
waste,[8047] and [I]barked[7111] my fig tree: he
hath made it clean bare, and cast *it* away;
the branches thereof are made white.

2 [a]Joel 2:2
3 [a]Ps. 78:4
4 [I]Hebr. *The residue of the palmerworm* [a]Deut. 28:38; Joel 2:25
5 [a]Isa. 32:10
6 [a]Prov. 30:25, 26, 27; Joel 2:2, 11, 25 [b]Rev. 9:8
7 [I]Hebr. laid *my fig tree for a barking* [a]Isa. 5:6

1:4 The palmerworm, locust, cankerworm, and caterpillar are probably not four different kinds of insect, but four stages in the growth of the locust. The verse emphasizes that the locusts would totally consume everything edible in the land. It is assumed that these were desert locusts, a type of locust that devastated Palestine as recently as A.D. 1915. They represent an unexplained metamorphosis from grasshoppers to their locust form. Furthermore, when their density reaches a certain level, a swarm of these insects will devour any green plants in its path. The plague of locusts (Ex. 10:1–19) had a significant impact on Egypt. The servants claimed that Egypt was "destroyed" (Ex. 10:7), and even Pharaoh called the plague "this death" (Ex. 10:17). Just as that plague mocked the Egyptian's pride in the fertility of their land, so this locust invasion would rebuke God's people, who had forgotten that their prosperity came from God (see Deut. 6:10–12; 8:10–14, 17–20).

8 [a]Lament like a virgin[1330] girded
with sackcloth for [b]the husband[1167] of
her youth.
9 [a]The meat offering[4503] and the
drink offering[5262] is cut off from the
house[1004] of the LORD; the priests,[3548]
the LORD's ministers,[8334] mourn.
10 The field[7704] is wasted,[7703] [a]the
land[127] mourneth;56 for the corn is
wasted: [b]the new wine is [I]dried up,[3001]
the oil[3323] languisheth.
11 [a]Be ye ashamed, O ye husbandmen;406 howl, O ye vinedressers, for the
wheat and for the barley; because the
harvest of the field is perished.[6]
12 [a]The vine is dried up, and the fig
tree languisheth; the pomegranate tree,
the palm tree also, and the apple tree,
even all the trees of the field, are withered: because [b]joy is withered away[3001]
from the sons of men.[120]
13 [a]Gird yourselves, and lament, ye
priests: howl, ye ministers of the
altar:[4196] come, lie all night in sackcloth,
ye ministers of my God:[430] for [b]the
meat offering and the drink offering is
withholden4513 from the house of your
God.
14 [a]Sanctify[6942] ye a fast, call[7121] [b]a
[I]solemn assembly,[6116] gather[622] the
elders[2205] *and* [c]all the inhabitants of the
land *into* the house of the LORD your
God, and cry[2199] unto the LORD.
🔑 15 [a]Alas for the day[3117] for [b]the day
of the LORD *is* at hand, and as a
destruction[7701] from the Almighty[7706]
shall it come.
16 Is not the meat cut off before our
eyes, *yea,* [a]joy and gladness from the
house of our God?
17 The [I]seed is rotten under their
clods, the garners214 are laid desolate,[8074]
the barns are broken down;[2040] for the
corn is withered.
18 How do [a]the beasts groan! the
herds of cattle are perplexed, because
they have no pasture; yea, the flocks of
sheep are made desolate.[816]
19 O LORD, [a]to thee will I cry:[7121] for
[b]the fire hath devoured the [I]pastures[4999]
of the wilderness, and the flame hath
burned all the trees of the field.
20 The beasts of the field [a]cry also
unto thee: for [b]the rivers of waters are
dried up,[3001] and the fire hath devoured
the pastures of the wilderness.

8 [a]Isa. 22:12 [b]Prov. 2:17; Jer. 3:4
9 [a]Joel 1:13; 2:14
10 [I]Or, *ashamed* [a]Jer. 12:11; 14:2 [b]Isa. 24:7; Joel 1:12
11 [a]Jer. 14:3, 4
12 [a]Joel 1:10 [b]Isa. 24:11; Jer. 48:33; Ps. 4:7; Isa. 9:3
13 [a]Jer. 4:8; Joel 1:8 [b]Joel 1:9
14 [I]Or, day of *restraint* [a]2Chr. 20:3, 4; Joel 2:15, 16 [b]Lev. 23:36 [c]2Chr. 20:13
15 [a]Jer. 30:7 [b]Isa. 13:6, 9; Joel 2:1
16 [a]Deut. 12:6, 7; 16:11, 14, 15
17 [I]Hebr. *grains*
18 [a]Hos. 4:3
19 [I]Or, *habitations* [a]Ps. 50:15 [b]Jer. 9:10; 2:3
20 [a]Job 38:41; Ps. 104:21; 145:15 [b]1Kgs. 17:7; 18:5

The Locusts Are a Warning About The Day of the LORD

2 🔑[a]Blow[8628] ye the [I]trumpet in Zion,
and [b]sound an alarm[7321] in my
holy[6944] mountain: let all the inhabitants
of the land tremble:[7264] for [c]the day[3117]
of the LORD cometh, for *it is* nigh at
hand;
2 [a]A day of darkness[2822] and of
gloominess,[653] a day of clouds[6051] and
of thick darkness,[6205] as the morning
spread upon the mountains: [b]a great
people[5971] and a strong; [c]there hath not
been[1961] ever[5769] the like, neither shall be
any more after it, *even* to the years of
many generations.[1755]
3 [a]A fire devoureth before them; and

1 [I]Or, *cornet* [a]Jer. 4:5; Joel 2:15 [b]Num. 10:5, 9 [c]Joel 1:15; Obad. 1:15; Zeph. 1:14, 15
2 [I]Hebr. *of generation and generation* [a]Amos 5:18, 20 [b]Joel 1:6; 2:5, 11, 25 [c]Ex. 10:14
3 [a]Joel 1:19, 20

🔑 **1:15** The "Day of the LORD" is also mentioned in Joel 2:1, 11, 31; 3:14 (see also Amos 5:18, 20; Obad. 1:15; Zeph. 1:7, 14, 18; 2:2; and Mal. 4:5). For more information on the "Day of the LORD" and related phrases, see the note on Zephaniah 1:7.

🔑 **2:1–11** Some scholars suggest that this is a continuation of the description of the locust attack. However, the terminology is inappropriate for describing locust swarms, but is found elsewhere in obvious eschatological contexts. The most acceptable approach is that Joel begins chapter one with the immediate arrival of the locust swarm. Then in chapter two he focuses on the greater judgment and destruction of the "Day of the LORD." The "great people" (v. 2) correspond to those mentioned in the fifth trumpet judgment of Revelation 9:1–11, and verse ten is particularly full of terms that are not normally associated with locusts ("earth shall quake"), but are found elsewhere in eschatological passages (cf. Is. 34:4; Matt. 24:49; Rev. 8:12). The locust swarm, nevertheless, can legitimately be considered part of the "Day of the LORD," since the highlight of that day is God's judgment, and the locusts are a direct judgment from God upon Judah.

behind them a flame burneth: the land[776] *is* as [b]the garden of Eden before them, [c]and behind them a desolate[8077] wilderness; yea, and nothing shall escape[6413] them.

4 [a]The appearance of them *is* as the appearance of horses; and as horsemen, so shall they run.

5 [a]Like the noise of chariots on the tops[7218] of mountains shall they leap, like the noise of a flame of fire that devoureth the stubble, [b]as a strong$_{6099}$ people set in battle array.

6 Before their face the people shall be much pained:[2342] [a]all faces shall gather[6908] [I]blackness.[6289]

7 They shall run like mighty men;$_{1368}$ they shall climb[5927] the wall like men of war; and they shall march every one[376] on his ways,[1870] and they shall not break their ranks:[734]

8 Neither shall one thrust another;[251] they shall walk every one[1397] in his path: and *when* they fall[5307] upon the [I]sword, they shall not be wounded.

9 They shall run to and fro$_{8264}$ in the city; they shall run upon the wall, they shall climb up upon the houses;[1004] they shall [a]enter in at the windows [b]like a thief.

10 [a]The earth[776] shall quake[7264] before them; the heavens$_{8064}$ shall tremble:[7493] [b]the sun and the moon shall be dark,[6937] and the stars shall withdraw[622] their shining:

11 [a]And the LORD shall utter his voice before [b]his army:[2428] for his camp[4264] *is* very great: [c]for *he is* strong that executeth[6213] his word:[1697] for the [d]day[3117] of the LORD *is* great and very terrible;[3372] and [e]who can abide it?

The LORD's Mercy

🔑 12 Therefore also now, saith$_{5002}$ the LORD, [a]turn[7725] ye *even* to me with all your heart,$_{3824}$ and with fasting, and with weeping, and with mourning:

13 And [a]rend$_{7167}$ your heart, and not [b]your garments, and turn unto the LORD your God:[430] for he *is* [c]gracious[2587] and merciful, slow[750] to anger,[639] and of great kindness,[2617] and repenteth[5162] him of the evil.[7451]

14 [a]Who knoweth[3045] *if* he will return[7725] and repent,[5162] and leave[7604] [b]a blessing[1293] behind him; *even* [c]a meat offering[4503] and a drink offering[5262] unto the LORD your God?

15 [a]Blow the trumpet in Zion, [b]sanctify[6942] a fast, call a solemn assembly:[6116]

16 Gather[622] the people, [a]sanctify the congregation,[6951] [b]assemble[6908] the elders,[2205] [c]gather the children, and those that suck the breasts: [d]let the bridegroom go forth of his chamber, and the bride out of her closet.

17 Let the priests,[3548] the ministers[8334] of the LORD, weep [a]between the porch and the altar,[4196] and let them say,[559] [b]Spare thy people, O LORD, and give not thine heritage[5159] to reproach,[2781] that the heathen[1471] should [I]rule[4910] over them: [c]wherefore should they say among the people, Where *is* their God?

🔑 18 Then will the LORD [a]be jealous[7065] for his land, [b]and pity his people.

19 Yea, the LORD will answer and say unto his people, Behold, I will send you [a]corn, and wine, and oil,[3323] and ye shall

3 [b]Gen. 2:8; 13:10; Isa. 51:3 [c]Zech. 7:14
4 [a]Rev. 9:7
5 [a]Rev. 9:9 [b]Joel 2:2
6 [I]Hebr. *pot* [a]Jer. 8:21; Lam. 4:8; Nah. 2:10
8 [I]Or, *dart*
9 [a]Jer. 9:21 [b]John 10:1
10 [a]Ps. 18:7 [b]Isa. 13:10; Ezek. 32:7; Joel 2:31; Joel 3:15; Matt. 24:29
11 [a]Jer. 25:30; Joel 3:16; Amos 1:2 [b]Joel 2:25 [c]Jer. 50:34; Rev. 18:8 [d]Jer. 30:7; Amos 5:18; Zeph. 1:15 [e]Num. 24:23; Mal. 3:2
12 [a]Jer. 4:1; Hos. 12:6; 14:1
13 [a]Ps. 34:18; 51:17 [b]Gen. 37:34; 2Sam. 1:11; Job 1:20 [c]Ex. 34:6; Ps. 86:5, 15; Jon. 4:2
14 [a]Josh. 14:12; 2Sam. 12:22; 2Kgs. 19:4; Amos 5:15; Jon. 3:9; Zeph. 2:3 [b]Isa. 65:8; Hag. 2:19 [c]Joel 1:9, 13
15 [a]Num. 10:3; Joel 2:1 [b]Joel 1:14
16 [a]Ex. 19:10, 22 [b]Joel 1:14 [c]2Chr. 20:13 [d]1Cor. 7:5
17 [I]Or, *use a byword against them* [a]Ezek. 8:16; Matt. 23:35 [b]Ex. 32:11, 12; Deut. 9:26-29 [c]Ps. 42:10; 79:10; 115:2; Mic. 7:10
18 [a]Zech. 1:14; 8:2 [b]Deut. 32:36; Isa. 60:10
19 [a]Joel 1:10; Mal. 3:10-12

🔑 **2:12–14** Although the preceding prophecy dealt with future events (Joel 2:1–11), the Lord is pleading with Israel to repent right then. The swarm of locusts could have still been averted by a swift, genuine, and heartfelt repentance (Joel 2:13). God is not going back on His word here. Though the ultimate purpose for exiling, regathering, and purging His people will still be carried out (see note on Ezek. 36:22–38), God is always ready to respond to sincere repentance. The case is similar to the events mentioned in the Book of Jonah. God ultimately destroyed Nineveh as He had said (after they returned to their wickedness; see both Zephaniah and Nahum); but at the time of Jonah, He acknowledged the repentance of the Ninevites and spared their city (Jon. 3:5–10).

🔑 **2:18–27** This passage speaks of God's future work of restoring the land. The Lord will "have pity" on His people and remove the plagues by which He had punished them (v. 25; Is. 40:1, 2). Then they, as well as the world, will know that God is in their midst (cf. Ezek. 48:35).

be satisfied[7646] therewith: and I will no more make you a reproach[2781] among the heathen:

20 But [a]I will remove far off from you [b]the northern *army,* and will drive him into a land barren[6723] and desolate, with his face [c]toward the east sea, and his hinder part [d]toward the utmost sea, and his stink shall come up,[5927] and his ill savour shall come up, because [I]he hath done[6213] great things.

21 Fear not, O land;[127] be glad and rejoice: for the LORD will do great things.

22 Be not afraid, [a]ye beasts of the field:[7704] [b]for the pastures of the wilderness do spring, for the tree beareth her fruit, the fig tree and the vine do yield their strength.[2428]

23 Be glad then, ye children[1121] of Zion, and [a]rejoice in the LORD your God: for he hath given you [I]the former rain [II]moderately,[6666] and he [b]will cause to come down for you [c]the rain, the former rain, and the latter rain in the first *month.*

24 And the floors shall be full of wheat, and the fats shall overflow with wine and oil.

25 And I will restore[7999] to you the years [a]that the locust[697] hath eaten, the cankerworm,[3218] and the caterpiller,[2625] and the palmerworm,[1501] [b]my great army which I sent among you.

26 And ye shall [a]eat in plenty, and be satisfied, and praise[1984] the name of the LORD your God, that hath dealt[6213] wondrously[6318] with you: and my people shall never be ashamed.[954]

27 [a]And ye shall know[3045] that I *am* [b]in the midst[7130] of Israel, and *that* [c]I am the LORD your God, and none else: and my people shall never be ashamed.

🔑 28 [a]And it shall come to pass afterward, *that* I [b]will pour out[8210] my spirit[7307] upon all flesh;[1319] [c]and your sons[1121] and [d]your daughters shall prophesy,[5012] your old men[2205] shall dream dreams, your young men shall see[7200] visions:[2384]

29 And also upon [a]the servants[5650] and upon the handmaids in those days will I pour out my spirit.

30 And [a]I will shew wonders[4159] in the heavens and in the earth, blood,[1818] and fire, and pillars of smoke.

31 [a]The sun shall be turned[2015] into darkness,[2822] and the moon into blood, [b]before the great and the terrible day of the LORD come.

32 And it shall come to pass, *that* [a]whosoever shall call[7121] on the name of the LORD shall be delivered:[4422] for [b]in mount Zion and in Jerusalem shall be

20 [I]Hebr. *he hath magnified to do* [a]Ex. 10:19 [b]Jer. 1:14 [c]Ezek. 47:18; Zech. 14:8 [d]Deut. 11:24
22 [a]Joel 1:18, 20 [b]Zech. 8:12; Joel 1:19
23 [I]Or, *a teacher of righteousness* [II]Hebr. *according to righteousness* [a]Isa. 41:16; 61:10; Hab. 3:18; Zech. 10:7 [b]Lev. 26:4; Deut. 11:14; 28:12 [c]James 5:7
25 [a]Joel 1:4 [b]Joel 2:11
26 [a]Lev. 26:5; Ps. 22:26; Lev. 26:26; Mic. 6:14
27 [a]Joel 3:17 [b]Lev. 26:11, 12; Ezek. 37:26, 27, 28 [c]Isa. 45:5, 21, 22; Ezek. 39:22, 28
28 [a]Isa. 44:3; Ezek. 39:29; Acts 2:17 [b]Zech. 12:10; John 7:39 [c]Isa. 54:13 [d]Acts 21:9
29 [a]1Cor. 12:13; Gal. 3:28; Col. 3:11
30 [a]Matt. 24:29; Mark 13:24; Luke 21:11, 25
31 [a]Isa. 13:9, 10; Joel 2:10; 3:1, 15; Matt. 24:29; Mark 13:24; Luke 21:25; Rev. 6:12 [b]Mal. 4:5
32 [a]Rom. 10:13 [b]Isa. 46:13; 59:20; Obad. 1:17; Rom. 11:26

🔑 **2:28–32** There is a great controversy over when this prophecy was or will be fulfilled. Some people believe that the "first stage" of this prophecy was fulfilled at Pentecost. The verses were cited by Peter at Pentecost (Acts 2:17–21) in response to the question from the multitude, "What meaneth this?" (Acts 2:12). They claim that Peter connected the events of that day with Joel's prophecy dealing with the coming "Day of the LORD" (Joel 2:31). However, many of the parts of this prophecy were not fulfilled in Acts: sons and daughters did not predict; young men, as a group, did not see visions; and old men did not dream dreams (cf. Joel 2:28). The passage in Acts does not even follow the grammatical formula used for the fulfillment of portions of the Old Testament (cf. Acts 7:37; 8:32; 15:15). Those who believe that Pentecost was the "first stage" claim Peter was saying that only the first part of Joel's prophecy was being fulfilled.

Others claim that none of this prophecy was fulfilled at Pentecost, and that it was used by Peter as an example of how the work of the Holy Spirit may be marked by extraordinary phenomena. Peter was merely responding to those who said that they were drunk. His emphasis was that he was calling "on the name of the LORD" (Acts 2:21; Joel 2:32).

The fulfillment of this prophecy, or the second stage of its fulfillment, will be evident in the Second Coming of Christ at the end of the Great Tribulation. The day of darkness and gloom, along with wonders in the heavens, will follow the opening of the sixth seal (Joel 2:2, 30, 31, cf. Rev. 6:12).

deliverance,[6413] as the LORD hath said, and in [c]the remnant[8300] whom the LORD shall call.

The LORD Will Judge the Nations

3 For, behold, [a]in those days,[3117] and in that time,[6256] when I shall bring again[7725] the captivity[7622] of Judah and Jerusalem,

2 [a]I will also gather[6908] all nations,[1471] and will bring them down into [b]the valley of Jehoshaphat, and [c]will plead[8199] with them there for my people[5971] and *for* my heritage[5159] Israel, whom they have scattered among the nations, and parted my land.[776]

3 And they have [a]cast lots for my people; and have given a boy for an harlot,[2181] and sold a girl for wine, that they might drink.

4 Yea, and what have ye to do with me, [a]O Tyre, and Zidon, and all the coasts of Palestine? [b]will ye render[7999] me a recompence? and if ye recompense[1580] me, swiftly *and* speedily will I return[7725] your recompence upon your own head;[7218]

5 Because ye have taken my silver and my gold, and have carried into your temples[1964] my goodly[2896] [I][a]pleasant things:[4261]

6 The children[1121] also of Judah and the children of Jerusalem have ye sold unto [I]the Grecians, that ye might remove them far from their border.

7 Behold, [a]I will raise[5782] them out of the place whither ye have sold them, and will return your recompence upon your own head:

8 And I will sell your sons[1121] and your daughters into the hand[3027] of the children[1121] of Judah, and they shall sell them to the [a]Sabeans, to a people[1471] [b]far off: for the LORD hath spoken[1696] *it.*

9 [a]Proclaim[7121] ye this among the Gentiles;[1471] [I]Prepare[6942] war, wake up the mighty men,[582] let all the men of war draw near;[5066] let them come up:[5927]

10 [a]Beat[3807] your plowshares into swords,[2719] and your [I]pruninghooks into spears: [b]let the weak say,[559] I *am* strong.

11 [a]Assemble[5789] yourselves, and come, all ye heathen,[1471] and gather yourselves together round about: thither [I]cause [b]thy mighty ones to come down, O LORD.

12 Let the heathen be wakened, [a]and come up to the valley of Jehoshaphat: for there will I sit to [b]judge[8199] all the heathen round about.

13 [a]Put ye in the sickle, for [b]the harvest is ripe:[1310] come, get you down; for the [c]press is full, the fats[3342] overflow; for their wickedness[7451] *is* great.

14 Multitudes,[1995] multitudes in [a]the valley of [I]decision: for [b]the day[3117] of the LORD *is* near in the valley of decision.[2742]

15 The [a]sun and the moon shall be darkened,[6937] and the stars shall withdraw[622] their shining.

Blessings for the LORD's People

16 The LORD also shall [a]roar out of Zion, and utter his voice from Jerusalem; and [b]the heavens[8064] and the earth shall shake:[7493] [c]but the LORD *will be* the [I]hope[4268] of his people, and the strength[4581] of the children of Israel.

17 So [a]shall ye know[3045] that I *am* the LORD your God dwelling[7931] in Zion, [b]my holy[6944] mountain: then shall Jerusalem be [I]holy, and there shall[5674] no [c]strangers[2114] pass[5674] through her any more.

18 And it shall come to pass in that day, *that* the mountains shall [a]drop down[5197] new wine, and the hills shall

32 [c]Isa. 11:11, 16; Jer. 31:7; Mic. 4:7; 5:3, 7, 8; Rom. 9:27; 11:5, 7
1 [a]Jer. 30:3; Ezek. 38:14
2 [a]Zech. 14:2-4 [b]2Chr. 20:26; Joel 3:12 [c]Isa. 66:16; Ezek. 38:22
3 [a]Obad. 1:11; Nah. 3:10
4 [a]Amos 1:6, 9 [b]Ezek. 25:15-17
5 [I]Hebr. *desirable* [a]Dan. 11:38
6 [I]Hebr. *the sons of the Grecians*
7 [a]Isa. 43:5, 6; 49:12; Jer. 23:8
8 [a]Ezek. 23:42 [b]Jer. 6:20
9 [I]Hebr. *Sanctify* [a]Isa. 8:9, 10; Jer. 46:3, 4; Ezek. 38:7
10 [I]Or, *scythes* [a]Isa. 2:4; Mic. 4:3 [b]Zech. 12:8
11 [I]Or, *the LORD shall bring down* [a]Joel 3:2 [b]Ps. 103:20; Isa. 13:3
12 [a]Joel 3:2 [b]Ps. 96:13; 98:9; 110:6; Isa. 2:4; 3:13; Mic. 4:3
13 [a]Matt. 13:39; Rev. 14:15, 18 [b]Jer. 51:33; Hos. 6:11 [c]Isa. 63:3; Lam. 1:15; Rev. 14:19, 20
14 [I]Or, *concision,* or, *threshing* [a]Joel 3:2 [b]Joel 2:1
15 [a]Joel 2:10, 31
16 [I]Hebr. *place of repair,* or, *harbor* [a]Jer. 25:30; Joel 2:11; Amos 1:2 [b]Hag. 2:6 [c]Isa. 51:5, 6
17 [I]Hebr. *holiness* [a]Joel 2:27 [b]Dan. 11:45; Obad. 1:16; Zech. 8:3 [c]Isa. 35:8; 52:1; Nah. 1:15; Zech. 14:21; Rev. 21:27
18 [a]Amos 9:13

3:2, 14 These verses speak of the time to come when the nations of the earth will gather together in the valley of Jehoshaphat for the purpose of fighting against Jesus Christ and His armies (Rev. 19:19).

flow with milk, [b]and all the rivers of Judah shall [I]flow with waters, and [c]a fountain shall come forth of the house[1004] of the LORD, and shall water [d]the valley of Shittim.

19 [a]Egypt shall be a desolation,[8077] and [b]Edom shall be a desolate wilderness, for the violence[2555] *against* the children of Judah, because they have shed[8210] innocent blood in their land.

20 But Judah shall [I]dwell [a]for ever, and Jerusalem from generation to generation.

21 For I will [a]cleanse[5352] their blood *that* I have not cleansed: [I][b]for the LORD dwelleth in Zion.

18 [b]Isa. 30:25 [I]Hebr. *go* [c]Ps. 46:4; Ezek. 47:1; Zech. 14:8; Rev. 22:1 [d]Num. 25:1

19 [a]Isa. 19:1-22 [b]Jer. 49:17; Ezek. 25:12, 13; Amos 1:11; Obad. 1:10

20 [I]Or, *abide* [a]Amos 9:15

21 [I]Or, *even I the LORD that dwelleth in Zion* [a]Isa. 4:4 [b]Ezek. 48:35; Joel 3:17; Rev. 21:3

The Book of

AMOS

The name Amos means "a burden," which is the key word of the book. It is an appropriate name for one suddenly taken from his humble country roots and given the burden of serving as God's prophet (Amos 7:14, 15). Although Amos was from the town of Tekoa in Judah (see note on Amos 1:1), most of his ministry was carried out in the Northern Kingdom (Israel). Amos is believed to have prophesied between the years of 765 and 755 B.C., during the reign of Jeroboam II. The first verse suggests that at least two years passed between the time that he received the vision of chapter one and when he wrote it down.

Amos was contemporary with the prophets Hosea, Micah, Isaiah, and Jonah. Amos' simple, rural upbringing is apparent in the frequent references to and images drawn from country life. Although he had no formal training, his prophecy contains passages of great literary beauty and oratorical skill.

His pleas to the people to repent and predictions of the destruction of Israel made him very unpopular because he ministered at the peak of Israel's material and political success. They were enjoying a prosperous reign under Jeroboam II, who had expanded Israel's territory and secured it from external threats. However, as Hosea observed and Moses predicted (Deut. 6:4–10; Hos. 2:5–13), this prosperity caused the people to forget God.

Amos strongly denounced the rich and privileged classes who were using their power to exploit the poor. Amos cited several flagrant violations of specific social and legal stipulations in the Law of Moses (Amos 2:6–8; 4:1; 5:7, 10–12; 8:5–7). He also condemned the false religion practiced at the altar at Bethel (Amos 3:14; 4:4; 5:5, 6; 7:9, 10). As a result, Amaziah, the false high priest of Bethel rigorously opposed him (Amos 7:10–17).

God Judges Israel's Neighbours

1 🔑The <u>words</u>[1697] of Amos, [a]who
was among the herdmen of [b]Tekoa,
which he <u>saw</u>[2372] concerning Israel [c]in
the <u>days</u>[3117] of Uzziah king of Judah,
and in the days of [d]Jeroboam the <u>son</u>[1121]
of Joash king of Israel, two years before
the [e]<u>earthquake</u>.[7494]

1 [a]Amos 7:14
[b]2Sam. 14:2;
2Chr. 20:20
[c]Hos. 1:1
[d]Amos 7:10
[e]Zech. 14:5
2 [a]Jer. 25:30;
Joel 3:16
[b]1Sam. 25:2;
Isa. 33:9
3 [1]Or, *yea, for four* [a]Isa.
8:4; 17:1;
Jer. 49:23; Zech. 9:1

2 And he <u>said</u>,[559] The LORD will [a]roar
from Zion, and utter his voice from
Jerusalem; and the <u>habitations</u>[4999] of the
shepherds shall mourn, and the <u>top</u>[7218] of
[b]Carmel <u>shall wither</u>.[3001]
🔑3 Thus saith the LORD; For three
<u>transgressions</u>[6588] of [a]Damascus, [1]and for

🔑 **1:1, 2** Tekoa was a hilly area about twelve miles south of Jerusalem. While earthquakes are not uncommon in Palestine, this one must have been particularly severe because it was mentioned by Zechariah more than 200 years later (Zech. 14:5). Since Amos refers to the earthquake as a known event, at least two years have elapsed since he began to prophesy.

🔑 **1:3—2:16** Amos demonstrates great rhetorical skill in the way he prepared his audience for the point of his message. He first pronounced judgment on the enemies of Israel who were not related to them: Damascus (Syria), Gaza (Philistia), and Tyre. He then moved to his ultimatum by announcing judgments on the enemies of Israel who were also descendants of Abraham: Edom, Ammon, and Moab. Next, he mentioned Judah, Israel's brother kingdom. By this time Amos probably had his audience agreeing with him and feeling pleased with the way God was carrying out His judgment against these enemies of Israel. Then Amos pronounced the same judgment upon Israel (Amos 2:6–16). The expression "for three . . . and for four" is a Hebrew numeric parallelism. The numbers are poetic figures, not specific quantitative measures of the countries' sins, and signify that their sins were innumerable.

four, I will not [II][b]turn away[7725] *the punishment* thereof; [c]because they have threshed Gilead with threshing instruments of iron:

4 [a]But I will send a fire into the house[1004] of Hazael, which shall devour the palaces[759] of Ben–hadad.

5 I will break[7665] also the [a]bar of Damascus, and cut off[3772] the inhabitant from the plain of Aven,[205] and him that holdeth the sceptre[7626] from the house of Eden: and [b]the people[5971] of Syria shall go into captivity[1540] [c]unto Kir, saith the LORD.

6 Thus saith the LORD; For three transgressions of [a]Gaza, and for four, I will not turn away *the punishment* thereof; because they [I][b]carried away captive[1540] the whole[8003] captivity,[1546] [c]to deliver *them* up to Edom:

7 [a]But I will send a fire on the wall of Gaza, which shall devour the palaces[759] thereof:

8 And I will cut off the inhabitant [a]from Ashdod, and him that holdeth the sceptre from Ashkelon, and I will [b]turn[7725] mine hand[3027] against Ekron: and [c]the remnant[7611] of the Philistines shall perish,[6] saith the Lord[136] GOD.

9 Thus saith the LORD; For three transgressions of [a]Tyrus, and for four, I will not turn away *the punishment* thereof; [b]because they delivered up[5462] the whole captivity to Edom, and remembered[2142] not [I][c]the brotherly[251] covenant:[1285]

10 [a]But I will send a fire on the wall of Tyrus, which shall devour the palaces thereof.

11 Thus saith the LORD; For three transgressions of [a]Edom, and for four, I will not turn away *the punishment* thereof; because he did pursue [b]his brother [c]with the sword,[2719] and [I]did cast off[7843] all pity,[7356] [d]and his anger[639] did tear perpetually,[5703] and he kept[8104] his wrath[5678] for ever:[5331]

12 But [a]I will send a fire upon Teman, which shall devour the palaces of Bozrah.

13 Thus saith the LORD; For three transgressions of [a]the children[1121] of Ammon, and for four, I will not turn away *the punishment* thereof; because they have [I][b]ripped up the women with child of Gilead, [c]that they might enlarge their border:

14 But I will kindle a fire in the wall of [a]Rabbah, and it shall devour the palaces thereof, [b]with shouting[8643] in the day of battle, with a tempest in the day of the whirlwind:

15 And [a]their king shall go into captivity,[1473] he and his princes[8269] together, saith the LORD.

2 Thus saith the LORD; For three transgressions[6588] of [a]Moab, and for four, I will not turn away[7725] *the punishment* thereof; because he [b]burned[8313] the bones[6106] of the king of Edom into lime:

2 But I will send a fire upon Moab, and it shall devour the palaces[759] of [a]Kirioth: and Moab shall die with tumult,[7588] [b]with shouting, *and* with the sound of the trumpet:

3 And I will cut off[3772] [a]the judge[8199] from the midst thereof, and will slay[2026] all the princes[8269] thereof with him, saith the LORD.

4 Thus saith the LORD; For three transgressions of Judah, and for four, I will not turn away *the punishment* thereof; [a]because they have despised[3988] the law[8451] of the LORD, and have not kept[8104] his commandments,[2706] and [b]their lies[3577] caused them to err,[8582] [c]after the which their fathers[1] have walked:

5 [a]But I will send a fire upon Judah, and it shall devour the palaces of Jerusalem.

He Will Judge Israel Too

6 Thus saith the LORD; For three transgressions of Israel, and for four, I will not turn away *the punishment* thereof; because [a]they sold the righteous[6662] for silver, and the poor for a pair of shoes;

3 IIOr, *convert it*, or, *let it be quiet* [b]Amos 1:6 [c]2Kgs. 10:33; 13:7
4 [a]Jer. 17:27; 49:27; Amos 1:7, 10, 12; 2:2, 5
5 [a]Jer. 51:30; Lam. 2:9; [b]2Kgs. 16:9 [c]Amos 9:7
6 IOr, *carried them away with an entire captivity* [a]2Chr. 28:18; Isa. 14:29; Jer. 47:4, 5; Ezek. 25:15; Zeph. 2:4 [b]Amos 1:9 [c]2Chr. 21:16, 17; Joel 3:6
7 [a]Jer. 47:1
8 [a]Zeph. 2:4; Zech. 9:5, 6 [b]Ps. 81:14 [c]Jer. 47:4; Ezek. 25:16
9 IHebr. *the covenant of brethren* [a]Isa. 23:1; Jer. 47:4; Joel 3:4, 5 [b]Amos 1:6 [c]2Sam. 5:11; 1Kgs. 5:1; 9:11-14
10 [a]Amos 1:4, 7-9
11 IHebr. *corrupted his compassions* [a]Isa. 21:11; 34:5; Jer. 49:8-22; Ezek. 25:12-14; 35:2-12; Joel 3:19; Obad. 1:1-16; Mal. 1:4 [b]Gen. 27:41; Deut. 23:7; Mal. 1:2 [c]2Chr. 28:17 [d]Ezek. 35:5
12 [a]Obad. 1:9, 10
13 IOr, *divided the mountains* [a]Jer. 49:1, 2; Ezek. 25:2; Zeph. 2:9 [b]Hos. 13:16 [c]Jer. 49:1
14 [a]Deut. 3:11; 2Sam. 12:26; Jer. 49:2; Ezek. 25:5 [b]Amos 2:2
15 [a]Jer. 49:3

1 [a]Ezek. 25:8; Zeph. 2:8 [b]2Kgs. 3:27
2 [a]Jer. 48:41 [b]Amos 1:14
3 [a]Num. 24:17; Jer. 48:7
4 [a]Lev. 26:14, 15; Neh. 1:7; Dan. 9:11 [b]Isa. 28:15; Jer. 16:19, 20; Rom. 1:25 [c]Ezek. 20:13, 16, 18, 24, 30
5 [a]Jer. 17:27; Hos. 8:14
6 [a]Lev. 25:35-40; Deut. 24:7; 1Sam. 29:21; Amos 8:6

7 That pant[7602] after the dust[6083] of the earth[776] on the head[7218] of the poor, and [a]turn aside the way[1870] of the meek: [b]and a man[376] and his father[1] will go in unto the *same* [I]maid, [c]to profane[2490] my holy[6944] name:

8 And they lay *themselves* down upon clothes [a]laid to pledge[2254] [b]by every altar,[4196] and they drink the wine of [I]the condemned[6064] *in* the house[1004] of their god.[430]

9 Yet destroyed[8045] I the [a]Amorite before them, [b]whose height *was* like the height of the cedars, and he *was* strong as the oaks; yet I [c]destroyed his fruit from above, and his roots from beneath.

10 Also [a]I brought you up[5927] from the land[776] of Egypt, and [b]led you forty years through the wilderness, to possess[3423] the land of the Amorite.

11 And I raised up of your sons[1121] for prophets,[5030] and of your young men for [a]Nazarites.[5139] *Is it* not even thus, O ye children[1121] of Israel? saith[5002] the LORD.

12 But ye gave the Nazarites wine to drink; and commanded[6680] the prophets, [a]saying,[559] Prophesy[5012] not.

13 [a]Behold, [I]I am pressed under you, as a cart is pressed *that is* full of sheaves.

14 [a]Therefore the flight shall perish[6] from the swift, and the strong[2389] shall not strengthen his force, [b]neither shall the mighty deliver[4422] [I]himself:

15 Neither shall he stand that handleth the bow; and *he that is* swift of foot shall not deliver *himself:* [a]neither shall he that rideth the horse deliver himself.

16 And *he that is* [I]courageous[3820] among the mighty shall flee away naked[6174] in that day,[3117] saith the LORD.

The Work of a Prophet

3 Hear this word[1697] that the LORD hath spoken[1696] against you, O children[1121] of Israel, against the whole family[4940] which I brought up[5927] from the land[776] of Egypt, saying,[559]

2 [a]You only have I known[3045] of all the families of the earth:[127] [b]therefore I will [I]punish[6485] you for all your iniquities.[5771]

3 Can two walk together, except they be agreed?[3529]

4 Will a lion roar in the forest, when he hath no prey? will a young lion [I]cry out of his den, if he have taken nothing?

5 Can a bird fall[5307] in a snare[6341] upon the earth,[776] where no gin[4170] *is* for him? shall *one* take up[5927] a snare from the earth, and have taken nothing at all?

6 Shall a trumpet be blown[8628] in the city, and the people[5971] [I]not be afraid?[2729] [a]shall there be evil[7451] in a city, [II]and the LORD hath not done[6213] *it?*

7 Surely the Lord[136] GOD will do nothing but [a]he revealeth[1540] his secret[5475] unto his servants[5650] the prophets.[5030]

8 [a]The lion hath roared, who will not fear?[3372] the Lord GOD hath spoken, [b]who can but prophesy?[5012]

Samaria Is Doomed

9 Publish[8085] in the palaces[759] at Ashdod, and in the palaces in the land of Egypt, and say, Assemble[622] yourselves upon the mountains of Samaria, and behold[7200] the great tumults[4103] in the midst thereof, and the [I]oppressed in the midst thereof.

7 [I]Or, *young woman* [a]Isa. 10:2; Amos 5:12 [b]Lev. 18:6-20; 19:29; 20:10; Ezek. 22:11 [c]Lev. 20:3; Ezek. 36:20; Rom. 2:24
8 [I]Or, *such as have fined,* or, *mulcted* [a]Ex. 22:26; Deut. 24:13 [b]Ezek. 23:41; 1Cor. 8:10; 10:21
9 [a]Num. 21:24; Deut. 2:31; Josh. 24:8 [b]Num. 13:28, 32, 33 [c]Isa. 5:24; Mal. 4:1
10 [a]Ex. 12:51; Mic. 6:4 [b]Deut. 2:7; 8:2
11 [a]Num. 6:2; Judg. 13:5
12 [a]Isa. 30:10; Jer. 11:21; Amos 7:12, 13; Mic. 2:6
13 [I]Or, *I will press your place, as a cart full of sheaves presseth* [a]Isa. 1:14
14 [I]Hebr. *his soul,* or, *life* [a]Jer. 9:23; Amos 9:1-4 [b]Ps. 33:16
15 [a]Ps. 33:17
16 [I]Hebr. *strong of his heart*

2 [I]Hebr. *visit upon* [a]Deut. 7:6; 10:15; Ps. 147:19, 20 [b]Dan. 9:12; Matt. 11:22; Luke 12:47; Rom. 2:9; 1Pet. 4:17
4 [I]Hebr. *give forth his voice*
6 [I]Or, *not run together* [II]Or, *and shall not the LORD do* somewhat [a]Isa. 45:7
7 [a]Gen. 6:13; 18:17; Ps. 25:14; John 15:15
8 [a]Amos 1:2 [b]Acts 4:20; 5:20, 29; 1Cor. 9:16
9 [I]Or, *oppressions*

3:2 The Hebrew word *yada'* (3045), which is translated "known" in this verse, denotes far more than mere knowledge, particularly when used of God. This indicates knowledge accompanied by special attention or affection (see Jer. 1:5).

3:6 The word "evil" would be better translated "disaster" or "calamity." It does not speak of moral evil, but of misfortune. Nevertheless, it is sometimes translated "evil" because it refers to the disastrous consequences of sin as in this case.

10 For they [a]know[3045] not to do[6213] right,[5228] saith the LORD, who store up violence[2555] and [I]robbery[7701] in their palaces.

🔑 11 Therefore thus saith the Lord GOD; [a]An adversary *there shall be* even round about the land; and he shall bring down thy strength[5797] from thee, and thy palaces shall be spoiled.

12 Thus saith the LORD; As the shepherd [I]taketh out[5337] of the mouth[6310] of the lion two legs, or a piece of an ear;[241] so shall the children of Israel be taken out that dwell in Samaria in the corner of a bed, and [II]in Damascus *in* a couch.

13 Hear ye, and testify[5749] in the house[1004] of Jacob, saith[5002] the Lord GOD,[430] the God of hosts,[6635]

14 That in the day[3117] that I shall [II]visit[6485] the transgressions[6588] of Israel upon him I will also visit the altars[4196] of Bethel: and the horns of the altar shall be cut off, and fall to the ground.[776]

15 And I will smite[5221] [a]the winter house with [b]the summer house; and [c]the houses of ivory shall perish,[6] and the great houses shall have an end,[5486] saith the LORD.

4 🔑Hear this word,[1697] ye [a]kine[6510] of Bashan, that *are* in the mountain of Samaria, which oppress the poor, which crush the needy, which say to their masters,[113] Bring, and let us drink.

2 [a]The Lord[136] GOD hath sworn[7650] by his holiness,[6944] that, lo, the days shall come upon you, that he will take you away[5375] [b]with hooks, and your posterity[319] with fishhooks.

3 And [a]ye shall go out at the breaches, every *cow at that which is* before her; and [I]ye shall cast[7993] *them* into the palace, saith the LORD.

Israel Won't Learn the Lesson

4 [a]Come to Bethel, and transgress;[6586] at [b]Gilgal multiply[7235] transgression; and [c]bring your sacrifices[2077] every morning, [d]*and* your tithes[4643] after [I]three years:

5 [a]And [I]offer a sacrifice[6999] of thanksgiving[8426] with leaven,[2557] and proclaim[7121] *and* publish[8085] [b]the free offerings:[5071] [c]for [II]this liketh[157] you, O ye children[1121] of Israel, saith[5002] the Lord GOD.

6 And I also have given you cleanness[5356] of teeth in all your cities, and want of bread in all your places: [a]yet have ye not returned[7725] unto me, saith the LORD.

7 And also I have withholden[4513] the rain from you, when *there were* yet three months to the harvest: and I caused it to rain upon one city, and caused it not to rain upon another city: one piece[2513] was rained upon, and the piece whereupon it rained not withered.[3001]

8 So two *or* three cities wandered[5128] unto one city, to drink water; but they were not satisfied: [a]yet have ye not returned unto me, saith the LORD.

9 [a]I have smitten[5221] you with blasting and mildew: [I]when your gardens and your vineyards and your fig trees and your olive trees increased, [b]the palmerworm devoured *them:* yet have ye not returned unto me, saith the LORD.

10 I have sent among you the pestilence[1698] [I][a]after the manner[1870] of Egypt: your young men have I slain[2026]

10 [I]Or, *spoil* [a]Jer. 4:22
11 [a]2Kgs. 17:3, 6; 18:9-11
12 [I]Hebr. *delivereth* [II]Or, *on the bed's feet*
14 [I]Or, *punish Israel for*
15 [a]Jer. 36:22 [b]Judg. 3:20 [c]1Kgs. 22:39
1 [a]Ps. 22:12; Ezek. 39:18
2 [a]Ps. 89:35 [b]Jer. 16:16; Hab. 1:15
3 [I]Or, *ye shall cast away the things of the palace* [a]Ezek. 12:5, 12
4 [I]Hebr. *three years of days* [a]Ezek. 20:39 [b]Hos. 4:15; 12:11; Amos 5:5 [c]Num. 28:3, 4 [d]Deut. 14:28
5 [I]Hebr. *offer by burning* [II]Hebr. *so ye love* [a]Lev. 7:13; 23:17 [b]Lev. 22:18, 21; Deut. 12:6 [c]Ps. 81:12
6 [a]Isa. 26:11; Jer. 5:3; Amos 4:8, 9; Hag. 2:17
8 [a]Amos 4:6, 10, 11
9 [I]Or, *the multitude of your gardens did the palmerworm* [a]Deut. 28:22; Hag. 2:17 [b]Joel 1:4; 2:25
10 [I]Or, *in the way* [a]Ex. 9:3, 6; 12:29; Deut. 28:27, 60; Ps. 78:50

🔑 **3:11–15** These verses serve as the summary of Amos' message of judgment. The two evils Israel had committed were false worship at Bethel and materialism.

🔑 **4:1–3** The "kine [cows] of Bashan," east of the Sea of Galilee, were known for their fine quality. They metaphorically refer to the upper class women of Samaria who felt that there was nothing wrong with oppressing the poor. In fact, verse one suggests that some of the oppressions practiced by their husbands were done to satisfy their demands. Amos warned that they would indeed be treated like cattle, when the captors of Samaria would sort them out for slavery.

with the sword,[2719] [II][b]and have taken away[7628] your horses; and I have made[5927] the stink of your camps[4264] to come up[5927] unto your nostrils:[639] [c]yet have ye not returned unto me, saith the LORD.

11 I have overthrown[2015] *some* of you, as God[430] overthrew [a]Sodom and Gomorrah, [b]and ye were as a firebrand plucked[5337] out of the burning:[8316] [c]yet have ye not returned unto me, saith the LORD.

12 Therefore thus will I do[6213] unto thee, O Israel: *and* because I will do this unto thee, [a]prepare[3559] to meet thy God, O Israel.

13 For, lo, he that formeth[3335] the mountains, and createth[1254] the [I]wind,[7307] [a]and declareth[5046] unto man[120] what *is* his thought, [b]that maketh[6213] the morning darkness,[5890] [c]and treadeth upon the high places[1116] of the earth,[776] [d]The LORD,[3068] The God of hosts,[6635] *is* his name.

Come Back, Israel!

5 Hear ye this word[1697] which I [a]take up[5375] against you, *even* a lamentation, O house[1004] of Israel.

2 The virgin[1330] of Israel is fallen;[5307] she shall no more rise: she is forsaken[5203] upon her land;[127] *there is* none to raise her up.

3 For thus saith the Lord[136] GOD; The city that went out *by* a thousand shall leave[7604] an hundred, and that which went forth *by* an hundred shall leave ten, to the house of Israel.

4 For thus saith the LORD unto the house of Israel, [a]Seek[1875] ye me, [b]and ye shall live:[2421]

5 But seek not [a]Bethel, nor enter into Gilgal, and pass[5674] not to [b]Beer–sheba: for Gilgal shall surely go into captivity,[1540] and [c]Bethel shall come to nought.[205]

6 [a]Seek the LORD, and ye shall live; lest he break out like fire in the house of Joseph, and devour *it,* and *there be* none to quench *it* in Bethel.

7 Ye who [a]turn[2015] judgment[4941] to wormwood,[3939] and leave off[3240] righteousness in the earth,[776]

8 *Seek him* that maketh[6213] the [a]seven stars and Orion, and turneth the shadow of death[6757] into the morning, [b]and maketh the day dark[2821] with night:[3915] that [c]calleth[7121] for the waters of the sea, and poureth them out[8210] upon the face of the earth: [d]The LORD *is* his name:

9 That strengtheneth[1082] the [I]spoiled[7701] against the strong,[5794] so that the spoiled shall come against the fortress.

10 [a]They hate him that rebuketh in the gate, and they [b]abhor[8581] him that speaketh uprightly.[8549]

11 Forasmuch therefore as your treading *is* upon the poor, and ye take from him burdens[4864] of wheat: [a]ye have built houses of hewn stone,[1496] but ye shall not dwell in them; ye have planted [I]pleasant vineyards, but ye shall not drink wine of them.

12 For I know[3045] your manifold transgressions[6588] and your mighty sins:[2403] [a]they afflict the just,[6662] they take [I]a bribe,[3724] and they [b]turn aside the poor in the gate *from their right.*

13 Therefore [a]the prudent shall keep silence in that time;[6256] for it *is* an evil[7451] time.

14 Seek good,[2896] and not evil, that ye may live:[2421] and so the LORD, the God[430] of hosts,[6635] shall be with you, [a]as ye have spoken.

15 [a]Hate the evil, and love[157] the good, and establish judgment in the gate: [b]it may be that the LORD God of hosts will be gracious[2603] unto the remnant[7611] of Joseph.

16 Therefore the LORD, the God of hosts, the Lord, saith thus; Wailing *shall be* in all streets; and they shall say[559] in all the highways, Alas! alas! and they shall call[7121] the husbandman[406] to mourning, and [a]such as are skilful[3045] of lamentation to wailing.

17 And in all vineyards *shall be* wailing: for [a]I will pass through thee, saith the LORD.

---

10 [II]Hebr. *with the captivity of your horses* [b]2Kgs. 13:7 [c]Amos 4:6

11 [a]Gen. 19:24, 25; Isa. 13:19; Jer. 49:18 [b]Zech. 3:2; Jude 1:23 [c]Amos 4:6

12 [a]Ezek. 13:5; 22:30; Luke 14:31, 32

13 [I]Or, *spirit* [a]Ps. 139:2; Dan. 2:28 [b]Amos 5:8; 8:9 [c]Deut. 32:13; 33:29; Mic. 1:3 [d]Isa. 47:4; Jer. 10:16; Amos 5:8; 9:6

1 [a]Jer. 7:29; Ezek. 19:1; 27:2

4 [a]2Chr. 15:2; Jer. 29:13; Amos 5:6 [b]Isa. 55:3

5 [a]Amos 4:4 [b]Amos 8:14 [c]Hos. 4:15; 10:8

6 [a]Amos 5:4

7 [a]Amos 6:12

8 [a]Job 9:9; 38:31 [b]Ps. 104:20 [c]Job 38:34; Amos 9:6 [d]Amos 4:13

9 [I]Hebr. *spoil*

10 [a]Isa. 29:21 [b]1Kgs. 22:8

11 [I]Hebr. *vineyards of desire* [a]Deut. 28:30, 38, 39; Mic. 6:15; Zeph. 1:13; Hag. 1:6

12 [I]Or, *a ransom* [a]Amos 2:6 [b]Isa. 29:21; Amos 2:7

13 [a]Amos 6:10

14 [a]Mic. 3:11

15 [a]Ps. 34:14; 97:10; Rom. 12:9 [b]Ex. 32:30; 2Kgs. 19:4; Joel 2:14

16 [a]Jer. 9:17

17 [a]Ex. 12:12; Nah. 1:12

🔑 18 [a]Woe unto you that desire[183] the day of the LORD! to what end *is* it for you? [b]the day[3117] of the LORD *is* darkness,[2822] and not light.[216]

19 [a]As if a man[376] did flee from a lion, and a bear met[6293] him; or went into the house, and leaned his hand[3027] on the wall, and a serpent[5175] bit him.

20 *Shall* not the day of the LORD *be* darkness, and not light? even very dark,[651] and no brightness in it?

21 [a]I hate, I despise[3988] your feast days,[2282] and [b]I will not [I]smell[7306] in your solemn assemblies.[6116]

22 [a]Though ye offer[5927] me burnt offerings[5930] and your meat offerings,[4503] I will not accept[7521] *them:* neither will I regard the [I]peace offerings[8002] of your fat beasts.

23 Take thou away[5493] from me the noise of thy songs;[7892] for I will not hear[8085] the melody of thy viols.5035

24 [a]But let judgment [I]run down[1556] as waters, and righteousness as a mighty386 stream.

25 [a]Have ye offered[5066] unto me sacrifices[2077] and offerings[4503] in the wilderness forty years, O house of Israel?

26 But ye have borne[5375] [I]the tabernacle[5522] [a]of your Moloch and Chiun your images,[6754] the star of your god,[430] which ye made[6213] to yourselves.

27 Therefore will I cause you to go into captivity[1540] [a]beyond Damascus, saith the LORD, [b]whose name *is* The God of hosts.

Israel Will Be Destroyed

6 Woe [a]to them *that* [I]*are* at ease7600 in Zion, and trust[982] in the mountain of Samaria, *which are* named[5344] [II][b]chief[7225] of the nations,[1471] to whom the house[1004] of Israel came!

2 [a]Pass[5674] ye unto [b]Calneh, and see;[7200] and from thence go ye to [c]Hamath the great: then go down to [d]Gath of the Philistines: [e]*be they* better[2896] than these kingdoms?[4467] or their border greater than your border?

3 Ye that [a]put far away the [b]evil[7451] day,[3117] [c]and cause[5066] [d]the [I]seat of violence[2555] to come near;[5066]

4 That lie upon beds of ivory, and stretch themselves upon their couches, and eat the lambs[3733] out of the flock, and the calves out of the midst of the stall;

5 [a]That chant to the sound[6310] of the viol, *and* invent[2803] to themselves instruments of musick,[7892] [b]like David;

6 That drink [I]wine in bowls, and anoint[4886] themselves with the chief ointments:[8081] [a]but they are not grieved for the [II]affliction[7667] of Joseph.

7 Therefore now shall they go captive[1540] with the first[7218] that go captive, and the banquet of them that stretched themselves shall be removed.[5493]

8 [a]The Lord[136] GOD hath sworn[7650] by himself, saith the LORD the God[430] of hosts,[6635] I abhor[8374] [b]the excellency1347 of Jacob, and hate[8130] his palaces:[759] therefore will I deliver up the city with all [I]that is therein.

9 And it shall come to pass, if there remain[3498] ten men[582] in one house, that they shall die.

10 And a man's uncle shall take him up, and he that burneth him, to bring out the bones[6106] out of the house, and shall say unto him that *is* by the sides of the house, *Is there* yet *any* with thee? and he shall say, No. Then shall he say, [a]Hold thy tongue: [b]for [I]we may not make mention[2142] of the name of the LORD.

11 For, behold, [a]the LORD commandeth,[6680] [b]and he will smite[5221] the great house with [I]breaches, and the little house with clefts.

18 [a]Isa. 5:19; Jer. 17:15; Ezek. 12:22, 27; 2Pet. 3:4 [b]Jer. 30:7; Joel 2:2; Zeph. 1:15
19 [a]Jer. 48:44
21 [I]Or, *smell your holy days* [a]Prov. 21:27; Isa. 1:11-16; Jer. 6:20; Hos. 8:13 [b]Lev. 26:31
22 [I]Or, *thank offerings* [a]Isa. 66:3; Mic. 6:6, 7
24 [I]Hebr. *roll* [a]Hos. 6:6; Mic. 6:8
25 [a]Deut. 32:17; Josh. 24:14; Ezek. 20:8, 16, 24; Acts 7:42, 43; Isa. 43:23
26 [I]Or, *Siccuth your king* [a]1Kgs. 11:33
27 [a]2Kgs. 17:6 [b]Amos 4:13

1 [I]Or, *are secure* [II]Or, *firstfruits* [a]Luke 6:24 [b]Ex. 19:5
2 [a]Jer. 2:10 [b]Isa. 10:9 [c]2Kgs. 18:34 [d]2Chr. 26:6 [e]Nah. 3:8
3 [I]Or, *habitation* [a]Ezek. 12:27; [b]Amos 5:18; 9:10 [c]Amos 5:12; Amos 6:12 [d]Ps. 94:20
5 [a]Isa. 5:12 [b]1Chr. 23:5
6 [I]Or, *in bowls of wine* [II]Hebr. *breach* [a]Gen. 37:25
8 [I]Hebr. *the fullness thereof* [a]Jer. 51:14; Heb. 6:13, 17 [b]Ps. 47:4; Ezek. 24:21; Amos 8:7
10 [I]Or, *they will not, or, have not* [a]Amos 5:13 [b]Amos 8:3
11 [I]Or, *droppings* [a]Isa. 55:11 [b]Amos 3:15

🔑 **5:18–20** This passage reveals Israel's false perspective in regard to God protecting them because they had the temple (see note on Jer. 7:2–15). The people were taking for granted that the "Day of the LORD" would be their day of triumph. Amos reminded them, however, that because of their unbelief and wickedness, it would be a day of judgment for them, as well as for the other nations. See note on Zephaniah 1:7.

12 Shall horses run upon the rock?
will *one* plow *there* with oxen? for
[a]ye have turned[2015] judgment[4941] into
gall,7219 and the fruit of righteousness
into hemlock:3939
13 Ye which rejoice in a thing of
nought, which say, Have we not taken to
us horns by our own strength?[2392]
14 But, behold, [a]I will raise up
against you a nation, O house of Israel,
saith the LORD the God of hosts; and they
shall afflict3905 you from the [b]entering in
of Hemath unto the [I]river of the wilderness.[6160]

Three Visions: How Israel Will Be Destroyed

7 Thus hath[7200] the Lord[136] GOD
shewed[7200] unto me; and, behold, he
formed[3335] [I]grasshoppers1462 in the beginning of the shooting up[5927] of the latter growth; and, lo, *it was* the latter
growth after the king's mowings.
2 And it came to pass, *that* when
they had made an end[3615] of eating
the grass of the land,[776] then I said,[559]
O Lord GOD, forgive,[5545] I beseech thee:
[Ia]by whom shall Jacob arise? for he *is*
small.
3 [a]The LORD repented[5162] for this: It
shall not be, saith the LORD.
4 Thus hath the Lord GOD shewed
unto me: and, behold, the Lord GOD
called[7121] to contend[7378] by fire, and it
devoured the great deep,8415 and did eat
up a part.
5 Then said I, O Lord GOD, cease, I
beseech thee: [a]by whom shall Jacob arise?
for he *is* small.
6 The LORD repented for this: This
also shall not be, saith the Lord GOD.
7 Thus he shewed me: and, behold,
the Lord stood[5324] upon a wall *made* by
a plumbline,594 with a plumbline in his
hand.[3027]
8 And the LORD said unto me, Amos,
what seest[7200] thou? And I said, A
plumbline. Then said the Lord, Behold, [a]I
will set a plumbline in the midst of my
people[5971] Israel: [b]I will not again
pass[5674] by them any more:
9 [a]And the high places[1116] of Isaac
shall be desolate,[8074] and the sanctuaries[4720] of Israel shall be laid
waste;[2717] and [b]I will rise against the
house[1004] of Jeroboam with the
sword.[2719]

Amos and Amaziah

10 Then Amaziah [a]the priest[3548] of
Bethel sent to [b]Jeroboam king of Israel,
saying,[559] Amos hath conspired against
thee in the midst[7130] of the house of
Israel: the land is not able to bear3557 all
his words.[1697]
11 For thus Amos saith, Jeroboam
shall die[4191] by the sword, and Israel
shall surely be led away captive[1540] out
of their own land.[127]
12 Also Amaziah said unto Amos, O
thou seer,[2374] go, flee thee away into the
land of Judah, and there eat bread, and
prophesy[5012] there:
13 But [a]prophesy not again any more

12 [a]Hos. 10:4; Amos 5:7
14 [I]Or, *valley* [a]Jer. 5:15 [b]Num. 34:8; 1Kgs. 8:65
1 [I]Or, *green worms*
2 [I]Or, *who of (or, for,) Jacob shall stand?* [a]Isa. 51:19
3 [a]Deut. 32:36; Amos 7:6; Jon. 3:10; James 5:16
5 [a]Amos 7:2, 3
8 [a]2Kgs. 21:13; Isa. 28:17; 34:11; Lam. 2:8 [b]Amos 8:2; Mic. 7:18
9 [a]Gen. 26:23; 46:1; Amos 5:5; 8:14; Beer-sheba [b]2Kgs. 15:10
10 [a]1Kgs. 12:32 [b]2Kgs. 14:23
13 [a]Amos 2:12

7:7–9 The "plumbline" was to serve as the measure of Israel's sin to reveal how far she had gone astray. Although the Lord complied with Amos' first two requests to stay His judgment, destruction was now certain, and captivity by the Assyrians was imminent (Amos 7:17).

7:10 The phrase "the land is not able to bear all his words" referred to Amos' preaching, which was intolerable to those who held positions of leadership. Amos spoke out against the unfair practices by which the rich were oppressing the poor. When Amos said that the rich would be judged for their injustices, the poor people began to support Amos' message. Amaziah and other leaders in the Northern Kingdom of Israel saw this as a direct threat to their authority.

7:12–15 Amos is emphasizing his background to Amaziah the priest, who had called him a "seer" (v. 12) or a "professional prophet." Unlike many other prophets (e.g., Isaiah, Jeremiah, and Ezekiel), Amos had not been called to prophesy before birth, nor had he been trained in any prophetic schools (see note on 2 Kgs. 2:3, 5). The fact is, Amos already had a profession as a shepherd before God called him to go and prophesy.

at Bethel: [b]for it *is* the king's [I]chapel,[4720]
and it *is* the [II]king's court.[1004]
14 Then answered Amos, and said to
Amaziah, I *was* no prophet,[5030] neither
was I [a]a prophet's son;[1121] [b]but I *was* an
herdman, and a gatherer of [I]sycomore
fruit:
15 And the LORD took me [I]as I followed the flock, and the LORD said unto
me, Go, prophesy unto my people Israel.
16 Now therefore hear thou the word
of the LORD: Thou sayest, Prophesy not
against Israel, and [a]drop[5197] not *thy word*
against the house of Isaac.
17 [a]Therefore thus saith the LORD;
[b]Thy wife[802] shall be an harlot[2181] in the
city, and thy sons and thy daughters
shall fall[5307] by the sword, and thy
land shall be divided by line;[2256] and
thou shalt die in a polluted[2931] land: and
Israel shall surely go into captivity forth
of his land.

A Basket of Ripe Fruit

8 Thus hath[7200] the Lord[136] GOD
shewed[7200] unto me: and behold a
basket of summer fruit.
2 And he said,[559] Amos, what
seest[7200] thou? And I said, A basket of
summer fruit. Then said the LORD unto
me, [a]The end is come upon my people[5971]
of Israel; [b]I will not again pass[5674] by
them any more.
3 And [a]the songs[7892] of the tem-
ple[1964] [I]shall be howlings in that day,[3117]
saith[5002] the Lord GOD: *there shall be*
many dead bodies[6297] in every place;
[b]they shall cast *them* forth [II]with silence.

Israel's Doom Is Near

4 Hear this, O ye that [a]swallow
up[7602] the needy, even to make the poor
of the land[776] to fail,
5 Saying,[559] When will the [I]new
moon be gone,[5674] that we may sell
corn?[7668] and [a]the sabbath,[7676] that we
may [II]set forth wheat, [b]making the ephah
small, and the shekel great, and
[III][c]falsifying[5791] the balances by deceit?[4820]
6 That we may buy the poor for [a]sil-
ver, and the needy for a pair of shoes;
yea, and sell the refuse[4651] of the wheat?
7 The LORD hath sworn[7650] by [a]the
excellency of Jacob, Surely [b]I will never
forget any of their works.
8 [a]Shall not the land tremble[7264] for
this, and every one mourn that dwelleth
therein? and it shall rise up[5927] wholly as
a flood;[216] and it shall be cast out and
drowned, [b]as *by* the flood of Egypt.
9 And it shall come to pass in that
day, saith the Lord GOD, [a]that I will cause
the sun to go down at noon, and I will
darken[2821] the earth[776] in the clear[216]
day:
10 And I will turn[2015] your feasts[2282]
into mourning, and all your songs into
lamentation; [a]and I will bring up[5927] sackcloth upon all loins, and baldness upon
every head;[7218] [b]and I will make[7760] it as
the mourning of an only[3173] *son,* and the
end[319] thereof as a bitter[4751] day.
11 Behold, the days come, saith the
Lord GOD, that I will send a famine in the
land, not a famine of bread, nor a thirst
for water, but [a]of hearing[8085] the
words[1697] of the LORD:
12 And they shall wander from sea
to sea, and from the north even to the
east, they shall run to and fro[7751] to seek
the word of the LORD, and shall not find
it.
13 In that day shall the fair virgins[1330] and young men faint for thirst.
14 They that [a]swear[7650] by [b]the
sin[819] of Samaria, and say, Thy god,[430]
O Dan, liveth; and, The [I]manner[1870]

13 [I]Or, *sanctuary* [II]Hebr. *house of the kingdom* [b]1Kgs. 12:32; 13:1
14 [I]Or, *wild figs* [a]1Kgs. 20:35; 2Kgs. 2:5; 4:38; 6:1 [b]Amos 1:1; Zech. 13:5
15 [I]Hebr. *from behind*
16 [a]Ezek. 21:2; Mic. 2:6
17 [a]Jer. 28:12; 29:21, 25, 31, 32 [b]Isa. 13:16; Lam. 5:11; Hos. 4:13; Zech. 14:2

2 [a]Ezek. 7:2 [b]Amos 7:8
3 [I]Hebr. *shall howl* [II]Hebr. *be silent* [a]Amos 5:33 [b]Amos 6:9, 10
4 [a]Ps. 14:4; Prov. 30:14
5 [I]Or, *month* [II]Hebr. *open* [III]Hebr. *perverting the balances of deceit* [a]Neh. 13:15, 16 [b]Mic. 6:10, 11 [c]Hos. 12:7
6 [a]Amos 2:6
7 [a]Amos 6:8 [b]Hos. 8:13; 9:9
8 [a]Hos. 4:3 [b]Amos 9:5
9 [a]Job 5:14; Isa. 13:10; 59:9, 10; Jer. 15:9; Mic. 3:6
10 [a]Isa. 15:2, 3; Jer. 48:37; Ezek. 7:18; 27:31 [b]Jer. 6:26; Zech. 12:10
11 [a]1Sam. 3:1; Ps. 74:9; Ezek. 7:26
14 [I]Hebr. *way:* Acts 9:2; 18:25; 19:9, 23; 24:14 [a]Hos. 4:15 [b]Deut. 9:21

8:1–3 The image of the "basket of summer fruit" shows that Israel is ripe for judgment.

8:11, 12 Many see this as an eschatological reference because of the language in the preceding verses. It does not imply a "famine" of words to hear, but a lack of those who truly have a message from God. This could be said of the situation in the world today—many voices claim to speak for God, but few are faithful to His Word.

[c]of Beer–sheba liveth;[2416] even they shall fall,[5307] and never rise up again.

Israel Can't Escape the LORD

9 I saw[7200] the Lord[136] standing[5324] upon the altar:[4196] and he said,[559] Smite[5221] the [I]lintel[3730] of the door, that the posts may shake:[7493] and [II][a]cut[1214] them in the head,[7218] all of them; and I will slay[2026] the last[319] of them with the sword:[2719] [b]he that fleeth of them shall not flee away, and he that escapeth of them shall not be delivered.

2 [a]Though they dig into hell,[7585] thence shall mine hand[3027] take them; [b]though they climb up[5927] to heaven,[8064] thence will I bring them down:

3 And though they hide themselves in the top[7218] of Carmel, I will search[2664] and take them out thence; and though they be hid from my sight in the bottom of the sea, thence will I command[6680] the serpent,[5175] and he shall bite them:

4 And though they go into captivity[7628] before their enemies, [a]thence will I command the sword, and it shall slay[2026] them: and [b]I will set[7760] mine eyes upon them for evil,[7451] and not for good.[2896]

5 And the Lord GOD of hosts[6635] *is* he that toucheth[5060] the land,[776] and it shall [a]melt, [b]and all that dwell therein shall mourn: and it shall rise up[5927] wholly like a flood; and shall be drowned, as *by* the flood of Egypt.

6 *It is* he that buildeth his [I][a]stories in the heaven, and hath founded[3245] his [II]troop in the earth; he that [b]calleth[7121] for the waters of the sea, and poureth them out[8210] upon the face of the earth: [c]The LORD *is* his name.

7 *Are* ye not as children[1121] of the Ethiopians unto me, O children of Israel? saith the LORD. Have not I brought up[5927] Israel out of the land of Egypt? and the [a]Philistines from [b]Caphtor, and the Syrians from [c]Kir?

8 Behold, [a]the eyes of the Lord GOD *are* upon the sinful[2403] kingdom,[4467] and I [b]will destroy[8045] it from off the face of the earth;[127] saving that I will not utterly destroy the house[1004] of Jacob, saith the LORD.

9 For, lo, I will command, and I will [I]sift[5128] the house of Israel among all nations,[1471] like as *corn* is sifted in a sieve, yet shall not the least [II]grain fall[5307] upon the earth.

10 All the sinners[2400] of my people[5971] shall die[4191] by the sword, [a]which say, The evil shall not overtake[5066] nor prevent us.

Israel Will Be Brought Back

11 [a]In that day[3117] will I raise up the tabernacle[5521] of David that is fallen, and [I]close up the breaches thereof; and I will raise up his ruins, and I will build it as in the days of old:[5769]

12 [a]That they may possess[3423] the remnant[7611] of [b]Edom, and of all the heathen,[1471] [I]which are called by my name, saith the LORD that doeth[6213] this.

13 Behold, [a]the days come, saith the LORD, that the plowman shall overtake[5066] the reaper, and the treader of grapes him that [I]soweth seed;[2233] [b]and the mountains shall drop[5197] [II]sweet wine, and all the hills shall melt.

14 [a]And I will bring again[7725] the captivity[7622] of my people of Israel, and

14 [c]Amos 5:5;

1 [I]Or, *chapiter, or, knop* [II]Or, *wound them* [a]Ps. 68:21; Hab. 3:13 [b]Amos 2:14

2 [a]Ps. 139:8-14 [b]Job 20:6; Jer. 51:53; Obad. 1:4

4 [a]Lev. 26:33; Deut. 28:65; Ezek. 5:12 [b]Lev. 17:10; Jer. 44:11

5 [a]Mic. 1:4 [b]Amos 8:8

6 [I]Or, *spheres* [II]Hebr. *ascensions* [III]Or, *bundle* [a]Ps. 104:3, 13 [b]Amos 5:8 [c]Amos 4:13

7 [a]Jer. 47:4 [b]Deut. 2:23; Jer. 47:4 [c]Amos 1:5

8 [a]Amos 9:4 [b]Jer. 30:11; 31:35, 36; Obad. 1:16, 17

9 [I]Hebr. *cause to move* [II]Hebr. *stone*

10 [a]Amos 6:3

11 [I]Hebr. *hedge, or, wall* [a]Acts 15:16, 17

12 [I]Hebr. *upon who my name is called* [a]Obad. 1:19 [b]Num. 24:18

13 [I]Hebr. *draweth forth* [II]Or, *new wine* [a]Lev. 26:5 [b]Joel 3:18

14 [a]Jer. 30:3

9:9, 10 Amos is using the illustration of a "sieve" to show how God would sift out every evil thing that had been committed, and not one deed would pass through this judgment. The people were proud of their sin (v. 10). What they did not realize, however, was that God would ultimately judge them for all their sin.

9:11, 12 This passage speaks of "the remnant of Edom," which refers to a future time when God would deal directly with the Gentiles and bring to them salvation. James, who was the leader of the church in Jerusalem, quoted these verses to show how Amos' prophecy was being fulfilled in the great number of Gentiles who were believing on Christ (Acts 15:16, 17).

[b]they shall build the <u>waste</u>[8074] cities, and inhabit *them*; and they shall plant vineyards, and drink the wine thereof; they <u>shall</u> also <u>make</u>[6213] gardens, and eat the fruit of them.

14 [b]Isa. 61:4; 65:21; Ezek. 36:33-36
15 [a]Isa. 60:21; Jer. 32:41; Ezek. 34:28; Joel 3:20

15 And I will plant them upon their <u>land</u>,[127] and [a]they <u>shall</u> no more <u>be pulled up</u>[5428] out of their land which I have given them, saith the LORD thy <u>God</u>.[430]

The Book of OBADIAH

Obadiah is the shortest book in the Old Testament. The name Obadiah means "servant or worshiper of the Lord," and belonged to thirteen men in the Old Testament.

The evidence of the text best supports an early date for the prophecy. Since Edom is mentioned as having more than one ally (cf. Obad. 1:7, 11), the most likely time for this prophecy is during the reign of Jehoram (ca. 852–841 B.C.) when Jerusalem was plundered by the Philistines and Arabians (2 Chr. 21:16–19). The book definitely appears to have been written before Jeremiah (see Jer. 49:7–22).

This entire prophecy is a poem. The reader must be careful in his interpretation of this book to consider the Hebrew parallelism (see introduction to Job). This particular style of poetry reveals Obadiah's intense emotional involvement in what God had revealed.

The Edomites were a thorn in Israel's side, though they enjoyed special protection under the Law (see note on Gen. 27:39, 40). Herod the Great, who lived in New Testament times, was an Idumaean (a descendant of the Edomites). After Jerusalem's fall in A.D. 70, the Edomites vanish from history. Some suggest, however, that there will be a future resurgence of the Edomites.

Edom Will Be Humbled

THE vision[2377] of Obadiah. Thus saith the Lord[136] God [a]concerning Edom; [b]We have heard[8085] a rumour8052 from the LORD, and an ambassador6735 is sent among the heathen,[1471] Arise ye, and let us rise up against her in battle.

2 Behold, I have made thee small among the heathen: thou art greatly despised.

3 The pride[2087] of thine heart[3820] hath deceived thee, thou that dwellest[7931] in the clefts [a]of the rock, whose habitation *is* high; [b]that saith in his heart, Who shall bring me down to the ground?[776]

4 [a]Though thou exalt *thyself* as the eagle, and though thou [b]set[7760] thy nest among the stars, thence will I bring thee down, saith5002 the LORD.

5 If [a]thieves came to thee, if robbers[7703] by night, (how art thou cut off[1820]) would they not have stolen till they had enough? if the grapegatherers came to thee, [b]would they not leave[7604] [I]*some* grapes?

6 How are *the things* of Esau searched out2664 *how* are his hidden things sought up[1158]

7 All the men[582] of thy confederacy[1285] have brought thee *even* to the border: [I][a]the men that were at peace[7965] with thee have deceived thee, *and* prevailed against thee; [II]*they that eat* thy bread have laid[7760] a wound under thee: [b]*there is* none understanding [III]in him.

8 [a]Shall[6] I not in that day,[3117] saith the LORD, even destroy[6] the wise[2450] *men* out of Edom, and understanding out of the mount of Esau?

9 And thy [a]mighty *men,* O [b]Teman, shall be dismayed,[2865] to the end that every one of the mount of Esau may be cut off[3772] by slaughter.

10 For *thy* [a]violence[2555] against thy brother[251] Jacob shame[955] shall cover[3680] thee, and [b]thou shalt be cut off for ever.[5769]

1 [a]Isa. 21:11; 34:5; Ezek. 25:12-14; Joel 3:19; Mal. 1:3 [b]Jer. 49:14-20
3 [a]2Kgs. 14:7 [b]Isa. 14:13-15; Rev. 18:7
4 [a]Job 20:6; Jer. 49:16; 51:53; Amos 9:2 [b]Hab. 2:9
5 [I]Or, *gleanings* [a]Jer. 49:9 [b]Deut. 24:21; Isa. 17:6; 24:13
7 [I]Hebr. *the men of thy peace* [II]Hebr. the men *of thy bread* [III]Or, *of it* [a]Jer. 38:22 [b]Isa. 19:11, 12
8 [a]Job 5:12, 13; Isa. 29:14; Jer. 49:7
9 [a]Ps. 76:5; Amos 2:16 [b]Jer. 49:7
10 [a]Gen. 27:41; Ps. 137:7; Ezek. 25:12; 35:5; Amos 1:11 [b]Ezek. 35:9; Mal. 1:4

1:3 The word translated "rock" is from the Hebrew word *sela'* (5553), and is the name of the Edomite capital. The use of this word emphasizes the Edomites' feeling of security because of the narrow canyons that controlled access to their land.

1:10–14 These verses may not refer to one specific instance, but rather to a prophecy of future judgments of God on Edom, because of the evil he committed against his brother, Israel.

11 In the day that thou stoodest on the other side, in the day that the strangers[2114] [I]carried away captive[7617] his forces,[2428] and foreigners[5237] entered into his gates, and [a]cast lots upon Jerusalem, even thou *wast* as one of them.

12 But [I]thou shouldest not have [a]looked[7200] on [b]the day of thy brother in the day that he became a stranger;[5235] neither shouldest thou have [c]rejoiced over the children[1121] of Judah in the day of their destruction;[6] neither shouldest thou have [II]spoken[6310] proudly in the day of distress.

13 Thou shouldest not have entered into the gate of my people[5971] in the day of their calamity;[343] yea, thou shouldest not have looked on their affliction[7451] in the day of their calamity, nor have laid *hands* on their [I]substance[2428] in the day of their calamity;

14 Neither shouldest thou have stood in the crossway, to cut off those of his that did escape; neither shouldest thou have [I][a]delivered up those of his that did remain[8300] in the day of distress.

Israel Will Win!

🔑 15 [a]For the day[3117] of the LORD *is* near upon all the heathen: [b]as thou hast done, it shall be done[6213] unto thee: thy reward shall return[7725] upon thine own head.[7218]

16 [a]For as ye have drunk upon my holy[6944] mountain, *so* shall all the heathen drink continually,[8548] yea, they shall drink, and they shall [I]swallow down, and they shall be as though they had not been.

🔑 17 [a]But upon mount Zion [b]shall be [I]deliverance,[6413] and [II][c]there shall be holiness;[6944] and the house[1004] of Jacob shall possess[3423] their possessions.

18 And the house of Jacob [a]shall be a fire, and the house of Joseph a flame, and the house of Esau for stubble, and they shall kindle in them, and devour them; and there shall not be *any* remaining of the house of Esau; for the LORD hath spoken[1696] it.

19 And *they of* the south [a]shall possess the mount of Esau; [b]and *they of* the plain[8219] the Philistines: and they shall possess the fields[7704] of Ephraim, and the fields of Samaria: and Benjamin *shall possess* Gilead.

20 And the captivity[1546] of this host[2426] of the children of Israel *shall possess* that of the Canaanites, *even* [a]unto Zarephath; and the captivity of Jerusalem, [I]which *is* in Sepharad, [b]shall possess the cities of the south.[5045]

🔑 21 And [a]saviours[3467] shall come up[5927] on mount Zion to judge[8199] the mount of Esau; and the [b]kingdom shall be the LORD's.

11 [I]Or, *carried away his substance* [a]Joel 3:3; Nah. 3:10
12 [I]Or, *do not behold* [II]Hebr. *magnified thy mouth* [a]Ps. 22:17; 54:7; 59:10; Mic. 4:11; 7:10 [b]Ps. 37:13; 137:7 [c]Job 31:29; Prov. 17:5; 24:17, 18; Mic. 7:8
13 [I]Or, *forces*
14 [I]Or, *shut up* [a]Ps. 31:8
15 [a]Ezek. 30:3; Joel 3:14 [b]Ezek. 35:15; Hab. 2:8
16 [I]Or, *sup up* [a]Jer. 25:28, 29; 49:12; Joel 3:17; 1Pet. 4:17
17 [I]Or, *they that escape* [II]Or, *it shall be holy* [a]Joel 2:32 [b]Amos 9:8 [c]Joel 3:17
18 [a]Isa. 10:17; Zech. 12:6
19 [a]Amos 9:12 [b]Zeph. 2:7
20 [I]Or, shall possess *that which is in Sepharad* [a]1Kgs. 17:9, 10 [b]Jer. 32:44
21 [a]1Tim. 4:16; James 5:20 [b]Ps. 22:28; Dan. 2:44; 7:14, 27; Zech. 14:9; Luke 1:33; Rev. 11:15; 19:6

🔑 **1:15, 16** See note on Zephaniah 1:7 concerning the "Day of the LORD." Edom represents all gentile opposition to God's people. In Amos, the "Day of the LORD" is seen as a general reference to a time when Israel's sin will be judged (Amos 5:18–20, see note). However, it is also presented as a time for judgment upon the Gentiles. Some would suggest that Israel understood the "Day of the LORD" to be a day of deliverance, forgetting their need to be brought into a right relationship with God.

🔑 **1:17–20** The Book of Obadiah concludes with the millennial blessing to the people of Israel. At this time the tables will be turned, and Edom's persecution of Israel will be returned on them. God says that Israel will devour Edom "like a fire" as the Edomites are judged for the evil that they committed against God's people (v. 18, cf. Zech. 12:6). Furthermore, God speaks of a future time when Israel will actually occupy the full extent of its promised land, and the Edomites will be removed from the land that they seized from Israel after the Babylonian Captivity began in 586 B.C. (vv. 19, 20).

🔑 **1:21** In this verse the word translated "saviours" could better be translated "deliverers," referring to the deliverance of the land by the restored exiles from the Babylonian Captivity. Also, the term "judge" used here is the same word used to describe how the judges governed the people (Judg. 2:16). In other words, the land will be delivered and ruled.

The Book of

JONAH

The name Jonah means "dove." In 2 Kings 14:25, it is stated that Jonah was from Gath-hepher, about two miles northeast of Nazareth, and that he gave a prophecy that was fulfilled by Jeroboam II (793–752 B.C.). The Book of Jonah is unique in the Old Testament in that the entire prophecy is written in the third person. God commanded Jonah to prophesy against Nineveh, the capital of Assyria, at a time when the power of the Assyrian Empire was resurgent and posed a threat to Israel. For this reason Jonah was unwilling to speak to Nineveh. He hoped that God would destroy these people.

The book was written after Jonah returned from his mission, and had time to reflect on its significance. Some have called the Book of Jonah the "Acts of the Old Testament," because it graphically demonstrates that God is willing to have mercy on all who seek Him in humility and sincerity. The repentance of the people of Ninevah postponed the destruction of their city for roughly 150 years (until 612 B.C.)

Many critics dismiss the story of Jonah as a "myth" or "fable" because they reject the miraculous element of the great fish. This simply shows their inability to comprehend the supernatural nature of the God of the Bible. For one who can stay the sun or divide the Red Sea, controlling one fish is not a great problem. Jesus treated the book as a historical fact, comparing Jonah's time in the belly of the fish to His own time in the tomb (Matt. 12:40). Moreover, He affirmed that the repentance of the Ninevites was genuine and contrasted their reaction to the indifference of the scribes and Pharisees (Matt. 12:41; Luke 11:32).

Jonah Runs Away

1 Now the word[1697] of the LORD came
unto [1a]Jonah the son[1121] of Amittai,
saying,[559]

🔑2 Arise, go to Nineveh, that [a]great
city, and cry[7121] against it; for [b]their
wickedness[7451] is come up[5927] before me.

1 [a]2Kgs. 14:25; Matt. 12:39
2 [a]Gen. 10:11, 12; Jon. 3:2, 3; 4:11 [b]Gen. 18:20, 21; Ezra 9:6; James 5:4; Rev. 18:5
3 [a]Jon. 4:2 [b]Josh. 19:46; 2Chr. 2:16; Acts 9:36

🔑3 But Jonah [a]rose up to flee[1272] unto
Tarshish from the presence of the LORD,
and went down to [b]Joppa; and he found
a ship going to Tarshish: so he paid the
fare thereof, and went down into it, to go
with them unto Tarshish [c]from the presence of the LORD.

[c]Gen. 4:16; Job 1:12; 2:7

🔑 **1:2** Nineveh was the capital of the Assyrian Empire at various times during its history, including the time of Jonah's visit in the eighth century B.C. Within a few decades, Assyria became dominant in the Land of Palestine, Israel was carried into exile (722 B.C.), and Judah was nearly conquered (701 B.C.). This domination proved to be the peak of Assyrian power. By 612 B.C., the great city of Nineveh was in ruins, and by 609 B.C., the Assyrian Empire had vanished forever. Both Zephaniah (Zeph. 2:13) and Nahum (Nah. 3:5–7) prophesied this final destruction of Nineveh.

🔑 **1:3** Tarshish was a Phoenician mining town (located in modern day Spain) that was situated on the western extremity of the trade routes of the "ships of Tyre" (see note on 1 Kgs. 10:22). Nineveh was to the east of Israel. In other words, Jonah was going as far as he could in the opposite direction from the place God had sent him. Note the repeated use of "went down" in this verse, a phrase used in Jonah 2:6 to describe actions against God's leading or commands.

Also in this verse, the phrase "from the presence of the LORD" refers to Jonah's attempt to escape from the will of God. This does not mean that Jonah thought that God could not find him in Tarshish; but he may have felt that in leaving the place where God had called him, God would no longer desire to have him go to Nineveh. It is often the misconception of God's people today that there are some places where God is more evident than others. In the same manner, they feel that if they go far enough away from these places of God's "presence," He will no longer seek to use them.

4 But [a]the LORD [I]sent out a great wind[7307] into the sea, and there was a mighty tempest in the sea, so that the ship was [II]like[2803] to be broken.[7665]

5 Then the mariners were afraid,[3372] and cried[2199] every man[376] unto his god,[430] and [a]cast forth the wares[3627] that *were* in the ship into the sea, to lighten[7043] *it* of them. But Jonah was gone down [b]into the sides of the ship; and he lay, and was fast asleep.

6 So the shipmaster came[7126] to him, and said[559] unto him, What meanest thou, O sleeper? arise, [a]call[7121] upon thy God,[430] [b]if so be that God will think upon us, that we perish[6] not.

7 And they said every one to his fellow,[7453] Come, and let us [a]cast[5307] lots, that we may know[3045] for whose cause this evil[7451] *is* upon us. So they cast lots, and the lot fell[5307] upon Jonah.

8 Then said they unto him, [a]Tell[5046] us, we pray thee, for whose cause this evil *is* upon us; What *is* thine occupation?[4399] and whence comest thou? what *is* thy country?[776] and of what people[5971] *art* thou?

9 And he said unto them, I *am* an Hebrew; and I fear[3373] [I]the LORD,[3068] the God[430] of heaven,[8064] [a]which hath made[6213] the sea and the dry[3004] *land.*

10 Then were the men[582] [I]exceedingly afraid, and said unto him, Why hast thou done this? For the men knew[3045] that he fled from the presence of the LORD, because he had told them.

11 Then said they unto him, What shall we do[6213] unto thee, that the sea [I]may be calm unto us? for the sea [II]wrought, and was tempestuous.

12 And he said unto them, [a]Take me up,[5375] and cast me forth into the sea; so shall the sea be calm unto you: for I know that for my sake this great tempest *is* upon you.

13 Nevertheless the men [I]rowed hard to bring[7725] *it* to the land;[3004] [a]but they could not: for the sea wrought,[1980] and was tempestuous against them.

14 Wherefore they cried[7121] unto the LORD, and said, We beseech thee,[577] O LORD, we beseech thee, let us not perish[6] for this man's[376] life,[5315] and [a]lay not upon us innocent[5355] blood:[1818] for thou, O LORD, [b]hast done as it pleased[2654] thee.

15 So they took up Jonah, and cast him forth into the sea: [a]and the sea [I]ceased from her raging.[2197]

🔑 16 Then the men [a]feared[3372] the LORD exceedingly, and [I]offered[2076] a sacrifice[2077] unto the LORD, and made[5087] vows.[5088]

🔑 17 Now the LORD had prepared[4487] a great fish[1709] to swallow up[1104] Jonah. And [a]Jonah was in the [I]belly[4578] of the fish three days[3117] and three nights.

Jonah Is Thankful

2 🔑Then Jonah prayed[6419] unto the LORD his God[430] out of the fish's belly,

4 [I]Hebr. *cast forth* [II]Hebr. *thought to be broken* [a]Ps. 107:25

5 [a]Acts 27:18, 19, 38 [b]1Sam. 24:3

6 [a]Ps. 107:28 [b]Joel 2:14

7 [a]Josh. 7:14, 16; 1Sam. 10:20, 21; 14:41, 42; Prov. 16:33; Acts 1:26

8 [a]Josh. 7:19; 1Sam. 14:43

9 [I]Or, *JEHOVAH* [a]Ps. 146:6; Acts 17:24

10 [I]Hebr. *with great fear*

11 [I]Hebr. *may be silent from us* [II]Or, *grew more and more tempestuous* [III]Hebr. *went*

12 [a]John 11:50

13 [I]Hebr. *digged* [a]Prov. 21:30

14 [a]Deut. 21:8 [b]Ps. 115:3

15 [I]Hebr. *stood* [a]Ps. 89:9; Luke 8:24

16 [I]Hebr. *sacrificed a sacrifice unto the LORD and vowed vows* [a]Mark 4:41; Acts 5:11

17 [I]Hebr. *bowels* [a]Matt. 12:40; 16:4; Luke 11:30

🔑 **1:16** It is not known for certain whether these men were actually saved. Some suggest that the sacrifice of thanksgiving could have been offered to God in the same way that they offered sacrifices to all the other gods that they worshiped (Jon. 1:5). Others believe that the phrase "the men feared the LORD exceedingly" reflects not only the fear they felt, but also their joy because their lives had been spared.

🔑 **1:17** Throughout the Book of Jonah, God is said to have "prepared" things—a fish, a gourd, a worm, and a wind—to carry out His purposes in dealing with Jonah. The translation of the Hebrew word *mānāh* (4487), "prepared," in this context is misleading because it seems to imply that God created the fish instantly at that time. Rather, He just used things that were already in existence. Some would go further to say that God had created this fish for the sole purpose of using it to reprove Jonah. There is nothing in the Hebrew text that speaks to whether this fish was specially created.

🔑 **2:1–9** Jonah's prayer is a great affirmation of God's faithfulness and availability. Jonah realized that nothing could separate one of God's own from Him, and no situation could ever prevent a sincere prayer from being heard by God (cf. Rom. 8:33–35; James 5:16).

2 And said, I [a]cried[7121] [I]by reason of mine affliction6869 unto the LORD, [b]and he heard me; out of the belly[990] of [II][c]hell[7585] cried I, *and* thou heardest[8085] my voice.

3 [a]For thou hadst cast me into the deep, in the [I]midst3824 of the seas; and the floods compassed me about: [b]all thy billows and thy waves passed over[5674] me.

4 [a]Then I said, I am cast out of thy sight; yet I will look again [b]toward thy holy[6944] temple.[1964]

5 The [a]waters compassed me about, *even* to the soul:[5315] the depth closed me round about, the weeds were wrapped[2280] about my head.[7218]

6 I went down to the [I]bottoms of the mountains; the earth[776] with her bars *was* about me for ever:[5769] yet hast thou brought up[5927] my life[2416] [a]from [II]corruption,[7845] O LORD my God.

7 When my soul fainted within me I remembered[2142] the LORD: [a]and my prayer[8605] came in unto thee, into thine holy temple.

8 They that observe[8104] [a]lying[7723] vanities forsake[5800] their own mercy.[2617]

2 [I]Or, *out of mine affliction* [II]Or, *the grave* [a]Ps. 120:1; 130:1; 142:1; Lam. 3:55, 56 [b]Ps. 65:2 [c]Isa. 14:9

3 [I]Hebr. *heart* [a]Ps. 88:6 [b]Ps. 42:7

4 [a]Ps. 31:22 [b]1Kgs. 8:38

5 [a]Ps. 69:1; Lam. 3:54

6 [I]Hebr. *cuttings off* [II]Or, *the pit* [a]Ps. 16:10

7 [a]Ps. 18:6

8 [a]2Kgs. 17:15; Ps. 31:6; Jer. 10:8; 16:19

9 [a]Ps. 50:14, 23; 116:17, 18; Hos. 14:2; Heb. 13:15 [b]Ps. 3:8

3 [I]Hebr. *of God* [a]Gen. 30:8; Ps. 36:6; 80:10

4 [a]Deut. 18:22

5 [a]Matt. 12:41; Luke 11:32

9 But I will [a]sacrifice unto thee with the voice of thanksgiving;[8426] I will pay *that* that I have vowed.[5087] [b]Salvation[3444] *is* of the LORD.

10 And the LORD spake[559] unto the fish,[1709] and it vomited out Jonah upon the dry[3004] *land.*

Jonah Finally Obeys

3 And the word of the LORD came unto Jonah the second time, saying,

2 Arise, go unto Nineveh, that great city, and preach[7121] unto it the preaching that I bid thee.

🔑 3 So Jonah arose, and went unto Nineveh, according to the word[1697] of the LORD. Now Nineveh was an [I][a]exceeding[430] great city of three days'[3117] journey.

4 And Jonah began to enter into the city a day's journey, and [a]he cried,[7121] and said,[559] Yet forty days, and Nineveh shall be overthrown.[2015]

🔑 5 So the people[582] of Nineveh [a]believed[539] God,[430] and proclaimed[7121] a fast, and put on sackcloth, from the

🔑 **3:3** Scholars do not agree on what "a three days' journey" signifies. The most sensible meaning was that there was a group of three cities, Nineveh, Khorsabad, and Nimrud, which made up the "Nineveh triangle" where Jonah was supposed to preach. The name Nineveh was given because that would be the final and greatest of the three cities of Assyria, and it was against Nineveh that God's judgment would finally be carried out. In addition, Nineveh was in the center of the three cities. Quite possibly the king was actually residing at Khorsabad (Dur-Sharrukin), as this city was also the royal capital of Assyria at different times.

🔑 **3:5–9** Some suggest that the actions of the Ninevites demonstrated true repentance. The middle eastern custom of putting on sackcloth and ashes (Jon. 3:5, 6) was a sign of mourning. The calling of a fast showed their total dedication and commitment to be right before God. This was emphasized by the fact that they caused the animals to fast as well. Jonah's message from God had given them no reason to hope that He would withhold the punishment mentioned in verse four. They could only trust in the mercy of God (cf. Jon. 4:2).

Others feel that this was not necessarily true repentance. It may be similar to what the mariners expressed in their sacrifice to God (see note on Jon. 1:16). Those who hold to this view support the idea that the Ninevites were responding purely out of fear of their destruction.

Many have wondered why the Assyrians would respond to a Jewish prophet. The reason for this, according to rabbinic traditions, is that Nineveh had heard of Jonah's miraculous deliverance from the belly of the fish. This is very probable, since Jesus said that Jonah was a "sign" (miracle) to the men of Nineveh. He further explained that the "sign of Jonah" was the only sign that would be given the nation of Israel concerning Himself, just as Jonah spent three days and nights in the belly of the fish, He Himself would spend three days and nights in the "heart of the earth" or the grave (Matt. 12:39–41; Luke 11:29, 30, 32). Unlike the Ninevites, the Jews refused to repent even though Christ performed many signs and miracles (John 20:30, 31).

greatest of them even to the least of
them.
6 For word came[5060] unto the king
of Nineveh, and he arose from his
throne,[3678] and he laid[5674] his robe from
him, and covered[3680] *him* with sackcloth,
[a]and sat in ashes.
7 [a]And he caused *it* to be proclaimed[2199] and [I]published[559] through
Nineveh by the decree[2940] of the king
and his [II]nobles, saying, Let neither
man[120] nor beast, herd nor flock, taste
any thing: let them not feed, nor drink
water:
8 But let man and beast be covered[3680] with sackcloth, and cry[7121]
mightily[2394] unto God: yea, [a]let them
turn[7725] every one[376] from his evil[7451]
way,[1870] and from [b]the violence[2555] that
is in their hands.[3709]
9 [a]Who can tell[3045] *if* God will turn
and repent,[5162] and turn away[7725] from
his fierce anger,[639] that we perish[6] not?
🗝 10 [a]And God saw their works, that
they turned from their evil way; and God
repented of the evil, that he had said[1696]
that he would do[6213] unto them; and he
did *it* not.

Jonah Is Angry

4 But it displeased Jonah exceedingly,
and he was very angry.[2734]
2 And he prayed[6419] unto the LORD,
and said, I pray thee,[577] O LORD, *was* not
this my saying,[1697] when I was yet in
my country?[127] Therefore I [a]fled[1272] before unto Tarshish: for I knew[3045] that
thou *art* a [b]gracious[2587] God,[410] and merciful, slow[750] to anger,[639] and of great
kindness,[2617] and repentest[5162] thee of
the evil.[7451]
3 [a]Therefore now, O LORD, take, I beseech thee, my life[5315] from me; for [b]*it is*
better[2896] for me to die[4194] than to
live.[2416]
4 Then said the LORD, [I]Doest thou
well[3190] to be angry?[2734]
5 So Jonah went out of the city, and
sat on the east side of the city, and there
made[6213] him a booth,[5521] and sat under
it in the shadow, till he might see what
would become of the city.
🗝 6 And the LORD God[430] prepared[4487]
a gourd, and made *it* to come up[5927] over
Jonah, that it might be a shadow over his
head,[7218] to deliver[5337] him from his
grief.[7451] So Jonah [I]was exceeding glad of
the gourd.
7 But God prepared a worm when
the morning rose[5927] the next day, and
it smote[5221] the gourd that it withered.[3001]
8 And it came to pass, when the sun
did arise, that God prepared a [I]vehe-
ment[2759] east wind;[7307] and the sun
beat[5221] upon the head of Jonah, that he
fainted, and wished[7592] in himself to
die,[4191] and said, [a]*It is* better for me to
die than to live.
🗝 9 And God said to Jonah, [I]Doest thou
well to be angry for the gourd? And he
said, [II]I do well to be angry, *even* unto
death.

6 [a]Job 2:8
7 [I]Hebr. *said* [II]Hebr. *great men* [a]2Chr. 20:3; Joel 2:15
8 [a]Isa. 58:6 [b]Isa. 59:6
9 [a]2Sam. 12:22; Joel 2:14
10 [a]Jer. 18:8; Amos 7:3, 6
2 [a]Jon. 1:3 [b]Ex. 34:6; Ps. 86:5; Joel 2:13
3 [a]1Kgs. 19:4 [b]Jon. 4:8
4 [I]Or, *Art thou greatly angry*
6 [I]Hebr. *rejoiced with great joy*
8 [I]Or, *silent* [a]Jon. 4:3
9 [I]Or, *Art thou greatly angry* [II]Or, *I am greatly angry*

🗝 **3:10** God is immutable (He never changes, cf. Mal. 3:6). However, God interacts with men, and men do change. In this instance, God's ultimate intention towards Nineveh did not change—the city was later destroyed. Nevertheless, God saw that their actions were a response to Jonah's message of the city's impending destruction. This verse is one of great hope for God's people today. If God is able to make provision for these people of Nineveh by suspending His judgment on them for over one hundred years, God is surely able to grant mercy to a believer today. The phrase translated "repented of the evil" implies that God "temporarily removed the calamity" that He had promised to the city of Nineveh. See note on Amos 3:6.

🗝 **4:6, 9, 10** Jonah had made the gourd that God had given to him into an idol. The fact that he was angered by its being destroyed revealed that he was just concerned for himself. God's people today do this very thing, in that they seek pleasure in the material things of the world. God wants His people to focus their attention on Him and the accomplishment of His will (Col. 4:1, 2). As He did in the case of Jonah, God may remove all those material things that keep His people from maintaining a proper relationship with Him.

10 Then said the LORD, Thou hast
[I]had pity2347 on the gourd, for the which
thou hast not laboured, neither madest it
grow; which [II]came up in a night, and
perished[6] in a night:

🔑 11 And should not I spare2347 Nineveh, [a]that great city, wherein are more than
sixscore thousand persons[120] [b]that cannot
discern[3045] between their right hand and
their left hand; and *also* much [c]cattle?

10 [I]Or, *spared* [II]Hebr. *was the son of the night*

11 [a]Ezek. 1:2; 3:2, 3 [b]Deut. 1:39 [c]Ps. 36:6; 145:9

🔑 **4:11** By not including Jonah's response to God's question in this verse, the book ends with an effective challenge to each reader to consider whether their priorities are in conflict with God's priorities. Some would suggest that the phrase "discern between their right hand and their left hand" refers to the spiritual ignorance of the pagan inhabitants of Nineveh. Others say that the phrase refers to young children who were not old enough to make rational decisions. However, the latter seems unlikely in light of the fact that the population of the city would be unusually large for those times if the 120,000 included only children.

The Book of
MICAH

The name Micah means "who is like Jehovah?" He apparently makes a word play on this in verse eighteen of chapter seven where he asks, "Who is a God like unto thee?" There is none so just as the King of Kings, and yet none so merciful, who pardons "the remnant of his heritage."

Micah was a contemporary of Isaiah and both ministered in the Southern Kingdom (Judah). His ministry, however, began somewhat later than Isaiah's and may have ended earlier. Their social standings were quite different in that Isaiah was a nobleman who prophesied in the king's court and Micah was of humble origin and spoke to the common people. Nevertheless, the prophecies of both were of great importance. Although Micah came from the insignificant town of Moresheth, a village bordering on the Philistine territory (also called Moresheth-gath, Mic. 1:14), he foretold the fall of the capital cities of Judah and Israel and saw beyond the current Assyrian crisis to the Babylonian captivity. Furthermore, despite his seeming unimportance in Israel, he was exclusively chosen by God to reveal the birthplace of the Messiah (Mic. 5:2).

The kings under whose reigns Micah ministered (Mic. 1:1) ruled from 752–697 B.C. Like Amos, he spoke out strongly against immorality, social injustices, and the oppression of the poor by the rich (Mic. 2:1, 2, 8, 9; 3:2, 3, 11; 6:10–12). The key word in Micah is "hear." This indicates that God wanted Judah to be attentive to Micah's message.

The LORD Will Judge

1 🗝The word[1697] of the LORD that
came to [a]Micah the Morasthite in the
days[3117] of Jotham, Ahaz, *and* Hezekiah,
kings of Judah, [b]which he saw[2372] concerning Samaria and Jerusalem.
🗝2 [I]Hear,[8085] all ye people;[5971] [a]hear-
ken,[7181] O earth,[776] and [II]all that therein
is: and let the Lord[136] GOD [b]be witness
against you, the LORD from [c]his holy[6944]
temple.[1964]
3 For, behold, [a]the LORD cometh forth
out of his [b]place, and will come down,
and tread upon the [c]high places[1116] of
the earth.
4 And [a]the mountains shall be molten under him, and the valleys shall be
cleft, as wax before the fire, *and* as the
waters *that are* poured down[5064] [I]a steep
place.
5 For the transgression[6588] of Jacob
is all this, and for the sins[2403] of the
house[1004] of Israel. What *is* the transgression of Jacob? *is it* not Samaria? and
what *are* the high places of Judah? *are
they* not Jerusalem?
6 Therefore I will make[7760] Samaria
[a]as an heap[5856] of the field,[7704] *and* as
plantings of a vineyard: and I will pour
down the stones thereof into the valley,
and I will [b]discover[1540] the foundations[3247] thereof.
7 And all the graven images[6456]

1 [a]Jer. 26:18 [b]Amos 1:1
2 [I]Hebr. *Hear, ye people, all of them* [II]Hebr. *the fullness thereof* [a]Deut. 32:1; Isa. 1:2 [b]Ps. 50:7; Mal. 3:5 [c]Ps. 11:4; Jon. 2:7; Hab. 2:20
3 [a]Isa. 26:21 [b]Ps. 115:3 [c]Deut. 32:13; 33:29; Amos 4:13
4 [I]Hebr. *a descent* [a]Judg. 5:5; Ps. 97:5; Isa. 64:1-3; Amos 9:5; Hab. 3:6,10
6 [a]2Kgs. 19:25; Mic. 3:12 [b]Ezek. 13:14

🗝 **1:1** The city of Moresheth was located about twenty miles southwest of Jerusalem, and seventeen miles west of Tekoa, where Amos lived. Like several other prophets, Micah describes his messages from God as something he saw (e.g., Ezekiel, Daniel). This may reflect the total involvement of the prophet's physical senses with the message God was giving to him rather than an actual vision (cf. Mic. 1:8, and Dan. 7:28; 8:27). The messages from God were experienced, not just received.
🗝 **1:2–7** Since Micah was very concerned about social unrighteousness, it is not surprising that his prophecy was addressed to Samaria and Jerusalem (Mic. 1:1, 5). These cities were inhabited by the wealthiest and most privileged classes of society, and there was much inhumanity being committed against the less fortunate groups of people.

thereof shall be beaten to pieces,[3807]
and all the [a]hires$_{868}$ thereof shall be
burned[8313] with the fire, and all the
idols[6091] thereof will I lay[7760] desolate:[8077] for she gathered[6908] *it* of the hire
of an harlot,[2181] and they shall return[7725]
to the hire of an harlot.
🗝 8 Therefore [a]I will wail and howl, [b]I
will go stripped and naked:[6174] [c]I will
make[6213] a wailing like the dragons,[8577]
and mourning as the [I]owls.
🗝 9 For [I]her wound[4347] *is* incurable; for
[a]it is come$_{935}$ unto Judah; he is come[5060]
unto the gate of my people, *even* to
Jerusalem.
🗝 10 [a]Declare[5046] ye *it* not at Gath,
weep ye not at all: in the house of
[I]Aphrah [b]roll thyself in the dust.[6083]
11 Pass ye away,[5674] [I]thou [II]inhabitant
of Saphir, having thy [a]shame naked:[6181]
the inhabitant of [III]Zaanan came not forth
in the mourning of [IV]Beth–ezel; he shall
receive of you his standing.$_{5979}$
12 For the inhabitant of Maroth
[I]waited carefully[2342] for good:[2896] but
[a]evil[7451] came down from the LORD unto
the gate of Jerusalem.
13 O thou inhabitant of [a]Lachish,
bind the chariot to the swift beast: she *is*
the beginning[7225] of the sin to the daughter of Zion: for the transgressions of
Israel were found in thee.

7 [a]Hos. 2:5, 12
8 [I]Hebr. *daughters of the owl* [a]Isa. 21:3; 22:4; Jer. 4:19 [b]Isa. 20:2-4 [c]Job 30:29; Ps. 102:6
9 [I]Or, *she is grievously sick of her wounds* [a]2Kgs. 18:13; Isa. 8:7, 8
10 [I]That is, *Dust* [a]2Sam. 1:20 [b]Jer. 6:26
11 [I]Or, *thou that dwellest fairly* [II]Hebr. *inhabitress* [III]Or, *The country of flocks* [IV]Or, *A place near* [a]Isa. 20:4; 47:2, 3; Jer. 13:22; Nah. 3:5
12 [I]Or, *was grieved* [a]Amos 3:6
13 [a]2Kgs. 18:14, 17
14 [I]Or, *for* [II]That is, *A lie* [a]2Sam. 8:2; 2Kgs. 18:14-16 [b]Josh. 15:44
15 [I]Or, *the glory of Israel shall come* [a]Josh. 15:44 [b]2Chr. 11:7
16 [a]Job 1:20; Isa. 15:2; 22:12; Jer. 7:29; 16:6; 47:5; 48:37 [b]Lam. 4:5

14 Therefore shalt thou [a]give pres-
ents$_{7964}$ [I]to Moresheth–gath: the houses
of [II][b]Achzib *shall be* a lie$_{391}$ to the kings
of Israel.
15 Yet will I bring an heir$_{2423}$ unto
thee, O inhabitant of [a]Mareshah: [I]he shall
come unto [b]Adullam the glory[3519] of Israel.
16 Make thee [a]bald, and poll$_{1494}$ thee
for thy [b]delicate$_{8588}$ children;[1121] enlarge
thy baldness as the eagle; for they are
gone into captivity[1540] from thee.

What Will Happen to Those Who Hurt the Poor

2 Woe to them [a]that devise iniquity,[205]
and [b]work evil[7451] upon their beds!
when the morning is light,[216] they practise[6213] it, because [c]it is in the power[410]
of their hand.[3027]
2 And they covet[2530] [a]fields,[7704] and
take *them* by violence; and houses,[1004]
and take *them* away:[5375] so they [I]oppress
a man[1397] and his house, even a man[376]
and his heritage.[5159]
3 Therefore thus saith the LORD;
Behold, against [a]this family[4940] do I devise an evil, from which ye shall not remove your necks; neither shall ye go
haughtily: [b]for this time[6256] *is* evil.

1 [a]Hos. 7:6 [b]Ps. 36:4 [c]Gen. 31:29
2 [I]Or, *defraud* [a]Isa. 5:8
3 [a]Jer. 8:3 [b]Amos 5:13; Eph. 5:16

🗝 **1:8** It is not known whether Micah actually went around unclothed. Although the Hebrew word *'eryah* (6181), translated "nakedness" in verse eleven, always means "unacceptable nudity" (see Ezek. 16:7, 22, 39), the word *'arom* (6174) is translated "naked" in this verse and could be interpreted any number of ways. Some see it as a lack of clothing, whether it is partial or complete (Job 22:6), while others say it refers to being poorly dressed (Job 24:7, 10; Is. 58:7), or having no upper garment (1 Sam. 19:24).

🗝 **1:9** The "incurable wound" is a symbol used throughout the Old Testament that illustrates the hopeless condition of Israel brought about by their habitual sin (see Jer. 10:19; 14:17; 15:18; 30:12, 14; Hos. 5:13; Nah. 3:19). The phrase "is come unto the gate" probably refers to Sennacherib's invasion in 701 B.C., in which everything was conquered except Jerusalem (cf. note on Is. 8:8).

🗝 **1:10–16** The meanings of these city names echo the judgments that God will bring on them. For example, the "house of Aphrah" means literally "house of dust" (v. 10), which reflects the fact that all that will remain will be the ruins of the city. The name "Maroth" means "bitterness," signifying their response to receiving evil instead of good (v. 12). "Lachish" was considered an impregnable city; their trust was within themselves (the meaning of Lachish), and the irony is seen in that they were ultimately destroyed by God (v. 13). The name "Achzib" means "deceit" and was reflected in their action to the kings of Israel (v. 14). The reference to "Adullam" is significant in that the "heir" will come to the inhabitants of this city pronouncing judgment on the people of the nation, which is the precise meaning of the city's name (v. 15). While it is known that these cities mentioned were in northern Judah, their precise locations are unknown today.

4 In that day[3117] shall *one* [a]take
up[5375] a parable4912 against you, and [b]la-
ment [I]with a doleful5093 lamentation, *and*
say, We be utterly spoiled:[7703] [c]he hath
changed the portion of my people:[5971]
how hath he removed *it* from me!
[II]turning away[7725] he hath divided our
fields.
5 Therefore thou shalt have none that
shall [a]cast a cord[2256] by lot in the
congregation[6951] of the LORD.
6 [I][a]Prophesy[5197] ye not, *say they to*
them that prophesy: they shall not prophesy to them, *that* they shall not take5253
shame.3639
7 O *thou that art* named the house
of Jacob, is the spirit[7307] of the LORD
[I]straitened?7114 *are* these his doings? do
not my words[1697] do good[3190] to him that
walketh [II]uprightly?[3477]
8 Even [I]of late my people is risen
up as an enemy: ye pull off the robe
[II]with the garment from them that pass
by[5674] securely[983] as men averse[7725] from
war.
9 The [I]women of my people have ye
cast out from their pleasant houses; from
their children have ye taken away my
glory[1926] for ever.[5769]
10 Arise ye, and depart; for this *is*
not *your* [a]rest: because it is [b]polluted,[2930]
it shall destroy[2254] *you,* even with a sore
destruction.[2256]
11 If a man [I][a]walking in the spirit
and falsehood[8267] do lie,[3576] *saying,* I will
prophesy unto thee of wine and of
strong drink; he shall even be the
prophet[5197] of this people.
🔑 12 [a]I will surely assemble,[622] O Jacob,
all of thee; I will surely gather[6908] the
remnant[7611] of Israel; I will put[7760] them
together [b]as the sheep of Bozrah, as the
flock in the midst of their fold: [c]they
shall make great noise[1949] by reason of
the multitude of men.[120]
13 The breaker is come up[5927] before
them: they have broken up, and have
passed through the gate, and are gone
out by it: and [a]their king shall pass before them, [b]and the LORD on the head[7218]
of them.

God Blames Israel's Leaders

3 And I said,[559] Hear, I pray you, O
heads[7218] of Jacob, and ye
princes[7101] of the house of Israel; [a]*Is it*
not for you to know[3045] judgment?[4941]
2 Who hate[8130] the good,[2896] and
love[157] the evil;[7451] who pluck off their
skin[5785] from off them, and their flesh
from off their bones;[6106]
3 Who also [a]eat the flesh[7607] of my
people,[5971] and flay6584 their skin from
off them; and they break their bones, and
chop them in pieces, as for the pot, and
[b]as flesh[1320] within the caldron.
4 Then [a]shall they cry[2199] unto the
LORD, but he will not hear them: he will
even hide his face from them at that
time,[6256] as they have behaved themselves ill[7489] in their doings.
5 Thus saith the LORD [a]concerning
the prophets[5030] that make my people
err,[8582] that [b]bite with their teeth, and
cry,[7121] Peace;[7965] and [c]he that putteth
not into their mouths,[6310] they even
prepare[6942] war against him.
6 [a]Therefore night *shall be* unto you,
[I]that ye shall not have a vision;[2377] and
it shall be dark[2821] unto you, [II]that ye
shall not divine;[7080] [b]and the sun shall go
down over the prophets, and the day[3117]
shall be dark[6937] over them.
7 Then shall[954] the seers[2374] be
ashamed,[954] and the diviners[7080] confounded: yea, they shall all cover their
[I]lips;[8222] [a]for *there is* no answer of
God.[430]
8 But truly I am full of power3581
by the spirit[7307] of the LORD, and of
judgment, and of might,1369 [a]to declare[5046] unto Jacob his transgression,[6588]
and to Israel his sin.[2403]
9 Hear this, I pray you, ye heads of

4 [I]Hebr. *with a lamentation of lamentations* [II]Or, *instead of restoring* [a]Hab. 2:6 [b]2Sam. 1:17 [c]Mic. 1:15
5 [a]Deut. 32:8, 9
6 [I]Or, *Prophesy not as they prophesy* [II]Hebr. *Drop* [a]Isa. 30:10; Ezek. 21:2; Amos 2:12; 7:16
7 [I]Or, *shortened* [II]Hebr. *upright*
8 [I]Hebr. *yesterday* [II]Hebr. *over against a garment*
9 [I]Or, *wives*
10 [a]Deut. 12:9 [b]Lev. 18:25, 28; Jer. 3:2
11 [I]Or, *walk with the wind, and lie falsely* [a]Ezek. 13:3
12 [a]Mic. 4:6, 7 [b]Jer. 31:10 [c]Ezek. 36:37
13 [a]Hos. 3:5 [b]Isa. 52:12

1 [a]Jer. 5:4, 5
3 [a]Ps. 14:4 [b]Ezek. 11:3, 7
4 [a]Ps. 18:41; Prov. 1:28; Isa. 1:15; Ezek. 8:18; Zech. 7:13
5 [a]Isa. 56:10, 11; Ezek. 13:10; 22:25 [b]Mic. 2:11; Matt. 7:15 [c]Ezek. 13:18, 19
6 [I]Hebr. *from a vision* [II]Hebr. *from divining* [a]Isa. 8:20, 22; Ezek. 13:23; Zech. 13:4 [b]Amos 8:9
7 [I]Hebr. *upper lip* [a]Ps. 74:9; Amos 8:11
8 [a]Isa. 58:1

🔑 **2:12, 13** The "breaker," which literally means "one who breaks open," is a reference to Israel's Messiah (v. 13, cf. Ex. 19:22; Judg. 21:15).

the house of Jacob, and princes of the house of Israel, that abhor[8581] judgment, and pervert all equity.[3477]

10 [a]They build up Zion with [I][b]blood,[1818] and Jerusalem with iniquity.[5766]

11 [a]The heads thereof judge[8199] for reward, and [b]the priests[3548] thereof teach[3384] for hire,[4242] and the prophets thereof divine for money: [c]yet will they lean[8172] upon the LORD, [I]and say, *Is* not the LORD among[7130] us? none evil can come upon us.

12 Therefore shall Zion for your sake be [a]plowed *as* a field,[7704] [b]and Jerusalem shall become heaps, and [c]the mountain of the house as the high places[1116] of the forest.

The LORD Will Rule Everywhere

4 But [a]in the last[319] days[3117] it shall come to pass, *that* the mountain of the house[1004] of the LORD shall be established[3559] in the top[7218] of the mountains, and it shall be exalted[5385] above the hills; and people[5971] shall flow unto it.

2 And many nations[1471] shall come, and say, Come, and let us go up[5927] to the mountain of the LORD, and to the house of the God[430] of Jacob; and he will teach[3384] us of his ways,[1870] and we will walk in his paths:[734] for the law[8451] shall go forth[3318] of Zion, and the word[1697] of the LORD from Jerusalem.

3 And he shall judge[8199] among many people, and rebuke[3198] strong nations afar off; and they shall beat[3807] their swords[2719] into [a]plowshares, and their spears into [I]pruninghooks: nation shall not lift up[5375] a sword against nation, [b]neither shall they learn[3925] war any more.

4 [a]But they shall sit every man under his vine and under his fig tree; and none shall make *them* afraid:[2729] for the mouth[6310] of the LORD of hosts[6635] hath spoken[1696] *it.*

5 For [a]all people will walk every one in the name of his god,[430] and [b]we will walk in the name of the LORD our God[430] for ever[5769] and ever.[5703]

Israel Will Return From Captivity

6 In that day, saith[5002] the LORD, [a]will I assemble[622] her that halteth,[6761] [b]and I will gather[6908] her that is driven out, and her that I have afflicted;[7489]

7 And I will make[7760] her that halted [a]a remnant,[7611] and her that was cast far

10 [I]Hebr. *bloods* [a]Jer. 22:13 [b]Ezek. 22:27; Hab. 2:12; Zeph. 3:3

11 [I]Hebr. *saying* [a]Isa. 1:23; Ezek. 22:12; Hos. 4:18; Mic. 7:3 [b]Jer. 6:13 [c]Isa. 48:2; Jer. 7:4; Rom. 2:17

12 [a]Jer. 26:18; Mic. 1:6 [b]Ps. 79:1 [c]Mic. 4:2

1 [a]Isa. 2:2; Ezek. 17:22, 23

3 [I]Or, *scythes* [a]Isa. 2:4; Joel 3:10 [b]Ps. 72:7

4 [a]1Kgs. 4:25; Zech. 3:10

5 [a]Jer. 2:11 [b]Zech. 10:12

6 [a]Ezek. 34:16; Zeph. 3:19 [b]Ps. 147:2; Ezek. 34:13; 37:21

7 [a]Mic. 2:12; 5:3, 7, 8; 7:18

3:12 This verse is a prediction of the destruction that was soon to come upon Jerusalem. Jeremiah made mention of this prophecy by Micah as he was observing its fulfillment (Jer. 26:18).

4:1–5 Here is a glorious picture of the reign of the Messiah (see Rev. 20:6). Certainly the conditions described in these verses have not yet been fulfilled. Moreover, these conditions clearly relate to a physical earthly reign (from Zion, Jerusalem).

4:3 In this verse, the prophecy is made concerning One who will come and bring about an end to all warfare on earth. In Isaiah 9:6, this one is called the "Prince of Peace." It is clear that Micah was speaking about Jesus Christ who will bring all this to pass when He returns at his Second Coming (see note on 1 Thess. 5:2).

4:6–13 These verses describe the conditions in and around the Holy Land at the end of the Great Tribulation. Verses six through eight are God's promise to the city of Jerusalem. "In that day" is a key Old Testament equivalent of the "Day of the LORD" (see note on Zeph. 1:7), and often relates to the Tribulation and the millennial kingdom of Christ (see Is. 2:11, 17 [cf. Is. 2:12]; 4:2; 10:20; 11:10, 11; 12:1; Jer. 30:8; Ezek 30:9; 36:33). The phrase "in that day" is also used to refer to more immediate judgments, particularly as they are related to, or typical of, the judgments of the Day of the Lord (cf. Is. 7:17, 18).

Furthermore, Micah reviews the processes and results of the regathering of Israel. The initial sufferings of Israel are described using a common image of the Tribulation—the image of a woman in labor pains (vv. 9–13, cf. Is. 13:8; 66:7, 8; Jer. 4:31; 30:6; Hos. 13:13; Matt. 24:8 "sorrows"; 1 Thess. 5:3). It is important to remember that God is in control of all the circumstances surrounding the future of Israel (v. 13). In all the blessings that Israel will receive upon their restoration to the land, it will be made clear that it is the LORD Jehovah that prospers them.

off a strong nation: and the LORD [b]shall
reign over them in mount Zion from
henceforth, even for ever.
8 And thou, O tower of [I][a]the flock,
the strong hold of the daughter of Zion,
unto thee shall it come, even the first
dominion,[4475] the kingdom[4467] shall come
to the daughter of Jerusalem.
9 Now why dost thou cry out[7321]
aloud? [a]*is there* no king in thee? is[6]
[b]thy counselor[3289] perished?[6] for [c]pangs
have taken[2388] thee as a woman in travail.
10 Be in pain,[2342] and labour to bring
forth, O daughter of Zion, like a woman
in travail: for now shalt thou go forth
out of the city, and thou shalt dwell[7931]
in the field,[7704] and thou shalt go *even* to
Babylon; there shalt thou be delivered;[5337]
there the LORD shall redeem[1350] thee from
the hand[3709] of thine enemies.
11 [a]Now also many nations are gathered against thee, that say, Let her be
defiled,[2610] and let our eye [b]look[2372] upon
Zion.
12 But they know[3045] not [a]the
thoughts[4284] of the LORD, neither understand[995] they his counsel:[6098] for he
shall gather them [b]as the sheaves into
the floor.
13 [a]Arise and thresh, O daughter of
Zion: for I will make[7760] thine horn iron,
and I will make thy hoofs brass: and thou
shalt [b]beat in pieces many people: [c]and I
will consecrate[2763] their gain unto the
LORD, and their substance[2428] unto [d]the
LORD[113] of the whole earth.[776]

7 [b]Isa. 9:6; 24:23; Dan. 7:14, 27; Luke 1:33; Rev. 11:15
8 [I]Or, *Edar* [a]Gen. 35:21
9 [a]Jer. 8:19 [b]Isa. 13:8; 21:3; Jer. 30:6; 50:43
11 [a]Lam. 2:16 [b]Obad. 1:12; Mic. 7:10
12 [a]Isa. 55:8; Rom. 11:33 [b]Isa. 21:10
13 [a]Isa. 41:15, 16; Jer. 51:33 [b]Dan. 2:44 [c]Isa. 18:7; 23:18; 60:6, 9 [d]Zech. 4:14; 6:5

1 [a]Lam. 3:30; Matt. 5:39; 27:30
2 [I]Hebr. *the days of eternity* [a]Matt. 2:6; John 7:42 [b]1Sam. 23:23 [c]Ex. 18:25 [d]Gen. 49:10; Isa. 9:6 [e]Ps. 90:2; Prov. 8:22, 23; John 1:1
3 [a]Mic. 4:10 [b]Mic. 4:7
4 [I]Or, *rule* [a]Isa. 40:11; 49:10; Ezek. 34:23; Mic. 7:14 [b]Ps. 72:8; Isa. 52:13; Zech. 9:10; Luke 1:32
5 [I]Hebr. *princes of men* [a]Ps. 72:7; Isa. 9:6; Zech. 9:10; Luke 2:14; Eph. 2:14
6 [I]Hebr. *eat up* [II]Or, *with her own naked swords* [a]Gen. 10:8, 10, 11 [b]Luke 1:71

God Promises a Ruler From Bethlehem

5 Now gather thyself in troops,[1413]
O daughter of troops:[1416] he hath
laid[7760] siege against us: they shall
[a]smite[5221] the judge[8199] of Israel with a
rod[7626] upon the cheek.
2 But thou, [a]Bethlehem Ephratah,
though thou be little [b]among the [c]thou-
sands[505] of Judah, *yet* out of thee shall
he come forth unto me *that is* to be
[d]ruler[4910] in Israel; [e]whose goings forth
have been from of old,[6924] from [I]ever-
lasting.[3117,5769]
3 Therefore will he give them up,
until the time[6256] *that* [a]she which
travaileth[3205] hath brought forth: then
[b]the remnant[3499] of his brethren[251]
shall return[7725] unto the children of
Israel.
4 And he shall stand and [I][a]feed[7462]
in the strength of the LORD, in the
majesty[1347] of the name of the LORD his
God;[430] and they shall abide: for now
[b]shall he be great unto the ends of the
earth.[776]
5 And this *man* [a]shall be the
peace,[7965] when the Assyrian shall come
into our land:[776] and when he shall tread
in our palaces,[759] then shall we raise
against him seven shepherds, and eight
[I]principal[5257] men.[120]
6 And they shall [I]waste the land of
Assyria with the sword,[2719] and the land
of [a]Nimrod [II]in the entrances thereof: thus
shall he [b]deliver[5337] *us* from the Assyrian,

5:1, 2 Some feel that verse one is a reference to the humiliation of Zedekiah by Nebuchadnezzar (2 Kgs. 25); but in view of the obvious reference to the Messiah in verse two, it seems that it would be more appropriate to recognize the smitten "judge of Israel" as the Messiah. In fact, seven hundred years after the Book of Micah was written, it was still recognized as a prophecy of the Messiah. The chief priests and scribes quoted it to Herod when they were asked where Christ was to be born (Matt. 2:2–6). Later, Jesus' enemies attempted to use Micah 5:2 to prove that He was not the Messiah because they knew His hometown was Nazareth in Galilee (John 7:41, 42). This prophecy is important because it reveals that the Messiah is "from everlasting," an eternal Being (i.e., the "Son of God"). The Jews could not comprehend this aspect of the prophecy (Matt. 22:42).

5:3–9 This passage describes Israel's vindication at the end of the Tribulation. "The Assyrian" (v. 4, 5) represents Israel's enemies during the Tribulation, much as the "king of the north" and the "king of the south" take on eschatological meanings, corresponding to the fact that they are actual historical figures (see note on Dan. 11:1–20).

when he cometh into our land, and when
he treadeth1869 within our borders.
7 And [a]the remnant[7611] of Jacob
shall be in the midst of many people[5971]
[b]as a dew from the LORD, as the showers
upon the grass, that tarrieth[6960] not for
man,[376] nor waiteth[3176] for the sons[1121]
of men.
8 And the remnant of Jacob shall be
among the Gentiles[1471] in the midst of
many people as a lion among the beasts
of the forest, as a young lion among
the flocks of [I]sheep: who, if he go
through,[5674] both treadeth down,7429 and
teareth in pieces, and none can deliver.
9 Thine hand[3027] shall be lifted
up7311 upon thine adversaries, and all
thine enemies shall be cut off.[3772]
⚿ 10 [a]And it shall come to pass in that
day, saith the LORD, that I will cut off thy
horses out of the midst of thee, and I
will destroy[6] thy chariots:
11 And I will cut off the cities of thy
land, and throw down[2040] all thy strong
holds:
12 And I will cut off witchcrafts[3785]
out of thine hand; and thou shalt have no
more [a]soothsayers:[6049]
13 [a]Thy graven images[6456] also will
I cut off, and thy [I]standing images[4676]
out of the midst[7130] of thee; and thou
shalt [b]no more worship[7812] the work of
thine hands.
14 And I will pluck up thy groves[842]
out of the midst of thee: so will I
destroy[8045] thy [I]cities.
15 And I will [a]execute[6213] vengeance[5359] in anger[622] and fury[2534] upon
the heathen,[1471] such as they have not
heard.

The LORD's Case Against Israel

6 Hear[8085] ye now what the LORD
saith; Arise, contend[7378] thou [I]before
the mountains, and let the hills hear thy
voice.
2 [a]Hear ye, O mountains, [b]the LORD's
controversy,[7379] and ye strong foundations[4146] of [c]the earth: for the LORD hath
a controversy with his people,[5971] and he
will plead[3198] with Israel.
3 O my people, [a]what have I done
unto thee? and wherein have I wearied3811 thee? testify against me.
4 [a]For I brought thee up[5927] out of the
land of Egypt, and redeemed[6299] thee out
of the house of servants;[5650] and I sent before thee Moses, Aaron, and Miriam.
5 O my people, remember[2142] now
what [a]Balak king of Moab consulted,[3289]
and what Balaam the son[1121] of Beor answered him from [b]Shittim unto Gilgal;
that ye may know[3045] [c]the righteousness
of the LORD.
⚿ 6 Wherewith shall I come before the
LORD, *and* bow3721 myself before the high
God?[430] shall I come before him with
burnt offerings,[5930] with calves [I]of a year
old?
7 [a]Will the LORD be pleased[7521] with
thousands of rams, *or* with ten thousands[505] of [b]rivers of oil?[8081] [c]shall I give
my firstborn *for* my transgression,[6588]
the fruit of my [I]body[990] *for* the sin[2403] of
my soul?[5315]
⚿ 8 He hath [a]shewed[5046] thee, O
man,[120] what *is* good;[2896] and what doth
the LORD require1875 of thee, but [b]to
do[6213] justly,[4941] and to love[160] mercy,[2617]
and to [I]walk humbly with thy God?

7 [a]Mic. 5:3 [b]Deut. 32:2; Ps. 72:6; 110:3
8 [a]Or, *goats*
10 [a]Zech. 9:10
12 [a]Isa. 2:6
13 [I]Or, *statues* [a]Zech. 13:2 [b]Isa. 2:8
14 [I]Or, *enemies*
15 [a]Ps. 149:7; Mic. 5:8; 2Thess. 1:8

1 [I]Or, *with*
2 [a]Deut. 32:1; Ps. 50:1, 4; Isa. 1:2 [b]Hos. 12:2 [c]Isa. 1:18; 5:3, 4; 43:26; Hos. 4:1
3 [a]Jer. 2:5, 31
4 [a]Ex. 12:51; 14:30; 20:2; Deut. 4:20; Amos 2:10
5 [a]Num. 22:5; 23:7; 24:10, 11; Deut. 23:4, 5; Josh. 24:9, 10; Rev. 2:14 [b]Num. 25:1; 33:49; Josh. 4:19; 5:10 [c]Judg. 5:11
6 [I]Hebr. *sons of a year*
7 [I]Hebr. *belly* [a]Ps. 50:9; 51:16; Isa. 1:11 [b]Job 29:6 [c]2Kgs. 16:3; 21:6; 23:10; Jer. 7:31; 19:5; Ezek. 23:37
8 [a]Deut. 10:12; 1Sam. 15:22; Hos. 6:6; 12:6 [I]Hebr. *humble thyself to walk* [b]Gen. 18:19; Isa. 1:17

⚿ **5:10–15** Although this prophecy is primarily directed at Israel's enemies, it also applies to the ungodly that God will purge from among Israel.

⚿ **6:6, 7** The questions of God's people can show how far they have strayed from true faith in God. In response to God's "lawsuit," the people tried to decide what might win back God's favor. They were so spiritually ignorant that they even proposed offering a human sacrifice to please God (v. 7, cf. 2 Kgs. 3:27; 16:3; 2 Chr. 28:3; see also note on 2 Kgs. 23:10). They continued to sacrifice their children to the Canaanite gods throughout the days when Jeremiah and Ezekiel prophesied (Jer. 19:5; 32:35; Ezek. 23:37).

⚿ **6:8** In both the Old and New Testaments, God desired men to have a genuine, heartfelt relationship with Him. The underlying purpose of all the detailed observances required by the Mosaic

(continued on next page)

9 The LORD's voice crieth[7121] unto the city, and [I]*the man of* wisdom[8454] shall see[7200] thy name: hear ye the rod,[4294] and who hath appointed[3259] it.

10 [I]Are there yet the treasures of wickedness[7562] in the house of the wicked,[7563] and the [II][a]scant measure [b]*that* is abominable?[2194]

11 [I]Shall I count *them* pure[2135] with [a]the wicked balances, and with the bag of deceitful[4820] weights?

12 For the rich men thereof are full of violence,[2555] and the inhabitants thereof have spoken[1696] lies,[8267] and [a]their tongue *is* deceitful in their mouth.[6310]

13 Therefore also will I [a]make *thee* sick in smiting[5221] thee, in making *thee* desolate[8074] because of thy sins.

14 [a]Thou shalt eat, but not be satisfied; and thy casting down[3445] *shall be* in the midst of thee; and thou shalt take hold,[5253] but shalt not deliver; and *that* which thou deliverest[6403] will I give up to the sword.[2719]

15 Thou shalt [a]sow, but thou shalt not reap; thou shalt tread the olives, but thou shalt not anoint[5480] thee with oil; and sweet wine, but shalt not drink wine.

16 For [I]the statutes[2708] of [a]Omri are [b]kept,[8104] and all the works of the house of [c]Ahab, and ye walk in their counsels; that I should make thee [d]a [II]desolation,[8047] and the inhabitants thereof an hissing: therefore ye shall bear[5375] the [e]reproach[2781] of my people.

Israel Is Corrupt

7 Woe is me! for I am as [I]when they have gathered[625] the summer fruits, as [a]the grapegleanings of the vintage: *there is* no cluster to eat: [b]my soul[5315] desired[183] the firstripe fruit.

2 The [I][a]good[2623] *man* is perished[6] out of the earth: and *there is* none upright among men:[120] they all lie in wait for blood;[1818] [b]they hunt every man[376] his brother[251] with a net.

3 That they may do evil[7451] with both hands[3709] earnestly,[3190] [a]the prince[8269] asketh,[7592] [b]and the judge[8199] *asketh* for a reward;[7966] and the great *man,* he uttereth [I]his mischievous[1942] desire:[5315] so they wrap it up.

4 The best[2896] of them [a]*is* as a brier: the most upright *is sharper* than a thorn hedge: the day[3117] of thy watchmen *and* thy visitation[6486] cometh; now shall be their perplexity.

🔑 5 [a]Trust[539] ye not in a friend,[7453] put ye not confidence[982] in a guide:[441] keep[8104] the doors of thy mouth[6310] from her that lieth in thy bosom.

6 For [a]the son[1121] dishonoureth the father,[1] the daughter riseth up against her mother,[517] the daughter in law against her mother in law; a man's[376] enemies *are* the men[582] of his own house.[1004]

7 Therefore [a]I will look unto the LORD; I will wait[3176] for the God[430] of my salvation:[3468] my God will hear[8085] me.

8 [a]Rejoice not against me, O mine enemy: [b]when I fall,[5307] I shall arise; when I sit in darkness,[2822] [c]the LORD *shall be* a light[216] unto me.

9 [I]Or, *thy name shall see that which is* **10** [I]Or, Is there *yet unto every man a house of the wicked* [II]Hebr. *measure of leanness* [a]Amos 8:5 [b]Deut. 25:13-16; Prov. 11:1; 20:10, 23 **11** [I]Or, *Shall I be pure with* [a]Hos. 12:7 **12** [a]Jer. 9:3, 5, 6, 8 **13** [a]Lev. 26:16; Ps. 107:17, 18 **14** [a]Lev. 26:26; Hos. 4:10 **15** [a]Deut. 28:38-40; Amos 5:11; Zeph. 1:13; Hag. 1:6 **16** [I]Or, *he doth much keep the* [II]Or, *astonishment* [a]1Kgs. 16:25, 26 [b]Hos. 5:11 [c]1Kgs. 16:30; 21:25, 26; 2Kgs. 21:3 [d]1Kgs. 9:8; Jer. 19:8 [e]Isa. 25:8; Jer. 51:51; Lam. 5:1, 2

1 [I]Hebr. *the gatherings of summer* [a]Isa. 17:6; 24:13 [b]Isa. 28:4; Hos. 9:10 **2** [I]Or, *godly,* or, *merciful* [a]Ps. 12:1; 14:1, 3; Isa. 57:1 [b]Hab. 1:15 **3** [I]Hebr. *the mischief of his soul* [a]Hos. 4:18 [b]Isa. 1:23; Mic. 3:11 **4** [a]2Sam. 23:6, 7; Isa. 55:13; Ezek. 2:6 **5** [a]Jer. 9:4 **6** [a]Ezek. 22:7; Matt. 10:21, 35, 36; Luke 12:53; 21:16; 2Tim. 3:2, 3 **7** [a]Isa. 8:17 **8** [a]Prov. 24:17; Lam. 4:21 [b]Ps. 37:24; Prov. 24:16 [c]Ps. 27:1

(continued from previous page)
Law is summed up in these brief statements (Hos. 6:6). "Mercy" is translated from the Hebrew word *chēsēd* (2617), the closest Old Testament equivalent to the New Testament term "grace." This verse incorporates the two commandments that Jesus said were the most important: to love the Lord your God, and love your neighbor as yourself (cf. Deut. 6:4–9; Matt. 22:34–40).

🔑 **7:5–7** These statements made by Micah are reflected in the teaching that Christ gave to His disciples (Matt. 10:35–37). Jesus was showing how complete dedication to Him would bring about rejection from those close to them, even by those in their immediate family. The person who places family ahead of his service for Christ is called "unworthy" (Matt. 10:38). The assurance is given by Micah that it is worthwhile to trust completely in God for salvation. Resting in Him is the only way to find peace, especially when a believer's own family forsakes him or her (Heb. 13:5).

9 [a]I will bear[5375] the indignation[2197]
of the LORD, because I have sinned[2398]
against him, until he plead[7378] my
cause,[7379] and execute[6213] judgment[4941]
for me: [b]he will bring me forth to the
light, *and* I shall behold[7200] his righteousness.

10 [I]Then *she that is* mine enemy
shall see *it,* and [a]shame[955] shall cover[3680]
her which said unto me, [b]Where is the
LORD thy God? [c]mine eyes shall behold
her: now [II]shall she be trodden down [d]as
the mire of the streets.

11 *In* the day that thy [a]walls are to
be built, *in* that day shall the decree[2706]
be far removed.

12 *In* that day *also* [a]he shall come
even to thee from Assyria, [I]and *from* the
fortified cities, and from the fortress even
to the river, and from sea to sea, and
from mountain to mountain.

13 [I]Notwithstanding the land shall
be desolate[8077] because of them that
dwell therein, [a]for the fruit of their doings.

The LORD Loves Israel

14 [I]Feed thy people[5971] with thy
rod,[7626] the flock of thine heritage,[5159]
which dwell[7931] solitarily [a]*in* the wood, in
the midst of Carmel: let them feed *in*
Bashan and Gilead, as in the days of
old.[5769]

15 [a]According to the days of thy
coming out of the land of Egypt will
I shew[7200] unto him marvellous[6381]
things.

16 The nations[1471] [a]shall see and be
confounded[954] at all their might: [b]they
shall lay[7760] *their* hand[3027] upon *their*
mouth, their ears[241] shall be deaf.

17 They shall lick the [a]dust[6083] like
a serpent,[5175] [b]they shall move[7264] out of
their holes like [I]worms of the earth: [c]they
shall be afraid[6342] of the LORD our God,
and shall fear[3372] because of thee.

18 [a]Who *is* a God[410] like unto thee,
that [b]pardoneth[5375] iniquity,[5771] and
passeth[5674] by the transgression[6588] of
[c]the remnant[7611] of his heritage? [d]he
retaineth[2388] not his anger[639] for ever,[5703]
because he delighteth[2654] *in* mercy.[2617]

19 He will turn again, he will have
compassion[7355] upon us; he will subdue[3533] our iniquities; and thou wilt cast
all their sins[2403] into the depths of the
sea.

20 [a]Thou wilt perform the truth[571]
to Jacob, *and* the mercy to Abraham,
[b]which thou hast sworn[7650] unto our
fathers[1] from the days of old.[6924]

9 [a]Lam. 3:39 [b]Ps. 37:6 [c]Ps. 35:26 [d]Ps. 42:3, 10; 79:10; 115:2; Joel 2:17
10 [I]Or, *And thou wilt see her that is mine enemy, and cover her with shame* [II]Hebr. *she shall be for a treading down* [a]Mic. 4:11 [b]2Sam. 22:43; Zech. 10:5
11 [a]Amos 9:11
12 [I]Or, *even to* [a]Isa. 11:16; 19:23; 27:13; Hos. 11:11
13 [I]Or, *After that it hath been* [a]Jer. 21:14; Mic. 3:12
14 [I]Or, *Rule* [a]Ps. 28:9; Mic. 5:4 [b]Isa. 37:24
15 [a]Ps. 68:22; 78:12
16 [a]Isa. 26:11 [b]Job 21:5; 29:9
17 [I]Or, *creeping things* [a]Ps. 72:9; Isa. 49:23 [b]Ps. 18:45 [c]Jer. 33:9
18 [a]Ex. 15:11 [b]Ex. 34:6, 7; Jer. 50:20 [c]Mic. 4:7; 5:3, 7, 8 [d]Ps. 103:9; Isa. 57:16; Jer. 3:5
20 [a]Luke 1:72, 73 [b]Ps. 105:9, 10

7:18–20 Micah ends his prophecy by declaring that his total confidence was in God. Despite Israel's great sins, God indeed pardons iniquity and delights in "mercy" (Hebr., *chēsēd* [2617], also in v. 20). Not only does God forgive sins, but He casts them far away "into the depths of the sea" (v. 19, cf. Ps. 103:12). All this is based on God's unchanging promises to Abraham, Isaac, and Jacob (v. 20; see note on Gen. 12:1–3).

The Book of

NAHUM

Nahum means "comfort" or "consolation" (of God). This is thought-provoking since Nahum's entire message concerns the destruction of Nineveh. However, the Hebrew title (the first word of the Hebrew text), "Burden," is indicative of the content (see note on Nah. 1:1).

Nahum prophesied in the time between the Assyrian capture of No (Thebes) in Egypt (see Nah. 3:8–10), which is known to have occurred in 661 B.C., and the final destruction of Nineveh in 612 B.C. (Nah. 2:8–13). Since verse fifteen of chapter one suggests that the feasts were being observed in Judah, it is probable that he ministered during or just after Josiah's revival. This means he would have prophesied around 620 B.C., or about the time of Habakkuk, Zephaniah, and the early part of Jeremiah's ministry. Several scholars have suggested that Capernaum in Galilee was his birthplace, and was renamed Kaphar-Nahum in his honor. In any event, he moved to Judah and prophesied there. If it is true that he prophesied from Jerusalem, as many believe, then verses nine through thirteen of chapter one probably refer to the then recent siege of Jerusalem by Sennacherib.

Nahum's book has certain aspects of a "theodicy" (a defense of God). He provided answers to the questions of God's people: "Has God forsaken us? Why are the Assyrians prospering? Are God's promises empty?" Nahum affirms that God may be "slow to anger" (Nah. 1:3a), but He "will not at all acquit the wicked" (Nah. 1:3b). Moreover, God is indeed "a strong hold in the day of trouble" (Nah. 1:7). This is also a vital message for today—in the press of circumstance and misfortune, God's people are prone to forget that God is in control.

The LORD Is Angry With Nineveh

1 The burden[4853] [a]of Nineveh. The
book[5612] of the vision[2377] of Nahum
the Elkoshite.
2 [I]God[410] *is* [a]jealous, and [b]the
LORD[3068] revengeth; the LORD revengeth,
and [II]*is* furious;[2534] the LORD will take
vengeance[5358] on his adversaries, and he
reserveth *wrath* for his enemies.
3 The LORD *is* [a]slow[750] to anger,[639]
and [b]great in power,[3581] and will not at
all acquit[5352] *the wicked:* [c]the LORD *hath*
his way[1870] in the whirlwind and in the
storm, and the clouds[6051] *are* the dust[80]
of his feet.
4 [a]He rebuketh[1605] the sea, and
maketh it dry,[3001] and drieth up[2717] all
the rivers; [b]Bashan languisheth,[535] and
Carmel, and the flower of Lebanon languisheth.
5 [a]The mountains quake[7493] at him,
and [b]the hills melt,[4127] and [c]the earth is

1 [a]Zeph. 2:13 **2** [I]Or, *The LORD is a jealous God, and a revenger* [II]Hebr. *that hath fury* [a]Ex. 20:5; 34:14; Deut. 4:24; Josh. 24:19 [b]Deut. 32:35; Ps. 94:1; Isa. 59:18 **3** [a]Ex. 34:6, 7; Neh. 9:17; Ps. 103:8; Jon. 4:2 [b]Job 9:4 [c]Ps. 18:7; 97:2; Hab. 3:5, 11, 12 **4** [a]Ps. 106:9; Isa. 50:2; Matt. 8:26 [b]Isa. 33:9 **5** [a]Ps. 68:8 [b]Judg. 5:5; Ps. 97:5; Mic. 1:4 [c]2Pet. 3:10

1:1 When Nahum used the phrase "burden of Nineveh," he was referring to his prophecy concerning Assyria's destruction and the removal of their oppressive hand on the people of Judah. The word "burden" (*massa* [4853]) actually describes the military advancements that the Assyrians were making against Judah.

1:2, 3 The Hebrew word *qannow* (7072) is translated "jealous," and in this context implies that God is "zealous." Nahum is not ascribing human emotions to God; rather, the emphasis is on God's desire for righteousness. The idea here is similar to Jesus' display of anger when He cleared the temple of the moneychangers (John 2:17). Along these lines, God is also said to be "slow to anger." This statement reveals the fact that God may delay the time that He begins His judgment. One can be sure, however, that He will ultimately carry out His judgment.

burned[5375] at his presence, yea, the world, and all that dwell therein.

6 Who can stand before his indignation?[2195] and [a]who can [I]abide in the fierceness[2740] of his anger? [b]his fury[2534] is poured out like fire, and the rocks are thrown down[5422] by him.

7 [a]The LORD *is* good,[2896] a [I]strong hold in the day[3117] of trouble; and [b]he knoweth[3045] them that trust[2620] in him.

8 [a]But with an overrunning[5674] flood[7858] he will make[6213] an utter end[3617] of the place thereof, and darkness[2822] shall pursue his enemies.

9 [a]What do ye imagine[2803] against the LORD? [b]he will make an utter end: affliction shall not rise up the second time.

10 For while *they be* folden together [a]*as* thorns, [b]and while they are drunken *as* drunkards, [c]they shall be devoured as stubble fully dry.[3002]

11 There is *one* come out of thee, [a]that imagineth evil[7451] against the LORD, [I]a wicked[1100] counselor.[3289]

🗝 12 Thus saith the LORD; [I]Though *they be* quiet,[8003] and likewise many, yet thus [a]shall they be [II]cut down, when he shall [b]pass through.[5674] Though I have afflicted[6031] thee, I will afflict thee no more.

13 For now will I [a]break[7665] his yoke from off thee, and will burst thy bonds in sunder.

14 And the LORD hath given a commandment[6680] concerning thee, *that* no more of thy name be sown: out of the house[1004] of thy gods[430] will I cut off[3772] the graven image[6459] and the molten image:[4541] [a]I will make[7760] thy grave;[6913] for thou art vile.[7043]

15 Behold [a]upon the mountains the feet of him that bringeth good tidings,[1319] that publisheth[8085] peace[7965] O Judah, [I]keep thy solemn feasts,[2282] perform thy vows:[5088] [II][b]for the wicked[1100] shall no more pass[5674] through thee; [c]he is utterly cut off.

Nineveh Will Fall

2 [I]He [a]that dasheth in pieces is come up[5927] before thy face: [b]keep[5341] the munition,[4694] watch the way,[1870] make *thy* loins strong,[2388] fortify[553] *thy* power mightily.

2 [a]For the LORD hath turned away[7725] [I]the excellency of Jacob, as the excellency of Israel: for [b]the emptiers have emptied them out, and marred[7843] their vine branches.

3 The shield of his mighty men[1368] is made [a]red, the valiant[2428] men *are* [I]in scarlet: the chariots *shall be* with [II]flaming torches in the day[3117] of his preparation,[3559] and the fir trees shall be terribly shaken.

4 The chariots shall rage[1984] in the streets, they shall justle[8264] one against another in the broad ways: [I]they shall seem[4758] like torches, they shall run like the lightnings.

5 He shall recount[2142] his [I]worthies:[117] they shall stumble[3782] in their walk; they shall make haste to the wall thereof, and the [II]defence shall be prepared.[3559]

6 The gates of the rivers shall be opened, and the palace[1964] shall be [I]dissolved.[4127]

7 And [I]Huzzab[5324] shall be [II]led away captive,[1540] she shall be brought up, and her maids shall lead *her* as with the voice of [a]doves, tabering[8608] upon their breasts.[3824]

8 But Nineveh *is* [I]of old like a pool of water: yet they shall flee away. Stand, stand, *shall they cry*; but none shall [II]look back.

9 Take ye the spoil of silver, take the spoil of gold: [I]for *there is* none end of the store *and* glory[3519] out of all the [II]pleasant furniture.

10 She is empty, and void, and waste:

6 [I]Hebr. *stand up* [a]Mal. 3:2 [b]Rev. 16:1
7 [I]Or, *strength* [a]1Chr. 16:34; Ps. 100:5; Jer. 33:11; Lam. 3:25 [b]Ps. 1:6; 2Tim. 2:19
8 [a]Dan. 9:26; 11:10, 22, 40
9 [a]Ps. 2:1 [b]1Sam. 3:12
10 [a]2Sam. 23:6, 7 [b]Nah. 3:11 [c]Mal. 4:1
11 [I]Hebr. *a counselor of Belial* [a]2Kgs. 19:22, 23
12 [I]Or, *If they would have been at peace, so should they have been many, and so should they have been shorn, and he should have passed away* [II]Hebr. *shorn* [a]2Kgs. 19:35, 37 [b]Isa. 8:8; Dan. 11:10
13 [a]Jer. 2:20; 30:8
14 [a]2Kgs. 19:37
15 [I]Hebr. *feast* [II]Hebr. *Belial* [a]Isa. 52:7; Rom. 10:15 [b]Nah. 1:11, 12 [c]Nah. 1:14

1 [I]Or, *The disperser*, or, *hammer* [a]Jer. 50:23 [b]Jer. 51:11, 12; Nah. 3:14
2 [I]Or, *the pride of Jacob as the pride of Israel* [a]Isa. 10:12; Jer. 25:29 [b]Ps. 80:12; Hos. 10:1
3 [I]Or, *dyed scarlet* [II]Or, *fiery torches* [a]Isa. 63:2, 3
4 [I]Hebr. *their show*
5 [I]Or, *gallants* [II]Hebr. *covering*, or, *coverer*
6 [I]Or, *molten*
7 [I]Or, *that which was established*, or, *there was a stand made* [II]Or, *discovered* [a]Isa. 38:14; 59:11
8 [I]Or, *from the* days that *she* hath been [II]Or, *cause them to turn*
9 [I]Or, *and their infinite store* [II]Hebr. *vessels of desire*

🗝 **1:12** The Hebrew word *shalame* (8003) is translated "quiet" in this verse. There are some who suggest that by the context of the verse this word can also mean "full" or "complete."

and the [a]heart[3820] melteth, and [b]the knees smite together,[6375] [c]and much pain *is* in all loins, and [d]the faces of them all gather[6908] blackness.[6289]

11 Where *is* the dwelling of [a]the lions, and the feedingplace of the young lions, where the lion, *even* the old lion, walked, *and* the lion's whelp,[1482] and none made *them* afraid?[2729]

12 The lion did tear in pieces enough for his whelps, and strangled for his lionesses, and filled his holes with prey, and his dens with ravin.[2966]

13 [a]Behold, I *am* against thee, saith[5002] the LORD of hosts,[6635] and I will burn her chariots in the smoke, and the sword[2719] shall devour thy young lions: and I will cut off[3772] thy prey from the earth,[776] and the voice of [b]thy messengers[4397] shall no more be heard.[8085]

Woe to Nineveh

3 Woe to the [1][a]bloody[1818] city! it *is* all full of lies *and* robbery; the prey departeth not;

2 The noise of a whip, and [a]the noise of the rattling of the wheels,[212] and of the pransing[1725] horses, and of the jumping chariots.

3 The horseman lifteth up[5927] both [1]the bright sword[2719] and the glittering spear: and *there is* a multitude of slain,[2491] and a great number of carcases;[6297] and *there is* none end of *their* corpses;[1472] they stumble[3782] upon their corpses:

4 Because of the multitude of the whoredoms[2183] of the wellfavoured[2896,2580] harlot,[2181] [a]the mistress[1172] of witchcrafts,[3785] that selleth nations[1471] through her whoredoms, and families[4940] through her witchcrafts.

5 [a]Behold, I *am* against thee, saith[5002] the LORD of hosts;[6635] and [b]I will discover[1540] thy skirts upon thy face, [c]and I will shew[7200] the nations thy nakedness, and the kingdoms[4467] thy shame.

6 And I will cast abominable filth[8251] upon thee, and [a]make thee vile,[5034] and will set[7760] thee as [b]a gazingstock.[7210]

7 And it shall come to pass, *that* all they that look upon[7200] thee [a]shall flee from thee, and say, Nineveh is laid waste:[7703] [b]who will bemoan her? whence shall I seek comforters[5162] for thee?

8 [a]Art thou better[3190] than populous[527] [b]No, that was situate among the rivers, *that had* the waters round about it, whose rampart[2426] *was* the sea, *and* her wall *was* from the sea?

9 Ethiopia and Egypt *were* her strength, and *it was* infinite;[369,7097] Put and Lubim were [1]thy helpers.

10 Yet *was* she carried away,[1473] she went into captivity:[7628] [a]her young children also were dashed in pieces [b]at the top[7218] of all the streets: and they [c]cast lots for her honourable men,[3513] and all her great men were bound in chains.

11 Thou also shalt [a]be drunken: thou shalt be hid, thou also shalt seek strength[4581] because of the enemy.

12 All thy strong holds *shall be like* [a]fig trees with the firstripe figs: if they be shaken, they shall even fall[5307] into the mouth[6310] of the eater.

13 Behold, [a]thy people[5971] in the midst of thee *are* women: the gates of thy land[776] shall be set wide open unto thine enemies: the fire shall devour thy [b]bars.

14 Draw thee waters for the siege, [a]fortify[2388] thy strong holds: go into clay, and tread the morter, make strong[2388] the brickkiln.

15 There shall the fire devour thee; the sword shall cut thee off,[3772] it shall eat thee up like [a]the cankerworm: make thyself many as the cankerworm, make thyself many as the locusts.

10 [a]Isa. 13:7, 8 [b]Dan. 5:6 [c]Jer. 30:6 [d]Joel 2:6
11 [a]Job 4:10, 11; Ezek. 19:2-7
13 [a]Ezek. 29:3; 38:3; 39:1; Nah. 3:5 [b]2Kgs. 18:17, 19; 19:9, 23
1 [1]Hebr. *city of bloods* [a]Ezek. 22:2, 3; 24:6, 9; Hab. 2:12
2 [a]Jer. 47:3
3 [1]Hebr. *the flame of the sword, and the lightning of the spear*
4 [a]Isa. 47:9, 12; Rev. 18:2, 3
5 [a]Nah. 2:13 [b]Isa. 47:2, 3; Jer. 13:22, 26; Ezek. 16:37; Mic. 1:11 [c]Hab. 2:16
6 [a]Mal. 2:9 [b]Heb. 10:33
7 [a]Rev. 18:10 [b]Jer. 15:5
8 [a]Amos 6:2 [b]Jer. 46:25, 26; Ezek. 30:14-16
9 [1]Hebr. *in thy help*
10 [a]Ps. 137:9; Isa. 13:16; Hos. 13:16 [b]Lam. 2:19 [c]Joel 3:3; Obad. 1:11
11 [a]Jer. 25:17, 27; Nah. 1:10
12 [a]Rev. 6:13
13 [a]Jer. 50:37; 51:30 [b]Ps. 147:13; Jer. 51:30
14 [a]Nah. 2:1
15 [a]Joel 1:4

3:9 The specific locations of the countries of "Put" and "Lubim" are unclear from the details found in Scripture. It has been suggested that they were located in the region that makes up the modern day country of Lybia. They are frequently mentioned in association with Egypt and Ethiopia (2 Chr. 12:3; Ezek. 27:10).

16 Thou hast multiplied thy merchants above the stars of heaven:[8064] the cankerworm [I]spoileth, and flieth away.

17 [a]Thy crowned[4502] *are* as the locusts, and thy captains[2951] as the great grasshoppers, which camp in the hedges in the cold day, *but* when the sun ariseth they flee away, and their place is not known[3045] where they *are*.

18 [a]Thy shepherds slumber, O [b]king of Assyria: thy [I]nobles[117] shall dwell[7931] *in the dust:* thy people is [c]scattered upon the mountains, and no man gathereth[6908] *them.*

19 *There is* no [I]healing of thy bruise;[7667] [a]thy wound is grievous: [b]all that hear the bruit[8088] of thee shall clap the hands over thee: for upon whom hath not thy wickedness passed continually?

16 [I]Or, *spreadeth himself*
17 [a]Rev. 9:7
18 [I]Or, *valiant ones* [a]Ex. 15:16; Ps. 76:6 [b]Jer. 50:18; Ezek. 31:3 [c]1Kgs. 22:17
19 [I]Hebr. *wrinkling* [a]Mic. 1:9 [b]Lam. 2:15; Zeph. 2:15; Isa. 14:8

The Book of
HABAKKUK

Very little is known about Habakkuk except his name, which means either "the embracer" or "the wrestler." These meanings correspond to Habakkuk's "wrestling" with the question of why God would let evil go unpunished and then why He would bring calamity on His own people (Hab. 1:13), while at the same time he "embraced" salvation by faith (Hab. 3:18).

Most scholars accept 606 B.C. as an approximate date for his prophecy. This was just before the Battle of Carchemish, which established Babylon as the ruling power in the area of Palestine. Others believe the book was written in 655 B.C., during the reign of Manasseh, king of Judah.

Habakkuk was deeply troubled with the injustice that prevailed in his land (Hab. 1:3, 4), and was desirous that the Lord would act against it. However, when God informed him that the Chaldeans (i.e., Babylonians, cf. Dan. 3:8) would rise up to destroy Judah (Hab. 1:5–11), Habakkuk was not pleased. He questioned why God's people should perish at the hands of the heathen Chaldeans (Hab. 1:12–17). God's reply was "wait," consider who I am, and keep silent (Hab. 2:1–20). Habakkuk accepts this verdict and offers up a prayer that expresses his trust in God (Hab. 3:1–19).

The inquiries that Habakkuk made of God have been echoed by many of God's children down through the ages. The answers he received conclusively affirm that God is not accountable to any man. He is in no way obligated to comply with man's ideas of how He should handle situations. So often Christians pray as though they would control the hand of God, and direct the Almighty in his path. The answer of the Lord convinces Habakkuk that God is completely wise and sovereign in all his dealings.

Habakkuk Complains About Injustice

1 The burden[4853] which Habakkuk the
prophet[5030] did see.[2372]
🗝 2 O LORD, how long shall I cry,[7768]
[a]and thou wilt not hear[8085] *even* cry
out[2199] unto thee *of* violence,[2555] and thou
wilt not save[3467]
3 Why dost thou shew[7200] me iniquity,[205] and cause *me* to behold grievance?[5999] for spoiling[7701] and violence *are*
before me: and there are *that* raise up[5375]
strife[7379] and contention.
4 Therefore the law[8451] is slacked,[6313]
and judgment[4941] doth never[3808,5331] go
forth: for the [a]wicked[7563] doth compass
about the righteous;[6662] therefore [I]wrong
judgment proceedeth.
🗝 5 [a]Behold[7200] ye among the heathen,[1471] and regard, and wonder[8539] marvellously: for *I* will work a work in your

2 [a]Lam. 3:8

4 [I]Or, *wrested* [a]Job 21:7; Ps. 94:3; Jer. 12:1

5 [a]Isa. 29:14; Acts 13:41

🗝 **1:2–11** In this first round of exchanges between Habakkuk and God, Habakkuk inquired of God why the wickedness and injustices of the people of Judah were continuing without some sort of punishment (vv. 2–4). God replied that He would raise up a violent nation, the Chaldeans (better known as the Babylonians), to place the people of Judah in captivity (vv. 5–11). God often uses wicked people to test believers or to punish the ones who are wicked.

🗝 **1:5** This verse was used by Paul when he spoke in the synagogue in Antioch (Acts 13:40, 41). This was a prophecy regarding Israel's rejection of God as was seen in their idol worship. The "work" that God would perform among them was their captivity in Babylon. God placed them in exile to purify them from their sin of idolatry. Following that time, Israel never again fell into idolatry. Some say that the phrase "work a work in your days, which ye will not believe" refers to the ministry of Christ while He was on earth. He peformed many signs and miracles among the Jews, but they

(continued on next page)

days,[3117] *which* ye will not believe,[539] though it be told[5608] *you.*

6 For, lo, [I][a]I raise up the Chaldeans, *that* bitter[4751] and hasty4116 nation,[1471] which shall march through the [II]breadth of the land, to possess[3423] the dwellingplaces[4908] *that are* not theirs.

7 They *are* terrible366 and dreadful:[3372] [I]their judgment and their dignity7613 shall proceed of themselves.

8 Their horses also are swifter[7043] than the leopards, and are more [I]fierce than the [a]evening wolves: and their horsemen shall spread themselves, and their horsemen shall come from far; [b]they shall fly as the eagle *that* hasteth to eat.

9 They shall come all for violence: [I]their faces shall sup up4041 *as* the east wind, and they shall gather[622] the captivity[7628] as the sand.

10 And they shall scoff at the kings, and the princes[7336] shall be a scorn unto them: they shall deride every strong hold; for they shall heap dust,[6083] and take it.

11 Then shall2498 *his* mind[7307] change,2498 and he shall pass over,[5674] and offend,[816] [a]*imputing* this his power unto his god.[433]

🔑 12 [a]*Art* thou not from everlasting,[6924] O LORD my God,[430] mine Holy One?[6918] we shall not die.[4191] O LORD, [b]thou hast ordained[7760] them for judgment; and, O [I][c]mighty God, thou hast [II]established[3245] them for correction.[3198]

13 [a]*Thou art* of purer[2889] eyes than to behold[7200] evil,[7451] and canst not look on [I]iniquity:[5999] [b]wherefore lookest thou upon them that deal treacherously,[898] *and* holdest thy tongue when the wicked devoureth[1104] *the man that is* more righteous than he?

14 And makest[6213] men[120] as the fishes of the sea, as the [I]creeping things, *that have* no ruler[4910] over them?

15 They [a]take up[5927] all of them with the angle, they catch them in their net, and gather them in their drag:4365 therefore they rejoice and are glad.

16 Therefore [a]they sacrifice unto their net, and burn incense[6999] unto their drag; because by them their portion *is* fat,8082 and their meat [I]plenteous.1277

17 Shall they therefore empty their net, and not spare continually[8548] to slay[2026] the nations?

The LORD Answers Habakkuk

2 I will [a]stand upon my watch,[4931] and set me upon the [I]tower, [b]and will watch to see[7200] what he will say[1696] [II]unto me, and what I shall answer[7725] [III]when I am reproved.[8433]

🔑 2 And the LORD answered me, and said,[559] [a]Write the vision,[2377] and make *it* plain874 upon tables, that he may run that readeth[7121] it.

3 For [a]the vision *is* yet for an appointed time,[4150] but at the end it shall speak,[6315] and not lie:[3576] though it tarry, wait for it; because it will [b]surely come, it will not tarry.

6 [I]Fulfilled in 2Chr. 36:6 [II]Hebr. *breadths* [a]Deut. 28:49, 50; Jer. 5:15

7 [I]Or, *from them shall proceed the judgment of these, and the captivity of these*

8 [I]Hebr. *sharp* [a]Jer. 5:6; Zeph. 3:3 [b]Jer. 4:13

9 [I]Hebr. *the opposition of their faces toward the east*

11 [a]Dan. 5:4

12 [I]Hebr. *rock* [II]Hebr. *founded* [a]Ps. 90:2; 93:2; Lam. 5:19 [b]2Kgs. 19:25; Ps. 17:13; Isa. 10:5-7; Ezek. 30:25 [c]Deut. 32:4

13 [I]Or, *grievance* [a]Ps. 5:5 [b]Jer. 12:1

14 [I]Or, *moving*

15 [a]Jer. 16:6; Amos 4:2

16 [I]Hebr. *fat* [a]Deut. 8:17; Isa. 10:13; 37:24, 25

1 [I]Hebr. *fenced place* [II]Or, *in me* [III]Hebr. *upon my reproof,* or, *arguing* [a]Isa. 21:8, 11 [b]Ps. 85:8

2 [a]Isa. 8:1; 30:8

3 [a]Dan. 10:14; 11:27, 35 [b]Heb. 10:37

(continued from previous page)
refused to accept Him as their Messiah. Paul may have applied these words to the miracles and signs of the Lord Jesus and His disciples, as well as to the works that were done in Antioch and the growth of the church that came about thereafter.

🔑 **1:12—2:4** Habakkuk was confused by God's response in verses five through eleven, because he knew the cruelty and wickedness of the Chaldeans. How could a holy God use such an unholy and ruthless nation to punish men who were more righteous than they (Hab. 1:12–17)? Convinced that his complaint was justified, he waited in anticipation for God's reply (Hab. 2:1). It did not come right away, but God assured him that all would be understood soon. In the meantime, the righteous man should live by his faith (Hab. 2:2–4). This seems to have satisfied him, because he asked no more questions. In fact, his conclusion in chapter two verse twenty may be as much of a self-criticism as it is a statement of the holiness of God.

🔑 **2:2** See note on Jeremiah 36:2.

4 Behold, his soul[5315] *which* is lifted up[6075] is not upright in him: but the [a]just[6662] shall live[2421] by his faith.[530]

5 [I]Yea also, because he transgresseth[898] by wine, *he is* a proud man,[1397] neither keepeth at home, who enlargeth his desire[5315] [a]as hell,[7585] and *is* as death,[4194] and cannot be satisfied, but gathereth[622] unto him all nations,[1471] and heapeth[6908] unto him all people:[5971]

6 Shall not all these [a]take up[5375] a parable against him, and a taunting proverb[2420] against him, and say, [I]Woe to him that increaseth *that which is* not his! how long? and to him that ladeth[3513] himself with thick clay[5671]

7 Shall they not rise up suddenly that shall bite thee, and awake that shall vex[2111] thee, and thou shalt be for booties[4933] unto them?

8 [a]Because thou hast spoiled many nations, all the remnant[3499] of the people shall spoil thee; [b]because of men's[120] [I]blood,[1818] and *for* the violence[2555] of the land,[776] of the city, and of all that dwell therein.

9 Woe to him that [Ia]coveteth[1214] an evil covetousness[1215] to his house,[1004] that he may [b]set[7760] his nest on high, that he may be delivered[5337] from the [II]power[3709] of evil!

10 Thou hast consulted[3289] shame to thy house by cutting off many people, and hast sinned[2398] *against* thy soul.

11 For the stone shall cry out[2199] of the wall, and the [I]beam out of the timber shall [II]answer it.

12 Woe to him that buildeth a town with [Ia]blood, and stablisheth[3559] a city by iniquity[5766]

13 Behold, *is it* not of the LORD of hosts[6635] [a]that the people shall labour[3021] in the very fire, and the people shall weary themselves [I]for very vanity?

14 For the earth[776] shall be filled [I]with the [a]knowledge[3045] of the glory[3519] of the LORD, as the waters cover the sea.

15 Woe unto him that giveth his neighbour[7453] drink, that puttest[5595] thy [a]bottle to *him,* and makest *him* drunken also, that thou mayest [b]look[5027] on their nakedness!

16 Thou art filled[7646] [I]with shame for glory: [a]drink thou also, and let thy foreskin be uncovered:[6188] the cup of the LORD's right hand shall be turned unto thee, and shameful spewing[7022] *shall be* on thy glory.

17 For the violence of Lebanon shall cover thee, and the spoil[7701] of beasts, *which* made them afraid,[2865] [a]because of men's blood, and for the violence of the land, of the city, and of all that dwell therein.

18 [a]What profiteth the graven image[6459] that the maker[3335] thereof hath graven[6456] it; the molten image,[4541] and a [b]teacher of lies,[8267] that [I]the maker of his work[3336] trusteth[982] therein, to make[6213] [c]dumb idols?[457]

19 Woe unto him that saith to the wood, Awake; to the dumb stone, Arise, it shall teach[3384] Behold, it *is* laid over with gold and silver, [a]and *there is* no breath[7307] at all in the midst of it.

20 But [a]the LORD *is* in his holy[6944] temple:[1964] [Ib]let all the earth keep silence before him.

Habakkuk's Prayer

3 A prayer[8605] of Habakkuk the prophet [Ia]upon Shigionoth.

2 O LORD, I have heard[8085] [I]thy speech, *and* was afraid:[3372] O LORD, [IIa]revive[2421] thy work in the midst of the years, in the midst of the years

4 [a]John 3:36; Rom. 1:17; Gal. 3:11; Heb. 10:38
5 [I]Or, *How much more* [a]Prov. 27:20; 30:16
6 [a]Mic. 2:4
8 [I]Hebr. *bloods* [a]Isa. 33:1 [b]Hab. 2:17
9 [I]Or, *gaineth an evil gain* [II]Hebr. *palm of the hand* [a]Jer. 22:13; [b]Jer. 49:16; Obad. 1:4
11 [I]Or, *piece,* or, *fastening* [II]Or, *witness against it*
12 [I]Hebr. *bloods* [a]Jer. 22:13; Ezek. 24:9; Mic. 3:10; Nah. 3:1
13 [I]Or, *in vain* [a]Jer. 51:58
14 [I]Or, *by knowing the glory of the LORD* [a]Isa. 11:9
15 [a]Hos. 7:5; [b]Gen. 9:22
16 [I]Or, *more with shame than with glory* [a]Jer. 25:26, 27; 51:57
17 [a]Hab. 2:8
18 [I]Hebr. *the fashioner of his fashion* [a]Isa. 44:9, 10; 46:2 [b]Jer. 10:8, 14; Zech. 10:2 [c]Ps. 115:5; 1Cor. 12:2
19 [a]Ps. 135:17
20 [I]Hebr. *be silent all the earth before him* [a]Ps. 11:4; Zeph. 1:7; Zech. 2:13

1 [I]Or, *according to variable songs,* or, *tunes, called in Hebrew, Shigionoth*
2 [I]Hebr. *thy report,* or, *thy hearing* [II]Or, *preserve alive* [a]Ps. 85:6

2:4 Paul used this famous verse in his explanation of the principle that justification is by faith alone not by works (Rom. 1:17; Gal. 3:11; Eph. 2:8, 9).

3:1–19 This passage is a prayer psalm that was intended to be sung with stringed accompaniment. It is not a part of the interaction between Habakkuk and God in chapters one and two. Nevertheless, it harmonizes with the theme of the previous two chapters because it expresses a strong faith in God in spite of unfavorable circumstances.

make known; in wrath[7367] remember[2142] mercy.[7355]

3 God[433] came from [I]Teman, [a]and the Holy One[6918] from mount Paran. Selah. His glory[1935] covered[3680] the heavens,8064 and the earth was full of his praise.[8416]

4 And *his* brightness5051 was as the light;[216] he had [I]horns *coming* out of his hand:[3027] and there *was* the hiding of his power.

5 [a]Before him went the pestilence,[1698] and [Ib]burning coals went forth at his feet.

6 He stood, and measured the earth: he beheld,[7200] and drove asunder5425 the nations;[1471] [a]and the [b]everlasting[5703] mountains were scattered, the perpetual[5769] hills did bow: his ways *are* everlasting.[5769]

7 I saw[7200] the tents[168] of [I]Cushan [II]in affliction:[205] *and* the curtains of the land of Midian did tremble.[7264]

8 Was the LORD displeased[2734] against the rivers? *was* thine anger[639] against the rivers? *was* thy wrath[5678] against the sea, [a]that thou didst ride upon thine horses *and* [I]thy chariots of salvation?[3444]

9 Thy bow was made quite naked,5783 *according* to the oaths[7621] of the tribes,[4294] *even thy* word. Selah. [Ia]Thou didst cleave the earth with rivers.

10 [a]The mountains saw thee, *and* they trembled:[2342] the overflowing of the water passed by:[5674] the deep uttered his voice, *and* [b]lifted up[5375] his hands on high.

11 [a]The sun *and* moon stood still in their habitation: [I]at the light of thine [b]arrows they went, *and* at the shining5051 of thy glittering1300 spear.

12 Thou didst march through the land in indignation,[2195] [a]thou didst thresh the heathen[1471] in anger.

13 Thou wentest forth3318 for the salvation[3468] of thy people,[5971] *even* for salvation with thine anointed;[4899] [a]thou woundedst the head[7218] out of the house of the wicked,[7563] [I]by discovering the foundation[3247] unto the neck. Selah.

14 Thou didst strike through[5344] with his staves the head of his villages: they [I]came out as a whirlwind to scatter me: their rejoicing *was* as to devour the poor secretly.

15 [a]Thou didst walk through the sea with thine horses, *through* the [I]heap of great waters.

16 When I heard, [a]my belly[990] trembled; my lips[8193] quivered at the voice: rottenness entered into my bones,[6106] and I trembled in myself, that I might rest in the day[3117] of trouble: when he cometh up[5927] unto the people, he will [I]invade them with his troops.

17 Although the fig tree shall not blossom, neither *shall* fruit *be* in the vines; the labour of the olive shall [I]fail, and the fields shall yield[6213] no meat; the flock shall be cut off from the fold, and *there shall be* no herd in the stalls:

18 [a]Yet I will [b]rejoice5937 in the LORD, I will joy1523 in the God[430] of my salvation.

19 The LORD[3068] God[136] *is* [a]my strength,[2428] and he will make[7760] my feet like [b]hinds'355 *feet,* and he will make me to [c]walk upon mine high places.[1116] To the chief singer on my stringed instruments.

3 [I]Or, *the south* [a]Deut. 33:2; Judg. 5:4; Ps. 68:7
4 [I]Or, *bright beams out of his side*
5 [I]Or, *burning diseases* [a]Nah. 1:3 [b]Deut. 32:24; Ps. 18:8
6 [a]Nah. 1:5 [b]Gen. 49:26
7 [I]Or, *Ethiopia* [II]Or, *under affliction,* or, *vanity*
8 [I]Or, *thy chariots were salvation* [a]Deut. 33:26, 27; Ps. 68:4; 104:3; Hab. 3:15
9 [I]Or, *Thou didst cleave the rivers of the earth* [a]Ps. 78:15, 16; 105:41
10 [a]Ex. 19:16, 18; Judg. 5:4, 5; Ps. 68:8; 77:18; 114:4 [b]Ex. 14:22; Josh. 3:16
11 [I]Or, *thine arrows walked in the light* [a]Josh. 10:12, 13 [b]Josh. 10:11; Ps. 18:14; 77:17, 18
12 [a]Jer. 51:33; Amos 1:3; Mic. 4:13
13 [I]Hebr. *making naked* [a]Josh. 10:24; 11:8, 12; Ps. 68:21
14 [I]Hebr. *were tempestuous*
15 [I]Or, *mud* [a]Ps. 77:19
16 [I]Or, *cut them in pieces* [a]Ps. 119:120; Jer. 23:9
17 [I]Hebr. *lie*
18 [a]Job 13:15 [b]Isa. 41:16; 61:10
19 [a]Ps. 27:1 [b]2Sam. 22:34; Ps. 18:33 [c]Deut. 32:13; 33:29

The Book of

ZEPHANIAH

The lineage recorded for Zephaniah (Zeph. 1:1), the longest given for any prophet, traces his ancestry back to the righteous king Hezekiah. His noble ancestry may have given him access to the palace and made it possible for him to effectively reach the heart of young Josiah with his prophecies. However, since Zephaniah is not mentioned in any of the Historical Books of the Old Testament, it is not certain whether he held a position in the national administration. He prophesied during the reign of Josiah (640–608 B.C.), but before Josiah initiated his reforms in 631–621 B.C. (2 Chr. 34:3—35:19).

Zephaniah is a book of vivid contrasts. Compared to other prophets, he paints a darker picture of God's judgment, and a brighter picture of Israel's future glory. This extreme contrast reflects the divided religious loyalties of the people of Judah. Their worship of the Lord was often mixed with pagan practices that were abominable to God. God's judgment on this divided camp is called the "Day of the LORD" (see note on Zeph. 1:7) and makes up the theme of the book. The term is specifically referred to in 1:7–10, 14–16, 18; 2:2, 3; and 3:8, 11, 16.

Another key element of Zephaniah's teaching is the concept of a "remnant" that is protected in the "Day of the LORD" (Zeph. 2:7, 9; see note on 3:13). It is interesting that the meaning of Zephaniah's name, "the LORD hides," is closely associated with this aspect of his prophecy.

The Day of God's Anger Is Coming

1 The word[1697] of the LORD which
came unto Zephaniah the son[1121] of
Cushi, the son of Gedaliah, the son of
Amariah, the son of Hizkiah, in the
days[3117] of Josiah the son of Amon, king
of Judah.

2 [I]I will utterly consume[5486] all *things*
from off [II]the land,[127] saith[5002] the LORD.

3 [a]I will consume man[120] and beast;
I will consume the fowls of the
heaven,[8064] and the fishes of the sea, and
[b]the [I]stumblingblocks[4384] with the
wicked;[7563] and I will cut off[3772] man
from off the land, saith the LORD.

4 I will also stretch out mine
hand[3027] upon Judah, and upon all the inhabitants of Jerusalem; and [a]I will cut
off the remnant[7605] of Baal from this
place, *and* the name of [b]the Chemarims[3649] with the priests;[3548]

5 And them [a]that worship[7812] the
host[6635] of heaven upon the housetops;
[b]and them that worship *and* [c]that swear
[I]by the LORD, and that swear[7650] [d]by
Malcham;[4445]

6 And [a]them that are turned back
from the LORD; and *those* that [b]have not
sought[1245] the LORD, nor enquired[1875] for
him.

7 [a]Hold thy peace at the presence of

2 [I]Hebr. *By taking away I will make an end* [II]Hebr. *the face of the land*
3 [I]Or, *idols* [a]Hos. 4:3 [b]Ezek. 7:19; 14:3, 4, 7; Matt. 13:41
4 [a]2Kgs. 23:4, 5 [b]Hos. 10:5
5 [I]Or, *to the* LORD [a]2Kgs. 23:12; Jer. 19:13 [b]1Kgs. 18:21; 2Kgs. 17:33, 41 [c]Isa. 48:1; Hos. 4:15 [d]Josh. 23:7; 1Kgs. 11:33
6 [a]Isa. 1:4; Jer. 2:13, 17; 15:6 [b]Hos. 7:7
7 [a]Hab. 2:20; Zech. 2:13

1:7 The phrase "Day of the LORD" is one of the primary expressions in the Old Testament that is relevant to eschatological events. It properly refers to any time the Lord openly intervenes in the affairs of men. Thus it often can apply to two separate events in two different time periods. Zephaniah saw the fall of Jerusalem as "that time" that would occur very soon (v. 12), and therefore used terms such as "at hand" (v. 7) and "near" (v. 14). Yet, as is common in Old Testament prophecy, this imminent intervention of God becomes merged in the prophet's vision with the "Day of the LORD," God's ultimate intervention in the affairs of His people. At that time, He will judge the whole earth (vv. 2, 3; 3:8), purge Israel (Zeph. 3:11–13; see note on Ezek. 43:13–27), and then reestablish His people into their land (3:14–20). The apostate people of Israel and Judah had to be

(continued on next page)

the Lord[136] GOD: [b]for the day[3117] of the LORD *is* at hand: for [c]the LORD hath prepared[3559] a sacrifice,[2077] he hath [I]bid[6942] his guests.

8 And it shall come to pass in the day of the LORD's sacrifice, that I will [I]punish[6485] [a]the princes,[8269] and the king's children,[1121] and all such as are clothed with strange[5237] apparel.

9 In the same day also will I punish all those that leap on the threshold, which fill their masters'[113] houses[1004] with violence[2555] and deceit.[4820]

10 And it shall come to pass in that day, saith the LORD, *that there shall be* the noise of a cry from [a]the fish gate, and an howling from the second,4932 and a great crashing[7667] from the hills.

11 [a]Howl, ye inhabitants of Maktesh, for all the merchant people[5971] are cut down;[1820] all they that bear silver are cut off.[3772]

🔑 12 And it shall come to pass at that time,[6256] *that* I will search Jerusalem with candles,[5216] and punish the men[582] that are [I][a]settled on their lees:8105 [b]that say in their heart,3824 The LORD will not do good,[3190] neither will he do evil.[7489]

13 Therefore their goods[2428] shall become a booty,4933 and their houses a desolation:[8077] they shall also build houses, but [a]not inhabit *them;* and they shall plant vineyards, but [b]not drink the wine thereof.

14 [a]The great day[3117] of the LORD *is* near, *it is* near, and hasteth greatly, *even* the voice of the day of the LORD: the mighty man shall cry there bitterly.[4751]

15 [a]That day[3117] *is* a day of wrath,[5678] a day of trouble6869 and distress,4691 a day of wasteness[7722] and desolation, a day of darkness[2822] and gloominess,[653] a day of clouds[6051] and thick darkness,[6205]

16 A day of [a]the trumpet and alarm against the fenced cities, and against the high towers.

17 And I will bring distress6887 upon men,[120] that they shall [a]walk like blind men, because they have sinned[2398] against the LORD: and [b]their blood[1818] shall be poured out[8210] as dust,[6083] and their flesh[3894] [c]as the dung.

18 [a]Neither their silver nor their gold shall be able to deliver[5337] them in the day[3117] of the LORD's wrath; but the whole land[776] shall be [b]devoured by the fire of his jealousy:[7068] for [c]he shall make[6213] even a speedy[926] riddance[3617] of all them that dwell in the land.

Israel's Neighbours Are Doomed

2 [a]Gather yourselves together,7197 yea, gather together, O nation[1471] [I]not desired;

2 Before the decree[2706] bring forth, *before* the day pass[5674] [a]as the chaff, before [b]the fierce anger[639] of the LORD come upon you, before the day[3117] of the LORD's anger come upon you.

🔑 3 [a]Seek ye the LORD, [b]all ye meek of the earth,[776] which have wrought6466 his judgment;[4941] seek righteousness, seek meekness: [c]it may be ye shall be hid in the day of the LORD's anger.

7 [I]Hebr. *sanctified,* or, *prepared* [b]Isa. 13:6 [c]Isa. 34:6; Jer. 46:10; Ezek. 39:17; Rev. 19:17

8 [I]Hebr. *visit upon* [a]Jer. 39:6

10 [a]2Chr. 33:14

11 [a]James 5:1

12 [I]Hebr. *curded,* or, *thickened* [a]Jer. 48:11; Amos 6:1 [b]Ps. 94:7

13 [a]Deut. 28:30, 39; Amos 5:11 [b]Mic. 6:15

14 [a]Joel 2:1, 11

15 [a]Isa. 22:5; Jer. 30:7; Joel 2:2, 11; Amos 5:18; Zeph. 1:18

16 [a]Jer. 4:19

17 [a]Deut. 28:29; Isa. 59:10 [b]Ps. 79:3 [c]Ps. 83:10; Jer. 9:22; 16:4

18 [a]Prov. 11:4; Ezek. 7:19 [b]Zeph. 3:8 [c]Zeph. 1:2, 3

1 [I]Or, *not desirous* [a]Joel 2:16

2 [a]Job 21:18; Ps. 1:4; Isa. 17:13; Hos. 13:3 [b]2Kgs. 23:26

3 [a]Ps. 105:4; Amos 5:6 [b]Ps. 76:9 [c]Joel 2:14; Amos 5:15; Jon. 3:9

(continued from previous page)
constantly reminded that the Day of the LORD would be a time of judgment, and for the ungodly, a time of utter darkness (see notes on Jer. 30:3—31:26; Amos 5:18–20; 1 Thess. 5:2).

The "sacrifice" mentioned here refers to Christ's atoning work on the cross of Calvary (Heb. 10:12). In the phrase "bid his guests," God is inviting His people to accept this offering and come into a right relationship with Him (Matt. 10:6; 15:24).

🔑 **1:12** The promise in this verse may be used to condemn the philosophy of the Deists in that God will punish those who merely acknowledge His existence and do not believe that He is involved in the affairs of this world, that He neither judges nor blesses the actions of men. To God, this is the same as denying Him (cf. Heb. 11:6). See the note on Ezekiel 8:7–18.

🔑 **2:3** Those who already had an inclination to serve God are challenged here to seek the Lord even more earnestly. The judgment would still come upon the land, but they would be hidden. This

(continued on next page)

4 For [a]Gaza shall be forsaken,[5800] and Ashkelon a desolation:[8077] they shall drive out Ashdod [b]at the noon day, and Ekron shall be rooted up.

5 Woe unto the inhabitants of [a]the sea coast,[2256] 3220 the nation of the Cherethites! the word[1697] of the LORD *is* against you; O [b]Canaan, the land of the Philistines, I will even destroy[6] thee, that there shall be no inhabitant.

6 And the sea coast shall be dwellings *and* cottages 3741 for shepherds, [a]and folds for flocks.

7 And the coast shall be for [a]the remnant[7611] of the house[1004] of Judah; they shall feed thereupon: in the houses of Ashkelon shall they lie down in the evening: [I]for the LORD their God[430] shall [b]visit[6485] them and [c]turn away[7725] their captivity.[7622]

8 [a]I have heard[8085] the reproach[2781] of Moab, and [b]the revilings of the children[1121] of Ammon, whereby they have reproached my people,[5971] and [c]magnified *themselves* against their border.

9 Therefore *as* I live,[2416] saith 5002 the LORD of hosts,[6635] the God of Israel, Surely [a]Moab shall be as Sodom, and [b]the children of Ammon as Gomorrah, [c]*even* the breeding 4476 of nettles, and saltpits, and a perpetual[5769] desolation: [d]the residue[7611] of my people[1471] shall spoil them, and the remnant[3499] of my people shall possess[5157] them.

10 This shall they have [a]for their pride, because they have reproached 2778 and magnified *themselves* against the people of the LORD of hosts.

11 The LORD *will be* terrible[3372] unto them: for he will [I]famish all the gods[430] of the earth; [a]and *men* shall worship[7812] him, every one[376] from his place, *even* all [b]the isles of the heathen.[1471]

12 [a]Ye Ethiopians also, ye *shall be* slain 2491 by [b]my sword.[2719]

13 And he will stretch out his hand[3027] against the north, and [a]destroy[6] Assyria; and will make[7760] Nineveh a desolation, *and* dry like a wilderness.

14 And [a]flocks shall lie down in the midst of her, all [b]the beasts[2416] of the nations: both the [Ic]cormorant and the bittern shall lodge in the [II]upper lintels 3730 of it; *their* voice shall sing in the windows; desolation *shall be* in the thresholds: [III]for he shall uncover the [d]cedar work.

15 This *is* the rejoicing city [a]that dwelt carelessly,[983] [b]that said in her heart, I *am*, and *there is* none beside me: how is she become a desolation,[8047] a place for beasts to lie down in! every one that passeth[5674] by her [c]shall hiss, *and* [d]wag 5128 his hand.

Jerusalem Will Be Saved

3 Woe to [I]her that is filthy 4754 and polluted, to the oppressing[3238] city!

2 She [a]obeyed[8085] not the voice; she [b]received not [I]correction;[4148] she trusted 982 not in the LORD; she drew not near[7126] to her God.[430]

3 [a]Her princes[8269] within[7130] her *are* roaring lions; her judges[8199] *are* [b]evening wolves; they gnaw not the bones till the morrow.

4 Her [a]prophets[5030] *are* light *and* treacherous persons:[582] her priests[3548] have polluted[2490] the sanctuary,[6944] they have done [b]violence[2554] to the law.[8451]

4 [a]Jer. 47:4, 5; Ezek. 25:15; Amos 1:6-8; Zech. 9:5, 6 [b]Jer. 6:4; 15:8
5 [a]Ezek. 25:16 [b]Josh. 13:3
6 [a]Isa. 17:2; Zeph. 2:14
7 [I]Or, *when* [a]Isa. 11:11; Mic. 4:7; 5:7, 8; Hag. 1:12; 2:2; Zeph. 2:9 [b]Ex. 4:31; Luke 1:68 [c]Ps. 126:1; Jer. 29:14; Zeph. 3:20
8 [a]Jer. 48:27; Ezek. 25:8 [b]Ezek. 25:3, 6 [c]Jer. 49:1
9 [a]Isa. 15; Jer. 48; Ezek. 25:9; Amos 2:1 [b]Amos 1:13 [c]Gen. 19:25; Deut. 29:23; Isa. 13:19; 34:12; Jer. 49:18; 50:40 [d]Zeph. 2:7
10 [a]Isa. 16:6; Jer. 48:29
11 [I]Hebr. *make lean* [a]Mal. 1:11; John 4:21 [b]Gen. 10:5
12 [a]Isa. 18:1; 20:4; Jer. 46:9; Ezek. 30:9 [b]Ps. 17:13
13 [a]Isa. 10:12; Ezek. 31:3; Nah. 1:1; 2:10; 3:15, 18
14 [I]Or, *pelican* [II]Or, *knops, threshold* [III]Or, *when he hath uncovered* [a]Zeph. 2:6 [b]Isa. 13:21, 22 [c]Isa. 34:11, 14 [d]Jer. 22:14
15 [a]Isa. 47:8 [b]Rev. 18:7 [c]Job 27:23; Lam. 2:15; Ezek. 27:36 [d]Nah. 3:19

1 [I]Or, *gluttonous*
2 [I]Or, *instruction* [a]Jer. 22:21 [b]Jer. 5:3
3 [a]Ezek. 22:27; Mic. 3:9-11 [b]Hab. 1:8
4 [a]Jer. 23:11, 32; Lam. 2:14; Hos. 9:7 [b]Ezek. 22:26

(continued from previous page)
might refer to some special protection under God's providence (cf. Jer. 15:11; 39:17; 45:5), or to the fact that they are hidden in Him unto eternal life.

2:8, 9 Moab and Ammon were descendants of Lot, Abraham's nephew. They were judged with special harshness for their offenses against Israel. The absorption of the territories of Ammon and Moab is clearly presupposed in the millennial land allocations (Ezek. 45:1–25; 47:13—48:35).

2:13 This verse foretells the fall of Nineveh and the destruction of Assyria. It is also representative of the judgment to come on all of Israel's end-time enemies (see note on Mic. 5:3–9). The city of Nineveh fell approximately twenty years after this prophecy was given.

5 [a]The just[6662] LORD [b]*is* in the
midst[7130] thereof; he will not do[6213]
iniquity:[5766] [I]every morning doth he bring
his judgment[4941] to light,[216] he faileth
not; but [c]the unjust[5767] knoweth[3045] no
shame.
6 I have cut off[3772] the nations:[1471]
their [I]towers are desolate;[8074] I made their
streets waste,[2717] that none passeth
by:[5674] their cities are destroyed,[6658] so
that there is no man,[376] that there is none
inhabitant.
7 [a]I said, Surely thou wilt fear[3372]
me, thou wilt receive instruction;[4148] so
their dwelling should not be cut off,
howsoever I punished[6485] them: but they
rose early, *and* [b]corrupted[7843] all their doings.
8 Therefore [a]wait ye upon me,
saith[5002] the LORD, until the day[3117] that
I rise up to the prey: for my determination *is* to [b]gather[622] the nations, that I
may assemble[6908] the kingdoms,[4467] to
pour[8210] upon them mine indignation,[2195]
even all my fierce anger:[639] for all the
earth[776] [c]shall be devoured with the fire
of my jealousy.[7068]
9 For then will I turn[2015] to the
people[5971] [a]a pure[1305] [I]language,[8193] that
they may all call upon the name of the
LORD, to serve[5647] him with one [II]consent.
10 [a]From beyond the rivers of
Ethiopia my suppliants,[6286] *even* the
daughter of my dispersed, shall bring
mine offering.[4503]
11 In that day shalt thou not be
ashamed[954] for all thy doings, wherein
thou hast transgressed[6586] against me:
for then I will take away[5493] out of the
midst of thee them that [a]rejoice in thy
pride, and thou shalt no more be haughty
[I]because of my holy[6944] mountain.
12 I will also leave[7604] in the midst
of thee [a]an afflicted and poor people, and
they shall trust[2620] in the name of the
LORD.
🔑 13 [a]The remnant[7611] of Israel [b]shall
not do iniquity, [c]nor speak[1696] lies;[3577]
neither shall a deceitful tongue be found
in their mouth:[6310] for [d]they shall feed
and lie down, and none shall make *them*
afraid.[2729]
14 [a]Sing, O daughter of Zion;
shout,[7321] O Israel; be glad and rejoice
with all the heart,[3820] O daughter of
Jerusalem.
15 The LORD hath taken away[5493] thy
judgments, he hath cast out thine enemy:
[a]the king[4428] of Israel, *even* the LORD, [b]*is*
in the midst of thee: thou shalt not
see[7200] evil[7451] any more.
16 In that day [a]it shall be said[559] to
Jerusalem, Fear thou not: *and to* Zion,
[b]Let not thine hands[3027] be [I]slack.[7503]
🔑 17 The LORD thy God [a]in the midst
of thee *is* mighty; he will save,[3467]

5 [I]Hebr. *morning by morning* [a]Deut. 32:4 [b]Zeph. 3:15, 17; Mic. 3:11 [c]Jer. 3:3; 6:15; 8:12
6 [I]Or, *corners*
7 [a]Jer. 8:6 [b]Gen. 6:12
8 [a]Ps. 27:14; 37:34; Prov. 20:22; [b]Joel 3:2; [c]Zeph. 1:18
9 [I]Hebr. *lip* [II]Hebr. *shoulder* [a]Isa. 19:18
10 [a]Ps. 68:31; Isa. 18:1, 7; 60:4; Mal. 1:11; Acts 8:27
11 [I]Hebr. *in my holy* [a]Jer. 7:4; Mic. 3:11; Matt. 3:9
12 [a]Isa. 14:32; Zech. 11:11; Matt. 5:3; 1Cor. 1:27, 28; James 2:5
13 [a]Mic. 4:7; Zeph. 2:7 [b]Isa. 60:21 [c]Isa. 63:8; Rev. 14:5 [d]Zeph. 34:28; Mic. 4:4; 7:14
14 [a]Isa. 12:6; 54:1; Zech. 2:10; 9:9
15 [a]John 1:49 [b]Ezek. 48:35; Zeph. 5:17; Rev. 7:15; 21:3, 4
16 [I]Or, *faint* [a]Isa. 35:3, 4 [b]Heb. 12:12
17 [a]Zeph. 3:15

🔑 **3:13** The concept of the "Remnant" represents a spiritual entity within the national body of Israel. As early as Elijah's day God made note of "seven thousand in Israel, all the knees which have not bowed unto Baal, and every mouth which hath not kissed him" (1 Kgs. 19:18). Here the term "remnant" has an immediate reference to the righteous ones living in Jerusalem. Remnant also refers to the group of God's people who would return after the Babylonian Exile; Isaiah's son's name has this reference as well as an eschatological one (see Is. 1:9; note on Is. 8:1–4). Such a reference to a remnant is also found in Haggai (Hag. 1:12, 14; 2:2). However, the most common figure is that eschatological "remnant" that will be regathered at the end of the Great Tribulation to reign with King Messiah (Is. 10:20–22; 11:11, 16; 46:3; Jer. 31:7; Joel 2:32; Mic. 2:12; 5:3, 7, 8; Zeph. 2:7, 9; Zech. 8:6, 12; Rev. 12:17). With regard to the New Testament, those Jews who have accepted Jesus Christ as savior are also called "a remnant" (Rom. 9:27 [quoting Is. 10:22]; 11:5), inasmuch as they prefigure God's ultimate remnant.

🔑 **3:17–19** These verses describe the blessings of God's presence, power, and protection to His chosen people. He promises them that they will be restored to their land and that all those who had persecuted Israel will be punished. God also reveals how He would make their fame known once again throughout the world. The ultimate fulfillment of these blessings will occur during the millennial reign of Christ (Rev. 21:3, 7, 12).

(continued on next page)

[b]he will rejoice7797 over thee with joy; [I]he
will rest2790 in his love,160 he will joy1524
over thee with singing.
18 I will gather622 *them that* [a]*are* sorrowful for the solemn assembly,4150 *who*
are of thee, *to whom* [I]the reproach2781 of
it *was* a burden.4864
19 Behold, at that time6256 I will
undo6213 all that afflict thee: and I will
save3467 her that [a]halteth, and gather6908
her that was driven out; and I will get7760
them praise8416 and fame8034 in every
land776 where they have been put to
shame.
20 At that time [a]will I bring you
again, even in the time that I gather you:
for I will make you a name and a praise
among all people of the earth, when I
turn back7725 your captivity7622 before
your eyes, saith the LORD.

17 [I]Hebr. *he will be silent* [b]Deut. 30:9; Isa. 62:5; 65:19; Jer. 32:41
18 [I]Hebr. *the burden upon it was reproach* [a]Lam. 2:6
19 [a]Ezek. 34:14; Mic. 4:6, 7
20 [a]Isa. 11:12; 27:12; 56:8; Ezek. 28:25; 37:12; Amos 9:14

(continued from previous page)

For the believer, these promises can provide comfort as well. In a world of turmoil and persecution, God reveals His presence ("I will never leave thee, nor forsake thee"; Heb. 13:5b), power ("I have written . . . because ye are strong . . . and ye have overcome the wicked one"; 1 John 2:14b), and protection ("no man is able to pluck them out of my Father's hand"; John 10:29).

The Book of

HAGGAI

Haggai is the first of the prophets who spoke to the exiles after they had returned to Palestine. Because of the precise dates given for each prophetic message, the events of this book may be dated more accurately than perhaps any other book in the whole Bible. Darius, who is mentioned for the first two dates, was the Babylonian king that removed the interdict for the rebuilding of the temple (521 B.C.). Haggai ministered in 520 B.C. between the months of August and December. He delivered four messages during this time (Hag. 1:1–15 [some divide this into two messages at v. 12]; 2:1–9; 2:10–19; 2:20–23). From the comments in verse three of chapter two, it seems likely that Haggai was born before Solomon's Temple was destroyed in 586 B.C. He was, therefore, a very old man at the time he prophesied, and his death may account for the brevity of his ministry.

His ministry had a single focus: urging God's people to be obedient, especially in the rebuilding of the temple. The Exiles had returned under Zerubbabel in 536 B.C., but opposition from the surrounding rulers (see Ezra 4:1–24) and self-centered thinking (Hag. 1:2–4) kept the returned exiles from doing any more than laying the foundation for the temple (Ezra 3:8–13). Haggai and Zechariah were raised up by God to promote a spirit of revival among His people (see Ezra 5:1; 6:14). Haggai's first message was one of challenge, but the rest were concerned with encouraging the people and their leaders in the work, and reminding them of the consequences of previous disobedience. Following Haggai's ministry, work on the temple was begun again, and completed in 516 B.C. It is not known whether Haggai lived to see its completion.

The Appeal to Rebuild the Temple

1 🗝In [a]the second year of Darius the
king,[4428] in the sixth month, in the
first day of the month, came the word[1697]
of the LORD [I]by[3027] Haggai the
prophet[5030] unto [b]Zerubbabel the son[1121]
of Shealtiel, [II]governor[6346] of Judah, and
to [c]Joshua the son of [d]Josedech, the high
priest,[3548] saying,[559]
2 Thus speaketh the LORD of
hosts,[6635] saying, This people[5971] say,
The time[6256] is not come, the time that
the LORD's house[1004] should be built.
3 Then came the word of the LORD
[a]by Haggai the prophet, saying,
4 [a]*Is it* time for you, O ye, to dwell
in your cieled[5603] houses, and this house
lie waste?[2720]
5 Now therefore thus saith the LORD
of hosts; [I][a]Consider your ways.[1870]
6 Ye have [a]sown much, and bring in
little; ye eat, but ye have not enough; ye
drink, but ye are not filled with drink; ye
clothe you, but there is none warm; and
[b]he that earneth wages earneth wages *to*
put it into a bag [I]with holes.[5344]
7 Thus saith the LORD of hosts;
Consider your ways.
8 Go up[5927] to the mountain, and
bring wood, and build the house; and I
will take pleasure[7521] in it, and I will be
glorified,[3513] saith the LORD.

1 [I]Hebr. *by the hand of Haggai* [II]Or, *captain* [a]Ezra 4:24; 5:1; Zech. 1:1 [b]1Chr. 3:17, 19; Ezra 3:2; Matt. 1:12; Luke 3:27 [c]Ezra 3:2; 5:2 [d]1Chr. 6:15
3 [a]Ezra 5:1
4 [a]2Sam. 7:2; Ps. 132:3
5 [I]Hebr. *Set your heart on your ways* [a]Lam. 3:40; Hag. 1:7
6 [I]Hebr. *pierced through* [a]Deut. 28:38; Hos. 4:10; Mic. 6:14, 15; Hag. 2:16 [b]Zech. 8:10

🗝 **1:1–12** Haggai's first message is a stirring challenge to the people through their political and spiritual leaders, Zerubbabel and Joshua. The people looked to the decoration of their own houses (v. 4) while doing nothing for God's "house." Haggai twice says "consider" your ways (vv. 5, 7). This literally means to "put upon your heart," and speaks of a firm resolve (cf. Dan. 1:8). By these words, God is informing them that their neglect of the temple has resulted in His judgment on them (vv. 6–9); their self-centered efforts will not satisfy because God is not blessing. Their first priority should have been to glorify God, and this devotion should be evident in the life of believers today (v. 8, cf. John 15:8; Eph. 1:6). See note on Zephaniah 3:13 concerning the "remnant."

9 [a]Ye looked for much, and, lo, *it* *came* to little; and when ye brought *it* home,[1004] [b]I did [I]blow[5301] upon it. Why? saith[5002] the LORD of hosts. Because of mine house that *is* waste, and ye run every man[376] unto his own house.

10 Therefore [a]the heaven[8064] over you is stayed from dew, and the earth[776] is stayed *from* her fruit.

11 And I [a]called for[7121] a drought upon the land,[776] and upon the mountains, and upon the corn, and upon the new wine, and upon the oil,[3323] and upon *that* which the ground[127] bringeth forth, and upon men,[120] and upon cattle, and [b]upon all the labour of the hands.[3709]

12 [a]Then Zerubbabel the son of Shealtiel, and Joshua the son of Josedech, the high priest, with all the remnant[7611] of the people, obeyed[8085] the voice of the LORD their God,[430] and the words of Haggai the prophet, as the LORD their God had sent him, and the people did fear[3372] before the LORD.

13 Then spake[559] Haggai the LORD's messenger[4397] in the LORD's message unto the people, saying, [a]I *am* with you, saith the LORD.

14 And [a]the LORD stirred up[5782] the spirit of Zerubbabel the son of Shealtiel, [b]governor of Judah, and the spirit of Joshua the son of Josedech, the high priest, and the spirit of all the remnant of the people; [c]and they came and did[6213] work[4399] in the house of the LORD of hosts, their God,

15 In the four and twentieth day of the sixth month, in the second year of Darius the king.

9 [I]Or, *blow it away* [a]Hag. 2:16 [b]Hag. 2:17
10 [a]Lev. 26:19; Deut. 28:23; 1Kgs. 8:35
11 [a]1Kgs. 17:1; 2Kgs. 8:1 [b]Hag. 2:17
12 [a]Ezra 5:2
13 [a]Matt. 28:20; Rom. 8:31
14 [a]2Chr. 36:22; Ezra 1:1 [b]Hag. 2:21 [c]Ezra 5:2, 8

God's Glory Will Again Fill the Temple

2 In the seventh *month,* in the one and twentieth *day* of the month, came the word[1697] of the LORD [I]by[3027] the prophet[5030] Haggai, saying,[559]

🗝 2 Speak[559] now to Zerubbabel the son of Shealtiel, governor[6346] of Judah, and to Joshua the son of Josedech, the high priest, and to the residue[7611] of the people,[5971] saying,

3 [a]Who *is* left[7604] among you that saw[7200] this house[1004] in her first glory?[3519] and how do ye see it now? [b]*is* *it* not in your eyes in comparison of it as nothing?

4 Yet now [a]be strong,[2388] O Zerubbabel, saith[5002] the LORD; and be strong, O Joshua, son of Josedech, the high priest;[3548] and be strong, all ye people of the land,[776] saith the LORD, and work:[6213] for I *am* with you, saith the LORD of hosts:[6635]

5 [a]*According to* the word that I covenanted[3772] with you when ye came out of Egypt, so [b]my spirit[7307] remaineth among you: fear[3372] ye not.

🗝 6 For thus saith the LORD of hosts; [a]Yet once, it *is* a little while, and [b]I will shake[7493] the heavens,[8064] and the earth,[776] and the sea, and the dry[2724] *land;*

🗝 7 And I will shake all nations,[1471]

1 [I]Hebr. *by the hand of*
3 [a]Ezra 3:12 [b]Zech. 4:10
4 [a]Zech. 8:9
5 [a]Ex. 29:45, 46 [b]Neh. 9:20; Isa. 63:11
6 [a]Hag. 2:21; Heb. 12:26 [b]Joel 3:16

🗝 **2:2–4** Quite possibly, the problem at this time was similar to the situation in Ezra 3:8–13. Those who had seen the original size and splendor of Solomon's Temple (which Nebuchadnezzar destroyed in 586 B.C.) could not help but see how much smaller and less ornate this temple would be, and seeing such grew discouraged.

🗝 **2:6–9** God, throughout this passage, is called the "LORD of hosts" (which literally means, "Lord of armies"). What a comforting name for the people of Israel, who felt that they were a tiny, powerless province of Persia. God confirmed that His "Spirit" was in their midst, according to the original covenant at Mount Sinai, by which they became God's people (Hag. 2:5). Doubtless that such "shaking" as is mentioned in this verse may have occurred at that time in the Persian Empire; yet these words have a much greater significance. The eschatological meaning is manifested in that God will shake "all nations" (Hag. 2:7), a reference to worldwide judgment.

🗝 **2:7** The interpretation of the phrase "the desire of all nations" is much disputed. Some versions translate the phrase "they will come with the wealth of all nations." This is supported by the con-

(continued on next page)

[a]and the desire[2532] of all nations shall come: and I will fill this house with glory, saith the LORD of hosts.

8 The silver *is* mine, and the gold *is* mine, saith the LORD of hosts.

9 [a]The glory of this latter house shall be greater than of the former, saith the LORD of hosts: and in this place will I give [b]peace,[7965] saith the LORD of hosts.

10 In the four and twentieth *day* of the ninth *month,* in the second year of Darius, came the word of the LORD by Haggai the prophet, saying,

11 Thus saith the LORD of hosts; [a]Ask[7592] now the priests *concerning* the law,[8451] saying,

12 If one[376] bear[5375] holy[6944] flesh[1319] in the skirt of his garment, and with his skirt do touch bread, or pottage,[5138] or wine, or oil,[8081] or any meat, shall it be holy?[6942] And the priests answered and said,[559] No.

13 Then said Haggai, if *one that is* [a]unclean[2931] by a dead body[5315] touch[5060] any of these, shall it be unclean? And the priests answered and said, It shall be unclean.

14 Then answered Haggai, and said, [a]So *is* this people, and so *is* this nation before me, saith the LORD; and so *is* every work of their hands;[3027] and that which they offer[7126] there *is* unclean.

15 And now, I pray you, [a]consider from this day[3117] and upward, from before a stone was laid[7760] upon a stone in the temple[1964] of the LORD:

16 Since those *days* were, [a]when *one* came to an heap of twenty *measures,* there were *but* ten: when *one* came to the pressfat[3342] for to draw out fifty *vessels* out of the press, there were *but* twenty.

17 [a]I smote[5221] you with blasting and with mildew and with hail [b]in all the labours of your hands; [c]yet ye *turned* not to me, saith the LORD.

18 Consider[7760][3824] now from this day and upward, from the four and twentieth day of the ninth *month, even* from [a]the day that the foundation of the LORD's temple was laid,[3245] consider *it.*

19 [a]Is the seed[2233] yet in the barn? yea, as yet the vine, and the fig tree, and the pomegranate, and the olive tree, hath not brought forth: from this day will I bless[1288] *you.*

20 And again the word of the LORD came unto Haggai in the four and twentieth *day* of the month, saying,

21 Speak to Zerubbabel, [a]governor of Judah, saying, [b]I will shake[7493] the heavens and the earth;

22 And [a]I will overthrow[2015] the throne[3678] of kingdoms,[4467] and I will

7 [a]Gen. 49:10; Mal. 3:1
9 [a]John 1:14 [b]Ps. 85:8, 9; Luke 2:14; Eph. 2:14
11 [a]Lev. 10:10, 11; Deut. 33:10; Mal. 2:7
13 [a]Num. 19:11
14 [a]Titus 1:15
15 [a]Hag. 1:5
16 [a]Hag. 1:6, 9; Zech. 8:10
17 [a]Deut. 28:22; 1Kgs. 8:37; Amos 4:9; Hag. 1:9 [b]Hag. 1:11 [c]Jer. 5:3; Amos 4:6, 8-11
18 [a]Zech. 8:9
19 [a]Zech. 8:12
21 [a]Hag. 1:14 [b]Hag. 2:6, 7; Heb. 12:26
22 [a]Dan. 2:44; Matt. 24:7

(continued from previous page)
struction of the sentence in Hebrew. The verb "shall come" is plural, and thus the word "desire" cannot refer to an individual person. This verse is best understood as a reference to the nations that will one day bring their offerings to God to be consecrated for His service.

2:10–19 This third message of encouragement is based on holiness. Personal holiness comes only by conscious effort, and sinfulness spreads and increases in one's life unless it is effectively combatted. This was evident in the lives of the Israelites. Their sinfulness in certain areas had affected all of their activities (Hag. 2:14). However, since they had now repented and laid the foundation for the temple in obedience to the message Haggai had delivered previously, God asked if they were ready for a harvest, because He was now going to bless their harvest (Hag. 2:19).

2:18 This verse is Haggai's plea to the people to keep in mind the motives for their labor. Previously, the people of Israel were guilty of being slothful in their service (Hag. 2:14–16). The result was God's punishment (Hag. 2:17). The prophet calls them to renew their vigor in accomplishing the task that God had called them to, namely the rebuilding of the temple. In the midst of the believer's service for God, he or she should remember to perform every task, keeping in mind that God desires diligence and integrity (Eph. 6:5, 6).

2:20–23 Completing the temple would not strengthen Zerubbabel's political power in the Persian Empire, so Haggai is given another message for this servant of God. As a descendant of David,
(continued on next page)

destroy[8045] the strength[2392] of the kingdoms of the heathen;[1471] and [b]I will overthrow the chariots, and those that ride in
them; and the horses and their riders
shall come down, every one[376] by the
sword[2719] of his brother.[251]

22 [b]Mic. 5:10; Zech. 4:6; 9:10

23 [a]Song 8:6; Jer. 22:24 [b]Isa. 42:1; 43:10

23 In that day,[3117] saith the LORD of
hosts, will I take thee, O Zerubbabel, my
servant,[5650] the son of Shealtiel, saith the
LORD, [a]and will make[7760] thee as a
signet:[2368] for [b]I have chosen[977] thee,
saith the LORD of hosts.

(continued from previous page)

He was in the kingly line of the coming Messiah. God had removed Jeconiah from the throne (Jer. 22:24), pronouncing a curse on him that none of his sons would ever again rule on the throne of David until the Messiah came (see note on Jer. 22:24–30).

The Book of

ZECHARIAH

The ministry of Zechariah, which began in 520 B.C., overlapped that of Haggai (Zech 1:1, cf. Hag. 1:1; 2:20), but continued long after Haggai ceased to prophesy. The meaning of Zechariah's name, "the LORD remembers," is also the theme of the book. The meanings of his ancestors' names (Zech. 1:1), Berechiah, "the LORD blesses," and Iddo, "the appointed time," are reflected in the messages that God gave to him as well. Zechariah was of the priestly line, since Iddo is listed as the head of a returning priestly family (Neh. 12:4, 16).

Zechariah, like Haggai, had a ministry of encouragement. There is, however, one fundamental difference between their messages. After challenging the people to proceed with the rebuilding of the temple, Haggai focused primarily on God's immediate presence and the blessings that were at hand. Zechariah, on the other hand, focuses on the ultimate glorification of Israel through the coming of the Messiah. Zechariah addresses both the first and second coming of Jesus, but clearly demonstrates that the first advent is a necessary preparation for the second. Some examples of this are: 1) The use of the "BRANCH" motif (chaps. 3, 6) emphasizes Jesus' humanity and service, and yet is unquestionably linked to the previous uses in Isaiah and Jeremiah where His deity and kingship are stressed (Is. 4:2; 11:1–5; 53:2; see note on Jer. 23:5–8); 2) The betrayal and crucifixion of Christ is connected with Israel's repentance (Zech. 11:12–13; 12:10, cf. 12:10–14:9); 3) The divine Shepherd is first smitten (cf. Zech 13:7 with Is. 40:11; Jer. 31:10; Ezek 34:5–23; Matt. 25:32; John 10:14, 15).

Chapters one through eight are full of apocalyptic imagery (see introductions to Dan. and Ezek.). Chapters nine through fourteen have more poetic imagery. Messianic pictures found throughout the book form a strong argument for its unity.

A Call to Come Back To the LORD

1 In the eighth month, [a]in the second year of Darius, came the word[1697] of the LORD [b]unto Zechariah, the son[1121] of Berechiah, the son of Iddo the prophet,[5030] saying,[559]

2 The LORD hath been[7107] [I]sore[7110] displeased[7107] with your fathers.[1]

3 Therefore say thou unto them, Thus saith[5002] the LORD of hosts;[6635] Turn[7725] [a]ye unto me, saith the LORD of hosts, and I will turn unto you, saith the LORD of hosts.

4 Be ye not as your fathers, [a]unto whom the former prophets have cried,[7121] saying, Thus saith the LORD of hosts; [b]Turn ye now from your evil[7451] ways,[1870] and *from* your evil doings: but they did not hear,[8085] nor hearken[7181] unto me, saith the LORD.

5 Your fathers, where *are* they? and the prophets, do they live[2421] for ever?[5769]

6 But [a]my words[1697] and my statutes,[2706] which I commanded[6680] my servants[5650] the prophets, did they not [I]take hold of your fathers? and they returned[7725] and said,[559] [b]Like as the LORD of hosts thought[2161] to do unto us, according to our ways, and according to our doings, so hath he dealt[6213] with us.

🔑 7 Upon the four and twentieth day of

1 [a]Ezra 4:24; Hag. 1:1 [b]Ezra 5:1; Matt. 23:35
2 [I]Hebr. *with displeasure*
3 [a]Jer. 25:5; 35:15; Mic. 7:19; Mal. 3:7; Luke 15:20; James 4:8
4 [a]2Chr. 36:15, 16 [b]Isa. 31:6; Jer. 3:12; 18:11; Ezek. 18:30; Hos. 14:1
6 [I]Or, *overtake* [a]Isa. 55:1 [b]Lam. 1:18; 2:17

🔑 **1:7–17** This is the first of Zechariah's eight night visions (Zech. 1:7—6:8) and is significant because the "angel of the LORD" (a phrase used throughout the Old Testament) is a reference to a

(continued on next page)

the eleventh month, which *is* the month
Sebat, in the second year of Darius, came
the word of the LORD unto Zechariah, the
son of Berechiah, the son of Iddo the
prophet, saying,
8 I saw[7200] by night, and behold [a]a
man[376] riding upon a red[122] horse, and
he stood among the myrtle trees that
were in the bottom; and behind him *were*
there [b]red horses, [I]speckled,[8320] and
white.
9 Then said I, O my lord,[113] what
are these? And the angel[4397] that talked
with me said unto me, I will shew[7200]
thee what these *be*.
10 And the man that stood among
the myrtle trees answered and said,
[a]These *are they* whom the LORD hath sent
to walk to and fro through the earth.[776]
11 [a]And they answered the angel of
the LORD that stood among the myrtle
trees, and said, We have walked to and
fro through the earth, and, behold, all the
earth sitteth still, and is at rest.[8252]
12 Then the angel of the LORD answered and said, [a]O LORD of hosts, how
long wilt thou not have mercy[7355] on
Jerusalem and on the cities of Judah,
against which thou hast had indignation[2194] [b]these threescore and ten years?
13 And the LORD[3068] answered the
angel that talked with me *with* [a]good
words *and* comfortable[5150] words.
14 So the angel that communed with
me said unto me, Cry[7121] thou, saying,
Thus saith the LORD of hosts; I am
[a]jealous[7065] for Jerusalem and for Zion
with a great jealousy.[7068]
15 And I am very sore displeased
with the heathen[1471] *that are* at ease: for
[a]I was but a little displeased, and they
helped forward the affliction.[7451]
16 Therefore thus saith the LORD;
[a]I am returned[7725] to Jerusalem with
mercies:[7356] my house[1004] shall be built in
it, saith the LORD of hosts, and [b]a line
shall be stretched forth upon Jerusalem.
17 Cry yet, saying, Thus saith the
LORD of hosts; My cities through
[I]prosperity[2896] shall yet be spread
abroad;[6327] [a]and the LORD shall yet
comfort[5162] Zion, and [b]shall yet choose[977]
Jerusalem.
🗝 18 Then lifted I up[5375] mine eyes,
and saw, and behold four horns.
19 And I said unto the angel that
talked with me, What *be* these? And he
answered me, [a]These *are* the horns which
have scattered Judah, Israel, and Jerusalem.
20 And the LORD shewed me four
carpenters.[2796]

8 [I]Or, *bay* [a]Josh. 5:13; Rev. 6:4 [b]Zech. 6:2-7
10 [a]Heb. 1:14
11 [a]Ps. 103:20, 21
12 [a]Ps. 102:13; Rev. 6:10 [b]Jer. 25:11, 12; Dan. 9:2; Zech. 7:5
13 [a]Jer. 29:10
14 [a]Joel 2:18; Zech. 8:2
15 [a]Isa. 47:6
16 [a]Isa. 12:1; 54:8; Zech. 2:10; 8:3 [b]Zech. 2:1, 2
17 [I]Hebr. *good* [a]Isa. 51:3 [b]Isa. 14:1; Zech. 2:12; 3:2
19 [a]Ezra 4:1, 4, 7; 5:3

(continued from previous page)
preincarnate appearance of Jesus Christ (see note on Ex. 23:20–23). The rider of the red horse symbolizes war and the end of peace on the earth (Rev. 6:4). The myrtle trees symbolize Israel (Zech. 1:10, 11). The earth has been patrolled by four angels of God and found to be "at rest" (Zech. 1:11). This means not only that the earth is at peace, but that the insignificance of the nation of Israel will continue. This causes the angel of the LORD to question "O LORD of hosts, how long?" (Zech. 1:12, on "LORD of hosts" see note on Hag. 2:6–9). God's answer was that He was going to direct His anger at those nations who chastened Jerusalem (Zech. 1:15). For Jerusalem, however, there was a word of immediate (and ultimate) comfort and exaltation (Zech. 1:16, 17). Note how the measuring line has now been transformed from a symbol of judgment (see note on Amos 7:7–9 on the word "plumbline") into a positive symbol of blessing (Zech. 1:16). The building of God's house (Zech. 1:16) obviously refers to the building of the temple at that time, and assurance was given that it would be completed.

🗝 **1:18–21** This second vision emphasizes that the Gentiles that have afflicted God's people will suffer the judgment of God. Though the text speaks of those afflicted and scattered Israel, Judah, and Jerusalem, these descriptions could just as well refer to Assyria and Babylon, and to Egypt and Ethiopia who were their allies. Therefore, these "four horns" are general references to any nation who would potentially pose a threat to Israel. The "four carpenters" (v. 20) are representative of God's intervention, destroying anyone who attacks His people. They may represent supernatural intervention (cf. Dan. 10:13, 20; 11:1), or simply other earthly kingdoms used by God to overthrow Judah's oppressors.

21 Then said I, What come these to do? And he spake, saying, These *are* the horns which have scattered Judah, so that no man did lift up[5375] his head:[7218] but these are come to fray[2729] them, to cast out the horns of the Gentiles,[1471] which [a]lifted up *their* horn over the land[776] of Judah to scatter it.

A Man With a Measuring Line

2 🔑 I lifted up[5375] mine eyes again, and looked,[7200] and behold [a]a man[376] with a measuring line[2256] in his hand.[3027]

2 Then said I, Whither goest thou? And he said unto me, [a]To measure Jerusalem, to see[7200] what *is* the breadth thereof, and what *is* the length thereof.

3 And, behold, the angel[4397] that talked with me went forth, and another angel went out to meet him,

4 And said unto him, Run, speak[1696] to this young man, saying,[559] [a]Jerusalem shall be inhabited *as* towns without walls for the multitude of men[120] and cattle therein:

5 For I, saith[5002] the LORD, will be unto her [a]a wall of fire round about, [b]and will be the glory[3519] in the midst of her.

6 Ho, ho, *come forth,* and flee [a]from the land[776] of the north, saith the LORD: for I have [b]spread you abroad as the four winds[7307] of the heaven,[8064] saith the LORD.

7 [a]Deliver thyself, O Zion, that dwellest *with* the daughter of Babylon.

8 For thus saith the LORD of hosts;[6635] After the glory hath he sent me unto the nations[1471] which spoiled you: for he that [a]toucheth[5060] you toucheth the apple of his eye.

9 For, behold, I will [a]shake[5130] mine hand upon them, and they shall be a spoil to their servants:[5647] and [b]ye shall know[3045] that the LORD of hosts hath sent me.

10 [a]Sing and rejoice, O daughter of Zion: for, lo, I come, and I [b]will dwell[7931] in the midst of thee, saith the LORD.

11 [a]And many nations shall be joined to the LORD [b]in that day,[3117] and shall be [c]my people:[5971] and I will dwell in the midst of thee, and [d]thou shalt know that the LORD of hosts hath sent me unto thee.

12 And the LORD shall [a]inherit[5157] Judah his portion in the holy[6944] land,[127] and [b]shall choose[977] Jerusalem again.

13 [a]Be silent, O all flesh,[1320] before the LORD: for he is raised up [b]out of [I][c]his holy habitation.

Clean Clothes for the High Priest

3 🔑 And he shewed[7200] me [a]Joshua the high priest[3548] standing before the angel[4397] of the LORD, and [I][b]Satan[7854] standing at his right hand [II]to resist him.

2 And the LORD said[559] unto Satan, [a]The LORD rebuke[1605] thee, O Satan; even the LORD that [b]hath chosen[977] Jerusalem rebuke thee: [c]*is* not this a brand plucked[5337] out of the fire?

3 Now Joshua was clothed with [a]filthy garments, and stood before the angel.

4 And he answered and spake unto those that stood before him, saying, Take

21 [a]Ps. 75:4, 5
1 [a]Ezek. 40:3
2 [a]Rev. 11:1; 21:15, 16
4 [a]Jer. 31:27; Ezek. 36:10, 11
5 [a]Isa. 26:1; Zech. 9:8 [b]Isa. 60:19; Rev. 21:23
6 [a]Isa. 48:20; 52:11; Jer. 1:14; 50:8; 51:6, 45 [b]Deut. 28:64; Ezek. 17:21
7 [a]Rev. 18:4
8 [a]Deut. 32:10; Ps. 17:8; 2Thess. 1:6
9 [a]Isa. 11:15; 19:16 [b]Zech. 4:9
10 [a]Isa. 12:6; 54:1; Zeph. 3:14 [b]Lev. 26:12; Ezek. 37:27; Zech. 8:3; John 1:14; 2Cor. 6:16
11 [a]Isa. 2:2, 3; 49:22; 60:3; Zech. 8:22, 23 [b]Zech. 3:10 [c]Ex. 12:49 [d]Ezek. 33:33; Zech. 2:9
12 [a]Deut. 32:9 [b]Zech. 1:17
13 [I]Hebr. *the habitation of his holiness* [a]Hab. 2:20; Zeph. 1:7 [b]Ps. 68:5; Isa. 57:15 [c]Deut. 26:15, Isa. 63:15

1 [I]That is, *an adversary* [II]Hebr. *to be his adversary* [a]Hag. 1:1 [b]Ps. 109:6; Rev. 12:10
2 [a]Jude 1:9 [b]Zech. 1:17; Rom. 8:33 [c]Amos 4:11; Rom. 11:5; Jude 1:23
3 [a]Isa. 64:6

🔑 **2:1–13** This third of Zechariah's visions stresses that the final exaltation of Jerusalem will exceed anything it has previously known. Jerusalem will be overrun with people and cattle like an unwalled town (Zech. 2:4). More than this, the Lord will be the "glory" within the city (Zech. 2:5). Many nations will join themselves to God's people (vv. 10, 11). This latter statement may be referring to God expanding His kingdom to include the Gentiles (Acts 13:45, 46; 28:28).

🔑 **3:1–10** This fourth vision focuses on Joshua, the high priest. However, it is clear that Joshua is a symbol of what God is going to do; namely, to bring forth His servant, "the BRANCH" (v. 8; see note on Jer. 23:5–8). The removal of Joshua's iniquity (v. 4) is symbolic of the national cleansing from sin that is coming to Israel (cf. Is. 66:8; Ezek. 36:24–33).

away[5493] the filthy garments from him. And unto him he said, Behold,[7200] I have caused[5674] thine iniquity[5771] to pass[5674] from thee, [a]and I will clothe thee with change of raiment.

5 And I said, Let them set[7760] a fair[2889] [a]mitre[6797] upon his head.[7218] So they set a fair mitre upon his head, and clothed him with garments. And the angel of the LORD stood by.

6 And the angel of the LORD protested[5749] unto Joshua, saying,

7 Thus saith the LORD of hosts;[6635] If thou wilt walk in my ways,[1870] and if thou wilt [a]keep[8104] my [I]charge,[4931] then thou shalt also [b]judge[1777] my house,[1004] and shalt also keep my courts, and I will give thee [II]places to walk among these that [c]stand by.

8 Hear now, O Joshua the high priest, thou, and thy fellows[7453] that sit before thee: for they *are* [I][a]men[582] wondered at:[4159] for, behold, I will bring forth [b]my servant[5650] the [c]BRANCH.[6780]

9 For behold the stone that I have laid before Joshua; [a]upon one stone *shall be* [b]seven eyes: behold, I will engrave the graving[6603] thereof, saith the LORD of hosts, and [c]I will remove[4185] the iniquity of that land[776] in one day.[3117]

10 [a]In that day, saith the LORD of hosts, shall ye call[7121] every man[376] his neighbour[7453] [b]under the vine and under the fig tree.

The Lampstand and the Olive Trees

4 And [a]the angel[4397] that talked with me came again,[7725] and waked me, [b]as a man[376] that is wakened out of his sleep,

2 And said[559] unto me, What seest[7200] thou? And I said, I have looked, and behold [a]a candlestick all *of* gold, [I]with a bowl upon the top[7218] of it, [b]and his seven lamps[5216] thereon, and [II]seven pipes to the seven lamps, which *are* upon the top thereof:

3 [a]And two olive trees by it, one upon the right *side* of the bowl, and the other upon the left *side* thereof.

4 So I answered and spake to the angel that talked with me, saying, What *are* these, my lord?[113]

5 Then the angel that talked with me answered and said unto me, Knowest[3045] thou not what these be? And I said, No, my lord.

🗝 6 Then he answered and spake unto me, saying, This *is* the word[1697] of the LORD unto Zerubbabel, saying, [a]Not by [I]might,[2428] nor by power,[3581] but by my Spirit[7307] saith the LORD of hosts.[6635]

7 Who *art* thou, [a]O great mountain? before Zerubbabel *thou shalt become* a plain: and he shall bring forth [b]the headstone[7222][68] *thereof* [c]*with* shoutings, *crying,* Grace,[2580] grace unto it.

8 Moreover the word of the LORD came unto me, saying,

9 The hands[3027] of Zerubbabel [a]have laid the foundation of this house;[1004] his hands [b]shall also finish[1214] it; and [c]thou shalt know that the [d]LORD of hosts hath sent me unto you.

10 For who hath despised[937] the day of [a]small things?[6996] [I]for they shall rejoice,[8056] and shall see the [II]plummet in the hand of Zerubbabel *with* those seven; [b]they *are* the eyes of the LORD, which run to and fro[7751] through the whole earth.

11 Then answered I, and said unto him, What *are* these [a]two olive trees upon the right *side* of the candlestick and upon the left *side* thereof?

12 And I answered again, and said unto him, What *be these* two olive branches which [I]through the two golden

4 [a]Isa. 61:10; Luke 15:22; Rev. 19:8
5 [a]Ex. 29:6; Zech. 6:11
7 [I]Or, *ordinance* [II]Hebr. *walks* [a]Lev. 8:35; 1Kgs. 2:3; Ezek. 44:16 [b]Deut. 17:9; Mal. 2:7 [c]Zech. 4:14; 6:5
8 [I]Hebr. *men of wonder, or, sign* [a]Ps. 71:7; Isa. 8:18; 20:3; Ezek. 12:11; 24:24 [b]Isa. 42:1; 49:3, 5; 52:13; 53:11; Ezek. 34:23, 24 [c]Isa. 4:2; 11:1; Jer. 23:5; 33:15; Zech. 6:12
9 [a]Ps. 118:22; Isa. 28:16 [b]Zech. 4:10; Rev. 5:6 [c]Jer. 31:34; 50:20; Mic. 7:18, 19; Zech. 13:1
10 [a]Zech. 2:11 [b]1Kgs. 4:25; Isa. 36:16; Mic. 4:4

1 [a]Zech. 2:3 [b]Dan. 8:18
2 [I]Hebr. *with her bowl* [II]Or, *seven several pipes to the lamps* [a]Ex. 25:31; Rev. 1:12 [b]Ex. 25:37; Rev. 4:5
3 [a]Zech. 4:11, 12; Rev. 11:4
6 [I]Or, *army* [a]Hos. 1:7
7 [a]Jer. 51:25; Matt. 21:21 [b]Ps. 118:22 [c]Ezra 3:11, 13
9 [a]Ezra 3:10 [b]Ezra 6:15 [c]Zech. 2:9, 11; 6:15 [d]Isa. 48:16; Zech. 2:8
10 [I]Or, *since the seven eyes of the LORD shall rejoice* [II]Hebr. *stone of tin* [a]Hag. 2:3 [b]2Chr. 16:9; Prov. 15:3; Zech. 3:9
11 [a]Zech. 4:3
12 [I]Hebr. *by the hand*

🗝 **4:6** This famous verse describes the source of Zerubbabel's sufficiency; it is God's "Spirit" that will sustain him, even though he is the governor of a seemingly insignificant province of the vast Persian Empire. Zerubbabel is also assured that he will complete the temple he had begun to build (Zech. 4:9).

pipes [II]empty [III]the golden *oil* out of themselves?

13 And he answered me and said, Knowest thou not what these *be*? And I said, No, my lord.

14 Then said he, [a]These *are* the two [I]anointed[3323] ones, [b]that stand by [c]the Lord[113] of the whole earth.

The Flying Scroll

5 🔑Then I turned,[7725] and lifted up[5375] mine eyes, and looked, and behold a flying [a]roll.[4039]

2 And he said unto me, What seest thou? And I answered, I see a flying roll; the length thereof *is* twenty cubits, and the breadth thereof ten cubits.

3 Then said he unto me, This *is* the [a]curse[423] that goeth forth over the face of the whole earth:[776] for [I]every one that stealeth shall be cut off *as* on this side according to it; and every one that sweareth[7650] shall be cut off *as* on that side according to it.

4 I will bring it forth, saith the LORD of hosts,[6635] and it shall enter into the house[1004] of the thief, and into the house of [a]him that sweareth falsely[8267] by my name: and it shall remain in the midst of his house, and [b]shall consume it with the timber thereof and the stones thereof.

🔑5 Then the angel[4397] that talked with me went forth, and said unto me, Lift up[5375] now thine eyes, and see[7200] what *is* this that goeth forth.

6 And I said, What *is* it? And he said, This *is* an ephah that goeth forth. He said moreover, This *is* their resemblance through all the earth.

7 And, behold, there was lifted up a [I]talent of lead: and this *is* a woman[802] that sitteth in the midst of the ephah.

8 And he said, This *is* wickedness.[7564] And he cast it into the midst of the ephah; and he cast the weight[68] of lead upon the mouth[6310] thereof.

9 Then lifted I up mine eyes, and looked, and, behold, there came out two women, and the wind[7307] *was* in their wings; for they had wings like the wings of a stork: and they lifted up the ephah between the earth and the heaven.[8064]

10 Then said I to the angel that talked with me, Whither do these bear the ephah?

🔑11 And he said unto me, To [a]build it an house in [b]the land of Shinar: and it shall be established,[3559] and set there upon her own base.[5178]

The Four Chariots

6 And I turned,[7725] and lifted up[5375] mine eyes, and looked,[7200] and, behold, there came four chariots out from between two mountains; and the mountains *were* mountains of brass.[5178]

2 In the first chariot *were* [a]red[122] horses; and in the second chariot [b]black horses;

3 And in the third chariot [a]white horses; and in the fourth chariot grisled[1261] and [I]bay[554] horses.

4 Then I answered [a]and said unto the angel[4397] that talked with me, What *are* these, my lord?[113]

🔑5 And the angel answered and said unto me, [a]These *are* the four [I]spirits[7307] of the heavens,[8064] which go forth from

4:12 [II]Or, *empty out of themselves* oil into *the gold* [III]Hebr. *the gold*
14 [I]Hebr. *sons of oil* [a]Rev. 11:4 [b]Zech. 3:7; Luke 1:19 [c]Josh. 3:11, 13; Zech. 6:5
5:1 [a]Ezek. 2:9
3 [I]Or, *every one of this* people *that stealeth holdeth* himself *guiltless, as it* doth [a]Mal. 4:6
4 [a]Lev. 19:12; Zech. 8:17; Mal. 3:5 [b]Lev. 14:45
7 [I]Or, *weighty piece*
11 [a]Jer. 29:5, 28 [b]Gen. 10:10
6:2 [a]Zech. 1:8; Rev. 6:4 [b]Rev. 6:5
3 [I]Or, *strong* [a]Rev. 6:2
4 [a]Zech. 5:10
5 [I]Or, *winds* [a]Ps. 104:4; Heb. 1:7, 14

🔑 **5:1–4** The word "roll" in verse one refers to God's Word, and the two sins mentioned violate commandments from each of the two tables of the Law (v. 3, cf. Ex. 32:15).
🔑 **5:5–11** This vision pictures the removal of wickedness from God's land. For Joshua the priest and Zerubbabel, this presented a challenge to make sure the land was purged of wickedness. This would be impossible for them without God's assistance (seen in "lifted up the ephah," v. 9).
🔑 **5:11** "Shinar" is an old name for Babylon that normally represented the city as a place of evil (Gen. 10:10; 11:2; Is. 11:11; Dan. 1:2, cf. Rev. 18:1–24).
🔑 **6:5** The interpretation of this last vision (Zech. 6:1–8) is seen in the statement in verse five, that these chariots are "four spirits of heaven." These are not the world empires of Daniel (see note on Dan. 7:1–28). The "chariots" in this passage symbolize God's power directed earthward for the purpose of judgment (cf. Ps. 68:17; Is. 66:15).

[b]standing before the Lord[113] of all the earth.[776]

6 The black horses which *are* therein go forth into [a]the north country;[776] and the white go forth after them; and the grisled go forth toward the south country.

7 And the bay went forth, and sought to go that they might [a]walk to and fro through the earth: and he said, Get you hence, walk to and fro through the earth. So they walked to and fro through the earth.

8 Then cried[2199] he upon me, and spake[1696] unto me, saying,[559] Behold,[7200] these that go toward the north country have quieted[5117] my [a]spirit in the north country.

9 And the word of the LORD came unto me, saying,

10 Take of *them of* the captivity,[1473] *even* of Heldai, of Tobijah, and of Jedaiah, which are come from Babylon, and come thou the same day, and go into the house[1004] of Josiah the son of Zephaniah;

11 Then take silver and gold, and make[6213] [a]crowns, and set[7760] *them* upon the head of Joshua the son of Josedech, the high priest;[3548]

12 And speak unto him, saying, Thus speaketh the LORD of hosts,[6635] saying, Behold [a]the man whose name *is* The [b]BRANCH;[6780] and he shall [I]grow up out of his place, [c]and he shall build the temple[1964] of the LORD:

13 Even he shall build the temple of the LORD; and he [a]shall bear[5375] the glory,[1935] and shall sit and rule[4910] upon his throne;[3678] and [b]he shall be a priest upon his throne: and the counsel[6098] of peace[7965] shall be between them both.

14 And the crowns shall be to Helem, and to Tobijah, and to Jedaiah, and to Hen the son of Zephaniah, [a]for a memorial[2146] in the temple of the LORD.

15 And [a]they *that are* far off shall come and build in the temple of the LORD, and [b]ye shall know[3045] that the LORD of hosts hath sent me unto you. And *this* shall come to pass, if ye will diligently obey[8085] the voice of the LORD your God.[430]

Insincere Fasting Reproved

7 And it came to pass in the fourth year of king[4428] Darius, *that* the word[1697] of the LORD came unto Zechariah in the fourth *day* of the ninth month, *even* in Chisleu;

2 When they had sent unto the house of God[410] Sherezer and Regem–melech, and their men,[582] [I]to pray before the LORD,

3 *And* to [a]speak unto the priests[3548] which *were* in the house of the LORD of hosts,[6635] and to the prophets,[5030] saying, Should I weep[1058] in [b]the fifth month, separating myself,[5144] as I have done these so many years?

4 Then came the word of the LORD of hosts unto me, saying,

5 Speak unto all the people[5971] of the land, and to the priests, saying, When ye [a]fasted[6684] and mourned[5594] in the fifth [b]and seventh *month,* [c]even those seventy years, did ye at all fast [d]unto me, *even* to me?

6 And when ye did eat, and when ye did drink, [I]did not ye eat *for yourselves,* and drink *for yourselves?*

7 [I]*Should* ye not *hear* the words which the LORD hath cried[7121] [II]by the former[7223] prophets, when Jerusalem was inhabited and in prosperity, and the cities thereof round about her, when *men* inhabited [a]the south and the plain?

8 And the word of the LORD came unto Zechariah, saying,

9 Thus speaketh the LORD of hosts, saying, [I][a]Execute[8199] true[571] judgment,[4941] and shew[6213] mercy[2617] and compassions[7356] every man[376] to his brother:[251]

10 And [a]oppress not the widow, nor the fatherless, the stranger,[1616] nor the poor; [b]and let none of you imagine[2803]

5 [b]1Kgs. 22:19; Dan. 7:10; Zech. 4:14; Luke 1:19
6 [a]Jer. 1:14
7 [a]Gen. 13:17; Zech. 1:10
8 [a]Judg. 8:3; Eccl. 10:4
11 [a]Ex. 28:36; 29:6; Lev. 8:9; Zech. 3:5
12 [I]Or, *branch up from under him* [a]Luke 1:78; John 1:45 [b]Zech. 3:8 [c]Zech. 4:9; Matt. 16:18; Eph. 2:20-22; Heb. 3:3
13 [a]Isa. 22:24 [b]Ps. 110:4; Heb. 3:1
14 [a]Ex. 12:14; Mark 14:9
15 [a]Isa. 57:19; 60:10; Eph. 2:13, 19 [b]Zech. 2:9; 4:9

2 [I]Hebr. *to entreat the face of the LORD* 1Sam. 13:12; Zech. 8:21
3 [a]Deut. 17:9-11; 33:10; Mal. 2:7 [b]Jer. 52:12; Zech. 8:19
5 [a]Isa. 58:5 [b]Jer. 41:1; Zech. 8:19 [c]Zech. 1:12 [d]Rom. 14:6
6 [I]Or, be *not ye they that*
7 [I]Or, Are *not these the words* [II]Hebr. *by the hand of* [a]Jer. 17:26
9 [I]Hebr. *Judge judgment of truth* [a]Isa. 58:6, 7; Jer. 7:23; Mic. 6:8; Zech. 8:16; Matt. 23:23
10 [a]Ex. 22:21, 22; Deut. 24:17; Isa. 1:17; Jer. 5:28 [b]Ps. 36:4; Mic. 2:1; Zech. 8:17

6:9–15 See notes on Jeremiah 23:5–8 and Zechariah 3:1–10.

evil[7451] against his brother in your
heart.3824
11 But they refused[3985] to hear-
ken,[7181] and [I][a]pulled away the shoulder,
and [II][b]stopped[3513] their ears, that they
should not hear.
12 Yea, they made[7760] their
[a]hearts[3820] *as* an adamant stone,8068 [b]lest
they should hear the law,[8451] and the
words which the LORD of hosts hath sent
in his spirit[7307] [I]by the former prophets:
[c]therefore came a great wrath[7110] from
the LORD of hosts.
13 Therefore it is come to pass, *that*
as he cried,[7121] and they would not hear;
so [a]they cried, and I would not hear, saith
the LORD of hosts:
14 But [a]I scattered them with a
whirlwind5590 among all the nations[1471]
[b]whom they knew[3045] not. Thus [c]the land
was desolate[8074] after them, that no man
passed through[5674] nor returned:[7725] for
they laid[7760] [d]the [I]pleasant land desolate.[8047]

Jerusalem Will Be Blessed

8 🗝Again the word of the LORD of
hosts[6635] came *to me,* saying,
2 Thus saith the LORD of hosts; [a]I
was jealous[7065] for Zion with great
jealousy,[7068] and I was jealous for her
with great fury.[2534]
3 Thus saith the LORD; [a]I am
returned[7725] unto Zion, and [b]will
dwell[7931] in the midst of Jerusalem: and
Jerusalem [c]shall be called[7121] a city of
truth;[571] and [d]the mountain of the LORD
of hosts [e]the holy[6944] mountain.
4 Thus saith the LORD of hosts;
[a]There shall yet old men[2205] and old
women dwell in the streets of Jerusalem,
and every man[376] with his staff in his
hand[3027] [I]for very age.
5 And the streets of the city shall be
full of boys and girls playing in the
streets thereof.
6 Thus saith the LORD of hosts; If it
be [I]marvellous[6381] in the eyes of the
remnant[7611] of this people[5971] in these
days,[3117] [a]should it also be marvellous in
mine eyes? saith the LORD of hosts.
7 Thus saith the LORD of hosts;
Behold, [a]I will save[3467] my people from
the east country,[776] and from [I][b]the west
country;
8 And I will bring them, and they
shall dwell in the midst of Jerusalem:
[a]and they shall be my people, and I will
be their God,[430] [b]in truth and in righteousness.
9 Thus saith the LORD of hosts; [a]Let
your hands[3027] be strong,[2388] ye that
hear[8085] in these days these words by the
mouth of [b]the prophets,[5030] which *were* in
[c]the day *that* the foundation of the house
of the LORD of hosts was laid,[3245] that
the temple[1964] might be built.
10 For before these days [I]there was
[a]no hire for man,[120] nor any hire for
beast; [b]neither *was there any* peace[7965] to
him that went out or came in because of
the affliction: for I set all men every
one[376] against his neighbour.[7453]
11 But now I *will* not *be* unto the
residue[7611] of this people as in the former days, saith the LORD of hosts.

11 [I]Hebr. *they gave a backsliding shoulder* [II]Hebr. *made heavy* [a]Neh. 9:29; Jer. 7:24; Hos. 4:16 [b]Acts 7:57
12 [I]Hebr. by the hand of [a]Ezek. 11:19; 36:26 [b]Neh. 9:29, 30 [c]2Chr. 36:16; Dan. 9:11
13 [a]Prov. 1:24-28; Isa. 1:15; Jer. 11:11; 14:12; Mic. 3:4
14 [I]Hebr. *land of desire* [a]Deut. 4:27; 28:64; Ezek. 36:19; Zech. 2:6 [b]Deut. 28:33 [c]Lev. 26:22 [d]Dan. 8:9

2 [a]Nah. 1:2; Zech. 1:14
3 [a]Zech. 1:16 [b]Zech. 2:10 [c]Isa. 1:21, 26 [d]Isa. 2:2, 3 [e]Jer. 31:23
4 [I]Hebr. *for multitude of days* [a]1Sam. 2:31; Isa. 65:20, 22; Lam. 2:20; 5:11-14
6 [I]Or, *hard,* or, *difficult* [a]Gen. 18:14; Luke 1:37; 18:27; Rom. 4:21
7 [I]Hebr. *the country of the going down of the sun* [a]Isa. 11:11, 12; 43:5, 6; Ezek. 37:21; Amos 9:14, 15 [b]Ps. 50:1; 113:3; Mal. 1:11
8 [a]Jer. 30:22; 31:1, 33; Zech. 13:9 [b]Jer. 4:2
9 [a]Hag. 2:4; Zech. 8:18 [b]Ezra 5:1, 2 [c]Hag. 2:18
10 [I]Or, *the hire of man became nothing* [a]Hag. 1:6, 9, 10; 2:16 [b]2Chr. 15:5

🗝 **8:1–23** This chapter looks at the positive prospect of God's future blessings. It opens with a distinct declaration that God is dwelling in the city of Jerusalem, and that Judah is exalted among the nations and made holy (v. 3, cf. Is. 1:21; 2:2, 3; Zech. 2:10; Rev. 21:3). God then asks a rhetorical question to see if anyone thinks it would be too difficult for Him to achieve this act (Zech. 8:6). Next, He reveals that the situation of Jerusalem is carried out in connection with the regathering of His people from their worldwide dispersion (8:7, 8), and His reidentification with them (see note on Hos. 1:10—2:1). Because of this, the people were to obey the prophets God had placed among them, and to deal honestly with one another (8:9–16). Their fasts would ultimately be turned into feasts of joy and gladness, with many nations seeking to come to the Lord in Jerusalem (vv. 19–23, cf. Is. 2:2, 3; 25:7; 49:6, 22, 23; 60:3–12; Zech. 14:16; Rev. 21:24–27). To be a Jew in that day will bring honor, not reviling (v. 23).

12 [a]For the seed[2233] *shall be* [I]prosperous;[7965] the vine shall give her fruit, and [b]the ground[776] shall give her increase, and [c]the heavens[8064] shall give their dew; and I will cause the remnant of this people to possess[5157] all these *things*.

13 And it shall come to pass, *that* as ye were [a]a curse[7045] among the heathen,[1471] O house of Judah, and house of Israel; so will I save[3467] you, and [b]ye shall be a blessing:[1293] fear[3372] not, *but* [c]let your hands be strong.

14 For thus saith the LORD of hosts; [a]As I thought[2161] to punish[7489] you, when your fathers[1] provoked me to wrath, saith the LORD of hosts, [b]and I repented[5162] not:

15 So again have I thought in these days to do well[3190] unto Jerusalem and to the house of Judah: fear ye not.

16 These *are* the things that ye shall do;[6213] [a]Speak[1696] ye every man the truth to his neighbour; [I]execute[8199] the judgment[4941] of truth and peace in your gates:

17 [a]And let none of you imagine[2803] evil[7451] in your hearts[3824] against his neighbour; and [b]love[157] no false[8267] oath:[7621] for all these *are things* that I hate,[8130] saith the LORD.

18 And the word of the LORD of hosts came unto me, saying,

19 Thus saith the LORD of hosts; [a]The fast of the fourth *month*, [b]and the fast of the fifth, [c]and the fast of the seventh, [d]and the fast of the tenth, shall be to the house of Judah [e]joy and gladness, and cheerful[2896] [I]feasts;[4150] [f]therefore love[157] the truth and peace.

20 Thus saith the LORD of hosts; *It shall* yet *come to pass*, that there shall come people, and the inhabitants of many cities:

21 And the inhabitants of one *city* shall go to another, saying, [a]Let us go [I]speedily [II]to pray[2470] before the LORD,

12 [I]Hebr. *of peace* [a]Hos. 2:21, 22; Joel 2:22; Hag. 2:19 [b]Ps. 67:6 [c]Hag. 1:10
13 [a]Jer. 42:18 [b]Gen. 12:2; Ruth 4:11, 12; Isa. 19:24, 25; Zeph. 3:20; Hag. 2:19 [c]Zech. 8:9
14 [a]Jer. 31:28 [b]2Chr. 36:16; Zech. 1:6
16 [I]Hebr. *judge truth, and the judgment of peace* [a]Zech. 7:9; 8:19; Eph. 4:25
17 [a]Prov. 3:29; Zech. 7:10 [b]Zech. 5:3, 4
19 [I]Or, *solemn,* or, *set times* [a]Jer. 52:6, 7 [b]Jer. 52:12, 13; Zech. 7:3, 5 [c]2Kgs. 25:25; Jer. 41:1, 2 [d]Jer. 52:4 [e]Esth. 8:17; Isa. 35:10 [f]Zech. 8:16
21 [I]Or, *continually;* Hebr. *going* [II]Hebr. *to entreat the face of the LORD* Zech. 7:2 [a]Isa. 2:3; Mic. 4:1, 2
22 [a]Isa. 60:3; 66:23
23 [a]Isa. 3:6; 4:1 [b]1Cor. 14:25
1 [a]Jer. 23:33 [b]Amos 1:3 [c]2Chr. 20:12; Ps. 145:15
2 [a]Jer. 49:23 [b]Isa. 23; Amos 1:9 [c]1Kgs. 17:9; Ezek. 28:21; Obad. 1:20 [d]Ezek. 28:3
3 [a]Job 27:16; Ezek. 28:4, 5
4 [a]Isa. 23:1 [b]Ezek. 26:17
5 [a]Jer. 47:1, 5; Zeph. 2:4
6 [a]Amos 1:8
7 [I]Hebr. *bloods*

and to seek the LORD of hosts: I will go also.

22 Yea, [a]many people and strong[6099] nations[1471] shall come to seek the LORD of hosts in Jerusalem, and to pray before the LORD.

23 Thus saith the LORD of hosts; In those days[3117] *it shall come to pass,* that ten men[582] shall [a]take hold[2388] out of all languages of the nations, even shall take hold of the skirt of him that is a Jew, saying, We will go with you: for we have heard[8085] [b]*that* God *is* with you.

Judgment on Israel's Enemies

9 🗝The [a]burden[4853] of the word[1697] of the LORD in the land[776] of Hadrach, and [b]Damascus *shall be* the rest[4496] thereof: when [c]the eyes of man,[120] as of all the tribes[7626] of Israel, *shall be* toward the LORD.

2 And [a]Hamath also shall border thereby; [b]Tyrus, and [c]Zidon, though it be very [d]wise.

3 And Tyrus did build herself a strong hold, and [a]heaped up silver as the dust,[6083] and fine gold as the mire of the streets.

4 Behold, [a]the Lord[136] will cast her out,[3423] and he will smite[5221] [b]her power[2428] in the sea; and she shall be devoured with fire.

5 [a]Ashkelon shall see[7200] *it,* and fear;[3372] Gaza also *shall see it,* and *be* very sorrowful,[2342] and Ekron; for her expectation shall be ashamed; and the king shall perish[6] from Gaza, and Ashkelon shall not be inhabited.

6 And a bastard shall dwell [a]in Ashdod, and I will cut off[3772] the pride of the Philistines.

7 And I will take away[5493] his [I]blood out of his mouth, and his abominations[8251] from between his teeth: but he that remaineth,[7604] even he, *shall be* for our God,[430] and he shall be as a

🗝 **9:1–8** This first "burden" of Zechariah uses Syria, Philistia, and Phoenicia to represent all of Israel's eschatological enemies, much the same way that the nation of Assyria was used in Micah's prophecy (see note on Mic. 5:3–9).

governor[441] in Judah, and Ekron as a Jebusite.

8 And [a]I will encamp about mine house[1004] because of the army, because of him that passeth by,[5674] and because of him that returneth:[7725] and [b]no oppressor shall pass[5674] through them any more: for now [c]have I seen[7200] with mine eyes.

A King in Zion

9 [a]Rejoice greatly, O daughter of Zion; shout,[7321] O daughter of Jerusalem: behold, [b]thy King[4428] cometh unto thee: he *is* just,[6662] and [I]having salvation; lowly,6041 and riding upon an ass, and upon a colt the foal[1121] of an ass.

10 And I [a]will cut off[3772] the chariot from Ephraim, and the horse from Jerusalem, and the battle bow shall be cut off: and he shall speak[1696] [b]peace[7965] unto the heathen:[1471] and his dominion[4915] *shall be* [c]from sea *even* to sea, and from the river *even* to the ends of the earth.[776]

11 As for thee also, [I][a]by the blood of thy covenant[1285] I have sent forth thy [b]prisoners out of the pit[953] wherein *is* no water.

12 Turn[7725] you to the strong hold, [a]ye prisoners of hope: even to day do I declare[5046] *that* [b]I will render[7725] double unto thee;

13 When I have bent Judah for me, filled the bow with Ephraim, and raised up thy sons,[1121] O Zion, against thy sons, O Greece, and made[7760] thee as the sword[2719] of a mighty man.

14 And the LORD shall be seen[7200] over them, and [a]his arrow shall go forth as the lightning: and the Lord GOD shall blow the trumpet, and shall go [b]with whirlwinds of the south.

15 The LORD[3068] of hosts[6635] shall defend them; and they shall devour, and [I]subdue with sling stones; and they shall drink, *and* make a noise as through wine; and they [II]shall be filled like bowls, *and* as [a]the corners of the altar.[4196]

16 And the LORD their God shall save[3467] them in that day[3117] as the flock of his people:[5971] for [a]*they shall be as* the stones of a crown,[5145] [b]lifted up as an ensign upon his land.[127]

17 For [a]how great *is* his goodness,[2898] and how great *is* his beauty! [b]corn shall make the young men [I]cheerful,5107 and new wine the maids.[1330]

The LORD Will Deliver

10 [a]Ask[7592] ye [a]of the LORD [b]rain [c]in the time[6256] of the latter rain; *so* the LORD shall make[6213] [I][d]bright clouds, and give them showers of rain, to every one[376] grass in the field.[7704]

2 For the [a]idols[8655] have spoken[1696] vanity,[205] and the diviners[7080] have seen[2372] a lie,[8267] and have told[1696]

8 [a]Ps. 34:7; Zech. 2:5 [b]Isa. 60:18; Ezek. 28:24 [c]Ex. 3:7
9 [I]Or, *saving himself* [a]Isa. 62:11; Zech. 2:10; Matt. 21:5; John 12:15 [b]Jer. 23:5; 30:9; Luke 19:38; John 1:49
10 [a]Hos. 1:7; 2:18; Mic. 5:10; Hag. 2:22 [b]Eph. 2:14, 17 [c]Ps. 72:8
11 [I]Or, *whose covenant* is *by blood* [a]Ex. 24:8; Heb. 10:29; 13:20 [b]Isa. 42:7; 51:14; 61:1
12 [a]Isa. 49:9 [b]Isa. 61:7
14 [a]Ps. 18:14; 77:17; 144:6
15 [I]Or, *subdue the stones of the sling* [II]Or, *shall fill both the bowls* [a]Lev. 4:18, 25; Deut. 12:27
16 [a]Isa. 62:3; Mal. 3:17 [b]Isa. 11:12
17 [I]Or, *grow,* or, *speak* [a]Ps. 31:19 [b]Joel 3:18; Amos 9:14

1 [I]Or, *lightnings* [a]Jer. 14:22 [b]Deut. 11:14 [c]Job 29:23; Joel 2:23 [d]Jer. 10:13
2 [a]Judg. 17:5; Jer. 10:8; Hab. 2:18

9:9–17 This section of Zechariah's first burden looks at the coming King of Zion, the Messiah. It begins with the scene of Christ's triumphal entry into Jerusalem (cf. Matt. 21:4–7; Mark 11:7; Luke 19:38; John 12:14, 15). The prophecy merely says that Jerusalem's king would come, and does not discuss the people's reception of Him. Jesus' entry into Jerusalem and the people's rejection of Him marks the end of Daniel's sixty-ninth week (see note on Dan. 9:24–27). Zechariah's prophecy then continues with a discussion of God's dealing with Israel in the seventieth week of Daniel. In the end times, Israel will no longer rely on military power ("cut off the chariot," v. 10a, cf. vv. 15, 16), but on the "Prince of Peace" (cf. Is. 9:6), who will exercise worldwide dominion ("from sea even to sea," v. 10b). Verse eleven speaks of the regathering of Israel (cf. Is. 24:17–23). God also speaks of His rendering "double" to Israel. This has two purposes: a double punishment for sin (cf. Is. 40:2) and a double blessing (cf. vv. 16b, 17).

10:1–8 This section speaks of God's future blessing of Israel. It begins by considering Israel's previous dependence on idols, and God's desire that they forsake them. He also pronounces judgment on the people and particularly their leaders, who are referred to as "false shepherds" (vv. 2, 3a). God then speaks of "visiting" His flock, in the sense of restoration and blessing. The images of the "corner" and "nail" appear (v. 4, "corner," see note on Is. 8:14, cf. Is. 28:16; Zech. 4:7; 1 Pet. 2:6–8), denoting the blessing and strengthening that will occur during the Millennium. This section ends with a statement of regathering (v. 8).

false[7723] dreams; they [b]comfort[5162] in
vain: therefore they went their way[5265] as
a flock, they [I]were troubled, [c]because
there was no shepherd.
3 Mine anger[639] was kindled[2734]
against the shepherds, [a]and I [I]pun-
ished[6485] the goats: for the LORD of
hosts[6635] [b]hath visited[6485] his flock the
house[1004] of Judah, and [c]hath made[7760]
them as his goodly[1935] horse in the battle.
4 Out of him came forth [a]the corner,[6438] out of him [b]the nail, out of him
the battle bow, out of him every oppressor together.
5 And they shall be as mighty *men,*
which [a]tread down *their enemies* in the
mire of the streets in the battle: and they
shall fight, because the LORD *is* with
them, and [I]the riders on horses shall be
confounded.[3001]
6 And I will strengthen the house of
Judah, and I will save[3467] the house of
Joseph, and [a]I will bring them again to
place them; for I [b]have mercy[7355] upon
them: and they shall be as though I had
not cast them off: for I *am* the LORD their
God,[430] and [c]will hear them.
7 And *they of* Ephraim shall be like
a mighty *man,* and their [a]heart[3820] shall
rejoice as through wine: yea, their
children[1121] shall see[7200] *it,* and be glad;
their heart shall rejoice in the LORD.
8 I will [a]hiss for them, and gather[6908]
them; for I have redeemed[6299] them: [b]and
they shall increase as they have increased.
9 And [a]I will sow them among the
people:[5971] and they shall [b]remember[2142]
me in far countries; and they shall
live[2421] with their children, and turn
again.[7725]
10 [a]I will bring them again[7725] also
out of the land[776] of Egypt, and gather
them out of Assyria; and I will bring
them into the land of Gilead and
Lebanon; and [b]*place* shall not be found
for them.
11 [a]And he shall pass[5674] through the
sea with affliction, and shall smite[5221]
the waves in the sea, and all the deeps
of the river shall dry up:[3001] and [b]the
pride of Assyria shall be brought down,
and [c]the sceptre[7626] of Egypt shall
depart away.[5493]
12 And I will strengthen them in the
LORD; and [a]they shall walk up and down
in his name, saith the LORD.

The Foolish Shepherds

11 Open [a]thy doors, O Lebanon, that
the fire may devour thy cedars.
2 Howl, fir tree; for the cedar is
fallen;[5307] because the [I]mighty[117] are
spoiled:[7703] howl, O ye oaks of Bashan;
[a]for [II]the forest of the vintage is come
down.
3 *There is* a voice of the howling of
the shepherds; for their glory[155] is
spoiled: a voice of the roaring of young
lions; for the pride[1347] of Jordan is
spoiled.
4 Thus saith the LORD my God;[430]
[a]Feed the flock of the slaughter;[2028]
5 Whose possessors slay[2026] them,
and [a]hold themselves not guilty:[816] and
they that sell them [b]say, Blessed[1288] *be*

2 [I]Or, *answered that* [b]Job 13:4 [c]Ezek. 34:5
3 [I]Hebr. *visited upon* [a]Ezek. 34:17 [b]Luke 1:68 [c]Song 4:9
4 [a]Num. 24:17; 1Sam. 14:38; Isa. 19:13 [b]Isa. 22:23
5 [I]Or, *they shall make the riders on horses ashamed* [a]Ps. 18:42
6 [a]Jer. 3:18; Ezek. 37:21 [b]Hos. 1:7 [c]Zech. 13:9
7 [a]Ps. 104:15; Zech. 9:15
8 [a]Isa. 5:26 [b]Isa. 49:19; Ezek. 36:37
9 [a]Hos. 2:23 [b]Deut. 30:1
10 [a]Isa. 11:11, 16; Hos. 11:11 [b]Isa. 49:20
11 [a]Isa. 11:15, 16 [b]Isa. 14:25 [c]Ezek. 30:13
12 [a]Mic. 4:5

1 [a]Zech. 10:10
2 [I]Or, *gallants* [II]Or, *the defensed forest* [a]Isa. 32:19
4 [a]Zech. 11:7
5 [a]Jer. 2:3; 50:7 [b]Deut. 29:19; Hos. 12:8

10:9–12 This short section recounts God's activities in the eschatological regathering of Israel. As in other prophetic passages, Assyria and Egypt are used to symbolize all of the countries into which God has scattered His people (see note on Dan. 11:36).

11:4–8 These verses discuss Israel's rejection of the true Shepherd, Jesus. They first rejected Him in favor of rulers who did not care for them, and became a "flock of the slaughter" (vv. 4, 7). The two staffs, "Beauty" and "Bands," signify millennial blessings (v. 7, cf. v. 14). The cutting of the staffs shows that Israel would forfeit these blessings by their rejection of the Messiah. As Ezekiel and Isaiah had done with some of their prophecies, Zechariah acted out his message. He tended this doomed flock (v. 7), and particularly the poor and afflicted, picturing those who possessed true faith (cf. Zech. 11:11). The three shepherds (v. 8) refer to the three classes of leaders God gave His people: the prophets (some suggest "teachers of the Law"), the priests, and the kings (representative of civil government).

the LORD; for I am rich: and their own shepherds pity them not.

6 For I will no more pity the inhabitants of the land,[776] saith the LORD: but, lo, I will [I]deliver[4672] the men[120] every one[376] into his neighbour's[7453] hand,[3027] and into the hand of his king: and they shall smite[3807] the land, and out of their hand I will not deliver *them.*

7 And I will [a]feed the flock[6629] of slaughter, [I]*even* you, [b]O poor of the flock. And I took unto me two staves; the one I called[7121] Beauty,[5278] and the other I called [II]Bands;[2254] and I fed the flock.

8 Three shepherds also I cut off [a]in one month; and my soul[5315] [I]lothed[7114] them, and their soul also abhorred[973] me.

9 Then said I, I will not feed you: [a]that that dieth,[4191] let it die; and that that is to be cut off, let it be cut off; and let the rest[7604] eat every one[802] the flesh[1319] [I]of another.[7468]

10 And I took my staff, *even* Beauty, and cut it asunder,[1438] that I might break[6565] my covenant[1285] which I had made[3772] with all the people.[5971]

11 And it was broken in that day:[3117] and [I]so [a]the poor of the flock that waited upon me knew that it *was* the word[1697] of the LORD.

🔑 12 And I said unto them, [I]If ye think good, give *me* my price; and if not, forbear. So they [a]weighed for my price thirty *pieces* of silver.

13 And the LORD said unto me, Cast it unto the [a]potter:[3335] a goodly price that I was prised[3365] at of them. And I took the thirty *pieces* of silver, and cast them to the potter in the house[1004] of the LORD.

14 Then I cut asunder mine other staff, *even* [I]Bands, that I might break the brotherhood[264] between Judah and Israel.

🔑 15 And the LORD said unto me, [a]Take unto thee yet the instruments of a foolish[196] shepherd.

16 For, lo, I will raise up a shepherd in the land, *which* shall not visit[6485] those that be [I]cut off, neither shall seek[1245] the young one, nor heal that that is broken,[7665] nor [II]feed that that standeth still:[5324] but he shall eat the flesh of the fat, and tear their claws in pieces.

17 [a]Woe to the idol[457] shepherd that leaveth[5800] the flock! the sword[2719] *shall be* upon his arm, and upon his right eye: his arm shall be clean dried up,[3001] and his right eye shall be utterly darkened.

Jerusalem's Enemies to Be Destroyed

12 🔑The burden[4853] of the word[1697] of the LORD for Israel, saith the LORD, [a]which stretcheth forth the heavens,[8064] and layeth the foundation of the earth,[776] and [b]formeth[3335] the spirit[7307] of man[120] within[7130] him.

2 Behold, I will make[7760] Jerusalem [a]a cup of [I]trembling[7478] unto all the people[5971] round about, [II]when they shall be in the siege both against Judah *and* against Jerusalem.

3 [a]And in that day[3117] will I make Jerusalem [b]a burdensome stone for all

6 [I]Hebr. *make to be found*
7 [a]Zech. 11:4 [I]Or, *verily the poor* [II]Or, *Binders* [b]Zeph. 3:12; Matt. 11:5
8 [I]Hebr. *was straitened for them* [a]Hos. 5:7
9 [I]Hebr. *of his fellow,* or, *neighbor* [a]Jer. 15:2; 43:11
11 [I]Or, *the poor of the flock certainly knew* [a]Zeph. 3:12; Zech. 11:7
12 [I]Hebr. *If* it be *good in your eyes* [a]Matt. 26:15; Ex. 21:32
13 [a]Matt. 27:9, 10
14 [I]Or, *Binders*
15 [a]Ezek. 34:2-4
16 [I]Or, *hidden* [II]Or, *bear*
17 [a]Jer. 23:1; Ezek. 34:2; John 10:12, 13

1 [a]Isa. 42:5; 44:24; 45:12, 18; 48:13 [b]Num. 16:22; Eccl. 12:7; Isa. 57:16; Heb. 12:9
2 [I]Or, *slumber,* or, *poison* [II]Or, *and also against Judah shall he be which shall be in siege against Jerusalem* [a]Isa. 51:17, 22, 23
3 [a]Ezek. 12:4, 6, 8, 9, 11; 13:1; 14:4, 6, 8, 9, 13 [b]Matt. 21:44

🔑 **11:12, 13** These verses speak of Judas Iscariot's betrayal of Jesus. According to the Mosaic Law, thirty shekels was the price that the owner of an ox was to give for compensation in the event that it gored another man's slave (Ex. 21:32). Even a quality slave brought twice this amount. The irony of Zechariah's words is heightened by describing the price as "goodly" (cf. Matt. 26:14–16). The blood-price of Christ did indeed go to the potter for his field (see note on Matt. 27:9, 10).

🔑 **11:15–17** This section is a description of the Antichrist that will come. Some would translate the word "foolish" as "impious," making a negative moral connotation. No other person mentioned in prophecy matches this description except the Antichrist (cf. Rev. 13:4–18). Note, however, that the prophecy ends with the doom of the Antichrist (v. 17).

🔑 **12:1–9** This second "burden" of Zechariah focuses on the the final siege of Jerusalem and God's judgment on the nations that have attacked Judah. Though "all the nations" are involved in the attack (v. 9), the empowerment of the Lord will enable His people to triumph over them (vv. 3–8). The "cup" is a symbol for God's wrath (Zech. 12:2, cf. Is. 51:17, 22; Jer. 13:13; 25:15–17, 27, 28; 51:7). See notes on Micah 4:6–13 and Zephaniah 1:7 concerning the phrase "in that day."

people:[1471] all that burden themselves with it shall be cut in pieces, though all the people of the earth be gathered together[622] against it.

4 In that day,[3117] saith the LORD, [a]I will smite[5221] every[3605] horse with astonishment, and his rider with madness: and I will open mine eyes upon the house of Judah, and will smite every horse of the people with blindness.

5 And the governors[441] of Judah shall say in their heart,[3820] [I][a]The inhabitants of Jerusalem *shall be* my strength in the LORD of hosts[6635] their God.[430]

6 In that day will I make the governors of Judah [a]like an hearth of fire among the wood, and like a torch of fire in a sheaf; and they shall devour all the people round about, on the right hand and on the left: and Jerusalem shall be inhabited again in her own place, *even* in Jerusalem.

7 The LORD also shall save[3467] the tents[168] of Judah first, that the glory[8597] of the house of David and the glory of the inhabitants of Jerusalem do not magnify *themselves* against Judah.

8 In that day shall the LORD defend the inhabitants of Jerusalem; and [a]he that is [I]feeble among them at that day shall be as David; and the house of David *shall be* as God, as the angel[4397] of the LORD before them.

9 And it shall come to pass in that day, *that* I will seek to [a]destroy all the nations[1471] that come against Jerusalem.

🔑 10 [a]And I will pour[8210] upon the house of David, and upon the inhabitants of Jerusalem, the spirit of grace[2580] and of supplications:[8469] and they shall [b]look[5027] upon me whom they have pierced,[1856] and they shall mourn[5594] for him, [c]as one mourneth for *his* only[3173] *son,* and shall be in bitterness for him, as one that is in bitterness for *his* firstborn.

11 In that day shall there be a great [a]mourning in Jerusalem, [b]as the mourning of Hadad–rimmon in the valley of Megiddon.

12 [a]And the land[776] shall mourn, every family[4940] apart; the family of the house of David apart,[905] and their wives apart; the family of the house of [b]Nathan apart, and their wives apart;

13 The family of the house of Levi apart, and their wives apart; the family [I]of Shimei apart, and their wives apart;

14 All the families that remain,[7604] every family apart, and their wives apart.

13 🔑In [a]that day[3117] there shall be [b]a fountain opened to the house[1004] of David and to the inhabitants of Jerusalem for sin[2403] and for [I]uncleanness.[5079]

2 And it shall come to pass in that day, saith the LORD of hosts,[6635] *that* I will [a]cut off[3772] the names of the idols[6091] out of the land,[776] and they shall no more be remembered:[2142] and also I will cause [b]the prophets[5030] and the unclean[2932] spirit[7307] to pass out of the land.

3 And it shall come to pass, *that* when any[376] shall yet prophesy, then his father[1] and his mother[517] that begat him shall say unto him, Thou shalt not live;[2421] for thou speakest[1696] lies[8267] in the name of the LORD: and his father and his mother that begat him [a]shall thrust him through when he prophesieth.[5012]

4 And it shall come to pass in that day, *that* [a]the prophets shall be ashamed[1954] every one[376] of his vision,[2384] when he hath prophesied; neither shall they wear [I][b]a rough garment to deceive:

12:4 [a]Ps. 76:6; Ezek. 38:4

5 [I]Or, There is *strength to me and to the inhabitants* [a]Joel 3:16

6 [a]Obad. 1:18

8 [I]Hebr. *fallen* [a]Joel 3:10

9 [a]Hag. 2:22; Zech. 12:3

10 [a]Jer. 31:9; 50:4; Ezek. 39:29; Joel 2:28 [b]John 19:34, 37; Rev. 1:7 [c]Jer. 6:26; Amos 8:10

11 [a]Acts 2:37 [b]2Kgs. 23:29; 2Chr. 35:24

12 [a]Matt. 24:30; Rev. 1:7 [b]2Sam. 5:14; Luke 3:31

13 [I]Or, *of Simeon*

13:1 [I]Hebr. *separation for uncleanness* [a]Zech. 12:3 [b]Heb. 9:14; 1Pet. 1:19; Rev. 1:5

2 [a]Ex. 23:13; Josh. 23:7; Ps. 16:4; Ezek. 30:13; Hos. 2:17; Mic. 5:12, 13 [b]2Pet. 2:1

3 [a]Deut. 13:6, 8; 18:20

4 [I]Hebr. *garment of hair* [II]Hebr. *to lie* [a]Mic. 3:6, 7 [b]2Kgs. 1:8; Isa. 20:2; Matt. 3:4

🔑 **12:10–14** The chronology in this section does not flow with the rest of the book. This passage looks at the spiritual impact that the Lord's physical return will have on the people. This event will complete the deliverance from the siege of Jerusalem (see note on 12:1–9). The use of the phrase "I will pour upon . . . the inhabitants of Jerusalem, the spirit of grace and of supplications" graphically depicts the sorrow that will follow the realization of the Jews that they killed their Messiah.

🔑 **13:1–5** See note on Daniel 9:24–27.

5 [a]But he shall say, I *am* no prophet,
I *am* an husbandman; for man[120] taught
me to keep cattle[7069] from my youth.
6 And *one* shall say unto him, What
are these wounds[4347] in[996] thine
hands?[3027] Then he shall answer, *Those*
with which I was wounded[5221] *in* the
house of my friends.[157]

The LORD's Shepherd Will Be Struck Down

7 Awake, O sword,[2719] against [a]my
shepherd, and against the man[1397] [b]*that*
is my fellow,[5997] saith the LORD of hosts:
[c]smite[5221] the shepherd, and the sheep
shall be scattered: and I will turn[7725]
mine hand upon [d]the little ones.
8 And it shall come to pass, *that* in
all the land, saith the LORD, two parts[6310]
therein shall be cut off *and* die;[1478] [a]but
the third shall be left[3498] therein.
9 And I will bring the third part
[a]through the fire, and will [b]refine[6884]
them as silver is refined, and will try
them as gold is tried:[974] [c]they shall
call[7121] on my name, and I will hear
them: [d]I will say, It *is* my people:[5971] and
they shall say,[559] The LORD *is* my God.[430]

The LORD Will Rule

14 Behold, [a]the day[3117] of the LORD
cometh, and thy spoil shall be divided in the midst[7130] of thee.
2 For [a]I will gather[622] all nations[1471]
against Jerusalem to battle; and the city
shall be taken, and [b]the houses[1004]
rifled,[8155] and the women ravished; and
half of the city shall go forth into
captivity,[1473] and the residue[3499] of the
people[5971] shall not be cut off[3772] from
the city.
3 Then shall the LORD go forth, and
fight against those nations, as when he
fought in the day of battle.
4 And his feet shall stand in that day
[a]upon the mount of Olives, which *is* before Jerusalem on the east, and the mount
of Olives shall cleave[1234] in the midst
thereof toward the east and toward the
west, [b]*and there shall be* a very great
valley;[1516] and half of the mountain shall
remove toward the north, and half of it
toward the south.
5 And ye shall flee *to* the valley of
[I]the mountains; [II]for the valley of the
mountains shall reach unto Azal: yea, ye
shall flee, like as ye fled from before the
[a]earthquake[7494] in the days of Uzziah
king of Judah: [b]and the LORD my God[430]
shall come, *and* [c]all the saints[6918] with
thee.
6 And it shall come to pass in that
day, [I]*that* the light[216] shall not be [II]clear,
nor [III]dark:
7 But [a]it shall be [b]one day [c]which
shall be known[3045] to the LORD, not day,
nor night: but it shall come to pass, *that*
at [d]evening time[6256] it shall be light.
8 And it shall be in that day, *that*
living[2416] [a]waters shall go out from
Jerusalem; half of them toward the
[Ib]former sea, and half of them toward
the hinder sea: in summer and in winter
shall it be.
9 And the LORD shall be [a]king[4428]
over all the earth:[776] in that day[3117] shall
there be [b]one LORD,[3068] and his name one.
10 All the land[776] shall be [I]turned
[a]as a plain[6160] from Geba to Rimmon
south of Jerusalem: and it shall be lifted
up, and [IIb]inhabited in her place, from
Benjamin's gate unto the place of the
first gate, unto the corner gate, [c]and *from*
the tower of Hananeel unto the king's
winepresses.
11 And *men* shall dwell in it, and
there shall be [a]no more utter destruction;[2764] [b]but Jerusalem [I]shall be
safely[983] inhabited.
🔑12 And this shall be the plague

5 [a]Amos 7:14
7 [a]Isa. 40:11; Ezek. 34:23 [b]John 10:30; 14:10, 11; Phil. 2:6 [c]Matt. 26:31; Mark 14:27 [d]Matt. 18:10, 14; Luke 12:32
8 [a]Rom. 11:5
9 [a]Isa. 48:10 [b]1Pet. 1:6, 7 [c]Ps. 50:15; 91:15; Zech. 10:6 [d]Ps. 144:15; Jer. 30:22; Ezek. 11:20; Hos. 2:23; Zech. 8:8

1 [a]Isa. 13:9; Joel 2:31; Acts 2:20
2 [a]Joel 3:2 [b]Isa. 13:16
4 [a]Ezek. 11:23 [b]Joel 3:12, 14
5 [I]Or, *my mountains* [II]Or, *when he shall touch the valley of the mountains to the place he separated* [a]Amos 1:1 [b]Matt. 16:27; 24:30, 31; 25:31; Jude 1:14 [c]Joel 3:11
6 [I]Or, it shall not be clear in some places, and dark in other places of the world [II]Hebr. *precious* [III]Hebr. *thickness*
7 [I]Or, *the day shall be one* [a]Rev. 22:5 [b]Matt. 24:36 [c]Isa. 30:26; 60:19, 20; Rev. 21:23
8 [I]Or, *eastern* [a]Ezek. 47:1; Joel 3:18; Rev. 22:1 [b]Joel 2:20
9 [a]Dan. 2:44; Rev. 11:15 [b]Eph. 4:5, 6
10 [I]Or, *compassed* [II]Or, *shall abide* [a]Isa. 40:4 [b]Zech. 12:6 [c]Neh. 3:1; 12:39; Jer. 31:38
11 [I]Or, *shall abide* [a]Jer. 31:40 [b]Jer. 23:6

🔑 **14:12–15** This section gives a description of the way God will smite those who have attacked Jerusalem. Several commentators have noted a similarity between the description in verse twelve and the effects of severe radiation exposure. Nevertheless, it cannot be proven that this section refers to nuclear devastation, rather than to some particularly swift acting and devastating disease.

wherewith the LORD will smite[5062] all the people that have fought[6633] against Jerusalem; Their flesh[1319] shall consume away[4743] while they stand upon their feet, and their eyes shall consume away in their holes, and their tongue shall consume away in their mouth.[6310]

13 And it shall come to pass in that day, *that* [a]a great tumult[4103] from the LORD shall be among them; and they shall lay hold[2388] every one[376] on the hand[3027] of his neighbour,[7453] and [b]his hand shall rise up[5927] against the hand of his neighbour.

14 And [I]Judah also shall fight [II]at Jerusalem; [a]and the wealth[2428] of all the heathen[1471] round about shall be gathered together,[622] gold, and silver, and apparel, in great abundance.

15 And [a]so shall be the plague of the horse, of the mule, of the camel, and of the ass, and of all the beasts that shall be in these tents,[4264] as this plague.

🔑 16 And it shall come to pass, *that* every one that is left[3498] of all the nations which came against Jerusalem shall even [a]go up[5927] from year to year to worship the King, the LORD of hosts,[6635] and to keep [b]the feast[2282] of tabernacles.[5521]

17 [a]And it shall be, *that* whoso will not come up[5927] of *all* the families[4940] of the earth unto Jerusalem to worship the King, the LORD of hosts, even upon them shall be no rain.

18 And if the family of Egypt go not up, and come not, [I][a]that *have* no *rain;* there shall be the plague,[4046] wherewith the LORD will smite the heathen that come not up to keep the feast of tabernacles.

19 This shall be the [I]punishment[2403] of Egypt, and the punishment of all nations that come not up to keep the feast of tabernacles.

20 In that day shall there be upon the [I]bells of the horses, [a]HOLINESS[6944] UNTO THE LORD; and the pots in the LORD's house shall be like the bowls before the altar.[4196]

21 Yea, every pot in Jerusalem and in Judah shall be holiness unto the LORD of hosts: and all they that sacrifice[2076] shall come and take of them, and seethe therein: and in that day there shall be no more the [a]Canaanite in [b]the house of the LORD of hosts.

13 [a]1Sam. 14:15, 20 [b]Judg. 7:22; 2Chr. 20:23; Zech. 38:21

14 [I]Or, *thou also, O Judah, shalt* [II]Or, *against* [a]Zech. 39:10, 17

15 [a]Zech. 14:12

16 [a]Isa. 60:6, 7, 9; 66:23 [b]Lev. 23:34, 43; Neh. 8:14; Hos. 12:9; John 7:2

17 [a]Isa. 60:12

18 [I]Hebr. *upon whom* there is *not* [a]Deut. 11:10

19 [I]Or, *sin*

20 [I]Or, *bridles* [a]Isa. 23:18

21 [a]Isa. 35:8; Joel 3:17; Rev. 21:27; 22:15 [b]Eph. 2:19-22

🔑 **14:16–21** The emphasis on the Feast of Tabernacles is significant (v. 19). Just as the original festival celebrated the end of wandering in the wilderness, so this festival will celebrate the final end of Israel's wandering. The severe penalty for failure to comply with the wishes of the Messiah (vv. 17–19) shows how He will rule with a "rod of iron" (Ps. 2:9). The fact that non-Israelites are also punished demonstrates again the universal extent of Messiah's reign. The book ends with a reiteration of the holiness of the Messiah's city (vv. 20, 21). The expression "HOLINESS UNTO THE LORD," which was formerly inscribed on Aaron's headdress (v. 20, cf. Ex. 28:36, 38), will then be used to describe the most common items in the city. The word "Canaanite" is used to represent any unclean, dishonest, or morally impure person (v. 21).

The Book of
MALACHI

Malachi either means "my messenger" or is an abbreviated form of "the messenger of the Lord." His prophecy is clearly later than those of Haggai and Zechariah. The reconstruction of the temple had been complete long enough for abuses to creep into the sacrificial system (Mal. 1:7–10; 3:8). Moreover, the overall spiritual state of the people seems to have been in decline: divorce was widespread (Mal. 2:14), mixed marriages were being contracted (Mal. 2:10–12), and tithes had been neglected (Mal. 3:8–10). The book, therefore, must be dated sometime after Nehemiah's return to the Persian court in 433 B.C., probably before 400 B.C. Malachi's dialectic style is unique among the prophets. He first makes an assertion, then states a question from his hearers, and, finally, offers a response proving the original assertion. This style of argumentation or rhetoric became very popular in Judaism and is seen in the Talmud and Mishnah.

The Book of Malachi ends with a prophetic statement regarding John the Baptist, a forerunner of the Messiah (Mal. 3:1–6). The Jews in the intertestamental period recognized that the prophets had ceased from Israel. When they cleansed the temple following Antiochus IV Epiphanes' abomination in 165 B.C. (Dan. 8:13; 11:31; see note on Ezek. 43:13–27), they set the polluted stones aside "until a prophet should arise" to tell them what to do with them (according to 1 Maccabees 4:46).

The LORD *Loves Jacob*

1 The burden[4853] of the word[1697] of
the LORD to Israel [I]by Malachi.
2 [a]I have loved[157] you, saith the
LORD. Yet ye say, Wherein hast thou
loved us? *Was* not Esau Jacob's
brother?[251] saith the LORD: yet [b]I loved
Jacob,
3 And I hated[8130] Esau, and [a]laid[7760]
his mountains and his heritage[5159]
waste[8077] for the dragons[8568] of the
wilderness.
4 Whereas Edom saith, We are impoverished, but we will return[7725] and
build the desolate places;[2723] thus saith
the LORD of hosts,[6635] They shall build,
but I will throw down;[2040] and they shall
call[7121] them, The border of wickedness,[7564] and, The people[5971] against
whom the LORD hath indignation[2194] for
ever.[5769]
5 And your eyes shall see,[7200] and
ye shall say, [a]The LORD will be magnified
from the border of Israel.
6 A son[1121] [a]honoureth[3513] *his*
father,[1] and a servant[5650] his master:[113]
[b]if then I *be* a father, where *is* mine
honour?[3519] and if I *be* a master, where
is my fear?[4172] saith the LORD of hosts
unto you, O priests,[3548] that despise my
name. [c]And ye say, Wherein have we despised thy name?
7 [I]Ye offer [a]polluted bread upon mine
altar;[4196] and ye say,[559] Wherein have we

1 [I]Hebr. *by the hand of Malachi*
2 [a]Deut. 7:8; 10:15 [b]Rom. 9:13
3 [a]Jer. 49:18; Ezek. 35:3, 4, 7, 9, 14, 15; Obad. 1:10
5 [a]Ps. 35:27
6 [a]Ex. 20:12 [b]Luke 6:46 [c]Mal. 2:14, 17; 3:7, 8, 13
7 [I]Or, *Bring unto* [a]Deut. 15:21

1:1–14 This chapter contains God's rebuke of Israel. However, before He begins to reprove them, He affirms His past and present love for Israel. He uses the comparison of Jacob and Esau, and moves from His choice of Jacob (v. 2) and rejection of Esau, to the current situation regarding Edom (vv. 3, 4). God then turns to the offenses that His people have committed. His initial focus is on the priests (vv. 6–9), those who ought to have set the example. They have been offering diseased or defective animals (vv. 7, 8, 13, 14), and thereby "despising" God and His table (vv. 6, 7, 12).

polluted thee? In that ye say, [b]The table of the LORD *is* contemptible.

8 And [a]if ye offer5066 the blind [I]for sacrifice,2076 *is it* not evil?7451 and if ye offer the lame and sick, *is it* not evil? offer7126 it now unto thy governor;6346 will he be pleased7521 with thee, or [b]accept5375 thy person? saith the LORD of hosts.

9 And now, I pray you, beseech [I]God410 that he will be gracious2603 unto us: [a]this hath been [II]by your means:3027 will he regard5375 your persons? saith the LORD of hosts.

10 Who *is there* even among you that would shut the doors *for nought?* [a]neither do ye kindle *fire* on mine altar for nought.2600 I have no pleasure2656 in you, saith the LORD of hosts, [b]neither will I accept an offering4503 at your hand.3027

11 For [a]from the rising of the sun even unto the going down of the same my name *shall be* great [b]among the Gentiles;1471 [c]and in every place [d]incense6999 *shall be* offered unto my name, and a pure2889 offering: [e]for my name *shall be* great among the heathen,1471 saith the LORD of hosts.

12 But ye have profaned2490 it, in that ye say, [a]The table of the LORD *is* polluted; and the fruit thereof, *even* his meat, *is* contemptible.

13 Ye said also, Behold, what a weariness4972 *is it!* [I]and ye have snuffed at it, saith the LORD of hosts; and ye brought *that which was* torn, and the lame, and the sick; thus ye brought an offering: [a]should I accept this of your hand? saith the LORD.

14 But cursed779 *be* [a]the deceiver, [I]which hath in his flock a male,2145 and voweth,5087 and sacrificeth2076 unto the LORD136 a corrupt thing:7843 for [b]I *am* a great King,4428 saith the LORD of hosts, and my name *is* dreadful3372 among the heathen.

7 [b]Ezek. 41:22; Mal. 1:12
8 [I]Hebr. *to sacrifice* [a]Lev. 22:22; Deut. 15:21; Mal. 8:14 [b]Job 42:8
9 [I]Hebr. *the face of God* [II]Hebr. *from your hand* [a]Hos. 13:9
10 [a]1Cor. 9:13 [b]Isa. 1:11; Jer. 6:20; Amos 5:21
11 [a]Ps. 113:3; Isa. 59:19 [b]Isa. 60:3, 5 [c]John 4:21, 23; 1Tim. 2:8 [d]Rev. 8:3 [e]Isa. 66:19, 20
12 [a]Mal. 1:7
13 [I]Or, *whereas ye might have blown it away* [a]Lev. 22:20
14 [I]Or, *in whose flock is* [a]Mal. 1:8 [b]Ps. 47:2; 1Tim. 6:15
2 [a]Lev. 26:14; Deut. 28:15
3 [I]Or, *reprove* [II]Hebr. *scatter* [III]Or, *it shall take you away to it* [a]1Kgs. 14:10
5 [a]Num. 25:12; Ezek. 34:25; 37:26 [b]Deut. 33:8, 9
6 [a]Deut. 33:10 [b]Jer. 23:22; James 5:20
7 [a]Lev. 10:11; Deut. 17:9, 10; 24:8; Ezra 7:10; Jer. 18:18; Hag. 2:11, 12 [b]Gal. 4:14
8 [I]Or, *fall in the law* [a]1Sam. 2:17; Jer. 18:15 [b]Neh. 13:29
9 [a]1Sam. 2:30 [I]Or, *lifted up the face against*
10 [a]1Cor. 8:6; Eph. 4:6 [b]Job 31:15

Israel Is Unfaithful

2 🗝And now, O ye priests,3548 this commandment4687 *is* for you.

2 [a]If ye will not hear,8085 and if ye will not lay7760 *it* to heart,3820 to give glory3519 unto my name, saith the LORD of hosts,6635 I will even send a curse779 upon you, and I will curse your blessings:1293 yea, I have cursed them already, because ye do not lay *it* to heart.

3 Behold, I will [I]corrupt1605 your seed,2233 and [II]spread dung upon your faces, *even* the dung of your solemn feasts;2282 and [III]*one* shall [a]take you away5375 with it.

4 And ye shall know3045 that I have sent this commandment unto you, that my covenant1285 might be with Levi, saith the LORD of hosts.

5 [a]My covenant was with him of life2416 and peace;7965 and I gave them to him [b]*for* the fear4172 wherewith he feared3373 me, and was afraid2865 before my name.

6 [a]The law8451 of truth571 was in his mouth,6310 and iniquity5766 was not found in his lips:8193 he walked with me in peace and equity,4334 and did [b]turn many away7725 from iniquity.5771

7 [a]For the priest's lips should keep8104 knowledge,1847 and they should seek the law at his mouth: [b]for he *is* the messenger4397 of the LORD of hosts.

8 But ye are departed5493 out of the way;1870 ye [a]have caused many to [I]stumble3782 at the law; [b]ye have corrupted7843 the covenant of Levi, saith the LORD of hosts.

9 Therefore [a]have I also made you contemptible and base before all the people,5971 according as ye have not kept my ways, but [I]have been partial in the law.

10 [a]Have we not all one father? [b]hath1254 not one God410 created1254 us? why do we deal treacherously898 every

🗝 **2:1–10** God warns the priests that they will be singled out for shame (vv. 2, 3) if they do not serve and teach without partiality (vv. 6–9). Besides this, they have acted improperly in their marriage relationships (cf. Mal. 1:10–16). Verse ten speaks of offenses against Jewish brothers; verse eleven condemns the making of mixed marriages (cf. Ezra 9:1, 2).

man[376] against his brother, by profaning[2490] the covenant of our fathers?[1]

11 Judah hath dealt treacherously, and an abomination[8441] is committed[6213] in Israel and in Jerusalem; for Judah hath profaned the holiness[6944] of the LORD which he [I]loved,[157] [a]and hath married[1166] the daughter of a strange[5236] god.[410]

12 The LORD will cut off[3772] the man[376] that doeth[6213] this, [I]the master 5782 and the scholar, 6030 out of the tabernacles[168] of Jacob, [a]and him that offereth an offering[4503] unto the LORD of hosts.

13 And this have ye done again, covering[3680] the altar[4196] of the LORD with tears, with weeping, and with crying out, insomuch that he regardeth not the offering any more, or receiveth *it* with good will[7522] at your hand.[3027]

14 Yet ye say, Wherefore? Because the LORD hath been witness[5749] between thee and [a]the wife[802] of thy youth, against whom thou hast dealt treacherously: [b]yet *is* she thy companion, and the wife of thy covenant.[1285]

15 And [a]did not he make[6213] one? Yet had he the [I]residue[7605] of the spirit.[7307] And wherefore one? That he might seek [II][b]a godly[430] seed.[2233] Therefore take heed[8104] to your spirit, and let none deal [III]treacherously against the wife of his youth.

16 For [a]the LORD,[3068] the God[430] of Israel, saith [I]that he hateth[8130] [II]putting away: 7971 for *one* covereth[3680] violence[2555] with his garment, saith the LORD of hosts: therefore take heed to your spirit, that ye deal not treacherously.

Judgment Day Is Near

17 [a]Ye have wearied the LORD with your words.[1697] Yet ye say, Wherein have we wearied *him?* When ye say, Every one that doeth[6213] evil[7451] *is* good[2896] in the sight of the LORD, and he delighteth[2654] in them; or, Where *is* the God of judgment?[4941]

3 🗝Behold, [a]I will send my messenger,[4397] and he shall [b]prepare the way[1870] before me: and the Lord,[113] whom ye seek, shall suddenly come to his temple,[1964] [c]even the messenger of the covenant,[1285] whom ye delight[2655] in: behold, [d]he shall come, saith the LORD of hosts.[6635]

2 But who may abide [a]the day[3117] of his coming? and [b]who shall stand when he appeareth?[7200] for [c]he *is* like a refiner's[6884] fire, and like fullers'[3526] soap:

3 And [a]he shall sit *as* a refiner and purifier[2891] of silver: and he shall purify the sons[1121] of Levi, and purge[2212] them as gold and silver, that they may [b]offer unto the LORD an offering[4503] in righteousness.

4 Then [a]shall the offering of Judah and Jerusalem be pleasant 6149 unto the LORD, as in the days of old,[5769] and as in [I]former years.

5 And I will come near[7126] to you to judgment;[4941] and I will be a swift witness against the sorcerers,[3784] and against the adulterers, 5003 [a]and against false[8267] swearers,[7650] and against those that [I]oppress the hireling in *his* wages, the widow, and the fatherless, and that turn aside the stranger[1616] *from his right,* and fear[3372] not me, saith the LORD of hosts.

Robbing God

6 For I *am* the LORD, [a]I change 8138 not; [b]therefore ye sons of Jacob are not consumed.[3615]

---

11 [I]Or, *ought to love* [a]Ezra 9:1; 10:2; Neh. 13:23

12 [I]Or, *him that waketh, and him that answereth* [a]Neh. 13:28, 29

14 [a]Prov. 5:18 [b]Prov. 2:17

15 [I]Or, *excellency* [II]Hebr. *a seed of God* [III]Or, *unfaithfully* [a]Matt. 19:4, 5 [b]Ezra 9:2; 1Cor. 7:14

16 [I]Or, *if he hate her, put her away* [II]Hebr. *to put away* [a]Deut. 24:1; Matt. 5:32; 19:8

17 [a]Isa. 43:24; Amos 2:13; Mal. 3:13-15

1 [a]Matt. 11:10; Mark 1:2; Luke 1:76; 7:27 [b]Isa. 40:3 [c]Isa. 63:9 [d]Hag. 2:7

2 [a]Mal. 4:1 [b]Rev. 6:17 [c]Isa. 4:4; Matt. 3:10-12

3 [a]Isa. 1:25; Zech. 13:9 [b]1Pet. 2:5

4 [I]Or, *ancient* [a]Mal. 1:11

5 [a]Zech. 5:4; James 5:4, 12 [I]Or, *defraud*

6 [a]Num. 23:19; Rom. 11:29; James 1:17 [b]Lam. 3:22

🗝 **3:1–3** This is a prediction of the ministry of John the Baptist. Following the description of John's ministry in verse one, Malachi announces the One for whom John will minister: "the Lord, whom you seek, shall suddenly come to his temple." This may have included all of the appearances of Jesus in the temple, both as a baby (Luke 2:21–24) and as one who cleansed it (John 2:13–22). Amos prophesied, however, that the Lord would first purge and judge Israel (Amos 5:18–22; cf. note on Ezek. 43:13–27).

7 Even from the days of [a]your fathers[1] ye are gone away[5493] from mine ordinances,[2706] and have not kept[8104] *them.* [b]Return[7725] unto me, and I will return unto you, saith the LORD of hosts. [c]But ye said, Wherein shall we return?

8 Will a man[120] rob God?[430] Yet ye have robbed me. But ye say, Wherein have we robbed thee? [a]In tithes[4643] and offerings.

9 Ye *are* cursed[779] with a curse: for ye have robbed me, *even* this whole nation.[1471]

10 [a]Bring ye all the tithes into [b]the storehouse, that there may be meat in mine house,[1004] and prove[974] me now herewith, saith the LORD of hosts, if I will not open you the [c]windows of heaven,[8064] and [I][d]pour you out a blessing,[1293] that *there shall* not *be room* enough *to receive it.*

11 And I will rebuke[1605] [a]the devourer for your sakes, and he shall not [I]destroy[7843] the fruits of your ground;[127] neither shall your vine cast her fruit before the time in the field,[7704] saith the LORD of hosts.

12 And all nations shall call you blessed:[833] for ye shall be [a]a delightsome[2656] land,[776] saith the LORD of hosts.

13 [a]Your words[1697] have been stout[2388] against me, saith the LORD. Yet ye say, What have we spoken *so much* against thee?

14 [a]Ye have said, It *is* vain[7723] to serve[5647] God: and what profit *is it* that we have kept [I]his ordinance,[4931] and that we have walked [II]mournfully[6941] before the LORD of hosts?

15 And now [a]we call the proud[2086] happy; yea, they that work[6213] wickedness[7564] [I]are set up;[1129] yea, *they that* [b]tempt[974] God are even delivered.[4422]

16 Then they [a]that feared[3373] the LORD [b]spake often one[376] to another:[7453] and the LORD hearkened,[7181] and heard *it,* and [c]a book[5612] of remembrance[2146] was written before him for them that feared the LORD, and that thought upon his name.

17 And [a]they shall be mine, saith the LORD of hosts, in that day when I make up[6213] my [I][b]jewels;[5459] and [c]I will spare them, as a man[376] spareth his own son that serveth[5647] him.

18 [a]Then shall ye return, and discern[7200] between the righteous[6662] and the wicked,[7563] between him that serveth God and him that serveth him not.

The LORD's Day Is Coming

4 For, behold, [a]the day[3117] cometh, that shall burn as an oven; and all [b]the proud, yea, and all that do[6213] wickedly,[7564] shall be [c]stubble: and the day that cometh shall burn them up, saith the LORD of hosts,[6635] that it shall [d]leave[5800] them neither root nor branch.

2 But unto you that [a]fear[3373] my

7 [a]Acts 7:51 [b]Zech. 1:3 [c]Mal. 1:6
8 [a]Neh. 13:10, 12
10 [I]Hebr. *empty out* [a]Prov. 3:9, 10 [b]1Chr. 26:20; 2Chr. 31:11; Neh. 10:38; 13:12 [c]Gen. 7:11; 2Kgs. 7:2 [d]2Chr. 31:10
11 [I]Hebr. *corrupt* [a]Amos 4:9
12 [a]Dan. 8:9
13 [a]Mal. 2:17
14 [I]Hebr. *his observation* [II]Hebr. *in black* [a]Job 21:14, 15; 22:17; Ps. 73:13; Zeph. 1:12
15 [I]Hebr. *are built* [a]Ps. 73:12; Mal. 2:17 [b]Ps. 95:9
16 [a]Ps. 66:16; Mal. 4:2 [b]Heb. 3:13 [c]Ps. 56:8; Isa. 65:6; Rev. 20:12
17 [I]Or, *special treasure* [a]Ex. 19:5; Deut. 7:6; Ps. 135:4; Titus 2:14; 1Pet. 2:9 [b]Isa. 62:3 [c]Ps. 103:13
18 [a]Ps. 58:11

1 [a]Joel 2:31; Mal. 3:2; 2Pet. 3:7 [b]Mal. 3:18 [c]Obad. 1:18 [d]Amos 2:9
2 [a]Mal. 3:16

3:7–15 This passage is often used by those who advocate "storehouse tithing"; that is, bringing the "tithe" into God's storehouse (the local church), rather than giving it anywhere else. They suggest that gifts to ministries other than the local church should be above the "tithe." Certainly the "storehouse" in Malachi represents the temple or a building in the temple complex. However, the Old Testament "tithe" or "tenth" cannot be reasonably equated with ten percent of gross salary or wages that most people earn today. Above all, giving should be a matter between the Holy Spirit and the believer, not a regulation. The "tithe" may be an adequate guide for determining how much some people could give (indeed, for many in a prosperous society, it is probably an inadequate level), but the amount of giving must be a personal decision. The Apostle Paul wrote that God examines the motives for the giving, not the amount (2 Cor. 9:7).

4:1–6 Malachi concludes his prophecy with a prediction of the "coming of Elijah." One must understand that Malachi 3:1 is explicitly cited in the New Testament as directly referring to John the Baptist, and he certainly ministered when Jesus first "came to His temple." On the other hand, Malachi 4:5, 6 is cited with reference to John the Baptist only because he came in "the spirit and power of Elijah" (Luke 1:17). In Matthew 17:10, Jesus makes a distinction between the Elijah who is yet to come, and John who came already (Matt. 17:11). See note on 1 Thessalonians 5:2.

name shall the [b]Sun of righteousness
arise with healing in his wings; and ye
shall go forth, and grow up6335 as calves
of the stall.
3 [a]And ye shall tread down the
wicked;[7563] for they shall be ashes
under the soles[3709] of your feet in the
day that I shall do *this,* saith the LORD of
hosts.
4 Remember[2142] ye the [a]law[8451] of
Moses my servant,[5650] which I commanded[6680] unto him [b]in Horeb for all
Israel, *with* [c]the statutes[2706] and judgments.[4941]
5 Behold, I will send you [a]Elijah the
prophet[5030] [b]before the coming of the
great and dreadful[3372] day of the LORD:
6 And he shall turn[7725] the heart[3820]
of the fathers[1] to the children,[1121] and
the heart of the children to their fathers,
lest I come and [a]smite[5521] the earth[776]
with [b]a curse.[2764]

2 [b]Luke 1:78; Eph. 5:14; 2Pet. 1:19; Rev. 2:28
3 [a]2Sam. 22:43; Mic. 7:10; Zech. 10:5
4 [a]Ex. 20:3 [b]Deut. 4:10 [c]Ps. 147:19
5 [a]Matt. 11:14; 17:11; Mark 9:11; Luke 1:17 [b]Joel 2:31
6 [a]Zech. 14:12 [b]Zech. 5:3

The NEW TESTAMENT *Of Our Lord and Saviour* Jesus Christ

The Gospel Accor to

MATTHW

Matthew, whose name means "gift of Jehovah," left h pation of collecting taxes (Matt. 9:9–13) in order to follow Jesus. In Luke 5:27–32, Matthe a banquet for Jesus before becoming one of the Twelve Apostles (Matt. 10:3). He was a itness of Jesus' entire ministry.

The four Gospels (Matthew, Mark, Luke, and John) forı que kind of written document. They present four complementary views of the life of Jesus from these four Gospels, there are only a few writings in the contemporary historians, Jos nd Tacitus, which discuss the life and activities of Jesus. Several scholars suggest that t ur were written down, under the inspiration of the Holy Spirit, because the number of ng eyewitnesses to Jesus' life were dwindling.

From early times, Matthew's book has been placed at th ning of the New Testament. The approximate date for its writing is A.D. 58–68. There is s idence that it was originally written in Hebrew or that Matthew made one copy in Hebre one in Greek.

The large number of Old Testament quotations used ir ook seem to indicate that Matthew directed his writing primarily toward a Jewish audi He lays great stress on the Old Testament passages that identify Jesus as the Messiah (, the long-awaited King of Israel. For the most part, the narrative is chronological, though n portions of the material are grouped according to subject matter (e.g., the Sermon on unt, chaps. 5—7, and the parables in chap. 13). In Matthew's presentation of the life of the central theme is that He is the King of the long-awaited kingdom of God.

Of the fifteen parables and twenty miracles recorded in the l of Matthew, ten of the parables and three of the miracles are not mentioned in the oth pels. In addition, the account of the saints who came back to life at Christ's resurrectio t. 27:51, 52), the sealing of Jesus' tomb, and the posting of the Roman guard outside it (7:62–66) are exclusively recorded in the Gospel of Matthew.

Genealogy of Jesus (Luke 3:23–38)

1 The book[976] of the [a]generation[1078] of Jesus Christ,[5547] [b]the son of David, [c]the son of Abraham.

2 [a]Abraham begat[1080] Isaac; and [b]Isaac begat Jacob; and [c]Jacob begat Judas and his brethren;

3 And [a]Judas begat Phares and Zara of Thamar; and [b]Phares begat Esrom; and Esrom begat Aram;

4 And Aram begat Aminadab; and Aminadab begat Naasson; and Naasson begat Salmon;

5 And Salmon begat Booz of Rachab; and Booz begat Obed of Ruth; and Obed begat Jesse;

6 And [a]Jesse begat David the king;[935] and [b]David the king begat Solomon of her *that had been the wife* of Urias;

7 And [a] on begat Roboam; and Roboam beg a; and Abia begat Asa;

8 And begat Josaphat; and Josaphat beg am; and Joram begat Ozias;

9 And O begat Joatham; and Joatham beg az; and Achaz begat Ezekias;

10 And [a]E s begat Manasses; and Manasses Amon; and Amon begat Josias;

11 And [a]Jos egat Jechonias and his brethren,[80] a the time they were [b]carried away to lon:

12 And after were brought to Babylon, [a]Jechoni gat Salathiel; and Salathiel begat [b]Z bel;

13 And Zorob egat Abiud; and

1 [a]Luke 3:23 [b]Ps. 132:11; Isa. 11:1; Jer. 23:5; Matt. 22:42; John 7:42; Acts 2:30; 13:23; Rom. 1:3 [c]Gen. 12:3; 22:18; Gal. 3:16
2 [a]Gen. 21:2, 3 [b]Gen. 25:26 [c]Gen. 29:35
3 [a]Gen. 38:27-30 [b]Ruth 4:18-22; 1Chr. 2:5, 9-16
6 [a]1Sam. 16:1; 17:12 [b]2Sam. 12:24
7 [a]1Chr. 3:10
10 [a]2Kgs. 20:21; 1Chr. 3:13
11 [a]1Chr. 3:15, 16 [b]2Kgs. 24:14-16; 25:11; 2Chr. 36:10, 20; Jer. 27:20; 39:9; 52:11, 15, 28-30; Dan. 1:2
12 [a]1Chr. 3:17, 19 [b]Ezra ; Neh. 12:1; Hag. 1:1

Abiud begat Eliakim; and Eliakim be
Azor;
14 And Azor begat Sadoc; and Sa
begat Achim; and Achim begat Eliu
15 And Eliud begat Eleazar;
Eleazar begat Matthan; and Ma
begat Jacob;
16 And Jacob begat Joseph
husband[435] of Mary, of whom was
Jesus, who is called Christ.[5547]
17 So all the generations
Abraham to David *are* fourteen
tions; and from David until the c
away into Babylon *are* fourteen
tions;[1074] and from the carryir
into Babylon unto Christ *are* en
generations.

The Birth of Jesus (Luke 2:1–7)

18 Now the [a]birth[1083] of J hrist
was on this wise: When as other
Mary was espoused[3423] to Jo efore
they came together, she was with
child [b]of the Holy Ghost.[415]
19 Then Joseph her hus being a
just[1342] *man,* and not willing o make
her a publick example, was ed [ainf]to
put her away[630] privily.[297]
20 But while he tho n these
things, behold, the angel the Lord
appeared[5316] unto him in eam, saying, Joseph, thou son of l, fear[5399]
not to take unto[3880] thee thy wife:
[a]for that which [aptp]is [I]con [1080] in her
is of the Holy Ghost.
21 [a]And she shall g forth a
son,[5207] and thou shalt is name[3686]
[I]JESUS: for [b]he shave[4982] his
people[2992] from their s
22 Now all this [pfi]lone,[1096] that
it might be fulfilled[41] ich was spoken of the Lord by t phet, saying,
23 [a]Behold, a [art]3933 shall be
with child, and shall g forth a son,
and [I]they shall call h me Emmanuel,
which being interpre s, God[2316] with
us.

[a]Luke 1:27 uke 1:35

9 [a]Deut. 24:1

20 [I]Gr. *begotten* [a]Luke 1:35

21 [I]That is, *SAVIOUR,* Hebr. [a]Luke 1:31 [b]Acts 4:12; 5:31; 13:23, 38

23 [I]Or, *his name shall be called* [a]Isa. 7:14

25 [a]Ex. 13:2; Luke 2:7, 21

1 [a]Luke 2:4, 6, 7 [b]Gen. 10:30; 25:6; 1Kgs. 4:30

2 [a]Luke 2:11 [b]Num. 24:17; Isa. 60:3

4 [a]2Chr. 36:14 [b]2Chr. 34:13 [c]Mal. 2:7

6 [I]Or, *feed* [a]Mic. 5:2; John 7:42 [b]Rev. 2:27

24 Then Joseph being raised from
sleep did as the angel of the Lord had
bidden[4367] him, and took unto[3880] him
his wife:
🔑 25 And [ipf]knew her not till she had
brought forth [a]her firstborn[4416] son: and
he called his name JESUS.

The Visit of the Magi

2 Now when [a]Jesus was born in Bethlehem of Judaea in[1722] the days[2250]
of Herod the king,[935] behold, there came
wise men [b]from the east to Jerusalem,
2 Saying, [a]Where is he that [aptp]is
born[5088] King[935] of the Jews? for we
[ao]have seen[1492] [b]his star in the east, and
[ao]are come[2064] to worship him.
3 When Herod the king had heard[191]
these things, he was troubled, and all
Jerusalem with[3326] him.
4 And when he had gathered[4863] all
[a]the chief priests[749] and [b]scribes[1122] of
the people together, [c]he demanded of
them where Christ [pin]should be born.
5 And they said unto him, In Bethlehem of Judaea: for thus [pfip]it is written
by the prophet,[4396]
6 [a]And thou Bethlehem, *in* the
land[1093] of Juda, art not least among[1722]
the princes of Juda: for out of thee shall
come a Governor,[2233] [b]that shall [I]rule my
people Israel.
7 Then Herod, when he had priv-
ily[2977] called the wise men, enquired of
them diligently what time[5550] the star
[ppt]appeared.[5316]
8 And he [apt]sent them to Bethlehem,
and said, [apt]Go and [aim]search diligently
for the young child; and when ye have
found *him,* bring me word again,[518] that
I [apt]may come[2064] and worship him also.
9 When they had heard the king, they
departed; and, lo, the star, which they
saw[1492] in the east, [ipf]went before them, till
it [apt]came and stood over where the young
child was.
10 When they saw the star, they
rejoiced[5463] with exceeding great joy.[5479]

🔑 **1:25** See note olossians 1:15.

11 And when they [apt]were come into the house,[3614] they saw the young child with Mary his mother, and [apt]fell down,[4098] and [ao]worshipped him: and when they [apt]had opened their treasures, [a]they [I]presented unto him gifts;[1435] gold, and frankincense,[3030] and myrrh.[4666]

12 And [aptp]being warned of God[5537] [a]in a dream that they should not return to Herod, they departed into their own country another[243] way.[3598]

God Warns Joseph

13 And when they [apt]were departed, behold, the angel of the Lord appeareth[5316] to Joseph in a dream, saying, [apt]Arise, and take[3880] the young child and his mother, and flee into Egypt, and be thou there until I bring thee word: for Herod will seek the young child to destroy[622] him.

14 When he [apt]arose, he took[3880] the young child and his mother by night, and departed into Egypt:

15 And was there until the death[5054] of Herod: that it might be fulfilled which was spoken of the Lord by the prophet, saying, [a]Out of Egypt have I [ao]called my son.

16 Then Herod, when he [apt]saw that he was mocked of the wise men, [aop]was exceeding wroth,[2373] and [apt]sent forth,[649] and slew all the children that were in Bethlehem, and in all the coasts thereof, from two years old and under,[2736] according to the time[5550] which he had diligently enquired of the wise men.

17 Then was fulfilled that which was spoken by [a]Jeremy the prophet, saying,

18 In Rama was there a voice[5456] heard,[191] lamentation, and weeping, and great mourning, Rachel weeping *for* her children, and would not be comforted, because they are not.

19 But when Herod [apt]was dead,[5053] behold, an angel of the Lord appeareth in a dream to Joseph in Egypt,

20 Saying, [aptp]Arise, and take[3880] the young child and his mother, and go into the land[1093] of Israel: for they [pfi]are dead[2348] which [ppt]sought the young child's life.

21 And he [aptp]arose, and took[3880] the young child and his mother, and came into the land of Israel.

22 But when he [apt]heard that Archelaus [pin]did reign[936] in Judaea in the room of his father[3962] Herod, he was afraid[5399] to go thither: notwithstanding, [aptp]being warned of God[5537] in a dream, he turned aside [a]into the parts of Galilee:

23 And he [apt]came and dwelt[2730] in a city called [a]Nazareth: that it might be fulfilled [b]which was spoken by the prophets, He shall be called a Nazarene.

The Preaching of John (Mark 1:1–8; Luke 3:1–9, 15–17; John 1:19–28)

3 In[1722] those days [pin]came [a]John the Baptist,[910] preaching[2784] [b]in the wilderness of Judaea,

2 And saying, [pim]Repent[3340] ye: for [a]the kingdom[932] of heaven [pfi]is at hand.[1448]

3 For this is he that was spoken of by the prophet Esaias, saying, [a]The voice[5456] of one crying in the wilderness, [aim][b]Prepare ye the way[3598] of the [an]Lord, [pim]make[4160] his paths straight.

4 And [a]the same John [ipf][b]had[2192] his raiment of camel's hair, and a leathern girdle[2223] about his loins; and his meat was [c]locusts and [d]wild honey.

5 [a]Then [ipf]went out to him Jerusalem, and all Judaea, and all the region round about Jordan,

6 [a]And [ipf]were baptized[907] of him in Jordan, confessing[1843] their sins.[266]

7 But when he [apt]saw many of the Pharisees and Sadducees [ppt]come to his baptism,[908] he said unto them, [a]O generation of vipers, who [ao]hath warned you to flee from [b]the wrath[3709] to come?[3195]

8 [aim]Bring forth therefore fruits meet[514] for [art]repentance:[3341]

9 And [aosi]think not to say within yourselves, [a]We have Abraham to *our* father:[3962] for I say unto you, that God is able[1410] of these stones to raise up children unto Abraham.

---

11 [I]Or, *offered* [a]Ps. 72:10; Isa. 60:6

12 [a]Matt. 1:20

15 [a]Hos. 11:1

17 [a]Jer. 31:15

22 [a]Matt. 3:13; Luke 2:39

23 [a]John 1:45 [b]Judg. 13:5; 1Sam. 1:11

1 [a]Mark 1:4, 15; Luke 3:2, 3; John 1:28 [b]Josh. 14:10

2 [a]Dan. 2:44; Matt. 4:17; 10:7

3 [a]Isa. 40:3; Mark 1:3; Luke 3:4; John 1:23 [b]Luke 1:76

4 [a]Mark 1:6 [b]2Kgs. 1:8; Zech. 13:4 [c]Lev. 11:22 [d]1Sam. 14:25, 26

5 [a]Mark 1:5; Luke 3:7

6 [a]Acts 19:4, 18

7 [a]Matt. 12:34; 23:33; Luke 3:7-9 [b]Rom. 5:9; 1Thess. 1:10

9 [a]John 8:33, 39; Acts 13:26; Rom. 4:1, 11, 16

10 And now also the axe [pin]is laid[2749] unto the root of the trees: [a]therefore every tree which [ppt]bringeth not forth good fruit is hewn down,[1581] and cast[906] into the fire.

🔑 11 [a]I indeed baptize[907] you with water unto repentance:[3341] but he that [ppt]cometh after me is mightier than I, whose shoes[5266] I am[1510] not worthy[2425] to bear: [b]he [ft]shall baptize you with the [an]Holy Ghost,[4151] and *with* fire:

12 [a]Whose fan *is* in his hand, and he [ft]will throughly purge his floor, and [ft]gather his wheat into the garner;[596] but he [ft]will [b]burn up the chaff with unquenchable fire.

Jesus Is Baptized by John (Mark 1:9–11; Luke 3:21, 22)

13 [a]Then cometh Jesus [b]from Galilee to Jordan unto John, to be baptized of him.

14 But John [ipf]forbad him, saying, I have need to be baptized of thee, and comest thou to me?

15 And Jesus answering[611] said unto him, Suffer *it to be so* now: for thus it becometh us to fulfil[4137] all righteousness.[1343] Then he suffered him.

16 [a]And Jesus, when he was baptized, went up[305] straightway[2117] out of the water: and, lo, the heavens were opened unto him, and he saw [b]the Spirit of God descending[2597] like a dove, and lighting upon him:

17 [a]And lo a voice[5456] from heaven, saying, [b]This is my beloved[27] Son,[5207] in whom I [ao]am well pleased.[2106]

Jesus Is Tempted By the Devil (Mark 1:12, 13; Luke 4:1–13)

4 Then was [a]Jesus led up of [b]the spirit[4151] into the wilderness [aifp]to be tempted[3985] of the devil.[1228]

2 And when he had fasted[3522] forty days and forty nights, he [ao]was afterward an hungred.[3983]

3 And when the tempter[3985] came to him, he said, If thou be the [an]Son of God, command that these stones be made[1096] bread.

4 But he answered[611] and said, [pfip]It is written,[1125] [a]Man[444] [fm]shall not live[2198] by bread alone, but by every word[4487] that [ppt]proceedeth out of the mouth of God.

5 Then the devil taketh him up[3880] [a]into the holy city, and [pin]setteth[2476] him on [art]a pinnacle of the temple,[2411]

6 And saith unto him, If thou be the [an]Son of God, cast[906] thyself down:[2736] for [pfip]it is written,[1125] [a]He shall give his angels charge[1781] concerning thee: and in *their* hands they shall bear thee up,[142] lest at any time thou [asba]dash[4350] thy foot against a stone.

7 Jesus said unto him, It is written[1125] again, [a]Thou [ft]shalt not tempt[1598] the Lord thy God.

8 Again, the devil [pin]taketh him up[3880] into an exceeding high mountain, and [pin]sheweth him all the kingdoms[932] of the world, and the glory[1391] of them;

9 And [pin]saith unto him, All these things will I give thee, if thou [apt]wilt fall down[4098] and [asba]worship me.

10 Then saith Jesus unto him, Get thee hence, Satan:[4567] for [pfip]it is written,[1125] [a]Thou shalt worship the [an]Lord thy God, and him only shalt thou serve.[3000]

11 Then the devil leaveth him, and, behold, [a]angels came and [ipf]ministered[1247] unto him.

Jesus Teaches the People (Mark 1:14, 15; Luke 4:14, 15)

12 [a]Now when Jesus had heard that John was [l]cast into prison, he departed into Galilee;

13 And leaving Nazareth, he came and [ao]dwelt[2730] in Capernaum, which is upon the sea coast, in the borders of Zabulon and Nephthalim:

10 [a]Matt. 7:19; Luke 13:7, 9; John 15:6
11 [a]Mark 1:8; Luke 3:16; John 1:15, 26, 33; Acts 1:5; 11:16; 19:4 [b]Isa. 4:4; 44:3; Mal. 3:2; Acts 2:3, 4; 1Cor. 12:13
12 [a]Mal. 3:3 [b]Mal. 4:1; Matt. 13:30
13 [a]Mark 1:9; Luke 3:21 [b]Matt. 2:22
16 [a]Mark 1:10 [b]Isa. 11:2; 42:1; Luke 3:22; John 1:32, 33
17 [a]John 12:28 [b]Ps. 2:7; Isa. 42:1; Matt. 12:18; 17:5; Mark 1:11; Luke 9:35; Eph. 1:6; Col. 1:13; 2Pet. 1:17
1 [a]Mark 1:12, 13; Luke 4:1-13 [b]1Kgs. 18:12; Ezek. 3:14; 8:3; 11:1, 24; 40:2; 43:5; Acts 8:39
4 [a]Deut. 8:3
5 [a]Neh. 11:1, 18; Isa. 48:2; 52:1; Matt. 27:53; Rev. 11:2
6 [a]Ps. 91:11, 12
7 [a]Deut. 6:16
10 [a]Deut. 6:13; 10:20; Josh. 24:14; 1Sam. 7:3
11 [a]Heb. 1:14
12 [l]Or, *delivered up* [a]Mark 1:14; Luke 3:20; 4:14, 31; John 4:43

🔑 **3:11** See notes on Acts 1:5.

14 That it might be fulfilled which was spoken by Esaias the prophet, saying,

15 [a]The land[1093] of Zabulon, and the land of Nephthalim, *by* the way[3598] of the sea, beyond Jordan, Galilee of the Gentiles;

16 [a]The people which [ppt]sat in darkness[4655] saw great light;[5457] and to them which [ppt]sat in the region and shadow of death[2288] light [ao]is sprung up.

17 [a]From that time Jesus [ao]began[756] to preach,[2784] and to say, [pim][b]Repent:[3340] for the kingdom[932] of heaven [pf]is at hand.[1448]

Jesus Calls Four Fishermen (Mark 1:16–20; Luke 5:1–11)

18 [a]And Jesus, walking by the sea of Galilee, saw two brethren, Simon [ppp][b]called Peter, and Andrew his brother, casting[906] a net[293] into the sea: for they were fishers.

19 And he saith unto them, Follow me, and [a]I will make[4160] you fishers of men.[444]

20 [a]And they straightway[2112] [apt]left[863] *their* nets,[1350] and followed[190] him.

21 [a]And going on from thence, he saw other[243] two brethren, James *the son* of Zebedee, and John his brother, in a [art]ship with Zebedee their father,[3962] mending[2675] their nets;[1350] and he called them.

22 And they immediately left[863] the ship and their father, and followed him.

Jesus Ministers to a Great Multitude

23 And Jesus [ipf]went about all Galilee, [a]teaching[1321] in their synagogues, and preaching[2784] [b]the gospel[2098] of the kingdom, [c]and healing[2323] all manner of sickness[3554] and all manner of disease[3119] among the people.

24 And his fame[189] went throughout all Syria: and they brought[4374] unto him all sick people that [ppt]were taken with[4912] divers[4164] diseases[3554] and torments, and [ppt]those which were possessed with devils,[1139] and those which were lunatic, and those that had the palsy;[3885] and he [ao]healed[2323] them.

25 [a]And there followed[190] him great multitudes of people from Galilee, and *from* Decapolis, and *from* Jerusalem, and *from* Judaea, and *from* beyond Jordan.

The Beatitudes (Luke 6:20–26)

5 🗝And seeing the multitudes, [a]he went up[305] into a mountain: and when he [apt]was set, his disciples[3101] came[4334] unto him:

15 [a]Isa. 9:1, 2
16 [a]Isa. 42:7; Luke 2:32
17 [a]Mark 1:14, 15 [b]Matt. 3:2; 10:7
18 [a]Mark 1:16-18; Luke 5:2 [b]John 1:42
19 [a]Luke 5:10, 11
20 [a]Mark 10:28; Luke 18:28
21 [a]Mark 1:19, 20; Luke 5:10
23 [a]Matt. 9:35; Mark 1:21, 39; Luke 4:15, 44 [b]Matt. 24:14; Mark 1:14 [c]Mark 1:34
25 [a]Mark 3:7
1 [a]Mark 3:13

🗝 **5:1–12** The Greek word translated "blessed" is *makárioi* (3107), which means to be "fully satisfied." In Classical Greek, the word referred to a state of blessedness in the hereafter. In the New Testament, however, the term is used of the joy that comes from salvation (cf. Ps. 51:12). This satisfaction is not the result of favorable circumstances in life. It comes only from being indwelt by Christ. Therefore, it would be wrong to translate *makárioi* as "happy" (derived from the English word "hap") because that word is connected with luck or favorable circumstances.

Blessedness is not static, but progressive. This progress depends upon the fulfillment of the conditions set down in these Beatitudes: 1) "The poor in spirit" (*ptōchoís* [4434], v. 3) indicates a "helpless" person as opposed to *pénēs* (3993), which means "poor, but able to help oneself." The first step toward blessedness is a realization of one's own spiritual helplessness. 2) "They that mourn" (v. 4) are those who sorrow for their sins and the sins of others. 3) The "meek" ones are willing to see themselves as they really are (v. 5). This concept they have of themselves is evidenced in their submission to God and His Word, as well as in their dealings with others. 4) "They which do hunger" (v. 6; from the Greek, *hoi peinōntes* [3983]) could be better rendered "the hungering ones." This indicates a constant and recurrent satisfaction with God's righteousness; the nourishment received from being filled is expended in hungering anew for another filling. 5) The "merciful" are characterized by a caring attitude for those who are in misery (v. 7). They take the heartaches of others

(continued on next page)

2 And he [apt]opened his mouth, and [ipf]taught them, saying,

3 [aj][a]Blessed[3107] *are* the poor[4434] in [art]spirit:[4151] for theirs is the kingdom[932] of heaven.[3772]

4 [a]Blessed *are* they that [ppt]mourn:[3996] for they [fp]shall be comforted.

5 [a]Blessed *are* the meek:[4239] for they shall inherit[2816] the earth.

6 Blessed *are* they which [ppt]do hunger and [ppt]thirst after [art]righteousness:[1343] [a]for they [fp]shall be filled.

🔑 7 Blessed *are* the merciful:[1655] [a]for they [fp]shall obtain mercy.

8 [a]Blessed *are* the pure[2513] in heart:[2588] for [b]they shall see God.[2316]

9 Blessed *are* the peacemakers:[1518] for they shall be called the [an]children[5207] of God.

🔑 10 [a]Blessed *are* they which [pfpp]are persecuted for righteousness' sake: for theirs is the kingdom of heaven.

11 [a]Blessed are ye, when *men* [aosb]shall revile you, and [aosb]persecute *you,* and [aosb]shall say all manner of [b]evil[4487] against you falsely, for my sake.

12 [pim][a]Rejoice,[5463] and [pim]be exceeding glad:[21] for great *is* your reward[3408] in heaven:[3772] for [b]so persecuted they the prophets[4396] which were before you.

Salt and Light
(Mark 9:50; Luke 14:34, 35)

13 Ye are the salt of the earth: [a]but if the salt [asbp]have lost his savour,[3471] wherewith [fp]shall it be salted?[233] it is thenceforth good[2480] for nothing, but [aifp]to be cast[906] out, and [pip]to be trodden under foot of men.

14 [a]Ye are the light[5457] of the world.[2889] A city that [ppt]is set[2749] on an hill cannot [aifp]be hid.

15 Neither [pin]do men [a]light[2545] a candle, and put[5087] it under a bushel, but on a candlestick; and it giveth light unto all that are in the house.

16 [aim]Let your light so shine[2989] before men, [a]that they [aosb]may see your good works, and [aosb][b]glorify[1392] your Father which is in heaven.

Teaching About the Law

17 [a]Think not that I [ao]am come [ainf]to destroy the law,[3551] or the prophets:[4396] I am not come to destroy,[2647] but [ainf]to fulfil.[4137]

18 For verily[281] I say unto you, [a]Till heaven[3772] and earth[1093] pass, one jot[2503] or one tittle[2762] shall in no wise pass from the law,[3551] till all be fulfilled.[1096]

19 [a]Whosoever therefore shall break[3089] one of these least commandments, and [aosb]shall teach[1321] men so, he shall be called the least in the kingdom of heaven: but whosoever [aosb]shall do and [aosb]teach *them,* the same [fp]shall be called great in the kingdom of heaven.

20 For I say unto you, That except your righteousness shall exceed [a]*the*

3 [a]Luke 6:20; Ps. 51:17; Prov. 16:19; 29:23; Isa. 57:15; 66:2
4 [a]Isa. 61:2, 3; Luke 6:21; John 16:20; 2Cor. 1:7; Rev. 21:4
5 [a]Ps. 37:11 [b]Rom. 4:13
6 [a]Isa. 55:1; 65:13
7 [a]Ps. 41:1; Matt. 6:14; Mark 11:25; 2Tim. 1:16; Heb. 6:10; James 2:13
8 [a]Ps. 15:2; 24:4; Heb. 12:14 [b]1Cor. 13:12; 1John 3:2, 3
10 [a]2Cor. 4:17; 2Tim. 2:12; 1Pet. 3:14
11 [a]Luke 6:22 [b]1Pet. 4:14
12 [a]Luke 6:23; Acts 5:41; Rom. 5:3; James 1:2; 1Pet. 4:13 [b]2Chr. 36:16; Neh. 9:26; Matt. 23:34, 37; Acts 7:52; 1Thess. 2:15
13 [a]Mark 9:50; Luke 14:34, 35
14 [a]Prov. 4:18; Phil. 2:15
15 [a]Mark 4:21; Luke 8:16; 11:33
16 [a]1Pet. 2:12 [b]John 15:8; 1Cor. 14:25
17 [a]Rom. 3:31; 10:4; Gal. 3:24
18 [a]Luke 16:17
19 [a]James 2:10
20 [a]Rom. 9:31; 10:3

(continued from previous page)
and make them their own. 6) "Purity of heart" can only be acquired through the continuous cleansing that believers experience when they have fulfilled the previous conditions of blessedness (v. 8). The purer a person becomes, the more clearly he can see God. 7) A "peacemaker" is not simply someone who tries to stop the feuding between nations and people (v. 9). It is a believer that has experienced the peace of God and who brings that peace to his fellow human beings. 8) Being "persecuted for righteousness' sake" causes a person to reach the highest level of the satisfaction of blessedness (v. 10).

This state of blessedness begins the very moment that a person believes on Jesus Christ for salvation. This is demonstrated by the fact that the promises concerning the kingdom of heaven in verses three and ten are in the present tense. While in this life one may enjoy the results of implementing these truths, his or her ultimate condition of blessedness will be experienced in heaven (v. 12).

🔑 **5:7** See note on James 2:12, 13.
🔑 **5:10** See note on 2 Timothy 2:12, 13.

righteousness of the scribes and
Pharisees, ye shall [efn]in no case enter into
the kingdom of heaven.

Teaching About Anger

21 Ye [ao]have heard that it was said
[I]by them of old time,[744] [a]Thou shalt not
kill; and whosoever shall kill shall be in
danger of the judgment:[2920]
🗝 22 But [epn]I say unto you, That
[a]whosoever [ppp]is angry with his brother[80]
without a cause shall be in danger of the
judgment:[2920] and whosoever shall say to
his brother, [I][b]Raca,[4469] shall be in danger
of the council: but whosoever shall say,
Thou fool,[3474] shall be in danger of
hell[1067] fire.
23 Therefore [a]if thou [psa]bring[4374] thy
gift[1435] to the altar, and there [asbp]remem-
berest that thy brother[80] hath ought
against thee;
24 [a]Leave[863] there thy gift[1435] before
the altar, and go thy way; first[4412] be
reconciled[1259] to thy brother,[80] and then
come and offer[4374] thy gift.
25 [a]Agree[2132][2468] with thine adversary[476]
quickly, [b]whiles thou art in the way with
him; lest at any time the adversary
[aosb]deliver thee to the judge, and the
judge[2923] deliver thee to the officer, and
thou be cast[906] into prison.
26 Verily I say unto thee, Thou shalt
[efn]by no means come out thence, till thou
hast paid the uttermost[2078] farthing.[2835]

Sin Begins in the Heart

🗝 27 Ye [ao]have heard that it was said
by them of old time,[744] [a]Thou [ft]shalt not
commit adultery:
28 But [epn]I say unto you, That
whosoever [ppt][a]looketh on a woman [aipr]to
lust[1937] after her [ao]hath committed
adultery[3431] with her already in his
heart.[2588]
🗝 29 [a]And if thy right[1188] eye
[pin][I]offend[4624] thee, [aim][b]pluck it out, and
[aim]cast *it* from thee: for it is profitable[4851]
for thee that one of thy members should
perish, and not *that* thy whole body
should be cast into hell.[1067]
30 And if thy right[1188] hand [pin]of-
fend thee, [aim]cut it off, and [aim]cast[906] *it*
from thee: for it is profitable for thee that
one of thy members should perish, and
not *that* thy whole body should be cast
into hell.[1067]

Divorce
(Matt. 19:9; Mark 10:11, 12; Luke 16:18; Rom. 7:1–3; 1 Cor. 7)

🗝 31 It [aop]hath been said, [a]Whosoever
[asba]shall put away[630] his wife, [aim]let
him give[1325] her a writing of divorcement:[647]
32 But [epn]I say unto you, That
[a]whosoever shall put away[630] his wife,
saving for the cause of fornication,[4202]
causeth her [pip]to commit adultery:[3429] and
whosoever shall marry her [pfpp]that is
divorced[630] [pin]committeth adultery.

Oaths

33 Again, ye [ao]have heard that [a]it
[aop]hath been said by them of old time,[744]
[b]Thou shalt not forswear thyself, but
[c]shalt perform unto the Lord thine oaths:
34 But [epn]I say unto you, [a]Swear not
at all; neither by heaven;[3772] for it is
[b]God's[2316] throne:
35 Nor by the earth;[1093] for it is his

21 [I]Or, *to them* [a]Ex. 20:13; Deut. 5:17
22 [I]That is, *Vain fellow* [a]1John 3:15 [b]2Sam. 6:20; James 2:20
23 [a]Matt. 8:4; 23:19
24 [a]Job 42:8; Matt. 18:19; 1Tim. 2:8; 1Pet. 3:7
25 [a]Prov. 25:8; Luke 12:58, 59 [b]Ps. 32:6; Isa. 55:6
27 [a]Ex. 20:14; Deut. 5:18
28 [a]Job 31:1; Prov. 6:25; Gen. 34:2; 2Sam. 11:2
29 [I]Or, *do cause thee to offend* [a]Matt. 18:8, 9; Mark 9:43-47 [b]Matt. 19:12; Rom. 8:13; 1Cor. 9:27; Col. 3:5
31 [a]Deut. 24:1; Jer. 3:1; Matt. 19:3-12; Mark 10:2-12
32 [a]Matt. 19:9; Luke 16:18; Rom. 7:3; 1Cor. 7:10, 11
33 [a]Matt. 23:16 [b]Ex. 20:7; Lev. 19:12; Num. 30:2; Deut. 5:11 [c]Deut. 23:23
34 [a]Matt. 23:16, 18, 22; James 5:12 [b]Isa. 66:1

🗝 **5:22, 29, 30** See note on Matthew 8:11, 12.
🗝 **5:27–32** The person who "keeps on looking" (v. 28, from the Greek, *ho blépōn* [991]) is guilty of adultery in his or her heart. If a person continues to place himself or herself in a position to be tempted to sin, that person will continue to fall into sin.
🗝 **5:31, 32** A more literal translation of these two very difficult verses would be "And it was said, 'Whosoever dismisses his wife, let him give her a bill of divorcement.' But I say unto you that whosoever dismisses his wife except for reason of fornication [while she is his wife] commits adultery against her, and whosoever marries one who is unjustifiably dismissed is considered as committing adultery." See note on Matthew 19:3–9.

footstool: neither by Jerusalem; for it is [a]the city of the great King.[935]

36 Neither shalt thou swear by thy head, because thou canst not make[4160] one hair white or black.

37 [a]But [pim]let your communication be,[2077] Yea, yea; Nay, nay: for whatsoever is more[4053] than these cometh of evil.

Retaliation (Luke 6:29, 30)

38 Ye [ao]have heard that it [aop]hath been said, [a]An eye for an eye, and a tooth for a tooth:

39 But [epn]I say unto you, [a]That ye resist not evil:[4190] [b]but whosoever shall smite[4474] thee on thy right[1188] cheek, turn to him the other[243] also.

40 And if any man will [aifp]sue thee at the law,[2919] and take away thy coat,[5509] [aim]let him have[863] *thy* cloke also.

41 And whosoever [a]shall compel thee to go[29] a mile, go with[3326] him twain.1417

42 Give to him that [ppt]asketh thee, and [a]from him that would[2309] [ainf]borrow of thee [aosi]turn not thou away.[654]

Enemies (Luke 6:27, 28, 32–36)

43 Ye [ao]have heard that it [ao]hath been said, [a]Thou [ft]shalt love[25] thy neighbour,[4139] [b]and [ft]hate thine enemy.

44 But [epn]I say unto you, [pima]Love your enemies, [pim]bless them that [ppt]curse[2672] you, [pim]do good to them that [ppt]hate you, and [pim]pray [b]for them which [ppt]despitefully use you, and [ppt]persecute you;

45 That ye [asbm]may be[1096] the [an]children[5207] of your Father which is in heaven:[3772] for [a]he maketh his sun to [pin]rise on the evil and on the good,[18] and [pin]sendeth rain on the just[1342] and on the unjust.[94]

46 [a]For if ye [aosb]love them which [ppt]love you, what reward[3408] have ye? do not even the publicans5057 the same?

47 And if ye [aosb]salute your brethren[80] only, what [pin]do ye more[4053] than others? [pin]do not even the publicans so?

48 [fma]Be ye therefore perfect,[5046] even [b]as your Father which is in heaven[3772] is perfect.

35 [a]Ps. 48:2; 87:3

37 [a]Col. 4:6; James 5:12

38 [a]Ex. 21:24; Lev. 24:20; Deut. 19:21

39 [a]Prov. 20:22; 24:29; Luke 6:29; Rom. 12:17, 19; 1Cor. 6:7; 1Thess. 5:15; 1Pet. 3:9 [b]Isa. 50:6; Lam. 3:30

41 [a]Matt. 27:32; Mark 15:21

42 [a]Deut. 15:8, 10; Luke 6:30, 35

43 [a]Lev. 19:18 [b]Deut. 23:6; Ps. 41:10

44 [a]Luke 6:27, 35; Rom. 12:14, 20 [b]Luke 23:34; Acts 7:60; 1Cor. 4:12, 13; 1Pet. 2:23; 3:9

45 [a]Job 25:3

46 [a]Luke 6:32

48 [a]Gen. 17:1; Lev. 11:44; 19:2; Luke 6:36; Col. 1:28; 4:12; James 1:4; 1Pet. 1:15, 16 [b]Eph. 5:1

1 IOr, *righteousness* IIOr, *with* [a]Deut. 24:13; Ps. 112:9; Dan. 4:27; 2Cor. 9:9, 10

2 IOr, *cause not a trumpet to be sounded* [a]Rom. 12:8

4 [a]Luke 14:14

6 [a]2Kgs. 4:33

7 [a]Eccl. 5:2 [b]1Kgs. 18:26, 29

The Proper Manner of Almsgiving

6 [pim]Take heed that ye [pinf]do not your [I]alms before men, to be seen of them: otherwise ye have no [a]reward[3408] [II]of your Father which is in heaven.[3772]

2 Therefore [a]when thou [psa]doest *thine* alms, [aosiI]do not sound a trumpet4537 before thee, as the hypocrites[5273] do in the synagogues and in the streets, that they [asbp]may have glory[1392] of men. Verily281 I say unto you, They have[568] their reward.[3408]

3 But when thou [ppt]doest alms, [aim]let not thy left hand know[1097] what thy right hand[1188] doeth:

4 That thine alms may be in secret: and thy Father which [ppt]seeth in secret himself [a]shall reward thee openly.[1722,5318]

Prayer (Luke 11:2–4)

5 And when thou [psa]prayest, thou [fm]shalt not be2071 as the hypocrites[5273] *are:* for they love[5368] [pinf]to pray standing in[1722] the synagogues and in the corners of the streets, that they [asbm]may be seen[5316,302] of men. Verily I say[3004] unto you, They have[568] their reward.[3408]

6 But thou, when thou [psa]prayest,[4336] [a]enter into thy closet, and when thou hast shut thy door, [aim]pray to thy Father which is in secret; and thy Father [ppt]which seeth in secret shall reward thee openly.[1722,5318] 3588

7 But when ye [ppt]pray, [aosia]use not vain repetitions,[945] as the heathen[1482] *do:* [b]for they think[1380] that they shall be heard for their much speaking.

8 Be not ye therefore like unto them: for your Father knoweth what things ye have need of, before ye [aip]ask him.

9 After this manner therefore

[pim]pray[4336] ye: [a]Our Father[3962] which art
in heaven, [aipp]Hallowed be[37] thy name.[3686]
10 Thy kingdom[932] [aim]come. [a]Thy
will [aipp]be done[1096] in earth,[1093] [b]as *it is*
in heaven.
11 [aim]Give us this day our [a]daily
bread.[1967][740]
12 And [aim][a]forgive[863] us our
debts,[3783] as we forgive our debtors.[3781]
🗝 13 [a]And [aosi]lead us not into temptation,[3986] but [aim][b]deliver[4506] us from
[art]evil:[4190] [c]For thine is the kingdom, and
the power, and the glory, for ever.
Amen.[281]
14 [a]For if ye [aosb]forgive[863] men their
trespasses,[3900] your heavenly[3770] Father
will also forgive you:
15 But [a]if ye [asbm]forgive[863] not men
their trespasses, neither will your Father
forgive your trespasses.

Fasting

16 Moreover [a]when ye [psa]fast,[3522]
be[1096] not, as the hypocrites,[5273] of a sad
countenance: for they disfigure their
faces,[4383] that they [aosb]may appear[5316]
unto men [ppt]to fast. Verily I say unto you,
They have[568] their reward.[3408]
17 But thou, when thou [ppt]fastest,
[aim][a]anoint thine head,[2776] and [aim]wash[3538]
thy face;[4383]
18 That thou [aosb]appear not unto
men [ppt]to fast, but unto thy Father which
is in secret: and thy Father, which
[ppt]seeth in secret, shall reward thee
openly.[1722,5318][3588]

Treasures in Heaven (Luke 12:33, 34)

19 [pim][a]Lay not up for yourselves
treasures upon earth,[1093] where moth and
rust doth corrupt, and where thieves
break through and steal:
20 [a]But [pim]lay up for yourselves
treasures in heaven,[3772] where neither
moth nor rust doth corrupt, and where
thieves do not break through nor steal:
21 For where your treasure is, there
will your heart[2588] be also.

The Light of the World (Luke 11:34–36)

22 [a]The light of the body is the eye:
if therefore thine eye be single,[573] thy
whole body shall be full of light.
23 But if thine eye be evil, thy whole
body shall be full of darkness. If therefore the light[5457] that is in thee be
darkness,[4655] how great *is* that darkness!

Put God's Kingdom First (Luke 12:22–34; 16:13)

24 [a]No man can [pinf]serve two
masters:[2962] for either he will hate the
one, and love[25] the other;[2087] or else
he will hold[472] to the one, and despise the
other.[2087] [b]Ye cannot [pinf]serve[1398] God and
mammon.
25 Therefore I say unto you, [pim][a]Take
no thought for your life, what ye [aosb]shall
eat, or what ye [aosb]shall drink; nor yet for
your body,[4983] what ye [asbm]shall put on.
Is not the life more than meat, and the
body than raiment?
26 [aim][a]Behold[1519][1689] the fowls of the air:
for they sow not, neither do they reap,
nor gather into barns; yet your heavenly[3770] Father feedeth them. [pin]Are ye
not much better[1308] than they?
27 Which of you by [ppt]taking
thought can [ainf]add one cubit unto his
stature?

9 [a]Luke 11:2-4
10 [a]Matt. 26:39, 42; Acts 21:14 [b]Ps. 103:20, 21
11 [a]Job 23:12; Prov. 30:8
12 [a]Matt. 18:21, 22
13 [a]Matt. 26:41; Luke 22:40, 46; 1Cor. 10:13; 2Pet. 2:9; Rev. 3:10 [b]John 17:15 [c]1Chr. 29:11
14 [a]Mark 11:25, 26; Eph. 4:32; Col. 3:13
15 [a]Matt. 18:35; James 2:13
16 [a]Isa. 58:5
17 [a]Ruth 3:3; Dan. 10:3
19 [a]Prov. 23:4; 1Tim. 6:17; Heb. 13:5; James 5:1
20 [a]Matt. 19:21; Luke 12:33, 34; 18:22; 1Tim. 6:19; 1Pet. 1:4
22 [a]Luke 11:34, 36
24 [a]Luke 16:13 [b]Gal. 1:10; 1Tim. 6:17; James 4:4; 1John 2:15
25 [a]Ps. 55:22; Luke 12:22, 23; Phil. 4:6; 1Pet. 5:7
26 [a]Job 38:41; Ps. 147:9; Luke 12:24-34

🗝 **6:13** Why did the Lord teach His disciples to pray, "lead us not into temptation"? Does this in fact mean that God tempts people? When God allows one of His children to be tempted, it is for the purpose of proving to His child that he or she can rely on God's wisdom and strength. It is God's desire to give believers victory over the temptation and at the same time make them more experienced in the tactics of spiritual warfare against the devil. It is crucial to remember, however, that the actual enticement to sin is never generated by God; hence, no one can ever truthfully say that God has tempted him or her to sin (James 1:13).

28 And why take ye thought for raiment? [aim]Consider the lilies of the field, how they grow; they toil[2872] not, neither do they spin:

29 And yet I say unto you, That even Solomon in all his glory [aom]was not arrayed[4016] like one of these.

30 Wherefore, if God so clothe the grass of the field, [ppt]which to day is,[5607] and to morrow [ppp]is cast into the oven, *shall he* not much more *clothe* you, O ye of little faith?[3640]

31 Therefore [aosi]take no thought,[3309] saying, What shall we eat? or, What shall we drink? or, Wherewithal shall we be clothed?

32 (For after all these things do the Gentiles[1484] seek:) for your heavenly[3770] Father knoweth that ye have need[5535] of all these things.

33 But [pim a]seek ye first[4412] the kingdom of God, and his righteousness;[1343] and all these things shall be added unto you.

34 [aosi]Take therefore no thought[3309] for the morrow: for the morrow shall take thought for the things of itself. Sufficient unto the day *is* the evil[2549] thereof.

Judging Others (Luke 6:37, 38, 41, 42)

7 [pim]Judge[2919] [a]not, that ye [asbp]be not judged.[2919]

2 For with what judgment[2917] ye judge, ye shall be judged: [a]and with what measure ye mete,[3354] it shall be measured to you again.

3 [a]And why beholdest thou the mote that is in thy brother's eye, but considerest[2657] not the beam[1385] that is in thine own eye?

4 Or how wilt thou say to thy brother,[80] [aim]Let[863] me [aosb]pull out the mote[2595] out of thine eye; and, behold, a beam *is* in thine own eye?

5 Thou hypocrite,[5273] first[4412] [aim]cast out the beam out of thine own eye; and then shalt thou see clearly [ainf]to cast out the mote out of thy brother's eye.

6 [aosi a]Give not that which is holy[40] unto the dogs, neither [aosi]cast ye your pearls before swine, lest they trample them under their feet, and turn again and rend[4486] you.

33 [a]1Kgs. 3:13; Ps. 37:25; Mark 10:30; Luke 12:31; 1Tim. 4:8

1 [a]Luke 6:37; Rom. 2:1; 14:3, 4, 10, 13; 1Cor. 4:3, 5; James 4:11, 12

2 [a]Mark 4:24; Luke 6:38

3 [a]Luke 6:41, 42

6 [a]Prov. 9:7, 8; 23:9; Acts 13:45, 46

7 [a]Matt. 21:22; Mark 11:24; Luke 11:9, 10; 18:1; John 14:13; 15:7; 16:23, 24; James 1:5, 6; 1John 3:22; 5:14, 15

8 [a]Prov. 8:17; Jer. 29:12, 13

9 [a]Luke 11:11-13

11 [a]Gen. 6:5; 8:21

12 [a]Luke 6:31 [b]Lev. 19:18; Matt. 22:40; Rom. 13:8-10; Gal. 5:14; 1Tim. 1:5

13 [a]Luke 13:24

14 [I]Or, *How*

15 [a]Deut. 13:3; Jer. 23:16; Matt. 24:4, 5, 11, 24; Mark 13:22; Rom. 16:17, 18; Eph. 5:6; Col. 2:8; 2Pet. 2:1-3; 1John 4:1 [b]Mic. 3:5; 2Tim. 3:5 [c]Acts 20:29, 30

Seeking God's Help (Luke 11:9–13)

7 [pim a]Ask,[154] and it shall be given you; [pim]seek, and ye shall find;[2147] [pim]knock, and it shall be opened unto you:

8 For [a]every one that [ppt]asketh [pin]receiveth; and he that [ppt]seeketh [pin]findeth;[2147] and to him that [ppt]knocketh it [fp]shall be opened.

9 [a]Or what man[444] is there of you, whom if his son [aosb]ask[154] bread, will he give him a stone?

10 Or if he [aosb]ask a fish, will he give him a serpent?

11 If ye then, [a]being evil,[4190] know[1492] how [pinf]to give good[18] gifts[1390] unto your children, how much more shall your Father[3962] which is in heaven give good things to them that [ppt]ask him?

12 Therefore all things [a]whatsoever ye [psa]would that men [psa]should do to you, [pim]do ye even so to them: for [b]this is the law[3551] and the prophets.[4396]

The Narrow Way (Luke 13:24)

13 [aim a]Enter ye in at the strait[4728] gate: for wide *is* the gate, and broad *is* the way, that leadeth[520] to destruction,[684] and many there be which [ppt]go in thereat:

14 [I]Because strait *is* the gate, and narrow *is* the way, which [ppt]leadeth[520] unto life,[2222] and few there be that [ppt]find it.

Behaviour and Belief (Luke 6:43, 44)

15 [pim a]Beware of false prophets,[5578] [b]which come to you in sheep's clothing, but inwardly they are [c]ravening wolves.

16 [a]Ye [fm]shall know them by their fruits. [b]Do men gather grapes of thorns, or figs of thistles?

17 Even so [a]every[3956] good[18] tree bringeth forth good[2570] fruit; but a corrupt tree bringeth forth evil fruit.

18 A good[18] tree cannot [pinf]bring forth evil[4190] fruit, neither *can* a corrupt tree [pinf]bring forth good fruit.

19 [a]Every tree that [ppt]bringeth not forth[4160] good[2570] fruit is hewn down,[1581] and cast into the fire.

20 Wherefore by their fruits ye shall know them.

"I Never Knew You" (Luke 13:25–27)

🔑 21 Not every one that [ppt]saith unto me, [a]Lord, Lord, shall enter into the kingdom[932] of heaven; but he that doeth the will of my Father which is in heaven.

22 Many will say to me in that day,[2250] Lord, Lord, [ao]have we [a]not prophesied[4395] in thy name?[3686] and in thy name [ao]have cast out devils?[1140] and in thy name [ao]done many wonderful works?

23 And [a]then [ft]will I profess[3670] unto them, I never knew you: [pim][b]depart from me, ye that work[2038] iniquity.[458]

Build on a Firm Foundation (Luke 6:47–49)

24 Therefore [a]whosoever[3956,3748] heareth these sayings of mine, and doeth them, I will liken him unto a wise[5429] man, which [ao]built[3618] his house[3614] upon a rock:

25 And the rain descended,[2597] and the floods came, and the winds blew,[4154] and beat upon that house; and it fell[4098] not; for it [plpf]was founded upon a rock.

26 And every one that [ppt]heareth these sayings of mine, and [ppt]doeth them not, shall be likened unto a foolish man, which built[3618] his house[3614] upon the sand:

27 And the rain descended, and the floods came, and the winds blew,[4154] and beat upon[4350] that house; and it fell:[4098] and great was the fall of it.

28 And it came to pass, when Jesus had ended[4931] these sayings, [a]the people [ipf]were astonished at his doctrine:[1322]

29 [a]For he taught them as *one* having authority, and not as the scribes.[1122]

Jesus Heals Leprosy (Mark 1:40–45; Luke 5:12–16)

8 When he was come down from the mountain, great multitudes followed[190] him.

2 [a]And, behold, there [apt]came[2064] a leper and [ipf]worshipped him, saying, Lord, if thou wilt,[2309] thou canst [ainf]make me clean.[2511]

3 And Jesus [apt]put forth[1614] *his* hand, and touched him, saying, I will; be thou clean.[2511] And immediately his leprosy was cleansed.

4 And Jesus saith unto him, [a]See[3708] thou tell no man; but go thy way, shew thyself to the priest, and offer[4374] the gift[1435] that [b]Moses commanded,[4367] for a testimony unto them.

Healing a Centurion's Servant (Luke 7:1–10; John 4:43–54)

5 [a]And when Jesus was entered into Capernaum, there came unto him a centurion,[1543] beseeching him,

6 And saying, Lord, my servant[3816] [pfip]lieth[906] at home sick of the palsy,[3885] grievously tormented.

7 And Jesus saith unto him, I will come and [ft]heal[2323] him.

16 [a]Matt. 7:20; 12:30 [b]Luke 6:43, 44
17 [a]Jer. 11:19; Matt. 12:33
19 [a]Matt. 3:10; Luke 3:9; John 15:2, 6
21 [a]Hos. 8:2; Matt. 25:11, 12; Luke 6:46; 13:25; Acts 19:13; Rom. 2:13; James 1:22
22 [a]Num. 24:4; John 11:51; 1Cor. 13:2
23 [a]Matt. 25:12; Luke 13:25, 27; 2Tim. 2:19 [b]Ps. 5:5; 6:8; Matt. 25:41
24 [a]Luke 6:46-49
28 [a]Matt. 13:54; Mark 1:22; 6:2; Luke 4:32
29 [a]John 7:46
2 [a]Mark 1:40-45; Luke 5:12-16
4 [a]Matt. 9:30; Mark 5:43 [b]Lev. 14:3, 4, 10; Luke 5:14
5 [a]Luke 7:1-10

🔑 **7:21–23** See note on Matthew 8:11, 12.

8 The centurion [apt]answered and
said, Lord, [a]I am not worthy that thou
shouldest come under my roof: but
[b]speak the word[3056] only, and my servant
shall be healed.[2390]
9 For I am a man under authority,
having soldiers under me: and I say to
this *man,* Go, and he goeth; and to another, Come, and he cometh; and to my
servant, Do this, and he doeth *it.*
10 When Jesus heard *it,* he marvelled, and said to them that [ppt]followed,
Verily[281] I say unto you, I [ao]have not
found[2147] so great faith,[4102] no, not in
Israel.
🔑11 And I say unto you, That [a]many

8 [a]Luke 15:19, 21 [b]Ps. 107:20

11 [a]Gen. 12:3; Isa. 2:2, 3; 11:10; Mal. 1:11; Luke 13:29; Acts 10:45; 11:18; 14:27; Rom. 15:9; Eph. 3:6

🔑 **8:11, 12** Jesus has just commended the great faith of the Roman centurion, a Gentile who came seeking healing for his servant. The "children of the kingdom" in this instance, refers to unrepentant Jews who thought that their ancestry automatically entitled them to the kingdom of God (see John 8:31–59). In reality, however, these were false children of the kingdom (Matt. 7:21–23; 13:38; Luke 13:22–30). Those who come "from the east and west" are Gentiles who, like this centurion, exercise personal faith in Jesus Christ. The Jews thought that they were assured of special favor by God, but the Lord reminded them that they could be "last" in the kingdom of God, while those who thought themselves "last," such as publicans and prostitutes, would be "first" if they exercised faith in Him (Matt. 21:31). Furthermore, the unrepentant Jews would be "cast out" because of their hypocritical claim that they were the children and followers of Abraham. Abraham was the father of the faithful, and although these people were physical descendants of Abraham, they were not part of the family of faith.

The expression "outer darkness" occurs three times in the Bible (Matt. 8:12; 22:13; 25:30) and is always preceded by the definite article in Greek. It seems to have denoted an area outside a well-illuminated banquet hall where there was darkness (see the parable of the wedding feast in Matt. 22:1–14). The person who managed to sneak into the banquet hall without the proper garment was cast into "outer darkness," separated from the ongoing feast. In the first two instances, "outer darkness" refers to the place of suffering for unbelievers and is in contrast to the light where believers dwell (see 1 John 1:5–7). Unbelievers will be thrown into the furnace of fire, whereas believers will shine as the sun in the kingdom of the Father (Matt. 13:42, 43). The "outer darkness" in Matthew 8:12 and 22:13 is referring to *Géenna* (1067), the "place of burning" (Matt. 5:22, 29, 30; 10:28; 18:9, cf. note on Josh. 15:8).

The expression "outer darkness" in Matthew 25:30 occurs at the end of the parable of the talents, which emphasizes the necessity of serving Christ faithfully. However, the "outer darkness" of Matthew 25:30 may not refer to *Géenna*. Those who say that it does refer to the "place of burning" are persuaded that the servants mentioned here are merely members of the visible church, and therefore are not necessarily believers. Hence, those wicked servants who "hide their talents" are in fact unbelievers who are cast into hell (John 15:6; James 2:14–26). Others say that this parable does not refer to unbelievers or hypocrites at all but to those believers who neglect to exercise their God-given talents. The Lord calls such a servant *ponēré* (4190), "wicked" (Matt. 25:26), and *hoi katēraménoi* (2672), "cursed" (Matt. 25:41), despite the fact that he or she is one of the Lord's servants. This is similar to the instance where the Lord called Peter "Satan" (Matt. 16:23). Hence, these terms may also be applied to believers who have failed the Lord in their service. The words of Paul in 1 Corinthians 3:10–15 are in full support of the fact that the works of faith by God's servants will be tried as by fire. Therefore, in this instance, the "outer darkness" may be a reference to a place or position of far less rewards for the servants who proved themselves less diligent than those who used and exercised their talents to the fullest. Entrance into heaven is gained by accepting Christ's sacrifice for justification, but a person's rewards in heaven will be determined by what he did for Christ on earth (Matt. 5:3–12; 7:21–23; 10:15; Luke 6:20–26; 12:47, 48; Acts 10:4, 31; Rom. 2:1–16; 14:10–23; 1 Cor. 3:13; 4:5; 2 Cor. 5:10; 1 John 4:17; Rev. 20:11–15). The Christian's faithfulness to his or her tasks and responsibilities in the world is considered of such paramount importance that the same metaphor, the "outer darkness," that was used by the Lord to indicate the punishment of the unbeliever for his rejection of God's salvation is used of the believer who does not live in obedience to the light

(continued on next page)

shall come from the east and west,
and shall sit down with Abraham, and
Isaac, and Jacob, in the kingdom[932] of
heaven.
12 But [a]the children[5207] of the kingdom [fp][b]shall be cast out into [art]outer1857
darkness:[4655] there shall be weeping and
gnashing1030 of teeth.
13 And Jesus said unto the centurion,
Go thy way; and as thou [ao]hast be-
lieved,[4100] *so* [aipp]be it done[1096] unto thee.
And his servant was healed[2390] in[1722] the
selfsame hour.

Peter's Mother-In-Law Is Healed (Mark 1:29–34; Luke 4:38–41)

14 [a]And when Jesus was come into
Peter's house, he saw [b]his wife's mother
[pfpp]laid,[906] and [ppt]sick of a fever.
15 And he touched her hand, and the
fever left her: and she arose,[1453] and
[ipf]ministered[1247] unto them.
16 [a]When the even was come, they
brought unto him many that [ppt]were possessed with devils: and he cast out the
spirits[4151] with *his* word,[3056] and healed
all that were sick:
17 That it might be fulfilled which
was spoken by Esaias the prophet, saying, [a]Himself took our infirmities, and
bare *our* sicknesses.

Following Jesus (Luke 9:57–62)

18 Now when Jesus saw great multitudes about him, he gave commandment
to depart unto the other side.
19 [a]And a certain scribe came, and
said unto him, Master, I will follow[190]
thee whithersoever thou goest.
20 And Jesus saith unto him, The
foxes have holes, and the birds of
the air[3772] *have* nests; but the Son of
man[444] hath not where to lay *his*
head.[2776]
21 [a]And another[2087] of his disciples[3101] said unto him, Lord, [b]suffer2010
me first[4412] to go and bury my father.
22 But Jesus said unto him, Follow
me; and let[863] the dead[3498] bury their
dead.[3498]

Calming a Storm (Mark 4:35–41; Luke 8:22–25)

23 And when he was entered into a
[art]ship, his disciples[3101] followed him,
24 [a]And, behold, there arose a great
tempest[4578] in the sea, insomuch that the
ship [pip]was covered[2572] with the waves:
but he [ipf]was asleep.
25 And his disciples came to *him* and
awoke[1453] him, saying, Lord, save[4982] us:
we perish.
26 And he saith unto them, Why
are ye fearful, O ye of little faith?[3640]
Then [a]he arose, and rebuked the winds
and the sea; and there was[1096] a great
calm.
27 But the men marvelled,2296 saying, What manner of man is this,
that even the winds and the sea obey[5219]
him!

Healing the Demon-Possessed At Gergesenes (Mark 5:1–20; Luke 8:26–39)

28 [a]And when he [apt]was come to the
other side into the country of the
Gergesenes, there met him two possessed
with devils,[1139] coming out of the tombs,
exceeding fierce, so that no man
might[2480] pass by that way.[3598]
29 And, behold, they cried out, say-

12 [a]Matt. 21:43 [b]Matt. 13:42, 50; 22:13; 24:51; 25:30; Luke 13:28; 2Pet. 2:17; Jude 1:13
14 [a]Mark 1:29-31; Luke 4:38, 39 [b]1Cor. 9:5
16 [a]Mark 1:32-34; Luke 4:40, 41
17 [a]Isa. 53:4; 1Pet. 2:24
19 [a]Luke 9:57, 58
21 [a]Luke 9:59, 60 [b]1Kgs. 19:20
24 [a]Mark 4:37-41; Luke 8:23-25
26 [a]Ps. 65:7; 89:9; 107:29
28 [a]Mark 5:1-20; Luke 8:26-36

(continued from previous page)
he has received. In the case of the unbeliever, it will be a punishment of fire and burning (Matt. 13:30; John 15:6). In the case of the believer, it will be weeping or expressing sorrow over not having used the opportunities God provided. Though his tears will be wiped away (Rev. 7:17; 21:4), he will nonetheless suffer a loss of reward.

ing, What have we to do with thee, Jesus, thou Son of God? art thou come hither [ainf]to torment us before the time?

30 And there was a good way off from them an herd of many swine feeding.

31 So the devils[1142] [ipf]besought him, saying, If thou [pin]cast us out,[1544] suffer[2010] us to go away into the herd of swine.

32 And he said unto them, Go. And when they were come out, they went into the herd of swine: and, behold, the whole herd of swine ran violently down[2596] a steep place into the sea, and perished[599] in the waters.

33 And they that [ppt]kept them fled, and [apt]went their ways into the city, and told every thing, and what was befallen to the possessed of the devils.[1139]

34 And, behold, the whole city came out to meet Jesus: and when they saw him, [a]they besought *him* that he would depart[3327] out of their coasts.

Jesus Heals a Crippled Man (Mark 2:1–12; Luke 5:17–26)

9 And he [apt]entered into a ship, and passed over, [a]and came into his own city.

2 [a]And, behold, they [ipf]brought to him a man sick of the palsy,[3885] [pfpp]lying[906] on a bed: [b]and Jesus [apt]seeing their faith[4102] said unto the sick of the palsy; Son, be of good cheer; thy sins[266] [pfip]be forgiven[863] thee.

3 And, behold, certain of the scribes said within themselves, This *man* blasphemeth.[987]

4 And Jesus [apt][a]knowing their thoughts said, Wherefore think ye evil[4190] in your hearts?

5 For whether is easier, to say, *Thy* sins [pfip]be forgiven[863] thee; or to say, [aim]Arise,[1453] and [pim]walk?

6 But that ye may know that the Son of man hath power[1849] on earth[1093] [pinf]to forgive sins, (then saith he to the sick of the palsy,) [aptp]Arise, take up thy bed, and go unto thine house.[3624]

7 And he [aptp]arose,[1453] and departed to his house.[3624]

8 But when the multitudes saw *it,* they marvelled,[2296] and glorified[1392] God, which had given such power[1849] unto men.

Jesus Calls Matthew (Mark 2:13–17; Luke 5:27–32)

9 [a]And as Jesus passed forth from thence, he saw a man, named Matthew, sitting at the receipt of custom:[5058] and he saith unto him, [pim]Follow[190] me. And he [apt]arose,[450] and followed him.

10 [a]And it came to pass, as Jesus sat at meat in the house, behold, many publicans[5057] and sinners[268] [apt]came and [ipf]sat down with him and his disciples.[3101]

11 And when the Pharisees saw *it,* they said unto his disciples, Why eateth your Master with [a]publicans and [b]sinners?

12 But when Jesus heard *that,* he said unto them, They that be whole[2480] need not a physician,[2395] but they that are sick.

13 But [aptp]go ye and [aim]learn[3129] what *that* meaneth, [a]I will have[2309] mercy,[1656] and not sacrifice: for I am not come to call the [an]righteous,[1342] [b]but sinners[268] to repentance.[3341]

Fasting (Mark 2:18–22; Luke 5:33–39)

14 Then [pin]came[4334] to him the disciples[3101] of John, saying, [a]Why do we and the Pharisees fast[3522] oft, but thy disciples fast not?

15 And Jesus said unto them, Can [a]the children[5207] of the bridechamber mourn, as long as the bridegroom is with them? but the days will come, when the bridegroom shall be taken from them, and [b]then shall they fast.

16 No man putteth a piece of [l]new cloth unto an old garment, for that

34 [a]Deut. 5:25; 1Kgs. 17:18; Luke 5:8; Acts 16:39

1 [a]Matt. 4:13

2 [a]Mark 2:3; Luke 5:18 [b]Matt. 8:10

4 [a]Ps. 139:2; Matt. 12:25; Mark 12:15; Luke 5:22; 6:8; 9:47; 11:17

9 [a]Mark 2:14; Luke 5:27

10 [a]Mark 2:15-17; Luke 5:29-32

11 [a]Matt. 11:19; Luke 5:30; 15:2 [b]Gal. 2:15

13 [a]Hos. 6:6; Mic. 6:6-8; Matt. 12:7 [b]1Tim. 1:15

14 [a]Mark 2:18-22; Luke 5:33-35; 18:12

15 [a]John 3:29 [b]Acts 13:2, 3; 14:23; 1Cor. 7:5

16 [l]Or, *raw,* or *unwrought cloth*

which is put in to fill it up[4138][846] taketh from the garment, and the rent is made worse.

17 Neither do men put[906] new[3501] wine[3631] into old bottles: else the bottles break, and the wine runneth out, and the bottles [fm]perish:[622] but they put new wine into new bottles, and both are preserved.[4933]

Jesus Raises Jairus' Daughter (Mark 5:21–43; Luke 8:40–56)

18 [a]While he spake these things unto them, behold, there [apt]came a certain ruler,[758] and [ipf]worshipped him, saying, My daughter [ao]is even now dead:[5053] but [apt]come and lay thy hand upon her, and she shall live.[2198]

19 And Jesus arose, and followed him, and *so did* his disciples.[3101]

20 [a]And, behold, a woman, which was diseased with an issue of blood twelve years, [apt]came[4334] behind *him,* and touched the hem of his garment:

21 For she [ipf]said within herself, If I [asbm]may but touch[680] his garment, I shall be whole.[4982]

22 But Jesus turned him about,[1994] and when he saw her, he said, Daughter, be of good comfort; [a]thy faith [pfi]hath made thee whole.[4982] And the woman was made whole from that hour.

23 [a]And when Jesus came into the ruler's[758] house, and [apt]saw [b]the minstrels and the people making a noise,

24 He said unto them, [a]Give place: for the maid [ao]is not dead,[599] but [pin]sleepeth. And they laughed him to scorn.

25 But when the people were put forth, he [apt]went in, and took her by the hand, and the maid arose.

26 And [l]the fame hereof went abroad into all that land.[1093]

Jesus Heals Two Blind Men

27 And when Jesus [ppt]departed thence, two blind men followed him, crying, and saying, [a]*Thou* son of David, [aim]have mercy on us.

28 And when he was come into the house, the blind men came[4334] to him: and Jesus saith unto them, Believe[4100] ye that I am able to do this? They [pin]said unto him, Yea, Lord.

29 Then touched he their eyes, saying, According to[2596] your faith [aipp]be it unto you.

30 And their eyes were opened; and Jesus straitly charged[1690] them, saying, [a]See *that* no man know *it.*

31 [a]But they, when they were departed, spread abroad his fame in all that country.

Jesus Heals a Mute

32 [a]As they [ppt]went out, behold, they brought to him a dumb man possessed with a devil.

33 And when the devil[1140] was cast out, the dumb spake:[2980] and the multitudes marvelled,[2296] saying, It was never so seen in Israel.

34 But the Pharisees said, [a]He casteth out devils[1140] through the prince[758] of the devils.

Jesus' Compassion

35 [a]And Jesus [ipf]went about all the cities and villages, [b]teaching[1321] in their synagogues, and preaching[2784] the gospel[2098] of the kingdom,[932] and healing every sickness and every disease[3119] among the people.

36 [a]But when he saw the multitudes, he was moved with compassion on them, because they [pfpp][l]fainted, and [pfpp]were scattered abroad, [b]as sheep having no shepherd.[4166]

37 Then saith he unto his disciples, [a]The harvest truly *is* plenteous, but the labourers *are* few;

38 [aipp][a]Pray[1189] ye therefore the Lord of the harvest, that he [asba]will send forth labourers into his harvest.

18 [a]Mark 5:22-24; Luke 8:41, 42
20 [a]Mark 5:25; Luke 8:43
22 [a]Luke 7:50; 8:48; 17:19; 18:42
23 [a]Mark 5:38; Luke 8:51 [b]2Chr. 35:25
24 [a]Acts 20:10
26 [l]Or, *this fame*
27 [a]Matt. 15:22; 20:30, 31; Mark 10:47, 48; Luke 18:38, 39
30 [a]Matt. 8:4; 12:16; 17:9; Luke 5:14
31 [a]Mark 7:36
32 [a]Matt. 12:22; Luke 11:14
34 [a]Matt. 12:24; Mark 3:22; Luke 11:15
35 [a]Mark 6:6; Luke 13:22; [b]Matt. 4:23
36 [l]Or, *were tired and lay down* [a]Mark 6:34 [b]Num. 27:17; 1Kgs. 22:17; Ezek. 34:5; Zech. 10:2
37 [a]Luke 10:2; John 4:35
38 [a]2Thess. 3:1

Jesus Chooses Twelve Apostles (Mark 3:13–19; 6:7–13; Luke 6:12–16; 9:1–6)

10 🔑 And [apt][a]when he had called unto[4341] *him* his twelve disciples,[3101] he gave them power[1849] [I]*against* unclean spirits, [pinf]to cast them out, and [pinf]to heal[2323] all manner of sickness and all manner of disease.[3119]

2 Now the names[3686] of the twelve apostles[652] are these; The first, Simon, [a]who is called Peter, and Andrew his brother; James *the son* of Zebedee, and John his brother;

3 Philip, and Bartholomew; Thomas, and Matthew the publican;5057 James *the son* of Alphaeus, and Lebbaeus whose surname was Thaddaeus;

4 [a]Simon the Canaanite, and Judas [b]Iscariot, who also [apt]betrayed him.

5 These twelve Jesus [ao]sent forth,[649] and [apt]commanded them, saying, [aosi][a]Go not into the way[3598] of the Gentiles,[1484] and into *any* city of [b]the Samaritans [aosi]enter ye not:

6 [a]But go rather to the [b]lost[622] sheep of the house of Israel.

7 [a]And as ye go, [pim]preach,[2784] saying, [b]The kingdom[932] of heaven [pf]is at hand.[1448]

8 [pim]Heal[2323] the sick,[770] [pim]cleanse[2511] the lepers, raise[1453] the dead,[3498] [pim]cast out devils:1140 [a]freely ye [ao]have received, freely [aim]give.

9 [aosi][I][a]Provide neither gold, nor silver, nor [b]brass in your purses,

10 Nor scrip4082 for *your* journey, neither two coats, neither shoes, nor yet [I]staves:4464 [a]for the workman is worthy of his meat.

11 [a]And into whatsoever city or town ye shall enter, [aim]enquire who in it is worthy; and there abide till ye [aosb]go thence.

12 And when ye come into an house, [aim]salute it.

13 [a]And if the house be worthy, [aim]let your peace come[2064] upon it: [b]but if it be not worthy, [aipp]let your peace return[1994] to you.

14 [a]And whosoever shall not receive you, nor hear your words, when ye depart out of that house or city, [b]shake off the dust of your feet.

15 Verily281 I say unto you, [a]It shall be more tolerable414 for the land of Sodom and Gomorrha in the day of judgment,[2920] than for that city.

Christ's Disciples Should Expect Persecution (Mark 13:9–13; Luke 21:12–17)

16 [a]Behold, I send you forth as sheep in the midst of wolves: [b]be ye therefore wise[5429] as serpents, and [I][c]harmless[185] as doves.

17 But [pim]beware of men: for [a]they will deliver you up to the councils, and [b]they will scourge3146 you in their synagogues;

18 And [a]ye shall be brought before governors and kings[935] for my sake, for a testimony[3142] against them and the Gentiles.[1484]

19 [a]But when they [psa]deliver you up, [aosi]take no thought how or what ye shall speak: for [b]it shall be given you in that same hour what ye shall speak.

20 [a]For it is not ye that [ppt]speak, but the Spirit of your Father which [ppt]speaketh in you.

21 [a]And the brother shall deliver up the brother to death,[2288] and the father

1 [I]Or, over [a]Mark 3:13, 14; 6:7; Luke 6:13; 9:1
2 [a]John 1:42
4 [a]Luke 6:15; Acts 1:13 [b]John 13:26
5 [a]Matt. 4:15 [b]2Kgs. 17:24; John 4:9, 20
6 [a]Matt. 15:24; Acts 13:46 [b]Isa. 53:6; Jer. 50:6, 17; Ezek. 34:5, 6, 16; 1Pet. 2:25
7 [a]Luke 9:2 [b]Matt. 3:2; 4:17; Luke 10:9
8 [a]Acts 8:18, 20
9 [I]Or, *Get* [a]1Sam. 9:7; Mark 6:8; Luke 9:3; 10:4; 22:35 [b]Mark 6:8
10 [I]Gr. *a staff* [a]Luke 10:7; 1Cor. 9:7-10; 1Tim. 5:18
11 [a]Luke 10:8
13 [a]Luke 10:5 [b]Ps. 35:13
14 [a]Mark 6:11; Luke 9:5; 10:10, 11 [b]Neh. 5:13; Acts 13:51; 18:6
15 [a]Matt. 11:22, 24
16 [I]Or, *simple* [a]Luke 10:3 [b]Rom. 16:19; Eph. 5:15 [c]1Cor. 14:20; Phil. 2:15
17 [a]Matt. 24:9; Mark 13:9; Luke 12:11; 21:12 [b]Acts 5:40
18 [a]Acts 12:1; 24:10; 25:7, 23; 2Tim. 4:16
19 [a]Mark 13:11, 12, 13; Luke 12:11; 21:14, 15 [b]Ex. 4:12; Jer. 1:7
20 [a]2Sam. 23:2; Acts 4:8; 6:10; 2Tim. 4:17
21 [a]Mic. 7:6; Matt. 10:35, 36; Luke 21:16

🔑 **10:1–15** This concerns the special commission of the Twelve Apostles. They were given special instructions, and they were to focus their ministry on the Jews. What was said to these disciples at this time should not be assumed applicable to those who are commissioned by the Lord at other times. For instance, in Luke 22:36, the Lord sent his disciples on an extended mission to the Gentiles and gave them instructions that were in direct opposition to those He gave here in Matthew chapter ten. In addition to this, only certain of the general principles of the ministry that were given to Christ's disciples can be applied to the commissioning of believers in this day. For example, the gifts of healing and raising the dead (v. 8) were only given to some (1 Cor. 12:28, 29), not to all. See note on 1 Corinthians 12:31.

the child: and the children shall rise up against *their* parents, and cause them to be put to death.

22 And [a]ye shall be hated of all *men* for my name's[3686] sake: [b]but he that [apt]endureth[5278] to the end[5056] shall be saved.[4982]

23 But [a]when they [psa]persecute you in this city, [pim]flee ye into another:[243] for verily I say unto you, Ye shall [efn]not [I]have gone over[5055] the cities of Israel, [b]till the Son of man [aosb]be come.

24 [a]The disciple[3101] is not above *his* master,[1320] nor the servant above his lord.

25 It is enough for the disciple that he be as his master,[1320] and the servant as his lord. If [a]they have called[2564] the master of the house[3617] [I]Beelzebub, how much more *shall they call* them of his household?[3615]

Admonitions Against Fear (Luke 12:2–7)

26 [aosi]Fear[5399] them not therefore: [a]for there is nothing [pfpp]covered,[2572] that [fp]shall not be revealed;[601] and hid, that shall not be known.

27 What I tell you in darkness,[4653] *that* [aim]speak ye in light: and what ye hear in the ear, *that* [aim]preach[2784] ye upon the housetops.

🔑 28 [a]And [aosi]fear not them which [ppt]kill the body,[4983] but [ppt]are not able[1410] to kill the soul:[5590] but rather [aim]fear him which is able [ainf]to destroy[622] both soul and body in hell.[1067]

29 Are not two sparrows sold for a farthing?[787] and one of them [fm]shall not fall[4098] on the ground[1093] without your Father.[3962]

30 [a]But the very hairs of your head[2776] are all numbered.

31 [aosi]Fear ye not therefore, ye are of more value[1308] than many sparrows.

22 [a]Luke 21:17 [b]Dan. 12:12, 13; Matt. 24:13; Mark 13:13
23 [I]Or, *end*, or, *finish* [a]Matt. 2:13; 4:12; 12:15; Acts 8:1; 9:25; 14:6 [b]Matt. 16:28
24 [a]Luke 6:40; John 13:16; 15:20
25 [I]Gr. *Beelzebul* [a]Matt. 12:24; Mark 3:22; Luke 11:15; John 8:48, 52
26 [a]Mark 4:22; Luke 8:17; 12:2, 3
28 [a]Isa. 8:12, 13; Luke 12:4; 1Pet. 3:14
30 [a]1Sam. 14:45; 2Sam. 14:11; Luke 21:18; Acts 27:34
32 [a]Luke 12:8; Rom. 10:9, 10 [b]Rev. 3:5
33 [a]Mark 8:38; Luke 9:26; 2Tim. 2:12
34 [a]Luke 12:49, 51-53
35 [a]Mic. 7:6
36 [a]Ps. 41:9; 55:13; Mic. 7:6; John 13:18
37 [a]Luke 14:26
38 [a]Matt. 16:24; Mark 8:34; Luke 9:23; 14:27
39 [a]Matt. 16:25; Luke 17:33; John 12:25
40 [a]Matt. 18:5; Luke 9:48; 10:16; John 12:44; 13:20; Gal. 4:14
41 [a]1Kgs. 17:10; 18:4; 2Kgs. 4:8

Confessing Christ Before Men (Luke 12:8, 9)

32 [a]Whosoever therefore shall confess[3670] me before men,[444] [b]him [ft]will I confess[3670] also before my Father which is in heaven.

33 [a]But whosoever [asbm]shall deny[720] me before men, him will I also deny before my Father which is in heaven.

Change Brings Conflict (Luke 12:51–53; 14:26, 27)

34 [aosi][a]Think not that I am come [ainf]to send peace[1515] on earth: I came not [ainf]to send peace, but a sword.

35 For I [ao]am come [ainf]to set a man at variance[1369] [a]against his father, and the daughter against her mother, and the daughter in law against her mother in law.

36 And [a]a man's foes *shall be* they of his own household.[3615]

🔑 37 [a]He that [ppt]loveth[5368] father or mother more than me is not worthy of me: and he that loveth son or daughter more than me is not worthy of me.

38 [a]And he that taketh not his cross,[4716] and followeth[190] after me, is not worthy of me.

39 [a]He that [apt]findeth[2147] his life shall lose[622] it: and he that [apt]loseth his life[5590] for my sake shall find it.

Rewards for Service (Mark 9:41)

40 [a]He that [ppt]receiveth you receiveth me, and he that [ppt]receiveth me receiveth him that [apt]sent me.

41 [a]He that [ppt]receiveth a prophet[4396] in the name[3686] of a prophet shall receive a prophet's reward;[3408] and he that [ppt]receiveth a righteous man[1342] in the name of a righteous man shall receive a righteous man's reward.

🔑 **10:28** See note on Matthew 8:11, 12.
🔑 **10:37** See note on Micah 7:5–7.

42 [a]And whosoever [aosb]shall give to drink[4222] unto one of these little ones a cup of cold *water* only in the name of a disciple,[3101] verily I say unto you, he shall [efn]in no wise lose his reward.

Messengers From John the Baptist (Luke 7:18–35)

11 And it came to pass, when Jesus had made an end[5055] of commanding[1299] his twelve disciples,[3101] he departed thence [infg]to teach[1321] and [infg]to preach[2784] in their cities.

2 [a]Now when John had heard [b]in the prison the works[2041] of Christ, he sent two of his disciples,

3 And said unto him, Art thou [a]he [ppt]that should come,[2064] or [pin]do we look for[4328] another?[2087]

4 Jesus answered[611] and said unto them, [apt]Go and [aim]shew John again[518] those things which ye do hear and see:[991]

5 [a]The blind [pin]receive their sight,[308] and the lame walk, the lepers are cleansed, and the deaf hear,[191] the dead[3498] are raised up,[1453] and [b]the poor have the gospel preached[2097] to them.

6 And blessed[3107] is *he,* whosoever [asbp]shall not [a]be offended[4624] in me.

7 [a]And as they [ppt]departed, Jesus began [pinf]to say unto the multitudes concerning John, What went ye out into the wilderness to see? [b]A reed [ppt]shaken with the wind?

8 But what went ye out for to see? A man clothed in soft raiment? behold, they that [ppt]wear[5409] soft *clothing* are in kings' houses.[3624]

9 But what went ye out for to see? A prophet?[4396] yea, I say unto you, [a]and more[4055] than a prophet.

10 For this is *he,* of whom [pfip]it is written,[1125] [a]Behold, I send my messenger[32] before thy face,[4383] which shall prepare thy way before thee.

11 Verily[281] I say unto you, Among[1722] them that are born of women there [pfip]hath not risen[1453] a greater than John the Baptist:[910] notwithstanding he that is least in[1722] the kingdom[932] of heaven is greater than he.

42 [a]Matt. 18:5, 6; 25:40; Mark 9:41; Heb. 6:10

2 [a]Luke 7:18-23 [b]Matt. 14:3

3 [a]Gen. 49:10; Num. 24:17; Dan. 9:24; John 6:14

5 [a]Isa. 29:18; 35:4-6; 42:7; John 2:23; 3:2; 5:36; 10:25, 38; 14:11 [b]Ps. 22:26; Isa. 61:1; Luke 4:18; James 2:5

6 [a]Isa. 8:14, 15; Matt. 13:57; 24:10; 26:31; Rom. 9:32, 33; 1Cor. 1:23; 2:14; Gal. 5:11; 1Pet. 2:8

7 [a]Luke 7:24 [b]Eph. 4:14

9 [a]Matt. 14:5; 21:26; Luke 1:76; 7:26

10 [a]Mal. 3:1; Mark 1:2; Luke 1:76; 7:27

12 [I]Or, *is gotten by force, and they that thrust men* [a]Luke 16:16

13 [a]Mal. 4:6

14 [a]Mal. 4:5; Matt. 17:12; Luke 1:17

15 [a]Matt. 13:9; Luke 8:8; Rev. 2:7, 11, 17, 29; 3:6, 13, 22

16 [a]Luke 7:31

19 [a]Matt. 9:10 [b]Luke 7:35

20 [a]Luke 10:13-16

21 [a]Jon. 3:7, 8

23 [a]Isa. 14:13; Lam. 2:1

24 [a]Matt. 10:15

12 [a]And from the days of John the Baptist until now the kingdom of heaven [I]suffereth violence,[971] and the violent take it by force.[726]

13 [a]For all the prophets and the law prophesied[4395] until John.

14 And if ye will [ainf]receive *it,* this is [a]Elias, which was for to come.[3195,2064]

15 [a]He that [ppt]hath ears to hear,[191] [pim]let him hear.[191]

16 [a]But whereunto shall I liken this generation? It is like unto children[3808] sitting in the markets,[58] and calling unto their fellows,

17 And saying, We [ao]have piped unto you, and ye [aom]have not danced;[3738] we have mourned[2354] unto you, and ye [aom]have not lamented.[2875]

18 For John came neither eating nor drinking, and they say, He hath a devil.[1140]

19 The Son of man came eating and drinking, and they say, Behold a man gluttonous, and a winebibber,[3630] [a]a friend of publicans[5057] and sinners.[268] [b]But wisdom[4678] [aop]is justified[1344] of her children.

Jesus Condemns Certain Cities (Luke 10:13–15)

20 [a]Then began he [pinf]to upbraid[3679] the cities wherein most of his mighty works were done, because they repented[3340] not:

21 Woe unto thee, Chorazin! woe unto thee, Bethsaida! for if the mighty works, which were done in[1722] you, had been done in Tyre and Sidon, they would have repented long ago[3819] [a]in sackcloth[4526] and ashes.

22 But I say unto you, It shall be more tolerable[414] for Tyre and Sidon at the day of judgment,[2920] than for you.

23 And thou, Capernaum, [a]which [aptp]art exalted unto heaven, shalt be brought down to hell:[86] for if the mighty works, which have been done in thee, had been done in Sodom, it [ao]would have remained[3306] until this day.

24 But I say unto you, [a]That it shall be more tolerable[414] for the land of

Sodom in the day of judgment,[2920] than for thee.

Rest in Jesus (Luke 10:21, 22)

25 [a]At that time Jesus answered and said, I thank[1843] thee, O Father, Lord of heaven and earth,[1093] because [b]thou [ao]hast hid these things from the wise[4680] and prudent, [c]and [ao]hast revealed[601] them unto babes.[3516]

26 Even so, Father: for so it seemed good[2107] in thy sight.

27 [a]All things are delivered unto me of my Father: and no man knoweth the Son, but the Father; [b]neither knoweth any man the Father, save the Son, and *he* to whomsoever the Son will reveal[601] *him.*

28 Come unto me, all *ye* that [ppt]labour and [pfpp]are heavy laden,[5412] and I [ft]will give you rest.[373]

29 [aim]Take[142] my yoke upon you, [a]and [aim]learn[3129] of me; for I am meek[4235] and [b]lowly in heart:[2588] [c]and ye shall find[2147] rest[372] unto your souls.[5590]

30 [a]For my yoke *is* easy,[5543] and my burden[5413] is light.

Jesus Is Lord Over the Sabbath Day (Mark 2:23–28; Luke 6:1–5)

12 At that time [a]Jesus went on the sabbath day[4521] through the corn; and his disciples[3101] were an hungred,[3983] and began[756] to pluck the ears of corn, and to eat.

2 But when the Pharisees saw *it,* they said unto him, Behold, thy disciples do that which is not lawful [pinf]to do upon the sabbath day.

3 But he said unto them, Have ye not read[314] [a]what David did, when he was an hungred,[3983] and they that were with him;

4 How he entered into the house of God,[2316] and did eat [a]the shewbread,[4286,740,3588] which was not lawful for him to eat, neither for them which were with him, [b]but only for the priests?

5 Or [ao]have ye not read[314] in the [a]law, how that on the sabbath days the priests in the temple[2411] profane[953] the sabbath, and are blameless?

6 But I say unto you, That in this place is [a]*one* greater than the temple.[2411]

7 But if ye had known what *this* meaneth, [a]I will have[2309] mercy,[1656] and not sacrifice, ye [ao]would not have condemned[2613] the guiltless.

8 For the Son of man is Lord even of the sabbath day.

Jesus Heals a Man With a Withered Hand (Mark 3:1–6; Luke 6:6–11)

9 [a]And when he was departed thence, he went[2064] into their synagogue:

10 And, behold, there was a man which had *his* hand withered. And they asked[1905] him, saying, [a]Is it lawful to heal on the sabbath days? that they might accuse[2723] him.

11 And he said unto them, What man shall there be among you, that shall have one sheep, and [a]if it fall into a pit on the sabbath day, will he not lay hold on it, and lift *it* out?[1453]

12 How much then [pin]is a man better[1308] than a sheep? Wherefore it is lawful to do well on the sabbath days.

13 Then saith he to the man, Stretch forth[1614] thine hand. And he stretched *it* forth; and it was restored[600] whole,[5199] like as the other.[243]

14 Then [a]the Pharisees [apt]went out, and [1]held a council against him, how they might destroy him.

God's Servant

15 But when Jesus knew *it,* [a]he withdrew himself from thence: [b]and great multitudes followed him, and he healed them all;

16 And [a]charged them that they should not make him known:[5318]

17 That it might be fulfilled which was spoken by Esaias the prophet, saying,

18 [a]Behold my servant,[3816] whom I

---

25 [a]Luke 10:21 [b]Ps. 8:2; 1Cor. 1:19, 27; 2:8; 2Cor. 3:14 [c]Matt. 16:17
27 [a]Matt. 28:18; Luke 10:22; John 3:35; 13:3; 17:2; 1Cor. 15:27 [b]John 1:18; 6:46; 10:15
29 [a]John 13:15; Phil. 2:5; 1Pet. 2:21; 1John 2:6 [b]Zech. 9:9; Phil. 2:7, 8 [c]Jer. 6:16
30 [a]1John 5:3
1 [a]Deut. 23:25; Mark 2:23; Luke 6:1
3 [a]1Sam. 21:6
4 [a]Ex. 25:30; Lev. 24:5 [b]Ex. 29:32, 33; Lev. 8:31; 24:9
5 [a]Num. 28:9; John 7:22
6 [a]2Chr. 6:18; Mal. 3:1
7 [a]Hos. 6:6; Mic. 6:6-8; Matt. 9:13
9 [a]Mark 3:1; Luke 6:6
10 [a]Luke 13:14; 14:3; John 9:16
11 [a]Ex. 23:4, 5; Deut. 22:4
14 [1]Or, *took counsel* [a]Matt. 27:1; Mark 3:6; Luke 6:11; John 5:18; 10:39; 11:53
15 [a]Matt. 10:23; Mark 3:7 [b]Matt. 19:2
16 [a]Matt. 9:30
18 [a]Isa. 42:1

[ao]have chosen;[140] my beloved, [b]in whom my soul [ao]is well pleased:[2106] I will put my spirit upon him, and he shall shew[518] judgment[2920] to the Gentiles.

19 He shall not strive, nor cry; neither [ft]shall any man hear[191] his voice in the streets.

20 A bruised reed shall he not break,[2608] and smoking flax shall he not quench, till he send forth judgment[2920] unto victory.

21 And in his name shall the Gentiles trust.[1679]

The Power of God Over the Devil (Mark 3:20–30; Luke 11:14–23; 12:10)

22 [a]Then was brought unto him one possessed with a devil, blind, and dumb: and he healed him, insomuch that the blind and dumb both spake and saw.

23 And all the people [ipf]were amazed,[1839] and said, Is not this the son of David?

24 [a]But when the Pharisees heard *it,* they said, This *fellow* doth not cast out devils,[1140] but by [I]Beelzebub the prince of the devils.

25 And Jesus [a]knew their thoughts, and said unto them, Every kingdom[932] divided against itself is brought to desolation; and every city or house divided against itself [fp]shall not stand:[2476]

26 And if Satan cast out Satan,[4567] he [aop]is divided against himself; how shall then his kingdom stand?

27 And if I by Beelzebub cast out devils,[1140] by whom do your children cast *them* out? therefore they shall be your judges.[2923]

28 But if I cast out devils by the Spirit of God, then [a]the kingdom of God [ao]is come unto you.

29 [a]Or else how can one [ainf]enter into a strong man's house, and [ainf]spoil his goods, except he first bind the strong man? and then he will spoil his house.

18 [b]Matt. 3:17; 17:5
22 [a]Matt. 9:32; Mark 3:11; Luke 11:14
24 [I]Gr. *Beelzebul* [a]Matt. 9:34; Mark 3:22; Luke 11:15
25 [a]Matt. 9:4; John 2:25; Rev. 2:23
28 [a]Dan. 2:44; 7:14; Luke 1:33; 11:20; 17:20, 21
29 [a]Isa. 49:24; Luke 11:21-23
31 [a]Mark 3:28; Luke 12:10; Heb. 6:4-6; 10:26, 29; 1John 5:16 [b]Acts 7:51
32 [a]Matt. 11:19; 13:55; John 7:12, 52 [b]1Tim. 1:13
33 [a]Matt. 7:17; Luke 6:43, 44
34 [a]Matt. 3:7; 23:33 [b]Luke 6:45
38 [a]Matt. 16:1; Mark 8:11; Luke 11:16, 29; John 2:18; 1Cor. 1:22
39 [a]Isa. 57:3; Matt. 16:4; Mark 8:38; John 4:48

30 He that is not with me is against me; and he that [ppt]gathereth not with me scattereth abroad.

🔑 31 Wherefore I say unto you, [a]All manner of sin[266] and blasphemy[988] shall be forgiven unto men: [b]but the blasphemy *against* the *Holy* Ghost[4151] shall not be forgiven unto men.

32 And whosoever [aosb][a]speaketh a word against the Son of man, [b]it shall be forgiven him: but whosoever [aosb]speaketh against the Holy Ghost, it shall not be forgiven him, neither in this world, neither in the *world* to come.

A Tree Is Known by Its Fruit (Luke 6:43–45)

33 Either [aim]make the tree good, and [a]his fruit good; or else [aim]make the tree corrupt, and his fruit corrupt: for the tree is known by *his* fruit.

34 O [a]generation of vipers, how can ye, being evil,[4190] [pinf]speak good things?[18] [b]for out of the abundance[4051] of the heart[2588] the mouth speaketh.

35 A good [art]man out of the good treasure of the heart bringeth forth good things: and an evil man out of the evil treasure bringeth forth evil things.

36 But I say unto you, That every idle[692] word[4487] that men shall speak, they shall give account[3056] thereof in the day of judgment.[2920]

37 For by thy words thou shalt be justified,[1344] and by thy words thou shalt be condemned.[2613]

The Desire for Signs Is Rebuked (Mark 8:11, 12; Luke 11:29–32)

38 [a]Then certain of the scribes[1122] and of the Pharisees answered,[611] saying, Master, we would[2309] [ainf]see a sign from thee.

39 But he answered and said unto them, An evil and [a]adulterous generation seeketh after a sign; and there shall no

🔑 **12:31, 32** See notes on Mark 3:28, 29 and Hebrews 6:1–6.

sign be given to it, but the sign of the prophet Jonas:

40 [a]For as Jonas was three days and three nights in the whale's[2785] belly; so shall the Son of man be three days and three nights in the heart[2588] of the earth.

41 [a]The [an]men of Nineveh shall rise in judgment[2920] with this generation, and [b]shall condemn[2632] it: [c]because they repented[3340] at the preaching[2782] of Jonas; and, behold, a greater than Jonas *is* here.

42 [a]The queen of the south shall rise up in the judgment[2920] with this generation, and shall condemn[2632] it: for she came from the uttermost parts of the earth to hear the wisdom of Solomon; and, behold, a greater than Solomon *is* here.

The Unclean Spirit Returns (Luke 11:24–26)

43 [a]When the unclean spirit [aosb]is gone out of a man, [b]he walketh through dry places, seeking rest,[372] and findeth none.

44 Then he saith, I will return[1994] into my house from whence I came out; and when he is come, he findeth *it* empty, [pfpp]swept, and [pfpp]garnished.

45 Then goeth he, and taketh with himself seven other[2087] spirits more wicked[4191] than himself, and they enter in and dwell[2730] there: [a]and the last[2078] *state* of that man is worse than the first. Even so shall it be also unto this wicked generation.

The True Family of Jesus (Mark 3:31–35; Luke 8:19–21)

46 While he yet [ppt]talked to the people, [a]behold, *his* mother and [b]his brethren[80] [plpf]stood[2476] without,[1854] desiring to speak with him.

40 [a]Jon. 1:17
41 [a]Luke 11:32 [b]Jer. 3:11; Ezek. 16:51, 52; Rom. 2:27 [c]Jon. 3:5
42 [a]1Kgs. 10:1; 2Chr. 9:1; Luke 11:31
43 [a]Luke 11:24 [b]Job 1:7; 1Pet. 5:8
45 [a]Heb. 6:4; 10:26; 2Pet. 2:20-22
46 [a]Mark 3:31; Luke 8:19-21 [b]Matt. 13:55; Mark 6:3; John 2:12; 7:3, 5; Acts 1:14; 1Cor. 9:5; Gal. 1:19
50 [a]John 15:14; Gal. 5:6; 6:15; Col. 3:11; Heb. 2:11
1 [a]Mark 4:1
2 [a]Luke 8:4 [b]Luke 5:3
3 [a]Luke 8:5
8 [a]Gen. 26:12
9 [a]Matt. 11:15; Mark 4:9

47 Then one said unto him, Behold, thy mother and thy brethren stand without, desiring to speak with thee.

48 But he answered and said unto him that told him, Who is my mother? and who are my brethren?

49 And he [apt]stretched forth his hand toward his disciples,[3101] and said, Behold my mother and my brethren!

50 For [a]whosoever shall do the will of my Father[3962] which is in heaven,[3772] the same is my brother, and sister, and mother.

The Parable of the Sower (Mark 4:1–9; Luke 8:4–8)

13 The same day [apt]went Jesus out of the house, [a]and [ipf]sat by the sea side.

2 [a]And great multitudes were gathered together unto him, so that [b]he [apt]went into a ship, and [aifp]sat; and the whole multitude [plpf]stood[2476] on the shore.

3 And he spake many things unto them in parables,[3850] saying, [a]Behold, a sower went forth to sow;

4 And when he [aie]sowed, some *seeds* fell[4098] by the way side, and the fowls came and devoured them up:

🔑5 Some fell upon stony places, where they had not much earth:[1093] and forthwith[2112] they sprung up, because they [aid]had no deepness of earth:

6 And when the sun was up, they were scorched; and because they had no root, they withered away.

7 And some fell among thorns; and the thorns sprung up,[305] and choked them:

8 But other fell into good ground,[1093] and [ipf]brought forth fruit, some [a]an hundredfold, some sixtyfold, some thirtyfold.

9 [a]Who hath ears to hear, let him hear.

🔑 **13:5–7** See note on Luke 8:13.

The Reason for Parables (Mark 4:10–12; Luke 8:9, 10)

🔑 10 And the disciples came, and said unto him, Why speakest thou unto them in parables?

11 He answered and said unto them, Because [a]it is given unto you [ainf]to know the mysteries3466 of the kingdom932 of heaven, but to them it [pfip]is not given.1325

12 [a]For whosoever hath, to him shall be given, and he shall have more abundance:4052 but whosoever hath not, from him shall be taken away even that he hath.

13 Therefore speak I to them in parables: because they seeing991 see991 not; and hearing they hear not, neither do they understand.

14 And in them is fulfilled378 the prophecy4394 of Esaias, which [ppt]saith, [a]By [nn]hearing189 ye [ft]shall hear,191 and [asba]shall not understand;4920 and [ppt]seeing991 ye [ft]shall see,991 and shall not perceive:3708

15 For this people's heart is waxed gross,3975 and *their* ears [a]are dull of [ao]hearing, and their eyes they [ao]have closed; lest at any time they [aosb]should see with *their* eyes, and hear with *their* ears, and [aosb]should understand with *their* heart, and [aosb]should be converted,1994 and I [fm]should heal2390 them.

16 But [a]blessed3107 *are* your eyes, for they see: and your ears, for they hear.

17 For verily281 I say unto you, [a]That many prophets and righteous1342 *men* [ao]have desired1937 [ainf]to see *those things* which ye see, and [ao]have not seen1492 *them;* and [ainf]to hear *those things* which ye hear, and [ao]have not heard191 *them.*

The Parable of the Sower Explained (Mark 4:13–20; Luke 8:11–15)

18 [aim][a]Hear ye therefore the parable of the [apt]sower.

19 When any one [ppt]heareth the word3056 [a]of the kingdom, and [ppt]understandeth *it* not, then cometh the wicked4190 *one,* and catcheth away726 that which [pfpp]was sown in his heart. This is he which [aptp]received seed by the way side.

20 But he that [aptp]received the seed into stony places, the same is he that [ppt]heareth the word,3056 and anon2117 [a]with joy5479 [ppt]receiveth it;

21 Yet hath he not root in himself, but dureth2076 for a while: for when tribulation2347 or persecution ariseth because of the word,3056 by and by [a]he [pinp]is offended.

22 [a]He also that [aptp]received seed [b]among the thorns is he that [ppt]heareth the word; and the care of this world, and the deceitfulness of riches, choke the word,3056 and he becometh unfruitful.

23 But he that [aptp]received seed into the good ground1093 is he that [ppt]heareth the word,3056 and [ppt]understandeth *it;* which also beareth fruit, and bringeth forth, some an hundredfold, some sixty, some thirty.

11 [a]Matt. 11:25; 16:17; Mark 4:11; 1Cor. 2:10; 1John 2:27
12 [a]Matt. 25:29; Mark 4:25; Luke 8:18; 19:26
14 [a]Isa. 6:9; Ezek. 12:2; Mark 4:12; Luke 8:10; John 12:40; Acts 28:26, 27; Rom. 11:8; 2Cor. 3:14, 15
15 [a]Heb. 5:11
16 [a]Matt. 16:17; Luke 10:23, 24; John 20:29
17 [a]Heb. 11:13; 1Pet. 1:10, 11
18 [a]Mark 4:14; Luke 8:11
19 [a]Matt. 4:23
20 [a]Isa. 58:2; Ezek. 33:31, 32; John 5:35
21 [a]Matt. 11:6; 2Tim. 1:15
22 [a]Matt. 19:23; Mark 10:23; Luke 18:24; 1Tim. 6:9; 2Tim. 4:10 [b]Jer. 4:3

🔑 **13:10–17** The key to understanding this difficult passage is found in Jesus' motive for using parables. Since the parables were given to explain spiritual truths, those who had already rejected Jesus did not have divinely enlightened minds with which to perceive these truths, and no amount of explanation would make them understand (1 Cor. 1:27; 2:14, cf. Rom. 7:13). They could watch and hear Jesus with their physical eyes and ears, but they were not capable of understanding the truth in their heart because they had rejected Him (2 Cor. 4:3, 4). Verse twelve simply explains the principle that those who accept the true light they have been given will receive even more light, while those who turn away from the light will continue to be increasingly shrouded in darkness. The word "for" at the beginning of verse fifteen should be understood as having the same meaning as "because." In other words, the people do not hear and see because their heart is full of wickedness; consequently, they fail to understand the truth that has been given them. They are so opposed to God's message that they harden themselves against it lest they should happen to understand it and ask forgiveness of God. Once they reject Jesus, they also reject the possibility of understanding the parables that Jesus told (Is. 55:6–8).

The Wheat and Tares

24 Another parable put he forth unto them, saying, The kingdom of heaven [aop]is likened unto a man which [apt]sowed good seed[4690] in his field:

25 But while men [aie]slept, his enemy came and sowed tares$_{2215}$ among[303,3319] the wheat, and went his way.

26 But when the blade was sprung up, and brought forth fruit, then appeared[5316] the tares also.

27 So the servants[1401] of the householder came and said unto him, Sir,[2962] didst not thou sow good seed[4690] in thy field? from whence then hath it tares?

28 He said unto them, An enemy [ao]hath done this. The servants said unto him, Wilt thou then that we [apt]go and [aosb]gather them up?

29 But he said, Nay; lest while ye [ppt]gather up the tares, ye [aosb]root up also the wheat with them.

30 Let[863] both [pinf]grow together until the harvest: and in the time[2540] of harvest I will say to the reapers, Gather ye together first the tares, and bind them in bundles to burn them: but [aima][a]gather[4863] the wheat into my barn.

A Mustard Seed (Mark 4:30–32; Luke 13:18–21)

31 Another parable put he forth unto them, saying, [a]The kingdom of heaven is like to a grain of mustard seed, which a man [apt]took, and sowed in his field:

32 Which indeed is the least of all seeds:[4690] but when it is grown, it is the greatest among herbs, and becometh a tree, so that the birds of the air[3772] [ainf]come and [pinf]lodge in the branches thereof.

Leaven (Mark 4:33, 34)

33 [a]Another parable spake he unto them; The kingdom[932] of heaven[3772] is like unto leaven, which a woman took, and hid in three measures of meal, till the whole was leavened.

Parables Explained

34 [a]All these things [ao]spake Jesus unto the multitude in parables;[3850] and without a parable [ipf]spake he not unto them:

35 That it might be fulfilled which was spoken by the prophet,[4396] saying, [a]I will open my mouth in parables; [b]I will utter things which [pfpp]have been kept secret$_{2928}$ from the foundation[2602] of the world.[2889]

36 Then Jesus [apt]sent[863] the multitude away, and went into the house: and his disciples[3101] came unto him, saying, Declare unto us the parable of the tares$_{2215}$ of the field.

37 He answered and said unto them, He that [ppt]soweth the good seed[4690] is the Son of man;

38 [a]The field is the world;[2889] the good seed are the children[5207] of the kingdom;[932] but the tares are [b]the children of the wicked *one;*

39 The enemy that [apt]sowed them is the devil;[1228] [a]the harvest is the end[4930] of the world; and the reapers are the angels.

40 As therefore the tares are gathered and burned in the fire; so shall it be in the end of this world.

41 The Son of man shall send forth his angels, [a]and they shall gather out of his kingdom[932] all [1]things that offend, and them which [ppt]do iniquity;[458]

42 [a]And shall cast them into a fur-

30 [a]Matt. 3:12
31 [a]Isa. 2:2, 3; Mic. 4:1; Mark 4:30-32; Luke 13:18, 19
33 [a]Luke 13:20, 21
34 [a]Mark 4:33, 34
35 [a]Ps. 78:2 [b]Rom. 16:25, 26; 1Cor. 2:7; Eph. 3:9; Col. 1:26
38 [a]Matt. 24:14; 28:19; Mark 16:15, 20; Luke 24:47; Rom. 10:18; Col. 1:6 [b]Gen. 3:15; John 8:44; Acts 13:10; 1John 3:8
39 [a]Joel 3:13; Rev. 14:15
41 [1]Or, *scandals* [a]Matt. 18:7; 2Pet. 2:1, 2
42 [a]Matt. 3:12; Rev. 19:20; 20:10

13:24–30 Compare this parable with the parable of the fish (Matt. 13:47–50).

13:31, 32 The analogy of the mustard seed vividly contrasts the size of the seed with the great results it produces. In these verses, Jesus was explaining that even though at that time the influence of the kingdom of heaven seemed small and insignificant, it would eventually have far reaching effects just like the tree that grows from a mustard seed.

13:34, 35 See note on Matthew 13:10–17.

13:38, 42, 43 See note on Matthew 8:11, 12.

nace of fire: [b]there shall be wailing and gnashing[1030] of teeth.

43 [a]Then shall the righteous[1342] shine forth as the sun in the kingdom of their Father. [b]Who hath ears [pinf]to hear, [pim]let him hear.

A Buried Treasure

44 Again, the kingdom of heaven is like unto treasure [pfpp]hid in a field; the which when a man [apt]hath found, he [ao]hideth, and for joy thereof goeth and [a]selleth all that he hath, and [b]buyeth[59] that field.

The Pearl of Great Price

45 Again, the kingdom[932] of heaven is like unto a merchant[1713] man, seeking goodly pearls:

46 Who, when he had found [a]one pearl of great price, went and sold all that he had, and bought[59] it.

A Large Net

🗝 47 Again, the kingdom[932] of heaven[3772] is like unto a net,[4522] that was cast into the sea, and [apta]gathered of every kind:

48 Which, when it was full,[4137] they [apt]drew to shore, and [apt]sat down, and gathered the good into vessels, but cast the bad away.

49 So shall it be at the end[4930] of the world: the angels shall come forth, and [a]sever[873] the wicked from among[3319] the just,[1342]

50 [a]And shall cast them into the furnace of fire: there shall be wailing and gnashing[1030] of teeth.

The Householder's Treasure

51 Jesus saith unto them, Have ye understood all these things? They say unto him, Yea, Lord.

42 [b]Matt. 8:12; 13:50
43 [a]Dan. 12:3; 1Cor. 15:42, 43, 58 [b]Matt. 13:9
44 [a]Phil. 3:7, 8 [b]Isa. 55:1; Rev. 3:18
46 [a]Prov. 2:4; 3:14, 15; 8:10, 19
47 [a]Matt. 22:10
49 [a]Matt. 25:32
50 [a]Matt. 13:42
52 [a]Song 7:13
54 [a]Matt. 2:23; Mark 6:1; Luke 4:16, 23
55 [a]Isa. 49:7; Mark 6:3; Luke 3:23; John 6:42 [b]Matt. 12:46 [c]Mark 15:40
57 [a]Matt. 11:6; Mark 6:3, 4 [b]Luke 4:24; John 4:44
58 [a]Mark 6:5, 6
1 [a]Mark 6:14; Luke 9:7
2 [1]Or, *are wrought by him*
3 [a]Mark 6:17; Luke 3:19, 20

52 Then said he unto them, Therefore every scribe[1122] *which is* instructed[3100] unto the kingdom[932] of heaven[3772] is like unto a man *that is* an householder, which bringeth forth out of his treasure [a]*things* new[2537] and old.[3820]

Jesus Rejected at Nazareth (Mark 6:1–6; Luke 4:16–30)

53 And it came to pass, *that* when Jesus had finished[5055] these parables, he departed thence.

54 [a]And when he was come into his own country, he [ipf]taught them in their synagogue, insomuch that they [pinf]were astonished, and [pinf]said, Whence hath this *man* this wisdom, and *these* mighty works?

🗝 55 [a]Is not this the carpenter's son? is not his mother called Mary? and [b]his brethren,[80] [c]James, and Joses, and Simon, and Judas?

56 And his sisters, are they not all with us? Whence then hath this *man* all these things?

57 And they [ipfa]were offended in him. But Jesus said unto them, [b]A prophet[4396] is not without honour, save in his own country, and in his own house.

58 And [a]he [ao]did not many mighty works there because of their unbelief.[570]

The Death of John the Baptist (Mark 6:14–29; Luke 9:7–9)

14 At that time [a]Herod the tetrarch[5076] heard of the fame[189] of Jesus,

2 And said unto his servants,[3816] This is John the Baptist;[910] he [aop]is risen[1453] from the dead; and therefore mighty works [pini]do shew forth[1754] themselves in him.

3 [a]For Herod [apt]had laid hold on John, and bound him, and put[5087] *him* in

🗝 **13:47–50** This is similar to the parable of the wheat and the tares (Matt. 13:24–30). The separation of the wicked from among the righteous will ultimately be done by the angels, not by believers. Until that time, the true believers will co-exist, perhaps unknowingly, with unbelievers in the visible church here on earth.

🗝 **13:55** See the introduction to the Book of Jude.

prison[5438] for Herodias' sake, his brother Philip's wife.

4 For John said unto him, [a]It is not lawful for thee [pinf]to have her.

5 And when he [ppt]would[2309] [ainf]have put him to death, he feared[5399] the multitude, [a]because they counted him as a prophet.[4396]

6 But when Herod's birthday was kept,[71] the daughter of Herodias danced [I]before them, and pleased Herod.

7 Whereupon he promised[3670] with[3326] an oath[3727] to give her whatsoever she would ask.

8 And she, being before instructed of her mother, said, Give me here John Baptist's head in a charger.

9 And the king[935] was sorry:[3076] nevertheless for the oath's sake, and them which sat with him at meat, he commanded *it* to be given *her.*

10 And he sent, and beheaded John in the prison.[5438]

11 And his head was brought in a charger, and given to the damsel: and she brought *it* to her mother.

12 And his disciples [apt]came, and took up the body,[4983] and buried it, and [apt]went and told Jesus.

Jesus Feeds the Five Thousand (Mark 6:30–44; Luke 9:10–17; John 6:1–14)

13 [a]When Jesus heard *of it,* he departed thence by ship into a desert place apart:[2596,2398] and when the people had heard *thereof,* they followed him on foot out of the cities.

14 And Jesus [apt]went forth, and saw a great multitude, and [a]was moved with compassion toward them, and he healed their sick.[732]

15 [a]And when it was evening, his disciples came to him, saying, This is a desert place, and the time[5610] is now past; send the multitude away,[630] that they [apt]may go into the villages, and buy[59] themselves victuals.[1033]

16 But Jesus said unto them, They need not depart; [aim]give ye them to eat.

17 And they say unto him, We have here but five loaves, and two fishes.

18 He said, Bring[5342] them hither to me.

19 And he [apt]commanded the multitude to sit down on the grass, and [apt]took the five loaves, and the two fishes, and [apt]looking up[308] to heaven, [a]he blessed,[2127] and [apt]brake,[2806] and gave the loaves to *his* disciples, and the disciples[3101] to the multitude.

20 And they did all eat, and were filled: and they took up of the fragments[2801] that remained twelve baskets full.[4134]

21 And they that [ppt]had eaten were about[5616] five thousand men,[435] beside women and children.

Walking on Water (Mark 6:45–52; John 6:15–21)

22 And straightway[2112] Jesus constrained[315] his disciples[3101] to get into a ship, and to go before[4254] him unto the other side, while he sent the multitudes away.

23 [a]And when he had sent the multitudes away, he went up into a mountain apart[2596,2398] [ainf]to pray: [b]and when the evening was come, he was there alone.

24 But the ship was now in the midst[3319] of the sea, tossed with waves: for the wind was contrary.

25 And in the fourth watch of the night Jesus went unto them, walking on the sea.

26 And when the disciples saw him [a]walking on the sea, they were troubled, saying, It is a spirit; and they cried out for fear.[5401]

27 But straightway Jesus spake unto them, saying, Be of good cheer; it is I; [pim]be not afraid.[5399]

28 And Peter answered him and said, Lord, if it be thou, bid me come unto thee on the water.

29 And he said, Come. And when Peter was come down out of the ship, he walked on the water, to go to Jesus.

30 But when he [ppt]saw the wind

---

4 [a]Lev. 18:16; 20:21

5 [a]Matt. 21:26; Luke 20:6

6 [I]Gr. *in the midst*

13 [a]Matt. 10:23; 12:15; Mark 6:32; Luke 9:10; John 6:1, 2

14 [a]Matt. 9:36; Mark 6:34

15 [a]Mark 6:35; Luke 9:12; John 6:5

19 [a]Matt. 15:36

23 [a]Mark 6:46 [b]John 6:16

26 [a]Job 9:8

[l]boisterous, he was afraid;[5399] and [apt]beginning to sink, he cried, saying, Lord, save me.

31 And immediately Jesus [apt]stretched forth *his* hand, and [ao]caught[1949] him, and said unto him, O thou of little faith,[3640] wherefore didst thou doubt?

32 And when they were come into the ship, the wind ceased.[2869]

33 Then they that were in the ship [apt]came and worshipped him, saying, Of a truth [a]thou art the [an]Son of God.

Jesus Heals the Sick at Gennesaret (Mark 6:53–56)

34 [a]And when they were gone over, they came into the land of Gennesaret.

35 And when the men of that place had knowledge of him, they sent out into all that country round about, and brought unto him all that were diseased;[2560,2192]

🗝 36 And [ipf]besought him that they [asbm]might only touch[680] the hem of his garment: and [a]as many as touched were made perfectly whole.[1295]

God's Command Or Man's Tradition? (Mark 7:1–23)

15 Then [a]came to Jesus scribes[1122] and Pharisees, which were of Jerusalem, saying,

2 [a]Why do thy disciples[3101] transgress[3845] [b]the tradition[3862] of the elders?[4245] for they wash not their hands when they eat bread.

3 But he answered and said unto them, Why do ye also transgress[3845] the commandment of God by your tradition?

4 For God commanded, saying, [a]Honour thy [art]father and [art]mother: and, he that [ppt]curseth father or mother, [pim]let him die[5053] the death.

5 But ye say, Whosoever shall say to *his* [art]father or *his* [art]mother, [a]*It is* a gift,[1435] by whatsoever thou mightest be profited by me;

6 And honour not his father or his mother, *he shall be free.* Thus have ye made the commandment of God of none effect by your tradition.

7 *Ye* [a]hypocrites, well did Esaias prophesy[4395] of you, saying,

8 [a]This people draweth nigh unto me with their mouth, and honoureth me with *their* lips; but their heart[2588] is[568] far from me.

9 But in vain[3155] they do worship[4576] me, [a]teaching *for* doctrines[1319] the commandments[1778] of men.[444]

10 [a]And he [apt]called the multitude, and said unto them, [pim]Hear, and [pim]understand:

11 [a]Not that which [ppt]goeth into the mouth defileth[2840] a man; but that which [ppt]cometh out of the mouth, this defileth a man.

12 Then [apt]came his disciples, and said unto him, Knowest thou that the Pharisees were offended, after they heard this saying?[3056]

13 But he answered and said, [a]Every plant, which my heavenly[3770] Father [ao]hath not planted,[5452] shall be rooted up.

14 Let them alone: [a]they be blind leaders of the blind. And if the blind lead the blind, both shall fall[4098] into the ditch.

15 [a]Then answered Peter and said unto him, Declare unto us this parable.[3850]

16 And Jesus said, [a]Are ye also yet without understanding?[801]

17 Do not ye yet understand,[3539] that [a]whatsoever [ppt]entereth in at the mouth goeth into the belly, and is cast out into the draught?[856]

18 But [a]those things which proceed out of the mouth come forth from the heart; and they defile the man.

19 [a]For out of the heart proceed evil[4190] thoughts,[1261] murders, adulteries, fornications,[4202] thefts, false witness, blasphemies:[988]

30 [l]Or, *strong*
33 [a]Ps. 2:7; Matt. 16:16; 26:63; Mark 1:1; Luke 4:41; John 1:49; 6:69; 11:27; Acts 8:37; Rom. 1:4
34 [a]Mark 6:53
36 [a]Matt. 9:20; Mark 3:10; Luke 6:19; Acts 19:12
1 [a]Mark 7:1
2 [a]Mark 7:5 [b]Col. 2:8
4 [a]Ex. 20:12; Lev. 19:3; Deut. 5:16; Prov. 23:22; Eph. 6:2 [b]Ex. 21:17; Lev. 20:9; Deut. 27:16; Prov. 20:20; 30:17
5 [a]Mark 7:11, 12
7 [a]Mark 7:6
8 [a]Isa. 29:13; Ezek. 33:31
9 [a]Isa. 29:13; Col. 2:18-22; Titus 1:14
10 [a]Mark 7:14
11 [a]Acts 10:15; Rom. 14:14, 17, 20; 1Tim. 4:4; Titus 1:15
13 [a]John 15:2; 1Cor. 3:12-15
14 [a]Isa. 9:16; Mal. 2:8; Matt. 23:16; Luke 6:39
15 [a]Mark 7:17
16 [a]Matt. 16:9; Mark 7:18
17 [a]1Cor. 6:13
18 [a]James 3:6
19 [a]Gen. 6:5; 8:21; Prov. 6:14; Jer. 17:9; Mark 7:21

🗝 **14:36** See note on Philippians 2:6–8.

20 These are *the things* which [ppt]defile a [art]man: but to eat with unwashen hands defileth not a [art]man.

The Faith of a Gentile Woman (Mark 7:24–30)

21 [a]Then Jesus [apt]went thence, and departed into the coasts of Tyre and Sidon.

22 And, behold, a woman of Canaan [apt]came out of the same coasts, and [ao]cried unto him, saying, Have mercy on me, O Lord, *thou* son of David; my daughter [pinp]is grievously vexed with a devil.[1139]

23 But he answered her not a word. And his disciples [apt]came and [ipf]besought him, saying, [aim]Send her away;[630] for she crieth after us.

24 But he answered and said, [a]I [aop]am not sent[649] but unto the lost[622] sheep of the house of Israel.

25 Then [apt]came she and [ipf]worshipped him, saying, Lord, help me.

26 But he answered and said, It is not meet[2570] to take the children's bread, and to cast *it* to [art a]dogs.

27 And she said, Truth, Lord:[2962] yet the dogs eat of the crumbs which [ppt]fall[4098] from their masters'[2962] table.

28 Then Jesus answered and said unto her, O woman, great *is* thy faith:[4102] be it unto thee even as thou wilt.[2309] And her daughter was made whole[2390] from that very hour.

Jesus Heals Many

29 [a]And Jesus [apt]departed from thence, and came nigh [b]unto[3844] the sea of Galilee; and [apt]went up into a mountain, and sat down there.

30 [a]And great multitudes came unto him, having with them *those that were* lame, blind, dumb, maimed, and many others, and cast them down at Jesus' feet; and he healed them:

31 Insomuch that the multitude wondered,2296 when they [ppt]saw the dumb to [ppt]speak, the maimed to be whole,[5199] the lame to [ppt]walk, and the blind to [ppt]see: and they glorified[1392] the God of Israel.

21 [a]Mark 7:24

24 [a]Matt. 10:5, 6; Acts 3:25, 26; 13:46; Rom. 15:8

26 [a]Matt. 7:6; Phil. 3:2

29 [a]Mark 7:31 [b]Matt. 4:18

30 [a]Isa. 35:5, 6; Matt. 11:5; Luke 7:22

32 [a]Mark 8:1

33 [a]2Kgs. 4:43

36 [a]Matt. 14:19 [b]1Sam. 9:13; Luke 22:19

39 [a]Mark 8:10

1 [a]Matt. 12:38; Mark 8:11; Luke 11:16; 12:54-56; 1Cor. 1:22

Jesus Feeds Four Thousand (Mark 8:1–10)

32 [a]Then Jesus [apt]called his disciples[3101] *unto him,* and said, I have compassion on the multitude, because they continue with[4357] me now three days,[2250] and have nothing to eat: and I will not send them away fasting,3523 lest they faint in the way.

33 [a]And his disciples say unto him, Whence should we have so much bread in the wilderness, as to fill so great a multitude?

34 And Jesus saith unto them, How many loaves have ye? And they said, Seven, and a few little fishes.

35 And he commanded the multitude to sit down on the ground.

36 And [a]he took the seven loaves and the fishes, and [apt b]gave thanks, and brake[2806] *them,* and [ao]gave to his disciples, and the disciples to the multitude.

37 And they did all eat, and were filled: and they took up of the broken[2801] *meat* that was left seven baskets full.[4134]

38 And they that did eat were four thousand men,[435] beside women and children.

39 [a]And he [apt]sent away[630] the multitude, and took ship, and came into the coasts of Magdala.

Understanding the Times (Mark 8:11–13; Luke 12:54–56)

16 The [a]Pharisees also with the Sadducees came, and tempting[3985] desired him that he would shew them a sign from heaven.

2 He answered and said unto them, When it is evening, ye say, *It will be* fair weather: for the sky is red.

3 And in the morning, *It will be* foul weather to day: for the sky is red and lowering. O *ye* hypocrites,[5273] ye can [pinf]discern[1252] the face[4383] of the sky; but can ye not *discern* the signs of the times?[2540]

4 [a]A wicked[4190] and adulterous generation seeketh after a sign; and there [fp]shall no sign be given[1325] unto it, but the sign of the prophet Jonas. And he left them, and departed.

Pharisees and Sadducees and Their Influence (Mark 8:14–21)

5 And [a]when his disciples[3101] were come to the other side, they had forgotten to take bread.

6 Then Jesus said unto them, [a]Take heed and beware of the leaven[2219] of the Pharisees and of the Sadducees.

7 And they [ipf]reasoned[1260] among themselves, saying, *It is* because we have [ao]taken no bread.

8 *Which* when Jesus perceived, he said unto them, O ye of little faith,[3640] why reason ye among yourselves, because ye [ao]have brought no bread?

9 [pin][a]Do ye not yet understand,[3539] neither remember the five loaves of the five thousand, and how many baskets ye took up?

10 [a]Neither the seven loaves of the four thousand, and how many baskets ye took up?

11 How is it that ye do not understand that I spake *it* not to you concerning bread, that ye [pinf]should beware of the leaven of the Pharisees and of the Sadducees?

4 [a]Matt. 12:39
5 [a]Mark 8:14
6 [a]Luke 12:1
9 [a]Matt. 14:17; John 6:9
10 [a]Matt. 15:34
13 [a]Mark 8:27; Luke 9:18
14 [a]Matt. 14:2; Luke 9:7-9
16 [a]Matt. 14:33; Mark 8:29; Luke 9:20; John 6:69; 11:27; Acts 8:37; 9:20; Heb. 1:2, 5; 1John 4:15; 5:5
17 [a]Eph. 2:8 [b]1Cor. 2:10; Gal. 1:16
18 [a]John 1:42 [b]Eph. 2:20; Rev. 21:14 [c]Job 38:17; Ps. 9:13; 107:18; Isa. 38:10
19 [a]Matt. 18:18; John 20:23

12 Then understood they how that he bade *them* not beware of the leaven of bread, but of the doctrine of the Pharisees and of the Sadducees.

Jesus Is the Messiah (Mark 8:27–30; Luke 9:18–21)

13 When Jesus came into the coasts of Caesarea Philippi, he [ipf]asked[2065] his disciples,[3101] saying, [a]Whom do men say that I the Son of man am?

14 And they said, [a]Some *say that thou art* John the Baptist:[910] some, Elias; and others, Jeremiah, or one of the prophets.[4396]

15 He saith unto them, But whom say ye that I am?

16 And Simon Peter answered and said, [a]Thou art the Christ,[5547] the Son of the living[2198] God.[2316]

17 And Jesus answered and said unto him, Blessed[3107] art thou, Simon Bar–jona: [a]for flesh[4561] and blood[129] [ao]hath not revealed[601] *it* unto thee, but [b]my Father[3962] which is in heaven.[3772]

🔑 18 And I say also unto thee, That [a]thou art Peter, and [b]upon this rock I will build[3618] my church;[1577] and the [anc]gates of hell[86] [ft]shall not prevail against[2729] it.

19 [a]And I will give unto thee the keys of the kingdom[932] of heaven:[3772] and [n]whatsoever thou [aosb]shalt bind[1210] on earth [fm]shall be [pfpp]bound[1210] in heaven: and whatsoever thou shalt loose

🔑 **16:18, 19** A more accurate translation of verse nineteen from the Greek is, "And I will give thee the keys of the kingdom of the heavens. And whatever thou shalt bind on the earth shall be as having been bound in the heavens; and whatever thou shalt loose on the earth shall be as having been loosed in the heavens." Before these verses can be correctly understood, a distinction must be made between the "church" (v. 18) and the kingdom of the heavens (v. 19). The Church is representative of the body of believers here on earth while the kingdom of the heavens is made up of both the earthly and heavenly realms. The teaching here is that those things which are conclusively decided by God in the kingdom of heaven are emulated by the Church on earth. The Church is made up of true believers who acknowledge the deity of Jesus Christ as Peter did. Christ is the "Rock" upon which the Church is built (1 Cor. 3:11). There is no reference made here to the binding or loosing of persons. One can note that this speaks exclusively of things because of the neuter gender of the indefinite pronouns *hó* (3739), "whatever," in verse nineteen, and *hósa* (3745), "whatever," in Matthew 18:18. Believers can never make conclusive decisions about things, but can only confirm those decisions which have already been made by God Himself in the context of His kingdom both on earth and in heaven. The two verbs, *dedeménon* (from *déō* [1210]) and *leluménon* (3089), are both perfect passive participles that should have been translated respectively as "having been bound" and "having been loosed" already in the heavens.

on earth[1093] [fm]shall be [pfpp]loosed[3089] in heaven.

20 [a]Then charged he his disciples that they [aosb]should tell no man that he was Jesus the Christ.

Jesus Must Die (Mark 8:31–9:1; Luke 9:22–27)

21 From that time forth began Jesus [pinf][a]to shew unto his disciples, how that he must go unto Jerusalem, and suffer[3958] many things of the elders[4245] and chief priests and scribes, and be killed, and be raised again the third day.

22 Then Peter [apt]took[4355] him, and began [pinf]to rebuke[2008] him, saying, [I]Be it far[2436] from thee, Lord: this shall [efn]not be unto thee.

23 But he turned, and said unto Peter, Get thee behind me, [a]Satan:[4567] [b]thou art an offence unto me: for thou savourest[5426] not the things that be of God, but those that be of men.

24 [a]Then said Jesus unto his disciples, If any *man* will come after me, [aim]let him deny[533] himself, and [aim]take up[142] his cross,[4716] and [pim]follow[190] me.

25 For [a]whosoever will [ainf]save[4982] his life[5590] shall lose[622] it: and whosoever [aosb]will lose[622] his life for my sake shall find it.

26 For what is a man profited, if he shall gain the whole world, and lose his own soul?[5590] or [a]what shall a man give in exchange[465] for his soul?

27 For [a]the Son of man shall [pinf]come in[1722] the glory[1391] of his Father [b]with his angels; [c]and then he shall reward every man according to his [sg]works.[4234]

28 Verily[281] I say unto you, [a]There be some standing[2476] here, which shall [efn]not taste[1089] of death,[2288] till they see the Son of man coming in his kingdom.

The Transfiguration (Mark 9:2–13; Luke 9:28–36)

17 And [a]after six days[2250] Jesus taketh Peter, James, and John his brother, and [pin]bringeth them up[399] into an high mountain apart,[2596,2398]

2 And was transfigured[3339] before them: and his face[4383] did shine as the sun, and his raiment [aom]was white as the light.

3 And, behold, there appeared unto them Moses and Elias talking with him.

4 Then answered[611] Peter, and said unto Jesus, Lord, it is good for us to be here: if thou [pin]wilt, let us make here three tabernacles;[4633] one for thee, and one for Moses, and one for Elias.

5 [a]While he yet [ppt]spake, behold, a bright cloud overshadowed them: and behold a voice out of the cloud, [ppt]which said, [b]This is my beloved[27] Son, [c]in whom I [ao]am well pleased;[2106] [pim][d]hear ye him.

6 [a]And when the disciples[3101] heard *it,* they fell on their face,[4383] and were sore[4970] afraid.

7 And Jesus [apt]came and [a]touched them, and said, Arise, and be not afraid.

8 And when they had lifted up[1869] their eyes, they saw no man, save Jesus only.

9 And as they [ppt]came down from the mountain, [a]Jesus charged them, saying, Tell the vision[3705] to no man, until the Son of man [asba]be risen again[450] from the dead.

10 And his disciples asked[1905] him, saying, [a]Why then say the scribes[1122] that Elias must first [ainf]come?

11 And Jesus answered and said unto them, Elias truly [pin]shall first come,[2064] and [a]restore[600] all things.

12 [a]But I say unto you, That Elias [ao]is come already, and they [ao]knew him not, but [ao][b]have done unto him whatsoever they [ao]listed.[2309] Likewise [c]shall also the Son of man [pinf]suffer of them.

13 [a]Then the disciples understood that he spake unto them of John the Baptist.[910]

Jesus Heals a Boy Possessed With a Demon (Mark 9:14–29; Luke 9:37–43)

14 [a]And when they were come to the multitude, there came to him a *certain* man, kneeling down to him, and saying,

---

20 [a]Matt. 17:9; Mark 8:30; Luke 9:21
21 [a]Matt. 20:17; Mark 8:31; 9:31; 10:33; Luke 9:22; 18:31; 24:6, 7
22 [I]Gr. *Pity thyself*
23 [a]2Sam. 19:22 [b]Rom. 8:7
24 [a]Matt. 10:38; Mark 8:34; Luke 9:23; 14:27; Acts 14:22; 1Thess. 3:3; 2Tim. 3:12
25 [a]Luke 17:33; John 12:25
26 [a]Ps. 49:7, 8
27 [a]Matt. 26:64; Mark 8:38; Luke 9:26 [b]Dan. 7:10; Zech. 14:5; Matt. 25:31; Jude 1:14 [c]Job 34:11; Ps. 62:12; Prov. 24:12; Jer. 17:10; 32:19; Ro 2:6; 1Cor. 3:8; 2Cor. 5:10; 1Pet. 1:17; Rev. 2:23; 22:12
28 [a]Mark 9:1; Luke 9:27

1 [a]Mark 9:2; Luke 9:28
5 [a]2Pet. 1:17 [b]Matt. 3:17; Mark 1:11; Luke 3:22 [c]Isa. 42:1 [d]Deut. 18:15, 19; Acts 3:22, 23
6 [a]2Pet. 1:18
7 [a]Dan. 8:18; 9:21; 10:10, 18
9 [a]Matt. 16:20; Mark 8:30; 9:9
10 [a]Mal. 4:5; Matt. 11:14; Mark 9:11
11 [a]Mal. 4:6; Luke 1:16, 17; Acts 3:21
12 [a]Matt. 11:14; Mark 9:12, 13 [b]Matt. 14:3, 10 [c]Matt. 16:21
13 [a]Matt. 11:14
14 [a]Mark 9:14; Luke 9:37

15 Lord, have mercy on my son: for he is lunatic, and sore[2560] vexed: for ofttimes he falleth into the fire, and oft into the water.

16 And I brought him to thy disciples, and they [aop]could not [ainf]cure him.

17 Then Jesus answered and said, O faithless[571] and perverse generation, how long shall I be with you? how long shall I suffer you? bring[5342] him hither to me.

18 And Jesus rebuked the devil; and he departed out of him: and the child was cured from that very hour.

19 Then came the disciples to Jesus apart,[2596,2398] and said, Why [aop]could not we [ainf]cast him out?[1544]

20 And Jesus said unto them, Because of your unbelief:[570] for verily[281] I say unto you, [a]If ye have faith[4102] as a grain of mustard seed, ye shall say unto this mountain, Remove[3327] hence to yonder place; and it shall remove; and nothing shall be impossible[101] unto you.

21 Howbeit[1161] this kind goeth not out but by prayer and fasting.[3521]

Jesus Prophesies of His Death And Resurrection (Mark 9:30–32; Luke 9:43–45)

22 [a]And while they abode[390] in Galilee, Jesus said unto them, The Son of man shall be betrayed into the hands of men:

23 And they shall kill him, and the third day he shall be raised again. And they [aop]were exceeding sorry.[3076]

Tax Money in the Mouth of a Fish

24 And [a]when they were come to Capernaum, they that received tribute *money* came to Peter, and said, Doth not your master pay[5055] tribute?

25 He saith, Yes. And when he was come into the house, Jesus prevented him, saying, What thinkest thou, Simon? of whom do the kings of the earth take custom[5056] or tribute? of their own children, or of strangers?

26 Peter saith unto him, Of strangers. Jesus saith unto him, Then are the children free.

27 Notwithstanding, lest we [aosb]should offend[4624] them, go thou to the sea, and cast an hook, and take up[142] the fish that first cometh up; and when thou hast opened his mouth, thou shalt find a piece of money: that take, and give unto them for me and thee.

Humble Yourself As a Little Child (Mark 9:33–37; Luke 9:46–48)

18 At [a]the same time came the disciples unto Jesus, saying, Who is the greatest in the kingdom[932] of heaven?

2 And Jesus [apt]called a little child unto him, and set[2476] him in the midst of them,

3 And said, Verily[281] I say unto you, [a]Except ye be converted,[4762] and become as little children, ye shall [efn]not enter into the kingdom of heaven.

4 [a]Whosoever therefore shall humble himself as this little child, the same is greatest in the kingdom of heaven.

5 And [a]whoso shall receive one such little child in my name[3686] receiveth me.

Stumblingblocks (Mark 9:42–48; Luke 17:1, 2)

6 [a]But whoso [asba]shall offend[4624] one of these little ones which [ppt]believe[4100] in me, it were better for him that a millstone were hanged about his neck, and *that* he were drowned in the depth[3989] of the sea.[2281]

7 Woe unto the world because of offences! for [a]it must needs[318] be that offences[4625] [ainf]come; but [b]woe to that man by whom the offence cometh!

8 [a]Wherefore if thy hand or thy foot [pin]offend[4624] thee, cut them off, and cast *them* from thee: it is better for thee to enter into life[2222] halt or maimed, rather than having two hands or two feet to be cast into [art]everlasting fire.

20 [a]Matt. 21:21; Mark 11:23; Luke 17:6; 1Cor. 12:9; 13:2
22 [a]Matt. 16:21; 20:17; Mark 8:31; 9:30, 31; 10:33; Luke 9:22, 44; 18:31; 24:6, 7
24 [a]Mark 9:33
1 [a]Mark 9:33; Luke 9:46; 22:24
3 [a]Ps. 131:2; Matt. 19:14; Mark 10:14; Luke 18:16; 1Cor. 14:20; 1Pet. 2:2
4 [a]Matt. 20:27; 23:11
5 [a]Matt. 10:42; Luke 9:48
6 [a]Mark 9:42; Luke 17:1, 2
7 [a]Luke 17:1; 1Cor. 11:19 [b]Matt. 26:24
8 [a]Matt. 5:29, 30; Mark 9:43, 45

9 And if thine eye [pin]offend thee,
pluck it out, and cast *it* from thee: it is
better for thee to enter into life with one
eye, rather than having two eyes to be
cast into [art]hell[1067] [art]fire.

Parable of a Lost Sheep (Luke 15:3–7)

10 Take heed that ye [aosi]despise not
one of these little ones; for I say unto
you, That in heaven [a]their angels do always [b]behold the face of my Father
which is in heaven.[3772]
11 [a]For the Son of man [ao]is come
[ainf]to save[4982] that which was lost.[622]
12 [a]How think ye? if a man have an
hundred sheep, and one of them be gone
astray, doth he not [apt]leave the ninety and
nine, and [aptp]goeth into the mountains,
and [pin]seeketh that which [ppp]is gone
astray?
13 And if so be that he find it, verily I say unto you, he rejoiceth[5463] more
of that *sheep,* than of the ninety and
nine which [pfpp]went not astray.
14 Even so it is not the will[2307] of
your Father which is in heaven, that
one of these little ones [asbm]should perish.[622]

When One Brother Sins Against Another (Luke 17:3)

15 Moreover [a]if thy brother [asba]shall
trespass[264] against thee, go and tell him
his fault between thee and him alone: if
he [asba]shall hear thee, [b]thou [ao]hast gained
thy brother.
16 But if he [asba]will not hear[191] *thee,*
then take with thee one or two more, that
in [a]the mouth of two or three witnesses[3144] every word[4487] may be established.[2476]
17 And if he shall neglect to hear
them, tell *it* unto the church: but if he
neglect to hear the church,[1577] let him be
unto thee as an [a]heathen man[1482] and a
publican.5057
18 Verily I say unto you, [n][a]What-
soever ye [asba]shall bind[1210] on earth[1093]
[fm]shall be bound[1210] in heaven: and
[n]whatsoever ye [aosb]shall loose on earth
shall be loosed[3089] in heaven.
19 [a]Again I say unto you, That if
two of you shall agree on earth[1093] as
touching any thing that they [asbm]shall
ask, [b]it [fm]shall be done for them of my
Father which is in heaven.
20 For where two or three are gathered together in my name, there am I in
the midst[3319] of them.

Forgiving Others

21 Then [apt]came Peter to him, and
said, Lord,[2962] how oft shall my brother
sin against me, and I forgive him? [a]till
seven times?
22 Jesus saith unto him, I say not
unto thee, Until seven times: [a]but, Until
seventy times seven.
23 Therefore [aop]is the kingdom of
heaven likened3666 unto a certain king,
which [ao]would [ainf]take account of his servants.
24 And when he had begun to
reckon, one was brought unto him, which
owed[3781] him ten thousand [I]talents.
25 But forasmuch as he had not to
pay, his lord[2962] commanded him [a]to be
sold, and his wife, and children, and all
that he had, and payment to be made.
26 The servant therefore [apt]fell down,
and [ipf]worshipped him, saying, Lord,
[aim]have patience[3114] with me, and I will
pay thee all.
27 Then the lord of that servant
[aptp]was moved with compassion, and
loosed[630] him, and forgave him the
debt.
28 But the same servant [apt]went out,
and found one of his fellowservants,[4889]
which [ipf]owed[3784] him an hundred
pence:1220 and he [apt]laid hands on him,

10 [a]Ps. 34:7; Zech. 13:7; Heb. 1:14 [b]Esth. 1:14; Luke 1:19
11 [a]Luke 9:56; 19:10; John 3:17; 12:47
12 [a]Luke 15:4
15 [a]Lev. 19:17; Luke 17:3 [b]James 5:20; 1Pet. 3:1
16 [a]Deut. 17:6; 19:15; John 8:17; 2Cor. 13:1; Heb. 10:28
17 [a]Rom. 16:17; 1Cor. 5:9; 2Thess. 3:6, 14; 2John 1:10
18 [a]Matt. 16:19; John 20:23; 1Cor. 5:4
19 [a]Matt. 5:24 [b]1John 3:22; 5:14
21 [a]Luke 17:4
22 [a]Matt. 6:14; Mark 11:25; Col. 3:13
24 [I]*A talent is 750 ounces of silver*
25 [a]2Kgs. 4:1; Neh. 5:8
26 [I]Or, *besought him*

18:9, 12 See note on Matthew 8:11, 12.
18:15–17 See note on 1 Timothy 1:20.

and [ipf]took *him* by the throat, saying, Pay me that thou owest.

29 And his fellowservant [apt]fell down at his feet, and [ipf]besought him, saying, [aim]Have patience[3114] with me, and I will pay thee all.

30 And he [ipf]would[2309] not: but [apt]went and [ao]cast him into prison, till he should pay the debt.[3784]

31 So when his fellowservants saw what was done, they were very sorry, and [apt]came and told unto their lord all that was done.

32 Then his lord, after that he had called him, [pin]said unto him, O thou wicked[4190] servant, I forgave thee all that debt,[3782] because thou desiredst me:

33 Shouldest not thou also have had compassion on thy fellowservant, even as I had pity on thee?

34 And his lord [aptp]was wroth,[3710] and delivered him to the tormentors, till he should pay all that was due[3784] unto him.

35 [a]So likewise shall my heavenly[2032] Father do also unto you, if ye from your hearts[2588] [aosb]forgive not every one[1538] his brother their trespasses.[3900]

Divorce
(Matt. 5:27–32; Mark 10:1–12; Luke 16:18; Rom. 7:1–3; 1 Cor. 7)

19 And it came to pass, [a]*that* when Jesus had finished these sayings, he departed from Galilee, and came into the coasts of Judaea beyond Jordan;

2 [a]And great multitudes followed him; and he healed them there.

🔑 3 The Pharisees also came unto him, tempting[3985] him, and saying unto him, Is it lawful for a man to put away[630] his wife for[2596] every cause?[156]

4 And he answered and said unto them, Have ye not read, [a]that he which [apt]made *them* at the beginning [ao]made them male and female,[2338]

5 And said, [a]For this cause shall a man leave father and mother, and shall cleave to his wife: and [b]they twain[1417] shall be one flesh?

6 Wherefore they are no more twain, but one flesh. What therefore God hath joined together, let not man put asunder.

7 They say unto him, [a]Why did Moses then command to give a writing of divorcement,[647] and to put her away?[630]

8 He saith unto them, Moses because[4314] of the hardness of your hearts[4641] suffered you to put away[630] your wives: but from the beginning it [pfi]was not so.

9 [a]And I say unto you, Whosoever shall put away[630] his wife, except *it be* for fornication,[4202] and shall marry another, [pin]committeth adultery: and whoso marrieth her [pfpp]which is put away [pin]doth commit adultery.

35 [a]Prov. 21:13; Matt. 6:12; Mark 11:26; James 2:13

1 [a]Mark 10:1; John 10:40

2 [a]Matt. 12:15

4 [a]Gen. 1:27; 5:2; Mal. 2:15

5 [a]Gen. 2:24; Mark 10:5-9; Eph. 5:31 [b]1Cor. 6:16; 7:2

7 [a]Deut. 24:1; Matt. 5:31

9 [a]Matt. 5:32; Mark 10:11; Luke 16:18; 1Cor. 7:10, 11

🔑 **19:3–9** It is assumed many times when these and similar verses (Matt. 5:32; Luke 16:18) are read that the one who is divorced should not remarry. However, in the situations that Jesus dealt with, the person that was put away was innocent. Jesus was addressing the issue here of a spouse divorcing a mate with the mere excuse that the desire to be married to that particular person was gone. The only just cause for divorce is fornication. Consequently, anyone who was unjustly divorced acquired the false stigma that they were guilty of moral misconduct. For this reason, the Lord insisted that the Old Testament provision (Deut. 24:1–4) be adhered to: the person that unjustly dismisses an innocent mate ought to clear them of guilt by providing them with a bill of divorcement. In the case that the dismissed spouse was guilty of fornication, the Mosaic Law required that he or she be stoned (Deut. 22:21), making a bill of divorcement unnecessary. Divorce papers issued by a judge in today's society should not be equated with the Old Testament bill of divorcement.

A careful reading of two passages in the Old Testament will reveal how the Lord determined who was the guilty party (Num. 5; Deut. 22). The Lord concerns Himself only with the innocent party and not with one who is merely able to secure a legal divorce. It is important to remember that Jesus never forbad the innocent party to remarry. In fact, Jesus accepted that this person might remarry because He stated in Matthew 5:32 that the spouse who initiated the divorce causes the innocent one to commit adultery (i.e., when they marry someone else).

10 His disciples say unto him, [a]If the case of the man be so with *his* wife, it [pin]is not good[4851] to marry.

11 But he said unto them, [a]All *men* cannot receive this saying, save *they* to whom it is given.

12 For there are some eunuchs, which were so born from *their* mother's womb: and there are some eunuchs, which were made eunuchs of men: and [a]there be eunuchs, which have made themselves eunuchs for the kingdom[932] of heaven's sake. He that [ppt]is able [pinf]to receive *it,* let him receive *it.*

Who Will Enter God's Kingdom? (Mark 10:13–16; Luke 18:15–17)

13 [a]Then were there brought unto him little children, that he should put *his* hands on them, and pray: and the disciples rebuked[2008] them.

14 But Jesus said, Suffer[863] little children, and forbid$_{2967}$ them not, to come unto me: for [a]of such is the kingdom[932] of heaven.

15 And he [apt]laid *his* hands on them, and departed thence.

The Rich Young Man (Mark 10:17–31; Luke 18:18–30)

16 [a]And, behold, one came and said unto him, [b]Good[18] Master, what good thing shall I do, that I may have eternal life?[2222]

17 And he said unto him, Why callest thou me good? *there is* none good but one, *that is,* God: but if thou wilt[2309] enter into life, [aim]keep[5083] the commandments.

18 He saith unto him, Which? Jesus said, [a]Thou shalt do no murder, Thou shalt not commit adultery, Thou shalt not steal, Thou shalt not bear false witness,

19 [pim][a]Honour thy father and *thy* mother: and, [b]Thou shalt love[25] thy neighbour[4139] as thyself.

20 The young man saith unto him, All these things [aom]have I kept[5442] from my youth[3503] up: what lack I yet?

21 Jesus said unto him, If thou wilt be perfect,[5046] [a]go *and* sell that thou hast, and give to the poor, and thou shalt have treasure in heaven: and come *and* follow[190] me.

22 But when the young man heard that saying,[3056] he went away sorrowful: for he had great possessions.

23 Then said Jesus unto his disciples, Verily$_{281}$ I say unto you, That [a]a rich man shall hardly enter into the kingdom[932] of heaven.[3772]

24 And again I say unto you, It is easier for a camel to go through the eye of a needle, than for a rich man [ainf]to enter into the kingdom of God.

25 When his disciples heard *it,* they were exceedingly amazed, saying, Who then can be saved?

26 But Jesus [apt]beheld$_{1689}$ *them,* and said unto them, With men this is impossible; but [a]with God all things are possible.

🔑 27 [a]Then answered Peter and said unto him, Behold, [b]we have forsaken all, and followed thee; what shall we have therefore?

28 And Jesus said unto them, Verily I say unto you, That ye which [apt]have followed me, in the regeneration[3824] when the Son of man shall sit in the throne of his glory,[1391] [a]ye also shall sit upon twelve thrones, judging[2919] the twelve tribes of Israel.

29 [a]And every one that [ao]hath forsaken houses, or brethren,[80] or sisters, or father, or mother, or wife, or children, or lands, for my name's[3686] sake, shall receive an hundredfold, and shall inherit[2816] everlasting life.

30 [a]But many *that are* first shall be last;[2078] and the last *shall be* first.

10 [a]Prov. 21:19
11 [a]1Cor. 7:2, 7, 9, 17
12 [a]1Cor. 7:32, 34; 9:5, 15
13 [a]Mark 10:13; Luke 18:15
14 [a]Matt. 18:3
16 [a]Mark 10:17; Luke 18:18 [b]Luke 10:25
18 [a]Ex. 20:13; Deut. 5:17
19 [a]Matt. 15:4 [b]Lev. 19:18; Matt. 22:39; Rom. 13:9; Gal. 5:14; James 2:8
21 [a]Matt. 6:20; Luke 12:33; 16:9; Acts 2:45; 4:34, 35; 1Tim. 6:18, 19
23 [a]Matt. 13:22; Mark 10:24; 1Cor. 1:26; 1Tim. 6:9, 10
26 [a]Gen. 18:14; Job 42:2; Jer. 32:17; Zech. 8:6; Luke 1:37; 18:27
27 [a]Mark 10:28; Luke 18:28 [b]Deut. 33:9; Matt. 4:20; Luke 5:11
28 [a]Matt. 20:21; Luke 22:28, 29, 30; 1Cor. 6:2, 3; Rev. 2:26
29 [a]Mark 10:29, 30; Luke 18:29, 30
30 [a]Matt. 20:16; 21:31, 32; Mark 10:31; Luke 13:30

🔑 **19:27** See note on Matthew 20:1–16.

The Parable of the Labourers

20 🔑For the kingdom[932] of heaven is like unto a man *that is* an householder,[3617] which went out early in the morning [ainf]to hire labourers into his vineyard.

2 And when he had agreed with the labourers for a penny[1220] a day, he sent[649] them into his vineyard.

3 And he [apt]went out about the third hour,[5610] and saw others [pfp]standing idle[692] in the marketplace,[58]

4 And said unto them; Go ye also into the vineyard, and whatsoever is right[1342] I will give you. And they went their way.

5 Again he [apt]went out about the sixth and ninth hour, and did likewise.

6 And about the eleventh hour he [apt]went out, and found others [pfp]standing idle, and saith unto them, Why [pfi]stand ye here all the day[2250] idle?

7 They say unto him, Because no man [aom]hath hired us. He saith unto them, Go ye also into the vineyard; and whatsoever is right, *that* shall ye receive.

8 So when even was come, the lord of the vineyard saith unto his steward, Call[2564] the labourers, and give them *their* hire,[3408] beginning from the last unto the first.

9 And when they [apt]came that *were hired* about the eleventh hour, they received every man a penny.

10 But when the first came, they supposed that they should have received more; and they likewise received every man a penny.

11 And when they had received *it,* they murmured against the goodman of the house,[3617]

12 Saying, These last [aoI]have wrought *but* one hour, and thou [ao]hast made them equal unto us, which [apt]have borne the burden and heat of the day.

13 But he answered one of them, and said, Friend, I [pin]do thee no wrong:[91] didst not thou agree with me for a penny?

14 Take[142] *that* thine *is,* and go thy way: I will give unto this last, even as unto thee.

15 [a]Is it not lawful for me [ainf]to do what I will with mine [pl]own? [b]Is thine eye evil,[4190] because I am good?[18]

16 [a]So the last[2078] shall be first, and the first last: [b]for many be called,[2822] but few chosen.

Jesus Will Rise From the Dead (Mark 10:32–34; Luke 18:31–34)

17 [a]And Jesus going up to Jerusalem took the twelve disciples apart in the way, and said unto them,

18 [a]Behold, we go up to Jerusalem; and the Son of man shall be betrayed unto the chief priests and unto the

12 [1]Or, *have continued one hour only*

15 [a]Rom. 9:21 [b]Deut. 15:9; Prov. 23:6; Matt. 6:23

16 [a]Matt. 19:30 [b]Matt. 22:14

17 [a]Mark 10:32; Luke 18:31; John 12:12

18 [a]Matt. 16:21

🔑 **20:1–16** The meaning of this parable is related to Peter's question in Matthew 19:27. The lesson that Jesus is teaching with this parable hinges upon the distinction between those laborers who were hired (vv. 1, 2), and those who were not (vv. 3–7). The first group of workers was hired to do twelve hours of work (6 a.m. to 6 p.m.) for a specific sum of money. All the others were not hired, but called with a promise from the householder that he would reward them justly according to his own estimation. The translation of verse nine causes a serious misunderstanding of this parable because the word "hired" is inserted. It should be translated: "And those having come about the eleventh hour each received one *dēnárion*." A *dēnárion* (1220) was a coin that denoted the regularly accepted pay for a normal twelve-hour day of work. Those who agreed to earn one *dēnárion* for twelve hours of work set their own price for their work and that is what they received. The Lord wants His servants (Christians) to follow the example of the other workers. Those who serve the Lord and leave the size of the reward up to Him will always be given far more than if they insist on knowing how much they will receive before they begin. It is significant that Jesus did not refer to the hired man as a "dear friend," which would have been indicated by *philós* (5384). Instead He called him *hetaī́ros* (2083), which is used to describe a comrade or acquaintance. Jesus called Judas *hetaī́ros* in Gethsemane just before He was arrested (Matt. 26:50; see 11:16; 22:12).

scribes,[1122] and they shall condemn[2632]
him to death,
19 [a]And shall deliver him to the
Gentiles[1484] [aies]to mock, and [aies]to
scourge,3146 and [aies]to crucify[4717] *him:*
and the third day he shall rise again.[450]

The Mother of James and John Makes a Request (Mark 10:35–45)

20 [a]Then came to him the mother of
[b]Zebedee's children with her sons, worshipping *him,* and desiring a certain
thing of him.
21 And he said unto her, What wilt
thou? She saith unto him, Grant that
these my two sons [aosb][a]may sit, the one
on thy right hand,[1188] and the other on
the left, in thy kingdom.
22 But Jesus answered and said, Ye
know not what ye ask. Are ye able to
drink of [a]the cup that I shall [pinf]drink of,
and to be baptized[907] with [b]the baptism[908] that I am baptized with? They
say unto him, We are able.
23 And he saith unto them, [a]Ye shall
drink indeed of my cup, and be baptized
with the baptism that I am baptized with:
but to sit on my right hand,[1188] and on
my left, is not mine to [b]give, but *it shall
be given to them* for whom it [pfip]is prepared of my Father.
24 [a]And when the ten heard *it,* they
were moved with indignation against the
two brethren.
25 But Jesus called them *unto him,*
and said, Ye know that the princes[758] of
the Gentiles[1484] exercise dominion over
them, and they that are great exercise
authority upon them.
26 But [a]it shall not be so among you:
but [b]whosoever [psa]will[2309] be great
among you, [pim]let him be[2077] your minister;[1249]
27 [a]And whosoever [psa]will[2309] be
chief among you, [pim]let him be[2077] your
servant:
28 [a]Even as the [b]Son of man came
not [aifp]to be ministered unto, [c]but [ainf]to
minister, and [ainf][d]to give his life[5590] a
ransom[3083] [e]for[473] many.

Jesus Heals Two Blind Men (Mark 10:46–52; Luke 18:35–43)

29 [a]And as they [ppt]departed from
Jericho, a great multitude followed him.
30 And, behold, [a]two blind men sitting by the way side, when they heard
that Jesus passed by, cried out, saying,
Have mercy on us, O Lord, *thou* son of
David.
31 And the multitude rebuked them,
because they [aosb]should hold their peace:
but they [ipf]cried the more, saying, [aim]Have
mercy on us, O Lord, *thou* son of David.
32 And Jesus [apt]stood still, and called
them, and said, What will ye that I shall
do unto you?
33 They say unto him, Lord, that our
eyes [asbp]may be opened.
34 So Jesus [aptp]had compassion *on
them,* and touched their eyes: and immediately their eyes received sight,308 and
they followed him.

Jesus Enters Jerusalem (Mark 11:1–11; Luke 19:28–38; John 12:12–19)

21 And [a]when they drew nigh unto
Jerusalem, and were come to
Bethphage, unto [b]the mount of Olives,
then sent Jesus two disciples,
2 Saying unto them, Go into the village over against you, and straight-
way2112 ye shall find an ass tied, and a
colt with[3326] her: [apt]loose[3089] *them,* and
bring *them* unto me.
3 And if any *man* say ought unto
you, ye shall say, The Lord hath need of
them; and straightway he will send them.
4 All this [pfi]was done,[1096] that it
might be fulfilled[4137] which was spoken
by the prophet, saying,
5 [a]Tell ye the daughter of Sion,
Behold, thy king[935] cometh unto thee,
meek,[4239] and [pfp]sitting[1910] upon an ass,
and a colt the foal of an ass.
6 [a]And the disciples [aptp]went, and
[apt]did as Jesus commanded4367 them,
7 And brought the ass, and the colt,
and [a]put on them their clothes, and they
set *him* thereon.

19 [a]Matt. 27:2; Mark 15:1, 16; Luke 23:1; John 18:28-37; Acts 3:13

20 [a]Mark 10:35 [b]Matt. 4:21

21 [a]Matt. 19:28

22 [a]Matt. 26:39, 42; Mark 14:36; Luke 22:42; John 18:11 [b]Luke 12:50

23 [a]Acts 12:2; Rom. 8:17; 2Cor. 1:7; Rev. 1:9 [b]Matt. 25:34

24 [a]Mark 10:41; Luke 22:24, 25

26 [a]1Pet. 5:3 [b]Matt. 23:11; Mark 9:35; 10:43

27 [a]Matt. 18:4

28 [a]John 13:4 [b]Phil. 2:7 [c]Luke 22:27; John 13:14 [d]Isa. 53:10, 11; Dan. 9:24, 26; John 11:51, 52; 1Tim. 2:6; Titus 2:14; 1Pet. 1:19 [e]Matt. 26:28; Rom. 5:15, 19; Heb. 9:28

29 [a]Mark 10:46; Luke 18:35

30 [a]Matt. 9:27

1 [a]Mark 11:1; Luke 19:29 [b]Zech. 14:4

5 [a]Isa. 62:11; Zech. 9:9; John 12:15

6 [a]Mark 11:4

7 [a]2Kgs. 9:13

8 And a very great multitude[3793] spread their garments in the way; [a]others [ipf]cut down[2875] branches from the trees, and [ipf]strawed4766 *them* in the way.

9 And the multitudes that [ppt]went before,[4254] and that [ppt]followed,[190] [ipf]cried, saying, [a]Hosanna to the son of David: [b]Blessed[2127] *is* he that [ppt]cometh in the name of the Lord;[2962] Hosanna in the highest.

10 [a]And when he was come into Jerusalem, all the city was moved, saying, Who is this?

11 And the multitude [ipf]said, This is Jesus [a]the prophet[4396] of Nazareth of Galilee.

Jesus Cleanses the Temple (Mark 11:15–19; Luke 19:45–48)

12 [a]And Jesus went into the temple of God, and cast out all them that [ppt]sold and [ppt]bought in the temple,[2411] and overthrew the tables of the [b]moneychangers, and the seats of them that [ppt]sold doves,

13 And said unto them, [pfip]It is written, [a]My house shall be called the house[3624] of prayer; [b]but ye [ao]have made it a den of thieves.

14 And the blind and the lame came to him in the temple; and he healed them.

15 And when the chief priests and scribes saw the wonderful things[2297] that he did, and the children crying in the temple, and saying, Hosanna to the son of David; they were sore displeased,23

16 And said unto him, Hearest thou what these say? And Jesus saith unto them, Yea; [ao]have ye never read,[314] [a]Out of the mouth of babes[3516] and sucklings thou [aom]hast perfected[2675] praise?[136]

8 [a]Lev. 23:40; John 12:13
9 [a]Ps. 118:25 [b]Ps. 118:26; Matt. 23:39
10 [a]Mark 11:15; Luke 19:45; John 2:13, 15
11 [a]Matt. 2:23; Luke 7:16; John 6:14; 7:40; 9:17
12 [a]Mark 11:11; Luke 19:45; John 2:15 [b]Deut. 14:25
13 [a]Isa. 56:7 [b]Jer. 7:11; Mark 11:17; Luke 19:46
16 [a]Ps. 8:2
17 [a]Mark 11:11; John 11:18
18 [a]Mark 11:12
19 [l]Gr. *one fig tree* [a]Mark 11:13
20 [a]Mark 11:20
21 [a]Matt. 17:20; Luke 17:6 [b]James 1:6 [c]1Cor. 13:2
22 [a]Matt. 7:7; Mark 11:24; Luke 11:9; James 5:16; 1John 3:22; 5:14
23 [a]Mark 11:27; Luke 20:1 [b]Ex. 2:14; Acts 4:7; 7:27

17 And he [apt]left them, and went out of the city into [a]Bethany; and he lodged there.

Jesus and the Unfruitful Fig Tree (Mark 11:12–14, 20–24)

18 [a]Now in the morning as he [ppt]returned into the city, he hungered.3983

19 [a]And when he saw [l]a fig tree in the way, he came to it, and found nothing thereon, but leaves only, and [pin]said unto it, [asbm]Let no fruit grow[1096] on thee henceforward for ever. And presently the fig tree withered away.

20 [a]And when the disciples saw *it,* they marvelled, saying, How soon [aop]is the fig tree withered away3583

21 Jesus answered and said unto them, Verily281 I say unto you, [a]If ye have faith,[4102] and [asbp][b]doubt[1252] not, ye shall not only do this *which is done* to the fig tree, [c]but also if ye shall say unto this mountain, Be thou removed, and be thou cast into the sea; it shall be done.

22 And [a]all things, whatsoever ye [asba]shall ask in prayer, believing,[4100] ye shall receive.

The Chief Priests Enquire About Jesus' Authority (Mark 11:27–33; Luke 20:1–8)

23 [a]And when he was come into the temple, the chief priests and the elders of the people came unto him as he [ppt]was teaching, and [b]said, By what authority doest thou these things? and who gave thee this authority?

24 And Jesus answered and said unto them, I also will ask[2065] you one thing,

---

21:18–22 The Lord did not curse the barren tree because it failed to provide food for His hunger, but because it had leaves and no fruit. Fig trees in that area yield fruit in both June and August, and it is normal for the figs to hang on the trees through the winter. New fruit grows right over the old and out of the old shoots. Consequently, fruit can normally be found on the trees all year round. This particular fig tree is symbolic of Israel, which produced leaves but bore no fruit (Is. 63:7; 64:12; 65:3–7). The Lord was entering Jerusalem where He would experience his final public rejection by Israel. Despite the fact that Jesus had adequately demonstrated that He was indeed God incarnate, they still refused to accept Him as such (vv. 21, 22). The withering of the fig tree illustrates the result of the Jews as a people rejecting Christ as their Messiah.

which if ye [aosb]tell me, I in like wise will tell you by what authority I do these things.

25 The baptism[908] of John, whence was it? from heaven,[3772] or of men?[444] And they [ipf]reasoned with themselves, saying, If we shall say, From heaven; he will say unto us, Why did ye not then believe[4100] him?

26 But if we shall say, Of men; we fear[5399] the people; [a]for all hold John as a prophet.

27 And they answered Jesus, and said, We cannot tell. And he said unto them, Neither tell I you by what authority I do these things.

The Parable of the Two Sons

28 But what think ye? A *certain* man had two sons; and he [apt]came to the first, and said, Son, [aim]go [pim]work[2038] to day in my vineyard.

29 He answered and said, I will[2309] not: but afterward he [aptp]repented,[3338] and went.

30 And he [apt]came to the second, and said likewise. And he answered and said, I *go,* sir:[2962] and went not.

31 Whether of them twain 1417 did the will of *his* father? They say unto him, The first. Jesus saith unto them, [a]Verily I say unto you, That the publicans 5057 and the harlots go into[4254] the kingdom[932] of God before[4254] you.

32 For [a]John came unto you in the way[3598] of righteousness,[1343] and ye believed[4100] him not; [b]but the publicans and the harlots believed him: and ye, when ye [apt]had seen *it,* repented[3338] not afterward, that ye [infg]might believe him.

The Wicked Husbandmen (Mark 12:1–12; Luke 20:9–19)

33 [aim]Hear another parable: There was a certain householder, [a]which planted a vineyard, and hedged it round about, and digged a winepress in it, and built a tower, and let it out to husbandmen, 1092 and [b]went into a far country:

34 And when the time[2540] of the fruit drew near, he sent his servants to the husbandmen, [a]that they [ainf]might receive the fruits of it.

35 [a]And the husbandmen [apt]took his servants, and beat one, and killed another, and stoned another.

36 Again, he sent other servants more than the first: and they did unto them likewise.

37 But last of all he sent unto them his son, saying, They will reverence 1788 my son.

38 But when the husbandmen saw the son, they said among themselves, [a]This is the heir; [b]come, let us kill him, and [aosi]let us seize on[2722] his inheritance.[2817]

39 [a]And they [apt]caught him, and cast *him* out of the vineyard, and slew *him.*

40 When the lord[2962] therefore of the vineyard [aosb]cometh, what will he do unto those husbandmen?

41 [a]They say unto him, [b]He will miserably destroy those wicked men, [c]and will let out *his* vineyard unto other husbandmen, which shall render him the fruits in their seasons.[2540]

42 Jesus saith unto them, [a]Did ye never read in the scriptures,[1124] The stone which the builders rejected,[593] the same [aop]is become the head[2776] of the corner: this is the Lord's doing, and it is marvellous in our eyes?

43 Therefore say I unto you, [a]The kingdom of God shall be taken from you, and given to a nation bringing forth the fruits thereof.

44 And whosoever [apt][a]shall fall on this stone [fp]shall be broken: but on whomsoever it [asba]shall fall, [b]it [ft]will grind him to powder.

45 And when the chief priests and Pharisees [apt]had heard his parables, they perceived that he [pin]spake of them.

46 But when they [ppt]sought [ainf]to lay hands on him, they feared[5399] the multitude, because [a]they [ipf]took him for a prophet.

26 [a]Matt. 14:5; Mark 6:20; Luke 20:6

31 [a]Luke 7:29, 50

32 [a]Matt. 3:1-3 [b]Luke 3:12, 13

33 [a]Ps. 80:9; Song 8:11; Isa. 5:1; Jer. 2:21; Mark 12:1; Luke 20:9 [b]Matt. 25:14, 15

34 [a]Song 8:11, 12

35 [a]2Chr. 24:21; 36:16; Neh. 9:26; Matt. 5:12; 23:34, 37; Acts 7:52; 1Thess. 2:15; Heb. 11:36, 37

38 [a]Ps. 2:8; Heb. 1:2 [b]Ps. 2:2; Matt. 26:3; 27:1; John 11:53; Acts 4:27

39 [a]Matt. 26:50-56; Mark 14:46-49; Luke 22:54-62; John 18:12-14; Acts 2:23

41 [a]Luke 20:16 [b]Luke 21:24; Heb. 2:3 [c]Acts 13:46; 15:7; 18:6; 28:28

42 [a]Ps. 118:22; Isa. 28:16; Mark 12:10; Luke 20:17; Acts 4:11; Eph. 2:20; 1Pet. 2:6, 7

43 [a]Matt. 8:12

44 [a]Isa. 8:14, 15; Zech. 12:3; Luke 20:18; Rom. 9:33; 1Pet. 2:8 [b]Isa. 60:12; Dan. 2:44

46 [a]Matt. 21:11; Luke 7:16; John 7:40

The Wedding Banquet (Luke 14:15–24)

22 🔑And Jesus answered[611] [a]and spake unto them again by parables,[3850] and said,

2 The kingdom[932] of heaven is like unto a certain king, which made a marriage[1062] for his son.

3 And sent forth his servants to call them [pfpp]that were bidden[2564] to the wedding:[1062] and they [ipf]would not [ainf]come.[2064]

4 Again, he sent forth other servants, saying, Tell them which [pfpp]are bidden, Behold, I [ao]have prepared my dinner: [a]my oxen and *my* fatlings *are* killed,[2380] and all things *are* ready: come unto the marriage.[1062]

5 But they [apt]made light of *it,* and went their ways, one to his farm, another to his merchandise:

6 And the remnant [apt]took his servants, and [ao]entreated *them* spitefully,[5195] and slew *them.*

7 But when the king heard *thereof,* he was wroth:[3710] and he [apt]sent forth [a]his armies, and destroyed those murderers,[5406] and burned up their city.

8 Then saith he to his servants, The wedding is ready, but they which [pfpp]were bidden were not [a]worthy.

9 Go ye therefore into the highways, and as many as ye shall find, bid to the marriage.[1062]

10 So those servants [apt]went out into the highways,[3598] and [a]gathered together all as many as they found, both bad[4190] and good:[18] and the wedding was furnished with [ppt]guests.

11 And when the king came in to see the guests, he saw there a man [a]which [pfpp]had not on a wedding garment:

12 And he saith unto him, Friend, how camest thou in hither not having[2192] a wedding garment? And he was speechless.

13 Then said the king to the servants, Bind[1210] him hand and foot, and take him away,[142] and cast *him* [a]into outer darkness;[4655] there [fm]shall be weeping and gnashing[1030] of teeth.

14 [a]For many are called,[2822] but few *are* chosen.

Jesus and Taxes (Mark 12:13–17; Luke 20:20–26)

15 [a]Then [apt]went the Pharisees, and took counsel how they might entangle him in *his* talk.[3056]

16 And they [pin]sent out unto him their disciples with the Herodians, saying, Master, we know that thou art true, and teachest the way[3598] of God in truth,[225] neither carest thou for any *man:* for thou regardest not the person[4383] of men.

17 Tell us therefore, What thinkest thou? Is it lawful to give tribute unto Caesar, or not?

18 But Jesus [apt]perceived their wickedness,[4189] and said, Why tempt[3985] ye me, *ye* hypocrites?

19 Shew me the tribute money. And they brought unto him a penny.

20 And he saith unto them, Whose *is* this image[1504] and superscription?

21 They say unto him, Caesar's. Then saith he unto them, [a]Render therefore unto Caesar the things which are Caesar's; and unto God the things that are God's.

22 When they had heard *these words,* they marvelled, and [apt]left him, and went their way.

Questions Concerning the Resurrection (Mark 12:18–27; Luke 20:27–40)

23 [a]The same day came to him the Sadducees, [b]which [ppt]say that there is no resurrection,[386] and asked[1905] him,

24 Saying, Master, [a]Moses said, If a man die,[599] having no children, his brother shall marry his wife, and raise up[450] seed[4690] unto his brother.

1 [a]Luke 14:16; Rev. 19:7, 9
4 [a]Prov. 9:2
7 [a]Dan. 9:26; Luke 19:27
8 [a]Matt. 10:11, 13; Acts 13:46
10 [a]Matt. 13:38, 47
11 [a]2Cor. 5:3; Eph. 4:24; Col. 3:10, 12; Rev. 3:4; 16:15; 19:8
13 [a]Matt. 8:12
14 [a]Matt. 20:16
15 [a]Mark 12:13; Luke 20:20
21 [a]Matt. 17:25; Rom. 13:7
23 [a]Mark 12:18; Luke 20:27 [b]Acts 23:8
24 [a]Deut. 25:5

🔑 **22:1–14** See note on Matthew 8:11, 12.

25 Now there were with us seven brethren: and the first, when he had married a wife, deceased, and, having no issue,[4690] left his wife unto his brother:

26 Likewise the second also, and the third, unto the seventh.

27 And last of all the woman died[599] also.

28 Therefore in the resurrection whose wife shall she be of the seven? for they all had her.

29 Jesus answered and said unto them, Ye do err, [a]not knowing the scriptures,[1124] nor the power of God.

30 For in the resurrection they neither marry, nor are given in marriage, but [a]are as the angels[32] of God in heaven.[3772]

31 But as touching the resurrection of the dead, [ao]have ye not read[314] that which was spoken unto you by God, saying,

32 [a]I am the God of Abraham, and the God of Isaac, and the God of Jacob? [art]God is not the [an]God of the [an]dead, but of the [an]living.

33 And when the multitude heard *this,* [a]they were astonished at his doctrine.

The Great Commandment (Mark 12:28–34; Luke 10:25–28)

34 [a]But when the Pharisees had heard that he [ao]had put the Sadducees to silence, they [aop]were gathered together.

35 Then one of them, *which was* a [a]lawyer,[3544] asked *him a question,* tempting[3985] him, and saying,

36 Master, which *is* the great commandment in the law?

37 Jesus said unto him, [a]Thou [ft]shalt love the Lord thy God with all thy heart, and with all thy soul,[5590] and with all thy mind.[1271]

38 This is the first and great commandment.

39 And the second *is* like[3664] unto it, [a]Thou [ft]shalt love thy neighbour[4139] as thyself.

40 [a]On these two commandments hang all the law and the prophets.

David's Lord (Mark 12:35–37; Luke 20:41–44)

41 [a]While the Pharisees were gathered together, Jesus asked[1905] them,

42 Saying, What think ye of Christ? whose son is he? They say unto him, *The son* of David.

43 He saith unto them, How then doth David in spirit call him Lord, saying,

44 [a]The LORD said unto my Lord, Sit thou on my right hand,[1188] till I [aosb]make thine enemies thy footstool?

45 If David then [pin]call him Lord, how is he his son?

46 [a]And no man was able to answer him a word, [b]neither durst any *man* from that day forth [ainf]ask[1905] him any more *questions.*

Jesus Condemns the Scribes And Pharisees (Mark 12:38–40; Luke 11:37–52; 20:45–47)

23 Then spake Jesus to the multitude, and to his disciples,

2 Saying, [a]The scribes[1122] and the Pharisees [ao]sit in Moses' seat:

3 All therefore whatsoever they [aosb]bid you [pinf]observe, *that* [pim]observe[5083] and [pim]do; but[1161] [pim]do not ye after their works: for [a]they say, and do not.

4 [a]For they bind heavy burdens[5413] and grievous to be borne, and lay *them* on men's shoulders; but they *themselves* will not [ainf]move them with one of their fingers.

5 But [a]all their works they do for [aipr]to be seen of men: [b]they make broad their phylacteries,[5440] and enlarge the borders of their garments,

6 [a]And love[5368] the uppermost rooms at feasts, and the chief seats in the synagogues,

7 And greetings in the markets,[58] and [pip]to be called of men, Rabbi, Rabbi.

8 [a]But [aosi]be not ye called[2564] Rabbi: for one is your Master,[2519] *even* Christ; and all ye are brethren.[80]

9 And call no *man* your father[3962]

29 [a]John 20:9
30 [a]1John 3:2
32 [a]Ex. 3:6, 16; Mark 12:26; Luke 20:37; Acts 7:32; Heb. 11:16
33 [a]Matt. 7:28
34 [a]Mark 12:28
35 [a]Luke 10:25
37 [a]Deut. 6:5; 10:12; 30:6; Luke 10:27
39 [a]Lev. 19:18; Matt. 19:19; Mark 12:31; Luke 10:27; Ro 13:9; Gal. 5:14; James 2:8
40 [a]Matt. 7:12; 1Tim. 1:5
41 [a]Mark 12:35; Luke 20:41
44 [a]Ps. 110:1; Acts 2:34; 1Cor. 15:25; Heb. 1:13; 10:12, 13
46 [a]Luke 14:6 [b]Mark 12:34; Luke 20:40
2 [a]Neh. 8:4, 8; Mal. 2:7; Mark 12:38; Luke 20:45
3 [a]Rom. 2:17-24
4 [a]Luke 11:46; Acts 15:10; Gal. 6:13
5 [a]Matt. 6:1, 2, 5, 16 [b]Num. 15:38; Deut. 6:8; 22:12; Prov. 3:3
6 [a]Mark 12:38, 39; Luke 11:43; 20:46; 3John 1:9
8 [a]James 3:1; 2Cor. 1:24; 1Pet. 5:3

upon the earth:[1093] [a]for one is your Father, which is in heaven.

10 Neither [aosi]be ye called[2564] masters:[2519] for one is your Master,[2519] *even* Christ.

11 But [a]he that is greatest among you shall be your servant.

12 [a]And whosoever shall exalt himself shall be abased;[5013] and he that shall humble himself shall be exalted.

13 But [a]woe unto you, scribes[1122] and Pharisees, hypocrites! for ye shut up the kingdom[932] of heaven against men: for ye neither go in *yourselves,* neither suffer[863] ye them that are entering to go in.

14 Woe unto you, scribes and Pharisees, hypocrites! [a]for ye devour widows' houses,[3614] and for a pretence [ppt]make long prayer: therefore ye shall receive the greater[4055] damnation.[2917]

15 Woe unto you, scribes and Pharisees, hypocrites! for ye compass sea[2281] and land [ainf]to make[4160] one proselyte,[4339] and when he is made, ye make him twofold more the child[5207] of hell[1067] than yourselves.

16 Woe unto you, [a]*ye* blind guides, which say, [b]Whosoever shall swear by the temple, it is nothing; but whosoever shall swear by the gold of the temple, he is a debtor!

17 *Ye* fools and blind: for whether is greater, the gold, [a]or the temple that [ppt]sanctifieth the gold?

18 And, Whosoever [aosb]shall swear by the altar, it is nothing; but whosoever [aosb]sweareth by the gift[1435] that is upon it, he is [I]guilty.

19 *Ye* fools and blind: for whether *is* greater, the gift, or [a]the altar that sanctifieth the gift?

20 Whoso therefore [apt]shall swear by the altar, sweareth by it, and by all things thereon.

21 And whoso [apt]shall swear by the temple, sweareth by it, and by [a]him that [ppt]dwelleth[2730] therein.

22 And he that [apt]shall swear by heaven, sweareth by [a]the throne of God, and by him that [ppt]sitteth thereon.

23 Woe unto you, scribes and Pharisees, hypocrites! [a]for ye pay tithe of mint and [I]anise[432] and cummin, and [ao][b]have omitted the weightier *matters* of the law,[3551] judgment,[2920] mercy,[1656] and faith:[4102] these ought ye [ainf]to have done, and not [pinf]to leave[863] the other undone.

24 *Ye* blind guides, which [ppt]strain at a gnat, and [ppt]swallow a camel.

25 Woe unto you, scribes and Pharisees, hypocrites! [a]for ye make clean[2511] the outside of the cup and of the platter, but within they are full of extortion[724] and excess.

26 *Thou* blind Pharisee, [aim]cleanse first that *which is* within the cup and platter, that the outside of them [aosb]may be clean also.

27 Woe unto you, scribes and Pharisees, hypocrites! [a]for ye are like unto whited sepulchres,[5028] which indeed appear beautiful[5611] outward, but are within full of dead *men's* bones, and of all uncleanness.[167]

28 Even so ye also outwardly appear[5316] righteous[1342] unto men, but within ye are full of hypocrisy and iniquity.[458]

29 [a]Woe unto you, scribes and Pharisees, hypocrites! because ye build the tombs of the prophets, and garnish[2885] the sepulchres[3419] of the righteous,

30 And say, If we had been in the days[2250] of our fathers,[3962] we would not have been partakers[2844] with them in the blood[129] of the prophets.

31 Wherefore ye be witnesses[3140] unto yourselves, that [a]ye are the children[5207] of them which [apt]killed the prophets.

32 [aim][a]Fill ye up[4137] then the measure of your fathers.[3962]

33 *Ye* serpents, *ye* [a]generation of vipers, how [asba]can ye escape[5343] the damnation[2920] of hell?[1067]

34 [a]Wherefore, behold, I send unto you prophets, and wise men,[4680] and scribes:[1122] and [b]*some* of them ye [ft]shall kill and crucify;[4717] and [c]*some* of them [ft]shall ye scourge[3146] in your synagogues, and persecute *them* from city to city:

9 [a]Mal. 1:6
11 [a]Matt. 20:26, 27
12 [a]Job 22:29; Prov. 15:33; 29:23; Luke 14:11; 18:14; James 4:6; 1Pet. 5:5
13 [a]Luke 11:52
14 [a]Mark 12:40; Luke 20:47; 2Tim. 3:6; Titus 1:11
16 [a]Matt. 15:14; 23:24 [b]Matt. 5:33, 34
17 [a]Ex. 30:29
18 [I]Or, *debtor,* or, *bound*
19 [a]Ex. 29:37
21 [a]1Kgs. 8:13; 2Chr. 6:2; Ps. 26:8; 132:14
22 [a]Ps. 11:4; Matt. 5:34; Acts 7:49
23 [I]Gr. *dill* [a]Luke 11:42 [b]1Sam. 15:22; Hos. 6:6; Mic. 6:8; Matt. 9:13; 12:7
25 [a]Mark 7:4; Luke 11:39
27 [a]Luke 11:44; Acts 23:3
29 [a]Luke 11:47
31 [a]Acts 7:51, 52; 1Thess. 2:15
32 [a]Gen. 15:16; 1Thess. 2:16
33 [a]Matt. 3:7; 12:34
34 [a]Matt. 21:34, 35; Luke 11:49 [b]Acts 5:40; 7:58, 59; 22:19 [c]Matt. 10:17; 2Cor. 11:24, 25

35 [a]That upon you may come all the
righteous blood[129] [ppt]shed upon the earth,
[b]from the blood of righteous Abel unto
[c]the blood of Zacharias son of Barachias,
whom ye slew between the temple and
the altar.
36 Verily[281] I say unto you, All these
things shall come upon this generation.

Christ Weeps Over Jerusalem (Luke 13:34, 35)

37 [a]O Jerusalem, Jerusalem, *thou* that
[ppt]killest the prophets, [b]and [ppt]stonest
them which [pfpp]are sent unto thee, how
often [ao]would[2309] [c]I [ainf]have gathered thy
children together,[1996] even as a hen
gathereth[1996] her chickens [d]under *her*
wings, and ye [ao]would not!
38 Behold, your house is left unto
you desolate.
39 For I say unto you, Ye shall [efn]not
see me henceforth, till ye shall say,
[a]Blessed[2127] *is* he that cometh in the
[an]name of the [an]Lord.

The Destruction of the Temple And the Last Days (Mark 13:1, 2; Luke 21:5, 6)

24 And [a]Jesus went out, and departed from the temple:[2411] and
his disciples came to *him* for to shew
him the buildings[3619] of the temple.
2 And Jesus said unto them, See ye
not all these things? verily[281] I say unto
you, [a]There [asbp]shall not be left[863] here
one stone upon another, that [fp]shall not
be thrown down.[2647]

Coming Woes (Mark 13:3–13; Luke 21:7–19)

3 And as he sat upon the mount of
Olives, [a]the disciples came unto him privately, saying, [b]Tell us, when shall these
things be? and what *shall be* the sign of
thy coming, and of the end[4930] of the
world?
4 And Jesus answered and said unto
them, [pim][a]Take heed[991] that no man
[aosb]deceive you.
5 For [a]many shall come in my
name,[3686] saying, I am Christ; [b]and shall
deceive many.
6 And ye shall hear of wars and rumours of wars:[4171] [pim]see that ye be not
troubled: for all *these things* must come
to pass,[1096] but the end is not yet.
7 For [a]nation[1484] shall rise[1453]
against nation, and kingdom against
kingdom: and there shall be famines,[3042]
and pestilences, and earthquakes, in
divers places.[2596] [5117]

35 [a]Rev. 18:24 [b]Gen. 4:8; 1John 3:12 [c]2Chr. 24:20, 21
37 [a]Luke 13:34 [b]2Chr. 24:21 [c]Deut. 32:11, 12 [d]Ps. 17:8; 91:4
39 [a]Ps. 118:26; Matt. 21:9
1 [a]Mark 13:1; Luke 21:5
2 [a]1Kgs. 9:7; Jer. 26:18; Mic. 3:12; Luke 19:44
3 [a]Mark 13:3 [b]1Thess. 5:1
4 [a]Eph. 5:6; Col. 2:8, 18; 2Thess. 2:3; 1John 4:1
5 [a]Jer. 14:14; 23:21, 25; Matt. 24:24; John 5:43 [b]Matt. 24:11
7 [a]2Chr. 15:6; Isa. 19:2; Hag. 2:22; Zech. 14:13

24:3 See note on 1 Thessalonians 2:19.

24:4—25:46 This passage is known as the Olivet Discourse. Jesus begins this discourse in response to the disciples' questions in verse three. Their first inquiry was an attempt to ascertain when the destruction of the temple in Jerusalem, of which Christ had spoken (Matt. 24:3, cf. vv. 1, 2), would take place. Their second query concerned Christ's Second Coming and the end of the world. Some scholars feel that Jesus only responded to this second question.

There are two different views on how this passage relates to end time events. Some theologians suggest that this entire portion of Matthew relates exclusively to eschatological events. They propose that chapter twenty-four should be divided into four parts: the first half of the Great Tribulation (vv. 4–14), the second half of the Tribulation (vv. 15–28), the signs of Christ's coming (vv. 29–31), and the illustrations of the sudden end of the world (vv. 32–51). They also suggest that chapter twenty-five is an exhortation to God's people to be watchful for the coming of the events previously mentioned in chapter twenty-four.

On the other hand, there are those who believe that not all of the things Christ mentioned in these two chapters necessarily refer to eschatological events. These people suggest that chapter twenty-four opens with a general description of the events that will mark the end of the world (vv. 4–14), revealing the deceit and rampant sin that will be evident on the earth. Then, they propose that Christ sets forth the signs that will precede the end of the world (vv. 15–28). These "signs" are divided into two categories: Jerusalem's destruction (vv. 15–22) and God's restrained judgment

(continued on next page)

8 All these *are* the beginning of sorrows.[5604]

9 [a]Then shall they deliver you up to be [nn]afflicted, and shall kill you: and ye shall be hated of all nations for my name's sake.

10 And then shall many [a]be offended, and shall betray one another, and shall hate one another.

11 And [a]many false prophets shall rise, and [b]shall deceive many.

12 And because iniquity[458] shall abound, the love of many shall wax cold.[5594]

13 [a]But he that [apt]shall endure[5278] unto the end,[5056] the same shall be saved.[4982]

14 And this [a]gospel[2098] of the kingdom[932] [b]shall be preached[2784] in all the world[3625] for a witness unto all nations; and then shall the end come.

The Great Tribulation (Mark 13:14–23; Luke 21:20–24)

15 [a]When ye therefore shall see the abomination[946] of desolation, spoken of by [b]Daniel the prophet, stand in the holy[40] place, ([c]whoso [ppt]readeth, let him understand:[3539])

16 Then let them which be in Judaea flee into the mountains:

17 Let him which is on the housetop not come down to take any thing out of his house:

18 Neither let him which is in the field [aim]return[1994] back [ainf]to take his clothes.

19 And [a]woe unto them that [ppt]are with child, and to them that [ppt]give suck in those days!

20 But [pim]pray[4336] ye that your flight be not in the winter, neither on the sabbath day:[4521]

21 For [a]then shall be great tribulation,[2347] such as [pfi]was not since the beginning of the world to this time, no, [efn]nor ever shall be.

22 And except those days should be shortened, there should no flesh[4561] [aop]be saved: [a]but for the elect's[1588] sake those days shall be shortened.

23 [a]Then if any man shall say unto you, Lo, here *is* Christ, or there; [aosi]believe *it* not.

24 For [a]there shall arise[1453] false Christs,[5580] and false prophets, and shall shew great signs and wonders; insomuch that, [b]if *it were* possible, they [ainf]shall deceive the very elect.

25 Behold, I have told you before.

26 Wherefore if they [asba]shall say unto you, Behold, he is in the desert; go not forth: behold, *he is* in the secret chambers; [aosi]believe *it* not.

27 [a]For as the lightning cometh out of the east, and shineth[5316] even unto the west; so shall also the coming[3952] of the Son of man be.

28 [a]For wheresoever the carcase is, there will the eagles be gathered together.

Christ Is Coming Again (Mark 13:24–27; Luke 21:25–28)

29 [a]Immediately after the tribulation of those days [b]shall the sun be darkened, and the moon shall not give her light,[5338] and the stars shall fall from heaven, and the powers of the heavens shall be shaken:

30 [a]And then shall appear the sign of the Son of man in heaven:[3772] [b]and then shall all the tribes of the earth mourn,

9 [a]Matt. 10:17; Mark 13:9; Luke 21:12; John 15:20; 16:2; Acts 4:2, 3; 7:59; 12:1-4; 1Pet. 4:16; Rev. 2:10, 13
10 [a]Matt. 11:6; 13:57; 2Tim. 1:15; 4:10, 16
11 [a]Matt. 7:15; Acts 20:29; 2Pet. 2:1 [b]1Tim. 4:1
13 [a]Matt. 10:22; Mark 13:13; Heb. 3:6, 14; Rev. 2:10
14 [a]Matt. 4:23; 9:35 [b]Rom. 10:18; Col. 1:6, 23
15 [a]Mark 13:14; Luke 21:20 [b]Dan. 9:27; 12:11 [c]Dan. 9:23, 25
19 [a]Luke 23:29
21 [a]Dan. 9:26; 12:1; Joel 2:2
22 [a]Isa. 65:8, 9; Zech. 14:2, 3
23 [a]Mark 13:21; Luke 17:23; 21:8
24 [a]Deut. 13:1; Matt. 24:5, 11; 2Thess. 2:9, 10, 11; Rev. 13:13 [b]John 6:37; 10:28, 29; Rom. 8:28, 29, 30; 2Tim. 2:19
27 [a]Luke 17:24
28 [a]Job 39:30; Luke 17:37
29 [a]Dan. 7:11, 12 [b]Isa. 13:10; Ezek. 32:7; Joel 2:10, 31; 3:15; Amos 5:20; 8:9; Mark 13:24; Luke 21:25; Acts 2:20; Rev. 6:12
30 [a]Dan. 7:13 [b]Zech. 12:12

(continued from previous page)
on the earth during the Church Age (vv. 23–28). This chapter closes with the fulfillment of the events that mark the end of the world, as well as Christ's gathering of His people and the Battle of Armageddon (vv. 29–44, cf. Rev. 19:11–21). The proponents of this view also hold that Matthew 24:45—25:46 gives the details regarding the future judgment of the visible church (24:45–51) and of mankind (25:1–46).

24:15 See notes on 2 Thessalonians 2:3–8 and Revelation 13:1–18.

24:22, 31 See notes on Ephesians 1:4, 5 and 1 Thessalonians 2:19.

[c]and they shall see the Son of man coming in the clouds of heaven with[3326]
power and great glory.[1391]
31 [a]And he shall send his angels
[I]with[3326] a great sound[5456] of a trumpet,
and they shall gather together[1996] his
elect from the four winds, from one [pl]end
of heaven to the [pl]other.

The Lesson of the Fig Tree (Mark 13:28–31; Luke 21:29–33)

32 Now [aim]learn [a]a parable[3850] of the
fig tree; When his branch [asbm]is yet tender, and [psa]putteth forth leaves, ye know
that summer *is* nigh:[1451]
33 So likewise ye, when ye shall see
all these things, know [a]that [I]it is near,[1451]
even at the doors.
34 Verily I say unto you, [a]This
generation[1074] shall [efn]not pass, till all
these things be fulfilled.
35 [art][a]Heaven and [art]earth[1093] [fm]shall
pass away, but my words shall [efn]not
pass away.

The Time of Christ's Coming Is Unknown (Mark 13:32–37; Luke 17:26–30, 34–36)

36 [a]But of that day and hour
knoweth no *man,* no, not the angels[32] of
heaven, [b]but my Father[3962] only.
37 But as the days of Noe *were,* so
shall also the coming[3952] of the Son of
man be.
38 [a]For as in the days that were before the flood they were [ppt]eating and
[ppt]drinking, [ppt]marrying and [ppt]giving in
marriage, until the day that Noe entered
into the ark,
39 And knew not until the flood
came, and took them all away; so shall
also the coming[3952] of the Son of man
be.
40 [a]Then shall two be in the field;
the one [pinp]shall be taken,[3880] and the
other [pinp]left.
41 Two *women shall be* [ppt]grinding at
the mill; the one [pinp]shall be taken,[3880]
and the other [pinp]left.
42 [pim][a]Watch therefore: for ye know
not what hour your Lord doth come.
43 [a]But know this, that if the goodman of the house[3617] had known in what
watch the thief[2812] [pin]would come, he
would have watched, and [ao]would not
have suffered[302][1439] his house [aifp]to be broken up.
44 [a]Therefore [pim]be ye also ready: for
in such an hour as ye think not the Son
of man cometh.

Faithful and Unfaithful Servants (Luke 12:41–48)

45 [a]Who then is a faithful and
wise[5429] servant,[1401] whom his lord
[ao]hath made ruler[2525] over his household,[2322] to give them meat in due
season?[2540]
46 [a]Blessed[3107] *is* that servant, whom
his lord when he [apt]cometh shall find so
doing.
47 Verily I say unto you, That [a]he
shall make him ruler[2525] over all his
goods.[5224]
48 But and if that evil servant shall
say in his heart, My lord delayeth his
[ainf]coming;
49 And shall begin [pinf]to smite[5180] *his*
fellowservants,[4889] and [pinf]to eat and
[pinf]drink with the [ppt]drunken;
50 The lord of that servant shall
come in a day when he looketh[4328] not
for *him,* and in an hour that he is not
aware of,
51 And shall [I]cut him asunder, and
appoint[5087] *him* his portion with the hypocrites: [a]there shall be weeping and
gnashing[1030] of teeth.

The Ten Virgins

25 Then shall the kingdom[932] of
heaven be likened unto ten vir-

30 [c]Matt. 16:27; Mark 13:26; Rev. 1:7
31 [I]Or, *with a trumpet, and a great voice* [a]Matt. 13:41; 1Cor. 15:52; 1Thess. 4:16
32 [a]Luke 21:29
33 [I]Or, *he* [a]James 5:9
34 [a]Matt. 16:28; 23:36; Mark 13:30; Luke 21:32
35 [a]Ps. 102:26; Isa. 51:6; Jer. 31:35, 36; Matt. 5:18; Mark 13:31; Luke 21:33; Heb. 1:11
36 [a]Mark 13:32; Acts 1:7; 1Thess. 5:2; 2Pet. 3:10 [b]Zech. 14:7
38 [a]Gen. 6:3, 4, 5; 7:5; Luke 17:26; 1Pet. 3:20
40 [a]Luke 17:34-37
42 [a]Matt. 25:13; Mark 13:32-37; Luke 21:36
43 [a]Luke 12:39; 1Thess. 5:2; 2Pet. 3:10; Rev. 3:3; 16:15
44 [a]Matt. 25:13; 1Thess. 5:6
45 [a]Luke 12:42; Acts 20:28; 1Cor. 4:2; Heb. 3:5
46 [a]Rev. 16:15
47 [a]Matt. 25:21, 23; Luke 22:29
51 [I]Or, *cut him off* [a]Matt. 8:12; 25:30

24:36 See note on Philippians 2:6–8.

gins,3933 which [apt]took their lamps, and went forth to meet [a]the bridegroom.

2 [a]And five of them were wise,[5429] and five *were* foolish.

3 They that *were* foolish [apt]took their lamps, and took no oil with them:

4 But the wise took oil in their vessels with their lamps.

5 While the bridegroom [ppt]tarried, [a]they all slumbered and [ipf]slept.

6 And at midnight[3319,3571] [a]there [pfi]was a cry made, Behold, the bridegroom cometh; go ye out to meet him.

7 Then all those virgins arose, and [a]trimmed their lamps.

8 And the foolish said unto the wise, Give us of your oil; for our lamps [pin]are [I]gone out.

9 But the wise answered, saying, *Not so;* lest there be not enough for us and you: but [pim]go ye rather to them that [ppt]sell, and [aim]buy for yourselves.

10 And while they went to buy, the bridegroom came; and they that were ready went in with him to the marriage:[1062] and [a]the door was shut.

11 Afterward [pin]came also the other virgins, saying, [a]Lord, Lord, open to us.

12 But he answered and said, Verily281 I say unto you, [a]I know[1492] you not.

13 [pim][a]Watch therefore, for ye know neither the day nor the hour wherein the Son of man cometh.

The Talents
(Luke 19:11–27)

🗝 14 [a]For *the kingdom of heaven is* [b]as a man travelling into a far country, *who* called[2564] his own servants, and delivered unto them his goods.

15 And unto one he gave five talents, to another two, and to another one; [a]to every man according to his several ability; and straightway2112 took his journey.

16 Then he that had received the five talents [apt]went and traded[2038] with the same, and made *them* other five talents.

17 And likewise he that *had received* two, he also gained other two.

18 But he that had received one went and digged in the earth,[1093] and hid his lord's money.

19 After a long time[5550] the lord of those servants cometh, and reckoneth with them.

20 And so he that had received five talents [apt]came and brought other five talents, saying, Lord, thou deliveredst unto me five talents: behold, I have gained beside them five talents more.

21 His lord said unto him, Well done,[2095] *thou* good[18] and faithful[4103] servant: thou hast been faithful[4103] over a few things, [a]I will make thee ruler[2525] over many things: enter thou into [b]the joy[5479] of thy lord.

22 He also that had received two talents [apt]came and said, Lord, thou deliveredst unto me two talents: behold, I have gained two other talents beside them.

23 His lord said unto him, [a]Well done,[2095] good and faithful[4103] servant; thou hast been faithful over a few things, I will make thee ruler[2525] over many things: enter thou into the joy[5479] of thy lord.

24 Then he which had received the one talent [apt]came and said, Lord, I knew thee that thou art an hard[4642] man, reaping where thou [ao]hast not sown,4687 and gathering where thou [ao]hast not strawed:1287

25 And I [aptp]was afraid, and [apt]went and hid thy talent in the earth: lo, *there* thou hast *that is* thine.

26 His lord answered and said unto him, *Thou* wicked[4190] and slothful servant, thou knewest that I reap where I sowed not, and gather where I [ao]have not strawed:1287

27 Thou [ipf]oughtest[1163] therefore to have put my money to the exchangers, and *then* at my [apt]coming I should have received mine own with usury.

28 Take therefore the talent from

1 [a]Eph. 5:29, 30; Rev. 19:7; 21:2, 9
2 [a]Matt. 13:47; 22:10
5 [a]1Thess. 5:6
6 [a]Matt. 24:31; 1Thess. 4:16
7 [a]Luke 12:35
8 [I]Or, *going out*
10 [a]Luke 13:25
11 [a]Matt. 7:21-23
12 [a]Ps. 5:5; Hab. 1:13; John 9:31
13 [a]Matt. 24:42, 44; Mark 13:33, 35; Luke 21:36; 1Cor. 16:13; 1Thess. 5:6; 1Pet. 5:8; Rev. 16:15
14 [a]Luke 19:12 [b]Matt. 21:33
15 [a]Rom. 12:6; 1Cor. 12:7, 11, 29; Eph. 4:11
21 [a]Matt. 24:47; 25:34, 46; Luke 12:44; 22:29, 30 [b]2Tim. 2:12; Heb. 12:2; 1Pet. 1:8
23 [a]Matt. 25:21

🗝 **25:14–30** See notes on Matthew 8:11, 12 and Luke 19:11–27.

him, and give *it* unto him which [ppt]hath ten talents.

29 [a]For unto every one that hath shall be given, and he shall have abundance: but from him that [ppt]hath not shall be taken away even that which he hath.

30 And [aim]cast ye the unprofitable[888] servant [a]into [art]outer darkness:[4655] there shall be weeping and gnashing[1030] of teeth.

Concerning the Future Judgment

31 [a]When the Son of man shall come in his glory,[1391] and all the holy angels with him, then shall he sit upon the throne of his glory:

32 And [a]before him shall be gathered all nations:[1484] and [b]he shall separate[873] them one from another, as a shepherd[4166] divideth *his* sheep from the goats:

33 And he shall set the sheep on his right hand,[1188] but the goats on the left.

34 Then shall the King[935] say unto them on his right hand, Come, ye blessed[2127] of my Father, [aim][a]inherit[2816] the kingdom [b]prepared for you from the foundation[2602] of the world:

35 [a]For I was an hungred,[3983] and ye gave me meat: I was thirsty, and ye gave me drink: [b]I was a stranger, and ye [ao]took me in:[4863]

36 [a]Naked,[1131] and ye clothed me: I was sick,[770] and ye visited[1980] me: [b]I was in prison, and ye came unto me.

37 Then shall the righteous[1342] answer him, saying, Lord, when saw we thee [ppt]an hungred,[3983] and fed *thee?* or [ppt]thirsty, and gave *thee* drink?

38 When saw we thee a stranger, and took *thee* in? or naked, and clothed *thee?*

39 Or when saw we thee sick,[772] or in prison, and came unto thee?

40 And the King[935] shall [apt]answer and say unto them, Verily I say unto you, [a]Inasmuch as ye have done *it* unto one of the least of these my brethren,[80] ye [ao]have done *it* unto me.

41 Then shall he say also unto them on the left hand, [pim][a]Depart from me, ye cursed,[2672] [b]into [art]everlasting fire, prepared for [c]the devil and his angels:[32]

42 For I [ao]was an hungred,[3983] and ye gave me no [ainf]meat: I [ao]was thirsty, and ye gave me no drink:

43 I was a stranger, and ye [ao]took me not in:[4863] naked,[1131] and ye clothed me not: sick, and in prison, and ye visited[1980] me not.

44 Then shall they also answer him, saying, Lord, when saw we thee [ppt]an hungred,[3983] or [ppt]athirst, or a stranger, or naked, or sick, or in prison, and did not minister unto[1247] thee?

45 Then shall he answer them, saying, Verily I say unto you, [a]Inasmuch as ye did *it* not to one of the least of these, ye did *it* not to me.

46 And [a]these shall go away into everlasting punishment:[2851] but the righteous[1342] into life[2222] eternal.

The Leaders Plot to Kill Jesus (Mark 14:1, 2; Luke 22:1, 2; John 11:45–53)

26 And it came to pass, when Jesus had finished all these sayings,[3056] he said unto his disciples,

2 [a]Ye know that after two days is *the feast of* the passover,[3957] and the Son of man is betrayed to be crucified.[4717]

3 [a]Then assembled together[4863] the chief priests, and the scribes, and the elders[4245] of the people, unto the palace of the high priest, who was called Caiaphas,

4 And consulted that they might take Jesus by subtilty, and kill *him.*

5 But they said, Not on the feast *day,* lest there be an uproar among the people.[2992]

Jesus Anointed at Bethany (Mark 14:3–9; John 12:1–8)

6 [a]Now when Jesus was[1096] in [b]Bethany, in the house of Simon the leper,

7 There came unto him a woman having an alabaster box of very precious ointment, and poured it on his head, as he [ppt]sat *at meat.*

29 [a]Matt. 13:12; Mark 4:25; Luke 8:18; 19:26; John 15:2
30 [a]Matt. 8:12; 24:51
31 [a]Zech. 14:5; Matt. 16:27; 19:28; Mark 8:38; Acts 1:11; 1Thess. 4:16; 2Thess. 1:7; Jude 1:14; Rev. 1:7
32 [a]Rom. 14:10; 2Cor. 5:10; Rev. 20:12 [b]Ezek. 20:38; 34:17, 20; Matt. 13:49
34 [a]Rom. 8:17; 1Pet. 1:4, 9; 3:9; Rev. 21:7 [b]Matt. 20:23; Mark 10:40; 1Cor. 2:9; Heb. 11:16
35 [a]Isa. 58:7; Ezek. 18:7; James 1:27 [b]Heb. 13:2; 3John 1:5
36 [a]James 2:15, 16 [b]2Tim. 1:16
40 [a]Prov. 14:31; 19:17; Matt. 10:42; Mark 9:41; Heb. 6:10
41 [a]Ps. 6:8; Matt. 7:23; Luke 13:27 [b]Matt. 13:40, 42 [c]2Pet. 2:4; Jude 1:6
45 [a]Prov. 14:31; 17:5; Zech. 2:8; Acts 9:5
46 [a]Dan. 12:2; John 5:29
2 [a]Mark 14:1; Luke 22:1; John 13:1
3 [a]Ps. 2:2; John 11:47; Acts 4:25-28
6 [a]Mark 14:3; John 11:1, 2; 12:3 [b]Matt. 21:17

8 [a]But when his disciples saw *it,* they had indignation, saying, To what purpose *is* this waste?[684]

9 For this ointment might have been sold for much, and given to the poor.

10 When Jesus understood *it,* he said unto them, Why trouble[2873] ye the woman? for she [aom]hath wrought[2038] a good work[2041] upon me.

11 [a]For ye have the poor always with you; but [b]me ye have not always.

12 For in that she [apt]hath poured this ointment on my body, she did *it* for my burial.

13 Verily[281] I say unto you, Wheresoever this gospel[2098] shall be preached[2784] in the whole world,[2889] *there* shall also this, that this woman [ao]hath done, be told for a memorial of her.

Judas Agrees to Betray Jesus (Mark 14:10, 11; Luke 22:3–6)

14 [a]Then one of the twelve, called [b]Judas Iscariot, [aptp]went unto the chief priests,

15 And said *unto them,* [a]What will[2309] ye [ainf]give me, and I will deliver him unto you? And they covenanted[2476] with him for thirty pieces of silver.

16 And from that time he [ipf]sought opportunity[2120] to betray him

Jesus Eats the Passover With His Disciples (Mark 14:12–21; Luke 22:7–14, 21–23; John 13:21–30)

17 [a]Now the first *day* of the *feast of* unleavened bread[106] the disciples came to Jesus, saying unto him, Where wilt thou that we prepare for thee to eat the passover?

18 And he said, Go into the city to such a man, and say unto him, The Master saith, My time[2540] is at hand;[1451] I [pin]will keep the passover at thy house with my disciples.

19 And the disciples did as Jesus had appointed them; and they made ready the passover.

8 [a]John 12:4

11 [a]Deut. 15:11; John 12:8 [b]Matt. 18:20; 28:20; John 13:33; 14:19; 16:5, 28; 17:11

14 [a]Mark 14:10; Luke 22:3; John 13:2, 30 [b]Matt. 10:4

15 [a]Zech. 11:12; Matt. 27:3

17 [a]Ex. 12:6, 18; Mark 14:12; Luke 22:7

20 [a]Mark 14:17-21; Luke 22:14; John 13:21

23 [a]Ps. 41:9; Luke 22:21; John 13:18

24 [a]Ps. 22; Isa. 53; Dan. 9:26; Mark 9:12; Luke 24:25, 26, 46; Acts 17:2, 3; 26:22, 23; 1Cor. 15:3 [b]John 17:12

26 [I]Many Greek texts read *gave thanks* [a]Mark 14:22; Luke 22:19 [b]1Cor. 11:23-25 [c]Mark 6:41 [d]1Cor. 10:16

27 [a]Mark 14:23

28 [a]Ex. 24:8; Lev. 17:11 [b]Jer. 31:31 [c]Matt. 20:28; Rom. 5:15; Heb. 9:22

29 [a]Mark 14:25; Luke 22:18 [b]Acts 10:41

30 [I]Or, *psalm* [a]Mark 14:26

31 [a]Mark 14:27; John 16:32 [b]Matt. 11:6 [c]Zech. 13:7

20 [a]Now when the even was come, he sat down with the twelve.

21 And as they [ppt]did eat, he said, Verily I say unto you, that one of you shall betray me.

22 And they [ppt]were exceeding sorrowful,[3076] and began every one of them to say unto him, Lord, is it [epn]I?

23 And he answered[611] and said, [a]He that [apt]dippeth[1686] *his* hand with me in the dish, the same shall betray me.

24 The Son of man goeth [a]as [pfip]it is written of him: but [b]woe unto that man by whom the Son of man is betrayed! it had been good for that man if he had not been born.

25 Then Judas, which betrayed him, answered[611] and said, Master, is it [epn]I? He [pin]said unto him, Thou [ao]hast said.

The Lord's Supper (Mark 14:22–26; Luke 22:15–20; 1 Cor. 11:23–25)

26 [a]And as they [ppt]were eating, [b]Jesus [apt]took bread, and [apt][I][c]blessed[2127] *it,* and brake *it,* and [ipf]gave *it* to the disciples, and said, Take, eat; [d]this is my body.[4983]

27 And he [apt]took the cup, and [apt]gave thanks,[2168] and gave *it* to them, saying, [aim][a]Drink ye all of it;

28 For [a]this is my blood[129] [b]of the new[2537] testament,[1242] which [ppt]is shed [c]for many for the remission of sins.[266]

29 But [a]I say unto you, I will [efn]not drink henceforth of this fruit of the vine, [b]until that day when I [psa]drink it new with you in my Father's kingdom.[932]

30 [a]And when they had sung an [I]hymn, they went out into the mount of Olives.

Prediction About Peter's Denial (Mark 14:27–31; Luke 22:31–34; John 13:36–38)

31 Then saith Jesus unto them, [a]All ye shall [b]be offended because of me this night: for [pfip]it is written, [c]I will smite[3960]

the shepherd,[4166] and the sheep of the flock[4167] shall be scattered abroad.

32 But after I am risen again, [a]I will go before[4254] you into Galilee.

33 Peter answered and said unto him, Though all *men* shall be offended because of thee, *yet* will I never be offended.

34 Jesus said unto him, [a]Verily I say unto thee, That this night, before the cock [ainf]crow,5455 thou [fm]shalt deny[533] me thrice.

35 Peter said unto him, Though I should die[599] with thee, yet [fm]will I not deny[533] thee. Likewise also said all the disciples.

Jesus Prays in Gethsemane (Mark 14:32–42; Luke 22:39–46)

36 [a]Then cometh Jesus with them unto a place called Gethsemane, and saith unto the disciples, Sit ye here, while I [apt]go and pray[4336] yonder.

37 And he [apt]took with him Peter and [a]the two sons of Zebedee, and began to be sorrowful[3076] and very heavy.

38 Then saith he unto them, [a]My soul[5590] is exceeding sorrowful, even unto death: tarry ye here, and watch with me.

39 And he [apt]went4281 a little farther, and fell[4098] on his face, and [ppt][a]prayed,[4336] saying, [b]O my Father,[3962] if it be possible, [aim][c]let this cup pass3928 from me: nevertheless [d]not as [epn]I will, but as [epn]thou *wilt.*

40 And he cometh unto the disciples, and findeth them [ppt]asleep, and saith unto Peter, What, [ao]could[2480] ye not [ainf]watch with me one hour?

41 [pim][a]Watch and [pim]pray, that ye [aosb]enter not into temptation:[3986] the spirit[4151] indeed *is* willing, but the flesh[4561] *is* weak.[772]

42 He went away again the second time, and prayed, saying, O my Father,[3962] if this cup may not [ainf]pass away from me, except I drink it, thy will[2307] be done.

43 And he [apt]came and [pin]found them [ppt]asleep again: for their eyes were [pfpp]heavy.

44 And he [apt]left them, and [apt]went away again, and prayed[4336] the third time, [apt]saying the same words.

45 Then cometh he to his disciples, and saith unto them, Sleep on now, and [pim]take *your* rest: behold, the hour[5610] [pfi]is at hand, and the Son of man [pp]is betrayed into the hands of sinners.[268]

46 Rise, [pim]let us be going:[71] behold, he [pfi]is at hand that [ppt]doth betray me.

Jesus Is Arrested (Mark 14:43–50; Luke 22:47–53; John 18:3–12)

47 And [a]while he yet spake, lo, Judas, one of the twelve, came, and with him a great multitude with swords and staves, from the chief priests and elders of the people.

48 Now he that [ppt]betrayed him gave them a sign, saying, Whomsoever I shall kiss,[5368] that same is he: [aim]hold him fast.[2902]

49 And forthwith2112 he [apt]came to Jesus, and said, Hail,[5463] master; [a]and kissed him.

50 And Jesus said unto him, [a]Friend, wherefore art thou come? Then came they, and laid hands on Jesus, and took him.

51 And, behold, [a]one of them which were with Jesus [apt]stretched out *his* hand, and drew his sword, and [apt]struck a [art]servant of the high priest's, and smote off851 his ear.

52 Then said Jesus unto him, Put up again[654] thy sword into his place: [a]for all they that [apt]take the sword shall perish[622] with the sword.

53 Thinkest thou that I cannot now [ainf]pray to my Father,[3962] and he shall presently give me [a]more than twelve legions of angels?

54 But how then shall the scriptures be fulfilled, [a]that thus it must be?

55 In that same hour said Jesus to the multitudes, [ao]Are ye come out1831 as against a thief[3027] with swords and staves for to take me? I [ipf]sat daily with you teaching in the temple,[2411] and ye laid no hold on me.

32 [a]Matt. 28:7, 10, 16; Mark 14:28; 16:7

34 [a]Mark 14:30; Luke 22:34; John 13:38

36 [a]Mark 14:32-35; Luke 22:39; John 18:1

37 [a]Matt. 4:21

38 [a]John 12:27

39 [a]Mark 14:36; Luke 22:42; Heb. 5:7 [b]John 12:27 [c]Matt. 20:22 [d]John 5:30; 6:38; Phil. 2:8

41 [a]Mark 13:33; 14:38; Luke 22:40, 46; Eph. 6:18

47 [a]Mark 14:43; Luke 22:47; John 18:3; Acts 1:16

49 [a]2Sam. 20:9

50 [a]Ps. 41:9; 55:13

51 [a]John 18:10

52 [a]Gen. 9:6; Rev. 13:10

53 [a]2Kgs. 6:17; Dan. 7:10

54 [a]Isa. 53:7; Matt. 26:24; Luke 24:25, 44, 46

56 But all this was done, that the [a]scriptures[1124] of the prophets might be fulfilled. Then [b]all the disciples [apt]forsook[863] him, and fled.

Jesus Is Brought Before Caiaphas (Mark 14:53–65; Luke 22:54, 55, 63–71; John 18:12–14, 19–24)

57 [a]And they that had laid hold on Jesus [ao]led *him* away$_{520}$ to Caiaphas the high priest,[749] where the scribes[1122] and the elders were assembled.

58 But Peter [ipf]followed him afar off unto the high priest's[749] palace, and [apt]went in, and sat with[3326] the servants,[5257] to see the end.[5056]

59 Now the chief priests, and elders,[4245] and all the council, [ipf]sought false witness against Jesus, to put him to death;

60 But found none: yea, though [a]many false witnesses [apt]came, *yet* found they none. At the last [apt]came [b]two false witnesses,

61 And said, This *fellow* said, [a]I am able to destroy[2647] the temple[3485] of God, and to build it in three days.

62 [a]And the high priest[749] [apt]arose, and said unto him, Answerest thou nothing? what *is it which* these witness against thee?

63 But [a]Jesus [ipf]held his peace. And the high priest [aptp]answered[611] and said unto him, [b]I adjure$_{1844}$ thee by[2596] the living[2198] God, that thou tell us whether thou be the Christ,[5547] the Son of God.

64 Jesus saith unto him, Thou [ao]hast said: nevertheless I say unto you, [a]Hereafter shall ye see the Son of man [b]sitting on the right hand[1188] of power, and coming in the clouds of heaven.[3772]

🗝 65 [a]Then the high priest rent$_{1284}$ his clothes,[2440] saying, He [ao]hath spoken blasphemy;[987] what further need have we of witnesses?[3144] behold, now ye [ao]have heard his blasphemy.[988]

66 What think ye? They [apt]answered and said, [a]He is guilty$_{1777}$ of death.

67 [a]Then did they spit in his face, and buffeted him; and others [ao]smote *him* with [I]the palms of their hands,[4474]

68 Saying, [a]Prophesy unto us, thou Christ, Who is he that smote$_{3817}$ thee?

Peter Denies Jesus (Mark 14:66–72; Luke 22:56–62; John 18:15–18, 25–27)

69 [a]Now Peter [ipf]sat without$_{1854}$ in the palace: and a damsel came unto him, saying, Thou also wast$_{2258}$ with Jesus of Galilee.

70 But he denied[720] before *them* all, saying, I know not what thou sayest.

71 And when he was gone out into the porch, another *maid* saw him, and [pin]said unto them that were there, This *fellow* was also with Jesus of Nazareth.

72 And again he denied with an oath,$_{3727}$ I [pin]do not know[1492] the man.

73 And after a while came unto *him* they that stood by, and said to Peter, Surely thou also art *one* of them; for thy [a]speech$_{2981}$ bewrayeth thee.

74 Then [a]began he to curse and to swear, *saying,* I know[1492] not the man. And immediately the cock crew.

75 And Peter remembered the word[4487] of Jesus, which [pfp]said unto him, [a]Before the cock [ainf]crow, thou shalt deny[533] me thrice. And he [apt]went out, and wept bitterly.

Jesus Is Delivered to Pilate (Mark 15:1; Luke 23:1, 2; John 18:28–32)

27 When the morning was come, [a]all the chief priests[749] and elders of the people took counsel against Jesus to put him to death:

2 And when they [apt]had bound[1210]

56 [a]Lam. 4:20; Matt. 26:54 [b]John 18:15

57 [a]Mark 14:53; Luke 22:54; John 18:12, 13, 24

60 [a]Ps. 27:12; 35:11; Mark 14:55; Acts 6:13 [b]Deut. 19:15 [c]Matt. 27:40; John 2:19

62 [a]Mark 14:60

63 [a]Isa. 53:7; Matt. 27:12, 14 [b]Lev. 5:1; 1Sam. 14:24, 26

64 [a]Dan. 7:13; Matt. 16:27; 24:30; 25:31; Luke 21:27; John 1:51; Rom. 14:10; 1Thess. 4:16; Rev. 1:7 [b]Ps. 110:1; Acts 7:55

65 [a]2Kgs. 18:37; 19:1

66 [a]Lev. 24:16; John 19:7

67 [I]Or, *rods* [a]Isa. 50:6; 53:3; Matt. 27:30 [b]Luke 22:63; John 19:3

68 [a]Mark 14:65; Luke 22:64

69 [a]Mark 14:66; Luke 22:55; John 18:16, 17, 25

73 [a]Luke 22:59

74 [a]Mark 14:71

75 [a]Matt. 26:34; Mark 14:30; Luke 22:61, 62; John 13:38

1 [a]Ps. 2:2; Mark 15:1; Luke 22:66; 23:1; John 18:28

🗝 **26:65, 66** See note on Mark 3:28, 29.

him, they led *him* away, and [a]delivered him to Pontius Pilate the governor.

The Death of Judas (Acts 1:18, 19)

3 [a]Then Judas, which [ppt]had betrayed him, when he saw that he was condemned,[2632] [aptp]repented himself,[3338] and brought again[654] the thirty pieces of silver to the chief priests[749] and elders,

4 Saying, I [ao]have sinned[264] in that I [apt]have betrayed the innocent [an]blood.[129] And they said, What *is that* to us? see thou *to that.*

5 And he [apt]cast down the pieces of silver in the temple,[3485] [a]and departed, and [apt]went and hanged himself.

6 And the chief priests [apt]took the silver pieces, and said, It is not lawful for [ainf]to put them into the treasury, because it is the price of blood.

7 And they [apt]took counsel, and bought with them the potter's field, to bury strangers in.

8 Wherefore that field was called, [a]The [an]field of blood, unto this day.

🗝 9 Then was fulfilled that which was spoken by Jeremy the prophet, saying, [a]And they took the thirty pieces of silver, the price of him that [pfpp]was valued, [I]whom they of the children of Israel did value;

10 And gave them for the potter's field, as the Lord[2962] appointed me.

2 [a]Matt. 20:19; Acts 3:13

3 [a]Matt. 26:14, 15

5 [a]2Sam. 17:23; Acts 1:18

8 [a]Acts 1:19

9 [I]Or, *whom they bought of the children of Israel* [a]Zech. 11:12, 13

11 [a]Mark 15:2; Luke 23:3; John 18:33 [b]John 18:37; 1Tim. 6:13

12 [a]Matt. 26:63; John 19:9

13 [a]Matt. 26:62; John 19:10

15 [a]Mark 15:6; Luke 23:17; John 18:39

Jesus Is Brought to Pilate (Mark 15:2–5; Luke 23:3–5; John 18:33–38)

11 And Jesus stood before the governor: [a]and the governor asked[1905] him, saying, Art thou the King of the Jews? And Jesus said unto him, [b]Thou sayest.

12 And when he [aie]was accused of the chief priests and elders, [a]he answered[611] nothing.

13 Then [pin]said Pilate unto him, [a]Hearest thou not how many things they witness against thee?

14 And he answered him to never a word;[4487] insomuch that the governor [pinf]marvelled greatly.

Jesus Sentenced to Death (Mark 15:6–15; Luke 23:13–25; John 18:39–19:16)

15 [a]Now at *that* feast the governor [plpf]was wont[1486] [pinf]to release[630] unto the people a prisoner, whom they [ipf]would.

16 And they had then a notable prisoner, called Barabbas.

17 Therefore when they were gathered together, Pilate said unto them, Whom will ye that I release unto you? Barabbas, or Jesus which is called Christ?[5547]

18 For he knew that for envy they [ao]had delivered him.

19 When he was set down on the judgment seat, his wife sent unto him, saying, Have thou nothing to do with that

---

🗝 **27:9, 10** Although Matthew states that he is quoting the prophet Jeremiah, actually the prophet Zechariah wrote these words. Some suggest that in fact Jeremiah did make a prophecy in regards to the purchase of a field for a certain amount of money, but their efforts are supported only by speculation. Others have suggested that since Jewish tradition holds that Zechariah prophesied "in the spirit of Jeremiah," it is possible that Matthew was supporting that idea when he mentioned this prophecy. Although Jeremiah could have spoken these words without writing them down, they were in fact spoken and written by Zechariah. Another view that explains Matthew's statement is that in the older method of dividing the books of the Old Testament the third section contained the books of the prophets beginning with the Book of Jeremiah. Since Zechariah's prophecy is found within this section, it is possible that Matthew was referring to a prophecy within that particular division of the Old Testament, as many Jews used the first book or the first words of a scroll to refer metonymously to the whole. In any event, it is clear that the one who made this prophecy accurately predicted the events that occurred between the death of Christ and His burial.

just man:[1342] for I [ao]have suffered many things this day in a dream because of him.

20 [a]But the chief priests and elders persuaded[3982] the multitude that they should ask Barabbas, and destroy[622] Jesus.

21 The governor answered and said unto them, Whether of the twain[1417] will ye that I release unto you? They said, Barabbas.

22 Pilate saith unto them, What shall I do then with Jesus which is called Christ? *They* all say unto him, [aipp]Let him be crucified.[4717]

23 And the governor said, Why, what evil [ao]hath he done?[4160] But they [ipf]cried out the more,[4057] saying, Let him be crucified.

24 When Pilate saw that he could prevail nothing, but *that* rather a tumult was made, he [apt][a]took water, and [ao]washed *his* hands before the multitude, saying, I am innocent of the blood of this just person: see ye *to it.*

25 Then answered all the people, and said, [a]His blood[129] *be* on us, and on our children.

26 Then released[630] he Barabbas unto them: and when [a]he had scourged[5417] Jesus, he delivered *him* to be crucified.

Jesus Is Mocked by the Soldiers (Mark 15:16–20; John 19:2, 3)

27 [a]Then the soldiers of the governor [apt]took[3880] Jesus into the [I]common hall, and gathered unto him the whole band *of soldiers.*

28 And they [apt]stripped him, and [a]put on him a scarlet robe.[5511]

29 [a]And when they had platted[4120] a crown of[1537] thorns, they put *it* upon his head, and a reed in his right hand: and they [apt]bowed the knee before him, and [ipf]mocked him, saying, Hail,[5463] King of the Jews!

30 And [a]they [apt]spit upon him, and took the reed, and [ipf]smote[5180] him on the head.

31 And after that they had mocked him, they took the robe[5511] off from him, and put his own raiment on him, [a]and [ao]led him away[520] to crucify *him.*

Jesus' Crucifixion (Mark 15:21–32; Luke 23:26–43; John 19:17–27)

32 [a]And as they came out, [b]they found[2147] a man of Cyrene, Simon by name: him they compelled[29] to bear[142] his cross.[4716]

33 [a]And when they were come unto a place called Golgotha, that is to say, a place of a skull,

34 [a]They gave him vinegar to drink [pfpp]mingled with gall: and when he had tasted[1089] *thereof,* he would not drink.

35 [a]And they [apt]crucified him, and parted his garments, [ppt]casting lots:[2819] that it might be fulfilled which was spoken by the prophet, [b]They parted my garments among them, and upon my vesture[2441] did they cast lots.

36 [a]And sitting down they [ipf]watched[5083] him there;

37 And [a]set up over his head his accusation[156] written, THIS IS JESUS THE KING[935] OF THE JEWS.

38 [a]Then were there two thieves[3027] [pinp]crucified with him, one on the right hand,[1188] and another on the left.

39 And [a]they that [ppt]passed by [ipf]reviled[987] him, wagging[2795] their heads,

40 And saying, [a]Thou that [ppt]destroyest[2647] the temple, and [ppt]buildest *it* in[1722] three days, save[4982] thyself. [b]If thou be the Son of God, come down from the cross.[4716]

41 Likewise also the chief priests[749] [ppt]mocking *him,* with the scribes and elders,[4245] said,

42 He saved others; himself he cannot [ainf]save. If he be the King of Israel, [aim]let him now come down from the cross,[4716] and we will believe[4100] him.

43 [a]He [pfi]trusted[3982] in God; [aim]let him deliver[4506] him now, if he will have[2309] him: for he said, I am the Son of God.

44 [a]The thieves also, which were crucified with[4957] him, [ipf]cast the same in his teeth.

20 [a]Mark 15:11; Luke 23:18; John 18:40; Acts 3:14
24 [a]Deut. 21:6
25 [a]Deut. 19:10; Josh. 2:19; 2Sam. 1:16; 1Kgs. 2:32; Acts 5:28
26 [a]Isa. 53:5; Mark 15:15; Luke 23:16, 24, 25; John 19:1, 16
27 [I]Or, *governor's house* [a]Mark 15:16; John 19:2
28 [a]Luke 23:11
29 [a]Ps. 69:19; Isa. 53:3
30 [a]Isa. 50:6; Matt. 26:67
31 [a]Isa. 53:7
32 [a]Num. 15:35; 1Kgs. 21:13; Acts 7:58; Heb. 13:12 [b]Mark 15:21; Luke 23:26
33 [a]Mark 15:22; Luke 23:33; John 19:17
34 [a]Ps. 69:21; Matt. 27:48
35 [a]Mark 15:24; Luke 23:34; John 19:24 [b]Ps. 22:18
36 [a]Matt. 27:54
37 [a]Mark 15:26; Luke 23:38; John 19:19
38 [a]Isa. 53:12; Mark 15:27; Luke 23:32, 33; John 19:18
39 [a]Ps. 22:7; 109:25; Mark 15:29; Luke 23:35
40 [a]Matt. 26:61; John 2:19 [b]Matt. 26:63
43 [a]Ps. 22:8
44 [a]Mark 15:32; Luke 23:39

Jesus' Death (Mark 15:33–41; Luke 23:44–49; John 19:28–30)

45 [a]Now from the sixth hour there was darkness[4655] over all the land unto the ninth hour.

46 And about the ninth hour [a]Jesus cried with a loud voice, saying, Eli, Eli, lama sabachthani? that is to say, [b]My God, my God, why hast thou forsaken me?

47 Some of them that [pfp]stood there, when they heard *that,* said, This *man* calleth for Elias.

48 And straightway2112 one of them ran, and [apt]took a sponge, [a]and [apt]filled *it* with vinegar, and [apt]put *it* on a reed, and [ipf]gave him to drink.4222

49 The rest said, Let be, let us see whether Elias will come to save him.

50 [a]Jesus, when he had cried again with a loud voice, yielded up[863] the ghost.[4151]

51 And, behold, [a]the veil of the temple[3485] was rent4977 in twain1417 from the top[509] to the bottom; and the earth did quake, and the rocks rent;

52 And the graves were opened; and many bodies of the saints[40] [pfpp]which slept arose,

53 And [apt]came out of the graves after his resurrection,[1454] and went into the holy[40] city, and appeared unto many.

54 [a]Now when the centurion, and they that were with him, watching[5083] Jesus, [apt]saw the earthquake, and those things that [apt]were done, they feared greatly, saying, Truly this was the Son of God.

55 And many women were there beholding afar off, [a]which followed[190] Jesus from Galilee, ministering unto him:

56 [a]Among which was Mary Magdalene, and Mary the mother of James and Joses, and the mother of Zebedee's children.

The Burial of Jesus (Mark 15:42–47; Luke 23:50–56; John 19:38–42)

57 [a]When the even [apt]was come, there came a rich man of Arimathaea, named Joseph, who also himself [ao]was Jesus' disciple:[3100]

58 He [apt]went to Pilate, and begged the body[4983] of Jesus. Then Pilate commanded the body to be delivered.

59 And when Joseph had taken the body, he wrapped it in a clean[2513] linen cloth,

60 And [a]laid it in his own new tomb, which he [ao]had hewn out2998 in the rock: and he [apt]rolled a great stone to the door of the sepulchre,3419 and departed.

61 And there was Mary Magdalene, and the other Mary, sitting over against the sepulchre.5028

62 Now the next day, that followed the day of the preparation, the chief priests and Pharisees came together unto Pilate,

63 Saying, Sir,[2962] we [aop]remember that that deceiver said, while he [ppt]was yet alive,[2198] [a]After three days I [pin]will rise again.

64 Command therefore that the sepulchre be made sure until the third day, lest his disciples [apt]come by night, and steal him away, and say unto the people,[2992] He [aop]is risen from the dead: so the last error shall be worse than the first.

65 Pilate said unto them, Ye have a watch: go your way, [aim]make *it* as sure805 as ye can.[1492]

66 So they [apt]went, and [ao]made the sepulchre sure,805 [a]sealing the stone, and setting a watch.

Jesus Is Risen (Mark 16:1–8; Luke 24:1–12; John 20:1–10)

28 In the [a]end of the sabbath,4521 as it began to dawn toward the first *day* of the week, came Mary Magdalene [b]and the other Mary to see the sepulchre.5028

2 And, behold, there [aomI]was a great earthquake: for [a]the angel of the Lord [apt]descended from heaven,[3772] and [apt]came and rolled back the stone from the door, and sat upon it.

3 [a]His countenance[2397] was like lightning, and his raiment white as snow:

---

45 [a]Amos 8:9; Mark 15:33; Luke 23:44
46 [a]Heb. 5:7 [b]Ps. 22:1
48 [a]Ps. 69:21; Mark 15:36; Luke 23:36; John 19:29
50 [a]Mark 15:37; Luke 23:46
51 [a]Ex. 26:31; 2Chr. 3:14; Mark 15:38; Luke 23:45
54 [a]Matt. 27:36; Mark 15:39; Luke 23:47
55 [a]Luke 8:2, 3
56 [a]Mark 15:40
57 [a]Mark 15:42; Luke 23:50; John 19:38
60 [a]Isa. 53:9
63 [a]Matt. 16:21; 17:23; 20:19; 26:61; Mark 8:31; 10:34; Luke 9:22; 18:33; 24:6, 7; John 2:19
66 [a]Dan. 6:17
1 [a]Mark 16:1; Luke 24:1; John 20:1 [b]Matt. 27:56
2 [I]Or, *had been* [a]Mark 16:5; Luke 24:4; John 20:12
3 [a]Dan. 10:6

4 And for fear[5401] of him the keepers[5083] did shake, and became as dead *men.*

5 And the angel answered and said unto the women, Fear[5399] not ye: for I know that ye seek Jesus, which [pfpp]was crucified.

6 He is not here: for he [ao]is risen, [a]as he said. Come, see the place where the Lord [ipf]lay.

7 And [aptp]go quickly, and tell his disciples that he is risen from the dead; and, behold, [a]he goeth before[4254] you into Galilee; there shall ye see him: lo, I [ao]have told you.

8 And they [apt]departed quickly from the sepulchre[3419] with[3326] fear and great joy; and did run to bring his disciples word.

9 And as they went to tell his disciples, behold, [a]Jesus met them, saying, All hail.[5463] And they [apt]came and held him by the feet, and worshipped him.

10 Then [pin]said Jesus unto them, [pim]Be not afraid:[5399] go tell [a]my brethren[80] that they go into Galilee, and there shall they see me.

11 Now when they were going, behold, some of the watch [apt]came into the city, and shewed unto the chief priests all the things that were done.

12 And when they were assembled with the elders, and had taken counsel, they gave large money unto the soldiers,

13 Saying, [aim]Say ye, His disciples [apt]came by night, and stole him *away* while we slept.

14 And if this come to the governor's ears, we will persuade[3982] him, and secure you.

15 So they [apt]took the money, and did as they were taught:[1321] and this saying[3056] [aop]is commonly reported among the Jews until this day.

The Great Commission (Mark 16:14–18; Luke 24:36–49; John 20:19–23; Acts 1:9–11)

16 Then the eleven disciples[3101] went away into Galilee, into a mountain [a]where Jesus had appointed[5021] them.

17 And when they saw him, they worshipped him: but some doubted.

18 And Jesus [apt]came and spake unto them, saying, [a]All power[1849] [aop]is given unto me in heaven and in earth.[1093]

🔑 19 [aptp][a]Go ye therefore, and [aim][I][b]teach[3100] all nations, baptizing them in the name[3686] of the Father,[3962] and of the Son, and of the Holy[40] Ghost:[4151]

20 [a]Teaching[1321] them to observe all things whatsoever I [aom]have commanded you: and, lo, I am with you alway, *even* unto the end[4930] of the world. Amen.[281]

6 [a]Matt. 12:40; 16:21; 17:23; 20:19
7 [a]Matt. 26:32; Mark 16:7
9 [a]Mark 16:9; John 20:14
10 [a]John 20:17; Rom. 8:29; Heb. 2:11
16 [a]Matt. 26:32; 28:7
18 [a]Dan. 7:13, 14; Matt. 11:27; 16:28; Luke 1:32; 10:22; John 3:35; 5:22; 13:3; 17:2; Acts 2:36; Rom. 14:9; 1Cor. 15:27; Eph. 1:10, 21; Phil. 2:9, 10; Heb. 1:2; 2:8; 1Pet. 3:22; Rev. 17:14
19 [I]Or, *make disciples,* or, *Christians of all nations* [a]Mark 16:15 [b]Isa. 52:10; Luke 24:47; Acts 2:38, 39; Rom. 10:18; Col. 1:23
20 [a]Acts 2:42

🔑 **28:19** See notes on Mark 16:16 and 1 Corinthians 10:2.

The Gospel According to Mark

MARK

The name Mark is actually a surname, his common name being John (Acts 12:12; 13:5; 2 Tim. 4:11). Since he was related to Barnabas (Col. 4:10), Mark may have been a Levite (Acts 4:36).

Mark traveled with the Apostle Paul and Barnabas on their first missionary journey (Acts 12:25), but he turned back (Acts 13:13). For this reason, Paul refused to consider taking him along on the second missionary journey (Acts 15:36–39). Paul and Barnabas had such a strong disagreement about the matter that they decided to go different directions, Paul with Silas and Barnabas with Mark. Paul and Mark were later reconciled (Col. 4:10; Phile. 1:24), and Paul came to regard Mark as one who was "profitable . . . for the ministry" (2 Tim. 4:11).

The contents of the book and extra-biblical sources indicate that Mark's Gospel was written for the benefit of those who lived outside Palestine. These people who had not witnessed the events of Jesus life would profit most from Mark's emphasis on the supernatural power of the Christ. His actions, rather than His words, are given the most attention, particularly the miracles He performed to demonstrate His divinity. The narrative moves swiftly from one stirring scene of Jesus' ministry to another without interruption. The rapid pace can be seen in the frequent use of the transitional Greek word *euthéō* (2117), meaning "immediately" or "straightway" (used 42 times).

It is generally accepted and supported by the writings of the church historians that Peter was Mark's source for the information contained in his Gospel. Since the book was probably written from Rome immediately after Peter's death, the date for its writing is presumed to be A.D. 67 or 68. The Gospel of Mark has about ninety-three percent of its material repeated in Matthew and Luke, many times using the same words. The details that Mark gives in his brief account, however, are more graphic than in the other accounts, helping readers unfamiliar with the area to visualize the events.

The Preaching of John the Baptist (Matt. 3:1–12; Luke 3:1–9, 15–17; John 1:19–28)

1 The beginning of the gospel[2098] of
Jesus Christ,[5547] [a]the Son of God;[2316]
2 As [pfip]it is written in the
prophets,[4396] [a]Behold, I send my messenger[32] before thy face, which shall prepare
thy way[3598] before thee.
3 [a]The voice of one crying in the
wilderness, [aim]Prepare ye the way of the
Lord, [pim]make his paths straight.
4 [a]John did [ppt]baptize[907] in the wilderness, and [ppt]preach[2784] the baptism[908]
of repentance[3341] [I]for[1519] the [an]remis-
sion[859] of sins.
5 [a]And there [ipf]went out unto him
all the land of Judaea, and they of
Jerusalem, and [ipf]were all baptized[907] of
him in the river of Jordan, confessing[1843]
their sins.
6 And John was [a]clothed with camel's
hair, and with a girdle[2223] of a skin about
his loins; and he [ppt]did eat [b]locusts and
wild honey;
7 And [ipf]preached,[2784] saying, [a]There
cometh one mightier than I after me, the
latchet[2438] of whose shoes I am not worthy to [apt]stoop down[2955] and [ainf]unloose.[3089]
🔑 8 [a]I indeed [ao]have baptized you with
water: but he [ft]shall baptize you [b]with
the Holy Ghost.

1 [a]Matt. 14:33; Luke 1:35; John 1:34
2 [a]Mal. 3:1; Matt. 11:10; Luke 7:27
3 [a]Isa. 40:3; Matt. 3:3; Luke 3:4; John 1:15, 23
4 [I]Or, *unto* [a]Matt. 3:1; Luke 3:3; John 3:23
5 [a]Matt. 3:5
6 [a]Matt. 3:4 [b]Lev. 11:22
7 [a]Matt. 3:11; John 1:27; Acts 13:25
8 [a]Acts 1:5; 11:16; 19:4 [b]Isa. 44:3; Joel 2:28; Acts 2:4; 10:45; 11:15, 16; 1Cor. 12:13

🔑 **1:8** See note on Acts 1:5.

Jesus Is Baptized
(Matt. 3:13–17; Luke 3:21, 22)

9 [a]And it came to pass in those days,
that Jesus came from Nazareth of Galilee, and was baptized[907] of John in Jordan.
10 [a]And straightway[2112] coming up
out of the water, he saw the heavens
[I]opened, and the Spirit like a dove descending upon him:
11 And there came a voice from
heaven, *saying,* [a]Thou art my beloved[27]
Son, in whom I [ao]am well pleased.

Jesus Is Tempted By the Devil
(Matt. 4:1–11; Luke 4:1–13)

12 [a]And immediately the Spirit driveth him into the wilderness.
13 And he was there in the wilderness forty days, [ppt]tempted[3985] of
Satan;[4567] and was with the wild
beasts;[2342] and the angels [ipf]ministered
unto him.

Jesus Begins His Ministry In Galilee
(Matt. 4:12–17; Luke 4:14, 15)

14 [a]Now after that John was put in
prison, Jesus came into Galilee, [b]preach-
ing[2784] the gospel[2098] of the kingdom[932]
of God,
15 And saying, [a]The time[2540] [pfip]is
fulfilled,[4137] and [b]the kingdom[932] of God
[pfi]is at hand:[1448] [pim]repent[3340] ye, and
[pim]believe[4100] the gospel.

Jesus Calls Four Fishermen
(Matt. 4:18–22; Luke 5:1–11)

16 [a]Now as he [ppt]walked by the sea
of Galilee, he saw Simon and Andrew
his brother casting a net[293] into the sea:
for they were fishers.
17 And Jesus said unto them, Come
ye after me, and I will make you to become fishers of men.[444]

18 And straightway [a]they [apt]forsook
their nets,[1350] and followed him.
19 [a]And when he had gone a little
farther thence, he saw James the *son* of
Zebedee, and John his brother, who also
were in the ship mending[2675] their nets.
20 And straightway he called them:
and they [apt]left their father Zebedee in
the ship with the hired servants,[3411] and
went after him.

The Man With an Unclean Spirit
(Luke 4:31–37)

21 [a]And they [pinp]went into Capernaum; and straightway on the sabbath
day[4521] he [apt]entered into the synagogue,
and [ipf]taught.
22 [a]And they [ipf]were astonished at
his doctrine: for he taught them as one
that [ppt]had authority, and not as the
scribes.[1122]
23 [a]And there was in their synagogue a man with an unclean spirit; and
he cried out,
24 Saying, Let *us* alone; [a]what have
we to do with thee, thou Jesus of Nazareth? art thou come to destroy us? I
know thee who thou art, the Holy One of
God.
25 And Jesus [a]rebuked him, saying,
Hold thy peace, and come out of him.
26 And when the unclean spirit [a]had
torn him, and [apt]cried with a loud voice,
he came out of him.
27 And they were all amazed, insomuch that they [pinf]questioned among
themselves, saying, What thing is this?
what new[2537] doctrine *is* this? for with
authority commandeth[2004] he even the
unclean spirits, and they do obey[5219]
him.
28 And immediately his fame spread
abroad throughout all the region round
about Galilee.

Jesus Heals Many
(Matt. 8:14–17; Luke 4:38–41)

29 [a]And forthwith, when they were
come out of the synagogue, they entered

9 [a]Matt. 3:13; Luke 3:21
10 [I]Or, *rent* [a]Matt. 3:16; John 1:32
11 [a]Ps. 2:7; Matt. 3:17; Mark 9:7
12 [a]Matt. 4:1; Luke 4:1
14 [a]Matt. 4:12 [b]Matt. 4:23
15 [a]Dan. 9:25; Gal. 4:4; Eph. 1:10 [b]Matt. 3:2; 4:17
16 [a]Matt. 4:18; Luke 5:4
18 [a]Matt. 19:27; Luke 5:11
19 [a]Matt. 4:21
21 [a]Matt. 4:13; Luke 4:31
22 [a]Matt. 7:28
23 [a]Luke 4:33
24 [a]Matt. 8:29
25 [a]Mark 1:34
26 [a]Mark 9:20
29 [a]Matt. 8:14; Luke 4:38

into the house of Simon and Andrew, with James and John.

30 But Simon's wife's mother lay2621 sick of a fever,4445 and anon2112 they tell him of her.

31 And he came and took her by the hand, and lifted her up;[1453] and immediately the fever left her, and she [ipf]ministered[1247] unto them.

32 [a]And at even, when the sun did set, they brought[5342] unto him all that were diseased,[2192,2560] and them that [ppt]were possessed with devils.[1139]

33 And all the city was gathered together1996 at the door.

34 And he healed many that were sick[2192,2560] of divers4164 diseases, and cast out many devils;1140 and [a]suffered not the devils1140 [1]to speak, because they knew him.

Jesus Ministers in All of Galilee (Luke 4:42–44)

35 And [a]in the morning, rising up[450] a great while before day, he went out, and departed into a solitary place, and there [ipf]prayed.

36 And Simon and they that were with him followed after him.

37 And when they had found him, they [pin]said unto him, All *men* seek for thee.

38 And he [pin]said unto them, [a]Let us go[71] into the next towns, that I may preach[2784] there also: for [b]therefore came I forth.

39 [a]And he preached in their synagogues throughout all Galilee, and [ppt]cast out devils.1140

Jesus Cleanses a Leper (Matt. 8:1–4; Luke 5:12–16)

40 [a]And there came a leper to him, beseeching him, and kneeling down to him, and saying unto him, If thou wilt, thou canst make me clean.

41 And Jesus, moved with compassion, put forth *his* hand, and touched him, and saith unto him, I will; be thou clean.

42 And as soon as he had spoken, immediately the leprosy departed from him, and he was cleansed.

43 And he [apt]straitly charged1690 him, and forthwith sent him away;

44 And saith unto him, See thou say nothing to any man: but go thy way, shew thyself to the priest, and offer for thy cleansing those things [a]which Moses commanded,4367 for a testimony unto them.

45 [b]But he went out, and began to publish[2784] *it* much, and to blaze abroad1310 the matter, insomuch that Jesus could no more openly enter into the city, but was without1854 in desert places: [c]and they [ipf]came to him from every quarter.

Jesus Heals a Crippled Man (Matt. 9:1–8; Luke 5:17–26)

2 And again [a]he entered into Capernaum after *some* days; and it was noised[191] that he was in the house.

2 And straightway2112 many were gathered together, insomuch that there was no room to receive *them,* no, not so much as about the door: and he preached[2980] the word[3056] unto them.

3 And they come unto him, bringing one sick of the palsy,3885 [ppt]which was borne of four.

4 And when they [ppt]could not come nigh[4331] unto him for the press, they uncovered the roof where he was: and when they had broken *it* up, they let down the bed wherein the sick of the palsy lay.

5 When Jesus saw their faith,[4102] he [pin]said unto the sick of the palsy, Son, thy sins [pfip]be forgiven thee.

6 But there were certain of the scribes sitting there, and reasoning[1260] in their hearts,

7 Why doth this *man* thus speak blasphemies? [a]who can forgive sins but God only?

---

32 [a]Matt. 8:16; Luke 4:40

34 [1]Or, *to say that they knew him* [a]Mark 3:12; Luke 4:41; Acts 16:17, 18

35 [a]Luke 4:42

38 [a]Luke 4:43 [b]Isa. 61:1; John 16:28; 17:4

39 [a]Matt. 4:23; Luke 4:44

40 [a]Matt. 8:2; Luke 5:12

44 [a]Lev. 14:3, 4, 10; Luke 5:14

45 [a]Luke 5:15; Mark 2:13

1 [a]Matt. 9:1; Luke 5:18

7 [a]Job 14:4; Isa. 43:25

8 And immediately [a]when Jesus perceived in his spirit[4151] that they so [pin]reasoned within themselves, he said unto them, Why reason ye these things in your hearts?

9 [a]Whether is it easier to say to the sick of the palsy, *Thy* sins [pfip]be forgiven thee; or to say, Arise, and take up thy bed, and [pim]walk?

10 But that ye [aosb]may know[1492] that the Son of man hath power[1849] on earth[1093] to forgive[863] sins, (he saith to the sick of the palsy,)

11 I say unto thee, Arise, and take up thy bed, and go thy way into thine house.

12 And immediately he arose, [apt]took up the bed, and went forth before them all; insomuch that they [pinf]were all amazed,[1839] and [pinf]glorified[1392] God, saying, We never saw it on this fashion.

Jesus Calls Levi (Matt. 9:9–13; Luke 5:27–32)

13 [a]And he went forth again by the sea side; and all the multitude [ipf]resorted unto him, and he [ipf]taught them.

14 [a]And as he [ppt]passed by, he saw Levi the *son* of Alphaeus sitting [I]at the receipt of custom,[5058] and said unto him, Follow me. And he arose[450] and followed him.

15 [a]And it came to pass, that, as Jesus sat at meat in his house, many publicans[5057] and sinners[268] [ipf]sat also together with Jesus and his disciples: for there were many, and they followed him.

16 And when the scribes and Pharisees saw him [ppt]eat with publicans and sinners,[268] they said unto his disciples, How is it that he eateth and drinketh with publicans and sinners?[268]

17 When Jesus heard *it,* he saith unto them, [a]They that are whole[2480] have no need of the physician,[2395] but they that are sick: I came not to call the righteous,[1342] but sinners[268] to repentance.[3341]

Jesus' Teaching on Fasting (Matt. 9:14–17; Luke 5:33–39)

18 [a]And the disciples[3101] of John and of the Pharisees [ppt]used to fast:[3522,2258] and they come and say unto him, Why do the disciples of John and of the Pharisees fast, but thy disciples fast not?

19 And Jesus said unto them, Can the children[5207] of the bridechamber [pinf]fast, while the bridegroom is with them? as long as they have the bridegroom with them, they cannot [pinf]fast.

20 But the days will come, when the bridegroom shall be taken away from them, and then shall they fast in those days.

21 No man also seweth a piece of [I]new cloth on an old garment: else the new piece that filled it up[4138] taketh away from the old, and the rent[4978] is made worse.[5501]

22 And no man putteth[906] new[3501] wine[3631] into old bottles: else the new wine doth burst the bottles, and the wine is spilled, and the bottles will be marred: but new wine must be put into new bottles.

Jesus Is Lord Over the Sabbath Day (Matt. 12:1–8; Luke 6:1–5)

23 [a]And it came to pass, that he [pinf]went through the corn fields on the sabbath day;[4521] and his disciples began, as they went,[4160,3598] [b]to pluck the ears of corn.

24 And the Pharisees said unto him, Behold, why do they on the sabbath day that which is not lawful?

25 And he said unto them, Have ye never read [a]what David did, when he had need, and was an hungred,[3983] he, and they that were with him?

26 How he went into the house of God[2316] in the days of Abiathar the high priest, and did eat the shewbread,[4286,720,3588] [a]which is not lawful to eat but for the priests, and gave also to them which were with him?

27 And he said unto them, The sab-

8 [a]Matt. 9:4
9 [a]Matt. 9:5
13 [a]Matt. 9:9
14 [I]Or, *at the place where the custom was received* [a]Matt. 9:9; Luke 5:27
15 [a]Matt. 9:10
17 [a]Matt. 9:12, 13; 18:11; Luke 5:31, 32; 19:10; 1Tim. 1:15
18 [a]Matt. 9:14; Luke 5:33
21 [I]Or, *raw,* or, *unwrought*
23 [a]Matt. 12:1; Luke 6:1 [b]Deut. 23:25
25 [a]1Sam. 21:6
26 [a]Ex. 29:32, 33; Lev. 24:9

bath was made for man,[444] and not man for the sabbath:

28 Therefore [a]the Son of man is Lord also of the sabbath.

Jesus Heals a Man On the Sabbath Day (Matt. 12:9–14; Luke 6:6–11)

3 And [a]he entered again into the synagogue; and there was a man there which had a withered hand.

2 And they [ipf]watched him, whether he [ft]would heal him on the sabbath day;[4521] that they might accuse him.

3 And he saith unto the man which had the withered hand, [I]Stand forth.

4 And he saith unto them, Is it lawful [ainf]to do good[15] on the sabbath days, or [ainf]to do evil?[2554] to save[4982] life, or to kill? But they [ipf]held their peace.

5 And when he had looked round about on[4017] them with anger,[3709] being grieved for the [I]hardness[4457] of their hearts, he saith unto the man, Stretch forth thine hand. And he stretched *it* out: and his hand was restored[600] whole[5199] as the other.

6 [a]And the Pharisees [apt]went forth, and straightway[2112] [ipf]took counsel with [b]the Herodians against him, how they might destroy him.

A Multitude Follows Jesus by the Sea

7 But Jesus withdrew himself with his disciples to the sea: and a great multitude from Galilee followed him, [a]and from Judaea,

8 And from Jerusalem, and from Idumaea, and *from* beyond Jordan; and they about Tyre and Sidon, a great multitude, when they had heard what great things he did, came unto him.

9 And he spake to his disciples, that a small ship should wait on[4342] him because of the multitude, lest they should throng him.

10 For he had healed many; insomuch that they [pinf][I]pressed upon him for to [asbm]touch him, as many as had plagues.

11 [a]And unclean spirits, when they [ipf]saw him, [ipf]fell down before him, and [ipf]cried, saying, [b]Thou art the Son of God.

12 And [a]he straitly[4183] [ipf]charged them that they [aosb]should not make[4160] him known.[5318]

Jesus Chooses Twelve Apostles (Matt. 10:1–4; Luke 6:12–16)

13 [a]And he goeth up into a mountain, and calleth *unto him* whom he [ipf]would: and they came unto him.

14 And he ordained[4160] twelve, that they should be with him, and that he [psa]might send them forth[649] [pinf]to preach,[2784]

15 And [pinf]to have power[1849] [pinf]to heal [art]sicknesses, and to cast out [art]devils:[1140]

16 And Simon [a]he surnamed Peter;

17 And James the *son* of Zebedee, and John the brother of James; and he surnamed them Boanerges, which is, The sons[5207] of thunder:

18 And Andrew, and Philip, and Bartholomew, and Matthew, and Thomas, and James the *son* of Alphaeus, and Thaddaeus, and Simon the Canaanite,

19 And Judas Iscariot, which also betrayed him: and they [pin]went into an house.

Jesus and Beelzebub (Matt. 12:22–32; Luke 11:14–23; 12:10)

20 And the multitude cometh together again, [a]so that they could not so much as eat bread.

21 And when his [I]friends heard *of it*, they went out to lay hold on him: [a]for they said, He [ao]is beside himself.[1839]

22 And the scribes which [apt]came down from Jerusalem [ipf]said, [a]He hath Beelzebub, and by the prince of the devils[1140] casteth he out devils.[1140]

---

28 [a]Matt. 12:8

1 [a]Matt. 12:9; Luke 6:6

3 [I]Gr. *Arise, stand forth in the midst*

5 [I]Or, *blindness*

6 [a]Matt. 12:14 [b]Matt. 22:16

7 [a]Luke 6:17

10 [I]Or, *rushed*

11 [a]Mark 1:23, 24; Luke 4:41 [b]Matt. 14:33; Mark 1:1

12 [a]Matt. 12:16; Mark 1:25, 34

13 [a]Matt. 10:1; Luke 6:12; 9:1

16 [a]John 1:42

20 [a]Mark 6:31

21 [I]Or, *kinsmen* [a]John 7:5; 10:20

22 [a]Matt. 9:34; 10:25; Luke 11:15; John 7:20; 8:48, 52; 10:20

23 [a]And he [apt]called them *unto him,*
and [ipf]said unto them in parables, How
can Satan [pinf]cast out Satan?[4567]
24 And if a kingdom be divided
against itself, that kingdom cannot
stand.[2476]
25 And if a house be divided against
itself, that house cannot stand.[2476]
26 And if Satan [ao]rise up[450] against
himself, and be divided, he cannot stand,
but hath an end.
27 [a]No man can enter into a strong
man's house, and [ainf]spoil his goods, except
he will first bind the strong man;
and then he will spoil his house.
🔑 28 [a]Verily[281] I say unto you, All
sins[265] shall be forgiven unto the sons of
men, and blasphemies[988] wherewith soever
they shall blaspheme:
29 But he that shall blaspheme[987]
against the Holy Ghost[4151] hath never
forgiveness, but is in danger of[1777] eternal
damnation:[2920]
30 Because they said, He hath an unclean
spirit.

23 [a]Matt. 12:25
27 [a]Isa. 49:24; Matt. 12:29
28 [a]Matt. 12:31; Luke 12:10; 1John 5:16
31 [a]Matt. 12:46; Luke 8:19
1 [a]Matt. 13:1; Luke 8:4

Jesus' Mother and Brothers (Matt. 12:46–50; Luke 8:19–21)

31 [a]There came then his brethren[80]
and his mother, and, standing without,[1854]
sent unto him, calling him.
32 And the multitude [ipf]sat about
him, and they said unto him, Behold, thy
mother and thy brethren without seek for
thee.
33 And he answered them, saying,
Who is my mother, or my brethren?
34 And he [aptp]looked[4017] round
about on them which [ppt]sat about him,
and said, Behold my mother and my
brethren!
35 For whosoever shall do the will of
God, the same is my brother, and my sister,
and mother.

The Parable of the Sower (Matt. 13:1–9; Luke 8:4–8)

4 And [a]he began again [pinf]to teach[1321]
by the sea side: and there was gath-

🔑 **3:28, 29** Christ is here answering the accusation that had been made against Him that the miracle He performed (the casting out a demon) was done by the power of Beelzebub, who was the chief of the demons (see Matt. 12:22–30; Mark 3:20–27). By their accusation, these men were calling the Holy Spirit a "devil" or "an unclean spirit" (vv. 22, 30). In fact, the work of the devil is designed to counter the work done by the Holy Spirit (John 16:8). The attitude of these scribes revealed their complete rejection of Christ's power and authority as the Son of God.

The "blasphemy against the Holy Spirit" to which Christ referred in verse twenty-nine was said to be unforgivable (Matt. 12:31, 32 and Luke 12:10). Matthew 12:32 says, "It shall not be forgiven him, neither in this age, neither in the world to come." The verb *ouk aphethēsetai*, translated "shall not be forgiven," is in the passive punctiliar future, which means that it will not be forgiven by God, and in particular by Jesus Christ, at any specific time in the future. Matthew says, "shall not be forgiven him," which might better be stated "will not be removed from him." Stated positively, it means it will be counted against him, hindering him from entrance into heaven.

Of the three passages in the Gospels where this is discussed, only Mark 3:29 has the concluding phrase, "but is in danger of eternal damnation." Literally, the Greek text says, "but he is guilty of eternal judgment." The Greek word is *enochós* (1777), meaning "something that is held fast or bound." Therefore, *enochós* means that one is deserving of the punishment (see Matt. 26:66; Mark 14:64). One should observe that the verb *estīn* (from *eimī*, [1510]) is in the present tense, meaning that this guilt is always upon anyone who does not recognize the Holy Spirit as the power behind the work of Christ. The last phrase of Mark 3:29 in some Greek texts is *aiōíou,* which means "eternal judgment or condemnation." In other manuscripts, instead of *kríseōs*, "judgment," the word *hamartēmatos* is used, connoting the "individual sin or the result of sin." This agrees with the meaning of *hamartēmata* found in verse twenty-eight in the phrases "all sins" and "whatever blasphemies." The adjective *aiōníou* (166) refers to the eternal judgment, namely that judgment that will take effect in the future, especially in the "age" to come (see 2 Thess. 1:9; Jude 1:7).

The Holy Spirit represented the manifestation of the power that Christ possessed. By denying this power, these scribes were guilty of a sin for which there was no forgiveness. See note on Hebrews 10:26, 27.

ered unto him a great multitude, so that he [apt]entered into a ship, and [pinf]sat in the sea; and the whole multitude was by the sea on the land.

2 And he [ipf]taught them many things by parables,[3850] [a]and [ipf]said unto them in his doctrine,[1322]

3 [pim]Hearken; Behold, there went out a sower [infg]to sow:

4 And it came to pass, as he [aie]sowed, [n]some fell by the way side, and the fowls of the air came and devoured it up.

5 And [n]some fell on stony ground, where it [ipf]had not much earth; and immediately it sprang up, because it [aid]had no depth of earth:

6 But when the sun [apt]was up, it was scorched; and because it had no root, it withered away.

7 And [n]some fell among thorns, and the thorns grew up, and choked it, and it yielded no fruit.

8 And [n]other fell on [art]good [art]ground, [a]and [ipf]did yield fruit that [ppt]sprang up[305] and [ppt]increased; and [ipf]brought forth,[5342] some thirty, and some sixty, and some an hundred.

9 And he said unto them, He that hath ears to hear, [pim]let him hear.[191]

Why Jesus Taught in Parables (Matt. 13:10–17; Luke 8:9, 10)

🔑 10 [a]And when he was alone, they that were about him with the twelve asked[2065] of him the parable.[3850]

11 And he said unto them, Unto you it [pfip]is given [ainf]to know the mystery[3466] of the kingdom[932] of God: but unto [a]them that are without,[1854] all *these* things are done in parables:

12 [a]That [ppt]seeing they [psa]may see, and not [aosb]perceive; and [ppt]hearing they [psa]may hear, and not [psa]understand; lest at any time they [aosb]should be converted,[1994] and *their* sins[265] [asbp]should be forgiven them.

Explanation of the Parable of the Sower (Matt. 13:18–23; Luke 8:11–15)

13 And he said unto them, Know ye not this parable? and how then will ye know all parables?

14 [a]The sower soweth the word.[3056]

15 And these are they by the way side, where the word is sown; but when they [aosb]have heard, Satan cometh immediately, and taketh away the word that [pfpp]was sown in their hearts.

16 And these are they likewise which [ppp]are sown on stony ground; who, when they [aosb]have heard the word, immediately receive it with gladness;

17 And have no root in themselves, and so endure but for a time: afterward, when affliction or persecution [aptp]ariseth for the word's[3056] sake, immediately they are offended.

18 And these are they which [ppp]are sown among thorns; such as [ppt]hear the word,

19 And the cares of this world, [a]and the deceitfulness of riches, and the lusts of other things entering in, choke the word, and it becometh unfruitful.

20 And these are they which [aptp]are sown on [art]good ground; such as hear the word, and receive[3858] *it,* and bring forth fruit, some thirtyfold, some sixty, and some an hundred.

A Light Under a Bushel (Luke 8:16–18)

21 [a]And he said unto them, Is a candle brought[2064] to be put under a bushel, or under a bed? and not to be set on a candlestick?

22 [a]For there is nothing hid, which shall not be manifested;[5319] neither was any thing kept secret, but that it [aosb]should come[2064] abroad.

23 [a]If any man have ears to hear, [pim]let him hear.[191]

24 And he said unto them, [pim]Take

2 [a]Mark 12:38
8 [a]John 15:5; Col. 1:6
10 [a]Matt. 13:10; Luke 8:9, 10
11 [a]1Cor. 5:12; Col. 4:5; 1Thess. 4:12; 1Tim. 3:7
12 [a]Isa. 6:9; Matt. 13:14; Luke 8:10; John 12:40; Acts 28:26; Rom. 11:8
14 [a]Matt. 13:19
19 [a]1Tim. 6:9, 17
21 [a]Matt. 5:15; Luke 8:16; 11:33
22 [a]Matt. 10:26; Luke 12:2
23 [a]Matt. 11:15; Mark 4:9

🔑 **4:10–12** See note on Matthew 13:10–17.

heed what ye hear: [a]with what measure ye mete,[3354] it shall be measured to you: and unto you that [ppt]hear shall more be given.

25 [a]For he that hath, to him shall be given: and he that hath not, from him shall be taken even that which he hath.

The Parable of the Growth Of the Seed

26 And he said, [a]So is the kingdom[932] of God, as if a man [aosb]should cast seed into the ground;

27 And [psa]should sleep, and [psmp]rise night and day, and the seed should spring and grow up, he knoweth not how.

28 For the earth[1093] bringeth forth fruit of herself; first the blade, then the ear, after that the full[4134] corn in the ear.

29 But when the fruit is [I]brought forth, immediately [a]he putteth in[649] the sickle, because the harvest [pf]is come.

The Parable of the Mustard Seed (Matt. 13:31, 32; Luke 13:18, 19)

30 And he said, [a]Whereunto shall we liken the kingdom of God? or with what comparison[3850] shall we compare[3846] it?

31 *It is* like a grain of mustard seed, which, when it is sown in the earth, is less than all the seeds that be in the earth:

32 But when it is sown, it groweth up,[305] and becometh greater than all herbs, and shooteth out great branches; so that the fowls of the air may [pinf]lodge under the shadow of it.

Jesus' Use of Parables (Matt. 13:34, 35)

33 [a]And with many such parables[3850] [ipf]spake he the word unto them, as they were able [pinf]to hear *it.*

34 But without a parable spake he not unto them: and when they were alone,[2596,2398] he [ipf]expounded all things to his disciples.

Jesus Calms a Storm (Matt. 8:23–27; Luke 8:22–25)

35 [a]And the same day, when the even was come, he saith unto them, Let us pass over unto the other side.

36 And when they had sent away[863] the multitude, they took him even as he was in the ship. And there were also with him other[243] little ships.

37 And there arose a great storm[2978] of wind, and the waves [ipf]beat into the ship, so that it [pinf]was now full.

38 And he was in the hinder part of the ship, [ppt]asleep on a pillow: and they awake him, and say unto him, Master, carest thou not that we perish?[622]

39 And he arose, and rebuked the wind, and said unto the sea, Peace, be still. And the wind ceased,[2869] and there was a great calm.

40 And he said unto them, Why are ye so fearful? how is it that ye have no faith?[4102]

41 And they feared exceedingly, and said one to another, What manner of man is this, that even the wind and the sea obey[5219] him?

Healing the Gadarene Demoniac (Matt. 8:28–34; Luke 8:26–39)

5 And [a]they came over unto the other side of the sea, into the country of the Gadarenes.

2 And when he was come out of the ship, immediately there met him out of the tombs a man with an unclean[169] spirit,

3 Who had *his* dwelling[2731] among the tombs; and no man could bind[1210] him, no, not with chains:

4 Because that he had been often bound with fetters and chains, and

24 [a]Matt. 7:2; Luke 6:38
25 [a]Matt. 13:12; 25:29; Luke 8:18; 19:26
26 [a]Matt. 13:24
29 [I]Or, *ripe* [a]Rev. 14:15
30 [a]Matt. 13:31; Luke 13:18; Acts 2:41; 4:4; 5:14; 19:20
33 [a]Matt. 13:34; John 16:12
35 [a]Matt. 8:18, 23; Luke 8:22
1 [a]Matt. 8:28; Luke 8:26

the chains had been plucked asunder
by him, and the fetters broken in pieces:
neither [ipf]could[2480] any *man* [ainf]tame
him.
5 And always,1275 night and day,
he was in the mountains, and in the
tombs, crying, and cutting himself with
stones.
6 But when he saw Jesus afar off, he
ran and worshipped him,
7 And [apt]cried with a loud voice, and
said, What have I to do with thee, Jesus,
thou Son of the most high God? I
adjure3726 thee by God, that thou [aosi]tor-
ment me not.
8 For he said unto him, Come out of
the man, *thou* unclean[169] spirit.
9 And he asked him, What *is* thy
name? And he answered, saying, My
name *is* Legion: for we are many.
10 And he [ipf]besought him much that
he [aosb]would not send them away[649] out
of the country.
11 Now there was there nigh unto[4314]
the mountains a great herd of swine
feeding.
12 And all the devils[1142] besought
him, saying, Send us into the swine, that
we may enter into them.
13 And forthwith Jesus gave them
leave. And the unclean[169] spirits [apt]went
out, and entered into the swine: and
the herd ran violently down[2596] a steep
place into the sea, (they were about[5613]
two thousand;) and [ipf]were choked in the
sea.
14 And they that [ppt]fed the swine
fled, and told[312] *it* in the city, and in the
country. And they went out to see what
it was that was done.
15 And they come to Jesus, and see
him that [ppp]was possessed with the devil,
and had the legion, sitting, and clothed,
and in his right mind:4993 and they were
afraid.
16 And they that saw *it* told[1334] them
how it befell to him that was possessed
with the devil, and *also* concerning the
swine.
17 And [a]they began to pray him to
depart out of their coasts.
18 And when he [apt]was come into the

17 [a]Matt. 8:34; Acts 16:39
18 [a]Luke 8:38
21 [a]Matt. 9:1; Luke 8:40
22 [a]Matt. 9:18; Luke 8:41
25 [a]Lev. 15:25; Matt. 9:20
30 [a]Luke 6:19; 8:46

ship, [a]he that had been possessed with
the devil prayed him that he might be
with him.
19 Howbeit1161 Jesus suffered him
not, but saith unto him, Go home to thy
friends, and tell[312] them how great things
the Lord hath done for thee, and [ao]hath
had compassion on thee.
20 And he departed, and began to
publish[2784] in Decapolis how great things
Jesus [ao]had done for him: and all *men*
[ipf]did marvel.2296

Jesus Raises Jairus' Daughter (Matt. 9:18–26; Luke 8:40–56)

21 [a]And when Jesus was passed over
again by ship unto the other side, much
people gathered unto him: and he was
nigh unto the sea.
22 [a]And, behold, there cometh one of
the rulers of the synagogue,752 Jairus by
name; and when he saw him, he [pin]fell at
his feet,
23 And [ipf]besought him greatly, saying, My little daughter lieth at the point
of death: *I pray thee,* [apt]come and [aosb]lay
thy hands on her, that she may be
healed;[4982] and she shall live.[2198]
24 And *Jesus* went with him; and
much people [ipf]followed him, and
[ipf]thronged him.
25 And a certain woman, [a]which had
an issue of blood[129] twelve years,
26 And had suffered many things of
many physicians,2395 and had spent all
that she had, and was nothing bettered,
but rather [apt]grew worse,
27 When she had heard of Jesus,
[apt]came in the press behind, and touched
his garment.
28 For she said, If I may touch but
his clothes, I shall be whole.[4982]
29 And straightway2112 the fountain[4077] of her blood[129] was dried up;
and she felt in *her* body that she was
healed[2390] of that plague.
30 And Jesus, immediately [apt]know-
ing in himself that [a]virtue had gone out
of him, [aptp]turned him about[1994] in the
press, and said, Who touched my clothes?

31 And his disciples said unto him, Thou seest the multitude thronging thee, and sayest thou, Who touched me?

32 And he [ipf]looked round about[4017] to see her that had done this thing.

33 But the woman [aptp]fearing and [ppt]trembling, knowing what was done in her, came and fell down before him, and told him all the truth.[225]

34 And he said unto her, Daughter, [a]thy faith[4102] hath made thee whole;[4982] go in peace,[1515] and be whole[5199] of thy plague.

35 [a]While he yet [ppt]spake, there [pin]came from the ruler of the synagogue's *house certain* which said, Thy daughter [ao]is dead: why troublest thou the Master any further?

36 As soon as Jesus heard the word that was spoken, he saith unto the ruler of the synagogue, [pim]Be not afraid,[5399] only [pim]believe.[4100]

37 And he suffered no man to follow him, save Peter, and James, and John the brother of James.

38 And he cometh to the house of the ruler of the synagogue, and seeth the tumult, and them that [ppt]wept and [ppt]wailed greatly.

39 And when he was come in, he saith unto them, Why make ye this ado, and weep? the damsel [ao]is not dead,[599] but [a]sleepeth.

40 And they [ipf]laughed him to scorn. [a]But when he had put them all out, he taketh the father and the mother of the damsel, and them that were with him, and entereth in where the damsel was lying.

41 And he [apt]took the damsel by the hand, and said unto her, Talitha cumi; which is, being interpreted, Damsel, I say unto thee, arise.

42 And straightway the damsel arose, and [ipf]walked; for she was *of the age* of twelve years. And they were astonished[1839] with a great astonishment.[1611]

43 And [a]he charged them straitly[4183] that no man should know it; and commanded that something should be given her to eat.

Jesus Is Rejected in His Own Home Town (Matt. 13:53–58; Luke 4:16–30)

6 And [a]he went out from thence, and came into his own country; and his disciples[3101] follow him.

2 And when the sabbath day[4521] was come, he began [pinf]to teach in the synagogue: and many hearing *him* [ipf]were astonished, saying, [a]From whence hath this *man* these things? and what wisdom *is* this which [aptp]is given unto him, that even such mighty works are wrought by his hands?

⊶ 3 Is not this the carpenter, the son of Mary, [a]the [an]brother[80] of James, and Joses, and of Juda, and Simon? and are not his sisters here with us? And they [ipf][b]were offended at him.

4 But Jesus said unto them, [a]A prophet[4396] is not without honour, but in his own country, and among his own kin, and in his own house.

5 [a]And he [ipf]could there [ainf]do no mighty work, save that he [apt]laid his hands upon a few sick folk,[732] and healed *them.*

6 And [a]he [ipf]marvelled because of their unbelief.[570] [b]And he [ipf]went round about the villages, teaching.

The Mission of the Twelve (Matt. 10:1, 5–15; Luke 9:1–6)

7 [a]And he called *unto him* the twelve, and began [pinf]to send them forth by two and two; and [ipf]gave them power[1849] over [art]unclean spirits;

8 And commanded[3853] them that they should take[142] nothing for *their* jour-

34 [a]Matt. 9:22; Mark 10:52; Acts 14:9
35 [a]Luke 8:49
39 [a]John 11:11
40 [a]Acts 9:40
43 [a]Matt. 8:4; 9:30; 12:16; 17:9; Mark 3:12; Luke 5:14
1 [a]Matt. 13:54; Luke 4:16
2 [a]John 6:42
3 [a]Matt. 12:46; Gal. 1:19 [b]Matt. 11:6
4 [a]Matt. 13:57; John 4:44
5 [a]Gen. 19:22; 32:25; Matt. 13:58; Mark 9:23
6 [a]Isa. 59:16 [b]Matt. 9:35; Luke 13:22
7 [a]Matt. 10:1; Mark 3:13, 14; Luke 9:1

⊶ **6:3** See general remarks in the introduction to the Book of Jude.

ney, save a staff only; no scrip,4082 no bread, no money in *their* purse;

9 But [a]*be* shod5265 with sandals; and not put on two coats.

10 [a]And he said unto them, In what place soever ye [aosb]enter into an house, there abide till ye [aosb]depart from that place.

11 [a]And whosoever shall not receive you, nor hear you, when ye [ppt]depart thence, [aim][b]shake off the dust under your feet for a testimony against them. Verily281 I say unto you, It shall be more tolerable414 for Sodom [I]and Gomorrha in the day of judgment,[2920] than for that city.

12 And they [apt]went out, and preached[2784] that men [aosb]should repent.[3340]

13 And they [ipf]cast out many devils, [a]and [ipf]anointed with oil many that were sick,[732] and [ipf]healed *them.*

Herod Is Confused About Jesus (Matt. 14:1–12; Luke 9:7–9)

14 [a]And king Herod heard *of him;* (for his name[3686] was spread abroad:[5318]) and he said, That John the Baptist[907] was risen from the dead, and therefore mighty works do shew forth[1754] themselves in him.

15 [a]Others[243] said, That it is Elias. And others said, That it is a prophet,[4396] or as one of the prophets.

16 [a]But when Herod heard *thereof,* he said, It is John, whom I beheaded: he [aop]is risen from the dead.

17 For Herod himself [apt]had sent forth and laid hold upon John, and bound him in prison for Herodias' sake, his brother Philip's wife: for he had married her.

18 For John had said unto Herod, [a]It is not lawful for thee to have thy brother's wife.

19 Therefore Herodias had [I]a quarrel against[1758] him, and [ipf]would have [ainf]killed him; but she could not:

20 For Herod [ipf][a]feared[5399] John, knowing that he was a just[1342] man and an holy,[40] and [ipf][I]observed[4933] him; and when he heard him, he [ipf]did many things, and [ipf]heard him gladly.

21 [a]And when a convenient day was come, that Herod [b]on his birthday [ipf]made a supper to his lords, high captains, and chief *estates* of Galilee;

22 And when the daughter of the said Herodias came in, and [apt]danced, and [apt]pleased Herod and them that sat with him, the king said unto the damsel, [aim]Ask of me whatsoever thou wilt, and I will give *it* thee.

23 And he sware unto her, [a]Whatsoever thou shalt ask of me, I will give *it* thee, unto the half of my kingdom.[932]

24 And she [apt]went forth, and said unto her mother, What shall I ask? And she said, The head of John the Baptist.[910]

25 And she [apt]came in straightway2112 with haste unto the king, and asked, saying, I will that thou give me by and by in a charger4094 the head of John the Baptist.

26 [a]And the king was exceeding sorry; *yet* for his oath's sake, and for their sakes which sat with him, he would not reject her.

27 And immediately the king [apt]sent [I]an executioner, and commanded[2004] his head to be brought: and he [apt]went and beheaded him in the prison,

28 And brought his head in a charger, and gave it to the damsel: and the damsel gave it to her mother.

29 And when his disciples heard *of it,* they came and took up[142] his corpse, and laid[5087] it in a tomb.

Jesus Feeds the Five Thousand (Matt. 14:13–21; Luke 9:10–17; John 6:1–14)

30 [a]And the apostles[652] [pin]gathered themselves together unto Jesus, and told him all things, both what they [ao]had done, and what they [ao]had taught.

31 [a]And he said unto them, Come ye yourselves apart into a desert place, and [pim]rest a while: for [b]there were many com-

---

9 [a]Acts 12:8
10 [a]Matt. 10:11; Luke 9:4; 10:7, 8
11 [I]Gr. *or* [a]Matt. 10:14; Luke 10:10 [b]Acts 13:51; 18:6
13 [a]James 5:14
14 [a]Matt. 14:1; Luke 9:7
15 [a]Matt. 16:14; Mark 8:28
16 [a]Matt. 14:2; Luke 3:19
18 [a]Lev. 18:16; 20:21
19 [I]Or, *an inward grudge*
20 [I]Or, *kept him,* or, *saved hi* [a]Matt. 14:5; 21:26
21 [a]Matt. 14:6 [b]Gen. 40:20
23 [a]Esth. 5:3, 6; 7:2
26 [a]Matt. 14:9
27 [I]Or, *one of his guard*
30 [a]Luke 9:10
31 [a]Matt. 14:13 [b]Mark 3:20

ing and going, and they had no leisure so much as to eat.

32 [a]And they departed into a desert place by ship privately.

33 And the people saw them departing, and many knew him, and ran afoot thither out of all cities, and outwent them, and came together unto him.

34 [a]And Jesus, when he came out, saw much people, and was moved with compassion toward them, because they were as sheep not having a shepherd:[4166] and [b]he began to teach them many things.

35 [a]And when the day[5610] was now far spent, his disciples [apt]came unto him, and [pin]said, This is a desert place, and now the time[5610] *is* far passed:

36 Send them away, that they [apt]may go into the country round about, and into the villages, and buy themselves bread:[740] for they have nothing to eat.

37 He [aptp]answered and said unto them, Give ye them to eat. And they say unto him, [apt][a]Shall we go[565] and buy two hundred pennyworth[1220] of bread, and give them to eat?

38 He saith unto them, How many loaves have ye? go and see. And when they knew, they say, [a]Five, and two fishes.

39 And he commanded[2004] them to make all sit down by companies upon the green grass.

40 And they sat down in ranks, by[303] hundreds, and by fifties.

41 And when he had taken the five loaves and the two fishes, he [apt]looked up to heaven, [a]and [ao]blessed,[2127] and brake the loaves, and [ipf]gave *them* to his disciples to set before them; and the two fishes divided he among them all.

42 And they did all eat, and were filled.

43 And they took up[142] twelve baskets full of the fragments,[2801] and of the fishes.

44 And they that did eat of the loaves were about five thousand men.

32 [a]Matt. 14:13

34 [a]Matt. 9:36; 14:14 [b]Luke 9:11

35 [a]Matt. 14:15; Luke 9:12

37 [a]Num. 11:13, 22; 2Kgs. 4:43

38 [a]Matt. 14:17; Luke 9:13; John 6:9; Matt. 15:34; Mark 8:5

41 [a]1Sam. 9:13; Matt. 26:26

45 [I]Or, *over against Bethsaida* [a]Matt. 14:22; John 6:17

47 [a]Matt. 14:23; John 6:16, 17

48 [a]Luke 24:28

52 [a]Mark 8:17, 18 [b]Mark 3:5; 16:14

53 [a]Matt. 14:34

Jesus Walks on Water
(Matt. 14:22–33; John 6:15–21)

45 [a]And straightway[2112] he constrained[315] his disciples[3101] to get into the ship, and to go to the other side before [I]unto Bethsaida, while he sent away the people.

46 And when he had sent them away,[657] he departed into a mountain [aifp]to pray.

47 [a]And when even was come, the ship was in the midst of the sea, and he alone on the land.

48 And he [ao]saw them toiling in rowing; for the wind was contrary unto them: and about the fourth watch of the night he cometh unto them, walking upon the sea, and [a]would have passed by them.

49 But when they saw him walking upon the sea, they supposed[1380] it had been a spirit,[5326] and cried out:

50 For they all saw him, and were troubled. And immediately he talked with them, and saith unto them, Be of good cheer: it is [epn]I; [pim]be not afraid.[5399]

51 And he went up unto them into the ship; and the wind ceased:[2869] and they [ipf]were[1839] sore[3029] amazed[1839] in themselves beyond measure,[4053] and [ipf]wondered.

52 For [a]they considered[4920] not *the miracle* of the loaves: for their [b]heart was hardened.[4456]

Jesus Heals in Gennesaret
(Matt. 14:34–36)

53 [a]And when they had passed over, they came into the land of Gennesaret, and drew to the shore.

54 And when they were come out of the ship, straightway[2112] they [apt]knew him,

55 And ran through that whole region round about, and began to carry about in beds those that were sick, where they heard he was.

56 And whithersoever he [ipf]entered, into villages, or cities, or country, they laid[5087] the sick in the streets, and

besought[3870] him that [a]they [asbm]might
touch if it were but the border of his
garment: and as many as [ipf]touched [I]him
[ipf]were made whole.

God's Command Or Man's Tradition? (Matt. 15:1–20)

7 Then [a]came together unto him the
Pharisees, and certain of the
scribes,[1122] which [apt]came from Jerusalem.
2 And when they saw some of his
disciples[3101] [ppt]eat bread with [I]defiled,[2839]
that is to say, with unwashen, hands, they
found fault.
3 For the Pharisees, and all the Jews,
except they wash[3538] *their* hands [I]oft, eat
not, holding the tradition[3862] of the
elders.[4245]
4 And *when they come* from the
market,[58] except they [asbm]wash,[907] they
eat not. And many other things[243] there
be, which they [ao]have received [pinf]to hold,
as the [pl]washing[909] of cups, and pots,
brasen vessels, and of [I]tables.
5 [a]Then the Pharisees and scribes
[pin]asked him, Why walk not thy disciples
according to[2596] the tradition of the
elders, but eat bread with unwashen
hands?
6 He answered and said unto them,
Well hath Esaias prophesied[4395] of you
hypocrites, as it is written, [a]This people
honoureth me with *their* lips, but their
heart[2588] is[568] far from me.
7 Howbeit[1161] in vain[3155] do they
worship[4576] me, teaching *for* doctrines[1319]
the commandments[1778] of men.
8 For [apt]laying aside the commandment of God, ye hold the tradition of
men, *as* the [pl]washing[909] of pots and
cups: and many other such like things ye
do.
9 And he said unto them, Full
well ye [I]reject the commandment of
God, that ye [aosb]may keep your own
tradition.
10 For Moses said, [pim][a]Honour thy father and thy mother; and, [b]Whoso

56 [I]Or, *it* [a]Matt. 9:20; Mark 5:27, 28; Acts 19:12

1 [a]Matt. 15:1

2 [I]Or, *common*

3 [I]Or, *diligently: up to the elbow*

4 [I]Or, *beds*

5 [a]Matt. 15:2

6 [a]Isa. 29:13; Matt. 15:8

9 [I]Or, *frustrate*

10 [a]Ex. 20:12; Deut. 5:16; Matt. 15:4 [b]Ex. 21:17; Lev. 20:9; Prov. 20:20

11 [a]Matt. 15:5; 23:18

14 [a]Matt. 15:10

16 [a]Matt. 11:15

17 [a]Matt. 15:15

21 [a]Gen. 6:5; 8:21; Matt. 15:19

22 [I]Gr. *covetousnesses, wickednesses*

[ppt]curseth father or mother, let him die
the death:
11 But ye say, If a man shall say to
his [art]father or [art]mother, *It is* [a]Corban,[2878]
that is to say, a gift,[1435] by whatsoever
thou mightest be profited by me; *he shall
be free.*
12 And ye suffer him no more to
do[4160] ought[3762] for his father or his
mother;
13 Making the word[3056] of God of
none effect through your tradition, which
ye have delivered: and many such like
things do ye.

Evil Comes From the Heart

14 [a]And when he had called all the
people *unto him,* he said unto them,
[pim]Hearken unto me every one *of you,*
and [pim]understand:
15 There is nothing from without[1855]
a man, that entering into him can defile
him: but the things which [ppt]come out of
him, those are they that [ppt]defile the man.
16 [a]If any man have ears [pinf]to hear,
[pim]let him hear.[191]
17 [a]And when he was entered into
the house from the people, his disciples
[ipf]asked him concerning the parable.[3850]
18 And he saith unto them, Are ye so
without understanding[801] also? Do ye not
perceive,[3539] that whatsoever thing from
without[1855] [ppt]entereth into the man, *it*
cannot [ainf]defile him;
19 Because it entereth not into his
heart, but into the belly, and goeth out
into the draught,[856] purging[2511] all
meats?
20 And he said, That which
[ppt]cometh out of the man, that defileth
the man.
21 [a]For from within, out of the heart
of men, proceed evil thoughts,[1261] adulteries, fornications,[4202] murders,
22 Thefts, [I]covetousness,[4124] wickedness,[4189] deceit, lasciviousness,[766] an
evil[4190] eye, blasphemy,[988] pride, foolishness:
23 All these evil things come from
within, and defile the man.

Jesus Honours a Syrophoenician Woman's Faith (Matt. 15:21–28)

24 [a]And from thence he [apt]arose, and went into the borders of Tyre and Sidon, and entered into an house, and [ipf]would have no man know *it,* but he could not be hid.

25 For a *certain* woman, whose young daughter had an unclean spirit,[4151] [apt]heard of him, and [apt]came and fell at his feet:

26 The woman was a [I]Greek, a Syrophenician by nation; and she [ipf]besought him that he [aosb]would cast forth the devil[1140] out of her daughter.

27 But Jesus said unto her, Let the children first [aifp]be filled: for it is not meet[2570] to take the children's bread, and [ainf]to cast *it* unto the dogs.

28 And she answered and said unto him, Yes, Lord: yet the dogs under the table eat of the children's crumbs.

29 And he said unto her, For this saying go thy way; the devil [pfi]is gone out of thy daughter.

30 And when she was come to her house, she found the devil gone out, and her daughter laid upon the bed.

Jesus Heals a Deaf and Dumb Man

31 [a]And again, departing from the coasts of Tyre and Sidon, he came unto the sea of Galilee, through[303] the midst[3319] of the coasts of Decapolis.

32 And [a]they bring[5342] unto him one that was deaf, and had an impediment in his speech; and they beseech him to put his hand upon him.

33 And he [apt]took[618] him aside from the multitude, and put[906] his fingers into his ears, and [a]he [apt]spit, and touched his tongue;[1100]

34 And [apt][a]looking up to heaven, [b]he sighed, and saith unto him, Ephphatha, that is, Be opened.

24 [a]Matt. 15:21
26 [I]Or, *Gentile*
31 [a]Matt. 15:29
32 [a]Matt. 9:32; Luke 11:14
33 [a]Mark 8:23; John 9:6
34 [a]Mark 6:41; John 11:41; 17:1 [b]John 11:33, 38
35 [a]Isa. 35:5, 6; Matt. 11:5
36 [a]Mark 5:43
1 [a]Matt. 15:32
5 [a]Matt. 15:34; Mark 6:38
7 [a]Matt. 14:19; Mark 6:41
10 [a]Matt. 15:39

35 [a]And straightway[2112] his ears[189] were opened, and the string of his tongue was loosed, and he [ipf]spake plain.

36 And [b]he charged them that they should tell no man: but the more he [ipf]charged them, so much the more a great deal they [ipf]published[2784] *it;*

37 And [ipf]were[1605] beyond measure[5249] astonished,[1605] saying, He hath done all things well: he maketh both the deaf to hear, and the dumb[216] to speak.[2980]

Jesus Feeds the Four Thousand (Matt. 15:32–39)

8 In those days [a]the multitude being very great, and having nothing to eat, Jesus [apt]called his disciples[3101] *unto him,* and saith unto them,

2 I have compassion on the multitude, because they [pin]have now been with[4357] me three days, and have nothing to eat:

3 And if I send them away fasting[3523] to their own houses, they will faint by the way: for divers[5100] of them came from far.

4 And his disciples answered him, From whence can a man satisfy these *men* with bread here in the wilderness?

5 [a]And he [ipf]asked them, How many loaves have ye? And they said, Seven.

6 And he commanded the people to sit down on the ground: and he [apt]took the seven loaves, and [apt]gave thanks,[2168] and brake, and [ipf]gave to his disciples to set before *them;* and they did set *them* before the people.

7 And they had a few small fishes: and [a]he [apt]blessed,[2127] and commanded to set them also before *them.*

8 So they did eat, and were filled: and they took up of the broken[2801] *meat* that was left[4051] seven baskets.

9 And they that had eaten were about[5613] four thousand: and he sent them away.

10 And [a]straightway he [apt]entered

into a ship with his disciples, and came into the parts of Dalmanutha.

The Pharisees Demand a Sign (Matt. 16:1–4)

11 [a]And the Pharisees came forth, and began to question with him, seeking of him a sign from heaven, tempting[3985] him.

12 And he [apt]sighed deeply in his spirit, and saith, Why doth this generation seek after a sign? verily[281] I say unto you, There shall no sign be given unto this generation.

13 And he [apt]left them, and [apt]entering into the ship again departed to the other side.

The Leaven of the Pharisees And of Herod (Matt. 16:5–12)

14 [a]Now *the disciples* [aom]had forgotten to take bread, neither had they in the ship with them more than one loaf.

15 [a]And he [ipf]charged them, saying, Take heed,[3708] beware[991] of the leaven[2219] of the Pharisees, and *of* the leaven of Herod.

16 And they reasoned among themselves, saying, *It is* [a]because we have no bread.

17 And when Jesus knew *it,* he saith unto them, Why reason ye, because ye have no bread? [a]perceive[3539] ye not yet, neither understand?[4920] have ye your heart yet hardened?

18 Having eyes, see ye not? and having ears, hear ye not? and do ye not remember?

19 [a]When I brake the five loaves among five thousand, how many baskets full of fragments[2801] took ye up? They say unto him, Twelve.

20 And [a]when the seven among four thousand, how many baskets full[4138] of fragments[2801] took ye up? And they said, Seven.

21 And he said unto them, How is it that [a]ye do not understand?

11 [a]Matt. 12:38; 16:1; John 6:30
14 [a]Matt. 16:5
15 [a]Matt. 16:6; Luke 12:1
16 [a]Matt. 16:7
17 [a]Mark 6:52
19 [a]Matt. 14:20; Mark 6:43; Luke 9:17; John 6:13
20 [a]Matt. 15:37; Mark 8:8
21 [a]Mark 6:52; 8:17
23 [a]Mark 7:33
26 [a]Matt. 8:4; 5:43
27 [a]Matt. 16:13; Luke 9:18
28 [a]Matt. 14:2
29 [a]Matt. 16:16; John 6:69; 11:27
30 [a]Matt. 16:20
31 [a]Matt. 16:21; 17:22; Luke 9:22

Jesus Heals a Blind Man at Bethsaida

22 And he cometh to Bethsaida: and they bring a blind man unto him, and [pin]besought him to touch him.

23 And he [apt]took[1949] the blind man by the hand, and led[1806] him out of the town; and when [a]he had spit on his eyes, and [apt]put his hands upon him, he asked him if he saw ought.

24 And he [apt]looked up,[308] and [ipf]said, I see men as trees, walking.

25 After that he put *his* hands again upon his eyes, and made him look up: and he was restored,[600] and saw[1689] every man clearly.

26 And he sent him away to his house, saying, Neither go into the town, [a]nor tell *it* to any in the town.

Peter's Declaration That Jesus Is the Messiah (Matt. 16:13–20; Luke 9:18–21)

27 [a]And Jesus went out, and his disciples, into the towns of Caesarea Philippi: and by the way he asked his disciples, saying unto them, Whom do men say that I am?

28 And they answered, [a]John the Baptist:[910] but some *say,* Elias; and others, One of the prophets.

29 And he saith unto them, But whom say ye that I am? And Peter answereth and saith unto him, [a]Thou art the Christ.[5547]

30 [a]And he charged them that they should tell no man of him.

Jesus Predicts His Death And Resurrection (Matt. 16:21–28; Luke 9:22–27)

31 And [a]he began to teach them, that the Son of man must suffer many things, and be rejected[593] of the elders,[4245] and *of* the chief priests, and scribes, and be killed, and after three days rise again.

32 And he [ipf]spake that saying

openly. And Peter [apt]took[4355] him, and began to rebuke him.

33 But when he had turned about[1994] and [apt]looked on his disciples, he rebuked Peter, saying, Get thee behind me, Satan:[4567] for thou savourest not the things that be of God, but the things that be of men.

34 And when he had called the people *unto him* with his disciples[3101] also, he said unto them, [a]Whosoever [pin]will [pinf]come after me, [aim]let him deny[533] himself, and [aim]take up his cross,[4716] and [pim]follow[190] me.

35 For [a]whosoever [psa]will [ainf]save his life[5590] [ft]shall lose it; but whosoever [aosb]shall lose his life for my sake and the gospel's,[2098] the same [ft]shall save it.

36 For what [ft]shall it profit[5623] a man, if he [aosb]shall gain the whole world, and [aosb]lose his own soul?[5590]

37 Or what [ft]shall a man give[1325] in exchange[465] for his soul?

38 [a]Whosoever therefore [asbp][b]shall be ashamed of me and of my words in[1722] this adulterous and sinful[268] generation; of him also [fp]shall the Son of man be ashamed,[1870] when he [aosb]cometh in[1772] the glory[1391] of his Father with the holy angels.

9 And he said unto them, [a]Verily[281] I say unto you, That there be some of them that [pfp]stand here, which shall not taste[1089] of death,[2288] till they have seen [b]the kingdom[932] of God [pfp]come with power.

The Transfiguration (Matt. 17:1–13; Luke 9:28–36)

2 [a]And after six days Jesus taketh *with him* Peter, and James, and John, and leadeth them up[399] into an high mountain apart by themselves: and he was transfigured[3339] before them.

3 And his raiment became shining, exceeding [a]white as snow; so as no fuller[1102] on earth[1093] can white them.

4 And there appeared unto them Elias with Moses: and they were talking with Jesus.

5 And Peter answered[611] and said to Jesus, Master, it is good for us to be here: and let us make three tabernacles;[4633] one for thee, and one for Moses, and one for Elias.

6 For he wist not what to say; for they were sore afraid.[1630]

7 And there was a cloud that [ppt]overshadowed them: and a voice came out of the cloud, saying, This is my beloved[27] Son:[5207] [pim]hear him.

8 And suddenly, when they had looked round about,[4017] they saw no man any more, save Jesus only with themselves.

9 [a]And as they [ppt]came down from the mountain, he charged them that they should tell[1334] no man what things they had seen, till the Son of man [aosb]were risen from the dead.

10 And they kept that saying with themselves, questioning one with another what the [ainf]rising from the dead should mean.

11 And they asked him, saying, Why say the scribes [a]that Elias must[1163] first [ainf]come?

12 And he answered and told them, Elias verily[3303] [apt]cometh first, and restoreth[600] all things; and [a]how it is written of the Son of man, that he must suffer many things, and [b]be set at nought.[1847]

13 But I say unto you, That [a]Elias [pfi]is indeed come,[2064] and they have done unto him whatsoever they listed, as it is written of him.

Jesus Heals a Boy With an Unclean Spirit (Matt. 17:14–20; Luke 9:37–43)

14 [a]And when he came to *his* disciples,[3101] he saw a great multitude about them, and the scribes[1122] questioning with them.

15 And straightway[2112] all the people, when they beheld him, were greatly amazed, and running to *him* [ipf]saluted him.

34 [a]Matt. 10:38; 16:24; Luke 9:23; 14:27
35 [a]John 12:25
38 [a]Matt. 10:33; Luke 9:26; 12:9 [b]Rom. 1:16; 2Tim. 1:8; 2:12
1 [a]Matt. 16:28; Luke 9:27 [b]Matt. 24:30; 25:31; Luke 22:18
2 [a]Matt. 17:1; Luke 9:28
3 [a]Dan. 7:9; Matt. 28:3
9 [a]Matt. 17:9
11 [a]Mal. 4:5; Matt. 17:10
12 [a]Ps. 22:6; Isa. 53:2-9; Dan. 9:26 [b]Luke 23:11; Phil. 2:7
13 [a]Matt. 11:14; 17:12; Luke 1:17
14 [a]Matt. 17:14; Luke 9:37

16 And he asked the scribes, What question ye [I]with them?

17 And [a]one of the multitude answered[611] and said, Master, I [ao]have brought unto thee my son, which [ppt]hath a dumb[216] spirit;

18 And wheresoever he [aosb]taketh[2638] him, he [I]teareth him: and he foameth, and gnasheth[5149] with his teeth, and pineth away:[3583] and I spake to thy disciples that they should cast him out; and they could[2480] not.

19 He answereth him, and saith, O faithless[571] generation, how long shall I be with you? how long shall I suffer[430] you? bring him unto me.

20 And they brought him unto him: and [a]when he saw him, straightway[2112] the spirit[4151] tare him; and he [apt]fell[4098] on the ground, and [ipf]wallowed foaming.

21 And he asked his father, How long is it ago since this came unto him? And he said, Of a child.

22 And ofttimes it [ao]hath cast him into the fire, and into the waters, to [aosb]destroy[622] him: but if thou canst do any thing, [aptp]have compassion on us, and help us.

23 Jesus said unto him, [a]If thou canst [ainf]believe,[4100] all things *are* possible to him that [ppt]believeth.

24 And straightway the father of the child cried out, and said with tears, Lord, I believe; [pim]help thou mine unbelief.[570]

25 When Jesus saw that the people came running together, he rebuked[2008] the foul spirit, saying unto him, *Thou* dumb[216] and deaf spirit, [epn]I charge thee, [aim]come out of him, and [aosi]enter no more into him.

26 And *the spirit* cried, and [apt]rent[4682] him sore,[4183] and came out of him: and he was as one dead; insomuch that many said, He [ao]is dead.

27 But Jesus [apt]took him by the hand, and lifted him up;[1453] and he arose.

28 [a]And when he was come into the house, his disciples[3101] [ipf]asked him privately, Why [aop]could not we [ainf]cast him out?

16 [I]Or, *among yourselves*

17 [a]Matt. 17:14; Luke 9:38

18 [I]Or, *dasheth him*

20 [a]Mark 1:26; Luke 9:42

23 [a]Matt. 17:20; Mark 11:23; Luke 17:6; John 11:40

28 [a]Matt. 17:19

31 [a]Matt. 17:22; Luke 9:44

33 [a]Matt. 18:1; Luke 9:46; 22:24

35 [a]Matt. 20:26, 27; Mark 10:43

36 [a]Matt. 18:2; Mark 10:16

37 [a]Matt. 10:40; Luke 9:48

38 [a]Num. 11:28; Luke 9:49

29 And he said unto them, This kind can [ainf]come forth by nothing, but by prayer and fasting.[3521]

Jesus Predicts His Death And Resurrection (Matt. 17:22, 23; Luke 9:43–45)

30 And they departed thence, and [ipf]passed through Galilee; and he [ipf]would not that any man should know *it.*

31 [a]For he [ipf]taught[1321] his disciples,[3101] and said unto them, The Son of man [pp]is delivered into the hands of men, and they shall kill him; and after that he is killed, he shall rise the third day.

32 But they [ipf]understood not[50] that saying,[4487] and [ipf]were afraid [ainf]to ask him.

The Greatness of Humility (Matt. 18:1–5; Luke 9:46–48)

33 [a]And he came to Capernaum: and [apt]being[1096] in the house he asked them, What was it that ye [ipf]disputed[1260] among yourselves by the way?

34 But they [ipf]held their peace: for by the way they [aop]had disputed among themselves, who *should be* the greatest.

35 And he sat down, and called the twelve, and saith unto them, [a]If any man desire to be first, *the same* shall be last[2078] of all, and servant of all.

36 And [a]he [apt]took a child, and set[2476] him in the midst of them: and when he had taken him in his arms, he said unto them,

37 Whosoever shall receive one of such children in my name,[3686] receiveth me: and [a]whosoever [asbm]shall receive me, receiveth not me, but him that sent me.

Others Who Work in the Name of Christ (Luke 9:49, 50)

38 [a]And John answered him, saying, Master, we saw one casting out[1544] devils[1140] in thy name, and he followeth

not us: and we forbad him, because he followeth not us.

39 But Jesus said, [pim]Forbid him not: [a]for there is no man which shall do a miracle in my name, that can lightly [ainf]speak evil of me.

40 For [a]he that is not against us is on our part.

41 [a]For whosoever [aosb]shall give you a cup of water to drink in my name, because ye belong to Christ,[5547] verily I say unto you, he shall not lose[622] his reward.[3408]

Entrapments (Matt. 18:6–9; Luke 17:1, 2)

42 [a]And whosoever [aosb]shall offend[4624] one of *these* little ones that [ppt]believe in me, it is better for him that a millstone were hanged about his neck, and he were cast into the sea.[2281]

43 [a]And if thy hand [psa]offend thee, [aim]cut it off: it is better for thee [ainf]to enter into life[2222] maimed, than having two hands [ainf]to go into [art]hell,[1067] into the fire that never shall be quenched:

44 [a]Where their worm dieth not, and the fire [pinp]is not quenched.[4570]

45 And if thy foot [psa]offend thee, [aim]cut it off: it is better for thee [ainf]to enter halt into life, than having two feet to be cast into hell,[1067] into the fire that never shall be quenched:

46 Where their worm dieth not, and the fire [pinp]is not quenched.[4570]

47 And if thine eye [psa]offend thee, pluck it out: it is better for thee [ainf]to enter into the kingdom[932] of God with one eye, than having two eyes to be cast into [art]hell[1067] [art]fire:

48 Where their [art]worm dieth not, and the fire [pinp]is not quenched.[4570]

49 For every one shall be salted with fire, [a]and every sacrifice shall be salted with salt.

50 [a]Salt *is* good:[2570] but if the salt [asbm]have lost his saltness, wherewith will ye season it? [pim][b]Have salt in yourselves, and [pim][c]have peace one with another.

39 [a]1Cor. 12:3
40 [a]Matt. 12:30
41 [a]Matt. 10:42
42 [a]Matt. 18:6; Luke 17:1
43 [1]Or, *cause thee to offend* [a]Deut. 13:6; Matt. 5:29; 18:8
44 [a]Isa. 66:24
47 [1]Or, *cause thee to offend*
49 [a]Lev. 2:13; Ezek. 43:24
50 [a]Matt. 5:13; Luke 14:34 [b]Eph. 4:29; Col. 4:6 [c]Rom. 12:18; 14:19; 2Cor. 13:11; Heb. 12:14

Divorce (Matt. 5:27–32; 19:1–12; Luke 16:18; Rom. 7:1–3; 1 Cor. 7)

10 And [a]he arose from thence, and cometh into the coasts of Judaea by the farther side of Jordan: and the people resort unto him again; and, as he was wont,[1486] he [ipf]taught[1321] them again.

2 [a]And the Pharisees came to him, and asked him, Is it lawful for a man[435] to put away[630] *his* wife? tempting[3985] him.

3 And he answered and said unto them, What did Moses command you?

4 And they said, [a]Moses suffered to write[1125] a bill[975] of divorcement,[647] and to put *her* away.[630]

5 And Jesus answered and said unto them, For the hardness of your heart[4641] he wrote you this precept.

6 But from the beginning of the creation[2937] [a]God made them male and female.[2338]

7 [a]For this cause shall a man leave his father and mother, and cleave[4347] to his wife;

8 And they twain[1417] shall be one flesh: so then they are no more twain, but one flesh.

9 What therefore God [ao]hath joined together, [pim]let not man[444] put asunder.

10 And in the house his disciples[3101] asked him again of the same *matter*.

11 And he saith unto them, [a]Whosoever [aosb]shall put away[630] his wife, and [aosb]marry another, [pin]committeth adultery against her.

12 And if a woman [asba]shall put away[630] her husband, and [asbp]be married to another, she [pin]committeth adultery.

Who Will Enter God's Kingdom? (Matt. 19:13–15; Luke 18:15–17)

13 [a]And they brought young children to him, that he [asbm]should touch them: and *his* disciples[3101] [ipf]rebuked those that [ppt]brought *them*.

1 [a]Matt. 19:1; John 10:40; 11:7
2 [a]Matt. 19:3
4 [a]Deut. 24:1; Matt. 5:31; 19:7
6 [a]Gen. 1:27; 5:2
7 [a]Gen. 2:24; 1Cor. 6:16; Eph. 5:31
11 [a]Matt. 5:32; 19:9; Luke 16:18; Rom. 7:3; 1Cor. 7:10, 11
13 [a]Matt. 19:13; Luke 18:15

14 But when Jesus saw *it,* he was
much displeased, and said unto them,
Suffer the little children to come unto me,
and forbid them not: for [a]of such is the
kingdom[932] of God.
15 Verily281 I say unto you, [a]Who-
soever shall not receive the kingdom[932] of
God as a little child, he shall not enter
therein.
16 And he [apt]took them up in his
arms, [ppt]put[5087] *his* hands upon them,
and blessed[2127] them.

The Rich Man Tested (Matt. 19:16–30; Luke 18:18–30)

17 [a]And when he was gone forth into
the way, there [ppt]came one running, and
[apt]kneeled to him, and asked him, Good[18]
Master, what shall I do that I may inherit[2816] eternal life?[2222]
18 And Jesus said unto him, Why
callest thou me good? *there is* none good
but one, *that is,* God.
19 Thou knowest the commandments, [a]Do not commit adultery, Do not
kill, Do not steal, Do not bear false witness, Defraud650 not, Honour thy father
and mother.
20 And he answered and said unto
him, Master, all these have I observed
from my youth.[3503]
21 Then Jesus [apt]beholding1689 him
loved[25] him, and said unto him, One
thing thou lackest: go thy way, sell whatsoever thou hast, and give to the poor,
and thou shalt have [a]treasure in
heaven:[3772] and come, [apt]take up the
cross,[4716] and [pim]follow me.
22 And he [apt]was sad at that saying,
and went away [ppt]grieved: for he had
great possessions.
23 [a]And Jesus [apt]looked round
about,4017 and saith unto his disciples,
How hardly shall they that [ppt]have
riches[5536] enter into the kingdom[932] of
God!
24 And the disciples [ipf]were astonished at his words. But Jesus answereth
again, and saith unto them, Children, how
hard is it for them [a]that [pfp]trust[3982] in
riches [ainf]to enter into the kingdom of
God!
25 It is easier for a camel [ainf]to go
through the eye of a needle, than for a
rich man [ainf]to enter into the kingdom of
God.
26 And they [ipf]were astonished out of
measure,4057 saying among themselves,
Who then can be saved?[4982]
27 And Jesus looking upon1689 them
saith, With men *it is* impossible, but not
[a]with God: for with God all things are
possible.
28 [a]Then Peter began to say unto
him, Lo, we [ao]have left all, and [ao]have followed thee.
29 And Jesus answered and said,
Verily I say unto you, There is no man
that [ao]hath left house, or brethren,[80] or
sisters, or father, or mother, or wife, or
children, or lands, for my sake, and the
gospel's,[2098]
30 [a]But he shall receive[2983] an hundredfold now in this time, houses, and
brethren, and sisters, and mothers, and
children, and lands, with persecutions;
and in the world[165] to come[2064] eternal
life.[2222]
31 [a]But many *that are* first shall be
last;[2078] and the last first.

Jesus Will Rise From the Dead (Matt. 20:17–19; Luke 18:31–34)

32 [a]And they were in the way going
up to Jerusalem; and Jesus went before
them: and they [ipf]were amazed; and as
they followed, they [ipf]were afraid. [b]And he
[apt]took again the twelve, and began to
tell them what things should [pinf]happen
unto him,
33 *Saying,* Behold, we go up to
Jerusalem; and the Son of man shall be
delivered unto the chief priests, and unto
the scribes;[1122] and they shall condemn
him to death, and shall deliver him to the
Gentiles:
34 And they shall mock him, and
shall scourge3146 him, and shall spit upon
him, and shall kill him: and the third day
he shall rise again.

14 [a]1Cor. 14:20; 1Pet. 2:2
15 [a]Matt. 18:3
17 [a]Matt. 19:16; Luke 18:18
19 [a]Ex. 20; Rom. 13:9
21 [a]Matt. 6:19, 20; 19:21; Luke 12:33; 16:9
22 [a]Matt. 19:23; Luke 18:24
24 [a]Job 31:24; Ps. 52:7; 62:10; 1Tim. 6:17
27 [a]Jer. 32:17; Matt. 19:26; Luke 1:37
28 [a]Matt. 19:27; Luke 18:28
30 [a]2Chr. 25:9; Luke 18:30
31 [a]Matt. 19:30; 20:16; Luke 13:30
32 [a]Matt. 20:17; Luke 18:31 [b]Mark 8:31; 9:31; Luke 9:22; 18:31

James and John Request Special Positions (Matt. 20:20–28)

35 [a]And James and John, the sons of Zebedee, come unto him, saying, Master, we would that thou [aosb]shouldest do for us whatsoever we shall desire.

36 And he said unto them, What would ye that I [ainf]should do for you?

37 They said unto him, Grant unto us that we may sit, one on thy right hand,[1188] and the other on thy left hand, in thy glory.[1391]

38 But Jesus said unto them, Ye know not what ye ask: can ye drink of the cup that I drink of? and be baptized[907] with the baptism[908] that I am baptized[907] with?

39 And they said unto him, We can. And Jesus said unto them, Ye shall indeed drink of the cup that I drink of; and with the baptism that I am baptized[907] withal shall ye be baptized:[907]

40 But [ainf]to sit on my right hand[1188] and on my left hand is not mine to give; but *it shall be given to them* for whom it is prepared.

41 [a]And when the ten heard *it,* they began [pinf]to be much displeased with James and John.

42 But Jesus called them *to him,* and saith unto them, [a]Ye know that they which [pptl]are accounted [pinf]to rule over[757] the Gentiles exercise lordship over them; and their great ones exercise authority upon them.

43 [a]But so shall it not be among you: but whosoever will be great among you, shall be your minister:[1249]

44 And whosoever of you will be the chiefest, shall be servant of all.

45 For even [a]the Son of man came not [aifp]to be ministered unto,[1247] but [ainf]to minister, and [b]to give his life[5590] a ransom[3083] for many.

The Healing of Blind Bartimaeus (Matt. 20:29–34; Luke 18:35–43)

46 [a]And they came to Jericho: and as he [ppt]went out of Jericho with his disciples[3101] and a great[2425] number of people, blind Bartimaeus, the son of Timaeus, [ipf]sat by the highway side begging.[4319]

47 And when he heard that it was Jesus of Nazareth, he began to cry out, and say, Jesus, *thou* son of David, have mercy on me.

48 And many [ipf]charged him that he should hold his peace: but he [ipf]cried the more a great deal, *Thou* son of David, have mercy on me.

49 And Jesus stood still, and commanded him [aifp]to be called. And they call the blind man, saying unto him, Be of good comfort, rise; he calleth thee.

50 And he, casting away his garment, [apt]rose, and came to Jesus.

51 And Jesus answered and said unto him, What wilt thou that I should do unto thee? The blind man said unto him, Lord, that I might receive my sight.

52 And Jesus said unto him, Go thy way; [a]thy faith[4102] [pfi]hath [I]made thee whole.[4982] And immediately he received his sight, and [ipf]followed Jesus in the way.

Jesus Enters Jerusalem (Matt. 21:1–11; Luke 19:28–40; John 12:12–19)

11 And [a]when they [pin]came nigh to Jerusalem, unto Bethphage and Bethany, at the mount of Olives, he sendeth forth two of his disciples,[3101]

2 And saith unto them, Go your way into the village over against you: and as soon as ye [ppp]be entered into it, ye shall find a colt tied, whereon never man sat; [apt]loose[3089] him, and bring[71] *him.*

3 And if any man [aosb]say unto you, Why do ye this? say ye that the Lord hath need of him; and straightway[2112] he will send him hither.

4 And they [ao]went their way, and found the colt tied by[4314] the door without[1854] in a place where two ways met; and they loose[3089] him.

5 And certain of them that [pfp]stood there said unto them, What do ye, loosing the colt?

---

35 [a]Matt. 20:20
41 [a]Matt. 20:24
42 [I]Or, *think good* [a]Luke 22:25
43 [a]Matt. 20:26, 28; Mark 9:35; Luke 9:48
45 [a]John 13:14; Phil. 2:7 [b]Matt. 20:28; 1Tim. 2:6; Titus 2:14
46 [a]Matt. 20:29; Luke 18:35
52 [I]Or, *saved thee* [a]Matt. 9:22; Mark 5:34
1 [a]Matt. 21:1; Luke 19:29; John 12:14

6 And they said unto them even as Jesus [aom]had commanded: and they let them go.

7 And they brought the colt to Jesus, and cast their garments on him; and he sat upon him.

8 [a]And many spread their garments in the way: and others [ipf]cut down[2875] branches off the trees, and [ipf]strawed 4766 *them* in the way.

9 And they that went before,[4254] and they that followed, cried, saying, [a]Hosanna; 5614 Blessed[2127] *is* he that [ppp]cometh in the name of the Lord:

10 Blessed *be* the kingdom[932] of our father David, that cometh in the name of the Lord: [a]Hosanna in the highest.

11 [a]And Jesus entered into Jerusalem, and into the temple:[2411] and when he had looked round about upon 4017 all things, and now the eventide was come, he went out unto Bethany with the twelve.

The Fruitless Fig Tree (Matt. 21:18, 19)

12 [a]And on the morrow, when they were come from Bethany, he was hungry:

13 [a]And seeing a fig tree afar off having leaves, he came, if haply 686 he might find anything thereon: and when he [apt]came to it, he found nothing but leaves; for the time[2540] of figs was not *yet.*

14 And Jesus answered and said unto it, No man eat fruit of thee hereafter for ever. And his disciples[3101] heard *it.*

Jesus Cleanses the Temple (Matt. 21:12–17; Luke 19:45–48; John 2:13–22)

15 [a]And they come to Jerusalem: and Jesus went into the temple,[2411] and [aom]began to cast out them that sold and bought in the temple, and overthrew the tables of the moneychangers, and the seats of them that sold doves;

16 And [ipf]would not suffer[863] that any man should carry *any* vessel through the temple.

8 [a]Matt. 21:8
9 [a]Ps. 118:26
10 [a]Ps. 148:1
11 [a]Matt. 21:12
12 [a]Matt. 21:18
13 [a]Matt. 21:19
15 [a]Matt. 21:12; Luke 19:45; John 2:14
17 [I]Or, *a house of prayer for all nations* [a]Isa. 56:7 [b]Jer. 7:11
18 [a]Matt. 21:45, 46; Luke 19:47 [b]Matt. 7:28; Mark 1:22; Luke 4:32
20 [a]Matt. 21:19
23 [a]Matt. 17:20; 21:21; Luke 17:6
24 [a]Matt. 7:7; Luke 11:9; John 14:13; 15:7; 16:24; James 1:5, 6
25 [a]Matt. 6:14; Col. 3:13
26 [a]Matt. 18:35
27 [a]Matt. 21:23; Luke 20:1

17 And he taught, saying unto them, [pfip]Is it not written, [a]My house shall be called [I]of all nations the house of prayer? but [epn][b]ye have made it a den of thieves.

18 And [a]the scribes[1122] and chief priests[749] heard *it,* and sought how they might destroy[622] him: for they feared him, because [b]all the people was astonished at his doctrine.[1322]

19 And when even was come, he went out of the city.

"Have Faith in God" (Matt. 21:20, 22)

20 [a]And in the morning, as they [ppp]passed by, they saw the fig tree dried up from the roots.

21 And Peter [aptp]calling to remembrance 363 saith unto him, Master, behold, the fig tree which thou cursedst[2672] is withered away.

22 And Jesus answering saith unto them, Have faith[4102] in God.

23 For [a]verily 281 I say unto you, That whosoever shall say unto this mountain, [aipp]Be thou removed,[142] and [aipp]be thou cast[906] into the sea; and shall not doubt[1252] in his heart, but shall believe[4100] that those things which he saith shall come to pass; he shall have whatsoever he saith.

24 Therefore I say unto you, [a]What things soever ye desire, when ye pray,[4336] believe that ye receive *them,* and ye shall have *them.*

25 And when ye stand praying, [a]forgive,[863] if ye have ought[5100] against any: that your Father also which is in heaven[3772] may forgive you your trespasses.[3900]

26 But [a]if [epn]ye do not forgive, neither will your Father which is in heaven forgive your trespasses.

Where Did Christ's Authority Come From? (Matt. 21:23–27; Luke 20:1–8)

27 And they [pin]come[2064] again 3825 to Jerusalem: [a]and as he was walking in the

temple,[2411] there come to him the chief priests,[749] and the scribes, and the elders,[4245]

28 And say unto him, By what authority[1849] doest thou these things? and who gave thee this authority to do these things?

29 And Jesus answered and said unto them, [epn]I will also ask of you one [I]question, and answer me, and I will tell you by what authority I do these things.

30 The baptism[908] of John, was *it* from heaven,[3772] or of men? answer me.

31 And they [ipf]reasoned[3049] with themselves, saying, If we shall say, From heaven; he will say, Why then did ye not believe him?

32 But if we shall say, Of men; they feared the people: for [a]all *men* counted John, that he was a prophet[4396] indeed.

33 And they answered and said unto Jesus, We cannot tell. And Jesus answering saith unto them, Neither do [epn]I tell you by what authority I do these things.

The Parable of the Vineyard And the Tenants (Matt. 21:33–46; Luke 20:9–19)

12 And [a]he began to speak unto them by parables.[3850] A *certain* man planted a vineyard, and set an hedge about *it,* and digged *a place for* the winefat, and built a tower, and let it out to husbandmen,[1092] and went into a far country.

2 And at the season[2540] he sent to the husbandmen a servant,[1401] that he might receive from the husbandmen of the fruit of the vineyard.

3 And they [apt]caught *him,* and beat him, and sent *him* away[649] empty.

4 And again he sent[649] unto them another servant; and at him they [apt]cast stones,[3036] and wounded *him* in the head, and sent *him* away[649] shamefully handled.

5 And again he sent another; and him they killed, and many others; [ppt]beating some, and [ppt]killing some.

6 Having yet therefore one son,[5207] his wellbeloved,[27] he sent him also last unto them, saying, They will reverence[1788] my son.

7 But those husbandmen said among themselves, This is the heir;[2818] come, let us kill him, and the inheritance[2817] shall be ours.

8 And they took him, and killed *him,* and cast *him* out of the vineyard.

9 What shall therefore the lord[2962] of the vineyard do? he [fm]will come and [ft]destroy the husbandmen, and will give the vineyard unto others.

10 And have ye not read this scripture;[1124] [a]The stone which the builders rejected[593] is become the head of the corner:

11 This was the Lord's[2962] doing, and it is marvellous in our eyes?

12 [a]And they sought to lay hold on him, but feared the people: for they knew that he had spoken the parable against[4314] them: and they left him, and went their way.

Jesus and Taxes (Matt. 22:15–22; Luke 20:20–26)

13 [a]And they send unto him certain of the Pharisees and of the Herodians, to [aosb]catch him in *his* words.

14 And when they were come, they say unto him, Master, we know that thou art true, and carest for no man: for thou regardest not the person[4383] of men, but teachest the way[3598] of God in truth:[225] Is it lawful to give tribute to Caesar, or not?

15 [aosi]Shall we give,[1325] or shall we not give? But he, knowing their hypocrisy, said unto them, Why tempt[3985] ye me? bring me a penny,[1220] that I may see *it.*

16 And they brought *it.* And he saith unto them, Whose *is* this image[1504] and superscription? And they said unto him, Caesar's.

17 And Jesus answering said unto them, Render to Caesar the things that

29 [I]Or, *thing*
32 [a]Matt. 3:5; 14:5; Mark 6:20
1 [a]Matt. 21:33; Luke 20:9
10 [a]Ps. 118:22
12 [a]Matt. 21:45, 46; Mark 11:18; John 7:25, 30, 44
13 [a]Matt. 22:15; Luke 20:20

are Caesar's, and to God the things that are God's. And they marvelled at him.

Life After the Resurrection (Matt. 22:23–33; Luke 20:27–40)

18 [a]Then come unto him the Sadducees, [b]which say there is no resurrection;[386] and they asked him, saying,

19 Master, [a]Moses wrote[1125] unto us, If a man's brother[80] die, and leave *his* wife *behind him,* and leave[863] no children, that his brother should take his wife, and raise up[1817] seed[4690] unto his brother.

20 Now there were seven brethren:[80] and the first took a wife, and dying left[863] no seed.[4690]

21 And the second took her, and died, neither left he any seed: and the third likewise.

22 And the seven had her, and left no seed: last of all the woman died also.

23 In the resurrection therefore, when they shall rise,[450] whose wife shall she be of them? for the seven had her to wife.

24 And Jesus answering said unto them, Do ye not therefore err, because ye [pfpp]know not the scriptures, neither the power of God?

25 For when they shall rise[450] from the dead, they neither marry, nor are given in marriage; but [a]are as the angels[32] which are in heaven.[3772]

26 And as touching the dead, that they rise: have ye not read in the book of Moses, how in the bush God spake unto him, saying, [epn][a]I *am* the God of Abraham, and the God of Isaac, and the God of Jacob?

27 He is not the God of the dead, but the God of the living:[2198] [epn]ye therefore do greatly err.

The Great Commandment (Matt. 22:34–40; Luke 10:25–28)

28 [a]And one of the scribes[1122] came, and having heard them reasoning together, and perceiving that he had an-

18 [a]Matt. 22:23; Luke 20:27 [b]Acts 23:8

19 [a]Deut. 25:5

25 [a]1Cor. 15:42, 49, 52

26 [a]Ex. 3:6

28 [a]Matt. 22:35

29 [a]Deut. 6:4; Luke 10:27

31 [a]Lev. 19:18; Matt. 22:39; Rom. 13:9; Gal. 5:14; James 2:8

32 [a]Deut. 4:39; Isa. 45:6, 14; 46:9

33 [a]1Sam. 15:22; Hos. 6:6; Mic. 6:6-8

34 [a]Matt. 22:46

35 [a]Matt. 22:41; Luke 20:41

36 [a]2Sam. 23:2 [b]Ps. 110:1

38 [a]Mark 4:2 [b]Matt. 23:1-12; Luke 20:46

swered them well, asked him, Which is the first commandment of all?

29 And Jesus answered him, The first of all the commandments *is,* [a]Hear, O Israel; The Lord our God is one Lord:

30 And thou shalt love[25] the Lord thy God with all thy heart, and with all thy soul,[5590] and with all thy mind,[1271] and with all thy strength:[2479] this *is* the first commandment.

31 And the second *is* like,[3664] *namely* this, [a]Thou [ft]shalt love[25] thy neighbour[4139] as thyself. There is none other[243] commandment greater than these.

32 And the scribe said unto him, Well, Master, thou hast said the truth:[225] for there is one God;[2316] [a]and there is none other[243] but he:

33 And [pinf]to love him with all the heart and with all the understanding, and with all the soul, and with all the strength, and to love *his* neighbour as himself, [a]is more than all whole burnt offerings and sacrifices.

34 And when Jesus saw that he answered discreetly,[3562] he said unto him, Thou art not far from the kingdom[932] of God. [a]And no man after that durst[5111] ask him *any question.*

David's Lord (Matt. 22:41–46; Luke 20:41–44)

35 [a]And Jesus answered and said, while he [ppt]taught in the temple,[2411] How say the scribes[1122] that Christ is the son of David?

36 For David himself said [a]by the Holy Ghost,[4151] [b]the LORD said to my Lord, Sit thou on my right hand, till I [aosb]make[5087] thine enemies thy footstool.

37 David therefore himself calleth him Lord; and whence is he *then* his son? And the common people heard[191] him gladly.

Jesus Denounces the Scribes (Matt. 23:1–36; Luke 20:45–47)

38 And [a]he said unto them in his doctrine,[1322] [b]Beware[991] of the

scribes,[1122] which [pptc]love[2309] to go in long clothing, and *love* salutations in the marketplaces,

39 And the chief seats in the synagogues,[4864] and the uppermost rooms at feasts:

40 [a]Which [ppt]devour[2719] widows' houses,[3614] and for a pretence [ppt]make long prayers:[4336] these shall receive greater damnation.[2917]

The Widow's Offering (Luke 21:1–4)

41 [a]And Jesus sat over against the treasury, and beheld how the people cast money [b]into the treasury: and many that were rich cast in much.

42 And there [apt]came a certain poor widow, and she threw in two mites,[3016] which make a farthing.[2835]

43 And he called *unto him* his disciples, and saith unto them, Verily[281] I say unto you, That [a]this poor widow hath cast more in, than all they which have cast into the treasury:

44 For all *they* did cast in of their [ppt]abundance; but she of her want[5304] did cast in all that she had, [a]*even* all her living.

The Destruction of the Temple And the Last Days (Matt. 24:1, 2; Luke 21:5, 6)

13 And [a]as he [ppp]went out of the temple,[2411] one of his disciples[3101] saith unto him, Master, see what manner of stones and what buildings[3619] *are here!*

2 And Jesus answering said unto him, Seest thou these great buildings? [a]there shall [efn]not be left[863] one stone upon another, that shall not be thrown down.[2647]

Forthcoming Woes (Matt. 24:3–14; Luke 21:7–19)

3 And as he sat upon the mount of Olives over against the temple, Peter and James and John and Andrew asked him privately,

4 [a]Tell us, when shall these things be? and what *shall be* the sign when all these things shall [pip]be fulfilled?[4931]

5 And Jesus answering them began to say, [a]Take heed lest any *man* deceive you:

6 For many shall come in my name,[3686] saying, [epn]I am *Christ;* and shall deceive many.

7 And when ye shall hear of wars[4171] and rumours of wars, be ye not troubled: for *such things* must needs be; but the end[5056] *shall* not *be* yet.

8 For nation [fp]shall rise[1453] against nation, and kingdom against kingdom: and there shall be earthquakes in divers[2596] places, and there shall be famines and troubles:[5016] [a]these *are* the beginnings of sorrows.[5604]

9 But [a]take heed to yourselves: for they shall deliver you up to councils; and in the synagogues[4864] ye shall be beaten: and ye shall be brought before rulers and kings for my sake, for a testimony against them.

10 And [a]the gospel[2098] must first [aifp]be published[2784] among all nations.

11 [a]But when they shall lead[71] *you,* and deliver you up, take no thought beforehand what ye shall speak, neither do ye premeditate: but whatsoever shall be given you in that hour, that speak ye: for it is not [epn]ye that speak, [b]but the Holy Ghost.[4151]

12 Now [a]the brother[80] shall betray the brother to death,[2288] and the father the son; and children shall rise up against *their* parents, and shall cause them to be put to death.

13 [a]And ye shall be hated of all *men* for my name's sake: but [b]he that [apt]shall endure unto the end,[5056] the same shall be saved.[4982]

The Great Tribulation (Matt. 24:15–28; Luke 21:20–24)

14 [a]But when ye shall see the abomination[946] of desolation, [b]spoken of

---

38 [c]Luke 11:43
40 [a]Matt. 23:14
41 [a]Luke 21:1 [b]2Kgs. 12:9
43 [a]2Cor. 8:12
44 [a]Deut. 24:6; 1John 3:17
1 [a]Matt. 24:1; Luke 21:5
2 [a]Luke 19:44
4 [a]Matt. 24:3; Luke 21:7
5 [a]Jer. 29:8; Eph. 5:6; 1Thess. 2:3
8 [a]Matt. 24:8
9 [a]Matt. 10:17, 18; 24:9; Rev. 2:10
10 [a]Matt. 24:14
11 [a]Matt. 10:19; Luke 12:11; 21:14 [b]Acts 2:4; 4:8, 31
12 [a]Mic. 7:6; Matt. 10:21; 24:10; Luke 21:16
13 [a]Matt. 24:9; Luke 21:17 [b]Dan. 12:12; Matt. 10:22; 24:13; Rev. 2:10
14 [a]Matt. 24:15 [b]Dan. 9:27

by Daniel the prophet, [pfp]standing where it ought not, (let him that readeth understand,) then [c]let them that be in Judaea flee to the mountains:

15 And let him that is on the housetop not go down into the house, neither enter *therein,* to take any thing out of his house:

16 And let him that is in the field not turn back again for to take up his garment.

17 [a]But woe to them that are with child, and to them that [ppt]give suck[2337] in those days!

18 And pray ye that your flight be not in the winter.

19 [a]For *in* those days shall be affliction, such as [pfi]was[1096] not from the beginning of the creation[2937] which God created[2936] unto this time, [efn]neither shall be.

20 And except that the Lord[2962] had shortened those days, no flesh[4561] should be saved:[4982] but for the elect's[1588] sake, whom he hath chosen, he hath shortened the days.

21 [a]And then if any man shall say to you, Lo, here *is* Christ;[5547] or, lo, *he is* there; believe *him* not:

🔑 22 For false Christs[5580] and false prophets shall rise,[1453] and shall shew signs and wonders, [aipr]to seduce,[635] if *it were* possible, even the elect.

23 But [a]take [epn]ye heed:[991] behold, I have foretold you all things.

Christ Is Coming Again (Matt. 24:29–31; Luke 21:25–28)

24 [a]But in those days, after that tribulation, the sun shall be darkened, and the moon shall not give her light,[5338]

25 And the stars of heaven[3772] shall fall, and the powers that are in heaven shall be shaken.

26 [a]And then shall they see the Son of man coming in the clouds with great power and glory.[1391]

27 And then shall he send his angels, and shall gather together[1996] his elect from the four winds, from the uttermost part of the earth to the uttermost part of heaven.

The Parable of the Fig Tree (Matt. 24:32–35; Luke 21:29–33)

28 [a]Now learn a parable of the fig tree; When her branch is yet tender, and putteth forth leaves, ye know that summer is near:

29 So ye in like manner, when ye shall see these things [ppp]come to pass,[1096] know that it is nigh, *even* at the doors.

30 Verily[281] I say unto you, that this generation shall [efn]not pass, till all these things be done.

31 Heaven[3772] and earth[1093] shall pass away: but [a]my words shall [efn]not pass away.

Time of Christ's Return Unknown (Matt. 24:36–44)

🔑 32 But of that day and *that* hour [pin]knoweth no man, no, not the angels[32] which are in heaven,[3772] neither the Son,[5207] but the Father.[3962]

33 [a]Take ye heed,[991] watch and pray: for ye know not when the time[2540] is.

34 [a]*For the Son of man is* as a man taking a far journey, who left his house, and gave authority to his servants,[1401] and to every man his work, and commanded[1781] the porter[2377] to watch.

35 [a]Watch ye therefore: for ye know not when the master[2962] of the house cometh, at even, or at midnight, or at the cockcrowing, or in the morning:[4404]

36 Lest [apt]coming suddenly he find you sleeping.

37 And what I say unto you I say unto all, Watch.

14 [c]Luke 21:21
17 [a]Luke 21:23; 23:29
19 [a]Dan. 9:26; 12:1; Joel 2:2; Matt. 24:21
21 [a]Matt. 24:23; Luke 17:23; 21:8
23 [a]2Pet. 3:17
24 [a]Dan. 7:10; Zeph. 1:15; Matt. 24:29-31; Luke 21:25
26 [a]Dan. 7:13, 14; Matt. 16:27; 24:30; Mark 14:62; Acts 1:11; 1Thess. 4:16; 2Thess. 1:7, 10; Rev. 1:7
28 [a]Matt. 24:32; Luke 21:29-33
31 [a]Isa. 40:8
33 [a]Matt. 24:42; 25:13; Luke 12:40; 21:34; Rom. 13:11; 1Thess. 5:6
34 [a]Matt. 24:45; 25:14
35 [a]Matt. 24:42, 44

🔑 **13:22, 32** See note on Philippians 2:6–8.

The Plot to Kill Jesus (Matt. 26:1–5; Luke 22:1, 2; John 11:45–53)

14 After [a]two days was *the feast of*
the passover,[3957] and of unleavened bread:[106] and the chief priests[749]
and the scribes[1122] sought how they
might take him by craft, and put *him* to
death.
2 But they said, Not on the feast *day,*
lest there be an uproar of the people.

The Anointing of Jesus at Bethany (Matt. 26:6–13; John 12:1–8)

3 [a]And being in Bethany in the house
of Simon the leper, as he [ppp]sat at meat,
there came a woman having an alabaster
box[211] of ointment of [l]spikenard[4101,3487]
very precious; and she brake the box, and
poured *it* on[2596] his head.
4 And there were some that had indignation within themselves, and said, Why
was this waste[684] of the ointment made?
5 For it might have been sold for
more than[1883] three hundred [l]pence,[1220]
and have been given to the poor. And
they [ipf]murmured against[1690] her.
6 And Jesus said, Let her alone;[863]
why trouble ye her? she hath wrought[2038]
a good[2570] work[2041] on me.
7 For [a]ye have the poor with you always, and whensoever ye will ye may do
them good: but me ye have not always.
8 She hath done what she could: she
is come aforehand[4301] to anoint[3462] my
body to the burying.
9 Verily[281] I say unto you, Wheresoever this gospel[2098] [asbp]shall be
preached[2784] throughout the whole
world,[2889] *this* also that she hath done shall
be spoken of for a memorial[3422] of her.

Judas Agrees on a Price To Betray Jesus (Matt. 26:14–16; Luke 22:3–6)

10 [a]And Judas Iscariot, one of the
twelve, went unto the chief priests,[749] to
[aosb]betray[3860] him unto them.
11 And when they heard *it,* they
were glad,[5463] and promised[1861] to give
him money. And he sought how he might
conveniently betray him.

Jesus Eats the Passover With His Disciples (Matt. 26:17–25; Luke 22:7–14, 21–23; John 13:21–30)

12 [a]And the first day of unleavened
bread,[106] when they [ipf][l]killed[2380] the
passover,[3957] his disciples[3101] said unto
him, Where wilt thou that we go and
prepare that thou mayest eat the
passover?
13 And he sendeth forth two of his
disciples, and saith unto them, Go ye into
the city, and there shall meet you a
man[444] bearing a pitcher of water: follow
him.
14 And wheresoever he shall go in,
say ye to the goodman of the house,[3617]
The Master saith, Where is the guestchamber, where I shall eat the passover
with my disciples?
15 And [epn]he will shew you a large
upper room [pfpp]furnished *and* prepared:
there make ready for us.
16 And his disciples went forth, and
came into the city, and found as he had
said unto them: and they made ready the
passover.
17 [a]And in the evening he cometh
with the twelve.
18 And as they sat and did eat,
Jesus said, Verily[281] I say unto you, One
of you which eateth with me shall betray
me.
19 And they began to be sorrow-
ful, and [pinf]to say unto him one by one,
Is it [epn]I? and another[243] *said, Is* it
[epn]I?
20 And he answered and said unto
them, *It is* one of the twelve, that
dippeth[1686] with me in the dish.
21 [a]The Son of man indeed goeth, as
it is written of him: but woe to that man
by whom the Son of man is betrayed!
good[2570] were it for that man if he had
never been born.

1 [a]Matt. 26:2; Luke 22:1; John 11:55; 13:1

3 [l]Or, *pure nard,* or, *liquid nard* [a]Matt. 26:6; John 12:1, 3; Luke 7:37

5 [l]Matt. 18:28

7 [a]Deut. 15:11

10 [a]Matt. 26:14; Luke 22:3, 4

12 [l]Or, *sacrificed* [a]Matt. 26:17; Luke 22:7

17 [a]Matt. 26:20-25

21 [a]Matt. 26:24; Luke 22:22

The Lord's Supper (Matt. 26:26–30; Luke 22:15–20; 1 Cor. 11:23–25)

22 [a]And as they did eat, Jesus [apt]took[2983] bread, and [apt]blessed,[2127] and brake *it,* and gave to them, and said, Take, eat: this is my body.[4983]

23 And he [apt]took the cup, and when he had given thanks, he gave *it* to them: and they all drank of it.

24 And he said unto them, This is my blood[129] of the new[2537] testament,[1242] which [ppp]is shed1632 for many.

25 Verily281 I say unto you, I will drink no more of the fruit1081 of the vine, until that day that I drink it new in the kingdom[932] of God.

26 [a]And when they [apt]had sung an [1]hymn,5214 they went out into the mount of Olives.

Jesus Predicts Peter's Denial (Matt. 26:31–35; Luke 22:31–34; John 13:36–38)

27 [a]And Jesus saith unto them, All ye shall be offended because of me this night: for it is written, [b]I will smite the shepherd, and the sheep shall be scattered.

28 But [a]after that I [aime]am risen,[1453] I will go before you into Galilee.

29 [a]But Peter said unto him, Although all shall be offended, yet *will* not I.

30 And Jesus saith unto him, Verily281 I say unto thee, That this day, *even* in this night, before the cock crow twice, thou shalt deny[533] me thrice.

31 But he spake the more vehemently,[4053] If I should[1163] die with thee, I will [efn]not deny[533] thee in any wise. Likewise also said they all.

Jesus in Gethsemane (Matt. 26:36–46; Luke 22:39–46)

32 [a]And they came to a place which was named Gethsemane: and he saith to his disciples,[3101] Sit ye here, while I shall pray.

33 And he taketh with him Peter and James and John, and began [pip]to be sore amazed,1568 and to be very heavy;

34 And saith unto them, [a]My soul[5590] is exceeding sorrowful unto death: tarry[3306] ye here, and watch.

35 And he [apt]went forward4281 a little, and fell on the ground, and prayed that, if it were possible, the hour[5610] might pass from him.

36 And he said, [a]Abba,5 Father, [b]all things *are* possible unto thee; take away this cup from me: [c]nevertheless not what [epn]I will, but what [epn]thou wilt.

37 And he cometh, and findeth them sleeping, and saith unto Peter, Simon, [pin]sleepest2518 thou? couldest not thou watch one hour?

38 Watch ye and pray, lest ye enter into temptation.[3986] [a]The spirit[4151] truly *is* ready, but the flesh[4561] *is* weak.[772]

39 And again he went away, and prayed, and [apt]spake the same words.

40 And when he returned, he found them asleep again, (for their eyes were heavy,) neither wist[1492] they what to answer him.

41 And he cometh the third time, and saith unto them, Sleep on now, and take *your* rest: [pin]it is enough,[566] [a]the hour is come; behold, the Son of man is betrayed into the hands of sinners.[268]

42 [a]Rise up, [psa]let us go;[71] lo, he that betrayeth me is at hand.

Jesus Is Arrested (Matt. 26:47–56; Luke 22:47–53; John 18:2–12)

43 [a]And immediately, while he yet spake, cometh Judas, one of the twelve, and with[3326] him a great multitude with[3326] swords and staves,3586 from the chief priests and the scribes and the elders.[4245]

44 And he that [ppt]betrayed3860 him had given them a token,4953 saying, Whomsoever I shall kiss,[5368] that same is he; take him, and lead *him* away safely.

45 And as soon as he was come, he

---

22 [a]Matt. 26:26; Luke 22:19; 1Cor. 11:23
26 [1]Or, *psalm* [a]Matt. 26:30
27 [a]Matt. 26:31 [b]Zech. 13:7
28 [a]Mark 16:7
29 [a]Matt. 26:33, 34; Luke 22:33, 34; John 13:37, 38
32 [a]Matt. 26:36; Luke 22:39; John 18:1
34 [a]John 12:27
36 [a]Rom. 8:15; Gal. 4:6 [b]Heb. 5:7 [c]John 5:30; 6:38
38 [a]Rom. 7:23; Gal. 5:17
41 [a]John 13:1
42 [a]Matt. 26:46; John 18:1, 2
43 [a]Matt. 26:47; Luke 22:47; John 18:3

goeth straightway[2112] to him, and saith, Master, master; and kissed him.

46 And they laid their hands on him, and took him.

47 And one of them that stood by [apt]drew[4685] a sword, and smote a servant[1401] of the high priest, and cut off his ear.

48 [a]And Jesus answered and said unto them, Are ye come out, as against a thief,[3027] with swords and *with* staves to take me?

49 I was daily with you in the temple[2411] teaching, and ye took me not: but [a]the scriptures [asbp]must be fulfilled.[4137]

50 [a]And they all [apt]forsook[863] him, and fled.

51 And there followed him a certain young man, having a linen cloth cast about *his* naked[1131] *body;* and the young men [pin]laid hold on[2902] him:

52 And he left the linen cloth, and fled from them naked.[1131]

Jesus Is Brought to Caiaphas (Matt. 26:57–68; Luke 22:54, 55, 63–71; John 18:13, 14, 19–24)

53 [a]And they led Jesus away to the high priest: and with him were assembled all the chief priests and the elders[4245] and the scribes.[1122]

54 And Peter followed him afar off, even into the palace of the high priest: and he sat with the servants,[5257] and warmed himself at the fire.

55 [a]And the chief priests and all the council sought for witness[3141] against Jesus [aies]to put him to death;[2289] and found none.

56 For many bare false witness against him, but their witness agreed not together.

57 And there arose certain, and bare false witness against him, saying,

58 We heard him say, [a]I will destroy this temple[3485] that is made with hands, and within three days I will build another made without hands.

59 But neither so did their witness agree together.

60 [a]And the high priest stood up[450] in the midst,[3319] and asked Jesus, saying, Answerest thou nothing? what *is it which* these [pin]witness against[2649] thee?

61 But [a]he held his peace, and answered nothing. [b]Again the high priest asked him, and said unto him, Art [epn]thou the Christ,[5547] the Son[5207] of the Blessed?[2128]

62 And Jesus said, [epn]I am: [a]and ye shall see the Son of man sitting on the right hand[1188] of power,[1411] and coming in the clouds of heaven.[3772]

63 Then the high priest rent[1284] his clothes,[5509] and saith, What need we any further witnesses?[3144]

64 Ye have heard[191] the blasphemy:[988] what think[5316] ye? And they all condemned him to be guilty[1777] of death.

65 And some began [pinf]to spit on[1716] him, and [pinf]to cover[4028] his face,[4383] and [pinf]to buffet[2852] him, and to say unto him, Prophesy: and the servants[5257] did strike[906] him with the palms of their hands.

Peter Denies Jesus (Matt. 26:69–75; Luke 22:56–62; John 18:15–18, 25–27)

66 [a]And as Peter was beneath[2736] in the palace, there cometh one of the maids of the high priest:

67 And when she saw Peter warming himself, she [apt]looked upon[1689] him, and said, And thou also wast[2258] with Jesus of Nazareth.

68 But he denied,[720] saying, I know not, neither understand I what thou sayest. And he went out into the porch; and the cock crew.

48 [a]Matt. 26:55; Luke 22:52
49 [a]Ps. 22:6; Isa. 53:7-10; Luke 22:37; 24:44
50 [a]Ps. 88:8; Mark 14:27
53 [a]Matt. 26:57; Luke 22:54; John 18:13
55 [a]Matt. 26:59
58 [a]Mark 15:29; John 2:19
60 [a]Matt. 26:62
61 [a]Isa. 53:7 [b]Matt. 26:63
62 [a]Matt. 24:30; 26:64; Luke 22:69
66 [a]Matt. 26:58, 69; Luke 22:55; John 18:16

14:51, 52 Some scholars feel that the young man mentioned here is Mark himself.
14:58 See note on 2 Corinthians 5:1.
14:64 See note on Mark 3:28, 29.

69 [a]And a maid saw him again, and began [pinf]to say to them that stood by, This is *one* of them.

70 And he denied[720] it again. [a]And a little after, they that stood by said again to Peter, Surely thou art *one* of [epn]them: [b]for thou art a Galilaean, and thy speech2981 agreeth *thereto.*

71 But he began to curse[332] and to swear, *saying,* I know[1492] not this man of whom ye speak.

72 [a]And the second time the cock crew. And Peter [aop]called to mind363 the word[4487] that Jesus said unto him, Before the cock crow twice, thou shalt deny[533] me thrice. And [l]when he thought thereon, he wept.

Jesus Is Brought to Pilate (Matt. 27:1, 2, 11–14; Luke 23:1–5; John 18:28–38)

15 And [a]straightway2112 in the morning the chief priests[749] held a consultation with the elders[4245] and scribes[1122] and the whole council, and bound Jesus, and carried *him* away,667 and delivered *him* to Pilate.

2 [a]And Pilate asked him, Art [epn]thou the King of the Jews? And he answering said unto him, [epn]Thou sayest *it.*

3 And the chief priests accused him of many things: but he answered nothing.

4 [a]And Pilate asked him again, saying, Answerest thou nothing? behold how many things they [pin]witness against2649 thee.

5 [a]But Jesus yet answered nothing; so that Pilate marvelled.

Jesus Sentenced to Death (Matt. 27:15–26; Luke 23:13–25; John 18:39–19:16)

6 Now [a]at *that* feast he [ipf]released[630] unto them one prisoner, whomsoever they desired.

7 And there was *one* named Barabbas, *which lay* bound with them that had made insurrection with him, who [plpf]had committed[4160] murder in the insurrection.[4714]

8 And the multitude crying aloud began [pinf]to desire[154] *him to do* as he had ever done unto them.

9 But Pilate answered them, saying, Will ye that I release unto you the King of the Jews?

10 For he knew that the chief priests[749] had delivered him for envy.

11 But [a]the chief priests moved the people, that he should rather release Barabbas unto them.

12 And Pilate answered and said again unto them, What [pin]will[2309] ye then that I shall do *unto him* whom ye [pin]call[3004] the King[935] of the Jews?

13 And they cried out again, Crucify[4717] him.

14 Then Pilate said unto them, Why, what evil hath he done? And they cried out the more exceedingly, Crucify him.

15 [a]And *so* Pilate, willing to content the people, released Barabbas unto them, and delivered Jesus, when he had scourged5417 *him,* to be crucified.

The Soldiers Mock Jesus (Matt. 27:27–31; John 19:2, 3)

16 [a]And the soldiers led him away into the hall, called Praetorium; and they call together[4779] the whole band.

17 And they clothed him with purple, and [apt]platted4120 a crown of thorns, and put it about his *head,*

18 And began to salute him, Hail,[5463] King of the Jews!

19 And they smote[5180] him on the head with a reed, and did spit upon him, and bowing[5087] *their* knees worshipped him.

20 And when they had mocked him, they took off the purple from him, and put his own[2398] clothes on him, and led him out1806 to [aosb]crucify[4717] him.

Jesus Is Crucified (Matt. 27:32–44; Luke 23:26–43; John 19:17–27)

21 [a]And they compel[29] one Simon a Cyrenian, who passed by, coming out of

69 [a]Matt. 26:71; Luke 22:58; John 18:25
70 [a]Matt. 26:73; Luke 22:59; John 18:26 [b]Acts 2:7
72 [l]Or, *he wept abundantly,* or, *he began to weep* [a]Matt. 26:75
1 [a]Ps. 2:2; Matt. 27:1; Luke 22:66; 23:1; John 18:28; Acts 3:13; 4:26
2 [a]Matt. 27:11
4 [a]Matt. 27:13
5 [a]Isa. 53:7; John 19:9
6 [a]Matt. 27:15; Luke 23:17; John 18:39
11 [a]Matt. 27:20; Acts 3:14
15 [a]Matt. 27:26; John 19:1, 16
16 [a]Matt. 27:27
21 [a]Matt. 27:32; Luke 23:26

the country,[68] the father of Alexander and Rufus, to bear[142] his cross.

22 [a]And they bring him unto the place Golgotha, which is, being interpreted, The place of a skull.

23 [a]And they gave him to drink wine [pfpp]mingled with myrrh:[4669] but he received *it* not.

24 And when they had crucified him, [a]they parted his garments, casting lots upon them, what every man should take.

25 And [a]it was the third hour, and they crucified him.

26 And [a]the superscription of his accusation [pfpp]was written over, THE KING[935] OF THE JEWS.

27 And [a]with him they crucify[4717] two thieves;[3027] the one on his right hand, and the other on his left.

28 And the scripture[1124] was fulfilled, which saith, [a]And he was numbered[3049] with the transgressors.[459]

29 And [a]they that [ppp]passed by[3899] railed[987] on him, wagging[2795] their heads, and saying, Ah, [b]thou that destroyest the temple,[3485] and buildest *it* in three days,

30 Save[4982] thyself, and come down from the cross.

31 Likewise also the chief priests mocking said among themselves with the scribes, He saved others; himself he cannot save.

32 Let Christ[5547] the King of Israel descend now from the cross,[4716] that we may see and believe. And [a]they that [pfpp]were crucified with[4957] him reviled him.

The Death of Jesus (Matt. 27:45–56; Luke 23:44–49; John 19:28–30)

33 And [a]when the sixth hour was come, there was darkness[4655] over the whole land until the ninth hour.

34 And at the ninth hour Jesus cried with a loud voice, saying, [a]Eloi, Eloi, lama sabachthani? which is, being interpreted, My God, my God, why hast thou forsaken me?

35 And some of them that stood by, when they heard *it*, said, Behold, he calleth Elias.

36 And [a]one ran and filled a sponge full of vinegar, and put *it* on a reed, and [b]gave him to drink, saying, Let alone; let us see whether Elias will come to take him down.

37 [a]And Jesus [apt]cried[863] with a loud voice, and gave up the ghost.[1606]

38 And [a]the veil of the temple[3485] was rent[4977] in twain[1417] from the top[509] to the bottom.

39 And [a]when the centurion, which stood over against him, saw that he so cried out, and gave up the ghost, he said, Truly this man was the Son of God.

40 [a]There were also women looking on [b]afar off: among whom was Mary Magdalene, and Mary the mother of James the less and of Joses, and Salome;

41 (Who also, when he was in Galilee, [ipfa]followed[190] him, and [ipf]ministered[1247] unto him;) and many other women which came up with him unto Jerusalem.

Joseph of Arimathea (Matt. 27:57–61; Luke 23:50–56; John 19:38–42)

42 [a]And now when the even was come, because it was the preparation, that is, the day before the sabbath,[4315]

43 Joseph of Arimathaea, an honourable counselor, which also [ppp][a]waited for[4327][2258] the kingdom[932] of God, came, and went in boldly unto Pilate, and craved the body of Jesus.

44 And Pilate marvelled if he were already dead:[2348] and calling *unto him* the centurion, he asked him whether he had been any while[3819] dead.

45 And when he knew *it* of the centurion, he gave the body to Joseph.

46 [a]And he bought fine linen, and took him down, and wrapped him in the linen, and laid him in a sepulchre[3419] which was hewn[2998] out of a rock, and rolled a stone unto the door of the sepulchre.

47 And Mary Magdalene and Mary *the mother* of Joses [ipf]beheld[2334] where he was laid.

22 [a]Matt. 27:33; Luke 23:33; John 19:17
23 [a]Matt. 27:34
24 [a]Ps. 22:18; Luke 23:34; John 19:23
25 [a]Matt. 27:45; Luke 23:44; John 19:14
26 [a]Matt. 27:37; John 19:19
27 [a]Matt. 27:38
28 [a]Isa. 53:12; Luke 22:37
29 [a]Ps. 22:7 [b]Mark 14:58; John 2:19
32 [a]Matt. 27:44; Luke 23:39
33 [a]Matt. 27:45; Luke 23:44
34 [a]Ps. 22:1; Matt. 27:46
36 [a]Matt. 27:48; John 19:29 [b]Ps. 69:21
37 [a]Matt. 27:50; Luke 23:46; John 19:30
38 [a]Matt. 27:51; Luke 23:45
39 [a]Matt. 27:54; Luke 23:47
40 [a]Matt. 27:55; Luke 23:49 [b]Ps. 38:11
41 [a]Luke 8:2, 3
42 [a]Matt. 27:57; Luke 23:50; John 19:38
43 [a]Luke 2:25, 38
46 [a]Matt. 27:59, 60; Luke 23:53; John 19:40

Jesus Is Risen (Matt. 28:1–8; Luke 24:1–12; John 20:1–10)

16 And [a]when the sabbath[4521] [apt]was past,[1230] Mary Magdalene, and Mary the *mother* of James, and Salome, [b]had bought sweet spices, that they might come and anoint[218] him.

2 [a]And very early in the morning the first *day* of the week, they came unto the sepulchre[3419] at the rising of the sun.

3 And they said among themselves, Who shall roll us away the stone from the door of the sepulchre?

4 And when they looked, they saw that the stone [pfip]was rolled away:[617] for it was very great.

5 [a]And entering into the sepulchre, they saw a young man sitting on the right side, clothed in a long white garment; and they were affrighted.[1568]

6 [a]And he saith unto them, Be not affrighted: Ye seek Jesus of Nazareth, which was crucified:[4717] he [aop]is risen;[1453] he is not here: behold the place where they laid him.

7 But go your way, tell his disciples[1301] and Peter that he goeth before you into Galilee: there shall ye see him, [a]as he said unto you.

8 And they went out quickly, and fled from the sepulchre; for they trembled and were amazed:[1611] [a]neither said they any thing to any *man;* for they [ipf]were afraid.[5399]

1 [a]Matt. 28:1; Luke 24:1; John 20:1 [b]Luke 23:56
2 [a]Luke 24:1; John 20:1
5 [a]Luke 24:3; John 20:11, 12
6 [a]Matt. 28:5-7
7 [a]Matt. 26:32; Mark 14:28
8 [a]Matt. 28:8; Luke 24:9
9 [a]John 20:14 [b]Luke 8:2
10 [a]Luke 24:10; John 20:18
11 [a]Luke 24:11
12 [a]Luke 24:13
14 [I]Or, *together* [a]Luke 24:36; John 20:19; 1Cor. 15:5
15 [a]Matt. 28:19; John 15:16 [b]Col. 1:23
16 [a]John 3:18, 36; Acts 2:38; 16:30-32; Rom. 10:9; 1Pet. 3:21

Jesus Appears to Mary Magdalene (Matt. 28:9, 10; John 20:11–18)

9 Now when *Jesus* was risen[450] early the first[4413] *day* of the week, [a]he appeared first to Mary Magdalene, [b]out of whom he had cast seven devils.[1140]

10 [a]*And* she went and told them that had been with him, as they [ppt]mourned[3996] and [ppt]wept.[2799]

11 [a]And they, when they [apt]had heard[191] that he was alive,[2198] and had been seen of her, believed not.[569]

The Appearance to Two Disciples (Luke 24:13–35)

12 After that he appeared[5319] in another[2087] form[3444] [a]unto two of them, as they [ppt]walked,[4043] and went into the country.

13 And they went and told *it* unto the residue: neither believed they them.

The Great Commission (Matt. 28:16–20; Luke 24:36–49; John 20:19–23; Acts 1:6–8)

14 [a]Afterward he appeared[5319] unto the eleven as they sat [I]at meat, and upbraided[3679] them with their unbelief[570] and hardness of heart,[4641] because they believed not them which had seen him after he was risen.[1453]

15 [a]And he said unto them, [apt]Go[4198] ye into all the world,[2889] [b]and preach[2784] the gospel[2098] to every creature.[2937]

🔑 16 [a]He that [apt]believeth[4100] and is

🔑 **16:16** The word "believeth" is *pisteúsas* (from *pisteúō* [4100]), an aorist participle referring to one who has believed at some time in the past. Also, *baptistheís* (907), translated "is baptized," is an aorist participle but in the passive voice. This form refers to an act of outward obedience, in this case, baptism. Therefore, the translation should be, "He who believed and who was baptized shall be saved." However, the Lord adds, "he that believeth not shall be damned." It should be noted that this negative statement does not include a reference to baptism, making it clear that what saves a person is living faith in Jesus Christ. Ephesians 2:8 states it this way, "For by grace are ye saved through faith." The word "saved" is translated from the Greek word *sesōsménoi,* which is a perfect passive participle. It means that this salvation took place at some point in the past and is continuing on in the present, being accomplished by Jesus Christ Himself. If baptism were necessary for salvation, the Greek text of Ephesians 2:8 and many others verses would have been "ye are saved through faith and baptism." There are examples in the New Testament of people who

(continued on next page)

baptized[907] shall be saved;[4982] [b]but he
that believeth not[569] shall be damned.[2632]

17 And these signs[4592] shall follow
them that [apt]believe;[4100] [a]In my
name[3686] shall they cast out devils;[1140]
[b]they shall speak[2980] with new[2537]
tongues;[1100]

18 [a]They shall take up serpents;
and if they drink any deadly thing, it
shall [efn]not hurt them; [b]they shall lay
hands on the sick,[732] and they shall recover.

16 [b]John 12:48
17 [a]Luke 10:17; Acts 5:16; 8:7; 16:18; 19:12 [b]Acts 2:4; 10:46; 19:6; 1Cor. 12:10, 28
18 [a]Luke 10:19; Acts 28:5 [b]Acts 5:15, 16; 9:17; 28:8; James 5:14, 15
19 [a]Acts 1:2, 3 [b]Luke 24:51 [c]Ps. 110:1; Acts 7:55
20 [a]Acts 5:12; 14:3; 1Cor. 2:4, 5; Heb. 2:4

The Ascension of Jesus (Luke 24:50–53; Acts 1:9, 11)

19 So then [a]after the Lord had spoken unto them, he was [b]received up[353]
into heaven,[3772] and [c]sat on the right
hand[1188] of God.

20 And they [apt]went forth,[1831] and
preached[2784] every where, the Lord working with *them,* [a]and confirming[950] the
word[3056] with signs[4592] following.
Amen.[281]

(continued from previous page)
were baptized for selfish reasons, rather than for the purpose of demonstrating their inner, saving faith in Christ (Luke 3:7–9, the Pharisees; Acts 8:9–25, Simon). Baptism is a distinct act of obedience apart from salvation. This is clarified by the order in which the words "believe" and "baptize" occur in the text (cf. Matt. 28:19 [note here that the word "teaching" precedes the mentioning of "baptism"]; Acts 2:38; 10:44–48).

16:17 The verb "believe" here in Greek is in the aorist tense *pisteúsasi* (4100), which refers to those who did believe, not those who would believe at that time or in the future. See note on 1 Corinthians 14:1–3.

The Gospel According to
LUKE

There is little doubt that the author of this Gospel is Luke, "the beloved physician" (Col. 4:14). He was a Gentile who is thought to have been a native of Antioch. He accompanied the Apostle Paul from Troas on his second missionary journey but remained in Philippi until Paul returned there on his last known missionary expedition (Acts 20:6). They seem to have been close companions up until Paul's death (2 Tim. 4:11). Paul referred to him as his "fellowlabourer" in Philemon 1:24. The introductory remarks (Luke 1:1–4) indicate that there were other written accounts of the events surrounding Jesus' life, death, and resurrection that existed at the time this book was written. Apparently, as Luke gathered a wealth of information from "eye-witnesses" that he had come in contact with while traveling with Paul, the Holy Spirit burdened his heart with the need to compose another narrative. Indeed, Luke does provide a more complete history than the other Gospels. He records twenty miracles of Jesus as well as twenty-three parables, eighteen of which appear only in his account.

The Gospel of Luke also gives special attention to prayer. The combined Gospels record that Christ prayed a total of fifteen different times. Luke records eleven of these instances (each of the other Gospels include four or less [some of the prayers are repeated]), as well as a significant portion of Christ's teaching on prayer that is not recorded in the other Gospels.

The book is thought to have been written sometime between the years A.D. 58 and 60. It is generally agreed that Luke intended his Gospel to be available to the public, particularly the Greek public, even though it was initially written to Theophilus (Luke 1:3). The information that is included and the way that the material is presented indicates that Luke was appealing to the Greek mindset. The vocabulary and style are so refined that Luke's Gospel has been favorably compared to various Classical Greek writings.

Jesus is portrayed in the Gospel of Luke as the long-awaited Messiah, the Savior of all mankind. Special emphasis is placed upon the kindness of Jesus toward women, the weak and poor, outcasts, and those who were suffering.

1 Forasmuch as many [ao]have taken
in hand [aifm]to set forth in order[392]
a declaration of those things [pfpp]which
are most surely believed[4135] among
us,
2 [a]Even as they delivered them unto
us, which [b]from the beginning were eyewitnesses, and ministers[5257] of the
word;[3056]
3 [a]It seemed good to me also, [pfp]hav-
ing had perfect understanding of all
things from the very first,[509] to write
unto thee [b]in order, [c]most excellent
Theophilus,
4 [a]That thou mightest know the certainty of those things, wherein thou
[aop]hast been instructed.

2 [a]Heb. 2:3; 1Pet. 5:1; 2Pet. 1:16; 1John 1:1 [b]Mark 1:1; John 15:27

3 [a]Acts 15:19, 25, 28; 1Cor. 7:40 [b]Acts 11:4; Acts 1:1

4 [a]John 20:31

5 [a]Matt. 2:1 [b]1Chr. 24:10, 19; Neh. 12:4, 17

6 [a]Gen. 7:1; 17:1; 1Kgs. 9:4; 2Kgs. 20:3; Job 1:1; Acts 23:1; 24:16; Phil. 3:6

The Birth of John the Baptist

5 There was [a]in the days[2250] of
Herod, the king of Judaea, a certain
priest named Zacharias, [b]of the course
of Abia: and his wife *was* of the daughters of Aaron, and her name *was* Elisabeth.
6 And they were both [a]righteous[1342]
before God,[2316] walking in all the commandments and ordinances[1345] of the
Lord blameless.[273]
7 And they had no child, because
that Elisabeth was barren, and they
both were *now* well stricken[4260] in
years.
8 And it came to pass, that while he

[aie]executed the priest's office before God [a]in the order[5010] of his course,

9 According to the custom of the priest's office, his lot was [a]to burn incense when he went into the temple[3485] of the Lord.

10 [a]And the whole multitude of the people[2992] were praying[4336] without[1854] at the time[5610] of incense.

11 And there appeared unto him an angel[32] of the Lord standing on the right side of [a]the altar of incense.

12 And when Zacharias saw *him,* [a]he was troubled, and fear[5401] fell upon him.

13 But the angel said unto him, Fear[5399] not, Zacharias: for thy prayer [aop]is heard; and thy wife Elisabeth [ft]shall bear[1080] thee a son,[5207] and [a]thou shalt call his name John.

14 And thou shalt have joy and gladness;[20] and [a]many [fm]shall rejoice[5463] at his birth.[1083]

15 For he shall be great in the sight of the Lord, and [a]shall drink neither wine nor strong drink;[4608] and he shall be filled with the Holy Ghost,[4151] [b]even from his mother's womb.

16 [a]And many of the children[5207] of Israel [ft]shall he turn[1994] to the Lord their God.

17 [a]And he shall go before him in the spirit[4151] and power of Elias, to turn the hearts[2588] of the fathers to the children, and the disobedient[545] [I]to the wisdom of the just; to make ready a people prepared for the Lord.

18 And Zacharias said unto the angel, [a]Whereby shall I know this? for I am an old man, and my wife well stricken in years.

19 And the angel answering said unto him, I am [a]Gabriel, that [pfp]stand in the presence of God; and [aop]am sent[649] to speak unto thee, and [ainf]to shew thee these glad tidings.[2097]

20 And, behold, [a]thou shalt be dumb, and not [ppt]able [ainf]to speak, until the day that these things shall be performed, because thou [ao]believest[4100] not my words,[3056] which shall be fulfilled in their season.[2540]

21 And the people waited for[4328] Zacharias, and [ipf]marvelled that he [aie]tarried so long in the temple.

22 And when he came out, he could not speak[2980] unto them: and they perceived that he had seen a vision in the temple: for he beckoned unto them, and [ipf]remained speechless.

23 And it came to pass, that, as soon as [a]the days of his ministration[3009] were accomplished, he departed to his own house.

24 And after those days his wife Elisabeth conceived, and [ipf]hid herself five months, saying,

25 Thus hath the Lord dealt with me in the days wherein he looked on[1896] *me,* to [a]take away my reproach among men.

The Angel Appears to Mary

26 And in the sixth month the angel[32] Gabriel was sent from God unto a city of Galilee, named[3686] Nazareth,

27 To a virgin[3933] [a]espoused[3423] to a man whose name was Joseph, of the house[3624] of David; and the virgin's name *was* Mary.

28 And the angel came in unto her, and said, [a]Hail,[5463] *thou that art* [pfpI][b]highly favoured,[5487] [c]the Lord *is* with thee: [pfp]blessed[2127] *art* thou among women.

29 And when she saw *him,* [a]she [aop]was troubled at his saying, and cast in her mind[1260] what manner of salutation this should be.

30 And the angel said unto her, [pim]Fear[5399] not, Mary: for thou [ao]hast found[2147] favour[5485] with God.

31 [a]And, behold, thou shalt conceive in thy womb, and bring forth a son,[5207] and [b]shalt call his name JESUS.

32 He shall be great, [a]and shall be called the Son of the Highest: and [b]the Lord God shall give unto him the throne of his father[3962] David:

33 [a]And he [ft]shall reign[936] over the house[3624] of Jacob for ever; and of his kingdom[932] there shall be no end.[5056]

34 Then said Mary unto the angel,

8 [a]1Chr. 24:19; 2Chr. 8:14; 31:2

9 [a]Ex. 30:7, 8; 1Sam. 2:28; 1Chr. 23:13; 2Chr. 29:11

10 [a]Lev. 16:17; Rev. 8:3, 4

11 [a]Ex. 30:1

12 [a]Judg. 6:22; 13:22; Dan. 10:8; Luke 1:29; 2:9; Acts 10:4; Rev. 1:17

13 [a]Luke 1:60, 63

14 [a]Luke 1:58

15 [a]Num. 6:3; Judg. 13:4; Luke 7:33 [b]Jer. 1:5; Gal. 1:15

16 [a]Mal. 4:5, 6

17 [I]Or, *by* [a]Mal. 4:5; Matt. 11:14; Mark 9:12

18 [a]Gen. 17:17

19 [a]Dan. 8:16; 9:21-23; Matt. 18:10; Heb. 1:14

20 [a]Ezek. 3:26; 24:27

23 [a]2Kgs. 11:5; 1Chr. 9:25

25 [a]Gen. 30:23; Isa. 4:1; 54:1, 4

27 [a]Matt. 1:18; Luke 2:4, 5

28 [I]Or, *graciously accepted,* or, *much graced* [a]Dan. 9:23; 10:29 [b]Luke 1:3 [c]Judg. 6:12

29 [a]Luke 1:12

31 [a]Isa. 7:14; Matt. 1:21 [b]Luke 2:21

32 [a]Mark 5:7 [b]2Sam. 7:11, 12; Ps. 132:11; Isa. 9:6, 7; 16:5; Jer. 23:5; Rev. 3:7

33 [a]Dan. 2:44; 7:14, 27; Obad. 1:21; Mic. 4:7; John 12:34; Heb. 1:8

How shall this be, seeing I know[1097] not
a man?
35 And the angel answered and said
unto her, [a]The [an]Holy Ghost shall come
upon thee, and the power of the Highest
shall overshadow thee: therefore also that
holy thing[40] which shall be born of thee
shall be called [b]the [an]Son of God.
36 And, behold, thy cousin Elisabeth,
she [pfp]hath also conceived[4815] a son in
her old age: and this is the sixth month
with her, who [ppp]was called barren.
37 For [a]with God nothing [ft]shall be
impossible.[101]
38 And Mary said, Behold the handmaid of the Lord; be it unto me according to thy word.[4487] And the angel departed from her.

Mary Visits Elisabeth

39 And Mary arose in those days,
and went into the hill country with haste,
[a]into a city of Juda;
40 And entered into the house of
Zacharias, and saluted Elisabeth.
41 And it came to pass, that, when
Elisabeth heard the salutation of Mary,
the babe[1025] leaped in her womb;
and Elisabeth was filled with the Holy
Ghost:
42 And she spake out with a loud
voice, and said, [pfpa]Blessed[2127] *art* thou
among women, and [pfp]blessed *is* the fruit
of thy womb.
43 And whence *is* this to me, that

35 [a]Matt. 1:20 [b]Matt. 14:33; 26:63, 64; Mark 1:1; John 1:34; 20:31; Acts 8:37; Rom. 1:4
37 [a]Gen. 18:14; Jer. 32:17; Zech. 8:6; Matt. 19:26; Mark 10:27; Luke 18:27; Rom. 4:21
39 [a]Josh. 21:9-11
42 [a]Judg. 5:24; Luke 1:28
45 [I]Or, *which believed that there*
46 [a]1Sam. 2:1; Ps. 34:2, 3; 35:9; Hab. 3:18
48 [a]1Sam. 1:11; Ps. 138:6 [b]Mal. 3:12; Luke 11:27
49 [a]Ps. 71:19; 126:2, 3 [b]Ps. 111:9
50 [a]Gen. 17:7; Ex. 20:6; Ps. 103:17, 18
51 [a]Ps. 98:1; 118:15; Isa. 40:10; 51:9; 52:10 [b]Ps. 33:10; 1Pet. 5:5
52 [a]1Sam. 2:6-10; Job 5:11; Ps. 113:6
53 [a]1Sam. 2:5; Ps. 34:10

the mother of my Lord should come to
me?
44 For, lo, as soon as the voice of
thy salutation sounded in mine ears, the
babe leaped in my womb for joy.[20]
45 And blessed[3107] *is* she [I]that believed: for there shall be a performance[5050] of those things which
[pfpp]were told her from the Lord.

Mary's Song of Praise

46 And Mary said, [a]My soul[5590]
[pin]doth magnify the Lord,
47 And my spirit [ao]hath rejoiced[21] in
God my Saviour.[4990]
🔑 48 For [a]he [ao]hath regarded[1914] the
low estate[5014] of his handmaiden: for, behold, from henceforth [b]all generations
shall call me blessed.[3106]
49 For he that is mighty [aoa]hath done
to me great things;[3167] and [b]holy[40] *is* his
name.
50 And [a]his mercy[1656] *is* on them
that fear[5399] him from generation to generation.
51 [a]He [ao]hath shewed strength with
his arm; [b]he [ao]hath scattered the
proud[5244] in the imagination[1271] of their
hearts.
52 [a]He [ao]hath put down[2507] the
mighty[1413] from *their* seats, and exalted
them of low degree.
53 [a]He [ao]hath filled the hungry with
good things;[18] and the rich he [ao]hath sent
empty away.

🔑 **1:48** This verse contains one of the most misunderstood words of the New Testament. It is the word *makários*, which is used repeatedly in the Beatitudes. The verb form that corresponds to the adjective *makários*, "blessed" (*makarízō* [3106]), is used here. The translation says "all generations shall call me blessed," but the Greek says *makarioúsi*, the future of *makarízō*, which in reality means "they shall bless me." In James 5:11, the verb *makarízō* is mistranslated as "we count them happy which endure." *Makariótēs* has absolutely nothing to do with happiness; "blessedness" is an inner quality granted by God. The Greek words for "happiness," in the Classic writings, *eudaímōn* and *eutuchēs*, "lucky," never occur in the New Testament. The Lord never promised good luck or favorable circumstances to the believer, but *makariótēs*, "blessedness." See note on Matthew 5:1–12.

One should note that the word translated "blessed" in verse forty-two is not *makária*, but is a totally different word, *eulogēménē* (2127), which in its literal meaning is "eulogized, well spoken of." When one blesses (*eulogéō*) God, he is speaking well of Him, which is equal to praising or thanking Him. When, however, a person asks God to bless another, he is not asking Him to approve the plans that have been made, but to use providence and the work of the Holy Spirit to affect his heart and life.

54 He [ao]hath holpen[482] his servant Israel, [a]in [ainf]remembrance of *his* mercy;

55 [a]As he spake to our fathers, to Abraham, and to his seed[4690] for ever.[165, 1519, 3588]

56 And Mary abode[3306] with her about three months, and returned to her own house.

John Is Born

57 Now Elisabeth's full time[5550] [aop]came that she [infg]should be delivered;[5088] and she brought forth[1080] a son.

58 And her neighbours and her cousins heard how the Lord [ao]had shewed great mercy upon her; and [a]they [ipf]rejoiced with her.

59 And it came to pass, that [a]on the eighth day they came [ainf]to circumcise[4059] the child; and they called him Zacharias, after the name of his father.

60 And his mother answered and said, [a]Not *so;* but he shall be called John.

61 And they said unto her, There is none of thy kindred that is called by this name.

62 And they [ipf]made signs to his father, how he would have him called.

63 And he asked for a writing table, and wrote,[1125] saying, [a]His name is John. And they marvelled all.

64 [a]And his mouth was opened immediately, and his tongue *loosed,* and he [ipf]spake, and [ppt]praised[2127] God.

65 And fear[5401] came on all that dwelt round about them: and all these [I]sayings[4487] [ipf]were noised abroad[1255] throughout all [a]the hill country of Judea.

66 And all they that [apt]heard *them* [a]laid *them* up in their hearts,[2588] saying, What manner of child[3813] shall this be! And [b]the hand of the Lord was with him.

The Prophecy of Zacharias

67 And his father Zacharias [a]was filled with the [an]Holy [an]Ghost, and prophesied,[4395] saying,

68 [a]Blessed[2128] *be* the Lord God of Israel; for [b]he [ao]hath visited[1980] and redeemed[4160,3085] his people,

69 [a]And [ao]hath raised up an horn of salvation[4991] for us in the house of his servant[3816] David;

70 [a]As he spake by the mouth of his holy prophets, which have been since the world began:

71 That we should be [nn]saved[4991] from our enemies, and from the hand of all that [ppt]hate us;

72 [ainf][a]To perform the mercy[1656] *promised* to our fathers, and [aifp]to remember his holy[40] covenant;[1242]

73 [a]The oath[3727] which he sware to our father Abraham,

74 That he would grant unto us, that we [aptp]being delivered[4506] out of the hand of our enemies [pinf]might [a]serve[3000] him without fear,

75 [a]In holiness[3742] and righteousness[1343] before him, all the days of our life.

76 And thou, child, shalt be called the prophet of the Highest: for [a]thou shalt go before the face[4383] of the Lord to prepare his ways;[3598]

77 To give knowledge[1108] of salvation[4991] unto his people [I][a]by the remission[859] of their sins,

78 Through the [I]tender mercy[1656] of our God; whereby the [II]dayspring from on high [aom]hath visited[1980] us,

79 [ainf][a]To give light[2014] to them that [ppt]sit in darkness[4655] and *in* the shadow of death, [infg]to guide our feet into the way of peace.

80 And [a]the child [ipf]grew, and [ipf]waxed strong[2901] in spirit,[4151] and [b]was in the deserts till the day of his shewing unto Israel.

The Birth of Jesus (Matt. 1:18–25)

2 And it came to pass in those days, that there went out a decree[1378] from Caesar Augustus, that all the world[3625] [pip]should be [I]taxed.

2 ([a]*And* this taxing was first[4413] made when Cyrenius was governor of Syria.)

---

54 [a]Ps. 98:3; Jer. 31:3, 20
55 [a]Gen. 17:19; Ps. 132:11; Rom. 11:28; Gal. 3:16
58 [a]Luke 1:14
59 [a]Gen. 17:12; Lev. 12:3
60 [a]Luke 1:13
63 [a]Luke 1:13
64 [a]Luke 1:20
65 [I]Or, *things* [a]Luke 1:39
66 [a]Luke 2:19, 51 [b]Gen. 39:2; Ps. 80:17; 89:21; Acts 11:21
67 [a]Joel 2:28
68 [a]1Kgs. 1:48; Ps. 41:13; 72:18; 106:48 [b]Ex. 3:16; 4:31; Ps. 111:9; Luke 7:16
69 [a]Ps. 132:17
70 [a]Jer. 23:5, 6; 30:10; Dan. 9:24; Acts 3:21; Rom. 1:2
72 [a]Lev. 26:42; Ps. 98:3; 105:8, 9; 106:45; Ezek. 16:60; Luke 1:54
73 [a]Gen. 12:3; 17:4; 22:16, 17; Heb. 6:13, 17
74 [a]Rom. 6:18, 22; Heb. 9:14
75 [a]Jer. 32:39, 40; Eph. 4:24; 2Thess. 2:13; 2Tim. 1:9; Titus 2:12; 1Pet. 1:15; 2Pet. 1:4
76 [a]Isa. 40:3; Mal. 3:1; 4:5; Matt. 11:10; Luke 1:17
77 [I]Or, *for* [a]Mark 1:4; Luke 3:3
78 [I]Or, *bowels of the mercy* [II]Or, *sunrising,* or, *branch* Num. 24:17; Isa. 11:1; Zech. 3:8; 6:12; Mal. 4:2
79 [a]Isa. 9:2; 42:7; 49:9; Matt. 4:16; Acts 26:18
80 [a]Luke 2:40 [b]Matt. 3:1; 11:7
1 [I]Or, *enrolled*
2 [a]Acts 5:37

3 And all [ipf]went [pip]to be taxed, every one into his own[2398] city.

4 And Joseph also went up from Galilee, out of the city of Nazareth, into Judaea, unto [a]the city of David, which is called Bethlehem; ([b]because he was of the house[3624] and lineage[3965] of David:)

5 [aifp]To be taxed with Mary [a]his espoused[3423] wife, being great with child.

6 And so it was, that, while they were there, the days were accomplished that she should be delivered.

🔑 7 And [a]she brought forth her firstborn[4416] son,[5207] and [ao]wrapped him in swaddling clothes,[4683] and laid him in a manger;[5336] because there was no room for them in the inn.

The Shepherds and the Angels

8 And there were in the same country shepherds[4166] abiding in the field, keeping[5442] [I]watch[5438] over their flock[4167] by night.

9 And, lo, the angel[32] of the Lord came upon them, and the glory[1391] of the Lord shone round about them: [a]and they were sore[3173] afraid.[5401]

10 And the angel said unto them, [pim]Fear[5399] not: for, behold, I bring you good tidings of great joy,[5479] [a]which shall be to all people.[2992]

11 [a]For unto you [aop]is born[5088] this day in the city of David [b]a Saviour,[4990] [c]which is Christ[5547] the [an]Lord.

12 And this *shall be* a [art]sign unto you; Ye shall find the babe[1025] wrapped in swaddling clothes, lying[2749] in a manger.

13 [a]And suddenly there was with the angel a multitude of the heavenly[3770] host[4756] praising[134] God,[2316] and saying,

14 [a]Glory[1391] to God in the highest, and on earth [b]peace,[1515] [c]good will[2107] toward men.[444]

15 And it came to pass, as the angels [ao]were gone away from them into heaven, the shepherds[444, 4166] said one to another, Let us now go even unto Bethlehem, and see this thing[4487] which is come to pass, which the Lord hath made known unto us.

16 And they came [apt]with haste, and found[429] Mary, and Joseph, and the babe[1025] lying[2749] in a manger.

17 And when they had seen *it,* they made known abroad[1232] the saying[4487] which was told them concerning this child.

18 And all they that heard *it* wondered at those things which were told them by the shepherds.[4166]

19 [a]But Mary [ipf]kept all these things, and [ppt]pondered *them* in her heart.

20 And the shepherds returned,[1994] glorifying[1392] and praising[134] God for all the things that they [ao]had heard and [ao]seen, as it was told unto them.

21 [a]And when eight days were accomplished[4130] for the [infg]circumcising[4059] of the child, his name was called [b]JESUS, which was so named of the angel[32] before he [infg]was conceived in the womb.

Jesus Is Dedicated in the Temple

22 And when [a]the days of her purification[2512] according to[2596] the law[3551] of Moses were accomplished, they [ao]brought him to Jerusalem, to present *him* to the Lord;

23 (As it is written[1125] in the law of the Lord, [a]Every male that [ppt]openeth the womb shall be called holy[40] to the Lord;[2962])

24 And to offer a sacrifice[2378] according to [a]that which is said in the law of the Lord, A pair of turtledoves, or two young[3502] pigeons.

25 And, behold, there was a man in Jerusalem, whose name *was* Simeon; and the same man *was* just[1342] and devout,[2126] [a]waiting for[4327] the consolation[3874] of Israel: and the [an]Holy [an]Ghost was upon him.

4 [a]1Sam. 16:1, 4; John 7:42 [b]Matt. 1:16; Luke 1:27
5 [a]Matt. 1:18; Luke 1:27
7 [a]Matt. 1:25
8 [I]Or, *the night watches*
9 [a]Luke 1:12
10 [a]Gen. 12:3; Matt. 28:19; Mark 1:15; Luke 2:31, 32; 24:47; Col. 1:23
11 [a]Isa. 9:6 [b]Matt. 1:21 [c]Matt. 1:16; 16:16; Luke 1:43; Acts 2:36; 10:36; Phil. 2:11
13 [a]Gen. 28:12; 32:1, 2; Ps. 103:20, 21; 148:2; Dan. 7:10; Heb. 1:14; Rev. 5:11
14 [a]Luke 19:38; Eph. 1:6; 3:10, 21; Rev. 5:13 [b]Isa. 57:19; Luke 1:79; Rom. 5:1; Eph. 2:17; Col. 1:20 [c]John 3:16; Eph. 2:4, 7; 2Thess. 2:16; 1John 4:9, 10
19 [a]Gen. 37:11; Luke 1:66; 2:51
21 [a]Gen. 17:12; Lev. 12:3; Luke 1:59 [b]Matt. 1:21, 25; Luke 1:31
22 [a]Lev. 12:2-4, 6
23 [a]Ex. 13:2; 22:29; 34:19; Num. 3:13; 8:17; 18:15
24 [a]Lev. 12:2, 6, 8
25 [a]Isa. 40:1; Mark 15:43; Luke 2:38

🔑 **2:7** See note on Colossians 1:15-18.

26 And it [pfpp]was revealed[5537] unto him by the [art]Holy Ghost, that he should not [a]see[1492] death,[2288] before he [aosb]had seen[1492] the Lord's Christ.

27 And he came [a]by the Spirit into the temple:[2411] and when the parents brought in[1521] the child Jesus, to do for him after the custom of the law,

28 Then took he him up[1209] in his arms, and blessed[2127] God, and said,

29 Lord,[1203] [a]now [pin]lettest thou thy servant depart[630] in peace, according to thy word:[4487]

30 For mine eyes [ao][a]have seen thy salvation,[4992]

31 Which thou [ao]hast prepared before the face[4383] of all people;[2992]

32 [a]A light[5457] to lighten[602] the Gentiles, and the glory of thy people Israel.

33 And Joseph and his mother marvelled at those things which [ppp]were spoken of him.

34 And Simeon blessed them, and said unto Mary his mother, Behold, this *child* [pin]is set[2749] for the [a]fall and rising again[386] of many in Israel; and for [b]a sign which [ppp]shall be spoken against;

35 (Yea, [a]a sword shall pierce through thy own soul[5590] also,) that the thoughts[1261] of many hearts [asbp]may be revealed.[601]

36 And there was one Anna, a prophetess,[4398] the daughter of Phanuel, of the tribe of Aser: she was of a great age, and [apt]had lived[2198] with an husband seven years from her virginity;

37 And she *was* a widow of about fourscore and four years, which [ipf]departed[868] not from the temple,[2411] but [ppt]served[3000] *God* with fastings[3521] and prayers [a]night and day.

38 And she coming in that instant[5610] [ipf]gave thanks likewise unto the Lord, and [ipf]spake of him to all them that [ppt][a]looked for[4327] redemption[3085] in [I]Jerusalem.

The Return to Nazareth

39 And when they [ao]had performed[5055] all things according to the law of the Lord, they returned into Galilee, to their own city Nazareth.

40 [a]And the child [ipf]grew, and [ipf]waxed strong[2901] in spirit,[4151] [ppp]filled with wisdom:[4678] and the [an]grace[5485] of God was upon him.

Jesus Speaks With The Leaders in the Temple

41 Now his parents [ipf]went to Jerusalem [a]every year at the feast of the passover.[3957]

42 And when he was twelve years old, they went up to Jerusalem after the custom of the feast.

43 And when they [apt]had fulfilled[5048] the days, as they [aie]returned, the child Jesus tarried behind[5278] in Jerusalem; and Joseph and his mother knew not *of it.*

44 But they, [apt]supposing him to have been in the company, went[2064] a day's journey;[3598] and they [ipf]sought him among *their* kinsfolk and [pl]acquaintance.[1110]

45 And when they found him not, they turned back again to Jerusalem, seeking him.

46 And it came to pass, that after three days they found him in the temple,[2411] sitting in the midst[3319] of the doctors,[1320] both hearing them, and asking them questions.

47 And [a]all that [ppt]heard him were astonished at his understanding and answers.[612]

48 And when they saw him, they were amazed: and his mother said unto him, Son,[5043] why [ao]hast thou thus dealt[4160] with us? behold, thy father[3962] and I [ipf]have sought[2212] thee sorrowing.

49 And he said unto them, How is it that ye [ipf]sought me? wist[1492] ye not that I must be about [a]my Father's[3962] business?

50 And [a]they understood not the saying[4487] which he spake unto them.

51 And he went down with them, and came to Nazareth, and was subject unto[5293] them: but his mother [ipf][a]kept[1301] all these sayings in her heart.[2588]

52 And Jesus [ipf][a]increased[4298] in wis-

26 [a]Ps. 89:48; Heb. 11:5
27 [a]Matt. 4:1
29 [a]Gen. 46:30; Phil. 1:23
30 [a]Isa. 52:10; Luke 3:6
32 [a]Isa. 9:2; 42:6; 49:6; 60:1-3; Matt. 4:16; Acts 13:47; 28:28
34 [a]Isa. 8:14; Hos. 14:9; Matt. 21:44; Rom. 9:32, 33; 1Cor. 1:23, 24; 2Cor. 2:16; 1Pet. 2:7, 8 [b]Acts 28:22
35 [a]Ps. 42:10; John 19:25
37 [a]Acts 26:7; 1Tim. 5:5
38 [I]Or, *Israel* [a]Mark 15:43; Luke 1:25; 24:21
40 [a]Luke 1:80; 2:52
41 [a]Ex. 23:15, 17; 34:23; Deut. 16:1, 16
47 [a]Matt. 7:28; Mark 1:22; Luke 4:22, 32; John 7:15, 46
49 [a]John 2:16
50 [a]Luke 9:45; 18:34
51 [a]Dan. 7:28; Luke 2:19
52 [a]1Sam. 2:26; Luke 2:40

dom[4678] and [I]stature, and in favour[5485] with God[2316] and man.[444]

John the Baptist Preaches (Matt. 3:1–12; Mark 1:1–8; John 1:19–28)

3 Now in the fifteenth year of the reign of Tiberius Caesar, Pontius Pilate being governor of Judaea, and Herod being tetrarch[5075] of Galilee, and his brother Philip tetrarch of Ituraea and of the region of Trachonitis, and Lysanias the tetrarch of Abilene,

2 [a]Annas and Caiaphas being the high priests, the word[4487] of God came unto John the son of Zacharias in the wilderness.

3 [a]And he came into all the country about Jordan, preaching[2784] the [an]baptism[908] of repentance[3341] [b]for the [an]remission[859] of sins;

4 As it is written[1125] in the book[976] of the words of Esaias the prophet, saying, [a]The voice of one crying in the wilderness, Prepare ye the way[3598] of the Lord, [pim]make his paths straight.

5 Every valley shall be filled, and every mountain and hill shall be brought low; and the crooked shall be made straight, and the rough ways *shall be* made smooth;

6 And [a]all flesh[4561] shall see the salvation[4992] of God.[2316]

7 Then said he to the multitude that [ppt]came forth [aifp]to be baptized[907] of him, [a]O generation of vipers, who hath warned you [ainf]to flee from the wrath[3709] to come?

8 [aim]Bring forth therefore fruits [I]worthy of repentance,[3341] and [aosi]begin not [pinf]to say within yourselves, We have Abraham to *our* father:[3962] for I say unto you, That God is able of these stones to raise up children[5043] unto Abraham.

9 And now also the axe [pin]is laid[2749] unto the root of the trees: [a]every tree therefore which [ppt]bringeth not forth good fruit is hewn down,[1581] and cast into the fire.

10 And the people asked him, saying, [a]What shall we do then?

11 He answereth and saith unto them, [a]He that hath two coats, let him impart to him that [ppt]hath none; and he that hath meat,[1033] [pim]let him do[4160] likewise.

12 Then [a]came also publicans[5057] to be baptized, and said unto him, Master, what shall we do?

13 And he said unto them, [pim][a]Exact no more than that which [pfpp]is appointed[1299] you.

14 And the soldiers likewise [ipf]demanded of him, saying, And what shall we do? And he said unto them, [aosi][I]Do violence to no man, [a]neither [aosi]accuse *any* falsely; and [pim]be content with your [II]wages.[3800]

15 And as the people were [I]in expectation, and all men [ppt][II]mused[1260] in their hearts[2588] of John, whether he were the Christ,[5547] or not;

🔑 16 John answered, saying unto *them* all, [a]I indeed baptize[907] you with water; but one mightier than I cometh, the latchet[2438] of whose shoes I am not worthy to unloose: he [ft]shall baptize you with the [an]Holy Ghost[4151] and with fire:

17 Whose fan *is* in his hand, and he will throughly purge his floor, and [a]will gather the wheat into his garner;[596] but the chaff he will burn with fire unquenchable.

18 And many other things in his [ppt]exhortation [ipf]preached[2097] he unto the people.

19 [a]But Herod the tetrarch,[5076] being reproved by him for Herodias his brother Philip's wife, and for all the evils[4190] which Herod [ao]had done,

20 Added yet this above all, that he shut up John in prison.

John Baptizes Jesus (Matt. 3:13–17; Mark 1:9–11)

21 Now when all the people [aie]were baptized,[907] [a]it came to pass, that Jesus

52 [I]Or, *age*

2 [a]John 11:49, 51; 18:13; Acts 4:6

3 [a]Matt. 3:1; Mark 1:4 [b]Luke 1:77

4 [a]Isa. 40:3; Matt. 3:3; Mark 1:3; John 1:23

6 [a]Ps. 98:2; Isa. 52:10; Luke 2:10

7 [a]Matt. 3:7

8 [I]Or, *meet for*

9 [a]Matt. 7:19

10 [a]Acts 2:37

11 [a]Luke 11:41; 2Cor. 8:14; James 2:15, 16; 1John 3:17; 4:20

12 [a]Matt. 21:32; Luke 7:29

13 [a]Luke 19:8

14 [I]Or, *Put no man in fear* [II]Or, *allowance* [a]Ex. 23:1; Lev. 19:11

15 [I]Or, *in suspense* [II]Or, *reasoned,* or, *debated*

16 [a]Matt. 3:11

17 [a]Mic. 4:12; Matt. 13:30

19 [a]Matt. 14:3; Mark 6:17

21 [a]Matt. 3:13; John 1:32

🔑 **3:16** See note on Acts 1:5.

also [aptp]being baptized, and praying, the heaven[3772] [aifp]was opened,

22 And the Holy Ghost [ainf]descended in a bodily[4984] shape[1491] like a dove upon him, and a voice [ainf]came from heaven,[3772] which said, Thou art my beloved[27] Son;[5207] in thee I [ao]am well pleased.

The Genealogy of Jesus (Matt. 1:1–17)

23 And Jesus himself began to be [a]about[5616] thirty years of age, being (as [ipf]was supposed) [b]the [an]son[5207] of Joseph, which was *the son* of Heli,

24 Which was *the son* of Matthat, which was *the son* of Levi, which was *the son* of Melchi, which was *the son* of Janna, which was *the son* of Joseph,

25 Which was *the son* of Mattathias, which was *the son* of Amos, which was *the son* of Naum, which was *the son* of Esli, which was *the son* of Nagge,

26 Which was *the son* of Maath, which was *the son* of Mattathias, which was *the son* of Semei, which was *the son* of Joseph, which was *the son* of Juda,

27 Which was *the son* of Joanna, which was *the son* of Rhesa, which was *the son* of Zorobabel, which was *the son* of Salathiel, which was *the son* of Neri,

28 Which was *the son* of Melchi, which was *the son* of Addi, which was *the son* of Cosam, which was *the son* of Elmodam, which was *the son* of Er,

29 Which was *the son* of Jose, which was *the son* of Eliezer, which was *the son* of Jorim, which was *the son* of Matthat, which was *the son* of Levi,

30 Which was *the son* of Simeon, which was *the son* of Juda, which was *the son* of Joseph, which was *the son* of Jonan, which was *the son* of Eliakim,

31 Which was *the son* of Melea, which was *the son* of Menan, which was *the son* of Mattatha, which was *the son* of [a]Nathan, [b]which was *the son* of David,

32 [a]Which was *the son* of Jesse, which was *the son* of Obed, which was *the son* of Booz, which was *the son* of Salmon, which was *the son* of Naasson,

33 Which was *the son* of Aminadab, which was *the son* of Aram, which was *the son* of Esrom, which was *the son* of Phares, which was *the son* of Juda,

34 Which was *the son* of Jacob, which was *the son* of Isaac, which was *the son* of Abraham, [a]which was *the son* of Thara, which was *the son* of Nachor,

35 Which was *the son* of Saruch, which was *the son* of Ragau, which was *the son* of Phalec, which was *the son* of Heber, which was *the son* of Sala,

36 [a]Which was *the son* of Cainan, which was *the son* of Arphaxad, [b]which was *the son* of Sem, which was *the son* of Noe, which was *the son* of Lamech,

37 Which was *the son* of Mathusalah, which was *the son* of Enoch, which was *the son* of Jared, which was *the son* of Maleleel, which was *the son* of Cainan,

38 Which was *the son* of Enos, which was *the son* of Seth, which was *the son* of Adam, [a]which was *the son* of God.[2316]

The Devil Tempts Jesus (Matt. 4:1–11; Mark 1:12, 13)

4 🗝And [a]Jesus being full of the [an]Holy[40] [an]Ghost[4151] returned from Jordan, and [ipf][b]was led by the Spirit[4151] into the wilderness,

2 [ppp]Being forty days tempted[3985] of the devil.[1228] And [a]in those days he did eat nothing: and when they [aptp]were ended,[4931] he afterward hungered.[3983]

3 And the devil said unto him, If thou be the Son[5207] of God,[2316] command this stone that it be made bread.

4 And Jesus answered him, saying, [a]It is written, That man[444] shall not live[2198] by bread alone, but by every word[4487] of God.

5 And the devil, [apt]taking him up into an high mountain, shewed unto him all the kingdoms of the world in a moment of time.[5550]

23 [a]Num. 4:3, 35, 39, 43, 47 [b]Matt. 13:55; John 6:42
31 [a]Zech. 12:12 [b]2Sam. 5:14; 1Chr. 3:5
32 [a]Ruth 4:18-22; 1Chr. 2:10-12
34 [a]Gen. 11:24, 26
36 [a]Gen. 11:12 [b]Gen. 5:6-26; 11:10-26
38 [a]Gen. 5:1, 2
1 [a]Matt. 4:1; Mark 1:12 [b]Luke 2:27; 4:14
2 [a]Ex. 34:28; 1Kgs. 19:8
4 [a]Deut. 8:3

🗝 **4:1–13** See note on Genesis 22:1.

6 And the devil said unto him, All this power[1849] will I give thee, and the glory[1391] of them: for [a]that [pfip]is delivered unto me; and to whomsoever I will I give it.

7 If thou therefore [aosb]wilt [I]worship me, all shall be thine.

8 And Jesus answered and said unto him, Get thee behind me, Satan: for [a]it is written, Thou shalt worship the Lord thy God, and him only shalt thou serve.

9 [a]And he brought him to Jerusalem, and set him on a pinnacle of the temple,[2411] and said unto him, If thou be the Son of God, cast thyself down[2736] from hence:

10 For [a]it is written, He shall give his angels charge over thee, [infg]to keep thee:

11 And in *their* hands they shall bear thee up, lest at any time thou [aosb]dash[4350] thy foot against a stone.

12 And Jesus answering said unto him, [a]It is said, Thou [ft]shalt not tempt[1598] the [an]Lord thy God.

13 And when the devil had ended[4931] all the [an]temptation,[3986] he departed[868] from him [a]for a season.[2540]

Jesus Reads the Scriptures (Matt. 4:12–17; Mark 1:14, 15)

14 [a]And Jesus returned [b]in the power of the Spirit into [c]Galilee: and there went out a fame of him through[2596] all the region round about.

15 And he [ipf]taught in their synagogues, being glorified[1392] of all.

Jesus' Rejection at Nazareth (Matt. 13:53–58; Mark 6:1–6)

16 And he came to [a]Nazareth, where he had been brought up: and, as his custom was, [b]he went into the synagogue on the sabbath[4521] day, and stood up for to read.

17 And there was delivered unto him the book[975] of the prophet Esaias. And when he had opened the book, he found the place where it was written,

18 [a]The Spirit[4151] of the Lord *is* upon me, because he [ao]hath anointed me [pinf]to preach the gospel[2097] to the poor; he [pfi]hath sent me [ainf]to heal[2390] the brokenhearted, [ainf]to preach[2784] deliverance[859] to the captives,[164] and recovering of sight[309] to the blind, to set at liberty them that are bruised,

19 [ainf]To preach the acceptable[1184] year[1763] of the Lord.

20 And he [apt]closed the book,[975] and he [apt]gave *it* again to the minister,[5257] and sat down. And the eyes of all them that were in the synagogue were fastened on him.

21 And he began [pinf]to say unto them, This day is this scripture[1124] fulfilled in your ears.

22 And all [ipf]bare him witness,[3140] and [ipfa]wondered at the gracious[5485] words which [ppt]proceeded out of his mouth. And they said, [b]Is not this Joseph's son?

23 And he said unto them, Ye will surely say unto me this proverb,[3850] Physician,[2395] [aim]heal thyself: whatsoever we have heard [apt]done[1096] in [a]Capernaum, [aim]do[4160] also here in [b]thy country.

24 And he said, Verily[281] I say unto you, No [a]prophet[4396] is accepted[1184] in his own country.

25 But I tell you of a truth, [a]many widows were in Israel in the days[2250] of Elias, when the heaven was shut up three years and six months, when great famine was throughout all the land;

26 But unto none of them was Elias sent, save unto Sarepta, *a city* of Sidon, unto a woman *that was* a widow.

27 [a]And many lepers were in Israel in the time of Eliseus the prophet; and none of them was cleansed, saving Naaman the Syrian.

28 And all they in the synagogue, when they heard these things, were filled with wrath,[2372]

29 And rose up, and thrust him out of the city, and led[71] him unto the [I]brow of the hill whereon their city was built, that they might cast him down headlong.

6 [a]John 12:31; 14:30; Rev. 13:2, 7
7 [I]Or, *fall down before me*
8 [a]Deut. 6:13; 10:20
9 [a]Matt. 4:5
10 [a]Ps. 91:11
12 [a]Deut. 6:16
13 [a]John 14:30; Heb. 4:15
14 [a]Matt. 4:12; John 4:43 [b]Luke 4:1 [c]Acts 10:37
16 [a]Matt. 2:23; 13:54; Mark 6:1 [b]Acts 13:14; 17:2
18 [a]Isa. 61:1
22 [a]Ps. 45:2; Matt. 13:54; Mark 6:2; Luke 2:47 [b]John 6:42
23 [a]Matt. 4:13; 11:23 [b]Matt. 13:54; Mark 6:1
24 [a]Matt. 13:57; Mark 6:4; John 4:44
25 [a]1Kgs. 17:9; 18:1; James 5:17
27 [a]2Kgs. 5:14
29 [I]Or, *edge*

30 But he [apt][a]passing through the midst[3319] of them [ipf]went his way,

The Man With an Unclean Spirit (Mark 1:21–28)

31 And [a]came down to Capernaum, a city of Galilee, and taught[1321] them on the sabbath days.

32 And they [ipf]were astonished at his doctrine: [a]for his word[3056] was with power.[1849]

33 [a]And in the synagogue there was a man, which had a spirit[4151] of an unclean devil,[1140] and cried out with a loud voice,

34 Saying, [I]Let *us* alone; what have we to do with thee, *thou* Jesus of Nazareth? [ao]art thou come[2064] [ainf]to destroy us? [a]I know thee who thou art; [b]the Holy One[40] of God.[2316]

35 And Jesus rebuked him, saying, Hold thy peace, and come out of him. And when the devil had thrown him in the midst, he came out of him, and hurt him not.[3367]

36 And they were all amazed, and [ipf]spake among themselves, saying, What a word *is* this! for with authority[1849] and power[1411] he commandeth[2004] the unclean spirits, and they come out.

37 And the fame of him [ipf]went out into every place of the country round about.

Jesus Heals Many (Matt. 8:14–17; Mark 1:29–34)

38 [a]And he arose out of the synagogue, and entered into Simon's house. And Simon's wife's mother was taken with[4912] a great fever; and they [ao]besought him for her.

39 And he stood over her, and rebuked the fever; and it left her: and immediately she arose and ministered[1247] unto them.

40 [a]Now when the sun was setting, all they that had any sick[770] with divers[4164] diseases brought them unto him; and he [apt]laid his hands on every one of them, and healed them.

41 [a]And devils also came out of many, crying out, and saying, Thou art [art]Christ[5547] the Son of God. And [b]he rebuking *them* suffered them not [pinfI]to speak: for they knew that he was [art]Christ.

Jesus Preaches in the Synagogues of Galilee (Mark 1:35–39)

42 [a]And when it was day, he [apt]departed and went into a desert place: and the people [ipf]sought him, and came unto him, and stayed[2722] him, that he should not [infg]depart from them.

43 And he said unto them, I must [ainf]preach[2097] the kingdom[932] of God[2316] to other cities also: for therefore am I sent.

44 [a]And he preached[2784] in the synagogues[4864] of Galilee.

Jesus Calls His Disciples (Matt. 4:18–22; Mark 1:16–20)

5 And [a]it came to pass, that, as the people pressed upon him [infg]to hear[191] the word[3056] of God, he stood by the lake of Gennesaret,

2 And saw two ships standing by the lake: but the fishermen [apt]were gone out of them, and [ao]were washing[637] *their* nets.[1350]

3 And he [apt]entered into one of the ships, which was Simon's, and prayed him that he would thrust out a little from the land. And he sat down, and [ipf]taught[1321] the people out of the ship.

4 Now when he [aom]had left[3973] speaking, he said unto Simon, [a]Launch out into the deep, and let down your nets for a draught.[61]

5 And Simon answering said unto him, Master, we [apt]have toiled[2872] all the night, and [ao]have taken nothing: nevertheless at thy word[4487] I will let down the net.

6 And when they had this done, they inclosed a great multitude of fishes: and their net [ipf]brake.

7 And they beckoned[2656] unto *their*

30 [a]John 8:59; 10:39
31 [a]Matt. 4:13; Mark 1:21
32 [a]Matt. 7:28, 29; Titus 2:15
33 [a]Mark 1:23
34 [I]Or, *Away* [a]Luke 4:41 [b]Ps. 16:10; Dan. 9:24; Luke 1:35
38 [a]Matt. 8:14; Mark 1:29
40 [a]Matt. 8:16; Mark 1:32
41 [I]Or, *to say that they knew him to be Christ* [a]Mark 1:34; 3:11 [b]Mark 1:25, 34; Luke 4:34, 35
42 [a]Mark 1:35
44 [a]Mark 1:39
1 [a]Matt. 4:18; Mark 1:16
4 [a]John 21:6

partners,3353 which were in the other ship, that they should come and help them. And they came, and filled both the ships, so that they began to sink.

8 When Simon Peter saw *it,* he fell down at Jesus' knees, saying, [a]Depart from me; for I am a sinful[268] man, O Lord.

9 For he was astonished, and all that were with him, at the draught of the fishes which they had taken:

10 And so *was* also James, and John, the sons of Zebedee, which were partners[2844] with Simon. And Jesus said unto Simon, [pim]Fear[5399] not; [a]from henceforth thou shalt catch men.

11 And when they had brought their ships to land,[1093] [a]they [apt]forsook all, and followed him.

Jesus Cleanses a Leper (Matt. 8:1–4; Mark 1:40–45)

12 [a]And it came to pass, when he was in a certain city, behold a man full of leprosy: who seeing Jesus [apt]fell on *his* face, and besought[1189] him, saying, Lord, if thou wilt, thou canst make me clean.

13 And he [apt]put forth *his* hand, and touched him, saying, I will: be thou clean. And immediately the leprosy departed from him.

14 [a]And he charged him to tell no man: but go, and shew thyself to the priest, and offer for thy cleansing,[2512] [b]according as Moses commanded,4367 for a testimony unto them.

15 But so much the more [ipf]went there a fame[3056] abroad of him: [a]and great multitudes [ipf]came together [pinf]to hear, and [pip]to be healed by him of their infirmities.[769]

16 [a]And he withdrew himself into the wilderness, and [ppt]prayed.

Jesus Heals a Paralytic (Matt. 9:1–8; Mark 2:1–12)

17 And it came to pass on a certain day, as he was teaching, that there were Pharisees and doctors of the law3547 sitting by, which were come out of every town of Galilee, and Judaea, and Jerusalem: and the power of the Lord was *present* [aies]to heal[2390] them.

18 [a]And, behold, men [ppt]brought in a bed a man[444] which was taken with a palsy:3886 and they [ipf]sought *means* to bring him in, and to lay *him* before him.

19 And when they could not find by what *way* they might bring him in because of the multitude, they went upon the housetop, and let him down through the tiling with *his* couch into the midst[3319] before Jesus.

20 And when he saw their faith,[4102] he said unto him, Man, thy sins [pfip]are forgiven[863] thee.

21 [a]And the scribes and the Pharisees began to reason, saying, Who is this which speaketh blasphemies?[988] [b]Who can [pinf]forgive sins, but God[2316] alone?

22 But when Jesus perceived their thoughts, he answering said unto them, What reason[1260] ye in your hearts?

23 Whether is easier, to say, Thy sins [pfip]be forgiven thee; or to say, Rise up and [pim]walk?

24 But that ye may know that the Son of man[444] hath power[1849] upon earth[1093] [pinf]to forgive[863] sins, (he said unto the sick of the palsy,) I say unto thee, Arise, and [apt]take up thy couch, and [pim]go into thine house.

25 And immediately he [apt]rose up before them, and [apt]took up that whereon he lay, and [ao]departed to his own house, glorifying[1392] God.

26 And they were all amazed,[1611] and they [ipf]glorified God, and were filled with fear,[5401] saying, We [ao]have seen strange things[3861] to day.

Jesus Calls Levi (Matt. 9:9–13; Mark 2:13–17)

27 [a]And after these things he went forth, and saw a publican,5057 named

8 [a]2Sam. 6:9; 1Kgs. 17:18
10 [a]Matt. 4:19; Mark 1:17
11 [a]Matt. 4:20; 19:27; Mark 1:18; Luke 18:28
12 [a]Matt. 8:2; Mark 1:40
14 [a]Matt. 8:4 [b]Lev. 14:4, 10, 21, 22
15 [a]Matt. 4:25; Mark 3:7; John 6:2
16 [a]Matt. 14:23; Mark 6:46
18 [a]Matt. 9:2; Mark 2:3
21 [a]Matt. 9:3; Mark 2:6, 7 [b]Ps. 32:5; Isa. 43:25
27 [a]Matt. 9:9; Mark 2:13, 14

Levi, sitting at the receipt of custom: and he said unto him, [pim]Follow me.

28 And he [apt]left all, [apt]rose up, and followed him.

29 [a]And Levi made him a great feast[1403] in his own house: and [b]there was a great company of publicans$_{5057}$ and of others that sat down with them.

30 But their scribes and Pharisees [ipf]murmured against his disciples,[3101] saying, Why do ye eat and drink with publicans and sinners?[268]

31 And Jesus answering said unto them, They that are whole need not a physician;$_{2395}$ but they that are sick.

32 [a]I came not to call the righteous,[1342] but sinners[268] to repentance.[3341]

The Question Concerning Fasting (Matt. 9:14–17; Mark 2:18–22)

33 And they said unto him, [a]Why do the disciples of John fast$_{3522}$ often, and make prayers, and likewise *the disciples* of the Pharisees; but thine eat and drink?

34 And he said unto them, Can ye make the children[5207] of the bridechamber [pinf]fast, while the bridegroom is with them?

35 But the days[2250] will come, when the bridegroom shall be taken away from them, and then shall they fast in those days.

36 [a]And he [ipf]spake also a parable unto them; No man putteth a piece of a new[2537] garment upon an old; if otherwise, then both the new [pin]maketh a rent,$_{4977}$ and the piece that was *taken* out of the new agreeth not with the old.

37 And no man putteth new wine[3631] into old bottles; else the new wine will burst the bottles, and be spilled, and the bottles shall perish.

38 But new wine must be put into new bottles; and both are preserved.[4933]

39 No man also having drunk old *wine* straightway$_{2112}$ desireth new: for he saith, The old[3820] is better.[5543]

29 [a]Matt. 9:10; Mark 2:15 [b]Luke 15:1
32 [a]Matt. 9:13; 1Tim. 1:15
33 [a]Matt. 9:14; Mark 2:18
36 [a]Matt. 9:16, 17; Mark 2:21, 22
1 [a]Matt. 12:1; Mark 2:23
2 [a]Ex. 20:10
3 [a]1Sam. 21:6
4 [a]Lev. 24:9
6 [a]Matt. 12:9; Mark 3:1; Luke 13:14; 14:3; John 9:16

Jesus Is Lord Over the Sabbath (Matt. 12:1–8; Mark 2:23–28)

6 And [a]it came to pass on the second sabbath$_{4521}$ after the first, that he [pinf]went through the corn fields; and his disciples[3101] [ipf]plucked the ears of corn, and [ipf]did eat, rubbing *them* in *their* hands.

2 And certain of the Pharisees said unto them, Why do ye that [a]which [pin]is not lawful$_{1832}$ to do on the sabbath days?

3 And Jesus answering them said, Have ye not read so much as this, [a]what David did, when himself [ao]was an hungred,$_{3983}$ and they which were with him;

4 How he went into the house[3624] of God,[2316] and did take and eat the shewbread,[4286]$_{3588,720}$ and gave also to them that were with him; [a]which it is not lawful to eat but for the priests alone?

5 And he said unto them, That the Son of man is Lord[2962] also of the sabbath.

The Man With a Withered Hand (Matt. 12:9–14; Mark 3:1–6)

6 [a]And it came to pass also on another sabbath, that he entered into the synagogue[4864] and [pinf]taught:[1321] and there was a man whose right[1188] hand was withered.

7 And the scribes[1122] and Pharisees [ipf]watched[3906] him, whether he [ft]would heal on the sabbath day; that they [aosb]might find an accusation[2724] against him.

8 But he knew their thoughts, and said to the man which [ppt]had the withered hand, Rise up, and stand forth in the midst.[3319] And he arose and stood forth.

9 Then said Jesus unto them, I will ask you one thing; Is it lawful on the sabbath days [ainf]to do good,[15] or [ainf]to do evil?[2554] [ainf]to save[4982] life, or [ainf]to destroy *it?*

10 And looking round about upon$_{4017}$ them all, he said unto the man, Stretch forth thy hand. And he did so: and his

hand [aop]was restored[600] whole[5199] as the other.

11 And they were filled with madness;[454] and [ipf]communed[1255] one with another what they might do to Jesus.

Jesus Chooses The Twelve Disciples (Matt. 10:1–4; Mark 3:13–19)

12 [a]And it came to pass in those days, that he went out into a mountain [ainf]to pray, and continued all night in prayer to God.

13 And when it was day, he called *unto him* his disciples:[3101] [a]and of them he [apt]chose twelve, whom also he named apostles;[652]

14 Simon, ([a]whom he also named Peter,) and Andrew his brother, James and John, Philip and Bartholomew,

15 Matthew and Thomas, James the *son* of Alphaeus, and Simon called Zelotes,

16 And Judas [a]*the brother* of James, and Judas Iscariot, which also was the traitor.

Jesus Ministers to a Great Multitude (Matt. 4:23–25)

17 And he came down with them, and stood in the plain, and the company of his disciples,[3101] [a]and a great multitude of people out of all Judaea and Jerusalem, and from the sea coast of Tyre and Sidon, which came to hear him, and to be healed of their diseases;

18 And they that [ppp]were vexed[3791] with unclean spirits: and they [ipf]were healed.

19 And the whole multitude [ipf a]sought [pinf]to touch him: for [b]there [ipf]went virtue out of[3844] him, and [ipf]healed[2390] *them* all.

Blessings and Woes (Matt. 5:1–12)

20 And he [apt]lifted up his eyes on his disciples, and said, [a]Blessed[3107] *be ye* poor:[4434] for yours is the kingdom[932] of God.

21 [a]Blessed *are ye* that [ppt]hunger now: for ye shall be filled. [b]Blessed *are ye* that [ppt]weep now: for ye shall laugh.

22 [a]Blessed are ye, when men [aosb]shall hate you, and when they [aosb b]shall separate[873] you *from their company,* and [aosb]shall reproach *you,* and [aosb]cast out your name as evil,[4190] for the Son of man's sake.

23 [pim a]Rejoice ye in that day, and [aim]leap for joy: for, behold, your reward[3408] *is* great in heaven:[3772] for [b]in the like manner [ipf]did their fathers unto the prophets.[4396]

24 [a]But woe unto you [b]that are rich for [c]ye have received[568] your consolation.[3874]

25 [a]Woe unto you that [pfpp]are full for ye shall hunger. [b]Woe unto you that [ppt]laugh now! for ye shall mourn and weep.

26 [a]Woe unto you, when all men[444] shall speak well of you! for so [ipf]did their fathers to the false prophets.

Love Your Enemies (Matt. 5:38–48; 7:12)

27 [a]But I say unto you which [ppt]hear, [pim]Love[25] your enemies, [pim]do good to them which [ppt]hate you,

28 [pim]Bless them that [ppt]curse[2672] you, and [a]pray for them which [ppt]despitefully use you.

29 [a]And unto him that [ppt]smiteth[5180] thee on the *one* cheek offer also the other; [b]and him that [ppt]taketh away thy cloke [aosi]forbid not *to take thy* coat[5509] also.

30 [pim a]Give to every man that [ppt]asketh of thee; and of him that [ppt]taketh away thy goods [pim]ask *them* not again.[523]

31 [a]And as ye would that men [psa]should do to you, [pim]do ye also to them likewise.

32 [a]For if ye love them which [ppt]love you, what thank have ye? for sinners[268] also love those that [ppt]love them.

33 And if ye [psa]do good[15] to them

12 [a]Matt. 14:23
13 [a]Matt. 10:1
14 [a]John 1:42
16 [a]Jude 1:1
17 [a]Matt. 4:25; Mark 3:7
19 [a]Matt. 14:36 [b]Mark 5:30; Luke 8:46
20 [a]Matt. 5:3; 11:5; James 2:5
21 [a]Isa. 55:1; 65:13; Matt. 5:6 [b]Isa. 61:3; Matt. 5:4
22 [a]Matt. 5:11; 1Pet. 2:19; 3:14; 4:14 [b]John 16:2
23 [a]Matt. 5:12; Acts 5:41; Col. 1:24; James 1:2 [b]Acts 7:51
24 [a]Amos 6:1; James 5:1 [b]Luke 12:21 [c]Matt. 6:2, 5, 16; Luke 16:25
25 [a]Isa. 65:13 [b]Prov. 14:13
26 [a]John 15:19; 1John 4:5
27 [a]Ex. 23:4; Prov. 25:21; Matt. 5:44; Luke 6:35; Rom. 12:20
28 [a]Luke 23:34; Acts 7:60
29 [a]Matt. 5:39 [b]1Cor. 6:7
30 [a]Deut. 15:7, 8, 10; Prov. 21:26; Matt. 5:42
31 [a]Matt. 7:12
32 [a]Matt. 5:46

which [ppt]do good[15] to you, what thank have ye? for sinners[268] also do even the same.

34 [a]And if ye [psa]lend *to them* of whom ye hope[1679] [ainf]to receive,618 what thank have ye? for sinners also lend to sinners, to [aosb]receive as much again.

35 But [a]love ye your enemies, and [pim]do good,[15] and [pim][b]lend, [ppt]hoping for nothing again;[560] and your reward[3408] shall be great, and [c]ye shall be the [an]children[5207] of the Highest: for he is kind[5543] unto the unthankful and *to* the evil.

36 [pim][a]Be ye therefore merciful, as your Father[3962] also is merciful.

Judging Others (Matt. 7:1–5)

37 [pim][a]Judge[2919] not, and ye shall not be judged: [pim]condemn[2613] not, and ye shall not be condemned: [pim]forgive,[630] and ye shall be forgiven:

38 [pim][a]Give, and it shall be given unto you; good measure, [pfpp]pressed down, and [pfpp]shaken together, and [ppp]running over, shall men give into your [b]bosom. For [c]with the same measure that ye mete3354 withal it shall be measured to you again.

39 And he spake a parable unto them, [a]Can the [sg]blind [pinf]lead the [sg]blind? shall they not both fall into the ditch?

40 [a]The disciple[3101] is not above his master:[1320] but every one [I]that [pfpp]is perfect[2675] shall be as his master.[1320]

41 [a]And why beholdest thou the mote that is in thy brother's eye, but perceivest not the beam that is in thine own[2398] eye?

42 Either how canst thou say to thy brother, Brother, let me pull out the mote2595 that is in thine eye, when thou thyself [ppt]beholdest not the beam that is in thine own eye? Thou hypocrite, [a]cast out first the beam1385 out of thine own eye, and then shalt thou see clearly [ainf]to pull out the mote that is in thy brother's eye.

Bearing Fruit (Matt. 7:17–20; 12:34, 35)

43 [a]For a good tree [ppt]bringeth not forth[4160] corrupt fruit; neither doth a corrupt tree bring forth good fruit.

44 For [a]every tree [pinp]is known by his own[2398] fruit. For of thorns men do not gather figs, nor of a bramble bush gather they grapes.

45 [a]A good[18] man out of the good treasure of his heart bringeth forth that which is good; and an evil man out of the evil treasure of his heart bringeth forth4393 that which is evil: for [b]of the abundance[4051] of the heart his mouth speaketh.

The Two Foundations (Matt. 7:24–27)

46 [a]And why call ye me, Lord, Lord, and do not the things which I say?

47 [a]Whosoever [ppt]cometh to me, and [ppt]heareth my sayings, and [ppt]doeth them, I will shew you to whom he is like:

48 He is like a man [ppt]which built an house, and digged deep, and laid[5087] the foundation on a rock: and when the flood [apt]arose, the stream beat vehemently4366 upon that house, and could[2480] not shake it: for it was founded upon a rock.

49 But he that [apt]heareth, and [apt]doeth not, is like a man that without a foundation [apt]built an house upon the earth; against which the stream did beat vehemently, and immediately it fell; and the ruin of that house was great.

Jesus Heals the Centurion's Servant (Matt. 8:5–13; John 4:43–54)

7 Now when he [ao]had ended[4137] all his sayings in the audience of the people, [a]he entered into Capernaum.

2 And a certain centurion's1543 servant,[1401] who was dear unto him, was sick,[2560] and ready to die.

3 And when he heard of Jesus, he sent unto him the elders[4245] of the Jews,

---

34 [a]Matt. 5:42

35 [a]Luke 6:27 [b]Ps. 37:26; Luke 6:30 [c]Matt. 5:45

36 [a]Matt. 5:48

37 [a]Matt. 7:1

38 [a]Prov. 19:17 [b]Ps. 79:12 [c]Matt. 7:2; Mark 4:24; James 2:13

39 [a]Matt. 15:14

40 [I]Or, *shall be perfected as his master* [a]Matt. 10:24; John 13:16; 15:20

41 [a]Matt. 7:3

42 [a]Prov. 18:17

43 [a]Matt. 7:16, 17

44 [a]Matt. 12:33

45 [a]Matt. 12:35 [b]Matt. 12:34

46 [a]Mal. 1:6; Matt. 7:21; 25:11; Luke 13:25

47 [a]Matt. 7:24

1 [a]Matt. 8:5

beseeching him that he [apt]would come and [aosb]heal[1295] his servant.

4 And when they came to Jesus, they [ipf]besought him instantly, saying, That he was worthy for whom he should do this:

5 For he loveth[25] our nation,[1484] and he [ao]hath built us a synagogue.

6 Then Jesus [ipf]went with them. And when he was[568] now not far from the house, the centurion sent friends to him, saying unto him, Lord, [pim]trouble not thyself: for I am not worthy that thou [aosb]shouldest enter under my roof:

7 Wherefore neither thought I myself worthy [ainf]to come unto thee: but [aim]say in a word,[3056] and my servant[3816] shall be healed.

8 For I also am a man set[5021] under authority,[1849] having under me soldiers, and I say unto one, [aipp]Go, and he goeth; and to another, [pim]Come, and he cometh; and to my servant, [aim]Do this, and he doeth *it*.

9 When Jesus heard these things, he marvelled at him, and turned him about, and said unto the people that [ppt]followed him, I say unto you, I [ao]have not found[2147] so great faith,[4102] no, not in Israel.

10 And they that were sent, [apt]returning to the house, found the servant [ppt]whole that had been sick.

The Raising of the Widow's Son at Nain

11 And it came to pass the day after, that he [ipf]went into a city called Nain; and many of his disciples[3101] [ipf]went with him, and much people.

12 Now when he came nigh[1448] to the gate of the city, behold, there was a dead man carried out, the only[3439] son[5207] of his mother, and she was a widow: and much people of the city was with her.

13 And when the Lord saw her, he had compassion on her, and said unto her, [pim]Weep not.

14 And he came and touched the [I]bier: and they that [ppt]bare *him* stood still. And he said, Young man, I say unto thee, [a]Arise.

15 And he that was dead sat up, and began to speak. And he delivered him to his mother.

16 [a]And there came a fear[5401] on all: and they [ipf]glorified[1392] God, saying, [b]That a great prophet[4396] [pfip]is risen up among us; and, [c]That God [aom]hath visited[1980] his people.

17 And this rumour[3056] of him went forth throughout all Judaea, and throughout all the region round about.

Jesus Talks About John the Baptist (Matt. 11:2–19)

18 [a]And the disciples[3101] of John shewed him of all these things.

19 And John calling *unto him* two of his disciples sent *them* to Jesus, saying, Art thou he that [ppt]should come?[2064] or look we for another?[243]

20 When the men were come unto him, they said, John Baptist[910] hath sent us unto thee, saying, Art thou he that should come? or look we for another?[243]

21 And in that same hour he cured many of *their* infirmities and plagues, and of evil[4190] spirits; and unto many *that were* blind he gave[5483] sight.

22 [a]Then Jesus answering said unto them, [apt]Go your way, and [aim]tell[518] John what things ye [ao]have seen and [ao]heard; [b]how that the blind see, the lame walk, the lepers are cleansed, the deaf hear, the dead are raised, [c]to the poor the gospel is preached.[2097]

23 And blessed[3107] is *he,* whosoever [asbp]shall not be offended[4624] in me.

24 [a]And when the messengers[32] of John were departed, he began [pinf]to speak unto the people concerning John, What went ye out into the wilderness for to see? A reed shaken with the wind?

25 But what went ye out for to see? A man clothed in soft raiment?[2440] Behold, they which are gorgeously[1741] apparelled,[2441] and live[5225] delicately,[5172] are in kings' courts.

26 But what went ye out for to see?

14 [I]Or, *coffin* [a]Luke 8:54; John 11:43; Acts 9:40; Rom. 4:17

16 [a]Luke 1:65 [b]Luke 24:19; John 4:19; 6:14; 9:17 [c]Luke 1:68

18 [a]Matt. 11:2

22 [a]Matt. 11:4 [b]Isa. 35:5 [c]Luke 4:18

24 [a]Matt. 11:7

A prophet?[4396] Yea, I say unto you, and much more[4055] than a prophet.

27 This is *he,* of whom it is written, [a]Behold, I send my messenger before thy face, which shall prepare thy way[3598] before thee.

28 For I say unto you, Among those that are born of women there is not a greater prophet than John the Baptist: but he that is least in the kingdom[932] of God is greater than he.

29 And all the people that heard *him,* and the publicans,[5057] justified[1344] God, [aptp][a]being baptized[907] with the baptism[908] of John.

30 But the Pharisees and lawyers[3544] [I]rejected [a]the counsel[1012] of God [II]against themselves, being not baptized of him.

31 And the Lord said, [a]Whereunto then shall I liken the men of this generation?[1074] and to what are they like?

32 They are like unto children sitting in the marketplace, and calling one to another, and saying, We [ao]have piped unto you, and ye [aom]have not danced;[3738] we [ao]have mourned[2354] to you, and ye [ao]have not wept.[2799]

33 For [a]John the Baptist came neither eating bread nor drinking wine; and ye say, He hath a devil.[1140]

34 The Son of man is come eating and drinking; and ye say, Behold a gluttonous man, and a winebibber,[3630] a friend of publicans[5057] and sinners[268]

35 [a]But wisdom[4678] [aop]is justified[1344] of all her children.

Jesus Forgives a Sinful Woman

36 [a]And one of the Pharisees [ipf]desired him that he would eat with him. And he went into the Pharisee's house, and sat down to meat.

37 And, behold, a woman in the city, which was a sinner,[268] when she knew that *Jesus* sat at meat in the Pharisee's house, [apt]brought an alabaster box[211] of ointment,

38 And [apt]stood at his feet behind *him* weeping, and began [pinf]to wash his feet with tears, and [ipf]did wipe *them* with the hairs of her head, and [ipf]kissed his feet, and [ipf]anointed[218] *them* with the ointment.

39 Now when the Pharisee which had bidden[2564] him saw *it,* he spake within himself, saying, [a]This man, if he were a prophet,[4396] would have known who and what manner of woman *this is* that toucheth him: for she is a sinner.

40 And Jesus answering[611] said unto him, Simon, I have somewhat to say unto thee. And he saith, Master, say on.

41 There was a certain creditor which had two debtors: the one [ipf]owed five hundred [a]pence,[1220] and the other[2087] fifty.

42 And when they [ppt]had nothing [ainf]to pay, he frankly forgave[5483] them both. Tell me therefore, which of them [ft]will love[25] him most?

43 Simon answered and said, I suppose[5274] that *he,* to whom he forgave[5483] most. And he said unto him, Thou [ao]hast rightly judged.[2919]

44 And he turned to the woman, and said unto Simon, Seest thou this woman? I entered into thine house, thou gavest me no water for my feet: but she [ao]hath washed my feet with tears, and wiped *them* with the hairs of her head.

45 Thou gavest me no kiss: but this woman since the time I came in, [ao]hath not ceased[1257] to [ppt]kiss my feet.

46 [a]My head with oil[1637] thou didst not anoint: but this woman hath anointed my feet with ointment.[3464]

47 [a]Wherefore I say unto thee, Her sins, which are many, [pfip]are forgiven; for she loved[25] much: but to whom little is forgiven, *the same* loveth little.

48 And he said unto her, [a]Thy sins are forgiven.

49 And they that sat at meat with him began [pinf]to say within themselves, [a]Who is this that forgiveth sins also?

50 And he he said to the woman, [a]Thy faith [pfi]hath saved[4982] thee; [pim]go in peace.

---

27 [a]Mal. 3:1
29 [a]Matt. 3:5; Luke 3:12
30 [I]Or, *frustrated* [II]Or, *within themselves* [a]Acts 20:27
31 [a]Matt. 11:16
33 [a]Matt. 3:4; Mark 1:6; Luke 1:15
35 [a]Matt. 11:19
36 [a]Matt. 26:6; Mark 14:3; John 11:2
39 [a]Luke 15:2
41 [a]Matt. 18:28
46 [a]Ps. 23:5
47 [a]1Tim. 1:14
48 [a]Matt. 9:2; Mark 2:5
49 [a]Matt. 9:3; Mark 2:7
50 [a]Matt. 9:22; Mark 5:34; 10:52; Luke 8:48; 18:42

8 And it came to pass afterward, that he [ipf]went throughout every city and village, preaching[2784] and shewing the glad tidings[2097] of the kingdom[932] of God: and the twelve *were* with him,

2 And [a]certain women, which had been healed of evil[4190] spirits and infirmities, Mary called Magdalene, [b]out of whom [plpf]went[1831] seven devils,[1140]

3 And Joanna the wife of Chuza Herod's steward, and Susanna, and many others, which [ipf]ministered[1247] unto him of their substance.[5224]

The Parable of the Sower (Matt. 13:1–9; Mark 4:1–9)

4 [a]And when much people [ppt]were gathered together, and [ppt]were come to him out of every city, he spake by a parable:[3850]

5 A sower went out [infg]to sow his seed: and as he [aie]sowed, some fell by the way side; and it was trodden down, and the fowls of the air[3772] devoured it.

6 And some fell upon a [art]rock; and as soon as it [aptp]was sprung up,[5453] it withered away, because it [aid]lacked moisture.

7 And some fell among[3319][1722] [art]thorns; and the thorns sprang up with it, and choked it.

🔑 8 And other fell on [art]good[18] ground, and sprang up, and bare fruit an hundredfold. And when he had said these things, he cried, He that [ppt]hath ears to hear, [pim]let him hear.[191]

2 [a]Matt. 27:55, 56 [b]Mark 16:9
4 [a]Matt. 13:2; Mark 4:1
9 [a]Matt. 13:10; Mark 4:10
10 [a]Isa. 6:9; Mark 4:12
11 [a]Matt. 13:18; Mark 4:14

The Reason for Parables (Matt. 13:10–17; Mark 4:10–12)

9 [a]And his disciples [ipf]asked him, saying, What might this parable be?

10 And he said, Unto you it [pfip]is given [ainf]to know the mysteries[3466] of the kingdom[932] of God: but to [art]others in parables; [a]that [ppt]seeing[991] they [psa]might not see,[991] and [ppt]hearing[191] they [psa]might not understand.[4920]

Explanation of the Parable Of the Sower (Matt. 13:18–23; Mark 4:13–20)

🔑 11 [a]Now the parable is this: The seed is the word[3056] of God.[2316]

12 Those by the way side are they that [apt]hear; then cometh the devil,[1228] and taketh away the word out of their hearts,[2588] lest they [apt]should believe[4100] and [asbp]be saved.[4982]

🔑 13 They on the rock *are they,* which, when they [aosb]hear,[191] receive the word with joy;[5479] and these have no root, which for a while[2540] believe, and in time[2540] of temptation[3986] fall away.[868]

14 And that which [apt]fell among thorns are they, which, when they [apt]have heard, [ppt]go forth, and [pinp]are choked with cares and riches and pleasures of *this* life,[979] and bring no fruit to perfection.[5052]

15 But that on the good[2570] ground are they, which in an honest and good[18] heart,[2588] having heard the word, keep[2722] *it,* and bring forth fruit with patience.[5281]

🔑 **8:8, 11** See note on Matthew 13:10–17.

🔑 **8:13** There is a category of people who can be confused with true believers. These are those who appear to have been saved, but that have reverted to the world and continue in its ways. For instance, the phrase "which, when they hear, receive the word with joy; and these have no root; which for a while believe" denotes a different meaning for the word "believe." It should not be confused with the exercise of true faith in Jesus Christ that transforms a person's life. This "belief" is merely an intellectual assent. True faith is not simply giving reference to a repentant heart, but to an obedient heart toward God that causes them to do righteousness and to hate sin (Rom. 5:19). These who have no deep roots are the ones who profess faith in God, but do not profess Christ. See notes on 2 Thessalonians 2:3; Hebrews 6:1–6; and 1 John 3:6–9.

A Light Not to Be Hidden (Mark 4:21–25)

16 [a]No man, when he [apt]hath lighted a candle,[3088] covereth it with a vessel, or putteth *it* under a bed; but setteth *it* on a candlestick, that they which enter in [psa]may see[991] the light.

17 [a]For nothing is secret,2927 that shall not be made manifest; neither *any thing* hid,614 that shall not be known and come abroad.

18 Take heed therefore how ye [pin]hear: [a]for whosoever hath, to him shall be given; and whosoever hath not, from him shall be taken even that which he [I]seemeth[1380] to have.

16 [a]Matt. 5:15; Mark 4:21; Luke 11:33

17 [a]Matt. 10:26; Luke 12:2

18 [I]Or, *thinketh that he hath* [a]Matt. 13:12; 25:29; Luke 19:26

Jesus' Mother and Brothers (Matt. 12:46–50; Mark 3:31–35)

19 [a]Then [aom]came3854 to him *his* mother and his brethren, and [ipf]could not come at4940 him for the press.[3793]

20 And it was told him *by certain* which [ppt]said, Thy mother and thy brethren [pfi]stand without, desiring [ainf]to see[1492] thee.

21 And he [aptp]answered and said unto them, My mother and my brethren are these which [ppt]hear the word of God, and [ppt]do[4160] it.

19 [a]Matt. 12:46; Mark 3:31

Jesus Calms a Storm (Matt. 8:23–27; Mark 4:35–41)

22 [a]Now it came to pass on a certain day, that he went into a ship with his disciples: and he said unto them, Let us go over unto the other side of the lake. And they launched forth.321

23 But as they sailed he fell asleep: and there came down a storm2978 of wind on the lake; and they [ipf]were filled[4845] *with water,* and [ipf]were in jeopardy.2793

24 And they [apt]came[4334] to him, and awoke him, saying, Master,1988 master, we perish. Then he [apt]arose, and rebuked the wind and the raging2830 of the water: and they ceased, and there was a calm.

25 And he said unto them, Where is your faith? And they being afraid wondered, saying one to another,[240,4314] What manner of man is this! for he commandeth[2004] even the winds and water, and they [pin]obey him.

22 [a]Matt. 8:23; Mark 4:35

Jesus Heals the Gadarene Demoniac (Matt. 8:28–34; Mark 5:1–20)

26 [a]And they arrived at the country of the Gadarenes, which is over against Galilee.

27 And when he went forth to land, there met him out of the city a certain man, which [ipf]had devils long time,[5550] and [ipf]ware no [sg]clothes,[2440] neither [ipf]abode in *any* house, but in the tombs.

28 When he saw Jesus, he [apt]cried out, and fell down before him, and with a loud voice said, What have I to do with thee, Jesus, *thou* Son of God most high? I beseech[1189] thee, [aosi]torment928 me not.

29 (For he [ao]had commanded the unclean spirit to come out of the man. For oftentimes[5550] 4183 it [plpf]had caught him: and he was kept [ipf]bound with chains and in fetters; and he [ppt]brake the bands, and [ipf]was driven1643 of the devil[1142] into the wilderness.)

30 And Jesus asked him, saying, What is thy name? And he said, Legion: because many devils [ao]were entered into him.

31 And they [ipf]besought him that he [aosb]would not command[2004] them to go out [a]into the deep.12

32 And there was there an herd of many swine feeding on the mountain: and they [ipf]besought him that he [aosb]would suffer2010 them to enter into them. And he suffered them.

33 Then [apt]went the devils1140 out of the man, and entered into the swine: and the herd ran violently down a steep place into the lake, and [aop]were choked.638

34 When they that [ppt]fed *them* [apt]saw what was done, they fled, and went and told *it* in the city and in the country.

35 Then they went out to see what

26 [a]Matt. 8:28; Mark 5:1

31 [a]Rev. 20:3

was done; and came to Jesus, and found the man, out of whom the devils were departed, sitting at the feet of Jesus, clothed, and [ppt]in his right mind:4993 and they were afraid.

36 They also which saw *it* told them by what means he that was possessed of the devils [aop]was healed.[4982]

37 [a]Then the whole multitude of the country of the Gadarenes round about [ao][b]besought him to depart from them; for they [ipf]were taken[4912] with great fear:[5401] and he [apt]went up into the ship, and returned back again.

38 Now [a]the man out of whom the devils [plpf]were departed [ipf]besought[1189] him that he might be with him: but Jesus sent him away, saying,

39 Return to thine own house, and [pim]shew[1334] how great things God [ao]hath done unto thee. And he went his way, and [ppt]published[2784] throughout[2596] the whole city how great things Jesus had done unto him.

Jesus Raises Jairus' Daughter (Matt. 9:18–26; Mark 5:21–43)

40 And it came to pass, that, when Jesus was returned, the people *gladly* received[588] him: for they were all waiting for him.

41 [a]And, behold, there came a man named Jairus, and he was[5225] a ruler[758] of the synagogue:[4864] and he [apt]fell down at Jesus' feet, and [ipf]besought him that he would [ainf]come into his house:

42 For he had one only[3439] daughter, about twelve years of age, and she [ipf]lay a dying. But as he [aie]went the people [ipf]thronged him.

43 [a]And a woman having an issue of blood twelve years, which [apt]had spent all her living[979] upon physicians,2395 neither could [aifp]be healed[2323] of any,

44 Came behind *him,* and touched the border of his garment: and immediately her issue4511 of blood[129] [ao]stanched.[2476]

45 And Jesus said, Who [apt]touched me? When all [ppt]denied,[720] Peter and they that were with him said, Master, the multitude throng[4912] thee and press *thee,* and sayest thou, Who touched me?

46 And Jesus said, Somebody [aom]hath touched me: for I perceive that [a]virtue[1411] [apt]is gone out of me.

47 And when the women saw that she was not hid, she came trembling, and [apt]falling down before him, she declared[518] unto him before all the people for what cause[156] she had touched him, and how she was healed immediately.

48 And he said unto her, Daughter, [pim]be of good comfort: thy faith [pfi]hath made thee whole;[4982] [pim]go in peace.[1515]

49 [a]While he yet [ppt]spake, there cometh one from the ruler of the synagogue's *house,* saying to him, Thy daughter [pfi]is dead;[2348] [pim]trouble not the Master.

50 But when Jesus heard *it,* he answered him, saying, [pim]Fear[5399] not: [pim]believe only, and she [fp]shall be made whole.

51 And when he came into the house, he suffered no man to go in, save Peter, and James, and John, and the father and the mother of the maiden.[3816]

52 And all [ipf]wept, and [ipf]bewailed[2875] her: but he said, [pim]Weep not; she [ao]is not dead,[599] [a]but sleepeth.

53 And they [ipf]laughed him to scorn, knowing that she was dead.

54 And he [apt]put them all out, and [apt]took her by the hand, and called, saying, Maid,[3816] [pim][a]arise.

55 And her spirit[4151] came again, and she arose straightway:3916 and he commanded[1299] to give her meat.

56 And her parents were astonished: but [a]he charged them that they should tell no man what was done.

The Twelve Apostles Are Sent Forth (Matt. 10:5–15; Mark 6:7–13)

9 Then [a]he [apt]called[4779] his twelve disciples[3101] together,[4779] and gave them power and authority over all devils, and [pinf]to cure diseases.

37 [a]Matt. 8:34 [b]Acts 16:39
38 [a]Mark 5:18
41 [a]Matt. 9:18; Mark 5:22
43 [a]Matt. 9:20
46 [a]Mark 5:30; Luke 6:19
49 [a]Mark 5:35
52 [a]John 11:11, 13
54 [a]Luke 7:14; John 11:43
56 [a]Matt. 8:4; 9:30; Mark 5:43
1 [a]Matt. 10:1; Mark 3:13; 6:7

2 And [a]he sent[649] them [pinf]to preach[2784] the kingdom[932] of God,[2316] and [pinf]to heal the sick.

3 [a]And he said unto them, [pim]Take nothing for *your* journey, neither staves,[4464] nor scrip,[4082] neither bread, neither money; neither have two coats apiece.

4 [a]And whatsoever house ye [asbp]enter into, there [pim]abide, and thence [pim]depart.

5 [a]And whosoever will not receive you, when ye [ppt]go out of that city, [aim][b]shake off the very dust from your feet for a testimony[3142] against them.

6 [a]And they departed, and [ipf]went through the towns, preaching the gospel,[2097] and healing everywhere.

Herod Disturbed (Matt. 14:1–12; Mark 6:14–29)

7 [a]Now Herod the tetrarch[5076] heard of all that [ppt]was done by him: and he [ipf]was perplexed, because that it [aid]was said of some, that John [pfip]was risen from the dead;

8 And of some, that Elias [aop]had appeared; and of others, that one of the old prophets[4396] [ao]was risen again.

9 And Herod said, John [ao]have I beheaded:[607] but who is this, of whom I hear such things? [a]And he [ipf]desired [ainf]to see him.

Jesus Feeds Five Thousand People (Matt. 14:13–21; Mark 6:30–44; John 6:1–14)

10 [a]And the apostles,[652] when they were returned, told[1334] him all that they [ao]had done. [b]And he took them, and went aside privately into a desert place belonging to the city called Bethsaida.

11 And the people, when they knew *it,* followed him: and he [apt]received[1209] them, and [ipf]spake unto them of the kingdom[932] of God, and [ipf]healed them that had need of healing.[2322]

12 [a]And when the day began to wear away, then [apt]came the twelve, and said unto him, Send the multitude away, that they [apt]may go into the towns and country round about, and [aosb]lodge,[2647] and [aosb]get victuals:[1979] for we are here in a desert place.

13 But he said unto them, Give ye them to eat. And they said, We have no more but five loaves and two fishes; except we should go and [aosb]buy meat for all this people.

14 For they were about five thousand men. And he said to his disciples,[3101] Make them sit down by[303] fifties in a company.

15 And they did so, and made them all sit down.

16 Then he [apt]took the five loaves and the two fishes, and [apt]looking up to heaven, he blessed[2127] them, and brake, and [ipf]gave to the disciples to set before the multitude.

17 And they did eat, and were all filled: and there was taken up of fragments[2801] that remained to them twelve baskets.

Peter's Confession (Matt. 16:13–19; Mark 8:27–29)

18 [a]And it came to pass, as he was alone praying, his disciples[3101] were with him: and he asked them, saying, Whom say the people that I am?

19 They answering said, [a]John the Baptist;[910] but some *say,* Elias; and others *say,* that one of the old prophets[4396] [ao]is risen again.

20 He said unto them, But whom say ye that I am? [a]Peter answering said, The Christ[5547] of God.[2316]

Jesus Predicts His Death and Resurrection (Matt. 16:20–28; Mark 8:30–9:1)

21 [a]And he [apt]straitly charged[2008] them, and commanded[3853] *them* [ainf]to tell no man that thing;

22 Saying, [a]The Son of man must

2 [a]Matt. 10:7, 8; Mark 6:12; Luke 10:1, 9
3 [a]Matt. 10:9; Mark 6:8; Luke 10:4; 22:35
4 [a]Matt. 10:11; Mark 6:10
5 [a]Matt. 10:14 [b]Acts 13:51
6 [a]Mark 6:12
7 [a]Matt. 14:1; Mark 6:14
9 [a]Luke 23:8
10 [a]Mark 6:30 [b]Matt. 14:13
12 [a]Matt. 14:15; Mark 6:35; John 6:1, 5
18 [a]Matt. 16:13; Mark 8:27
19 [a]Matt. 14:2; Luke 9:7, 8
20 [a]Matt. 16:16; John 6:69
21 [a]Matt. 16:20
22 [a]Matt. 16:21; 17:22

suffer many things, and [aifp]be rejected[593] of the elders[4245] and chief priests[749] and scribes,[1122] and be slain, and be raised the third day.

23 [a]And he [ipf]said to *them* all, If any *man* will come after me, [aipp]let him deny[533] himself, and [aim]take up his cross[4716] daily, and [pim]follow me.

24 For whosoever [psa]will [ainf]save[4982] his life[5590] [ft]shall lose[622] it: but whosoever [aosb]will lose[622] his life for my sake, the same shall save it.

🗝 25 [a]For what is a man advantaged, if he [apt]gain the whole world, and [apt]lose himself, or [aptp]be cast away?

26 [a]For whosoever [asbp]shall be ashamed of me and of my words, of him shall the Son of man be ashamed, when he shall come in his own glory,[1391] and *in his* [art]Father's, and of the holy angels.[32]

27 [a]But I tell you of a truth, there be some [pfp]standing here, which [fm]shall not taste[1089] of death,[2288] till they [aosb]see the kingdom[932] of God.[2316]

The Transfiguration (Matt. 17:1–8; Mark 9:2–8)

28 [a]And it came to pass about an eight days after these [I]sayings, he [apt]took Peter and John and James, and went up into a mountain [ainf]to pray.

29 And as he prayed, the fashion[1491] of his countenance[4383] was altered,[2087] and his raiment[2441] *was* white *and* glistering.1823

30 And, behold, there [ipf]talked with him two men, which were Moses and Elias:

31 Who [aptp]appeared in glory,[1391] and [ipf]spake of his decease1841 which he should accomplish[4137] at Jerusalem.

32 But Peter and they that were with him [a]were heavy with sleep: and when they [apt]were awake, they saw his glory,[1391] and the two men that [pfp]stood with[4921] him.

33 And it came to pass, as they departed from him, Peter said unto Jesus, Master, it is good for us to be here: and let us make three tabernacles;4633 one for thee, and one for Moses, and one for Elias: not knowing what he said.

34 While he thus [ppt]spake, there came a cloud, and overshadowed them: and they feared as they [aie]entered into the cloud.

35 And there came a voice out of the cloud, saying, [a]This is my beloved[27] Son:[5207] [pim][b]hear[191] him.

36 And when the voice was past, Jesus was found alone. [a]And they [ao]kept *it* close, and told no man in those days any of those things which they [pfp]had seen.[3708]

Jesus Heals a Boy With An Unclean Spirit (Matt. 17:14–18; Mark 9:14–27)

37 [a]And it came to pass, that on the next day, when they [apt]were come down from the hill, much people met him.

38 And, behold, a man of the company[3793] cried out, saying, Master, I beseech[1189] thee, look1914 upon my son: for he is mine only child.[3439]

39 And, lo, a spirit[4151] taketh him, and he suddenly crieth out; and it teareth him that he foameth again, and bruising him hardly departeth from him.

40 And I besought[1189] thy disciples to cast him out; and they could not.

41 And Jesus answering said, O faithless[571] and perverse generation, how long shall I be with you, and suffer[430] you? Bring[4317] thy son hither.

42 And as he was yet a coming, the devil threw him down, and tare *him.* And Jesus rebuked the unclean[169] spirit,[4151] and healed the child, and delivered him again to his father.

Jesus Again Foretells His Death (Matt. 17:22, 23; Mark 9:30–32)

43 And they [ipf]were all amazed at the mighty power of God. But while

23 [a]Matt. 10:38; 16:24; Mark 8:34; Luke 14:27
25 [a]Matt. 16:26; Mark 8:36
26 [a]Matt. 10:33; Mark 8:38; 2Tim. 2:12
27 [a]Matt. 16:28; Mark 9:1
28 [I]Or, *things* [a]Matt. 17:1; Mark 9:2
32 [a]Dan. 8:18; 10:9
35 [a]Matt. 3:17 [b]Acts 3:22
36 [a]Matt. 17:9
37 [a]Matt. 17:14; Mark 9:14, 17

🗝 **9:25** See note on Hebrews 6:1–6.

they [ppt]wondered every one at all things which Jesus did, he said unto his disciples,

44 [a]Let these sayings sink down into your ears: for the Son of man shall be delivered into the hands of men.

45 [a]But they [ipf]understood not[50] this saying, and it was hid from them, that they [asbm]perceived[143] it not: and they [ipf]feared [ainf]to ask[2065] him of that saying.

Jesus Sets a Child Before His Disciples (Matt. 18:1–5; Mark 9:33–37)

46 [a]Then there arose a reasoning[1261] among them, which of them should be greatest.

47 And Jesus, perceiving the thought[1261] of their heart,[2588] [apt]took[1949] a child, and set[2476] him by him,

48 And said unto them, [a]Whosoever [asbm]shall receive[1209] this child in my name receiveth me: and whosoever [asbm]shall receive me receiveth him that [apt]sent me: [b]for he that is least among you all, the same shall be great.

Others Who Work in Christ's Name (Mark 9:38–40)

49 [a]And John answered and said, Master, we saw one casting out devils[1140] in thy name; and we forbad him, because he followeth not with us.

50 And Jesus said unto him, [pim]Forbid *him* not: for [a]he that is not against us is for us.

A Samaritan Village Refuses to Receive Jesus

51 And it came to pass, when the time [aie]was come[4845] that [a]he should be received up,[354] he stedfastly set[4741] his face to go to Jerusalem,

52 And sent messengers before his face:[4383] and they went, and entered into a village of the Samaritans, to make ready for him.

44 [a]Matt. 17:22
45 [a]Mark 9:32; Luke 2:50; 18:34
46 [a]Matt. 18:1; Mark 9:34
48 [a]Matt. 10:40; 18:5; Mark 9:37; John 12:44; 13:20 [b]Matt. 23:11, 12
49 [a]Num. 11:28; Mark 9:38
50 [a]Matt. 12:30; Luke 11:23
51 [a]Mark 16:19; Acts 1:2
53 [a]John 4:4, 9
54 [a]2Kgs. 1:10, 12
56 [a]John 3:17; 12:47
57 [a]Matt. 8:19
59 [a]Matt. 8:21
61 [a]1Kgs. 19:20
1 [a]Matt. 10:1; Mark 6:7
2 [a]Matt. 9:37, 38; John 4:35 [b]2Thess. 3:1

53 And [a]they did not receive him, because his face was as though he would go to Jerusalem.

54 And when his disciples[3101] James and John saw *this,* they said, Lord, wilt thou that we command fire to come down from heaven, and consume them, even as [a]Elias did?

55 But he turned, and rebuked them, and said, Ye know not what manner of spirit ye are of.

56 For [a]the Son of man [ao]is not come[2064] [ainf]to destroy[622] men's lives,[5590] but [ainf]to save *them.* And they went to another[2087] village.

God's Kingdom Must Be First (Matt. 8:19–22)

57 [a]And it came to pass, that, as they [ppt]went in the way, a certain *man* said unto him, Lord,[2962] I [ft]will follow[190] thee whithersoever thou goest.

58 And Jesus said unto him, Foxes have holes, and birds of the air *have* nests; but the Son of man hath not where to [psa]lay *his* head.

59 [a]And he said unto another, [pim]Follow me. But he said, Lord, suffer[2010] me first to go and [ainf]bury my father.

60 Jesus said unto him, Let the dead bury their dead: but [apt]go thou and [pim]preach[1229] the kingdom[932] of God.[2316]

61 And another also said, Lord, [a]I [ft]will follow[190] thee; but let me first [ainf]go bid them farewell,[657] which are at home at my house.

62 And Jesus said unto him, No man, having put his hand to the plough, and looking back, is fit for the kingdom of God.

Jesus Sends the Seventy

10 After these things the Lord appointed other seventy also, and [a]sent them two and[303] two before his face into every city and place, whither he himself [ipf]would [pinf]come.

2 Therefore said he unto them, [a]The harvest truly *is* great, but the labourers *are* few: [aipp][b]pray[1189] ye therefore the

Lord of the harvest, that he [psa]would send forth labourers into his harvest.

3 Go your ways: [a]behold, I send you forth as lambs among wolves.

4 [pim][a]Carry neither purse,[905] nor scrip,[4082] nor shoes: and [aosi][b]salute no man by the way.

5 [a]And into whatsoever house ye [psmp]enter, first [pim]say, Peace *be* to this house.

6 And if the son[5207] of peace be there, your peace [fm]shall rest[1879] upon it: if not, it shall turn to you again.

7 [a]And in the same house [pim]remain, [ppt][b]eating and [ppt]drinking such things as they give: for [c]the labourer is worthy of his hire.[3408] [pim]Go[3327] not from house to house.

8 And into whatsoever city ye [psmp]enter, and they [psmp]receive you, [pim]eat such things as are set before you:

9 [a]And [pim]heal the sick that are therein, and say unto them, [b]The kingdom[932] of God [pf]is come nigh[1448] unto you.

10 But into whatsoever city ye [psmp]enter, and they [psmp]receive you not, [apt]go your ways out into the streets of the same, and [aim]say,

11 [a]Even the very dust of your city, which cleaveth[2853] on us, we do wipe off against you: notwithstanding [pim]be ye sure of this, that the kingdom of God [pf]is come nigh unto you.

12 But I say unto you, that [a]it shall be more tolerable[414] in that day[2250] for Sodom, than for that city.

Woes to Unrepentant Cities (Matt. 11:20–24)

13 [a]Woe unto thee, Chorazin! woe unto thee, Bethsaida! [b]for if the mighty works[1411] [aom]had been done in Tyre and Sidon, which [apt]have been done in you, they had a great while ago[3819] [ao]repented,[3340] sitting in sackcloth[4526] and ashes.

14 But it shall be more tolerable[414] for Tyre and Sidon at the judgment,[2920] than for you.

3 [a]Matt. 10:16
4 [a]Matt. 10:9, 10; Mark 6:8; Luke 9:3 [b]2Kgs. 4:29
5 [a]Matt. 10:12
7 [a]Matt. 10:11 [b]1Cor. 10:27 [c]Matt. 10:10; 1Cor. 9:4; 1Tim. 5:18
9 [a]Luke 9:2 [b]Matt. 3:2; 4:17; 10:7; Luke 10:11
11 [a]Matt. 10:14; Luke 9:5; Acts 13:51; 18:6
12 [a]Matt. 10:15; Mark 6:11
13 [a]Matt. 11:21 [b]Ezek. 3:6
15 [a]Matt. 11:23 [b]Gen. 11:4; Deut. 1:28; Isa. 14:13; Jer. 51:53 [c]Ezek. 26:20; 32:18
16 [a]Matt. 10:40; Mark 9:37; John 13:20 [b]1Thess. 4:8 [c]John 5:23
17 [a]Luke 10:1
18 [a]John 12:31; 16:11; Rev. 9:1; 12:8, 9
19 [a]Mark 16:18; Acts 28:5
20 [a]Ex. 32:32; Ps. 69:28; Isa. 4:3; Dan. 12:1; Phil. 4:3; Heb. 12:23; Rev. 13:8; 20:12; 21:27
21 [a]Matt. 11:25
22 [a]Matt. 28:18; John 3:35; 5:27; 17:2 [b]John 1:18; 6:44, 46
23 [a]Matt. 13:16
24 [a]1Pet. 1:10

15 [a]And thou, Capernaum, which [apt]art [b]exalted to heaven,[3772] [fp][c]shalt be thrust down to hell.[86]

16 [a]He that [ppt]heareth[191] you heareth[191] me; and [b]he that [ppt]despiseth you despiseth me; [c]and he that [ppt]despiseth me despiseth him that sent me.

The Return of the Seventy

17 And [a]the seventy returned again with joy,[5479] saying, Lord, even the devils[1140] [pinp]are subject unto[5293] us through thy name.[3686]

18 And he said unto them, [a]I [ipf]beheld[2334] Satan as lightning [apt]fall from heaven.[3772]

19 Behold, [a]I give unto you [art]power [infg]to tread[3961] on serpents and scorpions, and over all the power[1411] of the enemy: and nothing shall [efn]by any means hurt[91] you.

20 Notwithstanding in this rejoice not, that the spirits are subject unto[5293] you; but rather rejoice, because [a]your names [aop]are written in heaven.[3772]

Jesus Praises God (Matt. 11:25–27; 13:16, 17)

21 [a]In that hour Jesus rejoiced[21] in spirit, and said, I thank[1843] thee, O Father,[3962] Lord[2962] of heaven and earth, that thou [ao]hast hid these things from the wise[4680] and prudent,[4908] and [ao]hast revealed[601] them unto babes:[3516] even so, Father; for so it seemed good[2107] in thy sight.

22 [a]All things [aop]are delivered to me of my Father: and [b]no man knoweth who the Son[5207] is, but the Father; and who the Father is, but the Son, and *he* to whom the Son will [ainf]reveal *him.*

23 And he turned him unto *his* disciples,[3101] and said privately, [a]Blessed[3107] *are* the eyes which [ppt]see the things that ye see:

24 For I tell you, [a]that many prophets[4396] and kings [ao]have desired [ainf]to see those things which ye see, and [ao]have not seen[1492] *them;* and [ainf]to hear

those things which ye hear, and [ao]have not heard[191] *them.*

A Good Samaritan

25 And, behold, a certain lawyer[3544] stood up, and [ppt]tempted[1598] him, saying, [a]Master,[1320] what [ft]shall I do to inherit[2816] eternal[166] life?[2222]

26 He said unto him, What is written[1125] in the law?[3551] how readest thou?

27 And he answering said, [a]Thou [ft]shalt love[25] the Lord[2962] thy God[2316] with all thy heart,[2588] and with all thy soul,[5590] and with all thy strength,[2479] and with all thy mind;[1271] and [b]thy neighbour[4139] as thyself.

28 And he said unto him, Thou [aop]hast answered right: this do, and [a]thou [fm]shalt live.[2198]

29 But he, willing [pinf]to [a]justify[1344] himself, said unto Jesus, And who is my neighbour?[4139]

30 And Jesus answering5274 said, A certain *man* [ipf]went down from Jerusalem to Jericho, and fell among thieves,[3027] which [apt]stripped him of his raiment, and [apt]wounded *him,* and departed, [apt]leaving[863] *him* half dead.

31 And by chance there [ipf]came down a certain priest[2409] that way: and when he [apt]saw him, [a]he passed by on the other side.

32 And likewise a Levite,3019 when he was at[2596] the place, [apt]came and [apt]looked *on him,* and passed by on the other side.

33 But a certain [a]Samaritan,4541 as he [ppt]journeyed, came where he was: and when he saw him, he had compassion4697 *on him,*

34 And [apt]went to *him,* and bound up his wounds, pouring in oil[1637] and wine, and [apt]set him on his own beast, and brought him to an inn, and took care of him.

35 And on the morrow when he [apt]departed, he [apt]took out1544 two [a]pence,1220 and gave *them* to the host, and said unto him, Take care of him; and whatsoever thou [aosb]spendest more, when I [aie]come again, I will repay thee.

36 Which now of these three, thinkest thou, [pfin]was neighbour unto him that fell among the thieves?

37 And he said, He that [apt]shewed mercy[1656] on him. Then said Jesus unto him, [pim]Go, and [pim]do thou likewise.

Visiting Martha and Mary

38 Now it came to pass, as they [aie]went, that he entered into a certain village: and a certain woman named [a]Martha received[5264] him into her house.

39 And she had a sister called Mary, [a]which also [apt b]sat at Jesus' feet, and [ipf]heard[191] his word.[3056]

40 But Martha [ipf]was cumbered4049 about much serving,[1248] and came to him, and said, Lord, dost thou not care that my sister [ao]hath left me [pinf]to serve[1247] alone? bid her therefore that she [asbm]help me.

41 And Jesus answered and said unto her, Martha, Martha, thou art careful and troubled about many things:

42 But [a]one thing is needful: and Mary [aom]hath chosen that good[18] part, which shall not be taken away from her.

Jesus Teaches the Disciples How to Pray (Matt. 6:9–15; 7:7–11)

11 And it came to pass, that, as he was praying in a certain place, when he ceased, one of his disciples[3101] said unto him, Lord, teach us [pinf]to pray, as John also taught[1321] his disciples.

🔑 2 And he said unto them, When ye pray, say, [a]Our Father[3962] which art in heaven,[3772] [aipp]Hallowed be[37] thy name. Thy kingdom[932] [aim]come. Thy will [aipp]be done, as in heaven,[3772] so in earth.[1093]

25 [a]Matt. 19:16; 22:35
27 [a]Deut. 6:5 [b]Lev. 19:18
28 [a]Lev. 18:5; Neh. 9:29; Ezek. 20:11, 13, 21; Rom. 10:5
29 [a]Luke 16:15
31 [a]Ps. 38:11
33 [a]John 4:9
35 [a]Matt. 20:2
38 [a]John 11:1; 12:2, 3
39 [a]1Cor. 7:32–34; Luke 8:35; Acts 22:3
42 [a]Ps. 27:4
2 [a]Matt. 6:9

🔑 **11:2–4** See the note on Matthew 6:13.

3 [pim]Give us [I]day by day our daily[1967] bread.

4 And [aim]forgive[863] us our sins; for we also forgive every one that [ppt]is indebted[3784] to us. And [aosi]lead us not into temptation;[3986] but [aim]deliver[4506] us from[art] evil.[4190]

🔑 5 And he said unto them, Which of you shall have a friend, and shall go unto him at midnight, and say unto him, Friend, lend[5531] me three loaves;

6 For a friend of mine [I]in his journey [aom]is come to me, and I have nothing to set before him?

7 And he from within shall answer and say, Trouble me not: the door [pfip]is now shut,2808 and my children are with me in bed; I cannot [apt]rise and [ainf]give thee.

8 I say unto you, [a]Though he will not [apt]rise and [ft]give him, because he is his friend, yet because of his importunity[335] he will [apt]rise and give him as many as he needeth.

🔑 9 [a]And [epn]I say unto you, [pim]Ask,[154] and it shall be given you; [pim]seek, and ye shall find; [pim]knock, and it shall be opened unto you.

10 For every one that [ppt]asketh receiveth;[2983] and he that [ppt]seeketh2212 findeth;[2147] and to him that [ppt]knocketh it shall be opened.

11 [a]If a son [ft]shall ask bread of any of you that is a father, will he give him a stone? or if *he ask* a fish, will he for a fish give him a serpent?

12 Or if he [aosb]shall ask an egg, will he [I]offer him a scorpion?

13 If ye then, being evil,[4190] know[1492] how to give good[18] gifts[1390] unto your children:[5043] how much more shall *your* heavenly [art]Father[3962] give the [an]Holy Spirit to them that [ppt]ask him?

Jesus and Beelzebub (Matt. 12:22–30; Mark 3:20–27)

🔑 14 [a]And he was casting out a devil,1140 and it was dumb. And it came to pass, when the devil [apt]was gone out, the dumb spake;[2980] and the people wondered.

15 But some of them said, [a]He casteth out devils1140 through [Ib]Beelzebub the chief of the devils.

16 And others,[2087] tempting[3985] *him,* [ipfa]sought of him a sign from heaven.

17 [a]But [b]he, knowing their thoughts,[1270] said unto them, Every kingdom[932] [aptp]divided against itself is brought to desolation; and a house[3624] *divided* against a house falleth.

18 If Satan[4567] also [aop]be divided against himself, how shall his kingdom stand? because ye say that I [pinf]cast out devils1140 through Beelzebub.

19 And if I by Beelzebub cast out devils, by whom do your sons cast *them* out? therefore shall they be your judges.

20 But if I [a]with the finger of God[2316] cast out devils, no doubt the kingdom of God [ao]is come upon you.

3 [I]Or, *for the day*
6 [I]Or, *out of his way*
8 [a]Luke 18:1
9 [a]Matt. 7:7; 21:22; Mark 11:24; John 15:7; James 1:6; 1John 3:22
11 [a]Matt. 7:9
12 [I]Gr. *give*
14 [a]Matt. 9:32; 12:22
15 [I]Gr. *Beelzebul* [a]Matt. 9:34; 12:24 [b]Luke 11:18, 19
16 [a]Matt. 12:38; 16:1
17 [a]Matt. 12:25; Mark 3:24 [b]John 2:25
20 [a]Ex. 8:19

🔑 **11:5–13** This parable deals with the responsibility of the Christian. When someone comes at midnight and asks for bread, the believer should not be indifferent. The Lord spoke this parable to teach Christians that they should earnestly pray on behalf of others and their needs. God wants to satisfy those prayers through us and give us the joy of being intercessors for others.

🔑 **11:9** The word that is translated "ask" is *aiteíte* (from *aitéō* [154]). This is the word that the Lord uses when He asks for something from His Father (John 14:16). In the same context, when it comes to the disciples asking something from the Father, the verb *aitéō* is used (vv. 13, 14). "Asking in prayer" means coming to the Lord as would a beggar to a generous person. One should not demand anything from God. If God's children will only trust Him for their needs, God will give them their requests. Many times, however, people ask for things that are not according to His will. God will give only what is eternally "good," (*agathón*, [18]) and according to the execution of His plan and timetable for the whole world (Eccl. 3:11) "Good" for the believer may not be what the believer wants, but it is what God has established to execute His plan and bring the believer into a closer relationship with Him. See note on James 5:14, 15.

🔑 **11:14–32** See note on Mark 3:28, 29.

21 [a]When a strong man armed [psa]keepeth[5442] his palace, his goods are in peace:[1515]

22 But [a]when a stronger than he [apt]shall come upon him, and overcome[3528] him, he taketh from him all his armour wherein he trusted,[3982] and divideth his spoils.

23 [a]He that is not with me is against me: and he that [ppt]gathereth not with me scattereth.

The Return of the Unclean Spirit (Matt. 12:43–45)

24 [a]When the unclean[169] spirit[4151] [aosb]is gone out of a man, he walketh through dry places, seeking rest;[372] and finding none, he saith, I will return unto my house whence I came out.

25 And when he [apt]cometh,[2064] he findeth *it* swept and garnished.

26 Then goeth he, and taketh *to him* seven other[2087] spirits more wicked[4191] than himself; and they enter in, and dwell[2730] there: and [a]the last[2078] *state* of that man[444] is worse than the first.

True Blessedness

27 And it came to pass, as he [aie]spake these things, a certain woman of the company [apt]lifted up her voice, and said unto him, [a]Blessed[3107] *is* the womb that [apt]bare thee, and the paps[3149] which thou [ao]hast sucked.

28 But he said, Yea [a]rather, blessed[3107] *are* they that [ppt]hear the word[3056] of God, and [ppt]keep[5442] it.

The Demand for a Sign (Matt. 12:38–42; Mark 8:12)

29 [a]And when the people were gathered thick together, he began [pinf]to say, This is an evil[4190] generation:[1074] they seek a sign;[4592] and there [fp]shall no sign be given[1325] it, but the sign of Jonas the prophet.[4396]

30 For as [a]Jonas was a sign unto the

21 [a]Matt. 12:29; Mark 3:27
22 [a]Isa. 53:12; Col. 2:15
23 [a]Matt. 12:30
24 [a]Matt. 12:43
26 [a]John 5:14; Heb. 6:4; 10:26; 2Pet. 2:20
27 [a]Luke 1:28, 48
28 [a]Matt. 7:21; Luke 8:21; James 1:25
29 [a]Matt. 12:38, 39
30 [a]Jon. 1:17; 2:10
31 [a]1Kgs. 10:1
32 [a]Jon. 3:5
33 [a]Matt. 5:15; Mark 4:21; Luke 8:16
34 [a]Matt. 6:22
36 [I]Gr. *a candle by its bright shining*
38 [a]Mark 7:3
39 [a]Matt. 23:25

Ninevites, so shall also the Son of man be to this generation.

31 [a]The queen of the south shall rise up in the judgment[2920] with the men of this generation,[1074] and condemn[2632] them: for she came from the utmost parts of the earth [ainf]to hear[191] the wisdom of Solomon; and, behold, a greater than Solomon *is* here.

32 The men of Nineveh shall rise up in the judgment with this generation, and [ft]shall condemn[2632] it: for [a]they repented[3340] at the preaching[2782] of Jonas; and, behold, a greater than Jonas *is* here.

Light Should Not Be Hidden (Matt. 5:15; 6:22, 23)

33 [a]No man, when he [apt]hath lighted a candle, putteth *it* in a secret place, neither under a bushel, but on a candlestick, that they which [ppt]come in [psa]may see the light.[5338]

34 [a]The light of the body is the eye: therefore when thine eye is single,[573] thy whole body also is full of light; but when *thine eye* is evil,[4190] thy body also *is* full of darkness.

35 [pim]Take heed[4648] therefore that the light[5457] which is in thee be not darkness.[4655]

36 If thy whole body therefore *be* full of light, having no part dark, the whole shall be full of light, as when [I]the bright shining of a candle [psa]doth give thee light.[5461]

Jesus Denounces the Pharisees And the Lawyers (Matt. 23:1–36; Mark 12:38–40; Luke 20:45–47)

37 And as he spake, a certain Pharisee besought him to dine with him: and he went in, and sat down to meat.

38 And [a]when the Pharisee [apt]saw *it*, he marvelled that he [aop]had not first washed[907] before dinner.

39 [a]And the Lord said unto him, Now do ye Pharisees make clean[2511] the outside of the cup and the platter; but

[b]your inward part is full of ravening[724] and wickedness.[4189]

40 *Ye* fools, did not he that [apt]made that which is without1855 [ao]make that which is within also?

41 [a]But rather give alms[1654] [I]of such things as ye have; and, behold, all things are clean[2513] unto you.

42 [a]But woe unto you, Pharisees for ye tithe586 mint2238 and rue4076 and all manner of herbs, and pass over judgment[2920] and the love[26] of God: these ought ye [ainf]to have done, and not [pinf]to leave the other undone.[863]

43 [a]Woe unto you, Pharisees! for ye love[25] the uppermost seats in the synagogues,[4864] and [art]greetings in the markets.

44 [a]Woe unto you, scribes[1122] and Pharisees, hypocrites[5273] [b]for ye are as [art]graves which appear not, and the men that [ppt]walk over *them* are not aware *of them.*

45 Then answered one of the lawyers,[3544] and said unto him, Master, thus saying thou reproachest5195 us also.

46 And he said, Woe unto you also, *ye* lawyers! [a]for ye [pin]lade5412 men with burdens[5413] grievous to be borne, and ye yourselves touch not the burdens with one of your fingers.

47 [a]Woe unto you! for ye build the sepulchres3419 of the prophets,[4396] and your fathers[3962] killed them.

48 Truly ye bear witness[3140] that ye allow the deeds[2041] of your fathers: for they indeed killed them, and ye build their sepulchres.

49 Therefore also said the wisdom[4678] of God, [a]I will send them prophets and apostles,[652] and *some* of them they shall slay and persecute:

50 That the blood[129] of all the prophets, which [ppt]was shed from the foundation[2602] of the world,[2889] [asbp]may be required of this generation;

51 [a]From the blood[129] of Abel unto [b]the blood of Zacharias, which [aptp]perished between the altar and the temple:[3624] verily[3483] I say unto you, It shall be required of this generation.

52 [a]Woe unto you, lawyers! for ye [ao]have taken away the key of knowledge:[1108] ye entered not in yourselves, and them that [ppt]were entering in ye [aoI]hindered.

53 And as he said these things unto them, the scribes and the Pharisees began [pinf]to urge[1758] *him* vehemently,1171 and [pinf]to provoke him to speak653 of many things:

54 Laying wait for him, and [a]seeking to catch something out of his mouth, that they might accuse him.

Hypocrisy Will Be Revealed

12 In [a]the mean time, when there were gathered together an innumerable multitude of people, insomuch that they [pinf]trode2662 one upon another, he began to say unto his disciples first of all, [b]Beware ye of the leaven[2219] of the Pharisees, which is hypocrisy.5272

2 [a]For there is nothing covered, that [fp]shall not be revealed;[601] neither hid, that shall not be known.

3 Therefore whatsoever ye have spoken in darkness[4653] shall be heard in the light; and that which ye have spoken in the ear in closets [fp]shall be proclaimed[2784] upon the housetops.

Fear God (Matt. 10:28–31)

4 [a]And I say unto you [b]my friends, [aosi]Be not afraid[5399] of them that [ppt]kill the body,[4983] and after that [ppt]have no more4055 that they [ainf]can do.

5 But I will forewarn you whom ye [asbp]shall fear: [aipp]Fear[5399] him, which after he [aime]hath killed [ppt]hath power[1849] [ainf]to cast into hell;[1067] yea, I say unto you, Fear him.

6 Are not five sparrows sold for two [I]farthings,787 and not one of them is forgotten before God?

7 But even the very hairs of your head [pfi]are all numbered.705 [pim]Fear not therefore: ye are of more value1308 than many sparrows.

39 [b]Titus 1:15
41 [I]Or, *as you are able* [a]Isa. 58:7; Dan. 4:27; Luke 12:33
42 [a]Matt. 23:23
43 [a]Matt. 23:6; Mark 12:38, 39
44 [a]Matt. 23:27 [b]Ps. 5:9
46 [a]Matt. 23:4
47 [a]Matt. 23:29
49 [a]Matt. 23:34
51 [a]Gen. 4:8 [b]2Chr. 24:20, 21
52 [I]Or, *forbade* [a]Matt. 23:13
54 [a]Mark 12:13
1 [a]Matt. 16:6; Mark 8:15 [b]Matt. 16:12
2 [a]Matt. 10:26; Mark 4:22; Luke 8:17
4 [a]Isa. 51:7, 8, 12, 13; Jer. 1:8; Matt. 10:28 [b]John 15:14, 15
6 [a]Matt. 10:29

Confessing Christ Before Men (Matt. 10:32, 33; 10:19, 20; 12:32)

8 [a]Also I say unto you, Whosoever [aosb]shall confess[3670] me before men, him shall the Son of man also confess[3670] before the angels[32] of God:

9 But he that [apt]denieth[720] me before men [fp]shall be denied[533] before the angels of God.

⊶ 10 And [a]whosoever shall speak a word against the Son of man, it [fp]shall be forgiven[863] him: but unto him that [apt]blasphemeth[987] against the Holy Ghost[4151] it shall not be forgiven.

11 [a]And when they bring you unto the synagogues,[4864] and *unto* magistrates,[746] and powers,[1849] take ye no thought how or what thing ye [asbm]shall answer, or what ye [aosb]shall say:

12 For the Holy Ghost [ft]shall teach[1321] you in the same hour what ye ought to say.

A Prosperous Farmer

13 And one of the company said unto him, Master,[1320] speak to my brother,[80] that he divide the inheritance[2817] with me.

14 And he said unto him, [a]Man, who made[2525] me a judge[1348] or a divider over you?

15 And he said unto them, [pima]Take heed, and [pim]beware of covetousness: for a man's life consisteth not in the abundance of the things which he possesseth.

16 And he spake a parable[3850] unto[4314] them, saying, The ground of a certain rich man [ao]brought forth plentifully:

17 And he [ipf]thought[1260] within himself, saying, What shall I do, because I have no room where to bestow my fruits?

18 And he said, This will I do: I will pull down my barns, and build greater; and there will I bestow all my fruits and my goods.[18]

19 And I will say to my soul,[5590] [a]Soul, thou hast much goods [ppt]laid up[2749] for many years; [pim]take thine ease, [aim]eat, [aim]drink, *and* [pim]be merry.[2165]

20 But God said unto him, *Thou* fool, this night [I][a]thy soul[5590] shall be required[523] of thee: [b]then whose shall those things be, which thou [ao]hast provided?

21 So *is* he that [ppt]layeth up treasure for himself, [a]and [ppt]is not rich[4147] toward God.

Christ Warns Against Earthly Anxiety (Matt. 6:25–34)

22 And he said unto his disciples,[3101] Therefore I say unto you, [pima]Take no thought for your life,[5590] what ye [aosb]shall eat; neither for the body, what ye [asbm]shall put on.

23 The life is more than meat, and the body *is more* than raiment.[1742]

24 [aim]Consider[2657] the ravens: for they neither sow nor reap; which neither have storehouse nor barn; and [a]God[2316] feedeth them: how much more [pin]are ye better[1308] than the fowls?

25 And which of you with taking thought can [ainf]add to his stature one cubit?[4083]

26 If ye then be not able to do that thing which is least, why take ye thought for the rest?

27 [aim]Consider the lilies how they grow: they toil not, they spin[3514] not; and yet I say unto you, that Solomon in all his glory [aom]was not arrayed[4016] like one of these.

28 If then God so clothe the grass, which is to day in the field, and to morrow [ppp]is cast into the oven; how much more *will he clothe* you, O ye of little faith?[3640]

29 And seek not ye what ye shall eat, or what ye shall drink, [I]neither be ye of doubtful mind.

30 For all these things do the nations

8 [a]Matt. 10:32; Mark 8:38; 2Tim. 2:12; 1John 2:23

10 [a]Matt. 12:31, 32; Mark 3:28; 1John 5:16

11 [a]Matt. 10:19; Mark 13:11; Luke 21:14

14 [a]John 18:36

15 [a]1Tim. 6:7-10

19 [a]Eccl. 11:9; 1Cor. 15:32; James 5:5

20 [I]Or, *do they require thy soul* [a]Job 20:22; 27:8; Ps. 52:7; James 4:14 [b]Ps. 39:6; Jer. 17:11

21 [a]Matt. 6:20; Luke 12:33; 1Tim. 6:18, 19; James 2:5

22 [a]Matt. 6:25

24 [a]Job 38:41; Ps. 147:9

29 [I]Or, *live not in careful suspense*

⊶ **12:10** See notes on Mark 3:28, 29.

of the world[2889] seek after: and your Father[3962] knoweth that ye have need of these things.

31 [a]But rather [pim]seek ye the kingdom[932] of God; and all these things shall be added unto you.

32 [pim]Fear[5399] not, little flock;[4168] for [a]it is your Father's good pleasure[2106] [ainf]to give you the kingdom.

33 [aim][a]Sell that ye have, and give alms;[1654] [aim][b]provide yourselves bags which [ppt]wax not old,[3822] a treasure in the heavens[3772] that faileth not, where no thief approacheth, neither moth corrupteth.

34 For where your treasure2344 is, there will your heart[2588] be also.

Watchful Servants (Matt. 24:45–51)

35 [a]Let your loins be [pfpp]girded about, and [b]*your* lights burning;

36 And ye yourselves like unto men that [ppt]wait for[4327] their lord,[2962] when he will return from the wedding;[1062] that when he [apt]cometh and [apt]knocketh, they [aosb]may open unto him immediately.

37 [a]Blessed[3107] *are* those servants,[1401] whom the lord when he cometh shall find watching: verily281 I say unto you, that he [fm]shall gird4024 himself, and make them to sit down to meat, and [ft]will [apt]come forth and serve[1247] them.

38 And if he shall come in the second watch, or come in the third watch, and find *them* so, blessed[3107] are those servants.

39 [a]And this [pim]know, that if the goodman of the house[3617] had known what hour the thief [pin]would come, he would have watched, and not [ao]have suffered[863] his house to be broken through.

40 [a]Be[1096] ye therefore ready also: for the Son of man cometh at an hour when ye think not.

31 [a]Matt. 6:33
32 [a]Matt. 11:25, 26
33 [a]Matt. 19:21; Acts 2:45; 4:34 [b]Matt. 6:20; Luke 16:9; 1Tim. 6:19
35 [a]Eph. 6:14; 1Pet. 1:13 [b]Matt. 25:1-13
37 [a]Matt. 24:46
39 [a]Matt. 24:43; 1Thess. 5:2; 2Pet. 3:10; Rev. 3:3; 16:15
40 [a]Matt. 24:44; 25:13; Mark 13:33; Luke 21:34, 36; 1Thess. 5:6; 2Pet. 3:12
42 [a]Matt. 24:45; 25:21; 1Cor. 4:2
44 [a]Matt. 24:47
45 [a]Matt. 24:48
46 [I]Or, *cut him off* [a]Matt. 24:51
47 [a]Num. 15:30; Deut. 25:2; John 9:41; 15:22; Acts 17:30; James 4:17
48 [a]Lev. 5:17; 1Tim. 1:13
49 [a]Luke 12:51
50 [a]Matt. 20:22; Mark 10:38

The Duties of Christ's Ministers

41 Then Peter said unto him, Lord,[2962] speakest thou this parable unto us, or even to all?

42 And the Lord said, [a]Who then is that faithful[4103] and wise[5429] steward, whom *his* lord [ft]shall make[2525] ruler over his household,2322 [infg]to give *them their* portion of meat in due season?[2540]

43 Blessed *is* that servant, whom his lord when he cometh shall find so doing.

44 [a]Of a truth I say unto you, that he will make him ruler over all that he hath.

45 [a]But and if that servant [aosb]say in his heart, My lord delayeth his [pinf]coming; and shall begin [pinf]to beat[5180] the menservants[3816] and maidens, and [pinf]to eat and [pinf]drink, and [pip]to be drunken;

46 The lord of that servant will come in a day when he looketh not for *him,* and at an hour when he is not aware, and [ft]will [I][a]cut him in sunder,1371 and [ft]will appoint[5087] him his portion with the unbelievers.[571]

🗝 47 And [a]that servant, which [ainf]knew his lord's will, and [apt]prepared not *himself,* neither [apt]did according to his will, shall be beaten with many *stripes.*

48 [a]But he that knew not, and did commit things worthy of stripes, shall be beaten with few *stripes.* For unto whomsoever much [aop]is given, of him shall be much required: and to whom men [aom]have committed much, of him they will ask the more.4055

No Compromise (Matt. 10:34–36)

49 [a]I am come to send fire on the earth; and what will I, if it [aop]be already kindled?381

50 But [a]I have a baptism[908] to be baptized[907] with; and how [pin]am I

🗝 **12:47, 48** See note on Matthew 8:11, 12.

[l]straitened[4912] till it [asbp]be accomplished[5055]

51 [a]Suppose ye that I [ao]am come [ainf]to give peace[1515] on earth?[1093] I tell you, Nay; [b]but rather division:[1267]

52 [a]For from henceforth there shall be five in one house divided, three against two and two against three.

53 The father shall be divided against the [an]son, and the [an]son against the [an]father; the [an]mother against the [an]daughter, and the [an]daughter against the [an]mother; the [an]mother in law against her [an]daughter in law, and the daughter in law against her mother in law.

Discerning the Time (Matt. 16:2, 3)

54 And he [ipf]said also to the people, [a]When ye see a cloud [ppt]rise out of the west, straightway[2112] ye say, There cometh a shower; and so it is.

55 And when *ye see* the south wind [ppt]blow,[4154] ye say, There will be heat; and it cometh to pass.

56 *Ye* hypocrites,[5273] ye can [pinf]discern[1381] the face[4383] of the sky[3772] and of the earth;[1093] but how is it that ye do not discern this time?[2540]

Being Reconciled With Your Accuser (Matt. 5:25, 26)

57 Yea, and why even of yourselves judge[2919] ye not what is right?[1342]

58 [a]When thou goest with thine adversary[476] to the magistrate,[758] [b]*as thou art* in the way, give diligence that thou [pfin]mayest be delivered[525] from him; lest he hale[2694] thee to the judge, and the judge [aosb]deliver thee to the officer, and the officer [psa]cast thee into prison.

59 I tell thee, thou shalt not depart thence, till thou hast paid the very last [a]mite.[3016]

A Call to Repentance

13 🔑There were present at that season some that [ppt]told[518] him of the Galilaeans, whose blood[129] Pilate [ao]had mingled with their sacrifices.[2378]

2 And Jesus answering said unto them, Suppose ye that these Galilaeans were sinners[268] above all the Galilaeans, because they [pf]suffered such things?

3 I tell you, Nay: but, except ye [psa]repent,[3340] ye [fm]shall all likewise perish.[622]

4 Or those eighteen, upon whom the tower in Siloam fell,[4098] and slew them, think ye that they were [a]sinners[3781] above all men that dwelt[2730] in Jerusalem?

5 I tell you, Nay: but, except ye [psa]repent, ye shall all likewise perish.

The Parable of the Barren Fig Tree

6 He [ipf]spake also this parable;[3850] [a]A certain *man* had a fig tree planted in his vineyard; and he came and sought fruit thereon, and found none.

7 Then said he unto the dresser of his vineyard, Behold, these three years I come seeking fruit on this fig tree, and find none: cut it down; why cumbereth[2673] it the ground?

8 And he answering said unto him, Lord, [aim]let it alone[863] this year also, till I shall dig about it, and dung[906] [2874] *it:*

9 And if it [aosb]bear fruit, *well:* and if not, *then* after that thou shalt cut it down.

The Healing of a Crippled Woman On the Sabbath

10 And he was teaching[1321] in one of the synagogues[4864] on the sabbath.[4521]

50 [l]Or, *pained*

51 [a]Matt. 10:34; Luke 12:49 [b]Mic. 7:6; John 7:43; 9:16; 10:19

52 [a]Matt. 10:35

54 [a]Matt. 16:2

58 [a]Prov. 25:8; Matt. 5:25 [b]Ps. 32:6; Isa. 55:6

59 [l]Mark 12:42

4 [l]Or, *debtors* [a]Matt. 18:24; Luke 11:4

6 [a]Isa. 5:2; Matt. 21:19

🔑 **13:1–5** The Jews of the first century believed that all suffering was a result of God's judgment on sin (see note on Job 2:11–13). This concept is shared by many Christians today when they attempt to answer the question, "Why do the righteous suffer?" The Scripture teaches that God allows temporal disasters to happen for various reasons—one of which is to lead people to repentance. Although God may punish sin with suffering, suffering may also be part of a testing or learning process.

11 And, behold, there was a woman
which had a spirit[4151] of infirmity[769]
eighteen years, and was bowed together,
and [ppt]could in no wise [ainf]lift up[352] *her-*
self.

12 And when Jesus saw her, he
called *her to him,* and said unto her,
Woman, thou [pfip]art loosed[630] from thine
infirmity.

13 [a]And he laid *his* hands on her:
and immediately she [aop]was made
straight,[461] and [ipf]glorified[1392] God.

14 And the ruler of the synagogue[752]
[ppt]answered with indignation, because
that Jesus [ao]had healed on the sabbath
day, and said unto the people, [a]There are
six days in which men ought [pinf]to
work:[2038] in them therefore [ppt]come
and [pin]be healed, and [b]not on the sabbath
day.

15 The Lord then answered him, and
said, *Thou* hypocrite,[5273] [a]doth not each
one of you on the sabbath loose[3089] his
ox or *his* ass from the stall, and [apt]lead
him away to [pin]watering?

16 And ought not this woman, [a]being
a daughter of Abraham, whom Satan[4567]
[ao]hath bound, lo, these eighteen years,
[aifp]be loosed[3089] from this bond on the
sabbath day?

17 And when he [ppt]had said these
things, all his adversaries [ipf]were
ashamed: and all the people [ipf]rejoiced for
all the glorious things that [ppp]were done
by him.

The Parables of the Mustard Seed and the Leaven (Matt. 13:31–33; Mark 4:30–32)

18 [a]Then said he, Unto what is the
kingdom[932] of God[2316] like? and whereunto shall I resemble it?

19 It is like a grain of mustard seed,
which a man [apt]took, and [ao]cast into his
garden; and it [ao]grew, and [aom]waxed[1096]
a great tree; and the fowls of the air[3772]
lodged in the branches of it.

13 [a]Mark 16:18; Acts 9:17
14 [a]Ex. 20:9 [b]Matt. 12:10; Mark 3:2; Luke 6:7; 14:13
15 [a]Luke 14:5
16 [a]Luke 19:9
18 [a]Matt. 13:31; Mark 4:30
21 [I]Matt. 13:33
22 [a]Matt. 9:35; Mark 6:6
24 [a]Matt. 7:13 [b]John 7:34; 8:21; 13:33; Rom. 9:31
25 [a]Ps. 32:6; Isa. 55:6 [b]Matt. 25:10 [c]Luke 6:46 [d]Matt. 7:23; 25:12
27 [a]Matt. 7:23; 25:41; Luke 13:25 [b]Ps. 6:8; Matt. 25:41
28 [a]Matt. 8:12; 13:42; 21:51 [b]Matt. 8:11
30 [a]Matt. 19:30; 20:16; Mark 10:31

20 And again he said, Whereunto
shall I liken the kingdom[932] of God?[2316]

21 It is like leaven,[2219] which a
woman [apt]took and hid in three [a]mea-
sures[4568] of meal, till the whole [aop]was
leavened.[2220]

"The Strait Gate" (Matt. 7:13, 14, 21–23)

22 [a]And he [ipf]went through the cities
and villages, teaching, and journeying toward Jerusalem.

23 Then said one unto him, Lord, are
there few that [ppp]be saved?[4982] And he
said unto them,

24 [pima]Strive[75] [ainf]to enter in at the
strait[4728] gate: for [b]many, I say unto you,
will seek to enter in, and shall not be
able.

25 [a]When once the master of the
house [asbp]is risen up, and [aosb][b]hath shut
to the door, and ye [asbm]begin [pfin]to stand
without,[1854] and [pinf]to knock at the door,
saying, [c]Lord, Lord, open unto us; and he
shall answer and say unto you, [d]I know
you not whence ye are:

26 Then shall ye begin [pinf]to say,
We [ao]have eaten and [ao]drunk in thy presence, and thou [ao]hast taught in our
streets.

🗝 27 [a]But he shall say, I tell you, I
know you not whence ye are; [aim][b]de-
part[868] from me, all *ye* workers of iniquity.[93]

28 [a]There shall be weeping and
gnashing[1030] of teeth, [b]when ye shall
see Abraham, and Isaac, and Jacob,
and all the prophets,[4396] in the kingdom[932] of God,[2316] and you *yourselves*
[ppt]thrust out.

29 And they shall come from the
east, and *from* the west, and from the
north, and *from* the south, and shall sit
down in the kingdom of God.

30 [a]And, behold, there are last[2078]
which shall be first, and there are first
which shall be last.

🗝 **13:27–30** See notes on Matthew 8:11, 12 and 2 Thessalonians 2:3.

Jesus Laments Over Jerusalem (Matt. 23:37–39)

31 The same day there came certain of the Pharisees, saying unto him, [aim]Get thee out, and [pim]depart hence: for Herod will kill thee.

32 And he said unto them, [aptp]Go ye, and tell that fox, Behold, I cast out devils,[1140] and I do[2005] cures[2392] to day and to morrow, and the third *day* [a]I [pin]shall be perfected.[5048]

33 Nevertheless I must [pinf]walk to day, and to morrow, and the *day* following: for it cannot be[1735] that a prophet[4396] [ainf]perish out of Jerusalem.

34 [a]O Jerusalem, Jerusalem, which [ppt]killest the prophets, and [ppt]stonest them that [pfpp]are sent unto thee; how often [ao]would[2309] I [ainf]have gathered thy children together, as a hen *doth gather* her brood under *her* wings, and ye [ao]would not!

35 Behold, [a]your house [pin]is left unto you desolate: and verily[281] I say unto you, Ye shall not see me, until *the time* come when ye shall say, [b]Blessed[2127] *is* he that [ppt]cometh in the name of the Lord.[2962]

Jesus Heals a Man On the Sabbath Day

14 And it came to pass, as he [aie]went into the house of one of the chief Pharisees to eat bread on the sabbath day,[4521] that they watched[3906] him.

2 And, behold, there was a certain man before him which had the dropsy.[5203]

3 And Jesus answering spake unto the lawyers[3544] and Pharisees, saying, [a]Is it lawful [pinf]to heal on the sabbath day?

4 And they [ao]held their peace.[2270] And he took *him,* and healed him, and let him go;

5 And answered them, saying, [a]Which of you [fm]shall have an ass or an ox fallen[1706] into a pit,[5421] and will not straightway[2212] pull him out on the sabbath day?

6 And they could not [ainf]answer him again[470] to these things.

Jesus Teaches Humility

7 And he put forth a parable[3850] to those which [pfpp]were bidden,[2564] when he [ppt]marked how they [ipf]chose out the chief rooms; saying unto them,

8 When thou [asbp]art bidden of any *man* to a wedding,[1062] sit not down in the highest room; lest a more honourable man than thou [pfpp]be bidden of him;

9 And he that bade[2564] thee and him [apt]come and say to thee, Give this man place; and thou begin with shame[152] [pinf]to take[2722] the lowest[2078] room.

10 [a]But when thou art bidden, [apt]go and sit down in the lowest room; that when he that [pfp]bade thee [aosb]cometh, he may say unto thee, Friend, go up higher:[511] then shalt thou have worship in the presence of them that [ppt]sit at meat with thee.

11 [a]For whosoever [ppt]exalteth himself shall be abased; and he that [ppt]humbleth himself shall be exalted.

12 Then [ipf]said he also to him that [pfp]bade him, When thou makest a dinner or a supper, [pim]call not thy friends, nor thy brethren, neither thy kinsmen, nor *thy* rich neighbours; lest they also bid thee again, and a recompence be made thee.

13 But when thou makest a feast,[1403] [pim]call [a]the poor, the maimed, the lame, the blind:

14 And thou shalt be blessed;[3107] for they cannot recompense thee: for thou shalt be recompensed at the resurrection[386] of the just.[1342]

The Parable of the Great Banquet (Matt. 22:1–10)

15 And when one of them that sat at meat with him heard these things, he said unto him, [a]Blessed[3107] *is* he that shall eat bread in the kingdom[932] of God.[2316]

16 [a]Then said he unto him, A certain

32 [a]Heb. 2:10
34 [a]Matt. 23:37
35 [a]Lev. 26:31, 32; Ps. 69:25; Isa. 1:7; Dan. 9:27; Mic. 3:12 [b]Ps. 118:26; Matt. 21:9; Mark 11:10; Luke 19:38; John 12:13
3 [a]Matt. 12:10
5 [a]Ex. 23:5; Deut. 22:4; Luke 13:15
10 [a]Prov. 25:6, 7
11 [a]Job 22:29; Ps. 18:27; Prov. 29:23; Matt. 23:12; Luke 18:14; James 4:6; 1Pet. 5:5
13 [a]Neh. 8:10, 12
15 [a]Rev. 19:9
16 [a]Matt. 22:2

man made a great supper, and bade many:

17 And [a]sent his <u>servant</u>[1401] at supper time to say to them that were bidden, [pim]Come; for all things are now ready.

18 And they all with one *consent* [aom]began [pinf]<u>to make excuse</u>.[3868] The first said unto him, I [ao]have bought a piece of ground, and I must needs [ainf]go and [ainf]see it: I pray thee have me [pfpp]<u>excused</u>.[3868]

19 And another said, I have bought five yoke of oxen, and I go [ainf]to prove them: I pray thee have me excused.

20 And another said, I [ao]have married a wife, and therefore I cannot [ainf]come.

21 So that servant [apt]came, and [ao]shewed his <u>lord</u>[2962] these things. Then the master of the house [aptp]being angry said to his servant, Go out quickly into the streets and lanes of the city, and bring in hither the poor, and the maimed, and the halt, and the blind.

22 And the servant said, Lord, it [pfi]is done as thou [ao]<u>hast commanded</u>,[2004] and yet there is room.

23 And the lord said unto the servant, Go out into the highways and <u>hedges</u>,[5418] and <u>compel</u>[315] *them* to come in, that my house may be filled.

24 For I say unto you, [a]That none of those men which [pfpp]were bidden [fm]<u>shall taste</u>[1089] of my <u>supper</u>.[1173]

Love Jesus More Than Yourself

🔑 25 And there went great multitudes with him: and he turned, and said unto them,

26 [a]If any *man* come to me, [b]and <u>hate</u>[3404] not his father, and mother, and wife, and children, and brethren, and sisters, [c]yea, and his own <u>life</u>[5590] also, he cannot be my <u>disciple</u>.[3101]

27 And [a]whosoever doth not bear his <u>cross</u>,[4716] and come after me, cannot be my disciple.

28 For [a]which of you, intending to build a tower, [apt]sitteth not down first, and counteth the cost, whether he have *sufficient* to finish *it?*

29 <u>Lest haply</u>,[3379] after he [apt]hath laid the foundation, and [ppt]is not able [ainf]to finish *it,* all that [ppt]behold *it* [aosb]begin [pinf]to mock him,

30 Saying, This man began to build, and [ao]<u>was</u> not <u>able</u>[2480] [pinf]to finish.

31 Or what king, going [ainf]to make war against another king, [apt]sitteth not down first, and consulteth whether he be able with ten thousand [ainf]to meet him that cometh against him with twenty thousand?

32 Or else, while the other is yet a great way off, he [apt]sendeth an <u>ambassage</u>,[4242] and <u>desireth</u>[2065] conditions of <u>peace</u>.[1515]

33 So likewise, whosoever he be of you that [pin]<u>forsaketh</u>[657] not all that he hath, he cannot be my disciple.

Salt
(Matt. 5:13; Mark 9:50)

34 [a]Salt *is* <u>good</u>:[2570] but if the salt [asbp]<u>have lost</u> his <u>savour</u>,[3471] wherewith shall it be seasoned?

35 It is neither fit for the land, nor yet for the <u>dunghill</u>;[2874] *but* men cast it out. He that [ppt]hath ears to hear, [pim]<u>let</u> him <u>hear</u>.[191]

The Lost Sheep
(Matt. 18:12–14)

15 Then [a]<u>drew near</u>[1448][2258] unto him all the <u>publicans</u>[5057] and <u>sinners</u>[268] for to hear him.

17 [a]Prov. 9:2, 5
24 [a]Matt. 21:43; 22:8; Acts 13:46
26 [a]Deut. 13:6; 33:9; Matt. 10:37 [b]Rom. 9:13 [c]Rev. 12:11
27 [a]Matt. 16:24; Mark 8:34; Luke 9:23; 2Tim. 3:12
28 [a]Prov. 24:27
34 [a]Matt. 5:13; Mark 9:50
1 [a]Matt. 9:10

🔑 **14:25–33** In light of Matthew 10:37, the word "hate" in verse twenty-six should be understood as loving one's relatives less than the Lord. The phrase, "that forsaketh not" (v. 33), does not refer to the abandonment of one's belongings, but the proper prioritization of them. The Greek word is *apotássetai* ([657], the middle voice of *apotássō*, "to properly arrange." It refers to believers who are worthy of Christ and know how to properly arrange their life so that Christ is given the preeminence (see note on Micah 7:5–7).

2 And the Pharisees and scribes[1122] murmured, saying, This man receiveth[4327] sinners, [a]and eateth with them.

3 And he spake this parable[3850] unto them, saying,

4 [a]What man of you, having an hundred sheep, if he [apt]lose[622] one of them, doth not leave the ninety and nine in the wilderness, and go after that which [pfp]is lost, until he find it?

5 And when he hath found *it,* he layeth *it* on his shoulders, rejoicing.[5463]

6 And when he cometh home, he calleth together[4779] *his* friends and neighbours, saying unto them, [aim]Rejoice[4796] with me; for I [ao]have found my sheep [a]which [pfpp]was lost.[622]

7 I say unto you, that likewise joy[5479] shall be in heaven[3772] over one sinner that [ppt]repenteth,[3340] [a]more than over ninety and nine just[1342] persons, which need no repentance.[3341]

The Lost Coin

8 Either what woman having ten pieces of silver, if she [aosb]lose one piece, doth not light a candle, and sweep the house, and seek diligently till she [aosb]find *it?*

9 And when she hath found *it,* she calleth *her* friends and *her* neighbours together,[4779] saying, [aim]Rejoice with[4796] me; for I [ao]have found the piece which I [ao]had lost.[622]

10 Likewise, I say unto you, there is joy[5479] in the presence of the angels[32] of God[2316] over one sinner[268] that repenteth.[3340]

The Lost Son

11 And he said, A certain man had two sons:[5207]

12 And the younger of them said to *his* father,[3962] Father, [aim]give me the portion of goods that [ppt]falleth *to me.* And he divided[1244] unto them [a]*his* living.[979]

13 And not many days after the younger son [apt]gathered all together,[4863] and took his journey into a far country, and there wasted his substance[3776] with riotous[811] living.[2198]

14 And when he had spent all, there arose a mighty famine in that land; and he began [pinf]to be in want.[5302]

15 And he went and joined himself to a citizen of that country; and he sent him into his fields [pinf]to feed swine.

16 And he [ipf]would fain[1937] [ainf]have filled[1072] his belly with the husks that the swine [ipf]did eat: and no man [ipf]gave unto him.

17 And when he came[2064] to himself, he said, How many hired servants[3407] of my father's have bread enough and to spare,[4052] and I perish[622] with hunger!

18 I will arise and go to my father, and will say unto him, Father, I [ao]have sinned[264] against heaven,[3772] and before thee,

19 And am no more worthy [aifp]to be called thy son: [aim]make[4160] me as one of thy hired servants.[3407]

20 And he arose, and came to his father. But [a]when he was[568] yet a great way off, his father saw him, and had compassion,[4697] and [apt]ran, and fell on his neck, and [ao]kissed him.

21 And the son said unto him, Father, I [ao]have sinned against heaven, [a]and in thy sight, and am no more worthy to be called thy son.

22 But the father said to his servants,[1401] [aim]Bring forth the best robe, and put *it* on him; and put a ring on his hand, and shoes on *his* feet:

23 And [apt]bring hither the fatted calf, and [aim]kill[2380] *it;* and let us [apt]eat, and [aosi]be merry:[2165]

24 [a]For this my son was dead,[3498] and [ao]is alive again;[326] he was lost,[622] and [aop]is found.[2147] And they began [pinf]to be merry.[2165]

25 Now his elder[4245] son was in the field: and as he [ppt]came and drew nigh[1448] to the house, he heard musick and dancing.

26 And he [apt]called one of the servants,[3816] and [ipf]asked what these things meant.

2 [a]Acts 11:3; Gal. 2:12
4 [a]Matt. 18:12
6 [a]1Pet. 2:10, 25
7 [a]Luke 5:32
12 [a]Mark 12:44
20 [a]Acts 2:39; Eph. 2:13, 17
21 [a]Ps. 51:4
24 [a]Luke 15:32; Eph. 2:1; 5:14; Rev. 3:1

27 And he said unto him, Thy brother[80] is come; and thy father [ao]hath killed[2380] the fatted calf, because he [ao]hath received618 him safe and sound.

28 And he was angry, and would not go in: therefore [apt]came his father out, and [ipf]intreated[3870] him.

29 And he answering said to *his* father, Lo, these many years [pin]do I serve[1398] thee, neither transgressed3928 I at any time thy commandment:[1785] and yet thou never gavest me a kid, that I [asbp]might make merry[2165] with my friends:

🔑 30 But as soon as this thy son [ao]was come, which [apt]hath devoured thy living with harlots, thou [ao]hast killed[2380] for him the fatted calf.

31 And he said unto him, Son, thou art ever with me, and all that I have is thine.

32 It [ipf]was meet[1163] that we [aifp]should make merry,[2165] and [aifb]be glad:[5463] [a]for this thy brother was dead,[3498] and [ao]is alive again;326 and was lost,[622] and [aop]is found.[2147]

The Parable of The Unrighteous Steward

16 And he said also unto his disciples,[3101] There was a certain rich man, which had a steward;[3623] and the same [aop]was accused[1225] unto him that he [ppt]had wasted his goods.

2 And he called him, and said unto him, How is it that I hear this of thee? [aim]give an [art]account of thy stewardship;[3622] for thou mayest [pinf]be no longer steward.3621

3 Then the steward said within himself, What shall I do? for my lord[2962] taketh away from me the stewardship: I cannot [pinf]dig; [pinf]to beg[1871] I am ashamed.

4 I am resolved what to do, that, when I [asbp]am put out[3179] of the stewardship, they [asbm]may receive me into their houses.

5 So he [apt]called every one of his lord's debtors *unto him,* and [ipf]said unto the first, how much owest thou unto my lord?

6 And he said, An hundred measures of oil. And he said unto him, Take thy bill,[1121] and sit down quickly, and write[1125] fifty.

7 Then said he to another, And how much owest thou? And he said, An hundred measures2884 of wheat. And he said unto him, Take thy bill, and write[1125] fourscore.

🔑 8 And the lord[2962] commended the unjust[93] steward, because he [ao]had done wisely: for the children[5207] of this world[165] are in their generation wiser[5429] than [a]the children of light.[5457]

9 And [epn]I say unto you, [aim][a]Make to yourselves friends of[1537] the [I]mammon[3126] of unrighteousness;[93] that, when ye [aosb]fail, they [asbm]may receive you into everlasting[166] habitations.4633

10 [a]He that is faithful[4103] in that which is least is faithful also in much: and he that is unjust[94] in the least is unjust[94] also in much.

11 If therefore ye [aom]have not been[1096] faithful in the unrighteous[94] [I]mammon,[3126] who [ft]will commit to your trust[4100] the true[228] *riches?*

12 And if ye have not been faithful

32 [a]Luke 15:24
8 [a]John 12:36; Eph. 5:8; 1Thess. 5:5
9 [I]Or, *riches* [a]Dan. 4:27; Matt. 6:19; 19:21; Luke 11:41; 1Tim. 6:17-19
10 [a]Matt. 25:21; Luke 19:17
11 [I]Or, *riches*

🔑 **15:30** The elder son would not accept his younger brother because his brother had associated himself with harlots, although he repented. In the case of such prodigal sons and daughters, Christians today sometimes act like the "older son," when they should follow the example of the father.

🔑 **16:8** The words "wisely" and "wiser" are translations of the Greek word *phronímōs* (5430) and its derivative *phronimōtepoi* (5429). This word must be distinguished from *sophós* (4680), a Greek word that is translated "wise." Both words refer to the use of intelligence and the wise use of one's means to accomplish something. The difference lies in the ends that one is attempting to accomplish. The word *sophós* is used only when the thing that will be accomplished is good, but the word *phronímōs* is most often used when the end that will be accomplished is evil.

in that which is another man's,[245] who shall give you that which is your own?

13 [a]No servant[3610] can [pinf]serve[1398] two masters:[2962] for either he will hate the one, and love[25] the other; or else he [fm]will hold to[472] the one, and despise the other.[2087] Ye cannot [pinf]serve[1398] God[2316] and mammon.[3126]

14 And the Pharisees also, [a]who were covetous, [ipf]heard all these things: and they [ipf]derided him.

15 And he said unto them, Ye are they which [ppt][a]justify[1344] yourselves before men; but [b]God knoweth your hearts:[2588] for [c]that which is highly esteemed among men is abomination[946] in the sight of God.

The Law and the Kingdom of God

16 [a]The law[3551] and the prophets[4396] *were* until John: since that time the kingdom[932] of God[2316] [pin]is preached,[2097] and every man presseth[971] into it.

17 [a]And it is easier for heaven[3772] and earth[1093] [ainf]to pass, than one tittle[2762] of the law [ainf]to fail.[4098]

Divorce
(Matt. 5:27–32; 19:1–12; Mark 10:1–12; Rom. 7:1–3; 1 Cor. 7)

🗝 18 [a]Whosoever [ppt]putteth away[630] his wife, and [ppt]marrieth another,[2087] [pin]committeth adultery: and whosoever [ppt]marrieth her that [pfpp]is put away from *her* husband [pin]committeth adultery.

The Rich Man and Lazarus

🗝 19 There was a certain rich man, which [ipf]was clothed in purple and fine linen, and [ppt]fared[2165] sumptuously[2988] every day:

20 And there was a certain beggar[4434] named Lazarus, which [plpf]was laid[906] at his gate, [pfpp]full of sores,

21 And desiring[1937] [aifp]to be fed with the crumbs which [ppt]fell from the rich man's table: moreover the dogs[2965] [ppt]came and [ipf]licked his sores.

22 And it came to pass, that the beggar [ainf]died, and [aifp]was carried[667] by the angels into Abraham's bosom: the rich man also died, and was buried;

23 And in hell[86] he [apt]lift up his eyes, being[5225] in torments, and seeth Abraham afar off, and Lazarus in his bosom.[2859]

24 And he [apt]cried and said, Father Abraham, [aim]have mercy on me, and [aim]send Lazarus, that he [aosb]may dip[911] the tip of his finger in water, and [aosb][a]cool[2711] my tongue;[1100] for I [pin][b]am tormented[3600] in this flame.

25 But Abraham said, Son, [a]remember that thou in thy lifetime[2222] [ao]receivedst[618] thy good things,[18] and likewise Lazarus evil things: but now he is comforted,[3870] and thou art tormented.

26 And beside all this, between us and you there is a great gulf[5490] [pfip]fixed: so that they which [ppt]would [aimf]pass from hence to you cannot; neither [psa]can they pass[1276] to us, that *would come* from thence.

27 Then he said, I pray thee therefore, father, that thou [aosb]wouldest send him to my father's house:

28 For I have five brethren;[80] that he [psa][a]may testify[1263] unto them, lest they also come into this place of torment.

29 Abraham saith unto him, [a]They have Moses and the prophets;[4396] [aim]let them hear[191] them.

30 And he said, Nay, father Abraham: but if one [asbp]went unto them from the dead,[3498] they [ft]will repent.[3340]

31 And he said unto him, If they [pin]hear not Moses and the prophets, [a]neither [fp]will they be persuaded,[3982] though one [aosb]rose[450] from the dead.

13 [a]Matt. 6:24
14 [a]Matt. 23:14
15 [a]Luke 10:29 [b]Ps. 7:9 [c]1Sam. 16:7
16 [a]Matt. 4:17; 11:12, 13; Luke 7:29
17 [a]Ps. 102:26, 27; Isa. 40:8; 51:6; Matt. 5:18; 1Pet. 1:25
18 [a]Matt. 5:32; 19:9; Mark 10:11; 1Cor. 7:10, 11
24 [a]Zech. 14:12 [b]Isa. 66:24; Mark 9:44-50
25 [a]Job 21:13; Luke 6:24
29 [a]Isa. 8:20; 34:16; John 5:39, 45; Acts 15:21; 17:11
31 [a]John 12:10, 1:11

🗝 **16:18** See note on Matthew 19:3–9.

🗝 **16:19–31** See note on 2 Corinthians 12:1–10.

Always Forgive
(Matt. 18:6, 7, 21, 22; Mark 9:42)

17 Then said he unto the disciples,[3101] [a]It is impossible but that offences[4625] [infg]will come: but woe *unto him,* through whom they come!

2 It were better for him that a millstone were hanged about his neck, and he [pfip]cast into the sea, than that he [aosb]should offend[4624] one of these little ones.

3 [pim]Take heed4337 to yourselves: [a]If thy brother [aosb]trespass[264] against thee, [aim][b]rebuke him; and if he [aosb]repent,[3340] [aim]forgive[863] him.

4 And if he [aosb]trespass[264] against thee seven times in a day, and seven times in a day [aosb]turn again to thee, saying, I repent; thou shalt forgive him.

5 And the apostles[652] said unto the Lord,[2962] [aim]Increase our faith.[4102]

6 [a]And the Lord said, If ye [pin]had faith[4102] as a grain of mustard seed, ye [ipf]might say unto this sycamine tree, [aipp]Be thou plucked up by the root,1610 and [aipp]be thou planted5452 in the sea; and it [ao]should obey[5219] you.

7 But which of you, having a servant[1401] [ppt]plowing or [ppt]feeding cattle, will say unto him by and by, when he [apt]is come from the field, [apt]Go and [aim]sit down to meat?

8 And will not rather say unto him, [aim]Make ready wherewith I may sup, and [apt]gird thyself, [a]and [pim]serve[1247] me, till I [aosb]have eaten and [aosb]drunken; and afterward thou shalt eat and drink?

9 Doth he thank that servant because he did the things that were commanded[1299] him? I [I]trow[1380] not.

10 So likewise ye, when ye [aosb]shall have done all those things which are [aptp]commanded[1299] you, [pim]say, We are [a]unprofitable[888] servants: we have done that which was our duty to do.

Jesus Cleanses Ten Lepers

11 And it came to pass, [a]as he [aie]went to Jerusalem, that he [ipf]passed through the midst[3319] of Samaria and Galilee.

12 And as he [ppt]entered into a certain village, there met him ten men that were lepers, [a]which stood afar off:

13 And they lifted up *their* voices, and [ppt]said, Jesus, Master, [aim]have mercy on us.

14 And when he saw *them,* he said unto them, [apt][a]Go [aim]shew yourselves unto the priests.[2409] And it came to pass, that, as they [aie]went, they [aop]were cleansed.[2511]

15 And one of them, when he saw that he was healed, turned back, and with a loud voice [ppt]glorified[1392] God,

16 And fell down on *his* face at his feet, giving him thanks:[2168] and he was a Samaritan.

17 And Jesus answering said, [aop]Were there not ten cleansed?[2511] but where *are* the nine?

18 There are not found that [apt]returned [ainf]to give glory[1391] to God, save this stranger.[241]

19 [a]And he said unto him, [apt]Arise, [pim]go thy way: thy faith [pfi]hath made thee whole.[4982]

The Kingdom of God
(Matt. 24:23–28, 37–41)

20 And when he was demanded of the Pharisees, when the kingdom[932] of God should come, he answered them and said, The kingdom[932] of God[2316] cometh not [I]with observation:[3907]

21 [a]Neither shall they say, Lo here or, lo there! for, behold, [b]the kingdom of God is [I][c]within you.

22 And he said unto the disciples,[3101] [a]The days[2250] will come, when ye shall desire[1937] to see one of the days of the Son of man, and ye shall not see *it.*

23 [a]And they shall say to you, See here; or, see there: [aosi]go not after *them,* nor [aosi]follow *them.*

When Jesus Comes Again

24 [a]For as the lightning, that [ppt]lighteneth out of the one *part* under heaven, shineth unto the other *part* under

---

1 [a]Matt. 18:6, 7; Mark 9:42; 1Cor. 11:19
3 [a]Matt. 18:15, 21 [b]Lev. 19:17; Prov. 17:10; James 5:19
6 [a]Matt. 17:20; 21:21; Mark 9:23; 11:23
8 [a]Luke 12:37
9 [I]Or, *think*
10 [a]Job 22:3; 35:7; Ps. 16:2; Matt. 25:30; Rom. 3:12; 11:35; 1Cor. 9:16, 17; Phile. 1:11
11 [a]Luke 9:51, 52; John 4:4
12 [a]Lev. 13:46
14 [a]Lev. 13:2; 14:2; Matt. 8:4; Luke 5:14
19 [a]Matt. 9:22; Mark 5:34; 10:52; Luke 7:50; 8:48; 18:42
20 [I]Or, *with outward show*
21 [I]Or, *among you* [a]Luke 17:23 [b]Rom. 14:17 [c]John 1:26
22 [a]Matt. 9:15; John 17:12
23 [a]Matt. 24:23; Mark 13:21; Luke 21:8
24 [a]Matt. 24:27

heaven; so shall also the Son of man be
in his day.
25 [a]But first must he [ainf]suffer many
things, and [aifp]be rejected[593] of this generation.[1074]
26 [a]And as it was in the days of
Noe, so shall it be also in the days of the
Son of man.
27 They [ipf]did eat, they [ipf]drank, they
[ipf]married wives, they [ipf]were given in
marriage, until the day that Noe [ao]en-
tered into the ark, and the flood came,
and destroyed[622] them all.
28 Likewise also as it was in the
days[2250] of Lot; they [ipf]did eat, they
[ipf]drank, they [ipf]bought, they [ipf]sold, they
[ipf]planted, they [ipf]builded;
29 But [a]the same day that Lot went
out of Sodom it [ao]rained fire and brimstone[2303] from heaven,[3772] and destroyed
them all.
30 Even thus shall it be in the day
when the Son of man [pin][a]is revealed.[601]
31 In that day, he [a]which shall
be upon the housetop, and his stuff in
the house, [aim]let him not come down[2597]
[ainf]to take it away:[142] and he that is in the
field, [aim]let him likewise not return[1994]
back.
32 [pim][a]Remember Lot's wife.
33 [a]Whosoever [aosb]shall seek [ainf]to
save[4982] his life[5590] [aosb]shall lose[622] it; and
whosoever [aosb]shall lose his life shall preserve it.
34 [a]I tell you, in that night there shall
be two *men* in one bed; the one [fp]shall
be taken,[3880] and the other[2087] shall be
left.
35 Two *women* shall be grinding together; the [f]one [fp]shall be taken,[3880] and
the other left.
36 Two *men* shall be in the field;
the [m]one shall be taken, and the [m]other
left.
37 And they answered and said
unto him, [a]Where, Lord? And he said
unto them, Wheresoever the body *is,*
thither will the eagles[105] be gathered together.

25 [a]Mark 8:31; 9:31; 10:33; Luke 9:22
26 [a]Gen. 7; Matt. 24:37
29 [a]Gen. 19:16, 24
30 [a]2Thess. 1:7
31 [a]Matt. 24:17; Mark 13:15
32 [a]Gen. 19:26
33 [a]Matt. 10:39; 16:25; Mark 8:35; Luke 9:24; John 12:25
34 [a]Matt. 24:40, 41; 1Thess. 4:17
37 [a]Job 39:30; Matt. 24:28

1 [a]Luke 11:5; 21:36; Rom. 12:12; Eph. 6:18; Col. 4:2; 1Thess. 5:17
2 [I]Gr. *in a certain city*
5 [a]Luke 11:8
7 [a]Rev. 6:10
8 [a]Heb. 10:37; 2Pet. 3:8, 9
9 [I]Or, *as being righteous* [a]Luke 10:29; 16:15
11 [a]Ps. 135:2 [b]Isa. 1:15; 58:2; Rev. 3:17

The Importunate Widow: A Lesson in Prayer

18 And he spake a parable[3850] unto
them *to this end,* that men ought
[a]always [pinf]to pray, and not [pinf]to faint;[1573]
2 Saying, There was [I]in a city a
judge,[2923] [ppt]which feared[5399] not God,[2316]
neither [ppt]regarded[1788] man:[444]
3 And there was a widow in that
city; and she [ipf]came unto him, saying,
[aim]Avenge[1556] me of mine adversary.[476]
4 And he [ao]would not for a while:[5550]
but afterward he said within himself,
Though I fear not God, nor regard[1788]
man;
5 [a]Yet because this widow troubleth
me, I will avenge her, lestby her continual[1519,5056] [ppt]coming she [psa]weary me.
6 And the Lord[2962] said, [aim]Hear
what the unjust[93] judge saith.
🔑 7 And [a]shall not God avenge[4160,1557]
his own elect,[1588] which [ppt]cry day and
night unto him, though he [ppt]bear
long[3114] with them?
8 I tell you [a]that he will avenge them
speedily. Nevertheless when the Son of
man [apt]cometh,[2064] shall he find faith[4102]
on the earth?[1093]

The Parable of the Pharisee and The Tax Collector

9 And he spake this parable[3850] unto
certain [a]which trusted[3982] in themselves
[I]that they were righteous,[1342] and [ppt]de-
spised others:
10 Two men went up into the tem-
ple[2411] [ainf]to pray; the one a Pharisee, and
the other a publican.[5057]
11 The Pharisee [a]stood and prayed
thus with himself, [b]God, I thank[2168]
thee, that I am not as other men *are,*
extortioners,[727] unjust,[94] adulterers, or
even as this publican.
12 I fast[3522] twice in the week, I give
tithes[586] of all that I possess.
13 And the publican, [pfp]standing afar
off, [ipf]would not [ainf]lift up so much as *his*

🔑 **18:7** See note on Ephesians 1:4, 5.

eyes unto heaven,[3772] but [ipf]smote[5180] upon his breast, saying, God [aipp]be merciful[2433] to me a [art]sinner.[268]

14 I tell you, this man went down to his house [pfpp]justified[1344] *rather* than the other: [a]for every one that [ppt]exalteth himself shall be abased;[5013] and he that [ppt]humbleth himself shall be exalted.

Jesus Blesses Little Children (Matt. 19:13–15; Mark 10:13–16)

15 [a]And they [ipf]brought unto him also infants,[1025] that he [psmp]would touch them: but when *his* disciples[3101] [apt]saw *it,* they [ao]rebuked them.

16 But Jesus called them *unto him,* and said, [aim]Suffer[863] little [art]children to [pinf]come unto me, and [pim]forbid them not: for [a]of such is the kingdom[932] of God.[2316]

17 [a]Verily[281] I say unto you, Whosoever [asbm]shall not receive the kingdom of God as a little child [aosb]shall in no wise enter[1525] therein.

How to Inherit Eternal Life (Matt. 19:16–30; Mark 10:17–31)

18 [a]And a certain ruler asked him, saying, Good[18] Master, what [ft]shall I do to inherit[2816] eternal[166] life?[2222]

19 And Jesus said unto him, Why callest thou me good? none *is* good, save one, *that is,* God.[2316]

20 Thou knowest the commandments,[1785] [aosi][a]Do not commit adultery,[3431] [aosi]Do not kill,[5407] [aosi]Do not steal,[2813] [aosi]Do not bear false witness,[5576] [pim][b]Honour thy father and thy mother.

21 And he said, All these have I kept from my youth[3503] up.

22 Now when Jesus heard these things, he said unto him, Yet lackest thou one thing: [aim][a]sell all that thou hast, and [aim]distribute unto the poor, and thou shalt have treasure in heaven:[3772] and come, [pim]follow me.

23 And when he heard this, he was very sorrowful: for he was very rich.

24 And when Jesus saw that he was very sorrowful, he said, [a]How hardly shall they that [ppt]have riches[5536] enter into the kingdom[932] of God[2316]

25 For it is easier for a camel [ainf]to go through a needle's eye, than for a rich man [ainf]to enter into the kingdom of God.

26 And they that heard *it* said, Who then can [aifp]be saved?[4982]

27 And he said, [a]The things which are impossible with men are possible with God.

28 [a]Then Peter said, Lo, we [ao]have left all, and [ao]followed thee.

29 And he said unto them, Verily[281] I say unto you, [a]There is no man that [ao]hath left house, or parents, or brethren,[80] or wife, or children, for the kingdom of God's sake,

30 [a]Who [aosb]shall not receive[618] manifold more in this present time, and in the world [ppt]to come[2064] life everlasting.

Jesus Foretells His Resurrection (Matt. 20:17–19; Mark 10:32–34)

31 [a]Then he took *unto him* the twelve, and said unto them, Behold, we go up to Jerusalem, and all things that are written by the prophets[4396] concerning the Son of man shall be accomplished.

32 For [a]he shall be delivered unto the Gentiles, and shall be mocked, and spitefully entreated,[5195] and spitted on:

33 And they [apt]shall scourge[3146] *him,* and put him to death: and the third day he shall rise again.

34 [a]And they understood[4920] none of these things: and this saying was hid from them, neither [ipf]knew they the things which [ppp]were spoken.

Jesus Heals a Blind Beggar (Matt. 20:29–34; Mark 10:46–52)

35 [a]And it came to pass, that as he was [aie]come nigh[1448] unto Jericho, a certain blind man sat by the way side begging:[4319]

36 And hearing the multitude [ppt]pass by, he asked what it meant.

37 And they told him, that Jesus of Nazareth passeth by.

---

14 [a]Job 22:29; Matt. 23:12; Luke 14:11; James 4:6; 1Pet. 5:5, 6
15 [a]Matt. 19:13; Mark 10:13
16 [a]1Cor. 14:20; 1Pet. 2:2
17 [a]Mark 10:15
18 [a]Matt. 19:16; Mark 10:17
20 [a]Ex. 20:12, 16; Deut. 5:16-20; Rom. 13:9 [b]Eph. 6:2; Col. 3:20
22 [a]Matt. 6:19, 20; 19:21; 1Tim. 6:19
24 [a]Prov. 11:28; Matt. 19:23; Mark 10:23
27 [a]Jer. 32:17; Zech. 8:6; Matt. 19:26; Luke 1:37
28 [a]Matt. 19:27
29 [a]Deut. 33:9
30 [a]Job 42:10
31 [a]Matt. 16:21; 17:22; 20:17; Mark 10:32
32 [a]Matt. 27:2; 23:1; John 18:28; Acts 3:13
34 [a]Mark 9:32; Luke 2:50; 9:45; John 10:6; 12:16
35 [a]Matt. 20:29; Mark 10:46

38 And he cried, saying, Jesus, *thou* son[5207] of David, [aim]have mercy on me.

39 And they which [ppt]went before [ipf]rebuked[2008] him, that he [aosb]should hold his peace: but he [ipf]cried so much the more, *Thou* son of David, have mercy on me.

40 And Jesus stood, and commanded him [aifp]to be brought unto him: and when he [apt]was come near, he asked him,

41 Saying, What wilt thou that I shall do unto thee? And he said, Lord, that I may receive my sight.

42 And Jesus said unto him, Receive thy sight: [a]thy faith[4102] [pfi]hath saved thee.

43 And immediately he received his sight, and [ipf]followed him, [a]glorifying[1392] God: and all the people, when they saw *it,* gave praise[136] unto God.

The Conversion of Zacchaeus

19 And *Jesus* [apt]entered and [ipf]passed through Jericho.

2 And, behold, *there was* a man named Zacchaeus, which was the chief among the publicans,754 and he was rich.

3 And he [ipf]sought [ainf]to see Jesus who he was; and could not for the press,[3793] because he was little of stature.

4 And he [apt]ran before, and climbed up into a sycomore tree to see him: for he was [pinf]to pass that *way.*

5 And when Jesus came to the place, he [apt]looked up, and saw him, and said unto him, Zacchaeus, [apt]make haste, and come down; for to day I must [ainf]abide at thy house.

6 And he made haste, and came down, and received[5264] him joyfully.

7 And when they saw *it,* they all murmured, saying, [a]That he was gone [ainf]to be guest[2647] with a man that is a sinner.[268]

8 And Zacchaeus stood, and said unto the Lord; Behold, Lord, the half of my goods I give to the poor; and if I [ao]have taken any thing from any man by [a]false accusation, [b]I restore *him* fourfold.

9 And Jesus said unto him, This day [ao]is salvation come[1096] to this house,[3624] forsomuch as [a]he also is [b]a son of Abraham.

10 [a]For the Son of man [ao]is come [ainf]to seek and [ainf]to save[4982] that which [pfp]was lost.[622]

The Parable of the Ten Pounds (Matt. 25:14–30)

11 And as they [ppt]heard these things, he [apt]added4369 and spake a parable,[3850] because he [aid]was nigh to Jerusalem, and because [a]they thought that the kingdom[932] of God[2316] [pin]should immediately appear.

12 [a]He said therefore, A certain nobleman went into a far country [ainf]to receive for himself a kingdom, and [ainf]to return.

13 And he [apt]called his ten servants, and delivered them ten pounds, and said unto them, [aim]Occupy till I come.

14 [a]But his citizens [ipf]hated him, and sent a message after him, saying, We will not have this *man* [ainf]to reign over us.

15 And it came to pass, that when he [aie]was returned, having received the kingdom, then he commanded these servants to be called unto him, to whom he [ao]had

42 [a]Luke 17:19
43 [a]Luke 5:26; Acts 4:21; 11:18
7 [a]Matt. 9:11; Luke 5:30
8 [a]Luke 3:14 [b]Ex. 22:1; 1Sam. 12:3; 2Sam. 12:6
9 [a]Rom. 4:11, 12, 16; Gal. 3:7 [b]Luke 13:16
10 [a]Matt. 18:11; Matt. 10:6; 15:24
11 [a]Acts 1:6
12 [a]Matt. 25:14; Mark 13:34
14 [a]John 1:11

19:11–27 The difference between this parable and the parable of the talents in Matthew 25:14–30 is that in Luke's parable, the nobleman gave equally one pound to each person, but in the parable in Matthew, he bestowed unequal endowments. He expects the proper yield proportionate to His endowment. This is in confirmation of Paul's statement in 1 Corinthians 4:7: "and what hast thou that thou didst not receive? now if thou didst receive it, why dost thou glory as if thou hadst not received it?" All things have been received from God. None can say that he or she has received nothing. No matter how much or how little one has, it must always be remembered that it has come from God, and that every person is responsible to Him for the way he or she uses what the Lord has given.

given the [I]money, that he might know how much every man had gained by trading.

16 Then came the first, saying, Lord,[2962] thy pound [ao]hath gained ten pounds.

17 And he said unto him, Well, thou good[18] servant:[1401] because thou [aom]hast been [a]faithful in a very little, have thou authority over ten cities.

18 And the second came,[2064] saying, Lord, thy pound [ao]hath gained five pounds.

19 And he said likewise to him, Be thou also over five cities.

20 And another came, saying, Lord, behold, *here is* thy pound, which I have kept laid up in a napkin:

21 [a]For I [ipf]feared thee, because thou art an austere[840] man: thou takest up that thou [ao]layedst not down,[5087] and reapest that thou [ao]didst not sow.[4687]

22 And he saith unto him, [a]Out of thine own mouth will I judge[2919] thee, *thou* wicked[4190] servant. [b]Thou knewest that I was an austere man, [ppt]taking up that I laid not down, and reaping that I did not sow:

23 Wherefore then gavest not thou my [I]money into the bank, that at my coming I might have required mine own with usury?[5110]

24 And he said unto them that stood by, Take from him the pound, and give *it* to him that hath ten pounds.

25 (And they said unto him, Lord, he hath ten pounds.)

26 For I say unto you, [a]That unto every one which [ppt]hath shall be given; and from him that hath not, even that he [pin]hath shall be taken away from him.

27 But those mine enemies, which would not that I should [aifp]reign over them, bring hither,[5602] and slay *them* before me.

Jesus Enters Jerusalem (Matt. 21:1–11; Mark 11:1–11; John 12:12–19)

28 And when he had thus spoken, [a]he [ipf]went before, ascending up to Jerusalem.

29 [a]And it came to pass, when he [ao]was come nigh to Bethphage and Bethany, at the mount called *the mount* of Olives, he sent two of his disciples,[3101]

30 Saying, Go ye into the village over against *you;* in the which at your entering ye shall find a colt[4454] tied, whereon yet never man sat: loose him, and bring *him hither.*

31 And if any man ask[2065] you, Why do ye loose *him?* thus shall ye say unto him, Because the Lord[2962] hath need of him.

32 And they that were sent went their way, and found even as he had said unto them.

33 And as they [ppt]were loosing the colt, the owners[2962] thereof said unto them, Why loose ye the colt?

34 And they said, The Lord hath need of him.

35 And they brought him to Jesus: [a]and they cast their garments upon the colt, and they set Jesus thereon.

36 [a]And as he went, they [ipf]spread their clothes in the way.

37 And when he was come nigh, even now at[4314] the descent of the mount of Olives, the whole multitude of the disciples began to [ppt]rejoice and [pinf]praise[134] God with a loud voice for all the mighty works[1411] that they had seen;

38 Saying, [a]Blessed[2127] *be* the King[935] that cometh in the name of the Lord: [b]peace[1515] in heaven, and glory[1391] in the highest.

39 And some of the Pharisees from among the multitude said unto him, Master,[1320] rebuke thy disciples.[3101]

40 And he answered and said unto them, I tell you that, if these should hold their peace, [a]the stones would immediately cry out.

41 And when he was come near, he beheld the city, and [a]wept over it,

42 Saying, If thou hadst known, even thou, at least in this thy day, the things *which belong* unto thy peace but now they [aop]are hid from thine eyes.

43 For the days shall come upon thee, that thine enemies shall [a]cast a

15 [I]Gr. *silver*
17 [a]Matt. 25:21; Luke 16:10
21 [a]Matt. 25:24
22 [a]2Sam. 1:16; Job 15:6; Matt. 12:37 [b]Matt. 25:26
23 [I]Gr. *silver*
26 [a]Matt. 13:12; 25:29; Mark 4:25; Luke 8:18
28 [a]Mark 10:32
29 [a]Matt. 21:1; Mark 11:1
35 [a]2Kgs. 9:13; Matt. 21:7; Mark 11:7; John 12:14
36 [a]Matt. 21:8
38 [a]Ps. 118:26; Luke 13:35 [b]Luke 2:14; Eph. 2:14
40 [a]Hab. 2:11
41 [a]John 11:35
43 [a]Isa. 29:3, 4; Jer. 6:3, 6; Luke 21:20

trench about thee, and compass thee round, and [ft]keep thee in[4912] on every side,

44 And [a]shall lay thee even with the ground, and thy children within thee; and [b]they [ft]shall not leave[863] in thee one stone upon another; [c]because thou knewest not the time[2540] of thy visitation.[1984]

The Cleansing of the Temple (Matt. 21:12–17; Mark 11:15–19; John 2:13–22)

45 [a]And he went into the temple,[2411] and began [pinf]to cast out them that [ppt]sold therein, and them that [ppt]bought;

46 Saying unto them, [a]It is written, My house is the house of prayer: but [b]ye have made it a den of thieves.

47 And he taught[1321] 2258 daily in the temple. But [a]the chief priests[749] and the scribes[1122] and the chief of the people [ipf]sought [ainf]to destroy[622] him,

48 And [ipf]could not find[2147] what they might do: for all the people [ipf]I[a]were very attentive 1582 to [ppt]hear him.

Jesus' Authority Questioned (Matt. 21:23–27; Mark 11:27–33)

20 And [a]it came to pass, *that* on one of those days, as he [ppt]taught[1321] the people in the temple,[2411] and [ppt]preached the gospel,[2097] the chief priests[749] and the scribes[1122] came upon *him* with the elders,[4245]

2 And spake unto him, saying, Tell us, [a]by what authority[1849] doest thou these things? or who is he that [apt]gave thee this authority?

3 And he answered and said unto them, I [ft]will also ask[2065] you one thing, and answer me:

4 The baptism[908] of John, was it from heaven,[3772] or of men?

5 And they reasoned with themselves, saying, If we shall say, From heaven; he will say, Why then believed ye him not?

6 But and if we say, Of men; all the people will stone us: [a]for they be persuaded[3982] that John was a prophet.[4396]

7 And they answered, that they could not tell whence *it was.*

8 And Jesus said unto them, Neither tell I you by what authority I do these things.

The Parable of the Husbandmen (Matt. 21:33–46; Mark 12:1–12)

9 Then began he to speak to the people this parable;[3850] [a]A certain man planted a vineyard, and let it forth to husbandmen, 1092 and went into a far country for a long time.[5550]

10 And at the season[2540] he sent a servant[1401] to the husbandmen, that they should give him of the fruit of the vineyard: but the husbandmen [apt]beat him, and sent *him* away empty.

11 And again he sent another servant: and they beat him also, and [apt]entreated *him* shamefully, and sent *him* away empty.

12 And again he sent a third: and they [apt]wounded him also, and [ao]cast *him* out. 1544

13 Then said the lord of the vineyard, What shall I do? I will send my beloved son: it may be they will reverence 1788 *him* when they see him.

14 But when the husbandmen saw him, they [ipf]reasoned[1260] among themselves, saying, This is the heir: come, let us kill him, that the inheritance may be ours.

15 So they cast him out of the vineyard, and killed *him.* What therefore shall the lord[2962] of the vineyard do unto them?

16 He shall come and destroy these husbandmen, and shall give the vineyard to others. And when they heard *it,* they said, God forbid.[1096] 3361

17 And he [apt]beheld 1689 them, and said, What is this then that is written, [a]The [an]stone which the builders rejected,[593] the same [ao]is become the head[2776] of the corner?

18 Whosoever [apt]shall fall upon that stone shall be broken; but [a]on whomsoever it shall fall, it will grind him to powder.

44 [a]1Kgs. 9:7, 8; Mic. 3:12 [b]Matt. 24:2; Mark 13:2; Luke 21:6 [c]Dan. 9:24; Luke 1:68, 78; 1Pet. 2:12

45 [a]Matt. 21:12; Mark 11:11, 15; John 2:14, 15

46 [a]Isa. 56:7 [b]Jer. 7:11

47 [a]Mark 11:18; John 7:19; 8:37

48 IOr, *hanged on him,* [a]Acts 16:14

1 [a]Matt. 21:23

2 [a]Acts 4:7; 7:27

6 [a]Matt. 14:5; 21:26; Luke 7:29

9 [a]Matt. 21:33; Mark 12:1

17 [a]Ps. 118:22; Matt. 21:42

18 [a]Dan. 2:34, 35; Matt. 21:44

19 And the chief priests[749] and the scribes[1122] the same hour sought to lay hands on him; and they feared the people: for they perceived that he had spoken this parable against them.

Paying Tribute
(Matt. 22:15–22; Mark 12:13–17)

20 [a]And they [apt]watched[3906] *him,* and sent forth spies, which [ppt]should feign[5271] themselves just men,[1342] that they might take hold of[1949] his [sg]words,[3056] that so they might deliver him unto the power[746] and authority[1849] of the governor.

21 And they asked him, saying, [a]Master,[1320] we know that thou sayest and teachest[1321] rightly, neither acceptest thou the person *of any,* but teachest the way[3598] of God[2316] [I]truly:

22 Is it lawful for us to give tribute[5411] unto Caesar, or no?

23 But he [apt]perceived[2657] their craftiness, and said unto them, Why tempt[3985] ye me?

24 Shew me a [a]penny.[1220] Whose image[1504] and superscription hath it? They answered and said, Caesar's.

25 And he said unto them, Render therefore unto Caesar the things which be Caesar's, and unto God the things which be God's.

26 And they could not take hold of[1949] his words before the people: and they [apt]marvelled at his answer,[612] and held their peace.

Is There a Resurrection?
(Matt. 22:23–33; Mark 12:18–27)

27 [a]Then came to *him* certain of the Sadducees, [b]which [ppt]deny that there is any resurrection;[386] and they asked him,

28 Saying, Master,[1320] [a]Moses wrote unto us, If any man's brother die, having a wife, and he die without children, that his brother should take his wife, and raise up[1817] seed[4690] unto his brother.

20 [a]Matt. 22:15
21 [I]Or, *of a truth* [a]Matt. 22:16; Mark 12:14
24 [a]Matt. 18:28
27 [a]Matt. 22:23; Mark 12:18 [b]Acts 23:6, 8
28 [a]Deut. 25:5
36 [a]1Cor. 15:42, 49, 52; 1John 3:2 [b]Rom. 8:23
37 [a]Ex. 3:6
38 [a]Rom. 6:10, 11
41 [a]Matt. 22:42; Mark 12:35
42 [a]Ps. 110:1; Acts 2:34

29 There were therefore seven brethren:[80] and the first took a wife, and died[599] without children.

30 And the second took her to wife, and he died childless.

31 And the third took her; and in like manner the seven also: and they left no children, and died.

32 Last of all the woman died also.

33 Therefore in the resurrection[386] whose wife of them is she? for seven had her to wife.

34 And Jesus answering said unto them, The children of this world marry, and are given in marriage:

35 But they which [aptp]shall be accounted worthy to obtain[5177] that world, and the resurrection from the dead, neither marry, nor are given in marriage:

36 Neither can they die any more: for [a]they are equal unto the angels;[2465] and are the children of God, [b]being the children[5207] of the resurrection.

37 Now that the dead[3498] [pinp]are raised,[1453] [a]even Moses shewed at the bush, when he calleth the Lord[2962] the God of Abraham, and the God of Isaac, and the God of Jacob.

38 For he is not a God of the dead,[3498] but of the living:[2198] for [a]all live[2198] unto him.

39 Then certain of the scribes[1122] answering said, Master, thou [ao]hast well said.[2036]

40 And after that they [ipf]durst[5111] not [pinf]ask him any *question at all.*

David's Lord
(Matt. 22:41–46; Mark 12:35–37)

41 And he said unto them, [a]How say they that [art]Christ[5547] is David's son?

42 And David himself saith in the book of Psalms, [a]The LORD[2962] said unto my Lord,[2962] Sit thou on my right hand,[1188]

43 Till I make thine enemies thy footstool.

44 David therefore calleth him Lord, how is he then his son?[5207]

Jesus Denounces the Scribes (Matt. 23:1–36; Mark 12:38–40; Luke 11:37–54)

45 [a]Then in the audience of all the
people he said unto his disciples,[3101]
46 [a]Beware of the scribes,[1122] which
[ppt]desire [pinf]to walk in long robes, and
[ppt][b]love[5368] greetings in the markets, and
the highest seats in the synagogues,[4864]
and the chief rooms at feasts;
47 [a]Which devour widows' hous-
es,[3614] and for a shew make long prayers:
the same shall receive greater damnation.[2917]

The Widow's Offering (Mark 12:41–44)

21 And he [apt]looked up, [a]and saw
the rich men casting their gifts[1435]
into the treasury.
2 And he saw also a certain poor
widow casting in thither[1563] two
[a]mites.[3016]
3 And he said, Of a truth I say unto
you, [a]that this poor widow [ao]hath cast in
more than they all:
4 For all these have of their abundance[4052] cast in unto the offerings[1435] of
God: but she of her penury[5303] hath cast
in all the living[979] that she had.

The Temple Will Be Destroyed (Matt. 24:1, 2; Mark 13:1, 2)

5 [a]And as some [ppt]spake of the temple,[2411] how it [pfip]was adorned with
goodly stones and gifts,[334] he said,
6 *As for* these things which ye behold, the days will come, in the which
[a]there shall not be left one stone upon another, that shall not be thrown down.

Signs and Persecutions (Matt. 24:3–14; Mark 13:3–13)

7 And they asked him, saying,
Master,[1320] but when shall these things
be? and what sign *will there be* when
these things shall come to pass?
8 And he said, [a]Take heed[991] that ye
be not deceived: for many shall come in
my name,[3686] saying, I am *Christ;* [I][b]and
the time [pfi]draweth near: [aosi]go ye not
therefore after them.
9 But when ye shall hear of wars
and commotions,[181] [aosi]be not terrified:[4422]
for these things must first come to pass;
but the end[5056] *is* not by and by.
10 [a]Then said he unto them, Nation[1484] shall rise against nation, and
kingdom[932] against kingdom:
11 And great earthquakes shall be in
divers[2596] places, and famines, and pestilences;[3061] and fearful sights and great
signs shall there be from heaven.
12 [a]But before all these, they shall
lay their hands on you, and persecute
you, delivering *you* up to the synagogues,[4864] and [b]into prisons, [c]being
brought before kings[935] and rulers [d]for
my name's sake.
13 And [a]it shall turn to you for a
testimony.[3142]
14 [a]Settle *it* therefore in your
hearts,[2588] not to meditate before what
ye shall answer:
15 For I will give you a mouth and
wisdom, [a]which all your adversaries shall
not be able [ainf]to gainsay[471] nor resist.
16 [a]And ye shall be betrayed both by
parents, and brethren, and kinsfolks, and
friends; and [b]*some* of you shall they
cause to be put to death.
17 And [a]ye shall be hated of all *men*
for my name's sake.
18 [a]But there shall not an hair of
your head perish.
19 In your patience[5281] [aim]possess ye
your souls.[5590]

The Destruction of Jerusalem Foretold (Matt. 24:15–21; Mark 13:14–19)

20 [a]And when ye shall see Jerusalem [ppp]compassed with armies, then

45 [a]Matt. 23:1; Mark 12:38
46 [a]Matt. 23:5 [b]Luke 11:43
47 [a]Matt. 23:14
1 [a]Mark 12:41
2 [a]Mark 12:42
3 [a]2Cor. 8:12
5 [a]Matt. 24:1; Mark 13:1
6 [a]Luke 19:44
8 [a]Matt. 24:4; Mark 13:5; Eph. 5:6; 2Thess. 2:3 [I]Or, *and, The time* [b]Matt. 3:2; 4:17
10 [a]Matt. 24:7
12 [a]Mark 13:9; Rev. 2:10 [b]Acts 4:3; 5:18; 12:4; 16:24 [c]Acts 25:23 [d]1Pet. 2:13
13 [a]Phil. 1:28; 2Thess. 1:5
14 [a]Matt. 10:19; Mark 13:11; Luke 12:11
15 [a]Acts 6:10
16 [a]Mic. 7:6; Mark 13:12 [b]Acts 7:59; 12:2
17 [a]Matt. 10:22
18 [a]Matt. 10:30
20 [a]Matt. 24:15; Mark 13:14

21:1–38 See note on Matthew 24:4—25:46 concerning the Olivet Discourse.

[aim]know that the desolation thereof [pfi]is nigh.

21 Then let them which are in Judaea [pim]flee to the mountains; and let them which are in the midst of it [pim]depart out; and let not them that are in the countries [pim]enter thereinto.

22 For these be the days of vengeance,[1557] that [a]all things which are written may be fulfilled.

23 [a]But woe unto them that are with child, and to them that give suck, in those days! for there shall be great distress[318] in the land, and wrath[3709] upon this people.

24 And they [fm]shall fall[4098] by the edge of the sword, and shall be led away captive into all nations:[1484] and Jerusalem shall be trodden down[3961] of the Gentiles, [a]until the times[2540] of the Gentiles [asbp]be fulfilled.[4137]

Jesus Will Return (Matt. 24:29–31; Mark 13:24–27)

25 [a]And there shall be signs[4592] in the sun, and in the moon, and in the stars; and upon the earth[1093] distress of nations, with perplexity;[640] the sea and the waves roaring;

26 Men's hearts failing[674] them for fear,[5401] and for looking after[4329] those things which are coming on the earth:[3625] [a]for the powers[1411] of heaven[3772] shall be shaken.

27 And then shall they see the Son of man [a]coming in a cloud with power and great glory.[1391]

28 And when these things begin to come to pass, then look up,[352] and lift up[1869] your heads; for [a]your redemption[629] draweth nigh.[1448]

The Parable of the Fig Tree (Matt. 24:32–35; Mark 13:28–31)

29 [a]And he spake to them a parable;[3850] Behold the fig tree, and all the trees;

30 When they now [aosb]shoot forth, ye [ppt]see and know of your own selves that summer is now nigh at hand.[1451]

31 So likewise ye, when ye [aosb]see these things [ppt]come to pass, know ye that the kingdom[932] of God[2316] is nigh at hand.

32 Verily[281] I say unto you, This generation[1074] [aosb]shall not pass away,[3928] till all [asbm]be fulfilled.[1096]

33 [a]Heaven and earth[1093] shall pass away: but my words[3056] shall not pass away.

Be Watchful

34 And [a]take heed to yourselves, lest at any time your hearts be overcharged with surfeiting,[2897] and drunkenness,[3178] and cares of this life, and *so* that day come upon you unawares.[160]

35 For [a]as a snare[3803] shall it come on all them that [ppt]dwell on the face[4383] of the whole earth.

36 [pim][a]Watch ye therefore, and [ppt][b]pray[1189] always, that ye may be accounted worthy to escape all these things that shall come to pass, and [c]to stand before the Son of man.

37 [a]And in the day time he was teaching[1321] in the temple;[2411] and [b]at night he [ppt]went out, and abode in the mount that is called *the mount* of Olives.

38 And all the people [ipf]came early in the morning to him in the temple, for [pinf]to hear him.

Passover Is Near (Matt. 26:1–5, 14–16; Mark 14:1, 2, 10, 11; John 11:45–53)

22 Now [a]the feast of unleavened bread[106] [ipf]drew nigh, which is called the Passover.[3957]

2 And [a]the chief priests[749] and scribes[1122] [ipf]sought how they [aosb]might kill him; for they [ipf]feared[5399] the people.

3 [a]Then entered Satan[4567] into Judas surnamed Iscariot, being of the number of the twelve.

22 [a]Dan. 9:26; 27; Zech. 11:1
23 [a]Matt. 24:19
24 [a]Dan. 9:27; 12:7; Rom. 11:25
25 [a]Matt. 24:29; Mark 13:24; 2Pet. 3:10, 12
26 [a]Matt. 24:29
27 [a]Matt. 24:30; Rev. 1:7; 14:14
28 [a]Rom. 8:10, 23
29 [a]Matt. 24:32; Mark 13:28
33 [a]Matt. 24:35
34 [a]Rom. 13:13; 1Thess. 5:6; 1Pet. 4:7
35 [a]1Thess. 5:2; 2Pet. 3:10; Rev. 3:3; 16:15
36 [a]Matt. 24:42; 25:13; Mark 13:33 [b]Luke 18:1 [c]Ps. 1:5; Eph. 6:13
37 [a]John 8:1, 2 [b]Luke 22:39
1 [a]Matt. 26:2; Mark 14:1
2 [a]Ps. 2:2; John 11:47; Acts 4:27
3 [a]Matt. 26:14; Mark 14:10; John 13:2, 27

4 And he went his way, and communed with the chief priests and captains, how he might betray him unto them.

5 And they were glad, and [a]covenanted to give him money.

6 And he promised,[1843] and [ipf]sought opportunity[2120] to betray him unto them [I]in the absence of the multitude.

The Preparation of the Passover (Matt. 26:17–25; Mark 14:12–21; John 13:21–30)

7 [a]Then came[2064] the day of unleavened bread,[106] when the passover$_{3957}$ must be killed.

8 And he sent Peter and John, saying, [aptp]Go and [aim]prepare us the passover, that we may eat.

9 And they said unto him, Where wilt thou that we prepare?

10 And he said unto them, Behold, when ye are entered into the city, there shall a man meet you, bearing a pitcher of water; follow him into the house where he entereth in.

11 And ye shall say unto the goodman of the house,[3614] The Master[1320] saith unto thee, Where is the guestchamber, where I shall eat the passover with my disciples?[3101]

12 And he shall shew you a large upper room furnished: there make ready.

13 And they went, and found as he had said unto them: and they made ready the passover.

The True Meaning Of the Passover Meal (Matt. 26:26–30; Mark 14:22–26; 1 Cor. 11:23–25)

14 [a]And when the hour was come, he sat down, and the twelve apostles[652] with him.

15 And he said unto them, [I]With desire I [ao]have desired[1937] to eat this passover with you before I suffer:

16 For I say unto you, I [aosb]will not any more eat$_{5315}$ thereof, [a]until it be fulfilled in the kingdom[932] of God.[2316]

17 And he [apt]took the [an]cup, and [apt]gave thanks, and said, Take this, and divide *it* among yourselves:

18 For [a]I say unto you, I [aosb]will not drink$_{4095}$ of the fruit of the vine, until the kingdom of God shall come.

19 [a]And he [apt]took bread, and [apt]gave thanks, and brake *it,* and gave unto them, saying, This is my body[4983] which is [ppp]given for you: [b]this [pim]do in remembrance[364] of me.

20 Likewise also the cup after supper, saying, [a]This cup *is* the new testament[1242] in my blood,[129] which [ppt]is shed$_{1632}$ for you.

21 [a]But, behold, the hand of him that [ppt]betrayeth me *is* with me on the table.

22 [a]And truly the Son of man goeth, [b]as it [pfpp]was determined:[3724] but woe unto that man by whom he is betrayed!

23 [a]And they began to enquire among themselves, which of them it was that should [pinf]do[4238] this thing.

Who Is the Greatest?

🔑 24 [a]And there was also a strife among them, which of them should be accounted the greatest.

25 [a]And he said unto them, The kings of the Gentiles exercise lordship over them; and they that [ppt]exercise authority upon them are called benefactors.

26 [a]But ye *shall* not *be* so: [b]but he that is greatest among you, let him be as the younger; and he that [ppt]is chief,[2233] as he that [ppt]doth serve.

27 [a]For whether *is* greater, he that [ppt]sitteth at meat,$_{345}$ or he that [ppt]serveth? *is* not he that sitteth at meat? but [b]I am among you as he that serveth.

5 [a]Zech. 11:12
6 [I]Or, without tumult
7 [a]Matt. 26:17; Mark 14:12
14 [a]Matt. 26:20; Mark 14:17
15 [I]Or, *I have heartily desired*
16 [a]Luke 14:15; Acts 10:41; Rev. 19:9
18 [a]Matt. 26:29; Mark 14:25
19 [a]Matt. 26:26; Mark 14:22 [b]1Cor. 11:24
20 [a]1Cor. 10:16
21 [a]Ps. 41:9; Matt. 26:21, 23; Mark 14:18; John 13:21, 26
22 [a]Matt. 26:24 [b]Acts 2:23; 4:28
23 [a]Matt. 26:22; John 13:22, 25
24 [a]Mark 9:34; Luke 9:46
25 [a]Matt. 20:25; Mark 10:42
26 [a]Matt. 20:26; 1Pet. 5:3 [b]Luke 9:48
27 [a]Luke 12:37 [b]Matt. 20:28; John 13:13, 14; Phil. 2:7

🔑 **22:24–34** See note on 1 Peter 2:17.

28 Ye are they which [pfp]have continued with[3326] me in [a]my temptations.[3986]

29 And [a]I appoint[1303] unto you a kingdom,[932] as my Father hath appointed unto me;

30 That [a]ye [psa]may eat and [psa]drink at my table in my kingdom, [b]and sit on thrones judging the twelve tribes of Israel.

Peter's Denial Foretold (Matt. 26:31–35; Mark 14:27–31; John 13:36–38)

31 And the Lord[2962] said, Simon, Simon, behold,2400 [a]Satan[4567] [aom]hath desired[1809] *to have* you, that he may [infg][b]sift *you* as wheat:

32 But [a]I [aop]have prayed[1189] for thee, that thy faith[4102] [aosb]fail1587 not: [b]and when thou [apt]art converted,[1994] strengthen thy brethren.

33 And he said unto him, Lord,[2962] I am ready [pinf]to go with thee, both into prison,[5438] and to death.[2288]

34 [a]And he said, I tell thee, Peter, the cock shall not crow this day, before that thou shalt thrice deny that thou knowest me.

Christ's Servants Will Lack Nothing

35 [a]And he said unto them, When I sent you without purse, and scrip,4082 and shoes, lacked ye any thing? And they said, Nothing.

36 Then said he unto them, But now, he that hath a purse, let him take *it,* and likewise *his* scrip: and he that hath no sword, let him sell his garment, and buy one.

37 For I say unto you, that this that is written must yet [aifp]be accomplished[5055] in me, [a]And he [aop]was reckoned[3049] among the [an]transgressors:[459] for the things concerning me have an end.[5056]

38 And they said, Lord, behold, here *are* two swords. And he said unto them, It is enough.[2425]

Jesus' Prayer on the Mount of Olives (Matt. 26:36–46; Mark 14:32–42)

39 [a]And he came out, and [b]went, as he was wont,[2596] 1485 to the mount of Olives; and his disciples also followed him.

40 [a]And when he was at the place, he said unto them, [pim]Pray that ye [ainf]enter not into temptation.[3986]

41 [a]And he was withdrawn from them about a stone's cast, and kneeled down, and [ipf]prayed,

42 Saying, Father,[3962] if thou be willing, [aim]remove this cup from me: nevertheless [a]not my will,[2307] but thine, be done.

43 And there appeared [a]an angel[32] unto him from heaven,[3772] strengthening him.

44 [a]And being in an agony[74] he [ipf]prayed more earnestly:1617 and his sweat was as it were great drops of blood falling down to the ground.

45 And when he rose up from prayer, and was come to his disciples,[3101] he found them sleeping for sorrow,

46 And said unto them, Why sleep ye? [apt]rise and [pima]pray, lest ye [aosb]enter into temptation.[3986]

Judas Betrays the Lord (Matt. 26:47–56; Mark 14:43–50; John 18:3–11)

47 And while he yet spake, [a]behold a multitude, and he that was called Judas, one of the twelve, went before them, and drew near[1448] unto Jesus [ainf]to kiss[5368] him.

48 But Jesus said unto him, Judas, betrayest thou the Son of man with a kiss?

49 When they which were about him saw what would follow, they said unto him, Lord, shall we smite with the sword?

50 And [a]one of them smote the servant of the high priest, and cut off his right ear.

51 And Jesus answered and said, Suffer ye thus far. And he [apt]touched his ear, and healed[2390] him.

28 [a]Heb. 4:15
29 [a]Matt. 24:47; Luke 12:32; 2Cor. 1:7; 2Tim. 2:12
30 [a]Matt. 8:11; Luke 14:15; Rev. 19:9 [b]Ps. 49:14; Matt. 19:28; 1Cor. 6:2; Rev. 3:21
31 [a]1Pet. 5:8 [b]Amos 9:9
32 [a]John 17:9, 11, 15 [b]Ps. 51:13; John 21:15-17
34 [a]Matt. 26:34; Mark 14:30; John 13:38
35 [a]Matt. 10:9; Luke 9:3; 10:4
37 [a]Isa. 53:12; Mark 15:28
39 [a]Matt. 26:36; Mark 14:32; John 18:1 [b]Luke 21:37
40 [a]Matt. 6:13; 26:41; Mark 14:38; Luke 22:46
41 [a]Matt. 26:39; Mark 14:35
42 [a]John 5:30; 6:38
43 [a]Matt. 4:11
44 [a]John 12:27; Heb. 5:7
46 [a]Luke 22:40
47 [a]Matt. 26:47; Mark 14:43; John 18:3
50 [a]Matt. 26:51; Mark 14:47; John 18:10

52 [a]Then Jesus said unto the chief priests,[749] and captains of the temple,[2411] and the elders,[4245] which [apt]were come to him, [pfi]Be ye come out,[1831] as against a thief,[3027] with swords and staves?[3586]

53 When I was daily with you in the temple, ye stretched forth no hands against me: [a]but this is your hour, and the power[1849] of darkness.[4655]

Peter's Denial of Jesus (Matt. 26:57, 58, 69–75; Mark 14:53, 54, 66–72; John 18:12–18, 25–27)

54 [a]Then took they him, and led *him,* and brought him into the high priest's[749] house. [b]And Peter [ipf]followed afar off.

55 [a]And when they had kindled a fire in the midst of the hall, and were set down together, Peter sat down among them.

56 But a certain maid beheld him as he [ppt]sat[2521] by the fire, and [apt]earnestly looked[816] upon him, and said, This man was also with him.

57 And he denied[720] him, saying, Woman, I know[1492] him not.

58 [a]And after a little while another saw him, and said, Thou art also of them. And Peter said, Man, I am not.

59 [a]And about the space of one hour after another [ipf]confidently affirmed, saying, Of a truth this *fellow* also was with him: for he is a Galilaean.

60 And Peter said, Man, I know[1492] not what thou sayest. And immediately, while he yet [ppt]spake, the cock crew.

61 And the Lord turned, and looked upon[1689] Peter. [a]And Peter remembered the word[3056] of the Lord, how he had said unto him, [b]Before the cock [ainf]crow, thou [fm]shalt deny[533] me thrice.

62 And Peter went out, and wept bitterly.

Mocking and Beating of Jesus (Matt. 26:67, 68; Mark 14:65)

63 [a]And the men that [ppt]held[4912] Jesus [ipf]mocked him, and [ppt]smote *him.*

64 And when they had blindfolded him, they [ipf]struck[5180] him on the face, and [ipf]asked him, saying, Prophesy,[4395] who is it that [apt]smote thee?

65 And many other things [ppt]blasphemously[987] [ipf]spake they against him.

Jesus Before the Council (Matt. 26:59–66; Mark 14:55–64; John 18:19–24)

66 [a]And as soon as it was day, [b]the elders[4244] of the people and the chief priests[749] and the scribes[1122] came together, and led him into their council, saying,

67 [a]Art thou the Christ?[5547] tell us. And he said unto them, If I tell you, ye [aosb]will not believe:[4100]

68 And if I also ask *you,* ye will not answer me, nor let *me* go.

69 [a]Hereafter shall the Son of man [ppt]sit on the right hand[1188] of the power[1411] of God.[2316]

70 Then said they all, Art thou then the Son[5207] of God?[2316] And he said unto them, [a]Ye say that I am.

71 [a]And they said, What need we any further witness?[3141] for we ourselves [ao]have heard[191] of his own mouth.

Jesus Brought Before Pilate (Matt. 27:1, 2, 11–14; Mark 15:1–5; John 18:28–38)

23 And [a]the whole multitude of them [apt]arose, and [ao]led him unto Pilate.

2 And they began [pinf]to accuse him, saying, We found this *fellow* [a]perverting the nation, and [b]forbidding [pinf]to give tribute[5411] to Caesar, saying [c]that he himself is Christ[5547] a King.[935]

3 [a]And Pilate asked him, saying, Art thou the King of the Jews? And he answered him and said, Thou sayest *it.*

4 Then said Pilate to the chief priests and *to* the people, [a]I find no fault in this man.

5 And they [ipf]were the more fierce, saying, He stirreth up the people, teach-

52 [a]Matt. 26:55; Mark 14:48
53 [a]John 12:27
54 [a]Matt. 26:57 [b]Matt. 26:58; John 18:15
55 [a]Matt. 26:69; Mark 14:66; John 18:17, 18
58 [a]Matt. 26:71; Mark 14:69; John 18:25
59 [a]Matt. 26:73; Mark 14:70; John 18:26
61 [a]Matt. 26:75; Mark 14:72 [b]Matt. 26:34, 75; John 13:38
63 [a]Matt. 26:67, 68; Mark 14:65
66 [a]Matt. 27:1 [b]Acts 4:26; 22:5
67 [a]Matt. 26:63; Mark 14:61
69 [a]Matt. 26:64; Mark 14:62; Heb. 1:3; 8:1
70 [a]Matt. 26:64; Mark 14:62
71 [a]Matt. 26:65; Mark 14:63
1 [a]Matt. 27:2; Mark 15:1; John 18:28
2 [a]Acts 17:7 [b]Matt. 17:27; 22:21; Mark 12:17 [c]John 19:12
3 [a]Matt. 27:11; 1Tim. 6:13
4 [a]1Pet. 2:22

ing throughout[2596] all Jewry, beginning from Galilee to this place.

Jesus Before Herod

6 When Pilate heard of Galilee, he asked whether the man were a Galilaean.

7 And as soon as he knew that he belonged unto [a]Herod's jurisdiction,[1849] he sent him to Herod, who himself also was at Jerusalem at that time.

8 And when Herod saw Jesus, he was exceeding glad: for [a]he was desirous[2309] to see him of a long *season,* because [b]he [aid]had heard many things of him; and he [ipf]hoped[1679] to have seen some miracle[4592] [ppt]done by him.

9 Then he [ipf]questioned with him in many words; but he answered him nothing.

10 And the chief priests[749] and scribes[1122] stood and vehemently2159 [ppt]accused him.

11 [a]And Herod with his men of war [apt]set him at nought,1848 and mocked *him,* and arrayed him in a gorgeous robe, and sent him again to Pilate.

12 And the same day [a]Pilate and Herod were made friends together: for before they were at enmity2189 between themselves.

Jesus Sentenced to Die (Matt. 27:15–26; Mark 15:6–15; John 18:39–19:16)

13 [a]And Pilate, when he had called together[4779] the chief priests and the rulers[758] and the people,

14 Said unto them, [a]Ye [ao]have brought this man unto4374 me, as one that [ppt]perverteth[654] the people: and, behold, [b]I, [apt]having examined *him* before you, have found no fault in this man touching those things whereof ye accuse him:

15 No, nor yet Herod: for I sent you to him; and, lo, nothing worthy of death[2288] is done unto him.

16 [a]I will therefore [apt]chastise[3811] him, and release *him.*

17 ([a]For of necessity[318] he [ipf]must [pinf]release one unto them at the feast.)

18 And [a]they cried out all at once, saying, [pim]Away with this *man,* and release[630] unto us Barabbas:

19 (Who for a certain sedition[4714] [apt]made in the city, and for murder, [pfpp]was cast into prison.)

20 Pilate therefore, willing to release Jesus, spake again to them.

21 But they [ipf]cried, saying, Crucify[4717] *him,* crucify him.

22 And he said unto them the third time, Why, what evil [ao]hath he done?[4160] I have found no cause of death in him: I will therefore chastise him, and let *him* go.

23 And they [ipf]were instant with loud voices, requiring that he [aifp]might be crucified. And the voices of them and of the chief priests [ipf]prevailed.2729

24 And [a]Pilate [1b]gave sentence that it should be as they required.[155]

25 And he released unto them him that for sedition and murder [pfpp]was cast into prison, whom they [ipf]had desired; but he delivered Jesus to their will.[2307]

The Way to the Cross (Matt. 27:32–44; Mark 15:21–32; John 19:17–27)

26 [a]And as they led him away, they laid hold upon[1949] one Simon, a Cyrenian, coming out of the country, and on him they laid the cross,[4716] that he might bear *it* after Jesus.

27 And there [ipf]followed him a great company of people, and of women, which also [ipf]bewailed[2875] and [ipf]lamented[2354] him.

28 But Jesus turning unto them said, Daughters of Jerusalem, [pim]weep not for me, but [pim]weep for yourselves, and for your children.[5043]

29 [a]For, behold, the days[2250] are coming, in the which they shall say, Blessed[3107] *are* the barren, and the

7 [a]Luke 3:1
8 [a]Luke 9:9 [b]Matt. 14:1; Mark 6:14
11 [a]Isa. 53:3
12 [a]Acts 4:27
13 [a]Matt. 27:23; Mark 15:14; John 18:38; 19:4
14 [a]Luke 23:1, 2 [b]Luke 23:4
16 [a]Matt. 27:26; John 19:1
17 [a]Matt. 27:15; Mark 15:6; John 18:39
18 [a]Acts 3:14
24 [1]Or, *assented* [a]Matt. 27:26; Mark 15:15; John 19:16 [b]Ex. 23:2
26 [a]Matt. 27:32; Mark 15:21; John 19:17
29 [a]Matt. 24:19; Luke 21:23

wombs that never bare,[1080] and the paps3149 which never gave suck.

30 [a]Then shall they begin to say to the mountains, [aim]Fall[4098] on us; and to the hills, [aim]Cover[2572] us.

31 [a]For if they do these things in a green tree, what shall be done in the dry?

32 [a]And there were also two other, malefactors,[2557] [ipf]led with him [aifp]to be put to death.

33 And [a]when they were come to the place, which is called [I]Calvary, there they crucified[4717] him, and the malefactors, one on the right hand, and the other on the left.

34 Then [ipf]said Jesus, Father,[3962] [aim][a]forgive[863] them; for [b]they know[1492] not what they do.[4160] And [c]they [ppt]parted his raiment,[2440] and [ao]cast lots.

35 And [a]the people stood beholding.[2334] And the [b]rulers also with them [ipf]derided *him,* saying, He saved[4982] others; [aim]let him save[4982] himself, if he be Christ,[5547] the chosen of God.[2316]

36 And the soldiers also [ipf]mocked him, coming to him, and offering him vinegar,

37 And saying, If thou be the king[935] of the Jews, save[4982] thyself.

38 [a]And a superscription also was written over him in letters[1121] of Greek, and Latin, and Hebrew, THIS IS THE KING[935] OF THE JEWS.

39 [a]And one of the malefactors which [aptp]were hanged [ipf]railed on him, saying, If thou be Christ,[5547] save[4982] thyself and us.

40 But the other answering [ipf]rebuked[2008] him, saying, Dost not thou fear God, seeing thou art in the same condemnation?[2917]

41 And we indeed justly;[1346] for we receive618 the due reward of our deeds but this man [ao]hath done[4238] nothing amiss.824

42 And he [ipf]said unto Jesus, Lord,[2962] [aipp]remember me when thou [aosb]comest into thy kingdom.[932]

43 And Jesus said unto him, Verily281 I say unto thee, To day shalt thou be with me in paradise.3857

The Death of Jesus (Matt. 27:45–56; Mark 15:33–41; John 19:28–30)

44 [a]And it was about the sixth hour, and there was a darkness[4655] over all the [I]earth[1093] until the ninth hour.

45 And the sun was darkened, and [a]the veil of the temple[3485] [aop]was rent4977 in the midst.

46 And when Jesus had cried with a loud voice, he said, [a]Father, into thy hands I commend[3908] my spirit:[4151] [b]and having said thus, he gave up the ghost.1606

47 [a]Now when the centurion1543 saw what [apt]was done, he glorified[1392] God, saying, Certainly this was a righteous[1342] man.

48 And all the people that [apt]came together to that sight,2335 beholding[2334] the things which were done, [ppt]smote[5180] their breasts,4738 and [ipf]returned.

49 [a]And all his acquaintance,[1110] and the women that followed him from Galilee, stood afar off, beholding these things.

The Burial of Jesus (Matt. 27:57–61; Mark 15:42–47; John 19:38–42)

50 [a]And, behold, *there was* a man named Joseph, a counselor;1010 *and he was* a good[18] man, and a just:[1342]

51 (The same had not consented to the counsel[1012] and deed4234 of them;) *he was* of Arimathaea, a city of the Jews: [a]who also himself waited for[4327] the kingdom[932] of God.[2316]

52 This *man* went unto Pilate, and begged the body of Jesus.

53 [a]And he took it down, and wrapped it in linen, and laid it in a

30 [a]Isa. 2:19; Hos. 10:8; Rev. 6:16; 9:6

31 [a]Prov. 11:31; Jer. 25:29; Ezek. 20:47; 21:3, 4; 1Pet. 4:17

32 [a]Isa. 53:12; Matt. 27:38

33 [I]Or, *The place of a skull* [a]Matt. 27:33; Mark 15:22; John 19:17, 18

34 [a]Matt. 5:44; Acts 7:60; 1Cor. 4:12 [b]Acts 3:17 [c]Matt. 27:35; Mark 15:24; John 19:23

35 [a]Ps. 22:17; Zech. 12:10 [b]Matt. 27:39; Mark 15:29

38 [a]Matt. 27:37; Mark 15:26; John 19:19

39 [a]Matt. 27:44; Mark 15:32

44 [I]Or, *land* [a]Matt. 27:45; Mark 15:33

45 [a]Matt. 27:51; Mark 15:38

46 [a]Ps. 31:5; 1Pet. 2:23 [b]Matt. 27:50; Mark 15:37; John 19:30

47 [a]Matt. 27:54; Mark 15:39

49 [a]Ps. 38:11; Matt. 27:55; Mark 15:40; John 19:25

50 [a]Matt. 27:57; Mark 15:42; John 19:38

51 [a]Mark 15:43; Luke 2:25, 38

53 [a]Matt. 27:59; Mark 15:46

23:43 See note on 2 Corinthians 12:1–10.

sepulchre3418 that was hewn in stone,2991 wherein never man before was laid.

54 And that day was [a]the preparation, and the sabbath4521 [ipf]drew on.

55 And the women also, [a]which came with him from Galilee, [apt]followed after, and [b]beheld the sepulchre,3419 and how his body was laid.

56 And they returned, and [a]prepared spices and ointments; and rested[2270] the sabbath day4521 [b]according to the commandment.[1785]

The Resurrection of Jesus
(Matt. 28:1–10; Mark 16:1–8; John 20:1–10)

24 Now [a]upon the first *day* of the week, very early in the morning, they came unto the sepulchre,3418 [b]bringing the spices which they [ao]had prepared, and certain *others* with them.

2 [a]And they found the stone [pfpp]rolled away from the sepulchre.3419

3 [a]And they entered in, and found not the body of the Lord Jesus.

4 And it came to pass, as they [aie]were much perplexed thereabout, [a]behold, two men stood by them in shining garments:

5 And as they [apt]were afraid, and [ppt]bowed down *their* faces to the earth, they said unto them, Why seek ye [1]the living[2198] among the dead?[3498]

6 He is not here, but [aop]is risen:[1453] [aipp][a]remember how he spake unto you when he was yet in Galilee,

7 Saying, the Son of man must [aifp]be delivered into the hands of sinful[268] men,[444] and [aifp]be crucified,[4717] and the third day [ainf]rise again.[450]

8 And [a]they remembered his words,[4487]

9 [a]And returned from the sepulchre,3419 and told all these things unto the eleven, and to all the rest.

10 It was Mary Magdalene, and [a]Joanna, and Mary *the mother* of James, and other *women that were* with them, which [ipf]told these things unto the apostles.[652]

11 [a]And their words seemed[5316] to them as idle tales, and they [ipf]believed them not.[569]

12 [a]Then arose Peter, and ran unto the sepulchre; and [apt]stooping down,3879 he beheld the linen clothes [ppt]laid[2749] by themselves, and departed, wondering in himself at that which [pfp]was come to pass.[1096]

The Road to Emmaus
(Mark 16:12, 13)

13 [a]And, behold, two of them went that same day to a village called3686 Emmaus, which was from Jerusalem *about* threescore furlongs.4712

14 And they [ipf]talked together of all these things which [pfp]had happened.

15 And it came to pass, that, while they [aie]communed *together* and [aie]reasoned, [a]Jesus himself [apt]drew near, and [ipf]went with them.

16 But [a]their eyes [ipf]were holden[2902] that they [infg]should not know1921 him.

17 And he said unto them, What manner of communications[3056] *are* these that ye have one to another, as ye [ppt]walk, and are sad?

18 And the one of them, [a]whose name was Cleopas, answering said unto him, Art thou only a stranger[3939] in Jerusalem, and [ao]hast not known[1097] the things which are [apt]come to pass there in these days?

19 And he said unto them, What things? And they said unto him, Concerning Jesus of Nazareth, [a]which was a prophet[4396] [b]mighty in deed[2041] and word[3056] before God and all the people:

20 [a]And how the chief priests and our rulers delivered him to be condemned[2917] to death,[2288] and [ao]have crucified[4717] him.

21 But we [ipf]trusted[1679] [a]that it had been he which [ppt]should have [pinf]redeemed[3084] Israel: and beside[4862] all this, to day is[71] the third day since these things were done.

22 Yea, and [a]certain women also of

54 [a]Matt. 27:62
55 [a]Luke 8:2 [b]Mark 15:47
56 [a]Mark 16:1 [b]Ex. 20:10
1 [a]Matt. 28:1; Mark 16:1; John 20:1 [b]Luke 23:56
2 [a]Matt. 28:2; Mark 16:4
3 [a]Mark 16:5; Luke 24:23
4 [a]John 20:12; Acts 1:10
5 [1]Or, *him that liveth*
6 [a]Matt. 16:21; 17:23; Mark 8:31; 9:31; Luke 9:22
8 [a]John 2:22
9 [a]Matt. 28:8; Mark 16:10
10 [a]Luke 8:3
11 [a]Mark 16:11; Luke 24:25
12 [a]John 20:3, 6
13 [a]Mark 16:12
15 [a]Matt. 18:20; Luke 24:36
16 [a]John 20:14; 21:4
18 [a]John 19:25
19 [a]Matt. 21:11; Luke 7:16; John 3:2; 4:19; 6:14; Acts 2:22 [b]Acts 7:22
20 [a]Luke 23:1; Acts 13:27, 28
21 [a]Luke 1:68; 2:38; Acts 1:6
22 [a]Matt. 28:8; Mark 16:10; Luke 24:9, 10; John 20:18

our company [ao]made us astonished,[1839] which were early at the sepulchre;[3419]

23 And when they found not his body, they came, saying, that they [pfin]had also seen[3708] a vision of angels,[32] which said that he [pinf]was alive.[2198]

24 And [a]certain of them which were with us went to the sepulchre, and found *it* even so as the women had said: but him they saw[1492] not.

25 Then he said unto them, O fools,[453] and slow[1021] of heart [infg]to believe[4100] all that the prophets[4396] [ao]have spoken:

26 [a]Ought not Christ[5547] [ainf]to have suffered these things, and [ainf]to enter into his glory?[1391]

27 [a]And beginning at [b]Moses and [c]all the prophets, he [ipf]expounded[1329] unto them in all the scriptures[1124] the things concerning himself.

28 And they drew nigh unto the village, whither they [ipf]went: and [a]he [ipf]made as though he would have [pinf]gone further.

29 But [a]they constrained him, saying, Abide with[3326] us: for it is toward[4314] evening, and the day [pfi]is far spent. And he went in [infg]to tarry with them.

30 And it came to pass, as he sat at meat[2625] with them, [a]he [apt]took bread, and blessed *it,* and [apt]brake, and [ipf]gave to them.

31 And their eyes were opened, and they knew him; and he [Ia]vanished out of their sight.

32 And they said one to another, Did not our heart[2588] burn within us, while he [ipf]talked with us by the way, and while he [ipf]opened to us the scriptures?

33 And they rose up the same hour, and returned to Jerusalem, and found the eleven gathered together, and them that were with them,

34 Saying, The Lord [aop]is risen[1453] indeed, and [aopa]hath appeared to Simon.

35 And they [ipf]told[1834] what things *were done* in the way, and how he [aop]was known[1097] of them in breaking[2800] of bread.

24 [a]Luke 24:12

26 [a]Luke 24:46; Acts 17:3; 1Pet. 1:11

27 [a]Luke 24:45 [b]Gen. 3:15; 22:18; 26:4; 49:10; Num. 21:9; Deut. 18:15 [c]Ps. 16:9, 10; 22; 132:11; Isa. 7:14; 9:6; 40:10, 11; 50:6; 53; Jer. 23:5; 33:14, 15; Ezek. 34:23; 37:25; Dan. 9:24; Mic. 7:20; Mal. 3:1; 4:2; John 1:45

28 [a]Gen. 32:26; 42:7; Mark 6:48

29 [a]Gen. 19:3; Acts 16:15

30 [a]Matt. 14:19

31 [I]Or, *ceased to be seen of them* [a]Luke 4:30; John 8:59

34 [a]1Cor. 15:5

36 [a]Mark 16:14; John 20:19; 1Cor. 15:5

37 [a]Mark 6:49

39 [a]John 20:20, 27

41 [a]Gen. 45:26 [b]John 21:5

43 [a]Acts 10:41

44 [a]Matt. 16:21; 17:22; 20:18; Mark 8:31; Luke 9:22; 18:31; Luke 24:6

45 [a]Acts 16:14

46 [a]Luke 24:26; Isa. 50:6; 53:2-12; Acts 17:3

47 [a]Dan. 9:24; Acts 13:38, 46; 1John 2:12 [b]Gen. 12:3; Ps. 22:27; Isa. 49:6, 22; Jer. 31:34; Hos. 2:23; Mic. 4:2; Mal. 1:11

48 [a]John 15:27; Acts 1:8, 22; 2:32; 3:15

49 [a]Isa. 44:3; Joel 2:28; John 14:16, 26; 15:26; 16:7; Acts 1:4; 2:1-4

Jesus Appears to the Disciples (Matt. 28:16–20; Mark 16:14–18; John 20:19–23; Acts 1:6–8)

36 [a]And as they thus [ppt]spake, Jesus himself stood in the midst of them, and saith unto them, Peace[1515] *be* unto you.

37 But they [aptp]were terrified and affrighted,[1719] and [ipf]supposed that they [pinf]had seen a [a]spirit.[4151]

38 And he said unto them, Why are ye troubled? and why do thoughts[1261] arise in your hearts?[2588]

39 Behold my hands and my feet, that it is I myself: [a]handle[5584] me, and see; for a spirit[4151] hath not flesh[4561] and bones, as ye see me have.

40 And when he had thus spoken, he shewed them *his* hands and *his* feet.

41 And while they yet [ppt]believed not[569] [a]for joy, and [ppt]wondered, he said unto them, [b]Have ye here any meat?

42 And they gave him a piece of a broiled fish, and of an honeycomb.

43 [a]And he took *it,* and did eat before them.

44 And he said unto them, [a]These *are* the words[3056] which I spake unto you, while I was yet with you, that all things must [aifp]be fulfilled,[4137] which [pfpp]were written in the law[3551] of Moses, and *in* the prophets,[4396] and *in* the psalms,[5568] concerning me.

45 Then [a]opened he their understanding,[3563] that they [infg]might understand[4920] the scriptures,[1124]

46 And said unto them, [a]Thus [pfip]it is written,[1125] and thus it behoved[1163] Christ[5547] [aifp]to suffer,[3958] and [ainf]to rise[450] from the dead[3498] the third day:

47 And that repentance[3341] and [a]remission[859] of sins [aifp]should be preached[2784] in his name [b]among all nations, beginning at Jerusalem.

48 And [a]ye are witnesses of these things.

49 [a]And, behold, I send the promise[1860] of my Father upon you: but [aim]tarry ye in the city of Jerusalem, until ye [asbm]be endued with power from on high.

The Ascension of Jesus (Mark 16:19, 20; Acts 1:9–11)

50 And he [ao]led[1806] them out [a]as far
as to Bethany, and he [apt]lifted up[1869] his
hands, and blessed them.
51 [a]And it came to pass, while
he [aie]blessed them, he [ao]was parted
from them, and [ipf]carried up[399] into
heaven.[3772]
52 [a]And they [apt]worshipped him, and
[ao]returned to Jerusalem with great joy:
53 And were continually [a]in the
temple,[2411] praising[134] and blessing[2127]
God. Amen.[281]

50 [a]Acts 1:12
51 [a]2Kgs. 2:11; Mark 16:19; John 20:17; Acts 1:9; Eph. 4:8
52 [a]Matt. 28:9, 17
53 [a]Acts 2:46; 5:42

The Gospel According to

JOHN

The Apostle John is believed to have written this book about the year A.D. 90 in the city of Ephesus in Asia. John's name is never mentioned in the book, but it is assumed that he is referring to himself when he speaks of the disciple "whom Jesus loved" and who leaned against the bosom of Jesus (John 13:23; 20:2). He and the Apostle James were the sons of Zebedee, but Jesus surnamed them the "sons of thunder" (Mark 3:17) and included them in the "inner circle" of apostles (Matt. 17:1; Mark 5:37; Luke 8:51). Jesus also entrusted His aged mother to John (John 19:26, 27). John was the first of the disciples to believe that Jesus rose from the dead (John 20:8) and the first to recognize Him on the shore of the Sea of Galilee (John 21:1–7).

This account of Jesus' life is very different from the Synoptic Gospels (Matthew, Mark, and Luke). The purpose of this Gospel, stated near the end of the book (John 20:30, 31), is to present the signs and wonders that Jesus performed so that those who read it will believe that He is "the Christ, the Son of God." Each of the incidents recorded in the Gospel of John is specifically included to prove that Jesus is indeed the Son of God.

The literary style is simple and easy to understand. Each incident and discourse of Jesus is treated as an isolated event or statement, rather than being incorporated into an overall framework. The same majestic truths that appear in the other Gospels are repeated in intricate parallelisms.

Several miracles mentioned in the Gospel of John are not mentioned in the other Gospels: Jesus' turning the water into wine (John 2:1–12); the healing of the nobleman's son (John 4:46–54); the healing of the paralytic at the pool of Bethesda (John 5:1–9); the healing of the blind man (John 9:1–7); the raising of Lazarus (John 11:38–44); and the second drought of fishes (John 21:4–6). Furthermore, the Gospel of John allows us to determine the approximate length of Jesus' public ministry (about three and a half years) by the number of times that Passover was celebrated (John 2:23; 6:4; 11:55).

The Gospel of John may be divided into the following chronological portions: the preexistence of Christ (John 1:1–18); His first year of ministry (John 1:19—4:54); His popularity during the second year (chap. 5); the opposition against Him in His third year of ministry (John 6:1—12:11); the passion week (John 12:12—19:42); and the forty days following His resurrection (chaps. 20; 21).

The Word Became Flesh

1 ⊶In the beginning[746] [ipf][a]was the
Word,[3056] and the Word [ipf]was [b]with
[art]God,[2316] [c]and the Word [ipf]was God.
2 [a]The same [ipf]was in the beginning[746] with [art]God.
3 [a]All things[3956] [ao]were made[1096] by
him; and without him [ao]was not any
thing made[1096] that [pfi]was made.
4 [a]In him [ipf]was life;[2222] and [b]the life
[ipf]was the light[5457] of men.

1 [a]Col. 1:17; 1John 1:1; Rev. 1:2; 19:13 [b]John 17:5; 1John 1:2 [c]Phil. 2:6; 1John 5:7 **2** [a]Gen. 1:1 **3** [a]Ps. 33:6; John 1:10; Eph. 3:9; Col. 1:16; Heb. 1:2; Rev. 4:11 **4** [a]John 5:26; 1John 5:11 [b]John 8:12; 9:5; 12:35, 46

⊶ **1:1–17** John is the only writer who begins his story of Jesus Christ with His eternal existence rather than the time He appeared on earth. *Lógos* (3056), the word given to describe His existence at the beginning, is the "intelligence." He originated everything that is, and then He became the Word, which is the expression that explains that Intelligence and is undiscoverable except through the revelation of God and the Scriptures (Rom. 1:20).

(continued on next page)

5 And [a]the light [pin]shineth[5316] in
[art]darkness;[4653] and the darkness [ao]com-
prehended[2638] it not.
6 [a]There [aom]was a man [pfpp]sent from
God, whose name *was* John.
7 [a]The same [ao]came for a witness,[3141]
to [aosb]bear witness[3140] of the Light, that
all *men* through him [aosb]might believe.
8 He [ipf]was not that [art]Light, but
was sent to [aosb]bear witness of that
[art]Light.
🔑 9 [a]*That* [ipf]was the true Light, which
[pin]lighteth[5461] every man that [ppt]cometh
into the world.
10 He [ipf]was in the world,[2889] and
[a]the world [aom]was made[1096] by him, and
the world [ao]knew[1097] him not.
11 [a]He [ao]came unto [ajn-m]his own,[2398][3588]
and [ajn-m]his own [ao]received[3880] him not.
🔑 12 But [a]as many as received him, to
them [ao]gave he [1]power[1849] [ainf]to become[1096] the sons[5043] of God,[2316] *even* to
them that [ppt]believe[4100] on his name:[3686]
13 [a]Which were born, not of
[pl]blood,[129] nor of the [an]will[2307] of the
[an]flesh,[4561] nor of the [an]will of man,[435]
but of God.

14 [a]And the Word[3056] [aom][b]was
made[1096] [c]flesh,[4561] and [ao]dwelt among
us, (and [d]we [aom]beheld his glory,[1391] the
glory as of the only begotten[3439] of the
[an]Father,) [e]full[4134] of grace[5485] and
truth.[225]
15 [a]John [pin]bare witness of him, and
cried, saying, This was he of whom I
spake, [b]He that [ppt]cometh after me [pf]is
preferred before[1715] me: [c]for he [ipf]was before me.
16 And of his [a]fulness[4138] [ao]have
all we [ao]received,[2983] and grace for[473]
grace.
17 For [a]the law[3551] was given by
Moses, *but* [b]grace and [c]truth[225] came by
Jesus Christ.[5547]
🔑 18 [a]No man [pfi]hath seen[3708] God
at any time; [b]the only begotten[3439]
Son,[5207] which [ppt]is in the bosom of the
Father,[3962] he [aom]hath declared[1834]
him.

5 [a]John 3:19
6 [a]Mal. 3:1; Matt. 3:1; Luke 3:2; John 1:33
7 [a]Acts 19:4
9 [a]John 1:4; Isa. 49:6; 1John 2:8
10 [a]John 1:3; Heb. 1:2; 11:3
11 [a]Luke 19:14; Acts 3:26; 13:46
12 [1]Or, *the right, or, privilege* [a]Isa. 56:5; Rom. 8:15; Gal. 3:26; 2Pet. 1:4; 1John 3:1
13 [a]John 3:5; James 1:18; 1Pet. 1:23
14 [a]Matt. 1:16, 20; Luke 1:31, 35; 2:7; 1Tim. 3:16 [b]Rom. 1:3; Gal. 4:4 [c]Heb. 2:11, 14, 16, 17 [d]Isa. 40:5; Matt. 17:2; John 2:11; 11:40; 2Pet. 1:17 [e]Col. 1:19; 2:3, 9
15 [a]John 1:32; 3:32; 5:33 [b]Matt. 3:11; Mark 1:7; Luke 3:16; John 1:27, 30; 3:31 [c]John 8:58; Col. 1:17
16 [a]John 3:34; Eph. 1:6-8; Col. 1:19; 2:9, 10
17 [a]Ex. 20:1-17; Deut. 4:44; 5:1; 33:4 [b]Rom. 3:24; 5:21; 6:14 [c]John 8:32; 14:6
18 [a]Ex. 33:20; Deut. 4:12; Matt. 11:27; Luke 10:22; John 6:46; 1Tim. 1:17; 6:16; 1John 4:12, 20 [b]John 1:14; 3:16, 18; 1John 4:9

(continued from previous page)

There are two main verbs used throughout this passage that serve to contrast what Jesus had always been and what He became at His incarnation. There is *ēn*, the imperfect tense of *eimí* (1510), "to be," which in this context could have been better translated as "had been." Thus, a paraphrase of the first verse would be: "Before there was any beginning, the Word had been, and the Word has been toward the God, and God had been the Word." This verb *ēn* is found in every instance in this context where the Person of Jesus Christ is referred to in His eternal state of being (vv. 1, 2, 4, 8, 9, 10, 15). See notes on Philippians 2:6–8 and 1 John 1:5–10. The second verb is *egéneto* (the aorist form of *gínomai* [1096]), "to become." It refers to becoming something that one was not before. Thus, in verse fourteen John says, "And the Word *became* flesh." The Lord Jesus, at a particular time in the past, became that which He was not before, a physical being. This verb is in the aorist, *egéneto* (John 1:3, 6, 10, 14, 17) and is also found in the perfect, *gégone* (John 1:3, 15). The aorist usage refers to some historical time in the past as the beginning of this new state. The perfect tense implies a continuing existence in a new state.

🔑 **1:9** See notes on Matthew 13:10–17 and Hebrews 6:1–6.

🔑 **1:12** See note on Hebrews 6:1–6.

🔑 **1:18** In the Greek New Testament, this verse begins with the word "God" (*Théon* [2316]), without the definite article. It therefore refers to God as Spirit (John 4:24). John is declaring that no created being has ever seen God in His essence as Spirit. This first statement is to be connected with verse one, which also speaks of Jesus Christ in His self-existence as an eternal and infinite Spirit. Then, to show the very special relationship of the Son to the Father, He is called *monogenēs* (3439). The word is translated "only begotten," thus giving the false idea that, in His eternal state, He was generated by the Father. The second part of verse eighteen declares that this unique Son, or "unique God" (as some manuscripts have it), who has always been in the bosom of the Father,

(continued on next page)

The Testimony of John the Baptist (Matt. 3:1–12; Mark 1:7, 8; Luke 3:15–17)

19 And this is [a]the record[3141] of John, when the Jews sent priests[2409] and Levites from Jerusalem to ask[2065] him, Who art thou?

🔑 20 And [a]he confessed,[3670] and denied[720] not; but confessed, I am not the Christ.

21 And they asked[2065] him, What then? Art thou [a]Elias? And he saith, I am not. Art thou [1b]that prophet?[4396] And he answered, No.

22 Then said they unto him, Who art thou? that we may give an answer[612] to them that sent us. What sayest thou of thyself?

23 [a]He said, I *am* the voice of one crying in the wilderness, [aim]Make straight the way[3598] of the Lord, as [b]said the prophet Esaias.

24 And they which [pfpp]were sent were of the Pharisees.

25 And they asked[2065] him, and said unto him, Why baptizest[907] thou then, if thou be not that Christ, nor Elias, neither that [art]prophet?

26 John answered them, saying, [a]I baptize with water: [b]but there [pfi]standeth one among you, whom ye know not;

27 [a]He it is, who coming after me [pfi]is preferred before me, whose shoe's latchet[2438] I am not worthy to [aosb]unloose.

28 These things were done[1096] [a]in Bethabara beyond Jordan, where John was baptizing.

The Lamb of God

29 The next day John seeth Jesus coming unto him, and saith, Behold [a]the Lamb[286] of God, [b]which [ppt]taketh away[142] the sin[266] of the world.

30 [a]This is he of whom I said, After me cometh a man which [pfi]is preferred before[1715] me: for he was before me.

31 And I knew him not: but that he [asbp]should be made manifest[5319] to Israel, [a]therefore [ao]am I come[2064] baptizing with water.

32 [a]And John bare record, saying, I [pfip]saw the Spirit descending from heaven like a dove, and it [ao]abode upon him.

🔑 33 And I knew him not: but he that [apt]sent me [pinf]to baptize[907] with water, the same said unto me, Upon whom thou [aosb]shalt see the Spirit descending, and remaining on him, [a]the same is he which [ppt]baptizeth with the [an]Holy Ghost.

34 And I saw, and [pfi]bare record that this is the Son[5207] of God.[2316]

The First Disciples

35 Again the next day after John [plpf]stood, and two of his disciples;[3101]

36 And looking upon[1689] Jesus as he walked, he saith, [a]Behold the Lamb[286] of God!

19 [a]John 5:33
20 [a]Luke 3:15; John 3:28; Acts 13:25
21 [1]Or, *a prophet* [a]Mal. 4:5; Matt. 17:10 [b]Deut. 18:15, 18
23 [a]Matt. 3:3; Mark 1:3; Luke 3:4; John 3:28 [b]Isa. 40:3
26 [a]Matt. 3:11 [b]Mal. 3:1
27 [a]John 1:15, 30; Acts 19:4
28 [a]Judg. 7:24; John 10:40
29 [a]Ex. 12:3; Isa. 53:7; John 1:36; Acts 8:32; 1Pet. 1:19; Rev. 5:6-10 [b]Isa. 53:11; 1Cor. 15:3; Gal. 1:4; Heb. 1:3; 2:17; 9:28; 1Pet. 2:24; 3:18; 1John 2:2; 3:5; 4:10; Rev. 1:5
30 [a]John 1:15, 27
31 [a]Mal. 3:1; Matt. 3:6; Luke 1:17, 76, 77; 3:3, 4
32 [a]Matt. 3:16; Mark 1:10; Luke 3:22; John 5:32
33 [a]Matt. 3:11; Acts 1:5; 2:4; 10:44; 19:6
36 [a]John 1:29

(continued from previous page)
manifested the Godhead and made Him understood. This second declaration of verse eighteen agrees with verse fourteen which speaks of the incarnation of the *Lógos*, the "Word." See note on Colossians 1:15–18.

🔑 **1:20, 21** In these verses, the priests and Levites wanted to know whether John the Baptist was the Messiah, a reincarnation of the prophet Elijah, or "that Prophet." The Jews understood, according to Scripture, that a prophet would come and speak of delivering the people of Israel from all their oppression (see notes on Deut. 18:15–19 and Mal. 4:1–6). The fact that John the Baptist denied being Elijah is significant because the Jews believed that Elijah would be the forerunner of the Messiah. John's appearance certainly resembled Elijah's, and even the angel Gabriel that appeared to Zechariah, John's father, pointed out that he would come "in the spirit and power of Elijah" (Luke 1:17). However, John's answer to the priests and Levites was intended to show them that he was simply a messenger of God, not a reincarnation of Elijah or any other prophet.

🔑 **1:33** See note on Acts 1:5.

37 And the two disciples heard him [ppt]speak, and they followed Jesus.

38 Then Jesus turned, and saw them following, and saith unto them, What seek ye? They said unto him, Rabbi, (which is to say, being interpreted, Master,[1320]) where [I]dwellest thou?

39 He saith unto them, [pim]Come and [aim]see. They came and saw where he dwelt,[3306] and abode[3306] with him that day: for it was about[5613] the tenth hour.

40 One of the two which [apt]heard John *speak,* and [apt]followed him, was [a]Andrew, Simon Peter's brother.[80]

41 He first[4413] findeth his own[2398] brother Simon, and saith unto him, We [pfi]have found the Messias,3323 which is, being interpreted, the Christ.[5547]

42 And he brought him to Jesus. And when Jesus beheld1689 him, he said, Thou art Simon the son of Jona: [a]thou shalt be called Cephas, which is by interpretation,2059 [I]A stone.

Jesus Calls Philip and Nathanael

43 The day following Jesus would [ainf]go forth into Galilee, and findeth Philip, and saith unto him, [pim]Follow me.

44 Now [a]Philip was of Bethsaida, the city of Andrew and Peter.

45 Philip findeth [a]Nathanael, and saith unto him, We [pfi]have found him, of whom [b]Moses in the law,[3551] and the [c]prophets,[4396] did write,[1125] Jesus [d]of Nazareth, the son of Joseph.

46 And Nathanael said unto him, [a]Can there any good thing[18] come out of Nazareth? Philip saith unto him, [pim]Come and [aim]see.[1492]

47 Jesus saw Nathanael coming to him, and saith of him, Behold [a]an Israelite indeed, in whom is no guile1388

48 Nathanael saith unto him, Whence knowest thou me? Jesus answered and said unto him, Before that Philip [aip]called thee, when thou wast5607 under the fig tree, I saw thee.

49 Nathanael answered and saith unto him, Rabbi, [a]thou art the Son[5207] of God;[2316] thou art [b]the King[935] of Israel.

38 [I]Or, *abidest*

40 [a]Matt. 4:18

42 [I]Or, *Peter* [a]Matt. 16:18

44 [a]John 12:21

45 [a]John 21:2 [b]Gen. 3:15; 49:10; Deut. 18:18; Luke 24:27 [c]Isa. 4:2; 7:14; 9:6; 53:2; Mic. 5:2; Zech. 6:12; 9:9; Luke 24:27 [d]Matt. 2:23; Luke 2:4

46 [a]John 7:41, 42, 52

47 [a]Ps. 32:2; 73:1; John 8:39; Rom. 2:28, 29; 9:6

49 [a]Matt. 14:33 [b]Matt. 21:5; 27:11, 42; John 18:37; 19:3

51 [a]Gen. 28:12; Matt. 4:11; Luke 2:9, 13; 22:43; 24:4; Acts 1:10

1 [a]Josh. 19:28

4 [a]John 19:26 [b]2Sam. 16:10; 19:22 [c]John 7:6

6 [a]Mark 7:3

9 [a]John 4:46

11 [a]John 1:14

50 Jesus answered and said unto him, Because I said unto thee, I saw thee under the fig tree, believest[4100] thou? thou shalt see greater things than these.

51 And he saith unto him, Verily,281 verily, I say unto you, [a]Hereafter ye shall see heaven open, and the angels[32] of God ascending and descending upon the Son[5207] of man.[444]

The First Miracle

2 And the third day there was a marriage[1062] in [a]Cana of Galilee; and the mother of Jesus was there:

2 And both Jesus was called, and his disciples,[3101] to the marriage.

3 And when they [apt]wanted wine, the mother of Jesus saith unto him, They have no wine.

4 Jesus saith unto her, [a]Woman, [b]what have I to do with thee? [c]mine hour is not yet come.

5 His mother saith unto the servants,[1249] Whatsoever he saith unto you, do *it.*

6 And there were set[2749] there six waterpots of stone, [a]after the manner of the purifying[2512] of the Jews, containing two or three firkins3355 apiece.[303]

7 Jesus saith unto them, Fill the waterpots with water. And they filled them up to the brim.[507]

8 And he saith unto them, [aim]Draw out now, and [pim]bear unto the governor of the feast. And they [ao]bare *it.*

9 When the ruler of the feast [aom]had tasted[1089] [a]the water that [pfpp]was made[1096] wine,[3631] and knew not whence it was: (but the servants which [pfp]drew the water knew;) the governor of the feast called the bridegroom,

10 And saith unto him, Every man at the beginning doth set forth[5087] good wine; and when men [asbp]have well drunk, then that which is worse: *but* thou [pfi]hast kept the good wine until now.

11 This beginning of miracles did Jesus in Cana of Galilee, [a]and manifested forth[5319] his glory;[1391] and his disciples believed[4100] on him.

12 After this he went down to Capernaum, he, and his mother, and [a]his brethren,[80] and his disciples: and they continued[3306] there not many days.

Jesus Goes to the Temple (Matt. 21:12, 13; Mark 11:15–18; Luke 19:45, 46)

13 [a]And the Jews' passover[3957] was at hand, and Jesus went up to Jerusalem,

14 [a]And found in the temple[2411] those that [ppt]sold oxen and sheep and doves, and the changers of money sitting:

15 And when he had made a scourge[5416] of small cords, he drove them all out of the temple, and the sheep, and the oxen; and poured out the changers' money, and overthrew the tables;

16 And said unto them that sold doves, Take these things hence; [pim]make not [a]my Father's[3962] house an house of merchandise.

17 And his disciples[3101] remembered that it was written, [a]The zeal[2205] of thine house[3624] [ao]hath eaten me up.[2719]

18 Then answered the Jews and said unto him, [a]What sign[4592] shewest thou unto us, seeing that thou doest these things?

19 Jesus answered and said unto them, [a]Destroy[3089] this temple,[3485] and in three days I [ft]will raise it up.[1453]

20 Then said the Jews, Forty and six years [aop]was this temple in building, and wilt thou rear it up in three days?

21 But he [ipf]spake [a]of the temple of his body.[4983]

22 When therefore he [aop]was risen[1453] from the dead, [a]his disciples remembered that he [ipf]had said this unto them; and they believed[4100] the scripture,[1124] and the word[3056] which Jesus had said.

23 Now when he was in Jerusalem at the passover,[3957] in the feast *day,* many believed[4100] in his name,[3686] when they [ppt]saw[2334] the miracles[4592] which he did.

🔑 24 But Jesus [ipf]did not commit[4100] himself unto them, because he [aid]knew[1097] all *men,*

25 And needed not that any [aosb]should testify of man: for [a]he [ipf]knew what was in man.

Nicodemus

3 There was a man of the Pharisees, named Nicodemus, a ruler[758] of the Jews:

🔑 2 [a]The same came to Jesus by night,

12 [a]Matt. 12:46
13 [a]Ex. 12:14; Deut. 16:1, 16; John 1:23; 5:1; 6:4; 11:55
14 [a]Matt. 21:12; Mark 11:15; Luke 19:45
16 [a]Luke 2:49
17 [a]Ps. 69:9
18 [a]Matt. 12:38; John 6:30
19 [a]Matt. 26:61; 27:40; Mark 14:58; 15:29
21 [a]Col. 2:9; Heb. 8:2; 1Cor. 3:16; 6:19; 2Cor. 6:16
22 [a]Luke 24:8
25 [a]1Sam. 16:7; 1Chr. 28:9; Matt. 9:4; Mark 2:8; John 6:64; 16:30; Acts 1:24; Rev. 2:23
2 [a]John 7:50; 19:39

🔑 **2:24** Christ was performing many miracles in Jerusalem, and as a result, many people believed on Him. The phrase "did not commit himself to them" is significant because it reveals that only Christ knew if these people were sincere. Most commentators agree that this verse speaks of those who believed on Christ, yet because Christ knew their true intentions, He saw the hypocrisy and shallowness of their faith. The word "commit" would be better understood if it were translated "trust." Evidently, Christ was sorrowful at the knowledge of the hypocrisy of their faith. Others feel that these people were in fact unbelievers who only accepted those things that they had seen with their eyes. A good illustration of such people is found in Christ's "Parable of the sower," represented by the seed that fell on stony ground. See notes on Luke 8:13 and 1 John 3:6–9.

🔑 **3:2** The question that arises from an examination of this verse is why Nicodemus came to Christ at night. Some scholars suggest that Nicodemus was a timid man, and because he was a religious leader among the Pharisees, he was afraid to be seen with Jesus for fear that his associates would criticize him. Others say that this view lacks substantiation because it was too early in Christ's ministry for Him to have received such opposition as to warrant Nicodemus' speaking with Him at night. They propose that Christ was simply too busy during the day to have made time to meet with Nicodemus. Still another view suggests that Nicodemus was the one who was busy during the day, being a member of the Sanhedrin, and he would have only had time to meet with Jesus at night. Whatever his motive was for coming to Christ when he did, Nicodemus later confessed Jesus before the other Pharisees and leaders of the Jews (John 7:50, 51).

and said unto him, Rabbi, we know that
thou art a teacher [pfi]come from God:[2316]
for [b]no man can do these miracles[4592]
that thou doest, except [c]God be with him.
3 Jesus answered and said unto him,
Verily,[281] verily, I say unto thee, [a]Except
a man [asbp]be born[1080] [I]again,[509] he cannot [ainf]see[1492] the kingdom[932] of God.
4 Nicodemus saith unto him, How
can a man be born when he is old? can
he [ainf]enter the second time into his
mother's womb, and be born?
5 Jesus answered, Verily, verily, I say
unto thee, [a]Except a man be born[1080] of
water and *of* the [an]Spirit,[4151] he cannot
enter into the kingdom of God.
6 That which [pfpp]is born of the
flesh[4561] is flesh; and that which is born
of the Spirit[4151] is spirit.[4151]
7 [aosi]Marvel not that I said unto thee,
Ye must be born[1080] [I]again.[509]
8 [a]The wind[4151] bloweth[4154] where it
[pin]listeth,[2309] and thou hearest the
sound[5456] thereof, but canst not tell
whence it cometh, and whither it goeth:
so is every one that [pfpp]is born of the
Spirit.[4151]
9 Nicodemus answered and said unto
him, [a]How can these things [ainf]be?
10 Jesus answered and said unto him,
Art thou a master[1320] of Israel, and
knowest not these things?
11 [a]Verily, verily, I say unto thee, We
speak that we do know, and testify[3140]
that we have seen; and [b]ye receive not
our witness.[3141]
12 If I [ao]have told you earthly
things,[1919] and ye believe[4100] not, how
[ft]shall ye believe,[4100] if I [aosb]tell you *of*
heavenly things?
13 And [a]no man [pfi]hath ascended up
to heaven,[3772] but he that [apt]came down
from heaven, *even* the Son[5207] of man[444]
which [ppt]is in heaven.
14 [a]And as Moses lifted up the serpent in the wilderness, even so [b]must the
Son of man [aifp]be lifted up:

🔑 15 That whosoever [ppt]believeth[4100] in
him [asbm]should not perish,[622] but [psa][a]have
eternal[166] life.[2222]
16 [a]For God[2316] so [ao]loved[25] the
world,[2889] that he gave his only begotten[3439] Son,[5207] that whosoever [ppt]be-
lieveth[4100] in him should not perish,[622]
but [psa]have everlasting[166] life.[2222]
17 [a]For God sent[649] not his Son into
the world to condemn[2919] the world; but
that the world through him [asbp]might be
saved.[4982]
18 [a]He that [ppt]believeth[4100] on him
[pinp]is not condemned:[2919] but he that
[ppt]believeth not [pfip]is condemned already,
because he [pfi]hath not believed[4100] in the
name[3686] of the only begotten Son of
God.
🔑 19 And this is the condemnation,[2920]
[a]that light[5457] [pfi]is come[2064] into the
world, and men[444] [ao]loved[25] [art]dark-
ness[4655] rather than [art]light, because their
deeds[2041] were evil.[4190]
20 For [a]every one that [ppt]doeth[4238]
evil[5337] hateth the light, neither cometh to
the light, lest his deeds should be
[I]reproved.
21 But he that [ppt]doeth truth[225]
cometh to the light, that his deeds
[asbp]may be made manifest,[5319] that they
are wrought[2038] in God.

Jesus Is Greater Than John

22 After these things came Jesus and
his disciples[3101] into the land of Judaea;
and there he [ipf]tarried with them, [a]and
[ipf]baptized.[907]
23 And John also was baptizing in
Aenon near to [a]Salim, because there was
much water there: [b]and they [ipf]came, and
[ipf]were baptized.
24 For [a]John was not yet cast into
prison.
25 Then there arose a question between *some* of John's disciples and the
Jews about purifying.[2512]

2 [b]John 9:16, 33; Acts 2:22 [c]Acts 10:38
3 [I]Or, *from above* [a]John 1:13; Gal. 6:15; Titus 3:5; James 1:18; 1Pet. 1:23; 1John 3:9
5 [a]Mark 16:16; Acts 2:38
7 [I]Or, *from above*
8 [a]Eccl. 11:5; 1Cor. 2:11
9 [a]John 6:52, 60
11 [a]Matt. 11:27; John 1:18; 7:16; 8:28; 12:49; 14:24 [b]John 3:32
13 [a]Prov. 30:4; John 6:33, 38, 51, 62; 16:28; Acts 2:34; 1Cor. 15:47; Eph. 4:9, 10
14 [a]Num. 21:9 [b]John 8:28; 12:32
15 [a]John 3:36; John 6:47
16 [a]Rom. 5:8; 1John 4:9
17 [a]Luke 9:56; John 5:45; 8:15; 12:47; 1John 4:14
18 [a]John 5:24; 6:40, 47; 20:31
19 [a]John 1:4, 9-11; 8:12
20 [I]Or, *discovered* [a]Job 24:13, 17; Eph. 5:13
22 [a]John 4:2
23 [a]1Sam. 9:4 [b]Matt. 3:5, 6
24 [a]Matt. 14:3

🔑 **3:15, 16** See notes on Ephesians 1:4, 5 and Hebrews 6:1–6.
🔑 **3:19** See note on 1 John 1:5–10.

26 And they came unto John, and said unto him, Rabbi, he that was with thee beyond Jordan, [a]to whom thou [pfi]barest witness,[3140] behold, the same baptizeth, and all *men* come to him.

27 John answered and said, [a]A man can [pinf][1]receive nothing, except it be given him from heaven.[3772]

28 Ye yourselves bear me witness, that I said, [a]I am not the Christ,[5547] but [b]that I am sent before him.

29 [a]He that [ppt]hath the bride is the bridegroom: but [b]the friend of the bridegroom, which [pfp]standeth and [ppt]heareth him, rejoiceth greatly because of the bridegroom's voice: this my joy therefore [pfip]is fulfilled.

30 He must [pinf]increase, but I *must* [pip]decrease.

31 [a]He that [ppt]cometh from above[509] [b]is above all: [c]he that is of the earth[1093] is earthly,[1093] and speaketh of the earth: [d]he that [ppt]cometh from heaven[3772] is above all.

32 And [a]what he hath seen and heard, that he testifieth;[3140] and no man receiveth his testimony.[3141]

33 He that [apt]hath received his testimony [ao][a]hath set to his seal that God is true.

34 [a]For he whom God [ao]hath sent[649] speaketh the words[4487] of God: for God giveth not the Spirit [b]by measure *unto him.*

35 [a]The Father loveth[25] the Son, and [pfi]hath given all things into his hand.

36 [a]He that [ppt]believeth[4100] on the Son hath everlasting life:[2222] and he that [ppt]believeth not[544] the Son shall not see life; but the wrath[3709] of God abideth on him.

A Samaritan Woman

4 When therefore the Lord[2962] knew how the Pharisees had heard that Jesus made and [a]baptized[907] more disciples[3101] than John,

2 (Though Jesus himself [ipf]baptized not, but his disciples,)

3 He left Judaea, and departed again into Galilee.

4 And he must needs [pinf]go through Samaria.

5 Then cometh he to a city of Samaria, which is called Sychar, near[4139] to the parcel of ground [a]that Jacob gave to his son Joseph.

6 Now Jacob's well was there. Jesus therefore, [pfp]being wearied with *his* journey, sat thus on the well: *and* it was about the sixth hour.

7 There cometh a woman of Samaria [ainf]to draw water: Jesus saith unto her, Give me to drink.

8 (For his disciples [plpf]were gone away unto the city to buy meat.)

9 Then saith the woman of Samaria unto him, How is it that thou, being a Jew, askest drink of me, which am a woman of Samaria? for [a]the Jews have no dealings with the Samaritans.

🗝 10 Jesus answered and said unto her, If thou knewest the gift of God, and

26 [a]John 1:7, 15, 27, 34
27 [1]Or, *take unto himself* [a]1Cor. 4:7; Heb. 5:4; James 1:17
28 [a]John 1:20, 27 [b]Mal. 3:1; Mark 1:2; Luke 1:17
29 [a]Matt. 22:2; 2Cor. 11:2; Eph. 5:25, 27; Rev. 21:9 [b]Song 5:1
31 [a]John 1:13; 8:23 [b]Matt. 28:18; John 1:15, 27; Rom. 9:5 [c]1Cor. 15:47 [d]John 6:33; 1Cor. 15:47; Eph. 1:21; Phil. 2:9
32 [a]John 1:11; 8:26; 15:15
33 [a]Rom. 3:4; 1John 5:10
34 [a]John 7:16 [b]John 1:16
35 [a]Matt. 11:27; 28:18; Luke 10:22; John 5:20, 22; 13:3; 17:2; Heb. 2:8
36 [a]Hab. 2:4; John 1:12; 6:47; 1:15, 16; Rom. 1:17; 1John 5:10
1 [a]John 3:22, 26
5 [a]Gen. 33:19; 48:22; Josh. 24:32
9 [a]2Kgs. 17:24; Luke 9:52, 53; Acts 10:28

🗝 **4:10** The important idea to glean from this verse is the meaning of the phrase, "the gift of God." Some believe that the gift refers to the statement by Christ that follows: "and who it is that saith to thee." They suggest that the word translated "and" should in fact be translated "namely," which would define the "gift of God" as the knowledge of who Jesus is and His reason for coming to earth. For the believer, this would provide the basis for the benefits that Christ gives to him and would reveal His willingness to meet all the believer's needs. Other scholars propose that the "gift" is the "living water" that Jesus was offering to the Samaritan woman. They suggest that there is a two-fold purpose to this water: first, it can refer to the spiritual, everlasting water for the soul (John 4:14, "eternal life"), while also applying to the literal water found in the well from which the Samaritan woman was going to draw. Yet a third view states that the "gift" is in fact Christ Himself. This idea is seen in the freeness with which the offer was made to the woman. Christ said, "If thou knewest . . . who it is that saith to thee . . . thou wouldest have asked of him." Christ did not come to earth because God felt that He owed something to mankind. This final view seems to be

(continued on next page)

who it is that saith to thee, Give me to drink; thou wouldest have asked of him, and he would have given thee [a]living[2198] water.

11 The woman saith unto him, Sir,[2962] thou hast nothing to draw with, and the well[5421] is deep: from whence then hast thou that [art]living water?

12 Art thou greater than our father Jacob, which gave us the well, and [ao]drank thereof himself, and his children, and his cattle?

13 Jesus answered and said unto her, Whosoever [ppt]drinketh of this water shall thirst again:

14 But [a]whosoever [aosb]drinketh of the water that I shall give him [aosb]shall never thirst;[1372] but the water that I shall give him [b]shall be in him a well[4077] of water springing up into everlasting[166] life.[2222]

15 [a]The woman saith unto him, Sir, give me this water, that I [psa]thirst not, neither [psa]come hither [pinf]to draw.

16 Jesus saith unto her, Go, call thy husband,[435] and come hither.

17 The woman answered and said, I have no husband. Jesus said unto her, Thou hast well said, I have no husband:

18 For thou hast had five husbands; and he whom thou now hast is not thy husband: in that saidst thou truly.

19 The woman saith unto him, Sir, [a]I perceive that thou art a prophet.[4396]

20 Our fathers [ao]worshipped[4352] in [a]this mountain; and ye say, that in [b]Jerusalem is the place where men ought [pinf]to worship.

21 Jesus saith unto her, Woman, [aim]believe me, the hour[5610] cometh, [a]when ye shall neither in this mountain, nor yet at Jerusalem, worship the Father.

22 Ye worship [a]ye know not what: we know what we worship: for [art][b]salvation[4991] is of the Jews.

23 But the hour cometh, and now is, when the true worshippers shall worship the Father[3962] in [a]spirit[4151] [b]and in truth:[225] for the Father seeketh such to [ppt]worship him.

24 [art][a]God *is* a Spirit:[4151] and they that [ppt]worship him must [pinf]worship *him* in spirit and in truth.[225]

25 The woman saith unto him, I know that Messias[3323] cometh, which is called Christ:[5547] when he [aosb]is come, [a]he [ft]will tell[312] us all things.

26 Jesus saith unto her, [a]I that [ppt]speak unto thee am *he.*

27 And upon this came his disciples, and marvelled that he [ipf]talked with the woman: yet no man said, What seekest thou? or, Why talkest thou with her?

28 The woman then left her waterpot, and went her way into the city, and saith to the men,

29 Come, see a man, [a]which told me all things that ever I did: is not this the Christ?

30 Then they went out of the city, and came unto him.

31 In the mean while his disciples[3101] [ipf]prayed him, saying, Master, eat.

32 But he said unto them, I have meat to eat that ye know not of.

33 Therefore [ipf]said the disciples one to another, Hath any man brought him *ought* to eat?

34 Jesus saith unto them, [a]My meat is to [psa]do the will[2307] of him that [apt]sent me, and to [aosb]finish[5048] his work.

35 Say not ye, There are yet four months, and *then* cometh harvest? behold, I say unto you, Lift up your eyes, and look on the fields; [a]for they are white already to harvest.

36 [a]And he that [ppt]reapeth receiveth wages,[3408] and gathereth fruit unto life[2222] eternal:[166] that both he that [ppt]soweth and he that [ppt]reapeth [psa]may rejoice together.

37 And herein is that saying[3056] true, One [ppt]soweth, and another[243] [ppt]reapeth.

10 [a]Isa. 12:3; 44:3; Jer. 2:13; Zech. 13:1; 14:8
14 [a]John 6:35, 58 [b]John 7:38
15 [a]John 6:34; 17:2, 3; Rom. 6:23; 1John 5:20
19 [a]Luke 7:16; 24:19; John 6:14; 7:40
20 [a]Judg. 9:7 [b]Deut. 12:5, 11; 1Kgs. 9:3; 2Chr. 7:12
21 [a]Mal. 1:11; 1Tim. 2:8
22 [a]2Kgs. 17:29 [b]Isa. 2:3; Luke 24:47; Rom. 9:4, 5
23 [a]Phil. 3:3 [b]John 1:17
24 [a]2Cor. 3:17
25 [a]John 1:29, 39
26 [a]Matt. 26:63, 64; Mark 14:61, 62; John 9:37
29 [a]John 4:25
34 [a]Job 23:12; John 6:38; 17:4; 19:30
35 [a]Matt. 9:37; Luke 10:2
36 [a]Dan. 12:3

(continued from previous page)
the most consistent since it shows the Person of Christ as the focal point of the gift, not anything that He brought with Him.

38 I sent you [pinf]to reap that whereon ye [pfi]bestowed no labour: other[243] men [pfi]laboured, and ye [pfi]are entered into their labours.

39 And many of the Samaritans of that city believed[4100] on him [a]for the saying of the woman, which testified, He told me all that ever I did.

40 So when the Samaritans were come unto him, they [ipf]besought him that he would [ainf]tarry with them: and he [ao]abode there two days.

41 And many more believed because of his own word;

42 And said unto the woman, Now we believe, not because of thy saying:2981 for [a]we have heard *him* ourselves, and know that this is indeed the Christ,[5547] the Saviour[4990] of the world.[2889]

Jesus Heals an Official's Son (Matt. 8:5–13; Luke 7:1–10)

43 Now after two days he departed thence, and went into Galilee.

44 For [a]Jesus himself testified, that a prophet[4396] hath no honour in his own country.

45 Then when he was come into Galilee, the Galilaeans received him, [a]having seen all the things that he did at Jerusalem at the feast: [b]for they also went unto the feast.

46 So Jesus came again into Cana of Galilee, [a]where he made the water wine. And there was a certain [I]nobleman,[937] whose son[5207] [ipf]was sick at Capernaum.

47 When he heard that Jesus was come out of Judaea into Galilee, he went unto him, and [ipf]besought him that he would come down, and heal his son: for he was at the point of death.

48 Then said Jesus unto him, [a]Except ye [aosb]see[1492] signs[4592] and wonders,[5059] ye [aosb]will not believe.[4100]

49 The nobleman saith unto him, Sir, come down ere4250 my child [ainf]die.

50 Jesus saith unto him, [pim]Go thy way; thy son liveth.[2198] And the man believed the word[3056] that Jesus had spoken unto him, and he went his way.

51 And as he was now going down, his servants[1401] met him, and told *him,* saying, Thy son[3816] liveth.[2198]

52 Then enquired he of them the hour when he [ao]began to amend.[2192] 2866 And they said unto him, Yesterday at the seventh hour the fever left[863] him.

53 So the father knew that *it was* at the same hour, in the which Jesus said unto him, Thy son liveth: and himself believed, and his whole house.[3614]

54 This *is* again the second miracle *that* Jesus did, when he was come out of Judaea into Galilee.

Jesus Heals a Sick Man On the Sabbath Day

5 After [a]this there was a feast of the Jews; and Jesus went up to Jerusalem.

2 Now there is at Jerusalem [a]by the sheep [I]*market* a pool, which is called in the Hebrew tongue Bethesda, having five porches.

3 In these [ipf]lay a great multitude of impotent folk,[770] of blind, halt, withered, waiting for[1551] the moving of the water.

4 For an angel[32] went down at a certain season[2540] into the pool, and troubled the water: whosoever then first[4413] after the troubling of the water stepped in was made whole[5199] of whatsoever disease3553 he had.[2722]

5 And a certain man was there, which [ppt]had[2192] an infirmity thirty and eight years.

6 When Jesus saw him [ppt]lie, and knew that he [pin]had been now a long time[5550] *in that case,* he saith unto him, Wilt thou be made whole?[5199]

7 The impotent man answered him, Sir, I have no man, when the water [asbp]is troubled, to [psa]put[906] me into the pool: but while I am coming, another[243] steppeth down before me.

8 Jesus saith unto him, [a]Rise, take up[142] thy bed,2895 and [pim]walk.

9 And immediately the man was made whole,[5199] and took up[142] his bed, and [ipf]walked: and [a]on the same day was the sabbath.4521

39 [a]John 4:29
42 [a]John 17:8; 1John 4:14
44 [a]Matt. 13:57; Mark 6:4; Luke 4:24
45 [a]John 2:23; 3:2 [b]Deut. 16:16
46 [I]Or, *courtier,* or, *ruler* [a]John 2:1, 11
48 [a]1Cor. 1:22
1 [a]Lev. 23:2; Deut. 16:1; John 2:13
2 [I]Or, gate [a]Neh. 3:1; 12:39
8 [a]Matt. 9:6; Mark 2:11; Luke 5:24
9 [a]John 9:14

10 The Jews therefore said unto him that [pfpp]was cured, It is the sabbath day: [a]it is not lawful for thee to carry *thy* bed.

11 He answered them, He that [apt]made[4160] me whole, the same said unto me, [aim]Take up thy bed, and [pim]walk.

12 Then asked[2065] they him, What man is that which said unto thee, Take up thy bed, and walk?

13 And he that was healed wist[1492] not who it was: for Jesus had conveyed himself away, [I]a multitude being in *that* place.

14 Afterward Jesus findeth him in the temple,[2411] and said unto him, Behold, thou [pfi]art made whole:[5199] [pim][a]sin[264] no more, lest a worse thing [asbm]come unto thee.

15 The man departed, and told[312] the Jews that it was Jesus, which [apt]had made[4160] him whole.

16 And therefore [ipf]did the Jews persecute[1377] Jesus, and [ipf]sought [ainf]to slay him, because he [ipf]had done these things on the sabbath day.

17 But Jesus answered them, [a]My Father[3962] [pin]worketh hitherto, and I [pin]work.

18 Therefore the Jews [ipfa]sought the more [ainf]to kill him, because he not only [ipf]had broken[3089] the sabbath, but said also that God was his[2398] Father, [b]making himself equal with God.

The Father and the Son

19 Then answered Jesus and said unto them, Verily,[281] verily, I say unto you, [a]The Son[5207] can [pinf]do nothing of himself, but what he [psa]seeth the Father [ppt]do: for what things soever he [psa]doeth, these also doeth the Son likewise.

20 For [a]the Father loveth[5368] the Son, and sheweth him all things that himself doeth: and he will shew him greater works[2041] than these, that ye [psa]may marvel.

21 For as the Father raiseth up[1453] the dead, and quickeneth[2227] *them;* [a]even so the Son quickeneth whom he will.

22 For the Father judgeth[2919] no man, but [pfia]hath committed all judgment[2920] unto the Son:

23 That all *men* should [psa]honour the Son, even as they honour the Father. [a]He that [ppt]honoureth not the Son honoureth not the Father which [apt]hath sent him.

24 Verily, verily, I say unto you, [a]He that [ppt]heareth my word, and [ppt]believeth[4100] on him that [apt]sent me, hath everlasting[166] life,[2222] and shall not come into condemnation;[2920] [b]but [pfi]is passed[3327] from death[2288] unto life.

25 Verily, verily, I say unto you, The hour is coming, and now is, when [a]the dead shall hear the voice of the Son[5207] of God: and they that [apt]hear shall live.[2198]

26 For as the Father hath life in himself; so [ao]hath he given[1325] to the Son [pinf]to have life in himself;

27 And [aoa]hath given him authority[1849] [pinf]to execute[4160] judgment[2920] also, [b]because he is the [an]Son of man.

28 [pim]Marvel not at this: for the hour[5610] is coming, in the which all that are in the graves shall hear his voice,

29 [a]And shall come forth; [b]they that [apt]have done good,[18] unto the [an]resurrection[386] of life; and they that [apt]have done[4238] evil,[5337] unto the [an]resurrection of damnation.[2920]

30 [epna]I can of mine own self [pinf]do nothing: as I hear, I judge: and my judgment[2920] is just;[1342] because [b]I seek not mine own will,[2307] but the will of the Father which [apt]hath sent me.

31 [a]If I bear witness of myself, my witness[3141] is not true.

32 [a]There is another that [ppt]beareth witness[3140] of me; and I know that the witness which he witnesseth of me is true.

33 Ye [pfi]sent unto John, [a]and he [pfi]bare witness unto the truth.[225]

34 But I receive not testimony[3141] from man: but these things I say, that ye [asbp]might be saved.[4982]

35 He was a burning and [a]a shining[5316] light:[3088] and [b]ye [ao]were willing for a season[5610] to [aifp]rejoice[21] in his light.[5457]

10 [a]Ex. 20:10; Neh. 13:19; Jer. 17:21-27; Matt. 12:2; Mark 2:24; 3:4; Luke 6:2; 13:14
13 [I]Or, *from the multitude that was*
14 [a]Matt. 12:45; John 8:11
17 [a]John 9:4; 14:10
18 [a]John 7:19 [b]John 10:30, 33; Phil. 2:6
19 [a]John 5:30; 9:4; 12:49; 14:10
20 [a]Matt. 3:17; John 3:35; 2Pet. 1:17
21 [a]Luke 7:14; 8:54; John 11:25, 43
22 [a]Matt. 11:27; 28:18; John 5:27; 3:35; 17:2; Acts 17:31; 1Pet. 4:5
23 [a]1John 2:23
24 [a]John 3:16, 18; 6:40, 47; 8:51; 20:31 [b]1John 3:14
25 [a]John 5:28; Eph. 2:1, 5; 5:14; Col. 2:13
27 [a]John 5:22; Acts 10:42; 17:31 [b]Dan. 7:13, 14
29 [a]Isa. 26:19; 1Cor. 15:52; 1Thess. 4:16 [b]Dan. 12:2; Matt. 25:32, 33, 46
30 [a]John 5:19 [b]Matt. 26:39; John 4:34; 6:38
31 [a]John 8:14; Rev. 3:14
32 [a]Matt. 3:17; 17:5; John 8:18; 1John 5:6, 7, 9
33 [a]John 1:15, 19, 27, 32
35 [a]2Pet. 1:19 [b]Matt. 13:20; 21:26; Mark 6:20

36 But [a]I have greater witness[3141] than *that* of John: for [b]the works[2041] which the Father [ao]hath given me to [aosb]finish,[5048] the same works that I do, bear witness of me, that the Father [pfi]hath sent me.

37 And the Father himself, which [apt]hath sent me, [pfi][a]hath borne witness of me. Ye [pfi]have neither heard[191] his voice at any time, [b]nor [pfi]seen[3708] his shape.[1491]

38 And ye have not his word[3056] abiding[3306] in you: for whom he [ao]hath sent, him ye believe not.

39 [a]Search the scriptures; for in them ye think ye have eternal life: and [b]they are they which [ppt]testify of me.

40 [a]And ye will not [ainf]come to me, that ye [psa]might have life.[2222]

41 [a]I receive not honour from men.

42 But I [pfi]know you, that ye have not the love[26] of God[2316] in you.

🔑 43 I [pfi]am come in my Father's name, and ye receive me not: if another shall come in his own[2398] name, him ye [fm]will receive.

44 [a]How can ye [ainf]believe, which [ppt]receive honour[1391] one of another, and seek not [b]the honour that *cometh* from God only?

45 [pim]Do not think[1380] that I [ft]will accuse[2723] you to the Father: [a]there is *one* that [ppt]accuseth you, *even* Moses in whom ye [pfi]trust.[1679]

46 For [ipf]had ye believed[4100] Moses, ye [ipf]would have believed me: [a]for he wrote of me.

47 But if ye believe not his writings,[1121] how shall ye believe my words?[4487]

Jesus Feeds the Five Thousand (Matt. 14:13–21; Mark 6:30–44; Luke 9:10–17)

6 After [a]these things Jesus went over the sea of Galilee, which is *the sea* of Tiberias.

2 And a great multitude [ipf]followed him, because they [ipf]saw his miracles[4592] which he did on them that were diseased.

3 And Jesus went up into a mountain, and there he [ipf]sat with his disciples.[3101]

4 [a]And the passover,[3957] a feast of the Jews, was nigh.

5 [a]When Jesus then [apt]lifted up *his* eyes, and [aptm]saw a great company come unto him, he saith unto Philip, Whence shall we buy bread, that these [psa]may eat?

6 And this he said to [ppt]prove[3985] him: for he himself knew what he [ipf]would [pinf]do.

7 Philip answered him, [a]Two hundred pennyworth[1220] of bread is not sufficient for them, that every one of them may take a little.

8 One of his disciples, Andrew, Simon Peter's brother, saith unto him,

9 There is a lad here, which hath five barley loaves, and two small fishes: [a]but what are they among so many?

10 And Jesus said, [aim]Make the men [ainf]sit down. Now there was much grass in the place. So the men sat down, in number about five thousand.

11 And Jesus took the loaves; and when he had given thanks he distributed to the disciples, and the disciples to them that [ppt]were set down; and likewise of the fishes as much as they [ipf]would.

12 When they were filled, he said unto his disciples, Gather up the fragments[2801] that remain, that nothing be lost.

13 Therefore they gathered *them* together, and filled twelve baskets with the fragments of the five barley loaves, which remained over and above unto them that had eaten.

14 Then those men, when they had seen the miracle that Jesus did, said, This is of a truth [a]that [art]prophet[4396] that [ppt]should come into the world.

15 When Jesus therefore [apt]perceived that they [pin]would [pinf]come and [pinf]take him by force,[726] to [aosb]make him a

36 [a]1John 5:9 [b]John 3:2; 10:25; 15:24
37 [a]Matt. 3:17; 17:5; John 6:27; 8:18 [b]Deut. 4:12; John 1:18; 1Tim. 1:17; 1John 4:12
39 [a]Isa. 8:20; 34:16; Luke 16:29; John 5:46; Acts 17:11 [b]Deut. 18:15, 18; Luke 24:27; John 1:45
40 [a]John 1:11; 3:19
41 [a]John 5:34; 1Thess. 2:6
44 [a]John 12:43 [b]Rom. 2:29
45 [a]Rom. 2:12
46 [a]Gen. 3:15; 12:3; 18:18; 22:18; 49:10; Deut. 18:15, 18; John 1:45; Acts 26:22
1 [a]Matt. 14:15; Mark 6:35; Luke 9:10, 12
4 [a]Lev. 23:5, 7; Deut. 16:1; John 2:13; 5:1
5 [a]Matt. 14:14; Mark 6:35; Luke 9:12
7 [a]Num. 11:21, 22
9 [a]2Kgs. 4:43
14 [a]Gen. 49:10; Deut. 18:15, 18; Matt. 11:3; John 1:21; 4:19, 25; 7:40

🔑 **5:43** See note on Revelation 13:1–18.

king,[935] he departed again into a mountain himself alone.

Jesus Walks on Water (Matt. 14:22–27; Mark 6:45–52)

16 [a]And when even was *now* come, his disciples went down unto the sea,

17 And [apt]entered into a ship, and [ipf]went over the sea toward Capernaum. And it [plpf]was now dark,[4653] and Jesus [plpf]was not come[2064] to them.

18 And the sea [ipf]arose by reason of a great wind that [ppt]blew.[4154]

19 So when they [pfp]had rowed about[5613] five and twenty or thirty furlongs,[4712] they see Jesus [ppt]walking on the sea, and drawing nigh[1451] unto the ship: and they [aop]were afraid.[5399]

20 But he saith unto them, It is I; [pim]be not afraid.[5399]

21 Then they [ipf]willingly [ainf]received him into the ship: and immediately the ship was at the land whither they went.

22 The day following, when the people which [pfp]stood on the other side of the sea [apt]saw that there was none other boat there, save that one whereinto his disciples[3101] were entered, and that Jesus [ao]went not with his disciples into the boat, but *that* his disciples [ao]were gone away alone;

23 (Howbeit[1161] there came other boats from Tiberias nigh[1451] unto the place where they [ao]did eat bread, after that the Lord [apt]had given thanks:)

24 When the people therefore saw that Jesus was not there, neither his disciples, they also took shipping, and came to Capernaum, seeking for Jesus.

Everlasting Food—Jesus the Bread of Life

25 And when they [apt]had found him on the other side of the sea, they said unto him, Rabbi, when [pfi]camest thou hither?[5602]

26 Jesus answered them and said, Verily,[281] verily, I say unto you, Ye seek me, not because ye saw the [an]miracles, but because ye did eat of the loaves, and were filled.

27 [pim]ILabour[2038] not for the meat which [ppt]perisheth, but [a]for that meat which [ppt]endureth unto everlasting life,[2222] which the Son of man shall give unto you: [b]for him hath God the Father[3962] sealed.

28 Then said they unto him, What [psa]shall we do,[4160] that we [psmp]might work[2038] the works[2041] of God?

29 Jesus answered and said unto them, [a]This is the work of God, that ye [aosb]believe[4100] on him whom he [ao]hath sent.

30 They said therefore unto him, [a]What sign[4592] shewest thou then, that we [aosb]may see, and believe thee? what dost thou work?

31 [a]Our fathers did eat manna[3131] in the desert; as it is written, [b]He gave them bread[740] from heaven[3772] [ainf]to eat.

32 Then Jesus said unto them, Verily, verily, I say unto you, Moses [pfi]gave you not that bread from heaven;[3772] but my Father giveth you the true[228] bread from heaven.

33 For the bread of God[2316] is he which [ppt]cometh down from heaven, and [ppt]giveth life[2222] unto the world.[2889]

34 [a]Then said they unto him, Lord, evermore [aim]give us this bread.

35 And Jesus said unto them, [a]I am the bread of life: [b]he that [ppt]cometh[2064] to me [aosb]shall [efn]never hunger;[3983] and he that [ppt]believeth on me [aosb]shall never thirst.[1372]

36 [a]But I said unto you, That ye also [pfi]have seen me, and believe not.

37 [a]All that the Father[3962] giveth me shall come to me; and [b]him that [ppt]cometh to me I [aosb]will in no wise cast[1544] out.

38 For I came down from heaven,[3772] [a]not to [psa]do mine own will,[2307] [b]but the will of him that [apt]sent me.

39 And this is the Father's will which [apt]hath sent me, [a]that of all which he [pfi]hath given me I [aosb]should lose nothing, but [aosb]should raise it up again[450] at the last[2078] day.

40 And this is the will of him that [apt]sent me, [a]that every one which [ppt]seeth

---

16 [a]Matt. 14:23; Mark 6:47

27 IOr, *Work not* [a]John 6:54; John 4:14 [b]Matt. 3:17; 17:5; Mark 1:11; 9:7; Luke 3:22; 9:35; John 1:33; 5:37; 8:18; Acts 2:22; 2Pet. 1:17

29 [a]1John 3:23

30 [a]Matt. 12:38; 16:1; Mark 8:11; 1Cor. 1:22

31 [a]Ex. 16:15; Num. 11:7; Neh. 9:15; 1Cor. 10:3 [b]Ps. 78:24, 25

34 [a]John 4:15

35 [a]John 6:48, 58 [b]John 4:14; 7:37

36 [a]John 6:26, 64

37 [a]John 6:45 [b]Matt. 24:24; John 10:28, 29; 2Tim. 2:19; 1John 2:19

38 [a]Matt. 26:39; John 5:30 [b]John 4:34

39 [a]John 10:28; 17:12; 18:9

40 [a]John 6:27, 47, 54; John 3:15, 16; 4:14

the Son, and [ppt]believeth[4100] on him,
[psa]may have everlasting[166] life:[2222] and I
[aosb]will raise him up[450] at the last day.
41 The Jews then [ipf]murmured at
him, because he said, I am the bread
which [apt]came down from heaven.
42 And they said, [a]Is not this Jesus,
the son of Joseph, whose father and
mother we know? how is it then that he
saith, I [pfi]came down from heaven?
43 Jesus therefore answered and said
unto them, [pim]Murmur not among yourselves.
44 [a]No man can [ainf]come to me, except the Father which [apt]hath sent me
[aosb]draw[1670] him: and I will raise him up
at the last day.
45 [a]It is [pfpp]written[1125] in the prophets,[4396] And they shall be all taught of
God. [b]Every man therefore that [apt]hath
heard,[191] and [apt]hath learned[3129] of the
Father, cometh unto me.
46 [a]Not that any man [pfi]hath seen[3708]
the Father,[3962] [b]save[1508] he which is
of[3844] God, he [pfi]hath seen the Father.
47 Verily,[281] verily, I say unto you,
[a]He that [ppt]believeth on me hath everlasting life.
48 [a]I am that [art]bread of life.[2222]
49 [a]Your fathers did eat [art]manna[3131]
in the wilderness, and [ao]are dead.[599]
50 [a]This is the bread which [ppt]com-
eth down from heaven, that a man
[aosb]may eat thereof, and not [aosb]die.
51 I am the living[2198] bread [a]which
[apt]came down from heaven: if any man
[aosb]eat of this bread, he [ft]shall live[2198] for
ever:[1519,165] [3588] and [b]the bread that I will
give is my flesh,[4561] which I will give for
the life of the world.[2889]
52 The Jews therefore [ipfa]strove
among themselves, saying, [b]How can this
man [ainf]give us *his* flesh [ainf]to eat?
53 Then Jesus said unto them, Verily,
verily, I say unto you, [a]Except ye [aosb]eat
the flesh of the Son of man, and
[aosb]drink his blood,[129] ye have no life in
you.
54 [a]Whoso [ppt]eateth my flesh, and
[ppt]drinketh my blood, hath eternal
life; and I will raise him up at the last
day.

42 [a]Matt. 13:55; Mark 6:3; Luke 4:22
44 [a]Song 1:4; John 6:65
45 [a]Isa. 54:13; Jer. 31:34; Mic. 4:2; Heb. 8:10; 10:16 [b]John 6:37
46 [a]John 1:18; 5:37 [b]Matt. 11:27; Luke 10:22; John 1:18; 7:29; 8:19
47 [a]John 3:16, 18, 36; John 6:40
48 [a]John 6:33, 35
49 [a]John 6:31
50 [a]John 6:51, 58
51 [a]John 3:13 [b]Heb. 10:5, 10
52 [a]John 7:43; 9:16; 10:19 [b]John 3:9
53 [a]Matt. 26:26, 28
54 [a]John 6:27, 40, 63; John 4:14
56 [a]1John 3:24; 4:15, 16
58 [a]John 6:49-51
60 [a]Matt. 11:6; John 6:66
62 [a]Mark 16:19; John 3:13; Acts 1:9; Eph. 4:8
63 [a]2Cor. 3:6
64 [a]John 6:36 [b]John 2:24, 25; 13:11
65 [a]John 6:44, 45
66 [a]John 6:60
68 [a]Acts 5:20

55 For my flesh is meat indeed, and
my blood is drink indeed.
56 He that eateth my flesh, and drinketh my blood, [a]dwelleth[3306] in me, and
I in him.
57 As the living[2198] Father [ao]hath
sent me, and I live by the Father: so he
that [ppt]eateth me, even he shall live by
me.
58 [a]This is that [art]bread which
[apt]came down from heaven: not as your
fathers did eat [art]manna, and [ao]are dead:
he that [ppt]eateth of this bread [fm]shall
live[2198] for ever.
59 These things said he in the synagogue,[4864] as he [ppt]taught[1321] in Capernaum.

Many Disciples Desert Jesus

60 [a]Many therefore of his disciples,[3101] when they had heard *this,* said,
This is an hard[4642] saying;[3056] who can
[pinf]hear[191] it?
61 When Jesus knew in himself that
his disciples murmured at it, he said unto
them, Doth this offend[4624] you?
62 [a]*What* and if ye [psa]shall see the
Son of man [ppt]ascend up where he was
before?
63 [a]It is the spirit[4151] that [ppt]quick-
eneth;[2227] the flesh[4561] profiteth nothing:
the words that I speak unto you, *they* are
spirit,[4151] and *they* are life.[2222]
64 [a]But there are some of you that
believe not. For [b]Jesus knew from the beginning who they were that [ppt]believed
not, and who should betray him.
65 And he said, Therefore [a]said I
unto you, that no man can come unto
me, except it were given unto him of my
Father.
66 [a]From that *time* many of his
disciples[3101] went back, and [ipf]walked no
more with[3326] him.
67 Then said Jesus unto the twelve,
[pin]Will ye also [ainf]go away?
68 Then Simon Peter answered
him, Lord, to whom shall we go? thou
hast [a]the [an]words[4487] of eternal[166]
life.[2222]

69 [a]And we [pfi]believe[4100] and [pfi]are sure that thou art that Christ,[5547] the Son[5207] of the living[2198] God.[2316]

70 Jesus answered them, [aom][a]Have not I chosen[1586] you twelve, [b]and one of you is a devil?[1228]

71 He spake of Judas Iscariot *the son* of Simon: for he it was that [ipf]should[3195] [pinf]betray him, being one of the twelve.

Jesus at the Feast of Tabernacles

7 After these things Jesus [ipf]walked in Galilee: for he would not walk in Jewry,[2449] [a]because the Jews [ipf]sought to kill him.

2 [a]Now the Jews' feast of tabernacles[4634] was at hand.

3 [a]His brethren[80] therefore said unto him, Depart hence, and go into Judaea, that thy disciples[3101] also may see the works[2041] that thou doest.

4 For *there is* no man *that* doeth any thing in secret, and he himself seeketh to be known openly. If thou do these things, [aim]shew[5319] thyself to the world.

5 For [a]neither [ipf]did his brethren believe[4100] in him.

6 Then Jesus said unto them, [a]My time[2540] is not yet come: but your time is alway ready.

7 [a]The world[2889] cannot [pinf]hate you; but me it hateth, [b]because I testify[3140] of it, that the works thereof are evil.[4190]

8 Go ye up unto this feast: I go not up yet unto this feast; [a]for my time [pfip]is not yet full come.[4137]

9 When he had said these words unto them, he [ao]abode[3306] *still* in Galilee.

10 But when his brethren were gone up, then went he also up unto the feast, not openly, but as it were in secret.

11 Then [a]the Jews [ipf]sought him at the feast, and said, Where is he?

12 And [a]there was much murmuring among the people concerning him: for [b]some said, He is a good man:[18] others[243] said, Nay; but he deceiveth the people.

13 Howbeit[3305] no man [ipf]spake openly of him [a]for fear[5401] of the Jews.

14 Now about the midst of the feast Jesus went up into the temple,[2411] and [ipf]taught.[1321]

15 [a]And the Jews [ipf]marvelled, saying, How knoweth[1492] this man [I]letters,[1121] [pfp]having never learned?[3129]

16 Jesus answered them, and said, [a]My doctrine[1322] is not mine, but his that sent me.

17 [a]If any man [psa]will [pinf]do his will,[2307] he [fm]shall know[1097] of the doctrine, whether it be of God, or *whether* I speak of myself.

18 [a]He that [ppt]speaketh of himself [pin]seeketh his own glory:[1391] but he that seeketh his glory that sent him, the same is true, and no unrighteousness[93] is in him.

19 [pfi][a]Did not Moses give[1325] you the law,[3551] and *yet* none of you keepeth the law? [b]Why go ye about [ainf]to kill me?

20 The people answered and said, [a]Thou hast a devil:[1140] who goeth about to kill thee?

21 Jesus answered and said unto them, I have done one work,[2041] and ye all marvel.

22 [a]Moses therefore [pfi]gave unto you circumcision;[4061] (not because it is of Moses, [b]but of the fathers;) and ye on the sabbath day[4521] circumcise[4059] a man.

23 If a man on the sabbath day receive circumcision,[4061] [I]that the law of Moses [asbp]should not be broken;[3089] are ye angry at me, because [a]I [ao]have made a man every whit[3650] whole[5199] on the sabbath day?

24 [pim][a]Judge[2919] not according to the appearance, but judge[2919] [art]righteous[1342] judgment.[2920]

Divisions Concerning Who Christ Is

25 Then said some of them of Jerusalem, Is not this he, whom they seek to kill?

---

69 [a]Matt. 16:16; Mark 8:29; Luke 9:20; John 1:49; 11:27

70 [a]Luke 6:13 [b]John 13:27

1 [a]John 5:16, 18

2 [a]Lev. 23:34

3 [a]Matt. 12:46; Mark 3:31; Acts 1:14

5 [a]Mark 3:21

6 [a]John 2:4; 7:8, 30; 8:20

7 [a]John 15:19 [b]John 3:19

8 [a]John 7:6; 8:20

11 [a]John 11:56

12 [a]John 9:16; 10:19 [b]Matt. 21:46; Luke 7:16; John 6:14; 7:40

13 [a]John 9:22; 12:42; 19:38

15 [I]Or, *learning* [a]Matt. 13:54; Mark 6:2; Luke 4:22; Acts 2:7

16 [a]John 3:11; 8:28; 12:49; 14:10, 24

17 [a]John 8:43

18 [a]John 5:41; 8:50

19 [a]Ex. 24:3; Deut. 33:4; John 1:17; Acts 7:38 [b]Matt. 12:14; Mark 3:6; John 5:16, 18; 10:31, 39; 11:53

20 [a]John 8:48, 52; 10:20

22 [a]Lev. 12:3 [b]Gen. 17:10

23 [I]Or, *without breaking the law of Moses* [a]John 5:8, 9, 16

24 [a]Deut. 1:16, 17; Prov. 24:23; John 8:15; James 2:1

26 But, lo, he speaketh boldly, and they say nothing unto him. [aoa]Do the rulers know[1097] indeed that this is the very Christ?[5547]

27 [a]Howbeit[235] we know this man whence he is: but when Christ [psa]cometh, no man knoweth whence he is.

28 Then cried Jesus in the temple[2411] as he [ppt]taught,[1321] saying, [a]Ye both know[1492] me, and ye know whence I am: and [b]I [pfi]am not come[2064] of myself, but he that sent me [c]is true,[228] [d]whom ye know not.

29 But [a]I know him: for I am from him, and he [ao]hath sent me.

30 Then [a]they [ipf]sought [ainf]to take him: but [b]no man laid hands on him, because his hour[5610] [plpf]was not yet come.[2064]

31 And [a]many of the people believed[4100] on him, and said, When Christ [aosb]cometh, will he do more miracles[4592] than these which this *man* [ao]hath done?

Officers Sent to Arrest Jesus

32 The Pharisees heard that the people [ppt]murmured such things concerning him; and the Pharisees and the chief priests sent officers to take him.

33 Then said Jesus unto them, [a]Yet a little while[5550] am I with you, and *then* I go unto him that sent me.

34 Ye [a]shall seek me, and shall not find *me:* and where I am, *thither* ye cannot [ainf]come.

35 Then said the Jews among themselves, Whither will he go, that we shall not find him? will he go unto [a]the dispersed among the [I]Gentiles, and [pinf]teach[1321] the Gentiles?

36 What *manner of* saying is this that he said, Ye shall seek me, and shall not find *me:* and where I am, *thither* ye cannot come?

"Rivers of Living Water"

37 [a]In the last day, that great *day* of the feast, Jesus stood and cried, saying, [b]If any man thirst, let him come[2064] unto me, and [pim]drink.

38 [a]He that [ppt]believeth[4100] on me, as the scripture[1124] hath said, [b]out of his belly shall flow rivers of living[2198] water.

39 ([a]But this spake he of the Spirit, which they that [ppt]believe on him [ipf]should [pinf]receive: for the [an]Holy Ghost[4151] was not yet *given;* because that Jesus [aop]was not yet [b]glorified.[1392])

Division Among the People

40 Many of the people therefore, when they heard this saying, said, Of a truth this is [a]the Prophet.[4396]

41 Others said, [a]This is the Christ. But some said, [pin]Shall Christ come[2064] [b]out of Galilee?

42 [a]Hath not the scripture[1124] said, That Christ cometh of the seed[4690] of David, and out of the town of Bethlehem, [b]where David was?

43 So there was a division[4978] among the people because of him.

44 And [a]some of them [ipf]would [ainf]have taken him; but no man [ao]laid hands on him.

Unbelieving Rulers

45 Then came the officers to the chief priests and Pharisees; and they said unto them, Why have ye not brought him?

46 The officers answered, [a]Never man[444] spake like this man.

47 Then answered them the Pharisees, [pfip]Are ye also deceived?[4105]

48 [aoa]Have any of the rulers or of the Pharisees believed[4100] on him?

49 But this people who [ppt]knoweth[1097] not the law[3551] are cursed.

50 Nicodemus saith unto them, ([a]he that [apt]came [I]to Jesus by night, being one of them,)

51 [pina]Doth our law judge[2919] *any* [art]man, before it [aosb]hear him, and [aosb]know what he doeth?

26 [a]John 7:48
27 [a]Matt. 13:55; Mark 6:3; Luke 4:22
28 [a]John 8:14 [b]John 5:43; 8:42 [c]John 5:32; 8:26; Rom. 3:4 [d]John 1:18; 8:55
29 [a]Matt. 11:27; John 10:15
30 [a]Mark 11:18; Luke 19:47; 20:19; John 7:19; 8:37 [b]John 7:44; 8:20
31 [a]Matt. 12:23; John 3:2; 8:30
33 [a]John 13:33; 16:16
34 [a]Hos. 5:6; John 8:21; 13:33
35 [I]Or, *Greeks* [a]Isa. 11:12; James 1:1; 1Pet. 1:1
37 [a]Lev. 23:36 [b]Isa. 55:1; John 6:35; Rev. 22:17
38 [a]Deut. 18:15 [b]Prov. 18:4; Isa. 12:3; 44:3; John 4:14
39 [a]Isa. 44:3; Joel 2:28; John 16:7; Acts 2:17, 33, 38 [b]John 12:16; 16:7
40 [a]Deut. 18:15, 18; John 1:21; 6:14
41 [a]John 4:42; 6:69 [b]John 1:46; 7:52
42 [a]Ps. 132:11; Jer. 23:5; Mic. 5:2; Matt. 2:5; Luke 2:4 [b]1Sam. 16:1, 4
44 [a]John 7:30
46 [a]Matt. 7:29
48 [a]John 12:42; Acts 6:7; 1Cor. 1:20, 26; 2:8
50 [I]Gr. *to him* [a]John 3:2
51 [a]Deut. 1:17; 17:8-13; 19:15

52 They answered and said unto him, Art thou also of Galilee? Search, and look: for [a]out of Galilee [pfip]ariseth no prophet.

53 And every man went unto his own house.

A Woman Taken in Adultery

8 Jesus went unto the mount of Olives.

2 And early in the morning he came again into the temple,[2411] and all the people [ipf]came unto him; and he sat down, and [ipf]taught[1321] them.

3 And the scribes[1122] and Pharisees brought unto him a woman [pfpp]taken[2638] in adultery; and when they [apt]had set her in the midst,

4 They say unto him, Master, this woman [aop]was taken in [ppp]adultery, in the very act.

5 [a]Now Moses in the law[3551] commanded us, that such should [pip]be stoned: but what sayest thou?

6 This they said, tempting[3985] him, that they [psa]might have [pinf]to accuse him. But Jesus [apt]stooped[2955] down, and with *his* finger [ipf]wrote[1125] on the ground, *as though he heard them not.*

7 So when they continued asking him, he lifted up himself, and said unto them, [a]He that is without sin[361] among you, [aim]let him first cast[906] a stone at her.

8 And again he stooped down, and [ipf]wrote on the ground.

9 And they which [apt]heard *it,* [a]being convicted by *their own* conscience,[4893] [ipf]went out one by one, beginning at the eldest,[4245] *even* unto the last:[2078] and Jesus was left alone, and the woman standing in the midst.

10 When Jesus had lifted up himself, and saw none but the woman, he said unto her, Woman, where are those thine accusers?[2725] hath no man condemned[2632] thee?

11 She said, No man, Lord. And Jesus said unto her, [a]Neither [pin]do I condemn[2632] thee: [pim]go, and [pim][b]sin[264] no more.

Jesus Is the True Light

12 Then spake Jesus again unto them, saying, [a]I am the light[5457] of the world:[2889] he that [ppt]followeth[190] me [aosb]shall not walk[4043] in [art]darkness,[4653] but shall have the light of life.[2222]

13 The Pharisees therefore said unto him, [a]Thou bearest record of thyself; thy record[3141] is not true.

14 Jesus answered and said unto them, Though I bear record of myself, *yet* my record is true: for I know whence I came, and whither I go; but [a]ye cannot tell whence I come, and whither I go.

15 [a]Ye judge[2919] after the flesh;[4561] [b]I judge[2919] no man.

16 And yet if I judge,[2919] my judgment[2920] is true: for [a]I am not alone, but I and the Father[3962] that [apt]sent me.

17 [a]It is also written in your law,[3551] that the testimony[3141] of two men is true.

18 I am one that [ppt]bear witness of myself, and [a]the Father that [apt]sent me beareth witness of me.

19 Then said they unto him, Where is thy Father? Jesus answered, [a]Ye neither know me, nor my Father: [b]if ye had

52 [a]Isa. 9:1, 2; Matt. 4:15; John 1:46; 7:41
5 [a]Lev. 20:10; Deut. 22:22
7 [a]Deut. 17:7; Rom. 2:1
9 [a]Rom. 2:22
11 [a]Luke 9:56; 12:14; John 3:17 [b]John 5:14
12 [a]John 1:4, 5, 9; 3:19; 9:5; 12:35, 36, 46
13 [a]John 5:31
14 [a]John 7:28; 9:29
15 [a]John 7:24 [b]John 3:17; 12:47; 18:36
16 [a]John 8:29; 16:32
17 [a]Deut. 17:6; 19:15; Matt. 18:16; 2Cor. 13:1; Heb. 10:28
18 [a]John 5:37
19 [a]John 8:55; 16:3 [b]John 14:7

7:52 The Pharisees were challenging the statement that the people made in verse forty concerning Christ being "the Prophet." The Pharisee's argument was based on the assumption that in all of Scripture, no prophets ever came out of Galilee. When Nicodemus entreated the other Pharisees to consider Christ's words before determining whether or not He spoke the truth, they sought to confuse the issue and discredit Christ's ministry. However, their arguments were faulty. First of all, Christ did not grow up in Galilee; He was born in Bethlehem of Judah. The Pharisees probably made this assumption because Christ's followers were mostly from Galilee. Another mistake that they made was that they told Nicodemus to search the Scriptures; they had forgotten that there was a prophet that came from the area of Galilee. Jonah was called by God to go to Nineveh from the city of Gath-hepher (2 Kgs. 14:25).

8:12 See note on 1 John 1:5–10.

known me, ye should have known my Father also.

20 These words spake Jesus in [a]the treasury, as he taught in the temple: and [b]no man laid hands on him; for [c]his hour[5610] [plpf]was not yet come.[2064]

21 Then said Jesus again unto them, I go my way, and [a]ye shall seek me, and [fm][b]shall die[599] in your sins:[266] whither I go, ye cannot come.

22 Then said the Jews, Will he kill himself? because he saith, Whither I go, ye cannot come.

23 And he said unto them, [a]Ye are from beneath; I am from above:[507] [b]ye are of this world;[2889] I am not of this world.

24 [a]I said therefore unto you, that ye shall die in your sins: [b]for if ye [aosb]believe[4100] not that I am *he,* ye shall die in your sins.

25 Then said they unto him, Who art thou? And Jesus saith unto them, Even *the same* that I said unto you from the beginning.

26 I have many things [pinf]to say and [pinf]to judge[2919] of you: but [a]he that [apt]sent me is true;[227] and [b]I speak to the world those things which I [ao]have heard of him.

27 They understood not that he spake to them of the Father.

28 Then said Jesus unto them, When ye [aosb]have [a]lifted up the Son of man, [b]then shall ye know that I am *he,* and [c]*that* I do nothing of myself; but [d]as my Father [ao]hath taught[1321] me, I speak these things.

29 And [a]he that sent me is with me: [b]the Father [ao]hath not left[863] me alone; [c]for I do always those things that please[701] him.

30 As he [ppt]spake these words, [a]many believed[4100] on him.

20 [a]Mark 12:41 [b]John 7:30 [c]John 7:8

21 [a]John 7:34; 13:33 [b]John 8:24

23 [a]John 3:31 [b]John 15:19; 17:16; 1John 4:5

24 [a]John 8:21 [b]Mark 16:16

26 [a]John 7:28 [b]John 3:32; 15:15

28 [a]John 3:14; 12:32 [b]Rom. 1:4 [c]John 5:19, 30 [d]John 3:11

29 [a]John 14:10, 11 [b]John 8:16 [c]John 4:34; 5:30; 6:38

30 [a]John 7:31; 10:42; 11:45

32 [a]Rom. 6:14, 18, 22; 8:2; James 1:25; 2:12

33 [a]Lev. 25:42; Matt. 3:9; John 8:39

34 [a]Rom. 6:16, 20; 2Pet. 2:19

35 [a]Gal. 4:30

36 [a]Rom. 8:2; Gal. 5:1

37 [a]John 7:19; 8:40

38 [a]John 3:32; 5:19, 30; 14:10, 24

39 [a]Matt. 3:9; John 8:33 [b]Rom. 2:28; 9:7; Gal. 3:7, 29

40 [a]John 8:37 [b]John 8:26

41 [a]Isa. 63:16; 64:8; Mal. 1:6

42 [a]1John 5:1 [b]John 16:27; 17:8, 25 [c]John 5:43; 7:28, 29

The Truth Frees You

🔑 31 Then said Jesus to those Jews which [pfp]believed on him, If ye [aosb]continue in my word,[3056] *then* are ye my disciples[3101] indeed;

32 And ye shall know the truth,[225] and [a]the truth shall make you free.[1659]

33 They answered him, [a]We be Abraham's seed,[4690] and [pfi]were never in bondage[1398] to any man: how sayest thou, Ye shall be made free?[1658]

34 Jesus answered them, Verily,[281] verily, I say unto you, [a]Whosoever [ppt]committeth[4160] sin[266] is the [an]servant[1401] of sin.

35 And [a]the servant[1401] abideth[3306] not in the house for ever:[1519,165] [3588] *but* the Son[5207] abideth ever.

36 [a]If the Son therefore shall make you free, ye shall be free indeed.

37 I know that ye are Abraham's seed;[4690] but [a]ye seek to kill me, because my word hath no place in you.

38 [a]I speak that which I have seen with my Father: and ye do that which ye have seen with your father.

39 They answered and said unto him, [a]Abraham is our father. Jesus saith unto them, [b]If ye were Abraham's children,[5043] ye [ipf]would do the works of Abraham.

40 [a]But now ye seek [ainf]to kill me, a man that [pfi]hath told you the truth,[225] [b]which I have heard of God: this did not Abraham.

🔑 41 Ye do the deeds of your father.[3962] Then said they to him, We [pfip]be not born[1080] of fornication;[4202] [a]we have one Father, *even* God.

42 Jesus said unto them, [a]If God were your Father, ye [ipf]would love[25,302] me: [b]for I [ao]proceeded forth and came from God; [c]neither came I of myself, but he sent me.

🔑 **8:31, 32** See notes on Hebrews 6:1–6 and 1 John 3:6–9.

🔑 **8:41** These people believed they were God's "spiritual" children because they were Abraham's physical children. Christ stated that if the works that they were supposedly doing for God were genuine, they would have readily accepted Christ who was also performing God's work (cf. John 8:42). The truth was that their works were done deceitfully, revealing them to be children of the devil (John 8:44).

43 [a]Why do ye not understand my speech?[2981] *even* because ye cannot [pinf]hear[191] my word.[3056]

44 [a]Ye are of *your* father[3962] the devil,[1228] and the lusts of your father ye will[2309] [pinf]do. He was a murderer[443] from the beginning, and [b]abode[2476] not in the truth,[225] because there is no truth[225] in him. When he speaketh a lie,[5579] he speaketh of his own: for he is a liar,[5583] and the father of it.

45 And because I tell *you* the truth, ye believe me not.

46 Which of you convinceth[1651] me of sin?[266] And if I say the truth, why do ye not believe me?

47 [a]He that is of God heareth[191] God's words:[4487] ye therefore hear[191] *them* not, because ye are not of God.

48 Then answered the Jews, and said unto him, Say we not well that thou art a Samaritan, and [a]hast a devil?[1140]

49 Jesus answered, I have not a devil;[1140] but I honour my Father, and ye do dishonour me.

50 And [a]I seek not mine own glory:[1391] there is one that [ppt]seeketh and [ppt]judgeth.

51 Verily,[281] verily, I say unto you, [a]If a man [aosb]keep my saying, he [aosb]shall never see[2334] death.[2288]

52 Then said the Jews unto him, Now we [pfi]know that thou hast a devil.[1140] [a]Abraham [ao]is dead,[599] and the prophets;[4396] and thou sayest, If a man keep my saying, he [asbm]shall never taste[1089] of death.

53 Art thou greater than our father Abraham, which [ao]is dead? and the prophets [ao]are dead: whom makest thou thyself?

54 Jesus answered, [a]If I [psa]honour[1392] myself, my honour[1391] is nothing: [b]it is my Father that [ppt]honoureth me; of whom ye say, that he is your God:

55 Yet [a]ye [pfi]have not known[1097] him; but I know[1492] him: and if I should say, I know him not, I shall be a liar like unto you: but I know him, and keep his saying.

56 Your father Abraham [a]rejoiced[21] to see my day: [b]and he saw *it,* and was glad.

57 Then said the Jews unto him, Thou art not yet fifty years old, and hast thou seen Abraham?

58 Jesus said unto them, Verily, verily, I say unto you, Before Abraham [ainf]was, [a]I am.[1510]

59 Then [a]took they up stones to cast[906] at him: but Jesus hid himself, and went out of the temple,[2411] [apt][b]going through the midst of them, and so passed by.

A Man Born Blind

9 And as *Jesus* passed by, he saw a man which was blind from *his* birth.

2 And his disciples asked[2065] him, saying, Master, [a]who did sin,[264] this man, or his parents, that he was born blind?

3 Jesus answered, Neither [ao]hath this man sinned,[264] nor his parents: [a]but that the works of God [asbp]should be made manifest[5319] in him.

4 [a]I must [pinf]work[2038] the works of him that sent me, while it is day:[2250] the night cometh, when no man can work.

5 As long as I am in the world, [a]I am the light[5457] of the world.

6 When he had thus spoken, [a]he spat on the ground, and made clay of the spittle,[4427] and he [I]anointed[2025] the eyes of the blind man with the clay,

7 And said unto him, Go, wash[3538] [a]in the pool of Siloam, (which is by interpretation,[2059] Sent.) [b]He went his way therefore, and washed, and came seeing.

8 The neighbours therefore, and they which before had seen him that he was blind, said, Is not this he that [ppt]sat and [ppt]begged?[4319]

9 Some said, This is he: others[243] *said,* He is like him: *but* he said, I am *he.*

43 [a]John 7:17
44 [a]Matt. 13:38; 1John 3:8 [b]Jude 1:6
47 [a]John 10:26, 27; 1John 4:6
48 [a]John 7:20; 8:52; 10:20
50 [a]John 5:41; 7:18
51 [a]John 5:24; 11:26
52 [a]Zech. 1:5; Heb. 11:13
54 [a]John 5:31 [b]John 5:41; 16:14; 17:1; Acts 3:13
55 [a]John 7:28, 29
56 [a]Luke 10:24 [b]Heb. 11:13
58 [a]Ex. 3:14; Isa. 43:13; John 17:5, 24; Col. 1:17; Rev. 1:8
59 [a]John 10:31, 39; 11:8 [b]Luke 4:30
2 [a]John 9:34
3 [a]John 11:4
4 [a]John 4:34; 5:19, 36; 11:9; 12:35; 17:4
5 [a]John 1:5, 9; 3:19; 8:12; 12:35, 46
6 [I]*Or, spread the clay upon the eyes of the blind man* [a]Mark 7:33; 8:23
7 [a]Neh. 3:15 [b]2Kgs. 5:14

9:3 See note on Ezekiel 18:1–32.

10 Therefore said they unto him, How were thine eyes opened?

11 He answered and said, [a]A man that is called Jesus made clay, and anointed mine eyes, and said unto me, Go to the pool of Siloam, and wash: and I went and washed, and I [ao]received sight.[308]

12 Then said they unto him, Where is he? He said, I know[1492] not.

13 They brought to the Pharisees him that aforetime was blind.

14 And it was the sabbath day[4521] when Jesus made the clay, and opened his eyes.

15 Then again the Pharisees also asked[2065] him how he [ao]had received his sight. He said unto them, He put clay upon mine eyes, and I washed, and do see.

16 Therefore said some of the Pharisees, This man is not of God, because he keepeth[5083] not the sabbath day. Others[243] said, [a]How can a man that is a sinner[268] do such miracles?[4592] And [b]there was a division[4978] among them.

17 They say unto the blind man again, What sayest thou of him, that he [ao]hath opened thine eyes? He said, [a]He is a prophet.[4396]

18 But the Jews [ao]did not believe[4100] concerning him, that he had been blind, and [ao]received his sight, until they called the parents of him that had received his sight.

19 And they asked[2065] them, saying, Is this your son,[5207] who ye say was born blind? how then [pin]doth he now see?[991]

20 His parents answered them and said, We know that this is our son, and that he was born blind:

21 But by what means he now seeth, we know not; or who [ao]hath opened his eyes, we know not: he is of age; ask[2065] him: he shall speak for himself.

22 These *words* spake his parents, because [a]they feared the Jews: for the Jews had agreed already, that if any man [aosb]did confess[3670] that he was

11 [a]John 9:6, 7

16 [a]John 9:33; John 3:2 [b]John 7:12, 43; 10:19

17 [a]John 4:19; 6:14

22 [a]John 7:13; 12:42; 19:38; Acts 5:13 [b]John 9:34; John 16:2

24 [a]Josh. 7:19; 1Sam. 6:5 [b]John 9:16

29 [a]John 8:14

30 [a]John 3:10

31 [a]Job 27:9; 35:12; Ps. 18:41; 34:15; 66:18; Prov. 1:28; 15:29; 28:9; Isa. 1:15; Jer. 11:11; 14:12; Ezek. 8:18; Mic. 3:4; Zech. 7:13

33 [a]John 9:16

34 [1]Or, *excommunicated him* [a]John 9:2 [b]John 9:22

35 [a]Matt. 14:33; 16:16; Mark 1:1; John 10:36; 1John 5:13

37 [a]John 4:26

Christ,[5547] he [b]should be put out of the synagogue.[656]

23 Therefore said his parents, He is of age; ask him.

24 Then again called they the man that was blind, and said unto him, [a]Give God the praise:[1391] [b]we know that this man is a sinner.[268]

25 He answered and said, Whether he be a sinner *or no,* I know[1492] not: one thing I know, that, whereas I was blind, now I see.

26 Then said they to him again, What did he to thee? how opened he thine eyes?

27 He answered them, I have told you already, and ye did not hear: wherefore would ye [pinf]hear *it* again? will ye also [ainf]be his disciples?[3101]

28 Then they reviled[3058] him, and said, Thou art his disciple; but we are Moses' disciples.[3101]

29 We know that God spake unto Moses: *as for* this *fellow,* [a]we know not from whence he is.

30 The man answered and said unto them, [a]Why herein is a marvellous thing, that ye know not from whence he is, and *yet* he [ao]hath opened mine eyes.

31 Now we know that [a]God heareth[191] not sinners: but if any man be a worshipper of God,[2318] and [psa]doeth his will,[2307] him he heareth.[191]

32 Since the world began was it not heard that any man opened the eyes of one that was born blind.

33 [a]If this man were not of God, he could [pinf]do nothing.

34 They answered and said unto him, [a]Thou [aop]wast altogether born[1080] in sins,[266] and [pin]dost thou teach[1321] us? And they [1][b]cast him out.

35 Jesus heard that they had cast him out; and when he [apt]had found him, he said unto him, [pin]Dost thou believe[4100] on [a]the Son of God?

36 He answered and said, Who is he, Lord, that I [aosb]might believe on him?

37 And Jesus said unto him, Thou [pfi]hast both seen[3708] him, and [a]it is he that [ppt]talketh with thee.

38 And he said, Lord, I believe. And
he worshipped4352 him.
39 And Jesus said, [a]For judgment[2917]
I [ao]am come into this world,[2889] [b]that
they which [ppt]see not [psa]might see; and
that they which [ppt]see [asbm]might be made
blind.
40 And *some* of the Pharisees which
were with him heard these words [a]and
said unto him, Are we blind also?
41 Jesus said unto them, [a]If ye were
blind, ye should have no sin:[266] but now
ye say, We see; therefore your sin remaineth.[3306]

Jesus Is the Good Shepherd

10 Verily,281 verily, I say unto
you, He that [ppt]entereth not by
the door into the sheepfold, but [ppt]climb-
eth up some other way, the same is a
thief[2812] and a robber.[3027]
2 But he that entereth in by the door
is the shepherd of the sheep.
3 To him the porter2377 openeth; and
the sheep hear[191] his voice: and he calleth his own sheep by name, and [pin]lead-
eth them out.1806
4 And when he [aosb]putteth forth his
own sheep, he goeth before them, and the
sheep follow[190] him: for they know[1492]
his voice.
5 And a stranger will they not follow,
but will flee from him: for they know not
the voice of strangers.
6 This parable3942 [ao]spake Jesus unto
them: but they understood not what
things they were which he spake unto
them.
7 Then said Jesus unto them again,
Verily, verily, I say unto you, I am the
door of the sheep.
8 All that ever came before me are
thieves[2812] and robbers:[3027] but the sheep
did not hear[191] them.
9 [a]I am the door: by me if any man
[aosb]enter in, he [fp]shall be saved,[4982] and
shall go in and out, and find pasture.
10 The thief cometh not, but for to
steal, and to kill,[2380] and to destroy:[622] I
[ao]am come that they [psa]might have
life,[2222] and that they [psa]might have *it*
more abundantly.[4053]
11 [a]I am the good shepherd: the
good shepherd giveth his life[5590] for the
sheep.
12 But he that is an hireling, and not
the shepherd, whose own the sheep are
not, seeth[2334] the wolf coming, and
[a]leaveth the sheep, and fleeth: and the
wolf catcheth[726] them, and scattereth the
sheep.
13 The hireling fleeth, because he is
an hireling, and careth3199 not for the
sheep.
14 I am the good shepherd, and
[a]know[1097] my *sheep,* and [pinp]am
known[1097] of mine.
15 [a]As the Father [pin]knoweth[1097] me,
even so know[1097] I the Father: [b]and I lay
down my life[5590] for the sheep.
16 And [a]other[243] sheep I have, which
are not of this fold:833 them also I must
bring, and they [ft]shall hear my voice;
[b]and there shall be one fold, *and* one
shepherd.
17 Therefore doth my Father love
me, [a]because I lay down my life,[5590] that
I [asba]might take it again.
18 No man [pin]taketh it from me, but
I lay it down of myself. I have power[1849]
to lay it down, and I [a]have power to take
it again. [b]This commandment [ao]have I
received[2983] of my Father.
19 [a]There [aom]was a division[4978] there-

39 [a]John 3:17; 5:22, 27; 12:47 [b]Matt. 13:13
40 [a]Rom. 2:19
41 [a]John 15:22, 24
9 [a]John 14:6; Eph. 2:18
11 [a]Isa. 40:11; Ez. 34:12, 23; 37:24; Heb. 13:20; 1Pet. 2:25; 5:4
12 [a]Zech. 11:16, 17
14 [a]2Tim. 2:19
15 [a]Matt. 11:27 [b]John 15:13
16 [a]Isa. 56:8 [b]Ezek. 37:22; Eph. 2:14; 1Pet. 2:25
17 [a]Isa. 53:7, 8, 12; Heb. 2:9
18 [a]John 2:19 [b]John 6:38; 15:10; Acts 2:24, 32
19 [a]John 7:43; 9:16

9:39 Christ came into the world to open the spiritual eyes of some and to close others. The Jews were given the true light of Christ's message, but they chose to reject it. As a result, the message was later sent to the Gentiles. The Jews thought that simply because they were God's chosen people, they had no spiritual duties. They took pride in their ancestry and totally disregarded their own spiritual need. In this way, those who thought they saw the truth were made blind by the coming of the Messiah (see 1 Cor. 1:18–31).

10:1–21 See note on Mark 3:28, 29.

fore again among the Jews for these sayings.
20 And many of them [ipf]said, [a]He
hath a devil,[1140] and [pin]is mad;[3105] why
hear[191] ye him?
21 Others[243] [ipf]said, These are not
the words of him that [ppt]hath a devil.
[a]Can a devil[1140] [pinfb]open the eyes of the
blind?

The Believer's Assurance

🔑 22 And it was at Jerusalem the
feast of the dedication,[1456] and it was
winter.
23 And Jesus [ipf]walked in the temple[2411] [a]in Solomon's porch.
24 Then came the Jews round about
him, and said unto him, How long dost
thou [I]make us to doubt?[5590,142] If thou be
the Christ,[5547] tell us plainly.
25 Jesus answered them, I told you,
and ye [pin]believed[4100] not: [a]the works[2041]
that I do in my Father's name, they bear
witness[3140] of me.
26 But [a]ye believe not, because ye
are not of my sheep, as I said unto
you.
27 [a]My sheep hear[191] my voice, and
I know[1097] them, and they follow[190] me:
28 And I give unto them eternal[166]
life;[2222] and [a]they [asbm]shall never perish,[622] neither [ft]shall any *man* pluck[726]
them out of my hand.
🔑 29 [a]My Father, [b]which gave *them* me,
is greater than all; and no *man* is able
[pinf]to pluck[726] *them* out of my Father's
hand.
30 [a]I and *my* Father[3962] are [n]one.[1520]

31 Then [a]the Jews took up stones
again to stone him.
32 Jesus answered them, Many good
works[2041] [ao]have I shewed[1166] you from
my Father; for which of those works do
ye stone me?
33 The Jews answered him, saying,
For a good work we stone thee not;
but for blasphemy;[988] and because that
thou, being a man, [a]makest thyself
God.[2316]
34 Jesus answered them, [a]Is it not
written in your law,[3551] I said, Ye are
gods?[2316]
35 If he called them gods, [a]unto
whom the word[3056] of God came,
and the scripture[1124] cannot [aifp]be broken;[3089]
36 Say ye of him, [a]whom the Father
[ao]hath sanctified,[37] and [b]sent into the
world, Thou blasphemest; [c]because[3754] I
said, I am [d]the Son[5207] of God?
37 [a]If I do not the works of my
Father, believe me not.
38 But if I do, though ye [psa]believe
not me, [aima]believe the works: that ye may
know, and [aosb]believe, [b]that the Father *is*
in me, and I in him.
39 [a]Therefore they [ipf]sought again
[ainf]to take him: but he escaped out of
their hand,
40 And went away again beyond
Jordan into the place [a]where John at first
baptized;[907] and there he abode.[3306]
41 And many resorted unto him, and
said, John did no miracle:[4592] [a]but all
things that John spake of this man were
true.[227]
42 [a]And many believed on him there.

20 [a]John 7:20; 8:48, 52
21 [a]Ex. 4:11; Ps. 94:9; 146:8 [b]John 9:6, 7, 32, 33
23 [a]Acts 3:11; 5:12
24 [I]Or, *hold us in suspense?*
25 [a]John 3:2; 5:36; 10:38
26 [a]John 8:47; 1John 4:6
27 [a]John 10:4, 14
28 [a]John 6:37; 17:11, 12; 18:9
29 [a]John 14:28 [b]John 17:2, 6-10
30 [a]John 17:11, 22 [b]John 8:59
33 [a]John 5:18
34 [a]Ps. 82:6
35 [a]Rom. 13:1
36 [a]John 6:27 [b]John 3:17; 5:36, 37; 8:42 [c]John 5:17, 18; 10:30 [d]Luke 1:35; John 9:35, 37
37 [a]John 15:24
38 [a]John 5:36; 14:10, 11 [b]John 14:10, 11; 17:21
39 [a]John 7:30, 44; 8:59
40 [a]John 1:28
41 [a]John 3:30
42 [a]John 8:30; 11:45

🔑 **10:22** The Feast of Dedication was a ceremony of great importance to the Jewish people. It originated at the dedication of the temple after its desecration by Antiochus Epiphanes (see note on Ezek. 43:13–27). The Jews underwent severe persecution by this ruler. A number of years later, a priest named Mattathias led a revolt, later continued by his son Maccabeus, that ended this persecution. Following this victory, the temple in Jerusalem was cleansed, and a ceremony was held to mark its rededication. Jewish tradition records that the oil lamps that were lit as part of this celebration had only one day's supply of oil, but burned for eight days. This annual feast was marked by the lighting of candles and the chanting of the Hallel (Ps. 113—118), as well as the waving of palm branches. Since the Feast of Dedication was intended as a time of great rejoicing, all fasting and public mourning were prohibited.

🔑 **10:29–39** See note on Philippians 2:6–8.

Lazarus Dies

11 Now a certain *man* was sick, *named* Lazarus, of Bethany, the town of [a]Mary and her sister Martha.

2 ([a]It was *that* Mary which [apt]anointed[218] the Lord with ointment, and wiped his feet with her hair, whose brother Lazarus was sick.)

3 Therefore his sisters sent unto him, saying, Lord, behold, he whom thou lovest[5368] is sick.

4 When Jesus heard *that,* he said, This sickness is not unto death,[2288] [a]but for the glory[1391] of God, that the Son[5207] of God [asbp]might be glorified[1392] thereby.

5 Now Jesus [ipf]loved[25] Martha, and her sister, and Lazarus.

6 When he had heard therefore that he was sick, [a]he abode two days still in the same place where he was.

7 Then after that saith he to *his* disciples,[3101] Let us go into Judaea again.

8 *His* disciples say unto him, Master, [a]the Jews of late [ipf]sought to stone thee; and goest thou thither[1563] again?

9 Jesus answered, Are there not twelve hours in the day? [a]If any man [psa]walk in the day,[2250] he stumbleth[4350] not, because he seeth the light[5457] of this world.[2889]

10 But [a]if a man walk in the night, he stumbleth,[4350] because there is no light in him.

11 These things said he: and after that he saith unto them, Our friend Lazarus [pfip][a]sleepeth; but I go, that I may awake him out of sleep.

12 Then said his disciples, Lord, if he [pfip]sleep, he [fp]shall do well.[4982]

13 Howbeit[1161] Jesus [plpf]spake of his death: but they thought that he had spoken of taking of rest in sleep.

14 Then said Jesus unto them plainly, Lazarus [ao]is dead.[599]

15 And I am glad for your sakes that I was not there, to the intent ye [aosb]may believe;[4100] nevertheless let us go[71] unto him.

16 Then said Thomas, which is called Didymus, unto his fellowdisciples, Let us also go, that we may die with him.

17 Then when Jesus came, he found that he [ppt]had *lain* in the grave four days already.

18 Now Bethany was nigh unto[1451] Jerusalem, about[5613] fifteen furlongs[4712] off:

19 And many of the Jews [plpf]came to Martha and Mary, to comfort them concerning their brother.

20 Then Martha, as soon as she heard that Jesus was coming, went and met him: but Mary [ipf]sat *still* in the house.

21 Then said Martha unto Jesus, Lord, if thou [ipf]hadst been here, my brother[80] [plpf]had not died.[2348]

22 But I know,[1492] that even now, [a]whatsoever thou [aosb]wilt ask[154] of God, God will give *it* thee.

23 Jesus saith unto her, Thy brother [fm]shall rise again.[450]

24 Martha saith unto him, [a]I know that he shall rise again in the resurrection at the last[2078] day.

25 Jesus said unto her, I am the [a]resurrection,[386] and the [b]life:[2222] [c]he that [ppt]believeth[4100] in me, though he [aosb]were dead, yet [fm]shall he live:[2198]

26 And whosoever [ppt]liveth[2198] and [ppt]believeth in me [aosb]shall never die.[599] Believest thou this?

27 She saith unto him, Yea, Lord: [a]I [pfi]believe that thou art the Christ,[5547] the Son[5207] of God,[2316] which [ppt]should come into the world.[2889]

28 And when she had so said, she went her way, and called Mary her sister secretly, saying, The Master is come, and calleth for thee.

29 As soon as she heard *that,* she arose quickly, and came unto him.

30 Now Jesus [plpf]was not yet come[2064] into the town, but was in that place where Martha met him.

31 [a]The Jews then which were with her in the house, and [ppt]comforted her, when they [apt]saw Mary, that she rose up hastily and went out, followed her, saying, She goeth unto the grave to [aosb]weep there.

---

1 [a]Luke 10:38, 39

2 [a]Matt. 26:7; Mark 14:3; John 12:3

4 [a]John 9:3; 11:40

6 [a]John 10:40

8 [a]John 10:31

9 [a]John 9:4

10 [a]John 12:35

11 [a]Deut. 31:16; Dan. 12:2; Matt. 9:24; Acts 7:60; 1Cor. 15:18, 51

22 [a]John 9:31

24 [a]Luke 14:14; John 5:29

25 [a]John 5:21; 6:39, 40, 44 [b]John 1:4; 6:35; 14:6; Col. 3:4; 1John 1:1, 2; 5:11 [c]John 3:36; 1John 5:10-12

27 [a]Matt. 16:16; 4:42; John 6:14, 69

31 [a]John 11:19

32 Then when Mary was come where Jesus was, and [apt]saw him, she fell down at his feet, saying unto him, [a]Lord, if thou [ipf]hadst been here, my brother had not died.[599]

33 When Jesus therefore saw her weeping, and the Jews also weeping which came with her, he groaned in the spirit,[4151] and [I]was troubled,

34 And said, Where [pfi]have ye laid him? They said unto him, Lord, come and see.

35 [a]Jesus wept.

36 Then said the Jews, Behold how he [ipf]loved[5368] him!

37 And some of them said, Could not this man, [a]which [apt]opened the eyes of the blind, [ainf]have caused that even this man [aosb]should not have died?[599]

Jesus Brings Lazarus Back to Life

38 Jesus therefore again groaning in himself cometh to the grave. It was a cave, and a stone [ipf]lay upon it.

39 Jesus said, [aim]Take ye away[142] the stone. Martha, the sister of him that was dead, saith unto him, Lord, by this time he stinketh: for he hath been *dead* four days.

40 Jesus saith unto her, Said I not unto thee, that, if thou [aosb]wouldest believe,[4100] thou [fm]shouldest [a]see the glory[1391] of God?

41 Then they took away the stone *from the place* where the dead[2348] was [ppt]laid.[2749] And Jesus lifted up *his* eyes, and said, Father, I thank[2168] thee that thou [ao]hast heard[191] me.

42 And I knew that thou hearest me always: but [a]because of the people which [pfp]stand by I said *it,* that they [aosb]may believe[4100] that thou [ao]hast sent me.

43 And when he thus had spoken, he cried with a loud voice, Lazarus, come forth.

44 And he that was dead came forth, bound hand and foot with graveclothes: and [a]his face was [plpf]bound about with a napkin. Jesus saith unto them, Loose him, and let him go.

45 Then many of the Jews which [apt]came to Mary, [a]and had [apt]seen the things which Jesus did, believed[4100] on him.

46 But some of them went their ways to the Pharisees, and told them what things Jesus [ao]had done.

47 [a]Then gathered the chief priests[749] and the Pharisees a council, and [ipf]said, [b]What do we? for this man doeth many miracles.[4592]

48 If we [aosb]let him thus alone, all *men* will believe on him: and the Romans shall come and take away both our place and nation.[1484]

49 And one of them, *named* [a]Caiaphas, being the high priest[749] that same year, said unto them, Ye know nothing at all,

50 [a]Nor consider[1260] that it is expedient[4851] for us, that one man [aosb]should die[599] for the people, and that the whole nation [asbm]perish[622] not.

51 And this spake he not of himself: but being high priest that year, he prophesied[4395] that Jesus should [pinf]die[599] for that nation;

52 And [a]not for that nation only, [b]but that also he should gather together in [n]one the children[5043] of God[2316] that [pfpp]were scattered abroad.

53 Then from that day forth they took counsel together for to [aosb]put him to death.

54 Jesus [a]therefore [ipf]walked no more openly among the Jews; but went thence unto a country near to the wilderness, into a city called [b]Ephraim, and there continued with his disciples.[3101]

55 [a]And the Jews' passover[3957] was nigh at hand:[1451] and many went out of the country up to Jerusalem before the passover, [aosb]to purify[48] themselves.

56 [a]Then [ipf]sought they for Jesus, and [ipf]spake among themselves, as they [pfp]stood in the temple,[2411] What think ye, that he will not come to the feast?

32 [a]John 11:21
33 [I]Gr. *he troubled himself*
35 [a]Luke 19:41
37 [a]John 9:6
40 [a]John 11:4, 23
42 [a]John 12:30
44 [a]John 20:7
45 [a]John 2:23; 10:42; 12:11, 18
47 [a]Ps. 2:2; Matt. 26:3; Mark 14:1; Luke 22:2 [b]John 12:19; Acts 4:16
49 [a]Luke 3:2; John 18:14; Acts 4:6
50 [a]John 18:14
52 [a]Isa. 49:6; 1John 2:2 [b]John 10:16; Eph. 2:14-17
54 [a]John 4:1, 3; 7:1 [b]2Chr. 13:19
55 [a]John 2:13; 5:1; 6:4
56 [a]John 7:11

57 Now both the chief priests[749] and the Pharisees had given a commandment, that, if any man knew where he were, he should shew *it,* that they might take him.

Mary Anoints Jesus at Bethany (Matt. 26:6–13; Mark 14:3–9)

12 Then Jesus six days before the passover3957 came to Bethany, [a]where Lazarus was which had been dead,[2348] whom he raised from the dead.[3498]

2 [a]There they made him a supper; and Martha [ipf]served:[1247] but Lazarus was one of them that [ppp]sat at the table with him.

3 Then [apt]took [a]Mary a pound of ointment of spikenard, very costly, and anointed[218] the feet of Jesus, and wiped his feet with her hair: and the house [aop]was filled[4137] with the odour of the ointment.

4 Then saith one of his disciples,[3101] Judas Iscariot, Simon's *son,* which [ppt]should [pinf]betray him,

5 Why was not this ointment sold for three hundred pence,1220 and [aop]given to the poor?

6 This he said, not that he [ipf]cared for the poor; but because he was a thief,[2812] and [a]had the bag, and bare what [ppt]was put therein.

7 Then said Jesus, Let her alone: against the day of my burying [pfi]hath she kept[5083] this.

8 For [a]the poor always ye have with you; but me ye have not always.

9 Much people of the Jews therefore knew that he was there: and they came not for Jesus' sake only, but that they [aosb]might see[1492] Lazarus also, [a]whom he [ao]had raised[1453] from the dead.

10 [a]But the chief priests[749] consulted that they might put Lazarus also to death;

11 [a]Because that by reason of him many of the Jews [ipf]went away, and [ipf]believed[4100] on Jesus.

1 [a]John 11:1, 43
2 [a]Matt. 26:6; Mark 14:3
3 [a]Luke 10:38, 39; John 11:2
6 [a]John 13:29
8 [a]Matt. 26:11; Mark 14:7
9 [a]John 11:43, 44
10 [a]Luke 16:31
11 [a]John 11:45; 12:18
12 [a]Matt. 21:8; Mark 11:8; Luke 19:35-38
13 [a]Ps. 118:25, 26
14 [a]Matt. 21:7
15 [a]Zech. 9:9
16 [a]Luke 18:34 [b]John 7:39 [c]John 14:26
18 [a]John 12:11
19 [a]John 11:47, 48
20 [a]Acts 17:4 [b]1Kgs. 8:41, 42; Acts 8:27
21 [a]John 1:44

Jesus' Triumphal Entry Into Jerusalem (Matt. 21:1–11; Mark 11:1–11; Luke 19:28–40)

12 [a]On the next day much people that [apt]were come to the feast, when they heard that Jesus was coming to Jerusalem,

13 Took branches of palm trees, and went forth to meet him, and [ipf]cried, [a]Hosanna:5614 Blessed[2127] *is* the King[935] of Israel that [ppt]cometh in the name of the Lord.[2962]

14 [a]And Jesus, when he had found a young ass, sat thereon; as it is written,

15 [a]Fear[5399] not, daughter of Sion; behold, thy King cometh, sitting on an ass's colt.

16 These things [a]understood not his disciples at the first: [b]but when Jesus [aop]was glorified,[1392] [c]then remembered they that these things were written of him, and *that* they [ao]had done these things unto him.

17 The people therefore that was with him when he called Lazarus out of his grave, and raised him from the dead, [ipf]bare record.[3140]

18 [a]For this cause the people also met him, for that they heard that he had done this miracle.[4592]

19 The Pharisees therefore said among themselves, [a]Perceive ye how ye prevail nothing? behold, the world[2889] [ao]is gone after him.

Christ's Final Discourse To the People

20 And there [a]were certain Greeks among them [b]that [ppt]came up to [aosb]worship4352 at the feast:

21 The same came therefore to Philip, [a]which was of Bethsaida of Galilee, and [ipf]desired him, saying, Sir,[2962] we [pin]would [ainf]see[1492] Jesus.

22 Philip cometh and telleth Andrew: and again Andrew and Philip tell Jesus.

23 And Jesus answered them, saying,

[a]The hour[5610] [pfi]is come, that the Son of man [asbp]should be glorified.[1392]

24 Verily,281 verily, I say unto you, [a]Except a [art]corn2848 of [art]wheat [apt]fall into the ground and [aosb]die,[599] it abideth[3306] alone: but if it [aosb]die,[599] it bringeth forth[5342] much fruit.

25 [a]He that [ppt]loveth[5368] his life[5590] [ft]shall lose[622] it; and he that [ppt]hateth his life in this world shall keep[5442] it unto life[2222] eternal.[166]

26 If any man [psa]serve[1247] me, [pim]let him follow[190] me; and [a]where I am, there shall also my servant[1249] be: if any man serve me, him will5091 *my* Father[3962] honour.5091

27 [a]Now [pfip]is my soul troubled;5015 and what shall I say? Father, save[4982] me from this hour:[5610] [b]but for this cause came I unto this hour.

28 Father, glorify[1392] thy name. [a]Then came there a voice from heaven,[3772] *saying,* I have both glorified *it,* and will glorify *it* again.

29 The people therefore, that stood by, and [apt]heard[191] *it,* [ipf]said that it [pfin]thundered: others[243] said, An angel[32] [pfi]spake to him.

30 Jesus answered and said, [a]This voice [pfi]came not because of me, but for your sakes.

31 Now is the judgment[2920] of this world:[2889] now [fp]shall [a]the prince of this world be cast1544 out.

32 And I, [a]if I be lifted up from the earth, [ft]will draw[1670] [b]all *men* unto me.

33 [a]This he said, signifying what death[2288] he should die.[599]

34 The people answered him, [a]We [ao]have heard[191] out of the law[3551] that Christ abideth[3306] for ever:[1519,165] 3588 and how sayest thou, The Son of man must aifpbe lifted up? who is this Son of man?

35 Then Jesus said unto them, Yet a little while[5550] [a]is the light[5457] with you. [pim][b]Walk while ye have the light, lest darkness[4653] [aosb]come upon[2638] you: for [c]he that [ppt]walketh in darkness[4653] knoweth not whither he goeth.

36 While ye have [art]light, [pim]believe in the light, that ye [asbm]may be [a]the [an]children[5207] of light. These things spake Jesus, and departed, and [b]did hide himself from them.

Many People Believe, But Are Afraid

37 But though he [pfp]had done so many miracles[4592] before them, yet they [ipf]believed not on him:

38 That the saying of Esaias the prophet [asbp]might be fulfilled, which he spake, [a]Lord, who [ao]hath believed[4100] our report?[189] and to whom [aop]hath the arm of the Lord been revealed?[601]

39 Therefore they [ipf]could not [pinf]believe, because that Esaias said again,

40 [a]He [pfi]hath blinded their eyes, and [pfi]hardened[4456] their heart;[2588] that they [aosb]should not see[1492] with *their* eyes, nor [aosb]understand[3539] with *their* heart, and [asbp]be converted,[1994] and I [fm]should heal[2390] them.

41 [a]These things said Esaias, when he saw his glory,[1391] and spake of him.

42 Nevertheless among the chief rulers[758] also many believed[4100] on him; but [a]because of the Pharisees they [ipf]did not confess[3670] *him,* lest they should be put out of the synagogue:[656]

43 [a]For they loved[25] the praise[1391] of men[444] more than the praise[1391] of God.[2316]

44 Jesus cried and said, [a]He that [ppt]believeth[4100] on me, believeth not on me, but on him that [apt]sent me.

45 And [a]he that [ppt]seeth me seeth him that [apt]sent me.

46 [a]I [pfi]am come a light[5457] into the world,[2889] that whosoever [ppt]believeth on me [aosb]should not abide[3306] in [art]darkness.[4653]

47 And if any man [aosb]hear[191] my words,[4487] and [aosb]believe not, [a]I judge[2919]

---

23 [a]John 13:32; 17:1
24 [a]1Cor. 15:36
25 [a]Matt. 10:39; 16:25; Mark 8:35; Luke 9:24; 17:33
26 [a]John 14:3; 17:24; 1Thess. 4:17
27 [a]Matt. 26:38, 39; Luke 12:50; John 13:21 [b]Luke 22:53; John 18:37
28 [a]Matt. 3:17
30 [a]John 11:42
31 [a]Matt. 12:29; Luke 10:18; John 14:30; 16:11; Acts 26:18; 2Cor. 4:4; Eph. 2:2; 6:12
32 [a]John 3:14; 8:28 [b]Rom. 5:18; Heb. 2:9
33 [a]John 18:32
34 [a]Ps. 89:36, 37; 110:4; Isa. 9:7; 53:8; Ezek. 37:25; Dan. 2:44; 7:14, 27; Mic. 4:7
35 [a]John 1:9; 8:12; 9:5; 12:46 [b]Jer. 13:16; Eph. 5:8 [c]John 11:10; 1John 2:11
36 [a]Luke 16:8; Eph. 5:8; 1Thess. 5:5; 1John 2:9; 10:11 [b]John 8:59; 11:54
38 [a]Isa. 53:1; Rom. 10:16
40 [a]Isa. 6:9, 10; Matt. 13:14
41 [a]Isa. 6:1
42 [a]John 7:13; 9:22
43 [a]John 5:44
44 [a]Mark 9:37; 1Pet. 1:21
45 [a]John 14:9
46 [a]John 3:19; 8:12; 9:5, 39; 12:35, 36
47 [a]John 5:45; 8:15, 26

12:35 See note on 1 John 1:5–10.

him not: for [b]I came not to judge the world, but to save[4982] the world.

48 [a]He that [ppt]rejecteth me, and [ppt]receiveth not my words,[4487] hath one that [ppt]judgeth him: [b]the word that I have spoken, the same shall judge him in the last[2078] day.

49 For [a]I have not spoken of myself; but the Father which [apt]sent me, he gave me a commandment, [b]what I [aosb]should say, and what I should speak.

50 And I know that his commandment is life[2222] everlasting:[166] whatsoever I speak[2980] therefore, even as the Father said unto me, so I speak.

Jesus Washes His Disciples' Feet

13 Now [a]before the feast of the passover,[3957] when Jesus knew that [b]his hour[5610] [pfi]was come that he [aosb]should depart[3327] out of this world[2889] unto the Father, [apt]having loved[25] his [m]own which were in the world, he loved them unto the end.[5056]

2 And supper being ended, [a]the devil[1228] [pfp]having now put[906] into the heart[2588] of Judas Iscariot, Simon's *son,* to [aosb]betray him;

3 Jesus knowing[1492] [a]that the Father [pfi]had given all things into his hands, and [b]that he [ao]was come from God, and went to God;

4 [a]He riseth from supper, and laid aside[5087] his garments; and took a towel and girded himself.

5 After that he poureth water into a bason, and began [pinf]to wash[3538] the disciples' feet, and [pinf]to wipe *them* with the towel wherewith he was girded.

6 Then cometh he to Simon Peter: and Peter saith unto him, Lord, [a]dost thou wash my feet?

7 Jesus answered and said unto him, What [epn]I [pin]do thou knowest[1492] not now; [a]but thou [fm]shalt know[1097] hereafter.

🔑 8 Peter saith unto him, Thou [aosb]shalt never wash[3538] my feet. Jesus answered him, [a]If I wash thee not, thou hast no part with me.

9 Simon Peter saith unto him, Lord, not my feet only, but also *my* hands and *my* head.

10 Jesus saith to him, He that is washed needeth not save [ainf]to wash[3538] *his* feet, but is clean[2513] every whit:[3650] and [a]ye are clean, but not all.

11 For [a]he knew who [ppt]should betray him; therefore said he, Ye are not all clean.

12 So after he had washed their feet, and had taken his garments, and was set down again, he said unto them, Know ye what I have done to you?

13 [a]Ye call me Master[1320] and Lord:[2962] and ye say well; for *so* I am.

14 [a]If I then, *your* Lord and Master, [ao]have washed your feet; [b]ye also ought [pinf]to wash one another's feet.

15 For [a]I have given you an example, that ye [psa]should do as I have done to you.

16 [a]Verily,[281] verily, I say unto you,

47 [b]John 3:17
48 [a]Luke 10:16 [b]Deut. 18:19; Mark 16:16
49 [a]John 8:38; 14:10 [b]Deut. 18:18

1 [a]Matt. 26:2 [b]John 12:23; 17:1, 11
2 [a]Luke 22:3; John 13:27
3 [a]Matt. 11:27; 28:18; John 3:35; 17:2; Acts 2:36; 1Cor. 15:27; Heb. 2:8 [b]John 8:42; 16:28
4 [a]Luke 22:27; Phil. 2:7, 8
6 [a]Matt. 3:14
7 [a]John 13:12
8 [a]John 3:5; 1Cor. 6:11; Eph. 5:26; Titus 3:5; Heb. 10:22
10 [a]John 15:3
11 [a]John 6:64
13 [a]Matt. 23:8, 10; Luke 6:46; 1Cor. 8:6; 12:3; Phil. 2:11
14 [a]Luke 22:27 [b]Rom. 12:10; Gal. 6:1, 2; 1Pet. 5:5
15 [a]Matt. 11:29; Phil. 2:5; 1Pet. 2:21; 1John 2:6
16 [a]Matt. 10:24; Luke 6:40; John 15:20

🔑 **13:8** There are three major viewpoints regarding Jesus' statement in this verse. First, it has been suggested that in refusing to have Christ wash his feet, Peter was rejecting salvation from his sins. This opinion is based on the definition of the word translated "wash." It has been suggested that the "washing" represents free forgiveness or pardon from sin, the "newness of life," or both.

Another view proposes that Peter sought only physical cleansing as opposed to spiritual. In focusing on himself for this "cleansing," Peter missed the whole point to Christ's illustration—that is, humility.

A third interpretation of this passage reflects two particular perspectives on this verse. In the first place it states that Jesus was warning Peter that he would be disobeying the Lord if he did not allow Him to wash his feet. In other words, Peter would be standing apart from Christ, renouncing Him as Lord. It also emphasizes the importance of a person being washed spiritually. A person cannot enjoy the blessings that result from a close, personal walk with Jesus Christ without being spiritually cleansed. This last interpretation is best supported by the text because obedience to Christ is not the focus of the verses in context.

The servant[1401] is not greater than his lord;[2962] neither he that is sent greater than he that sent[3992] him.

17 [a]If ye know these things, happy[3107] are ye if ye [psa]do them.

18 I speak not of you all: I know whom I [aom]have chosen: but that the scripture [asbp]may be fulfilled, [a]He that [ppt]eateth bread with me [ao]hath lifted up[1869] his heel against me.

19 [I][a]Now I tell you before it [aip]come, that, when it [asbm]is come to pass, ye [aosb]may believe[4100] that I am *he*.

20 [a]Verily, verily, I say unto you, He that [ppt]receiveth whomsoever I send receiveth me; and he that receiveth me receiveth him that [apt]sent me.

Jesus Foretells His Betrayal (Matt. 26:20–25; Mark 14:17–21; Luke 22:21–23)

21 [a]When Jesus had thus said, [b]he was troubled in spirit,[4151] and testified,[3140] and said, Verily, verily, I say unto you, that [c]one of you shall betray me.

22 Then the disciples [ipf]looked one on another, doubting of whom he spake.

23 Now [a]there was leaning on Jesus' bosom[2859] one of his disciples, whom Jesus [ipf]loved.[25]

24 Simon Peter therefore beckoned to him, that he [ainf]should ask who it should be of whom he spake.

25 He then [apt]lying on Jesus' breast[4738] saith unto him, Lord, who is it?

26 Jesus answered, He it is, to whom I shall give a [I]sop,[5596] when I [apt]have dipped[911] *it*. And when he [apt]had dipped the sop, he gave *it* to Judas Iscariot, *the son* of Simon.

27 [a]And after the sop Satan entered into him. Then said Jesus unto him, That thou doest, [aim]do quickly.

28 Now no man at the table knew for what intent[4314,5101] he spake this unto him.

29 For some *of them* [ipf]thought, because [a]Judas had the bag,[1101] that Jesus had said unto him, Buy *those things* that we have need of against the feast; or, that he should give something to the poor.

30 He then having received the sop went immediately out: and it was night.

"Love One Another"

31 Therefore, when he was gone out, Jesus said, [a]Now [aop]is the Son of man glorified,[1392] and [b]God [aop]is glorified in him.

32 [a]If God be glorified in him, God shall also glorify him in himself, and [b]shall straightway[2117] glorify him.

33 Little children, yet a little while I am with you. Ye shall seek me: [a]and as I said unto the Jews, Whither I go, ye cannot come; so now I say to you.

34 [a]A new[2537] commandment I give unto you, That ye love[25] one another; as I [ao]have loved you, that ye also love one another.

35 [a]By this shall all *men* know that ye are my disciples,[3101] if ye [psa]have love[26] one to another.

Peter's Denial Predicted (Matt. 26:31–35; Mark 14:27–31; Luke 22:31–34)

36 Simon Peter said unto him, Lord, whither goest thou? Jesus answered him, Whither I go, thou canst not [ainf]follow me now; but [a]thou shalt follow me afterwards.

37 Peter said unto him, Lord, why cannot I [ainf]follow thee now? I will [a]lay down my life[5590] for thy sake.

38 Jesus answered him, Wilt thou lay down thy life for my sake? Verily, verily, I say unto thee, The cock [ft]shall not crow,[5455] till thou [asbm]hast denied[533] me thrice.

"I Go to Prepare a Place"

14 [pim]Let [a]not your heart be troubled:[5015] ye believe[4100] in God, believe[4100] also in me.

2 In my Father's house[3614] are many mansions:[3438] if *it were* not *so*, I would

17 [a]James 1:25

18 [a]Ps. 41:9; Matt. 26:23; John 13:21

19 [I]Or, *From henceforth* [a]John 14:29; 16:4

20 [a]Matt. 10:40; 25:40; Luke 10:16

21 [a]Matt. 26:21; Mark 14:18; Luke 22:21 [b]John 12:27 [c]Acts 1:17; 1John 2:19

23 [a]John 19:26; 20:2; 21:7, 20, 24

26 [I]Or, *morsel*

27 [a]Luke 22:3; 6:70

29 [a]John 12:6

31 [a]John 12:23 [b]John 14:13; 1Pet. 4:11

32 [a]John 17:1, 4-6 [b]John 12:23

33 [a]John 7:34; 8:21

34 [a]Lev. 19:18; 15:12, 17; Eph. 5:2; 1Thess. 4:9; James 2:8; 1Pet. 1:22; 1John 2:7, 8; 3:11, 23; 4:21

35 [a]1John 2:5; 4:20

36 [a]John 21:18; 2Pet. 1:14

37 [a]Matt. 26:33-35; Mark 14:29-31; Luke 22:33, 34

1 [a]John 14:27; 16:22, 23

have told you. [a]I go [ainf]to prepare a place for you.

3 And if I [aosb]go and prepare a place for you, [a]I will come again, and receive you unto myself; that [b]where I am, *there* ye may be also.

4 And whither I go ye know,[1492] and the way ye know.

5 Thomas saith unto him, Lord, we know not whither thou goest; and how can we know the way?

6 Jesus saith unto him, I am [a]the way,[3598] [b]the truth,[225] and [c]the life:[2222] [d]no man cometh unto the Father,[3962] but by me.

7 [a]If ye [plpf]had known[1097] me, ye should have known my Father also: and from henceforth ye know him, and [pfi]have seen[3708] him.

8 Philip saith unto him, Lord, shew us the Father, and it sufficeth us.

9 Jesus saith unto him, Have I been so long time[5550] with you, and yet hast thou not known me, Philip? [a]he that hath seen me hath seen the Father; and how sayest thou *then,* Shew us the Father?

10 Believest thou not that [a]I am in the Father, and the Father in me? the words[4487] that I speak unto you [b]I speak not of myself: but the Father that [ppt]dwelleth[3306] in me, he doeth the works.

11 [pim]Believe me that I *am* in the Father, and the Father in me: [a]or else [pim]believe me for the very works' sake.

12 [a]Verily,[281] verily, I say unto you, He that [ppt]believeth on me, the works that I do shall he do also; and greater *works* than these shall he do; because I go unto my Father.

13 [a]And whatsoever ye [aosb]shall ask[154] in my name,[3686] that will I do, that the Father [asbp]may be glorified[1392] in the Son.

🔑 14 If ye [aosb]shall ask[154] any thing in my name, I will do *it.*

The Holy Spirit Will Come

15 [a]If ye love[25] me, [aim]keep my commandments.

16 And I [ft]will pray[2065] the Father,[3962] and [a]he shall give you another Comforter,[3875] that he [psa]may abide[3306] with you for ever;[1519,165] [3588]

17 *Even* [a]the Spirit[4151] of truth; [b]whom the world[2889] cannot [ainf]receive, because it seeth him not, neither knoweth him: but ye know[1097] him; for he dwelleth with you, [c]and shall be in you.

18 [a]I [ft]will not leave[863] you [I]comfortless:[3737] [b]I [pin]will come[2064] to you.

19 Yet a little while, and the world seeth[2334] me no more; but [a]ye see me: [b]because I live,[2198] ye shall live also.

20 At that day ye shall know that [a]I *am* in my Father, and ye in me, and I in you.

21 [a]He that [ppt]hath my commandments, and [ppt]keepeth[5083] them, he it is that [ppt]loveth[25] me: and he that loveth me shall be loved of my Father, and I will love him, and will manifest myself to him.

22 [a]Judas saith unto him, not Iscariot, Lord, how is it that thou wilt [pinf]manifest thyself unto us, and not unto the world?

23 Jesus answered and said unto him, [a]If a man [psa]love me, he will keep my words: and my Father will love him, and [b]we will come unto him, and make our abode[3438] with him.

24 He that [ppt]loveth me not keepeth not my sayings: and [a]the word which ye hear is not mine, but the Father's which sent me.

25 These things [pfi]have I spoken[2980] unto you, being *yet* present with you.

26 But [a]the Comforter,[3875] *which is* the Holy Ghost,[4151] whom the Father[3962] will send in my name, [b]he [ft]shall teach[1321] you all things, and bring all things to your remembrance, whatsoever I have said unto you.

27 [a]Peace[1515] I leave with you, my peace I give unto you: not as the world[2889] giveth, give I unto you. [pim][b]Let not your heart be troubled,[5015] neither [pim]let it be afraid.[1168]

2 [a]John 13:33, 36
3 [a]John 14:18, 28; Acts 1:11 [b]John 12:26; 17:24; 1Thess. 4:17
6 [a]Heb. 9:8 [b]John 1:17; 8:32 [c]John 1:4; 11:25 [d]John 10:9
7 [a]John 8:19
9 [a]John 12:45; Col. 1:15; Heb. 1:3
10 [a]John 10:38; 17:21, 23; 14:20 [b]John 5:19; 7:16; 8:28; 12:49
11 [a]John 5:36; 10:38
12 [a]Matt. 21:21; Mark 16:17; Luke 10:17
13 [a]Matt. 7:7; 21:22; Mark 11:24; Luke 11:9; John 15:7, 16; 16:23, 24; James 1:5; 1John 3:22; 5:14
15 [a]John 14:21, 23; 15:10, 14; 1John 5:3
16 [a]John 15:26; 16:7; Rom. 8:15, 26
17 [a]John 15:26; 16:13; 1John 4:6 [b]1Cor. 2:14 [c]1John 2:27
18 [I]Or, *orphans* [a]Matt. 28:20 [b]John 14:3, 28
19 [a]John 16:16 [b]1Cor. 15:20
20 [a]John 14:10; 10:38; 17:21, 23, 26
21 [a]John 14:15, 23; 1John 2:5; 5:3
22 [a]Luke 6:16
23 [a]John 14:15 [b]1John 2:24; Rev. 3:20
24 [a]John 5:19, 38; 7:16; 8:28; 12:49; 14:10
25 [a]Luke 24:49; John 14:16; 15:26; 16:7 [b]John 2:22; 12:16; 16:13; 1John 2:20, 27
27 [a]Phil. 4:7; Col. 3:15 [b]John 14:1

🔑 **14:13–16** See note on Luke 11:9.

28 Ye have heard how [a]I said unto you, I go away, and come[2064] *again* unto you. If ye [ipf]loved me, ye [ao]would rejoice, because I said, [b]I go unto the Father: for [c]my Father is greater than I.

29 And [a]now I [pfi]have told you before it [ainf]come to pass, that, when it [aosb]is come to pass, ye [aosb]might believe.[4100]

30 Hereafter I will not talk much with you: [a]for the prince[758] of this world cometh, and hath nothing in me.

31 But that the world [aosb]may know that I love[25] the Father;[3962] and [a]as the Father gave me commandment, even so I do. Arise,[1453] let us go hence.

Jesus Is the True Vine

15 I am the true[228] vine, and my Father[3962] is the husbandman.1092

2 [a]Every branch in me that [ppt]beareth not fruit he taketh away: and every *branch* that beareth fruit, he purgeth[2508] it, that it [psa]may bring forth more fruit.

3 [a]Now ye are clean[2513] through the word[3056] which I [pfi]have spoken unto you.

4 [aim][a]Abide[3306] in me, and I in you. As the branch cannot bear fruit of itself, except it [aosb]abide[3306] in the vine; no more can ye, except ye [aosb]abide in me.

5 I am the vine, ye *are* the branches:[2814] He that [ppt]abideth in me, and I in him, the same bringeth forth much [a]fruit: for [b]without me ye can [pinf]do nothing.

6 If a man [aosb]abide not in me, [a]he [aop]is cast forth as a branch, and [aop]is withered; and men gather them, and cast *them* into the fire, and they are burned.

7 If ye [aosb]abide in me, and my words[4487] [aosb]abide in you, [a]ye [fm]shall ask what ye [psa]will, and it shall be done unto you.

8 [a]Herein [aop]is my Father glorified,[1392] that ye [psa]bear much fruit; [b]so shall ye be my disciples.[3101]

9 As the Father [ao]hath loved[25] me, so [ao]have I loved[25] you: [aim]continue[3306] ye in my love.[26]

10 [a]If ye [aosb]keep[5083] my commandments, ye [ft]shall abide[3306] in my love; even as I [pfi]have kept my Father's commandments, and abide in his love.

11 These things [pfi]have I spoken[2980] unto you, that my joy [aosb]might remain in you, and [a]*that* your joy [asbp]might be full.[4137]

12 [a]This is my commandment, That ye love[25] one another, as I have loved you.

13 [a]Greater love[26] hath no man than this, that a man [aosb]lay down his life[5590] for his friends.5384

14 [a]Ye are my friends, if ye [psa]do whatsoever I command you.

15 Henceforth I call you not servants;[1401] for the servant knoweth not what his lord[2962] doeth: but I [pfi]have called you friends; [a]for all things that I have heard of my Father I [ao]have made known[1107] unto you.

16 [a]Ye [aom]have not chosen[1586] me, but I have chosen you, and [ao][b]ordained[5087] you, that ye [psa]should go and [psa]bring forth fruit, and *that* your fruit [psa]should remain:[3306] that [c]whatsoever ye [aosb]shall ask of the Father in my name, he [aosb]may give it you.

28 [a]John 14:3, 18 [b]John 14:12; 16:16; 20:17 [c]John 5:18; 10:30; Phil. 2:6
29 [a]John 13:19; 16:4
30 [a]John 12:31; 16:11
31 [a]John 10:18; Phil. 2:8; Heb. 5:8
2 [a]Matt. 15:13
3 [a]John 13:10; 17:17; Eph. 5:26; 1Pet. 1:22
4 [a]Col. 1:23; 1John 2:6
5 [a]Hos. 14:8; Phil. 1:11; 4:13 [b]Acts 4:12
6 [a]Matt. 3:10; 7:19
7 [a]John 15:16; 14:13, 14; 16:23
8 [a]Matt. 5:16; Phil. 1:11 [b]John 8:31; 13:35
10 [a]John 14:15, 21, 23
11 [a]John 16:24; 17:13; 1John 1:4
12 [a]John 13:34; 1Thess. 4:9; 1Pet. 4:8; 1John 3:11; 4:21
13 [a]John 10:11, 15; Rom. 5:7, 8; Eph. 5:2; 1John 3:16
14 [a]Matt. 12:50; John 14:15, 23
15 [a]Gen. 18:17; John 17:26; Acts 20:27
16 [a]John 6:70; 13:18; 1John 4:10, 19 [b]Matt. 28:19; Mark 16:15; Col. 1:6 [c]John 14:13; 15:7

14:28 See note on Philippians 2:6–8.

15:4, 5, 7 The phrase, "abide in me," has been interpreted in several different ways, but all arrive at the same conclusion. Some feel that Christ was referring to the power that He would grant to those who would remain "in Christ." According to this view, the meaning of the phrase is seen in verses seven and nine. Christ desired that His disciples continue to obey the words that He had spoken to them so that their lives would be full of joy.

Another view continues the meaning of this phrase, suggesting that it reflects one's dependence on Christ, communion with Him, and obedience to Him. Remaining in these things will result in one's life becoming fruitful for Christ. For the believer, Christ alone can provide the grace and provision of needs in life. Thus, he must remain faithful to his service for the Lord and to the study of the Scriptures in order to bear fruit.

17 [a]These things I command[1781] you, that ye love[25] one another.

The Disciple of Christ Should Expect Persecution

18 [a]If the world[2889] hate you, ye know that it [pfi]hated me before[4412] *it hated* you.

19 [a]If ye were of the world, the world would [ipf]love[302][5368] his own: but [b]because ye are not of the world, but I [aom]have chosen you out of the world, therefore the world hateth you.

20 [pim]Remember the word that I said unto you, [a]The servant[1401] is not greater than his lord.[2962] If they [ao]have persecuted me, they will also persecute you; [b]if they [ao]have kept[5083] my saying,[3056] they will keep yours also.

21 But [a]all these things will they do unto you for my name's sake, because they know not him that sent me.

22 [a]If I had not come and spoken unto them, they [ipf]had not had[2192] sin:[266] [b]but now they have [I]no cloke for their sin.

23 [a]He that [ppt]hateth me hateth my Father also.

24 If I had not done among them [a]the works which none other man[243] [pfi]did, they [ipf]had not had[2192] sin: but now [pfi]have they both seen[3708] and [pfi]hated both me and my Father.

25 But *this cometh to pass,* that the word might be fulfilled that is written in their law,[3551] [a]They hated me without a cause.

26 [a]But when the Comforter[3875] [aosb]is come, whom I will send unto you from the Father,[3962] *even* the Spirit[4151] of truth,[225] which proceedeth from the Father, [b]he shall testify[3140] of me:

27 And [a]ye also [pin]shall bear witness,[3140] because [b]ye have been with me from the beginning.

17 [a]John 15:12
18 [a]John 3:1, 13
19 [a]1John 4:5, [b]John 17:14
20 [a]Matt. 10:24; Luke 6:40; John 13:16 [b]Ezek. 3:7
21 [a]Matt. 10:22; 24:9; John 16:3
22 [I]Or, *excuse* [a]John 9:41 [b]Rom. 1:20; James 4:17
23 [a]1John 2:23
24 [a]John 3:2; 7:31; 9:32
25 [a]Ps. 35:19; 69:4
26 [a]Luke 24:49; John 14:17, 26; 16:7, 13; Acts 2:33 [b]1John 5:6
27 [a]Luke 24:48; Acts 1:8, 21, 22; 2:32; 3:15; 4:20, 33; 5:32; 10:39; 13:31; 1Pet. 5:1; 2Pet. 1:16 [b]Luke 1:2; 1John 1:1, 2

16 These things have I spoken unto you, that ye [asbp][a]should not be offended.[4624]

2 [a]They shall put you out of the synagogues:[656] yea, the time[5610] cometh, [b]that whosoever [apt]killeth you [aosb]will think[1380] that he [pinf]doeth God service.[2999]

3 And [a]these things will they do unto you, because they [ao]have not known[1097] the Father, nor me.

4 But [a]these things have I told you, that when the time[5610] shall come, ye [psa]may remember that I told you of them. And [b]these things I said not unto you at the beginning, because I was with you.

The Work of the Holy Spirit

5 But now [a]I go my way to him that sent me; and none of you asketh[2065] me, Whither goest thou?

6 But because I [pfi]have said these things unto you, [a]sorrow [pfi]hath filled your heart.

7 Nevertheless I tell you the truth;[225] It [pfi]is expedient[4851] for you that I [aosb]go away: for if I [aosb]go not away, [a]the Comforter[3875] will not come unto you; but [b]if I [asbp]depart, I will send him unto you.

8 And when he is come, he [ft]will [I]reprove[1651] the world[2889] of sin,[266] and of righteousness,[1343] and of judgment:[2920]

9 [a]Of sin, because they believe[4100] not on me;

10 [a]Of righteousness, [b]because I go to my Father,[3962] and ye see[2334] me no more;

11 [a]Of judgment,[2920] because [b]the prince[758] of this world [pfip]is judged.[2919]

12 I have yet many things to say unto you, [a]but ye cannot [pinf]bear them now.

1 [a]Matt. 11:6; 24:10; 26:31
2 [a]John 9:22, 34; 12:42 [b]Acts 8:1; 9:1; 26:9-11
3 [a]John 15:21; Rom. 10:2; 1Cor. 2:8; 1Tim. 1:13
4 [a]John 13:19; 14:29 [b]Matt. 9:15
5 [a]John 7:33; 13:3; 14:28; 16:10, 16
6 [a]John 14:1; 16:22
7 [a]John 7:39; 14:16, 26; 15:26 [b]Acts 2:33; Eph. 4:8
8 [I]Or, *convince*
9 [a]Acts 2:22-37
10 [a]Acts 2:32 [b]John 3:14; 5:32
11 [a]Acts 26:18 [b]Luke 10:18; John 12:31; Eph. 2:2; Col. 2:15; Heb. 2:14
12 [a]Mark 4:33; 1Cor. 3:2; Heb. 5:12

16:7–15 See note on Mark 3:28, 29.

16:10 It has been suggested that the world being reproved of righteousness (John 16:8) means that the message of the need for accepting God's grace will be made known by the convicting power of the Holy Spirit (John 16:13). Along with the coming of the Holy Spirit, the ascension of Christ itself proves that He had finished the work He had set out to do.

13 Howbeit[1161] when he, [a]the Spirit[4151] of truth,[225] is come, [b]he [ft]will guide[3594] you into all [art]truth: for he shall not speak of himself; but whatsoever he [aosb]shall hear,[191] *that* [ft]shall he speak:[2980] and he will shew[312] you things to come.[2064]

14 He [ft]shall glorify[1392] [epn]me: for he shall receive of mine, and [ft]shall shew[312] *it* unto you.

15 [a]All things that the Father hath are mine: therefore said I, that he shall take of mine, and [ft]shall shew[312] *it* unto you.

16 [a]A little while, and ye shall not see me: and again, a little while, and ye shall see me, [b]because I go to the Father.

17 Then said *some* of his disciples[3101] among themselves, What is this that he saith unto us, A little while, and ye shall not see me: and again, a little while, and ye shall see me: and, Because I go to the Father?

18 They said therefore, What is this that he saith, A little while? we cannot tell what he saith.

19 Now Jesus knew that they [ipf]were desirous [pinf]to ask him, and said unto them, Do ye enquire among yourselves of that I said, A little while, and ye shall not see me: and again, a little while, and ye shall see me?

20 Verily,[281] verily, I say unto you, That ye shall weep and lament,[2354] but the world[2889] [fp]shall rejoice:[5463] and ye shall be sorrowful, but your sorrow shall be turned into joy.

21 [a]A woman when she is in travail[5088] hath sorrow, because her hour[5610] [ao]is come: but as soon as she [aosb]is delivered[1080] of the child, she remembereth no more the anguish,[2347] for joy that a man[444] [aop]is born[1080] into the world.

22 [a]And ye now therefore have sorrow: but I will see you again, and [b]your heart shall rejoice, and your joy no man taketh from you.

23 And in that day ye [ft]shall ask[2065] me nothing. [a]Verily, verily, I say unto you, Whatsoever ye [aosb]shall ask the Father in my name, he will give *it* you.

24 Hitherto[2193,737] [ao]have ye asked[154] nothing in my name: [pim]ask, and ye shall receive, [a]that your joy may be full.[4137]

Jesus Will Return to Heaven

25 These things have I spoken unto you in proverbs: but the time[5610] cometh, when I shall no more speak unto you in proverbs, but I shall shew you plainly of the Father.

26 [a]At that day ye [fm]shall ask[154] in my name: and I say not unto you, that I will pray[2065] the Father for you:

27 [a]For the Father himself loveth[5368] you, because ye [pfi]have loved me, and [pfi][b]have believed[4100] that I came out from God.

28 [a]I came forth from the Father,[3962] and [pfi]am come into the world: again, I leave[863] the world, and go to the Father.[3962]

29 His disciples said unto him, Lo, now speakest[2980] thou plainly, and speakest no [I]proverb.

30 Now are we sure[1492] that [a]thou knowest[1492] all things, and needest not that any man [psa]should ask[2065] thee: by this [b]we believe[4100] that thou camest forth from God.

31 Jesus answered them, Do ye now believe?[4100]

32 [a]Behold, the hour[5610] cometh, yea, [pfi]is now come,[2064] that ye [asbp]shall be scattered, [b]every man to [I]his own,[2398] and [aosb]shall leave[863] me alone: and [c]yet I am not alone, because the Father is with me.

🔑 33 These things I have spoken unto you, that [a]in me ye [psa]might have peace.[1515] [b]In the world ye shall have

13 [a]John 14:17; 15:26 [b]John 14:26; 1John 2:20, 27
15 [a]Matt. 11:27; John 3:35; 13:3; 17:10
16 [a]John 7:33; 13:33; 14:19; 16:10 [b]John 13:3; 16:28
21 [a]Isa. 26:17
22 [a]John 16:6 [b]Luke 24:41, 52; John 14:1, 27; 20:20; Acts 2:46; 13:52; 1Pet. 1:8
23 [a]Matt. 7:7; John 14:13; 15:16
24 [a]John 15:11
25 [I]Or, *parables*
26 [a]John 16:23
27 [a]John 14:21, 23 [b]John 3:13; 16:30; 17:8
28 [a]John 13:3
29 [I]Or, *parable*
30 [a]John 21:17 [b]John 16:27; 17:8
32 [I]Or, *his own home* [a]Matt. 26:31; Mark 14:27 [b]John 20:10 [c]John 8:29; 14:10, 11
33 [a]Isa. 9:6; John 14:27; Rom. 5:1; Eph. 2:14; Col. 1:20 [b]John 15:19-21; 2Tim. 3:12

🔑 **16:33** See note on 2 Timothy 1:12.

tribulation:[2347] [c]but [pim]be of good cheer; [d]I [pfi]have overcome the world.[2889]

Jesus' Intercessory Prayer

17 These words spake Jesus, and lifted up his eyes to heaven,[3772] and said, Father, [a]the hour[5610] [pfi]is come; [aim]glorify[1392] thy Son, that thy Son also [aosb]may glorify thee:

2 [a]As thou hast given him power[1849] over all flesh,[4561] that he [aosb]should give eternal[166] life[2222] to as many [b]as thou [pfi]hast given him.

3 And [a]this is [art]life eternal, that they might know thee [b]the only true[228] God, and Jesus Christ,[5547] [c]whom thou [ao]hast sent.[649]

4 [a]I [ao]have glorified thee on the earth: [b]I [ao]have finished[5048] the work [c]which thou gavest me to do.

🔑 5 And now, O Father, [aim]glorify thou me with thine own self with the glory[1391] [a]which I [ipf]had with thee before the world[2889] was.

6 [a]I [ao]have manifested[5319] thy name unto the men[444] [b]which thou [pfi]gavest me out of the world: thine they were, and thou gavest them me; and they [pfi]have kept thy word.[3056]

7 Now they have known that all things whatsoever thou hast given me are of thee.

8 For I [pfi]have given unto them the words[4487] [a]which thou gavest me; and they [ao]have received *them,* [b]and [ao]have known surely that I came out from thee, and they [ao]have believed[4100] that thou [ao]didst send[649] me.

9 I pray[2065] for them: [a]I pray not for the world, but for them which thou hast given me; for they are thine.

10 And all mine are thine, and [a]thine are mine; and I [pfip]am glorified[1392] in them.

🔑 11 [a]And now I am no more in the world,[2889] but these are in the world, and I come to thee. Holy[40] Father,[3962] [aim][b]keep[5083] through thine own name those whom thou hast given me, [c]that they may be [n]one, [d]as we *are.*

🔑 12 While I was with them in the world, [a]I [ipf]kept them in thy name: those that thou gavest me I [ao]have kept,[5442] and [b]none of them [aom]is lost, [c]but the son[5207] of perdition;[684] [d]that the scripture might be fulfilled.

13 And now come I to thee; and these things I speak in the world, that they [psa]might have my joy [pfpp]fulfilled in themselves.

14 [a]I have given them thy word; [b]and the world hath hated them, because they are not of the world, [c]even as I am not of the world.

15 I pray[2065] not that thou [aosb]shouldest take them out of the world, but [a]that thou [aosb]shouldest keep them from the evil.[4190]

16 [a]They are not of the world, even as I am not of the world.

17 [a]Sanctify[37] them through thy truth: [b]thy word[3056] is truth.[225]

18 [a]As thou [ao]hast sent[649] me into the world, even so have I also sent them into the world.

19 And [a]for their sakes I sanctify[37] myself, that they also might be sanctified through the [an]truth.

20 Neither pray[2065] I for these alone, but for them also which shall believe[4100] on me through their word;[3056]

🔑 21 [a]That they all [psa]may be [n]one; as [b]thou, Father, *art* in me, and I in thee, that they also may be [n]one in us: that the world [aosb]may believe that thou hast sent me.

22 And the glory[1391] which thou gavest me I have given them; [a]that they may be one, even as we are one:

33 [c]John 14:1 [d]Rom. 8:37; 1John 4:4; 5:4

1 [a]John 12:23; 13:32
2 [a]Dan. 7:14; Matt. 11:27; 28:18; John 3:35; 5:27; 1Cor. 15:25, 27; Phil. 2:10; Heb. 2:8 [b]John 6:37; 17:6, 9, 24
3 [a]Isa. 53:11; Jer. 9:24 [b]1Cor. 8:4; 1Thess. 1:9 [c]John 3:34; 5:36, 37; 6:29, 57; 7:29; 10:36; 11:42
4 [a]John 13:31; 14:13 [b]John 4:34; 5:36; 9:3; 19:30 [c]John 14:31; 15:10
5 [a]John 1:1, 2; 10:30; 14:9; Phil. 2:6; Col. 1:15, 17; Heb. 1:3, 10
6 [a]Ps. 22:22; John 16:26 [b]John 6:37, 39; 10:29; 15:19; 17:2, 9, 11
8 [a]John 8:28; 12:49; 14:10; John 16:27, 30; 17:25
9 [a]1John 5:19
10 [a]John 16:15
11 [a]John 13:1; 16:28 [b]1Pet. 1:5; Jude 1:1 [c]John 17:21-23 [d]John 10:30
12 [a]John 6:39; 10:28; Heb. 2:13 [b]John 18:9; 1John 2:19 [c]John 6:70; 13:18 [d]Ps. 109:8; Acts 1:20
14 [a]John 17:8 [b]John 15:18, 19; 1John 3:13 [c]John 18:23; 17:16
15 [a]Matt. 6:13; Gal. 1:4; 2Thess. 3:3; 1John 5:18
16 [a]John 17:14
17 [a]John 15:3; Acts 15:9; Eph. 5:26; 1Pet. 1:22 [b]2Sam. 7:28; Ps. 119:142, 151; John 8:40
18 [a]John 20:21 **19** [a]1Cor. 1:2, 30; 1Thess. 4:7; Heb. 10:10 **21** [a]John 10:16; 11:22, 23; Rom. 12:5; Gal. 3:28 [b]John 10:38; 14:11 **22** [a]John 14:20; 1John 1:3; 3:24

🔑 **17:5, 11, 21, 22** See note on Philippians 2:6–8.
🔑 **17:12** See note on 2 Thessalonians 2:3.

23 I in them, and thou in me, [a]that they may be made perfect[5048] in one; and that the world [psa]may know[1097] that thou hast sent me, and [ao]hast loved[25] them, as thou hast loved[25] me.

24 [a]Father, I will that they also, whom thou hast given me, be with me where I am; that they [psa]may behold[2334] my glory, which thou hast given me: [b]for thou lovedst me before the foundation[2602] of the world.[2889]

25 O righteous[1342] Father, [a]the world [ao]hath not known[1097] thee: but [b]I [ao]have known thee, and [c]these [ao]have known that thou hast sent me.

26 [a]And I [ao]have declared[1107] unto them thy name, and will declare *it:* that the love[26] [b]wherewith thou hast loved me may be in them, and I in them.

Jesus Prays in the Garden (Matt. 26:47–56; Mark 14:43–50; Luke 22:47–53)

18 When Jesus had spoken these words, [a]he went forth with his disciples[3101] over [b]the brook Cedron, where was a garden, into the which he entered, and his disciples.

2 And Judas also, which betrayed him, knew the place: [a]for Jesus ofttimes resorted thither[1563] with his disciples.

3 [a]Judas then, having received a band *of men* and officers from the chief priests[749] and Pharisees, cometh thither with lanterns and torches and weapons.

4 Jesus therefore, knowing all things that [ppt]should come[2064] upon him, went forth, and said unto them, Whom seek ye?

5 They answered him, Jesus of Nazareth. Jesus saith unto them, I am *he.* And Judas also, which [ppt]betrayed him, stood with them.

6 As soon then as he had said unto them, I am *he,* they went backward, and fell[4098] to the ground.

7 Then asked he them again, Whom seek ye? And they said, Jesus of Nazareth.

8 Jesus answered, I have told you that I am *he:* if therefore ye seek me, let these [pinf]go their way:

9 That the saying [asbp]might be fulfilled,[4137] which he spake, [a]Of them which thou gavest me [ao]have I lost[622] none.

10 [a]Then Simon Peter having[2192] a sword drew it, and smote[3817] the high priest's servant,[1401] and cut off his right ear. The servant's name was Malchus.

11 Then said Jesus unto Peter, Put up[906] thy sword into the sheath: [a]the cup which my Father hath given me, shall I [efn]not drink it?

Jesus Before the High Priest (Matt. 26:57, 58; Mark 14:53, 54; Luke 22:54)

12 Then the band and the captain and officers of the Jews took Jesus, and bound him,

13 And [a]led him away to [b]Annas first; for he was father in law to Caiaphas, which was the high priest[749] that same year.

14 [a]Now Caiaphas was he, which gave counsel to the Jews, that it [pin]was expedient[4851] that one man[444] [ainf]should die[622] for the people.

Peter Denies Jesus (Matt. 26:69, 70; Mark 14:66–68; Luke 22:55–57)

15 [a]And Simon Peter [ipf]followed Jesus, and *so* did another[243] disciple:[3101] that disciple was known[1110] unto the high priest, and went in with Jesus into the palace of the high priest.

16 [a]But Peter stood at[4314] the door without.[1854] Then went out that other disciple, which was known unto the high priest, and spake unto her that kept the door, and brought in Peter.

17 Then saith the damsel[3814] that kept the door unto Peter, Art not thou also *one* of this man's disciples? He saith, I am not.

18 And the servants[1401] and officers[5257] [plpf]stood there, who [pfp]had made a fire of coals; for it was cold: and they

23 [a]Col. 3:14
24 [a]John 12:26; 14:3; 1Thess. 4:17 [b]John 17:5
25 [a]John 15:21; 16:3 [b]John 7:29; 8:55; 10:15 [c]John 16:8, 27
26 [a]John 15:15; 17:6 [b]John 15:9
1 [a]Matt. 26:36; Mark 14:32; Luke 22:39 [b]2Sam. 15:23
2 [a]Luke 21:37; 22:39
3 [a]Matt. 26:47; Mark 14:43; Luke 22:47; Acts 1:16
9 [a]John 17:12
10 [a]Matt. 26:51; Mark 14:47; Luke 22:49, 50
11 [a]Matt. 20:22; 26:39, 42
13 [a]Matt. 26:57 [b]Luke 3:2
14 [a]John 11:50
15 [a]Matt. 26:58; Mark 14:54; Luke 22:54
16 [a]Matt. 26:69; Mark 14:66; Luke 22:54

[ipf]warmed themselves: and Peter [pfp]stood with them, and [ppt]warmed himself.

The High Priest Questions Jesus (Matt. 26:59–66; Mark 14:55–64; Luke 22:66–71)

19 The high priest then asked[2065] Jesus of his disciples,[3101] and of his doctrine.[1322]

20 Jesus answered him, [a]I spake openly to the world; [epn]I ever [ao]taught[1321] in the synagogue,[4864] and in the temple,[2411] whither[3699] the Jews always resort;[4905] and in secret [ao]have I said[2980] nothing.

21 Why [pin]askest[1905] thou me? ask them which [pfp]heard me, what I have said unto them: behold, they know[1492] what I said.

22 And when he had thus [apt]spoken, one of the officers[5257] which stood by [a]struck Jesus [I]with the palm of his hand, saying, Answerest thou the high priest so?

23 Jesus answered him, If I have spoken evil,[2560] bear witness of the evil: but if well, why smitest[1194] thou me?

24 [a]Now Annas [ao]had sent him bound unto Caiaphas the high priest.

Peter Denies Jesus Again (Matt. 26:71–75; Mark 14:69–72; Luke 22:58–62)

25 And Simon Peter stood and warmed himself. [a]They said therefore unto him, Art not thou also *one* of his disciples?[3101] He denied[720] *it,* and said, I am not.

26 One of the servants[1401] of the high priest, being *his* kinsman whose ear Peter cut off, saith, Did not I see thee in the garden with him?

27 Peter then denied again: and [a]immediately the cock crew.

Jesus Is Brought to Pilate (Matt. 27:1, 2, 11–14; Mark 15:1–5; Luke 23:1–5)

28 [a]Then led they Jesus from Caiaphas unto [b]the hall of judgment: and it was early; [c]and they themselves went not into the judgment hall, lest they [asbp]should be defiled; but that they [aosb]might eat the passover.[3957]

29 Pilate then went out unto them, and said, What accusation[2724] bring[5342] ye against this man?

30 They answered and said unto him, If he were not a malefactor,[2555] we would not have delivered him up unto thee.

31 Then said Pilate unto them, Take ye him, and [aim]judge[2919] him according to your law. The Jews therefore said unto him, It is not lawful for us [ainf]to put any man to death:

32 [a]That the saying of Jesus might be fulfilled, which he spake, signifying what death[2288] he [ipf]should [pinf]die.

33 [a]Then Pilate entered into the judgment hall again, and called Jesus, and said unto him, Art thou the King[935] of the Jews?

34 Jesus answered him, Sayest thou this thing of thyself, or did others tell it thee of me?

35 Pilate answered, Am I a Jew? Thine own nation and the chief priests[749] [ao]have delivered thee unto me: what [ao]hast thou done?[4160]

36 [a]Jesus answered, [b]My kingdom[932] is not of this world:[2889] if my kingdom were of this world, then [ipf]would[75] my servants[5257] fight,[75] that I [asbp]should not be delivered[3860] to the Jews: but now is my kingdom not from hence.

37 Pilate therefore said unto him, Art thou a king then? Jesus answered, Thou sayest that I am a king.[935] To this end [pfip]was I born,[1080] and for this cause [pfi]came I into the world, that I [aosb]should bear witness unto the truth.[225] Every one that [a]is of the truth heareth my voice.

Jesus Sentenced to Die (Matt. 27:15–31; Mark 15:6–20; Luke 23:13–25)

38 Pilate saith unto him, What is truth? And when he had said this, he went out again unto the Jews,[2453] and

20 [a]Matt. 26:55; Luke 4:15; John 7:14, 26, 28; 8:2
22 [I]Or, *with a rod* [a]Jer. 20:2; Acts 23:2
24 [a]Matt. 26:57
25 [a]Matt. 26:69, 71; Mark 14:69; Luke 22:58
27 [a]Matt. 26:74; Mark 14:72; Luke 22:60; John 13:38
28 [a]Matt. 27:2; Mark 15:1; Luke 23:1; Acts 3:13 [b]Matt. 27:27 [c]Acts 10:28; 11:3
32 [a]Matt. 20:19; John 12:32, 33
33 [a]Matt. 27:11
36 [a]1Tim. 6:13 [b]Dan. 2:44; 7:14; Luke 12:14; John 6:15; 8:15
37 [a]John 8:47; 1John 3:19; 4:6

saith unto them, [a]I find[2147] in him no
fault[156] *at all.*
39 [a]But ye have a custom, that
I should release unto you one at
the passover: will ye therefore that I
[aosb]release unto you the King of the
Jews?
40 [a]Then cried they all again, saying,
Not this man, but Barabbas. [b]Now
Barabbas was a robber.[3027]

Jesus Is Sent to Die on the Cross

19 Then [a]Pilate therefore took Jesus,
and scourged[3146] *him.*
2 And the soldiers [apt]platted[4120]
a crown of thorns, and put *it* on his
head, and they [ao]put on him a purple
robe,
3 And [ipf]said, Hail,[5463] King of the
Jews! and they [ipf]smote him with their
hands.
4 Pilate therefore went forth again,
and saith unto them, Behold, I bring him
forth to you, [a]that ye [aosb]may know that
I find[2147] no fault in him.
5 Then came Jesus forth, wearing[5409]
the crown of thorns, and the purple robe.
And *Pilate* saith unto them, Behold the
man!
6 [a]When the chief priests[749] therefore and officers[5257] saw him, they cried
out, saying, Crucify[4717] *him,* crucify *him.*
Pilate saith unto them, [aim]Take ye him,
and [aim]crucify *him:* for I find no fault in
him.
7 The Jews answered him, [a]We have
a law, and by our law he ought [ainf]to
die,[599] because [b]he made himself the
[an]Son[5207] of God.[2316]
8 When Pilate therefore heard that
saying, he [aop]was the more afraid;[5399]
9 And went again into the judgment
hall, and saith unto Jesus, Whence
art thou? [a]But Jesus gave him no answer.[612]
10 Then saith Pilate unto him,
Speakest thou not unto me? knowest
thou not that I have power[1849] [ainf]to crucify thee, and have power [ainf]to release
thee?
11 Jesus answered, [a]Thou couldest
have no power *at all* against me, except
it were [pfpp]given thee from above:[509]
therefore he that [ppt]delivered me unto
thee hath the greater sin.[266]
12 And from thenceforth Pilate
[ipf]sought [ainf]to release him: but the
Jews [ipf]cried out, saying, [a]If thou
[aosb]let this man go, thou art not
Caesar's friend:[5384] [b]whosoever [ppt]mak-
eth himself a king speaketh against
Caesar.
13 When Pilate therefore heard that
saying, he brought Jesus forth, and sat
down in the judgment seat in a place that
is called the Pavement, but in the Hebrew,
Gabbatha.[1042]
14 And [a]it was the preparation of
the passover,[3957] and about the sixth
hour: and he saith unto the Jews, Behold
your King!
15 But they cried out, Away with
him, away with *him,* crucify[4717] him.
Pilate saith unto them, Shall I crucify
your King? The chief priests answered,
[a]We have no king but Caesar.
16 [a]Then delivered he him therefore unto them to [asbp]be crucified. And
they took[3880] Jesus, and led *him*
away.

Jesus on the Cross (Matt. 27:32–44; Mark 15:21–32; Luke 23:26–43)

17 [a]And he bearing his cross[4716]
[b]went forth into a place called *the place*
of a skull, which is called in the Hebrew
Golgotha:[1115]
18 Where they crucified him, and
two other[243] with him, on either side one,
and Jesus in the midst.
19 And Pilate wrote[1125] a title,[5102]
and put *it* on the cross.[4716] And the writing[1125] was, [a]JESUS OF NAZARETH
THE KING[935] OF THE JEWS.
20 This title then read[314] many of
the Jews: for the place where Jesus was
crucified was nigh[1451] to the city: and it
was written in Hebrew, *and* Greek, *and*
Latin.
21 Then said the chief priests of the

38 [a]Matt. 27:24; Luke 23:4; John 19:4, 6
39 [a]Matt. 27:15; Mark 15:6; Luke 23:17
40 [a]Acts 3:14 [b]Luke 23:19
1 [a]Matt. 20:19; 27:26; Mark 15:15; Luke 18:33
4 [a]John 18:38; 19:6
6 [a]Acts 3:13
7 [a]Lev. 24:16 [b]Matt. 26:65; John 5:18; 10:33
9 [a]Isa. 53:7; Matt. 27:12, 14
11 [a]Luke 22:53; John 7:30
12 [a]Luke 23:2 [b]Acts 17:7
14 [a]Matt. 27:62
15 [a]Gen. 49:10
16 [a]Matt. 27:26, 31; Mark 15:15; Luke 23:24
17 [a]Matt. 27:31, 33; Mark 15:21, 22; Luke 23:26, 33 [b]Num. 15:36; Heb. 13:12
19 [a]Matt. 27:37; Mark 15:26; Luke 23:38

Jews to Pilate, [pim]Write not, The King of the Jews; but that he said, I am King of the Jews.

22 Pilate answered, What I have written I have written.

23 [a]Then the soldiers, when they [ao]had crucified Jesus, took his garments, and made four parts, to every soldier a part; and also *his* coat: now the coat was without seam, woven from the top[509] throughout.

24 They said therefore among themselves, [aosi]Let us not rend[4977] it, but [aosi]cast lots for it, whose it shall be: that the scripture [asbp]might be fulfilled,[4137] which [ppt]saith, [a]They parted my raiment[2440] among them, and for my vesture[2441] they did cast lots. These things therefore the soldiers did.

25 [a]Now there [plpf]stood by the cross[4716] of Jesus his mother, and his mother's sister, Mary the *wife* of [I][b]Cleophas, and Mary Magdalene.

26 When Jesus therefore saw his mother, and [a]the disciple[3101] standing by, whom he [ipf]loved,[25] he saith unto his mother, [b]Woman, behold thy son!

27 Then saith he to the disciple, Behold thy mother! And from that hour that disciple took her [a]unto his own[2398] *home.*

The Death of Jesus (Matt. 27:45–56; Mark 15:33–41; Luke. 23:44–49)

28 After this, Jesus knowing that all things [pfip]were now accomplished,[5055] [a]that the scripture[1124] [asbp]might be fulfilled,[5048] saith, I thirst.

29 Now there [ipf]was set[2749] a vessel full of vinegar: and [a]they [apt]filled a sponge with vinegar, and [apt]put *it* upon hyssop,[5301] and put *it* to his mouth.

30 When Jesus therefore had received the vinegar, he said, [pfip][a]It is finished:[5055] and he [apt]bowed his head, and gave up[3860] the ghost.[4151]

31 The Jews therefore, [a]because it was the preparation, [b]that the bodies should not remain upon the cross on the sabbath day,[4521] (for that sabbath day was an high day,) besought Pilate that their legs [asbp]might be broken,[2608] and *that* they [asbp]might be taken away.

32 Then came the soldiers, and brake[2608] the legs of the first, and of the other[243] which [aptp]was crucified with[4957] him.

33 But when they came to Jesus, and saw that he [pfp]was dead[2348] already, they brake not his legs:

34 But one of the soldiers with a spear pierced his side, and forthwith [a]came there out blood[129] and water.

35 And he that [pfp]saw *it* [pfi]bare record, and his record[3141] is true:[228] and he knoweth that he saith true, that ye [aosb]might believe.[4100]

36 For these things were done, [a]that the scripture [asbp]should be fulfilled,[4137] A bone of him shall not be broken.

37 And again another[2087] scripture[1124] saith, [a]They shall look on him whom they pierced.

The Burial of Jesus (Matt. 27:57–61; Mark 15:42–47; Luke 23:50–56)

38 [a]And after this Joseph of Arimathaea, being a disciple[3101] of Jesus, but [pfpp]secretly [b]for fear[5401] of the Jews, besought Pilate that he [aosb]might take away the body of Jesus: and Pilate gave *him* leave. He came therefore, and took the body of Jesus.

39 And there came also [a]Nicodemus, which at the first [apt]came to Jesus by night, and [ppt]brought a mixture of myrrh[4666] and aloes,[250] about an hundred pound *weight.*

40 Then took they the body of Jesus, and [a]wound[1210] it in linen clothes with the spices, as the manner of the Jews is [pinf]to bury.

41 Now in the place where he [aop]was crucified[4717] there was a garden; and in the garden a new sepulchre,[3419] wherein [aop]was never man yet laid.[5087]

42 [a]There laid they Jesus therefore

23 [a]Matt. 27:35; Mark 15:24; Luke 23:34
24 [a]Ps. 22:18
25 [I]Or, *Clopas* [a]Matt. 27:55; Mark 15:40; Luke 23:49 [b]Luke 24:18
26 [a]John 13:23; 20:2; 21:7, 20, 24 [b]John 2:4
27 [a]John 1:11; 16:32
28 [a]Ps. 69:21
29 [a]Matt. 27:48
30 [a]John 17:4
31 [a]Mark 15:42; John 19:42 [b]Deut. 21:23
34 [a]1John 5:6, 8
36 [a]Ex. 12:46; Num. 9:12; Ps. 34:20
37 [a]Ps. 22:16, 17; Zech. 12:10; Rev. 1:7
38 [a]Matt. 27:57; Mark 15:42; Luke 23:50 [b]John 9:22; 12:42
39 [a]John 3:1, 2; 7:50
40 [a]Acts 5:6
42 [a]Isa. 53:9

[b]because of the Jews' preparation *day;* for the sepulchre was nigh at hand.[1451]

The Resurrection of Jesus (Matt. 28:1–10; Mark 16:1–8; Luke 24:1–12)

20 The [a]first *day* of the week cometh Mary Magdalene early, when it was yet dark,[4653] unto the sepulchre,[3419] and seeth[991] the stone [pfpp]taken away from the sepulchre.

2 Then she runneth, and cometh to Simon Peter, and to the [a]other[243] disciple,[3101] whom Jesus [ipf]loved,[5368] and saith unto them, They [ao]have taken away the Lord[2962] out of the sepulchre, and we know not where they [ao]have laid him.

3 [a]Peter therefore went forth, and that other disciple,[3101] and came to the sepulchre.

4 So they [ipf]ran both together: and the other disciple did outrun Peter, and came first[4413] to the sepulchre.

5 And he [apt]stooping down,[3879] *and looking in,* saw [a]the linen clothes lying; yet went he not in.

6 Then cometh[2064] Simon Peter following him, and went into the sepulchre, and seeth[2334] the linen clothes [ppt]lie,

7 And [a]the napkin,[4676] that was about his head, not lying with the linen clothes, but wrapped together in a place by itself.

8 Then went in also that other disciple, which [apt]came first[4413] to the sepulchre, and he saw, and believed.[4100]

9 For as yet they [plpf]knew not the [a]scripture, that he must [ainf]rise again from the dead.[3498]

42 [b]John 19:31
1 [a]Matt. 28:1; Mark 16:1; Luke 24:1
2 [a]John 13:23; 19:26; 21:7, 20, 24
3 [a]Luke 24:12
5 [a]John 19:40
7 [a]John 11:44
9 [a]Ps. 16:10; Acts 2:25-31; 13:34, 35
11 [a]Mark 16:5
14 [a]Matt. 28:9; Mark 16:9 [b]Luke 24:16, 31; John 21:4
17 [a]Ps. 22:22; Matt. 28:10; Rom. 8:29; Heb. 2:11 [b]John 16:28 [c]Eph. 1:17
18 [a]Matt. 28:10; Luke 24:10

10 Then the disciples went away again unto their own home.

Jesus Appears to Mary Magdalene (Mark 16:9–11)

11 [a]But Mary [plpf]stood without[1854] at the sepulchre weeping: and as she [ipf]wept, she stooped down,[3879] *and looked* into the sepulchre,

12 And seeth two angels in white sitting, the one at[4314] the head, and the other at the feet, where the body of Jesus [ipf]had lain.

13 And they say unto her, Woman, why weepest thou? She saith unto them, Because they have taken away my Lord,[2962] and I know not where they [ao]have laid him.

14 [a]And when she had thus said, she turned herself back, and saw[2334] Jesus [pfp]standing, and [b]knew[1492] not that it was Jesus.

15 Jesus saith unto her, Woman, why weepest thou? whom seekest thou? She, supposing him to be the gardener, saith unto him, Sir,[2962] if thou [ao]have borne[941] him hence, tell me where thou [ao]hast laid him, and I will take him away.

16 Jesus saith unto her, Mary. She turned herself, and saith unto him, Rabboni;[4462] which is to say, Master.

🔑 17 Jesus saith unto her, [pim]Touch[680] me not; for I [pfi]am not yet ascended[305] to my Father: but [pim]go to [a]my brethren,[80] and [aim]say unto them, [b]I [pin]ascend unto my Father,[3962] and your Father; and *to* [c]my God,[2316] and your God.

18 [a]Mary Magdalene came and [ppt]told[518] the disciples[3101] that she [pfi]had

---

🔑 **20:17** The verb *háptou*, the present imperative of *haptōmai* (680), should be translated "do not continue touching me." The significance of Christ's statement is related to the fact that He had not ascended to His Father. Some suggest that Mary was attempting to show Christ that she desired for Him to remain in the world and not go to His Father. Christ's command to her to stop touching Him was His explanation to her that His life would no longer be the same as it was before His death. In this view, it has been stated that Christ would be ascending to His Father, which would complete His resurrected state. Others go a step further to say that this woman reflected the feelings of all of Christ's followers who desired to have Christ set up an earthly kingdom. This statement by the Lord was a reminder of His earlier statements about His ascension to His Father (cf. John 14).

seen the Lord, and *that* he had spoken these things unto her.

Jesus Appears to the Disciples (Matt. 28:16–20; Mark 16:14–18; Luke 24:36–49)

19 [a]Then the same day at evening, being the first *day* of the week, when the doors [pfpp]were shut where the disciples[3101] were assembled for fear[5401] of the Jews, came Jesus and stood in the midst, and saith unto them, Peace[1515] *be* unto you.

20 And when he had so said, he shewed unto them *his* hands and his side. [a]Then were the disciples glad, when they saw the Lord.

21 Then said Jesus to them again, Peace *be* unto you: [a]as *my* Father [pfi]hath sent[649] me, even so send I you.

🗝 22 And when he had said this, he breathed on *them,* and saith unto them, [aim]Receive ye the [an]Holy Ghost:[4151]

🗝 23 [a]Whose soever sins[266] ye [aosb]remit,[863] they [pinp]are remitted[863] unto them; *and* whose soever *sins* ye [psa]retain,[2902] they [pfip]are retained.[2902]

Thomas' Unbelief

24 But Thomas, one of the twelve, [a]called Didymus,[1324] was not with them when Jesus came.

25 The other[243] disciples[3101] therefore [ipf]said unto him, We have seen the Lord.[2962] But he said unto them, Except I [aosb]shall see[1492] in his hands the print[5179] of the nails, and put my finger into the print of the nails, and thrust my hand into his side, I [ft]will not believe.[4100]

26 And after eight days again his disciples were within, and Thomas with them: *then* came Jesus, the doors [pfpp]being shut, and stood in the midst, and said, Peace[1515] *be* unto you.

27 Then saith he to Thomas, Reach hither thy finger, and behold my hands; and [a]reach hither thy hand, and thrust *it* into my side: and be not faithless,[571] but [aj]believing.[4103]

28 And Thomas answered and said unto him, My Lord and my God.[2316]

29 Jesus saith unto him, Thomas, because thou hast seen me, thou hast believed: [a]blessed[3107] *are* they that [apt]have not seen,[1492] and *yet* [apt]have believed.

The Purpose of John's Gospel

30 [a]And many other signs[4592] truly did Jesus in the presence of his disciples, which are not written in this book:[975]

31 [a]But these [pfip]are written, that ye [aosb]might believe[4100] that Jesus is the Christ,[5547] the Son[5207] of God;[2316] [b]and that believing ye [psa]might have life[2222] through his name.[3686]

Jesus Appears in Galilee

21 After these things Jesus shewed[5319] himself again to the disciples[3101] at the sea of Tiberias; and on this wise shewed he *himself.*

2 There were together Simon Peter, and Thomas called Didymus, and [a]Nathanael of Cana in Galilee, and [b]the *sons* of Zebedee, and two other[243] of his disciples.

🗝 3 Simon Peter saith unto them, I go

19 [a]Mark 16:14; Luke 24:36; 1Cor. 15:5
20 [a]John 16:22
21 [a]Matt. 28:18; John 17:18, 19; 2Tim. 2:2; Heb. 3:1
23 [a]Matt. 16:19; 18:18
24 [a]John 11:16
27 [a]1John 1:1
29 [a]2Cor. 5:7; 1Pet. 1:8
30 [a]John 21:25
31 [a]Luke 1:4 [b]John 3:15, 16; 5:24; 1Pet. 1:8, 9
1 [a]John 1:45 [b]Matt. 4:21

🗝 **20:22** This was one of the many times that God "breathed," gave, or filled His people with the Holy Spirit. This giving or filling of the Holy Spirit should not be confused with the baptism in the Holy Spirit (see note on Acts 1:5) and the special advent of the Holy Spirit at Jerusalem, Caesarea, and Ephesus (Acts 2:1–13; 11:15–18; 19:1–7). See also note on 1 Corinthians 12:13.

🗝 **20:23** See note on Matthew 16:18, 19.

🗝 **21:3** Some have suggested that Peter's statement about going fishing is significant in that it marks his departure from service to the Lord back to his old profession as a fisherman. They say this was a result of his confusion about the circumstances that had previously transpired (i.e., Christ's death). Others, however, suggest that Peter and the other disciples had to have some form of livelihood until the power that Christ promised came on them.

a [pinf]fishing. They say unto him, We also go with thee. They went forth, and entered into a ship immediately: and that night they caught nothing.

4 But when the morning was now come, Jesus stood on the shore: but the disciples [a]knew[1492] not that it was Jesus.

5 Then [a]Jesus saith unto them, Children, have ye any meat?[4371] They answered him, No.

6 And he said unto them, [a]Cast the net[1350] on the right side of the ship, and ye shall find. They cast therefore, and now they were not able [ainf]to draw[1670] it for the multitude of fishes.

7 Therefore [a]that disciple whom Jesus [ipf]loved saith unto Peter, It is the Lord.[2962] Now when Simon Peter heard that it was the Lord, he girt[1241] *his* fisher's coat *unto him,* (for he was naked,[1131]) and [ao]did cast[906] himself into the sea.

8 And the other[243] disciples came in a little ship; (for they were not far from land,[1093] but as it were two hundred cubits,[4083]) dragging[4951] the net with fishes.

9 As soon then as they [ao]were come to land,[1093] they saw a fire of coals there, and fish laid thereon, and bread.

10 Jesus saith unto them, Bring of the fish which ye [ao]have now caught.[4084]

11 Simon Peter went up, and drew[1670] the net to land[1093] full of great fishes, an hundred and fifty and three: and for all there were so many, yet was not the net broken.

12 Jesus saith unto them, [a]Come *and* [aim]dine. And none of the disciples [ipf]durst[5111] [ainf]ask him, Who art thou? knowing[1492] that it was the Lord.

13 Jesus then cometh, and taketh [art]bread, and giveth them, and [art]fish likewise.

14 This is now [a]the third time that Jesus shewed[5319] himself to his disciples, after that he [aptp]was risen[1453] from the dead.[3498]

4 [a]John 20:14
5 [a]Luke 24:41
6 [a]Luke 5:4, 6, 7
7 [a]John 13:23; 20:2
12 [a]Acts 10:41
14 [a]John 20:19; 26
16 [a]Acts 20:28; Heb. 13:20; 1Pet. 2:25; 5:2, 4
17 [a]John 2:24, 25; 16:30
18 [a]John 13:36; Acts 12:3, 4
19 [a]2Pet. 1:14
20 [a]John 13:23, 25; 20:2
22 [a]Matt. 16:27, 28; 25:31; 1Cor. 4:5; 11:26; Rev. 2:25; 3:11; 22:7, 20

"Lovest Thou Me?"

15 So when they had dined, Jesus saith to Simon Peter, Simon, *son* of Jonas, lovest[25] thou me more than these? He saith unto him, Yea, Lord; thou knowest[1492] that I love[5368] thee. He saith unto him, Feed my lambs.[721]

16 He saith to him again the second time, Simon, *son* of Jonas, lovest[25] thou me? He saith unto him, Yea, Lord; thou knowest[1492] that I love[5368] thee. [a]He saith unto him, [pim]Feed[4165] my sheep.

17 He saith unto him the third time, Simon, *son* of Jonas, lovest[5368] thou me? Peter was grieved because he said unto him the third time, Lovest[5368] thou me? And he said unto him, Lord, [a]thou knowest[1097] all things; thou knowest that I love[5368] thee. Jesus saith unto him, Feed my sheep.

18 [a]Verily,[281] verily, I say unto thee, When thou wast[2258] [cd]young, thou [ipf]girdedst thyself, and [ipf]walkedst whither thou [ipf]wouldest: but when thou [aosb]shalt be old, thou shalt stretch forth thy hands, and another shall gird thee, and carry *thee* whither thou wouldest not.

19 This spake he, signifying [a]by what death[2288] he [ft]should glorify[1392] God. And when he had spoken this, he saith unto him, [pim]Follow[190] me.

20 Then Peter, [aptp]turning about, seeth the disciple[3101] [a]whom Jesus loved[25] following; which also leaned on his breast at supper, and said, Lord, which is he that [ppt]betrayeth thee?

21 Peter seeing him saith to Jesus, Lord,[2962] and what *shall* this man *do?*

22 Jesus saith unto him, If I [psa]will that he [pinf]tarry[3306] [a]till I come, what *is that* to thee? [pim]follow[190] thou me.

23 Then went this saying abroad among the brethren,[80] that that disciple [pin]should not die:[599] yet Jesus said not unto him, He shall not die; but, If I will that he tarry till I come, what *is that* to thee?

24 This is the disciple which [ppt]testifieth[3140] of these things, and [apt]wrote

these things: and [a]we <u>know</u>[1492] that his
<u>testimony</u>[3141] is true.
25 [a]And there are also many other
things which Jesus did, the which, if they
[psmp]<u>should be written</u>[1125] every one, [b]I
suppose that even the world itself could
not contain the books that [ppp]<u>should be</u>
<u>written</u>.[1125] <u>Amen</u>.[281]

24 [a]John 19:35; 3John 1:12

25 [a]John 20:30 [b]Amos 7:10

THE ACTS

of the Apostles

The Book of Acts was written by Luke, the physician, to Theophilus as a supplement to the Gospel of Luke (Acts 1:1, cf. Luke 1:1–3). The Gospel of Luke relates "all that Jesus began both to do and teach" (Acts 1:1). The Acts of the Apostles, on the other hand, begins with the Ascension of Jesus and tells the story of how the gospel was spread far beyond the confines of the Jewish community to the whole world. The statement of Jesus in Acts 1:8, "and ye shall be witnesses unto me both in Jerusalem, and in all Judea, and in Samaria, and unto the uttermost part of the earth," provides an excellent outline for the book.

The Book of Acts concludes rather abruptly with Paul's imprisonment in Rome. It is assumed that the reason for this unexpected closing is that Luke had recorded all the significant events known to him at that time. Hence, the date for the writing of the book is generally agreed to be about A.D. 61. It is clear from certain passages within the Book of Acts that the author was with the Apostle Paul on several occasions (Acts 16:10–17; 20:5—21:18; 27:1—28:16). In fact, many believe that Paul was referring to Luke in 2 Corinthians 8:18 when he mentions "the brother" who was praised "throughout all the churches."

Luke's purpose in writing Acts was not to give a complete history of the growth of the church, but only to list those events with which he was familiar. He does not record how the gospel spread to the east and south of Palestine, or why there were already believers in Damascus before Paul arrived. Nevertheless, the lives and ministries of the prominent individuals that Luke does include sufficiently demonstrate the shift of the evangelical concerns of Christianity from Jews to Gentiles.

1 The former treatise[3056] [aom]have I made,[4160] O [a]Theophilus, of all that Jesus began both [pinf]to do[4160] and [pinf]teach,[1321]

2 [a]Until the day in which he [aop]was taken up,[353] after that he through the [an]Holy Ghost[4151] [apt][b]had given commandments unto the apostles[652] whom he [ao]had chosen:[1586]

3 [a]To whom also he shewed himself alive[2198] after his [aime]passion[3958] by many infallible proofs,[5039] [ppt]being seen of them forty days, and speaking of the things pertaining to the kingdom[932] of God:[2316]

4 [a]And, being assembled together with *them,* commanded them that they should not depart from Jerusalem, but [pinf]wait for[4037] the promise[1860] of the Father,[3962] [b]which, *saith he,* ye [ao]have heard of me.

🔑 5 [a]For John truly [ao]baptized[907] with water; [b]but ye [fp]shall be baptized with the [an]Holy Ghost not many days hence.

The Holy Spirit Will Come

6 When they therefore [apt]were come together,[4905] they [ipf]asked of him, saying,

1 [a]Luke 1:3
2 [a]Mark 16:19; Luke 9:51; 24:51; Acts 1:9; 1Tim. 3:16 [b]Matt. 28:19; Mark 16:15; John 20:21; Acts 10:41, 42
3 [a]Mark 16:14; Luke 24:36; John 20:19, 26; 21:1, 14; 1Cor. 15:5
4 [a]Luke 24:43, 49 [b]Luke 24:49; John 14:16, 26, 27; 15:26; 16:7; Acts 2:33
5 [a]Matt. 3:11; Acts 11:16; 19:4 [b]Joel 3:18; Acts 2:4; 11:15

🔑 **1:5** Many times this is interpreted to mean that the Holy Spirit did the baptizing. The correct understanding of this, however, is that the Holy Spirit is the element of the baptism just as water was the element of the baptism of John. This is the fifth time that the phrase, "baptized with the Holy Ghost," occurs in the New Testament. In each of the previous four instances Jesus Christ is the One being baptized (see Matt. 3:11; Mark 1:8; Luke 3:16; John 1:33).

[a]Lord, wilt thou at this time[5550] [b]restore again[600] the kingdom[932] to Israel?

7 And he said unto them, [a]It is not for you [ainf]to know the times[5550] or the seasons,[2540] which the Father [aom]hath put in his own power.[1849]

8 [a]But ye shall receive [I]power,[1411] [b]after that the Holy Ghost [apt]is come upon you: and [c]ye shall be witnesses[3144] unto me both in Jerusalem, and in all Judaea, and in Samaria, and unto the uttermost part[2078] of the earth.

9 [a]And when he had spoken these things, while they [ppt]beheld, [b]he [aop]was taken up;[1869] and a cloud received[5274] him out of their sight.

10 And while they looked stedfastly toward heaven[3772] as he [ppt]went up, behold, two men[435] stood by them [a]in white apparel;

🔑 11 Which also said, [a]Ye men of Galilee, why stand ye gazing up[1689] into heaven?[3772] this same Jesus, which is taken up from you into heaven, [b]shall so come in like manner as ye [aom]have seen him [ppt]go into heaven.

Matthias Replaces Judas

12 [a]Then returned they unto Jerusalem from the mount called Olivet, which is from Jerusalem a sabbath day's[4521] journey.[3598]

13 And when they were come in, they went up [a]into an upper room, where abode[2258,2650] both [b]Peter, and James, and John, and Andrew, Philip, and Thomas, Bartholomew, and Matthew, James *the son* of Alphaeus, and [c]Simon Zelotes, and [d]Judas *the brother* of James.

14 [a]These all continued[4342] [2258] with one accord in prayer[4335] and supplication,[1162] with [b]the women, and Mary the mother of Jesus, and with [c]his brethren.[80]

15 And in those days Peter stood up in the midst of the disciples,[3101] and said, (the number [a]of names[3686] together were about[5613] an hundred and twenty,)

16 Men *and* brethren, this scripture[1124] must needs [aifp]have been fulfilled,[4137] [a]which the Holy Ghost[4151] by the mouth of David spake before concerning Judas, [b]which was guide to them that took Jesus.

17 For [a]he was numbered with us, and had obtained part[2819] of [b]this ministry.

18 [a]Now this man purchased a field with [b]the reward[3408] of iniquity;[93] and falling headlong, he burst asunder[2997] in the midst,[3319] and all his bowels[4698] gushed out.

19 And it was known[1110] unto all the dwellers[2730] at Jerusalem; insomuch as that field is called in their proper[2398] tongue, Aceldama, that is to say, The field of blood.[129]

20 For it is written in the book of Psalms, [a]Let his habitation[1886] be desolate,[2048] and let no man dwell therein: and [b]his [I]bishopric[1984] let another take.

21 Wherefore of these men which have companied with us all the time[5550] that the Lord Jesus went in and out among us,

22 [a]Beginning from the baptism[908] of John, unto that same day that [b]he was taken up from us, must one be ordained [c]to be a witness[3144] with us of his resurrection.[386]

23 And they appointed[2476] two, Joseph called [a]Barsabas, who was surnamed Justus, and Matthias.

24 And they prayed, and said, Thou, Lord, [a]which knowest the hearts[2589] of all *men,* shew whether of these two thou hast chosen,

25 [a]That he may take part[2819] of this ministry[1248] and apostleship,[651] from which Judas by transgression fell,[3845] that he might go to his own place.

26 And they gave forth their lots;[2819] and the lot fell[4098] upon Matthias; and he was numbered with the eleven apostles.[652]

6 [a]Matt. 24:3 [b]Isa. 1:26; Dan. 7:27; Amos 9:11
7 [a]Matt. 24:36; Mark 13:32; 1Thess. 5:1
8 [I]Or, *the power of the Holy Ghost coming upon you* [a]Acts 2:1, 4 [b]Luke 24:49 [c]Luke 24:48; John 15:27; Acts 1:22; 2:32
9 [a]Luke 24:51; John 6:32 [b]Acts 1:2
10 [a]Matt. 28:3; Mark 16:5; Luke 24:4; John 20:12; Acts 10:3, 30
11 [a]Acts 2:7; 13:31 [b]Dan. 7:13; Matt. 24:30; Mark 13:26; Luke 21:27; John 14:3; 1Thess. 1:10; 4:16; 2Thess. 1:10; Rev. 1:7
12 [a]Luke 24:52
13 [a]Acts 9:37, 39; 20:8 [b]Matt. 10:2-4 [c]Luke 6:15 [d]Jude 1:1
14 [a]Acts 2:1, 46 [b]Luke 23:49, 55; 24:10 [c]Matt. 13:55
15 [a]Rev. 3:4
16 [a]Ps. 41:9; John 13:18 [b]Luke 22:47; John 18:3
17 [a]Matt. 10:4; Luke 6:16 [b]Acts 1:25; 12:25; 20:24; 21:19
18 [a]Matt. 27:5, 7, 8 [b]Matt. 26:15; 2Pet. 2:15
20 [I]Or, *office,* or, *charge* [a]Ps. 69:25 [b]Ps. 109:8
22 [a]Mark 1:1 [b]Acts 1:9 [c]John 15:27; Acts 1:8; 4:33
23 [a]Acts 15:22
24 [a]1Sam. 16:7; 1Chr. 28:9; 29:17; Jer. 11:20; 17:10; Acts 15:8; Rev. 2:23
25 [a]Acts 1:17

🔑 **1:11** See notes on 1 Thessalonians 1:10; 2:19.

The Baptism of the Holy Spirit

2 🔑 And when [a]the day of Pentecost[4005] [aie]was fully come,[4845] [b]they were all with one accord in one place.

2 And suddenly there came a sound from heaven[3772] as of a rushing[5342] mighty wind,[4157] and [a]it filled all the house where they were sitting.

3 And there [aop]appeared unto them [ppt]cloven tongues[1100] like as of fire, and it sat upon each of them.

4 And [a]they were all filled with the [an]Holy Ghost,[4151] and began [pinf][b]to speak[2980] with other[2087] tongues,[1100] as the Spirit [ipf]gave them [pinf]utterance.

5 And there were dwelling[2730] at Jerusalem Jews, devout[2126] men, out of every nation[1484] under heaven.[3772]

6 Now [I]when this [apt]was noised[1096] abroad, the multitude came together, and were [II]confounded, because that every man [ipf]heard them [ppt]speak in his own language.[1258]

7 And they [ipf]were all amazed[1839] and [ipf]marvelled, saying one to another, Behold, are not all these which [ppt]speak [a]Galilaeans?

8 And how hear we every man in our own tongue,[1258] wherein we were born?

9 Parthians, and Medes, and Elamites, and the dwellers in Mesopotamia, and in Judaea, and Cappadocia, in Pontus, and Asia,

10 Phrygia, and Pamphylia, in Egypt, and in the parts of Libya about Cyrene, and strangers of Rome, Jews and proselytes,[4339]

11 Cretes and Arabians, we [pin]do hear[191] them [ppt]speak[2980] in our tongues[1100] the wonderful works[3167] of God.

12 And they [ipf]were all amazed,[1839] and [ipf]were in doubt, saying one to another, What meaneth this?

13 Others [ppt]mocking [ipf]said, These men are full of new wine.[1098]

Peter's Sermon

14 But Peter, standing up with the eleven, lifted up his voice, and said unto them, Ye men of Judaea, and all *ye* that dwell at Jerusalem, be this known[1110] unto you, and hearken to my words:[4487]

15 For these [pin]are not drunken,[3184] as ye suppose,[5274] [a]seeing it is *but* the third hour of the day.

16 But this is that which [pfpp]was spoken[2046] by the prophet Joel;

🔑 17 [a]And it shall come to pass in the last[2078] days, saith God, [b]I will pour out of my Spirit[4151] upon all flesh:[4561] and your sons and [c]your daughters [ft]shall prophesy,[4395] and your young men shall see visions,[3706] and your old men[4245] shall dream dreams:

18 And on my servants[1401] and on my handmaidens[1399] I will pour out in those days of my Spirit; [a]and they [ft]shall prophesy:[4395]

19 [a]And I will shew wonders[5059] in heaven above,[507] and signs[4592] in the earth beneath;[2736] blood, and fire, and vapour of smoke:

20 [a]The sun shall be turned into darkness,[4655] and the moon into blood,

1 [a]Lev. 23:15; Deut. 16:9; Acts 20:16 [b]Acts 1:14
2 [a]Acts 4:31
4 [a]Acts 1:5 [b]Mark 16:17; Acts 10:46; 19:6; 1Cor. 12:10, 28, 30; 13:1; 14:2
6 [I]Gr. *when this voice was made* [II]Or, *troubled in mind*
7 [a]Acts 1:11
15 [a]1Thess. 5:7
17 [a]Isa. 44:3; Ezek. 11:19; 36:27; Joel 2:28, 29; Zech. 12:10; John 7:38 [b]Acts 10:45 [c]Acts 21:9
18 [a]Acts 21:4, 9, 10; 1Cor. 12:10, 28; 14:1
19 [a]Joel 2:30, 31
20 [a]Matt. 24:29; Mark 13:24; Luke 21:25

🔑 **2:1–13** This is the fulfillment of Jesus' promise to send the Holy Spirit. The purpose of the coming of the Holy Spirit was to glorify Jesus Christ (John 16:7–14).

The Holy Spirit came on the day of Pentecost and filled not just a selected few, but every believer that was present in the upper room (Acts 2:4). One result of this baptism was that these people spoke in languages that they did not previously understand. In Acts 2:6, 8, the writer uses the Greek word *dialéktō* (1258), which referred to known and understood ethnic languages, or "dialects."

The "other tongues" mentioned in verse four should not be confused with the "unknown tongue" spoken by the Corinthians (see 1 Cor. 14:2, 4, 13, 19, 27). This "unknown tongue" is always in the singular and is accompanied by a singular personal pronoun. The Apostle Paul demanded that this unknown tongue always be interpreted. The tongues that were spoken in this passage, however, needed no interpreter because each man heard the message of the Lord in his own language.

🔑 **2:17** See note on Joel 2:28–32.

before that great and notable day of the
Lord [ainf]come:
21 And it shall come to pass, *that*
[a]whosoever [asbm]shall call on[1941] the
name[3686] of the Lord [fp]shall be saved.[4982]
22 Ye men of Israel, [aim]hear[191] these
words;[3056] Jesus of Nazareth, a man
[pfpp]approved of God among you [a]by miracles[1411] and wonders[5059] and signs, which
God did by him in the midst of you, as
ye yourselves also know:
23 Him, [a]being delivered by the
[pfpp]determinate[3724] counsel[1012] and foreknowledge[4268] of God, [b]ye [apt]have taken,
and by wicked[459] hands [apt]have crucified[4362] and [ao]slain:
24 [a]Whom God [ao]hath raised up,[450]
having loosed the pains[5604] of death:[2288]
because it was not possible that he
[pip]should be holden[2902] of it.
25 For David speaketh concern-
ing him, [a]I [ipf]foresaw[4308] the Lord[2962] always before my face, for he is on my
right hand,[1188] that I should not be
moved:
26 Therefore [ao]did my heart rejoice,[2165] and my tongue[1100] [aom]was
glad;[21] moreover also my flesh[4561] shall
rest in hope:[1680]
27 Because thou wilt not leave my
soul[5590] in hell,[86] neither wilt thou suffer
thine Holy One[3741] [ainf]to see[1492] corruption.[1312]
28 Thou [ao]hast made known to me
the ways[3598] of life;[2222] thou shalt make
me full of joy[2167] with thy countenance.[4383]
29 Men *and* brethren, let me freely
speak[2036] unto you [a]of the patriarch[3966]
David, that he [ao]is both dead[5053] and
buried, and his sepulchre[3418] is with us
unto this day.
30 Therefore being a prophet,[4396]
[a]and knowing that God [ao]had sworn with
an oath[3727] to him, that of the fruit of
his loins, according to the flesh,[4561] he
[finf]would raise up[450] Christ[5547] [ainf]to sit on
his throne;
31 He seeing this before spake of the
resurrection[386] of Christ, [a]that his
soul[5590] was not left in hell,[86] neither his
flesh[4561] did see corruption.
32 [a]This Jesus [ao]hath God raised
up,[450] [b]whereof we all are witnesses.[3144]
33 Therefore [a]being by the right
hand[1188] of God[2316] exalted,[5312] and
[apt][b]having received of the Father[3962] the
promise[1860] of the Holy Ghost,[4151] he
[ao][c]hath shed forth this, which ye now see
and hear.
34 For David [ao]is not ascended[305]
into the heavens:[3772] but he saith himself,
[a]The LORD[2962] said unto my Lord, Sit
thou on my right hand,
35 Until I [aosb]make thy foes thy footstool.
36 Therefore [pim]let all the house of
Israel know[1097] assuredly, that God
[ao][a]hath made[4160] that same Jesus, whom
ye [ao]have crucified,[4717] both Lord[2962] and
Christ.[5547]
37 Now when they heard *this,* [a]they
[aop]were pricked[2660] in their heart,[2588] and
said unto Peter and to the rest of the
apostles,[652] Men *and* brethren,[80] what
shall we do?
38 Then Peter said unto them,
[aim][a]Repent,[3340] and [aipp]be baptized[907] every one of you in the name[3686] of Jesus
Christ for the [an]remission[859] of sins,[266]

21 [a]Rom. 10:13
22 [a]John 3:2; 14:10, 11; Acts 10:38; Heb. 2:4
23 [a]Matt. 26:24; Luke 22:22; 24:44; Acts 3:18; 4:28 [b]Acts 5:30
24 [a]Acts 2:32; 3:15; 4:10; 10:40; 13:30, 34; 17:31; Rom. 4:24; 8:11; 1Cor. 6:14; 15:15; 2Cor. 4:14; Gal. 1:1; Eph. 1:20; Col. 2:12; 1Thess. 1:10; Heb. 13:20; 1Pet. 1:21
25 [a]Ps. 16:8
29 [a]1Kgs. 2:10; Acts 13:36
30 [a]2Sam. 7:12, 13; Ps. 132:11; Luke 1:32, 69; Rom. 1:3; 2Tim. 2:8
31 [a]Ps. 16:10; Acts 13:35
32 [a]Acts 2:24 [b]Acts 1:8
33 [a]Acts 5:31; Phil. 2:9; Heb. 10:12 [b]John 14:26; 15:26; 16:7, 13; Acts 1:4 [c]Acts 10:45; Eph. 4:8
34 [a]Ps. 110:1; Matt. 22:44; 1Cor. 15:25; Eph. 1:20; Heb. 1:13
36 [a]Acts 5:31
37 [a]Zech. 12:10; Luke 3:10; Acts 9:6; 16:30
38 [a]Luke 24:47; Acts 3:19

2:23 See note on Ephesians 1:4, 5.

2:38 The main verb in this verse is *metanoēsate* (3340), meaning "repent." This refers to that initial repentance of a sinner unto salvation. The verb translated "be baptized" is in the indirect passive imperative of *baptízō* (907), which means that it does not have the same force as the direct command to "repent." The preposition "for" in the phrase "for the remission of sins" in Greek is *eis* (1519), "unto." Literally, the phrase means "for the purpose of identifying you with the remission of sins." This same preposition is used in 1 Corinthians 10:2 in the phrase "and were all baptized unto [*eis*] Moses." These people were identifying themselves with the work and ministry of Moses. Repentance is something that concerns an individual and God, while baptism is intended to be a testimony to other people. That is why *baptisthētō,* "to be baptized," is in the passive voice indicating that one does not baptize himself, but he is baptized by another usually in the presence of others.

and ye shall receive the gift[1431] of the Holy Ghost.[4151]

39 For the promise[1860] is unto you, and [a]to your children, and [b]to all that are afar off, *even* as many as the Lord our God [asbm]shall call.[4341]

40 And with many other words [ipf]did he testify[1263] and [ipf]exhort,[3870] saying, [aipp]Save yourselves from this untoward generation.

41 Then they that gladly [apt]received[588] his word were baptized: and the same day there were added *unto them* about three thousand souls.[5590]

42 [a]And they continued stedfastly[4342] in the apostles'[652] doctrine[1322] and fellowship,[2842] and in breaking[2800] of bread, and in prayers.[4335]

"All Things Common"

43 And fear[5401] came upon every soul:[5590] and [a]many wonders[5059] and signs[4592] [ipf]were done by the apostles.

44 And all that [ppt]believed[4100] were together, and [ipf][a]had all things common;[2839]

45 And [ipf]sold their possessions and goods, and [ipf][a]parted them to all *men,* as every man had need.

46 [a]And they, continuing[4342] daily with one accord [b]in the temple,[2411] and [c]breaking[2806] bread from house to house, [ipf]did eat their meat with gladness[20] and singleness of heart,[2588]

47 Praising[134] God,[2316] and [a]having favour with all the people. And [b]the Lord[2962] [ipf]added to the church[1577] daily such as [ppp]should be saved.[4982]

The Healing of the Lame Man

3 Now Peter and John [ipf]went up together [a]into the temple[2411] at the hour of prayer,[4335] [b]*being* the ninth *hour.*

2 And [a]a certain man lame from his mother's womb was carried, whom they [ipf]laid daily at the gate of the temple which is called Beautiful,[5611] [infg][b]to ask[154] alms[1654] of them that [ppt]entered into the temple;

3 Who [apt]seeing Peter and John about[3195] to go into the temple [ipf]asked an alms.

4 And Peter, fastening his eyes upon him with John, said, Look on us.

5 And he [ipf]gave heed unto them, expecting[4328] [ainf]to receive something of them.

6 Then Peter said, Silver and gold have[5225] I none; but such as I have give I thee: [a]In the name[3686] of Jesus Christ[5547] of Nazareth rise up and walk.

7 And he took him by the right[1188] hand, and lifted *him* up: and immediately his feet and ankle bones received strength.

8 And he [a]leaping up stood, and [ipf]walked, and entered with them into the temple, walking, and leaping, and praising[134] God.

9 [a]And all the people saw him walking and praising God:

10 And they [ipf]knew that it was he which [ppt][a]sat for alms at the Beautiful[5611] gate of the temple: and they were filled with wonder[2285] and amazement[1611] at that which [pfp]had happened unto him.

Peter Addresses the People

11 And as the lame man [aptp]which was healed [ppt]held Peter and John, all the people ran together unto them in the porch [a]that is called Solomon's, greatly wondering.

12 And when Peter saw *it,* he answered unto the people, Ye men of Israel, why marvel[2296] ye at this? or why look ye so earnestly on us, as though by our own power[1411] or holiness[2150] we [pfp]had made this man [infg]to walk?

13 [a]The God of Abraham, and of Isaac, and of Jacob, the God of our fathers,[3962] [ao][b]hath glorified[1392] his Son[3816] Jesus; whom ye [c]delivered up, and [d]denied[720] him in the presence[4383] of Pilate, when he [apt]was determined[2919] [pinf]to let *him* go.

14 But ye denied[720] [a]the Holy One[40] [b]and the Just,[1342] and desired a murderer[5406] [aifp]to be granted[5483] unto you;

15 And killed the [I][a]Prince[747] of life,[2222] [b]whom God [ao]hath raised[1453]

39 [a]Joel 2:28; Acts 3:25 [b]Acts 10:45; 11:15, 18; 14:27; 15:3, 8, 14; Eph. 2:13, 17

42 [a]Acts 1:14; 2:46; Rom. 12:12; Eph. 6:18; Col. 4:2; Heb. 10:25

43 [a]Mark 16:17; Acts 4:33; 5:12

44 [a]Acts 4:32, 34

45 [a]Isa. 58:7

46 [a]Acts 1:14 [b]Luke 24:53; Acts 5:42 [c]Acts 20:7

47 [a]Luke 2:52; Acts 4:33; Rom. 14:18 [b]Acts 5:14; 11:24

1 [a]Acts 2:46 [b]Ps. 55:17

2 [a]Acts 14:8 [b]John 9:8

6 [a]Acts 4:10

8 [a]Isa. 35:6

9 [a]Acts 4:16, 21

10 [a]John 9:8

11 [a]John 10:23; Acts 5:12

13 [a]Acts 5:30 [b]John 7:39; 12:16; 17:1 [c]Matt. 27:2 [d]Matt. 27:20; Mark 15:11; Luke 23:18, 20, 21; John 18:40; 19:15; Acts 13:28

14 [a]Ps. 16:10; Mark 1:24; Luke 1:35; Acts 2:27; 4:27 [b]Acts 7:52; 22:14

15 [I]Or, *Author* [a]Heb. 2:10; 5:9; 1John 5:11 [b]Acts 2:24

from the dead;[3498] [c]whereof we are
witnesses.[3144]
16 [a]And his name[3686] through
faith[4102] in his name[3686] hath made this
man strong, whom ye see and know: yea,
the faith which is by him [ao]hath given
him this perfect soundness3647 in the
presence of you all.
17 And now, brethren, I wot[1492] that
[a]through[2596] ignorance[52] ye did[4238] *it,* as
did also your rulers.
18 But [a]those things, which God
[ao]before had shewed[4293] [b]by the mouth
of all his prophets,[4396] that Christ
[ainf]should suffer, he [ao]hath so fulfilled.[4137]
19 [aim][a]Repent[3340] ye therefore, and
[aim]be converted,[1994] that your sins[266]
[aies]may be blotted out,1813 when the
times[2540] of refreshing403 [aosb]shall come
from the presence[4383] of the Lord;[2962]
20 And he shall send Jesus
Christ,[5547] which [pfpp]before was
preached4296 unto you:
21 [a]Whom the heaven[3772] must
[ainf]receive until the times[5550] of [b]resti-
tution[605] of all things, [c]which God
[ao]hath spoken by the mouth of all his
holy[40] prophets[4396] since the world began.[165] 575
22 For Moses truly said unto the
fathers,[3962] [a]A prophet[4396] [ft]shall the Lord
your God raise up[450] unto you of your
brethren,[80] like unto me; him [fm]shall ye
hear[191] in all things whatsoever he shall
say unto you.
23 And it shall come to pass, *that*
every soul,[5590] which will not hear that
prophet, shall be destroyed from among
the people.
24 Yea, and all the prophets from
Samuel and those that follow after, as
many as have spoken, [ao]have likewise
foretold[4293] of these days.
25 [a]Ye are the [an]children[5207] of the
prophets, and of the covenant[1242] which
God made[1303] with our fathers, saying
unto Abraham, [b]And in thy seed[4690]
shall1757 all the kindreds[3965] of the earth
be blessed.1757
26 [a]Unto you first God, having raised
up his Son[3816] Jesus, [b]sent[649] him to
[ppt]bless[2127] you, [c]in [aie]turning away[654]
every one of you from his iniquities.[4189]

Peter and John Are Brought Before the Jewish Leaders

4 And as they [ppt]spake unto the people, the priests, and the [1][a]captain of
the temple, and the Sadducees, came
upon them,
2 [a]Being grieved1278 that they
[aid]taught[1321] the people,[2992] and
[aid]preached[2605] through Jesus the resurrection[386] from the dead.[3498]
3 And they laid hands on them, and
put *them* in[1519] hold[5084] unto[1519] the next
day: for it was now eventide.
4 Howbeit1161 many of them which
[apt]heard the word[3056] believed;[4100] and
the number of the men was about five
thousand.
5 And it came to pass on the mor-
row, that their rulers,[758] and elders,[4245]
and scribes,[1122]
6 And [a]Annas the high priest, and
Caiaphas, and John, and Alexander, and
as many as were of the kindred of the
high priest,[748] were gathered together at
Jerusalem.
7 And when they had set them in
the midst, they [ipf]asked, [a]By what
power,[1411] or by what name,[3686] have ye
done this?
8 [a]Then Peter, filled with the
[an]Holy Ghost,[4151] said unto them, Ye
rulers[758] of the people,[2992] and elders[4245]
of Israel,
9 If we this day be examined of the
good deed done to the impotent[772]
man,[444] by what means he [pfip]is made
whole;[4982]
10 Be it known unto you all, and
to all the people of Israel, [a]that by the
name of Jesus Christ[5547] of Nazareth,
whom ye crucified,[4717] [b]whom God
raised[1453] from the dead,[3498] *even* by him
doth this man stand here before you
whole.[5199]
11 [a]This is the stone which [aptp]was
set at nought1848 of you builders, which
is become the head of the corner.

15 [c]Acts 2:32
16 [a]Matt. 9:22; Acts 4:10; 14:9
17 [a]Luke 23:34; John 16:3; Acts 13:27; 1Cor. 2:8; 1Tim. 1:13
18 [a]Luke 24:44; Acts 26:22 [b]Ps. 22; Isa. 50:6; 53:5; Dan. 9:26; 1Pet. 1:10, 11
19 [a]Acts 2:38
21 [a]Acts 1:11 [b]Matt. 17:11 [c]Luke 1:70
22 [a]Deut. 18:15, 18, 19; Acts 7:37
25 [a]Acts 2:39; Rom. 9:4, 8; 15:8; Gal. 3:26 [b]Gen. 12:3; 18:18; 22:18; 26:4; 28:14; Gal. 3:8
26 [a]Matt. 10:5; 15:24; Luke 24:47; Acts 13:32, 33, 46 [b]Acts 3:22 [c]Matt. 1:21
1 [1]Or, *ruler* [a]Luke 22:4; Acts 5:24
2 [a]Matt. 22:23; Acts 23:8
6 [a]Luke 3:2; John 11:49; 18:13
7 [a]Ex. 2:14; Matt. 21:23; Acts 7:27
8 [a]Luke 12:11, 12
10 [a]Acts 3:6, 16 [b]Acts 2:24
11 [a]Ps. 118:22; Isa. 28:16; Matt. 21:42

12 [a]Neither is there salvation[4991] in any other: for there is none other name under heaven[3772] [pfpp]given among men,[444] whereby we must [aifp]be saved.[4982]

13 Now when they [ppt]saw the boldness of Peter and John, [a]and [apt]perceived[2638] that they were unlearned and ignorant[2399] men, they [ipf]marvelled; and they [ipf]took knowledge of them, that they had been with Jesus.

14 And beholding the man which [pfpp]was healed[2323] [a]standing with them, they could say nothing against it.

15 But when they had commanded them to go aside out of the council,4892 they [ao]conferred among themselves,

16 Saying, [a]What shall we do to these men? for that indeed a notable miracle[4592] [pfi]hath been done[1096] by them *is* [b]manifest[5318] to all them that dwell in Jerusalem; and we cannot [ainf]deny[720] *it.*

17 But that it spread no further among the people, let us straitly547 threaten them, that they [pinf]speak henceforth to no man in this name.

18 [a]And they called them, and commanded[3853] them not [pinf]to speak5350 at all nor [pinf]teach[1321] in the name[3686] of Jesus.

19 But Peter and John answered and said unto them, [a]Whether it be right[1342] in the sight of God[2316] [pinf]to hearken[191] unto you more than unto God, judge[2919] ye.

20 [a]For we cannot but speak[2980] the things which [b]we [ao]have seen[1492] and [ao]heard.[191]

21 So when they [apt]had further threatened them, they let them go, finding[2147] nothing how they might punish them, [a]because of the people: for all *men* [ipf]glorified[1392] God[2316] for [b]that which was done.

22 For the man was above forty years old, on whom this miracle[4592] of healing[2392] [plpf]was shewed.

The Apostles Seek Courage From God in Prayer

23 And being let go, [a]they went to their own company, and reported all that the chief priests[749] and elders[4245] had said unto them.

24 And when they heard that, they lifted up[142] their voice to God with one accord, and said, Lord,[1203] [a]thou *art* God,[2316] which hast made heaven,[3772] and earth,[1093] and the sea,[2281] and all that in them is:

25 Who by the mouth of thy servant[3816] David hast said, [a]Why [ao]did the heathen rage,5433 and the people[2992] imagine3191 vain things?[2756]

26 The kings[935] of the earth stood up, and the rulers[758] were gathered together against the Lord,[2962] and against his Christ.[5547]

27 For of [a]a truth[225] against [b]thy holy[40] child[3816] Jesus, [c]whom thou [ao]hast anointed,[5548] both Herod, and Pontius Pilate, with the Gentiles,[1484] and the people[2992] of Israel, were gathered together,

🔑 28 [a]For to do whatsoever thy hand and thy counsel[1012] determined before[4309] to be done.

29 And now, Lord, behold[1896] their threatenings: and grant unto thy servants,[1401] [a]that with all boldness they [pinf]may speak[2980] thy word,[3056]

30 By stretching forth thine hand to heal;[2392] [a]and that signs[4592] and wonders[5059] may be done [b]by the name[3686] of [c]thy holy[40] child[3816] Jesus.

31 And when they [aptp]had prayed,[1189] [a]the place was shaken where they were assembled together; and they were all filled with the [an]Holy Ghost,[4151] [b]and they [ipf]spake the word of God with boldness.

The Believers Had All Things Common

32 And the multitude of them that believed[4100] [a]were of one heart[2588] and of

12 [a]Matt. 1:21; Acts 10:43; 1Tim. 2:5, 6
13 [a]Matt. 11:25; 1Cor. 1:27
14 [a]Acts 3:11
16 [a]John 11:47 [b]Acts 3:9, 10
18 [a]Acts 5:40
19 [a]Acts 5:29
20 [a]Acts 1:8; 2:32 [b]Acts 22:15; 1John 1:1, 3
21 [a]Matt. 21:26; Luke 20:6, 19; 22:2; Acts 5:26 [b]Acts 3:7, 8
23 [a]Acts 12:12
24 [a]2Kgs. 19:15
25 [a]Ps. 2:1
27 [a]Matt. 26:3; Luke 22:2; 23:1, 8 [b]Luke 1:35 [c]Luke 4:18; John 10:36
28 [a]Acts 2:23; 3:18
29 [a]Acts 4:13, 31; 9:27; 13:46; 14:3; 19:8; 26:26; 28:31; Eph. 6:19
30 [a]Acts 2:43; 5:12 [b]Acts 3:6, 16 [c]Acts 4:27
31 [a]Acts 2:2, 4; 16:26 [b]Acts 4:29
32 [a]Acts 5:12; Rom. 15:5, 6; 2Cor. 13:11; Phil. 1:27; 2:2; 1Pet. 3:8

🔑 **4:28** See note on Ephesians 1:4, 5.

one soul:[5590] [b]neither said any *of them*
that ought of the things which he pos-
sessed5224 was his own;[2398] but they had
all things common.[2839]
33 And with [a]great power[1411] [ipf]gave
the apostles[652] [b]witness[3142] of the resurrection[386] of the Lord Jesus: and [c]great
grace[5485] was upon them all.
34 Neither was there any among
them that lacked: [a]for as many as
were[5225] possessors of lands or houses
[ppt]sold them, and [ipf]brought the prices of
the things that were sold,
35 [a]And [ipf]laid *them* down at the
apostles' feet: [b]and [ipf]distribution was
made unto every man according as he
had need.
36 And Joses, who by the apostles
was surnamed Barnabas, (which is, being
interpreted, The son[5207] of consolation,[3874]) a Levite, *and* of the country of
Cyprus,
37 [a]Having land, sold *it,* and brought
the money,[5536] and laid *it* at the apostles'
feet.

Ananias and Sapphira

5 But a certain man named
Ananias, with Sapphira his wife, sold
a possession,
2 And kept back[3557] *part* of the
price, his wife also being privy[4894] *to it,*
[a]and [apt]brought a certain part, and laid *it*
at the apostles'[652] feet.
3 [a]But Peter said, Ananias, why
[ao]hath [b]Satan filled[4137] thine heart [ainf1c]to
lie to the Holy[40] Ghost,[4151] and [ainf]to keep
back *part* of the price of the land?
4 Whiles it remained, was it not thine
own? and after it was sold, was it not in
thine own power?[1849] why hast thou conceived this thing in thine heart?[2588] thou
[aom]hast not lied5574 unto men,[444] but unto
God.[2316]
5 And Ananias hearing these words
[apt][a]fell down, and gave up the ghost:[1634]
and great fear[5401] came on all them that
[ppt]heard these things.
6 And the young men arose, [a]wound
him up, and carried *him* out, and buried
him.
7 And it was about the space of
three hours after, when his wife, not
knowing what was done, came in.
8 And Peter answered unto her, Tell
me whether ye sold the land for so much?
And she said, Yea, for so much.
9 Then Peter said unto her, How
is it that ye have agreed together
[ainf][a]to tempt[3985] the Spirit[4151] of the
Lord?[2962] behold, the feet of them
which have buried thy husband[435] *are*
at the door, and [ft]shall carry thee
out.1627
10 [a]Then fell she down[4098] straightway[3916] at his feet, and yielded up
the ghost:[1634] and the young men came
in, and found her dead,[3498] and, [apt]carry-
ing *her* forth,1627 buried *her* by her husband.
11 [a]And great fear came upon all the
church,[1577] and upon as many as [ppt]heard
these things.

"Many Signs and Wonders"

12 And [a]by the hands of the apostles[652] [ipf]were many signs and wonders
wrought[1096] among the people;[2992] ([b]and
they were all with one accord in
Solomon's porch.
13 And [a]of the rest [ipf]durst5111 no
man join himself to them: [b]but the people magnified them.
14 And [ppt]believers[4100] [ipf]were the
more added4369 to the Lord,[2962] multitudes both of men[435] and women.)
15 Insomuch that they [pinf]brought
forth1627 the sick[772] [1]into the streets,
and [pinf]laid *them* on beds and couches,
[a]that at the least the shadow of Peter

32 [b]Acts 2:44
33 [a]Acts 1:8 [b]Acts 1:22 [c]Acts 2:47
34 [a]Acts 2:45
35 [a]Acts 4:37; 5:2 [b]Acts 2:45; 6:1
37 [a]Acts 4:34, 35; 5:1, 2
2 [a]Acts 4:37
3 [1]Or, *to deceive* [a]Num. 30:2; Deut. 23:21; Eccl. 5:4 [b]Luke 22:3 [c]Acts 5:9
5 [a]Acts 5:10, 11
6 [a]John 19:40
9 [a]Matt. 4:7; Acts 5:3
10 [a]Acts 5:5
11 [a]Acts 2:43; 5:5; 19:17
12 [a]Acts 2:43; 14:3; 19:11; Rom. 15:19; 2Cor. 12:12; Heb. 2:4 [b]Acts 3:11; 4:32
13 [a]John 9:22; 12:42; 19:38 [b]Acts 2:47; 4:21
15 [1]Or, *in every street* [a]Matt. 9:21; 14:36; Acts 19:12

5:1–16 Ananias and Sapphira were not only guilty of lying to the Holy Spirit (v. 3, 9), but of hypocrisy and coveteousness as well. They were obviously concerned with what the other believers would think of them once they gave their gift. Christ also noted this characteristic among the Pharisees when he contrasted them to the widow who gave all she had (Luke 21:2, 3).

passing by [aosb]might overshadow some of them.

16 There [ipf]came also a multitude *out* of the cities round about unto Jerusalem, bringing [a]sick folks,[772] and them which [ppp]were vexed[3791] with unclean[169] spirits:[4151] and they [ipf]were healed[2323] every one.

The Apostles Are Arrested

17 [a]Then the high priest[749] rose up, and all they that were with him, (which is the sect[139] of the Sadducees,) and were filled with indignation,[2205]

18 [a]And laid their hands on the apostles,[652] and put them in the common[1219] prison.[5084]

19 But [a]the angel[32] of the Lord[2962] by night opened the prison doors, and brought them forth, and said,

20 [pim]Go, [aptp]stand and [pim]speak in the temple[2411] to the people [a]all the words[4487] of this life.[2222]

21 And when they heard *that,* they entered into the temple early in the morning, and [ipf]taught.[1321] [a]But the high priest came, and they that were with him, and called[4779] the council[4892] together,[4779] and all the senate[1087] of the children[5207] of Israel, and sent to the prison to have them brought.

22 But when the officers came, and found them not in the prison, they returned, and told,

23 Saying, The prison truly found we shut with all safety, and the keepers[5441] standing without[1854] before the doors: but when we had opened, we found no man within.

24 Now when the high priest and [a]the captain of the temple and the chief priests heard these things,[3056] they [ipf]doubted[1280] of them whereunto this would grow.

25 Then came one and told them, saying, Behold, the men whom ye put in prison are standing in the temple, and teaching the people.

26 Then went the captain with the officers, and brought[71] them without violence: [a]for they [ipf]feared the people, lest they [asbp]should have been stoned.

27 And when they had brought them, they set *them* before the council: and the high priest asked them,

28 Saying, [ao][a]Did not we straitly command[3853] you that ye [pinf]should not teach[1321] in this name? and, behold, ye [pfi]have filled Jerusalem with your doctrine,[1322] [b]and intend to bring[1863] this man's[444] [c]blood[129] upon[1863] us.

29 Then Peter and the *other* apostles[652] answered and said, [a]We ought [pinf]to obey[3980] God[2316] rather than men.[444]

30 [a]The God of our fathers[3962] raised up[1453] Jesus, whom ye slew and [apt][b]hanged on a tree.

31 [a]Him hath God exalted with his right hand[1188] *to be* [b]a Prince[747] and [c]a Saviour,[4990] [d]for [ainf]to give repentance[3341] to Israel, and forgiveness[859] of sins.[266]

32 And [a]we are his witnesses[3144] of these things;[4487] and *so is* also the Holy[40] Ghost,[4151] [b]whom God [ao]hath given to them that [ppt]obey him.

33 [a]When they [apt]heard *that,* they [ipf]were cut[1282] *to the heart,* and [ipf]took counsel to slay them.

34 Then stood there up one in the council,[4892] a Pharisee, named [a]Gamaliel, a doctor of the law,[3547] had in reputation among all the people, and commanded to put the apostles[652] forth a little space;

35 And said unto them, Ye men of Israel, take heed to yourselves what ye intend[3195] to do as touching[1909] these men.

36 For before these days rose up[450] Theudas, boasting himself to be somebody; to whom a number of men, about four hundred, joined themselves: who was slain; and all, as many as [ipf][1]obeyed[3982] him, were scattered, and brought to nought.

🗝 37 After this man rose up Judas of

16 [a]Mark 16:17, 18; John 14:12
17 [a]Acts 4:1, 2, 6
18 [a]Luke 21:12
19 [a]Acts 12:7; 16:26
20 [a]John 6:68; 17:3; 1John 5:11
21 [a]Acts 4:5, 6
24 [a]Luke 22:4; Acts 4:1
26 [a]Matt. 21:26
28 [a]Acts 4:18 [b]Acts 2:23, 36; 3:15; 7:52 [c]Matt. 23:35; 27:25
29 [a]Acts 4:19
30 [a]Acts 3:13, 15; 22:14 [b]Acts 10:39; 13:29; Gal. 3:13; 1Pet. 2:24
31 [a]Acts 2:33, 36; Phil. 2:9; Heb. 2:10; 12:2 [b]Acts 3:15 [c]Matt. 1:21 [d]Luke 24:47; Acts 3:26; 13:38; Eph. 1:7; Col. 1:14
32 [a]John 15:26, 27 [b]Acts 2:4; 10:44
33 [a]Acts 2:37; 7:54
34 [a]Acts 22:3
36 [1]Or, *believed*

🗝 **5:37, 38** See note on 2 Thessalonians 2:3.

Galilee in the days of the taxing, and
drew away[868] much people after him: he
also perished; and all, *even* as many as
obeyed him, were dispersed.
🔑 38 And now I say unto you, Refrain[868] from these men, and let them
alone: [a]for if this counsel[1012] or this work
be of men, it [fp]will come to nought:[2647]
39 [a]But if it be of God,[2316] ye cannot [ainf]overthrow[2647] it; lest haply[3379] ye
be found even [b]to fight against God.
40 And to him they agreed:[3982] and
when they [apt]had [a]called[4341] the apostles,[652] [b]and beaten *them,* they commanded that they should not speak[2980]
in the name[3686] of Jesus, and let them
go.
41 And they departed from the pres-
ence[4383] of the council,[4892] [a]rejoicing that
they were counted worthy [aifp]to suffer
shame for his name.
42 And daily [a]in the temple,[2411] and
in every house,[3624] [b]they [ipf]ceased not
to teach[1321] and preach[2097] Jesus
Christ.[5547]

Seven Are Chosen

6 And in those days, [a]when the number of the disciples[3101] [ppt]was multiplied, there arose a murmuring of the
[b]Grecians against the Hebrews, because
their widows [ipf]were neglected [c]in the
daily ministration.[1248]
2 Then the twelve called the multitude of the disciples *unto them,* and said,
[a]It is not reason[701] that we [apt]should leave
the word[3056] of God,[2316] and [pinf]serve tables.
3 Wherefore, brethren,[80] [aim][a]look ye
out[1980] among you seven men [ppp]of honest report,[3140] full of the [an]Holy[40]
Ghost[4151] and wisdom,[4678] whom we
[ft]may appoint[2525] over this business.[5532]

38 [a]Prov. 21:30; Isa. 8:10; Matt. 15:13

39 [a]Luke 21:15; 1Cor. 1:25 [b]Acts 7:51; 9:5; 23:9

40 [a]Acts 4:18 [b]Matt. 10:17; 23:34; Mark 13:9

41 [a]Matt. 5:12; Rom. 5:3; 2Cor. 12:10; Phil. 1:29; Heb. 10:34; James 1:2; 1Pet. 4:13, 16

42 [a]Acts 2:46 [b]Acts 4:20, 29

1 [a]Acts 2:41; 4:4; 5:14; 6:7 [b]Acts 9:29; 11:20 [c]Acts 4:35

2 [a]Ex. 18:17

3 [a]Deut. 1:13; Acts 1:21; 16:2; 1Tim. 3:7

4 [a]Acts 2:42

5 [a]Acts 11:24 [b]Acts 8:5, 26; 21:8 [c]Rev. 2:6, 15

6 [a]Acts 1:24 [b]Acts 8:17; 9:17; 13:3; 1Tim. 4:14; 5:22; 2Tim. 1:6

7 [a]Acts 12:24; 19:20; Col. 1:6 [b]John 12:42

10 [a]Ex. 4:12; Isa. 54:17; Luke 21:15; Acts 5:39

11 [a]1Kgs. 21:10, 13; Matt. 26:59, 60

4 But we [ft][a]will give ourselves continually[4342] to prayer,[4335] and to the ministry[1248] of the word.[3056]
5 And the saying pleased the whole
multitude: and they chose Stephen, [a]a
man full of faith[4102] and of the [an]Holy
Ghost, and [b]Philip, and Prochorus, and
Nicanor, and Timon, and Parmenas, and
[c]Nicolas a proselyte[4339] of Antioch:
6 Whom they set before the apos-
tles:[652] and [a]when they had prayed, [b]they
laid *their* hands on them.
7 And [a]the word of God [ipf]in-
creased;[837] and the number of the disciples [ipf]multiplied in Jerusalem greatly;
and a great company [b]of the priests
[ipf]were obedient[5219] to the faith.[4102]

Stephen Taken Prisoner

8 And Stephen, full of faith[4102] and
power,[1411] [ipf]did great wonders[5059] and
miracles[4592] among the people.
9 Then there arose[450] certain of the
synagogue,[4864] which is called *the synagogue* of the Libertines, and Cyrenians,
and Alexandrians, and of them of Cilicia
and of Asia, disputing with Stephen.
10 And [a]they were not able to resist
the wisdom and the spirit[4151] by which
he spake.
11 [a]Then they suborned[5260] men,
which [ppt]said, We [pfi]have heard him
[ppt]speak blasphemous[989] words against
Moses, and *against* God.
12 And they stirred up the people,[2992] and the elders,[4245] and the
scribes,[1122] and came upon *him,* and
caught him, and brought[71] *him* to the
council,
13 And set up false witnesses,[3144]
which said, This man ceaseth not to
speak blasphemous words against this
holy[40] place, and the law:[3551]

🔑 **5:38, 39** In the Greek New Testament the conditional clauses in these two verses begin with different words. Each word gives a distinctly different meaning to the clause it begins, but in English both words are translated "if." In verse thirty-eight, the clause, "for if this counsel or this work be of men," is introduced by the Greek word *eán* (1437), which signifies that Gamaliel thought that it was only a possibility that it was the work of the men. In verse thirty-nine, however, the word *ei* (1487) is used, which indicates that he was assuming that it was of God.

14 [a]For we have heard him say, that this Jesus of Nazareth shall [b]destroy this place, and [ft]shall change[236] the customs which Moses delivered us.

15 And all that sat in the council,[4892] looking stedfastly on him, saw his face as it had been the face of an angel.[32]

Stephen's Sermon

7 Then said the high priest,[749] Are these things so?

🔑 2 And he said, [a]Men,[435] brethren,[80] and fathers,[3962] hearken;[191] The God of glory[1391] [aop]appeared unto our father Abraham, when he was in Mesopotamia, before he [ainf]dwelt in Charran,

3 And said unto him, [a]Get thee out of thy country, and from thy kindred, and come into the land which I shall shew thee.

4 Then [a]came he out of the land of the Chaldeans, and dwelt in Charran: and from thence, when his father was dead, he removed him into this land, wherein ye now dwell.

5 And he gave him none inheritance[2817] in it, no, not *so much as* to set his foot on: [a]yet he [aom]promised[1861] that he [ainf]would give it to him for a possession, and to his seed[4690] after him, when *as yet* he had no child.

6 And God spake on this wise, [a]That his seed should sojourn[3941] in a strange[245] land; and that they [ft]should bring them into bondage, and [ft]entreat *them* evil[2559] [b]four hundred years.

7 And the nation[1484] to whom they [aosb]shall be in bondage[1398] will I judge, said God: and after that shall they come forth, and [a]serve me in this place.

8 [a]And he gave him the covenant[1242] of circumcision:[4061] [b]and so *Abraham* begat Isaac, and circumcised[4059] him the eighth day; [c]and Isaac *begat* Jacob; and [d]Jacob *begat* the twelve patriarchs.[3966]

9 [a]And the patriarchs, [apt]moved with envy, sold Joseph into Egypt: [b]but God was with him,

10 And delivered him out of all his afflictions,[2347] [a]and gave him favour and wisdom in the sight of Pharaoh king of Egypt; and he made[2525] him governor[2233] over Egypt and all his house.

11 [a]Now there came a dearth[3042] over all the land of Egypt and Chanaan, and great affliction: and our fathers [ipf]found no sustenance.

12 [a]But when Jacob heard that there was corn[4621] in Egypt, he sent out our fathers first.

13 [a]And at the second *time* Joseph [aop]was made known[319] to his brethren; and Joseph's kindred [aom]was made[1096] known[5318] unto Pharaoh.

🔑 14 [a]Then sent Joseph, and called[3333] his father Jacob to *him,* and [b]all his kindred, threescore and fifteen souls.[5590]

15 [a]So Jacob went down into Egypt, [b]and died, he, and our fathers,

16 And [a]were carried over into Sychem, and laid in [b]the sepulchre[3418] that Abraham bought for a sum of money of the sons of Emmor *the father* of Sychem.

17 But when [a]the time[5550] of the

14 [a]Acts 25:8 [b]Dan. 9:26
2 [a]Acts 22:1
3 [a]Gen. 12:1
4 [a]Gen. 11:31; 12:4, 5
5 [a]Gen. 12:7; 13:15; 15:3, 18; 17:8; 26:3
6 [a]Gen. 15:13, 16 [b]Ex. 12:40; Gal. 3:17
7 [a]Ex. 3:12
8 [a]Gen. 17:9-11 [b]Gen. 21:2-4 [c]Gen. 25:26 [d]Gen. 29:31; 30:5; 35:18, 23
9 [a]Gen. 37:4, 11, 28; Ps. 105:17 [b]Gen. 39:2, 21, 23
10 [a]Gen. 41:37; 42:6
11 [a]Gen. 41:54
12 [a]Gen. 42:1
13 [a]Gen. 45:4, 16
14 [a]Gen. 45:9, 27 [b]Gen. 46:27; Deut. 10:22
15 [a]Gen. 46:5 [b]Gen. 49:33; Ex. 1:6
16 [a]Ex. 13:19; Josh. 24:32 [b]Gen. 23:16; 33:19
17 [a]Gen. 15:13; Acts 7:6

🔑 **7:2–4** Some have suggested that there is a contradiction between this passage and Genesis 11:26, 32; 12:4. In his sermon, Stephen states that Abraham dwelt in Haran until his father (Terah) died, and then moved to Canaan. The Genesis account states that Terah was 70 years old when he begat his sons (Gen. 11:26), and that Abraham left Haran when he was 75 years old (Gen. 12:4). However, it also states that Terah died when he was 205 years old (Gen. 11:32). Some explain this 60-year gap by saying that Stephen had only the Samaritan Pentateuch to refer to as a source for historical events. They propose that this document was corrupted and simply contained inaccurate figures. Others suggest that Terah reverted to his old life of idolatry (cf. Josh. 24:2), and Abraham declared him spiritually dead by leaving him at Haran. Still others point out that Abraham was not necessarily the eldest son of Terah, but was listed first in Genesis 11:26 because of his prominence in Scripture. This could mean that many years separated the births of Terah's three sons, thus Stephen's statement is not in conflict.

🔑 **7:14** See note on Genesis 46:26, 27.

promise[1860] [ipf]drew nigh, which God
[ao]had sworn to Abraham, [b]the people
grew and multiplied in Egypt,
18 Till another[2087] king arose,[450]
which knew not Joseph.
19 The same [apt]dealt subtilly with[2686]
our kindred, and evil entreated[2559] our
fathers, [a]so that they [infg]cast out their
young children,[1025] to the end they
[aies]might not live.
20 [a]In which time[2540] Moses was
born, and [b]was [I]exceeding fair,[791] and
nourished up in his father's house three
months:
21 And [a]when he was cast out, Pharaoh's daughter took him up, and nourished him for her own son.
22 And Moses [aop]was learned[3811] in
all the wisdom of the Egyptians, and
was [a]mighty in words and in deeds.
23 [a]And when he was full forty
years old, it came[305] into his heart [ainf]to
visit[1980] his brethren the children of
Israel.
24 And seeing one *of them* [ppp]suffer
wrong,[91] he [ao]defended *him,* and avenged
him that [ppp]was oppressed, and [apt]smote
the Egyptian:
25 For he supposed his brethren
[pinf]would have understood how that God
by his hand [pin]would deliver[4991] them:
but they understood not.
26 [a]And the next day he [aop]shewed
himself unto them as they [ppt]strove, and
[ao]would have set them at one again, saying, Sirs, ye are brethren; why [pin]do ye
wrong[91] one to another?
27 But he that [ppt]did his neighbour
wrong [aom]thrust him away,[683] saying,
[a]Who made[2525] thee a ruler[758] and a
judge[1348] over us?
28 Wilt thou [ainf]kill me, as thou
[ao]diddest the Egyptian yesterday?
29 [a]Then fled Moses at this saying,
and was a stranger[3941] in the land of
Madian, where he begat two sons.
30 [a]And when forty years [aptp]were
expired, there [aop]appeared to him in the
wilderness of mount Sina an angel of
the Lord in a flame of fire in a bush.
31 When Moses [apt]saw *it,* he wondered at the sight:[3705] and as he [ppt]drew

17 [b]Ex. 1:7, 8, 9; Ps. 105:24, 25

19 [a]Ex. 1:22

20 [I]Or, *fair to God* [a]Ex. 2:2 [b]Heb. 11:23

21 [a]Ex. 2:3-10

22 [a]Luke 24:19

23 [a]Ex. 2:11, 12

26 [a]Ex. 2:13

27 [a]Luke 12:14; Acts 4:7

29 [a]Ex. 2:15, 22; 4:20; 18:3, 4

30 [a]Ex. 3:2

32 [a]Matt. 22:32; Heb. 11:16

33 [a]Ex. 3:5; Josh. 5:15

34 [a]Ex. 3:7

35 [a]Ex. 14:19; Num. 20:16

36 [a]Ex. 12:41; 33:1 [b]Ex. 7, 8, 9, 10, 11, 14; Ps. 105:27 [c]Ex. 14:21, 27, 28, 29 [d]Ex. 16:1, 35

37 [I]Or, *as myself* [a]Deut. 18:15, 18; Acts 3:22 [b]Matt. 17:5

38 [a]Ex. 19:3, 17 [b]Isa. 63:9; Gal. 3:19; Heb. 2:2 [c]Ex. 21:1; Deut. 5:27, 31; 33:4; John 1:17 [d]Rom. 3:2

40 [a]Ex. 32:1

41 [a]Deut. 9:16; Ps. 106:19

42 [a]Ps. 81:12; Ezek. 20:25, 39; Rom. 1:24; 2Thess. 2:11

near [ainf]to behold[2657] *it,* the voice of the
Lord[2962] came unto him,
32 *Saying,* [a]I *am* the God[2316] of thy
fathers, the God of Abraham, and the
God of Isaac, and the God of Jacob.
Then Moses trembled, and [ipf]durst not
[ainf]behold.
33 [a]Then said the Lord to him, Put
off thy shoes from thy feet: for the place
where thou standest is holy[40] ground.
34 [a]I have [apt]seen, I [ao]have seen the
affliction[2561] of my people which is in
Egypt, and I [ao]have heard their groaning,
and [ao]am come down [ainf]to deliver them.
And now come, I will send thee into
Egypt.
35 This Moses whom they refused,[720]
saying, Who [ao]made[2525] thee a ruler and
a judge[1348]? the same [ao]did God send[649]
to be a ruler and a deliverer[3086] [a]by the
hand of the [an]angel[32] which [aptp]appeared
to him in the bush.
36 [a]He brought them out, after that
he had [b]shewed wonders[5059] and
signs[4592] in the land of Egypt, [c]and in
the Red sea, [d]and in the wilderness forty
years.
37 This is that Moses, which said
unto the children of Israel, [a]A prophet[4396]
shall the Lord your God raise up unto
you of your brethren, [I]like unto me; [b]him
shall ye hear.
38 [a]This is he, that [apt]was in the
church[1577] in the wilderness with [b]the
angel which [ppt]spake to him in the mount
Sina, and *with* our fathers: [c]who received
the [ppt]lively[2198] [d]oracles[3051] [ainf]to give
unto us:
39 To whom our fathers [ao]would not
[ainf]obey,[5255][1096] but thrust *him* from them,
and in their hearts turned back again
into Egypt,
40 [a]Saying unto Aaron, Make us
gods[2316] to go before us: for *as for* this
Moses, which brought us out of the land
of Egypt, we wot[1492] not what [pfi]is become of him.
41 [a]And they made a calf in those
days, and offered sacrifice[2378] unto the
idol,[1497] and [ipf]rejoiced[2165] in the works of
their own hands.
42 Then [a]God turned,[4762] and gave

them up [pinf]to worship[3000] [b]the host[4756] of
heaven; as it is written in the book of the
prophets, [c]O ye house of Israel, [ao]have ye
offered[4374] to me slain beasts and sacrifices *by the space of* forty years in the
wilderness?
43 Yea, ye took up the tabernacle[4633]
of Moloch, and the star of your god
Remphan, figures[5179] which ye made [pinf]to
worship[4352] them: and I will carry you
away beyond Babylon.
44 Our fathers had the tabernacle of
witness[3142] in the wilderness, as he [aom]had
appointed,[1299] [I]speaking unto Moses, [a]that
he [ainf]should make it according to the fashion[5179] that he [plpf]had seen.
45 [a]Which also our fathers [I]that came
after[1237] brought in with Jesus into the
possession of the Gentiles, [b]whom God
drave out before the face[4383] of our fathers, unto the days of David;
46 [a]Who found[2147] favour before
God, and [ao][b]desired [ainf]to find a tabernacle for the God of Jacob.
47 [a]But Solomon built him an house.
48 Howbeit[235] [a]the most High dwelleth not in temples[3485] made with hands;
as saith the prophet,
49 [a]Heaven[3772] *is* my throne, and
earth[1093] *is* my footstool: what house[3624]
will ye build me? saith the Lord: or what
is the place of my rest?[2663]
50 Hath not my hand [ao]made all
these things?
51 Ye [a]stiffnecked and [b]uncircum-
cised[564] in heart and ears, ye do always
resist the Holy Ghost: as your fathers *did,*
so *do* ye.
52 [a]Which of the prophets[4396] have
not your fathers persecuted?[1377] and they
[ao]have slain them which [apt]shewed before[4293] of the coming of [b]the Just
One;[1342] of whom ye [pfip]have been now
the betrayers and murderers:
53 [a]Who [ao]have received the law by
the disposition[1296] of angels, and [ao]have
not kept[5442] *it.*

Stephen Is Put to Death

54 [a]When they [ppt]heard these
things, they [ipf]were cut to the heart,
and they [ipf]gnashed[1031] on him with *their*
teeth.
55 But he, [a]being full of the [an]Holy
Ghost,[4151] looked up stedfastly into
heaven, and saw the glory of God, and
Jesus standing on the right hand[1188] of
God,
56 And said, Behold, [a]I see the heavens [pfpp]opened, and the [b]Son of man
standing on the right hand of God.
57 Then they [apt]cried out with a loud
voice, and stopped[4912] their ears, and ran
upon him with one accord,
58 And [apt][a]cast *him* out of the city,
[b]and [ipf]stoned *him:* and [c]the witnesses[3144]
[aom]laid down their clothes at a young
man's feet, whose name was Saul.
59 And they [ipf]stoned Stephen, [a]call-
ing upon *God,* and saying, Lord Jesus,
[b]receive my spirit.[4151]
60 And he [apt][a]kneeled down, and
cried with a loud voice, [b]Lord, [aosi]lay[2476]
not this sin[266] to their charge. And when
he had said this, he fell asleep.

The Congregation Is Persecuted

8 And [a]Saul was consenting unto his
death. And at that time there was a
great persecution against the church[1577]
which was at Jerusalem; and [b]they were
all scattered abroad throughout the regions of Judaea and Samaria, except the
apostles.[652]
2 And devout[2126] men carried
Stephen *to his burial,* and [a]made great
lamentation over him.
3 As for Saul, [a]he [ipf]made havoc[3075]
of the church, entering into every house,
and haling[4951] men and women [ipf]com-
mitted *them* to prison.

The Gospel Proclaimed In Samaria

4 Therefore [a]they that were scattered
abroad went every where preaching[2097]
the word.[3056]
5 Then [a]Philip went down to the city

42 [b]Deut. 4:19; 17:3; 2Kgs. 17:16; 21:3; Jer. 19:13 [c]Amos 5:25, 26
44 [I]Or, *who spake* [a]Ex. 25:40; 26:30; Heb. 8:5
45 [I]Or, *having received* [a]Josh. 3:14 [b]Neh. 9:24; Ps. 44:2; 78:55; Acts 13:19
46 [a]1Sam. 16:1; 2Sam. 7:1; Ps. 89:19; Acts 13:22 [b]1Kgs. 8:17; 1Chr. 22:7; Ps. 132:4, 5
47 [a]1Kgs. 6:1; 8:20; 1Chr. 17:12; 2Chr. 3:1
48 [a]1Kgs. 8:27; 2Chr. 2:6; 6:18; Acts 17:24
49 [a]Isa. 66:1, 2; Matt. 5:34, 35; 23:22
51 [a]Ex. 32:9; 33:3; Isa. 48:4 [b]Lev. 26:41; Deut. 10:16; Jer. 4:4; 6:10; 9:26; Ezek. 44:9
52 [a]2Chr. 36:16; Matt. 21:35; 23:34, 37; 1Thess. 2:15 [b]Acts 3:14
53 [a]Ex. 20:1; Gal. 3:19; Heb. 2:2
54 [a]Acts 5:33
55 [a]Acts 6:5
56 [a]Ezek. 1:1; Matt. 3:16; Acts 10:11 [b]Dan. 7:13
58 [a]1Kgs. 21:13; Luke 4:29; Heb. 13:12 [b]Lev. 24:16 [c]Deut. 13:9, 10; 17:7; Acts 8:1; 22:20
59 [a]Acts 9:14 [b]Ps. 31:5; Luke 23:46
60 [a]Acts 9:40; 20:36; 21:5 [b]Matt. 5:44; Luke 6:28; 23:34

1 [a]Acts 7:58; 22:20 [b]Acts 11:19
2 [a]Gen. 23:2; 50:10; 2Sam. 3:31
3 [a]Acts 7:58; 9:1, 13, 21; 22:4; 26:10, 11; 1Cor. 15:9; Gal. 1:13; Phil. 3:6; 1Tim. 1:13

4 [a]Matt. 10:23; Acts 11:19 5 [a]Acts 6:5

of Samaria, and [ipf]preached[2784] Christ[5547] unto them.

6 And the people with one accord [ipf]gave heed unto those things which Philip [ppt]spake, [aie]hearing and [aie]seeing the miracles[4592] which he [ipf]did.

7 For [a]unclean[169] spirits,[4151] crying with loud voice, [ipf]came out of many that were possessed *with them:* and many taken with palsies,3886 and that were lame, were healed.

8 And there [aom]was great joy in that city.

9 But there was a certain man, called Simon, which beforetime in the same city [ppt][a]used sorcery,3096 and [ppt]bewitched[1839] the people[1484] of Samaria, [b]giving out that himself was some great one:

10 To whom they all [ipf]gave heed, from the least to the greatest, saying, This man is the great power of God.[2316]

11 And to him they [ipf]had regard, because that of long time[5550] he [aid]had bewitched them with sorceries.3095

12 But when they believed[4100] Philip preaching[2097] the things [a]concerning the kingdom[932] of God, and the name of Jesus Christ, they [ipf]were baptized,[907] both men and women.

13 Then Simon himself believed also: and when he was baptized, he continued[4342] with Philip, and [ipf]wondered,[1839] [ppt]beholding the [I]miracles[1411] and signs[4592] which [ppt]were done.

14 Now when the apostles[652] which were at Jerusalem [apt]heard that Samaria [pfi]had received the word[3056] of God, they sent unto them Peter and John:

15 Who, when they were come down, [ao]prayed for them, [a]that they [aosb]might receive the [an]Holy Ghost:[4151]

🔑 16 (For [a]as yet he was fallen upon none of them: only [b]they were baptized in [c]the name[3686] of the Lord Jesus.)

17 Then [ipf][a]laid they *their* hands on them, and they [ipf]received the [an]Holy Ghost.

18 And when Simon saw that through laying on of the apostles' hands the Holy Ghost [pinp]was given, he offered them money,[5536]

19 Saying, Give me also this power,[1849] that on whomsoever I [aosb]lay hands, he [psa]may receive the [an]Holy Ghost.

20 But Peter said unto him, Thy money694 perish with thee, because [a]thou [ao]hast thought that [b]the gift of God [pinf]may be purchased with money.

21 Thou hast neither part nor lot[2819] in this matter: for thy heart[2588] is not right in the sight of God.

22 [aim]Repent[3340] therefore of this thy wickedness,[2549] and [aipp]pray God, [a]if perhaps the thought[1963] of thine heart [fp]may be forgiven[863] thee.

23 For I perceive that thou art in [a]the gall[5521] of bitterness, and *in* the bond of iniquity.[93]

24 Then answered Simon, and said, [aipp][a]Pray[1189] ye to the Lord for me, that none of these things which ye [pfi]have spoken [aosb]come upon me.

25 And they, when they [apt]had testified[1263] and [apt]preached the word of the Lord, returned to Jerusalem, and preached the gospel[2097] in many villages of the Samaritans.

Philip and the Ethiopian Eunuch

26 And the angel[32] of the Lord spake unto Philip, saying, Arise, and [pim]go toward[2596] the south unto the way that goeth down from Jerusalem unto Gaza, which is desert.

27 And he arose and went: and, behold, [a]a man of Ethiopia, an eunuch[2135] of great authority[1413] under Candace queen of the Ethiopians, who had the charge of all her treasure, and [plpf][b]had come to Jerusalem for [ft]to worship,4352

28 Was returning, and sitting in his chariot [ipf]read Esaias the prophet.[4396]

7 [a]Mark 16:17
9 [a]Acts 13:6 [b]Acts 5:36
12 [a]Acts 1:3
13 [I]Gr. *signs and great miracles*
15 [a]Acts 2:38
16 [a]Acts 19:2 [b]Matt. 28:19; Acts 2:38 [c]Acts 10:48; 19:5
17 [a]Acts 6:6; 19:6; Heb. 6:2
20 [a]2Kgs. 5:16; Matt. 10:8 [b]Acts 2:38; 10:45; 11:17
22 [a]Dan. 4:27; 2Tim. 2:25
23 [a]Heb. 12:15
24 [a]Gen. 20:7, 17; Ex. 8:8; Num. 21:7; 1Kgs. 13:6; Job 42:8; James 5:16
27 [a]Zeph. 3:10 [b]John 12:20

🔑 **8:16** See note on 1 Corinthians 10:2.

29 Then the Spirit said unto Philip, Go near, and [aipp]join thyself to this chariot.

30 And Philip [apt]ran thither to *him,* and heard him [ppt]read the prophet Esaias, and said, Understandest thou what thou readest?

31 And he said, How [opt]can I, except some man [aosb]should guide me? And he desired[3870] Philip that he [apt]would come up and [ainf]sit with him.

32 The place of the scripture which he [ipf]read was this, [a]He was led as a sheep to the slaughter; and like a lamb[286] dumb before his shearer, so opened he not his mouth:

33 In his humiliation[5014] his judgment[2920] was taken away: and who [fm]shall declare[1334] his generation?[1074] for his life is taken from the earth.

34 And the eunuch answered Philip, and said, I pray thee, of whom speaketh the prophet this? of himself, or of some other man?

35 Then Philip opened his mouth, [a]and began at the same scripture,[1124] and preached[2097] unto him Jesus.

36 And as they [ipf]went on *their* way, they came unto a certain water: and the eunuch said, See, *here is* water; [a]what doth hinder me [aifp]to be baptized?[907]

37 And Philip said, [a]If thou believest[4100] with all thine heart, thou mayest. And he answered and said, [b]I believe that Jesus Christ[5547] is the Son[5207] of God.[2316]

38 And he commanded the chariot [ainf]to stand still:[2476] and they went down both into the water, both Philip and the eunuch; and he baptized him.

⊶ 39 And when they were come up out of the water, [a]the Spirit[4151] of the Lord caught away[726] Philip, that the eunuch saw him no more: and he [ipf]went on his way rejoicing.

40 But Philip was found at Azotus: and passing through he [ipf]preached[2097] in all the cities, till he came to Caesarea.

32 [a]Isa. 53:7, 8
35 [a]Luke 24:27; Acts 18:28
36 [a]Acts 10:47
37 [a]Matt. 28:19; Mark 16:16 [b]Matt. 16:16; John 6:69; 9:35, 38; 11:27; Acts 9:20; 1John 4:15; 5:5, 13
39 [a]1Kgs. 18:12; 2Kgs. 2:16; Ezek. 3:12, 14
1 [a]Acts 8:3; Gal. 1:13; 1Tim. 1:13
2 [l]Gr. *of the way* [a]Acts 19:9, 23
3 [a]Acts 22:6; 26:12; 1Cor. 15:8
4 [a]Matt. 25:40
5 [a]Acts 5:39
6 [a]Luke 3:10; Acts 2:37; 16:30
7 [a]Dan. 10:7; Acts 22:9; 26:13
10 [a]Acts 22:12
11 [a]Acts 21:39; 22:3

Paul's Conversion (Acts 22:6–16; 26:12–18)

9 And [a]Saul, yet breathing out threatenings and slaughter against the disciples[3101] of the Lord, [apt]went unto the high priest,

2 And desired of him letters to Damascus to the synagogues, that if he [aosb]found any [la]of this way,[3598] whether they were men or women, he [aosb]might bring them bound unto Jerusalem.

3 And [a]as he journeyed, he came near Damascus: and suddenly there shined round about him a light from heaven:

4 And he [apt]fell to the earth, and heard a voice saying unto him, Saul, Saul, [a]why persecutest thou me?

5 And he said, Who art thou, Lord?[2962] And the Lord said, I am Jesus whom thou persecutest: [a]*it is* hard for thee to kick against the pricks.[2759]

6 And he trembling and astonished said, Lord, [a]what wilt thou have me to do? And the Lord *said* unto him, Arise, and go into the city, and it shall be told thee what thou must do.

7 And [a]the men which [ppt]journeyed with him stood speechless, hearing a voice, but seeing no man.

8 And Saul arose from the earth; and when his eyes [pfpp]were opened, he [ipf]saw no man: but they [ppt]led him by the hand, and brought *him* into Damascus.

9 And he was three days without [ppt]sight, and neither did eat nor drink.

10 And there was a certain disciple at Damascus, [a]named Ananias; and to him said the Lord in a vision,[3705] Ananias. And he said, Behold, I *am here,* Lord.

11 And the Lord *said* unto him, Arise, and go into the street which is called Straight, and enquire in the house of Judas for *one* called Saul [a]of Tarsus: for, behold, he prayeth,

12 And [ao]hath seen in a vision[3705] a

⊶ **8:39** See note on 1 Thessalonians 4:17.

man named Ananias [apt]coming in, and
[apt]putting *his* hand on him, that he
[aosb]might receive his sight.[308]
13 Then Ananias answered, Lord, I
[pfi]have heard by many of this man, [a]how
much evil[2556] he [ao]hath done to thy
saints[40] at Jerusalem:
14 And here he hath authority[1849]
from the chief priests to bind all [a]that
[ppt]call on thy name.
15 But the Lord said unto him, [pim]Go
thy way: for [a]he is a chosen vessel unto
me, [infg]to bear my name before [b]the
Gentiles,[1484] and [c]kings, and the children
of Israel:
16 For [a]I will shew him how great
things he must [ainf]suffer[3958] for my
name's sake.
17 [a]And Ananias went his way, and
entered into the house; and [apt b]putting his
hands on him said, Brother Saul, the
Lord, *even* Jesus, that [aptp]appeared unto
thee in the way as thou [ipf]camest, [pfi]hath
sent me, that thou [aosb]mightest receive
thy sight,[308] and [asbp c]be filled with the
[an]Holy Ghost.
18 And immediately there fell from
his eyes as it had been scales: and he received sight forthwith, and arose, and
was baptized.[907]
19 And when he had received meat,
he was strengthened.[1765] [a]Then was Saul
certain days with the disciples[3101] which
were at Damascus.

Paul Preaches at Damascus

20 And straightway[2112] he
[ipf]preached[2784] Christ[5547] in the synagogues, [a]that he is the Son[5207] of God.[2316]
21 But all that [ppt]heard *him* [ipf]were
amazed, and [ipf]said; [a]Is not this he
that [apt]destroyed them which [ppt]called
on this name in Jerusalem, and
[plpf]came hither for that intent, that he
might bring them bound unto the chief
priests?
22 But Saul [ipf]increased the more in
strength,[1743] [a]and [ipf]confounded the Jews
which [ppt]dwelt at Damascus, [ppt]proving
that this is very Christ.[5547]

13 [a]Acts 9:1
14 [a]Acts 7:59; 9:21; 22:16; 1Cor. 1:2; 2Tim. 2:22
15 [a]Acts 13:2; 22:21; 26:17; Rom. 1:1; 1Cor. 15:10; Gal. 1:15; Eph. 3:7, 8; 1Tim. 2:7; 2Tim. 1:11 [b]Rom. 1:5; 11:13; Gal. 2:7, 8 [c]Acts 25:22, 23; 26:1
16 [a]Acts 20:23; 21:11; 2Cor. 11:23
17 [a]Acts 22:12, 13 [b]Acts 8:17 [c]Acts 2:4; 4:31; 8:17; 13:52
19 [a]Acts 26:20
20 [a]Acts 8:37
21 [a]Acts 8:3; 9:1; Gal. 1:13, 23
22 [a]Acts 18:28
23 [a]Acts 23:12; 25:3; 2Cor. 11:26
24 [a]2Cor. 11:32
25 [a]Josh. 2:15; 1Sam. 19:12
26 [a]Acts 22:17; Gal. 1:17, 18
27 [a]Acts 4:36; 13:2 [b]Acts 9:20, 22
28 [a]Gal. 1:18
29 [a]Acts 6:1; 11:20 [b]Acts 2Cor. 11:26
31 [a]Acts 8:1
32 [a]Acts 8:14

Paul's Escape

23 And after that many days [ipf]were
fulfilled, [a]the Jews took counsel [ainf]to kill
him:
24 [a]But their laying await was
known of Saul. And they [ipf]watched[3906]
the gates day and night to [aosb]kill him.
25 Then the disciples took him by
night, and [a]let *him* down by the wall in
a basket.

Paul Goes to Jerusalem

26 And [a]when Saul [apt]was come to
Jerusalem, he [ipf]assayed[3987] [pip]to join himself to the disciples: but they [ipf]were all
afraid[5399] of him, and [ppt]believed[4100] not
that he was a disciple.[3101]
27 But [a]Barnabas [apt]took[1949] him,
and brought[71] *him* to the apostles,[652] and
declared[1334] unto them how he [ao]had seen
the Lord in the way, and that he [ao]had
spoken to him, [b]and how he [ao]had
preached boldly[3955] at Damascus in the
name[3686] of Jesus.
28 And [a]he was with them coming in
and going out at Jerusalem.
29 And he [ppt]spake boldly in the
name of the Lord Jesus, and [ipf]disputed
against the [a]Grecians: [b]but they [ipf]went
about [ainf]to slay him.
30 *Which* when the brethren knew,
they brought him down to Caesarea, and
sent him forth to Tarsus.
31 [a]Then [ipf]had the churches[1577]
rest[1515] throughout all Judaea and Galilee
and Samaria, and [ppt]were edified; and
[ppt]walking in the fear[5401] of the Lord,
and in the comfort[3874] of the Holy Ghost,
[ipf]were multiplied.

Aeneas Healed

32 And it came to pass, as Peter
[ppt]passed [a]throughout all *quarters,* he
[ainf]came down also to the saints[40] which
[ppt]dwelt at Lydda.
33 And there he found a certain man
named Aeneas, which [ppt]had kept his bed
eight years, and was sick of the palsy.[3886]

34 And Peter said unto him, Aeneas,
[a]Jesus Christ maketh thee whole: arise,
and make thy bed. And he arose immediately.
35 And all that dwelt at Lydda and
[a]Saron saw him, and [b]turned[1994] to the
Lord.

Peter Raises Dorcas to Life

36 Now there was at Joppa a certain
disciple[3102] named Tabitha, which by interpretation[1329] is called Dorcas: this
woman was full[4134] [a]of good[18] works and
almsdeeds[1654] which she [ipf]did.
37 And it came to pass in those days,
that she [apt]was sick, and [ainf]died: whom
when they had washed, they laid *her* in
[a]an upper chamber.
38 And forasmuch as Lydda was
nigh to Joppa, and the disciples[3101] had
heard that Peter was there, they sent unto
him two men, desiring[3870] *him* that he
would not delay [ainf]to come to them.
39 Then Peter arose and went with
them. When he was come, they brought
him into the upper chamber: and all the
widows stood by him weeping, and shewing the coats and garments which Dorcas
[ipf]made, while she was with them.
40 But Peter [apt][a]put them all forth,
and [b]kneeled down, and prayed; and
[apt]turning *him* to the body [c]said, Tabitha,
arise. And she opened her eyes: and
when she [apt]saw Peter, she sat up.
41 And he gave her *his* hand, and
lifted her up, and when he had called
the saints and widows, presented her
alive.[2198]
42 And it was known throughout all
Joppa; [a]and many believed[4100] in the
Lord.
43 And it came to pass, that he
[ainf]tarried many days in Joppa with one
[a]Simon a tanner.

The Conversion of Cornelius

10 There was a certain man in
Caesarea called Cornelius, a
centurion of the band called the Italian
band,

34 [a]Acts 3:6, 16; 4:10
35 [a]1Chr. 5:16 [b]Acts 11:21
36 [a]1Tim. 2:10; Titus 3:8
37 [a]Acts 1:13
40 [a]Matt. 9:25 [b]Acts 7:60 [c]Mark 5:41, 42; John 11:43
42 [a]John 11:45; 12:11
43 [a]Acts 10:6
2 [a]Acts 8:2; 10:22; 22:12 [b]Acts 10:35
3 [a]Acts 10:30; 11:13
6 [a]Acts 9:43 [b]Acts 11:14
9 [a]Acts 11:5
11 [a]Acts 7:56; Rev. 19:11
14 [a]Lev. 11:4; 20:25; Deut. 14:3, 7; Ezek. 4:14
15 [a]Matt. 15:11; Acts 10:28; Rom. 14:14, 17, 20; 1Cor. 10:25; 1Tim. 4:4; Titus 1:15

2 [a]A devout[2152] *man,* and one that
[ppt][b]feared[5399] God with all his house,[3624]
which [ppt]gave much alms to the people,
and [ppt]prayed to God alway.
3 [a]He saw in a vision[3705] evidently
about the ninth hour of the day an
angel[32] of God [apt]coming in to him, and
[apt]saying unto him, Cornelius.
4 And when he looked on him, he
was afraid, and said, What is it, Lord?
And he said unto him, Thy prayers[4335]
and thine alms[1654] [ao]are come up for a
memorial before God.
5 And now send men to Joppa, and
call for *one* Simon, whose surname is
Peter:
6 He lodgeth with one [a]Simon a tanner, whose house is by the sea side:
[b]he shall tell thee what thou oughtest to
do.
7 And when the angel which spake
unto Cornelius was departed, he called
two of his household servants, and a devout soldier of them that waited on him
continually;[4342]
8 And when he [apt]had declared[1834]
all *these* things unto them, he sent them
to Joppa.
9 On the morrow, as they went on
their journey, and [ppt]drew nigh[1448] unto
the city, [a]Peter went up upon the housetop to pray about the sixth hour:
10 And he became very hungry,
and [ipf]would [ainf]have eaten:[1089] but
while they made ready, he fell into a
trance,[1611]
11 And [a]saw heaven opened, and
a certain vessel descending unto him,
as it had been a great sheet knit at the
four corners, and [ppp]let down to the
earth:
12 Wherein were all manner of four-
footed beasts of the earth, and wild
beasts,[2342] and creeping things, and fowls
of the air.
13 And there came a voice to him,
[apt]Rise, Peter; [aim]kill,[2380] and [aim]eat.
14 But Peter said, Not so, Lord;[2962]
[a]for I have never eaten any thing that is
common[2839] or unclean.[169]
15 And the voice *spake* unto him
again the second time, [a]What God [ao]hath

cleansed,[2511] *that* [pim]call not thou common.[2840]

16 This was done thrice: and the vessel was received up again into heaven.

17 Now while Peter [ipf]doubted in himself what this vision[3705] which he [ao]had seen [opt]should mean, behold, the men which [pfpp]were sent from Cornelius [apt]had made enquiry for Simon's house, and stood before the gate,

18 And called, and asked whether Simon, which was surnamed Peter, were lodged there.

19 While Peter [ppt]thought on the vision, [a]the Spirit[4151] said unto him, Behold, three men seek thee.

20 [apt][a]Arise therefore, and get thee down, and [pim]go with them, [ppt]doubting[1252] nothing: for I [pfi]have sent them.

21 Then Peter went down to the men which were sent unto him from Cornelius; and said, Behold, I am he whom ye seek: what *is* the cause[156] wherefore ye are come?

22 And they said, [a]Cornelius the centurion, a just[1342] man, and one that [ppt]feareth[5399] God, and [ppt][b]of good report[3140] among all the nation of the Jews, was warned from God[5537] by an holy angel [ainf]to send for thee into his house, and [ainf]to hear words[4487] of thee.

23 Then called he them in,[1528] and lodged *them.* And on the morrow Peter went away with them, [a]and certain brethren[80] from Joppa accompanied him.

24 And the morrow after they entered into Caesarea. And Cornelius waited for them, and [apt]had called together[4779] his kinsmen and near[316] friends.

25 And as Peter was coming in, Cornelius [apt]met him, and [apt]fell down at his feet, and worshipped *him.*

26 But Peter took him up, saying, [a]Stand up; I myself also am a man.[444]

27 And as he [ppt]talked with him, he went in, and found many that [pfp]were come together.

28 And he said unto them, Ye know how [a]that it is an unlawful thing[111] for a man that is a Jew [pinf]to keep company, or [pinf]come unto one of another nation;[246] but [b]God hath shewed me that I should not call any man common[2839] or unclean.[169]

29 Therefore came I *unto you* without gainsaying,[369] as soon as I [aptp]was sent for: I ask therefore for what intent[3056] ye [aom]have sent for me?

30 And Cornelius said, Four days ago I was fasting[3522] until this hour; and at the ninth hour I [apt]prayed in my house, and, behold, [a]a man stood before me [b]in bright clothing,

31 And said, Cornelius, [a]thy prayer [aop]is heard, [b]and thine alms[1654] are [aop]had in remembrance in the sight of God.

32 Send therefore to Joppa, and call hither[3333] Simon, whose surname is Peter; he is lodged in the house of *one* Simon a tanner by the sea side: who, when he cometh, shall speak unto thee.

33 Immediately therefore I sent to thee; and thou hast well done that thou [apt]art come. Now therefore are we all here present before God,[2316] [ainf]to hear all things that [pfpp]are commanded[4367] thee of God.

34 Then Peter opened *his* mouth, and said, [a]Of a truth I perceive[2638] that God[2316] is no respecter of persons:

35 But [a]in every nation he that [ppt]feareth[5399] him, and [ppt]worketh[2038] righteousness,[1343] is accepted[1184] with him.

36 The word[3056] which *God* sent unto the children[5207] of Israel, [a]preaching[2097] peace[1515] by Jesus Christ: ([b]he is Lord of all:)

37 That word,[4487] *I say,* ye know, which was published throughout all Judaea, and [a]began from Galilee, after the baptism[908] which John preached;[2784]

38 How [a]God anointed[5548] Jesus of Nazareth with the [an]Holy Ghost and with power: who went about doing good, and healing all that [ppp]were oppressed of the devil;[1228] [b]for God was with him.

39 And [a]we are witnesses[3144] of all

19 [a]Acts 11:12
20 [a]Acts 15:7
22 [a]Acts 10:1-8 [b]Acts 22:12
23 [a]Acts 10:45; 11:12
26 [a]Acts 14:14, 15; Rev. 19:10; 22:9
28 [a]John 4:9; 18:28; Acts 11:3; Gal. 2:12, 14 [b]Acts 15:8, 9; Eph. 3:6
30 [a]Acts 1:10 [b]Matt. 28:3; Mark 16:5; Luke 24:4
31 [a]Dan. 10:12; Acts 10:4-8 [b]Heb. 6:10
34 [a]Deut. 10:17; 2Chr. 19:7; Job 34:19; Rom. 2:11; Gal. 2:6; Eph. 6:9; Col. 3:25; 1Pet. 1:17
35 [a]Acts 15:9; Rom. 2:13, 27; 3:22, 29; 10:12, 13; 1Cor. 12:13; Gal. 3:28; Eph. 2:13, 18; 3:6
36 [a]Isa. 57:19; Eph. 2:14, 16, 17; Col. 1:20 [b]Matt. 28:18; Rom. 10:12; 1Cor. 15:27; Eph. 1:20, 22; 1Pet. 3:22; Rev. 17:14; 19:16
37 [a]Luke 4:14
38 [a]Luke 4:18; Acts 2:22; 4:27; Heb. 1:9 [b]John 3:2
39 [a]Acts 2:32

things which he did both in the land of the Jews, and in Jerusalem; [b]whom they slew and hanged on a tree:

40 Him [a]God raised up the third day, and shewed him openly;

41 [a]Not to all the people, but unto witnesses[3144] [pfpp]chosen before of God, *even* to us, [b]who [ao]did eat and [ao]drink with him after he [aime]rose from the dead.

42 And [a]he commanded us to preach[2784] unto the people, and [ainf]to testify[1263] [b]that it is he which [pfpp]was ordained[3724] of God *to be* the Judge[2923] [c]of quick[2198] and dead.

43 [a]To him give all the prophets[4396] witness, that through his name[3686] [b]whosoever [ppt]believeth[4100] in him [ainf]shall receive remission[859] of sins.[266]

The Gentiles Receive the Holy Spirit

🔑 44 While Peter yet spake these words, [a]the Holy Ghost fell on all them which [ppt]heard the word.[3056]

45 [a]And they of the circumcision[4061] [ajn]which believed[4103] were astonished, as many as came with Peter, [b]because that on the Gentiles also [pfip]was poured out the gift[1431] of the Holy Ghost.

46 For they [ipf]heard them [ppt]speak[2980] with tongues,[1100] and [ppt]magnify God. Then answered Peter,

47 Can any man [ainf]forbid water, that these [infg]should not be baptized,[907] which have [ao]received the Holy Ghost [a]as well as we?

🔑 48 [a]And he commanded[4367] them to be baptized [b]in the name[3686] of the Lord. Then prayed they him [ainf]to tarry certain days.

39 [b]Acts 5:30
40 [a]Acts 2:24
41 [a]John 14:17, 22; Acts 13:31 [b]Luke 24:30, 43; John 21:13
42 [a]Matt. 28:19, 20; Acts 1:8 [b]John 5:22, 27; Acts 17:31 [c]Rom. 14:9, 10; 2Cor. 5:10; 2Tim. 4:1; 1Pet. 4:5
43 [a]Isa. 53:11; Jer. 31:34; Dan. 9:24; Mic. 7:18; Zech. 13:1; Mal. 4:2; Acts 26:22 [b]Acts 15:9; 26:18; Rom. 10:11; Gal. 3:22
44 [a]Acts 4:31; 8:15-17; 11:15
45 [a]Acts 10:23 [b]Acts 11:18; Gal. 3:14
47 [a]Acts 11:17; 15:8, 9; Rom. 10:12
48 [a]1Cor. 1:17 [b]Acts 2:38; 8:16
2 [a]Acts 10:45; Gal. 2:12
3 [a]Acts 10:28 [b]Gal. 2:12
4 [a]Luke 1:3
5 [a]Acts 10:9

Peter Reports to the Jerusalem Church

11 And the apostles and brethren that were in Judaea heard that the Gentiles[1484] [aom]had also received[1209] the word[3056] of God.

2 And when Peter was come up to Jerusalem, [a]they that were of the circumcision [ipf]contended[1252] with him,

3 Saying, [a]Thou wentest in to men uncircumcised,[203] [b]and didst eat with them.

4 But Peter [apt]rehearsed *the matter* from the beginning, and expounded *it* [a]by order unto them, saying,

5 [a]I was in the city of Joppa praying: and in a trance[1611] I saw a vision,[3705] A certain vessel [ppt]descend, as it had been a great sheet, [ppt]let down from heaven[3772] by four corners;[746] and it came even to me:

6 Upon the which when I [apt]had fastened mine eyes, I [ipf]considered,[2657] and [ao]saw fourfooted beasts of the earth, and wild beasts,[2342] and creeping things, and fowls of the air.[3772]

7 And I heard a voice saying unto me, Arise, Peter; slay[2380] and eat.

8 But I said, Not so, Lord: for nothing common[2839] or unclean[169] hath at any time entered into my mouth.

9 But the voice answered me again from heaven, What God [ao]hath cleansed,[2511] *that* [pim]call not thou common.[2840]

10 And this was done three times: and all were drawn up again into heaven.

11 And, behold, immediately there [ao]were three men already come[2186] unto the house where I was, [pfpp]sent from Caesarea unto me.

🔑 **10:44–48** This is similar to the circumstances at Jerusalem and Samaria in that many believers were baptized in the Holy Spirit at the same time (cf. Acts 2:1–4; 8:14–17). The special manifestation of the Holy Spirit here that allowed these Gentiles to speak in tongues proved that God gave the Gentiles the same "gift" (v. 45) as the Jews. Notice that the baptism of the Holy Spirit took place prior to the water baptism and that apostles were present in each instance. "Spiritual" baptism is what actually places believers into the body of Christ, while water baptism only demonstrates to others that a person is in the body of Christ (1 Cor. 12:13). See notes on Acts 2:1–13 and 1 Corinthians 12:13; 14:1–3.

🔑 **10:48** See notes on Mark 16:16 and 1 Corinthians 10:2.

12 And [a]the Spirit[4151] bade me go with them, nothing doubting. Moreover [b]these six brethren[80] accompanied me, and we entered into the man's house:

13 [a]And he shewed us how he had seen an [art]angel[32] in his house, which stood and said unto him, Send men to Joppa, and call for Simon, whose surname is Peter;

14 Who shall tell thee words,[4487] whereby thou and all thy house [fp]shall be saved.[4982]

15 And as I [aie]began [pinf]to speak,[2980] the Holy Ghost[4151] fell on them, [a]as on us at the beginning.

16 Then remembered I the word of the Lord, how that he [ipf]said, [a]John indeed [ao]baptized[907] with water; but [b]ye shall be baptized with the [an]Holy Ghost.

17 [a]Forasmuch then as God gave them the like gift[1431] as *he did* unto us, [apt]who believed[4100] on the Lord Jesus Christ; [b]what was I, that I could [ainf]withstand God?

18 When they heard these things, they [ao]held their peace,[2270] and glorified[1392] God, saying, [a]Then hath God also to the Gentiles granted repentance[3341] unto life.[2222]

The New Believers In Antioch

19 [a]Now they which were scattered abroad upon the persecution[2347] that arose about Stephen travelled as far as Phenice, and Cyprus, and Antioch, preaching[2980] the word[3056] to none but unto the Jews only.

20 And some of them were men of Cyprus and Cyrene, which, when they were come to Antioch, spake unto [a]the Grecians, preaching[2097] the Lord Jesus.

21 And [a]the hand of the Lord was with them: and a great number [apt]believed,[4100] and [b]turned[1994] unto the Lord.

22 Then tidings[3056] of these things came unto the ears of the church[1577] which was in Jerusalem: and they sent forth [a]Barnabas, that he should go as far as Antioch.

23 Who, when he came, and had seen the grace[5485] of God, was glad, and [a]exhorted[3870] them all, that with purpose[4286] of heart[2588] they [pinf]would cleave unto[4357] the Lord.

24 For he was a good[18] man, and [a]full of the [an]Holy Ghost and of faith:[4102] [b]and much people was added unto the Lord.

25 Then departed Barnabas to [a]Tarsus, for to seek Saul:

26 And when he had found him, he brought him unto Antioch. And it came to pass, that a whole year they [aifp]assembled themselves [1]with the church,[1577] and [ainf]taught[1321] much people. And the disciples[3101] [ainf]were called[5537] Christians[5546] first in Antioch.

27 And in these days came [a]prophets[4396] from Jerusalem unto Antioch.

28 And there stood up one of them named [a]Agabus, and signified by the spirit that there should be great dearth[3042] throughout all the world:[3625] which came to pass in the days of Claudius Caesar.

29 Then the disciples, every man according to his [ipf]ability,[2141] determined[3724] [ainf]to send [a]relief unto the brethren[80] which [ppt]dwelt in Judaea:

30 [a]Which also they did, and sent it to the elders[4245] by the hands of Barnabas and Saul.

Peter Is Put in Jail

12 Now about that time[2540] Herod the king [1]stretched forth *his* hands to vex[2559] certain of the church.[1577]

2 And he killed James [a]the brother of John with the sword.

3 And because he saw it pleased[701] the Jews, he proceeded further to take Peter also. (Then were [a]the days of unleavened bread.[106])

4 And [a]when he [apt]had apprehended him, he put *him* in prison, and [apt]delivered[3860] *him* to four quaternions[5069] of

---

12 [a]John 16:13; Acts 10:19; 15:7 [b]Acts 10:23
13 [a]Acts 10:30
15 [a]Acts 2:4
16 [a]Matt. 3:11; John 1:26, 33; Acts 1:5; 19:4 [b]Isa. 44:3; Joel 2:28; 3:18
17 [a]Acts 15:8, 9 [b]Acts 10:47
18 [a]Rom. 10:12, 13; 15:9, 16
19 [a]Acts 8:1
20 [a]Acts 6:1; 9:29
21 [a]Luke 1:66; Acts 2:47 [b]Acts 9:35
22 [a]Acts 9:27
23 [a]Acts 13:43; 14:22
24 [a]Acts 6:5 [b]Acts 5:14; 11:21
25 [a]Acts 9:30
26 [1]Or, *in the church*
27 [a]Acts 2:17; 13:1; 15:32; 21:9; 1Cor. 12:28; Eph. 4:11
28 [a]Acts 21:10
29 [a]Rom. 15:26; 1Cor. 16:1; 2Cor. 9:1
30 [a]Acts 12:25
1 [1]Or, *began*
2 [a]Matt. 4:21; 20:23
3 [a]Ex. 12:14, 15; 23:15
4 [a]John 21:18

soldiers [pinf]to keep him; intending after Easter[3957] to bring him forth to the people.

5 Peter therefore [ipf]was kept in prison: but [Ia]prayer[4335] was made without ceasing[1618] of the church unto God for him.

Peter Delivered From Prison

6 And when Herod would have brought him forth, the same night Peter was [ppt]sleeping between two soldiers, bound with two chains: and the keepers before the door [ipf]kept[5083] the prison.

7 And, behold, [a]the angel[32] of the Lord came upon *him,* and a light shined in the prison:[3612] and he smote Peter on the side, and [ao]raised him up,[1453] saying, Arise up[450] quickly. And his chains fell off from *his* hands.

8 And the angel said unto him, Gird thyself, and bind on thy sandals. And so he did. And he saith unto him, Cast thy garment about thee, and [pim]follow me.

9 And he [apt]went out, and [ipf]followed him; and [a]wist[1492] not that it was true which was done by the angel; but [ipf]thought [b]he [pinf]saw a vision.[3705]

10 When they were past the first and the second ward,[5438] they came unto the iron gate that leadeth[5342] unto the city; [a]which [aop]opened to them of his own accord: and they went out, and passed on through one street; and forthwith the angel departed[868] from him.

11 And when Peter was come[1096] to himself, he said, Now I know of a surety, that [a]the Lord hath sent his angel, and [aom][b]hath delivered me out of the hand of Herod, and *from* all the expectation[4329] of the people of the Jews.

12 And when he had considered *the thing,* [a]he came to the house of Mary the mother of [b]John, whose surname was Mark; where many were gathered together [c]praying.

13 And as Peter [apt]knocked at the door of the gate, a damsel[3814] came [ainf][I]to hearken,[5219] named Rhoda.

14 And when she knew Peter's voice, she opened not the gate for gladness, but [apt]ran in, and told how Peter stood before the gate.

15 And they said unto her, Thou art mad. But she [ipf]constantly affirmed that it [pinf]was even so. Then [ipf]said they, [a]It is his angel.[32]

16 But Peter [ipf]continued [ppt]knocking: and when they had opened *the door,* and saw him, they were astonished.

17 But he, [a]beckoning unto them with the hand to hold their peace, declared[1334] unto them how the Lord had brought him out of the prison. And he said, Go shew these things unto James, and to the brethren.[80] And he departed, and went into another place.

18 Now as soon as it was day,[2250] there was no small stir among the soldiers, what [aom]was become of Peter.

19 And when Herod [apt]had sought for him, and [apt]found him not, he [apt]examined the keepers, and commanded that *they* should be put to death. And he went down from Judaea to Caesarea, and *there* [ipf]abode.

Herod Dies

20 And Herod was highly displeased with them of Tyre and Sidon: but they came with one accord to him, and, having [apt]made Blastus [I]the king's chamberlain their friend, [ipf]desired[154] peace; because [a]their country [aid]was nourished by the king's[937] *country.*

21 And upon a set[5002] day Herod, [apt]arrayed in royal[937] apparel, sat upon his throne, and [ipf]made an oration unto them.

22 And the people[1218] [ipf]gave a shout, *saying, It is* the voice of a god,[2316] and not of a man.

23 And immediately the angel of the Lord [a]smote him, because [b]he gave not God[2316] the glory:[1391] and he was eaten of worms, and gave up the ghost.[1634]

24 But [a]the word[3056] of God [ipf]grew and [ipf]multiplied.

25 And Barnabas and Saul returned

5 [I]Or, *instant and earnest prayer was made* [a]2Cor. 1:11; Eph. 6:18; 1Thess. 5:17

7 [a]Acts 5:19

9 [a]Ps. 126:1 [b]Acts 10:3, 17; 11:5

10 [a]Acts 16:26

11 [a]Ps. 34:7; Dan. 3:28; 6:22; Heb. 1:14 [b]Job 5:19; Ps. 33:18, 19; 34:22; 41:2; 97:10; 2Cor. 1:10; 2Pet. 2:9

12 [a]Acts 4:23 [b]Acts 15:37 [c]Acts 12:5

13 [I]Or, *to ask who was there*

15 [a]Gen. 48:16; Matt. 18:10

17 [a]Acts 13:16; 19:33; 21:40

20 [I]Gr. *that was over the king's bedchamber* [a]1Kgs. 5:9, 11; Ezek. 27:17

23 [a]1Sam. 25:38; 2Sam. 24:17 [b]Ps. 115:1

24 [a]Isa. 55:11; Acts 6:7; 19:20; Col. 1:6

from Jerusalem, when they [apt]had fulfilled[4137] *their* [I][a]ministry, and [b]took with them [c]John, whose surname was Mark.

Paul and Barnabas Are Chosen

13 🔑Now there were [a]in the church[1577] that was at Antioch certain prophets[4396] and teachers;[1320] as [b]Barnabas, and Simeon that was called Niger, and [c]Lucius of Cyrene, and Manaen, [I]which had been brought up with Herod the tetrarch,[5076] and Saul.

2 As they [ppt]ministered[3008] to the Lord, and [ppt]fasted,[3522] the Holy Ghost said, [aim][a]Separate[873] me Barnabas and Saul for the work[2041] [b]whereunto I [pfip]have called[4341] them.

3 And [a]when they had fasted and prayed, and laid *their* hands on them, they sent *them* away.

Ministry on Cyprus

4 So they, being sent forth by the Holy Ghost, departed unto Seleucia; and from thence they sailed to [a]Cyprus.

5 And when they were at Salamis, [a]they [ipf]preached[2605] the word[3056] of God in the synagogues of the Jews: and they had also [b]John to *their* minister.[5257]

6 And when they had gone through the isle unto Paphos, they found [a]a certain sorcerer,[3097] a false prophet, a Jew, whose name *was* Bar–jesus:

7 Which was with the deputy of the country, Sergius Paulus, a prudent man; who [apt]called for Barnabas and Saul, and desired [ainf]to hear the word[3056] of God.

8 But [a]Elymas the sorcerer (for so *is* his name by interpretation[3177]) [ipf]withstood them, seeking [ainf]to turn away the deputy from the faith.[4102]

9 Then Saul, (who also *is called* Paul,) [aptp][a]filled with the [an]Holy Ghost, [apt]set his eyes on him,

10 And said, O full of all subtilty[1388] and all mischief, [a]*thou* child[5207] of the devil,[1228] *thou* enemy of all righteousness,[1343] [fm]wilt thou not cease[3973] to [ppt]pervert the right ways[3598] of the Lord?

11 And now, behold, [a]the hand of the Lord *is* upon thee, and thou shalt be blind, not seeing the sun for a season.[2540] And immediately there fell on him a mist[887] and a darkness;[4655] and he [ppt]went about [ipf]seeking some to lead him by the hand.

12 Then the deputy, when he saw what was done, believed,[4100] being astonished at the doctrine[1322] of the Lord.

In Antioch of Pisidia

13 Now when Paul and his company loosed[321] from Paphos, they came to Perga in Pamphylia: and [a]John departing from them returned to Jerusalem.

14 But when they departed from Perga, they came to Antioch in Pisidia, and [a]went into the synagogue[4864] on the sabbath[4521] day, and sat down.

15 And [a]after the reading[320] of the law[3551] and the prophets[4396] the rulers of the synagogue[752] sent unto them, saying, *Ye* men *and* brethren, if ye have [b]any word of exhortation[3874] for the people, say on.

16 Then Paul [apt]stood up, and [apt][a]beckoning with *his* hand said, Men of Israel, and [b]ye that fear God,[2316] give audience.

17 The God of this people of Israel [a]chose our fathers, and exalted the people [b]when they dwelt as strangers in the land of Egypt, [c]and with an high[5308] arm brought he them out of it.

18 And [a]about the time[5550] of forty years [I][b]suffered he their manners in the wilderness.

19 And when [a]he had destroyed seven nations in the land of Chanaan,

25 [I]Or, *charge* [a]Acts 11:29, 30 [b]Acts 13:5, 13; 15:37 [c]Acts 12:12

1 [I]Or, *Herod's foster brother* [a]Acts 11:27; 14:26; 15:35 [b]Acts 11:22-26 [c]Rom. 16:21

2 [a]Num. 8:14; Acts 9:15; 22:21; Rom. 1:1; Gal. 1:15; 2:9 [b]Matt. 9:38; Acts 14:26; Rom. 10:15; Eph. 3:7, 8; 1Tim. 2:7; 2Tim. 1:11; Heb. 5:4

3 [a]Acts 6:6

4 [a]Acts 4:36

5 [a]Acts 13:46 [b]Acts 12:25; 15:37

6 [a]Acts 8:9

8 [a]Ex. 7:11; 2Tim. 3:8

9 [a]Acts 4:8

10 [a]Matt. 13:38; John 8:44; 1John 3:8

11 [a]Ex. 9:3; 1Sam. 5:6

13 [a]Acts 15:38

14 [a]Acts 16:13; 17:2; 18:4

15 [a]Luke 4:16; Acts 13:27 [b]Heb. 13:22

16 [a]Acts 12:17 [b]Acts 10:35; 12:26, 42, 43

17 [a]Deut. 7:6, 7 [b]Ex. 1:1; Ps. 105:23, 24; Acts 7:17 [c]Ex. 6:6; 13:14, 16

18 [I]Gr. *bore,* or, *fed them, as a nurse beareth,* or, *feedeth her child* [a]Ex. 16:35; Num. 14:33, 34; Ps. 95:9, 10; Acts 7:36 [b]Deut. 1:31

19 [a]Deut. 7:1

🔑 **13:1** The fact that Manaen "had been brought up with Herod the tetrarch" is also noted in Josephus' writings and the Talmud. According to these sources, Manaen was the son of a man named Essene who had gained favor and position with Herod the Great. As a result, Manaen was brought up in the king's court with Herod the Great's son Herod Antipas (the tetrarch).

[b]he [ao]divided their land to them by lot.[2624]

20 And after that [a]he gave *unto them* judges[2923] about the space of four hundred and fifty years, [b]until Samuel the prophet.

21 [a]And afterward they desired a king:[935] and God gave unto them Saul the son of Cis, a man of the tribe of Benjamin, by the space of forty years.

22 And [a]when he [apt]had removed[3179] him, [b]he raised up[1453] unto them David to be their king; to whom also he [apt]gave testimony, and said, [c]I have found David the *son* of Jesse, [d]a man after mine own heart,[2588] which shall fulfil all my will.[2307]

23 [a]Of this man's[4690] seed hath God according [b]to *his* promise[1860] raised unto Israel [c]a Saviour,[4990] Jesus:

24 [a]When John had first preached before[4383] [4253] his coming the baptism[908] of repentance[3341] to all the people of Israel.

25 And as John [ipf]fulfilled his course, he said, [a]Whom think[5282] ye that I am? I am not *he.* But, behold, there cometh one after me, whose shoes of *his* feet I am not worthy to loose.

26 Men *and* brethren, children of the stock of Abraham, and whosoever among you [ppt]feareth God, [a]to you is the word of this salvation[4991] sent.

27 For they that dwell at Jerusalem, and their rulers, [a]because they [apt]knew him not,[50] nor yet the voices of the prophets [b]which are read every sabbath day, [c]they [ao]have fulfilled *them* in [apt]condemning[2919] *him.*

28 [a]And though they [apt]found[2147] no cause of death *in him,* [b]yet desired they Pilate that he should be slain.

29 [a]And when they [ao]had fulfilled[5055] all that was written of him, [b]they [apt]took *him* down from the tree, and laid *him* in a sepulchre.[3419]

30 [a]But God raised him from the dead:[3498]

31 And [a]he [aop]was seen many days of them which [apt]came up with him [b]from Galilee to Jerusalem, [c]who are his witnesses[3144] unto the people.

32 And we [pin]declare unto you glad tidings,[2097] how that [a]the promise which was made unto the fathers,

33 God [pfi]hath fulfilled[1603] the same unto us their children, in that he [apt]hath raised up Jesus again; as it is also written in the second psalm, [a]Thou art my Son,[5207] this day [pfi]have I begotten[1080] thee.

34 And as concerning that he raised him up from the dead, *now* no more [pinf]to return to corruption, he said on this wise, [a]I will give you the sure[4103] mercies[3741] of David.

35 Wherefore he saith also in another[2087] *psalm,* [a]Thou shalt not suffer thine Holy One[3741] to see corruption.

36 For David, [I][a]after he had served his own generation[1074] by the will[1012] of God, [b]fell on sleep, and was laid unto his fathers, and saw corruption:

37 But he, whom God raised again, saw no corruption.

🔑 38 Be it known unto you therefore, men *and* brethren, that [a]through this man is preached[2605] unto you the forgiveness[859] of sins:[266]

39 And [a]by him all that [ppt]believe [pinp]are justified[1344] from all things, from which ye could not be justified by the law[3551] of Moses.

40 Beware[991] therefore, lest that [asbp]come upon you, which is spoken of in [a]the prophets;[4396]

41 Behold, ye despisers, and wonder, and perish: for I work a work in your days, a work which ye shall in no wise believe, though a man declare it unto you.

42 And when the Jews were gone out of the synagogue,[4864] the Gentiles [ipf]besought[3870] that these words[4487] might be preached to them [I]the next sabbath.

19 [b]Josh. 14:1, 2; Ps. 78:55 **20** [a]Judg. 2:16 [b]1Sam. 3:20 **21** [a]1Sam. 8:5; 10:1 **22** [a]1Sam. 15:23, 26, 28; 16:1; Hos. 13:11 [b]1Sam. 16:13; 2Sam. 2:4; 5:3 [c]Ps. 89:20 [d]1Sam. 13:14; Acts 7:46 **23** [a]Isa. 11:1; Luke 1:32, 69; Acts 2:30; Rom. 1:3 [b]2Sam. 7:12; Ps. 132:11 [c]Matt. 1:21; Rom. 11:26 **24** [a]Matt. 3:1; Luke 3:3 **25** [a]Matt. 3:11; Mark 1:7; Luke 3:16; John 1:20, 27 **26** [a]Matt. 10:6; Luke 24:47; Acts 3:26; 13:46 **27** [a]Luke 23:34; Acts 3:17; 1Cor. 2:8 [b]Acts 13:14, 15; 15:21 [c]Luke 24:20, 44; Acts 26:22; 28:23 **28** [a]Matt. 27:22; Mark 15:13, 14; Luke 23:21, 22; John 19:6, 15 [b]Acts 3:13, 14 **29** [a]Luke 18:31; 24:44; John 19:28, 30, 36, 37 [b]Matt. 27:59; Mark 15:46; Luke 23:53; John 19:38 **30** [a]Matt. 28:6; Acts 2:24; 3:13, 15, 26; 5:30 **31** [a]Matt. 28:16; Acts 1:3; 1Cor. 15:5, 6, 7 [b]Acts 1:11 [c]Acts 1:8; 2:32; 3:15; 5:32 **32** [a]Gen. 3:15; 12:3; 22:18; Acts 26:6; Rom. 4:13; Gal. 3:16 **33** [a]Ps. 2:7; Heb. 1:5; 5:5 **34** [a]Isa. 55:3 **35** [a]Ps. 16:10; Acts 2:31 **36** [I]*Or, after he had in his own age served the will of God* [a]Ps. 78:72; Acts 13:22 [b]1Kgs. 2:10; Acts 2:29 **38** [a]Jer. 31:34; Dan. 9:24; Luke 24:47; 1John 2:12 **39** [a]Isa. 53:11; Rom. 3:28; 8:3; Heb. 7:19 **40** [a]Isa. 29:14; Hab. 1:5 **42** [I]*Gr. in the week between, or, in the sabbath between*

🔑 **13:38, 39** See note on Romans 3:19, 20.

43 Now when the congregation[4864]
was broken up, many of the Jews and
religious[4576] proselytes[4339] followed Paul
and Barnabas: who, speaking to them,
[a]persuaded[3982] them to continue in [b]the
grace[5485] of God.
44 And the next[2064] sabbath day
came almost the whole city together to
hear the word[3056] of God.
45 But when the Jews saw the multitudes, they were filled with envy, and
[ipfa]spake against those things which
[ppt]were spoken by Paul, contradicting and
blaspheming.[987]
46 Then Paul and Barnabas [apt]waxed
bold,[3955] and said, [a]It was necessary[316]
that the word of God [aifp]should first have
been spoken[2980] to you: but [b]seeing ye
put it from you, and judge[2919] yourselves
unworthy of everlasting life,[2222] lo, [c]we
turn[4762] to the Gentiles.[1484]
47 For so [pfip]hath the Lord com-
manded[1781] us, *saying,* [a]I [pfi]have set[5087]
thee to be a light[5457] of the Gentiles, that
thou shouldest be for salvation unto the
ends[2078] of the earth.
48 And when the Gentiles [ppt]heard
this, they [ipf]were glad, and [ipf]glorified[1392]
the word of the Lord: [a]and as many as
[ipf]were ordained[5021] to eternal life [ao]be-
lieved.
49 And the word[3056] of the Lord
[ipf]was published[1308] throughout all the region.
50 But the Jews stirred up the
devout[4576] and honourable women,
and the chief men of the city, and
[a]raised persecution against Paul and
Barnabas, and expelled them out of their
coasts.
51 [a]But they [apt]shook off the dust of
their feet against them, and came[2064]
unto Iconium.
52 And the disciples[3101] [ipfa]were filled
with joy, and with the [an]Holy Ghost.

43 [a]Acts 11:23; 14:22 [b]Titus 2:11; Heb. 12:15; 1Pet. 5:12
45 [a]Acts 18:6; 1Pet. 4:4; Jude 1:10
46 [a]Matt. 10:6; Acts 3:26; 13:26; Rom. 1:16 [b]Ex. 32:10; Deut. 32:21; Isa. 55:5; Matt. 21:43; Rom. 10:19 [c]Acts 18:6; 28:28
47 [a]Isa. 42:6; 49:6; Luke 2:32
48 [a]Acts 2:47
50 [a]2Tim. 3:11
51 [a]Matt. 10:14; Mark 6:11; Luke 9:5; Acts 18:6
52 [a]Matt. 5:12; John 16:22; Acts 2:46

3 [a]Mark 16:20; Heb. 2:4
4 [a]Acts 13:3
5 [a]2Tim. 3:11
6 [a]Matt. 10:23
8 [a]Acts 3:2
9 [a]Matt. 8:10; 9:28, 29
10 [a]Isa. 35:6

Paul and Barnabas in Iconium

14 And it came to pass in Iconium,
that they [ainf]went both together[2596,846] into the synagogue of the
Jews, and so [ainf]spake, that a great multitude both of the Jews and also of the
Greeks [ainf]believed.[4100]
2 But the unbelieving[544] Jews stirred
up the Gentiles, and made[2559] their
minds[5590] evil affected[2559] against the
brethren.
🗝 3 Long time[5550] therefore abode they
speaking boldly in the Lord, [a]which
[ppt]gave testimony[3140] unto the word[3056] of
his grace,[5485] and [ppt]granted signs[4592]
and wonders[5059] [pinf]to be done by their
hands.
4 But the multitude of the city was
divided: and part held with the Jews, and
part with the [a]apostles.[652]
5 And when there was an assault[3730]
made both of the Gentiles, and also of
the Jews with their rulers, [ainfa]to use *them*
despitefully,[5195] and [ainf]to stone them,
6 They were ware[4894] of *it,* and [a]fled
unto Lystra and Derbe, cities of
Lycaonia, and into the region that lieth
round about:
7 And there they preached the
gospel.[2097]

In Lystra

8 [a]And there sat a certain man at
Lystra, impotent[102] in his feet, being a
cripple from his mother's womb, who
never had walked:
9 The same heard Paul speak: who
[apt]stedfastly beholding him, and [apta]per-
ceiving that he had faith[4102] [infg]to be
healed,[4982]
🗝 10 Said with a loud voice, [a]Stand
upright[3717] on thy feet. And he leaped
and [ipf]walked.
🗝 11 And when the people saw what

🗝 **14:3, 10** See note on 2 Timothy 4:20.

🗝 **14:11, 12** The names given to Paul and Barnabas were significant because the people were referring to them as their own heathen gods in human form. The reason that Paul and Barnabas did not refuse the people's worship immediately was that in the people's excitement after witnessing the miracle, they reverted back to speaking their native language which Paul and Barnabas did not understand.

Paul had done, they lifted up their voices, saying in the speech of Lycaonia, [a]The gods[2316] [ao]are come down to us [aptp]in the likeness[3666] of men.

12 And they called Barnabas, Jupiter; and Paul, Mercurius, because he was the chief[2233] speaker.

13 Then the priest of Jupiter, which was before their city, [apt]brought oxen and garlands unto the gates, [a]and [ipf]would [pinf]have done sacrifice with the people.

14 *Which* when the apostles,[652] Barnabas and Paul, heard *of,* [a]they [apt]rent[1284] their clothes, and ran in among the people,[3793] crying out,

15 And saying, Sirs, [a]why do ye these things? [b]We also are men of like passions with you, and [ppt]preach[2097] unto you that ye [pinf]should turn[1994] from [c]these vanities [d]unto the living[2198] God,[2316] [e]which made heaven,[3772] and earth,[1093] and the sea, and all things that are therein:

16 [a]Who in times past suffered all nations to walk in their own ways.[3598]

17 [a]Nevertheless he left not himself without witness, in that he [ppt]did good,[15] and [ppt][b]gave us rain from heaven, and fruitful seasons,[2540] filling our hearts with food and gladness.[2167]

18 And with these sayings scarce restrained[2664] they the people, that they [infg]had not done sacrifice[2380] unto them.

19 [a]And there came thither *certain* Jews from Antioch and Iconium, who [apt]persuaded[3982] the people, [b]and, [apt]having stoned Paul, drew[4951] *him* out of the city, [apt]supposing he [pfin]had been dead.

20 Howbeit,[1161] as the disciples stood round about him, he rose up, and came into the city: and the next day he departed with Barnabas to Derbe.

Returning to Antioch in Syria

21 And when they [apt]had preached the gospel[2097] to that city, [a]and [aoI]had taught[3100] many, they returned again to Lystra, and *to* Iconium, and Antioch,

22 Confirming the souls[5590] of the disciples, *and* [a]exhorting[3870] them [pinf]to continue[1696] in the faith, and that [b]we must through much tribulation[2347] [ainf]enter into the kingdom[932] of God.

23 And when they [apt]had [a]ordained[5500] them elders[4245] in every church,[1577] and had prayed with fasting,[3521] they commended them to the Lord, on whom they believed.

24 And after they had passed throughout Pisidia, they came to Pamphylia.

25 And when they had preached the word[3056] in Perga, they went down into Attalia:

26 And thence sailed to Antioch, [a]from whence they had been [b]recommended to the grace[5485] of God for the work[2041] which they fulfilled.

27 And when they were come, and had gathered the church[1577] together, [a]they rehearsed[312] all that God [ao]had done with them, and how he had [b]opened the door of faith[4102] unto the Gentiles.

28 And there they [ipf]abode long time with the disciples.[3101]

Is Circumcision Required?

15 And [a]certain men which came down from Judaea [ipf]taught[1321] the brethren,[80] *and said,* [b]Except ye [psmp]be circumcised[4059] [c]after the manner of Moses, ye cannot [aifp]be saved.[4982]

2 When therefore Paul and Barnabas had no small dissension[4714] and disputation[4803] with them, they determined that [a]Paul and Barnabas, and certain other of them, [pinf]should go up to Jerusalem unto the apostles[652] and elders[4245] about this question.

3 And [a]being brought on their way by the church,[1577] they [ipf]passed through Phenice and Samaria, [b]declaring[1555] the conversion[1995] of the Gentiles: and they [ipf]caused great joy unto all the brethren.

4 And when they were come to Jerusalem, they [aop]were received[588] of the church,[1577] and *of* the apostles and elders,[4245] and [a]they declared all things that God [ao]had done with them.

5 But there rose up[1817] certain of the sect[139] of the Pharisees which [pfp]be-

11 [a]Acts 8:10; 28:6

13 [a]Dan. 2:46

14 [a]Matt. 26:65

15 [a]Acts 10:26 [b]James 5:17; Rev. 19:10 [c]1Sam. 12:21; 1Kgs. 16:13; Jer. 14:22; Amos 2:4; 1Cor. 8:4 [d]1Thess. 1:9 [e]Gen. 1:1; Ps. 33:6; 146:6; Rev. 14:7

16 [a]Ps. 81:12; Acts 17:30; 1Pet. 4:3

17 [a]Acts 17:27; Rom. 1:20 [b]Lev. 26:4; Deut. 11:14; 28:12; Job 5:10; Ps. 65:10; 68:9; 147:8; Jer. 14:22; Matt. 5:45

19 [a]Acts 13:45 [b]2Cor. 11:25; 2Tim. 3:11

21 [I]Gr. *had made many disciples* [a]Matt. 28:19

22 [a]Acts 11:23; 13:43 [b]Matt. 10:38; 16:24; Luke 22:28, 29; Rom. 8:17; 2Tim. 2:11, 12; 3:12

23 [a]Titus 1:5

26 [a]Acts 13:1, 3 [b]Acts 15:40

27 [a]Acts 15:4, 12; 21:19 [b]1Cor. 16:9; 2Cor. 2:12; Col. 4:3; Rev. 3:8

1 [a]Gal. 2:12 [b]John 7:22; Acts 15:5; Gal. 5:2; Phil. 3:2; Col. 2:8, 11, 16 [c]Gen. 17:10; Lev. 12:3

2 [a]Gal. 2:1

3 [a]Rom. 15:24; 1Cor. 16:6, 11 [b]Acts 14:27

4 [a]Acts 14:27; 15:12; 21:19

lieved,[4100] saying, [a]That it was needful [pinf]to circumcise[4059] them, and [pinf]to command *them* [pinf]to keep the law of Moses.

6 And the apostles and elders[4245] came together for [ainf]to consider[1492] of this matter.[3056]

7 And when there had been much disputing, Peter rose up, and said unto them, [a]Men *and* brethren, ye know how that a good while ago God [aom]made choice among us, that the Gentiles by my mouth [ainf]should hear the word[3056] of the gospel,[2098] and [ainf]believe.

8 And God, [a]which knoweth the hearts,[2589] bare them witness, [apt][b]giving them the Holy Ghost, even as *he did* unto us;

9 [a]And [ao]put no difference[1252] between us and them, [apt][b]purifying[2511] their hearts[2588] by faith.[4102]

10 Now therefore why tempt[3985] ye God, [a]to put a yoke upon the neck of the disciples, which neither our fathers[3962] nor we were able [ainf]to bear?

11 But [a]we believe that through the grace of the Lord Jesus Christ we [aifp]shall be saved,[4982] even as they.

12 Then all the multitude kept silence, and gave audience[191] to Barnabas and Paul, declaring[1834] what miracles and wonders God [ao]had [a]wrought among the Gentiles[1484] by them.

13 And after they had [aime]held their peace,4601 [a]James answered, saying, Men[435] *and* brethren,[80] hearken unto me:

14 [a]Simeon [aom]hath declared[1834] how God at the first [aom]did visit[1980] the Gentiles, to take out of them a people for his name.

15 And to this agree the words of the prophets;[4396] as it is written,

16 [a]After this I will return, and will build again the tabernacle4633 of David, which is fallen down; and I will build again the ruins thereof, and I [ft]will set it up:[461]

17 That the residue2645 of men might seek after the Lord, and all the Gentiles, upon whom my name [pfip]is called,[1941] saith the Lord, who [ppt]doeth all these things.

18 Known[1110] unto God are all his works from the beginning of the world.

19 Wherefore [a]my sentence is,[2919] that we trouble not them, which from among the Gentiles [b]are turned to God:

🔑 20 But that we [ainf]write unto them, that they abstain[567] [a]from pollutions of idols,[1497] and [b]*from* fornication,4202 and *from* things strangled, [c]and *from* blood.

21 For Moses of old time hath in every city them that [ppt]preach[2784] him, [a]being read in the synagogues every sabbath day.4521

The Letter to Antioch

22 Then pleased it the apostles and elders,[4245] with the whole church, to send chosen men of their own company to Antioch with Paul and Barnabas; *namely,* Judas surnamed [a]Barsabas, and Silas, chief men among the brethren:

23 And they [apt]wrote *letters* by them after this manner; The apostles and elders and brethren *send* greeting[5463] unto the brethren which are of the Gentiles in Antioch and Syria and Cilicia:

24 Forasmuch as we have heard, that [a]certain which [apt]went out from us have troubled you with words, subverting your souls,[5590] saying, *Ye must* [pip]be circumcised,[4059] and [pinf]keep the law: to whom we gave no *such* commandment:

25 It seemed good unto us, being assembled with one accord, to send chosen men unto you with our beloved Barnabas and Paul,

26 [a]Men that [pfp]have hazarded their lives[5590] for the name of our Lord Jesus Christ.

27 We have sent therefore Judas and Silas, who [ppt]shall also tell[518] *you* the same things by [I]mouth.

28 For it seemed good[1380] to the Holy Ghost, and to us, [pinf]to lay upon you no greater burden than these necessary[1876] things;

🔑 29 [a]That ye abstain[567] from meats offered to idols,[1494] and [b]from blood,

5 [a]Acts 15:1
7 [a]Acts 10:20; 11:12
8 [a]1Chr. 28:9; Acts 1:24 [b]Acts 10:44
9 [a]Rom. 10:11 [b]Acts 10:15, 28, 43; 1Cor. 1:2; 1Pet. 1:22
10 [a]Matt. 23:4; Gal. 5:1
11 [a]Rom. 3:24; Eph. 2:8; Titus 2:11; 3:4, 5
12 [a]Acts 14:27
13 [a]Acts 12:17
14 [a]Acts 15:7
16 [a]Amos 9:11, 12
19 [a]Acts 15:28 [b]1Thess. 1:9
20 [a]Gen. 35:2; Ex. 20:3, 23; Ezek. 20:30; 1Cor. 8:1; 10:20, 28; Rev. 2:14, 20 [b]1Cor. 6:9, 18; Gal. 5:19; Eph. 5:3; Col. 3:5; 1Thess. 4:3; 1Pet. 4:3 [c]Gen. 9:4; Lev. 3:17; Deut. 12:16, 23
21 [a]Acts 13:15, 27
22 [a]Acts 1:23
24 [a]Acts 15:1; Gal. 2:4; 5:12; Titus 1:10, 11
26 [a]Acts 13:50; 14:19; 1Cor. 15:30; 2Cor. 11:23, 26
27 [I]Gr. *word*
29 [a]Acts 15:20; 21:25; Rev. 2:14, 20 [b]Lev. 17:14

🔑 **15:20, 29** See note on Ezekiel 33:25, 26.

and from things strangled, and from fornication: from which if ye [ppt]keep[1301] yourselves, ye shall do well, Fare ye well.

30 So when they were dismissed, they came to Antioch: and when they had gathered the multitude together, they delivered the epistle:[1992]

31 *Which* when they had read, they rejoiced for the [I]consolation.[3874]

32 And Judas and Silas, being prophets[4396] also themselves, [a]exhorted[3870] the brethren with many words, and confirmed *them.*

33 And after they had tarried *there* a space,[5550] they were let [a]go in peace[1515] from the brethren unto the apostles.

34 Notwithstanding it pleased Silas [ainf]to abide there still.

35 [a]Paul also and Barnabas [ipf]continued in Antioch, teaching[1321] and preaching[2097] the word[3056] of the Lord, with many others[2087] also.

Paul and Barnabas Separate

🗝 36 And some days after Paul said unto Barnabas, [aosi]Let us go again and visit[1980] our brethren [a]in every city where we [ao]have preached[2605] the word of the Lord, *and see* how they do.

37 And Barnabas determined to take with them [a]John, whose surname was Mark.

38 But Paul thought not good [ainf]to take him with them, [a]who [apt]departed[868] from them from Pamphylia, and [apt]went not with them to the work.[2041]

39 And the contention [ao]was so sharp between them, that they [ainf]departed asunder one from the other: and so Barnabas [apt]took Mark, and [ainf]sailed unto Cyprus;

40 And Paul chose Silas, and departed, [a]being recommended by the brethren unto the grace of God.

41 And he [ipf]went through Syria and Cilicia, [a]confirming the churches.[1577]

Timothy Joins Paul

16 Then came he to [a]Derbe and Lystra: and, behold, a certain disciple was there, [b]named Timotheus, [c]the son of a certain woman, which was a Jewess, and believed;[4103] but his father *was* a Greek:

2 Which [ipfa]was well reported of by the brethren[80] that were at Lystra and Iconium.

3 Him would Paul have [ainf]to go forth with him; and [a]took and circumcised[4059] him because of the Jews which were in those quarters: for they knew all that his father was a Greek.

4 And as they [ipf]went through the cities, they delivered them the decrees[1378] for [pinf]to keep, [a]that [pfpp]were ordained[2919] of the apostles[652] and elders[4245] which were at Jerusalem.

Paul's Vision of the Man of Macedonia

5 And [a]so were the churches[1577] established in the faith,[4102] and [ipf]increased in number daily.

6 Now when they had gone throughout Phrygia and the region of Galatia, and [aptp]were forbidden of the Holy Ghost[4151] [ainf]to preach[2980] the word[3056] in Asia,

7 After they were come to Mysia, they [ipf]assayed[3985] [pinf]to go into Bithynia: but the Spirit[4151] suffered them not.

8 And they passing by Mysia [a]came down to Troas.

9 And a vision[3705] [aop]appeared to Paul in the night; There stood a [a]man of Macedonia, and [ppt]prayed[3870] him, saying, [apt]Come over into Macedonia, and [aim]help us.

10 And after he had seen the vision, immediately we endeavoured to go [a]into Macedonia, assuredly gathering that the Lord [pfi]had called[4341] us for [ainf]to preach the gospel[2097] unto them.

31 IOr, *exhortation*
32 [a]Acts 14:22; 18:23
33 [a]1Cor. 16:11; Heb. 11:31
35 [a]Acts 13:1
36 [a]Acts 13:4, 13, 14, 51; 14:1, 6, 24, 25
37 [a]Acts 12:12, 25; 13:5; Col. 4:10; 2Tim. 4:11; Phile. 1:24
38 [a]Acts 13:13
40 [a]Acts 14:26
41 [a]Acts 16:5
1 [a]Acts 14:6 [b]Acts 19:22; Rom. 16:21; 1Cor. 4:17; Phil. 2:19; 1Thess. 3:2; 1Tim. 1:2; 2Tim. 1:2 [c]2Tim. 1:5
2 [a]Acts 6:3
3 [a]1Cor. 9:20; Gal. 2:3; 5:2
4 [a]Acts 15:28, 29
5 [a]Acts 15:41
8 [a]2Cor. 2:12; 2Tim. 4:13
9 [a]Acts 10:30
10 [a]2Cor. 2:13

🗝 **15:36** See introduction to 1 Timothy.

In Philippi

11 Therefore loosing from Troas, we came with a straight course to Samothracia, and the next *day* to Neapolis;

🔑 12 And from thence to [a]Philippi, which is [I]the chief[4413] city of that part of Macedonia, *and* a colony: and we were in that city abiding certain days.

13 And on the [I]sabbath[4521] we went out of the city by a river side, where prayer [ipf]was wont[3543] to be made; and we [apt]sat down, and [ipf]spake unto the women which [apt]resorted *thither.*

14 And a certain woman named Lydia, a seller of purple, of the city of Thyatira, which [ppp]worshipped[4576] God, [ipf]heard *us:* whose [a]heart[2588] the Lord opened, that she [pinf]attended unto the things which [ppp]were spoken of Paul.

15 And when she [aop]was baptized,[907] and her household, she besought[3870] *us,* saying, If ye [pf]have judged[2919] me to be faithful to the Lord,[2962] [apt]come into my house, and [aim]abide *there.* And [a]she constrained us.

Paul and Silas Imprisoned

16 And it came to pass, as we went to prayer, a certain damsel[3814] [a]possessed with a spirit[4151] of divination met us, which [ipf]brought her masters[2962] [b]much gain by soothsaying:[3132]

17 The same [apt]followed Paul and us, and [ipf]cried, saying, These men are the servants[1401] of the most high God,[2316] which shew[2605] unto us the way[3598] of salvation.[4991]

🔑 18 And this [ipf]did she many days. But Paul, [a]being grieved, turned[1994] and said to the spirit, I command thee in the name[3686] of Jesus Christ [ainf]to come out of her. [b]And he came out the same hour.

19 And [a]when her masters saw that the hope[1680] of their gains was gone, [b]they caught[1949] Paul and Silas, and [c]drew[1670] *them* into the [I]marketplace[58] unto the rulers,

20 And brought[4317] them to the magistrates, saying, These men, being Jews, [a]do exceedingly trouble our city,

21 And teach[2605] customs, which are not lawful for us [pinf]to receive,[3858] neither [pinf]to observe, being Romans.

22 And the multitude rose up together against them: and the magistrates [apt]rent off[4048] their clothes, [a]and [ipf]commanded [pinf]to beat *them.*

23 And when they [apt]had laid many stripes upon them, they cast *them* into prison, charging the jailer [pinf]to keep[5083] them safely:

24 Who, having received such a charge,[3852] thrust them into the inner prison, and made their feet fast in the stocks.

25 And at midnight Paul and Silas [ppt]prayed, and [ipf]sang praises[5214] unto God: and the prisoners [ipf]heard them.

26 [a]And suddenly there was a great earthquake, so that the foundations of the prison [aifp]were shaken: and immediately [b]all the doors were opened, and every one's bands were loosed.

27 And the keeper of the prison awaking out of his sleep, and seeing the prison doors [pfpp]open, he [apt]drew out his sword, and would have killed himself, supposing that the prisoners [pfin]had been fled.

28 But Paul cried with a loud voice, saying, Do thyself no harm: for we are all here.

29 Then he called for a light, and sprang in, and came trembling, and fell down before Paul and Silas,

30 And brought[4254] them out, and said, [a]Sirs,[2962] what must I do to be saved?

31 And they said, [aim][a]Believe[4100] on the Lord Jesus Christ, and thou [fp]shalt be saved,[4982] and thy house.

32 And they spake unto him the

12 [I]Or, *the first* [a]Phil. 1:1
13 [I]Gr. *sabbath day*
14 [a]Luke 24:45
15 [a]Gen. 19:3; 33:11; Judg. 19:21; Luke 24:29; Heb. 13:2
16 [a]1Sam. 28:7 [b]Acts 19:24
18 [a]Mark 1:25, 34 [b]Mark 16:17
19 [I]Or, *court* [a]Acts 19:25, 26 [b]2Cor. 6:5 [c]Matt. 10:18
20 [a]1Kgs. 18:17; Acts 17:6
22 [a]2Cor. 6:5; 11:23, 25; 1Thess. 2:2
26 [a]Acts 4:31 [b]Acts 5:19; 12:7, 10
30 [a]Luke 3:10; Acts 2:37; 9:6
31 [a]John 3:16, 36; 6:47; 1John 5:10

🔑 **16:12** See introduction to 1 Timothy.
🔑 **16:18** See note on 2 Timothy 4:20.

word of the Lord, and to all that were in his house.

33 And he took them the same hour of the night, and washed *their* stripes; and [aop]was baptized,[907] he and all his, straightway.[3916]

34 And when he had brought them into his house, [a]he set meat before them, and rejoiced,[21] [pfp]believing[4100] in God with all his house.[3832]

35 And when it was day, the magistrates sent the serjeants, saying, Let those men go.

36 And the keeper of the prison told this saying to Paul, The magistrates have sent to [asbp]let you go:[630] now therefore depart, and [pim]go in peace.[1515]

37 But Paul said unto them, They [apt]have beaten us openly uncondemned, [a]being Romans, and [ao]have cast *us* into prison; and now do they thrust us out privily?[2977] nay verily;[1063] but let them come themselves and fetch us out.

38 And the serjeants told[312] these words unto the magistrates: and they feared, when they heard that they were Romans.

39 And they came and besought them, and [apt]brought *them* out, and [ipfa]desired *them* [ainf]to depart out of the city.

40 And they went out of the prison, [a]and entered into *the house of* Lydia: and when they had seen the brethren, they comforted[3870] them, and departed.

In Thessalonica

17 🔑Now when they had passed through Amphipolis and Apollonia, they came to Thessalonica, where was a synagogue[4864] of the Jews:

2 And Paul, as his manner was, [a]went in unto them, and three sabbath days[4521] [ipf]reasoned with them out of the scriptures,[1124]

3 Opening and alleging, [a]that Christ[5547] must needs [ainf]have suffered, and [ainf]risen again from the dead; and that this Jesus, whom I preach[2605] unto you, is Christ.

4 [a]And some of them believed,[3982] and consorted with Paul and [b]Silas; and of the devout[4576] Greeks a great multitude, and of the chief women not a few.

5 But the Jews which [ppt]believed not,[544] [apt]moved with envy, [apt]took[4355] unto them certain lewd[4190] fellows of the baser sort,[60] and [apt]gathered a company, and [ipf]set all the city on an uproar, and [apt]assaulted the house of [a]Jason, and [ipf]sought [ainf]to bring them out[71] to the people.[1218]

6 And when they found them not, they drew[4951] Jason and certain brethren unto the rulers of the city, crying, [a]These that [apt]have turned the world upside down[387] are come hither also;

7 Whom Jason [pfip]hath received:[5264] and these all do contrary to the decrees of Caesar, [a]saying that there is another[2087] king,[935] *one* Jesus.

8 And they troubled the people and the rulers of the city, when they heard these things.

9 And when they [apt]had taken security of Jason, and of the other, they let them go.

In Berea

10 And [a]the brethren[80] immediately sent away Paul and Silas by night unto Berea: who coming *thither* went into the synagogue[4864] of the Jews.

11 These were more noble than those in Thessalonica, in that they received the word[3056] with all readiness of mind, and [ppta]searched the scriptures[1124] daily, whether those things were so.

12 Therefore many of them believed;[4100] also of honourable women which were Greeks, and of men, not a few.

13 But when the Jews of Thessalonica had knowledge that the word of God [aop]was preached[2605] of Paul

34 [a]Luke 5:29; 19:6
37 [a]Acts 22:25
39 [a]Matt. 8:34
40 [a]Acts 16:14
2 [a]Luke 4:16; Acts 9:20; 13:5, 14; 14:1; 16:13; 19:8
3 [a]Luke 24:26, 46; Acts 18:28; Gal. 3:1
4 [a]Acts 28:34 [b]Acts 15:22, 27, 32, 40
5 [a]Rom. 16:21
6 [a]Acts 16:20
7 [a]Luke 23:2; John 19:12; 1Pet. 2:13
10 [a]Acts 9:25; 17:14
11 [a]Isa. 34:16; Luke 16:29; John 5:39

🔑 **17:1–10** See introduction to 1 Thessalonians.

at Berea, they came thither also, and
[ppt]stirred up the people.
14 [a]And then immediately the
brethren sent away Paul to go as it were
to the sea: but Silas and Timotheus
abode[5278] there still.
15 And they that conducted[2525] Paul
brought him unto Athens: and [a]receiving
a commandment unto Silas and
Timotheus for to come to him with all
speed, they departed.

In Athens

16 Now while Paul waited for[1551]
them at Athens, [a]his spirit [ipf]was stirred
in him, when he [ppt]saw the city [I]wholly
given to idolatry.[2712]
17 Therefore [ipf]disputed he in the
synagogue with the Jews, and with the
devout persons,[4576] and in the market[58]
daily with them that [ppt]met with him.
18 Then certain philosophers of the
Epicureans, and of the Stoics, [ipf]encoun-
tered him. And some [ipf]said, What
will this babbler 4691 say? other some,
He seemeth to be a setter forth[2604]
of strange gods: 1140 because he
[ipf]preached[2097] unto them Jesus, and the
resurrection.[386]
19 And they took him, and brought[71]
him unto [I]Areopagus, saying, May we
know what this new[2537] doctrine,[1322]
whereof thou [ppp]speakest,[2980] *is?*
20 For thou bringest certain strange
things to our ears:[189] we would know
therefore what these things mean.
21 (For all the Athenians and
strangers which were there [ipf]spent their
time in nothing else,[2087] but either [pinf]to
tell, or [pinf]to hear some new thing.)
22 Then Paul stood in the midst of
[I]Mars' hill, and said, *Ye* men of Athens,
I perceive that in all things ye are too
superstitious.[1174]
23 For as I passed by, and [ppt]be-
held 333 your [I][a]devotions,[4574] I found an
altar with this inscription, TO THE UN-
KNOWN[57] GOD.[2316] Whom therefore ye
ignorantly[50] worship,[2151] him declare[2605]
I unto you.
24 [a]God that [apt]made the world[2889]
and all things therein, seeing that he is
[b]Lord[2962] of heaven[3772] and earth,[1093]
[c]dwelleth not in temples[3485] made with
hands;
25 Neither is worshipped with
men's[444] hands, [a]as though 4326 he
needed 4326 any thing, seeing [b]he [ppt]giveth
to all life,[2222] and breath,[4157] and all
things;
26 And hath made of one blood[129]
all nations[1484] of men for to dwell[2730] on
all the face[4383] of the earth, and [apt]hath
determined[3724] the times[2540] before appointed,[4384] and [a]the bounds of their
habitation; 2733
27 [a]That they should seek the Lord,
if haply 686 they [opt]might feel after him,
and [opt]find him, [b]though he be not far
from every one of us:
28 For [a]in him we live,[2198] and move,
and have our being; [b]as certain also of
your own poets have said, For we are
also his offspring.
29 Forasmuch then as we are the offspring of God, [a]we ought not to think
that the Godhead is like unto gold, or silver, or stone, graven[5480] by art and man's
device.
30 And [a]the times[5550] of this ignorance[52] God [apt]winked at;[5237] but [b]now
commandeth[3853] all men[444] every where
[pinf]to repent:[3340]
31 Because he hath appointed[2476]
a day, in the which [a]he will [pinf]judge[2919]
the world[3625] in righteousness[1343] by
that man[435] whom he [ao]hath ordained;[3724] *whereof* he hath [I]given
assurance[4102] unto all *men,* in that
[b]he [apt]hath raised[450] him from the
dead.[3498]
32 And when they heard of the resurrection[386] of the dead, some mocked:
and others said, We will hear thee again
of this *matter.*
33 So Paul departed from among
them.
34 Howbeit 1161 certain men
[aptp]clave 2853 unto him, and believed:
among the which *was* Dionysius the
Areopagite, and a woman named
Damaris, and others[2087] with them.

14 [a]Matt. 10:23
15 [a]Acts 18:5
16 [I]Or, *full of idols* [a]2Pet. 2:8
19 [I]Or, *Mars' hill*
22 [I]Or, *the court of the Areopagites*
23 [I]Or, *gods that ye worship* [a]2Thess. 2:4
24 [a]Acts 14:15 [b]Matt. 11:25 [c]Acts 7:48
25 [a]Ps. 50:8 [b]Gen. 2:7; Num. 16:22; Job 12:10; 27:3; 33:4; Isa. 42:5; 57:16; Zech. 12:1
26 [a]Deut. 32:8
27 [a]Rom. 1:20 [b]Acts 14:17
28 [a]Col. 1:17; Heb. 1:3 [b]Titus 1:12
29 [a]Isa. 40:18
30 [a]Acts 14:16; Rom. 3:25 [b]Luke 24:47; Titus 2:11, 12; 1Pet. 1:14; 4:3
31 [I]Or, *offered faith* [a]Acts 10:42; Rom. 2:16; 14:10 [b]Acts 2:24

In Corinth

18 After these things Paul departed from Athens and came to Corinth;

2 And found a certain Jew named [a]Aquila, born in Pontus, lately come from Italy, with his wife Priscilla; (because that Claudius had commanded[1299] all Jews to depart from Rome:) and came unto them.

3 And because he was of the same craft, he [ipf]abode with them, [a]and [ipf]wrought:[2038] for by their occupation they were tentmakers.

4 [a]And he [ipf]reasoned in the synagogue[4864] every sabbath,[4521] and persuaded the Jews and the Greeks.

🗝 5 And [a]when Silas and Timotheus were come from Macedonia, Paul [ipf]was [b]pressed[4912] in the spirit, and [ppt]testified[1263] to the Jews *that* Jesus [I]*was* Christ.

6 And [a]when they [ppt]opposed themselves, and [ppt]blasphemed, [b]he [apt]shook *his* raiment, and said unto them, [c]Your blood[129] *be* upon your own heads; [d]I *am* clean:[2513] [e]from henceforth I will go unto the Gentiles.[1484]

7 And he departed[3327] thence, and entered into a certain *man's* house, named Justus, *one* that [ppt]worshipped[4576] God, whose house joined hard to the synagogue.

8 [a]And Crispus, the chief ruler of the synagogue,[752] believed[4100] on the Lord with all his house; and many of the Corinthians hearing [ipf]believed, and [ipf]were baptized.[907]

9 Then [a]spake the Lord to Paul in the night by a vision,[3705] [pim]Be not afraid,[5399] but [pim]speak,[2980] and [aosi]hold not thy peace:[4623]

10 [a]For I am with thee, and no man shall set on thee [infg]to hurt[2559] thee: for I have much people in this city.

11 And he [I]continued *there* a year and six months, teaching[1321] the word[3056] of God among them.

12 And when Gallio was the deputy of Achaia, the Jews made insurrection with one accord against Paul, and brought him to the judgment seat,

13 Saying, This *fellow* persuadeth men [pinf]to worship[4576] God contrary[3844] to the law.[3551]

14 And when Paul was now about to open *his* mouth, Gallio said unto the Jews, [a]If it were a matter of wrong[92] or wicked[4190] lewdness, O *ye* Jews, reason[3056] would that I [aom]should bear with[430,302] you:

15 But if it be a question of words and names, and *of* your law, look ye *to it;* for I will be no judge of such *matters.*

16 And he drave them from the judgment seat.

17 Then all the Greeks [apt]took [a]Sosthenes, the chief ruler of the synagogue, and [ipf]beat[5180] *him* before the judgment seat. And Gallio cared for none of those things.

Paul Sails for Syria

18 And Paul *after this* [apt]tarried[4357] *there* yet a good while, and then [apt]took his leave[657] of the brethren, and sailed thence into Syria, and with him Priscilla and Aquila; having [a]shorn *his* head in [b]Cenchrea: for he had a vow.

19 And he came to Ephesus, and left them there: but he himself [apt]entered into the synagogue, and reasoned with the Jews.

20 When they [ppt]desired *him* to tarry longer time[5550] with them, he consented not;

21 But [aom]bade them farewell,[657] saying, [a]I must by all means keep this feast that [ppt]cometh[2064] in Jerusalem: but I will return again unto you, [b]if God will. And he sailed[321] from Ephesus.

22 And when he had landed at Caesarea, and gone up, and saluted[782] the church,[1577] he went down to Antioch.

23 And after he had spent some time *there,* he departed, and went over *all* the

2 [a]Rom. 16:3; 1Cor. 16:19; 2Tim. 4:19

3 [a]Acts 20:34; 1Cor. 4:12; 1Thess. 2:9; 2Thess. 3:8

4 [a]Acts 17:2

5 [a]Acts 17:14, 15 [b]Job 32:18; Acts 17:3; 18:28

6 [a]Acts 13:45; 1Pet. 4:4 [b]Neh. 5:13; Matt. 10:14; Acts 13:51 [c]Lev. 20:9, 11, 12; 2Sam. 1:16; Ezek. 18:13; 33:4 [d]Ezek. 3:18, 19; 33:9; Acts 20:26 [e]Acts 13:46; 28:28

8 [a]1Cor. 1:14

9 [a]Acts 23:11

10 [a]Jer. 1:18, 19; Matt. 28:20

11 [I]Gr. *remained there*

14 [a]Acts 23:29; 25:11, 19

17 [a]1Cor. 1:1

18 [a]Num. 6:18; Acts 21:24 [b]Rom. 16:1

21 [a]Acts 19:21; 20:16 [b]1Cor. 4:19; Heb. 6:3; James 4:15

🗝 **18:5** See introduction to 1 Thessalonians.

country of [a]Galatia and Phrygia in order,
[b]strengthening all the disciples.[3101]

Apollos Preaches at Ephesus

24 [a]And a certain Jew named
Apollos, born at Alexandria, an eloquent
man, *and* mighty in the scriptures, came
to Ephesus.
25 This man was instructed in the
way[3598] of the Lord; and being [a]fer-
vent in the spirit, he [ipf]spake and
[ipf]taught[1321] diligently the things of the
Lord, [b]knowing only the baptism[908] of
John.
26 And he began to speak boldly in
the synagogue:[4864] whom when Aquila
and Priscilla had heard, they took him
unto[4355] *them,* and expounded unto him
the way of God more perfectly.
27 And when he was disposed to
pass into Achaia, the brethren wrote,
[apt]exhorting the disciples [ainf]to receive[588]
him: who, when he was come, [a]helped
them much which [pfp]had believed[4100]
through grace:[5485]
28 For he mightily [ipf]convinced the
Jews, *and that* publickly, [ppt][a]shewing
by the scriptures that Jesus was
Christ.[5547]

In Ephesus

19 And it came to pass, that,
while [a]Apollos was at Corinth,
Paul having passed through the upper
coasts came to Ephesus: and finding certain disciples,[3101]
2 He said unto them, Have ye received the Holy Ghost[4151] since ye [apt]be-
lieved?[4100] And they said unto him, [a]We
have not so much as heard whether there
be any Holy Ghost.
3 And he said unto them, Unto what
then [aop]were ye baptized?[907] And they
said, [a]Unto John's baptism.
4 Then said Paul, [a]John verily[3303]
baptized with the baptism of repentance,[3341] saying unto the people, that
they [aosb]should believe on him which
should come after him, that is, on Christ
Jesus.
5 When they heard *this,* they were
baptized [a]in the name of the Lord
Jesus.
6 And when Paul had [a]laid *his* hands
upon them, the Holy Ghost came[2064] on
them; and [b]they [ipf]spake with tongues,[1100]
and [ipf]prophesied.[4395]
7 And all the men were about twelve.
8 [a]And he went into the synagogue,[4864] and [ipf]spake boldly for the
space of three months, disputing and
persuading the things [b]concerning the
kingdom[932] of God.
9 But [a]when divers[5100] [ipf]were hardened,[4645] and [ipf]believed not,[544] but
[ppt]spake evil [b]of that way[3598] before the
multitude, he departed[868] from them,
and separated[873] the disciples,[3101] disputing daily in the school of one Tyrannus.

23 [a]Gal. 1:2; 4:14; Acts 14:22; 15:32, 41
24 [a]1Cor. 1:12; 3:5, 6; 4:6; Titus 3:13
25 [a]Rom. 12:11 [b]Acts 19:3
27 [a]1Cor. 3:6
28 [a]Acts 9:22; 17:3; 18:5
1 [a]1Cor. 1:12; 3:5, 6
2 [a]1Sam. 3:7; Acts 8:16
3 [a]Acts 18:25
4 [a]Matt. 3:11; John 1:15, 27, 30; Acts 1:5; 11:16; 13:24, 25
5 [a]Acts 8:16
6 [a]Acts 6:6; 8:17 [b]Acts 2:4; 10:46
8 [a]Acts 17:2; 18:4 [b]Acts 1:3; 28:23
9 [a]2Tim. 1:15; 2Pet. 2:2; Jude 1:10 [b]Acts 9:2; 22:4; 24:14

19:1–7 This event took place in Ephesus, and it concerned the disciples of John the Baptist there. These people had received the baptism of John but not the baptism of the Holy Spirit, which would be consequent to their exercise of faith in the Lord. The statement that they made, "We have not so much as heard whether there be any Holy Ghost," reflects their lack of knowledge about the Holy Spirit's work or ministry, not their denial of His existence.

Many have pointed out that Paul asked these people if they had received the Holy Ghost "since" they believed. Their purpose is to show that Paul accepted the idea that some do not receive the Spirit until after salvation. It should be understood, however, that the Greek text does not support this translation. A literal rendering of the Greek would be: "Did you receive the Holy Spirit, having believed?" It is plain in verses four and five that these people had not believed in Jesus Christ but in the repentance that John the Baptist had preached. Thus there is no conflict here with the belief that all believers receive the Holy Spirit at salvation.

19:3, 5 See note on 1 Corinthians 10:2.

19:6 See notes on Acts 2:1–13; 1 Corinthians 14:1–3.

19:9 See note on 2 Thessalonians 2:3.

10 And [a]this continued by the space
of two years; so that all they which dwelt
in Asia heard the word[3056] of the Lord
Jesus, both Jews and Greeks.

The Sons of Sceva

🔑 11 And [a]God [ipf]wrought special miracles[1411] by the hands of Paul:
12 [a]So that from his body [pip]were
brought unto the sick handkerchiefs or
aprons, and the diseases [pip]departed[525]
from them, and the evil[4190] spirits [pinf]went
out of them.
13 [a]Then certain of the vagabond
Jews, exorcists,1845 [b]took upon them to
call over them which had evil spirits the
name of the Lord Jesus, saying, We
adjure3726 you by Jesus whom Paul preacheth.[2784]
14 And there were seven sons of *one*
Sceva, a Jew, *and* chief of the priests,[749]
which [ppt]did so.
15 And the evil spirit answered and
said, Jesus I know, and Paul I know; but
who are ye?
16 And the man in whom the evil
spirit was leaped on them, and [apt]over-
came them, and prevailed[2480] against
them, so that they [ainf]fled out of that
house naked[1131] and wounded.
17 And this was known to all the
Jews and Greeks also dwelling at
Ephesus; and [a]fear[5401] fell on them all,
and the name of the Lord Jesus [ipf]was
magnified.
18 And many that [pfp]believed[4100]
[ipf]came, and [ppt][a]confessed,[1843] and
[ppt]shewed their deeds.
19 Many of them also which used
curious arts4021 [apt]brought their books
together,[4851] and [ipf]burned them before
all *men:* and they counted the price of
them, and found *it* fifty thousand *pieces*
of silver.
20 [a]So mightily [ipf]grew the word[3056]
of God and [ipf]prevailed.[2480]

10 [a]Acts 20:31
11 [a]Mark 16:20; Acts 14:3
12 [a]2Kgs. 4:29; Acts 5:15
13 [a]Matt. 12:27 [b]Mark 9:38; Luke 9:49
17 [a]Luke 1:65; 7:16; Acts 2:43; 5:5, 11
18 [a]Matt. 3:6
20 [a]Acts 6:7; 12:24
21 [a]Rom. 15:25; Gal. 2:1 [b]Acts 20:22 [c]Acts 18:21; 23:11; Rom. 15:24-28
22 [a]Acts 13:5 [b]Rom. 16:23; 2Tim. 4:20
23 [a]2Cor. 1:8 [b]Acts 9:2
24 [a]Acts 16:16, 19
26 [a]Ps. 115:4; Isa. 44:10-20; Jer. 10:3
29 [a]Rom. 16:23; 1Cor. 1:14 [b]Acts 20:4; 27:2; Col. 4:10; Phile. 1:24

21 [a]After these things were ended,
Paul [b]purposed[5087] in the spirit,[4151] when
he [apt]had passed through Macedonia
and Achaia, to go to Jerusalem, saying,
After I have been there, [c]I must also see
Rome.
22 So he sent into Macedonia two of
[a]them that [ppt]ministered[1247] unto him,
Timotheus and [b]Erastus; but he himself
stayed in Asia for a season.[5550]

The Riot at Ephesus

23 And [a]the same time there arose
no small stir about [b]that way.[3598]
24 For a certain *man* named Demetrius, a silversmith, which made silver
shrines[3485] for Diana, [ipf]brought [a]no small
gain unto the craftsmen;5079
25 Whom he called together with the
workmen of like occupation, and said,
Sirs, ye know that by this craft we have
our wealth.
26 Moreover ye see and hear, that not
alone at Ephesus, but almost throughout
all Asia, this Paul hath persuaded and
turned away[3179] much people, saying
that [a]they be no gods,[2316] which are made
with hands:
27 So that not only this our craft
is in danger to be set at nought;557
but also that the temple[2411] of the great
goddess Diana [aifp]should be despised,
and her magnificence should be destroyed, whom all Asia and the world
worshippeth.
28 And when they heard *these sayings,* they were full of wrath,[2372] and
cried out, saying, Great *is* Diana of the
Ephesians.
🔑 29 And the whole city was filled
with confusion: and having caught
[a]Gaius and [b]Aristarchus, men of Macedonia, Paul's companions in travel,
they rushed with one accord into the
theatre.
30 And when Paul would have en-

🔑 **19:11** See note on 2 Timothy 4:20.
🔑 **19:29** See note on 3 John 1:1.

tered in unto the people, the disciples suffered him not.

31 And certain of the chief of Asia, which were his friends, [apt]sent unto him, [ipf]desiring *him* that he would not adventure himself into the theatre.

32 Some therefore [ipf]cried one thing, and some another: for the assembly[1577] was confused; and the more part knew not wherefore they were come together.

33 And they drew Alexander out of the multitude, the Jews putting him forward. And [a]Alexander [b]beckoned with the hand, and would have made his defence unto the people.

34 But when they knew that he was a Jew, all with one voice about the space of two hours cried out, Great *is* Diana of the Ephesians.

35 And when the townclerk[1122] had appeased the people, he said, *Ye* men of Ephesus, what man is there that knoweth not how that the city of the Ephesians is [I]a worshipper of the great goddess Diana, and of the *image* which fell down from Jupiter?

36 Seeing then that these things cannot be spoken against, ye ought to be quiet, and to do nothing rashly.

37 For ye have brought hither these men, which are neither robbers of churches,[2417] nor yet [ppt]blasphemers of your goddess.

38 Wherefore if Demetrius, and the craftsmen[5079] which are with him, have a matter against any man, [I]the law [pin]is open,[71] and there are deputies: [pim]let them implead[1458] one another.

39 But if ye enquire any thing concerning other matters, it shall be determined in a [I]lawful[1772] assembly.[1577]

40 For we are in danger [pinf]to be called in question[1458] for this day's uproar,[4714] there being no cause whereby we may give an account of this concourse.[4963]

41 And when he had thus spoken, he dismissed the assembly.[1577]

33 [a]1Tim. 1:20; 2Tim. 4:14 [b]Acts 12:17

35 [I]Gr. *the temple keeper*

38 [I]Or, *the court days are kept*

39 [I]Or, *ordinary*

1 [a]1Cor. 16:5; 1Tim. 1:3

3 [a]Acts 9:23; 23:12; 25:3; 2Cor. 11:26

4 [a]Acts 19:29; 27:2; Col. 4:10 [b]Acts 19:29 [c]Acts 16:1 [d]Eph. 6:21; Col. 4:7; 2Tim. 4:12; Titus 3:12 [e]Acts 21:29; 2Tim. 4:20

6 [a]Ex. 12:14, 15; 23:15 [b]Acts 16:8; 2Cor. 2:12; 2Tim. 4:13

7 [a]1Cor. 16:2; Rev. 1:10 [b]Acts 2:42, 46; 1Cor. 10:16; 11:20

8 [a]Acts 1:13

10 [a]1Kgs. 17:21; 2Kgs. 4:34

Paul's Journey to Macedonia And Greece

20 🔑And after the uproar was ceased, Paul [apt]called unto *him* the disciples,[3101] and [apt]embraced *them,* and [a]departed for to go into Macedonia.

2 And when he had gone over those parts, and [apt]had given them much exhortation,[3870] he came into Greece,

3 And *there* abode three months. And [a]when the Jews laid wait for him, as he was about to sail into Syria, he purposed[1096,1106] to return through Macedonia.

🔑4 And there accompanied him into Asia Sopater of Berea; and of the Thessalonians, [a]Aristarchus and Secundus; and [b]Gaius of Derbe, and [c]Timotheus; and of Asia, [d]Tychicus and [e]Trophimus.

5 These going before [ipf]tarried[3306] for us at Troas.

6 And we sailed away from Philippi after [a]the days of unleavened bread,[106] and came unto them [b]to Troas in five days; where we abode seven days.

Paul's Farewell Visit to Troas

7 And upon [a]the first *day* of the week, when the disciples came together [infg][b]to break[2806] bread, Paul [ipf]preached unto them, ready[3195] to depart on the morrow; and continued his speech until midnight.

8 And there were many lights [a]in the upper chamber, where they were gathered together.

9 And there sat in a window a certain young man named Eutychus, being fallen into a deep sleep: and as Paul was long preaching, he [aptp]sunk down with sleep, and fell down from the third loft, and [aop]was taken up[142] dead.

10 And Paul went down, and [a]fell

🔑 **20:1–5** See notes on 2 Timothy 4:20; 3 John 1:1.

🔑 **20:4, 5** See introduction to 1 Timothy and also notes on Colossians 4:7, 10; 3 John 1:1.

on him, and embracing *him* said, [b]Trouble not yourselves; for his life[5590] is in him.

11 When he therefore was come up again, and had broken bread, and eaten, and talked a long while, even till break of day,[827] so he departed.

12 And they brought the young man[3816] alive,[2198] and were not a little comforted.[3870]

From Troas to Miletus

13 And we went before to ship, and sailed unto Assos, there intending[3195] [pinf]to take in[353] Paul: for so [ipf]had[2258] he appointed,[1299] minding[3195] himself to go afoot.

14 And when he met with us at Assos, we [apt]took him in,[353] and came to Mitylene.

15 And we sailed thence, and came the next *day* over against Chios; and the next *day* we arrived[3846] at Samos, and tarried at Trogyllium; and the next *day* we came to Miletus.

16 For Paul [ao]had determined[2919] to sail by Ephesus, because he would not spend the time in Asia: for [a]he hasted, if it were possible for him, [b]to be at Jerusalem [c]the day of Pentecost.[4005]

Paul Meets With the Ephesian Elders

17 And from Miletus he [apt]sent to Ephesus, and called[3333] the elders[4245] of the church.[1577]

18 And when they were come to him, he said unto them, Ye know, [a]from the first day that I came[1910] into Asia, after what manner I have been with you at all seasons,[5550]

19 Serving[1398] the Lord with all humility of mind, and with many tears, and temptations,[3986] which befell me [a]by the lying in wait of the Jews:

20 *And* how [a]I kept back nothing that was profitable *unto you,* but [infg]have shewed[312] you, and have taught you publickly, and from house to house,

21 [a]Testifying[1263] both to the Jews, and also to the Greeks, [b]repentance[3341] toward God, and faith[4102] toward our Lord Jesus Christ.

22 And now, behold, [a]I go bound in the spirit unto Jerusalem, not knowing the things that shall befall me there:

23 Save that [a]the Holy Ghost witnesseth[1263] in every city, saying that bonds and afflictions [I]abide me.

24 But [a]none of these things move me, neither count I my life dear unto myself, [b]so that I [ainf]might finish[5048] my course with joy, [c]and the ministry,[1248] [d]which I have received of the Lord Jesus, [ainf]to testify[1263] the gospel[2098] of the grace[5485] of God.

25 And now, behold, [a]I know that ye all, among whom I have gone preaching[2784] the kingdom[932] of God, shall see my face no more.

26 Wherefore I take you to record[3143] this day, that I *am* [a]pure[2513] from the blood of all *men.*

27 For [a]I [aom]have not shunned[5288] [infg]to declare[312] unto you all [b]the counsel[1012] of God.

28 [a]Take heed therefore unto yourselves, and to all the flock,[4168] over the which the Holy Ghost [b]hath made[5087] you overseers,[1985] [pinf]to feed[4165] the church of God, [c]which he [aom]hath purchased [d]with his own blood.[129]

29 For I know this, that after my departing [a]shall grievous wolves enter in among you, not sparing the flock.[4168]

30 Also [a]of your own selves shall men arise, speaking perverse things, to draw away disciples after them.

31 Therefore watch, and [ppt]remember, [a]that by the space of three years I ceased not to warn[3560] every one night and day with tears.

32 And now, brethren, I commend you to God, and [a]to the word of his grace, which is able [ainfb]to build you up,[2026] and to give you [c]an inheritance[2817] among all them which are sanctified.[37]

33 [a]I have coveted no man's silver, or gold, or apparel.[2441]

34 Yea, ye yourselves know, [a]that these hands have ministered unto my

10 [b]Matt. 9:24

16 [a]Acts 18:21; 19:21; 21:4, 12 [b]Acts 24:17 [c]Acts 2:1; 1Cor. 16:8

18 [a]Acts 18:19; 19:1, 10

19 [a]Acts 20:3

20 [a]Acts 20:27

21 [a]Acts 18:5 [b]Mark 1:15; Luke 24:47; Acts 2:38

22 [a]Acts 19:21

23 [I]Or, *wait for me* [a]Acts 21:4, 11; 1Thess. 3:3

24 [a]Acts 21:13; Rom. 8:35; 2Cor. 4:16 [b]2Tim. 4:7 [c]Acts 1:17; 2Cor. 4:1 [d]Gal. 1:1; Titus 1:3

25 [a]Acts 20:38; Rom. 15:23

26 [a]Acts 18:6; 2Cor. 7:2

27 [a]Acts 20:20 [b]Luke 7:30; John 15:15; Eph. 1:11

28 [a]1Tim. 4:16; 1Pet. 5:2 [b]1Cor. 12:28 [c]Eph. 1:7, 14; Col. 1:14; Heb. 9:12; 1Pet. 1:19; Rev. 5:9 [d]Heb. 9:14

29 [a]Matt. 7:15; 2Pet. 2:1

30 [a]1Tim. 1:20; 1John 2:19

31 [a]Acts 19:10

32 [a]Heb. 13:9 [b]Acts 9:31 [c]Acts 26:18; Eph. 1:18; Col. 1:12; 3:24; Heb. 9:15; 1Pet. 1:4

33 [a]1Sam. 12:3; 1Cor. 9:12; 2Cor. 7:2; 11:9; 12:17

34 [a]Acts 18:3; 1Cor. 4:12; 1Thess. 2:9; 2Thess. 3:8

necessities,[5532] and to them that were with me.

35 I have shewed you all things, [a]how that so labouring ye ought [pinf]to support[482] the weak,[770] and to remember the words of the Lord Jesus, how he said, It is more blessed[3107] to give than to receive.

36 And when he had thus spoken, he [a]kneeled down, and prayed with them all.

37 And they all wept sore,[2425] and [apt][a]fell on Paul's neck, and [ipf]kissed him,

38 Sorrowing most of all for the words [a]which he spake, that they should see his face no more. And they [ipf]accompanied him unto the ship.

Paul's Voyage to Jerusalem

21 And it came to pass, that after we were gotten from them, and had launched, we came with a straight course unto Coos, and the *day* following unto Rhodes, and from thence unto Patara:

2 And finding a ship sailing over unto Phenicia, we went aboard,[1910] and set forth.[321]

3 Now when we had discovered Cyprus, we left it on the left hand, and [ipf]sailed into Syria, and landed[2609] at Tyre: for there the ship was to unlade her burden.

4 And finding[429] disciples, we tarried there seven days: [a]who [ipf]said to Paul through the Spirit, that he should not go up to Jerusalem.

5 And when we had accomplished[1822] those days, we departed and went our way; and they all brought us on our way, with wives and children, till *we were* out of the city: and [a]we kneeled down on the shore, and prayed.

6 And when we had taken our leave one of another, we took[1910,1519] ship; and they returned [a]home again.

7 And when we had finished *our* course from Tyre, we came to Ptolemais, and saluted the brethren, and abode with them one day.

8 And the next *day* we that were of Paul's company departed, and came unto Caesarea: and we entered into the house of Philip [a]the evangelist,[2099] [b]which was *one* of the seven; and abode with him.

9 And the same man had four daughters, virgins,[3933] [a]which [ppt]did prophesy.[4395]

10 And as we tarried *there* many days, there came down from Judaea a certain prophet,[4396] named [a]Agabus.

11 And when he was come unto us, he [apt]took Paul's girdle, and [apt]bound his own hands and feet, and said, Thus saith the Holy Ghost, [a]So shall the Jews at Jerusalem bind the man that owneth this girdle,[2223] and shall deliver *him* into the hands of the Gentiles.

12 And when we heard these things, both we, and they of that place, [ipf]besought[3870] him not to go up to Jerusalem.

13 Then Paul answered, [a]What mean ye to weep and to break mine heart? for I am ready not to be bound only, but also to die at Jerusalem for the name of the Lord Jesus.

14 And when he would not be persuaded,[3982] we ceased,[2270] saying, [a]The will[2307] of the Lord[2962] be done.

15 And after those days we took up our carriages, and [ipf]went up to Jerusalem.

16 There went with us also *certain* of the disciples[3101] of Caesarea, and [ppt]brought[71] with them one Mnason of Cyprus, an old[744] disciple, with whom we should lodge.

Paul Arrives in Jerusalem

17 [a]And when we were come to Jerusalem, the brethren received us gladly.

18 And the *day* following Paul went in with us unto [a]James; and all the elders[4245] were present.

19 And when he had saluted them, [a]he declared[1834] particularly what things God had wrought among the Gentiles[1484] [b]by his ministry.

35 [a]Rom. 15:1; 1Cor. 9:12; 2Cor. 11:9, 12; 12:13; Eph. 4:28; 1Thess. 4:11; 5:14; 2Thess. 3:8
36 [a]Acts 7:60; 21:5
37 [a]Gen. 45:14; 46:29
38 [a]Acts 20:25
4 [a]Acts 20:23; 21:12
5 [a]Acts 20:36
6 [a]John 1:11
8 [a]Eph. 4:11; 2Tim. 4:5 [b]Acts 6:5; 8:26, 40
9 [a]Joel 2:28; Acts 2:17
10 [a]Acts 11:28
11 [a]Acts 20:23; 21:33
13 [a]Acts 20:24
14 [a]Matt. 6:10; 26:42; Luke 11:2; 22:42
17 [a]Acts 15:4
18 [a]Acts 15:13; Gal. 1:19; 2:9
19 [a]Acts 15:4, 12; Rom. 15:18, 19 [b]Acts 1:17; 20:24

20 And when they heard *it,* they [ipf]glorified[1392] the Lord, and said unto him, Thou seest, brother, how many thousands of Jews there are[1526] which [pfp]believe;[4100] and they are[5225] all [a]zealous of the law:

21 And they are informed of thee, that thou teachest[1321] all the Jews which are among the Gentiles to forsake[646] Moses, saying that they [pinf]ought not to circumcise[4059] *their* children, neither to walk after the customs.

22 What is it therefore? the multitude must needs come together: for they will hear that thou [pf]art come.

23 Do therefore this that we say to thee: We have four men which have a vow on them;

24 Them take, and purify[48] thyself with them, and be at charges with them, that they may [a]shave *their* heads: and all may know that those things, whereof they were informed concerning thee, are nothing; but *that* thou thyself also walkest orderly, and [ppt]keepest the law.

25 As touching the Gentiles which [pfp]believe, [a]we have written *and* [apt]concluded[2919] that they [pinf]observe no such thing, save only that they [pinf]keep themselves from *things* offered to idols, and from blood, and from strangled, and from fornication.[4202]

26 Then Paul [apt]took the men, and the next day [aptp]purifying himself with them [a]entered into the temple,[2411] [b]to [ppt]signify[1229] the accomplishment[1604] of the days of purification,[49] until that an offering[4376] should be offered for every one of them.

The Riot and Paul's Arrest In the Temple

⊶ 27 And when the seven days were almost[3195] ended,[4931] [a]the Jews which were of Asia, when they saw him in the temple, [ipf]stirred up all the people, and [ao][b]laid hands on him,

28 Crying out, Men of Israel, help: This is the man,[444] [a]that [ppt]teacheth[1321] all *men* every where against the people, and the law,[3551] and this place: and further brought Greeks also into the temple, and hath polluted[2840] this holy[40] place.

29 (For they had seen before with him in the city [a]Trophimus an Ephesian, whom they supposed that Paul had brought into the temple.)

30 And [a]all the city was moved, and the people ran together: and they took Paul, and drew[1670] him out of the temple: and forthwith the doors were shut.

31 And as they went about to kill him, tidings came unto the chief captain of the band, that all Jerusalem was in an uproar.

32 [a]Who immediately took soldiers and centurions, and ran down unto them: and when they saw the chief captain and the soldiers, they left beating[5180] of Paul.

33 Then the chief captain came near, and took him, and [a]commanded *him* to be bound with two chains; and demanded who he was, and what he had done.

34 And some cried one thing, some another, among the multitude: and when he could not know the certainty for the tumult, he commanded him to be carried into the castle.

35 And when he came upon the stairs, so it was, that he was borne of the soldiers for the violence of the people.

36 For the multitude of the people followed after, crying, [a]Away with him.

Paul's Defence Before the Jews

37 And as Paul was to be led into the castle, he said unto the chief captain, May I speak unto thee? Who said, Canst thou speak Greek?

20 [a]Acts 22:3; Rom. 10:2; Gal. 1:14
24 [a]Num. 6:2, 13, 18; Acts 18:18
25 [a]Acts 15:20, 29
26 [a]Acts 24:18 [b]Num. 6:13
27 [a]Acts 24:18 [b]Acts 26:21
28 [a]Acts 24:5, 6
29 [a]Acts 20:4
30 [a]Acts 26:21
32 [a]Acts 23:27; 24:7
33 [a]Acts 20:23; 21:11
36 [a]Luke 23:18; John 19:15; Acts 22:22

⊶ **21:27–36** See note on 2 Timothy 4:20.

38 [a]Art not thou that Egyptian, which before these days [apt]madest an uproar,[387] and [apt]leddest out into the wilderness four thousand men that were murderers?[4607]

39 But Paul said, [a]I am a man *which am* a Jew of Tarsus, *a city* in Cilicia, a citizen of no mean city: and, I beseech[1189] thee, suffer me to speak unto the people.

40 And when he had given him licence, Paul stood on the stairs, and [a]beckoned with the hand unto the people. And when there was made a great silence, he spake unto *them* in the Hebrew tongue, saying,

22 Men,[435] [a]brethren,[80] and fathers,[3962] hear ye my defence[627] *which I make* now unto you.

2 (And when they heard that he spake in the Hebrew tongue to them, they kept the more silence: and he saith,)

3 [a]I am verily[3303] a man *which am* a Jew, born in Tarsus, *a city* in Cilicia, yet brought up in this city [b]at the feet of [c]Gamaliel, *and* taught[3811] [d]according to the perfect manner of the law of the fathers, and [e]was zealous toward God, [f]as ye all are this day.

4 [a]And I persecuted this way[3598] unto the death, binding and delivering into prisons both men and women.

5 As also the high priest doth bear me witness,[3140] and [a]all the estate[4244] of the elders: [b]from whom also I received letters unto the brethren, and went to Damascus, to bring them which were there bound unto Jerusalem, for to be punished.[5097]

Paul's Testimony of His Conversion

6 And [a]it came to pass, that, as I made my journey, and was come nigh unto Damascus about noon, suddenly there shone from heaven a great light round about me.

7 And I fell unto the ground, and heard a voice saying unto me, Saul, Saul, why persecutest thou me?

8 And I answered, Who art thou, Lord?[2962] And he said unto me, I am Jesus of Nazareth, whom thou persecutest.

9 And [a]they that were with me saw indeed the light, and were afraid; but they heard not the voice of him that [ppt]spake to me.

10 And I said, What shall I do, Lord? And the Lord said unto me, Arise, and go into Damascus; and there it shall be told thee of all things which are appointed[5021] for thee to do.

11 And when I [ipf]could not see[1689] for the glory[1391] of that light, being led by the hand of them that were with[4895] me, I came into Damascus.

12 And [a]one Ananias, a devout[2152] man according to the law, [ppt][b]having a good report[3140] of all the [c]Jews which dwelt *there,*

13 Came unto me, and stood, and said unto me, Brother Saul, receive thy sight. And the same hour I looked up upon him.

14 And he said, [a]The God of our fathers [b]hath chosen thee, that thou shouldest know his will, and [c]see [d]that Just One,[1342] and [e]shouldest hear the voice of his mouth.

15 [a]For thou shalt be his witness unto all men of [b]what thou hast seen and heard.

16 And now why tarriest thou? arise, and [aim]be baptized,[907] [a]and wash away[628] thy sins,[266] [apt][b]calling on the name of the Lord.

Paul Sent to the Gentiles

17 And [a]it came to pass, that, when I was come again to Jerusalem, even while I [ppt]prayed in the temple,[2411] I was in a trance;[1611]

18 And [a]saw him saying unto me, [b]Make haste, and get thee quickly out of Jerusalem: for they [fm]will not receive[3858] thy testimony[3141] concerning me.

38 [a]Acts 5:36
39 [a]Acts 9:11; 22:3
40 [a]Acts 12:17
1 [a]Acts 7:2
3 [a]Acts 21:39; 2Cor. 11:22; Phil. 3:5 [b]Deut. 33:3; 2Kgs. 4:38; Luke 10:39 [c]Acts 5:34 [d]Acts 26:5 [e]Acts 21:20; Gal. 1:14 [f]Rom. 10:2
4 [a]Acts 8:3; 26:9, 10, 11; Phil. 3:6; 1Tim. 1:13
5 [a]Luke 22:66; Acts 4:5 [b]Acts 9:2; 26:10, 12
6 [a]Acts 9:3; 26:12, 13
9 [a]Dan. 10:7; Acts 9:7
12 [a]Acts 9:17 [b]Acts 10:22 [c]1Tim. 3:7
14 [a]Acts 3:13; 5:30 [b]Acts 9:15; 26:16 [c]1Cor. 9:1; 15:8 [d]Acts 3:14; 7:52 [e]1Cor. 11:23; Gal. 1:12
15 [a]Acts 23:11 [b]Acts 4:20; 26:16
16 [a]Acts 2:38; Heb. 10:22 [b]Acts 9:14; Rom. 10:13
17 [a]Acts 9:26; 2Cor. 12:2
18 [a]Acts 22:14 [b]Matt. 10:14

19 And I said, Lord, [a]they know that I imprisoned[2252,5439] and [b]beat in every synagogue them that [ppt]believed[4100] on thee:

20 [a]And when the blood[129] of thy martyr[3144] Stephen [ipf]was shed, I also was standing by, and [b]consenting unto his death, and [ppt]kept the raiment of them that [ppt]slew him.

21 And he said unto me, Depart: [a]for I will send thee far hence unto the Gentiles.[1484]

Paul Before the Roman Court

22 And they [ipf]gave him audience[191] unto this word, and *then* lifted up their voices, and said, [a]Away with such a *fellow* from the earth: for it is not fit that [b]he should live.[2198]

23 And as they [ppt]cried out, and [ppt]cast off *their* clothes, and [ppt]threw dust into the air,

24 The chief captain commanded him to be brought into the castle,[3925] and bade that he should be examined by scourging;[3148] that he might know wherefore they [ipf]cried so against him.

25 And as they bound him with thongs, Paul said unto the centurion that stood by, [a]Is it lawful for you [pinf]to scourge[3147] a man that is a Roman, and uncondemned?

26 When the centurion heard *that,* he went and told the chief captain, saying, Take heed what thou doest: for this man is a Roman.

27 Then the chief captain came, and said unto him, Tell me, art thou a Roman? He said, Yea.

28 And the chief captain answered, With a great sum obtained I this freedom. And Paul said, But I was *free* born.

29 Then straightway[2112] they departed[868] from him which should have [I]examined him: and the chief captain also was afraid, after he knew that he was a Roman, and because he had bound him.

30 On the morrow, because he would have known the certainty wherefore he was accused of the Jews, he loosed him from *his* bands, and commanded the chief priests and all their council to appear, and [apt]brought Paul down,[2609] and set him before them.

Paul Speaks To the Sanhedrin

23 And Paul, earnestly beholding the council,[4892] said, Men[435] *and* brethren,[80] [a]I have lived in all good[18] conscience[4893] before God until this day.

2 And the high priest[749] Ananias commanded[2004] them that stood by him [a]to smite[5180] him on the mouth.

3 Then said Paul unto him, God shall smite thee, *thou* whited wall: for sittest thou to [ppt]judge[2919] me after the law,[3551] and [a]commandest me to be smitten contrary to the law?[3891]

4 And they that stood by said, Revilest[3058] thou God's high priest?

5 Then said Paul, [a]I wist not, brethren, that he was the high priest: for it is written, [b]Thou shalt not speak evil of the ruler of thy people.

6 But when Paul perceived that the one part were Sadducees, and the other Pharisees, he cried out in the council, Men *and* brethren, [a]I am a Pharisee, the son of a Pharisee: [b]of the hope[1680] and resurrection[386] of the dead I [pinp]am called in question.[2919]

7 And when he had so said, there arose a dissension[4714] between the Pharisees and the Sadducees: and the multitude was divided.

8 [a]For the Sadducees say that there is no resurrection, neither angel,[32] nor spirit:[4151] but the Pharisees confess[3670] both.

9 And there arose a great cry: and the scribes[1122] *that were* of the Pharisees' part [apt]arose, and [ipf]strove, saying, [a]We find no evil in this man: but [b]if a spirit or an angel hath spoken to him, [c]let us not fight against God.

10 And when there arose a great

19 [a]Acts 8:3; 22:4 [b]Matt. 10:17
20 [a]Acts 7:58 [b]Luke 11:48; Acts 8:1; Rom. 1:32
21 [a]Acts 9:15; 13:2, 46, 47; 18:6; 26:17; Rom. 1:5; 11:13; 15:16; Gal. 1:15, 16; 2:7, 8; Eph. 3:7, 8; 1Tim. 2:7; 2Tim. 1:11
22 [a]Acts 21:36 [b]Acts 25:24
25 [a]Acts 16:37
29 [I]Or, *tortured him*

1 [a]Acts 24:16; 1Cor. 4:4; 2Cor. 1:12; 4:2; 2Tim. 1:3; Heb. 13:18
2 [a]1Kgs. 22:24; Jer. 20:2; John 18:22
3 [a]Lev. 19:35; Deut. 25:1, 2; John 7:51
5 [a]Acts 24:17 [b]Ex. 22:28; Eccl. 10:20; 2Pet. 2:10; Jude 1:8
6 [a]Acts 26:5; Phil. 3:5 [b]Acts 24:15, 21; 26:6; 28:20
8 [a]Matt. 22:23; Mark 12:18; Luke 20:27
9 [a]Acts 25:25; 26:31 [b]Acts 22:7, 17, 18 [c]Acts 5:39

dissension,[4714] the chief captain, fearing[2125] lest Paul should have been pulled in pieces of them, commanded the soldiers to go down, and [ainf]to take him by force[726] from among them, and to bring *him* into the castle.

11 And [a]the night following the Lord[2962] stood by him, and said, Be of good cheer, Paul: for as thou hast testified[1263] of me in Jerusalem, so must thou bear witness[3140] also at Rome.

A Plot to Kill Paul

12 And when it was day, [a]certain of the Jews banded together, and [ao]bound themselves [I]under a curse,[332] saying that they would neither eat nor drink till they had killed Paul.

13 And they were more than forty which had made this conspiracy.

14 And they came to the chief priests and elders, and said, We have bound ourselves under a great curse, that we will eat[1089] nothing until we have slain Paul.

15 Now therefore ye with the council signify to the chief captain that he bring him down unto you to morrow, as though ye would enquire[1231] something more perfectly concerning him: and we, or ever he come near, are ready to kill him.

16 And when Paul's sister's son heard of their lying in wait, he went and entered into the castle, and told Paul.

17 Then Paul called one of the centurions unto *him,* and said, Bring this young man unto the chief captain: for he hath a certain thing to tell him.

18 So he took him, and brought *him* to the chief captain, and said, Paul the prisoner [apt]called me unto *him,* and prayed me to bring this young man unto thee, who hath something to say unto thee.

19 Then the chief captain took him by the hand, and went *with him* aside privately, and asked *him,* What is that thou hast to tell me?

20 And he said, [a]The Jews have agreed to desire thee that thou wouldest bring down Paul to morrow into the council, as though they would enquire somewhat of him more perfectly.

21 But [aosi]do not thou yield[3982] unto them: for there lie in wait for him of them more than forty men, which have bound themselves with an oath,[332] that they will neither eat nor drink till they have killed him: and now are they ready, looking for[4327] a promise[1860] from thee.

22 So the chief captain *then* let the young man depart, and charged *him, See thou* tell no man that thou hast shewed these things to me.

23 And he called unto *him* two centurions, saying, Make ready two hundred soldiers to go to Caesarea, and horsemen threescore and ten, and spearmen two hundred, at the third hour of the night;

24 And provide *them* beasts, that they may set Paul on, and [aosb]bring *him* safe[1295] unto Felix the governor.

25 And he [apt]wrote[1125] a letter after this manner:[5179]

26 Claudius Lysias unto the most excellent governor Felix *sendeth* greeting.[5463]

27 [a]This man [aptp]was taken of the Jews, and should have been killed of them: then came I with an army, and rescued him, [apt]having understood[3129] that he was a Roman.

28 [a]And when I would have known the cause wherefore they [ipf]accused[1458] him, I [ao]brought him forth[2609] into their council:

29 Whom I perceived to [ppp]be accused [a]of questions of their law,[3551] [b]but to have nothing laid to his charge[1462] worthy of death or of bonds.

30 And [a]when it was told me how that the Jews laid wait for the man, I sent straightway[1824] to thee, and [b]gave commandment to his accusers[2725] also to say before thee what *they had* against him. Farewell.

31 Then the soldiers, as it [pfpp]was commanded[1299] them, took Paul, and brought *him* by night to Antipatris.

32 On the morrow they left the

11 [a]Acts 18:9; 27:23, 24
12 [I]Or, *with an oath of execration* [a]Acts 22:21, 30; 25:3
20 [a]Acts 22:12
27 [a]Acts 21:33; 24:7
28 [a]Acts 22:30
29 [a]Acts 18:15; 25:19 [b]Acts 26:31
30 [a]Acts 24:20 [b]Acts 24:8; 25:6

horsemen to go with him, and returned to the castle:

33 Who, when they came to Caesarea, and delivered the epistle[1992] to the governor, presented Paul also before him.

34 And when the governor had read *the letter,* he asked of what province he was. And when he understood that *he was* of [a]Cilicia;

35 [a]I will hear thee, said he, when thine accusers are also come. And he commanded him to be kept in [b]Herod's judgment hall.

In Caesarea

24 And after [a]five days [b]Ananias the high priest[749] descended with the elders,[4245] and *with* a certain orator *named* Tertullus, who informed the governor against Paul.

2 And when he was called forth, Tertullus began to accuse *him,* saying, Seeing that by thee we enjoy great quietness,[1515] and that very worthy deeds are done unto this nation by thy providence,[4307]

3 We accept[588] *it* always, and in all places, most noble Felix, with all thankfulness.

4 Notwithstanding, that I be not further tedious unto thee, I pray[3870] thee that thou wouldest hear us of thy clemency[1932] a few words.

5 [a]For we [apt]have found this man *a* pestilent[3061] *fellow,* and a mover of sedition[4714] among all the Jews throughout the world, and a ringleader of the sect of the Nazarenes:

6 [a]Who also [ao]hath gone about[3985] to profane[953] the temple:[2411] whom we took, and would [b]have judged according to our law.

7 [a]But the chief captain Lysias came *upon us,* and with great violence took *him* away out of our hands,

8 [apt][a]Commanding his accusers[2725] to come unto thee: by examining of whom thyself mayest[1410] take knowledge of all these things, whereof we accuse him.

9 And the Jews also assented, saying that these things were so.

10 Then Paul, after that the governor had beckoned unto him to speak, answered, Forasmuch as I know that thou hast been of many years a judge unto this nation, I do the more cheerfully answer for myself:

11 Because that thou mayest understand, that there are yet but twelve days since I went up to Jerusalem [a]for to worship.

12 [a]And they neither found me in the temple disputing with any man, neither raising up the people, neither in the synagogues,[4864] nor in the city:

13 Neither can they prove the things whereof they now accuse me.

14 But this I confess[3670] unto thee, that after [a]the way[3598] which they call heresy,[139] so worship[3000] I the [b]God[2316] of my fathers, believing[4100] all things which are written in [c]the law[3551] and in the prophets:[4396]

15 And [a]have hope[1680] toward God, which they themselves also allow,[4327] [b]that there shall be a resurrection[386] of the dead,[3498] both of the just[1342] and unjust.[94]

16 And [a]herein do I exercise myself, to have always a conscience[4893] void of offence[677] toward[4314] God, and *toward* men.[444]

17 Now after many years [a]I came to bring alms to my nation, and offerings.[4376]

18 [a]Whereupon certain Jews from Asia found me purified[48] in the temple,[2411] neither with multitude, nor with tumult.

19 [a]Who ought to have been here before thee, and object, if they had ought against me.

20 Or else let these same *here* say, if they have found any evil doing[92] in me, while I stood before the council,

21 Except it be for this one voice, that I cried standing among them, [a]Touching the resurrection of the dead I [pinp]am called in question[2919] by you this day.

22 And when Felix heard these

34 [a]Acts 21:39
35 [a]Acts 24:1, 10; 25:16 [b]Matt. 27:27

1 [a]Acts 21:27 [b]Acts 23:2, 30, 35; 25:2
5 [a]Luke 23:2; Acts 6:13; 16:20; 17:6; 21:28; 1Pet. 2:12, 15
6 [a]Acts 21:28 [b]John 18:31
7 [a]Acts 21:33
8 [a]Acts 23:30
11 [a]Acts 21:26; 24:17
12 [a]Acts 25:8; 28:17
14 [a]Amos 8:14; Acts 9:2 [b]2Tim. 1:3 [c]Acts 26:22; 28:23
15 [a]Acts 23:6; 26:6, 7; 28:20 [b]Dan. 12:2; John 5:28, 29
16 [a]Acts 23:1
17 [a]Acts 11:29, 30; 20:16; Rom. 15:25; 2Cor. 8:4; Gal. 2:10
18 [a]Acts 21:26, 27; 26:21
19 [a]Acts 23:30; 25:16
21 [a]Acts 23:6; 28:20

things, having more perfect knowledge of *that* way,[3598] he deferred them, and said, When [a]Lysias the chief captain shall come down, I [fm]will know the uttermost[1231] of your matter.

23 And he [apt]commanded[1299] a centurion [pinf]to keep[5083] Paul, and to let *him* have liberty,[425] and [a]that he should forbid none of his acquaintance to minister or come unto him.

Felix and Drusilla

24 And after certain days, when Felix came with his wife Drusilla, which was a Jewess, he sent for Paul, and heard him concerning the faith[4102] in Christ.[5547]

25 And as he reasoned of righteousness,[1343] temperance,[1466] and judgment[2917] to come, Felix trembled, and answered, Go thy way for this time; when I have a convenient season,[2540] I [fm]will call[3333] for thee.

26 He hoped also that [a]money[5536] should have been given him of Paul, that he might loose him: wherefore he sent for him the oftener, and communed with him.

27 But after two years Porcius Festus came into Felix' room: and Felix, [a]willing to shew the Jews a pleasure, left Paul bound.

Paul Appears Before Festus

25 Now when Festus was come into the province, after three days he ascended from Caesarea to Jerusalem.

2 [a]Then the high priest and the chief of the Jews informed him against Paul, and [ipf]besought[3870] him,

3 And [ppt]desired favour[5485] against him, that he would send for him to Jerusalem, [a]laying wait in the way to kill him.

4 But Festus answered, that Paul [pinf]should be kept[5083] at Caesarea, and that he himself would depart shortly *thither.*

5 Let them therefore, said he, which among you are able, go down with *me,* and accuse this man, [a]if there be any wickedness in him.

6 And when he had tarried among them more than ten days, he went down unto Caesarea; and the next day sitting on the judgment seat commanded Paul to be brought.

7 And when he was come, the Jews which came down from Jerusalem stood round about, [a]and laid[5342] many and grievous complaints[157] against Paul, which they could not prove.

8 While he answered for himself, [a]Neither against the law[3551] of the Jews, neither against the temple,[2411] nor yet against Caesar, have I offended any thing at all.

9 But Festus, [a]willing to do the Jews a pleasure,[5485] answered Paul, and said, [b]Wilt thou go up to Jerusalem, and there [pinf]be judged[2919] of these things before me?

10 Then said Paul, I stand at Caesar's judgment seat, where I ought to be judged: to the Jews [ao]have I done no wrong,[91] as thou very well knowest.

11 [a]For if I [pin]be an offender,[91] or have committed any thing worthy of death, I refuse[3868] not to die: but if there be none of these things whereof these accuse me, no man may deliver[5483] me unto them. [b]I appeal unto Caesar.

12 Then Festus, when he had conferred with the council, answered, Hast thou appealed unto Caesar? unto Caesar shalt thou go.

Agrippa and Bernice

13 And after certain days king Agrippa and Bernice came unto Caesarea to salute Festus.

14 And when they had been there many days, Festus declared Paul's cause unto the king, saying, [a]There is a certain man left in bonds by Felix:

15 [a]About whom, when I was at Jerusalem, the chief priests[749] and the elders[4245] of the Jews informed *me,* desiring *to have* judgment[1349] against him.

16 [a]To whom I answered, It is not

---

22 [a]Acts 24:7
23 [a]Acts 27:3; 28:16
26 [a]Ex. 23:8
27 [a]Ex. 23:2; Acts 12:3; 25:9, 14
2 [a]Acts 24:1; 25:15
3 [a]Acts 23:12, 15
5 [a]Acts 18:14; 25:18
7 [a]Mark 15:3; Luke 23:2, 10; Acts 24:5, 13
8 [a]Acts 6:13; 24:12; 28:17
9 [a]Acts 24:27 [b]Acts 25:20
11 [a]Acts 18:14; 23:29; 25:25; 26:31 [b]Acts 26:32; 28:19
14 [a]Acts 24:27
15 [a]Acts 25:2, 3
16 [a]Acts 25:4, 5

the manner of the Romans [pinf]to deliver[5483] any man to die,[684] before that he which is accused have the accusers[2725] face to face,[2596,4383] and have licence to answer for himself concerning the crime laid against[1462] him.

17 Therefore, when they were come hither, [a]without any delay on the morrow I sat on the judgment seat, and commanded the man to be brought forth.

18 Against whom when the accusers[2725] stood up, they brought none accusation of such things as I supposed:[5282]

19 [a]But had certain questions against him of their own superstition,[1175] and of one Jesus, which was dead, whom Paul affirmed [pinf]to be alive.[2198]

20 And because [I]I doubted of such manner of questions, I [ipf]asked *him* whether he would go to Jerusalem, and there be judged of these matters.

21 But when Paul had appealed [aifp]to be reserved[5083] unto the [I]hearing[1233] of Augustus,[4575] I commanded him [pinf]to be kept[5083] till I might send him to Caesar.

22 Then [a]Agrippa said unto Festus, I would also hear the man myself. To morrow, said he, thou shalt hear him.

23 And on the morrow, when Agrippa was come, and Bernice, with great pomp,[5325] and was entered into the place of hearing, with the chief captains, and principal men of the city, at Festus' commandment Paul was brought forth.

24 And Festus said, King Agrippa, and all men which are here present with us, ye see this man, about whom [a]all the multitude of the Jews have dealt with me, both at Jerusalem, and *also* here, crying that he ought [b]not to live any longer.

25 But when I found[2638] that [a]he had committed nothing worthy of death, [b]and that he himself [apt]hath appealed[1941] to Augustus,[4575] I [ao]have determined[2919] to send him.

26 Of whom I have no certain thing to write unto my lord. Wherefore I [ao]have brought him forth[4254] before you, and specially before thee, O king Agrippa, that, after examination had, I might have somewhat [ainf]to write.[1125]

27 For it seemeth to me unreasonable to send a prisoner, and not withal[2532] to signify the crimes *laid* against him.

Paul Defends Himself Before Agrippa

26 Then Agrippa said unto Paul, Thou art permitted to speak for thyself. Then Paul stretched forth the hand, and answered for himself:

2 I think[2233] myself happy,[3107] king[935] Agrippa, because I shall answer for myself this day before thee touching[4012] all the things whereof I [pinp]am accused[1458] of the Jews:

3 Especially *because I know* thee to be expert[1109] in all customs and questions which are among the Jews: wherefore I beseech[1189] thee to hear me patiently.

4 My manner of life from my youth,[3503] which was at the first among mine own nation[1484] at Jerusalem, know all the Jews;

5 Which knew[4267] me from the beginning,[509] if they would[2309] testify, that after [a]the most straitest[196] sect[139] of our religion[2356] I [ao]lived a Pharisee.

6 [a]And now I stand and [ppt]am judged[2919] for the hope of [b]the promise[1860] made of God[2316] unto our fathers:

7 Unto which *promise* [a]our twelve tribes, instantly serving *God* [I][b]day and night, [c]hope to come. For which hope's sake, king Agrippa, I am accused of the Jews.

8 Why [pinp]should it be thought[2919] a thing incredible[571] with you, that God [pin]should raise[1453] the dead?[3498]

9 [a]I verily[3303] thought with myself, that I ought [ainf]to do many things contrary to the name[3686] of Jesus of Nazareth.

10 [a]Which thing I also did in Jerusalem: and many of the saints[40] did I shut up in prison, having received au-

---

17 [a]Acts 25:6
19 [a]Acts 18:15; 23:29
20 [I]Or, *I was doubtful how to inquire hereof*
21 [I]Or, *judgment*
22 [a]Acts 9:15
24 [a]Acts 25:2, 3, 7 [b]Acts 22:22
25 [a]Acts 23:9, 29; 26:31 [b]Acts 25:11, 12
5 [a]Acts 22:3; 23:6; 24:15, 21; Phil. 3:5
6 [a]Acts 23:6 [b]Gen. 3:15; 22:18; 26:4; 49:10; Deut. 18:15; 2Sam. 7:12; Ps. 132:11; Isa. 4:2; 7:14; 9:6; 40:10; Jer. 23:5; 33:14-16; Ezek. 34:23; 37:24; Dan. 9:24; Mic. 7:20; Acts 13:32; Rom. 15:8; Titus 2:13
7 [I]Gr. *night and day* [a]James 1:1 [b]Luke 2:37; 1Thess. 3:10; 1Tim. 5:5 [c]Phil. 3:11
9 [a]John 16:2; 1Tim. 1:13
10 [a]Acts 8:3; Gal. 1:13

thority [b]from the chief priests; and when they were put to death, I gave my voice against *them.*

11 [a]And I punished[5097] them oft in every synagogue, and [ipf]compelled[315] *them* to blaspheme;[987] and being exceedingly[4057] mad against them, I persecuted *them* even unto strange cities.

Paul Preaches To King Agrippa

12 [a]Whereupon as I [ppt]went to Damascus with authority[1849] and commission from the chief priests,

13 At midday, O king, I saw in the way a light from heaven, above the brightness of the sun, [apt]shining round about me and them which [ppt]journeyed with me.

14 And when we were all fallen to the earth, I heard a voice speaking unto me, and saying in the Hebrew tongue, Saul, Saul, why persecutest thou me? *it is* hard for thee to kick against the pricks.

15 And I said, Who art thou, Lord?[2962] And he said, I am Jesus whom thou persecutest.

16 But rise, and stand upon thy feet: for I [aop]have appeared unto thee for this purpose, [a]to make thee a minister[5257] and a witness[3144] both of these things which thou hast seen, and of those things in the which I will appear unto thee;

17 Delivering thee from the people, and *from* the Gentiles,[1484] [a]unto whom now I send thee,

18 [a]To open their eyes, *and* [infg][b]to turn[1994] *them* from darkness[4655] to light,[5457] and *from* the power[1849] of Satan[4567] unto God,[2316] [c]that they may receive[2983] forgiveness[859] of sins,[266] and [d]inheritance[2819] among them which [pfpp]are [e]sanctified[37] by faith[4102] that is in me.

19 Whereupon, O king Agrippa, I was not disobedient[545] unto the heavenly[3770] vision:[3701]

20 But [ipfa]shewed first unto them of Damascus, and at Jerusalem, and throughout all the coasts of Judaea, and *then* to the Gentiles, that they [pinf]should repent[3340] and [pinf]turn[1994] to God, and [ppt]do [b]works meet[514] for repentance.[3341]

21 For these causes [a]the Jews [apt]caught me in the temple,[2411] and [ipf]went about[3987] to kill *me.*

22 [apt]Having therefore obtained[5177] help of God, I continue unto this day, witnessing[3140] both to small and great, saying none other things than those [a]which the prophets[4396] and [b]Moses did say should come:

23 [a]That Christ[5547] should suffer,[3805] *and* [b]that he should be the first that should rise from the dead,[3498] and [c]should [pinf]shew[2605] light[5457] unto the people,[2992] and to the Gentiles.[1484]

24 And as he thus spake for himself, Festus said with a loud voice, Paul, [a]thou art beside thyself; much learning[1121] doth make thee mad.[3130]

25 But he said, I am not mad, most noble Festus; but speak forth the words[4487] of truth[225] and soberness.[4997]

26 For the king[935] knoweth of these things, before whom also I speak freely: for I am persuaded that none of these things are hidden from him; for this thing was not done in a corner.

27 King Agrippa, believest[4100] thou the prophets?[4396] I know that thou believest.

28 Then Agrippa said unto Paul, Almost thou persuadest me [ainf]to be[1096] a Christian.[5546]

29 And Paul said, [a]I would to God, that not only thou, but also all that hear me this day, were both almost, and altogether such as I am, except these bonds.

30 And when he had thus spoken, the king rose up, and the governor, and Bernice, and they that sat with them:

31 And when they were gone aside, they [ipf]talked between themselves, saying, [a]This man doeth nothing worthy of death or of bonds.

32 Then said Agrippa unto Festus, This man might have been set at liberty,

10 [b]Acts 9:14, 21; 22:5
11 [a]Acts 22:19
12 [a]Acts 9:3; 22:6
16 [a]Acts 22:15
17 [a]Acts 22:21
18 [a]Isa. 35:5; 42:7; Luke 1:79; John 8:12; 2Cor. 4:4; Eph. 1:18; 1Thess. 5:5 [b]2Cor. 6:14; Eph. 4:18; 5:8; Col. 1:13; 1Pet. 2:9, 25 [c]Luke 1:77 [d]Eph. 1:11; Col. 1:12 [e]Acts 20:32
20 [a]Acts 9:20, 22, 29; 11:26; 13, 14, 16-21 [b]Matt. 3:8
21 [a]Acts 21:30, 31
22 [a]Luke 24:27, 44; Acts 24:14; 28:23; Rom. 3:21 [b]John 5:46
23 [a]Luke 24:26, 46 [b]1Cor. 15:20; Col. 1:18; Rev. 1:5 [c]Luke 2:32
24 [a]2Kgs. 9:11; John 10:20; 1Cor. 1:23; 2:13, 14; 4:10
29 [a]1Cor. 7:7
31 [a]Acts 23:9, 29; 25:25

[a]if he [plpf]had not appealed unto[1941] Caesar.

The Prisoners Sail for Italy

27 And when [a]it [aop]was determined[2919] that we should sail into Italy, they delivered Paul and certain other prisoners unto *one* named Julius a centurion of Augustus'[4575] band.

🔑 2 And entering into[1910] a ship of Adramyttium, we launched, meaning to sail by the coasts of Asia; *one* [a]Aristarchus, a Macedonian of Thessalonica, being with us.

3 And the next *day* we touched[2609] at Sidon. And Julius [a]courteously[5364] entreated[5530] Paul, and gave *him* liberty to go unto his friends [ainf]to refresh himself.

🔑 4 And when we had launched from thence, we sailed under Cyprus, because the winds were contrary.

5 And when we had sailed over the sea[3989] of Cilicia and Pamphylia, we came to Myra, *a city* of Lycia.

6 And there the centurion found a ship of Alexandria sailing into Italy; and he put us therein.

7 And when we had sailed slowly many days, and scarce were come over against Cnidus, the wind not suffering us, we sailed under Crete, over against Salmone;

8 And, hardly passing it, came unto a place which is called The fair havens; nigh whereunto was the city *of* Lasea.

9 Now when much time[5550] was spent, and when sailing was now dangerous, [a]because the fast[3521] was now already past, Paul admonished *them,*

10 And said unto them, Sirs,[435] I perceive that this voyage will be with [1]hurt[5196] and much damage, not only of the lading[5414] and ship, but also of our lives.[5590]

11 Nevertheless the centurion [ipf]believed[3982] the master[2942] and the owner of the ship, more than those things which were spoken by Paul.

12 And because the haven was not commodious to winter in, the more part advised[5087,1012] to depart thence also, if by any means they might attain to Phenice, *and there* to winter; *which is* an haven of Crete, and lieth toward the southwest and northwest.

The Storm

13 And when the south wind blew softly, supposing[1380] that they had obtained *their* purpose,[4286] loosing[142] *thence,* they [ipf]sailed close by Crete.

🔑 14 But not long after there [1]arose[906] against[2596] it a tempestuous wind, called Euroclydon.

15 And when the ship was caught, and could not bear up into the wind, we let *her* drive.

16 And running under a certain island which is called Clauda, we had much work to come by the boat:

17 Which when they had taken up, they used[5530] helps, undergirding the ship; and, fearing lest they should fall into the quicksands, strake sail, and so [ipf]were driven.[5342]

18 And we being exceedingly tossed with a tempest, the next *day* they [ipf]lightened the ship;

19 And the third *day* [a]we cast out with our own hands the tackling[4631] of the ship.

20 And when neither sun nor stars in many days appeared,[2014] and no small tempest lay on *us,* all hope[1680] that we

32 [a]Acts 25:11
1 [a]Acts 25:12, 25
2 [a]Acts 19:29
3 [a]Acts 24:23; 28:16
9 [a]Lev. 23:27, 29
10 [1]Or, *injury*
14 [1]Or, *beat*
19 [a]Jon. 1:5

🔑 **27:2** See note on Colossians 4:10.

🔑 **27:4** The phrase, "the winds were contrary," refers to the unfavorable weather conditions that existed on the Mediterranean Sea during that time of year. The sailors brought the ship close to Cyprus in hopes that they might catch a good westerly headwind. This would have enabled them to get the ship into a harbor along the coast of Asia Minor before winter came.

🔑 **27:14** The word "Euroclydon" is a half-Greek, half-Latin term that sailors used to describe the strong northeasterly wind that blew the ship off course.

[infg]should be saved[4982] was then taken away.

21 But after long abstinence Paul stood forth in the midst of them, and said, Sirs,[435] ye should have hearkened unto me, and not have loosed from Crete, and to have gained this harm[5196] and loss.

22 And now I exhort you to be of good cheer: for there shall be no loss of *any man's* life among you, but of the ship.

23 [a]For there stood by me this night the [an]angel of God, whose I am, and [b]whom I serve,

24 Saying, Fear[5399] not, Paul; thou must be brought before Caesar: and, lo, God [pfip]hath given[5483] thee all them that sail with thee.

25 Wherefore, sirs, be of good cheer: [a]for I believe[4100] God, that it shall be even as it was told me.

26 Howbeit[1161] [a]we must be cast upon a certain island.

27 But when the fourteenth night was come, as we were driven up and down[1308] in Adria, about midnight the shipmen [ipf]deemed[5282] that they [pinf]drew near[4317] to some country;

28 And sounded, and found *it* twenty fathoms: and when they had gone a little further, they sounded again, and found *it* fifteen fathoms.[3712]

29 Then fearing lest we should have fallen upon rocks, they cast four anchors out of the stern, and wished for the day.[2250]

30 And as the shipmen were about to flee out of the ship, when they had let down the boat into the sea, under colour as though they would have cast anchors out[1614] of the foreship,

31 Paul said to the centurion and to the soldiers, Except these [aosb]abide in the ship, ye cannot be saved.

32 Then the soldiers cut off the ropes of the boat, and let her fall off.

33 And while the day[2250] was coming on, Paul [ipf]besought[3870] *them* all to take[3335] meat, saying, This day is the fourteenth day[2250] that ye have tarried and continued fasting,[777] having taken[4355] nothing.

34 Wherefore I pray[3870] you [ainf]to take[4355] *some* meat: for this is[5225] for[4314] your health:[4991] for [a]there shall not an hair fall from the head of any of you.

35 And when he had thus spoken, he [apt]took[2983] bread, and [a]gave thanks[2168] to God in presence of them all: and when he had broken *it,* he began to eat.

36 Then were they all of good cheer, and they also took[4355] *some* meat.

37 And we were in all in the ship two hundred threescore and sixteen [a]souls.[5590]

38 And when they [aptp]had eaten enough,[2880] [5160] they lightened the ship, and [ppt]cast out the wheat into the sea.

The Shipwreck

39 And when it was day,[2250] they [ipf]knew not the land: but they [ipf]discovered[2657] a certain creek with a shore, into the which they [aom]were minded, if it were possible, to thrust in the ship.

40 And when they had [I]taken up the anchors, they committed *themselves* unto the sea, and loosed the rudder bands, and hoised up[1869] the mainsail to the wind,[4154] and made[2722] toward shore.

41 And falling into a place where two seas met, [a]they ran the ship aground; and the forepart stuck fast, and remained unmoveable, but the hinder part [ipf]was broken[3089] with the violence of the waves.

42 And the soldiers' counsel[1012] was to kill the prisoners, lest any of them should swim out, and escape.

43 But the centurion, willing [ainf]to save[1295] Paul, kept them from *their* purpose; and commanded that they which could swim should cast *themselves* first *into the sea,* and get to land:

44 And the rest, some on boards, and some on *broken pieces* of the ship. And so it came to pass, [a]that they escaped all safe[1295] to land.

23 [a]Acts 23:11 [b]Dan. 6:16; Rom. 1:9; 2Tim. 1:3
25 [a]Luke 1:45; Rom. 4:20, 21; 2Tim. 1:12
26 [a]Acts 28:1
34 [a]1Kgs. 1:52; Matt. 10:30; Luke 12:7; 21:18
35 [a]1Sam. 9:13; Matt. 15:36; Mark 8:6; John 6:11; 1Tim. 4:3, 4
37 [a]Acts 2:41; 7:14; Rom. 13:1; 1Pet. 3:20
40 [I]Or, *cut the anchors, they left them in the sea*
41 [a]2Cor. 11:25
44 [a]Acts 27:22

On Malta

28 And when they [aptp]were escaped,[1295] then they knew that
[a]the island was called Melita.
2 And the [a]barbarous people[915]
shewed us no little[5177] kindness:[5363] for
they kindled a fire, and received us every
one, because of the present rain, and because of the cold.
3 And when Paul had gathered a
bundle of sticks, and laid *them* on the
fire, there came a viper out of the heat,
and fastened on his hand.
4 And when the barbarians[915] saw
the *venomous* beast[2342] hang on his hand,
they [ipf]said among themselves, No doubt
this man is a murderer, whom, though
he [aptp]hath escaped[1295] the sea, yet
vengeance[1349] suffereth not to live.
🔑 5 And he shook off the beast[2342] into
the fire, and [a]felt[3958] no harm.
6 Howbeit[1161] they [ipf]looked when he
should have swollen, or fallen down dead
suddenly: but after they [ppt]had looked a
great while, and [ppt]saw no harm [ppt]come
to him, they changed their minds, and
[a]said that he was a god.[2316]
7 In the same quarters were[5225] possessions of the chief man of the island,
whose name was Publius; who re-
ceived[324] us, and lodged us three days[2250]
courteously.
🔑 8 And it came to pass, that the father
of Publius lay sick[4912] of a fever and of
a bloody flux:[1420] to whom Paul entered
in, and [a]prayed, and [b]laid his hands on
him, and healed him.
9 So when this was done, others also,
which had diseases in the island, [ipf]came,
and [ipf]were healed:
10 Who also honoured us with many
[a]honours; and when we departed, they
laded *us* with such things as were necessary.
🔑 11 And after three months we departed in a ship of Alexandria, which
had wintered in the isle, whose sign was
Castor and Pollux.
12 And landing at Syracuse, we tarried *there* three days.[2250]
13 And from thence we fetched a
compass, and came to Rhegium: and after
one day the south wind blew, and we
came the next day to Puteoli:
14 Where we found brethren, and
[aop]were desired[3870] to tarry with them
seven days: and so we went[2064] toward
Rome.
15 And from thence, when the
brethren heard of us, they came to meet
us as far as Appii forum, and the three
taverns: whom when Paul saw, he
thanked[2168] God,[2316] and took courage.

Arrival in Rome

16 And when we came to Rome, the
centurion delivered the prisoners to the
captain of the guard: but [a]Paul was suffered to dwell by himself with a soldier
that [ppt]kept him.
17 And it came to pass, that after
three days Paul [ainf]called the chief of the
Jews together:[4779] and when they were
come together, he said unto them, Men
and brethren, [a]though I have committed
nothing against the people, or customs of
our fathers, yet [b]was I delivered prisoner
from Jerusalem into the hands of the
Romans.
18 Who, [a]when they had examined
me, would have let *me* go, because there
was no cause of death in me.
19 But when the Jews spake against
it, [a]I [aop]was constrained[315] [ainf]to appeal
unto[1941] Caesar; not that I had ought to
accuse my nation of.
20 For this cause therefore [ao]have I
called[3870] for you, to see *you,* and to speak
with *you*: because that [a]for the hope[1680] of
Israel I am bound with [b]this chain.
21 And they said[2036] unto him, We

1 [a]Acts 27:26
2 [a]Rom. 1:14; 1Cor. 14:11; Col. 3:11
5 [a]Mark 16:18; Luke 10:19
6 [a]Acts 14:11
8 [a]James 5:14, 15 [b]Mark 6:5; 7:32; 16:18; Luke 4:40; Acts 19:11, 12; 1Cor. 12:9, 28
10 [a]Matt. 15:6; 1Tim. 5:17
16 [a]Acts 24:25; 27:3
17 [a]Acts 24:12, 13; 25:8 [b]Acts 21:33
18 [a]Acts 22:24; 24:10; 25:8; 26:31
19 [a]Acts 25:11
20 [a]Acts 26:6, 7 [b]Acts 26:29; Eph. 3:1; 4:1; 6:20; 2Tim. 1:16; 2:9; Phile. 1:10, 13

🔑 **28:5, 8** See note on 2 Timothy 4:20.
🔑 **28:11** "Castor and Pollux" were twin brothers, the sons of the mythological god, Zeus. The "sign" mentioned in this verse was a figurehead of these two brothers on the front of the ship, which was believed to provide safety for those who traveled at sea.

neither received letters[1121] out of Judaea concerning thee, neither any of the brethren[80] that came shewed or spake any harm[4190] of thee.

22 But we desire to hear of thee what thou thinkest:[5426] for as concerning this sect,[139] we know that every where [a]it is spoken against.

23 And when they [apt]had appointed[5021] him a day, there came many to him into *his* lodging; [a]to whom he expounded and testified[1263] the kingdom[932] of God, persuading[3982] them concerning Jesus, [b]both out of the law[3551] of Moses, and *out of* the prophets, from morning till evening.

24 And [a]some [ipf]believed[3982] the things which were spoken, and some [ipf]believed not.[569]

25 And when they agreed not among themselves, they [ipf]departed,[630] after that Paul had spoken one word,[4487] Well spake the Holy Ghost[4151] by Esaias the prophet unto our fathers,

26 Saying, [a]Go unto this people, and say, Hearing[189] ye shall hear, and shall not understand; and seeing ye shall see, and not perceive:

27 For the heart[2588] of this people[2992] [aop]is waxed gross,[3975] and their ears are dull of hearing, and their eyes have they closed; lest they should see with *their* eyes, and hear with *their* ears, and understand[4920] with *their* heart, and [asba]should be converted,[1994] and I should heal them.

28 Be it known therefore unto you, that the salvation[4992] of God is sent [a]unto the Gentiles,[1484] and *that* they will hear it.

29 And when he had said these words, the Jews departed, and had great reasoning among themselves.

30 And Paul dwelt two whole years in his own hired house, and received[588] all that came in unto him,

31 [a]Preaching[2784] the kingdom of God, and teaching[1321] those things which concern the Lord Jesus Christ, with all confidence, no man forbidding him.

22 [a]Luke 2:34; Acts 24:5, 14; 1Pet. 2:12; 4:14

23 [a]Luke 24:27; Acts 17:3; 19:8 [b]Acts 26:6, 22

24 [a]Acts 14:4; 17:4; 19:9

26 [a]Isa. 6:9; Jer. 5:21; Ezek. 12:2; Matt. 13:14, 15; Mark 4:12; Luke 8:10; John 12:40; Rom. 11:8

28 [a]Matt. 21:41, 43; Acts 13:46, 47; 18:6; 22:21; 26:17, 18; Rom. 11:11

31 [a]Acts 4:31; Eph. 6:19

The Epistle of Paul to the

ROMANS

The Book of Romans was written by the Apostle Paul from the city of Corinth shortly after he wrote 2 Corinthians. Since it is known that the date of his arrival in Jerusalem on his third missionary journey was A.D. 58 or 59, and that he was preparing to leave for Jerusalem (Rom. 15:25, cf. Acts 20:16), Romans is believed to have been written in the spring of A.D. 56.

Although it is commonly believed that Peter founded the church at Rome, there is very little evidence for this. In fact, the evidence does not even give us enough information to suggest who was responsible for leading the believers in Rome. It is true, however, that the dispersion of the Jews led to a multitude of synagogues being established in the midst of Gentile populations throughout the Roman Empire. The apostles and many other converts to Christianity had ready access to these synagogues. During that period, the polytheistic religion of the Roman Empire was becoming increasingly unpopular, and there is a great deal of evidence that many became proselytes to Judiasm or began to worship the one true God. These were the most receptive to the message of the gospel since they did not have the hostile predisposition of the Jews, yet were also convinced that polytheism was false.

Paul was writing to a predominantly gentile audience (Rom. 1:13). His main concerns in writing the Book of Romans were to educate the believers in the basic doctrines related to salvation (chaps. 1—8) and to help them understand the unbelief of the Jews and how they benefited from it (chaps. 9—11). He also explained general principles of the Christian life that he wanted them to comprehend and put into practice (Rom. 12:1—15:13).

Introduction

1 Paul, a servant[1401] of Jesus
Christ,[5547] [a]called[2822] *to be* an apostle,[652] [b]separated[873] unto the gospel[2098]
of God,
2 ([a]Which he [aom]had promised
afore[4279] [b]by his prophets[4396] in the holy
scriptures,[1124])
3 Concerning his Son[5207] Jesus Christ
our Lord,[2962] [a]which was [b]made of the
seed[4690] of David according to[2596] the
flesh;[4561]
4 And [I][a]declared *to be* the [an]Son of
God[2316] with power, according [b]to the
spirit[4151] of holiness,[42] by the resurrection[386] from the dead:[3498]
5 By whom [a]we [ao]have received
grace[5485] and apostleship,[651] [I]for [b]obe-
dience[5218] to the faith[4102] among all nations, [c]for his name:[3686]
6 Among whom are ye also the
called[2822] of Jesus Christ:

1 [a]Acts 22:21; 1Cor. 1:1; Gal. 1:1; 1Tim. 1:11; 2:7; 2Tim. 1:11 [b]Acts 9:15; 13:2; Gal. 1:15
2 [a]Acts 26:6; Titus 1:2 [b]Rom. 3:21; 16:26; Gal. 3:8
3 [a]Matt. 1:6, 16; Luke 1:32; Acts 2:30; 2Tim. 2:8 [b]John 1:14; Gal. 4:4
4 [I]Gr. *determined* [a]Acts 13:33 [b]Heb. 9:14
5 [I]Or, *to the obedience of faith* [a]Rom. 12:3; 15:15; 1Cor. 15:10; Gal. 1:15; 2:9; Eph. 3:8 [b]Acts 6:7; Rom. 16:26 [c]Acts 9:15
7 [a]Rom. 9:24; 1Cor. 1:2; 1Thess. 4:7 [b]1Cor. 1:3; 2Cor. 1:2; Gal. 1:3

7 To all that be in Rome, beloved of
God, [a]called *to be* saints:[40] [b]Grace to you
and peace[1515] from God our Father,[3962]
and the Lord Jesus Christ.

The Gentiles' Need of Righteousness

8 First, [a]I thank[2168] my God through
Jesus Christ for you all, that [b]your faith
[pinp]is spoken of[2605] throughout the whole
world.[2889]
9 For [a]God is my witness,[3144] [b]whom
I serve [I]with my spirit[4151] in the gospel
of his Son, that [c]without ceasing I make
mention of you always in my prayers;
⊶ 10 [a]Making request, if by any means
now at length I might have a prosperous

8 [a]1Cor. 1:4; Phil. 1:3; Col. 1:3, 4; 1Thess. 1:2; Phile. 1:4; Rom. 16:19; 1Thess. 1:8 **9** [I]Or, *in my spirit,* John 4:23, 24; Phil. 3:3 [a]Rom. 9:1; 2Cor. 1:23; Phil. 1:8; 1Thess. 2:5 [b]Acts 27:23; 2Tim. 1:3 [c]1Thess. 3:10
10 [a]Rom. 15:23, 32; 1Thess. 3:10

⊶ **1:10** See note on 3 John 1:2.

journey [b]by the will of God to come unto you.

11 For I long to see you, that [a]I may impart unto you some spiritual gift,[5486] to the end ye may be established;

12 That is, that I [aifp]may be comforted together4837 [I]with you by [a]the mutual faith both of you and me.

13 Now I would not have you ignorant, brethren,[80] that [a]oftentimes I purposed[4388] to come unto you, (but [b]was let hitherto,) that I might have some [c]fruit [I]among you also, even as among other Gentiles.[1484]

14 [a]I am debtor[3781] both to the Greeks, and to the Barbarians;915 both to the wise,[4680] and to the unwise.[453]

15 So, as much as in me is, I am ready [ainf]to preach the gospel[2097] to you that are at Rome also.

16 For [a]I am not ashamed of the gospel[2098] of Christ: for [b]it is the power[1411] of God unto salvation[4991] to every one that [ppt]believeth;[4100] [c]to the Jew first, and also to the Greek.

17 For [a]therein is the righteousness[1343] of God [pinp]revealed[601] from faith[4102] to faith: as it is written, [b]The [sg]just[1342] [fm]shall live[2198] by faith.

Sin Will Be Punished

18 [a]For the wrath[3709] of God[2316] is [pinp]revealed from heaven[3772] against all ungodliness[763] and unrighteousness[93] of men,[444] who [ppt]hold[2722] the truth[225] in unrighteousness;[93]

19 Because [a]that which may be known[1110] of God is manifest[5318] [I]in them; for [b]God [ao]hath shewed[5319] *it* unto them.

20 For [a]the invisible things of him from the creation[2937] of the world[2889] are clearly seen, being understood[3539] by the things that are made, *even* his eternal[126] power and Godhead;[2305] [I]so that they are without excuse:

21 Because that, when they knew God, they glorified[1392] *him* not as God, neither [ao]were thankful;[2168] but [a]became vain[3154] in their imaginations, and their foolish heart[2588] was darkened.

22 [a]Professing themselves to be wise,[4680] they became fools,3471

23 And changed[236] the glory[1391] of the uncorruptible[862] [a]God into an image[1504] made like to[3667] corruptible man, and to birds, and fourfooted beasts, and creeping things.

24 [a]Wherefore God also gave them up to uncleanness[167] through the lusts of their own hearts, [b]to dishonour their own bodies [c]between themselves:

25 Who changed[3337] [a]the truth[225] of God[2316] [b]into a lie, and worshipped[4573] and served[3000] the creature[2937] [I]more than the Creator,[2936] who is blessed[2128] for ever. Amen.281

26 For this cause God gave them up unto [a]vile[819] affections:[3806] for even their women[2338] did change[3337] the natu-

10 [b]James 4:15
11 [a]Rom. 15:29
12 [I]Or, *in you* [a]Titus 1:4; 2Pet. 1:1
13 [I]Or, *in you* [a]Rom. 15:23 [b]Acts 16:7; 1Thess. 2:18 [c]Phil. 4:17
14 [a]1Cor. 9:16
16 [a]Ps. 40:9, 10; Mark 8:38; 2Tim. 1:8 [b]1Cor. 1:18; 15:2 [c]Luke 2:30, 31, 32; 24:47; Acts 3:26; 13:26, 46; Rom. 2:9
17 [a]Rom. 3:21 [b]Hab. 2:4; John 3:36; Gal. 3:11; Phil. 3:9; Heb. 10:38
18 [a]Acts 17:30; Eph. 5:6; Col. 3:6
19 [I]Or, *to them* [a]Acts 14:17 [b]John 1:9
20 [I]Or, *that they may be* [a]Ps. 19:14; Acts 14:17; 17:27
21 [a]2Kgs. 17:15; Jer. 2:5; Eph. 4:17, 18
22 [a]Jer. 10:14
23 [a]Deut. 4:16; Ps. 106:20; Isa. 40:18, 25; Jer. 2:11; Ezek. 8:10; Acts 17:29
24 [a]Ps. 81:12; Acts 7:42; Eph. 4:18, 19; 2Thess. 2:11, 12 [b]1Cor. 6:18; 1Thess. 4:4; 1Pet. 4:3 [c]Lev. 18:22
25 [I]Or, *rather* [a]1Thess. 1:9; 1John 5:20 [b]Isa. 44:20; Jer. 10:14; 13:25; Amos 2:4
26 [a]Lev. 18:22, 23; Eph. 5:12; Jude 1:10

1:17 The expression "from faith to faith" is merely an intensive form meaning "faith alone." Remembering that Paul was a Hebrew, see the note on Ecclesiastes 1:2 and compare the Hebrew form for superlative adjectives.

1:18 The expression "hold the truth in unrighteousness" does not mean that the men mentioned here actually possessed the truth but simply failed to put it into practice. *Katechō* (2722), the verb translated "hold," is better translated in this context "hold back" or "restrain." This use of the word is also found in 2 Thessalonians 2:6, 7, where *katechō* is translated "withholdeth" and "letteth," respectively. These ungodly men attempt to restrain the truth through unrighteousness.

1:20 The word translated "Godhead" is *theiótēs* (2305), which merely means "divinity," or the demonstrated power of the Godhead, not the essence and the character of the Godhead. By looking at nature, one can observe that God is indeed all-powerful, but creation does not necessarily reveal that He is an all-loving God of righteousness and justice. There is only so much of God that one can know from God's creation (Rom. 1:19). In order to know the essence of God as a triune Deity, one needs to receive His revelation by faith.

ral use[5540] into that which is against nature:

27 And likewise also the men, [apt]leaving the natural use of the woman, burned in their lust[3715] one toward another; men with men working that which is unseemly, and receiving[618] in themselves that recompence of their error which [ipf]was meet.[1163]

28 And even as they [ao]did not like[1381] [I]to retain God in *their* knowledge,[1922] God gave them over to [II]a reprobate[96] mind,[3563] [pinf]to do[4160] those things [a]which are not convenient;[2520]

29 Being filled with all unrighteousness, fornication,[4202] wickedness,[4189] covetousness, maliciousness;[2549] full of envy, murder, debate,[2054] deceit, malignity;[2550] whisperers,[5588]

30 Backbiters,[2637] haters of God, despiteful,[5197] proud,[5244] boasters,[213] inventors of evil things, disobedient[545] to parents,

31 Without understanding, covenantbreakers,[802] without natural affection,[794] implacable,[786] unmerciful:[415]

32 Who [apt][a]knowing the judgment[1345] of God, that they which [ppt]commit[4238] such things [b]are worthy of death, not only do the same, but [I][c]have pleasure in them that [ppt]do them.

God's Law

2 Therefore thou art [a]inexcusable, O man, whosoever thou art that [ppt]judgest:[2919] [b]for wherein thou judgest another, thou condemnest[2632] thyself; for thou that [ppt]judgest doest[4238] the same things.

2 But we are sure that the judgment[2917] of God[2316] is according to truth[225] against them which [ppt]commit such things.

3 And thinkest thou this, O man, that judgest them which do such things, and [ppt]doest the same, that thou [fm]shalt escape[1628] the judgment of God?

4 Or despisest thou [a]the riches of his goodness[5544] and [b]forbearance[463] and [c]longsuffering;[3115] [d]not knowing[50] that the goodness[5543] of God leadeth[71] thee to repentance?[3341]

5 But after thy hardness[4643] and impenitent[279] heart[2588] [a]treasurest up unto thyself wrath[3709] against the day of wrath and revelation[602] of the righteous judgment[1341] of God;

6 [a]Who will render to every man according to his deeds:[2041]

7 To them who by patient continuance in well[18] doing[2041] seek for glory and honour and immortality, eternal[166] life:[2222]

8 But unto them that are contentious, and [a]do not obey[544] the truth,[225] but [ppt]obey[3982] unrighteousness,[93] indignation[2372] and wrath,[3709]

9 Tribulation[2347] and anguish,[4730] upon every soul[5590] of man that [ppt]doeth evil,[2556] of the Jew [a]first, and also of the [I]Gentile;

10 [a]But glory,[1391] honour,[5092] and peace,[1515] to every man that [ppt]worketh[2038] good,[18] to the Jew first, and also to the [I]Gentile:

11 For [a]there is no respect of persons[4382] with God.

12 For as many as [ao]have sinned[264] without law [fm]shall also perish[622] without law:[460] and as many as have sinned in the law[3551] shall be judged by the law;

13 (For [a]not the hearers of the law *are* just[1342] before God, but the doers of the law [fp]shall be justified.[1344]

14 For when the Gentiles,[1484] which [ppt]have not the law, [psa]do by nature the things contained in the law, these, having not the law, are a law unto themselves:

15 Which shew the work[2041] of the law written in their hearts,[2588] [I]their conscience[4893] also bearing witness, and *their* thoughts[3053] [II]the mean while accusing[2723] or else excusing one another;)

16 [a]In the day when God [ft]shall judge[2919] the secrets of men [b]by Jesus Christ [c]according to my gospel.[2098]

Obeying God's Law

17 Behold, [a]thou art called a Jew, and [b]restest[1879] in the law, [c]and makest thy boast of God,

28 [I]Or, *to acknowledge* [II]Or, *a mind void of judgment* [a]Eph. 5:4
32 [I]Or, *consent with them* [a]Rom. 2:2 [b]Rom. 6:21 [c]Ps. 50:18; Hos. 7:3

1 [a]Rom. 1:20 [b]2Sam. 12:5, 6, 7; Matt. 7:1, 2; John 8:9
4 [a]Rom. 9:23; Eph. 1:7; 2:4, 7 [b]Rom. 3:25 [c]Ex. 34:6 [d]Isa. 30:18; 2Pet. 3:9, 15
5 [a]Deut. 32:34; James 5:3
6 [a]Job 34:11; Ps. 62:12; Prov. 24:12; Jer. 17:10; 32:19; Matt. 16:27; Rom. 14:12; 1Cor. 3:8; 2Cor. 5:10; Rev. 2:23; 20:12; 22:12
8 [a]Job 24:13; Rom. 1:18; 2Thess. 1:8
9 [I]Gr. *Greek* [a]Amos 3:2; Luke 12:47, 48; 1Pet. 4:17
10 [I]Gr. *Greek* [a]1Pet. 1:7
11 [a]Deut. 10:17; 2Chr. 19:7; Job 34:19; Acts 10:34; Gal. 2:6; Eph. 6:9; Col. 3:25; 1Pet. 1:17
13 [a]Matt. 7:21; James 1:22, 23, 25; 1John 3:7
15 [I]Or, *the conscience witnessing with them* [II]Or, *between themselves*
16 [a]Eccl. 12:14; Matt. 25:31; John 12:48; Rom. 3:6; 1Cor. 4:5; Rev. 20:12 [b]John 5:22; Acts 10:42; 17:31; 2Tim. 4:1, 8; 1Pet. 4:5 [c]Rom. 16:25; 1Tim. 1:11; 2Tim. 2:8
17 [a]Matt. 3:9; John 8:33; Rom. 9:6, 7; 2Cor. 11:22 [b]Mic. 3:11; Rom. 9:4 [c]Isa. 45:25; 48:2; John 8:41

18 And [a]knowest *his* [art]will,[2307] and [Ib]approvest the things that are more excellent, being instructed out of the law;

19 And [pfi][a]art confident[3982] that thou thyself art a guide of the blind, a light[5457] of them which are in darkness,[4655]

20 An instructor[3810] of the foolish, a teacher[1320] of babes,[3516] [a]which hast the form[3446] of knowledge and of the truth in the law.

21 [a]Thou therefore which [ppt]teachest another, teachest[1321] thou not thyself? thou that preachest[2784] a man should not steal, dost thou steal?

22 Thou that sayest a man should not commit adultery, dost thou commit adultery? thou that abhorrest[948] idols, [a]dost thou commit sacrilege?

23 Thou that [a]makest thy boast of the law, through breaking[3847] the law dishonourest thou God?

24 For the name of God [pinp]is blasphemed[987] among the Gentiles through you, as it is [a]written.

25 [a]For circumcision[4061] verily[3303] profiteth, if thou keep[4238] the law: but if thou be a breaker[3848] of the law, thy circumcision is made uncircumcision.[203]

26 Therefore [a]if the uncircumcision[203] keep the righteousness[1345] of the law, [fp]shall not his uncircumcision be counted[3049] for circumcision?

27 And shall not uncircumcision which is by nature, if it fulfil[5055] the law, [a]judge[2919] thee, who[3848] by the letter[1121] and circumcision dost transgress[3848] the law?

28 For [a]he is not a Jew, which is one outwardly;[1722,5318] neither *is that* circumcision, which is outward in the flesh:[4561]

29 But he *is* a Jew, [a]which is one inwardly; and [b]circumcision[4061] *is that* of the heart, [c]in the spirit, *and* not in the letter;[1121] [d]whose praise *is* not of men,[444] but of God.[2316]

3

What advantage[4053] then hath the Jew? or what profit *is there* of circumcision?[4061]

18 [I]Or, *triest the things that differ* [a]Deut. 4:8; Ps. 147:19, 20 [b]Phil. 1:10
19 [a]Matt. 15:14; 23:16, 17, 19, 24; John 9:34, 40, 41
20 [a]Rom. 6:17; 2Tim. 1:13; 3:5
21 [a]Ps. 50:16-22; Matt. 23:3-6
22 [a]Mal. 3:8
23 [a]Rom. 2:17
24 [a]2Sam. 12:14; Isa. 52:5; Ezek. 36:20, 23
25 [a]Gal. 5:3
26 [a]Acts 10:34, 35
27 [a]Matt. 12:41, 42
28 [a]Matt. 3:9; John 8:39; Rom. 9:6, 7; Gal. 6:15; Rev. 2:9
29 [a]1Pet. 3:4 [b]Phil. 3:3; Col. 2:11 [c]Rom. 7:6; 2Cor. 3:6 [d]1Cor. 4:5; 2Cor. 10:18; 1Thess. 2:4
2 [a]Deut. 4:7, 8; Ps. 147:19, 20; Rom. 2:18; 9:4
3 [a]Rom. 10:16; Heb. 4:2 [b]Num. 23:19; Rom. 9:6; 11:29; 2Tim. 2:13
4 [a]Job 40:8 [b]John 3:33 [c]Ps. 62:9; 116:11 [d]Ps. 51:4
5 [a]Rom. 6:19; Gal. 3:15
6 [a]Gen. 18:25; Job 8:3; 34:17
8 [a]Rom. 5:20; 6:1, 15
9 [I]Gr. *charged* [a]Rom. 1:28—2:4 [b]Rom. 3:23; Gal. 3:22
10 [a]Ps. 14:1-3; 53:1
13 [a]Ps. 5:9; Jer. 5:16 [b]Ps. 140:3
14 [a]Ps. 10:7
15 [a]Prov. 1:16; Isa. 59:7, 8

2 Much every way: chiefly,[4412] because that [a]unto them [aop]were committed[4100] the oracles[3051] of God.

3 For what if [a]some did not believe?[569] [b]shall their unbelief[570] make the faith[4102] of God without effect?

4 [a]God forbid:[3361,1096] yea, let [b]God be[1096] true, but [c]every man a liar; as it is written, [d]That thou [asbp]mightest be justified[1344,302] in thy sayings, and mightest overcome when thou art judged.[2919]

5 But if our unrighteousness[93] commend[4921] the righteousness[1343] of God, what shall we say? *Is* God unrighteous[94] who taketh[2018] vengeance?[3709] ([a]I speak as a man)

6 God forbid: for then [a]how [ft]shall God judge[2919] the world?

7 For if the truth[225] of God hath more abounded through my lie unto his glory;[1391] why yet am I also judged as a sinner?[268]

8 And not *rather,* (as we [pinp]be slanderously reported,[987] and as some affirm that we say,) [a]Let us do evil, that good[18] may come? whose damnation[2917] is just.[1738]

"All Have Sinned"

9 What then? are we better *than they*? No, in no wise: for we have before [I][a]proved both Jews and Gentiles, that [b]they are all under sin;[266]

10 As it is written, [a]There is none righteous,[1342] no, not one:

11 There is none that [ppt]understandeth, there is none that [ppt]seeketh after God.

12 They [ao]are all gone out of the way,[1578] they [aop]are together become unprofitable;[889] there is none that [ppt]doeth good,[5544] no, not one.

13 [a]Their throat *is* an open sepulchre; with their tongues they [ipf]have used deceit; [b]the poison of asps[785] *is* under their lips:

14 [a]Whose mouth *is* full of cursing[685] and bitterness:

15 [a]Their feet *are* swift to shed blood:

16 Destruction and misery *are* in their ways:[3598]

17 And the way of peace have they not known:

18 [a]There is no fear[5401] of God before their eyes.

🔑 19 Now we know that what things soever [a]the law[3551] saith, it saith to them who are under the law: that [b]every mouth may be stopped, and [c]all the world may become [I]guilty[5267] before God.

20 Therefore [a]by the deeds of the law there [fp]shall no flesh be justified[1344] in his sight: for [b]by the law *is* the knowledge of sin.[266]

The Only Way of Salvation

21 But now [a]the righteousness[1343] of God without the law [pfip]is manifested,[5319] [b]being witnessed by the law [c]and the prophets;

22 Even the righteousness of God *which is* by faith[4102] of Jesus Christ unto all and upon all them that [ppt]believe:[4100] for [a]there is no difference:

23 For [a]all [ao]have sinned,[264] and come short of the glory[1391] of God;

24 Being justified freely[1432] [a]by his grace[5485] [b]through the redemption[629] that is in Christ Jesus:

25 Whom God [aom]hath [I]set forth[4388] [a]*to be* a propitiation[2435] through faith [b]in his blood,[129] to declare his righteousness [c]for the [II]remission[3929] of [d]sins[265] that [pfp]are past, through the forbearance[463] of God;

26 To declare, *I say,* at this time[2540] his righteousness: that he might be just,[1342] and the justifier[1344] of him which believeth[1537,4102] in Jesus.

27 [a]Where *is* boasting then? It is excluded. By what law?[3551] of works?[2041] Nay: but by the law of faith.[4102]

28 Therefore we conclude[3049] [a]that a man[444] is justified[1344] by faith[4102] without the deeds[2041] of the law.

29 *Is he* the God of the Jews only? *is he* not also of the Gentiles?[1484] Yes, of the Gentiles also:

30 Seeing [a]*it is* one God, which shall justify the circumcision[4061] by faith, and uncircumcision[203] through faith.

31 Do we then make void the law through faith? God forbid:[3361,1096] yea, we establish the law.

4 What shall we say then that [a]Abraham our father,[3962] as pertaining to the flesh,[4561] hath found?

🔑 2 For if Abraham [aop]were [a]justified[1344] by works,[2041] he hath *whereof* to glory; but not before God.

3 For what saith the scripture?[1124] [a]Abraham believed[4100] God, and it was counted unto him for righteousness.[1343]

4 Now [a]to him that [ppt]worketh is[3049] the reward[3408] not reckoned[3049] of grace,[5485] but of debt.[3783]

🔑 5 But to him that worketh not, but

18 [a]Ps. 36:1 **19** [I]Or, *subject to the judgment of God* [a]John 10:34; 15:25 [b]Job 5:16; Ps. 107:42; Ezek. 16:63; Rom. 1:20; 2:1 [c]Rom. 2:2; 9:23 **20** [a]Ps. 143:2; Acts 13:39; Gal. 2:16; 3:11; Eph. 2:8, 9; Titus 3:5 **21** [a]Acts 15:11; Rom. 1:17; Phil. 3:9; Heb. 11:4-22 [b]John 5:46; Acts 26:22 [c]Rom. 1:2; 1Pet. 1:10 **22** [a]Rom. 10:12; Gal. 3:28; Col. 3:11 **23** [a]Rom. 3:9; 11:32; Gal. 3:22 **24** [a]Rom. 4:16; Eph. 2:8; Titus 3:5, 7 [b]Matt. 20:28; Eph. 1:7; Col. 1:14; 1Tim. 2:6; Heb. 9:12; 1Pet. 1:18, 19 **25** [I]Or, *foreordained* [II]Or, *passing over* [a]Lev. 16:15; 1John 2:2; 4:10 [b]Col. 1:20 [c]Acts 13:38, 39; 1Tim. 1:15 [d]Acts 17:30; Heb. 9:15 **27** [a]Rom. 2:17, 23; 4:2; 1Cor. 1:29, 31; Eph. 2:9 **28** [a]Acts 13:38, 39; Rom. 3:20-22; 8:3; Gal. 2:16 **30** [a]Rom. 10:12, 13; Gal. 3:8, 20, 28

1 [a]Isa. 51:2; Matt. 3:9; John 8:33, 39; 2Cor. 11:22 **2** [a]Rom. 3:20, 27, 28 **3** [a]Gen. 15:6; Gal. 3:6; James 2:23 **4** [a]Rom. 11:6

🔑 **3:19, 20** These verses form a key conclusion in Paul's argument regarding sin and righteousness. In the previous verses, Paul has quoted the Old Testament to demonstrate man's sinfulness (vv. 10–18). The "law" (v. 19), referring to the Old Testament, was designed to silence all mankind under the conviction that they have nothing to say against the charge of sin. Likewise, the law was intended to convince all men of their guilt, or liability to punishment, before God.

Paul concludes that since all men are guilty, they cannot be "justified" by their own personal character or conduct (v. 20). Justification is a legal term meaning to remove the guilt (liability to punishment) of the sinner. It does not involve making one inwardly holy, but merely declares that the demands of justice have been satisfied. Hence, there are no grounds for condemnation (Rom. 8:1). Not even obedience to the law can justify one before God, Paul reasons, because the very nature of the law is to prove to each person that he or she is sinful and deserves God's punishment. Thus, the purpose of the law is to lead people to renounce their own righteousness and trust in the imputation of Christ's righteousness as the only grounds for acceptance with God.

🔑 **4:2, 5, 8** See note on Romans 3:19, 20.

[ppt]believeth[4100] on him that [ppt]justifieth[1344] [a]the ungodly,[765] his faith[4102] [pinp]is counted[3049] for righteousness.

6 Even as David also describeth the blessedness of the man, unto whom God imputeth[3049] righteousness without works,[2041]

7 *Saying,* [a]Blessed[3107] *are* they whose iniquities[458] are forgiven, and whose sins[266] are covered.

8 Blessed *is* the man to whom the Lord [fm]will not impute[3049] sin.

9 *Cometh* this blessedness then upon the circumcision[4061] *only,* or upon the uncircumcision[203] also? for we say that faith[4102] was reckoned to Abraham for righteousness.

10 How [aop]was it then reckoned?[3049] when he was in circumcision, or in uncircumcision? Not in circumcision, but in uncircumcision.

11 And [a]he received the [an]sign[4592] of circumcision, a seal of the righteousness[1343] of the faith which *he had yet* being uncircumcised: that [b]he might be the father of all them that [ppt]believe, though they be not circumcised;[203] that righteousness[1343] might be imputed[3049] unto them also:

12 And the father of circumcision[4061] to them who are not of the circumcision only, but who also walk in the steps of that faith[4102] of our father Abraham, which *he had* being *yet* uncircumcised.

God's Promise

13 For the promise,[1860] that he should be the [a]heir[2818] of the world,[2889] *was* not to Abraham, or to his seed,[4690] through the law,[3551] but through the righteousness[1343] of faith.[4102]

14 For [a]if they which are of the law *be* heirs, faith [pfip]is made void,[2758] and the promise made of none effect:

15 Because [a]the law[3551] worketh wrath:[3709] for where no law is, *there is* no transgression.[3847]

16 Therefore *it is* of faith,[4102] that *it might be* [a]by grace;[5485] [b]to the end the promise might be sure[949] to all the seed;[4690] not to that only which is of the law,[3551] but to that also which is of the faith of Abraham; [c]who is the father[3962] of us all,

17 (As it is written, [a]I [pfi]have made[5087] thee a father of many nations,) [I]before him whom he believed, *even* God, [b]who [ppt]quickeneth[2227] the dead,[3498] and [ppt]calleth those [c]things which be not as though they were.

18 Who against hope[1680] believed[4100] in hope, that he might become the father of many nations, according to that which was spoken, [a]So shall thy seed[4690] be.

19 And [apt]being not weak[770] in faith, [a]he considered not his own body now dead, when he was about an hundred years old, neither yet the deadness[3500] of Sarah's womb:

20 He staggered[1252] not at the promise of God through unbelief;[570] but was strong in faith, giving glory[1391] to God;

21 And [apt]being fully persuaded[4135] that, what he [pfip]had promised,[1861] [a]he was able also [ainf]to perform.

22 And therefore it [aop]was imputed[3049] to him for righteousness.[1343]

23 Now [a]it was not written for his sake alone, that it was imputed to him;

24 But for us also, to whom it shall be imputed, if we believe[4100] [a]on him that [apt]raised up[1453] Jesus our Lord from the dead;

25 [a]Who was delivered for our offences,[3900] and [b]was raised again for our justification.[1347]

The Results of Justification

5 Therefore [aptp][a]being justified[1344] by faith,[4102] we have [b]peace[1515] with God through our Lord Jesus Christ:

2 [a]By whom also we [pfi]have access[4318] by faith into this grace[5485] [b]wherein we stand, and [c]rejoice in hope[1680] of the glory[1391] of God.

3 And not only *so,* but [a]we glory in tribulations also: [b]knowing that tribulation worketh patience;

4 [a]And patience, experience;[1382] and experience, hope:[1680]

---

5 [a]Josh. 24:2
7 [a]Ps. 32:1, 2
11 [a]Gen. 17:10 [b]Luke 19:9; Rom. 4:12, 16; Gal. 3:7
13 [a]Gen. 17:4-9; Gal. 3:29
14 [a]Gal. 3:18
15 [a]Rom. 3:20; 5:13, 20; 7:8-11; 1Cor. 15:56; 2Cor. 3:7, 9; Gal. 3:10, 19; 1John 3:4
16 [a]Rom. 3:24 [b]Gal. 3:22 [c]Isa. 51:2; Rom. 9:8
17 [I]Or, *like unto him* [a]Gen. 17:5 [b]Rom. 8:11; Eph. 2:1, 5 [c]Rom. 9:26; 1Cor. 1:28; 1Pet. 2:10
18 [a]Gen. 15:5
19 [a]Gen. 17:17; 18:11; Heb. 11:11, 12
21 [a]Ps. 115:3; Luke 1:37, 45; Heb. 11:19
23 [a]Rom. 15:4; 1Cor. 10:6, 11
24 [a]Acts 2:24; 13:30
25 [a]Isa. 53:5, 6; Rom. 3:25; 5:6; 8:32; 2Cor. 5:21; Gal. 1:4; Heb. 9:28; 1Pet. 2:24; 3:18 [b]1Cor. 15:17; 1Pet. 1:21

1 [a]Isa. 32:17; John 16:33; Rom. 3:28, 30 [b]Eph. 2:14; Col. 1:20
2 [a]John 10:9; 14:6; Eph. 2:18; 3:12; Heb. 10:19 [b]1Cor. 15:1 [c]Heb. 3:6
3 [a]Matt. 5:11, 12; Acts 5:41; 2Cor. 12:10; Phil. 2:17; James 1:2, 12; 1Pet. 3:14 [b]James 1:3
4 [a]James 1:12

5 [a]And hope maketh not ashamed; [b]because the love[26] of God [pfip]is shed abroad in our hearts[2588] by the [an]Holy Ghost[4151] which [aptp]is given unto us.

6 For when we were yet without strength,[772] [I]in due time[2540] [a]Christ died[599] for the ungodly.[765]

7 For scarcely for a righteous man[1342] will one die: yet peradventure[5029] for a good man[18] some would even dare to die.

8 But [a]God commendeth[4921] his love toward us, in that, while we were yet sinners,[268] Christ[5547] died for us.

9 Much more then, [aptp]being now justified[1344] [a]by his blood,[129] we [fp]shall be saved[4982] [b]from wrath[3709] through him.

10 For [a]if, when we were enemies, [b]we [aop]were reconciled[2644] to God by the death[2288] of his Son,[5207] much more, being reconciled, we shall be saved [c]by his life.[2222]

11 And not only *so,* but we also [ppt][a]joy in God through our Lord Jesus Christ, by whom we have now received the [I]atonement.[2643]

Christ and Adam Contrasted

12 Wherefore, as [a]by one man[444] sin[266] entered into the world,[2889] and [b]death by sin; and so death[2288] passed upon all men, [I]for that all have sinned:[264]

13 (For until the law[3551] sin[266] was in the world: but [a]sin[266] [pinp]is not imputed[1677] when there is no law.

14 Nevertheless death reigned[936] from Adam to Moses, even over them that had not sinned after the similitude[3667] of Adam's transgression,[3847] [a]who is the figure[5179] of him that was to come.

15 But not as the offence,[3900] so also *is* the free gift.[5486] For if through the offence of one many [ao]be dead, much more the grace[5485] of God, and the gift by grace, *which is* by one man, Jesus Christ, [ao]hath abounded[4052] [a]unto many.

16 And not as *it was* by one that sinned, *so is* the gift:[1434] for the judgment[2917] *was* by one to condemnation,[2631] but the free gift[5486] *is* of many offences unto justification.[1345]

17 For if [I]by one man's offence death[2288] reigned[936] by one; much more they which receive abundance[4050] of grace[5485] and of the gift[1431] of righteousness[1343] shall reign in life by one, Jesus Christ.)

18 Therefore as [I]by the offence of one *judgment came* upon all men to condemnation;[2631] even so [II]by the righteousness of one *the free gift came* [a]upon all men unto justification[1347] of life.[2222]

19 For as by one man's disobedience[3876] many [aop]were made[2525] sinners, so by the obedience[5218] of one shall many be made righteous.[1342]

20 Moreover [a]the law[3551] entered, that the offence might abound. But where sin abounded, grace[5485] did much [b]more abound:[5248]

21 That as sin hath reigned[936] unto death, even so might grace[5485] reign through righteousness[1343] unto eternal life by Jesus Christ our Lord.

Dead to Sin

6 What shall we say then? [a]Shall we continue in sin,[266] that grace[5485] [asba]may abound?

2 God forbid.[3361,1096] How shall[2198] we, that [ao]are [a]dead[599] to sin, live[2198] any longer therein?

🔑 3 Know ye not,[50] that [a]so many of us as [aop]were baptized[907] into Jesus Christ [b]were baptized into his death?[2288]

4 Therefore we [aop]are [a]buried with him by baptism[908] into death: that [b]like as Christ[5547] [aop]was raised up[1453] from the dead by [c]the glory[1391] of the Father, [d]even so we also [aosi]should walk in newness[2538] of life.[2222]

5 [a]For if we have been planted together[4854] in the likeness[3667] of his death,

5 [a]Phil. 1:20 [b]2Cor. 1:22; Gal. 4:6; Eph. 1:13, 14
6 [I]Or, *according to the time,* Gal. 4:4 [a]Rom. 4:25; 5:8
8 [a]John 15:13; 1Pet. 3:18; 1John 3:16; 4:9, 10
9 [a]Rom. 3:25; Eph. 2:13; Heb. 9:14; 1John 1:7 [b]Rom. 1:18; 1Thess. 1:10
10 [a]Rom. 8:32 [b]2Cor. 5:18, 19; Eph. 2:16; Col. 1:20, 21 [c]John 5:26; 14:19; 2Cor. 4:10, 11
11 [I]Or, *reconciliation,* [a]Rom. 2:17; 3:29, 30; Gal. 4:9
12 [I]Or, *in who* [a]Gen. 3:6; 1Cor. 15:21 [b]Gen. 2:17; Rom. 6:23; 1Cor. 15:21
13 [a]Rom. 4:15; 1John 3:4
14 [a]1Cor. 15:21, 22, 45
15 [a]Isa. 53:11; Matt. 20:28; 26:28
17 [I]Or, *by one offense*
18 [I]Or, *by one offense* [II]Or, *by one righteousness* [a]John 12:32; Heb. 2:9
20 [a]John 15:22; Rom. 3:20; 4:15; 7:8; Gal. 3:19, 23 [b]Luke 7:47; 1Tim. 1:14

1 [a]Rom. 3:8; 6:15; [b]Rom. 6:11; 7:4; Gal. 2:19; 6:14; Col. 3:3; 1Pet. 2:24
3 [a]Gal. 3:27 [b]1Cor. 15:29
4 [a]Col. 2:12 [b]Rom. 8:11; 1Cor. 6:14; 2Cor. 13:14 [c]John 2:11; 11:40 [d]Gal. 6:15; Eph. 4:22-24; Col. 3:10
5 [a]Phil. 3:10, 11

🔑 **6:3** See note on 1 Corinthians 10:2.

we shall be also *in the likeness* of *his* resurrection:[386]

6 Knowing this, that [a]our old[3820] man[444] [aop]is crucified[4957] with him, that [b]the body[4983] of sin[266] might be destroyed, that henceforth we [infg]should not serve[1398] sin.

7 For [a]he that [apt]is dead[599] [pfip]is [I]freed[1344] from sin.

8 Now [a]if we [ao]be dead with Christ, we believe[4100] that we [ft]shall also live with[4800] him:

9 Knowing that [a]Christ being raised from the dead[3498] dieth no more; death hath no more dominion over[2961] him.

10 For in that he died,[599] [a]he died unto sin once: but in that he liveth,[2198] [b]he liveth unto God.

11 Likewise reckon[3049] ye also yourselves to be [a]dead[3498] indeed unto sin, but [ppt][b]alive[2198] unto God through Jesus Christ our Lord.

12 [pim][a]Let not sin therefore reign[936] in your mortal body, that ye [aies]should obey[5219] it in the lusts thereof.

13 Neither [pim]yield ye your [a]members *as* [I]instruments of unrighteousness[93] unto sin: but [b]yield yourselves unto God, as those that [ppt]are alive from the dead, and your members *as* instruments of righteousness[1343] unto God.

14 For [a]sin shall not have dominion over you: for ye are not under the law,[3551] but under grace.[5485]

Servants to God

15 What then? [ft]shall we sin,[264] [a]because we are not under the law, but under grace? God forbid.[3361,1096]

16 Know ye not, that [a]to whom ye yield yourselves servants to obey,[5218] his servants[1401] ye are to whom ye obey; whether of sin[266] unto death,[2288] or of obedience[5218] unto righteousness?[1343]

17 But God be thanked, that ye were the servants of sin, but ye [ao]have obeyed[5219] from the heart[2588] [a]that form[5179] of doctrine[1322] [I]which was delivered you.

18 Being then [a]made free from sin, ye became the servants of righteousness.

6 [a]Gal. 2:20; 5:24; 6:14; Eph. 4:22; Col. 3:5, 9 [b]Col. 2:11

7 [I]Gr. *justified* [a]1Pet. 4:1

8 [a]2Tim. 2:11

9 [a]Rev. 1:18

10 [a]Heb. 9:27, 28 [b]Luke 20:38

11 [a]Rom. 6:2 [b]Gal. 2:19

12 [a]Ps. 19:13; 119:133

13 [I]Gr. *arms, or, weapons* [a]Rom. 7:5; Col. 3:5; James 4:1 [b]Rom. 12:1; 1Pet. 2:24; 4:2

14 [a]Rom. 7:4, 6; 8:2; Gal. 5:18

15 [a]1Cor. 9:21

16 [a]Matt. 6:24; John 8:34; 2Pet. 2:19

17 [I]Gr. *whereto ye were delivered* [a]2Tim. 1:13

18 [a]John 8:32; 1Cor. 7:22; Gal. 5:1; 1Pet. 2:16

20 [I]Gr. *to righteousness* [a]John 8:34

21 [a]Rom. 7:5 [b]Rom. 1:32

22 [a]John 8:32

23 [a]Gen. 2:17; Rom. 5:12; James 1:15 [b]Rom. 2:7; 5:17, 21; 1Pet. 1:4

2 [a]1Cor. 7:39

3 [a]Matt. 5:32

4 [a]Rom. 8:2; Gal. 2:19; 5:18; Eph. 2:15; Col. 2:14 [b]Gal. 5:22

5 [I]Gr. *passions* [a]Rom. 6:13 [b]Rom. 6:21; Gal. 5:19; James 1:15

19 I speak after the manner of men because of the infirmity of your flesh:[4561] for as ye [ao]have yielded your members servants to uncleanness[167] and to iniquity[458] unto iniquity; even so now [aim]yield your members servants to righteousness unto holiness.[38]

20 For when ye were [a]the [an]servants of sin, ye were free [I]from righteousness.

21 [a]What fruit had ye then in those things whereof ye are now ashamed? for [b]the end[5056] of those things *is* death.[2288]

22 But now [a]being made free from sin, and become servants to God, ye have your fruit unto holiness, and the end everlasting[166] life.[2222]

23 For [a]the wages[3800] of sin[266] *is* death;[2288] but [b]the gift[5486] of God *is* eternal[166] life[2222] through Jesus Christ our Lord.

Released From the Law

7 Know ye not,[50] brethren,[80] (for I speak to them that know the law,) how that the law[3551] [pin]hath dominion over[2961] a man as long as he liveth?[2198]

2 For [a]the woman which hath an husband [pfip]is bound[1210] by the law to *her* husband so long as he liveth; but if the husband [asba]be dead, she [pfi]is loosed from the law of *her* husband.

3 So then [a]if, while *her* husband liveth, she be married to another[2087] man, she [ft]shall be called[5537] an adulteress: but if her husband [asba]be dead, she is free[1658] from that law; so that she is no adulteress, though she be married to another man.

4 Wherefore, my brethren, ye also are [aop]become [a]dead to the law by the body of Christ; that ye should be married to another, *even* to him who [aptp]is raised[1453] from the dead,[3498] that we should [b]bring forth fruit unto God.

5 For when we were in the flesh,[4561] the [I]motions[3804] of sins, which were by the law, [ipfa]did work[1754] in our members [b]to bring forth fruit unto death.

6 But now we are delivered from the

law, [I][a]that [apt]being dead wherein we were
held;[2722] that we [pinf]should serve [b]in newness[2538] of spirit,[4151] and not *in* the
oldness[3821] of the letter.[1121]
7 What shall we say then? *Is* the
law[3551] sin?[266] God forbid.[3361,1096] Nay, [a]I
had not known[1097] sin, but by the law:
for I had not known [I]lust,[1939] except the
law had said, [b]Thou shalt not covet.[1937]
8 But [a]sin, [apt]taking occasion by the
commandment,[1785] wrought in me all
manner of concupiscence.[1939] For [b]with-
out the law sin *was* dead.[3498]
9 For I [ipf]was alive[2198] without the
law once: but when the commandment
[apt]came, sin revived, and I died.[599]
10 And the commandment, [a]which
was ordained to life,[2222] I found[2147] *to be*
unto death.[2288]
11 For sin, [apt]taking occasion by the
commandment, deceived me, and by it
slew *me*.
12 Wherefore [a]the law *is* holy,[40] and
the commandment holy, and just,[1342] and
good.[18]
13 Was then that which is good
made death unto me? God forbid. But
sin, that it might appear sin, working[2716]
death in me by that which is good; that
sin by the commandment might become
exceeding sinful.[268]

The Sin Nature Still Remains

14 For we know that the law is spiritual:[4152] but I am carnal,[4559] [a]sold under
sin.[266]
15 For that which I do I [I][a]allow not:
for [b]what I would, that do[4238] I not; but
what I hate, that do I.
16 If then I do that which I would
not, I consent unto the law that *it is* good.
🔑 17 Now then it is no more I that do
it, but sin that [ppt]dwelleth[3611] in me.
18 For I know that [a]in me (that is, in
my flesh,[4561]) dwelleth no good thing: for
to will is present with me; but *how* to perform that which is good I find not.
19 For the good[18] that I would I do
not: but the evil[2556] which I would not,
that I do.
20 Now if I do that I would not, it is
no more I that do it, but sin that
[ppt]dwelleth in me.
21 I find then a law,[3551] that, when I
[ppt]would[2309] [pinf]do good, evil [pin]is present
with me.
22 For I [a]delight in the law of
God[2316] after [b]the inward man:[444]
🔑 23 But [a]I see another[2087] law in [b]my
members, warring against the law of
my mind, and bringing me into captivity
to the law of sin which is in my members.
24 O wretched man that I am! who
[fm]shall deliver[4506] me from [I]the body of
this death?[2288]
25 [a]I thank God through Jesus
Christ[5547] our Lord.[2962] So then with the
mind[3563] I myself serve[1398] the law of
God; but with the flesh the law of sin.

No Condemnation Now

8 There is therefore now no condemnation[2631] to them which are in
Christ[5547] Jesus, who [ppt][a]walk not after
the flesh,[4561] but after the Spirit.[4151]
2 For [a]the law[3551] of [b]the Spirit of
life[2222] in Christ Jesus [ao]hath made me
free[1659] from [c]the law of sin[266] and
death.[2288]

6 [I]Or, *being dead to that* [a]Rom. 6:2; 7:4 [b]Rom. 2:29; 2Cor. 3:6

7 [I]Or, *concupiscence* [a]Rom. 3:20 [b]Ex. 20:17; Deut. 5:21; Acts 20:33; Rom. 13:9

8 [a]Rom. 4:15; 5:20 [b]1Cor. 15:56

10 [a]Lev. 18:5; Ezek. 20:11, 13, 21; 2Cor. 3:7

12 [a]Ps. 19:8; 119:38, 137; 1Tim. 1:8

14 [a]1Kgs. 21:20, 25; 2Kgs. 17:17

15 [I]Gr. *know* [a]Ps. 1:6 [b]Gal. 5:17

17 [a]Gen. 6:5; 8:21

22 [a]Ps. 1:2 [b]2Cor. 4:16; Eph. 3:16; Col. 3:9, 10

23 [a]Gal. 5:17 [b]Rom. 6:13, 19

24 [I]Or, *this body of death*

25 [a]1Cor. 15:57

1 [a]Rom. 8:4; Gal. 5:16, 25

2 [a]John 8:36; Rom. 6:18, 22; Gal. 2:19; 5:1 [b]1Cor. 15:45; 2Cor. 3:6 [c]Rom. 7:24, 25

🔑 **7:17–19** Paul's statement "Now then it is no more I that do it, but sin that dwelleth in me" (v. 17) should not be taken as an abdication of his responsibility for his actions. Instead, he reveals the inner conflict between his two natures. To will (v. 15; *thélō* [2309]) was his attitude, but to perform (*katergázomai* [2716], "to accomplish") that which is good Paul could not realize (v. 18). Paul bemoans that the good he desired, he did not do (*poiéō* [4160], stressing the object of an act), but the evil he did not desire was what he practiced (*prássō* [4238], emphasizing the means by which an act is accomplished).

🔑 **7:23** Paul further develops the concept of conflict between his new nature, in which he "rejoices with" (*sunēdomai* [4913]) the law of God, and his old nature, by which he is captivated (*aichmalōtízontá* [163]).

3 For [a]what the law could not do, in that it [ipf]was weak[770] through the flesh,[4561] [b]God [apt]sending his own Son[5207] in the likeness[3667] of sinful[266] flesh, and [I]for sin, condemned[2632] sin in the flesh:

4 That the righteousness[1345] of the law might be fulfilled in us, [a]who [ppt]walk not after the flesh, but after the Spirit.[4151]

5 For [a]they that are after the flesh [pin]do mind[5426] the things of the flesh;[4561] but they that are after the Spirit[4151] [b]the things of the Spirit.

6 For [Ia]to be carnally[4561] minded *is* death;[2288] but [II]to be spiritually minded *is* life[2222] and peace.[1515]

🗝 7 Because [Ia]the carnal mind *is* enmity[2189] against God: for it [pin]is not subject[5293] to the law[3551] of God, [b]neither indeed can be.

8 So then they that are in the flesh cannot [ainf]please God.

9 But ye are not in the flesh, but in the Spirit, if so be that [a]the [an]Spirit[4151] of God dwell[3611] in you. Now if any man have not [b]the [an]Spirit of Christ, he is none of his.

10 And if Christ[5547] *be* in you, the body[4983] *is* dead because of sin; but the Spirit[4151] *is* life because of righteousness.[1343]

11 But if the Spirit of [a]him that raised up[1453] Jesus from the dead dwell[3611] in you, [b]he that raised up Christ from the dead shall also quicken[2227] your mortal[2349] bodies [I]by his Spirit that [ppt]dwelleth in you.

12 [a]Therefore, brethren, we are debtors,[3781] not to the flesh, [infg]to live[2198] after the flesh.

13 For [a]if ye live after the flesh, ye shall die: but if ye through the Spirit do [b]mortify the deeds[4234] of the body, ye shall live.

14 For [a]as many as [pinp]are led[71] by the [an]Spirit of God, they are the [an]sons[5207] of God.[2316]

15 For [a]ye [ao]have not received[2983] the [an]spirit[4151] of bondage[1397] again [b]to fear;[5401] but ye have received the [anc]Spirit of adoption,[5206] whereby we cry, [d]Abba,[5] Father.[3962]

16 [a]The Spirit itself beareth witness with our spirit,[4151] that we are the [an]children[5043] of God:

17 And if children, then heirs;[2818] [a]heirs of God, and joint-heirs[4789] with Christ; [b]if so be that we suffer with[4841] *him,* that we may be also glorified together.[4888]

The Revelation of God's Glory Through Believers

18 For I reckon that [a]the sufferings[3804] of this present time[2540] *are* not worthy *to be compared* with the glory[1391] which shall be revealed in us.

19 For [a]the earnest expectation[603] of the creature waiteth for[553] the [b]manifestation[602] of the sons[5207] of God.

20 For [a]the creature [aop]was made subject[5293] to vanity,[3153] not willingly, but by reason of him who hath subjected[5293] *the same* in hope,[1680]

21 Because the creature itself also shall be delivered from the bondage[1397] of corruption into the glorious[1391] liberty of the children of God.

22 For we know that [Ia]the whole creation [b]groaneth and travaileth in pain together[4944] until now.

23 And not only *they,* but ourselves also, which have [a]the firstfruits of the Spirit, [b]even we ourselves groan within ourselves, [c]waiting for[553] the adoption,[5206] *to wit,* the [d]redemption[629] of our body.[4983]

24 For we [aop]are saved[4982] by hope:[1680] but [a]hope that [ppp]is seen is not hope: for what a man seeth, why doth he yet hope for?[1679]

25 But if we hope for that we see not, *then* do we with patience wait for[553] *it.*

26 Likewise the Spirit[4151] also

3 [I]Or, *by a sacrifice for sin* [a]Acts 13:39; Rom. 3:20; Heb. 7:18, 19; 10:1, 2, 10, 14 [b]2Cor. 5:21; Gal. 3:13
4 [a]Rom. 8:1
5 [a]John 3:6; 1Cor. 2:14 [b]Gal. 5:22, 25
6 [I]Gr. *the minding of the flesh* [II]Gr. *the minding of the Spirit* [a]Rom. 6:21; 8:7, 13; Gal. 6:8
7 [I]Gr. *the minding of the flesh* [a]James 4:4 [b]1Cor. 2:14
9 [a]1Cor. 3:16; 6:19 [b]John 3:34; Gal. 4:6; Phil. 1:19; 1Pet. 1:11
11 [I]Or, *because of his Spirit* [a]Acts 2:24 [b]Rom. 6:4, 5; 1Cor. 6:14; 2Cor. 4:14; Eph. 2:5
12 [a]Rom. 6:7, 14
13 [a]Rom. 8:6; Gal. 6:8 [b]Eph. 4:22; Col. 3:5
14 [a]Gal. 5:18
15 [a]1Cor. 2:12; Heb. 2:15 [b]2Tim. 1:7; 1John 4:18 [c]Isa. 56:5; Gal. 4:5, 6 [d]Mark 14:36
16 [a]2Cor. 1:22; 5:5; Eph. 1:13; 4:30
17 [a]Acts 26:18; Gal. 4:7 [b]Acts 14:22; Phil. 1:29; 2Tim. 2:11, 12
18 [a]2Cor. 4:17; 1Pet. 1:6, 7; 4:13
19 [a]2Pet. 3:13 [b]1John 3:2
20 [a]Gen. 3:19; Rom. 8:22
22 [I]Or, *every creature* [a]Mark 16:15; Col. 1:23 [b]Jer. 12:11
23 [a]2Cor. 5:5; Eph. 1:14 [b]2Cor. 5:2, 4 [c]Luke 20:36 [d]Luke 21:28; Eph. 4:30
24 [a]2Cor. 5:7; Heb. 11:1

🗝 **8:7** See note on Romans 3:19, 20.

helpeth our infirmities: for [a]we know not what we [aosb]should pray for as we ought: but [b]the Spirit itself maketh intercession[5241] for us with groanings which cannot be uttered.

27 And [a]he that [ppt]searcheth the hearts[2588] knoweth what *is* the mind[5427] of the Spirit, [I]because he maketh intercession[1793] for the saints[40] [b]according to *the will of* God.[2316]

🗝 28 And we know[1492] that all things work together[4903] for good[18] to them that [ppt]love[25] God, to them [a]who are the called[2822] according to *his* purpose.[4286]

29 For whom [a]he [ao]did foreknow,[4267] [b]he also [ao]did predestinate[4309] [c]*to be* conformed[4832] to the image[1504] of his Son,[5207] [d]that he might be the firstborn[4416] among many brethren.[80]

30 Moreover whom he did predestinate, them he also [a]called:[2564] and whom he called, them he also [b]justified:[1344] and whom he justified, them he also [c]glorified.[1392]

Nothing Separates the Believer From God's Love

31 What shall we then say to these things? [a]If God[2316] *be* for us, who *can be* against us?

32 [a]He that spared not his own[2398] Son, but [b]delivered him up for us all, how shall he not with him also freely give[5483] us all things?

🗝 33 Who [ft]shall lay any thing to the charge[1458] of God's elect?[1588] [a]*It is* God that justifieth.

34 [a]Who *is* he that [ppt]condemneth? *It is* Christ[5547] that died,[599] yea rather, that [aptp]is risen again,[1453] [b]who [pin]is even at the right hand[1188] of God, [c]who also maketh intercession[1793] for us.

35 Who shall separate us from the love[26] of Christ?[5547] *shall* tribulation,[2347] or distress,[4730] or persecution, or famine, or nakedness,[1132] or peril, or sword?

36 As it is written, [a]For thy sake we are killed all the day long; we [aop]are accounted[3049] as sheep for the slaughter.

37 [a]Nay, in all these things we are more than conquerors through him that loved[25] us.

38 For I am persuaded, that neither death,[2288] nor life, nor angels, nor [a]principalities,[746] nor powers, nor [pfp]things present,[1764] nor things to come,

39 Nor height, nor depth, nor any other creature,[2937] shall be able to separate us from the love of God, which is in Christ Jesus our Lord.

The People of Israel

9 I [a]say the truth[225] in Christ,[5547] I lie not, my conscience[4893] also bearing me witness in the [an]Holy Ghost,[4151]

2 [a]That I have great heaviness[3077] and continual[88] sorrow in my heart.

3 For [a]I [ipf]could wish that myself were [I]accursed[331] from Christ for my brethren,[80] my kinsmen according to the flesh:[4561]

4 [a]Who are Israelites; [b]to whom *pertaineth* the adoption,[5206] and [c]the glory,[1391] and [d]the [I]covenants,[1242] and [e]the giving of the law, and [f]the service[2999] *of God,* and [g]the promises;

5 [a]Whose *are* the fathers,[3962] and [b]of whom as concerning[2596] the flesh[4561] Christ *came,* [c]who is over all, God blessed[2128] for ever. Amen.[281]

6 [a]Not as though the word[3056] of God [pfi]hath taken none effect. For [b]they *are* not all Israel, which are of Israel:

7 [a]Neither, because they are the seed[4690] of Abraham, *are they* all children:[5043] but, In [b]Isaac shall thy seed be called.

8 That is, They which are the children of the flesh,[4561] these *are* not the

26 [a]Matt. 20:22; James 4:3 [b]Zech. 12:10; Eph. 6:18
27 [I]Or, *that* [a]1Chr. 28:9; Ps. 7:9; Prov. 17:3; Jer. 11:20; 17:10; 20:12; Acts 1:24; 1Thess. 2:4; Rev. 2:23 [b]1John 5:14
28 [a]Rom. 9:11, 23, 24; 2Tim. 1:9
29 [a]Ex. 33:12, 17; Ps. 1:6; Jer. 1:5; Matt. 7:23; Rom. 11:2; 2Tim. 2:19; 1Pet. 1:2 [b]Eph. 1:5, 11 [c]John 17:22; 2Cor. 3:18; Phil. 3:21; 1John 3:2 [d]Col. 1:15, 18; Heb. 1:6; Rev. 1:5
30 [a]Rom. 1:6; 9:24; Eph. 4:4; Heb. 9:15; 1Pet. 2:9 [b]1Cor. 6:11; John 17:22; Eph. 2:6
31 [a]Num. 14:9; Ps. 118:6
32 [a]Rom. 5:6, 10 [b]Rom. 4:25
33 [a]Isa. 50:8, 9; Rev. 12:10, 11
34 [a]Job 34:29 [b]Mark 16:19; Col. 3:1; Heb. 1:3; 8:1; 12:2; 1Pet. 3:22 [c]Heb. 7:25; 9:24; 1John 2:1
36 [a]Ps. 44:22; 1Cor. 15:30, 31; 2Cor. 4:11
37 [a]1Cor. 15:57; 2Cor. 2:14; 1John 4:4; 5:4, 5; Rev. 12:11
38 [a]Eph. 1:21; 6:12; Col. 1:16; 2:15; 1Pet. 3:22

1 [a]Rom. 1:9; 2Cor. 1:23; 11:31; 12:19; Gal. 1:20; Phil. 1:8; 1Tim. 2:7
2 [a]Rom. 10:1
3 [I]Or, *separated* [a]Ex. 32:32
4 [I]Or, *testaments* [a]Deut. 7:6 [b]Ex. 4:22; Deut. 14:1; Jer. 31:9 [c]1Sam. 4:21; 1Kgs. 8:11; Ps. 63:2; 78:61 [d]Acts 3:25; Heb. 8:8-10 [e]Ps. 147:19 [f]Heb. 9:1 [g]Acts 13:32; Rom. 3:2; Eph. 2:12
5 [a]Deut. 10:15; Rom. 11:28 [b]Luke 3:23; Rom. 1:3 [c]Jer. 23:6; John 1:1; Acts 20:28; Heb. 1:8; 1John 5:20
6 [a]Num. 23:19; Rom. 3:3 [b]John 8:39; Rom. 2:28, 29; 4:12, 16; Gal. 6:16
7 [a]Gal. 4:23 [b]Gen. 21:12; Heb. 11:18

🗝 **8:28, 29, 33** See note on Ephesians 1:4, 5.

children of God: but [a]the children of the promise[1860] [pinp]are counted[3049] for the seed.

9 For this *is* the word of promise, [a]At this time[2540] will I come, and Sarah shall have a son.[5207]

10 And not only *this;* but when [a]Rebecca also had[2192] conceived by one, *even* by our father Isaac;

🗝 11 (For *the children* being not yet born, neither [apt]having done[4238] any good[18] or evil, that the purpose[4286] of God according to election[1589] [psa]might stand,[3306] not of works,[2041] but of [a]him that [ppt]calleth;)

12 It was said unto her, [a]The [I]elder [ft]shall serve[1398] the [II]younger.

13 As it is written, [a]Jacob [ao]have I loved,[25] but Esau have I hated.

14 What shall we say then? [a]*Is there* unrighteousness[93] with God? God forbid.

15 For he saith to Moses, [a]I will have mercy on whom I will have mercy, and I will have compassion on whom I will have compassion.

16 So then *it is* not of him that [ppt]willeth, nor of him that [ppt]runneth, but of God that [ppt]sheweth mercy.

🗝 17 For [a]the scripture saith unto Pharaoh, [b]Even for this same purpose [ao]have I raised thee up,[1825] that I [asbm]might shew my power in thee, and that my name might be declared[1229] throughout all the earth.[1093]

18 Therefore hath he mercy on whom he will *have mercy,* and whom he will he hardeneth.[4645]

19 Thou wilt say then unto me, Why doth he yet find fault? For [a]who [pfi]hath resisted his will?[1013]

20 Nay but, O man, who art thou that [pptI][a]repliest against[470] God? [b]Shall the thing formed say to him that formed *it,* Why [ao]hast thou made[4160] me thus?

21 Hath not the [a]potter power[1849] over the clay, of the same lump to make [b]one vessel unto honour, and another unto dishonour?[819]

22 *What* if God, willing to shew *his* wrath,[3709] and [ainf]to make his power known,[1107] endured[5342] with much longsuffering [a]the vessels of wrath [pfppI][b]fitted[2675] to destruction:[684]

23 And that he [asba]might make known[1107] [a]the riches of his glory on the vessels of mercy,[1656] which he [ao]had [b]afore prepared unto glory,

24 Even us, whom he [ao]hath called, [a]not of the Jews only, but also of the Gentiles?[1484]

25 As he saith also in Osee, [a]I will call them my people,[2992] which were not my people; and her beloved,[25] which was not beloved.

26 [a]And it shall come to pass, *that* in the place where it was said unto them, Ye *are* not my people; there shall they be called the children of the living[2198] God.

8 [a]Gal. 4:28
9 [a]Gen. 18:10, 14
10 [a]Gen. 25:21
11 [a]Rom. 4:17; 8:28
12 [I]Or, *greater* [II]Or, *lesser* [a]Gen. 25:23
13 [a]Deut. 21:15; Prov. 13:24; Mal. 1:2, 3; Matt. 10:37; Luke 14:26; John 12:25
14 [a]Deut. 32:4; 2Chr. 19:7; Job 8:3; 34:10; Ps. 92:15
15 [a]Ex. 33:19
17 [a]Gal. 3:8, 22 [b]Ex. 9:16
19 [a]2Chr. 20:6; Job 9:12; 23:13; Dan. 4:35
20 [I]Or, *answerest again,* or, *disputest with God* [a]Job 33:13 [b]Isa. 29:16; 45:9; 64:8
21 [a]Prov. 16:4; Jer. 18:6 [b]2Tim. 2:20
22 [I]Or, *made up* [a]1Thess. 5:9 [b]1Pet. 2:8; Jude 1:4
23 [a]Rom. 2:4; Eph. 1:7; Col. 1:27 [b]Rom. 8:28-30
24 [a]Rom. 3:29
25 [a]Hos. 2:23; 1Pet. 2:10
26 [a]Hos. 1:10

🗝 **9:11–13** See notes on Psalm 5:5 and Ephesians 1:4, 5.

🗝 **9:17** God said of Pharaoh, in Exodus 4:21 and 7:13, "I will harden his heart, that he should not let the people go . . . And he hardened Pharaoh's heart, that he hearkened not unto him." The same phrase occurs in Exodus 9:12: "And the LORD hardened the heart of Pharaoh." However, the Scripture also declares that Pharaoh hardened his own heart (Ex. 8:15, 32; 9:34). Paul is here answering the objection in verse fourteen that some might bring against his doctrine, "Is there unrighteousness with God?" God claims and exercises His right, by reason of His sovereignty over humankind, to dispense His mercy as He sees fit (cf. Ex. 33:19). He did so in the case of Pharaoh. It is not that Pharaoh was "beyond" the help of God's mercy, nor that God made him wicked, but simply that God withheld His mercy and left him to his own wickedness.

In ancient Egypt, the Pharaohs themselves were frequently reverenced as gods. The Pharaoh that ruled during the time of Moses seems to have regarded himself as a deity capable of resisting Jehovah Himself. His attitude toward God is expressed in Exodus 5:2, "Who is the LORD, that I should obey his voice to let Israel go?" God exalted Himself by His mighty judgments upon Egypt and His mighty deliverance of Israel. Even the Philistines in Canaan knew about these judgments and feared God as a result (1 Sam. 4:8).

27 Esaias also crieth concerning Israel, [a]Though the number of the children[5207] of Israel be as the sand of the sea, [b]a remnant[2640] [fp]shall be saved:[4982]

28 For he [ppt]will finish[4931] [I]the work, and [ppt]cut *it* short in righteousness:[1343] [a]because a short work will the Lord make upon the earth.

29 And as Esaias said before, [a]Except the Lord[2962] of Sabaoth[4519] [ao]had left us a seed, [b]we [aop]had been as Sodoma, and [aop]been made like unto Gomorrha.

The Gentiles Are Called

30 What shall we say then? [a]That the Gentiles, which [ppt]followed not after righteousness,[1343] [ao]have attained[2638] to righteousness, [b]even the righteousness which is of faith.[4102]

31 But Israel, [a]which [ppt]followed after the law[3551] of righteousness, [ao][b]hath not attained[5348] to the law of righteousness.

32 Wherefore? Because *they sought it* not by faith, but as it were by the [an]works of the [an]law. For [a]they stumbled at[4350] that stumblingstone;

33 As it is written, [a]Behold, I lay in Sion a stumblingstone and rock of offence:[4625] and [b]whosoever [ppt]believeth[4100] on him shall not be [I]ashamed.

10 Brethren,[80] my heart's[2588] desire and prayer to God for Israel is, that they might be saved.[1519,4991]

2 For I bear them record [a]that they have a zeal[2205] of God, but not according to knowledge.[1922]

3 For they [ppt]being ignorant[50] of [a]God's righteousness,[1343] and [ppt]going about [ainf]to establish their own [b]righteousness,[1343] [aop]have not submitted[5293] themselves unto the righteousness of God.

4 For [a]Christ[5547] *is* the end[5056] of the law[3551] for righteousness to every one that [ppt]believeth.[4100]

The Method of Justification

5 For Moses describeth the righteousness which is of the law, [a]That the man which [apt]doeth those things [fm]shall live[2198] by them.

6 But the righteousness[1343] which is of faith[4102] speaketh on this wise, [a]Say not in thine heart,[2588] Who shall ascend into heaven?[3772] (that is, to bring Christ down[2609] *from above:*)

7 Or, Who shall descend into the deep? (that is, [ainf]to bring up Christ again[321] from the dead.)

8 But what saith it? [a]The word is nigh thee, *even* in thy mouth, and in thy heart:[2588] that is, the word[4487] of faith, which we preach;[2784]

🔑 9 That [a]if thou [asba]shalt confess[3670] with thy mouth the Lord[2962] Jesus, and [asba]shalt believe[4100] in thine heart that God [ao]hath raised[1453] him from the dead, thou [fp]shalt be saved.[4982]

10 For with the heart man believeth unto righteousness;[1343] and with the mouth confession is made[3670] unto salvation.[4991]

11 For the scripture saith, [a]Whosoever [ppt]believeth on him shall not be ashamed.

12 For [a]there is no difference between the Jew and the Greek: for [b]the same Lord over all [ppt][c]is rich unto all that [ppt]call upon[1941] him.

13 [a]For whosoever shall call [b]upon the name of the Lord shall be saved.

14 How then shall they call on him in whom they [ao]have not believed?[4100] and how shall they believe in him of whom they [ao]have not heard?[191] and how shall they hear [a]without a [ppt]preacher?[2784]

15 And how [ft]shall they preach,[2784] except they [asbp]be sent?[649] as it is written, [a]How beautiful[5611] are the feet of them that [ppt]preach the gospel[2097] of peace,[1515] and [ppt]bring glad tidings of good things![18]

16 But [a]they [ao]have not all obeyed[5219]

27 [a]Isa. 10:22, 23 [b]Rom. 11:5
28 [I]Or, *the account* [a]Isa. 28:22
29 [a]Isa. 1:9; Lam. 3:22 [b]Isa. 13:19; Jer. 50:40
30 [a]Rom. 4:11; 10:20 [b]Rom. 1:17
31 [a]Rom. 10:2; 11:7 [b]Gal. 5:4
32 [a]Luke 2:34; 1Cor. 1:23
33 [I]Or, *confounded* [a]Ps. 118:22; Isa. 8:14; 28:16; Matt. 21:42; Rom. 10:11; 1Pet. 2:6-8

2 [a]Acts 21:20; 22:3; Gal. 1:14; 4:17; Rom. 9:31
3 [a]Rom. 1:17; 9:30 [b]Phil. 3:9
4 [a]Matt. 5:17; Gal. 3:24
5 [a]Lev. 18:5; Neh. 9:29; Ezek. 20:11, 13, 21; Gal. 3:12
6 [a]Deut. 30:12, 13
8 [a]Deut. 30:14
9 [a]Matt. 10:32; Luke 12:8; Acts 8:37
11 [a]Isa. 28:16; 49:23; Jer. 17:7; Rom. 9:33
12 [a]Acts 15:9; Rom. 3:22; Gal. 3:28 [b]Acts 10:36; Rom. 3:29; 1Tim. 2:5 [c]Eph. 1:7; 2:4, 7
13 [a]Joel 2:32; Acts 2:21 [b]Acts 9:14
14 [a]Titus 1:3
15 [a]Isa. 52:7; Nah. 1:15
16 [a]Rom. 3:3; Heb. 4:2

🔑 **10:9** See note on Mark 3:28, 29.

the gospel.2098 For Esaias saith, [b]Lord, who [ao]hath believed [I]our [II]report?189

17 So then faith *cometh* by hearing,189 and hearing by the word4487 of God.2316

18 But I say, [ao]Have they not heard?191 Yes verily,3304 [a]their sound went into all the earth,1093 [b]and their words4487 unto the ends of the world.3625

19 But I say, Did not Israel know?1097 First Moses saith, [a]I [ft]will provoke you to jealousy3863 by *them that are* no people, *and* by a [b]foolish801 nation I will anger you.

20 But Esaias is very bold, and saith, [a]I was found of them that [ppt]sought me not; I was made manifest unto them that [ppt]asked not after me.

21 But to Israel he saith, [a]All day long I [ao]have stretched forth my hands unto a [ppt]disobedient544 and [ppt]gainsaying483 people.2992

God's Chosen People

11 I say then, [aom][a]Hath God cast away683 his people? God forbid.3361,1096 For [b]I also am an Israelite, of the seed of Abraham, *of* the tribe of Benjamin.

2 God hath not cast away his people2992 which he [a]foreknew.4267 Wot1492 ye not what the scripture saith of Elias? how he maketh intercession1793 to God against Israel, saying,

3 [a]Lord, they have killed thy prophets,4396 and digged down thine altars; and I [aop]am left alone, and they seek my life.5590

4 But what saith the answer of God5538 unto him? [a]I have reserved to myself seven thousand men, who have not bowed the knee to *the image of* Baal.

5 [a]Even so then at this present time2540 also there [pf]is a remnant3005 according to the election1589 of grace.5485

6 And [a]if by grace, then *is it* no more of works:2041 otherwise grace5485 is no more grace. But if *it be* of works, then is it no more grace:5485 otherwise work is no more work.

16 [I]Gr. *the hearing of us?* [II]Or, *preaching?* [b]Isa. 53:1; John 12:38
18 [a]Ps. 19:4; Matt. 24:14; 28:19; Mark 16:15; Col. 1:6, 23 [b]1Kgs. 18:10; Matt. 4:8
19 [a]Deut. 32:21; Rom. 11:11 [b]Titus 3:3
20 [a]Isa. 65:1; Rom. 9:30
21 [a]Isa. 65:2
1 [a]1Sam. 12:22; Jer. 31:37 [b]2Cor. 11:22; Phil. 3:5
2 [a]Rom. 8:29
3 [a]1Kgs. 19:10, 14
4 [a]1Kgs. 19:18
5 [a]Rom. 9:27
6 [a]Rom. 4:4, 5; Gal. 5:4; Deut. 9:4, 5
7 [I]Or, *hardened* [a]Rom. 9:31; 10:3 [b]2Cor. 3:14
8 [I]Or, *remorse* [a]Isa. 29:10 [b]Deut. 29:4; Isa. 6:9; Jer. 5:21; Ezek. 12:2; Matt. 13:14; John 12:40; Acts 28:26, 27
9 [a]Ps. 69:22
10 [a]Ps. 69:23
11 [a]Acts 13:46; 18:6; 22:18, 21; 28:24, 28; Rom. 10:19
12 [I]Or, *decay,* or, *loss*
13 [a]Acts 9:15; 13:2; 22:21; Rom. 15:16; Gal. 1:16; 2:2, 7-9; Eph. 3:8; 1Tim. 2:7; 2Tim. 1:11
14 [a]1Cor. 7:16; 9:22; 1Tim. 4:16; James 5:20
16 [a]Lev. 23:10; Num. 15:18-21
17 [I]Or, *for them* [a]Jer. 11:16 [b]Acts 2:39; Eph. 2:12, 13
18 [a]1Cor. 10:12

7 What then? [a]Israel [ao]hath not obtained2013 that which he seeketh for; but the election1589 hath obtained it, and the rest [aop]were [I][b]blinded.4456

8 (According as it is written, [a]God2316 [ao]hath given them the spirit4151 of [I]slumber, [b]eyes that they [infg]should not see,991 and ears that they [infg]should not hear;191) unto this day.

9 And David saith, [a]Let their table be made a snare, and a trap, and a stumblingblock,4625 and a recompence unto them:

10 [aipp][a]Let their eyes be darkened,4654 that they [infg]may not see,991 and [aim]bow down their back alway.

11 I say then, [ao]Have they stumbled4417 that they [aosb]should fall? God forbid:3361,1096 but *rather* [a]through their fall3900 salvation4991 *is come* unto the Gentiles,1484 for [aies]to provoke them to jealousy.3863

12 Now if the fall of them *be* the riches of the world,2889 and the [I]diminishing of them the riches4149 of the Gentiles; how much more their fulness?4138

Two Kinds of Branches

13 For I speak to you Gentiles, inasmuch as [a]I am the apostle652 of the Gentiles, I magnify1392 mine office:1248

14 If by any means I may provoke to emulation *them which are* my flesh,4561 and [asba][a]might save4982 some of them.

15 For if the casting away of them *be* the reconciling2643 of the world, what *shall* the receiving4356 *of them be,* but life2222 from the dead?3498

16 For if [a]the firstfruit536 *be* holy,40 the lump5445 *is* also *holy:* and if the root *be* holy, so *are* the branches.

17 And if [a]some of the branches be [aop]broken off, [b]and thou, being a wild olive tree, wert graffed in1461 [I]among them, and with them partakest of the root and fatness of the olive tree;

18 [pim][a]Boast not against the branches. But if thou boast, thou bearest not the root, but the root thee.

19 Thou wilt say then, The branches

[aop]were broken off, that I might be graffed in.

20 Well; because of unbelief[570] they were broken off, and thou [pf]standest by faith.[4102] [a]Be not highminded, but [b]fear:[5399]

21 For if God spared not the natural branches,[2798] *take heed* lest he also spare not thee.

22 Behold therefore the goodness and severity[663] of God: on them which [apt]fell,[4098] severity;[663] but toward thee, goodness,[5544] [a]if thou [aosb]continue in *his* goodness: otherwise [b]thou also shalt be cut off.

23 And they also, [a]if they abide not still in unbelief, shall be graffed in: for God is able [ainf]to graff them in again.

24 For if thou wert cut out[1581] of the olive tree which is wild by nature, and wert graffed contrary to nature into a good olive tree: how much more shall these, which be the natural *branches,* be graffed into their own olive tree?

"All Israel Shall Be Saved"

25 For I would not, brethren,[80] that ye should be ignorant[50] of this mystery,[3466] lest ye should be [a]wise[5429] in your own conceits; that [I][b]blindness[4457] in part is happened to Israel, [c]until the fulness[4138] of the Gentiles [asba]be come in.

26 And so all Israel [fp]shall be saved:[4982] as it is written, [a]There shall come out of Sion the [ppt]Deliverer,[4506] and shall turn away ungodliness[763] from Jacob:

27 [a]For this *is* my covenant[1242] unto them, when I shall take away their sins.[266]

28 As concerning[2596] the gospel,[2098] *they are* enemies for your sakes: but as touching[2596] the election,[1589] *they are* [a]beloved[27] for the fathers' sakes.

29 For the gifts[5486] and calling[2821] of God *are* [a]without repentance.

20 [a]Rom. 12:16 [b]Prov. 28:14; Isa. 66:2; Phil. 2:12
22 [a]1Cor. 15:2; Heb. 3:6, 14 [b]John 15:2
23 [a]2Cor. 3:16
25 [I]Or, *hardness* [a]Rom. 12:16 [b]Rom. 11:7; 2Cor. 3:14 [c]Luke 21:24; Rev. 7:9
26 [a]Isa. 59:20; Ps. 14:7
27 [a]Isa. 27:9; Jer. 31:31-34; Heb. 8:8; 10:16
28 [a]Deut. 7:8; 9:5; 10:15
29 [a]Num. 23:19
30 [I]Or, *obeyed* [a]Eph. 2:2; Col. 3:7
31 [I]Or, *obeyed*
32 [I]Or, *shut them all up together* [a]Rom. 3:9; Gal. 3:22
33 [a]Ps. 36:6 [b]Job 11:7; Ps. 92:5
34 [a]Job 15:8; Isa. 40:13; Jer. 23:18; 1Cor. 2:16 [b]Job 36:22
35 [a]Job 35:7; 41:11
36 [I]Gr. *him* [a]1Cor. 8:6; Col. 1:16 [b]Gal. 1:5; 1Tim. 1:17; 2Tim. 4:18; Heb. 13:21; 1Pet. 5:11; 2Pet. 3:18; Jude 1:25; Rev. 1:6

1 [a]2Cor. 10:1 [b]1Pet. 2:5 [c]Ps. 50:13, 14; Rom. 6:13, 16, 19; 1Cor. 6:13, 20 [d]Heb. 10:20
2 [a]1Pet. 1:14; 1John 2:15 [b]Eph. 1:18; 4:23; Col. 1:21, 22; 3:10 [c]Eph. 5:10, 17; 1Thess. 4:3
3 [I]Gr. *to sobriety* [a]Rom. 1:5; 15:15; 1Cor. 3:10; 15:10; Gal. 2:9; Eph. 3:2, 7, 8 [b]Prov. 25:27; Eccl. 7:16; Rom. 11:20 [c]1Cor. 12:7, 11; Eph. 4:7
4 [a]1Cor. 12:12; Eph. 4:16

30 For as ye [a]in times past have not [I]believed[544] God, yet [aop]have now obtained mercy[1653] through their unbelief:[543]

31 Even so [ao]have these also now not [I]believed,[544] that through your mercy[1656] they also [asbp]may obtain mercy.

32 For [a]God [ao]hath [I]concluded them all in unbelief, that he [asba]might have mercy upon all.

33 O the depth of the riches both of the wisdom[4678] and knowledge of God![2316] [a]how unsearchable *are* his judgments,[2917] and [b]his ways past finding out!

34 [a]For who hath known the mind of the Lord?[2962] or [b]who hath been his counselor?

35 Or [a]who hath first given to him, and it shall be recompensed unto him again?

36 For [a]of him, and through him, and to him, *are* all things: [b]to [I]whom *be* glory[1391] for ever. Amen.[281]

Exhortation to Practical Living

12 I [a]beseech[3870] you therefore, brethren,[80] by the mercies[3628] of God, [b]that ye [ainfc]present your bodies [d]a living[2198] sacrifice,[2378] holy,[40] acceptable[2101] unto God, *which is* your reasonable[3050] service.[2999]

2 And [pim][a]be not conformed[4964] to this world: but [pim][b]be ye transformed[3339] by the renewing[342] of your mind,[3563] that ye [aies]may [c]prove what *is* that good,[18] and acceptable,[2101] and perfect,[5046] will[2307] of God.

3 For I say, [a]through the grace[5485] given unto me, to every man that is among you, [b]not [pinf]to think *of himself* more highly than he ought [pinf]to think;[5426] but [pinf]to think[5426] [I]soberly,[4993] according as God [ao]hath dealt [c]to every man the measure of faith.[4102]

4 For [a]as we have many members in one body,[4983] and all members have not the same office:[4234]

12:3 See note on 1 Corinthians 4:6, 7.

5 So [a]we, *being* many, are one
body[4983] in Christ,[5547] and every one
members one of another.
🗝 6 [a]Having then gifts[5486] differing1313
[b]according to the grace[5485] that [aptp]is
given to us, whether [c]prophecy,[4394] *let us*
prophesy according to the proportion[356] of
faith;
7 Or ministry,[1248] *let us wait* on *our*
ministering:[1248] or [a]he that [ppt]teacheth,[1321]
on teaching;[1319]
8 Or [a]he that exhorteth,[3870] on exhortation:[3874] [b]he that [I]giveth, *let him do*
it [II]with simplicity;[572] [c]he that ruleth, with
diligence; he that sheweth mercy, [d]with
cheerfulness.
9 [a]*Let* love[26] *be* without dissimulation.[505] [ppt b]Abhor[655] that which is
evil;[4190] [ppp]cleave2853 to that which is
good.[18]
10 [a]*Be* kindly affectioned one to another [I]with brotherly love;[5360] [b]in honour
preferring[4285] one another;
11 Not slothful in business; [ppt]fervent
in spirit; serving[1398] the Lord;
12 [a]Rejoicing in hope;[1680] [ppt b]pa-
tient[5278] in tribulation; [c]continuing instant[4342] in prayer;
13 [a]Distributing[2841] to the necessity[5532] of saints;[40] [ppt b]given to hospitality.
14 [a]Bless[2127] them which [ppt]persecute
you: bless, and curse[2672] not.
15 [a]Rejoice with them that [ppt]do rejoice, and weep with them that [ppt]weep.
16 [a]*Be* of the same mind one toward
another. [b]Mind[5426] not high things, but
[pppI]condescend to men of low estate.
[pim c]Be not wise[5429] in your own conceits.
17 [ppt a]Recompense to no man evil for
evil. [ppt b]Provide[4306] things honest in the
sight of all men.[444]
18 If it be possible, as much as lieth
in you, [ppt a]live peaceably with all men.
🗝 19 Dearly beloved,[27] [ppt a]avenge[1556]
not yourselves, but *rather* [aim]give place
unto wrath:[3709] for it is written, [b]Ven-
geance[1557] *is* mine; I will repay, saith the
Lord.
20 [a]Therefore if thine enemy
[psa]hunger, [pim]feed him; if he thirst, [pim]give
him drink:4222 for in so doing thou shalt
heap coals of fire on his head.
21 [pim]Be not overcome3528 of evil,[2556]
but [pim]overcome evil with good.[18]

"Subject Unto the Higher Powers"

13 🗝 [pim]Let every soul [a]be subject[5293] unto the higher pow-
ers.[1849] For [b]there is no power but of
God:[2316] the powers that be are
[I]ordained[5021] of God.
2 Whosoever therefore [ppt]resisteth
[a]the power, resisteth the ordinance[1296] of
God: and they that resist shall receive to
themselves damnation.[2917]
3 For rulers are not a terror to good[18]
works, but to the evil.[2556] Wilt thou then
not [pinf]be afraid[5399] of the power? [pim a]do
that which is good, and thou shalt have
praise of the same:
4 For he is the minister[1249] of God to
thee for good. But if thou [psa]do that
which is evil, [pim]be afraid; for he beareth
not the sword in vain: for he is the minister of God, a revenger[1558] to *execute*
wrath[3709] upon him that [ppt]doeth[4238] evil.
5 Wherefore [a]*ye* must needs[318] [pip]be
subject, not only for wrath, [b]but also for
conscience[4893] sake.
6 For for this cause pay[5055] ye tribute[5411] also: for they are God's ministers,3011 [ppt]attending continually[4342]
upon this very thing.
7 [a]Render therefore to all their

5 [a]1Cor. 10:17; 12:20, 27; Eph. 1:23; 4:25
6 [a]1Cor. 12:4; 1Pet. 4:10, 11 [b]Rom. 12:3 [c]Acts 11:27; 1Cor. 12:10, 28; 13:2; 14:1, 6, 29, 31
7 [a]Acts 13:1; Gal. 6:6; Eph. 4:11; 1Tim. 5:17
8 I Or, *imparteth* II Or, *liberally,* 2Cor. 8:2 [a]Acts 15:32; 1Cor. 14:3 [b]Matt. 6:1, 2, 3 [c]Acts 20:28; 1Tim. 5:17; Heb. 13:7, 24; 1Pet. 5:2 [d]2Cor. 9:7
9 [a]1Tim. 1:5; 1Pet. 1:22 [b]Ps. 34:14; 36:4; 97:10; Amos 5:15
10 I Or, *in the love of the brethren* [a]Heb. 13:1; 1Pet. 1:22; 2:17; 3:8; 2Pet. 1:7 [b]Phil. 2:3; 1Pet. 5:5
12 [a]Luke 10:20; Rom. 5:2; 15:13; Phil. 3:1; 4:4; 1Thess. 5:16; Heb. 3:6; 1Pet. 4:13 [b]Luke 21:19; 1Tim. 6:11; Heb. 10:36; 12:1; James 1:4; 5:7; 1Pet. 2:19, 20 [c]Luke 18:1; Acts 2:42; 12:5; Eph. 6:18; Col. 4:2; 1Thess. 5:17
13 [a]1Cor. 16:1; 2Cor. 9:1, 12; Heb. 6:10; 13:16; 1John 3:17 [b]1Tim. 3:2; Titus 1:8; Heb. 13:2; 1Pet. 4:9
14 [a]Matt. 5:44; Luke 6:28; 23:34; Acts 7:60; 1Cor. 4:12; 1Pet. 2:23; 3:9
15 [a]1Cor. 12:26
16 I Or, *be contented with mean things* [a]Rom. 15:5; 1Cor. 1:10; Phil. 2:2; 3:16; 1Pet. 3:8 [b]Ps. 131:1, 2; Jer. 45:5 [c]Prov. 3:7; 26:12; Isa. 5:21; Rom. 11:25
17 [a]Prov. 20:22; Matt. 5:39; 1Thess. 5:15; 1Pet. 3:9 [b]Rom. 14:16; 2Cor. 8:21
18 [a]Mark 9:50; Rom. 14:19; Heb. 12:14
19 [a]Lev. 19:18; Prov. 24:29; Rom. 12:17 [b]Deut. 32:35; Heb. 10:30
20 [a]Ex. 23:4, 5; Prov. 25:21, 22; Matt. 5:44
1 I Or, *ordered* [a]Titus 3:1; 1Pet. 2:13 [b]Prov. 8:15, 16; Dan. 2:21; 4:32; John 19:11
2 [a]Titus 3:1
3 [a]1Pet. 2:14; 3:13
5 [a]Eccl. 8:2 [b]1Pet. 2:19
7 [a]Matt. 22:21; Mark 12:17; Luke 20:25

🗝 **12:6–8** See note on 1 Corinthians 12:1–11.
🗝 **12:19–21** See note on Psalm 109:1–29.
🗝 **13:1** See note on 1 Peter 2:17.

dues:[3782] tribute to whom tribute *is due;* custom[5056] to whom custom; fear to whom fear; honour to whom honour.

8 Owe no man any thing, but [pinf]to love one another: for [a]he that [ppt]loveth another[2087] [pfi]hath fulfilled[4137] the law.[3551]

9 For this, [a]Thou shalt not commit adultery, Thou shalt not kill, Thou shalt not steal, Thou shalt not bear false witness, Thou [ft]shalt not covet;[1937] and if *there be* any other commandment, it [pinp]is briefly comprehended[346] in this saying, namely, [b]Thou [ft]shalt love[25] thy neighbour[4139] as thyself.

10 Love[26] worketh[2038] no ill[2556] to his neighbour: therefore [a]love *is* the fulfilling[4138] of the law.

🔑 11 And that, knowing the time,[2540] that now *it is* high time [aifp][a]to awake[1453] out of sleep: for now *is* our salvation[4991] nearer than when we believed.[4100]

12 The night [ao]is far spent, the day[2250] [pfi]is at hand: [aosi][a]let us therefore cast off[659] the works of darkness,[4655] and [aosi][b]let us put on[1746] the armour of light.

13 [a]Let us walk [I]honestly, as in the day; [b]not in rioting[2970] and drunkenness,[3178] [c]not in chambering and wantonness,[766] [d]not in strife[2054] and envying.[2205]

14 But [aim][a]put ye on[1746] the Lord Jesus Christ, and [pim][b]make not provision[4307] for the flesh,[4561] to *fulfil* the lusts[1939] *thereof.*

"Why Dost Thou Judge Thy Brother?"

14 Him that [ppt][a]is weak[770] in the faith[4102] [pim]receive ye, *but* [I]not to doubtful[1261] disputations.[1253]

2 For one believeth[4100] that he [ainf][a]may eat all things: another, who [ppt]is weak,[770] eateth herbs.

3 [pim]Let not him that eateth despise[1848] him that [ppt]eateth not; and [a]let not him which eateth not judge[2919] him that eateth: for God [aom]hath received him.

4 [a]Who art thou that [ppt]judgest another man's[245] servant?[3610] to his own[2398] master[2962] he standeth or falleth.[4098] Yea, he [fp]shall be holden up:[2476] for God is able [ainf]to make him stand.[2476]

5 [a]One man esteemeth[2919] one day above another: another esteemeth[2919] every day *alike.* [pim]Let every man be [I]fully persuaded[4135] in his own mind.[3563]

6 He that [ppt][I][a]regardeth the day, regardeth *it* unto the Lord;[2962] and he that [ppt]regardeth not the day, to the Lord he doth not regard *it.* He that eateth, eateth to the Lord, for [b]he [pin]giveth God thanks;[2168] and he that eateth not, to the Lord he eateth not, and giveth God thanks.

7 For [a]none of us liveth[2198] to himself, and no man dieth[599] to himself.

8 For whether we live, we live unto the Lord; and whether we die, we die unto the Lord: whether we live therefore, or die, we are the Lord's.

9 For [a]to this end Christ[5547] both died, and rose,[450] and revived, that he [asba]might be [b]Lord both of the dead[3498] and living.

10 But why [pin]dost thou judge[2919] thy brother? or why [pin]dost thou set at nought[1848] thy brother? for [a]we shall all stand before the judgment seat of Christ.

11 For it is written, [a]As I live, saith the Lord, every knee shall bow to me, and every tongue [fm]shall confess[1843] to God.

12 So then [a]every one of us shall give account[3056] of himself to God.

The Christian's Liberty

13 [aosi]Let us not therefore judge[2919] one another any more: but judge[2919] this rather, that [a]no man [pinf]put a stumblingblock or an occasion to fall[4625] in *his* brother's[80] way.

14 I know, and am persuaded by the

8 [a]Rom. 13:10; Gal. 5:14; Col. 3:14; 1Tim. 1:5; James 2:8
9 [a]Ex. 20:13-17; Deut. 5:17-21; Matt. 19:18 [b]Lev. 19:18; Matt. 22:39; Mark 12:31; Gal. 5:14; James 2:8
10 [a]Matt. 22:40; Rom. 13:8
11 [a]1Cor. 15:34; Eph. 5:14; 1Thess. 5:5, 6
12 [a]Eph. 5:11; Col. 3:8 [b]Eph. 6:13; 1Thess. 5:8
13 [I]Or, *decently* [a]Phil. 4:8; 1Thess. 4:12; 1Pet. 2:12 [b]Prov. 23:20; Luke 21:34; 1Pet. 4:3 [c]1Cor. 6:9; Eph. 5:5 [d]James 3:14
14 [a]Gal. 3:27; Eph. 4:24; Col. 3:10 [b]Gal. 5:16; 1Pet. 2:11

1 [I]Or, *not to judge* his *doubtful thoughts* [a]Rom. 15:1, 7; 1Cor. 8:9, 11; 9:22
2 [a]Rom. 14:14; 1Cor. 10:25; 1Tim. 4:4; Titus 1:15
3 [a]Col. 2:16
4 [a]James 4:12
5 [I]Or, *fully assured* [a]Gal. 4:10; Col. 2:16
6 [I]Or, *observeth* [a]Gal. 4:10 [b]1Cor. 10:31; 1Tim. 4:3
7 [a]1Cor. 6:19, 20; Gal. 2:20; 1Thess. 5:10; 1Pet. 4:2
9 [a]2Cor. 5:15 [b]Acts 10:36
10 [a]Matt. 25:31, 32; Acts 10:42; 17:31; 2Cor. 5:10; Jude 1:14, 15
11 [a]Isa. 45:23; Phil. 2:10
12 [a]Matt. 12:36; Gal. 6:5; 1Pet. 4:5
13 [a]1Cor. 8:9, 13; 10:32

🔑 **13:11** See note on 1 Peter 1:5.

Lord Jesus, [a]that *there is* nothing [I]unclean[2839] of itself: but [b]to him that [ppt]esteemeth[3049] any thing to be [II]unclean, to him *it is* unclean.

15 But if thy brother [pin]be grieved[3076] with *thy* meat, now walkest thou not [I]charitably.[2596,26] [pim][a]Destroy not him with thy meat, for whom Christ died.

16 [a]Let not then your good[18] [pim]be evil spoken of:[987]

17 [a]For the kingdom[932] of God is not meat and drink; but righteousness,[1343] and peace,[1515] and joy[5479] in the [an]Holy Ghost.[4151]

18 For he that in these things [ppt]serveth[1398] Christ [a]*is* acceptable[2101] to God, and approved[1384] of men.

19 [psa][a]Let us therefore follow after[1377] the things which make for peace, and things wherewith [b]one may edify[3619] another.

20 [a]For meat [pim]destroy[2647] not the work[2041] of God. [b]All things indeed *are* pure;[2513] [c]but *it is* evil[2556] for that man who [ppt]eateth with offence.

21 *It is* good neither [ainf]to eat [a]flesh, nor [ainf]to drink wine,[3631] nor *any thing* whereby thy brother stumbleth, or is offended,[4624] or is made weak.

22 Hast thou faith?[4102] have *it* to thyself before God. [a]Happy[3107] *is* he that [ppt]condemneth[2919] not himself in that thing which he alloweth.

23 And he that [ppt][I]doubteth[1252] [pfip]is damned[2632] if he [aosb]eat, because *he eateth* not of faith: for [a]whatsoever *is* not of faith is sin.[266]

Edify One Another

15 We [a]then that are strong ought to bear the [b]infirmities[771] of the weak, and not [pinf]to please ourselves.

2 [pim][a]Let every one of us please[700] *his* neighbour for *his* good[18] [b]to edification.[3619]

3 [a]For even Christ[5547] pleased not himself: but, as it is written, [b]The reproaches of them that [ppt]reproached thee fell on me.

4 For [a]whatsoever things were written aforetime were written for our learning,[1319] that we through patience and comfort[3874] of the scriptures[1124] might have hope.[1680]

5 [a]Now the God of patience and consolation grant you to be likeminded[5426][846] one toward another [I]according to Christ Jesus:

6 That ye may [a]with one mind *and* one mouth glorify[1392] God, even the Father of our Lord Jesus Christ.

7 Wherefore [a]receive ye one another, [b]as Christ also received us to the glory[1391] of God.

8 Now I say that [a]Jesus Christ [pfin]was a minister[1249] of the circumcision[4061] for the truth[225] of God, [aies][b]to confirm[950] the promises[1860] *made* unto the fathers:

9 And [a]that the Gentiles[1484] [ainf]might glorify God for *his* mercy;[1656] as it is written, [b]For this cause I [fm]will confess[1843] to thee among the Gentiles, and sing unto thy name.[3686]

10 And again he saith, [aipp][a]Rejoice,[2165] ye Gentiles, with his people.

11 And again, [pim][a]Praise[134] the Lord, all ye Gentiles; and [aim]laud him, all ye people.

12 And again, Esaias saith, [a]There shall be a root of Jesse, and he that [ppt]shall rise[450] [pinf]to reign over[757] the Gentiles; in him [ft]shall the Gentiles trust.[1679]

13 Now the God of hope[1680] [opt]fill you with all [a]joy and peace in [aie]believing,[4100] that ye [aies]may abound in hope, through the power[1411] of the [an]Holy Ghost.[4151]

Paul's Diligence in Preaching The Gospel

14 And [a]I myself also [pfip]am persuaded of you, my brethren, that ye also are full of goodness,[19] [pfpp][b]filled with all knowledge, able[1410] also [pinf]to admonish[3560] one another.

15 Nevertheless, brethren, I have written the more boldly unto you in some sort, as putting you in mind, [a]because of the grace[5485] that [aptp]is given to me of God,

14 IGr. *common* IIGr. *common* [a]Acts 10:15; Rom. 14:2, 20; 1Cor. 10:25; 1Tim. 4:4; Titus 1:15 [b]1Cor. 8:7, 10
15 IGr. *according to charity* [a]1Cor. 8:11
16 [a]Rom. 12:17
17 [a]1Cor. 8:8
18 [a]2Cor. 8:21
19 [a]Ps. 34:14; Rom. 12:18 [b]Rom. 15:2; 1Cor. 14:12; 1Thess. 5:11
20 [a]Rom. 14:15 [b]Matt. 15:11; Acts 10:15; Rom. 14:14; Titus 1:15 [c]1Cor. 8:9-12
21 [a]1Cor. 8:13
22 [a]1John 3:21
23 IOr, *discerneth and putteth a difference between meats* [a]Titus 1:15

1 [a]Gal. 6:1 [b]Rom. 14:1
2 [a]1Cor. 9:19, 22; 10:24, 33; 13:5; Phil. 2:4, 5
3 [a]Matt. 26:39; John 5:30; 6:38 [b]Ps. 69:9
4 [a]Rom. 4:23, 24; 1Cor. 9:9, 10; 10:11; 2Tim. 3:16, 17
5 IOr, *after the example of* [a]Rom. 12:16; 1Cor. 1:10; Phil. 3:16
6 [a]Acts 4:24, 32
7 [a]Rom. 14:1, 3 [b]Rom. 5:2
8 [a]Matt. 15:24; John 1:11; Acts 3:25, 26; 13:46 [b]Rom. 3:3; 2Cor. 1:20
9 [a]John 10:16; Rom. 9:23 [b]Ps. 18:49
10 [a]Deut. 32:43
11 [a]Ps. 117:1
12 [a]Isa. 11:1, 10; Rev. 5:5; 22:16
13 [a]Rom. 12:12; 14:17
14 [a]2Pet. 1:12; 1John 2:21 [b]1Cor. 8:1, 7, 10
15 [a]Rom. 1:5; 12:3; Gal. 1:15; Eph. 3:7, 8

16 That [a]I [aies]should be the minister[3011] of Jesus Christ to the Gentiles,[1484] ministering the gospel[2098] of God, that the [I][b]offering up of the Gentiles might be acceptable,[2144] [pfpp]being sanctified[37] by the Holy Ghost.

17 I have therefore whereof I may glory through Jesus Christ [a]in those things which pertain to God.

18 For I will not dare [pinf]to speak of any of those things [a]which Christ [aom]hath not wrought[2716] by me, [b]to make the Gentiles obedient,[5218,1519] by word and deed,[2041]

19 [a]Through mighty[1411] signs[4592] and wonders,[5059] by the power[1411] of the Spirit[4151] of God; so that from Jerusalem, and round about unto Illyricum, I [pfin]have fully preached[4137] the gospel of Christ.

20 Yea, so [ppt]have I strived[5389] [pinf]to preach the gospel,[2097] not where Christ [aop]was named, [a]lest I [psa]should build upon another man's foundation:

21 But as it is written, [a]To whom he was not spoken of, they shall see: and they that have not heard shall understand.

22 For which cause also [a]I [ipf]have been [I]much hindered[1465] from coming to you.

23 But now having no more place in these parts, and [a]having a great desire these many years to come unto you;

24 Whensoever I take my journey into Spain, I will come to you: for I trust to see you in my journey, [a]and to be brought on my way thitherward[1563] by you, if first I be somewhat filled [I][b]with your *company.*

25 But now [a]I go unto Jerusalem to [ppt]minister unto[1247] the saints.[40]

26 For [a]it [ao]hath pleased[2106] them of Macedonia and Achaia to make a certain contribution[2842] for the poor saints which are at Jerusalem.

27 It hath pleased them verily;[1063] and their debtors they are. For [a]if the Gentiles [ao]have been made partakers[2841]

16 [I]Or, *sacrificing* [a]Rom. 11:13; Gal. 2:7, 8, 9; 1Tim. 2:7; 2Tim. 1:11 [b]Isa. 66:20; Phil. 2:17
17 [a]Heb. 5:1
18 [a]Acts 21:19; Gal. 2:8 [b]Rom. 1:5; 16:26
19 [a]Acts 19:11; 2Cor. 12:12
20 [a]2Cor. 10:13, 15, 16
21 [a]Isa. 52:15
22 [I]Or, *many ways,* or, *oftentimes* [a]Rom. 1:13; 1Thess. 2:17, 18
23 [a]Acts 19:21; Rom. 1:11; 15:32
24 [I]Gr. *with you* [a]Acts 15:3 [b]Rom. 15:32
25 [a]Acts 19:21; 20:22; 24:17
26 [a]1Cor. 16:1, 2; 2Cor. 8:1; 9:2, 12
27 [a]Rom. 11:17 [b]1Cor. 9:11; Gal. 6:6
28 [a]Phil. 4:17
29 [a]Rom. 1:11
30 [a]Phil. 2:1 [b]2Cor. 1:11; Col. 4:12
31 [I]Or, *are disobedient* [a]2Thess. 3:2 [b]2Cor. 8:4
32 [a]Rom. 1:10 [b]Acts 18:21; 1Cor. 4:19; James 4:15 [c]1Cor. 16:18; 2Cor. 7:13; 2Tim. 1:16; Phile. 1:7, 20
33 [a]Rom. 16:20; 1Cor. 14:33; 2Cor. 13:11; Phil. 4:9; 1Thess. 5:23; 2Thess. 3:16; Heb. 13:20

1 [a]Acts 18:18
2 [a]Phil. 2:29; 3John 1:5, 6
3 [a]Acts 18:2, 18, 26; 2Tim. 4:19
5 [a]1Cor. 16:19; Col. 4:15; Phile. 1:2 [b]1Cor. 16:15

of their spiritual things, [b]their duty is also to minister[3008] unto them in carnal things.[4559]

28 When therefore I [apt]have performed[2005] this, and [apt]have sealed to them [a]this fruit, I will come by you into Spain.

29 [a]And I am sure that, when I come unto you, I shall come in the fulness[4138] of the blessing[2129] of the gospel of Christ.

30 Now I beseech you, brethren, for the Lord Jesus Christ's sake, and [a]for the love[26] of the Spirit,[4151] [b]that ye [ainf]strive together with[4865] me in *your* prayers to God for me;

31 [a]That I [asbp]may be delivered[4506] from them that [ppt][I]do not believe[544] in Judaea; and that [b]my service which *I have* for Jerusalem [asbm]may be[1096] accepted[2144] of the saints;

32 [a]That I may come unto you with joy [b]by the will of God, and may with you be [c]refreshed.

33 Now [a]the God of peace[1515] *be* with you all. Amen.[281]

Greetings

16 ⊶I commend[4921] unto you Phebe our sister, which is a servant[1249] of the church[1577] which is at [a]Cenchrea:

2 [a]That ye [asbm]receive[4327] her in the Lord, as becometh saints,[40] and that ye [aosb]assist her in whatsoever business she [psa]hath need[5535] of you: for she [aop]hath been a succourer[4368] of many, and of myself also.

3 Greet [a]Priscilla and Aquila my helpers in Christ Jesus:

4 Who have for my life[5590] laid down their own necks: unto whom not only I [pin]give thanks,[2168] but also all the churches of the Gentiles.

5 Likewise *greet* [a]the church[1577] that is in their house. Salute[782] my wellbeloved Epaenetus, who is [b]the firstfruits[536] of Achaia unto Christ.

⊶ **16:1–4** See note on 1 Timothy 2:9–15.

6 Greet Mary, who bestowed much labour on us.

7 Salute Andronicus and Junia, my kinsmen, and my fellowprisoners, who are of note among the apostles,[652] who also [a]were in Christ before me.

8 Greet Amplias my beloved in the Lord.

9 Salute Urbane, our helper in Christ, and Stachys my beloved.

10 Salute Apelles approved[1384] in Christ. Salute them which are of Aristobulus' *household.*

11 Salute Herodion my kinsman. Greet them that be of the *household* of Narcissus, which are in the Lord.

12 Salute Tryphena and Tryphosa, who [ppt]labour in the Lord. Salute the beloved Persis, which laboured much in the Lord.

13 Salute Rufus [a]chosen in the Lord, and his mother and mine.

14 Salute Asyncritus, Phlegon, Hermas, Patrobas, Hermes, and the brethren[80] which are with them.

15 Salute Philologus, and Julia, Nereus, and his sister, and Olympas, and all the saints[40] which are with them.

16 [a]Salute one another with an holy[40] kiss. The churches[1577] of Christ salute you.

Exhortation to Unity

17 Now I beseech you, brethren, [pinf]mark[4648] them [a]which [ppt]cause divisions[1370] and offences contrary to the doctrine which ye [ao]have learned;[3129] and [aimb]avoid them.

18 For they that are such serve[1398] not our Lord Jesus Christ, but [a]their own belly; and [b]by good words and fair speeches[2129] deceive the hearts of the simple.[172]

19 For [a]your obedience[5218] [ao]is come abroad unto all *men.* I am glad therefore on your behalf: but yet I would have you [b]wise unto that which is good,[18] and [l]simple[185] concerning evil.

20 And [a]the God of peace[1515] [b]shall [l]bruise Satan under your feet shortly. [c]The grace of our Lord Jesus Christ *be* with you. Amen.[281]

21 [a]Timotheus my workfellow, and [b]Lucius, and [c]Jason, and [d]Sosipater, my kinsmen, salute you.

22 I Tertius, who wrote *this* epistle,[1992] salute you in the Lord.

23 [a]Gaius mine host, and of the whole church,[1577] saluteth you. [b]Erastus the chamberlain[3623] of the city saluteth you, and Quartus a brother.

24 [a]The grace of our Lord Jesus Christ *be* with you all. Amen.

25 Now [a]to him that is of [ppt]power [ainf]to stablish you [b]according to my gospel,[2098] and the preaching[2782] of Jesus Christ, [c]according to the revelation[602] of the mystery,[3466] [d]which [pfpp]was kept secret since the world began,

26 But [a]now [aptp]is made manifest,[5319] and by the scriptures[1124] of the prophets,[4397] according to the commandment[2003] of the everlasting[166] God, [aptp]made known[1107] to all nations for [b]the obedience[5218] of faith:[4102]

27 To [a]God only wise,[4680] *be* glory[1391] through Jesus Christ for ever. Amen.

7 [a]Gal. 1:22
13 [a]2John 1:1
16 [a]1Cor. 16:20; 2Cor. 13:12; 1Thess. 5:26; 1Pet. 5:14
17 [a]Acts 15:1, 5, 24; 1Tim. 6:3 [b]1Cor. 5:9, 11; 2Thess. 3:6, 14; 2Tim. 3:5; Titus 3:10; 2John 1:10
18 [a]Phil. 3:19; 1Tim. 6:5 [b]Col. 2:4; 2Tim. 3:6; Titus 1:10; 2Pet. 2:3
19 [l]Or, *harmless* [a]Rom. 1:8 [b]Matt. 10:16; 1Cor. 14:20
20 [l]Or, *tread* [a]Rom. 15:33 [b]Gen. 3:15 [c]Rom. 16:24; 1Cor. 16:23; 2Cor. 13:14; Phil. 4:23; 1Thess. 5:28; 2Thess. 3:18; Rev. 22:21
21 [a]Acts 16:1; Phil. 2:19; Col. 1:1; 1Thess. 3:2; 1Tim. 1:2; Heb. 13:23 [b]Acts 13:1 [c]Acts 17:5 [d]Acts 20:4
23 [a]1Cor. 1:14 [b]Acts 19:22; 2Tim. 4:20
24 [a]Rom. 16:20; 1Thess. 5:28
25 [a]Eph. 3:20; 1Thess. 3:13; 2Thess. 2:17; 3:3; Jude 1:24 [b]Rom. 2:16 [c]Eph. 1:9; 3:3-5; Col. 1:27 [d]1Cor. 2:7; Eph. 3:5, 9; Col. 1:26
26 [a]Eph. 1:9; 2Tim. 1:10; Titus 1:2, 3; 1Pet. 1:20 [b]Acts 6:7; Rom. 1:5; 15:18
27 [a]1Tim. 1:17; 6:16; Jude 1:25

16:23 See note on 3 John 1:1.

The First Epistle of Paul to the

CORINTHIANS

Corinth was an important cosmopolitan city located in the Roman province of Achaia (the southern part of modern-day Greece) on a large isthmus about fifty miles west of Athens. It was situated along a major trade route and had a thriving economy. For this reason, large numbers of sailors and merchants from every nation flocked to the city of Corinth. During the first century, it was one of the largest cities in the Roman Empire, and by the end of the second century it had become one of richest cities in the world.

Corinth was a strategic center of influence for the gospel since those travelers who heard the gospel there could carry it to all parts of the world. The city of Corinth, however, was one of the most wicked cities of ancient times. Immorality, unscrupulous business dealings, and pagan practices abounded. Of the scores of heathen religions that were practiced in the city, the most well-known was the worship of Aphrodite, the goddess of love and beauty. The temple of Aphrodite stood on the most prominent point in the city, a hill called Acrocorinth, and housed one thousand "temple prostitutes."

Paul was able to establish a church in Corinth during his eighteen month residence there (about A.D. 52–53) on his second missionary journey (Acts 18:1–11; 1 Cor. 2:1, 2). Paul lived and worked as a tentmaker with two other Jewish converts, Aquila and Priscilla, who had recently come from Rome (Acts 18:1, 2). When Paul left Corinth, a man named Apollos ministered there after Aquila and Priscilla had more completely expounded the gospel to him (Acts 18:26, 27; 19:1; see 1 Cor. 1:12; 16:12). Three years after this, Paul wrote this letter from Ephesus to the Corinthian believers. Later, Paul received a report from the members of the household of Chloe concerning the bad conduct of some in the church (1 Cor. 1:11). Many of the members had recently been converted from paganism and were having difficulty breaking habits of their former lifestyles. There were such deep divisions among them that some of the believers were bringing lawsuits against one another and allowing unbelieving judges to settle the disputes (chap. 6).

Paul reprimanded the church for failing to discipline certain of its members who were guilty of gross immorality (chap. 5). He also gave them counsel regarding some of the common marriage problems, and instructed them regarding the proper conduct of those who were unmarried (chap. 7). In addition, Paul discussed the eating of meats offered to idols (1 Cor. 8; 10:18–31), abuses of the Lord's Supper (1 Cor. 11:17–34), spiritual gifts (chaps. 12; 13), conduct in the formal assemblies for worship (1 Cor. 11:2–16; 14:1–40), and the resurrection (chap. 15).

1 Paul, [a]called[2822] *to be* an apostle[652] of
Jesus Christ[5547] [b]through the will[2307]
of God,[2316] and [c]Sosthenes *our* brother,[80]
2 Unto the church[1577] of God which
is at Corinth, [a]to them that [pfpp][b]are sanctified[37] in Christ Jesus, [c]called *to be*
saints,[40] with all that in every place
[ppt][d]call upon the name[3686] of Jesus Christ
[e]our Lord,[2962] [f]both theirs and ours:
3 [a]Grace *be* unto you, and peace,[1515]
from God our Father,[3962] and *from* the
Lord Jesus Christ.

1 [a]Rom. 1:1 [b]2Cor. 1:1; Eph. 1:1; Col. 1:1 [c]Acts 18:17
2 [a]Jude 1:1 [b]John 17:19; Acts 15:9 [c]Rom. 1:7; 2Tim. 1:9 [d]Acts 9:14, 21; 22:16; 2Tim. 2:22 [e]1Cor. 8:6 [f]Rom. 3:22; 10:12
3 [a]Rom. 1:7; 2Cor. 1:2; Eph. 1:2; 1Pet. 1:2
4 [a]Rom. 1:8

🔑 4 [a]I thank[2168] my God always on
your behalf, for the grace[5485] of God
which [aptp]is given you by Jesus Christ;
5 That in every thing ye are [aop]en-
riched by him, [a]in all utterance,[3056] and
in all knowledge;[1108]
6 Even as [a]the testimony[3142] of
Christ was confirmed in you:
7 So that ye [pip]come behind in no

5 [a]1Cor. 12:8; 2Cor. 8:7 **6** [a]1Cor. 2:1; 2Tim. 1:8; Rev. 1:2

🔑 **1:4–7** See note on 1 Corinthians 12:1–11.

gift; [a]waiting for[553] the [b]coming[602] of our
Lord Jesus Christ:
🔑 8 [a]Who [ft]shall also confirm[950] you
unto the end,[5056] [b]*that ye may be* blameless[410] in the day[2250] of our Lord Jesus
Christ.
9 [a]God *is* faithful,[4103] by whom ye
[aop]were called[2564] unto [b]the fellowship[2842]
of his Son[5207] Jesus Christ our Lord.

Exhortation to Unity

🔑 10 Now I beseech[3870] you, brethren,
by the name of our Lord Jesus Christ,
[a]that ye all speak the same thing, and
that there be no [I][b]divisions[4978] among
you; but *that* ye be [pfpp]perfectly joined
together[2675] in the same mind[3563] and in
the same judgment.[1106]
11 For it [aop]hath been declared unto
me of you, my brethren, by them *which
are of the house* of Chloe, that there are
contentions among you.
12 Now this I say, [a]that every one
of you saith, I am of Paul; and I of
[b]Apollos; and I of [c]Cephas; and I of
Christ.
🔑 13 [pfip][a]Is Christ divided?3307 was Paul
crucified for you? or [aop]were ye baptized[907] in the name of Paul?
🔑 14 I thank[2168] God that I baptized
none of you, but [a]Crispus and [b]Gaius;
15 Lest any should say that I had
baptized in mine own name.
16 And I baptized also the household
of [a]Stephanas: besides, I know not
whether I baptized any other.
17 For Christ sent me not [pinf]to baptize, but [pinf]to preach the gospel:[2097] [a]not
with wisdom of [I]words,[3056] lest the
cross[4716] of Christ [asbp]should be made of
none effect.[2758]

7 [a]Phil. 3:20; Titus 2:13; 2Pet. 3:12 [b]Col. 3:4
8 [a]1Thess. 3:13 [b]Col. 1:22; 1Thess. 5:23
9 [a]Isa. 49:7; 1Cor. 10:13; 1Thess. 5:24; 2Thess. 3:3; Heb. 10:23 [b]John 15:4; 17:21; 1John 1:3; 4:13
10 [I]Gr. *schisms* [a]Rom. 12:16; 15:5; 2Cor. 13:11; Phil. 2:2; 3:16; 1Pet. 3:8 [b]1Cor. 11:18
12 [a]1Cor. 3:4 [b]Acts 18:24; 19:1; 1Cor. 16:12 [c]John 1:42
13 [a]2Cor. 11:4; Eph. 4:5
14 [a]Acts 18:8 [b]Rom. 16:23
16 [a]1Cor. 16:15, 17
17 [I]Or, *speech* [a]1Cor. 2:1, 4, 13; 2Pet. 1:16
18 [a]2Cor. 2:15 [b]Acts 17:18; 1Cor. 2:14 [c]1Cor. 15:2 [d]Rom. 1:16; 1Cor. 1:24
19 [a]Job 5:12, 13; Isa. 29:14; Jer. 8:9
20 [a]Isa. 33:18 [b]Job 12:17, 20, 24; Isa. 44:25; Rom. 1:22
21 [a]Matt. 11:25; Luke 10:21; Rom. 1:20, 21, 28
22 [a]Matt. 12:38; 16:1; Mark 8:11; Luke 11:16; John 4:48
23 [a]Isa. 8:14; Matt. 11:6; 13:57; Luke 2:34; John 6:60, 66; Rom. 9:32; Gal. 5:11; 1Pet. 2:8 [b]1Cor. 1:18; 2:14

Paul Defends His Manner Of Preaching

18 For the preaching[3056] of the
cross is to [a]them that [ppt]perish[622] [b]fool-
ishness;3472 but unto us [c]which
[ppp]are saved[4982] it is the [d]power[1411] of
God.
19 For it is written, [a]I [ft]will destroy[622]
the wisdom[4678] of the wise,[4680] and will
bring to nothing the understanding of the
prudent.
20 [a]Where *is* the wise? where *is* the
scribe?[1122] where *is* the disputer of this
world?[165] [aob]hath not God made fool-
ish3471 the wisdom of this world?[2889]
21 [a]For after that in the wisdom of
God the world by wisdom knew not God,
it pleased[2106] God by the foolishness3472
of preaching[2782] [ainf]to save them that
[ppt]believe.[4100]
22 For the [a]Jews require a sign, and
the Greeks seek after wisdom:
23 But we preach[2784] Christ [pfpp]cru-
cified,[4717] [a]unto the Jews a stumbling
block,[4625] and unto the Greeks [b]foolish-
ness;3472
24 But unto them which are
[ajn]called,[2822] both Jews and Greeks, Christ
[a]the power[1411] of God, and [b]the wisdom[4678] of God.
25 Because the foolishness of God is
wiser than men;[444] and the weakness[772]
of God is stronger than men.
26 For ye see your calling,[2821]
brethren, how that [a]not many wise
men4860 after the flesh,[4561] not many
mighty, not many noble, *are called:*
27 But [a]God [aom]hath chosen the foolish things of the world[2889] to confound

24 [a]Rom. 1:4, 16; 1Cor. 1:18 [b]Col. 2:3 **26** [a]John 7:48 **27** [a]Ps. 8:2; Matt. 11:25; James 2:5

🔑 **1:8** See note on 1 Thessalonians 5:2.
🔑 **1:10–13** The Apostle Paul opens chapter one with a statement that believers are sanctified and secure in their position in Christ (vv. 2, 8). Then, in verse ten, Paul gives the occasion for his letter; that is, it had been reported to him that there were divisions in the church (v. 11). One such division concerned the leaders that the people followed. There were some who followed after Apollos, some after Peter, and some after Paul (cf. 1 Cor. 3:4, 5). Paul was exhorting these believers to be joined together in Christ, not to another man (see note on 1 Cor. 4:6, 7).
🔑 **1:13** See note on Mark 16:16 concerning baptism.
🔑 **1:14** See note on 3 John 1:1 concerning Gaius.

the wise; and God hath chosen the weak things of the world to confound the things which are mighty;

28 And base things of the world, and things [pfpp]which are despised, hath God chosen, *yea,* and [a]things which are not, [b]to bring to nought[2673] things that are:

29 [a]That no flesh[4561] [asbm]should glory[2744] in his presence.

30 But of him are ye in Christ Jesus, who of God is made unto us [a]wisdom,[4678] and [b]righteousness,[1343] and [c]sanctification,[38] and [d]redemption:[629]

31 That, according as it is written, [a]He that [ppt]glorieth, [pim]let him glory[2744] in the Lord.

The Power of God

2 And I, brethren, when I came to you, [a]came not with excellency of speech[3056] or of wisdom,[4678] declaring[2605] unto you the [b]testimony[3142] of God.

2 For I determined[2919] not [infg]to know[1492] any thing among you, [a]save Jesus Christ, and him crucified.[4717]

3 And [a]I was with you [b]in weakness, and in fear, and in much trembling.

4 And my speech[3056] and my preaching[2782] [a]*was* not with [I]enticing words[3056] of man's wisdom,[4678] [b]but in demonstration of the [an]Spirit[4151] and of power:[1411]

5 That your faith[4102] should not stand in the wisdom[4678] of men,[444] but [a]in the power of God.[2316]

True Wisdom

6 Howbeit[1161] we speak wisdom[4678] among them [a]that are [ajn]perfect:[5046] yet not [b]the wisdom[4678] of this world, nor of the princes of this world, [c]that [ppp]come to nought:[2673]

7 But we speak the [an]wisdom[4678] of God in a mystery,[3466] *even* the [pfpp]hidden *wisdom,* [a]which God ordained[4309] before the world[165] unto our glory:[1391]

8 [a]Which none of the princes of this world [pfi]knew: for [ao][b]had they known[1097] *it,* they would not have crucified the Lord of glory.

9 But as it is written, [a]Eye [ao]hath not seen,[1492] nor ear heard, neither [ao]have entered[305] into the heart of man, the things which God hath prepared for them that [ppt]love[25] him.

10 But [a]God [ao]hath revealed[601] *them* unto us by his Spirit: for the Spirit searcheth all things, yea, the deep things of God.

11 For what man knoweth[1492] the things of a man, [a]save the spirit[4151] of man which is in him? [b]even so the things of God knoweth no man, but the Spirit of God.

12 Now we [ao]have received, not the spirit of the world, but [a]the spirit which is of God; that we might know the things that [aptp]are freely given[5483] to us of God.

13 [a]Which things also we speak, not in the words which man's wisdom[4678] teacheth, but which the Holy Ghost[4151] teacheth; comparing[4793] spiritual things with spiritual.

🔑 14 [a]But the [an]natural[5591] man receiveth not the things of the Spirit of God: [b]for they are foolishness[3472] unto him: [c]neither can he [ainf]know *them,* because they are spiritually[4153] discerned.

15 [a]But he that is spiritual[4152] [I]judgeth all things, yet he himself is judged of no man.

16 [a]For who [ao]hath known the mind[3563] of the Lord,[2962] that he [I]may instruct him? [b]But we have the [an]mind of Christ.[5547]

28 [a]Rom. 4:17; 1Cor. 2:6
29 [a]Rom. 3:27; Eph. 2:9
30 [a]1Cor. 1:24 [b]Jer. 23:5, 6; Rom. 4:25; 2Cor. 5:21; Phil. 3:9 [c]John 17:19 [d]Eph. 1:7
31 [a]Jer. 9:23, 24; 2Cor. 10:17

1 [a]1Cor. 1:17; 1Cor. 1:4, 13; 2Cor. 10:10; 11:6 [b]1Cor. 1:6
2 [a]Gal. 6:14; Phil. 3:8
3 [a]Acts 18:1, 6, 12 [b]2Cor. 4:7; 10:1, 10; 11:30; 12:5, 9; Gal. 4:13
4 [I]Or, *persuasive* [a]1Cor. 1:17; 2:1; 2Pet. 1:16 [b]Rom. 15:19; 1Thess. 1:5
5 [a]2Cor. 4:7; 6:7
6 [a]1Cor. 14:20; Eph. 4:13; Phil. 3:15; Heb. 5:14 [b]1Cor. 1:20; 2:1, 13; 3:19; 2Cor. 1:12; James 3:15 [c]1Cor. 1:28
7 [a]Rom. 16:25, 26; Eph. 3:5, 9; Col. 1:26; 2Tim. 1:9
8 [a]Matt. 11:25; John 7:48; Acts 13:27; 2Cor. 3:14 [b]Luke 23:34; Acts 3:17; John 16:3
9 [a]Isa. 64:4
10 [a]Matt. 13:11; 16:17; John 14:26; 16:13; 1John 2:27
11 [a]Prov. 20:27; 27:19; Jer. 17:9 [b]Rom. 11:33, 34
12 [a]Rom. 8:15
13 [a]2Pet. 1:16; 1Cor. 1:17; 2:4
14 [a]Matt. 16:23 [b]1Cor. 1:18, 23 [c]Rom. 8:5-7; Jude 1:19
15 [I]Or, *discerneth* [a]Prov. 28:5; 1Thess. 5:21; 1John 4:1
16 [I]Gr. *shall* [a]Job 15:8; Isa. 40:13; Jer. 23:18; Rom. 11:34 [b]John 15:15 [c]1Cor. 2:15 [d]1Cor. 2:14 [e]Heb. 5:13

🔑 **2:14** The word translated "natural" from the Greek is *psuchikós* (5591), referring to the man who is governed only by his environment; namely, his natural or animal instincts, as a result of his fallen Adamic nature (Rom 5:12). This man is unable to understand spiritual truths because he does not possess the indwelling Spirit of God.

Jesus Is the Foundation

3 And I, brethren, [aop]could not [ainf]speak unto you as unto [a]spiritual,[4152] but as unto [b]carnal,[4559] *even* as unto [c]babes[3516] in Christ.

2 I [ao]have fed you with [a]milk,[1051] and not with meat:1033 [b]for hitherto ye [ipf]were not able[1410] *to bear it,* neither yet now are ye able.

3 For ye are yet carnal: for [a]whereas *there is* among you envying, and strife, and divisions,[1370] are ye not carnal, and walk [I]as men?

4 For while one saith, [a]I am of Paul; and another, I *am* of Apollos; are ye not carnal?

5 Who then is Paul, and who *is* Apollos, but [a]ministers[1249] by whom ye believed,[4100] [b]even as the Lord gave to every man?

6 [a]I [ao]have planted, [b]Apollos watered; [c]but God[2316] gave the increase.

7 So then [a]neither is he that [ppt]planteth any thing, neither he that [ppt]watereth; but God that [ppt]giveth the increase.

8 Now he that planteth and he that watereth are one: [a]and every man shall receive his own reward according to his own labour.

9 For [a]we are labourers together with God: ye are God's husbandry,1091 *ye are* [b]God's building.[3619]

10 [a]According to the grace[5485] of God which [aptp]is given unto me, as a wise[4680] masterbuilder, I [pf]have laid [b]the foundation, and another buildeth thereon. But [c]let every man take heed how he buildeth thereupon.[2026]

11 For other foundation2310 can no man lay than [a]that [ppt]is laid,[2749] [b]which is Jesus Christ.

12 Now if any man build[2026] upon this foundation gold, silver, precious stones, wood, hay, stubble;

13 [a]Every man's work[2041] shall be made manifest: for the day [b]shall declare it, because [c]it [pinp][I]shall be revealed[601] by fire; and the fire shall try every man's work of what sort it is.

14 If any man's work abide which he [ao]hath built thereupon, [a]he shall receive a reward.

15 If any man's work shall be burned, he shall suffer loss: but he himself [fp]shall be saved;[4982] [a]yet so as by fire.

16 [a]Know ye not that ye are the [an]temple[3485] of God,[2316] and *that* the Spirit[4151] of God dwelleth[3611] in you?

17 If any man [I]defile the temple of God, him shall God destroy; for the temple of God is holy,[40] which *temple* ye are.

18 [pim][a]Let no man deceive[1818] himself. If any man among you seemeth to be wise in this world, let him become a fool, that he may be wise.[4680]

19 For [a]the wisdom of this world is foolishness3472 with God. For it is written, [b]He [ppt]taketh the wise in their own craftiness.

20 And again, [a]The Lord knoweth the thoughts[1261] of the wise, that they are vain.

21 Therefore [a]let no man glory in men. For [b]all things are yours;

22 Whether Paul, or Apollos, or Cephas, or the world,[2889] or life,[2222] or death,[2288] or things present, or things to come; all are yours;

23 And [a]ye are Christ's;[5547] and Christ *is* God's.

4 🔑Let a man so account[3049] of us, as of [a]the ministers[5257] of Christ, [b]and stewards[3623] of the mysteries[3466] of God.

2 Moreover it is required in stewards, that a man be found faithful.[4103]

3 But with me it is a very small

2 [a]Heb. 5:12, 13; 1Pet. 2:2 [b]John 16:12
3 [I]Gr. *according to man* [a]1Cor. 1:11; 11:18; Gal. 5:20, 21; James 3:16
4 [a]1Cor. 1:12
5 [a]1Cor. 4:1; 2Cor. 3:3 [b]Rom. 12:3, 6; 1Pet. 4:11
6 [a]Acts 18:4, 8, 11; 1Cor. 4:15; 9:1; 15:1; 2Cor. 10:14, 15 [b]Acts 18:24, 27; 19:1 [c]1Cor. 1:30; 15:10; 2Cor. 3:5
7 [a]2Cor. 12:11; Gal. 6:3
8 [a]Ps. 62:12; Rom. 2:6; 1Cor. 4:5; Gal. 6:4, 5; Rev. 2:23; 22:12
9 [a]Acts 15:4; 2Cor. 6:1 [b]Eph. 2:20; Col. 2:7; Heb. 3:3, 4; 1Pet. 2:5
10 [a]Rom. 1:5; 12:3 [b]Rom. 15:20; 1Cor. 3:6; 4:15; Rev. 21:14 [c]1Pet. 4:11
11 [a]Isa. 28:16; Matt. 16:18; 2Cor. 11:4; Gal. 1:7 [b]Eph. 2:20
13 [I]Gr. *is revealed* [a]1Cor. 4:5 [b]1Pet. 1:7; 4:12 [c]Luke 2:35
14 [a]1Cor. 4:5
15 [a]Jude 1:23
16 [a]1Cor. 6:19; 2Cor. 6:16; Eph. 2:21, 22; Heb. 3:6; 1Pet. 2:5
17 [I]Or, *destroy*
18 [a]Prov. 3:7; Isa. 5:21
19 [a]1Cor. 1:20; 2:6 [b]Job 5:13
20 [a]Ps. 94:11
21 [a]1Cor. 1:12; 3:4-6; 4:6 [b]2Cor. 4:5, 15
23 [a]Rom. 14:8; 1Cor. 11:3; 2Cor. 10:7; Gal. 3:29

1 [a]Matt. 24:45; 1Cor. 3:5; 9:17; 2Cor. 6:4; Col. 1:25 [b]Luke 12:42; Titus 1:7; 1Pet. 4:10

🔑 **4:1** A steward (*oikonómos,* [3623]) is one who manages a house and is accountable to the owner. Christians are called "stewards" in that they have been entrusted with the "mysteries of God," which is the Gospel message. It is a responsibility for which believers are held accountable.

thing that I should be judged of you, or
of man's [1][a]judgment:[2250] yea, I judge not
mine own self.
4 For I know nothing by myself; [a]yet
[pfip]am I not hereby justified:[1344] but he
that [ppt]judgeth me is the Lord.
5 [a]Therefore judge[2919] nothing before
the time,[2540] until the Lord come, [b]who
both [ft]will bring to light[5461] the hidden
things of darkness,[4655] and [ft]will make
manifest[5319] the counsels[1012] of the
hearts:[2588] and [c]then shall every man
have praise of God.
6 And these things, brethren, [a]I
[ao]have in a figure transferred[3345] to myself and *to* Apollos for your sakes; [b]that
ye might learn in us not [pinf]to think[5426]
of men above that which is written, that
no one of you [c]be puffed up for one
against another.
7 For who [pin]maketh thee to differ[1252]
from another? and [a]what hast thou that
thou didst not receive? now if thou didst
receive *it,* why dost thou glory, as if thou
hadst not received *it?*
8 Now ye are full,[2880] [a]now ye [ao]are
rich, ye [ao]have reigned as kings without
us: and I would to God ye did reign, that
we also might reign with you.
9 For I think[1380] that God [ao]hath set
forth us the apostles last,[2078] [a]as it were
appointed to death: for [b]we [aop]are made
a spectacle unto the world, and to angels,
and to men.
10 [a]We *are* [b]fools for Christ's sake,
but ye *are* wise[5429] in Christ; [c]we *are*
weak,[772] but ye *are* strong; ye *are* honourable,[1741] but we *are* despised.
11 [a]Even unto this present hour we
both hunger, and thirst, and [b]are naked,
and [c]are buffeted, and have no certain
dwellingplace;[790]
12 [a]And labour, working[2038] with our
own hands: [b]being reviled,[3058] we bless;
being persecuted, we suffer[430] it:
13 Being defamed,[987] we intreat:[3870]
[a]we [aop]are made as the filth[4027] of the
world, *and are* the offscouring of all
things unto this day.
14 I write not these things to
shame[1788] you, but [a]as my beloved[27]
sons[5043] I warn[3560] *you.*
15 For though ye have ten thousand
instructors[3807] in Christ, yet *have ye* not
many fathers:[3962] for [a]in Christ Jesus I
[ao]have begotten[1080] you through the
gospel.[2098]
16 Wherefore I beseech you, [a]be ye
followers of me.
17 For this cause have I sent unto
you [a]Timotheus, [b]who is my beloved son,
and faithful[4103] in the Lord, who shall
bring you [c]into remembrance of my ways
which be in Christ, as I [d]teach[1321] every
where [e]in every church.[1577]
18 [a]Now some [aop]are puffed up, as
though I would not come to you.
19 [a]But I will come to you shortly, [b]if
the Lord will, and will know, not the
speech[3056] of them which are puffed up,
but the power.
20 For [a]the kingdom[932] of God *is* not
in word,[3056] but in power.[1411]
21 What will ye? [a]shall I come unto
you with a rod, or in love,[26] and *in* the
spirit[4151] of meekness?

Concerning Church Discipline

5 It is reported commonly *that there is*
fornication[4202] among you, and such

3 [1]Gr. *day* [a]1Cor. 3:13
4 [a]Job 9:2; Ps. 130:3; 143:2; Prov. 21:2; Rom. 3:20; 4:2
5 [a]Matt. 7:1; Rom. 2:1, 16; 14:4; 10, 13; Rev. 20:12 [b]1Cor. 3:13 [c]Rom. 2:29; 2Cor. 5:10
6 [a]1Cor. 1:12; 3:4 [b]Rom. 12:3 [c]1Cor. 3:21; 5:2, 6
7 [a]John 3:27; James 1:17; 1Pet. 4:10
8 [a]Rev. 3:17
9 [a]Ps. 44:22; Rom. 8:36; 1Cor. 15:30, 31; 2Cor. 4:11; 6:9 [b]Heb. 10:33
10 [a]1Cor. 2:3 [b]Acts 17:18; 26:24; 1Cor. 1:18; 2:14; 3:18 [c]2Cor. 13:9
11 [a]2Cor. 4:8; 11:23-27; Phil. 4:12 [b]Job 22:6; Rom. 8:35 [c]Acts 23:2
12 [a]Acts 18:3; 20:34; 1Thess. 2:9; 2Thess. 3:8; 1Tim. 4:10 [b]Matt. 5:44; Luke 6:28; 23:34; Acts 7:60; Rom. 12:14, 20; 1Pet. 2:23; 3:9
13 [a]Lam. 3:45
14 [a]1Thess. 2:11
15 [a]Acts 18:11; Rom. 15:20; 1Cor. 3:6; Gal. 4:19; Phile. 1:10; James 1:18
16 [a]1Cor. 11:1; Phil. 3:17; 1Thess. 1:6; 2Thess. 3:9
17 [a]Acts 19:22; 1Cor. 16:10; Phil. 2:19; 1Thess. 3:2 [b]1Tim. 1:2; 2Tim. 1:2 [c]1Cor. 11:2 [d]1Cor. 7:17 [e]1Cor. 14:33
18 [a]1Cor. 5:2
19 [a]Acts 19:21; 16:5; 2Cor. 1:15, 23 [b]Acts 18:21; Rom. 15:32; Heb. 6:3; James 4:15
20 [a]1Cor. 2:4; 1Thess. 1:5
21 [a]2Cor. 10:2; 13:10

4:6, 7 This difficult verse can be better understood when it is examined in its context. In the phrase "in a figure transferred to myself" Paul was implying that he was working out the divisions within the Corinthian congregation with Apollos (1 Cor. 1:10–13). This relationship was intended to be an example for them to follow in settling their divisions. Paul used his own humility as an example by not allowing others to place him on a pedestal. In verse seven, Paul gives the primary reason for not acknowledging the Corinthians' accolades. He intimates that all believers are servants of Christ, not of themselves (cf. Rom. 12:3, 16).
4:17 See the introduction to 1 Timothy.

fornication as is not so much as [a]named among the Gentiles,[1484] [b]that one should have his [c]father's wife.

2 [a]And ye are puffed up, and [ao]have not rather [b]mourned,[3996] that he that [apt]hath done this deed[2041] [asbp]might be taken away from among[3319] you.

3 [a]For I verily,3303 as absent in body, but present in spirit,[4151] [pfi]have judged[2919] already, as though I were present, *concerning* him that [apt]hath so done2716 this deed,

4 In the name of our Lord Jesus Christ, when ye are gathered together, and my spirit, [a]with[4862] the power[1411] of our Lord Jesus Christ,

5 [ainf][a]To deliver such an one unto [b]Satan[4567] for the destruction[3639] of the flesh,[4561] that the spirit [asbp]may be saved[4982] in the day[2250] of the Lord Jesus.

6 [a]Your glorying *is* not good. Know ye not that [b]a little leaven[2219] leaveneth[2220] the whole lump?

7 Purge out therefore the old leaven, that ye may be a new lump, as ye are unleavened.[106] For even [a]Christ[5547] our [b]passover3957 [aop]is sacrificed[2380] for us:

8 Therefore [aosi][a]let us keep the feast,1858 [b]not with old leaven, neither [c]with the leaven of malice[2549] and wickedness;[4189] but with the unleavened *bread* of sincerity[1505] and truth.[225]

9 I wrote unto you in an epistle1992 [a]not [pinf]to company with fornicators:4205

10 [a]Yet not altogether with the fornicators [b]of this world, or with the covetous, or extortioners, or with idolaters;[1496] for then must ye needs [ainf]go [c]out of the world.[2889]

11 But now I have written unto you not to keep company, [a]if any man that [ppp]is called a brother[80] be a fornicator,4205 or covetous, or an idolater, or a railer,3060 or a drunkard, or an extortioner; with such an one [b]no not to eat.

12 For what have I to do to judge [a]them also that are without?1854 do not ye judge [b]them that are within?

13 But them that are without God judgeth. Therefore [ft][a]put away from among yourselves that wicked person.[4190]

Concerning Believers and Legal Matters

6 Dare any of you, having a matter against another,[2087] go to law[2919] before the unjust,[94] and not before the saints?[40]

2 Do ye not know that [a]the saints [ft]shall judge[2919] the world?[2889] and if the world shall be judged by you, are ye unworthy to judge[2922] the smallest matters?

3 Know ye not that we shall [a]judge angels?[32] how much more things that pertain to this life?

4 [a]If then ye have judgments[2922] of things pertaining to this life, set them to judge who are least esteemed in the church.[1577]

5 I speak to your shame.[1791] Is it so, that there is not a wise man[4680] among you? no, not one that shall be able [ainf]to judge[1252] between[3319] his brethren?[80]

6 But brother goeth to law[2919] with brother, and that before the [an]unbelievers.[571]

7 Now therefore there is utterly a fault among you, because ye go to law one with another. [a]Why do ye not rather take wrong? why do ye not rather *suffer yourselves* to be defrauded?

8 Nay, ye do wrong, and defraud, [a]and that *your* brethren.

9 Know ye not that the unrighteous[94] [ft]shall not inherit[2816] the kingdom[932] of God? Be not deceived: [a]neither fornicators,4205 nor idolaters,[1496] nor adulterers, nor effeminate,3120 nor abusers of themselves with mankind,733

10 Nor thieves, nor covetous, nor drunkards, nor revilers, nor extortioners,[727] [ft]shall inherit[2816] the kingdom of God.

11 And such were [a]some of you: [b]but ye [aom]are washed,[628] but ye are sanctified,[37] but ye [aop]are justified[1344] in the name[3686] of the Lord Jesus, and by the Spirit[4151] of our God.

Abuses of Christian Liberty

12 [a]All things are lawful unto me, but all things [pin]are not [I]expedient:[4851] all

1 [b]Eph. 5:3 [c]Lev. 18:8; Deut. 22:30; 27:20 [d]2Cor. 7:12
2 [a]1Cor. 4:18 [b]2Cor. 7:7, 10
3 [a]Col. 2:5
4 [a]Matt. 16:19; 18:18; John 20:23; 2Cor. 2:10; 13:3, 10
5 [a]Job 2:6; Ps. 109:6; 1Tim. 1:20 [b]Acts 26:18
6 [a]1Cor. 3:21; 4:19; 5:2; James 4:16 [b]1Cor. 15:33; Gal. 5:9; 2Tim. 2:17
7 [a]Isa. 53:7; John 1:29; 1Cor. 15:3; 1Pet. 1:19; Rev. 5:6, 12 [b]John 19:14
8 [a]Ex. 12:15; 13:6 [b]Deut. 16:3 [c]Matt. 16:6, 12; Mark 8:15; Luke 12:1
9 [a]1Cor. 5:2, 7; 2Cor. 6:14; Eph. 5:11; 2Thess. 3:14
10 [a]1Cor. 10:27 [b]1Cor. 1:20 [c]John 17:15; 1John 5:19
11 [a]Matt. 18:17; Rom. 16:17; 2Thess. 3:6, 14; 2John 1:10 [b]Gal. 2:12
12 [a]Mark 4:11; Col. 4:5; 1Thess. 4:12; 1Tim. 3:7 [b]1Cor. 6:1-4
13 [a]Deut. 13:5; 17:7; 21:21; 22:21, 22, 24

2 [a]Ps. 49:14; Dan. 7:22; Matt. 19:28; Luke 22:30; Rev. 2:26; 3:21; 20:4
3 [a]2Pet. 2:4; Jude 1:6
4 [a]1Cor. 5:12
7 [a]Prov. 20:22; Matt. 5:39, 40; Luke 6:29; Rom. 12:17, 19; 1Thess. 5:15
8 [a]1Thess. 4:6
9 [a]1Cor. 15:50; Gal. 5:21; Eph. 5:5; 1Tim. 1:9; Heb. 12:14; 13:4; Rev. 22:15
11 [a]1Cor. 12:2; Eph. 2:2; 4:22; 5:8; Col. 3:7; Titus 3:3 [b]1Cor. 1:30; Heb. 10:22
12 IOr, *profitable* [a]1Cor. 10:23

things are lawful for me, but I will not
be brought under the power of any.
13 [a]Meats for the belly, and the belly
for meats: but God shall destroy both it
and them. Now the body[4983] *is* not for
fornication,4202 but [b]for the Lord;[2962] [c]and
the Lord for the body.
14 And [a]God hath both raised up[1453]
the Lord, and [ft]will also raise up[1825] us
[b]by his own power.
15 Know ye not that [a]your bodies are
the members of Christ?[5547] shall I then
take the members of Christ, and make
them the members of an harlot? God forbid.[3361,1096]
16 What? know ye not that he which
[ppt]is joined to an harlot is one body? for
[a]two, saith he, shall be one flesh.
17 [a]But he that [ppt]is joined unto the
Lord is one spirit.
18 [a]Flee fornication. Every sin[265] that
a man doeth is without the body; but he
that committeth fornication sinneth[264]
[b]against his own body.
19 What? [a]know ye not that your
body[4983] is the temple[3485] of the Holy[40]
Ghost[4151] *which is* in you, which ye have
of God, [b]and ye are not your own?
20 For [a]ye [aop]are bought[59] with a
price: therefore [aim]glorify[1392] God in your
body, and in your spirit, which are God's.

Concerning Marriage

7 Now concerning the things whereof
ye wrote unto me: [a]*It is* good for a
man[444] not [pinf]to touch[680] a woman.
2 Nevertheless, *to avoid* fornication,4202 let every man have his own wife,
and let every woman have her own husband.
3 [pima]Let the husband render591 unto
the wife [ppp]due benevolence:[2133] and likewise also the wife unto the husband.
4 The wife [pin]hath not power1850 of
her own body, but the husband: and likewise also the husband hath not power of
his own body, but the wife.
5 [pima]Defraud ye not one the other,
except *it be* with consent for a time,[2540]
that ye [psmp]may give yourselves to fast-
ing3521 and prayer;[4335] and [psa]come together again, that [b]Satan[4567] [psa]tempt[3985]
you not for your incontinency.192
6 But I speak this by permission,[4774]
[a]*and* not of commandment.[2003]
7 For [a]I would that all men were
[b]even as I myself. But [c]every man hath
his proper gift[5486] of God, one after this
manner, and another after that.
8 I say therefore to the unmarried
and widows, [a]It is good[2570] for them if
they [aosb]abide even as I.
9 But [a]if they cannot contain, [aim]let
them marry:1060 for it is better [ainf]to
marry than [pip]to burn.
10 And unto the [pfp]married I com-
mand, [a]*yet* not I, but the Lord, [aifp][b]Let not
the wife depart5563 from *her* husband:
11 But and if she [asbp]depart, [pim]let
her remain[3306] unmarried, or [aipp]be reconciled[2644] to *her* husband: and let not
the husband [pinf]put away[863] *his* wife.
12 But to the rest speak I, [a]not the
Lord: If any brother[80] hath a wife that
believeth not,[571] and she be pleased to
dwell with him, [pim]let him not put her
away.[863]
13 And the woman which hath an
husband that believeth not,[571] and if he
be pleased to dwell with her, [pim]let her
not leave[863] him.
14 For the unbelieving[571] husband
[pfip]is sanctified[37] by the wife, and the
unbelieving[571] wife [pfip]is sanctified by the
husband: else [pina]were your children
unclean;[169] but now are they holy.[40]
15 But if the [ajn]unbelieving[571] depart,
[pim]let him depart.5563 A brother or a sister [pfip]is not under bondage[1402] in such
cases: but God[2316] [pfi]hath called us [I][a]to
peace.[1515]
16 For what[5101] knowest thou, O
wife, whether thou [ft]shalt [a]save[4982] *thy*
husband? or [I]how knowest thou, O man,
whether thou shalt save *thy* wife?
17 But as God [ao]hath distributed to
every man, as the Lord[2962] [pfi]hath called
every one, so [pim]let him walk.4043 And
[a]so ordain[1299] I in all [art]churches.
18 [aop]Is any man called[2564] [pfpp]being
circumcised?[4059] [pim]let him not become
uncircumcised.[1986] Is any called in uncircumcision?[203] [a]let him not be circumcised.

13 [a]Matt. 15:17; Rom. 14:17; Col. 2:22, 23 [b]1Cor. 6:15, 19, 20; 1Thess. 4:3, 7 [c]Eph. 5:23
14 [a]Rom. 6:5, 8; 8:11; 2Cor. 4:14 [b]Eph. 1:19, 20
15 [a]Rom. 12:5; 1Cor. 12:27; Eph. 4:12, 15, 16; 5:30
16 [a]Gen. 2:24; Matt. 19:5; Eph. 5:31
17 [a]John 17:21-23; Eph. 4:4; 5:30
18 [a]Rom. 6:12, 13; Heb. 13:4 [b]Rom. 1:24; 1Thess. 4:4
19 [a]1Cor. 3:16; 2Cor. 6:16 [b]Rom. 14:7, 8
20 [a]Acts 20:28; 1Cor. 7:23; Gal. 3:13; Heb. 9:12; 1Pet. 1:18, 19; 2Pet. 2:1; Rev. 5:9

1 [a]1Cor. 7:8, 26
3 [a]Ex. 21:10; 1Pet. 3:7
5 [a]Ex. 19:15; 1Sam. 21:4, 5; Joel 2:16; Zech. 7:3 [b]1Thess. 3:5
6 [a]1Cor. 7:12, 25; 2Cor. 8:8; 11:17
7 [a]Acts 26:29; [b]1Cor. 9:5 [c]Matt. 19:12; 1Cor. 12:11
8 [a]1Cor. 7:1, 26
9 [a]1Tim. 5:14
10 [a]1Cor. 7:12, 25, 40 [b]Mal. 2:14, 16; Matt. 5:32; 19:6, 9; Mark 10:11, 12; Luke 16:18
12 [a]1Cor. 7:6
14 [a]Mal. 2:15
15 [I]Gr. *in peace* [a]Rom. 12:18; 14:19; 1Cor. 14:33; Heb. 12:14
16 [I]Gr. *what* [a]1Pet. 3:1
17 [a]1Cor. 4:17; 2Cor. 11:28
18 [a]Acts 15:1, 5, 19, 24, 28; Gal. 5:2

19 [a]Circumcision[4061] is nothing, and uncircumcision[203] is nothing, but [b]the keeping[5084] of the commandments[1785] of God.[2316]

20 [pim]Let every man abide[3306] in the same calling[2821] wherein he was called.

21 [aop]Art thou called[59] *being* a servant?[1401] [pim]care not for it: but if thou mayest be made free,[1658] use *it* rather.

22 For he that [aptp]is called in the Lord, *being* a servant, is [a]the Lord's freeman: likewise also he that is called, *being* free, is [b]Christ's[5547] servant.

23 [a]Ye [aop]are bought[59] with a price; be not ye the [an]servants of men.

24 Brethren, [a]let every man, wherein he [aop]is called, therein [pim]abide with God.

Concerning Virgins

25 Now concerning virgins[3933] [a]I have no commandment[2003] of the Lord: yet I give my judgment,[1106] as one [b]that [pfpp]hath obtained mercy of the Lord [c]to be faithful.[4103]

26 I suppose therefore that this is good[2570] for the present[1764] [I]distress,[318] *I say,* [a]that *it is* good for a man[444] so to be.

27 [pfip]Art thou bound[1210] unto a wife? seek not to be loosed. [pfip]Art thou loosed[3089] from a wife? seek not a wife.

28 But and if thou [aosb]marry, thou [ao]hast not sinned;[264] and if a virgin marry, she hath not sinned. Nevertheless such shall have trouble[2347] in the flesh:[4561] but I spare you.

29 But [a]this I say, brethren,[80] the time *is* [pfpp]short: it remaineth, that both they that [ppt]have wives be as though they had none;

30 And they that [ppt]weep, as though they wept not; and they that [ppt]rejoice, as though they rejoiced not; and they that [ppt]buy, as though they possessed[2722] not;

31 And they that [ppt]use[5530] this world,[2889] as not [a]abusing[2710] *it:* for [b]the fashion[4976] of this world passeth away.

32 But I would have you without carefulness. [a]He that is unmarried careth for the things [b]that belong to the Lord,[2962] how he may please the Lord:

33 But he that [apt]is married careth

19 [a]Gal. 5:6; 6:15 [b]John 15:14; 1John 2:3; 3:24
22 [a]John 8:36; Rom. 6:18, 22; Phile. 1:16 [b]1Cor. 9:21; Gal. 5:13; Eph. 6:6; 1Pet. 2:16
23 [a]1Cor. 6:20; 1Pet. 1:18, 19; Lev. 25:42
24 [a]1Cor. 7:20
25 [a]1Cor. 7:6, 10, 40; 2Cor. 8:8, 10 [b]1Tim. 1:16 [c]1Cor. 4:2; 1Tim. 1:12
26 [I]Or, *necessity* [a]1Cor. 7:1, 8
29 [a]Rom. 13:11; 1Pet. 4:7; 2Pet. 3:8, 9
31 [a]1Cor. 9:18 [b]Ps. 39:6; James 1:10; 4:14; 1Pet. 1:24; 4:7; 1John 2:17
32 [a]1Tim. 5:5 [b]1Cor. 7:34
34 [a]Luke 10:40
38 [a]Heb. 13:4
39 [a]Rom. 7:2 [b]2Cor. 6:14
40 [a]1Cor. 7:25 [b]1Thess. 4:8
1 [a]Acts 15:20, 29; 1Cor. 10:19 [b]Rom. 14:14, 22 [c]Rom. 14:3, 10
2 [a]1Cor. 13:8, 9, 12; Gal. 6:3; 1Tim. 6:4
3 [a]Ex. 33:12, 17; Nah. 1:7; Matt. 7:23; Gal. 4:9; 2Tim. 2:19

for the things that are of the world, how he may please *his* wife.

34 There [pfip]is difference *also* between a wife and a virgin. The unmarried woman [a]careth for the things of the Lord, that she may be holy[40] both in body[4983] and in spirit:[4151] but she that [apt]is married careth for the things of the world, how she may please *her* husband.

35 And this I speak for your own profit;[4851] not that I [aosb]may cast a snare upon you, but for that which is comely,[2158] and that ye may attend upon the Lord without distraction.

36 But if any man think that he [pinf]behaveth himself uncomely toward his virgin,[3933] if she pass the flower of *her* age, and need so require, [pim]let him do[4160] what he will, he sinneth not: [pim]let them marry.[264]

37 Nevertheless he that standeth stedfast in his heart,[2588] having no necessity, but hath power[1849] over his own will,[2307] and [pfi]hath so decreed[2919] in his heart that he will [infg]keep his virgin, doeth well.

38 [a]So then he that [ppt]giveth *her* in marriage doeth well; but he that giveth *her* not in marriage doeth better.[2908]

39 [a]The wife [pfip]is bound[1210] by the law[3551] as long[5550] as her husband liveth;[2198] but if her husband be dead,[2837] she is at liberty [aifp]to be married to whom she will; [b]only in the Lord.

40 But she is happier[3107] if she so [aosb]abide, [a]after my judgment:[1106] and [b]I think[1380] also that I have the [an]Spirit[4151] of God.[2316]

Things Offered to Idols

8 Now [a]as touching things offered unto idols,[1494] we know[1492] that we all have [b]knowledge.[1108] [c]Knowledge puffeth up, but charity[26] edifieth.[3618]

2 And [a]if any man think that he knoweth any thing, he [pfi]knoweth nothing yet as he ought [ainf]to know.

3 But if any man love[25] God, [a]the same [pfip]is known of him.

4 As concerning therefore the eating of those things that are offered in sacri-

fice unto idols,[1494] we know that [a]an idol[1497] *is* nothing in the world, [b]and that *there is* none other[2087] God[2316] but one.

5 For though there be that are [a]called gods,[2316] whether in heaven[3772] or in earth,[1093] (as there be gods many, and lords[2962] many,)

6 But [a]to us *there is but* one God, the Father,[3962] [b]of whom *are* all things, and we [I]in him; and [c]one Lord[2962] Jesus Christ, [d]by whom *are* all things, and we by him.

7 Howbeit[235] *there is* not in every man that knowledge: for some [a]with conscience[4893] of the idol unto this hour eat *it* as a thing offered unto an idol; and their conscience being weak is [b]defiled.[3435]

8 But [a]meat[1033] commendeth us not to God: for neither, if we eat, [I]are we the better; neither, if we eat not, [II]are we the worse.

9 But [a]take heed lest by any means this [I]liberty[1849] of yours become [b]a stumblingblock to them that [ppt]are weak.[770]

10 For if any man [aosb]see thee which [ppt]hast knowledge [ppt]sit at meat in the idol's temple, shall not [a]the conscience of him which is weak be [I]emboldened[3618] to eat those things which are offered to idols;

11 And [a]through thy knowledge shall the weak brother[80] perish, for whom Christ died?[599]

12 But [a]when ye [ppt]sin[264] so against the brethren, and [ppt]wound[5180] their weak conscience, ye sin against Christ.[5547]

13 Wherefore, [a]if meat [pin]make my brother to offend,[4624] I will eat no flesh[2907] while the world standeth, lest I [aosb]make my brother to offend.[4624]

The Necessity of Self-Denial

9 [a]Am I not an apostle?[652] am I not free?[1658] [pfi][b]have I not seen[3708] Jesus Christ our Lord?[2962] [c]are not ye my work[2041] in the Lord?

2 If I be not an apostle unto others, yet doubtless I am to you: for [a]the seal of mine apostleship[651] are ye in the Lord.

3 Mine answer to them that do examine me is this,

4 [a]Have we not power[1849] [ainf]to eat and [ainf]to drink?

5 Have we not power [pinf]to lead about[4013] a sister, a wife, as well as other apostles, and *as* [a]the brethren[80] of the Lord, and [b]Cephas?

6 Or I only and Barnabas, [a]have not we power [infg]to forbear working?[3361,2038]

7 Who [a]goeth a warfare any time at his own charges?[3800] who [b]planteth a vineyard, and eateth not of the fruit thereof? or who [c]feedeth[4165] a flock,[4167] and eateth not of the milk[1051] of the flock?

8 Say I these things as a man?[444] or saith not the law[3551] the same also?

9 For it is written in the law[3551] of Moses, [a]Thou shalt not muzzle the mouth of the ox that treadeth out the corn. [pin]Doth God take care[3199] for oxen?

10 Or saith he *it* altogether for our sakes? For our sakes, no doubt, *this* is written: that [a]he that ploweth should plow in hope; and that he that thresheth in hope[1680] should be partaker of his hope.

11 [a]If we [ao]have sown unto you spiritual things, *is it* a great thing if we shall reap your carnal things?[4559]

12 If others be partakers of *this* power over you, *are* not we rather? [a]Nevertheless we [aom]have not used[5530] this power; but suffer all things, [b]lest we [asba]should hinder the gospel[2098] of Christ.

13 [a]Do ye not know that they which [ppt]minister[2038] about holy things[2413] live *of the things* of the temple?[2411] and they which [ppt]wait at the altar are partakers with the altar?

14 Even so [ao][a]hath the Lord ordained[1299] [b]that they which preach[2605] the gospel should live[2198] of the gospel.

15 But [a]I [aom]have used none of these things: neither have I written these things, that it should be so done unto me: for [b]*it were* better for me to die, than

4 [a]Isa. 41:24; 1Cor. 10:19 [b]Deut. 4:39; 6:4; Isa. 44:8; Mark 12:29; 1Cor. 8:6; Eph. 4:6; 1Tim. 2:5
5 [a]John 10:34
6 [I]Or, *for him* [a]Mal. 2:10; Eph. 4:6 [b]Acts 17:28; Rom. 11:36 [c]John 13:13; Acts 2:36; 1Cor. 12:3; Eph. 4:5; Phil. 2:11 [d]John 1:3; Col. 1:16; Heb. 1:2
7 [a]1Cor. 10:28, 29 [b]Rom. 14:14, 23
8 [I]Or, *have we the more* [II]Or, *have we the less* [a]Rom. 14:17
9 [I]Or, *power* [a]Gal. 5:13 [b]Rom. 14:13, 20
10 [I]Gr. *edified* [a]1Cor. 10:28, 32
11 [a]Rom. 14:15, 20
12 [a]Matt. 25:40, 45
13 [a]Rom. 14:21; 2Cor. 11:29

1 [a]Acts 9:15; 13:2; 26:17; 2Cor. 12:12; Gal. 2:7, 8; 1Tim. 2:7; 2Tim. 1:11 [b]Acts 9:3, 17; 18:9; 22:14, 18; 23:11; 1Cor. 15:8 [c]1Cor. 3:6; 4:15
2 [a]2Cor. 3:2; 12:12
4 [a]1Cor. 9:14; 1Thess. 2:6; 2Thess. 3:9
5 [a]Matt. 13:55; Mark 6:3; Luke 6:15; Gal. 1:19 [b]Matt. 8:14
6 [a]2Thess. 3:8, 9
7 [a]2Cor. 10:4; 1Tim. 1:18; 6:12; 2Tim. 2:3; 4:7 [b]Deut. 20:6; Prov. 27:18; 1Cor. 3:6-8 [c]John 21:15; 1Pet. 5:2
9 [a]Deut. 25:4; 1Tim. 5:18
10 [a]2Tim. 2:6
11 [a]Rom. 15:27; Gal. 6:6
12 [a]Acts 20:33; 1Cor. 9:15, 18; 2Cor. 11:7, 9; 12:13; 1Thess. 2:6 [b]2Cor. 11:12
13 [a]Lev. 6:16, 26; 7:6; Num. 5:9, 10; 18:8-20; Deut. 10:9; 18:1
14 [a]Matt. 10:10; Luke 10:7 [b]Gal. 6:6; 1Tim. 5:17
15 [a]1Cor. 9:12; Acts 18:3; 20:34; 1Cor. 4:12; 1Thess. 2:9; 2Thess. 3:8 [b]2Cor. 11:10

that any man [asba]should make my glorying void.[2758]
16 For though I preach the
gospel,[2097] I have nothing to glory of: for
[a]necessity[318] [pin]is laid upon me; yea, woe
is unto me, if I preach not the gospel!
17 For if I do this thing willingly, [a]I
have a reward:[3408] but if against my will,
a [b]dispensation[3622] *of the gospel* [pfip]is
committed[4100] unto me.
18 What is my reward then? *Verily*
that, [a]when I [ppt]preach the gospel, I
[aosb]may make[5087] the gospel of Christ
without charge, that I [aies][b]abuse[2710] not
my power[1849] in the gospel.
19 For though I be [a]free[1658] from all
men, yet have [b]I [ao]made myself servant[1402] unto all, [c]that I [aosb]might gain
the more.
20 And [a]unto the Jews I became as a
Jew, that I might gain the Jews; to them
that are under the law,[3551] as under the
law, that I might gain them that are
under the law;
21 [a]To [b]them that are without law,[459]
as without law, ([c]being not without law
to God, but under the law[1772] to Christ,)
that I might gain them that are without
law.
22 [a]To the weak[772] became I as
weak, that I might gain the weak: [b]I [pf]am
made all things to all *men,* [c]that I
[asba]might by all means save[4982] some.
23 And this I do for the gospel's
sake, that I [asbm]might be partaker thereof
with *you.*
24 Know ye not that they which
[ppt]run in a race run all, but one receiveth
the prize? [a]So run, that ye [aosb]may obtain.[2638]
25 And every man that [ppt][a]striveth[75]
for the mastery is temperate in all things.
Now they *do it* to [aosb]obtain a corruptible
crown; but we [b]an incorruptible.[862]
26 I therefore so run, [a]not as uncertainly; so fight I, not as one that beateth
the air:
27 [a]But I keep under my body, and
[b]bring *it* into subjection:[1396] lest that by
any means, when I [apt]have preached[2784]
to others, I myself [asbm]should be [c]a castaway.[96]

Admonitions from Israel's History

10 Moreover, brethren, I would not
that ye should [pinf]be ignorant,[50]
how that all our fathers[3962] were under
[a]the cloud, and all passed through [b]the
sea;[2281]
🔑 2 And [aom]were all baptized[907]
unto[1519] Moses in the cloud and in the
sea;
3 And did all eat the same [a]spiri-
tual[4152] meat;[1033]
4 And did all drink the same [a]spiri-
tual drink: for they [ipf]drank of that spiritual Rock that [ppt][b]followed them: and
that Rock was Christ.[5547]
5 But with many of them God was
not well pleased:[2106] for they [a]were overthrown in the wilderness.
6 Now these things were our
examples,[5179] to the intent we should not
lust after evil things, as [a]they also
lusted.[1937]
7 [a]Neither be ye idolaters,[1496] as *were*
some of them; as it is written, [b]The people sat down to eat and drink, and rose
up to play.
8 [a]Neither let us commit fornication,[4203] as some of them committed, and
[b]fell[4098] in one day three and twenty
thousand.
9 Neither [psa]let us tempt[1598] Christ,
as [a]some of them also tempted,[3985] and
[b]were destroyed of serpents.
10 Neither murmur ye, as [a]some of
them also murmured, and [b]were destroyed of [c]the destroyer.

16 [a]Rom. 1:14
17 [a]1Cor. 3:8, 14 [b]1Cor. 4:1; Gal. 2:7; Phil. 1:17; Col. 1:25
18 [a]1Cor. 10:33; 2Cor. 4:5; 11:7 [b]1Cor. 7:31
19 [a]1Cor. 9:1 [b]Gal. 5:13 [c]Matt. 18:15; 1Pet. 3:1
20 [a]Acts 16:3; 18:18; 21:23
21 [a]Gal. 3:2 [b]Rom. 2:12, 14 [c]1Cor. 7:22
22 [a]Rom. 15:1; 2Cor. 11:29 [b]1Cor. 10:33 [c]Rom. 11:14; 1Cor. 7:16
24 [a]Gal. 2:2; 5:7; Phil. 2:16; 3:14; 2Tim. 4:7; Heb. 12:1
25 [a]Eph. 6:12; 1Tim. 6:12; 2Tim. 2:5; 4:7 [b]2Tim. 4:8; James 1:12; 1Pet. 1:4; 5:4; Rev. 2:10; 3:11
26 [a]2Tim. 2:5
27 [a]Rom. 8:13; Col. 3:5 [b]Rom. 6:18, 19 [c]Jer. 6:30; 2Cor. 13:5, 6

1 [a]Ex. 13:21; 40:34; Num. 9:18; 14:14; Deut. 1:33; Neh. 9:12, 19; Ps. 78:14; 105:39 [b]Ex. 14:22; Num. 33:8; Josh. 4:23; Ps. 78:13
3 [a]Ex. 16:15, 35; Neh. 9:15, 20; Ps. 78:24
4 [a]Ex. 17:6; Num. 20:11; Ps. 78:15 [b]Deut. 9:21; Ps. 105:41
5 [a]Num. 14:29, 32, 35; 26:64, 65; Ps. 106:26; Heb. 3:17; Jude 1:5
6 [a]Num. 11:4, 33, 34; Ps. 106:14
7 [a]1Cor. 10:14 [b]Ex. 32:6
8 [a]1Cor. 6:18; Rev. 2:14 [b]Num. 25:1, 9; Ps. 106:29
9 [a]Ex. 17:2, 7; Num. 21:5; Deut. 6:16; Ps. 78:18, 56; 95:9; 106:14 [b]Num. 21:6
10 [a]Ex. 16:2; 17:2; Num. 14:2, 29; 16:41 [b]Num. 14:37; 16:49 [c]Ex. 12:23; 2Sam. 24:16; 1Chr. 21:15

🔑 **10:2** In this verse, the word *baptízō* (907) means "to be identified with." In the exodus from Egypt, the Israelites identified with the work and purposes of their leader, Moses. See note on Mark 16:16.

11 Now all these things [ipf]happened unto them for [I]ensamples:[5179] and [a]they [aop]are written for our admonition,[3559] [b]upon whom the ends[5056] of the world are come.

12 Wherefore [pim][a]let him that thinketh he standeth take heed[991] lest he fall.[4098]

13 There hath no temptation[3986] taken you but such as is common to man: but [a]God *is* faithful,[4103] [b]who will not suffer you [aifp]to be tempted[3985] above that ye are able; but will with the temptation also [c]make a way to escape, that ye may be able [ainf]to bear *it.*

14 Wherefore, my dearly beloved, [a]flee from idolatry.[1495]

15 I speak as to [a]wise men;[5429] judge[2919] ye what I say.

16 [a]The cup of blessing[2129] which we bless,[2127] is it not the communion[2842] of the blood of Christ? [b]The bread which we break,[2806] is it not the communion of the body[4983] of Christ?[5547]

17 For [a]we *being* many are one bread, *and* one body: for we are all partakers of that one bread.

18 Behold [a]Israel [b]after the flesh:[4561] [c]are not they which [ppt]eat of the sacrifices partakers[2844] of the altar?

19 What say I then? [a]that the idol[1497] is any thing, or that which is offered in sacrifice to idols[1494] is any thing?

20 But *I say,* that the things which the Gentiles [a]sacrifice, they sacrifice to devils,[1140] and not to God:[2316] and I would not that ye should have fellowship[2844] with devils.

21 [a]Ye cannot [pinf]drink the cup of the Lord, and [b]the cup of devils: ye cannot be partakers[3348] of the Lord's table, and of the table of devils.

22 Do we [a]provoke the Lord to jealousy? [b]are we stronger than he?

23 [a]All things are lawful for me, but all things [pin]are not expedient:[4851] all things are lawful for me, but all things edify not.

24 [pim][a]Let no man seek[2212] his own, but every man another's[2087] *wealth.*

25 [a]Whatsoever [ppp]is sold in the shambles,[3111] *that* eat, asking no question for conscience[4893] sake:

26 For [a]the earth[1093] *is* the Lord's,[2962] and the fulness[4138] thereof.

27 If any of them that [ajn]believe not[571] bid you *to a feast,* and ye be disposed to go; [a]whatsoever is set before you, eat, asking no question for conscience sake.

28 But if any man say unto you, This is offered in sacrifice unto idols,[1494] eat not [a]for his sake that shewed it, and for conscience sake: for [b]the earth *is* the Lord's, and the fulness thereof:

29 Conscience, I say, not thine own, but of the other:[2087] for [a]why is my liberty[1657] judged[2919] of another[243] *man's* conscience?

30 For if I by [I]grace[5485] be a partaker,[3348] why am I evil spoken of[987] for that [a]for which I give thanks?[2168]

31 [a]Whether therefore ye eat, or drink, or whatsoever ye do, do all to the glory of God.

32 [a]Give none offence,[677] neither to the Jews, nor to the [I]Gentiles, nor to [b]the church[1577] of God:

33 Even as [a]I please[700] all *men* in all *things,* [b]not seeking mine own profit,[4851] but the *profit* of many, that they may be saved.[4982]

11 Be [a]ye followers of me, even as I also *am* of Christ.

God's Ordained Order

🔑 2 Now I praise you, brethren, [a]that ye remember me in all things, and [b]keep[2722] the [I][c]ordinances, as I delivered *them* to you.

11 [I]Or, *types* [a]Rom. 15:4; 1Cor. 9:10 [b]1Cor. 7:29; Phil. 4:5; Heb. 10:25, 37; 1John 2:18
12 [a]Rom. 11:20
13 [a]1Cor. 1:9 [b]Ps. 125:3; 2Pet. 2:9 [c]Jer. 29:11
14 [a]1Cor. 10:7; 2Cor. 6:17; 1John 5:21
15 [a]1Cor. 8:1
16 [a]Matt. 26:26, 28 [b]Acts 2:42, 46; 1Cor. 11:23, 24
17 [a]Rom. 12:5; 1Cor. 12:27
18 [a]Rom. 4:12; Gal. 16 [b]Rom. 4:1; 9:3, 5; 2Cor. 11:18 [c]Lev. 3:3; 7:15
19 [a]1Cor. 8:4
20 [a]Lev. 17:7; Deut. 32:17; Ps. 106:37; Rev. 9:20
21 [a]2Cor. 6:15, 16 [b]Deut. 32:38
22 [a]Deut. 32:21 [b]Ezek. 22:14
23 [a]1Cor. 6:12
24 [a]Rom. 15:1, 2; 1Cor. 10:33; 13:5; Phil. 2:4, 21
25 [a]1Tim. 4:4
26 [a]Ex. 19:5; Deut. 10:14; Ps. 24:1; 50:12; 1Cor. 10:28
27 [a]Luke 10:7
28 [a]1Cor. 8:10, 12 [b]Deut. 10:14; Ps. 24:1; 1Cor. 10:26
29 [a]Rom. 14:16
30 [I]Or, *thanksgiving* [a]Rom. 14:6; 1Tim. 4:3, 4
31 [a]Col. 3:17; 1Pet. 4:11
32 [I]Gr. *Greeks* [a]Rom. 14:13; 1Cor. 8:13; 2Cor. 6:3 [b]Acts 20:28; 1Cor. 11:22; 1Tim. 3:5
33 [a]Rom. 15:2; 1Cor. 9:19, 22 [b]1Cor. 10:24

1 [a]1Cor. 4:16; Eph. 5:1; Phil. 3:17; 1Thess. 1:6; 2Thess. 3:9 **2** [I]Or, *traditions* [a]1Cor. 4:17 [b]1Cor. 7:17 [c]2Thess. 2:15; 3:6

🔑 **11:2–16** Paul is writing here to the Corinthian Christians who customarily consented to Greek traditions (e.g., men had their heads uncovered and the women covered their heads, which was

(continued on next page)

3 But I would have you know, that [a]the head of every man[435] is Christ;[5547] and [b]the head[2776] of the woman *is* the man; and [c]the head of Christ *is* God.[2316]

4 Every man praying[4336] or [a]prophesying,[4395] having *his* head covered, dishonoureth his head.

5 But [a]every woman that [ppt]prayeth or [ppt]prophesieth with *her* head uncovered dishonoureth her head: for that is even all one as if she were [b]shaven.

6 For if the woman be not covered, let her also be shorn: but if it be [a]a shame for a woman to be shorn or shaven, [pim]let her be covered.[2619]

7 For a man indeed ought not [pinf]to cover *his* head, forasmuch as [a]he is the image[1504] and glory[1391] of God: but the woman is the glory of the man.

8 For [a]the man is not of the woman; but the woman of the man.

9 [a]Neither was the man created[2936] for the woman; but the woman for the man.

10 For this cause ought the woman [a]to have [I]power[1849] on *her* head [b]because of the angels.[32]

11 Nevertheless [a]neither is the man without the woman, neither the woman without the man, in the Lord.[2962]

12 For as the woman *is* of the man, even so *is* the man also by the woman; [a]but all things of God.

13 Judge[2919] in yourselves: is it comely[4241] that a woman [pinf]pray[4336] unto God uncovered?

🗝 14 Doth not even nature itself teach[1321] you, that, if a man have long hair, it is a shame[819] unto him?

15 But if a woman have long hair, it is a glory[1391] to her: for *her* hair [pfip]is given her for a covering.

16 But [a]if any man seem to be contentious, we have no such custom, [b]neither the churches[1577] of God.

The Lord's Supper

17 Now in this that I declare[3853] *unto you* I praise[1867] *you* not, that ye come together not for the better,[2909] but for the worse.

18 For first of all, when ye [ppt]come together in the church, [a]I hear that there be divisions[4978] among you; and I partly believe[4100] it.

19 For [a]there must be also [I]heresies[139] among you, [b]that they which are approved[1384] may be made manifest[5318] among you.

20 When ye come together therefore

3 [a]Eph. 5:23 [b]Gen. 3:16; 1Tim. 2:11, 12; 1Pet. 3:1, 5, 6 [c]John 14:28; 1Cor. 3:23; 15:27, 28; Phil. 2:7-9
4 [a]1Cor. 12:10, 28; 14:1
5 [a]Acts 21:9 [b]Deut. 21:12
6 [a]Num. 5:18; Deut. 22:5
7 [a]Gen. 1:26, 27; 5:1; 9:6
8 [a]Gen. 2:21, 22
9 [a]Gen. 2:18, 21, 23
10 [I]That is, *a covering, in sign that she is under the power of her husband* [a]Gen. 24:65 [b]Eccl. 5:6
11 [a]Gal. 3:28
12 [a]Rom. 11:36
16 [a]1Tim. 6:4 [b]1Cor. 7:17; 14:33
18 [a]1Cor. 1:10-12; 3:3
19 [I]Or, *sects* [a]Matt. 18:7; Luke 17:1; Acts 20:30; 1Tim. 4:1; 2Pet. 2:1, 2 [b]Luke 2:35; 1John 2:19; Deut. 13:3

(continued from previous page)
contrary to the Jewish tradition. Even to this day, Jewish men cover their heads at worship, while the women no longer do). The question that faced the Corinthians was what to do with the existing custom of their day. Paul's advice is to examine the symbolism of the custom and determine whether or not it is contrary to God's Word or His order in creation. Paul indicated that there is nothing wrong with this, for in creation God created man, and from man came the woman (see note on 1 Tim. 2:9–15). In spite of the fact that he prays without a covering, man still is accountable to Christ (v. 3). It is clear from verse eleven that men and women are equal in the Lord (Gal. 3:28 and 1 Pet. 3:7). Although there is equality in Christ, the husband is still the head of the family. It was God who caused there to be differences in males and females. Since this custom of head coverings revealed what was evident in the creative order of things, the Greek custom was not to be looked down on by those upholding Jewish traditions. In the event of having to choose between the two, the decision was left entirely up to the Corinthian believers (v. 13). The goal was to give the believers an opportunity to evaluate the customs and determine whether or not they are in accordance to God's word. Scripture teaches that existing customs, as long as they are not contrary to morals and Scripture, are to be adhered to for the sake of unity among the believers and not to be flaunted. See note on 1 Corinthians 14:33–40.

🗝 **11:14, 15** The verb *komáō* (2863) means "to have long hair." The passage continues: "But if a woman have long hair, it is a glory to her." A woman wearing her hair longer than a man's identifies her distinctively as a woman. See notes on 1 Corinthians 14:33–40 and 1 Timothy 2:9–15.

into one place, *this* is not [ainf]to eat the Lord's[2960] supper.

21 For in eating every one taketh before[4301] *other* his own supper: and one is hungry, and [a]another is drunken.

22 What? have ye not houses to eat and to drink in? or despise ye [a]the church[1577] of God, and [b]shame [I]them that [ppt]have not? What shall I say to you? shall I praise you in this? I praise *you* not.

23 For [a]I [ao]have received of the Lord that which also I delivered unto you, [b]That the Lord Jesus the *same* night in which he [ipf]was betrayed took bread:

24 And when he [apt]had given thanks,[2168] he brake[2806] *it,* and said, Take, eat: this is my body,[4983] which [ppp]is broken for you: this do in remembrance[364] of me.

25 After the same manner also *he took* the cup, when he [aime]had supped,[1172] saying, This cup is the new[2537] testament[1242] in my blood:[129] this do ye, as oft as ye drink *it,* in remembrance[364] of me.

26 For as often as ye eat this bread, and drink this cup, [I]ye do shew[2605] the Lord's[2962] death[2288] [a]till he come.[2064]

27 [a]Wherefore whosoever [psa]shall eat this bread, and [psa]drink *this* cup of the Lord, unworthily,[371] shall be guilty of[1777] the body and blood of the Lord.

28 But [pima]let a man examine[1381] himself, and so let him eat[2068] of *that* bread, and [pim]drink of *that* cup.

29 For he that [ppt]eateth and [ppt]drinketh unworthily,[371] eateth and drinketh [Ia]damnation[2917] to himself, not discerning[1252] the Lord's body.

30 For this cause many *are* weak and sickly[732] among you, and many sleep.

31 For [a]if we [ipf]would judge[1252] ourselves, we [ipf]should not be judged.[2919]

32 But when we are [ppp]judged, [a]we are chastened[3811] of the Lord, that we [asbp]should not be condemned[2632] with the world.[2889]

33 Wherefore, my brethren, when ye [ppt]come together to eat, tarry[1551] one for another.

34 And if any man [a]hunger, let him eat at [b]home; that ye come not together unto [I]condemnation.[2917] And the rest [fmc]will I set in order[1299] when [d]I come.

Spiritual Gifts

12 🗝Now [a]concerning spiritual *gifts,* brethren,[80] I would not have you ignorant.[50]

2 Ye know [a]that ye were Gentiles,[1484] [ppp]carried away unto these [b]dumb[880] idols,[1497] even as ye [ipf]were led.

3 Wherefore I [pin]give you to understand,[1107] [a]that no man speaking by the [an]Spirit[4151] of God calleth Jesus accursed:[331] and [b]*that* no man can say that Jesus is the Lord,[2962] but by the [an]Holy Ghost.[4151]

4 Now [a]there are diversities[1243] of gifts,[5486] but [b]the same Spirit.

5 [a]And there are differences[1243] of [I]administrations,[1248] but the same Lord.

6 And there are diversities[1243] of operations,[1755] but it is the same God [a]which [ppt]worketh[1754] all in all.

7 [a]But the manifestation[5321] of the Spirit [pinp]is given to every man[1538] to profit[4851] withal.

8 For to one is given by the Spirit [a]the word[3056] of wisdom;[4678] to another[243] [b]the word of knowledge[1108] by the same Spirit;

21 [a]2Pet. 2:13; Jude 1:12
22 [I]Or, *them that are poor?* [a]1Cor. 10:32 [b]James 2:6
23 [a]1Cor. 15:3; Gal. 1:1, 11, 12 [b]Matt. 26:26; Mark 14:22; Luke 22:19
26 [I]Or, *ye announce* [a]John 14:3; 21:22; Acts 1:11; 1Cor. 4:5; 15:23; 1Thess. 4:16; 2Thess. 1:10; Jude 1:14; Rev. 1:7
27 [a]Num. 9:10, 13; John 6:51, 63, 64; 13:27; 1Cor. 10:21
28 [a]2Cor. 13:5; Gal. 6:4
29 [I]Or, *judgment* [a]Rom. 13:2
31 [a]Ps. 32:5; 1John 1:9
32 [a]Ps. 94:12, 13; Heb. 12:5-11
34 [I]Or, *judgment* [a]1Cor. 11:21 [b]1Cor. 11:22 [c]1Cor. 7:17; Titus 1:5 [d]1Cor. 4:19

1 [a]1Cor. 14:1, 37
2 [a]1Cor. 6:11; Eph. 2:11, 12; 1Thess. 1:9; Titus 3:3; 1Pet. 4:3 [b]Ps. 115:5
3 [a]Mark 9:39; 1John 4:2, 3 [b]Matt. 16:17; John 15:26; 2Cor. 3:5
4 [a]Rom. 12:4; Heb. 2:4; 1Pet. 4:10 [b]Eph. 4:4
5 [I]Or, *ministries* [a]Rom. 12:6-8; Eph. 4:11
6 [a]Eph. 1:23
7 [a]Rom. 12:6-8; 1Cor. 14:26; Eph. 4:7; 1Pet. 4:10, 11
8 [a]1Cor. 2:6, 7 [b]1Cor. 1:5; 13:2; 2Cor. 8:7

🗝 **12:1–11** This is not a complete list of the gifts of the Holy Spirit (cf. Rom. 12:6–8 and Eph. 4:11, 12). These may have been specifically mentioned because they constituted a portion of the questions in the Corinthian's letter to Paul (1 Cor. 7:1). In 1 Corinthians 1:4–7, Paul is telling the Corinthians that the grace of God was given unto them in Christ Jesus, so that they would not be lacking in any spiritual gifts. Since every Christian has been given the Holy Spirit, he has the potential to demonstrate the particular gift which has been given to him. The intent of this passage is to first exhort the Corinthians to seek God's grace, then it will be revealed further through the manifestation of the gift that God will give to them.

9 [a]To <u>another</u>[2087] <u>faith</u>[4102] by the same Spirit; to <u>another</u>[243] [b]the [an]<u>gifts</u>[5486] of [pl]<u>healing</u> 2386 by the same Spirit;

10 [a]To <u>another</u>[243] the [pl]working of <u>miracles;</u>[1411] to another [b]<u>prophecy;</u>[4394] [c]to another [pl]<u>discerning</u>[1253] of spirits; to <u>another</u>[2087] [d]*divers* kinds of <u>tongues;</u>[1100] to <u>another</u>[243] the [an]<u>interpretation</u> 2058 of tongues:

11 But all these worketh that one and the selfsame Spirit, [a]<u>dividing</u>[1244] to every man severally [b]as he will.

One Body, Many Members

12 For [a]as the <u>body</u>[4983] is one, and hath many members, and all the members of that one body, being many, are one body: [b]so also *is* <u>Christ</u>.[5547]

🔑 13 For [a]by one Spirit [aop]<u>are</u> we all <u>baptized</u>[907] into one body, [b]whether *we be* Jews or [I]Gentiles, whether *we be* <u>bond</u>[1401] or <u>free;</u>[1658] and [aop][c]<u>have been</u> all <u>made to drink</u> 4222 into one Spirit.

14 For the <u>body</u>[4983] is not one member, but many.

15 If the foot shall say, Because I am not the hand, I am not <u>of</u>[1537] the body; is it <u>therefore</u>[3844] 5124 not of the body?

16 And if the ear shall say, Because I am not the eye, I am not of the body; is it <u>therefore</u>[3844] 5124 not of the body?

17 If the whole body *were* an eye, where *were* the <u>hearing</u>?[189] If the whole *were* hearing, where *were* the smelling?

18 But now [aom]<u>hath</u> [a]God <u>set</u>[5087] the members every one of them in the body, [b]as it hath pleased him.

19 And if they were all one member, where *were* the body?

20 But now *are they* many members, yet but one body.

21 And the eye cannot say unto the hand, I have no need of thee: nor again the head to the feet, I have no need of you.

22 Nay, much more those members of the body, which seem to be <u>more feeble</u>,[772] are <u>necessary</u>:[316]

23 And those *members* of the body, which we think to be less honourable, upon these we [I]bestow <u>more abundant</u> 4055 <u>honour;</u> 5092 and our uncomely *parts* have more abundant <u>comeliness</u>. 2157

24 For our <u>comely</u> 2158 *parts* have no need: but God [ao]hath tempered the body together, having given more abundant honour to that *part* which [ppt]lacked:

25 That there should be no [I]<u>schism</u>[4978] in the body; but *that* the members should have the same care one for another.

26 And whether one member suffer, all the members <u>suffer with</u>[4841] it; or one member [pinp]<u>be honoured</u>,[1392] all the members rejoice with it.

27 Now [a]ye are the <u>body</u>[4983] of <u>Christ</u>,[5547] and [b]members in particular.

28 And [a]God [aom]hath set some in the <u>church</u>,[1577] <u>first</u>[4412] [b]<u>apostles</u>,[652] secondarily [c]<u>prophets</u>,[4396] thirdly <u>teachers</u>,[1320] after that [d]<u>miracles</u>,[1411] then [e]<u>gifts</u>[5486] of <u>healings</u>, 2386 [f]<u>helps</u>,[484] [g]<u>governments</u>,[2941] [I]diversities of <u>tongues</u>.[1100]

29 *Are* all apostles? *are* all prophets? *are* all teachers? *are* all [I]workers of miracles?

30 Have all the <u>gifts</u>[5486] of [pl]healing? <u>do</u> all <u>speak</u>[2980] with tongues? <u>do</u> all <u>interpret</u>? 1329

Love

🔑 31 But [a]covet earnestly the <u>best</u>[2909] gifts: and yet shew I unto you a more excellent way.

9 [a]Matt. 17:19, 20; 1Cor. 13:2; 2Cor. 4:13 [b]Mark 16:1; James 5:14
10 [a]1Cor. 12:28, 29; Mark 16:17; Gal. 3:5 [b]Rom. 12:6; 1Cor. 13:2; 14:1 [c]1Cor. 14:29; 1John 4:1 [d]Acts 2:4; 10:46; 1Cor. 13:1
11 [a]Rom. 12:6; 1Cor. 7:7; 2Cor. 10:13; Eph. 4:7 [b]John 3:8; Heb. 2:4
12 [a]Rom. 12:4, 5; Eph. 4:4, 16 [b]1Cor. 12:27; Gal. 3:16
13 [I]Gr. *Greeks* [a]Rom. 6:5 [b]Gal. 3:28; Eph. 2:13, 14, 16; Col. 3:11 [c]John 6:63; 7:37-39
18 [a]1Cor. 12:28 [b]Rom. 12:3; 1Cor. 3:5; 12:11
23 [I]Or, *put on*
25 [I]Or, *division*
27 [a]Rom. 12:5; Eph. 1:23; 4:12; 5:23, 30; Col. 1:24 [b]Eph. 5:30
28 [I]Or, *kinds* [a]Eph. 4:11 [b]Eph. 2:20; 3:5 [c]Acts 13:1; Rom. 12:6 [d]1Cor. 12:10 [e]1Cor. 12:9 [f]Num. 11:17 [g]Rom. 12:8; 1Tim. 5:17; Heb. 13:17, 24 [h]1Cor. 12:10
29 [I]Or, *powers*
31 [a]1Cor. 14:1, 39

🔑 **12:13** This is the final time that the baptism of the Holy Spirit is used in the New Testament (see note on Acts 1:5).

🔑 **12:31** The "best gifts" mentioned here refer to those which are most useful. The Corinthian believers were desiring the gifts that would bring them the most acclaim and prestige among their fellow brethren in Christ (e.g., the gifts of tongues, prophecies, and knowledge, cf. 1 Cor. 13:8).

(continued on next page)

13 Though I speak with the
tongues[1100] of men[444] and of
angels,[32] and have not charity,[26] I [pfi]am
become *as* sounding brass, or a tinkling
cymbal.
2 And though I have *the gift of*
[a]prophecy,[4394] and understand[1492] all
mysteries,[3466] and all knowledge;[1108] and
though I have all faith,[4102] [b]so that I
[pinf]could remove[3179] mountains, and have
not charity, I am nothing.
3 And [a]though I bestow all my goods
to feed *the poor,* and though I give my
body[4983] to be burned, and have not charity, it profiteth me nothing.
4 [a]Charity suffereth long,[3114] *and* is
kind; charity envieth not; charity
[I]vaunteth not itself,[4068] is not puffed up,
5 Doth not behave itself unseemly,
[a]seeketh not her own, is not easily provoked, thinketh[3049] no evil;[2556]
6 [a]Rejoiceth[5463] not in iniquity,[93] but
[b]rejoiceth[4796] [I]in the truth;[225]
7 [a]Beareth[4722] all things, believeth[4100]
all things, hopeth[1679] all things, endureth[5278] all things.
⊶ 8 Charity[26] never faileth:[1601] but
whether *there be* prophecies,[4394] they
shall fail;[2673] whether *there be*
tongues,[1100] they shall cease; whether
there be knowledge,[1108] it shall vanish
away.
9 [a]For we know[1097] in part, and we
prophesy[4395] in part.
⊶ 10 But when that which is perfect[5046]
[aosb]is come,[2064] then that which is in part
shall be done away.
11 When I was a child,[3516] I [ipf]spake
as a child, I [ipf]understood[5426] as a child,
I [ipfI]thought as a child: but when I
[pfi]became a man,[435] I [pfi]put away child-
ish[3516] things.
12 For [a]now we see through a glass,
darkly; but then [b]face to face: now I know
in part; but then shall I know even as
also I [aop]am known.
13 And now abideth[3306] faith,[4102]
hope,[1680] charity,[26] these three; but the
greatest of these *is* charity.

Concerning Speaking in Tongues

14 ⊶Follow after charity,[26] and [a]de-
sire spiritual[4152] *gifts,* [b]but rather
that ye may prophesy.[4395]
2 For he that [ppt][a]speaketh[2980] in an
unknown tongue[1100] speaketh not unto
men, but unto God:[2316] for no man
[I][b]understandeth[191] *him;* howbeit[1161] in the
[an]spirit[4151] he speaketh mysteries.[3466]
3 But he that [ppt]prophesieth[4395]
speaketh unto men *to* edification,[3619] and
exhortation,[3874] and comfort.[3889]
4 He that speaketh in an *unknown*
tongue edifieth[3618] himself; but he that
prophesieth edifieth the church.[1577]
5 I would that ye all [pinf]spake with
tongues, but rather that ye [psa]prophesied:
for greater *is* he that [ppt]prophesieth than

2 [a]1Cor. 12:8-10; 14:1; Matt. 7:22 [b]Matt. 17:20; Mark 11:23; Luke 17:6
3 [a]Matt. 6:1, 2
4 IOr, *is not rash* [a]Prov. 10:12; 1Pet. 4:8
5 [a]1Cor. 10:24; Phil. 2:4
6 IOr, *with the truth* [a]Ps. 10:3; Rom. 1:32 [b]2John 1:4
7 [a]Rom. 15:1; Gal. 6:2; 2Tim. 2:24
9 [a]1Cor. 8:2
11 IOr, *reasoned*
12 [a]2Cor. 3:18; 5:7; Phil. 3:12 [b]Matt. 18:10; 1John 3:2

1 [a]1Cor. 12:31 [b]Num. 11:25, 29
2 IGr. *heareth* [a]Acts 2:4; 10:46 [b]Acts 22:9

(continued from previous page)
Instead, Paul urged them to "covet" (earnestly desire) the gifts that would best benefit the cause of Christ, not themselves. In chapter thirteen, Paul further explains that the gifts must be done in love for Christ, not for self.

⊶ **13:8, 10** It is clear from these verses that tongues no longer continue today. The phrase "when that which is perfect is come" refers to the written revelation of Scripture. When this revelation was completed, there was no need for the temporary gifts (e.g., tongues, prophecies, and knowledge), which were given in order to substantiate the message that the apostles were preaching.

⊶ **14:1–3** One observation needs to be made. In these three historical occurrences (Acts 2:4, 6, 8; 10:46; 19:6) speaking in tongues refers to dialects, or languages (*hēterai* [2087]) other than the ones known by the speakers. When the word "tongue" is used in the singular, *glōssa* ([1100], cf. 1 Cor. 14:2, 4, 13, 19, 26, 27), it refers to the Corinthian ecstatic utterance. In 1 Corinthians 14:9, it refers to the physical tongue of man, and in 1 Corinthians 14:23, being in the plural with a plural pronoun, it refers to the Corinthian ecstatic utterances. The whole thesis of the Apostle Paul is that no one should be speaking in the presence of other human beings unless the hearers can understand what is being said. See note on 1 Corinthians 14:33–40.

he that speaketh with tongues, except he [psa]interpret, that the church[1577] [asba]may receive edifying.[3619]

6 Now, brethren, if I come unto you speaking[2980] with tongues,[1100] what shall I profit you, except I shall speak to you either by [a]revelation,[602] or by knowledge,[1108] or by prophesying,[4394] or by doctrine?

7 And even things without life[895] giving sound, whether pipe or harp, except they give a distinction in the sounds, how shall it be known what is piped or harped?

8 For if the trumpet give an uncertain sound, who shall prepare himself to the battle?

9 So likewise ye, except ye utter by the tongue words easy to be understood, how shall it be known what is spoken? for ye shall speak into the air.

10 There are, it may be, so many kinds of voices in the world, and none of them *is* without signification.

11 Therefore if I know not the meaning[1411] of the voice, I shall be unto him that [ppt]speaketh a barbarian,[915] and he that [ppt]speaketh *shall be* a barbarian unto me.

12 Even so ye, forasmuch as ye are zealous [I]of spiritual[4151] *gifts,* seek that ye [psa]may excel to the edifying of the church.[1577]

13 Wherefore let him that speaketh in an *unknown* tongue[1100] [pim]pray that he may interpret.

14 For if I pray in an *unknown* tongue, my spirit[4151] prayeth, but my understanding is unfruitful.

15 What is it then? I will pray with the spirit,[4151] and I will pray with the understanding also: [a]I will sing[5567] with the spirit, and I will sing [b]with the understanding also.

16 Else when thou shalt bless[2127] with the spirit, how shall he that [ppt]occupieth[378] the room of the unlearned[2399] say Amen[281] [a]at thy giving of thanks, seeing he understandeth not what thou sayest?

17 For thou verily[3303] givest thanks well, but the other[2087] is not edified.[3618]

6 [a]1Cor. 14:26

12 [I]Gr. *of spirits*

15 [a]Eph. 5:19; Col. 3:16 [b]Ps. 47:7

16 [a]1Cor. 11:24

20 [I]Gr. *perfect, or, of a ripe age* [a]Ps. 131:2; Matt. 11:25; 18:3; 19:14; Rom. 16:19; 1Cor. 3:1; Eph. 4:14; Heb. 5:12, 13 [b]Matt. 18:3; 1Pet. 2:2 [c]1Cor. 2:6

21 [a]John 10:34 [b]Isa. 28:11, 12

23 [a]Acts 2:13

25 [a]Isa. 45:14; Zech. 8:23

26 [a]1Cor. 12:8-10; 14:6 [b]1Cor. 12:7; 2Cor. 12:19; Eph. 4:12

18 I thank[2168] my God, I speak[2980] with tongues[1100] more than ye all:

19 Yet in the church[1577] I had rather speak five words with my understanding,[3563] that *by my voice* I might teach[2727] others[243] also, than ten thousand words in an *unknown* tongue.[1100]

20 Brethren, [a]be not children in understanding:[5424] howbeit[235] in malice[2549] [b]be ye children,[3515] but in understanding be [I][c]men.[5046]

21 [a]In the law[3551] it is [b]written, With *men of* other tongues[2084] and other lips will I speak[2980] unto this people;[2992] and yet for all that [fm]will they not hear[1522] me, saith the Lord.

22 Wherefore tongues[1100] are for a sign,[4592] not to them that [ppt]believe,[4100] but to them that [ajn]believe not:[571] but prophesying[4394] *serveth* not for them that [ajn]believe not, but for them which [ppt]believe.

23 If therefore the whole church[1577] [asba]be come together into one place, and all speak with tongues, and there come in *those that are* unlearned,[2399] or unbelievers,[571] [a]will they not say that ye are mad?

24 But if all prophesy, and there come in one that believeth not, or *one* unlearned, he is convinced of all, he is judged[350] of all:

25 And thus are the secrets of his heart[2588] made manifest;[5318] and so [apt]falling down on *his* face he will worship God, and [ppt]report [a]that God is in you of a truth.

Do Things Properly and Orderly

26 How is it then, brethren?[80] when ye come together, every one of you hath a psalm,[5568] [a]hath a doctrine,[1322] hath a tongue,[1100] hath a revelation,[602] hath an interpretation.[2058] [b]Let all things be done unto edifying.

27 If any man speak in an *unknown* tongue,[1100] *let it be* by[2596] two, or at the most *by* three, and *that* by[303] course; and let one interpret.[1329]

28 But if there be no interpreter, let

him keep silence in the church;[1577] and
[pim]let him speak[2980] to himself, and to
God.[2316]
29 Let the prophets[4396] speak two or
three, and [pim][a]let the other judge.[1252]
30 If *any thing* be revealed[601] to another that sitteth by, [a]let the first[4413] hold
his peace.
31 For ye may all prophesy one
by[2596] one, that all may learn,[3129] and all
may be comforted.[3870]
32 And [a]the spirits[4151] of the
prophets[4396] [pinp]are subject[5293] to the
prophets.
🔑 33 For God is not *the author* of confusion,[181] but of peace,[1515] [a]as in all
churches[1577] of the saints.[40]
34 [pim][a]Let your women keep silence[4601] in the churches: for it is not permitted unto them to speak; but [b]*they are
commanded* [pip]to be under obedience,[5293]
as also saith the [c]law.[3551]
35 And if they will learn[3129] any
thing, [pim]let them ask[1905] their husbands
at home: for it is a shame for women to
speak in the church.
36 What? came the word[3056] of God
out from you? or came it unto you only?
37 [a]If any man think himself to be
a prophet,[4396] or spiritual,[4152] let him acknowledge that the things that I write[1125]
unto you are the commandments[1785] of
the Lord.[2962]
38 But if any man be ignorant,[50] let
him be ignorant.
39 Wherefore, brethren, [a]covet to
prophesy,[4395] and forbid not [pinf]to
speak[2980] with tongues.[1100]
40 [a]Let all things be done decently[2156] and in order.[5010]

A Summary of the Gospel

15 Moreover, brethren,[80] I declare[1107]
unto you the gospel[2098] [a]which I
preached[2097] unto you, which also ye
[ao]have received, and [b]wherein ye stand;
2 [a]By which also ye [pinp]are saved,[4982]

29 [a]1Cor. 12:10
30 [a]1Thess. 5:19, 20
32 [a]1John 4:1
33 [a]1Cor. 11:16
34 [a]1Tim. 2:11, 12 [b]1Cor. 11:3; Eph. 5:22; Col. 3:18; Titus 2:5; 1Pet. 3:1 [c]Gen. 3:16
37 [a]2Cor. 10:7; 1John 4:6
39 [a]1Cor. 12:31; 1Thess. 5:20
40 [a]1Cor. 14:33 [b]Gal. 1:11 [c]Rom. 5:2
2 [a]Rom. 1:16; 1Cor. 1:21

🔑 **14:33–40** The question frequently asked concerning this portion of Scripture is "Does the Apostle Paul forbid women to speak at all or to pray or prophesy in church?" The main verse that constitutes the foundation of all that Paul says in 1 Corinthians 14:33, "For God is not the author of confusion but of peace, as in all the churches of the saints." The instruction of Paul is found in verse thirty-nine: "Therefore, my brethren, desire earnestly to prophesy," meaning "be zealous about giving forth the word of God." In verse forty, Paul states, "But let all things be done decently and in order." This as a principle applies to all the churches (v. 34) although it was born out of a practice existing only in Corinth. When Paul says, "Let the women keep silent in the churches," (v. 34), it was not an instruction to men in general not to permit any woman to speak in church, but to husbands to guide and teach their own wives lest they produce confusion and disturbance in a meeting. This may have resulted from the exercising of a gift that they thought they had and were anxious to externalize. One cannot take Paul's indirect imperative in 1 Corinthians 14:34 as absolute. It must be taken in conjunction with what follows: "for they are not permitted to speak." The word "speak" should be taken to mean "uttering sounds that are incoherent and not understood by others." Paul says that instead it is better to have silence. Paul uses the same word "keep silent" to admonish a man who speaks in an unknown tongue without an interpreter (vv. 28, 30). What Paul is saying is that only one man must speak at a time, for if two speak at once, there will be confusion. The phrase, "let him keep silent" is then qualified to the woman (v. 34). Under no circumstances does the injunction of Paul indicate that women should not utter a word at any time during the church service. The issue is not men versus women, but it is confusion versus order. In God's sight, it makes no difference who causes the confusion. It is a shame for any woman to bring confusion into the local church (v. 35), even as it is for any man to do so. Furthermore, the word *gunaíkes* (1135) should not be translated as "women" in its generic sense, but as "wives" (v. 34). It is wives who should submit (*hupotássomai*, [5293]) to their own husbands (v. 35, from *ándras* [435]). The whole argument is not the subjection of women to men in general, but of wives to their own husbands in the family unit that has been ordained by God (see note on 1 Tim. 2:9–15). Paul states the principle that the duty of the husbands is to restrain their own wives from outbursts during the worship service. Whenever Paul speaks of submissiveness by a woman, it is always on the part of a wife to her own husband. See note on Titus 2:1–5.

if ye [I]keep in memory[2722] [II]what I [aom]preached unto you, unless [b]ye have believed[4100] in vain.

3 For [a]I delivered unto you first of all that [b]which I also received, how that Christ[5547] died for our sins[266] [c]according to the scriptures;[1124]

4 And that he was buried, and that he [pfip]rose again[1453] the third day [a]according to the scriptures:

5 [a]And that he was seen of Cephas, then [b]of the twelve:

6 After that, he was seen of above[1883] five hundred brethren at once; of whom the greater part remain[3306] unto this present, but some [ao]are fallen asleep.

7 After that, he was seen of James; then [a]of all the apostles.[652]

8 [a]And last of all he was seen of me also, as of one born out of due time.

9 For I am [a]the least of the apostles, that am not meet[2425] to be called an apostle, because [b]I persecuted the church[1577] of God.

10 But [a]by the grace[5485] of God I am what I am: and his grace[5485] which *was bestowed* upon me was not in vain; but [b]I laboured more abundantly than they all: [c]yet not I, but the grace[5485] of God which was with[4862] me.

11 Therefore whether *it were* I or they, so we preach,[2784] and so ye believed.

12 Now if Christ[5547] be preached[2784] that he rose from the dead,[3498] how say some among you that there is no resurrection[386] of the dead?

13 But if there be no resurrection of the dead, [a]then [pfip]is Christ not risen:[1453]

14 And if Christ be not risen, then *is* our preaching[2782] vain, and your faith[4102] *is* also vain.

15 Yea, and we are found false witnesses [gc]of God; because [a]we have testified of God that he raised up[1453] Christ: whom he raised not up, if so be that the dead rise not.

16 For if the dead rise not, then is not Christ raised:

17 And if Christ be not raised, your faith *is* vain; [a]ye are yet in your sins.[266]

18 Then they also which [aptp]are fallen asleep in Christ [aom]are perished.[622]

19 [a]If in this life only we have hope[1679] in Christ, we are of all men most miserable.[1652]

20 But now [a]is Christ risen from the dead, *and* become [b]the firstfruits[536] of them that [pfp]slept.

21 For [a]since by man *came* death,[2288] [b]by man *came* also the resurrection[386] of the dead.[3498]

22 For as in Adam all die,[599] even so in Christ [fp]shall all be made alive.[2227]

23 But [a]every man in his own order:[5001] Christ the firstfruits; afterward they that are Christ's at his coming.[3952]

24 Then *cometh* the end,[5056] when he [asba]shall have delivered up [a]the kingdom[932] to God,[2316] even the Father;[3962] when he [asba]shall have put down all rule[746] and all authority[1849] and power.[1411]

25 For he must [pinf]reign,[936] [a]till he [asba]hath put all enemies under his feet.

26 [a]The last enemy *that* [pinp]shall be destroyed *is* death.

27 For he [ao][a]hath put[5293] all things under his feet. But when he [aosb]saith all things [pfip]are put under *him, it is* manifest that he is excepted, which [apt]did put all things under him.

28 [a]And when all things [asbp]shall be subdued unto[5293] him, then [b]shall the Son[5207] also himself be subject unto him that put all things under him, that God may be all in all.

29 Else what shall they do which [ppp]are baptized[907] for the dead, if the dead rise not at all? why [pinp]are they then baptized[907] for the dead?

30 And [a]why stand we in jeopardy every hour?

31 I protest by your [a]rejoicing which I have in Christ Jesus our Lord, [b]I die daily.

32 If after the manner of men [a]I [ao]have fought with beasts at Ephesus, what advantageth it me, if the dead rise not? [b]let us eat and drink; for to morrow we die.

2 IOr, *hold fast* IIGr. *by what speech* [b]Gal. 3:4
3 [a]1Cor. 11:2, 23 [b]Gal. 1:12 [c]Ps. 22:15; Isa. 53:5, 6; Dan. 9:26; Zech. 13:7; Luke 24:26, 46; Acts 3:18; 26:23; 1Pet. 1:11; 2:24
4 [a]Ps. 2:7; 16:10; Isa. 53:10; Hos. 6:2; Luke 24:26, 46; Acts 2:25-31; 13:33-35; 26:22, 23; 1Pet. 1:11
5 [a]Luke 24:34 [b]Matt. 28:17; Mark 16:14; Luke 24:36; John 20:19, 26; Acts 10:41
7 [a]Luke 24:50; Acts 1:3, 4
8 [a]Acts 9:4, 17; 22:14, 18; 1Cor. 9:1
9 [a]Eph. 3:8 [b]Acts 8:3; 9:1; Gal. 1:13; Phil. 3:6; 1Tim. 1:13
10 [a]Eph. 3:7, 8 [b]2Cor. 11:23; 12:11 [c]Matt. 10:20; Rom. 15:18, 19; 2Cor. 3:5; Gal. 2:8; Eph. 3:7; Phil. 2:13
13 [a]1Thess. 4:14
15 [a]Acts 2:24, 32; 4:10, 33; 13:30
17 [a]Rom. 4:25
19 [a]2Tim. 3:12
20 [a]1Pet. 1:3 [b]Acts 26:23; 1Cor. 15:23; Col. 1:18; Rev. 1:5
21 [a]Rom. 5:12, 17 [b]John 11:25; Rom. 6:23
23 [a]1Cor. 15:20; 1Thess. 4:15-17
24 [a]Dan. 7:14, 27
25 [a]Ps. 110:1; Acts 2:34, 35; Eph. 1:22; Heb. 1:13; 10:13
26 [a]2Tim. 1:10; Rev. 20:14
27 [a]Ps. 8:6; Matt. 28:18; Heb. 2:8; 1Pet. 3:22
28 [a]Phil. 3:21 [b]1Cor. 3:23; 11:3
30 [a]2Cor. 11:26; Gal. 5:11

31 [a]1Thess. 2:19 [b]Rom. 8:36; 1Cor. 4:9; 2Cor. 4:10, 11; 11:23 **32** [a]2Cor. 1:8 [b]Eccl. 2:24; Isa. 22:13; 56:12; Luke 12:19

33 Be not deceived: [a]evil communications[3657] corrupt good[5543] manners.

34 [a]Awake to righteousness,[1346] and [pim]sin[264] not; [b]for some have not the knowledge[56] of God:[2316] [c]I speak *this* to your shame.[1791]

Resurrection Promised

35 But some *man* will say, [a]How are the dead raised up? and with what body[4983] do they come?

36 *Thou* fool, [a]that which thou sowest [pinp]is not quickened,[2227] except it [aosb]die:[599]

37 And that which thou sowest, thou sowest not that body that shall be, but bare[1131] grain, it [opt]may chance[5177] of wheat, or of some other *grain:*

38 But God giveth it a body as it hath pleased him, and to every seed[4690] his own body.

39 All flesh[4561] *is* not the same flesh: but *there is* one[243] *kind of* flesh of men, another[243] flesh of beasts, another[243] of fishes, *and* another[243] of birds.

40 *There are* also celestial bodies,[4983] and bodies terrestrial:[1919] but the glory[1391] of the celestial *is* one,[2087] and the *glory* of the terrestrial *is* another.[2087]

41 *There is* one[243] glory of the sun, and another[243] glory of the moon, and another[243] glory of the stars: for *one* star differeth from[1308] *another* star in glory.

42 [a]So also *is* the resurrection[386] of the dead.[3498] It [pinp]is sown in corruption; it [pinp]is raised[1453] in incorruption:

43 [a]It is sown in dishonour;[819] it is raised in glory: it is sown in weakness;[769] it is raised in power:[1411]

44 It is sown a natural[5591] body;[4983] it is raised a spiritual body. There is a natural body, and there is a spiritual body.

45 And so it is written, The first[4413] man Adam [a]was made[1096] a living[2198] soul;[5590] [b]the last Adam *was made* [c]a [ppt]quickening[2227] spirit.[4151]

46 Howbeit[235] that *was* not first which is spiritual,[4152] but that which is natural;[5591] and afterward that which is spiritual.

47 [a]The first man *is* of the earth,[1093] [b]earthy:[5517] the second man *is* the Lord[2962] [c]from heaven.[3772]

48 *As* is the earthy, such *are* they also that are earthy: [a]and as *is* the heavenly, such *are* they also that are heavenly.

49 And [a]as we [ao]have borne[5409] the image[1504] of the earthy, [b]we [ft]shall also bear[5409] the image of the heavenly.

50 Now this I say, brethren, that [a]flesh[4561] and blood[129] cannot [ainf]inherit[2816] the kingdom[932] of God; neither doth corruption[5356] inherit incorruption.[861]

🔑 51 Behold, I shew you a mystery;[3466] [a]We shall not all sleep, [b]but we [fp]shall all be changed,[236]

52 In a moment, in the twinkling of an eye, at the last trump: [a]for the trumpet shall sound, and the dead shall be raised incorruptible,[862] and we shall be changed.

53 For this corruptible must [ainf]put on incorruption, and [a]this mortal[2349] *must* put on immortality.[110]

54 So when this corruptible [asbm]shall have put on incorruption, and this mortal [asbm]shall have put on immortality, then shall be brought to pass the saying that is written, [a]Death[2288] [aop]is swallowed up in victory.[3534]

55 [a]O death, where *is* thy sting? O [I]grave,[86] where *is* thy victory?

56 The sting of death *is* sin;[266] and [a]the strength of sin *is* the law.[3551]

57 [a]But thanks[5485] *be* to God, which [ppt]giveth us [b]the victory through our Lord Jesus Christ.

58 [a]Therefore, my beloved[27] brethren,[80] [pim]be ye stedfast, unmoveable, always [ppt]abounding in the work[2041] of the Lord, forasmuch as ye know [b]that your labour[2873] is not in vain[2756] in the Lord.

33 [a]1Cor. 5:6
34 [a]Rom. 13:11; Eph. 5:14 [b]1Thess. 4:5 [c]1Cor. 6:5
35 [a]Ezek. 37:3
36 [a]John 12:24
42 [a]Dan. 12:3; Matt. 13:43
43 [a]Phil. 3:21
45 [a]Gen. 2:7 [b]Rom. 5:14 [c]John 5:21; 6:33, 39, 40, 54, 57; Phil. 3:21; Col. 3:4
47 [a]John 3:31 [b]Gen. 2:7; 3:19 [c]John 3:13, 31
48 [a]Phil. 3:20, 21
49 [a]Gen. 5:3 [b]Rom. 8:29; 2Cor. 3:18; 4:11; Phil. 3:21; 1John 3:2
50 [a]Matt. 16:17; John 3:3, 5
51 [a]1Thess. 4:15-17 [b]Phil. 3:21
52 [a]Zech. 9:14; Matt. 24:31; John 5:25; 1Thess. 4:16
53 [a]2Cor. 5:4
54 [a]Isa. 25:8; Heb. 2:14, 15; Rev. 20:14
55 [I]Or, *hell* [a]Hos. 13:14
56 [a]Rom. 4:15; 5:13; 7:5, 13
57 [a]Rom. 7:25 [b]1John 5:4, 5
58 [a]2Pet. 3:14 [b]1Cor. 3:8

🔑 **15:51, 52** See note on 1 Thessalonians 4:17.

Concerning the Collection From the Churches

16 ⊶Now concerning [a]the collection
for the saints,[40] as I [ao]have given
order[1299] to the churches[1577] of Galatia,
even so [aim]do ye.
⊶2 [a]Upon the first *day* of the week
let every one of you [pim]lay[5087] by him
in [ppt]store, as *God* [psmp]hath prospered
him, that there be no gatherings when I
come.
3 And when I [asbm]come, [a]whomso-
ever ye [aosb]shall approve by *your* letters,
them will I send [ainf]to bring[667] your
[b]liberality[5485] unto Jerusalem.
4 [a]And if it be meet[514] that I [infg]go
also, they shall go with me.
5 Now I will come unto you, [a]when I
shall pass through Macedonia: for I do
pass through Macedonia.
6 And it may be that I will abide,[3887]
yea, and winter with you, that ye [aosb]may
[a]bring me on my journey whithersoever
I go.
7 For I will not see you now by the
way; but I trust[1679] to tarry a while[5550]
with you, [a]if the Lord permit.
8 But I will tarry at Ephesus until
Pentecost.[4005]
9 For [a]a great door and effectual is
opened unto me, and [b]*there are* many adversaries.
⊶10 Now [a]if Timotheus come, see that
he may be with you without fear: for [b]he
worketh the work[2041] of the Lord, as I
also *do.*
11 [aosi][a]Let no man therefore despise[1848] him: but conduct him forth [b]in
peace,[1515] that he may come unto me: for
I look for[1551] him with the brethren.
12 As touching *our* brother [a]Apollos,
I greatly desired[3870] him to come unto
you with the brethren: but his will was
not at all to come at this time; but he
will come when he shall have convenient
time.
13 [a]Watch ye, [b]stand fast in the
faith,[4102] quit you like men,[407] [c]be
strong.[2901]
14 [a]Let all your things be done with
charity.[26]
15 I beseech[3870] you, brethren, (ye
know [a]the house[3614] of Stephanas, that it
is [b]the firstfruits[536] of Achaia, and *that*
they [ao]have addicted[5021] themselves to
[c]the ministry of the saints,)
16 [a]That ye submit yourselves[5293]
unto such, and to every one that
[ppt]helpeth with *us,* and [ppt][b]laboureth.
17 I am glad of the coming of Stephanas and Fortunatus and Achaicus: [a]for
that which was lacking on your part they
[ao]have supplied.[378]
18 [a]For they [ao]have refreshed my
spirit[4151] and yours: therefore [b]ac-
knowledge ye them that are such.
19 The churches[1577] of Asia salute[782]
you. Aquila and Priscilla salute you much
in the Lord, [a]with the church that is in
their house.
20 All the brethren greet you.
[a]Greet[782] ye one another with an holy[40]
kiss.
21 [a]The salutation[783] of *me* Paul
with mine own hand.
22 If any man [a]love[5368] not the Lord
Jesus Christ, [b]let him be Anathema[331]
[c]Maran–atha.[3134]
23 [a]The grace[5485] of our Lord Jesus
Christ *be* with you.
24 My love[26] *be* with you all in Christ
Jesus. Amen.[281]

1 [a]Acts 11:29; 24:17; Rom. 15:26; 2Cor. 8:4; 9:1, 12; Gal. 2:10
2 [a]Acts 20:7; Rev. 1:10
3 [a]2Cor. 8:19 [b]2Cor. 8:4, 6, 19
4 [a]2Cor. 8:4, 19
5 [a]Acts 19:21; 2Cor. 1:16
6 [a]Acts 15:3; 17:15; 21:5; Rom. 15:24; 2Cor. 1:16
7 [a]Acts 18:21; 1Cor. 4:19; James 4:15
9 [a]Acts 14:27; 2Cor. 2:12; Col. 4:3; Rev. 3:8 [b]Acts 19:9
10 [a]Acts 19:22; 1Cor. 4:17 [b]Rom. 16:21; Phil. 2:20, 22; 1Thess. 3:2
11 [a]1Tim. 4:12 [b]Acts 15:33
12 [a]1Cor. 1:12; 3:5
13 [a]Matt. 24:42; 25:13; 1Thess. 5:6; 1Pet. 5:8 [b]1Cor. 15:1; Phil. 1:27; 4:1; 1Thess. 3:8; 2Thess. 2:15 [c]Eph. 6:10; Col. 1:11
14 [a]1Cor. 14:1; 1Pet. 4:8
15 [a]1Cor. 1:16 [b]Rom. 16:5 [c]2Cor. 8:4; 9:1; Heb. 6:10
16 [a]Heb. 13:17 [b]Heb. 6:10
17 [a]2Cor. 11:9; Phil. 2:30; Phile. 1:13
18 [a]Col. 4:8 [b]Phil. 2:29; 1Thess. 5:12
19 [a]Rom. 16:5, 15; Phile. 1:2
20 [a]Rom. 16:16
21 [a]Col. 4:18; 2Thess. 3:17
22 [a]Eph. 6:24 [b]Gal. 1:8, 9 [c]Jude 1:14, 15
23 [a]Rom. 16:20

⊶ **16:1–4** See notes on Colossians 4:7 and 2 Timothy 4:20.
⊶ **16:2** See note on Malachi 3:7–15.
⊶ **16:10, 11** See the introduction to 1 Timothy.

The Second Epistle of Paul to the

CORINTHIANS

Paul had established the church at Corinth during his first stay there and later wrote the first letter to them concerning the dishonorable behavior of some of its members. Apparently Paul paid them another visit, which was not very pleasant, between the first time he stayed there and the time that this letter was written (2 Cor 12:14; 13:1). As he traveled through Macedonia (northern Greece) on his way to Corinth (located in Achaia or southern Greece), he met with Titus and discovered that his first letter to the Corinthian church had been received and accomplished much good (2 Cor. 7:5–11). Nevertheless, there were still some serious problems in the church at Corinth, including a faction in the congregation who denied that Paul was truly an apostle of Jesus. As a result, Paul immediately wrote this letter, probably from Philippi, and sent it on ahead with Titus (see 2 Cor. 8:16, 17; 9:2–4). This is believed to have been written about A.D. 54 or 55, only eight months to a year after the writing of the Book of 1 Corinthians. Paul spent the next winter in Corinth as he had planned (Acts 20:2, 3; 1 Cor. 16:5, 6).

The Apostle Paul's intense emotions and fiery personality are more evident in this letter than in any other epistle. The Book of 2 Corinthians has only a vague systematic form, and except for Paul's letter to Philemon, has the least emphasis on doctrinal issues. He shared some of his personal experiences, such as the vision in which he was "caught up into the third heaven" (2 Cor. 12:1–4) and his "thorn in the flesh" (2 Cor. 12:7–9).

Paul warned the Corinthians about certain doctrinal errors, instructed them in matters of duty as Christians, and expressed joy that they had heeded his instructions in the first letter. He also defended his authority as an apostle against the attacks of legalistic teachers who sought to disrupt his work. The main theme of the Book of 2 Corinthians is that one should always be faithful to Christ.

1 Paul, an [a]apostle[652] of Jesus
Christ[5547] by the will[2307] of God,[2316]
and Timothy *our* brother,[80] unto the
church[1577] of God which is at Corinth,
[b]with all the saints[40] which are in all
Achaia:
2 [a]Grace[5485] *be* to you and peace[1515]
from God our Father,[3962] and *from* the
Lord[2962] Jesus Christ.

"The God of All Comfort"

3 [a]Blessed[2128] *be* God, even the
Father of our Lord Jesus Christ, the Father of mercies, and the God of all
comfort;[3874]
4 Who [ppt]comforteth[3870] us in all our
tribulation, that we may be able [pinf]to
comfort them which are in any trouble,[2347] by the comfort[3874] wherewith we
ourselves are comforted of God.
5 For as [a]the sufferings[3804] of Christ
abound[4052] in us, so our consolation[3874]
also aboundeth by Christ.
6 And whether we be afflicted,
[a]*it is* for your consolation and salvation,[4991] which [ppt][1]is effectual[1754] in the
enduring of the same sufferings which
we also suffer:[3958] or whether we be comforted, *it is* for your consolation and salvation.
7 And our hope of you *is* stedfast,[949]
knowing, that [a]as ye are partakers[2844] of
the sufferings, so *shall ye be* also of the
consolation.
8 For we would not, brethren, have
you ignorant[50] of [a]our trouble which
came to us in Asia, that we were pressed
out of measure, above strength, insomuch
that we [aifp]despaired even of life:[2198]
9 But we [pfi]had the sentence[610] of
death[2288] in ourselves, that we should
[a]not trust[3982] in ourselves, but in God
which [ppt]raiseth[1453] the dead:[3498]

1 [a]1Cor. 1:1; Eph. 1:1; Col. 1:1; 1Tim. 1:1; 2Tim. 1:1 [b]Phil. 1:1; Col. 1:2

2 [a]Rom. 1:7; 1Cor. 1:3; Gal. 1:3; Phil. 1:2; Col. 1:2; 1Thess. 1:1; 2Thess. 1:2; Phile. 1:3

3 [a]Eph. 1:3; 1Pet. 1:3

5 [a]Acts 9:4; 2Cor. 4:10; Col. 1:24

6 [1]Or, *is wrought* [a]2Cor. 4:15

7 [a]Rom. 8:17; 2Tim. 2:12

8 [a]Acts 19:23; 1Cor. 15:32; 16:9

9 [a]Jer. 17:5, 7

10 [a]Who [aom]delivered[4506] us from so great a death, and doth deliver: in whom we trust[1679] that he will yet deliver *us;*

11 Ye also [ppt][a]helping together by prayer for us, that [b]for the gift[5486] *bestowed* upon us by the means of many persons[4383] [asbp]thanks may be given[2168] by many on our behalf.

Paul's Sincerity

12 For our rejoicing is this, the testimony[3142] of our conscience,[4893] that in simplicity and [a]godly sincerity,[1505] [b]not with fleshly[4559] wisdom, but by the grace[5485] of God, we [aop]have had our conversation[390] in the world, and more abundantly[4056] to you-ward.[5209]

13 For we write none other things unto you, than what ye read or acknowledge; and I trust ye shall acknowledge even to the end;[5056]

🗝 14 As also ye have acknowledged us in part, [a]that we are your rejoicing, even as [b]ye also *are* ours in the day[2250] of the Lord Jesus.

15 And in this confidence[4006] [a]I [ipf]was minded [ainf]to come unto you before, that ye might have [b]a second [I]benefit;[5485]

16 And to pass by you into Macedonia, and [a]to come again out of Macedonia unto you, and of you to be brought on my way toward Judaea.

17 When I therefore [ppt]was thus minded,[1011] did I use lightness? or the things that I purpose, do I purpose [a]according to[2596] the flesh, that with me there should be yea yea, and nay nay?

18 But *as* God *is* true,[4103] our word[3056] toward you was not yea and nay.

🗝 19 For [a]the Son[5207] of God, Jesus Christ,[5547] who [aptp]was preached[2784] among you by us, *even* by me and Silvanus and Timotheus, [aom]was not yea and nay, [b]but in him [pfi]was yea.

20 [a]For all the promises[1860] of God in him *are* yea, and in him Amen,[281] unto the glory[1391] of God by us.

21 Now he which [ppt]stablisheth[950] us with you in Christ, and [apt][a]hath anointed[5548] us, *is* God;

22 Who [apt][a]hath also sealed[4972] us, and [apt][b]given the earnest[728] of the Spirit[4151] in our hearts.[2588]

23 Moreover [a]I call[1941] God for a record[3144] upon my soul,[5590] [b]that to spare you I came not as yet unto Corinth.

24 Not for [a]that we have dominion over your faith,[4102] but are helpers of your joy:[5479] for [b]by faith ye [pfi]stand.

2 But I determined[2919] this with myself, [a]that I would not come again to you in heaviness.

2 For if I make you sorry,[3076] who is he then that [ppt]maketh me glad,[2165] but the same which [ppp]is made sorry[3076] by me?

3 And I wrote[1125] this same unto you, lest, when I came, [a]I should have sorrow from them of whom I ought [pinf]to rejoice; [b]having confidence[3982] in you all, that my joy[5479] is *the joy* of you all.

4 For out of much affliction and anguish of heart I wrote unto you with many tears; [a]not that ye [asbp]should be grieved, but that ye [aosb]might know the love[26] which I have more abundantly unto you.

Forgiveness for a Penitent Man

5 But [a]if any [pfi]have caused grief,[3076] he hath not [pfi][b]grieved me, but in part: that I may not [psa]overcharge you all.

6 Sufficient[2425] to such a man *is* this [I]punishment, which *was inflicted* [a]of many.

7 [a]So that contrariwise ye *ought* rather [ainf]to forgive[5483] *him,* and [ainf]comfort[3870] *him,* lest perhaps such a one

10 [a]2Pet. 2:9
11 [a]Rom. 15:30; Phil. 1:19; Phile. 1:22 [b]2Cor. 4:15
12 [a]2Cor. 2:17; 4:2 [b]1Cor. 2:4, 13
14 [a]2Cor. 5:12 [b]Phil. 2:16; 4:1; 1Thess. 2:19, 20
15 [I]Or, *grace* [a]1Cor. 4:19 [b]Rom. 1:11
16 [a]1Cor. 16:5, 6
17 [a]2Cor. 10:2
19 [a]Mark 1:1; Luke 1:35; Acts 9:20 [b]Heb. 13:8
20 [a]Rom. 15:8, 9
21 [a]1John 2:20, 27
22 [a]Eph. 1:13; 4:30; 2Tim. 2:19; Rev. 2:17 [b]2Cor. 5:5; Eph. 1:14
23 [a]Rom. 1:9; 2Cor. 11:31; Gal. 1:20; Phil. 1:8 [b]1Cor. 4:21; 2Cor. 2:3; 12:20; 13:2, 10
24 [a]1Cor. 3:5; 1Pet. 5:3 [b]Rom. 11:20; 1Cor. 15:1
1 [a]2Cor. 1:23; 12:20, 21; 13:10
3 [a]2Cor. 12:21 [b]2Cor. 7:16; 8:22; Gal. 5:10
4 [a]2Cor. 7:8, 9, 12
5 [a]1Cor. 5:1 [b]Gal. 4:12
6 [I]Or, *censure* [a]1Cor. 5:4, 5; 1Tim. 5:20
7 [a]Gal. 6:1

🗝 **1:14** See note on 1 Thessalonians 5:2.
🗝 **1:19** See the introduction to 1 Timothy.

[asbp]should be swallowed up with over-
much4055 sorrow.
8 Wherefore I beseech3870 you that
ye [ainf]would confirm *your* love26 toward
him.
9 For to this end also did I write,1125
that I [aosb]might know the proof1382 of
you, whether ye be [a]obedient5255 in all
things.
10 To whom ye forgive5483 any
thing, I *forgive* also: for if I [pfi]forgave
any thing, to whom I [pfi]forgave *it,* for
your sakes *forgave I it* [I]in the person4383
of Christ;
11 Lest Satan4567 [asbp]should get an
advantage of us: for we are not ig-
norant50 of his devices.3540
12 Furthermore, [a]when I came to
Troas to *preach* Christ's gospel,2098 and
[b]a door [pfpp]was opened unto me of the
Lord,
13 [a]I [pfi]had no rest425 in my spirit,4151
because I [ainf]found not Titus my brother:
but [apt]taking my leave657 of them, I went
from thence into Macedonia.

Victory in Christ

14 Now thanks5485 *be* unto God,
which always [ppt]causeth us to triumph
in Christ, and [ppt]maketh manifest5319 [a]the
savour of his knowledge1108 by us in
every place.
15 For we are unto God a sweet
savour of Christ, [a]in them that [ppp]are
saved,4982 and [b]in them that [ppp]perish:622
16 [a]To the [pl]one *we are* the savour of
death2288 unto death; and to the [pl]other
the savour of life2222 unto life. And [b]who
is sufficient2425 for these things?
17 For we are not as many, which
[ppt][a]corrupt2585 the word3056 of God: but
as [b]of sincerity,1505 but as of God, in the
sight of God speak2980 we in Christ.

A New Ministry

3 Do [a]we begin again [pinf]to commend
ourselves? or need we, as some
others, [b]epistles1992 of commendation to
you, or *letters* of commendation from
you?

2 [a]Ye are our epistle [pfpp]written in our
hearts,2588 [ppp]known and [ppp]read of all
men:
3 *Forasmuch as ye are* manifestly
declared5319 to be the [an]epistle of Christ
[aptp][a]ministered1247 by us, [pfpp]written1449
not with ink, but with the [an]Spirit4151 of
the [an]living2198 God; not [b]in tables of
stone, but [c]in fleshy4560 tables of the
heart.2588
4 And such trust4006 have we
through Christ to God-ward:
5 [a]Not that we are sufficient2425
of ourselves [ainf]to think any thing as of
ourselves; but [b]our sufficiency2426 *is* of
God;
6 Who also [ao]hath made us able2427
[a]ministers1249 of [b]the [an]new2537 testament;1242 not [c]of the [an]letter,1121 but of
the [an]spirit:4151 for [d]the letter killeth, [e]but
the spirit [I]giveth life.
7 But if [a]the ministration of
death,2288 [b]written1121 *and* engraven in
stones, was glorious,1391 [c]so that the chil-
dren5207 of Israel [pinf]could not [ainf]sted-
fastly behold816 the face of Moses for the
glory of his countenance;4383 which *glory*
[ppp]was to be done away:
8 How shall not [a]the ministration of
the spirit be rather glorious?
9 For if the ministration of con-
demnation2633 *be* glory,1391 much more
doth the ministration [a]of righteous-
ness1343 exceed in glory.
10 For even that which [pfpp]was
made glorious had no glory in this respect, by reason of the glory that [ppt]ex-
celleth.
11 For if that which [ppp]is done away
was glorious, much more that which
[ppt]remaineth *is* glorious.
12 Seeing then that we [ppt]have such
hope,1680 [a]we use great [I]plainness of
speech:
13 And not as Moses, [a]*which* [ipf]put
a veil over his face, that the children
of Israel [aipr]could not stedfastly look816
to [b]the end5056 of that which [ppp]is abolished:
14 But [a]their minds3540 [aop]were
blinded:4456 for until this day remaineth
the same vail [ppp]untaken away in the

---

9 [a]2Cor. 7:15; 10:6
10 [I]Or, *in the sight*
12 [a]Acts 16:8; 20:6 [b]1Cor. 16:9
13 [a]2Cor. 7:5, 6
14 [a]Song 1:3
15 [a]1Cor. 1:18 [b]2Cor. 4:3
16 [a]Luke 2:34; John 9:39; 1Pet. 2:7, 8 [b]1Cor. 15:10; 2Cor. 3:5, 6
17 [a]2Cor. 4:2; 11:13; 2Pet. 2:3 [b]2Cor. 1:12; 4:2

1 [a]2Cor. 5:12; 10:8, 12; 12:11 [b]Acts 18:27
2 [a]1Cor. 9:2
3 [a]1Cor. 3:5 [b]Ex. 24:12; 34:1 [c]Ps. 40:8; Jer. 31:33; Ezek. 11:19; 36:26; Heb. 8:10
5 [a]John 15:5; 2Cor. 2:16 [b]1Cor. 15:10; Phil. 2:13 [c]1Cor. 3:5; 15:10; 2Cor. 5:18; Eph. 3:7; Col. 1:25, 29; 1Tim. 1:11, 12; 2Tim. 1:11
6 [I]Or, *quickeneth* [a]Jer. 31:31; Matt. 26:28; Heb. 8:6, 8 [b]Rom. 2:27, 29; 7:6 [c]Rom. 3:20; 4:15; 7:9-11; Gal. 3:10 [d]John 6:23; Rom. 8:2
7 [a]Rom. 7:10 [b]Ex. 34:1, 28; Deut. 10:1 [c]Ex. 34:29, 30, 35
8 [a]Gal. 3:5
9 [a]Rom. 1:17; 3:21
12 [I]Or, *boldness* [a]2Cor. 7:4; Eph. 6:19
13 [a]Ex. 34:33, 35 [b]Rom. 10:4; Gal. 3:23
14 [a]Isa. 6:10; Matt. 13:11, 14; John 12:40; Acts 28:26; Rom. 11:7, 8, 25; 2Cor. 4:4

reading[320] of the old[3820] testament;[1242] which *vail* is done away in Christ.[5547]

15 But even unto this day, when Moses is read, the vail is upon their heart.[2588]

16 Nevertheless [a]when it [aosb]shall turn to the Lord,[2962] [b]the vail [pinp]shall be taken away.[4014]

17 Now [a]the Lord is that [art]Spirit: and where the Spirit[4151] of the Lord *is,* there *is* liberty.[1657]

18 But we all, with [pfpp]open face beholding [a]as in a glass [b]the glory of the Lord, [pin][c]are changed[3339] into the same image from glory to glory, *even* as [I]by the [an]Spirit of the [an]Lord.

Never Give Up

4 Therefore seeing we have [a]this ministry,[1248] [b]as we [aop]have received mercy, we faint[1573] not;

2 But [aom]have renounced the hidden things of [I][a]dishonesty,[152] not walking in craftiness, [b]nor handling[1389] the word[3056] of God deceitfully;[1389] but [c]by manifestation[5321] of the truth [d]commending[4921] ourselves to every man's conscience[4893] in the sight of God.[2316]

3 But if our gospel[2098] be hid, [a]it is hid[2572] to them that [ppp]are lost:[622]

4 In whom [a]the god[2316] of this world[165] [ao][b]hath blinded the minds[3540] of them which believe not,[571] lest [c]the light[5462] of the glorious[1391] gospel[2098] of Christ, [d]who is the [an]image[1504] of God, [aies]should shine[826] unto them.

5 [a]For we preach[2784] not ourselves, but Christ[5547] Jesus the [an]Lord;[2962] and [b]ourselves your servants[1401] for Jesus' sake.

6 For God,[2316] [a]who [apt]commanded the light[5457] [ainf]to shine out of darkness,[4655] [ao]hath [b]shined in our hearts,[2588] to *give* [c]the light[5462] of the knowledge of the glory[1391] of God in the face of Jesus Christ.

7 But we have this treasure in [a]earthen vessels, [b]that the excellency of the power[1411] may be of God, and not of us.

8 *We are* [ppp][a]troubled on every side, yet not [ppp]distressed; *we are* [ppp]perplexed, but [I]not [ppp]in despair;[1820]

9 [ppp]Persecuted, but not [ppp]forsaken;1459 [ppp][a]cast down, but not [ppp]destroyed;[622]

10 [a]Always [ppt]bearing about in the body[4983] the dying[3500] of the Lord Jesus, [b]that the life[2222] also of Jesus [asbp]might be made manifest[5319] in our body.

🔑 11 For we which live [a]are alway delivered unto death[2288] for Jesus' sake, that the life also of Jesus [asbp]might be made manifest in our mortal[2349] flesh.

12 So then [a]death worketh[1754] in us, but life[2222] in you.

13 We having [a]the same spirit[4151] of faith,[4102] according as it is written, [b]I believed,[4100] and therefore have I spoken; we also believe, and therefore speak;

14 Knowing that [a]he which [apt]raised up the Lord Jesus shall raise up us also by Jesus, and shall present *us* with you.

15 For [a]all things *are* for your sakes, that [b]the [apt]abundant grace[5485] might through the thanksgiving of many [aosb]redound4052 to the glory of God.

16 For which cause we faint[1573] not; but though our outward man[444] perish, yet [a]the inward *man* is renewed[341] day[2250] by day.

17 For [a]our light affliction, which is but for a moment, worketh for us a far more exceeding *and* eternal[166] weight of glory;[1391]

18 [a]While we [ppt]look not at[4648] the things which [ppp]are seen, but at the things which are not seen: for the things which are seen *are* temporal;4340 but the things which are not seen *are* eternal.[166]

16 [a]Ex. 34:34; Rom. 11:23, 26 [b]Isa. 25:7
17 [a]1Cor. 15:45; 2Cor. 3:6
18 [I]Or, *of the LORD the Spirit* [a]1Cor. 13:12 [b]2Cor. 4:4, 6; 1Tim. 1:11 [c]Rom. 8:29; 1Cor. 15:49; Col. 3:10

1 [a]2Cor. 3:6 [b]1Cor. 7:25; 1Tim. 1:13
2 [I]Gr. *shame* [a]Rom. 1:16; 6:21 [b]2Cor. 2:17; 1Thess. 2:3, 5 [c]2Cor. 6:4, 7; 7:14 [d]2Cor. 5:11
3 [a]1Cor. 1:18; 2Cor. 2:15; 1Thess. 2:10
4 [a]John 12:31; 14:30; 16:11; Eph. 6:12 [b]Isa. 6:10; John 12:40; 2Cor. 3:14 [c]2Cor. 3:8, 9, 11, 18; 4:6 [d]John 1:18; 12:45; 14:9; Phil. 2:6; Col. 1:15; Heb. 1:3
5 [a]1Cor. 1:13, 23; 10:33 [b]1Cor. 9:19; 2Cor. 1:24
6 [a]Gen. 1:3 [b]2Pet. 1:19 [c]2Cor. 4:4; 1Pet. 2:9
7 [a]2Cor. 5:1 [b]1Cor. 2:5; 2Cor. 12:9
8 [I]Or, *not altogether without help,* or, *means* [a]2Cor. 7:5
9 [a]Ps. 37:24
10 [a]1Cor. 15:31; 2Cor. 1:5, 9; Gal. 6:17; Phil. 3:10 [b]Rom. 8:17; 2Tim. 2:11, 12; 1Pet. 4:13
11 [a]Ps. 44:22; Rom. 8:36; 1Cor. 15:31, 49
12 [a]2Cor. 13:9
13 [a]Rom. 1:12; 2Pet. 1:1 [b]Ps. 116:10
14 [a]Rom. 8:11; 1Cor. 6:14
15 [a]1Cor. 3:21; 2Cor. 1:6; Col. 1:24; 2Tim. 2:10 [b]2Cor. 1:11; 8:19; 9:11, 12
16 [a]Rom. 7:22; Eph. 3:16, Col. 3:10; 1Pet. 3:4
17 [a]Matt. 5:12; Rom. 8:18; 1Pet. 1:6; 5:10
18 [a]Rom. 8:24; 2Cor. 5:7; Heb. 11:1 [b]Job 4:19; 2Cor. 4:7; 2Pet. 1:13, 14

🔑 4:11 See note on 2 Timothy 1:12.

5 🔑For we know that if [a]our
earthly[1919] house[3614] of *this* taber-
nacle4636 [asbp]were dissolved, we have
a building[3619] of God, an house not
made with hands, eternal[166] in the heavens.[3772]
2 For in this [a]we groan, [ppt]earnestly
desiring1971 [ainf]to be clothed upon with
our house3613 which is from heaven:[3772]
3 If so be that [apt][a]being clothed we
shall not be found naked.[1131]
🔑4 For we that are in *this* tabernacle
do groan, [ppp]being burdened: not for that
we would [ainf]be unclothed, but [ainf][a]clothed
upon, that mortality[2349] [asbp]might be
swallowed up of life.[2222]
5 Now [a]he that [apt]hath wrought us
for the selfsame thing *is* God, who also
[apt][b]hath given unto us the earnest[728] of
the Spirit.[4151]
6 Therefore *we are* always [ppt]confi-
dent, knowing that, whilst we [ppt]are at
home in the body,[4983] we are absent from
the Lord:[2962]
7 (For [a]we walk by faith,[4102] not by
sight:[1491])
8 We are confident, *I say,* and [a]will-
ing rather [ainf]to be absent from the body,
and [ainf]to be present with the Lord.
9 Wherefore we [I]labour, that, whether
present or absent, we may be accepted[2101] of him.
10 [a]For we must all [aifp]appear[5319] before the judgment seat968 of Christ;[5547]
[b]that every one [asbm]may receive the
things *done* in *his* body, according to[4314]
that he [ao]hath done,[4238] whether *it be*
good[18] or bad.[2556]

Paul Defends Himself

11 Knowing therefore [a]the terror[5401]
of the Lord,[2962] we persuade men;[444] but
[b]we [pfip]are made manifest[5319] unto God;

2 [a]Rom. 8:23
3 [a]Rev. 3:18; 16:15
4 [a]1Cor. 15:53, 54
5 [a]Isa. 29:23; Eph. 2:10 [b]Rom. 8:23; 2Cor. 1:22; Eph. 1:14; 4:30
7 [a]Rom. 8:24, 25; 1Cor. 13:12; 2Cor. 4:18; Heb. 11:1
8 [a]Phil. 1:23
9 [I]Or, *endeavor*
10 [a]Matt. 25:31, 32; Rom. 14:10 [b]Rom. 2:6; Gal. 6:7; Eph. 6:8; Col. 3:24, 25; Rev. 22:12
11 [a]Job 31:23; Heb. 10:31; Jude 1:23 [b]2Cor. 4:2

🔑 **5:1** What Paul is saying here is that the spirit is the real person, not the body. The body is represented by the Greek word *skēnon* (4633) "tent." Paul explains that though this earthly body ("house") will be "dissolved," God has promised that there will be a "building of God." This is a description of the death of the mortal body, yet it is intended to be encouragement for the believer as he or she looks at death. The word that is translated "building" is the Greek word *oikodomēn* (3619), which refers to "the process of building something." God is building a new house for the believer's spirit, which will be disembodied at the point of death, leaving the body here on earth. This indicates that God will create something completely new. Then Paul uses the word *oikían* (3614), "dwelling place," which refers to the completion of the "eternal body." There are two qualities of this new body that must be understood. First, it will be similar to the present one and identifiable, yet not identical because it will be produced by God. The word translated "not made with hands" is *acheiropoíēton* (886). This is the same word that the Lord used in Mark 14:58 when He spoke of destroying the temple, which was made by the hands of men, and in three days, building another, not made by man. Christ was speaking of His body following His resurrection. Although His own body was "made of a woman" (Gal. 4:4) at His birth, yet no human being was involved at the time of His resurrection. The believer's human body will have the same outcome. The first time, when one is born into this world, the body is physically produced. However, at the resurrection by Christ of the righteous dead (1 Thess. 4:15–17), God will change them to new, glorified bodies (1 Cor. 15:50–57). The second quality of this new body is that it is going to be "eternal," translated from the Greek word *aiōnion* (166). This idea of eternality focuses on what characterizes God Himself. The life that is given to believers at salvation is the promise of eternal life (*aiōnios* [166], *zōē* [2222]), denoting not only a period of time, but also the quality of the life. This life can never be lost or taken away once a person accepts Jesus Christ as Lord and Savior. The word *aiōnios*, however, is always related to time using the form *aiōn* (165), "age or generation." One must consider its usage in 2 Corinthians 4:17, 18, where contrast is made between "the things which are seen [and] are temporal," the affliction the Corinthians were then undergoing and the "more exceeding and eternal weight of glory." Therefore, *aiōnios* means that which is not temporal, cannot be lost, nor destroyed. Paul gives the location of this "life to be" as "in the heavens" (see also 1 Cor. 8:5; 15:57; 2 Cor. 5:2; 12:2). Paul recognized this place to be where God is and where the believer will find his ultimate rest (1 Thess. 4:17, 18).

🔑 **5:4** See note on 2 Timothy 1:12.

and I trust also [pfi]are made manifest in your consciences.[4893]

12 For [a]we commend not ourselves again unto you, but [ppt]give you occasion [b]to glory on our behalf, that ye may have somewhat to *answer* them which [ppt]glory [I]in appearance, and not in heart.

13 For [a]whether we be beside ourselves,[1839] *it is* to God: or whether we be sober,[4993] *it is* for your cause.

14 For the love[26] of Christ constraineth[4912] us; because we thus [apt]judge,[2919] that [a]if one died[599] for all, then [ao]were all dead:[599]

15 And *that* he died for all, [a]that they which [ppt]live[2198] should not henceforth live unto themselves, but unto him which [apt]died for them, and [aptp]rose again.[1453]

16 [a]Wherefore henceforth know[1492] we no man after the flesh: yea, though we have known Christ after the flesh, [b]yet now henceforth know we *him* no more.

17 Therefore if any man [a]*be* in Christ, *he is* [b]a new[2537] creature:[2937] [art][c]old things are passed away; behold, all things [pfi]are become new.

18 And all things *are* of God, [a]who [apt]hath reconciled[2644] us to himself by Jesus Christ, and hath [apt]given to us the ministry[1248] of reconciliation;[2643]

19 To wit, that [a]God was in Christ,[5547] reconciling[2644] the world[2889] unto himself, not imputing[3049] their trespasses[3900] unto them; and [apt]hath [I]committed unto us the word[3056] of reconciliation.[2643]

20 Now then we are [a]ambassadors[4243] for Christ, as [b]though God [ppt]did beseech *you* by us; we pray *you* in Christ's stead, [aipp]be ye reconciled[2644] to God.

21 For [a]he [ao]hath made him *to be* sin[266] for us, who knew[1097] no sin; that we [psa]might be made [b]the [an]righteousness[1343] of God in him.

The Apostle's Fidelity and Love

6 We then, as [a]workers together *with him,* [b]beseech *you* also [c]that ye [ainf]receive not the grace[5485] of God in vain.[2756]

2 (For he saith, [a]I [ao]have heard thee in a time[2540] accepted,[1184] and in the day[2250] of salvation[4991] [ao]have I succoured[997] thee: behold, now *is* the accepted[2144] time; behold, now *is* the day of salvation.)

3 [a]Giving no offence in any thing, that the ministry[1248] be not blamed:

4 But in all *things* [I][a]approving[4921] ourselves [b]as the ministers[1249] of God, in much patience,[5281] in afflictions,[2347] in necessities, in distresses,[4730]

5 [a]In stripes, in imprisonments, in tumults,[181] in labours, in watchings, in fastings;[3521]

6 By pureness,[54] by knowledge, by longsuffering,[3115] by kindness,[5544] by the [an]Holy Ghost,[4151] by love[26] unfeigned,[505]

7 [a]By the word[3056] of truth,[225] by [b]the power[1411] of God, by [c]the armour of righteousness[1343] on the right hand[1188] and on the left,

8 By honour[1391] and dishonour,[819] by evil report and good report: as deceivers, and *yet* true;

9 As [ppp]unknown, and [a]*yet* [ppp]well known;[191] [b]as dying, and, behold, we live;[2198] [c]as chastened,[3811] and not killed;

10 As sorrowful, yet alway rejoicing; as poor, yet making many rich; as having nothing, and *yet* possessing[2722] all things.

11 O *ye* Corinthians, our mouth is open unto you, [a]our heart[2588] is enlarged.

12 Ye are not straitened[4729] in us, but [a]ye are straitened in your own bowels.[4698]

13 Now for a recompence in the same, ([a]I speak as unto *my* children,) be ye also enlarged.

14 [a]Be ye not [ppt]unequally yoked together[2086] with unbelievers: for [b]what fellowship[3352] hath righteousness[1343] with unrighteousness?[458] and what communion[2842] hath light[5457] with darkness?[4655]

15 And what concord hath Christ with Belial? or what part hath he that believeth[4103] with[3326] an infidel?[571]

16 And what agreement hath the

12 [I]Gr. *in the face* [a]2Cor. 3:1 [b]2Cor. 1:14
13 [a]2Cor. 11:1, 16, 17; 12:6, 11
14 [a]Rom. 5:15
15 [a]Rom. 6:11, 12; 14:7, 8; 1Cor. 6:19; Gal. 2:20; 1Thess. 5:10; 1Pet. 4:2
16 [a]Matt. 12:50; John 15:14; Gal. 5:6; Phil. 3:7, 8; Col. 3:11 [b]John 6:63
17 [a]Rom. 8:9; 16:7; Gal. 6:15 [b]Gal. 5:6; 6:15 [c]Isa. 43:18, 19; 65:17; Eph. 2:15; Rev. 21:5
18 [a]Rom. 5:10; Eph. 2:16; Col. 1:20; 1John 2:2; 4:10
19 [I]Gr. *put in us* [a]Rom. 3:24, 25
20 [a]Job 33:23; Mal. 2:7; 2Cor. 3:6; Eph. 6:20 [b]2Cor. 6:1
21 [a]Isa. 53:6, 9, 12; Gal. 3:13; 1Pet. 2:22, 24; 1John 3:5 [b]Rom. 1:17; 5:19; 10:3

1 [a]1Cor. 3:9 [b]2Cor. 5:20 [c]Heb. 12:15
2 [a]Isa. 49:8
3 [a]Rom. 14:13; 1Cor. 9:12; 10:32
4 [I]Gr. *commending* [a]2Cor. 4:2 [b]1Cor. 4:1
5 [a]2Cor. 11:23
7 [a]2Cor. 4:2; 7:14 [b]1Cor. 2:4 [c]2Cor. 10:4; Eph. 6:11, 13; 2Tim. 4:7
9 [a]2Cor. 4:2; 5:11; 11:6 [b]1Cor. 4:9; 2Cor. 1:9; 4:10, 11 [c]Ps. 118:18
11 [a]2Cor. 7:3
12 [a]2Cor. 12:15
13 [a]1Cor. 4:14
14 [a]Deut. 7:2, 3; 1Cor. 5:9; 7:39 [b]1Sam. 5:2, 3; 1Kgs. 18:21; 1Cor. 10:21; Eph. 5:7, 11

temple[3485] of God with[3326] idols?[1497] for [a]ye are the temple of the living[2198] God; as God hath said, [b]I will dwell in them, and walk in *them*; and I will be their God, and they shall be my people.[2992]

17 [a]Wherefore [aim]come out from among[3319] them, and [aipp]be ye separate,[873] saith the Lord, and [pim]touch not the unclean[169] *thing;* and I will receive[1523] you,

18 [a]And will be a Father[3962] unto you, and ye shall be my sons[5207] and daughters, saith the Lord Almighty.[3841]

7 Having [a]therefore these promises, dearly beloved,[27] let us cleanse[2511] ourselves from all filthiness[3436] of the flesh[4561] and spirit,[4151] perfecting[2005] holiness[42] in the fear[5401] of God.

The Former Letter

2 [aim]Receive us; we [ao]have wronged no man, we [ao]have corrupted no man, [a]we [ao]have defrauded[4122] no man.

3 I speak not *this* to condemn[2633] *you:* for [a]I have said before, that ye are in our hearts [aies]to die and [aies]live with *you.*

4 [a]Great *is* my boldness of speech toward you, [b]great *is* my glorying of you: [c]I [pfip]am filled with comfort,[3874] I am exceeding joyful[5479] in all our tribulation.

5 For, [a]when we [apt]were come into Macedonia, our flesh had no rest,[425] but [b]we [ppp]were troubled on every side; [c]without[1855] *were* fightings, within *were* fears.

6 Nevertheless [a]God, that [ppt]comforteth[3870] those that are cast down, comforted us by [b]the coming of Titus;

7 And not by his coming only, but by the consolation[3874] wherewith he was comforted in you, when he [ppt]told[312] us your earnest desire, your mourning, your fervent mind toward me; so that I [ainf]rejoiced the more.

8 For though I made you sorry[3076] with a letter, I [pin]do not repent,[3338] [a]though I did repent: for I perceive that the same epistle[1992] [ao]hath made you sorry, though *it were* but for a season.[5610]

9 Now I rejoice, not that ye were made sorry, but that ye sorrowed[3076] to repentance:[3341] for ye were made sorry [l]after a godly[2316] manner, that ye [asbp]might receive damage by us in nothing.

10 For [a]godly sorrow worketh repentance[3341] to salvation[4991] not to be repented of: [b]but the sorrow of the world[2889] worketh death.

11 For behold this selfsame thing, that ye [aifp]sorrowed after a godly[2316] sort, what carefulness it [aom]wrought[2716] in you, yea, *what* clearing of yourselves, yea, *what* indignation, yea, *what* fear, yea, *what* vehement desire,[1972] yea, *what* zeal, yea, *what* revenge[1557] In all *things* ye have approved[4921] yourselves to be clear in this matter.

12 Wherefore, though I wrote unto you, *I did it* not for his cause that had done the wrong,[91] nor for his cause that suffered wrong, [a]but that our care for you in the sight of God might appear[5319] unto you.

13 Therefore we were comforted in your comfort:[3874] yea, and exceedingly the more joyed we for the joy of Titus, because his spirit [pfip][a]was refreshed by you all.

🔑 14 For if I [pfi]have boasted any thing to him of you, I [aop]am not ashamed;[2617] but as we spake all things to you in truth, even so our boasting, which *I made* before Titus, is found a truth.

15 And his [l][a]inward affection is more abundant toward you, whilst he [ppt]remembereth [b]the obedience[5218] of you all, how with fear[5401] and trembling[5156] ye [aom]received him.

16 I rejoice therefore that [a]I have confidence in you in all *things.*

16 [a]1Cor. 3:16; 6:19; Eph. 2:21, 22; Heb. 3:6 [b]Ex. 29:45; Lev. 26:12; Jer. 31:33; 32:38; Ezek. 11:20; 36:28; 37:26; Zech. 8:8; 13:9
17 [a]Isa. 52:11; 2Cor. 7:1; Rev. 18:4
18 [a]Jer. 31:1, 9; Rev. 21:7

1 [a]2Cor. 6:17, 18; 1John 3:3
2 [a]Acts 20:33; 2Cor. 12:17
3 [a]2Cor. 6:11, 12
4 [a]2Cor. 3:12 [b]1Cor. 1:4; 2Cor. 1:14 [c]2Cor. 1:4; Phil. 2:17; Col. 1:24
5 [a]2Cor. 2:13 [b]2Cor. 4:8 [c]Deut. 32:25
6 [a]2Cor. 1:4 [b]2Cor. 2:13
8 [a]2Cor. 2:4
9 [l]Or, *according to God*
10 [a]2Sam. 12:13; Matt. 26:75 [b]Prov. 17:22
12 [a]2Cor. 2:4
13 [a]Rom. 15:32
15 [l]Gr. *bowels* [a]2Cor. 6:12 [b]2Cor. 2:9; Phil. 2:12
16 [a]2Thess. 3:4; Phile. 1:8, 21

🔑 **7:14, 15** See the introduction to Titus.

The Macedonian Saints

8 Moreover, brethren, we do you to wit[1107] of the grace[5485] of God [pfpp]bestowed on the churches of Macedonia;

2 How that in a great trial[1382] of affliction the abundance[4050] of their joy[5479] and [a]their deep poverty abounded[4052] unto the riches of their [1b]liberality.[572]

3 For to *their* power,[1411] I bear record, yea, and beyond *their* power *they were* willing of themselves;

4 Praying[1189] us with much intreaty[3874] that we would receive the gift,[5485] and *take upon us* [a]the fellowship[2842] of the ministering[1248] to the saints.[40]

5 And *this they did,* not as we hoped,[1679] but first gave their own selves to the Lord,[2962] and unto us by the will of God.[2316]

6 Insomuch that [a]we [ainf]desired Titus, that as he had begun, so he [aosb]would also finish[2005] in you the same [b]grace also.

7 Therefore, as [a]ye abound in every *thing, in* faith,[4102] and utterance,[3056] and knowledge,[1108] and *in* all diligence,[4710] and *in* your love[26] to us, *see* [b]that ye [psa]abound in this grace also.

8 [a]I speak not by commandment,[2003] but by occasion of the forwardness[4710] of others, and to [ppt]prove the sincerity of your love.

9 For ye know the grace[5485] of our Lord Jesus Christ,[5547] [a]that, though he was rich, yet for your sakes he [ao]became poor, that ye through his poverty [aosb]might be rich.

10 And herein [a]I give *my* advice:[1106] for [b]this is expedient[4851] for you, who have begun before, not only to do, but also to be [1c]forward a year ago.

11 Now therefore [aim]perform[2005] the [ainf]doing *of it;* that as *there was* a readiness to will,[2309] so *there may be* a performance also out of that which ye have.

2 [1]Gr. *simplicity* [a]Mark 12:44 [b]2Cor. 9:11
4 [a]Acts 11:29; 24:17; Rom. 15:25, 26; 1Cor. 16:1, 3, 4; 2Cor. 9:1
6 [a]2Cor. 8:17; 12:18 [b]2Cor. 8:4, 19
7 [a]1Cor. 1:5; 12:13 [b]2Cor. 9:8
8 [a]1Cor. 7:6
9 [a]Matt. 8:20; Luke 9:58; Phil. 2:6, 7
10 [1]Gr. *willing* [a]1Cor. 7:25 [b]Prov. 19:17; Matt. 10:42; 1Tim. 6:18, 19; Heb. 13:16 [c]2Cor. 9:2
12 [a]Mark 12:43, 44; Luke 21:3
15 [a]Ex. 16:18
17 [a]2Cor. 8:6
18 [a]2Cor. 12:18
19 [a]1Cor. 16:3, 4 [b]2Cor. 8:4, 6, 7; 9:8 [c]2Cor. 4:15
21 [a]Rom. 12:17; Phil. 4:8; 1Pet. 2:12

12 For [a]if there be first a willing mind, *it is* accepted[2144] according to that a man [psa]hath, *and* not according to that he hath not.

13 For *I mean* not that other men be eased,[425] and ye burdened:

14 But by an equality, *that* now at this time[2540] your abundance[4051] *may be a supply* for their want, that their abundance also may be *a supply* for your want:[5303] that there may be equality:

15 As it is written, [a]He that *had gathered* much [ao]had nothing over;[4121] and he that *had gathered* little [ao]had no lack.[1641]

Paul Receives a Report from Titus and Another Brother

🗝 16 But thanks[5485] *be* to God, which [ppt]put the same earnest care into the heart[2588] of Titus for you.

17 For indeed he accepted [a]the exhortation; but being more forward, of his own accord he went unto you.

18 And we [ao]have sent with him [a]the brother,[80] whose praise *is* in the gospel[2098] throughout all the churches;[1577]

19 And not *that* only, but [aptp]who was also [a]chosen[5500] of the churches to travel with us with this [b]grace, which [ppp]is administered by us [c]to the glory[1391] of the same Lord, and *declaration of* your ready mind:

20 Avoiding[4724] this, that no man [aosb]should blame us in this abundance[100] which is administered by us:

21 [a]Providing[4306] for honest things, not only in the sight of the Lord,[2962] but also in the sight of men.[444]

22 And we [ao]have sent with[4842] them our brother, whom we [ao]have often times proved[1381] diligent in many things, but now much more diligent, upon the great confidence[4006] which *I have* in you.

23 Whether *any do enquire* of Titus, *he is* my partner[2844] and fellowhelper concerning you: or our brethren *be*

🗝 **8:16–23** See the introduction to Titus.

enquired of, they are [a]the messengers[652] of the churches, *and* the glory of Christ.

24 Wherefore [aim]shew ye to them, and before[4383] the churches, the proof of your love,[26] and of our [a]boasting on your behalf.

Free and Cheerful Giving

9 For as touching [a]the ministering[1248] to the saints,[40] it is superfluous[4053] for me to write[1125] to you:

2 For I know [a]the forwardness[4288] of your mind, [b]for which I boast of you to them of Macedonia, that [c]Achaia [pfip]was ready a year ago; and your zeal[2205] [ao]hath provoked very many.

3 [a]Yet have I sent the brethren,[80] lest our boasting of you [asbp]should be in vain[2758] in this behalf; that, as I said, ye may be ready:

4 Lest haply[3381] if they of Macedonia come with me, and find you unprepared, we (that we say not, ye) [asbp]should be ashamed in this same confident[5287] boasting.

5 Therefore I thought[2233] it necessary [ainf]to exhort[3870] the brethren, that they would go before unto you, and make up beforehand[4294] your [I][a]bounty,[2129] [II]whereof ye had notice before,[4293] that the same might be ready, as *a matter of* bounty, and not as *of* covetousness.

6 [a]But this *I say,* He which [ppt]soweth sparingly shall reap also sparingly; and he which soweth bountifully[2129] shall reap also bountifully.

7 Every man according as he purposeth in his heart, *so let him give;* [a]not grudgingly, or of necessity:[318] for [b]God loveth[25] a cheerful giver.

8 [a]And God *is* able [ainf]to make[4052] all grace[5485] abound[4052] toward you; that ye, always having all sufficiency in all *things,* [psa]may abound to every good[18] work:[2041]

9 (As it is written, [a]He [ao]hath dispersed abroad; he [ao]hath given to the poor:[3993] his righteousness[1343] remaineth[3306] for ever.[165,1519] [3588]

10 Now he that [a]ministereth seed[4690] to the sower both [opt]minister bread for *your* food, and [opt]multiply your seed sown, and [opt]increase the fruits of your [b]righteousness;)

11 Being enriched in every thing to all [a]bountifulness,[572] [b]which causeth through us thanksgiving to God.

12 For the administration[1248] of this service[3009] not only [a]supplieth the want[5303] of the saints, but is abundant[4052] also by many thanksgivings unto God;

13 While by the experiment[1382] of this ministration[1248] they [ppt][a]glorify[1392] God for your professed[3671] subjection[5292] unto the gospel[2098] of Christ, and for *your* liberal[572] [b]distribution[2842] unto them, and unto all *men;*

14 And by their prayer for you, [ppt]which long after[1971] you for the [ppt]exceeding [a]grace of God in you.

15 Thanks[5485] *be* unto God [a]for his unspeakable gift.

Paul's Self-Vindication

10 Now [a]I Paul myself beseech[3870] you by the meekness and gentleness[1932] of Christ, [b]who [I]in presence *am* base among you, but being absent[548] am bold toward you:

2 But I beseech[1189] *you,* [a]that I [ainf]may not be bold[2292] when I am present with that confidence,[4006] wherewith I think[3049] [ainf]to be bold against some, which [ppt][I]think of us as if we [ppt]walked according to the flesh.[4561]

3 For though we walk in the flesh, we do not war after the flesh:

4 ([a]For the weapons [b]of our warfare *are* not carnal,[4559] but [c]mighty through God [d]to the pulling down of strong holds;)

5 [a]Casting down [I]imaginations,[3053] and every high thing that exalteth itself against the knowledge[1108] of God, and bringing into captivity every thought[3540] to the obedience[5218] of Christ;

6 [a]And having in a readiness [ainf]to revenge[1556] all disobedience,[3876] when [b]your obedience is fulfilled.

7 [a]Do ye look on things after the outward appearance?[4383] [b]If any man

23 [a]Phil. 2:25
24 [a]2Cor. 7:14; 9:2

1 [a]Acts 11:29; Rom. 15:26; 1Cor. 16:1; 2Cor. 8:4; Gal. 2:10
2 [a]2Cor. 8:19 [b]2Cor. 8:24 [c]2Cor. 8:10
3 [a]2Cor. 8:6, 17, 18, 22
5 [I]Gr. *blessing* [II]Or, *which hath been so much spoken of before* [a]Gen. 33:11; 1Sam. 25:27; 2Kgs. 5:15
6 [a]Prov. 11:24; 19:17; 22:9; Gal. 6:7, 9
7 [a]Deut. 15:7 [b]Ex. 25:2; 35:5; Prov. 11:25; Rom. 12:8; 2Cor. 8:12
8 [a]Prov. 11:24, 25; 28:27; Phil. 4:19
9 [a]Ps. 112:9
10 [a]Isa. 55:10 [b]Hos. 10:12; Matt. 6:1
11 [a]2Cor. 8:2 [b]2Cor. 1:11; 4:15
12 [a]2Cor. 8:14
13 [a]Matt. 5:16 [b]Heb. 13:16
14 [a]2Cor. 8:1 [b]James 1:17

1 [I]Or, *in outward appearance* [a]Rom. 12:1 [b]2Cor. 10:10; 12:5, 7, 9
2 [I]Or, *reckon* [a]1Cor. 4:21; 2Cor. 13:2, 10
4 [a]Eph. 6:13; 1Thess. 5:8 [b]1Tim. 1:18; 2Tim. 2:3 [c]Acts 7:22; 1Cor. 2:5; 2Cor. 6:7; 13:3, 4 [d]Jer. 1:10
5 [I]Or, *reasonings* [a]1Cor. 1:19; 3:19
6 [a]2Cor. 13:2, 10 [b]2Cor. 2:9; 7:15
7 [a]John 7:24; 2Cor. 5:12; 11:18 [b]1Cor. 14:37; 1John 4:6

trust[3982] to himself that he is Christ's, [pim]let him of himself think[3049] this again, that, as he *is* Christ's, even so *are* [c]we Christ's.

8 For though I [aosb]should boast somewhat more [a]of our authority,[1849] which the Lord hath given us for edification,[3619] and not for your destruction,[2506] [b]I should not be ashamed:

9 That I [aosb]may not seem[1380] as if I [pinf]would terrify you by letters.

10 For *his* letters, [I]say they, *are* weighty and powerful; but [a]*his* bodily presence *is* weak,[772] and *his* [b]speech[3056] contemptible.

11 Let such an one [pim]think this, that, such as we are in word[3056] by letters when we are absent,[548] such *will we be* also in deed[2041] when we are present.

12 [a]For we dare not [ainf]make ourselves of the number,[1469] or [ainf]compare[4793] ourselves with some that [ppt]commend themselves: but they [ppt]measuring themselves by themselves, and [ppt]comparing themselves among themselves, [I]are not wise.

13 [a]But we will not boast of things without *our* measure, but according to the measure of the rule which God [ao]hath distributed to us, a measure [ainf]to reach even unto you.

14 For we stretch not ourselves beyond *our measure,* as though we [ppt]reached not unto you: [a]for we are come as far as to you also in *preaching* the gospel[2098] of Christ:

15 Not [ppt]boasting of things without *our* measure, *that is,* [a]of other men's labours; but [ppt]having hope,[1680] when your faith[4102] [ppp]is increased, that we [aifp]shall be enlarged by you according to our rule abundantly,[1519,4050]

7 [c]1Cor. 3:23; 9:1; 2Cor. 11:23
8 [a]2Cor. 13:10 [b]2Cor. 7:14; 12:6
10 [I]Gr. *saith he* [a]1Cor. 2:3, 4; 2Cor. 10:1; 12:5, 7, 9; Gal. 4:13 [b]1Cor. 1:17; 2:1, 4; 2Cor. 11:6
12 [I]Or, *understand* it *not* [a]2Cor. 3:1; 5:12
13 [a]2Cor. 10:15
14 [a]1Cor. 3:5, 10; 4:15; 9:1
15 [a]Rom. 15:20
17 [a]Isa. 65:16; Jer. 9:24; 1Cor. 1:31
18 [a]Prov. 27:2 [b]Rom. 2:29; 1Cor. 4:5
1 [I]Or, *ye do bear with me* [a]2Cor. 5:13; 11:16
2 [a]Gal. 4:17, 18 [b]Hos. 2:19, 20; 1Cor. 4:15 [c]Col. 1:28 [d]Lev. 21:13
3 [a]Gen. 3:4; John 8:44 [b]Eph. 6:24; Col. 2:4, 8, 18; 1Tim. 1:3; 4:1; Heb. 13:9; 2Pet. 3:17
4 [a]Gal. 1:7, 8
5 [a]1Cor. 15:10; 2Cor. 12:11; Gal. 2:6
6 [a]1Cor. 1:17; 2:1, 13; 2Cor. 10:10 [b]Eph. 3:4 [c]2Cor. 4:2; 5:11; 12:12
7 [a]Acts 18:3; 1Cor. 9:6, 12; 2Cor. 10:1

16 [ainf]To preach the gospel[2097] in the *regions* beyond you, *and* not [ainf]to boast in another man's line of things made ready to our hand.

17 [a]But he that glorieth,[2744] [pim]let him glory[2744] in the Lord.

18 For [a]not he that [ppt]commendeth[4921] himself is approved,[1384] but [b]whom the Lord commendeth.

11 Would to God ye [ipf]could bear with[430] me a little in [a]*my* folly: and indeed [I]bear with me.

2 For I am [a]jealous over you with godly[2316] jealousy: for [b]I [aom]have espoused[718] you to one husband, [c]that I [ainf]may present *you* [d]*as* a chaste[53] virgin[3933] to Christ.

3 But I fear,[5399] lest by any means, as [a]the serpent [ao]beguiled Eve through his subtilty,[3834] so your minds[3540] [asbp][b]should be corrupted from the simplicity[572] that is in Christ.

4 For if he that cometh preacheth[2784] another[243] Jesus, whom we have not preached, or *if* ye receive another[2087] spirit,[4151] which ye [ao]have not received,[2983] or [a]another[2087] gospel,[2098] which ye [aom]have not accepted,[1209] ye [ipf]might well bear with[430] *him.*

🗝 5 For I suppose[3049] [a]I [pfin]was[5302] not a whit[3367] behind[5302] the very chiefest apostles.[521]

6 But though [a]*I be* rude[2399] in speech,[3056] yet not [b]in knowledge;[1108] but [c]we [aptp]have been throughly made manifest[5319] among you in all things.

7 [ao]Have I committed[4160] an offence [a]in [ppt]abasing myself that ye [asbp]might be exalted, because I [ao]have preached[2097] to you the gospel of God[2316] freely?

🗝 **11:5** The phrase "very chiefest" is a translation of the Greek word *hupérlian* (5244), meaning "exceedingly great." Some believe that this word is an indication that Paul was equal in authority and station to the Twelve Apostles. Hence, Paul declared in Galatians 2:6 that he was equal with Peter in every respect. Others suggest that Paul used this word to speak sarcastically of those people who wanted to be seen as outstanding apostles, who thought their words should be regarded as more valid than those of the Twelve Apostles of Jesus Christ (cf. 2 Cor. 12:11). The context indicates that there were those in Corinth who wanted to impose their views over Paul's teaching. It is to these "false apostles" that Paul makes reference (see also 2 Cor. 11:13–15).

8 I [ao]robbed other[243] churches,[1577]
[apt]taking wages[3800] *of them,* to do you
service.[1248]
9 And when I was present with you,
and [aptp]wanted, [a]I [ao]was chargeable to no
man: for that which was lacking to me
[b]the brethren[80] which came from
Macedonia [ao]supplied:[4322] and in all
things I [ao]have kept myself [c]from being
burdensome unto you, and *so* will I keep
myself.
10 [a]As the truth[225] of Christ is in
me, [I][b]no man shall stop me of this boasting in the regions of Achaia.
11 Wherefore? [a]because I love[25] you
not? God knoweth.[1492]
12 But what I do, that I will do, [a]that
I may cut off occasion from them which
[ppt]desire occasion; that wherein they
glory, they may be found even as we.
13 For such [a]*are* false apostles,[5570]
[b]deceitful workers, transforming themselves[3345] into the [an]apostles of
Christ.[5547]
14 And no marvel; for Satan[4567] himself is transformed into [a]an angel[32] of
light.[5457]
15 Therefore *it is* no great thing if
his ministers[1249] also be transformed as
the [a]ministers[1249] of righteousness;[1343]
[b]whose end[5056] shall be according to their
works.[2041]

Paul's Apostolic Labours and Sufferings

16 [a]I say again, [aosi]Let no man
think[1380] me a fool; if otherwise, yet as
a fool [I]receive me, that I may boast myself a little.
17 That which I speak, [a]I speak *it*
not after the Lord,[2962] but as it were foolishly, [b]in this confidence[5287] of boasting.
18 [a]Seeing that many glory after the
flesh,[4561] I will glory also.
19 For ye suffer[430] fools gladly, [a]see-
ing ye *yourselves* are wise.[5429]
20 For ye suffer, [a]if a man bring you
into bondage,[2615] if a man devour *you,*
if a man take *of you,* if a man exalt
himself,1869 if a man smite you on the
face.
21 I speak as concerning[2596] reproach,[819] [a]as though we [ao]had been
weak.[770] Howbeit1161 [b]whereinsoever any
is bold, (I speak foolishly,) I am bold also.
22 Are they Hebrews? [a]so *am* I. Are
they Israelites? so *am* I. Are they the
seed[4690] of Abraham? so *am* I.
23 Are they ministers[1249] of Christ?
(I speak as a [ppt]fool) I *am* more; [a]in
labours[2873] more abundant, [b]in stripes
above measure, in prisons more frequent,
[c]in deaths oft.
24 Of the Jews five times [ao]received
I [a]forty *stripes* save[3844] one.
25 Thrice [aop]was I [a]beaten4463 with
rods, [b]once [aop]was I stoned,[3034] thrice I
[ao][c]suffered shipwreck, a night and a day
I [pfi]have been in the deep;
26 *In* journeyings often, *in* perils of
waters, *in* perils of robbers,[3027] [a]*in* perils
by *mine own* countrymen, [b]*in* perils by
the heathen, *in* perils in the city, *in* perils in the wilderness, *in* perils in the sea,
in perils among false brethren;[5569]
27 In weariness[2873] and painful-
ness,[3449] [a]in watchings often, [b]in hunger
and thirst, in fastings3521 often, in cold
and nakedness.[1132]
28 Beside those things that are without, that which cometh upon[1999] me daily,
[a]the care of all the churches.
29 [a]Who is weak,[770] and I am not
weak? who is offended, and I burn not?
30 If I must needs [pinf]glory, [a]I will
glory of the things which concern mine
infirmities.
31 [a]The God and Father of our Lord
Jesus Christ, [b]which is blessed[2128] for
evermore, knoweth[1492] that I lie not.
32 [a]In Damascus the governor under
Aretas the king [ipf]kept the city of the
Damascenes with a garrison,5432 [ppt]de-
sirous [ainf]to apprehend me:
33 And through a window in a basket [aop]was I let down5465 by the wall,
and [ao]escaped his hands.

9 [a]Acts 20:33; 2Cor. 12:13; 1Thess. 2:9; 2Thess. 3:8, 9 [b]Phil. 4:10, 15, 16 [c]2Cor. 12:14, 16
10 [I]Gr. *this boasting shall not be stopped in me* [a]Rom. 9:1 [b]1Cor. 9:15
11 [a]2Cor. 6:11; 7:3; 12:15
12 [a]1Cor. 9:12
13 [a]Acts 15:24; Rom. 16:18; Gal. 1:7; 6:12; Phil. 1:15; 2Pet. 2:1; 1John 4:1; Rev. 2:2 [b]2Cor. 2:17; Phil. 3:2; Titus 1:10, 11
14 [a]Gal. 1:8
15 [a]2Cor. 3:9 [b]Phil. 3:19
16 [I]Or, *suffer* [a]2Cor. 11:1; 12:6, 11
17 [a]1Cor. 7:6, 12 [b]2Cor. 9:4
18 [a]Phil. 3:3, 4
19 [a]1Cor. 4:10
20 [a]Gal. 2:4; 4:9
21 [a]2Cor. 10:10 [b]Phil. 3:4
22 [a]Acts 22:3; Rom. 11:1; Phil. 3:5
23 [a]1Cor. 15:10 [b]Acts 9:16; 20:23; 21:11; 2Cor. 6:4, 5 [c]1Cor. 15:30-32; 2Cor. 1:9, 10; 4:11; 6:9
24 [a]Deut. 25:3
25 [a]Acts 16:22 [b]Acts 14:19 [c]Acts 27:41
26 [a]Acts 9:23; 13:50; 14:5; 17:5; 20:3; 21:31; 23:10, 11; 25:3 [b]Acts 14:5; 19:23
27 [a]Acts 20:31; 2Cor. 6:5 [b]1Cor. 4:11
28 [a]Acts 20:18; Rom. 1:14
29 [a]1Cor. 8:13; 9:22
30 [a]2Cor. 12:5, 9, 10
31 [a]Rom. 1:9; 9:1; 2Cor. 1:23; Gal. 1:20; 1Thess. 2:5 [b]Rom. 9:5
32 [a]Acts 9:24, 25

11:26 See note on Galatians 2:4 concerning the "false brethren" that Paul had encountered.

Paul's Vision

12 🔑It is not expedient for me doubtless to glory. [I]I will come to visions and revelations of the Lord.

2 I knew[1492] a man [a]in Christ above fourteen years ago, (whether in the body,[4983] I cannot tell; or whether out of the body,[4983] I cannot tell: God knoweth;) such an one [aptp][b]caught up[726] to the third heaven.[3772]

3 And I knew such a man, (whether in the body, or out of the body,[4983] I cannot tell: God knoweth;)

4 How that he [aop]was caught up into [a]paradise,[3857] and [ao]heard unspeakable words,[4487] which it is not [I]lawful for a man [ainf]to utter.

5 Of such an one will I glory: [a]yet of myself I will not glory, but in mine infirmities.

6 For [a]though I would desire [ainf]to glory, I shall not be a fool; for I will say the truth: but *now* I forbear, lest any man [asbm]should think[3049] of me above that which he seeth me *to be,* or *that* he heareth of me.

Evidences of Paul's Apostleship

7 And lest I [psmp]should be exalted above measure through the abundance of the revelations, there [aop]was given to me a [a]thorn in the flesh,[4561] [b]the messenger[32] of Satan[4566] to [psa]buffet me, lest I should be exalted above measure.

8 [a]For this thing I [ao]besought[3870] the Lord thrice, that it [aosb]might depart from me.

9 And he said unto me, My grace[5485] is sufficient for thee: for my strength is made perfect[5048] in weakness. Most gladly therefore [a]will I rather glory in my infirmities, [b]that the power[1411] of Christ [aosb]may rest upon me.

10 Therefore [a]I take pleasure[2106] in infirmities, in reproaches,[5196] in necessities,[318] in persecutions, in distresses[4730] for Christ's sake: [b]for when I am weak, then am I strong.

🔑 11 I [pfi]am become [a]a fool in [ppt]glorying; ye [ao]have compelled me: for I [ipf]ought [pip]to have been commended[4921] of you: for [b]in nothing [ao]am I behind[5302] the very chiefest apostles, though [c]I [pin]be nothing.

12 [a]Truly the signs[4592] of an [art]apostle[652] [aop]were wrought[2716] among you in all patience, in signs, and wonders,[5059] and mighty deeds.[1411]

13 [a]For what is it wherein ye [aop]were inferior to other churches,[1577] except *it be* that [b]I myself was not burdensome to you? [aim]forgive[5483] me [c]this wrong.[93]

14 [a]Behold, the third time I am ready to come to you; and I will not be burdensome to you: for [b]I seek not yours, but you: [c]for the children[5043] ought not [pinf]to lay up for the parents, but the parents for the children.

15 And [a]I will very gladly spend and be spent [b]for [I]you; though [c]the more abundantly I [ppt]love[25] you, the less I be loved.

16 But be it so, [a]I did not burden you: nevertheless, being crafty, I caught you with guile.[1388]

17 [a]Did I [ao]make a gain of you by any of them whom I [pfi]sent unto you?

🔑 18 [a]I desired[3870] Titus, and with *him* I sent a [art][b]brother. Did Titus make a gain of you? [ao]walked we not in the same spirit?[4151] *walked we* not in the same steps?

19 [a]Again, think ye that we excuse

1 [I]Gr. *For I will come*
2 [a]Rom. 16:7; 2Cor. 5:17; Gal. 1:22 [b]Acts 22:17
4 [I]Or, *possible* [a]Luke 23:43
5 [a]2Cor. 11:30
6 [a]2Cor. 10:8; 11:16
7 [a]Ezek. 28:24; Gal. 4:13, 14 [b]Job 2:7; Luke 13:16
8 [a]Deut. 3:23-27; Matt. 26:44
9 [a]2Cor. 11:30 [b]1Pet. 4:14
10 [a]Rom. 5:3; 2Cor. 7:4 [b]2Cor. 13:4
11 [a]2Cor. 11:1, 16, 17 [b]2Cor. 11:5; Gal. 2:6-8 [c]1Cor. 3:7; 15:8, 9; Eph. 3:8
12 [a]Rom. 15:18, 19; 1Cor. 9:2; 2Cor. 4:2; 6:4; 11:6
13 [a]1Cor. 1:7 [b]1Cor. 9:12; 2Cor. 11:9 [c]2Cor. 11:7
14 [a]2Cor. 13:1 [b]Acts 20:33; 1Cor. 10:33 [c]1Cor. 4:14, 15
15 [I]Gr. *your souls* [a]Phil. 2:17; 1Thess. 2:8 [b]John 10:11; 2Cor. 1:6; Col. 1:24; 2Tim. 2:10 [c]2Cor. 6:12, 13
16 [a]2Cor. 11:9
17 [a]2Cor. 7:2
18 [a]2Cor. 8:6, 16, 22 [b]2Cor. 8:18
19 [a]2Cor. 5:12

🔑 **12:1–10** The Apostle Paul reveals his unique experience of being "caught up to the third heaven." Although the person mentioned in verse two is not named, it is obvious from verse seven that Paul is speaking about himself. Perhaps Paul mentioned this experience to the Corinthians because they were bragging about their own spiritual visions and gifts. Paul wanted to demonstrate to the Corinthians that he had a spiritual experience far superior to anything they had encountered. Yet, Paul was modest about his experience (seen in the use of the third person). This was to serve as an example to the Corinthians.

🔑 **12:11** See note on 2 Corinthians 11:5.

🔑 **12:18** See the introduction to Titus.

ourselves unto you? [b]we speak before God in Christ: [c]but *we do* all things, dearly beloved,[27] for your edifying.

20 For I fear,[5399] lest when I come, I shall not find you such as I would, and *that* [a]I [asbp]shall be found unto you such as ye would not: lest *there be* debates,[2054] envyings,[2205] wraths,[2372] strifes, backbitings,[2636] whisperings, swellings, tumults:[181]

21 *And* lest, when I come again, my God [aosb][a]will humble me among you, and *that* I shall bewail[3996] many [b]which [pfp]have sinned already, and [apt]have not repented[3340] of the uncleanness[167] and [c]fornication[4202] and lasciviousness[766] which they [ao]have committed.

Paul's Desire to Visit Corinth Again

13 This *is* [a]the third *time* I am coming to you. [b]In the mouth of two or three witnesses[3144] shall[2476] every word[4487] be established.[2476]

2 [a]I [pfi]told you before,[4280] and [pin]foretell you, as if I were present, the second time; and being absent[548] now I write to them [b]which [pfp]heretofore have sinned,[4258] and to all other, that, if I come again, [c]I will not spare:

3 Since ye seek a proof[1382] of Christ [a]speaking in me, which to you-ward is not weak, but is mighty[1414] [b]in you.

4 [a]For though he was crucified[4717] through weakness,[769] yet [b]he liveth[2198] by the power[1411] of God.[2316] For [c]we also are weak in him, but we shall live with him by the power of God toward you.

5 [pim][a]Examine[3985] yourselves, whether ye be in the faith;[4102] [pim]prove[1381] your own selves. Know ye not your own selves, [b]how that Jesus Christ[5547] is in you, except ye be [c]reprobates?[96]

6 But I trust that ye shall know that we are not reprobates.

7 Now I pray to God that ye [ainf]do no evil;[2556] not that we [asbp]should appear approved,[1384] but that ye [psa]should do that which is honest, though [a]we be as reprobates.

8 For we can do nothing against the truth,[225] but for the truth.

9 For we are glad, [a]when we [psa]are weak, and ye are strong: and this also we wish, [b]*even* your perfection.[2676]

10 [a]Therefore I write these things being absent,[548] lest being present [b]I [asbm]should use sharpness, [c]according to the power[1849] which the Lord[2962] [ao]hath given me to edification,[3619] and not to destruction.[2506]

11 Finally, brethren, farewell.[5463] [pim]Be perfect, [pim]be of good comfort, [pim][a]be of one mind, [pim]live in peace; and the God of love[26] [b]and peace[1515] shall be with you.

12 [aim][a]Greet[782] one another with an holy[40] kiss.

13 All the saints[40] salute[782] you.

14 [a]The grace[5485] of the Lord Jesus Christ, and the love of God, and [b]the communion[2842] of the Holy Ghost, *be* with you all. Amen.[281]

19 [b]Rom. 9:1; 2Cor. 11:31 [c]1Cor. 10:33
20 [a]1Cor. 4:21; 2Cor. 10:2; 13:2, 10
21 [a]2Cor. 2:1, 4 [b]2Cor. 13:2 [c]1Cor. 5:1

1 [a]2Cor. 12:14 [b]Num. 35:30; Deut. 17:6; 19:15; Matt. 18:16; John 8:17; Heb. 10:28
2 [a]2Cor. 10:2 [b]2Cor. 12:21 [c]2Cor. 1:23
3 [a]Matt. 10:20; 1Cor. 5:4; 2Cor. 2:10 [b]1Cor. 9:2
4 [a]Phil. 2:7, 8; 1Pet. 3:18 [b]Rom. 6:4 [c]2Cor. 10:3, 4
5 [a]1Cor. 11:28 [b]Rom. 8:10; Gal. 4:19 [c]1Cor. 9:27
7 [a]2Cor. 6:9
9 [a]1Cor. 4:10; 2Cor. 11:30; 12:5, 9, 10 [b]1Thess. 3:10
10 [a]1Cor. 4:21; 2Cor. 2:3; 10:2; 12:20, 21 [b]Titus 1:13 [c]2Cor. 10:8
11 [a]Rom. 12:16, 18; 15:5; 1Cor. 1:10; Phil. 2:2; 3:16; 1Pet. 3:8 [b]Rom. 15:33
12 [a]Rom. 16:16; 1Cor. 16:20; 1Thess. 5:26; 1Pet. 5:14
14 [a]Rom. 16:24 [b]Phil. 2:1

The Epistle of Paul to the

GALATIANS

It is generally accepted that Paul visited the Galatian believers twice before he wrote this epistle. During his absence, teachers came from Palestine, called "Judaizers," and insisted that these Gentile believers could not be true Christians until they submitted to the Jewish ordinance of circumcision. Furthermore, they maintained that the Galatians must adhere to the Law of Moses. These naive Galatian Christians accepted their teachings just as enthusiastically as they had Paul's preaching. The purpose of the Book of Galatians is to combat this vicious heresy in which the work of Christ was considered insufficient for salvation.

The first way Paul chose to do this was to disprove the Judaizers' claim that he was not a true apostle. They maintained that since he was not one of the twelve original apostles, he must have received his teachings and doctrines from the other apostles. Paul showed that he was equal with the original apostles because he received his doctrine from a revelation straight from Jesus Christ (Gal. 1:11–19). He had even rebuked the Apostle Peter when there was a dispute over whether he, as a Jew, should be allowed to disregard the Mosaic Law (Gal. 2:11–14).

Once he had established his apostolic authority, he proved that men are justified by faith in Christ's atoning work rather than by the works of the Law (Gal. 2:15—4:15). This leads into his final topic of being led by the Spirit (Gal. 5:16—6:10). The threat of the Judaizers came to an end at the fall of Jerusalem in A.D. 70. Prior to that time, Jewish Christians were considered by many to be a sect (Acts 24:5), or a new branch of Judaism.

1 Paul, an apostle,[652] ([a]not of men,[444]
neither by man, but [b]by Jesus
Christ,[5547] and God[2316] the Father,[3962]
[c]who [apt]raised[1453] him from the dead;[3498])
🔑 2 And all the brethren[80] [a]which are
with me, [b]unto the churches[1577] of
Galatia:
3 [a]Grace *be* to you and peace[1515]

1 [a]Gal. 1:11, 12 [b]Acts 9:6; 22:10, 15, 21; 26:16; Titus 1:3 [c]Acts 2:24
2 [a]Phil. 2:22; 4:21 [b]1Cor. 16:1
3 [a]Rom. 1:7; 1Cor. 1:3; 2Cor. 1:2; Eph. 1:2; Phil. 1:2; Col. 1:2; 1Thess. 1:1; 2Thess. 1:2; 2John 1:3

🔑 **1:2** There are two views as to the location and identification of these Galatian believers. The disagreement revolves around what Paul meant when he used the term "Galatian." Some say that he was referring to the people living in the Roman Province of Galatia, while others believe he was addressing a group of believers who were mainly of Gallic descent. Both theories have their own set of suppositions with respect to when the book was written, the place from which it was written, and the time periods in which other details mentioned in the book took place.

The area of northern Galatia (which included the chief cities of Ancyra, Tavium, and Pessinus) was conquered by the Gauls in the third century B.C. and existed as an independent nation for about two hundred years. During this period, however, the Gallic people were absorbed into the native populace. If Paul was using the term "Galatian" in the racial sense, he was referring to those who had descended from the Gauls. In accordance with this assumption, it is suggested that Paul visited this church on his second and third missionary journeys (Acts 16:6; 18:23), and wrote this epistle from either Ephesus or Corinth during his last journey.

Those who hold the South Galatia Theory suggest that Paul used the term "Galatian" to refer to those who lived in the Roman province of Galatia, which was established in 25 B.C. In that year, King Amyntas, of the old kingdom of Galatia, bequeathed his kingdom to Rome. This province covered the southern part of central Asia Minor and encompassed the cities of Iconium, Lystra, Antioch of Pisidia, and Derbe. If this theory is true, it is likely that Paul visited these believers on his first missionary journey (Acts 13; 14), and then again during his later travels. A reasonable date for the writing of the book then would be about A.D. 55 or 56 or sometime between his first and second missionary journeys. According to this theory, the cities of Corinth and Antioch in Syria are the most likely places for Paul to have written the book.

from God the Father, and *from* our Lord
Jesus Christ,
4 [a]Who [apt]gave himself for our
sins,[266] that he [asbm]might deliver us [b]from
this present evil world,[165] according to
the will[2307] of God and our Father:
5 To whom *be* glory[1391] for ever and
ever. Amen.[281]

The One True Gospel

🔑6 I marvel that ye are so soon removed [a]from him that [apt]called you into
the grace[5485] of Christ unto another[2087]
gospel:[2098]
7 [a]Which is not another; but there
be some [b]that [ppt]trouble you, and
[ppt]would [ainf]pervert[3344] the gospel[2098] of
Christ.
8 But though [a]we, or an angel[32] from
heaven,[3772] [psa]preach any other gospel[2097]
unto you than that which we [aom]have
preached[2097] unto you, let him be accursed.[331]
9 As we [pfi]said before, so [pin]say I now
again, if any *man* preach any other
gospel unto you [a]than that ye [ao]have received, let him be accursed.
10 For [a]do I now [b]persuade[3982]
men,[444] or God?[2316] or [c]do I seek [pinf]to
please men? for if I yet [ipf]pleased men, I
should not be the servant[1401] of Christ.

Paul's Call to the Ministry

11 [a]But I certify[1107] you, brethren,[80]
that the gospel[2098] which [aptp]was
preached[2097] of me is not after man.
12 For [a]I neither received it of
man,[444] neither was I taught[1321] *it,* but
[b]by the revelation[602] of Jesus Christ.
13 For ye have heard of my conversation[391] in time past in the Jews' religion, how that [a]beyond measure I
[ipf]persecuted the church[1577] of God, and
[ipf][b]wasted[4199] it:
14 And [ipf]profited in the Jews' religion[2454] above many my [l]equals in mine
own nation,[1085] [a]being more exceedingly
zealous [b]of the traditions[3862] of my fathers.
15 But when it pleased[2106] God, [a]who
[apt]separated[873] me from my mother's
womb, and [aptp]called[2564] *me* by his
grace,[5485]
16 [ainf][a]To reveal[601] his Son in me,
that [b]I [psmp]might preach[2097] him among
the heathen;[1484] immediately I conferred
not with [c]flesh[4561] and blood:[129]
17 Neither went I up to Jerusalem to
them which were apostles[652] before me;
but I went into Arabia, and returned
again unto Damascus.
18 Then after three years [a]I went up
to Jerusalem to see Peter, and abode with
him fifteen days.
19 But [a]other[2087] of the apostles
saw I none, save [b]James the Lord's[2962]
brother.
20 Now the things which I write[1125]
unto you, [a]behold, before God, I lie not.
21 [a]Afterwards I came into the regions of Syria and Cilicia;
22 And was unknown[50] by face
[a]unto the churches[1577] of Judaea which
[b]were in Christ:
23 But they had heard only, That he
which [ppt]persecuted us in times past now
preacheth[2097] the faith[4102] which once he
[ipf]destroyed.
24 And they [ipf]glorified[1392] God in
me.

In Jerusalem

2 Then fourteen years after [a]I went up
again to Jerusalem with Barnabas,
and took Titus with *me* also.

4 [a]Matt. 20:28; Rom. 4:25; Gal. 2:20; Titus 2:14 [b]Isa. 65:17; John 15:19; 17:14; Heb. 2:5; 6:5; 1John 5:19
6 [a]Gal. 5:8
7 [a]2Cor. 11:4 [b]Acts 15:1, 24; 2Cor. 2:17; 11:13; Gal. 5:10, 12
8 [a]1Cor. 16:22
9 [a]Deut. 4:2; 12:32; Prov. 30:6; Rev. 22:18
10 [a]1Thess. 2:4 [b]1Sam. 24:7; Matt. 28:14; 1John 3:19 [c]1Thess. 2:4; James 4:4
11 [a]1Cor. 15:1
12 [a]1Cor. 15:1, 3; Gal. 1:1 [b]Eph. 3:3
13 [a]Acts 9:1; 22:4; 26:11; 1Tim. 1:13 [b]Acts 8:3
14 [l]Gr. *equals in years* [a]Acts 22:3; 26:9; Phil. 3:6 [b]Jer. 9:14; Matt. 15:2; Mark 7:5
15 [a]Isa. 49:1, 5; Jer. 1:5; Acts 9:15; 13:2; 22:14, 15; Rom. 1:1
16 [a]2Cor. 4:6 [b]Acts 9:15; 22:21; 26:17, 18; Rom. 11:13; Eph. 3:8 [c]Matt. 16:17; 1Cor. 15:50; Eph. 6:12
18 [a]Acts 9:26
19 [a]1Cor. 9:5 [b]Matt. 13:55; Mark 6:3
20 [a]Rom. 9:1
21 [a]Acts 9:30
22 [a]1Thess. 2:14 [b]Rom. 16:7
1 [a]Acts 15:2

🔑 **1:6–8** The context of the Book of Galatians indicates that a different gospel from the one Paul preached had penetrated the church in Galatia. Paul calls this "another gospel," and the Greek word for "different" in verse six is *héteron* (2087), which means qualitatively different. However, in verse seven, Paul uses an entirely different word, which is also translated "another." It is *állō* (243), which means "another of the same kind." The true Gospel of Christ can be declared in different ways by different people, but its truth can never be altered.

2 And I went up by revelation,[602] [a]and communicated unto them that gospel[2098] which I preach[2784] among the Gentiles,[1484] but privately to them which were of reputation, lest by any means [b]I [psa]should run, or [ao]had run, in vain.

3 But neither Titus, who was with me, being a Greek, [aop]was compelled [aifp]to be circumcised:[4059]

4 And that because of [a]false brethren[5569] unawares brought in,[3920] who came in privily[3922] to spy out our [b]liberty[1657] which we have in Christ Jesus, [c]that they [asbm]might bring us into bondage:[2615]

5 To whom we gave place by subjection,[5292] no, not for an hour; that [a]the truth[225] of the gospel[2098] [aosb]might continue with you.

6 But of these [a]who seemed to be somewhat, (whatsoever they were, it maketh no matter[1308] to me: [b]God accepteth[2983] no man's person:) for they who seemed *to be somewhat* [aomc]in conference added[4323] nothing to me:

7 But contrariwise, [a]when they saw that the gospel of the uncircumcision[203] [pfip][b]was committed[4100] unto me, as *the gospel* of the circumcision[4061] *was* unto Peter;

8 (For he that [apt]wrought effectually in Peter to the apostleship[651] of the circumcision,[4061] [a]the same was [b]mighty in me toward the Gentiles:)

9 And when James, Cephas, and John, who seemed to be [a]pillars, [apt]perceived [b]the grace[5485] that was given unto me, they gave to me and Barnabas the right hands[1188] of fellowship;[2842] that we *should go* unto the heathen, and they unto the circumcision.

10 Only *they would* that we [psa]should remember the poor; [a]the same which I also [ao]was forward [ainf]to do.

Paul Confronts Peter

11 [a]But when Peter [ao]was come to Antioch, I [ao]withstood him to the face,[4383] because he was to be blamed.[2607]

12 For before that certain [aip]came from James, [a]he [ipf]did eat with the Gentiles:[1484] but when they were come, he [ipf]withdrew and [ipf]separated[873] himself, fearing[5399] them which were of the circumcision.[4061]

13 And the other Jews dissembled likewise with him; insomuch that Barnabas also was carried away with their dissimulation.[5272]

14 But when I saw that they walked not uprightly according to [a]the truth[225] of the gospel,[2098] I said unto Peter [b]before *them* all, [c]If thou, being a Jew, livest after the manner of Gentiles,[1483] and not as do the Jews, why compellest thou the Gentiles to live as do the Jews?

15 [a]We *who are* Jews by nature, and not [b]sinners[268] of the Gentiles,

16 [a]Knowing that a man[444] is not

2 [a]Acts 15:12 [b]Phil. 2:16; 1Thess. 3:5
4 [a]Acts 15:1, 24; 2Cor. 11:26 [b]Gal. 3:25; 5:1, 13 [c]2Cor. 11:20; Gal. 4:3, 9
5 [a]Gal. 2:14; 3:1; 4:16
6 [a]Gal. 6:3 [b]Acts 10:34; Rom. 2:11 [c]2Cor. 12:11
7 [a]Acts 13:46; Rom. 1:5; 11:13; 1Tim. 2:7; 2Tim. 1:11 [b]1Thess. 2:4
8 [a]Acts 9:15; 13:2; 22:21; 26:17, 18; 1Cor. 15:10; Gal. 1:16; Col. 1:29 [b]Gal. 3:5
9 [a]Matt. 16:18; Eph. 2:20; Rev. 21:14 [b]Rom. 1:5; 12:3, 6; 15:15; 1Cor. 15:10; Eph. 3:8
10 [a]Acts 11:30; 24:17; Rom. 15:25; 1Cor. 16:1
11 [a]Acts 15:35
12 [a]Acts 10:28; 11:3
14 [a]Gal. 2:5 [b]1Tim. 5:20 [c]Acts 10:28; 11:3
15 [a]Acts 15:10, 11 [b]Matt. 9:11; Eph. 2:3, 12
16 [a]Acts 13:38, 39

2:3 See the introduction to Titus.

2:4 In this verse, Paul is warning the church in Galatia that some were endeavoring to bring the Christians under the Law of Moses. Although Paul circumcised Timothy, who was half Jew and half Gentile (Acts 16:3), he did not yield to pressure to circumcise Titus. Had Titus voluntarily chosen to be circumcised, it would have been acceptable.

Judaizers were teaching that Christians should still be under obligation to keep the law. Paul calls them *pareisáktous* (3920), which is translated "unawares brought in." These people had infiltrated the church secretly, without declaring from the start who they were or what they intended to do. This does not indicate that they were brought in by the church itself, but that they managed to deceive them and enter the fellowship. Paul calls these intruders "false brethren," *pseudadélphoi* (5569), the same term that Paul used in 2 Corinthians 11:26 speaking of himself being "in dangers among false brethren." In other words, these false brethren became violently opposed to Paul. The phrase "who came in privily" is from the Greek word *pareisélthon*, which also indicates the deceitfulness of these people who joined the local church in Galatia in order to spread their own form of legalism.

2:16 See notes on Romans 3:19, 20 and James 2:14–19.

justified[1344] by the works[2041] of the law,[3551] but [b]by the faith[4102] of Jesus Christ, even we [ao]have believed[4100] in Jesus Christ, that we [asbp]might be justified[1344] by the faith of Christ, and not by the works of the law: for [c]by the works of the law shall no flesh[4561] be justified.

17 But if, while we [ppt]seek [aifp]to be justified by Christ, we ourselves also [aop]are found[2147] [a]sinners,[268] *is* therefore Christ the minister[1249] of sin?[266] God forbid.[1096,3361]

18 For if I build again the things which I destroyed, I make[4921] myself a transgressor.[3848]

19 For I [a]through the law [ao][b]am dead[599] to the law, that I [aosb]might [c]live[2198] unto God.

20 I [pfip]am [a]crucified[4957] with Christ:[5547] nevertheless I live; yet not I, but Christ liveth in me: and the life which I now live in the flesh[4561] [b]I live by the faith[4102] of the Son[5207] of God, [c]who [apt]loved[25] me, and [apt]gave himself for me.

21 I do not frustrate the grace[5485] of God: for [a]if righteousness[1343] *come* by the law,[3551] then Christ [ao]is dead[599] in vain.[1432]

The Experience of the Galatians

3 O foolish[453] Galatians, [a]who [ao]hath bewitched you, that ye should not obey[3982] [b]the truth,[225] before whose eyes Jesus Christ [aop]hath been evidently set forth, [pfpp]crucified[4717] among you?

2 This only would I learn[3129] of you, Received ye [a]the Spirit[4151] by the works[2041] of the law,[3551] [b]or by the hearing[189] of faith?[4102]

3 Are ye so foolish? [apt][a]having begun in the Spirit, are ye now made perfect[2005] by [b]the flesh?[4561]

4 [ao][a]Have ye suffered[3958] so many things in vain?[1500] if *it be* yet in vain.

5 He therefore [a]that [ppt]ministereth to you the Spirit, and [ppt]worketh miracles[1411] among you, *doeth he it* by the works[2041] of the law,[3551] or by the hearing[189] of faith?[4102]

6 Even as [a]Abraham believed[4100] God, and it was [l]accounted to him for righteousness.[1343]

7 Know ye therefore that [a]they which are of faith, the same are the children[5207] of Abraham.

8 And [a]the scripture,[1124] [apt]foreseeing[4275] that God would justify[1344] the heathen[1484] through faith,[4102] [ao]preached before the gospel[4283] unto Abraham, *saying,* [b]In thee shall all nations[1484] be blessed.

9 So then they which be of faith are blessed[2127] with faithful[4103] Abraham.

10 For as many as are of the [an]works[2041] of the [an]law[3551] are under the [an]curse:[2671] for it is written, [a]Cursed[1944] *is* every one that continueth[1696] not in all things which are written in the book[975] of the law to do them.

🔑 11 But [a]that no man is justified[1344] by the [an]law in the sight of God, *it is* evident: for, [b]The just[1342] shall live[2198] by faith.[4102]

12 And [a]the law is not of faith: but, [b]The man[444] that [apt]doeth them shall live[2198] in them.

13 [a]Christ[5547] hath redeemed[1805] us from the curse[2671] of the law, [apt]being made a curse for us: for it is written, [b]Cursed[1944] *is* every one that hangeth on a tree:

14 [a]That the blessing[2129] of Abraham [aosb]might come on the Gentiles[1484] through Jesus Christ;[5547] that we [aosb]might receive [b]the promise[1860] of the Spirit[4151] through faith.[4102]

15 Brethren, I speak after the manner of men; [a]Though *it be* but a man's covenant,[1242] yet *if it be* [pfpp]confirmed, no man disannulleth, or addeth thereto.

16 Now [a]to Abraham and his seed[4690] [aop]were the promises made.[4483] He saith not, And to seeds,[4690] as of many; but as of one, And to thy seed, which is [b]Christ.[5547]

16 [b]Rom. 1:17; 3:22, 28; 8:3; Gal. 3:24; Heb. 7:18, 19 [c]Ps. 143:2; Rom. 3:20; Gal. 3:11
17 [a]1John 3:8, 9
19 [a]Rom. 8:2 [b]Rom. 6:14; 7:4, 6; [c]Rom. 6:11; 2Cor. 5:15; 1Thess. 5:10; Heb. 9:14; 1Pet. 4:2
20 [a]Rom. 6:6; Gal. 5:24; 6:14 [b]2Cor. 5:15; 1Thess. 5:10; 1Pet. 4:2 [c]Gal. 1:4; Eph. 5:2; Titus 2:14
21 [a]Gal. 3:21; 5:4; Heb. 7:11; Rom. 11:6

1 [a]Gal. 5:7 [b]Gal. 2:14; 5:7
2 [a]Acts 2:38; 8:15; 10:47; 15:8; Gal. 3:14; Eph. 1:13; Heb. 6:4 [b]Rom. 10:16, 17
3 [a]Gal. 4:9 [b]Heb. 7:16; 9:10
4 [a]Heb. 10:35, 36; 2John 1:8
5 [a]2Cor. 3:8
6 [l]Or, *imputed* [a]Gen. 15:6; Rom. 4:3, 9, 21, 22; James 2:23
7 [a]John 8:39; Rom. 4:11, 12, 16
8 [a]Rom. 9:17; Gal. 3:22 [b]Gen. 12:3; 18:18; 22:18; Acts 3:25
10 [a]Deut. 27:26; Jer. 11:3
11 [a]Gal. 2:16 [b]Hab. 2:4; Rom. 1:17; Heb. 10:38
12 [a]Rom. 4:4, 5; 10:5, 6; 11:6 [b]Lev. 18:5; Neh. 9:29; Ezek. 20:11; Rom. 10:5
13 [a]Rom. 8:3; 2Cor. 5:21; Gal. 4:5 [b]Deut. 21:23
14 [a]Rom. 4:9, 16 [b]Isa. 32:15; 44:3; Jer. 31:33; 32:40; Ezek. 11:19; 36:27; Joel 2:28, 29; Zech. 12:10; John 7:39; Acts 2:33
15 [a]Heb. 9:17
16 [a]Gen. 12:3, 7; 17:7; Gal. 3:8 [b]1Cor. 12:12

🔑 **3:11, 12** See note on James 2:14–19.

17 And this I say, *that* the covenant, that [pfpp]was confirmed before of God in Christ, the law, [a]which [pfp]was four hundred and thirty years after, cannot disannul, [b]that it [aies]should make[2673] the promise[1860] of none effect.[2673]

18 For if [a]the inheritance[2817] *be* of the law,[3551] [b]*it is* no more of promise: but God [pfi]gave[5483] *it* to Abraham by promise.

The Purpose of the Law

19 Wherefore then *serveth* the law?[3551] [a]It was added because of transgressions,[3847] till [b]the seed[4690] [aosb]should come to whom the [pfip]promise was made;[1861] *and it was* [aptp][c]ordained[1299] by angels[32] in the hand [d]of a mediator.[3316]

20 Now a mediator is not *a mediator* of one, [a]but God is one.

21 *Is* the law then against the promises of God? God forbid:[1096,3361] [a]for if there [aop]had been a law given[1325] which could have[1410] [ainf]given life, verily[3689] righteousness[1343] should have been by the law.

22 But [a]the scripture [ao]hath concluded [b]all under sin,[266] [c]that the promise by faith of Jesus Christ [asbp]might be given to them that [ppt]believe.[4100]

23 But before faith [aip]came, we [ipf]were kept under the law, [pfpp]shut up unto the faith[4102] which should afterwards [aifp]be revealed.

24 Wherefore [a]the law [pfi]was our schoolmaster[3807] *to bring us* unto Christ,[5547] [b]that we [asbp]might be justified[1344] by faith.

25 But after that faith [apt]is come, we are no longer under a schoolmaster.

26 For ye [a]are all the children[5207] of God[2316] by faith in Christ Jesus.

27 For [a]as many of you as [aop]have been baptized[907] into Christ [aom][b]have put on Christ.

17 [a]Ex. 12:40, 41 [b]Rom. 4:13, 14; Gal. 3:21 **18** [a]Rom. 8:17 [b]Rom. 4:14 **19** [a]John 15:22; Rom. 4:15; 5:20; 7:8, 13 [b]1Tim. 1:9 [c]Gal. 3:16 [d]Acts 7:53; Heb. 2:2 [e]Ex. 20:19, 21, 22; Deut. 5:5, 22, 23, 27, 31; John 1:17; Acts 7:38; 1Tim. 2:5 **20** [a]Rom. 3:29, 30 **21** [a]Gal. 2:21 **22** [a]Gal. 3:8 [b]Rom. 3:9, 19, 23; 11:32 [c]Rom. 4:11, 12, 16 **24** [a]Matt. 5:17; Rom. 10:4; Col. 2:17; Heb. 9:9, 10 [b]Acts 13:39; Gal. 2:16 **26** [a]John 1:12; Rom. 8:14-16; Gal. 4:5; 1John 3:1, 2 **27** [a]Rom. 6:3 [b]Rom. 13:14 **28** [a]Rom. 10:12; 1Cor. 12:13; Gal. 5:6; Col. 3:11 [b]John 10:16; 17:20, 21; Eph. 2:14-16; 4:4, 15 **29** [a]Gen. 21:10, 12; Rom. 9:7; Heb. 11:18 [b]Rom. 8:17; Gal. 4:7, 28; Eph. 3:6, 8

3 [a]Gal. 2:4; 4:9; 5:1; Col. 2:8, 20; Heb. 9:10 **4** [a]Gen. 49:10; Dan. 9:24; Mark 1:15; Eph. 1:10 [b]John 1:14; Rom. 1:3; Phil. 2:7; Heb. 2:14 [c]Gen. 3:15; Isa. 7:14; Mic. 5:3; Matt. 1:23; Luke 1:31, 2:7 [d]Matt. 5:17; Luke 2:27 **5** [a]Matt. 20:28; Gal. 3:13; Eph. 1:7; Titus 2:14; Heb. 9:12; 1Pet. 1:18, 19 [b]John 1:12; Gal. 3:26; Eph. 1:5

28 [a]There is neither Jew nor Greek, there is neither bond[1401] nor free,[1658] there is neither male[730] nor female:[2338] for ye are all [b]one in Christ Jesus.

29 And [a]if ye *be* Christ's, then are ye Abraham's seed,[4690] and [b]heirs[2818] according to the promise.[1860]

The Believer's Inheritance

4 Now I say, *That* the heir,[2818] as long as he is a child,[3516] differeth nothing from[1308] a servant,[1401] though he be lord[2962] of all;

2 But is under tutors and governors until the time appointed[4287] of the father.[3962]

3 Even so we, when we were children,[3516] [a]were in bondage under the elements[4747] of the world:[2889]

4 But [a]when the fulness[4138] of the time [ao]was come,[2064] God[2316] sent forth his Son,[5207] [apt][b]made [c]of a woman, [apt][d]made under the law,[3551]

5 [aosb][a]To redeem[1805] them that were under the law, [b]that we [aosb]might receive[618] the adoption of sons.[5206]

6 And because ye are sons, God [ao]hath sent forth [a]the Spirit[4151] of his Son into your hearts,[2588] crying, Abba,[5] Father.[3962]

7 Wherefore thou art no more a servant, but a son; [a]and if a son, then an heir[2818] of God through Christ.[5547]

8 Howbeit[235] then, [a]when ye knew not God,[2316] [b]ye [ao]did service[1398] unto them which by nature are no gods.[2316]

9 But now, [a]after that ye have known[1097] God, or rather [aptp]are known of God, [b]how turn ye [I]again to [c]the weak[772] and beggarly [II][d]elements,[4747]

6 [a]Rom. 5:5; 8:15 **7** [a]Rom. 8:16, 17; Gal. 3:29 **8** [a]Eph. 2:12; 1Thess. 4:5 [b]Rom. 1:25; 1Cor. 12:2; Eph. 2:11, 12; 1Thess. 1:9 **9** [I]Or, *back* [II]Or, *rudiments* [a]1Cor. 8:3; 13:12; 2Tim. 2:19 [b]Gal. 3:3; Col. 2:20 [c]Rom. 8:3; Heb. 7:18 [d]Gal. 4:3

3:17 See note on Genesis 15:13–16.

3:22 See notes on Luke 8:13; Hebrews 6:1–6; 10:26, 27; and 1 John 3:6–9.

3:28 See note on 1 Timothy 2:9–15 concerning a woman's conduct in the church.

whereunto ye desire again[3825] [pinf]to be in
bondage?[1398]
10 [a]Ye observe[3906] days, and months,
and times,[2540] and years.
11 I am afraid[5399] of you, [a]lest I
[pfi]have bestowed upon you labour in vain.
12 Brethren,[80] I beseech you, [pim]be as
I *am;* for I *am* as ye *are:* [a]ye [ao]have not
injured[91] me at all.
13 Ye know[1492] how [a]through infirmity of the flesh I preached the gospel[2097] unto you [b]at the first.
14 And my temptation[3986] which was
in my flesh[4561] ye despised not, nor rejected; but received me [a]as an angel[32] of
God, *even* [b]as Christ Jesus.
15 [I]Where is then the blessedness ye
spake of? for I bear you record, that, if
it had been possible, ye [apt]would have
plucked out your own eyes, and [ao]have
given them to me.
16 [pfi]Am I therefore become[1096]
your enemy, [a]because I [ppt]tell you the
truth?[226]
17 They [a]zealously affect[2206] you, *but*
not well; yea, they would [ainf]exclude [I]you,
that ye [psa]might affect them.
18 But *it is* good [pip]to be zealously affected always in *a* good *thing,* and not
only when I am present with you.
19 [a]My little children, of whom I
travail in birth[5605] again until Christ[5547]
[asbp]be formed[3445] in you,
20 I desire to be present with you
now, and to change[236] my voice; for [I]I
stand in doubt of you.

Isaac and Ishmael

21 [pim]Tell me, ye that [ppt]desire to be
under the [an]law,[3551] do ye not hear the
law?
22 For it is written, that Abraham
had two sons,[5207] [a]the one by a bondmaid, [b]the other by a freewoman.
23 But he *who was* of the bond-
woman [pfip][a]was born after the flesh;[4561]
[b]but he of the freewoman *was* by promise.[1860]
24 Which things are an allegory:[238]
for these are the two covenants;[1242] the
one from the mount [I][a]Sinai, which
[ppt]gendereth[1080] to bondage,[1397] which is
Agar.
25 For this Agar is mount Sinai in
Arabia, and answereth to Jerusalem
which now is, and is in bondage[1398] with
her children.
26 But [a]Jerusalem which is above[507]
is free, which is the mother of us all.
27 For it is written, [aipp][a]Rejoice,[2165]
thou barren that [ppt]bearest not; [aim]break
forth and [aim]cry, thou that [ppt]travailest[5605]
not: for the desolate hath many more
children than she which hath an husband.
28 Now we, brethren, as Isaac was,
are [a]the children[5043] of promise.[1860]
29 But as then [a]he that [aptp]was born
after the flesh [ipf]persecuted him *that was*
born after the Spirit, [b]even so *it is* now.
30 Nevertheless what saith [a]the
scripture?[1124] [b]Cast out the bondwoman
and her son: for [c]the son of the bondwoman shall not be heir[2816] with the son
of the freewoman.
31 So then, brethren, we are not children[5043] of the bondwoman, [a]but of the
free.

Privileges of Christian Liberty

5 [pim]Stand fast therefore in [a]the liberty[1657] wherewith Christ[5547] [ao]hath
made us free,[1659] and [pim]be not entangled
again [b]with[1758] the yoke of bondage.[1397]
2 Behold, I Paul say unto you, that [a]if
ye [psmp]be circumcised,[4059] Christ shall
profit you nothing.
3 For I testify[3143] again to every man
that [ppp]is circumcised,[4059] [a]that he is a
debtor[3781] to do the whole law.[3551]
🔑 4 [a]Christ [aop]is become of no effect unto
you, whosoever of you are justified[1344]

10 [a]Rom. 14:5; Col. 2:16
11 [a]Gal. 2:2; 5:2, 4; 1Thess. 3:5
12 [a]2Cor. 2:5
13 [a]1Cor. 2:3; 2Cor. 11:30; 12:7, 9 [b]Gal. 1:6
14 [a]2Sam. 19:27; Zech. 12:8; Mal. 2:7 [b]Matt. 10:40; Luke 10:16; John 13:20; 1Thess. 2:13
15 [I]Or, *What was then*
16 [a]Gal. 2:5, 14
17 [I]Or, *us* [a]Rom. 10:2; 2Cor. 11:2
19 [a]1Cor. 4:15; Phile. 1:10; James 1:18
20 [I]Or, *I am perplexed for you*
22 [a]Gen. 16:15 [b]Gen. 21:2
23 [a]Rom. 9:7, 8 [b]Gen. 18:10, 14; 21:1, 2; Heb. 11:11
24 [I]Gr. *Sina* [a]Deut. 33:2
26 [a]Isa. 2:2; Heb. 12:22; Rev. 3:12; 21:2, 10
27 [a]Isa. 54:1
28 [a]Acts 3:25; Rom. 9:8; Gal. 3:29
29 [a]Gen. 21:9 [b]Gal. 5:11; 6:12
30 [a]Gal. 3:8, 22 [b]Gen. 21:10, 12 [c]John 8:35
31 [a]John 8:36; Gal. 5:1, 13

1 [a]John 8:32; Rom. 6:18; 1Pet. 2:16 [b]Acts 15:10; Gal. 2:4; 4:9
2 [a]Acts 15:1; 16:3
3 [a]Gal. 3:10
4 [a]Rom. 9:31, 32; Gal. 2:21

🔑 **5:4** This text is often misused to teach that the phrase "fall from grace" means that a person can lose his or her salvation. In the context of verses one through three, Paul is teaching how de-

(continued on next page)

by the law; [b]ye [ao]are fallen from grace.[5485]
5 For we through the Spirit [a]wait
for[553] the hope[1680] of righteousness[1343]
by faith.[4102]
6 For [a]in Jesus Christ neither circumcision[4061] availeth[2480] any thing, nor
uncircumcision;[203] but [b]faith[4102] which
[ppt]worketh[1754] by love.[26]
7 Ye [ipf][a]did run well; [b]who did hinder
you that ye [pip]should not obey[3982] the
truth?[225]
8 This persuasion *cometh* not of him
[a]that [ppt]calleth you.
9 [a]A little leaven[2219] leaveneth[2220] the
whole lump.
10 [a]I have confidence[3982] in you
through the Lord, that ye will be[5426] none
otherwise[243] minded:[5426] but [b]he that
[ppt]troubleth you [c]shall bear his judgment,[2917] whosoever he be.
11 [a]And I, brethren, if I yet
preach[2784] circumcision, [b]why do I yet
suffer persecution? then is [c]the offence[4625]
of the cross[4716] [pfip]ceased.
12 [a]I would they [fm]were even cut
off[609] [b]which [ppt]trouble[387] you.
13 For, brethren, ye [aop]have been
called unto liberty;[1657] only *use* [a]not liberty for an occasion to the flesh,[4561] but
[b]by love [pim]serve[1398] one another.
14 For [a]all the law [pinp]is fulfilled in
one word,[3056] *even* in this; [b]Thou shalt
love[25] thy neighbour as thyself.
15 But if ye bite and devour one another, [pim]take heed that ye [asbp]be not
consumed[355] one of another.
16 *This* I say then, [pim][a]Walk[4043] in
the Spirit,[4151] and ye [asba]shall not fulfil[5055] the lust[1939] of the flesh.[4561]
17 For [a]the flesh lusteth[1937] against
the Spirit, and the Spirit against the flesh:
and these are contrary the one to the

4 [b]Heb. 12:15
5 [a]Rom. 8:24, 25; 2Tim. 4:8
6 [a]1Cor. 7:19; Gal. 3:28; 6:15; Col. 3:11 [b]1Thess. 1:3; James 2:18, 20, 22
7 [a]1Cor. 9:24 [b]Gal. 3:1
8 [a]Gal. 1:6
9 [a]1Cor. 5:6; 15:33
10 [a]2Cor. 2:3; 8:22 [b]Gal. 1:7 [c]2Cor. 10:6
11 [a]Gal. 6:12 [b]1Cor. 15:30; Gal. 4:29; 6:17 [c]1Cor. 1:23
12 [a]Josh. 7:25; 1Cor. 5:13; Gal. 1:8, 9 [b]Acts 15:1, 2, 24
13 [a]1Cor. 8:9; 1Pet. 2:16; 2Pet. 2:19; Jude 1:4 [b]1Cor. 9:19; Gal. 6:2
14 [a]Matt. 7:12; 22:40; James 2:8 [b]Lev. 19:18; Matt. 22:39; Rom. 13:8, 9
16 [a]Rom. 6:12; 8:1, 4, 12; 13:14; Gal. 5:25; 1Pet. 2:11
17 [a]Rom. 7:23; 8:6, 7 [b]Rom. 7:15, 19
18 [a]Rom. 6:14; 8:2
19 [a]1Cor. 3:3; Eph. 5:3; Col. 3:5; James 3:14, 15
21 [a]1Cor. 6:9; Eph. 5:5; Col. 3:6; Rev. 22:15
22 [a]John 15:2; Eph. 5:9 [b]Col. 3:12; James 3:17 [c]Rom. 15:14 [d]1Cor. 13:7
23 [a]1Tim. 1:9
24 [I]Or, *passions* [a]Rom. 6:6; 13:14; Gal. 2:20; 1Pet. 2:11
25 [a]Rom. 8:4, 5; Gal. 5:16
26 [a]Phil. 2:3

other: [b]so that ye cannot do the things
that ye [psa]would.
18 But [a]if ye [pinp]be led[71] of the
Spirit, ye are not under the law.
19 Now [a]the works[2041] of the flesh
are manifest,[5318] which are *these;*
Adultery, fornication,[4202] uncleanness,[167]
lasciviousness,[766]
20 Idolatry,[1495] witchcraft, [pl]hatred,
[pl]variance,[2054] emulations,[2205] [pl]wrath,[2372]
[pl]strife, seditions,[1370] heresies,[139]
21 Envyings, murders, [pl]drunken-
ness,[3178] revellings,[2970] and such like:[3664]
of the which I [pin]tell you before,[4302] as I
[ao]have also told *you* in time past,[4275] that
[a]they which [ppt]do[4238] such things shall
not inherit[2816] the kingdom[932] of God.
22 But [a]the fruit of the Spirit is
love,[26] joy,[5479] peace,[1515] longsuffering,
[b]gentleness,[5544] [c]goodness,[19] [d]faith,
23 Meekness, temperance: [a]against
such there is no law.
24 And they that are Christ's [ao][a]have
crucified[4717] the flesh[4561] with the
[I]affections[3804] and lusts.
25 [a]If we live[2198] in the Spirit, [psa]let
us also walk[4748] in the Spirit.
26 [psa][a]Let us not be[1096] desirous of
vain glory, [ppt]provoking one another,
[ppt]envying one another.

The Practice of Love

6 Brethren, [a]if a man[444] [asbp]be overtaken[4301] in a fault,[3900] ye [b]which are
spiritual, [pim]restore[2675] such an one [c]in
the spirit[4151] of meekness; [ppt]consider-
ing[4648] thyself, [d]lest thou also [asbp]be
tempted.[3985]

1 [a]Rom. 14:1; 15:1; Heb. 12:13; James 5:19 [b]1Cor. 2:15; 3:1 [c]1Cor. 4:21; 2Thess. 3:15; 2Tim. 2:25 [d]1Cor. 7:5; 10:12

(continued from previous page)
pending on the Law of Moses for salvation makes Christ's work on the cross meaningless. Then in verse four, he speaks about those who think they can justify themselves through the law. Because these individuals chose to obey the law for salvation, they have no room for Jesus Christ and His grace. The key to understanding the phrase "you are fallen from grace" is seen in the verb *ex-epésate* (1601), which is better translated "have fallen." It does not mean that the grace of God was evident at one time, and then was lost. Rather, this person deviates from the true path of grace by choosing justification by law instead of by grace. Grace has a law associated with it, but the law has no grace, only restrictions (see Rom. 2:12; 7:7). See note on James 2:14–19.

2 [pima]Bear ye one another's burdens,
and so [aim]fulfil[378] [b]the law[3551] of
Christ.
3 For [a]if a man think himself to be
something, when [b]he is nothing,[3367] he
deceiveth himself.
4 But [a]let every man [pim]prove his
own work,[2041] and then shall he have rejoicing in himself alone, and [b]not in
another.[2087]
5 For [a]every man shall bear his own
burden.[5413]
6 [pima]Let[2841] him that [ppp]is taught
in the word[3056] communicate[2841] unto
him that [ppt]teacheth[2727] in all good
things.[18]

Law of Sowing and Reaping

7 [pima]Be not deceived;[4105] [b]God[2316] is
not mocked: for [c]whatsoever a man[444]
[psa]soweth, that shall he also reap.
8 [a]For he that [ppt]soweth to his
flesh[4561] shall of the flesh reap corruption;[5356] but he that soweth to the
Spirit shall of the Spirit reap life[2222] everlasting.[166]
9 And [psaa]let us not be weary[1573] in
well[2570] [ppt]doing:[4160] for in due[2398] season[2540] we shall reap, [b]if we [ppp]faint[1590]
not.
10 [a]As we have therefore opportu-
nity,[2540] [psab]let us do[2038] good[18] unto all
men, especially unto them who are of
[c]the household[3609] of faith.[4102]

2 [a]Rom. 15:1; Gal. 5:13; 1Thess. 5:14 [b]John 13:14, 15, 34; 15:12; James 2:8; 1John 4:21
3 [a]Rom. 12:3; 1Cor. 8:2; Gal. 2:6 [b]2Cor. 3:5; 12:11
4 [a]1Cor. 11:28; 2Cor. 13:5 [b]Luke 18:11
5 [a]Rom. 2:6; 1Cor. 3:8
6 [a]Rom. 15:27; 1Cor. 9:11, 14
7 [a]1Cor. 6:9; 15:33 [b]Job 13:9 [c]Luke 16:25; Rom. 2:6; 2Cor. 9:6
8 [a]Job 4:8; Prov. 11:18; 22:8; Hos. 8:7; 10:12; Rom. 8:13; James 3:18
9 [a]1Cor. 15:58; 2Thess. 3:13 [b]Matt. 24:13; Heb. 3:6, 14; 10:36; 12:3, 5; Rev. 2:10
10 [a]John 9:4; 12:35 [b]1Thess. 5:15; 1Tim. 6:18; Titus 3:8 [c]Eph. 2:19; Heb. 3:6
12 [a]Gal. 2:3, 14 [b]Phil. 3:18 [c]Gal. 5:11
14 [a]Phil. 3:3, 7, 8 [b]Rom. 6:6; Gal. 2:20
15 [a]1Cor. 7:19; Gal. 5:6; Col. 3:11 [b]2Cor. 5:17
16 [a]Ps. 125:5 [b]Phil. 3:16 [c]Rom. 2:29; 4:12; 9:6-8;

Paul's Closing Remarks

11 Ye see how large a letter[1121] I
have written[1125] unto you with mine own
hand.
12 As many as desire [ainf]to make a
fair shew[2146] in the flesh,[4561] [a]they constrain you [pip]to be circumcised;[4059] [b]only
lest they [psmp]should [c]suffer persecution
for the cross[4716] of Christ.
13 For neither they themselves who
[ppp]are circumcised keep[5442] the law;[3551]
but desire [pip]to have you circumcised,[4059]
that they [aosb]may glory in your flesh.
14 [a]But God forbid[1096,3361] that I
[pinf]should glory, save in the cross of our
Lord Jesus Christ, by whom the world[2889]
[pfip]is [b]crucified[4717] unto me, and I unto
the world.
15 For [a]in Christ Jesus neither circumcision[4061] availeth[2480] any thing, nor
uncircumcision,[203] but [b]a new[2537] creature.[2937]
16 [a]And as many as walk [b]accord-
ing to this rule, peace[1515] *be* on them,
and mercy,[1656] and upon [c]the Israel of
God.
🔑 17 From henceforth [pim]let no man
trouble[3930,2873] me: for [a]I bear in my
body[4983] the marks of the Lord Jesus.
18 Brethren, [a]the grace[5485] of our
Lord Jesus Christ *be* with your spirit.
Amen.[281]

Gal. 3:7, 9, 29; Phil. 3:3 Gal. 5:11; Col. 1:24
17 [a]2Cor. 1:5; 4:10; 11:23;
18 [a]2Tim. 4:22; Phile. 1:25

🔑 **6:17** See note on 2 Timothy 1:12.

The Epistle of Paul to the

EPHESIANS

Ephesus was the capital of the chief province of Asia. It was located about one mile from the Aegean Sea. The temple of Diana (Artemis) was important to the commerce of the city because the Mediterranean world considered it to be such a sacred and impeccable institution that it became the chief banking establishment in all of Asia Minor. The great number of pilgrims that came to worship at the temple also bolstered the economy in Ephesus. In fact, the population is believed to have exceeded a quarter million.

Paul came to Ephesus during his second missionary journey with Aquila and Priscilla but journeyed on to Jerusalem by himself not long afterward (Acts 18:18–21). On his next missionary journey, Paul spent three years in Ephesus (Acts 19). He had so much influence on the people there that the craftsmen who manufactured silver shrines for Diana incited a riot against him, concerned that their trade would become obsolete (Acts 19:24–29). As a result, Paul left Ephesus, traveling to Macedonia (Acts 20:1). Upon a return trip to Jerusalem, he requested that the elders of the Ephesian congregation meet with him at Miletus, a city located thirty-five miles to the south, so that he could bid them his last farewell (Acts 20:16–38).

The Book of Ephesians was probably written by Paul during his imprisonment in Rome (ca. A.D. 60–64), about the same time that he wrote Colossians and Philemon. The content of the Book of Ephesians is very similar to that of Colossians; both stress doctrine and give instruction in practical Christian duties. One difference between them, however, is that Colossians portrays Christ as the head of the Church, while Ephesians goes on to display Jesus as the ascended, glorified Christ. Also, in Colossians Paul attacks the gnostic heresy; but in Ephesians, Paul examines the splendor of Christ in glory.

The major theme of this letter is that the Church (*ekklēsía* [1577]) is the body of Christ (Eph. 1:22, 23; 2:15, 16). Paul also metaphorically spoke of the Church as a building of which Christ is the chief cornerstone (Eph. 2:20–22) and compared the Church to a bride who will soon be united with Christ (Eph. 5:21–33). The key idea is that a body has individual parts that must operate as a unit. God's plan is to bring all believers together (Eph. 1:10) with Christ as the head (Eph. 1:22, 23).

1 🔑 Paul, an apostle[652] of Jesus
Christ [a]by the will[2307] of God,[2316] [b]to
the saints[40] which are at Ephesus, [c]and
to the faithful[4103] in Christ Jesus:
2 [a]Grace[5485] *be* to you, and peace,[1515]
from God our Father,[3962] and *from* the
[an]Lord[2962] Jesus Christ.[5547]

1 [a]2Cor. 1:1 [b]Rom. 1:7; 2Cor. 1:1 [c]1Cor. 4:17; Eph. 6:21; Col. 1:2
2 [a]Gal. 1:3; Titus 1:4
3 [a]2Cor. 1:3; 1Pet. 1:3 [b]Eph. 6:12

The Blessings of Redemption

3 [a]Blessed[2128] *be* the God and Father of our Lord Jesus Christ, who
[apt]hath blessed us with all spiritual[4152]
[sg]blessings[2129] in [b]heavenly *places* in
Christ:

🔑 **1:1** The words "at Ephesus" do not appear in several important Greek manuscripts. Consequently, many believe that this letter was not originally sent to the congregation at Ephesus, but was meant to be circulated to the many Gentile churches in Asia. This would explain why Paul would completely omit any personal greetings to believers with whom he had spent three years (Acts 19). Scholars believe that it eventually became known as the Epistle to the Ephesians because the church in Ephesus was the mother church from which the letter would have been distributed to the other churches in Asia.

4 According as [a]he [aom]hath chosen
us in him [b]before the foundation of the
world,[2889] that we should [c]be holy[40] and
without blame[299] before him in love:
5 [apt][a]Having predestinated[4309] us
unto [b]the adoption of children[5206] by
Jesus Christ to himself, [c]according to the
good pleasure of his will,[2307]
6 To the praise of the glory[1391] of
his grace,[5485] [a]wherein he [ao]hath made
us accepted[5487] in [b]the beloved.[25]
7 [a]In whom we have redemption[629]
through his blood,[129] the forgiveness[859] of
sins,[3900] according to [b]the riches of his
grace;[5485]
8 Wherein he [ao]hath abounded toward us in all wisdom[4678] and prudence;[5428]
9 [apt][a]Having made known unto us the
mystery[3466] of his will,[2307] according to
his good pleasure[2107] [b]which he [aom]hath
purposed[4388] in himself:
10 That in the dispensation[3622] of
[a]the fulness[4138] of times[2540] [b]he [ainf]might
gather together in one[346] [c]all things in
Christ,[5547] both which are in [I]heaven,[3772]
and which are on earth;[1093] *even* in
him:
11 [a]In whom also we [aop]have obtained
an inheritance,[2820] [aptp][b]being predestinated[4309] according to [c]the purpose[4286]
of him who [ppt]worketh[1754] all things after
the counsel[1012] of his own will:
12 [a]That we should be to the
praise[1868] of his glory,[1391] [b]who [pfp]first
trusted in Christ.
13 In whom ye also *trusted,* after
[apt]that ye heard [a]the word[3056] of truth,[225]
the gospel[2098] of your salvation:[4991] in
whom also after that ye [apt]believed,[4100]
[b]ye [aop]were sealed[4972] with that holy[40]
Spirit[4151] of promise,[1860]
14 [a]Which is the earnest[728] of our
inheritance[2817] [b]until the redemption[629] of
[c]the purchased possession, [d]unto the
praise of his glory.
15 Wherefore I also, [a]after I heard of
your faith[4102] in the Lord[2962] Jesus, and
love[26] unto all the saints,[40]
16 [a]Cease not to [ppt]give thanks[2168]
for you, [ppt]making mention of you in my
prayers;[4335]
17 That [a]the God of our Lord Jesus
Christ, the Father[3962] of glory, [b]may give
unto you the [an]spirit[4151] of wisdom[4678]

4 [a]Rom. 8:28; 2Thess. 2:13; 2Tim. 1:9; James 2:5; 1Pet. 1:2; 2:9 [b]1Pet. 1:2, 20 [c]Luke 1:75; Eph. 2:10; 5:27; Col. 1:22; 1Thess. 4:7; Titus 2:12 **5** [a]Rom. 8:29, 30; Eph. 11:11 [b]John 1:12; Rom. 8:15; 2Cor. 6:18; Gal. 4:5; 1John 3:1 [c]Matt. 11:26; Luke 12:32; 1Cor. 1:21; Eph. 1:9 **6** [a]Rom. 3:24; 5:15 [b]Matt. 3:17; 17:5; John 3:35; 10:17 **7** [a]Acts 20:28; Rom. 3:24; Col. 1:14; Heb. 9:12; 1Pet. 1:18, 19; Rev. 5:9 [b]Rom. 2:4; 3:24; 9:23; Eph. 2:7; 3:8, 16; Phil. 4:19 **9** [a]Rom. 16:25; Eph. 3:4, 9; Col. 1:26 [b]Eph. 3:11; 2Tim. 1:9 **10** [I]Gr. *the heavens* [a]Gal. 4:4; Heb. 1:2; 9:10; 1Pet. 1:20 [b]1Cor. 3:22, 23; 11:3; Eph. 2:15; 3:15 [c]Phil. 2:9, 10; Col. 1:20 **11** [a]Acts 20:32; 26:18; Rom. 8:17; Col. 1:12; 3:24; Titus 3:7; James 2:5; 1Pet. 1:4 [b]Eph. 1:5 [c]Isa. 46:10, 11 **12** [a]Eph. 1:6, 14; 2Thess. 2:13 [b]James 1:18 **13** [a]John 1:17; 2Cor. 6:7 [b]2Cor. 1:22; Eph. 4:30 **14** [a]2Cor. 1:22; 5:5 [b]Luke 21:28; Rom. 8:23; Eph. 4:30 [c]Acts 20:28 [d]Eph. 1:6, 12; 1Pet. 2:9 **15** [a]Col. 1:4; Phile. 1:5 **16** [a]Rom. 1:9; Phil. 1:3, 4; Col. 1:3, 1Thess. 1:2; 2Thess. 1:3 **17** [a]John 20:17 [b]Col. 1:9

1:4, 5 There are two words in this passage that must be examined in order to explain the much debated subject of God's election and predestination. The first is found in verse four, "he has chosen," a translation of the Greek word *exeléxatō* (1586) meaning "chosen out of." In this context, this word means that at one particular time in the past, God chose individuals for salvation (Matt. 24:31; Luke 18:7; Rom. 8:33; 2 Tim. 2:10; James 2:5).

The second verb is in verse five: *proorísas* (4309), "to determine beforehand or predestinate" (cf. Acts 4:28; Rom. 8:29; 9:11; 1 Pet. 1:2, 20). It is interesting that Peter referred to the concept of predestination in his sermon on the day of Pentecost. He said (speaking of Christ), "Him, being delivered by the determinate counsel and foreknowledge of God, ye have taken, and by wicked hands have crucified and slain." The concept of free choice is here coupled with the responsibility for one's own actions. God delivered up His Son, and man was given the choice of what they would do with Christ. They chose to crucify Him, leaving them with the responsiblity for their act.

In 1 John 2:2 the writer states, "And he is the propitiation for our sins, (i.e., believers) and not for ours only, but also for the sins of the whole world." Therefore, the ministry of Christ that He did on the cross was intended for all. Repeatedly, God says that "whosoever believeth in Him" can obtain salvation (John 3:16–18, 36; Acts 10:43). To come to Christ is an invitation to all, and all who hear the gospel are responsible and without excuse if they do not accept Christ.

1:11 See note on Ephesians 1:4, 5.

1:13, 14 The phrase "the earnest of our inheritance" refers to the act of the Holy Spirit whereby He makes a pledge, providing assurance for the believer of an eternal life in Christ, which he must accept by faith.

and revelation[602] [c]in the knowledge[1922] of him:

18 [a]The eyes of your understanding[1271] [pfpp]being enlightened;[5461] that ye may know what is [b]the hope[1680] of his calling,[2821] and what the riches of the glory[1391] of his [c]inheritance in the saints,

19 And what *is* the exceeding greatness of his power[1411] to us-ward who [ppt]believe, [a]according to the working of his mighty[2479] power,[2904]

20 Which he [ao]wrought[1754] in Christ, when [a]he raised[1453] him from the dead,[3498] and [ao][b]set *him* at his own right hand[1188] in the heavenly *places,*

21 [a]Far above all [b]principality, and power,[1849] and might,[1411] and dominion,[2963] and every name[3686] that [ppp]is named, not only in this world,[165] but also in that which is to come:[3195]

22 And [ao][a]hath put[5293] all *things* under his feet, and gave him *to be* [b]the head[2776] over all *things* to the church,[1577]

23 [a]Which is his body,[4983] [b]the fulness[4138] of him [c]that filleth all in all.

Salvation From Sin

2 And [a]you *hath he quickened,* [b]who were dead[3498] in trespasses[3900] and sins;[266]

2 [a]Wherein in time past ye walked according to the course[165] of this world,[2889] according to [b]the prince of the power[1849] of the air, the spirit[4151] that now [ppt]worketh[1754] in [c]the children[5207] of disobedience:[543]

3 [a]Among whom also we all [aop]had our conversation[390] in times past in [b]the lusts[1939] of our flesh,[4561] [ppt]fulfilling the desires[2307] of the flesh and of the mind;[1271] and [c]were by nature[5449] the [an]children[5043] of wrath,[3709] even as others.

4 But God,[2316] [a]who is rich[4145] in mercy,[1656] for his great love[26] wherewith he loved[25] us,

5 [a]Even when we were dead[3498] in sins,[3900] [ao]hath [b]quickened us together[4806] with Christ, ([c]by grace[5485] ye are saved;[4982])

6 And hath raised *us* up together, and [ao]made *us* sit together [a]in heavenly *places* in Christ[5547] Jesus:

7 That in the ages[165] to come he [asbm]might shew the [ppt]exceeding riches of his grace in *his* [a]kindness[5544] toward us through Christ Jesus.

🔑 8 [a]For by grace[5485] are ye saved[4982] [b]through faith;[4102] and that not of yourselves: *it is* [c]the gift[1435] of God:

9 [a]Not of works,[2041] lest any man [asbm]should boast.

10 For we are [a]his workmanship, [aptp]created[2936] in Christ Jesus unto good[18] works, [b]which God [ao]hath before [l]ordained that we [aosb]should walk in them.

No Longer Strangers

11 Wherefore [pim][a]remember, that ye *being* in time past Gentiles[1484] in the flesh, who [ppp]are called Uncircumcision[203] by that which [ppp]is called [b]the Circumcision[4061] in the flesh made by hands;

12 [a]That at that time[2540] ye were without Christ, [b]being aliens[526] from the commonwealth of Israel, and strangers from [c]the covenants[1242] of promise,[1860] [d]having no hope,[1680] [e]and without God in the world:[2889]

13 [a]But now in Christ Jesus ye who sometimes were [b]far off [aop]are made nigh[1451] by the blood[129] of Christ.

14 For [a]he is our peace,[1515] [b]who [apt]hath made both one, and [apt]hath broken down[3089] the middle wall of partition *between us;*

17 [c]Col. 2:2
18 [a]Acts 26:18 [b]Eph. 2:12; 4:4 [c]Eph. 1:11
19 [a]Eph. 3:7; Col. 1:29; 2:12
20 [a]Acts 2:24, 33 [b]Ps. 110:1; Acts 7:55, 56; Col. 3:1; Heb. 1:3; 10:12
21 [a]Phil. 2:9, 10; Col. 2:10; Heb. 1:4 [b]Rom. 8:38; Col. 1:16; 2:15
22 [a]Ps. 8:6; Matt. 28:18; 1Cor. 15:27; Heb. 2:8 [b]Eph. 4:15, 16; Col. 1:18; Heb. 2:7
23 [a]Rom. 12:5; 1Cor. 12:12, 27; Eph. 4:12; 5:23, 30; 30; Col. 1:18, 24 [b]Col. 2:9 [c]1Cor. 12:6; Eph. 4:10; Col. 3:11

1 [a]John 5:24; Col. 2:13 [b]Eph. 1:5; 4:18
2 [a]1Cor. 6:11; Eph. 4:22; Col. 1:21; 3:7; 1John 5:19 [b]Eph. 6:12 [c]Eph. 5:6; Col. 3:6
3 [a]Titus 3:3; 1Pet. 4:3 [b]Gal. 5:16 [c]Ps. 51:5; Rom. 5:12, 14
4 [a]Rom. 10:12; Eph. 1:7; 2:7
5 [a]Rom. 5:6, 8, 10; Eph. 2:1 [b]Rom. 6:4, 5; Col. 2:12, 13; 3:1, 3 [c]Acts 15:11; Eph. 2:8; Titus 3:5
6 [a]Eph. 1:20
7 [a]Titus 3:4
8 [a]Rom. 3:24; Eph. 2:5; 2Tim. 1:9 [b]Rom. 4:16 [c]Matt. 16:17; John 6:44, 65; Rom. 10:14, 15, 17; Eph. 1:19; Phil. 1:29
9 [a]Rom. 3:20, 27, 28; 4:2; 9:11, 11:6; 1Cor. 1:29-31; 2Tim. 1:9; Titus 3:5
10 [l]Or, *prepared* [a]Deut. 32:6; Ps. 100:3; Isa. 19:25; 29:23; 44:21; John 3:3, 5; 1Cor. 3:9; 2Cor. 5:5, 17; Eph. 4:24; Titus 2:14 [b]Eph. 1:4
11 [a]1Cor. 12:2; Eph. 5:8; Col. 1:21; 2:13 [b]Rom. 2:28, 29; Col. 2:11
12 [a]Eph. 4:18; Col. 1:21 [b]Ezek. 13:9; John 10:16
12 [c]Rom. 9:4, 8 [d]1Thess. 4:13 [e]Gal. 4:8; 1Thess. 4:5
13 [a]Gal. 3:28 [b]Acts 2:39; Eph. 2:17
14 [a]Mic. 5:5; John 16:33; Acts 10:36; Rom. 5:1; Col. 1:20 [b]John 10:16; Gal. 3:28

🔑 **2:8** See note on Mark 16:16.

15 [apt][a]Having abolished [b]in his
flesh[4561] the enmity,2189 *even* the law[3551]
of commandments[1785] *contained* in ordinances;[1378] for to make[2936] in himself
of twain1417 one [c]new[2537] man,[444] *so*
making peace;[1515]
16 And that he [asba]might [a]reconcile
both unto God in one body[4983] by the
cross,[4716] [apt][b]having slain the enmity2189
[I]thereby:
17 And came [a]and [aom]preached[2097]
peace[1515] to you which were afar off, and
to [b]them that were nigh.[1451]
18 For [a]through him we both have
access[4318] [b]by one Spirit[4151] unto the
Father.[3962]
19 Now therefore ye are no more
strangers and foreigners,[3941] but [a]fellow-
citizens with the saints,[40] and of [b]the
household[3609] of God;
20 And [aptp]are [a]built [b]upon[2026] the
foundation of the [c]apostles[652] and
prophets,[4396] Jesus Christ himself being
[d]the chief corner *stone;*
21 [a]In whom all the building[3619]
[ppp]fitly framed together groweth unto [b]an
holy[40] temple[3485] in the Lord:[2962]
22 [a]In whom ye also are builded
together4925 for an habitation2732 of God
through the Spirit.

God's Plan

3 For this cause I Paul, [a]the prisoner of
Jesus Christ [b]for you Gentiles,[1484]
2 If ye [ao]have heard of [a]the dispensation[3622] of the grace[5485] of God
[b]which [aptp]is given me to you-ward:5209
3 [a]How that [b]by revelation[602] [c]he
[ao]made known[1107] unto me the mystery;[3466] ([d]as I wrote afore in few
words,
4 Whereby, when ye [ppt]read, ye may
[ainf]understand[3539] my knowledge [a]in the
mystery[3466] of Christ)
5 [a]Which in other[2087] ages [aop]was not
made known[1107] unto the sons[5207] of
men,[444] [b]as it [aop]is now revealed[601] unto
his holy[40] apostles[652] and prophets[4396] by
the Spirit;
6 That the Gentiles[1484] [a]should be fel-
lowheirs,[4789] and [b]of the same body,[4954]
and [c]partakers4830 of his promise[1860] in
Christ by the gospel:[2098]
7 [a]Whereof I was made a minis-
ter,[1249] [b]according to the gift[1431] of
the grace[5485] of God [aptp]given unto me
by [c]the effectual working of his
power.[1411]
8 Unto me, [a]who am less than the
least of all saints,[40] is this grace[5485]
given, that [b]I [ainf]should preach[2097] among
the Gentiles [c]the unsearchable riches of
Christ;[5547]
9 And [ainf]to make all *men* see[5461]
what *is* the fellowship[2842] of [a]the mystery,[3466] [b]which from the beginning
of the world [pfpp]hath been hid in God,
[c]who [apt]created[2936] all things by Jesus
Christ:
10 [a]To the intent that now [b]unto the
principalities[746] and powers[1849] in heavenly *places* [asbp][c]might be known by the
church[1577] the manifold wisdom[4678] of
God,
11 [a]According to the eternal[165] purpose[4286] which he purposed in Christ
Jesus our Lord:
12 In whom we have boldness and
[a]access[4318] [b]with confidence[4006] by the
faith[4102] of him.
13 [a]Wherefore I desire that ye
[pinf]faint[1573] not at my tribulations [b]for
you, [c]which is your glory.[1391]

Paul's Prayer for the Ephesians

14 For this cause I bow my knees
unto the Father[3962] of our Lord Jesus
Christ,
15 Of whom [a]the whole family[3965] in
heaven[3772] and earth[1093] is named,
16 That he would grant you, [a]ac-
cording to the riches of his glory,[1391]
[aifp][b]to be strengthened2901 with might by
his Spirit[4151] in [c]the inner man;[444]

15 [a]Col. 2:14, 20 [b]Col. 1:22 [c]2Cor. 5:17; Gal. 6:15; Eph. 4:24
16 [I]Or, *in himself* [a]Col. 1:20-22 [b]Rom. 6:6; 8:3; Col. 2:14
17 [a]Isa. 57:19; Zech. 9:10; Acts 2:39; 10:36; Rom. 5:1; Eph. 2:13, 14 [b]Ps. 148:14
18 [a]John 10:9; 14:6; Rom. 5:2; Eph. 3:12; Heb. 4:16; 10:19, 20; 1Pet. 3:18 [b]1Cor. 12:13; Eph. 4:4
19 [a]Phil. 3:20; Heb. 12:22, 23 [b]Gal. 6:10; Eph. 3:15
20 [a]1Cor. 3:9, 10; Eph. 4:12; 1Pet. 2:4, 5 [b]Matt. 16:18; Gal. 2:9; Rev. 21:14 [c]1Cor. 12:28; Eph. 4:11 [d]Ps. 118:22; Isa. 28:16; Matt. 21:42
21 [a]Eph. 4:15, 16 [b]1Cor. 3:17; 6:19; 2Cor. 6:16
22 [a]1Pet. 2:5

1 [a]Acts 21:33; 28:17, 20; Eph. 4:1; 6:20; Phil. 1:7, 13, 14, 16; Col. 4:3, 18; 2Tim. 1:8; 2:9; Phile. 1:1, 9 [b]Gal. 5:11; Col. 1:24; 2Tim. 2:10
2 [a]Rom. 1:5; 11:13; 1Cor. 4:1; Eph. 4:7; Col. 1:25 [b]Acts 9:15; 13:2; Rom. 12:3; Gal. 1:16; Eph. 3:8
3 [a]Acts 22:17, 21; 26:17, 18 [b]Gal. 1:12 [c]Rom. 16:25; Col. 1:26, 27 [d]Eph. 1:9, 10
4 [a]1Cor. 4:1; Eph. 6:19
5 [a]Acts 10:28; Rom. 16:25; Eph. 3:5 [b]Eph. 2:20
6 [a]Gal. 3:28, 29; Eph. 2:14 [b]Eph. 2:15, 16 [c]Gal. 3:14
7 [a]Rom. 15:16; Col. 1:23, 25 [b]Rom. 1:5 [c]Rom. 15:18; Eph. 1:19; Col. 1:29
8 [a]1Cor. 15:9; 1Tim. 1:13, 15 [b]Gal. 1:16; 2:8; 1Tim. 2:7; 2Tim. 1:11 [c]Eph. 1:7; Col. 1:27
9 [a]Eph. 1:9; 3:3 [b]Rom. 16:25; Eph. 3:5; 1Cor. 2:7; Col. 1:26 [c]Ps. 33:6; John 1:3; Col. 1:16; Heb. 1:2
10 [a]1Pet. 1:12 [b]Rom. 8:38; Eph. 1:21; Col. 1:16; 1Pet. 3:22 [c]1Cor. 2:7; 1Tim. 3:16
11 [a]Eph. 1:9
12 [a]Eph. 2:18 [b]Heb. 4:16
13 [a]Acts 14:22; Phil. 1:14; 1Thess. 3:3 [b]Eph. 3:1 [c]2Cor. 1:6
15 [a]Eph. 1:10; Phil. 2:9-11
16 [a]Rom. 9:23; Eph. 1:7; Phil. 4:19; Col. 1:27 [b]Eph. 6:10; Col. 1:11 [c]Rom. 7:22; 2Cor. 4:16

17 [a]That Christ[5547] [ainf]may dwell[2730]
in your hearts[2588] by faith,[4102] that ye,
[pfpp][b]being rooted and [pfpp]grounded in
love,[26]
18 [aosb][a]May be able [ainf]to comprehend[2638] with all saints[40] [b]what *is* the
breadth, and length, and depth, and
height;
19 And [ainf]to know[1097] the love[26] of
Christ, which [ppt]passeth knowledge,[1108]
that ye might be filled [a]with all the fulness[4138] of God.
20 Now [a]unto him that is [ppt]able [ainf]to
do exceeding abundantly[4053] [b]above all
that we ask[154] or think,[3539] [c]according to
the power[1411] that [ppt]worketh[1754] in us,
21 [a]Unto him *be* glory[1391] in the
church[1577] by Christ Jesus throughout all
ages,[1074] world without end.[165] Amen.[281]

Oneness

4 I therefore, [a]the prisoner [I]of the
Lord, beseech you that ye
[ainf][b]walk[4043] worthy of the vocation[2821]
wherewith ye [aop]are called,[2564]
2 [a]With all lowliness and meekness,
with longsuffering,[3115] [ppt]forbearing[430]
one another in love;[26]
3 Endeavouring [pinf]to keep the unity
of the Spirit[4151] [a]in the bond of
peace.[1515]
🔑 4 [a]There is one body,[4983] and [b]one
Spirit, even as ye [aop]are called in one
[c]hope[1680] of your calling;[2821]
5 [a]One Lord,[2962] [b]one faith,[4102] [c]one
baptism,[908]
6 [a]One God[2316] and Father[3962] of all,
who *is* above all, and [b]through all, and in
you all.
7 But [a]unto every one of us [aop]is
given grace[5485] according to the measure
of the gift of Christ.[5547]
🔑 8 Wherefore he saith, [a]When he
[apt]ascended[305] up on high, [b]he [ao]led captivity captive,[162] and gave gifts[1390] unto
men.[444]
9 ([a]Now that he ascended, what is it
but that he also [ao]descended[2597] first into
the lower[2737] parts of the earth?
10 He that descended is the same

17 [a]John 14:23; Eph. 2:22 [b]Col. 1:23; 2:7
18 [a]Eph. 1:18 [b]Rom. 10:3, 11, 12
19 [a]John 1:16; Eph. 1:23; Col. 2:9, 10
20 [a]Rom. 16:25; Jude 1:24 [b]1Cor. 2:9 [c]Eph. 3:7; Col. 1:29
21 [a]Rom. 11:36; 16:27; Heb. 13:21

1 [I]Or, *in the Lord* [a]Eph. 3:1; Phile. 1:1, 9 [b]Phil. 1:27; Col. 1:10; 1Thess. 2:12
2 [a]Acts 20:19; Gal. 5:22, 23; Col. 3:12, 13
3 [a]Col. 3:14
4 [a]Rom. 12:5; 1Cor. 12:12, 13; Eph. 2:16 [b]1Cor. 12:4, 11 [c]Eph. 1:18
5 [a]1Cor. 1:13; 8:6; 12:5; 2Cor. 11:4 [b]Eph. 4:13; Jude 1:3 [c]Gal. 3:27, 28; Heb. 6:6
6 [a]Mal. 2:10; 1Cor. 8:6; 12:6 [b]Rom. 11:36
7 [a]Rom. 12:3, 6; 1Cor. 12:11 **8** [a]Ps. 68:18 [b]Judg. 5:12; Col. 2:15 **9** [a]John 3:13; 6:33, 62

🔑 **4:4** This verse begins with the statement, "There is one body." Paul is emphasizing the unity of believers, specifically that Jews and Gentiles are equal in Christ. Gentiles could become Christians without having to conform to Jewish traditions. However, many Jewish Christians, who had always been prejudiced against the Gentiles, thought they were not true followers of the Messiah unless they were first circumcised, and then were obedient to the Law of Moses. The tendency for Jews was to see themselves as the center of God's plan of salvation instead of placing Christ there. Paul taught that they should view the Gentiles as their brothers in Christ, on an equal level. God is sovereign over all races, cultures, problems of humanity (e.g., social and family situations), and even the unseen beings (Eph. 3:10). God's chosen people, having been set free from sin and made to be equals by Jesus' death and resurrection, must live in the unity of Christ.

🔑 **4:8–10** This passage discusses in detail Christ's incarnation, resurrection, and ascension. In verse nine, Paul uses the phrase "Now that he ascended" to emphasize the fact that Christ ascended to heaven following his resurrection. The verse continues by stating that if Christ ascended, he obviously had to have come ("descended") to earth at a previous time. Therefore, the "descent" of Jesus "into the lower parts of the earth" is His incarnation, making it possible for Him to experience death. The "ascent" is His ascension from earth to heaven after His resurrection (John 8:23; 16:28).

In verse eight, there is some controversy over what Christ is actually "leading captive." However, the meaning of this passage is simple: Christ defeated sin and death by His resurrection, taking them captive and rendering them powerless as would a king after a victory over his enemies. The "gifts" (i.e., eternal life and forgiveness of sin) that are given to believers were consequent to Christ's defeat of sin and death. The analogy is that Christ is sharing the spoils of His ultimate victory over Satan with those who have received Him. In Psalm 68:18, David is expressing the same idea of God Almighty obtaining victory over His enemies and leading them away as captives. The gifts given

(continued on next page)

also [a]that ascended up far above all heavens, [b]that he [aosb]might [I]fill all things.)
🔑 11 [a]And he gave some, apostles;[652]
and some, prophets;[4396] and some,
[b]evangelists;[2099] and some, [c]pastors[4166]
and [d]teachers;[1320]
12 [a]For the perfecting of the saints,[40]
for the work[2041] of the ministry,[1248] [b]for
the edifying of [c]the body of Christ:
13 Till we all [aosb]come in the unity of
the faith, [a]and of the knowledge[1922] of
the Son[5207] of God, unto [b]a perfect[5046]
man, unto the measure of the stature of
the fulness[4138] of Christ:
14 That we *henceforth* be no more
[a]children,[3516] [ppt][b]tossed to and fro, and
[ppt]carried about with every [c]wind of doctrine,[1319] by the sleight[2940] of men, *and*
cunning craftiness, [d]whereby they lie in
wait to deceive;
15 But [ppt][a]speaking the truth[226] in
love,[26] [aosi][b]may grow up into him in all
things, [c]which is the head,[2776] *even* Christ:
16 [a]From whom the whole body[4983]
fitly [ppp]joined together and [ppp]compacted
by that which every joint supplieth, according to the effectual working in the
measure of every part, maketh increase
of the body unto the edifying of itself in
love.

A New Way of Thinking

17 This I say therefore, and testify[3143] in the Lord, that [a]ye henceforth
[pinf]walk[4043] not as other[3062] Gentiles[1484]
walk, [b]in the vanity[3153] of their mind,[3563]
18 [a]Having the understanding[1271]
darkened, [b]being [pfpp]alienated[526] from the
life[2222] of God through the ignorance[52]
that is in them, because of the
[I][c]blindness[4457] of their heart:[2588]
19 [a]Who [pfp]being past feeling [ao][b]have
given themselves over unto lasciviousness,[766] to work all uncleanness[167]
with greediness.

10 IOr, *fulfill* aActs 1:9, 11; 1Tim. 3:16; Heb. 4:14; 7:26; 8:1; 9:24 bActs 2:33
11 a1Cor. 12:28; Eph. 2:20 bActs 21:8; 2Tim. 4:5 cActs 20:28 dRom. 12:7
12 a1Cor. 12:7 b1Cor. 14:26 cEph. 1:23; Col. 1:24
13 aCol. 2:2 b1Cor. 14:20; Col. 1:28
14 aIsa. 28:9; 1Cor. 14:20 bHeb. 13:9 cMatt. 11:7 dRom. 16:18; 2Cor. 2:17
15 aZech. 8:16; 2Cor. 4:2; Eph. 4:25; 1John 3:18 bEph. 1:22; 2:21 cCol. 1:18
16 aCol. 2:19
17 aEph. 2:1-3; 4:22; Col. 3:7; 1Pet. 4:3 bRom. 1:21
18 IOr, *hardness* aActs 26:18 bEph. 2:12; Gal. 4:8; 1Thess. 4:5 cRom. 1:21
19 a1Tim. 4:2 bRom. 1:24, 26; 1Pet. 4:3
21 aEph. 1:13
22 aCol. 2:11; 3:8, 9; Heb. 12:1; 1Pet. 2:1 bEph. 2:2, 3; 4:17; Col. 3:7; 1Pet. 4:3 cRom. 6:6
23 aRom. 12:2; Col. 3:10
24 IOr, *holiness of truth* aRom. 6:4; 2Cor. 5:17; Gal. 6:15; Eph. 6:11; Col. 3:10 bEph. 2:10
25 aZech. 8:16; Eph. 4:15; Col. 3:9 bRom. 12:5
26 aPs. 4:4; 37:8
27 a2Cor. 2:10, 11; James 4:7; 1Pet. 5:9
28 IOr, *to distribute* aActs 20:35; 1Thess. 4:11; 2Thess.

20 But ye [ao]have not so learned[3129]
Christ;[5547]
21 [a]If so be that ye [ao]have heard him,
and [ao]have been taught by him, as the
truth[225] is in Jesus:
22 That ye [ainf][a]put off concerning
[b]the former conversation[391] [c]the old[3820]
man,[444] which is corrupt according to the
deceitful lusts;
23 And [a]be renewed[365] in the
spirit[4151] of your mind;[3563]
24 And that ye [ainf][a]put on the new[2537]
man,[444] which after God [aptp][b]is created[2936] in righteousness[1343] and [I]true[225]
holiness.[3742]
25 Wherefore [apt]putting away lying,
[pim][a]speak[2980] every man truth[225] with his
neighbour: for [b]we are members one of
another.
26 [pim][a]Be ye angry, and [pim]sin[264] not:
[pim]let not the sun go down[1931] upon your
wrath:[3950]
27 [a]Neither [pim]give place to the
devil.[1228]
28 Let him that [ppt]stole steal no
more: but rather [pim][a]let him labour,[2872]
working with *his* hands the thing which
is good,[18] that he [psa]may have [pinf][I]to give
[b]to him that [ppt]needeth.
29 [a]Let no corrupt[4550] communication[3056] proceed out of your mouth, but
[b]that which is good [I]to the use of edifying,[3619] [c]that it [aosb]may minister[1325]
grace[5485] unto the [ppt]hearers.
30 And [pim][a]grieve[3076] not the holy[40]
Spirit[4151] of God, [b]whereby ye [aop]are
sealed[4972] unto the day of [c]redemption.[629]
31 [a]Let all bitterness, and wrath,[2372]
and anger,[3709] and clamour, and [b]evil
speaking,[988] [aipp]be put away from you,
[c]with all malice:[2549]

3:8, 11, 12 bLuke 3:11 **29** IOr, *to edify profitably* aMatt. 12:36; Eph. 5:4; Col. 3:8 bCol. 4:6; 1Thess. 5:11 cCol. 3:16 **30** aIsa. 7:13; 63:10; Ezek. 16:43; 1Thess. 5:19 bEph. 1:13 cLuke 21:28; Rom. 8:23; Eph. 1:14 **31** aCol. 3:8, 19 bTitus 3:2; James 4:11; 1Pet. 2:1 cTitus 3:3

(continued from previous page)
by Christ (Eph. 4:8) include those things that are given to enable a Christian to live a more victorious life for Christ while on earth.
🔑 **4:11, 12** See note on 1 Corinthians 12:1–11.

32 And [pima]be ye kind[5543] one to another, tenderhearted, [b]forgiving[5483] one another, even as God for Christ's sake [aom]hath forgiven you.

Walk in Love

5 [pim]Be [a]ye therefore followers of God, as dear children:[5043]

2 And [pima]walk4043 in love,[26] [b]as Christ also [ao]hath loved[25] us, and [ao]hath given himself for us an offering4376 and a sacrifice[2378] to God [c]for a sweetsmelling savour.

3 But [a]fornication,4202 and all uncleanness,[167] or covetousness,[4124] [pimb]let it not be once named[3687] among you, as becometh saints;[40]

4 [a]Neither filthiness, nor foolish talking,[3473] nor jesting,[2160] [b]which are not convenient:[433] but rather giving of thanks.

5 For this ye know, that [a]no whoremonger,4205 nor unclean person,[169] nor covetous man, [b]who is an idolater,[1496] [c]hath any inheritance[2817] in the kingdom[932] of Christ and of God.

6 [pima]Let no man deceive538 you with vain[2756] words:[3056] for because of these things [b]cometh the wrath[3709] of God [c]upon the children of [1d]disobedience.[543]

7 [pim]Be not ye therefore partakers4830 with them.

8 [a]For ye were sometimes darkness,[4655] but now *are ye* [b]light[5457] in the Lord: [pim]walk as [c]children of light:

9 (For [a]the fruit of the Spirit[4151] *is* in all goodness[19] and righteousness[1343] and truth;[225])

10 [ppta]Proving what is acceptable[2101] unto the Lord.

11 And [pima]have no fellowship[4790] with [b]the unfruitful works of darkness, but rather [pimc]reprove *them.*

12 [a]For it is a shame even [pinf]to speak of those things which [ppp]are done of them in secret.

13 But [a]all things that [ppp]are reproved are made manifest[5319] by the light: for whatsoever doth make manifest is light.

32 [a]2Cor. 2:10; Col. 3:12, 13 [b]Matt. 6:14; Mark 11:25
1 [a]Matt. 5:45, 48; Luke 6:36; Eph. 4:32
2 [a]John 13:34; 15:12; 1Thess. 4:9; 1John 3:11, 23; 4:21 [b]Gal. 1:4; 2:20; Heb. 7:27; 9:14, 26; 10:10, 12; 1John 3:16 [c]Gen. 8:21; Lev. 1:9; 2Cor. 2:15
3 [a]Rom. 6:13; 1Cor. 6:18; 2Cor. 12:21; Eph. 4:19, 20; Col. 3:5; 1Thess. 4:3 [b]1Cor. 5:1
4 [a]Matt. 12:35; Eph. 4:29 [b]Rom. 1:28
5 [a]1Cor. 6:9; Gal. 5:19, 21 [b]Col. 3:5; 1Tim. 6:17 [c]Gal. 5:21; Rev. 22:15
6 1Or, *unbelief* [a]Jer. 29:8; Matt. 24:4; Col. 2:4, 8, 18; 2Thess. 2:3 [b]Rom. 1:18 [c]Eph. 2:2 [d]Col. 3:6
8 [a]Isa. 9:2; Matt. 4:16; Acts 26:18; Rom. 1:21; Eph. 2:11, 12; 4:18; Titus 3:3; 1Pet. 2:9 [b]John 8:12; 12:46; 2Cor. 3:18; 4:6; 1Thess. 5:5; 1John 2:9 [c]Luke 16:8; John 12:36
9 [a]Gal. 5:22
10 [a]Rom. 12:2; Phil. 1:10; 1Thess. 5:21; 1Tim. 2:3
11 [a]1Cor. 5:9, 11; 10:20; 2Cor. 6:14; 2Thess. 3:6, 14 [b]Rom. 6:21; 13:12; Gal. 6:8 [c]Lev. 19:17; 1Tim. 5:20
12 [a]Rom. 1:24, 26; Eph. 5:3
13 [a]John 3:20, 21; Heb. 4:13
14 [a]Isa. 60:1; Rom. 13:11, 12; 1Cor.

14 Wherefore he saith, [pima]Awake[1453] thou that [ppt]sleepest, and [aimb]arise[450] from the dead,[3498] and Christ shall give thee light.

15 [pima]See then that ye walk circumspectly, not as fools, but as wise,[4680]

16 [a]Redeeming[1805] the time,[2540] [b]because the days are evil.[4190]

17 [a]Wherefore [pim]be ye not unwise, but [b]understanding[4920] [c]what the will[2307] of the Lord *is.*

18 And [pima]be not drunk3182 with wine,[3631] wherein is excess;[810] but [pim]be filled with the Spirit;[4151]

19 [ppt]Speaking[2980] to yourselves [a]in psalms[5568] and hymns[5215] and spiritual songs,[5603] singing and making melody in your heart[2588] to the Lord;

20 [a]Giving thanks[2168] always for all things unto God and the Father [b]in the name of our Lord Jesus Christ;

Husbands and Wives

🔑 21 [a]Submitting[5293] yourselves one to another in the fear[5401] of God.

22 [a]Wives, [pim]submit[5293] yourselves unto your own husbands,[435] [b]as unto the Lord.[2962]

23 For [a]the husband is the head of the wife, even as [b]Christ[5547] is the head[2776] of the church:[1577] and he is the saviour[4990] of [c]the body.[4983]

24 Therefore as the church is subject unto[5293] Christ, so *let* the wives *be* to their own husbands [a]in every thing.

25 [a]Husbands, [pim]love[25] your wives, even as Christ also loved the church, and [b]gave himself for it;

15:34; 1Thess. 5:6 [b]John 5:25; Rom. 6:4, 5; Eph. 2:5; Col. 3:1 **15** [a]Col. 4:5 **16** [a]Gal. 6:10; Col. 4:5 [b]Eccl. 11:2; 12:1; John 12:35; Eph. 6:13 **17** [a]Col. 4:5 [b]Rom. 12:2 [c]1Thess. 4:3; 5:18 **18** [a]Prov. 20:1; 23:20, 30; Isa. 5:11, 22; Luke 21:34 **19** [a]1Cor. 14:26; Col. 3:16; James 5:13 **20** [a]Ps. 34:1; Isa. 63:7; Col. 3:17; 1Thess. 5:18; 2Thess. 1:3 [b]Heb. 13:15; 1Pet. 2:5; 4:11 **21** [a]Phil. 2:3; 1Pet. 5:5 **22** [a]Gen. 3:16; 1Cor. 14:34; Col. 3:18; Titus 2:5; 1Pet. 3:1 [b]Eph. 6:5 **23** [a]1Cor. 11:3 [b]Eph. 1:22, 4:15; Col. 1:18 [c]Eph. 1:23 **24** [a]Col. 3:20, 22; Titus 2:9 **25** [a]Col. 3:19; 1Pet. 3:7 [b]Acts 20:28; Gal. 1:4; 2:20; Eph. 5:2

🔑 **5:21, 22** See notes on 1 Corinthians 14:33–40 and 1 Timothy 2:9–15.

26 That he [asba]might sanctify[37] and [apt]cleanse[2511] it [a]with the washing[3067] of water [b]by the word,[4487]

27 [a]That he [aosb]might present it to himself a glorious[1741] church,[1577] [b]not having spot,[4695] or wrinkle, or any such thing; [c]but that it should be holy[40] and without blemish.[299]

28 So ought men [pinf]to love their wives as their own bodies.[4983] He that [ppt]loveth his wife loveth himself.

29 For no man ever yet hated his own flesh;[4561] but nourisheth and cherisheth it, even as the Lord the church:

30 For [a]we are members of his body, of his flesh, and of his bones.

31 [a]For this cause shall a man[444] leave his father and mother, and shall be joined unto his wife, and they [b]two shall be one flesh.

32 This is a great mystery:[3466] but I speak concerning Christ and the church.[1577]

33 Nevertheless [pim][a]let every one of you in particular so love[25] his wife even as himself; and the wife *see* that she [psmp][b]reverence[5399] *her* husband.

Children and Parents

6 Children,[5043] [a]obey[5219] your parents in the Lord:[2962] for this is right.[1342]

2 [a]Honour thy father[3962] and mother;[3384] which is the first commandment with promise;[1860]

3 That it [asbm]may be well with thee, and thou mayest live long on the earth.[1093]

4 And, [a]ye fathers, [pim]provoke not your children to wrath:[3949] but [b]bring them up in the nurture and admonition[3559] of the Lord.[2962]

Servants and Masters

5 [a]Servants,[1401] [pim]be obedient[5219] to them that are *your* masters[2962] according to the flesh, [b]with fear and trembling, [c]in singleness[572] of your heart,[2588] as unto Christ;

6 [a]Not with eyeservice,[3787] as menpleasers;[441] but as the servants[1401] of Christ, doing the will[2307] of God from the heart;[5590]

7 With good will[2133] doing service,[1398] as to the Lord,[2962] and not to men:[444]

8 [a]Knowing that whatsoever good thing[18] any man [aosb]doeth, the same shall he receive of the Lord, [b]whether *he be* bond[1401] or free.[1658]

9 And, ye [a]masters, [pim]do the same things unto them, [b]forbearing threatening: knowing that [I][c]your Master[2962] also is in heaven;[3772] [d]neither is there respect of persons[4382] with him.

The Christian's Armour

10 Finally, my brethren,[80] [pim]be strong[1743] in the Lord, and [a]in the power[2904] of his might.[2479]

11 [aim][a]Put on the whole armour of God, that ye may be able to stand against the wiles[3180] of the devil.[1228]

12 For we wrestle not against [a]flesh[4561] and blood,[129] but against [b]principalities,[746] against powers,[1849] against [c]the rulers[2888] of the darkness[4655] of this world,[165] against [I]spiritual[4152] wickedness[4189] in [II]high *places*.

13 [a]Wherefore [aim]take unto[353] you the whole armour of God, that ye [asbp]may be able [ainf]to withstand[436] [b]in the evil[4190] day,[2250] and [c]having done all, [ainf]to stand.[2476]

14 [aim]Stand therefore, [a]having your loins[3751] girt about[4024] with truth,[225] and [apt][b]having on the breastplate of righteousness;[1343]

15 [a]And your feet shod[5265] with the preparation of the gospel[2098] of peace;[1515]

16 Above all, [apt]taking[353] [a]the shield of faith,[4102] wherewith ye shall be able [ainf]to quench all the fiery darts of the wicked.[4190]

17 And [aim][a]take the helmet of salvation,[4992] and [b]the sword of the Spirit,[4151] which is the word[4487] of God:

26 [a]John 3:5; Titus 3:5; Heb. 10:22; 1John 5:6 [b]John 15:3; 17:17
27 [a]2Cor. 11:2; Col. 1:22 [b]Song 4:7 [c]Eph. 1:4
30 [a]Gen. 2:23; Rom. 12:5; 1Cor. 6:15; 12:27
31 [a]Gen. 2:24; Matt. 19:5; Mark 10:7, 8 [b]1Cor. 6:16
33 [a]Eph. 5:25; Col. 3:19 [b]1Pet. 3:6

1 [a]Prov. 23:22; Col. 3:20
2 [a]Ex. 20:12; Deut. 5:16; 27:16; Jer. 35:18; Ezek. 22:7; Mal. 1:6; Matt. 15:4; Mark 7:10
4 [a]Col. 3:21 [b]Gen. 18:19; Deut. 4:9; 6:7, 20; 11:19; Ps. 78:4; Prov. 19:18; 22:6; 29:17
5 [a]Col. 3:22; 1Tim. 6:1; Titus 2:9; 1Pet. 2:18 [b]2Cor. 7:15; Phil. 2:12 [c]1Chr. 29:17; Col. 3:22
6 [a]Col. 3:22, 23
8 [a]Rom. 2:6; 2Cor. 5:10; Col. 3:24 [b]Gal. 3:28; Col. 3:11
9 [I]Some texts read, *both your and their Master* [a]Col. 4:1 [b]Lev. 25:43 [c]John 13:13; 1Cor. 7:22 [d]Rom. 2:11; Col. 3:25
10 [a]Eph. 1:19; 3:16; Col. 1:11
11 [a]Rom. 13:12; 2Cor. 6:7; Eph. 6:13; 1Thess. 5:8
12 [I]Or, *wicked spirits* [II]Or, *heavenly* [a]Matt. 16:17; 1Cor. 15:50 [b]Rom. 8:38; Eph. 1:21; Col. 2:15 [c]Luke 22:53, John 12:31; 14:30; Eph. 2:2; Col. 1:13
13 [a]2Cor. 10:4; Eph. 6:11 [b]Eph. 5:16
14 [a]Isa. 11:5; Luke 12:35; 1Pet. 1:13 [b]Isa. 59:17; 2Cor. 6:7; 1Thess. 5:8
15 [a]Isa. 52:7; Rom. 10:15
16 [a]1John 5:4
17 [a]Isa. 59:17; 1Thess. 5:8 [b]Heb. 4:12; Rev. 1:16; 2:16; 19:15

18 [a]Praying[4336] always[2540] with all
prayer and supplication[1162] in the Spirit,
and [b]watching thereunto with all per-
severance4343 and [c]supplication for all
saints,[40]
19 [a]And for me, that utterance[3056]
[opt]may be given unto me, that I may open
my mouth [b]boldly, [ainf]to make known[1107]
the mystery[3466] of the gospel,
20 For which [a]I am an ambas-
sador4243 [1b]in bonds: that therein [c]I
[asbm]may speak boldly, as I ought[1163] [ainf]to
speak.

Benediction

21 But [a]that ye also may know my
affairs, *and* how I do, [b]Tychicus, a
beloved[27] brother[80] and faithful[4103] minister[1249] in the Lord, shall make known
to you all things:
22 [a]Whom I have sent unto you for
the same purpose, that ye [aosb]might know
our affairs, and *that* he [aosb]might comfort
your hearts.[2588]
23 [a]Peace *be* to the brethren, and
love[26] with faith,[4102] from God the Father
and the Lord Jesus Christ.
24 Grace *be* with all them that
[ppt]love[25] our Lord Jesus Christ [1a]in sincerity. Amen.281

18 [a]Luke 18:1; Rom. 12:12; Col. 4:2; 1Thess. 5:17 [b]Matt. 26:41; Mark 13:33 [c]Eph. 1:16; Phil. 1:4; 1Tim. 2:1 **19** [a]Acts 4:29; Col. 4:3; 2Thess. 3:1 [b]2Cor. 3:12 **20** [1]Or, *in a chain* [a]2Cor. 5:20 [b]Acts 26:29; 28:20; Eph. 3:1; Phil. 1:7, 13, 14; 2Tim. 1:16; 2:9; Phile. 1:10 [c]Acts 28:31; Phil. 1:20; 1Thess. 2:2 **21** [a]Col. 4:7 [b]Acts 20:4; 2Tim. 4:12; Titus 3:12

22 [a]Col. 4:8 **23** [a]1Pet. 5:14 **24** [1]Or, *with incorruption* [a]Titus 2:7

6:21, 22 See note on Colossians 4:7.

The Epistle of Paul to the

PHILIPPIANS

The city of Philippi was named for Philip of Macedon, the father of Alexander the Great, who seized the city in 358 B.C. from the Thracians. Later, Octavius (Augustus Caesar) made Philippi a Roman colony. It was a principal city on the great Egnation Way in Macedonia (this highway extended from Rome to Byzantium), and traders from both eastern and western countries stopped there often. This made it a strategic place for the spreading of the gospel.

In the early portion of Paul's second missionary journey, the Lord indicated that He wanted Paul to preach the gospel in Macedonia (Acts 16:9, 10). Apparently there were no synagogues in the city, because on the Sabbath Paul went out of the city and down to the bank of the river where he found Lydia and a number of other women who accepted what he had to say (Acts 16:13, 14). After Lydia and her family had been baptized, she asked Paul and his companions to stay at her house (Acts 16:15). Later, Paul and Silas were imprisoned for casting the unclean spirit out of a slave girl (Acts 16:16–25). This led to the salvation of the jailor and his family (Acts 16:26–34). Paul may have visited them again when he journeyed from Ephesus to Macedonia, because he spent the spring with them (Acts 20:1, 6; 2 Cor. 2:12, 13). The church that Paul established there was probably the first in all of Europe. The Apostle Paul is thought to have written this letter to the Philippians during his first Roman imprisonment (ca. A.D. 60–62).

Paul, who was a tentmaker by trade (Acts 18:3), ordinarily refused to receive any financial assistance from the churches (2 Cor. 11:7–9). However, he did accept gifts from the Philippian brethren when he was in Thessalonica (Phil. 4:16, 18). Epaphroditus brought another gift to Paul during his imprisonment in Rome (Phil. 4:18). While Epaphroditus was there, he became severely sick and nearly died. He did recover, however, and carried this letter back to Philippi (Phil. 2:25–30).

Although there is no development of one particular theme, the concept of the all-sufficiency of Christ is found throughout the book. Christ gives meaning to life and causes people to serve Him even to their death (Phil. 1:20, 21).

1 Paul and Timotheus, the servants[1401]
of Jesus Christ,[5547] to all the saints[40]
[a]in Christ Jesus which are at Philippi,
with the bishops[1985] and deacons:[1249]
2 [a]Grace[5485] *be* unto you, and
peace,[1515] from God[2316] our Father,[3962]
and *from* the Lord[2962] Jesus Christ.
3 [a]I thank[2168] my God upon every
[I]remembrance of you,
4 Always in every prayer[1162] of mine
for you all making request[1162] with
joy,[5479]
5 [a]For your fellowship[2842] in the
gospel[2098] from the first day until now;
⊶ 6 Being confident[3982] of this very
thing, that he which [apt]hath begun [a]a
good[18] work in you [I]will perform[2005] *it*
[b]until the day[2250] of Jesus Christ:

1 [a]1Cor. 1:2
2 [a]Rom. 1:7; 2Cor. 1:2; 1Pet. 1:2
3 [I]Or, *mention* [a]Rom. 1:8, 9; 1Cor. 1:4; Eph. 1:15, 16; Col. 1:3; 1Thess. 1:2; 2Thess. 1:3
5 [a]Rom. 12:13; 15:26; 2Cor. 8:1; Phil. 4:14, 15
6 [I]Or, *will finish* it [a]John 6:29; 1Thess. 1:3 [b]Phil. 1:10
7 [I]Or, *ye have me in your heart* [II]Or, *partakers with me of grace* [a]2Cor. 3:2; 7:3 [b]Eph. 3:1; 6:20; Col. 4:3, 18; 2Tim. 1:8

7 Even as it is meet for me [pinf]to
think this of you all, because [I]I have you
[a]in my heart; inasmuch as both in [b]my
bonds, and in [c]the defence and confirmation[951] of the gospel,[2098] [d]ye all are
[II]partakers of my grace.
8 For [a]God is my record,[3144] [b]how
greatly I long after you all in the bowels[4698] of Jesus Christ.
9 And this I pray, [a]that your love[26]
[psa]may abound yet more and more in
knowledge[1922] and *in* all judgment;[144]
⊶ 10 That [a]ye [aies]may approve things
that are excellent;[1308] [b]that ye may be

[c]Phil. 1:17 [d]Phil. 4:14 **8** [a]Rom. 1:9; 9:1; Gal. 1:20; 1Thess. 2:5 [b]Phil. 2:26; 4:1 **9** [a]1Thess. 3:12; Phile. 1:6 **10** [a]Rom. 2:18; 12:2; Eph. 5:10 [b]Acts 24:16; 1Thess. 3:13; 5:23

⊶ **1:6, 10** See note on 1 Thessalonians 5:2.

sincere[1506] and without offence[677] [c]till the day of Christ;

11 [pfpp]Being filled with the fruits of righteousness,[1343] [a]which are by Jesus Christ, [b]unto the glory[1391] and praise[1868] of God.

Paul Glories in His Affliction

12 But I would ye should [pinf]understand,[1097] brethren,[80] that the things *which happened* unto me [pfi]have fallen out[2064] rather unto the furtherance of the gospel;

13 So that my bonds in Christ are manifest[5318] [a]in all the palace, and in all other *places;*

14 And many of the brethren in the Lord, waxing confident[3982] by my bonds, are much more bold [pinf]to speak the word[3056] without fear.

15 Some indeed preach[2784] Christ even of envy and [a]strife; and some also of good will:

16 The [pl]one preach[2605] Christ of contention, not sincerely, supposing [pinf]to add affliction to my bonds:

17 But the [pl]other of love, knowing that I am set[2749] for [a]the defence of the gospel.

18 What then? notwithstanding, every way, whether in pretence, or in truth,[225] Christ is preached; and I therein do rejoice,[5463] yea, and will rejoice.

19 For I know that this shall turn to my salvation[4991] [a]through your prayer, and the supply of [b]the Spirit of Jesus Christ,

20 According to my [a]earnest expectation[603] and *my* hope,[1680] that [b]in nothing I shall be ashamed, but *that* [c]with all boldness, as always, *so* now also Christ[5547] shall be magnified in my body,[4983] whether *it be* by life,[2222] or by death.[2288]

21 For to me [pinf]to live[2198] *is* Christ, and [ainf]to die[599] *is* gain.

22 But if I [pinf]live in the flesh,[4561] this *is* the fruit of my labour:[2041] yet what I shall choose[138] I wot[1107] not.

23 For [a]I am in a strait[4912] betwixt two, having a desire [aies]to [b]depart, and to be with Christ; which is far better:

24 Nevertheless [ainf]to abide in the flesh *is* more needful for you.

25 And [a]having this confidence,[3982] I know that I shall abide and continue with you all for your furtherance and joy[5479] of faith;[4102]

26 That [a]your rejoicing [psa]may be more abundant in Jesus Christ for me by my coming to you again.

27 Only [pim][a]let your conversation be[4176] as it becometh the gospel of Christ: that whether I [apt]come and [apt]see you, or else be absent,[548] I may hear of your affairs, [b]that ye stand fast in one spirit,[4151] [c]with one mind[5590] [ppt][d]striving together for the faith of the gospel;

28 And in nothing [ppt]terrified by your [ppt]adversaries: [a]which is to them an evident token of perdition,[684] [b]but to you of salvation, and that of God.

29 For unto you [a]it [aop]is given[5483] in the behalf of Christ, [b]not only [pinf]to believe[4100] on him, but also [pinf]to suffer[3958] for his sake;

30 [a]Having the same conflict[73] [b]which ye saw in me, and now hear *to be* in me.

Exhortation to Be Like Christ

2 If *there be* therefore any consolation[3874] in Christ, if any comfort of love,[26] [a]if any fellowship[2842] of the [an]Spirit, if any [b]bowels[4698] and mercies,[3628]

2 [aim][a]Fulfil[4137] ye my joy,[5479] [b]that ye [psa]be likeminded, having the same love, *being* of one accord,[4861] of one [ppt]mind.[5426]

3 [a]*Let* nothing *be done* through strife or vainglory; but [b]in lowliness of mind [ppt]let each esteem[2233] other [ppt]better than themselves.

4 [pim][a]Look[4648] not every man on his own things, but every man also on the things of others.

5 [a]Let this mind be in you, which was also in Christ[5547] Jesus:

10 [c]1Cor. 1:8
11 [a]John 15:4, 5; Eph. 2:10; Col. 1:6 [b]John 15:8; Eph. 1:12, 14
13 [a]Phil. 4:22
15 [a]Phil. 2:3
17 [a]Phil. 1:7
19 [a]2Cor. 1:11 [b]Rom. 8:9
20 [a]Rom. 8:19 [b]Rom. 5:5 [c]Eph. 6:19, 20
23 [a]2Cor. 5:8 [b]2Tim. 4:6
25 [a]Phil. 2:24
26 [a]2Cor. 1:14; 5:12
27 [a]Eph. 4:1; Col. 1:10; 1Thess. 2:12; 4:1 [b]Phil. 4:1 [c]1Cor. 1:10 [d]Jude 1:3
28 [a]2Thess. 1:5 [b]Rom. 8:17; 2Tim. 2:11
29 [a]Acts 5:41; Rom. 5:3 [b]Eph. 2:8
30 [a]Col. 2:1 [b]Acts 16:19; 1Thess. 2:2
1 [a]2Cor. 13:14 [b]Col. 3:12
2 [a]John 3:29 [b]Rom. 12:16; 15:5; 1Cor. 1:10; 2Cor. 13:11; Phil. 1:27; 3:16; 4:2; 1Pet. 3:8
3 [a]Gal. 5:26; Phil. 1:15, 16; James 3:14 [b]Rom. 12:10; Eph. 5:21; 1Pet. 5:5
4 [a]1Cor. 10:24, 33; 13:5
5 [a]Matt. 11:29; John 13:15; 1Pet. 2:21; 1John 2:6

🔑 6 Who, [a]being[5225] in the form[3444] of God,[2316] [ao][b]thought it not robbery[725] to be equal[2470] with God:

7 [a]But [ao]made himself of no reputation,[2758] and [apt]took upon him the form[3444] [b]of a servant,[1401] and [apt][c]was made in the likeness[3667] of men:[444]

8 And [aptp]being found in fashion[4976] as a man, he [ao]humbled[5013] himself, and [apt][a]became obedient[5255] unto death,[2288] even the death of the cross.[4716]

9 Wherefore God also [ao][a]hath highly exalted him, and [aom][b]given[5483] him a name[3686] which is above every name:

10 [a]That at the name of Jesus every knee [asba]should bow, of *things* in heaven,[2032] and *things* in earth,[1919] and *things* under the earth;

11 And *that* [a]every tongue [asbm]should confess[1843] that Jesus Christ *is* Lord,[2962] to the glory[1391] of God the Father.[3962]

6 [a]John 1:1, 2; 17:5; 2Cor. 4:4; Col. 1:15; Heb. 1:3 [b]John 5:18; 10:33
7 [a]Ps. 22:6; Isa. 53:3; Dan. 9:26; Mark 9:12; Rom. 15:3 [b]Isa. 42:1; 49:3, 6; 52:13; 53:11; Ezek. 34:23, 24; Zech. 3:8; Matt. 20:28; Luke 22:27 [c]John 1:14; Rom. 1:3; 8:3; Gal. 4:4; Heb. 2:14, 17
8 [a]Matt. 26:39, 42; John 10:18; Heb. 5:8; 12:2
9 [a]John 17:1, 2, 5; Acts 2:33; Heb. 2:9 [b]Eph. 1:20, 21; Heb. 1:4
10 [a]Isa. 45:23; Matt. 28:18; Rom. 14:11; Rev. 5:13
11 [a]John 13:13; Acts 2:36; Rom. 14:9; 1Cor. 8:6; 12:3

"Work Out Your Own Salvation"

12 Wherefore, my beloved,[27] [a]as ye [ao]have always obeyed,[5219] not as in my presence only, but now much more in my absence, [pim]work out your own salvation[4991] with [b]fear[5401] and trembling.[5156]

13 For [a]it is God which [ppt]worketh in you both [pinf]to will[2309] and [pinf]to do[1754] of *his* good pleasure.

14 [pim]Do all things [a]without murmurings and [b]disputings:[1261]

15 That ye [asba]may be blameless[273] and harmless,[185] [a]the sons[5043] of God, without rebuke, [b]in the midst of [c]a crooked and perverse nation,[1074] among whom [d]ye shine[5316] as lights[5458] in the world;[2889]

12 [a]Phil. 1:5 [b]Eph. 6:5
13 [a]2Cor. 3:5; Heb. 13:21 **14** [a]1Cor. 10:10; 1Pet. 4:9 [b]Rom. 14:1 **15** [a]Matt. 5:45; Eph. 5:1 [b]1Pet. 2:12 [c]Deut. 32:5 [d]Matt. 5:14, 16; Eph. 5:8

🔑 **2:6–8** This passage deals with the deity of Jesus Christ, which was evidenced prior to His incarnation and continued even through His death on the cross.

In comparing verse six of this passage with John 10:30, one can note that Christ is equal to God. In addition to this fact, He proved in His incarnation and death that He was still deity. In other words, in becoming a human being, Christ did not become less than deity. In speaking to His disciples, Jesus said, "My Father, which gave them me, is greater than all; and no man is able to pluck them out of the Father's hand. I and my Father are one" (John 10:29, 30). Because Christ is equal with God, those who would seek to "snatch" His true followers out of His hand would also be able to remove them out of God's hand as well.

Therefore, Paul states in Philippians 2:6, 7 that Christ "thought it not robbery to be equal with God: but made himself of no reputation." What is to be understood here is that Christ merely relinquished the glory that He had due to the fact that He was deity. Prior to His death, He asked the Father to glorify Him in a position next to God with the glory that He had even before the world was created (John 17:5). If Christ had come to the earth with an emphasis on His equality with God and all that entailed, the world would have only wondered at Him, not received Him as Savior. The Lord lacked recognition and glory by men while He was on earth as the Incarnate God. However, Christ never lost His position as God.

The phrase in verse seven, "took upon him the form of a servant," should be understood as "having taken," which denotes that He became as a servant in man's likeness at His incarnation, and that he did not possess that form before that time. His purpose in coming as a man was to die for the sins of mankind. The key idea to consider is that Christ was and is who He claimed to be—God. He appeared in the form of man so that He could die in order to satisfy the Law's judgment against man's sin (1 John 2:2). The fact that He came as a human being did not remove His position in heaven, but allowed Him to carry out His Father's will. Christ was still equal with the Father, even while He was dying on the cross. In fact, Jesus experienced all the feelings that exist in the human body, yet He never allowed those things to block His mindset away from the cross or lead to sin (Heb. 4:15).

The last verse of this passage illustrates true humility in action. It is said of Christ that "he humbled himself, and became obedient unto death." This obedience resulted in the humility that Christ displayed in willingly going to the cross. At that time He was fully God, yet He set aside that glory in order to accomplish the Father's will.

16 Holding forth the word[3056] of life;[2222] that [a]I [pre,nn]may rejoice in the day[2250] of Christ, that [b]I [ao]have not run[5413] in vain, neither [ao]laboured in vain.

17 Yea, and if [a]I be [I]offered upon the sacrifice [b]and service[3009] of your faith,[4102] [c]I joy,[5463] and rejoice[4796] with you all.

18 For the same cause also do ye joy, and rejoice with me.

19 [I]But I trust[1679] in the Lord Jesus to send [a]Timotheus shortly unto you, that I also [psa]may be of good comfort, when I [apt]know your state.

20 For I have no man [a]likeminded,[2473] who will naturally care for your state.

21 For all [a]seek their own, not the things which are Jesus Christ's.

22 But ye know the proof[1382] of him, [a]that, as a son with the father, he [ao]hath served[1398] with me in the gospel.[2098]

23 Him therefore I hope[1679] to send presently, so soon as I shall see[872] how it will go with me.

24 But [a]I trust[3982] in the Lord that I also myself shall come shortly.

25 Yet I supposed it necessary[316] to send to you [a]Epaphroditus, my brother,[80] and companion in labour, and [b]fellowsoldier, [c]but your messenger,[652] and [d]he that ministered[3011] to my wants.[5532]

26 [a]For he longed after you all, and [ppt]was full of heaviness, because that ye [ao]had heard that he [ao]had been sick.

27 For indeed he was sick nigh unto death:[2288] but God [ao]had mercy on him; and not on him only, but on me also, lest I [aosb]should have sorrow upon sorrow.

28 I sent him therefore the more carefully, that, when ye see him again, ye [asba]may rejoice, and that I may be the less sorrowful.

29 Receive[4327] him therefore in the Lord with all gladness; and [pimI][a]hold such in reputation:

30 Because for the work[2041] of Christ he [ao]was nigh unto death, not [apt]regarding his life,[5590] [a]to [aosb]supply[378] your lack of service[3009] toward me.

16 [a]2Cor. 1:14; 1Thess. 2:19 [b]Gal. 2:2; 1Thess. 3:5
17 [I]Gr. *poured forth* [a]2Tim. 4:6 [b]Rom. 15:16 [c]2Cor. 7:4; Col. 1:24
19 [I]Or, *Moreover* [a]Rom. 16:21; 1Thess. 3:2
20 [a]Ps. 55:13
21 [a]1Cor. 10:24, 33; 13:5; 2Tim. 4:10, 16
22 [a]1Cor. 4:17; 1Tim. 1:2; 2Tim. 1:2
24 [a]Phil. 1:25; Phile. 1:22
25 [a]Phil. 4:18 [b]Phile. 1:2 [c]2Cor. 8:23 [d]2Cor. 11:9; Phil. 4:18
26 [a]Phil. 1:8
29 [I]Or, *honor such* [a]1Cor. 16:18; 1Thess. 5:12; 1Tim. 5:17
30 [a]1Cor. 16:17; Phil. 4:10

1 [a]2Cor. 13:11; Phil. 4:4; 1Thess. 5:16
2 [a]Isa. 56:10; Gal. 5:15 [b]2Cor. 11:13 [c]Rom. 2:28; Gal. 5:2
3 [a]Deut. 10:16; 30:6; Jer. 4:4; Rom. 2:29; 4:11, 12; Col. 2:11 [b]John 4:23, 24; Rom. 7:6 [c]Gal. 6:14
4 [a]2Cor. 11:18, 21
5 [a]Gen. 17:12 [b]2Cor. 11:22 [c]Rom. 11:1 [d]2Cor. 11:22 [e]Acts 23:6; 26:4, 5
6 [a]Acts 22:3; Gal. 1:13, 14 [b]Acts 8:3; 9:1 [c]Rom. 10:5 [d]Luke 1:6
7 [a]Matt. 13:44
8 [a]Isa. 53:11; Jer. 9:23, 24; John 17:3; 1Cor. 2:2; Col. 2:2
9 [a]Rom. 10:3, 5 [b]Rom. 1:17; 3:21, 22; 9:30; 10:3, 6; Gal. 2:16
10 [a]Rom. 6:3-5; 8:17; 2Cor. 4:10, 11; 2Tim. 2:11, 12; 1Pet. 4:13
11 [a]Acts 26:7

Count All Gain As Loss

3 Finally, my brethren,[80] [a]rejoice[5463] in the Lord. [pinf]To write the same things to you, to me indeed *is* not grievous, but for you *it is* safe.

2 [pim][a]Beware[991] of dogs, beware of [b]evil workers, [c]beware of the concision.[2699]

3 For we are [a]the circumcision,[4061] [b]which [ppt]worship God in the [an]spirit, and [pptc]rejoice in Christ Jesus, and have no confidence[3982] in the flesh.[4561]

4 Though [a]I [ppt]might also have[2192] confidence[4006] in the flesh. If any other man thinketh that he hath whereof he might trust[3982] in the flesh, I more:

5 [a]Circumcised[4061] the eighth day, [b]of the stock of Israel, *of* [c]the tribe of Benjamin, [d]an Hebrew of the Hebrews; as touching the law,[3551] [e]a Pharisee;

6 [a]Concerning[2596] zeal, [b]persecuting the church;[1577] [c]touching[2596] the righteousness[1343] which is in the law, [d]blameless.[273]

7 But [a]what things were gain to me, those I [pfip]counted loss for Christ.[5547]

8 Yea doubtless, and I count all things *but* loss [a]for the excellency of the knowledge of Christ Jesus my Lord:[2962] for whom I [aop]have suffered the loss of all things, and do count them *but* dung,[4657] that I may win Christ,

9 And be found in him, not having [a]mine own righteousness,[1343] which is of the law,[3551] but [b]that which is through the faith[4102] of Christ, the righteousness which is of God by faith:

10 That I [infg]may know[1097] him, and the power[1411] of his resurrection,[386] and [a]the fellowship[2842] of his sufferings,[3804] [ppp]being made conformable[4833] unto his death;[2288]

11 If by any means I might [a]attain unto the resurrection[1815] of the dead.[3498]

2:16 See note on 1 Thessalonians 5:2.

"The High Calling of God"

12 Not as though I [ao]had already [a]attained,[2983] either [pfip]were already [b]perfect:[5048] but I follow after, if that I may apprehend[2638] that for which also I [aop]am apprehended of Christ Jesus.

13 Brethren, I count[3049] not myself [pfin]to have apprehended: but *this* one thing *I do,* [a]forgetting those things which are behind, and [b]reaching forth unto those things which are before,

14 [a]I press toward the mark[4649] for the prize of [b]the high[507] calling[2821] of God in Christ Jesus.

15 [psa]Let[5426] us therefore, as many as be [a]perfect,[5046] [b]be thus minded:[5426] and if in any thing ye be otherwise[2088] minded,[5426] God shall reveal[601] even this unto you.

16 Nevertheless, whereto we [ao]have already attained,[5348] [pinf a]let us walk [b]by the same rule,[2583] [pinf c]let us mind[5426] the same thing.

17 Brethren, [a]be followers together of me, and [pim]mark[4648] them which [ppt]walk so as [b]ye have us for an ensample.[5179]

18 (For many walk, of whom I [ipf]have told you often, and now tell you even weeping, *that they are* [a]the enemies of the cross[4716] of Christ:

19 [a]Whose end[5056] *is* destruction,[684] [b]whose God *is their* belly, and *whose* [c]glory[1391] *is* in their shame,[152] [d]who [ppt]mind[5426] earthly things.[1919])

20 For [a]our conversation is in heaven;[3772] [b]from whence also we [c]look for[553] the Saviour,[4990] the Lord[2962] Jesus Christ:[5547]

21 [a]Who shall change[3345] our vile[5014] body,[4983] that it [aies]may be fashioned like unto[4832] his glorious[1391] body, [b]according to the working whereby he [infg]is able [c]even [ainf]to subdue[5293] all things unto himself.

"Rejoice in the Lord"

4 Therefore, my brethren[80] dearly beloved[27] and [a]longed for, [b]my joy[5479] and crown, so [c]stand fast in the Lord, *my* dearly beloved.

2 I beseech Euodias, and beseech Syntyche, [a]that they be of the same mind[5426] in the Lord.

3 And I intreat[2065] thee also, true yokefellow, [pim]help those women which [a]laboured with me in the gospel,[2098] with Clement also, and *with* other my fellowlabourers, whose names[3686] *are* in [b]the book[976] of life.[2222]

4 [a]Rejoice[5463] in the Lord alway: *and* again I say, Rejoice.

5 [aipp]Let[1097] your moderation[1933] be known[1097] unto all men.[444] [a]The Lord *is* at hand.[1451]

6 [pim a]Be careful for nothing;[3367] but in every thing by prayer[4335] and supplication[1162] with thanksgiving let your requests[155] [pim]be made known[1107] unto God.

7 And [a]the peace[1515] of God, which [ppt]passeth all understanding,[3563] shall keep your hearts[2588] and minds[3540] through Christ Jesus.

8 Finally, brethren, whatsoever things are true,[227] whatsoever things *are* [I]honest,[4586] whatsoever things *are* just,[1342] whatsoever things *are* pure,[53] whatsoever things *are* lovely,[4375] [a]whatsoever things *are* of good report;[2163] if *there be* any virtue,[703] and if *there be* any praise,[1868] [pim]think on these things.

9 [a]Those things, which ye [ao]have both learned,[3129] and [ao]received, and [ao]heard, and [ao]seen in me, [pim]do:[4238] and [b]the God of peace[1515] shall be with you.

Contentment

10 But I rejoiced in the Lord greatly, that now at the last [a]your [pinf]care[5426] of me [aoI]hath flourished again; wherein ye were also careful,[5426] but ye [ipf]lacked opportunity.

11 Not that I speak in respect of want:[5304] for I [ao]have learned,[3129] in whatsoever state I am, *therewith* [a]to be content.

12 [a]I know both how [pip]to be abased,[5013] and I know how [pinf]to abound:

12 [a]1Tim. 6:12 [b]Heb. 12:23
13 [a]Ps. 45:10; Luke 9:62; 2Cor. 5:16 [b]1Cor. 9:24, 26; Heb. 6:1
14 [a]2Tim. 4:7, 8; Heb. 12:1 [b]Heb. 3:1
15 [a]1Cor. 2:6; 14:20 [b]Gal. 5:10
16 [a]Rom. 12:16; 15:5 [b]Gal. 6:16 [c]Phil. 2:2
17 [a]1Cor. 4:16; 11:1; Phil. 4:9; 1Thess. 1:6 [b]1Pet. 5:3
18 [a]Gal. 1:7; 2:21; 6:12; Phil. 1:15, 16
19 [a]2Cor. 11:15; 2Pet. 2:1 [b]Rom. 16:18; 1Tim. 6:5; Titus 1:11 [c]Hos. 4:7; 2Cor. 11:12; Gal. 6:13 [d]Rom. 8:5
20 [a]Eph. 2:6, 19; Col. 3:1, 3 [b]Acts 1:11 [c]1Cor. 1:7; 1Thess. 1:10; Titus 2:13
21 [a]1Cor. 15:43, 48, 49; Col. 3:4; 1John 3:2 [b]Eph. 1:19 [c]1Cor. 15:26, 27

1 [a]Phil. 1:8 [b]2Cor. 1:14; Phil. 2:16; 1Thess. 2:19, 20 [c]Phil. 1:27
2 [a]Phil. 2:2; 3:16
3 [a]Rom. 16:3; Phil. 1:27 [b]Ex. 32:32; Ps. 69:28; Dan. 12:1; Luke 10:20; Rev. 3:5; 13:8; 20:12; 21:27
4 [a]Rom. 12:12; Phil. 3:1; 1Thess. 5:16; 1Pet. 4:13
5 [a]Heb. 10:25; James 5:8, 9; 1Pet. 4:7; 2Pet. 3:8, 9
6 [a]Ps. 55:22; Prov. 16:3; Matt. 6:25; Luke 12:22; 1Pet. 5:7
7 [a]John 14:27; Rom. 5:1; Col. 3:15
8 [I]Or, *venerable* [a]1Thess. 5:22
9 [a]Phil. 3:17 [b]Rom. 15:33; 16:20; 1Cor. 14:33; 2Cor. 13:11; 1Thess. 5:23; Heb. 13:20
10 [I]Or, *is revived* [a]2Cor. 11:9
11 [a]1Tim. 6:6, 8
12 [a]1Cor. 4:11; 2Cor. 6:10; 11:27

every where and in all things I [pfip]am instructed both to be full and to be hungry,
both to abound and to suffer need.

13 I can do all things [a]through
Christ**[5547]** which [ppt]strengtheneth me.

14 Notwithstanding ye have well
done, that [a]ye [apt]did communicate**[4790]**
with my affliction.

15 Now ye Philippians know also,
that in the beginning of the gospel, when
I departed from Macedonia, [a]no
church**[1577]** communicated**[2841]** with me as
concerning giving**[1394]** and receiving,**[3028]**
but ye only.

16 For even in Thessalonica ye sent
once and again unto my necessity.

17 Not because I desire a gift:**[1390]** but
I desire [a]fruit that [ppt]may abound to your
account.**[3056]**

13 [a]John 15:5; 2Cor. 12:9

14 [a]Phil. 1:7

15 [a]2Cor. 11:8, 9

17 [a]Rom. 15:28; Titus 3:14

18 [a]Phil. 2:25 [b]Heb. 13:16 [c]2Cor. 9:12

19 [a]Ps. 23:1; 2Cor. 9:8 [b]Eph. 1:7; 3:16

20 [a]Rom. 16:27; Gal. 1:5

21 [a]Gal. 1:2

22 [a]Phil. 1:13

23 [a]Rom. 16:24

18 But I have**[568]** all, and abound: I
[pfip]am full, [apt]having received [a]of Epaphroditus the things *which were sent* from
you, [b]an odour of a sweet smell, [c]a sacri-
fice**[2378]** acceptable,**[1184]** wellpleasing**[2101]** to
God.

19 But my God [a]shall supply**[4137]** all
your need [b]according to his riches in
glory**[1391]** by Christ Jesus.

20 [a]Now unto God and our Father**[3962]**
be glory for ever**[165,1519]**[3588] and ever.**[165]**[3588]
Amen.[281]

21 [aim]Salute[782] every saint**[40]** in Christ
Jesus. The brethren [a]which are with me
greet you.

22 All the saints salute you, [a]chiefly
they that are of Caesar's household.

23 [a]The grace of our Lord Jesus
Christ *be* with you all. Amen.

The Epistle of Paul to the

COLOSSIANS

The town of Colosse was located on a ridge overlooking the Lycus River valley in central Asia Minor. At the time of Paul's writing, its neighboring cities, Laodicea and Hierapolis, were becoming more important while Colosse was in a period of decline. Travelers were using a newer road that went through the other two cities but bypassed Colosse. Churches were established in all three of these cities by Epaphras (Col. 4:12, 13) and Timothy, but Paul never visited the believers there personally (Col. 2:1). However, he did tell Philemon, a native of Colosse, that he was hoping to visit him (Phile. 1:22).

Paul is believed to have written to the Colossians about A.D. 60 during his first imprisonment in Rome. While most agree that it was written about the same time as Philemon, Ephesians, and Philippians, it is not certain which was written first. Epaphras (also a native of Colosse) came to visit Paul in prison and gave him a report not only of the progress being made there but also of the problem with false teachers who had gained a foothold in the church. Paul sent the letter back with Onesimus (Philemon's slave) and Tychicus (Col. 4:7–9), but for some unknown reason Epaphras did not return at that time (Col. 4:12).

Paul's purpose in writing this letter was to refute the heretical teaching that was influencing the Colossian church. Paul's references to circumcision, food regulations, and feast days (Col. 2:11–16) indicate that this heresy involved Judaistic tendencies. It differed from the heresy in Galatia in that it integrated an early form of Gnostic philosophy, which consisted of ascetic ideas (Col. 2:20–23) and the worship of angels as intermediaries between God and man (Col. 2:18, 19). Supposedly, one could achieve perfection by progressing through a number of initiations and levels of wisdom in spiritual mysteries.

Instead of refuting the false teaching point by point, Paul shows that all things are fulfilled in the person of Christ. He stresses that all wisdom and spiritual understanding can be found in the God-Man who redeemed them and now holds authority over all things (Col. 1:9—2:19). He then goes on to explain the relationship of "mortifying" the deeds of the flesh to being alive through the Spirit (Col. 2:20—3:17). Finally, he gives practical injunctions for Christian behavior (Col. 3:18—4:6).

1 Paul, [a]an apostle[652] of Jesus
Christ[5547] by the will[2307] of God,[2316]
and Timotheus *our* brother,[80]
2 To the saints[40] [a]and faithful[4103]
brethren in Christ which are at Colosse:
[b]Grace[5485] *be* unto you, and peace,[1515]
from God our Father[3962] and the Lord[2962]
Jesus Christ.

The Progress of the Gospel

3 [a]We give thanks[2168] to God and the
Father of our Lord Jesus Christ, praying[4336] always for you,

1 [a]Eph. 1:1
2 [a]1Cor. 4:17; Eph. 6:21 [b]Gal. 1:3
3 [a]1Cor. 1:4; Eph. 1:16; Phil. 1:3; 4:6
4 [a]Eph. 1:15; Col. 1:19; Phile. 1:5 [b]Heb. 6:10
5 [a]2Tim. 4:8; 1Pet. 1:4
6 [a]Matt. 24:14; Mark 16:15; Rom. 10:18; Col. 1:23 [b]Mark 4:8; John 15:16; Phil. 1:11 [c]2Cor. 6:1; Eph. 3:2; Titus 2:11; 1Pet. 5:12
7 [a]Col. 4:12; Phile. 1:23

🔑4 [a]Since we heard of your faith[4102] in
Christ Jesus, and of [b]the love[26] *which ye*
have to all the saints.
5 For the hope[1680] [a]which [ppt]is laid
up for you in heaven,[3772] whereof ye
heard before in the word[3056] of the
truth[225] of the gospel;[2098]
6 Which is come unto you, [a]as *it is*
in all the world;[2889] and [b]bringeth forth
fruit, as *it doth* also in you, since the day
ye heard *of it,* and knew[1921] [c]the
grace[5485] of God in truth:
🔑7 As ye also learned[3129] of
[a]Epaphras our dear fellowservant,[4889]

🔑 **1:4–8** See introduction to Colossians.

🔑 **1:7** Epaphras (also mentioned in Col. 4:12 and Phile. 1:23) was one of Paul's friends and as-

(continued on next page)

who is for you [b]a faithful[4103] minister[1249]
of Christ;
8 Who also declared unto us your
[a]love[26] in the Spirit.[4151]
🗝 9 [a]For this cause we also, since the
day we heard *it,* do not cease to
pptpray[4336] for you, and to pptdesire [b]that
ye asbpmight be filled with [c]the knowledge[1922] of his will[2307] [d]in all wisdom[4678]
and spiritual[4152] understanding;[4907]
10 [a]That ye ainfmight walk[4043] worthy of the Lord [b]unto all pleasing,[699]
[c]being fruitful in every good[18] work,
and increasing in the knowledge[1922] of
God;
11 [a]Strengthened[1412] with all
might,[1411] according to his glorious[1391]
power,[2904] [b]unto all patience[5281] and long-
suffering [c]with joyfulness;[5479]
12 [a]Giving thanks[2168] unto the
Father, which apthath made us meet[2427] to
be partakers of [b]the inheritance[2819] of
the saints in light:[5457]
13 Who aomhath delivered[4506] us
from [a]the power[1849] of darkness,[4655] [b]and
aohath translated[3179] *us* into the kingdom[932] of [I]his dear[26] Son:[5207]
14 [a]In whom we have redemption[629]
through his blood,[129] *even* the forgiveness[859] of sins:[266]

The Preeminence of Christ

🗝 15 Who is [a]the image[1504] of the invisible God,[2316] [b]the firstborn[4416] of
every creature:
16 For [a]by him aopwere all things
created,[2936] that are in heaven,[3772] and
that are in earth,[1093] visible and invisible,
whether *they be* thrones, or [b]domin-
ions,[2963] or principalities,[746] or powers:[1849] all things were created[2936] [c]by
him, and for him:
17 [a]And he is before all things, and
by him all things pficonsist.[4921]
18 And [a]he is the head of the
body,[4983] the church:[1577] who is the beginning,[746] [b]the firstborn[4416] from the
dead; that in all *things* he might have
the preeminence.
19 For it pleased[2106] *the Father* that
[a]in him should all fulness[4138] ainfdwell;[2730]
20 And, apt[a]having made peace
through the blood of his cross,[4716] [b]by
him ainfto reconcile[604] [c]all things unto
himself; by him, *I say,* whether *they be*
things in earth,[1093] or things in
heaven.[3772]
21 And you, [a]that were sometime
pfppalienated[526] and enemies [I]in *your*
mind[1271] [b]by wicked[4190] works, yet now
aohath he reconciled[604]
22 [a]In the body[4983] of his flesh[4561]
through death,[2288] ainf[b]to present you
holy[40] and unblameable[299] and unreproveable in his sight:
23 If ye continue in the faith[4102]

7 [b]2Cor. 11:23; 1Tim. 4:6
8 [a]Rom. 15:30
9 [a]Eph. 1:15, 16; Col. 1:3, 4 [b]1Cor. 1:5 [c]Rom. 12:2; Eph. 5:10, 17 [d]Eph. 1:8
10 [a]Eph. 4:1; Phil. 1:27; 1Thess. 2:12 [b]1Thess. 4:1 [c]John 15:16; 2Cor. 9:8; Phil. 1:11; Titus 3:1; Heb. 13:21
11 [a]Eph. 3:16; 6:10 [b]Eph. 4:2 [c]Acts 5:41; Rom. 5:3
12 [a]Eph. 5:20; Col. 3:15 [b]Acts 26:18; Eph. 1:11
13 [I]Gr. *the Son of his love* [a]Eph. 6:12; Heb. 2:14; 1Pet. 2:9 [b]1Thess. 2:12; 2Pet. 1:11 [c]Matt. 3:17; Eph. 1:6
14 [a]Eph. 1:7
15 [a]2Cor. 4:4; Heb. 1:3 [b]Rev. 3:14
16 [a]John 1:3; 1Cor. 8:6; Eph. 3:9; Heb. 1:2 [b]Rom. 8:38; Eph. 1:21; Col. 2:10, 15; 1Pet. 3:22 [c]Rom. 11:36; Heb. 2:10
17 [a]John 1:1, 3; 17:5; 1Cor. 8:6
18 [a]1Cor. 11:3; Eph. 1:10, 22; 4:15; 5:23 [b]Acts 26:23; 1Cor. 15:20, 23; Rev. 1:5
19 [a]John 1:16, 3:34; Col. 2:9; 3:11
20 [a]Eph. 2:14-16 [b]2Cor. 5:18 [c]Eph. 1:10
21 [I]Or, *by your mind in wicked works* [a]Eph. 2:1, 2, 12, 19; 4:18 [b]Titus 1:15, 16
22 [a]Eph. 2:15, 16 [b]Luke 1:75, Eph. 1:4; 5:27; 1Thess. 4:7; Titus 2:14; Jude 1:24

(continued from previous page)
sociates, called by him a "fellow bondservant" and "fellow prisoner." Epaphras evangelized the cities of the Lycus Valley in Phrygia under Paul's direction and founded the churches of Colosse, Hierapolis, and Laodicea. Later, he visited Paul in prison in Rome, and it was his news of the conditions in the churches of the Lycus Valley that caused Paul to write the Book of Colossians.

🗝 **1:9** The heresy that prevailed in Colosse as well as in other contemporary churches was Gnosticism (see note on Col. 2:8–23).

🗝 **1:15–18** In the first verse of this passage, Jesus Christ is presented as the image of God, the invisible One (John 1:18). *Eikōn* (1504) "image," always assumes a prototype (the original form from which it is drawn), not merely a thing it resembles (e.g., the reflection of the sun in the water is an *eikōn*). Paul was telling the Colossians here that Jesus Christ has a "prototype," God the Father who is invisible. The relationship between Christ and the Father God is not coincidental (see the notes on John 1:18 and Phil. 2:6–8).

The other significant word is *prōtótokos* (4416), translated as "firstborn." What it means in this passage is that Christ holds the same relation to all creation as God the Father, because He is above all creation.

[pfpp][a]grounded and settled, and *be* [b]not [ppt]moved away from the hope[1680] of the gospel,[2098] which ye [ao]have heard, *and* [c]which was preached[2784] [d]to every creature[2937] which is under heaven; [e]whereof I Paul [aom]am made a minister;[1249]

Exhortation to Stedfastness

24 [a]Who now rejoice in my sufferings[3804] [b]for you, and fill up [c]that which is behind of the afflictions of Christ[5547] in my flesh[4561] for [d]his body's[4983] sake, which is the church:[1577]

25 Whereof I am made a minister, according to [a]the dispensation[3622] of God which [aptp]is given to me for you, [ainf]to fulfil[4137] the word[3056] of God;

26 *Even* [a]the mystery[3466] which [pfpp]hath been hid from ages[165] and from generations,[1074] [b]but now [aop]is made manifest[5319] to his saints:[40]

27 [a]To whom God [ao]would [ainf]make known[1107] what *is* [b]the riches of the glory[1391] of this mystery[3466] among the Gentiles;[1484] which is Christ[5547] in you, [c]the hope[1680] of glory:

28 Whom we preach,[2605] [ppt][a]warning[3560] every man,[444] and teaching[1321] every man in all wisdom;[4678] [b]that we [aosb]may present every man perfect[5046] in Christ Jesus:

29 [a]Whereunto I also labour, [b]striving[75] [c]according to his working, which [ppt]worketh[1754] in me mightily.

23 [a]Eph. 3:17; Col. 2:7 [b]John 15:6 [c]Rom. 10:18 [d]Col. 1:6 [e]Acts 1:17; 2Cor. 3:6; 4:1; 5:18; Eph. 3:7; Col. 1:25; 1Tim. 2:7
24 [a]Rom. 5:3; 2Cor. 7:4 [b]Eph. 3:1, 13 [c]2Cor. 1:5, 6; Phil. 3:10; 2Tim. 1:8; 2:10 [d]Eph. 1:23
25 [a]1Cor. 9:17; Gal. 2:7; Eph. 3:2; Col. 1:23
26 [a]Rom. 16:25; 1Cor. 2:7; Eph. 3:9 [b]Matt. 13:11; 2Tim. 1:10
27 [a]2Cor. 2:14 [b]Rom. 9:23; Eph. 1:7; 3:8 [c]1Tim. 1:1
28 [a]Acts 20:20, 27, 31 [b]2Cor. 11:2; Eph. 5:27; Col. 1:22
29 [a]1Cor. 15:10 [b]Col. 2:1 [c]Eph. 1:19; 3:7, 20

1 [a]Phil. 1:30; Col. 1:29; 1Thess. 2:2
2 [a]2Cor. 1:6 [b]Col. 3:14 [c]Phil. 3:8; Col. 1:9
3 [a]1Cor. 1:24; 2:6, 7; Eph. 1:8; Col. 1:9
4 [a]Rom. 16:18; 2Cor. 11:13; Eph. 4:14; 5:6; Col. 2:8, 18
5 [a]1Cor. 5:3; 1Thess. 2:17 [b]1Cor. 14:40 [c]1Pet. 5:9

Warnings Against Errors

2 For I would that ye knew what great [a]conflict[73] I have for you, and *for* them at Laodicea, and *for* as many as have not seen my face in the flesh;

2 [a]That their hearts might be comforted, [aptp][b]being knit together in love,[26] and unto all riches of the full assurance[4136] of understanding, [c]to the acknowledgement[1922] of the mystery of God,[2316] and of the Father,[3962] and of Christ;[5547]

3 [a]In whom are hid all the treasures of wisdom[4678] and knowledge.[1108]

4 And this I say, [a]lest any man [psmp]should beguile[3884] you with enticing words.

5 For [a]though I be absent[548] in the flesh,[4561] yet am I with you in the spirit,[4151] joying and beholding [b]your order,[5010] and the [c]stedfastness of your faith[4102] in Christ.

6 [a]As ye [ao]have therefore received[3880] Christ Jesus the Lord,[2962] *so* [pim]walk ye in him:

7 [pfpp][a]Rooted and [ppp]built up[2026] in him, and [ppp]stablished[950] in the faith,[4102] as ye [aop]have been taught,[1321] [ppt]abounding therein with thanksgiving.

🗝 8 [a]Beware[991] lest any man [ppt]spoil you through philosophy and vain[2756] de-

6 [a]1Thess. 4:1; Jude 1:3 **7** [a]Eph. 2:21, 22; 3:17; Col. 1:23 **8** [a]Jer. 29:8; Rom. 16:17; Eph. 5:6; Col. 2:18; Heb. 13:9

🗝 **2:8–23** Gnosticism is derived from the Greek word *gnōsis* (1108), meaning "knowledge." This heresy was repudiated not only by the writers of many New Testament epistles, but also by the church fathers, who lived in the period after the early church. It is the church fathers that give a knowledge of Gnosticism's general tenets.

The Gnostics separated matter from thought. They concluded that matter was evil, and formulated the idea that the possession of knowledge was the only requirement for salvation. This is why they did not want to attribute humanity to Jesus Christ because to them, material things were evil. Docetism resulted, which taught that the body of Christ was something that appeared material, but was in reality only spiritual. Such a belief led to an immoral life, for since the spirit was separate from the physical body, they ignored their responsibility for the actions done in the body. This is the reason why Paul stressed that "in him [Jesus Christ, as He appeared on earth], dwelleth all the fulness of the Godhead bodily" (v. 9). Jesus *was* truly God in the flesh (John 1:14). As a result of the philosophical concept of the evil of the body, the Gnostics ignored or diminished the significance of the historic facts of the ministry, death, and resurrection of Jesus Christ as not being real but simply apparent. To them, all the secrets of God were in the mind, or appearing in an im-

(continued on next page)

ceit, after [b]the tradition[3862] of men,[444] after the [I][c]rudiments[4747] of the world,[2889] and not after Christ.[5547]

9 For [a]in him dwelleth all the fulness[4138] of the Godhead[2320] bodily.

10 [a]And ye are complete in him, [b]which is the head[2776] of all [c]principality[746] and power:[1849]

11 In whom also ye [aop]are [a]circumcised[4059] with the circumcision[4061] made without hands, in [b]putting off the body[4983] of the sins[266] of the flesh[4561] by the circumcision of Christ:

12 [aptp][a]Buried with him in baptism,[908] wherein also [b]ye [aop]are risen with *him* through [c]the faith[4102] of the operation of God, [d]who [apt]hath raised[1453] him from the dead.[3498]

13 [a]And you, being dead in your sins[3900] and the uncircumcision[203] of your flesh, [ao]hath he quickened together[4806] with him, having forgiven[5483] you all trespasses;[3900]

14 [apt][a]Blotting out the handwriting of ordinances[1378] that was against us, which was contrary to us, and [pfi]took it out of the way,[3319] [apt]nailing it to his cross;[4716]

15 *And* [apt][a]having spoiled [b]principalities[746] and powers,[1849] he [ao]made a shew of them openly, [apt]triumphing over them in it.

16 [pim]Let no man therefore [a]judge[2919] you [I][b]in meat, or in drink, or in respect [c]of an holyday, or of the new moon, or of the sabbath[4521] *days:*

17 [a]Which are a shadow of things to come; but the body[4983] *is* of Christ.

18 [pim][a]Let no man beguile you of your reward[2603] [b]in a voluntary humility and worshipping[2356] of angels,[32] intruding into those things [c]which he [pfi]hath not seen,[3708] vainly [ppp]puffed up by his fleshly mind,[3563]

19 And not holding [a]the Head,[2776] from which all the body[4983] by joints and bands [ppp]having nourishment ministered, and [ppp]knit together, increaseth with the increase of God.

Legalism

20 Wherefore if ye [ao]be [a]dead[599] with Christ from [b]the [I]rudiments[4747] of the world,[2889] [c]why, as though living[2198] in the world, are ye subject to ordinances,[1379]

21 ([aosi][a]Touch[680] not; [aosi]taste[1089] not; [aosi]handle[2345] not;

22 Which all are to perish with the using;[671]) [a]after the commandments[1778] and doctrines[1319] of men?[444]

23 [a]Which things have indeed a shew[3056] of wisdom[4678] in [b]will worship, and humility, and [I]neglecting of the body;[4983] not in any honour to the satisfying of the flesh.[4561]

"Renewed in Knowledge"

3 If ye then [aop][a]be risen with Christ, [pim]seek those things which are above,[507] where [b]Christ sitteth on the right hand[1188] of God.

2 Set your [I]affection on[5426] things above,[507] not on things on the earth.[1093]

3 [a]For ye [ao]are dead,[599] [b]and your life[2222] is hid with Christ in God.

4 [a]When Christ, *who is* [b]our life,

8 [I]Or, *elements* [b]Matt. 15:2; Gal. 1:14; Col. 2:22 [c]Gal. 4:3, 9; Col. 2:20
9 [a]John 1:14; Col. 1:19
10 [a]John 1:16 [b]Eph. 1:20, 21; 1Pet. 3:22 [c]Col. 1:16
11 [a]Deut. 10:16; 30:6; Jer. 4:4; Rom. 2:29; Phil. 3:3 [b]Rom. 6:6; Eph. 4:22; Col. 3:8, 9
12 [a]Rom. 6:4 [b]Col. 3:1 [c]Eph. 1:19; 3:7 [d]Acts 2:24
13 [a]Eph. 2:1, 5, 6, 11
14 [a]Eph. 2:15, 16
15 [a]Gen. 3:15; Ps. 68:18; Isa. 53:12; Matt. 12:29; Luke 10:18; 11:22; John 12:31; 16:11; Eph. 4:8; Heb. 2:14 [b]Eph. 6:12
16 [I]Or, *for eating and drinking* [a]Rom. 14:3, 10, 13 [b]Rom. 14:2, 17; 1Cor. 8:8 [c]Rom. 14:5; Gal. 4:10
17 [a]Heb. 8:5; 9:9; 10:1
18 [a]Col. 2:4 [b]Col. 2:23 [c]Ezek. 13:1; 1Tim. 1:7
19 [a]Eph. 4:15, 16
20 [I]Or, *elements* [a]Rom. 6:3, 5; 7:4, 6; Gal. 2:19; Eph. 2:15 [b]Col. 2:8 [c]Gal. 4:3, 9
21 [a]1Tim. 4:3
22 [a]Isa. 29:13; Matt. 15:9; Titus 1:14
23 [I]Or, *punishing* [a]1Tim. 4:8 [b]Col. 2:18

1 [a]Rom. 6:5; Eph. 2:6; Col. 2:12 [b]Rom. 8:34; Eph. 1:20 **2** [I]Or, *mind*
3 [a]Rom. 6:2; Gal. 2:20; Col. 2:20 [b]2Cor. 5:7; Col. 1:5
4 [a]1John 3:2 [b]John 11:25; 14:6

(continued from previous page)
material identity. The result was a complete denial of sexual and other bodily appetites (i.e., acceptable behavior could range from virtual asceticism to unrestrained indulgence of the body [vv. 20–23]).

In this passage, Paul countered the teaching that stressed the way to holiness was through asceticism. He emphasized that spirituality is not achieved by self-centered efforts to control the passions, but by putting on Christ, "setting one's affections on Him," and in so doing, removing all that is contrary to His will (vv. 20–23; Col. 3:1–17). Furthermore, as far as immaterial knowledge is concerned, true wisdom is not found in a man-made philosophy (v. 8). See note on Colossians 1:15–18.

[asbp]shall appear,[5319] then shall ye also appear with him [c]in glory.[1391]

🔑 5 [aim][a]Mortify therefore [b]your members which are upon the earth; [c]fornication, uncleanness,[167] inordinate affection,[3806] [d]evil concupiscence,[1939] and covetousness,[4124] [e]which is idolatry:[1495]

6 [a]For which things' sake the wrath[3709] of God cometh on [b]the children of disobedience:[543]

7 [a]In the which ye also walked some time, when ye [ipf]lived[2198] in them.

8 [a]But now ye also [aim]put off all these; anger,[3709] wrath,[2372] malice,[2549] blasphemy,[988] [b]filthy communication out of your mouth.

9 [pim][a]Lie not one to another, [b]seeing that ye [apt]have put off the old man[444] with his deeds;[4234]

10 And [apt]have put on the new[3501] *man,* which [ppp][a]is renewed[341] in knowledge[1922] [b]after the image[1504] of him that [apt][c]created him:

11 Where there is neither [a]Greek nor Jew, circumcision[4061] nor uncircumcision,[203] Barbarian,[915] Scythian, bond[1401] *nor* free:[1658] [b]but Christ[5547] *is* all, and in all.

12 [aim][a]Put on therefore, [b]as the elect[1588] of God, holy[40] and beloved,[25] [c]bowels[4698] of mercies,[3628] kindness,[5544] humbleness of mind, meekness, longsuffering;

13 [a]Forbearing[430] one another, and forgiving[5483] one another, if any man [psa]have a [l]quarrel against any: even as Christ forgave you, so also *do* ye.

14 [a]And above all these things [b]*put on* charity,[26] which is the [c]bond of perfectness.[5047]

15 And [pim]let [a]the peace[1515] of God [pim]rule in your hearts,[2588] [b]to the which also ye [aop]are called [c]in one body;[4983] [d]and be ye thankful.[2170]

4 [c]1Cor. 15:43; Phil. 3:21
5 [a]Rom. 8:13; Gal. 5:24 [b]Rom. 6:13 [c]Eph. 5:3 [d]1Thess. 4:5 [e]Eph. 5:5
6 [a]Rom. 1:18; Eph. 5:6; Rev. 22:15 [b]Eph. 2:2
7 [a]Rom. 6:19, 20; 7:5; 1Cor. 6:11; Eph. 2:2; Titus 3:3
8 [a]Eph. 4:22; Heb. 12:1; James 1:21; 1Pet. 2:1 [b]Eph. 4:29; 5:4
9 [a]Lev. 19:11; Eph. 4:25 [b]Eph. 4:22, 24
10 [a]Rom. 12:2 [b]Eph. 4:23, 24 [c]Eph. 2:10
11 [a]Rom. 10:12; 1Cor. 12:13; Gal. 3:28; 5:6; Eph. 6:8 [b]Eph. 1:23
12 [a]Eph. 4:24 [b]1Thess. 1:4; 1Pet. 1:2; 2Pet. 1:10 [c]Gal. 5:22; Eph. 4:2, 32; Phil. 2:1
13 [l]Or, *complaint* [a]Mark 11:25; Eph. 4:2, 32
14 [a]1Pet. 4:8 [b]John 13:34; Rom. 13:8; Eph. 5:2; Col. 2:2; 1Thess. 4:9; 1Tim. 1:5; 1John 3:23; 4:21 [c]Eph. 4:3
15 [a]Rom. 14:17; Phil. 4:7 [b]1Cor. 7:15 [c]Eph. 2:16, 17; 4:4 [d]Col. 2:7; 3:17
16 [a]1Cor. 14:26; Eph. 5:19 [b]Col. 4:6
17 [a]1Cor. 10:31 [b]Rom. 1:8; Eph. 5:20; Col. 1:12; 2:7; 1Thess. 5:18; Heb. 13:15
18 [a]Eph. 5:22; Titus 2:5; 1Pet. 3:1 [b]Eph. 5:3
19 [a]Eph. 5:25, 28, 33; 1Pet. 3:7 [b]Eph. 4:31

🔑 16 Let the word[3056] of Christ dwell in you richly in all wisdom;[4678] teaching[1321] and admonishing[3560] one another [a]in psalms[5568] and hymns[5215] and spiritual[4152] songs,[5603] singing [b]with grace[5485] in your hearts[2588] to the Lord.

17 And [a]whatsoever ye [psa]do in word[3056] or deed,[2041] *do* all in the name[3686] of the Lord Jesus, [b]giving[2168] thanks to God and the Father by him.

Domestic Duties

🔑 18 [a]Wives, [pim]submit yourselves[5293] unto your own husbands, [b]as it is fit in the Lord.

19 [a]Husbands, [pim]love[25] *your* wives, and [pim]be not [b]bitter[4087] against them.

20 [a]Children, [pim]obey[5219] *your* parents [b]in all things: for this is well pleasing[2101] unto the Lord.[2962]

21 [a]Fathers, [pim]provoke[2042] not your children *to anger,* lest they [psa]be discouraged.

22 [a]Servants,[1401] obey[5219] [b]in all things *your* masters[2962] [c]according to the flesh; not with eyeservice,[3787] as menpleasers;[441] but in singleness[572] of heart, fearing[5399] God:

23 [a]And whatsoever ye [psa]do, [pim]do *it* heartily,[1537,5590] as to the Lord, and not unto men;[444]

24 [a]Knowing that of the Lord ye shall receive[618] the reward of the inheritance:[2817] [b]for ye serve[1398] the Lord[2962] Christ.[5547]

25 But he that [ppt]doeth wrong[91] shall receive for the wrong which he hath done; and [a]there is no respect of persons.[4382]

20 [a]Eph. 6:1 [b]Eph. 5:24; Titus 2:9 **21** [a]Eph. 6:4 **22** [a]Eph. 6:5; 1Tim. 6:1; Titus 2:9; 1Pet. 2:18 [b]Col. 3:20 [c]Phile. 1:16 **23** [a]Eph. 6:6, 7 **24** [a]Eph. 6:8 [b]1Cor. 7:22 **25** [a]Deut. 10:17; Rom. 2:11; Eph. 6:9; 1Pet. 1:17

🔑 **3:5** This verse also combats the teaching of Gnosticism that the physical body is evil. Since it is evil in itself and cannot be redeemed from its evil ways, it might as well do whatever it wants. This is the reason that Paul says, "Mortify therefore your members which are upon the earth [meaning 'bring them under control and treat them as though they were dead']."

🔑 **3:16** The expression "the word (*lógos* [3056]) of Christ" refers to the revelation which Jesus Christ brought into the world (see note on John 1:1–17).

🔑 **3:18, 19** See note on 1 Timothy 2:9–15 concerning a woman's conduct in the home.

Sundry Admonitions

4 [a]Masters,[2962] give unto *your* servants[1401] that which is just[1342] and
equal;[2471] knowing that ye also have a
Master[2962] in heaven.[3772]
2 [a]Continue[4342] in prayer,[4335] and
[ppt]watch in the same [b]with thanksgiving;
3 [a]Withal[260] praying[4336] also for us,
that God [aosb]would [b]open unto us a door
of utterance,[3056] [ainf]to speak [c]the mystery[3466] of Christ, [d]for which I am also
in bonds:
4 That I [aosb]may make it manifest,[5319] as I ought to speak.
5 [a]Walk[4043] in wisdom[4678] toward
them that are without,[1854] [b]redeeming[1805]
the time.[2540]
6 Let your speech[3056] *be* alway [a]with
grace,[5485] [b]seasoned with salt, [c]that ye
may know how ye ought [pinf]to answer
every man.
🗝 7 [a]All my state shall Tychicus declare[1107] unto you, *who is* a beloved
brother, and a faithful[4103] minister[1249]
and fellowservant[4889] in the Lord:[2962]
8 [a]Whom I have sent unto you for
the same purpose, that he might know
your estate, and [aosb]comfort your
hearts;[2588]
9 With [a]Onesimus, a faithful and
beloved[27] brother,[80] who is *one* of you.
They shall make known[1107] unto you all
things which *are done* here.
🗝 10 [a]Aristarchus my fellowprisoner saluteth you, and [b]Marcus, sister's son to
Barnabas, (touching whom ye received
commandments: if he come unto you, receive him;)
11 And Jesus, which is called Justus,
who are of the circumcision.[4061] These
only *are my* fellowworkers unto the kingdom[932] of God, which have been a comfort unto me.
12 [a]Epaphras, who is *one* of you, a
servant[1401] of Christ, saluteth[782] you, always [I][b]labouring fervently[75] for you in
prayers, that ye [aosb]may stand [c]perfect
and [pfpp]complete in all the will[2307] of
God.
13 For I bear him record, that he
hath a great zeal for you, and them *that*
are in Laodicea, and them in Hierapolis.
14 [a]Luke, the beloved physician,[2395]
and [b]Demas, greet you.
15 Salute the brethren which are in
Laodicea, and Nymphas, and [a]the
church[1577] which is in his house.
16 And when [a]this epistle[1992] is
read[314] among you, cause that it be read
also in the church of the Laodiceans; and
that ye likewise read the *epistle* from
Laodicea.
17 And say to [a]Archippus, Take heed
to [b]the ministry[1248] which thou hast received in the Lord, that thou fulfil[4137] it.
18 [a]The salutation by the hand of me
Paul. [b]Remember my bonds. [c]Grace *be*
with you. Amen.[281]

1 [a]Eph. 6:9
2 [a]Luke 18:1; Rom. 12:12; Eph. 6:18; 1Thess. 5:17, 18 [b]Col. 2:7; 3:15
3 [a]Eph. 6:19; 2Thess. 3:1 [b]1Cor. 16:9; 2Cor. 2:12 [c]Matt. 13:11; 1Cor. 4:1; Eph. 6:19; Col. 1:26; 2:2 [d]Eph. 6:20; Phil. 1:7
5 [a]Eph. 5:15; 1Thess. 4:12 [b]Eph. 5:16
6 [a]Eccl. 10:12; Col. 3:16 [b]Mark 9:50 [c]1Pet. 3:15
7 [a]Eph. 6:21
8 [a]Eph. 6:22
9 [a]Phile. 1:10
10 [a]Acts 19:29; 20:4; 27:2; Phile. 1:24 [b]Acts 15:37; 2Tim. 4:11
12 [I]Or, *striving* [a]Col. 1:7; Phile. 1:23 [b]Rom. 15:30 [c]Matt. 5:48; 1Cor. 2:6; 14:20; Phil. 3:15; Heb. 5:14
14 [a]2Tim. 4:11 [b]2Tim. 4:10; Phile. 1:24
15 [a]Rom. 16:5; 1Cor. 16:19
16 [a]1Thess. 5:27
17 [a]Phile. 1:2 [b]1Tim. 4:6
18 [a]1Cor. 16:21; 2Thess. 3:17 [b]Heb. 13:3 [c]Heb. 13:25

🗝 **4:7** Tychicus was an Ephesian who accompanied Paul to Jerusalem, doubtless as a delegate of his church carrying the collection (Acts 20:4, cf. 1 Cor. 16:1–4), and was well trusted by Paul (Eph. 6:21). He was Paul's personal representative to the churches in Colosse and Ephesus (Eph. 6:21, 22). Paul sent him to Crete as a messenger to Titus (Titus 3:12), and then he went on a mission to the church at Ephesus (2 Tim. 4:12).

🗝 **4:10** The first reference to Aristarchus in Acts 19:29 describes him as being Paul's fellow traveler when the two were seized by the Ephesian mob. In Acts 20:4, he accompanied Paul to Jerusalem, probably as a Thessalonian church delegate with the collection. Acts 27:2 refers to him as one of Paul's companions when he sailed to Rome. He possibly rejoined Paul and became His fellow prisoner, alternating with Epaphras in voluntary imprisonment (Phile. 1:23, 24).

The First Epistle of Paul to the

THESSALONIANS

The city of Thessalonica was ideally situated along the Egnatian Way on the western side of the Chalcidic peninsula. It was the chief seaport of ancient Macedonia and an important commercial and military center.

After Paul and Silas were forced to leave Philippi, they traveled along the Egnatian Way to Thessalonica (Acts 16:39—17:1) where Paul taught in the synagogue for three sabbaths. They were forced to leave the city when antagonistic Jews, after stirring up the people of Thessalonica, brought some of the believers before the city officials and accused them of promoting treasonous ideas (Acts 17:5–10). The believers there came under great persecution following this uproar. Paul, feeling that he had not had enough time to ground them in Christian doctrine, desired to return to Thessalonica, but was hindered by Satan (1 Thess. 2:17, 18). Consequently, he sent Timothy to complete the work he had begun (1 Thess. 3:1, 2).

The Book of 1 Thessalonians was probably written by the Apostle Paul between the years A.D. 50 and 51 when Timothy returned to him in Corinth (Acts 18:5). He brought good news of their steadfastness and zeal in propagating the gospel (1 Thess. 3:6). Nevertheless, he reported that there were some ethical problems (1 Thess. 3:4–7), as well as some eschatological misconceptions. The Thessalonian believers were concerned that those believers who had already died would miss Christ's coming. Paul assured them that those who had died would be caught up to meet the Lord just like those who are alive at His coming (1 Thess. 4:13–18). Despite these problems and the persecution that they had faced, the church at Thessalonica had faithfully spread the gospel (1 Thess. 1:8).

1 Paul, and [a]Silvanus, and Timotheus, unto the church[1577] of the Thessalonians *which is* in God[2316] the Father[3962] and *in* the Lord[2962] Jesus Christ:[5547] [b]Grace[5485] *be* unto you, and peace,[1515] from God our Father, and the Lord Jesus Christ.

The Power of the Gospel

2 [a]We give thanks[2168] to God always for you all, making mention of you in our prayers;[4335]

3 [a]Remembering without ceasing [b]your work[2041] of faith,[4102] [c]and labour[2873] of love,[26] and patience[5281] of hope[1680] in our Lord Jesus Christ, in the sight of God and our Father;

4 Knowing, brethren[80] [I]beloved,[25] [a]your election[1589] of God.

5 For [a]our gospel[2098] came not unto you in word[3056] only, but also in power,[1411] and [b]in the [an]Holy Ghost,[4151] [c]and in much assurance;[4136] as [d]ye know what manner of men we were among you for your sake.

6 And [a]ye became followers of us, and of the Lord, [apt]having received the word[3056] in much affliction, [b]with joy of the [an]Holy Ghost:

7 So that ye [ainf]were ensamples[5179] to all that [ppt]believe[4100] in Macedonia and Achaia.

8 For from you [pfip][a]sounded out the word of the Lord not only in Macedonia and Achaia, but also [b]in every place your faith to God-ward [pfi]is spread abroad; so that we need not [pinf]to speak any thing.

9 For they themselves shew of us [a]what manner of entering in we had unto you, [b]and how ye turned to God[2316] from idols[1497] to serve[1398] the living[2198] and true[228] God;

10 And [pinf][a]to wait for his Son[5207] [b]from heaven,[3772] [c]whom he raised[1453]

1 [a]2Cor. 1:19; 2Thess. 1:1; 1Pet. 5:12 [b]Eph. 1:2
2 [a]Rom. 1:8; Eph. 1:16; Phile. 1:4
3 [a]1Thess. 2:13 [b]John 6:29; Gal. 5:6; 1Thess. 3:6; 2Thess. 1:3, 11; James 2:17 [c]Rom. 16:6; Heb. 6:10
4 [I]Or, *beloved of God, your election* [a]Col. 3:12; 2Thess. 2:13
5 [a]Mark 16:20; 1Cor. 2:4; 4:20 [b]2Cor. 6:6 [c]Col. 2:2; Heb. 2:3 [d]1Thess. 2:1, 5, 10, 11; 2Thess. 3:7
6 [a]1Cor. 4:16; 11:1; Phil. 3:17; 1Thess. 2:14; 2Thess. 3:9 [b]Acts 5:41; Heb. 10:34
8 [a]Rom. 10:18 [b]Rom. 1:8; 2Thess. 1:4
9 [a]1Thess. 2:1 [b]1Cor. 12:2; Gal. 4:8
10 [a]Rom. 2:7; Phil. 3:20; Titus 2:13; 2Pet. 3:12; Rev. 1:7 [b]Acts 1:11; 1Thess. 4:16; 2Thess. 1:7 [c]Acts 2:24

from the dead,[3498] *even* Jesus, which [ppt]delivered[4506] us [d]from the wrath[3709] to come.[2064]

2 For [a]yourselves, brethren,[80] know our entrance in unto you, that it [pfi]was not in vain:[2756]

2 But even after that we had suffered before, and were shamefully entreated,[5195] as ye know, at [a]Philippi, [b]we were bold in our God [c]to speak unto you the gospel[2098] of God [d]with much contention.[73]

3 [a]For our exhortation[3874] *was* not of deceit, nor of uncleanness,[167] nor in guile:[1388]

4 But as [a]we were allowed of God [b]to be put in trust with[4100] the gospel, even so we speak; [c]not as pleasing men,[444] but God, [d]which [ppt]trieth our hearts.[2588]

5 For [a]neither at any time used we flattering words,[3056] as ye know, nor a cloke of covetousness; [b]God *is* witness:[3144]

6 [a]Nor of men [ppt]sought we glory,[1391] neither of you, nor *yet* of others, when [b]we might[1410] have been [c]burdensome, [d]as the apostles[652] of Christ.

7 But [a]we were gentle[2261] among you, even as a nurse[5162] cherisheth her children:[5043]

8 So being affectionately desirous of you, we were willing[2106] [a]to have imparted unto you, not the gospel of God only, but also [b]our own souls,[5590] because ye [pfip]were dear unto us.

9 For ye remember, brethren, our labour[2873] and travail:[3449] for [a]labouring[2038] night and day, [b]because we would not be chargeable unto any of you, we preached[2784] unto you the gospel of God.

10 [a]Ye *are* witnesses,[3144] and God *also,* [b]how holily[3743] and justly[1346] and unblameably we behaved ourselves among you that [ppt]believe:[4100]

11 As ye know how we [ppt]exhorted and [ppt]comforted and [ppt]charged[3140] every one of you, as a father[3962] *doth* his children,[5043]

12 [a]That ye [aies]would walk worthy of God, [b]who [ppt]hath called[2564] you unto his kingdom[932] and glory.[1391]

13 For this cause also thank we God [a]without ceasing, because, when ye received the word of God which ye heard of us, ye received *it* [b]not *as* the word of men,[444] but as it is in truth, the word[3056] of God,[2316] which effectually worketh[1754] also in you that [ppt]believe.

14 For ye, brethren, became followers [a]of the churches[1577] of God which in Judaea are in Christ Jesus: for [b]ye also [ao]have suffered like things of your own countrymen, [c]even as they *have* of the Jews:

15 [a]Who both [apt]killed the Lord Jesus, and [b]their own prophets,[4396] and [apt]have [I]persecuted us; and they [ppt]please not God, [c]and are contrary to all men:

16 [a]Forbidding us to speak to the Gentiles[1484] that they [asbp]might be saved,[4982] [aies][b]to fill up[378] their sins[266] alway: [c]for the wrath[3709] [ao]is come upon them to the uttermost.[5056]

17 But we, brethren, [aptp]being taken from you for a short[5610] time[2540] [a]in presence, not in heart,[2588] endeavoured the more abundantly [b]to see your face with great desire.

18 Wherefore we would have come unto you, even I Paul, once and again; but [a]Satan[4567] hindered us.

19 For [a]what *is* our hope, or joy,[5479]

10 [d]Matt. 3:7; Rom. 5:9; 1Thess. 5:9
1 [a]1Thess. 1:5, 9
2 [a]Acts 16:22 [b]1Thess. 1:5 [c]Acts 17:2 [d]Phil. 1:30; Col. 2:1
3 [a]2Cor. 7:2; 1Thess. 2:5; 2Pet. 1:16
4 [a]1Cor. 7:25; 1Tim. 1:11, 12 [b]1Cor. 9:17; Gal. 2:7; Titus 1:3 [c]Gal. 1:10 [d]Prov. 17:3; Rom. 8:27
5 [a]Acts 20:33; 2Cor. 2:17; 4:2; 7:2; 12:17 [b]Rom. 1:9
6 [a]John 5:41, 44; 12:43; 1Tim. 5:17 [b]1Cor. 9:4, 6, 12, 18; 2Cor. 10:1, 2, 10, 11; 13:10; 2Thess. 3:9; Phile. 1:8, 9 [c]2Cor. 11:9; 12:13, 14; 2Thess. 3:8 [d]1Cor. 9:1, 2, 5
7 [a]1Cor. 2:3; 9:22; 2Cor. 13:4; 2Tim. 2:24
8 [a]Rom. 1:11; 15:29 [b]2Cor. 12:15
9 [a]Acts 20:34; 1Cor. 4:12; 2Cor. 11:9; 2Thess. 3:8 [b]2Cor. 12:13, 14
10 [a]1Thess. 1:5 [b]2Cor. 7:2; 2Thess. 3:7
12 [a]Eph. 4:1; Phil. 1:27; Col. 1:10; 1Thess. 4:1 [b]1Cor. 1:9; 1Thess. 5:24; 2Thess. 2:14; 2Tim. 1:9
13 [a]1Thess. 1:3 [b]Matt. 10:40; Gal. 4:14; 2Pet. 3:2
14 [a]Gal. 1:22 [b]Acts 17:5, 13 [c]Heb. 10:33, 34

15 [I]Or, *chased us out* [a]Acts 2:23; 3:15; 5:30; 7:52 [b]Matt. 5:12; 23:34, 37; Luke 13:33, 34; Acts 7:52 [c]Esth. 3:8 **16** [a]Luke 11:52; Acts 13:50; 14:5, 19; 17:5, 13; 18:12; 19:9; 22:21, 22 [b]Gen. 15:16; Matt. 23:32 [c]Matt. 24:6, 14 **17** [a]1Cor. 5:3; Col. 2:5 [b]1Thess. 3:10 **18** [a]Rom. 1:13; 15:22 **19** [a]2Cor. 1:14; Phil. 2:16; 4:1

2:19 The word *parousía* (3952), translated "coming" in this verse, basically means "presence" or "arrival" (1 Cor. 16:17; 2 Cor. 7:7). Thus, the same Jesus who ascended to heaven will come again in a bodily presence (Acts 1:11) at the end of the age (Matt. 24:3). He will come in power and glory to destroy the Antichrist and evil (2 Thess. 2:8).

The return of Christ will also be a "revelation" or a "removing the cover" from something that is

(continued on next page)

or [b]crown of [I]rejoicing? *Are* not even ye in the presence of our Lord Jesus Christ [c]at his coming?[3952]

20 For ye are our glory and joy.

"Stand Fast in the Lord"

3 Wherefore [a]when we [ppt]could no longer forbear,4722 [b]we thought it good[2106] to be left at Athens alone;

2 And sent [a]Timotheus, our brother,[80] and minister[1249] of God, and our fellowlabourer in the gospel[2098] of Christ, to establish you, and to comfort you concerning your faith:[4102]

3 [a]That no man [pip]should be moved by these afflictions: for yourselves know that [b]we [pin]are appointed[2749] thereunto.

4 [a]For verily,2532 when we were with you, we [ipf]told you before that we should [pip]suffer tribulation; even as it came to pass, and ye know.

5 For this cause, [a]when I [ppt]could no longer forbear,4722 I sent to know your faith, [b]lest by some means the [ppt]tempter[3985] [ao]have tempted you, and [c]our labour[2873] be in vain.[2756]

6 [a]But now when Timotheus came from you unto us, and brought us good tidings[2097] of your faith and charity,[26] and that ye have good[18] remembrance of us always, desiring greatly to see us, [b]as we also *to see* you:

7 Therefore, brethren, [a]we were comforted over you in all our affliction and distress by your faith:

8 For now we live,[2198] if ye [a]stand fast in the Lord.

19 IOr, *glorying* [b]Prov. 16:31 [c]1Cor. 15:23; 1Thess. 3:13; Rev. 1:7; 22:12

1 [a]1Thess. 3:5 [b]Acts 17:15
2 [a]Rom. 16:21; 1Cor. 16:10; 2Cor. 1:19
3 [a]Eph. 3:13 [b]Acts 9:16; 14:22; 20:23; 21:11; 1Cor. 4:9; 2Tim. 3:12; 1Pet. 2:21
4 [a]Acts 20:24
5 [a]1Thess. 3:1 [b]1Cor. 7:5; 2Cor. 11:3 [c]Gal. 2:2; 4:11; Phil. 2:16
6 [a]Acts 18:1, 5 [b]Phil. 1:8
7 [a]2Cor. 1:4; 7:6, 7, 13
8 [a]Phil. 4:1
9 [a]1Thess. 1:2
10 [a]Acts 26:7; 2Tim. 1:3 [b]Rom. 1:10, 11; 15:32 [c]1Thess. 2:17 [d]2Cor. 13:9, 11; Col. 4:12
11 IOr, *guide* [a]Mark 1:3
12 [a]1Thess. 4:10 [b]1Thess. 4:9; 5:15; 2Pet. 1:7
13 [a]1Cor. 1:8; Phil. 1:10; 1Thess. 5:23; 2Thess. 2:17; 1John 3:20, 21 [b]Zech. 14:5; Jude 1:14

1 [a]Phil. 1:27; Col. 2:6 [b]1Thess. 2:12 [c]Col. 1:10
3 [a]Rom. 12:2; Eph. 5:17 [b]Eph. 5:27 [c]1Cor. 6:15, 18; Eph. 5:3; Col. 3:5
4 [a]Rom. 6:19; 1Cor. 6:15, 18
5 [a]Rom. 1:24, 26; Col. 3:5

9 [a]For what thanks can we render to God again for you, for all the joy wherewith we joy for your sakes before our God;

10 [a]Night and day [b]praying exceedingly[4053] [c]that we might see your face, [d]and might perfect[2675] that which is lacking in your faith?

11 Now God himself and our Father,[3962] and our Lord[2962] Jesus Christ,[5547] [I][a]direct our way[3598] unto you.

12 And the Lord[2962] [opt][a]make you to increase4121 and [opt]abound in love[26] [b]one toward another, and toward all *men,* even as we *do* toward you:

🔑 13 To the end he [aies]may [a]stablish4741 your hearts unblameable[273] in holiness[42] before God, even our Father, at the coming[3952] of our Lord Jesus Christ [b]with all his saints.[40]

Sanctification

4 Furthermore then we beseech you, brethren, and exhort[3870] *you* by the Lord Jesus, [a]that as ye [ao]have received of us [b]how ye ought [pinf]to walk [c]and [pinf]to please God, *so* ye [psa]would abound more and more.

2 For ye know what commandments[3852] we gave you by the Lord Jesus.

3 For this is [a]the will[2307] of God, *even* [b]your sanctification, [c]that ye [pinf]should abstain[567] from fornication:4202

🔑 4 [a]That every one of you should know how to possess his vessel in sanctification and honour;

5 [a]Not in the lust[3806] of concupis-

(continued from previous page)

hidden, noted by the Greek word *apokálupsis* (602), disclosure. The power and glory that Christ now possesses will be unveiled and disclosed to the world (1 Pet. 4:13). Christ is now reigning as Lord at God's right hand (Heb. 12:2), sharing God's throne (Rev. 3:21). Although His authority is not discernible to the world, it will be made visible by His *apokálupsis*, "revelation."

Another word that is related to the Second Coming of the Lord is *epipháneia* (2015), which means "a manifestation." In Ancient Greek, the word was used especially to refer to the appearance of gods and of the manifestation of divine power or providence. However, in the New Testament, it is used of the appearing of the manifestation of Jesus Christ on earth (2 Thess. 2:8; 2 Tim. 1:10; 4:1, 8; Titus 2:13).

🔑 **3:13** See note on 1 Thessalonians 2:19.

🔑 **4:4–7** See the introduction to 1 Thessalonians.

cence,[1939] [b]even as the Gentiles [c]which
know not God:
6 [a]That no *man* [pinf]go beyond[5233] and
[pinfI]defraud his brother [II]in *any* matter: because that the Lord [b]*is* the avenger[1558] of
all such, as we also have forewarned you
and testified.[1263]
7 For God [ao]hath not called[2564] us
unto uncleanness,[167] [a]but unto holiness.[38]
8 [a]He therefore that [pptI]despiseth, despiseth not man, but God, [b]who [apt]hath
also given1325 unto us his holy[40]
Spirit.[4151]
9 But as touching brotherly love[5360]
[a]ye need not that I write unto you: for [b]ye
yourselves are taught of God [pinfc]to love[25]
one another.
10 [a]And indeed ye do it toward all
the brethren which are in all Macedonia:
but we beseech[3870] you, brethren, [b]that ye
[pinf]increase more and more;
11 And that ye [pinf]study [pinf]to be
quiet,[2270] and [pinfa]to do[4238] your own business, and [pinfb]to work with your own
hands, as we commanded you;
12 [a]That ye [psa]may walk honestly toward them that are without,1854 and *that*
ye [psa]may have lack [I]of nothing.

Christ's Return

13 But I would not have you to be
ignorant,[50] brethren, concerning them
which [pfpp]are asleep, that ye [psa]sorrow
not, [a]even as others [b]which have no
hope.[1680]
14 For [a]if we believe[4100] that Jesus
died[599] and rose again,[450] even so [b]them
also which [apt]sleep in Jesus will God
bring with him.
15 For this we say unto you [a]by
the word[3056] of the Lord, that [b]we
which [ppt]are alive[2198] *and* [ppp]remain
unto the coming[3952] of the Lord
[asba]shall not prevent5348 them which
[apt]are asleep.
16 For [a]the Lord himself shall descend[2597] from heaven[3772] with a shout,
with the voice of the archangel,[743] and
with [b]the trump of God: [c]and the
dead[3498] in Christ shall rise[450] first:
17 [a]Then we which [ppt]are alive *and*
[ppp]remain [fp]shall be caught up[726] together
with them [b]in the clouds, to meet the
Lord in the air: and so [c]shall we ever be
with the Lord.
18 [a]Wherefore [pimI]comfort[3870] one another with these words.

"A Thief in the Night"

5 But of [a]the times[5550] and the seasons,[2540] brethren, [b]ye have no need
that I write[1125] unto you.
2 For yourselves know perfectly that
[a]the day[2250] of the Lord[2962] so cometh as
a thief in the night.

5 [b]Eph. 4:17, 18 [c]1Cor. 15:34; Gal. 4:8; Eph. 2:12; 4:18; 2Thess. 1:8 **6** [I]Or, *oppress, or, overreach* [II]Or, *in the matter* [a]Lev. 19:11, 13; 1Cor. 6:8 [b]2Thess. 1:8 **7** [a]Lev. 11:44; 19:2; 1Cor. 1:2; Heb. 12:14; 1Pet. 1:14, 15 **8** [I]Or, *rejecteth* [a]Luke 10:16 [b]1Cor. 2:10; 7:40; 1John 3:24 **9** [a]1Thess. 5:1 [b]Jer. 31:34; John 6:45; 14:26; Heb. 8:11; 1John 2:20, 27 [c]Matt. 22:39; John 13:34; 15:12; Eph. 5:2; 1Pet. 4:8; 1John 3:11, 23; 4:21 **10** [a]1Thess. 1:7 [b]1Thess. 3:12 **11** [a]2Thess. 3:11; 1Pet. 4:15 [b]Acts 20:35; Eph. 4:28; 2Thess. 3:7, 8, 12 **12** [I]Or, *of no man* [a]Rom. 13:13; 2Cor. 8:21; Col. 4:5; 1Pet. 2:12 **13** [a]Lev. 19:28; Deut. 14:1, 2; 2Sam. 12:20 [b]Eph. 2:12 **14** [a]1Cor. 15:13 [b]1Cor. 15:18, 23; 1Thess. 3:13 **15** [a]1Kgs. 13:17, 18; 20:35 [b]1Cor. 15:51

16 [a]Matt. 24:30, 31; Acts 1:11; 2Thess. 1:7 [b]1Cor. 15:52 [c]1Cor. 15:23, 52 **17** [a]1Cor. 15:51 [b]Acts 1:9; Rev. 11:12 [c]John 12:26; 14:3; 17:24 **18** [I]Or, *exhort* [a]1Thess. 5:11 **1** [a]Matt. 24:3, 36; Acts 1:7 [b]1Thess. 4:9 **2** [a]Matt. 24:43, 44; 25:13; Luke 12:39, 40; 2Pet. 3:10; Rev. 3:3; 16:15

4:13–18 See the introduction to 1 Thessalonians and the note on 1 Thessalonians 2:19.

4:15 The word here that is translated "prevent" is derived from the Greek verb *phthánō* (5348), which means "to anticipate, to be before." Also in this verse, the dead are called, "them which are asleep." The Greek word used is *koimēthéntas* (2837), "to sleep or slumber." In this verse, it refers to the body being asleep, not the soul.

4:17 There are two important Greek words in this verse. The first is *harpagēsómetha,* translated "caught up." This refers to a specific moment in the future when believers will be caught up by Jesus Christ, as He descends from heaven. The other word is "meet," translated from the Greek phrase *eis apántēsin* (1519, 529), which means "to come into the presence of, to meet." This occurs after the dead have been raised (1 Thess. 4:14–16). Then the bodies of those who are alive will be transformed into new bodies (see note on 2 Cor. 5:1).

5:2 The "Day of the Lord" holds an important place in prophecy. Amos declared that the "Day" signified judgment for Israel (cf. Is. 2:12–22; Ezek. 13:5; Joel 1:15; 2:1, 11; Zeph. 1:14; Zech. 13:1; see note on Zeph. 1:7).

Several prophets refer to it as God's "day of judgment" upon individual nations such as Babylon

(continued on next page)

3 For when they [psa]shall say, Peace[1515] and safety;[803] then [a]sudden destruction[3639] cometh upon them, [b]as travail[5604] upon a woman with child; and they shall not escape.
4 [a]But ye, brethren, are not in darkness,[4655] that that day [aosb]should overtake[2638] you as a thief.
5 Ye are all [a]the [an]children[5207] of light,[5457] and the [an]children of the day: we are not of the night, nor of darkness.
6 [a]Therefore [psa]let us not sleep,[2518] as *do* others; but [psab]let us watch[1127] and [psa]be sober.
7 For [a]they that [ppt]sleep sleep in the night; and they that [ppp]be drunken [b]are drunken in the night.
8 But let us, who are of the day, [psa]be sober, [apta]putting on the breastplate of faith[4102] and love;[26] and for an helmet, the hope[1680] of salvation.[4991]
9 For [a]God [aom]hath not appointed[5087] us to wrath,[3709] [b]but to obtain salvation by our Lord Jesus Christ,
10 [a]Who [apt]died for us, that, whether we [psa]wake or [psa]sleep, we [asba]should live[2198] together with him.
11 [a]Wherefore [I]comfort[3870] yourselves together, and edify one another, even as also ye do.

Final Instructions

12 And we beseech you, brethren, [a]to know[1492] them which [ppt]labour among you, and [ppt]are over you in the Lord, and [ppt]admonish[3560] you;
13 And [pinf]to esteem[2233] them very highly in love for their work's[2041] sake. [a]*And* [pim]be at peace among yourselves.
14 Now we [I]exhort[3870] you, brethren, [pima]warn[3560] them that are [II]unruly,[813] [pimb]comfort the feebleminded,[3642] [c]support[472] the weak,[772] [d]be patient[3114] toward all *men.*
15 [a]See[3708] that none [aosb]render evil[2556] for evil unto any *man;* but ever [pimb]follow that which is good,[18] both among yourselves, and to all *men.*
16 [pima]Rejoice[5463] evermore.
17 [pima]Pray[4336] without ceasing.[89]
18 [a]In every thing [pim]give thanks: for this is the will[2307] of God in Christ Jesus concerning you.
19 [pima]Quench not the Spirit.[4151]
20 [pima]Despise not prophesyings.[4394]
21 [pima]Prove all things; [b]hold fast[2722] that which is good.

3 [a]Isa. 13:6-9; Luke 17:27-29; 21:34, 35; 2Thess. 1:9 [b]Jer. 13:21; Hos. 13:13 **4** [a]Rom. 13:12, 13; 1John 2:8 **5** [a]Eph. 5:8 **6** [a]Matt. 25:5 [b]Matt. 24:42; 25:13; Rom. 13:11-13; 1Pet. 5:8 **7** [a]Luke 21:34, 36; Rom. 13:13; 1Cor. 15:34; Eph. 5:14 [b]Acts 2:15 **8** [a]Isa. 59:17; Eph. 6:14, 16, 17 **9** [a]Rom. 9:22; 1Thess. 1:10; 1Pet. 2:8; Jude 1:4 [b]2Thess. 2:13, 14 **10** [a]Rom. 14:8, 9; 2Cor. 5:15 **11** [I]Or, *exhort* [a]1Thess. 4:18 **12** [a]1Cor. 16:18; Phil. 2:29; 1Tim. 5:17; Heb. 13:7, 17 **13** [a]Mark 9:50 **14** [I]Or, *beseech* [II]Or, *disorderly* [a]2Thess. 3:11, 12 [b]Heb. 12:12 [c]Rom. 14:1; 15:1; Gal. 6:1, 2 [d]Gal. 5:22; Eph. 4:2; Col. 3:12; 2Tim. 4:2 **15** [a]Lev. 19:18; Prov. 20:22; 24:29; Matt. 5:39, 44; Rom. 12:17; 1Cor. 6:7; 1Pet. 3:9 [b]Gal. 6:10; 1Thess. 3:12 **16** [a]2Cor. 6:10; Phil. 4:4 **17** [a]Luke 18:1; 21:36; Rom. 12:12; Eph. 6:18; Col. 4:2; 1Pet. 4:7 **18** [a]Eph. 5:20; Col. 3:17 **19** [a]Eph. 4:30; 1Tim. 4:14; 2Tim. 1:6; 1Cor. 14:30 **20** [a]1Cor. 14:1, 39 **21** [a]1Cor. 2:11, 15; 1John 4:1 [b]Phil. 4:8

(continued from previous page)
(Is. 13:6–9), Egypt (Jer. 46:10), Edom (Obad. 1:8), and many other nations (Joel 2:31; 3:14; Obad. 1:15). Thus, the Day of the Lord represents the occasion when Jehovah will actively and openly intervene to punish sin.

During the time period of the Day of the Lord, there will be those who truly repent and are saved, but those who remain enemies of the Lord, whether Jews or Gentiles, will be punished.

In the New Testament, the Day of the Lord is related to the Second Coming of Christ. So also is the phrase "the Day of our Lord Jesus Christ" (1 Cor. 1:8; 5:5; Phil. 1:6, 10; 2:16; 2 Thess. 2:2). Both expressions, the "Day of the Lord" and the "Day of Christ," refer to time periods of judgment by Christ. The Day of the Lord will include the time of the Great Tribulation (cf. Rev. 6—20). It also refers to the liberation by Christ of His Church. Zechariah 14:1–4 explains that the events of the Second Advent are included in the program of the Day of the Lord. Thus, the Day of the Lord and the Day of Christ occur simultaneously. For the Church, it is the rapture; and for the unbelieving world, it is the beginning of judgment and the Tribulation. If the Day of the Lord began after the Second Advent, it could not come as a "thief in the night," unexpected and unheralded, since that particular advent is preceded by signs (1 Thess. 5:2; 2 Pet. 3:10). Consequently, the only way these events could occur unexpectedly would be for them to begin immediately after the rapture of the Church. The Day of the Lord, therefore, is that extended period of time when God begins to deal with Israel after the rapture of the church. It also continues through the Second Advent and the millennial age, preceding the creation of the new heaven and new earth.

22 [pim][a]Abstain[567] from all appearance[1491] of evil.[4190]

🗝 23 And [a]the very God of peace[1515] [opt][b]sanctify[37] you wholly;[3651] and *I pray God* your whole[3648] spirit and soul[5590] and body[4983] [opt][c]be preserved blameless[274] unto the coming[3952] of our Lord Jesus Christ.

24 [a]Faithful[4103] *is* he that [ppt]calleth you, who also will do *it*.

25 Brethren, [a]pray for us.

26 [aim][a]Greet[782] all the brethren[80] with an holy kiss.

27 I [I]charge you by the Lord that [a]this epistle[1992] be read unto all the holy brethren.

28 [a]The grace of our Lord Jesus Christ *be* with you. Amen.[281]

22 [a]1Thess. 4:12
23 [a]Phil. 4:9 [b]1Thess. 3:13 [c]1Cor. 1:8
24 [a]1Cor. 1:9; 10:13; 2Thess. 3:3
25 [a]Col. 4:3; 2Thess. 3:1
26 [a]Rom. 16:16
27 [I]Or, *adjure* [a]Col. 4:16; 2Thess. 3:14
28 [a]Rom. 16:20, 24; 2Thess. 3:18

🗝 **5:23** See the note on Ecclesiastes 12:7 concerning the material and immaterial parts of the body and the note on 1 Thessalonians 2:19 concerning the Second Coming of Christ.

The Second Epistle of Paul to the

THESSALONIANS

This second letter of Paul to the Thessalonians was written about A.D. 51–52, and was sent from Corinth soon after his first letter. Some members of the congregation in Thessalonica did not have a clear understanding of Paul's teaching concerning the "Day of the Lord" in his first epistle to them (1 Thess. 5:1–11). There was also a misunderstanding among some of the people regarding the imminent return of the Lord Jesus. They apparently had misinterpreted the meaning of the phrase "as a thief in the night" (1 Thess. 5:2) and confused the concepts of the suddenness of the Lord's coming with its immediacy. They thought that since Christ would be coming soon, there was no point in continuing to work. When the people encountered increased persecution, they felt that the "Day of the Lord" had already come and they had somehow missed Christ's return.

Paul corrects them in this second epistle by explaining that certain events must take place before Christ will return. For example, he states that there will be a worldwide rebellion against God, led by one who will represent the epitome of lawlessness and anarchy (2 Thess. 2:3–9). Moreover, Paul tells the believers in Thessalonica not to live at the expense of others, but to return to the Lord's work (2 Thess. 3:10–12).

In summary, the Thessalonians were apprehensive about the persistent persecution that they were enduring (2 Thess. 1:4, 5). Paul wrote this letter to comfort and exhort these believers to continue serving the Lord in spite of the hardships.

1 Paul, [a]and Silvanus, and Timotheus, unto the church[1577] of the Thessalonians [b]in God[2316] our Father[3962] and the Lord[2962] Jesus Christ:[5547]

2 [a]Grace[5485] unto you, and peace,[1515] from God our Father and the Lord Jesus Christ.

We Know You Are Suffering

3 [a]We [pin]are bound [pinf]to thank[2168] God always for you, brethren, as it is meet,514 because that your faith groweth exceedingly, and the charity[26] of every one of you all toward each other aboundeth;

4 So that [a]we ourselves [pinf]glory in you in the churches of God [b]for your patience and faith [c]in all your persecutions and tribulations that ye endure:[430]

5 *Which is* [a]a manifest token of the righteous[1342] judgment[2920] of God, that ye [aies]may be counted worthy of the kingdom[932] of God, [b]for which ye also suffer:[3958]

6 [a]Seeing *it is* a righteous thing with God [ainf]to recompense tribulation to them that [ppt]trouble you;

🗝 7 And to you who [ppp]are troubled [a]rest[425] with us, when [b]the Lord Jesus shall be revealed[602] from heaven[3772] with [I]his mighty angels,[32]

8 [a]In flaming fire taking vengeance on them [b]that know not God, and [c]that [ppt]obey[5219] not the gospel[2098] of our Lord Jesus Christ:

9 [a]Who shall be punished with everlasting[166] destruction[3639] from the presence of the Lord, and [b]from the glory[1391] of his power;

10 [a]When he shall come to be glorified[1740] in his saints,[40] [b]and to be admired2296 in all them that [apt]believe[4100] (because our testimony[3142] among you was believed) in that day.[2250]

11 Wherefore also we pray always

1 [a]2Cor. 1:19 [b]1Thess. 1:1
2 [a]1Cor. 1:3
3 [a]1Thess. 1:2, 3; 3:6, 9; 2Thess. 2:13
4 [a]2Cor. 7:14; 9:2; 1Thess. 2:19, 20 [b]1Thess. 1:3 [c]1Thess. 2:14
5 [a]Phil. 1:28 [b]1Thess. 2:14
6 [a]Rev. 6:10
7 [I]Gr. *the angels of his power* [a]Rev. 14:13 [b]1Thess. 4:16; Jude 1:14
8 [a]Heb. 10:27; 12:29; 2Pet. 3:7; Rev. 21:8 [b]Ps. 79:6; 1Thess. 4:5 [c]Rom. 2:8
9 [a]Phil. 3:19; 2Pet. 3:7 [b]Deut. 33:2; Isa. 2:19; 2Thess. 2:8
10 [a]Ps. 89:7 [b]Ps. 68:35

🗝 **1:7** See note on 1 Thessalonians 2:19.

for you, that our God [aosb]would [a]count you worthy of *this* calling, and [aosb]fulfil all the good pleasure[2107] of *his* goodness,[19] and [b]the work[2041] of faith with power:

12 [a]That the name of our Lord Jesus Christ may be glorified[1740] in you, and ye in him, according to the grace of our God and the Lord Jesus Christ.

"The Day of Christ"

2 🔑Now we beseech you, brethren, [a]by the coming[3952] of our Lord Jesus Christ, [b]and *by* our gathering together[1997] unto him,

🔑2 [a]That ye [aies]be not soon shaken[4531] in mind,[3563] or be troubled, neither by spirit,[4151] nor by word,[3056] nor by letter as from us, as that the day[2250] of Christ [pfi]is at hand.[1764]

🔑3 [aosi][a]Let no man deceive[1818] you by any means: for *that day shall not come,* [b]except there [aosb]come[2064] a falling away[646] first, and [c]that man[444] of sin[266] [asbp]be revealed, [d]the son[5207] of perdition;[684]

4 Who [ppt]opposeth[480] and [ppt][a]exalteth himself [b]above all that [ppp]is called God, or that is worshipped;[4574] so that he as God [ainf]sitteth in the temple[3485] of God, [ppt]shewing himself that he is God.[2316]

5 Remember ye not, that, when I was yet with you, I [ipf]told you these things?

🔑6 And now ye know what [ppt]withholdeth[2722] that he [aies]might be revealed in his time.[2540]

7 For [a]the mystery[3466] of iniquity[458] doth already work:[1754] only he who now [ppt]letteth[2722] *will let,* until he [asbm]be taken out of the way.

🔑8 And then [fp]shall that Wicked be revealed,[601] [a]whom the Lord[2962] shall consume [b]with the spirit[4151] of his mouth, and shall destroy [c]with the brightness[2015] of his coming:

🔑9 *Even him,* whose coming is [a]after the working of Satan[4567] with all

11 [a]2Thess. 1:5 [b]1Thess. 1:3
12 [a]1Pet. 1:7; 4:14

1 [a]1Thess. 4:16 [b]Matt. 24:31; Mark. 13:27; 1Thess. 4:17
2 [a]Matt. 24:4; Eph. 5:6; 1John 4:1
3 [a]Matt. 24:4; Eph. 5:6 [b]1Tim. 4:1 [c]Dan. 7:25; 1John 2:18; Rev. 13:11 [d]John 17:12
4 [a]Isa. 14:13; Ezek. 28:2, 6, 9 [b]Dan. 7:25; 11:36; Rev. 13:6 [c]1Cor. 8:5
7 [a]1John 2:18; 4:3
8 [a]Dan. 7:10, 11 [b]Job. 4:9; Isa. 11:4; Hos. 6:5; Rev. 2:16; 19:15, 20, 21 [c]2Thess. 1:8, 9; Heb. 10:27
9 [a]John 8:41; Eph. 2:2; Rev. 18:23

🔑 **2:1** See note on 1 Thessalonians 2:19.
🔑 **2:2** See note on 1 Thessalonians 5:2.
🔑 **2:3–12** See note on Revelation 13:1–18.
🔑 **2:3–9** The "man of sin" is called the Antichrist in other Scripture passages (1 John 2:18; 4:3; 2 John 1:7). The preposition *antí* (473), "against," indicates this man's opposition to, not a replacement of Christ (Dan. 7:7, 8, 21; Matt. 24:15; Rev. 13:1–18). The characteristic of this individual is that he "opposeth and exalteth himself above all that is called God, or that is worshipped" (v. 4). He will be a miracle worker and even claim to be God. His coming will be "after the working of Satan" (v. 9), but it will not be Satan. It is clear that Paul thinks that Satan is not concerned with the past, but with the future. Paul does not see the world evolving gradually into a perfected state, but the fact of evil continuing right up until the end. At that time, evil will make its greatest challenge to good, and the forces of evil will be led by a mysterious figure. This person will be empowered by Satan and is the instrument of Satan's climactic challenge to the things of God. Paul predicts that Christ will consume the "man of sin . . . with the spirit of his mouth" (vv. 3, 8). At that time, Satan and all of his conspirators will be defeated.
🔑 **2:6, 7** Paul refers here to the Holy Spirit as the restraining force in this world, restricting the many little "antichrists" existing today (1 John 2:18), as well as the final Antichrist. In verse six, the Holy Spirit is called *tó katéchon* (3588, 2722) or "that (which) withholdeth." This uses the neuter gender and corresponds to the phrase *tó Pneúma* (3588, 4151), "the Spirit," also in the neuter (John 14:26). In verse seven, it is *hó katéchōn*, "he who letteth," denoting that the Antichrist will never be able to do anything without the specific permission of the Holy Spirit. Of course, verse seven does not refer to a departure of the Holy Spirit, but to the removal of His restraining power. This will allow Satan and the Antichrist to have free reign on the earth, but whatever happens will help to further God's plan according to His own timetable.
🔑 **2:8** See note on 1 Thessalonians 2:19.
🔑 **2:9** In this verse there are three words that explain supernatural manifestations or miracles: *dúnamis* (1411), *sēmeíon* (4592), and *téras* (5059). Observe how the miracles mentioned in this verse *(continued on next page)*

power[1411] and [b]signs[4592] and lying wonders,[5059]

🔑 10 And with all deceivableness of unrighteousness in [a]them that [ppt]perish; because they [ao]received not the love[26] of the truth,[225] that they [aies]might be saved.[4982]

11 And [a]for this cause God shall send them strong delusion, [b]that they should believe[4100] a lie:

12 That they all [asbp]might be damned[2919] who [apt]believed not the truth, but [apt][a]had pleasure[2106] in unrighteousness.[93]

Stand Firm

13 But [a]we [pin]are bound [pinf]to give thanks[2168] alway to God for you, brethren beloved[25] of the Lord, because God [aom][b]hath [c]from the beginning chosen[138] you to salvation[4991] [d]through sanctification[38] of the Spirit and belief of the truth:

14 Whereunto he called you by our gospel,[2098] to [a]the obtaining of the glory of our Lord Jesus Christ.

15 Therefore, brethren, [a]stand fast, and hold [b]the traditions 3862 which ye [aop]have been taught,[1321] whether by word,[3056] or our epistle. 1992

16 [a]Now our Lord Jesus Christ himself, and God, even our Father, [b]which [apt]hath loved[25] us, and [apt]hath given *us* everlasting consolation[3874] and [c]good[18] hope through grace,[5485]

17 [opt]Comfort[3870] your hearts,[2588] [a]and [opt]stablish 4741 you in every good word and work.[2041]

3

Finally, brethren, [a]pray for us, that the word[3056] of the Lord[2962] [psa][1]may have *free* course, and [psmp]be glorified,[1392] even as *it is* with you:

2 And [a]that we [asbp]may be delivered[4506] from unreasonable and wicked[4190] men:[444] [b]for all *men* have not faith.[4102]

3 But [a]the Lord is faithful,[4103] who shall stablish you, and [b]keep *you* from [art]evil.[4190]

4 And [a]we have confidence[3982] in the Lord touching you, that ye both do and will do the things which we command[3853] you.

5 And [a]the Lord [opt]direct your hearts[2588] into the love[26] of God, and into [b]the patient waiting for Christ.[5547]

"Be Not Weary in Well Doing"

6 Now we command you, brethren,[80] in the name[3686] of our Lord Jesus Christ, [a]that ye [pim]withdraw yourselves[4724] [b]from every brother that [ppt]walketh [c]disorderly, 814 and not after [d]the tradition 3862 which he received of us.

7 For yourselves know [a]how ye ought [pinf]to follow us: for [b]we behaved not ourselves disorderly[812] among you;

8 Neither did we eat any man's bread for nought; 1432 but [ppt][a]wrought[2038] with labour and travail[3449] night and day, that we [aipr]might not be chargeable 1912 to any of you:

9 [a]Not because we have not power,[1849] but to [aosb]make [b]ourselves an ensample[5179] unto you [aies]to follow us.

10 For even when we were with you, this we [ipf]commanded you, [a]that if any would not [pinf]work,[2038] neither [pim]should he eat. 2068

11 For we hear that there are some [a]which [ppt]walk among you disorderly, 814 [b]working not at all, but [ppt]are busybodies.

12 [a]Now them that are such we command[3853] and exhort[3870] by our Lord Jesus Christ, [b]that with quietness 2271 they [ppt]work, and [psa]eat their own bread.

---

9 [b]Deut. 13:1; Matt. 24:24; Rev. 13:13; 19:20
10 [a]2Cor. 2:15; 4:3
11 [a]Rom. 1:24; 1Kgs. 22:22; Ezek. 14:9 [b]Matt. 24:5, 11; 1Tim. 4:1
12 [a]Rom. 1:32
13 [a]2Thess. 1:3 [b]1Thess. 1:4 [c]Eph. 1:4 [d]Luke 1:75; 1Pet. 1:2
14 [a]John 17:22; 1Thess. 2:12; 1Pet. 5:10
15 [a]1Cor. 16:13; Phil. 4:1 [b]1Cor. 11:2; 2Thess. 3:6
16 [a]2Thess. 1:1, 2 [b]1John 4:10; Rev. 1:5 [c]1Pet. 1:3
17 [a]1Cor. 1:8; 1Thess. 3:13; 1Pet. 5:10

1 [1]Gr. *may run* [a]Eph. 6:19; Col. 4:3; 1Thess. 5:25
2 [a]Rom. 15:31 [b]Acts 28:24; Rom. 10:16
3 [a]1Cor. 1:9; 1Thess. 5:24 [b]John 17:15; 2Pet. 2:9
4 [a]2Cor. 7:16; Gal. 5:10
5 [a]1Chr. 29:18 [b]1Thess. 1:3
6 [a]Rom. 16:17; 2Thess. 3:14; 1Tim. 6:5; 2John 1:10 [b]1Cor. 5:11, 13 [c]1Thess. 4:11; 5:14; 2Thess. 3:11, 12, 14 [d]2Thess. 2:15
7 [a]1Cor. 4:16; 11:1; 1Thess. 1:6, 7 [b]1Thess. 2:10
8 [a]Acts 18:3; 20:34; 2Cor. 11:9; 1Thess. 2:9
9 [a]1Cor. 9:6; 1Thess. 2:6 [b]2Thess. 3:7
10 [a]Gen. 3:19; 1Thess. 4:11
11 [a]2Thess. 3:6 [b]1Thess. 4:11; 1Tim. 5:13; 1Pet. 4:15
12 [a]1Thess. 4:11 [b]Eph. 4:28

(continued from previous page)
are accomplished by the power of Satan. Miracle working is not necessarily evidence of God's power (Acts 19:13, cf. Ex. 7:22).

🔑 **2:10–12** See note on Revelation 7:1–17.

13 But ye, brethren, [aosi][I][a]be not
weary[1573] in [ppt]well doing.
14 And if any man obey[5219] not our
word[3056] [I]by this epistle,1992 [pim]note that
man, and [pim][a]have no company4874 with
him, that he [asbp]may be ashamed.1788
15 [a]Yet [pim]count *him* not as an enemy,
[b]but [pim]admonish[3560] *him* as a brother.
16 Now [a]the Lord of peace[1515] himself [opt]give1325 you peace always by all
means. The Lord *be* with you all.
17 [a]The salutation783 of Paul with
mine own hand, which is the [an]token[4592]
in every epistle:1992 so I write.[1125]
18 [a]The grace of our Lord Jesus
Christ *be* with you all. Amen.281

13 [I]Or, *faint not* [a]Gal. 6:9
14 [I]Or, *signify that man by this epistle* [a]Matt. 18:17; 1Cor. 5:9, 11; 2Thess. 3:6
15 [a]Lev. 19:17; 1Thess. 5:14 [b]Titus 3:10
16 [a]Rom. 15:33; 16:20; 1Cor. 14:33; 2Cor. 13:11; 1Thess. 5:23
17 [a]1Cor. 16:21; Col. 4:18
18 [a]Rom. 16:24

The First Epistle of Paul to

TIMOTHY

The two epistles to Timothy and the one to Titus, because of their special instruction for church leaders, are commonly known as the Pastoral Epistles. It is generally believed that they were written just before Paul's martyrdom, about A.D. 66. In these letters, Paul records his thoughts and feelings as he prepared to pass his ministry on to others.

Timothy's mother was a Jew, and his father was a Greek (Acts. 16:1). By the time of Paul's second missionary journey, Timothy's mother had also become a Christian. His mother and grandmother had instructed him in the Old Testament (2 Tim. 1:5).

Timothy was a native of Lystra (Acts 16:1) and was highly esteemed by his Christian brethren both in Lystra and Iconium (Acts 16:2). He came to know the Lord through Paul's ministry in Lystra on his first missionary journey. During the second journey, Paul and Silas added Timothy to their party (Acts 15:36–41). To avoid criticism from the Jews, Timothy was circumcised by Paul before they set out on their journey.

Paul sent Timothy back to Thessalonica as his repesentative (1 Thess. 3:1, 2) when he was hindered by Satan from going there himself (1 Thess. 2:17, 18). The next time he is mentioned, Paul is sending him away from Ephesus with Erastus on another important mission to Macedonia (Acts 19:22). From there, he was to proceed to Corinth (1 Cor. 4:17). Apparently, Timothy was of a timid nature because Paul encouraged the believers in Corinth to accept him (1 Cor. 16:10, 11, cf. 1 Tim. 4:12).

Timothy also accompanied Paul on the journey to Jerusalem (Acts 20:4, 5) and was with Paul in Rome when he wrote three of the Prison Epistles (Phil. 1:1; 2:19; Col. 1:1; Phile. 1:1). After his release from prison, Paul became engaged in further ministry in the East, and left Timothy at Ephesus (1 Tim. 1:3) to deal with the false teachers, supervise public worship, and aid the church in the appointment of officials. Paul hoped to eventually rejoin Timothy, but wrote this letter because he feared that he might be delayed. The second letter to Timothy was written after Paul was arrested again and put on trial for his life (see the introduction to 2 Timothy). There is no indication as to whether Timothy visited Paul as he had requested. In fact, nothing else is known about Timothy except that he himself became a prisoner (Heb. 13:23).

Paul was writing to Timothy to instruct him on how to deal with the growing problem of false teachers that was evident in the church at Ephesus. The fact that these false teachers had infiltrated the church in Ephesus was a sad fulfillment of Paul's prediction nearly five years earlier (Acts 20:28–30). Paul urged Timothy to boldly withstand these evil men by upholding the truth of the Scripture.

1 Paul, an apostle**652** of Jesus Christ**5547**
[a]by the commandment**2003** [b]of
God**2316** our Saviour,**4990** and Lord Jesus
Christ, [c]*which is* our hope;**1680**

2 Unto [a]Timothy, [b]*my* own son**5043** in
the faith:**4102** [c]Grace,**5485** mercy,**1656** *and*
peace,**1515** from God our Father**3962** and
Jesus Christ our Lord.

1 [a]Acts 9:15; Gal. 1:1, 11 [b]1Tim. 2:3; 4:10; Titus 1:3; 2:10; 3:4; Jude 1:25 [c]Col. 1:27
2 [a]Acts 16:1; 1Cor. 4:17; Phil. 2:19; 1Thess. 3:2 [b]Titus 1:4 [c]Gal. 1:3; 2Tim. 1:2; 1Pet. 1:2

False Doctrine

🗝 3 As I besought thee to abide still4537
at Ephesus, [a]when I [ppt]went4198 into
Macedonia, that thou [aosb]mightest charge
some [b]that they teach**2085** no other doctrine,

3 [a]Acts 20:1, 3; Phil. 2:24 [b]Gal. 1:6, 7; 1Tim. 6:3, 10

🗝 **1:3** See the introduction to 1 Timothy.

4 [a]Neither [pinf]give heed to fables[3454]
and endless genealogies,[1076] [b]which
minister[3930] questions, rather than
godly edifying3620 which is in faith:[4102] *so*
do.
5 Now [a]the end[5056] of the commandment[3852] is charity[26] [b]out of a
pure[2513] heart,[2588] and *of* a good[18] conscience,[4893] and *of* faith unfeigned:[505]
6 From which some [apt]having
swerved [ao]have turned aside unto [a]vain
jangling;3150
7 Desiring to be teachers of the law;
[a]understanding[3539] neither what they say,
nor whereof they affirm.[1226]
8 But we know that [a]the law[3551] *is*
good,[2570] if a man use it lawfully;
9 [a]Knowing this, that the law [pin]is not
made[2749] for a righteous[1342] man, but for
the lawless[459] and disobedient,[506] for the
ungodly[765] and for sinners,[268] for un-
holy462 and profane,[952] for murderers of
fathers and murderers of mothers, for
manslayers,
10 For whoremongers,4205 for them
that defile themselves with mankind,
for menstealers, for liars, for perjured
persons, and if there be any other[2087]
thing that is contrary [a]to sound[5198] doctrine;[1319]
11 According to the glorious[1391]
gospel[2098] of [a]the blessed[3107] God, [b]which
was committed[4100] to my trust.

Paul's Personal Expression of Thanksgiving to God

12 And I thank[5485] Christ Jesus our
Lord, [a]who [apt]hath enabled me, [b]for that
he counted me faithful,[4103] [aptc]putting me
into the ministry;[1248]
13 [a]Who was before a blasphemer,[989]
and a persecutor, and injurious:[5197] but I
[aop]obtained mercy, because [b]I did *it* [ppt]ig-
norantly[50] in unbelief.[570]
14 [a]And the grace[5485] of our Lord
[ao]was exceeding abundant [b]with faith[4102]
[c]and love[26] which is in Christ Jesus.
15 [a]This *is* a faithful[4103] saying,[3056]
and worthy of all acceptation,[594] that
[b]Christ Jesus came into the world[2889] [ainf]to
save[4982] sinners;[268] of whom I am chief.
16 Howbeit235 for this cause [a]I [aop]ob-
tained mercy, that in me first Jesus Christ
might shew forth all longsuffering, [b]for a
pattern[5296] to them which [ppt]should hereafter [pinf]believe[4100] on him to life[2222] everlasting.[166]
17 Now unto [a]the King[935] eternal,[165]
[b]immortal,[862] [c]invisible, [d]the only wise[4680]
God,[2316] [e]*be* honour and glory[1391] for ever
and ever. Amen.281
18 This charge[3852] [a]I commit unto
thee, son Timothy, [b]according to the
prophecies[4394] which [ppt]went before[4254]
on thee, that thou by them [psmp]mightest
[c]war a good warfare;
🔑 19 [a]Holding faith,[4102] and a good[18]
conscience;[4893] which some [apt]having put
away concerning faith [ao]have [b]made shipwreck:
20 Of whom is [a]Hymenaeus and
[b]Alexander; whom I [ao]have [c]delivered
unto Satan,[4567] that they [asbp]may
learn[3811] not [pinf]to [d]blaspheme.[987]

4 [a]1Tim. 4:7; 6:4, 20; 2Tim. 2:14, 16, 23; Titus 1:14; 3:9 [b]1Tim. 6:4
5 [a]Rom. 13:8, 10; Gal. 5:14 [b]2Tim. 2:22
6 [a]1Tim. 6:4, 20
7 [a]1Tim. 6:4
8 [a]Rom. 7:12
9 [a]Gal. 3:19; 5:23
10 [a]1Tim. 6:3; 2Tim. 4:3; Titus 1:9; 2:1
11 [a]1Tim. 6:15 [b]1Cor. 9:17; Gal. 2:7; Col. 1:25; 1Thess. 2:4; 1Tim. 2:7; 2Tim. 1:11; Titus 1:3
12 [a]2Cor. 12:9 [b]1Cor. 7:25 [c]2Cor. 3:5, 6; 4:1; Col. 1:25
13 [a]Acts 8:3; 9:1; 1Cor. 15:9; Phil. 3:6 [b]Luke 23:34; John 9:39, 41; Acts 3:17; 26:9
14 [a]Rom. 5:20; 1Cor. 15:10 [b]2Tim. 1:13 #$Luke 7:47
15 [a]1Tim. 3:1; 4:9; 2Tim. 2:11; Titus 3:8 [b]Matt. 9:13; Mark 2:17; Luke 5:32; 19:10; Rom. 5:8; 1John 3:5
16 [a]2Cor. 4:1 [b]Acts 13:39
17 [a]Ps. 10:16; 145:13; Dan. 7:14; 1Tim. 6:15, 16 [b]Rom. 1:23 [c]John 1:18; Heb. 11:27; 1John 4:12 [d]Rom. 16:27; Jude 1:25 [e]1Chr. 29:11
18 [a]1Tim. 6:13, 14, 20; 2Tim. 2:2 [b]1Tim. 4:14 [c]1Tim. 6:12; 2Tim. 2:3; 4:7
19 [a]1Tim. 3:9 [b]1Tim. 6:9
20 [a]2Tim. 2:17 [b]2Tim. 4:14 [c]1Cor. 5:5 [d]Acts 13:45

🔑 **1:19, 20** In encouraging Timothy to be strengthened in the Christian warfare, Paul reminds him of the inseparable relation of faith and a good conscience. Those who are constantly doubting and questioning, have come to this point by thrusting away the pricks of their conscience. Such men were Hymenaeus and Alexander, whose doubt and immoral character had led them to blasphemy, to contradict and revile the doctrines of grace. Paul says that these men had been "delivered unto Satan." This is not merely some mental "giving up," convinced that his concern and prayers were to no end. Likewise, it does not indicate that Paul, through some supernatural power, delivered them over to be tormented by Satan, whether such torment be given in this life or the next. Instead, Paul has excluded them from the local fellowship of believers. Until they would repent of their wicked deeds, they would be left outside of the fellowship of God's people, so that Satan might buffet them.

Pray for Those in Authority

2 🔑I exhort therefore, that, first[4412]
of all, supplications,[1162] prayers,[4335]
intercessions,[1783] *and* giving of thanks,
[pip]be made for all men;[444]
2 [a]For kings,[935] and [b]*for* all that are
in authority;[5247] that we [psa]may lead a
quiet and peaceable[2272] life[979] in all
godliness[2150] and honesty.[4587]
3 For this *is* [a]good[2570] and acceptable[587] in the sight [b]of God our Saviour;[4990]
4 [a]Who will have all men[444] [aifp]to be
saved,[4982] [b]and [ainf]to come unto the
knowledge[1922] of the truth.[225]
5 [a]For *there is* one God,[2316] and [b]one
mediator[3316] between God and men, the
[an]man Christ Jesus;
6 [a]Who gave himself a ransom[487] for
all, [I][b]to be testified[3142] [c]in due[2398]
time.[2540]
7 [a]Whereunto I [aop]am ordained[5087] a
preacher,[2783] and an apostle,[652] ([b]I speak
the truth[225] in Christ, *and* lie not;) [c]a
teacher[1320] of the Gentiles[1484] in faith[4102]
and verity.[225]
8 I will therefore that men[435] [pinf]pray
[a]every where, [b]lifting up[1869] holy[3741]
hands, without wrath[3709] and doubting.[1261]
🔑9 In like manner also, that [a]women
[pinf]adorn themselves in modest[2887] apparel, with shamefacedness[127] and sobriety;[4997] not with [I]broided hair, or gold, or
pearls, or costly array;[2441]

2 [a]Ezra 6:10; Jer. 29:7 [b]Rom. 13:1
3 [a]Rom. 12:2; 1Tim. 5:4 [b]1Tim. 1:1; 2Tim. 1:9
4 [a]Ezek. 18:23; John 3:16, 17; Titus 2:11; 2Pet. 3:9 [b]John 17:3; 2Tim. 2:25
5 [a]Rom. 3:29, 30; 10:12; Gal. 3:20 [b]Heb. 8:6; 9:15
6 [I]Or, *a testimony* [a]Matt. 20:28; Mark 10:45; Eph. 1:7; Titus 2:14 [b]1Cor. 1:6; 2Thess. 1:10; 2Tim. 1:8 [c]Rom. 5:6; Gal. 4:4; Eph. 1:9; 3:5; Titus 1:3
7 [a]Eph. 3:7, 8; 2Tim. 1:11 [b]Rom. 9:1 [c]Rom. 11:13; 15:16; Gal. 1:16
8 [a]Mal. 1:11; John 4:21 [b]Ps. 134:2; Isa. 1:15
9 [I]Or, *plaited* [a]1Pet. 3:3

🔑 **2:1, 2** These remarks are designed to encourage believers to pray for kings and all those in authority over them, whether such leaders are believers or unbelievers (see note on 1 Peter 2:17). The object of the prayer is explained, "That we may lead a tranquil and quiet life." Praying for a person does not necessarily involve approving of his or her personality or actions.

🔑 **2:9–15** These verses indicate that women were full and active members in the early church (cf. 1 Cor. 11:4, 5; Titus 2:1–10). From an examination of 1 Corinthians 11:2–16, it is also clear that both wives and husbands could pray and prophesy in the worship service (see note on 1 Cor. 14:33–40). In all this discussion, Paul's chief concern was that by having shorn hair or a shaven head a woman would be of immoral character, because in this manner she dishonors God, her husband's character, and herself. Peter also had something to say concerning the witness of women and their conduct at home (1 Pet. 3:1–7). In marital relationships, a woman is not presented as having any fewer rights over her husband than a husband has over his wife. The key to understanding what the Apostle Paul is teaching is that women should not try to appear or act like men. In addition to this, they should not attempt to usurp the position of their husbands in the home and in the church. God has appointed specific tasks for both women and for men. Childbearing is reserved for women, just as the role of a husband is set aside for men. Paul emphatically states that these were differences created by God Himself.

Furthermore, in Galatians 3:28, Paul made it clear that there are no distinctions between male and female in Christ. He indicates that there are differences between the sexes, but no distinctions of believers in Christ. Moreover, Paul explains that the general attitude of Christians should not be to flaunt one's customs, even if they are the proper ones. If the acceptable code of behavior indicates a definite distinction between the manner of dress of a man and a woman, adhere to that which will characterize one's own gender. In addition to this, differentiation should exist between women and men by the method of hair grooming or style, and it is necessary to maintain that accepted distinction. Paul's other concern is that a woman should not dress in a provocative manner, bringing the lustful attention of men to herself. A Christian woman should be one man's wife, and in like manner, a Christian man should be one woman's husband (1 Cor. 7:2).

In 1 Timothy chapter two, the Apostle Paul is concerned about women appearing modest in their clothing. In verse nine, the Greek word *sōphrosúnē* (4997; cf. v. 15) provides the clue for the interpretation of this difficult passage. This Greek word, translated "sobriety," means "the voluntary limitation of one's freedom of thought and behavior," or "sober mindedness." The truth is that in Christianity women became free and equal to their husbands. Nevertheless, there was always a danger that they might take this freedom beyond the limitations that God had placed when He ap-

(continued on next page)

10 [a]But (which becometh women professing[1861] godliness[2317]) with good[18] works.[2041]

11 [pim]Let the woman learn[3129] in silence[2271] with all subjection.[5292]

12 But [a]I suffer not a woman [pinf]to teach,[1321] [b]nor to usurp authority[831] over the [an]man,[435] but to be in silence.[2271]

13 For [a]Adam [aop]was first formed,[4111] then Eve.

14 And [a]Adam was not deceived, but the woman [aptp]being deceived [pfi]was in the transgression.[3847]

15 Notwithstanding she shall be saved[4982] in childbearing, if they [aosb]continue[3306] in faith[4102] and charity[26] and holiness[38] with sobriety.[4997]

10 [a]1Pet. 3:4
12 [a]1Cor. 14:34 [b]Eph. 5:24
13 [a]Gen. 1:27; 2:18, 22; 1Cor. 11:8, 9
14 [a]Gen. 3:6; 2Cor. 11:3

(continued from previous page)
pointed man as head over woman in the marital relationship. No two people or things can be exactly the same. The inherent differences in people and things must be recognized by a *sōphrōn,* or a "sober minded" person. This is one who recognizes his or her abilities and limitations, and is mindful of the proper behavior in certain given circumstances.

There are numerous references in the Scripture where women are recognized as friends and coworkers in the gospel (Rom. 16:1–4). Peter refers to women as "heirs together of the grace of life" (1 Pet. 3:7). In one such instance, Paul does not differentiate between Priscilla and her husband Aquila, rather he refers to them both with the same word, *sunergoús* (4904), meaning "fellow workers" (Rom. 16:3). He does not distinguish between the work each can do because one is male and the other female (cf. Rom. 16:21; Phile. 1:24).

To function properly, everything needs a person in the position of leadership, especially a family. The marriage unit consists of two people that have two distinct personalities. These two require a "headship," that being the man according to God's creation and ordinance. In 1 Timothy 2:11, there are several key words that show how a wife should convey a proper relationship to her husband. The first of these terms is *gunē* (1135), which, depending on the context, may indicate a woman in general or a wife. The close relationship of this word with the word *andrós* (from *anēr* [435]), meaning "husband," not simply "man," requires that the word *gunē* be translated "wife." The subsequent term to consider is *hēsuchía* (2271), translated "silence." In the New Testament it occurs numerous times referring to tranquility or the state of being undisturbed. This should be the understanding in this verse. One must bear in mind here that during the era of time when Paul was writing, it was usually men who were the ones to receive an education. If this word meant "complete silence," women would never have the opportunity to ask questions or increase their knowledge of the Scriptures. Simply speaking, the wife ought to be displaying a tranquil spirit in her attempt to learn. The final word of key importance in understanding the "silence" mentioned in this verse is *hupotagē* (5292) meaning "to place in proper order," translated "subjection." Paul wanted to express the idea that in the wife's desire to learn, she should respect her husband's position over her in Christ (cf. 1 Cor. 11:3).

The phrase in 1 Timothy 1:12, "But I suffer not a woman to teach" should be understood as "But I suffer not a *wife* to teach." The discussion continues drawing contrasts between the Greek words for wife and for husband. The usage of *gunē* in this verse must be translated as "a wife," corresponding to the reference in verse eleven. *Andrós* (435) is translated as "man" in verse twelve, but it is better rendered "husband" when the usage of this Greek word occurs in relation to a discussion of wives. Furthermore, the word for "teach" in this verse is the Greek infinitive *didáskein* (1321). In this instance, it means "to teach continuously." The situation refers to the home, an assembly, or anywhere the husband and wife may be interacting together. If this injunction is not heeded, the position of the husband as the head will be undermined, and will not be in accordance with God's ordained order in creation. A wife should place limitations on her speech. Paul does not want women to be lackluster or even mute, but to be careful lest they go beyond the bounds of accepted propriety.

Moreover, the word translated "to usurp authority over" is the Greek word *authenteín* (831). Essentially, a wife's private or public life should be beyond reproach and never undermine the position that her husband has been given by God. Also, a wife should never encroach upon the role of her husband. In verse thirteen, Paul explains why this is so: "For Adam was first formed, then Eve." This is not because the husband is better, more intelligent, or more worthy than she; rather, it is the order originally ordained by God, for her to respect. See note on Titus 2:1–5.

Qualifications to Be an Overseer

3 This [a]*is* a true[4103] saying,[3056] If a man desire the office of a [b]bishop,[1984] he desireth[1937] a good[2570] [c]work.[2041]

🔑 2 [a]A bishop[1985] then must be blameless,[423] [b]the [an]husband[435] of one wife, vigilant,3524 sober,[4998] |of good behaviour,[2887] given to hospitality, [c]apt to teach;[1317]

3 |[a]Not given to wine, [b]no striker, [c]not greedy of filthy lucre;146 but [d]patient,1933 not a brawler, not covetous;

4 One that [ppt]ruleth well his own house, [a]having his children[5043] in subjection5292 with all gravity;[4587]

5 (For if a man know not how to rule his own house, how shall he take care of the church[1577] of God?[2316])

6 Not |a novice,[3504] lest [aptp]being lifted up with pride[5187] [a]he fall into the condemnation[2917] of the devil.[1228]

7 Moreover he must have a good[2570] report[3141] [a]of them which are without;1855 lest he [aosb]fall into reproach [b]and the snare of the devil.

Qualifications for Servants

8 Likewise *must* [a]the deacons[1249] *be* grave,[4586] not double-tongued, [b]not given to much wine,[3631] not greedy of filthy lucre;146

9 [a]Holding the mystery[3466] of the faith[4102] in a pure[2513] conscience.[4893]

10 And [pim]let these also first be proved;[1381] then [pim]let them use the office of a deacon,[1247] being *found* blameless.[410]

11 [a]Even so *must their* wives *be* grave,[4586] not slanderers,[1228] sober, faithful in all things.

12 Let the deacons be the [an]husbands[435] of one wife, ruling their children[5043] and their own houses well.

13 For [a]they that have |used the office of a deacon[1247] well purchase to themselves a good[2570] degree, and great boldness in the faith[4102] which is in Christ Jesus.

14 These things write I unto thee, hoping to come unto thee shortly:

15 But if I tarry long, that thou mayest know how thou oughtest [pinf]to behave thyself [a]in the house of God, which is the church[1577] of the living[2198] God, the pillar and |ground of the truth.[225]

16 And without controversy[3672] great is the mystery[3466] of godliness:[2150] [a]God was manifest[5319] in the flesh,[4561] [aop][b]justified[1344] in the Spirit, [aop][c]seen of angels, [aop][d]preached[2784] unto the Gentiles,[1484] [aop][e]believed on[4100] in the world, [aop][f]received up into glory.[1391]

Apostasy

4 🔑Now the Spirit[4151] [a]speaketh expressly, that [b]in the latter times[2540] some shall depart[868] from the faith,[4102] giving heed [c]to seducing spirits,[4151] [d]and doctrines[1319] of devils;1140

2 [a]Speaking lies in hypocrisy; [b]having their conscience[4893] [pfpp]seared with a hot iron;

3 [a]Forbidding to marry, [b]*and commanding* [pinf]to abstain[567] from meats, which God [ao]hath created [c]to be received [d]with thanksgiving of them which [ajn]believe[4103] and [pfp]know the truth.[225]

1 [a]1Tim. 1:15 [b]Acts 20:28; Phil. 1:1 [c]Eph. 4:12
2 |Or, *modest* [a]Titus 1:6 [b]1Tim. 5:9 [c]2Tim. 2:24
3 |Or, *Not ready to quarrel, and offer wrong, as one in wine* [a]1Tim. 3:8; Titus 1:7 [b]2Tim. 2:24 [c]1Pet. 5:2 [d]2Tim. 2:24
4 [a]Titus 1:6
6 |Or, *one newly come to the faith* [a]Isa. 14:12
7 [a]Acts 22:12; 1Cor. 5:12; 1Thess. 4:12 [b]1Tim. 6:9; 2Tim. 2:26
8 [a]Acts 6:3 [b]Lev. 10:9; Ezek. 44:21; 1Tim. 3:3
9 [a]1Tim. 1:19
11 [a]Titus 2:3
13 |Or, *ministered* [a]Matt. 25:21
15 |Or, *stay* [a]Eph. 2:21, 22; 2Tim. 2:20
16 [a]John 1:14; 1John 1:2 [b]Matt. 3:16; John 1:32, 33; 15:26; 16:8, 9; Rom. 1:4; 1Pet. 3:18; 1John 5:6 [c]Matt. 28:2; Mark 16:5; Luke 2:13; 24:4; John 20:12; Eph. 3:10; 1Pet. 1:12 [d]Acts 10:34; 13:46, 48; Rom. 10:18; Gal. 2:8; Eph. 3:5, 6, 8; Col. 1:27, 28; 1Tim. 2:7 [e]Col. 1:6, 23 [f]Luke 24:51; Acts 1:9; 1Pet. 3:22

1 [a]John 16:13; 2Thess. 2:3; 2Tim. 3:1; 2Pet. 3:3; 1John 2:18; Jude 1:4, 18 [b]1Pet. 1:20 [c]2Tim. 3:13; 2Pet. 2:1; Rev. 16:14 [d]Dan. 11:35, 37, 38; Rev. 9:20 **2** [a]Matt. 7:15; Rom. 16:18; 2Pet. 2:3 [b]Eph. 4:19 **3** [a]1Cor. 7:28, 36, 38; Col. 2:20, 21; Heb. 13:4 [b]Rom. 14:3, 17; 1Cor. 8:8 [c]Gen. 1:29; 9:3 [d]Rom. 14:6; 1Cor. 10:30

🔑 **3:2** The phrase "husband of one wife" does not mean that the bishop or the deacon was never married before else it would exclude a remarried widower (see 1 Tim. 3:12). Furthermore, it does not mean that in order to become a bishop or a deacon, one must be married.

In Romans 7:1–3, the Apostle Paul placed no restrictions upon a widower to remarry. The meaning of this phrase is that the bishop or the deacon should not be married to more than one woman simultaneously. In the Greek, *miás gunaikós* (3391, 1135), meaning "of one woman," would have been better translated "a one-woman husband." The total context speaks of the moral conduct of the bishop and the deacon. He should be a man totally dedicated to his wife and not flirtatious (cf. Titus 1:6).

🔑 **4:1–3** See note on 2 Thessalonians 2:3.

4 For [a]every creature[2938] of God *is* good,[2570] and nothing to be refused, if it [ppmp]be received[2983] with thanksgiving:

5 For it is sanctified[37] by the word[3056] of God and prayer.[1783]

Be an Example

6 If thou [ppt]put the brethren[80] in remembrance of these things, thou shalt be a good[2570] minister[1249] of Jesus Christ, [ppta]nourished up in the words of faith[4102] and of good doctrine,[1319] whereunto thou [pfi]hast attained.

7 But [pima]refuse[3868] profane[952] and old wives' fables,[3454] and [pimb]exercise thyself *rather* unto godliness.[2150]

8 For [a]bodily[4984] exercise profiteth [I]little: [b]but godliness is profitable unto all things, [c]having promise of the life that now is, and of that which is to come.[3195]

9 [a]This *is* a faithful[4103] saying[3056] and worthy of all acceptation.[594]

10 For therefore [a]we both labour and suffer reproach, because we [pfib]trust[1679] in the living[2198] God, [c]who is the Saviour[4990] of all men,[444] specially of those that believe.

11 [a]These things [pim]command[3853] and [pim]teach.[1321]

🔑 12 [pima]Let no man despise[2706] thy youth;[3503] but [pimb]be thou an example of the believers,[4103] in word,[3056] in conversation,391 in charity,[26] in spirit,[4151] in faith,[4102] in purity.[47]

13 Till I come, give attendance to reading,[320] to exhortation,[3874] to doctrine.[1319]

🔑 14 [pima]Neglect not the gift[5486] that is in thee, which was given thee [b]by prophecy,[4394] [c]with the laying on of the hands of the presbytery.[4244]

4 [a]Rom. 14:14, 20; 1Cor. 10:25; Titus 1:15
6 [a]2Tim. 3:14, 15
7 [a]1Tim. 1:4; 6:20; 2Tim. 2:16, 23; 4:4; Titus 1:14 [b]Heb. 5:14
8 [I]Or, *for a little time* [a]1Cor. 8:8; Col. 2:23 [b]1Tim. 6:6 [c]Ps. 37:4; 84:11; 112:2, 3; 145:19; Matt. 6:33; 19:29; Mark 10:30; Rom. 8:28
9 [a]1Tim. 1:15
10 [a]1Cor. 4:11, 12 [b]1Tim. 6:17 [c]Ps. 36:6; 107:2, 6
11 [a]1Tim. 6:2
12 [a]1Cor. 16:11; Titus 2:15 [b]Titus 2:7; 1Pet. 5:3
14 [a]2Tim. 1:6 [b]1Tim. 1:18 [c]Acts 6:6; 8:17; 13:3; 19:6; 1Tim. 5:22; 2Tim. 1:6
15 [I]Or, *in all things*
16 [a]Acts 20:28 [b]Ezek. 33:9 [c]Rom. 11:14; 1Cor. 9:22; James 5:20

1 [a]Lev. 19:32
3 [a]1Tim. 5:5, 16
4 [I]Or, *kindness* [a]Gen. 45:10, 11; Matt. 15:4; Eph. 6:1, 2 [b]1Tim. 2:3
5 [a]1Cor. 7:32 [b]Luke 2:37; 18:1 [c]Acts 26:7
6 [a]James 5:5
7 [a]1Tim. 1:3; 4:11; 6:17
8 [a]Isa. 58:7; Gal. 6:10 [b]2Tim. 3:5; Titus 1:16 [c]Matt. 18:17
9 [a]Luke 2:36; 1Tim. 3:2
10 [a]Acts 16:15; Heb. 13:2; 1Pet. 4:9

15 [pim]Meditate upon these things; give thyself wholly to them; that thy profiting may appear[5318] [I]to all.

16 [a]Take heed unto thyself, and unto the doctrine; continue in them: for in doing this thou shalt both [b]save[4982] thyself, and [c]them that [ppt]hear thee.

More Instructions

5 [aosi]Rebuke [a]not an elder,[4245] but [pim]intreat *him* as a father;[3962] *and* the younger men as brethren;[80]

2 The elder women as mothers; the younger as sisters, with all purity.[47]

3 [pim]Honour widows [a]that are widows indeed.

4 But if any widow have children or nephews, [pim]let them learn[3129] first [pinf]to shew [I]piety[2151] at home, and [pinfa]to requite their parents: [b]for that is good and acceptable[587] before God.

5 [a]Now she that is a widow indeed, and desolate, [pfi]trusteth[1679] in God, and [b]continueth[4357] in supplications[1162] and prayers[4335] [c]night and day.

6 [a]But she that [ppt]liveth in pleasure[4684] [pfi]is dead[2348] while she [ppt]liveth.[2198]

7 [a]And these things [pim]give in charge, that they may be blameless.[423]

8 But if any provide not for[4306] his own, [a]and specially for those of his own house,[3609] 3588 [b]he [pfip]hath denied the faith,[4102] [c]and is worse than an infidel.[571]

🔑 9 [pim]Let not a widow be taken into the number2639 under threescore years old, [a]having been the wife of one man,

10 Well reported of for good[2570] works;[2041] if she [ao]have brought up children, if she [ao]have [a]lodged strangers, if

---

🔑 **4:12** A comparison of this verse and Titus 2:15 suggests that Titus may have been older and more mature than Timothy, in that he had been the stronger of the two during the difficulties in Corinth (1 Cor. 16:10; 2 Cor. 7:13–15). Titus volunteered readily for the delicate task of leading a church (2 Cor. 8:17), and he was full of affection and enthusiasm for the Corinthian brethren (2 Cor. 7:15). He was one who shared in Paul's spirit and example (2 Cor. 12:18). In this case, Paul was exhorting Timothy to continue on and not allow men to undermine his abilities. Paul understood the difficulty in being a leader, and his advice to Timothy was for him to lead by example.

🔑 **4:14** See note on 2 Timothy 1:6.

🔑 **5:9** See note on 1 Timothy 3:2 concerning a woman having one husband.

she [ao]have [b]washed the saints'[40] feet, if she [ao]have relieved the afflicted, if she [ao]have diligently followed every good[18] work.[2041]

11 But the younger widows refuse:[3868] for when they [aosb]have begun to wax wanton against$_{2691}$ Christ, they will [pinf]marry;

12 Having damnation,[2917] because they [ao]have cast off their first faith.[4102]

13 [a]And withal$_{260}$ they learn *to be* idle,[692] wandering about from house to house; and not only idle, but tattlers also and busybodies, speaking things which they ought[1163] not.

14 [a]I will therefore that the younger women [pinf]marry, bear children, guide the house,$_{3616}$ [b]give none occasion to the adversary to speak reproachfully.

15 For some are already turned aside after Satan.

16 If any man or woman that believeth[4103] have widows, [pim]let them relieve$_{1884}$ them, and let not the church[1577] be charged; that it [asba]may relieve [a]them that are widows indeed.

17 [a]Let the elders[4245] that [pfp]rule well [pim][b]be counted worthy of double honour,$_{5092}$ especially they who [ppt]labour in the word[3056] and doctrine.[1319]

18 For the scripture saith, [a]Thou shalt not muzzle the ox that treadeth out the corn. And, [b]The labourer *is* worthy of his reward.[3408]

19 Against an elder [pim]receive[3858] not an accusation,[2724] but [a]before two or three witnesses.[3144]

20 [a]Them that [ppt]sin[264] [pim]rebuke before all, [b]that others also may fear.[5401]

21 [a]I charge[1263] *thee* before God, and the Lord Jesus Christ, and the elect[1588] angels,[32] that thou [aosb]observe these things [1]without preferring one before another,[4299] doing nothing by partiality.

22 [pim][a]Lay hands suddenly on no man, [b]neither [pim]be partaker[2841] of other men's sins:[266] [pim]keep thyself pure.[53]

23 Drink no longer water, but [pim]use a little wine[3631] [a]for thy stomach's sake and thine often infirmities.

24 [a]Some men's sins are open beforehand, going before[4254] to judgment;[2920] and some *men* they follow after.

25 Likewise also the good works *of some* are manifest beforehand; and they that are otherwise[247] cannot be hid.

6 Let as many [a]servants[1401] as are under the yoke count their own masters[1203] worthy of all honour, [b]that the name[3686] of God and *his* doctrine[1319] [psmp]be not blasphemed.[987]

2 And they that have believing[4103] masters, [pim]let them not despise[2706] *them,* [a]because they are brethren; but rather [pim]do *them* service,[1398] because they are [1]faithful[4103] and beloved,[27] [ppt]partakers[482] of the benefit. [b]These things teach and exhort.

Healthy Teaching

3 If any man [a]teach otherwise,[2085] and consent[4334] [b]not to wholesome words, *even* the words of our Lord Jesus Christ, [c]and to the doctrine[1319] which is according to[2596] godliness;[2150]

4 He [pfip]is proud,[5187] [a]knowing nothing, but doting$_{3552}$ about [b]questions and strifes of words, whereof cometh envy, strife, railings,[988] evil[4190] surmisings,[5283]

5 [a]Perverse disputings$_{3859}$ of [b]men of corrupt minds,[3563] and [pfpp]destitute of the truth,[225] [c]supposing that gain is godliness:[2150] [d]from such [pim]withdraw thyself.[868]

6 But [a]godliness with contentment is great gain.

7 For [a]we [ao]brought nothing into *this* world,[2889] *and it is* certain we can [ainf]carry nothing out.$_{1627}$

8 And [a]having food and raiment let us be therewith content.

9 But [a]they that [ppt]will [pinf]be rich fall into temptation[3986] [b]and a snare, and *into* many foolish[453] and hurtful lusts,[1939] [c]which drown men[444] in destruction[3639] and perdition.[684]

10 [a]For the love of money is the root of all evil:[2556] which while some [ppt]coveted after, they [aop]have [1]erred from the faith,[4102] and [ao]pierced themselves through with many sorrows.

---

10 [b]Gen. 18:4; 19:2; Luke 7:38, 44; John 13:5, 14
13 [a]2Thess. 3:11
14 [a]1Cor. 7:9 [b]1Tim. 6:1; Titus 2:8
16 [a]1Tim. 5:3, 5
17 [a]Rom. 12:8; 1Cor. 9:10, 14; Gal. 6:6; Phil. 2:29; 1Thess. 5:12, 13; Heb. 13:7, 17 [b]Acts 28:10
18 [a]Deut. 25:4; 1Cor. 9:9 [b]Lev. 19:13; Deut. 24:14, 15; Matt. 10:10; Luke 10:7
19 [a]Deut. 19:15
20 [a]Gal. 2:11, 14; Titus 1:13 [b]Deut. 13:11
21 [1]Or, *without prejudice* [a]1Tim. 6:13; 2Tim. 2:14; 4:1
22 [a]Acts 6:6; 13:3; 1Tim. 4:14; 2Tim. 1:6 [b]2John 1:11
23 [a]Ps. 104:15
24 [a]Gal. 5:19

1 [a]Eph. 6:5; Col. 3:22; Titus 2:9; 1Pet. 2:18 [b]Isa. 52:5; Rom. 2:24; Titus 2:5, 8
2 [1]Or, *believing* [a]Col. 4:1 [b]1Tim. 4:11
3 [a]1Tim. 1:3 [b]1Tim. 1:10; 2Tim. 1:13; 4:3; Titus 1:9 [c]Titus 1:1
4 [a]1Cor. 8:2; 1Tim. 1:7 [b]1Tim. 1:4; 2Tim. 2:23; Titus 3:9
5 [a]1Cor. 11:16; 1Tim. 1:6 [b]2Tim. 3:8 [c]Titus 1:11; 2Pet. 2:3 [d]Rom. 16:17; 2Tim. 3:5
6 [a]Ps. 37:16; Prov. 15:16; 16:8; Heb. 13:5
7 [a]Job. 1:21; Ps. 49:17; Prov. 27:24; Eccl. 5:15
8 [a]Gen. 28:20; Heb. 13:5
9 [a]Prov. 15:27; 20:21; 28:20; Matt. 13:22; James 5:1 [b]1Tim. 3:7 [c]1Tim. 1:19
10 [1]Or, been seduced [a]Ex. 23:8; Deut. 16:19

"Fight the Good Fight"

11 [a]But thou, [b]O man[444] of God, flee
these things; and follow after righteousness,[1343] godliness,[2150] faith,[4102] love,[26]
patience,[5281] meekness.[4236]
12 [a]Fight[75] the good[2570] fight[73] of
faith, [b]lay hold on[1949] eternal[166] life,[2222]
whereunto thou [aop]art also called,[2564]
[c]and [ao]hast professed[3670] a [art]good[2570]
profession[3671] before many witnesses.[3144]
13 [a]I give thee charge in the sight of
God, [b]who [ppt]quickeneth[2227] all things,
and *before* Christ Jesus, [c]who before
Pontius Pilate [apt]witnessed a [art]good
[I]confession;[3671]
14 That thou [ainf]keep *this* commandment without spot,[784] unrebukeable,[423]
[a]until the appearing[2015] of our Lord Jesus
Christ:
15 Which in his[2398] times[2540] he shall
shew, *who is* [a]the blessed[3107] and only
Potentate,[1413] [b]the King[935] of [ppt]kings,[936]
and Lord[2962] of [ppt]lords;[2961]
16 [a]Who only [ppt]hath immortality,[110]
dwelling[3611] in the light[5457] which no
man can approach unto; [b]whom no man
[ao]hath seen, nor can [ainf]see: [c]to whom *be*
honour[5092] and power[2904] everlasting.[166]
Amen.[281]
17 [pim]Charge them that are rich in
this world,[165] that they [pinf]be not high-
minded;[5309] [a]nor [pfin]trust[1679] in [Ib]uncer-
tain riches, but in [c]the living[2198] God,
[d]who [ppt]giveth us richly all things to
enjoy;
18 That they [pinf]do good,[14] that [a]they
be [pinf]rich in good works, [b]ready to distribute, [c]willing to communicate;[2843]
19 [ppta]Laying up in store for themselves a good foundation against the time
to come,[3195] that they [asbm]may [b]lay hold
on eternal life.
20 O Timothy, [aima]keep that which
is committed to thy trust, [b]avoiding
profane[952] *and* vain babblings,[2757] and
oppositions of science[1108] falsely so
called:
21 Which some professing[1861]
[aoa]have erred concerning the faith. Grace
be with thee. Amen.

11 [a]2Tim. 2:22 [b]Deut. 33:1; 2Tim. 3:17
12 [a]1Cor. 9:25, 26; 1Tim. 1:18; 2Tim. 4:7 [b]Phil. 3:12, 14; 1Tim. 6:19 [c]Heb. 13:23
13 [I]Or, *Profession* [a]1Tim. 5:21 [b]Deut. 32:39; 1Sam. 2:6; John 5:21 [c]Matt. 27:11; John 18:37; Rev. 1:5; 3:14
14 [a]Phil. 1:6, 10; 1Thess. 3:13; 5:23
15 [a]1Tim. 1:11, 17 [b]Rev. 17:14; 19:16
16 [a]1Tim. 1:17 [b]Ex. 33:20; John 6:46 [c]Eph. 3:21; Phil. 4:20; Jude 1:25; Rev. 1:6; 4:11; 7:12
17 [I]Gr. *uncertainty of riches* [a]Job 31:24; Ps. 52:7; 62:10; Mark 10:24; Luke 12:21 [b]Prov. 23:5 [c]1Thess. 1:9; 1Tim. 3:15; 4:10 [d]Acts 14:17; 17:25
18 [a]Luke 12:21; 1Tim. 5:10; Titus 3:8; James 2:5 [b]Rom. 12:13 [c]Gal. 6:6; Heb. 13:16 **19** [a]Matt. 6:20; 19:21 [b]1Tim. 6:12 **20** [a]2Tim. 1:14; Titus 1:9; Rev. 3:3 [b]1Tim. 1:4, 6; 4:7; 2Tim. 2:14, 16, 23; Titus 1:14; 3:9 **21** [a]1Tim. 1:6, 19; 2Tim. 2:18

The Second Epistle of Paul to

TIMOTHY

Paul wrote this second letter to Timothy (see introduction to 1 Timothy) from a prison in Rome toward the close of his life (2 Tim. 1:8). This would place the date of the writing of this letter toward the end of A.D. 66. The Book of Acts concludes with Paul being placed under house arrest (Acts 28:30–31), but there is evidence in the Book of 2 Timothy that Paul was imprisoned a second time (2 Tim. 4:16–18). Most scholars believe that Paul was acquitted in the first trial and subsequently returned to Greece and Asia Minor to continue his missionary work. It is suggested that he was arrested again, taken back to Rome, and imprisoned in what is known as the Mamertine prison. This is evident from the fact that John Mark, who was present during Paul's first imprisonment (Col. 4:10), was not with Paul at the time he wrote 2 Timothy. Some believe that the second time Paul was imprisoned, he was being held for a much more serious charge (2 Tim. 2:9) than the one he was imprisoned for the first time. Paul believed that his death was near, but he was satisfied that he had done his best (2 Tim. 4:6–8).

Paul wrote this letter to encourage Timothy in the work of the ministry. Timothy would encounter persecution and turmoil in dealing with false teachers in his congregation. Paul urged him to exercise his spiritual gifts (2 Tim. 1:6), to boldly face suffering "as a good soldier of Jesus Christ" (2 Tim. 2:3), to deal wisely with false teachers in his church (2 Tim. 2:14–26), and to continue to exhibit a strong testimony for Christ in the wake of the apostasy and wickedness in the world (2 Tim. 3:1–9).

Some suggest that Paul was writing a more personal letter to Timothy because of the fact that he was expecting to die soon. The style of the epistle is less didactic than Paul's first letter to Timothy. Paul talks to Timothy as a father who would soon be leaving his son. The references to Timothy's own spiritual heritage and call to the ministry (1 Tim. 1:3, 5, 6) reveal how Paul reflected on his own influence on Timothy's life.

1 Paul, [a]an apostle ***652*** of Jesus Christ by the will ***2307*** of God, ***2316*** according to [b]the promise ***1860*** of life ***2222*** which is in Christ ***5547*** Jesus,

2 [a]To Timothy, *my* dearly beloved ***27*** son: ***5043*** Grace, ***5485*** mercy, ***1656*** *and* peace, ***1515*** from God the Father ***3962*** and Christ Jesus our Lord. ***2962***

"Stir Up the Gift of God"

3 [a]I thank ***5485*** God, [b]whom I serve ***3000*** from *my* forefathers with pure ***2513*** conscience, ***4893*** that [c]without ceasing ***88*** I have remembrance of thee in my prayers night and day;

4 [a]Greatly desiring to see thee, [pfpp]being mindful of thy tears, that I [asbp]may be filled with joy;

5 When I call to remembrance ***5280*** [a]the unfeigned ***505*** faith ***4102*** that is in thee, which dwelt first in thy grandmother Lois, and [b]thy mother Eunice; and I am persuaded that in thee also.

🗝 6 Wherefore I put thee in remembrance [a]that thou [pinf]stir up the gift ***5486*** of

1 [a]2Cor. 1:1 [b]Eph. 3:6; Titus 1:2; Heb. 9:15

2 [a]1Tim. 1:2

3 [a]Rom. 1:8; Eph. 1:16 [b]Acts 22:3; 23:1; 24:14; 27:23; Rom. 1:9; Gal. 1:14 [c]1Thess. 1:2; 3:10

4 [a]2Tim. 4:9, 21

5 [a]1Tim. 1:5; 4:6 [b]Acts 16:1

6 [a]1Thess. 5:19; 1Tim. 4:14

🗝 **1:6** Paul mentions a "gift," which Timothy possessed as a result of the "putting on" of his hands on him. It is identical to the word used by Paul to describe the gifts (*chárismata* [5486]) of the Spirit (1 Cor. 12:1–11). This gift mentioned in 2 Timothy 1:6 is not identified in any specific detail. Undoubtedly, this particular gift that came upon Timothy was the outcome of his ordination to the ministry of the gospel in 1 Timothy 4:14. In this verse, Paul speaks of "the presbytery" having participated in Timothy's ordination. This is an indication that in a local church in addition to the pastor acting as an elder, there should be "a presbytery," or better, a body of elders, known as presbyters.

God, which is in thee by the putting on of my hands.

7 For [a]God [ao]hath not given[1325] us the [an]spirit[4151] of fear;[1167] [b]but of power,[1411] and of love,[26] and of a sound mind.[4995]

8 [aosi][a]Be not thou therefore ashamed[1870] of [b]the testimony[3142] of our Lord, nor of me [c]his prisoner: [d]but [aim]be thou partaker of the afflictions[4777] of the gospel[2098] according to the power of God;

🔑 9 [a]Who [apt]hath saved[4982] us, and [apt][b]called *us* with an holy[40] calling,[2821] [c]not according to our works,[2041] but [d]according to his own purpose[4286] and grace,[5485] which [aptp]was given us in Christ Jesus [e]before the world began,

10 But [aptp][a]is now made manifest[5319] by the appearing[2015] of our Saviour[4990] Jesus Christ, [b]who [apt]hath abolished death,[2288] and [apt]hath brought life and immortality to light[5461] through the gospel:

11 [a]Whereunto I [aop]am appointed[5087] a preacher,[2783] and an apostle,[652] and a teacher[1320] of the Gentiles.[1484]

🔑 12 [a]For the which cause I also suffer these things: nevertheless I am not ashamed: [b]for I know[1492] whom I [pfi]have believed,[4100] and am persuaded that he is able [ainf]to [c]keep that which I have committed unto him [d]against that day.

13 [a]Hold fast [b]the form[5296] of [c]sound[5198] words,[3056] [d]which thou [ao]hast heard of me, [e]in faith and love which is in Christ Jesus.

14 [a]That good thing which was committed unto thee [aim]keep by the [an]Holy Ghost[4151] [b]which [ppt]dwelleth in us.

7 [a]Rom. 8:15 [b]Luke 24:49; Acts 1:8
8 [a]Rom. 1:16 [b]1Tim. 2:6; Rev. 1:2 [c]Eph. 3:1; Phil. 1:7 [d]Col. 1:24; 2Tim. 4:5
9 [a]1Tim. 1:1; Titus 3:4 [b]1Thess. 4:7; Heb. 3:1 [c]Rom. 3:20; 9:11; Titus 3:5 [d]Rom. 8:28 [e]Rom. 16:25; Eph. 1:4; 3:11; Titus 1:2; 1Pet. 1:20
10 [a]Rom. 16:26; Eph. 1:9; Col. 1:26; Titus 1:3; 1Pet. 1:20 [b]1Cor. 15:54, 55; Heb. 2:14
11 [a]Acts 9:15; Eph. 3:7, 8; 1Tim. 2:7; Titus 4:17
12 [a]Eph. 3:1; Titus 2:9 [b]1Pet. 4:19 [c]1Tim. 6:20 [d]2Tim. 1:18; 4:8
13 [a]2Tim. 3:14; Titus 1:9; Heb. 10:23; Rev. 2:25 [b]Rom. 2:20; 6:17 [c]1Tim. 1:10; 6:3 [d]2Tim. 2:2 [e]1Tim. 1:14
14 [a]1Tim. 6:20 [b]Rom. 8:11
15 [a]Acts 19:10 [b]2Tim. 4:10, 16
16 [a]Matt. 5:7 [b]2Tim. 4:19 [c]Phile. 1:7 [d]2Tim. 1:8 [e]Acts 28:20; Eph. 6:20
18 [a]Matt. 25:34-40 [b]2Thess. 1:10; 2Tim. 2:12 [c]Heb. 6:10

1 [a]1Tim. 1:2; 2Tim. 1:2 [b]Eph. 6:10

15 This thou knowest, that [a]all they which are in Asia [aop]be [b]turned away from[654] me; of whom are Phygellus and Hermogenes.

16 The Lord [opt][a]give mercy[1656] unto [b]the house of Onesiphorus; [c]for he oft refreshed[404] me, and [d]was not ashamed of [e]my chain:

17 But, when he was[1096] in Rome, he sought me out very diligently, and found *me.*

18 The Lord [opt]grant unto him [a]that he [ainf]may find[2147] mercy[1656] of the Lord [b]in that day:[2250] and in how many things he [c]ministered unto[1247] me at Ephesus, thou knowest very well.

The Christian Warfare

2 Thou therefore, [a]my son,[5043] [pim][b]be strong[1743] in the grace that is in Christ Jesus.

2 [a]And the things that thou [ao]hast heard of me among many witnesses,[3144] [b]the same [aim]commit thou to faithful[4103] men,[444] who shall be [c]able to teach[1321] others[2087] also.

3 [a]Thou therefore [aim]endure hardness,[2553] [b]as a good soldier of Jesus Christ.

4 [a]No man that [ppt]warreth entangleth himself with the affairs of *this* life;[979] that he [aosb]may please him who [apt]hath chosen him to be a soldier.

2 [a]2Tim. 1:13; 3:10, 14 [b]1Tim. 1:18 [c]1Tim. 3:2; Titus 1:9 **3** [a]2Tim. 1:8; 4:5 [b]1Tim. 1:18 **4** [a]1Cor. 9:25

🔑 **1:9** In this verse, the Greek word *próthesin* (4286) is translated "purpose," but actually means "God's intention beforehand" (see note on Ephesians 1:4, 5 dealing with God's election of believers to salvation and grace).

🔑 **1:12** Paul states, "I also suffer." This does not mean that he was suffering due to some sin in his own life. Rather, it is an inevitable part of the life of the Christian because he has the same mortal and corruptible body as unbelievers (Rom. 6:12; 8:11; 1 Cor. 15:53, 54; 2 Cor. 4:11; 5:4). The word *thnētón* (2349), "mortal," appearing in all previous verses referenced, deals only with believers. The word translated "corruptible," is the Greek word *phthartón* (5349), referring to the deterioration of the human body (Rom. 1:23; 1 Cor. 15:53, 54). The use of this word makes it clear that upon receiving Christ, the physical body of the believer does not become exempt from mortality or corruptibility. Suffering may also come as a result of persecution from the world because the Christian does not conform to its standards. However, Christ will ultimately overcome (John 16:33; Gal. 6:17; 2 Tim. 3:12). Therefore, Paul states, "I also suffer these things, nevertheless I am not ashamed."

5 And [a]if a man also [psa]strive for masteries, *yet* is he not crowned, except he [aosb]strive lawfully.

6 [I][a]The husbandman1092 that [ppt]laboureth must [pinf]be first partaker[3335] of the fruits.

7 [pim]Consider[3539] what I say; and the Lord [opt]give thee understanding in all things.

8 [pim]Remember that Jesus Christ [a]of the seed[4690] of David [pfpp][b]was raised[1453] from the dead[3498] [c]according to my gospel:[2098]

9 [a]Wherein I suffer trouble,[2553] as an evil doer,[2557] [b]*even* unto bonds; [c]but the word[3056] of God [pfip]is not bound.[1210]

10 Therefore [a]I endure[5278] all things for the elect's[1588] sakes, [b]that they [aosb]may also obtain5177 the salvation[4991] which is in Christ Jesus with eternal glory.[1391]

11 [a]*It is* a faithful[4103] saying:[3056] For [b]if we [ao]be dead with *him,* we shall also live with *him:*

12 [a]If we suffer,[5278] we shall also reign with *him:* [b]if we deny[720] *him,* he also will deny us:

13 [a]If we believe not,[569] *yet* he abideth faithful: [b]he cannot [ainf]deny himself.

Be a Good Example

14 Of these things [pim]put *them* in remembrance,5279 [a]charging[1263] *them* before the Lord [b]that they [pinf]strive not about words3054 to no profit,[5539] *but* to the subverting of the [ppt]hearers.

15 Study [ainf]to shew thyself approved[1384] unto God, a workman that needeth not to be ashamed, rightly dividing[3718] the word of truth.

16 But [a]shun profane[952] *and* vain babblings:[2757] for they will increase unto more ungodliness.[763]

17 And their word will eat as doth a [I]canker:1044 of whom is [a]Hymenaeus and Philetus;

18 Who [a]concerning the truth [ao]have erred, [b]saying that the resurrection[386] [pfin]is past already; and overthrow the faith[4102] of some.

19 Nevertheless [a]the foundation of God [pfi]standeth [I]sure, having this seal, The Lord [ao][b]knoweth them that are his. And, Let every one that [ppt]nameth the name[3686] of Christ [aim]depart[868] from iniquity.[93]

20 [a]But in a great house there are not only vessels of gold and of silver, but also of wood and of earth; [b]and some to honour, and some to dishonour.[819]

21 [a]If a man therefore [aosb]purge himself from these, he shall be a vessel unto honour, sanctified,[37] and meet for[2173] the master's[1203] use,[2173] *and* [pfpp][b]prepared unto every good[18] work.[2041]

22 [pim]Flee also youthful lusts: but [pim][a]follow righteousness,[1343] faith,[4102] charity,[26] peace,[1515] with them that [ppt][b]call on[1941] the Lord [c]out of a pure[2513] heart.[2588]

23 But [a]foolish[3474] and unlearned[521] questions [pim]avoid,[3868] knowing that they do gender[1080] strifes.

24 And [a]the servant[1401] of the Lord must not [pinf]strive; but be gentle[2261] unto all *men,* [b]apt to teach,[1317] [I]patient,[420]

25 [a]In meekness instructing[3811] those that [ppt]oppose themselves; [b]if God peradventure [aosb]will give them repentance[3341] [c]to the [an]acknowledging[1922] of the [an]truth;

26 And *that* they [aosb]may [I]recover

5 [a]1Cor. 9:25, 26
6 [I]Or, *The husbandman, laboring first, must be partaker of the fruits* [a]1Cor. 9:10
8 [a]Acts 2:30; 13:23; Rom. 1:3, 4 [b]1Cor. 15:1, 4, 20 [c]Rom. 2:16
9 [a]Acts 9:16; 2Tim. 1:12 [b]Eph. 3:1; Phil. 1:7; Col. 4:3, 18 [c]Acts 28:31; Eph. 6:19, 20; Phil. 1:13, 14
10 [a]Eph. 3:13; Col. 1:24 [b]2Cor. 1:6
11 [a]1Tim. 1:15 [b]Rom. 6:5, 8; 2Cor. 4:10
12 [a]Rom. 8:17; 1Pet. 4:13 [b]Matt. 10:33; Mark 8:38; Luke 12:9
13 [a]Rom. 3:3; 9:6 [b]Num. 23:19
14 [a]1Tim. 5:21; 6:13; 2Tim. 4:1 [b]1Tim. 1:4; 6:4; Titus 3:9, 11
16 [a]1Tim. 4:7; 6:20; Titus 1:14
17 [I]Or, *gangrene* [a]1Tim. 1:20
18 [a]1Tim. 6:21 [b]1Cor. 15:12
19 [I]Or, *steady* Num. 16:5 [a]Matt. 24:24; Rom. 8:35; 1John 2:19 [b]Nah. 1:7; John 10:14, 27
20 [a]1Tim. 3:15 [b]Rom. 9:21
21 [a]Isa. 52:11 [b]2Tim. 3:17; Titus 3:1
22 [a]1Tim. 6:11 [b]Acts 9:14; 1Cor. 1:2 [c]1Tim. 1:5; 4:12
23 [a]1Tim. 1:4; 4:7; 6:4; 2Tim. 2:16; Titus 3:9
24 [I]Or, *forbearing* [a]Titus 3:2 [b]1Tim. 3:2, 3; Titus 1:9
25 [a]Gal. 6:1; 1Tim. 6:11; 1Pet. 3:15 [b]Acts 8:22 [c]1Tim. 2:4; 2Tim. 3:7; Titus 1:1
26 [I]Gr. *awake*

2:10 See note on Ephesians 1:4, 5 dealing with the subject of election.

2:12, 13 In this passage, Paul is encouraging Timothy that though he is suffering in this life, there is the prospect of future blessing. The believer who continues trusting in Christ, remaining faithful to his call, certainly will receive a blessed reward in heaven. On the other hand, those who are unfaithful to the call of Christ (i.e., those who "deny" or "believe not") will receive his just reward as well, namely, judgment from God. The phrase "yet he abideth faithful" means that Christ will be true to His promise of judgment on those who are unfaithful to Him.

themselves [a]out of the snare of the devil,[1228] who [pfpp]are [II]taken captive2221 by him at his will.[2307]

The Last Times

3 This know also, that [a]in the last[2078] days perilous times[2540] shall come.[1764]

2 For men shall be [a]lovers of their own selves,[5367] [b]covetous, [c]boasters,[213] [d]proud,[5244] [e]blasphemers,[989] [f]disobedient[545] to parents, unthankful, unholy,462

3 [a]Without natural affection,[794] [b]trucebreakers,[786] [c]false accusers,[1228] [d]incontinent,193 fierce, despisers of those that are good,[865]

4 [a]Traitors, heady,4312 highminded,[5187] [b]lovers of pleasures more than lovers of God;

5 Having a form[3446] of godliness,[2150] but [pfp][a]denying[720] the power[1411] thereof: [b]from such turn away.

6 For [a]of this sort are they which [ppt]creep into houses, and [ppt]lead captive silly women laden with sins,[266] led away[71] with divers4164 lusts,[1939]

7 Ever learning,[3129] and never able [ainf][a]to come to the knowledge[1922] of the truth.[225]

8 [a]Now as Jannes and Jambres withstood Moses, so do these also resist the truth: [b]men of [pfpp]corrupt minds,[3563] [c]reprobate[96] concerning the faith.[4102]

9 But they shall proceed no further: for their folly[454] shall be manifest unto all *men,* [a]as theirs also was.

Live a Godly Life

10 [a]But [I]thou [pfi]hast fully known my doctrine,[1319] manner of life, purpose,[4286] faith,[4102] longsuffering,[3115] charity,[26] patience,[5281]

11 Persecutions, afflictions, which came unto me [a]at Antioch, [b]at Iconium, [c]at Lystra; what persecutions I endured: but [d]out of *them* all the Lord delivered[4506] me.

26 IIGr. *taken alive* [a]1Tim. 3:7
1 [a]1Tim. 4:1; 2Tim. 4:3; 2Pet. 3:3; 1John 2:18; Jude 1:18
2 [a]Phil. 2:21 [b]2Pet. 2:3 [c]Jude 1:16 [d]1Tim. 6:4 [e]1Tim. 1:20; 2Pet. 2:12; Jude 1:10 [f]Rom. 1:30
3 [a]Rom. 1:31 [b]Rom. 1:31 [c]Titus 2:3 [d]2Pet. 3:3
4 [a]2Pet. 2:10 [b]Phil. 3:19; 2Pet. 2:13; Jude 1:4, 19
5 [a]1Tim. 5:8; Titus 1:16 [b]2Thess. 3:6; 1Tim. 6:5
6 [a]Matt. 23:14; Titus 1:11
7 [a]1Tim. 2:4
8 [a]Ex. 7:11 [b]1Tim. 6:5 [c]Rom. 1:28; 2Cor. 13:5; Titus 1:16
9 [a]Ex. 7:12; 8:18; 9:11
10 IOr, *thou hast been a diligent follower of* [a]Phil. 2:22; 1Tim. 4:6
11 [a]Acts 13:45, 50 [b]Acts 14:2, 5 [c]Acts 14:19 [d]Ps. 34:19; 2Cor. 1:10; 2Tim. 4:17
12 [a]Ps. 34:19; Matt. 16:24; John 17:14; Acts 14:22; 1Cor. 15:19; 1Thess. 3:3
13 [a]2Thess. 2:11; 1Tim. 4:1; 2Tim. 2:16
14 [a]2Tim. 1:13; 2:2
15 [a]John 5:39
16 [a]2Pet. 1:20, 21 [b]Rom. 15:4
17 [a]1Tim. 6:11 [b]2Tim. 2:21

1 [a]1Tim. 5:21; 6:13; 2Tim. 2:14 [b]Acts 10:42
2 [a]1Tim. 5:20; Titus 1:13; 2:15 [b]1Tim. 4:13
3 [a]2Tim. 3:1 [b]1Tim. 1:10 [c]2Tim. 3:6
4 [a]1Tim. 1:4; 4:7; Titus 1:14

🗝 12 Yea, and [a]all that [ppt]will [pinf]live[2198] godly2153 in Christ Jesus shall suffer persecution.

13 [a]But evil[4190] men and seducers shall wax4298 worse and worse, deceiving, and being deceived.

14 But [a]continue thou in the things which thou [ao]hast learned and hast been assured of,[4104] knowing of whom thou hast learned *them;*

15 And that from a child[1025] thou hast known[1492] [a]the holy[2413] scriptures,[1121] which are able[1410] [ainf]to make thee wise4679 unto salvation[4991] through faith[4102] which is in Christ Jesus.

16 [a]All scripture *is* given by inspiration of God, [b]and *is* profitable for doctrine,[1319] for reproof,[1650] for correction,[1882] for instruction[3809] in righteousness:[1343]

17 [a]That the man[444] of God[2316] may be perfect,[739] [pfpp][b]throughly furnished[1822] unto all good[18] works.[2041]

4 I [a]charge[1263] *thee* therefore before God, and the Lord Jesus Christ, [b]who shall judge[2919] the quick[2198] and the dead[3498] at his appearing[2015] and his kingdom;[932]

2 [aim]Preach[2784] the word;[3056] [aim]be instant in season, out of season; [aim]reprove, [aim][a]rebuke, [aim][b]exhort[3870] with all longsuffering and doctrine.[1322]

3 [a]For the time[2540] will come when they will not endure[430] [b]sound[5198] doctrine;[1319] [c]but after their own lusts[1939] shall they heap to themselves teachers,[1320] having itching ears;

4 And they shall turn away[654] *their* ears[189] from the truth,[225] and [a]shall be turned unto fables.[3454]

5 But watch thou in all things, [aim][a]endure afflictions,[2553] do the work[2041] of [b]an evangelist,[2099] [I]make full proof[4135] of thy ministry.[1248]

5 IOr, *fulfill* [a]2Tim. 1:8; 2:3 [b]Rom. 15:19; Col. 1:25; 4:17

🗝 **3:12** See note on 2 Timothy 1:12.

6 For [a]I am now ready to be offered,
and the time of [b]my departure [pfi]is at
hand.
7 [a]I [pfip]have fought[75] a good[2570]
fight,[73] I [pfi]have finished *my* course, I
[pfi]have kept the faith:[4102]
8 Henceforth there is laid up for me
[a]a crown of righteousness,[1343] which the
Lord, the righteous[1342] judge,[2923] shall
give me [b]at that day:[2250] and not to me
only, but unto all them also that [pfp]love[25]
his appearing.[2015]

Paul's Closing Words

9 Do thy diligence to come shortly
unto me:
🔑 10 For [a]Demas [ao]hath forsaken[1459]
me, [apt][b]having loved this present
world,[165] and is departed unto Thessalonica; Crescens to Galatia, Titus unto
Dalmatia.
11 [a]Only [b]Luke is with me. [apt]Take[353]
[c]Mark, and bring[71] him with thee: for he
is profitable[2173] to me for the ministry.[1248]
🔑 12 And [a]Tychicus [ao]have I sent[649] to
Ephesus.
13 The cloke that I left at Troas with
Carpus, when thou comest, bring *with
thee,* and the books, *but* especially the
parchments.
14 [a]Alexander the coppersmith [ao]did
me much evil: [b]the Lord [opt]reward him according to his works:[2041]
15 Of whom be thou ware[5442] also;
for he [pfi]hath greatly withstood[436] our
words.
16 At my first[4413] answer no man
[aom]stood with me, [a]but all *men* [ao]for-
sook[1459] me: [b]*I pray God* that it [opt]may
not be laid to their charge.[3049]
17 [a]Notwithstanding the Lord stood
with me, and strengthened me; [b]that by
me the preaching[2782] might be fully
known,[4135] and *that* all the Gentiles
might hear: and I was delivered[4506] [c]out
of the mouth of the lion.
18 [a]And the Lord shall deliver me
from every evil[4190] work,[2041] and will
preserve[4982] *me* unto his heavenly kingdom:[932] [b]to whom *be* glory[1391] for ever
and ever. Amen.[281]
19 Salute [a]Prisca and Aquila, and
[b]the household of Onesiphorus.
🔑 20 [a]Erastus abode at Corinth: but
[b]Trophimus have I left at Miletum
sick.
21 [a]Do thy diligence to come before
winter. Eubulus greeteth thee and
Pudens, and Linus, and Claudia, and all
the brethren.
22 [a]The Lord Jesus Christ *be* with
thy spirit. Grace *be* with you. Amen.

6 [a]Phil. 2:17 [b]Phil. 1:23; 2Pet. 1:14
7 [a]1Cor. 9:24, 25; Phil. 3:14; 1Tim. 6:12; Heb. 12:1
8 [a]1Cor. 9:25; James 1:12; 1Pet. 5:4; Rev. 2:10 [b]2Tim. 1:12
10 [a]Col. 4:14; Phile. 1:24 [b]1John 2:15
11 [a]2Tim. 1:15 [b]Col. 4:14; Phile. 1:24 [c]Acts 12:25; 15:37; Col. 4:10
12 [a]Acts 20:4; Eph. 6:21; Col. 4:7; Titus 3:12
14 [a]Acts 19:33; 1Tim. 1:20 [b]2Sam. 3:39; Ps. 28:4; Rev. 18:6
16 [a]2Tim. 1:15 [b]Acts 7:60
17 [a]Matt. 10:19; Acts 23:11; 27:23 [b]Acts 9:15; 26:17, 18; Eph. 3:8 [c]Ps. 22:21; 2Pet. 2:9
18 [a]Ps. 121:7 [b]Rom. 11:36; Gal. 1:5; Heb. 13:21
19 [a]Acts 18:2; Rom. 16:3 [b]2Tim. 1:16
20 [a]Acts 19:22; Rom. 16:23 [b]Acts 20:4; 21:29
21 [a]2Tim. 4:9
22 [a]Gal. 6:18; Phile. 1:25

🔑 **4:10** See the introduction to Titus.

🔑 **4:12** See note on Colossians 4:7.

🔑 **4:20** Trophimus was an Ephesian Christian who accompanied Paul to Europe after the riot in Ephesus. He returned to Ephesus, but later left to wait for Paul at Troas. He continued with Paul on his journey to Jerusalem as one of the delegates of the Asian churches bringing the collection for the church leaders there (Acts 20:1–5, cf. 1 Cor. 16:1–4). In Jerusalem, however, Jewish pilgrims from Asia recognized Trophimus in Paul's company. Then, finding Paul in the temple with four other men, they presumed that Paul had introduced Trophimus there (Acts 21:27–36). To take him beyond the court of the Gentiles would be to risk the penalty of death. The incident initiated a riot and was followed by Paul's arrest.

The Epistle of Paul to

TITUS

Titus was most likely a Gentile from Macedonia (Gal. 2:3) who was led to Christ by Paul (Titus 1:4). Titus was with Paul in Jerusalem (Gal. 2:1) when some dogmatic, Jewish brethren insisted that Titus should be circumcised. Paul would not allow it (Gal. 2:3–5) because this would have suggested that all non-Jewish Christians were second-class citizens in the church.

Titus remained as Paul's traveling companion and may have been with Paul when he wrote the letter to the Galatians. After Paul's release from his first imprisonment in Rome, Titus traveled with Paul to do mission work in the East. They landed at Crete and evangelized several towns (Titus 1:5). However, since Paul was unable to stay, he left Titus on Crete to complete the organization of congregations in that region. Titus met with considerable opposition and insubordination in the church, especially from the Jews (Titus 1:10). It is quite possible that Titus had written to Paul to report this problem and ask for spiritual advice. Paul responded with this short letter encouraging him to complete the process of organization, to ordain elders, to exercise his own authority firmly, and to teach sound doctrine while avoiding unnecessary strife.

Paul asked Titus to join him at Nicopolis (Titus 3:12), where he planned to spend the winter. It is probable that Titus was dispatched from there on a new mission to Dalmatia (2 Tim. 4:10).

The letter was probably delivered by Zenas and Apollos (Titus 3:13). It is believed, however, that Paul penned this sometime between his first and second imprisonments in Rome (ca. A.D. 64) when he was in the city of Nicopolis (Titus 3:12). This was about the same time that the Book of 1 Timothy was written. The instructive tone of this epistle to Titus is similar to that of Paul's first letter to Timothy. Both Titus and Timothy endured much criticism from false teachers during their ministries. Paul exhorts Titus to continue to preach sound doctrine (Titus 2:1) and to use wise judgment concerning the appointing of leaders in the church (Titus 1:5–9).

1 Paul, a servant[1401] of God,[2316] and
an apostle[652] of Jesus Christ, according to the faith[4102] of God's elect,[1588]
and [a]the acknowledging[1922] of the
truth[225] [b]which is after godliness;[2150]
2 [a]In hope[1680] of eternal[166] life,[2222]
which God,[2316] [b]that cannot lie, promised[1861] [c]before the world[166] began;
3 [a]But hath in due times[2540] manifested[5319] his word[3056] through preaching,[2782] [b]which [aop]is committed unto me
[c]according to the commandment[2003] of
God our Saviour;[4990]
4 To [a]Titus, [b]*mine* own son[5043] after
[c]the common[2839] faith: [d]Grace, mercy,
and peace, from God the Father[3962]
and the Lord[2962] Jesus Christ[5547] our Saviour.

The Qualifications Of an Elder

🔑 5 For this cause left I thee in Crete,
that thou [aosb]shouldest [a]set in order[1930]
the things that are [I]wanting, and [aosb][b]or-
dain[2525] elders[4245] in every city, as I
[aom]had appointed[1299] thee:
🔑 6 [a]If any be blameless,[410] [b]the husband[435] of one wife, [c]having faithful[4103]
children[5043] not accused of riot[810] or unruly.[506]
7 For a bishop[1985] must be blameless, as [a]the steward[3623] of God; not self-
willed, not soon angry,[3711] [b]not given to

1 [a]2Tim. 2:25 [b]1Tim. 3:16; 6:3 **2** [a]2Tim. 1:1; Titus 3:7 [b]Num. 23:19; 2Tim. 2:13 [c]Rom. 16:25; 2Tim. 1:9; 1Pet. 1:20 **3** [a]2Tim. 1:10 [b]1Thess. 2:4; 1Tim. 1:11 [c]1Tim. 1:1; 2:3; 4:10 **4** [a]2Cor. 2:13; 7:13; 8:6, 16, 23; 12:18; Gal. 2:3 [b]1Tim. 1:2 [c]Rom. 1:2; 2Cor. 4:13; 2Pet. 1:1 [d]Eph. 1:2; Col. 1:2; 1Tim. 1:2; 2Tim. 1:2 **5** [I]Or, *left undone* [a]1Cor. 11:34 [b]Acts 14:23; 2Tim. 2:2 **6** [a]1Tim. 3:2 [b]1Tim. 3:12 [c]1Tim. 3:4, 12 **7** [a]Matt. 24:45; 1Cor. 4:1, 2 [b]Lev. 10:9; Eph. 5:18; 1Tim. 3:3, 8

🔑 **1:5** See the introduction to Titus.
🔑 **1:6** See note on 1 Timothy 3:2.

wine, no striker, [c]not given to filthy
lucre;146
8 [a]But a lover of hospitality, a lover
of [I]good men,[5358] sober,[4998] just,[1342]
holy,[3741] temperate;1468
9 [a]Holding fast[472] [b]the faithful
word[3056] [I]as he hath been taught,[1322] that
he may be able [c]by sound doctrine both
[pinf]to exhort[3870] and to convince[1651] the
[ppt]gainsayers.483
10 For [a]there are many unruly[506] and
vain talkers[3151] and [b]deceivers, [c]specially
they of the circumcision:[4061]
11 Whose mouths must [pinf]be
stopped, [a]who subvert whole houses,
teaching things which they ought not,
[b]for filthy lucre's2771 sake.
12 [a]One of themselves, *even* a
prophet[4396] of their own, said, The
[an]Cretians *are* alway liars, evil beasts,
slow[692] bellies.
13 This witness[3141] is true.
[a]Wherefore [pim]rebuke them sharply,
that they [psa]may be [b]sound in the
faith;[4102]
14 [a]Not giving heed to Jewish fables,[3454] and [b]commandments of men,
that [ppt]turn from[654] the truth.[225]
15 [a]Unto the pure[2513] all things *are*
pure: but [b]unto them that [pfpp]are defiled
and [ajn]unbelieving[571] *is* nothing pure; but
even their mind[3563] and conscience[4893]
[pfip]is defiled.
16 They profess[3670] that they know
God; but [a]in works they deny[720] *him,*
being abominable,[947] and disobedient,[545]
[b]and unto every good[18] work[2041] reprobate.[96]

Teach Sound Doctrine

2 🔑But speak[2980] thou the things
which become [a]sound[5198] doctrine:
2 That the aged men be sober,3524
grave,[4586] temperate,[4998] [ppt][a]sound in
faith,[4102] in charity,[26] in patience.[5281]
3 [a]The aged women likewise, that
they be in behaviour as becometh
[I]holiness,[2412] not false accusers,[1228] not
[pfpp]given to much wine,[3631] teachers of
good things;
4 That they [psa]may teach[4994] the
young[3501] women to be sober,[4994] [a]to love
their husbands, to love their children,
5 *To be* discreet,[4998] chaste,[53] keepers
at home,[3626] good,[18] [a]obedient[5293] to their
own husbands, [b]that the word[3056] of God
[psmp]be not blasphemed.[987]
6 Young men likewise exhort[3870]
[pinf]to be [I]sober minded.4993
7 [a]In all things shewing thyself a
pattern[5179] of good[2570] works:[2041] in doctrine[1319] *shewing* uncorruptness, gravity,
[b]sincerity,
8 [a]Sound[5199] speech,[3056] that cannot
be condemned;[176] [b]that he that is of the
contrary part [asbp][c]may be ashamed,1788
having no evil[5337] thing [pinf]to say of you.
9 *Exhort* [a]servants[1401] to be obedient
unto their own masters,[1203] *and* to please
them well[2101] [b]in all *things;* not answering again;
10 Not purloining,[3557] but [ppt]shewing
all good fidelity;[4102] [a]that they [psa]may
adorn the doctrine[1319] of God our
Saviour[4990] in all things.
11 For [a]the grace[5485] of God that
bringeth salvation[4992] [aop][b]hath appeared[2014] to all men,[444]
12 Teaching[3811] us [a]that, [apt]deny-
ing[720] ungodliness[763] [b]and worldly[2886]
lusts,[1939] we [aosb]should live soberly,4996
righteously,[1346] and godly,2153 in this
present world;[165]

7 [c]1Tim. 3:3, 8; 1Pet. 5:2
8 [I]Or, *good things* [a]1Tim. 3:2
9 [I]Or, *in teaching* [a]2Thess. 2:15; 2Tim. 1:13 [b]1Tim. 1:15; 4:9; 6:3; 2Tim. 2:2 [c]1Tim. 1:10; 6:3; 2Tim. 4:3; Titus 2:1
10 [a]1Tim. 1:6 [b]Rom. 16:18 [c]Acts 15:1
11 [a]Matt. 23:14; 2Tim. 3:6 [b]1Tim. 6:5
12 [a]Acts 17:28
13 [a]2Cor. 13:10; 2Tim. 4:2 [b]Titus 2:2
14 [a]1Tim. 1:4; 4:7; 2Tim. 4:4 [b]Isa. 29:13; Matt. 15:9; Col. 2:22
15 [a]Luke 11:39-41; Rom. 14:14, 20; 1Cor. 6:12; 10:23, 35; 1Tim. 4:3, 4 [b]Rom. 14:23
16 [a]2Tim. 3:5; Jude 1:4 [b]Rom. 1:28; 2Tim. 3:8

1 [a]1Tim. 1:10; 6:3; 2Tim. 1:13; Titus 1:9
2 [a]Titus 1:13
3 [I]Or, *holy women* [a]1Tim. 2:9, 10; 3:11; 1Pet. 3:3, 4
4 [a]1Tim. 5:14
5 [a]1Cor. 14:34; Eph. 5:22; Col. 3:18; 1Tim. 2:11; 1Pet. 3:1, 5 [b]Rom. 2:24; 1Tim. 6:1
6 [I]Or, *discreet*
7 [a]1Tim. 4:12; 1Pet. 5:3 [b]Eph. 6:24
8 [a]1Tim. 6:3 [b]Neh. 5:9; 1Tim. 5:14; 1Pet. 2:12, 15; 3:16 [c]2Thess. 3:14
9 [a]Eph. 6:5; Col. 3:22; 1Tim. 6:1, 2; 1Pet. 2:18 [b]Eph. 5:24
10 [a]Matt. 5:16; Phil. 2:15
11 [a]Rom. 5:15; Titus 3:4, 5; 1Pet. 5:12 [b]Luke 3:6; John 1:9; 1Tim. 2:4
12 [a]Luke 1:75; Rom. 6:19; Eph. 1:4; Col. 1:22; 1Thess. 4:7 [b]1Pet. 4:2; 1John 2:16

🔑 **2:1–5** In verse four, the word "sober" is the Greek verb *sōphronízō* (4994). It means "to be sober minded or to voluntarily place limitations on one's own freedom." Some have mistakenly thought that the Apostle Paul inferred that women should not teach at all in the church (1 Cor. 14:34–40; 1 Tim. 2:12). However, Paul instructs Titus to teach the older women (v. 3) as well as the older men (v. 2). In addition, he urges the aged women to be "teachers of good things" (v. 3). Those older women who evidence spiritual maturity are to teach the younger women, both in the church and at home, by counsel and by example. See note on 1 Timothy 2:9–15.

13 ppt[a]Looking for[4327] that blessed [b]hope,[1680] and the glorious[1391] [c]appearing[2015] of the great God[2316] and our Saviour[4990] Jesus Christ;[5547]

14 [a]Who gave himself for us, that he asbmmight redeem[3084] us from all iniquity,[458] [b]and aosbpurify[2511] unto himself [c]a peculiar[4041] people, [d]zealous of good[2570] works.[2041]

15 These things speak, and [a]exhort, and rebuke with all authority. [b]Let no man despise thee.

God's Mercy Remembered

3 Put them in mind [a]to be subject[5293] to principalities[746] and powers,[1849] pinfto obey magistrates, [b]to be ready to every good[18] work,[2041]

2 pinf[a]To speak evil[987] of no man, [b]to be no brawlers, *but* [c]gentle, shewing all [d]meekness unto all men.

3 For [a]we ourselves also were sometimes foolish,[453] disobedient,[545] deceived, serving[1398] divers4164 lusts[1939] and pleasures, living in malice[2549] and envy, hateful, *and* hating one another.

4 But after that [a]the kindness[5544] and love[5363] of [b]God our Saviour[4990] toward man aopappeared,[2014]

5 [a]Not by works of righteousness[1343] which we aohave done, but according to his mercy[1656] he saved[4982] us, by [b]the washing[3067] of regeneration,[3824] and renewing[342] of the anHoly[40] Ghost;[4151]

6 [a]Which he shed on us [I]abundantly through Jesus Christ our Saviour;[4990]

7 [a]That aptpbeing justified[1344] by his grace,[5485] [b]we asbmshould be made heirs[2818] [c]according to the hope[1680] of eternal[166] life.[2222]

8 [a]*This is* a faithful[4103] saying,[3056] and these things I will that thou pinfaffirm constantly,[1226] that they which pfphave believed[4100] in God psamight be careful pinf[b]to maintain good works. These things are good and profitable unto men.

9 But pim[a]avoid foolish[3474] questions, and genealogies,[1076] and contentions, and strivings[3163] about the law; [b]for they are unprofitable and vain.

10 A man that is an heretick[141] [a]after the first and second admonition[3559] pim[b]reject;[3868]

11 Knowing that he that is such pfpis subverted, and sinneth,[264] [a]being condemned of himself.[843]

Conclusion

12 When I shall send Artemas unto thee, or [a]Tychicus, be diligent ainfto come unto me to Nicopolis: for I pfihave determined[2919] there to winter.

13 Bring Zenas the lawyer and [a]Apollos on their journey diligently, that nothing psabe wanting unto them.

14 And pimlet ours also learn[3129] pinf[a]to [I][b]maintain good works for necessary[316] uses, that they be [c]not unfruitful.

15 All that are with me salute782 thee. Greet782 them that pptlove[5368] us in the faith.[4102] Grace *be* with you all. Amen.281

2:13 [a]1Cor. 1:7; Phil. 3:20; 2Pet. 3:12 [b]Acts 24:15; Col. 1:5, 23; Titus 1:2; 3:7 [c]Col. 3:4; 2Tim. 4:1, 8; Heb. 9:28; 1Pet. 1:7; 1John 3:2
14 [a]Gal. 1:4; 2:20; Eph. 5:2; 1Tim. 2:6 [b]Heb. 9:14 [c]Ex. 15:16; 19:5; Deut. 7:6; 14:2; 26:18; 1Pet. 2:9 [d]Eph. 2:10; Titus 3:8
15 [a]2Tim. 4:2 [b]1Tim. 4:12

3:1 [a]Rom. 13:1; 1Pet. 2:13 [b]Col. 1:10; 2Tim. 2:21; Heb. 13:21
2 [a]Eph. 4:31 [b]2Tim. 2:24, 25 [c]Phil. 4:5 [d]Eph. 4:2; Col. 3:12
3 [a]1Cor. 6:11; Eph. 2:1; Col. 1:21; 3:7; 1Pet. 4:3
4 [a]Titus 2:11 [b]1Tim. 2:3
5 [a]Rom. 3:20; 9:11; 11:6; Gal. 2:16; Eph. 2:4, 8, 9; 2Tim. 1:9 [b]John 3:3, 5; Eph. 5:26; 1Pet. 3:21
6 [I]Gr. *richly* [a]Ezek. 36:25; Joel 2:28; John 1:16; Acts 2:33; 10:45; Rom. 5:5
7 [a]Rom. 3:24; Gal. 2:16; Titus 2:11 [b]Rom. 8:23, 24 [c]Titus 1:2
8 [a]1Tim. 1:15; Titus 1:9 [b]Titus 2:14; 3:1, 14
9 [a]1Tim. 1:4; 2Tim. 2:23; Titus 1:14 [b]2Tim. 2:14
10 [a]2Cor. 13:2 [b]Matt. 18:17; Rom. 16:17; 2Thess. 3:6, 14; 2Tim. 3:5; 2John 1:10 **11** [a]Acts 13:46
12 [a]Acts 20:4; 2Tim. 4:12 **13** [a]Acts 18:24
14 [I]Or, *profess honest trades* [a]Titus 3:8 [b]Eph. 4:28 [c]Rom. 15:28; Phil. 1:11; 4:17; Col. 1:10; 2Pet. 1:8

3:1 See note on 1 Peter 2:17.
3:7 See note on Romans 3:19, 20.
3:12, 13 See the introduction to Titus.

The Epistle of Paul to

PHILEMON

The Epistle to Philemon was a private letter written by Paul during his first imprisonment in Rome (A.D. 62). The focus of the letter is to give a proper understanding of the Hebrew fugitive law found in Deuteronomy 23:15, 16. It reveals how Paul acted in strict accordance with the requirements of the law in dealing with Onesimus, a slave who had run away from Philemon. First, Paul gave him shelter in his own hired house. He did not betray him as a fugitive, nor did he send word to Philemon to come to Rome to take Onesimus back. Furthermore, Paul instructed Onesimus in the gospel, eventually leading him to salvation in Christ (Phile. 1:10). He then sent Onesimus back to Philemon as a trusted messenger and brother in Christ, bearing a request for Philemon to grant Onesimus his freedom (Phile. 1:12). Paul did not accuse Onesimus of wrongdoing by running away from Philemon. Instead, Paul stated that it was by the merciful providence of God that he had departed from Philemon. Paul desired for Philemon to receive Onesimus back no longer as a servant, but as a beloved brother and partner in Christ (Phile. 1:15–17).

Some suggest that Onesimus had stolen something from Philemon and had run away because he was afraid of the punishment he would receive. Paul graciously offered to repay this and any debts that Onesimus owed to Philemon (Phile. 1:18). It is commonly believed that Onesimus was received by Philemon and forgiven his debt, just as Paul had expected (Phile. 1:21).

1 Paul, [a]a prisoner of Jesus Christ,[5547] and Timothy *our* brother,[80] unto Philemon our dearly beloved,[27] [b]and fellowlabourer,

2 And to *our* beloved Apphia, and [a]Archippus [b]our fellowsoldier, and to [c]the church[1577] in thy house:[3624]

3 [a]Grace[5485] to you, and peace,[1515] from God[2316] our Father[3962] and the Lord[2962] Jesus Christ.

Paul's Expression of Thanksgiving

4 [a]I thank[2168] my God, making mention of thee always in my prayers,[4335]

5 [a]Hearing of thy love[26] and faith,[4102] which thou hast toward the Lord Jesus, and toward all saints;[40]

6 That the communication[2842] of thy faith may become effectual [a]by the acknowledging of every good thing[18] which is in you in Christ Jesus.

7 For we have great joy[5485] and consolation[3874] in thy love, because the bowels[4698] of the saints [pfip][a]are refreshed by thee, brother.

1 [a]Eph. 3:1; 4:1; 2Tim. 1:8; Phile. 1:9 [b]Phil. 2:25
2 [a]Col. 4:17 [b]Phil. 2:25 [c]Rom. 16:5; 1Cor. 16:19
3 [a]Eph. 1:2
4 [a]Eph. 1:16; 1Thess. 1:2; 2Thess. 1:3
5 [a]Eph. 1:15; Col. 1:4
6 [a]Phil. 1:9, 11
7 [a]2Cor. 7:13; 2Tim. 1:16; Phile. 1:20
8 [a]1Thess. 2:6
9 [a]Phile. 1:1
10 [a]Col. 4:9 [b]1Cor. 4:15; Gal. 4:19
13 [a]1Cor. 16:17; Phil. 2:30
14 [a]2Cor. 9:7

Onesimus

8 Wherefore, [a]though I might be much bold in Christ to enjoin[2004] thee that which is convenient,[433]

9 Yet for love's sake I rather beseech[3870] *thee,* being such an one as Paul the aged, [a]and now also a prisoner of Jesus Christ.

10 I beseech thee for my son[5043] [a]Onesimus, [b]whom I [ao]have begotten[1080] in my bonds:

11 Which in time past was to thee unprofitable,[890] but now profitable[2173] to thee and to me:

12 Whom I [ao]have sent again: thou therefore [aim]receive him, that is, mine own bowels:[4698]

13 Whom I [ipf]would have [pinf]retained[2722] with me, [a]that in thy stead he [psa]might have ministered[1247] unto me in the bonds of the gospel:[2098]

14 But without thy mind [ao]would I [ainf]do nothing; [a]that thy benefit[18] should not be as it were of necessity,[318] but willingly.

15 [a]For perhaps he therefore [aop]departed for a season,[5610] that thou [psa]shouldest receive[568] him for ever;

16 Not now as a servant, but above a servant,[1401] [a]a brother[80] beloved, specially to me, but how much more unto thee, [b]both in the flesh and in the Lord?

17 If thou count me therefore [a]a partner,[2844] receive him as myself.

18 If he [ao]hath wronged[91] thee, or oweth *thee* ought, [pim]put that on mine account;[1677]

19 I Paul [ao]have written *it* with mine own hand, I will repay *it:* albeit I do not say to thee how thou owest unto me even thine own self besides.

20 Yea, brother, [opt]let me have[3685] joy of thee in the Lord: [aim][a]refresh my bowels in the Lord.

21 [a]Having confidence in thy obedience[5218] I wrote unto thee, knowing that thou wilt also do more than I say.

22 But withal[260] [pim]prepare me also a lodging: for [a]I trust that [b]through your prayers I shall be given[5483] unto you.

23 There salute[782] thee [a]Epaphras, my fellowprisoner in Christ Jesus;

24 [a]Marcus, [b]Aristarchus, [c]Demas, [d]Lucas, my fellowlabourers.

25 [a]The grace of our Lord Jesus Christ *be* with your spirit. Amen.[281]

15 [a]Gen. 45:5, 8
16 [a]Matt. 23:8; 1Tim. 6:2 [b]Col. 3:22
17 [a]2Cor. 8:23
20 [a]Phile. 1:7
21 [a]2Cor. 7:16
22 [a]Phil. 1:25; 2:24 [b]2Cor. 1:11
23 [a]Col. 1:7; 4:12
24 [a]Acts 12:12, 25 [b]Acts 19:29; 27:2; Col. 4:10 [c]Col. 4:14 [d]2Tim. 4:11
25 [a]2Tim. 4:22

1:23 See notes on Colossians 1:7 and 4:10.

The Epistle to the

HEBREWS

The author of the Book of Hebrews is unknown. Martin Luther suggested that Apollos was the author. This is based on Acts 18:24–28, where Apollos is referred to as a well-read, Hellenistic Jew from Alexandria in Egypt. Tertullian (writing in A.D. 150–230) said that Hebrews was a letter of Barnabas. Adolf Harnack and J. Rendel Harris speculated that it was written by Priscilla (or Prisca). William Ramsey suggested that it was done by Philip. However, the traditional position is that the Apostle Paul wrote Hebrews. From the very beginning, the eastern church attributed the letter to him, but the western church did not accept this until the fourth century. Eusebius (A.D. 263–339) believed that Paul wrote it, but Origen (ca. A.D. 185–254) was not positive of Pauline authorship. About the end of the second century, Clement of Alexandria thought that Paul had originally written the letter in the Hebrew language and that it was later translated by Luke or by someone else into Greek. Notwithstanding, the recipients of the letter knew who the author was and recognized his credibility in writing the work.

There is also uncertainty as to the exact date of the writing of Hebrews. Numerous references to the temple in Jerusalem seem to place the date of writing prior to the fall of Jerusalem in A.D. 70 (Heb. 10:11; 13:10, 11).

The purpose of the epistle was to reassure Jewish Christians that their faith in Jesus as the Messiah was secure and legitimate. Also, it was intended to prepare them for the impending disaster of the Roman destruction of Jerusalem. The temple, with its system of animal sacrifices, and the office of the priest, would soon be done away with, just as Jesus had predicted. The Book of Hebrews explains that there was no more need for a priest to intercede before God on an individual's behalf, since Christ's death provided believers with direct access to God's throne (Heb. 4:14–16; 10:19–22). Furthermore, the blood of Christ now continually takes away sin (Heb. 9:18–26).

The Book of Hebrews is easily divided into two major sections: the first deals with doctrinal issues (Heb. 1:1—10:18), and the second focuses on practical living (Heb. 10:19—13:25). In addition, it contains several warnings to Jewish Christians not to revert back to Judaism and that system of worship (Heb. 10:39). It was evident that these believers were weak in their faith; when they should have been teaching others, they themselves still required teaching. The writer urges them to grow and not remain as "babes" in Christ (Heb. 5:12–14). A major theme in the book, often expressed by the words "better" and "great," is the superiority and preeminence of Christ (Heb. 1:4; 2:3; 4:14; 7:19, 22; 8:6; 9:11, 23; 10:32, 34, 35; 11:16, 34, 40; 12:1; 13:20).

God Has Spoken Through His Son

1 God,[2316] who at sundry times[4181]
and [a]in divers manners4187
[apt]spake[2980] in time past[3819] unto the
fathers[3962] by the prophets,[4396]
2 Hath [a]in these last[2078] days [b]spoken
unto us by *his* Son,[5207] [c]whom he [ao]hath
appointed[5087] heir[2818] of all things, [d]by
whom also he made[4160] the worlds;[165]
3 [a]Who being the brightness[541] of
his glory,[1391] and the express image[5481]
of his person,[5287] and [b]upholding[5342] all
things by the word[4487] of his power,[1411]
[c]when he had by himself [apt]purged our
sins,[266] [d]sat down on the right hand[1188]
of the Majesty on high;

Christ Is Greater Than the Angels

4 Being [apt]made so much better[2909]
than the angels,[32] as [a]he [pfi]hath by inheritance obtained[2816] a more excel-
lent1313 name[3686] than they.
5 For unto which of the angels said

1 [a]Num. 12:6, 8 **2** [a]Deut. 4:30; Gal. 4:4; Eph. 1:10 [b]John 1:17; 15:15; Heb. 2:3 [c]Ps. 2:8; Matt. 21:38; 28:18; John 3:35; Rom. 8:17 [d]John 1:3; 1Cor. 8:6; Col. 1:16 **3** [a]John 1:14; 14:9; 2Cor. 4:4; Col. 1:15 [b]John 1:4; Col. 1:17; Rev. 4:11 [c]Heb. 7:27; 9:12, 14, 26 [d]Ps. 110:1; Eph. 1:20; Heb. 8:1; 10:2; 12:2; 1Pet. 3:22 **4** [a]Eph. 1:21; Phil. 2:9, 10

he at any time, [a]Thou art my son,[5207] this day [pfi]have I begotten[1080] thee? And again, [b]I will be to him a Father, and he shall be to me a Son?

🗝 6 And again, when he [aosb]bringeth in1521 [a]the first begotten[4416] into the world, he saith, [b]And [aim]let all the angels of God worship4352 him.

7 And [I]of the angels he saith, [a]Who [ppt]maketh his angels spirits,[4151] and his ministers3011 a flame of fire.

8 But unto the Son *he saith,* [a]Thy throne, O God, *is* for ever[165,1519][3588] and ever: a sceptre4464 of [I]righteousness2118 *is* the sceptre of thy kingdom.[932]

9 Thou [ao]hast loved[25] righteousness,[1343] and [ao]hated iniquity;[458] therefore God, *even* thy God, [ao][a]hath anointed[5548] thee with the oil[1637] of gladness[20] above thy fellows.3353

10 And, [a]Thou, Lord, in the beginning[746] [ao]hast laid the foundation of the earth; and the heavens are the works of thine hands:

11 [a]They [fm]shall perish;[622] but thou remainest; and they all shall wax old[3822] as doth a garment;

12 And as a vesture4018 shalt thou fold them up, and they [fp]shall be changed:[236] but thou art the same, and thy years shall not fail.

13 But to which of the angels said he at any time, [a]Sit on my right hand,[1188] until I make thine enemies thy footstool?

14 [a]Are they not all ministering3010 spirits,[4151] [ppp]sent forth to minister[1248] for them who [ppt]shall be [pinf][b]heirs of[2816] salvation?[4991]

2

Therefore we ought to give the more earnest heed to the things which we [aptp]have heard, lest at any time we should [aosb][I]let *them* slip.3901

2 For if the word[3056] [aptp][a]spoken by angels[32] [aom]was stedfast,[949] and [b]every transgression[3847] and disobedience[3876] received a just[1738] recompence of reward;[3405]

3 [a]How shall we escape, if we [apt]neglect so great salvation;[4991] [b]which at the first began [pip]to be spoken by the Lord, and was [c]confirmed[950] unto us by them that [apt]heard *him;*

4 [a]God also [ppt]bearing *them* witness, [b]both with signs[4592] and wonders,[5059] and with divers4164 miracles,[1411] and [I][c]gifts[3311] of the [an]Holy Ghost, [d]according to his own will?

Christ Is Preeminent

5 For unto the angels [ao]hath he not put in subjection[5293] [a]the world[3625] to come,[3195] whereof we speak.

6 But one in a certain place testified,[1263] saying, [a]What is man,[444] that thou art mindful of him? or the son of man, that thou visitest[1980] him?

7 Thou madest him [I]a little lower than the angels; thou [ao]crownedst him with glory[1391] and honour, and [ao]didst set him over the works of thy hands:

8 [a]Thou [ao]hast put all things in subjection[5293] under his feet. For in that he [aie]put all in subjection[5293] under him, he left nothing *that is* not put under[506] him. But now [b]we see not yet all things [pfpp]put under him.

9 But we see Jesus, [a]who [pfpp]was made a little lower than the angels [I]for the suffering[3804] of death,[2288] [pfpp][b]crowned with glory and honour; that he by the grace[5485] of God [asbm]should taste[1089] death [c]for every man.

10 [a]For it became him, [b]for whom *are* all things, and by whom *are* all things, in [apt]bringing many sons unto glory, [ainf]to make [c]the captain of their salvation [d]perfect[5048] through sufferings.

11 For [a]both he that [ppt]sanctifieth[37] and they who are sanctified [b]*are* all of

5 [a]Ps. 2:7; Acts 13:33; Heb. 5:5 [b]2Sam. 7:14; 1Chr. 22:10; 28:6; Ps. 89:26, 27
6 [a]Rom. 8:29; Col. 1:18; Rev. 1:5 [b]Ps. 97:7; 1Pet. 3:22
7 [I]Gr. *unto* [a]Ps. 104:4
8 [I]Gr. *rightness, or, straightness* [a]Ps. 45:6, 7
9 [a]Isa. 61:1; Acts 4:27; 10:38
10 [a]Ps. 102:25-28
11 [a]Isa. 34:4; 51:6; Matt. 24:35; 2Pet. 3:7, 10; Rev. 21:1
13 [a]Ps. 110:1; Matt. 22:44; Mark 12:36; Luke 20:42; Heb. 1:3; 10:12
14 [a]Gen. 19:16; 32:1, 2, 24; Ps. 34:7; 91:11; 103:20, 21; Dan. 3:28; 7:10; 10:11; Matt. 18:10; Luke 1:19; 2:9, 13; Acts 12:7; 27:23 [b]Rom. 8:17; Titus 3:7; James 2:5; 1Pet. 3:7

1 [I]Gr. *run out as leaking vessels*
2 [a]Deut. 33:2; Ps. 68:17; Acts 7:53; Gal. 3:19 [b]Num. 15:30, 31; Deut. 4:3; 17:2, 5, 12; 27:26
3 [a]Heb. 10:28, 29; 12:25 [b]Matt. 4:17; Mark 1:14; Heb. 1:2 [c]Luke 1:2
4 [I]Or, *distributions* [a]Mark 16:20; Acts 14:3; 19:11; Rom. 15:18, 19; 1Cor. 2:4 [b]Acts 2:22, 43 [c]1Cor. 12:4, 7, 11 [d]Eph. 1:5, 9
5 [a]Heb. 6:5; 2Pet. 3:13
6 [a]Job 7:17; Ps. 8:4; 144:3
7 [I]Or, *a little while inferior to*
8 [a]Matt. 28:18; 1Cor. 15:27; Eph. 1:22; Heb. 1:13 [b]1Cor. 15:25
9 [I]Or, *by* [a]Phil. 2:7, 8, 9 [b]Acts 2:33 [c]John 3:16; 12:32; Rom. 5:18; 8:32; 2Cor. 5:15; 1Tim. 2:6; 1John 2:2; Rev. 5:9
10 [a]Luke 24:46 [b]Rom. 11:36 [c]Acts 3:15; 5:31; Heb. 12:2 [d]Luke 13:32; Heb. 5:9
11 [a]Heb. 10:10, 14 [b]Acts 17:26

🗝 **1:6** See note on Colossians 1:15–18.

one: for which cause [c]he is not ashamed to call them brethren,[80]

12 Saying, [a]I [ft]will declare[518] thy name[3686] unto my brethren, in the midst of the church[1577] will I sing praise unto thee.

13 And again, [a]I will put my trust[3982] in him. And again, [b]Behold I and the children [c]which God [ao]hath given me.

14 Forasmuch then as the children [pfi]are partakers[2841] of flesh[4561] and blood,[129] he [a]also himself likewise [ao]took part of the same; [b]that through death he [asba]might destroy him that [ppt]had the power of death, that is, the devil;[1228]

15 And [aosb]deliver[525] them who [a]through fear[5401] of death were all their lifetime[2198] subject to[1777] bondage.[1397]

16 For verily[1222] [I]he [pin]took not on[1949] *him the nature of* angels; but he [pin]took on *him* the seed[4690] of Abraham.

17 Wherefore in all things it [ipf]behoved[3780] him [aifp][a]to be made like unto *his* brethren,[80] that he [asbm]might be [b]a merciful and faithful[4103] high priest[749] in things *pertaining* to God, [aies]to make reconciliation for[2433] the sins[266] of the people.[2992]

18 [a]For in that he himself [pfi]hath suffered being tempted,[3985] he is able [ainf]to succour[997] them that are tempted.

Superior to Moses

3 Wherefore, holy[40] brethren,[80] partakers[3353] of [a]the heavenly calling,[2821] [aim]consider[2657] [b]the Apostle[652] and High Priest[749] of our profession,[3671] Christ[5547] Jesus;

2 Who was faithful[4103] to him that [apt][I][a]appointed him, as also [b]Moses *was faithful* in all his house.

3 For this *man* [pfip]was counted worthy of more glory[1391] than Moses, inasmuch as [a]he who [apt]hath builded the house hath more honour than the house.

4 For every house is builded by some *man;* but [a]he that [apt]built all things *is* God.[2316]

5 [a]And Moses verily[3303] *was* faithful in all his house, as [b]a servant, [c]for a testimony of those things which were to be spoken after;

6 But Christ as [a]a son[5207] over his own house; [b]whose house are we, [c]if we [aosb]hold fast[2722] the confidence and the rejoicing of the hope[1680] firm[949] unto the end.[5056]

7 Wherefore (as [a]the Holy Ghost saith, [b]To day if ye [aosb]will hear[191] his voice,

8 [psa]Harden[4645] not your hearts,[2588] as in the provocation, in the day of temptation[3986] in the wilderness:

9 When your fathers tempted[3985] me, proved me, and saw my works forty years.

10 Wherefore I [ao]was grieved with that generation,[1074] and said, They do alway err in *their* heart; and they [ao]have not known[1097] my ways.

11 So I [ao]sware in my wrath,[3709] [I]They shall not enter into my rest.[2663])

12 Take heed, brethren, lest there be in any of you an evil[4190] heart[2588] of unbelief,[570] [aie]in departing[868] from the living[2198] God.

13 But exhort[3870] one another daily, while it is called To day; lest any of you [asbp]be hardened[4645] through the deceitfulness of sin.

14 For we [pfi]are made partakers[3353] of Christ,[5547] [a]if we [aosb]hold[2722] the beginning of our confidence[5287] stedfast unto the end;[5056]

15 While it is said, [a]To day if ye [asba]will hear his voice, harden[4645] not your hearts, as in the provocation.[3894]

16 [a]For some, when they had heard, did provoke:[3893] howbeit[235] not all that came out of Egypt by Moses.

17 But with whom [ao]was he grieved[4360] forty years? *was it* not with them that [apt]had sinned,[264] [a]whose carcases fell[4098] in the wilderness?

11 [c]Matt. 28:10; John 20:17; Rom. 8:29
12 [a]Ps. 22:22, 25
13 [a]Ps. 18:2; Isa. 12:2 [b]Isa. 8:18 [c]John 10:29; 17:6, 9-12
14 [a]John 1:14; Rom. 8:3; Phil. 2:7 [b]1Cor. 15:54, 55; Col. 2:15; 2Tim. 1:10
15 [a]Luke 1:74; Rom. 8:15; 2Tim. 1:7
16 [I]Gr. *he taketh not hold of angels, but of the seed of Abraham he taketh hold*
17 [a]Phil. 2:7 [b]Heb. 4:15; 5:1, 2
18 [a]Heb. 4:15, 16; 5:2; 7:25

1 [a]Rom. 1:7; 1Cor. 1:2; Eph. 4:1; Phil. 3:14; 2Thess. 1:11; 2Tim. 1:9; 2Pet. 1:10 [b]Rom. 15:8; Heb. 2:17; 4:14; 5:5; 6:20; 8:1; 9:11; 10:21
2 [I]Gr. *made* [a]1Sam. 12:6 [b]Num. 12:7; Heb. 3:5
3 [a]Zech. 6:12; Matt. 16:18
4 [a]Eph. 2:10; 3:9; Heb. 1:2
5 [a]Heb. 3:2 [b]Ex. 14:31; Num. 12:7; Deut. 3:24; Josh. 1:2; 8:31 [c]Deut. 18:15, 18, 19
6 [a]Heb. 1:2 [b]1Cor. 3:16; 6:19; 2Cor. 6:16; Eph. 2:21, 22; 1Tim. 3:15; 1Pet. 2:5 [c]Matt. 10:22; 24:13; Rom. 5:2; Col. 1:23; Heb. 3:14; 6:11; 10:35
7 [a]2Sam. 23:2; Acts 1:16 [b]Ps. 95:7; Heb. 3:15
11 [I]Gr. *If they shall enter*
14 [a]Heb. 3:6
15 [a]Heb. 3:7
16 [a]Num. 14:2, 4, 11, 24, 30; Deut. 1:34, 36, 38
17 [a]Num. 14:22, 29; 26:65; Ps. 106:26; 1Cor. 10:5; Jude 1:5

3:12 See note on 2 Thessalonians 2:3.

18 And [a]to whom sware he that they should not enter into his rest,[2663] but to them that [apt]believed not?[544]

19 [a]So we see that they could not [ainf]enter in because of unbelief.[570]

The Saints' Everlasting Rest

4 [aosi]Let [a]us therefore fear,[5399] lest, a promise[1860] being left *us* of [ainf]entering into his rest,[2663] any of you [psa]should seem [pfin]to come short of it.

2 For unto us was the gospel preached,[2097] as well as unto them: but [I]the word[3056] preached[189] did not profit them, [II]not [pfpp]being mixed with faith[4102] in them that [apt]heard *it.*

3 [a]For we which [apt]have believed[4100] do enter into [art]rest,[2663] as he said, [b]As I have sworn in my wrath,[3709] if they shall enter into my rest: although the works[2041] [aptp]were finished from the foundation of the world.

4 For he spake in a certain place of the seventh *day* on this wise, [a]And God [ao]did rest[2664] the seventh day from all his works.

5 And in this *place* again, If they shall enter into my rest.

6 Seeing therefore it remaineth that some must enter therein, [a]and they to whom [I]it [aptp]was first preached[2097] entered not in because of unbelief:[543]

7 Again, he limiteth[3724] a certain day, saying in David, To day, after so long a time; as it is said, [a]To day if ye [asba]will hear his voice, [psa]harden[4645] not your hearts.[2588]

8 For if [I]Jesus [ao]had given them rest,[2664] then would he not afterward [ipf]have spoken of another day.

9 There remaineth therefore a [I]rest to the people of God.

10 For he that [apt]is entered into his rest,[2663] he also [ao]hath ceased[2664] from his own works, as God *did* from his.

11 Let us labour therefore [ainf]to enter into that rest, lest any man [aosb]fall [a]after the same example of [I]unbelief.[543]

12 For the word[3056] of God *is* [a]quick,[2198] and powerful, and [b]sharper than any [c]twoedged sword, piercing even to the dividing asunder[3311] of soul[5590] and spirit,[4151] and of the joints and marrow, and *is* [d]a discerner[2924] of the thoughts[1761] and intents[1771] of the heart.[2588]

13 [a]Neither is there any creature[2937] that is not manifest in his sight: but all things *are* naked[1131] [b]and opened unto the eyes of him with whom we have to do.

Jesus, the Great High Priest

14 Seeing then that we have [a]a great high priest,[749] [b]that [pfp]is passed into the heavens,[3772] Jesus the Son[5207] of God,[2316] [psa][c]let us hold fast[2902] *our* profession.[3671]

15 For [a]we have not an high priest which cannot [ainf]be touched with the feeling of[4834] our infirmities; but [pfpp][b]was in all points tempted[3985] like as *we are,* [c]yet without sin.[266]

16 [a]Let us therefore come[4334] boldly unto the throne of grace,[5485] that we [asba]may obtain mercy,[1656] and [aosb]find grace[5485] to help in time of need.

5 For every high priest[749] taken from among men [a]is ordained[2525] for men [b]in things *pertaining* to God, [c]that he [psa]may offer both gifts[1435] and sacrifices[2378] for sins:[266]

2 [a]Who [I]can have compassion[3356] on the [ppt]ignorant,[50] and on them that [ppp]are out of the way;[4105] for that [b]he himself also is compassed with infirmity.

3 And [a]by reason hereof he ought, as for the people, so also for himself, [pinf]to offer for sins.

4 [a]And no man taketh this honour unto himself, but he that [ppp]is called of God, as [b]*was* Aaron.

5 [a]So also Christ glorified[1392] not himself [aifp]to be made an high priest; but he that [apt]said unto him, [b]Thou art my Son, to day [pfi]have I begotten[1080] thee.

6 As he saith also in another *place,* [a]Thou *art* a priest for ever after[2596] the order[5010] of Melchisedec.

---

18 [a]Num. 14:30; Deut. 1:34, 35
19 [a]Heb. 4:6

1 [a]Heb. 12:15
2 [I]Gr. *the word of hearing* [II]Or, *because they were not united by faith to*
3 [a]Heb. 3:14 [b]Ps. 95:11; Heb. 3:11
4 [a]Gen. 2:2; Ex. 20:11; 31:17
6 [I]Or, *the gospel was first preached* [a]Heb. 3:19
7 [a]Ps. 95:7; Heb. 3:7
8 [I]That is, *Joshua*
9 [I]Or, *keeping of a sabbath*
11 [I]Or, *disobedience* [a]Heb. 3:12, 18, 19
12 [a]Isa. 49:2; Jer. 23:29; 2Cor. 10:4, 5; 1Pet. 1:23 [b]Prov. 5:4 [c]Eph. 6:17; Rev. 1:16; 2:16 [d]1Cor. 14:24, 25
13 [a]Ps. 33:13, 14; 90:8; 139:11, 12 [b]Job 26:6; 34:21; Prov. 15:11
14 [a]Heb. 3:1 [b]Heb. 7:26; 9:12, 24 [c]Heb. 10:23
15 [a]Isa. 53:3; Heb. 2:18 [b]Luke 22:28 [c]2Cor. 5:21; Heb. 7:26; 1Pet. 2:22; 1John 3:5
16 [a]Eph. 2:18; 3:12; Heb. 10:19, 21, 22

1 [a]Heb. 8:3 [b]Heb. 2:17 [c]Heb. 8:3, 4; 9:9; 10:11; 11:4
2 [I]Or, *can reasonably bear with* [a]Heb. 2:18; 4:15 [b]Heb. 7:28
3 [a]Lev. 4:3; 9:7; 16:6, 15, 16, 17; Heb. 7:27; 9:7
4 [a]2Chr. 26:18; John 3:27 [b]Ex. 28:1; Num. 16:5, 40; 1Chr. 23:13
5 [a]John 8:54 [b]Ps. 2:7; Heb. 1:5
6 [a]Ps. 110:4; Heb. 7:17, 21

7 Who in the days of his flesh,[4561] when he [apt]had [a]offered up prayers[1162] and supplications[2428] [b]with strong crying and tears unto him [c]that was able [pinf]to save[4982] him from death,[2288] and [aptp]was heard [I][d]in that he feared;[2124]

8 [a]Though he were a Son,[5207] yet learned[3129] he [b]obedience[5218] by the things which he suffered;

9 And [aptp][a]being made perfect,[5048] he became the author[159] of eternal[166] salvation[4991] unto all them that [ppt]obey[5219] him;

10 [aptp]Called[4316] of God an high priest[749] [a]after[2596] the order[5010] of Melchisedec.

11 Of whom [a]we have many things to say, and hard to be uttered, seeing ye [pfi]are [b]dull of hearing.

12 For when for the time[5550] ye [ppt]ought to be teachers,[1320] ye have need that one [infg]teach[1321] you again which *be* [a]the first principles[4747] of the oracles[3051] of God; and [pfi]are become such as [ppt]have need of [b]milk,[1051] and not of strong meat.

13 For every one that [ppt]useth[3348] milk[1051] [I]*is* unskilful in the word of righteousness:[1343] for he is [a]a babe.[3516]

14 But strong meat belongeth to them that are [I][a]of full age,[5046] *even* those who by reason [II]of use have their senses[145] [pfpp]exercised [b]to discern[1253] both good and evil.

6 Therefore [apt][a]leaving [I]the principles of the doctrine of Christ, [psmp]let us go on[5342] unto perfection;[5047] not

7 [I]Or, *for his piety* [a]Matt. 26:39, 42, 44; Mark 14:36, 39; John 17:1 [b]Ps. 22:1; Matt. 27:46, 50; Mark 15:34, 37 [c]Matt. 26:53; Mark 14:36 [d]Matt. 26:37; Mark 14:33; Luke 22:43; John 12:27
8 [a]Heb. 3:6 [b]Phil. 2:8
9 [a]Heb. 2:10; 11:40
10 [a]Heb. 5:6; 6:20
11 [a]John 16:12; 2Pet. 3:16 [b]Matt. 13:15
12 [a]Heb. 6:1 [b]1Cor. 3:1-3
13 [I]Gr. *hath no experience* [a]1Cor. 13:11; 14:20; Eph. 4:14; 1Pet. 2:2
14 [I]Or, perfect [II]Or, *of a habit,* or, *perfection*

[a]1Cor. 2:6; Eph. 4:13; Phil. 3:15 [b]Isa. 7:15; 1Cor. 2:14, 15 **1** [I]Or, *the word of the beginning of Christ* [a]Phil. 3:12-14; Heb. 5:12

6:1–6 The goal of the Christian is expressed fully by the Greek word *teleiótēta* (5047), which is translated "perfection" (v. 1). The idea being explained here is that the believer is to pursue a state of maturity, instead of going back to the initial rudiments of Christianity and basic faith (v. 2). The phrase "laying again a foundation" refers to the idea that if a Christian could lose his salvation, he would need to be regenerated again and again.

In laying the groundwork for this passage, there needs to be a proper understanding of the controversial section in verses four through six. The key idea is that the whole passage is hypothetical. For the sake of argument, one must accept the supposition that one can undergo the process of salvation, and then "fall away" (v. 6), or lose his salvation. The explanation in the following verses is designed to show the oddity of this idea (v. 4). The nature of the impossibility is tied directly to the infinitive in verse six "to renew" (*anakainízein* [340]). In the Greek text, there are five participles that must be explained thoroughly in order to properly understand this passage.

The first of these participles, which appears in verse four, is the Greek word *phōtisthéntas* (5461). This term is translated "those who were once enlightened." However, it should be rendered "having been enlightened," noting the usage of the passive voice. The latter meaning reveals that the salvation process is initiated by God giving "light" to every man (John 1:9).

The next phrase to consider in this salvation process, also found in verse four, is "and have tasted of the heavenly gift." This too could be better expressed "having tasted" (the Greek word is *geusaménous* [1089]). In this case, the middle voice is used to reveal that a person is responding to the light God has given. The focus changes to man's responsibility in initiating a reaction to his "enlightened state." This fact is always clear in the salvation process: God offers the gift, but man must take the initiative to receive it (John 1:12; 3:16).

The third participle is *genēthéntas* (v. 4, from *gínomai* [1096]), translated "were made." This also should be rendered in the passive voice as "having been made," indicating a result of man's receiving the gift of God. Connected with the phrase "partakers of the Holy Ghost," this participle expresses that by virtue of the receiving, one is made a partaker. Therefore, the Holy Spirit is involved in the process by coming to indwell the believer. However, the Holy Spirit not only works in the indwelling, but it is also indicated that the divine revelation and conviction processes previous to salvation are the result of the activity of the Holy Spirit.

In examining the fourth Greek participle (found in verse five), *geusaménous* (cf. v. 4), one should

(continued on next page)

[ppt]laying again the foundation of repentance[3341] [b]from dead[3498] works,[2041] and of faith[4102] toward God,

2 [a]Of the doctrine[1322] of baptisms,[909] [b]and of laying on of hands, [c]and of resurrection[386] of the dead, [d]and of eternal[166] judgment.[2917]

3 And this will we do, [a]if God [psa]permit.

4 For [a]*it is* impossible for those [b]who [aptp]were once enlightened,[5461] and [apt]have tasted[1089] of [c]the heavenly gift, and [aptp][d]were made partakers[3353] of the [an]Holy Ghost,[4151]

5 And [apt]have tasted the good[2570] word[4487] of God, and the powers[1411] of [a]the world[165] to come,[3195]

6 If they [apt]shall fall away,[3895] [pinf]to renew[340] them again unto repentance; [a]seeing they [ppt]crucify[388] to themselves the Son[5207] of God[2316] afresh, and [ppt]put *him* to an open shame.[3856]

7 For the earth[1093] which [apt]drinketh in the rain that [ppt]cometh oft upon it, and [ppt]bringeth forth herbs meet[2111] for them [I]by whom it is dressed, [a]receiveth[3335] blessing[2129] from God:

8 [a]But that which [ppt]beareth[1627] thorns and briers *is* rejected,[96] and *is* nigh unto cursing;[2671] whose end[5056] *is* to be burned.

9 But, beloved, we are persuaded better things of you, and things that accompany salvation,[4991] though we thus speak.

10 [a]For [b]God *is* not unrighteous [ainf]to forget [c]your work[2041] and labour of love,[26] which ye [aom]have shewed toward his name, in that ye [apt]have [d]ministered to the saints,[40] and [ppt]do minister.

11 And we desire[1937] that [a]every one of you [pinf]do shew the same diligence [b]to the full assurance of hope[1680] unto the end:[5056]

12 That ye [asbm]be not slothful,[3576] but followers of them who through faith and patience [a]inherit[2816] the promises.[1860]

God Keeps His Promises

13 For when God [apt]made promise[1861] to Abraham, because he [ipf]could [ainf]swear by[2596] no greater, [a]he [ao]sware by[2596] himself,

14 Saying, Surely blessing I will bless thee, and multiplying I will multiply thee.

1 [b]Heb. 9:14
2 [a]Acts 19:4, 5 [b]Acts 8:14-17; 19:6 [c]Acts 17:31, 32 [d]Acts 24:25; Rom. 2:16
3 [a]Acts 18:21; 1Cor. 4:19
4 [a]Matt. 12:31, 32; Heb. 10:26; 2Pet. 2:20, 21; 1John 5:16 [b]Heb. 10:32 [c]John 4:10; 6:32; Eph. 2:8 [d]Gal. 3:2, 5; Heb. 2:4
5 [a]Heb. 2:5
6 [a]Heb. 10:29
7 IOr, *for* [a]Ps. 65:10
8 [a]Isa. 5:6
10 [a]Prov. 14:31; Matt. 10:42; 25:40; John 13:20 [b]Rom. 3:4; 2Thess. 1:6, 7 [c]1Thess. 1:3 [d]Rom. 15:25; 2Cor. 8:4; 9:1, 12; 2Tim. 1:18
11 [a]Heb. 3:6, 14 [b]Col. 2:2
12 [a]Heb. 10:36
13 [a]Gen. 22:16, 17; Ps. 105:9; Luke 1:73

(continued from previous page)

consider that the same interpretation is intended by the middle voice in the phrase "having tasted." It appears in this form to reveal to man his responsibility to God's word. The believer is not merely accountable to simply follow the "good word of God," he or she is also urged to understand God's future plan to exercise His "power" (v. 5, *dúnameis* [1411]) to benefit the believer as well. The word for "power" here refers to miracles which God will perform in believers, not of the impending judgment and destruction to come.

Now one must turn his attention back to the phrase in verse four, "it is impossible," and combine it with the Greek infinitive *anakainizein* (340), meaning "to renew again" (v. 6). Applied to verse six, this word refers to a repentance that is qualitatively new and different. If a different form of repentance was needed, Christ would also have to die on the cross a second time. This, however, is inconsistent with the context of the rest of Hebrews (cf. Heb. 9:28; 10:11, 12). The teaching is clear: Christ died once for man's sin. If His death was insufficient, there would be no security for believers. This is precisely why the writer of Hebrews uses this illustration. In philosophical language, this form of reasoning is called *reductio ad absurdum* (a reduction to an absurdity). From a false assumption one deduces absurd conclusions. It would be false to assume a believer could fall, because his repentance, based on Christ's death, would be invalidated. There would be no security, and Christ would need to be crucified again.

The difficulty of these verses is removed by recognizing when the actual decision to follow Christ becomes true salvation. A person is saved at the point of genuine acceptance of God's gift of "light," and then he or she is received by God (Eph. 1:6). God ultimately judges every human heart and knows those who are truly repentant. The decision for salvation is made ineffective when it is based on emotions and one's own abilities (2 Thess. 2:13). See note on 1 John 3:6–9.

15 And so, after he [apt]had patiently endured,[3114] he obtained the promise.

16 For men verily[3303] swear by[2596] the greater:[3187] and [a]an oath[3727] for confirmation[951] *is* to them an end of all strife.

17 Wherein God, willing more abundantly [ainf]to shew unto [a]the heirs[2818] of promise [b]the immutability[276] of his counsel,[1012] [aoI]confirmed[3315] *it* by an oath:

18 That by two immutable[276] things, in which *it was* impossible for God [ainf]to lie, we [psa]might have a strong consolation, who [apt]have fled for refuge [ainf]to lay hold upon[2902] the hope[1680] [a]set before us:

19 Which *hope* we have as an anchor of the soul,[5590] both sure and stedfast,[949] [a]and which [ppt]entereth into that within the veil;

20 [a]Whither the forerunner[4274] is for us entered, *even* Jesus, [apt][b]made an high priest[749] for ever after the order[5010] of Melchisedec.

Superior to Melchisedec

7 🗝For this [a]Melchisedec, king of Salem, priest of the most high God, who [apt]met Abraham returning from the slaughter of the kings,[935] and [apt]blessed him;

2 To whom also Abraham [ao]gave a tenth part of all; first [ppp]being by interpretation[2059] King of righteousness,[1343] and after that also King of Salem, which is, King[935] of peace;[1515]

3 Without father, without mother, [I]without descent, having neither beginning of days, nor end[5056] of life;[2222] but [pfpp]made like unto the Son of God; abideth[3306] a priest continually.

4 Now [pim]consider[2334] how great this man *was,* [a]unto whom even the patriarch[3966] Abraham gave the tenth of the spoils.

5 And verily[3303] [a]they that are of the sons of Levi, who [ppt]receive the office of the priesthood, have a commandment to take tithes of the people according to the law, that is, of their brethren, though they [pfp]come out of the loins of Abraham:

6 But he whose [pptI]descent is not counted[1075] from them received tithes of Abraham, [a]and [pfi]blessed [b]him that had the promises.[1860]

7 And without all contradiction the less is blessed of the better.

8 And here men that [ppt]die receive tithes; but there he *receiveth them,* [a]of whom it [ppt]is witnessed that he liveth.[2198]

9 And as I may so say, Levi also, who [ppt]receiveth tithes, [pfip]payed tithes in Abraham.

10 For he was yet in the loins of his father, when Melchisedec met him.

11 [a]If therefore perfection[5050] were by the Levitical priesthood,[2420] (for under it the people [plpf]received the law,) what further need *was there* that another[2087] priest[2409] [pinf]should rise[450] after the order[5010] of Melchisedec, and not [pip]be called after the order of Aaron?

12 For the priesthood [ppp]being changed, there is made of necessity a change also of the law.

13 For he of whom these things are spoken [pfi]pertaineth[3348] to another[2087] tribe, of which no man [pfi]gave attendance at the altar.

14 For *it is* evident that [a]our Lord [pfi]sprang out of Juda; of which tribe Moses [ao]spake nothing concerning priesthood.

15 And it is yet far more evident: for that after the similitude[3665] of Melchisedec there ariseth[450] another[2087] priest,

16 [a]Ex. 22:11
17 [I]Gr. *interposed himself by an oath* [a]Heb. 11:9 [b]Rom. 11:29
18 [a]Heb. 12:1
19 [a]Lev. 16:15; Heb. 9:7
20 [a]Heb. 4:14; 8:1; 9:24 [b]Heb. 3:1; 5:6, 10; 7:17
1 [a]Gen. 14:18
3 [I]Gr. *without pedigree*
4 [a]Gen. 14:20
5 [a]Num. 18:21, 26
6 [I]Or, *pedigree* [a]Gen. 14:19 [b]Rom. 4:13; Gal. 3:16
8 [a]Heb. 5:6; 6:20
11 [a]Gal. 2:21; Heb. 7:18, 19; 8:7
14 [a]Isa. 11:1; Matt. 1:3; Luke 3:33; Rom. 1:3; Rev. 5:5

🗝 **7:1–28** This chapter describes the similarities in priestly ministries of Melchisedec and Christ. This arises from an examination of verse eleven where the writer of Hebrews reveals that Christ, being after the priestly order of Melchisedec (v. 17), has a different ministry than those priests who followed the order of Aaron. Since the Law of Moses had not been established during Melchisedec's day, Christ's ministry, being separate from that of the Law, was in fact similar to Melchisedec's. See note on Genesis 14:18–20 concerning the suggested identities of Melchisedec.

16 Who [pfi]is made, not after the [an]law[3551] of a carnal[4559] commandment,[1785] but after the power of an endless life.[2222]

17 For he testifieth, [a]Thou *art* a priest for ever after the order of Melchisedec.

18 For there is verily a disannulling of the commandment [ppt]going before[4254] for [a]the weakness[772] and unprofitableness thereof.

19 For [a]the law[3551] [ao]made nothing perfect,[5048] [I][b]but the bringing in of [c]a better[2909] hope[1680] *did;* by the which [d]we draw nigh[1448] unto God.

20 And inasmuch as not without an oath *he was made priest:*

21 (For those priests were made [I]without an oath;[3728] but this with an oath by him that said unto him, [a]The Lord [ao]sware and [fp]will not repent,[3338] Thou *art* a priest for ever[165,1519][3588] after the order of Melchisedec:)

22 By so much [pfi][a]was Jesus made[1096] a surety of a better testament.[1242]

23 And they truly were many priests, because they [aid]were not suffered [pinf]to continue[3887] by reason of death:[2288]

24 But this *man,* because he [aid]continueth[3306] ever, hath [I]an unchangeable[531] priesthood.

25 Wherefore he is able also [pinf]to save[4982] them [I]to the uttermost[3838] that [ppt]come unto God by him, seeing he ever [ppt]liveth [aies][a]to make intercession for them.

26 For such an high priest [ipf]became us, [a]*who is* holy,[3741] harmless,[172] undefiled,[283] [pfpp]separate from [art]sinners,[268] [b]and [apt]made higher than the heavens;

27 Who needeth not daily, as those high priests, [pinf]to offer up sacrifice,[2378] [a]first for his own sins,[266] [b]and then for the people's: for [c]this he did once, when he [apt]offered up[399] himself.

28 For the law maketh[2525] [a]men high priests which have infirmity; but the word of the oath, which was since the law, *maketh* the [an]Son, [b]who [pfpp]is [I]consecrated[5048] for evermore.

Christ Supercedes the Levitical System

8 Now of the things which we have spoken *this is* the sum: We have such an high priest, [a]who [ao]is set on the right hand[1188] of the throne of the Majesty in the heavens;[3772]

2 A minister[3011] [I]of [a]the sanctuary,[39] and of [b]the true[228] tabernacle,[4633] which the Lord[2962] [ao]pitched, and not man.[444]

3 For [a]every high priest[749] is ordained[2525] [aies]to offer gifts[1435] and sacrifices:[2378] wherefore [b]*it is* of necessity that this man have somewhat also to [aosb]offer.

4 For if he were on earth,[1093] he should not be a priest, seeing that [I]there are priests that [ppt]offer gifts according to the law:[3551]

5 Who serve[3000] unto the example and [a]shadow of heavenly things, as Moses [pfip]was admonished of God[5537] when he was about [pinf]to make[2005] the tabernacle: [b]for, See, saith he, *that* thou make all things according to the pattern[5179] [aptp]shewed to thee in the mount.

6 But now [pfi][a]hath he obtained[5177] a more excellent[1313] ministry,[3009] by how much also he is the mediator[3316] of a better[2909] [I]covenant,[1242] which [pfip]was established upon better promises.[1860]

Better Promises

7 [a]For if that first *covenant* had been faultless,[273] then should no place [ipf]have been sought for the second.

8 For finding fault with them, he saith, [a]Behold, the days come, saith the Lord, when I will make[4931] a new[2537] covenant with the house of Israel and with the house of Judah:

9 Not according to the covenant that I made with their fathers in the day when I [apt]took them by the hand [ainf]to lead them out of the land of Egypt; because they continued[1696] not in my covenant, and I [ao]regarded them not, saith the Lord.

10 For [a]this *is* the covenant that I will make[1303] with the house of Israel after those days, saith the Lord; I [ppt]will [I]put my laws[3551] into their mind,[1271] and

17 [a]Ps. 110:4; Heb. 5:6, 10; 6:20

18 [a]Rom. 8:3; Gal. 4:9

19 [I]Or, *but it was the bringing in* [a]Acts 13:39; Rom. 3:20, 21, 28; 8:3; Gal. 2:16; Heb. 9:9 [b]Gal. 3:24 [c]Heb. 6:18; 8:6 [d]Rom. 5:2; Eph. 2:18; 3:12; Heb. 4:16; 10:19

21 [I]Or, *without swearing of an oath* [a]Ps. 110:4

22 [a]Heb. 8:6; 9:15; 12:24

24 [I]Or, *which passeth not from one to another*

25 [I]Or, *evermore* [a]Rom. 8:34; 1Tim. 2:5; Heb. 9:24; 1John 2:1

26 [a]Heb. 4:15 [b]Eph. 1:20; 4:10; Heb. 8:1

27 [a]Lev. 9:7; 16:6, 11; Heb. 5:3; 9:7 [b]Lev. 16:15 [c]Rom. 6:10; Heb. 9:12, 28; 10:12

28 [I]Gr. *perfected* [a]Heb. 5:1, 2; Heb. 2:10; 5:9

1 [a]Eph. 1:20; Col. 3:1; Heb. 1:3; 10:12; 12:2

2 [I]Or, *of holy things* [a]Heb. 9:8, 12, 24 [b]Heb. 9:11

3 [a]Heb. 5:1 [b]Eph. 5:2; Heb. 9:14

4 [I]Or, *they are priests*

5 [a]Col. 2:17; Heb. 9:23; 10:1 [b]Ex. 25:40; 26:30; 27:8; Num. 8:4; Acts 7:44

6 [I]Or, *testament* [a]2Cor. 3:6, 8, 9; Heb. 7:22

7 [a]Heb. 7:11, 18

8 [a]Jer. 31:31-34

10 [I]Gr. *give* [a]Heb. 10:16

write[1924] them [II]in their hearts:[2588] and [b]I will be to them a God,[2316] and they shall be to me a people:[2992]

11 And [a]they [asba]shall not teach[1321] every man his neighbour, and every man his brother,[80] saying, [aim]Know[1097] the Lord:[2962] for all shall know[1492] me, from the least to the greatest.

12 For I [fm]will be merciful[2436] to their unrighteousness,[93] [a]and their sins[266] and their iniquities[458] will I remember [efn]no more.

13 [a]In that he saith, A new[2537] *covenant,* he [pfi]hath made the first old.[3822] Now that which [ppp]decayeth[3822] and [ppt]waxeth old[1095] *is* ready to vanish away.

A New Covenant

9 Then verily[3303] the first *covenant* [ipf]had also [I]ordinances[1345] of divine service,[2999] and [a]a worldly[2886] sanctuary.[39]

2 [a]For there [aop]was a tabernacle made;[2680] the first, [b]wherein *was* [c]the candlestick,[3087] and [d]the table, and the shewbread; which is called [I]the sanctuary.[39]

3 [a]And after the second vail, the tabernacle which is called the Holiest of all;[39]

4 Which had the golden censer, and [a]the ark of the covenant [pfpp]overlaid round about with gold, wherein *was* [b]the golden pot that had manna,[3131] and [c]Aaron's rod that [apt]budded, and [d]the tables of the covenant;[1242]

5 And [a]over it the cherubims[5502] of glory[1391] shadowing the mercyseat;[2435] of which we cannot now [pinf]speak particularly.[2596,3313]

6 Now when these things [pfpp]were thus ordained,[2680] [a]the priests went always into the first tabernacle, accomplishing[2005] the service[2999] *of God.*

7 But into the second *went* the high priest alone [a]once every year, not without blood,[129] [b]which he offered for himself, and *for* the errors[51] of the people:[2992]

8 [a]The Holy Ghost this [ppt]signifying, that [b]the way into the holiest of all[39] [pfin]was not yet made manifest,[5319] while as the first tabernacle was yet standing:[4714]

9 Which *was* a figure[3850] for the time then [pfp]present, in which were offered both gifts[1435] and sacrifices,[2378] [a]that could not [ainf]make him that did the service perfect,[5048] as pertaining to the conscience;[4893]

10 *Which stood* only in [a]meats and drinks, and [b]divers[1313] washings,[909] [c]and carnal[4561] [I]ordinances,[1345] [ppt]imposed *on them* until the time[2540] of reformation.[1357]

The Blood of Christ

11 But Christ[5547] [apt]being come [a]an high priest[749] [b]of good things[18] to come, [c]by a greater and more perfect[5046] tabernacle,[4633] not made with hands, that is to say, not of this building;[2937]

12 Neither [a]by the blood of goats and calves, but [b]by his own blood[129] he entered in [c]once into the holy place,[39] [apt d]having obtained eternal[166] redemption[3085] *for us.*

13 For if [a]the blood[129] of bulls and of goats, and [b]the ashes of an heifer sprinkling[4472] the unclean,[2840] sanctifieth[37] to the purifying[2514] of the flesh:[4561]

14 How much more [a]shall the blood[129] of Christ,[5547] [b]who through the eternal Spirit[4151] [ao c]offered himself without [I]spot[299] to God, [d]purge[2511] your conscience[4893] from [e]dead[3498] works[2041] [aies f]to serve[3000] the living[2198] God?[2316]

15 [a]And for this cause [b]he is the mediator[3316] of the [an]new[2537] testament,[1242] [c]that by means of death,[2288] for the redemption[629] of the transgressions[3847] *that were* under the first testament, [d]they which are called[2564] [aosb]might receive the promise[1860] of eternal[166] inheritance.[2817]

16 For where a testament *is,* there must also of necessity [I]be[5342] the death of the testator.[1303]

17 For [a]a testament[1242] *is* of force[949] after men are dead: otherwise it is of no

10 [II]Or, *upon* [b]Zech. 8:8
11 [a]Isa. 54:13; John 6:45; 1John 2:27
12 [a]Rom. 11:27; Heb. 10:17
13 [a]2Cor. 5:17

1 [I]Or, *ceremonies* [a]Ex. 25:8
2 [I]Or, *holy* [a]Ex. 26:1 [b]Ex. 26:35; 40:4 [c]Ex. 25:31 [d]Ex. 25:23, 30; Lev. 24:5, 6
3 [a]Ex. 26:31, 33; 40:3, 21; Heb. 6:19
4 [a]Ex. 25:10; 26:33; 40:3, 21 [b]Ex. 16:33, 34 [c]Num. 17:10 [d]Ex. 25:16, 21; 34:29; 40:20; Deut. 10:2, 5; 1Kgs. 8:9, 21; 2Chr. 5:10
5 [a]Ex. 25:18, 22; Lev. 16:2; 1Kgs. 8:6, 7
6 [a]Num. 28:3; Dan. 8:11
7 [a]Ex. 30:10; Lev. 16:2, 11, 12, 15, 34; Heb. 9:25 [b]Heb. 5:3; 7:27
8 [a]Heb. 10:19, 20 [b]John 14:6
9 [a]Gal. 3:21; Heb. 7:18, 19; 10:1, 11
10 [I]Or, *rites,* or, *ceremonies* [a]Lev. 11:2; Col. 2:16 [b]Num. 19:7 [c]Eph. 2:15; Col. 2:20; Heb. 7:16
11 [a]Heb. 3:1 [b]Heb. 10:1 [c]Heb. 8:2
12 [a]Heb. 10:4 [b]Acts 20:28; Eph. 1:7; Col. 1:14; 1Pet. 1:19; Rev. 1:5; 5:9 [c]Zech. 3:9; Heb. 9:26, 28; 10:10 [d]Dan. 9:24
13 [a]Lev. 16:14, 16 [b]Num. 19:2, 17
14 [I]Or, *fault* [a]1Pet. 1:19; 1John 1:7; Rev. 1:5 [b]Rom. 1:4; 1Pet. 3:18 [c]Eph. 5:2; Titus 2:14; Heb. 7:27 [d]Heb. 1:3; 10:22 [e]Heb. 6:1 [f]Luke 1:74; Rom. 6:13, 22; 1Pet. 4:2
15 [a]1Tim. 2:5 [b]Heb. 7:22; 8:6; 12:24 [c]Rom. 3:25; 5:6; 1Pet. 3:18 [d]Heb. 3:1
16 [I]Or, *be brought in* **17** [a]Gal. 3:15

strength[2480] at all while the testator liveth.[2198]

18 [a]Whereupon neither the first *testament* [pfip]was [I]dedicated[1457] without blood.[129]

19 For when Moses had spoken every precept to all the people[2992] according to the law,[3551] [a]he [apt]took the blood[129] of calves and of goats, [b]with water, and [I]scarlet wool, and hyssop,[5301] and sprinkled[4472] both the book, and all the people,

20 Saying, [a]This *is* the blood of the testament which God [aom]hath enjoined unto you.

21 Moreover [a]he sprinkled[4472] with blood both the tabernacle,[4633] and all the vessels of the ministry.[3009]

22 And almost all things [pinp]are by the law purged[2511] with blood; and [a]without shedding of blood[130] is no remission.[859]

A Better Sacrifice

23 *It was* therefore necessary that [a]the patterns of things in the heavens[3772] [pip]should be purified[2511] with these; but the heavenly things themselves with better sacrifices than these.

24 For [a]Christ [ao]is not entered[1525] into the holy places[39] made with hands, *which are* the figures[499] of [b]the true;[228] but into heaven[3772] itself, now [aifp][c]to appear in the presence of God for us:

25 Nor yet that he should offer himself often, as [a]the high priest entereth into the holy place[39] every year with blood[129] of others;[245]

26 For then must he often [ainf]have suffered since the foundation of the world:[2889] but now [a]once [b]in the end[4930] of the world[165] [pfip]hath he appeared[5319] to put away sin[266] by the sacrifice[2378] of himself.

27 [a]And as it is appointed unto men[444] once [ainf]to die,[599] [b]but after this the judgment:[2920]

🔑 28 So [a]Christ[5547] [aptp]was once [b]offered[4374] [aies]to bear[399] the [an]sins [c]of many; and unto them that [ppt][d]look for[553] him shall he appear the second time without sin unto salvation.[4991]

Christ's Sacrifice Once for All

10 For the law[3551] having [a]a shadow [b]of good things[18] to come,[3195] *and* not the very image[1504] of the things, [c]can never with those sacrifices[2378] which they offered year by year continually [ainf]make the comers thereunto [d]perfect.[5048]

2 For then [I]would they not [aom]have ceased to [ppp]be offered? because that the [ppt]worshippers[3000] once [pfpp]purged[2508] should have had no more conscience[4893] of sins.[266]

3 [a]But in those *sacrifices there is* a remembrance again[364] *made* of sins every year.

4 For [a]*it is* not possible that the blood[129] of bulls and of goats [pinf]should take away sins.

5 Wherefore when he cometh into the world, he saith, [a]Sacrifice and offering[4376] thou [ao]wouldest[2309] not, but a body[4983] [aomI]hast thou prepared[2675] me:

6 In burnt offerings and *sacrifices* for sin thou [ao]hast had no pleasure.[2106]

7 Then said I, Lo, I come (in the volume of the book it is written of me,) [infg]to do thy will,[2307] O God.

8 Above[511] when he said, Sacrifice and offering and burnt offerings and *offering* for sin thou wouldest not, neither hadst pleasure *therein;* which are offered by the law;[3551]

9 Then said he, Lo, I come to do thy will, O God. He taketh away the first, that he [aosb]may establish the second.

10 [a]By the which will we are sanctified[37] [b]through the offering of the body of Jesus Christ[5547] once *for all.*

🔑 11 And every priest[2409] standeth [a]daily ministering[3008] and offering often-

18 [I]Or, *purified* [a]Ex. 24:6
19 [I]Or, *purple* [a]Ex. 24:5, 6, 8; Lev. 16:14, 15, 18 [b]Lev. 14:4, 6, 7, 49, 51, 52
20 [a]Ex. 24:8; Matt. 26:28
21 [a]Ex. 29:12, 36; Lev. 8:15, 19; 16:14-16, 18, 19
22 [a]Lev. 17:11
23 [a]Heb. 8:5
24 [a]Heb. 6:20 [b]Heb. 8:2 [c]Rom. 8:34; Heb. 7:25; 1John 2:1
25 [a]Heb. 9:7
26 [a]Heb. 9:12; Heb. 7:27; 10:10; 1Pet. 3:18 [b]1Cor. 10:11; Gal. 4:4; Eph. 1:10
27 [a]Gen. 3:19; Eccl. 3:20 [b]2Cor. 5:10; Rev. 20:12, 13
28 [a]Rom. 6:10; 1Pet. 3:18 [b]1Pet. 2:24; 1John 3:5 [c]Matt. 26:28; Rom. 5:15 [d]Titus 2:13; 2Pet. 3:12

1 [a]Col. 2:17; Heb. 8:5; 9:23 [b]Heb. 9:11 [c]Heb. 9:9 [d]Heb. 10:14
2 [I]Or, *they would have ceased to be offered, because*
3 [a]Lev. 16:21; Heb. 9:7
4 [a]Mic. 6:6, 7; Heb. 9:13; Heb. 10:11
5 [I]Or, *thou hast fitted me* [a]Ps. 40:6; 50:8; Isa. 1:11; Jer. 6:20; Amos 5:21, 22
10 [a]John 17:19; Heb. 13:12 [b]Heb. 9:12
11 [a]Num. 28:3; Heb. 7:27

🔑 **9:28** See note on Hebrews 6:1–6.

🔑 **10:11, 12** See the introduction to Hebrews.

times the same sacrifices, [b]which can never [ainf]take away[4014] sins:

12 [a]But this man, after he [apt]had offered one sacrifice[2378] for sins[266] for ever,[1519][1336,3588] sat down on the right hand[1188] of God;

13 From henceforth [ppt]expecting[1551] [a]till his enemies [asbp]be made his footstool.

14 For by one offering[4376] [a]he [pfi]hath perfected[5048] for ever them that [ppp]are sanctified.

15 *Whereof* the Holy Ghost[4151] also is a witness[3140] to us: for after that he [aime]had said before,

16 [a]This *is* the covenant[1242] that I will make[1303] with them after those days, saith the Lord, I [ppt]will put my laws into their hearts,[2588] and in their minds[1271] will I write[1924] them;

17 [I]And their sins[266] and iniquities[458] will I remember no more.

18 Now where remission[859] of these *is, there is* no more offering for sin.

The Believer's Access to God

19 Having therefore, brethren,[80] [Ia]boldness[3954] to enter [b]into the holiest[39] by the blood[129] of Jesus,

20 By [a]a new and living[2198] way,[3598] which he hath [I]consecrated[1457] for us, [b]through the veil, that is to say, his flesh;

21 And *having* [a]an high priest over [b]the house of God;

22 [psaa]Let us draw near[4334] with a true[228] heart[2588] [b]in full assurance of faith,[4102] having our hearts [pfpp]sprinkled[4472] [c]from an evil[4190] conscience,[4893] and [d]our bodies [pfpp]washed with pure[2513] water.

23 [psaa]Let us hold fast[2722] the profession[3671] of *our* faith[1680] without wavering; (for [b]he *is* faithful[4103] that [apt]promised;[1861])

24 And [psa]let us consider[2657] one another to provoke[3948] unto love[26] and to good[2570] works:[2041]

25 [a]Not [ppt]forsaking[1459] the assembling of ourselves together,[1997] as the manner of some *is;* but exhorting[3870] *one another:* and [b]so much the more, as ye see [c]the day approaching.

🔑 26 For [a]if we [ppt]sin[264] wilfully [b]after that we [aime]have received the knowledge[1922] of the truth,[225] there remaineth no more sacrifice for sins,[266]

27 But a certain fearful looking for[1561] of judgment[2920] and [a]fiery indignation, which [pinf]shall devour the adversaries.

28 [a]He that [apt]despised Moses' law[3551] died[599] without mercy[3628] [b]under two or three witnesses:[3144]

29 [a]Of how much sorer[5501] punishment,[5098] suppose ye, shall he be thought worthy, who [apt]hath trodden under foot the Son[5207] of God,[2316] and [aptb]hath counted the blood[129] of the covenant,[1242] wherewith he was sanctified, an unholy[2839] thing, [c]and [apt]hath done despite unto the Spirit[4151] of grace?[5485]

30 For we know[1492] him that hath said, [a]Vengeance[1557] *belongeth* unto me, I will recompense, saith the Lord. And again, [b]The Lord[2962] shall judge[2919] his people.[2992]

31 [a]*It is* a fearful thing [ainf]to fall into the hands of the living[2198] God.

32 But [a]call to remembrance the former days, in which, [b]after ye [aptp]were illuminated,[5461] ye endured [c]a great fight of afflictions;

33 Partly, whilst ye [ppp]were made [a]a gazingstock[2301] both by reproaches and afflictions; and partly, whilst [b]ye

11 [b]Heb. 10:4
12 [a]Col. 3:1; Heb. 1:3
13 [a]Ps. 110:1; Acts 2:35; 1Cor. 15:25; Heb. 1:13
14 [a]Heb. 10:1
16 [a]Jer. 31:33, 34; Heb. 8:10, 12
17 [I]Some texts have, *Then he said, And their*
19 [I]Or, *liberty* [a]Rom. 5:2; Eph. 2:18; 3:12 [b]Heb. 9:8, 12
20 [I]Or, *new made* [a]John 10:9; 14:6; Heb. 9:8 [b]Heb. 9:3
21 [a]Heb. 4:14 [b]1Tim. 3:15
22 [a]Heb. 4:16 [b]Eph. 3:12; James 1:6; 1John 3:21 [c]Heb. 9:14 [d]Ezek. 36:25; 2Cor. 7:1
23 [a]Heb. 4:14 [b]1Cor. 1:9; 10:13; 1Thess. 5:24; 2Thess. 3:3; Heb. 11:11
25 [a]Acts 2:42; Jude 1:19 [b]Rom. 13:11 [c]Phil. 4:5; 2Pet. 3:9, 11, 14
26 [a]Num. 15:30; Heb. 6:4 [b]2Pet. 2:20, 21
27 [a]Ezek. 36:5; Zeph. 1:18; 3:8; 2Thess. 1:8; Heb. 12:29
28 [a]Heb. 2:2 [b]Deut. 17:2, 6; 19:15; Matt. 18:16; John 8:17; 2Cor. 13:1
29 [a]Heb. 2:3; 12:25 [b]1Cor. 11:29; Heb. 13:20 [c]Matt. 12:31, 32; Eph. 4:30
30 [a]Deut. 32:35; Rom. 12:19 [b]Deut. 32:36; Ps. 50:4; 135:14
31 [a]Luke 12:5
32 [a]Gal. 3:4; 2John 1:8 [b]Heb. 6:4 [c]Phil. 1:29, 30; Col. 2:1
33 [a]1Cor. 4:9 [b]Phil. 1:7; 4:14; 1Thess. 2:14

🔑 **10:26, 27** The key idea expressed in these verses is that there will be no restitution made for one who willfully rejects Christ. The emphasis is seen in the Greek word *oukéti* (3765), which is translated "no more." Once Christ is rejected, there cannot be another sacrifice on the cross in order to forgive that individual (see notes on Mark 3:28, 29 and Heb. 6:1–6). The only consequence for such a person is "judgment and fiery indignation," reflecting God's judgment for sin (v. 27). This refers to the ultimate punishment for the one who has received the knowledge of God's truth, but chosen to forsake it (cf. Rom. 1:21, 25).

[aptp]became companions[2844] of them that
[ppt]were so used.390
34 For ye [ao]had compassion[4834] of
me [a]in my bonds, and [ao][b]took[4327] joyfully
the spoiling[724] of your goods, knowing
[I]in yourselves that [c]ye have in heaven[3772]
a better[2909] and an enduring[3306] sub-
stance.5223
35 [aosi]Cast not away therefore your
confidence, [a]which hath great recompence
of reward.[3405]
36 [a]For ye have need of patience,
that, after ye [apt]have done the will[2307] of
God, [b]ye might receive the promise.[1860]
37 For [a]yet a little while, and [b]he that
[ppt]shall come will come, and will not
tarry.
38 Now [a]the just[1342] [fm]shall live[2198]
by faith:[4102] but if *any man* [asbm]draw
back, my soul[5590] [pin]shall have no pleasure[2106] in him.
39 But we are not of them [a]who
draw back unto perdition;[684] but of them
that [b]believe[4102] to the saving4047 of the
soul.[5590]

"By Faith"

11 Now faith[4102] is the [I]substance[5287]
of [ppp]things hoped for,[1679] the
evidence[1650] [a]of things not [ppp]seen.
2 For [a]by it the elders[4245] [aop]obtained
a good report.[3140]
3 Through faith we understand[3539]
that [a]the worlds[165] were framed[2675] by
the word[4487] of God,[2316] so that things
which [ppp]are seen [aies]were not made[1096]
of things which [ppp]do appear.
🔑 4 By faith [a]Abel [ao]offered unto God
a more excellent sacrifice[2378] than Cain,
by which he [aop]obtained witness that he
was righteous,[1342] God testifying of his
gifts:[1435] and by it he [apt]being dead[599]
[I][b]yet speaketh.[2980]
🔑 5 By faith [a]Enoch [aop]was trans-
lated3346 that he [infg]should not see[1492]
death;[2288] and [ipf]was not found,[2147] because God [ao]had translated him: for before his translation he [pfip]had this testimony,[3140] that he [pfin]pleased[2100] God.
6 But without faith *it is* impossible
[ainf]to please *him:* for he that [ppt]cometh[4334]
to God must [ainf]believe[4100] that he is, and
that he is a rewarder[3406] of them that
[ppt]diligently seek him.
7 By faith [a]Noah, [aptp]being warned
of God[5537] of things not [ppp]seen as yet,
[aptp][I]moved with fear,[2125] [b]prepared an ark
to the saving[4991] of his house; by the
which he condemned[2632] the world,[2889]
and became heir[2818] of [c]the righteousness[1343] which is by faith.
8 By faith [a]Abraham, when he
[ppp]was called [ainf]to go out into a place
which he [ipf]should after [pinf]receive for an
inheritance,[2817] [ao]obeyed;[5219] and he
[ao]went out, not knowing whither he went.
9 By faith he sojourned[3939] in the
land of promise, as *in* a strange country,[245] [apt][a]dwelling in tabernacles4633 with
Isaac and Jacob, [b]the heirs with him[4789]
of the same promise:[1860]
10 For he [ipf]looked for[1551] [a]a city
which hath foundations, [b]whose
builder5079 and maker[1217] *is* God.[2316]
11 Through faith also [a]Sarah herself
received strength to conceive[2602] seed,[4690]
and [ao][b]was delivered of a child[5088] when
she was past[3844] age, because she judged
him [c]faithful[4103] who [apt]had promised.[1861]
🔑 12 Therefore sprang there even of
one, and [a]him [pfpp]as good as dead,[3499] [b]*so
many* as the stars of the sky[3772] in multitude, and as the sand which is by the
sea shore innumerable.
13 These all died[599] [I]in faith,[4102] [a]not
having received the promises,[1860] but
[b]having seen them afar off, and were persuaded of *them,* and [apt]embraced *them,*
and [apt][c]confessed[3670] that they were
strangers3581 and pilgrims[3927] on the
earth.[1093]

34 [I]Or, *that ye have in your selves,* or, *for yourselves* [a]Phil. 1:7; 2Tim. 1:16 [b]Matt. 5:12; Acts 5:41; James 1:2 [c]Matt. 6:20; 19:21; Luke 12:33; 1Tim. 6:19
35 [a]Matt. 5:12; 10:32
36 [a]Luke 21:19; Gal. 6:9; Heb. 12:1 [b]Col. 3:24; Heb. 9:15; 1Pet. 1:9
37 [a]Luke 18:8; 2Pet. 3:9 [b]Hab. 2:3, 4
38 [a]Rom. 1:17; Gal. 3:11
39 [a]2Pet. 2:20, 21 [b]Acts 16:30, 31; 1Thess. 5:9; 2Thess. 2:14
1 [I]Or, *ground,* or, *confidence* [a]Rom. 8:24, 25; 2Cor. 4:18; 5:7
2 [a]Heb. 11:39
3 [a]Gen. 1:1; Ps. 33:6; John 1:3; Heb. 1:2; 2Pet. 3:5
4 [I]Or, *is yet spoken of* [a]Gen. 4:4; 1John 3:12 [b]Gen. 4:10; Matt. 23:35; Heb. 12:24
5 [a]Gen. 5:22, 24
7 [I]Or, *being wary* [a]Gen. 6:13, 22 [b]1Pet. 3:20 [c]Rom. 3:22; 4:13; Phil. 3:9
8 [a]Gen. 12:1, 4; Acts 7:2-4
9 [a]Gen. 12:8; 13:3, 18; 18:1, 9 [b]Heb. 6:17
10 [a]Heb. 12:22; 13:14; Heb. 3:4
11 [a]Gen. 17:19; 18:11, 14; 21:2 [b]Luke 1:36 [c]Rom. 4:21; Heb. 10:23
12 [a]Rom. 4:19 [b]Gen. 22:17; Rom. 4:18
13 [I]Gr. *according to faith* [a]Heb. 11:39 [b]Heb. 11:27; John 8:56 [c]Gen. 23:4; 47:9; 1Chr. 29:15; Ps. 39:12; 119:19; 1Pet. 1:17; 2:11

🔑 **11:4** See note on Genesis 4:3–7.
🔑 **11:5** See note on Genesis 5:22, 24.
🔑 **11:12** See note on Genesis 25:1, 2.

14 For they that [ppt]say such things [a]declare plainly that they seek a country.

15 And truly, if they [ipf]had been mindful of that *country* from whence they came out, they might have had opportunity [ainf]to have returned.

16 But now they desire a better[2909] *country,* that is, an heavenly: wherefore God is not ashamed [a]to be called their God:[2316] for [b]he [ao]hath prepared for them a city.

🔑 17 By faith [a]Abraham, when he [ppp]was tried,[3985] offered up[4374] Isaac: and he that [apt]had received[324] the promises [b]offered up his only begotten[3439] *son,*

18 [I]Of whom it was said, [a]That in Isaac shall thy seed be called:

19 [apt]Accounting[3049] that God [a]*was* able [pinf]to raise *him* up,[1453] even from the dead;[3498] from whence also he [aom]received him in a figure.[3850]

20 By faith [a]Isaac blessed[2127] Jacob and Esau concerning things to come.

🔑 21 By faith Jacob, when he [ppt]was a dying, [a]blessed both the sons of Joseph; and [b]worshipped, *leaning* upon the top of his staff.

22 By faith [a]Joseph, when he [ppt]died, [I]made mention of the departing of the children of Israel; and gave commandment concerning his bones.

23 By faith [a]Moses, when he was born, was hid three months of his parents,[3962] because they saw *he was* a proper[791] child; and they [aop]were not afraid[5399] of the king's [b]commandment.[1297]

24 By faith [a]Moses, when he was come to years, refused[720] to be called the son of Pharaoh's daughter;

25 [a]Choosing[138] rather to suffer affliction with the people[2992] of God, than to enjoy the pleasures of sin[266] for a season;

26 [apt]Esteeming [a]the reproach [I]of Christ[5547] greater riches than the treasures in Egypt: for he [ipf]had respect[578] unto [b]the recompence of the reward.[3405]

27 By faith [a]he forsook Egypt, not [apt]fearing[5399] the wrath[2372] of the king: for he endured,[2594] as [b]seeing him who is invisible.

28 Through faith [a]he kept the passover,[3957] and the sprinkling of blood, lest he that [ppt]destroyed the firstborn[4416] [asba]should touch[2345] them.

29 By faith [a]they passed through the Red sea as by dry *land:* which the Egyptians assaying to do[3984,2983] were drowned.

30 By faith [a]the walls of Jericho fell down,[4098] after they were compassed about seven days.

🔑 31 By faith [a]the harlot Rahab perished not with them [I]that believed not,[544] when [b]she [apt]had received the spies with peace.[1515]

32 And what shall I more say? for the time[5550] [ft]would fail me to [ppt]tell[1334] of [a]Gideon, and *of* [b]Barak, and *of* [c]Samson, and *of* [d]Jephthae; *of* [e]David also, and [f]Samuel, and *of* the prophets:[4396]

33 Who through faith subdued[2610] kingdoms,[932] wrought[2038] righteousness,[1343] [a]obtained promises,[1860] [b]stopped the mouths of lions,

34 [a]Quenched the violence of fire, [b]escaped the edge of the sword, [c]out of weakness were made strong, waxed[1096] valiant in fight, [d]turned to flight the armies of the aliens.[245]

35 [a]Women received their dead[3498] raised to life again: and others were [b]tortured, not accepting[4327] deliverance; that they [aosb]might obtain a better[2909] resurrection:[386]

36 And others had trial[3984] of *cruel* mockings and scourgings,[3148] yea, moreover [a]of bonds and imprisonment:

🔑 37 [a]They were stoned, they were

14 [a]Heb. 13:14
16 [a]Ex. 3:6, 15; Matt. 22:32; Acts 7:32 [b]Phil. 3:20; Heb. 13:14
17 [a]Gen. 22:1, 9 [b]James 2:21
18 [I]Or, *To* [a]Gen. 21:12; Rom. 9:7
19 [a]Rom. 4:17, 19, 21
20 [a]Gen. 27:27, 39
21 [a]Gen. 48:5, 16, 20 [b]Gen. 47:31
22 [I]Or, *remembered* [a]Gen. 50:24, 25; Ex. 13:19
23 [a]Ex. 2:2; Acts 7:20 [b]Ex. 1:16, 22
24 [a]Ex. 2:10, 11
25 [a]Ps. 84:10
26 [I]Or, *for Christ* [a]Heb. 13:13 [b]Heb. 10:35
27 [a]Ex. 10:28, 29; 12:37; 13:17, 18 [b]Heb. 11:13
28 [a]Ex. 12:21
29 [a]Ex. 14:22, 29
30 [a]Josh. 6:20
31 [I]Or, *that were disobedient* [a]Josh. 6:23; James 2:25 [b]Josh. 2:1
32 [a]Judg. 6:11 [b]Judg. 4:6 [c]Judg. 13:24 [d]Judg. 11:1; 12:7 [e]1Sam. 16:1, 13; 17:45 [f]1Sam. 1:20; 12:20
33 [a]2Sam. 7:11 [b]Judg. 14:5, 6; 1Sam. 17:34, 35; Dan. 6:22
34 [a]Dan. 3:25 [b]1Sam. 20:1; 1Kgs. 19:3; 2Kgs. 6:16 [c]2Kgs. 20:7; Job 42:10; Ps. 6:8 [d]Judg. 15:8, 15; 1Sam. 14:13; 17:51, 52; 2Sam. 8:1
35 [a]1Kgs. 17:22; 2Kgs. 4:35 [b]Acts 22:25
36 [a]Gen. 39:20; Jer. 20:2; 37:15
37 [a]1Kgs. 21:13; 2Chr. 24:21; Acts 7:58; 14:19

🔑 **11:17–19** See note on Genesis 22:1.
🔑 **11:21** See note on Genesis 47:31.
🔑 **11:31** See note on Joshua 2:1.
🔑 **11:37** See the introduction to Isaiah.

sawn asunder, were tempted,[3985] were slain with the sword: [b]they wandered about [c]in sheepskins and goatskins; [ppp]being destitute, [ppp]afflicted, [ppp]tormented;

38 (Of whom the world[2889] was not worthy:) they wandered in deserts, and *in* mountains, and [a]*in* dens and caves of the earth.[1093]

39 And these all, [a]having obtained a good report[3140] through faith, received not the promise:[1860]

40 God having [1]provided [a]some better thing for us, that they without us [asbp]should not be [b]made perfect.[5048]

Exhortations to Follow Christ

12 Wherefore seeing we also are compassed about with so great a cloud of witnesses,[3144] [apt][a]let us lay aside[659] every weight, and the sin[266] which doth so easily beset *us,* and [psa][b]let us run[5143] [c]with patience[5281] the race[73] that [ppt]is set before us,

2 Looking[872] unto Jesus the [1]author[747] and finisher[5051] of *our* faith;[4102] [a]who for the joy[5479] that [ppt]was set before him endured[5278] the cross,[4716] [apt]despising the shame,[152] and [b]is set down at the right hand[1188] of the throne of God.

3 [a]For [aim]consider him that [pfp]endured such contradiction of sinners[268] against himself, [b]lest ye [aosb]be wearied[2577] and faint in your minds.[5590]

4 [a]Ye have not yet resisted unto blood, striving[464] against sin.

5 And ye have forgotten the exhortation[3874] which speaketh unto you as unto children,[5207] [a]My son,[5207] despise not thou the chastening of the Lord,[2962] nor faint when thou [ppp]art rebuked of him:

6 For [a]whom the Lord loveth[25] he chasteneth, and scourgeth[3146] every son whom he receiveth.[3858]

7 [a]If ye endure chastening, God dealeth[4374] with you as with sons; for what son is he whom the father[3962] chasteneth not?

8 But if ye be without chastisement, [a]whereof all are partakers,[3353] then are ye bastards,[3541] and not sons.[5207]

9 Furthermore we have had fathers[3962] of our flesh which corrected[3810] *us,* and we [ipf]gave *them* reverence:[1788] shall we not much rather be in subjection[5293] unto [a]the Father[3962] of spirits,[4151] and live?[2198]

10 For they verily[3303] for a few days [ipf]chastened *us* [1]after their own pleasure; but he for *our* profit,[4851] [a]that *we* [aies]might be partakers of his holiness.[41]

11 Now no chastening for the present seemeth to be joyous, but grievous: nevertheless afterward it yieldeth [a]the peaceable fruit of righteousness[1343] unto them which [pfpp]are exercised thereby.

Exhortations to Holiness

12 Wherefore [a]lift up[461] the hands which hang down, and the feeble knees;

13 [a]And make [1]straight[3717] paths for your feet, lest that which is lame be turned out of the way; [b]but let it rather be healed.

14 [a]Follow peace[1515] with all *men,* and holiness,[38] [b]without which no man shall see the Lord:

15 [a]Looking diligently[1983] [b]lest any man [ppt][1]fail[5302] of the grace[5485] of God; [c]lest any root of bitterness springing[5453] up[507] trouble *you,* and thereby many be defiled;

16 [a]Lest there *be* any fornicator,[4205] or profane person,[952] as Esau, [b]who for one morsel of meat sold his birthright.

17 For ye know how that afterward, [a]when he [ppt]would have [ainf]inherited[2816] the blessing,[2129] he was rejected:[593] [b]for he found no [1]place of repentance,[3341] though he [apt]sought it carefully with tears.

18 For ye [pfi]are not come[4334] unto [a]the mount that [ppp]might be touched, and that [pfpp]burned with fire, nor unto blackness,[1105] and darkness,[4655] and tempest,[2366]

19 And the sound of a trumpet, and

37 [b]2Kgs. 1:8; Matt. 3:4 [c]Zech. 13:4
38 [a]1Kgs. 18:4; 19:9
39 [a]Heb. 2:13
40 [1]Or, *foreseen* [a]Heb. 7:22; 8:6 [b]Heb. 5:9; 12:23; Rev. 6:11

1 [a]Col. 3:8; 1Pet. 2:1 [b]1Cor. 9:24; Phil. 3:13, 14 [c]Rom. 12:12; Heb. 10:36
2 [1]Or, *beginner* [a]Luke 24:26; Phil. 2:8; 1Pet. 1:11 [b]Ps. 110:1; Heb. 1:3, 13; 8:1; 1Pet. 3:22
3 [a]Matt. 10:24, 25; John 15:20 [b]Gal. 6:9
4 [a]1Cor. 10:13; Heb. 10:32, 33, 34
5 [a]Job 5:17; Prov. 3:11
6 [a]Ps. 94:12; 119:75; Prov. 3:12; James 1:12; Rev. 3:19
7 [a]Deut. 8:5; 2Sam. 7:14; Prov. 13:24; 19:18; 23:13
8 [a]Ps. 73:15; 1Pet. 5:9
9 [a]Num. 16:22; 27:16; Job 12:10; Eccl. 12:7; Isa. 42:5; 57:16; Zech. 12:1
10 [1]Or, *as seemed good* [a]Lev. 11:44; 19:2; 1Pet. 1:15, 16
11 [a]James 3:18
12 [a]Job 4:3, 4; Isa. 35:3
13 [1]Or, *even* [a]Prov. 4:26, 27 [b]Gal. 6:1
14 [a]Ps. 34:14; Rom. 12:18; 14:19; 2Tim. 2:22 [b]Matt. 5:8; 2Cor. 7:1; Eph. 5:5
15 [1]Or, *fall from* [a]2Cor. 6:1 [b]Gal. 5:4 [c]Deut. 29:18; Heb. 3:12
16 [a]Eph. 5:3; Col. 3:5; 1Thess. 4:3 [b]Gen. 25:33
17 [1]Or, *way to change his mind* [a]Gen. 27:34, 36, 38 [b]Heb. 6:6
18 [a]Ex. 19:12, 18, 19; 20:18; Deut. 4:11; 5:22; Rom. 6:14; 8:15; 2Tim. 1:7

the voice of words;[4487] which *voice* they that heard [a]intreated[3868] that the word should not be spoken to them any more:

20 (For they [ipf]could not endure[5342] that which [ppp]was commanded, [a]And if so much as a beast[2342] [aosb]touch the mountain, it shall be stoned, or thrust through with a dart:

21 [a]And so terrible was the sight, *that* Moses said, I exceedingly fear and quake:)

22 But ye [pfi]are come [a]unto[4334] mount Sion, [b]and unto the city of the living God, the heavenly Jerusalem, [c]and to an innumerable company of angels,

23 To the general assembly[3831] and church[1577] of [a]the [pl]firstborn,[4416] [b]which [pfpp]are [I]written in heaven,[3772] and to God[2316] [c]the Judge[2923] of all, and to the spirits[4151] of just men[1342] [pfpp][d]made perfect,[5048]

24 And to Jesus [a]the mediator[3316] of the [an]new[3501] [I]covenant,[1242] and to [b]the blood of sprinkling,[4473] that [ppt]speaketh[2980] better things[2909] [c]than *that of* Abel.

25 See that ye [aosb]refuse[3868] not him that [ppt]speaketh. For [a]if they escaped not who refused him that [ppt]spake[5537] on earth, much more *shall not* we *escape,* if we turn away from[654] him that *speaketh* from heaven:

26 [a]Whose voice then shook the earth:[1093] but now he [pfi]hath promised,[1861] saying, [b]Yet once more I shake not the earth only, but also heaven.

27 And this *word,* Yet once more, signifieth [a]the removing of those things that [ppp][I]are shaken, as of things that [pfpp]are made, that those things which cannot [ppp]be shaken [aosb]may remain.

28 Wherefore we receiving a kingdom[932] which cannot be moved, [I]let us have grace,[5485] whereby we [psa]may serve[3000] God acceptably[2102] with reverence[127] and godly fear:[2124]

29 For [a]our God *is* a consuming fire.

Social and Religious Duties

13 Let [a]brotherly love[5360] continue.
2 [a]Be not forgetful to [apt]entertain strangers:[5381] for thereby [b]some have entertained angels[32] unawares.[2990]

3 [a]Remember them that are in bonds, as bound with them; *and* them which [ppp]suffer adversity, as being yourselves also in the body.

4 Marriage[1062] *is* honourable in all, and the bed undefiled:[283] [a]but whoremongers[4205] and adulterers God will judge.[2919]

5 *Let your* conversation *be* without covetousness; *and* [a]*be* content with such things as ye have: for he [pfi]hath said, [b]I will never leave thee, nor forsake thee.

6 So that we may boldly say, [a]The Lord *is* my helper, and I [fp]will not fear[5399] what man[444] shall do unto me.

7 [a]Remember them which [I]have the rule over[2233] you, who [ao]have spoken[2980] unto you the word[3056] of God: [b]whose faith follow, considering[333] the end of *their* conversation.

8 Jesus Christ[5547] [a]the same yesterday, and to day, and for ever.

9 [a]Be not carried about with divers[4164] and strange[3581] doctrines.[1322] For *it is* a good thing[2570] that the heart [pinf]be established with grace;[5485] [b]not with meats, which [aop]have not profited[5623] them that [apt]have been occupied therein.

10 [a]We have an altar, whereof they have no right[1849] to eat which [ppt]serve[3000] the tabernacle.[4633]

11 For [a]the bodies[4983] of those beasts,[2226] whose blood[129] is brought[1533] into the sanctuary[39] by the high priest[749] for sin,[266] are burned without[1854] the camp.

12 Wherefore Jesus also, that he [asba]might sanctify[37] the people[2992] with his own blood,[129] [a]suffered without the gate.

13 Let us go forth therefore unto him without the camp, bearing[5342] [a]his reproach.

14 [a]For here have we no continuing city, but we seek one to come.

19 [a]Ex. 20:19; Deut. 5:5, 25; 18:16
20 [a]Ex. 19:13
21 [a]Ex. 19:16
22 [a]Gal. 4:26; Rev. 3:12; 21:2, 10 [b]Phil. 3:20 [c]Deut. 33:2; Ps. 68:17
23 [I]Or, *enrolled* [a]Ex. 4:22; James 1:18; Rev. 14:4 [b]Luke 10:20; Phil. 4:3; Rev. 13:8 [c]Gen. 18:25; Ps. 94:2 [d]Phil. 3:12; Heb. 11:40
24 [I]Or, *testament* [a]Heb. 8:6; 9:15 [b]Ex. 24:8; Heb. 10:22; 1Pet. 1:2 [c]Gen. 4:10; Heb. 11:4
25 [a]Heb. 2:2, 3; 3:17; 10:28, 29
26 [a]Ex. 19:18 [b]Hag. 2:6
27 [I]Or, *may be shaken* [a]Ps. 102:26; Matt. 24:35; 2Pet. 3:10; Rev. 21:1
28 [I]Or, *let us hold fast*
29 [a]Ex. 24:17; Deut. 4:24; 9:3; Ps. 50:3; 97:3; Isa. 66:15; 2Thess. 1:8; Heb. 10:27

1 [a]Rom. 12:10; 1Thess. 4:9; 1Pet. 1:22; 2:17; 3:8; 4:8; 2Pet. 1:7; 1John 3:11; 4:7, 20, 21
2 [a]Matt. 25:35; Rom. 12:13; 1Tim. 3:2; 1Pet. 4:9 [b]Gen. 18:3; 19:2
3 [a]Matt. 25:36; Rom. 12:15; 1Cor. 12:26; Col. 4:18; 1Pet. 3:8
4 [a]1Cor. 6:9; Gal. 5:19, 21; Eph. 5:5; Col. 3:5, 6; Rev. 22:15
5 [a]Matt. 6:25, 34; Phil. 4:11, 12; 1Tim. 6:6, 8 [b]Gen. 28:15; Deut. 31:6, 8; Josh. 1:5; 1Chr. 28:20; Ps. 37:25
6 [a]Ps. 27:1; 56:4, 11, 12; 118:6
7 [I]Or, *are the guides* [a]Heb. 13:17 [b]Heb. 6:12

8 [a]John 8:58; Heb. 1:12; Rev. 1:4 9 [a]Eph. 4:14; 5:6; Col. 2:4, 8; 1John 4:1 [b]Rom. 14:17; Col. 2:16; 1Tim. 4:3 10 [a]1Cor. 9:13; 10:18 11 [a]Ex. 29:14; Lev. 4:11, 12, 21; 6:30; 9:11; 16:27; Num. 19:3 12 [a]John 19:17, 18; Acts 7:58 13 [a]Heb. 11:26; 1Pet. 4:14 14 [a]Mic. 2:10; Phil. 3:20; Heb. 11:10, 16; 12:22

15 [a]By him therefore let us offer [b]the sacrifice[2378] of praise[133] to God continually, that is, [c]the fruit of *our* lips Igiving thanks[3670] to his name.[3686]

16 [a]But to do good and to communicate[2842] forget not: for [b]with such sacrifices God is well pleased.[2100]

17 [a]Obey[3982] them that Ihave the rule over[2233] you, and submit[5226] yourselves: for [b]they watch for your souls,[5590] as they that must give account,[3056] that they [psa]may do it with joy,[5479] and not with [ppt]grief: for that *is* unprofitable for you.

18 [pim][a]Pray for us: for we trust[3982] we have [b]a good conscience,[4893] in all things willing [pinf]to live honestly.

19 But I beseech *you* [a]the rather[4056] [ainf]to do this, that I [asbp]may be restored[600] to you the sooner.

"Jesus, that Great Shepherd"

20 Now [a]the God of peace,[1515] [b]that [apt]brought again from the dead our Lord Jesus, [c]that great shepherd[4166] of the sheep, [d]through the blood[129] of the everlasting[166] Icovenant,[1242]

21 [opt][a]Make you perfect[2675] in every good[18] work[2041] [aies]to do his will, [ppt][b]working in you that which is wellpleasing[2101] in his sight, through Jesus Christ; [c]to whom *be* glory[1391] for ever[165,1519][3588] and ever. Amen.[281]

22 And I beseech you, brethren,[80] suffer[430] the word of exhortation:[3874] for [a]I have written a letter unto you in few words.

23 Know ye that [a]*our* brother Timothy [b]is set at liberty;[630] with whom, if he come shortly, I will see you.

24 Salute[782] all them [a]that have the rule over[2233] you, and all the saints.[40] They of Italy salute you.

25 [a]Grace *be* with you all. Amen.

15 IGr. *confessing to* [a]Eph. 5:20; 1Pet. 2:5 [b]Lev. 7:12; Ps. 50:14, 23; 69:30, 31; 107:22; 116:17 [c]Hos. 14:2 **16** [a]Rom. 12:13 [b]2Cor. 9:12; Phil. 4:18; Heb. 6:10 **17** IOr, *guide* [a]Phil. 2:29; 1Thess. 5:12; 1Tim. 5:17; Heb. 13:7 [b]Ezek. 3:17; 33:2, 7; Acts 20:26, 28 **18** [a]Rom. 15:30; Eph. 6:19; Col. 4:3; 1Thess. 5:25; 2Thess. 3:1 [b]Acts 23:1; 24:16; 2Cor. 1:12 **19** [a]Phile. 1:22 **20** IOr, *testament* [a]Rom. 15:33; 1Thess. 5:23 [b]Acts 2:24, 32; Rom. 4:24; 8:11; 1Cor. 6:14; 15:15; 2Cor. 4:14; Gal. 1:1; Col. 2:12; 1Thess. 1:10; 1Pet. 1:21 [c]Isa. 40:11; Ezek. 34:23; 37:24; John 10:11, 14; 1Pet. 2:25; 5:4 [d]Zech. 9:11; Heb. 10:29 **21** IOr, *doing* [a]2Thess. 2:17; 1Pet. 5:10 [b]Phil. 2:13 [c]Gal. 1:5; 2Tim. 4:18; Rev. 1:6 **22** [a]1Pet. 5:12 **23** [a]1Thess. 3:2 [b]1Tim. 6:12 **24** [a]Heb. 13:7-17 **25** [a]Titus 3:15

The Epistle of

JAMES

James was the oldest half-brother of the Lord Jesus (Matt. 13:55). He witnessed Christ's appearance following His resurrection (1 Cor. 15:7), and he was among those who assembled together following the Ascension, to await the coming of the Holy Spirit (Acts 1:14). Later, James became a leader of the believers in Jerusalem (Acts 12:17; Gal. 1:18, 19). Even Paul took his advice on how to deal with the new Gentile converts (Acts 21:18–26). James kept the potentially explosive situation concerning Gentile evangelism under control. In addition, he helped draft a very tolerant letter to the Gentile Christians in Antioch regarding their status (Acts 15:13–19). James was cognizant of Paul's ministry to the Gentiles, but concentrated his own efforts on winning his Jewish brethren to faith in Jesus.

The phrase "to the twelve tribes which are scattered abroad" (James 1:1) is a symbolic reference to the Jews in general (cf. James 1:2, 18). The phrase "scattered abroad" denotes those Jews who were living outside of Palestine, due in great part to the intense persecution of Christians living in Jerusalem (Acts 8:1). Since the letter was written in the Greek language, it is logical to assume that these Jews had been scattered far enough north to have ended up in a locale chiefly populated by Greek speaking peoples (Acts 11:19).

Most scholars suggest that this book was written shortly before James' martyrdom in A.D. 62. There are some, however, who place the time of writing closer to the time of the Jerusalem council in A.D. 46.

The Book of James is a simple, yet organized and logical treatise on the ethical aspects of the Christian life. This fact, along with the realization that the book is largely composed of general exhortations and admonitions, has led some to call the Book of James the "New Testament Book of Proverbs." The major theme of the book is James' appeal to the believer that true faith results in outward acts of obedience and righteousness (James 1:22).

1 [a]James, [b]a servant[1401] of God[2316] and of the Lord[2962] Jesus Christ,[5547] [c]to the twelve tribes [d]which are scattered abroad, greeting.[5463]

The Prayer of Faith

2 My brethren,[80] [aim][a]count it all joy[5479] [b]when ye [aosb]fall into divers[4164] temptations;[3986]

3 [a]Knowing *this,* that the trying[1383] of your faith[4102] worketh patience.

4 But let patience[5281] have *her* perfect[5046] work,[2041] that ye may be perfect and entire,[3648] wanting nothing.

5 [a]If any of you lack wisdom,[4678] [b]let him ask[154] of God,[2316] that [ppt]giveth to all *men* liberally, and [ppt]upbraideth[3679] not; and [c]it shall be given him.

6 [a]But [pim]let him ask[154] in faith, nothing wavering.[1252] For he that wavereth is like a wave of the sea [ppp]driven with the wind and [ppp]tossed.

7 For let not that man think that he shall receive any thing of the Lord.

8 [a]A double minded[1374] man *is* unstable[182] in all his ways.[3598]

9 [pim]Let the brother of low degree [I]rejoice[2744] in that he is exalted:

10 But the rich, in that he is made low:[5014] because [a]as the flower of the grass he shall pass away.

11 For the sun [ao]is no sooner risen[393] with a burning heat, but it [ao]withereth the grass, and the flower thereof [ao]falleth, and the grace of the fashion[4383] of it [aom]perisheth: so also shall the rich man fade away[3133] in his ways.

1 [a]Acts 12:17; 15:13; Gal. 1:19; 2:9; Jude 1:1 [b]Titus 1:1 [c]Acts 26:7 [d]Deut. 32:26; John 7:35; Acts 2:5; 8:1; 1Pet. 1:1
2 [a]Matt. 5:12; Acts 5:41; Heb. 10:34; 1Pet. 4:13, 16 [b]1Pet. 1:6
3 [a]Rom. 5:3
5 [a]1Kgs. 3:9, 11, 12; Prov. 2:3 [b]Matt. 7:7; 21:22; Mark 11:24; Luke 11:9; John 14:13; 15:7; 16:23 [c]Jer. 29:12; 1John 5:14, 15
6 [a]Mark 11:24; 1Tim. 2:8
8 [a]James 4:8
9 [I]Or, *glory*
10 [a]Job 14:2; Ps. 37:2; 90:5, 6; 102:11; 103:15; Isa. 40:6; 1Cor. 7:31; James 4:14; 1Pet. 1:24; 1John 2:17

Enduring Tests

12 [a]Blessed[3107] *is* the man that endureth[5278] temptation:[3986] for when he is tried,[1384] he shall receive [b]the crown of life,[2222] [c]which the Lord [aom]hath promised[1861] to them that [ppt]love[25] him.

🔑 13 Let no man say when he is tempted,[3985] I [pinp]am tempted of God: for God cannot be tempted with [I]evil,[2556] neither tempteth he any man:

14 But every man is tempted, when he [ppp]is drawn away of his own lust,[1939] and [ppp]enticed.

15 Then [a]when lust [apt]hath conceived, it bringeth forth[5088] sin:[266] and sin, when it [aptp]is finished, [b]bringeth forth[616] death.[2288]

16 [pim]Do not err,4105 my beloved brethren.

17 [a]Every good[18] gift[1394] and every perfect[5046] gift[1434] is from above,[509] and cometh down from the Father[3962] of lights,[5457] [b]with whom is no variableness, neither shadow of turning.

18 [a]Of his own will begat[616] he us with the word[3056] of truth,[225] [b]that we should be a kind of [c]firstfruits[536] of his creatures.[2938]

Be Doers of the Word

19 Wherefore, my beloved[27] brethren,[80] [a]let every man[444] be swift [aies]to hear, [b]slow[1021] [aies]to speak, [c]slow to wrath:[3709]

20 For the wrath[3709] of man[435] worketh not the righteousness[1343] of God.

21 Wherefore [apta]lay apart all filthiness and superfluity[4050] of naughtiness,[2549] and [aim]receive with meekness[4240] the engrafted1721 word, [b]which is able [ainf]to save[4982] your souls.[5590]

22 But [pima]be ye doers of the word,[3056] and not hearers only, deceiving your own selves.

23 For [a]if any be a hearer of the word, and not a doer, he is like unto a man beholding his natural[1078] face[4383] in a glass:

24 For he [ao]beholdeth himself, and [pfi]goeth his way, and straightway[2112] [aom]forgetteth what manner of man he was.

25 But [a]whoso [apt]looketh3879 into the perfect[5046] [b]law[3551] of liberty,[1657] and [apt]continueth[3887] *therein,* he being not a forgetful hearer, but a doer of the work, [c]this man shall be blessed[3107] in his [I]deed.

26 If any man among you seem to be religious,[2357] and [ppta]bridleth not his tongue, but [ppt]deceiveth his own heart,[2588] this man's religion2356 *is* vain.

27 Pure[2513] religion and undefiled[283] before God[2316] and the Father[3962] is this, [pinfa]To visit[1980] the fatherless and widows in their affliction,[2347] [b]*and* [pinf]to keep himself unspotted[784] from the world.[2889]

Respect for Others

2 My brethren,[80] have not the faith[4102] of our Lord Jesus Christ, [a]*the Lord* of glory,[1391] with [b]respect of persons.

2 For if there [aosb]come unto your [I]assembly[4864] a man with a gold ring, in goodly apparel, and there [aosb]come in also a poor man in vile4508 raiment;

3 And ye [asba]have respect to him that weareth the gay2986 clothing, and [aosb]say unto him, Sit thou here [I]in a good place; and [aosb]say to the poor, Stand thou there, or sit here under my footstool:

4 [aop]Are ye not then partial[1252] in yourselves, and [aom]are become judges of evil[4190] thoughts?[1261]

🔑 5 Hearken, my beloved brethren, [aoma]Hath not God chosen[1586] the poor of this world[2889] [b]rich in faith,[4102] and heirs[2818] of [I]the kingdom[932] [c]which he [aom]hath promised[1861] to them that [ppt]love[25] him?

12 [a]Job 5:17; Prov. 3:11, 12; Heb. 12:5; Rev. 3:19 [b]1Cor. 9:25; 2Tim. 4:8; James 2:5; 1Pet. 5:4; Rev. 2:10 [c]Matt. 10:22; 19:28, 29; James 2:5
13 [I]Or, *evils*
15 [a]Job 15:35; Ps. 7:14 [b]Rom. 6:21, 23
17 [a]John 3:27; 1Cor. 4:7 [b]Num. 23:19; 1Sam. 15:29; Mal. 3:6; Rom. 11:29
18 [a]John 1:13; 3:3; 1Cor. 4:15; 1Pet. 1:23 [b]Eph. 1:12 [c]Jer. 2:3; Rev. 14:4
19 [a]Eccl. 5:1 [b]Prov. 10:19; 17:27; Eccl. 5:2 [c]Prov. 14:17; 16:32; Eccl. 7:9
21 [a]Col. 3:8; 1Pet. 2:1 [b]Acts 13:26; Rom. 1:16; 1Cor. 15:2; Eph. 1:13; Titus 2:11; Heb. 2:3; 1Pet. 1:9
22 [a]Matt. 7:21; Luke 6:46; 11:28; Rom. 2:13; 1John 3:7
23 [a]Luke 6:47; James 2:14
25 [I]Or, *doing* [a]2Cor. 3:18 [b]James 2:12 [c]John 13:17
26 [a]Ps. 34:13; 39:1; 1Pet. 3:10
27 [a]Isa. 1:16, 17; 58:6, 7; Matt. 25:36 [b]Rom. 12:2; James 4:4; 1John 5:18

1 [a]1Cor. 2:8 [b]Lev. 19:15; Deut. 1:17; 16:19; Prov. 24:23; 28:21; Matt. 22:16; James 2:9; Jude 1:16
2 [I]Gr. *synagogue*
3 [I]Or, *well,* or, *seemly*
5 [I]Or, *that* [a]John 7:48; 1Cor. 1:26, 28 [b]Luke 12:21; 1Tim. 6:18; Rev. 2:9 [c]Ex. 20:6; 1Sam. 2:30; Prov. 8:17; Matt. 5:3; Luke 6:20; 12:32; 1Cor. 2:9; 2Tim. 4:8; James 1:12

🔑 **1:13–15** See note on Genesis 22:1 concerning God "tempting" Abraham.
🔑 **2:5** See note on Ephesians 1:4, 5.

6 But [a]ye [ao]have despised the poor.
Do not rich men oppress you, [b]and
draw[1670] you before the judgment
seats?[2922]
7 Do not they blaspheme[987] that worthy name[3686] by the which ye [aptp]are
called?[1941]
8 If ye [pin]fulfil[5055] the royal[937]
law[3551] according to the scripture,[1124]
[a]Thou shalt love[25] thy neighbour[4139] as
thyself, ye do well:
9 But [a]if ye [pin]have respect to persons,[4380] ye commit[2038] sin,[266] and [ppp]are
convinced of the law[3551] as transgressors.[3848]
10 For whosoever [ft]shall keep the
whole law, and yet offend in one *point,*
[a]he [pfi]is guilty[1777] of all.
11 For [1]he that said, [aosi][a]Do not commit adultery,[3431] said also, [aosi]Do not
kill.[5407] Now if thou commit no adultery,
yet if thou kill, thou [pfi]art become a transgressor of the law.
12 So speak[2980] ye, and so do, as
they that shall [pip]be judged[2919] by [a]the
law[3551] of liberty.[1657]
13 For [a]he shall have judgment[2920]
without mercy,[448] that [apt]hath shewed no
mercy;[1656] and [b]mercy rejoiceth against
judgment.

"Faith Without Works Is Dead"

14 [a]What *doth it* profit, my brethren,
though a man [psa]say he hath faith,[4102]
and [psa]have not works?[2041] can faith
save[4982] him?

6 [a]1Cor. 11:22 [b]Acts 13:50; 17:6; 18:12; James 5:6
8 [a]Lev. 19:18; Matt. 22:39; Rom. 13:8, 9; Gal. 5:14; 6:2
9 [a]James 2:1
10 [a]Deut. 27:26; Matt. 5:19; Gal. 3:10
11 [1]Or, *that law which said* [a]Ex. 20:13, 14
12 [a]James 1:25 [b]Job 22:6; Prov. 21:13; Matt. 6:15; 18:35; 25:41, 42 [c]1John 4:17, 18
14 [a]Matt. 7:26; James 1:23

2:12, 13 The literal translation of these two verses is "Thus speak and thus do, as if you are going to be judged by a law of freedom or liberality." James tells us here that the believer is going to be judged (2 Cor. 5:10). The Judge, of course, is Jesus Christ. However, He is not going to be absolutely rigid, but He is going to exercise liberality or generosity in many cases toward those who are judged. In verse thirteen, James explains how this judgment is going to be determined: "For judgment will be merciless to one who has shown no mercy." This explains the fifth Beatitude in Matthew 5:7, "Blessed are the merciful, for they shall receive mercy." The Judge's generosity toward a believer will be in proportion to the amount of mercy that believer showed while on earth. If he or she showed no mercy, that one will receive no mercy. Entrance into heaven is a result of the work that Christ alone did, yet the believer's enjoyment of heaven and its rewards will be reflected in what he or she did for Christ in the life of faith on earth. Then follows the last part of James 2:13, which literally translated says, "Mercy or mercifulness boasts against judgment." This means that the believer whose life has been full of mercifulness will face the Judge unafraid, because the Judge in His liberality will take into account the mercy that the believer demonstrated on earth.

2:14–19 In Romans 3:20, Paul says, "By the works of the law no flesh will be justified." On the other hand, James 2:21–24 apparently states that man is not justified by faith only but also by works. The difficulty of the seeming contradiction is accentuated by the statement of Paul himself in Romans 2:13, "The doers of the law will be justified." How can these two statements be reconciled?

James 2:14 does not say, "What doth it profit . . . though a man have faith?" rather, "What use is it, my brethren, if a man says he has faith." A mere profession of faith does not mean the possession of faith or the natural accompaniments of faith. Faith that is not accompanied by its inevitable and expectant fruits of faith is no faith at all. It is a mockery, and James calls such a faith "dead."

Moreover, Paul speaks of a true, living faith that purifies the heart and works by love (Gal. 5:6). James in this instance speaks of a profession or presumption of faith, barren and destitute of good fruit. Such a faith is dead (v. 17); it is a "faith" like the devils may have (v. 19). It consists only of an intellectual belief of God's being or existence, not consenting to His offer of salvation through repentance and turning from sin nor relying on His promises. When Paul speaks of faith, he speaks of it as including the works of faith. When James speaks of faith, in this instance, he speaks of false faith that does not result in the works of faith. When any apostle speaks of works resulting from faith, inherent in those works is included the faith that is the only way whereby those works can be produced. When they speak of fruit, the whole process of the development of the fruit is included. When works, however, are spoken about as the works not resulting from faith, they are by their very

(continued on next page)

15 [a]If a brother or sister be naked, and destitute of daily food,

16 And [a]one of you [aosb]say unto them, Depart in peace,[1515] be *ye* warmed and filled; notwithstanding ye [aosb]give them not those things which are needful to the body; what *doth it* profit?

17 Even so faith, if it [psa]hath not works, is dead,[3498] being [I]alone.

18 Yea, a man may say, Thou hast faith, and I have works: shew me thy faith [I]without thy works, [a]and I will shew thee my faith by my works.

19 Thou believest[4100] that there is one God;[2316] thou doest well: [a]the devils[1140] also believe, and tremble.

20 But wilt thou know, O vain[2756] man, that faith without works is dead?

21 Was not Abraham our father justified[1344] by works, [a]when he [apt]had offered Isaac his son upon the altar?

22 [I]Seest thou [a]how faith [ipf]wrought with his works, and by works [aop]was faith made perfect?[5048]

23 And the scripture was fulfilled which saith, [a]Abraham believed[4100] God, and it [aop]was imputed[3049] unto him for righteousness:[1343] and he was called [b]the Friend of God.

24 Ye see then how that by works[2041] a man [pinp]is justified, and not by faith[4102] only.

25 Likewise also [a]was not Rahab the harlot justified by works, when she had received[5264] the messengers, and had sent *them* out another[2087] way?

26 For as the body[4983] without the [I]spirit[4151] is dead,[3498] so faith without works is dead also.

Control the Tongue

3 My brethren, [pim][a]be not many masters,[1320] [b]knowing that we shall

15 [a]Job 31:19, 20; Luke 3:11
16 [a]1John 3:18
17 [I]Gr. *by itself*
18 [I]Some texts read, *by thy works* [a]James 3:13
19 [a]Matt. 8:29; Mark 1:24; 5:7; Luke 4:34; Acts 16:17; 19:15
21 [a]Gen. 22:9, 12
22 [I]Or, *Thou seest* [a]Heb. 11:17
23 [a]Gen. 15:6; Rom. 4:3; Gal. 3:6 [b]2Chr. 20:7; Isa. 41:8
25 [a]Josh. 2:1; Heb. 11:31
26 [I]Or, *breath*

1 [I]Or, *judgment* [a]Matt. 23:8, 14; Rom. 2:20, 21; 1Pet. 5:3 [b]Luke 6:37
2 [a]1Kgs. 8:46; 2Chr. 6:36; Prov. 20:9; Eccl. 7:20; 1John 1:8 [b]Ps. 34:13; James 1:26; 1Pet. 3:10 [c]Matt. 12:37
3 [a]Ps. 32:9
5 [I]Or, *wood* [a]Prov. 12:18; 15:2 [b]Ps. 12:3; 73:8, 9
6 [I]Gr. *wheel* [a]Prov. 16:27 [b]Matt. 15:11, 18-20; Mark 7:15, 20, 23
7 [I]Gr. *nature* [II]Gr. *nature of man*
8 [a]Ps. 140:3
9 [a]Gen. 1:26; 5:1; 9:6
11 [I]Or, *hole*

receive the greater [I]condemnation.[2917]

2 For [a]in many things we offend all. [b]If any man offend not in word,[3056] [c]the same *is* a perfect[5046] man, *and* able also [ainf]to bridle the whole body.

3 Behold, [a]we put bits in the horses' mouths, that they may obey[3982] us; and we turn about their whole body.[4983]

4 Behold also the ships, which though *they be* so great, and *are* driven of fierce winds, yet are they turned about with a very small helm, whithersoever the governor [psmp]listeth.

5 Even so [a]the tongue[1100] is a little member, and [b]boasteth great things. Behold, how great [I]a matter a little fire kindleth!

6 And [a]the tongue *is* a fire, a world of iniquity;[93] so is[2525] the tongue among our members, that [b]it defileth[4695] the whole body, and [ppt]setteth on fire the [I]course of nature;[1078] and it [ppp]is set on fire of hell.[1067]

7 For every [I]kind of beasts, and of birds, and of serpents, and of things in the sea, [pfip]is tamed, and [pfip]hath been tamed of [II]mankind:

8 But the tongue can no man [ainf]tame; *it is* an unruly evil, full of deadly poison.

9 Therewith bless we God, even the Father; and therewith curse[2672] we men, [a]which [pfpp]are made after the similitude[3669] of God.

10 Out of the same mouth proceedeth blessing[2129] and cursing.[2671] My brethren, these things ought[5534] not so to be.

11 Doth a fountain send forth at the same [I]place sweet *water* and bitter?

12 Can the fig tree, my brethren, [ainf]bear olive berries? either a vine, figs? so *can* no fountain both [ainf]yield salt water and fresh.

(continued from previous page)

nature the false fruits of a nonexistent faith. One cannot have the fruits of faith that are true and real without true and real faith, no more than oranges can come from pine trees.

This sort of reasoning would shed light upon a statement concerning baptism that results from the exercise of living faith in Jesus Christ (see 1 Pet. 3:21). It is not actually the baptism that saves, because the act of physical baptism without the antecedent of living, spiritual faith in Christ is nothing but an empty and ineffective act (see note on Mark 16:16).

True Wisdom Comes From God

13 [a]Who *is* a wise man[4680] and endued with knowledge among you? [aim]let him shew[1166] out of a good[2570] conversation[391] [b]his works[2041] [c]with meekness[4240] of wisdom.[4678]

14 But if ye have [a]bitter envying and strife in your hearts,[2588] [b]glory not, and lie not against the truth.[225]

15 [a]This wisdom[4678] [ppt]descendeth not from above, but *is* earthly,[1919] [I][b]sensual,[5591] devilish.

16 For [a]where envying and strife *is,* there *is* [I]confusion[181] and every evil[5337] work.

17 But [a]the wisdom that is from above[509] is first pure,[53] then peaceable, gentle,[1933] *and* easy to be intreated, full of mercy[1656] and good[18] fruits, [I]without partiality,[87] [b]and without hypocrisy.[505]

18 [a]And the fruit of righteousness[1343] is sown in peace[1515] of them that [ppt]make peace.

Warnings Against Loving the World

4 From whence *come* wars and [I]fightings among you? *come they* not hence, *even* of your [II][a]lusts [b]that [ppt]war in your members?

2 Ye lust,[1937] and have not: ye [I]kill, and desire to have, and cannot obtain: ye fight and war, yet ye have not, because ye [aid]ask[154] not.

3 [a]Ye ask, and receive[2983] not, [b]because ye ask amiss,[2560] that ye may consume *it* upon your [I]lusts.[2237]

4 [a]Ye adulterers and adulteresses, know ye not that [b]the friendship of the world[2889] is enmity[2189] with God? [c]whosoever therefore will be a friend of the world is[2076] the enemy of God.

🔑5 Do ye think that the scripture[1124] saith in vain, [a]The spirit[4151] that dwelleth in us lusteth [I]to envy?

6 But he giveth more grace.[5485] Wherefore he saith, [a]God resisteth the proud,[5244] but giveth grace[5485] unto the humble.[5011]

7 [aipp]Submit[5293] yourselves therefore to God. [aim][a]Resist the devil,[1228] and he will flee from you.

8 [aim][a]Draw nigh[1448] to God, and he will draw nigh to you. [aim][b]Cleanse[2511] *your* hands, *ye* sinners;[268] and [aim][c]purify[48] *your* hearts,[2588] *ye* [d]double minded.[1374]

9 [aim][a]Be afflicted, and [aim]mourn,[3996] and [aim]weep: let your laughter be turned to mourning, and *your* joy[5479] to heaviness.

10 [aipp][a]Humble yourselves in the sight of the Lord, and he shall lift you up.

Cautions Concerning Criticism

11 [pim][a]Speak not evil[2635] one of another, brethren. He that [ppt]speaketh evil of *his* brother, [b]and [ppt]judgeth[2919] his brother, speaketh evil of the law, and judgeth the law: but if thou judge[2919] the law, thou art not a doer of the law, but a judge.

12 There is one lawgiver, [a]who is able[1410] [ainf]to save[4982] and [ainf]to destroy:[622] [b]who art thou that judgest[2919] another?[2087]

"If the Lord Will"

13 [a]Go to now, ye that [ppt]say, To day or to morrow we will go into such a city, and continue there a year, and buy and sell, and get gain:

14 Whereas ye know not what *shall*

13 [a]Gal. 6:4 [b]James 2:18 [c]James 1:21
14 [a]Rom. 13:13 [b]Rom. 2:17, 23
15 [I]Or, *natural* [a]Phil. 3:19; James 1:17 [b]Jude 1:19
16 [I]Gr. *tumult,* or, *unquietness* [a]1Cor. 3:3; Gal. 5:20
17 [I]Or, *without wrangling* [a]1Cor. 2:6, 7 [b]Rom. 12:9; 1Pet. 1:22; 2:1; 1John 3:18
18 [a]Prov. 11:18; Hos. 10:12; Matt. 5:9; Phil. 1:11; Heb. 12:11

1 [I]Or, *brawlings* [II]Or, *pleasures* [a]James 4:3 [b]Rom. 7:23; Gal. 5:17; 1Pet. 2:11
2 [I]Or, *envy*
3 [I]Or, *pleasures* [a]Job 27:9; 35:12; Ps. 18:41; Prov. 1:28; Isa. 1:15; Jer. 11:11; Mic. 3:4; Zech. 7:13 [b]Ps. 66:18; 1John 3:22; 5:14
4 [a]Ps. 73:27 [b]1John 2:15 [c]John 15:19; 17:14; Gal. 1:10
5 [I]Or, *enviously* [a]Gen. 6:5; 8:21; Num. 11:29; Prov. 21:10
6 [a]Job 22:29; Ps. 138:6; Prov. 3:34; 29:23; Matt. 23:12; Luke 1:52; 14:11; 18:14; 1Pet. 5:5
7 [a]Eph. 4:27; 6:11; 1Pet. 5:9
8 [a]2Chr. 15:2 [b]Isa. 1:16 [c]1Pet. 1:22; 1John 3:3 [d]James 1:8
9 [a]Matt. 5:4
10 [a]Job 22:29; Matt. 23:12; Luke 14:11; 18:14; 1Pet. 5:6

11 [a]Eph. 4:31; 1Pet. 2:1 [b]Matt. 7:1; Luke 6:37; Rom. 2:1; 1Cor. 4:5 **12** [a]Matt. 10:28 [b]Rom. 14:4, 13
13 [a]Prov. 27:1; Luke 12:18 [b]Job 7:7; Ps. 102:3; James 1:10; 1Pet. 1:24; 1John 2:17

🔑 **4:5** The solution to this difficult verse is to recognize that the word "spirit" is not referring to the Holy Spirit, but to the fallen spirit of man (that which is responsible for man's propensity to sin; cf. Rom 5:12). The fallen spirit in man "lusteth" (*epipotheí* [1971]) toward envy. This envy manifests itself in selfishness and malice.

be on the morrow. For what *is* your life?[2222] [a]It is even a vapour, that appeareth for a little time, and then vanisheth away.

15 For that ye *ought* to say, [a]If the Lord will, we shall live,[2198] and do this, or that.

16 But now ye rejoice in your boastings:[212] [a]all such rejoicing is evil.[4190]

17 Therefore [a]to him that knoweth[1492] [pinf]to do[4160] good,[2570] and [ppt]doeth *it* not, to him it is sin.[266]

Warnings to the Rich

5 Go [a]to now, *ye* rich men, weep and howl for your miseries that shall come upon *you*.

2 Your riches are corrupted, and [a]your garments are motheaten.

3 Your gold and silver is cankered; and the rust of them shall be a witness[3142] against you, and shall eat your flesh as it were fire. [a]Ye [ao]have heaped treasure together for the last[2078] days.

4 Behold, [a]the hire[3408] of the labourers who [aptp]have reaped down your fields, which is of you kept back by fraud, crieth: and [b]the cries of them which have reaped are entered into the ears of the Lord[2962] of sabaoth.[4519]

5 [a]Ye [ao]have lived in pleasure[5171] on the earth, and [ao]been wanton; ye [ao]have nourished your hearts, as in a day of slaughter.

6 [a]Ye have condemned[2613] *and* killed the just;[1342] *and* he doth not resist you.

15 [a]Acts 18:21; 1Cor. 4:19; 16:7; Heb. 6:3
16 [a]1Cor. 5:6
17 [a]Luke 12:47; John 9:41; 15:22; Rom. 1:20, 21, 32; 2:17, 18, 23

1 [a]Prov. 11:28; Luke 6:24; 1Tim. 6:9
2 [a]Job 13:28; Matt. 6:20; James 2:2
3 [a]Rom. 2:5
4 [a]Lev. 19:13; Job 24:10, 11; Jer. 22:13; Mal. 3:5 [b]Deut. 24:15
5 [a]Job 21:13; Amos 6:1, 4; Luke 16:19, 25; 1Tim. 5:6
6 [a]James 2:6
7 [1]Or, *Be long patient,* or, *Suffer with long patience* [a]Deut. 11:14; Jer. 5:24; Hos. 6:3; Joel 2:23; Zech. 10:1
8 [a]Phil. 4:5; Heb. 10:25, 37; 1Pet. 4:7 [b]James 4:11 [c]Matt. 24:33; 1Cor. 4:5
10 [a]Matt. 5:12; Heb. 11:35
11 [a]Ps. 94:12; Matt. 5:10, 11; 10:22 [b]Job 1:21, 22; 2:10 [c]Job 42:10 [d]Num. 14:18; Ps. 103:8
12 [a]Matt. 5:34
13 [a]Eph. 5:19; Col. 3:16

Patience Exhorted

7 [1]Be patient[3114] therefore, brethren,[80] unto the coming of the Lord. Behold, the husbandman[1092] waiteth for[1551] the precious fruit of the earth, and [ppt]hath long patience[3114] for it, until he receive [a]the early and latter rain.

8 [aim]Be ye also patient;[3114] stablish your hearts: [a]for the coming[3952] of the Lord [pfi]draweth nigh.

9 [a]Grudge not one against another, brethren, lest ye [asbp]be condemned: behold, the judge[2923] [b]standeth before the door.

10 [a]Take, my brethren, the prophets,[4396] who have spoken in the name[3686] of the Lord, for an example of suffering affliction,[2552] and of patience.[3115]

11 Behold, [a]we count them happy[3106] which [ppt]endure.[5278] Ye have heard of [b]the patience of Job, and have seen [c]the end[5056] of the Lord; that [d]the Lord is very pitiful, and of tender mercy.

12 But above all things, my brethren, [a]swear not, neither by heaven,[3772] neither by the earth,[1093] neither by any other[243] oath:[3727] but let your yea be yea; and *your* nay, nay; lest ye [aosb]fall into condemnation.

13 Is any among you afflicted?[2553] [pim]let him pray.[4336] Is any merry? [pim][a]let him sing psalms.[5567]

14 Is any sick among you? [aim]let him call for[4341] the elders[4245] of the church;[1577] and [aim]let them pray[4336] over

---

4:17 See note on 1 John 3:6–9.

5:7, 8 Since numerous references to rain in the Old Testament are accompanied by the expression "early" or "latter" (Deut. 11:14; Job 29:23; Prov. 16:15; Jer. 3:3; Hos. 6:3; Joel 2:23), it stands to reason that the analogy James is making in this passage relates to the severe weather patterns that existed in early Palestine.

5:11 See notes on Job 1:21, 22; 38:1—42:6.

5:14, 15 The key question that arises from this passage is whether Christianity prohibits the use of medicine. In the original Greek text, verse fourteen began with a statement rather than a question, and should be rendered "Someone among you is sick." James begins the discussion with the fact that there is sickness in the world and the Christian is not exempt from it. In the examination of this verse, one can conclude that the initiative to call the elders of the church to the sick believer's bedside must come from the believer himself. At the time of the apostolic church, its elders performed many duties. One such task was treating sick people in whatever manner possible.

(continued on next page)

him, [apt][a]anointing[218] him with oil in the
name of the Lord:
15 And the prayer2171 of faith[4102]
shall save[4982] the sick,[2577] and the Lord
shall raise him up; [a]and if he have committed sins,[266] they shall be forgiven[863]
him.
16 [pim]Confess[1843] *your* faults[3900] one
to another, and [pim]pray one for another,
that ye [asbp]may be healed. [a]The [ppt]effec-
tual fervent[1754] prayer[1162] of a righteous[1342] man availeth[2480] much.
17 Elias was a man[444] [a]subject to like
passions as we are, and [b]he [ao]prayed[4336]
[I]earnestly[4335] that it [infg]might not rain:1026
[c]and it rained not on the earth by the
space of three years and six months.
18 And [a]he prayed again, and the
heaven[3772] gave rain, and the earth
brought forth her fruit.
19 Brethren, [a]if any of you [asbp]do err
from the truth,[225] and one convert[1994] him;
20 Let him know, that he which
[apt]converteth the sinner[268] from the error
of his way [a]shall save a soul[5590] from
death,[2288] and [b]shall hide[2572] a multitude
of sins.[266]

14 [a]Mark 6:13; 16:18 **15** [a]Isa. 33:24; Matt. 9:2 **16** [a]Gen. 20:17; Num. 11:2; Deut. 9:18, 19, 20; Josh. 10:12; 1Sam. 12:18; 1Kgs. 13:6; 2Kgs. 4:33; 19:15, 20; 20:2, 4; Ps. 10:17; 34:15; 145:18; Prov. 15:29; 28:9; John 9:31; 1John 3:22 **17** [I]Or, *in his prayer* [a]Acts 14:15 [b]1Kgs. 17:1 [c]Luke 4:25 **18** [a]1Kgs. 18:42, 45

19 [a]Matt. 18:15 **20** [a]Rom. 11:14; 1Cor. 9:22; 1Tim. 4:16 [b]Prov. 10:12; 1Pet. 4:8

(continued from previous page)

This verse reads, "let them pray over him, anointing him with oil in the name of the Lord." The order in which these two things were to be performed is clarified in the Greek text. The word translated "anointing him" is the aorist participle *aleípsantes* (from *aleíphō* [218]). This term describes an act which preceded the prayer and should be translated "having anointed." Therefore, this instance denotes the application of medicine first, then the elders are commanded to pray for the sick person.

In addition to this, prayer is to be made "in the name of the Lord," not necessarily the anointing act. This is explained by the aorist imperative verb, *proseuxásthōsan* (from *proseúchomai* [4336]) translated "let them pray." Also the verb *proskalesásthō* (from *proskaléomai* [4341]), meaning "let him call," denotes the aorist tense. In both cases reference is made to one action at one point in the past, not a repetitive connotation. The participle, *aleípsantes*, does not refer back to the main verb or the main action in the clause. The application of medicine can be rendered by both believers and unbelievers, but prayer as an exercise of faith is the key to seeking God's will in regard to healing. Furthermore, the phrase "in the name of the Lord" does not refer to a matter of habit by which one must close his prayers. Rather, it indicates a willingness to place prayer and any answer to prayer into the sovereign will and purpose of God. In John 14:13, the Lord said, "And whatsoever ye shall ask in my name, that will I do, that the Father may be glorified in the Son." It is true that believers do not always receive the things for which they ask, even perfect health. However, there is coming a time when the bodies of Christians are going to be redeemed (Rom. 8:23), and they will be given glorified, resurrected ones (1 Cor. 15:51–54). Also, the "name of the Lord" indicates His character and purpose. For instance, if a parent were to say to a child, "Respect my name," he is requiring obedience to do what he commands. In the same way, the Lord gives His children the freedom to pray for all that they would wish the Heavenly Father to grant to them. However, He knows and gives the best according to His will. God's best may be sickness and privation, instead of health and wealth, but it is designed to bring the believer into a closer walk with Him (Rom. 8:28).

Ultimately, it is God that does the healing for both believers and unbelievers, with or without the use of medicine. Often times, God heals even when prayer is not offered. In the case of the believer there must be the realization that the prayer of faith to God has power. While He is a sovereign God, He is also a prayer-hearing and prayer-answering God. In verse fifteen, James explains the believer's assurance: "And the prayer of faith shall save the sick, and the Lord shall raise him up."

The First Epistle of

PETER

The Apostle Peter was the most prominent disciple during the ministry of Jesus and had a tremendous impact on the early church. The first twelve chapters of Acts are devoted to his ministry and to the development of the church in the East where he was the dominant figure. Paul mentioned him in 1 Corinthians (1 Cor. 1:12; 3:22; 9:5; 15:5) and Galatians (Gal. 1:18; 2:7–9, 11, 14), and Peter wrote two New Testament books. This first letter is addressed to the five Roman provinces in Asia Minor (modern-day Turkey) north of the Taurus Mountains (1 Pet. 1:1).

This letter was written to encourage the believers to endure the intense persecution that was prevalent in the area and to prepare the readers for the difficult times ahead of them. The first empire-wide persecution of Christians did not come until A.D. 249 under the brutal emperor Decius, but local persecutions many times were quite severe. One in particular took place early in the second century in Bithynia, one of the provinces to which Peter wrote (1 Pet. 1:1). A letter was sent from Pliny, governor of Bithynia, to the Roman emperor Trajan, in A.D. 112. He explained that he had been executing people who confessed that they were Christians. Trajan's reply expressed his approval of Pliny's policy, but instructed him to set free those Christians who would renounce their faith and worship the Roman gods. Since 1 Peter was most likely written in the A.D. 60's, persecution of the severest kind was yet to come. Peter used Jesus' own suffering as the cornerstone of his exhortation. Likewise, Peter admonished believers to suffer as "Christians," not as lawbreakers.

1 Peter, an apostle[652] of Jesus
Christ,[5547] to the strangers[3927] [a]scattered
throughout Pontus, Galatia,
Cappadocia, Asia, and Bithynia,
🔑 2 [a]Elect[1588] [b]according to the
foreknowledge[4268] of God[2316] the Father,[3962]
[c]through sanctification[38] of the
Spirit,[4151] unto obedience[5218] and [d]sprinkling[4473]
of the blood[129] of Jesus Christ:
[e]Grace[5485] unto you, and peace,[1515] be
multiplied.

Heaven Is Worth the Wait

3 [a]Blessed[2128] *be* the God and Father
of our Lord[2962] Jesus Christ, which
[b]according to his abundant mercy[1656]
[apt][c]hath begotten us again[313] unto a
[ppt]lively[2198] hope[1680] [d]by the resurrection[386]
of Jesus Christ from the
dead,[3498]
4 To an inheritance[2817] incorruptible,[862]
and undefiled,[283] [a]and that fadeth
not away,[263] [pfpp][b]reserved[5083] in
heaven[3772] [I]for you,
🔑 5 [a]Who [ppp]are kept by the power[1411]
of God[2316] through faith[4102] unto salvation[4991]
ready [aifp]to be revealed[601] in
the last time.[2540]
6 [a]Wherein ye greatly rejoice,[21]

1 [a]John 7:35; Acts 2:5, 9, 10; James 1:1
2 [a]Eph. 1:4; 1Pet. 2:9 [b]Rom. 8:29; 11:2 [c]2Thess. 2:13 [d]Heb. 10:22; 12:24 [e]Rom. 1:7; 2Pet. 1:2; Jude 1:2 [f]2Cor. 1:3; Eph. 1:3 [g]Titus 3:5 [h]John 3:3, 5; James 1:18 [i]1Cor. 15:20; 1Thess. 4:14; 1Pet. 3:21
4 [I]Or, *for us* [a]1Pet. 5:4 [b]Col. 1:5; 2Tim. 4:8
5 [a]John 10:28, 29; 17:11, 12, 15; Jude 1:1
6 [a]Matt. 5:12; Rom. 12:12; 2Cor. 6:10; 1Pet. 4:13

🔑 **1:2** See note on Ephesians 1:4, 5.

🔑 **1:5** The phrase "who are kept by the power of God" refers to believers (1 Pet. 1:3). These also have become heirs of a resurrection body (1 Pet. 1:4), and their inheritance is reserved in heaven. The sense in which the perfect participle, *tetērēménēn* (meaning "reserved," and derived from *tēréō* [5083]), is used denotes that the act was made possible by Christ sometime in the past and is now being kept by Him until the proper time of delivery. Also, the purpose of the protection indicated in verse five is related to the believer's future liberation noted in the phrase, "kept by the power of God . . . unto salvation" (Rom. 8:23; 13:11).

though now [b]for a season, if need[1163] be,
[c]ye [aptp]are in heaviness through manifold
temptations:[3986]
🔑 7 That [a]the trial[1383] of your faith,[4102]
being much more precious than of gold
that perisheth, though [b]it [ppp]be tried[1381]
with fire, [asbp][c]might be found[2147] unto
praise and honour and glory[1391] at the
appearing[602] of Jesus Christ:
8 [a]Whom having not seen, ye love;[25]
[b]in whom, though now ye [ppt]see *him* not,
yet believing,[4100] ye rejoice with joy[5479]
unspeakable and full of glory:[1392]
9 Receiving [a]the end[5056] of your
faith, *even* the salvation[4991] of *your*
souls.[5590]
10 [a]Of which salvation the prophets[4396] [ao]have enquired and searched
diligently, who prophesied[4395] of the
grace[5485] *that should come* unto you:
11 Searching what, or what manner
of time [a]the Spirit[4151] of Christ[5547] which
was in them [ipf]did signify, when it
[ppt]testified beforehand [b]the sufferings
of Christ, and the glory that should follow.
12 [a]Unto whom it was revealed,[601]
that [b]not unto themselves, but unto us
they [ipf]did minister[1247] the things, which
are now reported unto you by them that
[apt]have preached the gospel[2097] unto you
with [c]the [an]Holy Ghost[4151] sent down
from heaven;[3772] [d]which things the angels[32] desire[1937] to look[3879] into.

Exhortation to Holiness

🔑 13 Wherefore [apta]gird up the loins[3751]
of your mind,[1271] [pptb]be sober, and
[aim]hope [I]to the end[5049] for the grace[5485]
that is to [ppp]be brought unto you [c]at the
revelation[602] of Jesus Christ;
14 As obedient[5218] children,[5043] [a]not
fashioning[4964] yourselves according to the
former lusts[1939] [b]in your ignorance:[52]
15 [a]But as he which [apt]hath called
you is holy,[40] so be ye holy in all manner of conversation;[391]

6 [b]2Cor. 4:17; 1Pet. 5:10 [c]James 1:2
7 [a]James 1:3, 12; 1Pet. 4:12 [b]Job 23:10; Ps. 66:10; Prov. 17:3; Isa. 48:10; Zech. 13:9; 1Cor. 3:13 [c]Rom. 2:7, 10; 1Cor. 4:5; 2Thess. 1:7-12
8 [a]1John 4:20 [b]John 20:29; 2Cor. 5:7; Heb. 11:1, 27
9 [a]Rom. 6:22
10 [a]Gen. 49:10; Dan. 2:44; Hag. 2:7; Zech. 6:12; Matt. 13:17; Luke 10:24; 2Pet. 1:19-21
11 [a]1Pet. 3:19; 2Pet. 1:21 [b]Ps. 22:6; Isa. 53:3; Dan. 9:26; Luke 24:25, 26, 44, 46; John 12:41; Acts 26:22, 23
12 [a]Dan. 9:24; 12:9, 13 [b]Heb. 11:13, 39, 40 [c]Acts 2:4 [d]Ex. 25:20; Dan. 8:13; 12:5, 6; Eph. 3:10
13 IGr. *perfectly* [a]Luke 12:35; Eph. 6:14 [b]Luke 21:34; Rom. 13:13; 1Thess. 5:6, 8; 1Pet. 4:7; 5:8 [c]Luke 17:30; 1Cor. 1:7; 2Thess. 1:7
14 [a]Rom. 12:2; 1Pet. 4:2 [b]Acts 17:30; 1Thess. 4:5
15 [a]Luke 1:74, 75; 2Cor. 7:1; 1Thess. 4:3, 4, 7; Heb. 12:14; 2Pet. 3:11
16 [a]Lev. 11:44; 19:2; 20:7
17 [a]Deut. 10:17; Acts 10:34; Rom. 2:11 [b]2Cor. 7:1; Phil. 2:12; Heb. 12:28 [c]2Cor. 5:6; Heb. 11:13; 1Pet. 2:11
18 [a]1Cor. 6:20; 7:23 [b]Ezek. 20:18; 1Pet. 4:3
19 [a]Acts 20:28; Eph. 1:7; Heb. 9:12, 14; Rev.

16 Because it is written, [a]Be ye holy;
for I am holy.
17 And if ye call on the Father,[3962]
[a]who without respect of persons[678]
[ppt]judgeth[2919] according to every man's
work,[2041] [aipp][b]pass the time[5550] of your
[c]sojourning[3940] *here* in fear:[5401]
18 Forasmuch as ye know [a]that ye
[aop]were not redeemed[3084] with corruptible things, *as* silver and gold, from your
vain conversation [b]*received* by tradition
from your fathers;[3970]
19 But [a]with the precious blood of
Christ,[5547] [b]as of a lamb without blemish[299] and without spot:[784]
🔑 20 [a]Who verily [pfpp]was foreordained[4267] before the foundation of the
world,[2889] but was manifest[5319] in these
last[2078] times for you,
21 Who by him [ppt]do believe[4100] in
God, [a]that [apt]raised[1453] him up from the
dead,[3498] and [b]gave him glory;[1391] that
your faith[4102] and hope[1680] might be in
God.[2316]
22 Seeing ye [pfpa]have purified[48] your
souls[5590] in obeying[5218] the truth through
the [an]Spirit[4151] unto unfeigned[505] [b]love of
the brethren,[5360] *see that ye* [aim]love[25] one
another with a pure[2513] heart[2588] fervently:[1619]
23 [a]Being born again,[313] not of corruptible seed, but of incorruptible, [b]by
the word[3056] of God, [ppt]which liveth[2198]
and [ppt]abideth[3306] for ever.[165,1519] [3588]
24 For [a]all flesh[4561] *is* as grass, and
all the glory of man as the flower of
grass. The grass [aop]withereth, and the
flower thereof [ao]falleth away:
25 [a]But the word[4487] of the Lord[2962]

5:9 [b]Ex. 12:5; Isa. 53:7; John 1:29, 36; 1Cor. 5:7
20 [a]Rom. 3:25; 16:25, 26; Eph. 3:9, 11; Col. 1:26; 2Tim. 1:9, 10; Titus 1:2, 3; Rev. 13:8 [b]Gal. 4:4; Eph. 1:10; Heb. 1:2; 9:26 **21** [a]Acts 2:24 [b]Matt. 28:18; Acts 2:33; 3:13; Eph. 1:20; Phil. 2:9; Heb. 2:9; 1Pet. 3:22 **22** [a]Acts 15:9 [b]Rom. 12:9, 10; 1Thess. 4:9; 1Tim. 1:5; Heb. 13:1; 1Pet. 2:17; 3:8; 4:8; 2Pet. 1:7; 1John 3:18; 4:7, 21 **23** [a]John 1:13; 3:5 [b]James 1:18; 1John 3:9 **24** [a]Ps. 103:15; Isa. 40:6; 51:12; James 1:10 **25** [a]Ps. 102:12, 26; Isa. 40:8; Luke 16:17

🔑 **1:7, 13** See note on 1 Thessalonians 2:19.
🔑 **1:20** See note on Ephesians 1:4, 5.

endureth[3306] for ever. [b]And this is the word which [aptp]by the gospel is preached[2097] unto you.

The People of God

2 Wherefore [apt][a]laying aside all malice,[2549] and all guile,1388 and hypocrisies, and envies, and all evil speakings,

2 [a]As newborn[738] babes,[1025] [aim]desire the sincere[97] [b]milk[1051] of the word,[3050] that ye [asbp]may grow thereby:

3 If so be ye [aom]have [a]tasted[1089] that the Lord *is* gracious.[5543]

4 To whom coming, *as unto* a living[2198] stone, [pfpp][a]disallowed[593] indeed of men, but chosen[1588] of God, *and* precious,

5 [a]Ye also, as [ppt]lively[2198] stones, [I]are built up [b]a spiritual house, [c]an holy[40] priesthood,2406 to offer up [d]spiritual sacrifices,[2378] [e]acceptable[2144] to God by Jesus Christ.

6 Wherefore also it is contained in the scripture,[1124] [a]Behold, I lay in Sion a chief corner stone, elect,[1588] precious: and he that [ppt]believeth[4100] on him shall [efn]not be confounded.

7 Unto you therefore which [ppt]believe *he is* [I]precious: but unto them which [ppt]be disobedient,[544] [a]the stone which the builders disallowed,[593] the same is made the head of the corner,

8 [a]And a stone of stumbling, and a rock of offence,[4625] [b]*even to them* which stumble[4350] at the word,[3056] [ppt]being disobedient: [c]whereunto also they were appointed.

9 But ye *are* [a]a chosen generation, [b]a royal priesthood, [c]an holy nation,[1484] [I][d]a peculiar[1519] 4047 people;[2992] that ye [asbp]should shew forth[1804] the [II]praises of him who [apt]hath called you out of [e]darkness[4655] into his marvellous light:[5457]

10 [a]Which in time past *were* not a people,[2992] but *are* now the people of God: which [pfpp]had not obtained mercy,[1653] but now [aptp]have obtained mercy.

11 Dearly beloved, I beseech[3870] *you* [a]as strangers[3941] and pilgrims,[3927] [pinf][b]abstain[567] from fleshly lusts,[1939] [c]which war against the soul;[5590]

12 [a]Having your conversation391 honest among the Gentiles:[1484] that, whereas they speak against[2635] you as evildoers,[2555] [b]they may by *your* good works, which they [apt]shall behold,2029 [aosb]glorify[1392] God [c]in the day[2250] of visitation.[1984]

13 [aipp][a]Submit yourselves[5293] to every ordinance[2937] of man for the Lord's sake: whether it be to the king,[935] as supreme;

14 Or unto governors, as unto them that [ppp]are sent by him [a]for the punishment[1557] of evildoers,[2555] and [b]for the praise of them that do well.

15 For so is the will[2307] of God, that [a]with [ppt]well doing[15] ye may put to silence the ignorance[56] of foolish men:

16 [a]As free, and not [I]using *your* liberty[1657] for a cloke of maliciousness,[2549] but as [b]the servants[1401] of God.

🔑 17 [aim][I][a]Honour all *men.* [pim][b]Love[25]

25 [b]John 1:1, 14; 1John 1:1, 3

1 [a]Eph. 4:22, 25, 31; Col. 3:8; Heb. 12:1; James 1:21; 5:9; 1Pet. 4:2
2 [a]Matt. 18:3; Mark 10:15; Rom. 6:4; 1Cor. 14:20; 1Pet. 1:23 [b]1Cor. 3:2; Heb. 5:12, 13
3 [a]Ps. 34:8; Heb. 6:5
4 [a]Ps. 118:22; Matt. 21:42; Acts 4:11
5 [I]Or, *be ye built* [a]Eph. 2:21, 22 [b]Heb. 3:6 [c]Isa. 61:6; 66:21; 1Pet. 2:9 [d]Hos. 14:2; Mal. 1:11; Rom. 12:1; Heb. 13:15, 16 [e]Phil. 4:18; 1Pet. 4:11
6 [a]Isa. 28:16; Rom. 9:33
7 [I]Or, *an honor* [a]Ps. 118:22; Matt. 21:42; Acts 4:11
8 [a]Isa. 8:14; Luke 2:34; Rom. 9:33 [b]1Cor. 1:23 [c]Ex. 9:16; Rom. 9:22; 1Thess. 5:9; Jude 1:4
9 [I]Or, *a purchased people* [II]Or, *virtues* [a]Deut. 10:15; 1Pet. 1:2 [b]Ex. 19:5, 6; Rev. 1:6; 5:10 [c]John 17:19; 1Cor. 3:17; 2Tim. 1:9 [d]Deut. 4:20; 7:6; 14:2; 26:18, 19; Acts 20:28; Eph. 1:14; Titus 2:14 [e]Acts 26:18; Eph. 5:8; Col. 1:13; 1Thess. 5:4, 5
10 [a]Hos. 1:9, 10; 2:23; Rom. 9:25
11 [a]1Chr. 29:15; Ps. 39:12; 119:19; Heb. 11:13; 1Pet. 1:17 [b]Rom. 13:14; Gal. 5:16 [c]James 4:1
12 [I]Or, *wherein* [a]Rom. 12:17; 2Cor. 8:21; Phil. 2:15; Titus 2:8; 1Pet. 3:16 [b]Matt. 5:16 [c]Luke 19:44
13 [a]Matt. 22:21; Rom. 13:1; Titus 3:1
14 [a]Rom. 13:4 [b]Rom. 13:3
15 [a]Titus 2:8; 1Pet. 2:12
16 [I]Gr. *having* [a]Gal. 5:1, 13 [b]1Cor. 7:22
17 [I]Or, *Esteem* [a]Rom. 12:10; Phil. 2:3 [b]Heb. 13:1; 1Pet. 1:22

🔑 **2:17** The Christian's submission to authority figures is the theme of this verse. People normally object to those whose rule is tyrannical, oppressive, and ungodly. While the Bible does not condone tyranny or oppression, it is taught, as evidenced by this verse, that believers should respect the established authorities.

At the time Peter was writing these words, there was not one king that professed Christianity. Hence, the recipients of Peter's first epistle were governed by a pagan king. No doubt Peter had fully explained to them that Christ had abolished forever the ideas of kingship and lordship among His followers. Peter's advice to them was not to be rebellious toward the governing powers under

(continued on next page)

the brotherhood.[81] [pim][c]Fear[5399] God. [pim]Honour the king.[935]

Subjection to Authority

18 [a]Servants,[3610] *be* subject to *your* masters[1203] with all fear;[5401] not only to the good[18] and gentle,1933 but also to the froward.[4646]

19 For this *is* [a]thankworthy,[5485] if a man for conscience[4893] toward God endure grief, suffering wrongfully.

20 For [a]what glory *is it,* if, when ye [ppp]be buffeted2852 for your faults,[264] ye shall take it patiently?[5278] but if, when ye [ppt]do well,[15] and [ppt]suffer *for it,* ye take it patiently, this *is* acceptable[5485] with God.

21 For [a]even hereunto [aop]were ye called:[2564] because [b]Christ[5547] also suffered [I]for us, [c]leaving us an example,[5261] that ye should follow his steps:

22 [a]Who did no sin,[266] neither was guile found in his mouth:

23 [a]Who, when he [ppp]was reviled,[3058] reviled not again; when he [ppt]suffered, he threatened not; but [ipf][I][b]committed *himself* to him that judgeth[2919] righteously:[1346]

24 [a]Who his own self bare399 our sins in his own body[4983] [I]on the tree, [b]that we, [apt]being dead[581] to sins, [aosb]should live[2198] unto righteousness:[1343] [c]by whose stripes ye [aop]were healed.[2390]

25 For [a]ye were as sheep going astray; but are now returned [b]unto the Shepherd[4166] and Bishop[1985] of your souls.[5590]

Advice to Wives and Husbands

3 ⚷Likewise, [a]ye wives, *be* in subjection[5293] to your own husbands; that, if any obey not[544] the word,[3056] [b]they also [fp]may without the word [c]be won by the conversation391 of the wives;

2 [a]While they [apt]behold2029 your chaste[53] conversation *coupled* with fear.

3 [a]Whose adorning[2889] let it not be that outward *adorning* of plaiting1708 the hair, and of wearing of gold, or of putting on of apparel;

4 But *let it be* [a]the hidden man of the heart,[2588] in that which is not corruptible,[862] *even the ornament* of a meek[4239] and quiet2272 spirit,[4151] which is in the sight of God of great price.

5 For after this manner in the old time the holy[40] women also, who [ppt]trusted[1679] in God, [ipf]adorned themselves, being in subjection unto their own husbands:

6 Even as Sarah obeyed[5219] Abraham, [a]calling him lord:[2962] whose [I]daughters ye [aop]are, as long as ye [ppt]do well,[15] and [ppt]are not afraid[5399] with any amazement.

7 [a]Likewise, ye husbands, [ppt]dwell with4924 *them* according to knowledge,[1108] giving honour unto the wife, [b]as unto the weaker[772] vessel, and as being heirs together[4789] of the grace[5485] of life;[2222] [c]that your prayers[4335] [aies]be not hindered.1581

The Blessedness of Suffering for Righteousness' Sake

8 Finally,[5056] [a]*be ye* all of one mind, having compassion one of another,[4835] [b]love as brethren,[5361] [c]*be* pitiful, *be* courteous:

9 [a]Not rendering evil[2556] for evil, or railing for railing: but contrariwise bless-

17 [c]Prov. 24:21; Matt. 22:21; Rom. 13:7
18 [a]Eph. 6:5; Col. 3:22; 1Tim. 6:1; Titus 2:9
19 [a]Matt. 5:10; Luke 6:32; Rom. 13:5; 1Pet. 2:20; 3:14
20 [a]1Pet. 3:14; 4:14, 15
21 [I]Some read, *for you* [a]Matt. 16:24; Acts 14:22; 1Thess. 3:3; 2Tim. 3:12 [b]1Pet. 3:18 [c]John 13:15; Phil. 2:5; 1John 2:6
22 [a]Isa. 53:9; Luke 23:41; John 8:46; 2Cor. 5:21; Heb. 4:15
23 [I]Or, *committed his cause* [a]Isa. 53:7; Matt. 27:39; John 8:48, 49; Heb. 12:3 [b]Luke 23:46
24 [I]Or, *to* [a]Isa. 53:4-6, 11; Matt. 8:17; Heb. 9:28 [b]Rom. 6:2, 11; 7:6 [c]Isa. 53:5
25 [a]Isa. 53:6; Ezek. 34:6 [b]Ezek. 34:23; 37:24; John 10:11, 14, 16; Heb. 13:20; 1Pet. 5:4

1 [a]1Cor. 14:34; Eph. 5:22; Col. 3:18; Titus 2:5 [b]1Cor. 7:16 [c]Matt. 18:15; 1Cor. 9:19-22
2 [a]1Pet. 2:12
3 [a]1Tim. 2:9; Titus 2:3
4 [a]Ps. 45:13; Rom. 2:29; 7:22; 2Cor. 4:16
6 [I]Gr. *children* [a]Gen. 18:12
7 [a]1Cor. 7:3; Eph. 5:25; Col. 3:19 [b]1Cor. 12:23; 1Thess. 4:4 [c]Job 42:8; Matt. 5:23, 24; 18:19
8 [a]Rom. 12:16; 15:5; Phil. 3:16 [b]Rom. 12:10; Heb. 13:1; 1Pet. 2:17 [c]Eph. 4:32; Col. 3:12
9 [a]Prov. 17:13; 20:22; Matt. 5:39; Rom. 12:14, 17; 1Cor. 4:12; 1Thess. 5:15

(continued from previous page)

which they lived. Rather, they were to submit quietly to their rulers, giving due honor and respect to them. The result would be that they would not have the reputation of being rebels, whereby shame might be brought on Christ's name. Furthermore, they would be able to receive the protection and privileges of the kingdom if they needed them. See note on Titus 3:1.

⚷ **3:1–4** See note on 1 Timothy 2:9–15 concerning the conduct of women.

ing;[2127] knowing that ye [aop]are thereunto called,[2564] [b]that ye should inherit[2816] a blessing.

10 For [a]he that will [pinf]love[25] life,[2222] and see[1492] good[18] days, [b]let him refrain his tongue from evil, and his lips that they [infg]speak no guile:[1388]

11 [aim]Let him [a]eschew[1578] evil, and [aim]do good; [aim][b]let him seek[2212] peace,[1515] and [aim]ensue it.

12 For the eyes of the Lord[2962] *are* over the righteous,[1342] [a]and his ears *are open* unto their prayers:[1162] but the face of the Lord *is* against them that [ppt]do evil.

13 [a]And who *is* he that will harm[2559] you, if ye [asbm]be followers of that which is good?

14 [a]But and if ye [opt]suffer for righteousness'[1343] sake, happy[3107] *are ye:* and [aosi][b]be not afraid[5399] of their terror, neither [aosi]be troubled;

15 But [aim]sanctify[37] the Lord God in your hearts:[2588] and [a]*be* ready always to *give* an answer to every man that [ppt]asketh you a reason of the hope[1680] that is in you with meekness[4240] and [I]fear:[5401]

16 [a]Having a good[18] conscience;[4893] [b]that, whereas they speak evil of[3635] you, as of evildoers,[2555] they [asbp]may be ashamed that [ppt]falsely accuse your good conversation[391] in Christ.

17 For *it is* better,[2909] if the will[2307] of God be so, that ye [pinf]suffer for [ppt]well doing,[15] than for [ppt]evil doing.[2554]

18 For Christ also [ao]hath [a]once suffered[3958] for sins, the just[1342] for the unjust,[94] that he [aosb]might bring[4317] us to God, [b]being put to death [c]in the flesh,[4561] but [d]quickened[2227] by the Spirit:[4151]

🗝 19 By which also he went and [a]preached[2784] unto the spirits[4151] [b]in prison;

20 Which sometime [apt]were disobedient,[544] [a]when once the longsuffering[3115] of God [ipf]waited[1551] in the days of Noah, while [b]the ark [ppp]was a preparing, [c]wherein few, that is, eight souls[5590] were saved[1295] by water.

🗝 21 [a]The like figure[499] whereunto *even* baptism[908] [pin]doth also now save[4982] us (not the putting away of [b]the filth of the flesh, [c]but the answer of a good conscience toward God,) [d]by the resurrection[386] of Jesus Christ:

9 [b]Matt. 25:34
10 [a]Ps. 34:12 [b]James 1:26; 1Pet. 2:1, 22; Rev. 14:5
11 [a]Ps. 37:27; Isa. 1:16, 17; 3John 1:11 [b]Rom. 12:18; 14:19; Heb. 12:14 [c]John 9:31; James 5:16
13 [a]Prov. 16:7; Rom. 8:28
14 [a]Matt. 5:10-12; James 1:12; 1Pet. 2:19; 4:14 [b]Isa. 8:12, 13; Jer. 1:8; John 14:1, 27
15 [I]Or, *reverence* [a]Ps. 119:46; Acts 4:8; Col. 4:6; 2Tim. 2:25
16 [a]Heb. 13:18 [b]Titus 2:8; 1Pet. 2:12
18 [a]Rom. 5:6; Heb. 9:26, 28; 1Pet. 2:21; 4:1 [b]2Cor. 13:4 [c]Col. 1:21, 22 [d]Rom. 1:4; 8:11
19 [a]1Pet. 1:12; 4:6 [b]Isa. 42:7; 49:9; 61:1
20 [a]Gen. 6:3, 5, 13 [b]Heb. 11:7 [c]Gen. 7:7; 8:18; 2Pet. 2:5
21 [a]Eph. 5:26 [b]Titus 3:5 [c]Rom. 10:10 [d]1Pet. 1:3

🗝 **3:19** One common interpretation of this passage is that subsequent to Christ's death, possibly before His resurrection, His disembodied spirit went to the unseen world and there preached to the disobedient dead. This interpretation is based on the reference to the dead during the days of Noah. However, there is no justification at all that such a small number of people who lived during the span of about 120 years should be singled out from the great mass of mankind for so singular and great a blessing. Many who hold such a theory of interpretation extend it to include the theory of the doctrine of probation after death, meaning that the impenitent dead have a second chance. Nowhere in Scripture is there any indication that those who die unrepentant have a second chance.

In this verse, it is simply stated that Christ preached. It does not describe what message He might have preached. Every time the word *kērússō* (2784), "preach," occurs it does not necessarily mean "to preach the Gospel." The glorious result of Christ being put to death, "the just for the unjust," was not merely the attainment of a resurrection body; for Peter goes on to say, "By which also he went and preached unto spirits in prison." Whatever the nature of this preaching may have been, it had to take place between His death and resurrection. There is certainly no need to put an arbitrary interpretation on the words "spirits in prison," as referring simply to those who had passed to the unseen world, because the ungodly are constantly spoken of in Scripture as being in a state of imprisonment, bondage, or captivity. If, therefore, this passage does not refer to certain individuals but to the declaration of Christ's victory over death and hell, then the meaning of the phrase "preached unto spirits in prison" is clarified. See note on Ephesians 4:8–10.

🗝 **3:21** The expression "baptism doth also now save" should be understood in light of verse twenty: "eight souls were saved by water." Noah and his family, being in the ark, were able to pass safely "through" the waters (seen in the Greek word *diá* [1223]). In the same way, the term "baptism" (v. 21) should be understood as the visible representation of deliverance through Christ, just as the

(continued on next page)

22 Who [aptp]is gone into heaven,[3772] and [a]is on the right hand[1188] of God; [b]angels[32] and authorities[1849] and powers[1411] [aptp]being made subject unto[5293] him.

4

Forasmuch then [a]as Christ [aptp]hath suffered for us in the flesh,[4561] [aim]arm yourselves likewise with the same mind:[1771] for [b]he that hath suffered in the flesh hath ceased from sin;

2 [a]That he no longer [aies][b]should live the rest of *his* time[5550] in the flesh[4561] to the lusts[1939] of men, [c]but to the will[2307] of God.

3 [a]For the time [pfp]past of *our* life[979] may suffice us [b]to have wrought the will[2307] of the Gentiles, when we [pfp]walked in lasciviousness,[766] lusts,[1939] excess of wine, revellings,[2970] banquetings,[4224] and abominable[111] idolatries:[1495]

4 Wherein they think it strange that ye [ppt]run not with *them* to the same excess of riot,[810] [a]speaking evil[987] of *you:*

5 Who shall give account to him that is ready [ainf][a]to judge[2919] the quick[2198] and the dead.[3498]

6 For for this cause [aop][a]was the gospel preached[2097] also to them that are dead, that they [asbp]might be judged according to men in the flesh, but [psa]live[2198] according to God in the spirit.[4151]

7 But [a]the end[5056] of all things [pfi]is at hand: [aim][b]be ye therefore sober,4993 and [aim]watch unto prayer.[4335]

8 [a]And above all things [ppt]have fervent[1618] charity[26] among yourselves: for [b]charity [I]shall cover[2572] the multitude of sins.[266]

9 [a]Use hospitality one to another [b]without grudging.

10 [a]As every man [ao]hath received the gift,[5486] *even so* [ppt]minister[1247] the same one to another, [b]as good stewards[3623] of [c]the manifold grace[5485] of God.

11 [a]If any man speak,[2980] *let him speak* as the oracles[3051] of God; [b]if any man minister, *let him do it* as of the ability which God giveth: that [c]God in all things [psmp]may be glorified[1392] through Jesus Christ, [d]to whom be praise[1391] and dominion[2904] for ever 165,1519 3588 and ever. Amen.281

Believers Should Not Be Ashamed

12 Beloved, think it not strange concerning [a]the fiery trial which is to try[3986] you, as though some strange thing [ppt]happened unto you:

🔑 13 [a]But rejoice,[5463] inasmuch as [b]ye are partakers[2841] of Christ's sufferings;[3804] [c]that, when his glory[1391] shall be revealed, ye may be glad[5463] also with exceeding joy.[21]

14 [a]If ye be reproached for the name[3686] of Christ,[5547] happy[3107] *are ye;* for the spirit[4151] of glory and of God[2316] resteth upon you: [b]on their part he is evil spoken of,[987] but on your part he is glorified.

15 But [pim][a]let none of you suffer[3958] as a murderer,[5406] or *as* a thief, or *as* an evildoer,[2555] [b]or as a busybody in other men's matters.[244]

16 Yet if *any man suffer* as a Christian,[5546] [pim]let him not be ashamed;153 [a]but [pim]let him glorify[1392] God on this behalf.

17 For the time[2540] *is come* [a]that judgment[2917] [ainf]must begin at the house[3624] of God: and [b]if *it* first *begin* at us, [c]what shall the end[5056] *be* of them that [ppt]obey not[544] the gospel[2098] of God?

22 [a]Ps. 110:1; Rom. 8:34; Eph. 1:20; Col. 3:1; Heb. 1:3 [b]Rom. 8:38; 1Cor. 15:24; Eph. 1:21

1 [a]1Pet. 3:18 [b]Rom. 6:2, 7; Gal. 5:24; Col. 3:3, 5 **2** [a]Rom. 14:7; 1Pet. 2:1 [b]Gal. 2:20; 1Pet. 1:14 [c]John 1:13; Rom. 6:11; 2Cor. 5:15; James 1:18 **3** [a]Ezek. 44:6; 45:9; Acts 17:30 [b]Eph. 2:2; 4:17; 1Thess. 4:5; Titus 3:3; 1Pet. 1:14 **4** [a]Acts 13:45; 18:6; 1Pet. 3:16 **5** [a]Acts 10:42; 17:31; Rom. 14:10, 12; 1Cor. 15:51, 52; 2Tim. 4:1; James 5:9 **6** [a]1Pet. 3:19 **7** [a]Matt. 24:13, 14; Rom. 13:12; Phil. 4:5; Heb. 10:25; James 5:8; 2Pet. 3:9, 11; 1John 2:18 [b]Matt. 26:41; Luke 21:34; Col. 4:2; 1Pet. 1:13; 5:8 **8** [I]Or, *will* [a]Col. 3:14; Heb. 13:1 [b]Prov. 10:12; 1Cor. 13:7; James 5:20 **9** [a]Rom. 12:13; Heb. 13:2 [b]2Cor. 9:7; Phil. 2:14; Phile. 1:14 **10** [a]Rom. 12:6; 1Cor. 4:7 [b]Matt. 24:45; 25:14, 21; Luke 12:42; 1Cor. 4:1, 2; Titus 1:7 [c]1Cor. 12:4; Eph. 4:11 **11** [a]Jer. 23:22 [b]Rom. 12:6-8; 1Cor. 3:10 [c]Eph. 5:20; 1Pet. 2:5 [d]1Tim. 6:16; 1Pet. 5:11; Rev. 1:6 **12** [a]1Cor. 3:13; 1Pet. 1:7 **13** [a]Acts 5:41; James 1:2 [b]Rom. 8:17; 2Cor. 1:7; 4:10; Phil. 3:10; Col. 1:24; 2Tim. 2:12; 1Pet. 5:1, 10; Rev. 1:9 [c]1Pet. 1:5, 6 **14** [a]Matt. 5:11; 2Cor. 12:10; James 1:12; 1Pet. 2:19, 20; 3:14 [b]1Pet. 2:12; 3:16 **15** [a]1Pet. 2:20 [b]1Thess. 4:11; 1Tim. 5:13 **16** [a]Acts 5:41 **17** [a]Isa. 10:12; Jer. 25:29; 49:12; Ezek. 9:6; Mal. 3:5 [b]Luke 23:31 [c]Luke 10:12, 14

(continued from previous page)
ark represented deliverance from the waters of the Flood. When a person accepts Christ, he is saved; when the believer is baptized, he is identified with the One who has delivered him (i.e., Jesus Christ). See note on Mark 16:16.

🔑 **4:13** See note on 1 Thessalonians 2:19.

18 [a]And if the righteous[1342] scarcely be saved,[4982] where shall[5316] the ungodly[765] and the sinner[268] appear?[5316]

19 Wherefore let them that [ppt]suffer according to the will[2307] of God [pim][a]commit the keeping of their souls[5590] *to him* in well doing,16 as unto a faithful[4103] Creator.[2939]

Exhortations to Elders

5 The elders[4245] which are among you I exhort,[3870] who am also [a]an elder,[4850] and [b]a witness of the sufferings of Christ, and also [c]a partaker[2844] of the glory[1391] that shall be revealed:

2 [a]Feed[4165] the flock[4168] of God [I]which is among you, taking the oversight[1983] *thereof,* [b]not by constraint, but willingly; [c]not for filthy lucre,147 but of a ready mind;

3 Neither as [a]being lords over [b]*God's* heritage,[2819] but [c]being ensamples[5179] to the flock.[4168]

4 And when [a]the chief Shepherd[750] [aptp]shall appear,[5319] ye shall receive [b]a crown of glory [c]that fadeth not away.[262]

5 Likewise, ye younger, submit[5293] yourselves unto the [pl]elder.[4245] Yea, [a]all *of you* be subject[5293] one to another, and [aim]be clothed with humility: for [b]God resisteth the proud,[5244] and [c]giveth grace[5485] to the humble.

6 [a]Humble yourselves therefore under the mighty2900 hand of God, that he may exalt you in due time:[2540]

7 [apt][a]Casting all your care upon him; for he careth for you.

8 [aim][a]Be sober, [aim]be vigilant; because [b]your adversary[476] the devil,[1228] as a roaring lion, walketh about, [ppt]seeking whom he [aosb]may devour:

9 [a]Whom resist stedfast in the faith,[4102] [b]knowing that the same afflictions are accomplished[2005] in your brethren[81] that are in the world.[2889]

10 But the God[2316] of all grace,[5485] [a]who hath called us unto his eternal[166] glory[1391] by Christ Jesus, after that ye [apt]have suffered[3958] [b]a while, [opt][c]make you perfect,[2675] [d]stablish,4741 strengthen,[4599] settle *you.*

11 [a]To him *be* glory[1391] and dominion[2904] for ever[165,1519] 3588 and ever. Amen.281

12 [a]By Silvanus, a faithful[4103] brother[80] unto you, as I suppose,[3049] I have [b]written briefly, exhorting, and testifying[1957] [c]that this is the true grace of God wherein ye stand.

13 The *church that is* at Babylon, elected together with[4899] *you,* saluteth782 you; and *so doth* [a]Marcus my son.[5207]

14 [a]Greet782 ye one another with a kiss of charity.[26] [b]Peace[1515] *be* with you all that are in Christ Jesus. Amen.

18 [a]Prov. 11:31; Luke 23:31 **19** [a]Ps. 31:5; Luke 23:46; 2Tim. 1:12

1 [a]Phile. 1:9 [b]Luke 24:48; Acts 1:8, 22; 5:32; 10:39 [c]Rom. 8:17, 18; Rev. 1:9 **2** [I]Or, *as much as in you is* [a]John 21:15, 16, 17; Acts 20:28 [b]1Cor. 9:17 [c]1Tim. 3:3, 8; Titus 1:7 [d]Ezek. 34:4; Matt. 20:25, 26; 1Cor. 3:9; 2Cor. 1:24 [e]Ps. 33:12; 74:2 [f]Phil. 3:17; 2Thess. 3:9; 1Tim. 4:12; Titus 2:7 **4** [a]Heb. 13:20 [b]1Cor. 9:25; 2Tim. 4:8; James 1:12 [c]1Pet. 1:4 **5** [a]Rom. 12:10; Eph. 5:21; Phil. 2:3 [b]James 4:6 [c]Isa. 57:15; 66:2 **6** [a]James 4:10 **7** [a]Ps. 37:5; 55:22; Matt. 6:25; Luke 12:11, 22; Phil. 4:6; Heb. 13:5 **8** [a]Luke 21:34, 36; 1Thess. 5:6; 1Pet. 4:7 [b]Job 1:7; 2:2; Luke 22:31; Rev. 12:12 **9** [a]Eph. 6:11, 13; James 4:7 [b]Acts 14:22; 1Thess. 3:3; 2Tim. 3:12; 1Pet. 2:21

10 [a]1Cor. 1:9; 1Tim. 6:12 [b]2Cor. 4:17; 1Pet. 1:6 [c]Heb. 13:21; Jude 1:24 [d]2Thess. 2:17; 3:3
11 [a]1Pet. 4:11; Rev. 1:6 **12** [a]2Cor. 1:19 [b]Heb. 13:22 [c]Acts 20:24; 1Cor. 15:1; 2Pet. 1:12
13 [a]Acts 12:12, 25 **14** [a]Rom. 16:16; 1Cor. 16:20; 2Cor. 13:12; 1Thess. 5:26 [b]Eph. 6:23

The Second Epistle of

PETER

The Book of 2 Peter is similar in both order and content to the Book of Jude (2 Pet. 2:1—3:3, cf. Jude 1:3–18). Peter, however, issues a warning concerning the false teachers that eventually would come, while Jude states that they were already present. It is reasonable to conclude from the phrase, "to them that have obtained like precious faith with us" (2 Pet. 1:1), that Peter was writing to Gentile believers. Though it is possible that Peter was addressing the same group of believers to whom 1 Peter was written (1 Pet. 3:1), some believe that it was addressed to an entirely different group. This second letter of Peter was particularly directed against the gnostic and antinomian philosophies. Gnostics taught that in addition to believing in Christ, one must also receive the *gnōsis* or esoteric knowledge (see note on Col. 2:8–23). Peter refuted this idea by stressing the fact that they had already received the true knowledge (2 Pet. 1:16–21).

Antinomians believe that since salvation was by grace alone, the requirements of the moral law are irrelevant. Peter devotes the second chapter to attacking the licentious lifestyle that naturally resulted among those who held this belief. In the third chapter, Peter reproves them for their skepticism about Christ's return. Within this discussion, Peter gives one of the most detailed descriptions of end-time events in all of Scripture. The delay of Jesus' return is only apparent, he explains, because God does not exist within the concept of time (2 Pet. 3:8). Peter also tells them that when the Day of the Lord comes, it will be accompanied by the total destruction of the physical universe (2 Pet. 3:10–12, cf. Rev. 21:1).

1 [I][a]Simon Peter, a servant[1401] and an apostle[652] of Jesus Christ,[5547] to them that have obtained [b]like precious faith[4102] with us through the righteousness[1343] [II][c]of God[2316] and our Saviour[4990] Jesus Christ:

2 [a]Grace[5485] and peace[1515] be multiplied unto you through the knowledge[1922] of God, and of Jesus our Lord,[2962]

"Great and Precious Promises"

3 According as his divine[2304] power[1411] hath given unto us all things that *pertain* unto life[2222] and godliness,[2150] [a]through the knowledge[1922] of him [b]that [apt]hath called us [I]to glory[1391] and virtue:[703]

4 [a]Whereby are given unto us exceeding great and precious promises:[1862] that by these ye might be [b]partakers[2844] of the divine nature,5449 [c]having escaped the corruption that is in the world[2889] through lust.[1939]

5 And beside this, [a]giving all diligence, add to your faith[4102] virtue; and to virtue[703] [b]knowledge;[1108]

6 And to knowledge temperance;1466 and to temperance patience;[5281] and to patience godliness;

7 And to godliness[2150] brotherly kindness; and [a]to brotherly kindness[5360] charity.[26]

8 For if these things be[5225] in you, and [ppt]abound, they make[2525] *you that ye shall* neither *be* [I]barren[692] [a]nor unfruitful in the knowledge[1922] of our Lord Jesus Christ.

9 But he that lacketh these things [a]is blind, and [ppt]cannot see afar off, and hath forgotten that he was [b]purged from his old[3819] sins.[266]

10 Wherefore the rather, brethren, give diligence [pinfa]to make your calling[2821] and election[1589] sure:[949] for if ye [ppt]do these things, [b]ye [asba]shall never fall:4417

11 For so an entrance shall be ministered unto you abundantly into the everlasting[166] kingdom[932] of our Lord and Saviour Jesus Christ.

1 IOr, *Symeon* IIGr. *of our God and Savior* [a]Acts 15:14 [b]Rom. 1:12; 2Cor. 4:13; Eph. 4:5; Titus 1:4 [c]Titus 2:13
2 [a]Dan. 4:1; 6:25; 1Pet. 1:2; Jude 1:2
3 IOr, *by* [a]John 17:3 [b]1Thess. 2:12; 4:7; 2Thess. 2:14; 2Tim. 1:9; 1Pet. 2:9; 3:9
4 [a]2Cor. 7:1 [b]2Cor. 3:18; Eph. 4:24; Heb. 12:10; 1John 3:2 [c]2Pet 2:18, 20
5 [a]2Pet. 3:18 [b]1Pet. 3:7
7 [a]Gal. 6:10; 1Thess. 3:12; 5:15; 1John 4:21
8 IGr. *idle* [a]John 15:2; Titus 3:14
9 [a]1John 2:9, 11 [b]Eph. 5:26; Heb. 9:14; 1John 1:7
10 [a]1John 3:19 [b]2Pet. 3:17

12 Wherefore [a]I will not be negligent [pinf]to put you always in remembrance 5279 of these things, [b]though ye know[1492] *them,* and be established in the present truth.[225]

13 Yea, I think it meet,[1342] [a]as long as I am in this tabernacle, 4638 [b]to stir you up by putting *you* in remembrance;[5280]

14 [a]Knowing that shortly I must put off *this* my tabernacle, even as [b]our Lord Jesus Christ hath shewed me.

15 Moreover I will endeavour that ye may be able after my decease to have these things always in remembrance.

"A More Sure Word of Prophecy"

🔑 16 For we [apt]have not followed 1811 [a]cunningly devised 4679 fables,[3454] when we made known[1107] unto you the power[1411] and coming[3952] of our Lord Jesus Christ, but [aptp][b]were eyewitnesses 2030 of his majesty.

17 For he [apt]received from God the Father[3962] honour 5092 and glory,[1391] when there [aptp]came such a voice to him from the excellent glory, [a]This is my beloved[27] Son,[5207] in whom I am well pleased.[2106]

18 And this voice which [aptp]came from heaven[3772] we heard, when we were with him in [a]the holy[40] mount.

19 We have also a more sure[949] word[3056] of prophecy;[4397] whereunto ye do well that ye [ppt]take heed, as unto [a]a light that [ppt]shineth[5316] in a dark place, until the day [aosb]dawn, and [b]the day star [aosb]arise in your hearts:[2588]

20 Knowing this first,[4412] that [a]no prophecy[4394] of the scripture[1124] is of any private[2398] interpretation. 1955

21 For [a]the prophecy[4394] came not [I]in old time by the will[2307] of man:[444] [b]but holy[40] men[444] of God spake[2980] *as they were* moved[5342] by the [an]Holy Ghost.[4151]

Warnings Against False Teachers

2 But [a]there were false prophets also among the people,[2992] even as [b]there shall be false teachers[5572] among you, who privily shall bring in 3919 damnable[684] heresies,[139] even [c]denying[720] the Lord[1203] [d]that bought[59] them, [e]and bring upon themselves swift destruction.[684]

2 And many shall follow their [I]pernicious ways;[684] by reason of whom the way[3598] of truth[225] shall be evil spoken of.[987]

3 And [a]through covetousness shall they with feigned 4112 words [b]make merchandise of you: [c]whose judgment[2917] now of a long time lingereth not, and their damnation[684] slumbereth not.

4 For if God spared not [a]the angels[32] [b]that [apt]sinned,[264] but [apt][c]cast *them* down to hell,[5020] and delivered *them* into chains of darkness, 2217 to [ppp]be reserved[5083] unto judgment;[2920]

5 And spared not the old world,[2889] but saved [a]Noah the eighth *person,* [b]a preacher[2783] of righteousness,[1343] [apt][c]bringing in the flood upon the world of the ungodly;[765]

6 And [a]turning the cities of Sodom and Gomorrha into ashes condemned[2632] *them* with an overthrow, [pfp][b]making *them* an ensample unto those that after should live ungodly;[764]

7 And [a]delivered[4506] just[1342] Lot, vexed 2669 with the filthy[766] conversation 391 of the wicked:

8 (For that righteous man[1342] dwelling among them, [a]in seeing and hearing, [ipf]vexed *his* righteous soul[5590] from day to day with *their* unlawful[459] deeds;)

9 [a]The Lord knoweth[1492] how to deliver the godly[2152] out of temptations,[3986] and [pinf]to reserve[5083] the unjust[94] unto the day of judgment to [ppp]be punished:

10 But chiefly [a]them that [ppt]walk after the flesh[4561] in the lust[1939] of uncleanness,[3394] and [ppt]despise [I]government.[2963] [b]Presumptuous *are they,* self-

12 [a]Rom. 15:14, 15; Phil. 3:1; 2Pet. 3:1; 1John 2:21; Jude 1:5 [b]1Pet. 5:12; 2Pet. 3:17
13 [a]2Cor. 5:1, 4; [b]1Pet. 3:1
14 [a]Deut. 4:21, 22; 31:14; 2Tim. 4:6 [b]John 21:18, 19
16 [a]1Cor. 1:17; 2:1, 4; 2Cor. 2:17; 4:2 [b]Matt. 17:1, 2; Mark 9:2; John 1:14; 1John 1:1; 4:14
17 [a]Matt. 3:17; 17:5; Mark 1:11; 9:7; Luke 3:22; 9:35
18 [a]Ex. 3:5; Josh. 5:15; Matt. 17:6
19 [a]Ps. 119:105; John 5:35 [b]2Cor. 4:4, 6; Rev. 2:28; 22:16
20 [a]Rom. 12:6
21 [I]Or, *at any time* [a]2Tim. 3:16; 1Pet. 1:11 [b]2Sam. 23:2; Luke 1:70; Acts 1:16; 3:18

1 [a]Deut. 13:1 [b]Matt. 24:11; Acts 20:30; 1Cor. 11:19; 1Tim. 4:1; 2Tim. 3:1-5; 1John 4:1; Jude 1:18 [c]Jude 1:4 [d]1Cor. 6:20; Gal. 3:13; Eph. 1:7; Heb. 10:29; 1Pet. 1:18; Rev. 5:9 [e]Phil. 3:19
2 [I]Some texts read *lascivious*
3 [a]Rom. 16:18; 2Cor. 12:17, 18; 1Tim. 6:5; Titus 1:11 [b]2Cor. 2:17; 2Pet. 1:16 [c]Deut. 32:35; Jude 1:4, 15
4 [a]Job 4:18; Jude 1:6 [b]John 8:44; 1John 3:8 [c]Luke 8:31; Rev. 20:2, 3
5 [a]Gen. 7:1, 7, 23; Heb. 11:7; 1Pet. 3:20 [b]1Pet. 3:19 [c]2Pet. 3:6

6 [a]Gen. 19:24; Deut. 29:23; Jude 1:7 [b]Num. 26:10
7 [a]Gen. 19:16 **8** [a]Ps. 119:139, 158; Ezek. 9:4
9 [a]Ps. 34:17, 19; 1Cor. 10:13 **10** [I]Or, *dominion*
[a]Jude 1:4, 7, 8, 10, 16 [b]Jude 1:8

🔑 **1:16** See note on 1 Thessalonians 2:19.

willed, they are not afraid to [ppt]speak evil of[987] dignities.[1391]

11 Whereas [a]angels,[32] which are greater in power[2479] and might,[1411] bring not railing[989] accusation[2920] [I]against them before the Lord.[2962]

12 But these, [a]as natural brute beasts,[2226] made[1080] to be taken and destroyed, speak evil[987] of the things that they understand not;[50] and shall utterly perish in their own corruption;

13 [a]And shall receive the reward[3408] of unrighteousness,[93] *as* they that [ppt]count it pleasure [b]to riot[5172] in the day time. [c]Spots[4695] *they are* and blemishes,[3470] sporting themselves[1792] with their own deceivings while [d]they feast with you;

14 Having eyes full of [I]adultery, and that cannot cease[180] from sin;[266] beguiling[1185] unstable souls:[5590] [a]an heart[2588] they have exercised with covetous practices; cursed[2671] children:[5043]

15 Which have forsaken the right[2117] way, and are gone astray, [apt]following the way of [a]Balaam *the son* of Bosor, who loved[25] the wages[3408] of unrighteousness;

16 But was rebuked for his iniquity:[3892] the dumb ass speaking with man's[444] voice forbad the madness of the prophet.[4396]

17 [a]These are wells without water, clouds that are carried with a tempest;[2978] to whom the mist[2217] of darkness[4655] [pfip]is reserved[5083] for ever.[165,1519,3588]

18 For when [a]they [ppt]speak great swelling *words* of vanity,[3153] they allure through the lusts[1939] of the flesh,[4561] *through much* wantonness,[766] those that [b]were [I]clean escaped from them who live in error.

19 While they [ppt]promise[1861] them [a]liberty,[1657] they themselves are [b]the servants[1401] of corruption: for of whom a man is overcome, of the same is he brought in bondage.

20 For [a]if after they [apt][b]have escaped the pollutions[3393] of the world[2889] [c]through the knowledge[1922] of the Lord[2962] and Saviour[4990] Jesus Christ,[5547] they [aptp]are again entangled therein, and overcome, the latter end[2078] is worse with them than the beginning.

21 For [a]it had been better[2909] for them not [pfin]to have known the way[3598] of righteousness,[1343] than, after they [apt]have known *it,* [ainf]to turn from the holy[40] commandment[1785] delivered unto them.

🔑 22 But it is happened unto them according to the true proverb, [a]The dog *is* [apt]turned to his own vomit again; and the sow that was washed to her wallowing in the mire.[1004]

Exhortations to Stedfastness

3 This second epistle,[1992] beloved, I now write[1125] unto you; in *both* which [a]I stir up your pure[1506] minds[1271] by way of remembrance:[5280]

2 That ye may be mindful of the words which were spoken before by the holy prophets,[4396] [a]and of the commandment of us the apostles[652] of the Lord[2962] and Saviour:[4990]

3 [a]Knowing[1097] this first,[4412] that there shall come in the last[2078] days scoffers, [b]walking after their own lusts,[1939]

4 And saying, [a]Where is the promise[1860] of his coming?[3952] for since the fathers fell asleep,[2837] all things continue as *they were* from the beginning of the creation.[2937]

5 For this they willingly[2309] are ignorant of, that [a]by the word[3056] of God the heavens[3772] were of old, and the earth[1093] [I][b]standing[4921] out of the water and in the water:

🔑 6 [a]Whereby the world[2889] that then was, [aptp]being overflowed with water, perished.[622]

11 [I]Some texts read, *against themselves* [a]Jude 1:9
12 [a]Jer. 12:3; Jude 1:10
13 [a]Phil. 3:19 [b]Rom. 13:13 [c]Jude 1:12 [d]1Cor. 11:20, 21
14 [I]Gr. *an adulteress* [a]Jude 1:11
15 [a]Num. 22:5, 7, 21, 23, 28; Jude 1:11
17 [a]Jude 1:12, 13
18 [I]Or, *for a little,* or, *a while* [a]Jude 1:16 [b]Acts 2:40; 2Pet. 1:4; 2Pet. 2:20
19 [a]Gal. 5:13; 1Pet. 2:16 [b]John 8:34; Rom. 6:16
20 [a]Matt. 12:45; Luke 11:26; Heb. 6:4-8; 10:26, 27 [b]2Pet. 1:4; 2Pet. 2:18 [c]2Pet. 1:2
21 [a]Luke 12:47, 48; John 9:41; 15:22
22 [a]Prov. 26:11

1 [a]2Pet. 1:13
2 [a]Jude 1:17
3 [a]1Tim. 4:1; 2Tim. 3:1; Jude 1:18 [b]2Pet. 2:10
4 [a]Isa. 5:19; Jer. 17:15; Ezek. 12:22, 27; Matt. 24:48; Luke 12:45
5 [I]Gr. *consisting* [a]Gen. 1:6, 9; Ps. 33:6; Heb. 11:3 [b]Ps. 24:2; 136:6; Col. 1:17
6 [a]Gen. 7:11, 21-23; 2Pet. 2:5

🔑 **2:22** The dog and pig mentioned in this verse may symbolize temporary external changes resulting from conformity to a false profession of faith. Contrastly, a sheep is designated as the one representing a true believer with a living faith in Jesus Christ (John 10:1–21). This faith is indicated by the fruits of his or her faith. See note on James 2:14–19.

🔑 **3:6, 7** See note on 1 Peter 3:21.

7 But [a]the heavens and the earth, which are now, by the same word are kept in store, [ppp]reserved[5083] unto [b]fire against the day[2250] of judgment[2920] and perdition[684] of ungodly[765] men.[444]

8 But, beloved, be not ignorant of this one thing, that one day[2250] *is* with the Lord[2962] as a thousand years, and [a]a thousand years as one day.

9 [a]The Lord [pin]is not slack[1019] concerning his promise,[1860] as some men count slackness;[1022] but [b]is longsuffering[3114] to us-ward, [c]not willing that any should perish, but [d]that all should come to repentance.[3341]

🔑 10 But [a]the day of the Lord will come as a thief in the night; in the which [b]the heavens shall pass away with a great noise, and the elements[4747] [fp]shall melt[3089] [ppp]with fervent heat, the earth also and the works[2041] that are therein shall be burned up.

11 *Seeing* then *that* all these things [ppp]shall be dissolved,[3089] what manner *of persons* ought ye to be [a]in *all* holy[40] conversation[391] and godliness,[2150]

12 [a]Looking for and [I]hasting unto the coming of the day of God, wherein the heavens being on fire shall [b]be dissolved, and the elements [fp]shall [c]melt [ppp]with fervent heat?

13 Nevertheless we, according to his promise,[1862] look for [a]new[2537] heavens and a new earth, wherein dwelleth[2730] righteousness.[1343]

14 Wherefore, beloved, seeing that ye [ppt]look for such things, be diligent [a]that ye [aifp]may be found of him in peace,[1515] without spot,[784] and blameless.

15 And account *that* [a]the longsuffering of our Lord *is* salvation;[4991] even as our beloved brother Paul also according to the wisdom given unto him hath written unto you;

16 As also in all *his* epistles,[1992] [a]speaking in them of these things; in which are some things hard to be understood,[1425] which they that are unlearned and unstable wrest, as *they do* also the other scriptures,[1124] unto their own destruction.[684]

17 Ye therefore, beloved, [a]seeing ye [ppt]know *these things* before,[4267] [b]beware[5442] lest ye also, being led away with the error[4106] of the wicked,[113] [aosb]fall from your own stedfastness.

18 [a]But grow in grace,[5485] and *in* the knowledge[1108] of our Lord and Saviour Jesus Christ. [b]To him *be* glory[1391] both now and for ever.[165,1519] [2250] Amen.[281]

7 [a]2Pet. 3:10 [b]Matt. 25:41; 2Thess. 1:8 **8** [a]Ps. 90:4 **9** [a]Hab. 2:3; Heb. 10:37 [b]Isa. 30:18; 1Pet. 3:20; 2Pet. 3:15 [c]Ezek. 18:23, 32; 33:11 [d]Rom. 2:4; 1Tim. 2:4 **10** [a]Matt. 24:43; Luke 12:39; 1Thess. 5:2; Rev. 3:3; 16:15 [b]Ps. 102:26; Isa. 51:6; Matt. 24:35; Mark 13:31; Rom. 8:12; Heb. 1:11; Rev. 20:11; 21:1 **11** [a]1Pet. 1:15 **12** [I]Or, *hasting the coming* [a]1Cor. 1:7; Titus 2:13 [b]Ps. 50:3; Isa. 34:4 [c]Mic. 1:4; 2Pet. 3:10 **13** [a]Isa. 65:17; 66:22; Rev. 21:1, 27 **14** [a]1Cor. 1:8; 15:58; Phil. 1:10; 1Thess. 3:13; 5:23 **15** [a]Rom. 2:4; 1Pet. 3:20; 2Pet. 3:9 **16** [a]Rom. 8:19; 1Cor. 15:24; 1Thess. 4:15 **17** [a]Mark 13:23; 2Pet. 1:12 [b]Eph. 4:14; 2Pet. 1:10, 11; 2:18

18 [a]Eph. 4:15; 1Pet. 2:2 [b]2Tim. 4:18; Rev. 1:6

🔑 **3:10** See note on 1 Thessalonians 5:2.

The First Epistle of
JOHN

The similarities between this epistle and the Gospel of John provide conclusive evidence that the author of 1 John was the Apostle John (see introduction to the Gospel of John). The use of words like "truth," "light," and phrases like "in the light," and "born of God" in 1 John reveal the significant resemblances in structure, style, and vocabulary to John's Gospel. It is also significant that John's anonymity is as evident in his epistles as it was in his Gospel (see introduction to John). He never uses his authority as an apostle in substantiating his message, but begins this first epistle much the same way as with the Gospel of John (1 John 1:1, 2, cf. John 1:1, 2, 14). This differs from both Paul's and Peter's writings where they use their authority as apostles of Christ to give weight to their message.

John was writing this epistle to believers, namely to those who were members of the churches of Asia Minor. Because the letter addresses such broad moral topics, it is clear that John's goal was to provide direction for those Christians who faced new challenges to their faith. At this time, there was an emergence of various groups whose teachings opposed Christianity. These people infiltrated the church, and there were many who gave in to their denial of the key fundamentals of Christianity (e.g., Christ's deity and resurrection). As opposition to the believers' faith arose, John encouraged them to continue walking in fellowship with Christ so as to not be drawn into false beliefs (1 John 1:5—2:2).

The Book of 1 John is believed to have been written in approximately A.D. 90. There are several ways that this date can be substantiated. First, there are no references by John to any persecutions of believers. From an examination of church history during the first century A.D., one may observe that there were no significant widespread persecutions on Christians until the reign of the Roman emperor Trajan (A.D. 98–117). Second, if the date were closer to A.D. 70, John would certainly have had reason to refer to the catastrophic events surrounding the destruction of the city of Jerusalem and the temple. However, an examination of the focus of John's epistle makes it obvious that he is instructing believers concerning the heresies that were being spread among them, not concerning some disaster that had come as a result of political events. Hence, the infiltration of these corrupt ideas that the church was experiencing was most likely from gentile influences, not Jewish opposition. Thus, this would most certainly place the date of writing much later than A.D. 70.

The Book of 1 John is easily divided into four major sections. John seeks first to warn believers concerning indifference to morality and sin (1 John 1:1—2:11). Next, he admonishes concerning a love for the things of the world as opposed to a love for the things of Christ (1 John 2:12–28). A third section deals with the importance of exhibiting a pure and righteous love, especially with regard to a brother or sister in Christ (1 John 2:29—3:22). Finally, John reveals that a true faith in Christ as the Son of God is the foundation on which all of Christianity is based (1 John 3:23—5:21).

1 That [a]which was from the beginning,
which we [pfi]have heard, which we
[pfi]have seen with our eyes, [b]which we
[aom]have looked upon, and [c]our hands
[ao]have handled,[5584] of the Word[3056] of
life;[2222]
2 (For [a]the life [aop][b]was manifested,[5319] and we [pfi]have seen *it*, [c]and
[pin]bear witness, [d]and [pin]shew[518] unto you
that eternal life, [e]which was with the
Father,[3962] and [aop]was manifested unto
us;)
3 [a]That which we have seen and

1 [a]John 1:1; 1John 2:13 [b]John 1:14; 2Pet. 1:16; 1John 4:14 [c]Luke 24:39; John 20:27
2 [a]John 1:4; 11:25; 14:6 [b]Rom. 16:26; 1Tim. 3:16; 1John 3:5 [c]John 21:24; Acts 2:32 [d]1John 5:20 [e]John 1:1, 2
3 [a]Acts 4:20

heard declare[518] we unto you, that ye also
[psa]may have fellowship[2842] with us: and
truly [b]our fellowship *is* with the Father,
and with his Son[5207] Jesus Christ.[5547]
4 And these things write[1125] we unto
you, [a]that your joy[5479] may be full.[4137]

"Walk in the Light"

🔑 5 [a]This then is the message[1860]
which we have heard of him, and declare[312] unto you, that [b]God[2316] is
light,[5457] and in him is no darkness[4653] at
all.
6 [a]If we say that we have fellowship
with him, and walk[4043] in darkness,[4655]
we lie, and do not the truth:[225]
7 But if we walk in the light, as he
is in the light, we have fellowship one
with another, and [a]the blood[129] of Jesus
Christ his Son cleanseth[2511] us from all
sin.[266]
8 [a]If we say that we have no sin,[266]
we deceive ourselves, [b]and the truth is
not in us.
9 [a]If we [psa]confess[3670] our sins, he is
faithful[4103] and just[1342] to [aosb]forgive[863]
us *our* sins, and to [aosb][b]cleanse[2511] us
from all unrighteousness.[93]
10 If we [aosb]say that we [pfi]have not
sinned,[264] we make him a liar, and his
word[3056] is not in us.

2 🔑My little children,[5040] these
things write[1125] I unto you, that ye
[aosb]sin[264] not. And if any man [aosb]sin,
[a]we have an advocate[3875] with the
Father,[3962] Jesus Christ[5547] the righteous:[1342]
2 And [a]he is the propitiation[2434] for
our sins:[266] and not for ours only, but
[b]also for *the sins of* the whole world.[2889]

The Believer's Assurance

3 And hereby we [pin]do know that we
[pfi]know him, if we keep[5083] his commandments.[1785]
4 [a]He that saith, I [pfi]know him, and

3 [b]John 17:21; 1Cor. 1:9; 1John 2:24
4 [a]John 15:11; 16:24; 2John 1:12
5 [a]1John 3:11 [b]John 1:9; 8:12; 9:5; 12:35, 36
6 [a]2Cor. 6:14; 1John 2:4
7 [a]1Cor. 6:11; Eph. 1:7; Heb. 9:14; 1Pet. 1:19; 1John 2:2; Rev. 1:5
8 [a]1Kgs. 8:46; 2Chr. 6:36; Job 9:2; 15:14; 25:4; Prov. 20:9; Eccl. 7:20; James 3:2; [b]1John 2:4
9 [a]Ps. 32:5; Prov. 28:13 [b]Ps. 51:2; 1John 1:7

1 [a]Rom. 8:34; 1Tim. 2:5; Heb. 7:25; 9:24
2 [a]Rom. 3:25; 2Cor. 5:18; 1John 1:7; 4:10 [b]John 1:29; 4:42; 11:51, 52; 1John 4:14
4 [a]1John 1:6; 4:20

🔑 **1:5–10** This passage describes God's nature and the relation that humankind has to God. "God is light" depicts the essence of His character in holiness and purity (v. 5). To understand this concept, one must examine who God is in relation to humankind. Man and woman are the creation of God and must acknowledge God's superiority over them. However, man was created in God's image (Gen. 1:27), a reflection of God Himself. As a result of Adam and Eve's fall into sin, their relationship with God was broken (Rom. 3:10–12, 23; 5:12). In order to restore humankind into fellowship with God, He sent His Son, Jesus Christ, who is also in God's image (though He was not created), to give His life so men and women could come back into a right relationship with God (see note on Col. 1:15–18). To walk in darkness (v. 6; cf. John 3:19), would be to continue in sin. On the other hand, to walk in light is to have continuous fellowship with God (v. 7, cf. John 8:12).

In this passage, there are three false appeals that people make regarding their sin before God. First, they claim that they have fellowship with God, when in reality they are living apart from God in their sin (v. 6). This reveals their indifference to morality with regard to their relationship to God. John states that in fact, such a person does not possess the truth because he or she has not been cleansed from sin (v. 7). Second, people suggest that they do not even have sin (v. 8). In this attitude is the denial of any consequence for wrong actions by an individual. This is a rejection that there is a sin nature within that person. On the other hand, if a person will acknowledge his or her sinfulness, confessing before God (i.e., saying the same thing as God says about sin), then that person can receive forgiveness and be brought back to a proper relationship to God. The final plea that people make is an actual denial that sin is even present in their life. They essentially say that they are not in any way practicing sin. Even though by His death Christ satisfied God's wrath on the believer's sin (1 John 2:1, 2), the sin nature still remains within every person. Therefore, he or she must realize that there must be a desire to continue in a right relationship with God by confession of sin.

It is obvious that the people John is speaking of in this passage are believers. He is urging them to seek proper fellowship with God, realizing that they have been purchased by God through Christ's death on the cross (1 Cor. 6:20).

🔑 **2:1** See note on 1 John 3:6–9.

[ppt]keepeth not his commandments, [b]is a liar, and the truth[225] is not in him.

5 But [a]whoso [psa]keepeth his word,[3056] [b]in him verily[230] is the love[26] of God [pfip]perfected: [c]hereby know we that we are in him.

6 [a]He that saith he [pinf]abideth in him [b]ought himself also so [pinf]to walk, even as he walked.

Exhortations to Brotherly Love

7 Brethren, [a]I write no new[2537] commandment unto you, but an old commandment [b]which ye [ipf]had from the beginning. The old commandment is the word which ye [ao]have heard from the beginning.

8 Again, [a]a new commandment I write unto you, which thing is true in him and in you: [b]because the darkness[4653] is past, and [c]the true[228] light[5457] now shineth.[5316]

9 [a]He that saith he is in the light, and [ppt]hateth his brother,[80] is in darkness even until now.

10 [a]He that [ppt]loveth[25] his brother abideth in the light, and [b]there is none [l]occasion of stumbling in him.

11 But he that [ppt]hateth his brother is in darkness, and [a]walketh in darkness, and knoweth not whither he goeth, because that darkness [ao]hath blinded his eyes.

12 I write unto you, little children, because [a]your sins[266] [pfip]are forgiven[863] you for his name's[3686] sake.

13 I write unto you, fathers,[3962] because ye [pfi]have known[1097] him [a]*that is* from the beginning. I write unto you, young men, because ye [pfi]have overcome the wicked one.[4190] I [ao]write unto you, little children, because ye [pfi]have known the Father.

14 I have written unto you, fathers, because ye have known him *that is* from the beginning. I have written unto you, young men, because [a]ye are strong, and the word[3056] of God abideth in you, and ye [pfi]have overcome the wicked one.

"Love Not the World"

15 [pim][a]Love[25] not the world,[2889] neither the things *that are* in the world. [b]If any man love the world, the love[26] of the Father is not in him.

16 For all that *is* in the world, the lust of the flesh,[4561] [a]and the lust of the eyes, and the pride[212] of life,[979] is not of the Father, but is of the world.

17 And [a]the world passeth away, and the lust[1939] thereof: but he that [ppt]doeth the will[2307] of God abideth[3306] for ever.[165,1519] [3588]

The Promise of Eternal Life

18 [a]Little children, [b]it is the last[2078] time:[5610] and as ye [ao]have heard that [c]antichrist[500] [pin]shall come, [d]even now [pfi]are there many antichrists; whereby we know [e]that it is the last time.

19 [a]They went out from us, but they were not of us: for [b]if they had been of us, they would *no doubt* [plpf]have continued with us: but *they went out,* [c]that they [asbp]might be made manifest[5319] that they were not all of us.

20 But [a]ye have an unction[5545] [b]from the Holy One, and [c]ye know[1492] all things.

21 I have not written unto you because ye know not the truth,[225] but because ye know it, and that no lie is of the truth.

22 [a]Who is a liar but he that [ppt]denieth[720] that Jesus is the Christ?[5547] He is antichrist, that denieth the Father[3962] and the Son.[5207]

23 [a]Whosoever denieth the Son, the same hath not the Father: [*but*] [b]*he that acknowledgeth the Son hath the Father also.*

24 Let that therefore abide in you, [a]which ye [ao]have heard from the beginning. If that which ye have heard from the beginning [aosb]shall remain in you, [b]ye also shall continue in the Son, and in the Father.

25 [a]And this is the promise[1860] that he [aom]hath promised[1861] us, *even* eternal[166] life,[2222]

---

4 [b]1John 1:8
5 [a]John 14:21, 23 [b]1John 4:12 [c]1John 4:13
6 [a]John 15:4, 5 [b]Matt. 11:29; John 13:15; 1Pet. 2:21
7 [a]2John 1:5 [b]1John 3:11
8 [a]John 13:34; 15:12 [b]Rom. 13:12; Eph. 5:8; 1Thess. 5:5, 8 [c]John 1:9; 8:12; 12:35
9 [a]1Cor. 13:2; 2Pet. 1:9; 1John 3:14, 15
10 [l]Gr. *scandal* [a]1John 3:14 [b]2Pet. 1:10
11 [a]John 12:35
12 [a]Luke 24:47; Acts 4:12; 10:43; 13:38; 1John 1:7
13 [a]1John 1:1
14 [a]Eph. 6:10
15 [a]Rom. 12:2 [b]Matt. 6:24; Gal. 1:10; James 4:4
16 [a]Eccl. 5:11
17 [a]1Cor. 7:31; James 1:10; 4:14; 1Pet. 1:24
18 [a]John 21:5 [b]Heb. 1:2 [c]2Thess. 2:3; 2Pet. 2:1; 1John 4:3 [d]Matt. 24:5, 24; 2John 1:7 [e]1Tim. 4:1; 2Tim. 3:1
19 [a]Deut. 13:13; Ps. 41:9; Acts 20:30 [b]Matt. 24:24; John 6:37; 10:28, 29; 2Tim. 2:19 [c]1Cor. 11:19
20 [a]2Cor. 1:21; Heb. 1:9; 1John 2:27 [b]Mark 1:24; Acts 3:14 [c]John 10:4, 5; 14:26; 16:13; 1John 2:27
22 [a]1John 4:3; 2John 1:7
23 [a]John 15:23; 2John 1:9 [b]John 14:7, 9, 10; 1John 4:15
24 [a]2John 1:6 [b]John 14:23; 1John 1:3
25 [a]John 17:3; 1John 1:2; 5:11

26 These *things* have I written unto you [a]concerning them that [ppt]seduce you.

27 But [a]the anointing[5545] which ye [ao]have received of him abideth[3306] in you, and [b]ye need not that any man [psa]teach[1321] you: but as the same anointing [c]teacheth you of all things, and is truth, and is no lie, and even as it hath taught you, ye shall abide in [I]him.

28 And now, little children,[5040] [pim]abide in him; that, [a]when he [asbp]shall appear,[5319] we [psa]may have confidence, [b]and not [asbp]be ashamed before him at his coming.[3952]

29 [a]If ye know that he is righteous, [I]ye know that [b]every one that [ppt]doeth righteousness[1343] [pfip]is born[1080] of him.

Evidences of a True Believer

3 Behold, what manner of love[26] the Father[3962] [pfi]hath bestowed upon us, that [a]we [asbp]should be called the sons[5043] of God:[2316] therefore the world[2889] knoweth[1097] us not, [b]because it knew him not.

2 Beloved, [a]now are we the sons of God, and [b]it [aop]doth not yet appear[5319] what we shall be: but we know that, when he shall appear, [c]we shall be like him; for [d]we shall see him as he is.

3 [a]And every man that [ppt]hath this hope[1680] in him purifieth[48] himself, even as he is pure.

4 Whosoever [ppt]committeth sin[266] transgresseth also the law: for [a]sin is the transgression of the law.[458]

5 And ye know[1492] [a]that he was manifested[5319] [b]to [aosb]take away[142] our sins;[266] and [c]in him is no sin.

🗝 6 Whosoever [ppt]abideth[3306] in him sinneth[264] not: [a]whosoever [ppt]sinneth

26 [a]1John 3:7; 2John 1:7
27 [a]1John 2:20 [b]Jer. 31:33, 34; Heb. 8:10, 11 [c]John 14:26; 16:13; 1John 2:20
27 [I]Or, *it*
28 [a]1John 3:2 [b]1John 4:17
29 [I]Or, *know ye* [a]Acts 22:14 [b]1John 3:7, 10

1 [a]John 1:12 [b]John 15:18, 19; 16:3; 17:25
2 [a]Isa. 56:5; Rom. 8:15; Gal. 3:26; 4:6; 1John 5:1 [b]Rom. 8:18; 2Cor. 4:17 [c]Rom. 8:29; 1Cor. 15:49; Phil. 3:21; Col. 3:4; 2Pet. 1:4 [d]Job 19:26; Ps. 16:11; Matt. 5:8; 1Cor. 13:12; 2Cor. 5:7
3 [a]1John 4:17
4 [a]Rom. 4:15; 1John 5:17

5 [a]1John 1:2 [b]Isa. 53:5, 6, 11; 1Tim. 1:15; Heb. 1:3; 9:26; 1Pet. 2:24 [c]2Cor. 5:21; Heb. 4:15; 9:28; 1Pet. 2:22 **6** [a]1John 2:4; 4:8; 3John 1:11

🗝 **3:6–9** In this passage, John examines the question of whether the person "born of God" can commit sin. In verse six, The apostle writes, "Whosoever abideth in him sinneth not," and in verse eight, "He that committeth sin is of the devil." Furthermore, in verse nine there is an emphatic declaration: "Whosoever is of God doth not commit sin . . . and he cannot sin." If it were possible for a Christian to sin, there would appear to be a contradiction in these portions of Scripture. In this instance, John says if it is not possible for those who are really born again to sin, there must be very few genuine Christians. Every believer still possesses a fallen, sin nature, as well as the indwelling Holy Spirit. Also, the doctrine of eternal security is evident in Scripture (John 1:12; 10:28; Rom. 8:38, 39). Though they may fall into sin, the believer's eternal salvation is not affected (see note on 1 Thess. 2:3–9).

Antinomians (derived from the Greek words *antí* [473], "against," and *nómos* [3551], "law") contend that the covenant of grace was not established based on conditions. The result is that no person can be held accountable to any moral law. It is only required of them that they believe, then they can then live as they please. The perfectionists go so far as to say that the sin nature has been eradicated as though surgically removed. John was warning believers against this form of thinking, that they not continue in sin, but abide in righteousness (vv. 8, 9). Moreover, the apostle exposes these doctrines in the command, "My little children, these things write I unto you, that ye sin not. And if any man sin, we have an advocate with the Father, Jesus Christ the righteous" (1 John 2:1). This is not the proper rendering of this verse. It should denote the mere action of a sin, not the idea of habitually sinning. John explains that even he was capable of committing sin, not in a habitual sense, but as one particular action. The phrase, used here in verse nine, "does not commit sin" is in the present tense denoting continuous action. On the other hand, in chapter two, verse one, John uses the aorist tense, speaking of one point in the past when a sin was committed.

Furthermore, there were those who taught that mere intellectual knowledge and assent to the Christian faith was enough to make one acceptable to God, even though he or she lived impure lives. Therefore, John reiterates in verse seven that only those who continued in righteousness (*ho poión*, [4160], a participle phrase meaning "the one habitually doing"), were considered righteous. They were not only making the righteousness and holy life of Christ the object of their trust, but also the pattern of their walk and practice.

(continued on next page)

[pfi]hath not seen[3708] him, neither [pfi]known him.

7 Little children,[5040] [pim][a]let no man deceive[4105] you: [b]he that [ppt]doeth righteousness[1343] is righteous, even as he is righteous.[1342]

8 [a]He that [ppt]committeth sin is of the devil; for the devil[1228] sinneth from the beginning. For this purpose the Son of God was manifested,[5319] [b]that he [aosb]might destroy[3089] the works[2041] of the devil.

9 [a]Whosoever [pfpp]is born[1080] of God doth not commit sin; for [b]his seed[4690] remaineth in him: and he cannot [pinf]sin, because he [pfip]is born of God.

10 In this the children[5043] of God[2316] are manifest,[5318] and the children[5043] of the devil: [a]whosoever [ppt]doeth not righteousness is not of God, [b]neither he that [ppt]loveth[25] not his brother.[80]

Love in Deed and Truth

11 For [a]this is the [I]message[31] that ye heard from the beginning, [b]that we [psa]should love one another.

12 Not as [a]Cain, *who* was of that wicked one,[4190] and slew his brother. And wherefore [ao]slew he him? Because his own works were evil,[4190] and his brother's righteous.

13 Marvel not, my brethren, if [a]the world hate you.

14 [a]We know that we [pfi]have passed from death[2288] unto life,[2222] because we love the brethren. [b]He that [ppt]loveth not *his* brother abideth in death.

15 [a]Whosoever [ppt]hateth his brother is a murderer: and ye know that [b]no murderer hath eternal life [ppt]abiding in him.

16 [a]Hereby [pfi]perceive we the love[26] *of God,* because he laid down his life[5590] for us: and we ought to lay down *our* lives for the brethren.

17 But [a]whoso [psa]hath this world's good,[979] and [psa]seeth his brother [ppt]have need, and [aosb]shutteth up his bowels[4698] *of compassion* from him, [b]how dwelleth the love of God in him?

18 My little children, [psa][a]let us not love in word,[3056] neither in tongue;[1100] but in deed[2041] and in truth.

19 And hereby we know[1097] [a]that we are of the truth, and shall [I]assure[3982] our hearts before him.

20 [a]For if our heart[2588] [psa]condemn[2607] us, God is greater than our heart, and knoweth all things.

21 [a]Beloved, if our heart condemn us not, [b]*then* have we confidence[3954] toward God.

22 And [a]whatsoever we [psa]ask,[154] we receive of him, because we keep[5083] his commandments,[1785] [b]and do those things that are pleasing[701] in his sight.

23 [a]And this is his commandment, That we [aosb]should believe[4100] on the name[3686] of his Son[5207] Jesus Christ, [b]and [psa]love[25] one another, [c]as he gave us commandment.

7 [a]1John 2:26 [b]Ezek. 18:5-9; Rom. 2:13; 1John 2:29
8 [a]Matt. 13:38; John 8:44 [b]Gen. 3:15; Luke 10:18; John 16:11; Heb. 2:14
9 [a]1John 5:18 [b]1Pet. 1:23
10 [a]1John 2:29 [b]1John 4:8
11 [I]Or, *commandment* [a]1John 1:5; 2:7 [b]John 13:34; 15:12; 1John 3:23; 1John 4:7, 21; 2John 1:5
12 [a]Gen. 4:4, 8; Heb. 11:4; Jude 1:11
13 [a]John 15:18, 19; 17:14; 2Tim. 3:12
14 [a]1John 2:10 [b]1John 2:9, 11
15 [a]Matt. 5:21, 22; 1John 4:20 [b]Gal. 5:21; Rev. 21:8
16 [a]John 3:16; 15:13; Rom. 5:8; Eph. 5:2, 25; 1John 4:9, 11
17 [a]Deut. 15:7; Luke 3:11 [b]1John 4:20
18 [a]Ezek. 33:31; Rom. 12:9; Eph. 4:15; James 2:15, 16; 1Pet. 1:22
19 [I]Gr. *persuade* [a]John 18:37; 1John 1:8
20 [a]1Cor. 4:4
21 [a]Job 22:26 [b]Heb. 10:22; 1John 2:28; 4:17
22 [a]Ps. 34:15; 145:18, 19; Prov. 15:29; Jer. 29:12; Matt. 7:8; 21:22; Mark 11:24; John 14:13; 15:7; 16:23, 24; James 5:16; 1John 5:14 [b]John 8:29; 9:31
23 [a]John 6:29; 17:3 [b]Matt. 22:39; John 13:34; 15:12; Eph. 5:2; 1Thess. 4:9; 1Pet. 4:8; 1John 3:11; 1John 4:21 [c]1John 2:8, 10

(continued from previous page)

John's idea of committing sin on a permanent, habitual basis is further explained in 3 John 1:11, "He that doeth good is of God: But he that doeth evil hath not seen God." There are two participial nouns in this verse, *ho agathopoiōn* (215), meaning "the one being a doer of good, a benevolent person," and *ho kakopoiōn* (2554), referring to "the one doing evil, a malicious person." This is the same usage found in 1 John 3:7, "he that doeth righteousness is righteous." John does not imply that merely acting good will make one righteous. A person is an artisan who has acquired a skill and works at that trade as his calling or occupation. Hence, the correct translation of 1 John. 3:8 should be, "The one who practices sin." The expression, "he cannot sin," (1 John 3:9) simply means the true believer cannot sin habitually, deliberately, easily and maliciously (e.g., Cain sinned out of hatred of goodness, 1 John 3:12). John does not ignore the existence of the sinful nature in the believer, which exists as a mortal in a corrupt world. Consequently, John states in 1 John. 1:8: "If we say that we have no sin, we deceive ourselves, and the truth is not in us."

24 And [a]he that [ppt]keepeth his commandments [b]dwelleth in him, and he in him. And [c]hereby we know that he abideth[3306] in us, by the Spirit[4151] which he hath given us.

"Try the Spirits"

4 Beloved, [a]believe[4100] not every spirit,[4151] but [b]try the spirits whether they are of God: because [c]many false prophets [pfi]are gone out into the world.[2889]

2 Hereby know ye the Spirit of God: [a]Every spirit that confesseth[3670] that Jesus Christ[5547] is come in the flesh is of God:

🗝 3 And [a]every spirit that confesseth[3670] not that Jesus Christ [pfp]is come in the flesh is not of God: and this is that *spirit* of antichrist,[500] whereof ye [pfi]have heard that it should come; and [b]even now already is it in the world.

4 [a]Ye are of God, little children, and have overcome them: because greater is he that is in you, than [b]he that is in the world.

5 [a]They are of the world: therefore speak they of the world, and [b]the world heareth them.

6 We are of God: [a]he that [ppt]knoweth[1097] God heareth[191] us; he that is not of God heareth not us. Hereby know we [b]the spirit of truth,[225] and the spirit of error.[4106]

"God Is Love"

7 [a]Beloved, [psa]let us love[25] one another: for love[26] is of God; and every one that [ppt]loveth [pfp]is born[1080] of God, and knoweth God.

8 He that loveth not [aoa]knoweth not God; for [b]God is love.

9 [a]In this was manifested[5319] the love of God toward us, because that God [pfi]sent his only begotten[3439] Son[5207] into the world, [b]that we [aosb]might live[2198] through him.

24 [a]John 14:23; 15:10; 1John 4:12 [b]John 17:21 [c]Rom. 8:9; 1John 4:13
1 [a]Jer. 29:8; Matt. 24:4 [b]1Cor. 14:29; 1Thess. 5:21; Rev. 2:2 [c]Matt. 24:5, 24; Acts 20:30; 1Tim. 4:1; 2Pet. 2:1; 1John 2:18; 2John 1:7
2 [a]1Cor. 12:3; 1John 5:1
3 [a]1John 2:22; 2John 1:7 [b]2Thess. 2:7; 1John 2:18, 22
4 [a]1John 5:4 [b]John 12:31; 14:30; 16:11; 1Cor. 2:12; Eph. 2:2; 6:12
5 [a]John 3:31 [b]John 15:19; 17:14
6 [a]John 8:47; 10:27; 1Cor. 14:37; 2Cor. 10:7 [b]Isa. 8:20; John 14:17
7 [a]1John 3:10, 11, 23
8 [a]1John 2:4; 3:6 [b]1John 4:16
9 [a]John 3:16; Rom. 5:8; 8:32; 1John 3:16 [b]1John 5:11
10 [a]John 15:16; Rom. 5:8, 10; Titus 3:4 [b]1John 2:2
11 [a]Matt. 18:33; John 15:12, 13; 1John 3:16
12 [a]John 1:18; 1Tim. 6:16; 1John 4:20 [b]1John 2:5; 1John 4:18
13 [a]John 14:20; 1John 3:24
14 [a]John 1:14; 1John 1:1, 2 [b]John 3:17
15 [a]Rom. 10:9; 1John 5:1, 5
16 [a]1John 4:8 [b]1John 3:24; 1John 4:12
17 [I]Gr. *love with us* [a]James 2:13; 1John 2:28; 3:19, 21 [b]1John 3:3
18 [a]1John 4:12
20 [a]1John 2:4; 3:17 [b]1John 4:12
21 [a]Matt. 22:37, 39; John 13:34; 15:12; 1John 3:23

10 Herein is love, [a]not that we loved God, but that he loved us, and sent[649] his Son [b]*to be* the propitiation[2434] for our sins.[266]

11 Beloved, [a]if God so loved us, we ought also [pinf]to love one another.

12 [a]No man [pfip]hath seen God at any time. If we [psa]love one another, God dwelleth[3306] in us, and [b]his love is perfected[5048] in us.

13 [a]Hereby know we that we dwell in him, and he in us, because he [pfi]hath given us of his Spirit.

14 And [a]we have seen and do testify that [b]the Father [pfi]sent[649] the Son *to be* the Saviour[4990] of the world.[2889]

15 [a]Whosoever [aosb]shall confess[3670] that Jesus is the Son of God, God dwelleth in him, and he in God.

16 And we [pfi]have known and [pfi]believed the love that God hath to us. [a]God is love;[26] and [b]he that [ppt]dwelleth in love dwelleth in God, and God in him.

17 Herein is [I]our love [pfip]made perfect,[5048] that [a]we [psa]may have boldness in the day[2250] of judgment:[2920] [b]because as he is, so are we in this world.

18 There is no fear[5401] in love; but perfect[5046] love casteth out fear: because fear hath torment.[2851] He that [ppt]feareth[5399] [pfip][a]is not made perfect[5048] in love.

19 We love[25] him, because he first loved us.

20 [a]If a man say, I love God, and hateth his brother,[80] he is a liar: for he that [ppt]loveth not his brother whom he [pfi]hath seen, how can he love God [b]whom he [pfi]hath not seen?[3708]

21 And [a]this commandment[1785] have we from him, That he who [ppt]loveth God love his brother also.

The Believer's Victory

5 Whosoever [ppt][a]believeth[4100] that [b]Jesus is the Christ[5547] [pfip]is [c]born[1080]

1 [a]John 1:12 [b]1John 2:22, 23; 4:2, 5 [c]John 1:13

🗝 **4:3** See notes on 2 Thessalonians 2:3–9.

of God: [d]and every one that [ppt]loveth[25] him that [apt]begat[1080] loveth him also that [pfpp]is begotten[1080] of him.

2 By this we know that we love the children[5043] of God,[2316] when we love God, and keep[5083] his commandments.

3 [a]For this is the love[26] of God, that we keep his commandments: and [b]his commandments are not grievous.

4 For [a]whatsoever [pfpp]is born[1080] of God overcometh3528 the world:[2889] and this is the victory that [apt]overcometh the world,[2889] *even* our faith.[4102]

5 Who is he that [ppt]overcometh the world, but [a]he that [ppt]believeth that Jesus is the Son[5207] of God?[2316]

6 This is he that [apt]came [a]by water and blood, *even* Jesus Christ; not by water only, but by water and blood.[129] [b]And it is the Spirit that [ppt]beareth witness, because the Spirit[4151] is truth.[225]

7 For there are three that bear record[3140] in heaven,[3772] the Father,[3962] [a]the Word,[3056] and the Holy Ghost:[4151] [b]and these three are one.

8 And there are three that [ppt]bear witness in earth,[1093] the spirit, and the water, and the blood: and these three agree in one.

9 If we receive [a]the witness[3141] of men,[444] the witness of God is greater: [b]for this is the witness of God which he [pfi]hath testified of his Son.

10 He that [ppt]believeth on the Son of God [a]hath the witness in himself: he that believeth not God [pfi][b]hath made him a liar; because he [pfi]believeth not the record[3141] that God [pfi]gave of his Son.

11 [a]And this is the record, that God [ao]hath given to us eternal[166] life,[2222] and [b]this life is in his Son.

12 [a]He that [ppt]hath the Son hath life; *and* he that hath not the Son of God hath not life.

God Answers Prayer

13 [a]These things [ao]have I written[1125] unto you that [ppt]believe on the name[3686] of the Son of God; [b]that ye may know that ye have eternal life, and that ye [psa]may believe on the name of the Son of God.

14 And this is the confidence[3954] that we have [1]in him, that, [a]if we [psa]ask any thing according to his will, he heareth[191] us:

15 And if we know that he hear us, whatsoever we ask,[154] we know that we have the petitions[155] that we desired[154] of him.

16 If any man see his brother [ppt]sin[264] a sin[266] *which is* not unto death,[2288] he shall ask, and [a]he shall give him life for them that sin not unto death. [b]There is a sin unto death: [c]I do not say that he [aosb]shall pray for it.

17 [a]All unrighteousness[93] is sin: and there is a sin not unto death.

18 We know that [a]whosoever [pfpp]is born[1080] of God sinneth not; but he that [aptp]is begotten[1080] of God [b]keepeth himself, and that wicked one[4190] toucheth[680] him not.

19 *And* we know that we are of God, and [a]the whole world[2889] lieth[2749] in wickedness.[4190]

20 And we know that the Son of God is come, and [pfia]hath given us an understanding,[1271] [b]that we [psa]may know[1097] him that is true,[228] and we are in him that is true, *even* in his Son Jesus Christ. [c]This is the true God, [d]and eternal life.

21 Little children,[5040] [a]keep yourselves from idols.[1497] Amen.281

1 [d]John 15:23
3 [a]John 14:15, 21, 23; 15:10; 2John 1:6 [b]Mic. 6:8; Matt. 11:30
4 [a]1John 3:9; 4:4
5 [a]1Cor. 15:57; 1John 4:15
6 [a]John 19:34 [b]John 14:17; 15:26; 16:13; 1Tim. 3:16
7 [a]John 1:1; Rev. 19:13 [b]John 10:30
9 [a]John 8:17, 18 [b]Matt. 3:16, 17; 17:5
10 [a]Rom. 8:16; Gal. 4:6 [b]John 3:33; 5:38
11 [a]1John 2:25 [b]John 1:4; 1John 4:9
12 [a]John 3:36; 5:24
13 [a]John 20:31 [b]1John 1:1, 2
14 [1]Or, *concerning him* [a]1John 3:22
16 [a]Job 42:8; James 5:14, 15 [b]Matt. 12:31, 32; Mark 3:29; Luke 12:10; Heb. 6:4, 6; 10:26 [c]Jer. 7:16; 14:11; John 17:9
17 [a]1John 3:4
18 [a]1Pet. 1:23; 1John 3:9 [b]James 1:27
19 [a]Gal. 1:4
20 [a]Luke 24:45 [b]John 17:3 [c]Isa. 9:6; 44:6; 54:5; John 20:28; Acts 20:28; Rom. 9:5; 1Tim. 3:16; Titus 2:13; Heb. 1:8 [d]1John 5:11, 12, 13
21 [a]1Cor. 10:14

The Second Epistle of

JOHN

The Apostle John is unmistakably the author of this book (see introduction to 1 John). It was probably written about the same time as the Book of 1 John (A.D. 85–90) and may have been addressed to some of the same people. The "elect lady and her children" (2 John 1:1) may be a reference to an actual lady and her children, but many scholars contend that this is a cryptic way of addressing a church to safeguard against the letter falling into the hands of those who were hostile to the Church.

The purpose of the book was to warn against false teachers who commonly traveled from church to church spreading heresy. John instructed that these people should not even receive ordinary hospitality from those in the church (2 John 1:10, 11). Another objective of the Book of 2 John was to inform the recipients of his plans to visit them soon. This is also given as the reason for the brevity of the letter (2 John 1:12).

1 The elder[4245] unto the elect[1588] lady and her children,[5043] [a]whom I love[25] in the truth;[225] and not I only, but also all they that [pfp]have known [b]the truth;

2 For the truth's sake, which dwelleth in us, and shall be with us for ever.[165,1519] [3588]

3 [a]Grace [I]be with you, mercy,[1656] *and* peace,[1515] from God[2316] the Father,[3962] and from the Lord[2962] Jesus Christ,[5547] the Son[5207] of the Father, [b]in truth and love.

"Love One Another"

4 I rejoiced greatly that I [pfi]found of thy children[5043] [ppt][a]walking[4043] in truth, as we [ao]have received a commandment from the Father.

5 And now I beseech thee, lady, [a]not as though I [ppt]wrote a new[2537] commandment unto thee, but that which we [ipf]had from the beginning, [b]that we [psa]love one another.

6 And [a]this is love,[26] that we [psa]walk after his commandments. This is the commandment, That, [b]as ye [ao]have heard from the beginning, ye [psa]should walk in it.

Exhortation to Stedfastness

🗝 7 For [a]many deceivers [ao]are entered into the world, [b]who [ppt]confess[3670] not that Jesus Christ[5547] [ppt]is come in the flesh.[4561] [c]This is a deceiver and an antichrist.[500]

8 [a]Look to yourselves, [b]that we [aosb]lose not those things which we have [I]wrought,[2038] but that we [aosb]receive[618] a full[4134] reward.[3408]

9 [a]Whosoever [ppt]transgresseth,[3845] and [ppt]abideth not in the doctrine[1322] of Christ, hath not God. He that abideth[3306] in the doctrine of Christ, he hath both the Father and the Son.

10 If there come any unto you, and bring not this doctrine, receive him not into *your* house, [a]neither bid him God speed:[5463]

11 For he that [ppt]biddeth[3004] him God speed is partaker[2841] of his evil[4190] deeds.[2041]

12 [a]Having many things to write unto you, I [aop]would not *write* with paper and ink: but I trust to come unto you, and speak [I]face to face, [b]that [II]our joy may be full.

13 [a]The children of thy elect sister greet thee. Amen.[281]

1 [a]1John 3:18; 2John 1:3; 3John 1:1 [b]John 8:32; Gal. 2:5, 14; 3:1; 5:7; Col. 1:5; 2Thess. 2:13; 1Tim. 2:4; Heb. 10:26
3 [I]Gr. *shall be* [a]1Tim. 1:2 [b]2John 1:1
4 [a]3John 1:3
5 [a]1John 2:7, 8; 3:11 [b]John 13:34; 15:12; Eph. 5:2; 1Pet. 4:8; 1John 3:23
6 [a]John 14:15, 21; 15:10; 1John 2:5; 5:3 [b]1John 2:24
7 [a]1John 4:1 [b]1John 4:2, 3 [c]1John 2:22; 4:3
8 [I]Or, *gained* [a]Mark 13:9 [b]Gal. 3:4; Heb. 10:32, 35
9 [a]1John 2:23
10 [a]Rom. 16:17; 1Cor. 5:11; 16:22; Gal. 1:8, 9; 2Tim. 3:5; Titus 3:10
12 [I]Gr. *mouth to mouth* [II]Or, *your* *#$3John 1:13* [a]John 17:13; 1John 1:4
13 [a]1Pet. 5:13

🗝 **1:7** See note on 2 Thessalonians 2:3–9.

The Third Epistle of

JOHN

The Book of 3 John was written by the Apostle John who calls himself "the elder." It is closely related to the books of 1 and 2 John (see introductions to these books) in that they deal with similar subjects and were all written about the same time (ca. A.D. 85–90). John addressed this letter to Gaius, a leader in the congregation of a church that John had most likely helped to establish. The purpose of this epistle was to encourage Gaius to continue to help those who were spreading the gospel and teaching the truth (3 John 1:5–8). John also wanted to express his displeasure about the offensive behavior of Diotrephes, a man who refused to accept John and was mistreating other believers (3 John 1:9). Furthermore, he revealed his intention to visit the church there himself and reprove this selfish and indifferent man to his face (3 John 1:10).

1 🔑The elder[4245] unto the wellbeloved[27] Gaius, [a]whom I love[25] [I]in
the truth.[225]
🔑2 Beloved,[27] I [I]wish above all
things that thou [pinf]mayest prosper and
[pinf]be in health, even as thy soul[5590] prospereth.
3 For I rejoiced[5463] greatly, when the
brethren[80] came and [ppt]testified of the
truth that is in thee, even as [a]thou walkest[4043] in the truth.
4 I have no greater joy[5479] than to
hear that [a]my children[5043] [ppt]walk in
truth.

Concerning Helping Others

5 Beloved, thou [pin]doest faithfully[4103]
whatsoever thou doest[2038] to the brethren,
and to strangers;
6 Which [ao]have borne witness of thy
charity[26] before the church:[1577] whom if

1 [I]Or, *truly* [a]2 John 1:1
2 [I]Or, *pray*
3 [a]2 John 1:4
4 [a]1 Cor. 4:15; Phile. 1:10

🔑 **1:1** Originally from Macedonia, Gaius was one of Paul's companions who was caught during a riot in Ephesus (Acts 19:29). He was also among those who accompanied Paul to Jerusalem, perhaps as an official delegate of his church in Derbe, and was a member of the party which awaited Paul at Troas (Acts 20:4, 5). He was baptized by Paul in Corinth (1 Cor. 1:14). His house was used as a regular meeting place for the congregation; in fact, Paul stayed with him during one of his visits to Corinth (Rom. 16:23). John is commending Gaius for his good hospitality, as well as expressing his desire to see him shortly (3 John 1:14).

🔑 **1:2** There are some who misapply this verse to mean that it is God's will for His children to always prosper and be in good health, which would give credence to the belief in a "health and wealth gospel." However, the writer is conveying nothing more than a wish to Gaius that this letter might find him well and in good health.

There are several words in this verse that are mistranslated in the KJV. For instance, the preposition *perí* (4012) should be rendered "concerning" or "about," rather than "above." John is not stating that prosperity and wealth should be considered the important priorities of one's life. The verb *eúchomaí* (2172) merely expresses a wish, not the promise of an Apostle to a fellow believer. The word translated "prosper" is *euodoústhai* (a present infinitive from *euodóō* [2137]). Essentially, this word means to have a good and safe journey throughout one's life (cf. Rom. 1:10). In 1 Corinthians 16:2, Paul used it in regard to God's benevolence toward Christians. Although it is translated "as God hath prospered him," one should accept the idea that prospering does not necessarily mean to gain riches. Rather, one should understand that the Lord will make sufficient provision for the believer's material needs, and the idea of wealth should not be interpreted here. The third word of importance in this verse is *hugiaínein* (5198), "to be healthy." Likewise, this is not a guarantee that Gaius is going to be healthy, but simply a wish.

thou bring forward on their journey after a godly sort,[2316] [516] thou shalt do well:

7 Because that for his name's[3686] sake they went forth, [a]taking nothing of the Gentiles.[1484]

8 We therefore ought [pinf]to receive such, that we might be fellowhelpers to the truth.

🗝 9 I wrote[1125] unto the church: but Diotrephes, who loveth to have the preeminence among them, receiveth us not.

10 Wherefore, if I come, I will remember his deeds[2041] which he doeth, prating against[5396] us with malicious[4190] words: and not content therewith, neither doeth he himself receive the brethren, and forbiddeth them that would, and casteth *them* out of the church.

7 [a]1Cor. 9:12, 15

11 [a]Ps. 37:27; Isa. 1:16, 17; 1Pet. 3:11 [b]1John 2:29; 3:6, 9

12 [a]1Tim. 3:7 [b]John 21:24

13 [a]2John 1:12

14 [I]Gr. *mouth to mouth*

11 Beloved,[27] [a]follow not that which is evil,[2556] but that which is good.[18] [b]He that [ppt]doeth good[15] is of God:[2316] but he that [ppt]doeth evil[2554] [pfi]hath not seen[3708] God.

12 Demetrius [a]hath good report[3140] of all *men,* and of the truth itself: yea, and we *also* bear record; [b]and ye know[1492] that our record[3141] is true.

Benediction

13 [a]I had many things to write, but I will not with ink and pen write unto thee:

14 But I trust I shall shortly see thee, and we shall speak[2980] [I]face to face. Peace *be* to thee. *Our* friends salute[782] thee. Greet[782] the friends by name.

🗝 **1:9** Diotrephes was an ambitious person who resisted the authority of the elders in the church. He attacked them publicly, and forbade the reception of John and his adherents. Also, whether by formal excommunication or physical violence, he excluded those who received them.

The Epistle of

JUDE

The author of this letter is identified as "Jude, the servant of Jesus Christ, and brother of James" (Jude 1:1). In the early church, there was only one James who could be referred to in this way without further specification; namely, "James, the Lord's brother" (Gal. 1:19, see introduction to James). This Jude was most likely the same one who was listed as one of the half-brothers of the Lord Jesus (Matt. 13:55; Mark 6:3; Acts 1:13).

There are differing views concerning the recipients of the Book of Jude. Some scholars feel that he wrote to believers in the churches of Asia Minor, to whom also the Book of 2 Peter was directed. Others support the view that Jude wrote to believers in Palestine who would have been familiar with the references to Jewish history (Jude 1:7–11).

Little is known of the circumstances of those to whom Jude addresses this letter, and no one knows the precise time when the book was written. It has been suggested that the Book of 2 Peter sparked the ideas that Jude wrote in his epistle (2 Pet. 2:1—3:3, cf. Jude 1:3–18). Consequently, Jude is thought to have written this book after Peter's death, but before the destruction of Jerusalem (A.D. 70).

Both Peter and Jude were alarmed at the great number of false teachers that were being accepted in the churches (see introduction to 2 Peter). Serious apostasy, similar to the one of which Paul had spoken (cf. Acts 20:29–31), seems to have been prevalent in Jude's day (Jude 1:4). Therefore, Jude urged these believers to "earnestly contend for the faith which was once delivered unto the saints" (Jude 1:3).

1 Jude, the servant[1401] of Jesus
Christ,[5547] and [a]brother of James, to
them that are sanctified[37] by God[2316] the
Father,[3962] and [b]preserved[5083] in Jesus
Christ, *and* [c]called.[2822]

2 Mercy[1656] unto you, and [a]peace,[1515]
and love,[26] be multiplied.

Warnings From History to the Ungodly

3 Beloved,[27] when I gave all diligence
to write unto you [a]of the common[2839]
salvation,[4991] it was needful[318] for me to
write unto you, and exhort[3870] *you* that
[b]ye should earnestly contend[1864] for the
faith[4102] which was once delivered unto
the saints.[40]

4 [a]For there are certain men crept in
unawares,3921 [b]who were before of old
ordained to this condemnation,[2917] ungodly men,[765] [c]turning [d]the grace[5485] of
our God into lasciviousness,[766] and [e]deny-

1 [a]Luke 6:16; Acts 1:13 [b]John 17:11, 12, 15; 1Pet. 1:5 [c]Rom. 1:7
2 [a]1Pet. 1:2; 2Pet. 1:2
3 [a]Titus 1:4 [b]Phil. 1:27; 1Tim. 1:18; 6:12; 2Tim. 1:13; 4:7
4 [a]Gal. 2:4; 2Pet. 2:1 [b]Rom. 9:21, 22; 1Pet. 2:8 [c]2Pet. 2:10 [d]Titus 2:11; Heb. 12:15 [e]Titus 1:16; 2Pet. 2:1; 1John 2:22
5 [a]1Cor. 10:9 [b]Num. 14:29, 37; 26:64; Ps. 106:26; Heb. 3:17, 19
6 [I]Or, *principality* [a]John 8:44 [b]2Pet. 2:4 [c]Rev. 20:10
7 [I]Gr. *other* [a]Gen. 19:24; Deut. 29:23; 2Pet. 2:6
8 [a]2Pet. 2:10 [b]Ex. 22:28

ing[720] the only Lord[1203] God, and our
Lord Jesus Christ.

5 I will therefore put you in remembrance, though ye once knew this,
how that [a]the Lord, having saved[4982] the
people out of the land of Egypt, afterward [b]destroyed them that believed[4100]
not.

6 And [a]the angels[32] which kept not
their [I]first estate, but [apt]left their own habitation,3613 [b]he [pfi]hath reserved[5083] in everlasting[126] chains under darkness2217 [c]unto
the judgment[2920] of the great day.[2250]

7 Even as [a]Sodom and Gomorrha,
and the cities about them in like manner,
[apt]giving themselves over to fornication,1608 and [apt]going after [I]strange[2087]
flesh,[4561] are set forth for an example,
suffering the vengeance[1349] of eternal[166]
fire.

8 [a]Likewise also these *filthy* dreamers
defile the flesh, despise dominion,[2963] and
[b]speak evil of[987] dignities.[1391]

9 Yet [a]Michael the archangel,[743] when contending[1252] with the devil[1228] he [ipf]disputed about the body of Moses, [b]durst not bring against[2018] him a railing[988] accusation,[2920] but said, [c]The Lord rebuke thee.

10 [a]But these speak evil of those things which they know not: but what they know naturally, as brute beasts, in those things they corrupt themselves.

11 Woe unto them! for they [ao]have gone in the way[3598] [a]of Cain, and [b]ran greedily after the error of Balaam for reward,[3408] and perished[622] [c]in the gainsaying[485] of Core.

12 [a]These are spots in your [b]feasts of charity,[26] when they [ppt]feast with you, feeding themselves without fear: [c]clouds *they are* without water, [d]carried about of winds; trees whose fruit withereth, without fruit, twice dead,[599] [e]plucked up by the roots;

13 [a]Raging waves of the sea, [b]foaming out their own shame;[152] wandering stars, [c]to whom is reserved[5083] the blackness[2217] of darkness[4655] for ever.[165,1519][3588]

14 And Enoch also, [a]the seventh from Adam, prophesied of these, saying, Behold, [b]the Lord [ao]cometh with ten thousands of his saints,

15 To execute judgment[2920] upon all, and to convince all that are ungodly among them of all their ungodly[763] deeds[2041] which they have ungodly committed,[764] and of all their [a]hard *speeches* which ungodly sinners[268] have spoken against him.

16 These are murmurers, complainers, walking[4198] after their own lusts;[1939]

9 [a]Dan. 10:13; 12:1; Rev. 12:7 [b]2Pet. 2:11 [c]Zech. 3:2
10 [a]2Pet. 2:12
11 [a]Gen. 4:5; 1John 3:12 [b]Num. 22:7, 21; 2Pet. 2:15 [c]Num. 16:1
12 [a]2Pet. 2:13 [b]1Cor. 11:21 [c]Prov. 25:14; 2Pet. 2:17 [d]Eph. 4:14 [e]Matt. 15:13
13 [a]Isa. 57:20 [b]Phil. 3:19 [c]2Pet. 2:17
14 [a]Gen. 5:18 [b]Deut. 33:2; Dan. 7:10; Zech. 14:5; Matt. 25:31; 2Thess. 1:7; Rev. 1:7
15 [a]1Sam. 2:3; Ps. 31:18; 94:4; Mal. 3:13
16 [a]2Pet. 2:18 [b]Prov. 28:21; James 2:1, 9
17 [a]2Pet. 3:2
18 [a]1Tim. 4:1; 2Tim. 3:1; 4:3; 2Pet. 2:1; 3:3
19 [a]Prov. 18:1; Ezek. 14:7; Hos. 4:14; 9:10; Heb. 10:25 [b]1Cor. 2:14; James 3:15
20 [a]Col. 2:7; 1Tim. 1:4 [b]Rom. 8:26; Eph. 6:18
21 [a]Titus 2:13; 2Pet. 3:12
23 [a]Rom. 11:14; 1Tim. 4:16 [b]Amos 4:11; Zech. 3:2; 1Cor. 3:15 [c]Zech. 3:4, 5; Rev. 3:4
24 [a]Rom. 16:25; Eph. 3:20 [b]Col. 1:22
25 [a]Rom. 16:27; 1Tim. 1:17; 2:3

and [a]their mouth speaketh great swelling *words,* [b]having men's persons in admiration because of advantage.

"Keep Yourselves in the Love of God"

17 [a]But, beloved, remember ye the words[4487] which were spoken before of the apostles[652] of our Lord Jesus Christ;

18 How that they [ipf]told you [a]there should be mockers in the last[2078] time,[5550] who should walk after their own ungodly[763] lusts.

19 These be they [a]who separate[592] themselves, [b]sensual,[5591] having not the Spirit.

20 But ye, beloved, [a]building up yourselves on[2026] your most holy[40] faith, [b]praying in the Holy Ghost,[4151]

21 Keep[5083] yourselves in the love[26] of God, [a]looking for the mercy[1656] of our Lord Jesus Christ unto eternal[166] life.[2222]

22 And of some have compassion, making a difference:[1252]

23 And others [a]save[4982] with fear,[5401] [b]pulling[726] *them* out of the fire; hating even [c]the garment spotted[4695] by the flesh.[4561]

24 [a]Now unto him that is able [ainf]to keep[5442] you from falling, and [b]to present *you* faultless[299] before the presence of his glory[1391] with exceeding joy,[20]

25 [a]To the only wise[4680] God our Saviour,[4990] *be* glory and majesty, dominion[2904] and power,[1849] both now and ever.[165] Amen.[281]

1:9 This records an otherwise unknown incident of a dispute between Michael the archangel and the devil concerning the burial of Moses' body. The Holy Spirit related this incident through Jude to tell us that the archangel Michael did not bring a railing accusation against the devil, but said, "The Lord rebuke you." He wanted to show that neither believers nor angels will be able to put the devil out of commission, but that the time of his demise will soon come. It is said of him in Revelation 20:2 that he will be bound for a thousand years during Christ's millennial kingdom, and that finally, he is going to be cast into the lake of fire and brimstone (Rev. 20:10).

1:14–16 In this passage, Jude quotes from the apocryphal Book of Enoch. Although this book was not included in the canon of Scripture, early church historians wrote that the church accepted it as a reliable source of information. Therefore, it is plausible to conclude that Jude, writing under the inspiration of the Holy Spirit, used this prophecy of Enoch as a means of describing those false teachers who sought to lead believers astray from the true faith in Christ.

THE REVELATION

to John

The author of the Book of Revelation is the Apostle John (Rev. 1:1, 9; 21:2; 22:8; see the introductions to John's Gospel and 1 John). The title of the book describes the content and purpose of John's writing. The word "Revelation" means "to take the cover off," from the Greek word *apokálupsis* (602). It is the uncovering or unveiling of the glory of Christ and of future events (1 Thess 1:19).

Revelation was addressed to the churches of Asia Minor (Rev. 1:4) specifically named in chapters two and three. This book was written at a time when these churches were undergoing persecution and difficulty. The two most important such periods were during the reigns of Nero in A.D. 37–68 and Domitian in A.D. 81–96.

There are four views on the interpretation of the Book of Revelation. The first is the preterist view. It interprets the events and visions as belonging to the past, particularly to the Roman Empire of the first century A.D. The proponents of this view explain the highly symbolic nature of the book as John's endeavor to hide the real meaning of what he was saying from the general populace, making it relative to the believers who lived at that time. It is very unlikely that this view is correct in light of the prophetic nature of the book (Rev. 1:3). Some of the descriptions are of future events and cannot possibly be identified as historical ones.

The second view is the future historical view, maintaining that Revelation is a panoramic view of history from the first century A.D. to the Second Coming of Christ. However, this position is unsubstantiated because historians have been unable to identify precise events in history which would answer particular visions that are symbolized.

The third view is the symbolic (allegorical) view which contends that Revelation portrays the continuing conflict between the forces of good and evil throughout the span of human history. According to this view, the book was designed to give encouragement because good will triumph in the end.

The fourth view is the futuristic view, maintaining that from chapter four to the end of the book, Revelation deals with end-time events. According to this view, Revelation is not concerned with the events of John's own day as much as later historical events, particularly those things that will take place in connection with the Second Coming of Christ. The proponents of this view would outline Revelation as follows (cf. Rev. 1:19): chapter one deals with the past; chapters two and three discuss things that were present at that time; chapters four through twenty-two speak of things that are yet to come, which things include the "Day of the Lord" as well as the Second Coming of Christ (cf. Rev. 4:1).

1 🗝The Revelation*602* of Jesus
Christ,*5547* [a]which God*2316* gave unto
him, to shew unto his servants*1401* things
which [b]must shortly come to pass; and
[c]he sent and signified *it* by his angel*32*
unto his servant John:
2 [a]Who bare record of the word*3056*

1 [a]John 3:32; 8:26; 12:49 [b]Rev. 1:3; 4:1 [c]Rev. 22:16
2 [a]1Cor. 1:6; Rev. 1:9; 6:9; 12:17

🗝 **1:1** There are some who interpret the phrase, "must shortly come to pass," to mean that the events of the Book of Revelation have already taken place. They suggest that John wrote about things that happened either in his lifetime or the lifetime of those in the churches to which he was writing. The problem with this view is that in Revelation 22:7, Jesus said He Himself was coming "quickly." This is the same Greek word that is translated "shortly" here in chapter one. Therefore, if these things have already taken place, Christ has already come and there is no hope for believers.
This verse should be understood to mean that the events in the book will occur "soon" in God's

(continued on next page)

of God, and of the testimony[3141] of Jesus
Christ, and of all things [b]that he saw.
3 [a]Blessed[3107] *is* he that [ppt]readeth,
and they that [ppt]hear the words of this
prophecy,[4394] and [ppt]keep those things
which are written therein: for [b]the
time[2540] *is* at hand.

"To the Seven Churches"

4 John to the seven churches[1577]
which are in Asia: Grace[5485] *be* unto you,
and peace,[1515] from him [a]which is, and
[b]which was, and which is to come; [c]and
from the seven Spirits[4151] which are before his throne;
🔑 5 And from Jesus Christ, [a]*who is* the
faithful[4103] witness,[3144] *and* the [b]first begotten[4416] of the dead,[3498] and [c]the prince[758]
of the kings[935] of the earth.[1093] Unto him
[d]that [apt]loved[25] us, [e]and [apt]washed us from
our sins[266] in his own blood,[129]
6 And [ao]hath [a]made us kings[935] and
priests[2409] unto God and his Father; [b]to
him *be* glory[1391] and dominion[2904] for
ever[165,1519][3588] and ever. Amen.[281]
7 [a]Behold, he cometh with clouds;
and every eye shall see him, and [b]they
also which pierced him: and all kindreds
of the earth shall wail[2875] because of
him. Even so, Amen.
8 [a]I am Alpha[1] and Omega,[5598] the
beginning[746] and the ending,[5056] saith the
Lord, [b]which is, and which was, and
which is to come, the Almighty.[3841]

John on the Isle of Patmos

9 I John, who also am your brother,[80]
and [a]companion in tribulation,[2347] and [b]in
the kingdom[932] and patience[5281] of Jesus
Christ, [ao]was in the isle that is called
Patmos, [c]for the word[3056] of God, and for
the testimony[3141] of Jesus Christ.

10 [a]I [ao]was in the Spirit[4151] on [b]the
Lord's[2960] day,[2250] and heard behind me
[c]a great voice, as of a trumpet,
11 Saying, [a]I am Alpha and Omega,
[b]the first[4413] and the last:[2078] and,
What thou seest, write[1125] in a book, and
send *it* unto the seven churches which
are in Asia; unto Ephesus, and unto Smyrna, and unto Pergamos, and unto Thyatira, and unto Sardis, and unto
Philadelphia, and unto Laodicea.
12 And I turned to see the voice that
[ao]spake[2980] with me. And being turned,
[a]I saw seven golden candlesticks;
13 [a]And in the midst of the seven
candlesticks [b]*one* like unto the Son[5207] of
man,[444] [c]clothed with a garment down to
the foot,[4158] and [d]girt about[4314] the
paps[3149] with a golden girdle.[2223]
14 His head and [a]*his* hairs *were* white
like wool, as white as snow; and [b]his eyes
were as a flame of fire;
15 [a]And his feet like unto fine
brass, as if they burned in a furnace;
and [b]his voice as the sound of many waters.
16 [a]And he [ppt]had in his right[1188]
hand seven stars: and [b]out of his mouth
went a sharp twoedged sword: [c]and
his countenance[3799] *was* as the sun
shineth[5316] in his strength.[1411]
17 And [a]when I saw him, I fell at his
feet as dead. And [b]he laid his right hand
upon me, saying unto me, Fear[5399] not; [c]I
am the first[4413] and the last:[2078]
🔑 18 [a]*I am* he that liveth,[2198] and was
dead;[3498] and, behold, [b]I am alive[2198] for
evermore,[165,1519][3588] Amen;[281] and [c]have
the keys of hell[86] and of death.[2288]

2 [b]1John 1:1
3 [a]Luke 11:28; Rev. 22:7 [b]Rom. 13:11; James 5:8; 1Pet. 4:7; Rev. 22:10
4 [a]Ex. 3:14; Rev. 1:8 [b]John 1:1 [c]Zech. 3:9; 4:10; Rev. 3:1; 4:5; 5:6
5 [a]John 8:14; 1Tim. 6:13; Rev. 3:14 [b]1Cor. 15:20; Col. 1:18 [c]Eph. 1:20; Rev. 17:14; 19:16 [d]John 13:34; 15:9; Gal. 2:20 [e]Heb. 9:14; 1John 1:7
6 [a]1Pet. 2:5, 9; Rev. 5:10; 20:6 [b]1Tim. 6:16; Heb. 13:21; 1Pet. 4:11; 5:11
7 [a]Dan. 7:13; Matt. 24:30; 26:64; Acts 1:11 [b]Zech. 12:10; John 19:37
8 [a]Isa. 41:4; 44:6; 48:12; Rev. 1:11, 17; 2:8; 21:6; 22:13 [b]Rev. 1:4; 4:8; 11:17; 16:5
9 [a]Phil. 1:7; 4:14; 2Tim. 1:8 [b]Rom. 8:17; 2Tim. 2:12 [c]Rev. 1:2; 6:9
10 [a]Acts 10:10; 2Cor. 12:2; Rev. 4:2; 17:3; 21:10 [b]John 20:26; Acts 20:7; 1Cor. 16:2 [c]Rev. 4:1; 10:8
11 [a]Rev. 1:8 [b]Rev. 1:17
12 [a]Ex. 25:37; Zech. 4:2; Rev. 1:20
13 [a]Rev. 2:1 [b]Ezek. 1:26; Dan. 7:13; 10:16; Rev. 14:14 [c]Dan. 10:5 [d]Rev. 15:6
14 [a]Dan. 7:9 [b]Dan. 10:6; Rev. 2:18; 19:12
15 [a]Ezek. 1:7; Dan. 10:6; Rev. 2:18 [b]Ezek. 43:2; Dan. 10:6; Rev. 14:2; 19:6 **16** [a]Rev. 1:20; 2:1; 3:1 [b]Isa. 49:2; Eph. 6:17; Heb. 4:12; Rev. 2:12, 16; 19:15, 21 [c]Acts 26:13; Rev. 10:1 **17** [a]Ezek. 1:28 [b]Dan. 8:18; 10:10 [c]Isa. 41:4; 44:6; 48:12; Rev. 1:11; 2:8; 22:13
18 [a]Rom. 6:9 [b]Rev. 4:9; 5:14 [c]Ps. 68:20; Rev. 20:1

(continued from previous page)
view of time. He is relating these events to infinite time frames. The human mind is only able to relate to those things which he can see and understand. Hence, the proper way to interpret this verse is to realize that when these events do happen (though the specific time is unknown to believers but known to God), they will occur suddenly and quickly.

🔑 **1:5** See note on Colossians 1:15–18.

🔑 **1:18** See note on Ephesians 4:8–10.

19 Write[1125] [a]the things which thou hast seen, [b]and the things which are, [c]and the things which shall be hereafter;

20 The mystery[3466] [a]of the seven stars which thou sawest in my right hand, [b]and the seven golden candlesticks. The seven stars are [c]the angels[32] of the seven churches:[1577] and [d]the seven candlesticks which thou sawest are the seven churches.

Ephesus

2 🗝Unto the angel[32] of the church[1577] of Ephesus write; These things saith [a]he that [ppt]holdeth the seven stars in his right hand,[1188] [b]who [ppt]walketh in the midst of the seven golden candlesticks;

2 [a]I know thy works,[2041] and thy labour, and thy patience, and how thou canst not bear them which are evil:[2556] and [b]thou [aom]hast tried[3985] them [c]which say they are apostles,[652] and are not, and hast found them liars:

3 And hast borne, and hast patience,[5281] and for my name's sake hast laboured, and [pfi]hast [a]not fainted.[2577]

4 Nevertheless I have *somewhat* against thee, because thou hast left thy first love.[26]

5 Remember therefore from whence thou [pfi]art fallen, and repent,[3340] and do the first works;[2041] [a]or else I will come unto thee quickly, and will remove thy candlestick out of his place, except thou [aosb]repent.

6 But this thou hast, that thou hatest the deeds[2041] of [a]the Nicolaitanes, which I also hate.

7 [a]He that hath an ear, let him hear what the Spirit[4151] saith unto the churches; To him that [ppt]overcometh will I give [b]to eat of [c]the tree of life,[2222] which is in the midst of the paradise[3857] of God.

Smyrna

🗝8 And unto the angel[32] of the church[1577] in Smyrna write; These things saith [a]the first[4413] and the last,[2078] which was dead,[3498] and is alive;[2198]

9 [a]I know thy works, and tribulation, and poverty, (but thou art [b]rich) and *I know* the blasphemy[988] of [c]them which say they are Jews, and are not, [d]but *are* the synagogue[4864] of Satan.[4567]

10 [a]Fear[5399] none of those things which thou shalt suffer: behold, the devil[1228] shall cast *some* of you into prison, that ye [asbp]may be tried;[3985] and ye shall have tribulation[2347] ten days: [b]be thou faithful[4103] unto death,[2288] and I will give thee [c]a crown of life.[2222]

11 [a]He that [ppt]hath an ear, let him hear what the Spirit saith unto the churches; He that [ppt]overcometh [asbp]shall not be hurt[91] of [b]the second death.[2288]

Pergamos

🗝12 And to the angel[32] of the church[1577] in Pergamos write; These things saith [a]he which hath the sharp sword with two edges;

19 [a]Rev. 1:12 [b]Rev. 2:1 [c]Rev. 4:1
20 [a]Rev. 1:16 [b]Rev. 1:12 [c]Mal. 2:7; Rev. 2:1 [d]Zech. 4:2; Matt. 5:15; Phil. 2:15
1 [a]Rev. 1:16, 20 [b]Rev. 1:13
2 [a]Ps. 1:6; Rev. 2:9, 13, 19; 3:1, 8, 15 [b]1John 4:1 [c]2Cor. 11:13; 2Pet. 2:1
3 [a]Gal. 6:9; Heb. 12:3, 5
5 [a]Matt. 21:41, 43
6 [a]Rev. 2:15
7 [a]Matt. 11:15; 13:9, 43; Rev. 2:11, 17, 29; 3:6, 13, 22; 13:9 [b]Rev. 22:2, 14 [c]Gen. 2:9
8 [a]Rev. 1:8, 17, 18
9 [a]Rev. 2:2 [b]Luke 12:21; 1Tim. 6:18; James 2:5 [c]Rom. 2:17, 28, 29; 9:6 [d]Rev. 3:9
10 [a]Matt. 10:22 [b]Matt. 24:13 [c]James 1:12; Rev. 3:11
11 [a]Rev. 2:7; 13:9 [b]Rev. 20:14; 21:8
12 [a]Rev. 1:16

🗝 **2:1—3:22** These chapters contain letters to the seven churches. These were local churches in Asia Minor.

🗝 **2:1–7** Ephesus was sixty miles northeast of the Isle of Patmos, where the Apostle John was writing, and thirty-five miles South of modern Izmir.

🗝 **2:8–11** Smyrna (modern-day Izmir) was thirty-five miles north of Ephesus. It was the most splendid of the seven cities and was the pride of Asia. Emperor worship developed in this city, and the Christians there suffered greatly because they would not worship Caesar. Polycarp, the bishop of the church in Smyrna, was martyred here in A.D. 156 because he refused to call Caesar "Lord."

🗝 **2:12–17** The city of Pergamus (or Pergamos) was fifteen miles from the Aegean Coast and seventy miles north of Smyrna. An immense altar to Zeus, the chief of the Greek mythological gods, stood on the Acropolis (the upper or higher part of the city) one thousand feet above the plain. This may be what is being referred to as "Satan's seat" (v. 13).

13 [a]I know thy works, and where
thou dwellest, *even* [b]where Satan's4567
seat *is:* and thou holdest fast my name,
and aomhast not denied720 my faith,4102
even in those days wherein Antipas
was my faithful4103 martyr,3144 who
was slain among you, where Satan
dwelleth.

14 But I have a few things against
thee, because thou hast there them that
ppthold the doctrine1322 of [a]Balaam, who
ipftaught1321 Balac ainfto cast a stum-
blingblock4625 before the children5207 of
Israel, [b]to eat things sacrificed unto idols,
[c]and to commit fornication.4203

15 So hast thou also them that
ppthold the doctrine [a]of the Nicolaitanes,
which thing I hate.

16 Repent;3340 or else I will come
unto thee quickly, and [a]will fight against
them with the sword of my mouth.

17 [a]He that hath an ear, let him hear
what the Spirit saith unto the churches;
To him that pptovercometh will I give
to eat of the hidden manna,3131 and
will give him a white stone, and in the
stone [b]a new2537 name3686 written, which
no man knoweth saving he that pptre-
ceiveth *it.*

Thyatira

🔑 18 And unto the angel32 of the
church1577 in Thyatira write; These
things saith the Son5207 of God,2316 [a]who
ppthath his eyes like unto a flame of fire,
and his feet *are* like fine brass;

19 [a]I know thy works, and charity,26
and service,1248 and faith,4102 and
thy patience,5281 and thy works;2041
and the last2078 *to be* more than the
first.4413

20 Notwithstanding I have a few
things against thee, because thou suffer-
est that woman [a]Jezebel, which calleth
herself a prophetess,4398 to teach1321 and
to seduce my servants1401 [b]to commit fornication, and to eat things sacrificed unto
idols.

21 And I gave her space5550 [a]to
repent3340 of her fornication; and she repented not.

22 Behold, I will cast her into a bed,
and them that pptcommit adultery with
her into great tribulation,2347 except they
repent of their deeds.2041

23 And I will kill her children with
death; and all the churches shall know
that [a]I am he which pptsearcheth the
reins3510 and hearts:2588 and [b]I will give
unto every one of you according to your
works.2041

24 But unto you I say, and unto the
rest in Thyatira, as many as have not
this doctrine,1322 and which aohave not
known1097 the depths of Satan,4567 as
they speak; [a]I ftwill put upon you none
other burden.

25 But [a]that which ye have *already*
hold fast till I come.

26 And he that overcometh, and
keepeth [a]my works unto the end,5056 [b]to
him will I give power1849 over the na-
tions:1484

27 [a]And he shall rule4165 them with
a rod of iron; as the vessels of a potter
shall they be broken to shivers:4937 even
as I received of my Father.3962

28 And I will give him [a]the morning
star.

29 [a]He that hath an ear, let him hear
what the Spirit saith unto the churches.

Sardis

3 🔑 And unto the angel32 of the
church1577 in Sardis write; These
things saith he [a]that ppthath the seven
Spirits4151 of God, and the seven stars; [b]I
know thy works,2041 that thou hast a

13 [a]Rev. 2:2 [b]Rev. 2:9
14 [a]Num. 24:14; 25:1; 31:16; 2Pet. 2:15; Jude 1:11 [b]Acts 15:29; 1Cor. 8:9, 10; 10:19, 20; Rev. 2:20 [c]1Cor. 6:13
15 [a]Rev. 2:6
16 [a]Isa. 11:4; 2Thess. 2:8; Rev. 1:16; 19:15, 21
17 [a]Rev. 2:7, 11 [b]Rev. 3:12; 19:12
18 [a]Rev. 1:14, 15
19 [a]Rev. 2:2
20 [a]1Kgs. 16:31; 21:25; 2Kgs. 9:7 [b]Ex. 34:15; Acts 15:20, 29; 1Cor. 10:19, 20; Rev. 2:14
21 [a]Rom. 2:4; Rev. 9:20
23 [a]1Sam. 16:7; 1Chr. 28:9; 29:17; 2Chr. 6:30; Ps. 7:9; Jer. 11:20; 17:10; 20:12; John 2:24, 25; Acts 1:24; Rom. 8:27 [b]Ps. 62:12; Matt. 16:27; Rom. 2:6; 14:12; 2Cor. 5:10; Gal. 6:5; Rev. 20:12
24 [a]Acts 15:28
25 [a]Rev. 3:11
26 [a]John 6:29; 1John 3:23 [b]Matt. 19:28; Luke 22:29, 30; 1Cor. 6:3; Rev. 3:21; 20:4
27 [a]Ps. 2:8, 9; 49:14; Dan. 7:22; Rev. 12:5; 19:15
28 [a]2Pet. 1:19; Rev. 22:16
29 [a]Rev. 2:7

1 [a]Rev. 1:4, 16; 4:5; 5:6 [b]Rev. 2:2

🔑 **2:18–29** Thyatira was the least important of the seven cities that are mentioned and was about halfway between Pergamum and Sardis. It was more important commercially than politically.

🔑 **3:1–6** Sardis was fifty miles due east of Smyrna and thirty miles southeast of Thyatira. The richest man living, Croesus, reigned here. The city was devastated by an earthquake in A.D. 17, but was later rebuilt.

name[3686] that thou livest,[2198] [c]and art
dead.[3498]
2 Be watchful, and strengthen the
things which remain that are ready to
die: for I have not found thy works
perfect[4137] before God.
3 [a]Remember therefore how thou
[pfi]hast received and heard, and [pim]hold
fast, and [aim][b]repent.[3340] [c]If therefore thou
[asba]shalt not watch,[1127] I will come on
thee as a thief, and thou shalt [efn]not know
what hour I will come upon thee.
4 Thou hast [a]a few names[3686] even in
Sardis which [ao]have not [b]defiled[3435] their
garments; and they shall walk with me
[c]in white: for they are worthy.
5 He that [ppt]overcometh, [a]the same
shall be clothed in white raiment; and I
will not [b]blot out his name out of the
[c]book[976] of life,[2222] but [d]I will confess[1843]
his name before my Father,[3962] and be-
fore his angels.
6 [a]He that hath an ear, [aim]let him
hear[191] what the Spirit saith unto the
churches.

Philadelphia

🔑 7 And to the angel[32] of the
church[1577] in Philadelphia write; These
things saith [a]he that is holy,[40] [b]he that is
true,[228] he that hath [c]the key of David,
[d]he that [ppt]openeth,[455] and no man
[pin]shutteth; and [pin][e]shutteth, and no man
openeth;
8 [a]I know thy works:[2041] behold, I
have set before thee [b]an open door,
and no man can [ainf]shut it: for thou hast
a little strength, and [ao]hast kept my
word,[3056] and [aom]hast not denied[720] my
name.[3686]
9 Behold, I will make [a]them of the
synagogue[4864] of Satan,[4567] which say
they are Jews, and are not, but do lie; behold, [b]I will make them to come and
worship[4352] before thy feet, and to know
that I have loved[25] thee.
10 Because thou hast kept the
word[3056] of my patience,[5281] [a]I also will
keep thee from the hour[5610] of temptation,[3986] which shall come[2064] upon [b]all
the world,[3625] to try[3985] them that dwell
[c]upon the earth.[1093]
11 Behold, [a]I come quickly: [b]hold that
fast which thou hast, that no man take
[c]thy crown.[4735]
12 Him that overcometh will I make
[a]a pillar in the temple[3485] of my God,
and he shall go no more out: and [b]I will
write[1125] upon him the name[3686] of my
God, and the name of the city of my
God, *which is* [c]new[2537] Jerusalem, which
cometh down out of heaven[3772] from my
God: [d]and *I will write upon him* my
new[2537] name.
13 [a]He that hath an ear, [aim]let him
hear[191] what the Spirit saith unto the
churches.

Laodicea

🔑 14 And unto the angel[32] of the
church[1577] [I]of the Laodiceans write;
[a]These things saith the Amen,[281] [b]the
faithful[4103] and true[228] witness,[3144] [c]the
beginning[746] of the creation[2937] of God;
15 [a]I know thy works,[2041] that thou
art neither cold nor hot: I would thou
wert[1498] cold or hot.
16 So then because thou art lukewarm, and neither cold nor hot, I will
spue[1692] thee out of my mouth.
17 Because thou sayest, [a]I am rich,
and increased with goods, and have need

1 [c]Eph. 2:1, 5; 1Tim. 5:6
3 [a]1Tim. 6:20; 2Tim. 1:13; Rev. 3:11 [b]Rev. 3:19 [c]Matt. 24:42, 43; 25:13; Mark 13:33; Luke 12:39, 40; 1Thess. 5:2, 6; 2Pet. 3:10; Rev. 16:15
4 [a]Acts 1:15 [b]Jude 1:23 [c]Rev. 4:4; 6:11; 7:9, 13
5 [a]Rev. 19:8 [b]Ex. 32:32; Ps. 69:28 [c]Phil. 4:3; Rev. 13:8; 17:8; 20:12, 21:27 [d]Matt. 10:32; Luke 12:8
6 [a]Rev. 2:7
7 [a]Acts 3:14 [b]1John 5:20; Rev. 1:5; 3:14; 6:10; 19:11 [c]Isa. 22:22; Luke 1:32; Rev. 1:18 [d]Matt. 16:19 [e]Job 12:14
8 [a]Rev. 3:1 [b]1Cor. 16:9; 2Cor. 2:12
9 [a]Rev. 2:9 [b]Isa. 49:23; 60:14
10 [a]2Pet. 2:9 [b]Luke 2:1 [c]Isa. 24:17
11 [a]Phil. 4:5; Rev. 1:3; 22:7, 12, 20 [b]Rev. 2:25; 3:3 [c]Rev. 2:10
12 [a]1Kgs. 7:21; Gal. 2:9 [b]Rev. 2:17; 14:1; 22:4 [c]Gal. 4:26; Heb. 12:22; Rev. 21:2, 10 [d]Rev. 22:4
13 [a]Rev. 2:7
14 IOr, *in Laodicea* [a]Isa. 65:16 [b]Rev. 1:5; 3:7; 19:11; 22:6 [c]Col. 1:15
15 [a]Rev. 3:1
17 [a]Hos. 12:8; 1Cor. 4:8

🔑 **3:7–13** The city of Philadelphia was built in a dangerous volcanic area located about twenty-eight miles southeast of Sardis. It was completely destroyed by an earthquake in A.D. 17. Emperor Tiberius required no taxes from its citizens for five years to allow them funds to rebuild the city.

🔑 **3:14–22** Laodicea was located about forty miles southeast of Philadelphia and one hundred miles east of Ephesus. It was known as a banking center and had a famous medical school. The city is in complete ruins today.

🔑 **3:14** In this verse, the Lord Jesus Christ is called "the beginning of the creation of God." In this instance, the Greek word *archē* (746), translated "beginning," literally refers to Him as the originator or cause of creation.

of nothing; and knowest not that thou art
wretched, and miserable,[1652] and poor,
and blind, and naked:[1131]
18 I counsel thee [ainf][a]to buy of me
gold tried in the fire, that thou [aosb]mayest
be rich; and [b]white raiment, that thou
mayest be clothed, and *that* the shame[152]
of thy nakedness[1132] [asbp]do not appear;[5319] and anoint thine eyes with eyesalve, that thou mayest see.
19 [a]As many as I love,[5368] I rebuke[1651] and chasten:[3811] [aim]be zealous
therefore, and [aim]repent.[3340]
20 Behold, [a]I stand at the door, and
knock: [b]if any man [aosb]hear my voice,
and [aosb]open the door, [c]I will come in to
him, and will sup[1172] with him, and he
with me.
21 To him that [ppt]overcometh [a]will I
grant [ainf]to sit with me in my throne, even
as I also overcame, and [ao]am set down
with my Father[3962] in his throne.
22 [a]He that [ppt]hath an ear, [aim]let him
hear[191] what the Spirit saith unto the
churches.

The Throne in Heaven

4 After this I looked, and, behold, a
door *was* [pfpp]opened in heaven:[3772]
and [a]the first voice which I heard *was* as
it were of a trumpet talking with me;
which said, [b]Come up hither, [c]and I will
shew thee things which must be hereafter.
2 And immediately [a]I [ao]was in the
spirit:[4151] and, behold, [b]a throne [ipf]was
set[2749] in heaven, and *one* [ppt]sat on the
throne.
3 And he that sat was to look
upon3706 like a jasper and a sardine
stone: [a]and *there was* a rainbow round
about the throne, in sight3706 like unto an
emerald.
4 [a]And round about the throne *were*
four and twenty seats: and upon the
seats I saw four and twenty elders[4245]
sitting, [b]clothed in white raiment;[2440]
[c]and they had on their heads crowns of
gold.
5 And out of the throne proceeded
[a]lightnings and thunderings and voices:
[b]and *there were* seven lamps of fire burning before the throne, which are [c]the
seven Spirits of God.
6 And before the throne *there was* [a]a
sea of glass like unto crystal: [b]and in the
midst of the throne, and round about the
throne, *were* four beasts[2226] full of eyes
before [c]and behind.
7 [a]And the first beast *was* like a lion,
and the second beast like a calf, and
the third beast had a face as a man,
and the fourth beast *was* like a flying
eagle.
8 And the four beasts [ipf]had each[303]
of them [a]six wings about *him;* and *they
were* full of eyes [b]within: and they rest
not day and night, saying, [c]Holy,[40] holy,
holy, [d]Lord[2962] God[2316] Almighty,3841
[e]which was, and is, and is to come.
9 And when those beasts [ft]give
glory[1391] and honour and thanks to him
that [ppt]sat on the throne, [a]who [ppt]liv-
eth[2198] for ever[165] and ever,
10 [a]The four and twenty elders[4245]
[ft]fall down before him that sat on the
throne, [b]and [pin]worship him that liveth
for ever and ever, [c]and [pin]cast their
crowns[4735] before the throne, saying,
11 [a]Thou art worthy, O Lord, [ainf]to
receive glory and honour and power:
[b]for thou [ao]hast created[2936] all things, and
for thy pleasure they are and were created.

The Seven-Sealed Book

5 And I saw in the right hand[1188] of
him that [ppt]sat on the throne [a]a
book975 written within and on the backside, [pfpp][b]sealed with seven seals.
2 And I saw a strong angel[32] proclaiming[2784] with a loud voice, Who is
worthy514 [ainf]to open the book, and [ainf]to
loose[3089] the seals thereof?
3 And no man [a]in heaven,[3772] nor in
earth, neither under the earth,[1093] [ipf]was
able [ainf]to open the book, neither [pinf]to look
thereon.
4 And I [ipf]wept much, because no
man was found[2147] worthy to open
and to read the book, neither to look
thereon.

18 [a]Isa. 55:1; Matt. 13:44; 25:9 [b]2Cor. 5:3; Rev. 7:13; 16:15; 19:8
19 [a]Job 5:17; Prov. 3:11, 12; Heb. 12:5, 6; James 1:12
20 [a]Song 5:2 [b]Luke 12:37 [c]John 14:23
21 [a]Matt. 19:28; Luke 22:30; 1Cor. 6:2; 2Tim. 2:12; Rev. 2:26, 27
22 [a]Rev. 2:7

1 [a]Rev. 1:10 [b]Rev. 11:12 [c]Rev. 1:19; 22:6
2 [a]Rev. 1:10; 17:3; 21:10 [b]Isa. 6:1; Jer. 17:12; Ezek. 1:26; 10:1; Dan. 7:9
3 [a]Ezek. 1:28
4 [a]Rev. 11:16 [b]Rev. 3:4, 5; 6:11; 7:9, 13, 14; 19:14 [c]Rev. 4:10
5 [a]Rev. 8:5; 16:18 [b]Ex. 37:23; 2Chr. 4:20; Ezek. 1:13; Zech. 4:2 [c]Rev. 1:4; 3:1; 5:6
6 [a]Ex. 38:8; Rev. 15:2 [b]Ezek. 1:5 [c]Rev. 4:8
7 [a]Num. 2:2; Ezek. 1:10; 10:14
8 [a]Isa. 6:2 [b]Rev. 4:6 [c]Isa. 6:3 [d]Rev. 1:8 [e]Rev. 1:4
9 [a]Rev. 1:18; 5:14; 15:7
10 [a]Rev. 5:8, 14 [b]Rev. 4:9 [c]Rev. 4:4
11 [a]Rev. 5:12 [b]Gen. 1:1; Acts 17:24; Eph. 3:9; Col. 1:16; Rev. 10:6

1 [a]Ezek. 2:9, 10 [b]Isa. 29:11; Dan. 12:4
3 [a]Rev. 5:13

5 And one of the elders[4245] saith unto me, [pim]Weep not: behold, [a]the Lion of the tribe of Juda, [b]the Root of David, [ao]hath prevailed to open the book, [c]and to loose[3089] the seven seals thereof.

6 And I beheld, and, lo, in the midst of the throne and of the four beasts,[2226] and in the midst of the elders, stood [a]a Lamb[721] as it [pfpp]had been slain, having seven horns and [b]seven eyes, which are [c]the seven Spirits[4151] of God sent forth into all the earth.[1093]

7 And he came and took the book out of the right hand[1188] [a]of him that sat upon the throne.

8 And when he [ao]had taken the book, [a]the four beasts and four *and* twenty elders fell down before the Lamb, having every one of them [sgb]harps, and golden vials full of [l]odours, [c]which are the prayers[4335] of saints.[40]

9 And [a]they [pin]sung a new[2537] song,[5603] saying, [b]Thou art worthy [ainf]to take the book, and [ainf]to open the seals thereof: [c]for thou wast slain,[4969] and [d]hast redeemed[59] us to God by thy blood[129] [e]out of every kindred,[5443] and tongue,[1100] and people,[2992] and nation;[1484]

10 [a]And [ao]hast made us unto our God kings[935] and priests:[2409] and we shall reign[936] on the earth.

11 And I beheld, and I heard the voice of many angels[32] [a]round about the throne and the beasts and the elders: and the number of them was [b]ten thousand times ten thousand, and thousands of thousands;

12 Saying with a loud voice, [a]Worthy[514] is the Lamb that [pfpp]was slain [ainf]to receive power,[1411] and riches,[4149] and wisdom,[4678] and strength,[2479] and honour,[5092] and glory,[1391] and blessing.[2129]

13 And [a]every creature[2938] which is in heaven,[3772] and on the earth,[1093] and under the earth, and such as are in the sea, and all that are in them, heard I saying, [b]Blessing, and honour, and glory, and power,[2904] *be* unto him [c]that [ppt]sitteth upon the throne, and unto the Lamb for ever and ever.

14 [a]And the four beasts [ipf]said, Amen.[281] And the four *and* twenty elders[4245] fell down and worshipped[4352] him [b]that liveth[2198] for ever[165,1519] [3588] and ever.

The Seven Seals Opened

6 ⚷And [a]I saw when the Lamb opened one of the seals, and I heard, as it were the noise[5456] of thunder, [b]one of the four beasts[2226] saying, Come and see.

2 And I saw, and behold [a]a white horse: [b]and he that [ppt]sat on him [ppt]had a bow; [c]and a crown was given unto him: and he went forth conquering, and to [aosb]conquer.

3 And when he [ao]had opened the second seal, [a]I heard the second beast say, Come and see.

4 [a]And there went out another horse *that was* red: and *power* was given to him that sat thereon [ainf]to take peace[1515] from the earth,[1093] and that they [aosb]should kill one another: and there was given unto him a great sword.

5 And when he [ao]had opened the third seal, [a]I heard the third beast say, Come and see. And I beheld, and lo [b]a black horse; and he that [ppt]sat on him [ppt]had a pair of balances in his hand.

6 And I heard a voice in the midst of the four beasts say, A measure[5518] of wheat for a penny, and three measures of barley for a penny;[1220] and [a]*see* thou hurt[91] not the oil and the wine.

7 And when he [ao]had opened the fourth seal, [a]I heard the voice of the fourth beast say, Come and see.

8 [a]And I looked, and behold a pale horse: and his name that sat on him was Death,[2288] and Hell[86] [ipf]followed with him. And power[1849] was given [l]unto them over the fourth part of the earth, [ainfb]to kill

5 [a]Gen. 49:9, 10; Heb. 7:14 [b]Isa. 11:1, 10; Rom. 15:12; Rev. 22:16 [c]Rev. 5:1; 6:1
6 [a]Isa. 53:7; John 1:29, 36; 1Pet. 1:19; Rev. 5:9, 12; 13:8 [b]Zech. 3:9; 4:10 [c]Rev. 4:5
7 [a]Rev. 4:2
8 [l]Or, *incense* [a]Rev. 4:8, 10 [b]Rev. 14:2; 15:2 [c]Ps. 141:2; Rev. 8:3, 4
9 [a]Ps. 40:3; Rev. 14:3 [b]Rev. 4:11 [c]Rev. 5:6 [d]Acts 20:28; Rom. 3:24; 1Cor. 6:20; 7:23; Eph. 1:7; Col. 1:14; Heb. 9:12; 1Pet. 1:18, 19; 2Pet. 2:1; 1John 1:7; Rev. 14:4 [e]Dan. 4:1; 6:25; Rev. 7:9; 11:9; 14:6
10 [a]Ex. 19:6; 1Pet. 2:5, 9; Rev. 1:6; 20:6; 22:5
11 [a]Rev. 4:4, 6 [b]Ps. 68:17; Dan. 7:10; Heb. 12:22
12 [a]Rev. 4:11
13 [a]Phil. 2:10; Rev. 5:3 [b]1Chr. 29:11; Rom. 9:5; 16:27; 1Tim. 6:16; 1Pet. 4:11; 5:11; Rev. 1:6 [c]Rev. 6:16; 7:10
14 [a]Rev. 19:4 [b]Rev. 4:9, 10

1 [a]Rev. 5:5-7 [b]Rev. 4:7
2 [a]Zech. 6:3; Rev. 19:11 [b]Ps. 45:4, 5 [c]Zech. 6:11; Rev. 14:14
3 [a]Rev. 4:7
4 [a]Zech. 6:2
5 [a]Rev. 4:7 [b]Zech. 6:2
6 [a]Rev. 9:4
7 [a]Rev. 4:7
8 [l]Or, *to him* [a]Zech. 6:3 [b]Ezek. 14:21

⚷ **6:1–17** This chapter tells of the beginning of the time known as the "Day of the Lord" in which God's judgment will be poured out on the earth (see notes on Dan. 9:24–27 and 1 Thess. 5:2).

with sword, and with hunger, and with
death, [c]and with the beasts[2342] of the
earth.
9 And when he [ao]had opened the
fifth seal, I saw under [a]the altar[2379]
[b]the souls[5590] of them that were slain [c]for
the word[3056] of God, and for [d]the testimony which they [ipf]held:
10 And they cried with a loud voice,
saying, [a]How long, O Lord,[1203] [b]holy[40]
and true,[228] [pin][c]dost thou not judge[2919]
and avenge[1556] our blood[129] on them that
[ppt]dwell on the earth?
11 And [a]white robes were given unto
every one of them; and it was said unto
them, [b]that they [asbm]should rest yet for a
little season,[5550] until their fellowservants
also and their brethren, that should be
killed as they *were,* [fm]should be fulfilled.[4137]
12 And I beheld when he had opened
the sixth seal, [a]and, lo, there [ao]was a
great earthquake; and [b]the sun became
black as sackcloth[4526] of hair, and the
moon became as blood;
13 [a]And the stars of heaven fell unto
the earth, even as a fig tree casteth her
untimely figs, when she [ppp]is shaken of
a mighty wind.
14 [a]And the heaven[3772] departed as a
scroll when it [ppp]is rolled together; and
[b]every mountain and island were moved
out of their places.
15 And the kings[935] of the earth, and
the great men, and the rich men, and the
chief captains, and the mighty men, and
every bondman,[1401] and every free man,
[a]hid themselves in the dens and in the
rocks of the mountains;
16 [a]And said to the mountains and
rocks, Fall[4098] on us, and [aim]hide us from
the face of him that [ppt]sitteth on the
throne, and from the wrath[3709] of the
Lamb:
17 [a]For the great day[2250] of his
wrath [ao]is come; [b]and who shall be able
[aifp]to stand?

8 [c]Lev. 26:22

9 [a]Rev. 8:3; 9:13; 14:18 [b]Rev. 20:4 [c]Rev. 1:9 [d]2Tim. 1:8; Rev. 12:17; 19:10

10 [a]Zech. 1:12 [b]Rev. 3:7 [c]Rev. 11:18; 19:2

11 [a]Rev. 3:4, 5; 7:9, 14 [b]Heb. 11:40; Rev. 14:13

12 [a]Rev. 16:18 [b]Joel 2:10, 31; 3:15; Matt. 24:29; Acts 2:20

13 [a]Rev. 8:10; 9:1

14 [a]Ps. 102:26; Isa. 34:4; Heb. 1:12, 13 [b]Jer. 3:23; 4:24; Rev. 16:20

15 [a]Isa. 2:19

16 [a]Hos. 10:8; Luke 23:30; Rev. 10:6

17 [a]Isa. 13:6; Zeph. 1:14; Rev. 16:14 [b]Ps. 76:7

1 [a]Dan. 7:2 [b]Rev. 9:4

3 [a]Rev. 6:6; 9:4 [b]Ezek. 9:4; Rev. 14:1 [c]Rev. 22:4

4 [a]Rev. 9:16 [b]Rev. 14:1

The 144,000

7 And after these things I saw four
angels[32] standing on the four corners
of the earth,[1093] [a]holding the four winds
of the earth, [b]that the wind [psa]should not
blow[4154] on the earth, nor on the sea, nor
on any tree.
2 And I saw another angel ascending
from the east, having the seal of the
living God:[2316] and he cried with a
loud voice to the four angels, to whom it
was given [ainf]to hurt[91] the earth and the
sea,
3 Saying, [aosi][a]Hurt not the earth, neither the sea, nor the trees, till we [aosb]have
[b]sealed the servants[1401] of our God [c]in
their foreheads.
4 [a]And I heard the number of them
which [pfpp]were sealed: *and there were*
sealed [b]an hundred *and* forty *and* four
thousand of all the tribes of the children[5207] of Israel.
5 Of the tribe of Juda *were* sealed
twelve thousand. Of the tribe of Reuben
were sealed twelve thousand. Of the tribe
of Gad *were* sealed twelve thousand.
6 Of the tribe of Aser *were* sealed
twelve thousand. Of the tribe of Nepthalim *were* sealed twelve thousand. Of the
tribe of Manasses *were* sealed twelve
thousand.
7 Of the tribe of Simeon *were* sealed
twelve thousand. Of the tribe of Levi
were sealed twelve thousand. Of the tribe
of Issachar *were* sealed twelve thousand.

7:1–17 The events in this chapter will occur between the opening of the sixth and seventh seals. In this period there are two distinct groups mentioned: 1) The 144,000 servants of God that are sealed are representative of the twelve tribes of Israel. This does not mean that only 144,000 Israelites will be saved, but that 12,000 chosen in each tribe will be protected from the wrath of Satan and the Antichrist. 2) The great multitude that will be saved are described as "they which came out of the great tribulation, and have washed their robes, and made them white in the blood of the Lamb" (Rev. 7:14). It is clear from 2 Thessalonians 2:10–12, that those who hear the gospel before the Tribulation and reject it, will be doomed to spend an eternity without Christ.

8 Of the tribe of Zabulon *were* sealed twelve thousand. Of the tribe of Joseph *were* sealed twelve thousand. Of the tribe of Benjamin *were* sealed twelve thousand.

The Congregation in Heaven

9 After this I beheld, and, lo, [a]a great multitude, which no man [ipf]could number, [b]of all nations,[1484] and kindreds,[5443] and people,[2992] and tongues,[1100] stood before the throne, and before the Lamb,[721] [pfpp][c]clothed with white robes, and palms in their hands;

10 And cried with a loud voice, saying, [a]Salvation[4991] to our God[2316] [b]which sitteth upon the throne, and unto the Lamb.

11 [a]And all the angels stood round about the throne, and *about* the elders[4245] and the four beasts, and fell before the throne on their faces, and worshipped[4352] God,

12 [a]Saying, Amen:[281] Blessing,[2129] and glory,[1391] and wisdom,[4678] and thanksgiving,[2169] and honour,[5092] and power,[1411] and might,[2479] *be* unto our God[2316] for ever[165,1519][3588] and ever. Amen.

13 And one of the elders answered, saying unto me, What are these which [pfpp]are arrayed in [a]white robes? and whence came they?

14 And I said unto him, Sir,[2962] thou knowest. And he said to me, [a]These are they which [ppt]came out of great tribulation, and [ao]have [b]washed[4150] their robes, and made them white in the blood[129] of the Lamb.[721]

15 Therefore are they before the throne of God, and serve him day and night in his temple:[3485] and he that sitteth on the throne shall [a]dwell among them.

16 [a]They shall hunger no more, neither thirst any more; [b]neither shall the sun light on them, nor any heat.

17 For the Lamb which is in[303] the midst of the throne [a]shall feed[4165] them, and shall lead them unto living[2198] fountains[4077] of waters: [b]and God shall wipe away all tears from their eyes.

7:9 [a]Rom. 11:25 [b]Rev. 5:9 [c]Rev. 3:5, 18; 4:4; 6:11; 7:14
10 [a]Ps. 3:8; Isa. 43:11; Jer. 3:23; Hos. 13:4; Rev. 19:1 [b]Rev. 5:13
11 [a]Rev. 4:6
12 [a]Rev. 5:13, 14
13 [a]Rev. 7:9
14 [a]Rev. 6:9; 17:6 [b]Isa. 1:18; Zech. 3:3-5; Heb. 9:14; 1John 1:7; Rev. 1:5
15 [a]Isa. 4:5, 6; Rev. 21:3
16 [a]Isa. 49:10 [b]Ps. 121:6; Rev. 21:4
17 [a]Ps. 23:1; 36:8; John 10:11, 14 [b]Isa. 25:8; Rev. 21:4
8:1 [a]Rev. 6:1
2 [a]Matt. 18:10; Luke 1:19 [b]2Chr. 29:25-28
3 [1]Or, *add it to the prayers* [a]Rev. 5:8 [b]Ex. 30:1; Rev. 6:9
4 [a]Ps. 141:2; Luke 1:10
5 [a]Rev. 16:18 [b]2Sam. 22:8; 1Kgs. 19:11; Acts 4:31
7 [a]Ezek. 38:22 [b]Rev. 16:2 [c]Isa. 2:13; Rev. 9:4
8 [a]Jer. 51:25; Amos 7:4 [b]Rev. 16:3 [c]Ezek. 14:19
9 [a]Rev. 16:3

Silence in Heaven

8 🔑And [a]when he had opened the seventh seal, there [aom]was silence in heaven[3772] about[5613] the space of half an hour.

2 [a]And I saw the seven angels[32] which stood before God;[2316] [b]and to them were given seven trumpets.

3 And another angel came and stood at the altar,[2379] having a golden censer;[3031] and there was given unto him much incense, that he [asba]should [1]offer *it* with [a]the prayers[4335] of all saints[40] upon [b]the golden altar which was before the throne.

4 And [a]the smoke of the incense, *which came* with the prayers of the saints, ascended up before God out of the angel's hand.

5 And the angel took the censer, and filled it with fire of the altar, and cast *it* into the earth: and [a]there were voices, and thunderings, and lightnings, [b]and an earthquake.

The Seven Trumpets

6 And the seven angels which had the seven trumpets prepared themselves to sound.

7 The first angel[32] sounded, [a]and there followed hail and fire mingled with blood,[129] and they were cast [b]upon the earth: and the third part [c]of trees was burnt up, and all green grass was burnt up.

8 And the second angel[32] sounded, [a]and as it were a great mountain burning with fire was cast into the sea: [b]and the third part of the sea [c]became blood;

9 [a]And the third part of the crea-

🔑 **8:1–7** The silence in heaven that accompanies the opening of the seventh seal (v. 1) is in anticipation of the sounding of the seven trumpet judgments (v. 6).

tures[2938] which were in the sea, and had life,[5590] died; and the third part of the ships were destroyed.

10 And the third angel[32] sounded, [a]and there fell a great star from heaven, burning as it were a lamp, [b]and it fell upon the third part of the rivers, and upon the fountains[4077] of waters;

11 [a]And the name of the star is called Wormwood: [b]and the third part of the waters became wormwood;[894] and many men died of the waters, because they were made bitter.

12 [a]And the fourth angel[32] sounded, and the third part of the sun was smitten, and the third part of the moon, and the third part of the stars; so as the third part of them was darkened, and the day shone[5316] not for a third part of it, and the night likewise.

13 And I beheld, [a]and heard an angel flying through the midst of heaven, saying with a loud voice, [b]Woe, woe, woe, to the inhabiters of the earth[1093] by reason of the other voices of the trumpet of the three angels, which are yet to sound!

9 And the fifth angel[32] sounded, [a]and I saw a star [pfp]fall from heaven[3772] unto the earth:[1093] and to him was given the key of [b]the bottomless pit.[5421]

2 And he opened the bottomless pit; [a]and there arose a smoke out of the pit, as the smoke of a great furnace; and the sun and the air were darkened by reason of the smoke of the pit.

3 And there came out of the smoke [a]locusts upon the earth: and unto them was given power,[1849] [b]as the scorpions of the earth have power.

4 And it was commanded them [a]that they [asba]should not hurt[91] [b]the grass of the earth, neither any green thing, neither any tree; but only those men[444] which have not [c]the seal of God[2316] in their foreheads.

5 And to them it was given that they should not kill them, [a]but that they [asbp]should be tormented five months: and their torment *was* as the torment of a scorpion, when he striketh a man.[444]

6 And in those days [a]shall men seek death,[2288] and shall not find it; and shall desire to die,[599] and death shall flee from them.

7 And [a]the shapes[3667] of the locusts *were* like unto horses prepared unto battle; [b]and on their heads *were* as it were crowns like gold, [c]and their faces *were* as the faces of men.[444]

8 And they had hair as the hair of women, and [a]their teeth were as *the teeth* of lions.

9 And they had breastplates, as it were breastplates of iron; and the sound of their wings *was* [a]as the sound of chariots of many horses running to battle.

10 And they had tails like unto scorpions, and there were stings in their tails: [a]and their power[1849] *was* [ainf]to hurt men[444] five months.

11 [a]And they had a king[935] over them, *which is* [b]the angel[32] of the bottomless pit, whose name in the Hebrew tongue *is* Abaddon,[3] but in the Greek tongue hath *his* name [I]Apollyon.[623]

12 [a]One woe is past; *and,* behold, there come two woes more hereafter.

13 And the sixth angel[32] sounded, and I heard a voice from the four horns of the golden altar[2379] which is before God,[2316]

14 Saying to the sixth angel which [ipf]had the trumpet, Loose the four angels which [pfpp]are bound [a]in the great river Euphrates.

15 And the four angels were loosed, which [pfpp]were prepared for an hour, and a day, and a month, and a year, for to slay[615] the third part of men.

16 And [a]the number of the army [b]of the horsemen *were* two hundred thousand thousand: [c]and I heard the number of them.

17 And thus I saw the horses in the vision,[3706] and them that [ppt]sat on them, having breastplates of fire, and of jacinth,[5191] and brimstone:[2306] [a]and the heads of the horses *were* as the heads of lions; and out of their mouths issued fire and smoke and brimstone.

18 By these three was the third part

10 [a]Isa. 14:12; Rev. 9:1 [b]Rev. 16:4
11 [a]Ruth 1:20 [b]Ex. 15:23; Jer. 9:15; 23:15
12 [a]Isa. 13:10; Amos 8:9
13 [a]Rev. 14:6; 19:17 [b]Rev. 9:12; 11:14
1 [a]Luke 10:18; Rev. 8:10 [b]Luke 8:31; Rev. 9:2, 11; 17:8; 20:1
2 [a]Joel 2:2, 10
3 [a]Ex. 10:4; Judg. 7:12 [b]Rev. 9:10
4 [a]Rev. 6:6; 7:3 [b]Rev. 8:7 [c]Ex. 12:23; Ezek. 9:4; Rev. 7:3
5 [a]Rev. 9:10; 11:7
6 [a]Job 3:21; Isa. 2:19; Jer. 8:3; Rev. 6:16
7 [a]Joel 2:4 [b]Nah. 3:17 [c]Dan. 7:8
8 [a]Joel 1:6
9 [a]Joel 2:5, 7
10 [a]Rev. 9:5
11 [I]That is to say, *A destroyer* [a]Eph. 2:2 [b]Rev. 9:1
12 [a]Rev. 8:13
14 [a]Rev. 16:12
16 [a]Ps. 68:17; Dan. 7:10 [b]Ezek. 38:4 [c]Rev. 7:4
17 [a]1Chr. 12:8; Isa. 5:28, 29

of men killed,615 by the fire, and by the smoke, and by the brimstone, which [ppt]issued out of their mouths.

19 For their power[1849] is in their mouth, and in their tails: [a]for their tails *were* like unto serpents, and had heads, and with them they do hurt.[91]

20 And the rest of the men[444] which were not killed by these plagues [a]yet repented[3340] not of the works[2041] of their hands, that they [aosb]should not worship4352 [b]devils,1140 [c]and idols[1497] of gold, and silver, and brass, and stone, and of wood: which neither can [pinf]see, nor [pinf]hear, nor [pinf]walk:

21 Neither repented they of their murders, [a]nor of their sorceries,[5331] nor of their fornication,4202 nor of their thefts.

A Strong Angel

10 🗝And I saw another mighty angel[32] [ppt]come down from heaven,[3772] [pfpp]clothed with a cloud: [a]and a rainbow *was* upon his head, and [b]his face *was* as it were the sun, and [c]his feet as pillars of fire:

2 And he [ipf]had in his hand a little book open: [a]and he set his right[1188] foot upon the sea, and *his* left *foot* on the earth,

3 And cried with a loud voice, as *when* a lion roareth: and when he had cried, [a]seven thunders uttered their voices.

4 And when the seven thunders had uttered their voices, I was about to write:[1125] and I heard a voice from heaven saying unto me, [aim][a]Seal up those things which the seven thunders uttered, and write them not.

5 And the angel which I saw stand upon the sea and upon the earth [a]lifted up[142] his hand to heaven,

6 And sware by him that [ppt]liveth[2198] for ever[165,1519] 3588 and ever, [a]who created[2936] heaven, and the things that therein are, and the earth, and the things that therein are, and the sea, and the things which are therein, [b]that there should be time no longer:

7 But [a]in the days of the voice of the seventh angel, when he shall begin[3195] [pinf]to sound, the mystery of God [asbp]should be finished,[5055] as he [ao]hath declared[2097] to his servants[1401] the prophets.[4396]

8 And [a]the voice which I heard from heaven [ppt]spake unto me again, and [ppt]said, Go *and* take the little book which [pfpp]is open in the hand of the angel which standeth upon the sea and upon the earth.

9 And I went unto the angel, and said unto him, Give me the little book. And he said unto me, [aim][a]Take *it,* and [aim]eat it up; and it shall make thy belly bitter, but it shall be in thy mouth sweet as honey.

10 And I took the little book out of the angel's hand, and ate it up; [a]and it was in my mouth sweet as honey: and as soon as I [ao]had eaten it, [b]my belly [aop]was bitter.

11 And he said unto me, Thou must [ainf]prophesy[4395] again before many peoples,[2992] and nations,[1484] and tongues,[1100] and kings.[935]

The Two Prophets of God

11 🗝And there was given me [a]a reed like unto a rod: and the angel[32] stood, saying, [b]Rise,[1453] and measure the temple[3485] of God, and the altar,[2379] and them that [ppt]worship4352 therein.

2 But [a]the court which is without1855 the temple leave out, and measure it not;

19 [a]Isa. 9:15
20 [a]Deut. 31:29 [b]Lev. 17:7; Deut. 32:17; Ps. 106:37; 1Cor. 10:20 [c]Ps. 115:4; 135:15; Dan. 5:23
21 [a]Rev. 22:15
1 [a]Ezek. 1:28 [b]Matt. 17:2; Rev. 1:16 [c]Rev. 1:15
2 [a]Matt. 28:18
3 [a]Rev. 8:5
4 [a]Dan. 8:26; 12:4, 9
5 [a]Ex. 6:8; Dan. 12:7
6 [a]Neh. 9:6; Rev. 4:11; 14:7 [b]Dan. 12:7; Rev. 16:17
7 [a]Rev. 11:15
8 [a]Rev. 10:4
9 [a]Jer. 15:16; Ezek. 2:8; 3:1-3
10 [a]Ezek. 3:3 [b]Ezek. 2:10
1 [a]Ezek. 40:3; Zech. 2:1; Rev. 21:15 [b]Num. 23:18
2 [a]Ezek. 40:17, 20

🗝 **10:1–11** The events in this chapter will occur between the sixth and the seventh trumpets. The words of the seven thunders were the only thing that John was not permitted to reveal.

🗝 **11:1–12** The exact identity of these two witnesses is unknown. There is speculation that they will be either Moses and Elijah, or Enoch and Elijah.

[b]for it is given unto the Gentiles:[1484] and the holy[40] city shall they [c]tread under foot[3961] [d]forty *and* two months.

3 And [1]I will give *power* unto my two [a]witnesses,[3144] [b]and they shall prophesy [c]a thousand two hundred *and* threescore days, clothed in sackcloth.[4526]

4 These are the [a]two olive trees, and the two candlesticks standing before the God[2316] of the earth.

5 And if any man will [ainf]hurt[91] them, [a]fire proceedeth out of their mouth, and devoureth their enemies: [b]and if any man will [ainf]hurt them, he must in this manner be killed.

6 These [a]have power[1849] [ainf]to shut heaven,[3772] that it rain not in the days of their prophecy:[4394] and [b]have power[1849] over waters [pinf]to turn them to blood,[129] and [ainf]to smite the earth with all plagues, as often as they will.

7 And when they [a]shall have finished their testimony,[3141] [b]the beast[2342] that [ppt]ascendeth [c]out of the bottomless pit [d]shall make war against them, and shall overcome them, and kill[615] them.

8 And their dead bodies *shall lie* in the street of [a]the great city, which spiritually[4153] is called Sodom and Egypt, [b]where also our Lord[2962] was crucified.[4717]

9 [a]And they of the people[2992] and kindreds[5443] and tongues[1100] and nations[1484] shall see their dead bodies three days and an half, [b]and shall not suffer their dead bodies to be put in graves.

10 [a]And they that [ppt]dwell upon the earth shall rejoice over them, and make merry, [b]and shall send gifts[1435] one to another; [c]because these two prophets[4396] tormented them that dwelt on the earth.

11 [a]And after three days and an half [b]the Spirit[4151] of life[2222] from God entered into them, and they stood upon their feet; and great fear[5401] fell upon them which [ppt]saw them.

12 And they heard a great voice from heaven saying unto them, Come up hither. [a]And they ascended up to heaven [b]in a cloud; [c]and their enemies beheld them.

13 And the same hour [ao][a]was there a great earthquake, [b]and the tenth part of the city fell, and in the earthquake were slain [c]of men seven thousand: and the remnant[3062] were affrighted,[1719] [d]and gave glory[1391] to the God[2316] of heaven.

Christ Will Rule For Ever

14 [a]The second woe is past; *and,* behold, the third woe cometh quickly.

15 And [a]the seventh angel sounded; [b]and there [ao]were great voices in heaven, saying, [c]The kingdoms[932] of this world[2889] are become *the kingdoms* of our Lord,[2962] and of his Christ;[5547] [d]and he shall reign[936] for ever[165,1519 3588] and ever.

16 And [a]the four and twenty elders,[4245] which [ppt]sat before God on their seats, fell upon their faces, and worshipped[4352] God,

17 Saying, We give thee thanks[2168], O Lord[2962] God[2316] Almighty,[3841] [a]which art, and wast, and art to come; because thou [pfi]hast taken to thee thy great power,[1411] [b]and [ao]hast reigned.[936]

18 [a]And the nations were angry, and thy wrath[3709] [ao]is come, [b]and the time[2540] of the dead,[3498] that they should be judged,[2919] and that thou [ainf]shouldest give reward unto thy servants[1401] the prophets,[4396] and to the saints,[40] and them that [ppt]fear[5399] thy name,[3686] [c]small and great; [d]and [ainf]shouldest destroy[1311] them which [ppt][1]destroy the earth.[1093]

19 And [a]the temple[3485] of God was opened in heaven,[3772] and there was seen in his temple the ark of his testament:[1242] and [b]there [ao]were lightnings, and voices, and thunderings, and an earthquake, [c]and great hail.

A Woman Gives Birth to a Son

12 And there [aop]appeared a great [1]wonder in heaven;[3772] a woman clothed with the sun, and the moon under her feet, and upon her head a crown of twelve stars:

2 And she being with child cried, [a]travailing in birth,[5605] and pained to be delivered.[5088]

---

2 [b]Ps. 79:1; Luke 21:24 [c]Dan. 8:10 [d]Rev. 13:5
3 [1]Or, *I will give unto my two witnesses that they may prophesy* [a]Rev. 20:4 [b]Rev. 19:10 [c]Rev. 12:6
4 [a]Ps. 52:8; Jer. 11:16; Zech. 4:3, 11, 14
5 [a]2Kgs. 1:10, 12; Jer. 1:10; 5:14; Ezek. 43:3; Hos. 6:5 [b]Num. 16:29
6 [a]1Kgs. 17:1; James 5:16, 17 [b]Ex. 7:19
7 [a]Luke 13:32 [b]Rev. 13:1, 11; 17:8 [c]Rev. 9:2 [d]Dan. 7:21; Zech. 14:2
8 [a]Rev. 14:8; 17:1, 5; 18:10 [b]Heb. 13:12; Rev. 18:24
9 [a]Rev. 17:15 [b]Ps. 79:2, 3
10 [a]Rev. 12:12; 13:8 [b]Esth. 9:19, 22 [c]Rev. 16:10
11 [a]Rev. 11:9 [b]Ezek. 37:5, 9, 10, 14
12 [a]Isa. 14:13; Rev. 12:5 [b]Isa. 60:8; Acts 1:9 [c]2Kgs. 2:1, 5, 7
13 [a]Rev. 6:12 [b]Rev. 16:19 [c]Rev. 3:4 [d]Josh 7:19; Rev. 14:7; 15:4
14 [a]Rev. 8:13; 9:12; 15:1
15 [a]Rev. 10:7 [b]Isa. 27:13; Rev. 16:17; 19:6 [c]Rev. 12:10 [d]Dan. 2:44; 7:14, 18, 27
16 [a]Rev. 4:4; 5:8; 19:4
17 [a]Rev. 1:4, 8; 4:8; 16:5
17 [a]Rev. 19:6
18 [1]Or, *corrupt* [a]Rev. 11:2, 9 [b]Dan. 7:9, 10; Rev. 6:10 [c]Rev. 19:5 [d]Rev. 13:10; 18:6
19 [a]Rev. 15:5, 8 [b]Rev. 8:5; 16:18 [c]Rev. 16:21

1 [1]Or, *sign*
2 [a]Isa. 66:7; Gal. 4:19

3 And there appeared another [I]wonder in heaven; and behold [a]a great red dragon, [b]having seven heads and ten horns, [c]and seven crowns[1238] upon his heads.

4 And [a]his tail drew the third part [b]of the stars of heaven, [c]and did cast them to the earth: and the dragon stood [d]before the woman which was ready to be delivered, [e]for to devour her child[5043] as soon as it was born.

5 And she brought forth a man child, [a]who was [pinf]to rule[4165] all nations[1484] with a rod of iron: and her child was caught up[726] unto God, and *to* his throne.

6 And [a]the woman fled into the wilderness, where she hath a place [pfpp]prepared of God, that they [psa]should feed her there [b]a thousand two hundred *and* threescore days.

7 And there [aom]was war in heaven: [a]Michael and his angels[32] [ainf]fought [b]against the dragon; and the dragon fought and his angels,

8 And prevailed[2480] not; neither was their place found any more in heaven.

9 And [a]the great dragon was cast out, [b]that old serpent, called the Devil,[1228] and Satan,[4567] [c]which [ppt]deceiveth the whole world: [d]he was cast out into the earth,[1093] and his angels[32] were cast out with him.

10 And I heard a loud voice saying in heaven, [a]Now [aom]is come salvation,[4991] and strength,[1411] and the kingdom[932] of our God,[2316] and the power[1849] of his Christ:[5547] for the accuser[2725] of our brethren[80] is cast down, [b]which [ppt]accused[2723] them before our God day and night.

11 And [a]they overcame him by the blood[129] of the Lamb,[721] and by the word[3056] of their testimony;[3141] [b]and they loved[25] not their lives[5590] unto the death.[2288]

12 Therefore [a]rejoice,[2165] *ye* heavens,[3772] and ye that [ppt]dwell in them. [b]Woe to the inhabiters of the earth and of the sea! for the devil is come down unto you, having great wrath,[2372] [c]because he knoweth that he hath but a short time.[2540]

13 And when the dragon saw that he was cast unto the earth, he persecuted [a]the woman which brought forth the man *child*.

14 [a]And to the woman were given two wings of a great eagle, [b]that she might fly [c]into the wilderness, into her place, where she is nourished [d]for a time, and times, and half a time, from the face of the serpent.

15 And the serpent [a]cast out of his mouth water as a flood after the woman, that he might cause her to be carried away of the flood.

16 And the earth[1093] helped the woman, and the earth opened her mouth, and swallowed up the flood which the dragon cast out of his mouth.

17 And the dragon was wroth[3710] with the woman, [a]and went [ainf]to make war with the remnant[3062] of her seed,[4690] [b]which [ppt]keep[5083] the commandments[1785] of God, and [ppt]have [c]the testimony[3141] of Jesus Christ.

The Two Beasts

13 ⊶ And I stood upon the sand of the sea, and saw [a]a beast[2342] [ppt]rise up out of the sea, [b]having seven heads and ten horns, and upon his horns ten crowns,[1238] and upon his heads the [Ic]name of blasphemy.[988]

2 [a]And the beast which I saw was

3 [I]Or, *sign* [a]Rev. 17:3 [b]Rev. 17:9, 10 [c]Rev. 13:1
4 [a]Rev. 9:10, 19 [b]Rev. 17:18 [c]Dan. 8:10 [d]Rev. 12:2 [e]Ex. 1:16
5 [a]Ps. 2:9; Rev. 2:27; 19:15
6 [a]Rev. 12:4 [b]Rev. 11:3
7 [a]Dan. 10:13, 21; 12:1 [b]Rev. 12:3; 20:2
9 [a]Luke 10:18; John 12:31 [b]Gen. 3:1, 4; Rev. 20:2 [c]Rev. 20:3 [d]Rev. 9:1
10 [a]Rev. 11:15; 19:1 [b]Job 1:9; 2:5; Zech. 3:1
11 [a]Rom. 8:33, 34, 37; 16:20 [b]Luke 14:26
12 [a]Ps. 96:11; Isa. 49:13; Rev. 18:20 [b]Rev. 8:13; 11:10 [c]Rev. 10:6
13 [a]Rev. 12:5
14 [a]Ex. 19:4 [b]Rev. 12:6 [c]Rev. 17:3 [d]Dan. 7:25; 12:7
15 [a]Isa. 59:19
17 [a]Gen. 3:15; Rev. 11:7; 13:7 [b]Rev. 14:12 [c]1Cor. 2:1; 1John 5:10; Rev. 1:2, 9; 6:9; 20:4
1 [I]Or, *names* [a]Dan. 7:2, 7 [b]Rev. 12:3; 17:3, 9, 12 [c]Rev. 17:3
2 [a]Dan. 7:6

⊶ **13:1–18** The beasts that are mentioned in this chapter represent two key personalities involved in the last days. The first beast (vv. 1–10) represents the Antichrist, the future political ruler who will oppose God and those who follow Him (vv. 6, 7). The term "antichrist" only occurs in 1 John 2:18–22; 4:3; and 2 John 1:7. See the note on 2 Thessalonians 2:3–9 regarding the Antichrist.

The second beast (vv. 11–18) represents the false prophet, the future religious ruler who will seek to force the earth's inhabitants to worship the first beast (vv. 12, 15). Those who receive the mark of the beast on their right hand or on their forehead (v. 16) will be cast into the lake of fire (Rev. 14:9–11).

like unto a leopard, [b]and his feet were as
the feet of a bear, [c]and his mouth as the
mouth of a lion: and [d]the dragon gave
him his power,[1411] [e]and his seat, [f]and
great authority.[1849]
3 And I saw one of his heads [a]as it
were [pfppI]wounded to death;[2288] and his
deadly wound was healed: and [b]all the
world[1093] wondered after the beast.
4 And they worshipped[4352] the
dragon which [ao]gave power[1849] unto the
beast: and they worshipped the beast,
saying, [a]Who *is* like unto the beast? who
is able [ainf]to make war with him?
5 And there was given unto him [a]a
mouth speaking[2980] great things and
blasphemies;[988] and power was given
unto him [ainfI]to continue [b]forty *and* two
months.
6 And he opened his mouth in blasphemy[988] against God, [ainf]to blaspheme[987]
his name, [a]and his tabernacle,[4633] and
them that [ppt]dwell in heaven.[3772]
7 And it was given unto him [ainfa]to
make war with the saints,[40] and [ainf]to
overcome them: [b]and power[1849] was given
him over all kindreds,[5443] and
tongues,[1100] and nations.[1484]
8 And all that [ppt]dwell upon the
earth shall worship him, [a]whose
names[3686] [pfip]are not written[1125] in the
book[976] of life[2222] of the Lamb[721] slain
[b]from the foundation of the world.[2889]
9 [a]If any man have an ear, [aim]let him
hear.[191]
10 [a]He that leadeth into captivity
[pin]shall go into captivity: [b]he that killeth
with the sword must [aifp]be killed with the
sword. [c]Here is the patience[5281] and the
faith[4102] of the saints.
11 And I beheld another beast [a]com-
ing up out of the earth; and he had two
horns like a lamb, and he [ipf]spake as a
dragon.
12 And he exerciseth all the power of
the first beast before him, and causeth
the earth and them which [ppt]dwell therein
to [aosb]worship the first beast, [a]whose
deadly wound was healed.
13 And [a]he doeth great wonders, [b]so
that he [psa]maketh fire [pinf]come down from
heaven on the earth in the sight of men,
14 And [a]deceiveth them that [ppt]dwell
on the earth [b]by *the means of* those miracles which he had power [ainf]to do in the
sight of the beast; saying to them that
dwell on the earth, that they [ainf]should
make an image[1504] to the beast, which
had the wound by a sword, [c]and did
live.[2198]
15 And he [aop]had power [ainf]to give
[I]life[4151] unto the image of the beast, that
the image of the beast [asba]should both
speak,[2980] [a]and [aosb]cause that as many
as [asba]would not worship[4352] the image of
the beast [asbp]should be killed.
16 And he causeth all, both small
and great, rich and poor, free and
bond,[1401] [Ia]to [aosb]receive a mark[5480] in
their right hand, or in their foreheads:
17 And that no man [psmp]might
[ainf]buy or [ainf]sell, save he that had the
mark, or [a]the name of the beast, [b]or the
number of his name.
18 [a]Here is wisdom.[4678] Let him that
hath understanding [aim]count [b]the number
of the beast: [c]for it is the number of a
man; and his number *is* Six hundred
threescore *and* six.

Jesus and His People

14 And I looked, and, lo, [a]a Lamb[721]
stood on the mount Sion, and
with him [b]an hundred forty *and* four
thousand, [c]having his Father's[3962]
name[3686] [pfpp]written in their foreheads.
2 And I heard a voice from
heaven,[3772] [a]as the voice of many waters,
and as the voice of a great thunder: and
I heard the voice of [b]harpers harping
with their harps:
3 And [a]they [pin]sung as it were a
new[2537] song[5603] before the throne, and
before the four beasts, and the elders:[4245]
and no man [ipf]could [ainf]learn that song
[b]but the hundred *and* forty *and* four
thousand, which [pfpp]were redeemed[59]
from the earth.[1093]
4 These are they which were not
defiled[3435] with women; [a]for they are
virgins.[3933] These are they [b]which [ppt]fol-
low[190] the Lamb[721] whithersoever he
[psa]goeth. These [aopIc]were redeemed[59] from

2 [b]Dan. 7:5 [c]Dan. 7:4 [d]Rev. 12:9 [e]Rev. 16:10 [f]Rev. 12:4
3 [I]Gr. *slain* [a]Rev. 13:12, 14 [b]Rev. 17:8
4 [a]Rev. 18:18
5 [I]Or, *to make war* [a]Dan. 7:8, 11, 25; 11:36 [b]Rev. 11:2; 12:6
6 [a]John 1:14; Col. 2:9
7 [a]Dan. 7:21; Rev. 11:7; 12:17 [b]Rev. 11:18; 17:15
8 [a]Ex. 32:32; Dan. 12:1; Phil. 4:3; Rev. 3:5; 20:12, 15; 21:27 [b]Rev. 17:8
9 [a]Rev. 2:7
10 [a]Isa. 33:1 [b]Gen. 9:6; Matt. 26:52 [c]Rev. 14:12
11 [a]Rev. 11:7
12 [a]Rev. 13:3
13 [a]Deut. 13:1-3; Matt. 24:24; 2Thess. 2:9; Rev. 16:14 [b]1Kgs. 18:38; 2Kgs. 1:10, 12
14 [a]Rev. 12:9; 19:20 [b]2Thess. 2:9, 10 [c]2Kgs. 20:7
15 [I]Gr. *breath* [a]Rev. 16:2; 19:20; 20:4
16 [I]Gr. *to give them* [a]Rev. 14:9; 19:20; 20:4
17 [a]Rev. 14:11 [b]Rev. 15:2
18 [a]Rev. 17:9 [b]Rev. 15:2 [c]Rev. 21:17
1 [a]Rev. 5:6 [b]Rev. 7:4 [c]Rev. 7:3; 13:16
2 [a]Rev. 1:15; 19:6 [b]Rev. 5:8
3 [a]Rev. 5:9; 15:3 [b]Rev. 14:1
4 [I]Gr. *were bought* [a]2Cor. 11:2 [b]Rev. 3:4; 7:15, 17; 17:14 [c]Rev. 5:9

among men,[444] [d]*being* the firstfruits[536] unto God and to the Lamb.[721]

5 And [a]in their mouth was found no guile:1388 for [b]they are without fault[299] before the throne of God.

6 And I saw another angel[32] [ppt][a]fly in the midst of heaven, [b]having the everlasting[166] gospel[2098] [ainf]to preach[2097] unto them that [ppt]dwell on the earth, [c]and to every nation,[1484] and kindred,5443 and tongue,[1100] and [sg]people,[2992]

7 Saying with a loud voice, [aim][a]Fear[5399] God, and [aim]give glory[1391] to him; for the hour[5610] of his judgment[2920] [ao]is come: [b]and [aim]worship4352 him that [apt]made heaven, and earth, and the sea, and the fountains[4077] of waters.

8 And there followed[190] another angel, saying, [a]Babylon [ao]is fallen, is fallen, [b]that great city, because she [pf]made all nations drink4222 of the wine[3631] of the wrath[2372] of her fornication.4202

9 And the third angel followed them, saying with a loud voice, [a]If any man [pin]worship the beast and his image, and receive *his* mark[5480] in his forehead, or in his hand,

10 The same [a]shall drink of the wine of the wrath of God, which [pfpp]is [b]poured out without mixture into [c]the cup of his indignation;[3709] and [d]he shall be tormented with [e]fire and brimstone2303 in the presence of the holy[40] angels, and in the presence of the Lamb:

11 And [a]the smoke of their torment ascendeth up for ever[165,1519] 3588 and ever: and they have no rest[372] day nor night, who [ppt]worship the beast and his image, and whosoever receiveth the mark[5480] of his name.[3686]

12 [a]Here is the patience[5281] of the saints:[40] [b]here *are* they that [ppt]keep[5083] the commandments[1785] of God, and the faith[4102] of Jesus.

13 And I heard a voice from heaven saying unto me, [aim]Write,[1125] [a]Blessed[3107] *are* the dead[3498] [b]which [ppt]die[599] in the Lord[2962] from henceforth: Yea, saith the Spirit,[4151] [c]that they [asbm]may rest from their labours; and their works[2041] do follow[190] them.

The Time for Judgment

🗝 14 And I looked, and behold a white cloud, and upon the cloud *one* sat [a]like unto the Son[5207] of man,[444] [b]having on his head a golden crown, and in his hand a sharp sickle.

15 And another angel[32] [a]came out of the temple,[3485] crying with a loud voice to him that sat on the cloud, [b]Thrust in thy sickle, and reap: for the time[5610] [ao]is come for thee [infg]to reap; for the harvest [c]of the earth [aop]is [I]ripe.

16 And he that [ppt]sat on the cloud thrust[906] in his sickle on the earth;[1093] and the earth was reaped.

17 And another angel came out of the temple which is in heaven, he also having a sharp sickle.

18 And another angel came out from the altar,[2379] [a]which [ppt]had power[1849] over fire; and cried with a loud cry to him that had the sharp sickle, saying, [b]Thrust in thy sharp sickle, and gather the clusters of the vine of the earth; for her grapes [ao]are fully ripe.

19 And the angel thrust in[906] his sickle into the earth, and gathered the vine of the earth, and cast[906] *it* into [a]the great winepress of the wrath[2372] of God.[2316]

20 And [a]the winepress was trodden[3961] [b]without1854 the city, and blood[129] came out of the winepress, [c]even unto the horse bridles, by the space of a thousand *and* six hundred furlongs.4712

4 [d]James 1:18
5 [a]Ps. 32:2; Zeph. 3:13 [b]Eph. 5:27; Jude 1:24
6 [a]Rev. 8:13 [b]Eph. 3:9-11; Titus 1:2 [c]Rev. 13:7
7 [a]Rev. 11:18; 15:4 [b]Neh. 9:6; Ps. 33:6; 124:8; 146:5, 6; Acts 14:15; 17:24
8 [a]Isa. 21:9; Jer. 51:8; Rev. 18:2 [b]Jer. 51:7; Rev. 11:8; 16:19; 17:2, 5; 18:3, 10, 18, 21; 19:2
9 [a]Rev. 13:14-16
10 [a]Ps. 75:8; Isa. 51:17; Jer. 25:15 [b]Rev. 18:6 [c]Rev. 16:19 [d]Rev. 20:10 [e]Rev. 19:20
11 [a]Isa. 34:10; Rev. 19:3
12 [a]Rev. 13:10 [b]Rev. 12:17
13 [a]Eccl. 4:1, 2; Rev. 20:6 [b]1Cor. 15:18; 1Thess. 4:16 [c]2Thess. 1:7; Heb. 4:9, 10; Rev. 6:11
14 [a]Ezek. 1:26; Dan. 7:13; Rev. 1:13 [b]Rev. 6:2
15 [I]Or, *dried* [a]Rev. 16:17 [b]Joel 3:13; Matt. 13:39 [c]Jer. 51:33; Rev. 13:12
18 [a]Rev. 16:8 [b]Joel 3:13
19 [a]Rev. 19:15
20 [a]Isa. 63:3; Lam. 1:15 [b]Heb. 13:12; Rev. 11:8 [c]Rev. 19:14

🗝 **14:14–20** In this passage, the record is given of the Lord Jesus Christ's ultimate triumph over evil at the Battle of Armageddon. Although man has desperately tried to abolish war, the word of God clearly teaches that he will never be successful. In Matthew 24:6, the Lord said that there would be "wars and rumours of wars" until the Second Coming of Christ. At this time, the war to end all wars will take place, the Battle of Armageddon (cf. Is. 34:1–8; 63:1–6; Joel 2:1–11; 3:9–13; Zeph. 1:14–18; 3:8; Zech. 12:9–11; 14:1–3).

The Seven Plagues

15 [key]And [a]I saw another sign[4592] in heaven,[3772] great and marvellous, [b]seven angels having the seven last[2078] plagues; [c]for in them [aop]is filled up[5055] the wrath[2372] of God.[2316]

2 And I saw as it were [a]a sea of glass [b]mingled with fire: and them that [ppt]had gotten the victory over the beast,[2342] [c]and over his image, and over his mark,[5480] *and* over the number of his name, stand on the sea of glass, [d]having the harps of God.

3 And they sing [a]the song[5603] of Moses the servant[1401] of God, and the song of the Lamb, saying, [b]Great and marvellous *are* thy works, Lord[2962] God[2316] Almighty;3841 [c]just[1342] and true[228] *are* thy ways, thou King[935] of saints.[40]

4 [a]Who [asbp]shall not fear[5399] thee, O Lord, and [aosb]glorify[1392] thy name? for *thou* only *art* holy:[3741] for [b]all nations[1484] shall come and worship4352 before thee; for thy judgments[1345] [aop]are made manifest.[5319]

5 And after that I looked, and, behold, [a]the temple[3485] of the tabernacle4633 of the testimony[3142] in heaven was opened:

6 [a]And the seven angels came out of the temple, having the seven plagues, [b]clothed in pure[2513] and white linen, and having their breasts girded with golden girdles.2223

7 [a]And one of the four beasts gave unto the seven angels seven golden vials full of the wrath[2372] of God,[2316] [b]who liveth[2198] for ever[165,1519] 3588 and ever.

8 And [a]the temple was filled with smoke [b]from the glory[1391] of God, and from his power;[1411] and no man [ipf]was able [ainf]to enter into the temple, till the seven plagues of the seven angels [asbp]were fulfilled.[5055]

1 [a]Rev. 12:1, 3 [b]Rev. 16:1; 21:9 [c]Rev. 14:10
2 [a]Rev. 4:6; 21:18 [b]Matt. 3:11 [c]Rev. 13:15-17 [d]Rev. 5:8; 14:2
3 [a]Ex. 15:1; Deut. 31:30; Rev. 14:3 [b]Deut. 32:4; Ps. 111:2; 139:14 [c]Ps. 145:17; Hos. 14:9; Rev. 16:7
4 [a]Ex. 15:14-16; Jer. 10:7 [b]Isa. 66:23
5 [a]Num. 1:50; Rev. 11:19
6 [a]Rev. 15:1 [b]Ex. 28:6, 8; Ezek. 44:17, 18; Rev. 1:13
7 [a]Rev. 4:6 [b]1Thess. 1:9; Rev. 4:9; 10:6
8 [a]Ex. 40:34; 1Kgs. 8:10; 2Chr. 5:14; Isa. 6:4 [b]2Thess. 1:9

The Seven Vials of Wrath

16 And I heard a great voice out of the temple[3485] saying [a]to the seven angels,[32] Go your ways, and pour out the vials5357 [b]of the wrath[2372] of God upon the earth.[1093]

2 And the first went, and poured out his vial [a]upon the earth; and [b]there fell a noisome[2556] and grievous[4190] sore1668 upon the men [c]which [ppt]had the mark[5480] of the beast, and *upon* them [d]which [ppt]worshipped4352 his image.

3 And the second angel[32] poured out his vial [a]upon the sea; and [b]it became as the blood[129] of a dead[3498] *man:* [c]and every living[2198] soul[5590] died[599] in the sea.

4 And the third angel[32] poured out his vial [a]upon the rivers and fountains[4077] of waters; [b]and they became blood.

5 And I heard the angel of the waters say, [a]Thou art righteous,[1342] O Lord, [b]which art, and wast,[2258] and shalt be, because thou [ao]hast judged[2919] thus.

6 For [a]they [ao]have shed the blood[129] [b]of saints[40] and prophets,[4396] [c]and thou [ao]hast given them blood [ainf]to drink; for they are worthy.514

7 And I heard another out of the altar[2379] say, Even so, [a]Lord God Almighty,3841 [b]true[228] and righteous[1342] *are* thy judgments.[2920]

8 And the fourth angel[32] poured out his vial [a]upon the sun; [b]and power was given unto him [ainf]to scorch men with fire.

9 And men[444] were [1]scorched with great heat, and [a]blasphemed[987] the name[3686] of God, which hath power[1849] over these plagues: [b]and they repented[3340] not [ainfc]to give him glory.[1391]

10 And the fifth angel[32] poured out his vial [a]upon the seat of the beast; [b]and his kingdom[932] was full of darkness; [c]and they [ipf]gnawed their tongues for pain,[4192]

1 [a]Rev. 15:1 [b]Rev. 14:10; 15:7
2 [a]Rev. 8:7 [b]Ex. 9:9-11 [c]Rev. 13:16, 17 [d]Rev. 13:14
3 [a]Rev. 8:8 [b]Ex. 7:17, 20 [c]Rev. 8:9
4 [a]Rev. 8:10 [b]Ex. 7:20
5 [a]Rev. 15:3 [b]Rev. 1:4, 8; 4:8; 11:17
6 [a]Matt. 23:34, 35; Rev. 13:15 [b]Rev. 11:18; 18:20 [c]Isa. 49:26
7 [a]Rev. 15:3 [b]Rev. 13:10; 14:10; 19:2
8 [a]Rev. 8:12 [b]Rev. 9:17, 18; 14:18
9 [1]Or, *burned* [a]Rev. 16:11, 21 [b]Dan. 5:22, 23; Rev. 9:20 [c]Rev. 11:13; 14:7
10 [a]Rev. 13:2 [b]Rev. 9:2 [c]Rev. 11:10

[key] **15:1–8** This chapter describes the preparation for the pouring out of the seven vials (bowls) which will constitute the final expression of the wrath of God during the Tribulation.

The first expression of God's wrath is seen in the seven seals (Rev. 6:1–17). The seventh seal contains the seven trumpet judgments (Rev. 8:1–13; 9:1–21; 11:15–19). Then out of the seventh trumpet judgment comes the seven vials of God's wrath (Rev. 15:1; 16:1–21).

11 And [a]blasphemed the God of heaven[3772] because of their pains and [b]their sores, [c]and repented not of their deeds.[2041]

12 And the sixth angel[32] poured out his vial [a]upon the great river Euphrates; [b]and the water thereof was dried up, [c]that the way of the kings[935] of the east might be prepared.

13 And I saw three unclean [a]spirits[4151] like frogs *come* out of the mouth of [b]the dragon, and out of the mouth of the beast, and out of the mouth of [c]the false prophet.

14 [a]For they are the spirits[4151] of devils,[1142] [b]working miracles,[4592] *which* go forth unto the kings of the earth [c]and of the whole world,[3625] [ainf]to gather them to [d]the battle of that great day[2250] of God Almighty.[3841]

15 [a]Behold, I come as a thief. Blessed[3107] *is* he that [ppt]watcheth, and [ppt]keepeth his garments, [b]lest he [psa]walk naked,[1131] and they [psa]see his shame.

16 [a]And he gathered them together into a place called in the Hebrew tongue Armageddon.[717]

17 And the seventh angel[32] poured out his vial into the air; and there came a great voice out of the temple[3485] of heaven,[3772] from the throne, saying, [a]It is done.

18 And [a]there [aom]were voices, and thunders, and lightnings; [b]and there [aom]was a great earthquake, [c]such as [aom]was not since men[444] were upon the earth,[1093] so mighty an earthquake, *and* so great.

19 And [a]the great city [aom]was divided into three parts, and the cities of the nations fell: and great Babylon [b]came in remembrance before God, [ainfc]to give unto her the cup of the wine[3631] of the fierceness[2372] of his wrath.[3709]

20 And [a]every island fled away, and the mountains were not found.[2147]

21 [a]And there fell upon men a great hail out of heaven, *every stone* about the weight of a talent: and [b]men[444] blasphemed[987] God[2316] because of [c]the plague of the hail; for the plague thereof was exceeding great.

11 [a]Rev. 16:9, 21 [b]Rev. 16:2 [c]Rev. 16:9
12 [a]Rev. 9:14 [b]Jer. 50:38; 51:36 [c]Isa. 41:2, 25
13 [a]1John 4:1-3 [b]Rev. 12:3, 9 [c]Rev. 19:20; 20:10
14 [a]1Tim. 4:1; James 3:15 [b]2Thess. 2:9; Rev. 13:13, 14; 19:20 [c]Luke 2:1 [d]Rev. 17:14; 19:19; 20:8
15 [a]Matt. 24:43; 1Thess. 5:2; 2Pet. 3:10; Rev. 3:3 [b]2Cor. 5:3; Rev. 3:4, 18
16 [a]Rev. 19:19
17 [a]Rev. 21:6
18 [a]Rev. 4:5; 8:5; 11:19 [b]Rev. 11:13 [c]Dan. 12:1
19 [a]Rev. 14:8; 17:18 [b]Rev. 18:5 [c]Isa. 51:17, 22; Jer. 25:15, 16; Rev. 14:10
20 [a]Rev. 6:14
21 [a]Rev. 11:19 [b]Rev. 16:9, 11 [c]Ex. 9:23-25

1 [a]Rev. 21:9 [b]Rev. 16:19; 18:16, 17, 19 [c]Nah. 3:4; Rev. 19:2 [d]Jer. 51:13; Rev. 17:15
2 [a]Rev. 18:3 [b]Jer. 51:7; Rev. 14:8; 18:3
3 [a]Rev. 12:6, 14 [b]Rev. 12:3 [c]Rev. 13:1 [d]Rev. 17:9 [e]Rev. 17:12
4 [a]Rev. 18:12, 16 [b]Dan. 11:38 [c]Jer. 51:7; Rev. 18:6 [d]Rev. 14:8
5 [I]Or, *fornications* [a]2Thess. 2:7 [b]Rev. 11:8; 14:8; 16:19; 18:2, 10, 21 [c]Rev. 18:9; 19:2
6 [a]Rev. 18:24 [b]Rev. 13:15; 16:6 [c]Rev. 6:9, 10; 12:11
8 [a]Rev. 11:7; 13:1 [b]Rev. 13:10; 17:11 [c]Rev. 13:3 [d]Rev. 13:8
9 [a]Rev. 13:18 [b]Rev. 13:1

The Great Mystery

17 And there came [a]one of the seven angels[32] which had the seven vials,[5357] and talked with me, saying unto me, Come hither; [b]I will shew unto thee the judgment[2917] of [c]the great whore[4204] [d]that [ppt]sitteth upon many waters:

2 [a]With whom the kings[935] of the earth[1093] [ao]have committed fornication,[4203] and [b]the inhabitants of the earth [aop]have been made drunk with the wine of her fornication.

3 So he carried me away[667] in the spirit[4151] [a]into the wilderness: and I saw a woman [ppt]sit [b]upon a scarlet coloured beast, full of [c]names of blasphemy,[988] [d]having seven heads and [e]ten horns.

4 And the woman [a]was arrayed in purple and scarlet colour, [b]and decked[5558] with gold and precious stones and pearls, [c]having a golden cup in her hand [d]full of abominations[946] and filthiness[168] of her fornication:

5 And upon her forehead *was* a name[3686] written, [a]MYSTERY,[3466] BABYLON [b]THE GREAT, [c]THE MOTHER OF [I]HARLOTS[4204] AND ABOMINATIONS[946] OF THE EARTH.[1093]

6 And I saw [a]the woman [ppt]drunken [b]with the blood[129] of the saints,[40] and with the blood of [c]the martyrs[3144] of Jesus: and when I saw her, I wondered with great admiration.[2295]

7 And the angel said unto me, Wherefore didst thou marvel? I will tell thee the mystery of the woman, and of the beast that [ppt]carrieth her, which hath the seven heads and ten horns.

8 The beast that thou sawest was, and is not; and [a]shall ascend out of the bottomless pit, and [pinfb]go into perdition:[684] and they that [ppt]dwell on the earth [c]shall wonder, [d]whose names [pfip]were not written[1125] in the book[975] of life[2222] from the foundation of the world, when they [ppt]behold the beast that was, and is not, and yet is.

9 And [a]here *is* the mind which hath wisdom.[4678] [b]The seven heads are seven mountains, on which the woman sitteth.

10 And there are seven kings:[935] five are fallen, and one is, *and* the other [ao]is not yet come;[2064] and when he [aosb]cometh, he must [ainf]continue a short space.

11 And the beast that was, and is not, even he is the eighth, and is of the seven, [a]and goeth into perdition.

12 And [a]the ten horns which thou sawest are ten kings, which [ao]have received no kingdom[932] as yet; but receive power[1849] as kings one hour with the beast.

13 These have one mind,[1106] and shall give their power[1411] and strength[1849] unto the beast.

14 [a]These shall make war with the Lamb,[721] and the Lamb shall overcome them: [b]for he is Lord[2962] of lords, and King[935] of kings: [c]and they that are with him *are* called,[2822] and chosen, and faithful.[4103]

15 And he saith unto me, [a]The waters which thou sawest, where the whore sitteth, [b]are peoples,[2992] and multitudes, and nations,[1484] and tongues.[1100]

16 And the ten horns which thou sawest upon the beast, [a]these shall hate the whore, and shall make her desolate [b]and naked,[1131] and shall eat her flesh,[4561] and [c]burn her with fire.

17 [a]For God [ao]hath put in their hearts[2588] [ainf]to fulfil his will,[1106] and [ainf]to agree, and [ainf]give their kingdom unto the beast, [b]until the words[4487] of God [asbp]shall be fulfilled.[5055]

18 And the woman which thou sawest [a]is that great city, [b]which reigneth over the kings[935] of the earth.[1093]

The Fall of Babylon

18 And [a]after these things I saw another angel[32] [ppt]come down from heaven,[3772] having great power;[1849] [b]and the earth[1093] was lightened[5461] with his glory.[1391]

2 And he cried mightily with a strong voice, saying, [a]Babylon the great [aom]is fallen, is fallen, and [aom][b]is become the habitation2732 of devils,[1142] and the hold[5438] of every foul spirit,[4151] and [c]a cage[5438] of every unclean and hateful bird.

3 For all nations[1484] [pfi][a]have drunk of the wine of the wrath[2372] of her fornication,4202 and the kings of the earth [ao]have committed fornication with her, [b]and the merchants1713 of the earth are waxed rich[4147] through the [I]abundance of her delicacies.4764

4 And I heard another voice from heaven, saying, [a]Come out of her, my people,[2992] that ye [asba]be not partakers[4790] of her sins,[266] and that ye [aosb]receive not of her plagues.

5 [a]For her sins [aop]have reached unto heaven, and [b]God [ao]hath remembered her iniquities.[92]

6 [a]Reward her even as she rewarded you, and double unto her double according to her works:[2041] [b]in the cup which she [ao]hath filled [aim][c]fill to her double.

7 [a]How much she [ao]hath glorified[1392] herself, and lived deliciously,[4763] so much torment and sorrow [aim]give her: for she saith in her heart,[2588] I sit a [b]queen, and am no widow, and shall see [efn]no sorrow.

8 Therefore shall her plagues come [a]in one day, death,[2288] and mourning, and famine; and [b]she shall be utterly burned with fire: [c]for strong2478 *is* the Lord God who [apt]judgeth[2919] her.

9 And [a]the kings[935] of the earth,[1093] who [apt]have committed fornication and [apt]lived deliciously with her, [b]shall bewail2799 her, and lament[2875] for her, [c]when they [psa]shall see the smoke of her burning,

10 Standing afar off for the fear[5401] of her torment, saying, [a]Alas, alas that great city Babylon, that mighty city! [b]for in one hour is thy judgment[2920] come.

11 And [a]the merchants1713 of the earth [pin]shall weep and [pin]mourn over her; for no man buyeth their merchandise any more:

12 [a]The merchandise of gold, and silver, and precious stones, and of pearls, and fine linen, and purple, and silk, and scarlet, and all [I]thyine2367 wood, and all manner vessels of ivory, and all manner vessels of most precious wood, and of brass, and iron, and marble,

11 [a]Rev. 17:8
12 [a]Dan. 7:20; Zech. 1:18, 19, 21; Rev. 13:1
14 [a]Rev. 16:14; 19:19 [b]Deut. 10:17; 1Tim. 6:15; Rev. 19:16 [c]Jer. 50:44, 45; Rev. 14:4
15 [a]Isa. 8:7; Rev. 17:1 [b]Rev. 13:7
16 [a]Jer. 50:41, 42; Rev. 16:12 [b]Ezek. 16:37-44; Rev. 18:16 [c]Rev. 18:8
17 [a]2Thess. 2:11 [b]Rev. 10:7
18 [a]Rev. 16:19 [b]Rev. 12:4

1 [a]Rev. 17:1 [b]Ezek. 43:2
2 [a]Isa. 13:19; 21:9; Jer. 51:8; Rev. 14:8 [b]Isa. 13:21; 21:8; 34:14; Jer. 50:39; 51:37 [c]Isa. 14:23; 34:11; Mark 5:2, 3
3 [I]Or, *power* [a]Rev. 14:8; 17:2 [b]Isa. 47:15; Rev. 18:11, 15
4 [a]Isa. 48:20; 52:11; Jer. 50:8; 51:6, 45; 2Cor. 6:17
5 [a]Gen. 18:20, 21; Jer. 51:9; Jon. 1:2 [b]Rev. 16:19
6 [a]Ps. 137:8; Jer. 50:15, 29; 51:24, 49; 2Tim. 4:14; Rev. 13:10 [b]Rev. 14:10 [c]Rev. 16:19
7 [a]Ezek. 28:2 [b]Isa. 47:7, 8; Zeph. 2:15
8 [a]Isa. 47:9; Rev. 18:10 [b]Rev. 17:16 [c]Jer. 50:34; Rev. 11:17
9 [a]Ezek. 26:16, 17; Rev. 17:2; 18:3 [b]Jer. 50:46 [c]Rev. 18:18; 19:3
10 [a]Isa. 21:9; Rev. 14:8 [b]Rev. 18:17, 19
11 [a]Ezek. 27:27-36; Rev. 18:3
12 [I]Or, *sweet* [a]Rev. 17:4

13 And cinnamon, and odours, and ointments, and frankincense,3030 and wine, and oil, and fine flour, and wheat, and beasts, and sheep, and horses, and chariots, and [I]slaves,[4983] and [a]souls[5590] of men.[444]

14 And the fruits that thy soul lusted after[1939] [ao]are departed from thee, and all things which were dainty and goodly are departed from thee, and thou shalt find them [efn]no more at all.

15 [a]The merchants of these things, which [apt]were made rich by her, shall stand afar off for the fear[5401] of her torment, weeping and wailing,

16 And saying, Alas, alas that great city, [a]that was clothed in fine linen, and purple, and scarlet, and decked5558 with gold, and precious stones, and pearls!

17 [a]For in one hour so great riches is come to nought. And [b]every shipmaster, and all the company in ships, and sailors, and as many as trade[2038] by sea, stood afar off,

18 [a]And [ipf]cried when they [ppt]saw the smoke of her burning, saying, [b]What *city* *is* like unto this great city!

19 And [a]they cast dust on their heads, and cried, weeping and wailing, saying, Alas, alas, that great city, wherein were [ao]made rich all that had ships in the sea by reason of her costliness! [b]for in one hour is she made desolate.

20 [pima]Rejoice[2165] over her, *thou* heaven,[3772] and *ye* holy[40] apostles[652] and prophets;[4396] for [b]God hath avenged you on her.

21 And a mighty angel[32] took up a stone like a great millstone, and cast *it* into the sea, saying, [a]Thus with violence shall that great city Babylon be thrown down, and [asbpb]shall be found[2147] no more at all.

22 [a]And the voice of harpers, and musicians, and of pipers, and trumpeters, shall be heard [efn]no more at all in thee; and no craftsman,5079 of whatsoever craft *he be,* [asbp]shall be found any more in thee; and the sound of a millstone3458 shall be heard [efn]no more at all in thee;

23 [a]And the light of a candle shall shine [efn]no more at all in thee; [b]and the voice of the bridegroom and of the bride shall be heard [efn]no more at all in thee: for [c]thy merchants1713 were the great men of the earth;[1093] [d]for by thy sorceries[5331] were all nations[1484] deceived.

24 And [a]in her was found the blood[129] of prophets,[4396] and of saints,[40] and of all that [b]were slain upon the earth.

"The Testimony of Jesus"

19 🔑And after these things [a]I heard a great voice of much people in heaven,[3772] saying, Alleluia;239 [b]Salvation,[4991] and glory,[1391] and honour,5092 and power,[1411] unto the Lord[2962] our God:[2316]

2 For [a]true[228] and righteous[1342] *are* his judgments:[2920] for he [ao]hath judged[2919] the great whore,4204 which did corrupt the earth with her fornication,4202 and [aob]hath avenged[1556] the blood[129] of his servants[1401] at her hand.

3 And again they said, Alleluia. And [a]her smoke rose up for ever[165,1519] 3588 and ever.

4 And [a]the four and twenty elders[4245] and the four beasts fell down and worshipped4352 God that sat on the throne, saying, [b]Amen;281 Alleluia.239

5 And a voice came out of the throne, saying, [pima]Praise[134] our God,[2316] all ye his servants,[1401] and ye that [ppt]fear[5399] him, [b]both small and great.

6 [a]And I heard as it were the voice of a great multitude, and as the voice of many waters, and as the voice of mighty

13 [I]Or, *bodies* [a]Ezek. 27:13
15 [a]Rev. 18:3, 11
16 [a]Rev. 17:4
17 [a]Rev. 18:10 [b]Isa. 23:14; Ezek. 27:29
18 [a]Ezek. 27:30, 31; Rev. 18:9 [b]Rev. 13:4
19 [a]Josh. 7:6; 1Sam. 4:12; Job 2:12; Ezek. 27:30 [b]Rev. 18:8
20 [a]Isa. 44:23; 49:13; Jer. 51:48 [b]Luke 11:49, 50; Rev. 19:2
21 [a]Jer. 51:64 [b]Rev. 12:8; 16:20
22 [a]Isa. 24:8; Jer. 7:34; 16:9; 25:10; Ezek. 26:13
23 [a]Jer. 25:10 [b]Jer. 7:34; 16:9; 25:10; 33:11 [c]Isa. 23:8 [d]2Kgs. 9:22; Nah. 3:4; Rev. 17:2, 5
24 [a]Rev. 17:6 [b]Jer. 51:49
1 [a]Rev. 11:15 [b]Rev. 4:11; 7:10, 12; 12:10
2 [a]Rev. 15:3; 16:7 [b]Deut. 32:43; Rev. 6:10; 18:20
3 [a]Isa. 34:10; Rev. 14:11; 18:9, 18
4 [a]Rev. 4:4, 6, 10; 5:14 [b]1Chr. 16:36; Neh. 5:13; 8:6; Rev. 5:14
5 [a]Ps. 134:1; 135:1 [b]Rev. 11:18; 20:12
6 [a]Ezek. 1:24; 43:2; Rev. 14:2

🔑 **19:1–21** This passage, which is the climax to the whole Book of Revelation, begins with the Second Coming of Christ to the earth. Heaven is opened and a white horse appears, and the rider on its back, Jesus Christ, is called "Faithful and True" (v. 11). At this time, He will introduce true peace and righteousness, a stark contrast to the false peace brought by the first white horse and its rider, the Antichrist (Rev. 6:1–17).

thunderings, saying, Alleluia: for [b]the
Lord[2962] God[2316] omnipotent3841
[ao]reigneth.[936]
7 Let us be glad and rejoice, and
[aosi]give honour[1391] to him: for [a]the marriage[1062] of the Lamb [ao]is come, and his
wife [ao]hath made herself ready.2090
8 And [a]to her was granted that she
[asbm]should be arrayed in fine linen,
clean[2513] and [I]white: [b]for the fine linen is
the righteousness[1345] of saints.[40]
9 And he saith unto me, [aim]Write,[1125]
[a]Blessed[3107] *are* they which [pfpp]are called
unto the marriage[1062] supper of the
Lamb.[721] And he saith unto me, [b]These
are the true[228] sayings[3056] of God.
10 And [a]I fell at his feet [ainf]to wor-
ship4352 him. And he said unto me, [b]See
thou do it not: I am thy fellowservant,[4889]
and of thy brethren[80] [c]that [ppt]have the
testimony[3141] of Jesus: [aim]worship God:
for the testimony of Jesus is the spirit[4151]
of prophecy.[4394]

The Righteous Judge

11 [a]And I saw heaven [pfpp]opened,
and behold [b]a white horse; and he
that [ppt]sat upon him *was* [ppp]called
[c]Faithful[4103] and True, and [d]in righteousness[1343] he doth judge[2919] and make
war.
12 [a]His eyes *were* as a flame of fire,
[b]and on his head *were* many crowns;[1238]
[c]and he had a name written,[1125] that no
man knew, but he himself.
13 [a]And he *was* clothed with a vesture[2440] [pfpp]dipped[911] in blood:[129] and his
name[3686] [pinp]is called [b]The Word[3056] of
God.[2316]
14 [a]And the armies *which were* in
heaven[3772] [ipf]followed[190] him upon white
horses, [b]clothed in fine linen, white and
clean.[2513]
15 And [a]out of his mouth goeth a
sharp sword, that with it he [psa]should
smite the nations: and [b]he shall rule[4165]
them with a rod of iron: and [c]he treadeth[3961] the winepress[3631]3025 of the fierceness[2372] and wrath[3709] of Almighty3841
God.[2316]
16 And [a]he hath on *his* vesture
and on his thigh a name written,
[b]KING[935] OF KINGS, AND LORD[2962] OF
LORDS.
17 And I saw an angel[32] standing in
the sun; and he cried with a loud voice,
saying [a]to all the fowls that [ppt]fly in the
midst of heaven, [b]Come and [pim]gather
yourselves together unto the supper of
the great God;[2316]
18 [a]That ye [aosb]may eat the flesh[4561]
of kings,[935] and the flesh of captains,
and the flesh of mighty men, and the
flesh of horses, and of them that sit on
them, and the flesh of all *men, both* free
and bond,[1401] both small and great.
🔑 19 [a]And I saw the beast, and the
kings of the earth,[1093] and their armies,
gathered together [ainf]to make war against
him that sat on the horse, and against his
army.
20 [a]And the beast was taken, and
with him the false prophet that
[apt]wrought miracles[4592] before him, with
which he deceived them that [apt]had received the mark[5480] of the beast, and
[b]them that [ppt]worshipped4352 his image.
[c]These both were cast alive[2198] into a
lake of fire [d]burning with brimstone.2303
21 And the remnant3062 [a]were
slain615 with the sword of him that sat
upon the horse, which *sword* [apt]proceeded
out of his mouth: [b]and all the fowls [c]were
filled with their flesh.[4561]

The Millennial Kingdom

20 🔑And I saw an angel[32] [ppt]come
down from heaven,[3772] [a]having
the key of the bottomless pit and a great
chain in his hand.

6 [b]Rev. 11:15, 17; 12:10; 21:22
7 [a]Matt. 22:2; 25:10; 2Cor. 11:2; Eph. 5:32; Rev. 21:2, 9
8 [I]Or, *bright* [a]Ps. 45:13, 14; Ezek. 16:10; Rev. 3:18 [b]Ps. 132:9
9 [a]Matt. 22:2, 3; Luke 14:15, 16 [b]Rev. 21:5; 22:6
10 [a]Rev. 22:8 [b]Acts 10:26; 14:14, 15; Rev. 22:9 [c]1John 5:10; Rev. 12:17
11 [a]Rev. 15:5 [b]Rev. 6:2 [c]Rev. 3:14 [d]Isa. 11:4
12 [a]Rev. 1:14; 2:18 [b]Rev. 6:2 [c]Rev. 2:17; 19:16
13 [a]Isa. 63:2, 3 [b]John 1:1; 1John 5:7
14 [a]Rev. 14:20 [b]Matt. 28:3; Rev. 4:4; 7:9
15 [a]Isa. 11:4; 2Thess. 2:8; Rev. 1:16; 19:21 [b]Ps. 2:9; Rev. 2:27; 12:5 [c]Isa. 63:3; Rev. 14:19, 20
16 [a]Rev. 19:12 [b]Dan. 2:47; 1Tim. 6:15; Rev. 17:14
17 [a]Rev. 19:21 [b]Ezek. 39:17
18 [a]Ezek. 39:18, 20
19 [a]Rev. 16:16; 17:13, 14
20 [a]Rev. 16:13, 14 [b]Rev. 13:12, 15 [c]Rev. 20:10; Dan. 7:11 [d]Rev. 14:10; 21:8
21 [a]Rev. 19:15 [b]Rev. 19:17, 18 [c]Rev. 17:16
1 [a]Rev. 1:18; 9:1

🔑 **19:19, 20** See note on Revelation 13:1–18.
🔑 **20:1–15** In this chapter, Jesus Christ comes back to set up His millennial (one-thousand-year) reign on the earth (vv. 1–6). There are a number of prophetic references that describe a particular
(continued on next page)

2 And he laid hold on [a]the dragon, that old serpent, which is the Devil,[1228] and Satan,[4567] and bound[1210] him a thousand years,

3 And cast[906] him into the bottomless pit, and shut him up, and [a]set a seal upon him, [b]that he [aosb]should deceive the nations[1484] no more, till the thousand years [asbp]should be fulfilled:[5055] and after that he must [aifp]be loosed a little season.[5550]

4 And I saw [a]thrones, and they sat upon them, and [b]judgment[2917] was given unto them: and *I saw* [c]the souls[5590] of them that [pfpp]were beheaded for the witness[3141] of Jesus, and for the word[3056] of God, and [d]which [ao]had not worshipped[4352] the beast, [e]neither his image,[1504] neither had received *his* mark[5480] upon their foreheads, or in their hands; and they lived[2198] and [f]reigned[936] with Christ[5547] a thousand years.

5 But the rest of the dead[3498] lived not again until the thousand years [asbp]were finished.[5055] This *is* the first resurrection.[386]

6 Blessed[3107] and holy[40] *is* he that [ppt]hath part in the first resurrection:[386] on such [a]the second death[2288] hath no power,[1849] but they shall be [b]priests[2409] of God[2316] and of Christ,[5547] [c]and shall reign[936] with him a thousand years.

7 And when the thousand years [asbp]are expired,[5055] [a]Satan[4567] shall be loosed out of his prison,

8 And shall go out [ainfa]to deceive the nations[1484] which are in the four quarters of the earth, [b]Gog and Magog, [ainfc]to gather them together to battle: the number of whom *is* as the sand of the sea.

9 [a]And they went up on the breadth of the earth, and compassed the camp of the saints[40] about, and the beloved[25] city: and fire came down from God out of heaven, and devoured them.

10 [a]And the devil[1228] that [ppt]deceived them [aop]was cast into the lake of fire and brimstone,[2303] [b]where the beast and the false prophet *are,* and [c]shall be tormented day and night for ever[165,1519][3588] and ever.

The Final Judgment Day

11 And I saw a great white throne, and him that sat on it, from whose face [a]the earth[1093] and the heaven[3772] fled away; [b]and there was found no place for them.

12 And I saw the dead,[3498] [a]small and great, stand before God; [b]and the books[975] were opened: and another [c]book was opened, which is *the book* of life:[2222] and the dead were judged[2919] out of those things which [pfpp]were written in the books, [d]according to their works.[2041]

13 And the sea gave up the dead which were in it; [a]and death[2288] and hell[86] delivered up the dead which were in them: [b]and they were judged every man according to their works.[2041]

14 And [a]death and hell were cast into the lake of fire. [b]This is the second death.

15 And whosoever was not found [pfpp]written in the book[976] of life [a]was cast into the lake of fire.

The New Jerusalem

21 And [a]I saw a new[2537] heaven[3772] and a new[2537] earth:[1093] [b]for the first heaven and the first earth were passed away; and there was no more sea.

2 And I John saw [a]the holy[40] city,

2 [a]Rev. 12:9; 2Pet. 2:4; Jude 1:6
3 [a]Dan. 6:17 [b]Rev. 16:14, 16; 20:8
4 [a]Dan. 7:9, 22, 27; Matt. 19:28; Luke 22:30 [b]1Cor. 6:2, 3 [c]Rev. 6:9 [d]Rev. 13:12 [e]Rev. 13:15, 16 [f]Rom. 8:17; 2Tim. 2:12; Rev. 5:10
6 [a]Rev. 2:11; 21:8 [b]Isa. 61:6; 1Pet. 2:9; Rev. 1:6; 5:10 [c]Rev. 20:4
7 [a]Rev. 20:2
8 [a]Rev. 20:3, 10 [b]Ezek. 38:2; 39:1 [c]Rev. 16:14
9 [a]Isa. 8:8; Ezek. 38:9, 16
10 [a]Rev. 20:8 [b]Rev. 19:20 [c]Rev. 14:10, 11
11 [a]2Pet. 3:7, 10, 11; Rev. 21:1 [b]Dan. 2:35
12 [a]Rev. 19:5 [b]Dan. 7:10 [c]Ps. 69:28; Dan. 12:1; Phil. 4:3; Rev. 3:5; 13:8; 21:27 [d]Jer. 17:10; 32:19; Matt. 16:27; Rom. 2:6; Rev. 2:23; 20:13; 22:12
13 [a]Rev. 6:8 [b]Rev. 20:12
14 [a]1Cor. 15:26, 54, 55 [b]Rev. 20:6; 21:8
15 [a]Rev. 19:20

1 [a]Isa. 65:17; 66:22; 2Pet. 3:13; [b]Rev. 20:11
2 [a]Isa. 52:1; Gal. 4:26; Heb. 11:10; 12:22; 13:14; Rev. 3:12; 21:10

(continued from previous page)
time when Christ will establish a kingdom on the earth (2 Sam. 7:14–17; Ps. 24:1–10; Is. 2:1–4; 11:5–12; 35:1–10; Dan. 2:44). At this time, the unrighteous dead will be judged (v. 12).

20:2–10 See note on Jude 1:9.

21:1—22:5 In these final two chapters, the new heaven and new earth are described in detail. The word "new" is a translation of the Greek word *kainón* (2537), which means "qualitatively new." The new heaven and the new earth are not duplicates of the heaven and earth that now exist. Some have suggested that the new heaven and the new earth will be as this heaven and this earth were at their creation.

new Jerusalem, coming down from God out of heaven,[3772] [pfpp]prepared [b]as a bride [pfpp]adorned for her husband.

3 And I heard a great voice out of heaven saying, Behold, [a]the tabernacle of God[2316] *is* with men,[444] and he will dwell with them, and they shall be his people,[2992] and God[2316] himself shall be with them, *and be* their God.

4 [a]And God shall wipe away all tears from their eyes; and [b]there shall be no more death,[2288] [c]neither sorrow, nor crying, neither shall there be any more pain:[4192] for the former things [ao]are passed away.

5 And [a]he that [ppt]sat upon the throne said, [b]Behold, I make all things new.[2537] And he said unto me, Write:[1125] for [c]these words are true[228] and faithful.[4103]

6 And he said unto me, [a]It [pfi]is done. [b]I am Alpha[1] and Omega,[5598] the beginning[746] and the end.[5056] [c]I will give unto him that [ppt]is athirst of the fountain[4077] of the water of life[2222] freely.

7 He that [ppt]overcometh shall inherit[2816] [I]all things; and [a]I will be his God,[2316] and he shall be my son.[5207]

8 [a]But the fearful, and unbelieving,[571] and the abominable,[948] and murderers,[5406] and whoremongers,[4205] and sorcerers,[5332] and idolaters,[1496] and all liars, shall have their part in [b]the lake which [ppp]burneth with fire and brimstone:[2303] which is the second death.[2288]

The City Walls

9 And there came unto me one of [a]the seven angels[32] which had the seven vials[5357] full of the seven last plagues, and talked with me, saying, Come hither, I will shew thee [b]the bride, the Lamb's[721] wife.

10 And he carried me away[667] [a]in the spirit[4151] to a great and high mountain, and shewed me [b]that great city, the holy Jerusalem, descending out of heaven from God,

11 [a]Having the glory[1391] of God: and her light[5458] *was* like unto a stone most precious, even like a jasper stone, clear as crystal;

12 And [ppt]had a wall great and high, *and* had [a]twelve gates, and at the gates twelve angels, and names [pfpp]written thereon, which are *the names* of the twelve tribes of the children of Israel:

13 [a]On the east three gates; on the north three gates; on the south three gates; and on the west three gates.

14 And the wall of the city had twelve foundations, and [a]in them the names of the twelve apostles[652] of the Lamb.[721]

15 And he that [ppt]talked with me [a]had a golden reed to [aosb]measure the city, and the gates thereof, and the wall thereof.

16 And the city lieth foursquare, and the length is as large as the breadth: and he measured the city with the reed, twelve thousand furlongs.[4712] The length and the breadth and the height of it are equal.

17 And he measured the wall thereof, an hundred *and* forty *and* four cubits,[4083] *according to* the measure of a man,[444] that is, of the angel.[32]

18 And the building of the wall of it was *of* jasper: and the city *was* pure[2513] gold, like unto clear[2513] glass.

19 [a]And the foundations of the wall of the city *were* [pfpp]garnished with all manner of precious stones. The first foundation was jasper; the second, sapphire; the third, a chalcedony; the fourth, an emerald;

20 The fifth, sardonyx; the sixth, sardius; the seventh, chrysolyte; the eighth, beryl; the ninth, a topaz; the tenth, a chrysoprasus; the eleventh, a jacinth; the twelfth, an amethyst.

21 And the twelve gates *were* twelve pearls; every several gate was of one pearl: [a]and the street of the city *was* pure gold, as it were transparent glass.

22 [a]And I saw no temple[3485] therein: for the Lord[2962] God[2316] Almighty[3841] and the Lamb[721] are the temple of it.

23 [a]And the city had no need of the sun, neither of the moon, to [psa]shine[5316] in it: for the glory[1391] of God did lighten[5461] it, and the Lamb *is* the light[3088] thereof.

2 [b]Isa. 54:5; 61:10; 2Cor. 11:2
3 [a]Lev. 26:11, 12; Ezek. 43:7; 2Cor. 6:16; Rev. 7:15
4 [a]Isa. 25:8; Rev. 7:17 [b]1Cor. 15:26, 54; Rev. 20:14 [c]Isa. 35:10; 61:3; 65:19
5 [a]Rev. 4:2, 9; 5:1; 20:11 [b]Isa. 43:19; 2Cor. 5:17 [c]Rev. 19:9
6 [a]Rev. 16:17 [b]Rev. 1:8; 22:13 [c]Isa. 12:3; 55:1; John 4:10, 14; 7:37; Rev. 22:17
7 [I]Or, *these things* [a]Zech. 8:8; Heb. 8:10
8 [a]1Cor. 6:9, 10; Gal. 5:19-21; Eph. 5:5; 1Tim. 1:9; Heb. 12:14; Rev. 22:15 [b]Rev. 20:14, 15
9 [a]Rev. 15:1, 6, 7 [b]Rev. 19:7; 21:2
10 [a]Rev. 1:10; 17:3 [b]Ezek. 48; Rev. 21:2
11 [a]Rev. 21:23; 22:5
12 [a]Ezek. 48:31-34
13 [a]Ezek. 48:31-34
14 [a]Matt. 16:18; Gal. 2:9; Eph. 2:20
15 [a]Ezek. 40:3; Zech. 2:1; Rev. 11:1
19 [a]Isa. 54:11
21 [a]Rev. 22:2
22 [a]John 4:23
23 [a]Isa. 24:23; 60:19, 20; Rev. 21:11; 22:5

24 [a]And the nations of them which are saved[4982] shall walk in the light[5457] of it: and the kings[935] of the earth[1093] do bring their glory[1391] and honour[5092] into it.

25 [a]And the gates of it shall not be shut at all by day: for [b]there shall be no night there.

26 [a]And they shall bring the glory and honour of the nations[1484] into it.

27 And [a]there shall [efn]in no wise enter into it any thing that defileth,[2840] neither *whatsoever* [ppt]worketh abomination, or *maketh* a lie: but they which [pfpp]are written in the Lamb's [b]book[975] of life.[2222]

22 And he shewed me [a]a pure[2513] river of water of life,[2222] clear as crystal, proceeding out of the throne of God[2316] and of the Lamb.[721]

2 [a]In the midst of the street of it, and on either side of the river, *was there* [b]the tree of life, which [ppt]bare twelve *manner of* fruits, *and* [ppt]yielded her fruit every month: and the leaves of the tree *were* [c]for the healing[2322] of the nations.[1484]

3 And [a]there shall be no more curse: [b]but the throne of God and of the Lamb shall be in it; and his servants[1401] shall serve him:

4 And [a]they shall see his face; and [b]his name *shall be* in their foreheads.

5 [a]And there shall be no night there; and they need no candle, neither light of the sun; for [b]the Lord God giveth them light:[5461] [c]and they shall reign[936] for ever[165,1519] [3588] and ever.

Christ Is Coming Quickly

6 And he said unto me, [a]These sayings[3056] *are* faithful[4103] and true:[228] and the Lord God of the holy[40] prophets[4396] [b]sent his angel[32] [ainf]to shew unto his servants the things which must shortly [ainf]be done.

7 [a]Behold, I come quickly: [b]blessed[3107] *is* he that [ppt]keepeth the sayings of the prophecy[4394] of this book.[975]

8 And I John [ppt]saw these things, and [ppt]heard *them.* And when I [ao]had heard and [ao]seen, [a]I fell down [ainf]to worship[4352] before the feet of the angel which [ppt]shewed me these things.

9 Then saith he unto me, [a]See *thou do it* not: for I am thy fellowservant,[4889] and of thy brethren[80] the prophets,[4396] and of them which keep[5083] the sayings[3056] of this book: worship God.

10 [a]And he saith unto me, [aosi]Seal not the sayings of the prophecy of this book: [b]for the time[2540] is at hand.[1451]

11 [a]He that [ppt]is unjust,[91] [aim]let him be unjust[91] still: and he which is filthy, [aim]let him be filthy[4510] still: and he that is righteous, [aipp]let him be righteous[1344] still: and he that is holy,[40] [aipp]let him be holy[37] still.

12 [a]And, behold, I come quickly; and [b]my reward[3408] *is* with me, [ainfc]to give every man according as his work[2041] shall be.

13 [a]I am Alpha[1] and Omega,[5598] the beginning[746] and the end,[5056] the first[4413] and the last.[2078]

14 [a]Blessed[3107] *are* they that [ppt]do[4160] his commandments,[1785] that they may have right[1849] [b]to the tree of life,[2222] [c]and [asba]may enter in through the gates into the city.

15 For [a]without[1854] *are* [b]dogs, and sorcerers,[5333] and whoremongers,[4205] and murderers, and idolaters,[1496] and whosoever [ppt]loveth[5368] and [ppt]maketh a lie.

16 [a]I Jesus have sent mine angel[32] [ainf]to testify unto you these things in the churches.[1577] [b]I am the root and the offspring of David, *and* [c]the bright and morning star.

17 And the Spirit[4151] and [a]the bride say, Come.[2064] And let him that [ppt]heareth say, Come. [b]And let him that is [ppt]athirst [aim]come. And whosoever [ppt]will,[2309] [pim]let him take[2983] the water of life freely.

18 For I testify unto every man that [ppt]heareth the words[3056] of the prophecy[4394] of this book,[975] [a]If any man [psa]shall add unto these things, God shall

24 [a]Isa. 60:3, 5, 11; 66:12
25 [a]Isa. 60:11 [b]Isa. 60:20; Zech. 14:7; Rev. 22:5
26 [a]Rev. 21:24
27 [a]Isa. 35:8; 52:1; 60:21; Joel 3:17; Rev. 22:14, 15 [b]Phil. 4:3; Rev. 3:5; 13:8; 20:12

1 [a]Ezek. 47:1; Zech. 14:8
2 [a]Ezek. 47:12; Rev. 21:21 [b]Gen. 2:9; Rev. 2:7 [c]Rev. 21:24
3 [a]Zech. 14:11 [b]Ezek. 48:35
4 [a]Matt. 5:8; 1Cor. 13:12; 1John 3:2 [b]Rev. 3:12; 14:1
5 [a]Rev. 21:23, 25 [b]Ps. 36:9; 84:11 [c]Dan. 7:27; Rom. 5:17; 2Tim. 2:12; Rev. 3:21
6 [a]Rev. 19:9; 21:5 [b]Rev. 1:1
7 [a]Rev. 3:11; 22:10, 12, 20 [b]Rev. 1:3
8 [a]Rev. 19:10
9 [a]Rev. 19:10
10 [a]Dan. 8:26; 12:4, 9; Rev. 10:4 [b]Rev. 1:3
11 [a]Ezek. 3:27; Dan. 12:10; 2Tim. 3:13
12 [a]Rev. 22:7 [b]Isa. 40:10; 62:11 [c]Rom. 2:6; 14:12; Rev. 20:12
13 [a]Isa. 41:4; 44:6; 48:12; Rev. 1:8, 11; 21:6
14 [a]Dan. 12:12; 1John 3:24 [b]Rev. 2:7; 22:2 [c]Rev. 21:27
15 [a]1Cor. 6:9, 10; Gal. 5:19-21; Col. 3:6; Rev. 9:20, 21; 21:8 [b]Phil. 3:2
16 [a]Rev. 1:1 [b]Rev. 5:5 [c]Num. 24:17; Zech. 6:12; 2Pet. 1:19; Rev. 2:28
17 [a]Rev. 21:2, 9 [b]Isa. 55:1; John 7:37; Rev. 21:6
18 [a]Deut. 4:2; 12:32; Prov. 30:6

add unto him the plagues that [pfpp]are
written in this book:
19 And if any man [psa]shall take
away from the words of the book[976]
of this prophecy, [a]God shall take away
his part out of the book[976] of life,[2222]
and out of [b]the holy[40] city, and *from*
the things which [pfpp]are written in this
book.
20 He which [ppt]testifieth these things
saith, [a]Surely I come quickly. [b]Amen.[281]
[c]Even so, come, Lord[2962] Jesus.
21 [a]The grace[5485] of our Lord Jesus
Christ *be* with you all. Amen.

19 [a]Ex. 32:33; Ps. 69:28; Rev. 3:5; 13:8 [b]Rev. 21:2
20 [a]Rev. 22:12 [b]John 21:25 [c]2Tim. 4:8
21 [a]Rom. 16:20, 24; 2Thess. 3:18

BIBLE STUDY HELPS

GRAMMATICAL CODES TO THE GRAMMATICAL NOTATIONS

The grammatical codes, the small codes at the upper left of words in the New Testament text of this Bible, are listed alphabetically below. These codes represent grammatical constructions found in the Greek New Testament, which are listed after each code. The number(s) in parenthesis after each grammatical construction refer to the grammatical notations that explain the construction. For example, the future middle **fm**, is explained by notation **21** (the *Future Tense*) and notation **28** (the *Middle Voice*).

aid..........articular infinitive with *dia* **(10)**
aie..........articular infinitive with *en* **(12)**
aies........articular infinitive with *eis* **(11)**
aifp.........aorist infinitive passive **(9,25,33)**
aim.........aorist imperative **(4)**
aime.......articular infinitive with *meta* **(13)**
ainf.........aorist infinitive **(5,25)**
aip..........articular infinitive with *pro* **(14)**
aipp........aorist imperative passive **(4,33)**
aipr.........articular infinitive with *pros* **(15)**
ajn..........adjectival noun **(2)**
an...........anarthrous **(3)**
ao...........aorist **(9)**
aom........aorist middle **(9,28)**
aop.........aorist passive **(9,33)**
aosb.......aorist subjunctive **(7,43)**
aosi........aorist subjunctive used as an imperative **(8)**
apt..........aorist participle **(6,32)**
aptp.......aorist participle passive **(6,32,33)**
art..........article (definite) **(17)**
asba.......aorist subjunctive active **(7,43,1)**
asbm......aorist subjunctive middle **(7,43,28)**
asbp.......aorist subjunctive passive **(7,43,33)**
cd...........comparative degree **(16)**
efn..........emphatic future negative **(18)**
epn.........emphatic personal pronoun **(19)**
f.............feminine gender **(20)**
finf..........future infinitive **(21,25)**
fm...........future middle **(21,28)**
fp...........future passive **(21,33)**
ft............future tense **(21)**
gc...........genitive case **(22)**
infg.........infinitive with genitive article **(26)**
ipf...........imperfect **(23)**
m............masculine gender **(27)**
n.............neuter gender **(29)**
nn...........noun **(30)**
opt..........optative mood **(31)**
pf............perfect tense **(34)**
pfi...........perfect indicative **(34,24)**
pfin.........perfect infinitive **(34,25)**
pfip.........perfect indicative passive **(34,24,33)**
pfp..........perfect participle **(34,32)**
pfpp.......perfect passive participle **(34,33,32)**
pim.........present imperative **(37)**
pin..........present indicative **(41,24)**
pinf.........present infinitive **(38,25)**
pinp........present indicative passive **(41,24,33)**
pip..........present infinitive passive **(38,25,33)**
pl............plural **(36)**
plpf.........pluperfect **(35)**
pp...........present passive **(41,33)**
ppp.........present passive participle **(39,33,32)**
ppt..........present participle **(39)**
pred.......predicate **(44)**
psa.........present subjunctive active **(40,1)**
psmp......present subjunctive middle passive **(40,28,33)**
sg...........singular **(42)**

GRAMMATICAL NOTATIONS

GRAMMATICAL DEFINITIONS OF THE GRAMMATICAL CATEGORIES

1. The *Active Voice* represents the action as accomplished by the subject of the verb. In Greek it is to be distinguished from the *Middle Voice* **(28)** and *Passive Voice* **(33).** Examples: he came, they see, you have believed.

2. An *Adjectival Noun* **(ajn)** is an adjective used as a noun. Example: *makarioi,* "blessed," in the Beatitudes.

3. *Anarthrous* **(an)** refers to a word or group of words which appear without the definite article (*ho, he, to* [3588] "the." Greek has no indefinite article, "a" or "an," as in English. Sometimes it is best to translate an anarthrous word by supplying "a" or "an" before it. In fact, due to reasons of English style or Greek idiom, "the" is even an appropriate translation in some cases. Anarthrous constructions in Greek are most often intended to point out the quality of something. In most cases, supplying an English indefinite article to translate an anarthrous construction would be incorrect. Example: It is the difference between "God is a Spirit" and "God is Spirit" (John 4:24). See also *Definite Article* **(17).**

4. The *Aorist Imperative* **(aim)** means a command for doing something in the future that is a simple action. This is contrasted with the *Present Imperative* **(37),** which involves a command for a continuous or repetitive action.

5. The *Aorist Infinitive* **(ainf)** refers to simple action and not the linear action represented by the *Present Infinitive* **(38).** Examples: *elpizō*, "I hope," *grapsai* (aorist infinitive of *graphō*). *epistolēn humin* would be translated, "I hope to write a letter to you." It does not signify the time of action. See also *Infinitive* **(25).**

6. The *Aorist Participle* **(apt)** expresses simple action, as opposed to the continuous action of the *Present Participle* **(39).** It does not in itself indicate the time of the action. However, when its relationship to the main verb is temporal, it usually signifies action prior to that of the main verb. Example: "He took some bread, and after a blessing (aorist participle) He broke it" (Mark 14:22). See also *Participle* **(32).**

7. The *Aorist Subjunctive* **(aosb)** is to be distinguished from the *Present Subjunctive* **(40)** in that it refers to simple, undefined action, while the latter refers to continuous or repeated action. It does not signify the time of the action. See also *Subjunctive Mood* **(43).**

8. The *Aorist Subjunctive used as an imperative* **(aosi)** usually forbids an action which is not in progress and thus commands that it not be started. Example: *mē*, "not," *eisenegkēs*, "lead," in the aorist subjunctive (Matt. 6:13), indicates that when the Lord taught us to pray that God would not lead us into temptation, God was not already leading us into temptation. For the opposite of this, see *Present Imperative* **(37).**

9. The *Aorist Tense* **(ao)** is used for simple, undefined action. In the indicative mood the aorist tense usually denotes a simple act occurring in past time. It should be distinguished from the imperfect tense which signifies continuous action in past time. With few exceptions, whenever the aorist tense is used in any mood other than the indicative, the verb does not have any temporal significance. In other words, it refers only to the reality of an event or action.

10. The *Articular Infinitive with the preposition dia,* "because of" **(aid),** is used with the accusative article and denotes cause. Example: *dia,* "for," *to,* neuter accusative of the article, *einai,* the infinitive of *eimi,* "to be," *philos,* "friend" (Luke 11:8). The expression *dia to einai* is best translated "because he is." The whole construction, therefore, would be rendered "because he is a friend."

11. The *Articular Infinitive with the preposition eis,* "unto" **(aies),** is used with the accusative article and most commonly denotes purpose. Example: *eis,* "unto," *to,* the definite article in the neuter accusative, *thanatōsai,* "to kill," *auton,* "him" (Mark 14:55) would be translated, "in order to put him [Jesus] to death."

12. The *Articular Infinitive with the preposition en,* "in" **(aie),** is used with the dative article and usually expresses the time at which something occurs. It is usually translated "while" or "when." Example: *en,* "in," *tō,* "the," *hupagein,* "to go," *auton,* "him" (Luke 8:42). This is best translated, "while he was going" or "when he was going."

13. The *Articular Infinitive with the preposition meta,* "after" **(aime),** is used with the accusative article. Example: *meta,* "after," *to,* the neuter accusative article, *paradothēnai,* "to be delivered," *ton,* "the," *Ioannēn,* "John" (Mark 1:14) is best translated, "after John was arrested."

14. The *Articular Infinitive with the preposition pro,* "before" **(aip),** is used with the genitive article. Example: *eichon,* "I was having," *pro,* "before," *tou,* the genitive of the neuter *to,* "the," *ton,* "the" in the accusative, *kosmon,* "world" in the accusative, *einai,* the infinitive of *eimi,* "to be," *para,* "with," *soi,* "you" (John 17:5) would be translated, "(the glory which) I was having with you before [*pro*] the world was."

15. The *Articular Infinitive with the preposition pros,* "toward" **(aipr),** is used with the accusative article and usually denotes purpose. Example: *pros,* "toward," *to,* neuter definite article in the accusative, *dunasthai,* "to be able," *humas,* "you" (Eph. 6:11) would be translated, "in order that you may be able."

16. The *Comparative Degree* **(cd)** is used when two items are being compared, as opposed to three or more, when the superlative is used. In New Testament Greek, however, there is a tendency for the degree to move up one step. Hence, the positive degree can be used with the comparative meaning, the comparative with superlative meaning, and the superlative with elative meaning ("very"). Example: *meizōn,* "greater" (comparative degree), *toutōn,* "these," *hē,* "the," *agapē,* "love" (1 Cor. 13:13) should be translated "the greatest of these is love," since three items are being compared.

17. The *Definite Article* **(art)** in Greek is sometimes translated with the English definite article, "the." However, the function of the two is quite different. In English, the definite article serves merely to particularize, to refer to a particular object. In Greek, however, it serves to emphasize, to identify in some way, the person or thing it modifies. There is perhaps no other part of Greek grammar where the Greek idiom differs so greatly from the English. For instance, an English grammarian would never place the definite article before a personal proper noun (e.g., "the Thomas"), though in Greek it is very common. In Greek, the significance of the presence or absence of the definite article is often critical to the understanding of a passage, requiring the most intimate knowledge of Greek syntax. See also *Anarthrous* **(3).**

18. The *Emphatic Future Negative* **(efn)** is indicated by the negative particles *ou,* "not," and *mē,* "not," as if it were "not, not," a double negative. It is most often used with the *Aorist Subjunctive* **(7),** but sometimes with the future indicative and indicates strong future negation. Example: *ou,* "not," *mē,* "not," *parelthē,* "will pass away," *hē,* "the," *genea,* "generation," *autē,* "this" (Matt. 24:34) would be translated, "This generation will definitely not pass away."

19. The *Emphatic Personal Pronoun* **(epn)** is used when emphasis is being placed on a person. This is especially useful when the subject of a verb is being emphasized. Since the verb ending in Greek indicates the person and number of the subject, a personal pronoun subject is not usually expressed as a separate word. Hence, when the pronoun is used, it calls special attention to the subject. Example: It is the difference between *legō,* "I say," *humin,* "to you," "I say to you," and the way the passage actually reads, *egō,* emphatic personal pronoun, *legō,* "I say," *humin,* "to you;" i.e., "I myself say to you" (Matt. 5:22).

20. *Feminine Gender* **(f)** may refer to a female or to a noun which has no relation to gender. Examples: *hē gunē,* "the woman," *hē heortē,* "the feast."

21. The *Future Tense* **(ft)** is concerned with the time of action, not the kind of action, although the future by itself almost always refers to a punctiliar action.

22. The *Genitive case* **(gc)** is used primarily to indicate possession, although it has several other functions. Example of the possessive use: my mother's sister, the sister of my mother.

23. The *Imperfect Tense* **(ipf)** is only used in the indicative mood and refers to continuous or linear action in past time. It is to be distinguished from the aorist indicative (see *Aorist Tense* **[17]**), which conceives of an action in past time as simply having taken place. Example: The aorist *eschon* would be translated "I had," but the imperfect *eichon,* "I was having."

24. The *Indicative Mood* makes an assertion of fact and is used with all six Greek tenses. It is the only mood in which distinctions can regularly be made about the time when an action occurs. Examples: he will go, they had said, she saw.

25. The *Infinitive* is a verbal noun, which has many more uses in Greek than it does in English. However, its most common use is best translated by the English infinitive. Examples: to see, to go, to throw. See *Aorist Infinitive* **(5)** and *Present Infinitive* **(38).** See also notations **10–15** and **26** for special uses of the infinitive.

26. The *Infinitive with a genitive article* **(infg)** frequently denotes purpose. It has the same meaning as the *articular infinitive with eis* or *pros* **(11,15),** to denote purpose, but it does not have a preposition before it. Example: *zētein,* "seeking," *to,* "the," *paidion,* "child," *tou,* genitive article, *apolesai,* "to destroy," *auto,* "him" (Matt. 2:13) would be translated, "seeking the child to (in order to) destroy him."

27. *Masculine Gender* **(m)** may refer to a male or to a noun that has no relation to gender. Example: *huios,* "son," or *naos,* "temple."

28. The *Middle Voice* represents the subject as acting in some way upon himself or concerning himself. Since English does not have a middle voice, it is usually difficult to render the middle voice into smooth English.

29. *Neuter Gender* **(n)** may refer to a thing or to a noun which, though neuter, refers to a person. Examples: *hieron,* "temple" or *teknon,* "child." Hence, for example, the fact that *pneuma,* "spirit" or "Spirit" is neuter has no bearing on whether or not the Holy Spirit is a person.

30. A *Noun* **(nn)** is the name of anything. Examples: Peter, sister, justice.

31. The *Optative Mood* **(opt)** is rare in New Testament Greek. It is a weaker mood than the subjunctive and usually expresses a wish.

32. The *Participle* is a verbal adjective. It has a wide range of possible meanings, some of which can only be inferred from the context. It is often best translated by the English participle. Examples: having gone, seeing the multitude, receiving the gift.

33. The *Passive Voice* represents the subject as receiving the action of the verb and English usually uses a form of the verb "to be" to express the passive. However, a passive form may sometimes be translated by an intransitive verb in English. Example: The verb "to burn" in 1 Corinthians 7:9 could either be translated "be burned" or "burn," in the sense of "being inflamed."

34. The *Perfect Tense* **(pf)** represents an action that was completed in the past but has continuing results. It has no exact equivalent in English, but is usually best translated by using the auxiliary "has" or "have." Example: "It has been written," i.e. "It stands written."

35. The *Pluperfect Tense* **(plpf)** is like the *Perfect Tense* **(34),** except that the existing result of the action is also in past time. Usually the English auxiliary "had" is used when translating a pluperfect. However, it may also be used when translating an aorist.

36. The *Plural Number* **(pl)** in New Testament Greek, as in English, refers to two or more items. Example: twelve apostles, two brothers, forty years. See also *Singular Number* **(42).**

37. The *Present Imperative* **(pim)** is a command to do something in the future and involves continuous or repeated action. When it is negative and prohibits an action, it usually carries with it the implication of stopping an action that has been taking place. For the opposite of this, see *Aorist Subjunctive used as an imperative* **(8).**

38. The *Present Infinitive* **(pinf)** refers to continuous or repeated action, without implying anything about the time of the action. See also *Aorist Infinitive* **(5)** and *Infinitive* **(25).**

39. The *Present Participle* **(ppt)** expresses continuous or repeated action. It does not in itself indicate the time of the action, but when its relationship to the main verb is temporal, it usually signifies action contemporary with that of the main verb. Example: "While they were eating (present participle), . . . he broke (the bread)" (Mark 14:22). See also Aorist Participle **(6)** and *Participle* **(32).**

40. The *Present Subjunctive Mood* refers to continuous or repeated action, without implying anything about the time of the action. See also *Subjunctive Mood* **(43).**

41. The *Present Tense* **(24)** represents contemporaneous action, as opposed to action in the past or the future. It normally refers to continuous or repeated action. However, in the Indicative Mood **(24)** it may represent punctiliar action.

42. The *Singular Number* **(sg)** in Greek, as in English, refers to one of something. Examples: one woman, the seventh commandment. See also *Plural Number* **(36).**

43. The *Subjunctive Mood* makes an assertion about which there is some doubt, uncertainty, or indefiniteness. It is closely related to the future tense, which helps point up the fact that often the uncertainty only arises because the action has not yet occurred. An example of this is the *Emphatic Future Negative* **(18).** A Greek subjunctive cannot always be rendered precisely into good English. Examples: I would have come, had you been here, let us go.

44. The *Predicate* **(pred).** Every sentence has two parts: the subject which names the person or thing uppermost in mind and the predicate which makes an assertion about the subject. The predicate may be a noun (e.g., he is the *teacher*); a pronoun (e.g., I am *yours*); or a predicate adjective (e.g., *Theos ēn ho logos,* "the Word was God" (John 1:1c), where *ho logos*, "the word," with the definite article, is the subject and *Theos,* "God," is the predicate.

CONCORDANCE

to the Old and New Testaments

This concordance is a compilation of **key words** and **proper names** found in Scripture. They are formatted as follows: **Proper names** are followed by a pronunciation guide and defining or explanatory words or phrases. Definitions are denoted by italics. Words in all capital characters refer to words that occur elsewhere in this concordance. **Key words** are followed by portions of Scripture, along with their references, designed to give an example of how the word is used in its context. These words are abbreviated to their first letter in the Scriptures portions (e.g., "wash" is "**w**" [in boldface]). Verbs that occur in different forms will appear under the root of that word (e.g., "worked" will be under "work").

A

AARON a´-ron
light (s?) Ex 4:14

AARONITES a´-ron-ites
descendants of Aaron 1 Chr 12:27

ABADDON a-bad´-don
destruction Rev 9:11

ABAGTHA a-bag´-thah
given by fortune Esth 1:10

ABANA a´-ba-nah
stony 2 Kgs 5:12

ABARIM a´-ba-rim
regions beyond Num 27:12

ABASE
and **a** him that is high Ezek 21:26
walk in pride he is able to **a** Dan 4:37
exalteth himself shall be **a** Matt 23:12; Luke 14:11; 18:14
I know both how to be **a** Phil 4:12

ABATED
days the waters were **a** Gen 8:3
it shall be **a** from Lev 27:18
nor his natural force **a** Deut 34:7
Then their anger was **a** Judg 8:3

ABBA ab´-bah
father Mark 14:36

ABDA ab´-dah
servant 1 Kgs 4:6

ABDEEL ab´-de-el
same as ABDIEL Jer 36:26

ABDI ab´-di
servant of Jehovah 1 Chr 6:44

ABDIEL ab´-di-el
servant of God 1 Chr 5:15

ABDON ab´-don
servile Judg 12:13

ABED-NEGO a-bed´-ne-go
servant (worshiper) of Nebo Dan 1:7

ABEL a´-bel
1 *vanity* Gen 4:2
2 *A meadow* 2 Sam 20:14

ABEL-BETH-MAACHAH a-bel-beth-ma´-a-kah
meadow of the house of Maachah 1 Kgs 15:20

ABEL-MAIM a´-bel-ma´-im
meadow of the waters 2 Chr 16:4

ABEL-MEHOLAH a´-bel-me-ho´-lah
meadow of dancing Judg 7:22

ABEL-MIZRAIM a´-bel-miz-ra´-im
meadow of Egypt Gen 50:11

ABEL-SHITTIM a´-bel-shit´-im
meadow of Acacias Num 33:49

ABEZ a´-bez
whiteness Josh 19:20

ABHOR
made our savour to be **a** Ex 5:21
my inward friends **a** me Job 19:19
he wroth, and greatly **a** Israel Ps 78:59
thou hast cast off and **a** Ps 89:38
a all manner of meat Ps 107:18
I hate and **a** lying Ps 119:163
a of the Lord shall fall Prov 22:14
land that thou **a** Is 7:16
shall be an **a** unto all flesh Is 66:24
made thy beauty to be **a** Ezek 16:25
I **a** the excellency of Jacob Amos 6:8

ABI a´-bi
short for ABIAH 2 Kgs 18:2

ABI-ALBON a-bi-al´-bon
father of strength 2 Sam 23:31

ABIA a-bi´-ah
Gr. for ABIJAH Matt 1:7

ABIAH a-bi´-ah
same as ABIJAH 2 Kgs 18:2

ABIASAPH a-bi´-a-saf
father of gathering Ex 6:24

ABIATHAR a-bi´-a-thar
father of plenty 1 Sam 22:20

ABIB a´-bib
an ear of corn, or green ear Ex 13:4

ABIDAH a-bi´-dah
father of knowledge Gen 25:4

ABIDAN a-bi´-dan
father of a judge Num 1:11

ABIDE
let thy servant **a** instead Gen 44:33
a ye every man in his place Ex 16:29
he saw Israel **a** in his tents Num 24:2
a without the camp Num 31:19
shall not **a** with us 1 Sam 5:7
nor **a** in the paths thereof Job 24:13
who shall **a** in thy tabernacle? Ps 15:1
shall **a** under the shadow Ps 91:1
reproof of life **a** among Prov 15:31
the earth **a** for ever Eccl 1:4
If ye will still **a** in this land Jer 42:10
shall no man **a** Jer 49:18,33; 50:40
shalt **a** for me many days Hos 3:3
very terrible, and who can **a** it? Joel 2:11
there **a** till ye Matt 10:11; Mark 6:10
shepherds **a** in field Luke 2:8
there **a**, and thence depart Luke 9:4
to day I must **a** at thy house Luke 19:5
A with us Luke 24:29
wrath of God **a** on him John 3:36
have not his word **a** in you John 5:38
Comforter, that he may **a** John 14:16
A in me John 15:4
he that **a** in me John 15:5
a in my love John 15:10
come into my house, and **a** Acts 16:15
if any man's work **a** 1 Cor 3:14
now **a** faith, hope, charity 1 Cor 13:13
if we believe not, he **a** 2 Tim 2:13

ABIEL a´-bi-el
father of strength 1 Sam 9:1

ABIEZER a´-bi-e´-zer
father of help Josh 17:2

ABIEZRITE a´-bi-ez´-rite
a descendant of Abiezer Judg 6:11

ABIGAIL a´-bi-gale
father of exultation 1 Sam 25:14

ABIHAIL a´-bi-hale
father of strength Num 3:35

ABIHU a-bi´-hoo
He [God] is father Ex 6:23

ABIHUD a-bi´-hood
father of Judah 1 Chr 8:3

ABIJAH a-bi´-jah
father of Jehovah 1 Kgs 14:1

ABIJAM a-bi´-jam
another spelling of ABIJAH 1 Kgs 14:31

ABILENE a´-bi-le´-ne
a grassy place (?) Luke 3:1

ABILITY
They gave after their **a** Ezra 2:69
such as had **a** to stand Dan 1:4
according to his several **a** Matt 25:15
as of the **a** which God giveth 1 Pet 4:11

ABIMAEL a´-bi-ma´-el
father of Mael Gen 10:28

ABIMELECH a-bi´-me-lek
father of the king Gen 20:2

ABINADAB a-bi´-na-dab
father of nobility 1 Sam 7:1

ABINER ab´-ner
same as ABNER 1 Sam 14:50

ABINOAM a´-bi-no´-am
father of pleasantness Judg 4:6

ABIRAM a-bi´-ram
father of loftiness Num 16:1

ABISHAG a-bi´-shag
father of error (?) 1 Kgs 1:3

ABISHAI a´-bi-sha´-i
father of a gift 1 Sam 26:6

ABISHALOM a-bi´-sha-lom
same as ABSALOM 1 Kgs 15:2

ABISHUA a´-bi-shoo´-ah
father of welfare 1 Chr 6:4

ABISHUR a-bi´-shoor
of the wall 1 Chr 2:28

ABITAL a-bi´-tal
father of dew 2 Sam 3:4

ABITUB a-bi´-toob
father of goodness 1 Chr 8:11

ABIUD a-bi´-ood
Gr. for ABIHUD Matt 1:13

ABLE
Every man give as he is **a** Deut 16:17
no man hath been **a** to stand Josh 23:9
Who is **a** to stand? 1 Sam 6:20
who is **a** to judge 1 Kgs 3:9
who is **a** to build 2 Chr 2:6
a to stand before envy? Prov 27:4
land is not **a** to bear Amos 7:10
God is **a** of these stones Matt 3:9
Believe ye that I am **a** Matt 9:28
Are ye **a** to drink Matt 20:22
not **a** to do that thing Luke 12:26
not **a** to resist the wisdom Acts 6:10
promised he was **a** Rom 4:21
a to separate us Rom 8:39
tempted above that ye are **a** 1 Cor 10:13
a ministers of the new testament 2 Cor 3:6
a to comprehend with all saints Eph 3:18
a to even subdue all things Phil 3:21
a to succour them that are tempted Heb 2:18
a to save and to destroy James 4:12
a to keep you from falling Jude 1:24
a to open book Rev 5:3
who shall be **a** to stand? Rev 6:17

ABNER ab´-ner
father of light 1 Sam 14:50

ABOARD
we went **a** Acts 21:2

ABODE (n)
make our **a** with him John 14:23

ABODE (v)
his bow **a** in strength Gen 49:24
the Lord **a** on mount Sinai Ex 24:16
house of God, and **a** there Judg 21:2
Mary **a** with her Luke 1:56
and it **a** upon him John 1:32
and **a** with him that day John 1:39
and **a** not in the truth John 8:44
long time therefore **a**, Acts 14:3
he **a** with them, and wrought Acts 18:3

ABOLISH
the end of that which is **a** 2 Cor 3:13
a in his flesh the enmity Eph 2:15
Christ, who hath **a** death 2 Tim 1:10

ABOMINABLE
a in following idols 1 Kgs 21:26
How much more **a** Job 15:16
they have done **a** works Ps 14:1
have done **a** iniquity Ps 53:1
like an **a** branch Is 14:19
a things Is 65:4; Jer 16:18
this **a** thing that I hate Jer 44:4
they deny him, being **a** Titus 1:16
a idolatries 1 Pet 4:3

ABOMINATION
a unto the Egyptians Gen 43:32; 46:34
commit any of these **a** Lev 18:26
bring an **a** into Deut 7:26
after the **a** of nations Deut 18:9
because of these **a** Deut 18:12
all that do unrighteously are an **a** Deut 25:16
Israel also was had in **a** 1 Sam 13:4
a to the Lord Prov 3:32; 11:20
wickedness an **a** to my lips Prov 8:7
sacrifice is **a** Prov 15:8; 21:27
way of the wicked is an **a** Prov 15:9
thoughts of the wicked are an **a** Prov 15:26
even his prayer shall be **a** Prov 28:9
the residue thereof an **a** Is 44:19
put away thine **a** out of my sight Jer 4:1
when they had committed **a** Jer 6:15; 8:12
because of all thine **a** Ezek 5:9
desolate, because of all their **a** Ezek 33:29
shall place the **a** Dan 11:31
shall see the **a** of desolation Matt 24:15; Mark 13:14
esteemed among men is **a** Luke 16:15
whatsoever worketh **a** Rev 21:27

ABOUND
faithful man shall **a** Prov 28:20
that ye may **a** in hope Rom 15:13
always **a** in the work 1 Cor 15:58
sufferings of Christ **a** 2 Cor 1:5

ABOVE
thou shalt be **a** only Deut 28:13
is there from **a** Job 31:2
way of life is **a** to wise Prov 15:24
disciple is not **a** his master Matt 10:24
He that cometh from **a** is **a** all John 3:31
I am from **a** John 8:23
one day **a** another Rom 14:5
a that which is written 1 Cor 4:6
Jerusalem which is **a** is free Gal 4:26

ABRAHAM a´-bra-ham
father of a multitude Gen 17:5

ABRAM ab´-ram
high father Gen 11:26

ABSALOM ab´-sa-lom
father of peace 2 Sam 3:3

ABSENT
a in body 1 Cor 5:3
a from Lord 2 Cor 5:6
a in flesh Col 2:5

ABSTAIN
a from pollutions of idols Acts 15:20
a from all appearance of evil 1 Thess 5:22
a from fleshly lusts 1 Pet 2:11

ABSTINENCE
after long **a** Paul stood forth Acts 27:21

ABUNDANCE
out of the **a** of my complaint 1 Sam 1:16
sound of **a** of rain 1 Kgs 18:41
sacrifices in **a** 1 Chr 29:21
trusted in the **a** of riches Ps 52:7
a of peace Ps 72:7; Jer 33:6
loveth **a** with increase Eccl 5:10
a of rich will not suffer him Eccl 5:12
out of the **a** of the heart Matt 12:34; Luke 21:4
he shall have more **a** Matt 13:12
life consisteth not in the **a** Luke 12:15
of affliction the **a** of their joy 2 Cor 8:2
through **a** of the revelations 2 Cor 12:7

ABUNDANT
and distil upon man **a** Job 36:28
a utter the memory Ps 145:7
and much more **a** Is 56:12
laboured more **a** than they all 1 Cor 15:10
grace of our Lord was exceeding **a** 1 Tim 1:14
shed on us **a** Titus 3:6
ministered unto you **a** 2 Pet 1:11

ABUSE
use this world as not **a** 1 Cor 7:31
that I **a** not my power 1 Cor 9:18

ACCAD ak´-ad
fortress (?) Gen 10:10

ACCEPT
shalt thou not be **a**? Gen 4:7
a before the Lord Ex 28:38
a the work of his hands Deut 33:11
a in the sight of all 1 Sam 18:5
the Lord thy God **a** thee 2 Sam 24:23
a of the multitude Esth 10:3
will ye **a** his person? Job 13:8
him will I **a** Job 42:8
a the person of the wicked Prov 18:5
I will not **a** them Jer 14:12; Amos 5:22
supplication be **a** Jer 42:2
I will **a** Ezek 20:40; 43:27
should I **a** this? Mal 1:13
no prophet is **a** Luke 4:24
he that worketh righteousness is **a** Acts 10:35
be **a** of the saints Rom 15:31
we may be **a** of him 2 Cor 5:9

ACCESS
we have **a** by faith Rom 5:2
both have **a** by one Spirit Eph 2:18
have boldness and **a** Eph 3:12

ACCHO ak´-o
sand-heated Judg 1:31

ACCOMPLISH
a as a hireling Job 14:6
they **a** a diligent search Ps 64:6
desire **a** is sweet Prov 13:19
her warfare is **a** Is 40:2
straitened till it be **a** Luke 12:50
afflictions are **a** same 1 Pet 5:9

ACCORD
with one **a** Acts 1:14; 4:24; 8:6
being of one **a** Phil 2:2

ACCORDING
a as he hath promised Ex 12:25
a as the LORD hath blessed Deut 16:10
a to his ways Job 34:11; Jer 17:10; 32:19
a to works Matt 16:27; 2 Tim 4:14
a to the appearance John 7:24
the called **a** to his purpose Rom 8:28
gifts differing **a** to the grace Rom 12:6
a to that a man hath 2 Cor 8:12

ACCOUNT (n)
give **a** thereof in the day Matt 12:36
give **a** of thy stewardship Luke 16:2
give **a** of himself to God Rom 14:12
as they that must give **a** Heb 13:17

ACCOUNT (v)
a worthy to obtain Luke 20:35
a to him for righteousness Gal 3:6

ACCURSED
a thing Josh 6:18; 7:1; 22:20
wish that myself were **a** Rom 9:3
Spirit of God calleth Jesus **a** 1 Cor 12:3
let him be **a** Gal 1:8,9

ACCUSATION
from any man by false **a** Luke 19:8
receive not an **a** 1 Tim 5:19
railing **a** 2 Pet 2:11
bring against him railing **a** Jude 1:9

ACCUSE
A not a servant Prov 30:10
when he was **a**, he answered Matt 27:12
the same was **a** Luke 16:1
I will **a** you to the Father John 5:45
not **a** of riot or unruly Titus 1:6

ACELDAMA a-kel´-da-mah
field of blood Acts 1:19

ACHAIA a-ka´-yah
Greece Acts 18:12

ACHAICUS a-ka´-ik-us
belonging to Achaia 1 Cor 16:17

ACHAN a´-kan
troubler Josh 7:1

ACHAR a´-kar
same as ACHAN 1 Chr. 2:7

ACHAZ a´-kaz
Gr. for AHAZ Matt 1:9

ACHBOR ak´-bor
a mouse Gen 36:38

ACHIM a´-kim
short for JACHIN (?) Matt 1:14

ACHISH a´-kish
angry (?) 1 Sam 21:10

ACHMETHA ak´-me-thah
fortress (?) Ezra 6:2

ACHOR a´-kor
trouble Josh 7:24

ACHSA ak´-sah
same as ACHSAH 1 Chr 2:49

ACHSAH ak´-sah
anklet Josh 15:16

ACHSHAPH ak´-shaf
enchantment Josh 11:1

ACHZIB ak´-zib
deceit Josh 15:44

ACKNOWLEDGE
I **a** my sin Ps 32:5
in all thy ways **a** him Prov 3:6
Israel **a** us not Is 63:16
he that **a** the Son 1 John 2:23

ACQUAINT
A now thyself with him Job 22:21
art **a** with all my ways Ps 139:3
yet **a** my heart with wisdom Eccl 2:3
and **a** with grief Is 53:3

ACQUAINTANCE
mine **a** are verily estranged Job 19:13
a fear to mine **a** Ps 31:11
my guide, and mine **a** Ps 55:13

ACQUIT
thou wilt not **a** me Job 10:14
will not at all **a** the wicked Nah 1:3

ACTIONS
by him **a** are weighed 1 Sam 2:3

ACTIVITY
any men of **a** among them Gen 47:6

ADADAH a´-da-dah
festival (?) Josh 15:22

ADAH a´-dah
ornament Gen 4:19

ADAIAH a-da´-yah
whom Jehovah adorns 2 Kgs 22:1

ADALIA a´-da-li´-ah
upright (?) Esth 9:8

ADAM a´-dam
red Gen 2:19

ADAMAH a´-da-mah
red earth Josh 19:36

ADAMI a´-da-mi
human Josh 19:33

ADAR a´-dar
fire (?) Esth 3:7

ADBEEL ad´-be-el
miracle of God (?) Gen 25:13

ADDAN ad´-an
humble (?) Ezra 2:59

ADDAR ad´-ar
greatness (?) 1 Chr 8:3

ADDER
an **a** in the path Gen 49:17
like the deaf **a** Ps 58:4
tread upon the lion and **a** Ps 91:13
tongues like a serpent; **a** poison Ps 140:3
stingeth like and **a** Prov 23:32

ADDI ad´-i
ornament (?) Luke 3:28

ADDICTED
they have **a** themselves 1 Cor 16:15

ADDITION
certain **a** made of thin work 1 Kgs 7:29
at the side of every **a** 1 Kgs 7:30
everyone, and **a** round about 1 Kgs 7:36

ADDON ad´-on
same as ADDAN Neh 7:61

ADER a´-der
flock 1 Chr 8:15

ADIEL a´-di-el
ornament of God 1 Chr 4:36

ADIN a´-din
slender Ezra 2:15

ADINA a´-di-nah
same as ADIN 1 Chr 11:42

ADINO a´-di-no
same as ADIN (?) 2 Sam 23:8

ADITHAIM a´-dith-a´-im
twofold ornament Josh 15:36

ADJURE
Joshua **a** them at Josh 6:26
Saul had **a** the people 1 Sam 14:24
shall I **a** thee that 1 Kgs 22:16; 2 Chr 18:15
I **a** thee Matt 26:63; Mark 5:7
We **a** you by Jesus Acts 19:13

ADLAI ad´-la-i
just (?) 1 Chr 27:29

ADMAH ad´-mah
same as ADAMAH Gen 10:19

ADMATHA ad´-math-ah
earthly, dark-colored (?) Esth 1:14

ADMINISTRATION
differences of **a**, but 1 Cor 12:5
For the **a** of this service 2 Cor 9:12

ADMIRATION
men's persons in **a** Jude 1:16
I wondered with great **a** Rev 17:6

ADMONISH
Paul **a** them Acts 27:9
a one another Rom 15:14; Col 3:16
in the Lord, and **a** you 1 Thess 5:12
a him as a brother 2 Thess 3:15
Moses was **a** of God Heb 8:5

ADMONITION
written for our **a** 1 Cor 10:11
nurture and **a** of the Lord Eph 6:4
first and second **a**, reject Titus 3:10

ADNA ad´-nah
pleasure Ezra 10:30

ADNAH ad´-nah
same as ADNA 2 Chr 17:14

ADO
why make he this **a** Mark 5:39

ADONI-BEZEK a-do´-ni-be´-zek
lord of Bezek Judg 1:5

ADONI-ZEDEK a-do´-ni-ze´-dek
lord of justice Josh 10:1

ADONIJAH a´-do-ni´-jah
Jehovah is my Lord 2 Sam 3:4

ADONIKAM a´-do-ni´-kam
lord of enemies Ezra 2:13

ADONIRAM a´-do-ni´-ram
lord of height 1 Kgs 4:6

ADOPTION
received the Spirit of **a** Rom 8:15
waiting for the **a** Rom 8:23
to whom pertaineth **a** Rom 9:4
receive the **a** of sons Gal 4:5
unto the **a** of children Eph 1:5

ADORAIM a´-dor-a´-im
two chiefs (?) 2 Chr 11:9

ADORAM a-do´-ram
contracted from ADONIRAM 2 Sam 20:24

ADORN
bride **a** herself Is 61:10; Rev 21:2
women **a** 1 Tim 2:9; 1 Pet 3:3,5
a doctrine of God Titus 2:10

ADRAMMELECH ad-ram´-me-lek
Adar is king, or king of fire (?) 2 Kgs 17:31

ADRAMYTTIUM ad´-ra-mit´-ti-um
the mansion of death Acts 27:2

ADRIEL a´-dri-el
flock of God 1 Sam 18:19

ADULLAM a-dul´-am
justice of the people Josh 12:15

ADULLAMITE a-dul´-am-ite
a native of Adullam Gen 38:1

ADUMMIM a-dum´-im
the red (men?) Josh 15:7

ADVANCED
the LORD **a** Moses 1 Sam 12:6
Hammedatha the Agagite, and **a** him Esth 3:1
how he had **a** him Esth 5:11
the king **a** him Esth 10:2

ADVANTAGE
what is a man **a**? Luke 9:25
what **a**? Rom 3:1; 1 Cor 15:32
lest Satan should get an **a** 2 Cor 2:11

ADVENTURE
which would not **a** to set Deut 28:56
fought for you, and **a** his life Judg 9:17
would not **a** himself Acts 19:31

ADVERSARY
a to thine **a** Ex 23:22
stood in the way for an **a** Num 22:22
his **a** Deut 32:43; Ps 89:42; Is 59:18; Jer 46:10; Nah 1:2; Luke 13:17
neither **a** nor evil 1 Kgs 5:4
LORD stirred up an **a** 1 Kgs 11:14,23
that mine **a** had written Job 31:35
my **a** Ps 38:20; 69:19; 109:20,29; Is 1:24
how long shall the **a** reproach? Ps 74:10
who is mine **a** Is 50:8
thine **a** Is 64:2; Jer 30:16; Mic 5:9; Matt 5:25; Luke 12:58
a shall be round the land Amos 3:11
there are many **a** 1 Cor 16:9
terrified by your **a** Phil 1:28
give none occasion to the **a** 1 Tim 5:14
which shall devour **a** Heb 10:27

ADVERSITY
all **a** 2 Sam 4:9; 2 Chr 15:6

I shall never be in **a** Ps 10:6
day of **a** Prov 24:10; Eccl 7:14
brother is born for **a** Prov 17:17
bread of **a** Is 30:20
them which suffer **a** Heb 13:3

ADVERTISE
I will **a** thee Num 24:14
I thought to **a** thee Ruth 4:4

ADVICE
blessed be thy **a** 1 Sam 25:33
our **a** should not be first 2 Sam 19:43
what **a** give ye? 2 Chr 10:9
with good **a** make war Prov 20:18
herein I give my **a** 2 Cor 8:10

ADVISE
with the well **a** is wisdom Prov 13:10
the more part **a** to depart Acts 27:12

ADVISEMENT
upon **a** sent him away 1 Chr 12:19

AENEAS **e´-ne-as**
praiseworthy (?) Acts 9:33

AENON **e´-non**
springs John 3:23

AFAR OFF
not a God **a** Jer 23:23
I will save them from **a** Jer 46:27
followed him **a** Matt 26:58; Mark 14:54
promise to all that are **a** Acts 2:39
peace to you which were **a** Eph 2:17
having seen them **a** Heb 11:13

AFFAIRS
and **a** of the king 1 Chr 26:32
entangleth himself with the **a** 2 Tim 2:4

AFFECTED
a against the brethren Acts 14:2
zealously **a** Gal 4:17,18

AFFECTION
set mine **a** to the house 1 Chr 29:3
gave them up unto vile **a** Rom 1:26
without natural **a** Rom 1:31; 2 Tim 3:3
be kindly **a** one to another Rom 12:10
crucified flesh with the **a** Gal 5:24
Set your **a** on things above Col 3:2
inordinate **a** Col 3:5

AFFINITY
Solomon made **a** with Pharaoh 1 Kgs 3:1
and joined **a** with Ahab 2 Chr 18:1
join in **a** with the people Ezra 9:14

AFFIRM
whom Paul **a** to be alive Acts 25:19

AFFLICT
ye shall **a** your souls Lev 16:29,31; Num 29:7
Wherefore hast thou **a**? Num 11:11
Almighty hath **a** me Ruth 1:21
a the seed of David 1 Kgs 11:39
when thou dost **a** them 1 Kgs 8:35; 2 Chr 6:26
to him that is **a** pity Job 6:14
how thou didst **a** the people Ps 44:2
God shall hear, and **a** Ps 55:19
do justice to the **a** Ps 82:3
the days wherein thou hast **a** Ps 90:15
Before I was **a** Ps 119:67
maintain the cause of the **a** Ps 140:12
days of the **a** are evil Prov 15:15
neither oppress the **a** Prov 22:22
pervert the judgment of the **a** Prov 31:5
thou **a** and drunken Is 51:21
smitten of God, and **a** Is 53:4,7
O thou **a**, Is 54:11
in all their **a** he was **a** Is 63:9
the LORD hath **a** her Lam 1:5,12
I will **a** thee no more Nah 1:12
leave an **a** and poor people Zeph 3:12
a, it is for your consolation 2 Cor 1:6
if she have relieved the **a** 1 Tim 5:10
destitute, **a**, tormented Heb 11:37
Be **a**, and mourn, and weep James 4:9
Is any among you **a**? James 5:13

AFFLICTION
looked upon my **a** Gen 29:32; Ps 25:18
seen the **a** of my people Ex 3:7; Acts 7:34
bread of **a** Deut 16:3; 1 Kgs 22:27; 2 Chr 18:26
cry to thee in our **a** 2 Chr 20:9
in **a** when he was 2 Chr 33:12
a cometh not forth of the dust Job 5:6
days of **a** Job 30:16,27
cords of **a** Job 36:8
Many are the **a** of righteous Ps 34:19
this is my comfort in my **a** Ps 119:50
remember David, and all his **a** Ps 132:1
water of **a** Is 30:20
furnace of **a** Is 48:10
refuge in the day of **a** Jer 16:19
man that hath seen **a** Lam 3:1
in their **a** they will seek Hos 5:15
a or persecution ariseth Mark 4:17
bonds and **a** abide me Acts 20:23
out of much **a** and anguish 2 Cor 2:4
For our light **a** 2 Cor 4:17
great trial of **a** 2 Cor 8:2
add **a** to my bonds Phil 1:16
great fight of **a** Heb 10:32
suffer **a** with people of God Heb 11:25
and widows in their **a** James 1:27

AFFRIGHT
fearfulness **a** me Is 21:4
they were **a** Mark 16:5
be not **a**, ye seek Jesus Mark 16:6

AFOOT
and ran **a** thither Mark 6:33
minding himself to go **a** Acts 20:13

AFORETIME
prayed as he did **a** Dan 6:10
things were written **a** Rom 15:4

AFRAID
were sore **a** Gen 20:8; Ex 14:10; Mark 9:6; Luke 2:9
whosoever is fearful and **a** Judg 7:3
Saul was yet the more **a** 1 Sam 18:29
they all made us **a** Neh 6:9
that which I was **a** of is come Job 3:25
I am **a** of all my sorrows Job 9:28
of whom shall I be **a**? Ps 27:1
What time I am **a** Ps 56:3,11
a at thy tokens Ps 65:8
not be **a** for the terror Ps 91:5
a of evil tidings Ps 112:7
none shall make them **a** Is 17:2; Ezek 34:28; Mic 4:4; Zeph 3:13
be **a** of a man that shall die Is 51:12
be not **a** Matt 14:27; Mark 5:36; 6:50; John 6:20
a to ask him Mark 9:32
he was the more **a** John 19:8
I am **a** of you Gal 4:11
a of the king's commandment Heb 11:23

AFRESH
the Son of God **a** Heb 6:6

AFTERNOON
they tarried until **a** Judg 19:8

AFTERWARDS
a that David's heart smote 1 Sam 24:5
a receive me to glory Ps 73:24
deceit is sweet to a man, but **a** Prov 20:17
a build thine house Prov 24:27
wise man keepeth it in till **a** Prov 29:11
thou shalt follow me **a** John 13:36
a they that are Christ's 1 Cor 15:23

AGABUS **ag´-ab-us**
Gr. for HAGAB Acts 11:28

AGAG **a´-gag**
flaming (?) Num 24:7

AGAGITE **a´-gag-ite**
member of house of Agag Esth 3:1

AGAINST
spoken **a** Luke 2:34; Acts 19:36; 28:22

AGAR **a´-gar**
same as HAGAR Gal 4:24

AGED
a men Job 15:10; Titus 2:2
Paul the **a** Phile 1:9

AGEE **a´-gee**
fugitive (?) 2 Sam 23:11

AGES
in the **a** to come Eph 2:7
in other **a** was not Eph 3:5
Christ Jesus throughout the **a** Eph 3:21
hid from **a** Col 1:26

AGONE
three days **a** I fell sick 1 Sam 30:13

AGONY
being in an **a** he prayed Luke 22:44

AGREE
except they be **a** Amos 3:3
a with thine adversary Matt 5:25
two of you shall **a** Matt 18:19
witness **a** not Mark 14:56
to this **a** the words Acts 15:15
these three **a** in one 1 John 5:8

AGREEMENT
with hell are we at **a** Is 28:15
what **a** hath the temple 2 Cor 6:16

AGRIPPA **a-grip´-ah**
King Agrippa II (A.D. 27–ca. A.D. 100) Last of the Herods Acts 25:13

AGROUND
they ran the ship **a** Acts 27:41

AGUR **a´-goor**
an assembler Prov 30:1

AHA
a, our eye hath seen it Ps 35:21
say unto me, **a** Ps 40:15
their shame that say, **a** Ps 70:3
saith, **a**, I am warm Is 44:16
A, against my sanctuary Ezek 25:3
Jerusalem, **A**, she is broken Ezek 26:2
A, even the ancient Ezek 36:2

AHAB **a´-hab**
uncle 1 Kgs 16:29

AHARAH **a-har´-ah**
after the brother 1 Chr 8:1

AHARHEL **a-har´-hel**
behind the breastwork 1 Chr 4:8

AHASAI **a-haz´-a-i**
same as JAHZERAH (?) Neh 11:13

AHASBAI **a-has´-ba-i**
blooming 2 Sam 23:34

AHASUERUS **a-haz´-u-e´-rus**
king (?) Esth 1:1

AHAVA **a´-ha-va**
a place and a stream in Babylon Ezra 8:15

AHAZ **a´-haz**
possessor 2 Kgs 15:38

AHAZIAH a-haz-i´-ah
whom Jehovah upholds 1 Kgs 22:40

AHBAN ah´-ban
brotherly 1 Chr 2:29

AHER a´-her
following 1 Chr 7:12

AHI a´-hi
brother 1 Chr 5:15

AHIAH a-hi´-ah
brother of Jehovah 1 Sam 14:3

AHIAM a-hi´-am
brother of the mother (?) 2 Sam 23:33

AHIAN a-hi´-an
brotherly 1 Chr 7:19

AHIEZER a´-hi-e´-zer
brother of help Num 1:12

AHIHUD a-hi´-hood
a brother is praiseworthy (?) Num 34:27

AHIJAH a-hi´-jah
same as AHIAH 1 Kgs 11:29

AHIKAM a-hi´-kam
brother of the enemy 2 Kgs 22:12

AHILUD a-hi´-lood
brother of one born 2 Sam 8:16

AHIMAAZ a´-hi-ma´-az
brother of anger 2 Sam 15:27

AHIMAN a-hi´-man
brother of a gift Num 13:22

AHIMELECH a-hi´-me-lek
brother of the king 1 Sam 21:1

AHIMOTH a-hi´-moth
brother of death 1 Chr 6:25

AHINADAB a-hi´-na-dab
brother of a nobleman 1 Kgs 4:14

AHINOAM a´-hi-no´-am
brother of grace 1 Sam 14:50

AHIO a-hi´-o
brotherly 2 Sam 6:3

AHIRA a-hi´-rah
brother of a wicked man Num 1:15

AHIRAM a-hi´-ram
brother of a tall man Num 26:38

AHIRAMITE a-hi´-ram-ite
a descendant of Ahiram Num 26:38

AHISAMACH a-hi´-sa-mak
brother of aid Ex 31:6

AHISHAHAR a-hi´-sha-har
brother of the dawn 1 Chr 7:10

AHISHAR a-hi´-shar
brother of the singer 1 Kgs 4:6

AHITHOPHEL a-hi´-tho-fel
brother of impiety 2 Sam 15:12

AHITUB a-hi´-toob
brother of goodness 1 Sam 14:3

AHLAB ah´-lab
fertility Judg 1:31

AHLAI ah-la´-i
sweet (?) 1 Chr 2:31

AHOAH a-ho´-ah
same as AHIJAH (?) 1 Chr 8:4

AHOHITE a-hoh´-ite
a descendant of Ahoah 2 Sam 23:9

AHOLAH a-ho´-lah
(she has) her own tent Ezek 23:4

AHOLIAB a´-ho-li´-ab
father's tent Ex 31:6

AHOLIBAH a´-ho-li´-bah
my tent is in her Ezek 23:4

AHOLIBAMAH a´-ho-li-ba´-mah
tent of the high place Gen 36:2

AHUMAI a´-hoo-ma´-i
brother of (dweller near) water 1 Chr 4:2

AHUZAM a-hooz´-am
their possession 1 Chr 4:6

AHUZZATH a-hooz´-ath
possession Gen 26:26

AI a´-i
a heap of ruins Josh 7:2

AIAH ai´-ah
hawk 2 Sam 3:7

AIATH ai´-ath
ruins Is 10:28

AIJA ai´-jah
same as AI Neh 11:31

AIJALON ai´-ja-lon
place of gazelles Josh 21:24

AILETH
What **a** thee Gen 21:17; Judg 18:23; 1 Sam 11:5; 2 Sam 14:5; Is 22:1

AIN a´-in
an eye, fountain Num 34:11

AIR
no **a** can come between Job 41:16
as one that beateth the **a** 1 Cor 9:26
ye shall speak into the **a** 1 Cor 14:9
meet the Lord in the **a** 1 Thess 4:17

AJAH a´-jah
same as AIAH Gen 36:24

AJALON ad´-jal-on
same as AIJALON Josh 19:42

AKAN a´-kan
twisted Gen 36:27

AKKUB ak´-oob
insidious 1 Chr 3:24

AKRABBIM ak-rab´-im
scorpions Num 34:4

ALAMETH a-lam´-eth
covering 1 Chr 7:8

ALAMMELECH al-am´-me-lek
king's oak Josh 19:26

ALARM
a of war Jer 4:19; 49:2
sound **a** in holy mountain Joel 2:1

ALAS
a my master 2 Kgs 6:15
A, for all the evil Ezek 6:11

ALBEIT
a I have not spoken Ezek 13:7
a I do not say to thee Phile 1:19

ALEMETH a-lem´-eth
same as ALAMETH 1 Chr 8:36

ALEXANDER al´-ex-an´-der
defending men Mark 15:21

ALEXANDRIA al´-ex-an´-dri-a
city named after Alexander Acts 18:24

ALIAH a-li´-ah
same as ALVAH 1 Chr 1:51

ALIAN a-li´-an
same as ALVAN 1 Chr 1:40

ALIEN
sell it unto an **a** Deut 14:21
an **a** unto my mother's children Ps 69:8
a from the commonwealth Eph 2:12
armies of the **a** Heb 11:34

ALIENATED
her mind was **a** Ezek 23:17
being **a** from life Eph 4:18
sometime **a** and enemies Col 1:21

ALIKE
lie down **a** in the dust Job 21:26
fashioneth their hearts **a** Ps 33:15
all things cometh **a** to all Eccl 9:2

ALIVE
shall be presented **a** Lev 16:10
went down **a** into the pit Num 16:33
are **a** every one of you Deut 4:4
I kill, and I make **a** Deut 32:39
save soul **a** Ezek 13:18
heard that he was **a** Mark 16:11
son was dead, and is **a** Luke 15:24
angels, which said he was **a** Luke 24:23
shewed himself **a** Acts 1:3
a unto God Rom 6:11
all be made **a** 1 Cor 15:22
which are **a** and remain 1 Thess 4:15
I am **a** for evermore Rev 1:18

ALLEGING
Opening and **a**, that Christ Acts 17:3

ALLELUIA
much people in heaven, saying, **A** Rev 19:1

ALLON al´-on
an oak 1 Chr 4:37

ALLON-BACHUTH al-on-bak´-ooth
oak of weeping Gen 35:8

ALLOW
a the deeds of your fathers Luke 11:48
that which I do, I **a** not Rom 7:15
thing which he **a** Rom 14:22

ALLOWANCE
his **a** was a continual 2 Kgs 25:30

ALLURE
I will **a** her Hos 2:14
they **a** through the lusts 2 Pet 2:18

ALMIGHTY
by the name of God **a** Ex 6:3
Canst thou find out the **a**? Job 11:7
When **a** was yet with me Job 29:5
as the voice of the **A** Ezek 1:24; 10:5
which is to come, the **A** Rev 1:8; 4:8; 11:17

ALMODAD al-mo´-dad
extension (?) Gen 10:26

ALMON al´-mon
hidden Josh 21:18

ALMON-DIBLATHAIM al´-mon-dib´-lath-a´-im
hiding of the two cakes (?) Num 33:46

ALMS
do not your **a** before men Matt 6:1
rather give **a** of such things Luke 11:41
Sell that ye have, and give **a** Luke 12:33
gave much **a** to the people Acts 10:2

ALONE
bear all these people **a** Num 11:14
they two were **a** in the field 1 Kgs 11:29
escaped **a** to tell Job 1:15
a doeth great wonders Ps 136:4
not live by bread **a** Matt 4:4; Luke 4:4
Jesus was found **a** Luke 9:36
let it **a** this year also Luke 13:8

ALOTH a´-loth
yielding milk (?) 1 Kgs 4:16

ALPHA al´-fah
first letter of Gr. alphabet Rev 1:8

ALPHAEUS al-fee´-us
successor Matt 10:3

ALREADY
a of old time Eccl 1:10
I have cursed them **a** Mal 2:2
is condemned **a** John 3:18
we have **a** attained Phil 3:16

ALTAR
bring thy gift to the **a** Matt 5:23
swear by the **a** Matt 23:18
wait at the **a** 1 Cor 9:13; 10:18
we have an **a** Heb 13:10

ALTER
nor **a** the thing gone Ps 89:34
his countenance was **a** Luke 9:29

ALTOGETHER
a become filthy Ps 14:3; 53:3
a such a one as thyself Ps 50:21
he is **a** lovely Song 5:16

ALUSH a´-loosh
tumult of men Num 33:13

ALVAH al´-vah
high, tall, thick Gen 36:40

ALVAN al´-van
tall Gen 36:23

ALWAY
I would not live **a** Job 7:16
I am with you **a** Matt 28:20
rejoice in the Lord **a** Phil 4:4

ALWAYS
not **a** chide Ps 103:9
the poor **a** with you Matt 26:11
me ye have not **a** Mark 14:7; John 12:8

AMAD a´-mad
eternal people (?) Josh 19:26

AMAL a´-mal
labor, sorrow 1 Chr 7:35

AMALEK am´-al-ek
grandson of Esau Gen 36:12

AMALEKITES am-al´-ek-ites
descendants of Amalek Gen 14:7

AMAM a´-mam
metropolis (?) Josh 15:26

AMANA a-ma´-nah
fixed (?) Song 4:8

AMARIAH a´-mar-i´-ah
Jehovah has said 1 Chr 6:7

AMASA a´-mas-a
burden 2 Sam 17:25

AMASAI a´-mas-a´-i
burdensome 1 Chr 6:25

AMASHAI a´-mash-a´-i
same as AMASAI Neh 11:13

AMASIAH a´-mas-i´-ah
burden of Jehovah 2 Chr 17:16

AMAZED
they were exceedingly **a** Matt 19:25
a, and glorified God Mark 2:12
he began to be sore **a** Mark 14:33
a at the mighty power Luke 9:43

AMAZIAH a´-maz-i´-ah
Jehovah strengthens 2 Kgs 14:1

AMEND
A your ways Jer 7:3; 26:13
a your doings Jer 35:15
when he began to **a** John 4:52

AMI a´-mi
same as AMON Ezra 2:57

AMIABLE
How **a** are thy tabernacles Ps 84:1

AMINADAB a-mi´-na-dab
same as AMMINADAB Matt 1:4

AMISS
we have done **a** 2 Chr 6:37
which speak any thing **a** Dan 3:29
man hath done nothing **a** Luke 23:41
because ye ask **a** James 4:3

AMITTAI a-mit´-a-i
true 2 Kgs 14:25

AMMAH am´-ah
beginning, foundation 2 Sam 2:24

AMMI am´-i
my people Hos 2:1

AMMIEL am´-i-el
people of God Num 13:12

AMMIHUD am-i´-hood
people of praise (?) Num 1:10

AMMINADAB am-i´-na-dab
people of the prince Ex 6:23

AMMINADIB am-i´-na-dib
same as AMMINADAB Song 6:12

AMMISHADDAI am´-i-shad´-a-i
people of the Almighty Num 1:12

AMMIZABAD am-i´-za-bad
people of the giver 1 Chr 27:6

AMMON am´-on
son of my people (?) Gen 19:38

AMMONITE am´-on-ite
descendant of Ammon Deut 23:3

AMMONITESS am´-on-ite-ess
fem. of AMMONITE 2 Chr 12:13

AMNON am´-non
faithful 2 Sam 3:2

AMOK a´-mok
deep Neh 12:7

AMON a´-mon
faithful 2 Kgs 21:18

AMORITE am´-or-ite
mountaineer Gen 10:16

AMOS a´-mos
burden Amos 1:1

AMOZ a´-moz
strong Is 1:1

AMPHIPOLIS am-phi´-pol-is
around the city Acts 17:1

AMPLIAS am´-pli-as
short for Ampliatus, *enlarged* Rom 16:8

AMRAM am´-ram
people of the Highest Ex 6:18

AMRAMITES am´-ram-ites
the descendants of Amram Num 3:27

AMRAPHEL am´-ra-fel
one that divulges secrets (?) Gen 14:1

AMZI am´-zi
strong 1 Chr 6:46

ANAB a´-nab
a place fertile in grapes Josh 11:21

ANAH a´-nah
answer Gen 36:2

ANAHARATH a-na´-har-ath
gorge Josh 19:19

ANAIAH an-ai´-ah
Jehovah has answered Neh 8:4

ANAK a´-nak
long-necked (?) Num 13:22

ANAKIM a´-nak-im
tribe named for Anak Deut 1:28

ANAMIM a´-na-mim
a descendent of MIZRAIM Gen 10:13

ANAMMELECH a-nam´-me-lek
idol of the king, or Anu is king (?) 2 Kgs 17:31

ANAN a´-nan
a cloud Neh 10:26

ANANI an-a´-ni
short for ANANIAH 1 Chr 3:24

ANANIAH an-an-i´-ah
whom Jehovah covers Neh 3:23

ANANIAS an-an-i´-as
Gr. for HANANIAH Acts 5:1

ANATH a´-nath
an answer to prayer Judg 3:31

ANATHEMA an-ath´-em-ah
accursed 1 Cor 16:22

ANATHOTH a´-nath-oth
answers to prayer Josh 21:18

ANDREW an´-droo
manly Mark 1:29

ANDRONICUS an´-dro-ni´-kus
man-conquering Rom 16:7

ANEM a´-nem
same as EN-GAN-NIM (?) 1 Chr 6:73

ANER a´-ner
a young man (?) Gen 14:13

ANETHOTHITE a-neth´-oth-ite
a man of Anathoth 2 Sam 23:27

ANETOTHITE a-net´-oth-ite
same as ANETHOTHITE 1 Chr 27:12

ANGEL
the **a** which redeemed me Gen 48:16
a of Lord encampeth Ps 34:7
man did eat **a** food Ps 78:25
neither say before **a** Eccl 5:6
a of his presence saved them Is 63:9
he had power over the **a** Hos 12:4
the reapers are the **a** Matt 13:39
are as the **a** Mark 12:25
there appeared an **a** Luke 22:43
a went down at a certain John 5:4
It is his **a** Acts 12:15
we shall judge **a** 1 Cor 6:3
transformed into an **a** of light 2 Cor 11:14
word spoken by **a** Heb 2:2
nature of **a** Heb 2:16
entertained **a** unawares Heb 13:2
a desire to look into 1 Pet 1:12

ANGER
Cursed be their **a** Gen 49:7
slow to **a** Neh 9:17
not in thine **a** Ps 6:1; Jer 10:24
a endureth but a moment Ps 30:5
grievous words stir up **a** Prov 15:1
deferreth his **a** Prov 19:11
a resteth in the bosom Eccl 7:9
a, wrath, malice Col 3:8

ANGRY
God is **a** with the wicked Ps 7:11

he that is soon **a** Prov 14:17
no friendship with an **a** man Prov 22:24
so doth an **a** countenance Prov 25:23
Doest thou well to be **a**? Jon 4:4
is **a** with his brother Matt 5:22
are ye **a** at me? John 7:23
be ye **a**, and sin not Eph 4:26
not soon **a** Titus 1:7

ANGUISH
hearkened not unto Moses for **a** Ex 6:9
speak in the **a** of spirit Job 7:11
and **a** upon every soul Rom 2:9
out of much affliction and **a** 2 Cor 2:4

ANIAM a-ni´-am
sighing of the people 1 Chr 7:19

ANIM a´-nim
fountains Josh 15:50

ANNA an´-ah
grace Luke 2:36

ANNAS an´-as
Gr. for HANANIAH Luke 3:2

ANOINT
a not thyself 2 Sam 14:2
a the shield Is 21:5
a me to preach Is 61:1; Luke 4:18
a my body to the burying Mark 14:8
thou didst not **a** Luke 7:46
a the eyes of the blind man John 9:6
a the feet of Jesus John 12:3
a us is God 2 Cor 1:21
the same **a** teacheth 1 John 2:27
a thine eyes with eye salve Rev 3:18

ANOINTED
hand against the LORD's **a** 1 Sam 26:9

ANON
and **a** with joy Matt 13:20
and **a** they tell him Mark 1:30

ANOTHER
let **a** man praise thee Prov 27:2
a gospel 2 Cor 11:4; Gal 1:6
pray one for **a** James 5:16

ANSWER (n)
no **a** Job 19:16; 32:3; Mic 3:7; John 19:9
A soft **a** turneth Prov 15:1
a of the tongue Prov 16:1
a of a good conscience 1 Pet 3:21
be ready always to give an **a** 1 Pet 3:15

ANSWER (v)
multitude of words be **a** Job 11:2
wilt thou **a** Ps 65:5
I will not **a** Prov 1:28
a a matter before he heareth Prov 18:13
a not a fool Prov 26:4
money **a** all things Eccl 10:19
what ye shall **a** Luke 21:14
somewhat to **a** 2 Cor 5:12
how ye ought to **a** every man Col 4:6
not **a** again Titus 2:9

ANTICHRIST an´-ti-christ
instead of Christ 1 John 2:18

ANTIOCH an´-ti-ok
named for Antiochus, a general of Alexander the Great Acts 6:5

ANTIPAS an´-tip-as
contraction of Antipater, *against the father* Rev 2:13

ANTIPATRIS an´-tip-atr´-is
city named for Antipater, *against the father* Acts 23:31

ANTIQUITY
whose **a** is of ancient days Is 23:7

ANTOTHIJAH an´-to-thi´-jah
prayers answered by Jehovah (?) 1 Chr 8:24

ANTOTHITE an´-toth-ite
a man of Anathoth 1 Chr 11:28

ANUB a´-noob
bound together (?) 1 Chr 4:8

APELLES a-pel´-les
exclusion Rom 16:10

APHARSACHITES a´-far-sa-kites
official Ezra 5:6

APHARSATHCHITES a´-far-sath-kites
official Ezra 4:9

APHARSITES a´-far-sa-kites
official Ezra 4:9

APART
desert place **a** Matt 14:13
mountain **a** Matt 14:23; 17:1
Come ye yourselves **a** Mark 6:31

APHEK a´-fek
strength Josh 12:18

APHEKAH a´-fek-ah
same as APHEK Josh 15:53

APHIAH af-i´-ah
refreshed (?) 1 Sam 9:1

APHIK a´-fik
same as APHEK Judg 1:31

APHRAH af´-rah
dust Mic 1:10

APHSES af´-sees
dispersion 1 Chr 24:15

APOLLONIA ap´-ol-o´-ni-ah
belonging to Apollos Acts 17:1

APOLLOS ap-ol´-os
abbr. of Apollonius Acts 18:24

APOLLYON ap-ol´-yon
one that exterminates Rev 9:11

APPAIM ap-a´-im
the nostrils 1 Chr 2:30

APPARENTLY
even **a**, and not in dark Num 12:8

APPEAR
a before God? Ps 42:2
Let thy work **a** Ps 90:16
flowers **a** on the earth Song 2:12
a unto men to fast Matt 6:16
outwardly **a** righteous Matt 23:28
that it might **a** sin Rom 7:13
we must all **a** before 2 Cor 5:10
who is our life, shall **a** Col 3:4
a the second time without sin Heb 9:28
profiting may **a** to all 1 Tim 4:15

APPEARANCE
man looketh on the outward **a** 1 Sam 16:7
glory in **a** 2 Cor 5:12
abstain from all **a** of evil 1 Thess 5:22

APPEARING
until the **a** of our Lord 1 Tim 6:14
by the **a** of our Saviour 2 Tim 1:10
all them also that love his **a** 2 Tim 4:8
glorious **a** of the great God Titus 2:13
honour and glory at the **a** 1 Pet 1:7

APPEASE
I will **a** him Gen 32:20
slow to anger **a** strife Prov 15:18
town clerk had **a** Acts 19:35

APPERTAIN
with all that **a** unto them Num 16:30
to thee it doth **a** Jer 10:7

APPETITE
fill the **a** of the young Job 38:39
a man given to **a** Prov 23:2
yet the **a** is not filled Eccl 6:7
his soul hath **a** Is 29:8

APPHIA af´-yah
Gr. for Appia Phile 1:2

APPII FORUM ap´-py-i fo´-rum
marketplace of Appius Acts 28:15

APPLY
we may **a** our hearts Ps 90:12
a thine heart Prov 2:2; 22:17; 23:12
a mine heart Eccl 7:25

APPOINT
wearisome nights are **a** Job 7:3
thou hast **a** his bounds Job 14:5
house **a** for all living Job 30:23
preserve those **a** to die Ps 79:11
a him his portion Matt 24:51; Luke 12:46
seven men whom we may **a** Acts 6:3
not **a** us to wrath 1 Thess 5:9

APPREHEND
when he had **a** him Acts 12:4
desirous to **a** me 2 Cor 11:32
that I may **a** Phil 3:12

APPROACH
take delight in **a** to God Is 58:2
where no thief **a** Luke 12:33
light which no man can **a** 1 Tim 6:16
as ye see the day **a** Heb 10:25

APPROVE
a man **a** of God Acts 2:22
a in Christ Rom 16:10
a things that are excellent Phil 1:10
shew thyself **a** unto God 2 Tim 2:15

APT
a for war 2 Kgs 24:16
a to teach 1 Tim 3:2; 2 Tim 2:24

AQUILA ak´-wil-ah
an eagle Acts 18:2

AR ar
city Num 21:15

ARA a´-ra
lion (?) 1 Chr 7:38

ARAB a´-rab
ambush Josh 15:52

ARABAH a´-rab-ah
a plain Josh 18:18

ARABIA a-ra´-bi-a
a desert 1 Kgs 10:15

ARABIAN a-ra´-bi-an
a person from Arabia Neh 2:19

ARAD a´-rad
wild ass 1 Chr 8:15

ARAH a´-rah
wandering 1 Chr 7:39

ARAM a´-ram
height Gen 10:22

ARAMITESS a´-ram-ite-ess
female inhabitant of Aram 1 Chr 7:14

ARAN a´-ran
wild goat Gen 36:28

ARARAT a-ra´-rat
the curse of trembling Gen 8:4

ARAUNAH a-raw´-nah
calf (?) 2 Sam 24:18

ARBA ar´-bah
four Josh 14:15

ARBAH ar´-bah
variant spelling of ARBA Gen 35:27

ARBATHITE ar´-bath-ite
an inhabitant of Beth-arabah 1 Chr 11:32

ARBEL see BETH-ARBEL

ARBITE arb´-ite
an inhabitant of Arab 2 Sam 23:35

ARCHELAUS ar´-ke-la´-us
prince of the people (?) Matt 2:22

ARCHEVITES ar´-kev-ites
the men of Erech (?) Ezra 4:9

ARCHI ar´-ki
an inhabitant of Erech Josh 16:2

ARCHIPPUS ar-kip´-us
master of the horse Col 4:17

ARCHITE ark´-ite
a native of Erech 2 Sam 15:32

ARCTURUS ark-tu´-rus
the Great Bear and Little Bear constellations Job 9:9

ARD ard
fugitive (?) Gen 46:21

ARDITES ard´-ites
descendants of Ard Num 26:40

ARDON ar´-don
fugitive 1 Chr 2:18

ARELI a-re´-li
heroic Gen 46:16

ARELITES a´-rel-ites
descendants of Areli Num 26:17

AREOPAGITE a´-re-op´-ag-ite
a judge of the court of Areopagus Acts 17:34

AREOPAGUS a´-re-op´-ag-us
hill of Mars Acts 17:19

ARETAS ar´-e-tas
husbandman (?) 2 Cor 11:32

ARGOB ar´-gobe
a rocky district Deut 3:4

ARGUING
doth your **a** reprove Job 6:25

ARGUMENTS
fill my mouth with **a** Job 23:4

ARIDAI a-rid´-a-i
delight of Hari (?) Esth 9:9

ARIDATHA a-rid´-ath-ah
given by Hari (?) Esth 9:8

ARIEH a-ri´-eh
lion 2 Kgs 15:25

ARIEL a´-ri-el
lion of God Ezra 8:16

ARIGHT
his conversation **a** will I Ps 50:23
set not their heart **a** Ps 78:8
wise useth knowledge **a** Prov 15:2
it moveth itself **a** Prov 23:31

ARIMATHAEA a´-rim-ath-ee´-ah
same as RAMAH Matt 27:57

ARIOCH a´-ri-ok
servant of the moon-god Gen 14:1

ARISE
there **a** a little cloud 1 Kgs 18:44
a and build Neh 2:20
Let God **a** Ps 68:1
shall the dead **a** and praise thee? Ps 88:10
upright there **a** light Ps 112:4
Sun of righteousness **a** Mal 4:2
I say unto thee **a** Mark 2:11; Luke 7:14
I will **a** and go Luke 15:18
a from the dead Eph 5:14
daystar **a** in your hearts 2 Pet 1:19

ARISTARCHUS a-ris-tark´-us
best ruling Acts 19:29

ARISTOBULUS a-ris´-to-bewl´-us
best counselor Rom 16:10

ARKITE ark´-ite
fugitive (?) Gen 10:17

ARMAGEDDON ar´-ma-ged´-on
height of Megiddo Rev 16:16

ARMENIA ar-me´-ni-a
land of Aram 2 Kgs 19:37

ARMONI ar-mo´-ni
belonging to a palace 2 Sam 21:8

ARMY
I defy the **a** of Israel 1 Sam 17:10
Is there any number of his **a**? Job 25:3
compassed with **a** Luke 21:20
then came I with an **a** Acts 23:27
a of the aliens Heb 11:34

ARNAN ar´-nan
active 1 Chr 3:21

ARNON ar´-non
swift Num 21:13

AROD a´-rod
wild ass Num 26:17

ARODI a´-rod-i
same as AROD Gen 46:16

ARODITES a´-rod-ites
descendants of Arod Num 26:17

AROER ar´-o-er
ruins (?) Deut 2:36

AROERITE ar-o´-er-ite
a man of Aroer 1 Chr 11:44

ARPAD ar´-pad
support 2 Kgs 18:34

ARPHAD ar´-fad
same as ARPAD Is 36:19

ARRAY
shall **a** himself with the land Jer 43:12
not **a** like one of these Matt 6:29; Luke 12:27
or costly **a** 1 Tim 2:9
a in white robes Rev 7:13

ARROGANCY
let not **a** come out 1 Sam 2:3
pride, **a** and the evil way Prov 8:13
the **a** of the proud to cease Is 13:11
his loftiness, and his **a** Jer 48:29

ARROW
pierce them through with his **a** Num 24:8
thine **a** stick fast Ps 38:2
brake he the **a** of the bow Ps 76:3
a that flieth by day Ps 91:5
a sharp **a** Prov 25:18
a and death Prov 26:18
evil **a** of famine Ezek 5:16

ARTAXERXES ar´-ta-xerk´-ses
honored king (?) Ezra 4:7

ARTEMAS ar´-te-mas
short for Artemidorus (?) Titus 3:12

ARTIFICER
every **a** in brass and iron Gen 4:22
by the hands of **a** 1 Chr 29:5
a and builders gave they 2 Chr 34:11
cunning **a**, and the eloquent Is 3:3

ARTILLERY
Jonathan gave his **a** 1 Sam 20:40

ARUBOTH a-roob´-oth
windows 1 Kgs 4:10

ARUMAH a-room´-ah
elevated Judg 9:41

ARVAD ar´-vad
wandering Ezek 27:8

ARVADITES ar´-vad-ites
inhabitants of Arvad Gen 10:18

ARZA ar´-zah
earth 1 Kgs 16:9

ASA a´-sah
physician 1 Kgs 15:8

ASAHEL a´-sa-hel
whom God made 2 Sam 2:18

ASAHIAH a´-sah-i´-ah
Jehovah has made 2 Kgs 22:12

ASAIAH a-sai´-ah
same as ASAHIAH 1 Chr 4:36

ASAPH a´-saf
collector 2 Kgs 18:18

ASAREEL a´-sar-e´-el
whom God has bound 1 Chr 4:16

ASARELAH a´-sar-el´-ah
same as JESHARELAH 1 Chr 25:2

ASCEND
a on high Ps 68:18
Who shall **a** into heaven? Rom 10:6
he **a** up on high Eph 4:8
angels of God **a** John 1:51
no man hath **a** up to heaven John 3:13
I am not yet **a** John 20:17
a up before God Rev 8:4
they **a** up to heaven Rev 11:12

ASCRIBE
a ye greatness unto our God Deut 32:3
a righteousness to my Maker Job 36:3
A ye strength unto God Ps 68:34

ASENATH a´-se-nath
she who is of Neith (?), (a goddess of the Egyptians) Gen 41:45

ASER a-´-ser
same as ASHER Luke 2:36

ASHAMED
shall no man make thee **a**? Job 11:3
let none that wait on thee be **a** Ps 25:3
let me never be **a** Ps 31:1
their faces were not **a** Ps 34:5
ye shall not be **a** Is 45:17
but ye shall be **a** Is 65:13
As the thief is **a** Jer 2:26
Were they **a**? Jer 6:15; 8:12
a of your revenues Jer 12:13
plowmen were **a** Jer 14:4
to beg I am **a** Luke 16:3
not **a** of the gospel Rom 1:16
hope maketh not **a** Rom 5:5
believeth shall not be **a** Rom 9:33; 10:11
a of the testimony 2 Tim 1:8
needeth not to be **a** 2 Tim 2:15
not **a** to call them brethren Heb 2:11
not **a** to be called their God Heb 11:16
let him not be **a** 1 Pet 4:16

ASHAN a´-shan
smoke Josh 15:42

ASHBEA ash´-be-ah
I conjure 1 Chr 4:21

ASHBEL ash´-bel
blame (?) Gen 46:21

ASHBELITES ash´-bel-ites
the descendants of Ashbel Num 26:38

ASHCHENAZ ash´-ke-naz
same as ASHKENAZ 1 Chr 1:6

ASHDOD ash´-dod
a strong place Josh 15:46

ASHDODITES ash´-dod-ites
the inhabitants of Ashdod Neh 4:7

ASHDOTH-PISGAH ash´-doth-piz´-gah
springs of Pisgah Josh 12:3

ASHDOTHITES ash´-doth-ites
same as ASHDODITES Josh 13:3

ASHER ash´-er
fortunate, happy Gen 30:13

ASHERAH ash-er´-ah
same as ASHTORETH 2 Kgs 17:10

ASHERITES a´-sher-ites
descendants of Asher Judg 1:32

ASHIMA ash´-im-a
an unknown deity 2 Kgs 17:30

ASHKELON ash´-kel-on
migration Judg 14:19

ASHKENAZ ash´-ke-naz
a fire that spreads Gen 10:3

ASHNAH ash´-nah
strong Josh 15:33

ASHRIEL ash´-ri-el
same as ASRIEL 1 Chr 7:14

ASHTAROTH ash´-tar-oth
statues of Ashtoreth Josh 9:10

ASHTERATHITE ash-ter´-ath-ite
a native of Ashteoth 1 Chr 11:44

ASHTEROTH KARNAIM ash´-ter-oth kar-na´-im
Ashteroth of the two horns Gen 14:5

ASHTORETH ash-tor´-eth
she who enriches 1 Kgs 11:5

ASHUR a´-shur
black 1 Chr 2:24

ASHURITES a´-sher-ites
1 a region of Israel 2 Sam 2:9
2 an Arab tribe Ezek 27:6

ASIA a´-sia
a Roman province Acts 2:9

ASIDE
thou shalt set **a** that 2 Kgs 4:4
took him **a** from the multitude Mark 7:33
lay **a** every weight Heb 12:1

ASIEL a´-si-el
created by God 1 Chr 4:35

ASK
a of me Ps 2:8
A me of things to come Is 45:11
sought of them that **a** not Is 65:1
a, and it shall be given Matt 7:7; Luke 11:9
whatsoever ye **a** in prayer Matt 21:22
a of me whatsoever Mark 6:22
a in my name John 14:13
let him **a** of God James 1:5
a you **a** reason of the hope 1 Pet 3:15
whatsoever we **a** 1 John 3:22; 5:15

ASKELON as´-kel-on
same as ASHKELON Judg 1:18

ASLEEP
but he was **a** Matt 8:24
a on a pillow Mark 4:38
findeth them **a** Matt 26:40
he found them **a** again Mark 14:40
some are fallen **a** 1 Cor 15:6
them which are **a** 1 Thess 4:13,15
since the fathers fell **a** 2 Pet 3:4

ASNAH as´-nah
bramble Ezra 2:50

ASNAPPER as-nap´-er
same as ASSUR-BANI-PAL, *Assur has formed a son* Ezra 4:10

ASRIEL as´-ri-el
the prohibition of God Num 26:31

ASRIELITES as´-ri-el-ites
descendants of Asriel Num 26:31

ASS
Am not I thine **a**? Num 22:30
bridle for the **a** Prov 26:3
a his master's crib Is 1:3
burial of an **a** Jer 22:19
riding on **a** Zech 9:9
and sitting upon an **a** Matt 21:5
shall have an **a** fallen Luke 14:5
dumb **a** speaking 2 Pet 2:16

ASSAULT
province that would **a** them Esth 8:11
a the house of Jason Acts 17:5

ASSAY
a to join Acts 9:26
they **a** to go into Bithynia Acts 16:7
Egyptians **a** to do Heb 11:29

ASSHUR ash´-oor
the gracious One (?) Gen 10:22

ASSHURIM ash-oor´-im
Arabian tribe from Dedan Gen 25:3

ASSIGNED
portion **a** them of Pharaoh Gen 47:22
they **a** Bezer Josh 20:8
he **a** Uriah 2 Sam 11:16

ASSIR as´-eer
captive Ex 6:24

ASSIST
that ye **a** her Rom 16:2

ASSUR as´-ser
1 the people of ASSHUR Ezek 27:23
2 the land of ASSYRIA Ezra 4:2

ASSURANCE
effect of righteousness **a** Is 32:17
full **a** of understanding Col 2:2
in much **a** 1 Thess 1:5
full **a** of hope Heb 6:11

ASSURE
learned and hast been **a** 2 Tim 3:14
shall **a** our hearts 1 John 3:19

ASSWAGE
the waters **a** Gen 8:1
my lips should **a** your grief Job 16:5

ASSYRIA as-ir´-ya
land named for Asshur Gen 2:14

ASSYRIANS as-ir´-yans
inhabitants of Assyria Is 10:5

ASTAROTH as´-tar-oth
same as ASHTORETH Deut 1:4

ASTONIED
sat down **a** Ezra 9:3
upright men shall be **a** Job 17:8
the king was **a** Dan 3:24
was **a** for one hour Dan 4:19

ASTONISHED
a at his doctrine Matt 7:28; 22:33; Mark 1:22; 11:18; Luke 4:32
a at his understanding Luke 2:47
he was **a** Luke 5:9
made us **a** Luke 24:22
trembling and **a** Acts 9:6
they were **a** Acts 12:16
being **a** Acts 13:12

ASTONISHMENT
to **a** and to hissing 2 Chr 29:8
the wine of **a** Ps 60:3
a hath taken hold Jer 8:21

ASUPPIM a-soop´-im
collections 1 Chr 26:15

ASYNCRITUS a-sin´-krit-us
incomparable Rom 16:14

ATAD a´-tad
buckthorn Gen 50:10

ATARAH a´-tar-ah
a crown 1 Chr 2:26

ATAROTH-ADAR a´-tar-oth–ad-ar
same as ATAROTH-ADDAR Josh 18:13

ATAROTH-ADDAR a´-tar-oth-ad-ar
crowns of power Josh 16:5

ATER a´-ter
bound, shut up Ezra 2:16

ATHACH a´-thak
lodging-place 1 Sam 30:30

ATHAIAH a-thai´-ah
whom Jehovah made (?) Neh 11:4

ATHALIAH ath´-al-i´-ah
whom Jehovah has afflicted 2 Kgs 8:26

ATHENIANS ath-e´-ni-ans
natives of Athens Acts 17:21

ATHIRST
we saw thee hungered, or **a**, Matt 25:44
unto him that is **a** Rev 21:6
let him that is **a** Rev 22:17

ATHLAI ath´-la-i
short for ATHALIAH Ezra 10:28

ATONEMENT
day of **a** Lev 23:28; 25:9
wherewith shall I make the **a**? 2 Sam 21:3
we received the **a** Rom 5:11

ATROTH at´-roth
same as ATAROTH Num 32:35

ATTAI at´-a-i
opportune 1 Chr 2:35

ATTAIN
I cannot **a** unto it Ps 139:6
he **a** not unto the first three 2 Sam 23:19
a to righteousness Rom 9:30
I might **a** Phil 3:11

ATTALIA at´-ta-li´-a
named for Attalus, royal founder of the city Acts 14:25

ATTEND
a unto my cry Ps 17:1; 142:6
a to my words Prov 4:20

ATTENDANCE
give **a** to reading 1 Tim 4:13
man gave **a** at the altar Heb 7:13

ATTENT
be **a** unto the prayer 2 Chr 6:40
mine ears **a** unto the prayer 2 Chr 7:15

ATTENTIVE
Let thine ear now be **a** Neh 1:6
Hear **a** the noise Job 37:2
people were very **a** Luke 19:48

ATTIRE
or a bride her **a** Jer 2:32
in dyed **a** Ezek 23:15

AUDIENCE
in the **a** of our God 1 Chr 28:8
a of the people Luke 7:1
ye that fear God, give **a** Acts 13:16

AUGMENT
to **a** yet the fierce anger Num 32:14

AUGUSTUS aw-gust´-us
venerable Luke 2:1

AUSTERE
thou art an **a** man Luke 19:21

AUTHOR
not the **a** of confusion 1 Cor 14:33
came the **a** of eternal salvation Heb 5:9
Jesus the **a** and finisher Heb 12:2

AUTHORITY
as one having **a** Matt 7:29
I am a man under **a** Matt 8:9
By what **a** Matt 21:23
power and **a** over all devils Luke 9:1
have **a** over ten cities Luke 19:17
a to execute judgment John 5:27
all **a** and power 1 Cor 15:24
and all that are in **a** 1 Tim 2:2
to usurp **a** 1 Tim 2:12
rebuke with all **a** Titus 2:15
angels and **a** 1 Pet 3:22

AVAILETH
all this **a** me nothing Esth 5:13
righteous man **a** much James 5:16

AVA av´-va
iniquity, guilt 2 Kgs 17:24

AVEN a´-ven
nothingness Ezek 30:17

AVENGE
he will **a** the blood Deut 32:43
people **a** themselves Josh 10:13
the LORD **a** me 1 Sam 24:12
it is God that **a** me 2 Sam 22:48; Ps 18:47
a themselves Esth 8:13
a me of mine enemies Is 1:24
A me of mine adversary Luke 18:3

AVENGER
enemy and the **a** Ps 8:2
the Lord is the **a** 1 Thess 4:6

AVERSE
as men **a** from war Mic 2:8

AVIM av´-im
ruins Josh 18:23

AVITH a´-vith
ruin Gen 36:35

AVOID
a it, pass not by it Prov 4:15
a profane and vain babblings 1 Tim 6:20

AVOUCHED
Thou hast **a** the LORD Deut 26:17,18

AWAKE
when I **a**, with thy likeness Ps 17:15
as a dream when one **a** Ps 73:20
when shall I **a**? Prov 23:35
a, **a**, put on strength Is 51:9
a, ye drunkards Joel 1:5
a, O sword Zech 13:7
a, they saw his glory Luke 9:32
high time to **a** Rom 13:11
A to righteousness 1 Cor 15:34
A thou that sleepest Eph 5:14

AWARE
ever was I **a** song Song 6:12
and thou wast not **a** Jer 50:24
are not **a** of them Luke 11:44

AWE
Stand in **a** Ps 4:4; 33:8; 119:161

AWL
bore his ear through with an **a** Ex 21:6
take an **a**, and thrust it Deut 15:17

AXE
he had lifted up **a** Ps 74:5
Shall the **a** boast? Is 10:15
the **a** is laid unto the root Matt 3:10; Luke 3:9

AZAL a´-zal
going away Zech 14:5

AZALIAH a´-zal-i´-ah
whom Jehovah has reserved 2 Kgs 22:3

AZANIAH a´-zan-i´-ah
whom Jehovah hears Neh 10:9

AZARAEL a´-zar-a´-el
whom God helps Neh 12:36

AZAREEL a´-zar-e´-el
same as AZAREEL 1 Chr 12:6

AZARIAH a´-zar-i´-ah
whom Jehovah aids 2 Chr 22:6

AZAZ a´-zaz
strong 1 Chr 5:8

AZAZIAH a´-zaz-i´-ah
whom Jehovah strengthened 1 Chr 15:21

AZEKAH az´-ek-ah
dug over Josh 10:10

AZEL a´-zel
noble 1 Chr 8:37

AZEM a´-zem
strength, bone Josh 15:29

AZGAD az´-gad
strong in fortune Ezra 2:12

AZIEL az´-i-el
whom God strengthens 1 Chr 15:20

AZIZA a-zi´-zah
strong Ezra 10:27

AZMAVETH az-ma´-veth
strength (?) 2 Sam 23:31

AZMON az´-mon
robust Num 34:4

AZNOTH-TABOR az´-noth-ta´-bor
ears (summits) of Tabor Josh 19:34

AZOR a´-zor
helper Matt 1:13

AZOTUS a-zo´-tus
Gr. for ASHDOD Acts 8:40

AZRIEL az´-ri-el
help of God 1 Chr 5:24

AZRIKAM az-ri´-kam
help against an enemy 1 Chr 3:23

AZUBAH a-zoob´-ah
forsaken 1 Kgs 22:42

AZUR a´-zoor
same as AZOR Jer 28:1

AZZAH az´-ah
strong, fortified Deut 2:23

AZZAN az´-an
strong Num 34:26

AZZUR az´-oor
same as AZOR Neh 10:17

B

BAAL ba´-al
Phoenician sun-god,
lord, master, possessor Num 22:41

BAAL-BERITH ba´-al-be´-rith
lord of a covenant Judg 8:33

BAAL-GAD ba´-al-gad
lord of fortune Josh 11:17

BAAL-HAMON ba´-al-ha´-mon
lord of a multitude Song 8:11

BAAL-HANAN ba´-al-ha´-nan
lord of benignity Gen 36:38

BAAL-HAZOR ba´-al-ha´-zor
lord of a village 2 Sam 13:23

BAAL-HERMON ba´-al-her´-mon
lord of Hermon Judg 3:3

BAAL-MEON ba´-al-me´-on
lord of habitation Num 32:38

BAAL-PEOR ba´-al-pe´-or
lord of the opening Num 25:3

BAAL-PERAZIM ba´-al-pe-raz´-im
lord of breaches 2 Sam 5:20

BAAL-SHALISHA ba´-al-sha-lish´-ah
lord of the third part 2 Kgs 4:42

BAAL-TAMAR ba´-al-ta´-mar
lord of palm trees Judg 20:33

BAAL-ZEBUB ba´-al-ze´-boob
lord of flies 2 Kgs 1:2

BAAL-ZEPHON ba´-al-zeph´-on
lord of winter Ex 14:2

BAALAH ba´-al-ah
mistress Josh 15:10

BAALATH ba´-al-ath
same as BAALAH Josh 19:44

BAALATH-BEER ba´-al-ath-be´-er
owner of a well Josh 19:8

BAALE ba´-al-ay
pl. of BAAL 2 Sam 6:2

BAALI ba´-al-i
my lord Hos 2:16

BAALIM ba´-al-im
lords Judg 2:11

BAALIS ba´-al-is
exultation Jer 40:14

BAANA ba´-a-nah
Gr. for BAANAH 1 Kgs 4:12

BAANAH ba´-a-nah
son of oppression 2 Sam 4:2

BAARA ba´-a-rah
foolish 1 Chr 8:8

BAASEIAH ba´-as-i´-ah
work of Jehovah 1 Chr 6:40

BAASHA ba´-ash-ah
wicked (?) 1 Kgs 15:16

BABBLER
b is no better Eccl 10:11
What will this **b** say? Acts 17:18

BABBLING
Who hath **b**? Prov 23:29
profane and vain **b** 1 Tim 6:20; 2 Tim 2:16

BABE
out of the mouth of **b** Ps 8:2; Matt 21:16
their substance to their **b** Ps 17:14

b shall rule over them Is 3:4
revealed them unto **b** Matt 11:25; Luke 10:21
teacher of **b** Rom 2:20
b in Christ 1 Cor 3:1
newborn **b** 1 Pet 2:2

BABEL ba´-bel
confusion Gen 11:9

BABYLON bab´-il-on
Gr. for BABEL 2 Kgs 17:24

BABYLONISH bab´-il-one-ish
of, belonging to, Babylon Josh 7:21

BACA ba´-kah
weeping Ps 84:6

BACHRITES bak´-rites
descendants of Becher Num 26:35

BACK
he had turned his **b** 1 Sam 10:9
cast thy law behind their **b** Neh 9:26
plowed upon my **b** Ps 129:3
rod is for the **b** Prov 10:13
cast all my sins behind my **b** Is 38:17
gave my **b** to the smiters Is 50:6

BACKBITERS
B, haters of God Rom 1:30

BACKBITETH
b not his tongue Ps 15:3

BACKBITING
countenance a **b** tongue Prov 25:23
strifes, **b**, whisperings 2 Cor 12:20

BACKSLIDING
b Israel Jer 3:6,8,11,12
perpetual **b** Jer 8:5
our **b** are many Jer 14:7
as a **b** heifer Hos 4:16
bent to **b** from me Hos 11:7
will heal their **b** Hos 14:4

BACKWARD
let the shadow return **b** 2 Kgs 20:10
b, but I cannot perceive Job 23:8
driven **b** Ps 40:14
judgment is turned away **b** Is 59:14
went **b**, and not forward Jer 7:24

BAD
good or **b** Gen 31:24,29; Lev 27:12,14,33; Num 13:19; 24:13; 2 Cor 5:10

BADNESS
land of Egypt for **b** Gen 41:19

BAG
b of divers weights Deut 25:13; Mic 6:11
transgression sealed up in a **b** Job 14:17
lavish gold out of the **b** Is 46:6
b with holes Hag 1:6
b which wax not old Luke 12:33
a thief, and had the **b** John 12:6

BAHARUMITE ba-har´-oom-ite
an inhabitant of Bahurim 1 Chr 11:33

BAHURIM ba-hoor´-im
(town of) young men 2 Sam 16:5

BAJITH ba´-yith
a house Is 15:2

BAKBAKKAR bak-bak´-ar
searcher 1 Chr 9:15

BAKBUK bak´-book
a bottle Ezra 2:51

BAKBUKIAH bak´-book-i´-ah
emptying (wasting) of Jehovah Neh 11:17

BAKE
b unleavened bread Gen 19:3; 1 Sam 28:24
b unleavened cakes Ex 12:39

BAKER
his **b** had offended Gen 40:1
both me and the chief **b** Gen 41:10
and to be **b** 1 Sam 8:13
bread out of the **b** street Jer 37:21
oven heated by the **b** Hos 7:4

BALAAM ba´-lam
destruction (?) Num 22:5

BALAC ba´-lac
same as BALAK Rev 2:14

BALADAN ba´-la-dan
Baal (is) judge 2 Kgs 20:12

BALAH ba´-lah
decay Josh 19:3

BALAK ba´-lak
to make empty Num 22:2

BALANCE
just **b** Lev 19:36; Ezek 45:10
the **b** of the clouds Job 37:16
laid in the **b** Ps 62:9
false **b** Prov 11:1; 20:23
wicked **b** Mic 6:11
hills in a **b** Is 40:12
weigh silver in the **b** Is 46:6
a pair of **b** Rev 6:5

BALD
go up, thou **b** head 2 Kgs 2:23
every head shall be **b** Jer 48:37

BALDNESS
instead of well set hair **b** Is 3:24
to mourning, and to **b** Is 22:12
enlarge thy **b** as the eagle Mic 1:16

BALL
toss thee like a **b** Is 22:18

BALM
b in Gilead Jer 8:22

BAMAH ba´-mah
high place Ezek 20:29

BAMOTH ba´-moth
high places Num 21:19

BAMOTH-BAAL ba´-moth-ba´-al
high places of Baal Josh 13:17

BANDS
break their **b** asunder Ps 2:3
there are no **b** in their death Ps 73:4
with **b** of love Hos 11:4
and the other I called **b** Zech 11:7
whole **b** of soldiers Matt 27:27

BANI ba´-ni
built 2 Sam 23:36

BANISHED
not fetch home again his **b** 2 Sam 14:13
unto death, or to **b** Ezra 7:26
false burdens and causes of **b** Lam 2:14

BANK
money into the **b** Luke 19:23

BANNER
set up our **b** Ps 20:5

BANQUET
come this day unto the **b** Esth 5:4
companions make a **b** of him Job 41:6
b of them that stretched Amos 6:7

BAPTISM
be baptized with the **b** Matt 20:22; Mark 10:38
b of John Matt 21:25; Mark 11:30; Luke 7:29; 20:4; Acts 1:22; 18:25
b of repentance Mark 1:4; Luke 3:3; Acts 13:24; 19:4
buried with him by **b** Rom 6:4
One Lord, one faith, one **b** Eph 4:5
doctrine of **b** Heb 6:2

BAPTIZE
b you with the Holy Ghost Matt 3:11; Mark 1:8; Luke 3:16
I have need to be **b** Matt 3:14
Jesus, when he was **b** went up Matt 3:16
he that believeth and is **b** Mark 16:16
that came forth to be **b** Luke 3:7
publicans to be **b** Luke 3:12
Jesus being **b**, and praying Luke 3:21
being not **b** of him Luke 7:30
he that sent me to **b** John 1:33
tarried with them, and **b** John 3:22
Jesus made and **b** more John 4:1,2
repent, and be **b** Acts 2:38
gladly received word were **b** Acts 2:41
b, both men and women Acts 8:12
b in the name of the Lord Jesus Acts 8:16
what doth hinder me to be **b**? Acts 8:36
arose, and was **b** Acts 9:18
that these should not be **b**? Acts 10:47
b, and her household Acts 16:15,33
believed, and were **b** Acts 18:8
be **b**, and wash away thy sins Acts 22:16
were **b** into Jesus Rom 6:3
b in the name of Paul? 1 Cor 1:13
were all **b** unto Moses 1 Cor 10:2
all **b** into one body 1 Cor 12:13
b for the dead 1 Cor 15:29

BAR-JESUS bar-je´-sus
son of Jesus Acts 13:6

BAR-JONA bar-jo´-nah
son of Jona Matt 16:17

BARABBAS ba-rab´-as
son of a father Mark 15:7

BARACHEL ba´-rak-el
whom God blessed Job 32:6

BARACHIAS ba´-rak-i´-as
whom the LORD *blesses* Matt 23:35

BARAK ba´-rak
thunderbolt, lightning Judg 4:6

BARBARIANS
b saw the venomous beast Acts 28:4
him that speaketh a **b** Rom 1:14; 1 Cor 14:11

BARBAROUS
the **b** people shewed us Acts 28:2

BARBED
fill his skin with **b** irons Job 41:7

BARBER
take thee a **b** razor Ezek 5:1

BARE (n)
strip you, and make you **b** Is 32:11
I have made Esau **b** Jer 49:10

BARE (v)
b you on eagles' wings Ex 19:4
the LORD thy God **b** thee Deut 1:31
he **b** the sin of many Is 53:12
redeemed them; and he **b** them Is 63:9
b our sicknesses Matt 8:17
his own self **b** our sins 1 Pet 2:24

BARHUMITE bar´-hoom-ite
same as BAHARUMITE 2 Sam 23:31

BARIAH ba-ri´-ah
a fugitive 1 Chr 3:22

BARKED
vine waste, and **b** my fig tree Joel 1:7

BARKOS bar´-kos
painter (?) Ezra 2:53

BARN
gather it into thy **b** Job 39:12
nor gather into **b** Matt 6:26
gather the wheat into my **b** Matt 13:30
pull down my **b** Luke 12:18

BARNABAS bar´-na-bas
son of exhortation Acts 4:36

BARREL
meal in a **b** 1 Kgs 17:12

BARREN
and the ground is **b** 2 Kgs 2:19
fruitful land into **b** Ps 107:34
Sing, O **b** Is 54:1
neither be **b** nor unfruitful 2 Pet 1:8

BARS
down to the **b** of the pit Job 17:16
having neither **b** nor gates Ezek 38:11

BARSABAS bar´-sa-bas
son of Seba Acts 1:23

BARTHOLOMEW bar-thol´-o-mew
son of Talmai Matt 10:3

BARTIMAEUS bar´-ti-me´-us
son of Timai Mark 10:46

BARUCH ba´-rook
blessed Jer 32:12

BARZILLAI bar-zil´-a-i
of iron 2 Sam 17:27

BASE
children of **b** men Job 30:8
made you contemptible and **b** Mal 2:9
fellows of the **b** sort Acts 17:5
b things of the world 1 Cor 1:28
in presence am **b** 2 Cor 10:1

BASHAN ba´-shan
soft rich soil Num 21:33

BASHAN-HAVOTH-JAIR ba´-shan-hav´-oth-ja´-yir
Bashan of the villages of Jair Deut 3:14

BASHEMATH ba´-shem-ath
sweet-smelling Gen 26:34

BASKET
blessed be thy **b** Deut 28:5
b of summer fruit Amos 8:1
twelve **b** Matt 14:20; Mark 6:43; Luke 9:17; John 6:13
seven **b** Matt 15:37; Mark 8:8
how many **b**? Matt 16:9; Mark 8:19

BASMATH bas´-math
same as BASHEMATH 1 Kgs 4:15

BASON
poureth water into a **b** John 13:5

BATH-RABBIM bath-rab´-im
daughter of many Song 7:4

BATH-SHEBA bath´-she-bah
daughter of an oath 2 Sam 11:3

BATH-SHUA bath´-shoo-ah
same as BATH-SHEBA 1 Chr 3:5

BATHE
b himself in water Lev 15:5
b his flesh Lev 17:16; Num 19:7
shall be **b** in heaven Is 34:5

BATS
the lapwing, and the **b** Lev 11:19; Deut 14:18
to the moles and to the **b** Is 2:20

BATTLE
shouted for **b** 1 Sam 17:20
the **b** is the Lord's 1 Sam 17:47
when kings go forth to **b** 2 Sam 11:1
they cried to God in the **b** 1 Chr 5:20
strength unto the **b** Ps 18:39
in peace from the **b** Ps 55:18
nor the **b** to the strong, Eccl 9:11
sound of **b** Jer 50:22

BATTLEMENTS
make a **b** for thy roof Deut 22:8
take away her **b** Jer 5:10

BAY TREE
like a green **b** Ps 37:35

BAZLITH baz´-lith
making naked (?) Neh 7:54

BAZLUTH baz´-looth
same as BAZLITH Ezra 2:52

BEACON
left as a **b** Is 30:17

BEALIAH be´-al-i´-ah
whom Jehovah rules 1 Chr 12:5

BEALOTH be´-al-oth
pl. of BAALAH Josh 15:24

BEAM
Who layeth the **b** Ps 104:3
cast out the **b** Matt 7:5

BEAR (n)
cow and the **b** shall feed Is 11:7
We roar all like **b** Is 59:11
as a **b** that is bereaved Hos 13:8
and a **b** met him Amos 5:19

BEAR (v)
greater than I can **b** Gen 4:13
land was not able to **b** Gen 13:6
let me **b** the blame Gen 43:9
b their names before Lord Ex 28:12
not able to **b** Num 11:14; Deut 1:9
b witness 1 Kgs 21:10; Luke 11:48; John 1:7; 5:31; 8:18; 15:27; Acts 23:11; Rom 8:16; 1 John 1:2; 5:8
they shall **b** thee up Ps 91:12; Matt 4:6; Luke 4:11
wounded spirit who can **b**? Prov 18:14
clean that **b** vessels Is 52:11
b reproach of my youth Jer 31:19
b the yoke in his youth Lam 3:27
b the sin Ezek 23:49; Heb 9:28
not worthy to **b** Matt 3:11
b his cross Matt 27:32; Mark 15:21
cannot **b** them now John 16:12
b not the sword in vain Rom 13:4
b the infirmities of the weak Rom 15:1
b all things 1 Cor 13:7
shall also **b** the image 1 Cor 15:49
b his own burdens Gal 6:5
b in my body Gal 6:17

BEARD
your **b** be grown 2 Sam 10:5; 1 Chr 19:5
even Aaron's **b** Ps 133:2
upon thine head and upon thy **b** Ezek 5:1

BEARING
b precious seed Ps 126:6
b his cross John 19:17
conscience also **b** witness Rom 2:15
b about in the body 2 Cor 4:10
b his reproach Heb 13:13

BEAST
ask now the **b**, Job 12:7
counted as **b** Job 18:3
b that perish Ps 49:12
as a **b** before thee Ps 73:22
regardeth the life of his **b** Prov 12:10
no preeminence above a **b** Eccl 3:19
fought with **b** 1 Cor 15:32
every kind of **b** James 3:7
as natural brute **b** 2 Pet 2:12

BEAT
b their swords Is 2:4; Mic 4:3
b with many stripes Luke 12:47
as one that **b** the air 1 Cor 9:26

BEAUTIFUL
B for situation Ps 48:2
how **b** are the feet Is 52:7; Rom 10:15

BEAUTY
b of holiness 1 Chr 16:29; 2 Chr 20:21; Ps 29:2; 96:9; 110:3
to **b** the house of the Lord Ezra 7:27
behold the **b** of the Lord Ps 27:4
b to consume away Ps 39:11
perfection of **b** Ps 50:2
b is vain Prov 31:30

BEBAI be´-bai
void, empty Ezra 2:11

BECHER be´-ker
a young camel Gen 46:21

BECHORATH be-kor´-ath
offspring of the first birth 1 Sam 9:1

BECKON
he **b** unto them Luke 1:22
Peter therefore **b** to him John 13:24
b unto them with the hand Acts 12:17
Paul stood on the stairs, and **b** Acts 21:40

BECOMETH
holiness **b** thine house Ps 93:5
as **b** saints Rom 16:2; Eph 5:3
as **b** the gospel Phil 1:27
b holiness Titus 2:3

BED
my **b** shall comfort Job 7:13
in slumberings upon the **b** Job 33:15
I remember thee upon my **b** Ps 63:6
take up thy **b** Matt 9:6; Mark 2:9; John 5:11

BEDAD be´-dad
separation, part Gen 36:35

BEDAN be´-dan
son of Dan (?) 1 Sam 12:11

BEDEIAH be-di´-ah
servant of Jehovah Ezra 10:35

BEELIADA be-el´-ya-dah
whom Baal has known 1 Chr 14:7

BEELZEBUB be-el´-ze-bub
same as BAALZEBUB Matt 10:25

BEER be´-er
a well Num 21:16

BEER-ELIM be´-er-el´-im
well of heroes Is 15:8

BEER-LAHAI-ROI be´-er-la-ha´-i-ro´-i
well of vision (of God) to the living Gen 16:14

BEER-SHEBA be´-er-she´-bah
well of the oath Gen 21:31

BEERA be-er´-ah
same as BEER 1 Chr 7:37

BEERAH be-er´-ah
same as BEER 1 Chr 5:6

BEERI be´-er-i
man of the well Gen 26:34

BEEROTH be-er´-oth
wells Josh 9:17

BEEROTHITE be-er´-oth-ite
a native of Beeroth 2 Sam 23:37

BEES
chased you, as **b** do Deut 1:44
swarm of **b** and honey Judg 14:8
compassed me about like **b** Ps 118:12
for the **b** that is in the land Is 7:18

BEESH-TERAH be-esh´-te-rah
temple of Astarte (?) Josh 21:27

BEEVES
of the **b**, of the sheep Lev 22:19
of the persons, of the **b** Num 31:28

BEFALL
mischief **b** him Gen 42:4; 44:29
b you in the last days Gen 49:1
why then is all this **b** us? Judg 6:13
no evil **b** thee Ps 91:10
b the sons men **b** beasts Eccl 3:19

BEG
nor his seed **b** bread Ps 37:25
continually vagabonds and **b** Ps 109:10
shall he **b** in harvest Prov 20:4
to **b** I am ashamed Luke 16:3

BEGGARLY
weak and **b** elements Gal 4:9

BEGIN
b at my sanctuary Ezek 9:6
judgment must **b** 1 Pet 4:17

BEGINNING
Though thy **b** was small Job 8:7
b of wisdom Ps 111:10; Prov 9:10
word is true from the **b** Ps 119:160
end of a thing than the **b** Eccl 7:8
from the **b** it was not so Matt 19:8
b at Jerusalem Luke 24:47
hold the **b** of our confidence Heb 3:14

BEGOTTEN
this day have I **b** thee Ps 2:7; Acts 13:33; Heb 1:5
b us unto a lively hope 1 Pet 1:3

BEGUILE
wherefore then hast thou **b** me? Gen 29:25
b unstable souls 2 Pet 2:14

BEGUN
having **b** in the Spirit Gal 3:3
hath **b** a good work Phil 1:6

BEHALF
speak on God's **b** Job 36:2
in the **b** of Christ Phil 1:29

BEHAVE
b himself wisely 1 Sam 18:5,14
b ourselves valiantly 1 Chr 19:13
I will **b** myself wisely Ps 101:2
child shall **b** proudly Is 3:5
we **b** ourselves 1 Thess 2:10

BEHEADED
b John in the prison Matt 14:10
John, whom I **b** Mark 6:16
Herod said, John have I **b** Luke 9:9
were **b** for the witness of Jesus Rev 20:4

BEHEMOTH be-he´-moth
water-ox Job 40:15

BEHIND
not a hoof be left **b** Ex 10:26
things which are **b** Phil 3:13
fill up that which is **b** Col 1:24

BEHOLD
b the upright Ps 37:37
their angels do always **b** Matt 18:10
that they may **b** my glory John 17:24
b as in a glass 2 Cor 3:18

BEHOVED
thus it **b** Christ Luke 24:46
in all things it **b** him Heb 2:17

BEL bel
patron god of Babylon, *lord* Is 46:1

BELA be´-lah
destruction Gen 14:2

BELAH be´-lah
same as BELA Gen 46:21

BELAITES be´-la-ites
descendants of Bela Num 26:38

BELIAL be´-li-al
worthless Deut 13:13

BELIEVE
ere they **b** me? Num 14:11
B in the Lord your God 2 Chr 20:20
they **b** not in God Ps 78:22
simple **b** every word Prov 14:15
as thou hast **b**, so be it Matt 8:13
B ye that I am able Matt 9:28
down from the cross, and we will **b** Matt 27:42
only **b** Mark 5:36
if thou canst **b**, all things are possible Mark 9:23
ye not **b** Mark 11:31
b that ye receive them Mark 11:24
neither **b** they them Mark 16:13
most surely **b** Luke 1:1
which for a while **b** Luke 8:13
slow of heart to **b** Luke 24:25
b not for joy Luke 24:41
all men through him might **b** John 1:7
they **b** the scripture John 2:22
how shall ye **b**, if I tell you John 3:12
How can ye **b** which receive honour? John 5:44
how shall ye **b** my words? John 5:47
seen me, and **b** not John 6:36
neither did his brethren **b** John 7:5
of the Pharisees **b**, on him **b** John 7:48
b the works John 10:38
to the intent ye may **b** John 11:15
b in me shall never die John 11:26
all men will **b** John 11:48
b in the light John 12:36
the world may **b** John 17:21
I will not **b** John 20:25
have not seen, yet have **b** John 20:29
multitude of them that **b** Acts 4:32
all that **b** are justified Acts 13:39
ordained to eternal life **b** Acts 13:48
b in Gad with all his house Acts 16:34
father of all them that **b** Rom 4:11
against hope **b** in hope Rom 4:18
b on him shall not be ashamed Rom 9:33
how shall they **b**? Rom 10:14
wife that **b** not 1 Cor 7:12
we also **b**, and therefore speak 2 Cor 4:13
to them that **b** Gal 3:22
admired in all them that **b** 2 Thess 1:10
b to the saving of the soul Heb 10:39
must **b** that he is Heb 11:6
devils also **b**, and tremble James 2:19
b on him shall not be confounded 1 Pet 2:6

BELLY
upon thy **b** shalt thou go Gen 3:14
fill his **b** with the east wind Job 15:2
at the mouth goeth into the **b** Matt 15:17
but into the **b**, and goeth out into Mark 7:19
out of his **b** shall flow rivers of John 7:38
whose God is their **b** Phil 3:19

BELONGETH
To me **b** vengeance Deut 32:35
to whom vengeance **b** Ps 94:1
Vengeance **b** unto me, I will Heb 10:30

BELOVED
b of the Lord Deut 33:12
giveth his **b** sleep Ps 127:2
greatly **b** Dan 9:23; 10:11,19
b Son Matt 3:17; 17:5; Mark 1:11; 9:7; Luke 3:22; 9:35; 2 Pet 1:17
b for the fathers' sake Rom 11:28
accepted in the **b** Eph 1:6
b brother Col 4:9

BELSHAZZAR bel-shaz´-ar
Bel protects Dan 5:1

BELTESHAZZAR bel´-te-shaz´-ar
preserve his life Dan 1:7

BEMOAN
and they **b** him Job 42:11
or who shall **b** thee? Jer 15:5
who will **b** her? Nah 3:7

BEN ben
son 1 Chr 15:18

BEN-AMMI ben´-am´-i
son of my own kindred Gen 19:38

BEN-HADAD ben-ha´-dad
son of Hadad 1 Kgs 15:18

BEN-HAIL ben-ha´-yil
son of the host 2 Chr 17:7

BEN-HANAN ben-ha´-nan
son of one who is gracious 1 Chr 4:20

BEN-ONI ben-o´-ni
son of my sorrow Gen 35:18

BEN-ZOHETH ben-zo´-heth
son of Zoheth 1 Chr 4:20

BENAIAH ben-ai´-ah
whom Jehovah has built 2 Sam 8:18

BEND
the wicked **b** their bow Ps 11:2
them that afflicted thee shall come **b** Is 60:14
vine did **b** her roots toward him Ezek 17:7

BENE-BERAK be-ne´-be-rak
sons of Barak (lightning) Josh 19:45

BENE-JAAKAN be-ne-ja´-ak-an
son of Jaakan Num 33:31

BENEATH
depart from hell **b** Prov 15:24
hell from **b** is moved Is 14:9
ye are from **b** John 8:23

BENEFACTORS
called **b** Luke 22:25

BENEFIT
loadeth us with **b** Ps 68:19
partakers of the **b** 1 Tim 6:2

BENEVOLENCE
render unto the wife due **b** 1 Cor 7:3

BENINU be-ni´-noo
our son Neh 10:13

BENJAMIN ben´-ja-min
son of the right hand (fortunate) Gen 35:18

BENJAMITE ben´-jam-ite
of the tribe of Benjamin Judg 20:35

BENO ben´-o
his son 1 Chr 24:26

BEON be´-on
contracted from BAAL-MEON Num 32:3

BEOR be´-or
a torch Gen 36:32

BERA be´-rah
excellence Gen 14:2

BERACHAH be-rak´-ah
blessing 1 Chr 12:3

BERACHIAH be´-rak-i´-ah
whom the LORD hath blessed 1 Chr 6:39

BERAIAH be-rai´-ah
whom Jehovah created 1 Chr 8:21

BEREAVE
b of my children Gen 42:36; 43:14
b my soul of good Eccl 4:8
I will **b** them Jer 15:7

BEREA be-ree´-ah
heavy Acts 17:10

BERECHIAH be´-rek-i´-ah
same as BERACHIAH 1 Chr 3:20

BERED be´-red
hail Gen 16:14

BERI be´-ri
man of the well 1 Chr 7:36

BERIAH be-ri´-ah
in evil (?) Gen 46:17

BERIITES be-ri´-ites
descendants of Beriah Num 26:44

BERITES ber´-ites
descendants of Bichri 2 Sam 20:14

BERITH be´-rith
a covenant Judg 9:46

BERNICE ber-ni´-see
victorious Acts 25:13

BERODACH-BALADAN be´-ro-dak-bal´-a-dan
Berodach (Merodach) has given a son 2 Kgs 20:12

BEROTHAH be´-roth-ah
wells Ezek 47:16

BEROTHAI be´-roth-a-i
my wells 2 Sam 8:8

BEROTHITE be´-roth-ite
same as BEEROTHITE 1 Chr 11:39

BESAI be´-sa-i
sword, victory (?) Ezra 2:49

BESEECH
Hear, I **b** thee Job 42:4
centurion, **b** him Matt 8:5
I **b** thee, look; upon my son Luke 9:38
as though God did **b** you 2 Cor 5:20
b you that ye walk Eph 4:1
I rather **b** thee Phile 1:9

BESET
bulls of Bashan have **b** me Ps 22:12
Thou hast **b** me behind Ps 139:5
their doings have **b** them Hos 7:2
sin which doth so easily **b** us Heb 12:1

BESIDE
He is **b** himself Mark 3:21
thou art **b** thyself Acts 26:24
whether we **b** ourselves 2 Cor 5:13

BESIEGE
b thee in all thy gates Deut 28:52
b it and build great bulwarks Eccl 9:14
as a **b** city Is 1:8

BESODEIAH be´-sod-i´-ah
in the secret of the LORD Neh 3:6

BESOR be´-sor
cool 1 Sam 30:9

BESOUGHT
b the Lord Ex 32:11; Deut 3:23; 1 Kgs 13:6 2 Chr 33:12; Jer 26:19
devils **b** him Matt 8:31
b him that he would depart Matt 8:34
b him that he would tarry John 4:40
I **b** the Lord thrice 2 Cor 12:8

BEST
spared the **b** of the sheep 1 Sam 15:9,15
b state is altogether vanity Ps 39:5
b robe Luke 15:22
b gifts 1 Cor 12:31

BESTEAD
hardly **b** and hungry Is 8:21

BESTIR
thou shalt **b** thyself 2 Sam 5:24

BESTOW
to **b** my fruits Luke 12:17
grace which was **b** 1 Cor 15:10
I have **b** upon you labour in vain Gal 4:11
love the Father hath **b** 1 John 3:1

BETAH be´-tah
confidence 2 Sam 8:8

BETEN be´-ten
belly, hollow Josh 19:25

BETH-ANATH beth´-an-ath
echo Josh 19:38

BETH-ANOTH beth´-an-oth
house of (the goddess) Anath Josh 15:59

BETH-ARABAH beth-ar´-ab-ah
house of the desert Josh 15:6

BETH-ARAM beth-a´-ram
house of the height Josh 13:27

BETH-ARBEL beth-arb´-el
house of the ambush of God Hos 10:14

BETH-AVEN beth-a´-ven
house of vanity (i.e. of idols) Josh 7:2

BETH-AZMAVETH beth´-az-ma´-veth
house of strength Neh 7:28

BETH-BAAL-MEON beth´-ba´-al-me-on
house of Baal-meon Josh 13:17

BETH-BARAH beth-ba´-rah
same as BETH-ABARA Judg 7:24

BETH-BIREI beth-bir´-i
house of my creation 1 Chr 4:31

BETH-CAR beth´-kar
house of pasture 1 Sam 7:11

BETH-DAGON beth-da´-gon
house of Dagon Josh 15:41

BETH-DIBLATHAIM beth´-dib-la-tha´-im
house of the two cakes Jer 48:22

BETH-EMEK beth-e´-mek
house of the valley Josh 19:27

BETH-EZEL beth-e´-zel
house of firmness (?) Mic 1:11

BETH-GADER beth-ga´-der
house of the wall 1 Chr 2:51

BETH-GAMUL beth-ga´-mool
house of the weaned Jer 48:23

BETH-HACCEREM beth´-hak-er´-em
house of the vineyard Neh 3:14

BETH-HARAN beth-ha´-ran
same as BETH-ARAM Num 32:36

BETH-HOGLA beth-hog´-lah
same as BETH-HOGLAH Josh 15:6

BETH-HOGLAH beth-hog´-lah
house of the partridge Josh 18:19

BETH-HORON beth-ho´-ron
house of the hollow Josh 10:10

BETH-JESIMOTH beth-je-shim´-oth
house of the deserts Num 33:49

BETH-LEBAOTH beth´-le-ba´-oth
house of lionesses Josh 19:6

BETH-MAACHAH beth´-ma´-ak-ah
house of Maachah 2 Sam 20:14

BETH-MARCABOTH beth´-mar´-kab-oth
house of chariots Josh 19:5

BETH-MEON beth´-me´-on
house of habitation Jer 48:23

BETH-NIMRAH beth´-nim´-rah
house of sweet water Num 32:36

BETH-PALET beth´-pa´-let
house of escape, or of Pelet Josh 15:27

BETH-PAZZEZ beth´-paz´-ez
house of dispersion Josh 19:21

BETH-PEOR beth´-pe´-or
house (temple) of Peor Deut 3:29

BETH-PHELET beth´-fe´-let
same as BETH-PALET Neh 11:26

BETH-RAPHA beth´-ra´-fah
house of Rapha 1 Chr 4:12

BETH-REHOB beth´-re´-hob
house of Rehob Judg 18:28

BETH-SHAN beth´-shan
house of rest 1 Sam 31:10

BETH-SHEAN beth´-she´-an
same as BETHSHAN Josh 17:11

BETH-SHEMESH beth´-she´-mesh
house of the sun Josh 15:10

BETH-SHITTAH beth´-shit´-ah
house of acacias Judg 7:22

BETH-TAPPUAH beth´-tap-oo´-ah
house of apples Josh 15:53

BETH-ZUR beth´-zoor
house of the rock Josh 15:58

BETHABARA beth-ab´-ar-ah
house of passage John 1:28

BETHANY beth´-an-y
house of dates Matt 21:17

BETH-EL beth´-el
house of God Gen 12:8

BETHELITE beth´-el-ite
a native of Beth-el 1 Kgs 16:34

BETHER be´-ther
separation Song 2:17

BETHESDA beth-esd´-ah
house of mercy John 5:2

BETHINK
b themselves in the land 1 Kgs 8:47; 2 Chr 6:37

BETH-LEHEM beth´-le-hem
house of bread Gen 35:19

BETH-LEHEM EPHRATAH beth´-le-hem ef´-ra-tah
Bethlehem the fruitful (?) Mic 5:2

BETH-LEHEM-JUDAH beth´-le-hem-joo´-dah
Bethlehem of Judah Judg 17:7

BETHLEHEMITE beth´-le-hem-ite
a man of BETH-LEHEM 1 Sam 16:1

BETHPHAGE beth´-fa-jee
house of unripe figs Matt 21:1

BETHSAIDA beth´-sai´-dah
house of fishing Matt 11:21

BETHSHEMITE beth´-shem´-ite
a native of Bethshemesh 1 Sam 6:14

BETHUEL beth´-oo-el
house of God Gen 22:22

BETHUL beth´-ool
same as BETH-EL (?) Josh 19:4

BETIMES
they rose up **b** Gen 26:31
rising up **b**, and sending 2 Chr 36:15
rising **b** for a prey Job 24:5
loveth him chasteneth him **b** Prov 13:24

BETONIM be-to´-nim
pistachio nuts Josh 13:26

BETRAY
opportunity to **b** Matt 26:16
I have **b** the innocent blood Matt 27:4
night in which he was **b** 1 Cor 11:23

BETROTH
b them unto me for ever Hos 2:19,20

BETTER
to obey is **b** than sacrifice 1 Sam 15:22
I am not **b** than my fathers 1 Kgs 19:4
lovingkindness is **b** than life Ps 63:3
Two are **b** than one Eccl 4:9
former days were **b** than these Eccl 7:10
man **b** than a sheep Matt 12:12
he saith, The old is **b** Luke 5:39
each esteem other **b** than Phil 2:3
much **b** than the angels Heb 1:4
desire a **b** country Heb 11:16
b for them not to have known 2 Pet 2:21

BEULAH be-ool´-ah
married Is 62:4

BEWAIL
all wept and **b** her Luke 8:52
of women, which also **b** Luke 23:27
b many which have sinned 2 Cor 12:21

BEWARE
b, I pray thee, drink Judg 13:4
b lest he take thee away Job 36:18
b of the leaven Matt 16:6; Mark 8:15
b of the scribes Mark 12:38; Luke 20:46
b of covetousness Luke 12:15
b of dogs, **b** of evil workers Phil 3:2

BEWITCHED
and **b** the people of Samaria Acts 8:9
who hath **b** you Gal 3:1

BEWRAY
which **b** itself Prov 27:16
b it not Prov 29:24
b not him that wandereth Is 16:3
thy speech **b** thee Matt 26:73

BEYOND
I cannot go **b** the word Num 22:18
b their power 2 Cor 8:3
how that **b** measure I persecuted Gal 1:13
That no man go **b** 1 Thess 4:6

BEZAI be´-zai
short for BEZALEEL (?) Ezra 2:17

BEZALEEL be-zal´-e-el
in the shadow of God (?) Ex 31:2

BEZEK be´-zek
lightning (?) Judg 1:4

BEZER be´-zer
ore of precious metal Deut 4:43

BICHRI bik´-ri
young 2 Sam 20:1

BIDKAR bid´-kar
cleaver (?) 2 Kgs 9:25

BIER
David himself followed the **b** 2 Sam 3:31
came and touched the **b** Luke 7:14

BIGTHAN big´-than
given by God Esth 2:21

BIGTHANA big´-than-ah
same as BIGTHAN Esth 6:2

BIGVAI big´-va-i
happy, fortunate Ezra 2:2

BILDAD bil´-dad
son of contention (?) Job 2:11

BILEAM bil´-e-am
same as BALAAM (?) 1 Chr 6:70

BILGAH bil´-gah
cheerfulness 1 Chr 24:14

BILGAI bil´-ga-i
same as BILGAH Neh 10:8

BILHAH bil´-hah
modesty Gen 29:29

BILHAN bil´-han
modest Gen 36:27

BILLOWS
thy **b** have gone over me Ps 42:7
all thy **b** and thy waves Jon 2:3

BILSHAN bil´-shan
seeker (?) Ezra 2:2

BIMHAL bim´-hal
a descendant of Asher 1 Chr 7:33

BIND
b them continually upon thy heart Prov 6:21
b up the brokenhearted Is 61:1
b the strong man Matt 12:29; Mark 3:27
b on earth Matt 16:19; 18:18

BINEA bin´-ea
short for BAANA (?) 1 Chr 8:37

BINNUI bin´-oo-i
a building up Ezra 8:33

BIRD
neither the **b** of the air to rest 2 Sam 21:10
heritage is unto me as a speckled **b** Jer 12:9
b of the air have nests Matt 8:20; Luke 9:58

BIRSHA bir´-shah
with wickedness Gen 14:2

BIRTH
blind from his **b** John 9:1
of whom I travail in **b** Gal 4:19

BIRTHRIGHT
Sell me this day thy **b** Gen 25:31
he took away my **b** Gen 27:36
morsel of food sold his **b** Heb 12:16

BIRZAVITH bir´-za-vith
wounds (?) 1 Chr 7:31

BISHLAM bish´-lam
in peace Ezra 4:7

BISHOP
if a man desire the office of **b** 1 Tim 3:1
b must be blameless Titus 1:7

BIT
held in with **b** and bridle Ps 32:9
put **b** in the horses' mouths James 3:3

BITE
it **b** like a serpent Prov 23:32
that **b** with their teeth Mic 3:5
if ye **b** and devour one another Gal 5:15

BITHIAH bith-i´-ah
daughter (worshiper) of Jehovah 1 Chr 4:18

BITHRON bith´-ron
a broken place 2 Sam 2:29

BITHYNIA bi-thin´-i-a
a province in Asia Minor Acts 16:7

BITTER
b herbs Ex 12:8; Num 9:11
with **b** destruction Deut 32:24
writest **b** things Job 13:26
that put **b** for sweet Is 5:20
b to them that drink it Is 24:9
an evil thing and **b** Jer 2:19
wept **b** Matt 26:75; Luke 22:62
be not **b** against them Col 3:19

BITTERNESS
in **b** of my soul Job 10:1; Is 38:15
heart knoweth his own **b** Prov 14:10
in the gall of **b** Acts 8:23
all **b** and wrath be put away Eph 4:31
lest any root of **b** Heb 12:15

BIZJOTHJAH biz-joth´-jah
contempt of Jehovah Josh 15:28

BIZTHA biz´-thah
double gift (?) Esth 1:10

BLACK
make one hair white or **b** Matt 5:36
reserved the **b** of darkness Jude 1:13
lo a **b** horse Rev 6:5

BLADE
after the **b** Judg 3:22
When the **b** was sprung up Matt 13:26
first the **b**, then the ear Mark 4:28

BLAME (n)
bear the **b** Gen 43:9; 44:32
be holy and without **b** Eph 1:4

BLAME (v)
ministry be not **b** 2 Cor 6:3
no man should **b** us 2 Cor 8:20
because he was to be **b** Gal 2:11

BLAMELESS
be **b** in the day of our Lord 1 Cor 1:8
may be **b** and harmless Phil 2:15

BLASPHEME
enemies of the Lord to **b** 2 Sam 12:14
my name continually every day is **b** Is 52:5
This man **b** Matt 9:3
b against the Holy Ghost Mark 3:29
I compelled them to **b** Acts 26:11
name of God is **b** Rom 2:24
b that worthy name James 2:7

BLASPHEMY
All manner of sin and **b** Matt 12:31
He hath spoken **b** Matt 26:65
Who is this which speaketh **b**? Luke 5:21

BLAST
b with the east wind Gen 41:6
with **b**, and with mildew Deut 28:22
pestilence, **b**, mildew, locust 1 Kgs 8:37

BLASTUS blast´-us
a shoot Acts 12:20

BLAZE
to **b** abroad the matter Mark 1:45

BLEATING
hear the **b** of the flock Judg 5:16
What meaneth then this **b** 1 Sam 15:14

BLEMISH
Children in whom was no **b** Dan 1:4
holy and without **b** Eph 5:27
a lamb without **b** 1 Pet 1:19

BLESS
Oh that thou wouldest **b** me 1 Chr 4:10
b himself in the earth Is 65:16
b them that curse Matt 5:44; Luke 6:28

BLESSED
B shall thou be, in the city, Deut 28:3
memory of the just is **b** Prov 10:7
B are ye that sow Is 32:20
more **b** to give than to receive Acts 20:35
b for evermore 2 Cor 11:31
looking for that **b** hope Titus 2:13
B are the dead which die in Lord Rev 14:13

BLESSING
turned the curse into a **b** Deut 23:5; Neh 13:2
b of him that was ready to perish Job 29:13
b of Lord it maketh rich Prov 10:22
faithful man shall abound with **b** Prov 28:20
destroy it not, for a **b** is in it Is 65:8
I will curse your **b** Mal 2:2
pour you out a **b** Mal 3:10
fulness of the **b** of the gospel Rom 15:29
cup of **b** which we bless 1 Cor 10:16
proceedeth **b** and cursing James 3:10
honour and glory, and **b** Rev 5:12

BLIND (n)
I was eyes to the **b** Job 29:15
the **b** lead the **b** Matt 15:14; Luke 6:39

BLIND (v)
the gift **b** the wise Ex 23:8
their minds were **b** 2 Cor 3:14
darkness hath **b** 1 John 2:11

BLINDNESS
the **b** of their heart Eph 4:18

BLOOD
whoso sheddeth man's **b** Gen 9:6
b shall be upon head 1 Kgs 2:32
precious shall their **b** be in his sight Ps 72:14
garments rolled in **b** Is 9:5
the **b** of the souls Jer 2:34
land is full of **b** Ezek 9:9
his **b** shall be upon him Ezek 18:13; 33:5
buildeth a town with **b** Hab 2:12
issue of **b** Matt 9:20; Mark 5:25; Luke 8:43
flesh and **b** hath not revealed Matt 16:17
betrayed the innocent **b** Matt 27:4
His **b** be on us and on our children Matt 27:25
b of the new testament Mark 14:24
new testament in my **b** Luke 22:20; 1 Cor 11:25
great drops of **b** falling Luke 22:44
born, not of **b** John 1:13
drinketh my **b** John 6:54,56
from **b** Acts 15:20; 21:25
made of one **b** Acts 17:26
purchased with his own **b** Acts 20:28
through faith in his **b** Rom 3:25
justified by his **b** Rom 5:9
communion of the **b** 1 Cor 10:16
guilty of the body and **b** 1 Cor 11:27
flesh and **b** cannot inherit 1 Cor 15:50
redemption through his **b** Eph 1:7; Col 1:14
without shedding of **b** Heb 9:22
b of the covenant Heb 10:29
precious **b** of Christ 1 Pet 1:19
white in the **b** of the Lamb Rev 7:14; 12:11

BLOSSOM
shall **b** as the rose Is 35:1
fig tree shall not **b** Hab 3:17

BLOT
b out of book Ex 32:32; Ps 69:28
b out, as a thick cloud Is 44:22
that your sins may be **b** out Acts 3:19
B out the handwriting Col 2:14

BLUSH
b to lift up my face Ezra 9:6
neither could they **b** Jer 6:15; 8:12

BOANERGES bo´-an-er´-jes
sons of thunder Mark 3:17

BOAST (n)
make her **b** in the Lord Ps 34:2
makest thy **b** Rom 2:17,23

BOAST (v)
b himself as he that putteth it off 1 Kgs 20:11
b themselves Ps 49:6; 94:4
B not thyself of to morrow Prov 27:1
that I may **b** myself a little 2 Cor 11:16
lest any man should **b** Eph 2:9
b great things James 3:5

BOATS
none other **b** there John 6:22
work to come by **b** Acts 27:16
let down the **b** into the sea Acts 27:30

BOAZ bo´-az
fleetness Ruth 2:1

BOCHERU bo´-ke-roo
firstborn (?) 1 Chr 8:38

BOCHIM bo´-kim
weepers Judg 2:1

BODILY
descended in a **b** shape Luke 3:22
his **b** presence is weak 2 Cor 10:10
fulness of the Godhead **b** Col 2:9
b exercise profiteth little 1 Tim 4:8

BODY
worms destroy this **b** Job 19:26
thy flesh and thy **b** are consumed Prov 5:11
b should be cast into hell Matt 5:29
b full of light Matt 6:22
felt in her **b** that she was healed Mark 5:29
neither for the **b** Luke 12:22
wheresoever the **b** is Luke 17:37
the temple of his **b** John 2:21
from his **b** were brought Acts 19:12
b of sin might be destroyed Rom 6:6
b of this death Rom 7:24
your **b** a living sacrifice Rom 12:1
many members in one **b** Rom 12:4
I keep under my **b** 1 Cor 9:27
though I give my **b** to be burned 1 Cor 13:3
absent from the **b** 2 Cor 5:8
whether in the **b**, 2 Cor 12:2
I bear in my **b** the marks Gal 6:17
like unto his glorious **b** Phil 3:21
in his own **b** on the tree 1 Pet 2:24

BOHAN bo´-han
thumb (?) Josh 15:6

BOLDLY
he speaketh **b** John 7:26
us therefore come **b** unto the throne Heb 4:16

BOLDNESS
the **b** of his face changed Eccl 8:1
we have **b** and access Eph 3:12
have **b** in the day of judgment 1 John 4:17

BOND
in the **b** of iniquity Acts 8:23
b of peace Eph 4:3
b of perfectness Col 3:14

BONDAGE
never in **b** to any man John 8:33

BONDMAN
thou wast a **b** Deut 15:15; 16:12; 24:18

BONDWOMAN
Cast out this **b** Gen 21:10; Gal 4:30

BONE
neither shall ye break a **b** thereof Ex 12:46; Num 9:12
b full of sin Job 20:11
b as pieces of brass Job 40:18
the **b** broken may rejoice Ps 51:8
as rottenness in his **b** Prov 12:4
full of dead men's **b** Matt 23:27
spirit hath not flesh and **b** Luke 24:39

BOOK
printed in a **b** Job 19:23
adversary had written in **b** Job 31:35
the **b** of the Lord Is 34:16
b of remembrance Mal 3:16
when he had opened **b** Luke 4:17
could not contain the **b** John 21:25
b of life Phil 4:3; Rev 3:5; 13:8; 17:8; 20:12; 21:27
take away from the words of this **b** Rev 22:19

BOOTH
as a **b** that the keeper maketh Job 27:18
there made him a **b** Jon 4:5

BOOTY
the **b**, being the rest Num 31:32
camels shall be a **b** Jer 49:32
thou shalt be for **b** unto them Hab 2:7
goods shall become a **b** Zeph 1:13

BOOZ bo´-oz
same as BOAZ Matt 1:5

BORN
man **b** to trouble Job 5:7
b of a woman Job 14:1; 15:14; 25:4; Matt 11:11
this man was **b** there Ps 87:4
unto us a child is **b** Is 9:6
shall a nation be **b** at once? Is 66:8
b of God 1 John 4:7; 5:1,4,18
b again John 3:3; 1 Pet 1:23
b of the Spirit John 3:6,8
as of one **b** out of due time 1 Cor 15:8
as new **b** babes 1 Pet 2:2

BORNE
then I could have **b** it Ps 55:12
b our griefs Is 53:4
grievous to be **b** Matt 23:4; Luke 11:46

BORROW
thou shalt not **b** Deut 15:6; 28:12
wicked **b**,and payeth not Ps 37:21
the **b** is servant Prov 22:7
from him that would **b** Matt 5:42

BOSCATH bos´-kath
stony, elevated ground 2 Kgs 22:1

BOSOM
returned into mine own **b** Ps 35:13
take fire in his **b** Prov 6:27
carry them in his **b** Is 40:11
into Abraham's **b** Luke 16:22
in the **b** of the Father John 1:18
leaning on Jesus' **b** John 13:23

BOSOR bo´-sor
Gr. and Aramaic for BEOR 2 Pet 2:15

BOSSES
upon the thick **b** Job 15:26

BOTCH
with the **b** of Egypt Deut 28:27
sore **b** that cannot be healed Deut 28:35

BOTTLE
a **b** of milk Judg 4:19
a **b** of wine 1 Sam 1:24; 10:3; 16:20; 2 Sam 16:1
put tears into thy **b** Ps 56:8
b in the smoke Ps 119:83
new wine into old **b** Matt 9:17; Mark 2:22; Luke 5:37

BOUGH
Joseph is a fruitful **b** Gen 49:22
go over the **b** again Deut 24:20
cut down a **b** from the trees Judg 9:48
bring forth **b** like a plant Job 14:9
shadow of it, and the **b** Ps 80:10
top was among the thick **b** Ezek 31:3

BOUGHT
I have **b** a piece of ground Luke 14:18
ye are **b** with a price 1 Cor 6:20; 7:23
denying the Lord that **b** them 2 Pet 2:1

BOUND
being **b** in affliction Ps 107:10
b in the heart of a child Prov 22:15
I go **b** in the spirit Acts 20:22
Art thou **b** unto a wife? 1 Cor 7:27
word of God is not **b** 2 Tim 2:9
in bonds, as **b** with them Heb 13:3

BOUNTIFUL
a **b** eye shall be blessed Prov 22:9
nor the churl said to be **b** Is 32:5

BOUNTY
gave her of his royal **b** 1 Kgs 10:13
make up before hand your **b** 2 Cor 9:5

BOWELS
straitened in **b** 2 Cor 6:12
b of mercies Col 3:12
b of compassion 1 John 3:17

BOZEZ bo´-zez
shining 1 Sam 14:4

BOZKATH boz´-kath
same as BOSCATH Josh 15:39

BOZRAH boz´-rah
sheepfold Gen 36:33

BRACELET
saw the earring and the **b** Gen 24:30
brought **b**, and earrings, and rings Ex 35:22
The chains, and the **b** Is 3:19

BRAKE
he **b** in pieces 2 Kgs 23:14
blessed and **b** Matt 14:19; Mark 6:41; 14:22

BRAMBLE
trees unto the **b** Judg 9:14
nettles and **b** in the fortresses Is 34:13
nor of a **b** bush Luke 6:44

BRANCH
tender **b** thereof will not cease Job 14:7
righteous shall flourish as a **b** Prov 11:28
a righteous **B** Jer 23:5
lodge in **b** Matt 13:32; Luke 13:19
cut down **b** Matt 21:8; Mark 11:8

BRAND
set the **b** on fire Judg 15:5
a **b** plucked out of the fire Zech 3:2

BRASS
thou mayest dig **b** Deut 8:9
over thy head shall be **b** Deut 28:23
become a sounding **b** 1 Cor 13:1

BRAVERY
take away the **b** of their Is 3:18

BRAWLER
not a **b**, not covetous 1 Tim 3:3
to be no **b**, but gentle Titus 3:2

BRAY
Doth the wild ass **b** Job 6:5
Among the bushes they **b** Job 30:7
b a fool in a mortar Prov 27:22

BREACH
the repairer of the **b** Is 58:12
thy **b** is great like the sea Lam 2:13

BREAD
not live by **b** Deut 8:3; Matt 4:4; Luke 4:4
in giving them **b** Ruth 1:6
brought him **b** and flesh 1 Kgs 17:6
withholden **b** from the hungry Job 22:7
life abhorreth **b** Job 33:20
satisfy her poor with **b** Ps 132:15
b eaten in secret Prov 9:17
satisfied with **b** Prov 12:11; 20:13
eateth not **b** of idleness Prov 31:27
Cast thy **b** upon the waters Eccl 11:1
b shall be given, Is 33:16
money for that which is not **b** Is 55:2
b to the eater Is 55:10
stones be made **b** Matt 4:3
our daily **b** Matt 6:11
to take the children's **b** Matt 15:26; Mark 7:27
known of them in breaking **b** Luke 24:35
breaking of **b** Acts 2:42; 20:7; 27:35
any man's **b** for nought 2 Thess 3:8

BREAK
Until the day **b** Song 2:17; 4:6
bruised reed shall he not **b** Is 42:3; Matt 12:20
B up your fallow ground Jer 4:3; Hos 10:12
to weep and to **b** my heart Acts 21:13

BREATH
b of life Gen 2:7; 6:17; 7:15
Cease ye from man, whose **b** Is 2:22
I will cause **b** to enter Ezek 37:5
he giveth to all life, and **b** Acts 17:25

BREATHE
such a **b** out cruelty Ps 27:12
b upon the slain Ezek 37:9
he **b** on them, and saith John 20:22

BREECHES
make them linen **b** to cover Ex 28:42
linen **b** shall he put Lev 6:10
shall have linen **b** upon Lev 16:4
have linen **b** upon their loins Ezek 44:18

BRETHREN
all ye are **b** Matt 23:8
no man left house or **b** Mark 10:29
faithful **b** in Christ Col 1:2
because we love the **b** 1 John 3:14

BRIBE
have I received any **b**? 1 Sam 12:3
right hand is full of **b** Ps 26:10

BRICK
let us make **b** Gen 11:3
straw to make **b** Ex 5:7
b are fallen down Is 9:10
altars of **b** Is 65:3

BRIDE
as the **b** adorneth herself Is 61:10
a **b** her attire Jer 2:32
b adorned for her husband Rev 21:2
the Spirit and the **b** say Rev 22:17

BRIDEGROOM
to meet the **b** Matt 25:1
because of **b** voice John 3:29

BRIDLE
a **b** for the ass Prov 26:3
b not his tongue James 1:26
able to **b** the whole body James 3:2

BRIGANDINE
put on the **b** Jer 46:4
lifteth himself up in his **b** Jer 51:3

BRIGHT
b light which is in the clouds Job 37:21
b cloud overshadowed Matt 17:5
the **b** and morning star Rev 22:16

BRIGHTNESS
to the **b** of thy rising Is 60:3
righteousness go forth as **b** Is 62:1
b of his coming 2 Thess 2:8
the **b** of his glory Heb 1:3

BRINK
kine upon the **b** Gen 41:3
by the rivers **b** Ex 2:3; 7:15
come to the **b** of Josh 3:8

BROAD
thy commandment is exceeding **b** Ps 119:96
b is the way Matt 7:13
make **b** their phylacteries Matt 23:5

BROILED
piece of the **b** fish Luke 24:42

BROKEN
b heart Ps 34:18
scripture cannot be **b** John 10:35
bone of him shall not be **b** John 19:36
b down middle wall Eph 2:14

BROOD
hen doth gather her **b** Luke 13:34

BROOK
stones out of the **b** 1 Sam 17:40
panteth after the water **b** Ps 42:1
He shall drink of the **b** Ps 110:7

BROTH
put **b** in a pot Judg 6:19
and **b** of abominable things Is 65:4

BROTHER
b is born for adversity Prov 17:17
b to him that is a great waster Prov 18:9
b offended is harder to be won Prov 18:19
closer than a **b** Prov 18:24
neither child nor **b** Eccl 4:8
b shall deliver up the **b** Matt 10:21
b goeth to law with **b** 1 Cor 6:6
admonish him as a **b** 2 Thess 3:15

BROTHERLY
b love Rom 12:10; 1 Thess 4:9; Heb 13:1

BROW
thy **b** brass Is 48:4
unto the **b** of the hill Luke 4:29

BRUISE (n)
wounds, and **b**, and putrifying sores Is 1:6
Thy **b** is incurable Jer 30:12
all that hear the **b** of thee Nah 3:19

BRUISE (v)
b reed shall he not break Is 42:3; Matt 12:20
b for our iniquities Is 53:5

BRUIT
all that hear the **b** of thee Nah 3:19

BRUTISH
a **b** man knoweth not Ps 92:6
I am more **b** than any Prov 30:2
the pastors are become **b** Jer 10:21

BUCKET
water out of his **b** Num 24:7
as a drop of a **b** Is 40:15

BUCKLER
he is a **b** to all 2 Sam 22:31

my **b**, and the horn Ps 18:2
thy shield and **b** Ps 91:4
a **b** to them that walk Prov 2:7

BUD
brought forth **b** Num 17:8
when the **b** is perfect Is 18:5
earth bringeth forth her **b** Is 61:11
the **b** shall yield no meal Hos 8:7

BUFFET
spit in his face, and **b** him Matt 26:67
are naked, and **b** 1 Cor 4:11
messenger of Satan to **b** me 2 Cor 12:7
when ye be **b** for your faults 1 Pet 2:20

BUILD
labour in vain that **b** Ps 127:1
a time to **b** up Eccl 3:3
b the old waste places Is 58:12
b his house upon a rock Matt 7:24; Luke 6:48
began to **b** Luke 14:30
able to **b** you up Acts 20:32
lest I should **b** upon another man's Rom 15:20
if any man **b** on this foundation 1 Cor 3:12
in whom ye also are **b** together Eph 2:22

BUILDER
b rejected Mark 12:10; Luke 20:17; Acts 4:11; 1 Pet 2:7
whose **b** and maker is God Heb 11:10

BUILDING
ye are God's **b** 1 Cor 3:9
have a **b** of God 2 Cor 5:1
b fitly framed together Eph 2:21

BUKKI book´-i
abbr. of BUKKIAH Num 34:22

BUKKIAH book-i´-ah
proved of the LORD 1 Chr 25:4

BUL bool
rain 1 Kgs 6:38

BULRUSH
an ark of **b** Ex 2:3
even in vessels of **b** Is 18:2
bow down head as a **b** Is 58:5

BULWARK
appoint for walls and **b** Is 26:1

BUNAH boon´-ah
prudence 1 Chr 2:25

BUNDLE
every man's **b** of money Gen 42:35
bind them in **b** to burn Matt 13:30
gathered a **b** of sticks Acts 28:3

BUNNI boon´-i
built Neh 9:4

BURDEN
Cast thy **b** upon the Lord Ps 55:22
grasshopper shall be a **b** Eccl 12:5
my **b** is light Matt 11:30
borne the **b** and heat Matt 20:12
bind heavy **b** Matt 23:4
bear his own **b** Gal 6:5

BURDENSOME
make Jerusalem a **b** stone Zech 12:3
b unto you 2 Cor 11:9
we might have been **b** 1 Thess 2:6

BURIAL
he have no **b** Eccl 6:3
the **b** of an ass Jer 22:19
she did it for my **b** Matt 26:12
carried Stephen to his **b** Acts 8:2

BURN
while I was musing the fire **b** Ps 39:3
B lips and a wicked heart Prov 26:23
wickedness **b** as the fire Is 9:18
day that shall **b** as an oven Mal 4:1
bundles to **b** them Matt 13:30
b with fire unquenchable Luke 3:17
your lights **b** Luke 12:35
did not our heart **b**? Luke 24:32
he was a **b** and shining light John 5:35
give my body to be **b** 1 Cor 13:3
whose end is to be **b** Heb 6:8
lamps of fire **b** Rev 4:5
into a lake of fire **b** Rev 19:20

BURNT OFFERING
b and sin offering Ps 40:6
I hate robbery for **b** Is 61:8
your **b** are not acceptable Jer 6:20
knowledge of God more than **b** Hos 6:6
whole and sacrifices **b** Mark 12:33

BURST
ready to **b** like new bottles Job 32:19
thy presses shall **b** out Prov 3:10
new wine doth **b** the bottles Mark 2:22

BURY
to go and **b** my father Matt 8:21; Luke 9:59
let the dead **b** their dead Matt 8:22
b with him by baptism Rom 6:4
he was **b**, and that he rose again 1 Cor 15:4

BUSHEL
under a **b** Matt 5:15; Mark 4:21; Luke 11:33

BUSINESS
king's **b** requireth haste 1 Sam 21:8
do **b** in great waters Ps 107:23
diligent in his **b** Prov 22:29
about my Father's **b** Luke 2:49
not slothful in **b** Rom 12:11
to do your own **b** 1 Thess 4:11

BUTLER
b of the king of Egypt Gen 40:1
chief **b** unto Pharaoh Gen 41:9

BUTTER
B and honey shall he eat Is 7:15,22

BUY
b any soul with his money Lev 22:11
B the truth Prov 23:23
b and eat Is 55:1
and **b** for yourselves Matt 25:9
city to **b** meat John 4:8
we will **b** and sell, and get gain James 4:13
b of me gold Rev 3:18
no man might **b**, Rev 13:17
no man **b** her merchandise Rev 18:11

BUYER
it is naught, saith the **b** Prov 20:14
as with the **b**, so with the Is 24:2
let not the **b** rejoice Ezek 7:12

BUZ booz
contempt Gen 22:21

BUZI booz´-i
descended from Buz Ezek 1:3

BUZITE booz´-ite
a descendant of Buz Job 32:2

BY AND BY
b he is offended Matt 13:21
give me **b** in a charger Mark 6:25
will say unto him **b** Luke 17:7

BYWAYS
travellers through the **b** Judg 5:6

BYWORD
a **b** of the people Job 17:6
a **b** among the heathen Ps 44:14

C

CABBON kab´-on
cake Josh 15:40

CABINS
into the **c** Jer 37:16

CABUL kab´-ool
displeasing (?) Josh 19:27

CAESAREA PHILIPPI see´-zar-e´-a fil-ip´-i
named after Philip the tetrarch Matt 16:13

CAESAREA see´-zar-e´-a
named after Augustus Caesar Acts 8:40

CAGE
As a **c** is full of birds Jer 5:27
a **c** of every unclean Rev 18:2

CAIAPHAS kai´-a-fas
depression (?) Matt 26:3

CAIN kane
possession Gen 4:1

CAINAN ka-i´-nan
possessor Gen 5:9

CAKE
to every one a **c** of bread 2 Sam 6:19
make me thereof a little **c** first 1 Kgs 17:13

CALAH ka´-lah
holy gate (?) Gen 10:11

CALAMITY
day of my **c** Deut 32:35; 2 Sam 22:19; Ps 18:18
until these **c** be overpast Ps 57:1
I also will laugh at your **c** Prov 1:26
he that is glad at **c** Prov 17:5
foolish son is the **c** of his father Prov 19:13
brother's house in the day of thy **c** Prov 27:10

CALCOL kal´-kol
sustenance, maintenance 1 Chr 2:6

CALEB ka´-leb
a dog Num 26:65

CALEB-EPHRATAH ka´-leb-ef´-rat-ah
Caleb the fruitful 1 Chr 2:24

CALF
Made it a molten **c** Ex 32:4
the **c** and the young lion Is 11:6
bring hither the fatted **c** Luke 15:23

CAULKERS
in thee thy **c** Ezek 27:9,27

CALLING
c of God without repentance Rom 11:29
abide in the same **c** 1 Cor 7:20
the hope of his **c** Eph 1:18
prize of the high **c** Phil 3:14
worthy of this **c** 2 Thess 1:11
called us with a holy **c** 2 Tim 1:9
partakers of the heavenly **c** Heb 3:1
make your **c** and election sure 2 Pet 1:10

CALM
Maketh the storm a **c** Ps 107:29
sea be **c** unto us Jon 1:11
there was a great **c** Matt 8:26; Mark 4:39

CALNEH kal´-nay
all of them Gen 10:10

CALNO kal´-no
same as CALNEH Is 10:9

CALVARY kal´-va-ry
skull Luke 23:33

CALVES
render the **c** of our lips Hos 14:2
grow up as **c** of the stall Mal 4:2

CAMON ka´-mon
abounding in stalks Judg 10:5

CAMP (n)
which went before the **c** Ex 14:19
covered the **c** Ex 16:13
every man by his own **c** Num 1:52
Lord walketh in the midst of thy **c** Deut 23:14

CAMP (v)
I will **c** against thee Is 29:3
c against it round about Jer 50:29
which **c** in the hedges Nah 3:17

CANA ka´-nah
place of reeds John 2:1

CANAAN ka´-nan
low region Gen 9:18

CANAANITE ka´-nan-ite
a zealot Mark 3:18

CANAANITES ka´-nan-ites
inhabitants of Canaan Judg 1:1

CANAANITESS ka´-nan-ite-ess
fem. of CANAANITES 1 Chr 2:3

CANDACE kan´-da-see
title of queen-mother of Ethiopia Acts 8:27

CANDLE
his **c** shined upon my head Job 29:3
thou wilt light my **c** Ps 18:28
spirit of man is the **c** of the Lord Prov 20:27
search Jerusalem with **c** Zeph 1:12
lighted a **c** Luke 8:16; 11:33
c shall shine more Rev 18:23
need no **c**, neither light Rev 22:5

CANDLESTICK
a stool, and **c** 2 Kgs 4:10

CANNEH kan´-ay
same as CALNEH (?) Ezek 27:23

CAPERNAUM ka-per´-na-um
city of consolation (?) Matt 4:13

CAPHTHORIM kaf´-thor-im
same as CAPHTORIM 1 Chr 1:12

CAPHTOR kaf´-tor
a name for Crete (?) Deut 2:23

CAPHTORIM kaf´-tor-im
inhabitants of Caphtor Gen 10:14

CAPPADOCIA cap-pa-do´-shah
a province in Asia Minor Acts 2:9

CAPTIVE
firstborn of the **c** Ex 12:29
c exile hasteneth Is 51:14
O **c** daughter of Zion Is 52:2
taken **c** by him at his will 2 Tim 2:26
lead **c** silly women 2 Tim 3:6

CAPTIVITY
into **c** to the law of sin Rom 7:23
bringing into **c** every thought 2 Cor 10:5

CARCAS car´-cas
an eagle (?) Esth 1:10

CARCASE
look upon the **c** of the men Is 66:24
Wheresoever the **c** is Matt 24:28
Whose **c** fell in the wilderness Heb 3:17

CARCHEMISH kar´-kem-ish
fortress of Chemosh Jer 46:2

CARE (n)
nation that dwelleth without **c** Jer 49:31
c of this world Matt 13:22; Mark 4:19
choked with **c** Luke 8:14
have the same **c** one for another 1 Cor 12:25
the **c** of all the churches 2 Cor 11:28
casting all your **c** upon him 1 Pet 5:7

CARE (v)
no man **c** for my soul Ps 142:4
not that he **c** for the poor John 12:6
Gallio **c** for none of those things Acts 18:17
naturally **c** for your state Phil 2:20

CAREAH ka-re´-ah
bald 2 Kgs 25:23

CAREFUL
not be **c** in the year of drought Jer 17:8
we are not **c** to answer Dan 3:16
thou art **c** and troubled Luke 10:41
Be **c** for nothing Phil 4:6
he sought it **c** with tears Heb 12:17

CAREFULNESS
with trembling and **c** Ezek 12:18
have you without **c** 1 Cor 7:32
what **c** it wrought in you 2 Cor 7:11

CARELESS
how they dwelt **c** Judg 18:7
ye **c** daughters, give ear Is 32:9
that dwellest **c** Is 47:8; Ezek 39:6

CARMEL karm´-el
park Josh 12:22

CARMELITE karm´-el-ite
a native of Carmel 1 Sam 30:5

CARMELITESS karm´-el-ite-ess
fem. of CARMELITE 1 Sam 27:3

CARMI karm´-i
a vine-dresser Gen 46:9

CARMITES karm´-ites
descendants of Carmi Num 26:6

CARNAL
c sold under sin Rom 7:14
the **c** mind is enmity against God Rom 8:7
weapons of our warfare not **c** 2 Cor 10:4

CARPUS karp´-us
fruit (?) 2 Tim 4:13

CARRIAGE
cattle and **c** before them Judg 18:21
laid up his **c** Is 10:28
your **c** were heavy loaden Is 46:1
we took up our **c** Acts 21:15

CARRY
Spirit of the Lord shall **c** thee 1 Kgs 18:12
c them in his bosom Is 40:11
c our sorrows Is 53:4
c them all the days of old Is 63:9
men that **c** tales to shed blood Ezek 22:9
began to **c** about in beds Mark 6:55
not lawful for thee to **c** thy bed John 5:10
c thee whither thou wouldest not John 21:18
c about with every wind Eph 4:14
we can **c** nothing out 1 Tim 6:7
not **c** about with divers Heb 13:9
clouds that are **c** with a tempest 2 Pet 2:17
c about of winds Jude 1:12

CARSHENA kar´-shen-ah
pillage of war (?) Esth 1:14

CART
with a **c** rope Is 5:18
as a **c** is pressed Amos 2:13

CASE
in such a **c** Ps 144:15
in no **c** enter Matt 5:20
long time in that **c** John 5:6

CASIPHIA ka-sif´-yah
silver (?) Ezra 8:17

CASLUHIM kas´-loo-him
descendants from Egypt Gen 10:14

CAST
lot is **c** into the lap Prov 16:33
whole body should be **c** into hell Matt 5:29; Mark 9:45
one **c** out devils Mark 9:38; Luke 9:49
c their gifts into the treasury Luke 21:1
first **c** a stone at her John 8:7
C down imaginations 2 Cor 10:5
C all care upon him 1 Pet 5:7
love **c** out fear 1 John 4:18

CASTAWAY
lest I myself should be a **c** 1 Cor 9:27

CASTLE
and all their goodly **c** Num 31:10
like the bars of a **c** Prov 18:19
to be carried into the **c** Acts 21:34

CASTOR kas´-tor
A horseman, one of the sons of Zeus Acts 28:11

CATCH
to **c** the poor Ps 10:9
c away that which was sown Matt 13:19
henceforth thou shalt **c** men Luke 5:10
wolf **c** them and scattereth sheep John 10:12

CATTLE
their trade hath been to feed **c** Gen 46:32
Our **c** also shall go with us Ex 10:26
the **c** thereof ye shall take for prey Josh 8:2
c upon a thousand hills Ps 50:10

CAUGHT
ram **c** in a thicket by horns Gen 22:13
that night they **c** nothing John 21:3
c up to third heaven 2 Cor 12:2
I **c** you with guile 2 Cor 12:16
be **c** up together with them 1 Thess 4:17

CAUSE (n)
For this **c** shall a man leave Matt 19:5; Mark 10:7; Eph 5:31
For this **c** many are sickly 1 Cor 11:30
for this **c** I obtained mercy 1 Tim 1:16

CAUSE (v)
hath **c** his name to dwell Ezra 6:12
c his face to shine Ps 67:1
mark them which **c** divisions Rom 16:17

CAUSELESS
thou hast shed blood **c** 1 Sam 25:31
the curse **c** shall not come Prov 26:2

CEASE
poor shall never **c** out of the land Deut 15:11
the wicked **c** from troubling Job 3:17
He maketh wars to **c** Ps 46:9
strife **c** Prov 26:20
grinders **c** because they are few Eccl 12:3
I **c** not to warn Acts 20:31
tongues, they shall **c** 1 Cor 13:8
Pray without **c** 1 Thess 5:17
hath **c** from sin 1 Pet 4:1

CEDRON seed´-ron
same as KIDRON John 18:1

CELEBRATE
shall ye **c** your sabbath Lev 23:32
death cannot **c** thee Is 38:18

CELESTIAL
glory of the **c** is one 1 Cor 15:40

CENCHRAE sen´-kre-ah
millet, small pulse Acts 18:18

CEPHAS see´-fas
stone John 1:42

CEREMONIES
according to all the **c** Num 9:3

CERTAIN
no c dwelling place 1 Cor 4:11
a c fearful looking for of judgment Heb 10:27

CERTIFY
word from you to c me 2 Sam 15:28
But I c you, brethren Gal 1:11

CHAFF
burn up c with fire Matt 3:12; Luke 3:17

CHAIN
no, not with c Mark 5:3
his c fell off Acts 12:7
not ashamed of my c 2 Tim 1:16
into c of darkness 2 Pet 2:4
everlasting c under darkness Jude 1:6

CHALCOL kal´-kol
same as CALCOL 1 Kgs 4:31

CHALDEA kal-de´-ah
synonym for Babylonia Jer 50:10

CHALDEANS kal-de´-ans
inhabitants of Chaldea Job 1:17

CHALDEES kal-dees´
same as CHALDEANS Gen 11:28

CHALLENGETH
which another c to be his Ex 22:9

CHAMBER
Let us make a little c 2 Kgs 4:10
bridegroom coming out of his c Ps 19:5
enter thou into thy c Is 26:20
c of his imagery Ezek 8:12
in the secret c Matt 24:26
in an upper c Acts 9:37; 20:8

CHAMPION
their c was dead 1 Sam 17:4,51

CHANAAN ka´-nan
a form of CANAAN Acts 7:11

CHANCE
it was a c that happened 1 Sam 6:9
I happened by c 2 Sam 1:6
time and c happeneth Eccl 9:11
by c there came down Luke 10:31

CHANGE (n)
till my c come Job 14:14
them that are given to c Prov 24:21

CHANGE (v)
sweareth to his own hurt, and c not Ps 15:4
as a vesture shalt thou c them Ps 102:26
fine gold c Lam 4:1
I am the Lord, I c not Mal 3:6
c the glory of the uncorruptible God Rom 1:23
we shall all be c 1 Cor 15:51
are c into the same image 2 Cor 3:18

CHANT
C to the sound of the viol Amos 6:5

CHAPMEN
which c and merchants bought 2 Chr 9:14

CHARASHIM kar´-ash-im
craftsmen 1 Chr 4:14

CHARCHEMISH kar´-kem-ish
same as CARCHEMISH 2 Chr 35:20

CHARGE (n)
lay not this sin to their c Acts 7:60; 2 Tim 4:16
lay any thing to the c? Rom 8:33

CHARGE (v)
nor c God foolishly Job 1:22
angels he c with folly Job 4:18
Jesus c them Matt 9:30
c some that they teach 1 Tim 1:3
I c thee before God 1 Tim 5:21
C them that are rich 1 Tim 6:17

CHARGEABLE
lest we be c unto thee 2 Sam 13:25
I was c to no man 2 Cor 11:9
because we would not be c 1 Thess 2:9

CHARITY
now walkest thou not c Rom 14:15
put on c Col 3:14
c of every one 2 Thess 1:3
end of the commandment is c 1 Tim 1:5
faith, c, peace 2 Tim 2:22
sound in faith, in c Titus 2:2
c shall cover the multitude of sins 1 Pet 4:8
to brotherly kindness c 2 Pet 1:7
spots in your feasts of c Jude 1:12

CHARMER
Or a c, or a consulter Deut 18:11
harken to voice of c Ps 58:5

CHARRAN kar´-an
same as HARAN Acts 7:2

CHASE
you shall c a hundred Lev 26:8
one c a thousand Deut 32:30; Josh 23:10

CHASTE
present you as a c virgin 2 Cor 11:2
To be discreet, c, keepers at home Titus 2:5
behold your c conversation 1 Pet 3:2

CHASTEN
as a man c his son Deut 8:5
c me in thy hot displeasure Ps 6:1; 38:1
Blessed is the man whom thou c Ps 94:12
C thy son while there is hope Prov 19:18
as c, and not killed 2 Cor 6:9
whom the Lord loveth he c Heb 12:6
no c seemeth to be joyous Heb 12:11

CHASTISEMENT
seen the c of the Lord your God Deut 11:2
I have borne c Job 34:31
the c of our peace Is 53:5

CHATTER
Like a crane or a swallow, so did I c Is 38:14

CHEBAR ke´-bar
great (?) Ezek 1:1

CHEDORLAOMER ke´-dor-la´-o-mer
servant of (the god) Lagamar Gen 14:1

CHEEK
smite thee on thy right c Matt 5:39; Luke 6:29

CHEER
be of good c, I have overcome John 16:33
Be of good c Acts 23:11

CHEERFUL
maketh a c countenance Prov 15:13
God loveth a c giver 2 Cor 9:7

CHELAL ke´-lal
completion Ezra 10:30

CHELLUH kel´-oo
completed Ezra 10:35

CHELUB kel´-oob
bird-trap 1 Chr 4:11

CHELUBAI kel´-oob-a´-i
same as CALEB 1 Chr 2:9

CHEMARIMS kem´-ar-ims
persons dressed in black attire Zeph 1:4

CHEMOSH keem´-osh
subduer Num 21:29

CHENAANAH ke-na´-an-ah
fem. of Canaan 1 Kgs 22:11

CHENANI ke´-nane´-i
same as CHENANIAH (?) Neh 9:4

CHENANIAH ke´-nan-i´-ah
whom Jehovah supports 1 Chr 15:22

CHEPHAR-HAAMMONAI ke-far´-haam´-on-a´-i
village of the Ammonites Josh 18:24

CHEPHIRAH ke-fi´-rah
same as CAPHAR Josh 9:17

CHERAN ke´-ran
lute (?) Gen 36:26

CHERETHIMS ke´-reth-ims
Cretans (?) Ezek 25:16

CHERETHITES ke´-reth-ites
same as CHERETHIMS (?) 2 Sam 8:18

CHERISHETH
nourisheth and c it Eph 5:29
as a nurse c her children 1 Thess 2:7

CHERITH ke´-rith
gorge (?) 1 Kgs 17:3

CHERUB cher´-ub
blessing, or *strong* (?) Ezra 2:59

CHERUBIM cher´-oob-im
pl. of CHERUB Gen 3:24

CHESALON kes´-al-on
hope Josh 15:10

CHESED ke´-sed
conqueror (?) Gen 22:22

CHESIL ke´-sil
a fool Josh 15:30

CHESULLOTH ke-sool´-oth
confidences Josh 19:18

CHEZIB ke´-zib
false Gen 38:5

CHICKENS
gathereth her c under her wings Matt 23:37

CHIDE
was wroth, c with Laban Gen 31:36
Why c ye with me ? Ex 17:2
the people c with Moses Num 20:3
they did c with him sharply Judg 8:1
He will not always c Ps 103:9

CHIDON ki´-don
javelin 1 Chr 13:9

CHIEFEST
the c among ten thousand Song 5:10
you will be the c Mark 10:44
behind the very c apostles 2 Cor 11:5

CHILD
Do not sin against the c Gen 42:22
quieted myself, as a c Ps 131:2
Even a c is known by his doings Prov 20:11
Train up a c in way Prov 22:6
Foolishness is bound in the heart of a c Prov 22:15
unto us a c is born Is 9:6
c shall die a hundred years old Is 65:20
What manner of c Luke 1:66
come down ere my c die John 4:49
When I was a c 1 Cor 13:11
from a c thou hast known 2 Tim 3:15

CHILDREN
Are here all thy c? 1 Sam 16:11
Come, ye c, hearken unto me Ps 34:11
Instead of fathers shall be c Ps 45:16
thy c like olive plants Ps 128:3
I and the c Is 8:18; Heb 2:13
lying c, c that will not hear Is 30:9
c that will not lie Is 63:8
Rachel weeping for her c Jer 31:15; Matt 2:18
c teeth are set on edge Ezek 18:2
Then are the c free Matt 17:26

Suffer little **c** Matt 19:14; Luke 18:16
c of this world Luke 16:8
c of God Luke 20:36
c of light John 12:36; Eph 5:8; 1 Thess 5:5
the **c** of God Rom 8:16; Gal 3:26; 1 John 3:10
henceforth be no more **c** Eph 4:14
c of disobedience Eph 5:6; Col 3:6
c, obey your parents Eph 6:1; Col 3:20
having his **c** in subjection 1 Tim 3:4

CHILEAB kil´-e-ab
a form of CALEB (?) 2 Sam 3:3

CHILION kil´-yon
wasting away Ruth 1:2

CHILMAD kil´-mad
a city noted for trading with Tyre Ezek 27:23

CHIMHAM kim´-ham
longing 2 Sam 19:37

CHINNERETH kin´-er-eth
a lyre Josh 19:35

CHINNEROTH kin´-er-oth
pl. of CHINNERETH Josh 11:2

CHIOS ki´-os
an island in the Aegean Sea Acts 20:15

CHISLEU kis´-lew
the ninth month Neh 1:1

CHISLON kis´-lon
confidence, hope Num 34:21

CHISLOTH-TABOR kis´-loth-ta´-bor
flanks (?) *of Tabor* Josh 19:12

CHITTIM kit´-tim
descendants of Javan Num 24:24

CHIUN ki´-oon
image Amos 5:26

CHLOE klo´-ee
the first shoot of green grass 1 Cor 1:11

CHOICE
Saul, a **c** young man 1 Sam 9:2
God made **c** among us Acts 15:7

CHOKE
c the word Matt 13:22; Mark 4:19
are **c** with cares and riches Luke 8:14

CHOR-ASHAN kor-ash´-an
smoking furnace 1 Sam 30:30

CHORAZIN ko-ra´-zin
a town in Galilee Matt 11:21

CHOSE
c for his inheritance Ps 33:12
exalted one **c** out of the people Ps 89:19
rather to be **c** Prov 16:16; 22:1
death shall be **c** rather than life Jer 8:3
called, but few are **c** Matt 20:16; 22:14
hath **c** that good part Luke 10:42
they **c** out the chief rooms Luke 14:7
Ye have not **c** me John 15:16
he is a **c** vessel Acts 9:15
c in the Lord Rom 16:13
God hath **c** foolish things 1 Cor 1:27
as he hath **c** us Eph 1:4
c of God, and precious 1 Pet 2:4
a **c** generation 1 Pet 2:9

CHOZEBA ko´-ze-bah
deceiver 1 Chr 4:22

CHRIST krist
Gr. for MESSIAH, *the anointed* Matt 1:1
Thou art the **C** Matt 16:16
saying, I am **C** Matt 24:5
the Messiah, which is called **C** John 4:25
is not this the **C**? John 4:29
sure that thou art that **C** John 6:69
preach **C** Phil 1:15,16
the Spirit of **C** did signify 1 Pet 1:11
denieth that Jesus is the **C** 1 John 2:22
believeth that Jesus is the **C** 1 John 5:1
reigned with **C** a thousand years Rev 20:4
priests of God and of **C** Rev 20:6

CHRISTIAN
called **C** first in Antioch Acts 11:26
persuadest me to be a **C** Acts 26:28
man suffer as a **C** 1 Pet 4:16

CHUSHAN-RISHATHAIM koosh´-an-rish-a-tha´-im
blackness of the double crime Judg 3:8

CHUN choon
establishment 1 Chr 18:8

CHUZA koo´-za
modest, little Luke 8:3

CHURCH
tell it unto the **c** Matt 18:17
added to the **c** daily Acts 2:47
the **c** in the wilderness Acts 7:38
neither robbers of **c** Acts 19:37
feed the **c** of God Acts 20:28
greet the **c** Rom 16:5
keep silence in the **c** 1 Cor 14:28,34
the **c** is subject to Christ Eph 5:24
as Christ also loved the **c** Eph 5:25
head of the body the **c** Col 1:18
c of the firstborn Heb 12:23

CIELED
he **c** with fir tree 2 Chr 3:5
it is **c** with cedar Jer 22:14
dwell in your **c** houses Hag 1:4

CILICIA si-lish´-ya
modest, jug (?) Acts 15:23

CINNEROTH kin´-er-oth
same as CHINNEROTH 1 Kgs 15:20

CIRCLE
sitteth upon the **c** of the earth Is 40:22

CIRCUIT
went from year to year in **c** 1 Sam 7:16
walketh in the **c** of heaven Job 22:14
his **c** unto the ends of it Ps 19:6
according to his **c** Eccl 1:6

CIRCUMCISE
though they be not **c** Rom 4:11
if ye be **c**, Christ shall profit nothing Gal 5:2
C the eighth day Phil 3:5

CIRCUMCISION
what profit is there of **c**? Rom 3:1
Jesus Christ was a minister of **c** Rom 15:8
neither **c** availeth any thing Gal 5:6; 6:15
the **c**, which worship God Phil 3:3
c made without hands Col 2:11
c nor uncircumcision Col 3:11

CIRCUMSPECT
unto you be **c** Ex 23:13
that ye walk as **c**, not as fools Eph 5:15

CIS sis
same as KISH Acts 13:21

CISTERN
the wheel broken at the **c** Eccl 12:6
hewed them out **c** Jer 2:13

CITIZEN
joined himself to a **c** of that country Luke 15:15
his **c** hated him Luke 19:14
a **c** of no mean city Acts 21:39
but fellow **c** with the saints Eph 2:19

CITY
c for refuge Num 35:6
I may die in mine own **c** 2 Sam 19:37
make glad the **c** of God Ps 46:4
found no **c** to dwell in Ps 107:4
except the Lord keep **c** Ps 127:1
than he that taketh a **c** Prov 16:32
a little **c**, and few men Eccl 9:14
c of our solemnities Is 33:20
a **c** of truth Zech 8:3
c that is set on a hill Matt 5:14
all the **c** was moved Matt 21:10
tarry ye in the **c** Luke 24:49
great joy in that **c** Acts 8:8
a **c** which hath foundations Heb 11:10
the **c** of the living God Heb 12:22
no continuing **c** Heb 13:14
the **c** of the nations fell Rev 16:19
the beloved **c** Rev 20:9

CLAD
he had **c** himself 1 Kgs 11:29
was **c** with zeal as a cloke Is 59:17

CLAMOUR
wrath, and anger, and **c** Eph 4:31

CLAP
c your hands, all ye people Ps 47:1
Let the floods **c** their hands Ps 98:8
the trees of the field shall **c** Is 55:12
All that pass by **c** their hands Lam 2:15

CLAUDA klawd´-ah
a small island near CRETE Acts 27:16

CLAUDIA klawd´-yah
fem. of CLAUDIUS 2 Tim 4:21

CLAUDIUS klawd´-yus
Fourth of the Caesars (10 BC–AD 54) Acts 11:28

CLAWS
cleft into two **c** Deut 14:6
his nails as birds' **c** Dan 4:33
tear their **c** in pieces Zech 11:16

CLAY
thou hast made me as the **c** Job 10:9
bodies to bodies of **c** Job 13:12
I also am formed out of **c** Job 33:6
out of the miry **c** Ps 40:2
part of iron and part of **c** Dan 2:33
made **c** of the spitter John 9:6
power over the **c** Rom 9:21

CLEAN
may I not wash in them, and be **c** 2 Kgs 5:12
bring a **c** thing out of an unclean? Job 14:4
heavens are not **c** in his sight Job 15:15
He that hath **c** hands Ps 24:4
Create in me **c** heart Ps 51:10
his mercy **c** gone for ever? Ps 77:8
c in his own eyes Prov 16:2
wash ye, and make you **c** Is 1:16
be ye **c** that bear the vessels Is 52:11
will I sprinkle **c** water Ezek 36:25
thou canst make me **c** Matt 8:2; Mark 1:40; Luke 5:12
make **c** the outside Matt 23:25; Luke 11:39
all things are **c** unto you Luke 11:41
Ye are not all **c** John 13:11
c through word John 15:3
I am **c** Acts 18:6
arrayed in fine linen, **c** and white Rev 19:8

CLEANNESS
according to the **c** of my hands 2 Sam 22:21; Ps 18:20
given you **c** of teeth Amos 4:6

CLEANSE
c thou me from secret faults Ps 19:12
I have **c** my heart in vain Ps 73:13

blueness of a wound c away evil Prov 20:30
immediately his leprosy was c Matt 8:3
c the lepers Matt 10:8
c first that which is within Matt 23:26
none of them was c, saving Naaman Luke 4:27
Were there not ten c? Luke 17:17
What God hath c Acts 10:15; 11:9
let us c ourselves 2 Cor 7:1
C your hands, ye sinners James 4:8
c us from all sin 1 John 1:7

CLEAR (adj)
c shining after rain 2 Sam 23:4
be c when thou judgest Ps 51:4
c as crystal Rev 21:11; 22:1

CLEAR (v)
how shall we c ourselves? Gen 44:16
by no means c the guilty Ex 34:7

CLEARLY
saw every man c Mark 8:25
creation of the world c seen Rom 1:20

CLEAVE
c unto the Lord your God Josh 23:8
Ruth c unto her Ruth 1:14
his hand c unto the sword 2 Sam 23:10
shall c unto thee 2 Kgs 5:27
They c to their brethren Neh 10:29
tongue c to the roof Job 29:10; Ps 137:6; Ezek 3:26
My soul c unto the dust Ps 119:25
he that c wood shall be endangered Eccl 10:9
with purpose of heart they would c Acts 11:23
certain men c unto him Acts 17:34
c to that which is good Rom 12:9

CLEFTS
c of the rock Song 2:14; Is 2:21; Jer 49:16; Obad 1:3
little house with c Amos 6:11

CLEMENCY
hear of us thy c Acts 24:4

CLEMENT klem´-ent
kind, merciful Phil 4:3

CLEOPAS kle´-op-as
short for Cleopatros Luke 24:18

CLEOPHAS kle´-of-as
same as CLEOPAS John 19:25

CLIMB
but c up some other way John 10:1

CLODS
the c of the valley shall be sweet Job 21:33

CLOKE
let him have thy c Matt 5:40
a c of covetousness 1 Thess 2:5
a c of maliciousness 1 Pet 2:16

CLOSE (adj)
they kept it c Luke 9:36
they sailed c by Crete Acts 27:13

CLOSE (v)
c up the flesh Gen 2:21
hath c your eyes Is 29:10
their eyes have c Matt 13:15

CLOSET
enter into thy c Matt 6:6
in c shall be proclaimed Luke 12:3

CLOTH
covered it with a c 1 Sam 19:13
in a c behind the ephod 1 Sam 21:9
a piece of new c Matt 9:16; Mark 2:21

CLOTHE
pastures are c with flocks Ps 65:13
c himself with cursing Ps 109:18
c with righteousness Ps 132:9
c her priests with salvation Ps 132:16
drowsiness shall c a man Prov 23:21
household are c with scarlet Prov 31:21
c heavens with blackness Is 50:3
c me with the garments of salvation Is 61:10
c the grass Matt 6:30; Luke 12:28
Wherewithal shall we be c? Matt 6:31
man c in soft raiment? Matt 11:8; Luke 7:25
Naked, and ye c me Matt 25:36
c with camel's hair Mark 1:6
c, and in his right mind Mark 5:15; Luke 8:35
c him with purple Mark 15:17
c in purple and fine linen Luke 16:19
desiring to be c upon 2 Cor 5:2
be c with humility 1 Pet 5:5
that thou mayest be c Rev 3:18
woman c with the sun Rev 12:1
c with a vesture dipped in blood Rev 19:13

CLOTHES
c are not waxen old Deut 29:5; Neh 9:21
If I may touch but his c Mark 5:28
in swaddling c Luke 2:7
ware no c Luke 8:27
spread their c in the way Luke 19:36
linen c laid Luke 24:12
laid down their c at Saul's feet Acts 7:58
cried out, and cast off their c Acts 22:23

CLOTHING
her c is of wrought gold Ps 45:13
lambs are for thy c Prov 27:26
her c is silk and purple Prov 31:22
strength and honour are her c Prov 31:25
in my house is neither bread nor c Is 3:7
for durable c Is 23:18
garments of vengeance for c Is 59:17
in sheep's c Matt 7:15
love to go in long c Mark 12:38
a man stood before me in bright c Acts 10:30
to him that weareth gay c James 2:3

CLOUD
a pillar of a c Ex 13:21
a little c 1 Kgs 18:44
faithfulness reacheth unto the c Ps 36:5
C and darkness are round about him Ps 97:2
in the c pillar Ps 99:7
c drop down Prov 3:20
regardeth the c shall not reap Eccl 11:4
nor the c return after the rain Eccl 12:2
command the c Is 5:6
blotted out, as a thick c Is 44:22
fly as a c Is 60:8
Son of man with c Dan 7:13
goodness is as a morning c Hos 6:4
c overshadowed Matt 17:5
c of heaven with power Matt 24:30
fathers were under the c 1 Cor 10:1
in the c 1 Thess 4:17
c that are carried with a tempest 2 Pet 2:17
c they are without water Jude 1:12
he cometh with c Rev 1:7
white c Rev 14:14

CLOVEN
c hoof Deut 14:7
c tongues Acts 2:3

CLUSTER
wine is found in the c Is 65:8

CNIDUS kni´-dus
nettle (?) Acts 27:7

COAL
hot c Prov 6:28
heap c of fire Prov 25:22; Rom 12:20
fire of c John 18:18; 21:9

COAST
enlarge my c 1 Chr 4:10
depart out of their c Matt 8:34; Mark 5:17

COAT
take away thy c Matt 5:40
two c Matt 10:10; Mark 6:9
thy c also Luke 6:29
c was without seam John 19:23
fisher's c John 21:7
the c and garments which Dorcas Acts 9:39

COCK
before the c crows Matt 26:34; Mark 14:30
the c shall not crow Luke 22:34

COCKATRICE
hand on the c den Is 11:8
serpents' root shall come forth a c Is 14:29
hatch c eggs Is 59:5

COFFER
in a c by the side 1 Sam 6:8
the c with mice of gold 1 Sam 6:11
the c that was 1 Sam 6:15

COFFIN
he was put in a c Gen 50:26

COGITATIONS
my c much troubled me Dan 7:28

COL-HOZEH kol-ho´-zeh
every one that seeth Neh 3:15

COLD
by reason of the c Prov 20:4
c of snow in the time of harvest Prov 25:13
garment in c weather Prov 25:20
c waters to a thirsty soul Prov 25:25
cup of c water Matt 10:42
love of many wax c Matt 24:12
in c and nakedness 2 Cor 11:27
neither c nor hot Rev 3:15

COLLECTION
out of Jerusalem the c 2 Chr 24:6
concerning the c for the saints 1 Cor 16:1

COLLEGE
in Jerusalem in the c 2 Kgs 22:14; 2 Chr 34:22

COLOUR
c in the cup Prov 23:31
under c as though Acts 27:30

COLOSSE ko-los´-see
punishment, correction Col 1:2

COMELY
praise is c Ps 33:1
is it c that a woman pray 1 Cor 11:13

COMFORT (n)
be of good c Matt 9:22; Mark 10:49; Luke 8:48; 2 Cor 13:11
c of Holy Ghost Acts 9:31
patience and c of the scriptures Rom 15:4
God of all c 2 Cor 1:3
were comforted in your c 2 Cor 7:13
if any c of love Phil 2:1

COMFORT (v)
refused to be c Gen 37:35; Ps 77:2; Jer 31:15
rod and thy staff they c Ps 23:4
c ye, c ye, my people Is 40:1
the Lord hath c his people Is 49:13; 52:9
c all that mourn Is 61:2
As one whom his mother c Is 66:13
they shall be c Matt 5:4
he is c, and thou art tormented Luke 16:25
to c them concerning their brother John 11:19
able to c them 2 Cor 1:4
c one another with these words 1 Thess 4:18
c the feeble-minded 1 Thess 5:14

COMFORTABLE
shall now be **c**: for as an angel 2 Sam 14:17
good words and **c** words Zech 1:13

COMFORTABLY
Speak ye **c** to Jerusalem Is 40:2
and speak **c** unto her Hos 2:14

COMFORTER
miserable **c** are ye all Job 16:2
for **c**, but I found none Ps 69:20
another **c** John 14:16
when the **C** has come John 15:26
the **C** will not come John 16:7

COMFORTLESS
not leave you **c** John 14:18

COMMAND
he **c**, and it stood fast Ps 33:9
he **c** even the winds Luke 8:25
we **c** fire to come down Luke 9:54
whatsoever I **c** you John 15:14
c all men every where Acts 17:30

COMMANDER
a leader and a **c** to the people Is 55:4

COMMANDMENT
c are faithful Ps 119:86
c is exceedingly broad Ps 119:96
I love thy **c** Ps 119:127
thy **c** are my delight Ps 119:143
the **c** of men Matt 15:9; Mark 7:7
according to the **c** Luke 23:56
new **c** John 13:34; 1 John 2:7; 2 John 1:5
the law is holy, and the **c** Rom 7:12
by permission, and not of **c** 1 Cor 7:6; 2 Cor 8:8
first **c** with promise Eph 6:2
end of the **c** is charity 1 Tim 1:5

COMMEND
c the unjust steward Luke 16:8
into thy hands I **c** Luke 23:46
But if our unrighteousness **c** Rom 3:5
God **c** his love toward us Rom 5:8
meat **c** us not 1 Cor 8:8
c ourselves 2 Cor 3:1
c ourselves to every man's 2 Cor 4:2
that **c** himself is approved 2 Cor 10:18

COMMISSION
delivered the king's **c** Ezra 8:36
with authority and **c** Acts 26:12

COMMIT
C thy way unto the Lord Ps 37:5
have **c** two evils Jer 2:13
Jesus did not **c** himself John 2:24
hath **c** judgment John 5:22
were **c** the oracles of God Rom 3:2
hath **c** unto us the word of 2 Cor 5:19
keep that which is **c** to 1 Tim 6:20
c thou to faithful men 2 Tim 2:2
c himself to him that judgeth 1 Pet 2:23

COMMODIOUS
the haven was not **c** Acts 27:12

COMMON
it is **c** among men Eccl 6:1
the **c** people heard him gladly Mark 12:37
all things **c** Acts 2:44; 4:32
never eaten any thing that is **c** Acts 10:14
call not thou **c** Acts 10:15; 11:9
c to man 1 Cor 10:13

COMMOTION
a great **c** out of the north Jer 10:22
shall hear of wars and **c** Luke 21:9

COMMUNE
to **c** with thee Job 4:2
c with mine own heart Ps 4:4; 77:6; Eccl 1:16
angel that **c** with me Zech 1:14

COMMUNICATE
Let him that is taught in the word **c** Gal 6:6
willing to **c** 1 Tim 6:18
do good and to **c** Heb 13:16

COMMUNICATION
let your **c** be Matt 5:37
What manner of **c** Luke 24:17
evil **c** corrupt good manners 1 Cor 15:33
Let no corrupt **c** proceed Eph 4:29

COMMUNION
is it not the **c** 1 Cor 10:16
what **c** hath light 2 Cor 6:14
C of the Holy Ghost 2 Cor 13:14

COMPACT
a city that is **c** together Ps 122:3
joined together and **c** Eph 4:16

COMPANION
a **c** to owls Job 30:29
a **c** of all to them Ps 119:63
c of fools shall be destroyed Prov 13:20
c of riotous men Prov 28:7
the **c** of a destroyer Prov 28:24
Paul's **c** in travel Acts 19:29
brother and **c** in labour Phil 2:25

COMPANY
a **c** of prophets 1 Sam 10:5; 19:20
to the house of God in **c** Ps 55:14
great was the **c** of those Ps 68:11
sit down by **c** Mark 6:39
innumerable **c** of angels Heb 12:22

COMPARE
not to be **c** Prov 3:15; 8:11
what likeness will ye **c** unto him? Is 40:18
c me Is 46:5
c to fine gold Lam 4:2
not worthy to be **c** with the glory Rom 8:18
c spiritual things with spiritual 1 Cor 2:13

COMPARISON
in **c** of you Judg 8:2
in your eyes in **c** Hag 2:3
with what **c** shall we **c** Mark 4:30

COMPASS (n)
put it under the **c** of the altar Ex 27:5
marketh it out with a **c** Is 44:13

COMPASS (v)
sorrows of death **c** me Ps 18:4; 116:3
sorrows of hell **c** me 2 Sam 22:6; Ps 18:5
with favour wilt thou **c** him Ps 5:12
c me about with songs of deliverance Ps 32:7
mercy shall **c** him about Ps 32:10
c yourselves about with sparks Is 50:11
c sea and land Matt 23:15
Jerusalem **c** with armies Luke 21:20
he himself also is **c** with infirmity Heb 5:2
c about with a great cloud Heb 12:1

COMPASSION
that she should not have **c** Is 49:15
his **c** fail not Lam 3:22
yet will he have **c** Lam 3:32
moved with **c** Matt 9:36; 14:14; Mark 1:41; 6:34
c on thy fellowservant Matt 18:33
had **c** on Matt 20:34; Mark 5:19
have **c** on us and help us Mark 9:22
the Samaritan had **c** Luke 10:33
had **c** and ran Luke 15:20
I will have **c** on whom I will Rom 9:15
have **c** on the ignorant Heb 5:2
of one mind, having **c** 1 Pet 3:8
shutteth up his bowels of **c** 1 John 3:17
of some have **c**, making a difference Jude 1:22

COMPEL
c thee to go a mile Matt 5:41
c to bear his cross Matt 27:32
c them to come in Luke 14:23
c them to blaspheme Acts 26:11

COMPLAIN
c in the bitterness of my soul Job 7:11
Wherefore doth a living man **c**? Lam 3:39

COMPLAINT
to day is my **c** bitter Job 23:2
I poured out my **c** before him Ps 142:2

COMPLETE
seven sabbaths shall be **c** Lev 23:15
ye are **c** in him Col 2:10
stand perfect and **c** in all Col 4:12

COMPREHEND
we cannot **c** Job 37:5
c the dust of the earth Is 40:12
the darkness **c** it not John 1:5
able to **c** with all saints Eph 3:18

CONANIAH kon-an-i´-ah
same as CONONIAH 2 Chr 35:9

CONCEAL
prudent man **c** knowledge Prov 12:23
glory of God to **c** a thing Prov 25:2
publish, and **c** not Jer 50:2

CONCEIT
a high wall in his own **c** Prov 18:11
wise in his own **c** Prov 26:5; 28:11
in your own **c** Rom 11:25; 12:16

CONCEIVE
c mischief, brought forth falsehood Ps 7:14
in sin did my mother **c** me Ps 51:5
why hast thou **c** this thing Acts 5:4
when lust hath **c**, it bringeth forth James 1:15

CONCERNING
things **c** himself Luke 24:27
as **c** the flesh Christ came Rom 9:5
simple **c** evil Rom 16:19
c giving and receiving Phil 4:15
have erred **c** the faith 1 Tim 6:21
c the fiery trial 1 Pet 4:12

CONCISION
beware of the **c** Phil 3:2

CONCLUDE
we **c** that no man is justified Rom 3:28
God hath **c** them all Rom 11:32
scriptures hath **c** all Gal 3:22

CONCLUSION
hear the **c** of the whole Eccl 12:13

CONCORD
what **c** hath Christ 2 Cor 6:15

CONDEMN
I will say unto God, Do not **c** me Job 10:2
drink the wine of the **c** Amos 2:8
ye would not have **c** the guiltless Matt 12:7
by thy words shalt be **c** Matt 12:37
generation and **c** them Matt 12:42; Luke 11:31
shall **c** him to death Matt 20:18
when he saw that he was **c** Matt 27:3
all **c** him to be guilty Mark 14:64
c not, and ye shall not be **c** Luke 6:37
his Son into the world to **c** John 3:17
believeth not is **c** John 3:18
hath no man **c** thee? John 8:10
Neither do I **c** thee John 8:11
thou **c** thyself Rom 2:1
c sin in the flesh Rom 8:3
Who is he that **c**? Rom 8:34
that **c** not himself Rom 14:22
sound speech, that cannot be **c** Titus 2:8
Ye have **c** and killed the just James 5:6

lest ye be c James 5:9
if our heart c us not 1 John 3:21

CONDEMNATION
this is the c, that light John 3:19
therefore now no c to them Rom 8:1
the ministration of c 2 Cor 3:9
the c of the devil 1 Tim 3:6
lest ye fall into c James 5:12
of old ordained to this c Jude 1:4

CONDESCEND
c to men of low estate Rom 12:16

CONDITION
On this c will I make 1 Sam 11:2
desireth c of peace Luke 14:32

CONDUIT
by the c of the upper pool 2 Kgs 18:17; Is 36:2
made a pool, and a c 2 Kgs 20:20
at the end of the c Is 7:3

CONEY
And the c, because he cheweth Lev 11:5
the rocks for the c Ps 104:18
The c are but a feeble folk Prov 30:26

CONFECTION
a c after the art Ex 30:35
take your daughter to be c 1 Sam 8:13

CONFEDERACY
A c, neither fear ye Is 8:12
All the men of the c Obad 1:7

CONFEDERATE
these were c with Abram Gen 14:13
Syria is c with Ephraim Is 7:2

CONFERENCE
in c added nothing Gal 2:6

CONFERRED
immediately I c not Gal 1:16

CONFESS
whoso c and forsaketh Prov 28:13
c me before men Matt 10:32; Luke 12:8
if any man did c John 9:22
they did not c him John 12:42
Pharisees c both Acts 23:8
shall c with thy mouth Rom 10:9
every tongue shall c Rom 14:11
c that they were strangers Heb 11:13
C your faults one to another James 5:16
If we c our sins 1 John 1:9
Every spirit that c Christ 1 John 4:2
c that Jesus is the Son of God 1 John 4:15
I will c his name before my Father Rev 3:5

CONFESSION
with the mouth c is made Rom 10:10
witnessed a good c 1 Tim 6:13

CONFIDENCE
the c of all the ends of the earth Ps 65:5
than to put c in man Ps 118:8
In fear of the Lord is strong c Prov 14:26
in c shall be your strength Is 30:15
hath rejected thy c Jer 2:37
access with c by the faith Eph 3:12
no c in the flesh Phil 3:3,4
hold fast the c Heb 3:6,14
Cast not away therefore your c Heb 10:35
have we c toward God 1 John 3:21
this is the c that we have in him 1 John 5:14

CONFIDENT
in this will I be c Ps 27:3
the fool rageth, and is c Prov 14:16
we are always c 2 Cor 5:6
Being c of this very thing Phil 1:6

CONFIRM
c the feeble knees Is 35:3
c the word with signs Mark 16:20
C the souls of the disciples Acts 14:22
c the churches Acts 15:41
c the promises made unto the fathers Rom 15:8

CONFIRMATION
in the defence and c Phil 1:7
an oath of c Heb 6:16

CONFISCATION
to c of goods Ezra 7:26

CONFLICT
the same c which you saw in me Phil 1:30
what great c I have for you Col 2:1

CONFORM
also did predestinate to be c Rom 8:29
be not c to this world Rom 12:2

CONFOUND
and were not c Ps 22:5
ashamed and c Ps 40:14; 70:2
multitude came together, and were c Acts 2:6
c the Jews Acts 9:22

CONFUSED
with c noise Is 9:5
the assembly was c Acts 19:32

CONFUSION
unto us c of faces Dan 9:7
city was filled with c Acts 19:29
God is not the author of c 1 Cor 14:33

CONGEALED
depths were c in the heart Ex 15:8

CONGRATULATE
inquire of his welfare, and to c 1 Chr 18:10

CONGREGATION
all the c bade stone them Num 14:10
all the c said, Amen Neh 5:13
nor sinners in the c of the righteous Ps 1:5
in the c will I bless the Lord Ps 26:12
in the c of the dead Prov 21:16
sanctify the c Joel 2:16
when the c was broken up Acts 13:43

CONIAH ko-ni´-ah
contracted from JECONIAH Jer 22:24

CONONIAH kon-on-i´-ah
whom Jehovah has set up 2 Chr 31:12

CONQUERORS
more than c through him Rom 8:37
he went forth c, and to c Rev 6:2

CONSCIENCE
c void of offence Acts 24:16
c also bearing witness Rom 2:15; 2 Cor 1:12
for c sake Rom 13:5; 1 Cor 10:25,27,28
weak c 1 Cor 8:12
a good c 1 Tim 1:5,19; Heb 13:18; 1 Pet 3:16
faith in a pure c 1 Tim 3:9
c seared with hot iron 1 Tim 4:2
purge your c from dead works Heb 9:14
hearts sprinkled from an evil c Heb 10:22

CONSECRATE
to c his service 1 Chr 29:5
I will c Mic 4:13
who is c for evermore Heb 7:28
living way, which he hath c Heb 10:20

CONSENT
a thief, then thou c with him Ps 50:18
if sinners entice thee, c not Prov 1:10
to serve him with one c Zeph 3:9
with one c began to make excuse Luke 14:18

CONSIDER
When I c thy heavens Ps 8:3
blessed is he that c the poor Ps 41:1
c her palaces Ps 48:13
c this, ye that forget God Ps 50:22
c her ways, and be wise Prov 6:6
c diligently what is before thee Prov 23:1
pondereth the heart c it? Prov 24:12
and c not that poverty Prov 28:22
they c not that they do evil Eccl 5:1
in day of adversity c Eccl 7:14
my people doth not c Is 1:3
in the latter days ye shall c Jer 23:20; 30:24
it may be they will c Ezek 12:3
C your ways Hag 1:5,7
C lilies Matt 6:28; Luke 12:27
c not the beam Matt 7:3
c the ravens Luke 12:24
c thyself, lest thou also be tempted Gal 6:1
c the Apostle and High Priest Heb 3:1
Now c how great this man was Heb 7:4
c one another to provoke Heb 10:24
c him that endured Heb 12:3
c the end of their conversation Heb 13:7

CONSIST
a man's life c not Luke 12:15
by him all things c Col 1:17

CONSOLATION
Are the c of God small Job 15:11
ye have received your c Luke 6:24
the God of patience and c Rom 15:5
If there be therefore any c Phil 2:1
everlasting c 2 Thess 2:16
strong c Heb 6:18

CONSPIRACY
the c was strong 2 Sam 15:2
A c is found among the men Jer 11:9
which had made this c Acts 23:13

CONSTANTLY
if he be c to do 1 Chr 28:7
man that heareth speaketh c Prov 21:28
I will that thou affirm c Titus 3:8

CONSTRAIN
the spirit within me c me Job 32:18
they c him, Luke 24:29
the love of Christ c us 2 Cor 5:14

CONSULT
c against thy hidden ones Ps 83:3
c whether he be able Luke 14:31
c that they might put Lazarus John 12:10

CONSUME
bush was not c Ex 3:2
that shall c the eyes Lev 26:16
and c the sacrifice 1 Kgs 18:38
fire not blown shall c him Job 20:26
c away like a moth Ps 39:11
ye sons of Jacob are not c Mal 3:6
c them, even as Elijah did Luke 9:54
take heed that ye be not c Gal 5:15
that ye may c it upon your lusts James 4:3

CONSUMMATION
even until the c Dan 9:27

CONSUMPTION
c, and burning fever Lev 26:16
smite thee with a c Deut 28:22
the c decreed shall overflow Is 10:22

CONTAIN
heaven of heavens cannot c 1 Kgs 8:27; 2 Chr 2:6; 6:18
if they cannot c 1 Cor 7:9

CONTEMN
doth the wicked c God Ps 10:13
a vile person is c Ps 15:4
c the counsel of the Most High Ps 107:11
it c the rod of my son Ezek 21:10

CONTEMPT
wicked cometh, then also cometh c Prov 18:3
to shame and everlasting c Dan 12:2

CONTEMPTIBLE
The table of the Lord is c Mal 1:7
I also made you c and base Mal 2:9
and his speech c 2 Cor 10:10

CONTEND
I will c with him that c Is 49:25
who will c with me? Is 50:8
how canst thou c with horses? Jer 12:5

CONTENT
be c with your wages Luke 3:14
to be c Phil 4:11
let us be therewith c 1 Tim 6:8
be c with such things as ye have Heb 13:5

CONTENTION
lot causeth c to cease Prov 18:18
c of a wife Prov 19:13; 27:15
Who hath c? Prov 23:29
the c was so sharp Acts 15:39
there are c among you 1 Cor 1:11
preach Christ of c Phil 1:16
with much c 1 Thess 2:2
genealogies and c, and strivings Titus 3:9

CONTENTIOUS
than with a c and an angry woman Prov 21:19
so is a c man to kindle strife Prov 26:21
rainy day and a c woman are alike Prov 27:15
c, and do not obey the truth Rom 2:8
if any man seem to be c 1 Cor 11:16

CONTINUAL
merry heart hath a c feast Prov 15:15
with a c stroke Is 14:6
lest by her c coming Luke 18:5
c sorrow in my heart Rom 9:2

CONTINUALLY
praise shall c be Ps 34:1; 71:6
truth c preserve me Ps 40:11
I am c with thee Ps 73:23
Bind them c on thine heart Prov 6:21
my name c every day is blasphemed Is 52:5
were c in the temple Luke 24:53
give ourselves c to prayer Acts 6:4
abideth a priest c Heb 7:3

CONTINUANCE
of long c Deut 28:59
in C were fashioned Ps 139:16
in those is c, Is 64:5
who by patient c in well doing Rom 2:7

CONTINUE
as a shadow, and c not Job 14:2
name shall c as long as the sun Ps 72:17
c until night till wine inflame them Is 5:11
may c many days Jer 32:14
c all night in prayer Luke 6:12
have c with me in my temptation Luke 22:28
If ye c in my word John 8:31
c ye in my love John 15:9
c with one accord Acts 1:14
Peter c knocking Acts 12:16
to c in the grace of God Acts 13:43
exhorting them to c in the faith Acts 14:22
I c unto this day Acts 26:22
Shall we c in sin? Rom 6:1
c instant in prayer Rom 12:12
that c not in all things Gal 3:10
If ye c in the faith Col 1:23
c in them 1 Tim 4:16
not suffered to c by reason Heb 7:23
he c ever Heb 7:24
Let brotherly love c Heb 13:1
here have we no c city Heb 13:14
and c there a year James 4:13

all things c as they were 2 Pet 3:4
no doubt have c with us 1 John 2:19

CONTRADICTION
without c the less is blessed Heb 7:7
endured such c of sinners Heb 12:3

CONTRARIWISE
So that c ye ought rather forgive him 2 Cor 2:7
But c, when they saw Gal 2:7
but c blessing, knowing 1 Pet 3:9

CONTRARY
c to the law Acts 18:13
things c to the name of Jesus Acts 26:9
c the one to the other Gal 5:17
c to all men 1 Thess 2:15
c to sound doctrine 1 Tim 1:10
he that is of the c part Titus 2:8

CONTRIBUTION
make a c for the poor Rom 15:26

CONTRITE
of a c spirit Ps 34:18; Is 66:2
a broken and c heart Ps 51:17
that is of a c and humble spirit Is 57:15

CONTROVERSY
a c with the nations Jer 25:31
hath a c with his people Mic 6:2
without c great is the mystery 1 Tim 3:16

CONVENIENT
feed me with food c Prov 30:8
when I have a c season Acts 24:25
things which are not c Rom 1:28; Eph 5:4

CONVERSANT
strangers that were c among them Josh 8:35
as long as we were c with them 1 Sam 25:15

CONVERSATION
such as be of upright c Ps 37:14
that ordereth his c aright Ps 50:23
c be as it becometh the gospel Phil 1:27
our c is in heaven Phil 3:20
in word in c, in charity 1 Tim 4:12
c be without covetousness Heb 13:5
considering the end of their c Heb 13:7
in all manner of c 1 Pet 1:15; 2 Pet 3:11
from your vain c 1 Pet 1:18
your c honest among Gentiles 1 Pet 2:12
won by c of the wives 1 Pet 3:1
vexed with the filthy c 2 Pet 2:7

CONVERSION
declaring the c of the Gentiles Acts 15:3

CONVERT
perfect, c the soul Ps 19:7
with their heart, and c, and be healed Is 6:10
should be c Matt 13:15; Mark 4:12
be c, and I should heal John 12:40; Acts 28:27
Except ye be c Matt 18:3
when thou art c, strengthen thy Luke 22:32
Repent ye therefore, and be c Acts 3:19
and one c him James 5:19

CONVICTED
being c by their own conscience John 8:9

CONVINCE
Which of you c me of sin? John 8:46
able to c the gainsayers Titus 1:9

CONVOCATION
there shall be a holy c Ex 12:16
shall proclaim to be holy c Lev 23:2
have a holy c Num 28:26

COOL
in the c of the day Gen 3:8
c my tongue Luke 16:24

COOS ko´-os
summit Acts 21:1

COPY
write him a c of this law Deut 17:18
a c of the law of Moses Josh 8:32

CORD
holden with the c of his sins Prov 5:22
a threefold c Eccl 4:12
silver c be loosed Eccl 12:6
draw iniquity with c of vanity Is 5:18
lengthen thy c Is 54:2
with c of a man Hos 11:4
scourge of small c John 2:15

CORE ko´-re
Gr. for KORAH Jude 1:11

CORINTH kor´-inth
decoration, ornament Acts 18:1

CORINTHIANS kor-inth´-yans
inhabitants of Corinth Acts 18:8

CORN
c in Egypt Gen 42:2; Acts 7:12
treadeth out the c Deut 25:4; 1 Cor 9:9; 1 Tim 5:18
into the standing c Judg 15:5
like as a shock of c Job 5:26
in time their c increased Ps 4:7
prepared them c Ps 65:9
valleys are also covered over with c Ps 65:13
handful of c in the earth Ps 72:16
He that withholdeth c Prov 11:26
c shall make the young men cheerful Zech 9:17
pluck the ears of c Matt 12:1; Mark 2:23; Luke 6:1
full c in the ear Mark 4:28
a c of wheat fall into the ground John 12:24

CORNELIUS kor-ne´-li-as
of a horn Acts 10:1

CORNER
head stone of the c Ps 118:22
Christ himself being the chief c stone Eph 2:20
daughters may be as c stones Ps 144:12
a precious c stone Is 28:16
in c of the streets Matt 6:5
on the four c of the earth Rev 7:1

CORNET
on timbrels, and on c 2 Sam 6:5
sound of the c 1 Chr 15:28; Dan 3:5

CORPSE
they were all dead c 2 Kgs 19:35; Is 37:36
there is none end of their c Nah 3:3
came and took up his c Mark 6:29

CORRECT
whom the Lord loveth he c Prov 3:12
C thy son Prov 29:17
servant will not be c by words Prov 29:19
c me, but with judgment Jer 10:24
will c thee in measure Jer 30:11; 46:28
fathers of our flesh which c us Heb 12:9

CORRECTION
rod of c shall drive it Prov 22:15
receive c Jer 5:3; 7:28
for doctrine, for instruction, c 2 Tim 3:16

CORRUPT (adj)
a c tree Matt 7:17; Luke 6:43
off the old man, which is c Eph 4:22
Let no c communication Eph 4:29
men of c minds 1 Tim 6:5; 2 Tim 3:8

CORRUPT (v)
Lest ye c yourselves Deut 4:16
after my death ye will utterly c Deut 31:29
moth and rust doth c Matt 6:19
evil communications c 1 Cor 15:33
not as many, which c the word 2 Cor 2:17
we have c no man 2 Cor 7:2

your minds be c 2 Cor 11:3
your riches are c James 5:2

CORRUPTERS
children that are c Is 1:4
they are all c Jer 6:28

CORRUPTIBLE
image made like to c man Rom 1:23
obtain a c crown 1 Cor 9:25
this c must put on 1 Cor 15:53
not redeemed with c things 1 Pet 1:18

CORRUPTION
Holy One to see c Ps 16:10; 49:9; Acts 2:27; 13:35
brought up my life from c Jon 2:6
from the bondage of c Rom 8:21
sown in c 1 Cor 15:42
of the flesh reap c Gal 6:8
the c that is in the world 2 Pet 1:4
perish in their own c 2 Pet 2:12

CORRUPTLY
the people did yet c 2 Chr 27:2
We have dealt very c Neh 1:7

COSAM ko´-sam
divining Luke 3:28

COST
offer burnt offerings without c 1 Chr 21:24
sitteth not down first and counteth c? Luke 14:28

COTTAGE
c in the vineyard Is 1:8
dwellings and c for shepherds Zeph 2:6

COUCH
with his c into the midst Luke 5:19
take up thy c Luke 5:24
laid them on beds and c Acts 5:15

COULD
c have been done Is 5:4
but she c not Mark 6:19
She both done what she c Mark 14:8

COUNCIL
shall be in danger of the c Matt 5:22
deliver you up to the c Matt 10:17
set them before the c Acts 5:27
brought him to the c Acts 6:12

COUNSEL
brought their c to nought Neh 4:15
darkeneth c by words Job 38:2
hideth c without knowledge Job 42:3
c of the ungodly Ps 1:1
c of the LORD Ps 33:11; Prov 19:21
guide me with thy c Ps 73:24
set at nought all my c Prov 1:25
Where no c is, the people fall Prov 11:14
Without c purposes are disappointed Prov 15:22
nor c against the Lord Prov 21:30
wonderful in c Is 28:29
My c shall stand Is 46:10
Great in c, and mighty in work Jer 32:19
ashamed of his own c Hos 10:6
determinate c and foreknowledge Acts 2:23
thy c determined before Acts 4:28
if this c or this work be of men Acts 5:38
declare unto you all the c of God Acts 20:27
make manifest the c of the hearts 1 Cor 4:5
after the c of his own will Eph 1:11
the immutability of his c Heb 6:17
I c thee to buy of me gold Rev 3:18

COUNSELLER
in the multitude of c Prov 11:14; 15:22; 24:6
to the c of peace is joy Prov 12:20
is thy c perished? Mic 4:9
an honourable c Mark 15:43
who hath been his c? Rom 11:34

COUNT
c it to him for righteousness Gen 15:6
c as sheep for the slaughter Ps 44:22
is c wise Prov 17:28
field be c for a forest Is 32:15
they c him as a prophet Matt 14:5
c worthy Acts 5:41; 2 Thess 1:5; 1 Tim 5:17
neither c I my life dear Acts 20:24
c unto him for righteousness Rom 4:3
I c loss for Christ Phil 3:7
do c them but dung Phil 3:8
I c not myself to have apprehended Phil 3:13
c the blood Heb 10:29
c it all joy James 1:2
as some men c slackness 2 Pet 3:9

COUNTENANCE
look not on his c or 1 Sam 16:7
beautiful c 1 Sam 16:12
why is thy c sad? Neh 2:2
thou changest his c Job 14:20
light of thy c Ps 4:6; 44:3; 89:15; 90:8
merry heart maketh a cheerful c Prov 15:13
sharpeneth the c of his friend Prov 27:17
sadness of the c the heart Eccl 7:3
their c doth witness against them Is 3:9
hypocrites, of a sad c Matt 6:16
c was like lightning Matt 28:3
his c was altered Luke 9:29
his c was as the sun shineth Rev 1:16

COUNTRY
good news from a far c Prov 25:25
in his own c Matt 13:57; Mark 6:4; Luke 4:24; John 4:44
into a far c Matt 21:33; 25:14; Mark 12:1
do also here in thy c Luke 4:23
their c was nourished Acts 12:20
sojourned as in a strange c Heb 11:9
desire a better c Heb 11:16

COUNTRYMEN
in perils by mine own c 2 Cor 11:26
things of your own c 1 Thess 2:14

COUPLED
chaste conversation c with fear 1 Pet 3:2

COURAGE
of good c Deut 31:6,7,23; Ps 31:24
thanked God, and took c Acts 28:15

COURSE
may have free c 2 Thess 3:1
finished my c 2 Tim 4:7
setteth on fire the c of nature James 3:6

COURT
that he may dwell in thy c Ps 65:4
fainteth for the c of the Lord Ps 84:2
flourish in the c of our God Ps 92:13
into his c with praise Ps 100:4
to tread my c? Is 1:12
live delicately, are in kings' c Luke 7:25

COURTEOUSLY
Julius c entreated Paul Acts 27:3
lodged us three days c Acts 28:7

COUSIN
behold, thy c Elisabeth Luke 1:36
her neighbours and her c Luke 1:58

COVENANT
c of salt Num 18:19; 2 Chr 13:5
my c of peace Num 25:12
his c for ever Ps 105:8
ever be mindful of his c Ps 111:5
your c with death Is 28:18
they c with him Matt 26:15

the c which God made Acts 3:25
the adoption, and the glory, and the c Rom 9:4
strangers from c of promise Eph 2:12
mediator of a better c Heb 8:6
mediator of the new c Heb 12:24
blood of the everlasting c Heb 13:20

COVER
depths have c them Ex 15:5
will c thee with my hand Ex 33:22
c with a mantle 1 Sam 28:14
they c Haman's face Esth 7:8
whose sin is c Ps 32:1
violence c them as a garment Ps 73:6
He shall c thee with his feathers Ps 91:4
Thou c it with the deep Ps 104:6
violence c the mouth of the wicked Prov 10:6,11
love c all sins Prov 10:12
a prudent man c shame Prov 12:16
He that c a transgression seeketh love Prov 17:9
that c his sins shall not prosper Prov 28:13
no more c her slain Is 26:21
ship was c with the waves Matt 8:24
there is nothing c Matt 10:26; Luke 12:2
having his head c 1 Cor 11:4
if the woman be not c 1 Cor 11:6
ought not to c his head 1 Cor 11:7
charity shall c the multitude of sins 1 Pet 4:8

COVERING
Thick clouds are a c to him Job 22:14
have no c in the cold Job 24:7
destruction hath no c Job 26:6
any poor without c Job 31:19
c narrower than that he can wrap Is 28:20

COVERT
the c of thy wings Ps 61:4
a c from storm Is 4:6
thou a c to them Is 16:4
and a c from the tempest Is 32:2

COVET
He c greedily all the day Prov 21:26
c an evil covetousness Hab 2:9
I have c no man's silver Acts 20:33
c earnestly the best gifts 1 Cor 12:31
some c after, they have erred 1 Tim 6:10

COVETOUS
c man, who is an idolater Eph 5:5
lovers of their own selves, c, boasters 2 Tim 3:2
exercised with c practices 2 Pet 2:14

COVETOUSNESS
he that hateth c shall prolong Prov 28:16
their heart goeth after c Ezek 33:31
c, lasciviousness, and evil eye Mark 7:22
wickedness, c, maliciousness Rom 1:29
c, let it not be once named Eph 5:3
conversation be without c Heb 13:5
through c shall they with feigned 2 Pet 2:3

COW
whether it be c or ewe Lev 22:28
their c calveth Job 21:10
the c and the bear Is 11:7

COZ koz
thorn 1 Chr 4:8

COZBI kos´-bi
deceitful Num 25:15

CRACKLING
as the c of thorns Eccl 7:6

CRAFT
wise in their own c Job 5:13; 1 Cor 3:19
he perceived their c Luke 20:23
by this c we have our wealth Acts 19:25
our c is in danger Acts 19:27
not walking in c 2 Cor 4:2
cunning c whereby they lie Eph 4:14

CRAG
upon the c of the rock Job 39:28

CRANE
Like a c or a swallow Is 38:14
turtledove and the c Jer 8:7

CRASHING
a great c from the hills Zeph 1:10

CRAVE
his mouth c it of him Prov 16:26
c the body of Jesus Mark 15:43

CREATE
who hath c these things Is 40:26
c him for my glory Is 43:7
I c new heavens and a new earth Is 65:17
the Lord hath c a new thing Jer 31:22
that c wind Amos 4:13
hath not one God c us? Mal 2:10
neither was the man c for the woman 1 Cor 11:9
c in Christ Jesus Eph 2:10
after God is c in righteousness Eph 4:24
by him were all things c Col 1:16
which God hath c to be received 1 Tim 4:3

CREATION
beginning of the c God made Mark 10:6
c which God created unto this time Mark 13:19
from the c of the world Rom 1:20
the whole c groaneth Rom 8:22
from the beginning of the c 2 Pet 3:4

CREATOR
Remember now thy c Eccl 12:1
the C of the ends of the earth Is 40:28
served the creature more than the c Rom 1:25
unto a faithful C 1 Pet 4:19

CREATURE
preach the gospel to every c Mark 16:15
expectation of the c Rom 8:19
new c 2 Cor 5:17; Gal 6:15
firstborn of every c Col 1:15
every c of God is good 1 Tim 4:4

CREDITOR
Every c that lendeth ought Deut 15:2
the c is come to take 2 Kgs 4:1
which of my c is it Is 50:1
a certain c which had two debtors Luke 7:41

CREEK
a certain c with a shore Acts 27:39

CREEP
beasts of the forest c forth Ps 104:20
wherein are things c Ps 104:25
form of c things Ezek 8:10
Peter saw c things Acts 10:12
they which c into houses 2 Tim 3:6
certain men c in unawares Jude 1:4

CRESCENS kres´-ens
growing 2 Tim 4:10

CRETE kreet
carnal (?) Acts 27:7

CRETES kreets
same as CRETIANS Acts 2:11

CRETIANS kreet´-yans
inhabitants of Crete Titus 1:12

CREW
the cock c Matt 26:74; Mark 14:68; Luke 22:60

CRIB
abide by thy c Job 39:9
the c is clean Prov 14:4
his master's c Is 1:3

CRIMSON
in purple, and c, and blue 2 Chr 2:7
though they be red like c Is 1:18
thou clothest thyself with c Jer 4:30

CRIPPLE
c from his mother's womb Acts 14:8

CRISPUS krisp´-us
curled Acts 18:8

CROOKED
c cannot be made straight Eccl 1:15
c shall be made straight Is 40:4; Luke 3:5
make the c places straight Is 45:2
c paths Is 59:8
midst of a c and perverse nation Phil 2:15

CROSS
take up his c Matt 16:24; Mark 8:34; Luke 9:23
compelled to bear his c Matt 27:32
come down from the c Matt 27:40; Mark 15:30
there stood by the c John 19:25
c of Christ 1 Cor 1:17; Gal 6:12; Phil 3:18
preaching of the c 1 Cor 1:18
offence of the c Gal 5:11
glory, save in the c Gal 6:14
in one body by the c Eph 2:16
the death of the c Phil 2:8
peace through the blood of his c Col 1:20
nailing it to his c Col 2:14
endured the c Heb 12:2

CROUCH
shall come and c to him 1 Sam 2:36
He c, and humbleth himself Ps 10:10

CROWN (n)
taken the c from my head Job 19:9
a c of glory shall she deliver Prov 4:9
virtuous woman is a c Prov 12:4
prudent are c with knowledge Prov 14:18
hoary head is a c of glory Prov 16:31
children's children are the c of old men Prov 17:6
Woe to the c of pride Is 28:1
a c of thorns Matt 27:29; Mark 15:17; John 19:2
to obtain a corruptible c 1 Cor 9:25
my joy and c Phil 4:1
or c of rejoicing 1 Thess 2:19
not c, except he strive 2 Tim 2:5
a c of righteousness 2 Tim 4:8
c of life James 1:12; Rev 2:10
a c of glory 1 Pet 5:4
that no man take thy c Rev 3:11
cast their c before the throne Rev 4:10
on his head were many c Rev 19:12

CROWN (v)
c him with glory and honour Ps 8:5; Heb 2:7
Thou c the year Ps 65:11
c thee with loving kindness Ps 103:4

CRUCIFY
Let him be c Matt 27:22
C him Mark 15:13; Luke 23:21; John 19:6,15
wicked hands have c Acts 2:23
old man is c with him Rom 6:6
was Paul c for you? 1 Cor 1:13
we preach Christ c 1 Cor 1:23
save Jesus Christ, and him c 1 Cor 2:2
though he was c through weakness 2 Cor 13:4
I am c with Christ Gal 2:20
c among you Gal 3:1
have c the flesh Gal 5:24
the world is c unto me Gal 6:14
c to themselves Heb 6:6

CRUEL
with c hatred Ps 25:19
breathe out c Ps 27:12
full of the habitations of c Ps 74:20
thy years to the c Prov 5:9
c troubleth his own flesh Prov 11:17
tender mercies of the wicked are c Prov 12:10
Wrath is c Prov 27:4
jealousy is c Song 8:6
trials of c mockings Heb 11:36

CRUMBS
dogs eat of the c Matt 15:27
eat of the children's c Mark 7:28
fed with the c which fell Luke 16:21

CRUSE
the c of water 1 Sam 26:11
a c of honey 1 Kgs 14:3
a little oil in a c 1 Kgs 17:12
a c of water at his head 1 Kgs 19:6

CRUSH
they are c in the gate Job 5:4
forgetteth that the foot may c them Job 39:15

CRY (n)
c of the city went up to heaven 1 Sam 5:12
he heareth the c of the afflicted Job 34:28
forgetteth not c of the humble Ps 9:12
ears are open to their c Ps 34:15
stoppeth his ears at the c of the poor Prov 21:13
at midnight there was a c made Matt 25:6

CRY (v)
wherefore c thou unto me? Ex 14:15
upper lip, and shall c Unclean Lev 13:45
I delivered the poor that c Job 29:12
young ravens which c Ps 147:9
Doth not wisdom c Prov 8:1
C aloud, spare not Is 58:1
he shall not strive, nor c Matt 12:19
c the more Matt 20:31; Mark 10:48
elect, which c day and night Luke 18:7
Jesus stood and c if any man thirst John 7:37
c one thing, and some another Acts 19:32; 21:34

CRYING
soul spare for his c Prov 19:18
nor the voice of c Is 65:19
supplications with strong c and tears Heb 5:7
neither sorrow, nor c Rev 21:4

CRYSTAL
the c cannot equal it Job 28:17
colour of the terrible c Ezek 1:22
sea of glass like unto c Rev 4:6; 22:1

CUBIT
can add one c unto his stature Matt 6:27
add to his stature one c Luke 12:25

CUCUMBERS
the c, and the melon Num 11:5
as a lodge in a garden of c Is 1:8

CUMBER
bear your c, and your burden Deut 1:12
Martha was c about Luke 10:40
why c it the ground? Luke 13:7

CUMI koom´-i
arise Mark 5:41

CUNNING
let my right hand forget her c Ps 137:5
send for c women Jer 9:17
c craftiness Eph 4:14
not follow c devised fables 2 Pet 1:16

CUP
take the c of salvation Ps 116:13
c of cold water Matt 10:42
drink of my c Matt 20:22; Mark 10:39
clean the outside of the c Matt 23:25
took the c Matt 26:27; Mark 14:23; Luke 22:17; 1 Cor 11:25
let this c pass Matt 26:39

This c is the new testament Luke 22:20; 1 Cor 11:25
c which my Father hath given John 18:11
c of blessing which we bless 1 Cor 10:16
drink this c, ye do shew 1 Cor 11:26
drink this c of the Lord unworthily 1 Cor 11:27

CURDLED
c me like cheese Job 10:10

CURE
in that same hour he c many Luke 7:21
to c diseases Luke 9:1
I do c to day Luke 13:32

CURIOUS
the c girdle of the ephod Ex 28:8
and c wrought in the lowest Ps 139:15
used c arts Acts 19:19

CURRENT
c money with the merchant Gen 23:16

CURSE (n)
a blessing and a c Deut 11:26
turned the c into the blessing Deut 23:5
Ye are cursed with a c Mal 3:9
are under the c Gal 3:10
no more c Rev 22:3

CURSE (v)
not c the deaf Lev 19:14
How shall I c Num 23:8
c ye bitterly Judg 5:23
c God, and die Job 2:9
they c inwardly Ps 62:4
I will c your blessings Mal 2:2
bless them that c you Matt 5:44; Luke 6:28
he began to c Matt 26:74; Mark 14:71
fig tree which thou c Mark 11:21
who knoweth not the law are c John 7:49
C is every one that continueth not Gal 3:10
therewith c we men James 3:9

CUSH koosh
black Gen 10:6

CUSHAN koosh´-an
a form of CUSH Hab 3:7

CUSHI koosh´-i
the Cushites (Ethiopians) 2 Sam 18:21

CUSTOM
receipt of c Matt 9:9; Mark 2:14; Luke 5:27
do kings of earth take c ? Matt 17:25
his c was, he went into the synagogue Luke 4:16
ye have a c John 18:39
teach c which are not lawful Acts 16:21
c to whom c Rom 13:7
we have no such c 1 Cor 11:16

CUTH kooth
same as CUTHAH 2 Kgs 17:30

CUTHAH kooth´-ah
burning 2 Kgs 17:24

CUTTING
in c of stones, to set them Ex 31:35
c off of my days Is 38:10
crying, and c himself with stones Mark 5:5

CYMBAL
sounding brass, or a tinkling c 1 Cor 13:1

CYPRUS si´-prus
copper Acts 4:36

CYRENE si-reen´
a wall, the floor Matt 27:32

CYRENIAN si-reen´-yan
a native of Cyrene Acts 6:9

CYRENIUS si-reen´-yus
Gr. for the Rom. name Quirinus Luke 2:2

CYRUS si´-rus
the sun 2 Chr 36:22

D

DABAREH da´-bar-ay
pasture Josh 21:28

DABBASHETH dab-ash´-eth
hump of a camel Josh 19:11

DABERATH da´-ber-ath
same as DABAREH Josh 19:12

DAGGER
a d which had two edges Judg 3:16
took the d from his right thigh Judg 3:21
draw the d out of his belly Judg 3:22

DAGON da´-gon
fish Judg 16:23

DAILY
sorrow in my heart d Ps 13:2
d loadeth us Ps 68:19
I was d his delight Prov 8:30
d sacrifice Dan 8:11; 11:31; 12:11
our d bread Matt 6:11; Luke 11:3
take up cross d Luke 9:23
added to the church d Acts 2:47
the d ministration Acts 6:1
increased in number d Acts 16:5
searched the scriptures d Acts 17:11
I die d 1 Cor 15:31
destitute of d food James 2:15

DAINTY
let me not eat of their d Ps 141:4
Be not desirous of his d Prov 23:3

DALAIAH da-lai´-ah
whom Jehovah hath delivered 1 Chr 3:24

DALE
which is the king's d Gen 14:17
in the king's d 2 Sam 18:18

DALMANUTHA dal-ma-nu´-tha
a branch (?) Mark 8:10

DALPHON dal´-fon
proud (?) Esth 9:7

DAM
shall be with his d Ex 22:30
seven days under the d Lev 22:27
take the d with the young Deut 22:6

DAMAGE
drinketh d Prov 26:6
will be with hurt and much d Acts 27:10
receive d by us in nothing 2 Cor 7:9

DAMARIS dam´-ar-is
calf (?) Acts 17:34

DAMASCENES dam´-as-eens
people of Damascus 2 Cor 11:32

DAMASCUS dam-ask´-us
activity (?) Gen 14:15

DAMNABLE
bring in d heresies 2 Pet 2:1

DAMNATION
can ye escape the d of hell? Matt 23:33
in danger of eternal d Mark 3:29
the resurrection of d John 5:29
receive to themselves d Rom 13:2
eateth and drinketh d 1 Cor 11:29
their d slumbereth not 2 Pet 2:3

DAMNED
believeth not shall be d Mark 16:16
he that doubteth is d Rom 14:23
d who believed not the truth 2 Thess 2:12

DAMSEL
among them were the d playing Ps 68:25
given to the d Matt 14:11
d came to Peter Matt 26:69
the d is not dead Mark 5:39
charger, and gave it to the d Mark 6:28
the d that kept the door John 18:17
a d came to hearken Acts 12:13
d possessed with a spirit Acts 16:16

DAN dan
judge Gen 30:6

DAN-JAAN dan´-ja´-an
woodland (?) 2 Sam 24:6

DANCE (n)
praise his name in the d Ps 149:3
praise him with timbrel and d 150:4

DANCE (v)
David d before the Lord 2 Sam 6:14
their children d Job 21:11
a time to d Eccl 3:4
ye have not d Matt 11:17; Luke 7:32
daughter of Herodias d Matt 14:6

DANDLED
be d upon her knees Is 66:12

DANGER
in d of the judgment Matt 5:21
is in d of eternal damnation Mark 3:29
our craft is in d Acts 19:27

DANIEL dan´-yel
My God is judge Dan 1:6

DANITES dan´-ites
descendants of Dan Judg 13:2

DANNAH dan´-nah
judging Josh 15:49

DARA da´-rah
contracted from DARDA 1 Chr 2:6

DARDA dar´-dah
pearl of wisdom (?) 1 Kgs 4:31

DARE
some would even d to die Rom 5:7

DARIUS da-ri´-us
governor (?) Ezra 4:5

DARK
they grope in the d Job 12:25
Can he judge through the d cloud? Job 22:13
In the d they dig Job 24:16
d sayings Ps 49:4; Prov 1:6
wonders be known in the d Ps 88:12
shall not be clear, nor d Zech 14:6
early, when it was yet d John 20:1

DARKENED
Let their eyes be d Ps 69:23; Rom 11:10
be not d Eccl 12:2
look out of windows be d Eccl 12:3
sun be d Matt 24:29
sun was d Luke 23:45
foolish heart was d Rom 1:21
understanding d Eph 4:18

DARKNESS
of the thick d Deut 5:22
as the blind gropeth in d Deut 28:29
wicked shall be silent in d 1 Sam 2:9
d was under his feet 2 Sam 22:10; Ps 18:9
Lord will lighten my d 2 Sam 22:29
dwell in the thick d 1 Kgs 8:12; 2 Chr 6:1
d and the shadow of death Job 3:5; Ps 107:10
where the light is as d Job 10:22
waited for light, there came d Job 30:26
pestilence that walketh in d Ps 91:6
clouds and d are round about him Ps 97:2
to upright there ariseth light in the d Ps 112:4
d and the light are both alike Ps 139:12
put out in obscure d Prov 20:20

as far as light excelleth **d** Eccl 2:13
fool walketh in **d** Eccl 2:14
thy **d** be as the noon day Is 58:10
cover the earth, and gross **d** Is 60:2
day of clouds and of thick **d** Joel 2:2
body shall be full of **d** Matt 6:23
outer **d** Matt 8:12; 22:13; 25:30
What I tell in **d** Matt 10:27
light to them that sit in **d** Luke 1:79
the power of **d** Luke 22:53; Col 1:13
d over all the earth Luke 23:44
d comprehended it not John 1:5
loved **d** rather than light John 3:19
walk while ye have the light, lest **d** John 12:35
turn them from **d** to light Acts 26:18
works of **d** Rom 13:12; Eph 5:11
hidden things of **d** 1 Cor 4:5
light to shine out of **d** 2 Cor 4:6
what communion hath light with **d**? 2 Cor 6:14
rulers of the **d** of this world Eph 6:12
not of the night, nor of **d** 1 Thess 5:5
unto blackness and **d** Heb 12:18
out of **d** into his marvellous light 1 Pet 2:9
into chains of **d** 2 Pet 2:4
in him is no **d** at all 1 John 1:5
and walk in **d**, we lie 1 John 1:6
the **d** is past 1 John 2:8
hateth his brother, is in **d** 1 John 2:9
d hath blinded his eyes 1 John 2:11
kingdom was full of **d** Rev 16:10

DARKON dark´-on
scatterer (?) Ezra 2:56

DARLING
my **d** from the power Ps 22:20
my **d** from the lions Ps 35:17

DART
the spear, the **d**, nor the habergeon Job 41:26
Till a **d** strike through Prov 7:23
quench all the fiery **d** Eph 6:16

DASH
d them in pieces Ps 2:9:
shall be **d** to pieces Is 13:16; Hos 13:16
d thy foot Ps 91:12; Matt 4:6; Luke 4:11
that taketh and **d** thy little ones Ps 137:9

DATHAN da´-than
of a spring Num 16:1

DAUB
d it with slime Ex 2:3
others **d** it with untempered morter Ezek 13:10
prophets have **d** them Ezek 22:28

DAUGHTER
Whose **d** art thou? Gen 24:23,47
because of the **d** of Heth Gen 27:46
flesh of thy sons and thy **d** Deut 28:53
d of the Philistines rejoice 2 Sam 1:20
was unto him as a **d** 2 Sam 12:3
d were among thy honourable women Ps 45:9
our **d** may be as corner stones Ps 144:12
horseleech hath two **d** Prov 30:15
any **d** have done virtuously Prov 31:29
the **d** of musick Eccl 12:4
d of my people Is 22:4; Jer 6:14; 8:21; 9:1; Lam 2:11; 3:48
d riseth up against her mother Mic 7:6
d against the mother Matt 10:35; Luke 12:53
her **d** was made whole Matt 15:28
one only **d**, about twelve years of age Luke 8:42
d of Abraham Luke 13:16
refused to be called the son of Pharaoh's **d** Heb 11:24

DAVID da´-vid
beloved 1 Sam 16:19

DAWN
I prevented the **d** of the morning Ps 119:147
until the day **d** 2 Pet 1:19

DAY
I do remember my faults this **d** Gen 41:9
ask now of the **d** that are past Deut 4:32
come in a good **d** 1 Sam 25:8
this **d** is a **d** of good tidings 2 Kgs 7:9
full of **d** 1 Chr 23:1; 2 Chr 24:15
our **d** on the earth 1 Chr 29:15; Job 8:9
will they make an end in a **d** ? Neh 4:2
the **d** of a hireling Job 7:1
latter **d** upon the earth Job 19:25
reserved to the **d** of destruction Job 21:30
I said, D should speak Job 32:7
this **d** have I begotten thee Ps 2:7; Acts 13:33; Heb 1:5
D unto **d** uttereth speech Ps 19:2
a **d** in thy courts Ps 84:10
length of **d** Prov 3:2,16
and more unto the perfect **d** Prov 4:18
what a **d** may bring forth Prov 27:1
than the **d** of one's birth Eccl 7:1
while the evil **d** come not Eccl 12:1
in the **d** of visitation Is 10:3
keep it night and **d** Is 27:3
an acceptable **d** to the Lord? Is 58:5
an infant of **d** Is 65:20
despised the **d** of small things Zech 4:10
who may abide **d** of his coming? Mal 3:2
Many will say to me in that **d** Matt 7:22
that **d** and hour knoweth no man Matt 24:36
in a **d** when he looketh not Matt 24:50; Luke 12:46
the **d** nor the hour Matt 25:13
that **d** come upon you unawares Luke 21:34
raise it up again at the last **d** John 6:39
Abraham rejoiced to see my **d** John 8:56
while it is **d** John 9:4
he hath appointed a **d** Acts 17:31
wrath against the **d** of wrath Rom 2:5
esteemeth every **d** alike Rom 14:5
the **d** of salvation 2 Cor 6:2
perform it until the **d** of Christ Phil 1:6
d of the Lord 1 Thess 5:2; 2 Pet 3:10
children of the **d** 1 Thess 5:5
a thousand years as one **d** 2 Pet 3:8

DAYSMAN
and **d** betwixt us Job 9:33

DEAD
cuttings in your flesh for the **d** Lev 19:28
as ye have dealt with the **d** Ruth 1:8
d dog 1 Sam 24:14; 2 Sam 9:8; 16:9
forgotten as a **d** man Ps 31:12
d praise not the Lord Ps 115:17
knoweth not that the **d** are there Prov 9:18
the **d** which are already **d** Eccl 4:2
living dog is better than a **d** lion Eccl 9:4
d know not anything Eccl 9:5
D flies cause ointment Eccl 10:1
Thy **d** men shall live Is 26:19
Weep not for the **d** Jer 22:10
let the **d** bury their **d** Matt 8:22
not **d**, but sleepeth Matt 9:24; Mark 5:39; Luke 8:52
deaf hear, the **d** are raised Matt 11:5; Luke 7:22
not the God of the **d** Matt 22:32
full of **d** men's bones Matt 23:27
rising from the **d** should mean Mark 9:10
d, and is alive again Luke 15:24,32
though one rose from the **d** Luke 16:31
d shall hear John 5:25
eat manna in the wilderness, and are **d** John 6:49
though he were **d**, yet shall he live John 11:25
he that was **d** came forth John 11:44
Judge of quick and **d** Acts 10:42
first that should rise from the **d** Acts 26:23
d to sin Rom 6:2; 1 Pet 2:24
d to the law Rom 7:4; Gal 2:19
Lord both of the **d** and living Rom 14:9
the **d** rise not 1 Cor 15:15
How are the **d** raised 1 Cor 15:35
in God which raiseth **d** 2 Cor 1:9
then were all **d** 2 Cor 5:14
d in trespasses and sins Eph 2:1
arise from the **d** Eph 5:14
firstborn from the **d** Col 1:18
you, being **d** in your sins Col 2:13
d with Christ Col 2:20
d in Christ shall rise first 1 Thess 4:16
d while she liveth 1 Tim 5:6
For if we be **d** with him 2 Tim 2:11
quick and the **d** at his appearing 2 Tim 4:1
from **d** works Heb 6:1; 9:14
being **d** yet speaketh Heb 11:4
brought again from the **d** Heb 13:20
faith without works is **d** James 2:20,26
preached also to them that are **d** 1 Pet 4:6
twice **d** Jude 1:12
first-begotten of the **d** Rev 1:5
I am he that liveth, and was **d** Rev 1:18
a name that thou livest, and are **d** Rev 3:1
Blessed are the **d** Rev 14:13
rest of the **d** lived not again Rev 20:5
the **d**, small and great Rev 20:12
sea gave up the **d** Rev 20:13

DEADLY
drink any **d** thing Mark 16:18
full of **d** poison James 3:8

DEAF
like the **d** adder that stoppeth Ps 58:4
shall the **d** hear the words Is 29:18
the **d** hear Matt 11:5; Luke 7:22
the **d** to hear, and the dumb to speak Mark 7:37
Thou dumb and **d** spirit Mark 9:25

DEAL
neither **d** falsely Lev 19:11
d with you after your folly Job 42:8
D not foolishly Ps 75:4
they that **d** truly are his delight Prov 12:22
treacherous dealer **d** treacherously Is 21:2
he **d** unjustly Is 26:10
every one **d** falsely Jer 6:13; 8:10
have **d** treacherously against the Lord Hos 5:7
so hath he **d** with us Zech 1:6
the more a great **d** Mark 7:36; 10:48
why hast thou thus **d** with us? Luke 2:48
according as God hath **d** Rom 12:3

DEALING
I hear of your evil **d** 1 Sam 2:23
his violent **d** shall come down Ps 7:16
Jews have no **d** with the Samaritans John 4:9

DEAR
Is Ephraim my **d** son? Jer 31:20
neither count I my life **d** Acts 20:24
followers of God, as **d** children Eph 5:1
kingdom of his **d** Son Col 1:13
because ye were **d** unto us 1 Thess 2:8

DEARTH
If there be **d** in the land 2 Chr 6:28
buy corn, because of the **d** Neh 5:3
there should be great **d** Acts 11:28

DEATH
if these men die the common **d** Num 16:29
Let me die the **d** of the righteous Num 23:10
jeoparded lives unto the **d** Judg 5:18
soul was vexed unto **d** Judg 16:16
which he slew at his **d** were Judg 16:30
if ought but **d** part thee and me Ruth 1:17
the bitterness of **d** is past 1 Sam 15:32
but a step between me and **d** 1 Sam 20:3
in their **d** 2 Sam 1:23

waves of **d** compassed 2 Sam 22:5
long for **d**, but it cometh not Job 3:21
my soul chooseth strangling, and **d** Job 7:15
thou wilt bring me to **d** Job 30:23
in **d** there is no remembrance Ps 6:5
lest I sleep the sleep of **d** Ps 13:3
sorrows of **d** Ps 18:4; 116:3
shadow of **d** Ps 23:4; Ps 107:10; Is 9:2; Jer 2:6
our guide even unto **d** Ps 48:14
the issues from **d** Ps 68:20
shall not see **d** Ps 89:48
loose those that appointed to **d** Ps 102:20
d of his saints Ps 116:15
to the chambers of **d** Prov 7:27
they that hate me love **d** Prov 8:36
the righteous hath hope in his **d** Prov 14:32
deliver them that are drawn unto **d** Prov 24:11
love is strong as **d** Song 8:6
swallow up **d** in victory Is 25:8
d cannot celebrate thee Is 38:18
d shall be chosen rather than life Jer 8:3
d is come up into our windows Jer 9:21
no pleasure in the **d** Ezek 18:32; 33:11
O **d**, I will be thy plagues Hos 13:14
let him die the **d** Matt 15:4; Mark 7:10
not taste of **d** Matt 16:28; Mark 9:1; Luke 9:27
exceeding sorrowful even unto **d** Matt 26:38; Mark 14:34
lieth at the point of **d** Mark 5:23
should not see **d** Luke 2:26
into prison and to **d** Luke 22:33
passed from **d** unto life John 5:24; 1 John 3:14
shall never see **d** John 8:51
sickness not unto **d** John 11:4
signifying what **d** John 12:33; 18:32
having loosed the pains of **d** Acts 2:24
such things are worthy of **d** Rom 1:32
reconciled to God by the **d** Rom 5:10
d by sin, and so **d** passed Rom 5:12
d reigned from Adam to Moses Rom 5:14
in likeness of his **d** Rom 6:5
end of those things is **d** Rom 6:21
wages of sin is **d** Rom 6:23
law of sin and **d** Rom 8:2
life or **d** 1 Cor 3:22
shew the Lord's **d** till he come 1 Cor 11:26
by man came **d** 1 Cor 15:21
O **d**, where is thy sting? 1 Cor 15:55
sting of **d** is sin 1 Cor 15:56
sentence of **d** in ourselves 2 Cor 1:9
savour of **d** unto **d** 2 Cor 2:16
d worketh in us 2 Cor 4:12
in **d** oft 2 Cor 11:23
even the **d** of the cross Phil 2:8
of his flesh through **d**, to present you Col 1:22
taste **d** for every man Heb 2:9
through fear of **d** were Heb 2:15
bringeth forth **d** James 1:15
a sin unto **d** 1 John 5:16
keys of hell and of **d** Rev 1:18
be thou faithful unto **d** Rev 2:10
second **d** Rev 2:11; 20:14
his name that sat on him was **D** Rev 6:8
and **d** shall flee from them Rev 9:6
d and hell delivered up Rev 20:13
no more **d** Rev 21:4

DEBASE
didst **d** thyself even unto hell Is 57:9

DEBATE
ye fast for strife and **d** Is 58:4
murder, **d**, deceit, malignity Rom 1:29
lest there be **d**, envyings, wrath 2 Cor 12:20

DEBIR de´-ber
a recess Josh 10:3

DEBORAH deb´-or-ah
bee Judg 4:4

DEBT
pay thy **d**, and live 2 Kgs 4:7
the exaction of every **d** Neh 10:31
sureties for **d** Prov 22:26
forgave him the **d** Matt 18:27

DEBTOR
I am **d** both to the Greeks Rom 1:14
we are **d**, not to the flesh Rom 8:12
their **d** they are Rom 15:27
d to do the whole law Gal 5:3

DECAPOLIS de-ka´-pol-is
ten cities Matt 4:25

DECAY
bearers of burdens is **d** Neh 4:10
Now that which **d** and waxeth not Heb 8:13

DECEASE
spoke of his **d** Luke 9:31
able after my **d** to have these 2 Pet 1:15

DECEIT
mouth full of cursing and **d** and fraud Ps 10:7
words are of his mouth iniquity and **d** Ps 36:3
counsels of wicked are **d** Prov 12:5
Bread of **d** is sweet Prov 20:17
the **d** of their heart Jer 14:14
the house of Israel with **d** Hos 11:12
falsifying the balances by **d** Amos 8:5
houses with violence and **d** Zeph 1:9
they have used **d** Rom 3:13
false apostles, **d** workers 2 Cor 11:13
according to the **d** lusts Eph 4:22
vain **d**, after the tradition Col 2:8

DECEITFUL
d men shall not live out half their days Ps 55:23
kisses of an enemy are **d** Prov 27:6
favour is **d** and beauty vain Prov 31:30
The heart is **d** above all things Jer 17:9

DECEITFULLY
doeth the work of the Lord **d** Jer 48:10
handling the word of God **d** 2 Cor 4:2

DECEIVE
your heart be not **d** Deut 11:16
in whom thou trusteth **d** thee2 Kgs 19:10; Is 37:10
the **d** and the **d** are his Job 12:16
thou hast **d** me, and I was **d** Jer 20:7
D not yourselves Jer 37:9
pride of thine heart hath **d** thee Obad 1:3
d the very elect Matt 24:24
remember that that **d** said Matt 27:63
Nay, but he **d** the people John 7:12
Are ye also **d** ? John 7:47
Be not **d** 1 Cor 6:9; 15:33; Gal 6:7
as **d**, and yet true 2 Cor 6:8
whereby they lie in wait to **d** Eph 4:14
let no man **d** you Eph 5:6; 2 Thess 2:3
Adam was not **d** 1 Tim 2:14
worse and worse, **d**, and being **d** 2 Tim 3:13
no sin, we **d** ourselves 1 John 1:8
many **d** entered into the world 2 John 1:7

DECENTLY
all things be done **d** and in order 1 Cor 14:40

DECISION
valley of **d** Joel 3:14

DECK
D thyself with majesty Job 40:10
as a bridegroom **d** himself Is 61:10
though thou **d** thee with ornaments Jer 4:30
They **d** it with silver Jer 10:4

DECLARATION
the **d** of the greatness of Mordecai Esth 10:2
my **d** with your ears Job 13:17
in order a **d** of those things Luke 1:1
d of your ready mind 2 Cor 8:19

DECLARE
D his glory among the heathen 1 Chr 16:24; Ps 96:3
Who shall **d** his way to his face? Job 21:31
I would **d** unto him Job 31:37
I will **d** the decree Ps 2:7
d among the people his doings Ps 9:11
heavens **d** the glory of God Ps 19:1
shall it **d** thy truth? Ps 30:9
I have **d** thy faithfulness Ps 40:10
I will **d** what he hath done Ps 66:16
I will **d** for ever Ps 75:9
live, and **d** the works of the Lord Ps 118:17
shall **d** thy mighty acts Ps 145:4
they **d** their sin as Sodom Is 3:9
Who hath **d** from the beginning? Is 41:26
I **d** things that are right Is 45:19
D the end from the beginning Is 46:10
who shall **d** his generation? Is 53:8; Acts 8:33
d my glory among Gentiles Is 66:19
have **d** unto them thy name John 17:26
we **d** unto you glad tidings Acts 13:32
him **d** I unto you Acts 17:23
d unto you the counsel of God Acts 20:27
d to be the Son of God with power Rom 1:4
day shall **d** it 1 Cor 3:13

DECLINE
thou shalt not **d** from the sentence Deut 17:11
d neither to the right nor to the left 2 Chr 34:2
days like a shadow that **d** Ps 102:11
not **d** from thy law Ps 119:51

DECREASE
the waters **d** continually Gen 8:5
their cattle to **d** Ps 107:38
He must increase, but I must **d** John 3:30

DECREE
made a **d** for the rain Job 28:26
a **d** which shall not pass Ps 148:6
he gave to the sea his **d** Prov 8:29
delivered them the **d** Acts 16:4

DEDAN de´-dan
their breasts Gen 10:7

DEDANIM de´-dan-im
inhabitants of Dedan Is 21:13

DEDICATE
another man **d** it Deut 20:5
wholly **d** the silver to the Lord Judg 17:3
did they **d** to maintain the house 1 Chr 26:27

DEED
in very **d** Ex 9:16; 1 Sam 25:34; 26:4
by this **d** thou hast given 2 Sam 12:14
come upon us for our evil **d** Ezra 9:13
wipe not out my good **d** Neh 13:14
according to their **d** Ps 28:4; Jer 25:14; Rom 2:6
ye allow the **d** of your fathers Luke 11:48
due reward of our **d** Luke 23:41
a prophet mighty in **d** Luke 24:19
because their **d** were evil John 3:19
Ye do the **d** of your father John 8:41
mighty in word and in **d** Acts 7:22
by the **d** of law Rom 3:20
justified without **d** of the law Rom 3:28
put off the old man with his **d** Col 3:9
whatsoever ye do in word or **d** Col 3:17
shall be blessed in his **d** James 1:25
but in **d** and in truth 1 John 3:18

DEEMED
the shipmen **d** that they drew near Acts 27:27

DEEP
fountains of the great **d** Gen 7:11; 8:2
the **d** that coucheth beneath Deut 33:13
face of the **d** is frozen Job 38:30
maketh the **d** boil like a pot Job 41:31
thy judgments are a great **d** Ps 36:6
d calleth unto **d** Ps 42:7
In his hand are the **d** places Ps 95:4
his wonders in the **d** Ps 107:24
mouth of strange women is a **d** pit Prov 22:14
a whore is a **d** ditch Prov 23:27
led them through the **d** Is 63:13
no **d** of earth Matt 13:5
Launch out into the **d** Luke 5:4
digged **d**, and laid the foundations Luke 6:48
command them to go into the **d** Luke 8:31
the well is **d** John 4:11
d things of God 1 Cor 2:10

DEER
fallow **d** Deut 14:5; 1 Kgs 4:23

DEFAME
I heard the **d** of many Jer 20:10
Being **d**, we intreat 1 Cor 4:13

DEFEAT
d the counsel 2 Sam 15:34
had appointed to **d** 2 Sam 17:14

DEFENCE
the Almighty shall be thy **d** Job 22:25
my **d** is of God Ps 7:10
for God is my **d** Ps 59:9,17
Lord is our **d** Ps 89:18
wisdom is a **d**, money is a **d** Eccl 7:12
place of **d** shall be the munitions of rocks Is 33:16
in **d** of the Gospel Phil 1:17

DEFEND
shout for joy, because thou **d** them Ps 5:11
D the poor and fatherless Ps 82:3
Lord of hosts shall **d** them Zech 9:15
d him, and avenged Acts 7:24

DEFILE
every one that **d** Ex 31:14
blood it **d** the land Num 35:33
did the king **d** 2 Kgs 23:13
they have **d** the priesthood Neh 13:29
they have **d** by casting down Ps 74:7
thy holy temple have they **d** Ps 79:1
d with their own works Ps 106:39
your hands are **d** with blood Is 59:3
ye **d** my land Jer 2:7
eat their **d** bread Ezek 4:13
they have **d** my sanctuary Ezek 23:38
they **d** it by their own way Ezek 36:17
would not **d** himself Dan 1:8
d a man Matt 15:11
d the man Mark 7:15,20,23
lest they should be **d** John 18:28
If any man **d** the temple of God 1 Cor 3:17
conscience being weak is **d** 1 Cor 8:7
them that **d** themselves 1 Tim 1:10
conscience is **d** Titus 1:15
thereby many be **d** Heb 12:15
filthy dreamers **d** the flesh Jude 1:8
which have not **d** their garments Rev 3:4

DEFRAUD
whom have I **d**? 1 Sam 12:3
D not Mark 10:19
rather suffer yourselves to be **d** 1 Cor 6:7
ye do wrong, and **d** 1 Cor 6:8
D ye not one the other 1 Cor 7:5
we have **d** no man 2 Cor 7:2

DEGENERATE
turned into the **d** plant Jer 2:21

DEGREE
men of low **d** Ps 62:9
to themselves a good **d** 1 Tim 3:13
brother of low **d** rejoice James 1:9

DEHAVITES de´-hav-ites
the Aryan Da, a nomadic Persian tribe Ezra 4:9

DEKAR de´-kar
piercing 1 Kgs 4:9

DELAIAH de-lai´-ah
whom Jehovah has freed 1 Chr 24:18

DELAY
My lord **d** his coming Matt 24:48; Luke 12:45
that he would not **d** to come Acts 9:38

DELECTABLE
their **d** things shall not profit Is 44:9

DELICACY
abundance of her **d** Rev 18:3

DELICATE
Agag came unto him **d** 1 Sam 15:32
he that **d** bringeth up his servant Prov 29:21
no more be called tender and **d** Is 47:1
that did feed **d** are desolate Lam 4:5
live **d** are in kings' courts Luke 7:25

DELICIOUSLY
lived **d** Rev 18:7

DELIGHT (n)
Lord had a **d** in thy fathers Deut 10:15
the LORD as great **d** in burnt offerings? 1 Sam 15:22
I have no **d** in thee 2 Sam 15:26
shalt thou have **d** in the Almighty? Job 22:26
his **d** is in the law of the Lord Ps 1:2
to the excellent, in whom is all my **d** Ps 16:3
Thy testimonies also are my **d** Ps 119:24
thy law is my **d** Ps 119:77,174
thy commandments are my **d** Ps 119:143
I was daily his **d** Prov 8:30
my **d** were with the sons of men Prov 8:31
fool hath no **d** in understanding Prov 18:2
d is not seemly for a fool Prov 19:10
under his shadow with great **d** Song 2:3
call the sabbath a **d** Is 58:13

DELIGHT (v)
Will he **d** himself in the Almighty? Job 27:10
D thyself also in the Lord Ps 37:4
d themselves in abundance of peace Ps 37:11
thou **d** not in burnt offering Ps 51:16
thy comforts **d** my soul Ps 94:19
elect, in whom my soul **d** Is 42:1
soul **d** itself in fatness Is 55:2
the Lord **d** in thee Is 62:4
he **d** in mercy Mic 7:18
I **d** in the law of God Rom 7:22

DELIGHTSOME
ye shall be a **d** land Mal 3:12

DELILAH de-li´-lah
delicate Judg 16:4

DELIVER
am come down to **d** them Ex 3:8; Acts 7:34
congregation shall **d** the slayer Num 35:25
d out of my hand Deut 32:39; Is 43:13
able to **d** their lands? 2 Chr 32:13
shall **d** thee in six troubles Job 5:19
great ransom cannot **d** Job 36:18
d any by his great strength Ps 33:17
d my feet from falling Ps 56:13
d David his servant, from the hurtful Ps 144:10
forbear to **d** them Prov 24:11
by wisdom **d** the city Eccl 9:15
have I no power to **d**? Is 50:2
I am with thee to **d** thee Jer 1:8
I will **d** in that day Jer 39:17
is able to **d** Dan 3:17
set his heart on Daniel to **d** Dan 6:14
neither shall the mighty **d** Amos 2:14
escapeth of them shall not be **d** Amos 9:1
they that tempt God are even **d** Mal 3:15
d us from evil Matt 6:13; Luke 11:4
All things are **d** to me Matt 11:27; Luke 10:22
I will **d** him you Matt 26:15
being **d** by the determinate counsel Acts 2:23
was **d** for our offences Rom 4:25
we are **d** from the law Rom 7:6
shall be **d** Rom 8:21
d unto death for Jesus' sake 2 Cor 4:11
d me from every evil work 2 Tim 4:18
faith which was once **d** unto saints Jude 1:3

DELIVERANCE
had given **d** to Syria 2 Kgs 5:1
saved them by a great **d** 1 Chr 11:14
compass me with songs of **d** Ps 32:7
preach **d** to the captives Luke 4:18
not accepting **d** Heb 11:35

DELUSION
will choose their **d** Is 66:4
shall send them strong **d** 2 Thess 2:11

DEMAND
he **d** of them Matt 2:4
the soldiers likewise **d** of him Luke 3:14

DEMAS de´-mas
same as DEMETRIUS (?) Col 4:14

DEMETRIUS de-me´-tri-us
belonging to Demeter Acts 19:24

DEMONSTRATION
in **d** of the Spirit and of power 1 Cor 2:4

DEN
then the beasts go into **d** Job 37:8
hand on the cockatrice **d** Is 11:8
a **d** of robbers? Jer 7:11
a **d** of thieves Matt 21:13; Mark 11:17
in mountains, and in **d** Heb 11:38

DENOUNCE
I **d** unto you this day Deut 30:18

DENY
lest ye **d** your God Josh 24:27
lest I be full, and **d** thee Prov 30:9
d that there is any resurrection Luke 20:27
he cannot **d** himself 2 Tim 2:13
in works they **d** him Titus 1:16

DEPART
sceptre shall not **d** from Judah Gen 49:10
not wickedly **d** from my God 2 Sam 22:22; Ps 18:21
they say to God, **d** from us Job 21:14; 22:17
to **d** from evil is understanding Job 28:28
d from me, ye workers of iniquity Ps 6:8; Matt 7:23; Luke 13:27
d from evil, and do good Ps 34:14; 37:27
Egypt was glad when they **d** Ps 105:38
he may **d** from hell beneath Prov 15:24
when he is old, he will not **d** from it Prov 22:6
will not his foolishness **d** from him Prov 27:22
they need not **d** Matt 14:16
d from me, ye cursed Matt 25:41
lettest thou thy servant **d** in peace Luke 2:29
the devil **d** for a season Luke 4:13
them which are in the midst of it **d** Luke 21:21
that he should **d** out of this world John 13:1
besought that it might **d** from me 2 Cor 12:8
having a desire to **d**, Phil 1:23
some shall **d** from the faith 1 Tim 4:1
the name of Christ **d** from iniquity 2 Tim 2:19

DEPOSED
d from his kingly throne Dan 5:20

DEPRIVED
be **d** also of you both Gen 27:45

hath **d** her of wisdom Job 39:17
I am **d** of the residue Is 38:10

DEPTH
d saith, it is not in me Job 28:14
he layeth up the **d** in storehouses Ps 33:7
waters afraid, **d** also were troubled Ps 77:16
through the **d** as through wilderness Ps 106:9
they go down again to the **d** Ps 107:26
there were no **d,** I was brought forth Prov 8:24
The heaven for height, earth for **d** Prov 25:3
he were drowned in the **d** of sea Matt 18:6
it had no **d** of earth Mark 4:5
the **d** of the riches Rom 11:33

DEPUTED
no man **d** of the king 2 Sam 15:3

DEPUTY
a **d** was king 1 Kgs 22:47
with the **d** of the country Acts 13:7
Gallio was the **d** of Achaia Acts 18:12
and there are **d** Acts 19:38

DERBE der´-bee
juniper (?) Acts 14:6

DERIDE
they shall **d** every strong hold Hab 1:10
d him Luke 16:14; 23:35

DERISION
that are younger than I have me in **d** Job 30:1
the Lord shall have them in **d** Ps 2:4
a **d** to them that are round us Ps 44:13; 79:4
d daily Jer 20:7,8
I was a **d** to my people Lam 3:14

DESCEND
with them that **d** into the pit Ezek 26:20; 31:16
the rain **d,** and floods came Matt 7:25,27
Spirit **d** Mark 1:10; John 1:32,33
Christ **d** now from the cross Mark 15:32
who shall **d** into the deep? Rom 10:7
he that **d** is the same that ascended Eph 4:10
this wisdom **d** not from above James 3:15
great city **d** out of heaven from God Rev 21:10

DESCENT
at the **d** of the mount of Olives Luke 19:37
without **d** Heb 7:3
But he whose **d** is not counted Heb 7:6

DESCRIBE
and **d** it according the inheritance Josh 18:4
he **d** unto him the princes of Succoth Judg 8:14
David also **d** the blessedness of Rom 4:6
For Moses **d** the righteousness Rom 10:5

DESCRY
sent to **d** Beth-el Judg 1:23

DESERT
oft did they grieve him in **d** Ps 78:40
like an owl of the **d** Ps 102:6
the **d** shall rejoice Is 35:1
streams in the **d** Is 35:6; 43:19
in **d** a highway for our God Is 40:3
led us through land of **d** Jer 2:6
like the heath in the **d** Jer 17:6
people that dwell in the **d** Jer 25:24
Behold, he is in the **d** Matt 24:26
in the **d** till the day of his shewing Luke 1:80
aside privately into a **d** place Luke 9:10
did eat manna in the **d** John 6:31

DESERTS
render to them their **d** Ps 28:4
according to their **d** Ezek 7:27

DESERVE
the **d** of his hands Judg 9:16
less than our iniquities **d** Ezra 9:13

DESIRABLE
all of them **d** young men Ezek 23:6,12,23

DESIRE (n)
sought him with their whole **d** 2 Chr 15:15
My **d** is that Job may be tried Job 34:36
heart's **d** Ps 10:3; 21:2; Rom 10:1
he shall give thee the **d** of thine heart Ps 37:4
d upon mine enemies Ps 54:7; 59:10; 92:11
d of the wicked Ps 92:11; 112:10; 140:8
the **d** of every living thing Ps 145:16
the **d** of righteous Prov 10:24; 11:23
when the **d** cometh, it is a tree of life Prov 13:12
the **d** of a man is his kindness Prov 19:22
the **d** of the slothful killeth him Prov 21:25
d shall fail Eccl 12:5
the **d** of thine eyes Ezek 24:16
he uttereth his mischievous **d** Mic 7:3
enlargeth his **d** as hell Hab 2:5
the **D** of all nations shall come Hag 2:7
with **d** I have **d** to eat Luke 22:15
fulfilling the **d** of the flesh and mind Eph 2:3
having a **d** to depart Phil 1:23

DESIRE (v)
whatsoever thy soul **d** Deut 14:26
take as much as thy soul **d** 1 Sam 2:16
behold the king whom ye have **d** 1 Sam 12:13
servants who **d** to fear thy name Neh 1:11
I **d** to reason with God Job 13:3
More to be **d** are they than gold Ps 19:10
One thing have I **d** of the LORD Ps 27:4
that **d** life, and loveth many days Ps 34:12
Sacrifice and offering thou didst not **d** Ps 40:6
King greatly **d** thy beauty Ps 45:11
none upon earth I **d** besides thee Ps 73:25
unto their **d** haven Ps 107:30
thou canst **d** not to be compared Prov 3:15
soul of sluggard **d** and hath nothing Prov 13:4
whatsoever mine eyes **d** Eccl 2:10
no beauty that we should **d** him Is 53:2
I **d** mercy, and not sacrifice Hos 6:6
soul **d** first ripe fruit Mic 7:1
gather together, O nation not **d** Zeph 2:1
his brethren stood without **d** Matt 12:46
have **d** to see those things Matt 13:17
d a certain thing of him Matt 20:20
if any man **d** to be first Mark 9:35
do for us whatsoever we shall **d** Mark 10:35
what things ye **d,** Mark 11:24
prisoner, whomsoever they **d** Mark 15:6
d to see thee Luke 8:20
And he **d** to see him Luke 9:9
kings have **d** to see Luke 10:24
d to be fed with the crumbs Luke 16:21
which **d** to walk in long robes Luke 20:46
have **d** to eat this passover Luke 22:15
Satan hath **d** to have you Luke 22:31
d a murderer to be granted Acts 3:14
and **d** spiritual gifts 1 Cor 14:1
d to be clothed upon 2 Cor 5:2
ye **d** again to be in bondage Gal 4:9
ye that **d** to be under the law Gal 4:21
As many as **d** to make a fair Gal 6:12
I **d** that ye faint not Eph 3:13
not because I **d** a gift: but I **d** fruit Phil 4:17
he **d** a good work 1 Tim 3:1
they **d** a better country Heb 11:16
ye kill, and **d** to have James 4:2
the angels **d** to look into 1 Pet 1:12
newborn babes, **d** the sincere milk 1 Pet 2:2
we have the petitions that we **d** 1 John 5:15

DESIROUS
no **d** of his dainties Prov 23:3
d to see him Luke 23:8
they were **d** to ask him John 16:19
not be **d** of vainglory Gal 5:26

DESOLATE
for I am **d** and afflicted Ps 25:16
let them be **d** for a reward Ps 40:15
my heart within me is **d** Ps 143:4
more are the children of the **d** Is 54:1
shall thy land any more be termed **d** Is 62:4
be ye very **d,** saith the LORD Jer 2:12
d without man or beast Jer 32:43
altars may be laid waste and made **d** Ezek 6:6
abomination that maketh **d** Dan 11:31; 12:11
return and build the **d** places Mal 1:4
house is left unto you **d** Matt 23:38; Luke 13:35
Let his habitation be **d** Acts 1:20
widow indeed, and **d** 1 Tim 5:5
in one hour is she made **d** Rev 18:19

DESOLATION
they should become a **d** and a curse 2 Kgs 22:19
what **d** he hath made in the earth Ps 46:8
perpetual **d** Ps 74:3; Jer 25:9; Ezek 35:9
When your fear cometh as **d** Prov 1:27
d of the wicked Prov 3:25
raise up the former **d** Is 61:4
end of the war **d** are determined Dan 9:26
a day of wasteness and **d** Zeph 1:15
divided against itself is brought to **d** Matt 12:25; Luke 11:17
then know that the **d** thereof is nigh Luke 21:20

DESPAIR
shall **d** of me 1 Sam 27:1
cause my heart to **d** Eccl 2:20

DESPERATE
speeches of one that is **d** Job 6:26
day of grief and **d** sorrow Is 17:11
deceitful above all things, and **d** wicked Jer 17:9

DESPISE
ye have **d** the LORD Num 11:20
d the word Num 15:31; Prov 13:13; Is 5:24; 30:12
that **d** me shall be lightly esteemed 1 Sam 2:30
Hear, O God, for we are **d** Neh 4:4
so that they shall **d** their husbands Esth 1:17
d not thou the chastening Job 5:17; Heb 12:5
young children **d** me Job 19:18
God is mighty, and **d** not any Job 36:5
contrite heart, O God, thou wilt not **d** Ps 51:17
to shame, because God hath **d** them Ps 53:5
thou shalt **d** their image Ps 73:20
not **d** their prayer Ps 102:17
fools **d** wisdom Prov 1:7
d reproof Prov 1:30; 5:12
Men do not **d** a thief Prov 6:30
fool **d** his father's instruction Prov 15:5
foolish man **d** his mother Prov 15:20
refuseth instruction **d** his own soul Prov 15:32
he that **d** his ways shall die Prov 19:16
d to obey his mother Prov 30:17
poor man's wisdom is **d** Eccl 9:16
he that **d** the gain of oppressions Is 33:15
to him whom man **d** Is 49:7
and **d** among men Jer 49:15
they **d** my judgments Ezek 20:13,16
thou hast **d** mine holy things Ezek 22:8
they **d** the law of the Lord Amos 2:4
who hath **d** the day of small things? Zech 4:10
Wherein have we **d** thy name? Mal 1:6
hold to the one, and **d** the other Matt 6:24; Luke 16:13
d not one of these little ones Matt 18:10
he that **d** me **d** him that sent me Luke 10:16
righteous, and **d** others Luke 18:9
d thou the riches of his goodness Rom 2:4
things which are **d** 1 Cor 1:28
ye are honourable, but we are **d** 1 Cor 4:10

d ye the church of God 1 Cor 11:22
Let no man therefore **d** him 1 Cor 16:11
d not man, but God 1 Thess 4:8
D not prophesyings 1 Thess 5:20
Let no man **d** thy youth 1 Tim 4:12
not **d** them, because they are brethren 1 Tim 6:2
Let no man **d** thee Titus 2:15
endured the cross, **d** the shame Heb 12:2
ye have **d** the poor James 2:6

DESPISERS
Behold, ye **d**, and wonder Acts 13:41
d of those that are good 2 Tim 3:3

DESPITE
with all thy **d** against the land Ezek 25:6
taken vengeance with a **d** heart Ezek 25:15
with **d** minds Ezek 36:5
haters of God, **d**, proud Rom 1:30
hath done **d** unto Heb 10:29

DESPITEFULLY
which **d** use you Matt 5:44; Luke 6:28
to use them **d** Acts 14:5

DESTITUTE
will regard the prayer of the **d** Ps 102:17
Folly is joy to him that is **d** of wisdom Prov 15:21
d of the truth 1 Tim 6:5
being **d**, afflicted, tormented Heb 11:37

DESTROY
d the righteous with the wicked Gen 18:23
he shall be utterly **d** Ex 22:20
Let me alone, that I may **d** them Deut 9:14
lest I **d** you with them 1 Sam 15:6
d the LORD'S anointed 2 Sam 1:14
to **d** him without cause Job 2:3
yet thou dost **d** me Job 10:8
He hath **d** me on every side Job 19:10
worms **d** this body Job 19:26
seek after my soul to **d** it Ps 40:14
all the wicked will he **d** Ps 145:20
prosperity of fools shall **d** them Prov 1:32
is **d** for want of judgment Prov 13:23
that which **d** kings Prov 31:3
one sinner **d** much good Eccl 9:18
it is in his heart to **d** Is 10:7
nor **d** in all my holy mountain Is 11:9; 65:25
I will **d** the counsel thereof Is 19:3
a **d** storm Is 28:2
nor have mercy, but **d** them Jer 13:14
d them with double destruction Jer 17:18
unto the pastors that **d** and scatter Jer 23:1
with his **d** weapon in his hand Ezek 9:1
d souls, to get dishonest gain Ezek 22:27
he shall **d** wonderfully Dan 8:24
thou hast **d** thyself Hos 13:9
not come to **d**, but to fulfil Matt 5:17
fear him which is able to **d** Matt 10:28
they might **d** him Matt 12:14; Mark 3:6; 11:18
He will miserably **d** those Matt 21:41
and **d** those murderers Matt 22:7
ask Barabbas, and **d** Jesus Matt 27:20
art thou come to **d** us? Mark 1:24; Luke 4:34
d the husbandmen Mark 12:9; Luke 20:16
say, I will **d** this temple Mark 14:58
thou that **d** the temple Mark 15:29
to save life, or to **d** it? Luke 6:9
is not come to **d** men's lives Luke 9:56
flood came, and **d** them all Luke 17:27
D this temple John 2:19
D not him with thy meat Rom 14:15
God shall **d** both it and them 1 Cor 6:13
preacheth the faith which once he **d** Gal 1:23
if I build again the things which I **d** Gal 2:18
d with the brightness of his coming 2 Thess 2:8
d him that had the power Heb 2:14
able to save and to **d** James 4:12

d the works of the devil 1 John 3:8

DESTROYER
not suffer the **d** to come Ex 12:23
the **d** of our country Judg 16:24
in prosperity the **d** shall come Job 15:21
kept me from the paths of the **d** Ps 17:4
the companion of a **d** Prov 28:24

DESTRUCTION
death of his father to his **d** 2 Chr 22:4
heart was lifted up to his **d** 2 Chr 26:16
endure to see the **d** of my kindred Esth 8:6
neither shalt thou be afraid of **d** Job 5:21
how oft cometh their **d** Job 21:17
d hath no covering Job 26:6
Is not **d** to the wicked Job 31:3
d are come to a perpetual end Ps 9:6
into that very **d** let him fall Ps 35:8
thou castest them down to **d** Ps 73:18
turnest man to **d** Ps 90:3
the **d** that wasteth at noonday Ps 91:6
redeemeth thy life from **d** Ps 103:4
your **d** cometh as a whirlwind Prov 1:27
mouth of the foolish is near **d** Prov 10:14
d of the poor is their poverty Prov 10:15
want of people is the **d** of the prince Prov 14:28
Pride goeth before **d** Prov 16:18
he that exalteth his gate seeketh **d** Prov 17:19
A fool's mouth is his **d** Prov 18:7
Hell and **d** are never full Prov 27:20
such as are appointed to **d** Prov 31:8
the besom of **d** Is 14:23
The city of **d** Is 19:18
wasting and **d** are in their paths Is 59:7
nor **d** within thy borders Is 60:18
destroy them with double **d** Jer 17:18
d cometh; it cometh out of the north Jer 46:20
of great **d** Jer 50:22
d of the daughter of my people Lam 2:11; 3:48; 4:10
O grave, I will be thy **d** Hos 13:14
broad is the way, that leadeth to **d** Matt 7:13
D and misery are in their ways Rom 3:16
vessels of wrath fitted to **d** Rom 9:22
Whose end is **d** Phil 3:19
then sudden **d** cometh 1 Thess 5:3
punished with everlasting **d** 2 Thess 1:9
lusts, which drown men in **d** 1 Tim 6:9
bring upon themselves swift **d** 2 Pet 2:1
to their own **d** 2 Pet 3:16

DETAIN
let us **d** thee Judg 13:15
Though thou **d** me Judg 13:16
d before the Lord 1 Sam 21:7

DETERMINATE
delivered by the **d** counsel Acts 2:23

DETERMINATION
for my **d** is to gather Zeph 3:8

DETERMINE
pay as the judges **d** Ex 21:22
be sure that evil is **d** by him 1 Sam 20:7
Seeing his days are **d** Job 14:5
that that is **d** shall be done Dan 11:36
Son of man goeth, as it was **d** Luke 22:22
Pilate, when he was **d** to let him go Acts 3:13
hath **d** the times appointed Acts 17:26
I **d** not to know any thing 1 Cor 2:2

DETEST
thou shalt utterly **d** it Deut 7:26

DETESTABLE
d and abominable things Jer 16:18
sanctuary with all thy **d** things Ezek 5:11
their **d** things therein Ezek 7:20
all the **d** things thereof Ezek 11:18
nor with their **d** things Ezek 37:23

DEUEL doo´-el
same as REUEL (?) Num 1:14

DEVICE
wicked **d**, which he devised against Esth 9:25
let them be taken in the **d** Ps 10:2
maketh **d** of the people of none effect Ps 33:10
bringeth wicked **d** to pass Ps 37:7
be filled with their own **d** Prov 1:31
man of wicked **d** will he condemn Prov 12:2
many **d** in a man's heart Prov 19:21
no work, nor **d**, nor knowledge Eccl 9:10
will walk after our own **d** Jer 18:12
he shall forecast his **d** Dan 11:24
graven by art and man's **d** Acts 17:29
not ignorant of his **d** 2 Cor 2:11

DEVILISH
but is earthly, sensual, **d** James 3:15

DEVISE
d cunning works Ex 31:4; 35:35
to confusion that **d** my hurt Ps 35:4
He **d** mischief upon his bed Ps 36:4
against me do they **d** my hurt Ps 41:7
D not evil against thy neighbour Prov 3:29
he **d** mischief continually Prov 6:14
A heart that **d** wicked imaginations Prov 6:18
Do they not err that **d** evil Prov 14:22
man's heart **d** his way Prov 16:9
d wicked devices to destroy the poor Is 32:7
the liberal **d** liberal things Is 32:8
cunningly **d** fables 2 Pet 1:16

DEVOTE
as a field **d** Lev 27:21
a man shall **d** unto the LORD Lev 27:28
Every thing **d** in Israel Num 18:14
who is **d** to thy fear Ps 119:38

DEVOTIONS
beheld your **d** Acts 17:23

DEVOUR
Some evil beast hath **d** him Gen 37:20
thin ears **d** the seven rank Gen 41:7,24
d fire Ex 24:17; Is 29:6; 30:27,30; 33:14
fire from LORD **d** them Lev 10:2
d with burning heat Deut 32:24
sword **d** one as well as another 2 Sam 11:25
wood **d** more people than the sword **d** 2 Sam 18:8
fire out of his mouth **d** 2 Sam 22:9; Ps 18:8
death shall **d** his strength Job 18:13
beast of the field doth **d** it Ps 80:13
man who **d** that which is holy Prov 20:25
jaw teeth as knives, to **d** Prov 30:14
strangers **d** it in your presence Is 1:7
ye shall be **d** with the sword Is 1:20
your own sword hath **d** your prophets Jer 2:30
shame hath **d** the labour of our fathers Jer 3:24
that **d** thee shall be **d** Jer 30:16
fire shall **d** them Ezek 15:7
them through the fire to **d** them Ezek 23:37
it shall **d** palaces Hos 8:14; Amos 1:14; 2:2
A fire **d** before them Joel 2:3
the palmerworm **d** them Amos 4:9
d the man that is more righteous Hab 1:13
d by the fire of his jealousy Zeph 1:18
will rebuke the **d** for your sakes Mal 3:11
fowls came and **d** them Matt 13:4
d widows' houses Matt 23:14; Mark 12:40; Luke 20:47
which hath **d** thy living Luke 15:30
if a man **d** you 2 Cor 11:20
ye bite and **d** one another Gal 5:15
which shall **d** the adversaries Heb 10:27
seeking whom he may **d** 1 Pet 5:8

DEVOUT
just and **d** Luke 2:25
d men Acts 2:5; 8:2

DEW
let there be no **d** 2 Sam 1:21
we will light on him as the **d** falleth 2 Sam 17:12
there shall not be **d** nor rain 1 Kgs 17:1
who hath begotten the drops of **d**? Job 38:28
clouds drop down the **d** Prov 3:20
like a cloud of **d** in the heat of harvest Is 18:4
wet with the **d** of heaven Dan 4:15,23,33
as the early **d** it goeth away Hos 6:4
heaven over you is stayed from the **d** Hag 1:10

DIADEM
as a robe and a **d** Job 29:14
for a **d** of beauty Is 28:5
a royal **d** Is 62:3
Remove the **d** Ezek 21:26

DIAMOND
with the point of a **d** Jer 17:1
topaz, and the **d**, the beryl Ezek 28:13

DIANA di-an´-ah
Lat. for Gr. goddess Artemis Acts 19:24

DIBLAIM dib-la´-im
two cakes Hos 1:3

DIBLATH dib´-lath
same as RIBLAH (?) Ezek 6:14

DIBLATHAIM dib-lath-a´-im
same as DIBLAIM Num 33:46

DIBON di´-bon
wasting Num 21:30

DIBON-GAD di´-bon-gad
wasting of Gad Num 33:45

DIBRI dib´-ri
eloquent Lev 24:11

DID
he **d** not many mighty works Matt 13:58
all things that ever I **d** John 4:29
What **d** he to thee? John 9:26
works which none other man **d** John 15:24

DIDYMUS did´-im-us
twin John 11:16

DIE
surely **d** Gen 2:17; 20:7; 1 Sam 14:44; 22:16; 1 Kgs 2:37,42; Jer 26:8; Ezek 3:18; 33:8,14
lest ye **d** Gen 3:3; Lev 10:6; Num 18:32
before I **d** Gen 27:4; 45:28; Prov 30:7
smiteth a man, so that he **d** Ex 21:12
that **d** of itself Lev 7:24; 22:8; Deut 14:21
if these men **d** common death Num 16:29
Let me **d** the death of righteous Num 23:10
days approach that thou must **d** Deut 31:14
Where thou **d**, will I **d** Ruth 1:17
D Abner as a fool **d**? 2 Sam 3:33
shalt **d**, and not live 2 Kgs 20:1; Is 38:1
every man shall **d** for his own sin 2 Chr 25:4
curse God, and **d** Job 2:9
why **d** I not from the womb? Job 3:11
wisdom shall **d** with you Job 12:2
If a man **d**, shall he live again? Job 14:14
One **d** in his full strength Job 21:23
another **d** in the bitterness of his soul Job 21:25
I shall **d** in my nest Job 29:18
When shall he **d**, and his name perish? Ps 41:5
wise men **d**, likewise the fool Ps 49:10
when he **d** he shall carry nothing away Ps 49:17
He shall **d** without instruction Prov 5:23
fools **d** for want of wisdom Prov 10:21
d his expectation shall perish Prov 11:7
how **d** the wise man? Eccl 2:16
why shouldest thou **d** before thy time? Eccl 7:17
living know that they shall **d** Eccl 9:5
worm shall not **d** Is 66:24
why will ye **d**? Jer 27:13; Ezek 18:31; 33:11
this year thou shalt **d** Jer 28:16
thou shalt **d** in peace Jer 34:5
soul that sinneth, it shall **d** Ezek 18:4,20
no pleasure in death of him that **d** Ezek 18:32
wicked man shall **d** in his iniquity Ezek 33:8
they shall **d** Amos 6:9
sinners of my people shall **d** Amos 9:10
better for me to **d** than to live Jon 4:3,8
let him **d** the death Matt 15:4; Mark 7:10
woman **d** also Matt 22:27; Mark 12:22; Luke 20:32
d with thee Matt 26:35; Mark 14:31
ready to **d** Luke 7:2
that the beggar **d** Luke 16:22
can they **d** any more Luke 20:36
come down ere my child **d** John 4:49
my brother had not **d** John 11:21,32
even this man should not have **d** John 11:37
that one man **d** for the people John 18:14
that Jesus should **d** for that nation John 11:51
of wheat fall into the ground and **d** John 12:24
by our law he ought to **d** John 19:7
she was sick, and **d** Acts 9:37
to **d** at Jerusalem Acts 21:13
I refuse not to **d** Acts 25:11
for a righteous man will one **d** Rom 5:7
sin revived, and I **d** Rom 7:9
It is Christ that **d** Rom 8:34
no man **d** to himself Rom 14:7
Christ both **d**, rose, and revived Rom 14:9
for whom Christ **d** Rom 14:15; 1 Cor 8:11
Christ **d** for our sins 1 Cor 15:3
as in Adam all **d** 1 Cor 15:22
I **d** daily 1 Cor 15:31
not quickened, except it **d** 1 Cor 15:36
if one **d** for all 2 Cor 5:14
to **d** is gain Phil 1:21
we believe that Jesus **d** 1 Thess 4:14
Who **d** for us, that 1 Thess 5:10
here men that **d** receive tithes Heb 7:8
appointed unto men once to **d** Heb 9:27
These all **d** in faith Heb 11:13
that are ready to **d** Rev 3:2
shall desire to **d** Rev 9:6
the dead which **d** in the Lord Rev 14:13

DIET
there was a continual **d** Jer 52:34

DIFFER
gifts **d** according to the grace Rom 12:6
maketh thee to **d** from another 1 Cor 4:7
one star **d** from another I Cor 15:41
d nothing from a servant Gal 4:1

DIFFERENCE
put **d** between holy and unholy Lev 10:10
d between the unclean and the clean Lev 11:47
they have put no **d** between Ezek 22:26
put no **d** between us Acts 15:9
for there is no **d** Rom 3:22; 10:12

DIG
d a pit, and not cover it Ex 21:33
wells **d** Deut 6:11; Neh 9:25
thou mayest **d** brass Deut 8:9
ye **d** a pit for your friend Job 6:27
In the dark they **d** Job 24:16
d it, and is fallen Ps 7:15
they have **d** a pit Ps 57:6
hole of the pit whence ye are **d** Is 51:1
and **d** a winepress Matt 21:33
d in the earth, and hid Matt 25:18
till I shall **d** about it Luke 13:8
I cannot **d**, to beg I am ashamed Luke 16:3

DIGNITY
Folly set in great **d** Eccl 10:6
speak evil of **d** 2 Pet 2:10; Jude 1:8

DIKLAH dik´-lah
a palm tree Gen 10:27

DILEAN dil´-e-an
cucumber field (?) Josh 15:38

DILIGENCE
Keep thy heart will all **d** Prov 4:23
Do thy **d** to come shortly 2 Tim 4:9
I gave all **d** Jude 1:3

DILIGENT
take **d** heed to do the commandment Josh 22:5
accomplish a **d** search Ps 64:6
seek **d** till she find it Luke 15:8
taught **d** the things of the Lord Acts 18:25
he sought me out very **d** 2 Tim 1:17
Looking **d** lest any man fail Heb 12:15

DIM
his eye was not **d** Deut 34:7
eye also is **d** by reason of sorrow Job 17:7
gold become **d** Lam 4:1

DIMINISH
nor **d** ought from it Deut 4:2
Wealth gotten by vanity shall be **d** Prov 13:11
d of them the riches of Gentiles Rom 11:12

DIMNAH dim´-nah
dunghill Josh 21:35

DIMON di´-mon
same as DIBON Is 15:9

DIMONAH di-mo´-nah
same as DIBON (?) Josh 15:22

DINAH di´-nah
vindicated Gen 30:21

DINAITES di´-na-ites
the Armenian people Ezra 4:9

DINE
men shall **d** with me Gen 43:16
besought him to **d** Luke 11:37
when they had **d** John 21:15

DINHABAH din´-ha-bah
an Edomite city Gen 36:32

DINNER
a **d** of herbs Prov 15:17
I have prepared my **d** Matt 22:4
first washed before **d** Luke 11:38
makest a **d** or a supper Luke 14:12

DIONYSIUS di´-o-nis´-yus
belonging to Dionysus Acts 17:34

DIOTREPHES di-ot´-ref-ees
nourished by Zeus 3 John 1:9

DIP
priest shall **d** his finger Lev 4:6,17
d thy morsel in vinegar Ruth 2:14
d it in a honeycomb 1 Sam 14:27
d himself seven times in Jordan 2 Kgs 5:14
d his hand with me in the dish Matt 26:23
when he had **d** the sop John 13:26
a vesture **d** in blood Rev 19:13

DIRECT
he hath not **d** his words Job 32:14
He **d** it under the whole heaven Job 37:3
in the morning will I **d** my prayer Ps 5:3
O that my ways were **d** to keep Ps 119:5
he shall **d** thy paths Prov 3:6
of the perfect shall **d** his way Prov 11:5
the LORD **d** his steps Prov 16:9
as for the upright, he **d** his way Prov 21:29

wisdom is profitable to **d** Eccl 10:10
Who hath **d** the Spirit of the LORD Is 40:13
not in man that walketh to **d** his steps Jer 10:23
d your hearts into the love of God 2 Thess 3:5

DIRECTION
by the **d** of the lawgiver Num 21:18

DIRECTLY
her blood **d** before the tabernacle Num 19:4
the way **d** before the wall Ezek 42:12

DIRT
the **d** came out Judg 3:22
the **d** in the streets Ps 18:42
waters cast up mire and **d** Is 57:20

DISALLOWED
if her father **d** her Num 30:5
her husband **d** her on the day Num 30:8
a living stone, **d** indeed of men 1 Pet 2:4

DISANNUL
who shall **d** it? Is 14:27
no man **d**, or addeth Gal 3:15

DISAPPOINT
He **d** the devices Job 5:12
d him, cast him down Ps 17:13
Without counsel purposes are **d** Prov 15:22

DISCERN
can I **d** between good and evil? 2 Sam 19:35
that I may **d** between good and bad 1 Kgs 3:9
understanding to **d** judgment 1 Kgs 3:11
could not **d** the noise Ezra 3:13
could not **d** the form thereof Job 4:16
Cannot my taste **d** perverse things Job 6:30
I **d** among the youths Prov 7:7
wise man's heart **d** Eccl 8:5
cannot **d** between right Jon 4:11
d between the righteous and the wicked Mal 3:18
d the face of the sky Matt 16:3; Luke 12:56
they are spiritually **d** 1 Cor 2:14
not **d** the Lord's body 1 Cor 11:29
to another **d** of spirits 1 Cor 12:10
a **d** of the thoughts and intents Heb 4:12
exercised to **d** both good and evil Heb 5:14

DISCHARGE
cause them to be **d** there 1 Kgs 5:9
no **d** in that war Eccl 8:8

DISCIPLE
seal the law among my **d** Is 8:16
called unto him his twelve **d** Matt 10:1; Luke 6:13
d is not above his master Matt 10:24; Luke 6:40
in the name of a **d** Matt 10:42
thy **d** do that which is not lawful Matt 12:2
Why do thy **d** transgress the tradition Matt 15:2
to thy **d**, and they could not cure Matt 17:16
the **d** rebuked them Matt 19:13
took the twelve **d** apart Matt 20:17
sent out unto him their **d** Matt 22:16
passover with my **d** Mark 14:14; Luke 22:11
Likewise also said all the **d** Matt 26:35
all the **d** forsook him and fled Matt 26:56
tell his **d** that he is risen Matt 28:7
Say ye, his **d** came by night Matt 28:13
Why do the **d** of John Mark 2:18; Luke 5:33
he expounded all things to his **d** Mark 4:34
d eat bread with defiled Mark 7:2
walk not thy **d** according to tradition? Mark 7:5
Pharisees murmured against his **d** Luke 5:30
lifted up his eyes on his **d** Luke 6:20
as John also taught his **d** Luke 11:1
cannot be my **d** Luke 14:26,27,33
d began to rejoice and praise God Luke 19:37
Master, rebuke thy **d** Luke 19:39
his **d** believed on him John 2:11
Jesus himself baptized not, but his **d** John 4:2
his **d** were gone away alone John 6:22
many of his **d** went back John 6:66
thy **d** also may see the works John 7:3
then are ye my **d** indeed John 8:31
will ye also be his **d**? John 9:27
Thou art his **d**, we are Moses' **d** John 9:28
began to wash the **d** feet John 13:5
so shall ye be my **d** John 15:8
that **d** was known John 18:15
one of this man's **d**? John 18:17
a **d** of Jesus, but secretly for fear John 19:38
told the **d** she had seen the Lord John 20:18
d whom Jesus loved John 21:7,20
that that **d** should not die John 21:23
This is the **d** which testifieth John 21:24
slaughter against the **d** Acts 9:1
to join himself to the **d** Acts 9:26
d were called Christians first Acts 11:26
d came together to break bread Acts 20:7
to draw away **d** after them Acts 20:30
old **d**, with whom we should lodge Acts 21:16

DISCIPLINE
their ear to **d** Job 36:10

DISCLOSE
the earth also shall **d** her blood Is 26:21

DISCOMFITED
Lord **d** Sisera Judg 4:15
and **d** all the host Judg 8:12
lightning, and **d** them 2 Sam 22:15
his young men shall be **d** Is 31:8

DISCOMFITURE
there was a very great **d** 1 Sam 14:20

DISCONTENTED
every one that was **d** 1 Sam 22:2

DISCONTINUE
shalt **d** from thine heritage Jer 17:4

DISCORD
he soweth **d** Prov 6:14

DISCOURAGE
d ye the heart of the children of Israel? Num 32:7
fear not, neither be **d** Deut 1:21
our brethren have **d** our heart Deut 1:28
lest they be **d** Col 3:21

DISCOVER
we will **d** ourselves unto them 1 Sam 14:8
foundations of the world **d** 2 Sam 22:16; Ps 18:15
he **d** deep things Job 12:22
Who can **d** the face of his garment? Job 41:13
d not a secret to another Prov 25:9
your transgressions are **d** Ezek 21:24

DISCREET
d and wise Gen 41:33,39
he answered **d** Mark 12:34
To be **d**, chaste Titus 2:5

DISCRETION
guide his affairs with **d** Ps 112:5
which is without **d** Prov 11:22
instruct him to **d**, and doth teach Is 28:26
stretched out the heavens by his **d** Jer 10:12

DISDAINED
saw David, and **d** him 1 Sam 17:42
have **d** to set with the dogs Job 30:1

DISEASE
none of these **d** on thee Ex 15:26
upon thee all the **d** of Egypt Deut 28:60
recover of this **d** 2 Kgs 1:2; 8:8,9
in his **d** he sought not the Lord 2 Chr 16:12
By the great force of my **d** Job 30:18
who healeth all thy **d** Ps 103:3
vanity, and it is an evil **d** Eccl 6:2
d have ye not strengthened Ezek 34:4
pushed all the **d** with your horns Ezek 34:21

DISFIGURE
for they **d** their faces Matt 6:16

DISGRACE
do not **d** the throne of thy glory Jer 14:21

DISGUISE
d himself 1 Sam 28:8; 2 Chr 35:22
d thyself, that thou be not known 1 Kgs 14:2
I will **d** myself 1 Kgs 22:30; 2 Chr 18:29
d his face Job 24:15

DISH
butter in a lordly **d** Judg 5:25
as a man wipeth a **d** 2 Kgs 21:13
with me in the **d** Matt 26:23
that dippeth with me in the **d** Mark 14:20

DISHAN di´-shan
antelope (?) Gen 36:21

DISHON di´-shon
antelope (?) Gen 36:21

DISHONESTY
hidden things of **d** 2 Cor 4:2

DISHONOUR (n)
clothed with shame and **d** Ps 35:26
covered with reproach and **d** Ps 71:13
A wound and **d** shall he get Prov 6:33
one vessel to honour, another to **d** Rom 9:21
sown in **d** 1 Cor 15:43
by honour and **d** 2 Cor 6:8
some to honour, and some to **d** 2 Tim 2:20

DISHONOUR (v)
son **d** the father Mic 7:6
ye do **d** me John 8:49

DISINHERIT
d them, and will make Num 14:12

DISMAYED
fear not, neither be **d** Deut 31:8
nor be **d** Josh 10:25; 1 Chr 22:13; 2 Chr 20:17; Jer 23:4; Ezek 2:6
neither be thou **d** Josh 1:9; 8:1
be not afraid nor **d** 2 Chr 32:7
the heathen are **d** at them Jer 10:2
let them be **d**, but let not me be **d** Jer 17:18

DISMISSED
the priest **d** not the courses 2 Chr 23:8
when they were **d**, they came Acts 15:30
he **d** the assembly Acts 19:41

DISOBEDIENCE
by one man's **d** many Rom 5:19
the children of **d** Eph 2:2; 5:6
every transgression and **d** Heb 2:2

DISOBEDIENT
the **d** to the wisdom of the just Luke 1:17
not **d** unto the heavenly vision Acts 26:19
d to parents Rom 1:30; 2 Tim 3:2
for the lawless and **d** 1 Tim 1:9
ourselves were sometimes foolish, **d** Titus 3:3
unto them which be **d** 1 Pet 2:7
which sometime were **d** 1 Pet 3:20

DISORDERLY
every brother that walketh **d** 2 Thess 3:6
behaved not ourselves **d** among you 2 Thess 3:7
which walk among you **d**, working 2 Thess 3:11

DISPERSE
lips of the wise **d** knowledge Prov 15:7
will he go unto the **d**? John 7:35

DISPLAYED
that it may be **d** because Ps 60:4

DISPLEASE
it **d** the Lord Num 11:1
if it **d** thee, I will get me back Num 22:34
that David had done **d** the Lord 2 Sam 11:27

father had not **d** him at any time 1 Kgs 1:6
thou hast been **d** Ps 60:1
Lest the LORD see it, and it **d** him Prov 24:18
it **d** him that there was no judgment Is 59:15
it **d** Jonah exceedingly Jon 4:1
they were sore **d** Matt 21:15
he was much **d** Mark 10:14
much **d** with James and John Mark 10:41

DISPLEASURE
I was afraid of the anger and hot **d** Deut 9:19
though I do them a **d** Judg 15:3
vex them in his sore **d** Ps 2:5
hot **d** Ps 6:1; 38:1

DISPOSE
who hath **d** the whole world Job 34:13
know when God **d** them Job 37:15
but the **d** of thereof Prov 16:33
be **d** to go 1 Cor 10:27

DISPOSITION
received the law by the **d** of angels Acts 7:53

DISPOSSESS
ye shall **d** the inhabitants of the land Num 33:53
how can I **d** them Deut 7:17
the LORD God of Israel hath **d** the Judg 11:23

DISPUTATION
no small dissension and **d** with them Acts 15:2
but not to doubtful **d** Rom 14:1

DISPUTE
the righteous might **d** with him Job 23:7
that ye **d** of by the way Mark 9:33

DISPUTER
where is the **d** of this world? 1 Cor 1:20

DISQUIET
Why hast thou **d** me 1 Sam 28:15
why art thou **d** in me? Ps 42:5
d within me Ps 42:11; 43:5

DISSEMBLE
have also stolen, and **d** Josh 7:11
He that **d** with his lips Prov 26:24
ye **d** in your hearts Jer 42:20
the other Jews **d** likewise with him Gal 2:13

DISSENSION
had no small **d** and disputation Acts 15:2
there arose **d** between Acts 23:7

DISSIMULATION
Let love be without **d** Rom 12:9
carried away with their **d** Gal 2:13

DISSOLVE
host of heaven shall be **d** Is 34:4
make interpretations, and **d** doubts Dan 5:16
earthly house of this tabernacle were **d** 2 Cor 5:1
all these things shall be **d** 2 Pet 3:11
heavens being on fire shall be **d** 2 Pet 3:12

DISTAFF
her hands hold the **d** Prov 31:19

DISTIL
my speech shall **d** as the dew Deut 32:2
clouds do drop and **d** upon man Job 36:28

DISTINCTION
except they give a **d** 1 Cor 14:7

DISTINCTLY
book in the law of God **d** Neh 8:8

DISTRACT
suffer thy terrors I am **d** Ps 88:15
upon the Lord without **d** 1 Cor 7:35

DISTRESS
therefore is this **d** come upon us Gen 42:21
when ye are in **d**? Judg 11:7
every one in **d** 1 Sam 22:2
In my **d** I called 2 Sam 22:7; Ps 18:6
I called upon the LORD in **d** Ps 118:5; 120:1
redeemed my soul out of all **d** 1 Kgs 1:29
in the time of his **d** 2 Chr 28:22
Ye see the **d** that we are in Neh 2:17
out of their **d** Ps 107:6,13,19,28
when **d** and anguish cometh Prov 1:27
a strength to the needy in his **d** Is 25:4
day of **d** Obad 1:12,14
shall be great **d** in the land Luke 21:23
upon the earth **d** of nations Luke 21:25
tribulation, or **d**, or persecution Rom 8:35
good for the present **d** 1 Cor 7:26
in **d** 2 Cor 6:4; 12:10

DISTRIBUTE
office was to **d** unto their brethren Neh 13:13
God **d** sorrows in his anger Job 21:17
and **d** unto the poor Luke 18:22
given thanks, he **d** John 6:11
d to the necessity of the saints Rom 12:13
as God hath **d** to every man 1 Cor 7:17
your liberal **d** 2 Cor 9:13

DITCH
fallen into the **d** which he made Ps 7:15
both shall fall into the **d** Matt 15:14

DIVERS
sow thy vineyard with **d** seeds Deut 22:9
garment of **d** sorts Deut 22:11
not have in thy bag **d** weights Deut 25:13
d measures, a great and a small Deut 25:14
D weights, and **d** measures Prov 20:10,23
d diseases Matt 4:24; Mark 1:34; Luke 4:40
in **d** places Matt 24:7; Mark 13:8; Luke 21:11
for **d** of them came from far Mark 8:3
to another **d** kinds of tongues 1 Cor 12:10
led away with **d** lusts 2 Tim 3:6
fall into **d** temptations James 1:2

DIVERSE
laws are **d** from all people Esth 3:8

DIVERSITIES
d of operations 1 Cor 12:6

DIVIDE
d not the hoof Lev 11:4,5,6; Deut 14:7
an end of **d** the land Josh 19:49
D the living child in two 1 Kgs 3:25
innocent shall **d** they silver Job 27:17
d the spoil Ps 68:12; Prov 16:19; Is 9:3; 53:12
thy land shall be **d** by the line Amos 7:17
kingdom **d** Matt 12:25; Luke 11:17
d against himself Matt 12:26; Luke 11:18
that he **d** inheritance with me Luke 12:13
who made me a judge or a **d**? Luke 12:14
five in one house **d** Luke 12:52
father shall be **d** against the son Luke 12:53
he **d** unto them his living Luke 15:12
multitude of the city was **d** Acts 14:4
Is Christ **d**? 1 Cor 1:13
d to every man severally as he will 1 Cor 12:11
rightly **d** word of truth 2 Tim 2:15
piercing to the **d** asunder Heb 4:12

DIVINATION
neither is there any **d** against Israel Num 23:23
damsel possessed with a spirit of **d** Acts 16:16

DIVINE (adj)
A **d** sentence Prov 16:10
ordinances of **d** service Heb 9:1
his **d** power 2 Pet 1:3
partakers of the **d** nature 2 Pet 1:4

DIVINE (v)
a man as I can certainly **d**? Gen 44:15
d unto me by the familiar spirit 1 Sam 28:8
see vanity, and that **d** lies Ezek 13:9
they **d** a lie unto thee Ezek 21:29
prophets thereof **d** for money Mic 3:11

DIVINER
called for the priests and the **d** 1 Sam 6:2
maketh **d** mad Is 44:25
your **d** Jer 27:9; 29:8

DIVISION
will put a **d** between my people Ex 8:23
For the **d** of Reuben Judg 5:15
I tell you, Nay; but rather **d** Luke 12:51
d among the people because of him John 7:43
There was a **d** John 10:19
mark them which cause **d** Rom 16:17

DIZAHAB di´-za-hab
a place abounding in gold (?) Deut 1:1

DO
I will **d** Ruth 3:5
to **d** good in his life Eccl 3:12
I will also **d** it Is 46:11
what shall I **d** unto thee? Hos 6:4
men should **d** to you, **d** ye even so Matt 7:12
they say, and **d** not Matt 23:3
this **d,** and thou shalt live Luke 10:28
this **d** in remembrance Luke 22:19; 1 Cor 11:24
without me ye can **d** nothing John 15:5
what I would, that **d** I not Rom 7:15
what I **d,** that I will **d** 2 Cor 11:12
ye cannot **d** the things that ye would Gal 5:17
I can **d** all things through Christ Phil 4:13
with whom we have to **d** Heb 4:13

DOCTRINE
I give you good **d** Prov 4:2
make to understand **d** Is 28:9
the stock is a **d** of vanities Jer 10:8
teaching for **d** the commandments Matt 15:9; Mark 7:7
the **d** of the Pharisees Matt 16:12
new **d** Mark 1:27; Acts 17:19
shall know of the **d** John 7:17
continued stedfastly in the apostles' **d** Acts 2:42
filled Jerusalem with your **d** Acts 5:28
that form of **d** Rom 6:17
contrary to the **d** Rom 16:17
hath a **d** 1 Cor 14:26
every wind of **d** Eph 4:14
contrary to sound **d** 1 Tim 1:10
in the words of faith and good **d** 1 Tim 4:6
to reading, to exhortation, to **d** 1 Tim 4:13
take heed to thyself and unto the **d** 1 Tim 4:16
hast fully known my **d** 2 Tim 3:10
is profitable for **d** 2 Tim 3:16
exhort with all longsuffering and **d** 2 Tim 4:2
sound **d** both to exhort and to convince Titus 1:9
things which become sound **d** Titus 2:1
in **d** shewing uncorruptness Titus 2:7
adorn the **d** of God our Saviour Titus 2:10
principles of the **d** Heb 6:1
the **d** of baptisms Heb 6:2
carried about with divers and strange **d** Heb 13:9
abideth in the **d** of Christ 2 John 1:9

DODAI do´-da-i
loving 1 Chr 27:4

DODANIM do´-dan-im
a tribe related to JAVAN Gen 10:4

DODAVAH do´-dav-ah
love of Jehovah 2 Chr 20:37

DODO do´-do
same as DODAI 2 Sam 23:9

DOEG do´-eg
anxious 1 Sam 21:7

DOG
shall not a **d** move Ex 11:7
or the price of **d**, into the house Deut 23:18
as a **d** lappeth Judg 7:5
Am I a **d**? 1 Sam 17:43
upon such a dead **d** as I am 2 Sam 9:8
what, is thy servant a **d**? 2 Kgs 8:13
set with the **d** of my flock Job 30:1
darling from power of the **d** Ps 22:20
a noise like a **d** Ps 59:6
As a **d** returneth Prov 26:11
like one that taketh a **d** by the ears Prov 26:17
living **d** is better than a dead lion Eccl 9:4
they are all dumb **d** Is 56:10
as if he cut off a **d** neck Is 66:3
Give not that which is holy unto **d** Matt 7:6
the **d** eat of the crumbs Matt 15:27
Beware of **d** Phil 3:2
without are **d** Rev 22:15

DOING
fearful in praises, **d** wonders Ex 15:11
ceased not from their own **d** Judg 2:19
churlish and evil in his **d** 1 Sam 25:3
Arise therefore, and be **d** 1 Chr 22:16
I am **d** a great work Neh 6:3
terrible in his **d** toward the children Ps 66:5
talk of thy **d** Ps 77:12
the Lord's **d** Ps 118:23; Matt 21:42; Mark 12:11
shall find so **d** Matt 24:46; Luke 12:43
went about **d** good Acts 10:38
patient continuance in well **d** Rom 2:7
perform the **d** of it 2 Cor 8:11
weary in well **d** Gal 6:9; 2 Thess 3:13
d the will of God from the heart Eph 6:6
with well **d** ye may put to silence 1 Pet 2:15
suffer for well **d** 1 Pet 3:17
souls to him in well **d** 1 Pet 4:19

DOLEFUL
full of **d** creatures Is 13:21
lament with a **d** lamentation Mic 2:4

DOMINION
when thou shalt have the **d** Gen 27:40
shalt thou indeed have **d** over us? Gen 37:8
come he that shall have **d** Num 24:19
D and fear are with him Job 25:2
Canst thou set the **d** thereof? Job 38:33
d over the works of thy hands Ps 8:6
let them not have **d** over me Ps 19:13
d also from sea to sea Ps 72:8
let not any iniquity have **d** over me Ps 119:133
have had **d** over us Is 26:13
d is an everlasting **d** Dan 4:34; 7:14
princes of the Gentiles exercise **d** Matt 20:25
death hath no more **d** Rom 6:9
sin shall not have **d** Rom 6:14
law hath **d** over a man Rom 7:1
that we have **d** over your faith 2 Cor 1:24
and power, and might, and **d** Eph 1:21
whether they be thrones, or **d** Col 1:16

DOOR
sin lieth at the **d** Gen 4:7
every man at tent **d** Ex 33:8
took the **d** of the gate Judg 16:3
laid wait at neighbour's **d** Job 31:9
I opened my **d** to the traveller Job 31:32
the **d** of the shadow of death Job 38:17
Who can open the **d** of his face? Job 41:14
ye everlasting **d** Ps 24:7
opened the **d** of heaven Ps 78:23
keep the **d** of my lips Ps 141:3
come not nigh the **d** of her house Prov 5:8
at the coming in at the **d** Prov 8:3
As the **d** turneth upon his hinges Prov 26:14
d shall be shut in the streets Eccl 12:4
posts of the **d** moved Is 6:4
shut thy **d** about thee Is 26:20
for a **d** of hope Hos 2:15
would shut the **d** for nought? Mal 1:10
when thou hast shut thy **d** Matt 6:6
near, even at the **d** Matt 24:33; Mark 13:29
and the **d** was shut Matt 25:10
d of the sepulchre Matt 27:60; Mark 15:46
city was gathered together at the **d** Mark 1:33
not so much as about the **d** Mark 2:2
hath shut to the **d** Luke 13:25
by the **d** John 10:1,2
I am the **d** John 10:7,9
Peter stood at the **d** without John 18:16
damsel that kept the **d** John 18:17
when the **d** were shut John 20:19,26
at the **d**, and shall carry thee out Acts 5:9
opened the **d** of faith Acts 14:27
great **d** and effectual 1 Cor 16:9
d was opened unto me of the Lord 2 Cor 2:12
open unto us a **d** of utterance Col 4:3
judge standeth before the **d** James 5:9
set before thee an open **d** Rev 3:8
I stand at the **d** and knock Rev 3:20
behold, a **d** was opened in heaven Rev 4:1

DOPHKAH dof'-kah
a knocking Num 33:12

DOR dor
dwelling Josh 11:2

DORCAS dor'-kas
gazelle Acts 9:36

DOTE
and they shall **d** Jer 50:36
she **d** on her lovers Ezek 23:5
d about questions and strifes of words 1 Tim 6:4

DOTHAN do'-than
two wells or cisterns Gen 37:17

DOUBLE
take **d** money in hand Gen 43:12
he shall restore **d** Ex 22:4
worth a **d** hired servant Deut 15:18
a **d** portion of thy spirit 2 Kgs 2:9
a **d** heart 1 Chr 12:33; Ps 12:2
d for all her sins Is 40:2
recompense their iniquity and their sin **d** Jer 16:18
worthy of **d** honour 1 Tim 5:17
purify your hearts, ye **d**-minded James 4:8

DOUBT
thy life shall hang in **d** Deut 28:66
No **d** but ye are the people Job 12:2
shall **d** come again with rejoicing Ps 126:6
dissolving of **d** Dan 5:12
wherefore didst thou **d**? Matt 14:31
If ye have faith, and **d** not Matt 21:21
shall not **d** in his heart Mark 11:23
no **d** kingdom of God is come Luke 11:20
How long dost thou make us to **d**? John 10:24
d of them whereunto this would grow Acts 5:24
no **d** this man is a murderer Acts 28:4
he that **d** is damned if he eat Rom 14:23
I stand in **d** of you Gal 4:20
without wrath and **d** 1 Tim 2:8
would no **d** have continued 1 John 2:19

DOVE
that I had wings like a **d** Ps 55:6
mourn sore like **d** Is 59:11
as the **d** to their windows Is 60:8
and harmless as **d** Matt 10:16
them that sold **d** Matt 21:12; Mark 11:15

DOWN
till sun be **d** 2 Sam 3:35
again take root **d** 2 Kgs 19:30; Is 37:31
Let them wander up and **d** Ps 59:15
I am tossed up and **d** Ps 109:23
spirit of the beast that goeth **d** Eccl 3:21
walk up and **d** in his name Zech 10:12

DOWRY
with a good **d** Gen 30:20
never so much **d** and gift Gen 34:12
money according to the **d** of virgins Ex 22:17
The king desireth not any **d** 1 Sam 18:25

DRAG
gather them in their **d** Hab 1:15
burn incense unto their **d** Hab 1:16
d the net with fishes John 21:8

DRAGON
Their wine is the poison of **d** Deut 32:33
before the **d** well Neh 2:13
I am a brother to **d** Job 30:29
the **d** shalt thou trample Ps 91:13
Praise the Lord from the earth, ye **d** Ps 148:7
the **d** and the owls Is 43:20
a den of **d** Jer 9:11
the **d**, that old serpent Rev 20:2

DRANK
nor **d** any water three days and three 1 Sam 30:12
and **d** of his own cup 2 Sam 12:3
and he **d** of the brook 1 Kgs 17:6
of the wine which he **d** Dan 1:5
They **d**, wine, and praised the gods Dan 5:4
and they all **d** of it Mark 14:23
they **d**, they married wives Luke 17:27
d thereof himself John 4:12
for they **d** of that spiritual Rock 1 Cor 10:4

DRAUGHT
is cast out into the **d** Matt 15:17
goeth out into the **d** Mark 7:19
let down your nets for a **d** Luke 5:4
d of the fishes which they had taken Luke 5:9

DRAVE (v)
they **d** them heavily Ex 14:25
d them out from before you Josh 24:12; Judg 6:9

DRAW
he can **d** up Jordan Job 40:23
Canst thou **d** out leviathan? Job 41:1
D me not away with wicked Ps 28:3
wicked have **d** out the sword Ps 37:14
yet were they **d** swords Ps 55:21
my life **d** nigh unto the grave Ps 88:3
nor years **d** nigh Eccl 12:1
d iniquity with cords Is 5:18
d water out of the wells of salvation Is 12:3
with lovingkindness have I **d** thee Jer 31:3
d nigh unto me with their mouth Matt 15:8
the time **d** near Luke 21:8
your redemption **d** nigh Luke 21:28
thou hast nothing to **d** with John 4:11
thirst not, neither come hither to **d** John 4:15
the Father which hath set me **d** him John 6:44
will **d** all men unto me John 12:32
d near with a true heart Heb 10:22
if any man **d** back Heb 10:38
D nigh to God, and he will **d** James 4:8

DRAWER
thy wood unto the **d** of thy water Deut 29:11
wood and **d** of water Josh 9:21

DREAD
How **d** is this place! Gen 28:17
begin to put the **d** of thee Deut 2:25
the fear of you and the **d** of you Deut 11:25
let him be your **d** Is 8:13
the great and **d** day Mal 4:5

DREAM (n)
shall fly away as a **d** Job 20:8
In a **d**, in a vision Job 33:15
As a **d** when one awaketh Ps 73:20

a **d** cometh through Eccl 5:3
prophet that hath a **d** Jer 23:28

DREAM (v)
we were like them that **d** Ps 126:1
old men shall **d** dreams Joel 2:28; Acts 2:17

DREGS
but the **d** thereof Ps 75:8
thou hast drunken the **d** of the cup Is 51:17

DRESS
to **d** it and to keep it Gen 2:15
plant vineyards, and **d** them Deut 28:39
poor man's lamb, and **d** it 2 Sam 12:4

DREW
time **d** nigh that Israel must die Gen 47:29
because I **d** him out of the water Ex 2:10
Joshua **d** not his hand back Josh 8:26
man **d** a bow 1 Kgs 22:34; 2 Chr 18:33
Jehu **d** a bow with his full strength 2 Kgs 9:24
d them with cords of a man Hos 11:4
she **d** not near to her God Zeph 3:2
when the time of the fruit **d** near Matt 21:34
Jesus himself **d** near Luke 24:15
and **d** away much people Acts 5:37

DRINK (n)
Do not drink strong wine or strong **d** Lev 10:9
separate himself from wine and strong **d** Num 6:3
sheep, or for wine, or for strong **d** Deut 14:26
strong **d** Deut 29:6; Prov 20:1; 31:4,6
strong **d** shall be bitter Is 24:9
through strong **d** are out of the way Is 28:7
of wine and of strong **d** Mic 2:11
that giveth his neighbour **d** Hab 2:15
ye are not filled with **d** Hag 1:6
thirsty, and ye gave me **d** Matt 25:35
a Jew, askest **d** of me John 4:9
my blood is **d** indeed John 6:55
if he thirst, give him **d** Rom 12:20
kingdom of God is not meat and **d** Rom 14:17
same spiritual **d** 1 Cor 10:4
judge you in meat, or in **d** Col 2:16

DRINK (v)
What shall we **d**? Ex 15:24
no water for the people to **d** Ex 17:1
he would not **d** thereof 2 Sam 23:16
David would not **d** of it 1 Chr 11:18
d of the river of thy pleasures Ps 36:8
d of the wine of astonishment Ps 60:3
givest them tears to **d** Ps 80:5
shall **d** of the brook in the way Ps 110:7
D waters of thine own cistern Prov 5:15
Lest they **d**, and forget the law Prov 31:5
let him **d**, and forget his poverty Prov 31:7
d thy wine with merry heart Eccl 9:7
mighty to **d** wine Is 5:22
my servants shall **d**, but ye Is 65:13
give them wine to **d** Jer 35:2
We will **d** no wine Jer 35:6
unto this day they **d** none Jer 35:14
Thou shalt **d** also water by measure Ezek 4:11
d the wine of the condemned Amos 2:8
they shall **d**, and make a noise Zech 9:15
whosoever shall give to **d** Matt 10:42
Are ye able to **d**? Matt 20:22
saying, **D** ye all of it Matt 26:27
when I **d** it new Matt 26:29
except I **d** it Matt 26:42
shall give you cup of water to **d** Mark 9:41
can ye **d** of the cup Mark 10:38
if they **d** any deadly thing Mark 16:18
not **d** of the fruit Luke 22:18
Give me to **d** John 4:10
let him come unto me, and **d** John 7:37
shall I not **d** it? John 18:11
nor to **d** wine, nor anything Rom 14:21
did all **d** the same spiritual drink 1 Cor 10:4
as oft as ye **d** it 1 Cor 11:25
made to **d** into one Spirit 1 Cor 12:13

DRIVE
thou has **d** me out Gen 4:14
which shall **d** out the Hivite Ex 23:28
shouldest be **d** to worship them Deut 4:19
They **d** away the ass of the fatherless Job 24:3
They were **d** forth from among men Job 30:5
wicked is **d** away in his wickedness Prov 14:32
rod of correction shall **d** it Prov 22:15
north wind **d** away rain Prov 25:23
the LORD did **d** them Jer 46:15
shall **d** thee from men Dan 4:25
he was **d** from the sons of men Dan 5:21
the chaff that is **d** with the whirlwind Hos 13:3
was **d** of the devil Luke 8:29
wave of the sea **d** with the wind James 1:6

DROP (n)
small **d** of water Job 36:27
nations are as a **d** of a bucket Is 40:15

DROP (v)
doctrine shall **d** as the rain Deut 32:2
my speech **d** upon them Job 29:22
thy paths **d** fatness Ps 65:11
heavens also **d** at the presence of God Ps 68:8
idleness of the hands the house **d** Eccl 10:18
D down ye heavens Is 45:8
d thy word toward the south Ezek 20:46

DROSS
Take away the **d** from the silver Prov 25:4
potsherd covered with silver **d** Prov 26:23
silver is become **d** Is 1:22
purely purge away thy **d** Is 1:25
Israel is to me become **d** Ezek 22:18

DROUGHT
satisfy thy soul in **d** Is 58:11
careful in the year of **d** Jer 17:8
in the land of great **d** Hos 13:5
called for a **d** upon the land Hag 1:11

DROVE (n)
betwixt **d** and **d** Gen 32:16
by all this **d** which I met Gen 33:8

DROVE (v)
he **d** out the man Gen 3:24
Abram **d** them away Gen 15:11
he **d** them all out of the temple John 2:15

DROWN
d men in destruction and perdition 1 Tim 6:9

DROWSINESS
and **d** shall clothe a man with rags Prov 23:21

DRUNK
he made him **d** 2 Sam 11:13
was drinking himself **d** 1 Kgs 20:16
stagger like a **d** man Job 12:25; Ps 107:27
I am like a **d** man Jer 23:9
We have **d** our water for money Lam 5:4
makest him **d** also Hab 2:15
drink with the **d** Matt 24:29
these are not **d** Acts 2:15
one is hungry, and another is **d** 1 Cor 11:21
that be **d** are **d** in the night 1 Thess 5:7

DRUNKARD
he is a glutton, and a **d** Deut 21:20
d and the glutton shall come to poverty Prov 23:21
thorn goeth up into the hand of a **d** Prov 26:9
d, nor revilers, nor extortioners, shall 1 Cor 6:10

DRUNKENNESS
to add **d** to thirst Deut 29:19
not for **d** Eccl 10:17
shall be filled with **d** Ezek 23:33

DRUSILLA droo´-sil-lah
watered by the dew Acts 24:24

DRY
a broken spirit **d** the bones Prov 17:22
floods upon the **d** ground Is 44:3
through **d** places Matt 12:43; Luke 11:24
fountain of her blood was **d** up Mark 5:29

DUE
it is thy **d**, and thy sons' **d** Lev 10:13
rain in **d** season Lev 26:4
rain of your land in his **d** season Deut 11:14
meat in **d** season Ps 104:27; 145:15; Matt 24:45; Luke 12:42
word spoken in **d** season Prov 15:23
pay all that was **d** Matt 18:34
the **d** reward of our deeds Luke 23:41
in **d** time Christ died Rom 5:6
in **d** season we shall reap Gal 6:9

DULL
d of hearing Matt 13:15; Acts 28:27; Heb 5:11

DUMAH doom´-ah
silence Gen 25:14

DUMB
who maketh the **d** Ex 4:11
Open thy mouth for the **d** Prov 31:8
the tongue of the **d** sing Is 35:6
as a sheep before her shearers is **d** Is 53:7
a lamb **d** before his shearer Acts 8:32
they are all **d** dogs Is 56:10
d, and shalt not be to them a reprover Ezek 3:26
to the **d** stone, Arise, it shall teach Hab 2:19
d man Matt 9:32
the **d** to speak Mark 7:37
which hath a **d** spirit Mark 9:17

DUNG
lifteth up the beggar from the **d**-hill 1 Sam 2:8
the needy out of the **d**-hill Ps 113:7
fit for land nor yet for the **d**-hill Luke 14:35
count them but **d** Phil 3:8

DUNGEON
captive that was in the **d** Ex 12:29
cast him into the **d** Jer 38:6
life in the **d**, and cast a stone Lam 3:53

DURA doo´-rah
town Dan 3:1

DURABLE
d riches and righteousness Prov 8:18
for **d** clothing Is 23:18

DURST
neither **d** any man from that day Matt 22:46
no man after that **d** ask him Mark 12:34
they **d** not ask him Luke 20:40
none of disciples **d** ask John 21:12

DUST
Lord God formed man of the **d** Gen 2:7
d shalt thou eat Gen 3:14
d thou art Gen 3:19
which am but **d** and ashes Gen 18:27
lay up gold as **d** Job 22:24
repent in **d** and ashes Job 42:6
shall the **d** praise thee? Ps 30:9
and favour the **d** thereof Ps 102:14
remembereth that we are **d** Ps 103:14
all are of the **d**, and turn to **d** again Eccl 3:20
comprehended the **d** of the earth Is 40:12
d shall be the serpent's meat Is 65:25
he putteth his mouth in the **d** Lam 3:29
that sleep in the **d** Dan 12:2
lick the **d** like a serpent Mic 7:17
shake off the **d** of your feet Matt 10:14
Even the very **d** of your city Luke 10:11
and threw **d** into the air Acts 22:23

DUTY
the whole **d** of man Eccl 12:13
that which was our **d** to do Luke 17:10
their **d** is also to minister Rom 15:27

DWELL
cause his name to **d** there Deut 12:11
d between the cherubims 1 Sam 4:4; 2 Sam 6:2; 1 Chr 13:6
will **d** in the house of the Lord Ps 23:6
so shalt thou **d** in the land Ps 37:3
than to **d** in tents of wickedness Ps 84:10
here will I **d** Ps 132:14
for brethren to **d** together in unity Ps 133:1
shall **d** with the devouring fire? Is 33:14
he shall **d** on high Is 33:16
I **d** in the high and holy place Is 57:15
d in me, and I in him John 6:56
the Father that **d** in me John 14:10
d with you, and shall be in you John 14:17
sin that **d** in me Rom 7:17
in him **d** all the fulness of Godhead Col 2:9
word of Christ **d** in you richly Col 3:16
d in the light 1 Tim 6:16
wherein **d** righteousness 2 Pet 3:13
how **d** the love of God in him? 1 John 3:17
God **d** in us 1 John 4:12

DYED
ram's skins **d** red Ex 25:5
with **d** garments from Bozrah Is 63:1
exceeding in **d** attire Ezek 23:15

DYING
the **d** of Lord Jesus 2 Cor 4:10
as **d**, and, behold, we live 2 Cor 6:9

E

EACH
e one walking in his uprightness Is 57:2
e day for a year Ezek 4:6
it sat upon **e** of them Acts 2:3
let **e** esteem other Phil 2:3

EAGLE
how I bare you on **e** wings Ex 19:4
were swifter than **e** 2 Sam 1:23
youth is renewed like the **e** Ps 103:5
mount up with wings as **e** Is 40:31
e be gathered Matt 24:28; Luke 17:37

EAR (n)
tell in the **e** of thy son Ex 10:2
e shall tingle 2 Kgs 21:12; Jer 19:3
Let thine **e** now be attentive Neh 1:6
Doth not the **e** try words? Job 12:11
heard the fame thereof with our **e** Job 28:22
the **e** heard me, then it blessed me Job 29:11
heard of thee by the hearing of the **e** Job 42:5
cry came before him, even into his **e** Ps 18:6
his **e** are open unto their cry Ps 34:15
like the deaf adder that stoppeth her **e** Ps 58:4
He that planted the **e**, shall he not hear? Ps 94:9
They have **e**, but they hear not Ps 115:6; 135:17
liar giveth **e** to a naughty tongue Prov 17:4
e, and the seeing eye, the Lord hath made Prov 20:12
wise reprover upon an obedient **e** Prov 25:12
one that taketh a dog by the **e** Prov 26:17
nor the **e** filled with hearing Eccl 1:8
nor his **e** heavy, that it cannot hear Is 59:1
your **e** receive the word of his mouth Jer 9:20
a piece of an **e** Amos 3:12
what ye hear in the **e**, that preach Matt 10:27
e are dull of hearing Matt 13:15; Acts 28:27
your **e**, for they hear Matt 13:16
smote off his **e** Matt 26:51
put his fingers into his **e** Mark 7:33
having **e**, hear ye not? Mark 8:18
uncircumcised in heart and **e** Acts 7:51
strange things to our **e** Acts 17:20
nor **e** heard 1 Cor 2:9
e shall say, Because I am not the eye 1 Cor 12:16
having itching **e** 2 Tim 4:3
entered into the **e** of the Lord James 5:4
his **e** are open unto their prayers 1 Pet 3:12

EAR (v)
in **e** time and in harvest Ex 34:21
which is neither **e** or sown Deut 21:4
will set them to **e** his ground 1 Sam 8:12

EARLY
and that right **e** Ps 46:5
e will I seek thee Ps 63:1
satisfy us **e** with thy mercy Ps 90:14
seek me **e** Prov 1:28; 8:17
get up **e** to the vineyards Song 7:12
as the **e** dew Hos 6:4; 13:3
the **e** and latter rain James 5:7

EARNEST
the **e** of the Spirit 2 Cor 1:22; 5:5
the **e** of our inheritance Eph 1:14
to my **e** expectation and my hope Phil 1:20

EARNESTLY
As a servant **e** desireth the shadow Job 7:2
I do **e** remember him still Jer 31:20
do evil with both hands **e** Mic 7:3
in an agony he prayed more **e** Luke 22:44
the **e** expectation of the creature Rom 8:19
covet **e** the best gifts 1 Cor 12:31
e desiring to be clothed 2 Cor 5:2
e contend for the faith Jude 1:3

EARNETH
he that **e** wages Hag 1:6

EARS (of corn)
pluck the **e** Deut 23:25; Matt 12:1

EARTH
While the **e** remaineth Gen 8:22
Judge of all the **e** do right? Gen 18:25
all the **e** shall be filled with glory Num 14:21
the **e** open her mouth Num 16:30
hear, O **e**, the words of my mouth Deut 32:1
Lord of all the **e** Josh 3:11; Zech 6:5
going the way of all the **e** Josh 23:14
will God indeed dwell on the **e**? 1 Kgs 8:27
appointed time to man upon **e** Job 7:1
e is given into hand of the wicked Job 9:24
hangeth the **e** upon nothing Job 26:7
when I laid foundations of the **e** Job 38:4
Upon **e** there is not his like Job 41:33
excellent is thy name in all the **e** Ps 8:1
to the saints that are in the **e** Ps 16:3
his seed shall inherit the **e** Ps 25:13
the **e** is full of the goodness Ps 33:5
shall inherit the **e** Ps 37:9,11,22
not we fear, though the **e** be removed Ps 46:2
uttered his voice, the **e** melted Ps 46:6
desolations he hath made in the **e** Ps 46:8
will be exalted in the **e** Ps 46:10
shields of the **e** belong to God Ps 47:9
joy of the whole **e** Ps 48:2
glory be above all the **e** Ps 57:5
a God that judgeth in the **e** Ps 58:11
made the **e** to tremble Ps 60:2
lower parts of the **e** Ps 63:9
visitest the **e**, and waterest it Ps 65:9
e yield her increase Ps 67:6; Ezek 34:27
e shook, the heavens also dropped Ps 68:8
showers that water the **e** Ps 72:6
handful of corn in the **e** Ps 72:16
tongue walketh through the **e** Ps 73:9
none upon **e** that I desire besides thee Ps 73:25
Most High over all the **e** Ps 83:18
let the **e** be moved Ps 99:1
laid the foundation of the **e** Ps 102:25; 104:5; Is 48:13
the **e** is satisfied Ps 104:13
the **e** is full of thy riches Ps 104:24
seed shall be mighty upon the **e** Ps 112:2
e hath he given to children of men Ps 115:16
stranger in the **e** Ps 119:19
established the **e**, and it abideth Ps 119:90
he returneth to his **e** Ps 146:4
glory is above the **e** and heaven Ps 148:13
LORD founded the **e** Prov 3:19
or ever the **e** was Prov 8:23
he had not made the **e**, nor fields Prov 8:26
righteous shall be recompensed in the **e** Prov 11:31
for three things the **e** is disquieted Prov 30:21
little upon the **e** Prov 30:24
beast goeth downward to the **e** Eccl 3:21
profit of the **e** is for all Eccl 5:9
dust return to **e** Eccl 12:7
fruit of the **e** shall be excellent Is 4:2
e shall be full of the knowledge of the Is 11:9
e shall remove out of her place Is 13:13
e is utterly broken down Is 24:19
e also shall disclose her blood Is 26:21
let the **e** hear Is 34:1
sitteth upon the circle of the **e** Is 40:22
Creator of the ends of the **e** fainteth not Is 40:28
spreadeth abroad the **e** by myself Is 44:24
the **e** shall wax old Is 51:6
the **e** is my footstool Is 66:1
Shall the **e** be made to bring forth Is 66:8
man of contention to the whole **e** Jer 15:10
O **e**, **e**, **e**, hear the word of the LORD Jer 22:29
hath created a new thing in the **e** Jer 31:22
made the **e** by his power Jer 51:15
The LORD hath forsaken the **e** Ezek 9:9
the **e** shined with his glory Ezek 43:2
the **e** shall hear the corn Hos 2:22
bird fall in a snare upon the **e** Amos 3:5
darken the **e** in the clear day Amos 8:9
least grain fall upon the **e** Amos 9:9
e with her bars was about me Jon 2:6
ye strong foundations of the **e** Mic 6:2
good man is perished out of the **e** Mic 7:2
worms of the **e** Mic 7:17
e is burned at his presence Nah 1:5
e shall be filled with knowledge Hab 2:14
the **e** full of his praise Hab 3:3
e is stayed from her fruit Hag 1:10
run to and fro through the whole **e** Zech 4:10
smite the **e** with a curse Mal 4:6
meek, for they shall inherit the **e** Matt 5:5
Nor by the **e**; for it is his footstool Matt 5:35
treasure upon **e** Matt 6:19
power on **e** to forgive Matt 9:6; Mark 2:10; Luke 5:24
to send peace on **e** Matt 10:34
not much **e** Matt 13:5; Mark 4:5
shalt bind on **e** Matt 16:19; 18:18
call no man your father upon the **e** Matt 23:9
e bringeth forth fruit of herself Mark 4:28
less than all the seeds that be in the **e** Mark 4:31
no fuller on **e** can white them Mark 9:3
on **e** peace Luke 2:14
darkness over all the **e** Luke 23:44
of **e** is earthly, and speaketh of the **e** John 3:31
lifted up from the **e** John 12:32
I have glorified thee on the **e** John 17:4
life is taken from the **e** Acts 8:33
fell to the **e** Acts 9:4
Away with such a fellow from **e** Acts 22:22
sound went into all the **e** Rom 10:18
treasure in **e** vessels 2 Cor 4:7
not on things on the **e** Col 3:2
e which drinketh in the rain Heb 6:7
if he were on **e** Heb 8:4
refused him that spake on **e** Heb 12:25
voice then shook the **e** Heb 12:26
lived in pleasure on the **e** James 5:5

and the **e** brought forth her fruit James 5:18
the **e** also, and the works 2 Pet 3:10
we shall reign on the **e** Rev 5:10
Hurt not the **e** Rev 7:3
e was lightened with his glory Rev 18:1

EARTHLY
of earth is **e**, and speaketh of the earth John 3:31
first man is of the earth, **e** 1 Cor 15:47
earth, such are they also that are **e** 1 Cor 15:48
the image of the **e** 1 Cor 15:49
who mind **e** things Phil 3:19
is **e**, sensual, devilish James 3:15

EARTHQUAKE
after the wind an **e** 1 Kgs 19:11
fled from before the **e** Zech 14:5
e, in divers places Matt 24:7

EASY
but knowledge is **e** unto him Prov 14:6
For my yoke is **e** Matt 11:30
words **e** to be understood 1 Cor 14:9
and **e** to be intreated James 3:17

EAT
in the day that thou **e** Gen 2:17:
blood thereof, shall ye not **e** Gen 9:4
might not **e** bread with Hebrews Gen 43:32
that the poor of the people may **e** Ex 23:11
shall not be **e**, because it is holy Ex 29:34
shall not **e** any thing with the blood Lev 19:26
What shall we **e** the seventh year? Lev 25:20
e of the old corn of the land Josh 5:11,12
if haply people had **e** freely 1 Sam 14:30
had **e** no bread all the day 1 Sam 28:20
e, that thou mayest have strength 1 Sam 28:22
Arise and **e** 1 Kgs 19:5
They shall **e**, and shall leave thereof 2 Kgs 4:43
give thy son, that we may **e** him 2 Kgs 6:28
that we may **e**, and live Neh 5:2
my sighing cometh before I **e** Job 3:24
e without salt Job 6:6
meek shall **e** and be satisfied Ps 22:26
hath **e** me up Ps 69:9; John 2:17
have **e** ashes like bread Ps 102:9
e of the fruit of their own way Prov 1:31
e to satisfying of his soul Prov 13:25
they that love it shall **e** the fruit Prov 18:21
sittest to **e** with a ruler Prov 23:1
e thou honey, because it is good Prov 24:13
not good to **e** much honey Prov 25:27
e his own flesh Eccl 4:5
increase, they are increased that **e** Eccl 5:11
whether he **e** little or much Eccl 5:12
all his days also he **e** in darkness Eccl 5:17
power to **e** thereof Eccl 5:19; 6:2
thy princes **e** in the morning Eccl 10:16
princes **e** in due season Eccl 10:17
We will **e** our own bread Is 4:1
Butter and honey shall he **e** Is 7:15
lion shall **e** straw like the ox Is 11:7
worm shall **e** them like wool Is 51:8
e ye that which is good Is 55:2
words were found, and I did **e** them Jer 15:16
figs, which could not be **e** Jer 24:2
the fathers have **e** sour grapes Jer 31:29; Ezek 18:2
e this roll Ezek 3:1
e shall be by weight Ezek 4:10
e grass as oxen Dan 4:33
e, and not have enough Hos 4:10
have **e** the fruit of lies Hos 10:13
e your master with publicans and Matt 9:11
ears of corn, and to **e** Matt 12:1
which was not lawful for him to **e** Matt 12:4
give ye them to **e** Matt 14:16; Mark 6:37; Luke 9:13
to **e** with unwashen hands Matt 15:20
dogs **e** of the crumbs Matt 15:27
have nothing to **e** Matt 15:32; Mark 8:1
to **e** and drink with the drunken Matt 24:49
no leisure so much as to **e** Mark 6:31
no man **e** fruit of thee Mark 11:14
e such things as are set before you Luke 10:8
take thine ease, **e**, drink Luke 12:19
we have **e** and drunk in thy presence Luke 13:26
let us **e**, and be merry Luke 15:23
That ye may **e** and drink at my table Luke 22:30
he took it, and did **e** before them Luke 24:43
Master, **e** John 4:31
meat to **e** that he know not of John 4:32
because ye did **e** of the loaves John 6:26
can this man give us his flesh to **e**? John 6:52
except ye **e** the flesh John 6:53
did **e** their meat with gladness Acts 2:46
did neither **e** nor drink Acts 9:9
will **e** nothing until we have slain Paul Acts 23:14
one believeth that he may **e** all things Rom 14:2
e to the Lord Rom 14:6
who **e** with offence Rom 14:20
neither to **e** flesh nor to drink wine Rom 14:21
with such a one, no, not to **e** 1 Cor 5:11
e it as a thing offered unto an idol 1 Cor 8:7
if we **e** are we the better 1 Cor 8:8
e no flesh while the world standeth 1 Cor 8:13
Have we not power to **e** and to drink? 1 Cor 9:4
all **e** the same spiritual meat 1 Cor 10:3
e, asking no question 1 Cor 10:27
Whether therefore ye **e** 1 Cor 10:31
he that **e** and drinketh unworthily 1 Cor 11:29
not work, neither should he **e** 2 Thess 3:10
whereof they have no right to **e** Heb 13:10
e of the tree of life Rev 2:7
will I give to **e** of the hidden manna Rev 2:17
e the flesh of kings Rev 19:18

EBAL e´-bal
stony (?) Gen 36:23

EBED e´-bed
servant Judg 9:26

EBED-MELECH e´-bed-me´-lek
servant of the king Jer 38:7

EBEN-EZER e´-ben-e´-zer
stone of help 1 Sam 4:1

EBER e´-ber
the region beyond Gen 10:21

EBIASAPH e-bi´-a-saf
same as ABIASAPH 1 Chr 6:23

EBRONAH eb-ro´-nah
passage (?) Num 33:34

ED ed
witness Josh 22:34

EDAR e´-dar
flock Gen 35:21

EDEN e´-den
pleasantness Gen 2:8

EDER e´-der
same as EDAR 1 Chr 23:23

EDGE
do not whet the **e** Eccl 10:10

EDIFICATION
please his neighbour for his good to **e** Rom 15:2
prophesieth speaketh unto men to **e** 1 Cor 14:3

EDIFY
wherewith one may **e** another Rom 14:19
charity **e** 1 Cor 8:1
but all things **e** not 1 Cor 10:23
e himself, but he that prophesieth **e** 1 Cor 14:4

EDOM e´-dom
red Gen 25:30

EDOMITES e´-dom-ites
inhabitants of Edom Gen 36:9

EDREI ed´-re-i
strong Num 21:33

EFFECT
of none **e** Num 30:8; Ps 33:10; Matt 15:6; Mark 7:13; 1 Cor 1:17; Gal 5:4
the **e** of righteousness, quietness Is 32:17

EFFECTUAL
a great door and **e** is opened 1 Cor 16:9
the **e** working Eph 3:7; 4:16
e fervent prayer of a righteous man James 5:16

EFFEMINATE
adulterers, or **e**, nor abusers of 1 Cor 6:9

EGG
taste in the white of an **e** Job 6:6
leaveth her **e** in the earth Job 39:14
if he shall ask an **e** Luke 11:12

EGLAH eg´-lah
heifer 2 Sam 3:5

EGLAIM eg-la´-im
two pools Is 15:8

EGLON eg´-lon
circle Judg 3:12

EGYPT e´-jipt
black Gen 12:10

EGYPTIAN e-jip´-shan
a native of Egypt 1 Sam 30:11

EHI e´-hi
shortened form of AHIRAM Gen 46:21

EHUD e´-hud
joined together (?) Judg 3:15

EITHER
speak not to Jacob **e** good or bad Gen 31:24
prosper, **e** this or that Eccl 11:6
e he will hate the one Matt 6:24; Luke 16:13
on **e** side one John 19:18
on **e** side the river Rev 22:2

EKER e´-ker
same as ACHAR 1 Chr 2:27

EKRON ek´-ron
eradication Josh 13:3

EKRONITES ek´-ron-ites
inhabitants of Ekron Josh 13:3

EL-BETH-EL el-beth´-el
the house of God Gen 35:7

EL-ELOHE-ISRAEL el´-el-o´-he-iz´-ra-el
God, the God of Israel Gen 33:20

EL-PARAN el´-par-an
oak of Paran Gen 14:6

ELADAH el´-a-dah
whom God clothes 1 Chr 7:20

ELAH e´-lah
terebinth Gen 36:41

ELAM e´-lam
high land Gen 10:22

ELAMITES e´-lam-ites
inhabitants of Elam Ezra 4:9

ELASAH el´-a-sah
whom God made Ezra 10:22

ELATH e´-lath
a grove Deut 2:8

ELDAAH el´-da-ah
whom God called Gen 25:4

ELDAD el´-dad
whom God loves Num 11:26

ELDER
before the **e** of my people 1 Sam 15:30
aged men, much **e** than thy father Job 15:10
they were **e** than he Job 32:4
sitteth among the **e** of the land Prov 31:23
tradition of the **e** Matt 15:2; Mark 7:3
e that rule well be counted worthy 1 Tim 5:17
ordain **e** in every city Titus 1:5
the **e** obtained a good report Heb 11:2
call for the **e** of the church James 5:14
The **e** which are among you I exhort 1 Pet 5:1
submit yourselves unto the **e** 1 Pet 5:5

ELEAD el´-e-ad
whom God praises 1 Chr 7:21

ELEALEH el´-e-a´-lay
whither God ascends Num 32:3

ELEASAH el-e´-a-sah
same as ELASAH 1 Chr 2:39

ELEAZAR el-e-a´-zar
whom God aids Ex 6:23

ELECT
mine **e**, in whom my soul delighteth Is 42:1
mine **e** I have even called thee by name Is 45:4
mine **e** shall inherit Is 65:9
for the **e** sake Matt 24:22; Mark 13:20
deceive very **e** Matt 24:24
gather together his **e** Matt 24:31; Mark 13:27
avenge his own **e** Luke 18:7
to the charge of God's **e** Rom 8:33
as the **e** of God Col 3:12
the **e** angels 1 Tim 5:21
E according to the foreknowledge 1 Pet 1:2
cornerstone, **e**, precious 1 Pet 2:6

ELECTION
purpose of God according to **e** Rom 9:11
according to the **e** of grace Rom 11:5
your **e** of God 1 Thess 1:4
make your calling and **e** sure 2 Pet 1:10

ELEMENTS
bondage under the **e** of the world Gal 4:3
weak and beggarly **e** Gal 4:9
the **e** shall melt with fervent heat 2 Pet 3:10

ELEPH e´-lef
ox Josh 18:28

ELEVEN
his **e** sons Gen 32:22
and the **e** stars made obeisance Gen 37:9
he was numbered with the **e** Acts 1:26

ELHANAN el´-ha´-nan
whom God gave 2 Sam 21:19

ELI e´-li
height 1 Sam 1:3

ELI
Eli, Eli, lama sabachthani? Matt 27:46

ELIAB el-i´-ab
whose father is God Num 1:9

ELIADA el´-i´-a-dah
whom God cares for 2 Sam 5:16

ELIADAH el´-i´-a-dah
same as ELIADA 1 Kgs 11:23

ELIAH el-i´-ah
same as ELIJAH 1 Chr 8:27

ELIAHBA el-i´-a-bah
whom God hides 2 Sam 23:32

ELIAKIM el-i´-a-kim
whom God establishes 2 Kgs 18:18

ELIAM el-i´-am
same as AMMIEL 2 Sam 11:3

ELIAS el-i´-as
same as ELIJAH John 1:21

ELIASAPH el-i´-a-saf
whom God added Num 1:14

ELIASHIB el-i´-a-shib
whom God restores 1 Chr 24:12

ELIATHAH el-i´-a-thah
to whom God comes 1 Chr 25:4

ELIDAD el-i´-dad
whom God loves Num 34:21

ELIEL el-i´-el
to whom God is strength 1 Chr 5:24

ELIENAI el´-i-e-na´-i
unto Jehovah my eyes are raised (?) 1 Chr 8:20

ELIEZER el´-i-e´-zer
my God is help Gen 15:2

ELIHOENAI el´-i-ho´-e-na´-i
same as ELIOENAI Ezra 8:4

ELIHOREPH el´-i-ho´-ref
to whom God is the reward 1 Kgs 4:3

ELIHU el-i´-hoo
whose God is He 1 Sam 1:1

ELIJAH el-i´-jah
my God is Jehovah 1 Kgs 17:1

ELIKA el-i´-kah
whom God purifies (?) 2 Sam 23:25

ELIM eel´-im
oaks Ex 15:27

ELIMELECH el-i´-me-lek
to whom God is king Ruth 1:2

ELIOENAI el´-i-o´-e-na´-i
unto Jehovah my eyes are turned 1 Chr 3:23

ELIPHAL el´-i-fal
whom God judges 1 Chr 11:35

ELIPHALET el-i´-fa-let
to whom God is salvation 2 Sam 5:16

ELIPHAZ el´-i-faz
to whom God is strength Gen 36:4

ELIPHELEH el-i´-fe-lay
whom God distinguishes 1 Chr 15:18

ELIPHELET el-i´-fe-let
same as ELIPHALET 1 Chr 3:8

ELISABETH el-iz´-a-beth
same as ELISHEBA Luke 1:5

ELISEUS el-i´-se-us
same as ELISHA Luke 4:27

ELISHA el-i´-shah
to whom God is salvation 1 Kgs 19:16

ELISHAH el-i´-shah
God saves Gen 10:4

ELISHAMA el-i´-sha-mah
whom God hears Num 1:10

ELISHAPHAT el-i´-sha-fat
whom God judges 2 Chr 23:1

ELISHEBA el-i´-she-ba
to whom God is the oath Ex 6:23

ELISHUA el-i´-shoo´-ah
same as ELISHA 2 Sam 5:15

ELIUD el-i´-ood
God of Judah Matt 1:14

ELIZAPHAN el-i´-za-fan
whom God protects Num 3:30

ELIZUR el-i´-zoor
God is a rock Num 1:5

ELKANAH el´-ka´-nah
whom God possessed Ex 6:24

ELKOSHITE el´-kosh-ite
inhabitant of Elkosh Nah 1:1

ELLASAR el´-as-ar
a city of Mesopotamia Gen 14:1

ELMODAM el-mo´-dam
same as ALMODAD Luke 3:28

ELNAAM el´-na-am
whose pleasure God is 1 Chr 11:46

ELNATHAN el-na´-than
whom God gave 2 Kgs 24:8

ELOI
Eloi, Eloi, lama sabachthani? Mark 15:34

ELON e´-lon
oak Gen 26:34

ELON-BETH-HANAN e´-lon-beth´-ha´-nan
oak of the house of grace 1 Kgs 4:9

ELONITES e´-lon-ites
descendants of Elon Num 26:26

ELOQUENT
I am not **e** Ex 4:10
and the **e** orator Is 3:3
an **e** man, and mighty Acts 18:24

ELOTH e´-loth
same as ELATH 1 Kgs 9:26

ELPAAL el´-pa-al
to whom God is the reward 1 Chr 8:11

ELPALET el´-pa-let
same as ELIPHALET 1 Chr 14:5

ELTEKEH el´-te-kay
whose fear is God Josh 19:44

ELTEKON el´-te-kon
whose foundation is God Josh 15:59

ELTOLAD el´-to-lad
whose posterity is from God Josh 15:30

ELUL e´-lool
the sixth month of the year Neh 6:15

ELUZAI el´-oo-za´-i
God is my praises 1 Chr 12:5

ELYMAS el´-im-as
a wise man Acts 13:8

ELZABAD el´-za-bad
whom God gave 1 Chr 12:12

ELZAPHAN el´-za-fan
whom God protects Ex 6:22

EMBOLDEN
what **e** thee that thou answerest Job 16:3
which is weak be **e** to eat 1 Cor 8:10

EMBRACE
e the rock for want of a shelter Job 24:8
a time to **e** Eccl 3:5
were persuaded of them, and **e** them Heb 11:13

EMBROIDER
shalt **e** the coat of fine linen Ex 28:39
workman, and of the **e** Ex 35:35
an **e** n blue Ex 38:23

EMIMS eem´-ims
terrible men Gen 14:5

EMINENT
thine **e** place Ezek 16:24,31,39
high mountain an **e** Ezek 17:22

EMMANUEL em-an´-u-el
same as IMMANUEL Matt 1:23

EMMAUS em-a´-us
hot springs (?) Luke 24:13

EMMOR em´-or
same as HAMOR Acts 7:16

EMPIRE
be published throughout all his **e** Esth 1:20

EMPLOY
to **e** them in the siege Deut 20:19
were **e** in that work day and night 1 Chr 9:33
were **e** about this matter Ezra 10:15

EMPTY
sent me away now **e** Gen 31:42
ye shall not go **e** Ex 3:21
appear before me **e** Ex 23:15; 34:20
not let him go away **e** Deut 15:13
Thou hast sent widows away **e** Job 22:9
clouds **e** themselves on the earth Eccl 11:3
awaketh, and his soul is **e** Is 29:8
e from vessel to vessel Jer 48:11
the emptiers have **e** them out Nah 2:2
come, he findeth it **e** Matt 12:44

EMULATION
I may provoke to **e** Rom 11:14
hatred, variance, **e**, wrath Gal 5:20

ENDOR en´-dor
fountain of Dor Josh 17:11

EN-EGLAIM en´-eg-la´-im
fountain of two calves Ezek 47:10

EN-GANNIM en-gan´-im
fountain of gardens Josh 15:34

EN-GEDI en´-ged-i
fountain of the kid Josh 15:62

EN-HADDAH en-had´-ah
fountain of sharpness (swift) Josh 19:21

EN-HAKKORE en´-hak-o´-ree
fountain of him that calleth Judg 15:19

EN-HAZOR en-ha´-zor
fountain of the village Josh 19:37

EN-MISHPAT en-mish´-pat
fountain of judgment Gen 14:7

EN-RIMMON en´-rim´-on
fountain of the pomegranate Neh 11:29

EN-ROGEL en´-ro´-gel
fountain of the fuller Josh 15:7

EN-SHEMESH en´-she´-mesh
fountain of the sun Josh 15:7

EN-TAPPUAH en´-tap-oo´-ah
fountain of the apple tree Josh 17:7

ENABLED
who hath **e** me 1 Tim 1:12

ENAM e´-nam
two fountains Josh 15:34

ENAN e´-nan
having eyes Num 1:15

ENCAMP
Though a host should **e** against me Ps 27:3
angel of the LORD **e** round Ps 34:7

ENCOUNTERED
Stoics, **e** him Acts 17:18

ENCOURAGE
e him Deut 1:38; 3:28
They **e** themselves in an evil matter Ps 64:5

END
The **e** of all flesh is come before me Gen 6:13
in the **e** of the year Ex 23:16; Deut 11:12
let my last **e** be like his! Num 23:10
do thee good at thy latter **e** Deut 8:16
consider their latter **e** Deut 32:29
what is mine **e**, that I should prolong Job 6:11
thy latter **e** should greatly increase Job 8:7
Shall vain words have an **e**? Job 16:3
until the day and night come to an **e** Job 26:10
wickedness of the wicked come to an **e** Ps 7:9
destructions are come to a perpetual **e** Ps 9:6
the **e** of that man is peace Ps 37:37
make me to know mine **e** Ps 39:4
then understood I their **e** Ps 73:17
the same, and thy years have no **e** Ps 102:27
are at their wit's **e** Ps 107:27
an **e** of all perfection Ps 119:96
the **e** thereof are the ways of death Prov 14:12
in the **e** of the earth Prov 17:24
be wise in thy latter **e** Prov 19:20
lest thou know not what to do in the **e** Prov 25:8
from the beginning to the **e** Eccl 3:11
no **e** of all his labour Eccl 4:8
no **e** of all the people Eccl 4:16
that is the **e** of all men Eccl 7:2
Better is the **e** of a thing Eccl 7:8
the **e** of his talk is mischievous Eccl 10:13
of making many books there is no **e** Eccl 12:12
government and peace there shall be no **e** Is 9:7
Declaring the **e** from the beginning Is 46:10
what will ye do in the **e** thereof? Jer 5:31
the summer is **e** Jer 8:20
at his **e** shall be a fool Jer 17:11
to give you an expected **e** Jer 29:11
there is hope in thine **e** Jer 31:17
remembereth not her last **e** Lam 1:9
e is come Lam 4:18; Ezek 7:2
iniquity shall have an **e** Ezek 21:25
at the time of the **e** Dan 8:17
come to his **e**, and none shall help him Dan 11:45
What shall be the **e** of these things? Dan 12:8
go thou thy way till the **e** be Dan 12:13
at the **e** it shall speak Hab 2:3
endureth to the **e** Matt 10:22; Mark 13:13
the **e** of the world Matt 13:39; 24:3
the **e** is not yet Matt 24:6
then shall the **e** come Matt 24:14
gather from one **e** of heaven Matt 24:31
to see the **e** Matt 26:58
with you always, even unto the **e** Matt 28:20
cannot stand, but hath an **e** Mark 3:26
of his kingdom there shall be no **e** Luke 1:33
things concerning me have an **e** Luke 22:37
he loved them unto the **e** John 13:1
To this **e** was I born John 18:37
the **e** of those things is death Rom 6:21
the **e** everlasting life Rom 6:22
the **e** of the law for righteousness Rom 10:4
Whose **e** is destruction Phil 3:19
the **e** of the commandment 1 Tim 1:5
whose **e** is to be burned Heb 6:8
an **e** of all strife Heb 6:16
neither beginning of days nor **e** of life Heb 7:3
once in the **e** of the world Heb 9:26
the **e** of their conversation Heb 13:7
have seen the **e** of the Lord James 5:11
Receiving the **e** of your faith 1 Pet 1:9
be sober, and hope to the **e** 1 Pet 1:13
the **e** of all things is at hand 1 Pet 4:7
the **e** be of them that obey not 1 Pet 4:17
keepeth my works unto the **e** Rev 2:26
the beginning and the **e** Rev 21:6; 22:13

ENDANGER
cleaveth wood shall be **e** thereby Eccl 10:9
make me **e** my head to the king Dan 1:10

ENDEAVOUR
wickedness of their **e** Ps 28:4
E to keep the unity Eph 4:3
I will **e** 2 Pet 1:15

ENDLESS
fables and **e** geneaologies 1 Tim 1:4
power of an **e** life Heb 7:16

ENDUE
God hath **e** me with a good dowry Gen 30:20
e with prudence and understanding 2 Chr 2:12
until ye be **e** with power Luke 24:49
e with knowledge James 3:13

ENDURE
the children be able to **e** Gen 33:14
how can I **e** to see the evil Esth 8:6
hold it fast, but it shall not **e** Job 8:15
I could not **e** Job 31:23
LORD shall **e** for ever Ps 9:7; 104:31
weeping may **e** for a night Ps 30:5
goodness of God **e** continually Ps 52:1
as long as the sun and moon **e** Ps 72:5
His name shall **e** for ever Ps 72:17
his truth **e** to all generations Ps 100:5
his mercy **e** for ever Ps 106:1; 107:1; 118:1; 136:1; Jer 33:11
his righteousness **e** for ever Ps 111:3; 112:3,9
every one of thy righteous judgments **e** Ps 119:160
Thy name, O LORD, **e** for ever Ps 135:13
thy dominion **e** Ps 145:13
doth the crown **e** to every generation Prov 27:24
Can thine heart **e** Ezek 22:14
e to the end Matt 10:22; 24:13; Mark 13:13
root in himself, but **e** for a while Matt 13:21
so **e** but for a time Mark 4:17
meat which **e** unto everlasting life John 6:27
e with much longsuffering Rom 9:22
e all things 1 Cor 13:7
e hardness, as good soldier 2 Tim 2:3
they will not **e** sound doctrine 2 Tim 4:3
watch thou in all things, **e** afflictions 2 Tim 4:5
in heaven a better and an **e** substance Heb 10:34
If ye **e** chastening Heb 12:7
Blessed is the man that **e** temptation James 1:12
we count them happy which **e** James 5:11
the word of the Lord **e** for ever 1 Pet 1:25
conscience toward God **e** grief 1 Pet 2:19

ENEMY
I will be an **e** to thine **e** Ex 23:22
our **e** themselves being judges Deut 32:31
turned their backs before their **e** Josh 7:12
so let all thy **e** perish Judg 5:31
if a man find his **e**, will he let him go 1 Sam 24:19
Hast thou found me, O mine **e**? 1 Kgs 21:20
holdest me for thine **e**? Job 13:24
still the **e** and the avenger Ps 8:2
in the presence of mine **e** Ps 23:5
mine **e** are lively Ps 38:19
a strong tower from the **e** Ps 61:3
his **e** shall lick the dust Ps 72:9
wiser than mine **e** Ps 119:98
speak with the **e** in the gate Ps 127:5
I count them mine **e** Ps 139:22
maketh even his **e** to be at peace Prov 16:7
Rejoice not when thine **e** falleth Prov 24:17
kisses of an **e** are deceitful Prov 27:6
join his **e** together Is 9:11
When the **e** shall come in like a flood Is 59:19
he was turned to be their **e** Is 63:10
cause the **e** to entreat thee well Jer 15:11
wounded thee with the wound of an **e** Jer 30:14
man's **e** are the men of his own house Mic 7:6
hate thine **e** Matt 5:43
But I say unto you, Love your **e** Matt 5:44
his **e** sowed tares Matt 13:25
thine **e** shall cast a trench Luke 19:43
thou **e** of all righteousness Acts 13:10
if, when we were **e**, we were reconciled Rom 5:10
concerning the gospel, they are **e** Rom 11:28
If thine **e** hunger, feed him Rom 12:20
Am I therefore become your **e** Gal 4:16
the **e** of the cross Phil 3:18
e in your mind Col 1:21

count him not as an **e** 2 Thess 3:15
friend of the world is the **e** of God James 4:4

ENGAGED
who is this that **e** his heart Jer 30:21

ENGRAFTED
receive with meekness the **e** word James 1:21

ENGRAVE
I will **e** the graving Zech 3:9
written and **e** in stones 2 Cor 3:7

ENGRAVER
work of an **e** in stone Ex 28:11
all manner of work, of the **e** Ex 35:35
an **e**, and a cunning **e** Ex 38:23

ENJOY
e her sabbaths Lev 26:34; 2 Chr 36:21
e pleasure Eccl 2:1
soul **e** good Eccl 2:24
giveth us richly all things to **e** 1 Tim 6:17

ENLARGE
when the LORD shall **e** thy border Deut 12:20
thou hast **e** me Ps 4:1
troubles of heart are **e** Ps 25:17
when thou shalt **e** my heart Ps 119:32
hell hath **e** herself Is 5:14
our heart is **e** 2 Cor 6:11
we shall be **e** 2 Cor 10:15

ENLIGHTEN
of the LORD is pure, **e** the eyes Ps 19:8
eyes of your understaind being **e** Eph 1:18
those who were once **e** Heb 6:4

ENMITY
carnal mind is **e** Rom 8:7
having abolished in his flesh the **e** Eph 2:15
the world is **e** with God James 4:4

ENOCH **e´-nok**
experienced (?) Gen 4:17

ENOS **e´-nos**
man Gen 4:26

ENOSH **e´-nosh**
same as ENOS 1 Chr 1:1

ENOUGH
I have **e**, Gen 33:9,11
It is **e**, Gen 45:28; 2 Sam 24:16; 1 Kgs 19:4; 1 Chr 21:15; Mark 14:41; Luke 22:38
people bring much more than **e** Ex 36:5
shall have poverty **e** Prov 28:19
dogs which can never have **e** Is 56:11
will destroy till they have **e** Jer 49:9
eat, and not have **e** Hos 4:10
stolen till they had **e** Obad 1:5
room **e** to receive it Mal 3:10
e for the disciple Matt 10:25
lest there be not **e** Matt 25:9

ENRICH
king will **e** him 1 Sam 17:25
thou greatly **e** it Ps 65:9
thou didst **e** the kings Ezek 27:33
ye are **e** by him 1 Cor 1:5
Being **e** in every thing 2 Cor 9:11

ENSAMPLE
happened unto them for **e** 1 Cor 10:11
as ye have us for an **e** Phil 3:17
to make ourselves an **e** 2 Thess 3:9

ENSIGN
they set up their **e** Ps 74:4
lift up an **e** to the nations Is 5:26
which shall stand for an **e** Is 11:10
when he lifteth up an **e** Is 18:3
as an **e** on a hill Is 30:17

ENSNARED
lest the people be **e** Job 34:30

ENSUE
seek peace, and **e** it 1 Pet 3:11

ENTANGLE
They are **e** in the land Ex 14:3
how they might **e** him Matt 22:15
be not **e** again with the yoke of bondage Gal 5:1

ENTER
e into his gates with thanksgiving Ps 100:4
nation which keepeth the truth may **e** Is 26:2
e thou into thy chambers Is 26:20
mark well the **e** in of the house Ezek 44:5
prayest, **e** into thy closet Matt 6:6
E ye in at the strait gate Matt 7:13; Luke 13:24
better for thee to **e** into life Matt 18:8; Mark 9:43
if thou wilt **e** into life, keep Matt 19:17
e thou into the joy of thy lord Matt 25:21
we may **e** into the swine Mark 5:12
lest ye **e** into temptation Mark 14:38; Luke 22:46
feared as they **e** into the cloud Luke 9:34
what city ye **e** Luke 10:8,10
will seek to **e** Luke 13:24
can he **e** the second time John 3:4
ye are **e** into their labours John 4:38
e not by the door John 10:1
sin **e** into the world Rom 5:12
neither have **e** into the heart of man 1 Cor 2:9
shall not **e** into my rest Heb 3:11
he that is **e** into his rest Heb 4:10
forerunner is for us **e** Heb 6:20

ENTICE
E thy husband, that he may declare Judg 14:15
LORD said, Who shall **e** Ahab 2 Chr 18:19
if sinners **e** thee Prov 1:10

ENTIRE
that ye may be perfect and **e** James 1:4

ENTRANCE
The **e** of thy words giveth light Ps 119:130
so an **e** shall be ministered 2 Pet 1:11

ENTRY
keepers of the **e** 1 Chr 9:19
at the **e** of the city Prov 8:3
image of jealousy in the **e** Ezek 8:5
the chambers and the **e** Ezek 40:38

ENVIOUS
I was **e** at the foolish Ps 73:3
Be not thou **e** against evil men Prov 24:1,19

ENVIRON
shall **e** us around Josh 7:9

ENVY (n)
who is able to stand before **e**? Prov 27:4
e slayeth the silly one Job 5:2
e the rottenness of the bones Prov 14:30
and their **e** is now perished Eccl 9:6
for **e** they had delivered Matt 27:18
patriarchs, moved with **e** Acts 7:9
they were filled with **e** Acts 13:45; 17:5
full of **e**, murder Rom 1:29
preach Christ even of **e** Phil 1:15
whereof cometh **e** 1 Tim 6:4
living in malice and **e** Titus 3:3
spirit that dwelleth in us lusteth to **e** James 4:5

ENVY (v)
E thou not the oppressor Prov 3:31
let not thine heart **e** sinners Prov 23:17
for this a man is **e** of his neighbour Eccl 4:4
charity **e** not 1 Cor 13:4

ENVYING
not in strife and **e** Rom 13:13

among you **e**, and strife 1 Cor 3:3
lest there be debates, **e**, wraths 2 Cor 12:20
E, murders, drunkenness Gal 5:21

EPAENETUS **e-pe´-net-us**
laudable Rom 16:5

EPAPHRAS **ep´-af-ras**
a form of EPAPHRODITUS (?) Col 1:7

EPAPHRODITUS **ep-af´-ro-di´-tus**
handsome Phil 2:25

EPENETUS **e-pe´-net-us**
same as EPAENETUS Rom 16:5

EPHAI **e´-fa´-i**
languishing Jer 40:8

EPHER **e´-fer**
calf Gen 25:4

EPHES-DAMMIM **e´-fez-dam´-im**
boundary of blood 1 Sam 17:1

EPHESIANS **e-fe´-zi-ans**
inhabitants of Ephesus Acts 19:28

EPHESUS **ef´-es-us**
desirable Acts 18:19

EPHLAL **ef´-lal**
judgment 1 Chr 2:37

EPHPHATHA **ef´-ath-ah**
be opened Mark 7:34

EPHRAIM **ef´-ra-im**
fruitful (?) Gen 41:52

EPHRAIMITES **ef´-ra-im-ites**
inhabitants of Ephraim Judg 12:4

EPHRAIN **ef-ra´-in**
same as EPHRON 2 Chr 13:19

EPHRATH **ef´-rath**
short for EPHRATAH Gen 35:16

EPHRATAH **ef´-rat-ah**
fruitful (?) Ruth 4:11

EPHRATHITES **ef´-rath-ites**
inhabitants of Ephrath Ruth 1:2

EPHRON **ef´-ron**
of, or belonging to a calf Gen 23:8

EPICUREANS **ep´-ik-u-re´-ans**
followers of Epicurus Acts 17:18

EPISTLE
e of commendation to you 2 Cor 3:1
Ye are our **e** 2 Cor 3:2
to be the **e** of Christ 2 Cor 3:3
by word, or our **e** 2 Thess 2:15
obey not our word by this **e** 2 Thess 3:14
As also in all his **e** 2 Pet 3:16

EQUAL
eyes behold the things that are **e** Ps 17:2
a man mine **e**, my guide Ps 55:13
legs of the lame are not **e** Prov 26:7
or shall I be **e**? Is 40:25
Is not my way **e**? Ezek 18:25
their way is not **e** Ezek 33:17,20
hast made them **e** to us Matt 20:12
are **e** unto the angels Luke 20:36
e with God John 5:18; Phil 2:6
that which is just and **e** Col 4:1

EQUITY
the people with **e** Ps 98:9
judgment, and **e** Prov 1:3; 2:9
nor to strike princes for **e** Prov 17:26
in wisdom, and in knowledge, and in **e** Eccl 2:21

ER **er**
watchful Gen 38:3

ERAN **e´-ran**
one who watches Num 26:36

ERANITES e´-ran-ites
descendants of Eran Num 26:36

ERASTUS e-rast´-us
beloved Acts 19:22

ERECH e´-rek
length Gen 10:10

ERECTED
he e there an altar Gen 33:20

ERI e´-ri
same as ER Gen 46:16

ERITES er´-ites
descendants of Eri Num 26:16

ERR
people that do e in their heart Ps 95:10
do e from thy commandments Ps 119:21
lead thee cause thee to e Is 3:12
they e in vision Is 28:7
though fools, shall not e Is 35:8
e, not knowing the scriptures Matt 22:29
have e from the faith 1 Tim 6:10
have e concerning the faith 1 Tim 6:21
do not e, my beloved brethren James 1:16
if any do e from the truth James 5:19

ERRAND
until I have told mine e Gen 24:33
I have a secret e unto thee Judg 3:19

ERROR
Who can understand his e? Ps 19:12
it was an e Eccl 5:6
an e which proceedeth from the ruler Eccl 10:5
last e shall be worse than the first Matt 27:64
converteth the sinner from the e James 5:20
led away with the e of the wicked 2 Pet 3:17
the spirit of e 1 John 4:6

ESAIAS e´-sai-as
same as ISAIAH Matt 3:3

ESARHADDON e´-sar-had´-on
Ashur giveth a brother 2 Kgs 19:37

ESAU e´-saw
hairy Gen 25:25

ESCAPE
E for thy life Gen 19:17
let not one of them e 1 Kgs 18:40
thou shalt e in king's house Esth 4:13
they shall not e Job 11:20
e with the skin of my teeth Job 19:20
speaketh lies shall not e Prov 19:5
whoso pleaseth God shall e Eccl 7:26
how shall we e? Is 20:6
one that had e Ezek 33:21
that e of them shall not be delivered Amos 9:1
how can ye e the damnation of hell? Matt 23:33
worthy to e Luke 21:36
he e out of their hands John 10:39
they e all safe to land Acts 27:44
he e sea, yet vengeance Acts 28:4
How shall we e, if we neglect Heb 2:3
of fire, e the edge of sword Heb 11:34
if they e not who refused Heb 12:25
e corruption in the world 2 Pet 1:4
after they have e pollutions 2 Pet 2:20

ESCHEW
feared God and e evil Job 1:1
Let him e evil, and do good Pet 3:11

ESEK e´-sek
strife Gen 26:20

ESH-BAAL esh´-ba´-al
man of Baal 1 Chr 8:33

ESHBAN esh´-ban
reason, intelligence Gen 36:26

ESHCOL esh´-kol
cluster Gen 14:13

ESHEAN esh´-e-an
support (?) Josh 15:52

ESHEK e´-shek
oppression 1 Chr 8:39

ESHKALONITES esh´-ka-lon-ites
men of Ashkalon Josh 13:3

ESHTAOL esh´-ta-ol
petition (?) Josh 15:33

ESHTAULITES esh-ta´-ool-ites
inhabitants of Eshtaol 1 Chr 2:53

ESHTEMOA esh´-tem-o´-ah
obedience Josh 21:14

ESHTEMOH esh´-te-mo
same as ESHTEMOA Josh 15:50

ESHTON esht´-on
womanly 1 Chr 4:11

ESLI es´-li
same as AZALIAH (?) Luke 3:25

ESPECIALLY
men, e unto them who are Gal 6:10
e they who labour in the word 1 Tim 5:17
but e the parchments 2 Tim 4:13

ESPOUSE
I have e you to one husband 2 Cor 11:2

ESROM es´-rom
same as HEZRON Matt 1:3

ESTABLISH
and e my goings Ps 40:2
e work of our hands Ps 90:17
let thy ways be e Prov 4:26
lip of truth e for ever Prov 12:19
throne e by righteousness Prov 16:12
every purpose e by counsel Prov 20:18
by understanding is house e Prov 24:3
king by judgment e the land Prov 29:4
if ye will not believe, ye shall not be e Is 7:9
in mercy shall the throne be e Is 16:5
he e the world by his wisdom Jer 10:12; 51:15
every word may be e Matt 18:16
yea, we e the law Rom 3:31
to e their own righteousness Rom 10:3
the heart be e with grace Heb 13:9
be e in the present truth 2 Pet 1:12

ESTATE
remembered us in low e Ps 136:23
lo, I am come to great e Eccl 1:16
Herod made supper to chief e Mark 6:21
condescend to men of low e Rom 12:16
angels kept not first e Jude 1:6

ESTEEM
lightly e the Rock of his salvation Deut 32:15
despise me shall be lightly e 1 Sam 2:30
I am a poor man, and lightly e 1 Sam 18:23
I have e the words of his mouth Job 23:12
Will he e thy riches? Job 36:19
he e iron as straw Job 41:27
I e all thy precepts Ps 119:128
did e him smitten Is 53:4
e as earthen pitchers Lam 4:2
highly e among men Luke 16:15
one man e one day above another Rom 14:5
that e any thing unclean Rom 14:14
let each e other better Phil 2:3
e highly for work's sake 1 Thess 5:13
E the reproach of Christ greater riches Heb 11:26

ESTHER es´-ther
star Esth 2:7

ESTIMATE
the priest shall e it Lev 27:14

ESTIMATION
for the LORD by thy e Lev 27:2
according to thine e Num 18:16

ESTRANGED
mine acquaintance are verily e from me Job 19:13
They were not e from their lust Ps 78:30
forsaken me, and have e this place Jer 19:4
because they are all e from me Ezek 14:5

ETAM e´-tam
a place of ravenous creatures Judg 15:8

ETERNAL
the e God is thy refuge Deut 33:27
will make thee an e excellency Is 60:15
righteous into life e Matt 25:46
is in danger of e damnation Mark 3:29
that I may inherit e life? Mark 10:17; Luke 10:25; 18:18
in the world to come e life Mark 10:30
not perish, but have e life John 3:15
gathereth fruit unto life e John 4:36
in them ye think ye have e life John 5:39
drinketh my blood, hath e life John 6:54
thou hast the words of e life John 6:68
give unto them e life John 10:28
shall keep it unto life e John 12:25
give e life to as many John 17:2
this is life e, that they might know thee John 17:3
many as were ordained to e life Acts 13:48
and honour and immortality, e life Rom 2:7
reign through righteousness unto e life Rom 5:21
gift of God is e life Rom 6:23
and e weight of glory 2 Cor 4:17
things which are not seen are e 2 Cor 4:18
e in the heavens 2 Cor 5:1
According to the e purpose Eph 3:11
lay hold on e life 1 Tim 6:12,19
In hope of e life Titus 1:2; 3:7
author of e salvation Heb 5:9
e judgment Heb 6:2
promise of e inheritance Heb 9:15
called us unto his e glory by Christ 1 Pet 5:10
e life, which was with the Father 1 John 1:2
hath promised us, even e life 1 John 2:25
no murderer hath e life 1 John 3:15
that God hath given to us e life 1 John 5:11
know that ye have e life 1 John 5:13
This is the true God, and e life 1 John 5:20
vengeance of e fire Jude 1:7

ETERNITY
lofty One that inhabiteth e Is 57:15

ETHAM e´-tham
boundary of the sea (?) Ex 13:20

ETHAN e´-than
firmness 1 Kgs 4:31

ETHANIM eth´-an-im
incessant rains 1 Kgs 8:2

ETHBAAL eth-ba´-al
living with Baal 1 Kgs 16:31

ETHER e´-ther
plenty Josh 15:42

ETHIOPIA e´-thi-ope´-yah
(region of) *burnt faces* Gen 2:13

ETHIOPIAN e´-thi-ope´-yan
a native of Ethiopia Jer 13:23

ETHNAN eth´-nan
a gift 1 Chr 4:7

ETHNI eth´-ni
bountiful 1 Chr 6:41

EUBULUS eu-bew´-lus
good counselor 2 Tim 4:21

EUNICE eu-ni´-see
blessed with victory 2 Tim 1:5

EUODIAS eu-ode´-yas
success Phil 4:2

EUPHRATES eu-fra´-tes
the fertile river (?) Gen 2:14

EUROCLYDON eu-rok´-ly-don
strong wind from the northeast Acts 27:14

EUTYCHUS eu´-tyk-us
fortunate Acts 20:9

EVANGELIST
into the house of Philip the e Acts 21:8
some, e; and some, pastors Eph 4:11
do the work of an e 2 Tim 4:5

EVE ev
life Gen 3:20

EVENING
that eateth any food until e 1 Sam 14:24
bread and flesh in the e 1 Kgs 17:6
in the e it is cut down, and withereth Ps 90:6
to his labour until the e Ps 104:23
prayer as the e sacrifice Ps 141:2
in the e withhold not thine hand Eccl 11:6
shadows of the e are stretched out Jer 6:4
e wolves Hab 1:8; Zeph 3:3
at e time it shall be light Zech 14:7
the e was come, he was there alone Matt 14:23
it is toward e Luke 24:29

EVENT
one e happeneth to them all Eccl 2:14
there is one e to the righteous Eccl 9:2
there is one e to all Eccl 9:3

EVER
fire shall e be burning upon the altar Lev 6:13
he is e merciful, and lendeth Ps 37:26
our God for ever and e Ps 48:14
my sin is e before me Ps 51:3
trust in the mercy of God for ever and e Ps 52:8
so shall we e be with the Lord 1 Thess 4:17
e follow that which is good 1 Thess 5:15
e learning 2 Tim 3:7
he e liveth to make Heb 7:25

EVERLASTING
an e priesthood Ex 40:15; Num 25:13
from e to e, thou art God Ps 90:2
lead me in the way e Ps 139:24
I was set up from e Prov 8:23
righteous is an e foundation Prov 10:25
the e Father Is 9:6
in the LORD JEHOVAH is e strength Is 26:4
with e burnings Is 33:14
e joy Is 35:10; 51:11; 61:7
with an e salvation Is 45:17
with e kindness Is 54:8
for an e sign Is 55:13
an e name Is 56:5; 63:12
an e light Is 60:19
with an e love Jer 31:3
the e mountains Hab 3:6
into e fire Matt 18:8; 25:41
inherit e life Matt 19:29
into e punishment Matt 25:46
into e habitations Luke 16:9
in the world to come e life Luke 18:30
but have e life John 3:16,36
water springing up into e life John 4:14
hath e life John 5:24
meat which endureth to e life John 6:27
may have e life John 6:40
his commandment is life e John 12:50
unworthy of e life Acts 13:46
the end e life Rom 6:22
Spirit reap life e Gal 6:8
punished with e destruction 2 Thess 1:9
given us e consolation 2 Thess 2:16
reserved in e chains Jude 1:6
having the e gospel Rev 14:6

EVERMORE
Rejoice e 1 Thess 5:16
e give us this bread John 6:34

EVERY
e imagination of the thoughts of his heart Gen 6:5
neither shalt thou gather e grape Lev 19:10
e one of his fig tree 2 Kgs 18:31
pardon e one 2 Chr 30:18
till e one submit himself Ps 68:30
refrained my feet from e evil way Ps 119:101
e good path Prov 2:9
at e corner Prov 7:12
simple believeth e word Prov 14:15
e fool will be meddling Prov 20:3
E word of God is pure Prov 30:5
e purpose of the LORD Jer 51:29
by e word that proceedeth Matt 4:4
e one that asketh Matt 7:8; Luke 11:10
came to him from e quarter Mark 1:45
to e one which hath shall be given Luke 19:26
e knee shall bow to me, and Rom 14:11
bow to me, and e tongue confess Rom 14:11
bringing into captivity e thought 2 Cor 10:5
e name Eph 1:21; Phil 2:9
e creature of God 1 Tim 4:4
unto e good work 2 Tim 2:21
lay aside e weight Heb 12:1
e goodgift and e perfect gift James 1:17
e ordinance of man 1 Pet 2:13
believe not e spirit 1 John 4:1

EVERYONE
e that findeth me shall slay me Gen 4:14
alive e of you this day Deut 4:4
doth e speak of his glory Ps 29:9
For this shall e that is godly Ps 32:6
saith to e that he is a fool Eccl 10:3
e that loveth is born of God 1 John 4:7
robes were given unto e Rev 6:11

EVI e´-vi
desire Num 31:8

EVIDENCE
I subscribed the e Jer 32:10
the e of things not seen Heb 11:1

EVIDENT
Christ hath been e set forth Gal 3:1
it is e Gal 3:11
an e token of perdition Phil 1:28

EVIL
thoughts of his heart was only e Gen 6:5
few and e have the days Gen 47:9
repented of the e Ex 32:14; 2 Sam 24:16
eye e towards his brother Deut 28:54
eye shall be e toward the husband Deut 28:56
shall we not receive e? Job 2:10
looked for good, then e came Job 30:26
Depart from e Ps 34:14; 37:27; Prov 3:7
They rewarded me e Ps 35:12; 109:5
innumerable e have compassed Ps 40:12
e bow before the good Prov 14:19
beholding the e and the good Prov 15:3
Whoso rewardeth e for good Prov 17:13
that call e good, and good e Is 5:20
refuse the e and choose the good Is 7:15,16
have committed two e Jer 2:13
it is an e thing and bitter Jer 2:19
e, very e Jer 24:3
whether it be e, we will obey Jer 42:6
rise on the e and the good Matt 5:45
Sufficient unto the day is the e thereof Matt 6:34
If ye then, being e Matt 7:11; Luke 11:13
good tree cannot bring forth e Matt 7:18
Wherefore think e in your hearts? Matt 9:4
lightly speak e of me Mark 9:39
cast out your name as e Luke 6:22
kind unto the unthankful and the e Luke 6:35
e treasure of his heart bringeth forth e Luke 6:45
doeth e hateth the light John 3:20
If I have spoken e John 18:23
not speak e of the ruler Acts 23:5
the e which I would not Rom 7:19
Abhor that which is e Rom 12:9
Recompense to no man e for e Rom 12:17
overcome e with good Rom 12:21
appearance of e 1 Thess 5:22
the root of all e 1 Tim 6:10
every e work 2 Tim 4:18; James 3:16
speak e of no man Titus 3:2
an unruly e James 3:8
Not rendering e for e 1 Pet 3:9

EVILDOERS
Fret not thyself because of e Ps 37:1
a seed of e Is 1:4
they strengthen the hands of e Jer 23:14

EVIL-MERODACH e´-vil-me´-ro-dak
man of Merodach 2 Kgs 25:27

EXACT
shall not e it of his neighbour Deut 15:2
Ye e usury Neh 5:7
the e of every debt Neh 10:31
God e of thee less Job 11:6
E no more than what is Luke 3:13

EXALT
e as head above all 1 Chr 29:11
when the vilest men are e Ps 12:8
let us e his name together Ps 34:3
my horn shalt thou e Ps 92:10
e far above all gods Ps 97:9
E her, and she shall promote thee Prov 4:8
blessing of the upright the city is e Prov 11:11
he that is hasty of spirit e folly Prov 14:29
Righteousness e a nation Prov 14:34
he that e his gate Prov 17:19
e above the hills Is 2:2; Mic 4:1
every valley shall be e Is 40:4
e him that is low Ezek 21:26
e unto heaven Matt 11:23
e himself shall be abased Matt 23:12; Luke 14:11; 18:14
if a man e himself 2 Cor 11:20
e above measure 2 Cor 12:7
God also hath highly e him Phil 2:9
e himself above all that is called 2 Thess 2:4
he may e you in due time 1 Pet 5:6

EXAMINE
E me, O Lord Ps 26:2
If we this day be e Acts 4:9
e by scourging Acts 22:24,29
let a man e himself 1 Cor 11:28
E yourselves 2 Cor 13:5

EXAMPLE
I have given you an e John 13:15
be thou an e of the believers 1 Tim 4:12
also suffered for us, leaving us an e 1 Pet 2:21
an e, suffering the vengeance Jude 1:7

EXCEED
except your righteousness e Matt 5:20
righteousness doth e in glory 2 Cor 3:9

EXCEEDING
thy e great reward Gen 15:1
an e bitter cry Gen 27:34
is an e good land Num 14:7

so **e** proud 1 Sam 2:3
e glad with thy countenance Ps 21:6
unto God my **e** joy Ps 43:4
commandment is **e** broad Ps 119:96
e wise Prov 30:24
men feared the LORD **e** Jon 1:16
e glad of the gourd Jon 4:6
with **e** great joy Matt 2:10
an **e** high mountain Matt 4:8
Rejoice, and be **e** glad Matt 5:12
e fierce so that no man Matt 8:28
they were **e** sorry Matt 17:23
they were **e** amazed Matt 19:25
my soul is **e** sorrowful Matt 26:38; Mark 14:34
king was **e** sorry Mark 6:26
raiment became shining, **e** white Mark 9:3
he was **e** glad Luke 23:8
was **e** fair Acts 7:20
being **e** mad against them Acts 26:11
might become **e** sinful Rom 7:13
e and eternal weight of glory 2 Cor 4:17
e joyful in all our tribulation 2 Cor 7:4
e zealous of traditions Gal 1:14
the **e** greatness of his power Eph 1:19
the **e** riches of his grace Eph 2:7
able to do **e** abundantly Eph 3:20
your faith groweth **e** 2 Thess 1:3
e great and precious promises 2 Pet 1:4
with **e** joy Jude 1:24

EXCEL
thou shalt not **e** Gen 49:4
thou **e** them all Prov 31:29
wisdom **e** folly, as far as light **e** darkness Eccl 2:13
the glory that **e** 2 Cor 3:10

EXCELLENCY
the greatness of thine **e** Ex 15:7
not their **e** which is in them go away? Job 4:21
Shall not his **e** make you afraid? Job 13:11
will make thee an eternal **e** Is 60:15
not with **e** of speech 1 Cor 2:1
that the **e** of the power 2 Cor 4:7
loss for the **e** of the knowledge of Christ Phil 3:8

EXCELLENT
e in power Job 37:23
how **e** is thy name in all the earth! Ps 8:1,9
to the **e**, in whom is all my delight Ps 16:3
How **e** is thy lovingkindness, O God! Ps 36:7
I will speak of **e** things Prov 8:6
righteous is more **e** than his neighbour Prov 12:26
E speech becometh not a fool Prov 17:7
of an **e** spirit Prov 17:27
he hath done **e** things Is 12:5
e in working Is 28:29
an **e** spirit was in him Dan 6:3
things that are more **e** Rom 2:18
a more **e** way 1 Cor 12:31
from the **e** glory 2 Pet 1:17

EXCEPT
e thou bless me Gen 32:26
e their Rock had sold them Deut 32:30
E the LORD build house Ps 127:1
e they be agreed Amos 3:3
e your righteousness exceed Matt 5:20
E ye be converted Matt 18:3
e those days be shortened Matt 24:22
Jews, **e** they wash their hands oft Mark 7:3
e ye repent Luke 13:3
e God be with him John 3:2
E a man be born again John 3:5
E ye see signs and wonders John 4:48
E I shall see in his hands John 20:25
I am, **e** these bonds Acts 26:29
how shall they preach, **e** they be sent? Rom 10:15
e it die 1 Cor 15:36
e he strive lawfully 2 Tim 2:5

EXCESS
full of extortion and **e** Matt 23:25
not drunk with wine, wherein is **e** Eph 5:18
lusts, **e** of wine, revellings 1 Pet 4:3
the same **e** of riot 1 Pet 4:4

EXCHANGE
in **e** for his soul Matt 16:26; Mark 8:37
put money to the **e** Matt 25:27

EXCLUDE
Where is boasting then? It is **e** Rom 3:27
they would **e** you Gal 4:17

EXCUSE (n)
they are without **e** Rom 1:20

EXCUSE (v)
I pray thee have me **e** Luke 14:18
accusing or else **e** one another Rom 2:15
that we **e** ourselves unto you 2 Cor 12:19

EXECRATION
shall be an **e** Jer 42:18; 44:12

EXECUTE
he **e** the justice of the LORD Deut 33:21
e the priest's office 1 Chr 6:10; 24:2; Luke 1:8
known by the judgment which he **e** Ps 9:16
LORD **e** righteousness and judgment Ps 103:6
any that **e** judgment Jer 5:1
authority to **e** judgment John 5:27
minister of God, a revenger to **e** wrath Rom 13:4

EXERCISE
e myself in great matters Ps 131:1
e lovingkindness Jer 9:24
e dominion Matt 20:25
I **e** myself, to always have a conscience Acts 24:16
e thyself unto godliness 1 Tim 4:7
e to discern both good and evil Heb 5:14
unto them which are **e** thereby Heb 12:11
e with covetous practices 2 Pet 2:14

EXHORT
he that **e**, on exhortation Rom 12:8
These things teach and **e** 1 Tim 6:2
may be able by sound doctrine to **e** Titus 1:9
e and rebuke with all authority Titus 2:15
e one another Heb 3:13; 10:25

EXHORTATION
many other things in his **e** Luke 3:18
any word of **e** Acts 13:15
he that exhorteth, on **e** Rom 12:8
suffer the word of **e** Heb 13:22

EXILE
thou art a stranger, and also an **e** 2 Sam 15:19
The captive **e** hasteneth Is 51:14

EXPECTATION
the **e** of the poor Ps 9:18
my **e** is from him Ps 62:5
e of the wicked Prov 10:28; 11:23
ashamed of Ethiopia their **e** Is 20:5
such is our **e** Is 20:6
the earnest **e** of the creature Rom 8:19
my earnest **e** and my hope Phil 1:20

EXPEL
he shall **e** them from before you Josh 23:5
hate me, and **e** me out Judg 11:7
his banished be not **e** from him 2 Sam 14:14

EXPENCES
let the **e** be given out Ezra 6:4
forthwith **e** be given Ezra 6:8

EXPERIENCE
I have learned by **e** Gen 30:27
my heart had great **e** Eccl 1:16
And patience, **e**; and **e**, hope Rom 5:4

EXPLOITS
and he shall do **e** Dan 11:28,32

EXPOUND
e the riddle Judg 14:14,19
when they were alone, he **e** all things Mark 4:34
e unto them all the scriptures Luke 24:27

EXPRESS
the **e** image of his person Heb 1:3

EXPRESSLY
If I **e** say unto the lad 1 Sam 20:21
word of the LORD came **e** Ezek 1:3
the Spirit speaketh **e** 1 Tim 4:1

EXTEND
my goodness **e** not to thee Ps 16:2
be none to **e** mercy unto him Ps 109:12
I will **e** peace to her Is 66:12

EXTINCT
my days are **e** Job 17:1
they are **e**, they are quenched Is 43:17

EXTOL
I will **e** thee Ps 30:1; 145:1
e him that rideth Ps 68:4

EXTORTION
gained of thy neighbours by **e** Ezek 22:12
they are full of **e** and excess Matt 23:25

EXTORTIONER
Let the **e** catch all he hath Ps 109:11
the **e** is at an end Is 16:4
a drunkard, an **e** 1 Cor 5:11

EXTREME
with an **e** burning Deut 28:22
knoweth it not in great **e** Job 35:15

EYE
pleasant to the **e** Gen 3:6
e of them both were opened Gen 3:7
his **e** were dim Gen 27:1
His **e** shall be red with wine Gen 49:12
be to us instead of **e** Num 10:31
wilt thou put out the **e** of these men? Num 16:14
man whose **e** are open Num 24:3,15
behold it with thine **e** Deut 3:27
right in his own **e** Deut 12:8; Judg 17:6; 21:25
gift doth blind the **e** of the wise Deut 16:19
e shall look, and fail with longing Deut 28:32
kept him as the apple of his **e** Deut 32:10
his **e** was not dim Deut 34:7
e of all Israel are upon thee 1 Kgs 1:20
e may be open 1 Kgs 8:29; 2 Chr 6:20
whatsoever is pleasant in thine **e** 1 Kgs 20:6
LORD opened the **e** of the young man 2 Kgs 6:17
open the **e** of the young men 2 Kgs 6:20
e of the LORD run to and fro 2 Chr 16:9
neither shall thine **e** see all the evil 2 Chr 34:28
e of him that hath seen me Job 7:8
the **e** of wicked shall fail Job 11:20
what do thy **e** wink at Job 15:12
mine **e** shall behold, and not another Job 19:27
vulture's **e** hath not seen Job 28:7
his **e** seeth every precious thing Job 28:10
when the **e** saw me Job 29:11
I was **e** to the blind Job 29:15
caused the **e** of widow to fail Job 31:16
his **e** try the children of men Ps 11:4
In whose **e** a vile person Ps 15:4
enlightening the **e** Ps 19:8
e of LORD on them that fear him Ps 33:18
e of LORD on the righteous Ps 34:15; 1 Pet 3:12
no fear of God before his **e** Ps 36:1
Mine **e** fail Ps 69:3; 119:82,123; Lam 2:11
holdest mine **e** waking Ps 77:4
death, mine **e** from tears Ps 116:8

Open thou mine e Ps 119:18
not give sleep to mine e Ps 132:4
as smoke to the e Prov 10:26
the seeing e Prov 20:12
a bountiful e Prov 22:9
redness of e Prov 23:29
the e of man never satisfied Prov 27:20
The e that mocketh Prov 30:17
e is not satisfied with seeing Eccl 1:8
wise man's e are in his head Eccl 2:14
Better is the sight of the e than Eccl 6:9
for the e to behold the sun Eccl 11:7
I will hide mine e from you Is 1:15
hath closed your e Is 29:10
Thine e shall see the King in his beauty Is 33:17
Lift up your e on high Is 40:26
have e and see not Jer 5:21
mine e a fountain of tears Jer 9:1
mine e shall weep sore Jer 13:17
Let mine e run down with tears Jer 14:17
set mine e upon them for good Jer 24:6
let not the apple of thine e cease Lam 2:18
the desire of thine e Ezek 24:16,25
of purer e than to behold evil Hab 1:13
if thy right e offend thee Matt 5:29
blessed are your e Matt 13:16
to enter into life with one e Matt 18:9
Having e, see ye not? Mark 8:18
their e were holden Luke 24:16
not this man, which opened the e John 11:37
have plucked out your own e Gal 4:15
the e of your understanding Eph 1:18
Having e full of adultery 2 Pet 2:14
the lust of the e 1 John 2:16

EZAR e´-zar
treasure 1 Chr 1:38

EZBAI ez´-ba-i
from ELIAM (?) 1 Chr 11:37

EZBON ez´-bon
1 son of Gad Gen 46:16
2 form of OZNI Num 26:16
3 son of Bela 1 Chr 7:7

EZEKIAS ez´-ek-i´-as
same as HEZEKIAH Matt 1:9

EZEKIEL ez-e´-ki-el
whom God will strengthen Ezek 1:3

EZEL e´-zel
departure 1 Sam 20:19

EZEM e´-zem
bone 1 Chr 4:29

EZER e´-zer
help 1 Chr 4:4

EZION-GABER e´-zi-on-ga´-ber
same as EZION-GEBER Num 33:35

EZION-GEBER e´-zi-on-ge´-ber
the backbone of a man 1 Kgs 9:26

EZRA ez´-rah
help Ezra 7:1

EZRAHITE ez´-rah-ite
a descendant of Zerah 1 Kgs 4:31

EZRI ez´-ri
the help of Jehovah (?) 1 Chr 27:26

F

FABLES
Neither give heed to f 1 Tim 1:4
refuse profane and old wives' f 1 Tim 4:7
shall be turned to f 2 Tim 4:4
Not giving heed to Jewish f Titus 1:14
cunningly devised f 2 Pet 1:16

FACE
from thy f shall I be hid Gen 4:14
I have seen God f to f Gen 32:30
LORD spake to Moses f to f Ex 33:11
skin of his f shone Ex 34:29
put a vail on his f Ex 34:33
shall honour the f of the old man Lev 19:32
spit in his f, Deut 25:9
Dagon was fallen upon his f 1 Sam 5:3
staff upon the f of the child 2 Kgs 4:29,31
confusion of f Ezra 9:7; Dan 9:8
worshipped with their f to the ground Neh 8:6
curse thee to thy f Job 1:11; 2:5
spirit passed before my f Job 4:15
Wherefore hidest thou thy f Job 13:24; Ps 44:24
how long wilt thou hide thy f from me? Ps 13:1
hide not thy f Ps 27:9; 69:17; 102:2; 143:7
f were not ashamed Ps 34:5
look upon the f of thine anointed Ps 84:9
in water f answereth to f Prov 27:19
wisdom maketh his f to shine Eccl 8:1
grind the f of the poor Is 3:15
wipe away tears from off all f Is 25:8
set my f like a flint Is 50:7
their back unto me, and not their f Jer 2:27
their f harder than a rock Jer 5:3
all f turned into paleness? Jer 30:6
f as appearance of lightning Dan 10:6
testify to his f Hos 5:5
wash thy f Matt 6:17
messenger before thy f Matt 11:10; Mark 1:2; Luke 7:27
discern the f of the sky Matt 16:3; Luke 12:56
his f did shine as the sun Matt 17:2
do always behold the f of my Father Matt 18:10
before the f of all people Luke 2:31
set his f to go to Jerusalem Luke 9:51
struck him on the f Luke 22:64
then f to f 1 Cor 13:12
But we all, with open f 2 Cor 3:18
was unknown by f Gal 1:22
withstood him to the f Gal 2:11
beholding his natural f in a glass James 1:23
from whose f the earth Rev 20:11

FADE
whose leaf f Is 1:30
earth mourneth and f Is 24:4
the flower f Is 40:7
all do f as a leaf Is 64:6
and the leaf shall f Jer 8:13
whose leaf shall not f Ezek 47:12
shall the rich man f away James 1:11
that f not away 1 Pet 1:4; 5:4

FAIL
if money f Gen 47:16
thine eyes shall look and f Deut 28:32
There f not ought of any good thing Josh 21:45
Let no man's heart f because of him 1 Sam 17:32
there shall not f thee 1 Kgs 2:4; 8:25
neither shall the cruse of oil f 1 Kgs 17:14
take heed now that ye f not Ezra 4:22
As the waters f from the sea Job 14:11
My kinsfolk have f Job 19:14
the faithful f from among Ps 12:1
my strength f Ps 31:10; 38:10
doth his promise f Ps 77:8
suffer my faithfulness to f Ps 89:33
refuge f me Ps 142:4
his wisdom f him Eccl 10:3
desire shall f Eccl 12:5
the grass f Is 15:6
waters shall f Is 19:5
they all shall f together Is 31:3
cause the drink of the thirsty to f Is 32:6
the vintage shall f Is 32:10
no one of these shall f Is 34:16
eyes f with looking upward Is 38:14
tongue f for thirst Is 41:17
truth f Is 59:15
their eyes did f Jer 14:6
as waters that f Jer 15:18
I have caused wine to f Jer 48:33
his compassions f not Lam 3:22
our eyes as yet f Lam 4:17
every vision f Ezek 12:22
make the poor of the land to f Amos 8:4
labour of the olive shall f Hab 3:17
treasure in the heavens that f not Luke 12:33
when ye f, they may receive you Luke 16:9
one tittle of the law to f Luke 16:17
hearts f them for fear Luke 21:26
that thy faith f not Luke 22:32
Charity never f 1 Cor 13:8
thy years shall not f Heb 1:12
time would f me to tell Heb 11:32
lest any man f of the grace of God Heb 12:15

FAIN
he would f flee out of his hand Job 27:22
f have filled his belly Luke 15:16

FAINT (adj)
f, yet pursuing Judg 8:4
giveth power to the f Is 40:29
he drinketh no water, and is f Is 44:12
my heart is f Jer 8:18; Lam 1:22

FAINT (v)
came from field, and he was f Gen 25:29
Jacob's heart f Gen 45:26
now it is come upon thee, and thou f Job 4:5
I had f, unless I had believed Ps 27:13
their soul f in them Ps 107:5
if thou f in the day of adversity Prov 24:10
whole heart f Is 1:5
as when a standard bearer f Is 10:18
Creator of the ends of the earth f not Is 40:28
even youths shall f Is 40:30
walk, and not f Is 40:31
lest they f in the way Matt 15:32
pray, and not to f Luke 18:1
as we have received mercy, we f not 2 Cor 4:1
reap, if we f not Gal 6:9
wearied and f in your minds Heb 12:3
nor f when thou art rebuked Heb 12:5

FAIR
F weather cometh out of the north Job 37:22
f than the children of men Ps 45:2
f woman which is without discretion Prov 11:22
When he speaketh f, believe him not Prov 26:25
O thou f among women? Song 5:9; 6:1
f as the moon Song 6:10
even great and f, without inhabitant Is 5:9
in vain shalt thou make thyself f Jer 4:30
though they speak f words Jer 12:6
their countenances appeared f Dan 1:15
It will be f weather Matt 16:2
Moses was born and was exceeding f Acts 7:20
by good words and f speeches deceive Rom 16:18

FAITH
children in whom is no f Deut 32:20
ye of little f Matt 6:30; 8:26; 16:8; Luke 12:28
so great f Matt 8:10; Luke 7:9
seeing their f Matt 9:2; Mark 2:5; Luke 5:20
thy f hath made thee whole Matt 9:22; Mark 5:34; 10:52; Luke 8:48; 17:19
According to your f Matt 9:29
great is thy f Matt 15:28
f as a grain of mustard seed Matt 17:20
If ye have f, ye shall not only do this Matt 21:21

judgment, mercy, and f Matt 23:23
how is it that ye have no f? Mark 4:40
Have f in God Mark 11:22
Thy f hath saved thee Luke 7:50
Where is your f? Luke 8:25
Increase our f Luke 17:5
shall he find f on the earth? Luke 18:8
that thy f fail not Luke 22:32
the f which is by him Acts 3:16
a man full of f Acts 6:5
perceiving that he had f to be healed Acts 14:9
opened the door of f Acts 14:27
purifying their hearts by f Acts 15:9
established in the f Acts 16:5
sanctified by f Acts 26:18
for obedience to the f Rom 1:5
revealed from f to f Rom 1:17
by the law of f Rom 3:27
justified by f Rom 3:28; 5:1; Gal 2:16
f is counted for righteousness Rom 4:5
of the f of Abraham Rom 4:16
being not weak in f Rom 4:19
strong in f Rom 4:20
we have access by f Rom 5:2
the word of f, which we preach Rom 10:8
f cometh by hearing Rom 10:17
the measure of f Rom 12:3
according to the proportion of f Rom 12:6
weak in the f receive ye Rom 14:1
Hast thou f? Rom 14:22
whatsoever is not of f is sin Rom 14:23
your f should not stand in wisdom 1 Cor 2:5
though I have all f 1 Cor 13:2
now abideth f 1 Cor 13:13
and your f is also vain 1 Cor 15:14
stand fast in the f 1 Cor 16:13
same spirit of f 2 Cor 4:13
we walk by f 2 Cor 5:7
whether ye be in the f 2 Cor 13:5
I live by the f of Son of God Gal 2:20
by the hearing of f Gal 3:2
law is not of f Gal 3:12
before f came Gal 3:23
f which worketh by love Gal 5:6
the household of f Gal 6:10
access with confidence by the f of him Eph 3:12
dwell in your hearts by f Eph 3:17
One Lord, one f Eph 4:5
in the unity of the f Eph 4:13
the shield of f Eph 6:16
striving together for the f of the gospel Phil 1:27
If ye continue in the f Col 1:23
the stedfastness of your f Col 2:5
work of f 1 Thess 1:3; 2 Thess 1:11
the breastplate of f 1 Thess 5:8
all men have not f 2 Thess 3:2
my own son in the f 1 Tim 1:2
f unfeigned 1 Tim 1:5
if they continue in f 1 Tim 2:15
great boldness in the f 1 Tim 3:13
shall depart from the f 1 Tim 4:1
he hath denied the f 1 Tim 5:8
erred from the f 1 Tim 6:10
fight the good fight of f 1 Tim 6:12
reprobate concerning the f 2 Tim 3:8
I have kept the f 2 Tim 4:7
the f of God's elect Titus 1:1
not being mixed with f Heb 4:2
of f toward God Heb 6:1
f and patience inherit the promises Heb 6:12
in full assurance of f Heb 10:22
f is the substance of things hoped for Heb 11:1
By f Heb 11:4,5,7,8,9
without f it is impossible Heb 11:6
These all died in f Heb 11:13
through f subdued kingdoms Heb 11:33
a good report through f Heb 11:39
author and finisher of our f Heb 12:2
whose f follow Heb 13:7
the trying of your f James 1:3
let them ask in f James 1:6
My brethren, have not the f James 2:1
rich in f James 2:5
say he hath f and have not works James 2:14
f if it hath not works is dead James 2:17
thou hast f and I have works James 2:18
f wrought with his works James 2:22
the prayer of f shall save James 5:15
the end of your f 1 Pet 1:9
resist stedfast in the f 1 Pet 5:9
like precious f 2 Pet 1:1
add to your f virtue 2 Pet 1:5
overcometh the world, even our f 1 John 5:4
earnestly contend for the f Jude 1:3
your most holy f Jude 1:20
hast not denied my f Rev 2:13
service, and f, and thy patience Rev 2:19
patience and f of the saints Rev 13:10
the f of Jesus Rev 14:12

FAITHFUL

that are peaceable and f in Israel 2 Sam 20:19
a f man, and feared God Neh 7:2
his heart f before thee Neh 9:8
they were counted f Neh 13:13
the f fail from the children among men Ps 12:1
a f witness in heaven Ps 89:37
the f of the land Ps 101:6
all thy commandments are f Ps 119:86
f spirit concealeth Prov 11:13
f ambassador is health Prov 13:17
a f witness Prov 14:5; Is 8:2; Jer 42:5
a f man who can find Prov 20:6
a f messenger Prov 25:13
F are the wounds of a friend Prov 27:6
f man shall abound Prov 28:20
f city Is 1:21,26
Who then is a f and wise servant Matt 24:45; Luke 12:42
good and f servant Matt 25:21
f over a few things Matt 25:23
f also in much Luke 16:10
If ye have judged me f Acts 16:15
in stewards, that a man be found f 1 Cor 4:2
f in the Lord 1 Cor 4:17
blessed with f Abraham Gal 3:9
f minister Eph 6:21; Col 1:7; 4:7
F is he that calleth you 1 Thess 5:24
Lord is f, who shall stablish you 2 Thess 3:3
a f saying 1 Tim 1:15; 4:9; 2 Tim 2:11; Titus 3:8
f in all things 1 Tim 3:11
commit thou to f men 2 Tim 2:2
yet he abideth f 2 Tim 2:13
f high priest Heb 2:17
f to him that appointed him Heb 3:2
he is f that promised Heb 10:23
as unto a f Creator 1 Pet 4:19
he is f and just to forgive 1 John 1:9
be thou f unto death Rev 2:10
my f martyr Rev 2:13
called, and chosen, and f Rev 17:14
these words are true and f Rev 21:5

FAITHFULLY

in the fear of the LORD, f 2 Chr 19:9
men did the work f 2 Chr 34:12
let him speak my word f Jer 23:28
thou doest f whatsoever 3 John 1:5

FAITHFULNESS

no f in their mouths Ps 5:9
thy f reacheth unto the clouds Ps 36:5
declared thy f Ps 40:10
thy f in destruction Ps 88:11
nor suffer my f to fail Ps 89:33
thy f every night Ps 92:2
f the girdle of his reins Is 11:5
great is thy f Lam 3:23

FAITHLESS

O f and perverse generation Matt 17:17; Luke 9:41
f generation, how long Mark 9:19
be not f, but believing John 20:27

FALL (n)

haughty spirit before a f Prov 16:18
great was the f of it Matt 7:27
set for the f and rising again of many Luke 2:34
if the f of them be the riches Rom 11:12

FALL (v)

See ye f not out by the way Gen 45:24
brother be waxen and poor f in decay Lev 25:35
let none of his words f 1 Sam 3:19
how are the mighty f! 2 Sam 1:19,25,27
great man f this day 2 Sam 3:38
f now into the hands of the LORD 2 Sam 24:14
let me not f into the hand of man 1 Chr 21:13
to thy hurt that thou shouldest f 2 Kgs 14:10
deep sleep f on men Job 4:13; 33:15
let them f by their own counsels Ps 5:10
is f into the ditch Ps 7:15
lines are f unto me in pleasant places Ps 16:6
Though he f Ps 37:24
my feet from f Ps 56:13; 116:8
kings shall f down before him Ps 72:11
a thousand shall f at thy side Ps 91:7
a prating fool shall f Prov 10:8,10
Where no counsel is, the people f Prov 11:14
he that trusteth in riches shall f Prov 11:28
f into mischief Prov 13:17; 17:20; 24:16
just man f seven times Prov 24:16
Rejoice not when thine enemy f Prov 24:17
diggeth a pit shall f therein Prov 26:27; Eccl 10:8
woe to him that is alone when he f Eccl 4:10
where the tree f, there it shall be Eccl 11:3
How art thou f from heaven Is 14:12
as the leaf f off from the vine Is 34:4
the young men shall utterly f Is 40:30
young men shall f in her streets Jer 49:26; 50:30
let no lot f upon it Ezek 24:6
f down and worship Dan 3:5; Matt 4:9
f on us Hos 10:8; Luke 23:30; Rev 6:16
when I f Mic 7:8
the cedar is f Zech 11:2
shall not f to the ground Matt 10:29
f into pit on sabbath day Matt 12:11
shall f into the ditch Matt 15:14; Luke 6:39
f on this stone Matt 21:44
stars shall f from heaven Matt 24:29; Mark 13:25
in time of temptation f away Luke 8:13
Satan as lightning f from heaven Luke 10:18
to his own master he standeth or f Rom 14:4
occasion to f Rom 14:13
take heed lest he f 1 Cor 10:12
are f asleep 1 Cor 15:6,18
ye are f from grace Gal 5:4
f into the condemnation 1 Tim 3:6
lest he f into reproach 1 Tim 3:7
rich f into temptation 1 Tim 6:9
f after the same example of unbelief Heb 4:11
If they shall f away Heb 6:6
to f into the hands of the living God Heb 10:31
joy when ye f into temptation James 1:2
flower thereof f James 1:11; 1 Pet 1:24
lest ye f into condemnation James 5:12
ye shall never f 2 Pet 1:10
ye f from your own stedfastness 2 Pet 3:17

FALLING
- upholden him that was f Job 4:4
- except there come a f away first 2 Thess 2:3
- able to keep you from f Jude 1:24

FALLOW
- Break up your f ground Jer 4:3; Hos 10:12

FALSE
- bear f witness Ex 20:16; Deut 5:20; Matt 19:18
- shalt not raise a f report Ex 23:1
- It is f; tell us now 2 Kgs 9:12
- I hate every f way Ps 119:104,128
- thou f tongue? Ps 120:3
- f witness Prov 6:19; 12:17; 21:28; Matt 15:19; Mark 14:56,57
- A f balance Prov 11:1
- f Christs, and f prophets Matt 24:24; Mark 13:22
- f prophets shall rise Mark 13:22
- any man by f accusation Luke 19:8
- found f witnesses of God 1 Cor 15:15
- such are f apostles 2 Cor 11:13
- perils among f brethren 2 Cor 11:26
- f accusers 2 Tim 3:3; Titus 2:3

FALSEHOOD
- in your answers there remaineth f Job 21:34
- brought forth f Ps 7:14
- right hand of f Ps 144:8,11
- under f have we hid ourselves Is 28:15
- a seed of f Is 57:4
- words of f Is 59:13
- walking in the spirit and f Mic 2:11

FALSELY
- swear f Lev 6:3,5; Jer 5:2; 7:9; Zech 5:4
- prophesy f Jer 5:31; 29:9
- evil against you f, for my sake Matt 5:11
- science f so called 1 Tim 6:20

FAME
- we have heard the f of him Josh 9:9
- f of Solomon 1 Kgs 10:1; 2 Chr 9:1
- f in every land Zeph 3:19
- his f Matt 4:24; 9:31; Mark 1:28
- Herod heard of the f of Jesus Matt 14:1

FAMILIAR
- f friends have forgotten me Job 19:14
- mine own f friend Ps 41:9
- All my f watched for my halting Jer 20:10

FAMILY
- all the f of the earth be blessed Gen 12:3; 28:14
- return every man to his f Lev 25:10
- or f, or tribe, whose heart turneth Deut 29:18
- my f the least 1 Sam 9:21
- my father's f in Israel 1 Sam 18:18
- princes in their f 1 Chr 4:38
- setteth the solitary in f Ps 68:6
- one of a city, and two of a f Jer 3:14
- upon the f that call not Jer 10:25
- God of all the f of Israel Jer 31:1
- every f apart Zech 12:12
- whole f in heaven and earth Eph 3:15

FAMINE
- a f in the days of David 2 Sam 21:1
- If there be in the land f 1 Kgs 8:37
- sore f in Samaria 1 Kgs 18:2
- the LORD hath called for a f 2 Kgs 8:1
- In f he shall redeem thee Job 5:20
- At destruction and f thou shalt laugh Job 5:22
- to keep them alive in f Ps 33:19
- in the days of f they shall be satisfied Ps 37:19
- sword, the f, and the pestilence Jer 24:10; 29:17
- f, whereof ye were afraid, shall follow Jer 42:16
- because of the terrible f Lam 5:10
- evil arrows of f Ezek 5:16
- lay no f upon you Ezek 36:29
- not a f of bread Amos 8:11
- there shall be f Matt 24:7; Mark 13:8

FAMISH
- the land of Egypt was f Gen 41:55
- soul of the righteous to f Prov 10:3
- their honourable men are f Is 5:13
- he will f all the gods of the earth Zeph 2:11

FAMOUS
- be f in Beth-lehem Ruth 4:11
- be f in Israel Ruth 4:14
- men of valour, f men 1 Chr 5:24
- A man was f according as he Ps 74:5
- she became f among women Ezek 23:10

FAN
- with the shovel and the f Is 30:24
- f them with a f in the gates Jer 15:7
- fanners, that shall f her Jer 51:2
- Whose f is in his hand Matt 3:12

FAR
- that be f from thee Gen 18:25
- too f from thee Deut 12:21; 14:24
- f spent Judg 19:11; Mark 6:35; Luke 24:29
- Be it f from me 1 Sam 2:30; 22:15; 2 Sam 23:17
- children f from safety Job 5:4
- f away Job 11:14
- put my brethren f from me Job 19:13
- f be it from God Job 34:10
- judgments are f above out of his sight Ps 10:5
- be not f from me Ps 22:11; 35:22; 38:21; 71:12
- f above all gods Ps 97:9
- f as the east is from the west Ps 103:12
- f above rubies Prov 31:10
- sons from f Is 43:6; 60:9
- f from righteousness Is 46:12
- peace to him that is f off Is 57:19
- put f away the evil day Amos 6:3
- Be it f from thee, Lord Matt 16:22
- not f from the kingdom Mark 12:34
- as a man taking a f journey Mark 13:34
- they were not f from land John 21:8
- not f from every one of us Acts 17:27
- the night is f spent Rom 13:12
- a f more exceeding 2 Cor 4:17
- F above all principality Eph 1:21
- f off made nigh Eph 2:13
- f above all heavens Eph 4:10
- which is f better Phil 1:23
- it is yet f more evident Heb 7:15

FARE
- look how thy brethren f 1 Sam 17:18
- f sumptuously every day Luke 16:19

FAREWELL
- go bid them f Luke 9:61
- bade them f, saying Acts 18:21
- Finally, brethren, f 2 Cor 13:11

FARM
- to his f, another to his merchandise Matt 22:5

FARTHING
- till thou hast paid the utmost f Matt 5:26
- two sparrows sold for a f Matt 10:29
- two mites, which make a f Mark 12:42
- five sparrows sold for two f Luke 12:6

FASHION (n)
- never saw it on this f Mark 2:12
- the f of his countenance Luke 9:29
- the f of this world passeth 1 Cor 7:31
- found in f as a man Phil 2:8

FASHION (v)
- hands have made me and f Job 10:8; Ps 119:73
- did not one f us Job 31:15
- He f their hearts alike Ps 33:15
- in continuance were f Ps 139:16
- say to him that f it Is 45:9

FAST (n)
- wilt thou call this a f Is 58:5
- Is not this the f that I have chosen? Is 58:6
- Sanctify ye a f Joel 1:14

FAST (v)
- he is dead, wherefore should I f? 2 Sam 12:23
- he commanded, and it stood f Ps 33:9
- setteth f the mountains Ps 65:6
- Wherefore have we f Is 58:3
- ye f for strife Is 58:4
- did ye at all f unto me Zech 7:5
- when ye f, be not Matt 6:16
- appear not unto men to f Matt 6:18
- the children of the bridechamber f? Mark 2:19
- I f twice in the week Luke 18:12

FASTEN
- as nails f by the masters Eccl 12:11
- I will f him as a nail Is 22:23
- were f on him Luke 4:20
- when I had f mine eyes Acts 11:6

FASTING
- I humbled my soul with f Ps 35:13
- knees weak through f Ps 109:24
- upon the f day Jer 36:6
- send them away f Mark 8:3
- give yourselves to f and prayer 1 Cor 7:5
- in watchings, in f 2 Cor 6:5
- in f often 2 Cor 11:27

FAT
- shall eat the f of the land Gen 45:18
- his bread shall be f Gen 49:20
- Jeshurun waxed f, and kicked Deut 32:15
- eat the f, and drink the sweet Neh 8:10
- took strong cities and a f land Neh 9:25
- inclosed in their own f Ps 17:10
- shall be f and flourishing Ps 92:14
- heart is as f as grease Ps 119:70
- liberal soul shall be made f Prov 11:25
- soul of the diligent shall be made f Prov 13:4
- good report maketh the bones f Prov 15:30
- among his f ones leanness Is 10:16
- feast of f things Is 25:6
- by them their portion is f Hab 1:16

FATHER
- go to thy f in peace Gen 15:15
- a f of many nations Gen 17:4; Rom 4:17
- my f God, and I will exalt him Ex 15:2
- iniquity of f upon the children Ex 20:5; Num 14:18
- he that smiteth his f Ex 21:15
- he that curseth his f Ex 21:17
- be to me a f and a priest Judg 17:10
- who is their f? 1 Sam 10:12
- his f shewed kindness 2 Sam 10:2; 1 Chr 19:2
- not better than my f 1 Kgs 19:4
- my f, my f 2 Kgs 2:12; 13:14
- My f, shall I smite them? 2 Kgs 6:21
- know thou the God of thy f 1 Chr 28:9
- what I and my f have done 2 Chr 32:13
- Blessed be the LORD God of our f Ezra 7:27
- I was a f to the poor Job 29:16
- brought up with me as with a f Job 31:18
- Hath the rain a f? Job 38:28
- When my f and my mother forsake me Ps 27:10
- as all my f were Ps 39:12
- f of fatherless Ps 68:5
- your f tempted me Ps 95:9; Heb 3:9
- as a f pitieth his children Ps 103:13
- the instruction of a f Prov 4:1

I was my f son Prov 4:3
wise son maketh a glad f Prov 10:1; 15:20
the f of a fool hath no joy Prov 17:21
foolish son grief to his f Prov 17:25
The everlasting F Is 9:6
kings shall be thy nursing f Is 49:23
thou art our f Is 63:16; 64:8
cry unto me, my f Jer 3:4
I am a f to Israel Jer 31:9
f have eaten a sour grape Jer 31:29
as the soul of the f Ezek 18:4
set light by f and mother Ezek 22:7
if then I be a f, where is mine honour? Mal 1:6
Have we not all one f? Mal 2:10
your F which is in heaven Matt 5:16,45,48
your F knoweth Matt 6:8,32; Luke 12:30
Our F which art in heaven Matt 6:9; Luke 11:2
the will of my F Matt 7:21; 12:50
He that loveth f or mother Matt 10:37
behold the face of my F Matt 18:10
not the will of your F Matt 18:14
ye blessed of my F Matt 25:34
Abba, F Mark 14:36; Rom 8:15; Gal 4:6
about my F business Luke 2:49
as your F is also merciful Luke 6:36
of any of you that is a f Luke 11:11
it is your F good pleasure Luke 12:32
F, I have sinned Luke 15:21
send him to my f house Luke 16:27
F, if thou be willing Luke 22:42
F, forgive them Luke 23:34
F, into thy hands Luke 23:46
as of the only begotten of the f John 1:14
as the F raiseth up the dead John 5:21
the F judgeth no man John 5:22
even as they honour the F John 5:23
the F himself which hath sent me John 5:37
all that the F giveth me John 6:37
hath seen the F John 6:46; 14:9
we have one F, even God John 8:41
he is a liar, and the f of it John 8:44
I honour my F John 8:49
As the F knoweth me John 10:15
My F which gave them me John 10:29
F, save me from this hour John 12:27
F, glorify thy name John 12:28
depart out of this world unto the F John 13:1
no man cometh unto the F, but by me John 14:6
I will pray the F John 14:16; 16:26
my F is the husbandman John 15:1
whatsoever ye shall ask of the F John 15:16
because I go to the F John 16:16
I am come forth from the F John 16:28
the F is with me John 16:32
F, the hour is come John 17:1
I ascend unto my F, and your F John 20:17
so worship I the God of my f Acts 24:14
the f of all them that believe Rom 4:11
yet have we not many f 1 Cor 4:15
F of mercies, and the God of all comfort 2 Cor 1:3
zealous of the traditions of my f Gal 1:14
the time appointed of the f Gal 4:2
One God and F of all Eph 4:6
f, provoke not your children Eph 6:4
to the glory of God the F Phil 2:11
as a son with the f Phil 2:22
it pleased the F that in him Col 1:19
intreat him as a f 1 Tim 5:1
I will be to him a F Heb 1:5
Without f, without mother Heb 7:3
the F of spirits Heb 12:9
the F of lights James 1:17
since the f fell asleep 2 Pet 3:4
fellowship with the F 1 John 1:3
an advocate with the F 1 John 2:1
I write unto you, f 1 John 2:13
the love of the F is not in him 1 John 2:15
hath not the F 1 John 2:23
what manner of love the F hath 1 John 3:1
the F, the Word, and the Holy Ghost 1 John 5:7

FATHERLESS
the helper of the f Ps 10:14
the fields of the f Prov 23:10
they judge not the f Is 1:23
that they may rob the f Is 10:2
Leave thy f children Jer 49:11
in thee the f findeth mercy Hos 14:3
the f, and that turn aside the stranger Mal 3:5
visit the f and widows James 1:27

FATNESS
the f of thine house Ps 36:8
as with marrow and f Ps 63:5
thy paths drop f Ps 65:11
eyes stand out with f Ps 73:7
soul delight itself in f Is 55:2

FAULT
I do remember my f this day Gen 41:9
cleanse thou me from secret f Ps 19:12
find none occasion nor f Dan 6:4
tell him his f Matt 18:15
I find no f John 18:38; 19:4,6
Why doth he yet find f? Rom 9:19
overtaken in a f Gal 6:1
Confess your f James 5:16
are without f before the throne Rev 14:5

FAULTLESS
first covenant had been f Heb 8:7
present you f before the presence Jude 1:24

FAULTY
speak this thing as one which is f 2 Sam 14:13
shall they be found f Hos 10:2

FAVOUR
f in the sight of the keeper Gen 39:21
f in the sight of the Egyptians Ex 3:21; 11:3; 12:36
satisfied with f Deut 33:23
with f wilt thou compass him Ps 5:12
his f is life Ps 30:5
the set time to f her Ps 102:13
f the dust thereof Ps 102:14
A good man sheweth f Ps 112:5
Good understanding giveth f Prov 13:15
the king's f Prov 14:35; 19:12
obtaineth f of the LORD Prov 18:22
F is deceitful Prov 31:30
increased in f with God and man Luke 2:52
having f with all the people Acts 2:47

FAVOURABLE
Be f unto them for our sakes Judg 21:22
he will be f unto him Job 33:26
will he be f no more Ps 77:7
thou hast been f unto thy land Ps 85:1

FEAR (n)
the f of you and the dread Gen 9:2
f of God is not in this place Gen 20:11
f of thee upon the nations Deut 2:25
shall lay the f and the dread of you Deut 11:25
the f of him upon all nations 1 Chr 14:17
thou castest off f Job 15:4
He mocketh at f Job 39:22
in thy f will I worship Ps 5:7
f of the Lord is clean Ps 19:9
I will teach you the f of the Lord Ps 34:11
no f of God before his eyes Ps 36:1
in great f, where no f was Ps 53:5
f of the LORD is the beginning of wisdom Ps 111:10; Prov 9:10
mock when your f cometh Prov 1:26
not afraid of sudden f Prov 3:25
f of the LORD prolongeth days Prov 10:27
the f of the LORD is strong confidence Prov 14:26
f of the LORD is a fountain of life Prov 14:27
better is little with the f of the LORD Prov 15:16
f of the LORD tendeth to life Prov 19:23
f of man bringeth a snare Prov 29:25
f shall be in the way Eccl 12:5
neither fear ye their f Is 8:12
LORD shall give thee rest from f Is 14:3
f toward me is taught by the precept Is 29:13
a voice of trembling, of f, not of peace Jer 30:5
I will put my f in their hearts Jer 32:40
where is my f? Mal 1:6
they cried out for f Matt 14:26
hearts failing them for f Luke 21:26
for f of the Jews John 7:13; 19:38; 20:19
with you in weakness, and in f 1 Cor 2:3
what f, yea, what vehement desire 2 Cor 7:11
with f and trembling Eph 6:5; Phil 2:12
f of death Heb 2:15
moved with f Heb 11:7
with reverence and godly f Heb 12:28
feeding themselves without f Jude 1:12
others save with f Jude 1:23

FEAR (v)
I know that thou f God Gen 22:12
This do, and live, for I f God Gen 42:18
because the midwives f God Ex 1:21
F ye not, stand still, and see Ex 14:13
able men, such as f God Ex 18:21
F not, for God is come to prove Ex 20:20
that they may learn to f Deut 4:10
that they would f me Deut 5:29
f this glorious and fearful name Deut 28:58
thou shalt f day and night Deut 28:66
F before him, all the earth 1 Chr 16:30; Ps 96:9
and f God above many Neh 7:2
Doth Job f God for nought? Job 1:9
shalt be stedfast, thou shalt not f Job 11:15
whom shall I f? Ps 27:1
my heart shall not f Ps 27:3
laid up for them that f thee Ps 31:19
will not f what flesh can do Ps 56:4
Come and hear, all ye that f God Ps 66:16
unite my heart to f thy name Ps 86:11
Ye that f the LORD, trust Ps 115:11
They that f thee will be glad Ps 119:74
f the LORD, and depart Prov 3:7
Happy is the man that f always Prov 28:14
woman that f the Lord Prov 31:30
that men should f before him Eccl 3:14
but f thou God Eccl 5:7
as he that f an oath Eccl 9:2
F God, and keep his commandments Eccl 12:13
neither f ye their fear Is 8:12
to them that are of a fearful heart, f not Is 35:4
F thou not, I am with thee Is 41:10
F not, thou worm Jacob Is 41:14
Let us f the Lord Jer 5:24
would not f thee, O King of nations? Jer 10:7
they shall f and tremble Jer 33:9
f before the God of Daniel Dan 6:26
I said, Surely thou wilt f me Zeph 3:7
they that f the LORD spake Mal 3:16
unto you that f my name Mal 4:2
f not to take unto thee Matt 1:20
f him which is able to destroy Matt 10:28
f the multitude Matt 14:5; 21:46
we f the people Matt 21:26
they f exceedingly Mark 4:41
woman f and trembling Mark 5:33
they f him, because all the people Mark 11:18
f as they entered into the cloud Luke 9:34
F not, little flock Luke 12:32
judge, which f not God Luke 18:2
I f thee, because thou art Luke 19:21
Dost not thou f God? Luke 23:40

because they f the Jews John 9:22
just man, and one that f God Acts 10:22
f him, and worketh righteousness Acts 10:35
whosoever among you f God Acts 13:26
bondage again to f Rom 8:15
not highminded, but f Rom 11:20
I f, lest 2 Cor 11:3; 12:20
rebuke, that others may also f 1 Tim 5:20
heard in that he f Heb 5:7
I will not f what man Heb 13:6
He that f is not perfect in love 1 John 4:18

FEARFUL

f in praises Ex 15:11
to them that are of a f heart Is 35:4
Why are ye f? Matt 8:26
f looking for of judgment Heb 10:27
f thing to fall into the hands Heb 10:31

FEARFULNESS

F and trembling are come Ps 55:5
My heart panted, f affrighted me Is 21:4
f hath surprised the hypocrites Is 33:14

FEAST

hypocritical mockers in f Ps 35:16
merry heart hath a continual f Prov 15:15
the house of f Eccl 7:2; Jer 16:8
f is made for laughter Eccl 10:19
your appointed f my soul hateth Is 1:14
I despise your f days Amos 5:21
turn your f into mourning Amos 8:10
uppermost rooms at f Matt 23:6; Mark 12:39
Not on the f day Matt 26:5; Mark 14:2
after the custom of the f Luke 2:42
when thou makest a f Luke 14:13
go not up yet unto this f John 7:8
about the midst of the f John 7:14
that great day of the f John 7:37
we have need against the f John 13:29
I must by all means keep this f Acts 18:21
let us keep the f 1 Cor 5:8
bid you to a f 1 Cor 10:27

FEATHERS

wings and f unto the ostrich Job 39:13
cover thee with his f Ps 91:4
hairs were grown like eagles' f Dan 4:33

FED

which f me all my life long Gen 48:15
verily thou shalt be f Ps 37:3
f themselves, and f not my flock Ezek 34:8
an hungred, and f thee? Matt 25:37
I have f you with milk 1 Cor 3:2

FEEBLE

What do these f Jews? Neh 4:2
the f knees Job 4:4; Is 35:3; Heb 12:12
not one f person Ps 105:37
conies are but a f folk Prov 30:26
All hands shall be f Ezek 7:17; 21:7

FEED

trade hath been to f cattle Gen 46:32
commanded the ravens to f thee 1 Kgs 17:4
f him with the bread of affliction 1 Kgs 22:27
f them also, and lift them up for ever Ps 28:9
mouth of f on foolishness Prov 15:14
f me with food convenient Prov 30:8
lambs f after their manner Is 5:17
cow and the bear shall f Is 11:7
He f on ashes Is 44:20
strangers shall stand and f your flocks Is 61:5
The wolf and the lamb shall f Is 65:25
f you with knowledge Jer 3:15
f every one in his place Jer 6:3
Ephraim f on wind Hos 12:1
F the flock of the slaughter Zech 11:4
your heavenly Father f them Matt 6:26
and God f them Luke 12:24
F my lambs John 21:15
if thine enemy hunger, f him Rom 12:20
F the flock of God 1 Pet 5:2

FEEL

My father peradventure will f me Gen 27:12
if haply they might f after him Acts 17:27

FEELING

being past f Eph 4:19
touched with the f of our infirmities Heb 4:15

FEET

lawgiver from between his f Gen 49:10
I will pass through on my f Deut 2:28
f of the priests that bare the ark Josh 3:15
land whereon thy f have trodden Josh 14:9
she lay at his f Ruth 3:14
keep the f of his saints 1 Sam 2:9
my f did not slip 2 Sam 22:37; Ps 18:36
sound of his master's f 2 Kgs 6:32
he revived, and stood up on his f 2 Kgs 13:21
their f swelled not Neh 9:21
f was I to the lame Job 29:15
all things under his f Ps 8:6; 1 Cor 15:27; Eph 1:22
pierced my hands and my f Ps 22:16
set my f in a large room Ps 31:8
my f upon a rock Ps 40:2
my f from falling Ps 56:13; 116:8
suffered not our f to be moved Ps 66:9
my f were almost gone Ps 73:2
f have they, but they walk not Ps 115:7
a lamp unto my f Ps 119:105
Our f shall stand within thy gates Ps 122:2
f run to evil Prov 1:16; Is 59:7
Ponder the path of thy f Prov 4:26
Her f go down to death Prov 5:5
speaketh with his f Prov 6:13
and his f not be burned Prov 6:28
her f abide not in her house Prov 7:11
he that hasteth with his f Prov 19:2
washed my f; how shall I defile Song 5:3
How beautiful are thy f Song 7:1
tinkling with their f Is 3:16
with twain he covered his f Is 6:2
her own f shall carry her Is 23:7
the f of the poor Is 26:6
the f of him that bringeth Is 52:7; Nah 1:15
place of my f glorious Is 60:13
crush under his f all the prisoners Lam 3:34
stand upon thy f Ezek 2:1
shoes upon thy f Ezek 24:17,23
stamped with thy f Ezek 25:6
troublest the waters with thy f Ezek 32:2
with your f Ezek 34:18,19
f part of iron and part clay Dan 2:33
f like in colour to polished brass Dan 10:6
clouds are the dust of his f Nah 1:3
f shall stand on in that day Zech 14:4
trample them under their f Matt 7:6
dust of your f Matt 10:14; Mark 6:11; Luke 9:5
rather than having two hands or two f Matt 18:8
they came and held him by the f Matt 28:9
guide our f into the way of peace Luke 1:79
kissed his f, and anointed them Luke 7:38
sitting at the f of Jesus Luke 8:35
Mary, who also sat at Jesus' f Luke 10:39
Behold my hands and my f Luke 24:39
wiped his f with her hair John 11:2; 12:3
anointed the f of Jesus John 12:3
began to wash the disciples f John 13:5
dost thou wash my f? John 13:6
needeth not save to wash his f John 13:10
angel at the head, the other at the f John 20:12
f and ankle bones received strength Acts 3:7
at the apostles' f Acts 4:35,37; 5:2
f of them which have buried thy husband Acts 5:9
a man at Lystra, impotent in his f Acts 14:8
bound his own hands and f Acts 21:11
at the f of Gamaliel Acts 22:3
f swift to shed blood Rom 3:15
the f of them that preach Rom 10:15
bruise Satan under your f Rom 16:20
the head to the f, I have no need 1 Cor 12:21
your f shod with the preparation Eph 6:15
I fell at his f as dead Rev 1:17
f were as the f of a bear Rev 13:2
at his f to worship Rev 19:10
worship before the f of the angel Rev 22:8

FEIGN

f himself mad in their hands 1 Sam 21:13
prayer, that goeth not out of f lips Ps 17:1
with her whole heart, but f Jer 3:10
f themselves just men Luke 20:20

FELIX fe´-lix

happy Acts 23:24

FELL

his countenance f Gen 4:5
the wall f down flat Josh 6:20
fire of the Lord f, and consumed 1 Kgs 18:38
as one was f a beam 2 Kgs 6:5
there f a voice from heaven Dan 4:31
the lot f Jon 1:7
it f Matt 7:25; Luke 6:49
he f asleep Luke 8:23
f among thieves Luke 10:30
upon whom the tower in Siloam f Luke 13:4
from which Judas by transgression f Acts 1:25
lot f upon Matthias Acts 1:26
f on sleep Acts 13:36
since the fathers f asleep 2 Pet 3:4
cities of the nations f Rev 16:19

FELLOW

Wherefore smitest thou thy f? Ex 2:13
this f to play the madman 1 Sam 21:15
as one of the vain f 2 Sam 6:20
wherefore came this mad f 2 Kgs 9:11
oil of gladness above thy f Ps 45:7; Heb 1:9
one will lift up his f Eccl 4:10
the man that is my f Zech 13:7
calling unto their f Matt 11:16
begin to smite his f-servants Matt 24:49
This f said, I am able to destroy Matt 26:61
This f was also with Jesus Matt 26:71
found this f perverting Luke 23:2
as for this f John 9:29
lewd f of the baser sort Acts 17:5
Away with such a f Acts 22:22
this man a pestilent f Acts 24:5

FELLOWSHIP

in the apostles' doctrine and f Acts 2:42
called unto the f of his Son 1 Cor 1:9
not that ye should have f with devils 1 Cor 10:20
what f hath righteousness 2 Cor 6:14
the f of the mystery Eph 3:9
have no f with Eph 5:11
your f in the gospel Phil 1:5
if any f of the Spirit Phil 2:1
the f of his sufferings Phil 3:10
our f is with the Father 1 John 1:3
we have f one with another 1 John 1:7

FELT

even darkness which may be f Ex 10:21
they have beaten me, and I f it not Prov 23:35
she f in her body that she was healed Mark 5:29
into the harm, and f no harm Acts 28:5

FEMALE

made them male and f Matt 19:4; Mark 10:6
neither male nor f Gal 3:28

FENCED

hast f me with bones Job 10:11

He hath f up my way Job 19:8
he f it, and gathered Is 5:2

FERVENT
f in the spirit Acts 18:25
f in spirit Rom 12:11
f prayer of a righteous man James 5:16
with a pure heart f 1 Pet 1:22
melt with f heat 2 Pet 3:10,12

FESTUS fest´-us
joyful Acts 24:27

FETCH
must we f you water Num 20:10
I will f my knowledge from afar Job 36:3
I will f wine Is 56:12
come themselves and f us out Acts 16:37

FETTERS
bound him with f of brass Judg 16:21
feet they hurt with f Ps 105:18
with f of iron Ps 149:8
bound with f and chains Mark 5:4
with chains and in f Luke 8:29

FEW
they seemed unto him but a f days Gen 29:20
f and evil have the days Gen 47:9
to save by many or by f 1 Sam 14:6
left those f sheep in the wilderness? 1 Sam 17:28
borrow not a f 2 Kgs 4:3
but the people were f Neh 7:4
man is of f days Job 14:1
When a f years are come Job 16:22
let thy words be f Eccl 5:2
f there be that find it Matt 7:14
the labourers are f Matt 9:37; Luke 10:2
a f little fishes Matt 15:34
many called, but f chosen Matt 20:16
faithful over a f things Matt 25:21
laid his hands upon a f sick folk Mark 6:5
beaten with f stripes Luke 12:48
are there f that be saved? Luke 13:23
a f names even in Sardis Rev 3:4

FIELD
lying in the f Deut 21:1
give every one of you f 1 Sam 22:7
the f of the slothful Prov 24:30
that lay f to f Is 5:8
The f is the world Matt 13:38
treasure hid in a f Matt 13:44
look on the f John 4:35
who have reaped down your f James 5:4

FIERCE
anger, for it was f Gen 49:7
A nation of f countenance Deut 28:50
exceeding f Matt 8:28
and they were the more f Luke 23:5
f despisers of those that are good 2 Tim 3:3
driven of f winds James 3:4

FIERY
a f law for them Deut 33:2
a burning f furnace Dan 3:6
the f darts of the wicked Eph 6:16
judgment and f indignation Heb 10:27
concerning the f trial 1 Pet 4:12

FIG
vine and under his f tree 1 Kgs 4:25; Mic 4:4
every one of his f tree 2 Kgs 18:31; Is 36:16
the f tree shall not blossom Hab 3:17
grapes of thorns, or f of thistles? Matt 7:16
Behold the f tree Luke 21:29
Can the f tree James 3:12
casteth her untimely f Rev 6:13

FIGHT (n)
good f 1 Tim 6:12; 2 Tim 4:7
great f of afflictions Heb 10:32
valiant in f Heb 11:34

FIGHT (v)
f for you Ex 14:14; Deut 1:30; 3:22; 20:4
he it is that f for you Josh 23:10
f the battles of the Lord 1 Sam 25:28
f for your master's house 2 Kgs 10:3
f for your brethren, your sons Neh 4:14
my fingers to f Ps 144:1
then would my servants f John 18:36
f against God Acts 5:39; 23:9
so f I, not as one that beateth the air 1 Cor 9:26
ye f and war James 4:2

FIGHTINGS
without were f 2 Cor 7:5
wars and f among you James 4:1

FIGURE
similitude of any f Deut 4:16
who is the f of him Rom 5:14
a f for the time then present Heb 9:9
The like f whereunto even baptism 1 Pet 3:21

FILL
f with glory Num 14:21
f my mouth with arguments Job 23:4
open thy mouth wide, and I will f it Ps 81:10
they are f with good Ps 104:28
barns be f with plenty Prov 3:10
f with his own ways Prov 14:14
a fool when he is f with meat Prov 30:22
hath not f his days Is 65:20
shall be f Matt 5:6; Luke 6:21
Let the children first be f Mark 7:27
f with the Holy Ghost Luke 1:15; Acts 4:8; 9:17; 13:9
that my house may be f Luke 14:23
sorrow hath f your heart John 16:6
have f Jerusalem with your doctrine Acts 5:28
f our hearts with food and gladness Acts 14:17
f with all unrighteousness Rom 1:29
f with all knowledge Rom 15:14
him that f all in all Eph 1:23
f with all the fulness of God Eph 3:19
be f with the Spirit Eph 5:18
f with fruits of righteousness Phil 1:11
f up that which is behind Col 1:24
be ye warmed and f James 2:16
in them is f up the wrath of God Rev 15:1

FILTH
away the f of the daughters of Zion Is 4:4
as the f of the world 1 Cor 4:13

FILTHINESS
cleanse ourselves from all f of the flesh 2 Cor 7:1
Neither f, nor foolish talking Eph 5:4
lay apart all f James 1:21

FILTHY
much more abominable and f is man? Job 15:16
all together become f Ps 14:3
as f rags Is 64:6
clothed with f garments Zech 3:3
blasphemy, f communication Col 3:8
f lucre 1 Tim 3:3; Titus 1:7; 1 Pet 5:2
vexed with the f conversation 2 Pet 2:7
f dreamers Jude 1:8
he which is f let him be f Rev 22:11

FINALLY
F, brethren, farewell 2 Cor 13:11
F, my brethren, be strong Eph 6:10
F, my brethren, rejoice Phil 3:1
F, brethren, whatsoever things are true Phil 4:8
F, brethren, pray for us 2 Thess 3:1
F, be ye all of one mind 1 Pet 3:8

FIND
be sure your sin will f you out Num 32:23
past f out Job 9:10; Rom 11:33
where I might f him Job 23:3
life unto those that f them Prov 4:22
seek me early shall f me Prov 8:17
whoso f me f life Prov 8:35
f a wife, f a good thing Prov 18:22
thy hand f to do, do it Eccl 9:10
f it after many days Eccl 11:1
f thine own pleasure Is 58:13
f rest for your souls Jer 6:16
ye shall seek me, and f me Jer 29:13
seek, and ye shall f Matt 7:7; Luke 11:9
few there be that f it Matt 7:14
loseth his life for my sake shall f it Matt 10:39
as many as ye shall f Matt 22:9
he might f any thing thereon Mark 11:13
he f you sleeping Mark 13:36
until he f it Luke 15:4
shall he f faith on the earth? Luke 18:8
first f his own brother John 1:41
I f then a law, that, when I would Rom 7:21
f grace to help Heb 4:16

FINE
than much f gold Ps 19:10
an ornament of f gold Prov 25:12
is the most f gold changed! Lam 4:1
he bought f linen Mark 15:46

FINGER
This is the f of God Ex 8:19
written with the f of God Ex 31:18; Deut 9:10
little f shall be thicker 1 Kgs 12:10; 2 Chr 10:10
Bind them upon thy f Prov 7:3
the putting forth of the f Is 58:9
came forth f of a man's hand Dan 5:5
with one of their f Matt 23:4; Luke 11:46
the tip of his f Luke 16:24
with his f wrote on the ground John 8:6
put my f into the print of the nails John 20:25
Reach hither thy f John 20:27

FINISH
until thou hast f 1 Chr 28:20
So the wall was f Neh 6:15
to f Luke 14:28,29,30
and to f his work John 4:34
which the Father hath given me to f John 5:36
I have f the work John 17:4
It is f John 19:30
f my course Acts 20:24; 2 Tim 4:7
f in you the same grace 2 Cor 8:6
sin, when it is f James 1:15

FIRE
Behold the f and the wood Gen 22:7
bush burned with f Ex 3:2
that kindled the f shall make restitution Ex 22:6
f from the LORD Lev 10:2
pass through the f Lev 18:21; Deut 18:10; 2 Kgs 17:17; 23:10
brands on f, Judg 15:5
that answereth by f 1 Kgs 18:24
the LORD was not in the f 1 Kgs 19:12
answered him from heaven by f 1 Chr 21:26
musing the f burned Ps 39:3
they have cast f into thy sanctuary Ps 74:7
Can a man take f Prov 6:27
no wood is, there the f goeth out Prov 26:20
f; so is a contentious man to kindle Prov 26:21
as the fuel of the f Is 9:19
glorify ye the Lord in the f Is 24:15
walkest through the f Is 43:2
the melting f burneth Is 64:2
the LORD will come with f Is 66:15
by f and by his sword will Is 66:16
a burning f shut up in my bones Jer 20:9

your f be not in the winter Matt 24:20
turned to f the armies of the aliens Heb 11:34

FLINT
and oil out of the f rock Deut 32:13
horses' hoofs shall be counted like f Is 5:28
I set my face like a f Is 50:7
harder than f have I made thy forehead Ezek 3:9

FLOCK
f that was given thee, thy beautiful f? Jer 13:20
And ye my f, the f of my pasture Ezek 34:31
O poor of the f Zech 11:7
Fear not, little f Luke 12:32
and to all the f Acts 20:28
not sparing the f Acts 20:29
Feed the f of God 1 Pet 5:2
being examples to the f 1 Pet 5:3

FLOOD
other side of the f in old time Josh 24:2
He bindeth the f from overflowing Job 28:11
surely in f of great waters Ps 32:6
neither can f drown love Song 8:7
f upon the dry ground Is 44:3
enemy shall come in like a f Is 59:19
the f came, and the winds blew Matt 7:25
in days before the f Matt 24:38
knew not till f came Matt 24:39

FLOOR
gather as sheaves into the f Mic 4:12
will thoroughly purge his f Matt 3:12; Luke 3:17

FLOURISH
In his days shall the righteous f Ps 72:7
In the morning it f Ps 90:6
The righteous shall f like a palm tree Ps 92:12
a flower of the field, so he f Ps 103:15
the righteous shall f as branch Prov 11:28
the tabernacle of the upright f Prov 14:11
and the almond tree shall f Eccl 12:5
to see whether the vine f Song 6:11
let us see if the vine f Song 7:12
and have made dry tree to f Ezek 17:24
your care of me hath f again Phil 4:10

FLOW
his wind to blow, and the waters f Ps 147:18
the spices thereof may f out Song 4:16
and all nations shall f unto it Is 2:2
mountains might f down at thy presence Is 64:1
f together to the goodness of the Lord Jer 31:12
out of his belly shall f living water John 7:38

FLOWER
thine house shall die in f of their age 1 Sam 2:33
He cometh forth like a f Job 14:2
The f appear on earth Song 2:12
glorious beauty is a fading f Is 28:1
as the f of the field Is 40:6
f fadeth Is 40:7
and the f of Lebanon languisheth Nah 1:4
as the f of the grass James 1:10; 1 Pet 1:24

FLY
as sparks f upward Job 5:7
For then would I f away Ps 55:6
and we f away Ps 90:10
they f away as an eagle Prov 23:5
who are these that f as a cloud Is 60:8

FOAM
as the f upon the water Hos 10:7
and he f, and gnasheth with his teeth Mark 9:18
it teareth him that he f again Luke 9:39
waves of the sea, f out their own shame Jude 1:13

FOES
even mine enemies and my f Ps 27:2
hath not made my f to rejoice over me Ps 30:1
I will beat down his f before his face Ps 89:23

man's f shall be they Matt 10:36
I make thy f thy footstool Acts 2:35

FOLD (n)
shall be cut off from the f Hab 3:17
which are not of this f John 10:16

FOLD (v)
a little f of the hands to sleep Prov 6:10; 24:33
The fool f his hands Eccl 4:5

FOLK
The conies are but a feeble f Prov 30:26
and the f in the fire Jer 51:58
laid his hands upon a few sick f Mark 6:5
a great multitude of impotent f John 5:3

FOLLOW
hath f me fully Num 14:24
God, f him 1 Kgs 18:21
goodness and mercy shall f me Ps 23:6
My soul f hard after thee Ps 63:8
the players on instruments f after Ps 68:25
that f vain persons Prov 12:11
that they may f strong drink Is 5:11
if we f on to know the LORD Hos 6:3
took me as I f the flock Amos 7:15
F me Matt 4:19; 8:22; 9:9; 16:24; 19:21; Mark 2:14; 8:34; 10:21; Luke 5:27; 9:23,59; John 1:43
I will f thee Matt 8:19; Luke 9:57,61
we have left all, and have f thee Mark 10:28; Luke 18:28
as they f, they were afraid Mark 10:32
Peter f afar off Luke 22:54
and know me, and f me John 10:27
thou canst not f me now John 13:36
f after the things which make for peace Rom 14:19
that spiritual Rock that f them 1 Cor 10:4
F after charity 1 Cor 14:1
I f after Phil 3:12
ever f that which is good 1 Thess 5:15
some men they f after 1 Tim 5:24
f after righteousness 1 Tim 6:11; 2 Tim 2:22
F peace with all men Heb 12:14
whose faith f Heb 13:7
the glory that should f 1 Pet 1:11
that ye should f his steps 1 Pet 2:21
f the way of Balaam 2 Pet 2:15
they which f the Lamb Rev 14:4
their works do f them Rev 14:13

FOLLOWER
f of God, as dear children Eph 5:1
f of them who through faith Heb 6:12

FOLLY
and f is with him 1 Sam 25:25
his angels he charged with f Job 4:18
yet God layeth not f to them Job 24:12
lest I deal with you after your f Job 42:8
This their way is their f Ps 49:13
let them not turn again to f Ps 85:8
a fool layeth open his f Prov 13:16
the f of fools is deceitful Prov 14:8
The simple inherit f Prov 14:18
instruction of fools is f Prov 16:22
rather than a fool in his f Prov 17:12
Answer not a fool according to his f Prov 26:4
Answer fool according to his f Prov 26:5
wisdom, and to know madness and f Eccl 1:17
wisdom excelleth f Eccl 2:13
the wickedness of f Eccl 7:25
F is set in great dignity Eccl 10:6
bear with me a little in my f 2 Cor 11:1
their f shall be manifest 2 Tim 3:9

FOOD
tree was good for f Gen 3:6
her f, her raiment, and her duty Ex 21:10
in giving him f and raiment Deut 10:18

more than my necessary f Job 23:12
wilderness yieldeth f Job 24:5
did eat angels' f Ps 78:25
bring forth f out of the earth Ps 104:14
giveth f to all flesh Ps 136:25
gathereth her f in the harvest Prov 6:8
Much f is in the tillage of the poor Prov 13:23
with f convenient for me Prov 30:8
she bringeth her f from afar Prov 31:14
minister bread for your f 2 Cor 9:10
having f and raiment 1 Tim 6:8
desitute of daily f James 2:15

FOOL
Died Abner as a f dieth? 2 Sam 3:33
f hath said in his heart Ps 14:1; 53:1
unto the f, Deal not foolishly Ps 75:4
f despise wisdom Prov 1:7
shame shall be the promotion of f Prov 3:35
a prating f shall fall Prov 10:8,10
f die for want of wisdom Prov 10:21
sport to a f to do mischief Prov 10:23
the f shall be servant to the wise Prov 11:29
way of f is right in own eyes Prov 12:15
f wrath presently known Prov 12:16
f layeth open his folly Prov 13:16
companion of f shall be destroyed Prov 13:20
folly of f is deceit Prov 14:8
F make a mock at sin Prov 14:9
the f rageth, and is confident Prov 14:16
mouth of f poureth out foolishness Prov 15:2
a f despiseth his father's instruction Prov 15:5
the instruction of f is folly Prov 16:22
a f, when he holdeth his peace, is Prov 17:28
every f will be meddling Prov 20:3
a f uttereth all his mind Prov 29:11
f walketh in darkness Eccl 2:14
how dieth wise man? as the f Eccl 2:16
whether he shall be a wise man or a f? Eccl 2:19
f voice is known by multitude of words Eccl 5:3
A f also is full of words Eccl 10:14
wayfaring men, though f Is 35:8
at his end he shall be a f Jer 17:11
the prophet is a f Hos 9:7
shall say, thou f Matt 5:22
Ye f and blind Matt 23:17
Thou f, this night Luke 12:20
O f, and slow of heart Luke 24:25
let him become a f 1 Cor 3:18
Let no man think me a f 2 Cor 11:16
I am become a f in glorying 2 Cor 12:11
walk circumspectly, not as f, but as wise Eph 5:15

FOOLISH
O f people Deut 32:6
I have done very f 2 Sam 24:10; 1 Chr 21:8
as one of the f women Job 2:10
I was envious at the f Ps 73:3
Forsake the f, and live Prov 9:6
A f woman is clamorous Prov 9:13
the f plucketh it down Prov 14:1
A f son is grief Prov 17:25
neither be thou f Eccl 7:17
my people are f Jer 4:22
unto a f man Matt 7:26
their f heart was darkened Rom 1:21
hath not God made f 1 Cor 1:20
O f Galatians Gal 3:1
Are ye so f? Gal 3:3
nor f talking Eph 5:4
into many f and hurtful lusts 1 Tim 6:9
f and unlearned questions avoid 2 Tim 2:23
were sometimes f Titus 3:3
ignorance of f men 1 Pet 2:15

FOOLISHNESS
thou knowest my f Ps 69:5
F is bound in the heart of a child Prov 22:15
thought of f is sin Prov 24:9

FORGOTTEN
and hast f a sheaf Deut 24:19
hast f God that formed thee Deut 32:18
the needy shall not always be f Ps 9:18
God hath f: he hideth his face Ps 10:11
I am f as a dead man Ps 31:12
Why hast thou f me? Ps 42:9
If we have f the name of our God Ps 44:20
Hath God f to be gracious? Ps 77:9
in the days to come shall all be f Eccl 2:16
they were f in the city Eccl 8:10
the memory of them is f Eccl 9:5
thou hast f the God of thy salvation Is 17:10
thou shalt not be f of me Is 44:21
my Lord hath f me Is 49:14
the former troubles are f Is 65:16
my people have f me Jer 2:32; 18:15
f the Lord their God Jer 3:21
because thou hast f me Jer 13:25
ye have f the wickedness of your fathers Jer 44:9
they have f their resting place Jer 50:6
thou hast f me Ezek 22:12; 23:35
had f to take bread Matt 16:5; Mark 8:14
not one of them is f before God Luke 12:6
f that he was purged from old sins 2 Pet 1:9

FORM (n)
the earth was without f Gen 1:2; Jer 4:23
I could not discern the f Job 4:16
his f more than sons of men Is 52:14
the f of a man's hand Ezek 10:8
the f of his visage changed Dan 3:19
f of the fourth is like the Son of God Dan 3:25
he appeared in another f Mark 16:12
the f of knowledge and of the truth Rom 2:20
Who, being in the f of God Phil 2:6
took upon him the f of a servant Phil 2:7
Hold fast the f of sound words 2 Tim 1:13
Having a f of godliness 2 Tim 3:5

FORM (v)
hast forgotten God that f thee Deut 32:18
ancient times that I have f it 2 Kgs 19:25; Is 37:26
dead things are f from under the waters Job 26:5
his hand hath f the crooked serpent Job 26:13
I also am f out of the clay Job 33:6
thou hadst f the earth and the world Ps 90:2
He that f the eye shall he not see? Ps 94:9
The great God that f all things Prov 26:10
and he that f thee, O Israel Is 43:1
I have f him; yea Is 43:7
before me was there no God f Is 43:10
This people have I f for myself Is 43:21
Who hath f a god Is 44:10
I have f thee, thou art my servant Is 44:21
No weapon that is f against thee Is 54:17
behold, he f grasshoppers Amos 7:1
Shall the thing f say to him that f it Rom 9:20
until Christ be f in you Gal 4:19

FORMER
manner in f time Ruth 4:7
of the f age Job 8:8
where are thy f lovingkindnesses? Ps 89:49
no remembrance of f things Eccl 1:11
f days were better than these Eccl 7:10
Remember ye not the f things Is 43:18
Remember the f things of old Is 46:9
declared the f things from the beginning Is 48:3
measure their f work Is 65:7
f troubles are forgotten Is 65:16
f and the latter Jer 5:24
the f of all things Jer 10:16; 51:19
the latter and the f rain Hos 6:3
the rain, the f rain, and the latter Joel 2:23
greater than the f Hag 2:9
f prophets Zech 1:4; 7:7,12
as in the f days Zech 8:11
half of them toward the f sea Zech 14:8
as in f years Mal 3:4
concerning the f conversation Eph 4:22
for the f things are passed away Rev 21:4

FORSAKE
not f Deut 4:31; 31:6; 1 Chr 28:20
f not the Levite Deut 12:19
he f God which made him Deut 32:15
nor f thee Josh 1:5; Heb 13:5
f my sweetness Judg 9:11
if thou f him, he will cast thee off 1 Chr 28:9
if ye f him, he will f you 2 Chr 15:2
we will not f the house of our God Neh 10:39
Why is the house of God f? Neh 13:11
he f the fear of the Almighty Job 6:14
oppressed and hath f the poor Job 20:19
why hast thou f me? Ps 22:1; Matt 27:46; Mark 15:34
yet have I not seen the righteous f Ps 37:25
the LORD f not his saints Ps 37:28
f me not utterly Ps 119:8
f not the works of thine own hands Ps 138:8
f not law of thy mother Prov 1:8; 6:20
f the guide of her youth Prov 2:17
F her not, and she shall preserve thee Prov 4:6
and thy father's friend, f not Prov 27:10
a great f in the midst of the land Is 6:12
as a f bough Is 17:9
palaces shall be f Is 32:14
as a woman f Is 54:6
for a small moment have I f Is 54:7
no more be termed F Is 62:4
A city not f Is 62:12
f me the fountain of living waters Jer 2:13
every city shall be f Jer 4:29
we have f all Matt 19:27; Luke 5:11
that hath f houses Matt 19:29
f him, and fled Matt 26:56; Mark 14:50
they f their nets Mark 1:18
he be of you that f not all Luke 14:33
Persecuted, but not f 2 Cor 4:9
Demas hath f me 2 Tim 4:10
all men f me 2 Tim 4:16
Not f the assembling of ourselves Heb 10:25
by faith he f Egypt Heb 11:27

FORSWEAR
Thou shalt not f thyself Matt 5:33

FORTUNATUS for´-tu-na´-tus
prosperous 1 Cor 16:17

FORWARD
backward, and not f Jer 7:24
helped f the affliction Zech 1:15

FOUL
face is f with weeping Job 16:16
It will be f weather to day Matt 16:3
he rebuked the f spirit Mark 9:25
the hold of every f spirit Rev 18:2

FOUND
f it so quickly Gen 27:20
This have we f Gen 37:32
hath f out the iniquity Gen 44:16
a lion f him 1 Kgs 20:36
Hast thou f me, O mine enemy? 1 Kgs 21:20
I have f the book of the law 2 Kgs 22:8
good things f in thee 2 Chr 19:3
where shall wisdom be f? Job 28:12
I have f a ransom Job 33:24
when thou mayest be f Ps 32:6
iniquity be f to be hateful Ps 36:2
sparrow hath f a house Ps 84:3
Hast thou f honey? Prov 25:16
one man among a thousand have I f Eccl 7:28
this only have I f Eccl 7:29
but I f him whom my soul loveth Song 3:4
f of them that sought me not Is 65:1; Rom 10:20
thief is ashamed when he is f Jer 2:26
in thy skirts is f Jer 2:34
ten men were f Jer 41:8
but I f none Ezek 22:30
balances, and art f wanting Dan 5:27
iniquity was not f in his lips Mal 2:6
it was f upon a rock Matt 7:25
have not f so great faith Matt 8:10
f one pearl of great price Matt 13:46
f others standing idle Matt 20:6
f nothing thereon Matt 21:19
they f fault Mark 7:2
she f the devil gone out Mark 7:30
f them asleep Mark 14:40; Luke 22:45
they f him in the temple Luke 2:46
f the man Luke 8:35
f my sheep Luke 15:6
f the piece which I had lost Luke 15:9
was lost, and is f Luke 15:24,32
have f no fault Luke 23:14
f the stone rolled away Luke 24:2
f not the body Luke 24:3,23
we have f the Messiah John 1:41
our fathers f no sustenance Acts 7:11
if he f any of this way Acts 9:2
I f an altar Acts 17:23
I f to be unto death Rom 7:10
we ourselves also are f sinners Gal 2:17
f in fashion as a man Phil 2:8
was not f Heb 11:5
he f no place of repentance Heb 12:17
not f thy works perfect Rev 3:2
neither was their place f Rev 12:8
mountains were not f Rev 16:20

FOUNDATION
lay the f thereof in his firstborn Josh 6:26
whose f is in the dust Job 4:19
If the f be destroyed Ps 11:3
all the f of the earth Ps 82:5
Of old hast thou laid f of earth Ps 102:25
raze it, even to the f Ps 137:7
righteous is an everlasting f Prov 10:25
I lay in Zion for a f Is 28:16
the f of many generations Is 58:12
laid the f on a rock Luke 6:48
without a f Luke 6:49
upon another man's f Rom 15:20
I have laid the f 1 Cor 3:10
other f can no man lay 1 Cor 3:11
if any man build on this f 1 Cor 3:12
upon the f of the apostles and prophets Eph 2:20
in store for themselves a good f 1 Tim 6:19
the f of God standeth sure 2 Tim 2:19
not laying again the f of repentance Heb 6:1
a city which hath f Heb 11:10
the wall of the city had twelve f Rev 21:14

FOUNTAIN
f of the great deep broken up Gen 7:11
The f also of the deep Gen 8:2
of f and depths Deut 8:7
stop the waters of the f 2 Chr 32:3
the f of life Ps 36:9
let thy f be dispersed abroad Prov 5:16
no f abounding with water Prov 8:24
The law of the wise is a f of life Prov 13:14
fear of the Lord is a f of life Prov 14:27
as a troubled f and a corrupt spring Prov 25:26
the pitcher be broken at the f Eccl 12:6
a f sealed Song 4:12
a f of gardens Song 4:15
the f of living waters Jer 2:13; 17:13
and mine eyes a f of tears Jer 9:1
his f shall be dried up Hos 13:15
a f opened to the house of David Zech 13:1

Doth a f send forth James 3:11
so can no f yield James 3:12
shall lead them unto living f of water Rev 7:17
the sea, and f of waters Rev 14:7
of the f of life freely Rev 21:6

FRAGMENTS
Gather up the f that remain John 6:12
and filled twelve baskets with the f John 6:13

FRAIL
I may know how f I am Ps 39:4

FRAME
he could not f to pronounce it right Judg 12:6
which f mischief by a law Ps 94:20
shall the thing f say of him that f it Is 29:16
the building fitly f together Eph 2:21

FRANKLY
he f forgave them both Luke 7:42

FRAUD
mouth is full of cursing, deceit and f Ps 10:7
which is of you kept back by f James 5:4

FRAY
shall f them away Deut 28:26; Jer 7:33
these are come to f them Zech 1:21

FREE
but he shall be f at home one year Deut 24:5
none of you be f from being bondmen Josh 9:23
haply the people had eaten f 1 Sam 14:30
as many as were of a f heart 2 Chr 29:31
the king and his counsellers offered f Ezra 7:15
uphold me with thy f spirit Ps 51:12
F among the dead Ps 88:5
and to let the oppressed go f Is 58:6
I will love them f Hos 14:4
Then are the children f Matt 17:26
he shall be f Mark 7:11
and the truth shall make you f John 8:32
Ye shall be made f? John 8:33
If the Son shall make you f, John 8:36
ye shall be f indeed John 8:36
the f gift Rom 5:15
made f from sin Rom 6:18,22
ye were f from righteousness Rom 6:20
f from the law of sin and death Rom 8:2
am I not f? 1 Cor 9:1
For though I be f from all men 1 Cor 9:19
whether we be bond or f 1 Cor 12:13; Eph 6:8
bond nor f Gal 3:28; Col 3:11
wherewith Christ hath made us f Gal 5:1
word of the Lord may have f course 2 Thess 3:1
As f, and not using your liberty 1 Pet 2:16

FREELY
every tree of the garden thou mayest f eat Gen 2:16
offered f for the house of God Ezra 2:68
f ye have received, f give Matt 10:8
Being justified f by his grace Rom 3:24
not with him f give us all things Rom 8:32
the water of life f Rev 21:6; 22:17

FRESH
taste of f oil Num 11:8
My glory was f in me Job 29:20
flesh shall be f than a child's Job 33:25
both yield salt water and f James 3:12

FRET
F not thyself Ps 37:1,7,8; Prov 24:19
his heart f against the LORD Prov 19:3

FRIEND
as a man speaketh unto his f Ex 33:11
lovest thine enemies, and hatest thy f 2 Sam 19:6
ye dig a pit for your f Job 6:27
when he prayed for his f Job 42:10
as though he had been my f Ps 35:14
my own familiar f hath lifted Ps 41:9
Lover and f hast thou put far from me Ps 88:18
if thou be surety for thy f Prov 6:1
make sure thy f Prov 6:3
the rich hath many f Prov 14:20
whisperer separateth chief f Prov 16:28
f loveth at all times Prov 17:17
a f that sticketh closer than a brother Prov 18:24
Wealth maketh many f Prov 19:4
Faithful are the wounds of a f Prov 27:6
Thine own f and father's f forsake not Prov 27:10
man sharpeneth countenance of his f Prov 27:17
this is my f Song 5:16
seed of Abraham my f Is 41:8
a terror to all thy f Jer 20:4
trust ye not in a f Mic 7:5
wounded in the house of my f Zech 13:6
a f of publicans Matt 11:19; Luke 7:34
F, I do thee no wrong Matt 20:13
F, how camest thou hither Matt 22:12
F, wherefore art thou come? Matt 26:50
Go home to thy f Mark 5:19
which of you shall have a f Luke 11:5
because he is his f Luke 11:8
call not thy f Luke 14:12
calleth his f and neighbours Luke 15:6
f of the mammon Luke 16:9
Our f Lazarus sleepeth John 11:11
lay down his life for his f John 15:13
ye are my f, if ye do John 15:14
I have called you f John 15:15
thou art not Caesar's f John 19:12
he was called the F of God James 2:23
a f of the world James 4:4

FROWARD
a very f generation Deut 32:20
man that speaketh f things Prov 2:12
the f is abomination Prov 3:32
put away from thee a f mouth Prov 4:24
a f heart Prov 11:20; 17:20
a f man soweth strife Prov 16:28
The way of man is f Prov 21:8
snares are in the way of the f Prov 22:5

FRUIT
shewed them the f of the land Num 13:26
take of the first of all the f Deut 26:2
precious f brought forth Deut 33:14
yield f of increase Ps 107:37
the f of the womb is his reward Ps 127:3
My f is better than gold Prov 8:19
f of the righteous is a tree of life Prov 11:30
the f of his mouth Prov 12:14; 18:20
his f was sweet to my taste Song 2:3
with pleasant f Song 4:13,16
the f of their doings Is 3:10; Jer 17:10; 21:14; 32:19; Mic 7:13
fill the face of the world with f Is 27:6
the hasty f before the summer Is 28:4
I create the f of the lips Is 57:19
eaten the f of lies Hos 10:13
basket of summer f Amos 8:1
f of my body for the sin of soul Mic 6:7
neither shall f be in the vines Hab 3:17
earth is stayed from her f Hag 1:10
f meet for repentance Matt 3:8
by their f ye shall know them Matt 7:20
make the tree good, and his f good Matt 12:33
which also beareth f Matt 13:23
Let no f grow on thee Matt 21:19
when the time of the f drew near Matt 21:34
f of the vine Matt 26:29; Mark 14:25
earth bringeth forth f of herself Mark 4:28
the f of the vineyard Mark 12:2
he came and sought f thereon Luke 13:6
I come seeking f on this fig tree Luke 13:7
if it bear f, well Luke 13:9
f unto life eternal John 4:36
branch that beareth f John 15:2
branch cannot bear f of itself John 15:4
that ye bear much f John 15:8
that ye should go and bring forth f John 15:16
have some f among you Rom 1:13
What f had ye then Rom 6:21
bring forth f unto God Rom 7:4
the f of righteousness 2 Cor 9:10; Phil 1:11
the f of the Spirit Gal 5:22; Eph 5:9
this is the f of my labour Phil 1:22
I desire f that may abound Phil 4:17
bringeth forth f Col 1:6
first partaker of the f 2 Tim 2:6
peaceable f of righteousness Heb 12:11
the f of our lips Heb 13:15
full of mercy and good f James 3:17
waiteth for the precious f James 5:7
trees whose f withereth, without f Jude 1:12
yielded her f every month Rev 22:2

FRUSTRATE
to f their purpose Ezra 4:5
That f the tokens of the liars Is 44:25
do not f the grace of God Gal 2:21

FUEL
with burning and f of fire Is 9:5
into the fire for f Ezek 15:4
shalt be for f to the fire Ezek 21:32

FULFIL
f all thy counsel Ps 20:4
f all thy petitions Ps 20:5
he will f the desire of them Ps 145:19
to f all righteousness Matt 3:15
not come to destroy, but to f Matt 5:17
till all be f Matt 5:18
when all these things shall be f? Mark 13:4
shall be f in their season Luke 1:20
times of the Gentiles be f Luke 21:24
until it be f in the kingdom of God Luke 22:16
this my joy therefore is f John 3:29
And as John f his course Acts 13:25
God hath f the same unto us Acts 13:33
love is the f of the law Rom 13:10
all the law is f in one word Gal 5:14
so f the law of Christ Gal 6:2
f the desires of the flesh Eph 2:3
F ye my joy Phil 2:2
thou f it Col 4:17
f all the good pleasure 2 Thess 1:11
If ye f the royal law James 2:8

FULL
land became f of wickedness Lev 19:29
houses f of all good things Deut 6:11
f of the spirit of wisdom Deut 34:9
I went out f Ruth 1:21
mountain was f of horses 2 Kgs 6:17
for the f price 1 Chr 21:22,24
come to thy grave in a f age Job 5:26
a man f of talk Job 11:2
f of trouble Job 14:1
f of the sin of his youth Job 20:11
dieth in his f strength Job 21:23
I am f of matter Job 32:18
mouth f of cursing Ps 10:7; Rom 3:14
which is f of water Ps 65:9
f of the habitations of cruelty Ps 74:20
soul is f of troubles Ps 88:3
earth, O LORD, is f of thy mercy Ps 119:64
Happy is the man that hath his quiver f Ps 127:5
the f soul lotheth a honeycomb Prov 27:7
hell and destruction are never f Prov 27:20
Lest I be f, and deny thee Prov 30:9
yet the sea is not f Eccl 1:7
earth was f of his praise Hab 3:3
f of boys and girls Zech 8:5
f of light Matt 6:22; Luke 11:36
Woe unto you that are f! Luke 6:25

f of ravening Luke 11:39
f of grace and truth John 1:14
that your joy might be f John 15:11; 16:24
f of the Holy Ghost Acts 6:3; 7:55; 11:24
f of good works Acts 9:36
ye also are f of goodness Rom 15:14
Now ye are f 1 Cor 4:8
I am instructed to be f Phil 4:12
I am f Phil 4:18
make f proof of thy ministry 2 Tim 4:5
to them that are of f age Heb 5:14
with joy unspeakable and f of glory 1 Pet 1:8
f of the wrath of God Rev 15:7

FULLY
hath followed me f Num 14:24
heart is f set in them to do evil Eccl 8:11
Let every man be f persuaded Rom 14:5
I have f preached the gospel Rom 15:19
her grapes are f ripe Rev 14:18

FULNESS
f of joy Ps 16:11
of his f have we all received John 1:16
the f of the Gentiles Rom 11:25
the f of him that filleth all in all Eph 1:23
filled with all the f of God Eph 3:19
the stature of the f of Christ Eph 4:13
in him should all f dwell Col 1:19
the f of the Godhead bodily Col 2:9

FURIOUS
with a f man thou shalt not go Prov 22:24
a f man aboundeth in transgression Prov 29:22
the LORD revengeth, and is f Nah 1:2

FURNACE
LORD hath taken you out of f Deut 4:20
as silver tried in a f Ps 12:6
in the f of affliction Is 48:10
into a f of fire Matt 13:42

FURNISH
Can God f a table in the wilderness? Ps 78:19
the wedding was f with guests Matt 22:10
throughly f unto all good works 2 Tim 3:17

FURROWS
thou settlest the f thereof Ps 65:10
made long their f Ps 129:3
f of the field Hos 10:4; 12:11

FURTHER
they f the people Ezra 8:36
Hitherto shalt thou come, but no f Job 38:11
as though he would have gone f Luke 24:28
that it spread no f among the people Acts 4:17
But they shall proceed no f 2 Tim 3:9

FURY
until thy brother's f turn away Gen 27:44
F is not in me Is 27:4
my f, it upheld me Is 63:5
in f and in great wrath Jer 21:5
Take the wine cup of this f at my hand Jer 25:15
and I will cause my f to rest Ezek 21:17

G

GAAL ga´-al
loathing Judg 9:26

GAASH ga´-ash
shaking Josh 24:30

GABA ga´-bah
hill Josh 18:24

GABBAI gab´-a-i
a collector of tribute Neh 11:8

GABBATHA gab´-ath-ah
height John 19:13

GABRIEL ga´-bri-el
man of God Dan 8:16

GAD gad
a troop, good fortune Gen 30:11

GADARENES gad´-ar-eens
inhabitants of Gadara Mark 5:1

GADDI gad´-i
fortunate Num 13:11

GADDIEL gad´-i-el
fortune sent from God Num 13:10

GADI gad´-i
fortunate 2 Kgs 15:14

GADITES gad´-ites
persons belonging to the tribe of Gad Deut 3:12

GAHAM ga´-ham
sunburnt (?) Gen 22:24

GAHAR ga´-har
hiding place Ezra 2:47

GAIN (n)
Or is it g to him Job 22:3
greedy of g Prov 1:19
the g thereof than gold Prov 3:14
He that is greedy of g Prov 15:27
by usury and unjust g Prov 28:8
thou hast greedily g Ezek 22:12
dishonest g Ezek 22:13,27
divide the land for g Dan 11:39
consecrate their g unto the LORD Mic 4:13
hope of their g was gone Acts 16:19
no small g unto the craftsmen Acts 19:24
make a g of you? 2 Cor 12:18
to die is g Phil 1:21
g to me, those I counted loss Phil 3:7
supposing that g is godliness 1 Tim 6:5
godliness with contentment is great g 1 Tim 6:6

GAIN (v)
if he shall g the whole world Matt 16:26; Mark 8:36; Luke 9:25
thou hast g thy brother Matt 18:15
had also g other two Matt 25:17
had g by trading Luke 19:15
that I might g the more 1 Cor 9:19
that I might g the Jews 1 Cor 9:20

GAINSAY
able to g nor resist Luke 21:15
to convince the g Titus 1:9
perished in the g of Korah Jude 1:11

GAIUS ga´-yus
Gr. for Caius Acts 19:29

GALAL ga´-lal
worthy (?) 1 Chr 9:15

GALATIA ga-la´-shah
a place colonized by Gauls Acts 16:6

GALATIANS ga-la´-shans
inhabitants of Galatia Gal 3:1

GALEED gal´-e-ed
heap of witness Gen 31:47

GALILEE gal´-il-ee
circuit Josh 20:7

GALL
gave me also g for my meat Ps 69:21
the wormwood and the g Lam 3:19
vinegar to drink mingled with g Matt 27:34
thou art in the g of bitterness Acts 8:23

GALLIM gal´-im
heaps 1 Sam 25:44

GALLIO gal´-li-o
one who lives on milk Acts 18:12

GAMALIEL ga-ma´-li-el
benefit of God Num 1:10

GAMMADIMS gam´-ad-ims
warriors (?) Ezek 27:11

GAMUL ga´-mool
weaned 1 Chr 24:17

GAP
gone up into the g Ezek 13:5
stand in the g before me Ezek 22:30

GARDEN
as the g of the LORD Gen 13:10
as a g of herbs Deut 11:10; 1 Kgs 21:2
a g inclosed Song 4:12
blow upon my g Song 4:16
I am come into my g Song 5:1
gone down into his g Song 6:2,11
as a lodge in a g Is 1:8
as a g that hath no water Is 1:30
her desert like the g of the LORD Is 51:3
a watered g Is 58:11; Jer 31:12
as the g causeth the things Is 61:11
plant g, and eat the fruit Jer 29:5
in Eden the g of God Ezek 28:13
cedars in the g of God Ezek 31:8
is become like the g of Eden Ezek 36:35
land is as the g of Eden before them Joel 2:3
Did not I see thee in the g John 18:26
there was a g; and in the g John 19:41

GAREB ga´-reb
scabby 2 Sam 23:38

GARMENT
he left his g in her hand, and fled Gen 39:12
washed his g in wine Gen 49:11
a goodly Babylonish g Josh 7:21
old g upon them Josh 9:5
to receive g 2 Kgs 5:26
all the way was full of g 2 Kgs 7:15
How thy g are warm Job 37:17
They part my g among them Ps 22:18
wax old as a g Ps 102:26; Is 50:9; 51:6; Heb 1:11
with light as with a g Ps 104:2
coveredst it with the deep as with a g Ps 104:6
with cursing like as with his g Ps 109:18
Take his g that is surety Prov 20:16
a g in cold weather Prov 25:20
Who hath bound the waters in a g? Prov 30:4
Let thy g be always white Eccl 9:8
put on thy beautiful g Is 52:1
g of praise for the spirit of heaviness Is 61:3
the g of salvation Is 61:10
rend your heart, and not your g Joel 2:13
a rough g to deceive Zech 13:4
new cloth, unto an old g Matt 9:16; Mark 2:21
hem of g Matt 14:36; Luke 8:44
spread their g in the way Matt 21:8; Mark 11:8
wedding g Matt 22:11,12
enlarge the borders of their g Matt 23:5
parted his g, casting lots Matt 27:35; Mark 15:24
not turn back again to take up his g Mark 13:16
cast their g upon the colt Luke 19:35
let him sell his g Luke 22:36
in shining g Luke 24:4
shewing the coats and g Acts 9:39
your g are motheaten James 5:2
the g spotted by the flesh Jude 1:23
not defiled their g Rev 3:4
that watcheth, and keepeth his g Rev 16:15

GARMITE garm´-ite
bony 1 Chr 4:19

GARNER
That our g may be full Ps 144:13
the g are laid desolate Joel 1:17
gather his wheat into the g Matt 3:12

GARNISH
he hath **g** the heavens Job 26:13
findeth it empty, swept, and **g** Matt 12:44
g the sepulchres of the righteous Matt 23:29

GASHMU gash´-moo
same as GESHEM Neh 6:6

GATAM ga´-tam
puny Gen 36:11

GATE
the **g** of heaven Gen 28:17
posts of thy house, and on thy **g** Deut 6:9; 11:20
the **g** of righteousness Ps 118:19
exalteth his **g** seeketh destruction Prov 17:19
her husband known in the **g** Prov 31:23
open ye the **g**, that the righteous Is 26:2
the **g** of the grave Is 38:10
open before him the two-leaved **g** Is 45:1
thy **g** shall be open continually Is 60:11
walls Salvation, and thy **g** Praise Is 60:18
strait **g** Matt 7:13; Luke 13:24
g of hell shall not prevail Matt 16:18
suffered without the **g** Heb 13:12
g of it shall not be shut at all by day Rev 21:25

GATH gath
winepress Josh 11:22

GATH-HEPHER gath-he´-fer
winepress of the well 2 Kgs 14:25

GATH-RIMMON gath-rim´-on
winepress of the pomegranate Josh 19:45

GATHER
let them **g** all the food Gen 41:35
to him shall the **g** of the people be Gen 49:10
g, some more, some less Ex 16:17
shalt **g** but little in Deut 28:38
g thee from all nations Deut 30:3; Ezek 36:24
on the ground, which cannot be **g** 2 Sam 14:14
he cut off, and shut up, or **g** together Job 11:10
G not my soul with sinners Ps 26:9
knoweth not who shall **g** them Ps 39:6
in the summer, and **g** her food Prov 6:8
he that **g** in summer Prov 10:5
he that **g** by labour shall increase Prov 13:11
ye shall be **g** one by one Is 27:12
he shall **g** the lambs Is 40:11
Yet will I **g** others Is 56:8
g out the stones Is 62:10
g his wheat into garner Matt 3:12; Luke 3:17
nor **g** into barns Matt 6:26
Do men **g** grapes of thorns Matt 7:16
he that **g** not with me scattereth Matt 12:30; Luke 11:23
we go and **g** them up? Matt 13:28
lest while ye **g** up the tares Matt 13:29
shall **g** out of his kingdom Matt 13:41
before him shall be **g** all nations Matt 25:32
G up the fragments John 6:12
men **g** them, and cast John 15:6
that there be no **g** when I come 1 Cor 16:2
by our **g** together unto him 2 Thess 2:1

GAVE
The woman whom thou **g** me Gen 3:12
LORD **g** them rest Josh 21:44; 2 Chr 15:15
g him another heart 1 Sam 10:9
and **g** the sense Neh 8:8
the LORD **g** Job 1:21
He asked life of thee, and thou **g** it Ps 21:4
The Lord **g** the word Ps 68:11
unto God who **g** it Eccl 12:7
ye **g** the Nazarites wine Amos 2:12
who **g** thee this authority? Matt 21:23; Mark 11:28; Luke 20:2
ye **g** me meat Matt 25:35
no man **g** unto him Luke 15:16
My Father, who **g** them me John 10:29
as the Spirit **g** them utterance Acts 2:4
I **g** my voice against them Acts 26:10
God **g** them over Rom 1:28
God **g** the increase 1 Cor 3:6
g gifts unto men Eph 4:8
he **g** some apostles Eph 4:11

GAY
weareth the **g** clothing James 2:3

GAZA ga´-zah
same as AZZAH Gen 10:19

GAZATHITES ga´-zath-ites
inhabitants of Gaza Josh 13:3

GAZE
unto the LORD to **g** Ex 19:21
why sand ye **g** up into heaven Acts 1:11

GAZER ga´-zer
place cut off 2 Sam 5:25

GAZEZ ga´-zez
shearer 1 Chr 2:46

GAZITES ga´-zites
inhabitants of Gaza Judg 16:2

GAZZAM gaz´-am
eating up Ezra 2:48

GEBA ge´-bah
hill Josh 21:17

GEBAL ge´-bal
mountain Ps 83:7

GEBER ge´-ber
man 1 Kgs 4:13

GEBIM ge´-bim
trenches Is 10:31

GEDALIAH ged´-al-i´-ah
whom Jehovah has made great 2 Kgs 25:22

GEDEON ged´-e-on
same as GIDEON Heb 11:32

GEDER ged´-er
wall Josh 12:13

GEDERAH ged´-er-ah
enclosure, sheepfold Josh 15:36

GEDERATHITE ged-er´-ath-ite
an inhabitant of Gederah 1 Chr 12:4

GEDERITE ged´-er-ite
native of Geder 1 Chr 27:28

GEDEROTH ged´-er-oth
sheepfolds Josh 15:41

GEDEROTHAIM ged´-er-oth-a´-im
two sheepfolds Josh 15:36

GEDOR ged´-or
wall Josh 15:58

GEHAZI ge-ha´-zi
valley of vision 2 Kgs 4:12

GELILOTH gel-il´-oth
regions Josh 18:17

GEMALLI ge-mal´-i
possessor of camels Num 13:12

GEMARIAH gem´-ar-i´-ah
whom Jehovah has completed Jer 29:3

GENERATION
not one of these men of this evil **g** Deut 1:35
a perverse and crooked **g** Deut 32:5
God is in the **g** of the righteous Ps 14:5
accounted to the Lord for a **g** Ps 22:30
written for the **g** to come Ps 102:18
One **g** shall praise thy works Ps 145:4
crown endure to every **g** Prov 27:24
There is a **g** that curseth Prov 30:11
One **g** passeth away Eccl 1:4
from **g** to **g** it shall lie waste Is 34:10
children tell another **g** Joel 1:3
g of vipers Matt 3:7; 12:34; 23:33; Luke 3:7
in judgment with this **g** Matt 12:41
perverse **g** Matt 17:17
shall come on this **g** Matt 23:36
this **g** shall not pass Matt 24:34; Mark 13:30; Luke 21:32
are in their **g** wiser Luke 16:8
rejected of this **g** Luke 17:25
a chosen **g** 1 Pet 2:9

GENNESARET gen-es´-a-ret
garden of Hazor (?) Matt 14:34

GENTILES
By these were the isles of the **G** Gen 10:5
give thee for a light to the **G** Is 49:6
And the **G** shall come Is 60:3
now shall there be among the **G** Hos 8:8
Proclaim ye this among the **G** Joel 3:9
Go not into the way of the **G** Matt 10:5
unto the dispersed among the **G** John 7:35
bear my name before the **G** Acts 9:15
G besought that these words Acts 13:42
we turn to the **G** Acts 13:46
declaring conversion of the **G** Acts 15:3
from henceforth I will go unto the **G** Acts 18:6
is he not also of the **G**? Rom 3:29
salvation is come to the **G** Rom 11:11
as I am the apostle of the **G** Rom 11:13
not so much as named among the **G** 1 Cor 5:1
walk not as other **G** Eph 4:17
a teacher of the **G** 2 Tim 1:11
taking nothing of the **G** 3 John 1:7

GENTLE
we were **g** among you 1 Thess 2:7
be **g** unto all men 2 Tim 2:24
g, shewing all meekness Titus 3:2
is first pure, then peaceable, **g** James 3:17
not only to the good and **g** 1 Pet 2:18

GENUBATH je-noob´-ath
theft, robbery 1 Kgs 11:20

GERA ge´-ra
a grain Gen 46:21

GERAR ge´-rar
sojourning Gen 10:19

GERGESENES ger´-ge-seens
inhabitants of Gerasa Matt 8:28

GERIZIM ge-rize´-im
persons living in a desert Deut 11:29

GERSHOM ger´-shom
expulsion Ex 2:22

GERSHON ger´-shon
same as GERSHOM Gen 46:11

GERSHONITES ger´-shon-ites
descendants of Gershon Num 3:21

GESHAM ge´-sham
rain 1 Chr 2:47

GESHEM ge´-shem
stout (?) Neh 2:19

GESHUR ge´-shoor
bridge 2 Sam 3:3

GESHURI ge-shoor´-i
inhabitants of Geshur Deut 3:14

GESHURITES ge-shoor´-ites
same as GESHURI Josh 12:5

GETHER ge´-ther
dregs (?) Gen 10:23

GETHSEMANE geth-sem´-an-e
oil press Matt 26:36

GET
the man that g understanding Prov 3:13
with all thy getting g understanding Prov 4:7
He that g wisdom loveth his own soul Prov 19:8
so he that g riches Jer 17:11

GEUEL goo´-el
majesty of God Num 13:15

GEZER ge´-zer
precipice Josh 10:33

GEZRITES gez´-rites
dwelling in a desert land 1 Sam 27:8

GIAH gi´-ah
gushing forth 2 Sam 2:24

GIBBAR gib´-ar
a hero Ezra 2:20

GIBBETHON gib´-eth-on
a lofty place Josh 19:44

GIBEA gib´-e-ah
hill 1 Chr 2:49

GIBEAH gib´-e-ah
hill Josh 15:57

GIBEATH gib´-e-ath
hill Josh 18:28

GIBEON gib´-e-on
pertaining to a hill Josh 9:3

GIBEONITES gib´-e-on-ites
inhabitants of Gibeon 2 Sam 21:1

GIBLITES gib´-lites
inhabitants of Gebal Josh 13:5

GIDDALTI gid-al´-ti
I have increased 1 Chr 25:4

GIDDEL gid´-el
gigantic Ezra 2:47

GIDEON gid´-e-on
one who cuts down Judg 6:11

GIDEONI gid´-e-on-i
cutting down Num 1:11

GIDOM gi´-dom
a cutting off Judg 20:45

GIFT
g blindeth Ex 23:8; Deut 16:19
hath he given us any g? 2 Sam 19:42
nor taking of g 2 Chr 19:7
g for men Ps 68:18
kings of Sheba and Seba shall offer g Ps 72:10
though thou givest many g Prov 6:35
he that hateth g shall live Prov 15:27
a g is as a precious stone Prov 17:8
man's g maketh room for him Prov 18:16
a g in secret pacifieth anger Prov 21:14
the g of God Eccl 3:13; 5:19; John 4:10; Acts 8:20; Rom 6:23; Eph 2:8
a g destroyeth the heart Eccl 7:7
every one loveth g Is 1:23
bring thy g to the altar Matt 5:23
leave there thy g before the altar Matt 5:24
know how to give good g Matt 7:11; Luke 11:13
casting their g into the treasury Luke 21:1
some spiritual g Rom 1:11
g by grace Rom 5:15
g and calling of God are without Rom 11:29
g differing according to the grace Rom 12:6
his proper g of God 1 Cor 7:7
diversities of g 1 Cor 12:4
covet earnestly the best g 1 Cor 12:31
desire spiritual g 1 Cor 14:1
unspeakable g 2 Cor 9:15
not because I desire a g Phil 4:17
Neglect not the g 1 Tim 4:14
stir up the g 2 Tim 1:6
good gift and every perfect g James 1:17

GIHON gi´-hon
a river Gen 2:13

GILALAI gil´-al-a´-i
dungy (?) Neh 12:36

GILBOA gil-bo´-ah
bubbling fountain 1 Sam 28:4

GILEAD gil´-e-ad
hill of witness Gen 31:21

GILEADITE gil´-e-ad-ite
inhabitant of Gilead Judg 10:3

GILGAL gil´-gal
a circle Josh 4:19

GILOH gi´-lo
exile Josh 15:51

GILONITE gi´-lon-ite
an inhabitant of Giloh 2 Sam 15:12

GIMZO gim´-zo
a place abounding with sycamores 2 Chr 28:18

GINATH gi´-nath
garden 1 Kgs 16:21

GINNETHO gin´-eth-o
garden Neh 12:4

GINNETHON gin´-eth-on
same as GINNETHO Neh 10:6

GIRD
hast g me with strength 2 Sam 22:40; Ps 18:39
I g thee, though thou hast not Is 45:5
G yourselves, and lament Joel 1:13
having your loins g Eph 6:14

GIRDLE
righteousness shall be the g of his loins Is 11:5
a leathern g about his loins Matt 3:4
with a g of a skin Mark 1:6

GIRGASHITE gir´-gash-ite
dwelling in a clayish soil 1 Chr 1:14

GIRGASITE gir´-gas-ite
dwelling in a clayish soil Gen 10:16

GIRL
sold a g for wine Joel 3:3
boys and g playing in the streets Zech 8:5

GISPA gis´-pah
flattery Neh 11:21

GITTAH-HEPHER git´-tah-he´-fer
winepress of the well Josh 19:13

GITTAIM git´-a-im
two winepresses 2 Sam 4:3

GITTITES git´-ites
inhabitants of Gath Josh 13:3

GIVE
I will surely g the tenth Gen 28:22
rich shall not g more, and the poor shall not g less Ex 30:15
Thou shalt g him, and thine heart Deut 15:10
g as he is able Deut 16:17
of thine own have we g thee 1 Chr 29:14
to g us a reviving Ezra 9:9
I shall g thee the heathen Ps 2:8
in the grave who shall g thee thanks? Ps 6:5
LORD will g strength Ps 29:11
g thee the desires of thine heart Ps 37:4
the righteous sheweth mercy, and g Ps 37:21
LORD will g grace and glory Ps 84:11
I g myself unto prayer Ps 109:4
g me thine heart Prov 23:26
g seed to the sower Is 55:10
lambs as he shall be able to g Ezek 46:5
G to him that asketh Matt 5:42
G us this day our daily bread Matt 6:11
will he g him a stone? Matt 7:9
freely g Matt 10:8
it is g to you to know Matt 13:11; Mark 4:11
g in exchange Matt 16:26; Mark 8:37
and g to the poor Matt 19:21; Mark 10:21
not mine to g Matt 20:23; Mark 10:40
g to the poor Matt 26:9; Mark 14:5
G, and it shall be g Luke 6:38
G us day by day Luke 11:3
G me to drink John 4:7,10
All that the Father g me John 6:37
except it were g unto him John 6:65
I g unto them eternal life John 10:28
he should g something to the poor John 13:29
not as the world g, g I unto you John 14:27
such as I have g I thee Acts 3:6
will g ourselves continually to prayer Acts 6:4
more blessed to g Acts 20:35
he that g, let him do it Rom 12:8
rather g place unto wrath Rom 12:19
God that g the increase 1 Cor 3:7
God loveth a cheerful g 2 Cor 9:7
concerning g and receiving Phil 4:15
g attendance to reading 1 Tim 4:13
g thyself wholly to them 1 Tim 4:15
who g us richly 1 Tim 6:17
that g to all men liberally James 1:5
g more grace James 4:6
g grace to humble James 4:6
g all diligence 2 Pet 1:5

GIZONITE gi´-zon-ite
same as GUNITES 1 Chr 11:34

GLAD
he will be g in his heart Ex 4:14
g when they can find the grave Job 3:22
Therefore my heart is g Ps 16:9
humble shall hear, thereof, and be g Ps 34:2
make g the city of God Ps 46:4
maketh g the heart of man Ps 104:15
I was g when they said Ps 122:1
whereof we are g Ps 126:3
a wise son maketh a g father Prov 10:1; 15:20
let not thine heart be g Prov 24:17
they are g that thou hast done it Lam 1:21
make merry, and be g Luke 15:32
and was g John 8:56
I am g for your sakes John 11:15
seen the grace of God, was g Acts 11:23

GLADNESS
in the day of your g Num 10:10
with g of heart Deut 28:47
there was a very great g Neh 8:17
Thou hast put g in my heart Ps 4:7
the oil of g Ps 45:7; Heb 1:9
g for the upright Ps 97:11
they shall obtain joy, and g Is 35:10; 51:11
did eat their meat with g Acts 2:46
opened not the gate for g Acts 12:14
filling our hearts with food and g Acts 14:17

GLEAN
thou shalt not g thine vineyard Lev 19:10
thoroughly g the remnant of Israel Jer 6:9
would they not leave some g grapes Jer 49:9

GLISTERING
stones to be set, g stones 1 Chr 29:2
his raiment was white and g Luke 9:29

GLITTERING
whet my g sword Deut 32:41
the g sword cometh out of his gall Job 20:25
g spear and the shield Job 39:23
both the bright sword and the g spear Nah 3:3

GLOOMINESS
day of darkness and of **g** Joel 2:2; Zeph 1:15

GLORIFY
before all the people I will be **g** Lev 10:3
Whoso offereth praise **g** me Ps 50:23
g thy name Ps 86:9,12
g ye the LORD in the fires Is 24:15
I will **g** the house of my glory Is 60:7
I will be **g** in the midst of thee Ezek 28:22
hast thou not **g** Dan 5:23
g your Father which is in heaven Matt 5:16
they **g** the God of Israel Matt 15:31
being **g** of all Luke 4:15
because that Jesus was not yet **g** John 7:39
that the Son of God might be **g** John 11:4
Jesus was **g**, then remembered they John 12:16
Father, **g** thy name John 12:28
I have both **g** it, and will **g** it again John 12:28
God shall also **g** him John 13:32
Herein is my Father **g** John 15:8
g thy Son John 17:1
I have **g** thee on earth John 17:4
by what death he should **g** God John 21:19
they **g** him not as God Rom 1:21
suffer with him, that we may also be **g** Rom 8:17
them he also **g** Rom 8:30
g God in your body and your spirit 1 Cor 6:20
they **g** God in me Gal 1:24
to be **g** in his saints 2 Thess 1:10
so Christ **g** not himself Heb 5:5

GLORIOUS
g in holiness Ex 15:11
this **g** and fearful name Deut 28:58
all **g** within Ps 45:13
make his praise **g** Ps 66:2
blessed be his **g** name Ps 72:19
G things are spoken Ps 87:3
his rest shall be **g** Is 11:10
whose **g** beauty is a fading flower Is 28:1
place of my feet **g** Is 60:13
g in his apparel Is 63:1
to make thyself a **g** name Is 63:14
A **g** high throne Jer 17:12
in the **g** land Dan 11:16,41
in the **g** holy mountain Dan 11:45
rejoiced for all the **g** things done Luke 13:17
g liberty of the children of God Rom 8:21
ministration of the spirit be rather **g** 2 Cor 3:8
light of **g** gospel 2 Cor 4:4
a **g** church Eph 5:27
like unto his **g** body Phil 3:21
the **g** gospel of the blessed God 1 Tim 1:11
the **g** appearing of the great God Titus 2:13

GLORY
shew me thy **g** Ex 33:18
earth filled with **g** Num 14:21; Ps 72:19
thy **g** above the heavens Ps 8:1
my **g** rejoiceth Ps 16:9
the King of **g**? Ps 24:8,10
afterward receive me to **g** Ps 73:24
will give grace and **g** Ps 84:11
sing and give praise, even with my **g** Ps 108:1
the **g** of thy kingdom Ps 145:11
the wise shall inherit the **g** Prov 3:35
the **g** of children are their fathers Prov 17:6
the **g** of young men is their strength Prov 20:29
g of God to conceal Prov 25:2
men to search their own **g** is not **g** Prov 25:27
the whole earth is full of his **g** Is 6:3
where will ye leave your **g**? Is 10:3
even **g** to the righteous Is 24:16
my **g** will I not give to another Is 42:8
have created him for my **g** Is 43:7
will glorify the house of my **g** Is 60:7
my people have changed their **g** Jer 2:11
the **g** of all lands Ezek 20:6,15
To whom art thou thus like in **g** Ezek 31:18
kingdom, power, and strength, and **g** Dan 2:37
there was given him dominion and **g** Dan 7:14
change their **g** into shame Hos 4:7
I will fill this house with **g** Hag 2:7
that they may have **g** of men Matt 6:2
Solomon in all his **g** Matt 6:29; Luke 12:27
in the **g** of his Father Matt 16:27; Mark 8:38
sit in the throne of his **g** Matt 19:28
power and great **g** Matt 24:30; Luke 21:27
G to God in the highest Luke 2:14
he shall come in his own **g** Luke 9:26
appeared in **g**, and spake of his Luke 9:31
they saw his **g** Luke 9:32
to enter into his **g** Luke 24:26
we beheld his **g** John 1:14
manifested forth his **g** John 2:11
I seek not mine own **g** John 8:50
the **g** which I had with thee John 17:5
that they may behold my **g** John 17:24
he gave not God the **g** Acts 12:23
come short of the **g** of God Rom 3:23
not worthy to be compared with the **g** Rom 8:18
to whom be **g** Rom 11:36; Gal 1:5;
2 Tim 4:18; Heb 13:21
crucified the Lord of **g** 1 Cor 2:8
do all to the **g** of God 1 Cor 10:31
woman is the **g** of the man 1 Cor 11:7
long hair, it is a **g** to her 1 Cor 11:15
g of celestial is one, **g** of the terrestrial 1 Cor 15:40
raised in **g** 1 Cor 15:43
beholding as in a glass the **g** 2 Cor 3:18
eternal weight of **g** 2 Cor 4:17
the Father of **g** Eph 1:17
Unto him be **g** in the church Eph 3:21
whose **g** is in their shame Phil 3:19
according to his riches in **g** Phil 4:19
Christ in you, the hope of **g** Col 1:27
appear with him in **g** Col 3:4
the **g** of his power 2 Thess 1:9
received up into **g** 1 Tim 3:16
the brightness of his **g** Heb 1:3
in bringing many sons to **g** Heb 2:10
this man was counted worthy of more **g** Heb 3:3
joy unspeakable and full of **g** 1 Pet 1:8
the **g** that should follow 1 Pet 1:11
the **g** of man as the flower of grass 1 Pet 1:24
the Spirit of **g** and of God 1 Pet 4:14
called us unto his eternal **g** 1 Pet 5:10
voice to him from the excellent **g** 2 Pet 1:17
worthy to receive **g** Rev 4:11
Blessing, and **g**, and wisdom Rev 7:12
earth was lightened with his **g** Rev 18:1
g of God did lighten it Rev 21:23

GLORYING
Your **g** is not good 1 Cor 5:6
man should make my **g** void 1 Cor 9:15
great is my **g** of you 2 Cor 7:4
I am become fool in **g** 2 Cor 12:11

GNASH
g of teeth Matt 8:12; 13:42; 22:13;
24:51; 25:30; Luke 13:28
he foameth, and **g** with his teeth Mark 9:18

GNAT
Ye blind guides, that strain at a **g** Matt 23:24

GO
Let me **g**, for the day breaketh Gen 32:26
g forward Ex 14:15; Job 23:8
angel shall **g** before thee Ex 23:23; 32:34
presence **g** not with me Ex 33:15
whither thou **g**, I will **g** Ruth 1:16
Whither shall I **g** Ps 139:7
the way he should **g** Prov 22:6
three things which **g** well Prov 30:29
to **g** a mile, **g** with him twain Matt 5:41
I **g** sir, and went not Matt 21:30
g and do likewise Luke 10:37
I **g** unto my Father John 14:12

GOATH **go´-ath**
lowing Jer 31:39

GOB **gobe**
pit, cistern 2 Sam 21:18

GOD
walked with **G** Gen 5:22; 6:9
Thou **G** seest me Gen 16:13
hath power with **G** Gen 32:28
behold I die, but **G** shall be with you Gen 48:21
G is not a man, that he should lie Num 23:19
What hath **G** wrought! Num 23:23
what **G** is there in heaven or in earth Deut 3:24
The eternal **G** is thy refuge Deut 33:27
earth may know there is a **G** in Israel 1 Sam 17:46
if the LORD be **G**, follow him 1 Kgs 18:21
The LORD, he is the **G** 1 Kgs 18:39
How doth **G** know? Job 22:13; Ps 73:11
in his heart, there is no **G** Ps 14:1; 53:1
My **G**, my **G**, why hast
thou forsaken me Ps 22:1; Matt 27:46
this I know; for **G** is for me Ps 56:9
thou art **G** alone Ps 86:10; Is 37:16
for **G** is in heaven Eccl 5:2
Is there a **G** beside me? Is 44:8
for I am **G**, and there is none else Is 45:22; 46:9
for I am **G**, and not man Hos 11:9
whose name is The **G** of hosts Amos 5:27
arise, call upon thy **G** Jon 1:6
if so be that **G** will think upon us Jon 1:6
and walk humbly with thy **G** Mic 6:8
G with us Matt 1:23
G is not **G** of dead Matt 22:32
for there is one **G**, and none other Mark 12:32
hath set to his seal that **G** is true John 3:33
G is a Spirit John 4:24
he was come from **G**, and went to **G** John 13:3
and to my **G** and your **G** John 20:17
G forbid: yea, let **G** be true Rom 3:4
If **G** be for us Rom 8:31
G is faithful 1 Cor 1:9
but **G** is faithful 1 Cor 10:13
and report that **G** is in you 1 Cor 14:25
G is not the author of confusion 1 Cor 14:33
but **G** is one Gal 3:20
G is not mocked Gal 6:7
above all that is called **G** 2 Thess 2:4
G was manifest in the flesh 1 Tim 3:16
and I will be to them a **G** Heb 8:10
G is not ashamed Heb 11:16
to be called their **G** Heb 11:16
and to **G** the Judge of all Heb 12:23
that **G** is light 1 John 1:5
G is love 1 John 4:8,16
No man hath seen **G** 1 John 4:12
And we know that we are of **G** 1 John 5:19
and **G** himself shall be with them Rev 21:3
And **G** shall wipe away all tears Rev 21:4
and I will be his **G** Rev 21:7

GOD (an idol)
stolen my **g** Gen 31:30
make us **g**, which shall go before us Ex 32:1
these be thy **g** Ex 32:4
They chose new **g** Judg 5:8
if he be a **g**, let him plead Judg 6:31
cry unto the **g** which ye have chosen Judg 10:14
Micah had a house of **g** Judg 17:5
ye have taken away my **g** Judg 18:24
every nation made **g** 2 Kgs 17:29
feared the LORD, and served own **g** 2 Kgs 17:33
maketh a **g** and worshippeth it Is 44:15
pray to a **g** that cannot save Is 45:20
cried every man to his own **g** Jon 1:5

earth is full of the **g** of the LORD Ps 33:5
crownest the year with thy **g** Ps 65:11
the memory of thy great **g** Ps 145:7
proclaim every one his own **g** Prov 20:6
your **g** is as a morning cloud Hos 6:4
the riches of his **g** Rom 2:4
the **g** and severity of God Rom 11:22

GOSHEN go´-shen
drawing near (?) Gen 45:10

GOZAN go´-zan
who nourishes the body 2 Kgs 17:6

GOSPEL
according to my **g** Rom 2:16
if our **g** be hid 2 Cor 4:3
any other **g** Gal 1:8,9
the **g** of uncircumcision Gal 2:7
the hope of the **g** Col 1:23
g of the blessed God 1 Tim 1:11
everlasting **g** Rev 14:6

GOVERNMENT
the **g** shall be upon his shoulder Is 9:6
helps, **g**, diversities of tongues 1 Cor 12:28
lust of uncleanness, and despise **g** 2 Pet 2:10

GRACE
g is poured into thy lips Ps 45:2
an ornament of **g** Prov 1:9
and **g** to thy neck Prov 3:22
giveth **g** to the lowly Prov 3:34
crying, G, **g** unto it Zech 4:7
spirit of **g** and of supplications Zech 12:10
full of **g** and truth John 1:14
all we received, and **g** for **g** John 1:16
g and truth came by Jesus Christ John 1:17
great **g** was upon them all Acts 4:33
had seen the **g** Acts 11:23
the word of his **g** Acts 14:3
G to you, and peace Rom 1:7; 2 Thess 1:2; Phile 1:3
justified freely by his **g** Rom 3:24
not reckoned of **g**, but of debt Rom 4:4
access by faith into this **g** Rom 5:2
abundance of **g** Rom 5:17
where sin abounded, **g** did much more Rom 5:20
under **g** Rom 6:14,15
the election of **g** Rom 11:5
G be unto you 1 Cor 1:3; Phil 1:2; Col 1:2; 1 Thess 1:1; 1 Pet 1:2; Rev 1:4
G be to you, and peace 2 Cor 1:2; Gal 1:3; Eph 1:2
know the **g** of our Lord 2 Cor 8:9
able to make all **g** abound 2 Cor 9:8
My **g** is sufficient 2 Cor 12:9
and called me by his **g** Gal 1:15
ye are fallen from **g** Gal 5:4
by **g** ye are saved Eph 2:5,8
is this **g** given Eph 3:8
minister **g** unto the hearers Eph 4:29
G be with all them that love our Lord Eph 6:24
Let your speech be always with **g** Col 4:6
good hope through **g** 2 Thess 2:16
G, mercy, and peace 1 Tim 1:2; 2 Tim 1:2; Titus 1:4
the throne of **g** Heb 4:16
despite unto the Spirit of **g** Heb 10:29
g whereby we may serve God Heb 12:28
heart be established with **g** Heb 13:9
the **g** of the fashion of it James 1:11
he giveth more **g** James 4:6
heirs together of the **g** 1 Pet 3:7
giveth **g** to the humble 1 Pet 5:5
G and peace 2 Pet 1:2
grow in **g** 2 Pet 3:18
the **g** of our God into lasciviousness Jude 1:4

GRACIOUS
God be **g** to thee Gen 43:29
I will hear, for I am **g** Ex 22:27
I will be **g** to whom I will be **g** Ex 33:19
g, and merciful Neh 9:17,31
Hath God forgotten to be **g**? Ps 77:9
A **g** woman retaineth honour Prov 11:16
wait, that he may be **g** Is 30:18
the Lord GOD of hosts will be **g** Amos 5:15
I knew that thou art a **g** God Jon 4:2
wondered at the **g** words Luke 4:22
tasted that the Lord is **g** 1 Pet 2:3

GRAFF
wert **g** in among them Rom 11:17,24
be **g** in Rom 11:19,23

GRAIN
g of mustard seed Matt 13:31; 17:20; Mark 4:31; Luke 13:19; 17:6

GRANT
g you that ye may find rest Ruth 1:9
God **g** him that which he requested 1 Chr 4:10
g me the thing I long for Job 6:8
G that these my two sons Matt 20:21
G unto us that we may sit Mark 10:37
will I **g** to sit with me Rev 3:21

GRAPE
his clothes in the blood of the **g** Gen 49:11
drink the pure blood of the **g** Deut 32:14
vines with the tender **g** Song 2:13
looked that it should bring forth **g** Is 5:2
Yet gleaning **g** Is 17:6; 24:13
there shall be no **g** Jer 8:13
have eaten a sour **g** Jer 31:29; Ezek 18:2
the reaper, and the treader of **g** Amos 9:13

GRASS
as showers upon the **g** Deut 32:2
as **g** on house tops 2 Kgs 19:26; Ps 129:6
like rain upon the mown **g** Ps 72:6
like **g** which groweth up Ps 90:5
withered like **g** Ps 102:4,11
days are as **g** Ps 103:15
All flesh is as **g** Is 40:6; 1 Pet 1:24
if God so clothe the **g** Matt 6:30; Luke 12:28

GRAVE (adj)
must the deacons be **g** 1 Tim 3:8
That the aged men be sober, **g** Titus 2:2

GRAVE (n)
with sorrow to the **g** Gen 42:38; 44:31
no **g** in Egypt Ex 14:11
come to thy **g** in a full age Job 5:26
he that goeth to the **g** Job 7:9
hide me in the **g** Job 14:13
the **g** are ready for me Job 17:1
If I wait, the **g** is mine house Job 17:13
his soul draweth near to the **g** Job 33:22
in the **g** who shall give thanks? Ps 6:5
let them be silent in the **g** Ps 31:17
Like sheep they are laid in the **g** Ps 49:14
the power of the **g** Ps 49:15; Hos 13:14
nor wisdom, in the **g** Eccl 9:10
the **g** cannot praise thee Is 38:18
made his **g** with the wicked Is 53:9
O **g**, I will be thy destruction Hos 13:14
all that are in the **g** shall hear John 5:28
she goeth unto the **g** John 11:31
O **g**, where is thy victory? 1 Cor 15:55

GRAVE (v)
I have **g** thee upon the palms Is 49:16
that the maker thereof hath **g** it Hab 2:18

GRAVEL
his mouth shall be filled with **g** Prov 20:17
like the **g** Is 48:19
broken my teeth with **g** stones Lam 3:16

GRAVITY
in subjection with all **g** 1 Tim 3:4
shewing uncorruptness, **g**, sincerity Titus 2:7

GRAY
the beauty of old men is the **g** head Prov 20:29
g hairs are here and there upon him Hos 7:9

GREAT
make of thee a **g** nation Gen 12:2; 46:3
he also shall be **g** Gen 48:19
the heat of this **g** anger Deut 29:24
consider how **g** things 1 Sam 12:24
bid thee do some **g** thing 2 Kgs 5:13
for **g** is our God 2 Chr 2:5
I am doing a **g** work Neh 6:3
G men are not always wise Job 32:9
a **g** ransom Job 36:18
There were they in **g** fear Ps 14:5; 53:5
there is **g** reward Ps 19:11
how **g** is thy goodness! Ps 31:19
how **g** are thy works! Ps 92:5
How **g** is the sum of them! Ps 139:17
bringeth him before **g** men Prov 18:16
stand not in the place of **g** men Prov 25:6
g is your reward Matt 5:12
called **g** in kingdom of heaven Matt 5:19
pearl of **g** price Matt 13:46
g is thy faith Matt 15:28
whosoever will be **g** among you Matt 20:26
the **g** commandment Matt 22:36,38
the harvest truly is **g** Luke 10:2
a **g** gulf fixed Luke 16:26
that himself was some **g** one Acts 8:9
G is Diana Acts 19:28,34
g is the mystery 1 Tim 3:16
so **g** salvation Heb 2:3
so **g** a cloud of witnesses Heb 12:1
how **g** a matter a little fire kindleth! James 3:5

GREATER
punishment is **g** than I can bear Gen 4:13
waxed **g** and **g** 1 Chr 11:9; Esth 9:4
glory of this latter house shall be **g** Hag 2:9
g than he Matt 11:11; Luke 7:28
one **g** than the temple Matt 12:6
other commandment **g** than these Mark 12:31
shalt see **g** things John 1:50
Art thou **g** than our father John 4:12; 8:53
shew him **g** works than these John 5:20
My Father is **g** than all John 10:29
servant is not **g** than his lord John 13:16; 15:20
g works than these John 14:12
my Father is **g** than I John 14:28
G love hath no man John 15:13
the **g** part remain 1 Cor 15:6
he could swear by no **g** Heb 6:13
God is **g** than our hearts 1 John 3:20
g is he that is in you than he that is in the world 1 John 4:4
no **g** joy 3 John 1:4

GREATEST
it is **g** among herbs Matt 13:32
who is **g** in the kingdom of heaven? Matt 18:1,4
should be the **g** Mark 9:34; Luke 9:46
the **g** of these is charity 1 Cor 13:13

GREATLY
I have sinned **g** 2 Sam 24:10; 1 Chr 21:8
Obadiah feared the LORD **g** 1 Kgs 18:3
my heart **g** rejoiceth Ps 28:7
he is **g** exalted Ps 47:9
g to be feared in the assembly Ps 89:7
I was **g** afflicted Ps 116:10
thou art **g** beloved Dan 9:23
thou art **g** despised Obad 1:2
ye therefore do **g** err Mark 12:27

GREATNESS
the **g**, power, and glory 1 Chr 29:11
his **g** is unsearchable Ps 145:3
in the **g** of his folly Prov 5:23
travelling in **g** of strength Is 63:1
the exceeding **g** of his power Eph 1:19

GRECIA greesh´-ah
same as GREECE Dan 8:21

GRECIAN greesh´-an
a Jew who speaks Gr. Acts 11:20

GREECE grees
country of the Greeks Acts 20:2

GREEDILY
he coveteth **g** all the day Prov 21:26
had **g** gained of thy neighbours Ezek 22:12

GREEDINESS
to work all uncleanness and **g** Eph 4:19

GREEDY
g of gain Prov 1:19; 15:27
they are **g** dogs Is 56:11

GREEN
parched corn, nor **g** ears Lev 23:14
with seven **g** withs Judg 16:7
do these things in a **g** tree Luke 23:31

GRIEF
know his own sore and his own **g** 2 Chr 6:29
that my **g** were thoroughly weighed Job 6:2
life is spent with **g** Ps 31:10
in much wisdom is much **g** Eccl 1:18
acquainted with **g** Is 53:3
this is a **g**, and I must bear it Jer 10:19

GRIEVE
it **g** him at his heart Gen 6:6
be not **g** Gen 45:5
and to **g** thine heart 1 Sam 2:33
g him in the desert Ps 78:40
Forty years was I **g** Ps 95:10
doth not afflict willingly, nor **g** Lam 3:33
being **g** for the hardness Mark 3:5
went away **g** Mark 10:22
Peter was **g** John 21:17
brother be **g** with thy meat Rom 14:15
g not the holy Spirit of God Eph 4:30

GRIEVOUS
thing was very **g** in Abraham's sight Gen 21:11
a **g** mourning Gen 50:11
His ways are always **g** Ps 10:5
g words stir up anger Prov 15:1
his life shall be **g** Is 15:4
thy wound is **g** Jer 30:12; Nah 3:19
g to be borne Matt 23:4; Luke 11:46
to me indeed is not **g** Phil 3:1
g: nevertheless, afterward it yieldeth Heb 12:11
commandments are not **g** 1 John 5:3

GRIND
g the faces of the poor Is 3:15
took the young men to **g** Lam 5:13
it will **g** him to powder Matt 21:44; Luke 20:18

GROAN
God heard their **g** Ex 2:24
Men **g** from out of the city Job 24:12
How do the beasts **g**! Joel 1:18
whole creation **g** Rom 8:22
we ourselves **g** Rom 8:23
in this we **g** 2 Cor 5:2

GROPE
thou shalt **g** at noonday Deut 28:29
g in the noonday as in the night Job 5:14
They **g** in the dark without light Job 12:25
we **g** as if we had no eyes Is 59:10

GROSS
g darkness Is 60:2; Jer 13:16
this people's heart is waxed **g** Matt 13:15; Acts 28:27

GROUND
holy **g** Ex 3:5; Acts 7:33
trouble spring out of the **g** Job 5:6
parched **g** shall become a pool Is 35:7
break up your fallow **g** Jer 4:3; Hos 10:12
good **g** Matt 13:8; Luke 8:8
stony **g** Mark 4:16
why cumbereth it the **g**? Luke 13:7
bought a piece of **g** Luke 14:18
lay thee even with the **g** Luke 19:44
with his finger wrote on the **g** John 8:6

GROUNDED
being rooted and **g** in love Eph 3:17
continue in the faith **g** and settled Col 1:23

GROW
let them **g** into a multitude Gen 48:16
although he make it not to **g** 2 Sam 23:5
g like a cedar Ps 92:12
he shall **g** up before him Is 53:2
he shall **g** as the lily Hos 14:5
g up as calves of the stall Mal 4:2
Let both **g** together Matt 13:30
seed should spring and **g** up Mark 4:27
whereunto this would **g** Acts 5:24
g unto a holy temple Eph 2:21
may **g** up unto him Eph 4:15
your faith **g** exceedingly 2 Thess 1:3
that ye may **g** thereby 1 Pet 2:2
g in grace 2 Pet 3:18

GRUDGE
nor bear any **g** against the children Lev 19:18
hospitality one to another without **g** 1 Pet 4:9

GUDGODAH gud´-god-ah
thunder (?) Deut 10:7

GUEST
he hath bid his **g** Zeph 1:7
the wedding was furnished with **g** Matt 22:10
to be **g** with a man that is a sinner Luke 19:7

GUIDE (n)
our **g** even unto death Ps 48:14
having no **g**, overseer, or ruler Prov 6:7
the **g** of my youth Jer 3:4
ye blind **g** Matt 23:16,24

GUIDE (v)
meek will he **g** in judgment Ps 25:9
I will **g** thee with mine eye Ps 32:8
g me with thy counsel Ps 73:24
the LORD shall **g** thee Is 58:11
g our feet into the way of peace Luke 1:79
g you into all truth John 16:13

GUILE
in whose spirit there is no **g** Ps 32:2
lips from speaking **g** Ps 34:13
in whom is no **g**! John 1:47
I caught you with **g** 2 Cor 12:16
laying aside all malice, and all **g** 1 Pet 2:1
neither was **g** found in his mouth 1 Pet 2:22
his lips that they speak no **g** 1 Pet 3:10

GUILTLESS
will not hold him **g** Ex 20:7; Deut 5:11
we will be **g** Josh 2:19
are **g** before the LORD 2 Sam 3:28
ye would not have condemned the **g** Matt 12:7

GUILTY
verily **g** concerning our brother Gen 42:21
by no means clear the **g** Ex 34:7; Num 14:18
when he knoweth of it, he shall be **g** Lev 5:3
world may become **g** before God Rom 3:19

g of the body and blood 1 Cor 11:27
he is **g** of all James 2:10

GULF
there is a great **g** fixed Luke 16:26

GUNI goon´-i
painted with colors Gen 46:24

GUNITES goon´-ites
descendants of Guni Num 26:48

GUR goor
a young lion 2 Kgs 9:27

GUR-BAAL goor-ba´-al
dwelling of Baal 2 Chr 26:7

GUSH
till the blood **g** out upon them 1 Kgs 18:28
the waters **g** out Ps 78:20; 105:41
our eyelids **g** out with waters Jer 9:18

H

HAAHASHTARI ha´-a-hash´-tar-i
the muleteer (?) 1 Chr 4:6

HABAIAH hab´-a-i´-ah
whom Jehovah hides Ezra 2:61

HABAKKUK ha-bak´-ook
embrace Hab 1:1

HABAZINIAH hab´-az-in-i´-ah
lamp of Jehovah (?) Jer 35:3

HABITATION
unto thy holy **h** Ex 15:13
an house of **h** for thee 2 Chr 6:2
have loved the **h** Ps 26:8
From the place of his **h** Ps 33:14
Let their **h** be desolate Ps 69:25
full of the **h** of cruelty Ps 74:20
and judgment are the **h** of thy throne Ps 89:14
a city of **h** Ps 107:7
prepare a city for **h** Ps 107:36
he hath desired it for his **h** Ps 132:13
he blesseth the **h** of the just Prov 3:33
people dwell in a peaceable **h** Is 32:18
who shall enter into our **h**? Jer 21:13
the peaceable **h** are cut down Jer 25:37
everlasting **h** Luke 16:9
built together for a **h** of God Eph 2:22
but left their own **h** Jude 1:6

HABOR ha´-bor
joining together 2 Kgs 17:6

HACHALIAH hak-al-i´-ah
whom Jehovah disturbs Neh 1:1

HACHILAH hak´-i-lah
dark 1 Sam 23:19

HACHMONI hak´-mon-i
wise 1 Chr 27:32

HACHMONITE hak´-mon-ite
a descendant of Hachmoni 1 Chr 11:11

HADAD ha´-dad
fierce Gen 36:35

HADADEZER had-ad-e´-zer
whose help is fierce 2 Sam 8:3

HADADRIMMON had-ad-rim´-mon
invocation to the god Rimmon Zech 12:11

HADAR ha´-dar
enclosure Gen 25:15

HADAREZER had´-ar-e´-zer
same as HADADEZER 1 Chr 18:3

HADASHAH had-ash´-ah
new Josh 15:37

HADASSAH had-as´-ah
myrtle Esth 2:7

HADATTAH had-at´-ah
new Hazor Josh 15:25

HADID ha´-did
sharp Ezra 2:33

HADLAI had´-la-i
rest 2 Chr 28:12

HADORAM had-or´-am
noble honor Gen 10:27

HADRACH had´-rak
dwelling Zech 9:1

HAGAB ha´-gab
locust Ezra 2:46

HAGABA ha´-gab-ah
same as HAGAB Neh 7:48

HAGABAH ha´-gab-ah
same as HAGAB Ezra 2:45

HAGAR ha´-gar
flight Gen 16:3

HAGARENES hag´-ar-e´-nes
descendants of Hagar Ps 83:6

HAGARITES hag´-ar-ites
same as HAGARENES 1 Chr 5:10

HAGERITE hag´-er-ite
same as HAGARENES 1 Chr 27:31

HAGGAI hag´-a-i
festive Hag 1:1

HAGGERI hag´-er-i
wanderer 1 Chr 11:38

HAGGI hag´-i
same as HAGGERI Gen 46:16

HAGGIAH hag-i´-ah
festival of Jehovah 1 Chr 6:30

HAGGITES hag´-ites
the posterity of Haggi Num 26:15

HAGGITH hag´-ith
festive 2 Sam 3:4

HAI ha´-i
same as AI Gen 12:8

HAIL
the treasures of the **h** Job 38:22
h shall sweep away the refuge of lies Is 28:17

HAIR
bring down my gray **h** with sorrow Gen 42:38; 44:29
sling stones at **h** breadth Judg 20:16
the **h** of my flesh stood up Job 4:15
they are more than the **h** of my head Ps 40:12
raiment of camel's **h** Matt 3:4
John was clothed with camel's **h** Mark 1:6
cannot make one **h** white or black Matt 5:36
h of your head are all numbered Matt 10:30
long **h**, it is a shame to him 1 Cor 11:14
long **h** is a glory to her 1 Cor 11:15
broided **h** 1 Tim 2:9
plaiting the **h** 1 Pet 3:3

HAKKATAN hak´-at-an
the small Ezra 8:12

HAKKOZ hak´-oz
the thorn 1 Chr 24:10

HAKUPHA ha-koo´-fah
bent Ezra 2:51

HALAH ha´-lah
same as CALAH (?) 2 Kgs 17:6

HALAK ha´-lak
smooth Josh 11:17

HALE
lest he **h** thee to the judge Luke 12:58
h men and women Acts 8:3

HALHUL hal´-hool
opening (?) Josh 15:58

HALI ha´-li
necklace Josh 19:25

HALLOHESH hal-o´-hesh
same as HALOHESH Neh 10:24

HALLOW
I am the LORD which **h** you Lev 22:32
ye shall **h** the fiftieth year Lev 25:10
every man's **h** things Num 5:10
I have **h** this house 1 Kgs 9:3
but **h** ye the sabbath day Jer 17:22,24,27
And **h** my sabbaths Ezek 20:20; 44:24
H be thy name Matt 6:9

HALOHESH hal-o´-hesh
the enchanter Neh 3:12

HALT
How long **h** ye between two opinions? 1 Kgs 18:21
For I am ready to **h** Ps 38:17

HAM ham
warm Gen 9:18

HAMAN ha´-man
well-disposed Esth 3:1

HAMATH ha´-math
fortress Num 34:8

HAMATH-ZOBAH ha´-math-zo´-bah
fortress of Zobah 2 Chr 8:3

HAMATHITE ha´-math-ite
an inhabitant of Hamath Gen 10:18

HAMMATH ham´-ath
warm springs Josh 19:35

HAMMEDATHA ham-ed´-a-thah
given by the moon (?) Esth 3:1

HAMMELECH ham-me´-lek
the king Jer 36:26

HAMMOLEKETH ham´-mo-le´-keth
the queen 1 Chr 7:18

HAMMON ham´-on
warm Josh 19:28

HAMMOTH-DOR ham´-oth-dor
warm springs of Dor Josh 21:32

HAMON-GOG ham´-on-gog
mother of Gog Ezek 39:11

HAMONAH ha-mo´-nah
multitude Ezek 39:16

HAMOR ha´-mor
ass Gen 33:19

HAMUEL ham´-oo-el
heat (wrath) *of God* 1 Chr 4:26

HAMUL ha´-mool
who has experienced mercy Gen 46:12

HAMULITES ha´-mool-ites
descendants of Hamul Num 26:21

HAMUTAL ha-moo´-tal
refreshing like dew 2 Kgs 23:31

HANAMEEL han´-am-e´-el
a form of HANANEEL (?) Jer 32:7

HANAN ha´-nan
merciful 1 Chr 8:23

HANANEEL han´-an-e´-el
whom God graciously gave Neh 3:1

HANANI ha-na´-ni
same as HANANIAH (?) 1 Kgs 16:1

HANANIAH han´-an-i´-ah
whom Jehovah graciously gave 1 Chr 3:19

HAND
his **h** will be against every man Gen 16:12
thy **h** under my thigh Gen 24:2; 47:29
the **h** are the **h** of Esau Gen 27:22
in the power of my **h** to do you hurt Gen 31:29
h for **h**, foot for foot Ex 21:24; Deut 19:21
cover thee with my **h** while I pass Ex 33:22
Is the LORD's **h** waxed short? Num 11:23; Is 59:1
I would there were sword in mine **h** Num 22:29
might of my **h** hath gotten me this wealth Deut 8:17
from his right **h** went a fiery law Deut 33:2
My own **h** hath saved me Judg 7:2
the **h** of God was very heavy there 1 Sam 5:11
we shall know that it is not his **h** 1 Sam 6:9
of whose **h** have I received any bribe 1 Sam 12:3
he did put his life in his **h** 1 Sam 19:5
he strengthened his **h** in God 1 Sam 23:16
what evil is in mine **h**? 1 Sam 26:18
I have put my life in my **h** 1 Sam 28:21
the **h** of Joab with thee in all this? 2 Sam 14:19
me fall now into the **h** of the LORD 2 Sam 24:14; 1 Chr 21:13
ariseth a little cloud, like a man's **h** 1 Kgs 18:44
strike his **h** over the place 2 Kgs 5:11
could use the right **h** and the left 1 Chr 12:2
according to the good **h** of God Ezra 7:9; Neh 2:8
by the good **h** of our God Ezra 8:18
they gave their **h** Ezra 10:19
strengthened their **h** for this good work Neh 2:18
with an open letter in his **h** Neh 6:5
In whose **h** is the soul Job 12:10
for the **h** of God hath touched me Job 19:21
that thine own right **h** can save thee Job 40:14
at thy right **h** there are pleasures for evermore Ps 16:11
He that hath a clean **h** Ps 24:4
shall soon stretch out her **h** unto God Ps 68:31
establish thou the work of our **h** Ps 90:17
let my right **h** forget her cunning Ps 137:5
Length of days is in her right **h** Prov 3:16
and in the left **h** riches and honour Prov 3:16
a little folding of the **h** Prov 6:10; 24:33
that dealeth with a slack **h** Prov 10:4
though **h** join in **h** Prov 11:21; 16:5
the **h** of diligent shall bear rule Prov 12:24
a slothful man hideth his **h** Prov 19:24
slothful hideth his **h** in his bosom Prov 26:15
be thou not one of them that strike **h** Prov 22:26
that it was from the **h** of God Eccl 2:24
Whatsoever thy **h** findeth to do Eccl 9:10
withhold not thine **h** Eccl 11:6
who hath required this at your **h** Is 1:12
he hath stretched forth his **h** Is 5:25
his **h** is stretched out still Is 9:12; 10:4
this is the **h** that is stretched out Is 14:26
his **h** is stretched out Is 14:27
measured waters in the hollow of his **h** Is 40:12
another shall subscribe with his **h** Is 44:5
pleasure of LORD shall prosper in his **h** Is 53:10
keepeth his **h** from doing evil Is 56:2
they strengthen the **h** of evildoers Jer 23:14
shall the flocks pass under the **h** of him Jer 33:13
with his right **h** as an adversary Lam 2:4
The **h** of the pitiful women Lam 4:10
All **h** shall be feeble Ezek 7:17; 21:7
fill thine **h** with coals of fire Ezek 10:2
lo, he had given his **h** Ezek 17:18
none can stay his **h** Dan 4:35
stretched out his **h** with scorners Hos 7:5
do evil with both **h** earnestly Mic 7:3
Let not thine **h** be slack Zeph 3:16
What are these wounds in thine **h**? Zech 13:6

kingdom of heaven is at **h** Matt 3:2; 4:17; 10:7
Whose fan is in his **h** Matt 3:12; Luke 3:17
let not thy left **h** know Matt 6:3
if thy **h** or thy foot offend Matt 18:8; Mark 9:43
My time is at **h** Matt 26:18
he is at **h** that doth betray me Matt 26:46; Mark 14:42
sitting on the right **h** of power Mark 14:62
sat on the right **h** of God Mark 16:19
delivered into the **h** of men Luke 9:44
pluck them out of my **h** John 10:28
my Father's **h** John 10:29
behold my **h** John 20:27
reach hither thy **h** John 20:27
that these **h** have ministered Acts 20:34
a house not made with **h** 2 Cor 5:1
The LORD is at **h** Phil 4:5
to work with your own **h** 1 Thess 4:11
the day of Christ is at **h** 2 Thess 2:2
lifting up holy **h** 1 Tim 2:8
the **h** of the living God Heb 10:31
cleanse your **h** James 4:8
the end of all things is at **h** 1 Pet 4:7
our **h** have handled of the Word of life 1 John 1:1

HANDLE
they that **h** the pen of the writer Judg 5:14
but they **h** not Ps 115:7
He that **h** a matter wisely Prov 16:20
they that **h** the law Jer 2:8
sent him away shamefully **h** Mark 12:4
h me, and see Luke 24:39
nor **h** the Word of God deceitfully 2 Cor 4:2
taste not, **h** not Col 2:21
have **h** of the Word of life 1 John 1:1

HANDMAID
the son of thine **h** Ps 86:16; 116:16
a **h** that is heir to her mistress Prov 30:23
Behold the **h** of the LORD Luke 1:38

HANES ha´-nes
a city in Egypt Is 30:4

HANG
for he that is **h** is accursed Deut 21:23
h the earth upon nothing Job 26:7
We **h** our harps upon the willows Ps 137:2
millstone were **h** about his neck Matt 18:6; Mark 9:42; Luke 17:2
on these **h** all the law and the prophets Matt 22:40
went and **h** himself Matt 27:5
Cursed is everyone that **h** on a tree Gal 3:13
lift up the hands which **h** down Heb 12:12

HANIEL han´-i-el
favour of God 1 Chr 7:39

HANNAH han´-ah
gracious 1 Sam 1:2

HANNATHON han´-ath-on
gracious Josh 19:14

HANNIEL han´-i-el
same as HANIEL Num 34:23

HANOCH ha´-nok
same as ENOCH Gen 25:4

HANOCHITES ha´-nok-ites
descendants of Hanoch Num 26:5

HANUN ha´-noon
whom [God] pities 2 Sam 10:1

HAPHRAIM haf-ra´-im
two pits Josh 19:19

HAPLY
if **h** the people had eaten 1 Sam 14:30
if **h** he might find anything thereon Mark 11:13
h ye be found even to fight against God Acts 5:39
if **h** they might feel after him Acts 17:27

HAPPEN
it was a chance that **h** to us 1 Sam 6:9
There shall no evil **h** to the just Prov 12:21
and shew us what shall **h** Is 41:22
Therefore this evil is **h** Jer 44:23
tell them what thing should **h** to him Mark 10:32
all these things which had **h** Luke 24:14
blindness in part is **h** to Israel Rom 11:25
things **h** unto them for examples 1 Cor 10:11
the things which **h** unto me Phil 1:12
though some strange thing **h** unto you 1 Pet 4:12
h unto them according to the true proverb 2 Pet 2:22

HAPPY
H am I Gen 30:13
H art thou, O Israel Deut 33:29
h is the man whom God correcteth Job 5:17
h is the man that hath quiver full Ps 127:5
h shalt thou be Ps 128:2
H is that people Ps 144:15
h is the man that findeth wisdom Prov 3:13
h is everyone that retaineth her Prov 3:18
that hath mercy on the poor, **h** is he Prov 14:21
H is the man that feareth always Prov 28:14
are all they **h** that deal treacherously? Jer 12:1
now we call the proud **h** Mal 3:15
these things, **h** are ye if ye do them John 13:17
H is he that condemneth not himself Rom 14:22
we count them **h** that endure James 5:11
h are ye 1 Pet 3:14; 4:14

HARA ha´-ra
mountainous 1 Chr 5:26

HARADAH ha´-ra-dah
fear Num 33:24

HARAN ha´-ran
mountaineer Gen 11:27

HARARITE ha´-rar-ite
a mountaineer 2 Sam 23:11

HARBONA har-bo´-nah
same as HARBONAH Esth 1:10

HARBONAH har-bo´-nah
donkey-driver Esth 7:9

HARD
Is any thing too **h** for the LORD? Gen 18:14
cause that is too **h** Deut 1:17; 17:8
It shall not seem **h** to thee Deut 15:18
came to prove him with **h** questions 1 Kgs 10:1; 2 Chr 9:1
as **h** as a piece of nether millstone Job 41:24
way of the transgressors is **h** Prov 13:15
brother offended **h** is to be won Prov 18:19
there is nothing too **h** for thee Jer 32:17
Is there any thing too **h** for me Jer 32:27
to a people of **h** language Ezek 3:5,6
thou art a **h** man Matt 25:24
This is a **h** saying John 6:60
h for thee to kick against the pricks Acts 9:5; 26:14
many things to say, and **h** to be uttered Heb 5:11
some things **h** to be understood 2 Pet 3:16

HARDEN
I will **h** his heart Ex 4:21
I will **h** Pharaoh's heart Ex 7:3; 14:4
h the hearts of the Egyptians Ex 14:17
I would **h** myself in sorrow Job 6:10
who hath **h** himself against him? Job 9:4
A wicked man **h** his face Prov 21:29
he that **h** his heart shall fall Prov 28:14
that being often reproved **h** his neck Prov 29:1
h our heart from thy fear? Is 63:17
their heart was **h** Mark 6:52
your heart yet **h** Mark 8:17
blinded their eyes and **h** their heart John 12:40
when divers were **h** Acts 19:9

whom he will he **h** Rom 9:18
lest any of you be **h** Heb 3:13

HARDLY
Sarai dealt **h** with her Gen 16:6
a rich man shall **h** enter Matt 19:23
h shall they that have riches enter Mark 10:23; Luke 18:24

HARDNESS
grieved for the **h** of their hearts Mark 3:5
for their unbelief and **h** of heart Mark 16:14
endure **h**, as good soldier 2 Tim 2:3

HAREPH ha´-ref
plucking 1 Chr 2:51

HARETH ha´-reth
thicket 1 Sam 22:5

HARHAIAH har-hai´-ah
dried up (?) Neh 3:8

HARHAS har´-has
same as HASRAH 2 Kgs 22:14

HARHUR har´-hoor
inflammation Ezra 2:51

HARIM ha´-rim
flat-nosed 1 Chr 24:8

HARIPH ha´-rif
autumnal showers Neh 7:24

HARM
make amends for the **h** Lev 5:16
neither sought his **h** Num 35:23
I will no more do thee **h** 1 Sam 26:21
no **h** in the pot 2 Kgs 4:41
do my prophets no **h** 1 Chr 16:22; Ps 105:15
if he have done thee no **h** Prov 3:30
Do thyself no **h** Acts 16:28
he felt no **h** Acts 28:5

HARMLESS
wise as serpents, and **h** as doves Matt 10:16
ye may be blameless and **h** Phil 2:15
holy, **h**, undefiled Heb 7:26

HARNEPHER har-ne´-fer
descendant of Ashur 1 Chr 7:36

HAROD ha´-rod
terror Judg 7:1

HARODITE har´-od-ite
inhabitant of Harod 2 Sam 23:25

HAROEH ha-ro´-eh
the seer 1 Chr 2:52

HARORITE har´-or-ite
a form of HARODITE (?) 1 Chr 11:27

HAROSHETH ha-rosh´-eth
carving Judg 4:2

HARP
cunning player on a **h** 1 Sam 16:16
dark sayings upon the **h** Ps 49:4
hanged our **h** upon the willows Ps 137:2
h and the viol Is 5:12
joy of the **h** ceaseth Is 24:8
whether pipe or **h** 1 Cor 14:7
harping with their **h** Rev 14:2

HARSHA har´-shah
enchanter, magician Ezra 2:52

HART
the **h** panteth after the water Ps 42:1
shall the lame man leap as a **h** Is 35:6

HARUM ha´-room
high (?) 1 Chr 4:8

HARUMAPH ha-roo´-maf
flat-nosed Neh 3:10

HARUPHITE ha-roof´-ite
descendants of Hariph 1 Chr 12:5

HARUZ ha´-rooz
active 2 Kgs 21:19

HARVEST
seedtime and **h** Gen 8:22
the feast of **h** Ex 23:16
the firstfruits of wheat **h** Ex 34:22
when ye reap the **h** Lev 19:9
reap the **h** thereof Lev 23:10; Deut 24:19
Is it not wheat **h** to day? 1 Sam 12:17
Whose **h** the hungry eateth up Job 5:5
gathereth her food in **h** Prov 6:8
he that sleepeth in **h** Prov 10:5
cold of snow in the time of **h** Prov 25:13
as rain in **h** Prov 26:1
according to the joy in **h** Is 9:3
thy **h** is fallen Is 16:9
dew in heat of **h** Is 18:4
they shall eat up thine **h** Jer 5:17
appointed weeks of **h** Jer 5:24
The **h** is past, the summer ended Jer 8:20
the time of her **h** shall come Jer 51:33
the **h** is ripe Joel 3:13; Rev 14:15
the **h** is plenteous Matt 9:37
the LORD of the **h** Matt 9:38; Luke 10:2
in the time of **h** I will say Matt 13:30
in the sickle, because the **h** is come Mark 4:29
the **h** truly is great Luke 10:2
they are white already to **h** John 4:35

HASADIAH ha´-sad-i´-ah
whom Jehovah loves 1 Chr 3:20

HASENUAH ha´-se-noo´-ah
she that is hated 1 Chr 9:7

HASHABIAH ha´-shab-i´-ah
whom Jehovah esteems 1 Chr 6:45

HASHABNAH ha-shab´-nah
same as HASHABIAH (?) Neh 10:25

HASHABNIAH ha´-shab-ni´-ah
same as HASHABIAH Neh 3:10

HASHEM ha´-shem
fat 1 Chr 11:34

HASHMONAH hash-mo´-nah
fatness, fat soil Num 33:29

HASHUB hash´-oob
thoughtful Neh 3:11

HASHUBAH hash-oob´-ah
same as HASHUB 1 Chr 3:20

HASHUM hash´-oom
rich Ezra 2:19

HASHUPHA hash-oof´-ah
a form of HASUPHA Neh 7:46

HASRAH has´-rah
needy, lacking 2 Chr 34:22

HASSENAAH has´-en-a´-ah
the thorny Neh 3:3

HASSHUB hash´-oob
same as HASHUB 1 Chr 9:14

HASTE (n)
shall eat it in **h** Ex 12:11
king's business required **h** 1 Sam 21:8
I said in my **h** Ps 31:22; 116:11

HASTE (v)
he that **h** with his feet sinneth Prov 19:2
He that **h** to be rich Prov 28:22
it is near, and **h** greatly Zeph 1:14

HASTEN
captive exile **h** Is 51:14
will **h** it in his time Is 60:22
I will **h** my word Jer 1:12

HASTILY
An inheritance may be gotten **h** Prov 20:21
Go not forth **h** Prov 25:8

HASTY
he that is **h** of spirit exalteth folly Prov 14:29
h only to want Prov 21:5
seest thou a man that is **h** Prov 29:20
let not thine heart be **h** Eccl 5:2
Be not **h** Eccl 7:9

HASUPHA has-oof´-ah
made bare Ezra 2:43

HATACH ha´-tak
he that strikes (?) Esth 4:5

HATE
h they him Gen 37:4,5,8
shall not **h** thy brother Lev 19:17
but I **h** him 1 Kgs 22:8; 2 Chr 18:7
and love them that **h** the LORD 2 Chr 19:2
they that **h** the righteous shall be desolate Ps 34:21
ye that love the LORD, **h** evil Ps 97:10
Do not I **h** them, O LORD, that **h** thee? Ps 139:21
fools **h** knowledge? Prov 1:22
He that spareth his rod **h** his son Prov 13:24
The poor is **h** even of his neighbour Prov 14:20
he that **h** reproof shall die Prov 15:10
he that **h** gifts shall live Prov 15:27
I **h** life Eccl 2:17
a time to **h** Eccl 3:8
your appointed feasts my soul **h** Is 1:14
I **h** robbery for burnt offering Is 61:8
H the evil, and love the good Amos 5:15
Who **h** the good, and love the evil Mic 3:2
these are things that I **h** Zech 8:17
I loved Jacob, and **h** Esau Mal 1:3; Rom 9:13
do good to them that **h** you Matt 5:44; Luke 6:27
either he will **h** the one Matt 6:24
ye shall be **h** Matt 10:22; Mark 13:13; Luke 21:17
and shall **h** one another Matt 24:10
Blessed are ye when men shall **h** you Luke 6:22
and **h** not his father Luke 14:26
h the light John 3:20
The world cannot **h** you John 7:7
he that **h** his life John 12:25
if the world **h** you John 15:18; 1 John 3:13
they both seen and **h** John 15:24
no man ever yet **h** his own flesh Eph 5:29
h his brother 1 John 2:9,11; 3:15; 4:20

HATEFUL
found to be **h** Ps 36:2
h, and hating one another Titus 3:3

HATERS
h of the LORD Ps 81:15
Backbiters, **h** of God Rom 1:30

HATHATH ha´-thath
terror 1 Chr 4:13

HATIPHA ha´-ti-fah
seized Ezra 2:54

HATITA ha´-ti-tah
digging Ezra 2:42

HATTIL hat´-il
wavering Ezra 2:57

HATTUSH hat´-oosh
assembled (?) 1 Chr 3:22

HAUGHTY
thine eyes are upon the **h** 2 Sam 22:28
my heart is not **h** Ps 131:1
a **h** spirit before a fall Prov 16:18
proud and **h** scorner Prov 21:24

the **h** shall be humbled Is 10:33
no more be **h** because Zeph 3:11

HAURAN how´-ran
hollow land Ezek 47:16

HAVILAH ha-vil´-ah
sandy (?) Gen 10:7

HAVOTH-JAIR ha´-voth-ja´-ir
villages of Jair Num 32:41

HAZAEL ha´-za-el
whom God watches over 1 Kgs 19:15

HAZAIAH ha-zai´-ah
whom Jehovah watches over Neh 11:5

HAZAR-ADDAR ha´-zar-ad´-ar
Addar-town Num 34:4

HAZAR-ENAN ha´-zar-e´-nan
fountain-town Num 34:9

HAZAR-GADDAH ha´-zar-gad´-ah
luck-town Josh 15:27

HAZAR-HATTICON ha´-zar-hat´-ik-on
middle-town Ezek 47:16

HAZAR-SHUAL ha´-zar-shoo´-al
jackal-town Josh 15:28

HAZAR-SUSAH ha´-zar-soo´-sah
mare-town Josh 19:5

HAZAR-SUSIM ha´-zar-soo´-sim
horses-town 1 Chr 4:31

HAZARMAVETH ha´-zar-ma´-veth
death-town Gen 10:26

HAZAZON-TAMAR ha´-za-zon-ta´-mar
same as HAZEZON-TAMAR 2 Chr 20:2

HAZELELPONI haz´-lel-po´-ni
the shadow looking on me 1 Chr 4:3

HAZERIM ha´-zer-im
villages Deut 2:23

HAZEROTH ha´-zer-oth
same as HAZERIM Num 11:35

HAZEZON-TAMAR ha´-ze-zon-ta´-mar
pruning of the palm Gen 14:7

HAZIEL ha´-zi-el
the vision of God 1 Chr 23:9

HAZO ha´-zo
vision Gen 22:22

HAZOR ha´-zor
castle Josh 11:1

HEAD
it shall bruise thy **h** Gen 3:15
blood shall be on his **h** Josh 2:19
shall I be your **h**? Judg 11:9
away thy master from thy **h** to day 2 Kgs 2:3
he said unto his father, My **h**, my **h** 2 Kgs 4:19
Lift up your **h** Ps 24:7,9
caused men to ride over our **h** Ps 66:12
therefore shall he lift up the **h** Ps 110:7
oil, which shall not break my **h** Ps 141:5
Blessings are upon the **h** of the just Prov 10:6
on the **h** of him that selleth it Prov 11:26
coals of fire upon his **h** Prov 25:22; Rom 12:20
wise man's eyes are in his **h** Eccl 2:14
the whole **h** is sick Is 1:5
everlasting joy upon their **h** Is 35:10
to bow down his **h** as a bulrush Is 58:5
helmet of salvation upon his **h** Is 59:17; Eph 6:17
Oh that my **h** were waters Jer 9:1
covered their **h** Jer 14:3,4
Thou art this **h** of gold Dan 2:38
dust of the earth on the **h** Amos 2:7
cut them in the **h** Amos 9:1

no man did lift up his **h** Zech 1:21
neither shalt thou swear by thy **h** Matt 5:36
reviled him, wagging their **h** Matt 27:39
My **h** with oil thou didst not anoint Luke 7:46
not a hair of your **h** perish Luke 21:18
then look up, and lift up your **h** Luke 21:28
also my hands and my **h** John 13:9
the **h** of every man is Christ 1 Cor 11:3
dishonoureth his **h** 1 Cor 11:4
woman to have power on her **h** 1 Cor 11:10
[Christ] the **h** Eph 1:22; 4:15; Col 1:18
husband is the **h** of the wife Eph 5:23
not holding the **H** Col 2:19

HEAL
I am the LORD that **h** thee Ex 15:26
I wound, I **h** Deut 32:39
waters were **h** 2 Kgs 2:22
I will **h** thee 2 Kgs 20:5
O LORD, **h** me Ps 6:2
h my soul, for I have sinned Ps 41:4
who **h** all thy diseases Ps 103:3
sent his word, and **h** them Ps 107:20
convert and be **h** Is 6:10
with his stripes we are **h** Is 53:5
they have **h** also the hurt Jer 6:14
incurable which refuseth to be **h** Jer 15:18
H me, and I shall be **h** Jer 17:14
who can **h** thee? Lam 2:13
yet could he not **h** you Hos 5:13
he hath torn, and he will **h** us Hos 6:1
I will **h** their backslidings Hos 14:4
I will come and **h** him Matt 8:7
my servant shall be **h** Matt 8:8
to **h** all manner of sickness Matt 10:1
h the sick Matt 10:8; Luke 9:2; 10:9
lawful to **h** on the sabbath days? Matt 12:10; Luke 14:3
he would **h** on the sabbath day Mark 3:2; Luke 6:7
to **h** the brokenhearted Luke 4:18
Physician, **h** thyself Luke 4:23
power of the Lord was present to **h** Luke 5:17
that he would come down and **h** John 4:47
he that was **h** wist not John 5:13
beholding the man which was **h** Acts 4:14
they were **h** every one Acts 5:16
he had faith to be **h** Acts 14:9
let it rather be **h** Heb 12:13
pray for one another that ye may be **h** James 5:16
by whose stripes ye were **h** 1 Pet 2:24
his deadly wound was **h** Rev 13:3

HEALING
there is no **h** for us Jer 14:19
no **h** of thy bruise Nah 3:19
with **h** in his wings Mal 4:2
h all manner of sickness Matt 4:23
that had need of **h** Luke 9:11
the gifts of **h** 1 Cor 12:9,28,30
for the **h** of the nations Rev 22:2

HEALTH
Art thou in **h**, my brother? 2 Sam 20:9
the **h** of my countenance Ps 42:11; 43:5
thy saving **h** Ps 67:2
h to thy navel Prov 3:8
h to all their flesh Prov 4:22
h to the bones Prov 16:24
thy **h** shall spring forth Is 58:8
for a time of **h** Jer 8:15
h of the daughter of my people Jer 8:22
mayest prosper and be in **h** 3 John 1:2

HEAP
h mischiefs upon them Deut 32:23
I could **h** up words Job 16:4
Though he **h** up silver Job 27:16
he **h** up riches Ps 39:6
h coals of fire Prov 25:22; Rom 12:20
h on wood Ezek 24:10
they shall **h** dust Hab 1:10
h to themselves teachers 2 Tim 4:3
h treasure together for the last days James 5:3

HEAR
how then shall Pharaoh **h** me Ex 6:12
lowing of the oxen which I **h** 1 Sam 15:14
they shall **h** of thy great name 1 Kgs 8:42
O Baal, **h** us 1 Kgs 18:26
h the words of the great king 2 Kgs 18:28; Is 36:13
when thou **h** a sound of going 1 Chr 14:15
all that could **h** with understanding Neh 8:2
Oh that one would **h** me! Job 31:35
h my prayer Ps 4:1; 39:12; 54:2; 84:8; 102:1; 143:1
the LORD will **h** Ps 4:3
cause thine ear to **h** Ps 10:17
who, say they, doth **h**? Ps 59:7
the LORD will not **h** me Ps 66:18
I will **h** what God the LORD will speak Ps 85:8
h groaning of the prisoner Ps 102:20
the poor **h** not rebuke Prov 13:8
h the words of the wise Prov 22:17
more ready to **h**, than to give Eccl 5:1
better to **h** rebuke of the wise Eccl 7:5
h the conclusion of the whole matter Eccl 12:13
h, O heavens, and give ear Is 1:2
I will not **h** Is 1:15; Jer 11:14; 14:12
H, ye indeed but understand not Is 6:9
shall the deaf **h** the words of the book Is 29:18
h, ye that are far off Is 33:13
opening the ears, but he **h** not Is 42:20
h, and your soul shall live Is 55:3
he that **h**, let him **h** Ezek 3:27
h thy words, but they will not do them Ezek 33:31
whosoever **h** these sayings Matt 7:24
which ye do **h** and see Matt 11:4
the deaf **h** Matt 11:5; Luke 7:22
if he will not **h** thee Matt 18:16
shall **h** the voice of the Son of God John 5:25
as I **h**, I judge John 5:30
he that is of God **h** God's words John 8:47
God **h** not sinners John 9:31
I know thou **h** me always John 11:42
if any man **h** my words John 12:47
the word which ye **h** is not mine John 14:24
how **h** we every man Acts 2:8
whole city to **h** Acts 13:44
h without a preacher Rom 10:14
I **h** that there be divisions 1 Cor 11:18
save thyself, and them that **h** 1 Tim 4:16
swift to **h** James 1:19
the world **h** them 1 John 4:5
he that knoweth God **h** us 1 John 4:6
we know that he **h** us 1 John 5:15
let him **h** Rev 2:7; 3:6,13,22
if any man **h** my voice Rev 3:20

HEARD
they **h** the voice of the LORD Gen 3:8
God **h** the voice of the lad Gen 21:17
the house of Pharaoh **h** Gen 45:2
and have **h** their cry Ex 3:7
the LORD **h** it Num 11:1; 12:2
only ye **h** a voice Deut 4:12
nor any tool of iron **h** 1 Kgs 6:7
the fame which I **h** 1 Kgs 10:7
Hast thou not **h** long ago 2 Kgs 19:25; Is 37:26
exceedeth the fame which I **h** 2 Chr 9:6
the noise was **h** afar off Ezra 3:13
Jerusalem was **h** afar off Neh 12:43
Hast thou **h** the secret of God? Job 15:8
I have **h** many such things Job 16:2
but I am not **h** Job 19:7
how little a portion is **h** of him? Job 26:14
When the ear **h** me Job 29:11
the LORD hath **h** my supplication Ps 6:9
hast **h** the desire of the humble Ps 10:17
I sought the LORD, and he **h** Ps 34:4
But I, as a deaf man, **h** not Ps 38:13
thou, O God, hast **h** my vows Ps 61:5
I **h** a language that I understood not Ps 81:5
he hath **h** my voice Ps 116:1
the turtle dove is **h** Song 2:12
have ye not **h**? Is 40:21
hast thou not **h** Is 40:28
men have not **h** Is 64:4
weeping shall no more be **h** Is 65:19
Who hath **h** such a thing? Is 66:8
speaking but ye **h** not Jer 7:13
the rumour that shall be **h** Jer 51:46
We have **h** a rumour Obad 1:1
I **h**, but understood not Dan 12:8
we have **h** that God is with you Zech 8:23
the LORD hearkened, and **h** it Mal 3:16
they shall be **h** Matt 6:7
ye have **h** his blasphemy Matt 26:65
ye have **h** the blasphemy Mark 14:64
shall be **h** in the light Luke 12:3
we have **h** him ourselves John 4:42
as though he **h** them not John 8:6
I thank thee that thou hast **h** me John 11:41
many of them which **h** the word Acts 4:4
we have seen and **h** Acts 4:20; 1 John 1:3
the prisoners **h** them Acts 16:25
thou hast seen and **h** Acts 22:15
whom they have not **h** Rom 10:14
Have they not **h**? Rom 10:18
Eye hath not seen, nor ear **h** 1 Cor 2:9
h unspeakable words 2 Cor 12:4
If so be ye have **h** him Eph 4:21
learned, and received, and **h** Phil 4:9
things thou hast **h** of me 2 Tim 2:2
them that **h** Heb 2:3; 4:2
was **h** in that he feared Heb 5:7
we have **h** and seen 1 John 1:1
thou hast received and **h** Rev 3:3
I **h** a voice from heaven Rev 10:4; 14:2
I **h** another voice Rev 18:4

HEARER
the **h** of the law are just Rom 2:13
grace unto the **h** Eph 4:29
a **h** of the word James 1:23

HEARING
all Israel in their **h** Deut 31:11
neither voice, nor **h** 2 Kgs 4:31
by the **h** of the ear Job 42:5
The **h** ear Prov 20:12
nor the ear filled with **h** Eccl 1:8
h the words of the LORD Amos 8:11
h they hear not Matt 13:13
h a voice, but seeing no man Acts 9:7
faith cometh by **h** Rom 10:17
where were the **h**? 1 Cor 12:17
ye are dull of **h** Heb 5:11

HEARKEN
unto him ye shall **h** Deut 18:15
so will we **h** unto thee Josh 1:17
to **h** than the fat of rams 1 Sam 15:22
If a ruler **h** to lies Prov 29:12
h diligently unto me Is 55:2
O LORD, **h** and do Dan 9:19
H to me every one of you Mark 7:14

HEART
the **h** of a stranger Ex 23:9
serve him with all your **h** Deut 11:13; Josh 22:5

love the LORD thy God with all thy **h** Deut 13:3; Matt 22:37; Mark 12:30,33; Luke 10:27
circumcise thine **h** Deut 30:6
great searchings of **h** Judg 5:16
God gave him another **h** 1 Sam 10:9
serve the LORD with all your **h** 1 Sam 12:20
in truth with all your **h** 1 Sam 12:24
the LORD looketh on the **h** 1 Sam 16:7
an understanding **h** 1 Kgs 3:9,12
it was in the **h** of David 1 Kgs 8:17; 2 Chr 6:7
not perfect, as was the **h** of David 1 Kgs 11:4
not of double **h** 1 Chr 12:33
thou triest the **h** 1 Chr 29:17; Jer 11:20
he did it with all his **h** 2 Chr 31:21
his **h** was lifted up 2 Chr 32:25
nothing else but sorrow of **h** Neh 2:2
God maketh my **h** soft Job 23:16
the widow's **h** Job 29:13
said in his **h** Ps 10:6,11,13; 53:1
The fool hath said in his **h** Ps 14:1
my **h** shall not fear Ps 27:3
my **h** trusted in him Ps 28:7
the **h** is deep Ps 64:6
their **h** was not right Ps 78:37
Thy word have I hid in my **h** Ps 119:11
Let my **h** be sound Ps 119:80
Search me, O God, and know my **h** Ps 139:23
Keep thy **h** with all diligence Prov 4:23
The **h** knoweth his own bitterness Prov 14:10
king's **h** is in the hand of the LORD Prov 21:1
as he thinketh in his **h**, so is he Prov 23:7
songs to a heavy **h** Prov 25:20
h of her husband doth safely trust Prov 31:11
a wise man's **h** discerneth Eccl 8:5
them that are of a fearful **h** Is 35:4
no man layeth it to **h** Is 57:1; Jer 12:11
revive the **h** of the contrite Is 57:15
sing for joy of **h** Is 65:14
the reins of the **h** Jer 11:20; 20:12
The **h** is deceitful above all things Jer 17:9
mine **h** as a burning fire Jer 20:9
I will give them a **h** to know me Jer 24:7
who is this that engaged his **h** Jer 30:21
the pride of thine **h** Jer 49:16; Obad 1:3
the stony **h** Ezek 11:19
I will give them one **h** Ezek 11:19
a **h** of flesh Ezek 36:26
uncircumcised in **h** Ezek 44:7; Acts 7:51
Daniel purposed in his **h** Dan 1:8
rend your **h** Joel 2:13
their **h** as adamant stone Zech 7:12
if ye will not lay it to **h** Mal 2:2
he shall turn the **h** of fathers Mal 4:6
Blessed are the pure in **h** Matt 5:8
there will your **h** be also Matt 6:21; Luke 12:34
I am meek and lowly in **h** Matt 11:29
out of the **h** proceed evil thoughts Matt 15:19
if ye from your **h** forgive not Matt 18:35
Why reason ye these things in your **h**? Mark 2:8
hardness of your **h** Mark 10:5
hardness of **h** Mark 16:14
kept them in her **h** Luke 2:19
all these sayings in her **h** Luke 2:51
the good treasures of his **h** Luke 6:45
slow of **h** to believe Luke 24:25
Did not our **h** burn within us? Luke 24:32
Let not your **h** be troubled John 14:1,27
cut to the **h** Acts 5:33; 7:54
with purpose of **h** Acts 11:23
with the **h** man believeth Rom 10:10
the **h** of man 1 Cor 2:9
in fleshy tables of the **h** 2 Cor 3:3
glory in appearance, not in **h** 2 Cor 5:12
That Christ dwell in your **h** by faith Eph 3:17
making melody in your **h** Eph 5:19
doing the will of God from the **h** Eph 6:6
keep your **h** and minds Phil 4:7
in singleness of **h** Col 3:22
direct your **h** into the love of God 2 Thess 3:5
intents of the **h** Heb 4:12
draw near with true **h** Heb 10:22
the **h** be established Heb 13:9
strife in your **h** James 3:14
purify your **h** James 4:8
the hidden man of the **h** 1 Pet 3:4
sanctify the LORD God in your **h** 1 Pet 3:15

HEARTH
make cakes upon the **h** Gen 18:6
my bones are burned as a **h** Ps 102:3
fire from the **h** Is 30:14
there was fire on the **h** Jer 36:22

HEARTILY
whatsoever ye do, do **h** Col 3:23

HEAT
the **h** of this great anger Deut 29:24
nothing hid from **h** thereof Ps 19:6
two lie together, then they have **h** Eccl 4:11
a shadow in the daytime from the **h** Is 4:6
h upon herbs Is 18:4
dew in the **h** of harvest Is 18:4
neither shall the **h** nor sun smite them Is 49:10
as an oven **h** by the baker Hos 7:4
burden and **h** of the day Matt 20:12
sun is no sooner risen with burning **h** James 1:11
melt with fervent **h** 2 Pet 3:10

HEATH
like the **h** in the desert Jer 17:6
be like the **h** in the wilderness Jer 48:6

HEATHEN
Why do the **h** rage Ps 2:1
h for inheritance Ps 2:8
the **h** shall fear name of the LORD Ps 102:15
I will take you from among the **h** Ezek 36:24
ye were a curse among the **h** Zech 8:13
repetitions, as the **h** do Matt 6:7
as **h** man and a publican Matt 18:17

HEAVEN
the gate of **h** Gen 28:17
have talked with you from **h** Ex 20:22
make your **h** as iron Lev 26:19
the **h** and **h** of heavens Deut 10:14; 1 Kgs 8:27
the precious things of **h** Deut 33:13
the LORD make windows in **h** 2 Kgs 7:2
the **h** are not clean in his sight Job 15:15
Is not God in the height of **h**? Job 22:12
When I consider thy **h** Ps 8:3
looked down from **h** upon the Ps 14:2; 53:2
Whom have I in **h** but thee? Ps 73:25
who in **h** can be compared unto the LORD? Ps 89:6
thy word is settled in **h** Ps 119:89
when he prepared the **h** Prov 8:27
the **h** for height Prov 25:3
God is in **h** Eccl 5:2
will shake the **h** Is 13:13; Hag 2:6
meted out **h** with the span Is 40:12
new **h** and new earth Is 65:17; Rev 21:1
make cakes to the queen of **h** Jer 7:18
Do not I fill **h** and earth? Jer 23:24
If **h** above can be measured Jer 31:37
the **h** were opened Ezek 1:1; Matt 3:16
I will cover the **h** Ezek 32:7
clouds of **h** Dan 7:13
h over you is stayed from dew Hag 1:10
if I will not open windows of **h** Mal 3:10
Till **h** and earth pass Matt 5:18
Capernaum, which art exalted to **h** Matt 11:23
the powers of the **h** Matt 24:29
he saw the **h** opened Mark 1:10
stars of **h** shall fall Mark 13:25
not the angels which are in **h** Mark 13:32
I have sinned against **h** Luke 15:18
ye shall see **h** open John 1:51
bread from **h** John 6:31,32
none other name under **h** Acts 4:12
wrath of God is revealed from **h** Rom 1:18
eternal in the **h** 2 Cor 5:1
our house that is from **h** 2 Cor 5:2
an angel from **h**, preach Gal 1:8
things which are in **h** Eph 1:10
whole family in **h** Eph 3:15
your master also is in **h** Eph 6:9
our conversation is in **h** Phil 3:20
written in **h** Heb 12:23
three that bear record in **h** 1 John 5:7
door was opened in **h** Rev 4:1
throne was set in **h** Rev 4:2
silence in **h** Rev 8:1
a great wonder in **h** Rev 12:1

HEAVENLY
multitude of the **h** host Luke 2:13
I tell you of **h** things John 3:12
the **h** vision Acts 26:19
as is the **h**, such are they 1 Cor 15:48
in **h** places Eph 1:3; 2:6; 3:10
partakers of the **h** calling Heb 3:1
shadow of **h** things Heb 8:5
a **h** country Heb 11:16

HEAVINESS
I am full of **h** Ps 69:20
H in the heart Prov 12:25
the end of that mirth is **h** Prov 14:13
garment of praise for the spirit of **h** Is 61:3
joy to **h** James 4:9

HEAVY
Moses' hands were **h** Ex 17:12
sent to thee with **h** tidings 1 Kgs 14:6
the bondage was **h** Neh 5:18
hand **h** Job 33:7
songs to a **h** heart Prov 25:20
wine unto those of **h** hearts Prov 31:6
to undo the **h** burdens Is 58:6
all ye that labour and are **h** laden Matt 11:28
they bind **h** burdens Matt 23:4
to be sorrowful and very **h** Matt 26:37
their eyes were **h** Matt 26:43

HEBER he´-ber
1 same as EBER 1 Chr 5:13
2 *fellowship* Gen 46:17

HEBERITES he´-ber-ites
descendants of Heber Num 26:45

HEBREW he´-broo
1 the language spoken by the Jews John 19:20
2 a Jew Jer 34:9

HEBREWESS he´-broo-ess
a Jewess Jer 34:9

HEBREWS he´-broos
descendants of Eber Gen 40:15

HEBRON he´-bron
alliance Gen 13:18

HEBRONITES he´-bron-ites
the people of Hebron Num 3:27

HEDGE (n)
a **h** of thorns Prov 15:19
whoso breaketh a **h** Eccl 10:8
set a **h** about it Mark 12:1
the highways and **h** Luke 14:23

HEDGE (v)
whom God hath **h** in Job 3:23
He hath **h** me about Lam 3:7
I will **h** up thy ways Hos 2:6

HEED
took no **h** of the sword 2 Sam 20:10
by taking **h** thereto Ps 119:9
he gave good **h** Eccl 12:9
hearkened diligently with much **h** Is 21:7
let us not give **h** Jer 18:18
neither give **h** to fables 1 Tim 1:4
giving **h** to seducing spirits 1 Tim 4:1
give the more earnest **h** Heb 2:1

HEGAI he´-gai
meditation Esth 2:8

HEGE he´-ge
same as HEGAI Esth 2:3

HEIGHT
from the **h** of his sanctuary Ps 102:19
The heaven for **h** Prov 25:3
in the **h** above Is 7:11
the length, and depth, and **h** Eph 3:18

HEIR
we will destroy the **h** 2 Sam 14:7
handmaid that is **h** to her mistress Prov 30:23
This is the **h** Matt 21:38; Mark 12:7; Luke 20:14
h of God, joint-**h**, with Christ Rom 8:17
h according to the promise Gal 3:29
an **h** of God through Christ Gal 4:7
Gentiles should be fellow-**h** Eph 3:6
h according to hope of eternal life Titus 3:7
who shall be **h** of salvation Heb 1:14
the **h** of promise Heb 6:17
h of the righteousness Heb 11:7
h of the kingdom James 2:5
as **h** together of the grace 1 Pet 3:7

HELAH he´-lah
rust 1 Chr 4:5

HELAM he´-lam
stronghold 2 Sam 10:16

HELBAH hel´-bah
fatness Judg 1:31

HELBON hel´-bon
fertile Ezek 27:18

HELDAI hel´-da-i
terrestrial 1 Chr 27:15

HELEB he´-leb
fat, fatness 2 Sam 23:29

HELED he´-led
the world 1 Chr 11:30

HELEK he´-lek
portion Num 26:30

HELEKITES he´-lek-ites
descendants of Helek Num 26:30

HELEM he´-lem
a form of HELDAI 1 Chr 7:35

HELEPH he´-lef
exchange Josh 19:33

HELEZ he´-lez
liberation 2 Sam 23:26

HELI he´-li
Gr. for ELI Luke 3:23

HELKAI hel´-ka-i
a form of HILKIAH Neh 12:15

HELKATH hel´-kath
a portion Josh 19:25

HELKATH-HAZZURIM hel´-kath-haz´-oor-im
the field of swords (?) 2 Sam 2:16

HELL
shall burn unto the lowest **h** Deut 32:22
sorrows of **h** compassed me 2 Sam 22:6; Ps 18:5
deeper than **h** Job 11:8
H is naked before him Job 26:6
wicked shall be turned into **h** Ps 9:17
not leave my soul in **h** Ps 16:10; Acts 2:27
let them go down quick into **h** Ps 55:15
if I make my bed in **h** Ps 139:8
her steps take hold on **h** Prov 5:5
house is the way to **h** Prov 7:27
her guests are in the depths of **h** Prov 9:18
H and destruction before the LORD Prov 15:11
that he may depart from **h** beneath Prov 15:24
deliver his soul from **h** Prov 23:14
H and destruction are never full Prov 27:20
H from beneath is moved Is 14:9
with **h** are we at agreement Is 28:15
when I cast him down to **h** Ezek 31:16
shall speak out of the midst of **h** Ezek 32:21
Though they dig into **h** Amos 9:2
out of the belly of **h** Jon 2:2
enlargeth his desire as **h** Hab 2:5
in danger of **h** fire Matt 5:22
whole body should be cast into **h** Matt 5:29,30
destroy soul and body in **h** Matt 10:28
brought down to **h** Matt 11:23
gates of **h** shall not prevail Matt 16:18
two eyes to be cast into **h** Matt 18:9; Mark 9:47
more the child of **h** Matt 23:15
how can ye escape the damnation of **h**? Matt 23:33
hath power to cast into **h** Luke 12:5
in **h** he lift up Luke 16:23
his soul was not left in **h** Acts 2:31
set on fire of **h** James 3:6
cast them down to **h** 2 Pet 2:4

HELON he´-lon
strong Num 1:9

HELP (n)
an **h** meet for him Gen 2:18,20
the shield of thy **h** Deut 33:29
he was marvellously **h** 2 Chr 26:15
Is not my **h** in me? Job 6:13
he is our **h** and our shield Ps 33:20
the **h** of his countenance Ps 42:5
a very present **h** in trouble Ps 46:1
vain is the **h** of man Ps 60:11
laid **h** upon one that is mighty Ps 89:19
the hills, from whence cometh my **h** Ps 121:1
Our **h** is in the name of the LORD Ps 124:8
to whom will ye flee for **h**? Is 10:3
in me is thine **h** Hos 13:9
Having therefore obtained **h** of God Acts 26:22
grace to **h** in time of need Heb 4:16

HELP (v)
there is none to **h** Ps 22:11
They **h** every one his neighbour Is 41:6
LORD, **h** me Matt 15:25
h thou mine unbelief Mark 9:24
Men of Israel, **h** Acts 21:28

HELPER
The Lord is my **h** Heb 13:6

HEMAM he´-mam
same as HOMAM Gen 36:22

HEMAN he´-man
faithful 1 Kgs 4:31

HEMATH he´-math
1 *fortress* 1 Chr 2:55
2 same as HAMATH Amos 6:14

HEMDAN hem´-dan
pleasant Gen 36:26

HEN
as a **h** gathereth her chickens Matt 23:37
a **h** doth gather her brood Luke 13:34

HEN hen
favour Zech 6:14

HENA he´-na
troubling (?) 2 Kgs 18:34

HENADAD hen´-a´-dad
favour of Hadad (?) Ezra 3:9

HENCEFORTH
should not **h** live unto themselves 2 Cor 5:15
From **h** let no man trouble me Gal 6:17
H there is laid up for me a crown 2 Tim 4:8

HENOCH he´-nok
same as ENOCH 1 Chr 1:3

HEPHER he´-fer
pit Josh 12:17

HEPHERITES he´-fer-ites
descendants of Hepher Num 26:32

HEPHZI-BAH hef-zi´-bah
in whom is my delight 2 Kgs 21:1

HERES he´-res
the sun Judg 1:35

HERESH he´-resh
artificer 1 Chr 9:15

HERITAGE
h appointed unto him by God Job 20:29
a goodly **h** Ps 16:6; Jer 3:19
the **h** of those that fear Ps 61:5
children are a **h** of the LORD Ps 127:3
This is the **h** of the servants Is 54:17
the flock of thine **h** Mic 7:14
lords over God's **h** 1 Pet 5:3

HERMAS her´-mas
same as HERMES Rom 16:14

HERMES her´-mes
rock, refuge Rom 16:14

HERMOGENES her-mog´-e-nes
begotten of Hermes [Mercury] 2 Tim 1:15

HERMON her´-mon
lofty Deut 3:8

HERMONITES her´-mon-ites
inhabitants of Mount Hermon Ps 42:6

HEROD he´-rod
name of several kings of the Jews Matt 2:1

HERODIANS he-ro´-di-ans
partisans of the Herod family Matt 22:16

HERODIAS he-ro´-di-as
sister of Herod Agrippa I Matt 14:3

HERODION he-ro´-di-on
the song of Juno (?) Rom 16:11

HESED he´-sed
mercy 1 Kgs 4:10

HESHBON hesh´-bon
counting Num 21:25

HESHMON hesh´-mon
fatness Josh 15:27

HETH heth
father of the HITTITES Gen 10:15

HETHLON heth´-lon
hiding-place Ezek 47:15

HEZEKI hez´-ek-i
short for HIZKIAH 1 Chr 8:17

HEZEKIAH hez´-ek-i´-ah
the might of Jehovah 2 Kgs 18:1

HEZION hez´-yon
vision 1 Kgs 15:18

HEZIR he´-zir
swine 1 Chr 24:15

HEZRAI hez´-ra-i
enclosed wall 2 Sam 23:35

HEZRO hez´-ro
same as HEZRAI 1 Chr 11:37

HEZRON hez´-ron
same as HEZRAI Gen 46:12

HEZRONITES hez´-ron-ites
descendants of Hezron Num 26:6

HID
the LORD hath **h** it from me 2 Kgs 4:27
more than for **h** treasures Job 3:21
mine iniquity have I not **h** Ps 32:5
my sins are not **h** Ps 69:5
Thy word have I **h** in mine heart Ps 119:11
ye shall be **h** Zeph 2:3
h, that shall not be known Matt 10:26
now they are **h** from thine eyes Luke 19:42
h wisdom 1 Cor 2:7
if our gospel be **h** 2 Cor 4:3
your life is **h** with Christ Col 3:3
the **h** man of the heart 1 Pet 3:4
the **h** manna Rev 2:17

HIDDAI hid´-a-i
the rejoicing of Jehovah 2 Sam 23:30

HIDDEKEL hid-ek´-el
Gr. name for Tigris River Gen 2:14

HIDE
Shall I **h** from Abraham Gen 18:17
h me in the grave Job 14:13
he **h** his face Job 34:29; Ps 10:11
h me under the shadow of thy wings Ps 17:8
h me in his pavilion Ps 27:5
h them in secret of thy presence Ps 31:20
Wilt thou **h** thyself for ever Ps 89:46
darkness **h** not from thee Ps 139:12
I will **h** mine eyes from you Is 1:15
they **h** it not Is 3:9
h thyself Is 26:20
a man shall be as a **h** place Is 32:2
thou art a God that **h** thyself Is 45:15
no secret they can **h** from thee Ezek 28:3
h a multitude of sins James 5:20
h us from the face of him Rev 6:16

HIEL hi´-el
God liveth 1 Kgs 16:34

HIERAPOLIS hi´-e-ra´-pol-is
a sacred or holy city Col 4:13

HIGGAION hig-a´-yon
meditation Ps 9:16

HIGH
It is as **h** as heaven Job 11:8
stars, how **h** they are! Job 22:12
He beholdeth all **h** things Job 41:34
men of **h** degree are a lie Ps 62:9
Thou hast ascended on **h** Ps 68:18
as the heaven is **h** above the earth Ps 103:11
things too **h** for me Ps 131:1
Though the LORD be **h** Ps 138:6
it is **h** I cannot attain unto it Ps 139:6
afraid of that which is **h** Eccl 12:5
spirit poured upon us from on **h** Is 32:15
He shall dwell on **h** Is 33:16
as **h** as the eagle Jer 49:16
dayspring from on **h** Luke 1:78
power from on **h** Luke 24:49
Mind not **h** things Rom 12:16
it is **h** time Rom 13:11
for prize of the **h** calling Phil 3:14

HIGHER
heavens are **h** than the earth Is 55:9
Friend, go up **h** Luke 14:10
made **h** than the heavens Heb 7:26

HILEN hi´-len
same as HOLON 1 Chr 6:58

HILKIAH hilk-i´-ah
portion of Jehovah 2 Kgs 18:18

HILL
the everlasting **h** Gen 49:26
a land of **h** and valleys Deut 11:11
my King on my holy **h** Ps 2:6
who shall dwell in thy holy **h**? Ps 15:1
Who shall ascend into the **h** of the LORD? Ps 24:3
bring me unto thy holy **h** Ps 43:3
cattle upon a thousand **h** Ps 50:10
strength of the **h** is his Ps 95:4
I will lift up mine eyes unto the **h** Ps 121:1
before the **h** was I brought forth Prov 8:25
the **h** in a balance Is 40:12
salvation hoped for from the **h** Jer 3:23
to the **h**, fall on us Hos 10:8
city set on a **h** Matt 5:14

HILLEL hil´-el
praising Judg 12:13

HINDER
H me not Gen 24:56
who can **h** him? Job 9:12; 11:10
them that were entering in ye **h** Luke 11:52
what doth **h** me to be baptized? Acts 8:36
lest we should **h** the gospel 1 Cor 9:12
who did **h** you Gal 5:7
but Satan **h** us 1 Thess 2:18
that your prayers be not **h** 1 Pet 3:7

HINNOM hin´-ome
wailing Josh 15:8

HIRAH hi´-rah
nobility Gen 38:1

HIRAM hi´-ram
noble (?) 2 Sam 5:11

HIRE
thou shalt give him his **h** Deut 24:15
priests thereof teach for **h** Mic 3:11
give them their **h** Matt 20:8
labourer worthy of his **h** Luke 10:7
h of labourers which is kept back James 5:4

HIRED
in ship with **h** servants Mark 1:20
how many **h** servants Luke 15:17

HIRELING
like the days of a **h** Job 7:1
as a **h** looketh for the reward Job 7:2
accomplish, as a **h**, his day Job 14:6
that oppress the **h** Mal 3:5

HITHERTO
the LORD hath blessed me **h** Josh 17:14
H hath the LORD helped us 1 Sam 7:12
H shalt thou come Job 38:11
My Father worketh **h** John 5:17
H have ye asked nothing in my name John 16:24
h ye were not able to bear it 1 Cor 3:2

HITTITE hit´-tite
descendant of Heth Josh 11:3

HITTITES hit´-tites
plural of HITTITE Gen 15:20

HIVITES hive´-ites
villagers Ex 3:8

HIZKIAH hizk-i´-ah
might of Jehovah Zeph 1:1

HIZKIJAH hizk-i´-jah
same as HIZKIAH Neh 10:17

HOARY
think the deep to be **h** Job 41:32

HOBAB ho´-bab
beloved Num 10:29

HOBAH ho´-bah
a hiding-place Gen 14:15

HOD hode
splendor 1 Chr 7:37

HODAIAH ho-dai´-ah
praise of Jehovah 1 Chr 3:24

HODAVIAH ho´-dav-i´-ah
Jehovah is his praise 1 Chr 5:24

HODESH ho´-desh
new moon 1 Chr 8:9

HODEVAH ho´-de-vah
same as HODAVIAH Neh 7:43

HODIAH ho-di´-ah
same as HODAIAH 1 Chr 4:19

HODIJAH ho-di´-jah
same as HODIAH Neh 8:7

HOGLAH hog´-lah
partridge Num 26:33

HOHAM ho´-ham
woe to them (?) Josh 10:3

HOLD
h him in thine hand Gen 21:18
will not **h** him guiltless Ex 20:7; Deut 5:11
we **h** our peace 2 Kgs 7:9
if thou altogether **h** thy peace Esth 4:14
h in cords of affliction Job 36:8
thy right hand hath **h** me up Ps 18:35
By thee have I been **h** Ps 71:6
thou hast **h** me by my right hand Ps 73:23
H thou me up, and I shall be safe Ps 119:117
man of understanding **h** his peace Prov 11:12
a fool, when he **h** his peace Prov 17:28
the LORD thy God will **h** thy hand Is 41:13
for Zion's sake will I not **h** my peace Is 62:1
I cannot **h** my peace Jer 4:19
H thy tongue Amos 6:10
he will **h** to the one Matt 6:24
H thy peace, come out Mark 1:25; Luke 4:35
h the truth in unrighteousness Rom 1:18
let the first **h** his peace 1 Cor 14:30
H forth the word of life Phil 2:16
h such in reputation Phil 2:29
not **h** the Head Col 2:19
h fast that which is good 1 Thess 5:21
H faith and a good conscience 1 Tim 1:19
H the mystery of the faith 1 Tim 3:9
H fast the form of sound words 2 Tim 1:13
H fast the faithful word Titus 1:9
h the beginning of our confidence Heb 3:14
h fast our profession Heb 4:14; 10:23
thou **h** fast my name Rev 2:13
h fast till I come Rev 2:25
h fast, and repent Rev 3:3
h that fast which thou hast Rev 3:11

HOLE
child shall play on the **h** of the asp Is 11:8
h of the pit whence ye are digged Is 51:1
hide it there in a **h** of the rock Jer 13:4
a **h** in the wall Ezek 8:7
a bag with **h** Hag 1:6
foxes have **h** Matt 8:20; Luke 9:58

HOLIER
for I am **h** than thou Is 65:5

HOLIEST
called the **h** of all Heb 9:3
enter into the **h** by the blood Heb 10:19

HOLILY
God also, how **h** and just 1 Thess 2:10

HOLINESS
glorious in **h** Ex 15:11
H TO THE LORD Ex 28:36; 39:30; Zech 14:20
beauty of **h** 1 Chr 16:29; 2 Chr 20:21; Ps 29:2; 96:9; 110:3
at the remembrance of his **h** Ps 30:4; 97:12
the throne of his **h** Ps 47:8
God hath spoken in his **h** Ps 60:6; 108:7
h becometh thine house Ps 93:5
The way of **h** Is 35:8
habitation of thy **h** Is 63:15
the words of his **h** Jer 23:9
there shall be **h** Obad 1:17
in **h** and righteousness Luke 1:75
as though by our own **h** Acts 3:12
according to the Spirit of **h** Rom 1:4
fruit unto **h** Rom 6:22
perfecting **h** in the fear of God 2 Cor 7:1
created in righteousness and true **h** Eph 4:24
unblameable in **h** 1 Thess 3:13
called us to uncleanness, but unto **h** 1 Thess 4:7
continue in faith and charity and **h** 1 Tim 2:15
in behaviour as becometh **h** Titus 2:3
partakers of his **h** Heb 12:10
h, without which no man Heb 12:14

HOLLOW
touched the **h** of his thigh Gen 32:25
clave a **h** place Judg 15:19
waters in the **h** of his hand Is 40:12

HOLON ho´-lon
sandy Josh 15:51

HOLY
is **h** ground Ex 3:5
a **h** nation Ex 19:6; 1 Pet 2:9
sabbath day, to keep it **h** Ex 20:8
difference between **h** and unholy Lev 10:10
by ye **h** Lev 20:7
who is **h** Num 16:5
this is a **h** man of God 2 Kgs 4:9
the **h** seed Ezra 9:2; Is 6:13
from his **h** heaven Ps 20:6
thou art **h** O thou that inhabitest Ps 22:3
Preserve my soul, for I am **h** Ps 86:2
his **h** arm hath gotten him victory Ps 98:1
worship at his **h** hill Ps 99:9
and **h** in all his works Ps 145:17
who devoureth that which is **h** Prov 20:25
H, **h**, **h** is the LORD Is 6:3
make bare his **h** arm Is 52:10
Thy **h** cities are a wilderness Is 64:10
Our **h** and our beautiful house Is 64:11
no difference between the **h** and profane Ezek 22:26
with child of the **H** Ghost Matt 1:18
baptize you with the **H** Ghost Matt 3:11; Mark 1:8; Luke 3:16; John 1:33; Acts 1:5
Give not that which is **h** Matt 7:6
blasphemy against the **H** Ghost Matt 12:31
not ye that speak, but the **H** Ghost Mark 13:11
shall be filled with the **H** Ghost Luke 1:15
h thing which shall be born of thee Luke 1:35
H Ghost descended in bodily shape Luke 3:22
Jesus being full of the **H** Ghost Luke 4:1
H Ghost shall teach you Luke 12:12
the **H** Ghost was not yet given John 7:39
Comforter, which is the **H** Ghost John 14:26
H Father, keep through thine own name John 17:11
Receive ye the **H** Ghost John 20:22
after that the **H** Ghost is come Acts 1:8
all filled with the **H** Ghost Acts 2:4; 4:31
against thy **h** child Jesus Acts 4:27
to lie to the **H** Ghost and wisdom Acts 5:3
full of the **H** Ghost Acts 6:3
ye do always resist the **H** Ghost Acts 7:51
that they might receive **H** Ghost Acts 8:15
comfort of the **H** Ghost Acts 9:31
H Ghost fell on all Acts 10:44
received the **H** Ghost as well as we Acts 10:47
giving them the **H** Ghost Acts 15:8
seemed good to the **H** Ghost Acts 15:28
forbidden of the **H** Ghost Acts 16:6
Have ye received the **H** Ghost? Acts 19:2
H Ghost hath made you overseers Acts 20:28
in the **H** scriptures Rom 1:2
commandment **h**, and just, and good Rom 7:12
bearing me witness in **H** Ghost Rom 9:1
if the firstfruit be **h** Rom 11:16
a living sacrifice, **h**, acceptable unto God Rom 12:1
joy in the **H** Ghost Rom 14:17
with a **h** kiss Rom 16:16; 1 Cor 16:20; 2 Cor 13:12; 1 Thess 5:26
which the **H** Ghost teacheth 1 Cor 2:13
the temple of God is **h** 1 Cor 3:17
now are they **h** 1 Cor 7:14
communion of the **H** Ghost 2 Cor 13:14
be **h** and without blame Eph 1:4; 5:27
groweth unto a **h** temple in the Lord Eph 2:21
present you **h** and unblameable Col 1:22
elect of God, **h** and beloved Col 3:12
all the **h** brethern 1 Thess 5:27
lifting up **h** hands 1 Tim 2:8
called us with a **h** calling 2 Tim 1:9
the renewing of the **H** Ghost Titus 3:5
h brethren, partakers Heb 3:1
H Ghost sent down from heaven 1 Pet 1:12
h in all manner of conversation 1 Pet 1:15,16
a **h** priesthood 1 Pet 2:5
the **h** women also, who trusted 1 Pet 3:5
with him in the **h** mount 2 Pet 1:18
as they were moved by the **H** Ghost 2 Pet 1:21
saith he that is **h** Rev 3:7
O Lord, **h** and true Rev 6:10
h is he that hath part Rev 20:6
the **h** Jerusalem Rev 21:10
he that is **h**, let him be **h** Rev 22:11

HOMAM ho´-mam
destruction 1 Chr 1:39

HOME
and shall not be brought **h** Ex 9:19
born at **h** or born abroad Lev 18:9
free at **h** one year Deut 24:5
LORD hath brought me **h** again empty Ruth 1:21
fetch **h** again his banished 2 Sam 14:13
Come **h** with me 1 Kgs 13:7
tarry at **h** 2 Kgs 14:10; Ps 68:12
bring ark of God **h** 1 Chr 13:12
he will bring **h** thy seed Job 39:12
man goeth to his long **h** Eccl 12:5
at **h** there is as death Lam 1:20
when ye brought it **h** Hag 1:9
Go **h** to thy friends Mark 5:19
took her unto his own **h** John 19:27
went away again to their own **h** John 20:10
let him eat at **h** 1 Cor 11:34
ask their husbands at **h** 1 Cor 14:35
at **h** in the body 2 Cor 5:6
shew piety at **h** 1 Tim 5:4
keepers at **h** Titus 2:5

HONEST
an **h** and good heart Luke 8:15
men of **h** report Acts 6:3
Provide things **h** Rom 12:17
let us walk **h**, as in the day Rom 13:13
whatsoever things are **h** Phil 4:8
conversation **h** among the Gentiles 1 Pet 2:12

HONOUR (n)
promote thee unto the very great **h** Num 22:17
hath kept thee back from **h** Num 24:11
of them shall I be had in **h** 2 Sam 6:22
riches and **h** 1 Kgs 3:13
died full of days riches, and **h** 1 Chr 29:28
riches, wealth, or **h** 2 Chr 1:11,12
neither shall it be for thy **h** 2 Chr 26:18
wives shall give to their husbands **h** Esth 1:20
His sons come to **h** Job 14:21
lay mine **h** in the dust Ps 7:5
crowned him with glory and **h** Ps 8:5; Heb 2:7
place where thine **h** dwelleth Ps 26:8
man being in **h** abideth not Ps 49:12
H and majesty are before him Ps 96:6
this **h** have all his saints Ps 149:9
in her left hand riches and **h** Prov 3:16
she shall bring thee to **h** Prov 4:8
lest thou give thine **h** to others Prov 5:9
multitude of people is the king's **h** Prov 14:28
an **h** for a man to cease from strife Prov 20:3
the **h** of kings is to search out Prov 25:2
h is not seemly for a fool Prov 26:1
strength and **h** are her clothing Prov 31:25
God hath given riches, wealth, **h** Eccl 6:2
where is mine **h**? Mal 1:6
not without **h** Matt 13:57; Mark 6:4
I receive not **h** from men John 5:41
receive **h** one of another John 5:44
in well doing seek for glory and **h** Rom 2:7
h and peace to every man that worketh good Rom 2:10
in **h** preferring one another Rom 12:10
h to whom **h** Rom 13:7
By **h** and dishonour 2 Cor 6:8
not in any **h** to the satisfying Col 2:23
possess his vessel in sanctification and **h** 1 Thess 4:4
counted worthy of double **h** 1 Tim 5:17
masters worthy of all **h** 1 Tim 6:1
to whom be **h** and power everlasting 1 Tim 6:16
some to **h**, and some to dishonour 2 Tim 2:20
more **h** than the house Heb 3:3
no man taketh this **h** unto himself Heb 5:4
giving **h** unto the wife 1 Pet 3:7
to receive glory, and **h**, and power Rev 4:11; 5:12

HONOUR (v)
I will be **h** upon Pharaoh Ex 14:4
H thy father and mother Ex 20:12; Deut 5:16; Matt 19:19; Mark 7:10; Luke 18:20
h the face of the old man Lev 19:32
them that **h** me I will **h** 1 Sam 2:30
h me now 1 Sam 15:30
the king delight to do **h** Esth 6:6
he **h** them that fear the LORD Ps 15:4
H the LORD with thy substance Prov 3:9
better than he that **h** himself Prov 12:9
A son **h** his father Mal 1:6
h me with their lips Matt 15:8
h the Son as they **h** the Father John 5:23
H widows that are widows indeed 1 Tim 5:3
H all men 1 Pet 2:17

HONOURABLE
among thy **h** women Ps 45:9
the **h** man Is 3:3
ancient and **h**, he is the head Is 9:15
magnify the law, and make it **h** Is 42:21

HOPE (n)
spent without **h** Job 7:6
the hypocrite's **h** shall perish Job 8:13
where is now my **h**? Job 17:15
my **h** hath he removed Job 19:10
my flesh also shall rest in **h** Ps 16:9; Acts 2:26
my **h** is in thee Ps 39:7
let me not be ashamed of my **h** Ps 119:116
h deferred maketh the heart sick Prov 13:12
hath **h** in his death Prov 14:32

one is **h**, and another is drunken 1 Cor 11:21
instructed both to be full and to be **h** Phil 4:12

HUNT
as when one doth **h** a partridge 1 Sam 26:20
h them from every mountain Jer 16:16
h the souls of my people Ezek 13:18
they **h** every man his brother Mic 7:2

HUNTING
which he took in **h** Prov 12:27

HUPHAM hoo´-fam
inhabitant of the shore (?) Num 26:39

HUPHAMITES hoo´-fam-ites
descendants of Hupham Num 26:39

HUPPAH hoop´-ah
covering 1 Chr 24:13

HUPPIM hoop´-im
same as HUPHAM (?) Gen 46:21

HUR hoor
cavern Ex 17:10

HURAI hoo´-ra-i
a linen weaver (?) 1 Chr 11:32

HURAM hoo´-ram
variant spelling of Hiram 2 Chr 2:13

HURI hoo´-ri
linen-worker (?) 1 Chr 5:14

HURL
h at him by laying of wait Num 35:20
h stones and shooting arrows 1 Chr 12:2
as a storm **h** him out of his place Job 27:21

HURT (n)
that sweareth to his own **h** Ps 15:4
ruleth over another to his own **h** Eccl 8:9
have healed also the **h** slightly Jer 6:14; 8:11
for the **h** of the daughter of my people Jer 8:21
I will do you no **h** Jer 25:6
they have no **h** Dan 3:25
no manner of **h** was found upon him Dan 6:23

HURT (v)
shall not **h** nor destroy Is 11:9
deadly thing, it shall not **h** Mark 16:18
nothing shall by any means **h** you Luke 10:19
no man shall set on thee to **h** thee Acts 18:10
h not the oil and the wine Rev 6:6

HURTFUL
rebellious city, and **h** unto kings Ezra 4:15
servant from the **h** sword Ps 144:10
into many foolish and **h** lust 1 Tim 6:9

HUSBAND
a bloody **h** art thou Ex 4:25
Virtuous woman is a crown to her **h** Prov 12:4
her **h** doth safely trust Prov 31:11
Her **h** is known in the gates Prov 31:23
her **h** also, and he praiseth her Prov 31:28
thy Maker is thine **h** Is 54:5
Go, call thy **h** John 4:16
whether thou shalt save thy **h** 1 Cor 7:16
let them ask their **h** at home 1 Cor 14:35
Wives, submit yourselves unto your **h** Eph 5:22
H, love your wives Eph 5:25; Col 3:19
the **h** of one wife 1 Tim 3:12
to love their **h** Titus 2:4
obedient to their own **h** Titus 2:5
be in subjection to your **h** 1 Pet 3:1
ye **h**, dwell with them 1 Pet 3:7

HUSHAH hoo´-shah
haste 1 Chr 4:4

HUSHAI hoo´-sha-i
hasting 2 Sam 15:32

HUSHAM hoo´-sham
haste Gen 36:34

HUSHATHITE hoo´-shath-ite
inhabitant of Hushah 2 Sam 23:27

HUSHIM hoosh´-im
those who make haste Gen 46:23

HUZ hooz
same as UZ Gen 22:21

HUZZAB hooz´-ab
it is decreed Nah 2:7

HYMENAEUS hi´-men-e´-us
belonging to Hymen 2 Tim 2:17

HYMN
when they had sung a **h** Matt 26:30; Mark 14:26
Speaking to yourselves in psalms and **h** Eph 5:19
admonishing one another in psalms and **h** Col 3:16

HYPOCRISY
within ye are full of **h** Matt 23:28
he, knowing their **h** Mark 12:15
leaven of the Pharisees, which is **h** Luke 12:1
and without **h** James 3:17

HYPOCRITE
the **h** hope shall perish Job 8:13
the joy of the **h** but for a moment Job 20:5
the **h** in heart Job 36:13
every one is a **h** Is 9:17
as the **h** Matt 6:2,5,16
thou **h** Matt 7:5; Luke 6:42; 13:15
ye **h** Matt 15:7; 16:3; 22:18; Mark 7:6; Luke 12:56
woe unto you, scribes, and Pharisees, you **h** Matt 23:13; Luke 11:44
appoint him his portion with the **h** Matt 24:51

HYPOCRITICAL
With **h** mockers in feasts Ps 35:16
send him against a **h** nation Is 10:6

I

ICHABOD i´-ka-bod
inglorious 1 Sam 4:21

IBHAR ib´-har
whom God chooses 2 Sam 5:15

IBLEAM ib´-le-am
He destroys the people Josh 17:11

IBNEIAH ib-ni´-ah
whom Jehovah will build up 1 Chr 9:8

IBNIJAH ib-ni´-jah
same as IBNEIAH 1 Chr 9:8

IBRI ib´-ri
Hebrew 1 Chr 24:27

IBZAN ib´-zan
active (?) Judg 12:8

ICONIUM i-kon´-yum
image-like Acts 13:51

IDALAH id´-al-ah
snares (?) Josh 19:15

IDBASH id´-bash
honeyed 1 Chr 4:3

IDDO id´-do
1 *loving* 1 Chr 27:21
2 *seasonable* Zech 1:1

IDLE
they be **i** Ex 5:8
an **i** soul shall hunger Prov 19:15
eateth not bread of **i** Prov 31:27
every **i** word that men shall speak Matt 12:36
others standing **i** Matt 20:3,6

IDOL
all gods of the people are **i** 1 Chr 16:26; Ps 96:5
as if he blessed an **i** Is 66:3
they are mad upon their **i** Jer 50:38
Ephraim is joined to **i** Hos 4:17
abstain from pollutions of **i** Acts 15:20
we know that an **i** is nothing 1 Cor 8:4
with conscience of the **i** 1 Cor 8:7
ye turned to God from **i** 1 Thess 1:9
keep yourselves from **i** 1 John 5:21

IDUMAEA i-du-me´-ah
same as IDUMEA Mark 3:8

IDUMEA i-du-me´-ah
same as EDOM Is 34:5

IGAL i´-gal
whom God will avenge Num 13:7

IGDALIAH ig´-dal-i´-ah
whom Jehovah shall make great Jer 35:4

IGEAL i´-ge-al
same as IGAL 1 Chr 3:22

IGNORANCE
through **i** ye did it Acts 3:17
the times of this **i** God winked at Acts 17:30
through the **i** that is in them Eph 4:18
put to silence the **i** of foolish men 1 Pet 2:15

IGNORANT
so foolish was I, and **i** Ps 73:22
though Abraham be **i** of us Is 63:16
they were unlearned and **i** men Acts 4:13
being **i** of God's righteousness Rom 10:3
if any man be **i**, let him be **i** 1 Cor 14:38
not **i** of his devices 2 Cor 2:11
can have compassion on the **i** Heb 5:2
they willingly are **i** 2 Pet 3:5

IIM i´-im
ruins Num 33:45

IJE-ABARIM i-je-ab´-ar-im
ruinous heaps of Abarim Num 21:11

IJON i´-jon
a ruin 1 Kgs 15:20

IKKESH ik´-esh
perverseness of mouth 2 Sam 23:26

ILAI i´-la-i
most high 1 Chr 11:29

ILLYRICUM il-ir´-ik-um
province of Rome Rom 15:19

IMAGINATION
i of the thoughts of his heart Gen 6:5
i of man's heart is evil from his youth Gen 8:21
walketh after the **i** of mine heart Deut 29:19
understandeth all the **i** of thoughts 1 Chr 28:9
vain in their **i** Rom 1:21
Casting down **i** 2 Cor 10:5

IMAGINE
How long will ye **i** mischief Ps 62:3
What do ye **i** against the LORD? Nah 1:9
is one come out of thee, that **i** evil Nah 1:11
let none of you **i** evil Zech 7:10; 8:17

IMLA im´-lah
same as IMLAH 2 Chr 18:7

IMLAH im´-lah
whom [God] will fill up 1 Kgs 22:8

IMMANUEL im-an´-u-el
God with us Is 7:14

IMMER im´-er
talkative 1 Chr 9:12

IMMORTAL
i, invisible, the only wise God 1 Tim 1:17

IMMORTALITY
honour and i, eternal life Rom 2:7
this mortal shall put on i 1 Cor 15:53
Who only hath i dwelling in the light 1 Tim 6:16
brought life and i to light 2 Tim 1:10

IMNA im´-nah
whom [God] keeps back 1 Chr 7:35

IMNAH im´-nah
whom [God] assigns (?) 1 Chr 7:30

IMPART
neither hath he i to her understanding Job 39:17
let him i to him that hath none Luke 3:11
that I may i to you some spiritual gift Rom 1:11
we were willing to have i unto you 1 Thess 2:8

IMPEDIMENT
and had an i in his speech Mark 7:32

IMPENITENT
after thy hardness and i heart Rom 2:5

IMPLACABLE
without natural affection, i Rom 1:31

IMPOSE
shall not be lawful to i toll, tribute Ezra 7:24
ordinances, i on them until the time Heb 9:10

IMPOSSIBLE
with men it is i Matt 19:26; Mark 10:27
with God nothing shall be i Luke 1:37
things which are i with men
are possible with God Luke 18:27

IMPOTENT
lay a great multitude of i folk John 5:3
deed done to the i man Acts 4:9
i in his feet, being a cripple Acts 14:8

IMPOVERISH
greatly i because of the Midianites Judg 6:6
he that is so i that hath no oblation Is 40:20
they shall i thy fenced cities Jer 5:17

IMPRISONMENT
confiscation of goods, or to i Ezra 7:26
In stripes, in i, in tumults 2 Cor 6:5
moreover of bonds and i Heb 11:36

IMPUDENT
with an i face said unto him Prov 7:13
they are i children and stiffhearted Ezek 2:4; 3:7

IMPUTE
blood shall be i unto that man Lev 17:4
whom Lord i not iniquity Ps 32:2; Rom 4:8
i this his power unto his god Hab 1:11
sin is not i when there is no law Rom 5:13

IMRAH im´-rah
stubborn 1 Chr 7:36

IMRI im´-ri
eloquent 1 Chr 9:4

INDIA in´-di-ah
1 *great river* (?),
2 Hebr. for Indus Esth 1:1

INCLINE
i your heart unto the Lord Josh 24:23
That he may i our hearts unto him 1 Kgs 8:58
he i unto me, and heard my cry Ps 40:1
he hath i his ear unto me Ps 116:2
I my heart unto thy testimonies Ps 119:36
nor i their ear Jer 7:24; 11:8
neither i their ear Jer 17:23; 34:14

INCLOSED
They are i in their own fat Ps 17:10
the assembly of the wicked have i me Ps 22:16
they i a great multitude of fish Luke 5:6

INCONTINENT
Satan tempt you not for your i 1 Cor 7:5
i, fierce, despisers of those that are good 2 Tim 3:3

INCORRUPTIBLE
an i crown 1 Cor 9:25
an inheritance, i, and undefiled 1 Pet 1:4
i, by the word of God 1 Pet 1:23

INCREASE (n)
Take thou no usury of him, or i Lev 25:36
the land shall yield her i Lev 26:4
tithe all the i of thy seed Deut 14:22
tithe of thine i the same year Deut 14:28
Then shall the earth yield her i Ps 67:6
with the i of his lips shall he be filled Prov 18:20
loveth abundance with i, this is
also vanity Eccl 5:10
the i of his government Is 9:7
the earth shall yield her i Ezek 34:27
God gave the i 1 Cor 3:6
God that giveth the i 1 Cor 3:7

INCREASE (v)
thy latter end shall greatly i Job 8:7
their corn and their wine i Ps 4:7
riches i, set not your heart upon them Ps 62:10
Lord shall i you more and more Ps 115:14
A wise man will hear, and i learning Prov 1:5
teach a just man, and he will i Prov 9:9
There is that scattereth, and yet i Prov 11:24
he that i knowledge i sorrow Eccl 1:18
multiplied the nation, and not i the joy Is 9:3
them that have no might he i strength Is 40:29
I will i them with men like a flock Ezek 36:37
and knowledge shall be i Dan 12:4
he daily i lies and desolation Hos 12:1
i that which is not his Hab 2:6
Jesus i in wisdom and stature Luke 2:52
the word of God i Acts 6:7
in faith and i in number daily Acts 16:5
I am rich, and i with goods Rev 3:17

INCREDIBLE
thought a thing i with you Acts 26:8

INCURABLE
an i disease 2 Chr 21:18
my wound i Jer 15:18; Mic 1:9

INDEED
will God i dwell on the earth? 1 Kgs 8:27;
2 Chr 6:18
bless me i 1 Chr 4:10
a prophet i Mark 11:32
the Lord is risen i Luke 24:34
an Israelite i John 1:47
flesh is meat i, and my blood is drink i John 6:55
ye shall be free i John 8:36
that are widows i 1 Tim 5:3

INDIGNATION
wrath, i, and trouble Ps 78:49
till the i be overpast Is 26:20
Who can stand before his i? Nah 1:6
moved with i Matt 20:24
they had i Matt 26:8
yea, what i 2 Cor 7:11
fearful looking for of fiery i Heb 10:27
the cup of his i Rev 14:10

INDITING
my heart is i a good matter Ps 45:1

INDUSTRIOUS
that he was i 1 Kgs 11:28

INEXCUSABLE
thou art i, O man Rom 2:1

INFANT
as i which never saw light Job 3:16
an i of days Is 65:20
brought unto him also i Luke 18:15

INFIDEL
he that believeth with an i 2 Cor 6:15
is worse than an i 1 Tim 5:8

INFIRMITY
this is mine i Ps 77:10
spirit of man will sustain his i Prov 18:14
himself took our i Matt 8:17
the i of your flesh Rom 6:19
the Spirit also helpeth our i Rom 8:26
bear the i of the weak Rom 15:1
glory in mine i 2 Cor 12:5,10
wine for thine often i 1 Tim 5:23
touched with the feeling of our i Heb 4:15

INFLAME
till wine i them Is 5:11
I yourselves with idols Is 57:5

INFLICTED
which was i of many 2 Cor 2:6

INFLUENCES
thou bind the sweet i Job 38:31

INHABIT
One that i eternity Is 57:15
build houses, and i them Is 65:21
cities and i them Amos 9:14

INHABITANT
land eateth up i Num 13:32
curse bitterly the i Judg 5:23
cities wasted without i Is 6:11
i shall not say, I am sick Is 33:24
the i thereof are as grasshoppers Is 40:22
land without an i Jer 44:22

INHERIT
they shall i it for ever Ex 32:13
shall i the earth Ps 25:13
the meek shall i the earth Ps 37:11
the simple i folly Prov 14:18
shall i everlasting life Matt 19:29
i kingdom prepared Matt 25:34
i eternal life Mark 10:17;
Luke 10:25; 18:18
not i the kingdom 1 Cor 6:9;
15:50; Gal 5:21
when he would have i the blessing Heb 12:17

INHERITANCE
LORD is the portion of mine i Ps 16:5
shall choose our i for us Ps 47:4
An i may be gotten hastily Prov 20:21
Wisdom good with an i Eccl 7:11
the i shall be ours Mark 12:7
that he divide the i with me Luke 12:13
an i among all them which
are the sanctified Acts 20:32
earnest of our i Eph 1:14
promise of eternal i Heb 9:15

INIQUITY
visiting the i of the fathers Ex 20:5; 34:7;
Num 14:18; Deut 5:9
forgiving i and transgression Ex 34:7;
Num 14:18
they that plow i, and sow wickedness Job 4:8
to possess the i of my youth Job 13:26
if I have done i, I will do no more Job 34:32
pardon mine i, for it is great Ps 25:11
mine i have I not hid Ps 32:5
dost correct man for i Ps 39:11
I was shapen in i Ps 51:5
If I regard i in my heart Ps 66:18
add i to their i Ps 69:27
remember not against us former i Ps 79:8
thou hast set our i Ps 90:8
Who forgiveth all thine i Ps 103:3
not rewarded us according to our i Ps 103:10
because of their i, are afflicted Ps 107:17
They also do no i Ps 119:3
If thou, LORD, shouldest mark i Ps 130:3
He that soweth i shall reap vanity Prov 22:8
a people laden with i Is 1:4

thine i is taken away Is 6:7
her i is pardoned Is 40:2
he was bruised for our i Is 53:5
your i have separated between
you and your God Is 59:2
Your i turned away these things Jer 5:25
so i shall not be your ruin Ezek 18:30
canst not look on i Hab 1:13
because i shall abound Matt 24:12
purchased a field with the reward of i Acts 1:18
in the bond of i Acts 8:23
to i unto i Rom 6:19
the mystery of i 2 Thess 2:7
depart from i 2 Tim 2:19
a world of i James 3:6

INJURIOUS
and i: but I obtained mercy 1 Tim 1:13

INK
I wrote them with i in the book Jer 36:18
written not with i, but with the
Spirit of the living God 2 Cor 3:3
would not write with paper and i 2 John 1:12
will not with i and pen write 3 John 1:13

INN
gave his ass provender in the i Gen 42:27
came to pass by the way in the i Ex 4:24
was no room for them in the i Luke 2:7
brought him to an i Luke 10:34

INNOCENT
who ever perished, being i? Job 4:7
laugh at the trial of the i Job 9:23
the i shall divide the silver Job 27:17
i from the great transgression Ps 19:13
maketh haste to be rich shall not be i Prov 28:20
blood of the souls of the poor i Jer 2:34
with the blood of the i Jer 19:4

INNUMERABLE
as there are i before him Job 21:33
i evils have compassed me Ps 40:12
to an i company of angels Heb 12:22

INORDINATE
more corrupt in her i love Ezek 23:11
i affection, evil concupiscence Col 3:5

INQUIRE
people come unto me to i of God Ex 18:15
a man had i at the oracle 2 Sam 16:23
that we may i of the LORD by him 2 Kgs 3:11
returned and i early after God Ps 78:34
should I be i of at all by them? Ezek 14:3
I will not be i Ezek 20:3,31
I will yet for this be i of Ezek 36:37
nor i for him Zeph 1:6
i who in it is worthy Matt 10:11
the prophets have i 1 Pet 1:10

INQUISITION
judges shall make diligent i Deut 19:18
when i was made of the matter Esth 2:23
he maketh i for blood Ps 9:12

INSCRIPTION
I found an altar with this i Acts 17:23

INSPIRATION
the i of the Almighty giveth Job 32:8
All scripture is given by i of God 2 Tim 3:16

INSTANT
continuing i in prayer Rom 12:12
be i in season, out of season 2 Tim 4:2

INSTRUCT
thy good spirit to i them Neh 9:20
my reins also i me in the night season Ps 16:7
I will i thee and teach thee Ps 32:8
who i him Is 40:14
scribe which is i unto the kingdom Matt 13:52
in all things I am i both Phil 4:12

INSTRUCTION
thou hatest i Ps 50:17
fools despise wisdom and i Prov 1:7
take fast hold of i Prov 4:13
Hear i, and be wise Prov 8:33
Whoso loveth i loveth knowledge Prov 12:1
A fool despiseth his father's i Prov 15:5
the i of fools is folly Prov 16:22
I looked upon it, and received i Prov 24:32
for i in righteousness 2 Tim 3:16

INSTRUMENT
hath prepared the i of death Ps 7:13
a new sharp threshing i Is 41:15
can play well on an i Ezek 33:32
members as i of unrighteousness Rom 6:13

INTEGRITY
he holdeth fast his i Job 2:3
that God may know mine i Job 31:6
Let i and uprightness preserve me Ps 25:21
I have walked in i Ps 26:1
The i of the upright Prov 11:3
walketh in his i Prov 19:1; 20:7

INTENTS
performed the i of his heart Jer 30:24
thoughts and i of the heart Heb 4:12

INTERCESSION
made i for the transgressors Is 53:12
the Spirit itself maketh i Rom 8:26
ever liveth to make i Heb 7:25

INTERCESSOR
wondered that there was no i Is 59:16

INTERMEDDLE
a stranger doth not i with his joy Prov 14:10
seeketh and i with all wisdom Prov 18:1

INTREAT
I me not to leave thee Ruth 1:16
if a man sin against the LORD,
who shall i for him? 1 Sam 2:25
I i thy favour Ps 119:58
he shall be i of them Is 19:22
but i him as a father 1 Tim 5:1
easy to be i James 3:17

INTRUDING
i into those things which he
hath not seen Col 2:18

INVENTIONS
provoked him to anger with their i Ps 106:29
find out knowledge of witty i Prov 8:12
sought out many i Eccl 7:29

INVISIBLE
image of the i God Col 1:15
the King eternal, immortal, i 1 Tim 1:17
as seeing him who is i Heb 11:27

INWARD
wisdom in the i parts Job 38:36
truth in the i parts Ps 51:6
i thought of every one Ps 64:6
I will put my law in their i parts Jer 31:33
delight in the law of God after
the i man Rom 7:22
the i man is renewed 2 Cor 4:16

IPHEDEIAH if′-ed-i′-ah
whom Jehovah frees 1 Chr 8:25

IR eer
city 1 Chr 7:12

IR-NAHASH ir-na′-hash
snake-town 1 Chr 4:12

IR-SHEMESH ir′-she′-mesh
sun-town Josh 19:41

IRA i′-rah
watchful 2 Sam 20:26

IRAD i′-rad
descendant of Cain Gen 4:18

IRAM i′-ram
belonging to a city Gen 36:43

IRI i′-ri
same as IRAM 1 Chr 7:7

IRIJAH i-ri′-jah
whom Jehovah looks on Jer 37:13

IRON i′-ron
reverence Josh 19:38

IRPEEL ir′-pe-el
which God heals Josh 18:27

IRU i′-roo
same as IRAM 1 Chr 4:15

ISAAC i′-zak
laughter Gen 17:19

ISAIAH i-zai′-ah
salvation of Jehovah Is 1:1

ISCAH is′-kah
discerning, expectant (?) Gen 11:29

ISCARIOT is-kar′-i-ot
man of Kerioth Matt 10:4

ISH-BOSHETH ish-bo′-sheth
man of shame 2 Sam 2:8

ISH-TOB ish′-tobe
men of Tob 2 Sam 10:6

ISHBAH ish′-bah
praising 1 Chr 4:17

ISHBAK ish′-bak
he leaveth or relinquisheth (?) Gen 25:2

ISHBI-BENOB ish′-bi-ben′-obe
one who dwells at Nob 2 Sam 21:16

ISHI eesh′-i
my husband Hos 2:16

ISHI yish′-i
salutary 1 Chr 2:31

ISHIAH ish-i′-ah
whom Jehovah lends 1 Chr 7:3

ISHIJAH ish-i′-jah
same as ISHIA Ezra 10:31

ISHMA ish′-mah
desolation (?) 1 Chr 4:3

ISHMAEL ish′-ma-el
whom God hears Gen 16:15

ISHMAELITES ish′-ma-el-ites
descendants of Ishmael Judg 8:24

ISHMAIAH ish-mai′-ah
whom Jehovah hears 1 Chr 27:19

ISHMEELITES ish′-me-el-ites
same as ISHMAELITES Gen 37:25

ISHMERAL ish′-mer-a′-i
whom Jehovah keeps 1 Chr 8:18

ISHOD ish′-hode
man of glory 1 Chr 7:18

ISHPAN ish′-pan
cunning (?) 1 Chr 8:22

ISHUAH ish′-oo-ah
level Gen 46:17

ISHUAI ish′-oo-a′-i
same as ISUI 1 Chr 7:30

ISHUI ish′-oo-i
same as ISHUAH 1 Sam 14:49

ISMACHIAH is-mak-i´-ah
whom Jehovah upholds 2 Chr 31:13

ISMAIAH is-mai´-ah
same as ISHMAIAH 1 Chr 12:4

ISPAH is´-pah
bald 1 Chr 8:16

ISRAEL iz´-ra-el
soldier of God Gen 32:28

ISRAELITES iz´-ra-el-ites
descendants of Israel Ex 9:7

ISRAELITISH iz´-ra-el-ite-ish
after the fashion of an Israelite Lev 24:10

ISSACHAR is´-ak-ar
he is hired (?) Gen 30:18

ISSHIAH ish-hi´-ah
same as ISHIAH 1 Chr 24:21

ISSUES
belong the i from death Ps 68:20
out of it are the i of life Prov 4:23

ISUAH is´-oo-ah
same as ISHUAH 1 Chr 7:30

ISUI is´-oo-i
same as ISHUI Gen 46:17

ITALY it´-a-ly
abounding with calves (?) Acts 18:2

ITCHING
having i ears 2 Tim 4:3

ITHAI ith´-a-i
ploughman 1 Chr 11:31

ITHAMAR i´-tha-mar
island of palms Ex 6:23

ITHIEL ith´-i-el
God is with me Neh 11:7

ITHMAH ith´-mah
bereavedness 1 Chr 11:46

ITHNAN ith´-nan
perennial (?) Josh 15:23

ITHRA ith´-rah
excellence 2 Sam 17:25

ITHRAN ith´-ran
same as ITHRA Gen 36:26

ITHREAM ith´-re-am
remainder of the people 2 Sam 3:5

ITHRITE ith´-rite
descendants of Jether (?) 2 Sam 23:38

ITTAH-KAZIN it´-ah-ka´-zin
time of the chief Josh 19:13

ITTAI it´-a-i
same as ITHAI 2 Sam 15:19

ITURAEA i´-tu-re´-ah
a province, so named from Jetur Luke 3:1

IVAH i´-vah
same as AVA 2 Kgs 18:34

IZEHAR iz´-e-har
oil Num 3:19

IZEHARITES i´-ze-har´-ites
the descendants of Izehar Num 3:27

IZHAR iz-har
same as IZEHAR Ex 6:18

IZHARITES iz´-har-ites
same as IZEHARITES 1 Chr 26:23

IZRAHIAH iz-rah-i´-ah
whom Jehovah brought to light 1 Chr 7:3

IZRAHITE iz´-rah-ite
same as ZARHITE (?) 1 Chr 27:8

IZRI iz´-ri
a descendant of Jezer 1 Chr 25:11

J

JAAKAN ja´-ak-an
one who turns Deut 10:6

JAAKOBAH ja´-ak-o´-bah
same as JACOB 1 Chr 4:36

JAALA ja´-a-lah
wild she-goat Neh 7:58

JAALAH ja´-a-lah
same as JAALA Ezra 2:56

JAALAM ja´-a-lam
whom God hides Gen 36:5

JAANAI ja´-an-a´-i
whom Jehovah answers 1 Chr 5:12

JAARE-OREGIM ja´-ar-e-or´-eg-im
forests of the weavers 2 Sam 21:19

JAASAU ja´-a-saw
Jehovah maketh (?) Ezra 10:37

JAASIEL ja-as´-i-el
whom God created 1 Chr 27:21

JAAZANIAH ja´-az-an-i´-ah
whom Jehovah hears 2 Kgs 25:23

JAAZER ja´-a-zer
whom [God] aids Num 21:32

JAAZIAH ja´-za-i´-ah
whom Jehovah strengthens 1 Chr 24:26

JAAZIEL ja´-az´-i-el
whom God strengthens 1 Chr 15:18

JABAL ja´-bal
a stream, river Gen 4:20

JABBOK jab´-ok
pouring out Gen 32:22

JABESH ja´-besh
dry 2 Kgs 15:10

JABESH-GILEAD ja´-besh-gil´-e-ad
JABESH of Gilead Judg 21:8

JABEZ ja´-bez
causing pain 1 Chr 4:9

JABIN ja´-bin
whom He [God] considered Judg 4:2

JABNEEL jab´-ne-el
may God cause to be built Josh 15:11

JABNEH jab´-nay
which [God] causes to be built 2 Chr 26:6

JACHAN ja´-kan
troubled 1 Chr 5:13

JACHIN ja´-kin
whom [God] strengthens 1 Kgs 7:21

JACHINITES ja´-kin-ites
descendants of Jachin Num 26:12

JACOB ja´-kob
supplanter Gen 25:26

JADA ja´-dah
wise 1 Chr 2:28

JADAU ja´-daw
same as IDDO Ezra 10:43

JADDUA jad´-oo-ah
skilled Neh 10:21

JADON ja´-don
a judge Neh 3:7

JAEL ja´-el
same as JAALA Judg 4:17

JAGUR ja´-goor
a lodging Josh 15:21

JAH ja
poetic form of JEHOVAH Ps 68:4

JAHATH ja´-hath
grasping (?) 1 Chr 6:20

JAHAZ ja´-haz
a place trodden down Num 21:23

JAHAZA ja´-haz-ah
same as JAHAZ Josh 13:18

JAHAZAH ja´-haz-ah
same as JAHAZ Josh 21:36

JAHAZIAH ja´-haz-i´-ah
whom Jehovah watches over Ezra 10:15

JAHAZIEL ja-haz´-i-el
whom God watches over 1 Chr 16:6

JAHDAI jah´-da-i
whom Jehovah directs 1 Chr 2:47

JAHDIEL jah´-di-el
whom God makes glad 1 Chr 5:24

JAHDO jah´-do
union 1 Chr 5:14

JAHLEEL jah´-le-el
hoping in God Num 26:26

JAHLEELITES jah´-le-el-ites
descendants of Jahleel Num 26:26

JAHMAI jah´-ma-i
lusty 1 Chr 7:2

JAHZAH ja´-zah
same as JAHAZ 1 Chr 6:78

JAHZEEL jah´-ze-el
whom God allots Gen 46:24

JAHZEELITES jah´-ze-el-ites
descendants of Jahzeel Num 26:48

JAHZERAH jah´-zer-ah
may he bring back 1 Chr 9:12

JAHZIEL jah´-zi-el
same as JAHZEEL 1 Chr 7:13

JAIR ja´-er
[God] enlightens Num 32:41

JAIRITE ja´-er-ite
a descendant of Jair 2 Sam 20:26

JAIRUS ja-i´-rus
Gr. for JAIR Mark 5:22

JAKAN ja´-kan
same as JAAKAN 1 Chr 1:42

JAKEH ja´-kay
pious (?) Prov 30:1

JAKIM ja´-kim
[God] sets up 1 Chr 8:19

JALON ja´-lon
passing the night 1 Chr 4:17

JAMBRES jam´-brees
opposer (?) 2 Tim 3:8

JAMES
Eng. equivalent of JACOB Matt 4:21

JAMIN ja´-min
right hand Gen 46:10

JAMINITES ja´-min-ites
descendants of Jamin Num 26:12

JAMLECH jam´-lek
He makes to reign 1 Chr 4:34

JANGLING
turn aside from vain j 1 Tim 1:6

JANNA jan´-nah
a form of John (?) Luke 3:24

JANNES jan´-ees
an Egyptian Sorcerer 2 Tim 3:8

JANOAH ja-no´-ah
rest 2 Kgs 15:29

JANOHAH ja-no´-hah
same as JANOAH Josh 16:6

JANUM ja´-noom
sleep Josh 15:53

JAPHETH ja´-feth
extension Gen 5:32

JAPHIA ja-fi´-ah
splendid Josh 19:12

JAPHLET jaf´-let
may he deliver 1 Chr 7:32

JAPHLETI jaf-le´-ti
descendants of Japhlet Josh 16:3

JAPHO ja´-fo
beauty Josh 19:46

JARAH ja´-rah
honey 1 Chr 9:42

JAREB ja´-reb
contentious Hos 5:13

JARED ja´-red
descent Gen 5:15

JARESIAH ja´-res-i´-ah
whom Jehovah nourishes 1 Chr 8:27

JARIB ja´-rib
adversary 1 Chr 4:24

JARMUTH jar´-mooth
height Josh 10:3

JAROAH ja-ro´-ah
moon (?) 1 Chr 5:14

JASHEN ja´-shen
sleeping 2 Sam 23:32

JASHER ja´-sher
upright Josh 10:13

JASHOBEAM ja-shob´-e-am
the people return 1 Chr 11:11

JASHUB ja´-shoob
he returns Num 26:24

JASHUBI-LEHEM ja-shoob´-i-le´-hem
giving bread (?) 1 Chr 4:22

JASHUBITES ja´-shoob-ites
descendants of Jashub Num 26:24

JASIEL ja-si´-el
whom God made 1 Chr 11:47

JASON ja´-son
Graeco-Judaean equivalent of JOSHUA Acts 17:5

JATHNIEL jath´-ni-el
God gives 1 Chr 26:2

JATTIR jat´-yer
excelling Josh 15:48

JAVAN ja´-van
wine (?) Gen 10:2

JAZER ja´-zer
same as JAAZER Num 32:1

JAZIZ ja´-ziz
wanderer (?) 1 Chr 27:31

JEALOUS
j God Ex 20:5; 34:14; Deut 4:24; 5:9; 6:15; Josh 24:19
I have been very j for the LORD 1 Kgs 19:10,14
will be j for my holy name Ezek 39:25
I am j over you 2 Cor 11:2

JEALOUSY
provoked him to j Deut 32:16; 1 Kgs 14:22
j is the rage of a man Prov 6:34
j is cruel as the grave Song 8:6
in fire of j have I spoken Ezek 36:5
Do we provoke the Lord to j? 1 Cor 10:22

JEARIM je´-ar-im
forests Josh 15:10

JEATERAI je-at´-er-a´-i
same as ETHNI 1 Chr 6:21

JEBERECHIAH je-ber´-ek-i´-ah
whom Jehovah blesses Is 8:2

JEBUS je´-boos
a place trodden down (?) Judg 19:10

JEBUSI je´-boos-i
same as JEBUS Josh 18:16

JEBUSITES je´-boos-ites
the descendants of Jebus Num 13:29

JECAMIAH jek´-a-mi-ah
same as JEKAMIAH 1 Chr 3:18

JECHOLIAH jek´-ol-i´-ah
Jehovah is strong 2 Kgs 15:2

JECHONIAS jek´-on-i´-as
Gr. for JECONIAH Matt 1:11

JECOLIAH jek´-ol-i´-ah
same as JECHOLIAH 2 Chr 26:3

JECONIAH jek´-on-i´-ah
Jehovah establishes 1 Chr 3:16

JEDAIAH jed-ai´-ah
1 *Jehovah*—(?) 1 Chr 4:37
2 *Jehovah knoweth* 1 Chr 24:7

JEDIAEL jed´-i-a´-el
known of God 1 Chr 7:6

JEDIDAH jed-i´-dah
beloved 2 Kgs 22:1

JEDIDIAH jed´-id-i´-ah
beloved of Jehovah 2 Sam 12:25

JEDUTHUN jed-ooth´-oon
friendship (?) 1 Chr 16:38

JEEZER je-e´-zer
contracted from ABIEZER Num 26:30

JEEZERITES je-ez´-er-ites
descendants of Jeezer Num 26:30

JEGAR-SAHADUTHA je´-gar-sa-ha-doo´-thah
the heap of testimony Gen 31:47

JEHALELEEL je-hal´-el-e´-el
he praises God 1 Chr 4:16

JEHALELEL je-hal´-e-lel
same as JEHALELEEL 2 Chr 29:12

JEHDEIAH jed-i´-ah
whom Jehovah makes glad 1 Chr 24:20

JEHEZEKEL je-hez´-e-kel
same as EZEKIEL 1 Chr 24:16

JEHIAH je-hi´-ah
Jehovah lives 1 Chr 15:24

JEHIEL je-hi´-el
God liveth 1 Chr 15:18

JEHIELI je-hi´-el-i
my God liveth 1 Chr 26:21

JEHIZKIAH je´-hizk-i´-ah
same as HEZEKIAH 2 Chr 28:12

JEHOADAH je-ho´-a-dah
whom Jehovah adorns 1 Chr 8:36

JEHOADDAN je-ho´-ad-an
Jehovah is beauteous (?) 2 Kgs 14:2

JEHOAHAZ je-ho´-a-haz
whom Jehovah holds fast 2 Kgs 10:35

JEHOASH je-ho´-ash
Jehovah supports 2 Kgs 11:21

JEHOHANAN je-ho´-han-an
Jehovah is gracious 1 Chr 26:3

JEHOIACHIN je-ho´-ya-kin
Jehovah has established 2 Kgs 24:6

JEHOIADA je-ho´-ya-dah
Jehovah knoweth 2 Sam 8:18

JEHOIAKIM je-ho´-ya-kim
Jehovah has set up 2 Kgs 23:34

JEHOIARIB je-ho´-ya-rib
Jehovah will contend 1 Chr 9:10

JEHONADAB je-ho´-na-dab
Jehovah is bounteous 2 Kgs 10:15

JEHONATHAN je-ho´-na-than
same as JONATHAN 1 Chr 27:25

JEHORAM je-ho´-ram
Jehovah is high 1 Kgs 22:50

JEHOSHABEATH je-ho´-shab´-e-ath
Jehovah is the oath 2 Chr 22:11

JEHOSHAPHAT je-hosh´-af-at
whom Jehovah judges 1 Kgs 15:24

JEHOSHEBA je-ho´-she-bah
same as JEHOSHABEATH 2 Kgs 11:2

JEHOSHUA je-hosh´-oo-ah
same as JOSHUA Num 13:16

JEHOSHUAH je-hosh´-oo-ah
same as JOSHUA 1 Chr 7:27

JEHOVAH je-ho´-vah
the Eternal One Ex 6:3

JEHOVAH-JIREH je-ho´-vah-ji´-ray
Jehovah will provide Gen 22:14

JEHOVAH-NISSI je-ho´-vah-nis´-i
Jehovah my banner Ex 17:15

JEHOVAH-SHALOM je-ho´-vah-sha´-lom
Jehovah send peace Judg 6:24

JEHOZABAD je-ho´-za-bad
Jehovah gave 2 Kgs 12:21

JEHOZADAK je-ho´-za-dak
Jehovah is just 1 Chr 6:14

JEHU je´-hu
Jehovah is He (?) 1 Kgs 19:16

JEHUBBAH je-hoob´-ah
hidden 1 Chr 7:34

JEHUCAL je-hoo´-kal
Jehovah is mighty Jer 37:3

JEHUD je´-hood
praise Josh 19:45

JEHUDI je-hood´-i
a Jew Jer 36:14

JEHUDIJAH je-hood-i´-jah
a Jewess 1 Chr 4:18

JEHUSH je´-hoosh
to whom God hastens 1 Chr 8:39

JEIEL ji´-el
treasure of God (?) 1 Chr 5:7

JEKABZEEL je-kab´-ze-el
God gathers Neh 11:25

JEKAMEAM je´-ka-me´-am
he doth assemble the people 1 Chr 23:19

JEKAMIAH jek´-am-i´-ah
Jehovah gathers 1 Chr 2:41

JEKUTHIEL je-koo´-thi-el
the fear of God 1 Chr 4:18

JEMIMA je-mi´-mah
dove Job 42:14

JEMUEL jem-oo´-el
day of God Gen 46:10

JEPHTHAH jef´-tah
God opens Judg 11:1

JEPHUNNEH je´-foon´-eh
for whom it is prepared Num 13:6

JERAH je´-rah
the moon Gen 10:26

JERAHMEEL je-rah´-me-el
whom God loves 1 Chr 2:9

JERAHMEELITES je-rah´-me-el-ites
descendants of Jerahmeel 1 Sam 27:10

JERED je´-red
descent 1 Chr 1:2

JEREMAI jer´-em-a´-i
dwelling in heights Ezra 10:33

JEREMIAH jer-em-i´-ah
whom Jehovah has appointed Jer 1:1

JEREMIAS jer-em-i´-as
same as JEREMIAH Matt 16:14

JEREMOTH jer´-em-oth
high places 1 Chr 8:14

JEREMY jer´-em-ee
same as JEREMIAH Matt 2:17

JERIAH jer-i´-ah
whom Jehovah regards (?) 1 Chr 23:19

JERIBAI jer´-ib-a´-i
contentious 1 Chr 11:46

JERICHO jer´-ik-o
a fragrant place Num 22:1

JERIEL je-ri´-el
founded by God 1 Chr 7:2

JERIJAH jer-i´-jah
same as JERIAH 1 Chr 26:31

JERIMOTH jer´-i-moth
same as JEREMOTH 1 Chr 7:7

JERIOTH je-ri´-oth
curtains 1 Chr 2:18

JEROBOAM jer´-ob-o´-am
whose people are many 1 Kgs 11:26

JEROHAM je-ro´-ham
who is loved 1 Sam 1:1

JERUBBAAL je-roo´-ba-al
let Baal plead Judg 6:32

JERUBBESHETH je´-roo-be´-sheth
1 *let shame plead,*
2 another name for JERUBBAAL 2 Sam 11:21

JERUEL je-roo´-el
same as JERIEL 2 Chr 20:16

JERUSALEM je-roo´-sa-lem
founded in peace (?) Josh 10:1

JERUSHA je-roo´-shah
possession 2 Kgs 15:33

JERUSHAH je-roo´-shah
same as JERUSHA 2 Chr 27:1

JESAIAH je-sai´-ah
same as ISAIAH 1 Chr 3:21

JESHAIAH je-shai´-ah
same as ISAIAH 1 Chr 25:3

JESHANAH je-shan´-ah
old 2 Chr 13:19

JESHARELAH jesh´-ar-el´-ah
right before God (?) 1 Chr 25:14

JESHEBEAB je-sheb´-e-ab
father's seat 1 Chr 24:13

JESHER je´-sher
uprightness 1 Chr 2:18

JESHIMON je-shim´-on
the waste Num 21:20

JESHISHAI je-shi´-sha-i
like an old man 1 Chr 5:14

JESHOHAIAH je-sho´-ha-i´-ah
whom Jehovah humbles 1 Chr 4:36

JESHUA jesh´-oo-ah
Jehovah is salvation Ezra 2:2

JESHUAH jesh´-oo-ah
help 1 Chr 24:11

JESHURUN jesh-oor´-oon
righteous Deut 32:15

JESIAH je-si´-ah
Jehovah forgets 1 Chr 12:6

JESIMIEL je-sim´-i-el
whom God founds (?) 1 Chr 4:36

JESSE jes´-sy
gift (?) Ruth 4:17

JESTING
foolish talking, nor j Eph 5:4

JESUI je-soo´-i
same as ISHUA Num 26:44

JESUITES je´-soo-ites
descendants of Jesui Num 26:44

JESURUN je-soor´-oon
same as JESHURUN Is 44:2

JESUS je´-sus
Savior,
thou shalt call his name J Matt 1:21
J said unto her, I am the resurrection John 11:25
J wept John 11:35
same J, which is taken up from you Acts 1:11
the love of God, which is in Christ J Rom 8:39
name of J every knee should bow Phil 2:10
unto J the author and finisher Heb 12:2
J the mediator of the new covenant Heb 12:24
J Christ the same yesterday Heb 13:8
The testimony of J is the spirit of prophecy Rev 19:10
Even so, come, Lord J Rev 22:20

JETHER je´-ther
same as ITHRA Judg 8:20

JETHETH je´-theth
descendant of Edom Gen 36:40

JETHLAH jeth´-lah
lofty Josh 19:42

JETHRO jeth´-ro
same as ITHRA Ex 3:1

JETUR je´-toor
an enclosure Gen 25:15

JEUEL joo´-el
same as JEIEL 1 Chr 9:6

JEUSH je´-oosh
same as JEHUSH Gen 36:5

JEUZ je´-ooz
counselor 1 Chr 8:10

JEW joo
an Israelite Esth 2:5

JEWELS
adorneth herself with her j Is 61:10
when I make up my j Mal 3:17

JEWESS joo´-ess
a female Jew Acts 16:1

JEWISH joo´-ish
of or belonging to Jews Titus 1:14

JEWRY joo´-ry
Old Eng. name for Judea Dan 5:13

JEWS joos
inhabitants of Judea 2 Kgs 16:6

JEZANIAH jez´-an-i´-ah
Jehovah adorns (?) Jer 40:8

JEZEBEL jez´-e-bel
unmarried 1 Kgs 16:31

JEZER je´-zer
anything made Gen 46:24

JEZERITES je´-zer-ites
descendants of Jezer Num 26:49

JEZIAH jez-i´-ah
whom Jehovah assembles Ezra 10:25

JEZIEL jez-i´-el
the assembly of God 1 Chr 12:3

JEZLIAH jez-li´-ah
deliverance (?) 1 Chr 8:18

JEZOAR je-zo´-ar
splendid 1 Chr 4:7

JEZRAHIAH jez´-rah-i´-ah
Jehovah shines forth Neh 12:42

JEZREEL jez´-re-el
God scatters 1 Chr 4:3

JEZREELITE jez´-re-el-ite
an inhabitant of Jezreel 1 Kgs 21:6

JEZREELITESS jez´-re-el-ite-ess
fem. of JEZREELITE 1 Sam 27:3

JIBSAM jib´-sam
fragrant 1 Chr 7:2

JIDLAPH jid´-laf
weeping (?) Gen 22:22

JIMNA jim´-nah
same as IMNA Num 26:44

JIMNAH jim´-nah
same as IMNAH Gen 46:17

JIMNITES jim´-nites
descendants of Jimnah Num 26:44

JIPHTAH jif´-tah
same as JEPHTHAH Josh 15:43

JIPHTHAH-EL jif´-tah-el
which God opens Josh 19:14

JOAB jo´-ab
Jehovah is father 2 Sam 2:13

JOAH jo´-ah
Jehovah is brother 2 Kgs 18:18

JOAHAZ jo´-a-haz
whom Jehovah holds 2 Chr 34:8

JOANNA jo-an´-ah
Gr. for JOHANAN Luke 3:27

JOASH jo´-ash
whom Jehovah supports (?) 2 Kgs 11:2

JOATHAM jo´-ath-am
Gr. for JOTHAM Matt 1:9

JOB jobe
1 *a desert* Gen 46:13
2 *one persecuted* Job 1:1

JOBAB jo´-bab
a desert Gen 10:29

JOCHEBED jo´-ke-bed
Jehovah is glorious (?) Ex 6:20

JOED jo´-ed
for whom Jehovah is witness Neh 11:7

JOEL jo´-el
Jehovah is might Joel 1:1

JOELAH jo´-el-ah
He helps (?) 1 Chr 12:7

JOEZER jo´-e-zer
Jehovah is help 1 Chr 12:6

JOGBEHAH jog´-be-hah
lofty Num 32:35

JOGLI jo´-gli
an exile Num 34:22

JOHA jo´-hah
Jehovah lives (?) 1 Chr 8:16

JOHANAN jo-ha´-nan
Jehovah is gracious 2 Kgs 25:23

JOHN jon
Eng. spelling of Johanan Matt 3:1

JOIADA jo´-ya-dah
Jehovah knows Neh 12:10

JOIAKIM jo´-ya-kim
shortened from JEHOIAKIM Neh 12:10

JOIARIB jo´-ya-rib
whom Jehovah defends Ezra 8:16

JOIN
hand j in hand Prov 11:21; 16:5
to him that is j to all the living
there is hope Eccl 9:4
that j house to house Is 5:8
let us j ourselves to the LORD Jer 50:5
Ephraim is j to idols Hos 4:17
What therefore God hath j Matt 19:6; Mark 10:9
durst no man j himself Acts 5:13
perfectly j together in the same mind 1 Cor 1:10
j to the Lord 1 Cor 6:17
whole body fitly j together Eph 4:16

JOINT
out of j Gen 32:25; Ps 22:14; Prov 25:19
which every j supplieth Eph 4:16
of the j and marrow Heb 4:12

JOKDEAM jok´-de-am
burning of the people Josh 15:56

JOKIM jo´-kim
short for JEHOIAKIM 1 Chr 4:22

JOKMEAM jok´-me-am
the people are gathered together 1 Chr 6:68

JOKNEAM jok´-ne-am
possessed by the people Josh 12:22

JOKSHAN jok´-shan
fowler Gen 25:2

JOKTAN jok´-tan
small Gen 10:25

JOKTHEEL jok´-the-el
subdued by God Josh 15:38

JONA jo´-nah
Gr. spelling of JOHANAN John 1:42

JONADAB jo´-na-dab
same as JEHONADAB 2 Sam 13:3

JONAH jo´-nah
dove 2 Kgs 14:25

JONAN jo´-nan
contracted from JOHANAN Luke 3:30

JONAS jo´-nas
1 same as JONA John 21:15
2 Or, JONAH Matt 12:39

JONATHAN jo´-na-than
whom Jehovah gave 1 Sam 13:2

JOPPA jop´-ah
beauty (?) 2 Chr 2:16

JORAH jo´-rah
watering (?) Ezra 2:18

JORAI jo´-ra-i
archer (?) 1 Chr 5:13

JORAM jo´-ram
same as JEHORAM 2 Sam 8:10

JORDAN jor´-dan
flowing down Gen 13:10

JORIM jo´-rim
a form of JORAM (?) Luke 3:29

JORKOAM jor´-ko-am
spreading of the people (?) 1 Chr 2:44

JOSABAD jo´-sa-bad
same as JEHOZABAD 1 Chr 12:4

JOSAPHAT jo´-saf-at
Gr. for JEHOSHAPHAT Matt 1:8

JOSE jo´-se
an ancestor of Jesus Luke 3:29

JOSEDECH jo´-se-dek
same as JEHOZADAK Hag 1:1

JOSEPH jo´-sef
he shall add Gen 30:24

JOSES jo´-ses
Gr. for JOSEPH Matt 13:55

JOSHAH jo´-shah
Jehovah presents (?) 1 Chr 4:34

JOSHAPHAT jo´-sha-fat
short for JEHOSHAPHAT 1 Chr 11:43

JOSHAVIAH jo´-shav-i´-ah
same as JOSHAH 1 Chr 11:46

JOSHBEKASHAH josh´-be-ka´-shah
seat of hardship (?) 1 Chr 25:4

JOSHUA jo´-shoo-ah
Jehovah is salvation Num 14:6

JOSIAH jo-si´-ah
whom Jehovah heals 2 Kgs 21:24

JOSIAS jo-si´-as
Gr. for JOSIAH Matt 1:10

JOSIBIAH jos´-ib-i´-ah
to whom God gives a dwelling 1 Chr 4:35

JOSIPHIAH jos´-if-i´-ah
whom Jehovah will increase Ezra 8:10

JOTBAH jot´-bah
pleasantness (?) 2 Kgs 21:19

JOTBATH jot´-bath
same as JOTBAH Deut 10:7

JOTBATHAH jot´-ba-thah
same as JOTBAH Num 33:33

JOTHAM jo´-tham
Jehovah is upright Judg 9:5

JOURNEY (n)
or he is in a j 1 Kgs 18:27
For how long shall thy j be? Neh 2:6
Nor scrip for your j Matt 10:10
take nothing for thy j Mark 6:8; Luke 9:3
wearied with his j John 4:6

JOURNEY (v)
We are j unto the place Num 10:29

JOURNEYINGS
Thus were the j Num 10:28
In j often 2 Cor 11:26

JOY
not discern noise of the shout of j Ezra 3:13
j of the LORD is your strength Neh 8:10
the j of the hypocrite Job 20:5
widow's heart to sing for j Job 29:13
he shall see his face with j Job 33:26
sorrow is turned into j Job 41:22
fulness of j Ps 16:11
j cometh in the morning Ps 30:5
the j of the whole earth Ps 48:2
Restore unto me the j of thy salvation Ps 51:12
They that sow in tears shall reap in j Ps 126:5
prefer not Jerusalem above my chief j Ps 137:6
not intermeddle with his j Prov 14:10
It is j to the just to do judgment Prov 21:15
I withheld not my heart from any j Eccl 2:10
eat thy bread with j Eccl 9:7
not increased the j Is 9:3
with j shall ye draw water Is 12:3
j of the harp ceaseth Is 24:8
meek also shall increase their j Is 29:19
rejoice even with j and singing Is 35:2
with everlasting j Is 51:11
my servants shall sing for j of heart Is 65:14
thy word was unto me the j Jer 15:16
will turn their mourning into j Jer 31:13
the city of my j Jer 49:25
The j of the whole earth Lam 2:15
with j receiveth it Matt 13:20
for j thereof goeth and selleth Matt 13:44
the j of thy lord Matt 25:21,23
receive the word with j Luke 8:13
j shall be in heaven over one sinner Luke 15:7
there is j in the presence of angels Luke 15:10
they yet believed not for j Luke 24:41
this my j therefore is fulfilled John 3:29
that your j might be full John 15:11; 16:24
great j in that city Acts 8:8
finish my course with j Acts 20:24
helpers of your j 2 Cor 1:24
Fulfil ye my j Phil 2:2
for the j that was set before him Heb 12:2
count it all j when ye fall James 1:2
with j unspeakable 1 Pet 1:8
glad also with exceeding j 1 Pet 4:13
that our j may be full 2 John 1:12
presence of his glory with exceeding j Jude 1:24

JOYFUL
my soul shall be j in the Lord Ps 35:9
praise thee with j lips Ps 63:5
make a j noise Ps 66:1; 81:1; 95:1; 98:6
in day of prosperity be j Eccl 7:14
j in my house of prayer Is 56:7

JOZABAD jo´-za-bad
same as JEHOZABAD 1 Chr 12:20

JOZACHAR jo´-za-kar
whom Jehovah has remembered 2 Kgs 12:21

JOZADAK jo´-za-dak
same as JEHOZADAK Ezra 3:2

JUBAL joo´-bal
music (?) Gen 4:21

JUCAL joo´-kal
same as JEHUCAL Jer 38:1

JUDA joo´-dah
Same as JUDAH Luke 3:30

JUDAEA joo-de´-ah
land of the Jews Matt 2:1

JUDAH joo´-dah
praised Gen 29:35

JUDAS joo´-das
Gr. for JUDAH Matt 10:4

JUDE jood
abbr. for JUDAS Jude 1:1

JUDEA joo-de´-ah
same as JUDAEA Ezra 5:8

JUDGE (n)
the j of all the earth Gen 18:25; Ps 94:2
God is J himself Ps 50:6
a j of the widows Ps 68:5
the j asketh a reward Mic 7:3
who made me a j Luke 12:14
the unjust j Luke 18:6
the J of the quick and dead Acts 10:42
the Lord, the righteous j 2 Tim 4:8
to God the J of all Heb 12:23
the j standeth before the door James 5:9

JUDGE (v)
Lord j between me and thee Gen 16:5
Lord j the people Deut 32:36; Ps 7:8
he is a God that j in the earth Ps 58:11
j the fatherless Is 1:17
j not, that ye be not j Matt 7:1
thou hast rightly j Luke 7:43
j righteous judgment John 7:24
who art thou that j Rom 14:4

JUDGMENT
the j is God's Deut 1:17
shall not stand in the j Ps 1:5
I will sing of mercy and j Ps 101:1
j cometh from the Lord Prov 29:26
God will bring into j Eccl 11:9; 12:14
j will I lay to the line Is 28:17
taken from prison and from j Is 53:8
if there be any that executeth j Jer 5:1
correct with j, not in anger Jer 10:24
keep mercy and j Hos 12:6
in danger of the j Matt 5:21
Father committed all j to the Son John 5:22
for j I am come John 9:39
reprove the world of j John 16:8
reasoned of j to come Acts 24:25
we shall all stand before the j seat Rom 14:10
after this the j Heb 9:27
j must begin at home of God 1 Pet 4:17

JUDITH joo´-dith
1 *praiseworthy*
2 fem. of JEHUDI Gen 26:34

JULIA joo´-li-ah
fem. of JULIUS Rom 16:15

JULIUS joo´-li-us
downy Acts 27:1

JUNIA joo´-ni-ah
youth Rom 16:7

JUPITER joo´-pi-ter
supreme god of the Romans Acts 14:12

JUSHAB-HESED joo´-shab-he´-sed
whose love is returned 1 Chr 3:20

JUST
how should man be j with God? Job 9:2
God blesseth the habitation of the j Prov 3:33
path of j as shining light Prov 4:18
memory of j is blessed Prov 10:7
way of the j is uprightness Is 26:7
the j shall live by faith Hab 2:4; Rom 1:17;
Gal 3:11; Heb 10:38
sendeth rain on j and unjust Matt 5:45
recompensed at resurrection of j Luke 14:14
ninety and nine j persons Luke 15:7
resurrection both of j and unjust Acts 24:15
that he might be j Rom 3:26
whatsoever things are j Phil 4:8
a j recompence of reward Heb 2:2
spirits of j men made perfect Heb 12:23
the j for the unjust 1 Pet 3:18

JUSTICE
I would do j 2 Sam 15:4
j and judgment are the habitation Ps 89:14
by me princes decree j Prov 8:15
none calleth for j Is 59:4
execute judgment and j in the earth Jer 23:5
the habitation of j Jer 50:7

JUSTIFY
should a man full of talk be j? Job 11:2
How then can man be j with God? Job 25:4
be j when thou speakest Ps 51:4
in thy sight shall no man living be j Ps 143:2
which j the wicked for reward Is 5:23
wisdom is j of her children Matt 11:19;
Luke 7:35
by thy words thou shalt be j Matt 12:37
willing to j himself Luke 10:29
j rather than the other Luke 18:14
all that believe are j Acts 13:39
j freely by his grace Rom 3:24; Titus 3:7
being j by faith Rom 5:1
being now j by his blood Rom 5:9
man is not j by works of the law Gal 2:16
j in the Spirit 1 Tim 3:16

JUSTLY
but to do j, and to love mercy Mic 6:8
And we indeed j Luke 23:41
how holily and j and unblameably 1 Thess 2:10

JUSTUS just´-us
upright Acts 1:23

JUTTAH joot´-ah
extended Josh 15:55

K

KABZEEL kab´-ze-el
God has gathered Josh 15:21

KADESH ka´-desh
consecrated Gen 20:1

KADESH-BARNEA ka´-desh-bar´-nee-ah
consecrated Barnea Num 32:8

KADMIEL kad´-mi-el
eternity of God (?) Ezra 2:40

KADMONITES kad´-mon-ites
people of the east, orientals Gen 15:19

KALLAI kal-a´-i
swift Neh 12:20

KANAH ka´-nah
a place of reeds Josh 19:28

KAREAH ka-re´-ah
bald Jer 40:8

KARKAA kar-ka´-ah
floor Josh 15:3

KARKOR kar´-kor
plain (?) Judg 8:10

KARNAIM kar-na´-im
two horns Gen 14:5

KARTAH kar´-tah
city Josh 21:34

KARTAN kar´-tan
double city Josh 21:32

KATTATH kat´-ath
small (?) Josh 19:15

KEDAR ke´-dar
black-skinned Gen 25:13

KEDEMAH ke-de´-mah
eastward Gen 25:15

KEDEMOTH ke-de´-moth
eastern parts Josh 13:18

KEDESH ke´-desh
sanctuary Josh 12:22

KEEP
they shall k the way of the LORD Gen 18:19
The LORD bless thee, and k thee Num 6:24
He will k the feet of his saints 1 Sam 2:9
hath k me back from hurting thee 1 Sam 25:34
K me as the apple of the eye Ps 17:8
K thy tongue from evil Ps 34:13
to k thee in all thy ways Ps 91:11
he that k thee will not slumber Ps 121:3
except the Lord k the city Ps 127:1
k the door of my lips Ps 141:3
love her, she shall k thee Prov 4:6
k them in the midst of thine heart Prov 4:21
K thy heart with all diligence Prov 4:23
My son, k thy father's commandment Prov 6:20
a time to k Eccl 3:6
K thy foot when thou goest Eccl 5:1
Fear God, and k his commandments Eccl 12:13
Thou wilt k him in perfect peace Is 26:3
I will k it Is 27:3
will he k it to the end? Jer 3:5
let all the earth k silence Hab 2:20
what profit is it that we have k Mal 3:14
if thou wilt enter into life,
k the commandments Matt 19:17
that hear the word of God, and k it Luke 11:28
k thee in on every side Luke 19:43
k my saying John 8:51,52
hateth his life in this world shall k it John 12:25
If a man love me, he will k my words John 14:23
Father, k through thine own name John 17:11
thou shouldest k them from the evil John 17:15
delivered the decrees for to k Acts 16:4
k themselves from things offered
to idols Acts 21:25
let us k the feast 1 Cor 5:8
I k under my body 1 Cor 9:27
k the unity of the Spirit Eph 4:3
shall k your hearts and minds Phil 4:7
k thyself pure 1 Tim 5:22
k that which is committed 1 Tim 6:20
k himself unspotted James 1:27
k yourselves from idols 1 John 5:21
K yourselves in the love of God Jude 1:21
him that is able to k you from falling Jude 1:24
will k thee from the hour of temptation Rev 3:10
which k the sayings of this book Rev 22:9

KEEPER
The LORD is thy k Ps 121:5
when the k of the house shall tremble Eccl 12:3
they made me k of the vineyards Song 1:6
chaste, k at home Titus 2:5

KEHELATHAH ke´-he-la´-thah
assembly Num 33:22

KEILAH ki´-lah
sling (?) Josh 15:44

KELAIAH ke-lai´-ah
contempt (?) Ezra 10:23

KELITA ke-li´-tah
dwarf Neh 8:7

KEMUEL kem´-oo-el
congregation of God Gen 22:21

KENAN ke´-nan
same as CAINAN 1 Chr 1:2

KENATH ke´-nath
possession Num 32:42

KENAZ ke´-naz
hunting Gen 36:11

KENEZITE ke´-nez-ite
descendant of Kenaz Num 32:12

KENITE ke´-nite
maker of swords Gen 15:19

KENIZZITES ke´-niz-ites
same as KENEZITE Gen 15:19

KEREN-HAPPUCH ke´-ren-hap´-ook
horn of paint Job 42:14

KERIOTH ke´-ri-oth
cities Josh 15:25

KEROS ke´-ros
crook (?) Ezra 2:44

KETURAH ke-too´-rah
incense Gen 25:1

KEY
the **k** of the kingdom of heaven Matt 16:19
ye have taken away **k** of knowledge Luke 11:52
the **k** of hell and of death Rev 1:18

KEZIA ke-zi´-ah
cassia Job 42:14

KEZIZ ge´-ziz
cut off Josh 18:21

KIBROTH-HATTAAVAH kib´-roth-hat-ta´-a-vah
graves of lust Num 11:34

KIBZAIM kib-za´-im
two heaps Josh 21:22

KICK
Jeshurun waxes fat, and **k** Deut 32:15
Wherefore **k** ye at my sacrifice 1 Sam 2:29
hard for thee to **k** against the pricks Acts 9:5

KIDRON kid´-ron
turbid 2 Sam 15:23

KILL
to **k** us in the wilderness Num 16:13
Am I God, to **k** 2 Kgs 5:7
if they **k** us, we shall but die 2 Kgs 7:4
A time to **k** Eccl 3:3
k the body Matt 10:28; Luke 12:4
to save life, or to **k**? Mark 3:4
Jews sought the more to **k** him John 5:18
Why go ye about to **k** me? John 7:19
Will he **k** himself? John 8:22
For thy sake we are **k** all the day Rom 8:36
the letter **k** 2 Cor 3:6
chastened, and not **k** 2 Cor 6:9
ye **k**, and desire to have James 4:2
Ye have condemned and **k** the just James 5:6

KINAH ki´-nah
song of mourning, lamentation Josh 15:22

KIND
If thou be **k** to this people 2 Chr 10:7
k unto the unthankful and to the evil Luke 6:35
Charity suffereth long, and is **k** 1 Cor 13:4

KINDLE
his wrath is **k** but a little Ps 2:12
a contentious man to **k** strife Prov 26:21
in the sparks that ye have **k** Is 50:11
my repentings are **k** together Hos 11:8
what will I, if it be already **k**? Luke 12:49
how great a matter a little fire **k** James 3:5

KINDLY
if ye will deal **k** and truly Gen 24:49
spake **k** unto them Gen 50:21
the LORD deal **k** with you Ruth 1:8
Be **k** affectioned one to another Rom 12:10

KINDNESS
thou hast shewed more **k** Ruth 3:10
I also will requite you this **k** 2 Sam 2:6
shew him **k** for Jonathan's sake 2 Sam 9:1,7
merciful **k** Ps 117:2; 119:76
the righteous smite me, it shall be a **k** Ps 141:5
in her tongue is the law of **k** Prov 31:26
with everlasting **k** Is 54:8
I remember thee, the **k** of thy youth Jer 2:2
mercies, **k**, humbleness of mind, Col 3:12
to godliness, brotherly **k** 2 Pet 1:7

KINDRED
thy seed shall all the **k** Acts 3:25
all **k** of the earth shall wail Rev 1:7
thy blood out of every **k**, and tongue Rev 5:9
could number, of all nations, and **k** Rev 7:9

KING
the shout of a **k** is among them Num 23:21
to anoint a **k** over them Judg 9:8
no **k** in Israel Judg 17:6
now make us a **k** 1 Sam 8:5
we will have a **k** 1 Sam 8:19
God save the **k** 1 Sam 10:24; 2 Sam 16:16
bring him to the **k** of terrors Job 18:14
Is it fit to say to a **k**? Job 34:18
my **K** and my God Ps 5:2; 84:3
The LORD is **k** for ever Ps 10:16
let the **k** hear us when we call Ps 20:9
God is my **k** of old Ps 74:12
the **k** of the earth Ps 102:15
By me **k** reign Prov 8:15
He shall stand before **k** Prov 22:29
that which destroyeth **k** Prov 31:3
it is not for **k** to drink wine Prov 31:4
what can the man do that cometh after the **k**? Eccl 2:12
when thy **k** is a child! Eccl 10:16
Curse not the **k** Eccl 10:20
a **K** shall reign in righteousness Is 32:1
Thine eyes shall see the **K** in his beauty Is 33:17
k shall be thy nursing fathers Is 49:23
an everlasting **k** Jer 10:10
when the **k** came in to see the guests Matt 22:11
Blessed be the **K** that cometh Luke 19:38
saying that he himself is Christ a **k** Luke 23:2
by force, to make him a **k** John 6:15
Behold your **K**! John 19:14
We have no **k** but Caesar John 19:15
Now unto the **k** eternal 1 Tim 1:17
the **K** of **k**, and Lord of lords 1 Tim 6:15
made us **k** and priests Rev 1:6; 5:10
thou **K** of saints Rev 15:3

KINGDOM
a **k** of priests Ex 19:6
thine is the **k** 1 Chr 29:11; Matt 6:13
the **k** is the LORD'S Ps 22:28
his **k** ruleth over all Ps 103:19
the glorious majesty of his **k** Ps 145:12
that did shake **k** Is 14:16
his **k** is an everlasting **k** Dan 4:3
gospel of the **k** Matt 4:23; 9:35; 24:14
children of the **k** shall be cast out Matt 8:12
k divided against itself Matt 12:25; Mark 3:24; Luke 11:17
good seed are the children of the **k** Matt 13:38
inherit the **k** Matt 25:34
Father's good pleasure to give you the **k** Luke 12:32
I appoint unto you a **k** Luke 22:29
My **k** is not of this world John 18:36
restore again the **k** to Israel? Acts 1:6
when he shall have delivered up the **k** 1 Cor 15:24
into the **k** of his dear Son Col 1:13
unto his heavenly **k** 2 Tim 4:18
heirs of the **k** which he hath promised James 2:5
into the everlasting **k** 2 Pet 1:11

KIR kir
town 2 Kgs 16:9

KIR-HARASETH kir´-ha-ras´-eth
brick-town 2 Kgs 3:25

KIR-HARESETH kir´-ha-res´-eth
same as KIR-HARASETH Is 16:7

KIR-HARESH kir-har´-esh
same as KIR-HARASETH Is 16:11

KIR-HERES kir-her´-es
same as KIR-HARASETH Jer 48:31

KIRIATHAIM kir´-yath-a´-im
same as KIRJATHAIM Ezek 25:9

KIRIOTH kir´-i-oth
cities Amos 2:2

KIRJATH kir´-jath
city (?) Josh 18:28

KIRJATH-ARBA kir´-jath-ar´-bah
city of Arba Gen 23:2

KIRJATH-ARIM kir´-jath-ar´-im
contracted from KIRJATH-JEARIM Ezra 2:25

KIRJATH-BAAL kir´-jath-ba´-al
city of Baal Josh 15:60

KIRJATH-HUZOTH kir´-jath-hooz´-oth
city of streets Num 22:39

KIRJATH-JEARIM kir´-jath-je´-ar-im
city of woods Josh 9:17

KIRJATH-SANNAH kir´-jath-san´-ah
city of thorns Josh 15:49

KIRJATH-SEPHER kir´-jath-se´-fer
book-city Josh 15:15

KIRJATHAIM kir´-jath-a´-im
double city Num 32:37

KISH kish
bow 1 Sam 9:1

KISHI kish´-i
short for KUSHAIAH 1 Chr 6:44

KISHION kish´-i-on
hardness Josh 19:20

KISHON ki´-shon
tortuous Judg 4:7

KISON ki´-son
same as KISHON Ps 83:9

KISS (n)
the **k** of an enemy are deceitful Prov 27:6
Salute one another with a holy **k** Rom 16:16

KISS (v)
righteousness and peace have **k** each other Ps 85:10
k his feet, and anointed them Luke 7:38

KITHLISH kith´-lish
fortified Josh 15:40

KITRON kit´-ron
burning Judg 1:30

KITTIM kit´-tim
same as CHITTIM Gen 10:4

KNEW
LORD is in this place, and I **k** it not Gen 28:16
Before I formed thee in the belly I **k** thee Jer 1:5
I never **k** you, depart Matt 7:23
If thou **k** the gift of God John 4:10
who **k** no sin 2 Cor 5:21

KNOW
Samuel did not yet **k** the Lord 1 Sam 3:7
k thou the God of thy father 1 Chr 28:9
k thou it for thy good Job 5:27
we are but of yesterday, and **k** nothing Job 8:9
Make me to **k** my transgression Job 13:23

I **k** that my redeemer liveth Job 19:25
How doth God **k**? Job 22:13; Ps 73:11
make me to **k** mine end Ps 39:4
Be still, and **k** that I am God Ps 46:10
this I **k**; for God is for me Ps 56:9
he **k** our frame Ps 103:14
k my heart Ps 139:23
the living **k** that they shall die Eccl 9:5
k thou that for all these things Eccl 11:9
The ox **k** his owner Is 1:3
heart is deceitful above all things, who can **k** it? Jer 17:9
k the Lord, for they all shall **k** me Jer 31:34
k that there hath been a prophet Ezek 2:5
thou shalt **k** the Lord Hos 2:20
he **k** it not Hos 7:9
let not thy left hand **k** Matt 6:3
I **k** you not Matt 25:12
I **k** thee, who thou art Mark 1:24; Luke 4:34
unto you it is given to **k** Mark 4:11; Luke 8:10
If thou hadst **k** Luke 19:42
I **k** him not Luke 22:57
he shall **k** of the doctrine John 7:17
k my sheep, and am **k** of mine John 10:14
k not now, but thou shalt **k** hereafter John 13:7
If ye **k** these things John 13:17
shall all men **k** ye are my disciples John 13:35
It is not for you to **k** Acts 1:7
we **k** that all things work Rom 8:28
neither can he **k** them 1 Cor 2:14
we **k** in part 1 Cor 13:9
and to **k** the love of Christ Eph 3:19
I **k** whom I have believed 2 Tim 1:12
thou hast **k** the holy scriptures 2 Tim 3:15
He that saith, I **k** him 1 John 2:4
we **k** that, when he shall appear 1 John 3:2
I **k** thy works Rev 2:2,9,13,19; 3:1,8

KNOWLEDGE
wisdom and **k** 2 Chr 1:10,11,12
we desire not the **k** of thy ways Job 21:14
He that teacheth man **k** Ps 94:10
Such **k** is too wonderful Ps 139:6
that thou takest **k** of him Ps 144:3
Wise men lay up **k** Prov 10:14
k is easy unto him that understandeth Prov 14:6
He that hath **k** spareth his words Prov 17:27
a man of **k** increaseth strength Prov 24:5
nor have the **k** of the holy Prov 30:3
increaseth **k** increaseth sorrow Eccl 1:18
nor **k**, nor wisdom in the grave Eccl 9:10
the spirit of **k** Is 11:2
and taught him **k** Is 40:14
by his **k** shall my righteous servant justify many Is 53:11
God gave them **k** Dan 1:17
k shall be increased Dan 12:4
destroyed for lack of **k** Hos 4:6
the earth shall be filled with the **k** Hab 2:14
taken away the key of **k** Luke 11:52
took **k** of them Acts 4:13
more perfect **k** of that way Acts 24:22
zeal of God, but not according to **k** Rom 10:2
K puffeth up 1 Cor 8:1
k, it shall vanish away 1 Cor 13:8
some have not the **k** of God 1 Cor 15:34
love of Christ, which passeth **k** Eph 3:19
the excellency of the **k** of Christ Phil 3:8
treasures of wisdom and **k** Col 2:3
the **k** of the truth 1 Tim 2:4; 2 Tim 3:7
after we have received the **k** Heb 10:26
to virtue **k** 2 Pet 1:5
grow in grace, and in the **k** 2 Pet 3:18

KOA ko´-ah
prince Ezek 23:23

KOHATH ko´-hath
assembly Gen 46:11

KOHATHITES ko´-hath-ites
descendants of Kohath Num 3:27

KOLAIAH kol-ai´-ah
voice of Jehovah (?) Neh 11:7

KORAH ko´-rah
bald Num 16:1

KORAHITES ko´-rah-ites
descendants of Korah 1 Chr 9:19

KORATHITES ko´-rath-ites
same as KORAHITES Num 26:58

KORE ko´-re
partridge 1 Chr 9:19

KORHITE kor´-ite
same as KORATHITE 2 Chr 20:19

KOZ koz
thorn Ezra 2:61

KUSHAIAH kush-ai´-ah
bow of Jehovah 1 Chr 15:17

L

LAADAH la´-ad-ah
order (?) 1 Chr 4:21

LAADAN la´-ad-an
put in order (?) 1 Chr 7:26

LABAN la´-ban
white Gen 24:29

LABOUR (n)
yet is their strength l and sorrow Ps 90:10
to his l until evening Ps 104:23
he that gathereth by l shall increase Prov 13:11
In all l there is profit Prov 14:23
All things are full of l Eccl 1:8
what hath man of all his l Eccl 2:22
All the l of man is for his mouth Eccl 6:7
are entered into their l John 4:38
your l is not in vain 1 Cor 15:58
l of love 1 Thess 1:3; Heb 6:10
thy l, and thy patience Rev 2:2
they may rest from their l Rev 14:13

LABOUR (v)
Six days shalt thou l Ex 20:9; Deut 5:13
So we l in the work Neh 4:21
they l in vain Ps 127:1
our oxen may be strong to l Ps 144:14
He that l, l for himself Prov 16:26
L not to be rich Prov 23:4
for whom do I l? Eccl 4:8
The sleep of a l man is sweet Eccl 5:12
all ye that l Matt 11:28
L not for meat which perisheth John 6:27
For we are l together with God 1 Cor 3:9
rather let him l, working with his hands Eph 4:28
know them which l among you 1 Thess 5:12
they who l in word and doctrine 1 Tim 5:17

LACHISH la´-kish
impregnable Josh 10:3

LACK
what l I yet ? Matt 19:20
l ye any thing ? Luke 22:35
was there any among them that l Acts 4:34

LADEN
a people l with iniquity Is 1:4
labour and are heavy l Matt 11:28
captive silly women l with sins 2 Tim 3:6

LAEL la´-el
(devoted) to God Num 3:24

LAHAD la´-had
oppression 1 Chr 4:2

LAHAI-ROI la-hah´-i-ro´-i
to the living is sight Gen 24:62

LAHMAM lah´-mam
theirbread or *their war* Josh 15:40

LAHMI lah´-mi
warrior 1 Chr 20:5

LAISH la´-ish
lion 1 Sam 25:44

LAKUM la´-koom
fort (?) Josh 19:33

LAMA lam´-ah
why? Matt 27:46

LAMB
the l feed after their manner Is 5:17
The wolf also shall dwell with the l Is 11:6
as a l to the slaughter Is 53:7
Behold the L of God John 1:29,36
as of a l without blemish 1 Pet 1:19
stood a L as it had been slain Rev 5:6
by the blood of the L Rev 12:11
the throne of God and of the L Rev 22:1

LAME
feet was I to the l Job 29:15
legs of the l are not equal Prov 26:7
shall the l man leap Is 35:6
which is l be turned out of the way Heb 12:13

LAMECH la´-mek
destroyer Gen 4:18

LAMENT
ye have not l Matt 11:17
ye shall weep and l John 16:20
made great l over him Acts 8:2

LAMP
Thy word is a l unto my feet Ps 119:105
the l of the wicked shall be put out Prov 13:9
thereof as a l that burneth Is 62:1
which took their l, and went forth Matt 25:1

LAODICEA la-od-i-se´-ah
1 *people of justice*,
2 named after Laodice, wife of Antiochus II Col 2:1

LAODICEANS la´-od-i-se´-ans
inhabitants of Laodicea Col 4:16

LAP
number of them that l Judg 7:6
The lot is cast into the l Prov 16:33

LAPIDOTH la´-pid-oth
torches Judg 4:4

LASEA la-se´-ah
a city on the south side of Crete Acts 27:8

LASHA la´-shah
fissure Gen 10:19

LASHARON la-sha´-ron
of the plain Josh 12:18

LAST
let my l end be like his Num 23:10
At the l it biteth like a serpent Prov 23:32
l state of that man Matt 12:45; Luke 11:26
first shall be l Matt 19:30; Mark 10:31
the l day John 6:39; 11:24; 12:48

LATTER
stand at the l day upon the earth Job 19:25
wise in the l end Prov 19:20
glory of this l house Hag 2:9

LAUGH
I also will l at your calamity Prov 1:26
a time to l Eccl 3:4
for ye shall l Luke 6:21

LAW
all the words of the l Josh 8:34
the l of his God is in his heart Ps 37:31

thy l is within my heart Ps 40:8
I delight in thy l Ps 119:70
unless thy l had been my delight Ps 119:92
how I love thy l Ps 119:97
thy l do I love Ps 119:113,163
peace have they which l thy law Ps 119:165
the l of the wise is a fountain of life Prov 13:14
To the l and to the testimony Is 8:20
The l of truth was in his mouth Mal 2:6
come to destroy the l Matt 5:17
the weightier matters of the l Matt 23:23
Doth our l judge any man John 7:51
We have a l, and by our l John 19:7
are a l unto themselves Rom 2:14
by the deeds of the l Rom 3:20
the l is holy Rom 7:12
the l is spiritual Rom 7:14
the l that it is good Rom 7:16
what the l could not do Rom 8:3
the l was our schoolmaster Gal 3:24
all the l is fulfilled in one word Gal 5:14
against such there is no l Gal 5:23
so fulfil the l of Christ Gal 6:2
the l is not made for a righteous man 1 Tim 1:9
the l of a carnal commandment Heb 7:16
perfect l of liberty James 1:25
the royal l James 2:8

LAWFUL
which is not l to do Matt 12:2
it is not l for thee to carry thy bed John 5:10
All things are l unto me 1 Cor 6:12

LAWLESS
but for the l and disobedient 1 Tim 1:9

LAZARUS laz´-ar-us
Gr. for ELEAZAR Luke 16:20

LEAD
whither the LORD shall l you Deut 4:27; 28:37
he l me beside still waters Ps 23:2
l me in a plain path Ps 27:11
l me, and guide me Ps 31:3
l me to the rock that is higher than I Ps 61:2
there shall thy hand l me Ps 139:10
l me in the way everlasting Ps 139:24
when thou goest, it shall l thee Prov 6:22
a little child shall l them Is 11:6
I will l them in paths Is 42:16
which l thee by the way Is 48:17
l us not into temptation Matt 6:13; Luke 11:4
the blind l the blind Matt 15:14; Luke 6:39
seeking some to l him Acts 13:11
we may l a quiet and peaceable life 1 Tim 2:2

LEAF
sound of a shaken l shall chase them Lev 26:36
his l shall not wither Ps 1:3
we all do fade as a l Is 64:6
found nothing thereon, but l only Matt 21:19

LEAH le´-ah
languid Gen 29:16

LEAN
l not to thine own understanding Prov 3:5
l his hand on the wall Amos 5:19
yet will they l upon the LORD Mic 3:11
there was l on Jesus' bosom John 13:23
which also l on his breast at supper John 21:20

LEARN
l to fear the LORD Deut 31:13
will increase l Prov 1:5; 9:9
Lest thou l his ways Prov 22:25
L to do well Is 1:17
neither shall they l war Is 2:4; Mic 4:3
deliver to one that is l Is 29:11
hath l of the Father John 6:45
having never l John 7:15
l in all the wisdom of the Egyptians Acts 7:22
ye have not so l Christ Eph 4:20
in the things which thou hast l 2 Tim 3:14
yet l he obedience Heb 5:8

LEARNING
sweetness of the lips increaseth l Prov 16:21
much l doth make thee mad Acts 26:24
written for our l Rom 15:4

LEAST
one of these l commandments Matt 5:19
he that is l in the kingdom Matt 11:11; Luke 7:28
one of the l of these Matt 25:40,45
not able to do that thing which is l Luke 12:26
faithful in that which is l Luke 16:10
less than the l of all saints Eph 3:8

LEAVE
l his father and mother Gen 2:24; Mark 10:7; Eph 5:31
not l my soul in hell Ps 16:10; Acts 2:27
l me not Ps 27:9; 119:121
and not to l the other undone Matt 23:23
Peace I l with you John 14:27
I will never l thee Heb 13:5

LEBANAH leb´-an-ah
white Ezra 2:45

LEBANON leb´-an-on
the white (mountain) Deut 1:7

LEBAOTH leb´-a-oth
lionesses Josh 15:32

LEBBAEUS leb-e´-us
same as THADDAEUS Matt 10:3

LEBONAH leb-o´-nah
frankincense Judg 21:19

LECAH le´-kah
journey (?) 1 Chr 4:21

LEES
a feast of wines on the l Is 25:6
he hath settled on his l Jer 48:11
men that are settled on their l Zeph 1:12

LEHABIM le´-hab-im
descendants of Mizraim Gen 10:13

LEHI le´-hi
jaw-bone Judg 15:9

LEMUEL lem´-oo-el
(devoted) to God (?) Prov 31:1

LEND
thou shalt l unto many nations Deut 15:6
ever merciful, and l Ps 37:26
good man sheweth favour and l Ps 112:5
that hath pity on poor l unto the LORD Prov 19:17
the borrower is servant to the l Prov 22:7
if ye l to them of whom Luke 6:34

LESHEM le´-shem
precious stone Josh 19:47

LESS
the poor shall not give l Ex 30:15
God exacteth of thee l than thine iniquity deserveth Job 11:6
counted to him l than nothing Is 40:17

LETUSHIM le-toosh´-im
the hammered Gen 25:3

LEUMMIM le-oom´-im
peoples Gen 25:3

LEVI le´-vi
associate (?) Gen 29:34

LEVIATHAN le-vi´-a-than
a water monster Ps 104:26

LEVITES le´-vites
descendants of Levi Ex 6:25

LIARS
All men are l Ps 116:11
he is a l, and the father of it John 8:44
Cretians are always l, evil beasts Titus 1:12
hast found them l Rev 2:2
all l, shall have their part in the lake Rev 21:8

LIBERAL
The l soul shall be made fat Prov 11:25
vile person shall no more be called l Is 32:5
l deviseth l things Is 32:8

LIBERTINES lib´-ert-ines
freed-men Acts 6:9

LIBERTY
I will walk at l Ps 119:45
to proclaim l Is 61:1; Jer 34:8
to set at l Luke 4:18
glorious l of the children of God Rom 8:21
lest by any means this l of yours 1 Cor 8:9
the Spirit of the Lord is, there is l 2 Cor 3:17
Stand fast therefore in the l Gal 5:1
law of l James 1:25; 2:12

LIBNAH lib´-nah
whiteness Num 33:20

LIBNI lib´-ni
white Ex 6:17

LIBNITES lib´-nites
descendants of Libni Num 3:21

LIBYA lib´-ee-ah
1 to the Jews, the western part of lower Egypt Ezek 30:5
2 to the Romans, almost all of North Africa, west of Egypt Acts 2:10

LIFE
the breath of l Gen 2:7; 6:17; 7:22
the tree of l Gen 2:9; 3:24; Rev 2:7
I have set before thee this day l Deut 30:15
our l for yours Josh 2:14
bound in the bundle of l 1 Sam 25:29
shew me the path of l Ps 16:11
their portion in this l Ps 17:14; Eccl 9:9
not my l with bloody men Ps 26:9
the strength of my l Ps 27:1
in his favour is l Ps 30:5
what man is he that desireth l? Ps 34:12
the fountain of l Ps 36:9
With long l will I satisfy him Ps 91:16
even l for evermore Ps 133:3
So shall they be l unto thy soul Prov 3:22
whoso findeth me findeth l Prov 8:35
The way of l is above to the wise Prov 15:24
take no thought for your l Matt 6:25; Luke 12:22
to enter into l Matt 18:8; 19:17; Mark 9:43
a man's l consisteth not Luke 12:15
The l is more than meat Luke 12:23
in him was l John 1:4
passed from death unto l John 5:24; 1 John 3:14
as the Father hath l in himself John 5:26
will not come that ye might have l John 5:40
the bread of l John 6:48
I lay down my l John 10:15,17
the resurrection, and the l John 11:25
in newness of l Rom 6:4
l from the dead Rom 11:15
the savour of l unto l 2 Cor 2:16
the l which I now live Gal 2:20
alienated from the l of God Eph 4:18
your l is hid Col 3:3
promise of the l 1 Tim 4:8; 2 Tim 1:1
brought l and immortality to light 2 Tim 1:10
what is your l? James 4:14
the l was manifested 1 John 1:2
the pride of l 1 John 2:16

this l is in his Son 1 John 5:11
water of l Rev 22:1,17

LIGHT
Israel had l in their dwellings Ex 10:23
the l of the wicked Job 18:5
men see not the bright l Job 37:21
the l of thy countenance Ps 4:6; 90:8
The LORD is my l Ps 27:1
in thy l shall we see l Ps 36:9
l is sown for the righteous Ps 97:11
a l unto my path Ps 119:105
the l is sweet Eccl 11:7
darkness for l, and l for darkness Is 5:20
l of the moon shall be as the l of the sun Is 30:26
we wait for l Is 59:9
Arise, shine, for thy l is come Is 60:1
the l shall not be clear Zech 14:6
the l of the world Matt 5:14; John 8:12; 9:5
let your l so shine Matt 5:16
the l of the body is the eye Matt 6:22
and your l burning Luke 12:35
wiser than the children of l Luke 16:8
That was the true L John 1:9
l is come into the world John 3:19
hateth the l John 3:20
burning and a shining l John 5:35
Yet a little while is the l with you John 12:35
While ye have l, believe in the l John 12:36
turn them from darkness to l Acts 26:18
bring to l the hidden things 1 Cor 4:5
l of the glorious gospel 2 Cor 4:4
commanded the l to shine 2 Cor 4:6
an angel of l 2 Cor 11:14
l in the Lord: walk as children of l Eph 5:8
Christ shall give thee l Eph 5:14
in the l which no man can approach 1 Tim 6:16
a l that shineth in a dark place 2 Pet 1:19
God is l 1 John 1:5
walk in the l, as he is in the l 1 John 1:7
need no candle, neither l of the sun Rev 22:5

LIGHTNING
there were thunders and l Ex 19:16
as the l cometh out of the east Matt 24:27
I beheld Satan as l fall from heaven Luke 10:18

LIKENESS
when I awake, with thy l Ps 17:15
what l will ye compare Is 40:18
come down to us in the l of men Acts 14:11
planted together in the l of his death Rom 6:5
in the l of sinful flesh Rom 8:3
was made in the l of men Phil 2:7

LIKHI lik´-hi
fond of learning (?) 1 Chr 7:19

LIMIT
and l the Holy One of Israel Ps 78:41
he l a certain day Heb 4:7

LINE
The l are fallen Ps 16:6
l upon l Is 28:10
Judgment also will I lay to the l Is 28:17
the l of confusion Is 34:11
another man's l of things made ready 2 Cor 10:16

LINGER
while he l, the men laid hold Gen 19:16
except we had l Gen 43:10
now of a long time l not 2 Pet 2:3

LINUS li´-nus
flax 2 Tim 4:21

LIP
only her l moved 1 Sam 1:13
My l shall not speak wickedness Job 27:4
my l shall utter knowledge Job 33:3
flattering l Ps 12:2,3
our l are our own Ps 12:4
goeth not out of feigned l Ps 17:1
lying l Ps 31:18; 120:2; Prov 10:18; 12:22; 17:7
the l of the wise disperse knowledge Prov 15:7
l of a fool will swallow up himself Eccl 10:12
causing l of those asleep to speak Song 7:9
a man of unclean l Is 6:5
honoureth me with their l Matt 15:8

LITTLE
for a l space grace hath been shown Ezra 9:8
a l reviving in our bondage Ezra 9:8
how l a portion is heard Job 26:14
a l lower than the angels Ps 8:5; Heb 2:7
a l that a righteous man hath Ps 37:16
a l sleep, a l slumber, a l folding of the hands Prov 6:10; 24:33
Better is l with the fear of the LORD Prov 15:16
four things which are l on the earth Prov 30:24
here a l, and there a l Is 28:10
a very l thing Is 40:15; Ezek 16:47
bring in l Hag 1:6
l faith Matt 6:30; 8:26; 14:31; 16:8; Luke 12:28
l ones Matt 10:42; 18:6; Mark 9:42; Luke 17:2
to whom l is forgiven Luke 7:47
l of stature Luke 19:3
a l leaven 1 Cor 5:6; Gal 5:9
bodily exercise profiteth l 1 Tim 4:8
use a l wine 1 Tim 5:23

LIVE
O that Ishmael might l before thee! Gen 17:18
doth my father yet l? Gen 45:3
if a man do, he shall l Lev 18:5; Neh 9:29
not l by bread Deut 8:3; Matt 4:4; Luke 4:4
I would not l always Job 7:16
shall he l again? Job 14:14
I shall not die, but l Ps 118:17
make me to l Is 38:16
hear, and your soul shall l Is 55:3
he shall surely l Ezek 3:21; 18:9; 33:13
when thou wast in thy blood, L Ezek 16:6
we shall l in his sight Hos 6:2
the just shall l by his faith Hab 2:4
this do, and thou shalt l Luke 10:28
though he were dead, yet shall he l John 11:25
because I l, ye shall l also John 14:19
in him we l, and move Acts 17:28
l after the flesh Rom 8:12
whether we l, we l unto the Lord Rom 14:8
should l of the gospel 1 Cor 9:14
as dying, and, behold, we l 2 Cor 6:9
that I might l unto God Gal 2:19
If we l in the Spirit Gal 5:25
For me to l is Christ Phil 1:21
all that will l godly 2 Tim 3:12
If the Lord will, we shall l James 4:15
I am he that l, and was dead Rev 1:18
a name that thou l Rev 3:1

LIVELY
for they are l, and delivered Ex 1:19
received the l oracles to give unto us Acts 7:38
unto a l hope by the resurrection 1 Pet 1:3
l stones, are built up a spiritual house 1 Pet 2:5

LIVING
a l soul Gen 2:7
the land of the l Job 28:13; Ps 27:13; 52:5; 116:9
light of l Job 33:30; Ps 56:13
the book of the l Ps 69:28
the l will lay it to his heart Eccl 7:2
the l know that they shall die Eccl 9:5
l water Song 4:15; Jer 2:13; 17:13; Zech 14:8; John 4:10
the l, he shall praise thee Is 38:19
Wherefore doth a l man complain Lam 3:39
even all her l Mark 12:44
spent all her l Luke 8:43
I am the l bread John 6:51
a new and l way Heb 10:20

LO-AMMI lo-am´-i
not my people Hos 1:9

LO-DEBAR lo´-de-bar
without pasture (?) 2 Sam 9:4

LO-RUHAMAH lo´-ru´-ham-ah
not having obtained mercy Hos 1:6

LOAN
the l which is lent to the LORD 1 Sam 2:20

LOTHE
our soul l this light bread Num 21:5
I l it Job 7:16
they shall l themselves Ezek 6:9
l yourselves in your own sight Ezek 20:43; 36:31

LOD lode
strife (?) 1 Chr 8:12

LODGE
where thou l, I will l Ruth 1:16
righteousness l in it Is 1:21
if she have l strangers 1 Tim 5:10

LOFTY
nor mine eyes l Ps 131:1
The l looks of man shall be humbled Is 2:11
the high and l One Is 57:15

LOIS lo´-is
better 2 Tim 1:5

LONG
Which l for death Job 3:21
that God would grant the thing I l for! Job 6:8
my flesh l for thee in a dry and thirsty land Ps 63:1
My soul l, yea, even fainteth, for the courts of the LORD Ps 84:2
I have l for thy salvation Ps 119:174

LOOK
l not behind thee Gen 19:17
when he l upon it, shall live Num 21:8
he l upon men Job 33:27
and will l up Ps 5:3
They l unto him, and were lightened Ps 34:5
l upon the face of thine anointed Ps 84:9
he l for judgment Is 5:7
At that day shall a man l to his Maker Is 17:7
L unto me, and be saved Is 45:22
I l, and there was none to help Is 63:5
to this man will I l Is 66:2
We l for peace Jer 8:15; 14:19
l well to him Jer 39:12
I will l well unto thee Jer 40:4
Ye l for much Hag 1:9
do we l for another? Matt 11:3
in a day when he l not for Matt 24:50
l back, is fit for the kingdom Luke 9:62
came and l on him Luke 10:32
the Lord turned, and l upon Peter Luke 22:61
disciples l one on another John 13:22
said, L on us Acts 3:4
l ye out among you seven men Acts 6:3
we l not at the things seen 2 Cor 4:18
l on things after the outward appearance 2 Cor 10:7
L not every man on his own things Phil 2:4
L for that blessed hope Titus 2:13
he l for a city Heb 11:10
L unto Jesus Heb 12:2

angels desire to l into 1 Pet 1:12
L to yourselves 2 John 1:8

LOOSE
l the bands of Orion? Job 38:31
l those that are appointed to death Ps 102:20
thou hast l my bonds Ps 116:16
Or ever the silver cord be l Eccl 12:6
l on earth, shall be l in heaven Matt 16:19; 18:18
L him, and let him go John 11:44
having l the pains of death Acts 2:24
Art thou l from a wife? 1 Cor 7:27

LORD
the L, the L God, merciful Ex 34:6
the L he is God Deut 4:35
the L, he is the God 1 Kgs 18:39
The L our God is one L Deut 6:4
The L be with you Ruth 2:4; 2 Thess 3:16
It is the L 1 Sam 3:18; John 21:7
thou, art L alone Neh 9:6
whose God is the L Ps 33:12
Know ye that the L he is God Ps 100:3
This is the L doing Ps 118:23
one L, and his name one Zech 14:9
every one that saith unto me, L, L Matt 7:21
L, is it I? Matt 26:22
L also of the sabbath Mark 2:28; Luke 6:5
why call ye me L, L? Luke 6:46
Who is he, L? John 9:36
We have seen the L John 20:25
both L and Christ Acts 2:36
Who art thou, L? Acts 9:5; 26:15
One L Eph 4:5

LORDSHIP
Gentiles exercise l over them Mark 10:42; Luke 22:25

LOSE
shall l it Matt 10:39; 16:25; Mark 8:35; Luke 9:24
l his own soul Matt 16:26; Mark 8:36
I should l nothing John 6:39

LOSS
he shall suffer l 1 Cor 3:15
I counted l for Christ Phil 3:7

LOST
like a l sheep Ps 119:176
My people hath been l sheep Jer 50:6
our hope is l Ezek 37:11
l sheep of the house of Israel Matt 10:6; 15:24
to save that which was l Matt 18:11; Luke 19:10
that nothing be l John 6:12
none of them is l John 17:12
have I l none John 18:9

LOT
thou maintainest my l Ps 16:5
not rest upon the l of the righteous Ps 125:3
Cast in thy l among us Prov 1:14
l is cast into the lap Prov 16:33
l causeth contentions to cease Prov 18:18
stand in thy l Dan 12:13
neither part nor l in this matter Acts 8:21

LOT lot
veil Gen 11:27

LOTAN lo´-tan
veiling Gen 36:20

LOUD
shouted with a l shout Ezra 3:13
She is l and stubborn Prov 7:11
blesseth his friend with a l voice Prov 27:14
they were instant with l voices Luke 23:23

LOVE (n)
wonderful, passing the l of women 2 Sam 1:26
l covereth all sins Prov 10:12
Better a dinner of herbs where l is Prov 15:17
his banner over me was l Song 2:4
l is strong as death Song 8:6
loved thee with an everlasting l Jer 31:3
with bands of l Hos 11:4
l of many shall wax cold Matt 24:12
ye have not the l of God in you John 5:42
if ye have l one to another John 13:35
Greater l hath no man than this John 15:13
L worketh no ill Rom 13:10
the l of Christ constraineth us 2 Cor 5:14
God of l and peace shall be with you 2 Cor 13:11
the l of Christ, which passeth Eph 3:19
the l of money is the root of all evil 1 Tim 6:10
Let brotherly l continue Heb 13:1
l is of God 1 John 4:7
God is l 1 John 4:8,16
Herein is l, not that we loved God 1 John 4:10
There is no fear in l 1 John 4:18
thou hast left thy first l Rev 2:4

LOVE (v)
thou shalt l thy neighbour Lev 19:18; Matt 19:19; 22:39; Mark 12:31
l the LORD thy God Deut 6:5; 11:1; 19:9; 30:6; Matt 22:37; Mark 12:30; Luke 10:27
I will l thee, O Lord, my strength Ps 18:1
I have l the habitation of thy house Ps 26:8
l many days Ps 34:12
they that l his name Ps 69:36
ye that l the LORD Ps 97:10
As he l cursing Ps 109:17
they shall prosper that l thee Ps 122:6
I l them that l me Prov 8:17
A friend l at all times Prov 17:17
A time to l Eccl 3:8
my people l to have it so Jer 5:31
I have l thee with an everlasting love Jer 31:3
I will l them freely Hos 14:4
Hate the evil, and l the good Amos 5:15
but to l mercy, and to walk humbly Mic 6:8
L your enemies Matt 5:44; Luke 6:27
if ye l them which l you Matt 5:46
which of them will l him most? Luke 7:42
he whom thou l is sick John 11:3
That ye l one another John 15:12,17
l thou me? John 21:15,16,17
owe no man any thing, but to l Rom 13:8
Grace be with all them that l our Lord Eph 6:24
whom having not seen, ye l 1 Pet 1:8
L the brotherhood 1 Pet 2:17
We l him, because he first l us 1 John 4:19
As many as I l, I rebuke Rev 3:19

LOVELY
Saul and Jonathan were l 2 Sam 1:23
he is altogehter l Song 5:16
thou art unto them a very l song Ezek 33:32
whatsoever things are l Phil 4:8

LOVER
Hiram was ever a l of David 1 Kgs 5:1
L and friend hast thou put far Ps 88:18
l of pleasures more than l of God 2 Tim 3:4
a l of good men Titus 1:8

LOW
Who remembered us in our l estate Ps 136:23
condescend to men of l estate Rom 12:16
Let the brother of l degree James 1:9
in that he is made l James 1:10

LOWER
a little l than the angels Ps 8:5; Heb 2:7
into the l parts of the earth Ps 63:9; Eph 4:9

LOWEST
shall burn unto the l hell Deut 32:22
delivered my soul from the l hell Ps 86:13
with shame to take the l room Luke 14:9

LOWLINESS
all l and meekness Eph 4:2
l of mind let each esteem Phil 2:3

LOWLY
with the l is wisdom Prov 11:2
I am meek and l Matt 11:29

LUBIM loob´-im
the land or territory of the LUBIMS Nah 3:9

LUBIMS loob´-ims
same as LEHABIM 2 Chr 12:3

LUCAS loo´-cas
same as LUKE Phile 1:24

LUCIFER loo´-sif-er
light-bearer Is 14:12

LUCIUS loosh´-yus
a noble (?) Acts 13:1

LUD lood
strife (?) Gen 10:22

LUDIM lood´-im
pl. for LUD Gen 10:13

LUHITH loo´-hith
abounding in boards Is 15:5

LUKE luk
luminous, white Col 4:14

LUST
gave them up to their own hearts' l Ps 81:12
I had not known l Rom 7:7
with affections and l Gal 5:24
foolish and hurtful l 1 Tim 6:9
denying ungodliness and worldly l Titus 2:12
when he is drawn of his own l James 1:14
abstain from fleshly l 1 Pet 2:11
the l of the flesh 1 John 2:16
world passeth away, and the l thereof 1 John 2:17
walking after their own l Jude 1:16

LUZ looz
almond tree Gen 28:19

LYCAONIA li´-ka-o´-ni-ah
abounding in werewolves Acts 14:6

LYDDA lid´-ah
Gr. for LOD (?) Acts 9:32

LYDIA lid´-ee-ah
a standing pool Ezek 30:5

LYING
Let the l lips be put to silence Ps 31:18
I abhor l, but thy law do I love Ps 119:163
a l tongue Prov 6:17
a l tongue is but for a moment Prov 12:19
Trust ye not in l words Jer 7:4
putting away l Eph 4:25

LYSANIAS li-sa´-ni-as
ending sorrow Luke 3:1

LYSIAS lis´-yas
a loosing Acts 23:26

LYSTRA lis´-tra
that dissolves Acts 14:6

M

MAACAH ma´-ak-ah
same as MAACHAH 2 Sam 3:3

MAACHAH ma´-ak-ah
royal (?) 1 Kgs 2:39

MAACHATHI ma-ak´-a-thi
an inhabitant of Maachah Deut 3:14

MAACHATHITES ma-ak′-ath-ites
pl. of MAACHATHI — Josh 12:5

MAADAI ma′-ad-a′-i
adorned — Ezra 10:34

MAADIAH ma′-ad-i′-ah
ornament of Jehovah — Neh 12:5

MAAI ma-a′-i
compassionate (?) — Neh 12:36

MAALEH-ACRABBIM ma′-al-eh-ak′-rab-im
ascent of scorpions — Josh 15:3

MAARATH ma′-ar-ath
a treeless place — Josh 15:59

MAASEIAH ma′-as-i′-ah
work of Jehovah — Ezra 10:18

MAASIAI ma′-as-i-a′-i
same as AMASHAI (?) — 1 Chr 9:12

MAATH ma′-ath
small (?) — Luke 3:26

MAAZ ma′-az
wrath — 1 Chr 2:27

MAAZIAH ma′-az-i′-ah
consolation of Jehovah — 1 Chr 24:18

MACEDONIA mas-e-do′-nee-ah
a country north of Greece — Acts 16:9

MACEDONIAN mas-e-do′-nee-an
belonging to MACEDONIA — Acts 27:2

MACHBANAI mak′-ban-a-i
cloak — 1 Chr 12:13

MACHBENAH mak′-be-nah
clad with a cloak (?) — 1 Chr 2:49

MACHI ma′-ki
reduced, poor — Num 13:15

MACHIR ma′-kir
sold — Gen 50:23

MACHIRITES ma′-kir-ites
descendants of Machir — Num 26:29

MACHNADEBAI mak′-na-deb-a′-i
what is like the liberal (?) — Ezra 10:40

MACHPELAH mak-pe′-lah
a doubling — Gen 23:9

MAD
He hath a devil, and is **m** — John 10:20
being exceedingly **m** against them — Acts 26:11
much learning doth make thee **m** — Acts 26:24
will they not say that ye are **m** — 1 Cor 14:23

MADAI ma′-da-i
descendants of Japheth — Gen 10:2

MADE
Who **m** thee a prince — Ex 2:14
the day which the LORD hath **m** — Ps 118:24
LORD hath **m** all things for himself — Prov 16:4
He hath **m** every thing beautiful — Eccl 3:11
God hath **m** man upright — Eccl 7:29
all things hath mine hand **m** — Is 66:2
All things were **m** by him — John 1:3
he hath **m** him to be sin for us — 2 Cor 5:21
m nigh by the blood of Christ — Eph 2:13
I was **m** a minister — Eph 3:7
having **m** peace — Col 1:20
to be **m** like unto his brethren — Heb 2:17

MADIAN ma′-di-an
Gr. for MIDIAN — Acts 7:29

MADMANNAH mad′-man-ah
dunghill — Josh 15:31

MADMEN mad′-men
dungheap — Jer 48:2

MADMENAH mad′-men-ah
same as MADMEN — Is 10:31

MADON ma′-don
place of contention — Josh 11:1

MAGBISH mag′-bish
congregating — Ezra 2:30

MAGDALA mag′-dal-ah
tower — Matt 15:39

MAGDALENE mag′-dal-e′-ne
inhabitant of Magdala — Matt 27:56

MAGDIEL mag′-di-el
praise of God — Gen 36:43

MAGNIFY
This day will I begin to **m** thee — Josh 3:7
is man, that thou shouldest **m** him? — Job 7:17
m the LORD — Ps 34:3; Luke 1:46
m themselves — Ps 35:26; 38:16
thou hast **m** thy word above all — Ps 138:2
m the law — Is 42:21
the name of the Lord Jesus was **m** — Acts 19:17
I **m** mine office — Rom 11:13

MAGOG ma′-gog
descendants of Japheth — Gen 10:2

MAGOR-MISSABIB ma′-gor-mis′-a-bib
fear round about — Jer 20:3

MAGPIASH mag′-pi-ash
moth slayer (?) — Neh 10:20

MAHALAH mah′-hal-ah
disease — 1 Chr 7:18

MAHALALEEL ma-ha′-lal-e′-el
praise of God — Gen 5:12

MAHALATH mah′-al-ath
a musical instrument — Gen 28:9

MAHALI ma′-ha-li
weak — Ex 6:19

MAHANAIM ma′-han-a′-im
two camps — Gen 32:2

MAHANEH-DAN ma′-han-e-dan
camp of Dan — Judg 18:12

MAHARAI ma′-har-a′-i
impetuous — 2 Sam 23:28

MAHATH ma′-hath
taking hold (?) — 1 Chr 6:35

MAHAVITE ma′-hav-ite
marrow (?) — 1 Chr 11:46

MAHAZIOTH ma-haz′-i-oth
visions — 1 Chr 25:4

MAHER-SHALAL-HASH-BAZ ma′-her-sha′-lal-hash′-baz
the spoil hastens, the prey speeds — Is 8:1

MAHLAH mah′-lah
same as MAHALAH — Num 26:33

MAHLI mah′-li
same as MAHALI — 1 Chr 6:19

MAHLITES mah′-lites
descendants of Mahli — Num 3:33

MAHLON mah′-lon
a sick person — Ruth 1:2

MAHOL ma′-hol
a dance — 1 Kgs 4:31

MAIL
armed with a coat of **m** — 1 Sam 17:5

MAINTAIN
m their cause — 1 Kgs 8:45,49,59; 2 Chr 6:35,39
thou **m** my lot — Ps 16:5
to **m** good works — Titus 3:8,14

MAINTENANCE
we have **m** from the king's palace — Ezra 4:14
for the **m** of thy maidens — Prov 27:27

MAKAZ ma′-kaz
end (?) — 1 Kgs 4:9

MAKER
Shall a man be more pure than his **m** — Job 4:17
my **m** would soon take me away — Job 32:22
none saith, Where is God my **m** — Job 35:10
ascribe righteousness to my **M** — Job 36:3
kneel before the LORD our **m** — Ps 95:6
reproacheth his **M** — Prov 14:31; 17:5
the LORD is the **m** of them all — Prov 22:2
that striveth with his **m** — Is 45:9
forgettest the LORD thy **M** — Is 51:13
thy **M** is thine husband — Is 54:5
whose builder and **m** is God — Heb 11:10

MAKHELOTH mak′-hel-oth
assemblies — Num 33:25

MAKKEDAH mak′-ed-ah
place of shepherds (?) — Josh 10:10

MAKTESH mak′-tesh
a mortar — Zeph 1:11

MALACHI mal′-ak-i
the messenger of Jehovah — Mal 1:1

MALCHAM mal′-kam
their king — 1 Chr 8:9

MALCHI-SHUA malk′-i-shoo′-ah
king of aid — 1 Chr 8:33

MALCHIAH malk-i′-ah
Jehovah's king — 1 Chr 6:40

MALCHIEL malk′-i-el
God's king — Gen 46:17

MALCHIELITES malk′-i-el-ites
descendants of Malchiel — Num 26:45

MALCHIJAH malk-i′-jah
same as MALCHIAH — 1 Chr 9:12

MALCHIRAM malk-i′-ram
king of height (?) — 1 Chr 3:18

MALCHUS mal′-kus
Gr. for MALLUCH — John 18:10

MALELEEL mal′-el-el
same as MAHALALEEL — Luke 3:37

MALICIOUSNESS
covetousness, **m**, full of envy — Rom 1:29
for a cloke of **m** — 1 Pet 2:16

MALLOTHI mal′-lo-thi
my utterance — 1 Chr 25:4

MALLUCH mal′-ook
counselor — 1 Chr 6:44

MAMMON mam′-on
fullness — Matt 6:24

MAMRE mam′-re
fatness — Gen 14:13

MAN
the **m** is become as one of us — Gen 3:22
for **m** sake — Gen 8:21
God is not a **m** — Num 23:19
Should such a **m** as I flee? — Neh 6:11
m is born unto trouble — Job 5:7
seest thou as **m** seeth? — Job 10:4
vain **m** would be wise — Job 11:12
M that is born of a woman — Job 14:1
Art thou the first **m** that was born? — Job 15:7
m, that is a worm — Job 25:6
God is greater than **m** — Job 33:12
the **m** of earth — Ps 10:18
m being in honour abideth not — Ps 49:12
what **m** is he that liveth — Ps 89:48

thou turnest **m** to destruction Ps 90:3
m goeth forth to his labour Ps 104:23
I will not fear, what can **m** do? Ps 118:6
a good **m** obtaineth favour Prov 12:2
who knoweth what is good for **m** Eccl 6:12
cease ye from **m** Is 2:22
it is not in **m** to direct his steps Jer 10:23
I am the **m** that hath seen affliction Lam 3:1
I am God, and not **m** Hos 11:9
No **m** can serve Matt 6:24
tell no **m** Matt 8:4; Mark 8:30; Luke 5:14; 9:21
they saw no **m** Matt 17:8
No **m** hath seen God John 1:18; 1 John 4:12
Behold the **m** John 19:5
what **m** knoweth the things of a **m** 1 Cor 2:11
m is not of the woman 1 Cor 11:8
though our outward **m** perish 2 Cor 4:16
in fashion as a **m** Phil 2:8
the **m** Christ Jesus 1 Tim 2:5

MANAEN ma-na´-en
Gr. for MENAHEM Acts 13:1

MANAHATH ma-na´-hath
rest Gen 36:23

MANAHETHITES ma-na´-heth-ites
inhabitants of Manahath (?) 1 Chr 2:52

MANASSEH ma-nas´-ay
one who causes to forget Gen 41:51

MANASSES ma-nas´-es
Gr. for MANASSEH Matt 1:10

MANASSITES ma-nas´-ites
members of the tribe of Manasseh Deut 4:43

MANIFEST
which shall not be **m** Mark 4:22
and **m** forth his glory John 2:11
how is it thou wilt **m** thyself John 14:22
make **m** the counsels of the hearts 1 Cor 4:5
m the savour of his knowledge 2 Cor 2:14
the works of the flesh are **m** Gal 5:19
God was **m** in the flesh 1 Tim 3:16
good works of some are **m** beforehand 1 Tim 5:25
creature that is not **m** Heb 4:13
the life was **m** 1 John 1:2
he was **m** to take away our sins 1 John 3:5
In this was **m** the love of God 1 John 4:9

MANIFOLD
how **m** are thy works Ps 104:24
the **m** wisdom of God Eph 3:10
through **m** temptations 1 Pet 1:6
stewards of the **m** grace of God 1 Pet 4:10

MANNER
is this the **m** of man? 2 Sam 7:19
all **m** of store Ps 144:13
shall the lambs feed after their **m** Is 5:17
what **m** of man is this Matt 8:27; Mark 4:41; Luke 8:25
all **m** of sin and blasphemy shall be forgiven Matt 12:31
My **m** of life from my youth Acts 26:4
evil communications corrupt good **m** 1 Cor 15:33
as the **m** of some is Heb 10:25
forgetteth what **m** of man James 1:24
holy in all **m** of conversation 1 Pet 1:15
what **m** of persons ought ye to be 2 Pet 3:11

MANOAH ma-no´-ah
rest Judg 13:2

MANTLE
Elijah took his **m** 2 Kgs 2:8
rent his **m** Job 1:20
as with a **m** Ps 109:29

MAOCH ma´-ok
oppressed (?) 1 Sam 27:2

MAON ma´-on
habitation Josh 15:55

MAONITES ma´-on-ites
same as MEUNIM Judg 10:12

MAR
m the corners of thy beard Lev 19:27
that **m** the land 1 Sam 6:5
They **m** my path Job 30:13
visage was so **m** more than any man Is 52:14
the bottles will be **m** Mark 2:22

MARA ma´-rah
sad Ruth 1:20

MARAH ma´-rah
bitter Ex 15:23

MARALAH mar´-al-ah
trembling Josh 19:11

MARANATHA ma´-ran-ah´-thah
our Lord cometh 1 Cor 16:22

MARCUS mar´-kus
a large hammer Col 4:10

MARESHAH ma-resh´-ah
capital Josh 15:44

MARK
a large hammer Acts 12:12

MARK (n)
the LORD set a **m** upon Cain Gen 4:15
I press toward the **m** for the prize Phil 3:14

MARK (v)
m them which walk so Phil 3:17
Hast thou **m** the old way? Job 22:15
M the perfect man Ps 37:37
M ye well her bulwarks Ps 48:13
shouldest **m** iniquities Ps 130:3
thine iniquity is **m** before me Jer 2:22
who hath **m** his word? Jer 23:18

MAROTH mar´-oth
bitterness Mic 1:12

MARROW
bones are moistened with **m** Job 21:24
satisfied as with **m** and fatness Ps 63:5
m to thy bones Prov 3:8
and of the joints and **m** Heb 4:12

MARS' HILL
Eng. for AREOPAGUS Acts 17:22

MARSENA mar´-se-na
bitterness (?) Esth 1:14

MARTHA mar´-thah
lady Luke 10:38

MARVEL
he **m** Matt 8:10; Mark 6:6; Luke 7:9
all men did **m** Mark 5:20
m not John 3:7; 5:28; 1 John 3:13

MARVELLOUS
m things without number Job 5:9
m lovingkindness Ps 17:7
m in our eyes Ps 118:23; Matt 21:42; Mark 12:11
herein is a **m** thing John 9:30
into his **m** light 1 Pet 2:9

MARY ma´-ry
Gr. for MIRIAM Matt 1:16

MASH mash
same as MESHECH Gen 10:23

MASHAL ma´-shal
entreaty (?) 1 Chr 6:74

MASREKAH mas-rek´-ah
vineyard Gen 36:36

MASSA mas´-ah
burden Gen 25:14

MASSAH mas´-ah
temptation Ex 17:7

MASTER
sound of his **m** feet behind him 2 Kgs 6:32
if I be a **m**, where is my fear? Mal 1:6
the **m** and the scholar Mal 2:12
no man can serve two **m** Matt 6:24; Luke 16:13
disciple is not above his **m** Matt 10:24; Luke 6:40
for the disciple that he be as his **m** Matt 10:25
Doth not your **m** pay tribute? Matt 17:24
one is your **M**, even Christ Matt 23:8,10
M, is it I? Matt 26:25
why troublest thou the **M** Mark 5:35
M, it is good for us to be here Mark 9:5; Luke 9:33
M, what shall I do Mark 10:17; Luke 10:25
once the **m** of the house is risen Luke 13:25
Art thou a **m** of Israel John 3:10
The **m** is come, and calleth John 11:28
Ye call me **m**, and ye say well John 13:13
to his own **m** he standeth or falleth Rom 14:4
m according to the flesh Eph 6:5; Col 3:22
m, do the same things unto them Eph 6:9
ye also have a **M** in heaven Col 4:1
count their own **m** worthy of honour 1 Tim 6:1
that have believing **m** 1 Tim 6:2
be not many **m** James 3:1
Servants, be subject to your **m** 1 Pet 2:18

MASTERY
them that shout for **m** Ex 32:18
striveth for the **m** is temperate 1 Cor 9:25; 2 Tim 2:5

MATHUSALA ma-thoo´-sa-lah
Gr. for METHUSELAH Luke 3:37

MATRED ma´-tred
pushing forward Gen 36:39

MATRI ma´-tri
rainy 1 Sam 10:21

MATTAN mat´-an
a gift 2 Kgs 11:18

MATTANAH mat´-an-ah
same as MATTAN Num 21:18

MATTANIAH mat-an-i´-ah
gift of Jehovah 2 Kgs 24:17

MATTATHA mat´-ath-ah
Gr. for MATTANIAH Luke 3:31

MATTATHAH mat´-ath-ah
same as MATTANIAH Ezra 10:33

MATTATHIAS mat´-ath-i´-as
Gr. for MATTATHAH Luke 3:26

MATTENAI mat´-en-a´-i
liberal Ezra 10:33

MATTER
Arise, for this **m** belongeth unto thee Ezra 10:4
the root of the **m** is found in me Job 19:28
I am full of **m** Job 32:18
My heart is inditing a good **m** Ps 45:1
handleth a **m** wisely Prov 16:20
answereth a **m** before he heareth it Prov 18:13
that which hath wings shall tell the **m** Eccl 10:20
conclusion of the whole **m** Eccl 12:13
the weightier **m** Matt 23:23
If it were a **m** of wrong Acts 18:14
to judge the smallest **m** 1 Cor 6:2
how great a **m** a little fire kindleth! James 3:5

MATTHAN mat´-than
gift Matt 1:15

MATTHAT mat´-that
same as MATTHAN Luke 3:24

MATTHEW mat´-thew
Eng. for MATTATHIAH Matt 9:9

MATTHIAS math-i´-as
Gr. for MATTATHAH Acts 1:23

MATTITHIAH mat-ith-i´-ah
another form of MATTATHAH 1 Chr 9:31

MAZZAROTH maz´-ar-oth
the signs of the zodiac Job 38:32

ME-JARKON me´-jar´-kon
waters of yellowness Josh 19:46

MEAH me´-ah
a hundred Neh 3:1

MEAN (adj)
not stand before **m** men Prov 22:29
the **m** man Is 2:9; 5:15; 31:8
citizen of no **m** city Acts 21:39

MEAN (v)
What **m** ye by this Ex 12:26; Josh 4:6
What **m** the testimonies? Deut 6:20
Know ye not what these things **m** Ezek 17:12
the rising from the dead should **m** Mark 9:10

MEANS
by no **m** clear the guilty Ex 34:7; Num 14:18
can by any **m** redeem Ps 49:7
this hath been by your **m** Mal 1:9
shalt by no **m** come out Matt 5:26
nothing shall by any **m** hurt you Luke 10:19
by what **m** he now seeth John 9:21
lest by any **m** this liberty 1 Cor 8:9
that I might by all **m** save some 1 Cor 9:22
by any I might **m** attain Phil 3:11
give you peace always by all **m** 2 Thess 3:16

MEARAH me´-ar-ah
cave Josh 13:4

MEASURE (n)
divers **m** Deut 25:14; Prov 20:10
the **m** is longer than the earth Job 11:9
he weigheth the waters by **m** Job 28:25
the **m** of my days Ps 39:4
the dust of the earth in a **m** Is 40:12
correct thee in **m** Jer 30:11; 46:28
thou shalt drink also water by **m** Ezek 4:11
with what **m** ye mete Matt 7:2; Mark 4:24
three **m** of meal Matt 13:33; Luke 13:21
Fill ye up then the **m** of your fathers Matt 23:32
good **m**, pressed down Luke 6:38
giveth not the Spirit by **m** John 3:34
to every man the **m** of faith Rom 12:3
exalted above **m** 2 Cor 12:7
the **m** of the gift of Christ Eph 4:7
the **m** of the stature Eph 4:13
in the **m** of every part Eph 4:16
A **m** of wheat for a penny Rev 6:6
according to the **m** of a man Rev 21:17

MEASURE (v)
Who hath **m** the waters Is 40:12
Will I **m** former work into bosom Is 65:7
If heaven above can be **m** Jer 31:37
which cannot be **m** Hos 1:10
m themselves by themselves 2 Cor 10:12

MEAT
make me savoury **m** Gen 27:4
went in the strength of that **m** 1 Kgs 19:8
wander up and down for **m** Ps 59:15
they gave me also gall for my **m** Ps 69:21
he sent them **m** to the full Ps 78:25
m in due season Ps 145:15
dainties, for they are deceitful **m** Prov 23:3
a fool when filled with **m** Prov 30:22
giveth **m** to her household Prov 31:15
dust shall be the serpent's **m** Is 65:25
thy **m** which thou shalt eat Ezek 4:10
fruit thereof shall be for **m** Ezek 47:12
with the portion of the king's **m** Dan 1:8
their **m** is plenteous Hab 1:16
fields shall yield no **m** Hab 3:17
that there may be **m** Mal 3:10
life more than **m** Matt 6:25
workman is worthy of his **m** Matt 10:10
of the broken **m** Matt 15:37; Mark 8:8
ye gave me **m** Matt 25:35
he that hath **m** let him do likewise Luke 3:11
Have ye here any **m** Luke 24:41
I have **m** to eat John 4:32
m is to do the will of him that sent me John 4:34
labour not for the **m** that perisheth John 6:27
did eat **m** with gladness Acts 2:46
abstain from **m** offered to idols Acts 15:29
Destroy not him with thy **m** Rom 14:15
kingdom of God is not **m** and drink Rom 14:17
For **m** destroy not the work of God Rom 14:20
M for the belly 1 Cor 6:13
if **m** make my brother to offend 1 Cor 8:13
the same spiritual **m** 1 Cor 10:3
to abstain from **m** 1 Tim 4:3
not of strong **m** Heb 5:12,14
who for one morsel of **m** Heb 12:16

MEBUNNAI me-boon´-a´-i
built (?) 2 Sam 23:27

MECHERATHITE me-ker´-ath-ite
inhabitant of Mecherah (?) 1 Chr 11:36

MEDAD me´-dad
affectionate (?) Num 11:26

MEDAN me´-dan
contention Gen 25:2

MEDDLE
Why **m** to thy hurt 2 Kgs 14:10; 2 Chr 25:19
every fool will be **m** Prov 20:3
m not with him that flattereth Prov 20:19
m with strife Prov 26:17

MEDEBA me´-deb-ah
flowing water (?) Num 21:30

MEDES medes
inhabitants of Media 2 Kgs 17:6

MEDIA me´-di-ah
Gr. for MAADAI Esth 1:3

MEDITATE
Isaac went out to **m** Gen 24:63
thou shalt **m** therein Josh 1:8
in his law doth he **m** Ps 1:2
m on thee in the night watches Ps 63:6
I will **m** also of all thy works Ps 77:12; 143:5
Thine heart shall **m** terror Is 33:18
not to **m** before Luke 21:14
M upon these things 1 Tim 4:15

MEEK (adj)
Moses was very **m** Num 12:3
a **m** and quiet spirit 1 Pet 3:4

MEEK (n)
The **m** shall eat and be satisfied Ps 22:26
The **m** will he guide Ps 25:9
the **m** shall inherit the earth Ps 37:11
will beautify the **m** Ps 149:4
the **m** also shall increase their joy Is 29:19
good tidings unto the **m** Is 61:1
Blessed are the **m** Matt 5:5
for I am **m** Matt 11:29

MEEKNESS
by the **m** and gentleness of Christ 2 Cor 10:1
restore such a one in the spirit of **m** Gal 6:1
godliness, faith, love, patience, **m** 1 Tim 6:11
In **m** instructing 2 Tim 2:25
shewing all **m** unto all men Titus 3:2
give reason of hope in you with **m** 1 Pet 3:15

MEET (adj)
withholdeth more than is **m** Prov 11:24
not **m** to take the children's bread Matt 15:26
not **m** to be called an apostle 1 Cor 15:9

MEET (v)
to **m** the bridegroom Matt 25:1
to **m** the Lord in the air 1 Thess 4:17

MEGIDDO me-gid´-o
place of troops Josh 12:21

MEGIDDON me-gid´-on
same as MEGIDDO Zech 12:11

MEHETABEEL me-het´-ab-e´-el
masc. of MEHETABEL Neh 6:10

MEHETABEL me-het´-ab-el
God makes happy Gen 36:39

MEHIDA me-hi´-dah
conjunction, union Ezra 2:52

MEHIR me´-hir
price 1 Chr 4:11

MEHOLATHITE me-ho´-lath-ite
native of Meholah 1 Sam 18:19

MEHUJAEL me-hoo´-ja-el
struck by God Gen 4:18

MEHUMAN me´-hoom-an
faithful (?) Esth 1:10

MEHUNIM me-hoon´-im
same as MEUNIM Ezra 2:50

MEHUNIMS me-hoon´-ims
same as MEUNIM 2 Chr 26:7

MEJARKON me-jar´-kon
yellow waters Josh 19:46

MEKONAH me-ko´-nah
a base Neh 11:28

MELATIAH mel´-at-i´-ah
whom Jehovah freed Neh 3:7

MELCHI melk´-i
Gr. for MELCHIAH Luke 3:24

MELCHI-SHUA melk´-i-shoo´-ah
same as MALCHI-SHUA 1 Sam 14:49

MELCHIAH melk-i´-ah
Jehovah's king Jer 21:1

MELCHISEDEC Melk-is´-ed-ec
same as MELCHIZEDEK Heb 5:6

MELCHIZEDEK melk-iz´-ed-ek
king of righteousness Gen 14:18

MELEA mel´-e-ah
fullness (?) Luke 3:31

MELECH mel´-ech
king 1 Chr 8:35

MELICU mel´-i-koo
same as MALLUCH Neh 12:14

MELITA mel´-ee-tah
an island, now called Malta Acts 28:1

MELODY
make sweet **m** Is 23:16
the voice of **m** Is 51:3
hear the **m** of the viols Amos 5:23
singing and making **m** in your heart Eph 5:19

MELT
the earth **m** Ps 46:6
the hills **m** Ps 97:5
their soul is **m** Ps 107:26
He sendeth out his word, and **m** them Ps 147:18

every man's heart shall **m** Is 13:7
As when the **m** fire burneth Is 64:2

MELZAR mel´-zar
steward Dan 1:11

MEMBER
all my **m** were written Ps 139:16
Neither yield ye your **m** Rom 6:13,19
as we have many **m** Rom 12:4
bodies are the **m** of Christ 1 Cor 6:15
the tongue is a little **m** James 3:5
lusts that war in your **m** James 4:1

MEMORY
cut off the **m** of them Ps 109:15
utter the **m** of thy great goodness Ps 145:7
m of the just is blessed Prov 10:7
the **m** of them is forgotten Eccl 9:5

MEMPHIS mem´-fis
the place of good Hos 9:6

MEMUCAN me-mu´-can
certain, true (?) Esth 1:14

MEN
quit yourselves like **m** 1 Sam 4:9; 1 Cor 16:13
dwell with **m** 2 Chr 6:18
know themselves to be but **m** Ps 9:20
But ye shall die like **m** Ps 82:7
the strong **m** shall bow themselves Eccl 12:3
the Egyptians are **m**, and not God Is 31:3
shew yourselves **m** Is 46:8
do I now persuade **m** Gal 1:10
not as pleasing **m**, but God 1 Thess 2:4

MENAHEM me-na´-hem
comforter 2 Kgs 15:14

MENAN me´-nan
numbered Luke 3:31

MEND
iron and brass to **m** the house 2 Chr 24:12; 34:10
m their nets Matt 4:21; Mark 1:19

MENE me´-ne
numbered Dan 5:25

MENTION
make **m** of me to Pharoah Gen 40:14
I will make **m** of thy righteousness Ps 71:16
make **m** that his name is exalted Is 12:4
m the lovingkindnesses of the Lord Is 63:7
making **m** of you Rom 1:9; Eph 1:16; 1 Thess 1:2

MEONENIM me-o´-nen-im
augurs Judg 9:37

MEONOTHAI me-o´-noth-a´-i
my habitations 1 Chr 4:14

MEPHAATH me-fa´-ath
beauty Josh 13:18

MEPHIBOSHETH mef-ib´-osh-eth
destroying shame 2 Sam 4:4

MERAB me´-rab
increase 1 Sam 14:49

MERAIAH me-rai´-ah
rebellion Neh 12:12

MERAIOTH me-rai´-oth
rebellions 1 Chr 6:6

MERARI mer´-a-ri
bitter Gen 46:11

MERATHAIM mer´-ath-a´-im
rebellions Jer 50:21

MERCHANDISE
m of it is better than the **m** of silver Prov 3:14
her **m** and her hire shall be holiness Is 23:18
one to his farm, another to his **m** Matt 22:5

my father's house a house of **m** John 2:16
make **m** of you 2 Pet 2:3

MERCHANT
current money with the **m** Gen 23:16
whose **m** are princes Is 23:8
even thy **m** Is 47:15
the **m** of the earth Rev 18:3,11
thy **m** were great men of the earth Rev 18:23

MERCIFUL
ever **m**, and lendeth Ps 37:26
God be **m** unto us, and bless us Ps 67:1
m man doeth good to his own soul Prov 11:17
m men are taken away Is 57:1
for I am **m** Jer 3:12
Be ye therefore **m**, as your Father also is **m** Luke 6:36
God be **m** to me a sinner Luke 18:13
a **m** and faithful high priest Heb 2:17

MERCURIUS mer-cu´-ri-us
a pagan god of Rome (Gr. HERMES) Acts 14:12

MERCY
not worthy of the least of all the **m** Gen 32:10
will shew **m** on whom I will shew **m** Ex 33:19
Keeping **m** for thousands Ex 34:7
of great **m** Num 14:18; Ps 145:8
his **m** endureth for ever 1 Chr 16:34,41; 2 Chr 5:13; 7:3,6; Ezra 3:11; Ps 106:1; 107:1; 118:1; 136:1; Jer 33:11
Surely goodness and **m** shall follow Ps 23:6
according to thy **m** remember thou me Ps 25:7
Let thy **m**, O LORD, be upon us Ps 33:22
I trust in the **m** of God Ps 52:8
The God of my **m** Ps 59:10
nor his **m** from me Ps 66:20
Is his **m** clean gone for ever? Ps 77:8
M and truth are met together Ps 85:10
M shall be built up for ever Ps 89:2
satisfy us early with thy **m** Ps 90:14
I will sing of **m** Ps 101:1
thy **m** is great above the heavens Ps 108:4
for thy **m**, and for thy truth's sake Ps 115:1
The earth, O LORD, is full of thy **m** Ps 119:64
with the Lord there is **m** Ps 130:7
Let not **m** and truth forsake thee Prov 3:3
he that hath **m** on the poor Prov 14:21
m and truth Prov 16:6; 20:28
with great **m** will I gather thee Is 54:7
they are cruel, and have no **m** Jer 6:23
It is of the Lord's **m** Lam 3:22
there is no truth, nor **m** in the land Hos 4:1
I desired **m**, and not sacrifice Hos 6:6
reap in **m** Hos 10:12
in thee the fatherless find **m** Hos 14:3
but to do justly, and to love **m** Mic 6:8
he delighteth in **m** Mic 7:18
in wrath remember **m** Hab 3:2
they shall obtain **m** Matt 5:7
Son of David, have **m** on me Matt 9:27; Mark 10:47; Luke 18:38,39
He that shewed **m** Luke 10:37
m on whom I will have **m** Rom 9:15
of God that sheweth **m** Rom 9:16
by the **m** of God Rom 12:1
he that sheweth **m**, with cheerfulness Rom 12:8
the Father of **m** 2 Cor 1:3
God, who is rich in **m** Eph 2:4
I obtained **m** 1 Tim 1:13,16
that he may find **m** 2 Tim 1:18
obtain **m**, and find grace Heb 4:16
without **m**, that hath shown no **m** James 2:13
according to his abundant **m** 1 Pet 1:3

MERED me´-red
rebellion 1 Chr 4:17

MEREMOTH me´-rem-oth
elevations Ezra 8:33

MERES me´-res
worthy (?) Esth 1:14

MERIB-BAAL me´-ri-ba´-al
contender against Baal (?) 1 Chr 8:34

MERIBAH me´-reb-ah
water of strife Ex 17:7

MERODACH me´-ro-dak
Hebrew for proper name of BEL
contention, death Jer 50:2

MERODACH-BALADAN me´-ro-dak-bal´-a-dan
Merodach gives a son Is 39:1

MEROM me´-rom
a high place Josh 11:5

MERONOTHITE me-ro´-noth-ite
inhabitant of Meronoth 1 Chr 27:30

MEROZ me´-roz
refuge (?) Judg 5:23

MERRY
were **m** with him Gen 43:34
their hearts were **m** Judg 16:25
m heart maketh a cheerful countenance Prov 15:13
m heart hath a continual feast Prov 15:15
m heart doeth good like a medicine Prov 17:22
than to eat and to drink and be **m** Eccl 8:15
drink thy wine with a **m** heart Eccl 9:7
wine maketh **m** Eccl 10:19
Is any **m** James 5:13

MESECH me´-sech
same as MESHECH Ps 120:5

MESHA me´-shah
deliverance 2 Kgs 3:4

MESHACH me´-shak
who is what (the god) Aku is? Dan 1:7

MESHECH me´-shek
tall (?) Gen 10:2

MESHELEMIAH me-shel´-em-i´-ah
Jehovah repays 1 Chr 9:21

MESHEZABEEL me-shez´-a-be´-el
God delivers Neh 3:4

MESHILLEMITH me-shil´-em-ith
recompense 1 Chr 9:12

MESHILLEMOTH me-shil´-em-oth
retribution 2 Chr 28:12

MESHOBAB me-sho´-bab
brought back 1 Chr 4:34

MESHULLAM me-shool´-am
friend 2 Kgs 22:3

MESHULLEMETH me-shool´-em-eth
fem. of MESHULLAM 2 Kgs 21:19

MESOBAITE me-so´-ba-ite
inhabitant of Mesoba (?) 1 Chr 11:47

MESOPOTAMIA mes´-o-pot-a´-mi-ah
amidst the rivers Gen 24:10

MESSENGER
be a **m** with him Job 33:23
so is a faithful **m** to them Prov 25:13
as my **m** that I sent Is 42:19

MESSIAH mes-i´-ah
anointed Dan 9:25

MESSIAS mes-i´-as
Gr. for MESSIAH John 1:41

METE
and **m** out heaven with the span Is 40:12

with what measure ye **m** Matt 7:2; Mark 4:24
the same measure that ye **m** withal Luke 6:38

METHEG-AMMAH me´-theg-am´-ah
bridle of Ammah 2 Sam 8:1

METHUSAEL me-thoo´-sa-el
man of God Gen 4:18

METHUSELAH me-thoo´-se-lah
man of the dart (?) Gen 5:21

MEUNIM me-oon´-im
inhabitants of Maon (?) Neh 7:52

MEZAHAB me´-za-hab
water of gold Gen 36:39

MIAMIN mi´-ya-min
a form of MINIAMIN Ezra 10:25

MIBHAR mib´-har
choicest 1 Chr 11:38

MIBSAM mib´-sam
sweet odor Gen 25:13

MIBZAR mib´-zar
a fortress Gen 36:42

MICAH mi´-kah
a form of MICHAIAH Judg 17:1

MICAIAH mi-kai´-ah
a form of MICHAIAH 1 Kgs 22:8

MICHA mi´-kah
a form of MICHAIAH 2 Sam 9:12

MICHAEL mi´-ka-el
Who (is) like unto God? Dan 10:13

MICHAH mi´-kah
a form of MICHAIAH 1 Chr 24:24

MICHAIAH mi-kai´-ah
Who (is) like unto Jehovah? Neh 12:35

MICHAL mi´-kal
brook 1 Sam 14:49

MICHMAS mik´-mas
form of MICHMASH Ezra 2:27

MICHMASH mik´-mash
treasured 1 Sam 13:2

MICHMETHAH mik´-meth-ah
hiding place (?) Josh 16:6

MICHRI mik´-ri
precious (?) 1 Chr 9:8

MIDDIN mid´-in
extensions Josh 15:61

MIDDLE
wheel in the **m** of a wheel Ezek 1:16
hath broken down the **m** wall Eph 2:14

MIDIAN mid´-yan
strife Gen 25:2

MIDIANITES mid´-yan-ites
people of Midian Gen 37:28

MIDST
in the **m** of my days Ps 102:24
lieth down in **m** of the sea Prov 23:34
in the **m** of the week Dan 9:27
in the **m** of them Matt 18:2
there am I in the **m** Matt 18:20
stood in the **m** Luke 24:36
in the **m** of a crooked and perverse nation Phil 2:15
in the **m** of the paradise of God Rev 2:7
in the **m** of the throne Rev 4:6; 5:6; 7:17

MIGDAL-EL mig´-dal-el
tower of God Josh 19:38

MIGDAL-GAD mig´-dal-gad
tower of Gad Josh 15:37

MIGDOL mig´-dol
fortress, tower Ex 14:2

MIGHT
with all thy **m** Deut 6:5
the **m** of mine hand hath gotten Deut 8:17
David danced before the LORD with all his **m** 2 Sam 6:14
do it with thy **m** Eccl 9:10
to them that have no **m** Is 40:29
mighty man glory in his **m** Jer 9:23
their **m** hath failed Jer 51:30
not by **m**, nor by power Zech 4:6
strengthened with **m** Eph 3:16

MIGHTILY
cry **m** unto God Jon 3:8
he **m** convinced the Jews Acts 18:28
m grew the word of God Acts 19:20
which worketh in me **m** Col 1:29

MIGHTY
He was a **m** hunter Gen 10:9
to the help of the Lord against the **m** Judg 5:23
how are the **m** fallen 2 Sam 1:19,25
wise in heart and **m** in strength Job 9:4
m in battle Ps 24:8
thou hast a **m** arm Ps 89:13
help upon one that is **m** Ps 89:19
the **m** waves of the sea Ps 93:4
the **M** One of Israel Is 1:24; 30:29
m to drink wine Is 5:22
m to save Is 63:1
m in work Jer 32:19
neither shall the **m** deliver himself Amos 2:14
m works Matt 11:20; 13:54; 14:2; Mark 6:2
the **m** power of God Luke 9:43
prophet **m** in deed and word Luke 24:19
m in the scriptures Acts 18:24
not many **m** 1 Cor 1:26
m through God 2 Cor 10:4
the working of his **m** power Eph 1:19

MIGRON mig´-ron
a precipice Is 10:28

MIJAMIN mi´-ja-min
same as MINIAMIN 1 Chr 24:9

MIKLOTH mik´-loth
staves, lots 1 Chr 8:32

MIKNEIAH mik-ni´-ah
possession of Jehovah 1 Chr 15:18

MILALAI mil-al-a´-i
eloquent (?) Neh 12:36

MILCAH mil´-kah
counsel (?) Gen 11:29

MILCOM mil´-kom
same as MOLOCH 1 Kgs 11:5

MILETUM mi-le´-tum
same as MILETUS 2 Tim 4:20

MILETUS mi-le´-tus
red Acts 20:15

MILK
teeth white with **m** Gen 49:12
churning of **m** Prov 30:33
buy wine and **m** Is 55:1
whiter than **m** Lam 4:7
thy fruit, and they shall drink thy **m** Ezek 25:4
such as have need of **m** Heb 5:12
the sincere **m** of the word 1 Pet 2:2

MILLO mil´-o
a mound Judg 9:6

MIND (n)
the people had a **m** to work Neh 4:6
is in one **m**, and who can turn him? Job 23:13
Should it be according to thy **m** Job 34:33
as a dead man out of **m** Ps 31:12
A fool uttereth all his **m** Prov 29:11
whose **m** is stayed on thee Is 26:3
in his right **m** Mark 5:15; Luke 8:35
neither be ye of doubtful **m** Luke 12:29
the carnal **m** is enmity against God Rom 8:7
Be of the same **m** Rom 12:16
fully persuaded in his own **m** Rom 14:5
if there be first a willing **m** 2 Cor 8:12
of one **m** 2 Cor 13:11; Phil 2:2
in lowliness of **m** Phil 2:3
Let this **m** be in you Phil 2:5
shall keep your hearts and **m** Phil 4:7
men of corrupt **m** 1 Tim 6:5; 2 Tim 3:8
of a sound **m** 2 Tim 1:7
Put them in **m** to be subject Titus 3:1
the loins of your **m** 1 Pet 1:13
stir up your pure **m** 2 Pet 3:1

MIND (v)
the flesh do **m** the things of the flesh Rom 8:5
let us **m** the same thing Phil 3:16
who **m** earthly things Phil 3:19

MINDFUL
that thou art **m** of him Ps 8:4
ever be **m** of his covenant Ps 111:5
hast not been **m** of the Rock Is 17:10
ye be **m** of the words 2 Pet 3:2

MINGLE
to **m** strong drink Is 5:22
vinegar to drink **m** with gall Matt 27:34
Pilate had **m** with their sacrifices Luke 13:1

MINIAMIN min´-ya-min
on the right hand 2 Chr 31:15

MINISTER (n)
ye **m** of his Ps 103:21
his **m** a flaming fire Ps 104:4; Heb 1:7
men shall call you The **m** of God Is 61:6
the Lord's **m** mourn Joel 1:9
let him be your **m** Matt 20:26
he is the **m** of God to thee Rom 13:4
able **m** of the new testament 2 Cor 3:6
is therefore Christ the **m** of sin Gal 2:17
Whereof I was made a **m** Eph 3:7
a faithful **m** Eph 6:21; Col 1:7; 4:7
a good **m** 1 Tim 4:6

MINISTER (v)
the child did **m** unto the Lord 1 Sam 2:11
to **m** unto him for ever 1 Chr 15:2
thousand thousands **m** unto him Dan 7:10
not to be **m** unto, but to **m** Matt 20:28; Mark 10:45
angels **m** to him Mark 1:13
which **m** unto him of their substance Luke 8:3
these hands have **m** Acts 20:34

MINISTRATION
days of his **m** were accomplished Luke 1:23
were neglected in the daily **m** Acts 6:1
if the **m** of death 2 Cor 3:7
of this **m** they glorify God 2 Cor 9:13

MINISTRY
to the **m** of the word Acts 6:4
seeing we have this **m** 2 Cor 4:1
the **m** of reconciliation 2 Cor 5:18
that the **m** be not blamed 2 Cor 6:3
for the work of the **m** Eph 4:12
take heed to the **m** Col 4:17
make full proof of thy **m** 2 Tim 4:5

MINNI min´-i
Armenia Jer 51:27

MINNITH min´-ith
allotment Judg 11:33

MIPHKAD mif-kad
place of meeting Neh 3:31

MIRACLE
where be all his **m** Judg 6:13
which shall do a **m** in my name Mark 9:39
hoped to have seen some **m** Luke 23:8
This beginning of **m** John 2:11
This is again the second **m** John 4:54
said, John did no **m** John 10:41
God among you by **m** and signs Acts 2:22
to another, the working of **m** 1 Cor 12:10

MIRIAM mir´-yam
rebellion (?) Ex 15:20

MIRMA mir´-mah
fraud 1 Chr 8:10

MIRTH
required of us **m** Ps 137:3
end of that **m** is heaviness Prov 14:13
I will prove thee with **m** Eccl 2:1
in the house of **m** Eccl 7:4
I commended **m** Eccl 8:15

MIRY
out of the **m** clay Ps 40:2
the **m** places thereof Ezek 47:11
iron mixed with **m** clay Dan 2:41

MISCHIEF
conceive **m** Job 15:35; Ps 7:14; Is 59:4
m is in their hearts Ps 28:3
frameth **m** by a law Ps 94:20
It is as sport to a fool to do **m** Prov 10:23
he that seeketh **m** Prov 11:27
lips talk of **m** Prov 24:2
M shall come upon **m** Ezek 7:26
O full of all subtilty and all **m** Acts 13:10

MISERABLE
m comforters are ye all Job 16:2
of all men most **m** 1 Cor 15:19
thou art wretched, and **m**, and poor Rev 3:17

MISERY
drink, and remember his **m** no more Prov 31:7
the **m** of man is great upon him Eccl 8:6
days of her affliction and of her **m** Lam 1:7
howl for your **m** that shall come James 5:1

MISGAB mis´-gab
height Jer 48:1

MISHAEL mish´-a-el
Who is what God is? Ex 6:22

MISHAL mi´-shal
prayer Josh 21:30

MISHAM mi´-sham
cleansing 1 Chr 8:12

MISHEAL mi´-she-al
same as MISHAL Josh 19:26

MISHMA mish´-mah
report Gen 25:14

MISHMANNAH mish-man´-ah
fatness 1 Chr 12:10

MISHRAITES mish´-rah-ites
spread out (?) 1 Chr 2:53

MISPERETH mis-per´-eth
number Neh 7:7

MISREPHOTH-MAIM mis´-re-foth-ma´-im
burning of waters Josh 11:8

MITHCAH mith´-kah
place of sweetness Num 33:28

MITHNITE mith´-nite
gifts 1 Chr 11:43

MITHREDATH mith´-re-dath
given by Mithra Ezra 1:8

MITYLENE mit-i-le´-ne
capital of the island of Lesbos Acts 20:14

MIXED
thy wine **m** with water Is 1:22
not being **m** with faith Heb 4:2

MIZAR mi´-zar
smallness Ps 42:6

MIZPAH miz´-pah
a look out Gen 31:49

MIZPAR miz´-par
number Ezra 2:2

MIZPEH miz´-peh
watch-tower Josh 11:3

MIZRAIM miz-ra´-im
fortresses Gen 10:6

MIZZAH miz´-zah
fear Gen 36:13

MNASON na´-son
reminding (?) Acts 21:16

MOAB mo´-ab
progeny of a father Gen 19:37

MOABITES mo´-ab-ites
people of Moab Deut 2:9

MOABITESS mo´-ab-ite-ess
a lady of Moab Ruth 4:5

MOADIAH mo´-ad-i´-ah
festival of Jehovah Neh 12:17

MOCK
he seemed as one that **m** Gen 19:14
thou hast **m** me Num 22:29; Judg 16:10,13,15
Elijah **m** them 1 Kgs 18:27
they **m** the messengers of God 2 Chr 36:16
I will **m** when your fear cometh Prov 1:26
Whoso **m** the poor Prov 17:5
The eye that **m** at his father Prov 30:17
God is not **m** Gal 6:7

MOCKER
hypocritical **m** in feasts Ps 35:16
Wine is a **m** Prov 20:1
be ye not **m** Is 28:22
m in the last time Jude 1:18

MODERATION
Let your **m** be known Phil 4:5

MOISTURE
my **m** is turned into the drought Ps 32:4
because it lacked **m** Luke 8:6

MOLADAH mo´-lad-ah
birth Josh 15:26

MOULDY
their provision was dry and **m** Josh 9:5
behold, it is dry, and it is **m** Josh 9:12

MOLECH mo´-lek
Eng. for MOLOCH Lev 18:21

MOLID mo´-lid
begetter 1 Chr 2:29

MOLLIFIED
neither **m** with ointment Is 1:6

MOLOCH mo´-lok
king Amos 5:26

MOMENT
consume them in a **m** Num 16:21,45
try him every **m** Job 7:18
and in a **m** go down Job 21:13
his anger endureth but a **m** Ps 30:5
hide thyself as it were for a little **m** Is 26:20
I will water it every **m** Is 27:3
for a small **m** have I forsaken thee Is 54:7
in a **m** 1 Cor 15:52
affliction, which is but for a **m** 2 Cor 4:17

MONEY
Is it a time to receive **m** 2 Kgs 5:26
m is a defence Eccl 7:12
m answereth all things Eccl 10:19
redeemed without **m** Is 52:3
he that hath no **m** Is 55:1
Wherefore do ye spend **m** Is 55:2
tribute **m** Matt 17:24; 22:19
hid his lord's **m** Matt 25:18
Thy **m** perish with thee Acts 8:20
the love of **m** 1 Tim 6:10

MORASTHITE mo´-rasth-ite
native of Moresheth Jer 26:18

MORDECAI mor´-dek-a´-i
worshiper of Merodach (?) Esth 2:5

MOREH mo´-reh
archer Gen 12:6

MORESHETH-GATH mo-resh´-eth-gath
the possession of Gath Mic 1:14

MORIAH mor-i´-ah
provided by Jehovah Gen 22:2

MORROW
no thought for the **m** Matt 6:34
ye know not what shall be on the **m** James 4:14

MORSEL
have eaten my **m** myself Job 31:17
casteth forth his ice like **m** Ps 147:17
Better is a dry **m** Prov 17:1
who for one **m** of meat sold Heb 12:16

MORTAL
Shall **m** man be more just Job 4:17
your **m** body Rom 6:12; 8:11
this **m** must put on immortality 1 Cor 15:53

MORTER
slime had they for morter Gen 11:3
with untempered **m** Ezek 13:11,22,28

MORTIFY
do **m** the deeds of the body Rom 8:13
M therefore your members Col 3:5

MOSERA mo´-se-rah
bond Deut 10:6

MOSEROTH mo´-se-roth
bonds Num 33:30

MOSES mo´-zes
saved from the water Ex 2:10

MOTE
beholdest thou the **m** Matt 7:3; Luke 6:41

MOTHER
a **m** in Israel Judg 5:7; 2 Sam 20:19
Ahaziah walked in the way of his **m** 1 Kgs 22:52
his **m** was his counseller 2 Chr 22:3
to the worm, Thou art my **m** Job 17:14
a joyful **m** of children Ps 113:9
as one whom his **m** comforteth Is 66:13
As is the **m**, so is her daughter Ezek 16:44
Who is my **m** Matt 12:48; Mark 3:33
the **m** of Jesus John 2:1; Acts 1:14

MOUNT
the **m** of God Ex 18:5
They **m** up to heaven Ps 107:26
m up with wings as eagles Is 40:31

MOURN
into the grave unto **m** Gen 37:35
thou **m** at the last Prov 5:11
to comfort all that **m** Is 61:2
I will turn their **m** into joy Jer 31:13

Blessed are they that **m** Matt 5:4
shall all the tribes of the earth **m** Matt 24:30
you that laugh now for ye shall **m** Luke 6:25

MOURNER
feign thyself to be a **m** 2 Sam 14:2
the **m** go about the streets Eccl 12:5
the bread of **m** Hos 9:4

MOURNFULLY
we have walked **m** before the LORD Mal 3:14

MOUTH
mine own **m** shall condemn me Job 9:20
I will lay my hand upon my **m** Job 40:4
Out of the **m** of babes Ps 8:2; Matt 21:16
I will keep my **m** with a bridle Ps 39:1
My **m** shall speak of wisdom Ps 49:3
words of his **m** were smoother than butter Ps 55:21
open thy **m** wide Ps 81:10
the **m** of the foolish Prov 10:14; 14:3; 15:2
good by the fruit of his **m** Prov 13:2
keepeth his **m** Prov 13:3; 21:23
All the labour of man is for his **m** Eccl 6:7
This people draw near me with their **m** Is 29:13; Matt 15:8
with their **m** they shew much love Ezek 33:31
the law of truth was in his **m** Mal 2:6
the **m** speaketh Matt 12:34
I will open my **m** in parables Matt 13:35
I will give you a **m** and wisdom Luke 21:15
with the **m** confession is made Rom 10:10
Whose **m** must be stopped Titus 1:11
Out of the same **m** proceedeth James 3:10

MOVE
I shall not be **m** Ps 10:6; 16:8
all the city was **m** Matt 21:10; Acts 21:30
waiting for the **m** of the water John 5:3
in him we live, and **m** Acts 17:28
none of these things **m** me Acts 20:24

MOZA mo´-za
fountain 1 Chr 2:46

MOZAH mo´-zah
same as MOZA Josh 18:26

MUCH
he that gathered **m** Ex 16:18
ye take too **m** upon you Num 16:3
for she loved **m** Luke 7:47
unto whomsoever **m** is given Luke 12:48
faithful in **m** Luke 16:10

MULTIPLY
m the nation, and not increased the joy Is 9:3
when ye be **m** Jer 3:16
peace be **m** Dan 4:1; 6:25; 1 Pet 1:2; 2 Pet 1:2
Thou hast **m** thy merchants Nah 3:16

MULTITUDE
a **m** to do evil Ex 23:2
m of years should teach wisdom Job 32:7
in the **m** of thy mercy Ps 5:7; 69:13; 106:7
no king saved by the **m** of a host Ps 33:16
in the **m** of my thoughts Ps 94:19
in **m** of words there wanteth not sin Prov 10:19
in the **m** of counsellers Prov 11:14; 15:22; 24:6
through the **m** of business Eccl 5:3
a **m** of sins James 5:20; 1 Pet 4:8

MUPPIM moop´-im
same as SHEPHUPHAN (?) Gen 46:21

MURMURINGS
he heareth your **m** against the LORD Ex 16:7
heard the **m** of the children of Israel Num 14:27
Do all things without **m** and disputings Phil 2:14

MUSE
While I was **m** the fire burned Ps 39:3
I **m** on the work of thy hands Ps 143:5
all men **m** in their hearts Luke 3:15

MUSHI moo´-shi
withdrawn Ex 6:19

MUTTER
wizards that peep and that **m** Is 8:19
your tongue hath **m** perverseness Is 59:3

MUTUAL
by the **m** faith Rom 1:12

MYRA mi´-rah
balsam Acts 27:5

MYSIA my´-si-ah
a province in NW Asia Minor Acts 16:7

MYSTERY
to know the **m** of the kingdom Matt 13:11
the wisdom of God in a **m** 1 Cor 2:7
I shew you a **m** 1 Cor 15:51
This is a great **m** Eph 5:32

N

NAAM na´-am
pleasantness 1 Chr 4:15

NAAMAH na´-am-ah
pleasant Gen 4:22

NAAMAN na´-am-an
same as NAAM 2 Kgs 5:1

NAAMATHITE na-am´-ath-ite
inhabitant of Naamah Job 2:11

NAAMITES na´-am-ites
descendants of Naaman Num 26:40

NAARAH na´-ar-ah
a girl 1 Chr 4:5

NAARAI na´-ar-a´-i
youthful 1 Chr 11:37

NAARAN na´-ar-an
same as NAARAH 1 Chr 7:28

NAARATH na´-ar-ath
same as NAARAH Josh 16:7

NAASHON na-ash´-on
enchanter Ex 6:23

NAASSON na-as´-on
Gr. for NAASHON Matt 1:4

NABAL na´-bal
foolish 1 Sam 25:3

NABOTH na´-both
fruits (?) 1 Kgs 21:1

NACHON na´-kon
prepared 2 Sam 6:6

NACHOR na´-kor
same as NAHOR Josh 24:2

NADAB na´-dab
liberal Ex 6:23

NAGGE nag´-e
Gr. for NOGAH Luke 3:25

NAHALAL na´-hal-al
a pasture Josh 21:35

NAHALIEL na-hal´-i-el
valley of God Num 21:19

NAHALLAL na´-hal-al
same as NAHALAL Josh 19:15

NAHALOL na´-hal-ol
same as NAHALAL Judg 1:30

NAHAM na´-ham
consolation 1 Chr 4:19

NAHAMANI na´-ham-a´-ni
comforter Neh 7:7

NAHARAI na´-har-a´-i
one who snores 1 Chr 11:39

NAHARI na´-har-i
same as NAHARAI 2 Sam 23:37

NAHASH na´-hash
serpent 1 Sam 11:1

NAHATH na´-hath
descent Gen 36:13

NAHBI nah´-bi
hidden Num 13:14

NAHOR na´-hor
snorting Gen 11:22

NAHSHON nah´-shon
same as NAASHON Num 1:7

NAHUM na´-hoom
comforter Nah 1:1

NAIL
give us a **n** in his holy place Ezra 9:8
fasten him as a **n** in a sure place Is 22:23
put my finger into the print of the **n** John 20:25
n it to his cross Col 2:14

NAIN na´-in
pasture Luke 7:11

NAIOTH nai´-oth
habitations 1 Sam 19:18

NAKED
made them **n** unto their shame Ex 32:25
N came I out of my mother's womb Job 1:21
N, and ye clothed me Matt 25:36
are **n**, and are buffeted 1 Cor 4:11
we shall not be found **n** 2 Cor 5:3
things are **n** and opened unto the eyes Heb 4:13

NAKEDNESS
persecution, or famine, or **n** Rom 8:35
in cold and **n** 2 Cor 11:27
the shame of thy **n** do not appear Rev 3:18

NAME (n)
thou dost ask after my **n** Gen 32:29
this is my **n** for ever Ex 3:15
my **n** is in him Ex 23:21
what wilt thou do to thy great **n** Josh 7:9
in thy **n** we go 2 Chr 14:11
So didst thou get thee a **n** Neh 9:10
he shall have no **n** in the street Job 18:17
the **n** of the God of Jacob defend thee Ps 20:1
n of our God we will set up banners Ps 20:5
I will declare thy **n** Ps 22:22; Heb 2:12
According to thy **n** Ps 48:10
they that love his **n** Ps 69:36
holy and reverend is his **n** Ps 111:9
unto thy **n** give glory Ps 115:1
thy word above all thy **n** Ps 138:2
the **n** of the wicked shall rot Prov 10:7
the **n** of the Lord is a strong tower Prov 18:10
good **n** Prov 22:1; Eccl 7:1
thy **n** is as ointment poured forth Song 1:3
I am the Lord, that is my **n** Is 42:8
it shall be to the Lord for a **n** Is 55:13
an everlasting **n** Is 56:5; 63:12
whose **n** is Holy Is 57:15
called by a new **n** Is 62:2
there is none that calleth on thy **n** Is 64:7
thou art great, and thy **n** is great Jer 10:6
prophesy lies in my **n** Jer 14:14; 23:25
sworn by my great **n** Jer 44:26
walk up and down in his **n** Zech 10:12
one Lord, and his **n** one Zech 14:9
wherein have we despised thy **n** Mal 1:6
unto you that fear my **n** Mal 4:2
Hallowed be thy **n** Matt 6:9; Luke 11:2

for my **n** sake Matt 10:22; 19:29; Mark 13:13; Luke 21:12; John 15:21; Acts 9:16
in his **n** shall the Gentiles trust Matt 12:21
little child in my **n** Matt 18:5
gathered together in my **n** Matt 18:20
many shall come in my **n** Matt 24:5; Mark 13:6; Luke 21:8
what is thy **n** Mark 5:9; Luke 8:30
such children in my **n** Mark 9:37
do a miracle in my **n** Mark 9:39
receive this child in my **n** Luke 9:48
n are written in heaven Luke 10:20
if another shall come in his own **n** John 5:43
ye ask in my **n** John 14:13; 16:26
his **n** through faith in his **n** Acts 3:16
none other **n** under heaven Acts 4:12
that ye should not teach in this **n** Acts 5:28
worthy to suffer shame for his **n** Acts 5:41
every **n** that is named Eph 1:21
a **n** which is above every **n** Phil 2:9
whose **n** are in the book of life Phil 4:3
do all in the **n** of the Lord Jesus Col 3:17
obtained a more excellent **n** Heb 1:4
that worthy **n** James 2:7
holdest fast my **n** Rev 2:13
new **n** written, which no man knoweth Rev 2:17
thou hast a **n** that thou livest Rev 3:1
a few **n** even in Sardis Rev 3:4
the **n** of blasphemy Rev 13:1
Father's **n** written in their foreheads Rev 14:1

NAME (v)
that which hath been is **n** already Eccl 6:10
ye shall be **n** the priests of the LORD Is 61:6
not where Christ was **n** Rom 15:20
every one that **n** the name of Christ 2 Tim 2:19

NAOMI na´-om-i
pleasant Ruth 1:2

NAPHISH na´-fish
cheerful Gen 25:15

NAPHTALI naf´-tal-i
my wrestling Gen 30:8

NARCISSUS nar-sis´-us
benumbing Rom 16:11

NARROW
n than that he can wrap Is 28:20
too **n** by reason of the inhabitants Is 49:19
strait is the gate and **n** is the way Matt 7:14

NATHAN na´-than
gift 2 Sam 7:2

NATHAN-MELECH na´-than-me´-lek
gift of the king 2 Kgs 23:11

NATHANAEL na-than´-a-el
gift of God John 1:45

NATION
by these were the **n** divided Gen 10:32
wilt thou slay also a righteous **n** Gen 20:4
make of thee a greater **n** Num 14:12
one **n** in the earth is like thy people 2 Sam 7:23
driving out **n** from before thy people 1 Chr 17:21
Blessed is the **n** whose God is the LORD Ps 33:12
He hath not dealt so with any **n** Ps 147:20
Righteousness exalteth a **n** Prov 14:34
n shall not lift up sword against **n** Is 2:4; Mic 4:3
a **n** scattered and peeled Is 18:2
that the righteous **n** Is 26:2
come near, ye **n**, to hear Is 34:1
so shall he sprinkle many **n** Is 52:15
O King of **n** Jer 10:7
many **n** shall be joined to the Lord Zech 2:11
strong **n** shall come to seek the Lord Zech 8:22
n shall rise against **n** Matt 24:7; Mark 13:8; Luke 21:10
he loveth our **n** Luke 7:5
distress of **n** Luke 21:25
that the whole **n** perish not John 11:50
devout men, our of every **n** Acts 2:5
in every **n** he that feareth Acts 10:35
crooked and perverse **n** Phil 2:15
tongue, and people, and **n** Rev 5:9

NATIVITY
his **n**, in Ur of the Chaldees Gen 11:28
the land of our **n** Jer 46:16; Ezek 21:30; 23:15

NATURAL
nor his **n** force abated Deut 34:7
without **n** affection Rom 1:31; 2 Tim 3:3
the **n** man receiveth not 1 Cor 2:14

NATURE
Doth not even **n** itself teach 1 Cor 11:14
by **n** the children of wrath Eph 2:3
the **n** of angels Heb 2:16
partakers of the divine **n** 2 Pet 1:4

NOUGHT
it is **n**, saith the buyer Prov 20:14
spent my strength for **n** Is 49:4
ye have sold yourselves for **n** Is 52:3
shut the doors for **n** Mal 1:10
it will come to **n** Acts 5:38

NAUGHTINESS
thy pride, and the **n** of thine heart 1 Sam 17:28
shall be taken in their own **n** Prov 11:6
filthiness and superfluity of **n** James 1:21

NAUGHTY
A **n** person, a wicked man Prov 6:12
giveth ear to a **n** tongue Prov 17:4
the other basket had very **n** figs Jer 24:2

NAUM na´-oom
same as NAHUM Luke 3:25

NAY
communication be, Yea, yea; **N**, **n** Matt 5:37
there should be yea, yea, and **n**, **n** 2 Cor 1:17
word toward you was not yea and **n** 2 Cor 1:18
was not yea and **n** 2 Cor 1:19
your **n**, **n** lest ye fall James 5:12

NAZARENE naz´-ar-een
a native of Nazareth Matt 2:23

NAZARETH naz´-ar-eth
branch Luke 1:26

NAZARITE naz´-ar-ite
one separated Num 6:2

NEAH ne´-ah
of a slope Josh 19:13

NEAPOLIS ne-a´-po-lis
new city Acts 16:11

NEAR
knew not that evil was **n** Judg 20:34
trouble is **n** Ps 22:11
a people **n** unto him Ps 148:14
better is a neighbour that is **n** Prov 27:10
he is **n** that justifieth Is 50:8
call ye upon the Lord while he is **n** Is 55:6
the day of the Lord is **n** Obad 1:15; Zeph 1:14
it is **n**, even at the doors Matt 24:33
ye know that summer is **n** Mark 13:28

NEARIAH ne´-ar-i´-ah
servant of Jehovah 1 Chr 3:22

NEBAI neb-a´-i
fruitful Neh 10:19

NEBAIOTH ne-bai´-oth
high places 1 Chr 1:29

NEBAJOTH ne-ba´-joth
same as NEBAIOTH Gen 25:13

NEBALLAT ne-bal´-lat
a town inhabited by the Benjamites Neh 11:34

NEBAT ne´-bat
aspect 1 Kgs 11:26

NEBO ne´-bo
a lofty place Deut 32:49

NEBUCHADNEZZAR neb´-u-kad-nez´-ar
Nebo protect the crown 2 Kgs 24:1

NEBUCHADREZZAR neb´-u-kad-rez´-ar
same as NEBUCHADNEZZAR Jer 21:2

NEBUSHASBAN neb´-u-shas´-ban
Nebo will save me Jer 39:13

NEBUZAR-ADAN neb´-u-zar´-a-dan
Nebo gives posterity 2 Kgs 25:8

NECESSARY
of his mouth more than my **n** food Job 23:12
no greater burden than these **n** things Acts 15:28
laded us with such things as were **n** Acts 28:10
good works for **n** uses Titus 3:14

NECESSITY
distributing to the **n** of saints Rom 12:13
n is laid upon me 1 Cor 9:16
give, not grudgingly, or of **n** 2 Cor 9:7
benefit should not be as it were of **n** Phile 1:14

NECHO ne´-ko
conqueror (?) 2 Chr 35:20

NECHOH ne´-koh
only as part of Pharaoh–nechoh
same as NECHO 2 Kgs 23:29

NECK
bind them about thy **n** Prov 3:3; 6:21
millstone were hanged about his **n** Matt 18:6; Mark 9:42; Luke 17:2
fell on his **n** Luke 15:20
yoke upon the **n** of the disciples Acts 15:10

NEDABIAH ned´-ab-i´-ah
Jehovah is bountiful (?) 1 Chr 3:18

NEED (n)
he shall have no **n** of spoil Prov 31:11
what things ye have **n** of Matt 6:8
The Lord hath **n** of him Mark 11:3; Luke 19:31,34
as every man had **n** Acts 2:45
I have no **n** of thee 1 Cor 12:21
to abound and to suffer **n** Phil 4:12
God shall supply all your **n** Phil 4:19
grace to help in time of **n** Heb 4:16

NEED (v)
ye shall not **n** to fight 2 Chr 20:17
n not a physician Matt 9:12; Luke 5:31
They **n** not depart Matt 14:16
as many as he **n** Luke 11:8
that **n** not to be ashamed 2 Tim 2:15
ye have **n** that one teach you Heb 5:12
seeth his brother have **n** 1 John 3:17
and have **n** of nothing Rev 3:17
city had no **n** of the sun Rev 21:23

NEEDFUL
But one thing is **n** Luke 10:42
to abide in the flesh is more **n** Phil 1:24
things which are **n** to the body James 2:16

NEEDY
to thy poor, and to thy **n** Deut 15:11
They turn the **n** out of the way Job 24:4
the **n** shall not always be forgotten Ps 9:18
I am poor and **n** Ps 40:17; 70:5; 86:1; 109:22
let the poor and **n** praise thy name Ps 74:21
plead the cause of the poor and **n** Prov 31:9
when the poor and **n** seek water Is 41:17

NEGLECT
he shall **n** to hear them Matt 18:17
their widows were **n** Acts 6:1
N not the gift that is in thee 1 Tim 4:14
if we **n** so great salvation Heb 2:3

NEGLIGENT
My sons, be not now **n** 2 Chr 29:11
n to put you always in remembrance 2 Pet 1:12

NEGO ne'-go
same as NEBO Dan 1:7

NEHELAMITE ne-hel'-am-ite
dreamed Jer 29:24

NEHEMIAH ne'-hem-i'-ah
Jehovah comforts Neh 1:1

NEHUM ne'-hoom
consolation Neh 7:7

NEHUSHTA ne-hoosh'-tah
bronze 2 Kgs 24:8

NEHUSHTAN ne-hoosh'-tan
brazen 2 Kgs 18:4

NEIEL ni'-el
moved by God Josh 19:27

NEIGHBOUR
not unto thy **n**, Go and come again Prov 3:28
the poor is hated even of his own **n** Prov 14:20
his **n** findeth no favour Prov 21:10
envied of his **n** Eccl 4:4
useth his **n** service without wages Jer 22:13
that giveth his **n** drink Hab 2:15
Speak ye every man truth to his **n** Zech 8:16
who is my **n** Luke 10:29
nor thy rich **n** Luke 14:12

NEKEB ne'-keb
cavern Josh 19:33

NEKODA ne'-ko-dah
a herdman Ezra 2:48

NEMUEL nem'-oo-el
same as JEMUEL (?) Num 26:9

NEMUELITES nem-oo'-el-ites
descendants of Nemuel Num 26:12

NEPHEG ne'-feg
sprout Ex 6:21

NEPHISH ne'-fish
same as NAPHISH 1 Chr 5:19

NEPHISHESIM ne-fish'-es-im
same as NEPHUSIM Neh 7:52

NEPHTHALIM nef'-tha-lim
same as NAPHTALI Matt 4:13

NEPHTOAH nef-to'-ah
opened Josh 15:9

NEPHUSIM ne-foos'-im
expansions Ezra 2:50

NEPTHALIM nep'-tha-lim
same as NAPHTALI Rev 7:6

NER ner
light 1 Sam 14:50

NEREUS ne'-roos
liquid (?) Rom 16:15

NERGAL ner'-gal
lion 2 Kgs 17:30

NERGAL-SHAREZER ner'-gal-shar'-ez-er
Nergal protect the king Jer 39:3

NERI ne'-ri
Gr. for NERIAH Luke 3:27

NERIAH ner-i'-ah
lamp of Jehovah Jer 32:12

NEST
thou puttest thy **n** in a rock Num 24:21
As an eagle stirreth up her **n** Deut 32:11
I shall die in my **n** Job 29:18
the swallow a **n** for herself Ps 84:3
birds of the air have **n** Matt 8:20

NET
Let the wicked fall into their own **n** Ps 141:10
in vain the **n** is spread Prov 1:17
as the fishes that are taken in an evil **n** Eccl 9:12
they sacrifice unto their **n** Hab 1:16
kingdom of heaven is like unto a **n** Matt 13:47
they forsook their **n** Mark 1:18
at thy word I will let down the **n** Luke 5:5

NETHANEEL neth-an'-e-el
same as NATHANAEL Num 1:8

NETHANIAH neth'-an-i'-ah
whom Jehovah gave 2 Kgs 25:23

NETHER
shall take the **n** or the upper Deut 24:6
a piece of the **n** millstone Job 41:24

NETHINIMS neth'-in-ims
the appointed Neh 10:28

NETOPHAH net'-of-ah
dropping Ezra 2:22

NETOPHATHI net-of'-ath-i
an inhabitant of Netophah Neh 12:28

NETOPHATHITE net-of'-ath-ite
same as NETOPHATHI 2 Sam 23:28

NEVER
it shall **n** go out Lev 6:13
as infants which **n** saw light Job 3:16
he will **n** see it Ps 10:11
shall **n** be moved Ps 15:5; 30:6
n satisfied Prov 27:20; 30:15
which can **n** have enough Is 56:11
I **n** knew you Matt 7:23
it was **n** so seen in Israel Matt 9:33
yet will I **n** be offended Matt 26:33
We **n** saw it on this fashion Mark 2:12
hath **n** forgiveness Mark 3:29
if he had **n** been born Mark 14:21
shall **n** thirst John 4:14; 6:35
N man spake like this man John 7:46
shall **n** see death John 8:51
Charity **n** faileth 1 Cor 13:8
I will **n** leave thee Heb 13:5
ye shall **n** fail 2 Pet 1:10

NEW
if the Lord make a **n** thing Num 16:30
a **n** song Ps 33:3; 40:3; 96:1; 98:1; 144:9; 149:1; Is 42:10; Rev 5:9; 14:3
no **n** thing under the sun Eccl 1:9
n heavens and **n** earth Is 65:17
n every morning Lam 3:23
n cloth unto old garment Matt 9:16; Luke 5:36
things **n** and old Matt 13:52
what **n** doctrine is this Mark 1:27
A **n** commandment John 13:34; 1 John 2:7,8
to tell or to hear some **n** thing Acts 17:21
a **n** creature 2 Cor 5:17; Gal 6:15
n man Eph 2:15; 4:24; Col 3:10
n and living way Heb 10:20
a **n** name Rev 2:17; 3:12
I make all things **n** Rev 21:5

NEWLY
new gods that came **n** up Deut 32:17
had but **n** set the watch Judg 7:19

NEWNESS
walk in **n** of life Rom 6:4
serve in **n** of spirit Rom 7:6

NEWS
good **n** from a far country Prov 25:25

NEZIAH ne-zi'-ah
illustrious Ezra 2:54

NEZIB ne'-zib
garrison Josh 15:43

NIBHAZ nib'-haz
a pagan god 2 Kgs 17:31

NIBSHAN nib'-shan
level (?) Josh 15:62

NICANOR ni-ka'-nor
victorious Acts 6:5

NICODEMUS nik-o-de'-mus
victorious over the people John 3:1

NICOLAITANES nik'-o-la'-it-ans
named after Nicolas Rev 2:6

NICOLAS nik'-o-las
conqueror of the people Acts 6:5

NICOPOLIS nik-o'-pol-is
city of victory *Tit 3:12*

NIGER ni'-jer
black Acts 13:1

NIGH
but not **n** Num 24:17
the word is very **n** unto thee Deut 30:14
n unto them that are of a broken heart Ps 34:18
n unto all that call them Ps 145:18
made **n** by the blood of Christ Eph 2:13

NIGHT
a **n** to be much observed Ex 12:42
When shall I arise, and the **n** be gone Job 7:4
song in the **n** Job 35:10; Ps 77:6
weeping may endure for a **n** Ps 30:5
the terror by **n** Ps 91:5
moon and stars to rule by **n** Ps 136:9
the **n** shall be light about me Ps 139:11
the **n** of my pleasure Is 21:4
Watchman, what of the **n** Is 21:11
he continued all **n** in prayer Luke 6:12
n cometh, when no man can work John 9:4
walk in the **n**, he stumbleth John 11:10
The **n** is far spent Rom 13:12
cometh as a thief in the **n** 1 Thess 5:2; 2 Pet 3:10
no **n** there Rev 21:25; 22:5

NIMRAH nim'-rah
limpid (water) Num 32:3

NIMRIM nim'-rim
clear waters Is 15:6

NIMROD nim'-rod
rebellious (?) Gen 10:8

NIMSHI nim'-shi
discloser (?) 1 Kgs 19:16

NINEVE nin'-ev-eh
same as NINEVEH Luke 11:32

NINEVEH nin'-ev-ay
dwelling (?) Gen 10:11

NINEVITES nin'-ev-ites
inhabitants of Nineveh Luke 11:30

NISAN ni'-san
beginning, opening Neh 2:1

NISROCH nis'-rok
eagle (?) 2 Kgs 19:37

NO no
abode (?) Nah 3:8

NOADIAH no´-ad-i´-ah
whom Jehovah meets Neh 6:14

NOAH no´-ah
1 *rest* Gen 5:29
2 *wandering* Num 26:33

NOB nobe
high place 1 Sam 21:1

NOBAH no´-bah
a barking Num 32:42

NOBLE
their **n** put not their neck Neh 3:5
The **n** held their peace Job 29:10
planted thee a **n** vine Jer 2:21
n have sent their little ones to the waters Jer 14:3
were more **n** Acts 17:11
not many **n** 1 Cor 1:26

NOD node
flight, wandering Gen 4:16

NODAB no´-dab
nobility 1 Chr 5:19

NOE no-´e
Gr. for NOAH Matt 24:37

NOGAH no´-gah
brightness 1 Chr 3:7

NOHAH no´-hah
rest 1 Chr 8:2

NOISE
not discern the **n** of the shout of joy Ezra 3:13
joyful **n** Ps 66:1; 81:1; 95:1; 98:4; 100:1
n of great waters Ezek 1:24
pass away with a great **n** 2 Pet 3:10

NOISOME
the **n** pestilence Ps 91:3
the famine, and the **n** beast Ezek 14:21
a **n** and grievous sore Rev 16:2

NON none
same as NUN 1 Chr 7:27

NOPH nofe
same as MEMPHIS Is 19:13

NOPHAH no´-fah
windy Num 21:30

NOTHING
thou hast lacked **n** Deut 2:7
of that which doth cost me **n** 2 Sam 24:24
it is **n** with thee to help 2 Chr 14:11
unto them for whom **n** is prepared Neh 8:10
but of yesterday, and know **n** Job 8:9
he shall carry **n** away Ps 49:17
n shall offend them Ps 119:165
sluggard desireth, and hath **n** Prov 13:4
maketh himself rich, yet hath **n** Prov 13:7
Is it **n** to you Lam 1:12
n shall be impossible Matt 17:20; Luke 1:37
n but leaves Mark 11:13
hoping for **n** again Luke 6:35
they had **n** to pay Luke 7:42
without me ye can do **n** John 15:5
I know **n** by myself 1 Cor 4:4
as having **n** 2 Cor 6:10
we can do **n** against the truth 2 Cor 13:8
n to be refused 1 Tim 4:4
brought **n** into this world 1 Tim 6:7

NOURISH
I have **n** and brought up children Is 1:2
n up in words of faith 1 Tim 4:6
have **n** your hearts James 5:5

NOW
n it is come upon thee Job 4:5
but **n** have I kept thy word Ps 119:67
then was it better with me than **n** Hos 2:7
all things are **n** ready Luke 14:17
thou knowest not **n** John 13:7
ye cannot bear them **n** John 16:12
n I know in part 1 Cor 13:12
the life which I **n** live Gal 2:20
the life that **n** is 1 Tim 4:8
though **n** ye see him not 1 Pet 1:8
n are we the sons of God 1 John 3:2

NUMBER (n)
marvellous things without **n** Job 5:9; 9:10
Is there any **n** of his armies Job 25:3
more in **n** than the sand Ps 139:18
he telleth the **n** of the stars Ps 147:4
a great **n** believed Acts 11:21
increased in **n** daily Acts 16:5
the **n** of his name Rev 13:17

NUMBER (v)
he left **n** Gen 41:49
n ye the people 2 Sam 24:2
so teach us to **n** our days Ps 90:12
that which is wanting cannot be **n** Eccl 1:15
he was **n** with the transgressors Is 53:12; Mark 15:28
hairs of your head are all **n** Matt 10:30; Luke 12:7
multitude, which no man could **n** Rev 7:9

NUN noon
fish Ex 33:11

NURSE
Take this child away and **n** it Ex 2:9
daughters shall be **n** Is 60:4

NURTURE
bring them up in the **n** and admonition Eph 6:4

NYMPHAS nim´-fas
sacred to the muses Col 4:15

O

OBADIAH ob´-ad-i´-ah
worshiper of Jehovah Obad 1:1

OBAL o´-bal
hill (?) Gen 10:28

OBED-EDOM o´-bed-e´-dom
serving Edom 2 Sam 6:10

OBED o´-bed
worshiping [God] Ruth 4:17

OBEDIENCE
by the **o** of one Rom 5:19
the **o** of faith Rom 16:26
yet learned he **o** Heb 5:8

OBEDIENT
will we do, and be **o** Ex 24:7
wise reprover upon an **o** ear Prov 25:12
if ye shall be willing and **o** ye shall eat Is 1:19
o in all things 2 Cor 2:9
o unto death Phil 2:8
be **o** masters Titus 2:9
As **o** children 1 Pet 1:14

OBEISANCE
round about, and made **o** to my sheaf Gen 37:7
bowed down their heads and made **o** Gen 43:28
came nigh to him to do him **o** 2 Sam 15:5

OBEY
a blessing if ye **o** Deut 11:27
his voice will we **o** Josh 24:24
to **o** is better than sacrifice 1 Sam 15:22
O my voice, and I will be your God Jer 7:23
we ought to **o** God rather than men Acts 5:29
his servants ye are to whom ye **o** Rom 6:16
o your parents Eph 6:1; Col 3:20
that **o** not the gospel 2 Thess 1:8; 1 Pet 4:17
O them that have rule over you Heb 13:17
purified your souls in **o** the truth 1 Pet 1:22

OBIL o´-bil
camel keeper 1 Chr 27:30

OBJECT
have been there before thee, and **o** Acts 24:19

OBOTH o´-both
bottles (of skin) Num 21:10

OBSCURE
shall be put out in **o** darkness Prov 20:20

OBSCURITY
see out of **o**, and out of darkness Is 29:18
shall thy light rise in **o** Is 58:10
wait for light, but behold **o** Is 59:9

OBSERVATION
kingdom of God cometh not with **o** Luke 17:20

OBSERVE
his father **o** the saying Gen 37:11
is wise, and will **o** these things Ps 107:43
let thine eyes **o** my ways Prov 23:26
He that **o** the wind Eccl 11:4
that **o** lying vanities Jon 2:8
teaching them to **o** all things Matt 28:20
and **o** him Mark 6:20
all these have I **o** Mark 10:20

OBSERVER
useth divination, or an **o** of times Deut 18:10

OBSTINATE
his heart **o** that he might deliver Deut 2:30
art **o**, and thy neck is an iron sinew Is 48:4

OBTAIN
shall **o** favour of the LORD Prov 8:35
shall **o** joy and gladness Is 35:10; 51:11
worthy to **o** that world Luke 20:35
Having therefore **o** help of God Acts 26:22
So run that ye may **o** 1 Cor 9:24
to **o** salvation 1 Thess 5:9
I **o** mercy 1 Tim 1:13
o mercy, and find grace to help Heb 4:16
having **o** eternal redemption Heb 9:12
had not **o** mercy, but now have **o** 1 Pet 2:10
o like precious faith 2 Pet 1:1

OCCASION
great **o** to enemies 2 Sam 12:14
sought to find **o** Dan 6:4
sin, taking **o** by the commandment Rom 7:8
an **o** to fall in his brother's way Rom 14:13
give none **o** to the adversary 1 Tim 5:14

OCCUPATION
What is your **o**? Gen 46:33
by their **o** they were tent makers Acts 18:3
workman of like **o** Acts 19:25

OCCUPY
were in thee to **o** thy merchandise Ezek 27:9
said unto them, O till I come Luke 19:13

OCRAN ok´-ran
troublesome Num 1:13

ODED o´-ded
setting up (?) 2 Chr 15:1

ODOUR
filled with **o** of the ointment John 12:3
an **o** of a sweet smell Phil 4:18
golden vials full of **o** Rev 5:8

OFFENCE
yielding pacifieth great **o** Eccl 10:4
a rock of **o** Is 8:14; Rom 9:33; 1 Pet 2:8
thou art an **o** to me Matt 16:23
Woe unto the world because of **o**! Matt 18:7
conscience void of **o** Acts 24:16

that man who eateth with **o** Rom 14:20
Give none **o** 1 Cor 10:32; 2 Cor 6:3
without **o** till the day of Christ Phil 1:10

OFFEND
I will not **o** any more Job 34:31
nothing shall **o** them Ps 119:165
brother **o** is harder to be won Prov 18:19
if thine eye **o** thee Matt 5:29; 18:9; Mark 9:47
gather all things that **o** Matt 13:41
they were **o** in him Matt 13:57; Mark 6:3
all men shall be **o** because of thee Matt 26:33
whereby thy brother is **o** Rom 14:21
yet **o** in one point James 2:10

OFFENDER
my son Solomon shall be counted **o** 1 Kgs 1:21
make a man an **o** for a word Is 29:21
be an **o**, or have committed anything Acts 25:11

OFFER
people willingly **o** themselves Judg 5:2
Whoso **o** praise Ps 50:23
then come and **o** thy gift Matt 5:24
the one cheek **o** also the other Luke 6:29
things **o** unto idols 1 Cor 8:1,7
o in sacrifice unto idols 1 Cor 8:4; 10:19
o in the service of your faith Phil 2:17
now ready to be **o** 2 Tim 4:6
Christ once **o** to bear the sins of many Heb 9:28

OFFICE
into one of the priests' **o** 1 Sam 2:36
I magnify mine **o** Rom 11:13
the **o** of a bishop 1 Tim 3:1
the **o** of the priesthood Heb 7:5

OFFSCOURING
hast made us as the **o** and refuse Lam 3:45
the world, and are the **o** of all things 1 Cor 4:13

OFFSPRING
and his **o** shall not be satisfied Job 27:14
For we are also his **o** Acts 17:28
the root and the **o** of David Rev 22:16

OFTEN
being **o** reproved Prov 29:1
spake **o** one to another Mal 3:16
how **o** would I have gathered Matt 23:37; Luke 13:34
as **o** as ye eat 1 Cor 11:26
thine **o** infirmities 1 Tim 5:23

OG og
circle (?) Num 21:33

OHAD o′-had
might Gen 46:10

OHEL o′-hel
tent 1 Chr 3:20

OIL
with the **o** of gladness Ps 45:7; Heb 1:9
be anointed with fresh **o** Ps 92:10
o to make his face to shine Ps 104:15
o of joy for mourning Is 61:3
took no **o** with them Matt 25:3
pouring in **o** and wine Luke 10:34

OLD
waxed not **o** Deut 8:4; Neh 9:21
did eat of the **o** corn Josh 5:11
I have been young, and now am **o** Ps 37:25
when I am **o** Ps 71:18
when he is **o** he will not Prov 22:6
build the **o** waste places Is 58:12
ask for the **o** paths Jer 6:16
he saith, The **o** is better Luke 5:39
o things are passed away 2 Cor 5:17
God spared not the **o** world 2 Pet 2:5
o commandment is the word 1 John 2:7

that **o** serpent Rev 12:9; 20:2

OLIVET ol′-iv-et
place of olives 2 Sam 15:30

OLYMPAS o-limp′-as
bright (?) Rom 16:15

OMAR o′-mar
talkative Gen 36:11

OMEGA o′-meg-ah
last letter of the Gr. alphabet Rev 1:8

OMITTED
o the weightier matters of the law Matt 23:23

OMRI om′-ri
like a sheaf (?) 1 Kgs 16:16

ON on
the sun Gen 41:45

ONAM o′-nam
wealthy Gen 36:23

ONAN o′-nan
strong Gen 38:4

ONCE
yet but this **o** Gen 18:32
Let us go up at **o** Num 13:30
speaketh **o** Job 33:14; Ps 62:11
shall a nation be born at **o** Is 66:8
o enlightened Heb 6:4
o to die Heb 9:27

ONE
o of a thousand Job 9:3
o by **o** Eccl 7:27; Is 27:12
o thing thou lackest Mark 10:21
o thing is needful Luke 10:42
o thing I know John 9:25
that they may be **o** John 17:11,22
all **o** in Christ Gal 3:28
O Lord, **o** faith, **o** baptism Eph 4:5

ONESIMUS o-ne′-sim-us
profitable Col 4:9

ONESIPHORUS o′-nes-if′-o-rus
bringing profit 2 Tim 1:16

ONO o′-no
strong 1 Chr 8:12

OPEN
the earth **o** her mouth Num 16:30
I will **o** my dark saying Ps 49:4
o thou my lips Ps 51:15
o thy mouth wide Ps 81:10
thou **o** thine hand Ps 104:28
O thou mine eyes Ps 119:18
O thy mouth for the dumb Prov 31:8
he shall **o**, and none shall shut Is 22:22
To **o** the blind eyes Is 42:7
thy gates shall be **o** continually Is 60:11
never **o** thy mouth Ezek 16:63
o you the windows of heaven Mal 3:10
Lord **o** to us Matt 25:11; Luke 13:25
graves were **o** Matt 27:52
that is, Be **o** Mark 7:34
while he **o** to us the scriptures? Luke 24:32
then **o** he their understanding Luke 24:45
To **o** their eyes Acts 26:18
great door and effectual is **o** 1 Cor 16:9
o unto us a door of utterance Col 4:3

OPERATION
the **o** of his hands Ps 28:5; Is 5:12
there are diversities of **o** 1 Cor 12:6
through the faith of the **o** of God Col 2:12

OPHEL o′-fel
a hill 2 Chr 27:3

OPHIR o′-fir
ashes Gen 10:29

OPHNI of′-ni
man of the hill Josh 18:24

OPHRAH of′-rah
fawn 1 Chr 4:14

OPINION
How long halt ye between two **o**? 1 Kgs 18:21
and durst not shew you mine **o** Job 32:6

OPPORTUNITY
we have therefore **o**, let us do good Gal 6:10
ye were also careful, but ye lacked **o** Phil 4:10
might have had **o** to have returned Heb 11:15

OPPOSE
thou **o** thyself against me Job 30:21
o and exalteth himself above all 2 Thess 2:4
instructing those that **o** themselves 2 Tim 2:25

OPPOSITIONS
vain babblings, and **o** of science 1 Tim 6:20

OPPRESS
o a stranger Ex 23:9
ye shall not **o** one another Lev 25:14
whom have I **o** 1 Sam 12:3
man of the earth may no more **o** Ps 10:18
He that **o** the poor Prov 14:31; 22:16
A poor man that **o** the poor Prov 28:3
If ye **o** not the stranger Jer 7:6
he loveth to **o** Hos 12:7
o not the widow Zech 7:10

OPPRESSION
our labour, and our **o** Deut 26:7
Trust not in **o** Ps 62:10
deliver me from the **o** of man Ps 119:134
considered all the **o** Eccl 4:1
o maketh a wise man mad Eccl 7:7
trust in **o** Is 30:12

ORATOR
cunning artificer, and the eloquent **o** Is 3:3
a certain **o** named Tertullus Acts 24:1

ORDAIN
I will **o** a place for my people 1 Chr 17:9
hast thou **o** strength Ps 8:2
This he **o** in Joseph Ps 81:5
I have **o** a lamp for mine anointed Ps 132:17
thou wilt **o** peace for us Is 26:12
Tophet is **o** of old Is 30:33
I **o** thee a prophet Jer 1:5
o twelve Mark 3:14
o you, that ye should go and John 15:16
one be **o** to be a witness Acts 1:22
o of God to be the Judge Acts 10:42
o to eternal life Acts 13:48
o them elders Acts 14:23
o of the apostles Acts 16:4
by that man whom he hath **o** Acts 17:31
the powers that be are **o** of God Rom 13:1
it was **o** by angels Gal 3:19
good works which God hath before **o** Eph 2:10
of old **o** to this condemnation Jude 1:4

ORDER (n)
Set thine house in **o** 2 Kgs 20:1; Is 38:1
without any **o** Job 10:22
they cannot be reckoned up in **o** Ps 40:5
set them in **o** before thine eyes Ps 50:21
the **o** of Melchizedek Ps 110:4; Heb 5:6; 6:20; 7:11
decently and in **o** 1 Cor 14:40

ORDER (v)
How shall we **o** the child Judg 13:12
I would **o** my cause Job 23:4
we cannot **o** our speech Job 37:19
to him that **o** his conversation aright Ps 50:23

ORDINANCE
the **o** of their God — Is 58:2; Rom 13:2
we have kept his **o** — Mal 3:14
commandments contained in **o** — Eph 2:15
handwriting of **o** — Col 2:14
in carnal **o** — Heb 9:10

OREB **o´-reb**
raven — Judg 7:25

OREN **o´-ren**
pine tree — 1 Chr 2:25

ORNAN **or´-nan**
same as ARAUNAH — 1 Chr 21:15

ORPAH **orp´-ah**
hind (?) — Ruth 1:4

ORPHANS
We are **o** and fatherless — Lam 5:3

OSEE **o´-zee**
same as HOSEA — Rom 9:25

OSHEA **o-she´-ah**
same as JOSHUA — Num 13:8

OTHNI **oth´-ni**
powerful (?) — 1 Chr 26:7

OTHNIEL **oth´-ni-el**
powerful man of God — Josh 15:17

OUGHT
to know what Israel **o** to do — 1 Chr 12:32
these **o** ye to have done — Matt 23:23; Luke 11:42
o not Christ to have suffered — Luke 24:26
the place where men **o** to worship — John 4:20
we **o** to obey God — Acts 5:29
what we should pray for as we **o** — Rom 8:26
ye **o** to be teachers — Heb 5:12
these things **o** not so to be — James 3:10
what manner of persons **o** ye to be — 2 Pet 3:11

OURS
and the inheritance shall be **o** — Mark 12:7
both theirs and **o** — 1 Cor 1:2
also **o** in the day of the Lord Jesus — 2 Cor 1:14

OUT
be sure your sin will find you **o** — Num 32:23
are **o** of course — Ps 82:5
o of it are the issues of life — Prov 4:23
o of the abundance of the heart the mouth speaketh — Matt 12:34
o of them all the Lord delivered me — 2 Tim 3:11
instant in season, **o** of season — 2 Tim 4:2

OUTCAST
gathereth together the **o** of Israel — Ps 147:2
shall assemble the **o** of Israel — Is 11:12
the **o** in the land of Egypt — Is 27:13
they called thee an **o** — Jer 30:17

OUTGOINGS
the **o** of it shall be thine — Josh 17:18
thou makest the **o** of the morning — Ps 65:8

OUTRAGEOUS
Wrath is cruel, and anger is **o** — Prov 27:4

OUTRUN
the other disciple did **o** Peter — John 20:4

OUTSIDE
servant unto the **o** of the armed men — Judg 7:11
make clean the **o** of the cup — Matt 23:25

OUTSTRETCHED
with an **o** arm — Deut 26:8
with an **o** hand — Jer 21:5
my great power and by my **o** arm — Jer 27:5

OUTWARD
looketh on the **o** appearance — 1 Sam 16:7
though our **o** man perish — 2 Cor 4:16

OVERCHARGE
hearts be **o** with surfeiting — Luke 21:34
may not **o** you all — 2 Cor 2:5

OVERCOME
he shall **o** at the last — Gen 49:19
like a man whom wine hath **o** — Jer 23:9
I have **o** the world — John 16:33
Be not **o** of evil, but **o** evil — Rom 12:21
victory that **o** the world — 1 John 5:4
to him that **o** — Rev 2:7,17; 3:21

OVERMUCH
not **o** wicked, neither be thou foolish — Eccl 7:17
swallowed up with **o** sorrow — 2 Cor 2:7

OVERSEER
he made him **o** over his house — Gen 39:4
no guide, **o**, or ruler — Prov 6:7
o to feed the church of God — Acts 20:28

OVERSHADOW
a bright cloud **o** them — Matt 17:5
the Highest shall **o** thee — Luke 1:35
passing by might **o** some of them — Acts 5:15

OVERSIGHT
peradventure it was an **o** — Gen 43:12
the **o** of the outward business — Neh 11:16
among you, taking the **o** thereof — 1 Pet 5:2

OVERSPREAD
of them was the whole earth **o** — Gen 9:19
for the **o** of abominations — Dan 9:27

OVERTAKE
plowman shall **o** the reaper — Amos 9:13
if a man be **o** in a fault — Gal 6:1
day should **o** you as a thief — 1 Thess 5:4

OVERTHROW
utterly **o** them — Ex 23:24
God hath **o** me — Job 19:6
purposed to **o** my goings — Ps 140:4
wickedness **o** the sinner — Prov 13:6
Yet forty days, and Nineveh shall be **o** — Jon 3:4
if it be of God, ye cannot **o** it — Acts 5:39

OVERTURN
which **o** them in his anger — Job 9:5
they **o** the earth — Job 12:15
he **o** the mountains — Job 28:9
I will **o** — Ezek 21:27

OVERWHELM
ye **o** the fatherless — Job 6:27
when my heart is **o** — Ps 61:2
my spirit was **o** — Ps 77:3; 142:3

OVERWISE
neither make thyself **o** — Eccl 7:16

OWE
how much **o** thou — Luke 16:5,7
o no man any thing — Rom 13:8

OWN
after his **o** name — Num 32:42
of thine **o** have we given thee — 1 Chr 29:14
our lips are our **o** — Ps 12:4
even our **o** God shall bless us — Ps 67:6
do what I will with mine **o** — Matt 20:15
his **o**, and his **o** received him not — John 1:11
having loved his **o** — John 13:1
ye are not your **o** — 1 Cor 6:19

OWNER
the **o** of the ox shall be quit — Ex 21:28
the **o** of it shall accept thereof — Ex 22:11
riches kept for the **o** thereof — Eccl 5:13
The ox knoweth his **o** — Is 1:3

OZEM **o´-zem**
strength — 1 Chr 2:15

OZIAS **o-zi´-as**
Gr. for UZZIAH — Matt 1:8

OZNI **oz´-ni**
hearing — Num 26:16

OZNITES **oz´-nites**
descendants of Ozni — Num 26:16

P

PAARAI **pa´-ar-a´-i**
devoted to Peor (?) — 2 Sam 23:35

PACIFY
a wise man will **p** it — Prov 16:14
A gift in secret **p** anger — Prov 21:14
yeilding **p** great offences — Eccl 10:4
I am **p** toward thee — Ezek 16:63

PADAN-ARAM **pa´-dan-a´-ram**
the plain of Syria — Gen 25:20

PADON **pa´-don**
redemption — Ezra 2:44

PAGIEL **pa´-gi-el**
intervention of God — Num 1:13

PAHATH-MOAB **pa´-hath-mo´-ab**
governor of Moab — Ezra 2:6

PAI **pa´-i**
bleating — 1 Chr 1:50

PAIN
the **p** of hell gat hold upon me — Ps 116:3
having loosed the **p** of death — Acts 2:24
travaileth in **p** — Rom 8:22
neither shall there be any more **p** — Rev 21:4

PAINTED
She **p** her face — 2 Kgs 9:30
cedar, and **p** with vermilion — Jer 22:14
p thy eyes — Ezek 23:40

PALACE
consider her **p** — Ps 48:13
prosperity within thy **p** — Ps 122:7
the similitude of a **p** — Ps 144:12
entered into our **p** — Jer 9:21
a strong man armed keepeth his **p** — Luke 11:21
manifest in all the **p** — Phil 1:13

PALAL **pa´-lal**
judge — Neh 3:25

PALE
shall his face now wax **p** — Is 29:22
faces are turned into **p** — Jer 30:6
behold a **p** horse — Rev 6:8

PALESTINA **pal´-es-ti´-nah**
land of strangers (?) — Ex 15:14

PALLU **pal´-oo**
distinguished — Ex 6:14

PALLUITES **pal´-oo-ites**
descendants of Pallu — Num 26:5

PALM
upon the **p** of my hands — Is 49:16
the **p** of their hands — Matt 26:67; Mark 14:65
robes, and **p** in their hands — Rev 7:9

PALTI **pal´-ti**
deliverance of Jehovah — Num 13:9

PALTIEL **pal´-ti-el**
deliverance of God — Num 34:26

PALTITE **palt´-ite**
descendant of Palti — 2 Sam 23:26

PAMPHYLIA **pam-fil´-yah**
assemblage of mingled tribes (?) — Acts 27:5

PANT
heart **p**, and my strength faileth — Ps 38:10
the hart **p** after the water brooks — Ps 42:1
opened my mouth and **p** — Ps 119:131
that **p** after the dust of the earth — Amos 2:7

PAPHOS pa´-fos
capital of Roman province of Cyprus Acts 13:6

PARAH pa´-rah
heifer Josh 18:23

PARAN pa´-ran
cavernous Deut 33:2

PARBAR par´-bar
open apartment 1 Chr 26:18

PARDON
he will not **p** Ex 23:21
the LORD **p** thy servant 2 Kgs 5:18
the good LORD **p** every one 2 Chr 30:18
a God ready to **p** Neh 9:17
he will abundantly **p** Is 55:7

PARENTS
children shall rise up against their **p** Matt 10:21; Mark 13:12
no man that hath left house, or **p** Luke 18:29
ye shall be betrayed by **p** Luke 21:16
who did sin, this man, or his **p** John 9:2
disobedient to **p** Rom 1:30; 2 Tim 3:2
not to lay up for the **p**, but the **p** for the children 2 Cor 12:14
Children, obey your **p** Eph 6:1; Col 3:20

PARMASHTA par-mash´-tah
superior (?) Esth 9:9

PARMENAS par´-men-as
standing firm Acts 6:5

PARNACH par´-nak
descendant of Zebulun Num 34:25

PAROSH pa´-rosh
flea Ezra 2:3

PARSHANDATHA par´-shan-da´-thah
given to Persia (?) Esth 9:7

PART (n)
ye have no **p** in the LORD Josh 22:25,27
their inward **p** is very wickedness Ps 5:9
in the hidden **p**, thou shalt make me Ps 51:6
The LORD taketh my **p** Ps 118:7
dwell in the uttermost **p** Ps 139:9
he that is not against us is on our **p** Mark 9:40
that good **p** Luke 10:42
thou hast no **p** with me John 13:8
neither **p** nor lot Acts 8:21
what **p** hath he that believeth 2 Cor 6:15

PART (v)
if ought but death **p** thee and me Ruth 1:17
there was none to **p** them 2 Sam 14:6
They **p** my garments Ps 22:18
he was **p** from them Luke 24:51
p them to all men Acts 2:45

PARTAKER
hast been **p** with adulterers Ps 50:18
p of his hope 1 Cor 9:10
p with the altar 1 Cor 9:13
p of that one bread 1 Cor 10:17
p of the Lord's table 1 Cor 10:21
neither be **p** of other men's sins 1 Tim 5:22
p of the heavenly calling Heb 3:1
p of Christ's sufferings 1 Pet 4:13
a **p** of the glory 1 Pet 5:1
p of the divine nature 2 Pet 1:4

PARTIAL
have been **p** in the law Mal 2:9
doing nothing by **p** 1 Tim 5:21
Are ye not then **p** in yourselves James 2:4
fruits, without **p** James 3:17

PARTICULAR
body of Christ and members in **p** 1 Cor 12:27
in **p** so love his wife Eph 5:33

PARTITION
a **p** by the chains of gold 1 Kgs 6:21
wall of **p** between us Eph 2:14

PARTNER
is **p** with a thief hateth his own soul Prov 29:24
beckoned unto their **p** Luke 5:7
my **p** and fellow helper 2 Cor 8:23

PARUAH par-oo´-ah
flourishing 1 Kgs 4:17

PARVAIM parv-a´-im
oriental regions (?) 2 Chr 3:6

PAS-DAMMIM pas-dam´-im
short for EPHES-DAMMIM 1 Chr 11:13

PASACH pa´-sak
divider 1 Chr 7:33

PASEAH pa-se´-ah
lame 1 Chr 4:12

PASHUR pash´-oor
prosperity round about Jer 20:1

PASS
when I see the blood I will **p** over Ex 12:13
when thou **p** through the waters Is 43:2
let this cup **p** Matt 26:39
neither can they **p** to us Luke 16:26
fashion of this world **p** 1 Cor 7:31
old things are **p** away 2 Cor 5:17
love of Christ, which **p** knowledge Eph 3:19
which **p** all understanding Phil 4:7

PASSION
shewed himself alive after his **p** Acts 1:3
We also are men of like **p** Acts 14:15
a man subject to like **p** as we are James 5:17

PAST
as in months **p** Job 29:2
God requireth that which is **p** Eccl 3:15
the winter is **p** Song 2:11
the harvest is **p** Jer 8:20
of sins that are **p** Rom 3:25
ways **p** finding out Rom 11:33
being **p** feeling Eph 4:19

PASTOR
give you **p** according to mine heart Jer 3:15
being a **p** to follow thee Jer 17:16
Woe be unto **p** that destroy Jer 23:1
some **p**, and teachers Eph 4:11

PASTURE
of his **p**, and the sheep of his hand Ps 95:7
sheep of his **p** Ps 100:3
good **p**, and upon the high mountains Ezek 34:14
go in and out, and find **p** John 10:9

PATE
come down upon his own **p** Ps 7:16

PATH
there is a **p** which no fowl knoweth Job 28:7
shew me the **p** of life Ps 16:11
lead me in a plain **p** Ps 27:11
thy **p** drop fatness Ps 65:11
thy **p** in the great waters Ps 77:19
a light unto my **p** Ps 119:105
the **p** of the just Prov 4:18
we will walk in his **p** Is 2:3; Mic 4:2
in **p** that they have not known Is 42:16
restorer of **p** to dwell in Is 58:12
ask for the old **p** Jer 6:16
make his **p** straight Matt 3:3; Mark 1:3; Luke 3:4

PATARA pat´-a-ra
trodden under one's foot (?) Acts 21:1

PATHROS path´-ros
land of the south (?) Is 11:11

PATHRUSIM path-roos´-im
inhabitants of Pathros Gen 10:14

PATIENCE
have **p** with me Matt 18:26,29
bring forth fruit with **p** Luke 8:15
in your **p** possess ye your souls Luke 21:19
tribulation worketh **p** Rom 5:3
with **p** wait for it Rom 8:25
through **p** and comfort Rom 15:4
the God of **p** Rom 15:5
as ministers of God in much **p** 2 Cor 6:4
unto all **p** and long suffering Col 1:11
and **p** of hope 1 Thess 1:3
for your **p** 2 Thess 1:4
faith, love, **p**, meekness 1 Tim 6:11
sound in faith, in charity, in **p** Titus 2:2
ye have need of **p** Heb 10:36
run with **p** Heb 12:1
trying of your faith worketh **p** James 1:3
let **p** have her perfect work James 1:4
hath long **p** James 5:7
of suffering affliction and **p** James 5:10
ye have heard of the **p** of Job James 5:11
add to temperance **p** 2 Pet 1:6
thy **p** Rev 2:2,19
thou hast kept word of my **p** Rev 3:10
Here is the **p** Rev 13:10; 14:12

PATIENTLY
wait **p** for him Ps 37:7
I waited **p** for the LORD Ps 40:1
he had **p** endured Heb 6:15
for your faults, ye shall take it **p** 1 Pet 2:20

PATMOS pat´-mos
an island in the Aegean Sea Rev 1:9

PATROBAS pat´-ro-bas
father of life Rom 16:14

PATTERN
long suffering, for a **p** to them 1 Tim 1:16
a **p** of good works Titus 2:7
according to the **p** shown to thee Heb 8:5
the **p** of the things in the heavens Heb 9:23

PAU pa´-oo
same as PAI Gen 36:39

PAUL pawl
little Acts 13:9

PAULUS pawl´-us
same as PAUL Acts 13:7

PAVILION
his **p** round about him Ps 18:11
hide me in his **p** Ps 27:5
Keep them secretly in a **p** Ps 31:20
Spread his royal **p** over them Jer 43:10

PAY
let him **p** double Ex 22:7
water, then I will **p** for it Num 20:19
sell the oil, and **p** thy debt 2 Kgs 4:7
will **p** my vows Ps 22:25; 116:14
if thou hast nothing to **p** Prov 22:27
defer not to **p** it Eccl 5:4
I will **p** thee all Matt 18:26
P me that thou owest Matt 18:28
ye **p** tithe of mint Matt 23:23

PEACE
an answer of **p** Gen 41:16
give thee **p** Num 6:26
my covenant of **p** Num 25:12
proclaim **p** unto it Deut 20:10
thou shalt not seek their **p** Deut 23:6
p be to thine house 1 Sam 25:6
what hast thou to do with **p** 2 Kgs 9:19
Had Zimri **p**, who slew his master? 2 Kgs 9:31
beasts of the field shall be at **p** with thee Job 5:23
Acquaint thyself with him, and be at **p** Job 22:21

lay me down in **p** Ps 4:8
the LORD will bless his people with **p** Ps 29:11
seek **p**, and pursue it Ps 34:14
the end of that man is **p** Ps 37:37
will speak **p** unto his people Ps 85:8
Pray for the **p** of Jerusalem Ps 122:6
a time of **p** Eccl 3:8
keep him in perfect **p** Is 26:3
work of righteousness shall be **p** Is 32:17
I make **p**, and create evil Is 45:7
thy **p** been as a river Is 48:18
that publisheth **p** Is 52:7; Nah 1:15
The way of **p** they know not Is 59:8
saying **P**, **p**; when there is no **p** Jer 6:14; 8:11
we looked for **p** Jer 8:15; 14:19
thou shalt die in **p** Jer 34:5
they shall seek **p** Ezek 7:25
p be multiplied Dan 4:1; 6:25; 1 Pet 1:2; 2 Pet 1:2
in this place will I give **p** Hag 2:9
let your **p** come upon it Matt 10:13
to send **p** on earth Matt 10:34
have **p** one with another Mark 9:50
to guide our feet in the way of **p** Luke 1:79
on earth **p** Luke 2:14
things which belong to thy **p** Luke 19:42
p I leave with you, my **p** I give John 14:27
that in me ye might have **p** John 16:33
p, from God our Father Rom 1:7; 1 Cor 1:3; 2 Cor 1:2; Eph 1:2; Phil 1:2
we have **p** with God Rom 5:1
the gospel of **p** Rom 10:15; Eph 6:15
the things which make for **p** Rom 14:19
the God of **p** Rom 15:33; 16:20; Phil 4:9; Heb 13:20
author of confusion, but of **p** 1 Cor 14:33
live in **p** 2 Cor 13:11
he is our **p** Eph 2:14
p to you which were afar off Eph 2:17
in the bond of **p** Eph 4:3
p of God which passeth all understanding Phil 4:7
and **p** from God Col 1:2; 1 Thess 1:1; 2 Thess 1:2; Phile 1:3
let the **p** of God rule in your hearts Col 3:15
be at **p** among yourselves 1 Thess 5:13
Lord of **p** himself give you **p** always 2 Thess 3:16
King of **p** Heb 7:2
follow **p** with all men Heb 12:14
Depart in **p** James 2:16
fruit of righteousness is sown in **p** James 3:18
let him seek **p**, and ensue it 1 Pet 3:11
found of him in **p** 2 Pet 3:14

PEACEABLE
dwell in a **p** habitation Is 32:18
a quiet and **p** life 1 Tim 2:2
yieldeth the **p** fruit of righteousness Heb 12:11
pure, then **p**, gentle James 3:17

PEACEABLY
could not speak **p** unto him Gen 37:4
Comest thou **p** 1 Sam 16:4
one speaketh **p** to his neighbour Jer 9:8
live **p** with all men Rom 12:18

PEDAHEL pe´-dah-el
God redeemed Num 34:28

PEDAHZUR pe-dah´-zoor
the Rock redeemed Num 1:10

PEDAIAH pe-dah-i´-ah
whom Jehovah redeemed 1 Chr 27:20

PEELED
a nation scattered and **p** Is 18:2
every shoulder was **p** Ezek 29:18

PEEP
wizards that **p** and that mutter Is 8:19
or opened the mouth, or **p** Is 10:14

PEKAH pe´-kah
open-eyed 2 Kgs 15:25

PEKAHIAH pe´-kah-i´-ah
whose eyes Jehovah opened 2 Kgs 15:22

PEKOD pe´-kod
visitation Jer 50:21

PELAIAH pe´-la-i´-ah
whom Jehovah made distinguished 1 Chr 3:24

PELALIAH pe´-lal-i´-ah
whom Jehovah judged Neh 11:12

PELATIAH pe´-lat-i´-ah
whom Jehovah delivered Ezek 11:1

PELEG pe´-leg
division Gen 10:25

PELET pe´-let
liberation 1 Chr 2:47

PELETH pe´-leth
swiftness Num 16:1

PELETHITES pel´-eth-ites
runners 2 Sam 8:18

PELONITE pel´-o-nite
used of one of David's mighty men 1 Chr 11:27

PEN
with an iron **p** and lead in the rock Job 19:24
my tongue is the **p** of a ready writer Ps 45:1
written with a **p** of iron Jer 17:1
with ink and **p** 3 John 1:13

PENIEL pe´-ni-el
same as PENUEL Gen 32:30

PENINNAH pe-nin´-ah
coral 1 Sam 1:2

PENTECOST pen´-te-kost
fiftieth Acts 2:1

PENUEL pe´-noo-el
the face of God Gen 32:31

PENURY
the lips tendeth only to **p** Prov 14:23
She of her **p** hath cast in all the living Luke 21:4

PEOPLE
I will take you to me for a **p** Ex 6:7
to be unto him a **p** of inheritance Deut 4:20
to thyself thy **p** Israel 2 Sam 7:24
for a **p**, and for a name Jer 13:11
separated from other **p** Lev 20:24,26
Did ever **p** hear the voice of God Deut 4:33
O **p** saved by the Lord Deut 33:29
a **p** which I knew not 2 Sam 22:44
my **p** would not hearken Ps 81:11
happy is that **p** Ps 144:15
the ants are a **p** not strong Prov 30:25
a **p** laden with iniquity Is 1:4
a **p** of no understanding Is 27:11
p for thy life Is 43:4
blind **p** that have eyes Is 43:8
a **p** cometh from the north Jer 6:22; 50:41
of what **p** art thou Jon 1:8
a **p** prepared for the Lord Luke 1:17
purify unto himself a peculiar **p** Titus 2:14

PEOR pe´-or
point Num 23:28

PERAZIM pe-raz´-im
pl. of PEREZ Is 28:21

PERCEIVE
a heart to **p** Deut 29:4
we **p** that the LORD is among us Josh 22:31
I **p** him not Job 9:11
I cannot **p** him Job 23:8
see ye indeed, but **p** not Is 6:9
deeper speech than thou canst **p** Is 33:19
nor **p** by the ear Is 64:4
Jesus **p** their wickedness Matt 22:18
p ye not yet Mark 8:17
I **p** that virtue is gone out Luke 8:46
I **p** that thou art a prophet John 4:19
I **p** God is no respecter of persons Acts 10:34
Hereby **p** we the love of God 1 John 3:16

PERES pe´-res
divided Dan 5:28

PERESH pe´-resh
distinction 1 Chr 7:16

PEREZ pe´-rez
breach 1 Chr 27:3

PEREZ-UZZA pe´-rez-uz´-ah
same as PEREZ-UZZAH 1 Chr 13:11

PEREZ-UZZAH pe´-rez-uz´-ah
breach of Uzzah 2 Sam 6:8

PERFECT
Noah was a just man and **p** Gen 6:9
walk before me, and be thou **p** Gen 17:1
Thou shalt be **p** with the LORD Deut 18:13
his work is **p** Deut 32:4
his way is **p** 2 Sam 22:31; Ps 18:30
law of the LORD is **p** Ps 19:7
Mark the **p** man Ps 37:37
more and more unto the **p** day Prov 4:18
Thou wast **p** in thy ways Ezek 28:15
Be ye therefore **p** Matt 5:48
If thou wilt be **p** Matt 19:21
be made **p** in one John 17:23
p will of God Rom 12:2
wisdom among them that are **p** 1 Cor 2:6
strength is made **p** in weakness 2 Cor 12:9
unto a **p** man Eph 4:13
either were already **p** Phil 3:12
as many as be **p** Phil 3:15
present every man **p** Col 1:28
may stand **p** and complete Col 4:12
That the man of God may be **p** 2 Tim 3:17
salvation **p** through sufferings Heb 2:10
without us should not be made **p** Heb 11:40
spirits of just men made **p** Heb 12:23
make you **p** in every good work Heb 13:21
patience have her **p** work James 1:4
every good gift and **p** gift James 1:17
p law of liberty James 1:25
the same is a **p** man James 3:2
p love casteth out fear 1 John 4:18

PERFECTION
find out the Almighty unto **p** Job 11:7
an end of all **p** Ps 119:96
we wish, even your **p** 2 Cor 13:9
go on unto **p** Heb 6:1

PERFECTLY
ye shall consider it **p** Jer 23:20
the way of God more **p** Acts 18:26
but that ye be **p** joined 1 Cor 1:10

PERFECTNESS
which is the bond of **p** Col 3:14

PERFORM
not able to **p** it thyself alone Ex 18:18
half of the kingdom it shall be **p** Esth 5:6
cannot **p** their enterprise Job 5:12
unto thee shall the vow be **p** Ps 65:1
I have sworn, and I will **p** it Ps 119:106
zeal of the LORD of hosts will **p** this Is 9:7
shall **p** all my pleasure Is 44:28
p my good word Jer 29:10
able also to **p** Rom 4:21

to **p** that which is good I find not Rom 7:18
p it until the day of Christ Phil 1:6

PERFORMANCE
For there shall be a **p** of those things Luke 1:45
There may be a **p** also 2 Cor 8:11

PERGA per´-gah
citadel Acts 13:13

PERGAMOS per´-ga-mos
same as PERGA (?) Rev 1:11

PERIDA pe´-rid-ah
a recluse Neh 7:57

PERIL
gat our bread with the **p** of our lives Lam 5:9
famine, or nakedness, or **p** Rom 8:35
journeyings often, in **p** of waters 2 Cor 11:26

PERILOUS
last days **p** times shall come 2 Tim 3:1

PERISH
we die, we **p**, we all **p** Num 17:12
a Syrian ready to **p** Deut 26:5
who ever **p**, being innocent Job 4:7
blessing of him that was ready to **p** Job 29:13
all flesh shall **p** together Job 34:15
way of the ungodly shall **p** Ps 1:6
the wicked shall **p** Ps 37:20
like the beasts that **p** Ps 49:12
p at the rebuke of thy countenance Ps 80:16
They shall **p**, but thou shalt endure Ps 102:26
when the wicked **p** Prov 11:10
no vision, the people **p** Prov 29:18
strong drink unto him that is ready to **p** Prov 31:6
they shall come which were ready to **p** Is 27:13
truth is **p** Jer 7:28
God will think on us, that we **p** not Jon 1:6
let us not **p** for this man's life Jon 1:14
we **p** Matt 8:25; Luke 8:24
that one of these little ones should **p** Matt 18:14
shall **p** with the sword Matt 26:52
carest thou not that we **p** Mark 4:38
ye shall all likewise **p** Luke 13:3,5
I **p** with hunger Luke 15:17
shall not an hair of your head **p** Luke 21:18
labour not for the meat which **p** John 6:27
Thy money **p** with thee Acts 8:20
to **p** with the using Col 2:22
not willing that any should **p** 2 Pet 3:9

PERIZZITES per´-iz-ites
belonging to a village Gen 34:30

PERMISSION
I speak this by **p** 1 Cor 7:6

PERMIT
for it is not **p** unto them to speak 1 Cor 14:34
if the LORD **p** 1 Cor 16:7
we do, if God **p** Heb 6:3

PERNICIOUS
shall follow their **p** ways 2 Pet 2:2

PERPETUAL
for a **p** covenant Ex 31:16
their **p** possession Lev 25:34
destructions are come to a **p** end Ps 9:6
p desolations Ps 74:3; Jer 25:9; Ezek 35:9
a **p** backsliding Jer 8:5
Why is my pain **p** Jer 15:18
the **p** hills Hab 3:6

PERPETUALLY
heart shall be there **p** 1 Kgs 9:3; 2 Chr 7:16
anger did tear **p** Amos 1:11

PERPLEXED
and he was **p** Luke 9:7
as they were much **p** Luke 24:4
we are **p** 2 Cor 4:8

PERPLEXITY
treading down, and of **p** by the Lord Is 22:5
now shall be their **p** Mic 7:4
nations, with **p** Luke 21:25

PERSECUTE
Why do ye **p** me Job 19:22
save me from all them that **p** me Ps 7:1
p the poor Ps 10:2
p and take him; for there is none Ps 71:11
the enemy hath **p** my soul Ps 143:3
when men shall revile you and **p** you Matt 5:11
pray for them that use you and **p** you Matt 5:44
If they have **p** me John 15:20
why **p** thou me? Acts 9:4; 22:7; 26:14
I **p** this way unto the death Acts 22:4
I **p** them even unto strange cities Acts 26:11
being **p**, we suffer it 1 Cor 4:12
I **p** the church of God 1 Cor 15:9; Gal 1:13
P, but not forsaken 2 Cor 4:9
Concerning zeal, **p** the church Phil 3:6

PERSECUTION
p ariseth Matt 13:21; Mark 4:17
in **p** in distresses for Christ's sake 2 Cor 12:10
live godly in Christ Jesus shall suffer **p** 2 Tim 3:12

PERSEVERANCE
thereunto with all **p** Eph 6:18

PERSIA per´-si-ah
a country of western Asia 2 Chr 36:20

PERSIAN per´-shan
belonging to Persia Dan 6:28

PERSIS per´-sis
a Persian woman Rom 16:12

PERSON
which regardeth not **p** Deut 10:17
go to battle in thine own **p** 2 Sam 17:11
vile **p** Ps 15:4; Is 32:5,6
vain **p** Ps 26:4; Prov 12:11; 28:19
not one feeble **p** Ps 105:37
regardest not the **p** of men Matt 22:16; Mark 12:14
forgave I it in the **p** of Christ 2 Cor 2:10
the express image of his **p** Heb 1:3
what manner of **p** ought ye to be 2 Pet 3:11

PERSUADE
Who shall **p** Ahab 1 Kgs 22:20
by long forbearing is a prince **p** Prov 25:15
we will **p** him, and secure you Matt 28:14
almost thou **p** me Acts 26:28
Let every man be fully **p** Rom 14:5
we **p** men 2 Cor 5:11
do I now **p** men or God Gal 1:10
we are **p** better things of you Heb 6:9

PERTAIN
those things which **p** to God Rom 15:17
more things that **p** to this life 1 Cor 6:3
things that **p** unto life and godliness 2 Pet 1:3

PERUDA per´-ood-ah
same as PERIDA Ezra 2:55

PERVERSE
a **p** and crooked generation Deut 32:5
Cannot my taste discern **p** things Job 6:30
p lips put far from thee Prov 4:24
p heart shall be despised Prov 12:8
p tongue falleth into mischief Prov 17:20
thine heart shall utter **p** things Prov 23:33
midst of a crooked and **p** nation Phil 2:15

PERVERT
p the words of the righteous Deut 16:19
Doth God **p** judgment Job 8:3
he that **p** his ways shall be known Prov 10:9
The foolishness of man **p** his way Prov 19:3

they have **p** their way Jer 3:21
have **p** the words of the living God Jer 23:36
cease to **p** the right ways Acts 13:10
would **p** the gospel Gal 1:7

PESTILENCE
lest he fall upon us with **p** Ex 5:3
smite thee and thy people with **p** Ex 9:15
by the famine, and by the **p** Jer 42:17; 44:13

PESTILENT
found this man a **p** fellow Acts 24:5

PETER pe´-ter
a stone Matt 16:18

PETHAHIAH pe´-thah-i´-ah
whom Jehovah looses 1 Chr 24:16

PETHOR pe´-thor
cleft, opening Num 22:5

PETHUEL peth´-oo-el
God's opening (?) Joel 1:1

PETITION
the God of Israel grant thee thy **p** 1 Sam 1:17
one small **p** 1 Kgs 2:20
what is thy **p** Esth 5:6; 7:2; 9:12
whosoever shall ask a **p** Dan 6:7
maketh his **p** three times a day Dan 6:13

PEULTHAI pe´-ool-tha´-i
deed of Jehovah 1 Chr 26:5

PHALEC fa´-lek
Gr. for PELEG Luke 3:35

PHALLU fal´-oo
Eng. for PALLU Gen 46:9

PHALTI fal´-ti
deliverance of Jehovah 1 Sam 25:44

PHALTIEL fal´-ti-el
deliverance of God 2 Sam 3:15

PHANUEL fan-oo´-el
Gr. for PENUEL Luke 2:36

PHARAOH fa´-roh
the sun Gen 12:15

PHARES fa´-res
Gr. for PHAREZ Luke 3:33

PHAREZ fa´-rez
breach Gen 38:29

PHARISEES far´-is-ees
the separated Matt 5:20

PHAROSH fa´-rosh
same as PAROSH Ezra 8:3

PHARPAR far´-par
swift 2 Kgs 5:12

PHARZITES farz´-ites
descendants of Pharez Num 26:20

PHASEAH fa-se´-ah
same as PASEAH Neh 7:51

PHEBE fe´-be
moon Rom 16:1

PHENICE fe-ni´-see
palm tree Acts 27:12

PHENICIA fe-nish´-yah
land of palms Acts 21:2

PHICHOL fi´-kol
attentive (?) Gen 21:22

PHILADELPHIA fil´-a-delf´-yah
brotherly love Rev 1:11

PHILEMON fil-e´-mon
affectionate Phile 1:1

PHILETUS fil-e´-tus
beloved 2 Tim 2:17

PHILIP fil´-ip
lover of horses Matt 10:3

PHILIPPI fil-ip´-i
town named for Philip of Macedon Acts 16:12

PHILIPPIANS fil-ip´-yans
inhabitants of Philippi Phil 4:15

PHILISTIA fil-ist´-yah
the land of the Philistines Ps 60:8

PHILISTIM fil´-ist-im
wanderers Gen 10:14

PHILISTINES fil´-ist-ines
same as PHILISTIM Gen 21:34

PHILOLOGUS fil-o´-log-us
talkative Rom 16:15

PHILOSOPHY
spoil you through **p** and vain deceit Col 2:8

PHINEHAS fin´-e-as
serpent's mouth Num 25:7

PHLEGON fleg´-on
zealous, burning Rom 16:14

PHRYGIA fridg´-i-ah
a large province of Asia Minor Acts 2:10

PHURAH foor´-ah
branch (?) Judg 7:10

PHUT foot
a people related to the Egyptians Gen 10:6

PHUVAH foo´-vah
mouth Gen 46:13

PHYGELLUS fi-gel´-us
little fugitive 2 Tim 1:15

PI-BESETH pi-be´-seth
the city of (the goddess) Bast Ezek 30:17

PI-HAHIROTH pi´-ha-hi´-roth
where sedge grows Ex 14:2

PICTURES
destroy all their **p** Num 33:52
apples of gold in **p** Prov 25:11
upon all pleasant **p** Is 2:16

PIECE
a **p** of bread 1 Sam 2:36; Prov 6:26; 28:21
Samuel hewed Agag in **p** 1 Sam 15:33
rending it in **p** while there is none Ps 7:2
lest I tear you in **p** Ps 50:22
hammer that breaketh the rock in **p** Jer 23:29
one **p** was rained upon Amos 4:7
weighed for my price thirty **p** Zech 11:12
took the thirty **p** of silver Zech 11:13; Matt 27:9

PIERCE
into his hand and **p** it 2 Kgs 18:21; Is 36:6
whom they have **p** Zech 12:10; John 19:37
p themselves through with many sorrows 1 Tim 6:10

PILATE pi´-lat
armed with a javelin (?) Matt 27:2

PILDASH pil´-dash
steel (?) Gen 22:22

PILEHA pi´-le-hah
ploughman (?) Neh 10:24

PILLAR
the **p** thereof tremble Job 9:6
she hath hewn out her seven **p** Prov 9:1
Cephas and John, who seemed to be **p** Gal 2:9
the **p** and ground of the truth 1 Tim 3:15
Him that overcometh will I make a **p** Rev 3:12

PILLOW
put them for his **p** Gen 28:11
and put a **p** of goat's hair 1 Sam 19:13
women that sew **p** Ezek 13:18
asleep on a **p** Mark 4:38

PILTAI pil´-ta-i
whom Jehovah delivers Neh 12:17

PIN
will men take a **p** Ezek 15:3

PINE
shall they **p** away with them Lev 26:39
for these **p** away Lam 4:9
but ye shall **p** Ezek 24:23

PINON pi´-non
darkness Gen 36:41

PIPED
we have **p** unto you Matt 11:17; Luke 7:32
how shall it be known what it **p** 1 Cor 14:7

PIRAM pi´-ram
like a wild donkey Josh 10:3

PIRATHON pi´-rath-on
leader Judg 12:15

PIRATHONITE pi´-rath-on-ite
an inhabitant of Pirathon Judg 12:13

PISGAH piz´-gah
a part, boundary Num 21:20

PISIDIA pi-sid´-i-ah
a district in the province of Galatia Acts 13:14

PISON pi´-son
flowing stream (?) Gen 2:11

PISPAH pis´-pah
expansion 1 Chr 7:38

PIT
cast him into some **p** Gen 37:20
if a man shall dig a **p** Ex 21:33
into the **p** Num 16:30,33
deliver him from going down to the **p** Job 33:24
like them that go down into the **p** Ps 28:1
out of an horrible **p** Ps 40:2
mouth of a strange woman is a deep **p** Prov 22:14
shall fall himself into his own **p** Prov 28:10
the **p** of corruption Is 38:17
fall into a **p** on the sabbath Matt 12:11

PITCHER
Let down thy **p** Gen 24:14
lamps within the **p** Judg 7:16
or the **p** be broken Eccl 12:6
as earthen **p** Lam 4:2

PITHOM pi´-thom
abode of the setting sun (?) Ex 1:11

PITHON pi´-thon
simple (?) 1 Chr 8:35

PITIFUL
hands of the **p** Lam 4:10
Lord is very **p** and of tender mercy James 5:11
brethren, be **p** 1 Pet 3:8

PITY
thine eye shall have no **p** Deut 7:16
have **p** upon me, O ye my friends Job 19:21
I looked for some to take **p** Ps 69:20
he that hath **p** upon poor lendeth Prov 19:17
gather it for him that will **p** the poor Prov 28:8
they shall have no **p** on the fruit Is 13:18
in his **p** he redeemed them Is 63:9
I will not **p**, nor spare Jer 13:14
None eye **p** thee Ezek 16:5
that which your soul **p** Ezek 24:21
p his people Joel 2:18
their own shepherds **p** them not Zech 11:5
as I had **p** on thee Matt 18:33

PLACE
the **p** whereon thou standest is holy Ex 3:5; Josh 5:15
a **p** where there is no want Judg 18:10
strike his hand over the **p** 2 Kgs 5:11
p where we dwell is too strait for us 2 Kgs 6:1
the **p** where thine honour dwelleth Ps 26:8
Thou art my hiding **p** Ps 32:7; 119:114
thou shalt diligently consider his **p** Ps 37:10
the dark **p** of the earth Ps 74:20
our dwelling **p** Ps 90:1
his children have a **p** of refuge Prov 14:26
The eyes of the Lord are in every **p** Prov 15:3
All go unto one **p** Eccl 3:20
lay field to field, till there be no **p** Is 5:8
the **p** of my feet Is 60:13
where is the **p** of my rest Is 66:1
they shall feed every one in his **p** Jer 6:3
the LORD cometh forth out of his **p** Mic 1:3
p shall not be found for them Zech 10:10
in every **p** incense shall be offered Mal 1:11
see the **p** where the Lord lay Matt 28:6
into every city and **p** Luke 10:1
Give this man **p** Luke 14:9
my word hath no **p** in you John 8:37
knew the **p** John 18:2
with one accord in one **p** Acts 2:1
the **p** was shaken Acts 4:31
rather give **p** unto wrath Rom 12:19
Neither give **p** to the devil Eph 4:27
found no **p** of repentance Heb 12:17
there was found no **p** for them Rev 20:11

PLAGUE
I will bring seven times more **p** Lev 26:21
will make thy **p** wonderful Deut 28:59
when they see the **p** of that land Deut 29:22
every man the **p** of his own heart 1 Kgs 8:38
neither are they **p** like other men Ps 73:5
shall any **p** come nigh thy dwelling Ps 91:10
O death, I will be thy **p** Hos 13:14
that ye receive not of her **p** Rev 18:4
add unto him the **p** that are written Rev 22:18

PLAIN
Jacob was a **p** man Gen 25:27
lead me in a **p** path Ps 27:11
all **p** to him that understandeth Prov 8:9
the way of the righteous is made **p** Prov 15:19
rough places **p** Is 40:4
Write the vision, and make it **p** Hab 2:2

PLAINLY
the words of this law very **p** Deut 27:8
stammerers shall be ready to speak **p** Is 32:4
tell us **p** John 10:24
I shall shew you **p** of the Father John 16:25
now speakest thou **p** John 16:29

PLANES
he fitteth it with **p** Is 44:13

PLANT (n)
bring forth boughs like a **p** Job 14:9
children like olive **p** Ps 128:3
sons may be as **p** grown up Ps 144:12
his pleasant **p** Is 5:7
broken down the principal **p** Is 16:8
as a tender **p** Is 53:2
a **p** of renown Ezek 34:29
Every **p** which my heavenly Father hath not planted Matt 15:13

PLANT (v)
which the Lord hath **p** Num 24:6
will **p** them 2 Sam 7:10; 1 Chr 17:9
like a tree **p** Ps 1:3
vineyard which thy right hand hath **p** Ps 80:15
p in the house of the LORD Ps 92:13
he that **p** the ear Ps 94:9
I had **p** thee a noble vine Jer 2:21

being **p**, shall it prosper Ezek 17:10
be thou **p** in the sea Luke 17:6
if we have been **p** together Rom 6:5
I have **p** 1 Cor 3:6

PLATE
thou shalt make a **p** of pure gold Ex 28:36
they made the **p** of the holy crown Ex 39:30
silverspread into **p** is brought Jer 10:9

PLATTED
they had **p** a crown Matt 27:29
p a crown of thorns Mark 15:17
soldiers **p** a crown John 19:2
p the hair 1 Pet 3:3

PLATTER
of the **p** Matt 23:25
cup and the **p** Luke 11:39

PLAY
rose up to **p** Ex 32:6; 1 Cor 10:7
a man that can **p** well 1 Sam 16:17
I will **p** before the LORD 2 Sam 6:21
let us **p** the men 2 Sam 10:12
Wilt thou **p** with him Job 41:5
p skilfully with a loud noise Ps 33:3
the sucking child shall **p** Is 11:8
can **p** well on an instrument Ezek 33:32

PLEA
between **p** and **p** Deut 17:8

PLEAD
Will ye **p** for Baal? Judg 6:31
who shall set me a time to **p**? Job 9:19
Who is he that will **p** with me? Job 13:19
that one might **p** for a man Job 16:21
p against me with his great power? Job 23:6
p for the widow Is 1:17
The LORD standeth up to **p** Is 3:13
let us **p** together Is 43:26
nor any **p** for truth Is 59:4
I will yet **p** with you Jer 2:9
thou hast **p** the causes of my soul Lam 3:58
will **p** with them there for my people Joel 3:2

PLEASANT
p to the eyes Gen 3:6
were lovely and **p** in their lives 2 Sam 1:23
very **p** hast thou been to me 2 Sam 1:26
lines are fallen unto me in **p** places Ps 16:6
they despised the **p** land Ps 106:24
p it is for brethren to dwell together Ps 133:1
knowledge is **p** unto thy soul Prov 2:10
the words of the pure are **p** words Prov 15:26
P words are as a honeycomb Prov 16:24
p thing it is for the eyes Eccl 11:7
p fruits Song 4:13,16; 7:13
our **p** things are laid waste Is 64:11
a **p** child Jer 31:20
of one that hath a **p** voice Ezek 33:32
I ate no **p** bread Dan 10:3

PLEASANTNESS
ways of **p** Prov 3:17

PLEASE
the speech **p** the Lord 1 Kgs 3:10
then shalt thou be **p** with the sacrifices Ps 51:19
he hath done whatsoever he hath **p** Ps 115:3
when a man's ways **p** the Lord Prov 16:7
p themselves in the children of strangers Is 2:6
it **p** the LORD to bruise him Is 53:10
accomplish that which I **p** Is 55:11
Will the LORD be **p** with thousands of rams Mic 6:7
will he be **p** with thee? Mal 1:8
I do always those things that **p** him John 8:29
that are in the flesh cannot **p** God Rom 8:8
not to **p** ourselves Rom 15:1
even Christ **p** not himself Rom 15:3
p God by the foolishness of preaching 1 Cor 1:21
as I **p** all men in all things 1 Cor 10:33
do I seek to **p** men? Gal 1:10
without faith it is impossible to **p** him Heb 11:6

PLEASURE
hast **p** in uprightness 1 Chr 29:17
should do according to every man's **p** Esth 1:8
what **p** hath he in his house Job 21:21
never eateth with **p** Job 21:25
Is it any **p** to the Almighty Job 22:3
p for evermore Ps 16:11
hath **p** in the prosperity of his servants Ps 35:27
Do good in thy good **p** Ps 51:18
thy servants take **p** in her stones Ps 102:14
ye ministers of his, that do his **p** Ps 103:21
of all them that have **p** therein Ps 111:2
taketh **p** in them that fear him Ps 147:11
the Lord taketh **p** in his people Ps 149:4
He that loveth **p** shall be a poor man Prov 21:17
he hath no **p** in fools Eccl 5:4
I have no **p** in them Eccl 12:1
shall perform all my **p** Is 44:28
the **p** of the LORD shall prosper Is 53:10
in the day of your fast ye find **p** Is 58:3
doing thy **p** on my holy day Is 58:13
a vessel wherein is no **p** Jer 22:28; 48:38; Hos 8:8
Have I any **p** Ezek 18:23
I have no **p** in you, saith the LORD Mal 1:10
p of this life Luke 8:14
Father's good **p** Luke 12:32
the good **p** of his will Eph 1:5
both to will and to do of his good **p** Phil 2:13
she that liveth in **p** 1 Tim 5:6
lovers of **p** 2 Tim 3:4
my soul shall have no **p** in him Heb 10:38
the **p** of sin for a season Heb 11:25
chastened us after their own **p** Heb 12:10
Ye have lived in **p** on earth James 5:5
for thy **p** they are and were created Rev 4:11

PLEIADES pli´-ad-ees
(coming at) the sailing season (?) Job 9:9

PLENTEOUS
p in mercy Ps 86:5; 103:8
p redemption Ps 130:7
portion is fat, and their meat is **p** Hab 1:16
The harvest truly is **p** Matt 9:37

PLENTIFUL
send a **p** rain Ps 68:9
a **p** country Jer 2:7
the **p** field Jer 48:33

PLENTY
p of corn and wine Gen 27:28
p of silver Job 22:25
p of justice Job 37:23
barns be filled with **p** Prov 3:10

PLOW
they that **p** iniquity Job 4:8
not **p** by reason of the cold Prov 20:4
the **p** of the wicked is sin Prov 21:4
Doth plowman **p** all day to sow? Is 28:24

PLUCK
mayest **p** the ears with thine hand Deut 23:25
Then will I **p** them up 2 Chr 7:20
They **p** the fatherless from the breast Job 24:9
he shall **p** my feet out of the net Ps 25:15
P it out of thy bosom Ps 74:11
the foolish **p** it down with her hands Prov 14:1
a time to **p** up Eccl 3:2
my cheeks to them that **p** Is 50:6
yet would I **p** thee thence Jer 22:24
a firebrand **p** out Amos 4:11
offend thee, **p** it out Matt 5:29; 18:9; Mark 9:47
p the ears Matt 12:1; Mark 2:23; Luke 6:1
shall any **p** them out of my hand John 10:28

POCHERETH OF ZEBAIM po-ke´-reth of Ze-ba´-im
offspring of gazelles (?) Ezra 2:57

POINT
written with the **p** of iron Jer 17:1
in all **p** tempted Heb 4:15
yet offend in one **p** James 2:10

POLE
set it upon a **p** Num 21:8

POLICY
through his **p** Dan 8:25

POLISHED
made me a **p** shaft Is 49:2
their as **p** sapphire Lam 4:7
feet like in colour to **p** brass Dan 10:6

POLL
when he **p** his head 2 Sam 14:26
they shall only **p** their heads Ezek 44:20
p thee for thy delicate children Mic 1:16

POLLUX pol´-ux
1 *a boxer*
2 one of the Dioscuri (sons of Zeus) Acts 28:11

POMP
their **p**, and he that rejoiceth Is 5:14
Thy **p** is brought down to the grave Is 14:11
the **p** of the strong Ezek 7:24
the **p** of her strength Ezek 30:18
Bernice, with great **p** Acts 25:23

PONDER
P the path of thy feet Prov 4:26
Lest thou shouldest **p** Prov 5:6
the LORD, and **p** all his goings Prov 5:21

PONTIUS pon´-shus
belonging to the sea Matt 27:2

PONTUS pont´-us
sea Acts 2:9

POOL
the rain also filleth the **p** Ps 84:6
parched ground shall become a **p** Is 35:7
make the wilderness a **p** of water Is 41:18
by the sheep market a **p** John 5:2
wash in the **p** of Siloam John 9:7

POOR
the **p** shall not give less Ex 30:15
the **p** shall never cease Deut 15:11
none remained, save **p** sort 2 Kgs 24:14
the **p** of the earth hide Job 24:4
I was a father to the **p** Job 29:16
the **p** committeth himself unto thee Ps 10:14
This **p** man cried Ps 34:6
I am **p** Ps 40:17; 69:29; 70:5; 86:1; 109:22
rich and **p**, together Ps 49:2
becometh **p** that dealeth with a slack hand Prov 10:4
much food is in the tillage of the **p** Prov 13:23
The **p** useth intreaties Prov 18:23
rich and **p** meet together Prov 22:2
lest I be **p**, and steal Prov 30:9
When the **p** and needy seek water Is 41:17
sold the righteous for silver, and the **p** Amos 2:6
p of the flock Zech 11:7,11
Blessed are the **p** in spirit Matt 5:3
as **p**, yet making many rich 2 Cor 6:10
for your sakes he became **p** 2 Cor 8:9

POPULOUS
a nation, great, mighty, and **p** Deut 26:5
better than **p** Nah 3:8

PORATHA po´-rath-ah
having many chariots (?) Esth 9:8

PORTION
Is there yet any **p** Gen 31:14
one **p** above thy brethren Gen 48:22
the LORD'S **p** is his people Deut 32:9
a double **p** of thy spirit 2 Kgs 2:9
send **p** Neh 8:10; Esth 9:19
This is the **p** of a wicked man Job 20:29
their **p** is cursed Job 24:18
how little a **p** is heard of him? Job 26:14
what **p** of God is there from above? Job 31:2
this shall be the **p** of their cup Ps 11:6
The LORD is the **p** of mine inheritance Ps 16:5
have their **p** in this life Ps 17:14
my **p** for ever Ps 73:26
Thou art my **p**, O Lord Ps 119:57
a **p** to her maidens Prov 31:15
this was my **p** of all my labour Eccl 2:10
rejoice, for that is his **p** Eccl 3:22; 5:18; 9:9
power to eat thereof, and to take **p** Eccl 5:19
neither have they any more a **p** for ever Eccl 9:6
Give a **p** to seven Eccl 11:2
divide him a **p** with the great Is 53:12
they shall rejoice in their **p** Is 61:7
p of Jacob is not like them Jer 10:16; 51:19
my pleasant **p** a desolate wilderness Jer 12:10
every day a **p** Jer 52:34
with the **p** of the king's meat Dan 1:8
he hath changed the **p** of my people Mic 2:4
his **p** with the hypocrites Matt 24:51
their **p** of meat in due season Luke 12:42
his **p** with the unbelievers Luke 12:46
the **p** of goods that falleth Luke 15:12

POSSESS
thy seed shall **p** the gate Gen 22:17; 24:60
made to **p** months of vanity Job 7:3
p iniquities of my youth Job 13:26
the LORD **p** me in beginning Prov 8:22
I give tithes of all I **p** Luke 18:12
in patience **p** your souls Luke 21:19

POSSESSION
an everlasting **p** Gen 17:8; 48:4
good things in **p** Prov 28:10
great **p** Eccl 2:7; Matt 19:22; Mark 10:22
And sold their **p** Acts 2:45
redemption of the purchased **p** Eph 1:14

POSSIBLE
with God all things are **p** Matt 19:26; Mark 10:27
if it were **p** Mark 13:22
if it be **p**, let this cup pass from me Matt 26:39
all things are **p** to him that believeth Mark 9:23
all things are **p** unto thee Mark 14:36

POST
upon the **p** of thy house Deut 6:9
swifter than a **p** Job 9:25
One **p** shall run to meet Jer 51:31
that the **p** may shake Amos 9:1

POSTERITY
preserve you a **p** Gen 45:7
their **p** approve their sayings Ps 49:13
Let his **p** cut off Ps 109:13
not to his **p** Dan 11:4

POT
not any thing save a **p** of oil 2 Kgs 4:2
there is death in the **p** 2 Kgs 4:40
maketh the deep boil like a **p** Job 41:31
every **p** Zech 14:21
the washing of cups, and **p** Mark 7:4

POTENTATE
the blessed and only **P** 1 Tim 6:15

POTI-PHERAH pot´-i-fer´-ah
same as POTIPHAR Gen 41:45

POTIPHAR pot´-i-far
belonging to the sun Gen 37:36

POUND
delivered them ten **p** Luke 19:13
a **p** of ointment of spikenard John 12:3

POUR
Hast thou not **p** me out as milk Job 10:10
rock **p** me out rivers of oil Job 29:6
my soul is **p** out upon me Job 30:16
grace is **p** into thy lips Ps 45:2
p out your heart before him Ps 62:8
I will **p** out my Spirit Prov 1:23; Joel 2:28,29; Acts 2:17
as ointment **p** forth Song 1:3
p out a prayer when thy chastening Is 26:16
the spirit be **p** on us Is 32:15
I will **p** water on him that is thirsty Is 44:3
p out his soul unto death Is 53:12
my fury shall be **p** out Jer 7:20; 42:18
p out thine heart like water Lam 2:19
fury is **p** out like fire Nah 1:6
p you out a blessing Mal 3:10
p it on his head Matt 26:7; Mark 14:3
p out the changers' money John 2:15

POURTRAY
p upon it a city Ezek 4:1
p upon the wall Ezek 8:10; 23:14

POVERTY
come to **p** Gen 45:11; Prov 20:13
p come as one that travelleth Prov 6:11; 24:34
destruction of the poor is their **p** Prov 10:15
it tendeth to **p** Prov 11:24
P and shame shall be to him Prov 13:18
shall have **p** enough Prov 28:19
give me neither **p** nor riches Prov 30:8
Let him drink, and forget his **p** Prov 31:7

POWDER
ground it to **p** Ex 32:20
stamped it small to **p** 2 Kgs 23:6
grind him to **p** Matt 21:44

POWER
hast thou **p** with God Gen 32:28
glorious in **p** Ex 15:6
the pride of your **p** Lev 26:19
he that giveth thee **p** to get wealth Deut 8:18
God is my strength and **p** 2 Sam 22:33
the **p** and the glory 1 Chr 29:11; Matt 6:13
God hath **p** to help 2 Chr 25:8
him that is without **p** Job 26:2
from the **p** of the grave Ps 49:15
being girded with **p** Ps 65:6
Who knoweth **p** of thine anger? Ps 90:11
it is in the **p** of thine hand to do it Prov 3:27
in the **p** of the tongue Prov 18:21
p to eat thereof Eccl 5:19; 6:2
the word of a king is, there is **p** Eccl 8:4
he giveth **p** to the faint Is 40:29
full of **p** by the Spirit Mic 3:8
the hiding of his **p** Hab 3:4
Not by might, nor by **p** Zech 4:6
p on earth to forgive Matt 9:6; Mark 2:10
which had given such **p** to men Matt 9:8
in the clouds of heaven with **p** Matt 24:30
All **p** is given to me Matt 28:18
the **p** of the Highest Luke 1:35
All this **p** will I give thee Luke 4:6
Jesus returned in the **p** of the Spirit Luke 4:14
his word was with **p** Luke 4:32
the **p** of the Lord was present Luke 5:17
amazed at the mighty **p** of God Luke 9:43
that hath **p** to cast into hell Luke 12:5
magistrates and **p** Luke 12:11
your hour, and the **p** of darkness Luke 22:53
with **p** from on high Luke 24:49
p to become sons of God John 1:12
I have **p** to lay it down John 10:18
p over all flesh John 17:2
I have **p** to crucify thee John 19:10
p after that the Holy Ghost is come Acts 1:8
as though by our own **p** Acts 3:12
was it not in thine own **p**? Acts 5:4
this man is the great **p** of God Acts 8:10
Give me also this **p** Acts 8:19
from the **p** of Satan unto God Acts 26:18
his eternal **p** and Godhead Rom 1:20
that I might shew my **p** in thee Rom 9:17
Whosoever therefore resisteth the **p** Rom 13:2
it is raised in **p** 1 Cor 15:43
prince of the **p** of the air Eph 2:2
the effectual working of his **p** Eph 3:7
the **p** of his resurrection Phil 3:10
from the glory of his **p** 2 Thess 1:9
spirit of fear, but of **p**, and of love 2 Tim 1:7
form of godliness, but denying the **p** 2 Tim 3:5
destroy him that had the **p** of death Heb 2:14
the **p** of the world to come Heb 6:5
the **p** of an endless life Heb 7:16
to him will I give **p** Rev 2:26
receive glory and honour and **p** Rev 4:11

POWERFUL
voice of the LORD is **p** Ps 29:4
are weighty and **p** 2 Cor 10:10
word of God is quick, and **p** Heb 4:12

PRAISE (n)
fearful in **p** Ex 15:11
he is thy **p** and thy God Deut 10:21
sing **p** Judg 5:3; Ps 7:17; 9:2; 61:8; 104:33
above all blessing and **p** Neh 9:5
O thou that inhabitest the **p** of Israel Ps 22:3
My **p** shall be of thee Ps 22:25
p is comely Ps 33:1; 147:1
his **p** shall continually be in my mouth Ps 34:1
whoso offereth **p** glorifieth me Ps 50:23
P waiteth for thee Ps 65:1
make his **p** glorious Ps 66:2
O God of my **p** Ps 109:1
the **p** of all his saints Ps 148:14
so is a man to his **p** Prov 27:21
thy gates **P** Is 60:18
garment of **p** Is 61:3
a **p** in the earth Is 62:7
for a **p** Jer 13:11
How is the city of **p** Jer 49:25
the earth was full of his **p** Hab 3:3
a **p** among all people Zeph 3:20
Give God the **p** John 9:24
the **p** of men John 12:43
whose **p** is not of men Rom 2:29
thou shalt have **p** Rom 13:3
every man have **p** of God 1 Cor 4:5
whose **p** is in the gospel 2 Cor 8:18
p of the glory of his grace Eph 1:6
if there be any **p** Phil 4:8
offer the sacrifice of **p** Heb 13:15
p of them that do well 1 Pet 2:14
to whom be **p** and dominion 1 Pet 4:11

PRAISE (v)
whom thy brethren shall **p** Gen 49:8
none to be so much **p** 2 Sam 14:25
Shall the dust **p** thee? Ps 30:9
I shall yet **p** him Ps 42:5,11; 43:5
therefore shall the people **p** thee Ps 45:17
men will **p** thee when thou doest well Ps 49:18
my lips shall **p** thee Ps 63:3
Let the people **p** thee Ps 67:3,5
I will yet **p** thee more and more Ps 71:14
daily shall he be **p** Ps 72:15

The Lord shall **p** thee from evil Ps 121:7
p thy going out and thy coming in Ps 121:8
p the way of his saints Prov 2:8
Discretion shall **p** thee Prov 2:11
Mercy and truth **p** the king Prov 20:28
I will **p** them alive Jer 49:11
shall lose his life shall **p** it Luke 17:33

PRESS
I am **p** under you, as a cart is **p** Amos 2:13
they **p** upon him for to touch him Mark 3:10
good measure, **p** down Luke 6:38
every man **p** into it Luke 16:16
I **p** toward the mark Phil 3:14

PRESUME
the prophet which shall **p** to speak Deut 18:20
where is he, that durst **p** in his heart Esth 7:5

PRESUMPTUOUS
the soul that doeth ought **p** Num 15:30
Keep back thy servant also from **p** sins Ps 19:13
P are they, self-willed 2 Pet 2:10

PRETENSE
for a **p** make long prayer Matt 23:14; Mark 12:40
in **p** or in truth, Christ is preached Phil 1:18

PREVAIL
and hast **p** Gen 32:28
Moses held up his hand, that Israel **p** Ex 17:11
by strength shall no man **p** 1 Sam 2:9
let not man **p** Ps 9:19
Iniquities **p** against me Ps 65:3
if one **p** against him Eccl 4:12
gates of hell shall not **p** Matt 16:18
mightily grew the word of God and **p** Acts 19:20

PREVENT
snares of death **p** me 2 Sam 22:6; Ps 18:5
God of my mercy shall **p** me Ps 59:10
in the morning shall my prayer **p** thee Ps 88:13
I **p** the dawning of the morning Ps 119:147

PREY
Shall the **p** be taken from the mighty Is 49:24
for a **p** Jer 21:9; 38:2; 39:18; 45:5
shall no more be a **p** Ezek 34:22

PRICE
the **p** of his redemption Lev 25:52
buy it of thee at a **p** 2 Sam 24:24
kept back part of the **p** Acts 5:2
bought with a **p** 1 Cor 6:20; 7:23
of great **p** 1 Pet 3:4

PRICKS
remain of them shall be **p** in your eyes Num 33:55
for thee to kick against the **p** Acts 9:5; 26:14

PRIDE
from the **p** of man Ps 31:20
p, and arrogancy Prov 8:13
In the mouth of the foolish is a rod of **p** Prov 14:3
Woe to the crown of **p** Is 28:1
the **p** of thine heart Jer 49:16

PRIEST
p of most high God Gen 14:18; Heb 7:1
a kingdom of **p** Ex 19:6
I will raise me up a faithful **p** 1 Sam 2:35
p of them that are no gods 2 Chr 13:9
without a teaching **p** 2 Chr 15:3
clothe her **p** with salvation Ps 132:16
as with the people, so with the **p** Is 24:2
p and the prophet have erred Is 28:7
shall be named The **p** of the Lord Is 61:6
the **p** thereof teach for hire Mic 3:11
the **p** lips should keep knowledge Mal 2:7
shew yourselves unto the **p** Luke 17:14
p were obedient to the faith Acts 6:7
kings and **p** Rev 1:6; 5:10
thou shall be **p** of God Rev 20:6

PRIESTHOOD
an everlasting **p** Ex 40:15; Num 25:13
seek ye the **p** also Num 16:10
an unchangeable **p** Heb 7:24
an holy **p** 1 Pet 2:5
ye are a royal **p** 1 Pet 2:9

PRINCE
as a **p** hast thou power Gen 32:28
Who made thee a **p** Ex 2:14
to set them among **p** 1 Sam 2:8
a **p** and a great man 2 Sam 3:38
poureth contempt upon **p** Job 12:21; Ps 107:40
Where is the house of the **p**? Job 21:28
as a **p** would I go near unto him Job 31:37
make **p** in all the earth Ps 45:16
than to put confidence in **p** Ps 118:9
put not your trust in **p** Ps 146:3
p decree justice Prov 8:15
nor for **p** strong drink Prov 31:4
p walking as servants Eccl 10:7
thy **p** eat in the morning Eccl 10:16
thy **p** eat in due season Eccl 10:17
all her **p** shall be nothing Is 34:12
without a **p** Hos 3:4
by **p** of the devils Matt 9:34; 12:24; Mark 3:22
the **p** of this world John 12:31; 14:30; 16:11
and killed the **p** of life Acts 3:15
exalted to be a **p** and Saviour Acts 5:31
nor of the **p** of this world 1 Cor 2:6
none of the **p** of this world knew 1 Cor 2:8
the **p** of the power of the air Eph 2:2

PRINCIPAL
Wisdom is the **p** thing Prov 4:7
cast in the **p** wheat Is 28:25
captains, and **p** men of the city Acts 25:23

PRINCIPALITY
against **p**, and powers Eph 6:12
to be subject to **p** Titus 3:1

PRINCIPLES
first **p** of the oracles of God Heb 5:12
leaving the **p** of the doctrines of Christ Heb 6:1

PRINT
nor **p** any marks upon you Lev 19:28
a **p** upon the heels of my feet Job 13:27
they were **p** in a book Job 19:23
in his hands the **p** of the nails John 20:25

PRISCA pris´-kah
ancient 2 Tim 4:19

PRISCILLA pris-il´-ah
same as PRISCA Acts 18:2

PRISON
Bring my soul out of **p** Ps 142:7
out of **p** he cometh to reign Eccl 4:14
taken from **p** and from judgment Is 53:8
opening of the **p** Is 61:1
thou be cast into **p** Matt 5:25
John had heard in the **p** Matt 11:2
in **p**, and ye came unto me Matt 25:36
with thee both into **p**, and to death Luke 22:33
in **p** more frequent 2 Cor 11:23
spirits in **p** 1 Pet 3:19

PRISONER
the sighing of the **p** come before thee Ps 79:11
ye **p** of hope Zech 9:12
a notable **p**, called Barabbas Matt 27:16
For this cause, I Paul, the **p** Eph 3:1

PRIVATE
scripture is of any **p** interpretation 2 Pet 1:20

PRIVATELY
the disciples came unto him **p** Matt 24:3
his disciples asked him **p** Mark 9:28
and said **p**, Blessed are the eyes Luke 10:23
p to them which were of reputation Gal 2:2

PRIVILY
was minded to put her away **p** Matt 1:19
when he had **p** called the wise men Matt 2:7
do they thrust us out **p** Acts 16:37
came in **p** to spy out our liberty Gal 2:4
p shall bring in damnable heresies 2 Pet 2:1

PRIZE
but on receiveth the **p** 1 Cor 9:24
for the **p** of the high calling of God Phil 3:14

PROCEED
The thing **p** from the Lord Gen 24:50
that **p** out of the mouth of the LORD Deut 8:3; Matt 4:4
I will **p** no further Job 40:5
I will **p** to do a marvellous work Is 29:14
a law shall **p** from me Is 51:4
they **p** from evil to evil Jer 9:3
p out of the mouth Matt 15:18
I **p** forth John 8:42
p blessing and cursing James 3:10

PROCHORUS prok´-or-us
he that presides over the choir Acts 6:5

PROCLAIM
I will **p** the name of the Lord Ex 33:19
to **p** liberty to the captives Is 61:1
To **p** the acceptable year Is 61:2
the Lord hath **p** Is 62:11
p liberty every man to his neighbour Jer 34:15
p upon the housetops Luke 12:3

PROCURE
seeketh good **p** favour Prov 11:27
Hast thou not **p** this unto thyself Jer 2:17
thy doings have **p** these things Jer 4:18
we **p** great evil against our souls Jer 26:19
the prosperity that I **p** unto it Jer 33:9

PRODUCE
P your cause Is 41:21

PROFANE (adj)
prophet and priest are **p** Jer 23:11
no difference between the holy and **p** Ezek 22:26
unholy and **p** 1 Tim 1:9
refuse **p** and old wives' fables 1 Tim 4:7
avoiding **p** and vain babblings 1 Tim 6:20; 2 Tim 2:16
any **p** person Heb 12:16

PROFANE (v)
p the name of thy God Lev 18:21; 19:12; 21:6
priests in temple **p** the sabbath Matt 12:5
hath gone about to **p** temple Acts 24:6

PROFESS
P themselves to be wise Rom 1:22
glorify God for your **p** subjection 2 Cor 9:13
women **p** godliness 1 Tim 2:10
thou art also called, and hast **p** 1 Tim 6:12

PROFIT (n)
what **p** shall this birthright do to me? Gen 25:32
What **p** is it if we slay Gen 37:26
what **p** should we have if we pray Job 21:15
In all labour there is **p** Prov 14:23
What **p** Eccl 1:3; 3:9; 5:16
there was no **p** under the sun Eccl 2:11
p of the earth for all Eccl 5:9
there is **p** to them Eccl 7:11
things wherein there is no **p** Jer 16:19
what **p** is it that we have kept Mal 3:14
not seeking mine own **p**, but the **p** of many 1 Cor 10:33

about words to no **p** 2 Tim 2:14
for our **p** Heb 12:10

PROFIT (v)
vain things, which cannot **p** 1 Sam 12:21
and it **p** me not Job 33:27
It **p** a man nothing Job 34:9
Treasures of wickedness **p** nothing Prov 10:2
Riches **p** not in the day of wrath Prov 11:4
people that could not **p** Is 30:5
which teacheth thee to **p** Is 48:17
changed their glory for that which doth not **p** Jer 2:11
they shall not **p** this people Jer 23:32
what is a man **p**? Matt 16:26
given to every man to **p** withal 1 Cor 12:7
Christ shall **p** you nothing Gal 5:2
bodily exercise **p** little 1 Tim 4:8
the word preached did not **p** Heb 4:2

PROFITABLE
Can a man be **p** unto God Job 22:2
wisdom is **p** to direct Eccl 10:10
I kept back nothing that was **p** Acts 20:20
godliness is **p** unto all things 1 Tim 4:8
is **p** for doctrine 2 Tim 3:16

PROLONG
ye shall not **p** your days Deut 4:26; 30:18
mine end, that I should **p** my life? Job 6:11
The fear of the Lord **p** days Prov 10:27
days be **p** Eccl 8:12

PROMISE (n)
ye shall know my breach of **p** Num 14:34
hath not failed one word of all his good **p** 1 Kgs 8:56
Doth his **p** fail Ps 77:8
p of my Father Luke 24:49; Acts 1:4
p is unto you and to your children Acts 2:39
for the hope of the **p** Acts 26:6
the **p** made of none effect Rom 4:14
staggered not at the **p** Rom 4:20
the children of the **p** Rom 9:8
p of God in him are yea 2 Cor 1:20
Is the law then against the **p** of God? Gal 3:21
p of the life that now is 1 Tim 4:8
faith and patience inherit the **p** Heb 6:12
the **p** of eternal inheritance Heb 9:15
died in faith, not having received the **p** Heb 11:13
great and precious **p** 2 Pet 1:4
Where is the **p** of his coming? 2 Pet 3:4
not slack concerning his **p** 2 Pet 3:9

PROMISE (v)
will give you, according as he hath **p** Ex 12:25
up unto the place which the Lord **p** Num 14:40
as he hath **p** Deut 1:11
not able to bring them into the land which he **p** Deut 9:28
the land he **p** to give Deut 19:8
which the LORD your God **p** Josh 23:15
as he **p** him to give 2 Kgs 8:19
p to give him money Mark 14:11
had **p**, also he was able to perform Rom 4:21
he is faithful that **p** Heb 10:23
he hath **p** us, even eternal life 1 John 2:25

PROMOTE
Will **p** thee unto very great honour Num 22:17
I thought to **p** thee Num 24:11
Exalt her, and she shall **p** Prov 4:8

PROMOTION
For **p** cometh neither from the east Ps 75:6
shame shall be the **p** of fools Prov 3:35

PRONOUNCE
could not frame to **p** it right Judg 12:6
have **p** the word, saith the LORD Jer 34:5

PROOF
I might know the **p** of you 2 Cor 2:9
the **p** of your love 2 Cor 8:24
ye seek a **p** of Christ 2 Cor 13:3
ye know the **p** of him Phil 2:22
make full **p** of thy ministry 2 Tim 4:5

PROPER
I have of mine own **p** good 1 Chr 29:3
every man hath his own **p** gift 1 Cor 7:7
they saw that he was a **p** child Heb 11:23

PROPHECY
whether there be **p**, they shall fail 1 Cor 13:8
despise not **p** 1 Thess 5:20
sure word of **p** 2 Pet 1:19
p came not in old time 2 Pet 1:21
the words of this **p** Rev 1:3

PROPHESY
they **p**, and did not cease Num 11:25
he never **p** good unto me 2 Chr 18:7
p not unto us right things Is 30:10
prophets **p** falsely Jer 5:31
prophets **p** lies Jer 14:14
the prophet which **p** of peace Jer 28:9
P unto the wind Ezek 37:9
sons and daughters shall **p** Joel 2:28; Acts 2:17
who can but **p**? Amos 3:8
p not again any more Amos 7:13
I will **p** unto thee of wine Mic 2:11
P unto us, thou Christ Matt 26:68
P: and the servants did strike Mark 14:65
P, who is it that smote thee? Luke 22:64
let us **p** according to the proportion Rom 12:6
we **p** in part 1 Cor 13:9
covet to **p** 1 Cor 14:39

PROPHET
Aaron thy brother shall be thy **p** Ex 7:1
all the Lord's people were **p** Num 11:29
If there be a **p** among you Num 12:6
there arise among you a **p** or dreamer Deut 13:1
will raise up unto thee a **p** Deut 18:15
P shall the Lord your God raise up Acts 3:22; 7:37
there arose not a **p** Deut 34:10
Is Saul also among the **p**? 1 Sam 10:12; 19:24
there dwelt an old **p** in Beth-el 1 Kgs 13:11
I only, remain a **p** 1 Kgs 18:22
Is there not here a **p** 1 Kgs 22:7; 2 Kgs 3:11
he shall know that there is a **p** 2 Kgs 5:8
do my **p** no harm 1 Chr 16:22; Ps 105:15
believe his **p**, so shall ye prosper 2 Chr 20:20
there is no more any **p** Ps 74:9
mad, and maketh himself a **p** Jer 29:26
Where are now your **p** Jer 37:19
there hath been a **p** among them Ezek 2:5
the **p** is a fool Hos 9:7
I was no **p** Amos 7:14
the **p**, do they live for ever? Zech 1:5
Beware of false **p** Matt 7:15
that receiveth a **p** in the name of a **p** Matt 10:41
A **p** is not without honour Matt 13:57; Mark 6:4
ye build the tombs of the **p** Matt 23:29
be called the **p** of the Highest Luke 1:76
a great **p** is risen Luke 7:16
not a greater **p** than John Luke 7:28
if he were a **p**, would have known Luke 7:39
cannot be that a **p** perish out of Jerusalem Luke 13:33
which was a **p** mighty, in deed Luke 24:19
I perceive that thou art a **p** John 4:19
Of a truth this is the **p** John 7:40
out of Galilee ariseth no **p** John 7:52
believest thou the **p** Acts 26:27
are all **p**? 1 Cor 12:29
If any man think himself to be a **p** 1 Cor 14:37
the foundation of the apostles and **p** Eph 2:20
he gave some, apostles; and some, **p** Eph 4:11
Of which salvation the **p** inquired 1 Pet 1:10
of thy brethren the **p** Rev 22:9

PROPORTION
according to the **p** of everyone 1 Kgs 7:36
power, nor his comely **p** Job 41:12
according to the **p** of faith Rom 12:6

PROSPER
the LORD hath **p** my way Gen 24:56
the LORD made all that he did to **p** Gen 39:3
it shall not **p** Num 14:41
thou shalt not **p** in thy ways Deut 28:29
p thou, and build the house 1 Chr 22:11
believe his prophets, so shall ye **p** 2 Chr 20:20
God made him to **p** 2 Chr 26:5
p in their hands Ezra 5:8
The God of heaven will **p** us Neh 2:20
who hath hardened himself, and **p**? Job 9:4
fret not thyself because of him who **p** Ps 37:7
the ungodly, who **p** in the world Ps 73:12
they shall **p** that love thee Ps 122:6
he that covereth his sins shall not **p** Prov 28:13
knowest not whether shall **p** Eccl 11:6
pleasure of the Lord shall **p** Is 53:10
no weapon that is formed against thee shall **p** Is 54:17
it shall **p** in the thing Is 55:11
thou shalt not **p** in them Jer 2:37
wherefore doth the way of the wicked **p**? Jer 12:1
no man of his seed shall **p** Jer 22:30
shall it **p**? Ezek 17:9,10
shall he **p**, shall he escape? Ezek 17:15
as God hath **p** him 1 Cor 16:2
in health, even as thy soul **p** 3 John 1:2

PROSPERITY
thou shalt not seek their peace nor **p** Deut 23:6
say to him that liveth in **p** 1 Sam 25:6
in **p** the destroyer shall come Job 15:21
in my **p** I said, I shall never be moved Ps 30:6
when I saw the **p** of the wicked Ps 73:3
the **p** of fools shall destroy them Prov 1:32
In the day of **p** be joyful Eccl 7:14
I spake unto thee in thy **p** Jer 22:21

PROSPEROUS
he was a **p** man Gen 39:2
then thou shalt make thy way **p** Josh 1:8
the habitation of thy righteousness **p** Job 8:6
the seed shall be **p** Zech 8:12

PROTECTION
help you, and be your **p** Deut 32:38

PROTEST
The man did solemnly **p** Gen 43:3
earnestly **p** unto your fathers Jer 11:7
the LORD **p** unto Joshua Zech 3:6
I **p** by your rejoicing 1 Cor 15:31

PROUD
here shall thy **p** waves be stayed Job 38:11
every one that is **p**, and abase him Job 40:11
rewardeth the **p** doer Ps 31:23
respecteth not the **p** Ps 40:4
render a reward to the **p** Ps 94:2
him that hath a high look and **p** heart will not I suffer Ps 101:5
with the contempt of the **p** Ps 123:4
the **p** he knoweth afar off Ps 138:6
a **p** look Prov 6:17
LORD will destroy the house of the **p** Prov 15:25
p in heart is an abomination Prov 16:5
A high look, and a **p** heart Prov 21:4
patient in spirit is better than the **p** in spirit Eccl 7:8
he is a **p** man Hab 2:5
we call the **p** happy Mal 3:15
scattered the **p** Luke 1:51

he is **p**, knowing nothing 1 Tim 6:4
God resisteth the **p** James 4:6; 1 Pet 5:5

PROUDLY
in the thing wherein they dealt **p** Ex 18:11
Talk no more exceeding **p** 1 Sam 2:3
that they dealt **p** against them Neh 9:10
behave himself **p** against the ancient Is 3:5
spoken **p** in the day of distress Obad 1:12

PROVE
there he **p** them Ex 15:25
let me **p**, I pray thee but this once Judg 6:39
I have not **p** them 1 Sam 17:39
she came to **p** 1 Kgs 10:1; 2 Chr 9:1
Thou hast **p** mine heart Ps 17:3
I **p** thee at the waters Ps 81:7
when your fathers tempted me, **p** me Ps 95:9; Heb 3:9
p me now herewith Mal 3:10
I go to **p** them Luke 14:19
whom we have oftentimes **p** diligent 2 Cor 8:22
p your own selves 2 Cor 13:5
p all things 1 Thess 5:21

PROVERB
a **p**, and a byword Deut 28:37
I became a **p** to them Ps 69:11
set in order many **p** Eccl 12:9
every one that useth **p** Ezek 16:44
will surely say unto me this **p** Luke 4:23
speakest thou plainly, and speakest no **p** John 16:29

PROVIDE
God will **p** himself a lamb Gen 22:8
when shall I **p** for mine own house Gen 30:30
can he **p** flesh Ps 78:20
p neither gold, nor silver Matt 10:9
those things be, which thou hast **p**? Luke 12:20
p yourselves bags which wax not old Luke 12:33
p things honest Rom 12:17
if any **p** not for his own 1 Tim 5:8
having **p** some better thing for us Heb 11:40

PROVIDENCE
done unto this nation by thy **p** Acts 24:2

PROVISION
p for the way Gen 42:25; 45:21
I will abundantly bless her **p** Ps 132:15
make not **p** for the flesh Rom 13:14

PROVOCATION
doth not my eye continue in their **p**? Job 17:2
Harden not your heart as in the **p** Ps 95:8
presented the **p** of their offering Ezek 20:28

PROVOKE
obey his voice, and **p** him not Ex 23:21
How long will this people **p** me? Num 14:11
p me, and break my covenant Deut 31:20
they that **p** God are secure Job 12:6
p him at the sea Ps 106:7
p him to anger with their inventions Ps 106:29
p him to speak Luke 11:53
I will **p** you to jealousy Rom 10:19
is not easily **p** 1 Cor 13:5
p one another Gal 5:26
p not your children to wrath Eph 6:4
to **p** unto love and to good works Heb 10:24

PRUDENCE
endured with **p** and understanding 2 Chr 2:12
I wisdom dwell with **p** Prov 8:12
in all wisdom and **p** Eph 1:8

PRUDENT
a **p** man covereth shame Prov 12:16
a **p** man concealeth knowledge Prov 12:23
the **p** man looketh well to his going Prov 14:15
wise in heart shall be called **p** Prov 16:21
p wife is from the LORD Prov 19:14
p man foreseeth the evil Prov 22:3; 27:12
are **p** in their own sight Is 5:21
is counsel perished from the **p** Jer 49:7
p, and he shall know them Hos 14:9
things from wise and **p** Matt 11:25; Luke 10:21

PTOLEMAIS tol-em-a´-is
city of Ptolemy Acts 21:7

PUA poo´-ah
same as PHUVAH Num 26:23

PUAH poo´-ah
splendor Ex 1:15

PUBLICKLY
that **p**, shewing by the scriptures Acts 18:28
and have taught you **p** Acts 20:20

PUBLISH
I will **p** the name of the Lord Deut 32:3
p it not in the streets of Askelon 2 Sam 1:20
company of those that **p** it Ps 68:11
that **p** peace Is 52:7; Nah 1:15
began to **p** Mark 1:45; 5:20
p throughout the whole city Luke 8:39

PUBLIUS pub´-li-as
governor of the island of Malta Acts 28:7

PUDENS pu´-dens
shamefaced 2 Tim 4:21

PUFFETH
he **p** at them Ps 10:5
safety from him that **p** at them Ps 12:5
knowledge **p** up 1 Cor 8:1

PUHITES poo´-hites
descendants of Kirjath-Jearim 1 Chr 2:53

PUL pool
1 short for TIGLATH-PILESER (?) 2 Kgs 15:19
2 *son* (?) Is 66:19

PULL
p me in pieces Lam 3:11
shall no more be **p** up Amos 9:15
p away the shoulder Zech 7:11
p out the mote Matt 7:4; Luke 6:42
will **p** down barns Luke 12:18
p him out on the sabbath Luke 14:5
to the **p** down of strong holds 2 Cor 10:4
p them out of the fire Jude 1:23

PULPIT
stood upon a **p** of wood Neh 8:4

PULSE
lentiles, and parched **p** 2 Sam 17:28
give us **p** to eat Dan 1:12

PUNISH
p us less than our iniquities deserve Ezra 9:13
to **p** the just is not good Prov 17:26
I will **p** the world for their evil Is 13:11
Lord cometh to **p** the inhabitants Is 26:21
what wilt thou say when he shall **p** Jer 13:21
I **p** them oft in every synagogue Acts 26:11
p with everlasting destruction 2 Thess 1:9
unto the day of judgment to be **p** 2 Pet 2:9

PUNISHMENT
My **p** is greater than I can bear Gen 4:13
accept the **p** of their iniquity Lev 26:41
no **p** happen to thee 1 Sam 28:10
a man for the **p** of his sins Lam 3:39
For the **p** of the iniquity Lam 4:6
p of thine iniquity is accomplished Lam 4:22
shall bear the **p** of their iniquity Ezek 14:10
everlasting **p** Matt 25:46
of how much sorer **p** Heb 10:29
the **p** of evildoers 1 Pet 2:14

PUNITES poon´-ites
descendants of Pua Num 26:23

PUNON poon´-on
same as PINON Num 33:42

PUR poor
a lot Esth 3:7

PURCHASE
have I **p** to be my wife Ruth 4:10
thy congregation, which thou hast **p** Ps 74:2
p a field with reward of iniquity Acts 1:18
gift of God may be **p** with money Acts 8:20
he hath **p** with his own blood Acts 20:28
p to themselves a good degree 1 Tim 3:13

PURE
the **p** blood of the grape Deut 32:14
with the **p** thou wilt shew thyself **p** 2 Sam 22:27; Ps 18:26
Shall a man be more **p** than his maker? Job 4:17
If thou wert **p** and upright Job 8:6
My doctrine is **p** Job 11:4
my prayer is **p** Job 16:17
stars are not **p** in his sight Job 25:5
the words of the LORD are **p** Ps 12:6
commandment of the Lord is **p** Ps 19:8
Thy word is very **p** Ps 119:140
words of the **p** are pleasant Prov 15:26
I am **p** from my sin Prov 20:9
Shall I count them **p** Mic 6:11
will I turn to the people a **p** language Zeph 3:9
p from the blood of all men Acts 20:26
All things indeed are **p** Rom 14:20
whatsoever things are **p** Phil 4:8
p conscience 1 Tim 3:9; 2 Tim 1:3
keep thyself **p** 1 Tim 5:22
to the **p** all things are **p** Titus 1:15
P religion James 1:27
first **p**, then peaceable James 3:17
stir up your **p** minds 2 Pet 3:1
even as he is **p** 1 John 3:3
a **p** river of water of life Rev 22:1

PURELY
p purge away thy dross Is 1:25

PURENESS
the **p** of thy hands Job 22:30
He that loveth **p** of heart Prov 22:11
By **p**, by knowledge, by longsuffering 2 Cor 6:6

PURER
Nazarites were **p** than snow Lam 4:7
Thou art of **p** eyes than to behold evil Hab 1:13

PURGE
when he had **p** the land 2 Chr 34:8
P me with hyssop Ps 51:7
transgressions, thou shalt **p** them Ps 65:3
and purely **p** away thy dross Is 1:25
thy sin **p** Is 6:7
this iniquity shall not be **p** Is 22:14
I have **p** thee, and thou wast not **p** Ezek 24:13
p them as gold Mal 3:3
p his floor Matt 3:12; Luke 3:17
he **p** it, that it may bring forth John 15:2
P out therefore the old leaven 1 Cor 5:7
if a man **p** himself from these 2 Tim 2:21
p your conscience Heb 9:14
all things are by the law **p** with blood Heb 9:22

PURIFY
p unto himself a peculiar people Titus 2:14
p your hearts James 4:8
have **p** your souls 1 Pet 1:22

PURIM poor´-im
pl. of PUR Esth 9:26

PURITY
in spirit, in faith, in **p** 1 Tim 4:12
sisters, with all **p** 1 Tim 5:2

PURLOINING
Not **p**, but shewing all good fidelity Titus 2:10

PURPOSE (n)
my **p** are broken off Job 17:11
Every **p** is established by counsel Prov 20:18
To what **p** is this waste Matt 26:8
with **p** of heart Acts 11:23
the called according to his **p** Rom 8:28
p of God according to election Rom 9:11
according to the **p** Eph 1:11
eternal **p** which he purposed in Christ Eph 3:11

PURPOSE (v)
the LORD of hosts hath **p**, and who shall disannul? Is 14:27
I have **p** it, I will also do it Is 46:11

PURSE
let us all have one **p** Prov 1:14
silver, nor brass in your **p** Matt 10:9
no bread, no money in their **p** Mark 6:8
Carry neither **p**, nor scrip Luke 10:4

PURSUE
shall flee when none **p** Lev 26:17
avenger of blood **p** Deut 19:6; Josh 20:5
wilt thou **p** the dry stubble? Job 13:25
they **p** my soul Job 30:15
seek peace, and **p** it Ps 34:14
he that **p** evil, **p** it to his own death Prov 11:19
evil **p** sinners Prov 13:21
the sword shall **p** thee Jer 48:2

PUSH
ox were wont to **p** with his horn Ex 21:29
With these shalt thou **p** the Syrians 1 Kgs 22:11
they **p** away my feet Job 30:12

PUT
p not thine hand with the wicked Ex 23:1
p ten thousand to flight Lev 26:8; Deut 32:30
I **p** my life in my hands Judg 12:3
p me . . . into one of the priests' offices 1 Sam 2:36
to **p** my name there 1 Kgs 9:3
must he **p** to more strength Eccl 10:10
P me in remembrance Is 43:26
let not man **p** asunder Matt 19:6; Mark 10:9
p his hands upon them, and blessed Mark 10:16
p that on mine account Phile 1:18
I must **p** off this my tabernacle 2 Pet 1:14

PUT poot
same as PHUT 1 Chr 1:8

PUTEOLI poo-te´-o-li
wells Acts 28:13

PUTIEL poot´-i-el
afflicted of God (?) Ex 6:25

PUTRIFYING
wounds, and bruises, and **p** sores Is 1:6

Q

QUAKE
The earth shall **q** before them Joel 2:10
The mountains **q** at them Nah 1:5
earth did **q** and the rocks rent Matt 27:51
I exceedingly fear and **q** Heb 12:21

QUANTITY
all vessels of small **q** Is 22:24

QUARREL
avenge the **q** of my covenant Lev 26:25
he seeketh a **q** against me 2 Kgs 5:7
Herodias had a **q** against him Mark 6:19
any man have a **q** against any Col 3:13

QUARTER
leaven seen with thee in all thy **q** Ex 13:7
they came to him from every **q** Mark 1:45
four **q** of the earth Rev 20:8

QUARTUS kwart´-us
the fourth Rom 16:23

QUENCH
the fire was **q** Num 11:2
q not the light of Israel 2 Sam 21:17
Many waters cannot **q** love Song 8:7
shall not be **q** night nor day Is 34:10
smoking flax shall he not **q** Is 42:3; Matt 12:20
neither shall their fire be **q** Is 66:24
fire that never shall be **q** Mark 9:43
able to **q** all the fiery darts Eph 6:16
Q not the Spirit 1 Thess 5:19
Q the violence of fire Heb 11:34

QUESTION
to prove him with hard **q** 1 Kgs 10:1
that day forth ask him any more **q** Matt 22:46
ask of you one **q** Mark 11:29
asking no **q** for conscience sake 1 Cor 10:25
which minister **q** 1 Tim 1:4
doting about **q** 1 Tim 6:4
unlearned **q** avoid 2 Tim 2:23
avoid foolish **q**, and genealogies Titus 3:9

QUICK
go down **q** Num 16:30; Ps 55:15
of **q** understanding Is 11:3
Judge of **q** and dead Acts 10:42
the word of God is **q**, and powerful Heb 4:12

QUICKEN
shalt **q** me again Ps 71:20
q us, and we will call Ps 80:18
q thou me according to thy word Ps 119:25
q thou me in thy way Ps 119:37
thy word hath **q** me Ps 119:50
shall also **q** your mortal bodies Rom 8:11
that which thou sowest is not **q** 1 Cor 15:36
you hath he **q** Eph 2:1
q us together with Christ Eph 2:5
q together with him Col 2:13
death in the flesh, but **q** by the Spirit 1 Pet 3:18

QUICKLY
have turned aside **q** Ex 32:8
go **q** unto the congregation Num 16:46
come up to us **q**, and save us Josh 10:6
threefold cord is not **q** broken Eccl 4:12
Agree with thine adversary **q** Matt 5:25
Go out **q** into the streets and lanes Luke 14:21
That thou doest, do **q** John 13:27
repent, else I will come unto thee **q** Rev 2:5; 16
I come **q** Rev 3:11; 22:7,12
Surely I come **q** Rev 22:20

QUIET
glad because they be **q** Ps 107:30
words of wise men are heard in **q** Eccl 9:17
be **q**; fear not Is 7:4
The whole earth is at rest, and is **q** Is 14:7
in **q** resting places Is 32:18
a **q** habitation Is 33:20
sorrow on the sea; it cannot be **q** Jer 49:23
I will be **q** Ezek 16:42
ye ought to be **q** Acts 19:36
study to be **q** 1 Thess 4:11
a **q** and peaceable life 1 Tim 2:2
ornament of a meek and **q** spirit 1 Pet 3:4

QUIETLY
speak with him **q** 2 Sam 3:27
q wait for the salvation Lam 3:26

QUIETNESS
when he giveth **q** Job 34:29
Better is a dry morsel, and **q** Prov 17:1
Better is handful with **q** Eccl 4:6
in **q** and in confidence shall be Is 30:15
effect of righteousness, **q** Is 32:17

QUIT (adj)
shall he that smote him be **q** Ex 21:19
we will be **q** of thine oath Josh 2:20

QUIT (v)
Be strong and **q** yourselves 1 Sam 4:9
fast in faith **q** you like men 1 Cor 16:13

QUITE
hath **q** devoured also our money Gen 31:15
wisdom driven **q** from me Job 6:13
bow was made **q** naked Hab 3:9

QUIVER
the man that hath his **q** full Ps 127:5
their **q** is as an open sepulchre Jer 5:16
caused the arrows of his **q** to enter Lam 3:13

R

RAAMAH ra´-am-ah
trembling Gen 10:7

RAAMIAH ra´-am-i´-ah
trembling of Jehovah Neh 7:7

RAAMSES ra-am´-ses
same as RAMESES Ex 1:11

RAB-MAG rab´-mag
most exalted Jer 39:3

RAB-SARIS rab´-sar-is
chief eunuch 2 Kgs 18:17

RAB-SHAKEH rab´-sha-kay
chief of the cupbearers 2 Kgs 18:17

RABBAH rab´-ah
capital city Josh 13:25

RABBATH rab´-ath
same as RABBAH Deut 3:11

RABBI rab´-i
master Matt 23:7

RABBITH rab´-ith
populous Josh 19:20

RABBONI rab-o´-ni
my master John 20:16

RAB-MAG rab´-mag
1 *chief of the fortune-tellers* (?),
2 officer under NEBUCHADNEZZAR Num 26:16

RACA ra´-cah
worthless Matt 5:22

RACE
a strong man to run a **r** Ps 19:5
the **r** is not to the swift Eccl 9:11
they which run a **r** run all 1 Cor 9:24
the **r** that is set before us Heb 12:1

RACHAB ra´-kab
Gr. for RAHAB Matt 1:5

RACHAL ra´-kal
traffic 1 Sam 30:29

RACHEL ra´-chel
ewe Gen 29:6

RADDAI rad´-da-i
subduing 1 Chr 2:14

RAGAU ra´-gaw
Gr. for REU Luke 3:35

RAGE
Why do the heathen **r** Ps 2:1; Acts 4:25
the fool **r**, and is confident Prov 14:16

RAGING
Thou rulest the **r** of the sea Ps 89:9
strong drink is **r** Prov 20:1
the wind and the **r** of the water Luke 8:24
R waves of the sea Jude 1:13

RAGS
shall clothe a man with **r** Prov 23:21
our righteousness are as filthy **r** Is 64:6
cast clouts and old rotten **r** Jer 38:11

RAGUEL ra´-goo-el
friend of God Num 10:29

RAHAB ra´-hab
1 *broad* Josh 2:1
2 *violence* Ps 87:4

RAHAM ra´-ham
affection, tenderness 1 Chr 2:44

RAHEL ra´-hel
same as RACHEL Jer 31:15

RAIMENT
r to put on Gen 28:20
thy **r** waxed not old Deut 8:4
that he may sleep in his own **r** Deut 24:13
nor take a widow's **r** to pledge Deut 24:17
prepare **r** as the clay Job 27:16
I will stain all my **r** Is 63:3
clothe thee with change of **r** Zech 3:4
the body is more than **r** Matt 6:25
why take ye thought for **r**? Matt 6:28
a man clothed in soft **r** Matt 11:8; Luke 7:25
his **r** was white as the light Matt 17:2
having food and **r** let us be content 1 Tim 6:8
poor man in vile **r** James 2:2
white **r**, that thou mayest be clothed Rev 3:18

RAIN (n)
r was upon the earth forty days Gen 7:12
r in due season Lev 26:4; Deut 11:14; 28:12
drinketh water of the **r** of heaven Deut 11:11
my doctrine shall drop as the **r** Deut 32:2
clear shining after **r** 2 Sam 23:4
a sound of abundance of **r** 1 Kgs 18:41
a time of much **r** Ezra 10:13
who giveth **r** upon the earth Job 5:10
to the small **r** and to the great **r** Job 37:6
Hath the **r** a father? Job 38:28
like **r** upon the mown grass Ps 72:6
like clouds and wind without **r** Prov 25:14
the north wind driveth away **r** Prov 25:23
as **r** in harvest Prov 26:1
sweeping **r**, which leaveth no food Prov 28:3
if the clouds be full of **r** Eccl 11:3
nor the clouds return after the **r** Eccl 12:2
the **r** is over and gone Song 2:11
a covert from storm and from **r** Is 4:6
as the **r** cometh down Is 55:10
an overflowing **r** Ezek 38:22
he shall come unto us as the **r** Hos 6:3
r on the just and on the unjust Matt 5:45
the **r** descended, and floods came Matt 7:25

RAIN (v)
I will **r** bread from heaven Ex 16:4
shall **r** upon him while he is eating Job 20:23
upon the wicked he shall **r** snares Ps 11:6
and had **r** down manna upon them Ps 78:24
r upon in the day of indignation Ezek 22:24
till he come and **r** righteousness Hos 10:12

RAINY
continual dropping in a very **r** day Prov 27:15

RAISE
I will **r** them up a Prophet Deut 18:15; Acts 3:22
the LORD **r** up judges Judg 2:16,18
he **r** up the poor out of the dust 1 Sam 2:8; Ps 113:7
he **r** up himself, the mighty are afraid Job 41:25
r up all those that be bowed down Ps 145:14; 146:8
I have **r** him up in righteousness Is 45:13
in the third day he will **r** us up Hos 6:2
r the dead Matt 10:8; 11:5; Luke 7:22
be **r** the third day Matt 16:21; 17:23; Luke 9:22
in three days I will **r** it up John 2:19
I will **r** him up at last day John 6:39,40,44,54
whom God hath **r** up Acts 2:24,32; 3:15; 4:10; 5:30; 10:40; 13:30,33,34; 17:31; Rom 10:9; 1 Cor 6:14; 2 Cor 4:14; Gal 1:1; Eph 1:20
with you that God should **r** the dead? Acts 26:8
r again for our justification Rom 4:25
like as Christ was **r** up from the dead Rom 6:4
Spirit of him that **r** up Jesus Rom 8:11
will also **r** up us by his own power 1 Cor 6:14
he **r** up Christ: whom he **r** not up 1 Cor 15:15
then is not Christ **r** 1 Cor 15:16
if Christ be not **r** 1 Cor 15:17
How are the dead **r** up? 1 Cor 15:35
it is **r** in glory 1 Cor 15:43
God which **r** the dead 2 Cor 1:9
the Lord Jesus shall **r** up us also 2 Cor 4:14
hath **r** us up together Eph 2:6
that God was able to **r** him up Heb 11:19
women received their dead **r** to life Heb 11:35
and the Lord shall **r** him up James 5:15

RAKEM ra´-kem
variegated 1 Chr 7:16

RAKKATH rak´-ath
shore Josh 19:35

RAKKON rak´-on
same as RAKKATH Josh 19:46

RAM
r caught in a thicket Gen 22:13
the **r** of the atonement Num 5:8
a **r** of the flock for their trespass Ezra 10:19
a **r** which had two horns Dan 8:3

RAM ram
high Ruth 4:19

RAMA ra´-mah
Gr. for RAMAH Matt 2:18

RAMAH ra´-mah
high place Josh 18:25

RAMATH ra´-math
same as RAMAH Josh 19:8

RAMATH-LEHI ra´-math-le´-hi
height of Lehi Judg 15:17

RAMATH-MIZPEH ra´-math-miz´-peh
height of Mizpeh Josh 13:26

RAMATHAIM-ZOPHIM ra´-math-a´-im-zo´-phim
double high place of watchers 1 Sam 1:1

RAMATHITE ra´-math-ite
a native of Ramah 1 Chr 27:27

RAMESES ra´-me-sees
son of the sun Gen 47:11

RAMIAH ram-i´-ah
Jehovah is high Ezra 10:25

RAMOTH-GILEAD ra´-moth-gil´-yad
heights of Gilead 1 Kgs 4:13

RAMOTH ra´-moth
pl. of RAMAH 1 Chr 6:73

RAN
the fire **r** along upon the ground Ex 9:23
r into the midst of the congregation Num 16:47
have not sent these prophets, yet they **r** Jer 23:21

RANG
the earth **r** again 1 Sam 4:5
the city **r** again 1 Kgs 1:45

RANKS
light was against light in three **r** 1 Kgs 7:4
men of war, that could keep **r** 1 Chr 12:38
they shall not break their **r** Joel 2:7
they sat down in **r** Mark 6:40

RANSOM (n)
give for the **r** of his life Ex 21:30
every man a **r** for his soul Ex 30:12
I have found a **r** Job 33:24
a great **r** cannot deliver Job 36:18
nor give to God a **r** for him Ps 49:7
the **r** of a man's life are his riches Prov 13:8
the **r** of the LORD shall return Is 35:10
I gave Egypt for thy **r** Is 43:3
to give his life a **r** for many Matt 20:28; Mark 10:45
gave himself a **r** for all 1 Tim 2:6

RANSOM (v)
r him from the hand Jer 31:11
r them from the power of the grave Hos 13:14

RAPHA ra´-fah
giant (?) 1 Chr 8:37

RAPHU ra´-foo
healed Num 13:9

RARE
a **r** thing that the king requireth Dan 2:11

RASH
Be not **r** with thy mouth Eccl 5:2
do nothing **r** Acts 19:36

RATHER
death **r** than life Job 7:15
I had **r** be a doorkeeper Ps 84:10
go **r** to the lost sheep Matt 10:6
r fear him which is able Matt 10:28
go ye **r** to them that sell Matt 25:9
but **r** grew worse Mark 5:26
justified **r** than the other Luke 18:14
men loved darkness **r** than light John 3:19
we ought to obey God **r** than men Acts 5:29
Christ that died, yea **r**, that is risen Rom 8:34
r give place unto wrath Rom 12:19
Why do ye not **r** take wrong? 1 Cor 6:7
choosing **r** to suffer affliction Heb 11:25
let it **r** be healed Heb 12:13

RAVENING (adj)
a **r** and roaring lion Ps 22:13
inwardly they are **r** wolves Matt 7:15

RAVENING (v)
roaring lion **r** the prey Ezek 22:25

RAVENOUS
nor any **r** beast shall go up Is 35:9
calling a **r** bird from the east Is 46:11
I will give thee unto the **r** birds Ezek 39:4

RAZE
R it, **r** it, even to the foundation Ps 137:7

REACH
whose top may **r** unto heaven Gen 11:4
R hither thy finger John 20:27
a measure to **r** even unto you 2 Cor 10:13

READ
king shall **r** therein all the days Deut 17:19
seek ye out of the book of the LORD, and **r** Is 34:16
Have ye not **r** Matt 12:3; 19:4; 22:31; Mark 12:10; Luke 6:3
stood up for to **r** Luke 4:16
known and **r** of all men 2 Cor 3:2

READINESS
received the word with all **r** of mind Acts 17:11
there was a **r** to will 2 Cor 8:11
in a **r** to revenge all disobedience 2 Cor 10:6

READING
caused them to understand the **r** Neh 8:8
give attendance to **r** 1 Tim 4:13

READY
we ourselves will go **r** armed Num 32:17

a Syrian **r** to perish — Deut 26:5
seeing that thou hast no tidings **r** — 2 Sam 18:22
thou art a God **r** to pardon — Neh 9:17
He that is **r** to slip with his feet — Job 12:5
the graves are **r** for me — Job 17:1
blessing of him that was **r** to perish — Job 29:13
I am **r** to halt — Ps 38:17
the pen of a **r** writer — Ps 45:1
thou, LORD, art good, and **r** to forgive — Ps 86:5
r to die from my youth up — Ps 88:15
those that are **r** to be slain — Prov 24:11
drink unto him that is **r** to perish — Prov 31:6
be more **r** to hear — Eccl 5:1
they shall come which were **r** to perish — Is 27:13
tongue of the stammerers shall be **r** — Is 32:4
the LORD was **r** to save me — Is 38:20
if ye be **r** — Dan 3:15
all things are **r** — Matt 22:4; Luke 14:17
the wedding is **r** — Matt 22:8
be ye also **r** — Matt 24:44; Luke 12:40
they that were **r** went in — Matt 25:10
the spirit truly is **r** — Mark 14:38
I am **r** to go with thee — Luke 22:23
your time is always **r** — John 7:6
I am **r** not to be bound only — Acts 21:13
I am **r** to preach the gospel — Rom 1:15
declaration of your **r** mind — 2 Cor 8:19
Achaia was **r** a year ago — 2 Cor 9:2
r to distribute — 1 Tim 6:18
I am now **r** to be offered — 2 Tim 4:6
r to every good work — Titus 3:1
salvation **r** to be revealed in the last time — 1 Pet 1:5
be **r** always to give an answer — 1 Pet 3:15
not for filthy lucre, but of a **r** mind — 1 Pet 5:2
things which remaineth, that are **r** to die — Rev 3:2

REAIA re-ai´-ah
a form of REAIAH — 1 Chr 5:5

REAIAH re-ai´-ah
Jehovah has seen — 1 Chr 4:2

REAP
he that regardeth the clouds shall not **r** — Eccl 11:4
have sown wheat, but shall **r** thorns — Jer 12:13
they shall **r** the whirlwind — Hos 8:7
sow . . . in righteousness, **r** in mercy — Hos 10:12
thou shalt sow, but thou shalt not **r** — Mic 6:15
they sow not, neither **r** — Matt 6:26; Luke 12:24
I **r** where I sowed not — Matt 25:26; Luke 19:21
r that whereon ye bestowed no labour — John 4:38
if we shall **r** your carnal things? — 1 Cor 9:11
soweth sparingly shall **r** also sparingly — 2 Cor 9:6
man soweth that shall he also **r** — Gal 6:7
the cries of them which **r** — James 5:4

REASON (n)
I gave ear to your **r** — Job 32:11
seven men that can render a **r** — Prov 26:16
seek out wisdom, and the **r** of things — Eccl 7:25
bring forth your strong **r** — Is 41:21
a **r** of the hope that is in you — 1 Pet 3:15

REASON (v)
choose out my words to **r** with him? — Job 9:14
I desire to **r** with God — Job 13:3
Should he **r** with unprofitable talk? — Job 15:3
come now, and let us **r** together — Is 1:18
they **r** among themselves — Matt 16:7; 21:25; Mark 8:16; 11:31; Luke 20:5
What **r** ye in your hearts? — Luke 5:22
they communed together and **r** — Luke 24:15
as he **r** of righteousness — Acts 24:25

REASONABLE
which is your **r** service — Rom 12:1

REBA re´-bah
a fourth part — Num 31:8

REBECCA re-bek´-ah
Gr. for REBEKAH — Rom 9:10

REBEKAH re-bek´-ah
a noose — Gen 22:23

REBEL
only **r** not ye against the Lord — Num 14:9
doth **r** against thy commandment — Josh 1:18
will ye **r** against the king? — Neh 2:19
that **r** against the light — Job 24:13
they **r** not against his word — Ps 105:28
they have **r** against me — Is 1:2
they **r**, and vexed his holy Spirit — Is 63:10
we have transgressed and have **r** — Lam 3:42
though we have **r** against him — Dan 9:9

REBELLION
r is as the sin of witchcraft — 1 Sam 15:23
he addeth **r** unto his sin — Job 34:37
an evil man seeketh only **r** — Prov 17:11
thou hast taught **r** against the Lord — Jer 28:16

REBELLIOUS
a stubborn and **r** son — Deut 21:18
son of the perverse **r** woman — 1 Sam 20:30
let not the **r** exalt themselves — Ps 66:7
the **r** dwell in a dry land — Ps 68:6
princes are **r**, and companions of thieves — Is 1:23
people hath a revolting and a **r** heart — Jer 5:23

REBELS
a token against the **r** — Num 17:10
Hear now, ye **r**, must we fetch — Num 20:10
purge out from among you the **r** — Ezek 20:38

REBUKE (n)
this day is a day of trouble, and of **r** — 2 Kgs 19:3; Is 37:3
when thou with **r** dost correct — Ps 39:11
perish at the **r** of thy countenance — Ps 80:16
at thy **r** they fled — Ps 104:7
the poor heareth not **r** — Prov 13:8
open **r** is better than secret love — Prov 27:5
it is better to hear the **r** of wise — Eccl 7:5
one thousand shall flee at **r** of one — Is 30:17
for thy sake I have suffered **r** — Jer 15:15
without **r** — Phil 2:15

REBUKE (v)
r me not in thine anger — Ps 6:1; 38:1
r a wicked man getteth himself a blot — Prov 9:7
r a wise man, and he will love thee — Prov 9:8
he that **r** a man, afterwards shall find more favour — Prov 28:23
he shall **r** many people — Is 2:4; Mic 4:3
the LORD **r** thee — Zech 3:2; Jude 1:9
I will **r** the devourer for your sakes — Mal 3:11
he arose and **r** the wind — Matt 8:26; Mark 4:39; Luke 8:24
Peter took him, and began to **r** him — Matt 16:22; Mark 8:32
r the fever — Luke 4:39
brother trespass against thee, **r** him — Luke 17:3
Master, **r** thy disciples — Luke 19:39
r not an elder — 1 Tim 5:1
them that sin **r** before all — 1 Tim 5:20
r, exhort with all longsuffering — 2 Tim 4:2
r them sharply — Titus 1:13
nor faint when thou art **r** of him — Heb 12:5

RECALL
this I **r** to my mind — Lam 3:21

RECEIPT
sitting at the **r** of custom — Matt 9:9; Mark 2:14; Luke 5:27

RECEIVE
is it a time to **r** money — 2 Kgs 5:26
mine ear **r** a little — Job 4:12
r, I pray thee, the law from his mouth — Job 22:22
the LORD will **r** my prayer — Ps 6:9
he shall **r** me — Ps 49:15
hast **r** gifts for men — Ps 68:18
afterward **r** me to glory — Ps 73:24
if thou wilt **r** my words — Prov 2:1
she hath **r** of the Lord's hand double — Is 40:2
they **r** no correction — Jer 2:30
Ephraim shall **r** shame — Hos 10:6
r us graciously — Hos 14:2
the blind **r** their sight — Matt 11:5
if ye will **r** it, this is Elijah — Matt 11:14
whoso shall **r** one such little child — Matt 18:5
he that is able to **r** it, let him **r** it — Matt 19:12
ask in prayer, believing, ye shall **r** — Matt 21:22
but he **r** it not — Mark 15:23
he was **r** up into heaven — Mark 16:19
r you into everlasting habitations — Luke 16:9
R thy sight — Luke 18:42; Acts 22:13
his own **r** him not — John 1:11
to as many as **r** him — John 1:12
can **r** nothing, except it be given him — John 3:27
him ye will **r** — John 5:43
which **r** honour one of another — John 5:44
ask, and ye shall **r** — John 16:24
R ye the Holy Ghost — John 20:22
r my spirit — Acts 7:59
they **r** the Holy Ghost — Acts 8:17
shall **r** remission of sins — Acts 10:43
Have ye **r** the Holy Ghost — Acts 19:2
which I have **r** of the Lord Jesus — Acts 20:24
by whom we have now **r** the atonement — Rom 5:11
for God hath **r** him — Rom 14:3
r ye one another — Rom 15:7
every man shall **r** his own reward — 1 Cor 3:8
r of the Lord that which I delivered — 1 Cor 11:23
as we have **r** mercy, we faint not — 2 Cor 4:1
may **r** the things done in his body — 2 Cor 5:10
r us; we have wronged no man — 2 Cor 7:2
r him therefore in the Lord — Phil 2:29
as concerning giving and **r** — Phil 4:15
as ye have therefore **r** Christ — Col 2:6
r up into glory — 1 Tim 3:16
if it be **r** with thanksgiving — 1 Tim 4:4
whatsoever we ask, we **r** of him — 1 John 3:22

RECHAB re´-kab
horseman — 2 Sam 4:2

RECHABITES re´-kab-ites
descendants of Rechab — Jer 35:2

RECHAH re´-kah
side (?) — 1 Chr 4:12

RECKON
he shall **r** with him that bought him — Lev 25:50
they cannot be **r** up — Ps 40:5
when he had begun to **r** — Matt 18:24
lord of these servants cometh, and **r** with them — Matt 25:19
is the reward not **r** of grace — Rom 4:4
r ye also yourselves to be dead unto sin — Rom 6:11
I **r** that the sufferings of this present time — Rom 8:18

RECOMMENDED
had been **r** to the grace — Acts 14:26
r the bretheren — Acts 15:40

RECOMPENCE (n)
to me belongeth vengeance and **r** — Deut 32:35
vanity shall be his **r** — Job 15:31
days of **r** are come — Hos 9:7
will ye render me a **r**? — Joel 3:4
and a **r** be made thee — Luke 14:12
nor for a **r** in the same — 2 Cor 6:13
r of reward — Heb 2:2; 10:35; 11:26

RECOMPENSE (v)
he shall **r** his trespass Num 5:7
the LORD **r** thy work Ruth 2:12
why should the king **r** 2 Sam 19:36
he will **r** it, whether thou refuse Job 34:33
say not thou, I will **r** evil Prov 20:22
will **r**, even **r** into their bosom Is 65:6
will **r** them according to deeds Jer 25:14
for they cannot **r** thee Luke 14:14
it shall be **r** unto him again Rom 11:35
r to no man evil for evil Rom 12:17

RECONCILE
should he **r** himself unto his master? 1 Sam 29:4
so shall ye **r** the house Ezek 45:20
first be **r** to thy brother Matt 5:24
were enemies we were **r** to God Rom 5:10
that he might **r** both unto God Eph 2:16

RECORD (n)
my **r** is on high Job 16:19
the **r** of John, when the Jews sent John 1:19
ye know that our **r** i true 3 John 1:12

RECORD (v)
in all places where I **r** my name Ex 20:24
I call heaven and earth to **r** Deut 30:19; 31:28
thou bearest **r** of thyself John 8:13
I bear them **r** Rom 10:2
there are three that bear **r** 1 John 5:7

RECOUNT
he shall **r** his worthies Nah 2:5

RECOVER
he would **r** him of his leprosy 2 Kgs 5:3
that I may **r** strength Ps 39:13
to **r** the remnant of his people Is 11:11
will **r** my wool and my flax Hos 2:9
lay hands on sick, and they shall **r** Mark 16:18
r of sight to the blind Luke 4:18

RED
r pottage Gen 25:30
eyes shall be **r** with wine Gen 49:12
as **r** as blood 2 Kgs 3:22
the wine is **r**, it is full of mixture Ps 75:8
upon the wine when it is **r** Prov 23:31
though they be **r** like crimson Is 1:18
a vineyard of **r** wine Is 27:2
r in thine apparel Is 63:2
fair weather: for the sky is **r** Matt 16:2

REDEEM
Angel which **r** me Gen 48:16
I will **r** you Ex 6:6
people which thou hast **r** Ex 15:13
Who hath **r** my soul 2 Sam 4:9
neither is it in our power to **r** them Neh 5:5
our ability, have **r** our brethren the Jews Neh 5:8
in famine he shall **r** thee Job 5:20
r me from the hand of the mighty Job 6:23
r Israel, O God, out of all his troubles Ps 25:22
the LORD **r** the soul of his servants Ps 34:22
r us for thy mercies' sake Ps 44:26
none can by any means **r** his brother Ps 49:7
God will **r** my soul from the power of the grave Ps 49:15
he shall **r** their soul from deceit Ps 72:14
he shall **r** Israel Ps 130:8
Zion shall be **r** with judgment Is 1:27
the **r** shall walk there Is 35:9
return unto me: for I have **r** thee Is 44:22
hand shortened at all, that it cannot **r**? Is 50:2
r without money Is 52:3
have **r** them, yet they have spoken lies Hos 7:13
I will **r** them from death Hos 13:14
he hath visited and **r** his people Luke 1:68
he which should have **r** Israel Luke 24:21
r us from the curse of the law Gal 3:13
r them that were under the law Gal 4:5
that he might **r** us from all iniquity Titus 2:14
ye were not **r** with corruptible things 1 Pet 1:18
hast **r** us to God by thy blood Rev 5:9

REDEEMED
Let the **r** of the LORD say so Ps 107:2
the **r** of the LORD shall return Is 51:11
the year of my **r** is come Is 63:4

REDEEMER
I know that my **R** liveth Job 19:25
O LORD, my strength, and my **R** Ps 19:14
the high God their **r** Ps 78:35
their **r** is mighty Prov 23:11
our **r**, the LORD of hosts is his name Is 47:4
I the LORD am thy Saviour and thy **R** Is 49:26; 60:16
the **R** shall come to Zion Is 59:20
thou, O LORD, art our Father, our **R** Is 63:16

REDEMPTION
grant a **r** for the land Lev 25:24
the **r** of their soul is precious Ps 49:8
he sent **r** unto his people Ps 111:9
plenteous **r** Ps 130:7
the right of **r** is thine Jer 32:7
that looked for **r** in Jerusalem Luke 2:38
your **r** draweth nigh Luke 21:28
the **r** of our body Rom 8:23
sealed unto the day of **r** Eph 4:30

REDOUND
r to the glory of God 2 Cor 4:15

REED
a bruised **r** shall he not break Is 42:3; Matt 12:20
a staff of **r** to the house of Israel Ezek 29:6
a **r** shaken with the wind Matt 11:7; Luke 7:24

REELAIAH re´-el-ai´-ah
trembling caused by Jehovah Ezra 2:2

REFORMATION
until the time of **r** Heb 9:10

REFORMED
if ye will not be **r** Lev 26:23

REFRAIN
Joseph could not **r** himself Gen 45:1
I will not **r** my mouth Job 7:11
princes **r** talking Job 29:9
I have not **r** my lips Ps 40:9
r my feet from every evil way Ps 119:101
r thy foot from their path Prov 1:15
he that **r** his lips is wise Prov 10:19
r from these men Acts 5:38

REFRESH
he rested, and was **r** Ex 31:17
I will speak that I may be **r** Job 32:20
he **r** the soul of his masters Prov 25:13
they have **r** my spirit 1 Cor 16:18

REFUSE (n)
vile and **r** 1 Sam 15:9
as the offscouring and **r** Lam 3:45
sell the **r** of the wheat Amos 8:6

REFUSE (v)
he **r** to be comforted Gen 37:35
the LORD **r** to give me leave Num 22:13
I have **r** him 1 Sam 16:7
things that my soul **r** to touch Job 6:7
my soul **r** to be comforted Ps 77:2
r to walk in his law Ps 78:10
The stone which the builders **r** Ps 118:22
I have called, and ye **r** Prov 1:24
be wise, and **r** it not Prov 8:33
he that **r** reproof erreth Prov 10:17
shame . . . to him that **r** instruction Prov 13:18
r instruction despiseth his own soul Prov 15:32
his hands **r** to labour Prov 21:25
may know to **r** the evil Is 7:15,16
they **r** to return Jer 8:5
they **r** to know me Jer 9:6
which **r** to be healed Jer 15:18
if they **r** to take the cup Jer 25:28
if thou **r** to go forth Jer 38:21
they **r** to hearken Zech 7:11
this Moses whom they **r** Acts 7:35
nothing to be **r** 1 Tim 4:4
r profane and old wives' fables 1 Tim 4:7
the younger widows **r** 1 Tim 5:11
r to be called the son of Pharaoh Heb 11:24
r not him that speaketh Heb 12:25

REGARD
r not your stuff Gen 45:20
let them not **r** vain words Ex 5:9
which **r** not persons Deut 10:17
nor any to answer, nor any that **r** 1 Kgs 18:29
they perish for ever without any **r** it Job 4:20
nor **r** the rich more than the poor Job 34:19
neither **r** he the crying of the driver Job 39:7
they **r** not the works of the LORD Ps 28:5; Is 5:12
If I **r** iniquity in my heart Ps 66:18
He will **r** the prayer of the destitute Ps 102:17
he **r** their affliction Ps 106:44
no man **r** Prov 1:24
that thou mayest **r** discretion Prov 5:2
He will not **r** any ransom Prov 6:35
r the life of his beast Prov 12:10
he that **r** reproof Prov 13:18; 15:5
he that **r** the clouds shall not reap Eccl 11:4
he will no more **r** them Lam 4:16
r God of his fathers Dan 11:37
will he **r** your persons? Mal 1:9
r not the person of men Matt 22:16; Mark 12:14
feared not God, neither **r** man Luke 18:2
He that **r** the day, **r** it unto the LORD Rom 14:6

REGEM-MELECH re´-gem-me´-lek
friend of the king Zech 7:2

REGEM re´-gem
friend 1 Chr 2:47

REGISTER
sought their **r** among these Ezra 2:62; Neh 7:64
I found a **r** Neh 7:5

REHABIAH re´-hab-i´-ah
Jehovah enlarges 1 Chr 23:17

REHEARSE
r the righteous acts Judg 5:11
they **r** all that God had done Acts 14:27

REHOB re´-hob
street 2 Sam 8:3

REHOBOAM re´-hob-o´-am
who enlarges the people 1 Kgs 11:43

REHOBOTH re-hob´-oth
roominess Gen 10:11

REHUM re´-hoom
merciful Ezra 4:8

REI re´-i
friendly 1 Kgs 1:8

REIGN
Shalt thou indeed **r** over us? Gen 37:8
the LORD shall **r** for ever Ex 15:18; Ps 146:10
they that hate you shall **r** over you Lev 26:17
thou shalt **r** over many nations Deut 15:6
r thou over us Judg 9:8
Shall Saul **r** over us? 1 Sam 11:12
in whose stead thou has **r** 2 Sam 16:8
that the hypocrite **r** not Job 34:30
God **r** over the heathen Ps 47:8
the LORD **r** Ps 93:1; 96:10; 97:1; 99:1

by me kings **r** Prov 8:15
for a servant when he **r** Prov 30:22
out of prison he cometh to **r** Eccl 4:14
a King shall **r** in righteousness Is 32:1
that saith unto Zion, thy God **r** Is 52:7
r because thou closest thyself in cedar? Jer 22:15
a king shall **r** and prosper Jer 23:5
the LORD shall **r** over them Mic 4:7
will not have this man to **r** over us Luke 19:14
not that I should **r** over them Luke 19:27
death **r** from Adam to Moses Rom 5:14
death **r** by one Rom 5:17
as sin hath **r** unto death, even so might grace **r** Rom 5:21
Let not sin therefore **r** in your mortal body Rom 6:12
ye have **r** as kings without us 1 Cor 4:8
for he must **r** 1 Cor 15:25
If we suffer, we shall also **r** with him 2 Tim 2:12
we also shall **r** on the earth Rev 5:10
he shall **r** for ever and ever Rev 11:15
the Lord God omnipotent **r** Rev 19:6

REINS

he cleaveth my **r** asunder Job 16:13
my **r** be consumed within me Job 19:27
God trieth the hearts and **r** Ps 7:9
my **r** also instruct me Ps 16:7
prove me, try my **r** Ps 26:2
thus I was pricked in my **r** Ps 73:21
thou hast possessed my **r** Ps 139:13
my **r** shall rejoice Prov 23:16
faithfulness the girdle of his **r** Is 11:5
I am he which searcheth the **r** Rev 2:23

REJECT

have not **r** thee, but they have **r** me 1 Sam 8:7
ye have this day **r** your God 1 Sam 10:19
thou hast **r** the word of the LORD 1 Sam 15:23
r him from reigning over Israel 1 Sam 16:1
he is despised and **r** of men Is 53:3
the LORD hath **r** thy confidences Jer 2:37
the LORD hath **r** and forsaken the generation Jer 7:29
they have **r** the word of the LORD Jer 8:9
Hast thou utterly **r** Judah? Jer 14:19
thou hast utterly **r** us Lam 5:22
thou hast **r** knowledge, I will also **r** thee Hos 4:6
The stone which the builders **r** Matt 21:42; Mark 12:10; Luke 20:17
ye **r** the commandment of God Mark 7:9
and lawyers **r** the counsel of God Luke 7:30
be **r** of this generation Luke 17:25
the first and second admonition, **r** Titus 3:10
when he would have inherited the blessing, he was **r** Heb 12:17

REJOICE

ye shall **r** in all ye put your hand to Deut 12:7
thou shalt **r** in thy feast Deut 16:14
thou shalt **r** in every good thing Deut 26:11
the LORD will **r** over you Deut 28:63; 30:9
r over thee for good, as he **r** over thy fathers Deut 30:9
because I **r** in thy salvation 1 Sam 2:1
heart of them **r** that seek the Lord 1 Chr 16:10
let thy saints **r** in goodness 2 Chr 6:41
r at the sound of the organ Job 21:12
If I **r** because my wealth was great Job 31:25
r at destruction of him that hated me Job 31:29
r in his strength Job 39:21
r with trembling Ps 2:11
let all these that put their trust in thee **r** Ps 5:11
I will **r** in thy salvation Ps 9:14
r as a strong man to run a race Ps 19:5
our heart shall **r** in him Ps 33:21
in mine adversity they **r** Ps 35:15
that **r** at mine hurt Ps 35:26
otherwise they should **r** over me Ps 38:16
that the bones thou hast broken may **r** Ps 51:8
the righteous shall **r** when he seeth Ps 58:10
in the shadow of thy wings will I **r** Ps 63:7
let them **r** before God, yea, let them exceedingly **r** Ps 68:3
that thy people may **r** in thee Ps 85:6
in thy name shall they **r** all the day Ps 89:16
let the heavens **r** Ps 96:11
The LORD reigneth; let the earth **r** Ps 97:1
the LORD shall **r** in his works Ps 104:31
The righteous shall see it and **r** Ps 107:42
let thy servant **r** Ps 109:28
Let Israel **r** in him that made him Ps 149:2
who **r** to do evil Prov 2:14
r with the wife of thy youth Prov 5:18
thine heart be wise, my heart shall **r** Prov 23:15
father of the righteous shall greatly **r** Prov 23:24
she that bare thee shall **r** Prov 23:25
R not when thine enemy falleth Prov 24:17
righteous are in authority, the people **r** Prov 29:2
she shall **r** in time to come Prov 31:25
my heart **r** in all my labour Eccl 2:10
man to **r**, and to do good in his life Eccl 3:12
man should **r** in his own works Eccl 3:22; 5:19
R, O young man, in thy youth Eccl 11:9
as men **r** when they divide the spoil Is 9:3
noise of them that **r** endeth Is 24:8
poor among men shall **r** Is 29:19
the desert shall **r** Is 35:1
as the bridegroom **r** over the bride Is 62:5
him that **r** and worketh righteousness Is 64:5
my servants shall **r**, but ye shall be ashamed Is 65:13
when ye see this, your heart shall **r** Is 66:14
when thou doest evil, then thou **r** Jer 11:15
I will **r** over them to do them good Jer 32:41
that they may **r** and sleep Jer 51:39
let not the buyer **r** Ezek 7:12
which **r** in a thing of nought Amos 6:13
R not against me Mic 7:8
yet I will **r** in the Lord Hab 3:18
R greatly, O daughter of Zion Zech 9:9
he **r** more of that sheep Matt 18:13
many shall **r** at his birth Luke 1:14
R ye in that day, and leap for joy Luke 6:23
r, because your names are written in heaven Luke 10:20
in that hour Jesus **r** in spirit Luke 10:21
R with me Luke 15:6,9
willing for a season to **r** in his light John 5:35
Abraham **r** to see my day John 8:56
If ye loved me, ye would **r** John 14:28
ye shall weep and lament, but the world shall **r** John 16:20
I will see you again, and your heart shall **r** John 16:22
and **r** in hope of the glory of God Rom 5:2
R with them that do **r** Rom 12:15
they that **r**, as though they **r** not 1 Cor 7:30
R not in iniquity, but **r** in the truth 1 Cor 13:6
I therein do **r**, yea, and will **r** Phil 1:18
that I may **r** in the day of Christ Phil 2:16
Finally, my brethren, **r** in the Lord Phil 3:1
R in the Lord always: and again I say, **r** Phil 4:4
R evermore 1 Thess 5:16
let the brother of low degree **r** James 1:9
mercy **r** against judgment James 2:13
r with joy unspeakable 1 Pet 1:8

REJOICING

Fill my lips with **r** Job 8:21
declare his works with **r** Ps 107:22
voice of **r** and salvation is in the tabernacles of the righteous Ps 118:15
they are the **r** of my heart Ps 119:111
shall doubtless come again with **r** Ps 126:6
r in the habitable part of his earth Prov 8:31
I create Jerusalem a **r** Is 65:18
thy word was unto me the joy and **r** of mine heart Jer 15:16
This is the **r** city that dwelt carelessly Zeph 2:15
r that they were counted worthy Acts 5:41
R in hope Rom 12:12
as sorrowful, yet always **r** 2 Cor 6:10
what is our hope, or joy, or crown of **r**? 1 Thess 2:19

REKEM re´-kem

same as RAKEM Num 31:8

RELEASE

he made a **r** to the provinces Esth 2:18
Whom will ye that I **r** unto you? Matt 27:17
r Barabbas unto them Mark 15:11
have power to **r** thee? John 19:10

RELIEVE

then thou shalt **r** him Lev 25:35
he **r** the fatherless and widow Ps 146:9
r the oppressed Is 1:17
comforter that should **r** my soul is far from me Lam 1:16

RELIGION

straitest sect of our **r** Acts 26:5
in the Jews' **r** Gal 1:13
this man's **r** is vain James 1:26,27

RELIGIOUS

Jesus and **r** proselytes Acts 13:43
any man among you seem to be **r** James 1:26

RELY

they **r** upon the LORD God 2 Chr 13:18
not **r** on the LORD thy God 2 Chr 16:7
thou didst **r** on the LORD 2 Chr 16:8

REMAIN

while the earth **r** Gen 8:22
they that **r** fled to the mountain Gen 14:10
let nothing of it **r** until the morning Ex 12:10
r yet very much land to be possessed Josh 13:1
even I only, **r** a prophet of the LORD 1 Kgs 18:22
shall **r** in the tomb Job 21:32
the perfect shall **r** in it Prov 2:21
my wisdom **r** with me Eccl 2:9
this city shall **r** for ever Jer 17:25
there **r** but wounded men Jer 37:10
in the day of the LORD's anger none escaped nor **r** Lam 2:22
would have **r** until this day Matt 11:23
gather up the fragments that **r** John 6:12
ye say, we see; therefore your sin **r** John 9:41
While it **r**, was it not thine own? Acts 5:4
the greater part **r** unto this present 1 Cor 15:6
we which are alive and **r** unto the coming of the Lord 1 Thess 4:15
r therefore a rest to the people of God Heb 4:9
there **r** no more sacrifice for sins Heb 10:26
things which **r**, that are ready to die Rev 3:2

REMALIAH rem´-al-i´-ah

whom Jehovah adorned 2 Kgs 15:25

REMEDY

till there was no **r** 2 Chr 36:16
shall he be broken without **r** Prov 6:15
and that without **r** Prov 29:1

REMEMBER

yet did not the chief butler **r** Joseph Gen 40:23
I do **r** my faults this day Gen 41:9
R this day, in which ye came out from Egypt Ex 13:3
R the sabbath day Ex 20:8
r all the commandments of the LORD Num 15:39
r that thou wast a bondman Deut 5:15; 15:15; 16:12; 24:18,22
r all the way which the LORD thy God led thee Deut 8:2
R the days of old Deut 32:7

R his marvellous works 1 Chr 16:12
R me, O my God, concerning this Neh 13:14
O r that my life is wind Job 7:7
r it as waters that pass away Job 11:16
appoint me a set time, and r me Job 14:13
shall be no more r Job 24:20
maketh inquisition for blood, he r Ps 9:12
we will r the name of the LORD Ps 20:7
R, O LORD, thy tender mercies Ps 25:6
R not the sins of my youth Ps 25:7
When I r thee upon my bed Ps 63:6
I r God, and was troubled Ps 77:3
he r that they were but flesh Ps 78:39
r not against us former iniquities Ps 79:8
R how short my time is Ps 89:47
He hath r his covenant for ever Ps 105:8
have r thy name, O LORD, in the night Ps 119:55
Who r us in our low estate Ps 136:23
we wept, when we r Zion Ps 137:1
r his misery no more Prov 31:7
shall not much r the days of his life Eccl 5:20
let him r the days of darkness Eccl 11:8
R now thy Creator Eccl 12:1
we will r thy love Song 1:4
sing many songs, that thou mayest be r Is 23:16
R ye not the former things Is 43:18
thou hast lied, and hast not r me Is 57:11
the former shall not be r Is 65:17
I do earnestly r him still Jer 31:20
r the LORD afar off Jer 51:50
she r not her last end Lam 1:9
Then shalt thou r thy ways Ezek 16:61; 20:43; 36:31
and r not the brotherly covenant Amos 1:9
in wrath r mercy Hab 3:2
they shall r me in far countries Zech 10:9
Peter r the word of Jesus Matt 26:75
Son, r that thou in thy lifetime Luke 16:25
R Lot's wife Luke 17:32
Lord, r me when thou comest into thy kingdom Luke 23:42
And they r his words Luke 24:8
his disciples r John 2:22
R the word that I said unto you John 15:20
Then r I the word of the Lord Acts 11:16
r the words of the Lord Jesus Acts 20:35
we should r the poor Gal 2:10
R my bonds Col 4:18
R without ceasing your work of faith 1 Thess 1:3
R them that are in bonds Heb 13:3
R them which have the rule over you Heb 13:7
R therefore from whence thou art fallen Rev 2:5
R therefore how thou hast received Rev 3:3

REMEMBRANCE
bringing iniquity to r Num 5:15
no son to keep my name in r 2 Sam 18:18
come unto me to call my sin to r 1 Kgs 17:18
his r shall perish from the earth Job 18:17
in death there is no r of thee Ps 6:5
give thanks at r of his holiness Ps 30:4; 97:12
I call to r my song in the night Ps 77:6
the righteous shall be in everlasting r Ps 112:6
There is no r of former things Eccl 1:11
no r of the wise more than of the fool Eccl 2:16
put me in r Is 43:26
hast thou set up thy r Is 57:8
My soul hath them still in r Lam 3:20
calling to r the days of her youth Ezek 23:19
a book of r Mal 3:16
this do in r of me Luke 22:19; 1 Cor 11:24
bring all things to your r John 14:26
thine alms are had in r Acts 10:31
I have r of thee in my prayers 2 Tim 1:3
of these things put them in r 2 Tim 2:14

REMETH re´-meth
a high place Josh 19:21

REMIT
whosesoever sins ye r John 20:23

REMMON rem´-on
another form of RIMMON Josh 19:7

REMMON-METHOAR rem´-on-me´-tho-ar
stretching (to Neah) Josh 19:13

REMPHAN rem´-fan
same as CHIUN Acts 7:43

REMNANT
the r shall be the priest's Lev 5:13
lift up thy prayer for the r 2 Kgs 19:4; Is 37:4
leave us a r to escape Ezra 9:8
except the LORD of hosts had left unto us a very small r Is 1:9
to recover the r of his people Is 11:11
the r shall be very small and feeble Is 16:14
all the r of Judah Jer 44:28
yet will I leave a r Ezek 6:8
the r whom the LORD shall call Joel 2:32

REMOVE
shall not r thy neighbour's landmark Deut 19:14
r the mountains, and they know not Job 9:5
the rock is r out of his place Job 14:18
let not the hand of the wicked r me Ps 36:11
R thy stroke away from me Ps 39:10
will not we fear, though the earth be r Ps 46:2
I r his shoulder from the burden Ps 81:6
so far hath he r our transgressions from us Ps 103:12
R from me reproach Ps 119:22
as mount Zion, which cannot be r Ps 125:1
r thy foot from evil Prov 4:27
The righteous shall never be r Prov 10:30
r sorrow from thy heart Eccl 11:10
earth shall r out of her place Is 13:13
shall be r like a cottage Is 24:20
have r their heart far from me Is 29:13
the hills be r Is 54:10
then shalt thou not r Jer 4:1
thou hast r my soul far off from peace Lam 3:17
R hence to yonder place; and it shall r Matt 17:20
r this cup from me Luke 22:42
I marvel that ye are so soon r Gal 1:6
will r thy candlestick Rev 2:5

REND
will surely r the kingdom from thee 1 Kgs 11:11
that thou wouldest r the heavens Is 64:1
will r the caul of their heart Hos 13:8
r your heart and not your garments Joel 2:13
turn again and r you Matt 7:6

RENDER
r vengeance to mine enemies Deut 32:41
r to every man his righteousness 1 Sam 26:23
he will r unto man his righteousness Job 33:26
work of a man shall he r unto him Job 34:11
r to them their desert Ps 28:4
they also that r evil for good Ps 38:20
and r unto our neighbour sevenfold Ps 79:12
r a reward to the proud Ps 94:2
What shall I r unto the LORD Ps 116:12
r to every man according to his works? Prov 24:12; Rom 2:6
than seven men that can r a reason Prov 26:16
so will we r the calves of our lips Hos 14:2
will ye r me a recompence? Joel 3:4
I will r double Zech 9:12
r him the fruits in their seasons Matt 21:41
R unto Caesar Matt 22:21; Mark 12:17; Luke 20:25
r therefore to all their dues Rom 13:7
what thanks can we r 1 Thess 3:9
See that none r evil for evil 1 Thess 5:15
Not r evil for evil, or railing for railing 1 Pet 3:9

RENEW
thou r thy witnesses against me Job 10:17
my bow was r in my hand Job 29:20
and r a right spirit within me Ps 51:10
thy youth is r like the eagle's Ps 103:5
thou r the face of the earth Ps 104:30
They that wait upon the LORD shall r their strength Is 40:31
let the people r their strength Is 41:1
r our days as of old Lam 5:21
the inward man is r day by day 2 Cor 4:16
be r in the spirit of your mind Eph 4:23
the new man, which is r in knowledge Col 3:10
If they shall fall away, to r them again Heb 6:6

RENOUNCED
have r the hidden things of dishonesty 2 Cor 4:2

RENOWN
men of r Gen 6:4; Num 16:2
thy r went forth among the heathen Ezek 16:14
a plant of r Ezek 34:29

RENOWNED
the r of the congregation Num 1:16
the seed of evildoers shall never be r Is 14:20

RENT
Joseph is without doubt r in pieces Gen 37:33
wine bottles, old and r Josh 9:4
as he would have a r a kid Judg 14:6
the altar shall be r 1 Kgs 13:3
the cloud is not r under them Job 26:8
veil of the temple was r in twain Matt 27:51; Mark 15:38; Luke 23:45

REPAIR
of all Israel money to r the house 2 Chr 24:5
they shall r the waste cities Is 61:4

REPAY
he will r him to his face Deut 7:10
to the righteous good shall be r Prov 13:21
when I come again, I will r thee Luke 10:35
Vengeance is mine, I will r Rom 12:19
I will r it Phile 1:19

REPEATETH
he that r a matter separateth very friends Prov 17:9

REPENT
it r the LORD that he had made man Gen 6:6
lest peradventure the people r Ex 13:17
the LORD r of the evil Ex 32:14; 2 Sam 24:16; 1 Chr 21:15; Jer 18:8; 26:13,19; Joel 2:13
neither the son of man, that he should r Num 23:19
shall r himself for his servants Deut 32:36
for he is not a man that he should r 1 Sam 15:29
I abhor myself, and r in dust and ashes Job 42:6
let it r thee concerning thy servants Ps 90:13
r according to the multitude of his mercies Ps 106:45
LORD hath sworn, and will not r Ps 110:4; Heb 7:21
no man r him of his wickedness Jer 8:6
after that I was turned, I r Jer 31:19
they r at the preaching Matt 12:41; Luke 11:32
afterward he r and went Matt 21:29
except ye r Luke 13:3
likewise joy shall be in heaven over one sinner that r Luke 15:7
if he r, forgive him Luke 17:3
r therefore of this thy wickedness Acts 8:22
space to r of her fornication; and she r not Rev 2:21

REPENTANCE
r shall be hid from mine eyes Hos 13:14
fruits meet for r Matt 3:8; Luke 3:8; Acts 26:20

the goodness of God leadeth thee to **r** Rom 2:4
gifts and calling of God are without **r** Rom 11:29
r to salvation not to be repented of 2 Cor 7:10
not laying again the foundation of **r** Heb 6:1
to renew them again unto **r** Heb 6:6
no place of **r**, though he sought it Heb 12:17

REPHAEL re´-fa-el
whom God healed 1 Chr 26:7

REPHAH re´-fah
riches 1 Chr 7:25

REPHAIAH ref-ai´-ah
whom Jehovah healed 1 Chr 3:21

REPHAIM re-fa´-im
giants 2 Sam 5:18

REPHAIMS re-fa´-ims
same as REPHAIM Gen 14:5

REPHIDIM ref´-id-im
supports Ex 17:1

REPLENISH
r the earth Gen 1:28; 9:1
I have **r** every sorrowful soul Jer 31:25
I shall be **r**, now she is laid waste Ezek 26:2

REPLIEST
who art thou that **r** against God? Rom 9:20

REPORT (n)
their evil **r** Gen 37:2
Thou shalt not raise a false **r** Ex 23:1
an evil **r** of the land Num 13:32
it is no good **r** that I hear 1 Sam 2:24
it was a true **r** that I heard 1 Kgs 10:6; 2 Chr 9:5
a good **r** maketh the bones fat Prov 15:30
a vexation only to understand the **r** Is 28:19
Who hath believed our **r**? Is 53:1
men of honest **r** Acts 6:3
good **r** among all the nation of the Jews Acts 10:22
by evil **r** and good **r** 2 Cor 6:8
whatsoever things are of good **r** Phil 4:8
he must have a good **r** 1 Tim 3:7

REPORT (v)
It is **r** among the heathen Neh 6:6
R, say they, and we will **r** it Jer 20:10
saying is commonly **r** among the Jews Matt 28:15
well **r** of by the brethren Acts 16:2
r that God is in you 1 Cor 14:25

REPROACH (n)
God hath taken away my **r** Gen 30:23
that were a **r** unto us Gen 34:14
lay it for a **r** upon all Israel 1 Sam 11:2
that we be no more a **r** Neh 2:17
nor taketh up a **r** against his neighbour Ps 15:3
a **r** of men Ps 22:6
I was a **r** among all mine enemies Ps 31:11
a **r** to our neighbours Ps 44:13; 79:4; 89:41
the **r** of them that reproached thee Ps 69:9; Rom 15:3
put them to a perpetual **r** Ps 78:66
his **r** shall not be wiped away Prov 6:33
sin is a **r** to any people Prov 14:34
given Jacob to the curse, and Israel to **r** Is 43:28
fear ye not the **r** of men Is 51:7
I will bring an everlasting **r** upon you Jer 23:40
I did bear the **r** of my youth Jer 31:19
he is filled full with **r** Lam 3:30
I will make thee waste, and a **r** among the nations Ezek 5:14
it shall be a **r** and a taunt Ezek 5:15
ye shall bear the **r** of my people Mic 6:16
I speak as concerning **r** 2 Cor 11:21
in infirmities, in **r** for Christ's sake 2 Cor 12:10
lest he fall into **r** 1 Tim 3:7
we both labour and suffer **r** 1 Tim 4:10
Esteeming the **r** of Christ greater riches Heb 11:26
without the camp, bearing his **r** Heb 13:13

REPROACH (v)
the same **r** the Lord Num 15:30
r her not Ruth 2:15
Whom hast thou **r** 2 Kgs 19:22; Is 37:23
these ten times have ye **r** me Job 19:3
my heart shall not **r** me Job 27:6
As with a sword in my bones, mine enemies **r** me Ps 42:10
the voice of him that **r** Ps 44:16
how the foolish man **r** thee daily Ps 74:22
answer him that **r** me Ps 119:42; Prov 27:11
oppresseth the poor **r** his Maker Prov 14:31
If ye be **r** for the name of Christ 1 Pet 4:14

REPROACHFULLY
smitten me on the cheek **r** Job 16:10
to the adversary to speak **r** 1 Tim 5:14

REPROOF
astonished at his **r** Job 26:11
they despised all my **r** Prov 1:30
r of instruction are the way of life Prov 6:23
he that refuseth **r** erreth Prov 10:17
he that hateth **r** is brutish Prov 12:1
he that regardeth **r** is prudent Prov 15:5
The rod and **r** give wisdom Prov 29:15

REPROVE
r kings for their sakes 1 Chr 16:21; Ps 105:14
what doth your arguing **r**? Job 6:25
He will surely **r** you if ye do secretly accept persons Job 13:10
Will he **r** thee for fear Job 22:4
He that **r** God, let him answer it Job 40:2
I will not **r** thee for thy sacrifices Ps 50:8
let him **r** me; it shall be an excellent oil Ps 141:5
R not a scorner, lest he hate thee Prov 9:8
A scorner loveth not one that **r** him Prov 15:12
r one that hath understanding Prov 19:25
being often **r** hardeneth his neck Prov 29:1
lest he **r** thee, and thou be found a liar Prov 30:6
r with equity for the meek Is 11:4
thy backslidings shall **r** thee Jer 2:19
lest his deeds should be **r** John 3:20
he will **r** the world of sin John 16:8

REPROVER
a wise **r** upon an obedient ear Prov 25:12
shalt not be to them a **r** Ezek 3:26

REPUTATION
him that is in **r** for wisdom Eccl 10:1
had in **r** among all the people Acts 5:34
made himself of no **r** Phil 2:7
hold such in **r** Phil 2:29

REQUEST
I would desire a **r** of you Judg 8:24
the king granted him all his **r** Ezra 7:6
Oh that I might have my **r** Job 6:8
hast not withholden the **r** of his lips Ps 21:2
he gave them their **r** Ps 106:15
making **r** with joy Phil 1:4
let your **r** be made known Phil 4:6

REQUESTED
he **r** for himself that he might die 1 Kgs 19:4

REQUIRE
your blood of your lives will I **r** Gen 9:5
of my hand didst thou **r** it Gen 31:39
what doth the LORD thy God **r** of thee Deut 10:12; Mic 6:8
let the Lord himself **r** it Josh 22:23; 1 Sam 20:16
I will do to thee all that thou **r** Ruth 3:11
the king's business **r** haste 1 Sam 21:8
one thing I **r** of thee 2 Sam 3:13
whatsoever thou shalt **r** of me, that will I do 2 Sam 19:38
the Lord look upon it, and **r** it 2 Chr 24:22
restore them, and **r** nothing of them Neh 5:12
said in his heart, Thou wilt not **r** it Ps 10:13
sin offering hast thou not **r** Ps 40:6
they that wasted us **r** of us mirth Ps 137:3
Two things have I **r** of thee Prov 30:7
God **r** that which is past Eccl 3:15
who hath **r** this at your hand Is 1:12
his blood will I **r** at thine hand Ezek 3:18; 33:8
I will **r** my flock at their hand Ezek 34:10
may be **r** of this generation Luke 11:50
this night thy soul shall be **r** of thee Luke 12:20
of him shall be much **r** Luke 12:48
might have **r** mine own with usury Luke 19:23
the Jews **r** a sign 1 Cor 1:22
it is **r** in stewards, that a man be found faithful 1 Cor 4:2

REQUITE
will certainly **r** us Gen 50:15
Do ye thus **r** the LORD Deut 32:6
as I have done, so God hath **r** me Judg 1:7
I also will **r** you this kindness 2 Sam 2:6
that the LORD will **r** me good for this 2 Sam 16:12
to **r** their parents 1 Tim 5:4

REREWARD
the **r** came after the ark Josh 6:9
the God of Israel will be your **r** Is 52:12

RESCUE
r my soul from their destructions Ps 35:17
none shall **r** him Hos 5:14

RESEMBLANCE
this is their **r** through all the earth Zech 5:6

RESEMBLE
each one **r** the children of a king Judg 8:18
whereunto shall I **r** it? Luke 13:18

RESEN re´-sen
bridle Gen 10:12

RESERVE
Hast thou not **r** a blessing for me? Gen 27:36
gave to her that she had **r** Ruth 2:18
the wicked is **r** to day of destruction Job 21:30
have **r** against the time of trouble Job 38:23
Will he **r** his anger for ever? Jer 3:5
r unto us the appointed weeks of harvest Jer 5:24
I will pardon them whom I **r** Jer 50:20
he **r** wrath for his enemies Nah 1:2
r in heaven for you 1 Pet 1:4
to be **r** unto judgment 2 Pet 2:4
the **r** unto fire 2 Pet 3:7

RESHEPH re´-shef
flame 1 Chr 7:25

RESIDUE
they shall eat the **r** Ex 10:5
I am deprived of the **r** of my years Is 38:10
r of them will I deliver to the sword Jer 15:9
wilt thou destroy all the **r** of Israel Ezek 9:8
I will not be unto the **r** of this people as in the former days Zech 8:11
yet had he the **r** of the Spirit Mal 2:15
r of men might seek after the Lord Acts 15:17

RESIST
at his right hand to **r** him Zech 3:1
That ye **r** not evil Matt 5:39
shall not be able to gainsay nor **r** Luke 21:15
who hath **r** his will? Rom 9:19
whoso therefore **r** the power, **r** the ordinance of God Rom 13:2
God **r** the proud James 4:6; 1 Pet 5:5
R the devil, and he will flee from you James 4:7
whom **r** stedfast in the faith 1 Pet 5:9

RESORT

r ye thither unto us Neh 4:20
whereunto I may continually r Ps 71:3
Jesus ofttimes r thither John 18:2

RESPECT (n)

the LORD had r unto Abel Gen 4:4
God had r unto them Ex 2:25
have thou r unto the prayer 1 Kgs 8:28
there is no r of persons with God 2 Chr 19:7; Rom 2:11; Eph 6:9; Col 3:25
have r unto the covenant Ps 74:20
have r unto thy ways Ps 119:15
yet hath he r unto the lowly Ps 138:6
not good to have r of persons Prov 24:23; 28:21
his eyes shall have r to the Holy One Is 17:7
neither had r unto him that fashioned it Is 22:11
Not that I speak in r of want Phil 4:11

RESPECT (v)

shalt not r person of poor Lev 19:15
ye shall not r persons in judgment Deut 1:17
he r not any that are wise of heart Job 37:24

RESPITE

Pharaoh saw that there was r Ex 8:15
Give us seven days r 1 Sam 11:3

REST (n)

saw that r was good Gen 49:15
the sabbath of r Ex 31:15; 35:2; Lev 16:31; 23:3,32:25:4
my presence shall go with thee, and I will give thee r Ex 33:14
a year of r unto the land Lev 25:5
giveth you r from all your enemies Deut 12:10
the land had r fourscore years Judg 3:30
shall not I seek r for thee Ruth 3:1
a man of r; and I will give him r 1 Chr 22:9
hath he not given you r on every side? 1 Chr 22:18
to build a house of r 1 Chr 28:2
after they had r, they did evil Neh 9:28
had r from their enemies Esth 9:16
there the weary be at r Job 3:17
thou shalt take thy r in safety Job 11:18
when our r together is in the dust Job 17:16
then would I fly away, and be at r Ps 55:6
not enter into my r Ps 95:11; Heb 3:11
Return to thy r, O my soul Ps 116:7
Arise, O LORD, into thy r Ps 132:8
This is my r for ever Ps 132:14
his heart taketh not r in the night Eccl 2:23
his r shall be glorious Is 11:10
earth is at r Is 14:7; Zech 1:11
I will take my r Is 18:4
in returning and r shall ye be saved Is 30:15
where is the place of my r? Is 66:1
ye shall find r for your souls Jer 6:16
I will go to them that are at r Ezek 38:11
depart; for this is not your r Mic 2:10
I will give you r Matt 11:28
ye shall find r unto your souls Matt 11:29
seeking r, and finding none Matt 12:43; Luke 11:24
Sleep on now, and take your r Matt 26:45; Mark 14:41
of taking r in sleep John 11:13
then had the churches r Acts 9:31

REST (v)

he r on the seventh day Gen 2:2
when the spirit r upon them Num 11:25
people r themselves upon the words 2 Chr 32:8
there the prisoners r together Job 3:18
my flesh also shall r in hope Ps 16:9; Acts 2:26
R in the LORD Ps 37:7
anger r in bosom of fools Eccl 7:9
the spirit of the LORD shall r upon him Is 11:2
ye may cause the weary to r Is 28:12
like the troubled sea, when it cannot r Is 57:20
for Jerusalem's sake I will not r Is 62:1
the Spirit of the LORD caused him to r Is 63:14
r, and be still Jer 47:6
thou shalt r, and stand in thy lot Dan 12:13
the power of Christ may r upon me 2 Cor 12:9
they r not day and night Rev 4:8
r yet for a little season Rev 6:11
that they may r from their labours Rev 14:13

RESTORE

he shall r double Ex 22:4
r that which he took violently away Lev 6:4
thou shalt r it to him again Deut 22:2
He r my soul Ps 23:3
R unto me the joy of thy salvation Ps 51:12
I r that which I took not away Ps 69:4
I will r thy judges as at the first Is 1:26
r them to this place Jer 27:22
I will r health unto thee Jer 30:17
If the wicked r the pledge Ezek 33:15
Elijah truly shall first come and r all things Matt 17:11; Mark 9:12
I r him fourfold Luke 19:8
wilt thou at this time r again the kingdom to Israel? Acts 1:6
r such a one in the spirit of meekness Gal 6:1

RESTRAIN

nothing will be r from them Gen 11:6
people were r from bringing Ex 36:6
his sons made themselves vile, and he r them not 1 Sam 3:13
casteth off fear and r prayer before God Job 15:4
dost thou r wisdom to thyself? Job 15:8
the remainder of wrath shalt thou r Ps 76:10

RETAIN

Dost thou still r thine integrity? Job 2:9
happy is every one that r her Prov 3:18
Let thine heart r my words Prov 4:4
a gracious woman r honour Prov 11:16
no man hath power over the spirit to r the spirit Eccl 8:8
whosesoever sins ye r, they are r John 20:23

RETIRE

the men of Israel r in the battle Judg 20:39
r ye from him 2 Sam 11:15
r, stay not Jer 4:6

RETURN

unto dust shalt thou r Gen 3:19
the sea r to his strength Ex 14:27
fearful and afraid, let him r Judg 7:3
Intreat me not to leave thee, or to r Ruth 1:16
he shall not r to me 2 Sam 12:23
let the shadow r backward 2 Kgs 20:10
naked shall I r thither Job 1:21
he shall r no more Job 7:10
I go whence I shall not r Job 10:21; 16:22
he believeth not that he shall r out of darkness Job 15:22
he shall r to the days of his youth Job 33:25
my prayer r into mine own bosom Ps 35:13
his people r hither Ps 73:10
R, ye children of men Ps 90:3
they die, and r to their dust Ps 104:29
R unto thy rest, O my soul Ps 116:7
None that go unto her r again Prov 2:19
As a dog r to his vomit Prov 26:11
he that rolleth a stone, it will r upon him Prov 26:27
whence the rivers come, thither they r again Eccl 1:7
naked shall he r to go as he came Eccl 5:15
nor the clouds r after the rain Eccl 12:2
the dust r to earth, and the spirit shall r to God Eccl 12:7
if ye will inquire, inquire ye: r, come Is 21:12
ransomed of the LORD shall r Is 35:10; 51:11
r unto me, for I have redeemed thee Is 44:22
righteousness, and shall not r Is 45:23
it shall not r unto me void Is 55:11
If thou wilt r, O Israel, . . . r unto me Jer 4:1
let them r unto thee; but r not thou unto them Jer 15:19
shall r unto me with their whole heart Jer 24:7
a great company shall r thither Jer 31:8
r every man from his evil way Jer 36:3
he shall not r by the way Ezek 46:9
I will go and r to my first husband Hos 2:7
I will go and r to my place Hos 5:15
they r, but not to the most High Hos 7:16
that dwell under his shadow shall r Hos 14:7
Who knoweth if he will r and repent? Joel 2:14
yet have ye not r unto me Amos 4:6
I am r to Jerusalem with mercies Zech 1:16
I am r unto Zion, and will dwell Zech 8:3
R unto me, and I will r unto you Mal 3:7
Then shall ye r, and discern Mal 3:18
I will r into my house Matt 12:44; Luke 11:24
neither let him which is in the field r back Matt 24:18
apostles, when they were r, told them all Luke 9:10
the seventy r again with joy Luke 10:17
when he will r from the wedding Luke 12:36
not found that r to give glory to God Luke 17:18
now no more to r to corruption Acts 13:34
had opportunity to have r Heb 11:15
now r unto the Shepherd and Bishop of your souls 1 Pet 2:25

REU roo

same as RAGUEL Gen 11:18

REUBEN roo´-ben

behold a son (?) Gen 29:32

REUBENITES roo´-ben-ites

descendants of Reuben Num 26:7

REUEL roo´-el

friend of God 1 Chr 9:8

REUMAH room´-ah

exalted Gen 22:24

REVEAL

things which are r belong unto us Deut 29:29
the word of the LORD yet r unto him 1 Sam 3:7
the heaven shall r his iniquity Job 20:27
a talebearer r secrets Prov 11:13; 20:19
it was r in mine ears Is 22:14
the glory of the Lord shall be r Is 40:5
to whom is the arm of the Lord r? Is 53:1; John 12:38
my righteousness to be r Is 56:1
unto thee have I r my cause Jer 11:20
r unto them the abundance of peace Jer 33:6
he r the deep and secret things Dan 2:22
there is a God in heaven that r secrets Dan 2:28
he r his secret unto his servants the prophets Amos 3:7
nothing covered, that shall not be r Matt 10:26; Luke 12:2
hast r them unto babes Matt 11:25
flesh and blood hath not r it Matt 16:17
thoughts of many hearts may be r Luke 2:35
in the day when the Son of man is r Luke 17:30
righteousness of God is r Rom 1:17
wrath of God is r from heaven Rom 1:18
glory which shall be r in us Rom 8:18
God hath r them unto us by his Spirit 1 Cor 2:10
it shall be r by fire 1 Cor 3:13
if anything be r to another 1 Cor 14:30
to r his Son in me Gal 1:16
when the Lord Jesus shall be r 2 Thess 1:7
man of sin be r 2 Thess 2:3
that Wicked be r 2 Thess 2:8

RICHLY
dwell in you r in all wisdom Col 3:16
who giveth us r all things to enjoy 1 Tim 6:17

RIDDANCE
shalt not make clean r of the corners Lev 23:22
r of all them that dwell in the land Zeph 1:18

RIDDLE
put forth a r Judg 14:12; Ezek 17:2

RIDE
r on the high places of the earth Deut 32:13
who r upon the heaven Deut 33:26
ye that r on white asses Judg 5:10
slack not thy r for me 2 Kgs 4:24
causest me to r upon it Job 30:22
in thy majesty r prosperously Ps 45:4
hast caused men to r over our heads Ps 66:12
extol him that r upon the heavens Ps 68:4
the LORD r on a swift cloud Is 19:1

RIDER
his r shall fall backward Gen 49:17
the horse and his r hath he thrown into the sea Ex 15:1
scorneth the horse and his r Job 39:18
the r on horses shall be confounded Zech 10:5

RIDGES
waterest the r thereof Ps 65:10

RIGHT (adj)
led me in the r way Gen 24:48
just and r is he Deut 32:4
teach you the good and the r way 1 Sam 12:23
thy matters are good and r 2 Sam 15:3
gavest them r judgments Neh 9:13
How forcible are r words! Job 6:25
will not lay upon man more than r Job 34:23
The statutes of the LORD are r Ps 19:8
sceptre of thy kingdom is a r sceptre Ps 45:6
renew a r spirit within me Ps 51:10
he led them forth by the r way Ps 107:7
thy judgments are r Ps 119:75
I have led thee in r paths Prov 4:11
opening of my lips shall be r things Prov 8:6
The thoughts of the righteous are r Prov 12:5
The way of a fool is r in his own eyes Prov 12:15
There is a way that seemeth r Prov 14:12; 16:25
Every way of man is r in his own eyes Prov 21:2
kiss his lips that giveth a r answer Prov 24:26
prophesy not unto us r things Is 30:10
wholly a r seed Jer 2:21
that which is lawful and r Ezek 18:5,19; 33:14
the ways of the LORD are r Hos 14:9
they know not to do r Amos 3:10
whatsoever is r I will give you Matt 20:4
in his r mind Mark 5:15; Luke 8:35
thou hast answered r Luke 10:28
obey your parents in the Lord, for this is r Eph 6:1

RIGHT (n)
Shall not the Judge of all the earth do r? Gen 18:25
shalt do that which is r Deut 6:18; 12:25; 21:9
the r of the firstborn is his Deut 21:17
What r therefore have I yet to cry 2 Sam 19:28
ye have no portion, nor r Neh 2:20
Should I lie against my r? Job 34:6
giveth r to the poor Job 36:6
thou hast maintained my r Ps 9:4
Hear the r, O LORD Ps 17:1
the r of the poor Ps 140:12
great revenues without r Prov 16:8
that getteth riches, and not by r Jer 17:11
until he come whose r it is Ezek 21:27

RIGHTEOUS
thee have I seen r before me Gen 7:1
also destroy the r with the wicked? Gen 18:23
wilt thou slay also a r nation? Gen 20:4
she hath been more r than I Gen 38:26
perverteth the words of the r Ex 23:8
Let me die the death of the r Num 23:10
they shall justify the r Deut 25:1
Thou art more r than I 1 Sam 24:17
two men more r and better than he 1 Kgs 2:32
where were the r cut off? Job 4:7
though I were r, yet would I not answer Job 9:15
that he should be r Job 15:14
The r also shall hold on his way Job 17:9
thou art r? Job 22:3
there the r might dispute with him Job 23:7
Job hath said, I am r Job 34:5
the congregation of the r Ps 1:5
the LORD knoweth the way of the r Ps 1:6
the r God trieth the hearts Ps 7:9
what can the r do? Ps 11:3
The r cry, and the LORD heareth Ps 34:17
Many are the afflictions of the r Ps 34:19
a little that a r man hath Ps 37:16
the r sheweth mercy, and giveth Ps 37:21
have not seen the r forsaken Ps 37:25
The r shall inherit the land Ps 37:29
The mouth of the r speaketh wisdom Ps 37:30
salvation of the r is of the LORD Ps 37:39
never suffer the r to be moved Ps 55:22
there is a reward for the r Ps 58:11
not be written with the r Ps 69:28
The r shall flourish like the palm tree Ps 92:12
Light is sown for the r Ps 97:11
r shall be in everlasting remembrance Ps 112:6
rod of the wicked shall not rest upon the lot of the r Ps 125:3
the r shall give thanks Ps 140:13
let the r smite me Ps 141:5
the LORD loveth the r Ps 146:8
He layeth up sound wisdom for the r Prov 2:7
his secret is with the r Prov 3:32
not suffer the soul of the r to famish Prov 10:3
The mouth of a r man is a well of life Prov 10:11
labour of the r tendeth to life Prov 10:16
lips of r feed many Prov 10:21
desire of the r shall be granted Prov 10:24
the r is an everlasting foundation Prov 10:25
The r is delivered out of trouble Prov 11:8
When it goeth well with the r Prov 11:10
the root of the r shall not be moved Prov 12:3
r man regardeth the life of his beast Prov 12:10
to the r good shall be repayed Prov 13:21
r eateth to the satisfying of his soul Prov 13:25
among the r there is favour Prov 14:9
the r hath hope in his death Prov 14:32
In the house of the r is much treasure Prov 15:6
the way of the r is made plain Prov 15:19
R lips are the delight of kings Prov 16:13
the r runneth into it, and is safe Prov 18:10
the r are bold as a lion Prov 28:1
When the r are in authority, the people rejoice Prov 29:2
Be not r overmuch Eccl 7:16
one event to the r, and to the wicked Eccl 9:2
Say ye to the r, that it shall be well Is 3:10
songs, even glory to the r Is 24:16
raised up the r man from the east Is 41:2
shall my r servant justify Is 53:11
The r perisheth, and no man layeth it to heart Is 57:1
Thy people also shall be all r Is 60:21
raise unto David a r Branch Jer 23:5
with lies ye have made the heart of the r sad Ezek 13:22
they are more r than thou Ezek 16:52
The righteousness of the r shall not deliver Ezek 33:12
they sold the r for silver Amos 2:6
discern between the r and wicked Mal 3:18
to call the r Matt 9:13; Mark 2:17; Luke 5:32
r men have desired Matt 13:17
Then shall the r shine forth Matt 13:43
outwardly appear r unto men Matt 23:28
garnish the sepulchres of the r Matt 23:29
the r into life eternal Matt 25:46
they were both r before God Luke 1:6
trusted they were r, and despised others Luke 18:9
certainly this was a r man Luke 23:47
judge r judgment John 7:24
There is none r, no, not one Rom 3:10
For scarcely for a r man will one die Rom 5:7
many be made r Rom 5:19
it is a r thing with God 2 Thess 1:6
the Lord, the r Judge 2 Tim 4:8
obtained witness that he was r Heb 11:4
the eyes of the Lord are over the r 1 Pet 3:12
if the r scarcely be saved 1 Pet 4:18
vexed his r soul from day to day 2 Pet 2:8
Jesus Christ the r 1 John 2:1
righteousness is r, even as he is r 1 John 3:7
he that is r, let him be r still Rev 22:11

RIGHTEOUSLY
judge r Deut 1:16; Prov 31:9
shalt judge the people r Ps 67:4; 96:10
He that walketh r Is 33:15

RIGHTEOUSNESS
so shall my r answer for me Gen 30:33
offer sacrifices of r Deut 33:19
render unto every man his r 1 Sam 26:23; Job 33:26
return again, my r is in it Job 6:29
My r I hold fast Job 27:6
I put on r, and it clothed me Job 29:14
thou saidst, My r is more than God's Job 35:2
I will ascribe r to my Maker Job 36:3
O God of my r Ps 4:1
Offer the sacrifices of r Ps 4:5
he shall judge the world in r Ps 9:8
worketh r, and speaketh the truth Ps 15:2
as for me, I will behold thy face in r Ps 17:15
leadeth me in paths of r Ps 23:3
and r from the God of his salvation Ps 24:5
I have preached r Ps 40:9
thou lovest r Ps 45:7
heavens shall declare his r Ps 50:6
He shall judge thy people with r Ps 72:2
r and peace have kissed each other Ps 85:10
judgment shall return unto r Ps 94:15
r and judgment are the habitation of his throne Ps 97:2
his r endureth for ever Ps 111:3; 112:3,9
Open to me the gates of r Ps 118:19
Let thy priests be clothed with r Ps 132:9
durable riches and r Prov 8:18
but r delivereth from death Prov 10:2; 11:4
r of the perfect shall direct his way Prov 11:5
r of the upright shall deliver Prov 11:6
r tendeth to life Prov 11:19
In the way of r is life Prov 12:28
R exalteth a nation Prov 14:34
Better is a little with r Prov 16:8
the throne is established by r Prov 16:12
crown of glory, if it be found in the way of r Prov 16:31
a just man that perisheth in his r Eccl 7:15
r shall be the girdle of his loins Is 11:5
yet will he not learn r Is 26:10
a king shall reign in r Is 32:1
the work of r shall be peace Is 32:17
uphold thee with the right hand of my r Is 41:10
that are far from r Is 46:12
his r it sustained him Is 59:16
the Gentiles shall see thy r Is 62:2
our r are as filthy rags Is 64:6

THE LORD OUR R Jer 23:6
cause the Branch of r to grow Jer 33:15
The LORD hath brought forth our r Jer 51:10
righteous turneth away from his r Ezek 3:20; 18:24
deliver but their own souls by their r Ezek 14:14
r of the righteous shall be upon him Ezek 18:20
if he trust to his own r Ezek 33:13
break off thy sins by r Dan 4:27
r belongeth unto thee Dan 9:7
to bring in everlasting r Dan 9:24
they that turn many to r Dan 12:3
rain r upon you Hos 10:12
r as a mighty stream Amos 5:24
fruit of r into hemlock Amos 6:12
seek r Zeph 2:3
shall the Sun of r arise Mal 4:2
to fulfil all r Matt 3:15
hunger and thirst after r Matt 5:6
persecuted for r sake Matt 5:10
except your r shall exceed the r Matt 5:20
John came to you in the way of r Matt 21:32
In holiness and r before him Luke 1:75
reprove the world of sin, and of r John 16:8
worketh r Acts 10:35
thou enemy of all r Acts 13:10
as he reasoned of r Acts 24:25
the r of God Rom 1:17; 3:5; 10:3
to whom God imputeth r Rom 4:6
seal of the r of the faith Rom 4:11
which receive the gift of r Rom 5:17
by the r of one Rom 5:18
so might grace reign through r Rom 5:21
members as instruments of r Rom 6:13
ye were free from r Rom 6:20
the Spirit is life because of r Rom 8:10
the r which is of faith Rom 9:30
going about to establish their own r Rom 10:3
Christ is the end of the law for r Rom 10:4
with the heart man believeth unto r Rom 10:10
kingdom of God not meat and drink, but r Rom 14:17
made unto us wisdom, and r, and sanctification 1 Cor 1:30
Awake to r 1 Cor 15:34
that we might be made the r 2 Cor 5:21
the armour of r 2 Cor 6:7
what fellowship hath r with unrighteousness? 2 Cor 6:14
if r come by the law Gal 2:21
wait for the hope of r Gal 5:5
the breastplate of r Eph 6:14
filled with the fruits of r Phil 1:11
touching the r which is in the law, blameless Phil 3:6
not having mine own r Phil 3:9
follow after r 1 Tim 6:11
for instruction in r 2 Tim 3:16
laid up for me a crown of r 2 Tim 4:8
Not by works of r Titus 3:5
a sceptre of r Heb 1:8
unskilful in the word of r Heb 5:13
by interpretation, King of r Heb 7:2
heir of the r which is by faith Heb 11:7
wrought r Heb 11:33
the peaceable fruit of r Heb 12:11
wrath of man worketh not the r of God James 1:20
the fruit of r is sown in peace James 3:18
being dead to sins, should live unto r 1 Pet 2:24
a preacher of r 2 Pet 2:5
known the way of r 2 Pet 2:21
new earth, wherein dwelleth r 2 Pet 3:13
every one that doeth r 1 John 2:29

RIGHTLY
Is not he r named Jacob? Gen 27:36
Thou hast r judged Luke 7:43
thou sayest and teacheth r Luke 20:21
r dividing the word of truth 2 Tim 2:15

RIGOUR
children of Israel to serve with r Ex 1:13
not rule over him with r Lev 25:43
with r over him in thy sight Lev 25:53

RIMMON rim´-on
pomegranate 2 Sam 4:2

RIMMON-PAREZ rim´-on-pa´-rez
pomegranate of the breach Num 33:19

RINGLEADER
a r of the sect of the Nazarenes Acts 24:5

RINNAH rin´-ah
shout 1 Chr 4:20

RIOT
not in r and drunkenness Rom 13:13
having faithful children not accused of r or unruly Titus 1:6
the same excess of r, speaking evil 1 Pet 4:4
they that count it pleasure to r 2 Pet 2:13

RIPE
brought forth r grapes Gen 40:10
offer the first of thy r fruits Ex 22:29
whatsoever is first r in the land Num 18:13
Put in the sickle, for the harvest is r Joel 3:13
my soul desired the first r fruit Mic 7:1
for the harvest of the earth is r Rev 14:15

RIPHATH ri´-fath
descendants of Gomer Gen 10:3

RISE
ye shall r up early Gen 19:2
the sun was r upon the earth Gen 19:23
a Sceptre shall r out of Israel Num 24:17
ye are r up in your fathers' stead Num 32:14
commandeth the sun, and it r not Job 9:7
man lieth down, and r not Job 14:12
he r up, and no man is sure of life Job 24:22
What shall I do when God r up? Job 31:14
though war should r against me Ps 27:3
At midnight I will r to give thanks Ps 119:62
It is vain for you to r up early Ps 127:2
She r also while it is yet night Prov 31:15
he shall r up at the voice of the bird Eccl 12:4
Now will I r, saith the LORD Is 33:10
then shall thy light r in obscurity Is 58:10
the glory of the LORD is r upon thee Is 60:1
I spake unto you, r up early Jer 7:13; 26:5; 29:19; 35:15
r early and protesting Jer 11:7
fall and r no more Jer 25:27
and their r up; I am their musick Lam 3:63
his sun to r on the evil and the good Matt 5:45
until Son of man be r Matt 17:9
the third day he shall r again Matt 20:19; Mark 10:34; Luke 18:33
after I am r I will go before you Matt 26:32
R, let us be going Matt 26:46
should sleep, and r night and day Mark 4:27
r from the dead should mean Mark 9:10
r, he calleth thee Mark 10:49
this child is set for the fall and r Luke 2:34
I cannot r and give thee Luke 11:7
Why sleep ye? r and pray Luke 22:46
the Lord is r indeed Luke 24:34
Thy brother shall r again John 11:23
R, Peter, kill and eat Acts 10:13
r, and stand upon thy feet Acts 26:16
the first that should r from the dead Acts 26:23
Christ that died, yea rather, that is r Rom 8:34
if so be that the dead r not 1 Cor 15:15
but now is Christ r 1 Cor 15:20
If ye then be r with Christ Col 3:1
the dead in Christ shall r first 1 Thess 4:16

RISSAH ris´-ah
ruin Num 33:21

RITES
according to all the r of it Num 9:3

RITHMAH rith´-mah
broom Num 33:18

RIVER
upon their r Ex 7:19
city, and we will draw it into the r 2 Sam 17:13
r of Damascus better? 2 Kgs 5:12
He shall not see the r Job 20:17
He cutteth out r among the rocks Job 28:10
the rock poured me out r of oil Job 29:6
he drinketh up a r, and hasteth not Job 40:23
tree planted by the r Ps 1:3
the r of thy pleasures Ps 36:8
There is a r, the streams whereof shall make glad Ps 46:4
enrichest it with the r of God Ps 65:9
turneth r into a wilderness Ps 107:33
R of waters run down mine eyes Ps 119:136
by the r of Babylon Ps 137:1
All the r run into the sea Eccl 1:7
r of water in a dry place Is 32:2
through the r, they shall not overflow Is 43:2
r in the desert Is 43:19
then had thy peace been as a r Is 48:18
I will extend peace to her like a r Is 66:12
let tears run down like a r Lam 2:18
r of oil Mic 6:7
shall flow r of living water John 7:38
a pure r of water of life Rev 22:1

RIZPAH riz´-pah
hot coal 2 Sam 3:7

ROAD
Whither have ye made a r to day? 1 Sam 27:10

ROAR
let the sea r 1 Chr 16:32; Ps 96:11; 98:7
Though the waters thereof r Ps 46:3
young lions r after their prey Ps 104:21
We r are all like bears Is 59:11
Their voice r like the sea Jer 6:23
The LORD shall r from on high Jer 25:30
he shall r like a lion Hos 11:10
The LORD also shall r out of Zion Joel 3:16
Will a lion r in the forest Amos 3:4

ROARING
my r are poured out Job 3:24
as the r of a lion Prov 19:12; 20:2
as a r lion Prov 28:15
the sea and the waves r Luke 21:25
the devil as a r lion 1 Pet 5:8

ROAST
but r with fire Ex 12:9
slothful man r not Prov 12:27
he r and is satisfied Is 44:16

ROB
R not the poor Prov 22:22
that they may r the fatherless Is 10:2
have r their treasures Is 10:13
this is a people r and spoiled Is 42:22
give again that he had r Ezek 33:15
ye have r me Mal 3:8
I r other churches 2 Cor 11:8

ROBBER
tabernacles of r prosper Job 12:6
Jacob for a spoil, and Israel to the r? Is 42:24
become a den of r in your eyes? Jer 7:11
the same is a thief and a r John 10:1
came before me are thieves and r John 10:8
men are neither r of churches Acts 19:37
in perils of r 2 Cor 11:26

ROBBERY
thought it not **r** to be equal Phil 2:6

ROBE
cut off the skirt of Saul's **r** 1 Sam 24:4
my judgment was as a **r** Job 29:14
covered me with the **r** of righteousness Is 61:10
Bring forth the best **r** Luke 15:22
which desire to walk in long **r** Luke 20:46

ROBOAM rob-o´-am
Gr. for REHOBOAM Matt 1:7

ROCK
I will put thee in a clift of the **r** Ex 33:22
speak ye unto the **r** before their eyes Num 20:8
fetch you water out of this **r**? Num 20:10
from the top of the **r** I see him Num 23:9
thou puttest thy nest in a **r** Num 24:21
brought thee forth water out of the **r** Deut 8:15
He is the **R** Deut 32:4
lightly esteemed the **R** of his salvation Deut 32:15
Of the **R** that begat thee Deut 32:18
except their **R** had sold them Deut 32:30
their **r** is not as our **R** Deut 32:31
their **r** in whom they trusted Deut 32:37
neither is there any **r** like our God 1 Sam 2:2
The LORD is my **r** 2 Sam 22:2; Ps 18:2
The God of my **r** 2 Sam 22:3
who is a **r**, save our God? 2 Sam 22:32
the **R** of Israel spake 2 Sam 23:3
strong wind brake in pieces the **r** 1 Kgs 19:11
the **r** is removed out of his place Job 14:18
lead in the **r** for ever Job 19:24
embrace the **r** for want of a shelter Job 24:8
shall set me up upon a **r** Ps 27:5
thou art my **r** and my fortress Ps 31:3; 71:3
lead me to the **r** that is higher than I Ps 61:2
with honey out of the **r** Ps 81:16
yet make they their houses in the **r** Prov 30:26
art in the clefts of the **r** Song 2:14
a **r** of offence Is 8:14; Rom 9:33; 1 Pet 2:8
mindful of the **R** of thy strength Is 17:10
as the shadow of a great **r** Is 32:2
defence shall be the munitions of **r** Is 33:16
made their faces harder than a **r** Jer 5:3
hammer that breaketh the **r** in pieces Jer 23:29
the **r** are thrown down by him Nah 1:6
it was founded upon a **r** Matt 7:25; Luke 6:48
upon this **r** I will build my church Matt 16:18
and the **r** rent Matt 27:51
some fell upon a **r** Luke 8:6
that **R** was Christ 1 Cor 10:4
said to the mountains and **r**, fall on us Rev 6:16

ROD
Let him take his **r** away from me Job 9:34
neither is the **r** of God upon them Job 21:9
break them with a **r** of iron Ps 2:9
thy **r** and thy staff comfort me Ps 23:4
he that spareth his **r** Prov 13:24
the **r** of his anger shall fail Prov 22:8
beat him with thy **r** Prov 23:13
a **r** for the fool's back Prov 26:3
the **r** and reproof give wisdom Prov 29:15
as if the **r** should shake itself Is 10:15
shall come forth a **r** Is 11:1
the strong staff broken, and beautiful **r** Jer 48:17
cause you to pass under the **r** Ezek 20:37
hear ye the **r**, and who hath appointed it Mic 6:9
Thrice was I beaten with **r** 2 Cor 11:25

RODE
Absalom **r** upon a mule 2 Sam 18:9
when I and thou **r** together 2 Kgs 9:25
save the beast that I **r** upon Neh 2:12
he **r** upon a cherub Ps 18:10

ROGELIM ro´-gel-im
fullers 2 Sam 17:27

ROHGAH ro´-gah
outcry 1 Chr 7:34

ROLL
I have **r** away the reproach Josh 5:9
they **r** themselves upon me Job 30:14
garments **r** in blood Is 9:5
the heavens shall be **r** together Is 34:4
who shall **r** us away the stone from the door Mark 16:3
they found the stone **r** away Luke 24:2
departed as a scroll when it is **r** together Rev 6:14

ROMAMTI-EZER ro-mam´-ti-e´-zer
I have exalted help 1 Chr 25:4

ROME rom
strength (?) Acts 2:10

ROOF
under the shadow of my **r** Gen 19:8
make a battlement for thy **r** Deut 22:8
tongue cleaveth to the **r** of their mouth Job 29:10
tongue of the sucking child cleaveth to the **r** of his mouth Lam 4:4
cleave to the **r** of thy mouth Ezek 3:26
I am not worthy that thou shouldest come under my **r** Matt 8:8
they uncovered the **r** Mark 2:4

ROOM
is there **r** in thy father's house for us Gen 24:23
the LORD hath made **r** for us Gen 26:22
thou hast set my feet in a large **r** Ps 31:8
thou preparedst **r** before it Ps 80:9
A man's gift maketh **r** for him Prov 18:16
there shall not be **r** enough Mal 3:10
the uppermost **r** Matt 23:6; Mark 12:39; Luke 22:12
there was no **r** to receive them Mark 2:2
no **r** for them in the inn Luke 2:7
no **r** where to bestow Luke 12:17
how they chose out the chief **r** Luke 14:7
begin with shame to take the lowest **r** Luke 14:9
and yet there is **r** Luke 14:22

ROOT (n)
a **r** that beareth gall Deut 29:18
shall yet again take **r** downward 2 Kgs 19:30
I have seen the foolish taking **r** Job 5:3
His **r** are wrapped about the heap Job 8:17
The **r** thereof wax old in the earth Job 14:8
His **r** shall be dried up Job 18:16
the **r** of the matter Job 19:28
My **r** was spread out by the waters Job 29:19
r of the righteous shall not be moved Prov 12:3
r of the righteous yieldeth fruit Prov 12:12
their **r** shall be as rottenness Is 5:24
a Branch shall grow out of his **r** Is 11:1
there shall be a **r** of Jesse Is 11:10; Rom 15:12
them that come of Jacob to take **r** Is 27:6
shall again take **r** downward Is 37:31
as a **r** out of a dry ground Is 53:2
his **r** was by great waters Ezek 31:7
cast forth his **r** as Lebanon Hos 14:5
shall leave them neither **r** nor branch Mal 4:1
axe is laid unto the **r** of the trees Matt 3:10; Luke 3:9
because they had no **r** Matt 13:6
fig tree dried up from the **r** Mark 11:20
if the **r** be holy Rom 11:16
love of money is the **r** of all evil 1 Tim 6:10
lest any **r** of bitterness Heb 12:15
twice dead, plucked up by the **r** Jude 1:12
r and the offspring of David Rev 22:16

ROOT (v)
LORD **r** them out Deut 29:28
he shall **r** up Israel 1 Kgs 14:15
confidence shall be **r** out Job 18:14
let my offspring be **r** out Job 31:8
r out all mine increase Job 31:12
r thee out of the land of the living Ps 52:5
lest ye **r** up also the wheat Matt 13:29
hath not planted, shall be **r** up Matt 15:13
being **r** and grounded in love Eph 3:17
R and built up in him Col 2:7

ROSE (n)
I am the **r** of Sharon Song 2:1
blossom as the **r** Is 35:1

ROSE (v)
the sun **r** upon him as Gen 32:31
r up upon an heap Josh 3:16
though one **r** from the dead Luke 16:31
to this end Christ both died and **r** Rom 14:9
buried, and **r** the third day 1 Cor 15:4
which died for them, and **r** again 2 Cor 5:15

ROSH rosh
head Gen 46:21

ROT
make thy thigh to **r** Num 5:21
name of the wicked shall **r** Prov 10:7
chooseth a tree that will not **r** Is 40:20

ROTTEN
brass as **r** wood Job 41:27
old cast clouts and old **r** rags Jer 38:11
seed is **r** under their clods Joel 1:17

ROTTENNESS
as **r** in his bones Prov 12:4
envy the **r** of the bones Prov 14:30
their root shall be as **r** Is 5:24

ROUGH
stayeth his **r** wind Is 27:8
crooked shall be made straight, and the **r** places plain Is 40:4
wear a **r** garment to deceive Zech 13:4

ROUGHLY
spake **r** unto them Gen 42:7
the rich answereth **r** Prov 18:23

ROUND
there lay a **r** thing Ex 16:14
their **r** tires like the moon Is 3:18
compass thee **r** Luke 19:43

ROWED
the men **r** hard to bring it Jon 1:13
when they had **r** John 6:19

ROYAL
yield **r** dainties Gen 49:20
r wine in abundance Esth 1:7
r apparel Esth 5:1; 6:8; 8:15; Acts 12:21
fulfil the **r** law James 2:8
a **r** priesthood 1 Pet 2:9

RUBIES
price of wisdom is above **r** Job 28:18
wisdom is better than **r** Prov 8:11
her price is far above **r** Prov 31:10
more ruddy in body than **r** Lam 4:7

RUDDY
Now he was **r** 1 Sam 16:12
My beloved is white and **r** Song 5:10
more **r** in body than rubies Lam 4:7

RUDE
r in speech 2 Cor 11:6

RUDIMENTS
r of the world Col 2:8,20

RUFUS roo´-fus
red Mark 15:21

RUHAMAH roo´-ham-ah
obtained mercy Hos 2:1

RUIN
they were the **r** of him 2 Chr 28:23
hast brought his strong holds to **r** Ps 89:40
who knoweth the **r** of them both? Prov 24:22
a flattering mouth worketh **r** Prov 26:28
so iniquity shall not be your **r** Ezek 18:30
their **r** be multiplied Ezek 21:15
the **r** of that house was great Luke 6:49

RULE (n)
Jews had **r** over them Esth 9:1
wise servant shall have **r** Prov 17:2
servant to have **r** over princes Prov 19:10
no **r** over his own spirit Prov 25:28
thou never barest **r** over them Is 63:19
when he shall have put down all **r** 1 Cor 15:24
as many as walk according to this **r** Gal 6:16
them which have the **r** over you Heb 13:7

RULE (v)
to **r** the day Gen 1:16
thy husband, and he shall **r** over thee Gen 3:16
I will not **r** over you Judg 8:23
He that **r** over men must be just 2 Sam 23:3
He **r** by his power for ever Ps 66:7
Thou **r** the raging of the sea Ps 89:9
his kingdom **r** over all Ps 103:19
that **r** his spirit Prov 16:32
rich **r** over the poor Prov 22:7
him that **r** among fools Eccl 9:17
babes shall **r** over them Is 3:4
princes shall **r** in judgment Is 32:1
his arm shall **r** for him Is 40:10
shall no more **r** over the nations Ezek 29:15
he that **r**, with diligence Rom 12:8
peace of God **r** in your hearts Col 3:15
One that **r** well his own house 1 Tim 3:4
elders that **r** well 1 Tim 5:17

RULER
every one a **r** among them Num 13:2
having no guide, overseer, or **r** Prov 6:7
When thou sittest to eat with a **r** Prov 23:1
a wicked **r** over the poor people Prov 28:15
be thou our **r** Is 3:6
that is to be **r** in Israel Mic 5:2
I will make thee **r** Matt 25:21
Do the **r** know John 7:26
Have any of the **r** John 7:48
r are not a terror to good works Rom 13:3

RUMAH roo´-mah
height 2 Kgs 23:36

RUMOUR
I have heard a **r** Jer 49:14
r shall be upon **r** Ezek 7:26
wars and **r** of wars Matt 24:6; Mark 13:7

RUN
as a strong man to **r** a race Ps 19:5
my cup **r** over Ps 23:5
his word **r** very swiftly Ps 147:15
Draw me, we will **r** after thee Song 1:4
they shall **r**, and not be weary Is 40:31
shall **r** to thee Is 55:5
if thou hast **r** with the footmen Jer 12:5
One post shall **r** to meet another Jer 51:31
many shall **r** to and fro Dan 12:4
that he may **r** that readeth Hab 2:2
r, speak to this young man Zech 2:4
r over Luke 6:38
nor of him that **r** Rom 9:16
they which **r** in a race **r** all 1 Cor 9:24
I therefore so **r** 1 Cor 9:26
by any means I should **r**, or had
r in vain Gal 2:2
ye did **r** well Gal 5:7
let us **r** with patience Heb 12:1
that ye **r** not with them 1 Pet 4:4

RUNNING
the **r** of the foremost is like 2 Sam 18:27
the eyes of the Lord **r** to and fro 2 Chr 16:9

RUSH (n)
Can the **r** grow up without mire? Job 8:11
tail, branch and **r** Is 9:14; 19:15
shall be grass with reeds and **r** Is 35:7

RUSH (v)
nations shall **r** like the rushing
of many waters Is 17:13
the horse **r** into the battle Jer 8:6

RUSHING
a voice of a great **r**, saying Ezek 3:12
a **r** mighty wind Acts 2:2

RUST
where moth and **r** doth corrupt Matt 6:19,20
the **r** of them shall be a witness James 5:3

RUTH rooth
friendship (?) Ruth 1:4

S

SABACHTHANI sa-bac´-than-i
thou hast forsaken me Mark 15:34

SABAOTH sab-a´-oth
hosts Rom 9:29

SABBATH
number seven **s** of years Lev 25:8
it is neither new moon, nor **s** 2 Kgs 4:23
as she lay desolate she kept **s** 2 Chr 36:21
on the **s** it shall be opened Ezek 46:1
and the **s**, that we may set forth Amos 8:5
the **s** was made for man Mark 2:27
Son of man is Lord also of the **s** Mark 2:28; Luke 6:5
each one of you on the **s** loose Luke 13:15

SABEANS sab-e´-ans
inhabitants of Seba Is 45:14

SABTAH sab´-tah
rest (?) Gen 10:7

SABTECHA sab´-te-kah
descendants of Cush 1 Chr 1:9

SABTECHAH sab´-te-kah
same as SABTECHA Gen 10:7

SACAR sa´-kar
hire, reward 1 Chr 11:35

SACK
every man's money into his **s** Gen 42:25
money was in the mouth of his **s** Gen 43:21
opened every man his **s** Gen 44:11
the cup was found in Benjamin's **s** Gen 44:12
and took old **s** upon their asses Josh 9:4

SACRIFICE (n)
Jacob offered **s** Gen 31:54
Let us go and do **s** to the Lord Ex 5:17
people unto the **s** of their gods Num 25:2
Wherefore kick ye at my **s** 1 Sam 2:29
he doth bless the **s** 1 Sam 9:13
to obey is better than **s** 1 Sam 15:22
offer the **s** of righteousness Ps 4:5
s of joy Ps 27:6
S and offering thou didst not desire Ps 40:6
thou desires not **s** Ps 51:16
The **s** of God are a broken spirit Ps 51:17
bind the **s** with cords Ps 118:27
s of the wicked is an abomination Prov 15:8
than a house full of **s** with strife Prov 17:1
more acceptable to the Lord than **s** Prov 21:3
the **s** of fools Eccl 5:1
what purpose is the multitude of
your **s** unto me? Is 1:11
nor your **s** sweet unto me Jer 6:20
to do **s** continually Jer 33:18
daily **s** was taken away Dan 8:11
s and oblation to cease Dan 9:27
shall take away the daily **s** Dan 11:31
many days without a **s** Hos 3:4
I desired mercy, and not **s** Hos 6:6
bring your **s** every morning Amos 4:4
the Lord hath prepared a **s** Zeph 1:7
ye offer the blind for **s** Mal 1:8
I will have mercy, and not **s** Matt 9:13; 12:7
every **s** shall be salted Mark 9:49
all whole burnt offerings and **s** Mark 12:33
whose blood Pilate had mingled
with their **s** Luke 13:1
have ye offered me slain beasts and **s** Acts 7:42
and would have done **s** Acts 14:13
present your bodies a living **s** Rom 12:1
offered in **s** unto idols 1 Cor 8:4
is offered in **s** to idols 1 Cor 10:19
this is offered in **s** unto idols 1 Cor 10:28
a **s** to God for a sweetsmelling savour Eph 5:2
the **s** and service of your faith Phil 2:17
a **s** acceptable, well pleasing Phil 4:18
put away sin by the **s** of himself Heb 9:26
offered one **s** for sins Heb 10:12
there remaineth no more **s** for sin Heb 10:26
a more excellent **s** Heb 11:4
let us offer the **s** of praise Heb 13:15
with such **s** God is well pleased Heb 13:16
to offer up spiritual **s** 1 Pet 2:5

SACRIFICE (v)
he that **s** unto any god Ex 22:20
we do **s** unto him Ezra 4:2
will they **s**? Neh 4:2
I will freely **s** unto thee Ps 54:6
they **s** their sons and their daughters Ps 106:37
let them **s** the sacrifices of thanksgiving Ps 107:22
him that **s**, and to him that **s** not Eccl 9:2
that **s** in gardens Is 65:3
they **s** flesh for the sacrifices Hos 8:13
they **s** unto their net Hab 1:16
Christ our passover is **s** for us 1 Cor 5:7
the Gentiles **s**, they **s** to devils 1 Cor 10:20

SAD
Why is thy spirit so **s**, 1 Kgs 21:5
hypocrites of a **s** countenance Matt 6:16
he was **s** at that saying Mark 10:22
as ye walk, and are **s**? Luke 24:17

SADDLE
I will **s** me an ass 2 Sam 19:26
said unto his sons, S me an ass 1 Kgs 13:13

SADDUCEES sad´-u-sees
named for Zadok, founder of the sect Matt 3:7

SADOC sa´-dok
Gr. for ZADOK Matt 1:14

SAFE
Is the young man Absalom **s**? 2 Sam 18:29
their houses are **s** from fear Job 21:9
Hold thou me up, and I shall be **s** Ps 119:117
righteous runneth into it, and is **s** Prov 18:10
his trust in the Lord shall be **s** Prov 29:25
they shall be **s** in their land Ezek 34:27
they escaped all **s** to land Acts 27:44

SAFEGUARD
thou shalt be in **s** 1 Sam 22:23

SAFELY
he led them on **s** Ps 78:53
shall dwell **s** Prov 1:33
shalt thou walk in thy way **s** Prov 3:23
doth **s** trust in her Prov 31:11
will make them to lie down **s** Hos 2:18

SAFETY
I was not in **s** Job 3:26
His children are far from **s** Job 5:4

thou shalt take thy rest in s Job 11:18
in the multitude of counsellers
there is s Prov 11:14; 24:6
s is of the Lord Prov 21:31
when they say, Peace and s 1 Thess 5:3

SAIL (n)
they could not spread the s Is 33:23
thou spreadest forth to be thy s Ezek 27:7
and when s was now dangerous Acts 27:9

SAIL (v)
as they s, he fell asleep Luke 8:23

SAINTS
he will keep the feet of his s 1 Sam 2:9
to which of the s wilt thou turn? Job 5:1
he putteth no trust in his s Job 15:15
but to the s that are in the earth Ps 16:3
Sing unto the Lord, O ye s of his Ps 30:4
and forsaketh not his s Ps 37:28
gather my s together Ps 50:5
the congregation of the s Ps 89:5
be feared in the assembly of the s Ps 89:7
preserveth the souls of his s Ps 97:10
of the Lord is the death of his s Ps 116:15
let thy s shout for joy Ps 132:9
this honour have all his s Ps 149:9
the s of the most High shall take Dan 7:18
Then I heard one s speaking Dan 8:13
bodies of the s which slept arose Matt 27:52
much evil he hath done to thy s Acts 9:13
beloved of God, called to be s Rom 1:7
he maketh intercession for the s Rom 8:27
Distributing to the necessity of s Rom 12:13
receive her in the Lord as becometh s Rom 16:2
unjust, in Christ Jesus, called to be s 1 Cor 1:2
and not before the s? 1 Cor 6:1
the s shall judge the world? 1 Cor 6:2
concerning the collection for the s 1 Cor 16:1
the ministry of the s 1 Cor 16:15
his inheritance in the s Eph 1:18
fellow citizens with the s Eph 2:19
less than the least of all s Eph 3:8
perfecting of the s Eph 4:12
named among you, as becometh s Eph 5:3
the s in light Col 1:12
our Lord Jesus Christ with all his s 1 Thess 3:13
to be glorified in his s 2 Thess 1:10
if she have washed the s feet 1 Tim 5:10
was once delivered to the s Jude 1:3
the prayers of s Rev 5:8
offer it with the prayers of all s Rev 8:3
came with the prayers of the s Rev 8:4

SAKE
cursed is the ground for thy s Gen 3:17
the ground any more for man's s Gen 8:21
be well with me for thy s Gen 12:13
will spare all the place for their s Gen 18:26
the Lord hath blessed me for thy s Gen 30:27
Enviest thou for my s? Num 11:29
angry with me for your s Deut 1:37; 3:26; 4:21
kindness for Jonathan's s 2 Sam 9:1
deal gently for my s 2 Sam 18:5
for thy great mercies' s Neh 9:31
save me for thy mercies' s Ps 6:4; 31:16
of righteousness for his name's s Ps 23:3
for thy s are we killed Ps 44:22
he saved them for his name's s Ps 106:8
persecuted for righteousness' s Matt 5:10
govenors and kings for my s Matt 10:18
for the elect's s Matt 24:22; Mark 13:20
before rulers and kings for my s Mark 13:9; Luke 21:12
I am glad for your s John 11:15
thou lay down thy life for my s? John 13:38
also for conscience s Rom 13:5
no question for conscience s 1 Cor 10:25
for his body's s, which is the church Col 1:24
for their work's s 1 Thess 5:13
for thy stomach's s 1 Tim 5:23
for filthy lucre's s Titus 1:11
for the truth's s 2 John 1:2

SALA sa´-lah
Gr. for SALAH Luke 3:35

SALAH sa´-lah
sprout (?) Gen 10:24

SALAMIS sal´-a-mis
shaken, tossed Acts 13:5

SALATHIEL sa-la´-thi-el
Gr. for SHEALTIEL 1 Chr 3:17

SALCAH sal´-kah
road Josh 12:5

SALCHAH sal´-kah
same as SALCAH Deut 3:10

SALEM sa´-lem
peace Gen 14:18

SALIM sa´-lim
Gr. for SALEM John 3:23

SALLAI sal-a´-i
exaltation Neh 11:8

SALLU sal´-oo
same as SALLAI 1 Chr 9:7

SALMA sal´-mah
garment 1 Chr 2:11

SALMON sal´-mon
shady Ps 68:14

SALOME sal-o´-me
peace Mark 15:40

SALU sa´-loo
same as SALLU Num 25:14

SALUTATION
and love s in the marketplaces Mark 12:38
what manner of s this should be Luke 1:29
the s by the hand of me Col 4:18
the s of Paul with mine hand 2 Thess 3:17

SALUTE
and they will s thee 1 Sam 10:4
if thou meet any man, s him not 2 Kgs 4:29
began to s him, Hail, King of the Jews! Mark 15:18

SALVATION
I have waited for thy s Gen 49:18
see the s of the Lord Ex 14:13
he is become my s Ex 15:2
lightly esteemed the Rock of his s Deut 32:15
the Lord wrought s in Israel 1 Sam 11:13
who hath wrought this great s in Israel? 1 Sam 14:45
Lord wrought a great s for all 1 Sam 19:5
he is the tower of s for his king 2 Sam 22:51
shew forth from day to day his s 1 Chr 16:23
clothed with s 2 Chr 6:41
see the s of the Lord with you 2 Chr 20:17
S belongeth to the Lord Ps 3:8
I will rejoice in thy s Ps 9:14
Oh that the s of Israel were come Ps 14:7
thou art the God of my s Ps 25:5
my light and my s Ps 27:1
say unto my soul, I am thy s Ps 35:3
the s of the righteous is of the Lord Ps 37:39
declared thy faithfulness and s Ps 40:10
will I shew the s of God Ps 50:23
Restore unto me the joy of thy s Ps 51:12
my rock and my s Ps 62:6
He that is our God is the God of s Ps 68:20
hear me, in the truth of thy s Ps 69:13
let thy s, O God, set me up on high Ps 69:29
let such as love thy s say Ps 70:4
thy righteousness and thy s Ps 71:15
working s in the midst of the earth Ps 74:12
trusted not in his s Ps 78:22
his s is nigh them that fear him Ps 85:9
I satisfy him, and shew him my s Ps 91:16
shew forth his s from day to day Ps 96:2
all the ends of the earth have seen the s Ps 98:3
the cup of s Ps 116:13
and is become my s Ps 118:14
O Lord, even thy s Ps 119:41
My soul fainteth for thy s Ps 119:81
Mine eyes fail for thy s Ps 119:123
S is far from the wicked Ps 119:155
I have longed for thy s Ps 119:174
also clothe her priests with s Ps 132:16
that giveth s unto kings Ps 144:10
beautify the meek with s Ps 149:4
Behold, God is my s Is 12:2
the wells of s Is 12:3
s will God appoint for walls Is 26:1
our s also in time of trouble Is 33:2
and let them bring forth s Is 45:8
with an everlasting s Is 45:17
in a day of s have I helped thee Is 49:8
my s is gone forth Is 51:5
tidings of good, that publisheth s Is 52:7
ends of the earth shall see s Is 52:10
my s is near to come Is 56:1
for s, but it is far off Is 59:11
his arm brought s Is 59:16
an helmet of s upon his head Is 59:17
call thy walls S Is 60:18
the garments of s Is 61:10
the s thereof as a lamp Is 62:1
mine own arm brought s Is 63:5
in vain is s hoped for Jer 3:23
wait for the s of the Lord Lam 3:26
s is of the Lord Jon 2:9
and thy chariots of s Hab 3:8
I will joy in the God of my s Hab 3:18
he is just, and having s Zech 9:9
an horn of s for us Luke 1:69
give knowledge of s unto his people Luke 1:77
mine eyes have seen thy s Luke 2:30
all flesh shall see the s of God Luke 3:6
this day is s come to this house Luke 19:9
s is of the Jews John 4:22
Neither is there s in any other Acts 4:12
to you is the word of this s sent Acts 13:26
which shew unto us the way of s Acts 16:17
the power of God unto s Rom 1:16
confession is made to s Rom 10:10
now is our s nearer Rom 13:11
it is for your consolation and s 2 Cor 1:6
the day of s 2 Cor 6:2
sorrow worketh repentance to s 2 Cor 7:10
the gospel of your s Eph 1:13
the helmet of s Eph 6:17
this shall turn to my s Phil 1:19
but to you of s Phil 1:28
work out your own s Phil 2:12
for an helmet, the hope of s 1 Thess 5:8
to obtain s by our Lord Jesus Christ 1 Thess 5:9
chosen you to s through sanctification 2 Thess 2:13
wise unto s 2 Tim 3:15
grace of God that bringeth s Titus 2:11
for them who shall be heirs of s Heb 1:14
if we neglect so great s Heb 2:3
the captain of their s Heb 2:10
author of eternal s Heb 5:9
things that accompany s Heb 6:9
without sin unto s Heb 9:28
through faith unto s 1 Pet 1:5
your faith, even the s of your souls 1 Pet 1:9
of which s the prophets have inquired 1 Pet 1:10
longsuffering of the Lord is s 2 Pet 3:15

of the common s Jude 1:3
S to our God Rev 7:10

SAMARIA sa-ma´-ri-a
watch-mountain, watchtower 1 Kgs 13:32

SAMARITAN sa-mar´-i-tan
a native or inhabitant of Samaria Luke 10:33

SAME
sow wickedness, reap the s Job 4:8
thou art the s Ps 102:27
do not even the publicans the s? Matt 5:46
this s Jesus, which is taken up Acts 1:11
the s Lord over all Rom 10:12
Be of the s mind Rom 12:16
the s mind and in the s judgment 1 Cor 1:10
they be of the s mind in the Lord Phil 4:2
but thou art the s Heb 1:12
s yesterday, and to day, and for ever Heb 13:8

SAMGAR-NEBO sam´-gar-ne´-bo
Be gracious, Nebo Jer 39:3

SAMLAH sam´-lah
garment Gen 36:36

SAMOS sa´-mos
a height (?) Acts 20:15

SAMOTHRACIA sa´-mo-thra´-shah
Samos of Thrace Acts 16:11

SAMSON sam´-son
like the sun Judg 13:24

SAMUEL sam´-u-el
heard of God 1 Sam 1:20

SANBALLAT san-bal´-at
Sin (the moon) giveth life (?) Neh 2:10

SANCTIFY
s yourselves Lev 11:44
S yourselves therefore Lev 20:7
S yourselves against to morrow Num 11:18
people, s yourselves Josh 3:5
up, s the people Josh 7:13
s yourselves, and come with me 1 Sam 16:5
God shall be s in righteousness Is 5:16
I have commanded my s ones Is 13:3
they shall s my name Is 29:23
s themselves, and purify Is 66:17
I s thee and I ordained thee a prophet Jer 1:5
I will be s in you Ezek 20:41
s in them in the sight of the heathen Ezek 28:25
s ye a fast Joel 1:14
whom the Father hath s John 10:36
s them through thy truth John 17:17
for their sakes I s myself John 17:19
inheritance among all them that are s Acts 20:32
among them which are s Acts 26:18
being s by the Holy Ghost Rom 15:16
to them that are s 1 Cor 1:2
but now ye are s 1 Cor 6:11
husband is s by the wife 1 Cor 7:14
he might s and cleanse Eph 5:26
the very God of peace s you 1 Thess 5:23
it is s by the word of God 1 Tim 4:5
s, and meet for the master's use 2 Tim 2:21
he that s and they who are s Heb 2:11
by the which will we are s Heb 10:10
perfected for ever them that are s Heb 10:14
that he might s the people Heb 13:12
s the Lord God in your hearts 1 Pet 3:15
them that are s by God the Father Jude 1:1

SANCTUARY
in the S, O Lord Ex 15:17
let them make me a s Ex 25:8
work for the service of the s Ex 36:1,3,4
service of s belonging unto them Num 7:9
where are the vessels of the s Neh 10:39
they have cast fire into thy s Ps 74:7
beautify the place of my s Is 60:13
he hath abhorred his s Lam 2:7

SAND
be heavier than the s of the sea Job 6:3
stone is heavy, and s is weighty Prov 27:3
which built his house upon the s Matt 7:26

SANG
Then s Moses and the children Ex 15:1
the singers s loud Neh 12:42
the morning stars s together Job 38:7

SANK
they s into the bottom Ex 15:5

SANSANNAH san-san´-ah
palm branch Josh 15:31

SAP
trees of the Lord are full of s Ps 104:16

SAPH saf
threshold 2 Sam 21:18

SAPHIR saf´-ir
beautiful Mic 1:11

SAPPHIRA saf-i´-rah
Gr. for SAPHIR (fem.) Acts 5:1

SARA sa´-rah
same as SARAH Rom 9:9

SARAH sa´-rah
princess Gen 17:15

SARAI sa´-ra-i
contentious (?) Gen 11:29

SARAPH sa´-raf
burning 1 Chr 4:22

SARDIS sar´-dis
prince of joy Rev 1:11

SARDITES sard´-ites
descendants of Sered Num 26:26

SAREPTA sa-rep´-tah
Gr. for ZAREPHATH Luke 4:26

SARGON sar´-gon
[God] appoints the king Is 20:1

SARID sa´-rid
survivor Josh 19:10

SARON sa´-ron
Gr. for SHARON Acts 9:35

SARSECHIM sar´-se-kim
prince of the wardrobe (?) Jer 39:3

SARUCH sa´-rook
Gr. for SERUG Luke 3:35

SAT
wept, and s there before the Lord Judg 20:26
and s chief Job 29:25
I have not s with vain persons Ps 26:4
I s alone because of thy hand Jer 15:17
I s where they s Ezek 3:15
The people which s in darkness Matt 4:16
and s on the right hand of God Mark 16:19
he that was dead s up Luke 7:15
Mary which also s at Jesus' feet Luke 10:39
s thus on the well John 4:6
of fire, and it s upon each Acts 2:3

SATAN sa´-tan
adversary 1 Chr 21:1

SATIATE
I will s the soul of the priests Jer 31:14
For I have s the weary soul Jer 31:25
it shall be s and made drunk with their blood Jer 46:10

SATISFY
to s the desolate Job 38:27
I shall be s when I awake Ps 17:15
The meek shall eat and be s Ps 22:26
They shall be abundantly s with fatness Ps 36:8
in days of famine be s Ps 37:19
and grudge if they be not s Ps 59:15
my soul shall be s Ps 63:5
with honey should I have s thee Ps 81:16
s us early with thy mercy Ps 90:14
With long life will I s him Ps 91:16
Who s thy mouth with good Ps 103:5
the earth is s Ps 104:13
s them with bread from heaven Ps 105:40
he s the longing soul Ps 107:9
I will s her poor with bread Ps 132:15
if he steal to s his soul Prov 6:30
He that tilleth his land shall be s Prov 12:11
a good man shall be s from himself Prov 14:14
he that hath it shall abide s Prov 19:23
open thine eyes, and thou shalt be s Prov 20:13
three things that are never s Prov 30:15
the eye is not s with seeing Eccl 1:8
neither is his eye s with riches Eccl 4:8
shall not be s with silver Eccl 5:10
shall eat and not be s Is 9:20; Mic 6:14
travail of his soul, and be s Is 53:11
and s the afflicted soul Is 58:10
and s thy soul in drought Is 58:11
shall be s with my goodness Jer 31:14
yet thou couldest not be s Ezek 16:28
to drink water, but they were not s Amos 4:8
is as death, and cannot be s Hab 2:5

SAUL sawl
asked for 1 Sam 9:2

SAVE (besides, except)
who is God, s the Lord? 2 Sam 22:32
knoweth any man the Father, s the Son Matt 11:27
s in his own country Matt 13:57
s Jesus only Matt 17:8; Mark 9:8
s this stranger Luke 17:18
none is good, s one Luke 18:19
forty stripes s one 2 Cor 11:24
glory, s in the cross Gal 6:14

SAVE
to s your lives Gen 45:7
thou hast s our lives Gen 47:25
spoiled, and no man shall s thee Deut 28:29
O people, s by the Lord Deut 33:29
come up to us quickly, and s us Josh 10:6
wherewith shall I s Israel? Judg 6:15
may s us out of the hand of 1 Sam 4:3
How shall this man s us? 1 Sam 10:27
if there be no man to s us, we will come out to thee 1 Sam 11:3
no restraint to the Lord to s by many or by few 1 Sam 14:6
The king s us out of the hand of our enemies 2 Sam 19:9
s himself there, not once nor twice 2 Kgs 6:10
in thine hands, but s his life Job 2:6
he shall s the humble Job 22:29
s thou the arm that hath no strength? Job 26:2
God, which s the upright Ps 7:10
the Lord s his anointed Ps 20:6
and s such as be of a contrite spirit Ps 34:18
neither did their own arm s them Ps 44:3
s with thy right hand Ps 60:5
he shall s the children of the needy Ps 72:4
shall be s Ps 80:3; Prov 28:18; Jer 17:14; Matt 10:22; 24:13; Mark 13:13; 16:16; John 10:9; Acts 2:21; 16:31; Rom 5:9; 9:27; 10:9; 11:26
s thy servant that trusteth in thee Ps 86:2
s him from those that condemn Ps 109:31
S now, I beseech thee; send now Ps 118:25
s me; for I have sought thy precepts Ps 119:94
s me, and I shall keep thy testimonies Ps 119:146

thy right hand shall s me Ps 138:7
wait on the Lord, and he shall s thee Prov 20:22
your God will come and s you Is 35:4
I have declared, and have s Is 43:12
pray unto a god that cannot s Is 45:20
Look unto me, and be ye s Is 45:22
I will s thy children Is 49:25
Lord's hand not shortened, that it
cannot s Is 59:1
mighty to s Is 63:1
let them arise, if they can s Jer 2:28
the summer is ended, and we are not s Jer 8:20
but they shall not s Jer 11:12
as a mighty man that cannot s Jer 14:9
I am with thee to s thee Jer 15:20;
30:11; 42:11; 46:27
s me, and I shall be s Jer 17:14
I will s thee from afar Jer 30:10
flee, s your lives Jer 48:6
a nation that could not s us Lam 4:17
from his wicked way, to s his life Ezek 3:18
Therefore will I s my flock Ezek 34:22
I will s them by the Lord Hos 1:7
where is any other that may s thee
in all thy cities? Hos 13:10
cry to thee, and thou wilt not s Hab 1:2
he will s Zeph 3:17
s his people from their sins Matt 1:21
will s his life Matt 16:25;
Mark 8:35; Luke 9:24
to seek and to s that which was lost Matt 18:11;
Luke 19:10
Who then can be s? Matt 19:25; Mark
10:26; Luke 18:26
s thyself Matt 27:40; Mark 15:30
He s others: himself he cannot s Matt 27:42;
Mark 15:31
to s life, or to kill? Mark 3:4; Luke 6:9
Thy faith hath s thee Luke 7:50; 18:42
lest they should believe and be s Luke 8:12
not to destroy, but to s Luke 9:56
are there few that be s? Luke 13:23
let him s himself Luke 23:35
If thou be Christ, s thyself and us Luke 23:39
that the world might be s John 3:17
these things I say, that ye might be s John 5:34
I came not to judge, but to s John 12:47
such as should be s Acts 2:47
whereby we must be s Acts 4:12
after the manner of Moses, ye
cannot be s Acts 15:1
what must I do to be s? Acts 16:30
the centurion, willing to s Paul Acts 27:43
we are s by hope Rom 8:24
word, which is able to s your souls James 1:21
can faith s him? James 2:14
able to s and destroy James 4:12
the prayer of faith shall s the sick James 5:15
shall s a soul from death James 5:20
souls were s by water 1 Pet 3:20
if the righteous scarcely be s 1 Pet 4:18
others s with fear Jude 1:23

SAVIOUR
my refuge, my s 2 Sam 22:3
the Lord gave Israel a s 2 Kgs 13:5
They forgat God their s Ps 106:21
he shall send them a s Is 19:20
a just God and a S Is 45:21
all shall know I am thy S Is 49:26
so he was their S Is 63:8
he is the s of the body Eph 5:23
who is the S of all men 1 Tim 4:10

SAVOUR
salt have lost his s Matt 5:13; Luke 14:34

SAVOUREST
thou s not the things that be of God Matt 16:23

SAVOURY
make me s meat, such as I love Gen 27:4,14

SAW
and s the place afar off Gen 22:4
s certainly the the Lord was with thee Gen 26:28
they s not one another Ex 10:23
they s the God of Israel Ex 24:10
they s one another in the face 2 Chr 25:21
when the eye s me Job 29:11
the waters s thee Ps 77:16
also I s, that it was from hand of God Eccl 2:24
S ye him whom my soul loveth? Song 3:3
both spake and s Matt 12:22
they s no man Matt 17:8
if he s ought Mark 8:23
under the fig tree I s thee John 1:48
Abraham s my day John 8:56
glad when they s the Lord John 20:20

SAY
what shall I s unto them? Ex 3:13
teach thee what thou shalt s Ex 4:12
know what the Lord will s Num 22:19
what is this that ye s unto me Judg 18:24
what shall we s after this? Ezra 9:10
think not to s within yourselves Matt 3:9
many will s in that day Matt 7:22
do men s that I, the Son of man, am? Matt 16:13;
Mark 8:27
they s, and do not Matt 23:3
I have somewhat to s thee Luke 7:40
no man can s that Jesus 1 Cor 12:3

SAYING
the s pleased me well Deut 1:23
the s is good 1 Kgs 2:38
my dark s upon the harp Ps 49:4
utter dark s of old Ps 78:2
the dark s of the wise Prov 1:6
this s is commonly reported Matt 28:15
kept all these s in her heart Luke 2:51
herein is that s true John 4:37
a hard s; who can hear it? John 6:60

SCANT
s measure Mic 6:10

SCARCE
and Jacob was yet s gone Gen 27:30
s restrained they the people Acts 14:18

SCARCELY
For s for a righteous man will one die Rom 5:7
And if the righteous s be saved 1 Pet 4:18

SCARCENESS
bread without s Deut 8:9

SCAREST
Thou s me with dreams Job 7:14

SCATTER
lest we be s abroad Gen 11:4
I will s you among the heathen Lev 26:33
let thine enemies be s Num 10:35; Ps 68:1
brimstone shall be s upon his
habitation Job 18:15
he s his bright cloud Job 37:11
which s the east wind Job 38:24
s thou the people that delight in war Ps 68:30
the workers of iniquity shall be s Ps 92:9
he s the hoar frost Ps 147:16
there is that s, and yet increaseth Prov 11:24
s away evil with his eyes Prov 20:8
A wise king s the wicked Prov 20:26
all their flocks shall be s Jer 10:21
Woe be unto pastors that destroy
and s the sheep Jer 23:1
Israel is a s sheep Jer 50:17
sheep shall be s Zech 13:7;
Matt 26:31; Mark 14:27
s as sheep having no shepherd Matt 9:36
he that gathereth not with me s Matt 12:30;
Luke 11:23

SCENT
through the s of water it shall bud Job 14:9
his s is not changed Jer 48:11
s thereof shall be as the wine of Lebanon Hos 14:7

SCEVA se´-vah
left-handed Acts 19:14

SCHOLAR
the teacher as the s 1 Chr 25:8
master and the s, out of the tabernacles Mal 2:12

SCIENCE
understanding s, and such as had ability Dan 1:4
oppositions of s falsely so called 1 Tim 6:20

SCOFF
And they shall s at the kings Hab 1:10

SCORCH
when the sun was up, they were s Matt 13:6;
Mark 4:6
power was given unto him to s men Rev 16:8

SCORN (n)
s to lay hands on Mordecai alone Esth 3:6
a s and derision to them that are
round about us Ps 44:13; 79:4

SCORN (v)
My friends s me Job 16:20
An ungodly witness s judgment Prov 19:28

SCORNER
Reprove not a s Prov 9:8
a s heareth not rebuke Prov 13:1
Smite a s Prov 19:25
Judgments are prepared for s Prov 19:29
When the s is punished, the simple
is made wise Prov 21:11
the s is an abomination Prov 24:9
the s is consumed Is 29:20
he stretched out his hands with s Hos 7:5

SCOURGE (n)
the s of the tongue Job 5:21
If the s slay suddenly Job 9:23
the overflowing s Is 28:15
a s of small cords John 2:15

SCOURGE (v)
they will s you Matt 10:17; 23:34
is it lawful to s a man that is a Roman Acts 22:25
and s every son whom he receiveth Heb 12:6

SCRAPE
he shall cause the house to be s Lev 14:41
took him a potsherd to s himself withal Job 2:8
I will also s her dust from her Ezek 26:4

SCRIBE
a wise man and a s 1 Chr 27:32
Where is the s? Is 33:18
the pen of the s is in vain Jer 8:8
exceed the righteousness of the s Matt 5:20
as having authority, and not as the s Matt 7:29
every s instructed unto the kingdom Matt 13:52
beware of the s Mark 12:38; Luke 20:46

SCRIP
shepherd's bag which he had, even
in a s 1 Sam 17:40
Nor s for your journey Matt 10:10;
Luke 10:4; 22:35

SEARCH (n)
they accomplish a diligent s Ps 64:6; 77:6
I have not found it by secret s Jer 2:34

SEARCH (v)
that they may s the land Num 13:2
the Lord s all hearts 1 Chr 28:9
Canst thou by s find out God? Job 11:7
Is it good that he should s you out? Job 13:9

he prepared it, yea, and s it out Job 28:27
the cause which I knew not I s out Job 29:16
I gave ear to your reasons, whilst
ye s out what to say Job 32:11
can the number of his years be s out Job 36:26
Shall not God s this out? Ps 44:21
thou hast s me, and known me Ps 139:1
S me, O God, and know my heart Ps 139:23
honour of kings is to s out a matter Prov 25:2
men to s their own glory is not glory Prov 25:27
I gave my heart to s wisdom Eccl 1:13; 7:25
there is no s of his understanding Is 40:28
I the Lord s the heart Jer 17:10
when ye s for me with all your heart Jer 29:13
the foundations of the earth s out Jer 31:37
Let us s our ways, and turn Lam 3:40
none did s or seek after them Ezek 34:6
neither did my shepherds s for
my flock Ezek 34:8
I will s my sheep Ezek 34:11
I will s and take them out thence Amos 9:3
I will s Jerusalem with candles Zeph 1:12
S the scriptures John 5:39; Acts 17:11
he that s hearts knoweth my mind Rom 8:27
the Spirit s all things 1 Cor 2:10
which salvation prophets s diligently 1 Pet 1:10

SEARED
conscience s 1 Tim 4:2

SEASON
for signs, and s, and days Gen 1:14
give rain in his s Deut 28:12
for a long s without the true God 2 Chr 15:3
as a shock of corn in his s Job 5:26
that bringeth forth fruit in his s Ps 1:3
I cry in the night s Ps 22:2
appointed the moon for s Ps 104:19
word spoken in due s Prov 15:23
To every thing there is a s, and a time Eccl 3:1
know how to speak a word in s Is 50:4
former and latter rain in his s Jer 5:24
day and night in their s Jer 33:20
shower to come down in their s Ezek 34:26
changeth the times and s Dan 2:21
lives prolonged for a s Dan 7:12
my wine in the s thereof Hos 2:9
render the fruits in their s Matt 21:41
my words shall be fulfilled in their s Luke 1:20
at the s he sent servant Luke 20:10
desirous to see him of a long s Luke 23:8
angel went down at certain s John 5:4
willing for a s to rejoice John 5:35
not for you to know times and s Acts 1:7
not seeing the sun for a s Acts 13:11
a convenient s Acts 24:25
be instant in s 2 Tim 4:2
pleasures of sin for a s Heb 11:25

SEAT
thy s will be empty 1 Sam 20:18
that I might come even to his s Job 23:3
when I prepared my s in the street Job 29:7
the s of the scornful Ps 1:1
cause s of violence to come near Amos 6:3
s of them that sold doves Matt 21:12
scribes sit in Moses' s Matt 23:2
chief s in synagogues Matt 23:6; Mark 12:39

SEBA se´-bah
man (?) Gen 10:7

SEBAT se´-bat
rest (?) Zech 1:7

SECACAH sek´-ak-ah
enclosure Josh 15:61

SECHU se´-koo
watch-tower 1 Sam 19:22

SECRET (adj)
s things belong to God Deut 29:29
I have a s errand Judg 3:19
my name, seeing it is s Judg 13:18
cleanse me from s faults Ps 19:12
our s sins Ps 90:8
open rebuke better than s love Prov 27:5

SECRET (n)
come not into their s Gen 49:6
the s of wisdom Job 11:6
hast thou heard the s of God? Job 15:8
the s of God was upon my tabernacle Job 29:4
s of Lord is with them that fear him Ps 25:14
in s of his tabernacle will he hide Ps 27:5
when I was made in s Ps 139:15
his s is with the righteous Prov 3:32
bread eaten in s Prov 9:17
A gift in s pacifieth anger Prov 21:14
I have not spoken in s Is 45:19; 48:16
thy Father who seeth in s Matt 6:4
pray to thy Father who is in s Matt 6:6
he is in the s chambers Matt 24:26
in s have I said nothing John 18:20

SECRETLY
flee away s Gen 31:27
entice thee s, saying Deut 13:6
Commune with David s 1 Sam 18:22
Saul s practised mischief 1 Sam 23:9
for thou didst it s 2 Sam 12:12
a thing was s brought to me Job 4:12
if you s accept persons Job 13:10
my heart hath been s enticed Job 31:27
he lieth in wait s Ps 10:9
keep them s from the strife Ps 31:20
she called her sister s John 11:28
s for fear of the Jews John 19:38

SECT
the s of the Sadducees Acts 5:17
s of the Pharisees Acts 15:5
s of the Nazarenes Acts 24:5
straitest s of our religion Acts 26:5
as concerning this s, we know that Acts 28:22

SECUNDUS se-cun´-dus
second Acts 20:4

SECURE
And thou shalt be s Job 11:18
they that provoke God are s Job 12:6
we will persuade him, and s you Matt 28:14

SECURELY
seeing he dwelleth s by thee Prov 3:29
pass by s as men averse from war Mic 2:8

SEDUCE
shew signs and wonders, to s Mark 13:22
concerning them that s you 1 John 2:26
to s my servants Rev 2:20

SEE
came down to s the city Gen 11:5
you shall s my face no more Gen 44:23
I will go and s him before I die Gen 45:28
when I s the blood Ex 12:13
s the salvation of the Lord Ex 14:13
there shall no man s me, and live Ex 33:20
s the good land Deut 3:25
caused thee to s it Deut 34:4
open his eyes, that he may s 2 Kgs 6:17
s my zeal for the Lord 2 Kgs 10:16
mine eye shall no more s good Job 7:7
yet in my flesh shall I s God Job 19:26
to s the goodness of the Lord Ps 27:13
Come and s the works of God Ps 66:5
formed the eye, shall he not s Ps 94:9
lest they s with their eyes Is 6:10
eyes of them that s shall not be dim Is 32:3
shall s the king in his beauty Is 33:17

all flesh shall s it together Is 40:5
they shall s eye to eye Is 52:8
eyes, and s not Jer 5:21; Ezek 12:2
they shall s God Matt 5:8
we would s a sign Matt 12:38
s ye shall s Matt 13:14
s thou to that Matt 27:4
s the place where the Lord lay Matt 28:6
having eyes, s ye not? Mark 8:18
s here, or s there Luke 17:23
come and s John 1:39; 11:34; Rev 6:1
thou shalt s greater things John 1:50
I was blind, now I s John 9:25
that they which s not might s John 9:39
But we s Jesus Heb 2:9
though now we s him not 1 Pet 1:8
we shall s him as he is 1 John 3:2

SEED
enmity between thy s Gen 3:15
give us s Gen 47:19
it was like coriander s Ex 16:31
thou shalt not sow thy field mingled s Lev 19:19
ye shall sow your s in vain Lev 26:16
it is no place of s Num 20:5
unto them and to their s after them Deut 1:8
Egypt, where thou sowedst thy s Deut 11:10
tithe all the increase of your s Deut 14:22
shalt carry much s into the field Deut 28:38
bearing precious s Ps 126:6
in the morning sow thy s Eccl 11:6
the s of a homer shall yield Is 5:10
shalt thou make thy s to flourish Is 17:11
give s to the sower Is 55:10
the s which the Lord hath blessed Is 61:9
a noble vine wholly a right s Jer 2:21
the s is rotten Joel 1:17
overtake of grapes him that soweth s Amos 9:13
Is the s yet in the barn? Hag 2:19
the s shall be prosperous Zech 8:12
that he might seek a godly s Mal 2:15

SEEK
What s thou? Gen 37:15
I s my brethren: tell me Gen 37:15
that ye s not after your own heart Num 15:39
s ye the priesthood also? Num 16:10
if thou s him with all thy heart Deut 4:29
even unto his habitation shall ye s Deut 12:5
Thou shalt not s their peace Deut 23:6;
Ezra 9:12
shall I not s rest for thee Ruth 3:1
if thou s him, he will be found 1 Chr 28:9;
2 Chr 15:2
hast prepared thine heart to s God 2 Chr 19:3
Josiah began to s after God 2 Chr 34:3
we s your God, as ye do Ezra 4:2
s the welfare of the children of Israel Neh 2:10
I would s unto God Job 5:8
s unto God betimes Job 8:5
children shall s to please the poor Job 20:10
from thence she s the prey Job 39:29
hast not forsaken them that s thee Ps 9:10
countenance will not s after God Ps 10:4
s out his wickedness till thou find none Ps 10:15
any that did understand, and s God Ps 14:2
generation of them that s him Ps 24:6
I desired of the Lord, that will I s after Ps 27:4
S ye my face Ps 27:8
s peace, and pursue it Ps 34:14; 1 Pet 3:11
early will I s thee Ps 63:1
your heart shall live that s God Ps 69:32
that they may s thy name Ps 83:16
I will s thy good Ps 122:9
s me early, but they shall not find me Prov 1:28
those that s me early shall find me Prov 8:17
that diligently s good Prov 11:27
of them that s death Prov 21:6

they that go to s mixed wine Prov 23:30
I will s it yet again Prov 23:35
gave my heart to s and search Eccl 1:13; 7:25
I will s him whom my soul loveth Song 3:2
learn to do well, s judgment Is 1:17
should not a people s unto their God? Is 8:19
they shall s to the idols Is 19:3
S ye out of the book of the Lord Is 34:16
when the pour and needy s water Is 41:17
S ye me in vain Is 45:19
that s the truth, and I will pardon Jer 5:1
ye shall s me, and find when ye search Jer 29:13
Zion, whom no man s after Jer 30:17
this man s not welfare of this people Jer 38:4
them that wait for him, to the soul that s him Lam 3:25
they shall s peace Ezek 7:25
I will s that which was lost Ezek 34:16
to s by prayer, and supplications Dan 9:3
S ye me, and ye shall live Amos 5:4
S ye the Lord, all ye meek Zeph 2:3
they should s the law at his mouth Mal 2:7
after all these things do the Gentiles s Matt 6:32
s ye first the kingdom of God Matt 6:33
s, and ye shall find Matt 7:7
adulterous generation s after a sign Matt 12:39
I know that ye s Jesus Matt 28:5
All men s for thee Mark 1:37
s of him a sign from heaven Mark 8:11
I come s fruit Luke 13:7
many, I say unto you will s to enter in Luke 13:24
and s diligently till she find it Luke 15:8
is come to s and to save Luke 19:10
Why s ye the living among the dead? Luke 24:5
What s ye? John 1:38
the Father s such to worship him John 4:23
Is not this he, whom they s to kill? John 7:25
Ye shall s me, and shall not find me John 7:34
if . . . ye s me, let these go their way John 18:8
whom s thou? John 20:15
there is none that s after God Rom 3:11
the Greeks s after wisdom 1 Cor 1:22
Let no man s his own 1 Cor 10:24
s not her own 1 Cor 13:5
I s not yours, but you 2 Cor 12:14
all s their own Phil 2:21
s those things which are above Col 3:1
rewarder of them that diligently s him Heb 11:6
declare plainly that they s a country Heb 11:14
but we s one to come Heb 13:14
s whom he may devour 1 Pet 5:8
in those days shall men s death Rev 9:6

SEEM
he s as one that mocked Gen 19:14
they s to him but a few days Gen 29:20
S it but a small thing unto you Num 16:9
There is a way which s right Prov 14:12
taken even that which he s to have Luke 8:18
words s to them as idle tales Luke 24:11
If any among you s to be wise 1 Cor 3:18
if any man s to be contentious 1 Cor 11:16
you should s to come short Heb 4:1
no chastening for the present s to be joyous Heb 12:11

SEEMLY
Delight is not s for a fool Prov 19:10
so honour is not s for a fool Prov 26:1

SEEN
I have s God face to face Gen 32:30
Egyptians whom ye have s to day Ex 14:13
because I have s an angel Judg 6:22
What have they s in thine house 2 Kgs 20:15
mine eye hath s all this Job 13:1
the vulture's eye hath not s Job 28:7
yet have I not s the righteous forsaken Ps 37:25
years wherein we have s evil Ps 90:15
he hath not s the sun Eccl 6:5
have s a great light Is 9:2
neither hath the eye s Is 64:4; 1 Cor 2:9
who hath s such things? Is 66:8
to be s of them Matt 6:1
never so s in Israel Matt 9:33
till they have s the kingdom of God Mark 9:1
We have s strange things to day Luke 5:26
No man hath s God John 1:18
hast thou s Abraham? John 8:57
he that hath s me, hath s the Father John 14:9
when he had s the grace of God Acts 11:23
have I not s Jesus Christ our Lord? 1 Cor 9:1
whom no man hath s nor can see 1 Tim 6:16
evidence of things not s Heb 11:1
Whom having not s, ye love 1 Pet 1:8

SEETHE
Thou shalt not s a kid Ex 23:19
and s pottage for the sons 2 Kgs 4:38
let them s the bones of it therein Ezek 24:5

SEGUB se´-goob
elevated 1 Kgs 16:34

SEIR se´-ir
hairy Gen 14:6

SEIRATH se´-ir-ath
well-wooded Judg 3:26

SEIZE
let darkness s upon it Job 3:6
Let death s upon them Ps 55:15
fear hath s on her Jer 49:24
let us s on his inheritance Matt 21:38

SELA-HAMMAHLEKOTH se´-lah-ham-ah´-lek-oth
rock of escapes 1 Sam 23:28

SELA se´-lah
rock Is 16:1

SELAH se´-lah
forte (?), a musical direction Ps 3:2

SELED se´-led
exultation or burning 1 Chr 2:30

SELEUCIA se-lu´-si-a
brightness (?) Acts 13:4

SELF-WILLED
not s, not soon angry, not given Titus 1:7
Presemptuous are they, s 2 Pet 2:10

SELL
S me this day thy birthright Gen 25:31
Come, let us s him Gen 37:27
Ahab did s himself to work wickedness 1 Kgs 21:25
will ye even s your brethren? Neh 5:8
Buy the truth, and s it not Prov 23:23
I will s your sons and your daughters Joel 3:8
that we may s corn Amos 8:5
and s the refuse of the wheat Amos 8:6
s that thou hast Matt 19:21; Mark 10:21; Luke 12:33; 18:22
let him s his garment Luke 22:36
buy and s and get gain James 4:13

SELLER
as with the buyer, so with the s Is 24:2
buyer rejoice, not the s mourn Ezek 7:12
For the s shall not return Ezek 7:13
Lydia, a s of purple Acts 16:14

SEM sem
same as SHEM Luke 3:36

SEMACHIAH sem´-ak-i´-ah
whom Jehovah sustains 1 Chr 26:7

SEMEI sem´-e-i
Gr. for SHIMEI Luke 3:26

SENAAH sen-a´-ah
thorny (?) Ezra 2:35

SEND
he shall s his angel Gen 24:7
s me good speed this day Gen 24:12
by the hand of him whom thou wilt s Ex 4:13
if I s pestilence 2 Chr 7:13
S thee help from the sanctuary Ps 20:2
s out thy light and thy truth Ps 43:3
s now prosperity Ps 118:25
Whom shall I s, and who will go for us? Is 6:8
Here am I; s me Is 6:8
s forth labourers Matt 9:38; Luke 10:2
till he s forth judgment Matt 12:20
S her away, for she crieth after us Matt 15:23
that he might s them forth to preach Mark 3:14
whom the Father will s in my name John 14:26
believed that thou didst s me John 17:8
God s his own Son Rom 8:3

SENEH se´-nay
crag, thorn 1 Sam 14:4

SENIR se´-nir
coat of mail 1 Chr 5:23

SENNACHERIB sen-ak´-er-ib
Sin (the moon) multiplies brethren 2 Kgs 18:13

SENSUAL
above, but is earthly, s, devilish James 3:15
s, having not the Spirit Jude 1:19

SENT
have not I s thee? Judg 6:14
the skies s out a sound Ps 77:17
but s leanness into their soul Ps 106:15
He s his word, and healed them Ps 107:20
I have not s these prophets Jer 23:21
I am not s but unto lost sheep Matt 15:24
the will of him that s me John 4:34
work the works of him that s me John 9:4
know Jesus Christ whom thou hast s John 17:3
as soon as I was s for Acts 10:29
how shall they preach, except they be s? Rom 10:15
God s forth his Son Gal 4:4

SENTENCE
Let my s come forth Ps 17:2
A divine s in the lips of the king Prov 16:10
because s against an evil work Eccl 8:11
s of death in ourselves 2 Cor 1:9

SENUAH se-noo´-ah
bristling (?) Neh 11:9

SEORIM se-or´-im
barley 1 Chr 24:8

SEPARATE
s thyself, I pray thee, from me Gen 13:9
Thou shalt s three cities Deut 19:2
a whisperer s chief friends Prov 16:28
the poor is s from his neighbour Prov 19:4
he shall s them Matt 25:32
Who shall s us from love of God? Rom 8:35
be ye s 2 Cor 6:17
s from sinners Heb 7:26

SEPARATION
the days of his s Num 6:8
for a water of s Num 19:9
purified with the water of s Num 31:23
to make a s between Ezek 42:20

SEPHAR se´-far
a numbering Gen 10:30

SEPHARAD sef´-a-rad
1 *a descending book* (?),
2 *counting down* Obad 1:20

SEPHARVAIM se´-far-va´-im
twin Sipparas 2 Kgs 17:24

SERAH se´-rah
abundance Gen 46:17

SERAIAH ser-ai´-ah
soldier of Jehovah (?) 2 Sam 8:17

SERAPHIMS ser´-af-ims
burning ones Is 6:2

SERED se´-rad
fear Gen 46:14

SERGIUS sur´-ji-us
a Roman governor of Cyprus Acts 13:17

SERPENT
the s was more subtil Gen 3:1
Dan shall be a s by the way Gen 49:17
his hand formed the crooked s Job 26:13
like the poison of a s Ps 58:4
sharpened their tongues like a s Ps 140:3
At the last it biteth like a s Prov 23:32
breaketh a hedge, a s shall bite him Eccl 10:8
s will bite without enchantment Eccl 10:11
leviathonn the piercing s Is 27:1
dust shall be the s meat Is 65:25
I will send s, cockatrices among you Jer 8:17
I will command the s Amos 9:3
They shall lick dust like a s Mic 7:17
will he give him a s? Matt 7:10; Luke 11:11
be ye therefore wise as s Matt 10:16
Ye s, ye generation of vipers Matt 23:33
they shall take up s Mark 16:18
as Moses lifted up the s John 3:14
that old s, called the Devil Rev 12:9; 20:2

SERUG se´-roog
shoot Gen 11:20

SERVANT
a s of s shall he be Gen 9:25
the s is free Job 3:19
As a s earnestly desireth the shadow Job 7:2
I am thy s Ps 116:16; 119:125; 143:12
the borrower is s to the lender Prov 22:7
A s will not be corrected by words Prov 29:19
as with the s, so with his master Is 24:2
and the s as his lord Matt 10:25
good and faithful s Matt 25:21
that s, which knew his lord's will Luke 12:47
unprofitable s Luke 17:10
the s abideth not in house for ever John 8:35
s knoweth not what his lord doeth John 15:15
Art thou called being a s? 1 Cor 7:21
be not ye the s of men 1 Cor 7:23
S, be obedient Eph 6:5; Col 3:22; Titus 2:9; 1 Pet 2:18

SERVE
elder shall s the younger Gen 25:23
fear the Lord thy God, and s him Deut 6:13; 10:12,20; 11:13; 13:4; Josh 22:5; 24:14; 1 Sam 7:3; 12:14
choose you this day whom ye will s Josh 24:15
s him with a perfect heart 1 Chr 28:9
What is the Almighty, that we should s him? Job 21:15
A seed shall s him Ps 22:30
all nations shall s him Ps 72:11
I have not caused thee to s Is 43:23
thou hast made me to s with thy sins Is 43:24
so shall ye s strangers Jer 5:19
Thy God whom thou s continually Dan 6:16
to s him with one consent Zeph 3:9
spareth his son that s him Mal 3:17
between him that s God and him that Mal 3:18
No man can s two masters Matt 6:24
hath left me to s alone Luke 10:40
these many years do I s thee Luke 15:29
If any man s me, let him follow me John 12:26
leave word of God, and s tables Acts 6:2
henceforth we should not s sin Rom 6:6
by love s one another Gal 5:13
for ye s the Lord Christ Col 3:24
to s living and true God 1 Thess 1:9
s him day and night in his temple Rev 7:15

SERVICE
What mean ye by this s? Ex 12:26
then is willing to consecrate his s? 1 Chr 29:5
will think he doeth God s John 16:2
your reasonable s Rom 12:1
doing s, as to the Lord Eph 6:7
to supply your lack of s Phil 2:30

SET
the Lord s a mark upon Cain Gen 4:15
I do s my bow in the cloud Gen 9:13
I have s the land before thee Deut 1:8
s thy words in order Job 33:5
I have s the Lord always before me Ps 16:8
we will s up our banners Ps 20:5
he hath s his love upon me Ps 91:14
hath s the one over against the other Eccl 7:14
S me as a seal upon thine heart Song 8:6
A city that is s on a hill Matt 5:14
no man shall s on thee Acts 18:10
the hope s before us Heb 6:18

SETH seth
substitute Gen 4:25

SETHUR se´-thoor
hidden Num 13:13

SETTLED
and punish the men that are s Zeph 1:12
continue in the faith, grounded and s Col 1:23

SEVER
and have s you from other people Lev 20:26
And they shall s out men Ezek 39:14
S the wicked from among the just Matt 13:49

SEW
they s fig leaves together Gen 3:7
thou s up mine iniquity Job 14:17
A time to rend, a time to s Eccl 3:7
No man also s a piece of new cloth Mark 2:21

SHAALABBIN sha´-al-ab´-in
earths of foxes Josh 19:42

SHAALBIM sha-alb´-im
same as SHAALABBIN Judg 1:35

SHAALBONITE sha-alb´-on-ite
inhabitant of Shaalbim 2 Sam 23:32

SHAAPH sha´-af
anger (?) 1 Chr 2:47

SHAARAIM sha´-ar-a´-im
two gates 1 Sam 17:52

SHAASHGAZ sha-ash´-gaz
beauty's servant (?) Esth 2:14

SHABBETHAI shab´-eth-a´-i
born on the sabbath Ezra 10:15

SHACHIA sha´-ki-ah
lustful 1 Chr 8:10

SHADE
the Lord is thy s Ps 121:5

SHADOW
the s of my roof Gen 19:8
As a servant earnestly desireth the s Job 7:2
fleeth also as a s, and continueth not Job 14:2
all my members are as a s Job 17:7
under the s of the Almighty Ps 91:1
My days are like a s Ps 102:11; 144:4; Eccl 8:13
his vain life which he spendeth as a s Eccl 6:12
under his s with great delight Song 2:3
the s flee away Song 2:17; 4:6
for a s in the daytime Is 4:6
s from the heat Is 25:4
as the s of a great rock Is 32:2
in the s of his hand Is 49:2; 51:16
the s of the evening are stretched out Jer 6:4
Under his s we shall live Lam 4:20
that dwell under his s shall return Hos 14:7
the s of Peter might overshadow Acts 5:15
neither s of turning James 1:17

SHADRACH shad´-rak
decree of the moon-god (?) Dan 1:7

SHAFT
his s, and his branches Ex 25:31; 37:17
and made me a polished s Is 49:2

SHAGE sha´-ge
wanderer 1 Chr 11:34

SHAHARAIM sha´-har-a´-im
two dawns 1 Chr 8:8

SHAHAZIMAH sha-haz´-i-mah
lofty places Josh 19:22

SHAKE
as at other times before, and s myself Judg 16:20
The voice of the Lord s the wilderness Ps 29:8
the fruit thereof shall s like Lebanon Ps 72:16
when he ariseth to s terribly the earth Is 2:19
I will s the heavens Is 13:13; Joel 3:16; Hag 2:6,21
S thyself from the dust Is 52:2
I will s all nations Hag 2:7
A reed s with the wind Matt 11:7; Luke 7:24
good measure, pressed down, s together Luke 6:38
be not soon s in mind 2 Thess 2:2
I s not the earth only Heb 12:26
things which cannot be s Heb 12:27

SHALEM sha´-lem
safe, perfect Gen 33:18

SHALIM sha´-lim
foxes 1 Sam 9:4

SHALISHA sha´-lish-ah
a third part 1 Sam 9:4

SHALLECHETH shal-e´-keth
felling 1 Chr 26:16

SHALLUM shal´-oom
retribution 2 Kgs 15:10

SHALLUN shal´-oon
spoliation Neh 3:15

SHALMAI shal´-ma-i
peaceful (?) Ezra 2:46

SHALMAN shal´-man
short for SHALMANESER Hos 10:14

SHALMANESER shal´-man-e´-zer
be propitious 2 Kgs 17:3

SHAMA sha´-mah
obedient 1 Chr 11:44

SHAMARIAH sha´-mar-i´-ah
whom Jehovah guards 2 Chr 11:19

SHAME
turn my glory into s Ps 4:2
and put to s that Ps 35:4; 40:14
let them be put to s, and perish Ps 83:17
a son that causeth s Prov 10:5; 17:2
For your s ye shall have double Is 61:7
s hath covered our faces Jer 51:51
bear thine own s Ezek 16:52
some to s and everlasting contempt Dan 12:2
the unjust knoweth no s Zeph 3:5
with s to take the lowest room Luke 14:9
worthy to suffer s Acts 5:41

I speak this to your s 1 Cor 6:5; 15:34
a s even to speak of those things Eph 5:12
whose glory is in their s Phil 3:19
put him to an open s Heb 6:6
despising the s Heb 12:2

SHAMED sha´-med
destroyer 1 Chr 8:12

SHAMER sha´-mer
keeper 1 Chr 6:46

SHAMGAR sham´-gar
destroyer (?) Judg 3:31

SHAMHUTH sham´-hooth
notoriety (?) 1 Chr 27:8

SHAMIR sha´-mir
a thorn 1 Chr 24:24

SHAMMA sham´-ah
desert 1 Chr 7:37

SHAMMAH sham´-ah
same as SHAMMA Gen 36:13

SHAMMAI sham´-a-i
wasted 1 Chr 2:28

SHAMMOTH sham´-oth
deserts 1 Chr 11:27

SHAMMUA sham´-oo-ah
famous Num 13:4

SHAMMUAH sham´-oo-ah
same as SHAMMUA 2 Sam 5:14

SHAMSHERAI sham´-she-rai
conqueror 1 Chr 8:26

SHAPE
descended in a bodily s Luke 3:22
nor seen his s John 5:37
And the s of the locusts Rev 9:7

SHAPHAM sha´-fam
bald 1 Chr 5:12

SHAPHAN sha´-fan
coney 2 Kgs 22:3

SHAPHAT sha´-fat
judge Num 13:5

SHAPHER sha´-fer
pleasantness Num 33:23

SHARAI shar´-a-i
free Ezra 10:40

SHARAIM shar-a´-im
same as SHAARAIM Josh 15:36

SHARAR shar´-ar
firm 2 Sam 23:33

SHAREZER shar-e´-zer
[God] protect the king 2 Kgs 19:37

SHARON sha´-ron
plain 1 Chr 27:29

SHARONITE sha´-ron-ite
inhabitant of Sharon 1 Chr 27:29

SHARP
like a s razor, working deceitfully Ps 52:2
a sword, and a s arrow Prov 25:18
a new s threshing instrument Is 41:15
the contention was so s Acts 15:39
s than any two-edged sword Heb 4:12

SHARPEN
to s every man his share 1 Sam 13:20
to s the goads 1 Sam 13:21
have s their tongues like a serpent Ps 140:3
Iron s iron, so a man s the countenance of his friend Prov 27:17

SHASHAI shash-a´-i
pale Ezra 10:40

SHASHAK sha´-shak
activity (?) 1 Chr 8:14

SHAUL sha´-ool
same as SAUL Gen 46:10

SHAULITES sha´-ool-ites
family of Shaul Num 26:13

SHAVEH KIRIATHAIM sha´-vay kir-iath-a´-im
plain of Kiriathaim Gen 14:5

SHAVEH sha´-vah
plain Gen 14:17

SHAVSHA shav´-shah
same as SERAIAH 1 Chr 18:16

SHEAF
and hast forgot a s in the field Deut 24:19
after the reapers among the s Ruth 2:7
bringing his s with him Ps 126:6
he that bindeth s Ps 129:7

SHEAL she´-al
prayer Ezra 10:29

SHEALTIEL she-al´-ti-el
I asked from God Ezra 3:2

SHEAR-JASHUB she´-ar-ja´-shoob
the remnant shall return Is 7:3

SHEARERS
I have heard that thou hast s 1 Sam 25:7
a sheep before her s is dumb Is 53:7

SHEARIAH she´-ar-i´-ah
gate of Jehovah 1 Chr 8:38

SHEATH
sword, and drew it out of the s 1 Sam 17:51; Ezek 21:3
his sword again into the s thereof 1 Chr 21:27

SHEBA she´-bah
an oath 2 Sam 20:1

SHEBAH she´-bah
seven Gen 26:33

SHEBAM she´-bam
fragrance Num 32:3

SHEBANIAH she´-ban-i´-ah
whom Jehovah hides 1 Chr 15:24

SHEBARIM she-bar´-im
breaches Josh 7:5

SHEBER she´-ber
breaking 1 Chr 2:48

SHEBNA sheb´-nah
youth (?) 2 Kgs 18:18

SHEBUEL she-boo´-el
captive of God 1 Chr 23:16

SHECANIAH she´-kan-i´-ah
same as SHECHANIAH 1 Chr 24:11

SHECHANIAH she´-kan-i´-ah
Jehovah dwells 1 Chr 3:21

SHECHEM she´-kem
back, shoulder Gen 34:2

SHECHEMITES she´-kem-ites
inhabitants of Shechem Num 26:31

SHED
by man shall his blood be s Gen 9:6
s for many for the remission of sins Matt 26:28
love of God is s abroad in our hearts Rom 5:5
Which he s on us abundantly Titus 3:6
without s of blood is no remission Heb 9:22

SHEDEUR she´-de-oor
giving forth of light Num 1:5

SHEEP
Abel was a keeper of s Gen 4:2
s which have no shepherd Num 27:17; 1 Kgs 22:17; 2 Chr 18:16; Matt 9:36; Mark 6:34
What meaneth this bleating of s 1 Sam 15:14
Like s they are laid in the grave Ps 49:14
the s of his hand Ps 95:7; 100:3
All we like s have gone astray Is 53:6
pull them out like s for the slaughter Jer 12:3
My s wandered Ezek 34:6
false prophets in s clothing Matt 7:15
go rather to lost s Matt 10:6
then is a man better than a s Matt 12:12
by the door is the shepherd of the s John 10:2
good shepherd giveth his life for the s John 10:11
Feed my s John 21:16

SHEET
then I will give you thirty s Judg 14:12
as it had been a great s knit Acts 10:11; 11:5

SHEHARIAH she-har-i´-ah
Jehovah seeks 1 Chr 8:26

SHELAH she´-lah
petition Gen 38:5

SHELANITES she´-lan-ites
descendants of Shelah Num 26:20

SHELEMIAH she´-lem-i´-ah
whom Jehovah repays 1 Chr 26:14

SHELEPH she´-lef
drawing out Gen 10:26

SHELESH she´-lesh
triad 1 Chr 7:35

SHELOMI she-lo´-mi
peaceful Num 34:27

SHELOMITH she-lo´-mith
peacefulness Lev 24:11

SHELOMOTH she-lo´-moth
same as SHELOMITH 1 Chr 24:22

SHELTER
for want of a s Job 24:8
For thou hast been a s Ps 61:3

SHELUMIEL she-loom´-i-el
friend of God Num 1:6

SHEM shem
name Gen 5:32

SHEMA she´-mah
1 *echo* (?) Josh 15:26
2 *fame* 1 Chr 2:43

SHEMAAH she´-ma-ah
fame 1 Chr 12:3

SHEMAIAH she-mai´-ah
Jehovah has heard 1 Kgs 12:22

SHEMARIAH she´-mar-i´-ah
Jehovah guards 1 Chr 12:5

SHEMEBER shem-e´-ber
soaring on high (?) Gen 14:2

SHEMER she´-mer
guardian 1 Kgs 16:24

SHEMIDA shem´-i-dah
fame of wisdom Num 26:32

SHEMIDAH shem´-i-dah
same as SHEMIDA 1 Chr 7:19

SHEMIDAITES shem-id´-a-ites
descendants of Shemida Num 26:32

SHEMINITH she-mi´-nith
eighth 1 Chr 15:21

SHEMIRAMOTH she-mi´-ram-oth
most high name 1 Chr 15:18

SHEMUEL **she´-moo-el**
same as SAMUEL Num 34:20

SHEN **shen**
tooth 1 Sam 7:12

SHENAZAR **she-na´-zar**
protect, O moon-god (?) 1 Chr 3:18

SHENIR **she´-nir**
same as SENIR Deut 3:9

SHEPHAM **she´-fam**
nakedness Num 34:10

SHEPHATHIAH **she´-fat-i´-ah**
same as SHEPHATIAH 1 Chr 9:8

SHEPHATIAH **she´-fat-i´-ah**
whom Jehovah defends 2 Sam 3:4

SHEPHERD
s is an abomination unto the Egyptians Gen 46:34
The Lord is my s Ps 23:1
neither shall the s make their fold Is 13:20
He shall feed his flock like a s Is 40:11
they are s that cannot understand Is 56:11
will set up s over them which shall feed Jer 23:4
their s have caused them to go astray Jer 50:6
As the s taketh out of the mouth Amos 3:12
Woe to the idol s Zech 11:17
I am the good s John 10:14

SHEPHI **she´-fi**
baldness 1 Chr 1:40

SHEPHO **she´-fo**
same as SHEPHI Gen 36:23

SHEPHUPHAN **she´-foof-an**
serpent (?) 1 Chr 8:5

SHERAH **she´-rah**
consanguinity 1 Chr 7:24

SHEREBIAH **she´-reb-i´-ah**
heat of Jehovah Ezra 8:18

SHERESH **she´-resh**
root 1 Chr 7:16

SHEREZER **sher-e´-zer**
same as SHAREZER (?) Zech 7:2

SHESHACH **she´-shak**
same as BABEL Jer 25:26

SHESHAI **shesh´-a-i**
clothed in white (?) Num 13:22

SHESHAN **she´-shan**
lily (?) 1 Chr 2:31

SHESBAZZAR **shesh´-baz-zar**
perhaps same as ZERUBBABEL Ezra 1:8

SHETH **shayth**
tumult Num 24:17

SHETHAR **she´-thar**
star Esth 1:14

SHETHAR-BOZNAI **she´-thar-boz´-na´-i**
bright star Ezra 5:3

SHEVA **she´-vah**
vanity 2 Sam 20:25

SHIBBOLETH **shib´-ol-eth**
an ear of corn, or a flood Judg 12:6

SHIBMAH **shib´-mah**
fragrant Num 32:38

SHICRON **shik´-ron**
drunkenness Josh 15:11

SHIELD
was there a s or spear seen Judg 5:8
compass him as with a s Ps 5:12
he is our help and our s Ps 33:20; 59:11; 84:9
a sun and s Ps 84:11
his truth shall be thy s Ps 91:4
anoint the s Is 21:5
taking the s of faith Eph 6:16

SHIGIONOTH **shig´-i-o´-noth**
irregular Hab 3:1

SHIHON **shi´-hon**
ruin Josh 19:19

SHIHOR **shi´-hor**
black 1 Chr 13:5

SHIHOR-LIBNATH **shi´-hor-lib´-nath**
turbid stream of Libnath Josh 19:26

SHILHI **shil´-hi**
darter 1 Kgs 22:42

SHILHIM **shil´-him**
aqueducts Josh 15:32

SHILLEM **shil´-em**
requital Gen 46:24

SHILOAH **shi-lo´-ah**
outlet of water Is 8:6

SHILOH **shi´-lo**
rest Josh 18:1

SHILONI **shi´-lo-ni**
inhabitant of Shiloh Neh 11:5

SHILONITE **shi´-lo-nite**
same as SHILONI 1 Kgs 11:29

SHILSHAH **shil´-shah**
triad 1 Chr 7:37

SHIMEA **shim´-e-ah**
famous 1 Chr 3:5

SHIMEAH **shim´-e-ah**
same as SHEMAAH 2 Sam 13:3

SHIMEAM **shim´-e-am**
same as SHIMEAH 1 Chr 9:38

SHIMEATH **shim´-e-ath**
rumor 2 Kgs 12:21

SHIMEATHITE **shi´-me-ath-ite**
descendant of Shimeah 1 Chr 2:55

SHIMEI **shim´-e-i**
my fame Num 3:18

SHIMEON **shim´-e-on**
a hearkening Ezra 10:31

SHIMHI **shim´-hi**
same as SHIMEI 1 Chr 8:21

SHIMI **shim´-i**
same as SHIMEI Ex 6:17

SHIMITES **shim´-ites**
descendants of Shimei Num 3:21

SHIMMA **shim´-ah**
rumor 1 Chr 2:13

SHIMON **shi´-mon**
provision (?) 1 Chr 4:20

SHIMRATH **shim´-rath**
watchfulness 1 Chr 8:21

SHIMRI **shim´-ri**
watchful 1 Chr 4:37

SHIMRITH **shim´-rith**
vigilant 2 Chr 24:26

SHIMROM **shim´-rome**
same as SHIMRON 1 Chr 7:1

SHIMRON **shim´-rone**
watchful Gen 46:13

SHIMRONITES **shim´-ron-ites**
descendants of Shimron Num 26:24

SHIMSHAI **shim´-sha-i**
sunny Ezra 4:8

SHINAB **shi´-nab**
hostile (?) Gen 14:2

SHINAR **shi´-nar**
same as BABYLON (?) Gen 10:10

SHINE
the light shall s upon thy ways Job 22:28
When his candle s upon my head Job 29:3
oil to make his face to s Ps 104:15
the night s as the day Ps 139:12
light, that s more and more Prov 4:18
upon them hath the light s Is 9:2
Arise, s; for thy light is come Is 60:1
wise shall s as the brightness Dan 12:3
Let your light so s Matt 5:16
the righteous s as the sun Matt 13:43
God, who commanded the light to s 2 Cor 4:6

SHIPHI **shi´-fi**
abundant 1 Chr 4:37

SHIPHMITE **shif´-mite**
a native of Shephan 1 Chr 27:27

SHIPHRAH **shif´-rah**
beauty Ex 1:15

SHIPHTAN **shif´-tan**
judicial Num 34:24

SHISHA **shi´-shah**
brightness 1 Kgs 4:3

SHISHAK **shi´-shak**
illustrious 1 Kgs 11:40

SHITRAI **shit´-ra-i**
official 1 Chr 27:29

SHITTIM **shit´-im**
acacias Num 25:1

SHIZA **shi´-zah**
cheerful (?) 1 Chr 11:42

SHOA **sho´-ah**
opulent Ezek 23:23

SHOBAB **sho´-bab**
apostate 2 Sam 5:14

SHOBACH **sho´-bak**
pouring 2 Sam 10:16

SHOBAI **sho´-ba-i**
bright (?) Ezra 2:42

SHOBAL **sho´-bal**
stream Gen 36:20

SHOBEK **sho´-bek**
forsaker Neh 10:24

SHOBI **sho´-bi**
taking captive 2 Sam 17:27

SHOCHO **sho´-ko**
same as SHOCHOH 2 Chr 28:18

SHOCHOH **sho´-ko**
a hedge 1 Sam 17:1

SHOCK
burnt up both the s, and also the standing corn Judg 15:5
like as a s of corn cometh Job 5:26

SHOCO **sho´-ko**
same as SHOCHOH 2 Chr 11:7

SHOD
be s with sandals Mark 6:9
s with the preparation of the gospel Eph 6:15

SHOHAM **sho´-ham**
onyx 1 Chr 24:27

SHOMER **sho´-mer**
watchman 2 Kgs 12:21

SHOOT
they s out the lip Ps 22:7

to s their arrows, even bitter words Ps 64:3
s out thine arrows, and destroy them Ps 144:6

SHOPHACH sho´-fak
same as SHOBACH 1 Chr 19:16

SHOPHAN sho´-fan
baldness Num 32:35

SHORT
the light is s Job 17:12
triumphing of the wicked is s Job 20:5
Remember how s my time is Ps 89:47
come s of the glory of God Rom 3:23
the time is s 1 Cor 7:29

SHORTER
the bed is s Is 28:20

SHORTLY
s bring it to pass Gen 41:32
Now will I s pour out Ezek 7:8
bruise Satan under your feet s Rom 16:20

SHOUT
God is gone up with a s Ps 47:5
shall descend from heaven with a s 1 Thess 4:16

SHOWER
makest it soft with s Ps 65:10
as s that water the earth Ps 72:6
will cause the s to come in his season Ezek 34:26

SHUA shoo´-ah
wealth 1 Chr 2:3

SHUAH shoo´-ah
depression Gen 25:2

SHUAL shoo´-al
jackal 1 Chr 7:36

SHUBAEL shoo´-ba-el
same as SHEBUEL (?) 1 Chr 24:20

SHUHAM shoo´-ham
pitman (?) Num 26:42

SHUHAMITES shoo´-ham-ites
descendants of Shuham Num 26:42

SHUHITE shoo´-hite
a descendant of Shua Job 8:1

SHULAMITE shoo´-lam-ite
same as SHELOMITH Song 6:13

SHUMATHITES shoo´-math-ites
people of Shumah 1 Chr 2:53

SHUN
But s profhane and vain babblings 2 Tim 2:16

SHUNAMMITE shoon´-am-ite
an inhabitant of Shunem 1 Kgs 1:3

SHUNEM shoon´-em
two resting places Josh 19:18

SHUNI shoon´-i
quiet Gen 46:16

SHUNITES shoon´-ites
descendants of Shuni Num 26:15

SHUPHAM shoo´-fam
same as SHEPHUPHAM Num 26:39

SHUPHAMITES shoo´-fam-ites
descendants of Shupham Num 26:39

SHUPPIM shoop´-im
same as SHEPHUPHAM 1 Chr 7:12

SHUR shoor
a fort Gen 16:7

SHUSHAN shoo´-shan
lily (?) Neh 1:1

SHUT
the Lord s him in Gen 7:16
he shall open, and none shall s Is 22:22
they shall not be s day nor night Is 60:11

I am s up, I cannot go into house of the Lord Jer 36:5
he s out my prayer Lam 3:8

SHUTHALHITES shoo´-thal-ites
the descendants of Shuthelah Num 26:35

SHUTHELAH shoo-theel´-ah
plantation (?) Num 26:35

SIA si´-ah
assembly Neh 7:47

SIAHA si´-a-hah
council Ezra 2:44

SIBBECAI sib´-ek-a-i
entangling 1 Chr 11:29

SIBBECHAI sib´-ek-a-i
same as SIBBECAI 2 Sam 21:18

SIBMAH sib´-mah
same as SHIBMAH Josh 13:19

SIBRAIM sib-ra´-im
two hills (?) Ezek 47:16

SICHEM si´-kem
the shoulder blade Gen 12:6

SICK
maketh the heart s Prov 13:12
I was not s Prov 23:35
I am s of love Song 2:5
the whole head is s Is 1:5
made him s with bottles of wine Hos 7:5
s of a fever Matt 8:14
Is any s among you? James 5:14
prayer of faith shall save the s James 5:15

SICKNESS
make all his bed in his s Ps 41:3
much sorrow and wrath with his s Eccl 5:17
infirmities, and bare our s Matt 8:17

SIDDIM sid´-im
the plains Gen 14:3

SIDON si´-don
fishing Gen 10:15

SIDONIANS si-do´-ni-ans
inhabitants of Sidon Deut 3:9

SIFT
to s the nations with the sieve Is 30:28
I will s the house of Israel Amos 9:9
that he may s you as wheat Luke 22:31

SIGHT
this great s Ex 3:3
for the s of thine eyes Deut 28:34
Better is the s of the eyes Eccl 6:9
blind receive their s Matt 11:5; 20:34; Luke 7:21
it seemed good in thy s Matt 11:26; Luke 10:21
Receive thy s Luke 18:42; Acts 22:13
fearful s and great signs Luke 21:11
things honest in the s of all men Rom 12:17
walk by faith, not by s 2 Cor 5:7

SIGN
Ask thee a s of the Lord Is 7:11
for an everlasting s Is 55:13
I have set thee for a s Ezek 12:6
How great are his s! Dan 4:3
s of the times Matt 16:3
with s following Mark 16:20
for a s which shall be spoken against Luke 2:34
Except ye see s John 4:48
s which God did by him Acts 2:22
s and wonders may be done Acts 4:30

SIGNIFY
s what death he should die John 12:33
The Holy Ghost this s Heb 9:8
which was in them did s 1 Pet 1:11

SIHON si´-hon
brush Num 21:21

SIHOR si´-hor
same as SHICHOR Josh 13:3

SILAS si´-las
short for SILVANUS Acts 15:22

SILENCE
he had put the Sadducees to s Matt 22:34
Let the woman learn in s 1 Tim 2:11
ye may put to s 1 Pet 2:15

SILENT
s in darkness 1 Sam 2:9
be not s to me Ps 28:1
let them be s in the grave Ps 31:17
Be s, O all flesh, before the Lord Zech 2:13

SILLA sil´-ah
way, highway (?) 2 Kgs 12:20

SILLY
envy slayeth the s one Job 5:2
like a s dove without heart Hos 7:11
lead captive s women 2 Tim 3:6

SILOAH si-lo´-ah
same as SHILOAH Neh 3:15

SILOAM si-lo´-am
same as SHILOAH John 9:7

SILVANUS sil-vane´-us
of the forest 2 Cor 1:19

SILVER
s to be in Jerusalem as stones 1 Kgs 10:27
thou shalt have plenty of s Job 22:25
as s tried in a furnace Ps 12:6; 66:10
Receive my instruction, and not s Prov 8:10
He that loveth s shall not be satisfied Eccl 5:10
Thy s is become dross Is 1:22
Reprobate s shall men call them Jer 6:30
sit as a refiner and purifier of s Mal 3:3

SIMEON sim´-e-on
same as SHIMEON Gen 29:33

SIMILITUDE
the s of the Lord Num 12:8
saw no s Deut 4:12
after the s of a palace Ps 144:12
after the s of Adam's transgression Rom 5:14
made after the s of God James 3:9

SIMON si´-mon
same as SIMEON Matt 10:4

SIMPLE
making wise the s Ps 19:7
The Lord preserveth the s Ps 116:6
it giveth understanding unto the s Ps 119:130
the s pass on, and are punished Prov 22:3; 27:12
deceive the hearts of the s Rom 16:18

SIMRI sim´-ri
same as SHIMRI 1 Chr 26:10

SIN sin
clay Ex 16:1

SIN (n)
s lieth at the door Gen 4:7
died in his own s Num 27:3
put to death for his own s Deut 24:16; 2 Kgs 14:6; 2 Chr 25:4
searchest after my s Job 10:6
from presumptuous s Ps 19:13
Remember not the s of my youth Ps 25:7
whose s is covered Ps 32:1
I will be sorry for my s Ps 38:18
my s is ever before me Ps 51:3
our secret s Ps 90:8
hath not dealt with us after to our s Ps 103:10

holden with the cords of s Prov 5:22
In the multitude of words there wanteth not s Prov 10:19
Fools make a mock at s Prov 14:9
s is a reproach to any people Prov 14:34
they may add s to s Is 30:1
not remember thy s Is 43:25; 44:22
offering for s Is 53:10
bare the s of many Is 53:12
land was filled with s Jer 51:5
None of his s that he hath committed Ezek 33:16
They eat up the s of my people Hos 4:8
fruit of my body for the s of my soul Mic 6:7
all manner of s and blasphemy Matt 12:31
the s of the world John 1:29
He that is without s John 8:7
will reprove the world of s John 16:8
hath the greater s John 19:11
lay not this s to their charge Acts 7:60
wash away thy s Acts 22:16
where s abounded Rom 5:20
Shall we continue in s? Rom 6:1
I had not known s, but by the law Rom 7:7
whatsoever is not of faith is s Rom 14:23
made him to be s for us 2 Cor 5:21
that man of s 2 Thess 2:3
once offered to bear the s of many Heb 9:28
his own self bare our s 1 Pet 2:24

SIN (v)
Do not s against the child Gen 42:22
I have s Ex 9:27; 10:16; Num 22:34; Josh 7:20; 1 Sam 15:24; 26:21; 2 Sam 12:13; Job 7:20; Ps 41:4; Matt 27:4; Luke 15:18
if I s, then thou markest me Job 10:14
Stand in awe, and s not Ps 4:4
that I s not with my tongue Ps 39:1
he that s against me Prov 8:36
thy first father hath s Is 43:27
the soul that s, it shall die Ezek 18:4
now they s more and more Hos 13:2
how oft shall my brother s against me Matt 18:21
s no more John 5:14; 8:11
shall we s, because Rom 6:15
Awake to righteousness, and s not 1 Cor 15:34
Be ye angry, and s not Eph 4:26
he cannot s, because he is born of God 1 John 3:9

SINA si´-na
pointed Acts 7:30

SINAI si´-na-i
pointed Ex 19:1

SINCERE
that ye may be s and without offence Phil 1:10
desire the s milk of the word 1 Pet 2:2

SINCERITY
serve him in s and in truth Josh 24:14
the unleavened bread of s 1 Cor 5:8
love our Lord Jesus Christ in s Eph 6:24

SINFUL
for I am a s man Luke 5:8
delivered into the hands of s men Luke 24:7
become exceeding s Rom 7:13
the likeness of s flesh Rom 8:3

SINGING
come before his presence with s Ps 100:2
our tongue with s Ps 126:2
the time of the s of birds Song 2:12
s and making melody Eph 5:19

SINGLE
thine eye be s Matt 6:22; Luke 11:34

SINGLENESS
with gladness and s of heart Acts 2:46
in s of your heart, as unto Christ Eph 6:5; Col 3:22

SINIM sin´-im
Chinese (?) Is 49:12

SINITE sin´-ite
descendants of Canaan Gen 10:17

SINNER
men of Sodom were wicked and s Gen 13:13
nor standeth in way of s Ps 1:1
teach s in the way Ps 25:8
Gather not my soul with s Ps 26:9
s shall be converted Ps 51:13
if s entice thee Prov 1:10
Evil pursueth s Prov 13:21
one s destroyeth much good Eccl 9:18
The s in Zion are afraid Is 33:14
eat with publicans and s Matt 9:11; Mark 2:16; Luke 5:30; 15:2
but s to repentance Matt 9:13; Mark 2:17; Luke 5:32
a friend of publicans and s Matt 11:19; Luke 7:34
which was a s Luke 7:37
Suppose ye these Galileans were s Luke 13:2
over one s that repenteth Luke 15:7,10
be merciful to me a s Luke 18:13
a man that is a s John 9:16
Whether he be a s or no, I know not John 9:25
while we were yet s Rom 5:8
many were made s Rom 5:19
separate from s Heb 7:26

SION si´-on
same as ZION Deut 4:48

SIPHMOTH sif´-moth
bare places (?) 1 Sam 30:28

SIPPAI sip´-a-i
belonging to the doorstep (?) 1 Chr 20:4

SIRAH si´-rah
withdrawing 2 Sam 3:26

SIRION sir´-i-on
a coat of mail Deut 3:9

SISAMAI sis´-am-a´-i
fragrant (?) 1 Chr 2:40

SISERA si´-ser-ah
binding in chains (?) Judg 4:2

SISTER
my mother, and my s Job 17:14
wisdom, Thou art my s Prov 7:4
the same is my brother, and s Matt 12:50
the younger as s, with all purity 1 Tim 5:2

SIT
Why s we here till we die? 2 Kgs 7:3
They that s in the gate Ps 69:12
Such as s in darkness Ps 107:10
Their strength is to s still Is 30:7
Why do we s still? Jer 8:14
they s before thee as my people Ezek 33:31
they shall s every man under his vine Mic 4:4
he shall s as a refiner Mal 3:3
to s on my right hand Matt 20:23; Mark 10:37

SITNAH sit´-nah
contention Gen 26:21

SITUATION
the s of this city is pleasant 2 Kgs 2:19
Beautiful for s Ps 48:2

SIVAN si´-van
bright Esth 8:9

SKILFUL
every willing s man 1 Chr 28:21
play s with a loud noise Ps 33:3
s to destroy Ezek 21:31
s in all wisdom Dan 1:4

SKILL
nor yet favour to men of s Eccl 9:11
knowledge and s in all learning Dan 1:17
to give thee s and understanding Dan 9:22

SKIN
wist not that the s of his face shone Ex 34:29
S for s Job 2:4
Thou hast clothed me with s and flesh Job 10:11
though after my s worms destroy Job 19:26
Can the Ethiopian change his s Jer 13:23
cover you with s Ezek 37:6

SKIP
to s like a calf Ps 29:6
the mountains s like rams Ps 114:4
thou s for joy Jer 48:27

SKIRT
went down to the s of his garments Ps 133:2
in thy s is found the blood of the souls Jer 2:34
the s of him that is a Jew Zech 8:23

SLACK
he will not be s to him Deut 7:10
dealeth with a s hand Prov 10:4
Let not thine hands be s Zeph 3:16
The Lord is not s 2 Pet 3:9

SLAIN
I have s a man Gen 4:23
strong men have been s by her Prov 7:26
I shall be s in the streets Prov 22:13
those that are ready to be s Prov 24:11
thy s men are not s with the sword Is 22:2
shall no more cover her s Is 26:21
the s of the Lord shall be many Is 66:16
the s of the daughter of my people Jer 9:1
s with sword better than they that be s Lam 4:9
breathe upon these s Ezek 37:9
having s the enmity thereby Eph 2:16
a Lamb as it had been s Rev 5:6

SLAUGHTER
as sheep for the s Ps 44:22
brought as a lamb to the s Is 53:7; Jer 11:19
valley of s Jer 7:32; 19:6
every man a s weapon Ezek 9:2

SLAVE
is he a homeborn s Jer 2:14
chariots, and s, and souls of men Rev 18:13

SLAY
to s the righteous with the wicked Gen 18:25
If the scourge s suddenly Job 9:23
Though he s me Job 13:15

SLEEP (n)
deep s from the Lord 1 Sam 26:12
when deep s falleth Job 4:13; 33:15
lest I sleep the s of death Ps 13:3
giveth his beloved s Ps 127:2
thy s shall be sweet Prov 3:24
Yet a little s Prov 6:10; 24:33
Love not s, lest thou come to poverty Prov 20:13
The s of a labouring man is sweet Eccl 5:12
sleep a perpetual s Jer 51:39
heavy with s Luke 9:32
had spoken of taking of rest in s John 11:13
high time to awake out of s Rom 13:11

SLEEP (v)
wherein shall he s Ex 22:27
now shall I s in the dust Job 7:21
I will both lay me down in peace, and s Ps 4:8
shall neither slumber nor s Ps 121:4
they s not, except they have done Prov 4:16
when thou s, it shall keep thee Prov 6:22
he that s in harvest is a son that causeth shame Prov 10:5
I s, but my heart waketh Song 5:2
many of them that s in the dust Dan 12:2

not dead, but s Matt 9:24; Mark 5:39; Luke 8:52
while men s, the enemy came Matt 13:25
S on now, and take your rest Matt 26:45
coming suddenly he find you s Mark 13:36
Why s ye? rise and pray Luke 22:46
Our friend Lazarus s John 11:11
among you many s 1 Cor 11:30
We shall not all s 1 Cor 15:51
Awake thou that s Eph 5:14
them also which s in Jesus 1 Thess 4:14
let us not s, as do others 1 Thess 5:6
that, whether we wake or s 1 Thess 5:10

SLEIGHT
by the s of men and cunning craftiness Eph 4:14

SLEW
A woman s him Judg 9:54
s both the lion and the bear 1 Sam 17:36
Saul s his thousands 1 Sam 29:5
who s all these? 2 Kgs 10:9
When he s them, then they sought him Ps 78:34
He that killeth an ox is as if he s a man Is 66:3
whom he would he s Dan 5:19
whom ye s between temple and altar Matt 23:35
whom ye s and hanged on a tree Acts 5:30
kept the raiment of them that s him Acts 22:20
deceived me, and by it, s me Rom 7:11

SLIDE
their foot shall s in due time Deut 32:35
therefore I shall not s Ps 26:1
none of his steps shall s Ps 37:31
Israel s back as a backsliding Hos 4:16

SLIME
s had they for morter Gen 11:3
daubed it with s and with pitch Ex 2:3

SLIP
my feet did not s 2 Sam 22:37; Ps 18:36
He that is ready to s Job 12:5
that my footsteps s not Ps 17:5
when my foot s, they magnify themselves Ps 38:16
my steps had well nigh s Ps 73:2
we should let them s Heb 2:1

SLIPPERY
Let their way be dark and s Ps 35:6
Surely thou didst set them in s places Ps 73:18
shall be unto them as s ways Jer 23:12

SLOTHFUL
be not s to go, and to enter Judg 18:9
Thou wicked and s servant Matt 25:26
Not s in business Rom 12:11
That ye be not s Heb 6:12

SLOW
I am s of speech Ex 4:10
s to anger, and of great kindness Neh 9:17
s to wrath is of great understanding Prov 14:29
s of heart Luke 24:25

SLUMBER
that keepeth thee will not s Ps 121:3
nor s to thine eyelids Prov 6:4
Yet a little sleep, a little s Prov 6:10; 24:33
none shall s not sleep Is 5:27
loving to s Is 56:10
Thy shepherds s Nah 3:18
hath given them the spirit of s Rom 11:8

SMALL
s round thing, s as the frost Ex 16:14
every s matter they shall judge Ex 18:22
Seemeth it a s thing unto you Num 16:9
a s thing that thou hast brought us Num 16:13
even until it was as s as dust Deut 9:21
shall distil as the dew, as the s rain Deut 32:2
yet a s thing in thy sight, O Lord GOD 2 Sam 7:19
one s petition of thee 1 Kgs 2:20
inhabitants were of s power 2 Kgs 19:26
yet this was a s thing in thine eyes 1 Chr 17:17
thy beginning was s Job 8:7
Are the consolations of God s with thee? Job 15:11
he maketh s the drops of water Job 36:27
I am s and despised Ps 119:141
thy strength is s Prov 24:10
For a s moment Is 54:7
a s one a strong nation Is 60:22
I will make thee s among the heathen Jer 49:15
strong with a s people Dan 11:23
by whom shall Jacob arise? for he is s Amos 7:2
the day of s things Zech 4:10
a few s fishes Mark 8:7; John 6:9
no s stir Acts 12:18; 19:23
had no s dissension Acts 15:2
turned about with a very s helm James 3:4

SMART
shall s for it Prov 11:15

SMELL (n)
s of field which the Lord hath blessed Gen 27:27
noses have they, but they s not Ps 115:6
instead of sweet s Is 3:24
nor the s of fire Dan 3:27
hearing, where were the s? 1 Cor 12:17
an odour of a sweet s Phil 4:18

SMELL (v)
neither see, nor hear, nor eat, nor s Deut 4:28
he s the battle Job 39:25
thy garments s of myrrh Ps 45:8

SMITE
Wherefore s thou thy fellow? Ex 2:13
He that s a man Ex 21:12
I will not s him the second time 1 Sam 26:8
S this people 2 Kgs 6:18
shall I s them? 2 Kgs 6:21
The sun shall not s thee by day Ps 121:6
Let the righteous s me Ps 141:5
S a scorner Prov 19:25
he shall s thee with a rod Is 10:24
neither shall heat nor sun s them Is 49:10
gave my back to the s Is 50:6
s with the fist of wickedness Is 58:4
let us s him with the tongue Jer 18:18
giveth his cheek to him that s Lam 3:30
know that I am the Lord that s Ezek 7:9
prophesy, and s thine hands together Ezek 21:14
the knees s together Nah 2:10
s the shepherd, and the sheep shall Zech 13:7
lest I come and s the earth with a curse Mal 4:6
s thee on thy right cheek Matt 5:39
shall begin to s his fellow servants Matt 24:49
shall we s with the sword? Luke 22:49
why s thou me? John 18:23

SMITH
there was no s found 1 Sam 13:19
The s with the tongs Is 44:12
with the carpenters and s Jer 24:1

SMITTEN
that thou hast s Num 22:28
cause thee to be s Deut 28:25
wherefore hath the Lord s us 1 Sam 4:3
shouldest have s five or six times 2 Kgs 13:19
thou hast s all mine enemies Ps 3:7
My heart is s Ps 102:4
the gate is s with destruction Is 24:12
s of God Is 53:4
In vain have I s your children Jer 2:30
he hath s, and he will bind Hos 6:1
I have s you Amos 4:9

SMOKE
as the s of a furnace Gen 19:28
into s shall they consume away Ps 37:20
As s is driven away Ps 68:2
my days are consumed like s Ps 102:3
like a bottle in the s Ps 119:83
as s to the eyes Prov 10:26
the house was filled with s Is 6:4
the s thereof shall go up for ever Is 34:10
the heavens shall vanish away like s Is 51:6
These are a s in my nose Is 65:5
as the s out of a chimney Hos 13:3

SMOKING
behold a s furnace Gen 15:17
and the mountain s Ex 20:18
the s flax shall he not quench Is 42:3; Matt 12:20

SMOOTH
I am a s man Gen 27:11
five s stones 1 Sam 17:40; Is 57:6
speak unto us s things Is 30:10
rough ways shall be made s Luke 3:5

SMOTE
with his rod he s the rock twice Num 20:11
he s them hip and thigh Judg 15:8
David's heart s him 1 Sam 24:5
in my wrath I s thee Is 60:10
I s upon my thigh Jer 31:19
s you with blasting and with mildew Hag 2:17
Who is he that s thee? Matt 26:68; Luke 22:64
s upon his breast Luke 18:13
the angel of the Lord s him Acts 12:23

SMYRNA smir´-nah
myrrh Rev 1:11

SNARE
this man be a s unto us Ex 10:7
nor take it unto thee, lest thou be s Deut 7:25
that thou be not s by following them Deut 12:30
they shall be s and traps unto you Josh 23:13
which thing became a s unto Gideon Judg 8:27
that she may be a s 1 Sam 18:21
wherefore then layest thou a s 1 Sam 28:9
the s of death prevented me 2 Sam 22:6; Ps 18:5
he walketh upon a s Job 18:8
s are round about thee Job 22:10
on the wicked he shall rain s Ps 11:6
lay s for me Ps 38:12
commune of laying s privily Ps 64:5
Let their table become a s Ps 69:22
deliver thee from s of fowler Ps 91:3
the s is broken Ps 124:7
s with words of thy mouth Prov 6:2; 12:13
as a bird hasteth to the s Prov 7:23
the s of death Prov 13:14; 14:27
his lips are the s of his soul Prov 18:7
learn his ways, and get a s to thy soul Prov 22:25
bring city into a s Prov 29:8
fear of man bringeth a s Prov 29:25
s in an evil time Eccl 9:12
the pit, and the s are upon thee Is 24:17; Jer 48:43
Fear and a s is come upon us Lam 3:47
he shall be taken in my s Ezek 12:13
the prophet is a s Hos 9:8
Can a bird fall in a s Amos 3:5
as a s shall it come Luke 21:35
lest he fall into reproach and the s 1 Tim 3:7
fall into temptation and a s 1 Tim 6:9
out of the s of the devil 2 Tim 2:26

SNATCH
shall s on the right hand Is 9:20

SNOW
leprous as s Ex 4:6; Num 12:10; 2 Kgs 5:27
in the time of s 2 Sam 23:20
wherein the s is hid Job 6:16
wash myself with s water Job 9:30

Drought and heat consume the s waters Job 24:19
saith to the s, Be thou on the earth Job 37:6
the treasures of the s Job 38:22
I shall be whiter than s Ps 51:7
He giveth s like wool Ps 147:16
cold of s in the time of harvest Prov 25:13
As s in summer Prov 26:1
She is not afraid of the s Prov 31:21
your sins shall be white as s Is 1:18
as the s from heaven, and returneth not Is 55:10
Will a man leave the s of Lebanon Jer 18:14
Nazarites were purer than s Lam 4:7
garment was white as s Dan 7:9; Matt 28:3; Mark 9:3

SNUFFED
they s up the wind like dragons Jer 14:6
ye have s at it, saith the Lord Mal 1:13

SOAKED
land shall be s with blood Is 34:7

SOAP
take thee much s, yet Jer 2:22
fire, and like fullers' s Mal 3:2

SOBER
s, it is for your cause 2 Cor 5:13
let us watch and be s 1 Thess 5:6
s, of good behaviour, given to 1 Tim 3:2
good men, s, just, holy Titus 1:8
aged men be s Titus 2:2
teach the young women to be s Titus 2:4
be ye therefore s, and watch 1 Pet 4:7

SOCHO so´-ko
same as SHOCHO 1 Chr 4:18

SOCHOH so´-ko
same as SHOCHO 1 Kgs 4:10

SOCOH so´-ko
same as SHOCO Josh 15:35

SODI so´-di
an acquaintance Num 13:10

SODOM sod´-om
burning Gen 10:19

SODOMA sod´-o-ma
same as SODOM Rom 9:29

SOFT
God maketh my heart s Job 23:16
will he speak s words Job 41:3
thou makest it s with showers Ps 65:10
A s answer turneth away wrath Prov 15:1
a s tongue breaketh the bone Prov 25:15

SOFTLY
I will lead on s Gen 33:14
went s unto him Judg 4:21
in sackcloth, and went s 1 Kgs 21:27
I shall go s all my years Is 38:15

SOIL
planted in a good s Ezek 17:8

SOJOURN
This one fellow came in to s Gen 19:9
S in this land, and I will be with thee Gen 26:3
to s in the land are we come Gen 47:4
s there with a few, and became there a nation Deut 26:5
I go to s where I may find place Judg 17:9
s wheresoever thou canst s 2 Kgs 8:1
Woe is me, that I s Ps 120:5
feet shall carry her afar off to s Is 23:7
place whither ye desire to go and to s Jer 42:22
They shall no more s there Lam 4:15
By faith he s in land of promise Heb 11:9
pass the time of your s here in fear 1 Pet 1:17

SOJOURNER
I am a stranger and a s Gen 23:4; Ps 39:12

SOLD
for he hath s us Gen 31:15
whom ye s into Egypt Gen 45:4
The land shall not be s for ever Lev 25:23
shall not be s as bondmen Lev 25:42
possession, shall be s or redeemed Lev 27:28
be s unto thee and serve thee Deut 15:12
except their Rock had s them Deut 32:30
thou hast s thyself to work evil 1 Kgs 21:20
or shall they be s unto us? Neh 5:8
For we are s Esth 7:4
have ye s yourselves Is 50:1
Ye have s yourselves for nought Is 52:3
our wood is s unto us Lam 5:4
and s a girl for wine Joel 3:3
they s the righteous for silver Amos 2:6
Are not two sparrows s for a farthing? Matt 10:29
went and s all that he had Matt 13:46
his lord commanded him to be s Matt 18:25
cast out all them that s Matt 21:12; Mark 11:15
might have been s for much Matt 26:9; Mark 14:5
they bought, they s, they planted Luke 17:28
And s their possessions Acts 2:45
s under sin Rom 7:14
Whatsoever is s in the shambles 1 Cor 10:25

SOLDIER
to require of the king a band of s Ezra 8:22
having s under me Matt 8:9; Luke 7:8
And the s likewise demanded Luke 3:14
a devout s Acts 10:7
as a good s of Jesus Christ 2 Tim 2:3

SOLE
dove found no rest for the s of her foot Gen 8:9
s of his foot to the crown 2 Sam 14:25; Is 1:6

SOLEMN
upon the harp with a s sound Ps 92:3

SOLEMNITY
when a holy s is kept Is 30:29

SOLEMNLY
The man did s protest Gen 43:3
howbeit yet protest s unto them 1 Sam 8:9

SOLITARY
God setteth the s in families Ps 68:6
wandered in the wilderness in a s way Ps 107:4
The wilderness and s place shall be glad Is 35:1

SOLOMON sol´-om-on
peaceable 2 Sam 5:14

SOME
S evil beast Gen 37:20
and gathered, s more, s less Ex 16:17
found s good thing 1 Kgs 14:13
S trust in chariots Ps 20:7
I looked for s to take pity Ps 69:20
s to everlasting life, and s to shame Dan 12:2
S say thou art John the Baptist Matt 16:14; Mark 8:28; Luke 9:19
s doubted Matt 28:17
s of you that believe not John 6:64
S therefore cried one thing, and s another Acts 19:32; 21:34
what if s did not believe? Rom 3:3
s would even dare to die Rom 5:7
such were s of you 1 Cor 6:11
s have not the knowledge of God 1 Cor 15:34
s, prophets; and s, evangelists Eph 4:11
S men's sins are open 1 Tim 5:24
as the manner of s is Heb 10:25
as s men count slackness 2 Pet 3:9

SOMEBODY
S hath touched me Luke 8:46
boasting himself to be s Acts 5:36

SOMETIME
s were far off Eph 2:13
ye were s in darkness Eph 5:8
s alienated Col 1:21

SOMEWHAT
I have s to say 1 Kgs 2:14
these who seemed to be s Gal 2:6
I have s against thee Rev 2:4

SON
s of God Gen 6:2; Job 1:6; 2:1; 38:7; John 1:12; Phil 2:15; 1 John 3:1
his s come to honour Job 14:21
Kiss the S, lest he be angry Ps 2:12
save the s of thine handmaid Ps 86:16
the s of thine handmaid Ps 116:16
A wise s Prov 10:1; 13:1; 15:20
A foolish s Prov 17:25; 19:13
s of my womb? And what, s of my vows Prov 31:2
unto us a s is given Is 9:6
s of the morning Is 14:12
s of the house of the Rechabites Jer 35:5
s to pass through fire Ezek 20:31; 23:37
the s of the living God Hos 1:10
as a man spareth his s Mal 3:17
no man knoweth the S Matt 11:27
the carpenter's s Matt 13:55
This is my beloved S Matt 17:5
Christ, whose s is he? Matt 22:42
carpenter, the s of Mary Mark 6:3
Is not this Joseph's s? Luke 4:22
only s of his mother Luke 7:12
if the s of peace Luke 10:6
he also is a s of Abraham Luke 19:9
only begotten S John 1:18; 3:18
the S quickeneth whom he will John 5:21
the S abideth ever John 8:35
If the S therefore shall make you free John 8:36
the s of perdition John 17:12; 2 Thess 2:3
s of consolation Acts 4:36
in the gospel of his S Rom 1:9
God sending his own S Rom 8:3
conformed to the image of his S Rom 8:29
spared not his own S Rom 8:32
as my beloved s I warn you 1 Cor 4:14
the adoption of s Gal 4:5
if a s, then an heir Gal 4:7
the kingdom of his dear S Col 1:13
bringing many s unto glory Heb 2:10
Though he were a S, yet learned he obedience Heb 5:8
refused to be called the s Heb 11:24
scourgeth every s Heb 12:6
antichrist, that denieth the Father and the S 1 John 2:22
He that hath the S hath life 1 John 5:12

SONGS
now am I their s Job 30:9
who giveth s in the night Job 35:10
with s of deliverance Ps 32:7
Sing unto him a new s Ps 33:3; Is 42:10
he hath put a new s in my mouth Ps 40:3
I was the s of the drunkards Ps 69:12
my s in the night Ps 77:6
my s in house of my pilgrimage Ps 119:54
the Lord's s in a strange land Ps 137:4
that singeth s to an heavy heart Prov 25:20
sing many s Is 23:16
come to Zion with s Is 35:10
as a very lovely s Ezek 33:32
s of the temple Amos 8:3
psalms and hymns and spiritual s Eph 5:19; Col 3:16

SOON
How is it that ye are come so s to day? Ex 2:18

my maker would **s** take me away Job 32:22
shall **s** be cut down Ps 37:2
go astray as **s** as they be born Ps 58:3
Ethiopia shall **s** stretch out her hands Ps 68:31
it is **s** cut off Ps 90:10
They **s** forgat his works Ps 106:13
He that is **s** angry Prov 14:17

SOPATER so´-pa-ter
a good parentage Acts 20:4

SOPHERETH so-fer´-eth
scribe Ezra 2:55

SORE
one shall know his own **s** 2 Chr 6:29
wounds, and bruises, and putrifying **s** Is 1:6
laid at his gate, full of **s** Luke 16:20

SOREK so´-rek
choice vine Judg 16:4

SORROW
multiply thy **s** Gen 3:16
with **s** to the grave Gen 42:38; 44:29,31
I would harden myself in **s** Job 6:10
God distributeth **s** in his anger Job 21:17
s is turned into joy Job 41:22
having **s** in my heart daily? Ps 13:2
yet is their strength labour and **s** Ps 90:10
I found trouble and **s** Ps 116:3
to eat the bread of **s** Ps 127:2
maketh rich, addeth no **s** Prov 10:22
Who hath **s**? Prov 23:29
all his days are **s** Eccl 2:23
S is better than laughter Eccl 7:3
remove **s** from thy heart Eccl 11:10
day of grief and of desperate **s** Is 17:11
s and sighing shall flee away Is 35:10; 51:11
a man of **s** Is 53:3
thy **s** is incurable Jer 30:15
there is **s** on the sea Jer 49:23
any **s** like unto my **s** Lam 1:12
these are the beginning of **s** Matt 24:8; Mark 13:8
sleeping for **s** Luke 22:45
s hath filled your heart John 16:6
swallowed up with overmuch **s** 2 Cor 2:7
godly **s** worketh repentance 2 Cor 7:10
pierced themselves through with many **s** 1 Tim 6:10

SORROWFUL
woman of a **s** spirit 1 Sam 1:15
I am poor and **s** Ps 69:29
even in laughter the heart is **s** Prov 14:13
I have replenished every **s** soul Jer 31:25
I will gather them that are **s** Zeph 3:18
he went away **s** Matt 19:22; Luke 18:23
and he began to be **s** Matt 26:37
My soul is exceeding **s** Matt 26:38; Mark 14:34
ye shall be **s** John 16:20

SORRY
I will be **s** for my sin Ps 38:18
who shall be **s** for thee? Is 51:19

SORT
two of every **s** Gen 6:19
to offer so willingly after this **s** 1 Chr 29:14
God that can deliver after this **s** Dan 3:29
lewd fellows of the baser **s** Acts 17:5
ye sorrowed after a godly **s** 2 Cor 7:11; 3 John 1:6
of this **s** are they 2 Tim 3:6

SOSIPATER so-si´-pat-er
savior of a father Rom 16:21

SOSTHENES sos´-then-ees
of sound strength Acts 18:17

SOTAI so´-ta-i
deviator Ezra 2:55

SOTTISH
they are **s** children Jer 4:22

SOUGHT
he **s** where to weep Gen 43:30
the Lord met him, and **s** to kill him Ex 4:24
the Lord hath **s** him a man 1 Sam 13:14
we **s** him not after the due order 1 Chr 15:13
and **s** him, he was found of them 2 Chr 15:4
s him with their whole desire 2 Chr 15:15
in his disease he **s** not the Lord 2 Chr 16:12
as long as he **s** the Lord 2 Chr 26:5
I **s** the Lord, and he heard me Ps 34:4
In the day of my trouble I **s** the Lord Ps 77:2
s out of all them that have pleasure Ps 111:2
s out many inventions Eccl 7:29
preacher **s** to find acceptable words Eccl 12:10
thou shalt be called, **S** out Is 62:12
I am **s** of them that asked not Is 65:1
have not **s** the Lord Jer 10:21
they **s** their meat to relieve their souls Lam 1:19
I **s** for a man among them Ezek 22:30
neither have ye **s** that which was lost Ezek 34:4
s of him a sign from heaven Luke 11:16
he came and **s** fruit thereon Luke 13:6
s to see Jesus Luke 19:3
s it not by faith Rom 9:32
though he **s** it carefully with tears Heb 12:17

SOUL
man became a living **s** Gen 2:7
a ransom for his **s** Ex 30:12
with all your **s** Deut 11:13
thy friend, which is as thine own **s** Deut 13:6
with all thy **s** Deut 30:2; Matt 22:37
his **s** was grieved Judg 10:16
loved him as his own **s** 1 Sam 18:1; 20:17
with all their **s** 1 Kgs 8:48
set your heart and your **s** to seek the Lord 1 Chr 22:19
life unto the bitter in **s** Job 3:20
In whose hand is the **s** Job 12:10
if your **s** were in my **s** stead Job 16:4
what his **s** desireth, even that he doeth Job 23:13
wishing a curse to his **s** Job 31:30
his **s** draweth near unto the grave Job 33:22
To deliver their **s** from death Ps 33:19
redeemeth the **s** of his servants Ps 34:22
the redemption of their **s** is precious Ps 49:8
my **s** waiteth upon God Ps 62:1
my **s** thirsteth for thee Ps 63:1
the **s** of thy turtledove Ps 74:19
Bless the Lord, O my **s** Ps 103:1; 104:1
Return unto thy rest, O my **s** Ps 116:7
thou hast delivered my **s** from death Ps 116:8
Let my **s** live Ps 119:175
no man cared for my **s** Ps 142:4
The liberal **s** shall be made fat Prov 11:25
s be without knowledge Prov 19:2
cold waters to thirsty **s** Prov 25:25
hear, and your **s** shall live Is 55:3
satisfy the afflicted **s** Is 58:10
he hath delivered the **s** of the poor Jer 20:13
their **s** shall be as a watered garden Jer 31:12
all **s** are mine Ezek 18:4
they have devoured **s** Ezek 22:25
thou hast sinned against thy **s** Hab 2:10
to destroy both **s** and body Matt 10:28
lose his own **s** Matt 16:26; Mark 8:36
My **s** is exceeding sorrowful Matt 26:38; Mark 14:34
In your patience possess ye your **s** Luke 21:19
of one heart and of one **s** Acts 4:32
Let every **s** be subject Rom 13:1
that your whole spirit and **s** and body be preserved 1 Thess 5:23
an anchor of the **s** Heb 6:19
they watch for your **s** Heb 13:17

shall save a **s** from death James 5:20
which war against the **s** 1 Pet 2:11
commit the keeping of their **s** to him 1 Pet 4:19
beguiling unstable **s** 2 Pet 2:14
even as thy **s** prospereth 3 John 1:2

SOUND (adj)
s wisdom Prov 2:7; 3:21; 8:14
A **s** heart is the life of the flesh Prov 14:30
s doctrine 1 Tim 1:10; 2 Tim 4:3; Titus 1:9; 2:1
of a **s** mind 2 Tim 1:7
form of **s** words 2 Tim 1:13

SOUND (n)
the **s** of a shaken leaf Lev 26:36
s of abundance of rain 1 Kgs 18:41
a dreadful **s** is in his ears Job 15:21
that know the joyful **s** Ps 89:15
harp with a solemn **s** Ps 92:3
s of the grinding is low Eccl 12:4
s of battle is in the land Jer 50:22
s of a cry cometh from Babylon Jer 51:54
He heard the **s** of the trumpet Ezek 33:5
thou hearest the **s** thereof, but canst not tell John 3:8
suddenly there came a **s** from heaven Acts 2:2
their **s** went into all the earth Rom 10:18
an uncertain **s** 1 Cor 14:8

SOUND (v)
trumpet **s** long Ex 19:19
s an alarm in my holy mountain Joel 2:1
do not **s** a trumpet before thee Matt 6:2
from you **s** out word of the Lord 1 Thess 1:8

SOUR
the **s** grape is ripening Is 18:5
The fathers have eaten a **s** grape Jer 31:29; Ezek 18:2
Their drink is **s** Hos 4:18

SOW
plow iniquity, and **s** wickedness Job 4:8
Light is **s** for the righteous Ps 97:11
s in tears shall reap in joy Ps 126:5
he that **s** discord among the brethren Prov 6:19
he that observeth the wind shall not **s** Eccl 11:4
In morning **s** thy seed Eccl 11:6
Blessed are ye that **s** beside all waters Is 32:20
s not among thorns Jer 4:3
have **s** wheat, but shall reap thorns Jer 12:13
S to yourselves in righteousness, reap in mercy Hos 10:12
that no more of thy name be **s** Nah 1:14
Ye have **s** much, and bring in little Hag 1:6
they **s** not Matt 6:26
sower went forth to **s** Matt 13:3; Mark 4:3; Luke 8:5
He that **s** the good seed Matt 13:37
both he that **s** and he that reapeth John 4:36
that which thou **s** is not quickened 1 Cor 15:36
He which **s** sparingly 2 Cor 9:6
whatsoever a man **s**, that shall he also reap Gal 6:7

SOWER
that it may give seed to the **s** Is 55:10
Cut off the **s** from Babylon Jer 50:16
he that ministereth seed to the **s** 2 Cor 9:10

SPAIN spane
European country at western end of Mediterranean Rom 15:24

SPAKE
then **s** I with my tongue Ps 39:3
he **s** unadvisedly with his lips Ps 106:33
s often one to another Mal 3:16
Never man **s** like this man John 7:46
I **s** as a child 1 Cor 13:11
refused him that **s** on earth Heb 12:25

holy men of God s as they were moved by the Holy Ghost 2 Pet 1:21

SPAN
and meted out heaven with the s Is 40:12
and children of a s long? Lam 2:20

SPARE
I will s all the place for their sakes Gen 18:26
s me according to the greatness of thy mercy Neh 13:22
s me, that I may recover strength Ps 39:13
He that s his rod hateth his son Prov 13:24
let not thy soul s for his crying Prov 19:18
S thy people Joel 2:17
I will s them as a man s Mal 3:17
bread enough and to s Luke 15:17
s not his own Son Rom 8:32
if God s not the natural branches Rom 11:21
if God s not the angels that sinned 2 Pet 2:4

SPARK
trouble, as the s fly upward Job 5:7
the s of his fire shall not shine Job 18:5
the maker of it as a s Is 1:31
compass yourselves about with s Is 50:11

SPEAK
to s unto the Lord Gen 18:37
I know that he can s well Ex 4:14
spake to Moses as a man s unto his friend Ex 33:11
s ye unto the rock Num 20:8
a man cannot s to him 1 Sam 25:17
oh that God would s Job 11:5
Will ye s wickedly for God? Job 13:7
Days should s Job 32:7
God s once, yea, twice Job 33:14
If a man s, surely he shall be swallowed up Job 37:20
I will hear what God the Lord will s Ps 85:8
S not in the ears of a fool Prov 23:9
causing the lips of those that are asleep to s Song 7:9
s the language of Canaan Is 19:18
I that s in righteousness Is 63:1
while they are yet s, I will hear Is 65:24
I will not s any more in his name Jer 20:9
at the end it shall s Hab 2:3
S ye every man the truth Zech 8:16; Eph 4:25
s the word only, and my servant Matt 8:8
how or what ye shall s Matt 10:19; Mark 13:11
out of the abundance of the heart the mouth s Matt 12:34; Luke 6:45
every idle word that men shall s Matt 12:36
can lightly s evil of me Mark 9:39
when all men shall s well of you! Luke 6:26
We s that we do know John 3:11
that they s henceforth to no man in this name Acts 4:17
we cannot but s Acts 4:20
s forth the words of truth and soberness Acts 26:25
that ye all s the same thing 1 Cor 1:10
let him s to himself, and to God 1 Cor 14:28
we also believe, and therefore s 2 Cor 4:13
s the truth in love Eph 4:15
he being dead yet s Heb 11:4
that s better things than that of Abel Heb 12:24
slow to s James 1:19

SPEAR
nor s found in the hand of any 1 Sam 13:22
thou comest to me with a sword, and with a s 1 Sam 17:45
cutteth the s in sunder Ps 46:9
s into pruning hooks Is 2:4; Mic 4:3

SPECIAL
to be a s people unto himself Deut 7:6

God wrought s miracles by the hand of Paul Acts 19:11

SPECIALLY
Saviour of all men, s of those that believe 1 Tim 4:10
and s for those of his own house 1 Tim 5:8
a brother beloved, s to me Phile 1:16

SPECTACLE
we are made a s unto the world 1 Cor 4:9

SPEECH
earth was of one language, and of one s Gen 11:1
I am slow of s Ex 4:10
not in dark s Num 12:8
my s shall distil as dew Deut 32:2
Solomon's s pleased the Lord 1 Kgs 3:10
the s of one that is desperate Job 6:26
with s wherewith he can do no good Job 15:3
Day unto day uttereth s Ps 19:2
no s nor language where their voice Ps 19:3
Excellent s becometh not a fool Prov 17:7
thy s is comely Song 4:3
of a deeper s than thou canst perceive Is 33:19
thy s bewrayeth thee Matt 26:73
not with excellency of s 1 Cor 2:1
not the s of them which are puffed up 1 Cor 4:19
we use great plainness of s 2 Cor 3:12
his s contemptible 2 Cor 10:10
Let your s be always with grace Col 4:6
Sound s, that cannot be condemned Titus 2:8

SPEECHLESS
wedding garment? And he was s Matt 22:12
beckoned unto them, and remained s Luke 1:22
stood s, hearing a voice, but seeing no man Acts 9:7

SPEED
send me good s this day Gen 24:12

SPEEDILY
deliver me s Ps 31:2
hear me s Ps 69:17; 143:7
let thy tender mercies s prevent us Ps 79:8
when I call answer me s Ps 102:2
because sentence against an evil work is not executed s Eccl 8:11
thine health shall spring forth s Is 58:8
let us go s to pray Zech 8:21
he will avenge them s Luke 18:8

SPEND
They s their days in wealth Job 21:13
they shall s their days in prosperity Job 36:11
we s our years as a tale that is told Ps 90:9
Wherefore do ye s money for that which is not bread? Is 55:2
I will very gladly s and be spent for you 2 Cor 12:15

SPENT
water was s in the bottle Gen 21:15
and are s without hope Job 7:6
my life is s with grief Ps 31:10
I have s my strength for nought Is 49:4
s their time in nothing else Acts 17:21

SPILT
as water s on the ground 2 Sam 14:14

SPIN
women that were wise hearted did s Ex 35:25
they toil not, neither do they s Matt 6:28; Luke 12:27

SPIRIT
My s shall not always strive Gen 6:3
every one whom his s made willing Ex 35:21
take of the s which is upon thee Num 11:17
he had another s with him Num 14:24
the God of the s of all flesh Num 16:22; 27:16

a man in whom is the s Num 27:18
nor was there s in them any more Josh 5:1
there came forth a s 1 Kgs 22:21; 2 Chr 18:20
let a double portion of thy s be upon me 2 Kgs 2:9
gavest also thy good s to instruct them Neh 9:20
a s passed before my face Job 4:15
thou turnest thy s against God Job 15:13
whose s came from thee? Job 26:4
there is a s in man Job 32:8
Into thine hand I commit my s Ps 31:5; Luke 23:46
in whose s there is no guile Ps 32:2
renew a right s within me Ps 51:10
whose s was not stedfast Ps 78:8
Who maketh his angels s Ps 104:4; Heb 1:7
they provoked his s Ps 106:33
Whither shall I go from the s? Ps 139:7
the Lord weigheth the s Prov 16:2
and a haughty s before a fall Prov 16:18
he that ruleth his s better than he Prov 16:32
the humble in s Prov 29:23
Who knoweth the s of man that goeth upward Eccl 3:21
patient in s is better than the proud Eccl 7:8
no man that hath power over the s to retain the s Eccl 8:8
what is the way of the s Eccl 11:5
the s shall return unto God Eccl 12:7
s of judgment Is 4:4; 28:6
the s of wisdom Is 11:2; Eph 1:17
his s it hath gathered them Is 34:16
I have put my s upon him Is 42:1
a contrite and humble s Is 57:15
the s should fail before me Is 57:16
the S of the Lord God is upon me Is 61:1; Luke 4:18
So the s lifted me up Ezek 3:14; 8:3; 11:1
a new s Ezek 11:19; 18:31; 36:26
a man walking in the s and falsehood Mic 2:11
saying, It is a s Matt 14:26
the s indeed is willing Matt 26:41
S like a dove descending upon him Mark 1:10
they supposed it had been a s Mark 6:49
sighed deeply in his s Mark 8:12
The s truly is ready Mark 14:38
in the s and power of Elijah Luke 1:17
he came by the S into the temple Luke 2:27
her s came again Luke 8:55
ye know not what manner of s Luke 9:55
Jesus rejoiced in s Luke 10:21
for a s hath not flesh and bones Luke 24:39
I saw the S descending from heaven John 1:32
God giveth not the S by measure John 3:34
God is a S, and they that worship him John 4:24
It is the s that quickeneth John 6:63
S of truth John 14:17; 15:26; 16:13; 1 John 4:6
began to speak as the S gave them utterance Acts 2:4
not able to resist the wisdom and the s Acts 6:10
his s was stirred in him Acts 17:16
neither angel, nor s Acts 23:8
walk not after the flesh, but after the S Rom 8:1
the law of the S of life in Christ Rom 8:2
the S of him that raised up Jesus Rom 8:11
the S itself beareth witness Rom 8:16
the S itself maketh intercession for us Rom 8:26
fervent in s Rom 12:11
in demonstration of the S 1 Cor 2:4
the S searcheth all things 1 Cor 2:10
in the s of meekness 1 Cor 4:21; Gal 6:1
that is joined unto the Lord is one s 1 Cor 6:17
glorify God in body, and in your s 1 Cor 6:20
diversities of gifts, but the same S 1 Cor 12:4
to another discerning of s 1 Cor 12:10
in the s he speaketh mysteries 1 Cor 14:2

last Adam was made a quickening s 1 Cor 15:45
the letter killeth, but the s giveth life 2 Cor 3:6
where the S of the Lord is, there is liberty 2 Cor 3:17
having begun in the S Gal 3:3
Walk in the S Gal 5:16
the fruit of the S is love Gal 5:22
If we live in the S, let us walk in the S Gal 5:25
he that soweth to the S shall of the S reap life Gal 6:8
the s that now worketh in the children Eph 2:2
access by one S unto the Father Eph 2:18
a habitation of God through the S Eph 2:22
by his S in the inner man Eph 3:16
the unity of the S Eph 4:3
one body, and one S Eph 4:4
renewed in the s of your mind Eph 4:23
grieve not the holy S of God Eph 4:30
be filled with the S Eph 5:18
take sword of the S Eph 6:17
that ye stand fast in one s Phil 1:27
if any fellowship of the S Phil 2:1
your love in the S Col 1:8
absent in flesh, yet am I with you in the s Col 2:5
Quench not the S 1 Thess 5:19
through sanctification of the S 2 Thess 2:13; 1 Pet 1:2
justified in the S 1 Tim 3:16
giving heed to seducing s 1 Tim 4:1
in charity, in s, in faith 1 Tim 4:12
The Lord Jesus Christ be with thy s 2 Tim 4:22
ministering s, sent forth to minister Heb 1:14
dividing asunder of soul and s Heb 4:12
who through the eternal S offered himself Heb 9:14
in subjection to the Father of s Heb 12:9
to the s of just men made perfect Heb 12:23
the body without the s is dead James 2:26
The s that dwelleth in us lusteth James 4:5
ornament of a meek and quiet s 1 Pet 3:4
but quickened by the S 1 Pet 3:18
preached unto the s in prison 1 Pet 3:19
live according to God in the s 1 Pet 4:6
by the S which he hath given us 1 John 3:24
believe not every s, but try the s 1 John 4:1
Hereby know ye the S of God 1 John 4:2
every s that confesseth not 1 John 4:3
it is the S that beareth witness 1 John 5:6
the s, and the water, and the blood 1 John 5:8
sensual, having not the S Jude 1:19
I was in the S on the Lord's day Rev 1:10
hear what the S saith Rev 2:7,11,17,29; 3:6,13,22
I was in the S: and, behold, a throne Rev 4:2
the S of life from God entered Rev 11:11
Yea, saith the S Rev 14:13
the S and the bride say, Come Rev 22:17

SPIRITUAL
the s man is mad Hos 9:7
impart unto you some s gift Rom 1:11
For we know that the law is s Rom 7:14
partakers of their s things Rom 15:27
comparing s things with s 1 Cor 2:13
he that is s judgeth all things 1 Cor 2:15
could not speak unto you as unto s 1 Cor 3:1
all eat the same s meat 1 Cor 10:3
Now concerning s gifts 1 Cor 12:1
desire s gifts 1 Cor 14:1
it is raised a s body 1 Cor 15:44
that was not first which is s 1 Cor 15:46
ye which are s, restore such a one Gal 6:1
in psalms and hymns and s songs Eph 5:19
against s wickedness in high places Eph 6:12
holy priesthood, to offer up s sacrifices 1 Pet 2:5

SPIRITUALLY
but to be s minded is life Rom 8:6
because they are s discerned 1 Cor 2:14
which s is called Sodom and Egypt Rev 11:8

SPITE
thou beholdest mischief and s Ps 10:14

SPOIL (n)
necks of them that take the s Judg 5:30
people flew upon the s 1 Sam 14:32
of the s which they had brought 2 Chr 15:11
three days in gathering of the s 2 Chr 20:25
with the s clothed all that were naked 2 Chr 28:15
take the s of them for a prey Esth 3:13; 8:11
on the s laid they not their hand Esth 9:10
plucked the s out of his teeth Job 29:17
as one that findeth great s Ps 119:162
than to divide the s with the proud Prov 16:19
he shall have no need of s Prov 31:11
the s of the poor is in your houses Is 3:14
Who gave Jacob for a s Is 42:24
he shall divide the s with the strong Is 53:12

SPOIL (v)
ye shall s the Egyptians Ex 3:22
The stouthearted are s Ps 76:5
the little foxes, that s the vines Song 2:15
Woe to thee that s, and thou wast not s! Is 33:1
this is a people robbed and s Is 42:22
when thou art s, what wilt thou do? Jer 4:30
thou hast s many nations Hab 2:8
because the mighty are s Zech 11:2
having s principalities Col 2:15

SPOKEN
hath he s, and shall he not make it good? Num 23:19
out of my complaint and grief have I s 1 Sam 1:16
people answered and said, It is well s 1 Kgs 18:24
wouldest thou be s for to the king 2 Kgs 4:13
God hath s once Ps 62:11
my mouth hath s, when I was in trouble Ps 66:14
Glorious things are s of thee Ps 87:3
a word s in due season Prov 15:23
a word fitly s is like apples of gold Prov 25:11
take no heed unto all words that are s Eccl 7:21
I, even I, have s Is 48:15
What have we s so much against thee? Mal 3:13
shall be s of for a memorial of her Mark 14:9
for a sign which shall be s against Luke 2:34
these things cannot be s against Acts 19:36
your faith is s of throughout the whole world Rom 1:8
Let not then your good be evil s of Rom 14:16
the word s by angels was stedfast Heb 2:2

SPOKESMAN
he shall be thy s Ex 4:16

SPONGE
one of them ran, and took a s Matt 27:48
one ran and filled a s Mark 15:36
they filled a s with vinegar John 19:29

SPORT
Isaac was s with Rebekah Gen 26:8
Against whom do ye s yourselves? Is 57:4
s themselves with their own deceivings 2 Pet 2:13

SPOT
lambs of the first year without s Num 28:3,9,11; 29:17,26
their s is not the s of his children Deut 32:5
lift up thy face without s Job 11:15
or the leopard his s? Jer 13:23
glorious church, not having s Eph 5:27
keep this commandment without s 1 Tim 6:14
lamb without blemish and without s 1 Pet 1:19
in peace, without s, and blameless 2 Pet 3:14
These are s in your feasts of charity Jude 1:12

SPOUSE
Come with me from Lebanon, my s Song 4:8
my sister, my s Song 5:1
your s shall commit adultery Hos 4:13

SPRANG
fruit that s up and increased Mark 4:8
he called for a light, and s in Acts 16:29
our Lord s out of Judah Heb 7:14
Therefore s there even of one Heb 11:12

SPREAD
s abroad her wings Deut 32:11
s it before the Lord 2 Kgs 19:14; Is 37:14
which alone s out the heavens Job 9:8
s his cloud upon it Job 26:9
My root was s out by the waters Job 29:19
he s his light upon it Job 36:30
hast thou with him s out the sky? Job 37:18
He s a cloud for a covering Ps 105:39
they have s a net by the wayside Ps 140:5
when ye s forth your hands I will hide Is 1:15
they could not s the sail Is 33:23
s out hands all the day Is 65:2
they shall s them before the sun Jer 8:2
a place to s nets upon Ezek 26:14
s their garments Matt 21:8; Mark 11:8; Luke 19:36
But that it s no further Acts 4:17

SPRIGS
cut off the s with pruning hooks Is 18:5
branches, and shot forth s Ezek 17:6

SPRING (n)
about the s of the day 1 Sam 9:26
Hast thou entered into the s of the sea? Job 38:16
all my s are in thee Ps 87:7
He sendeth the s into valleys Ps 104:10
a troubled fountain, and a corrupt s Prov 25:26
like a s of water Is 58:11
seed should s and grow up Mark 4:27

SPRING (v)
S up, O well Num 21:17
neither doth trouble s out of the ground Job 5:6
before they s forth I tell you Is 42:9
a new thing, now it shall s forth Is 43:19
let righteousness s up together Is 45:8
thine health shall s forth Is 58:8

SPRINKLE
s dust upon their heads Job 2:12
So shall he s many nations Is 52:15
Then will I s clean water Ezek 36:25

SPROUT
a tree will s again Job 14:7

SPY
Moses sent to s out the land Num 13:16
to s secretly, saying, Go view Josh 2:1
who came in privily to s Gal 2:4

STABILITY
the s of thy times Is 33:6

STABLE
world also shall be s 1 Chr 16:30
a s for camels Ezek 25:5

STACHYS sta´-kis
an ear of corn Rom 16:9

STAFF
with my s I passed over Gen 32:10
your s in your hand Ex 12:11
bare it between two upon a s Num 13:23
put forth the end of the s Judg 6:21
that leaneth upon a s 2 Sam 3:29
lay my s upon the face of the child 2 Kgs 4:29
thou trustest upon the s 2 Kgs 18:21
thy rod and thy s they comfort me Ps 23:4
the stay and the s, the whole stay of bread Is 3:1

the s of his shoulder Is 9:4
the s in their hand is mine indignation Is 10:5
as if the s should lift up itself Is 10:15
Lord hath broken the s of the wicked Is 14:5
How is the strong s broken Jer 48:17
took my s, even Beauty Zech 11:10
save a s only Mark 6:8
leaning upon the top of his s Heb 11:21

STAGGER
s like a drunken man Job 12:25; Ps 107:27
they s, but not with strong drink Is 29:9

STAIN
and the shadow of death s it Job 3:5
to s the pride of all glory Is 23:9
I will s all my raiment Is 63:3

STAIRS
they went up with winding s 1 Kgs 6:8
Then stood up upon the s Neh 9:4
the secret places of the s Song 2:14

STAKES
not one of the s thereof Is 33:20
strengthen thy s Is 54:2

STALK
ears of corn came up upon one s Gen 41:5
and hid them with the s of flax Josh 2:6
reap the whirlwind: it hath no s Hos 8:7

STALL
there shall be no herd in the s Hab 3:17
grow up as calves of the s Mal 4:2

STAMMERING
with s lips and another tongue Is 28:11
of a s tongue Is 33:19

STAMP
and burnt it with fire, and s it Deut 9:21
I did s as the mire 2 Sam 22:43

STAND
s still, and see the salvation Ex 14:13; 2 Chr 20:17
Ye s this day all of you before the Lord Deut 29:10
s thou still a while 1 Sam 9:27
priests could not s to minister 1 Kgs 8:11; 2 Chr 5:14
before whom I s 1 Kgs 17:1; 18:15; 2 Kgs 3:14; 5:16
how then shall we s 2 Kgs 10:4
in Jerusalem and Benjamin to s to it 2 Chr 34:32
to s for their life Esth 8:11
lean upon his house, but it shall not s Job 8:15
he shall s at the latter day Job 19:25
nor s in the way of sinners Ps 1:1
the ungodly shall not s in the judgment Ps 1:5
S in awe, and sin not Ps 4:4
Why s thou afar off? Ps 10:1
who shall s in his holy place? Ps 24:3
The counsel of the Lord s for ever Ps 33:11
who may s in thy sight Ps 76:7
who will s up for me Ps 94:16
shall s at the right hand of the poor Ps 109:31
Our feet shall s within thy gates Ps 122:2
O Lord, who shall s? Ps 130:3
who can s before his cold? Ps 147:17
shall s before kings Prov 22:29
who is able to s before envy? Prov 27:4
s not in an evil thing Eccl 8:3
saith the Lord God, It shall not s Is 7:7; 8:10
I s continually upon the watchtower Is 21:8
your agreement with hell shall not s Is 28:18
the word of our God shall s for ever Is 40:8
S by thyself, come not near to me Is 65:5
S ye in the ways, and see, and ask for the old Jer 6:16
shall not want a man to s before me Jer 35:19
he shall s in the glorious land Dan 11:16
for thou shalt rest, and s in thy lot Dan 12:13
he shall s and feed in the strength Mic 5:4
S, s, shall they cry Nah 2:8
Satan s at his right hand to resist him Zech 3:1
who shall s when he appeareth? Mal 3:2
house divided against itself shall not s Matt 12:25; Mark 3:25
some s here, which shall not taste of death Matt 16:28
others s idle in the marketplace Matt 20:3
how shall his kingdom s Luke 11:18
this grace wherein we s Rom 5:2
God is able to make him s Rom 14:4
faith should not s in the wisdom of men 1 Cor 2:5
Watch ye, s fast in the faith 1 Cor 16:13
I s in doubt of you Gal 4:20
S fast therefore in the liberty Gal 5:1
having done all, to s Eph 6:13
s fast in one spirit Phil 1:27
s fast in the Lord Phil 4:1; 1 Thess 3:8
the foundation of God s sure 2 Tim 2:19
the judge s before the door James 5:9
I s at the door, and knock Rev 3:20
and who shall be able to s? Rev 6:17
I saw the dead, small and great, s before God Rev 20:12

STANDARD
set up my s to the people Is 49:22
Spirit of the Lord shall lift up a s against Is 59:19
lift up a s for the people Is 62:10
set up the s toward Zion Jer 4:6; 50:2; 51:12

STATE
man at his best s is altogether vanity Ps 39:5
last s of that man is worse Matt 12:45; Luke 11:26

STATURE
men of a great s Num 13:32
or on the height of his s 1 Sam 16:7
high ones of s shall be hewn down Is 10:33
the Sabeans, men of s, shall come Is 45:14
can add one cubit unto his s Matt 6:27; Luke 12:25
Jesus increased in wisdom and s Luke 2:52
he was little of s Luke 19:3
measure of the s of the fulness of Christ Eph 4:13

STATUTE
make them know the s of God Ex 18:16
a perpetual s Lev 3:17; 16:34; 24:9
s of the heathen 2 Kgs 17:8
s, and laws, by the hand of Moses Neh 9:14
The s of the Lord are right Ps 19:8
to declare my s Ps 50:16
my s more than the countries Ezek 5:6
s that were not good Ezek 20:25
walk in the s of life Ezek 33:15
my s, which I commanded Zech 1:6

STAVES
the lawgiver, with their s Num 21:18
Am I a dog, that thou comest with s 1 Sam 17:43
strike through with his s Hab 3:14
took unto me two s Zech 11:7
neither shoes, nor yet s Matt 10:10

STAY (n)
the Lord was my s 2 Sam 22:19; Ps 18:18
take away the s and staff Is 3:1

STAY (v)
neither s thou in all the plain Gen 19:17
ye shall s no longer Ex 9:28
the plague was s Num 16:48; 25:8; 2 Sam 24:25; 1 Chr 21:22; Ps 106:30
s now thine hand 2 Sam 24:16; 1 Chr 21:15
he will not s them Job 37:4
here shall thy proud waves be s Job 38:11
who can s the bottles of heaven Job 38:37
let no man s him Prov 28:17
whose mind is s on thee Is 26:3
he s his rough wind Is 27:8
s yourselves, and wonder Is 29:9
and perverseness, and s thereon Is 30:12
in the name of the Lord, and s upon his God Is 50:10
none can s his hand Dan 4:35
heaven over you is s from dew Hag 1:10

STEAD
risen up in your fathers' s Num 32:14
if your soul were in my soul's s Job 16:4
set others in their s Job 34:24
the wicked cometh in his s Prov 11:8
we pray you in Christ's s 2 Cor 5:20

STEDFAST
spirit was not s with God Ps 78:8
living God, and s for ever Dan 6:26
word spoken by angels was s Heb 2:2
our confidence s unto the end Heb 3:14
anchor of the soul, both sure and s Heb 6:19
Whom resist s in the faith 1 Pet 5:9

STEADY
his hands were s until the going down Ex 17:12

STEAL
flee away secretly, and s away? Gen 31:27
should we s out of thy lord's house Gen 44:8
if he s to satisfy his soul Prov 6:30
lest I be poor, and s Prov 30:9
that s my words every one from Jer 23:30
thieves break through and s Matt 6:19
thief cometh not, but for to s John 10:10

STEALTH
by s that day into the city 2 Sam 19:3

STEDFAST
spirit was not s with God Ps 78:8
living God, and s for ever Dan 6:26
word spoken by angels was s Heb 2:2
our confidence s unto the end Heb 3:14
anchor of the soul, both sure and s Heb 6:19
Whom resist s in the faith 1 Pet 5:9

STEEL
bow of s is broken 2 Sam 22:35
bow of s shall strike Job 20:24
the northern iron and the s Jer 15:12

STEEP
the s places shall fall Ezek 38:20
that are poured down a s place Mic 1:4
ran violently down a s place Matt 8:32; Mark 5:13; Luke 8:33

STEP
but a s between me and death 1 Sam 20:3
thou numberest my s Job 14:16
My foot hath held his s Job 23:11
I washed my s with butter Job 29:6
see my ways, and count all my s Job 31:4
If my s hath turned out of the way Job 31:7
The s of a good man are ordered Ps 37:23
none of his s shall slide Ps 37:31
nor have our s declined Ps 44:18
they mark my s Ps 56:6
my s had well nigh slipped Ps 73:2
set us in the way of his s Ps 85:13
Order my s in thy word Ps 119:133
thy s shall not be straitened Prov 4:12
her s take hold on hell Prov 5:5
the Lord directeth his s Prov 16:9
feet of the poor, and the s of the needy Is 26:6
not in man that walketh to direct his s Jer 10:23
walk in the s of that faith Rom 4:12
walked we not in same s 2 Cor 12:18
that ye should follow his s 1 Pet 2:21

My breath is s to my wife Job 19:17
a s punishment to the workers Job 31:3
the way of man is froward and s Prov 21:8
he may do his work his s work Is 28:21
not sent to people of a s speech Ezek 3:5
clothed with s apparel Zeph 1:8
We have seen s things to day Luke 5:26
bringest certain s things to our ears Acts 17:20
persecuted them even unto s cities Acts 26:11
with diverse and s doctrines Heb 13:9
they think it s that ye run not 1 Pet 4:4
think it not s concerning the fiery trial 1 Pet 4:12

STRANGER
I am a s and a sojourner Gen 23:4; Ps 39:12
ye know the heart of a s Ex 23:9
we are s before thee 1 Chr 29:15
no s passed among them Job 15:19
The s did not lodge in the street Job 31:32
For s are risen up against me Ps 54:3
let the s spoil his labour Ps 109:11
The Lord preserveth the s Ps 146:9
to deliver thee even from the s Prov 2:16
Lest s be filled with thy wealth Prov 5:10
only thine own, and not s with thee Prov 5:17
stricken thy hand with a s Prov 6:1
from the s which flattereth Prov 7:5
He that is surety for a s shall smart Prov 11:15
s doth not intermeddle with his joy Prov 14:10
Take his garment that is surety for a s Prov 20:16; 27:13
a s, and not thine own lips Prov 27:2
your land, s devour it Is 1:7
please themselves in the children of s Is 2:6
the s shall be joined with them Is 14:1
Neither let the son of the s Is 56:3
shouldest thou be as a s in the land? Jer 14:8
by the hand of s Ezek 28:10
S have devoured his strength Hos 7:9
I was a s, and ye took me in Matt 25:35
to give glory to God, save this s Luke 17:18
s from the covenants Eph 2:12
ye are no more s and foreigners Eph 2:19
that they were s and pilgrims Heb 11:13
be not forgetful to entertain s Heb 13:2

STRANGLED
s for his lionesses Nah 2:12
from fornication, and from things s Acts 15:20; 21:25

STREAM
the s had gone over our soul Ps 124:4
waters break out, and s in the desert Is 35:6
the Gentiles like a flowing s Is 66:12
righteousness as a mighty s Amos 5:24

STREET
she uttereth her voice in the s Prov 1:20
Go out quickly in the s Luke 14:21
the s of the city was pure gold Rev 21:21
In the midst of the s of it Rev 22:2

STRENGTH
The Lord is my s Ex 15:2; Ps 28:7; 118:14
thou hast trodden down s Judg 5:21
by s shall no man prevail 1 Sam 2:9
the S of Israel will not lie 1 Sam 15:29
If I speak of s, lo, he is strong Job 9:19
With him is wisdom and s Job 12:13
girded me with s Ps 18:32
the Lord is the s of my life Ps 27:1
The Lord will give s unto his people Ps 29:11
mighty man is not delivered by much s Ps 33:16
spare me, that I may recover s Ps 39:13
God is our refuge and s Ps 46:1; 81:1
his s is in the clouds Ps 68:34
God is the s of my heart Ps 73:26
the man whose s is in thee Ps 84:5
They go from s to s Ps 84:7
s and beauty are in his sanctuary Ps 96:6
strengthenedst me with s in my soul Ps 138:3
The way of the Lord is s Prov 10:29
Wisdom is better than s Eccl 9:16
princes eat in due season, for s Eccl 10:17
a s to the poor, a s to the needy Is 25:4
he increaseth s Is 40:29
awake, put on s Is 51:9
I will destroy the s of the kingdoms Hag 2:22
he hath shewed s with his arm Luke 1:51
when ye were without s Rom 5:6
the s of sin is the law 1 Cor 15:56
thou hast a little s Rev 3:8

STRENGTHEN
s himself against the Almighty Job 15:25
s thee out of Zion Ps 20:2
bread which s man's heart Ps 104:15
Wisdom s the wise Eccl 7:19
s ye the weak hands Is 35:3
when thou art converted, s thy brethren Luke 22:32
to be s with might Eph 3:16
all things through Christ which s me Phil 4:13

STRETCH
s out her hands unto God Ps 68:31
shorter than that a man can s himself Is 28:20
he hath s out the heavens Jer 10:12; 51:15
I have s out my hand over thee Ezek 16:27
S forth thine hand Matt 12:13

STRIKE
s hands Job 17:3; Prov 22:26
shall s through kings Ps 110:5
Till a dart s through his liver Prov 7:23

STRIVE
shall not always s Gen 6:3
S not with a man without a cause Prov 3:30
S to enter in at the strait gate Luke 13:24
If a man also s for the masteries 2 Tim 2:5
the servant of the Lord must not s 2 Tim 2:24

STRONG
be s 1 Sam 4:9; Is 35:4; Dan 10:19
if I speak of strength, lo, he is s Job 9:19
as a s man to run a race Ps 19:5
The Lord s and mighty Ps 24:8
be thou my s rock Ps 31:2
thou art my s refuge Ps 71:7
the rich man's wealth is his s city Prov 10:15
The name of the Lord is a s tower Prov 18:10
the battle to the s Eccl 9:11
for that he is s in power Is 40:26
first bind the s man Matt 12:29
s in faith Rom 4:20
we are weak, but ye are s 1 Cor 4:10
s delusion 2 Thess 2:11
of milk, and not of s meat Heb 5:12
we might have a s consolation Heb 6:18

STUBBLE
as the s before the wind Ps 83:13
conceive chaff, ye shall bring forth s Is 33:11
as driven s to his bow Is 41:2
I will scatter them as the s Jer 13:24

STUDY
that ye s to be quiet, and to do 1 Thess 4:11
s to shew thyself approved unto God 2 Tim 2:15

STUMBLE
they know not at what they s Prov 4:19
they s in judgment Is 28:7
we s at noonday Is 59:10
they shall s, and fall Jer 46:6; Dan 11:19
ye have caused many to s Mal 2:8
them which s at the word 1 Pet 2:8

SUAH **soo´-ah**
sweepings 1 Chr 7:36

SUBDUE
He shall s the people Ps 47:3
he will s our iniquities Mic 7:19
he is able to s all things Phil 3:21
Who through faith s kingdoms Heb 11:33

SUBJECT
devils are s unto us Luke 10:17
not s to the law of God Rom 8:7
creature was made s to vanity Rom 8:20
every soul be s unto the higher powers Rom 13:1
spirits of the prophets are s to the prophets 1 Cor 14:32
the Son also himself be s unto him 1 Cor 15:28
as the church is s unto Christ Eph 5:24
all their lifetime s to bondage Heb 2:15
a man s to like passions James 5:17
Servants, be s to your masters 1 Pet 2:18
powers being made s to him 1 Pet 3:22
all of you be s one to another 1 Pet 5:5

SUBMIT
s themselves 2 Sam 22:45
till every one s himself Ps 68:30
wives, s yourselves Eph 5:22
s yourselves therefore to God James 4:7
s yourselves to every ordinance of man 1 Pet 2:13

SUBSCRIBE
another shall s with his hand Is 44:5
and s evidences, and seal them Jer 32:44

SUBSTANCE
their s was great Gen 13:6
Bless, Lord, his s Deut 33:11
dissolvest my s Job 30:22
leave the rest of their s to their babes Ps 17:14
My s was not hid from thee Ps 139:15
Honour the Lord with thy s Prov 3:9
he that by usury and unjust gain increaseth his s Prov 28:8
give all the s Song 8:7
Thy s and thy treasures will I give Jer 15:13
I have found me out s Hos 12:8
their s unto the Lord of the whole earth Mic 4:13
ministered unto him of their s Luke 8:3
wasted his s Luke 15:13
a better and an enduring s Heb 10:34
the s of things hoped for Heb 11:1

SUBTIL
serpent was more s than any beast Gen 3:1
Jonadab was a very s man 2 Sam 13:3
s of heart Prov 7:10

SUBTILTY
Thy brother came with s Gen 27:35
might take Jesus by s Matt 26:4
O full of all s Acts 13:10

SUBVERT
s a man in his cause Lam 3:36
the s of the hearers 2 Tim 2:14
who s whole houses Titus 1:11
he that is such is s Titus 3:11

SUCCESS
have good s Josh 1:8

SUCCOTH **sook´-oth**
booths Gen 33:17

SUCCOTH-BENOTH **sook´-oth-ben´-oth**
supreme of the universe (?) 2 Kgs 17:30

SUCHATHITES **sook´-ath-ites**
inhabitant of Sucah 1 Chr 2:55

SUCK
s honey out of the rock Deut 32:13
s of the abundance of the seas Deut 33:19
he shall s the poison of asps Job 20:16
s the milk of the Gentiles Is 60:16

SUDDEN
s fear trouble thee Job 22:10
be not afraid of s fear Prov 3:25
s destruction cometh upon them 1 Thess 5:3

SUDDENLY
shall be s destroyed Prov 29:1
evil time, when it falleth s upon them Eccl 9:12
shall s come to his temple Mal 3:1
lest coming s he find you sleeping Mark 13:36
lay hands s on no man 1 Tim 5:22

SUFFER
s me that I may speak Job 21:3
shall never s the righteous to be moved Ps 55:22
nor s my faithfulness to fail Ps 89:33
an idle soul shall s hunger Prov 19:15
will not s him to sleep Eccl 5:12
s it to be so now Matt 3:15
s me first to go and bury my father Matt 8:21; Luke 9:59
s many things Matt 16:21; Mark 8:31; Luke 9:22
s little children to come Matt 19:14; Mark 10:14; Luke 18:16
neither s ye them that are entering to go in Matt 23:13
behoved Christ to s Luke 24:46; Acts 3:18
if so be that we s with him Rom 8:17
he shall s loss 1 Cor 3:15
will not s you to be tempted 1 Cor 10:13
whether one member s, all the members s with it 1 Cor 12:26
lest they should s persecution Gal 6:12
if we s, we shall also reign 2 Tim 2:12
shall s persecution 2 Tim 3:12
them which s adversity s Heb 13:3
Christ also s for us, leaving us an example 1 Pet 2:21
he that hath s in the flesh 1 Pet 4:1

SUFFICIENCY
in the fulness of his s he shall be in straits Job 20:22
our s is of God 2 Cor 3:5
always having all s in all things 2 Cor 9:8

SUFFICIENT
Lebanon is not s to burn Is 40:16
s unto the day is the evil thereof Matt 6:34
who is s for these things? 2 Cor 2:16

SUKKIIMS sook´-i-ims
nomads 2 Chr 12:3

SUM
how great is the s of them Ps 139:17
with a great s obtained I this freedom Acts 22:28
of the things which we have spoken this is the s Heb 8:1

SUMMER
s and winter Gen 8:22; Ps 74:17
provideth meat in s Prov 6:8; 30:25
he that gathereth in s is a wise son Prov 10:5
as snow in s Prov 26:1
the s is ended Jer 8:20
ye know s is nigh Matt 24:32; Mark 13:28

SUMPTUOUSLY
fared s every day Luke 16:19

SUN
s, stand thou still Josh 10:12
the s when he goeth forth in his might Judg 5:31
he is green before the s Job 8:16
that they may not see the s Ps 58:8
For the Lord God is a s and shield Ps 84:11
the s shall not smite thee by day Ps 121:6
there is no new thing under the s Eccl 1:9
a pleasant thing it is for the eyes to behold the s Eccl 11:7
while the s, or the light, or the moon Eccl 12:2
because the s hath looked upon me Song 1:6
clear as the s Song 6:10
her s is gone down while it was yet day Jer 15:9
s and the moon shall be darkened Joel 2:10; 3:15
the S of righteousness Mal 4:2
he maketh his s to rise on the evil Matt 5:45
then shall righteous shine as s Matt 13:43
let not the s go down on your wrath Eph 4:26

SUPERFLUITY
s of naughtiness James 1:21

SUPERSTITIOUS
in all things ye are too s Acts 17:22

SUPPLICATION
I have heard thy prayer and thy s 1 Kgs 9:3
I would make s to my judge Job 9:15
the Lord hath heard my s Ps 6:9
to seek by prayer and s Dan 9:3
spirit of grace and of s Zech 12:10
with all prayer and s in the Spirit Eph 6:18
when he had offered up prayers and s Heb 5:7

SUPPLY (n)
your abundance may be a s for their want 2 Cor 8:14
the s of the Spirit of Jesus Christ Phil 1:19

SUPPLY (v)
s your lack of service toward me Phil 2:30
my God shall s all your need Phil 4:19

SUPPORT
s the weak Acts 20:35; 1 Thess 5:14

SUPREME
to the king, as s 1 Pet 2:13

SUR soor
a turning away, departing 2 Kgs 11:6

SURE
be s your sin will find you out Num 32:23
no man is s of life Job 24:22
make s thy friend Prov 6:3
the s mercies of David Is 55:3; Acts 13:34
the foundation of God standeth s 2 Tim 2:19
a more s word of prophecy 2 Pet 1:19

SURPRISED
fearfulness has s the hypocrites Is 33:14
the strong holds are s Jer 48:41
how is the praise of the whole earth s Jer 51:41

SUSANCHITES soo´-sank-ites
inhabitants of Susa or Susinak Ezra 4:9

SUSANNA su-san´-ah
lily Luke 8:3

SUSI soo´-si
horseman Num 13:11

SUSTAIN
the Lord s me Ps 3:5
he shall s thee Ps 55:22
spirit of a man will s his infirmity Prov 18:14
his righteousness, it s him Is 59:16

SWEAR
that s to his own hurt Ps 15:4
he that s, as he that feareth an oath Eccl 9:2
every tongue shall s Is 45:23
shall s by the God of truth Is 65:16
thou shalt s, the Lord liveth, in truth Jer 4:2
because of s the land mourneth Jer 23:10
by s, and lying Hos 4:2
s falsely in making a covenant Hos 10:4
every one that s shall be cut off Zech 5:3
s not at all Matt 5:34; James 5:12
men verily s by the greater Heb 6:16

SWEAT
In the s of thy face Gen 3:19
anything that causeth s Ezek 44:18
his s was as it were great drops of blood Luke 22:44

SWEET
though wickedness be s in his mouth Job 20:12
we took s counsel together Ps 55:14
my meditation of him shall be s Ps 104:34
thy sleep shall be s Prov 3:24
stolen waters are s Prov 9:17
desire accomplished is s to the soul Prov 13:19
honeycomb, s to the soul Prov 16:24
to the hungry soul every bitter thing is s Prov 27:7
the sleep of a labouring man is s Eccl 5:12
truly the light is s Eccl 11:7
his fruit was s to my taste Song 2:3
put bitter for s, and s for bitter Is 5:20
make s melody Is 23:16
at the same place s water and bitter James 3:11

SWELLING
how wilt thou do in the s of Jordan? Jer 12:5
great s words 2 Pet 2:18; Jude 1:16

SWIFT
the race is not to the s Eccl 9:11
he that is s of foot shall not deliver himself Amos 2:15
their feet are s to shed blood Rom 3:15

SWIM
the iron did s 2 Kgs 6:6
waters to s in Ezek 47:5

SWOLLEN
when he should have s Acts 28:6

SWOON
the sucklings s in the streets Lam 2:11

SWORD
their tongue a sharp s Ps 57:4
nation shall not lift up s against nation Is 2:4
the s is without, and the pestilence Ezek 7:15
not to send peace, but a s Matt 10:34
a s shall pierce through thy own soul also Luke 2:35
he beareth not the s in vain Rom 13:4
the s of the Spirit Eph 6:17
sharper than any two-edged s Heb 4:12
out of his mouth went a sharp s Rev 1:16; 19:15
that killeth with the s must be killed with the s Rev 13:10

SYCHAR si´-kar
drunken (?) John 4:5

SYCHEM si´-kem
Gr. for SHECHEM Acts 7:16

SYENE si-e´-ne
opening Ezek 29:10

SYNAGOGUE
they have burned up all the s of God Ps 74:8
went into the s on the sabbath day Luke 4:16; Acts 13:14

SYNTYCHE sin´-ty-kee
fortunate Phil 4:2

SYRACUSE sir´-a-kyus
a city on the east coast of Sicily Acts 28:12

SYRIAN sir´-yan
inhabitant of Syria Gen 25:20

SYROPHOENICIAN si´-ro-fee-nish´-yan
Phoenician living in Syria Mark 7:26

T

TAANACH ta´-a-nak
castle (?) Josh 12:21

TAANATH-SHILOH ta´-a-nath-shi´-lo
fig tree of Shiloh (?) Josh 16:6

TABBAOTH tab´-a-oth
rings Ezra 2:43

TABBATH tab´-ath
pleasantness Judg 7:22

TABEAL tab´-e-al
God is good Is 7:6

TABEEL tab´-e-el
same as TABEAL Ezra 4:7

TABERAH tab´-er-ah
burning Num 11:3

TABERNACLE
abide in thy **t** Ps 15:1
in secret of his **t** shall he hide me Ps 27:5
How amiable are thy **t** Ps 84:1
a **t** that shall not be taken down Is 33:20

TABITHA tab´-ith-ah
gazelle Acts 9:36

TABLE
Thou preparest a **t** before me Ps 23:5
Let their **t** become a snare before them Ps 69:22
Can God furnish a **t** in the wilderness? Ps 78:19
like olive plants round about thy **t** Ps 128:3
she hath also furnished her **t** Prov 9:2
crumbs which fall from their masters' **t** Matt 15:27
yet the dogs under the **t** Mark 7:28
leave word of God, and serve **t** Acts 6:2
fleshy **t** of the heart 2 Cor 3:3

TABOR ta´-bor
height Josh 19:22

TABRIMON tab´-rim-on
Rimmon is good (?) 1 Kgs 15:18

TACHMONITE tak´-mon-ite
same as HACHMONITE (?) 2 Sam 23:8

TADMOR tad´-mor
city of palms (?) 1 Kgs 9:18

TAHAN ta´-han
camp Num 26:35

TAHANITES ta´-han-ites
descendants of Tahan Num 26:35

TAHAPANES ta-ha´-pa-nes
head of the land Jer 2:16

TAHATH ta´-hath
substitute 1 Chr 6:24

TAHPANHES ta´-pan-hes
same as TAHATH Jer 43:7

TAHREA tah-re´-ah
cunning (?) 1 Chr 9:41

TAKE
I will **t** you to me for a people Ex 6:7
t us for thine inheritance Ex 34:9
t advice, and speak your minds Judg 19:30
shall yet again **t** root downward 2 Kgs 19:30; Is 37:31
he knoweth the way that I **t** Job 23:10
t not thy holy spirit from me Ps 51:11
I will **t** the cup of salvation Ps 116:13
T us the foxes, the little foxes Song 2:15
the lame **t** the prey Is 33:23
t with you words Hos 14:2
thence shall mine hand **t** them Amos 9:2
T no thought Matt 6:25,31,34; 10:19; Mark 13:11; Luke 12:11
and why **t** ye thought Matt 6:28; Luke 12:26
T my yoke upon you Matt 11:29
forgotten to **t** bread Matt 16:5; Mark 8:14
then **t** with thee one or two more Matt 18:16
t that thine is, and go thy way Matt 20:14
T, eat; this is my body Matt 26:26; Mark 14:22; 1 Cor 11:24
forbid not to **t** thy coat also Luke 6:29
t thine ease, eat, drink, and be merry Luke 12:19
he shall **t** of mine John 16:15
Why do ye not rather **t** wrong? 1 Cor 6:7
how shall he **t** care of the church of God? 1 Tim 3:5
ye **t** it patiently 1 Pet 2:20
that no man **t** thy crown Rev 3:11

TALE
a **t** that is told Ps 90:9
words seemed to them as idle **t** Luke 24:11

TALITHA tal´-ith-ah
girl Mark 5:41

TALK
God doth **t** with man Deut 5:24
t of them when thou sittest in thine house Deut 6:7
and **t** deceitfully for him? Job 13:7
also **t** of thy righteousness Ps 71:24
and **t** of thy power Ps 145:11
let me **t** with thee of thy judgments Jer 12:1
and I will there **t** with thee Ezek 3:22
while he **t** with us by the way Luke 24:32
it is he that **t** with thee John 9:37

TALL
The people are greater and **t** Deut 1:28
people great, and many, and **t** Deut 2:10
cut down the **t** cedar trees 2 Kgs 19:23

TALMAI tal-ma´-i
abounding in furrows Num 13:22

TALMON tal´-mon
oppressed 1 Chr 9:17

TAMAH ta´-mah
joy Neh 7:55

TAMAR ta´-mar
a palm tree Gen 38:6

TAME
neither could any man **t** him Mark 5:4
t of mankind James 3:7
the tongue can no man **t** James 3:8

TAMMUZ tam´-ooz
son of life (?) Ezek 8:14

TANACH ta´-nak
same as TAANACH Josh 21:25

TANHUMETH tan-hoom´-eth
consolation 2 Kgs 25:23

TAPHATH ta´-fath
a drop (?) 1 Kgs 4:11

TAPPUAH tap-oo´-ah
apple 1 Chr 2:43

TARAH ta´-rah
station Num 33:27

TARALAH ta´-ra-lah
reeling (?) Josh 18:27

TARE
the king arose, and **t** his garments 2 Sam 13:31
out of the woods, and **t** forty and two children 2 Kgs 2:24
straightway the spirit **t** him Mark 9:20

TAREA ta-re´-ah
same as TAHREA 1 Chr 8:35

TARPELITES tar´-pel-ites
people of Tarpel Ezra 4:9

TARRY
t with him a few days Gen 27:44
out of Egypt, and could not **t** Ex 12:39
if we **t** till the morning light 2 Kgs 7:9
flee, and **t** not 2 Kgs 9:3
she that **t** at home divided the spoil Ps 68:12
he that telleth lies shall not **t** in my sight Ps 101:7
They that **t** long at the wine Prov 23:30
my salvation shall not **t** Is 46:13
that turneth aside to **t** for a night Jer 14:8
though it **t**, wait for it Hab 2:3
while the bridegroom **t** Matt 25:5
t ye here, and watch Mark 14:34
he went in to **t** with them Luke 24:29
t ye in city of Jerusalem, until ye be endued Luke 24:49
If I will that he **t** till I come John 21:22
why **t** thou? Acts 22:16
t one for another 1 Cor 11:33
and will not **t** Heb 10:37

TARSHISH tar´-shis
the sea coast Gen 10:4

THARSHISH thar´-shis
same as TARSHISH 1 Kgs 10:22

TARSUS tar´-sus
flat surface Acts 9:11

TARTAK tar´-takd
an Avvite deity 2 Kgs 17:31

TARTAN tar´-tan
military chief 2 Kgs 18:17

TASTE (n)
the **t** of it was as the **t** of fresh oil Num 11:8
is there any **t** in the white of egg? Job 6:6
how sweet are thy words unto my **t**! Ps 119:103
his **t** remained in him Jer 48:11

TASTE (v)
and the mouth **t** his meat? Job 12:11
as the mouth **t** meat Job 34:3
T and see that the Lord is good Ps 34:8
which shall not **t** of death Matt 16:28; Mark 9:1; Luke 9:27
were bidden shall **t** of my supper Luke 14:24
he shall never **t** of death John 8:52
Touch not; **t** not Col 2:21
t death for every man Heb 2:9
and have **t** of the heavenly gift Heb 6:4
ye have **t** that the Lord is gracious 1 Pet 2:3

TATNAI tat´-na-i
gift (?) Ezra 5:3

TATTLERS
t also and busybodies 1 Tim 5:13

TAUGHT
he **t** the men of Succoth Judg 8:16
thou hast **t** them the good way 2 Chr 6:27
such as **t** to sing praise 2 Chr 23:13
thou hast **t** me Ps 71:17; 119:102
he **t** me also, and said Prov 4:4
I have **t** thee in way of wisdom Prov 4:11
he still **t** the people knowledge Eccl 12:9
fear toward me is **t** by the precept of men Is 29:13
all thy children shall be **t** of Lord Is 54:13
as they **t** my people to swear by Baal Jer 12:16
I **t** them, rising up early Jer 32:33
man **t** me to keep cattle Zech 13:5
he **t** them as one having authority Matt 7:29; Mark 1:22
and did as they were **t** Matt 28; 15
thou hast **t** in our streets Luke 13:26
they shall be all **t** of God John 6:45
as my Father hath **t** me John 8:28
neither was I **t** it, but by the revelation of Jesus Christ Gal 1:12
let him that is **t** in the word Gal 6:6
if so be ye have been **t** by him Eph 4:21
traditions which ye have been **t** 2 Thess 2:15

TAUNT
t and curse Jer 24:9
a reproach and a t Ezek 5:15
a t proverb against him Hab 2:6

TEACH
and will t you what ye shall do Ex 4:15
that they may t their children Deut 4:10
t them diligently unto thy children Deut 6:7; 11:19
t us what we shall do unto the child Judg 13:8
I will t you the good way 1 Sam 12:23
he bade them t the children 2 Sam 1:18
without a t priest 2 Chr 15:3
t me, and I will hold my tongue Job 6:24
Shall not they t thee Job 8:10
they shall t thee Job 12:7
that which I see not t thou me Job 34:32
who t like him? Job 36:22
t me thy paths Ps 25:4
will he t sinners in the way Ps 25:8
T me thy way, O Lord Ps 27:11; 86:11
I will t you the fear of the Lord Ps 34:11
Then will I t transgressors Ps 51:13
So t us to number our days Ps 90:12
t him out of thy law Ps 94:12
he t with his fingers Prov 6:13
he will t us of his ways Is 2:3; Mic 4:2
Whom shall he t knowledge? Is 28:9
and doth t him discretion Is 28:26
I am the Lord thy God which t thee Is 48:17
and t your daughters wailing Jer 9:20
they shall t my people the difference Ezek 44:23
the priests thereof t for hire Mic 3:11
t all nations Matt 28:19
t us to pray Luke 11:1
the Holy Ghost shall t you Luke 12:12
dost thou t us? John 9:34
he shall t you all things John 14:26
they ceased not to t and preach Acts 5:42
he that t, on t Rom 12:7
I t everywhere in every church 1 Cor 4:17
Doth not even nature itself t you 1 Cor 11:14
by my voice I might t others also 1 Cor 14:19
t every man in all wisdom Col 1:28
t and admonishing one another Col 3:16
charge some that they t no other 1 Tim 1:3
I suffer not a woman to t 1 Tim 2:12
apt to t 1 Tim 3:2; 2 Tim 2:24
These things command and t 1 Tim 4:11
These things t and exhort 1 Tim 6:2
who shall be able to t others also 2 Tim 2:2
t things which they ought not Titus 1:11
t the young women to be sober Titus 2:4
T us that, denying ungodliness Titus 2:12
ye have need that one t you again Heb 5:12

TEACHER
the t as the scholar 1 Chr 25:8
more understanding than all my t Ps 119:99
have not obeyed the voice of my t Prov 5:13
thine eyes shall see thy t Is 30:20
a t of lies Hab 2:18
a t come from God John 3:2
a t of babes Rom 2:20
are all t? 1 Cor 12:29
and some, pastors and t Eph 4:11
desiring to be t of the law 1 Tim 1:7
t of good things Titus 2:3

TEAR
He t me in his wrath Job 16:9
He t himself in his anger Job 18:4
Lest he t my soul Ps 7:2
they did t me, and ceased not Ps 35:15
lest I t you in pieces Ps 50:22
will t and go away Hos 5:14

TEARS
I have seen thy t 2 Kgs 20:5; Is 38:5
mine eye poureth out t Job 16:20
I water my couch with my t Ps 6:6
hold not thy peace at my t Ps 39:12
t have been my meat Ps 42:3
put thou my t into thy bottle Ps 56:8
bread of t, and givest them t to drink Ps 80:5
mine eyes from t Ps 116:8
they that sow in t Ps 126:5
I will water thee with my t Is 16:9
the Lord God will wipe away t Is 25:8
and mine eyes a fountain of t Jer 9:1
and run down with t Jer 13:17; 14:17
and thine eyes from t Jer 31:16
her t are on her cheeks Lam 1:2
mine eyes do fail with t Lam 2:11
neither shall thy t run down Ezek 24:16
covering the altar of the Lord with t Mal 2:13
began to wash his feet with her t Luke 7:38
and with many t Acts 20:19
warn every one night and day with t Acts 20:31
being mindful of thy t 2 Tim 1:4
God shall wipe away all t Rev 7:17; 21:4

TEBAH te´-bah
slaughter Gen 22:24

TEBALIAH te-bal-i´-ah
whom Jehovah has immersed 1 Chr 26:11

TEBETH te´-beth
the tenth month Esth 2:16

TEDIOUS
that I be not further t unto thee Acts 24:4

TEETH
t white with milk Gen 49:12
flesh yet between their t Num 11:33
escaped with the skin of my t Job 19:20
As vinegar to the t Prov 10:26
sharp threshing instrument having t Is 41:15
childrens t are set on edge Jer 31:29; Ezek 18:2
I also have given you cleanness of t Amos 4:6

TEHAPHNEHES te-haph´-ne-hes
same as TAHAPANES Ezek 30:18

TEHINNAH te-hin´-ah
cry for mercy 1 Chr 4:12

TEKEL te´-kel
weighed Dan 5:25

TEKOA te-ko´-ah
sound of trumpet 1 Chr 2:24

TEKOAH te-ko´-ah
same as TEKOA 2 Sam 14:2

TEKOITE te-ko´-ite
inhabitant of Tekoah 2 Sam 23:26

TEL-ABIB tel-a´-bib
hill of ears of corn Ezek 3:15

TEL-HARESHA tel-har´-e-shah
forest-hill Neh 7:61

TEL-HARSA tel-har´-sah
same as TEL-HARESHA Ezra 2:59

TEL-MELAH tel-me´-lah
salt-hill Ezra 2:59

TELAH te´-lah
fracture 1 Chr 7:25

TELAIM te´-la-im
lambs 1 Sam 15:4

TELASSAR tel´-as´-ar
Assyrian hill Is 37:12

TELEM te´-lem
oppression Josh 15:24

TELL
t the stars Gen 15:5
T me, I pray thee, thy name Gen 32:29
T it not in Gath 2 Sam 1:20
t the towers thereof Ps 48:12
If I were hungry, I would not t thee Ps 50:12
who can t a man what shall be after him Eccl 6:12
what shall be after him, who can t him? Eccl 10:14
that which hath wings shall t the matter and repent Eccl 10:20
Who can t if God will turn and repent Jon 3:9
go and t him his fault Matt 18:15
t it unto the church Matt 18:17
neither t I you by what authority Matt 21:27; Luke 20:8
t them how great things Mark 5:19
We cannot t Mark 11:33
go ye and t that fox Luke 13:32
they could not t from whence it was Luke 20:7
canst not t whence it cometh John 3:8
if I t you of heavenly things? John 3:12
he will t us all things John 4:25
did others t it thee of me? John 18:34
either to t or hear some new thing Acts 17:21

TEMA te´-mah
a desert Gen 25:15

TEMAN te´-man
on the right hand Gen 36:11

TEMANI te´-man-i
descendants of Teman Gen 36:34

TEMANITE te´-man-ite
same as TEMANI Job 2:11

TEMENI te´-men-i
same as TEMANI 1 Chr 4:6

TEMPER
cakes unleavened t with oil Ex 29:2
t together, pure and holy Ex 30:35
oil, to t with the fine flour Ezek 46:14
God hath t the body 1 Cor 12:24

TEMPEST
he breaketh me with a t Job 9:17
fire and brimstone and a horrible t Ps 11:6
my escape from the windy storm and t Ps 55:8
a covert from the t Is 32:2
and darkness and t Heb 12:18
clouds that are carried with a t 2 Pet 2:17

TEMPESTUOUS
it shall be very t round about him Ps 50:3
the sea wrought, and was t Jon 1:11
there arose against it a t wind Acts 27:14

TEMPLE
he did hear my voice out of his t 2 Sam 22:7
within the t Neh 6:10
to inquire in his t Ps 27:4
in his t doth every one speak of his glory Ps 29:9
his train filled the t Is 6:1
songs of the t shall be howlings Amos 8:3
shall suddenly come to his t Mal 3:1
one greater than the t Matt 12:6
destroy this t John 2:19
Know ye not that ye are the t of God 1 Cor 3:16
ye are the t of the living God 2 Cor 6:16

TEMPORAL
the things which are seen are t 2 Cor 4:18

TEMPT
God did t Abraham Gen 22:1
wherefore do ye t the Lord? Ex 17:2
have t me now these ten times Num 14:22
Ye shall not t the Lord your God Deut 6:16; Matt 4:7; Luke 4:12
they t God in their heart Ps 78:18

I will not ask, neither will I **t** the Lord — Is 7:12
they that **t** God are even delivered — Mal 3:15
Why **t** ye me — Matt 22:18; Mark 12:15; Luke 20:23
and **t** him, saying — Luke 10:25
to **t** the Spirit of the Lord? — Acts 5:9
Now therefore why **t** ye God — Acts 15:10
to be **t** above that ye are able — 1 Cor 10:13
lest thou also be **t** — Gal 6:1
he himself hath suffered being **t** — Heb 2:18
in all points **t** like as we are — Heb 4:15
God cannot be **t** with evil — James 1:13
neither **t** he any man — James 1:13

TEMPTATION
lead us not into **t** — Matt 6:13
that ye enter not into **t** — Matt 26:41; Mark 14:38; Luke 22:46
in time of **t** fall away — Luke 8:13
There hath no **t** taken you — 1 Cor 10:13
my **t** which was in my flesh ye despised not — Gal 4:14
they that will be rich fall into **t** — 1 Tim 6:9
when ye fall into divers **t** — James 1:2
how to deliver the godly out of **t** — 2 Pet 2:9

TEND
As righteousness **t** to life — Prov 11:19
the talk of the lips **t** only to penury — Prov 14:23
The fear of the Lord **t** to life — Prov 19:23
The thoughts of the diligent **t** only to plenteousness — Prov 21:5

TENDER
the man that is **t** — Deut 28:54
as the small rain upon the **t** herb — Deut 32:2
thine heart was **t** — 2 Kgs 22:19; 2 Chr 34:27
the **t** branch will not cease — Job 14:7
t and only beloved in the sight of my mother — Prov 4:3
the vines with the **t** grapes — Song 2:13,15
whether the **t** grape appear — Song 7:12
thou shalt no more be called **t** — Is 47:1
he shall grow up before him as a **t** plant — Is 53:2
brought Daniel into favour and **t** love — Dan 1:9
through the **t** mercy of our God — Luke 1:78
the Lord is pitiful, and of **t** mercy — James 5:11

TENOR
according to the **t** of these words — Gen 43:7; Ex 34:27

TENT
How goodly are thy **t**, O Jacob — Num 24:5
fled every man into his **t** — 1 Sam 4:10; 2 Sam 18:17
to your **t**, O Israel — 1 Kgs 12:16
than to dwell in the **t** of wickedness — Ps 84:10
is removed from me as a shepherd's **t** — Is 38:12
Enlarge the place of thy **t** — Is 54:2
there is none to stretch forth my **t** — Jer 10:20

TENTH
I will surely give the **t** unto thee — Gen 28:22
the **t** shall be holy unto the Lord — Lev 27:32
But yet in it shall be a **t** — Is 6:13

TERAH te´-rah
a station (?) — Gen 11:24

TERAPHIM
and made an ephod and **t** — Judg 17:5
in these houses an ephod, and **t** — Judg 18:14
and the **t**, and the molten image — Judg 18:17,18
and he took the ephod, and the **t** — Judg 18:20
and without an ephod, and without **t** — Hos 3:4

TERESH te´-resh
severe (?) — Esth 2:21

TERRIBLE
it is a **t** thing that I will do with thee — Ex 34:10
that great and **t** wilderness — Deut 1:19; 8:15
a mighty God and **t** — Deut 7:21; 10:17; Neh 9:32
the great and **t** God — Neh 1:5; 4:14
done for thee these great and **t** things — Deut 10:21
like the countenance of an angel of God, very **t** — Judg 13:6
with God is **t** majesty — Job 37:22
The glory of his nostrils is **t** — Job 39:20
thy right hand shall teach thee **t** things — Ps 45:4
By **t** things in righteousness wilt thou answer us — Ps 65:5
How **t** art thou in thy works! — Ps 66:3
t in his doing toward the children of men — Ps 66:5
thou art **t** out of thy holy places — Ps 68:35
he is **t** to the kings of the earth — Ps 76:12
thy great and **t** name — Ps 99:3
the might of thy **t** acts — Ps 145:6
t as an army with banners — Song 6:4
the blast of the **t** ones is as a storm — Is 25:4
when thou didst **t** things — Is 64:3
redeem thee out of the hand of the **t** — Jer 15:21
day of the Lord is great and very **t** — Joel 2:11
so **t** was the sight — Heb 12:21

TERRIBLENESS
with great **t**, and with signs — Deut 26:8
a name of greatness and **t** — 1 Chr 17:21
Thy **t** hath deceived thee — Jer 49:16

TERRIBLY
he ariseth to shake **t** the earth — Is 2:19,21
the fir trees shall be **t** shaken — Nah 2:3

TERRIFY
let not his fear **t** me — Job 9:34
ye shall hear of wars and commotions, be not **t** — Luke 21:9
they were **t** and affrighted — Luke 24:37
in nothing **t** by adversaries — Phil 1:28

TERROR
the **t** of God was upon the cities — Gen 35:5
the sword without and **t** within — Deut 32:25
your **t** is fallen upon us — Josh 2:9
T shall make him afraid — Job 18:11
in the **t** of the shadow of death — Job 24:17
destruction from God was a **t** to me — Job 31:23
my **t** shall not make thee afraid — Job 33:7
the **t** of death are fallen upon me — Ps 55:4
they are utterly consumed with **t** — Ps 73:19
afraid for the **t** by night — Ps 91:5
Be not a **t** to me — Jer 17:17
I will make thee a **t** to thyself — Jer 20:4; Ezek 26:21
thou shalt be a **t** — Ezek 27:36; 28:19
rulers are not **t** to good works — Rom 13:3
Knowing therefore the **t** of the Lord — 2 Cor 5:11

TERTIUS ter´-shus
the third — Rom 16:22

TERTULLUS ter-tul´-us
same as TERTIUS — Acts 24:1

TESTIFY
one witness shall not **t** against any person — Num 35:30
this song shall **t** against them — Deut 31:21
seeing the Lord hath **t** against me — Ruth 1:21
thy mouth hath **t** against thee — 2 Sam 1:16
t against them by thy spirit — Neh 9:30
thine own lips **t** against thee — Job 15:6
our sins **t** against us — Is 59:12
pride of Israel doth **t** to his face — Hos 5:5; 7:10
wherein have I wearied thee? **t** against me — Mic 6:3
that he may **t** unto them — Luke 16:28
needed not that any should **t** of man — John 2:25
seen and heard, that he **t** — John 3:32
they which **t** of me — John 5:39
but me it hateth because I **t** of it — John 7:7
he shall **t** of me — John 15:26
the disciple which **t** of these things — John 21:24
as thou hast **t** of me in Jerusalem — Acts 23:11
to be **t** in due time — 1 Tim 2:6
t beforehand the sufferings of Christ — 1 Pet 1:11
we have seen and do **t** — 1 John 4:14

TESTIMONY
t which he testified against them — 2 Kgs 17:15
Thy **t** are very sure — Ps 93:5
I have kept thy **t** — Ps 119:22
Thy **t** are also my delight — Ps 119:24
I will speak of thy **t** also before kings — Ps 119:46
I turned my feet unto thy **t** — Ps 119:59
therefore I love thy **t** — Ps 119:119
Thy **t** are wonderful — Ps 119:129
Bind up the **t** — Is 8:16
to the law and to the **t** — Is 8:20
for a **t** against them — Matt 10:18; Mark 13:9
it shall turn to you for a **t** — Luke 21:13
and no man receiveth his **t** — John 3:32
we know that his **t** is true — John 21:24
t unto the word of his grace — Acts 14:3
declaring unto you the **t** of God — 1 Cor 2:1
the **t** of our conscience — 2 Cor 1:12
not thou therefore ashamed of the **t** — 2 Tim 1:8
before his translation he had this **t** — Heb 11:5

TETRARCH tet´-rark
ruler of a fourth part of a country — Matt 14:1

THADDAEUS thad-e´-us
Gr. for THEUDAS — Matt 10:3

THAHASH tha´-hash
seal (?) — Gen 22:24

THAMAH tha´-mah
laughter — Ezra 2:53

THAMAR tha´-mar
Gr. for TAMAR — Matt 1:3

THANK
I **t** thee, O Father — Matt 11:25; Luke 10:21
I **t** thee, that I am not like other men — Luke 18:11
I **t** thee that thou hast heard me — John 11:41
he **t** God, and took courage — Acts 28:15
I **t** my God always on your behalf — 1 Cor 1:4
we are bound to **t** God always — 2 Thess 1:3
I **t** Christ Jesus our Lord — 1 Tim 1:12

THANKS
companies of them that gave **t** — Neh 12:31
he took the cup, and gave **t** — Matt 26:27; Luke 22:17
coming in that instant gave **t** likewise unto the Lord — Luke 2:38
for he giveth God **t** — Rom 14:6
t be to God, who giveth us the victory — 1 Cor 15:57
t always for all things unto God — Eph 5:20
what **t** can we render to God again — 1 Thess 3:9
give glory and honour and **t** to him — Rev 4:9

THANKSGIVING
the voice of **t** — Ps 26:7
before his presence with **t** — Ps 95:2
t and the voice of melody — Is 51:3
offer a sacrifice of **t** — Amos 4:5
by prayer and supplication with **t** — Phil 4:6
watch in the same with **t** — Col 4:2
to be received with **t** — 1 Tim 4:3

THARA tha´-rah
Gr. for TERAH — Luke 3:34

THARSHISH thar´-shish
same as TARSHISH — 1 Kgs 10:22

THEBEZ the´-bez
brightness — Judg 9:50

THELASAR thel´-as-ar
same as TELASSAR — 2 Kgs 19:12

THEOPHILUS the-o´-fil-us
loved of God Luke 1:3

THESSALONICA thes´-al-on-i´-kah
conquest of Thessaly Acts 17:1

THEUDAS thoo´-das
praise (?) Acts 5:36

THICK
thou art grown t Deut 32:15
the mule went under the t boughs 2 Sam 18:9
he had lifted up axes on the t trees Ps 74:5
his top was among t boughs Ezek 31:3
him that ladeth himself with t clay Hab 2:6

THICKET
a ram caught in a t Gen 22:13
in the t of the forest Is 9:18
The lion is come up from his t Jer 4:7
they shall go into t Jer 4:29

THIEF
When thou sawest a t Ps 50:18
companions of t Is 1:23
As the t is asahmed Jer 2:26
enter at windows like a t Joel 2:9
and fell among t Luke 10:30
where no t approacheth Luke 12:33
the same is a t and a robber John 10:1
All that ever came before me are t and robbers John 10:8
Nor t, nor coveteous 1 Cor 6:10
let none of you suffer as a murderer, or as a t 1 Pet 4:15
come as a t 2 Pet 3:10; Rev 16:15

THIGH
I pray thee, thy hand under my t Gen 24:2; 47:29
he touched the hollow of his t Gen 32:25
he smote them hip and t Judg 15:8
every man hath his sword upon his t Song 3:8

THIMNATHAH thim´-nath-ah
portion Josh 19:43

THINK
t on me when it shall be well with thee Gen 40:14
t upon me, my God, for good Neh 5:19
poor and needy, yet the Lord t on me Ps 40:17
For as he t in his heart, so is he Prov 23:7
neither doth his heart t so Is 10:7
if so be that God will t upon us Jon 1:6
t not to say within yourselves Matt 3:9
they t that they shall be heard Matt 6:7
Wherefore t ye evil in your hearts? Matt 9:4
What t thou, Simon? Matt 17:25; 22:17
What t ye of Christ? Matt 22:42; 26:66; Mark 14:64
not to t of himself more highly than he ought to t Rom 12:3
let him that t he standeth 1 Cor 10:12
to t any thing as of ourselves 2 Cor 3:5
For if a man t himself to be something Gal 6:3
exceeding abundantly above all that we ask or t Eph 3:20
t on these things Phil 4:8
let not that man t he shall receive James 1:7
Beloved, t it not strange 1 Pet 4:12

THIRST (n)
to kill us and our children and our cattle with t Ex 17:3
to add drunkenness to t Deut 29:19
now I shall die for t Judg 15:18
to die by famine and by t 2 Chr 32:11
in my t they gave me vinegar Ps 69:21
and their tongue faileth for t Is 41:17
nor a t for water, but of hearing Amos 8:11
in hunger and t, in fastings often 2 Cor 11:27

THIRST (v)
My soul t for God Ps 42:2; 63:1; 143:6
They shall not hunger nor t Is 49:10
every one that t Is 55:1
and t after righteousness Matt 5:6
that I give him shall never t John 4:14
he that believeth on me shall never t John 6:35
if any man t, let him come unto me John 7:37
I t John 19:28
neither t anymore Rev 7:16

THIRSTY
in a dry and t land Ps 63:1; 143:6
hungry and t, their soul fainted Ps 107:5
as cold waters to a t soul Prov 25:25
brought water to him that was t Is 21:14
As when a t man dreameth Is 29:8
pour water on him that is t Is 44:3
but ye shall be t Is 65:13

THISTLE
thorns also and t shall it bring forth Gen 3:18
Let t grow instead of wheat Job 31:40
gather grapes of thorns, or figs of t? Matt 7:16

THOMAS tom´-as
a twin Matt 10:3

THORN
t in your sides Num 33:55; Judg 2:3
they are quenched as the fire of t Ps 118:12
way of the slothful man is as an hedge of t Prov 15:19
it was all grown over with t Prov 24:31
As a t goeth up into the hand of a drunkard Prov 26:9
the crackling of t under a pot Eccl 7:6
As the lily among t Song 2:2
as t cut up shall they be burned Is 33:12
and t shall come up in her palaces Is 34:13
Instead of the t shall come up the fir tree Is 55:13
sow not among t Jer 4:3
but shall reap t Jer 12:13
I will hedge up thy way with t Hos 2:6
t shall be in their tabernacles Hos 9:6
the t and the thistle shall come up on their altars Hos 10:8
most upright is sharper than t hedge Mic 7:4
there was given to me a t in the flesh 2 Cor 12:7

THOUGHT (n)
all the imaginations of the t 1 Chr 28:9
In t from the visions of the night Job 4:13
in the t of him that is at ease Job 12:5
no t can be withholden from thee Job 42:2
God is not in all his t Ps 10:4
and thy t which are to us-ward Ps 40:5
thy t are very deep Ps 92:5
The Lord knoweth the t of man Ps 94:11
In the multitude of my t Ps 94:19
thou understandest my t afar off Ps 139:2
How precious also are thy t unto me Ps 139:17
try me, and know my t Ps 139:23
The t of the righteous are right Prov 12:5
thy t shall be established Prov 16:3
The t of foolishness is sin Prov 24:9
and the unrighteous man his t Is 55:7
my t are not your t Is 55:8
they know not the t of the Lord Mic 4:12
[Jesus] knowing their t, said Matt 9:4; Luke 11:17
[Jesus] knew their t, and said Matt 12:25; Luke 6:8
Take no t Matt 6:25,31,34; 10:19; Mark 13:11; Luke 12:11,22
out of the heart proceed evil t Matt 15:19; Mark 7:21
t of many hearts may be revealed Luke 2:35
Jesus perceived their t Luke 5:22; 9:47
why do t arise in your hearts? Luke 24:38
if perhaps the t of thine heart may be forgiven thee Acts 8:22
The Lord knoweth the t of the wise 1 Cor 3:20
into captivity every t to the obedience of Christ 2 Cor 10:5
and is a discerner of the t and intents of the heart Heb 4:12
and are become judges of evil t James 2:4

THOUGHT (v)
I had not t to see thy face Gen 48:11
I t to promote thee unto great honour Num 24:11
as he t to have done unto his brother Deut 19:19
I t, He will surely come out to me 2 Kgs 5:11
they t to do me mischief Neh 6:2
We have t of thy lovingkindness Ps 48:9
t that I was altogether such an one as thyself Ps 50:21
When I t to know this Ps 73:16
I t on my ways Ps 119:59
if thou hast t evil Prov 30:32
as I have t, so shall it come to pass Is 14:24
I will repent of the evil that I t to do unto them Jer 18:8
as I t to punish you Zech 8:14
I t in these days to do well Zech 8:15
and that t upon his name Mal 3:16
But while he t on these things Matt 1:20
when he t thereon, he wept Mark 14:72
he t within himself, saying, What shall I do Luke 12:17
t the kingdom of God should immediately appear Luke 19:11
t he had spoken of taking of rest John 11:13
While Peter t on the vision Acts 10:19
Why should it be t a thing incredible Acts 26:8
I t as a child 1 Cor 13:11
t it not robbery to be equal with God Phil 2:6

THREAD
That I will not take from a t Gen 14:23
bind this line of scarlet t in the window Josh 2:18
as a t of tow is broken Judg 16:9

THREATEN
let us straitly t them Acts 4:17
do the same things unto them, forbearing t Eph 6:9
when he suffered, he t not 1 Pet 2:23

THREEFOLD
a t cord is not quickly broken Eccl 4:12

THRESH
thou shalt t the mountains Is 41:15
it is time to t her Jer 51:33
Arise and t Mic 4:13
thou didst t the heathen in anger Hab 3:12
t in hope 1 Cor 9:10

THRESHINGFLOOR
they rob the t 1 Sam 23:1
To buy the t of thee 2 Sam 24:21

THREW
So they t her down 2 Kgs 9:33
she t in two mites Mark 12:42
the devil t him down Luke 9:42
and t dust into the air Acts 22:23

THROAT
their t is an open sepulchre Ps 5:9
neither speak they through their t Ps 115:7
put a knife to their t Prov 23:2
took him by the t Matt 18:28

THRONE
the Lord's t is in heaven Ps 11:4
t of iniquity have fellowship with thee? Ps 94:20
there are set t of judgment Ps 122:5
his t is upholden by mercy Prov 20:28

heaven is my t Is 66:1; Acts 7:49
a glorious high t from the beginning Jer 17:12
his t was like the fiery flame Dan 7:9
the Son of man shall sit in the t
of his glory Matt 19:28; 25:31
whether they be t or dominions Col 1:16
come boldly unto the t of grace Heb 4:16
will I grant to sit with me in my t Rev 3:21
a t was set in heaven Rev 4:2
I saw a great white t Rev 20:11

THRONG
lest they should t him Mark 3:9
Thou seest the multitude t thee Mark 5:31
But as he went the people t him Luke 8:42
Master, the multitude t thee Luke 8:45

THROW
t down all thy strong holds Mic 5:11
They shall build, but I will t down Mal 1:4
that shall not be t down Matt 24:2

THRUST
God t him down, not man Job 32:13
neither shall one t another Joel 2:8
shall be t down to hell Luke 10:15
and you yourselves t out Luke 13:28
and t my hand into his side John 20:25
t in thy sickle, and reap Rev 14:15

THUMMIM thoom′-im
truth (?) Ex 28:30

TIBERIAS ti-be′-ri-as
a place named after Tiberius-Caesar John 6:1

TIBERIUS ti-be′-ri-us
1 stepson of Caesar Augustus
2 the second Roman emperor Luke 3:1

TIBHATH tib′-hath
butchery 1 Chr 18:8

TIBNI tib′-ni
made of straw (?) 1 Kgs 16:21

TIDAL ti′-dal
dread Gen 14:1

TIDINGS
afraid of evil t Ps 112:7
cursed be the man who brought t Jer 20:15
t out of the east Dan 11:44
glad t Luke 1:19; 2:10;
Acts 13:32; Rom 10:15

TIGLATH-PILESER tig′-lath-pil-e′-zer
my strength is the god Ninib (?) 2 Kgs 15:29

TIKVAH tik′-vah
expectation 2 Kgs 22:14

TIKVATH tik′-vath
same as TIKVAH 2 Chr 34:22

TILGATH-PILNESER til′-gath-pil-ne′-zer
same as TIGLATH-PILESER 1 Chr 5:6

TILL
not a man to t the ground Gen 2:5
t his land shall be satisfied Prov 12:11; 28:19
ye shall be t and sown Ezek 36:9

TILON ti′-lon
gift (?) 1 Chr 4:20

TIMAEUS ti-me′-us
polluted (?) Mark 10:46

TIME
the t drew nigh that Israel must die Gen 47:29
cut down out of t Job 22:16
I have reserved against the t of trouble Job 38:23
in a t when thou mayest be found Ps 32:6
shall not be ashamed in the evil t Ps 37:19
Lord will deliver him in t of trouble Ps 41:1
what t I am afraid Ps 56:3
in an acceptable t Ps 69:13; Is 49:8
Remember how short my t is Ps 89:47
and a t to every purpose Eccl 3:1
t and chance happeneth to them all Eccl 9:11
I the Lord, will hasten it in his t Is 60:22
thy t was the t of love Ezek 16:8
until a t and t and the dividing of t Dan 7:25
it is t to seek the Lord Hos 10:12
neither shall your vine cast her
fruit before the t Mal 3:11
discern the signs of the t Matt 16:3
knewest not the t of thy visitation Luke 19:44
the t of refreshing shall come Acts 3:19
the t of restitution of all things Acts 3:21
I have heard thee in a t accepted 2 Cor 6:2
Redeeming the t because the
days are evil Eph 5:16
grace to help in t of need Heb 4:16
or what manner of t 1 Pet 1:11
the t is at hand Rev 1:3
there should be t no longer Rev 10:6

TIMNA tim′-nah
unapproachable Gen 36:12

TIMNAH tim′-nah
a portion Josh 15:10

TIMNATH-HERES tim′-nath-he′-res
portion of the sun Judg 2:9

TIMNATH-SERAH tim′-nath-se′-rah
portion of the remainder Josh 19:50

TIMNATH tim′-nath
same as TIMNAH Gen 38:12

TIMNITE tim′-nite
a man of Timna Judg 15:6

TIMON ti′-mon
deeming worthy Acts 6:5

TIMOTHEUS tim-o′-the-us
same as TIMOTHY Rom 16:21

TIMOTHY tim′-oth-y
honoring God 2 Cor 1:1

TINGLE
everyone that heareth it shall t 1 Sam 3:11
his ears shall t 2 Kgs 21:12; Jer 19:8

TINKLING
making a t with their feet Is 3:16
t ornaments Is 3:18
sounding brass or a t symbol 1 Cor 13:1

TIPHSAH tif′-sah
passage 1 Kgs 4:24

TIRAS ti′-ras
crushing (?) Gen 10:2

TIRATHITES ti′-rath-ites
descendants of Tirah 1 Chr 2:55

TIRHAKAH tir′-ha-kah
distance (?) 2 Kgs 19:9

TIRHANAH tir′-han-ah
murmuring (?) 1 Chr 2:48

TIRIA tir′-i-ah
fear 1 Chr 4:16

TIRSHATHA tir-sha′-thah
the feared (?) Ezra 2:63

TIRZAH tir′-zah
pleasantness Num 26:33

TISHBITE tish′-bite
inhabitant of Tishbe 1 Kgs 17:1

TITUS ti′-tus
protected 2 Cor 2:13

TOAH to′-ah
low 1 Chr 6:34

TOB-ADONIJAH tob′-a-do-ni′-jah
good is my Lord Jehovah 2 Chr 17:8

TOB tobe
good Judg 11:3

TOBIAH tob-i′-ah
Jehovah is good Ezra 2:60

TOBIJAH tob-i′-jah
same as TOBIAH 2 Chr 17:8

TOCHEN to′-ken
a measure 1 Chr 4:32

TOGARMAH to-gar′-mah
rugged Gen 10:3

TOGETHER
the rich and poor meet t Prov 22:2
Can two walk t, except they be agreed? Amos 3:3
where two or three are gathered
t in my name Matt 18:20
all things work t for good Rom 8:28
shall be caught up t 1 Thess 4:17

TOHU to′-hoo
same as TOAH 1 Sam 1:1

TOI to′-i
wanderer 2 Sam 8:9

TOIL
work and t of our hands Gen 5:29
forget all my t Gen 41:51

TOLA to′-lah
worm Gen 46:13

TOLAD to′-lad
birth 1 Chr 4:29

TOLAITES to′-la-ites
descendants of Tola Num 26:23

TOLERABLE
t for the land of Sodom Matt 10:15; 11:24;
Mark 6:11
it shall be more t in that day
for Sodom Luke 10:12

TONGUE
hid from the scourge of the t Job 5:21
though he hide it under his t Job 20:12
Keep thy t from evil Ps 34:13
The t of the just is as choice silver Prov 10:20
t of the wise is health Prov 12:18
a lying t is but for a moment Prov 12:19
A wholesome t is a tree of life Prov 15:4
Death and life are in the power
of the t Prov 18:21
Whoso keepeth his t keepeth his soul Prov 21:23
a soft t breaketh the bone Prov 25:15
her t is the law of kindness Prov 31:26
and his t as a devouring fire Is 30:27
the t of the learned Is 50:4
they have taught their t to speak lies Jer 9:5
let us smite him with the t Jer 18:18
the string of his t was loosed Mark 7:35
and bridleth not his t James 1:26
the t is a little member James 3:5
the t is a fire James 3:6
the t can no man tame James 3:8
refrain his t from evil 1 Pet 3:10
let us not love in word, neither in t 1 John 3:18

TOOL
lift up thy t upon it Ex 20:25
fashioned it with a graving t Ex 32:4
thou shalt not lift up any iron t Deut 27:5
not any t of iron heard in the house 1 Kgs 6:7

TOOTH
Eye for eye t for t Ex 21:24; Matt 5:38
time of trouble is like a broken t Prov 25:19

TOPHEL to´-fel
lime Deut 1:1

TOPHET to´-fet
burning Is 30:33

TOPHETH to´-feth
same as TOPHET 2 Kgs 23:10

TORCHES
the chariots shall be with flaming **t** Nah 2:3
like a **t** of fire in a sheaf Zech 12:6
lanterns and **t** and weapons John 18:3

TORMAH torm´-ah
privily Judg 9:31

TORMENT
his eyes being in **t** Luke 16:23
because fear hath **t** 1 John 4:18
their **t** was as the **t** of a scorpion Rev 9:5
the smoke of their **t** ascendeth up Rev 14:11

TORN
surely he is **t** in pieces Gen 44:28
or is **t** in pieces Ezek 4:14
for he hath **t**, and he will heal us Hos 6:1

TOSS
I am **t** up and down Ps 109:23
and **t** thee like a ball Is 22:18
O thou afflicted, **t** with tempest Is 54:11
no more children, **t** to and fro Eph 4:14

TOU to´-oo
same as TOI 1 Chr 18:9

TOUCH
neither shall ye **t** it, lest ye die Gen 3:3
whose hearts God had **t** 1 Sam 10:26
t not mine anointed 1 Chr 16:22; Ps 105:15
there shall no evil **t** thee Job 5:19
The things that my soul refused to **t** Job 6:7
Lo, this hath **t** thy lips Is 6:7
and **t** my mouth Jer 1:9
he that **t** you, **t** the apple of his eye Zech 2:8
If I may but **t** his garment Matt 9:21
If I may but **t** his clothes Mark 5:28
that he should **t** them Mark 10:13; Luke 18:15
Jesus saith unto her, **T** me not John 20:17
t not the unclean thing 2 Cor 6:17

TOWER
my high **t** 2 Sam 22:3; Ps 18:2
a strong **t** from the enemy Ps 61:3
my high **t** and my deliverer Ps 144:2
The name of the Lord is a strong **t** Prov 18:10
where is he that counted the **t**? Is 33:18

TOWNCLERK
when the **t** had appeased Acts 19:35

TRACHONITIS tra-ko-ni´-tis
rugged Luke 3:1

TRAFFICK
the **t** of the spice merchants 1 Kgs 10:15
a land of **t** Ezek 17:4

TRAIN
came to Jerusalem with a very great **t** 1 Kgs 10:2
his **t** filled the temple Is 6:1

TRAITOR
which also was the **t** Luke 6:16
T, heady, highminded 2 Tim 3:4

TRAMPLE
the dragon shalt thou **t** Ps 91:13
and **t** them in my fury Is 63:3
lest they **t** them under their feet Matt 7:6

TRANQUILLITY
I may be a lengthening of thy **t** Dan 4:27

TRANSFORM
t by the renewing of your mind Rom 12:2
t themselves into the apostles of Christ 2 Cor 11:13
Satan himself is **t** into an angel of light 2 Cor 11:14
if his ministers also be **t** 2 Cor 11:15

TRANSGRESS
now do ye **t** the commandment of the Lord? Num 14:41
ye make the Lord's people to **t** 1 Sam 2:24
If ye **t**, I will scatter you abroad Neh 1:8
my mouth shall not **t** Ps 17:3
for a piece of bread that man will **t** Prov 28:21
the pastors also **t** against me Jer 2:8
thine iniquity, that thou hast **t** Jer 3:13
because he **t** by wine Hab 2:5

TRANSGRESSION
forgiving iniquity and **t** and sin Ex 34:7; Num 14:18
Saul died for his **t** 1 Chr 10:13
he mourned because of the **t** Ezra 10:6
why dost thou not pardon my **t** Job 7:21
Make me to know my **t** Job 13:23
My **t** is sealed up in a bag Job 14:17
I covered my **t** as Adam Job 31:33
I shall be innocent from the great **t** Ps 19:13
the sins of my youth nor my **t** Ps 25:7
Blessed is he whose **t** is forgiven Ps 32:1
thy tender mercies blot out my **t** Ps 51:1
as for our **t**, thou shalt purge them Ps 65:3
Fools, because of their **t** Ps 107:17
He that covereth a **t** seeketh love Prov 17:9
he that blotteth out thy **t** Is 43:25
blotted out, as a thick cloud, thy **t** Is 44:22
he was wounded for our **t** Is 53:5
for the **t** of my people was he stricken Is 53:8
shew my people their **t** Is 58:1
All his **t** that he hath committed Ezek 18:22
What is the **t** of Jacob? Mic 1:5

TRANSGRESSOR
Then will I teach **t** thy ways Ps 51:13
be not merciful to any wicked **t** Ps 59:5
the way of **t** is hard Prov 13:15
the **t** for the upright Prov 21:18
thou wast called a **t** from the womb Is 48:8
numbered with the **t** Is 53:12; Mark 15:28
reckoned among the **t** Luke 22:37

TRANSLATE
to **t** the kingdom 2 Sam 3:10
and hath **t** us into the kingdom Col 1:13
before his **t** he had his testimony Heb 11:5

TRAP
a **t** for him in the way Job 18:10
Let it become a **t** Ps 69:22
they set a **t**, they catch men Jer 5:26
Let their table be a snare, and a **t** Rom 11:9

TRAVAIL (n)
this sore **t** hath God given Eccl 1:13
days are sorrows, and his **t** grief Eccl 2:23
the **t** of his soul Is 53:11
remember, bretheren, our labour and **t** 1 Thess 2:9
with labour and **t** night and day 2 Thess 3:8

TRAVAIL (v)
he **t** with iniquity Ps 7:14
I **t** not, nor bring forth children Is 23:4
My little children, of whom I **t** Gal 4:19
the whole creation **t** in pain Rom 8:22

TRAVELLER
the **t** walked through byways Judg 5:6
a **t** unto the rich man 2 Sam 12:4
I opened my doors to the **t** Job 31:32

TREACHEROUS
the **t** dealer dealeth treacherously Is 21:2
an assembly of **t** men Jer 9:2
Her prophets are light and **t** persons Zeph 3:4

TREACHEROUSLY
dealest **t** and they dealt not **t** with thee Is 33:1
are all they happy that deal very **t**? Jer 12:1
her friends have dealt **t** with her Lam 1:2

TREAD
whereon the soles of your feet shall **t** Deut 11:24
when he **t** out the corn Deut 25:4; 1 Cor 9:9; 1 Tim 5:18
t down my life upon the earth Ps 7:5
through thy name will we **t** them Ps 44:5
he it is that shall **t** down our enemies Ps 60:12; 108:13
Thou shalt **t** upon the lion and adder Ps 91:13
t them down like the mire of the streets Is 10:6
the treaders shall **t** out no wine in their presses Is 16:10
I will **t** them in mine anger Is 63:3
none shall **t** with shouting Jer 48:33
ye must **t** down the residue of your pastures Ezek 34:18
loveth to **t** out corn Hos 10; 11
ye shall **t** down the wicked Mal 4:3

TREASURE
God of your father hath given you **t** Gen 43:23
ye shall be a peculiar **t** unto me Ex 19:5
Lord shall open unto thee his good **t** Deut 28:12
dig for it more than for hid **t** Job 3:21
the **t** of the snow Job 38:22
thou fillest with thy hid **t** Ps 17:14
Israel for his peculiar **t** Ps 135:4
searchest for her as for hid **t** Prov 2:4
I will fill their **t** Prov 8:21
T of wickedness profiteth nothing Prov 10:2
than great **t** and trouble therewith Prov 15:16
There is **t** to be desired Prov 21:20
the peculiar **t** of kings Eccl 2:8
neither is there any end of their **t** Is 2:7
I will give thee the **t** of darkness Is 45:3
we have **t** in the field Jer 41:8
waters abundant in **t** Jer 51:13
the **t** of gold and silver Dan 11:43
the **t** of wickedness Mic 6:10
where your **t** is there will your heart be Matt 6:21; Luke 12:34
out of the good **t** of the heart Matt 12:35
like unto **t** hid in a field Matt 13:44
out of his **t** things new and old Matt 13:52
thou shalt have **t** in heaven Matt 19:21; Mark 10:21; Luke 18:22
that layeth up **t** for himself Luke 12:21
we have this **t** in earthen vessels 2 Cor 4:7
the **t** of wisdom and knowledge Col 2:3
greater riches than the **t** in Egypt Heb 11:26
heaped **t** together for the last days James 5:3

TREASURER
I made **t** over the treasuries Neh 13:13
Go, get thee unto this **t** Is 22:15
the captains, the judges, the **t** Dan 3:2

TREASURY
they shall come into the **t** of the Lord Josh 6:19
the house of the king under the **t** Jer 38:11
not lawful for to put them into the **t** Matt 27:6

TREE
the **t** of the field is man's life Deut 20:19
there is hope of a **t** Job 14:7
wickedness shall be broken as a **t** Job 24:20
be like a **t** planted Ps 1:3; Jer 17:8
the **t** of the Lord are full of sap Ps 104:16
the place where the **t** falleth Eccl 11:3
Behold, I am a dry **t** Is 56:3
t of righteousness Is 61:3

What is the vine t more than any t Ezek 15:2
all the t of Eden Ezek 31:9

TREMBLE
t and be in anguish Deut 2:25
the earth t, and the heavens dropped Judg 5:4
Then the earth shook and t 2 Sam 22:8; Ps 18:7
assembled unto me every one that t Ezra 9:4
the pillars thereof t Job 9:6
the pillars of heaven t Job 26:11
rejoice with t Ps 2:11
thou hast made the earth to t Ps 60:2
lightened the world; the earth t and shook Ps 77:18
the earth saw and t Ps 97:4
the Lord reigneth, let the people t Ps 99:1
he looketh on the earth, and it t Ps 104:32
the keepers of the house shall t Eccl 12:3
the man that made the earth to t Is 14:16
that the nations may t at thy presence Is 64:2
ye that t at his word Is 66:5
will ye not t at my presence Jer 5:22
they shall fear and t Jer 33:9
Shall not the land t for this Amos 8:8
Felix t and answered Acts 24:25
devils also believe, and t James 2:19

TRENCH
he came to the t 1 Sam 17:20
Saul lay in the t 1 Sam 26:5
he made a t about the altar 1 Kgs 18:32
enemies shall cast a t about thee Luke 19:43

TRESPASS
What is my t? Gen 31:36
Forgive, I pray thee now the t Gen 50:17
rulers have been chief in this t Ezra 9:2
as goeth on still in his t Ps 68:21
if ye forgive men their t Matt 6:14
not imputing their t unto them 2 Cor 5:19
dead in t and sins Eph 2:1
having forgiven you all t Col 2:13

TRIAL
he will laugh at the t of the innocent Job 9:23
a great t of affliction 2 Cor 8:2
the t of your faith 1 Pet 1:7
fiery t which is to try you 1 Pet 4:12

TRIBES
not one feeble person among their t Ps 105:37
the t of the Lord Ps 122:4
they that are the stay of the t Is 19:13
my servant to raise up the t of Jacob Is 49:6
according to oaths of the t Hab 3:9
then shall all t of the earth mourn Matt 24:30

TRIBULATION
When thou art in t Deut 4:30
the time of your t Judg 10:14
when t or persecution ariseth Matt 13:21
then shall be great t Matt 24:21
In the world ye shall have t John 16:33
through much t enter into the kingdom of God Acts 14:22
t worketh patience Rom 5:3
Reloicing in hope, patient in t Rom 12:12

TRIBUTARY
there in shall be t unto thee Deut 20:11
Canaanites dwelt among them, and became t Judg 1:30
how is she become t! Lam 1:1

TRIBUTE
a servant unto t Gen 49:15
the Lord's t of the sheep Num 31:37
a t of a freewill offering Deut 16:10
shall not be lawful to impose toll, t, or custom Ezra 7:24
borrowed money for the king's t Neh 5:4
the slothful shall be under t Prov 12:24

TRIM
nor t his beard 2 Sam 19:24
Why t thou thy way to seek love? Jer 2:33
those virgins arose, and t Matt 25:7

TRIUMPH
he hath t gloriously Ex 15:1
let not mine enemies t Ps 25:2
I will t in the works of thy hands Ps 92:4
which always causeth us to t 2 Cor 2:14
a shew of them openly, t over them Col 2:15

TROAS tro´-as
a region around Troy Acts 16:8

TRODDEN
the old way which wicked men have t Job 22:15
thou hast t down all them that err Ps 119:118
and it shall be t down Is 5:5
I have t the winepress alone Is 63:3
now shall she be t down as mire Mic 7:10
and to be t under foot Matt 5:13
Jerusalem shall be t down of the Gentiles Luke 21:24
hath t under foot the Son of God Heb 10:29

TRODE
and t down the thistle 2 Kgs 14:9; 2 Chr 25:18
they t one upon another Luke 12:1

TROOP
I have run through a t 2 Sam 22:30; Ps 18:29
the t of robbers spoileth Hos 7:1

TROPHIMUS trof´-im-us
master of the house (?) Acts 20:4

TROUBLE (n)
many evils and t shall befall Deut 31:17
in my t I have prepared for the house of the Lord 1 Chr 22:14
let not all the t seem little before thee Neh 9:32
yet t came Job 3:26
neither doth t spring out of the ground Job 5:6
man is born unto t Job 5:7
He shall deliver thee in six t Job 5:19
of few days, and full of t Job 14:1
I weep for him that was in t Job 30:25
giveth quietness, who then can make t? Job 34:29
I have reserved against the time of t Ps 38:23
a refuge in times of t Ps 9:9
Be not far from me for t is near Ps 22:11
The t of my heart are enlarged Ps 25:17
Redeem Israel, O God, out of all his t Ps 25:22
in the time of t he shall hide me Ps 27:5
a very present help in t Ps 46:1
they are not in t as other men Ps 73:5
my soul is full of t Ps 88:3
T and anguish have taken hold on me Ps 119:143
Though I walk in the midst of t Ps 138:7
behold at eveningtide t Is 17:14
into the land of t and anguish Is 30:6
the former t are forgotten Is 65:16
they shall not labour in vain nor bring forth for t Is 65:23
in time of their t they will say, Arise, save us Jer 2:27
a time of health, and behold t Jer 8:15
such shall have t in the flesh 1 Cor 7:28
comfort them which are in t 2 Cor 1:4

TROUBLE (v)
Why hast thou t us? Josh 7:25
Art thou he that t Israel? 1 Kgs 18:17
I have not t Israel; but thou 1 Kgs 18:18
it toucheth thee, and thou art t Job 4:5
how are they increased that t me! Ps 3:1
I am so t that I cannot speak Ps 77:4
let not thy thoughts t thee Dan 5:10
the north shall t him Dan 11:44
see that ye be not t Matt 24:6
Why t ye the woman? Matt 26:10
into the pool and t the water John 5:4
he groaned in the spirit, and was t John 11:33
Now is my soul t John 12:27
he was t in spirit John 13:21
We are t on every side 2 Cor 4:8; 7:5
there be some that t you Gal 1:7
let no man t me Gal 6:17

TROUBLING
There the wicked cease from t Job 3:17
after the t of the water John 5:4

TRUCE-BREAKERS
Without natural affection, t 2 Tim 3:3

TRUE
we are t men Gen 42:11
tell me nothing but that which is t 1 Kgs 22:16
Israel hath been without the t God 2 Chr 15:3
right judgments, and t laws Neh 9:13
Thy word is t from the beginning Ps 119:160
A t witness delivereth souls Prov 14:25
the Lord is the t God Jer 10:10
we know that thou art t Matt 22:16; Mark 12:14
commit to your trust the t riches Luke 16:11
That was the t Light John 1:9
the t worshippers shall worship the Father John 4:23
If I bear witness of myself, my witness is not t John 5:31
my Father giveth you the t bread John 6:32
all things that John spake of this man were t John 10:41
I am the t vine John 15:1
they may know thee the only t God John 17:3
as deceivers, and yet t 2 Cor 6:8
God is created in t holiness Eph 4:24
bretheren, whatsoever things are t Phil 4:8
draw near with a t heart Heb 10:22
This is the t God, and eternal life 1 John 5:20

TRUST
Though he slay me, yet will I t in him Job 13:15
Wilt thou t him, because his strength is great? Job 39:11
O my God, I t in thee Ps 25:2
I t in the Lord Ps 31:6
T in the Lord Ps 37:3; 40:3; Prov 3:5
I t in thee Ps 55:23
I will t in thee Ps 56:3
T in him at all times Ps 62:8
t thou in the Lord Ps 115:9; Is 26:4
It is better to t in the Lord Ps 118:8
for in thee do I t Ps 143:8
my shield and he in whom I t Ps 144:2
He that t in his own heart is a fool Prov 28:26
let him t in the name of the Lord Is 50:10
let thy widows t in me Jer 49:11
T ye not in a friend Mic 7:5
he knoweth them that t in him Nah 1:7
He t in God; let him deliver him now Matt 27:43
parable unto certain which t in themselves Luke 18:9

TRUTH
a God of t and without iniquity Deut 32:4
speaketh the t in his heart Ps 15:2
thou desirest t in the inward parts Ps 51:6
his t shall be thy shield and buckler Ps 91:4
the t of the Lord endureth for ever Ps 117:2
I have chosen the way of t Ps 119:30
Buy the t and sell it not Prov 23:23
t is fallen in the streets Is 59:14
they are not valiant for the t Jer 9:3
Speak every man the t to his neighbour Zech 8:16
the law of t was in his mouth Mal 2:6
full of grace and t John 1:14

know the **t**, and the **t** shall make you free John 8:32
I am the way, the **t**, and the life John 14:6
Spirit of **t** is come he will guide you into all **t** John 16:13
Pilate saith unto him what is **t**? John 18:38
who hold the **t** in unrighteousness Rom 1:18
unleavened bread of sincerity and **t** 1 Cor 5:8
can do nothing against **t**, but for the **t** 2 Cor 13:8
speaking the **t** in love Eph 4:15
the pillar and ground of **t** 1 Tim 3:15
rightly dividing the word of **t** 2 Tim 2:15
if any of you err from the **t** James 5:19

TRY
God left him, to **t** him 2 Chr 32:31
when he hath **t** me, I shall come forth as gold Job 23:10
t my reins and my heart Ps 26:2
I will melt them and **t** them Jer 9:7
I will **t** them as gold is **t** Zech 13:9
the fire shall **t** every man's work 1 Cor 3:13
when he is **t**, he shall receive the crown James 1:12
t the spirits whether they are of God 1 John 4:1

TRYPHENA tri-fe´-nah
delicate Rom 16:12

TRYPHOSA tri-fo´-sah
delicate Rom 16:12

TUBAL-CAIN too´-bal-kane´
producer of weapons (?) Gen 4:22

TUBAL too´-bal
production (?) Gen 10:2

TURN
who can **t** him? Job 23:13
If he **t** not, he will whet his sword Ps 7:12
T you at my reproof Prov 1:23
t thou me, and I shall be **t** Jer 31:18
T thou us unto thee, O Lord, and we shall be **t** Lam 5:21
Repent, and **t** Ezek 14:6; 18:30
if thou warn the wicked of his way to **t** from it Ezek 33:9
Therefore **t** thou to thy God Hos 12:6
t ye even to me with all your heart Joel 2:12
T you to the strong hold, ye prisoners Zech 9:12
t to him the other also Matt 5:39
to **t** them from darkness to light Acts 26:18
from such **t** away 2 Tim 3:5

TWAIN
with **t** he covered his face Is 6:2
go with him **t** Matt 5:41
they **t** shall be one flesh Matt 19:5
to make of himself **t** one new man Eph 2:15

TWICE
God speaketh once, yea **t** Job 33:14
the cock crow **t** Mark 14:30
I fast **t** in the week Luke 18:12
without fruit, **t** dead Jude 1:12

TWINKLING
in the **t** of an eye 1 Cor 15:52

TWO-EDGED
sharp as a **t** sword Prov 5:4
any **t** sword, and piercing Heb 4:12

TYCHICUS tik´-ik-us
fortuitous Acts 20:4

TYRANNUS ti-ran´-us
tyrant Acts 19:9

TYRE tire
rock Josh 19:29

TYRUS ti´-rus
Latin name of TYRE Jer 25:22

U

UCAL oo´-kal
I shall prevail Prov 30:1

UEL oo´-el
will of God (?) Ezra 10:34

ULAI oo´-la-i
a river in Babylon Dan 8:2

ULAM oo´-lam
foremost 1 Chr 7:16

ULLA ool´-ah
yoke 1 Chr 7:39

UMMAH oom´-ah
community Josh 19:30

UNADVISEDLY
he spake **u** Ps 106:33

UNAWARES
that day come upon you **u** Luke 21:34
false brethren **u** brought in Gal 2:4
entertained angels **u** Heb 13:2
crept in **u** Jude 1:4

UNBELIEF
help thou mine **u** Mark 9:24
u make the faith of God without effect Rom 3:3
concluded them all in **u** Rom 11:32
evil heart of **u** Heb 3:12

UNBLAMEABLE
holy and **u** Col 1:22
stablish your hearts **u** 1 Thess 3:13

UNCERTAIN
give an **u** sound 1 Cor 14:8
nor trust in **u** riches 1 Tim 6:17

UNCLEAN
not call any man common or **u** Acts 10:28
nothing **u** Rom 14:14
touch not the **u** thing 2 Cor 6:17

UNCLOTHED
we would be **u** 2 Cor 5:4

UNCORRUPTNESS
in doctrine shewing **u** Titus 2:7

UNCTION
an **u** from the Holy One 1 John 2:20

UNDEFILED
blessed are the **u** Ps 119:1
pure religion and **u** James 1:27
an inheritance incorruptible, and **u** 1 Pet 1:4

UNDER
they are all **u** sin Rom 3:9
I keep **u** my body 1 Cor 9:27
u the curse Gal 3:10

UNDERSTAND
Who can **u** his errors? Ps 19:12
then **u** I their end Ps 73:17
I **u** more than the ancients Ps 119:100
thou **u** my thought afar off Ps 139:2
all plain to him that **u** Prov 8:9
how can a man then **u** his own way? Prov 20:24
though he **u** he will not answer Prov 29:19
hear ye indeed, but **u** not Is 6:9
a vexation only to **u** the report Is 28:19
he **u** and knoweth me Jer 9:24
thou didst set thine heart to **u** Dan 10:12
none of the wicked shall **u**, but the wise shall **u** Dan 12:10
Who is wise, and he shall **u** these things? Hos 14:9
Have ye **u** all these things? Matt 13:51
whoso readeth, let him **u** Matt 24:15
that they might **u** the scriptures Luke 24:45
Why do ye not **u** my speech? John 8:43
there is none that **u** Rom 3:11
they that have not heard shall **u** Rom 15:21
u all mysteries 1 Cor 13:2
I **u** as a child 1 Cor 13:11

UNDERSTANDING
in wisdom, and **u** Ex 31:3
your wisdom and your **u** Deut 4:6
hast asked for thyself **u** 1 Kgs 3:11
gave Solomon wisdom and **u** 1 Kgs 4:29
filled with wisdom, and **u** 1 Kgs 7:14
had **u** of the times 1 Chr 12:32
had **u** in visions 2 Chr 26:5
he hath counsel and **u** Job 12:13
taketh away the **u** of the aged Job 12:20
thou hast hid their heart from **u** Job 17:4
where is the place of **u**? Job 28:12
the Almighty giveth them **u** Job 32:8
who hath given **u** to the heart? Job 38:36
imparted to her **u** Job 39:17
sing ye praises with **u** Ps 47:7
meditation of my heart shall be of **u** Ps 49:3
give me **u** Ps 119:34, 73,125,144,169
I have more **u** than all my teachers Ps 119:99
through thy precepts I get **u** Ps 119:104
his **u** is infinite Ps 147:5
apply thine heart to **u** Prov 2:2
u shall keep thee Prov 2:11
lean not unto thine own **u** Prov 3:5
by **u** hath he established the heavens Prov 3:19
get wisdom, get **u** Prov 4:5
u put forth her voice? Prov 8:1
go in the way of **u** Prov 9:6
the knowledge of the Holy is **u** Prov 9:10
He that is slow to wrath is of great **u** Prov 14:29
U is a wellspring of life Prov 16:22
Wisdom is before him that hath **u** Prov 17:24
he that keepeth **u** shall find good Prov 19:8
u nor counsel against the Lord Prov 21:30
by **u** it is established Prov 24:3
have not the **u** of a man Prov 30:2
nor yet riches to men of **u** Eccl 9:11
rest upon him, the spirit of wisdom and **u** Is 11:2
it is a people of no **u** Is 27:11
u of their prudent men shall be hid Is 29:14
shewed to him the way of **u**? Is 40:14
there is no searching of his **u** Is 40:28
shall feed you with knowledge and **u** Jer 3:15
with thine **u** thou hast gotten thee riches Ezek 28:4
mine **u** returned Dan 4:34
Are ye also yet without **u**? Matt 15:16
are ye so without **u** Mark 7:18
with all the **u** Mark 12:33
astonished at his **u** Luke 2:47
then opened he their **u** Luke 24:45
bring to nothing the **u** of the prudent 1 Cor 1:19
I will pray with the **u** also 1 Cor 14:15
be not children in **u** 1 Cor 14:20
having the **u** darkened Eph 4:18
the peace of God, which passeth all **u** Phil 4:7

UNDERTAKE
u for me Is 38:14

UNDONE
he left nothing **u** Josh 11:15
I am **u** Is 6:5
not to leave the other **u** Matt 23:23; Luke 11:42

UNEQUAL
are not your ways **u**? Ezek 18:25,29; 2 Cor 6:14

UNFAITHFUL
dealt **u** like their fathers Ps 78:57
Confidence in an **u** man Prov 25:19

UNFEIGNED
by love **u** 2 Cor 6:6
of faith **u** 1 Tim 1:5

I call to remembrance the **u** faith 2 Tim 1:5
unto **u** love of the brethren 1 Pet 1:22

UNFRUITFUL
choke the word, and he becometh **u** Matt 13:22
the **u** works of darkness Eph 5:11
that they be not **u** Titus 3:14
u in the knowledge of our Lord 2 Pet 1:8

UNGODLINESS
revealed from heaven against all **u** Rom 1:18
shall turn away **u** from Jacob Rom 11:26
they will increase unto more **u** 2 Tim 2:16
denying **u** Titus 2:12

UNGODLY
Shouldest thou help the **u**? 2 Chr 19:2
God hath delivered me to the **u** Job 16:11
the counsel of the **u** Ps 1:1
the way of the **u** shall perish Ps 1:6
plead my cause against an **u** nation Ps 43:1
An **u** man diggeth up evil Prov 16:27
Christ died for the **u** Rom 5:6
where shall the **u** and the sinner appear? 1 Pet 4:18
perdition of **u** men 2 Pet 3:7

UNHOLY
put difference between holy and **u** Lev 10:10
for **u** and profane 1 Tim 1:9
unthankful, **u** 2 Tim 3:2
an **u** thing Heb 10:29

UNITE
be not thou **u** Gen 49:6
u my heart to fear thy name Ps 86:11

UNITY
brethren to dwell together in **u** Ps 133:1
endeavouring to keep the **u** of the Spirit Eph 4:3
come in the **u** of the faith Eph 4:13

UNJUST
u man Ps 43:1
the hope of **u** men perisheth Prov 11:7
he that by usury and **u** gain Prov 28:8
An **u** man is an abomination Prov 29:27
the **u** knoweth no shame Zeph 3:5
sendeth rain on the just and on the **u** Matt 5:45
hear what the **u** judge saith Luke 18:6
not as other men are, extortioners, **u** Luke 18:11
both of the just and **u** Acts 24:15
go to law before the **u** 1 Cor 6:1
the just for the **u** 1 Pet 3:18
he that is **u**, let him be **u** still Rev 22:11

UNKNOWN
inscription To The **U** God Acts 17:23
as **u**, and yet well known 2 Cor 6:9
was **u** by face unto the churches Gal 1:22

UNLAWFUL
ye know how that it is an **u** thing Acts 10:28
from day to day with their **u** deeds 2 Pet 2:8

UNLEARNED
perceived that they were **u** Acts 4:13
the room of the **u** 1 Cor 14:16
foolish and **u** questions avoid 2 Tim 2:23
they that are **u** and unstable wrest 2 Pet 3:16

UNMINDFUL
thou art **u** Deut 32:18

UNMOVEABLE
remained **u** Acts 27:41
be ye stedfast, **u** 1 Cor 15:58

UNNI oon´-i
depressed 1 Chr 15:18

UNPREPARED
find you **u** 2 Cor 9:4

UNPROFITABLE
u talk Job 15:3
cast ye the **u** servant Matt 25:30
we are **u** servants Luke 17:10

UNPUNISHED
the wicked shall not be **u** Prov 11:21
he shall not be **u** Prov 16:5
he that is glad at calamities shall not be **u** Prov 17:5
a false witness shall not be **u** Prov 19:5
should ye be utterly **u** Jer 25:29
thou shalt not go **u** Jer 49:12

UNQUENCHABLE
burn up the chaff with **u** fire Matt 3:12
the chaff he will burn with fire **u** Luke 3:17

UNREASONABLE
it seemeth to me **u** Acts 25:27
delivered from **u** and wicked men 2 Thess 3:2

UNREPROVEABLE
u in his sight Col 1:22

UNRIGHTEOUS
an **u** witness Ex 23:1
decree **u** decrees Is 10:1
the **u** man his thoughts Is 55:7
Is God **u** Rom 3:5
God is not **u** to forget your work Heb 6:10

UNRIGHTEOUSNESS
mammon of **u** Luke 16:9
hold the truth in **u** Rom 1:18
but obey **u** Rom 2:8
if our **u** commend righteousness Rom 3:5
instruments of **u** Rom 6:13
Is there **u** with God? Rom 9:14
what fellowship hath righteousness with **u**? 2 Cor 6:14
had pleasure in **u** 2 Thess 2:12
receive the reward of **u** 2 Pet 2:13
cleanse us from all **u** 1 John 1:9
all **u** is sin 1 John 5:17

UNRULY
warn them that are **u** 1 Thess 5:14
not accused of riot or **u** Titus 1:6
an **u** evil James 3:8

UNSAVOURY
Can that which is **u** be eaten Job 6:6

UNSEARCHABLE
doeth great things and **u** Job 5:9
his greatness is **u** Ps 145:3
how **u** are his judgments Rom 11:33
the **u** riches of Christ Eph 3:8

UNSEEMLY
working that which is **u** Rom 1:27
doth not behave itself **u** 1 Cor 13:5

UNSKILFUL
useth milk is **u** in the word Heb 5:13

UNSPEAKABLE
his **u** gift 2 Cor 9:15
heard **u** words 2 Cor 12:4
rejoice with joy **u** 1 Pet 1:8

UNSPOTTED
u from the world James 1:27

UNSTABLE
u as water Gen 49:4
u in all his ways James 1:8
beguiling **u** souls 2 Pet 2:14

UNTHANKFUL
kind unto the **u** Luke 6:35
u, unholy 2 Tim 3:2

UNWASHEN
eat with **u** hands Matt 15:20
with **u** hands Mark 7:2,5

UNWISE
O foolish people and **u** Deut 32:6
he is an **u** son Hos 13:13
both the wise, and to the **u** Rom 1:14
Wherefore be ye not **u** Eph 5:17

UNWORTHY
u of everlasting life Acts 13:46
u to judge the smallest matters 1 Cor 6:2

UPBRAID
Then began he to **u** the cities Matt 11:20
and **u** them with their unbelief Mark 16:14
to all men liberally, and **u** not James 1:5

UPHARSIN oo-far´-sin
and dividers Dan 5:25

UPHAZ oo-faz´
unknown location known for its gold Jer 10:9

UPHOLD
u me with thy free spirit Ps 51:12
with them that **u** my soul Ps 54:4
U me according unto thy word Ps 119:116
the Lord **u** all that fall Ps 145:14
I will **u** thee with the right hand Is 41:10
my servant, whom I **u** Is 42:1
there was none to **u** Is 63:5
u all things by the word of his power Heb 1:3

UPPERMOST
u rooms at feasts Matt 23:6; Mark 12:39
love the **u** seats Luke 11:43

UPRIGHT
u man is laughed to scorn Job 12:4
U men shall be astonished Job 17:8
then shall I be **u** Ps 19:13
Good and **u** is the Lord Ps 25:8
such as be of **u** conversation Ps 37:14
the **u** shall have dominion Ps 49:14
to shew that the Lord is **u** Ps 92:15
the assembly of the **u** Ps 111:1
unto the **u** there ariseth light Ps 112:4
that are **u** in their hearts Ps 125:4
the **u** shall dwell in the land Prov 2:21
The integrity of the **u** Prov 11:3
such as are **u** in their way Prov 11:20
the tabernacle of the **u** Prov 14:11
the prayer of the **u** is his delight Prov 15:8
the **u** shall have good things Prov 28:10
God hath made man **u** Eccl 7:29
the **u** love thee Song 1:4

UPRIGHTLY
Do ye judge **u**? Ps 58:1
I will judge **u** Ps 75:2
withhold from them that walk **u** Ps 84:11
He that walketh **u** Prov 10:9
man of understanding walketh **u** Prov 15:21
Whoso walketh **u** shall be saved Prov 28:18
and speaketh **u** Is 33:15

UPRIGHTNESS
in **u** of heart 1 Kgs 3:6
hast pleasure in **u** 1 Chr 29:17
the **u** of thy ways Job 4:6
to shew unto man his **u** Job 33:23
Let integrity and **u** preserve me Ps 25:21
lead me into the land of **u** Ps 143:10
Who leave the paths of **u** Prov 2:13

UPROAR
there be an **u** among the people Matt 26:5
lest there be an **u** of the people Mark 14:2
set all the city in an **u** Acts 17:5
all Jerusalem was in an **u** Acts 21:31

UPWARD
as the sparks fly **u** Job 5:7
the spirit of man that goeth **u** Eccl 3:21
mine eyes fail with looking **u** Is 38:14

UR oor
- *light* Gen 11:28

URBANE ur′-ban
- *pleasant* Rom 16:9

URGE
- he **u** him, and he took it Gen 33:11
- they **u** him till he was ashamed 2 Kgs 2:17
- the Pharisees began to **u** him Luke 11:53

URGENT
- the Egyptians were **u** Ex 12:33
- the king's commandment was **u** Dan 3:22

URI oo′-ri
- *fiery* Ex 31:2

URIAH oo-ri′-ah
- *light of Jehovah* 2 Sam 11:3

URIAS oo-ri′-as
- Gr. for URIAH Matt 1:6

URIEL oo′-ri-el
- *light of God* 1 Chr 6:24

URIJAH oo′-ri-jah
- same as URIAH 2 Kgs 16:10

URIM oo′-rim
- *light* Ex 28:30

USE
- **u** not vain repetitions Matt 6:7
- they that **u** this world 1 Cor 7:31
- **u** not liberty for an occasion Gal 5:13
- if a man **u** it lawfully 1 Tim 1:8

USURP
- nor to **u** authority over the man 1 Tim 2:12

UTHAI ooth′-a-i
- *helpful* 1 Chr 9:4

UTTER
- I will **u** dark sayings Ps 78:2
- Who can **u** the mighty acts Ps 106:2
- My lips shall **u** praise Ps 119:171
- she **u** her voice in the streets Prov 1:20
- thine heart shall **u** perverse things Prov 23:33
- A fool **u** all his mind Prov 29:11
- let not thine heart be hasty to **u** Eccl 5:2
- groanings which cannot be **u** Rom 8:26
- not lawful for a man to **u** 2 Cor 12:4
- and hard to be **u** Heb 5:11

UTTERANCE
- as the Spirit gave them **u** Acts 2:4

UTTERLY
- forsake me not **u** Ps 119:8
- I, even I, will **u** forget you Jer 23:39
- I will **u** consume all things Zeph 1:2
- shall **u** perish in their own 2 Pet 2:12

UTTERMOST
- till thou hast paid the **u** farthing Matt 5:26
- wrath is come upon them to the **u** 1 Thess 2:16
- able also to save them to the **u** Heb 7:25

UZ ooz
- *fertile* Gen 10:23

UZAI ooz′-a-i
- *hoped for* (?) Neh 3:25

UZAL ooz′-al
- *wanderer* Gen 10:27

UZZA ooz′-ah
- *strength* 2 Kgs 21:18

UZZAH ooz′-ah
- form of UZZA 2 Sam 6:3

UZZEN-SHERAH ooz-zen-she′-rah
- 1 *little ear,*
- 2 named for daughter of EPHRAIM 1 Chr 7:24

UZZI ooz′-i
- short for UZZIAH 1 Chr 6:5

UZZIA ooz-i′-ah
- form of UZZIAH 1 Chr 11:44

UZZIAH ooz-i′-ah
- *might of Jehovah* 2 Kgs 15:13

UZZIEL ooz′-i-el
- *power of God* Ex 6:18

UZZIELITES ooz′-i-el-ites
- descendants of Uzziel Num 3:27

V

VAGABOND
- Let his children be continually **v** Ps 109:10
- Then certain **v** Jews Acts 19:13

VAIN
- not regard **v** words Ex 5:9
- not take the name of the Lord thy God in **v** Ex 20:7; Deut 5:11
- it is not a **v** thing for you Deut 32:47
- as one of the **v** fellows 2 Sam 6:20
- they are but **v** words 2 Kgs 18:20; Is 36:5
- For **v** man would be wise Job 11:12
- Shall **v** words have an end? Job 16:3
- How then comfort ye me in **v** Job 21:34
- the people imagine a **v** thing Ps 2:1; Acts 4:25
- I have not sat with **v** persons Ps 26:4
- A horse is a **v** thing for safety Ps 33:17
- every man walketh in a **v** shew Ps 39:6
- **v** is the help of man Ps 60:11; 108:12
- hast thou made all men in **v**? Ps 89:47
- labour in **v** Ps 127:1; Is 49:4; 65:23
- followeth **v** persons Prov 12:11
- beauty is **v** Prov 31:30
- all the days of his **v** life Eccl 6:12
- Bring no more **v** oblations Is 1:13
- he created it not in **v** Is 45:18
- Seek ye me in **v** Is 45:19
- in **v** is salvation hoped for Jer 3:23
- the customs of the people are **v** Jer 10:3
- in **v** shalt thou use medicines Jer 46:11
- Ye have said, It is **v** to serve God Mal 3:14
- use not **v** repetitions Matt 6:7
- in **v** do they worship me Matt 15:9; Mark 7:7
- he beareth not the sword in **v** Rom 13:4
- unless ye have believed in **v** 1 Cor 15:2
- receive not the grace of God in **v** 2 Cor 6:1
- run in **v** Gal 2:2
- unruly and **v** talkers Titus 1:10
- this man's religion is **v** James 1:26
- from your **v** conversation 1 Pet 1:18

VAJEZATHA va′-je-za′-thah
- *strong as the wind* (?) Esth 9:9

VALIANT
- be thou **v** for me 1 Sam 18:17
- for thou art a **v** man 1 Kgs 1:42
- put down the inhabitants like a **v** man Is 10:13
- they are not **v** for the truth Jer 9:3
- waxed **v** in fight Heb 11:34

VALUE
- physicians of no **v** Job 13:4
- of more **v** Matt 10:31; Luke 12:7

VANIAH va-ni′-ah
- *distress* (?) Ezra 10:36

VANISH
- Heavens shall **v** Is 51:6
- shall **v** away 1 Cor 13:8
- ready to **v** away Heb 8:13

VANITY
- to possess months of **v** Job 7:3
- **v** shall be his recompence Job 15:31
- God will not hear **v** Job 35:13
- speak **v** every one with his neighbour Ps 12:2
- every man at his best state is altogether **v** Ps 39:5
- are **v** Ps 62:9
- Man is like to **v** Ps 144:4
- Wealth gotten by **v** Prov 13:11
- Remove far from me **v** Prov 30:8
- **V** of **v**, saith the preacher Eccl 1:2; 12:8
- many things that increase **v** Eccl 6:11
- childhood and youth are **v** Eccl 11:10
- with the sieve of **v** Is 30:28
- they have burned incense to **v** Jer 18:15
- shall weary themselves for very **v**? Hab 2:13
- from these **v** unto the living God Acts 14:15
- the creature was made subject to **v** Rom 8:20
- walk, in the **v** of their mind Eph 4:17
- great swelling words of **v** 2 Pet 2:18

VARIABLENESS
- with whom is no **v** James 1:17

VARIANCE
- man at **v** against Matt 10:35
- witchcraft, hatred, **v**, emulations Gal 5:20

VASHNI vash′-ni
- *strong* (?), perhaps not a proper name 1 Chr 6:28

VASHTI vash′-ti
- *beautiful* Esth 1:9

VAUNT
- lest Israel **v** themselves Judg 7:2
- charity **v** not itself 1 Cor 13:4

VEHEMENT
- a most **v** flame Song 8:6
- what **v** desire 2 Cor 7:11

VEIL
- the **v** of the temple was rent Matt 27:51
- this day remaineth the same **v** 2 Cor 3:14

VENGEANCE
- To me belongeth **v** Deut 32:35
- the day of **v** Prov 6:34; Is 61:2
- garments of **v** for clothing Is 59:17
- **v** suffereth not to live Acts 28:4
- the **v** of eternal fire Jude 1:7

VERILY
- are **v** guilty Gen 42:21
- **v** he is God Ps 58:11
- **V** I have cleansed Ps 73:13
- Elijah **v** cometh first Mark 9:12

VERITY
- the works of his hands are **v** Ps 111:7
- teacher of the Gentiles in faith and **v** 1 Tim 2:7

VESSEL
- There is not a **v** more 2 Kgs 4:6
- I am like a broken **v** Ps 31:12
- bring an offering in a clean **v** Is 66:20
- a **v** wherein is no pleasure Jer 22:28
- fall like a pleasant **v** Jer 25:34
- gathered the good into **v** Matt 13:48
- the wise took oil in their **v** Matt 25:4
- he is a chosen **v** unto me Acts 9:15
- the **v** of wrath Rom 9:22
- the **v** of mercy Rom 9:23
- we have this treasure in earthen **v** 2 Cor 4:7
- to possess his **v** in sanctification 1 Thess 4:4
- he shall be a **v** unto honour 2 Tim 2:21
- giving honour unto the wife, as unto the weaker **v** 1 Pet 3:7

VESTRY
- him that was over the **v** 2 Kgs 10:22

VESTURE
- arrayed him in **v** of fine linen Gen 41:42
- cast lots upon my **v** Ps 22:18
- as a **v** shall thou change them Ps 102:26
- upon my **v** did they cast lots Matt 27:35
- as a **v** shalt thou fold Heb 1:12
- a **v** dipped in blood Rev 19:13

VEX
neither v a stranger Ex 22:21
shall not v him Lev 19:33
and shall v you in the land Num 33:55
how will he then v himself 2 Sam 12:18
How long will ye v my soul Job 19:2
Judah shall not v Ephraim Is 11:13
I will also v the hearts of many Ezek 32:9
my daughter is grievously v Matt 15:22
v his righteous soul 2 Pet 2:8

VEXATION
all is vanity and v Eccl 1:14
of v of his heart Eccl 2:22
such as was in her v Is 9:1
a v only to understand Is 28:19
howl for v of spirit Is 65:14

VICTORY
v that day was turned to mourning 2 Sam 19:2
the v 1 Chr 29:11
hath gotten him the v Ps 98:1
send forth judgment unto v Matt 12:20
Death is swallowed up in v 1 Cor 15:54
v that overcometh the world, even our faith 1 John 5:4

VICTUALS
prepared for themselves any v Ex 12:39
the men took of their v Josh 9:14
v on the sabbath Neh 10:31
in the day wherein they sold v Neh 13:15
into villages, and buy themselves v Matt 14:15

VIEW
Go up and v the country Josh 7:2
and stood to v afar off 2 Kgs 2:7
and v the walls of Jerusalem Neh 2:13

VIGILANT
v, sober, of good behaviour 1 Tim 3:2
Be sober, be v 1 Pet 5:8

VILE
made themselves v 1 Sam 3:13
reputed v in your sight Job 18:3
I am v, what shall I answer thee? Job 40:4
v person Ps 15:4; Is 32:5; Dan 11:21
the precious from the v Jer 15:19
see, O Lord, for I am become v Lam 1:11
make thee v Nah 3:6
gave them up to v affections Rom 1:26
shall change our v body Phil 3:21
a poor man in v raiment James 2:2

VILLANY
Vile persons will speak v Is 32:6
they have committed v Jer 29:23

VINE
their v is of the v of Sodom Deut 32:32
eat anything that cometh of the v Judg 13:14
every man under his v 1 Kgs 4:25
eat ye every man of his own v 2 Kgs 18:31
a v out of Egypt Ps 80:8
Thy wife shall be as a fruitful v Ps 128:3
new wine mourneth, the v languisheth Is 24:7
Israel is an empty v Hos 10:1
they shall sit every man under his v Mic 4:4
fruit of the v Matt 26:29; Mark 14:25; Luke 22:18
I am the true v John 15:1

VINTAGE
they gather the v of the wicked Job 24:6
I have made their v shouting to cease Is 16:10
For the v shall fail Is 32:10
the grape gleanings of the v Mic 7:1

VIOL
The harp and the v Is 5:12
the noise of thy v Is 14:11

Chant to the sound of the v Amos 5:23; 6:5

VIOLENCE
earth was filled with v Gen 6:11
him that loveth v Ps 11:5
I have seen v and strife in the city Ps 55:9
weigh the v of your hands Ps 58:2
redeem their soul from deceit and v Ps 72:14
v covereth them as a garment Ps 73:6
drink the wine of v Prov 4:17
v covereth the mouth of the wicked Prov 10:6
because he had done no v Is 53:9
V shall no more be heard Is 60:18
they have filled the land with v Ezek 8:17
filled the midst of thee with v Ezek 28:16
store up v and robbery in their palaces Amos 3:10
spoiling and v are before me Hab 1:3
one covereth v with his garment Mal 2:16
the kingdom of heaven suffereth v Matt 11:12
Do v to no man Luke 3:14

VIOLENT
his v dealing Ps 7:16
v man Ps 18:48; 140:1; Prov 16:29

VIOLENTLY
He will surely v turn and toss thee Is 22:18
swine ran v down a steep place Matt 8:32; Mark 5:13

VIRGIN
a v shall conceive Is 7:14; Matt 1:23
O thou oppressed v Is 23:12
v daughter of Babylon Is 47:1
young man marrieth a v Is 62:5
for the v daughter of my people Jer 14:17

VIRTUE
v had gone out of him Mark 5:30
there went v out of him Luke 6:19
v has gone out of me Luke 8:46
if there be any v Phil 4:8

VIRTUOUS
thou art a v woman Ruth 3:11
v woman is a crown to her husband Prov 12:4
Who can find a v woman? Prov 31:10
daughters have done v Prov 31:29

VISAGE
his v was so marred Is 52:14
Their v is blacker than coal Lam 4:8
the form of his v was changed Dan 3:19

VISION
as a v of the night Job 20:8
Where there is no v, the people perish Prov 29:18
the valley of v Is 22:1
they err in v Is 28:7
prophets also find no v from the Lord Lam 2:9
I have multiplied v Hos 12:10
young men shall see v Joel 2:28; Acts 2:17
ashamed every one of his v Zech 13:4
Tell the v to no man Matt 17:9
they had also seen a v of angels Luke 24:23
not disobedient unto the heavenly v Acts 26:19

VISIT
God will surely v you Gen 50:24; Ex 13:19
v the iniquity of the fathers Ex 20:5; 34:7; Num 14:18; Deut 5:9
when I v, I will v their sin upon them Ex 32:34
how that the Lord had v his people Ruth 1:6
thou shalt v thy habitation Job 5:24
shouldest v him every morning Job 7:18
son of man, that thou v him Ps 8:4; Heb 2:6
v me with thy salvation Ps 106:4
Shall I not v for these things? Jer 5:9
I will v you, and perform my good word Jer 29:10
After many days thou shalt be v Ezek 38:8
I was sick, and ye v me Matt 25:36
God at the first did v the Gentiles Acts 15:14
To v the fatherless and widows James 1:27

VISITATION
thy v hath preserved Job 10:12
in the day of v Is 10:3; 1 Pet 2:12
the time of their v Jer 8:12; 10:15; 46:21; 50:27

VOCATION
worthy of the v Eph 4:1

VOICE
v of thy brother's blood Gen 4:10
The v is Jacob's v Gen 27:22
obey his v, provoke him not Ex 23:21
all the people answered with one v Ex 24:3
It is not the v of them that shout Ex 32:18
Did ever people hear the v of God Deut 4:33
nor make any noise with your v Josh 6:10
Is this thy v 1 Sam 24:16; 26:17
after the fire, a still small v 1 Kgs 19:12
there was neither v, nor hearing 2 Kgs 4:31
let no joyful v come therein Job 3:7
into the v of them that weep Job 30:31
a v roareth Job 37:4
canst thou thunder with a v like him? Job 40:9
My v shalt thou hear in the morning Ps 5:3
the v of my supplications Ps 31:22; 86:6
with the v of joy Ps 42:4
To day, if ye will hear his v Ps 95:7
the v of his word Ps 103:20
she uttereth her v in the streets Prov 1:20
not obeyed the v of my teachers Prov 5:13
and understanding put forth her v? Prov 8:1
my v is to the sons of man Prov 8:4
a fool's v is known Eccl 5:3
rise up at the v of the bird Eccl 12:4
The v of my beloved Song 2:8
the v of the turtle is heard Song 2:12
sweet is thy v Song 2:14
the v of my beloved that knocketh Song 5:2
exalt the v unto them Is 13:2
The v said, Cry Is 40:6
with a v of singing Is 48:20
with the v together shall they sing Is 52:8
v of weeping shall be no more heard Is 65:19
a v from the temple Is 66:6
the v of mirth, and the v of gladness Jer 7:34
the v of them that make merry Jer 30:19
A v of crying shall be Jer 48:3
a v of a multitude being at ease Ezek 23:42
one that hath a pleasant v Ezek 33:32
v was like a noise of many waters Ezek 43:2
lead her as with the v of doves Nah 2:7
v of one crying in the wilderness Matt 3:3; Mark 1:3; Luke 3:4
neither shall any man hear his v Matt 12:19
v of them and chief priests prevailed Luke 23:23
the dead shall hear the v of the Son of God John 5:25
sheep follow him, for they know his v John 10:4
they know not the v of strangers John 10:5
This v came not because of me John 12:30
Every one that is of the truth heareth my v John 18:37
and when she knew Peter's v Acts 12:14
I gave my v against them Acts 26:10
there are so many v in the world 1 Cor 14:10
that by my v I might teach others 1 Cor 14:19
now to change my v Gal 4:20
the v of the archangel 1 Thess 4:16
the dumb ass speaking with man's v 2 Pet 2:16
if any man hear my v Rev 3:20
lightnings and thunderings and a v Rev 4:5

VOID
without form, and v Gen 1:2; Jer 4:23
a nation v of counsel Deut 32:28
made v the covenant Ps 89:39
they have made v thy law Ps 119:126
v of wisdom Prov 11:12

it shall not return to me v Is 55:11
make v the counsel of Judah Jer 19:7
empty, and v, and waste Nah 2:10
a conscience v of offence Acts 24:16

VOLUME
in the v of the book Ps 40:7; Heb 10:7

VOLUNTARY
of his own v will Lev 1:3
a v offering Lev 7:16
peace offerings v unto the Lord Ezek 46:12
reward in a v humility Col 2:18

VOMIT
As a dog returneth to his v Prov 26:11; 2 Pet 2:22
drunken man staggereth in his v Is 19:14

VOPHSI vof'-si
expansion (?) Num 13:14

VOW (n)
vowed a v Gen 28:20; 31:13; Judg 11:30
beside your v Num 29:39
with her according to his v Judg 11:39
yearly sacrifice and his v 1 Sam 1:21
thou shalt pay thy v Job 22:27
I will pay my v Ps 22:25; 116:14
pay thy v unto the Most High Ps 50:14
Thy v are upon me, O God Ps 56:12
hast heard my v Ps 61:5
that I may daily perform my v Ps 61:8
unto thee shall the v be performed Ps 65:1
this day have I payed my v Prov 7:14
after v to make inquiry Prov 20:25
the son of my v Prov 31:2
When thou vowest a v unto God, defer not to pay Eccl 5:4
they shall v a v unto the Lord Is 19:21
for he had a v Acts 18:18
four men which have a v on them Acts 21:23

VOW (v)
if thou shalt forbear to v Deut 23:22
V, and pay unto the Lord your God Ps 76:11
and v unto the mighty God Ps 132:2

W

WAG
and w his head Jer 18:16
and w their head Lam 2:15
and w his hand Zeph 2:15

WAGES
what shall thy w be? Gen 29:15
Appoint me thy w Gen 30:28
changed my w ten times Gen 31:7
I will give thee thy w Ex 2:9
useth his neighbour's service without w Jer 22:13
earneth w to put in a bag with holes Hag 1:6
be content with your w Luke 3:14
he that reapeth receiveth w John 4:36
the w of sin is death Rom 6:23
the w of unrighteousness 2 Pet 2:15

WAGONS
take you w out of the land Gen 45:19
Two w and four oxen he gave Num 7:7
with chariots, w, and wheels Ezek 23:24

WAIL
w for the multitude Ezek 32:18
W shall be in all streets Amos 5:16
Therefore I will w and howl Mic 1:8
there shall be w and gnashing Matt 13:42
and them that w and w greatly Mark 5:38
all kindreds of the earth shall w Rev 1:7
fear of her torment, weeping and w Rev 18:15

WAIT
I have w for thy salvation Gen 49:18
by laying of w Num 35:20
should I w for the Lord any longer? 2 Kgs 6:33
will I w, till my change come Job 14:14
he is w for of the sword Job 15:22
If I w, the grave is mine house Job 17:13
and w, and kept silence Job 29:21
they w for me as for the rain Job 29:23
when I w for light, there came Job 30:26
none that w on thee be ashamed Ps 25:3
w on the Lord Ps 27:14; 37:34
our soul w for the Lord Ps 33:20
w patiently Ps 37:7
I will w on thy name Ps 52:9
my soul w upon God Ps 62:1
w thou only on God Ps 62:5
Praise w for thee, O God, in Sion Ps 65:1
mine eyes fail while I w for my God Ps 69:3
Let not them that w on thee Ps 69:6
These w all upon thee Ps 104:27
they w not for his counsel Ps 106:13
so our eyes w upon the Lord Ps 123:2
My soul w for the Lord Ps 130:6
but w on the Lord Prov 20:22
he that w on his master Prov 27:18
therefore will the Lord w Is 30:18
they that w upon the Lord shall renew Is 40:31
the isles shall w for his law Is 42:4
we w for light Is 59:9
prepared for him that w for him Is 64:4
in heart he layeth his w Jer 9:8
man should both hope and quietly w Lam 3:26
Blessed is he that w Dan 12:12
though it tarry, w for it Hab 2:3
poor of the flock that w upon me Zech 11:11
also w for the kingdom of God Mark 15:43
w for the consolation of Israel Luke 2:25
like unto men that w for their lord Luke 12:36
but w for promise of the Father Acts 1:4
w for the adoption Rom 8:23
then do we with patience w for it Rom 8:25
let us w on our ministering Rom 12:7
which w at the altar are partakers 1 Cor 9:13
w for the hope Gal 5:5
to w for his Son from heaven 1 Thess 1:10

WAKE
sleep a perpetual sleep, and not w Jer 51:39
Prepare war, w up the mighty men Joel 3:9
came again, and w me Zech 4:1
whether we w or sleep 1 Thess 5:10

WALK
w before me, and be thou perfect Gen 17:1
The Lord, before whom I w Gen 24:40
my fathers Abraham and Isaac did w Gen 48:15
whether they will w in my law Ex 16:4
the way wherein they must w Ex 18:20
I will w among you Lev 26:12
God w in midst of thy camp Deut 23:14
and w by the way Judg 5:10
Abner and his men w all that night 2 Sam 2:29
and he w upon a snare Job 18:8
he w in the circuit of heaven Job 22:14
by his light I w through darkness Job 29:3
though I w through the valley Ps 23:4
as for me, I will w in mine integrity Ps 26:11
W about Zion, and go round about her Ps 48:12
and w unto the house of God Ps 55:14
w before God in the light of the living? Ps 56:13
from them that w uprightly Ps 84:11
the pestilence that w in darkness Ps 91:6
who w upon the wings of the wind Ps 104:3
I will w before the Lord Ps 116:9
I will w at liberty Ps 119:45
though I w in the midst of trouble Ps 138:7
He that w uprightly w surely Prov 10:9
He that w with wise men shall be wise Prov 13:20
the poor that w in his integrity Prov 19:1
poor that w in his uprightness Prov 28:6
w uprightly shall be saved Prov 28:18
whoso w wisely, he shall be delivered Prov 28:26
the fool w in darkness Eccl 2:14
let us w in the light of the Lord Is 2:5
The people that w in darkness Is 9:2
Isaiah hath w naked and barefoot Is 20:3
saying, This is the way, w ye in it Is 30:21
the redeemed shall w there Is 35:9
that w in darkness, and hath no light? Is 50:10
w in the light of your fire Is 50:11
the good way, and w therein Jer 6:16
not in man that w to direct his steps Jer 10:23
thou hast w up and down Ezek 28:14
those that w in pride Dan 4:37
the just shall w in them Hos 14:9
can two w together Amos 3:3
to w humbly with thy God? Mic 6:8
even the old lion, w Nah 2:11
have w to and fro through the earth Zech 1:11
and that we have w mournfully Mal 3:14
Arise, and w? Matt 9:5
he w through dry places Matt 12:43
he w on the water Matt 14:29
Arise, and take up thy bed, and w? Mark 2:9
unto two of them, as they w Mark 16:12
Rise up and w? Luke 5:23
he w through dry places Luke 11:24
I must w to day, and to morrow Luke 13:33
Rise, take up thy bed, and w John 5:8
Take up thy bed, and w John 5:11,12
shall not w in darkness John 8:12
If any man w in the day John 11:9
rise up and w Acts 3:6
who also w in the steps of that faith Rom 4:12
w in newness of life Rom 6:4
who w not after the flesh, but after the Spirit Rom 8:1
we w by faith 2 Cor 5:7
as many as w according to this rule Gal 6:16
in time past ye w according to Eph 2:2
ordained that we should w in them Eph 2:10
w worthy of the vocation Eph 4:1
henceforth ye w not as other Gentiles Eph 4:17
w circumspectly Eph 5:15
mark them which w so as ye have Phil 3:17
many w, of whom I have told you Phil 3:18
That ye might w worthy of the Lord Col 1:10
which ye also w sometime Col 3:7
ye would w worthy of God 1 Thess 2:12
how ye ought to w 1 Thess 4:1
ye may w honestly 1 Thess 4:12
every brother that w disorderly 2 Thess 3:6
when we w in lasciviousness 1 Pet 4:3
w about, seeking whom he may devour 1 Pet 5:8
if we w in the light 1 John 1:7
to w, even as he w 1 John 2:6

WALKING
he knoweth thy w through this Deut 2:7
the moon w in brightness Job 31:26
w in the midst of the fire Dan 3:25
Jesus went to them, w on the sea Matt 14:25
I see men as trees, w Mark 8:24
w in the fear of the Lord Acts 9:31

WALL
branches run over the w Gen 49:22
the waters were a w unto them Ex 14:22
a w being on this side, Num 22:24
and a w on that side Num 22:24
have I leaped over a w 2 Sam 22:30; Ps 18:29
turned his face to the w 2 Kgs 20:2
and to make up this w? Ezra 5:3
So built we the w Neh 4:6
a bowing w shall ye be Ps 62:3
Peace be within thy w Ps 122:7
the stone w thereof was broken Prov 24:31

broken down, and without **w** Prov 25:28
salvation will God appoint for **w** Is 26:1
people that are on the **w** Is 36:11
We grope for the **w** Is 59:10
thou shalt call thy **w** Salvation Is 60:18
a hole in the **w** Ezek 8:7
of the **w** of the king's palace Dan 5:5
hand on the **w**, and a serpent bit Amos 5:19
the stone shall cry out of the **w** Hab 2:11
thou whited **w** Acts 23:3
the middle **w** of partition Eph 2:14

WALLOW
w thyself in ashes Jer 6:26
w yourselves in the ashes Jer 25:34
washed, to her **w** in the mire 2 Pet 2:22

WANDER
your children shall **w** Num 14:33
he that maketh the blind to **w** Deut 27:18
and causeth them to **w** Job 12:24
He **w** abroad for bread Job 15:23
they **w** for lack of meat Job 38:41
then would I **w** far off Ps 55:7
Let them **w** up and down Ps 59:15
let me not **w** from Ps 119:10
As a bird that **w** from her nest Prov 27:8
bewray not him that **w** Is 16:3
w every one to his quarter Is 47:15
Thus have they loved to **w** Jer 14:10
They have **w** as blind men Lam 4:14
My sheep **w** through all Ezek 34:6
cities **w** unto one city, to drink Amos 4:8

WANT (n)
and in **w** of all things Deut 28:48
a place where there is no **w** Judg 18:10
let all thy **w** lie upon me Judg 19:20
embrace the rock for **w** Job 24:8
If I have seen any perish for **w** Job 31:19
there is no **w** to them that fear him Ps 34:9
and **w** of bread in all your places Amos 4:6
she of her **w** did cast in all Mark 12:44
he began to be in **w** Luke 15:14
he that ministered to my **w** Phil 2:25

WANT (v)
I shall not **w** Ps 23:1
shall not **w** any good thing Ps 34:10
for him that **w** understanding Prov 9:4
of words there **w** not sin Prov 10:19
the belly of the wicked shall **w** Prov 13:25
he **w** nothing for his soul Eccl 6:2
none shall **w** her mate Is 34:16
we have **w** all things Jer 44:18
that they may **w** bread and water Ezek 4:17
when they **w** wine John 2:3
present with you, and **w**, I was 2 Cor 11:9

WANTON
stretched forth necks and **w** eyes Is 3:16
not in chambering and **w** Rom 13:13
begun to wax **w** against Christ 1 Tim 5:11
on the earth, and been **w** James 5:5

WAR (n)
There is a noise of **w** Ex 32:17
Shall your brethren go to **w** Num 32:6
he shall not go out to **w** Deut 24:5
then was **w** in the gates Judg 5:8
because the **w** was of God 1 Chr 5:22
changes and **w** are against me Job 10:17
against the day of battle and **w** Job 38:23
though **w** should rise against me Ps 27:3
He maketh **w** to cease Ps 46:9
w was in his heart Ps 55:21
scatter thou the people that delight in **w** Ps 68:30
with good advice make **w** Prov 20:18
a time of **w** Eccl 3:8
no discharge in that **w** Eccl 8:8
neither shall they learn **w** anymore Is 2:4; Mic 4:3
of Egypt, where we shall see no **w** Jer 42:14
as men averse from **w** Mic 2:8
w and rumours of **w** Matt 24:6; Mark 13:7
what king, going to make **w** Luke 14:31
of **w** and commotions Luke 21:9
From whence come **w** James 4:1
there was **w** in heaven Rev 12:7

WAR (v)
teacheth my hands to **w** 2 Sam 22:35; Ps 18:34; 144:1
If thy people go out to **w** 2 Chr 6:34
they that **w** against thee Is 41:12
we do not **w** after the flesh 2 Cor 10:3
w a good warfare 1 Tim 1:18
no man that **w** entangleth himself 2 Tim 2:4
lusts that **w** in your members James 4:1
ye fight and **w**, yet ye have not James 4:2
from fleshly lusts, which **w** 1 Pet 2:11

WARFARE
that her **w** is accomplished Is 40:2
weapons of our **w** are not carnal 2 Cor 10:4

WARM (adj)
how can one be **w** alone? Eccl 4:11
ye clothe you, but there is none **w** Hag 1:6

WARM (v)
there shall not be a coal to **w** at Is 47:14
and **w** himself at the fire Mark 14:54
stood with them and **w** himself John 18:18
be ye **w** and filled James 2:16

WARN
nor speaks to **w** the wicked Ezek 3:18
I ceased not to **w** everyone Acts 20:31
w them that are unruly 1 Thess 5:14

WASH
Go and **w** in Jordan 2 Kgs 5:10
may I not **w** in them, and be clean? 2 Kgs 5:12
if I **w** myself with snow water Job 9:30
thou **w** away the things which grow Job 14:19
When I **w** my steps with butter Job 29:6
I will **w** my hands in innocency Ps 26:6
W me throughly from mine iniquity Ps 51:2
w me, and I shall be whiter than snow Ps 51:7
and **w** my hands in innocency Ps 73:13
and yet is not **w** Prov 30:12
w with milk Song 5:12
W ye, make you clean Is 1:16
though thou **w** thee with nitre Jer 2:22
w thine heart Jer 4:14
neither wast thou **w** in water Ezek 16:4
anoint thine head, and **w** thy face Matt 6:17
took water, and **w** his hands Matt 27:24
except they **w** their hands oft Mark 7:3
began to **w** his feet with tears Luke 7:38
Go, **w** in the pool of Siloam John 9:7
and **w** their stripes Acts 16:33
w away thy sins Acts 22:16
but ye are **w** 1 Cor 6:11
our bodies **w** with pure water Heb 10:22
the sow that was **w** 2 Pet 2:22
w us from our sins Rev 1:5
have **w** their robes Rev 7:14

WASTE (adj)
in the **w** howling wilderness Deut 32:10
in former time desolate and **w** Job 30:3
and maketh it **w** Is 24:1
The field is **w** Joel 1:10

WASTE (v)
The barrel of meal shall not **w** 1 Kgs 17:14
The boar out of the wood doth **w** it Ps 80:13
nor for the destruction that **w** at noonday Ps 91:6

WATCH (n)
as a **w** in the night Ps 90:4
Mine eyes prevent the night **w** Ps 119:148
make the **w** strong Jer 51:12
I will stand upon my **w** Hab 2:1

WATCH (v)
The Lord **w** between me and thee Gen 31:49
dost thou not **w** over my sin? Job 14:16
The wicked **w** the righteous Ps 37:32
I **w**, and am as a sparrow Ps 102:7
they that **w** for the morning Ps 130:6
all that **w** for iniquity are cut off Is 29:20
my familiars **w** for my halting Jer 20:10
so will I **w** over them, to build Jer 31:28
I will **w** over them for evil Jer 44:27
the end is come: it **w** for thee Ezek 7:6
and will **w** to see what he will say Hab 2:1
W therefore, for ye know not Matt 24:42
W therefore; for ye know neither Matt 25:13
W and pray Matt 26:41; Mark 13:33
W ye therefore Mark 13:35; Luke 21:36
Therefore **w**, and remember Acts 20:31
let us **w** and be sober 1 Thess 5:6
for they **w** for your souls Heb 13:17

WATER (n)
The **w** is our's Gen 26:20
Unstable as **w** Gen 49:4
a land of brooks of **w** Deut 8:7
drinketh **w** of the rain of heaven Deut 11:11
and became as **w** Josh 7:5
as **w** spilt on the ground 2 Sam 14:14
Eat no bread, and drink no **w** 1 Kgs 13:22
w of affliction 1 Kgs 22:27; 2 Chr 18:26
which poured **w** on the hands 2 Kgs 3:11
brought **w** into the city 2 Kgs 20:20
as a stone into the mighty **w** Neh 9:11
Can the flag grow without **w**? Job 8:11
through the scent of **w** it will bud Job 14:9
The **w** wear the stones Job 14:19
which drinketh iniquity like **w**? Job 15:16
Thou hast not given **w** to the weary Job 22:7
bindeth up the **w** in his thick clouds Job 26:8
The **w** are hid as with a stone Job 38:30
I am poured out like **w** Ps 22:14
beside the still **w** Ps 23:2
He gathereth the **w** of the sea Ps 33:7
Though the **w** thereof roar Ps 46:3
a dry and thirsty land, where no **w** is Ps 63:1
w of a full cup are wrung out to them Ps 73:10
The **w** saw thee Ps 77:16
Their blood have they shed like **w** Ps 79:3
Then the **w** had overwhelmed us Ps 124:4
ye **w** that be above the heavens Ps 148:4
Drink **w** out of thine own cistern Prov 5:15
Stolen **w** are sweet Prov 9:17
is like deep **w** Prov 20:5
As cold **w** to a thirsty soul Prov 25:25
as in **w** face answereth to face Prov 27:19
Who hath bound the **w** in a garment? Prov 30:4
Cast thy bread upon the **w** Eccl 11:1
well of living **w** Song 4:15
Many **w** cannot quench love Song 8:7
thy wine mixed with **w** Is 1:22
the whole stay of **w** Is 3:1
as the **w** cover the sea Is 11:9; Hab 2:14
the **w** shall fail from the sea Is 19:5
w shall overflow the hiding place Is 28:17
Blessed are ye that sow beside all **w** Is 32:20
his **w** shall be sure Is 33:16
in the wilderness shall **w** break out Is 35:6
When the poor and needy seek **w** Is 41:17
When thou passest through the **w** Is 43:2
a path in the mighty **w** Is 43:16
I give **w** in the wilderness Is 43:20
I will pour **w** upon him that is thirsty Is 44:3
come ye to the **w** Is 55:1
whose **w** cast up mire and dirt Is 57:20
the fountain of living **w** Jer 2:13; 17:13

Oh that my head were **w** Jer 9:1
sent their little ones to the **w** Jer 14:3
Behold, **w** rise up out of the north Jer 47:2
that they may want bread and **w** Ezek 4:17
all knees shall be weak as **w** Ezek 7:17; 21:7
The **w** made him great Ezek 31:4
will I sprinkle clean **w** upon you Ezek 36:25
nor a thirst for **w** Amos 8:11
baptize you with **w** Matt 3:11; Mark 1:8; Luke 3:16; John 1:26
little ones a cup of cold **w** Matt 10:42
bid me come unto thee on the **w** Matt 14:28
he took **w**, and washed Matt 27:24
give you a cup of **w** Mark 9:41
filled with **w** Luke 8:23
the raging of the **w** Luke 8:24
dip the tip of his finger in **w** Luke 16:24
Except a man be born of **w** John 3:5
there was much **w** there John 3:23
Sir, give me this **w** John 4:15
waiting for the moving of the **w** John 5:3
flow rivers of living **w** John 7:38
came there out blood and **w** John 19:34
John truly baptized with **w** Acts 1:5; Acts 11:16
Can any man forbid **w** Acts 10:47
in perils of **w** 2 Cor 11:26
cleanse it with the washing of **w** Eph 5:26
eight souls were saved by **w** 1 Pet 3:20
wells without **w** 2 Pet 2:17
This is he that came by **w** 1 John 5:6
let him take the **w** of life freely Rev 22:17

WATER (v)
mist from the earth, and **w** Gen 2:6
that it was well **w** Gen 13:10
w it with thy foot, as a garden Deut 11:10
I **w** my couch with my tears Ps 6:6
as showers that **w** the earth Ps 72:6
he **w** the hills from his chambers Ps 104:13
He that **w**, shall be **w** Prov 11:25
I will **w** thee with my tears Is 16:9
I will **w** it every moment Is 27:3
but **w** the earth Is 55:10
I will also **w** with thy blood Ezek 32:6
Apollos **w**; but God gave the increase 1 Cor 3:6

WAVES
all thy **w** and thy billows Ps 42:7
the noise of their **w** Ps 65:7
when the **w** thereof arise Ps 89:9
the mighty **w** of the sea Ps 93:4
the **w** thereof are still Ps 107:29
thy righteousness as the **w** of the sea Is 48:18
though the **w** thereof toss Jer 5:22
shall smite the **w** in the sea Zech 10:11
Raging **w** of the sea Jude 1:13

WAX (n)
my heart is like **w** Ps 22:14
as **w** melteth before the fire Ps 68:2
The hills melted like **w** Ps 97:5
valleys shall be cleft, as **w** Mic 1:4

WAX (v)
my wrath shall **w** hot Ex 22:24
may **w** hot Ex 32:10
Is the Lord's hand **w** short? Num 11:23
raiment **w** not old Deut 8:4; 29:5
Jeshurun **w** fat, and kicked Deut 32:15
their clothes **w** not old Neh 9:21
shall **w** old like a garment Ps 102:26; Is 50:9; 51:6; Heb 1:11
the love of many shall **w** cold Matt 24:12
bags which **w** not old Luke 12:33

WAY
all flesh had corrupted his **w** Gen 6:12
seeing the Lord hath prospered my **w** Gen 24:56
will keep me in this **w** Gen 28:20
thy **w** is perverse Num 22:32
walk in his **w** Deut 8:6; 30:16; 1 Kgs 2:3; Ps 119:3; Is 42:24
the **w** of all the earth Josh 23:14; 1 Kgs 2:2
teach you the good and the right **w** 1 Sam 12:23
As for God, his **w** is perfect 2 Sam 22:31; Ps 18:30
all the **w** was full of garments 2 Kgs 7:15
thou hast taught them the good **w** 2 Chr 6:27
to seek of him a right **w** Ezra 8:21
to a man whose **w** is hid Job 3:23
a wilderness where there is no **w** Job 12:24; Ps 107:40
go the **w** whence I shall not return Job 16:22
fenced up my **w** Job 19:8
Hast thou marked the old **w** Job 22:15
he knoweth the **w** that I take Job 23:10
they know not the **w** thereof Job 24:13
Doth not he see my **w** Job 31:4
Where is the **w** where light dwelleth? Job 38:19
Lord knoweth the **w** of the righteous Ps 1:6
ye perish from the **w** Ps 2:12
the meek will he teach his **w** Ps 25:9
Teach me thy **w** Ps 27:11; 86:11
in a **w** that is not good Ps 36:4
Commit thy **w** unto the Lord Ps 37:5
I will take heed to my **w** Ps 39:1
This their **w** is their folly Ps 49:13
that thy **w** may be known Ps 67:2
He made a **w** to his anger Ps 78:50
they have not known my **w** Ps 95:10; Heb 3:10
behave myself wisely in a perfect **w** Ps 101:2
O that my **w** were directed Ps 119:5
I have chosen the **w** of truth Ps 119:30
I thought on my **w** Ps 119:59
all my **w** are before thee Ps 119:168
lead me in the **w** everlasting Ps 139:24
preserveth the **w** of his saints Prov 2:8
In all thy **w** acknowledge him Prov 3:6
Her **w** are **w** of pleasantness Prov 3:17
w of man are before the eyes of the Lord Prov 5:21
consider her **w**, and be wise Prov 6:6
the **w** of life Prov 6:23; 15:24; Jer 21:8
w of a fool is right in his own eyes Prov 12:15
The **w** of the slothful man Prov 15:19
When a man's **w** please the Lord Prov 16:7
Train up a child in the **w** Prov 22:6
guide thy heart in the **w** Prov 23:19
let thine eyes observe my **w** Prov 23:26
There is a lion in the **w** Prov 26:13
the **w** of the spirit Eccl 11:5
fears shall be in the **w** Eccl 12:5
he will teach us of his **w** Is 2:3; Mic 4:2
This is the **w**, walk ye in it Is 30:21
The **w** of holiness Is 35:8
My **w** is hid from the Lord Is 40:27
the blind by a **w** that they knew not Is 42:16
they would not walk in his **w** Is 42:24
I will direct all his **w** Is 45:13
neither are your **w** my **w** Is 55:8
delight to know my **w** Is 58:2
where is the good **w** Jer 6:16
every man according to his **w** Jer 17:10; 32:19
make your **w** and your doings good Jer 18:11
I will give them one heart and one **w** Jer 32:39
They shall ask the **w** to Zion Jer 50:5
to warn the wicked from his wicked **w** Ezek 3:18
are not my **w** equal? are not your **w** unequal? Ezek 18:29
march every one on his **w** Joel 2:7
the Lord hath his **w** in the whirlwind Nah 1:3
Consider your **w** Hag 1:5
he shall prepare the **w** before me Mal 3:1
broad is the **w**, that leadeth Matt 7:13
Go not into the **w** of the Gentiles Matt 10:5
teachest the **w** of God Matt 22:16; Mark 12:14; Luke 20:21
they will faint by the **w** Mark 8:3
spread their garments in the **w** Mark 11:8; Matt 21:8; Luke 19:36
when he was yet a great **w** off Luke 15:20
he was to pass that **w** Luke 19:4
but climbeth up some other **w** John 10:1
and the **w** ye know John 14:4
I am the **w**, the truth, and the life John 14:6
if he found any of this **w** Acts 9:2
how he had seen the Lord in the **w** Acts 9:27
shew unto us the **w** of salvation Acts 16:17
expounded unto him the **w** of God Acts 18:26
no small stir about that **w** Acts 19:23
after the **w** which they call heresy Acts 24:14
They are all gone out of the **w** Rom 3:12
his **w** past finding out! Rom 11:33
will make a **w** to escape 1 Cor 10:13
a more excellent **w** 1 Cor 12:31
took it out of the **w** Col 2:14
them that are out of the **w** Heb 5:2
the **w** into the holiest Heb 9:8
By a new and living **w** Heb 10:20
unstable in all his **w** James 1:8
the sinner from the error of his **w** James 5:20
many shall follow their pernicious **w** 2 Pet 2:2
Which have forsaken the right **w** 2 Pet 2:15
not to have known the **w** of righteousness 2 Pet 2:21
they have gone in the **w** of Cain Jude 1:11

WEAK
then shall I be **w** Judg 16:7
let not your hands be **w** 2 Chr 15:7
thou hast strengthened the **w** hands Job 4:3
I am **w** Ps 6:2
Art thou also become **w** as we? Is 14:10
Strengthen ye the **w** hands Is 35:3
all knees shall be **w** as water Ezek 7:17; 21:7
How **w** is thine heart! Ezek 16:30
let the **w** say, I am strong Joel 3:10
but the flesh is **w** Matt 26:41; Mark 14:38
ye ought to support the **w** Acts 20:35
being not **w** in faith Rom 4:19
it was **w** through the flesh Rom 8:3
w things of the world to confound 1 Cor 1:27
For this cause many are **w** 1 Cor 11:30
his bodily presence is **w** 2 Cor 10:10
Who is **w**, and I am not **w**? 2 Cor 11:29
when I am **w**, then am I strong 2 Cor 12:10
turn ye again to the **w** and beggarly Gal 4:9

WEAKNESS
the **w** of God 1 Cor 1:25
I was with you in **w** 1 Cor 2:3
it is sown in **w**, it is raised in power 1 Cor 15:43

WEALTH
he that giveth thee power to get **w** Deut 8:18
enemy in my habitation in all the **w** 1 Sam 2:32
thou hast not asked riches, **w** 2 Chr 1:11
seeking the **w** of his people Esth 10:3
They spend their days in **w** Job 21:13
If I rejoiced because my **w** was great Job 31:25
dost not increase **w** by their price Ps 44:12
They that trust in their **w** Ps 49:6
and leave their **w** to others Ps 49:10
W and riches shall be in his house Ps 112:3
Lest strangers be filled with thy **w** Prov 5:10
rich man's **w** is his strong city Prov 10:15; 18:11
W gotten by vanity Prov 13:11
W maketh many friends Prov 19:4
by this craft we have our **w** Acts 19:25
every man another's **w** 1 Cor 10:24

WEALTHY
out into a **w** place Ps 66:12
unto the **w** nation Jer 49:31

Who **w** their tongue like a sword Ps 64:3
do not **w** the edge Eccl 10:10

WHETHER
W of them twain did the will Matt 21:31
w is greater, the gold, or the temple Matt 23:17
w we live or die Rom 14:8
w in the body, I cannot tell, or out of the body 2 Cor 12:2

WHIP
hath chastised you with **w** 1 Kgs 12:11
A **w** for a horse Prov 26:3
The noise of a **w** Nah 3:2

WHIT
told him every **w**, and hid no thing 1 Sam 3:18
made man every **w** whole John 7:23
is clean every **w** John 13:10
I was not a **w** behind 2 Cor 11:5

WHITE
his teeth shall be **w** with milk Gen 49:12
leprous, **w** as snow Num 12:10
is there any taste in the **w** of an egg? Job 6:6
let thy garments be always **w** Eccl 9:8
my beloved is **w** and ruddy Song 5:10
they shall be **w** as snow Is 1:18
canst not make one hair **w** or black Matt 5:36
w already to harvest John 4:35
a **w** stone Rev 2:17
walk with me in **w** Rev 3:4

WHITED
like unto **w** sepulchres Matt 23:27
thou **w** wall Acts 23:3

WHITER
shall be **w** than snow Ps 51:7
w than milk Lam 4:7

WHITHER
Thy servant went no **w** 2 Kgs 5:25
W is thy beloved gone Song 6:1
not knowing **w** he went Heb 11:8

WHOLE
my life is yet **w** in me 2 Sam 1:9
this is the **w** duty of man Eccl 12:13
a vessel that cannot be made **w** Jer 19:11
it was **w** it was meet for no work Ezek 15:5
not that thy **w** body be cast into hell Matt 5:29
the **w** need not a physician Matt 9:12
till the **w** was leavened Matt 13:33; Luke 13:21
gain the **w** world Matt 16:26; Mark 8:36; Luke 9:25
that the **w** nation perish not John 11:50
if the **w** body were an eye 1 Cor 12:17
I pray God your **w** spirit 1 Thess 5:23
keep the **w** law James 2:10
for the sins of the **w** world 1 John 2:2
the **w** world lieth in wickedness 1 John 5:19

WHOLESOME
A **w** tongue is a tree of life Prov 15:4
consent not to **w** words 1 Tim 6:3

WHOLLY
dieth, being **w** at ease Job 21:23
planted thee a noble vine, **w** a right seed Jer 2:21
not **w** unpunished Jer 46:28
the city **w** given to idolatry Acts 17:16
sanctify you **w** 1 Thess 5:23
give thyself **w** to them 1 Tim 4:15

WHOMSOEVER
to **w** he will Dan 4:17,25,32
to **w** the Son will reveal him Matt 11:27
W shall fall upon that stone Matt 21:44; Luke 20:18
to **w** I will, I give it Luke 4:6
unto **w** much is given Luke 12:48

WHOSOEVER
w shall eat this bread 1 Cor 11:27
bear his judgment, **w** he be Gal 5:10
w will, let him take Rev 22:17

WICKED
destroy the righteous with the **w**? Gen 18:23
a thought in thy **w** heart Deut 15:9
the **w** shall be silent 1 Sam 2:9
dwelling place of the **w** shall come to nought Job 8:22
If I be **w**, why then labour I in vain? Job 9:29; 10:15
the **w** is reserved to destruction Job 21:30
let the wickedness of the **w** come to an end Ps 7:9
God is angry with the **w** Ps 7:11
the **w** shall be turned into hell Ps 9:17
The **w** walk on every side Ps 12:8
The **w** borroweth, and payeth not Ps 37:21
The **w** watcheth the righteous Ps 37:32
I have seen the **w** in great power Ps 37:35
The **w** are estranged from the womb Ps 58:3
how long shall the **w** triumph? Ps 94:3
see if there be any **w** way in me Ps 139:24
all the **w** will he destroy Ps 145:20
w shall fall by his own wickedness Prov 11:5
the **w** flee when no man pursueth Prov 28:1
be not overmuch **w** Eccl 7:17
I saw the **w** buried Eccl 8:10
he made his grave with the **w** Is 53:9
let the **w** forsake his way Is 55:7
the **w** are like the troubled sea Is 57:20
the heart is deceitful above all things, and desperately **w** Jer 17:9
have I any pleasure that the **w** should die? Ezek 18:23
O **w** man, thou shalt surely die Ezek 33:8
with **w** balances Mic 6:11
more **w** than himself Matt 12:45; Luke 11:26
sever the **w** from among the just Matt 13:49
w and slothful Matt 25:26
by **w** hands have crucified and slain Acts 2:23
put away from among yourselves that **w** person 1 Cor 5:13
the fiery darts of the **w** Eph 6:16
enemies of your mind by **w** works Col 1:21
then shall that **W** be revealed 2 Thess 2:8

WICKEDLY
Will you speak **w** for God? Job 13:7
God will not do **w** Job 34:12
they speak **w** Ps 73:8
speak against thee **w** Ps 139:20
the wicked shall do **w** Dan 12:10
all that do **w** Mal 4:1

WICKEDNESS
this great **w** Gen 39:9
how was this **w**? Judg 20:3
sell himself to work **w** 1 Kgs 21:25
they that plow iniquity, and sow **w**, reap the same Job 4:8
Is not thy **w** great? Job 22:5
let the **w** of the wicked come to an end Ps 7:9
the tents of **w** Ps 84:10
they eat the bread of **w** Prov 4:17
w is an abomination to my lips Prov 8:7
w overthroweth the sinner Prov 13:6
his **w** shall be shown Prov 26:26
the **w** of folly Eccl 7:25
w burneth as the fire Is 9:18
thou hast trusted in thy **w** Is 47:10
thine own **w** shall correct thee Jer 2:19
no man repented of his **w** Jer 8:6
Violence is risen up into a rod of **w** Ezek 7:11
I have driven him out for his **w** Ezek 31:11
Ye have ploughed **w** Hos 10:13
treasures of **w** in the house Mic 6:10
he said, This is **w** Zech 5:8
the border of **w** Mal 1:4
w, deceit, lasciviousness, an evil eye, Mark 7:22
full of ravening and **w** Luke 11:39
Being filled with all unrighteousness, fornication, **w** Rom 1:29
nor with the leaven of **w** 1 Cor 5:8
spiritual **w** in high places Eph 6:12
the whole world lieth in **w** 1 John 5:19

WIDE
they opened their mouth **w** Ps 35:21
this great and **w** sea Ps 104:25
w is the gate and broad is the way Matt 7:13

WIFE
the **w** of thy youth Prov 5:18
Whoso findeth a **w** findeth a good thing Prov 18:22
a prudent **w** is from the Lord Prov 19:14
the **w** whom thou lovest Eccl 9:9
I have married a **w** Luke 14:20
the unbelieving **w** is sanctified 1 Cor 7:14
the husband is the head of the **w** Eph 5:23
the bride, the Lamb's **w** Rev 21:9

WILES
For they vex you with their **w** Num 25:18
stand against the **w** of the devil Eph 6:11

WILFULLY
if we sin **w** Heb 10:26

WILL (n)
not the **w** of your Father Matt 18:14
whosoever shall do the **w** of God Mark 3:35
born, not of blood, nor of the **w** of the flesh John 1:13
to do the **w** of him that sent me John 4:34
the **w** of the Lord be done Acts 21:14

WILL (v)
I **w**, be thou clean Matt 8:3; Mark 1:41; Luke 5:13
not as I **w**, but as thou **w** Matt 26:39
to **w** is present with me Rom 7:18
both to **w** and to do Phil 2:13
I **w** that men pray every where 1 Tim 2:8
whosoever **w**, let him take Rev 22:17

WILLING
a **w** heart Ex 35:5
a perfect heart and a **w** mind 1 Chr 28:9
who then is **w** to consecrate his service 1 Chr 29:5
w in the day of thy power Ps 110:3
the spirit is **w** Matt 26:41
w rather to be absent 2 Cor 5:8
if there be first a **w** mind 2 Cor 8:12
w to communicate 1 Tim 6:18
not **w** that any should perish 2 Pet 3:9

WIN
and thought to **w** them for himself 2 Chr 32:1
he that **w** souls is wise Prov 11:30
that I may **w** Christ Phil 3:8

WIND
remember that my life is **w** Job 7:7
he shall inherit the **w** Prov 11:29
the north **w** driveth away rain Prov 25:23
gathered the **w** in his fists Prov 30:4
he that observeth the **w** Eccl 11:4
we have brought forth **w** Is 26:18
he stayeth his rough **w** Is 27:8
prophesy to the **w** Ezek 37:9
they have sown the **w** Hos 8:7
the mountains, and createth the **w** Amos 4:13
A reed shaken with the **w** Matt 11:7
The **w** bloweth where it listeth John 3:8
carried about with every **w** of doctrine Eph 4:14

WINDOWS
the **w** of heavens Gen 7:11
those that look out of the **w** Eccl 12:3

death is come up into our w Jer 9:21
open you the w of heaven Mal 3:10

WINGS
the shadow of thy w Ps 17:8; 36:7; 57:1
on the w of the wind Ps 18:10; 104:3
Oh that I had w like a dove! Ps 55:6
covert of thy w Ps 61:4
as the w of a dove Ps 68:13
under his w Ps 91:4
the w of the morning Ps 139:9
riches certainly make themselves w Prov 23:5
with healing in his w Mal 4:2

WINK
what do thy eyes w at Job 15:12
neither let them w with the eye Ps 35:19
He w with his eyes Prov 6:13
He that w with the eye Prov 10:10
of this ignorance God w Acts 17:30

WINTER
cold and heat, and summer and w Gen 8:22
w is past Song 2:11
flight not be in w Matt 24:20; Mark 13:18

WIPE
I will w Jerusalem as a man w a dish 2 Kgs 21:13
God will w away tears Is 25:8
wash his feet with tears, and did w them with the hairs Luke 7:38
wash the disciples feet and to w them John 13:5

WISDOM
they die even without w Job 4:21
w shall die with you Job 12:2
W is the principal thing Prov 4:7
better to get w than gold! Prov 16:16
He that getteth w loveth his own soul Prov 19:8
cease from thine own w Prov 23:4
in much w is much grief Eccl 1:18
of my hand I have done it, and by my w Is 10:13
the w of their wise men shall perish Is 29:14
rejected the word of the Lord; and what w is in them? Jer 8:9
the man of w shall see thy name Mic 6:9
w is justified of her children Matt 11:19
not with w of words 1 Cor 1:17
Christ the power of God, and the w of God 1 Cor 1:24
who of God is made unto us w 1 Cor 1:30
speak w among them that are perfect 1 Cor 2:6
w of this world is foolishness with God 1 Cor 3:19
not with fleshly w 2 Cor 1:12
that ye might be filled with the knowledge of his will in all w Col 1:9
walk in w toward them Col 4:5
If any of you lack w James 1:5
the w that is from above is pure James 3:17
to receive, power, and riches, and w Rev 5:12
Here is w Rev 13:18

WISE
to make one w Gen 3:6
the gift blindeth the w Ex 23:8
great nation is a w and understanding people Deut 4:6
O that they were w! Deut 32:29
I have given thee a w and understanding heart 1 Kgs 3:12
he is w in heart Job 9:4
For vain man would be w Job 11:12
he that is w may be profitable Job 22:2
Great men are not always w Job 32:9
Be w now therefore, O ye kings Ps 2:10
making w the simple Ps 19:7
he hath left off to be w Ps 36:3
when will ye be w? Ps 94:8
Whoso is w, and will observe Ps 107:43
A w man will hear Prov 1:5
a man of understanding shall attain w counsels Prov 1:5
Be not w in thine own eyes Prov 3:7
thou shalt be w for thyself Prov 9:12
he that winneth souls is w Prov 11:30
w in heart shall be called prudent Prov 16:21
A w king scattereth the wicked Prov 20:26
I said, I will be w Eccl 7:23
the w, and their works, are in the hand of God Eccl 9:1
The words of the w are as goads Eccl 12:11
I am the son of the w Is 19:11
they that be w shall shine Dan 12:3
be ye therefore w as serpents Matt 10:16
hast hid these things from the w Matt 11:25
I am debtor to the w Rom 1:14
Be not w in your own conceits Rom 12:16
Where is the w? 1 Cor 1:20
ye are w in Christ 1 Cor 4:10
w unto salvation 2 Tim 3:15

WISELY
charmers, charming never so w Ps 58:5
I will behave myself w Ps 101:2
that handleth a matter w Prov 16:20

WISER
for he was w than all men 1 Kgs 4:31
w than the children of light Luke 16:8
foolishness of God is w than men 1 Cor 1:25

WISH
more than heart could w Ps 73:7
I could w myself accursed Rom 9:3
I w above all things 3 John 1:2

WITHDRAW
If God will not w his anger Job 9:13
w thy foot from thy neighbour's Prov 25:17
w yourselves from every brother 2 Thess 3:6

WITHER
his leaf also shall not w Ps 1:3
they shall w as the green herb Ps 37:2
The grass w, the flower fadeth Is 40:7; 1 Pet 1:24
the fig tree w away Matt 21:19; Mark 11:21
trees whose fruit w Jude 1:12

WITHHOLD
W not thou thy tender mercies Ps 40:11
no good thing will he w Ps 84:11
W not good from them to whom it is due Prov 3:27
W not correction Prov 23:13
w not thy hand Eccl 11:6
your sins have w good things Jer 5:25

WITHSTAND
two shall w him Eccl 4:12
what was I, that I could w God? Acts 11:17
able to w in evil day Eph 6:13

WITNESS (n)
God is w betwixt Gen 31:50
this stone shall be a w Josh 24:27
my w is in heaven Job 16:19
as a faithful w in heaven Ps 89:37
A faithful w will not lie Prov 14:5
I have given him for a w to the people Is 55:4
The Lord be a true and faithful w Jer 42:5
for a w to all nations Matt 24:14
the same came for a w John 1:7
ye receive not our w John 3:11
I have greater w than that of John John 5:36
he left not himself without w Acts 14:17
conscience also bearing them w Rom 2:15
the w of God is greater 1 John 5:9
hath the w in himself 1 John 5:10

WITNESS (v)
heaven and earth to w Deut 4:26
countenance doth w against them Is 3:9
the Holy Ghost w in every city Acts 20:23
being w by the law and prophets Rom 3:21
before Pilate w a good confession 1 Tim 6:13

WITTY
knowledge of w inventions Prov 8:12

WOEFUL
the w day Jer 17:16

WOMAN
A w slew him Judg 9:54
pain as of a w in travail Ps 48:6; Is 13:8; Jer 4:31; 49:24
to keep thee from the evil w Prov 6:24
A foolish w is clamorous Prov 9:13
a virtuous w Prov 12:4
Every wise w buildeth her house Prov 14:1
with a brawling w in a wide house Prov 21:9
a w among all those have I not found Eccl 7:28
as a w forsaken Is 54:6
A w shall compass a man Jer 31:22
the heart of a w in her pangs Jer 48:41; 49:22
pangs as a w in travail Jer 50:43
whoso looketh on a w Matt 5:28
O w, great is thy faith Matt 15:28
the w died also Matt 22:27; Mark 12:22; Luke 20:32
Why trouble ye the w? Matt 26:10
there shall this, that this w hath done, be told Matt 26:13
W, what have I to do with thee? John 2:4
a w taken in adultery John 8:3
w, behold thy son! John 19:26
this w was full of good works Acts 9:36
the natural use of the w Rom 1:27
It is good for a man not to touch a w 1 Cor 7:1
the w is the glory of the man 1 Cor 11:7
God sent forth his Son, made of a w Gal 4:4
I suffer not a w to teach 1 Tim 2:12
the w being deceived 1 Tim 2:14

WOMB
blessings of the w Gen 49:25
the Lord had shut up her w 1 Sam 1:5
took me out of the w Ps 22:9
cast upon thee from the w Ps 22:10
the fruit of the w is his reward Ps 127:3
hast covered me in my mother's w Ps 139:13
how bones grow in the w Eccl 11:5
the Lord formed thee from the w Is 44:2; 49:5
a transgressor from the w Is 48:8
compassion on son of her w Is 49:15
give them miscarrying w Hos 9:14
blessed is the fruit of thy w Luke 1:42
Blessed is the w that bare thee Luke 11:27
Blessed are the barren, and the w that never bare Luke 23:29

WOMEN
Blessed above w Judg 5:24
the w answered one another 1 Sam 18:7
passing the love of w 2 Sam 1:26
among thy honourable w Ps 45:9
Give not thy strength to w Prov 31:3
pitiful w have sodden their children Lam 4:10
them that are born of w Matt 11:11
two w grinding at the mill Matt 24:41; Luke 17:35
blessed art thou among w Luke 1:28
Among those that are born of w Luke 7:28
Let your w keep silence 1 Cor 14:34
w adorn themselves 1 Tim 2:9
Let the w learn in silence 1 Tim 2:11
that the younger w marry 1 Tim 5:14
lead captive silly w 2 Tim 3:6
aged w in behaviour as becometh holiness Titus 2:3
W received their dead Heb 11:35

WONDER (n)
as a **w** unto many Ps 71:7
thou art the God that doest **w** Ps 77:14
Shall thy **w** be known in the dark? Ps 88:12
his **w** among all people Ps 96:3
his **w** in the deep Ps 107:24
walked barefoot for a sign and a **w** Is 20:3
I will do a marvellous work and a **w** Is 29:14
w in the heavens and in the earth Joel 2:30
I will shew **w** in heaven Acts 2:19
Except ye see signs and **w** John 4:48
that **w** may be done by the name Acts 4:30

WONDER (v)
Stay yourselves, and **w** Is 29:9
w that there was no intercessor Is 59:16
I **w** that there was none to uphold Is 63:5
regard, and **w** marvellously Hab 1:5
they are men **w** at Zech 3:8
all **w** at the gracious words Luke 4:22

WONDERFUL
thy love to me was **w** 2 Sam 1:26
things too **w** for me Job 42:3
Such knowledge is too **w** for me Ps 139:6
his name shall be called **W** Is 9:6
who is **w** in counsel Is 28:29

WONDERFULLY
I am fearfully and **w** made Ps 139:14
therefore she came down **w** Lam 1:9
and he shall destroy **w** Dan 8:24

WONDROUS
w works 1 Chr 16:9; Job 37:14; Ps 26:7; 75:1; 78:32; 105:2; 106:22; 119:27; 145:5; Jer 21:2
w things Ps 72:18; 86:10; 119:18

WONT
if the ox were **w** to push Ex 21:29
the governor was **w** to release Matt 27:15
as he was **w**, he taught them Mark 10:1
he went, as he was **w** Luke 22:39
where prayer was **w** to be made Acts 16:13

WOOD
Behold the fire and the **w** Gen 22:7
hewer of **w** Deut 29:11; Josh 9:21; Jer 46:22
the **w** devoured more people 2 Sam 18:8
as one cutteth and cleaveth **w** Ps 141:7
Where no **w** is, the fire goeth out Prov 26:20

WOOL
he giveth snow like **w** Ps 147:16
your sins shall be as **w** Is 1:18
hair like **w** Dan 7:9; Rev 1:14

WORD
every **w** that proceedeth out of the mouth Deut 8:3
the **w** is very nigh Deut 30:14; Rom 10:8
he multiplieth **w** Job 35:16
by **w** without knowledge Job 38:2
the Lord gave the **w** Ps 68:11
the **w** of truth Ps 119:43; 2 Cor 6:7; Eph 1:13; 2 Tim 2:15; James 1:18
A **w** fitly spoken Prov 25:11
an offender for a **w** Is 29:21
thine ears shall hear a **w** behind thee Is 30:21
the **w** is not in them Jer 5:13
nor the **w** from the prophet Jer 18:18
know whose **w** shall stand Jer 44:28
every **w** that proceedeth out of the mouth Matt 4:4
speak the **w** only Matt 8:8
every idle **w** that men shall speak Matt 12:36
every **w** may be established Matt 18:16
my **w** shall not pass away Matt 24:35
ashamed of me and of my **w** Mark 8:38; Luke 9:26
gracious **w** which proceeded Luke 4:22
a prophet mighty in deed and **w** Luke 24:19
In the beginning was the **W** John 1:1
the **w** that I speak unto you John 6:63
thou hast the **w** of eternal life John 6:68
the **w** which ye hear is not mine John 14:24
I have given unto them the **w** which thou gavest me John 17:8
any **w** of exhortation Acts 13:15
remember the **w** of the Lord Jesus Acts 20:35
the **w** of truth and soberness Acts 26:25
not in **w**, but in power 1 Cor 4:20
except ye utter by the tongue **w** easy to be understood 1 Cor 14:9
the **w** of reconciliation 2 Cor 5:19
all the law is fulfilled in one **w** Gal 5:14
him that is taught in the **w** Gal 6:6
deceive you with vain **w** Eph 5:6
Holding forth the **w** of life Phil 2:16
Let the **w** of Christ dwell in you Col 3:16
comfort one another with these **w** 1 Thess 4:18
nourished up in the **w** of faith 1 Tim 4:6
labour in the **w** and doctrine 1 Tim 5:17
strive not about **w** 2 Tim 2:14
in due times manifested his **w** Titus 1:3
Holding fast the faithful **w** Titus 1:9
by the **w** of his power Heb 1:3
the **w** preached did not profit Heb 4:2
the **w** of God is quick, and powerful Heb 4:12
is unskilful in the **w** Heb 5:13
And have tasted the good **w** of God Heb 6:5
the **w** of the oath Heb 7:28
worlds were framed by the **w** of God Heb 11:3
who have spoken unto you the **w** Heb 13:7
the engrafted **w** James 1:21
if any be a hearer of the **w** James 1:23
this is the **w** which by the gospel is preached 1 Pet 1:25
them which stumble at the **w** 1 Pet 2:8
a more sure **w** of prophecy 2 Pet 1:19
the **w** which were spoken 2 Pet 3:2
by the **w** of God the heavens were of old 2 Pet 3:5
by the same **w** are kept in store 2 Pet 3:7
whoso keepeth his **w** 1 John 2:5
let us not love in **w** 1 John 3:18
hast kept my **w** Rev 3:8
the **w** of my patience Rev 3:10
that were slain for the **w** Rev 6:9
take away from the **w** of the book Rev 22:19

WORK (n)
God ended his **w** Gen 2:2
shall comfort us concerning our **w** Gen 5:29
do all thy **w** Ex 20:9
Six days shall **w** be done Ex 35:2
do according to thy **w** Deut 3:24
the **w** of men's hands Deut 4:28; 2 Kgs 19:18; Ps 115:4; 135:15; Is 37:19
as every day's **w** required 1 Chr 16:37
in every **w** that he began 2 Chr 31:21
Let the **w** of this house of God alone Ezra 6:7
their nobles put not their necks to the **w** Neh 3:5
thou hast blessed the **w** of his hands Job 1:10
the **w** of thine hands Job 10:3; 14:15; Ps 143:5
w of a man shall he render unto him Job 34:11
the **w** of thy fingers Ps 8:3
wonderful **w** Ps 40:5; 78:4; 107:8; 111:4; Matt 7:22; Acts 2:11
I hate the **w** of them that turn aside Ps 101:3
man goeth forth unto his **w** Ps 104:23
The **w** of the Lord are great Ps 111:2
to practise wicked **w** Ps 141:4
whether his **w** be pure Prov 20:11
according to his **w** Prov 24:12; Matt 16:27; 2 Tim 4:14
let her own **w** praise her Prov 31:31
I have seen all the **w** that are done Eccl 1:14
destroy the **w** of thine hands Eccl 5:6
applied my heart unto every **w** Eccl 8:9
God now accepteth thy **w** Eccl 9:7
God shall bring every **w** into judgment Eccl 12:14
worship the **w** of their own hands Is 2:8; Jer 1:16
when the Lord hath performed his whole **w** Is 10:12
their **w** are in the dark Is 29:15
my **w** is with my God Is 49:4
I know their **w** and their thoughts Is 66:18
Great in counsel, and mighty in **w** Jer 32:19
I will never forget any of their **w** Amos 8:7
I will work a **w** in your days Hab 1:5
all their **w** they do for to be seen of men Matt 23:5
that we might work the **w** of God John 6:28
This is the **w** of God, that ye believe John 6:29
I have done one **w**, and ye all marvel John 7:21
w of God should be made manifest John 9:3
for which of those **w** do ye stone me John 10:32
I have finished the **w** John 17:4
w be of men, it will come to nought Acts 5:38
went not with them to the **w** Acts 15:38
imputeth righteousness without **w** Rom 4:6
grace, otherwise **w** is no more **w** Rom 11:6
For meat destroy not the **w** of God Rom 14:20
Every man's **w** shall be made manifest 1 Cor 3:13
by the **w** of the law Gal 2:16
Not of **w**, lest any man should boast Eph 2:9
the unfruitful **w** of darkness Eph 5:11
enemies in your mind by wicked **w** Col 1:21
in love for their **w** sake 1 Thess 5:13
not according to our **w** 2 Tim 1:9
in **w** they deny him Titus 1:16
from dead **w** Heb 6:1; 9:14
faith, if it hath not **w**, is dead, being alone James 2:17
shew me thy faith without thy **w** James 2:18
Was not Abraham our father justified by **w** James 2:21
w that are therein shall be burned up 2 Pet 3:10
destroy the **w** of the devil 1 John 3:8
keepeth my **w** to the end Rev 2:26
I have not found thy **w** perfect Rev 3:2
and their **w** do follow them Rev 14:13

WORK (v)
the Lord will **w** for us 1 Sam 14:6
sold thyself to **w** evil 1 Kgs 21:20
on the left hand, where he doth **w** Job 23:9
in heart ye **w** wickedness Ps 58:2
He that **w** deceit Ps 101:7
It is time for thee, Lord, to **w** Ps 119:126
I will **w**, and who shall let it? Is 43:13
w evil upon their beds Mic 2:1
they that **w** wickedness are set up Mal 3:15
Son, go **w** to day in my vineyard Matt 21:28
My Father **w** hitherto, and I **w** John 5:17
that we might **w** the works of God John 6:28
night cometh, when no man can **w** John 9:4
the law **w** wrath Rom 4:15
tribulation **w** patience Rom 5:3
all things **w** together for good Rom 8:28
it is the same God which **w** all in all 1 Cor 12:6
death **w** in us 2 Cor 4:12
faith which **w** by love Gal 5:6
who **w** all things after the counsel Eph 1:11
the spirit that now **w** Eph 2:2
w with his hands the thing which is good Eph 4:28
w out your own salvation Phil 2:12
w with your own hands 1 Thess 4:11
the trying of your faith **w** patience James 1:3

WORKMAN
the **w** made it Hos 8:6
a **w** that needeth not to be ashamed 2 Tim 2:15

WORLD
chased out of the **w** Job 18:18
from men of the **w** Ps 17:14
the **w** is mine Ps 50:12
the ungodly, who prosper in the **w** Ps 73:12
the **w** also is stablished Ps 93:1
he hath set the **w** in their heart Eccl 3:11
the **w** languisheth Is 24:4
all the kingdoms of the **w** Matt 4:8; Luke 4:5
the light of the **w** Matt 5:14
the cares of this **w** Matt 13:22; Mark 4:19
The field is the **w** Matt 13:38
in the end of the **w** Matt 13:40
gain the whole **w** Matt 16:26; Mark 8:36; Luke 9:25
the **w** to come Mark 10:30; Luke 18:30; Heb 2:5; 6:5
children of this **w** Luke 16:8; 20:34
He was in the **w** John 1:10
which taketh away the sin of the **w** John 1:29
God so loved the **w** John 3:16
the Saviour of the **w** John 4:42; 1 John 4:14
giveth life unto the **w** John 6:33
The **w** cannot hate you John 7:7
I am the light of the **w** John 8:12; 9:5
Now is the judgment of this **w** John 12:31
not to judge the **w**, but to save the **w** John 12:47
depart out of this **w** John 13:1
manifest thyself unto us, and not unto the **w** John 14:22
not as the **w** giveth, give I unto you John 14:27
the prince of this **w** cometh John 14:30
In the **w** ye shall have tribulation John 16:33
I pray not for the **w** John 17:9
w itself could not contain the books John 21:25
turned the **w** upside down Acts 17:6
be not conformed to this **w** Rom 12:2
the wisdom of this **w** 1 Cor 2:6
they that use this **w** as not abusing it 1 Cor 7:31
the god of this **w** hath blinded 2 Cor 4:4
this present evil **w** Gal 1:4
according to the course of this **w** Eph 2:2
without God in the **w** Eph 2:12
them that are rich in this **w** 1 Tim 6:17
having loved this present **w** 2 Tim 4:10
Of whom the **w** was not worthy Heb 11:38
unspotted from the **w** James 1:27
a **w** of iniquity James 3:6
spared not the old **w** 2 Pet 2:5
Love not the **w** 1 John 2:15
the **w** knoweth us not 1 John 3:1
the whole **w** lieth in wickedness 1 John 5:19

WORLDLY
denying ungodliness and **w** lusts Titus 2:12
divine service, and a **w** sanctuary Heb 9:1

WORM
My flesh is clothed with **w** Job 7:5
to the **w**, Thou art my mother Job 17:14
after my skin **w** destroy this body Job 19:26
and the **w** shall cover them Job 21:26
the **w** shall feed sweetly on him Job 24:20
man, that is a **w** Job 25:6
I am a **w**, and no man Ps 22:6
the **w** is spread under thee Is 14:11
Fear not, thou **w** Jacob Is 41:14
their **w** dieth not Mark 9:44,46,48

WORMWOOD
even this people, with **w** Jer 9:15
I will feed them with **w** Jer 23:15
who turn judgment to **w** Amos 5:7

WORSE
the rent is made **w** Matt 9:16; Mark 2:21
w than the first Matt 12:45; 27:64; Luke 11:26
nothing bettered, but rather grew **w** Mark 5:26
lest a **w** thing come unto thee John 5:14
not for the better, but for the **w** 1 Cor 11:17
he is **w** than an infidel 1 Tim 5:8
shall wax **w** and **w** 2 Tim 3:13
the latter end is **w** with them 2 Pet 2:20

WORSHIP
let us **w** and bow down Ps 95:6
w him, all ye gods Ps 97:7
w at his footstool Ps 99:5
shall **w** the Lord in the holy mount Is 27:13
did we make her cakes to **w** her? Jer 44:19
them that **w** the host of heaven Zeph 1:5
fall down and **w** me Matt 4:9
in vain they do **w** me Matt 15:9
Our fathers **w** in this mountain John 4:20
Ye **w** ye know not what John 4:22
must **w** in spirit and in truth John 4:24
came up to **w** John 12:20
Whom therefore ye ignorantly **w** Acts 17:23
so **w** I the God of my fathers Acts 24:14
w and served the creature more than the Creator Rom 1:25
he will **w** God 1 Cor 14:25

WORTH
make my speech nothing **w** Job 24:25
heart of the wicked is little **w** Prov 10:20
Woe **w** the day! Ezek 30:2

WORTHY
I am not **w** of the least Gen 32:10
ye are **w** to die 1 Sam 26:16
If he will shew himself a **w** man 1 Kgs 1:52
whose shoes I am not **w** to bear Matt 3:11
I am not **w** that thou shouldest come Matt 8:8
the workman is **w** of his meat Matt 10:10
loveth father or mother more than me is not **w** Matt 10:37
they which were bidden were not **w** Matt 22:8
fruits **w** of repentance Luke 3:8
not **w** to unloose Luke 3:16; John 1:27
he was **w** for whom he should do this Luke 7:4
the labourer is **w** of his hire Luke 10:7
things **w** of stripes Luke 12:48
no more **w** to be called thy son Luke 15:19
w to obtain that world Luke 20:35
very **w** deeds are done Acts 24:2
not **w** to be compared with the glory Rom 8:18
walk **w** Eph 4:1; Col 1:10; 1 Thess 2:12
Of whom the world was not **w** Heb 11:38
blaspheme that **w** name James 2:7
for they are **w** Rev 3:4

WOULD
I **w** there were a sword Num 22:29
Israel **w** none of me Ps 81:11
w none of my reproof Prov 1:25
They **w** none of my counsel Prov 1:30
whom he **w** he slew Dan 5:19
whatsoever ye **w** that men Matt 7:12
and calleth unto him whom he **w** Mark 3:13
what I **w**, that do I not Rom 7:15
I **w** that all men were even as I 1 Cor 7:7
I **w** thou wert cold or hot Rev 3:15

WOUND (n)
w for **w** Ex 21:25
My **w** is incurable Job 34:6
and bindeth up their **w** Ps 147:3
Who hath **w** without cause? Prov 23:29
Faithful are the **w** of a friend Prov 27:6
but **w** and bruises Is 1:6
my **w** incurable Jer 15:18
I will heal thee of thy **w** Jer 30:17
What are these **w** in thy hands? Zech 13:6
bound up his **w** Luke 10:34

WOUND (v)
I **w**, and I heal Deut 32:39
carry me out of the host; for I am **w** 1 Kgs 22:34; 2 Chr 18:33
he **w**, and his hands make whole Job 5:18
suddenly shall they be **w** Ps 64:7
my heart is **w** within me Ps 109:22
he was **w** for our transgressions Is 53:5

WOUNDED
she hath cast down many **w** Prov 7:26
a **w** spirit who can bear? Prov 18:14
there remained but **w** men Jer 37:10

WRAP
that he can **w** himself in it Is 28:20
so they **w** it up Mic 7:3
w together in a place by itself John 20:7

WRATH
feared the **w** of the enemy Deut 32:27
day of **w** Job 21:30; Prov 11:4; Zeph 1:15; Rom 2:5
Because there is **w**, beware Job 36:18
the **w** of man shall praise thee Ps 76:10
by thy **w** are we troubled Ps 90:7
w of a king is as messengers of death Prov 16:14
A man of great **w** shall suffer Prov 19:19
a fool's **w** is heavier Prov 27:3
W is cruel, and anger is outrageous Prov 27:4
much sorrow and **w** with his sickness Eccl 5:17
the day of the Lord cometh with **w** Is 13:9
in a little **w** I hid my face Is 54:8
he reserveth **w** for his enemies Nah 1:2
in **w** remember mercy Hab 3:2
from the **w** to come Matt 3:7; Luke 3:7
w against the day of **w** Rom 2:5
provoke not your children to **w** Eph 6:4
God hath not appointed us to **w** 1 Thess 5:9
lifting up holy hands, without **w** 1 Tim 2:8

WRATHFUL
let thy **w** anger take hold Ps 69:24
A **w** man stirreth up strife Prov 15:18

WREST
decline after many to **w** judgment Ex 23:2
Thou shalt not **w** judgment Deut 16:19
Every day they **w** my words Ps 56:5
unlearned and unstable **w** 2 Pet 3:16

WRESTLE
there **w** a man with him Gen 32:24
we **w** not against flesh and blood Eph 6:12

WRETCHED
O **w** man that I am! Rom 7:24
knowest not that thou art **w** Rev 3:17

WRING
w the dew out of the fleece Judg 6:38
wicked of the earth shall **w** them out Ps 75:8
w of the nose bringeth forth blood Prov 30:33

WRINKLE
thou hast filled me with **w** Job 16:8
glorious church, not having spot, or **w** Eph 5:27

WRITE
w them upon the table of thine heart Prov 3:3; 7:3
w grievousness which they have prescribed Is 10:1
few, that a child may **w** them Is 10:19
W ye this man childless Jer 22:30
w it in their hearts Jer 31:33; Heb 8:10
W the vision, and make it plain Hab 2:2

WRITING
the **w** was the **w** of God Ex 32:16
if ye believe not his **w** John 5:47

WRITTEN
Oh that my words were now **w** Job 19:23
not be **w** with the righteous Ps 69:28
and it was **w** within and without Ezek 2:10
because your names are **w** in heaven Luke 10:20
What I have **w** I have **w** John 19:22
w for our admonition 1 Cor 10:11
Ye are our epistle **w** in our hearts 2 Cor 3:2
a book **w** within and on the backside Rev 5:1
w in the Lamb's book of life Rev 21:27

WRONG
to him that did the **w** Ex 2:13
there is no **w** in mine hands 1 Chr 12:17
I cry out of **w**, but I am not heard Job 19:7
do no **w** Jer 22:3
Friend, I do thee no **w** Matt 20:13
Why do ye not rather take **w**? 1 Cor 6:7
forgive me this **w** 2 Cor 12:13
he that doeth **w** shall receive Col 3:25

WRONGFULLY
devices which ye **w** imagine Job 21:27
oppressed the stranger **w** Ezek 22:29
suffering **w** 1 Pet 2:19

WROTE
w over against the candlestick Dan 5:5
finger **w** on the ground John 8:6
Pilate **w** a title John 19:19
I **w** a new commandment 2 John 1:5

WROTH
Why art thou **w**? Gen 4:6
But Naaman was **w**, and went away 2 Kgs 5:11
thou hast been **w** with thine anointed Ps 89:38
I was **w** with my people Is 47:6
have I sworn that I would not be **w** Is 54:9
neither will I be always **w** Is 57:16
Be not **w** very sore Is 64:9
his lord was **w**, and delivered Matt 18:34

WROUGHT
What hath God **w**! Num 23:23
when he had **w** wonderfully 1 Sam 6:6
he hath **w** with God this day 1 Sam 14:45
with one of his hands **w** in the work Neh 4:17
this work was **w** of our God Neh 6:16
the hand of the Lord hath **w** this Job 12:9
who can say, Thou hast **w** iniquity? Job 36:23
hast **w** for them that trust in thee Ps 31:19
that which thou hast **w** for us Ps 68:28
curiously **w** in the lowest parts
of the earth Ps 139:15
I looked on all my hands had **w** Eccl 2:11
hast **w** all our works in us Is 26:12
Who hath **w** and done it Is 41:4
he **w** a work on the wheels Jer 18:3
I **w** for my name's sake Ezek 20:9
God hath **w** toward me Dan 4:2
These last have **w** but one hour Matt 20:12
she hath **w** a good work upon me Matt 26:10; Mark 14:6
manifest that they are **w** in God John 3:21
wonders God had **w** Acts 15:12
he abode with them, and **w** Acts 18:3
God **w** special miracles by the
hands of Paul Acts 19:11
w in me all manner of concupiscence Rom 7:8
things which Christ hath not **w** Rom 15:18
that hath **w** us for the selfsame thing 2 Cor 5:5
what carefulness it **w** in you 2 Cor 7:11
the signs of an apostle were **w** 2 Cor 12:12
he that **w** effectually in Peter Gal 2:8
Which he **w** in Christ Eph 1:20
but **w** with labour and travail 2 Thess 3:8
through faith subdued kingdoms,
w righteousness Heb 11:33
faith **w** with his works James 2:22
to have **w** the will of the Gentiles 1 Pet 4:3
lose not those things which we have **w** 2 John 1:8
the false prophet that **w** miracles Rev 19:20

WRUNG
the blood thereof shall be **w** out Lev 1:15
waters of a full cup are **w** out Ps 73:10
w them out Is 51:17

Y

YARN
and linen **y** 1 Kgs 10:28; 2 Chr 1:16

YEA
but let your communication be **y**, **y** Matt 5:37
there should be **y y**, and nay nay 2 Cor 1:17
let your **y** be **y**; and your nay, nay James 5:12

YEAR
and for seasons, days, and **y** Gen 1:14
keep this ordinance in his season
from **y** to **y** Ex 13:10
for all their sins once a **y** Lev 16:34
for it is a **y** of rest unto the land Lev 25:5
each day for a **y** shall ye bear
your iniquities Num 14:34
the **y** of release is at hand Deut 15:9
the third **y**, which is the **y** of tithing Deut 26:12
and brought it to him from **y** to **y** 1 Sam 2:19
and he went from **y** to **y** in circuit 1 Sam 7:16
there shall not be dew nor rain these **y** 1 Kgs 17:1
Are thy **y** as man's days? Job 10:5
number of **y** is hidden to the oppressor Job 15:20
multitude of **y** should teach wisdom Job 32:7
neither can the number of his **y** be
searched out Job 36:26
my **y** with sighing Ps 31:10
crownest the **y** with thy goodness Ps 65:11
the **y** of ancient times Ps 77:5
remember the **y** of the right hand Ps 77:10
their **y** in trouble Ps 78:33
for a thousand **y** in thy sight Ps 90:4
we spend our **y** as a tale that is told Ps 90:9
thy **y** shall have no end Ps 102:27
thy **y** unto the cruel Prov 5:9
y of the wicked shall be shortened Prov 10:27
according to the **y** of an hireling Is 21:16
I shall go softly all my **y** Is 38:15
to proclaim the acceptable **y** of the Lord Is 61:2
the **y** of my redeemed is come Is 63:4
even the **y** of their visitation Jer 11:23; 23:12; 48:44
have laid on thee the **y** of their iniquity Ezek 4:5
art come even unto thy **y** Ezek 22:4
in latter **y** thou shalt come into
the land Ezek 38:8
it shall be his to the **y** of liberty Ezek 46:17
to the **y** of many generations Joel 2:2
with calves of a **y** old? Mic 6:6
in the midst of the **y** make known Hab 3:2
as in former **y** Mal 3:4
To preach the acceptable **y** of the Lord Luke 4:19
let it alone this **y** also Luke 13:8
ye observe days and months and
times and **y** Gal 4:10
bound him a thousand **y** Rev 20:2

YEARLY
went up out of his city **y** to worship 1 Sam 1:3
for there is a **y** sacrifice 1 Sam 20:6
and the fifteenth day of the same, **y** Esth 9:21

YEARN
his bowels did **y** upon his brother Gen 43:30
her bowels **y** upon her son 1 Kgs 3:26

YELL
lions roared upon him and **y** Jer 2:15
they shall **y** as lions whelps Jer 51:38

YESTERDAY
for we are but of **y** Job 8:9
are but as **y** when it is past Ps 90:4
Jesus Christ the same **y** Heb 13:8

YIELD
not henceforth **y** unto thee her strength Gen 4:12
that it may **y** unto you the increase Lev 19:25
the land shall **y** her increase Lev 26:4
and **y** almonds Num 17:8
y yourselves to the Lord 2 Chr 30:8
it **y** much increase unto the kings Neh 9:37
then shall the earth **y** her increase Ps 67:6
plant vineyards, which may **y** fruits
of increase Ps 107:37
she caused him to **y** Prov 7:21
for **y** pacifieth great offences Eccl 10:4
if so be it **y**, the strangers shall
swallow it up Hos 8:7
fig tree and vine do **y** their strength Joel 2:22
and the fields shall **y** no meat Hab 3:17
when he had cried again, **y** up
the ghost Matt 27:50
but do not thou **y** unto them Acts 23:21
neither **y** ye your members unto sin Rom 6:13
but **y** yourselves unto God Rom 6:13
to whom ye **y** yourselves servants
to obey Rom 6:16
y the peaceable fruits of righteousness Heb 12:11

YOKE
his **y** from off thy neck Gen 27:40; Is 10:27
I have broken the bands of your **y** Lev 26:13
upon which never came **y** Num 19:2
shall put a **y** of iron upon thy neck Deut 28:48
on which there hath come no **y** 1 Sam 6:7
thy father made our **y** grievous 1 Kgs 12:4
thou hast broken the **y** of his burden Is 9:4
then shall his **y** depart from off them Is 14:25
that ye break every **y** Is 58:6
of old time I have broken thy **y** Jer 2:20
Make thee bonds and **y** Jer 27:2
broken the **y** of wood, but shall
make **y** of iron Jer 28:13
as a bullock unaccustomed to the **y** Jer 31:18
it is good for a man that he bear
the **y** in his youth Lam 3:27
take my **y** upon you Matt 11:29
for my **y** is easy Matt 11:30
put a **y** upon the neck of the disciples Acts 15:10
be not entangled with the **y** of bondage Gal 5:1
as many servants as are under the **y** 1 Tim 6:1

YONDER
I and the lad will go **y** Gen 22:5
while I meet the Lord **y** Num 23:15
Remove hence to **y** place Matt 17:20

YOUNG
there shall nothing cast their **y** Ex 23:26
ye shall not kill it and her **y** both
in one day Lev 22:28
shalt not take the dam with the **y** Deut 22:6
nor shew favour to the **y** Deut 28:50
toward her **y** one Deut 28:57
fluttereth over her **y** Deut 32:11
Solomon my son is **y**
and tender 1 Chr 22:5; 29:1
when Rehoboam was **y** and
tenderhearted 2 Chr 13:7
while he was yet **y**, he began to seek
after the God of David 2 Chr 34:3
when his **y** ones cry unto God Job 38:41
she is hardened against her **y** ones Job 39:16
I have been **y**, and now am old Ps 37:25
from following the ewes great with **y** Ps 78:71
where she may lay her **y** Ps 84:3
and to the **y** ravens which cry Ps 147:9
the **y** eagles shall eat it Prov 30:17
My beloved is like a roe or
a **y** hart Song 2:9; 8:14

their **y** ones shall lie down together Is 11:7
shall gently lead those that are with **y** Is 40:11
for the **y** of the flock and of the herd Jer 31:12
cropped off the top of his **y** twigs Ezek 17:4
When thou wast **y** thou girdedst thyself John 21:18
teach the **y** women to be sober Titus 2:4

YOUNGER
the elder shall serve the **y** Gen 25:23
that are **y** than I have me in derision Job 30:1
let him be as the **y** Luke 22:26
the **y** men as brethren 1 Tim 5:1
ye **y**, submit yourselves unto the elder 1 Pet 5:5

YOUNGEST
the **y** is this day with our father Gen 42:13
in his **y** son shall he set up the gates Josh 6:26; 1 Kgs 16:34

YOUTH
imagination of man's heart is evil from his **y** Gen 8:21
from our **y** until now Gen 46:34
he a man of war from his **y** 1 Sam 17:33
whose son is this **y**? 1 Sam 17:55
evil that befell thee from thy **y** 2 Sam 19:7
servant fear the Lord from my **y** 1 Kgs 18:12
to possess the iniquities of my **y** Job 13:26
His bones are full of the sin of his **y** Job 20:11
As I was in the days of my **y** Job 29:4
Upon my right hand rise the **y** Job 30:12
he shall return to the days of his **y** Job 33:25
they die in **y** Job 36:14
Remember not the sins of my **y** Ps 25:7
thou art my trust from my **y** Ps 71:5
thou hast taught me from my **y** Ps 71:17
ready to die from my **y** up Ps 88:15
The days of his **y** hast thou shortened Ps 89:45
thy **y** is renewed like the eagle's Ps 103:5
the dew of thy **y** Ps 110:3
so are children of the **y** Ps 127:4
have they afflicted me from my **y** Ps 129:1
as plants grown up in their **y** Ps 144:12
forsaketh the guide of her **y** Prov 2:17
rejoice with the wife of thy **y** Prov 5:18
Rejoice, O young man, in thy **y** Eccl 11:9
childhood and **y** are vanity Eccl 11:10
Remember now thy Creator in the days of thy **y** Eccl 12:1
wherein thou hast laboured from thy **y** Is 47:12
forget the shame of thy **y** Is 54:4
the kindness of thy **y** Jer 2:2
thou art the guide of my **y** Jer 3:4
this hath been thy manner from thy **y** Jer 22:21
bear the reproach of my **y** Jer 31:19
only done evil before me from their **y** Jer 32:30
hath been at ease from his **y** Jer 48:11
he bear the yoke in his **y** Lam 3:27
from my **y** up even till now Ezek 4:14
not remembered the days of thy **y** Ezek 16:22
as in the days of her **y** Hos 2:15
for husband of her **y** Joel 1:8
for man taught me to keep cattle from my **y** Zech 13:5
have I kept from my **y** up Matt 19:20; Mark 10:20; Luke 18:21
my manner of life from my **y** Acts 26:4
Let no man despise thy **y** 1 Tim 4:12

YOUTHFUL
flee also **y** lusts 2 Tim 2:22

Z

ZAANAIM **za´-an-a´-im**
wanderings (?) Judg 4:11

ZAANAN **za´-a-nan**
place of flocks Mic 1:11

ZAANANNIM **za´-a-nan´-im**
same as ZAANAIM Josh 19:33

ZAAVAN **za´-av-an**
disturbed Gen 36:27

ZABAD **za´-bad**
gift 1 Chr 2:36

ZABBAI **zab´-a-i**
humming Ezra 10:28

ZABBUD **zab´-ood**
given Ezra 8:14

ZABDI **zab´-di**
short for ZEBADIAH Josh 7:1

ZABDIEL **zab´-di-el**
the gift of God 1 Chr 27:2

ZABUD **za´-bood**
same as ZABBUD 1 Kgs 4:5

ZACCAI **zak-a´-i**
pure Ezra 2:9

ZACCHAEUS **zak-e´-us**
Gr. for ZACCAI Luke 19:2

ZACCHUR **zak´-oor**
mindful 1 Chr 4:26

ZACCUR **zak´-oor**
same as ZACCHUR Num 13:4

ZACHARIAH **zak´-ar-i´-ah**
whom Jehovah remembers 2 Kgs 14:29

ZACHARIAS **zak´-ar-i´-as**
Gr. for ZACHARIAH Matt 23:35

ZACHER **za´-ker**
memorial 1 Chr 8:31

ZADOK **za´-dok**
just 2 Sam 8:17

ZAHAM **za´-ham**
loathing 2 Chr 11:19

ZAIR **za´-ir**
small 2 Kgs 8:21

ZALAPH **za´-laf**
wound (?) Neh 3:30

ZALMON **zal´-mon**
shady 2 Sam 23:28

ZALMONAH **zal-mo´-nah**
same as ZALMON Num 33:41

ZALMUNNA **zal-moon´-ah**
shelter denied Judg 8:5

ZAMZUMMIMS **zam-zoom´-ims**
murmurmers Deut 2:20

ZANOAH **za-no´-ah**
marsh Josh 15:34

ZAPHNATH-PAANEAH **zaf´-nath-pa´-a-ne´-ah**
prince of the life of the age Gen 41:45

ZAPHON **za´-fon**
north Josh 13:27

ZARA **za´-rah**
Gr. for ZARAH Matt 1:3

ZARAH **za´-rah**
sunrise (?) Gen 38:30

ZAREAH **za´-re-ah**
hornet Neh 11:29

ZAREATHITES **za´-re-ath-ites**
inhabitants of Zareah 1 Chr 2:53

ZARED **za´-red**
exuberant growth Num 21:12

ZAREPHATH **zar´-ef-ath**
smelting furnace 1 Kgs 17:9

ZARETAN **za´-ret-an**
same as ZARTHAN Josh 3:16

ZARETH-SHAHAR **za´-reth-sha´-har**
the splendor of the morning Josh 13:19

ZARHITES **zar´-hites**
descendants of Zerah Num 26:13

ZARTANAH **zar´-ta-nah**
same as ZARTHAN 1 Kgs 4:12

ZARTHAN **zar´-than**
same as ZARETAN 1 Kgs 7:46

ZATTHU **zat´-thoo**
same as ZATTU Neh 10:14

ZATTU **zat´-oo**
irascible (?) Ezra 2:8

ZAVAN **za´-van**
same as ZAAVAN 1 Chr 1:42

ZAZA **za´-zah**
movement, abundance 1 Chr 2:33

ZEAL
sought to slay them in his **z** 2 Sam 21:2
see my **z** for the Lord 2 Kgs 10:16
the **z** of thine house Ps 69:9
my **z** hath consumed me Ps 119:139
the **z** of the Lord of hosts Is 9:7
clad with **z** as a cloke Is 59:17
where is thy **z** Is 63:15
I the Lord have spoken it in my **z** Ezek 5:13
the **z** of thine house John 2:17
they have a **z** of God Rom 10:2
your **z** hath provoked very many 2 Cor 9:2
concerning **z**, persecuting the church Phil 3:6
he hath a great **z** for you Col 4:13

ZEALOUS
he was **z** for my sake Num 25:11
they are all **z** of the law Acts 21:20
as ye are **z** of spiritual gifts 1 Cor 14:12
z of good works Titus 2:14
be **z** therefore, and repent Rev 3:19

ZEALOUSLY
z affect Gal 4:17

ZEBADIAH **zeb´-ad-i´-ah**
Jehovah hath given 1 Chr 8:15

ZEBAH **ze´-bah**
sacrifice Judg 8:5

ZEBAIM **ze-ba´-im**
same as ZEBOIM Ezra 2:57

ZEBEDEE **zeb´-ed-ee**
Gr. for ZEBADIAH Matt 4:21

ZEBINA **ze-bi´-nah**
bought Ezra 10:43

ZEBOIIM **ze-boy´-im**
gazelles Gen 14:2

ZEBOIM **ze-bo´-im**
1 same as ZEBOIIM Gen 10:19
2 *hyenas* 1 Sam 13:18

ZEBUDAH **ze-boo´-dah**
given 2 Kgs 23:36

ZEBUL **ze´-bool**
same as ZEBULUN Judg 9:28

ZEBULONITE **ze´-bool-on-ite**
descendants of Zebulun Judg 12:11

ZEBULUN **ze´-bool-oon**
habitation, dwelling Gen 30:20

ZEBULUNITES **ze´-bool-on-ites**
same as ZEBULONITES Num 26:27

ZECHARIAH **zek´-ar-i´-ah**
same as ZACHARIAH 2 Chr 24:20

ZEDAD ze´-dad
hunting (?) Num 34:8

ZEDEKIAH zed´-ek-i´-ah
justice of Jehovah 1 Kgs 22:11

ZEEB ze´-eb
wolf Judg 7:25

ZELAH ze´-lah
side Josh 18:28

ZELEK ze´-lek
fissure 2 Sam 23:37

ZELOPHEHAD ze-lo´-fe-had
fracture Num 26:33

ZELOTES ze-lo´-tees
1 *an emulator,*
2 Gr. for CANAAN Luke 6:15

ZELZAH zel´-zah
shade in the heat 1 Sam 10:2

ZEMARAIM zem´-ar-a´-im
two fleeces Josh 18:22

ZEMARITE zem´-ar-ite
descendants of Canaan Gen 10:18

ZEMIRA ze-mi´-rah
melody, a song 1 Chr 7:8

ZENAN ze´-nan
same as ZAANAN Josh 15:37

ZENAS ze´-nas
gift of Zeus Titus 3:13

ZEPHANIAH zef´-an-i´-ah
whom Jehovah hid 2 Kgs 25:18

ZEPHATH ze´-fath
watch-tower (?) Judg 1:17

ZEPHATHAH ze´-fath-ah
same as ZEPHATH 2 Chr 14:10

ZEPHI ze´-fi
same as ZEPHATH 1 Chr 1:36

ZEPHO ze´-fo
form of ZEPHI Gen 36:11

ZEPHON ze´-fon
a looking out Num 26:15

ZEPHONITES ze´-fon-ites
descendants of Zephon Num 26:15

ZER zer
flint (?) Josh 19:35

ZERAH ze´-rah
dawn 2 Chr 14:9

ZERAHIAH zer´-ah-i´-ah
whom Jehovah caused to rise 1 Chr 6:6

ZERED ze´-red
same as ZARED Deut 2:13

ZEREDA ze´-re-dah
cool 1 Kgs 11:26

ZEREDATHAH ze-red´-ath-ah
same as ZEREDA 2 Chr 4:17

ZERESH ze´-resh
gold (?) Esth 5:10

ZERETH ze´-reth
fissure, brightness (?) 1 Chr 4:7

ZERI ze´-ri
same as IZRI 1 Chr 25:3

ZEROR ze´-ror
bundle 1 Sam 9:1

ZERUAH ze´-roo-ah
leprous 1 Kgs 11:26

ZERUBBABEL ze-roob´-ab-el
scattered in Babylon Hag 1:1

ZERUIAH ze´-roo-i´-ah
cleft, divided 1 Sam 26:6

ZETHAM ze´-tham
olive 1 Chr 23:8

ZETHAN ze´-than
same as ZETHAM 1 Chr 7:10

ZIA zi´-ah
motion 1 Chr 5:13

ZIBA zi´-bah
planter 2 Sam 9:2

ZIBEON zib´-e-on
dyed Gen 36:2

ZIBIA zib´-i-ah
gazelle (?) 1 Chr 8:9

ZIBIAH zib´-i-ah
same as ZIBIA 2 Kgs 12:1

ZICHRI zik´-ri
famous 2 Chr 23:1

ZIDDIM zid´-im
sides Josh 19:35

ZIDKIJAH zid-ki´-jah
justice of Jehovah Neh 10:1

ZIDON zi´-don
fishing Gen 49:13

ZIDONIANS zi-done´-yans
inhabitants of Zidon Judg 10:12

ZIF zif
blossom 1 Kgs 6:1

ZIHA zi´-hah
drought Ezra 2:43

ZIKLAG zik´-lag
a city in southern Judah Josh 15:31

ZILLAH zil´-ah
shade Gen 4:19

ZILPAH zil´-pah
dropping Gen 29:24

ZILTHAI zil´-tha´-i
shady 1 Chr 8:20

ZIMMAH zim´-ah
planning 1 Chr 6:20

ZIMRAN zim´-ran
celebrated Gen 25:2

ZIMRI zim´-ri
same as ZIMBAN 1 Kgs 16:9

ZIN zin
thorn Num 13:21

ZINA zi´-nah
abundance (?) 1 Chr 23:10

ZION zi´-on
sunny 2 Sam 5:7

ZIOR zi´-or
smallness Josh 15:54

ZIPH zif
flowing 1 Chr 4:16

ZIPHAH zi´-fah
fem. of ZIPH 1 Chr 4:16

ZIPHION zif´-yon
same as ZEPHON Gen 46:16

ZIPHITES zif´-ites
same as ZIPHIM 1 Sam 23:19

ZIPHRON zif´-ron
sweet smell Num 34:9

ZIPPOR zip´-or
bird Num 22:2

ZIPPORAH zip´-or-ah
fem. of ZIPPOR Ex 2:21

ZITHRI zith´-ri
protection of Jehovah (?) Ex 6:22

ZIZ ziz
a flower 2 Chr 20:16

ZIZA zi´-zah
abundance 1 Chr 4:37

ZIZAH zi´-zah
fullness 1 Chr 23:11

ZOAN zo´-an
low region Num 13:22

ZOAR zo´-ar
smallness Gen 13:10

ZOBA zo´-bah
a plantation 2 Sam 10:6

ZOBAH zo´-bah
same as ZOBA 1 Sam 14:47

ZOBEBAH zo´-beb-ah
walking slowly 1 Chr 4:8

ZOHAR zo´-har
light Gen 23:8

ZOHELETH zo-he´-leth
serpentstone 1 Kgs 1:9

ZOHETH zo´-heth
strong (?) 1 Chr 4:20

ZOPHAH zo´-fah
a cruse (?) 1 Chr 7:35

ZOPHAI zo´-fa-i
honeycomb 1 Chr 6:26

ZOPHAR zo´-far
chatterer Job 2:11

ZOPHIM zo´-fim
watchers Num 23:14

ZORAH zo´-rah
a place of hornets Josh 19:41

ZORATHITES zo´-rath-ites
inhabitants of Zorah 1 Chr 4:2

ZOREAH zo´-re-ah
same as ZORAH Josh 15:33

ZORITES zor´-ites
same as ZORATHITES 1 Chr 2:54

ZOROBABEL zo-rob´-ab-el
Gr. for ZERUBBABEL Matt 1:12

ZUAR zoo´-ar
same as ZOAR Num 1:8

ZUPH zoof
flag, sedge 1 Sam 1:1

ZUR zoor
rock Num 25:15

ZURIEL zoor´-i-el
God is the Rock Num 3:35

ZURISHADDAI zoor´-i-shad-a´-i
whose Almighty is the Rock Num 1:6

ZUZIMS zoo´-zims
1 *beauty,*
2 perhaps same as ZAMZUMMIMS Gen 14:5

AMG's Annotated Strong's Hebrew Dictionary Of the Old Testament

Additional materials in this dictionary were taken from *The Complete Word Study Dictionary: Old Testament* by Warren Baker and Eugene Carpenter.

Transliteration of Hebrew Consonants

Hebrew Consonant	Name	Trans–literation	Phonetic Sound	Example
א	Aleph	’	Silent	Similar to h in honor
בּ	Beth	*b*	b	as in boy
ב	Veth	*b*	v	as in vat
גּ	Gimel	*g*	g	as in get
ג	Gimel	*g*	g	as in get
דּ	Daleth	*d*	d	as in do
ד	Daleth	*d*	d	as in do
ה	Hē	*h*	h	as in hat
ו	Waw	*v*	w	as in wait
ז	Zayin	*z*	z	as in zip
ח	Cheth	*ch*	ch	Similar to ch in the German *ach*
ט	Teth	*ṭ*	t	as in time
י	Yodh	*y*	y	as in you
כּ	Kaph	*k*	k	as in kit
כ	Chaph	*k*	ch	Similar to ch in the German *ach*
ל	Lamed	*l*	l	as in lit
מ	Mem	*m*	m	as in move
נ	Nun	*n*	n	as in not
ס	Samekh	*s*	s	as in see
ע	Ayin	‘	Silent	Similar to h in honor
פּ	Pē	*p*	p	as in put
פ	Phē	*ph*	f	as in phone
צ	Tsadde	*ts*	ts	as in wits
ק	Qoph	*q*	q	as in Qatar
ר	Resh	*r*	r	as in run
שׂ	Sin	*ś*	s	as in see
שׁ	Shin	*sh*	sh	as in ship
תּ	Taw	*t*	t	as in time
ת	Thaw	*th*	th	as in this

Transliteration of Hebrew Vowels

Hebrew Vowel	Name	Position	Transliteration	Sound
ְ	Shewa (Silent)	מְ	*Not transliterated or pronounced*	
ְ	Shewa (Vocal)	מְ	^{e}	u as in but
ַ	Pathah	מַ	*a*	a as in lad
ֲ	Hateph Pathah	מֲ	*ă*	a as in lad
ָ	Qamets	מָ	*â*	a as in car
ֳ	Hateph Qamets	מֳ	*ŏ*	a as in car
ֵי	Sere Yodh	מֵי	*êy*	ey as in prey
ֵ	Sere	מֵ	*ê*	ey as in prey
ֶ	Seghol	מֶ	*e*	e as in set
ֱ	Hateph Seghol	מֱ	*ĕ*	e as in set
ִי	Hiriq Yodh	מִי	*îy*	i as in machine
ִ	Hiriq	מִ	*i*	i as in pin
ָ	Qamets Qatan	מָ	*o*	o as in hop
ֹ	Holem	מֹ	*ô*	o as in go
וֹ	Holem	מוֹ	*ôw*	o as in go
ֻ	Qubbuts	מֻ	*u*	u as in put
וּ	Shureq	מוּ	*û*	u as in tune

Special Symbols

:— (*colon and one-em dash*) are used within each entry to mark the end of the discussion of syntax and meaning of the word under consideration, and to mark the beginning of the list of word(s) used to render it in translation.

() (*parentheses*) denote, in the translation renderings only, a word or syllable given in connection with the principal word it follows.

\+ (*addition symbol*) denotes a rendering in translation of one or more Hebrew words in connection with the one under consideration.

× (*multiplication symbol*) denotes a rendering within translation that results from an idiom peculiar to the Hebrew.

1. אָב, ’âb, *awb*; a primitive word; *father* in a literal and immediate, or figurative and remote application:—chief, (fore-) father ([-less]), × patrimony, principal. Comparative names in "Abi-".

A masculine noun meaning father, head of a household, ancestor, patron of a class, benevolence, respect, honour. This word is primarily used to mean either a human or spiritual father. There are numerous references to a father as a begetter or head of a household (Ge 24:40; Jos 14:1). When referring to an ancestor, this word can be collective; Naboth would not give up the inheritance of his fathers (1Ki 21:3). One of the most important meanings is God as Father (Isa 63:16). It can also mean originator of a profession or class; Jabal was called the father of nomadic farmers (Ge 4:20). A father is also one who bestows respect or honour (Jgs 17:10).

2. אַב, ’ab (Chaldee), *ab*; corresponding to 1:—father.

An Aramaic masculine noun meaning father or ancestor. The primary meaning is a male biological parent (Da 5:11, 13). In the plural, its meaning is ancestors or forefathers (Ezr 4:15). See the Hebrew cognate *’âb* (1).

3. אֵב, ’êb, *abe*; from the same as 24; a *green* plant:—greenness, fruit.

4. אֵב, ’êb (Chaldee), *abe*; corresponding to 3:—fruit.

5. אֲבַגְתָא, ’Âbagthâ’, *ab-ag-thaw´*; of foreign origin; *Abagtha*, a eunuch of Xerxes:—Abagtha.

6. אָבַד, ’âbad, *aw-bad´*; a primitive root; probably to *wander* away, i.e. *lose* oneself; by implication to *perish* (causative *destroy*):—break, destroy (-uction), + not escape, fail, lose, (cause to, make) perish, spend, × and surely, take, be undone, × utterly, be void of, have no way to flee.

A verb meaning to perish, to be lost, to wander, or, in a causative sense, to destroy, to reduce to some degree of disorder. It is used to signify God's destruction of evil, both threatened (Le 26:38) and realized (Nu 17:12[27]); Israel's destruction of the Canaanites and their altars (Nu 33:52; Dt 12:2, 3); the perishing of natural life (Ps 49:10[11]; 102:26[27]; Ecc 7:15); the perishing of abstract qualities such as wisdom and hope (Isa 29:14; La 3:18); and an item or animal being lost (Dt 22:3; Ecc 3:6).

7. אֲבַד, ’ăbad (Chaldee), *ab-ad´*; corresponding to 6:—destroy, perish.

An Aramaic verb meaning to perish, to be destroyed, or, in a causative sense, to destroy. This term is closely connected to death. It is used for the passing away of false gods (Jer 10:11); the execution of the Babylonian wise men (Da 2:12, 18, 24); the bodily destruction of Daniel's apocalyptic "beast" (Da 7:11). See the Hebrew cognate *’âbad* (6).

8. אֹבֵד, ’ôbêd, *o-bade´*; active participle of 6; (concrete) *wretched* or (abstract) *destruction*:—perish.

An abstract noun meaning destruction. The word is used this way only in Nu 24:20, 24 where Balaam prophesies the destruction of three nations or areas, one of which is Eber. If Eber refers to the Hebrews, then the destruction is not to be understood as absolute. Other occurrences of this form, although spelled identically, are used differently and are included under *’âbad* (6).

9. אֲבֵדָה, ’ăbêdâh, *ab-ay-daw´*; from 6; (concrete) something *lost*; (abstract) *destruction*, i.e. Hades:—lost. Compare 10.

A feminine noun meaning a lost object or possession. The term is employed only in a legal context in the Hebrew Bible (Ex 22:8; Le 6:4[5:23]; Dt 22:3). To keep a lost item in one's possession and lie about it to the rightful owner is listed among sins, such as deception concerning a deposit or pledge and robbery and fraud (Le 6:3[5:22]).

10. אֲבַדֹּה, ’ăbaddôh, *ab-ad-do´*; the same as 9, miswritten for 11; a *perishing*:—destruction.

A noun referring to the place of the dead, indistinguishable in meaning from *’ăbaddôwn* (11). This form occurs only in Pr 27:20 where, along with Sheol, it identifies death as a place that can always hold more just as the eyes of humans always want more. This word originally may have been *’ăbêdâh* (9) or *’ăbaddôwn* (11) but was changed in the transmission of the ancient manuscript.

11. אֲבַדּוֹן, ’ăbaddôwn, *ab-ad-done´*; intensive from 6; (abstract) a *perishing*; (concrete) Hades:—destruction.

A feminine noun meaning destruction (that is, death). It may also mean a place of destruction. It is used extensively in wisdom literature and connotes the abode of the dead. It commonly forms a word pair with *shᵉ’âl* (7594) (Job 26:6; Pr 15:11; 27:20) but is also linked with death (Job 28:22) and the grave (Ps 88:11[12]). See the Hebrew verb *’âbad* (6).

12. אַבְדָן, ’abdân, *ab-dawn´*; from 6; a *perishing*:—destruction.

A noun, probably masculine, meaning destruction. It occurs only in Est 9:5 where the Jews striking their enemies with the sword results in slaughter and destruction. A similar form, *’obdân* (13), also meaning destruction, occurs in Est 8:6 in a similar context: the desire of the Jews' enemies to bring destruction on them. These two forms may be identical.

13. אָבְדָן, ’obdân, *ob-dawn´*; from 6; a *perishing*:—destruction.

A masculine noun meaning destruction. This term conveys the slaughter of the Jews (Est 8:6; 9:5). See the Hebrew verb *’âbad* (6).

14. אָבָה, ’âbâh, *aw-baw´*; a primitive root; to *breathe* after, i.e. (figurative) to *be acquiescent*:—consent, rest content, will, be willing.

A verb meaning to be willing, to consent, to be acquiescent, to yield, to desire. Its primary meaning is to be positively inclined to respond to some authority or petition. The word is used to signify willingness or desire (Ge 24:5, 8; Jgs 19:25; 2Ch 21:7; Isa 30:15); agreement in principle (Jgs 11:17; 1Ki 20:8); consent to authority (Job 39:9; Isa 1:19); yielding, as to sin (Dt 13:8[9]; Pr 1:10); and, by extension, to be content (Pr 6:35; Ecc 7:8).

15. אָבֶה, ’âbeh, *aw-beh´*; from 14; *longing*:—desire.

16. אֵבֶה, ’êbeh, *ay-beh´*; from 14 (in the sense of *bending* toward); the *papyrus*:—swift.

17. אֲבוֹי, ’ăbôwy, *ab-o´ee*; from 14 (in the sense of *desiring*); *want*:—sorrow.

18. אֵבוּס, ’êbûws, *ay-booce´*; from 75; a *manger* or *stall*:—crib.

19. אִבְחָה, ’ibchâh, *ib-khaw´*; from an unused root (apparently meaning to *turn*); *brandishing* of a sword:—point.

20. אֲבַטִּיחַ, ’ăbaṭṭîyach, *ab-at-tee´-akh*; of uncertain derivation; a *melon* (only plural):—melon.

21. אֲבִי, ’Ăbîy, *ab-ee´*; from 1; *fatherly; Abi*, Hezekiah's mother:—Abi.

22. אֲבִיאֵל, ’Ăbîy’êl, *ab-ee-ale´*; from 1 and 410; *father* (i.e. *possessor*) *of God; Abiel*, the name of two Israelites:—Abiel.

23. אֲבִיאָסָף, ’Ăbîy’âsâph, *ab-ee-aw-sawf´*; from 1 and 622; *father of gathering* (i.e. *gatherer*); *Abiasaph*, an Israelite:—Abiasaph.

24. אָבִיב, ’Âbîyb, *aw-beeb´*; from an unused root (meaning to *be tender*); *green*, i.e. a young *ear* of grain; hence the name of the month *Abib* or Nisan:—Abib, ear, green ears of corn.

25. אֲבִי גִבְעוֹן, ’Ăbîy Gib‘ôwn, *ab-ee´ ghib-one´*; from 1 and 1391; *father* (i.e. *founder*) *of Gibon; Abi-Gibon*, perhaps an Israelite:—father of Gibeon.

26. אֲבִיגַיִל, ’Ăbîygayil, *ab-ee-gah´yil*; or shorter **אֲבִיגַל, ’Ăbîygal,** *ab-ee-gal´*; from 1 and 1524; *father* (i.e. *source*) *of joy; Abigail* or *Abigal*, the name of two Israelitesses:—Abigal.

27. אֲבִידָן, ’Ăbîydân, *ab-ee-dawn´*; from 1 and 1777; *father of judgment* (i.e. *judge*); *Abidan*, an Israelite:—Abidan.

28. אֲבִידָע, ’Ăbîydâ‘, *ab-ee-daw´*; from 1 and 3045; *father of knowledge* (i.e. *knowing*); *Abida*, a son of Abraham by Keturah:—Abida, Abidah.

29. אֲבִיָּה, ’Ăbîyyâh, *ab-ee-yaw´*; or prolonged **אֲבִיָּהוּ, ’Ăbîyyâhûw,** *ab-ee-yaw´-hoo*; from 1 and 3050; *father* (i.e. *worship-*

per) of Jah; Abijah, the name of several Israelite men and two Israelitesses:—Abiah, Abijah.

30. **אֲבִיהוּא, 'Ăbîyhûw',** *ab-ee-hoo´*; from 1 and 1931; *father* (i.e. *worshipper*) of *Him* (i.e. *God*); *Abihu*, a son of Aaron:—Abihu.

31. **אֲבִיהוּד, 'Ăbîyhûwd,** *ab-ee-hood´*; from 1 and 1935; *father* (i.e. *possessor*) *of renown*; *Abihud*, the name of two Israelites:—Abihud.

32. **אֲבִיהַיִל, 'Ăbîyhayil,** *ab-ee-hah´-yil*; or (more correctly) אֲבִיחַיִל, **'Ăbîychayil,** *ab-ee-khah´-yil*; from 1 and 2428; *father* (i.e. *possessor*) *of might*; *Abihail* or *Abichail*, the name of three Israelites and two Israelitesses:—Abihail.

33. **אֲבִי הָעֶזְרִי, 'Ăbîy hâ'Ezrîy,** *ab-ee´-haw-ez-ree´*; from 44 with the article inserted; *father of the Ezrite*; an *Abiezrite* or descendant of Abiezer:—Abiezrite.

34. **אֶבְיוֹן, 'ebyôwn,** *eb-yone´*; from 14, in the sense of *want* (especially in feeling); *destitute*:—beggar, needy, poor (man).

35. **אֲבִיּוֹנָה, 'ăbîyyôwnâh,** *ab-ee-yo-naw´*; from 14; provocative of *desire*; the *caper* berry (from its *stimulative* taste):—desire.

36. **אֲבִיטוּב, 'Ăbîyṭûwb,** *ab-ee-toob´*; from 1 and 2898; *father of goodness* (i.e. *good*); *Abitub*, an Israelite:—Abitub.

37. **אֲבִיטַל, 'Ăbîyṭal,** *ab-ee-tal´*; from 1 and 2919; *father of dew* (i.e. *fresh*); *Abital*, a wife of King David:—Abital.

38. **אֲבִיָּם, 'Ăbîyâm,** *ab-ee-yawm´*; from 1 and 3220; *father of* (the) *sea* (i.e. *seaman*); *Abijam* (or Abijah), a king of Judah:—Abijam.

39. **אֲבִימָאֵל, 'Ăbîymâ'êl,** *ab-ee-maw-ale´*; from 1 and an elsewhere unused (probably foreign) word; *father of Mael* (apparently some Arab tribe); *Abi-mael*, a son of Joktan:—Abimael.

40. **אֲבִימֶלֶךְ, 'Ăbîymelek,** *ab-ee-mel´-ek*; from 1 and 4428; *father of* (the) *king*; *Abimelek*, the name of two Philistine kings and of two Israelites:—Abimelech.

41. **אֲבִינָדָב, 'Ăbîynâdâb,** *ab-ee-naw-dawb´*; from 1 and 5068; *father of generosity* (i.e. *liberal*); *Abinadab*, the name of four Israelites:—Abinadab.

42. **אֲבִינֹעַם, 'Ăbîynô'am,** *ab-ee-no´-am*; from 1 and 5278; *father of pleasantness* (i.e. *gracious*); *Abinoam*, an Israelite:—Abinoam.

43. **אֶבְיָסָף, 'Ebyâsâph,** *eb-yaw-sawf´*; contracted from 23; *Ebjasaph*, an Israelite:—Ebiasaph.

44. **אֲבִיעֶזֶר, 'Ăbîy'ezer,** *ab-ee-ay´-zer*; from 1 and 5829; *father of help* (i.e. *helpful*); *Abiezer*, the name of two Israelites:—Abiezer.

45. **אֲבִי־עַלְבוֹן, 'Ăbîy-'albôwn,** *ab-ee al-bone´*; from 1 and an unused root of uncertain derivation; probably *father of strength* (i.e. *valiant*); *Abialbon*, an Israelite:—Abialbon.

46. **אָבִיר, 'âbîyr,** *aw-beer´*; from 82; *mighty* (spoken of God):—mighty (one).

47. **אַבִּיר, 'abbîyr,** *ab-beer´*; for 46:—angel, bull, chiefest, mighty (one), stout [-hearted], strong (one), valiant.

An adjective meaning mighty or strong. Used frequently as a noun, the word applies to God as the Mighty One (Ps 132:2, 5; Isa 1:24). It also designates angels (Ps 78:25); men (Ps 76:5); bulls (Ps 22:12[13]); and horses (Jer 8:16). When used to describe a person or a person's heart, it normally refers to a strength independent of or opposed to God (Job 34:20; Ps 76:5[6]; Isa 46:12). It is used once to mean chief of the shepherds (1Sa 21:7[8]).

48. **אֲבִירָם, 'Ăbîyrâm,** *ab-ee-rawm´*; from 1 and 7311; *father of height* (i.e. *lofty*); *Abiram*, the name of two Israelites:—Abiram.

49. **אֲבִישַׁג, 'Ăbîyshag,** *ab-ee-shag´*; from 1 and 7686; *father of error* (i.e. *blundering*); *Abishag*, a concubine of David:—Abishag.

50. **אֲבִישׁוּעַ, 'Ăbîyshûwa',** *ab-ee-shoo´-ah*; from 1 and 7771; *father of plenty* (i.e. *prosperous*); *Abishua*, the name of two Israelites:—Abishua.

51. **אֲבִישׁוּר, 'Ăbîyshûwr,** *ab-ee-shoor´*; from 1 and 7791; *father of* (the) *wall* (i.e. perhaps *mason*); *Abishur*, an Israelite:—Abishur.

52. **אֲבִישַׁי, 'Ăbîyshay,** *ab-ee-shah´ee*; or (shorter) אַבְשַׁי, **'Abshay,** *ab-shah´ee*; from 1 and 7862; *father of a gift* (i.e. probably *generous*); *Abishai*, an Israelite:—Abishai.

53. **אֲבִישָׁלוֹם, 'Ăbîyshâlôwm,** *ab-ee-shaw-lome´*; or (shortened) אַבְשָׁלוֹם, **'Abshâlôwm,** *ab-shaw-lome´*; from 1 and 7965; *father of peace* (i.e. *friendly*); *Abshalom*, a son of David; also (the fuller form) a later Israelite:—Abishalom, Absalom.

54. **אֶבְיָתָר, 'Ebyâthâr,** *eb-yaw-thawr´*; contracted from 1 and 3498; *father of abundance* (i.e. *liberal*); *Ebjathar*, an Israelite:—Abiathar.

55. **אָבַךְ, 'âbak,** *aw-bak´*; a primitive root; probably to *coil* upward:—mount up.

56. **אָבַל, 'âbal,** *aw-bal´*; a primitive root; to *bewail*:—lament, mourn.

57. **אָבֵל, 'âbêl,** *aw-bale´*; from 56; *lamenting*:—mourn (-er, -ing).

58. **אָבֵל, 'âbêl,** *aw-bale´*; from an unused root (meaning to *be grassy*); a *meadow*:—plain. Compare also the proper names beginning with Abel-.

59. **אָבֵל, 'Âbêl,** *aw-bale´*; from 58; a *meadow*; *Abel*, the name of two places in Palestine:—Abel.

60. **אֵבֶל, 'êbel,** *ay´-bel*; from 56; *lamentation*:—mourning.

61. **אֲבָל, 'ăbâl,** *ab-awl´*; apparently from 56 through the idea of *negation; nay*, i.e. *truly* or *yet*:—but, indeed, nevertheless, verily.

62. **אָבֵל בֵּית־מַעֲכָה, 'Âbêl Bêyth Mă'akâh,** *aw-bale´ bayth ma-a-kaw´*; from 58 and 1004 and 4601; *meadow of Beth-Maakah; Abel of Beth-maakah*, a place in Palestine:—Abel-beth-maachah, Abel of Beth-maachah.

63. **אָבֵל הַשִּׁטִּים, 'Âbêl hash-Shiṭṭîym,** *aw-bale´ hash-shit-teem´*; from 58 and the plural of 7848, with the article inserted; *meadow of the acacias; Abel hash-Shittim*, a place in Palestine:—Abel-shittim.

64. **אָבֵל כְּרָמִים, 'Âbêl Kᵉrâmîym,** *aw-bale´ ker-aw-meem´*; from 58 and the plural of 3754; *meadow of vineyards; Abel-Keramim*, a place in Palestine:—plain of the vineyards.

65. **אָבֵל מְחוֹלָה, 'Âbêl Mᵉchôwlâh,** *aw-bale´ mekh-o-law´*; from 58 and 4246; *meadow of dancing; Abel-Mecholah*, a place in Palestine:—Abel-meholah.

66. **אָבֵל מַיִם, 'Âbêl Mayim,** *aw-bale´ mah´-yim*; from 58 and 4325; *meadow of water; Abel-Majim*, a place in Palestine:—Abel-maim.

67. **אָבֵל מִצְרַיִם, 'Âbêl Mitsrayim,** *aw-bale´ mits-rah´-yim*; from 58 and 4714; *meadow of Egypt; Abel-Mitsrajim*, a place in Palestine:—Abel-mizraim.

68. **אֶבֶן, 'eben,** *eh´-ben*; from the root of 1129 through the meaning to *build; a stone*:—+ carbuncle, + mason, + plummet, [chalk-, hail-, head-, sling-] stone (-ny), (divers) weight (-s).

69. **אֶבֶן, 'eben** (Chaldee), *eh´-ben*; corresponding to 68:—stone.

70. **אֹבֶן, 'ôben,** *o´-ben*; from the same as 68; *a pair of stones* (only dual); a potter's *wheel* or a midwife's *stool* (consisting alike of two horizontal disks with a support between):—wheel, stool.

71. **אֲבָנָה, 'Ăbânâh,** *ab-aw-naw´*; perhaps feminine of 68; *stony; Abanah*, a river near Damascus:—Abana. Compare 549.

72. אֶבֶן הָעֵזֶר, 'Eben hâ'êzer, *eh´-ben haw-e´-zer*; from 68 and 5828 with the article inserted; *stone of the help; Eben-ha-Ezer*, a place in Palestine:—Ebenezer.

73. אַבְנֵט, 'abnêt, *ab-nate´*; of uncertain derivation; a *belt*:—girdle.

74. אַבְנֵר, 'Abnêr, *ab-nare´*; or (fully) אֲבִינֵר, **'Ăbîynêr,** *ab-ee-nare´*; from 1 and 5216; *father of light* (i.e. *enlightening*); *Abner*, an Israelite:—Abner.

75. אָבַס, 'âbas, *aw-bas´*; a primitive root; to *fodder*:—fatted, stalled.

76. אֲבַעְבֻּעָה, 'ăba'bu'âh, *ab-ah-boo-aw´*; (by reduplication) from an unused root (meaning to *belch* forth); an inflammatory *pustule* (as *eruption*):—blains.

77. אֶבֶץ, 'Ebets, *eh´-bets*; from an unused root probably meaning to *gleam; conspicuous; Ebets*, a place in Palestine:—Abez.

78. אִבְצָן, 'Ibtsân, *ib-tsawn´*; from the same as 76; *splendid; Ibtsan*, an Israelite:—Ibzan.

79. אָבַק, 'âbaq, *aw-bak´*; a primitive root; probably to *float* away (as vapor), but used only as denominative from 80; to *bedust*, i.e. *grapple*:—wrestle.

80. אָבָק, 'âbâq, *aw-bawk´*; from root of 79; light *particles* (as *volatile*):—(small) dust, powder.

A masculine noun meaning dust, especially extremely fine, powdery particles in contrast to the coarser dust or *'âphâr* (6083). It is used to signify the dust easily driven by the wind (Isa 5:24) and dust raised by the hooves of galloping horses (Eze 26:10). As a metaphor, it signifies the notion of utter insignificance (Isa 29:5); conditions of drought (Dt 28:24); and clouds as the dust of God's feet (Na 1:3).

81. אֲבָקָה, 'ăbâqâh, *ab-aw-kaw´*; feminine of 80:—powder.

82. אָבַר, 'âbar, *aw-bar´*; a primitive root; to *soar*:—fly.

83. אֵבֶר, 'êber, *ay-ber´*; from 82; a *pinion*:—[long-] wing (-ed).

84. אֶבְרָה, 'ebrâh, *eb-raw´*; feminine of 83:—feather, wing.

85. אַבְרָהָם, 'Abrâhâm, *ab-raw-hawm´*; contracted from 1 and an unused root (probably meaning to *be populous*); *father of a multitude; Abraham*, the later name of Abram:—Abraham.

86. אַבְרֵךְ, 'abrêk, *ab-rake´*; probably an Egyptian word meaning *kneel*:—bow the knee.

87. אַבְרָם, 'Abrâm, *ab-rawm´*; contracted from 48; *high father; Abram*, the original name of Abraham:—Abram.

88. אֹבֹת, 'ôbôth, *o-both´*; plural of 178; water-*skins; Oboth*, a place in the Desert:—Oboth.

89. אָגֵא, 'Âgê', *aw-gay´*; of uncertain derivation [compare 90]; *Agè*, an Israelite:—Agee.

90. אֲגַג, 'Ăgag, *ag-ag´*; or אֲגָג, **'Ăgâg,** *ag-awg´*; of uncertain derivation [compare 89]; *flame; Agag*, a title of Amalekitish kings:—Agag.

91. אֲגָגִי, 'Ăgâgîy, *ag-aw-ghee´*; patrial or patronymic from 90; an *Agagite* or descendant (subject) of Agag:—Agagite.

92. אֲגֻדָּה, 'ăguddâh, *ag-ood-daw´*; feminine passive participle of an unused root (meaning to *bind*); a *band, bundle, knot*, or *arch*:—bunch, burden, troop.

93. אֱגוֹז, 'ĕgôwz, *eg-oze´*; probably of Persian origin; a *nut*:—nut.

94. אָגוּר, 'Âgûwr, *aw-goor´*; passive participle of 103; *gathered* (i.e. *received* among the sages); *Agur*, a fanciful name for Solomon:—Agur.

95. אֲגוֹרָה, 'ăgôwrâh, *ag-o-raw´*; from the same as 94; probably something *gathered*, i.e. perhaps a *grain* or *berry*; used only of a small (silver) *coin*:—piece [of] silver.

96. אֶגֶל, 'egel, *eh´-ghel*; from an unused root (meaning to *flow* down or together as drops); a *reservoir*:—drop.

97. אֶגְלַיִם, 'Eglayim, *eg-lah´-yim*; dual of 96; a *double pond; Eglajim*, a place in Moab:—Eglaim.

98. אֲגַם, 'ăgam, *ag-am´*; from an unused root (meaning to *collect* as water); a *marsh*; hence a *rush* (as growing in swamps); hence a *stockade* of reeds:—pond, pool, standing [water].

99. אָגֵם, 'âgêm, *aw-game´*; probably from the same as 98 (in the sense of *stagnant* water); (figurative) *sad*:—pond.

100. אַגְמוֹן, 'agmôwn, *ag-mone´*; from the same as 98; a marshy *pool* [others from a different root, a *kettle*]; by implication a *rush* (as growing there); (collective) a *rope* of rushes:—bulrush, caldron, hook, rush.

101. אַגָּן, 'aggân, *ag-gawn´*; probably from 5059; a *bowl* (as *pounded* out hollow):—basin, cup, goblet.

102. אֲגַף, 'ăgâph, *ag-af´*; probably from 5062 (through the idea of *impending*); a *cover* or *heap*; i.e. (only plural) *wings* of an army, or *crowds* of troops:—bands.

103. אָגַר, 'âgar, *aw-gar´*; a primitive root; to *harvest*:—gather.

104. אִגְּרָא, 'iggᵉrâ' (Chaldee), *ig-ger-aw´*; of Persian origin; an *epistle* (as carried by a state courier or postman):—letter.

105. אֲגַרְטָל, 'ăgartâl, *ag-ar-tawl´*; of uncertain derivation; a *basin*:—charger.

106. אֶגְרֹף, 'egrôph, *eg-rofe´*; from 1640 (in the sense of *grasping*); the *clenched* hand:—fist.

107. אִגֶּרֶת, 'iggereth, *ig-eh´-reth*; feminine of 104; an *epistle*:—letter.

108. אֵד, 'êd, *ade*; from the same as 181 (in the sense of *enveloping*); a *fog*:—mist, vapor.

109. אָדַב, 'âdab, *aw-dab´*; a primitive root; to *languish*:—grieve.

110. אַדְבְּאֵל, 'Adbᵉ'êl, *ad-beh-ale´*; probably from 109 (in the sense of *chastisement*) and 410; *disciplined of God; Adbeël*, a son of Ishmael:—Adbeel.

111. אֲדַד, 'Ădad, *ad-ad´*; probably an orthographical variation for 2301; *Adad* (or Hadad), an Edomite:—Hadad.

112. אִדּוֹ, 'Iddôw, *id-do*; of uncertain derivation; *Iddo*, an Israelite:—Iddo.

113. אָדוֹן, 'âdôwn, *aw-done´*; or (shortened) אָדֹן, **'âdôn,** *aw-done´*; from an unused root (meaning to *rule*); *sovereign*, i.e. *controller* (human or divine):—lord, master, owner. Compare also names beginning with "Adoni-".

A masculine noun meaning lord or master. The most frequent usage is of a human lord, but it is also used of divinity. Generally, it carries the nuances of authority rather than ownership. When used of humans, it refers to authority over slaves (Ge 24:9; Jgs 19:11); people (1Ki 22:17); a wife (Ge 18:12; Am 4:1); or a household (Ge 45:8; Ps 105:21). When used of divinity, it frequently occurs with *yĕhôwâh* (3068), signifying His sovereignty (Ex 34:23; Jos 3:13; Isa 1:24). See the Hebrew noun *'ădônây* (136).

114. אַדּוֹן, 'Addôwn, *ad-done´*; probably intensive for 113; *powerful; Addon*, apparently an Israelite:—Addon.

115. אֲדוֹרַיִם, 'Ădôwrayim, *ad-o-rah´-yim*; dual from 142 (in the sense of *eminence*); *double mound; Adorajim*, a place in Palestine:—Adoraim.

116. אֱדַיִן, 'ĕdayin (Chaldee), *ed-ah´-yin*; of uncertain derivation; *then* (of time):—now, that time, then.

117. אַדִּיר, 'addîyr, *ad-deer´*; from 142; *wide* or (general) *large*; (figurative) *powerful*:—excellent, famous, gallant, glorious, goodly, lordly, mighty (-ier, one), noble, principal, worthy.

An adjective meaning excellent, majestic, lofty, or great. When describing physical objects, it often denotes strength of the waters of the sea (Ex 15:10; Ps 93:4); the precious value of a bowl (Jgs 5:25); or both the strength and beauty of trees (Eze 17:23; Zec 11:2). When describing humans, it refers to those who lead, either as rulers or royalty (Jer 14:3; 25:34–36; 30:21; Na 3:18). When describing God, this word describes His majestic power (1Sa 4:8; Ps 8:1[2], 9[10]; Isa 10:34) that is greater than the breakers of the sea (Ps 93:4).

118. אֲדַלְיָא, 'Ădalyâ', *ad-al-yaw´*; of Persian derivation; *Adalja*, a son of Haman:—Adalia.

119. אָדַם, 'âdam, *aw-dam´*; to *show blood* (in the face), i.e. *flush* or turn rosy:—be (dyed, made) red (ruddy).

A verb meaning to be red, ruddy, dyed red. It is used to describe people: Esau (Ge 25:25); David (1Sa 16:12; 17:42); and princes (La 4:7). As for things, it describes ram skins that were dyed red (Ex 25:5; 26:14; 35:7) and red wine (Pr 23:31). Metaphorically, this word describes sin as "red like crimson" (Isa 1:18).

120. אָדָם, 'âdâm, *aw-dawm´*; from 119; *ruddy*, i.e. a *human being* (an individual or the species, *mankind*, etc.):— × another, + hypocrite, + common sort, × low, man (mean, of low degree), person.

A masculine noun meaning a male, any human being, or generically the human race. The word is used to signify a man, as opposed to a woman (Ge 2:18; Ecc 7:28); a human (Nu 23:19; Pr 17:18; Isa 17:7); the human race in general (Ge 1:27; Nu 8:17; Ps 144:3; Isa 2:17); and the representative embodiment of humanity, as the appellation "son of man" indicates (Eze 2:1, 3). The first man used this word as a proper noun, "Adam" (Ge 2:20).

121. אָדָם, 'Âdâm, *aw-dawm´*; the same as 120; *Adam*, the name of the first man, also of a place in Palestine:—Adam.

122. אָדֹם, 'âdôm, *aw-dome´*; from 119; *rosy*:—red, ruddy.

A masculine adjective meaning red, ruddy, the colour of blood (red to reddish brown). The meaning of the word is best demonstrated in 2Ki 3:22, where the Moabites saw the sunrise reflecting off the water which the Lord had miraculously provided. The Moabites thought the water was "as red as blood." This word is also used to describe the colour of lentil stew (Ge 25:30); the health or attractiveness of a man (SS 5:10); the colour of garments (Isa 63:2); the colour of animals, like a red heifer (Nu 19:2) or chestnut or bay–coloured horses (Zec 1:8; 6:2).

123. אֱדֹם, 'Ědôm, *ed-ome´*; or (fully) אֱדוֹם, **'Ědôwm,** *ed-ome´*; from 122 *red* [see Ge 25:25]; *Edom*, the elder twin-brother of Jacob; hence the region (Idumæa) occupied by him:—Edom, Edomites, Idumea.

124. אֹדֶם, 'ôdem, *o´-dem*; from 119; *redness*, i.e. the *ruby, garnet*, or some other red gem:—sardius.

125. אֲדַמְדָּם, 'ădamdâm, *ad-am-dawm´*; reduplicated from 119; *reddish*:—(somewhat) reddish.

An adjective meaning reddish. This word is used only six times in the OT. It signifies the reddish appearance of leprosy on the skin (Le 13:19, 24, 42, 43); the mark of leprosy on a garment (Le 13:49); or the mark of leprosy within a house (Le 14:37). It is related to the verb *'âdam* (119), meaning to be red, and the adjective *'âdôm*, meaning red (122).

126. אַדְמָה, 'Admâh, *ad-maw´*; contraction for 127; *earthy; Admah*, a place near the Dead Sea:—Admah.

127. אֲדָמָה, 'ădâmâh, *ad-aw-maw´*; from 119; *soil* (from its general *redness*):—country, earth, ground, husband [-man] (-ry), land.

A feminine noun meaning dirt, ground, earth, clay. In the narrow sense of the word, it signifies the earth or clay God used to form man (Ge 2:7); dirt put on the head during mourning (2Sa 1:2; Ne 9:1); the ground itself (Ex 3:5); cultivated land (Ge 4:2; Zec 13:5). In a broader sense, it means the inhabited earth (Isa 24:21; Am 3:2). The first man, Adam, both came from the ground and was assigned the task of tending the ground (see Ge 2:7, 15).

128. אֲדָמָה, 'Ădâmâh, *ad-aw-maw´*; the same as 127; *Adamah*, a place in Palestine:—Adamah.

129. אֲדָמִי, 'Ădâmîy, *ad-aw-mee´*; from 127; *earthy; Adami*, a place in Palestine:—Adami.

130. אֱדֹמִי, 'Ědômîy, *ed-o-mee´*; or (fully) אֱדוֹמִי, **'Ědôwmîy,** *ed-o-mee´*; patronymically from 123; an *Edomite*, or descendant from (or inhabitant of) Edom:—Edomite. See 726.

131. אֲדֻמִּים, 'Ădummîym, *ad-oom-meem´*; plural of 121; *red* spots; *Adummim*, a pass in Palestine:—Adummim.

132. אַדְמֹנִי, 'admônîy, *ad-mo-nee´*; or (fully) אַדְמוֹנִי, **'admôwnîy,** *ad-mo-nee´*; from 119; *reddish* (of the hair or the complexion):—red, ruddy.

An adjective meaning red, ruddy. Esau is the prime example of someone who was red (Ge 25:25). The Edomites, or "red ones," descended from Esau. David is the other notable figure whose complexion was characterized as good-looking, bright-eyed, and ruddy (1Sa 16:12).

133. אַדְמָתָא, 'Admâthâ', *ad-maw-thaw´*; probably of Persian derivation; *Admatha*, a Persian nobleman:—Admatha.

134. אֶדֶן, 'eden, *eh´-den*; from the same as 113 (in the sense of *strength*); a *basis* (of a building, a column, etc.):—foundation, socket.

135. אַדָּן, 'Addân, *ad-dawn´*; intensive from the same as 134; *firm; Addan*, an Israelite:—Addan.

136. אֲדֹנָי, 'Ădônây, *ad-o-noy´*; an emphatic form of 113; the *Lord* (used as a proper name of God only):—(my) Lord.

A masculine noun used exclusively of God. An emphatic form of the word *'âdôwn* (113), this word means literally "my Lord" (Ge 18:3). It is often used in place of the divine name *YHWH* (3068), which was held by later Jewish belief to be too holy to utter. This designation points to the supreme authority or power of God (Ps 2:4; Isa 6:1). The word was often combined with the divine name to reinforce the notion of God's matchlessness (e.g., Eze 20:3; Am 7:6).

137. אֲדֹנִי־בֶזֶק, 'Ădônîy-Bezeq, *ad-o´-nee-beh´-zek*; from 113 and 966; *lord of Bezek; Adoni-Bezek*, a Canaanitish king:—Adoni-bezek.

138. אֲדֹנִיָּה, 'Ădônîyyâh, *ad-o-nee-yaw´*; original (prolonged) אֲדֹנִיָּהוּ, **'Ădônîyyâhûw,** *ad-o-nee-yaw´-hoo*; from 113 and 3050; *lord* (i.e. worshipper) of Jah; *Adonijah*, the name of three Israelites:—Adonijah.

139. אֲדֹנִי־צֶדֶק, 'Ădônîy-Tsedeq, *ad-o´-nee-tseh´-dek*; from 113 and 6664; *lord of justice; Adoni-Tsedek*, a Canaanitish king:—Adoni-zedec.

140. אֲדֹנִיקָם, 'Ădônîyqâm, *ad-o-nee-kawm´*; from 113 and 6965; *lord of rising* (i.e. *high*); *Adonikam*, the name of one or two Israelites:—Adonikam.

141. אֲדֹנִירָם, 'Ădônîyrâm, *ad-o-nee-rawm´*; from 113 and 7311; *lord of height; Adoniram*, an Israelite:—Adoniram.

142. אָדַר, 'âdar, *aw-dar*; a primitive root; to *expand*, i.e. *be great* or (figurative) *magnificent*:—(become) glorious, honourable.

A verb meaning to magnify, glorify, or, in the passive sense, to be magnified. Whereas the Hebrew noun *kâbôwd* (3519) pictures glory in terms of weight, this word pictures it in terms of size. The Hebrew word is used only three times in the OT: to celebrate God's power and holiness after the deliverance of Israel from Egypt (Ex 15:6, 11); and to describe the Law given on Sinai as great and glorious (Isa 42:21).

143. אֲדָר, 'Ădâr, *ad-awr´*; probably of foreign derivation; perhaps meaning *fire; Adar*, the 12th Hebrew month:—Adar.

144. אֲדָר, 'Ădâr (Chaldee), *ad-awr´*; corresponding to 143:—Adar.

145. אֶדֶר, 'eder, *eh´-der*; from 142; *amplitude*, i.e. (concrete) a *mantle*; also (figurative) *splendor*:—goodly, robe.

146. אַדָּר, 'Addâr, *ad-dawr´*; intensive from 142; *ample; Addar,* a place in Palestine; also an Israelite:—Addar.

147. אִדַּר, 'iddar (Chaldee), *id-dar´*; intensive from a root corresponding to 142; *ample,* i.e. a threshing-*floor*:—threshingfloor.

148. אֲדַרְגָּזֵר, 'ădargâzêr (Chaldee), *ad-ar´-gaw-zare´*; from the same as 147, and 1505; a *chief diviner,* or *astrologer*:—judge.

An Aramaic masculine noun meaning counselor. It is found only in the book of Daniel. When Nebuchadnezzar erected his statue for all to bow down to, he sent a decree to all the important people (i.e. satraps, administrators, counselors) to come for the dedication ceremony (Da 3:2, 3).

149. אַדְרַזְדָּא, 'adrazdâ' (Chaldee), *ad-raz-daw´*; probably of Persian origin; *quickly* or *carefully*:—diligently.

150. אֲדַרְכֹּן, 'ădarkôn, *ad-ar-kone´*; of Persian origin; a *daric* or Persian coin:—dram.

A noun meaning monetary value and weight. This word is used only in 1Ch 29:7, where David collected money for the first temple, and in Ezr 8:27, where it tells the weight of gold basins for use in the second temple. The word may refer to the Greek *drachma,* which weighed 4.3 grams, or to the Persian *daric,* which weighed about twice as much.

151. אֲדֹרָם, 'Ădôrâm, *ad-o-rawm´*; contraction for 141; *Adoram* (or Adoniram), an Israelite:—Adoram.

152. אַדְרַמֶּלֶךְ, 'Adrammelek, *ad-ram-meh´-lek*; from 142 and 4428; *splendor of* (the) *king; Adrammelek,* the name of an Assyrian idol, also of a son of Sennacherib:—Adrammelech.

153. אֶדְרָע, 'edrâ‘ (Chaldee), *ed-raw´*; an orthographical variation for 1872; an *arm,* i.e. (figurative) *power*:—force.

154. אֶדְרֶעִי, 'edre'îy, *ed-reh´-ee*; from the equivalent of 153; *mighty; Edrei,* the name of two places in Palestine:—Edrei.

155. אַדֶּרֶת, 'addereth, *ad-deh´-reth*; feminine of 117; something *ample* (as a *large* vine, a *wide* dress); also the same as 145:—garment, glory, goodly, mantle, robe.

156. אָדַשׁ, 'âdash, *aw-dash´*; a primitive root; to *tread* out (grain):—thresh.

157. אָהַב, 'âhab, *aw-hab´*; or **אָהֵב, 'âhêb,** *aw-habe´*; a primitive root; to *have affection* for (sexually or otherwise):—(be-) love (-d, -ly, -r), like, friend.

A verb meaning to love. The semantic range of the verb includes loving or liking objects and things such as bribes (Isa 1:23); wisdom (Pr 4:6); wine (Pr 21:17); peace, truth (Zec 8:19); or tasty food (Ge 27:4, 9, 14). The word also conveys love for other people (Ge 29:32; Ru 4:15; 1Ki 11:1); love for God (Ex 20:6; Ps 116:1); and also God's love of people (Dt 4:37; 1Ki 10:9; Hos 3:1).

158. אַהַב, 'ahab, *ah´-hab*; from 157; *affection* (in a good or a bad sense):—love (-r).

A masculine noun meaning love or lover. Both occurrences of this noun are in the plural. In Pr 5:19, it refers to marital love, while in Hos 8:9, the word refers to Israel's trust in foreign alliances rather than in God. The foreign nations are Israel's hired lovers.

159. אֹהַב, 'ôhab, *o´-hab*; from 156; meaning the same as 158:—love.

A masculine noun meaning loved one. It occurs twice in the Hebrew Bible, both times in the plural (Pr 7:18; Hos 9:10). Both occurrences are associated with illicit sexual relations.

160. אַהֲבָה, 'ahăbâh, *ă-hab-aw´*; feminine of 158 and meaning the same:—love.

A feminine noun meaning love. The word often signifies a powerful, intimate love between a man and a woman (Ge 29:20; SS 2:4, 5, 7); love between friends (2Sa 1:26); God's love for His people (Isa 63:9; Hos 3:1). Frequently, it is associated with forming a covenant, which enjoins loyalty (Dt 7:8). When used in an abstract way, the word designates a desirable personal quality, which connotes affection and faithfulness (Pr 15:17; 17:9).

161. אֹהַד, 'Ôhad, *o´-had*; from an unused root meaning to *be united; unity; Ohad,* an Israelite:—Ohad.

162. אֲהָהּ, 'âhâh, *ă-haw´*; apparently a primitive word expressing *pain* exclamatorily; *Oh!*:—ah, alas.

163. אַהֲוָא, 'Ahăvâ', *ă-hav-aw´*; probably of foreign origin; *Ahava,* a river of Babylonia:—Ahava.

164. אֵהוּד, 'Êhûwd, *ay-hood´*; from the same as 161; *united; Ehud,* the name of two or three Israelites:—Ehud.

165. אֱהִי, 'ĕhîy, *e-hee´*; apparently an orthographical variation for 346 *where*:—I will be (Hos 13:10, 14) [*which is often the rendering of the same Hebrew form from* 1961].

166. אָהַל, 'âhal, *aw-hal´*; a primitive root; to *be clear*:—shine.

167. אָהַל, 'âhal, *aw-hal´*; a denominative from 168; to *tent*:—pitch (remove) a tent.

168. אֹהֶל, 'ôhel, *o´-hel*; from 166; a *tent* (as *clearly* conspicuous from a distance):—covering, (dwelling) (place), home, tabernacle, tent.

A masculine noun meaning tent. It is used literally as a habitation of nomadic peoples and patriarchs (Ge 9:21; 25:27). It can be used figuratively for a dwelling (Ps 91:10; 132:3); or a people group (Ge 9:27; Jer 35:7; 49:29). As a generic collective, it describes cattle (Ge 4:20) or wickedness (Job 15:34; Ps 84:10[11]). The word is also employed in reference to the tabernacle, the "tent" (Nu 12:5, 10; Eze 41:1).

169. אֹהֶל, 'Ôhel, *o´-hel*; the same as 168; *Ohel,* an Israelite:—Ohel.

170. אָהֳלָה, 'Ohŏlâh, *ŏ-hol-aw´*; in form a feminine of 168, but in fact for **אָהֳלָהּ, 'Ohŏlâh,** *ŏ-hol-aw´*; from 168; *her tent* (i.e. idolatrous *sanctuary*); *Oholah,* a symbolical name for Samaria:—Aholah.

171. אָהֳלִיאָב, 'Ohŏlîy'âb, *ŏ´-hol-e-awb´*; from 168 and 1; *tent of* (his) *father; Oholiab,* an Israelite:—Aholiab.

172. אָהֳלִיבָה, 'Ohŏlîybâh, *ŏ´-hol-ee-baw´*; (similarly with 170) for **אָהֳלִיבָהּ, 'Ohŏlîybâh,** *ŏ´-hol-e-baw´*; from 168; *my tent (is) in her; Oholibah,* a symbolical name for Judah:—Aholibah.

173. אָהֳלִיבָמָה, 'Ohŏlîybâmâh, *ŏ´-hol-e-baw-maw´*; from 168 and 1116; *tent of* (the) *height; Oholibamah,* a wife of Esau:—Aholibamah.

174. אֲהָלִים, 'ăhâlîym, *â-haw-leem´*; or (feminine) **אֲהָלוֹת, 'ăhâlôwth,** *ă-haw-loth´*; of foreign origin; *aloe* wood (i.e. sticks):—(tree of lign-) aloes.

175. אַהֲרוֹן, 'Ahărôwn, *ă-har-one´*; of uncertain derivation; *Aharon,* the brother of Moses:—Aaron.

176. אוֹ, 'ôw, *o*; presumed to be the "constructive" or genitival form of **אַו, 'av,** *av,* shortened for 185 *desire* (and so probably in Pr 31:4); hence (by way of alternative) *or,* also *if*:—also, and, either, if, at the least, × nor, or, otherwise, then, whether.

177. אוּאֵל, 'Ûw'êl, *oo-ale´*; from 176 and 410; *wish of God; Uel,* an Israelite:—Uel.

178. אוֹב, 'ôwb, *obe*; from the same as 1 (apparently through the idea of *prattling* a father's name); probably a *mumble,* i.e. a water-*skin* (from its hollow sound); hence a *necromancer* (ventriloquist, as from a jar):—bottle, familiar spirit.

A masculine noun meaning a conjured spirit, a medium or necromancer; or a leather bottle. The primary use of the word is connected to the occult practice of necromancy or consulting the dead. It is used to signify a conjurer who professes to call up the dead by means of magic, especially to give revelation about future uncertainties (1Sa 28:7; Isa 8:19); a man or woman who has a familiar spirit (Le 20:27; 1Ch 10:13; Isa 29:4); the conjured spirit itself, particularly when speaking through the medium (1Sa 28:8; 2 Kgs 21:6; 2Ch 33:6). The Israelites were strictly forbidden from engaging in such practices or consulting mediums (Le 19:31; Dt 18:10–12). Interestingly, the word is used once to signify a leather bottle that may burst under pressure (Job 32:19). There is no convincing evidence that this particular reference has any occult connotations. Rather, the connection between the two divergent meanings of this Hebrew word is probably that a medium was seen as a "container" for a conjured spirit.

179. אוֹבִיל, 'Ôwbîyl, *o-beel´*; probably from 56; *mournful; Obil*, an Ishmaelite:—Obil.

180. אוּבָל, 'ûwbâl, *oo-bawl´*; or (shortened) אֻבָל, **'ubâl,** *oo-bawl´*; from 2986 (in the sense of 2988); a *stream*:—river.

181. אוּד, 'ûwd, *ood*; from an unused root meaning to *rake* together; a *poker* (for *turning* or *gathering* embers):—(fire-) brand.

182. אוֹדוֹת, 'ôwdôwth, *o-dōth´*; or (shortened) אֹדוֹת, **'ôdôwth,** *o-dōth´* (only thus in the plural); from the same as 181; *turnings* (i.e. *occasions*); (adverbial) on *account* of:—(be-) cause, concerning, sake.

183. אָוָה, 'âvâh, *aw-vaw´*; a primitive root; to *wish* for:—covet, (greatly) desire, be desirous, long, lust (after).

A verb meaning to desire, to be inclined. This word is used to signify coveting, as in the tenth commandment (Dt 5:21[18]; but *châmad* [2530] is used in Ex 20:17). The word may also signify acceptable desires for objects such as food or beauty (Ps 45:11[12]; Mic 7:1); as well as for righteousness and God (Isa 26:9; Mic 7:1). Both God and humans can be the subject of this word (Ps 132:13, 14).

184. אָוָה, 'âvâh, *aw-vaw´*; a primitive root; to *extend* or *mark* out:—point out.

185. אַוָּה, 'avvâh, *av-vaw´*; from 183; *longing*:—desire, lust after, pleasure.

186. אוּזַי, 'Ûwzay, *oo-zah´ee*; perhaps by permutation for 5813, *strong; Uzai*, an Israelite:—Uzai.

187. אוּזָל, 'Ûwzâl, *oo-zâwl´*; of uncertain derivation; *Uzal*, a son of Joktan:—Uzal.

188. אוֹי, 'ôwy, *ō´-ee*; probably from 183 (in the sense of *crying* out after); *lamentation*; also interjectional *Oh!*:—alas, woe.

189. אֱוִי, 'Ěvîy, *ev-ee´*; probably from 183; *desirous; Evi*, a Midianitish chief:—Evi.

190. אוֹיָה, 'ôwyâh, *o-yaw´*; feminine of 188:—woe.

191. אֱוִיל, 'ěvîyl, *ev-eel´*; from an unused root (meaning to be *perverse*); (figurative) *silly*:—fool (-ish) (man).

192. אֱוִיל מְרֹדַךְ, 'Ěvîyl Mᵉrôdak, *ev-eel´ mer-o-dak´*; of Chaldee derivation and probably meaning *soldier of Merodak; Evil-Merodak*, a Babylonian king:—Evil-merodach.

193. אוּל, 'ûwl, *ool*; from an unused root meaning to *twist*, i.e. (by implication) *be strong*; the *body* (as being *rolled* together); also *powerful*:—mighty, strength.

194. אוּלַי, 'ûwlay, *oo-lah´ee*; or (shortened) אֻלַי, **'ulay,** *oo-lah´ee*; from 176; *if not*; hence *perhaps*:—if so be, may be, peradventure, unless.

195. אוּלַי, 'Ûwlay, *oo-lah´ee*; of Persian derivation; the *Ulai* (or Eulæus), a river of Persia:—Ulai.

196. אֱוִלִי, 'ěvilîy, *ev-ee-lee´*; from 191; *silly, foolish*; hence (moral) *impious*:—foolish.

197. אוּלָם, 'ûwlâm, *oo-lawm´*; or (shortened) אֻלָם, **'ulâm,** *oo-lawm´*; from 481 (in the sense of *tying*); a *vestibule* (as *bound* to the building):—porch.

198. אוּלָם, 'Ûwlâm, *oo-lawm´*; apparently from 481 (in the sense of *dumbness*); *solitary; Ulam*, the name of two Israelites:—Ulam.

199. אוּלָם, 'ûwlâm, *oo-lawm´*; apparently a variation of 194; *however* or *on the contrary*:—as for, but, howbeit, in very deed, surely, truly, wherefore.

200. אִוֶּלֶת, 'ivveleth, *iv-veh´-leth*; from the same as 191; *silliness*:—folly, foolishly (-ness).

201. אוֹמָר, 'Ôwmâr, *o-mawr´*; from 559; *talkative; Omar*, a grandson of Esau:—Omar.

202. אוֹן, 'ôwn, *ōne*; probably from the same as 205 (in the sense of *effort*, but successful); *ability, power*, (figurative) *wealth*:—force, goods, might, strength, substance.

203. אוֹן, 'Ôwn, *ōne*; the same as 202; *On*, an Israelite:—On.

204. אוֹן, 'Ôwn, *ōne*; or (shortened) אֹן, **'Ôn,** *ōne*; of Egyptian derivation; *On*, a city of Egypt:—On.

205. אָוֶן, 'âven, *aw´-ven*; from an unused root perhaps meaning properly to *pant* (hence to *exert* oneself, usually in vain; to *come to naught*); strictly *nothingness*; also *trouble, vanity, wickedness*; specifically an *idol*:—affliction, evil, false, idol, iniquity, mischief, mourners (-ing), naught, sorrow, unjust, unrighteous, vain, vanity, wicked (-ness). Compare 369.

A masculine noun meaning nothingness, trouble, sorrow, evil, or mischief. The primary meaning is that of emptiness and vanity. It is used to signify empty or futile pursuits (Pr 22:8; Isa 41:29); nothingness, in the sense of utter destruction (Am 5:5); an empty word, implying falsehood or deceit (Ps 10:7; Pr 17:4; Zec 10:2); wickedness or one who commits iniquity (Nu 23:21; Job 22:15; Ps 14:4[5]; 36:4; 101:8; Isa 58:9; Mic 2:1); evil or calamity (Job 5:6; Pr 12:21; Jer 4:15); and great sorrow (Dt 26:14; Ps 90:10; Hos 9:4). In a metaphorical sense, the word is used once to signify an idol, strongly conveying the futility of worshiping an idol, which is, in fact, "nothing" (Isa 66:3).

206. אָוֶן, 'Âven, *aw´-ven*; the same as 205; *idolatry; Aven*, the contemptuous synonym of three places, one in Coele-Syria, one in Egypt (On), and one in Palestine (Bethel):—Aven. See also 204, 1007.

207. אוֹנוֹ, 'Ôwnôw, *o-no´*; or (shortened) אֹנוֹ, **'Ônôw,** *o-no´*; prolonged from 202; *strong; Ono*, a place in Palestine:—Ono.

208. אוֹנָם, 'Ôwnâm, *o-nawm´*; a variation of 209; *strong; Onam*, the name of an Edomite and of an Israelite:—Onam.

209. אוֹנָן, 'Ôwnân, *o-nawn´*; a variation of 207; *strong; Onan*, a son of Judah:—Onan.

210. אוּפָז, 'Ûwphâz, *oo-fawz´*; perhaps a corruption of 211; *Uphaz*, a famous gold region:—Uphaz.

211. אוֹפִיר, 'Ôwphîyr, *o-feer´*; or (shortened) אֹפִיר, **'Ôphîyr,** *o-feer´*; and אוֹפִר, **'Ôwphir,** *o-feer´*; of uncertain derivation; *Ophir*, the name of a son of Joktan, and of a gold region in the East:—Ophir.

212. אוֹפָן, 'ôwphân, *o-fawn´*; or (shortened) אֹפָן, **'ôphân,** *o-fawn´*; from an unused root meaning to *revolve*; a *wheel*:—wheel.

A masculine noun meaning wheel (although it is feminine in one usage). God caused the chariot wheels of the Egyptians to come off while they were chasing the Israelites through the Red Sea (Ex 14:25). This word is also used to describe the movable stands in Solomon's Temple (1Ki 7:30, 32, 33); the wheels of threshing carts (Pr 20:26; Isa 28:27); and the wheels of Ezekiel's chariot that supported the four living creatures (Eze 1:15, 16, 19–21).

213. אוּץ, 'ûwts, *oots*; a primitive root; to *press*; (by implication) to *be close, hurry, withdraw*:—(make) haste (-n, -y), labour, be narrow.

214. אוֹצָר, 'ôwtsâr, *o-tsaw´*; from 686; a *depository*:—armoury, cellar, garner, store (-house), treasure (-house) (-y).

215. אוֹר, **'ôwr,** *ore*; a primitive root; *to be* (causative *make*) *luminous* (literal and metaphorical):— × break of day, glorious, kindle, (be, en-, give, show) light (-en, -ened), set on fire, shine.

216. אוֹר, **'ôwr,** *ore*; from 215; *illumination* or (concrete) *luminary* (in every sense, including *lightning, happiness*, etc.):— bright, clear, + day, light (-ning), morning, sun.

A masculine noun meaning light. In a literal sense, it is used primarily to refer to light from heavenly bodies (Jer 31:35; Eze 32:7) but also for light itself (Ge 1:3; Ecc 12:2). The pillar of fire was a light for the wandering Israelites (Ex 13:21). One day God, who is clothed with light (a manifestation of His splendor), will replace the light of the heavens with His own light (Ps 104:2; Isa 60:19, 20; cf. Rev 21:23; 22:5). Light is always used as a positive symbol, such as for good fortune (Job 30:26); victory (Mic 7:8, 9); justice and righteousness (Isa 59:9); guidance (Ps 119:105); and a bearer of deliverance (Isa 49:6). Expressions involving light include the light of one's face, meaning someone's favour (Ps 44:3[4]); to see light, meaning to live (Ps 49:19[20]); and to walk in the light, meaning to live by God's known standards (Isa 2:5).

217. אוּר, **'ûwr,** *oor*; from 215; *flame*, hence (in the plural) the *East* (as being the region of light):—fire, light. See also 224.

A noun meaning fire. It refers to the fire of God's judgment (Isa 31:9) and God's destruction of the wicked (Eze 5:2). In Isa 44:16 and 47:14, the noun is used to speak of a form of idol worship.

218. אוּר, **'Ûwr,** *oor*; the same as 217; *Ur*, a place in Chaldea; also an Israelite:—Ur.

219. אוֹרָה, **'ôwrâh,** *o-raw´*; feminine of 216; *luminousness*, i.e. (figurative) *prosperity*; also a plant (as being *bright*):—herb, light.

A feminine noun meaning light, brightness, splendor, herbs. The primary stress of the word is on the life-giving properties. It is used to signify light (Ps 139:12); joyous well-being (Est 8:16); vibrant green herbs (2Ki 4:39). The word also conveys the quality of living (Isa 26:19).

220. אֲוֵרָה, **'ăvêrâh,** *av-ay-raw´*; by transposition for 723; a *stall*:—cote.

221. אוּרִי, **'Ûwrîy,** *oo-ree´*; from 217; *fiery; Uri*, the name of three Israelites:—Uri.

222. אוּרִיאֵל, **'Ûwrîy'êl,** *oo-ree-ale´*; from 217 and 410; *flame of God; Uriel*, the name of two Israelites:—Uriel.

223. אוּרִיָּה, **'Ûwrîyyâh,** *oo-ree-yaw´*; or (prolonged) אוּרִיָּהוּ, **'Ûwrîyyâhûw,** *oo-ree-yaw´-hoo*; from 217 and 3050; *flame of Jah; Urijah*, the name of one Hittite and five Israelites:—Uriah, Urijah.

224. אוּרִים, **'Ûwrîym,** *oo-reem´*; plural of 217; *lights; Urim*, the oracular brilliancy of the figures in the high priest's breastplate:—Urim.

A masculine plural noun, which occurs seven times in the OT, usually with "the Thummim." Our knowledge of the Urim and Thummim is limited. They were kept in the breastplate which the high priest wore over his heart (Ex 28:30; Le 8:8) and were given to the Levites as part of Moses' blessing (Dt 33:8). Some believe they were flat objects which were cast to determine the will of God, one providing a negative answer and the other a positive, much like casting lots. However, that is somewhat conjectural. Joshua received God's revelation by Eleazer's use of the Urim (Nu 27:21). God didn't answer Saul when he consulted the Lord with the use of the Urim (1Sa 28:6). The Urim and Thummim were also used to approve priestly qualifications (Ezr 2:63; Ne 7:65).

225. אוּת, **'ûwth,** *ooth*; a primitive root; probably to *come*, i.e. (implication) to *assent*:—consent.

226. אוֹת, **'ôwth,** *ōth*; probably from 225 (in the sense of *appearing*); a *signal* (literal or figurative), as a *flag, beacon, monument, omen, prodigy, evidence*, etc.:—mark, miracle, (en-) sign, token.

A masculine noun meaning sign, signal, mark, miracle. This word is used most often to describe awe-inspiring events: God's work to bring the Hebrew people out of Egypt (Ex 4:8, 9; Nu 14:22; Dt 7:19; Ps 78:43; Jer 32:20, 21); miracles verifying God's message (1Sa 2:34; 10:7, 9; Isa 7:11, 14). Moreover, this word may also denote signs from false prophets (Dt 13:1[2], 2[3]; Isa 44:25); circumstances demonstrating God's control (Dt 28:46; Ps 86:17). Associate meanings of the word denote physical emblems (Nu 2:2); a promise to remember (Ge 17:11; Dt 6:8; Jos 2:12; 4:6); an event to occur in the future (Isa 20:3; Eze 4:3).

227. אָז, **'âz,** *awz*; a demonstrative adverb; *at that time* or *place*; also as a conjunction, *therefore*:—beginning, for, from, hitherto, now, of old, once, since, then, at which time, yet.

An adverb meaning then, at that time, or since. This word may introduce something that used to be so (Ge 12:6); what happened next in a narrative (Ex 15:1); or what will happen in the future (Isa 35:5, 6). On occasion, it is also used as a preposition, such as in Ru 2:7: "Even from the morning" (KJV).

228. אֲזָא, **'ăzâ'** (Chaldee), *az-aw´*; or אֲזָה, **'ăzâh,** *az-aw´*; (Chaldee); to *kindle*; (by implication) to *heat*:—heat, hot.

229. אֶזְבַּי, **'Ezbay,** *ez-bah´ee*; probably from 231; *hyssop-like; Ezbai*, an Israelite:—Ezbai.

230. אֲזַד, **'ăzâd** (Chaldee), *az-awd´*; of uncertain derivation; *firm*:—be gone.

231. אֵזוֹב, **'êzôwb,** *ay-zobe´*; probably of foreign derivation; *hyssop*:—hyssop.

232. אֵזוֹר, **'êzôwr,** *ay-zore´*; from 246; something *girt*; a *belt*, also a *band*:—girdle.

233. אֲזַי, **'ăzay,** *az-ah´ee*; probably from 227; *at that time*:—then.

234. אַזְכָּרָה, **'azkârâh,** *az-kaw-raw´*; from 2142; a *reminder*; specifically *remembrance-offering*:—memorial.

235. אָזַל, **'âzal,** *aw-zal´*; a primitive root; to *go away*, hence to *disappear*:—fail, gad about, go to and fro [*but in Eze 27:19 the word is rendered* by *many* "from Uzal," *by others* "yarn"], be gone (spent).

236. אֲזַל, **'ăzal** (Chaldee), *az-al´*; the same as 235; to *depart*:— go (up).

237. אֶזֶל, **'ezel,** *eh´-zel*; from 235; *departure; Ezel*, a memorial stone in Palestine:—Ezel.

238. אָזַן, **'âzan,** *aw-zan´*; a primitive root; probably to *expand*; but used only as a denominative from 241; to *broaden out the ear* (with the hand), i.e. (by implication) to *listen*:—give (perceive by the) ear, hear (-ken). See 239.

A verb meaning to give an ear, to lend an ear, to listen, to hear. This word is almost always found in poetic texts of the OT and is often found in songs. The SS of Moses begins with an exhortation for the heavens to lend its ear (Dt 32:1); Jeremiah asked for the people of Israel to listen to his prophecy (Jer 13:15). God's people commonly asked the Lord to listen to their prayers and petitions; this significant use is found many times throughout the Book of Psalms (Ps 5:1[2]; 77:1[2]; 80:1[2]).

239. אָזַן, **'âzan,** *aw-zan´*; a primitive root [rather identical with 238 through the idea of *scales* as if two ears]; to *weigh*, i.e. (figurative) *ponder*:—give good heed.

240. אָזֵן, **'âzên,** *aw-zane´*; from 238; a *spade* or *paddle* (as having a *broad* end):—weapon.

241. אֹזֶן, **'ôzen,** *o´-zen*; from 238; *broadness*, i.e. (concrete) the *ear* (from its form in man):— + advertise, audience, + displease, ear, hearing, + show.

A masculine noun meaning ear. The word is often used metaphorically as an instrument of obedience (Pr 25:12) and intellect (Job 12:11; 13:1; Pr 18:15; Ecc 1:8). In Jer 6:10, the disobedient or inattentive are said to have uncircumcised ears. The Hebrew idiom for revealing something or making one aware is to open the ears (Ru 4:4; 1Sa 20:2, 12, 13; Isa 35:5).

242. **אֻזֵּן שֶׁאֱרָה, 'Uzzên She'ĕrâh,** *ooz-zane' sheh-er-aw'*; from 238 and 7609; *plat of Sheerah* (i.e. settled by him); *Uzzen-Sheërah*, a place in Palestine:—Uzzen-sherah.

243. **אַזְנוֹת תָּבוֹר, 'Aznôwth Tâbôwr,** *az-nōth' taw-bore'*; from 238 and 8396; *flats* (i.e. *tops*) *of Tabor* (i.e. situated on it); *Aznoth-Tabor*, a place in Palestine:—Aznoth-tabor.

244. **אָזְנִי, 'Oznîy,** *oz-nee'*; from 241; *having* (quick) *ears; Ozni*, an Israelite; also an *Oznite* (collective), his descendants:—Ozni, Oznites.

245. **אֲזַנְיָה, 'Ăzanyâh,** *az-an-yaw'*; from 238 and 3050; *heard* by *Jah; Azanjah*, an Israelite:—Azaniah.

246. **אֲזִקִּים, 'ăziqqîym,** *az-ik-keem'*; a variation for 2131; *manacles*:—chains.

247. **אָזַר, 'âzar,** *aw-zar'*; a primitive root; to *belt*:—bind (compass) about, gird (up, with).

248. **אֶזְרוֹעַ, 'ezrôwa',** *ez-ro'-ă*; a variation for 2220; the *arm*:—arm.

249. **אֶזְרָח, 'ezrâch,** *ez-rawkh'*; from 2224 (in the sense of *springing up*); a spontaneous *growth*, i.e. *native* (tree or persons):—bay tree, (home-) born (in the land), of the (one's own) country (nation).

250. **אֶזְרָחִי, 'Ezrâchîy,** *ez-raw-khee'*; patronymic from 2246; an *Ezrachite* or descendant of Zerach:—Ezrahite.

251. **אָח, 'âch,** *awkh*; a primitive word; a *brother* (used in the widest sense of literal relationship and metaphorical affinity or resemblance [like 1]):—another, brother (-ly), kindred, like, other. Compare also the proper names beginning with "Ah-" or "Ahi-".

A masculine noun meaning brother. The word is used not only of those with common parents but also of those with common ancestors. Thus, the descendants of Israel are brothers (Le 19:17; 25:46), as are two nations with common ancestors (Am 1:11, Ob 1:10, 12). It further describes a close friend outside the immediate physical family (2Sa 1:26).

252. **אַח, 'ach,** *akh*; corresponding to 251:—brother.

An Aramaic masculine noun meaning brother. It occurs only in Ezr 7:18 and is the equivalent of the Hebrew word *'âch* (251).

253. **אָח, 'âch,** *awkh*; a variation for 162; *Oh!* (expressive of grief or surprise):—ah, alas.

254. **אָח, 'âch,** *awkh*; of uncertain derivation; a fire-*pot* or chafing-dish:—hearth.

255. **אֹחַ, 'ôach,** *o'-akh*; probably from 253; a *howler* or lonesome wild animal:—doleful creature.

256. **אַחְאָב, 'Ach'âb,** *akh-awb'*; once (by contraction) אֶחָב, **'Echâb,** *ekh-awb'*; (Jer 29:22), from 251 and 1; *brother* [i.e. *friend*] *of* (his) *father; Achab*, the name of a king of Israel and of a prophet at Babylon:—Ahab.

257. **אַחְבָּן, 'Achbân,** *akh-bawn'*; from 251 and 995; *brother* (i.e. *possessor*) *of understanding; Achban*, an Israelite:—Ahban.

258. **אָחַד, 'âchad,** *aw-khad'*; perhaps a primitive root; to *unify*, i.e. (figurative) *collect* (one's thoughts):—go one way or other.

259. **אֶחָד, 'echâd,** *ekh-awd'*; a numeral from 258; probably *united*, i.e. *one*; or (as an ordinal) *first*:—a, alike, alone, altogether, and, any (-thing), apiece, a certain, [dai-] ly, each (one), + eleven, every, few, first, + highway, a man, once, one, only, other, some, together.

260. **אָחוּ, 'âchûw,** *aw'-khoo*; of uncertain (perhaps Egyptian) derivation; a *bulrush* or any marshy grass (particularly that along the Nile):—flag, meadow.

261. **אֵהוּד, 'Êchûwd,** *ay-khood'*; from 258; *united; Echud*, the name of three Israelites:—Ehud.

262. **אַחְוָה, 'achvâh,** *akh-vaw'*; from 2331 (in the sense of 2324); an *utterance*:—declaration.

263. **אַחֲוָה, 'achăvâh** (Chaldee), *akh-av-aw'*; corresponding to 262; *solution* (of riddles):—showing.

264. **אַחֲוָה, 'achăvâh,** *akh-av-aw'*; from 251; *fraternity*:—brotherhood.

A noun meaning brotherhood. It is used only in Zec 11:14 where it signifies the unity between Judah and Israel whose common ancestor is Jacob. The brotherhood is symbolically broken by Zechariah's breaking his staff.

265. **אֲחוֹחַ, 'Ăchôwach,** *akh-o'-akh*; by reduplication from 251; *brotherly; Achoach*, an Israelite:—Ahoah.

266. **אֲחוֹחִי, 'Ăchôwchîy,** *akh-o-khee'*; patronymically from 264; an *Achochite* or descendant of Achoach:—Ahohite.

267. **אֲחוּמַי, 'Ăchûwmay,** *akh-oo-mah'ee*; perhaps from 251 and 4325; *brother* (i.e. *neighbour*) *of water; Achumai*, an Israelite:—Ahumai.

268. **אָחוֹר, 'âchôwr,** *aw-khore'*; or (shortened) אָחֹר, **'âchôr,** *aw-khore'*; from 299; the *hinder* part; hence (adverbial) *behind, backward*; also (as facing north) the *West*:—after (-ward), back (part, -side, -ward), hereafter, (be-) hind (-er part), time to come, without.

269. **אָחוֹת, 'âchôwth,** *aw-khōth'*; irregular feminine of 251; a *sister* (used very widely [like 250], literal and figurative):—(an-) other, sister, together.

A feminine noun meaning sister. Besides a biological sister, it also refers to more intimate female relatives. SS of Solomon uses the word to refer to a bride (SS 4:9, 10, 12; 5:1, 2). In Nu 25:18, it is used as a generic term for female relatives. Poetically, it sometimes refers to a geographical location (Jer 3:7, 8, 10; Eze 16:45, 52). For inanimate objects, it can often be translated as the English word *another* (Ex 26:3, 5, 6, 17; Eze 1:9; 3:13).

270. **אָחַז, 'âchaz,** *aw-khaz'*; a primitive root; to *seize* (often with the accessory idea of holding in possession):— + be affrighted, bar, (catch, lay, take) hold (back), come upon, fasten, handle, portion, (get, have or take) possess (-ion).

271. **אָחָז, 'Âchâz,** *aw-khawz'*; from 270; *possessor; Achaz*, the name of a Jewish king and of an Israelite:—Ahaz.

272. **אֲחֻזָּה, 'ăchuzzâh,** *akh-ooz-zaw'*; feminine passive participle from 270; something *seized*, i.e. a *possession* (especially of land):—possession.

A feminine noun meaning possession, literally meaning something seized. The word usually refers to the possession of land, especially of the Promised Land (Ge 48:4; Dt 32:49). Because the Promised Land is "an everlasting possession" (Ge 17:8), this word often refers to land that is to pass down within families, never being permanently taken away (Le 25; Nu 27:4, 7, Eze 46:16–18). The Levites had God, instead of land, as their "possession" (Eze 44:28).

273. **אַחְזַי, 'Achzay,** *akh-zah'ee*; from 270; *seizer; Achzai*, an Israelite:—Ahasai.

274. **אֲחַזְיָה, 'Ăchazyâh,** *akh-az-yaw'*; or (prolonged) אֲחַזְיָהוּ, **'Ăchazyâhûw,** *akh-az-yaw'-hoo*; from 270 and 3050; *Jah has seized; Achazjah*, the name of a Jewish and an Israelite king:—Ahaziah.

275. **אֲחֻזָּם, 'Ăchuzzâm,** *akh-ooz-zawm'*; from 270; *seizure; Achuzzam*, an Israelite:—Ahuzam.

276. **אֲחֻזַּת, 'Ăchuzzath,** *akh-ooz-zath'*; a variation of 272; *possession; Achuzzath*, a Philistine:—Ahuzzath.

277. **אֲחִי, 'Ăchîy,** *akh-ee'*; from 251; *brotherly; Achi*, the name of two Israelites:—Ahi.

278. **אֵחִי, 'Êchîy,** *ay-khee´*; probably the same as 277; *Echi,* an Israelite:—Ehi.

279. **אֲחִיאָם, 'Ăchîy'âm,** *akh-ee-awm´*; from 251 and 517; *brother of* the *mother* (i.e. *uncle*); *Achiam,* an Israelite:—Ahiam.

280. **אֲחִידָה, 'ăchîydâh** (Chaldee), *akh-ee-daw´*; corresponding to 2420, an *enigma:*—hard sentence.

281. **אֲחִיָּה, 'Ăchîyyâh,** *akh-ee-yaw´*; or (prolonged) אֲחִיָּהוּ, **'Ăchîyyâhûw,** *akh-ee-yaw´-hoo*; from 251 and 3050; *brother* (i.e. *worshipper) of Jah; Achijah,* the name of nine Israelites:—Ahiah, Ahijah.

282. **אֲחִיהוּד, 'Ăchîyhûwd,** *akh-ee-hood´*; from 251 and 1935; *brother* (i.e. *possessor*) *of renown; Achihud,* an Israelite:—Ahihud.

283. **אַחְיוֹ, 'Achyôw,** *akh-yo´*; prolonged from 251; *brotherly; Achio,* the name of three Israelites:—Ahio.

284. **אֲחִיחֻד, 'Ăchîychud,** *akh-ee-khood´*; from 251 and 2330; *brother of a riddle* (i.e. *mysterious*); *Achichud,* an Israelite:—Ahihud.

285. **אֲחִיטוּב, 'Ăchîyṭûwb,** *akh-ee-toob´*; from 251 and 2898; *brother of goodness; Achitub,* the name of several priests:—Ahitub.

286. **אֲחִילוּד, 'Ăchîylûwd,** *akh-ee-lood´*; from 251 and 3205; *brother of* one *born; Achilud,* an Israelite:—Ahilud.

287. **אֲחִימוֹת, 'Ăchîymôwth,** *akh-ee-mōth´*; from 251 and 4191; *brother of death; Achimoth,* an Israelite:—Ahimoth.

288. **אֲחִימֶלֶךְ, 'Ăchîymelek,** *akh-ee-meh´-lek*; from 251 and 4428; *brother of* (the) *king; Achimelek,* the name of an Israelite and of a Hittite:—Ahimelech.

289. **אֲחִימַן, 'Ăchîyman,** *akh-ee-man´*; or אֲחִימָן, **'Ăchîymân,** *akh-ee-mawn´*; from 251 and 4480; *brother of a portion* (i.e. *gift*); *Achiman,* the name of an Anakite and of an Israelite:—Ahiman.

290. **אֲחִימַעַץ, 'Ăchîyma'ats,** *akh-ee-mah´-ats*; from 251 and the equivalent of 4619; *brother of anger; Achimaats,* the name of three Israelites:—Ahimaaz.

291. **אַחְיָן, 'Achyân,** *akh-yawn´*; from 251; *brotherly; Achjan,* an Israelite:—Ahian.

292. **אֲחִינָדָב, 'Ăchîynâdâb,** *akh-ee-naw-dawb´*; from 251 and 5068; *brother of liberality; Achinadab,* an Israelite:—Ahinadab.

293. **אֲחִינֹעַם, 'Ăchîynô'am,** *akh-ee-no´-am*; from 251 and 5278; *brother of pleasantness; Achinoam,* the name of two Israelitesses:—Ahinoam.

294. **אֲחִיסָמָךְ, 'Ăchîysâmâk,** *akh-ee-saw-mawk´*; from 251 and 5564; *brother of support; Achisamak,* an Israelite:—Ahisamach.

295. **אֲחִיעֶזֶר, 'Ăchîy'ezer,** *akh-ee-eh´-zer*; from 251 and 5828; *brother of help; Achiezer,* the name of two Israelites:—Ahiezer.

296. **אֲחִיקָם, 'Ăchîyqâm,** *akh-ee-kawm´*; from 251 and 6965; *brother of rising* (i.e. *high*); *Achikam,* an Israelite:—Ahikam.

297. **אֲחִירָם, 'Ăchîyrâm,** *akh-ee-rawm´*; from 251 and 7311; *brother of height* (i.e. *high*); *Achiram,* an Israelite:—Ahiram.

298. **אֲחִירָמִי, 'Ăchîyrâmîy,** *akh-ee-raw-mee´*; patronymically from 297; an *Achiramite* or descendants (collective) of Achiram:—Ahiramites.

299. **אֲחִירַע, 'Ăchîyra',** *akh-ee-rah´*; from 251 and 7451; *brother of wrong; Achira,* an Israelite:—Ahira.

300. **אֲחִישַׁחַר, 'Ăchîyshachar,** *akh-ee-shakh´-ar*; from 251 and 7837; *brother of* (the) *dawn; Achishachar,* an Israelite:—Ahishar.

301. **אֲחִישָׁר, 'Ăchîyshâr,** *akh-ee-shawr´*; from 251 and 7891; *brother of* (the) *singer; Achishar,* an Israelite:—Ahishar.

302. **אֲחִיתֹפֶל, 'Ăchîythôphel,** *akh-ee-tho´-fel*; from 251 and 8602; *brother of folly; Achithophel,* an Israelite:—Ahithophel.

303. **אַחְלָב, 'Achlâb,** *akh-lawb´*; from the same root as 2459; *fatness* (i.e. *fertile*); *Achlab,* a place in Palestine:—Ahlab.

304. **אַחְלַי, 'Achlay,** *akh-lah´ee*; the same as 305; *wishful; Achlai,* the name of an Israelitess and of an Israelite:—Ahlai.

305. **אַחֲלַי, 'achălay,** *ak-al-ah´ee*; or אַחֲלֵי, **'achălêy,** *akh-al-ay´*; probably from 253 and a variation of 3863; *would that!:*—O that, would God.

306. **אַחְלָמָה, 'achlâmâh,** *akh-law´-maw*; perhaps from 2492 (and thus *dream-stone*); a gem, probably the *amethyst:*—amethyst.

307. **אַחְמְתָא, 'Achmᵉthâ',** *akh-me-thaw´*; of Persian derivation; *Achmetha* (i.e. *Ecbatana*), the summer capital of Persia:—Achmetha.

308. **אֲחַסְבַּי, 'Ăchasbay,** *akh-as-bah´ee*; of uncertain derivation; *Achasbai,* an Israelite:—Ahasbai.

309. **אָחַר, 'âchar,** *aw-khar´*; a primitive root; to *loiter* (i.e. *be behind*); by implication to *procrastinate:*—continue, defer, delay, hinder, be late (slack), stay (there), tarry (longer).

310. **אַחַר, 'achar,** *akh-ar´*; from 309; probably the *hind* part; generally used as an adverb or conjunction, *after* (in various senses):—after (that, -ward), again, at, away from, back (from, -side), behind, beside, by, follow (after, -ing), forasmuch, from, hereafter, hinder end, + out (over) live, + persecute, posterity, pursuing, remnant, seeing, since, thence [-forth], when, with.

311. **אַחַר, 'achar** (Chaldee), *akh-ar´*; corresponding to 310; *after:*—[here-] after.

312. **אַחֵר, 'achêr,** *akh-air´*; from 309; probably *hinder;* generically *next, other,* etc.:—(an-) other (man), following, next, strange.

313. **אַחֵר, 'Achêr,** *akh-air´*; the same as 312; *Acher,* an Israelite:—Aher.

314. **אַחֲרוֹן, 'achăryôwn,** *akh-ar-one´*; or (shortened) אַחֲרֹן, **'achărôn,** *akh-ar-one´*; from 309; *hinder;* generically *late* or *last;* specifically (as facing the east) *western:*—after (-ward), to come, following, hind (-er, -ermost, -most), last, latter, rereward, ut(ter)most.

315. **אַחְרַח, 'Achrach,** *akh-rakh*; from 310 and 251; *after* (his) *brother; Achrach,* an Israelite:—Aharah.

316. **אֲחַרְחֵל, 'Ăcharchêl,** *akh-ar-kale´*; from 310 and 2426; *behind* (the) *intrenchment* (i.e. *safe*); *Acharchel,* an Israelite:—Aharhel.

317. **אָחֳרִי, 'ochŏrîy** (Chaldee), *okh-or-ee´*; from 311; *other:*—(an-) other.

318. **אָחֳרֵין, 'ochŏrêyn** (Chaldee), *okh-or-ane´*; or (shortened) אָחֳרֵן, **'ochŏrên,** *okh-or-ane´*; (Chaldee); from 317; *last:*—at last.

319. **אַחֲרִית, 'achărîyth,** *akh-ar-eeth´*; from 310; the *last* or *end,* hence the *future;* also *posterity:*—(last, latter) end (time), hinder (utter) -most, length, posterity, remnant, residue, reward.

A feminine noun meaning the end, last time, latter time (Ge 49:1; Nu 23:10; 24:14, 20; Dt 4:30; 8:16; 11:12; 31:29; 32:20, 29; Job 8:7; 42:12; Ps 37:37, 38; 73:17; 109:13; 139:9; Pr 5:4, 11; 14:12, 13; 16:25; 19:20; 20:21; 23:18, 32; 24:14, 20; 25:8; 29:21; Ecc 7:8; 10:13; Isa 2:2; 41:22; 46:10; 47:7; Jer 5:31; 12:4; 17:11; 23:20; 29:11; 30:24; 31:17; 48:47; 49:39; 50:12; La 1:9; Eze 23:25; 38:8, 16; Da 8:19, 23; 10:14; 11:4; 12:8; Hos 3:5; Am 4:2; 8:10; 9:1; Mic 4:1).

320. **אַחֲרִית, 'achărîyth** (Chaldee), *akh-ar-eeth´*; from 311; the same as 319; *later:*—latter.

321. **אָחֳרָן, 'ochŏrân** (Chaldee), *okh-or-awn´*; from 311; the same as 317; *other:*—(an-) other.

322. אֲחֹרַנִּית**, 'ăchôranníyth,** *akh-o-ran-neeth´*; prolonged from 268; *backwards*:—back (-ward, again).

323. אֲחַשְׁדַּרְפַּן**, 'ăchashdarpan,** *akh-ash-dar-pan´*; of Persian derivation; a *satrap* or governor of a main province (of Persia):—lieutenant.

324. אֲחַשְׁדַּרְפַּן**, 'ăchashdarpan** (Chaldee), *akh-ash-dar-pan´*; corresponding to 323:—prince.

A Chaldean noun meaning satrap. Satraps were officials who governed large provinces in Persia as representatives of the Persian sovereign. *Pechâh* (6346) denotes a smaller office within a satrapy. Daniel was one of three rulers over the satraps and became an object of their evil schemes (Da 6:1–4[2–5], 6[7], 7[8]; the word also occurs in Da 3:2, 3, 27). All occurrences of this Chaldean word are in the book of Daniel, but the Hebrew equivalent (323) is spelled the same and occurs in Ezra and Esther.

325. אֲחַשְׁוֵרוֹשׁ**, 'Ăchashvêrôwsh,** *akh-ash-vay-rōsh´*; or (shorter) אֲחַשְׁרֹשׁ**, 'Achashrôsh,** *akh-ash-rōsh´* (Est 10:1); of Persian origin; *Achashverosh* (i.e. Ahasuerus or Artaxerxes, but in this case Xerxes), the title (rather than name) of a Persian king:—Ahasuerus.

326. אֲחַשְׁתָּרִי**, 'ăchashtârîy,** *akh-ash-taw-ree´*; probably of Persian derivation; an *achastarite* (i.e. courier); the designation (rather than name) of an Israelite:—Haakashtari [*including the article*].

327. אֲחַשְׁתְּרָן**, 'ăchashtᵉrân,** *akh-ash-te-rawn´*; of Persian origin; a *mule*:—camel.

328. אַט**, 'aṭ,** *at*; from an unused root perhaps meaning to *move softly*; (as a noun) a *necromancer* (from their soft incantations), (as an adverb) *gently*:—charmer, gently, secret, softly.

An adverb meaning gently, with gentleness. It occurs five times (Ge 33:14; 2Sa 18:5; 1Ki 21:27; Job 15:11; Isa 8:6).

329. אָטָד**, 'âṭâd,** *aw-tawd*; from an unused root probably meaning to *pierce* or *make fast*; a *thorn*-tree (especially the *buckthorn*):—Atad, bramble, thorn.

330. אֵטוּן**, 'êṭûwn,** *ay-toon´*; from an unused root (probably meaning to *bind*); probably *twisted* (yarn), i.e. *tapestry*:—fine linen.

331. אָטַם**, 'âṭam,** *aw-tam´*; a primitive root; to *close* (the lips or ears); by analogy to *contract* (a window by bevelled jambs):—narrow, shut, stop.

332. אָטַר**, 'âṭar,** *aw-tar´*; a primitive root; to *close* up:—shut.

333. אָטֵר**, 'Âṭêr,** *aw-tare´*; from 332; *maimed; Ater*, the name of three Israelites:—Ater.

334. אִטֵּר**, 'iṭṭêr,** *it-tare*; from 332; *shut* up, i.e. *impeded* (as to the use of the right hand):— + left-handed.

335. אֵי**, 'êy,** *ay*; perhaps from 370; *where* hence *how*:—how, what, whence, where, whether, which (way).

336. אִי**, 'îy,** *ee*; probably identical with 335(through the idea of a *query*); *not*:—island (Job 22:30).

337. אִי**, 'îy,** *ee*; shortened from 188; *alas!*:—woe.

338. אִי**, 'îy,** *ee*; probably identical with 337 (through the idea of a *doleful* sound); a *howler* (used only in the plural), i.e. any solitary wild creature:—wild beast of the islands.

339. אִי**, 'îy,** *ee*; from 183; probably a *habitable* spot (as *desirable*); dry *land*, a *coast*, an *island*:—country, isle, island.

340. אָיַב**, 'âyab,** *aw-yab´*; a primitive root; to *hate* (as one of an opposite tribe or party); hence to *be hostile*:—be an enemy.

341. אֹיֵב**, 'ôyêb,** *o-yabe´*; or (fully) אוֹיֵב**, 'ôwyêb,** *o-yabe´*; active participle of 340; *hating*; an *adversary*:—enemy, foe.

342. אֵיבָה**, 'êybâh,** *ay-baw´*; from 340; *hostility*:—enmity, hatred.

A feminine noun meaning hostility, animosity, or ill will. It is used to signify acrimony, as between the woman and the serpent (Ge 3:15); malice that leads to violent acts against another (Nu 35:21); and the lingering hatred between mortal enemies (Eze 25:15; 35:5).

343. אֵיד**, 'êyd,** *ade*; from the same as 181 (in the sense of *bending* down); *oppression*; by implication *misfortune, ruin*:—calamity, destruction.

A masculine noun meaning calamity or disaster. The word refers to a time of trouble when a person is in special need of help (Pr 27:10); a calamity so severe that men and women should not rejoice or take selfish advantage of those whom the disaster renders helpless before God (Job 31:23; Pr 17:5; Ob 1:13). The calamity may result from a deliberate violation of principles (Pr 1:26) or a more explicit judgment of God (Jer 18:17). It may even befall a righteous person (2Sa 22:19; Ps 18:18[19]).

344. אַיָּה**, 'ayyâh,** *ah-yaw´*; perhaps from 337; the *screamer*, i.e. a *hawk*:—kite, vulture.

345. אַיָּה**, 'Ayyâh,** *ah-yaw´*; the same as 344; *Ajah*, the name of two Israelites:—Aiah, Ajah.

346. אַיֵּה**, 'ayyêh,** *ah-yay´*; prolonged from 335; *where*:—where.

347. אִיּוֹב**, 'Îyyôwb,** *ee-yobe´*; from 340; *hated* (i.e. *persecuted*); *Ijob*, the patriarch famous for his patience:—Job.

348. אִיזֶבֶל**, 'Îyzebel,** *ee-zeh´-bel*; from 336 and 2083; *chaste; Izebel*, the wife of king Ahab:—Jezebel.

349. אֵיךְ**, 'êyk,** *ake*; also אֵיכָה**, 'êykâh,** *ay-kaw´*; and אֵיכָכָה**, 'êykâkâh,** *ay-kaw´-kah*; prolonged from 335; *how* or *how!*; also *where*:—how, what.

350. אִי־כָבוֹד**, 'Îy-kâbôwd,** *ee-kaw-bode´*; from 336 and 3519; (there is) *no glory*, i.e. *inglorious; Ikabod*, a son of Phineas:—Ichabod.

351. אֵיכֹה**, 'êykôh,** *ay-kō*; probably a variation for 349, but not as an interrogative; *where*:—where.

352. אַיִל**, 'ayil,** *ah´-yil*; from the same as 193; probably *strength*; hence anything *strong*; specifically a *chief* (politically); also a *ram* (from his strength); a *pilaster* (as a strong support); an *oak* or other strong tree:—mighty (man), lintel, oak, post, ram, tree.

353. אֱיָל**, 'ěyâl,** *eh-yawl´*; a variation of 352; *strength*:—strength.

354. אַיָּל**, 'ayyâl,** *ah-yawl´*; an intensive form of 352 (in the sense of *ram*); a *stag* or male deer:—hart.

355. אַיָּלָה**, 'ayyâlâh,** *ah-yaw-law´*; feminine of 354; a *doe* or female deer:—hind.

356. אֵילוֹן**, 'Êylôwn,** *ay-lone´*; or (shortened) אֵלוֹן**, 'Êlôwn,** *ay-lone´*; or אֵילֹן**, 'Êylôn,** *ay-lone´*; from 352; *oak-grove; Elon*, the name of a place in Palestine, and also of one Hittite, two Israelites:—Elon.

357. אַיָּלוֹן**, 'Ayyâlôwn,** *ah-yaw-lone´*; from 354; *deer-field; Ajalon*, the name of five places in Palestine:—Aijalon, Ajalon.

358. אֵילוֹן בֵּית חָנָן**, 'Êylôwn Bêyth Chânân,** *ay-lone´ bayth-khaw-nawn´*; from 356, 1004, and 2603; *oak-grove of* (the) *house of favour; Elon of Beth-chanan*, a place in Palestine:—Elon-beth-hanan.

359. אֵילוֹת**, 'Êylôwth,** *ay-lōth´*; or אֵילַת**, 'Êylath,** *ay-lath´*; from 352; *trees* or a *grove* (i.e. palms); *Eloth* or *Elath*, a place on the Red Sea:—Elath, Eloth.

360. אֱיָלוּת**, 'ěyâlûwth,** *eh-yaw-looth´*; feminine of 353; *power*; by implication *protection*:—strength.

361. אֵילָם**, 'êylâm,** *ay-lawm´*; or (shortened) אֵלָם**, 'êlâm,** *ay-lawm´*; or (feminine) אֵלַמָּה**, 'êlammâh,** *ay-lam-maw´*; probably from 352; a *pillar-space* (or colonnade), i.e. a *pale* (or portico):—arch.

362. **אֵילִם, 'Êylim,** *ay-leem´*; plural of 352; palm-*trees; Elim*, a place in the Desert:—Elim.

363. **אִילָן, 'îylân** (Chaldee), *ee-lawn´*; corresponding to 356; a *tree*:—tree.

364. **אֵיל פָּארָן, 'Êyl Pâ'rân,** *ale paw-rawn´*; from 352 and 6290; *oak of Paran; El-Paran*, a portion of the district of Paran:—El-paran.

365. **אַיֶּלֶת, 'ayyeleth,** *ay-yeh´-leth*; the same as 355; a *doe*:—hind, Aijeleth.

366. **אָיֹם, 'âyôm,** *aw-yome´*; from an unused root (meaning to *frighten*); *frightful*:—terrible.

367. **אֵימָה, 'êymâh,** *ay-maw´*; or (shortened) אֵמָה, **'êmâh,** *ay-maw´*; from the same as 366; *fright*; (concrete) an *idol* (as a bugbear):—dread, fear, horror, idol, terrible, terror.

A feminine noun meaning fear, terror, dread, or horror. The basic meaning is that of fear. It is used to signify the dread of the darkness that fell on Abraham (Ge 15:12); a fear of hostile opponents (Jos 2:9; Ezr 3:3); the terror of the Lord's judgment (Ex 15:16; 23:27; Job 9:34); dread of the wrath of an earthly king (Pr 20:2); something fierce or fearsome (Job 39:20). In a metaphorical sense, it refers once to pagan idols (Jer 50:38).

368. **אֵימִים, 'Êymîym,** *ay-meem´*; plural of 367; *terrors; Emim*, an early Canaanitish (or Moabitish) tribe:—Emims.

369. **אַיִן, 'ayin,** *ay´-yin*; as if from a primitive root meaning to *be nothing* or *not exist*; a *nonentity*; generally used as a negative particle:—else, except, fail, [father-] less, be gone, in [-curable], neither, never, no (where), none, nor (any, thing), not, nothing, to nought, past, un [-searchable], well-nigh, without. Compare 370.

370. **אַיִן, 'ayin,** *ah-yin´*; probably identical with 369 in the sense of *query* (compare 336); *where* (only in connection with prepositional prefix, *whence*):—whence, where.

371. **אִין, 'îyn,** *een*; apparently a shortened form of 369; but (like 370) interrogative; is it *not*:—not.

372. **אִיעֶזֶר, 'Îy'ezer,** *ee-eh´-zer*; from 336 and 5828; *helpless; Iezer*, an Israelite:—Jeezer.

373. **אִיעֶזְרִי, 'Îy'ezrîy,** *ee-ez-ree´*; patronymically from 372; an *Iezrite* or descendant of Iezer:—Jezerite.

374. **אֵיפָה, 'êyphâh,** *ay-faw´*; or (shortened) אֵפָה, **'êphâh,** *ay-faw´*; of Egyptian derivation; an *ephah* or measure for grain; hence a *measure* in general:—ephah, (divers) measure (-s).

375. **אֵיפֹה, 'êyphôh,** *ay-fō´*; from 335 and 6311; *what place*; also (of time) *when*; or (of means) *how*:—what manner, where.

376. **אִישׁ, 'îysh,** *eesh*; contraction for 582 [or perhaps rather from an unused root meaning to *be extant*]; a *man* as an individual or a male person; often used as an adjunct to a more definite term (and in such cases frequently not expressed in translation):—also, another, any (man), a certain, + champion, consent, each, every (one), fellow, [foot-, husband-] man, (good-, great, mighty) man, he, high (degree), him (that is), husband, man [-kind], + none, one, people, person, + steward, what (man) soever, whoso (-ever), worthy. Compare 802.

A masculine noun meaning a man or an individual. It is also used to mean male or husband. This word does not indicate humankind but the male gender in particular. Its feminine counterpart is a woman or wife. In Hos 2:16[18], this word describes God's special relationship to Israel. He will be their protective husband, not their master. Curiously, the word is also used of animals (Ge 7:2), referring to a male and his mate.

377. **אִישׁ, 'îysh,** *eesh*; denominative from 376; to *be a man*, i.e. act in a manly way:—show (one) self a man.

378. **אִישׁ־בֹּשֶׁת, 'Îysh-Bôsheth,** *eesh-bō´-sheth*; from 376 and 1322; *man of shame; Ish-Bosheth*, a son of King Saul:—Ish-bosheth.

379. **אִישְׁהוֹד, 'Îyshhôwd,** *eesh-hode´*; from 376 and 1935; *man of renown; Ishod*, an Israelite:—Ishod.

380. **אִישׁוֹן, 'îyshôwn,** *ee-shone´*; diminutive from 376; the *little man* of the eye; the *pupil* or *ball*; hence the *middle* (of night):—apple [of the eye], black, obscure.

381. **אִישׁ־חַיִל, 'Îysh-Chayil,** *eesh-khah´-yil*; from 376 and 2428 *man of might*; by defective transcription (2Sa 23:20) אִישׁ־חַי, **'îysh-Chay,** *eesh-khah´ee*; as if from 376 and 2416; *living man; Ish-chail* (or *Ish-chai*), an Israelite:—a valiant man.

382. **אִישׁ־טוֹב, 'Îysh-Ṭôwb,** *eesh-tobe´*; from 376 and 2897; *man of Tob; Ish-Tob*, a place in Palestine:—Ish-tob.

383. **אִיתַי, 'îythay** (Chaldee), *ee-thah´ee*; corresponding to 3426; (properly) *entity*; used only as a particle of affirmation, there *is*:—art thou, can, do ye, have, it be, there is (are), × we will not.

384. **אִיתִיאֵל, 'Îythîy'êl,** *eeth-ee-ale´*; perhaps from 837 and 410; *God has arrived; Ithiel*, the name of an Israelite, also of a symbolical person:—Ithiel.

385. **אִיתָמָר, 'Îythâmâr,** *eeth-aw-mawr´*; from 339 and 8558; *coast of* the *palm*-tree; *Ithamar*, a son of Aaron:—Ithamar.

386. **אֵיתָן, 'êythân,** *ay-thawn´*; or (shortened) אֵתָן **'êthân,** *ay-thawn´*; from an unused root (meaning to *continue*); *permanence*; hence (concrete) *permanent*; specifically a *chieftain*:—hard, mighty, rough, strength, strong.

387. **אֵיתָן, 'Êythân,** *ay-thawn´*; the same as 386; *permanent; Ethan*, the name of four Israelites:—Ethan.

388. **אֵיתָנִים, 'Êythânîym,** *ay-thaw-neem´*; plural of 386; always with the article; the *permanent* brooks; *Ethanim*, the name of a month:—Ethanim.

389. **אַךְ, 'ak,** *ak*; akin to 403; a particle of affirmation, *surely*; hence (by limitation) *only*:—also, in any wise, at least, but, certainly, even, howbeit, nevertheless, notwithstanding, only, save, surely, of a surety, truly, verily, + wherefore, yet (but).

390. **אַכַּד, 'Akkad,** *ak-kad´*; from an unused root probably meaning to *strengthen*; a *fortress; Accad*, a place in Babylon:—Accad.

391. **אַכְזָב, 'akzâb,** *ak-zawb´*; from 3576; *falsehood*; by implication *treachery*:—liar, lie.

392. **אַכְזִיב, 'Akzîyb,** *ak-zeeb´*; from 391; *deceitful* (in the sense of a winter torrent which *fails* in summer); *Akzib*, the name of two places in Palestine:—Achzib.

393. **אַכְזָר, 'akzâr,** *ak-zawr´*; from an unused root (apparently meaning to *act harshly*); *violent*; by implication *deadly*; also (in a good sense) *brave*:—cruel, fierce.

394. **אַכְזָרִי, 'akzârîy,** *ak-zaw-ree´*; from 393; *terrible*:—cruel (one).

395. **אַכְזְרִיּוּת, 'akz^erîyyûwth,** *ak-ze-ree-ooth´*; from 394; *fierceness*:—cruel.

396. **אֲכִילָה, 'ǎkîylâh,** *ak-ee-law´*; feminine from 398; something *eatable*, i.e. *food*:—meat.

397. **אָכִישׁ, 'Âkîysh,** *aw-keesh´*; of uncertain derivation; *Akish*, a Philistine king:—Achish.

398. **אָכַל, 'âkal,** *aw-kal´*; a primitive root; to *eat* (literal or figurative):—× at all, burn up, consume, devour (-er, up), dine, eat (-er, up), feed (with), food, × freely, × in … wise (-deed, plenty), (lay) meat, × quite.

399. אֲכַל, **'ăkal** (Chaldee), *ak-al´*; corresponding to 398:—+ accuse, devour, eat.

400. אֹכֶל, **'ôkel,** *o´-kel*; from 398; *food*:—eating, food, meal [-time], meat, prey, victuals.

401. אֻכָל, **'Ukâl,** *oo-kawl´*; or אֻכָּל, **'Ukkâl,** *ook-kawl´*; apparently from 398; *devoured; Ucal*, a fancy name:—Ucal.

402. אָכְלָה, **'ôklâh,** *ok-law´*; feminine of 401; *food*:—consume, devour, eat, food, meat.

403. אָכֵן, **'âkên,** *aw-kane´*; from 3559 [compare 3651]; *firmly*; (figurative) *surely*; also (adversely) *but*:—but, certainly, nevertheless, surely, truly, verily.

404. אָכַף, **'âkaph,** *aw-kaf´*; a primitive root; apparently meaning to *curve* (as with a burden); to *urge*:—crave.

405. אֶכֶף, **'ekeph,** *eh´-kef*; from 404; a *load*; by implication a *stroke* (others *dignity*):—hand.

406. אִכָּר, **'ikkâr,** *ik-kawr´*; from an unused root meaning to *dig*; a *farmer*:—husbandman, ploughman.

407. אַכְשָׁף, **'Akshâph,** *ak-shawf´*; from 3784; *fascination; Acshaph*, a place in Palestine:—Achshaph.

408. אַל, **'al,** *al*; a negative particle [akin to 3808; *not* (the qualified negation, used as a deprecative); once (Job 24:25) as a noun, *nothing*:—nay, neither, + never, no, nor, not, nothing [worth], rather than.

409. אַל, **'al** (Chaldee), *al*; corresponding to 408:—not.

410. אֵל, **'êl,** *ale*; shortened from 352; *strength*; as adjective *mighty*; especially the *Almighty* (but used also of any *deity*):—God (god), × goodly, × great, idol, might (-y one), power, strong. Compare names in "-el."

A masculine noun meaning God, god, mighty one, hero. This is one of the most ancient terms for God, god, or deity. It appears most often in Genesis, Job, Psalms, and Isaiah and not at all in some books. The root meaning of the word mighty can be seen in Job 41:25[17] and Mic 2:1. This word is used occasionally of other gods (Ex 34:14; Dt 3:24; Ps 44:20[21]; Mal 2:11) but is most often used to mean the one true God (Ps 5:4[5]; Isa 40:18). It expresses various ideas of deity according to its context. The most common may be noted briefly: the holy God as contrasted to humans (Hos 11:9); the High God El (Ge 14:18; 16:13; Eze 28:2); the Lord (Yahweh) as a title of Israel according to the Lord's own claim (Ge 33:20; Isa 40:18); God or god in general (Ex 34:14; Dt 32:21; Mic 7:8); the God of Israel, the Lord (Nu 23:8; Ps 118:27); God (Job 5:8).

This word is used with various descriptive adjectives or attributes: *'êl* is God of gods (Ps 50:1); God of Bethel (Ge 35:7); a forgiving God (Ps 99:8). He is the holy God (Isa 5:16). Especially significant are the assertions declaring that *'êl* is with us, Immanuel (Isa 7:14); and He is the God of our salvation (Isa 12:2); a gracious God (Ne 9:31); a jealous God (Ex 20:5; 34:14). The closeness of this God is expressed in the hand of God (Job 27:11).

In the human realm, the word also designates men of power or high rank (Eze 31:11); mighty men (Job 41:25[17]); or mighty warriors (Eze 32:21). The word is used to designate superior and mighty things in nature, such as mighty or high mountains (Ps 36:6[7]), lofty, high cedars, or stars (Ps 80:10[11]; Isa 14:13).

In conjunction with other descriptive words, it occurs as *'êl shaday,* "God Almighty" (7706) (Ge 17:1; 28:3; Ex 6:3) or *'êl 'elyôwn,* "God Most High" (5945) (Ge 14:18, 19; Ps 78:35). Used with hand (*yâd*) in some settings, the word conveys power, strength (Ge 31:29; Dt 28:32; Pr 3:27), or ability.

411. אֵל, **'êl,** *ale*; a demonstrative particle (but only in a plural sense) *these* or *those*:—these, those. Compare 428.

412. אֵל, **'êl** (Chaldee), *ale*; corresponding to 411:—these.

413. אֵל, **'êl,** *ale*; (but used only in the shortened construction form אֶל, **'el,** *el*; a primitive particle, properly denoting motion *toward*, but occasionally used of a quiescent position, i.e. *near, with* or *among*; often in general, *to*:—about, according to, after, against, among, as for, at, because (-fore, -side), both ... and, by, concerning, for, from, × hath, in (-to), near, (out) of, over, through, to (-ward), under, unto, upon, whether, with (-in).

414. אֵלָא, **'Êlâ',** *ay-law´*; a variation of 424; *oak; Ela*, an Israelite:—Elah.

415. אֵל אֱלֹהֵי יִשְׂרָאֵל, **'Êl 'ĕlôhêy Yiśrâ'êl,** *ale el-o-hay´ yis-raw-ale´*; from 410 and 430 and 3478; the *mighty God of Jisrael; El-Elohi-Jisrael*, the title given to a consecrated spot by Jacob:—El-elohe-israel.

416. אֵל בֵּית־אֵל, **'Êl Bêyth-'Êl,** *ale bayth-ale´*; from 410 and 1008; the *God of Bethel; El-Bethel*, the title given to a consecrated spot by Jacob:—El-beth-el.

417. אֶלְגָּבִישׁ, **'elgâbîysh,** *el-gaw-beesh´*; from 410 and 1378; *hail* (as if a *great pearl*):—great hail [-stones].

418. אַלְגּוּמִּים, **'algûwmmîym,** *al-goom-meem´*; by transposition for 484; sticks of *algum* wood:—algum [trees].

419. אֶלְדָּד, **'Eldâd,** *el-dâd´*; from 410 and 1730; *God has loved; Eldad*, an Israelite:—Eldad.

420. אֶלְדָּעָה, **'Eldâ'âh,** *el-daw-aw´*; from 410 and 3045; *God of knowledge; Eldaah*, a son of Midian:—Eldaah.

421. אָלָה, **'âlâh,** *aw-law´*; a primitive root [rather identical with 422 through the idea of *invocation*]; to *bewail*:—lament.

422. אָלָה, **'âlâh,** *aw-law´*; a primitive root; proper to *adjure*, i.e. (usually in a bad sense) *imprecate*:—adjure, curse, swear.

A verb meaning to curse, to put under oath. It is used in many cases of persons bringing curses on themselves if they are guilty of doing wrong (Jgs 17:2). Similarly, *'âlâh* is used to prove someone's guilt or innocence. The person is guilty if the curse occurs but is innocent if the curse does not occur (1Ki 8:31; 2Ch 6:22). In 1Sa 14:24, the word is used to put someone under an oath. In Hosea, the word refers to a curse placed on a person who makes a covenant or treaty and does not keep his word (Hos 10:4).

423. אָלָה, **'âlâh,** *aw-law´*; from 422; an *imprecation*:—curse, cursing, execration, oath, swearing.

A feminine noun meaning an oath, a sworn covenant, or a curse. The word signifies an oath to testify truthfully (Le 5:1; 1Ki 8:31); a sworn covenant, bearing a curse if violated (Dt 29:19; Ne 10:29[30]); a curse from God for covenant violations (Dt 29:20; 2Ch 34:24; Da 9:11); God's judgment on sin (Dt 30:7; Isa 24:6; Zec 5:3); and that which is accursed because of unfaithfulness, such as an adulterous wife or the erring tribe of Judah (Nu 5:27; Jer 29:18; 42:18; 44:12).

424. אֵלָה, **'êlâh,** *ay-law´*; feminine of 352; an *oak* or other strong tree:—elm, oak, teil tree.

425. אֵלָה, **'Êlâh,** *ay-law´*; the same as 424; *Elah*, the name of an Edomite, of four Israelites, and also of a place in Palestine:—Elah.

426. אֱלָהּ, **'ĕlâh** (Chaldee), *el-aw´*; corresponding to 433; *God*:—God, god.

An Aramaic masculine noun meaning deity, divinity. This word can be used in a general sense to indicate a god (Da 3:15) or gods (Da 2:11; 3:12, 18, 25). In a specific sense, it signifies the God of Israel, namely, Yahweh (Ezr 5:1, 2, 8; 6:14; 7:15; Da 2:20, 28; 3:17).

427. אַלָּה, **'allâh,** *al-law´*; a variation of 424:—oak.

428. אֵלֶּה, **'êlleh,** *ale´-leh*; prolonged from 411; *these* or *those*:—an- (the) other; one sort, so, some, such, them, these (same), they, this, those, thus, which, who (-m).

429. אֵלֶּה, **'êlleh** (Chaldee), *ale´-leh*; corresponding to 428:—these.

430. אֱלֹהִים, **'ĕlôhîym,** *el-o-heem´*; plural of 433; *gods* in the ordinary sense; but specifically used (in the plural thus, especially with the article) of the supreme *God*; occasionally applied by way of deference to *magistrates*; and sometimes as a superlative:—angels, × exceeding, God (gods) (-dess, -ly), × (very) great, judges, × mighty.

A masculine plural noun meaning God, gods, judges, angels. Occurring more than 2,600 times in the OT, this word commonly designates the one true God (Ge 1:1) and is often paired with God's unique name *yĕhôwâh* (3068) (Ge 2:4; Ps 100:3). When the word is used as the generic designation of God, it conveys in Scripture that God is the Creator (Ge 5:1); the King (Ps 47:7[8]); the Judge (Ps 50:6); the Lord (Ps 86:12); and the Saviour (Hos 13:4). His character is compassionate (Dt 4:31); gracious (Ps 116:5); and faithful to His covenant (Dt 7:9). In fewer instances, this word refers to foreign gods, such as Dagon (1Sa 5:7) or Baal (1Ki 18:24). It also might refer to judges (Ex 22:8[7], 9[8]) or angels as gods (Ps 97:7). Although the form of this word is plural, it is frequently used as if it were singular—that is, with a singular verb (Ge 1:1–31; Ex 2:24). The plural form of this word may be regarded **(1)** as intensive to indicate God's fullness of power; **(2)** as majestic to indicate God's kingly rule; or **(3)** as an allusion to the Trinity (Ge 1:26). The singular form of this word *'ĕlôwah* (433) occurs only in poetry (Ps 50:22; Isa 44:8). The shortened form of the word is *'ēl* (410).

431. אֲלוּ, **'ălûw** (Chaldee), *al-oo´*; probably prolonged from 412; *lo!*:—behold.

432. אִלּוּ, **'illûw**, *il-loo´*; probably from 408; *nay*, i.e. (softened) *if*:—but if, yea though.

433. אֱלוֹהַּ, **'ĕlôwah**, *el-o´-ah*; rarely (shortened) אֱלֹהַּ, **'ĕlôah**, *el-o´-ah*; probably prolonged (emphatic) from 410; a *deity* or the *Deity*:—God, god. See 430.

A masculine noun meaning god or God. It is thought by some to be the singular of the noun *'ĕlôhiym* (430). This word is used of *yĕhôwâh* (3068) (Ps 18:31 [32]) and, with a negative, to describe what is not God (Dt 32:17). Most occurrences of this word are in the book of Job, where the speakers may not be Israelites and thus use other generic names for God (Job 3:4), of which this is one. It is used once in the name, "God of Jacob" (Ps 114:7) and once in the phrase, "God of forgiveness" (Ne 9:17).

434. אֱלוּל, **'ĕluwl**, *el-ool´*; for 457; good for *nothing*:—thing of nought.

435. אֱלוּל, **'Ĕlûwl**, *el-ool´*; probably of foreign derivation; *Elul*, the sixth Jewish month:—Elul.

436. אֵלוֹן, **'êlôwn**, *ay-lone´*; prolonged from 352; an *oak* or other strong tree:—plain. See also 356.

437. אַלּוֹן, **'allôwn**, *al-lone´*; a variation of 436:—oak.

438. אַלּוֹן, **'Allôwn**, *al-lone´*; the same as 437; *Allon*, an Israelite, also a place in Palestine:—Allon.

439. אַלּוֹן בָּכוּת, **'Allôwn Bâkûwth**, *al-lone´ baw-kooth´*; from 437 and a variation of 1068; *oak of weeping; Allon-Bakuth*, a monumental tree:—Allon-bachuth.

440. אֵלוֹנִי, **'Êlôwnîy**, *ay-lo-nee´*; or rather (shortened) אֵלֹנִי, **'Êlônîy**, *ay-lo-nee´*; patronymic from 438; an *Elonite* or descendants (collective) of Elon:—Elonites.

441. אַלּוּף, **'allûwph**, *al-loof´*; or (shortened) אַלֻּף, **'alluph**, *al-loof´*; from 502; *familiar*; a *friend*, also *gentle*; hence a *bullock* (as being tame; applied, although masculine, to a *cow*); and so a *chieftain* (as notable like neat cattle):—captain, duke, (chief) friend, governor, guide, ox.

An adjective meaning docile or a masculine noun meaning tame, friend, intimate, chief, captain. Even though the adjectival usage is rare, it is found in the well-known description, "Like a docile lamb to the slaughter" (Jer 11:19). In the nominal form, this word connotes the closest of companions; such companions can be separated by a whisperer (Pr 16:28). In another aspect, this term was used to describe a leader of a nation or group. Esau's descendants were listed as chiefs of Edom (Ge 36:15).

442. אָלוּשׁ, **'Âlûwsh**, *aw-loosh´*; of uncertain derivation; *Alush*, a place in the Desert:—Alush.

443. אֶלְזָבָד, **'Elzâbâd**, *el-zaw-bawd´*; from 410 and 2064; *God has bestowed; Elzabad*, the name of two Israelites:—Elzabad.

444. אָלַח, **'âlach**, *aw-lakh´*; a primitive root; to *muddle*, i.e. (figurative and intransitive) to *turn* (moral) *corrupt*:—become filthy.

445. אֶלְחָנָן, **'Elchânân**, *el-khaw-nawn´*; from 410 and 2603; *God* (is) *gracious; Elchanan*, an Israelite:—Elkanan.

446. אֱלִיאָב, **'Ĕlîy'âb**, *el-ee-awb´*; from 410 and 1; *God of* (his) *father; Eliab*, the name of six Israelites:—Eliab.

447. אֱלִיאֵל, **'Ĕlîy'êl**, *el-ee-ale´*; from 410 repeated; *God of* (his) *God; Eliel*, the name of nine Israelites:—Eliel.

448. אֱלִיאָתָה, **'Ĕlîy'âthâh**, *el-ee-aw-thaw´*; or (contracted) אֱלִיָּתָה, **'Ĕlîyyâthâh**, *el-ee-yaw-thaw´*; from 410 and 225; *God of* (his) *consent; Eliathah*, an Israelite:—Eliathah.

449. אֱלִידָד, **'Ĕlîydâd**, *el-ee-dawd´*; from the same as 419; *God of* (his) *love; Elidad*, an Israelite:—Elidad.

450. אֶלְיָדָע, **'Elyâdâ'**, *el-yaw-daw´*; from 410 and 3045; *God* (is) *knowing; Eljada*, the name of two Israelites and of an Aramaean leader:—Eliada.

451. אַלְיָה, **'alyâh**, *al-yaw´*; from 422 (in the original sense of *strength*); the *stout* part, i.e. the fat *tail* of the Oriental sheep:—rump.

452. אֵלִיָּה, **'Êlîyyâh**, *ay-lee-yaw´*; or prolonged אֵלִיָּהוּ, **'Êlîyyâhûw**, *ay-lee-yaw´-hoo*; from 410 and 3050; *God of Jehovah; Elijah*, the name of the famous prophet and of two other Israelites:—Elijah, Eliah.

453. אֱלִיהוּ, **'Ĕlîyhûw**, *el-ee-hoo´*; or (fully) אֱלִיהוּא, **'Ĕlîyhûw'**, *el-ee-hoo´*; from 410 and 1931; *God of him; Elihu*, the name of one of Job's friends, and of three Israelites:—Elihu.

454. אֶלְיְהוֹעֵינַי, **'Ely^e^hôw'êynay**, *el-ye-ho-ay-nah´ee*; or (shortened) אֶלְיוֹעֵינַי, **'Elyôw'êynay**, *el-yo-ay-nah´ee*; from 413 and 3068 and 5869; *toward Jehovah* (are) *my eyes; Elijehoenai* or *Eljoenai*, the name of seven Israelites:—Elihoenai, Elionai.

455. אֶלְיַחְבָּא, **'Elyachbâ'**, *el-yakh-baw´*; from 410 and 2244; *God will hide; Eljachba*, an Israelite:—Eliahbah.

456. אֱלִיחֹרֶף, **'Ĕlîychôreph**, *el-ee-kho´-ref*; from 410 and 2779; *God of autumn; Elichoreph*, an Israelite:—Elihoreph.

457. אֱלִיל, **'ĕlîyl**, *el-eel´*; apparently from 408; good for *nothing*, by analogy *vain* or *vanity*; specifically an *idol*:—idol, no value, thing of nought.

A masculine noun meaning worthlessness. The term is frequently used to describe false gods and idols (Le 19:4; Ps 96:5; Isa 2:8; Hab 2:18). Sometimes, this noun is used in a prepositional phrase, such as in Zec 11:17, where the Hebrew literally says "shepherd of worthlessness," and in Job 13:4, "physicians of worthlessness." In those verses, *'ĕlîyl* functions as an adjective.

458. אֱלִימֶלֶךְ, **'Ĕlîymelek**, *el-ee-meh´-lek*; from 410 and 4428; *God of* (the) *king; Elimelek*, an Israelite:—Elimelech.

459. אִלֵּין, **'illêyn** (Chaldee), *il-lane´*; or shorter אִלֵּן, **'illên**, *il-lane´*; prolonged from 412; *these*:—the, these.

460. אֶלְיָסָף, **'Elyâsâph**, *el-yaw-sawf´*; from 410 and 3254; *God* (is) *gatherer; Eljasaph*, the name of two Israelites:—Eliasaph.

461. אֱלִיעֶזֶר, **'Ĕlîy'ezer**, *el-ee-eh´-zer*; from 410 and 5828; *God of help; Eliezer*, the name of a Damascene and of ten Israelites:—Eliezer.

462. אֱלִיעֵינַי, **'Ĕlîy'êynay**, *el-ee-ay-nah´ee*; probably contraction for 454; *Elienai*, an Israelite:—Elienai.

463. אֱלִיעָם, **'Ĕlîy'âm,** *el-ee-awm´*; from 410 and 5971; *God of* (the) *people; Eliam,* an Israelite:—Eliam.

464. אֱלִיפַז, **'Ĕlîyphaz,** *el-ee-faz´*; from 410 and 6337; *God of gold; Eliphaz,* the name of one of Job's friends, and of a son of Esau:—Eliphaz.

465. אֱלִיפָל, **'Ĕlîyphâl,** *el-ee-fawl´*; from 410 and 6419; *God of judgment; Eliphal,* an Israelite:—Eliphal.

466. אֱלִיפְלֵהוּ, **'Ĕlîyph**e**lêhûw,** *el-ee-fe-lay´-hoo*; from 410 and 6395; *God of his distinction; Eliphelehu,* an Israelite:—Elipheleh.

467. אֱלִיפֶלֶט, **'Ĕlîyphelet,** *el-ee-feh´-let*; or (shortened) אֶלְפֶּלֶט, **'Elpelet,** *el-peh´-let*; from 410 and 6405; *God of deliverance; Eliphelet* or *Elpelet,* the name of six Israelites:—Eliphalet, Eliphelet, Elpalet.

468. אֱלִיצוּר, **'Ĕlîytsûwr,** *el-ee-tsoor´*; from 410 and 6697; *God of* (the) *rock; Elitsur,* an Israelite:—Elizur.

469. אֱלִיצָפָן, **'Ĕlîytsâphân,** *el-ee-tsaw-fawn´*; or (shortened) אֶלְצָפָן, **'Eltsâphân,** *el-tsaw-fawn´*; from 410 and 6845; *God of treasure; Elitsaphan* or *Eltsa-phan,* an Israelite:—Elizaphan, Elzaphan.

470. אֱלִיקָא, **'Ĕlîyqâ',** *el-ee-kaw´*; from 410 and 6958; *God of rejection; Elika,* an Israelite:—Elika.

471. אֶלְיָקִים, **'Elyâqîym,** *el-yaw-keem´*; from 410 and 6965; *God of raising; Eljakim,* the name of four Israelites:—Eliakim.

472. אֱלִישֶׁבַע, **'Ĕlîysheba',** *el-ee-sheh´-bah*; from 410 and 7651 (in the sense of 7650); *God of* (the) *oath; Elisheba,* the wife of Aaron:—Elisheba.

473. אֱלִישָׁה, **'Ĕlîyshâh,** *el-ee-shaw´*; probably of foreign derivation; *Elishah,* a son of Javan:—Elishah.

474. אֱלִישׁוּעַ, **'Ĕlîyshûwa',** *el-ee-shoo´-ah*; from 410 and 7769; *God of supplication* (or *of riches*); *Elishua,* a son of King David:—Elishua.

475. אֶלְיָשִׁיב, **'Elyâshîyb,** *el-yaw-sheeb´*; from 410 and 7725; *God will restore; Eljashib,* the name of six Israelites:—Eliashib.

476. אֱלִישָׁמָע, **'Ĕlîyshâmâ',** *el-ee-shaw-maw´*; from 410 and 8085; *God of hearing; Elishama,* the name of seven Israelites:—Elishama.

477. אֱלִישָׁע, **'Ĕlîyshâ',** *el-ee-shaw´*; contraction for 474; *Elisha,* the famous prophet:—Elisha.

478. אֱלִישָׁפָט, **'Ĕlîyshâphât,** *el-ee-shaw-fawt´*; from 410 and 8199; *God of judgment; Elishaphat,* an Israelite:—Elishaphat.

479. אִלֵּךְ, **'illêk** (Chaldee), *il-lake´*; prolonged from 412; *these:*—these, those.

480. אַלְלַי, **'allay,** *al-lah´ee*; by reduplication from 421; *alas!:*—woe.

481. אָלַם, **'âlam,** *aw-lam´*; a primitive root; to *tie* fast; hence (of the mouth) to be *tongue-tied:*—bind, be dumb, put to silence.

482. אֵלֶם, **'êlem,** *ay´-lem*; from 481; *silence* (i.e. mute justice):—congregation. Compare 3128.

483. אִלֵּם, **'illêm,** *il-lame´*; from 481; *speechless:*—dumb (man).

484. אַלְמֻגִּים, **'almuggiym,** *al-moog-gheem´*; probably of foreign derivation (used thus only in the plural); *almug* (i.e. probably sandal-wood) sticks:— almug trees. Compare 418.

485. אֲלֻמָּה, **'ălummâh,** *al-oom-maw´*; or (masculine) אָלֻם, **'âlum,** *aw-loom´*; passive participle of 481; something *bound*; a *sheaf:*—sheaf.

486. אַלְמוֹדָד, **'Almôwdâd,** *al-mo-dawd´*; probably of foreign derivation; *Almodad,* a son of Joktan:—Almodad.

487. אַלַּמֶּלֶךְ, **'Allammelek,** *al-lam-meh´-lek*; from 427 and 4428; *oak of* (the) *king; Allammelek,* a place in Palestine:—Alammelech.

488. אַלְמָן, **'almân,** *al-mawn´*; prolonged from 481 in the sense of *bereavement; discarded* (as a divorced person):—forsaken.

An adjective meaning forsaken or widowed. It occurs only in Jer 51:5, assuring Israel and Judah that, even in exile, they have not been forsaken by their God. Although this Hebrew word is similar to the Hebrew word for widow, the context of this verse does not support the idea that Israel is pictured as the wife of the Lord.

489. אַלְמֹן, **'almôn,** *al-mone´*; from 481 as in 488; *bereavement:*—widowhood.

490. אַלְמָנָה, **'almânâh,** *al-maw-naw´*; feminine of 488; a *widow*; also a *desolate* place:—desolate house (palace), widow.

A feminine noun meaning widow. The word occurs many times in the Law and the Prophets, where the well-being and care of the widow are the subject (Dt 14:29; Isa 1:17; Jer 7:6; Zec 7:10). Israel's concern for the widow was founded in the Lord's own concern (Ps 68:5[6]; 146:9; Pr 15:25; Jer 49:11). Figuratively, the term occurs twice in reference to a devastated city: Jerusalem (La 1:1) and Babylon (Isa 47:8).

491. אַלְמָנוּת, **'almânûwth,** *al-maw-nooth´*; feminine of 488; (concrete) a *widow*; (abstract) *widowhood:*—widow, widowhood.

492. אַלְמֹנִי, **'almônîy,** *al-mo-nee´*; from 489 in the sense of *concealment; some one* (i.e. *so and so,* without giving the name of the person or place):—one, and such.

493. אֶלְנַעַם, **'Elna'am,** *el-nah´-am*; from 410 and 5276; *God* (is his) *delight; Elnaam,* an Israelite:—Elnaam.

494. אֶלְנָתָן, **'Elnâthân,** *el-naw-thawn´*; from 410 and 5414; *God* (is the) *giver; Elnathan,* the name of four Israelites:—Elnathan.

495. אֶלָּסָר, **'Ellâsâr,** *el-law-sawr´*; probably of foreign derivation *Ellasar,* an early country of Asia:—Ellasar.

496. אֶלְעָד, **'El'âd,** *el-awd´*; from 410 and 5749; *God has testified; Elad,* an Israelite:—Elead.

497. אֶלְעָדָה, **'El'âdâh,** *el-aw-daw´*; from 410 and 5710; *God has decked; Eladah,* an Israelite:—Eladah.

498. אֶלְעוּזַי, **'El'ûwzay,** *el-oo-zah´ee*; from 410 and 5756 (in the sense of 5797); *God* (is) *defensive; Eluzai,* an Israelite:—Eluzai.

499. אֶלְעָזָר, **'El'âzâr,** *el-aw-zawr´*; from 410 and 5826; *God* (is) *helper; Elazar,* the name of seven Israelites:—Eleazar.

500. אֶלְעָלֵא, **'El'âlê',** *el-aw-lay´*; or (more properly) אֶלְעָלֵה, **'El'âlêh,** *el-aw-lay´*; from 410 and 5927; *God* (is) *going up; Elale* or *Elaleh,* a place east of the Jordan:—Elealeh.

501. אֶלְעָשָׂה, **'El'âśâh,** *el-aw-saw´*; from 410 and 6213; *God has made; Elasah,* the name of four Israelites:—Elasah, Eleasah.

502. אָלַף, **'âlaph,** *aw-lof´*; a primitive root, to *associate* with; hence to *learn* (and causative to *teach*):—learn, teach, utter.

A verb meaning to learn or, in a causative sense, to teach. The meaning apparently derives from a noun meaning association, familiarity, which leads to learning. This root idea appears in Pr 22:25 where association with an angry man causes one to learn his ways. Other usages mean to teach without obvious reference to learning by association (Job 15:5; 33:33; 35:11).

503. אָלַף, **'âlaph,** *aw-laf´*; denominative from 505; causative to *make a thousandfold:*—bring forth thousands.

A masculine verb meaning thousand. It presents the idea of bringing forth thousands or making a thousandfold. It comes from the noun *'eleph* (505) and is found only once in the OT. The psalmist asked God for his granaries to be filled and his sheep to bring forth thousands (Ps 144:13).

504. אֶלֶף, **'eleph,** *eh´-lef*; from 502; a *family*; also (from the sense of *yoking* or *taming*) an *ox* or *cow:*—family, kine, oxen.

505. אֶלֶף, 'eleph, *eh´-lef*; properly the same as 504; hence (an ox's head being the first letter of the alphabet, and this eventually used as a numeral) a *thousand*:—thousand.

A masculine noun meaning a thousand or clan. The word was commonly used for people, weights (including money), measures, and livestock (Jgs 8:26). Though the word is usually literal, sometimes it is used poetically to suggest a large number (Ge 24:60; Job 9:3). In a few cases, it carries the sense of an extended family or clan (Jgs 6:15).

506. אֲלַף, 'âlaph (Chaldee), *al-af´*; or אֶלֶף, **'eleph,** *eh´-lef*; (Chaldee); corresponding to 505:—thousand.

An Aramaic masculine noun meaning one thousand. This word is found only in the book of Daniel. For example, Belshazzar held a magnificent feast and invited the lords of the land, whose total number was one thousand (Da 5:1). Daniel had a dream of people ministering to the Ancient of Days; Daniel called these people the thousand thousands (Da 7:10).

507. אֶלֶף, 'Eleph, *eh´-lef*; the same as 505; *Eleph*, a place in Palestine:—Eleph.

508. אֶלְפַּעַל, 'Elpa'al, *el-pah´-al*; from 410 and 6466; *God* (is) *act; Elpaal*, an Israelite:—Elpaal.

509. אָלַץ, 'âlats, *aw-lats´*; a primitive root; to *press*:—urge.

510. אַלְקוּם, 'alqûwm, *al-koom´*; probably from 408 and 6965; a *non-rising* (i.e. *resistlessness*):—no rising up.

511. אֶלְקָנָה, 'Elqânâh, *el-kaw-naw´*; from 410 and 7069; *God has obtained; Elkanah*, the name of seven Israelites:—Elkanah.

512. אֶלְקֹשִׁי, 'Elqôshîy, *el-ko-shee´*; patrial from a name of uncertain derivation; an *Elkoshite* or native of Elkosh:—Elkoshite.

513. אֶלְתּוֹלַד, 'Eltôwlad, *el-to-lad´*; probably from 410 and a masculine form of 8435 [compare 8434]; *God* (is) *generator; Eltolad*, a place in Palestine:—Eltolad.

514. אֶלְתְּקֵא, 'Elteqê', *el-te-kay´*; or (more proper) אֶלְתְּקֵה, **'Elteqêh,** *el-te-kay´*; of uncertain derivation; *Eltekeh* or *Elteke*, a place in Palestine:—Eltekeh.

515. אֶלְתְּקֹן, 'Elteqôn, *el-te-kone´*; from 410 and 8626; *God* (is) *straight, Eltekon*, a place in Palestine:—Eltekon.

516. אַל תַּשְׁחֵת, 'Al tashchêth, *al tash-kayth´*; from 408 and 7843; *Thou must not destroy*; probably the opening words of a popular song:—Al-taschith.

517. אֵם, 'êm, *ame*; a primitive word; a *mother* (as the *bond* of the family); in a wide sense (both literal and figurative) [like 1]:—dam, mother, × parting.

A feminine noun meaning mother, a woman with children (Ex 20:12; Ps 35:14). The word may also signify a female ancestor, animals, or humans in general (Ge 3:20; 1Ki 15:13). A nation or city is sometimes viewed as the mother of its people. So in that sense, this word is sometimes used to refer to a nation (Isa 50:1; Hos 2:2[4], 5[7]).

518. אִם, 'im, *eem*; a primitive particle; used very widely as demonstrative, *lo!*; interrogative, *whether*; or conditional, *if, although*; also *Oh that!, when*; hence as a negative, *not*:—(and, can-, doubtless, if, that) (not), + but, either, + except, + more (-over, if, than), neither, nevertheless, nor, oh that, or, + save (only, -ing), seeing, since, sith, + surely (no more, none, not), though, + of a truth, + unless, + verily, when, whereas, whether, while, + yet.

519. אָמָה, 'âmâh, *aw-maw´*; apparently a primitive word; a *maid-servant* or female slave:—(hand-) bondmaid (-woman), maid (-servant).

520. אַמָּה, 'ammâh, *am-maw´*; prolonged from 517; properly a *mother* (i.e. *unit*) of measure, or the *fore-arm* (below the elbow), i.e. a *cubit*; also a door-*base* (as a *bond* of the entrance):—cubit, + hundred [*by exchange for* 3967], measure, post.

521. אַמָּה, 'ammâh (Chaldee), *am-maw´*; corresponding to 520:—cubit.

522. אַמָּה, 'Ammâh, *am-maw´*; the same as 520; *Ammah*, a hill in Palestine:—Ammah.

523. אֻמָּה, 'ummâh, *oom-maw´*; from the same as 517; a *collection*, i.e. community of persons:—nation, people.

A feminine noun meaning tribe, people. This word occurs three times in the Hebrew Bible (Ge 25:16; Nu 25:15; Ps 117:1) and is always plural. It is synonymous with *gôwy* (1471).

524. אֻמָּה, 'ummâh (Chaldee), *oom-maw´*; corresponding to 523:—nation.

An Aramaic feminine noun meaning nation. This word corresponds to the Hebrew word *'êm* (517) meaning mother, and when carried into the Aramaic, this word shifts to mean mother in a collective sense (i.e. nation). Often a nation is found in the expression "peoples, nations, and languages" (Da 3:4, 7; 4:1[3:31]; 5:19; 6:25[26]; 7:14; cf. Ezr 4:10). For example, after Shadrach, Meshach, and Abednego came through the fiery furnace, Nebuchadnezzar issued a decree to every people, language, and nation concerning the God of the Hebrews (Da 3:29).

525. אָמוֹן, 'âmôwn, *aw-mone´*; from 539, probably in the sense of *training; skilled*, i.e. an architect [like 542]:—one brought up.

A masculine noun meaning architect or craftsman. The word is used in Pr 8:30 as the personification of wisdom. Wisdom is portrayed as a craftsman at God's side, involved in designing the creation.

526. אָמוֹן, 'Âmôwn, *aw-mone´*; the same as 525; *Amon*, the name of three Israelites:—Amon.

527. אָמוֹן, 'âmôwn, *aw-mone´*; a variation for 1995; a *throng* of people:—multitude.

A masculine noun of uncertain derivation, meaning either a skilled craftsman or a throng of people. It is used only twice in the OT. In Pr 8:30, the sense is that of a master architect or artisan (525). The other appearance in Jer 52:15 seems to designate a general multitude of people.

528. אָמוֹן, 'Âmôwn, *aw-mone´*; of Egyptian derivation; *Amon* (i.e. Ammon or Amn), a deity of Egypt (used only as an adjunct of 4996):—multitude, populous.

A masculine noun meaning artisan or master craftsman. The legs of the beloved are said to be the work of an artisan (SS 7:1[2]). This word is also a proper name of an Egyptian god (Jer 46:25; Na 3:8). The Egyptian god was the local deity of Thebes but came to be the supreme god in Egypt.

529. אֵמוּן, 'êmûwn, *ay-moon´*; from 539; *established*, i.e. (figurative) *trusty*; also (abstract) *trustworthiness*:—faith (-ful), truth.

A masculine noun meaning trustworthiness, faithfulness, or dependability. It is used to signify the rare and beneficial quality of trustworthiness in an individual (Pr 13:17; 14:5; 20:6); the character of a righteous nation (Isa 26:2); and in a negative sense, a fundamental lack of dependability or faithfulness (Dt 32:20).

530. אֱמוּנָה, 'ĕmûwnâh, *em-oo-naw´*; or (shortened) אֱמֻנָה, **'ĕmunâh,** *em-oo-naw´*; feminine of 529; (literal) *firmness*; (figurative) *security*; (moral) *fidelity*:—faith (-ful, -ly, -ness, [man]), set office, stability, steady, truly, truth, verily.

A noun meaning truth, faithfulness. It is used to describe God's character and His actions in Dt 32:4. The psalmists often use this word in their praise of the Lord and His faithfulness (Ps 33:4; 100:5; 119:90). When people are faithful, good comes their way (2Ch 19:9; Pr 12:22; 28:20). The word *'emûnâh* is also used with righteousness to describe the character (Pr 12:17; Isa 59:4; Jer 5:1).

531. אָמוֹץ, 'Âmôwts, *aw-mohts´*; from 553; *strong; Amots*, an Israelite:—Amoz.

532. אָמִי, 'Âmîy, *aw-mee´*; an abbreviation for 526; *Ami*, an Israelite:—Ami.

533. **אַמִּיץ, ’ammîyts,** *am-meets´*; or (shortened) **אַמִּץ, ’ammits,** *am-meets´*; from 553; *strong* or (abstract) *strength:*—courageous, mighty, strong (one).

534. **אָמִיר, ’âmîyr,** *aw-meer´*; apparently from 559 (in the sense of *self-exaltation*); a *summit* (of a tree or mountain):—bough, branch.

535. **אָמַל, ’âmal,** *aw-mal´*; a primitive root; to *droop*; by implication to *be sick*, to *mourn*:—languish, be weak, wax feeble.

536. **אֻמְלַל, ’umlal,** *oom-lal´*; from 535; *sick*:—weak.

537. **אֲמֵלָל, ’ămêlâl,** *am-ay-lawl´*; from 535; *languid*:—feeble.

538. **אֲמָם, ’Ămâm,** *am-awm´*; from 517; *gathering* spot; *Amam*, a place in Palestine:—Amam.

539. **אָמַן, ’âman,** *aw-man´*; a primitive root; properly to *build up* or *support*; to *foster* as a parent or nurse; (figurative) to *render* (or *be*) *firm* or faithful, to *trust* or believe, to be *permanent* or quiet; moral to *be true* or certain; once (Isa 30:21; by interchange for 541) to *go to the right hand*:—hence assurance, believe, bring up, establish, + fail, be faithful (of long continuance, steadfast, sure, surely, trusty, verified), nurse, (-ing father), (put), trust, turn to the right.

A verb meaning to be firm, to build up, to support, to nurture, or to establish. The primary meaning is that of providing stability and confidence, like a baby would find in the arms of a parent. It is used to signify support of a pillar (2Ki 18:16); nurture and nourishment (Nu 11:12; Ru 4:16; thus, a nurse, 2Sa 4:4); cradling in one's arms (Isa 60:4); a house firmly founded (1Sa 2:35; 25:28); a secure nail that finds a solid place to grip (Isa 22:23); a lasting permanence (Ps 89:28[29]; with negative particle, Jer 15:18). Metaphorically, the word conveys the notion of faithfulness and trustworthiness, such that one could fully depend on (Dt 7:9; Job 12:20; Ps 19:7[8]; Isa 55:3; Mic 7:5). Therefore, the word can also signify certitude or assurance (Dt 28:66; Job 24:22; Hos 5:9) and belief, in the sense of receiving something as true and sure (Ge 15:6; Ex 4:5; 2Ch 20:20; Ps 78:22; Isa 53:1; Jnh 3:5).

540. **אֲמַן, ’ăman** (Chaldee), *am-an´*; corresponding to 539:—believe, faithful, sure.

An Aramaic verb meaning to trust in, to put one's faith in someone or something. This verb occurs only three times in the Hebrew Bible. In Da 6:23(24), it states that Daniel trusted in his God. In the other occurrences, the verb is in the form of a passive participle and functions as an adjective meaning trustworthy or faithful: the interpretation of the king's dream is trustworthy (Da 2:45); and Daniel is described as a faithful man without negligence or corruption (Da 6:4[5]).

541. **אָמַן, ’âman,** *aw-man´*; denominative from 3225; to take the *right hand* road:—turn to the right. See 539.

A verb meaning to go to the right or to use the right hand. This word is identical to *yâman* (3231) and is related to the noun *yĕmâniy* (3233), meaning right hand. In the OT, this word is always used with its opposite, *śâma'l*, meaning to go to the left or to use the left hand. Lot could choose which direction he wanted to go (Ge 13:9). God would guide Israel where they needed to go (Isa 30:21). God commanded Ezekiel to go the way God directed him (Eze 21:16[21]).

542. **אָמָּן, ’ommân,** *ow-mawn´*; from 539 (in the sense of *training*); an *expert*:—cunning workman.

543. **אָמֵן, ’âmên,** *aw-mane´*; from 539; *sure*; (abstract) *faithfulness*; adverb *truly*:—Amen, so be it, truth.

An adverb meaning verily or truly. The word is used more often as the declaration may it be so. It comes from a root meaning to confirm; to support; to be faithful. The major idea behind this word is constancy and reliability. It is used as a declaration to acknowledge affirmation of a statement (1Ki 1:36); acceptance of a curse (Ne 5:13); affirmation of a prophecy (Jer 28:6). It is also used in response to worship and praise (1Ch 16:36; Ne 8:6). The English word *amen* comes from this word and means, "I agree; may it be so."

544. **אֹמֶן, ’ômen,** *oh-men´*; from 539; *verity*:—truth.

545. **אָמְנָה, ’omnâh,** *om-naw´*; feminine of 544 (in the specific sense of *training*); *tutelage*:—brought up.

546. **אָמְנָה, ’omnâh,** *om-naw´*; feminine of 544 (in its usual sense); adverbial *surely*:—indeed.

An adverb meaning verily, truly, indeed. Abraham used this word to express that he was being truthful when he said Sarah was his sister (Ge 20:12)—although, in fact, he was lying. When Achan took loot from Jericho, he admitted his sin by saying he had indeed sinned against God (Jos 7:20).

547. **אֹמְנָה, ’ômᵉnâh,** *o-me-naw´*; feminine active participle of 544 (in the original sense of *supporting*); a *column*:—pillar.

548. **אֲמָנָה, ’ămânâh,** *am-aw-naw´*; feminine of 543; something *fixed*, i.e. a *covenant*, an *allowance*:—certain portion, sure.

A feminine noun meaning agreement, faith, support. It occurs in Ne 9:38[10:1] and 11:23. In Ne 9:38, it is the object of the verb *kârath* (3772), which is also used in the idiom "to make (lit., cut) a covenant," suggesting a possible semantic overlap.

549. **אֲמָנָה, ’Ămânâh,** *am-aw-naw´*; the same as 548; *Amanah*, a mountain near Damascus:—Amana.

550. **אַמְנוֹן, ’Amnôwn,** *am-nohn´*; or **אֲמִינוֹן, ’Ămîy-nôwn,** *am-ee-nohn´*; from 539; *faithful; Amnon* (or Aminon), a son of David:—Amnon.

551. **אָמְנָם, ’omnâm,** *om-nawm´*; adverbial from 544; *verily*:—indeed, no doubt, surely, (it is, of a) true (-ly, -th).

An adverb meaning admittedly, truly, or surely. The word is used to acknowledge that something is true but not the whole truth. Hezekiah admitted that Assyria destroyed other nations and their gods but claimed that it was because they were false gods (2Ki 19:17; Isa 37:18). Job admitted the truth of his friends' sayings but claimed that they did not see the whole truth (Job 9:2; 12:2, 19:4, 5). Eliphaz used the word to deny negative statements about God and himself (Job 34:12; 36:4).

552. **אֻמְנָם, ’umnâm,** *oom-nawm´*; an orthographic variation of 551:—in (very) deed; of a surety.

An interrogative particle meaning verily, truly, indeed. It always occurs in questions. An example is Ge 18:13, where Sarah doubted that she would have a child, "Shall I of a surety bear a child . . . ?"

553. **אָמַץ, ’âmats,** *aw-mats´*; a primitive root; to *be alert*, physically (on foot) or mentally (in courage):—confirm, be courageous (of good courage, steadfastly minded, strong, stronger), establish, fortify, harden, increase, prevail, strengthen (self), make strong (obstinate, speed).

554. **אָמֹץ, ’âmôts,** *aw-mohts´*; probably from 553; of a *strong* colour, i.e. *red* (others *fleet*):—bay.

555. **אֹמֶץ, ’ômets,** *o´-mets*; from 553; *strength*:—stronger.

556. **אַמְצָה, ’amtsâh,** *am-tsaw´*; from 553; *force*:—strength.

557. **אַמְצִי, ’Amtsîy,** *am-tsee´*; from 553; *strong; Amtsi*, an Israelite:—Amzi.

558. **אֲמַצְיָה, ’Ămatsyâh,** *am-ats-yaw´*; or **אֲמַצְיָהוּ, ’Ămatsyâhûw,** *am-ats-yaw´-hoo*; from 553 and 3050; *strength of Jah; Amatsjah*, the name of four Israelites:—Amaziah.

559. **אָמַר, ’âmar,** *aw-mar´*; a primitive root; to *say* (used with great latitude):—answer, appoint, avouch, bid, boast self, call, certify, challenge, charge, + (at the, give) command (-ment), commune, consider, declare, demand, × desire, determine, × expressly, × indeed, × intend, name, × plainly, promise, publish, report, require, say, speak (against, of), × still, × suppose, talk, tell, term, × that is, × think, use [speech], utter, × verily, × yet.

A verb meaning to say. It is translated in various ways depending on the context. It is almost always followed by a quotation. In addition to vocal speech, the word refers to thought as internal speech (2Sa

13:32; Est 6:6). Further, it also refers to what is being communicated by a person's actions along with his words (Ex 2:14; 2Ch 28:13).

560. אֲמַר, 'ămar (Chaldee), *am-ar´*; corresponding to 559:—command, declare, say, speak, tell.

An Aramaic verb meaning to say, to tell, to command. This root carries the same semantic range as its Hebrew cognate, *'âmar* (559) (Ezr 5:3, 15; Da 2:4; 3:24–26; 4:7–9[4–6]; 7:23).

561. אֵמֶר, 'êmer, *ay´-mer*; from 559; something *said*:—answer, × appointed unto him, saying, speech, word.

A masculine noun meaning word, speech, saying. The primary meaning is something said. The word is used like *dâbâr* (1697); however, it occurs (with the exception of Joshua 24:27) only in poetry, usually in the plural, often in the phrase "the words of my mouth" (Dt 32:1; Ps 19:14[15]). Words are seen as taking from their context qualities such as truth (Pr 22:21); beauty (Ge 49:21); deception (Isa 32:7); knowledge (Pr 23:12). This word may refer to God's words (Job 6:10; Ps 138:4) as well as people's words.

562. אֹמֶר, 'ômer, *o´-mer*; the same as 561:—promise, speech, thing, word.

A masculine noun meaning utterance, speech, word. It is used only in poetry in parallel constructions with *dâbâr* (1697), meaning word (Ps 19:3[4]; Pr 2:16; 4:10, 20); *millîm* (4405), meaning words (Job 32:12, 14; 33:3; 34:37); *mitswâh* (4687), meaning commandment (Job 23:12; Pr 2:1; 7:1).

563. אִמַּר, 'immar (Chaldee), *im-mar´*; perhaps from 560 (in the sense of *bringing forth*); a *lamb*:—lamb.

564. אִמֵּר, 'Immêr, *im-mare´*; from 559; *talkative; Immer*, the name of five Israelites:—Immer.

565. אִמְרָה, 'imrâh, *im-raw´*; or אֶמְרָה, **'emrâh,** *em-raw´*; feminine of 561, and meaning the same:—commandment, speech, word.

A feminine noun meaning word. This rare poetic term occurs more in Ps 119 than everywhere else combined. It is used in parallel with teaching, covenant, commandment, and voice (Dt 32:2; 33:9; Ps 119:172; Isa 28:23). This noun most often designates God's Word, which is the psalmist's guide for life and his basis for requesting God's kindness, graciousness, and deliverance (Ps 119:11, 41, 58, 76, 116, 133, 154, 170). The keeping of God's Word is a frequent topic in Scripture (Dt 33:9; Ps 119:67, 158; cf. Isa 5:24). God's Word is pure, sweeter than honey, and has been magnified with His name (Ps 119:103; 138:2; Pr 30:5).

566. אִמְרִי, 'Imrîy, *im-ree´*; from 564; *wordy; Imry*, the name of two Israelites:—Imri.

567. אֱמֹרִי, 'Ĕmôrîy, *em-o-ree´*; probably a patronymic from an unused name derived from 559 in the sense of *publicity*, i.e. prominence; thus a *mountaineer*; an *Emorite*, one of the Canaanitish tribes:—Amorite.

568. אֲמַרְיָה, 'Ămaryâh, *am-ar-yaw´*; or (prolonged) אֲמַרְיָהוּ, **'Ămaryâhûw,** *am-ar-yaw´-hoo*; from 559 and 3050; *Jah has said* (i.e. promised); *Amarjah*, the name of nine Israelites:—Amariah.

569. אַמְרָפֶל, 'Amrâphel, *am-raw-fel´*; of uncertain (perhaps foreign) derivation; *Amraphel*, a king of Shinar:—Amraphel.

570. אֶמֶשׁ, 'emesh, *eh´-mesh*; time *past*, i.e. *yesterday* or *last night*:—former time, yesterday (-night).

571. אֱמֶת, 'emeth, *eh´-meth*; contraction from 539; *stability*; (figurative) *certainty, truth, trustworthiness*:—assured (-ly), establishment, faithful, right, sure, true (-ly, -th), verity.

A feminine noun meaning truth, faithfulness. It is frequently connected with lovingkindness (Pr 3:3; Hos 4:1) and occasionally with other terms such as peace (2Ki 20:19); righteousness (Isa 48:1); and justice (Ps 111:7). To walk in truth is to conduct oneself according to God's holy standards (1Ki 2:4; 3:6; Ps 86:11; Isa 38:3). Truth was the barometer for measuring both one's word (1Ki 22:16; Da 11:2) and actions (Ge 24:49; Jos 2:14). Accordingly, God's words (Ps 119:160; Da 10:21) and actions (Ne 9:33) are characterized by this Hebrew term also. Indeed, God is the only God of truth (Ex 34:6; 2Ch 15:3; Ps 31:5[6]).

572. אַמְתַּחַת, 'amtachath, *am-takh´-ath*; from 4969; properly something *expansive*, i.e. a *bag*:—sack.

573. אֲמִתַּי, 'Ămittay, *am-it-tah´ee*; from 571; *veracious; Amittai*, an Israelite:—Amittai.

574. אֵמְתָנִי, 'êmtânîy (Chaldee), *em-taw-nee´*; from a root corresponding to that of 4975; well-*loined* (i.e. burly) or *mighty*:—terrible.

575. אָן, 'ân, *awn*; or אָנָה, **'ânâh,** *aw´-naw*; contraction from 370; *where*; hence *whither, when*; also *hither* and *thither*:— + any (no) whither, how, where, whither (-soever).

576. אֲנָא, 'ănâ', *an-aw´*; (Chaldee); or אֲנָה, **'ănâh,** *an-aw´*; (Chaldee); corresponding to 589; *I*:—I, as for me.

577. אָנָּא, 'ânnâ', *awn´-naw*; or אָנָּה, **'ânnâh,** *awn´-naw*; apparently contraction from 160 and 4994; *oh now!*:—I (me) beseech (pray) thee, O.

An interjection of entreaty meaning I beg you, ah now, alas, or oh. The primary use of the word is to intensify the urgency of request or the gravity of a given situation. It is used to signify the pressing desire for forgiveness (Ge 50:17); the great weight of sin (Ex 32:31); earnestness in prayer of petition (2Ki 20:3; Ne 1:5, Jnh 1:14).

578. אָנָה, 'ânâh, *aw-naw´*; a primitive root; to *groan*:—lament, mourn.

579. אָנָה, 'ânâh, *aw-naw´*; a primitive root [perhaps rather identical with 578 through the idea of *contraction* in anguish]; to *approach*; hence to *meet* in various senses:—befall, deliver, happen, seek a quarrel.

580. אֲנוּ, 'ănûw, *an-oo´*; contraction for 587; *we*:—we.

581. אִנּוּן, 'innûwn, *in-noon´*; (Chaldee); or (feminine) אִנִּין, **'innîyn,** *in-neen´*; (Chaldee); corresponding to 1992; *they*:—× are, them, these.

582. אֱנוֹשׁ, 'ĕnôwsh, *en-oshe´*; from 605; properly a *mortal* (and thus differing from the more dignified 120); hence a *man* in general (singly or collectively):—another, × [blood-] thirsty, certain, chap [-man], divers, fellow, × in the flower of their age, husband, (certain, mortal) man, people, person, servant, some (× of them), + stranger, those, + their trade. It is often unexpressed in the English Version, especially when used in apposition with another word. Compare 376.

A masculine noun meaning man. In the singular, this word occurs in poetry and prayers (2Ch 14:11[10]). This word may derive from *'ânash* (605), meaning to be weak or sick. In comparison to *'îsh* (376), which also means man, *'ĕnôwsh* often occurs in passages emphasizing man's frailty (Job 7:17; Ps 8:4[5]; 90:3). However, the plural of *'ĕnôwsh* serves as the plural of *'îsh* and occurs throughout the OT.

583. אֱנוֹשׁ, 'Ĕnôwsh, *en-ohsh´*; the same as 582; *Enosh*, a son of Seth:—Enos.

584. אָנַח, 'ânach, *aw-nakh´*; a primitive root; to *sigh*:—groan, mourn, sigh.

585. אֲנָחָה, 'ănâchâh, *an-aw-khaw´*; from 584; *sighing*:—groaning, mourn, sigh.

586. אֲנַחְנָא, 'ănachnâ', *an-akh´-naw*; (Chaldee); or אֲנַחְנָה, **'ănachnâh,** *an-akh-naw´*; (Chaldee); corresponding to 587; *we*:—we.

587. אֲנַחְנוּ, 'ănachnûw, *an-akh´-noo*; apparently from 595; *we*:—ourselves, us, we.

588. אֲנָחֲרָת, 'Ănâchărâth, *an-aw-kha-rawth´*; probably from the same root as 5170; a *gorge* or narrow pass; *Anacharath*, a place in Palestine:—Anaharath.

589. אֲנִי, 'ănîy, *an-ee´*; contraction from 595; *I*:—I, (as for) me, mine, myself, we, × which, × who.

590. אֳנִי, ’onîy, *on-ee´*; probably from 579 (in the sense of *conveyance*); a *ship* or (collective) a *fleet*:—galley, navy (of ships).

591. אֳנִיָּה, ’onîyyâh, *on-ee-yaw´*; feminine of 590; a *ship*:—ship (-men).

592. אֲנִיָּה, ’ănîyyâh, *an-ee-yaw´*; from 578; *groaning*:—lamentation, sorrow.

593. אֲנִיעָם, ’Ănîy‘âm, *an-ee-awm´*; from 578 and 5971; *groaning* of (the) *people; Aniam*, an Israelite:—Aniam.

594. אֲנָךְ, ’ănâk, *an-awk´*; probably from an unused root meaning to *be narrow*; according to most a plumb-*line*, and to others a *hook*:—plumb-line.

595. אָנֹכִי, ’ânôkîy, *aw-no-kee´*; (sometimes *aw-no´-kee*); a primitive pronoun; *I*:—I, me, × which.

596. אָנַן, ’ânan, *aw-nan´*; a primitive root; to *mourn*, i.e. *complain*:—complain.

597. אָנַס, ’ânas, *aw-nas´*; to *insist*:—compel.

598. אֲנַס, ’ănas (Chaldee), *an-as´*; corresponding to 597; (figurative) to *distress*:—trouble.

599. אָנַף, ’ânaph, *aw-naf´*; a primitive root; to *breathe* hard, i.e. *be enraged*:—be angry (displeased).

A verb meaning to be angry, enraged, or to breathe through the nose. The word derives its meaning from the heavy breathing and snorting typical of anger. It is used solely in reference to God's anger or severe displeasure with His people: Moses (Dt 1:37; 4:21); Aaron (Dt 9:20); Solomon (1Ki 11:9); and Israel (Dt 9:8; 1Ki 8:46; 2Ki 17:18; Ps 60:1[3]; 79:5) all provoked this divine anger. In Ps 2:12, this word is used in reference to the Messiah.

600. אֲנַף, ’ănaph (Chaldee), *an-af´*; corresponding to 639 (only in the plural as a singular); the *face*:—face, visage.

601. אֲנָפָה, ’ănâphâh, *an-aw-faw´*; from 599; an unclean bird, perhaps the *parrot* (from its *irascibility*):—heron.

602. אָנַק, ’ânaq, *aw-nak´*; a primitive root; to *shriek*:—cry, groan.

603. אֲנָקָה, ’ănâqâh, *an-aw-kaw´*; from 602; *shrieking*:—crying out, groaning, sighing.

604. אֲנָקָה, ’ănâqâh, *an-aw-kaw´*; the same as 603; some kind of lizard, probably the *gecko* (from its *wail*):—ferret.

605. אָנַשׁ, ’ânash, *aw-nash´*; a primitive root; to *be frail, feeble*, or (figurative) *melancholy*:—desperate (-ly wicked), incurable, sick, woeful.

606. אֱנָשׁ, ’ĕnâsh, *en-awsh´*; (Chaldee); or אֱנַשׁ, **’ĕnash,** *en-ash´*; (Chaldee); corresponding to 582; a *man*:—man, + whosoever.

An Aramaic masculine noun meaning man or mankind. This word is often used to differentiate man from deity. It can also be synonymous with human beings. The most frequent usage occurs in the book of Daniel. It is used in a general, collective sense to mean everyone (Ezr 6:11; Da 3:10); and in the phrase "son of man" to mean a human being (Da 7:13). See the related Hebrew noun *’ĕnôwsh* (582).

607. אַנְתָּה, ’antâh, *an-taw´*; (Chaldee); corresponding to 859; *thou*:—as for thee, thou.

608. אַנְתּוּן, ’antûwn, *an-toon´*; (Chaldee); plural of 607; *ye*:—ye.

609. אָסָא, ’Âsâ’, *aw-saw´*; of uncertain derivation; *Asa*, the name of a king and of a Levite:—Asa.

610. אָסוּךְ, ’âsûwk, *aw-sook´*; from 5480; *anointed*, i.e. an oil *flask*:—pot.

611. אָסוֹן, ’âsôwn, *aw-sone´*; of uncertain derivation; *hurt*:—mischief.

A masculine noun meaning mischief, evil, harm, hurt, or damage. It signifies potential danger during a journey (Ge 42:4, 38), bodily harm or personal loss (Ex 21:22, 23).

612. אֵסוּר, ’êsûwr, *ay-soor´*; from 631; a *bond* (especially *manacles* of a prisoner):—band, + prison.

613. אֱסוּר, ’ĕsûwr (Chaldee), *es-oor´*; corresponding to 612:—band, imprisonment.

614. אָסִיף, ’âsîyph, *aw-seef´*; or אָסִף, **’âsiph,** *aw-seef´*; from 622; *gathered*, i.e. (abstract) a *gathering* in of crops:—ingathering.

615. אָסִיר, ’âsîyr, *aw-sere´*; from 631; *bound*, i.e. a *captive*:—(those which are) bound, prisoner.

616. אַסִּיר, ’assîyr, *as-sere´*; for 615:—prisoner.

617. אַסִּיר, ’Assîyr, *as-sere´*; the same as 616; *prisoner; Assir*, the name of two Israelites:—Assir.

618. אָסָם, ’âsâm, *aw-sawm´*; from an unused root meaning to *heap* together; a *storehouse* (only in the plur.):—barn, storehouse.

619. אַסְנָה, ’Asnâh, *as-naw´*; of uncertain derivation; *Asnah*, one of the Nethinim:—Asnah.

620. אָסְנַפַּר, ’Ôsnappar, *os-nap-par´*; of foreign derivation; *Osnappar*, an Assyrian king:—Asnapper.

621. אָסְנַת, ’Âsᵉnath, *aw-se-nath´*; of Egyptian derivation.; *Asenath*, the wife of Joseph:—Asenath.

622. אָסַף, ’âsaph, *aw-saf´*; a primitive root; to *gather* for any purpose; hence to *receive, take away*, i.e. remove (destroy, leave behind, put up, restore, etc.):—assemble, bring, consume, destroy, fetch, gather (in, together, up again), × generally, get (him), lose, put all together, receive, recover [another from leprosy], (be) rereward, × surely, take (away, into, up), × utterly, withdraw.

A verb meaning to gather, to take away, to harvest. The meaning of the word varies depending on the context. The word can mean to gather people for different purposes (Ge 29:22; 42:17; Ex 3:16; 4:29). It is used of a nation collecting armies for fighting (Nu 21:23; Jgs 11:20; 1Sa 17:1; 2Sa 10:17); and the Lord taking away Rachel's disgrace of childlessness (Ge 30:23). Oftentimes it refers to gathering or harvesting food or gathering other objects, such as animals (Jer 12:9); quail (Nu 11:32); eggs (Isa 10:14); money (2Ki 22:4; 2Ch 24:11). The word also refers to death or burial, literally meaning to be gathered to one's people (Ge 25:8, 17; 35:29; 49:29, 33); to be gathered to one's fathers (Jgs 2:10); or to be gathered to one's grave (2Ki 22:20; 2Ch 34:28).

623. אָסָף, ’Âsâph, *aw-sawf´*; from 622; *collector; Asaph*, the name of three Israelites, and of the family of the first:—Asaph.

624. אָסֹף, ’âsôph, *aw-sof´*; passive participle of 622; *collected* (only in the plural), i.e. a *collection* (of offerings):—threshold, Asuppim.

A masculine noun meaning a collection, treasury, or storehouse. The primary meaning of the root is that which is gathered. It is used three times in the OT to signify the storehouses near the gates of a temple (1Ch 26:15, 17; Ne 12:25).

625. אֹסֶף, ’ôseph, *o´-sef*; from 622; a *collection* (of fruits):—gathering.

A masculine noun meaning a collection, ingathering, harvest. The Hebrew word especially refers to a harvest of summer fruit, as is depicted in Mic 7:1, "Gather the summer fruits" (NKJV). The prophet Isaiah is the other biblical author to use this term. In Isa 32:10, he states that the complacent people will be troubled and insecure because "the gathering will not come," but, then in Isa 33:4, the prophet uses the same word to refer to the Lord's spoil being collected like "the gathering of the caterpillar."

626. אֲסֵפָה, ’ăsêphâh, *as-ay-faw´*; from 622; a *collection* of people (only adverbial):—× together.

A feminine noun meaning a gathering or a collection. This word is related to *’âsaph* (622), which means to gather or collect. This particular word occurs only in Isa 24:22, "And they will be gathered together, as prisoners are gathered in the pit" (NKJV).

627. אֲסֻפָּה, 'ăsuppâh, *as-up-paw´*; feminine of 624; a *collection* of (learned) men (only in the plural):—assembly.

A feminine noun meaning council or assembly. It comes from a root meaning to gather. Although there are many usages of the different forms of the root, this particular word is used only once in the Hebrew Bible, and the usage is plural instead of singular. It is used with the word for master and can be translated as "the gathering of masters"; "the council of scholars"; or "the collected sayings of scholars" (Ecc 12:11).

628. אֲסַפְסֻף, 'ăsaphsuph, *as-af-soof´*; by reduplication from 624; *gathered up together*, i.e. a promiscuous *assemblage* (of people):—mixt multitude.

A masculine noun meaning a gathering or mixed multitude. This word is related to *'âsaph* (622), which means to gather or collect. It occurs only in Nu 11:4, "And the mixed multitude that was among them fell a lusting" (KJV).

629. אׇסְפַּרְנָא, 'osparnâ' (Chaldee), *os-par-naw´*; of Persian derivation; *diligently*:—fast, forthwith, speed (-ily).

630. אַסְפָּתָא, 'Aspâthâ', *as-paw-thaw´*; of Persian derivation; *Aspatha*, a son of Haman:—Aspatha.

631. אָסַר, 'âsar, *aw-sar´*; a primitive root; to *yoke* or *hitch*; by analogy to *fasten* in any sense, to *join* battle:—bind, fast, gird, harness, hold, keep, make ready, order, prepare, prison (-er), put in bonds, set in array, tie.

632. אֱסָר, 'ĕsâr, *es-awr´*; or אִסָּר, **'issâr,** *is-sawr´*; from 631; an *obligation* or *vow* (of abstinence):—binding, bond.

633. אֱסָר, 'ĕsâr (Chaldee), *es-awr´*; corresponding to 632 in a legal sense; an *interdict*:—decree.

634. אֵסַר־חַדּוֹן, 'Êsar-Chaddôwn, *ay-sar´ chad-dohn´*; of foreign derivation; *Esar-chaddon*, an Assyrian king:—Esar-haddon.

635. אֶסְתֵּר, 'Estêr, *es-tare´*; of Persian derivation; *Ester*, the Jewish heroine:—Esther.

636. אָע, 'â' (Chaldee), *aw*; corresponding to 6086; a *tree* or *wood*:—timber, wood.

637. אַף, 'aph, *af*; a primitive participle; meaning *accession* (used as an adverb or conjunction); *also* or *yea*; adversatively *though*:—also, + although, and (furthermore, yet), but, even, + how much less (more, rather than), moreover, with, yea.

638. אַף, 'aph (Chaldee), *af*; corresponding to 637:—also.

639. אַף, 'aph, *af*; from 599; properly the *nose* or *nostril*; hence the *face*, and occasionally a *person*; also (from the rapid breathing in passion) *ire*:—anger (-gry), + before, countenance, face, + forbearing, forehead, + [long-] suffering, nose, nostril, snout, × worthy, wrath.

A masculine noun meaning nose, nostril, and anger. These meanings are used together in an interesting wordplay in Pr 30:33. This word may, by extension, refer to the whole face, particularly in the expression, to bow one's face to the ground (Ge 3:19; 19:1; 1Sa 24:8[9]). To have length of nose is to be slow to wrath; to have shortness of nose is to be quick tempered (Pr 14:17, 29; Jer 15:14, 15). This Hebrew term is often intensified by being paired with another word for anger or by associating it with various words for burning (Nu 22:27; Dt 9:19; Jer 4:8; 7:20). Human anger is almost always viewed negatively with only a few possible exceptions (Ex 32:19; 1Sa 11:6; Pr 27:4). The anger of the Lord is a frequent topic in the OT. The OT describes how God is reluctant to exercise His anger and how fierce His anger is (Ex 4:14; 34:6; Ps 30:5[6]; 78:38; Jer 51:45).

640. אָפַד, 'âphad, *aw-fad´*; a primitive root [rather a denominative from 646]; to *gird* on (the ephod):—bind, gird.

641. אֵפֹד, 'Êphôd, *ay-fode´*; the same as 646 shorter; *Ephod*, an Israelite:—Ephod.

642. אֲפֻדָּה, 'ăphuddâh, *af-ood-daw´*; feminine of 646; a *girding* on (of the ephod); hence generally a *plating* (of metal):—ephod, ornament.

643. אַפֶּדֶן, 'appeden, *ap-peh´-den*; apparently of foreign derivation; a *pavilion* or palace-tent:—palace.

644. אָפָה, 'âphâh, *aw-faw´*; a primitive root; to *cook*, especially to *bake*:—bake, (-r, [-meats]).

645. אֵפוֹ, 'êphôw, *ay-fo´*; or אֵפוֹא, **'êphôw',** *ay-fo´*; from 6311; strictly a demonstrative participle, *here*; but used of time, *now* or *then*:—here, now, where.

646. אֵפוֹד, 'êphôwd, *ay-fode´*; rarely אֵפֹד, **'êphôd,** *ay-fode´*; probably of foreign derivation; a *girdle*; specifically the *ephod* or high priest's shoulder-piece; also generally an *image*:—ephod.

647. אֲפִיחַ, 'Ăphîyach, *af-ee´-akh*; perhaps from 6315; *breeze*; *Aphiach*, an Israelite:—Aphiah.

648. אָפִיל, 'âphîyl, *aw-feel´*; from the same as 651 (in the sense of *weakness*); *unripe*:—not grown up.

649. אַפַּיִם, 'Appayim, *ap-pah´-yim*; dual of 639; *two nostrils*; *Appajim*, an Israelite:—Appaim.

650. אָפִיק, 'âphîyq, *aw-feek´*; from 622; (properly) *containing*, i.e. a *tube*; also a *bed* or *valley* of a stream; also a *strong* thing or a *hero*:—brook, channel, mighty, river, + scale, stream, strong piece.

651. אָפֵל, 'aphêl, *aw-fale´*; from an unused root meaning to *set* as the sun; *dusky*:—very dark.

An adjective meaning dark or gloomy. This word is related to *'ôphel* (652), which means darkness or gloom. The only time this word occurs in the OT is in Am 5:20, "Shall not the day of the LORD be darkness, and not light? even very dark, and no brightness in it?" (KJV).

652. אֹפֶל, 'ôphel, *o´-fel*; from the same as 651; *dusk*:—darkness, obscurity, privily.

A masculine noun, used only in poetry to denote darkness, gloom, especially a thick darkness. Although the term can be used in reference to physical darkness (Job 28:3; Ps 91:6), it is more often used in a figurative sense to designate things like obscurity (Job 3:6); death (Job 10:22); evil (Job 23:17; 30:26; Ps 11:2). In Isa 29:18, the term has both a literal and a figurative meaning in reference to the blind.

653. אֲפֵלָה, 'ăphêlâh, *af-ay-law´*; feminine of 651; *duskiness*, (figurative) *misfortune*; (concrete) *concealment*:—dark, darkness, gloominess, × thick.

A feminine noun meaning darkness or gloominess. It signifies physical darkness: the plague of darkness (Ex 10:22); the naïve walking in darkness (Pr 7:9); the darkness which causes people to stumble and grope (Pr 4:19; Dt 28:29). Metaphorically, it is used to describe the calamity and misfortune that comes to the wicked (Isa 8:22; Jer 23:12) or the darkness of the day of the Lord (Joel 2:2; Zep 1:15).

654. אֶפְלָל, 'Ephlâl, *ef-lawl´*; from 6419; *judge*; *Ephlal*, an Israelite:—Ephlal.

655. אֹפֶן, 'ôphen, *o´-fen*; from an unused root meaning to *revolve*; a *turn*, i.e. a *season*:— + fitly.

656. אָפֵס, 'âphês, *aw-face´*; a primitive root; to *disappear*, i.e. *cease*:—be clean gone (at an end, brought to nought), fail.

657. אֶפֶס, 'ephes, *eh´-fes*; from 656; *cessation*, i.e. an *end* (especially of the earth); often used adverbially *no further*; also (like 6466) the *ankle* (in the dual), as being the extremity of the leg or foot:—ankle, but (only), end, howbeit, less than nothing, nevertheless (where), no, none (beside), not (any, -withstanding), thing of nought, save (-ing), there, uttermost part, want, without (cause).

658. אֶפֶס דַּמִּים, 'Ephes Dammîym, *eh´-fes dam-meem´*; from 657 and the plural of 1818; *boundary of blood* drops; *Ephes-Dammim*, a place in Palestine:—Ephes-dammim.

659. אֶפַע, 'epha', *eh´-fah*; from an unused root probably meaning to *breathe*; (properly) a *breath*, i.e. *nothing*:—of nought.

660. אֶפְעֶה, 'eph'eh, *ef-eh´*; from 659 (in the sense of *hissing*); an *asp* or other venomous serpent:—viper.

661. אָפַף, 'âphaph, *aw-faf´*; a primitive root; to *surround*:—compass.

662. אָפַק, 'âphaq, *aw-fak´*; a primitive root; to *contain*, i.e. (reflexive) *abstain*:—force (oneself), restrain.

663. אֲפֵק, 'Ăphêq, *af-ake´*; or אֲפִיק, **'Ăphîyq,** *af-eek´*; from 662 (in the sense of *strength*); *fortress; Aphek* (or *Aphik*), the name of three places in Palestine:—Aphek, Aphik.

664. אֲפֵקָה, 'Ăphêqâh, *af-ay-kaw´*; feminine of 663; *fortress; Aphekah*, a place in Palestine:—Aphekah.

665. אֵפֶר, 'êpher, *ay´-fer*; from an unused root meaning to *bestrew; ashes*:—ashes.

666. אֲפֵר, 'ăphêr, *af-ayr´*; from the same as 665 (in the sense of *covering*); a *turban*:—ashes.

667. אֶפְרֹחַ, 'ephrôach, *ef-ro´-akh*; from 6524 (in the sense of *bursting* the shell); the *brood* of a bird:—young (one).

668. אַפִּרְיוֹן, 'appiryôwn, *ap-pir-yone´*; probably of Egyptian derivation; a *palanquin*:—chariot.

669. אֶפְרַיִם, 'Ephrayim, *ef-rah´-yim*; dual of a masculine form of 672; *double fruit; Ephrajim*, a son of Joseph; also the tribe descended from him, and its territory:—Ephraim, Ephraimites.

670. אֲפָרְסַי, 'Ăphâr^{e}say (Chaldee), *af-aw-re-sah´*; of foreign origin (only in the plural); an *Apharesite* or inhabitant of an unknown region of Assyria:—Apharsite.

671. אֲפַרְסְכַי, 'Ăphars^{e}kay (Chaldee), *af-ar-sek-ah´ee*; or אֲפַרְסַתְכַי, **'Ăpharsathkay,** *af-ar-sath-kah´ee*; (Chaldee); of foreign origin (only in the plural); an *Apharsekite* or *Apharsathkite*, an unknown Assyrian tribe:—Apharsachites, Apharsath-chites.

672. אֶפְרָת, 'Ephrâth, *ef-rawth´*; or אֶפְרָתָה, **'Ephrâ-thâh,** *ef-raw´-thaw*; from 6509 *fruitfulness; Ephrath*, another name for Bethlehem; once (Ps 132:6) perhaps for *Ephraim*; also of an Israelite woman:—Ephrath, Ephratah.

673. אֶפְרָתִי, 'Ephrâthîy, *ef-rawth-ee´*; patrial from 672; an *Ephrathite* or an *Ephraimite*:—Ephraimite, Ephrathite.

674. אַפְּתֹם, 'app^{e}thôm (Chaldee), *ap-pe-thome´*; of Persian origin; *revenue*; others *at the last*:—revenue.

675. אֶצְבּוֹן, 'Etsbôwn, *ets-bone´*; or אֶצְבֹּן, **'Etsbôn,** *ets-bone´*; of uncertain derivation; *Etsbon*, the name of two Israelites:—Ezbon.

676. אֶצְבַּע, 'etsba', *ets-bah´*; from the same as 6648 (in the sense of *grasping*); some thing to *seize* with, i.e. a *finger*; by anal. a *toe*:—finger, toe.

677. אֶצְבַּע, 'etsba' (Chaldee), *ets-bah´*; corresponding to 676:—finger, toe.

678. אָצִיל, 'âtsîyl, *aw-tseel´*; from 680(in its secondary sense of *separation*); an *extremity* (Isa 41:9), also a *noble*:—chief man, noble.

A masculine noun designating side, corner, chief. This term can indicate the sides or borders of the earth, thereby referring to its extremities or remotest countries (Isa 41:9); or it can be used figuratively to mean nobles (Ex 24:11).

679. אַצִּיל, 'atstsîyl, *ats-tseel´*; from 680(in its primary sense of *uniting*); a *joint* of the hand (i.e. *knuckle*); also (according to some) a *party-wall* (Eze 41:8):—[arm] hole, great.

680. אָצַל, 'âtsal, *aw-tsal´*; a primitive root; (properly) to *join*; used only as a denominative from 681; to *separate*; hence to *select, refuse, contract*:—keep, reserve, straiten, take.

681. אֵצֶל, 'êtsel, *ay´-tsel*; from 680 (in the sense of *joining*); a *side*; (as a preposition) *near*:—at, (hard) by, (from) (beside), near (unto), toward, with. See also 1018.

682. אָצֵל, 'Âtsêl, *aw-tsale´*; from 680; *noble; Atsel*, the name of an Israelite, and of a place in Palestine:—Azal, Azel.

683. אֲצַלְיָהוּ, 'Ătsalyâhûw, *ats-al-yaw´-hoo*; from 680 and 3050 prolonged; *Jah has reserved; Atsaljah*, an Israelite:—Azaliah.

684. אֹצֶם, 'Ôtsem, *o´-tsem*; from an unused root probably meaning to *be strong; strength* (i.e. *strong*); *Otsem*, the name of two Israelites:—Ozem.

685. אֶצְעָדָה, 'ets'âdâh, *ets-aw-daw´*; a variation from 6807; properly a *step-chain*; by analolgy a *bracelet*:—bracelet, chain.

686. אָצַר, 'âtsar, *aw-tsar*; a primitive root; to *store* up:—(lay up in) store, (make) treasure (-r).

687. אֵצֶר, 'Êtser, *ay´-tser*; from 686; *treasure; Etser*, an Idumæan:—Ezer.

688. אֶקְדָּח, 'eqdâch, *ek-dawkh´*; from 6916; *burning*, i.e. a *carbuncle* or other fiery gem:—carbuncle.

689. אַקּוֹ, 'aqqôw, *ak-ko´*; probably from 602; *slender*, i.e. the *ibex*:—wild goat.

690. אֲרָא, 'Ărâ', *ar-aw´*; probably for 738; *lion; Ara*, an Israelite:—Ara.

691. אֶרְאֵל, 'er'êl, *er-ale´*; probably for 739; a *hero* (collective):—valiant one.

692. אַרְאֵלִי, 'Ar'êlîy, *ar-ay-lee´*; from 691; *heroic; Areli* (or an *Arelite*, collective), an Israelite and his descendants:—Areli, Arelites.

693. אָרַב, 'ârab, *aw-rab´*; a primitive root; to *lurk*:—(lie in) ambush (-ment), lay (lie in) wait.

694. אֲרָב, 'Ărâb, *ar-awb´*; from 693; *ambush; Arab*, a place in Palestine:—Arab.

695. אֶרֶב, 'ereb, *eh´-reb*; from 693; *ambuscade*:—den, lie in wait.

696. אֹרֶב, 'ôreb, *o´-reb*; the same as 695:—wait.

697. אַרְבֶּה, 'arbeh, *ar-beh´*; from 7235; a *locust* (from its rapid *increase*):—grasshopper, locust.

698. אָרְבָּה, 'orbâh, *or-baw´*; feminine of 696 (only in the plural); *ambuscades*:—spoils.

699. אֲרֻבָּה, 'ărubbâh, *ar-oob-baw´*; feminine participle passive of 693 (as if for *lurking*); a *lattice*; (by implication) a *window, dove-cot* (because of the pigeonholes), *chimney* (with its apertures for smoke), *sluice* (with openings for water):—chimney, window.

700. אֲרֻבּוֹת, 'Ărubbôwth, *ar-oob-both*; plural of 699; *Arubboth*, a place in Palestine:—Aruboth.

701. אַרְבִּי, 'Arbîy, *ar-bee´*; patrial from 694; an *Arbite* or native of Arab:—Arbite.

702. אַרְבַּע, 'arba', *ar-bah´*; masculine אַרְבָּעָה, **'ar-bâ'âh,** *ar-baw-aw´*; from 7251; *four*:—four.

703. אַרְבַּע, 'arba' (Chaldee), *ar-bah´*; corresponding to 702:—four.

704. אַרְבַּע, 'Arba', *ar-bah´*; the same as 702; *Arba*, one of the Anakim:—Arba.

705. אַרְבָּעִים, 'arbâ'îym, *ar-baw-eem´*; multiple of 702; *forty*:—forty.

706. אַרְבַּעְתַּיִם, **'arba'tayim,** *ar-bah-tah´-yim*; dual of 702; *fourfold*:—fourfold.

707. אָרַג, **'ârag,** *aw-rag´*; a primitive root; to *plait* or *weave*:—weaver (-r).

708. אֶרֶג, **'ereg,** *eh´-reg*; from 707; a *weaving*; a *braid*; also a *shuttle*:—beam, weaver's shuttle.

709. אַרְגֹּב, **'Argôb,** *ar-gobe´*; from the same as 7263; *stony; Argob*, a district of Palestine:—Argob.

710. אַרְגְּוָן, **'arg^evân,** *arg-ev-awn´*; a variation for 713; *purple*:—purple.

711. אַרְגְּוָן, **'arg^evân** (Chaldee), *arg-ev-awn´*; corresponding to 710:—purple.

712. אַרְגָּז, **'argâz,** *ar-gawz´*; perhaps from 7264 (in the sense of being *suspended*); a *box* (as a pannier):—coffer.

713. אַרְגָּמָן, **'argâmân,** *ar-gaw-mawn´*; of foreign origin; *purple* (the colour or the dyed stuff):—purple.

714. אַרְדְּ, **'Ard,** *ard*; from an unused root probably meaning to *wander; fugitive; Ard*, the name of two Israelites:—Ard.

715. אַרְדּוֹן, **'Ardôwn,** *ar-dohn´*; from the same as 714; *roaming; Ardon*, an Israelite:—Ardon.

716. אַרְדִּי, **'Ardîy,** *ar-dee´*; patronymic from 714; an *Ardite* (collectively) or descendants of Ard:—Ardites.

717. אָרָה, **'ârâh,** *aw-raw´*; a primitive root; to *pluck*:—gather, pluck.

718. אֲרוּ, **'ărûw** (Chaldee), *ar-oo´*; probably akin to 431; *lo!*:—behold, lo.

719. אַרְוַד, **'Arvad,** *ar-vad´*; probably from 7300; a refuge for the *roving; Arvad*, an island city of Palestine:—Arvad.

720. אֲרוֹד, **'Ărôwd,** *ar-ode´*; an orthographical variation of 719; *fugitive; Arod*, an Israelite:—Arod.

721. אַרְוָדִי, **'Arvâdîy,** *ar-vaw-dee´*; patrial from 719; an *Arvadite* or citizen of Arvad:—Arvadite.

722. אֲרוֹדִי, **'Ărôwdîy,** *ar-o-dee´*; patronymic from 721; an *Arodite* or descendant of Arod:—Arodi, Arodites.

723. אֻרְוָה, **'urvâh,** *oor-vaw´*; or, אֲרָיָה, **'ărâyâh,** *ar-aw-yah´*; from 717 (in the sense of *feeding*); a *herding-place* for an animal:—stall.

724. אֲרוּכָה, **'ărûwkâh,** *ar-oo-kaw´*; or אֲרֻכָה, **'ăru-kâh,** *ar-oo-kaw´*; feminine passive participle of 748 (in the sense of *restoring* to soundness); *wholeness* (literal or figurative):—health, made up, perfected.

A feminine noun meaning the healing of a wound, restoration, repair. The intuitive meaning is healing caused by the fleshly covering of a physical wound. It signifies the restoration of Israel, both the need for it (Jer 8:22) and the reality of it (Isa 58:8); and also the rebuilding of Jerusalem's walls that had been torn down (Jer 33:6).

725. אֲרוּמָה, **'Ărûwmâh,** *ar-oo-maw´*; a variation of 7316; *height; Arumah*, a place in Palestine:—Arumah.

726. אֲרוֹמִי, **'Ărôwmîy,** *ar-o-mee´*; a clerical error for 130; an *Edomite* (as in the margin):—Syrian.

727. אָרוֹן, **'ârôwn,** *aw-rone´*; or אָרֹן, **'ârôn,** *aw-rone´*; from 717 (in the sense of *gathering*); a *box*:—ark, chest, coffin.

A common noun meaning a box, chest, or ark. It is treated as masculine in some passages and as feminine in others. This word refers to the chest for collecting money offerings (2Ki 12:9[10], 10[11]); or the sarcophagus in which the mummy of Joseph was placed (Ge 50:26). In a sacred or cultic context, the term identifies the Ark of the Covenant (Nu 10:33), which at one time contained the tablets of the law (Dt 10:5); a copy of the Law which Moses had written (Dt 31:26); a pot of manna (Ex 16:33, 34); Aaron's rod (Nu 17:10). This word is often used with another word to denote the Ark of the Covenant: "the ark of the LORD your God" (Jos 4:5); "the ark of God" (1Sa 3:3); "the ark of the God of Israel" (1Sa 5:7); "the holy ark" (2Ch 35:3).

728. אֲרַוְנָה, **'Ăravnâh,** *ar-av-naw´*; or (by transposition) אוֹרְנָה, **'Ôwrnâh,** *ore-naw´*; or אַנִיָּה, **'Anîy-yâh,** *ar-nee-yaw´*; all by orthographical variation for 771; *Aravnah* (or *Arnijah* or *Ornah*), a Jebusite:—Araunah.

729. אָרַז, **'âraz,** *aw-raz´*; a primitive root; to be *firm*; used only in the passive participle as a denominative from 730; of *cedar*:—made of cedar.

730. אֶרֶז, **'erez,** *eh´-rez*; from 729; a *cedar* tree (from the tenacity of its roots):—cedar (tree).

731. אַרְזָה, **'arzâh,** *ar-zaw´*; feminine of 730; *cedar* wainscoting:—cedar work.

732. אָרַח, **'ârach,** *aw-rakh´*; a primitive root; to *travel*:—go, wayfaring (man).

733. אָרַח, **'Ârach,** *aw-rakh´*; from 732; *way-faring; Arach*, the name of three Israelites:—Arah.

734. אֹרַח, **'ôrach,** *o´-rakh*; from 732; a well trodden *road* (literal or figurative); also a *caravan*:—manner, path, race, rank, traveller, troop, [by-, high-] way.

A masculine noun meaning path, way, byway, or highway. It describes the literal path one walks on (Jgs 5:6); the path or rank one walks in (Joel 2:7). Figuratively, this word describes the path of an individual or course of life (Job 6:18); the characteristics of a lifestyle, good or evil (Ps 16:11); righteousness or judgment (Pr 2:13). It is further used to mean traveler or wayfarer (Job 31:32). In the plural, it means caravans or troops (Job 6:19).

735. אֲרַח, **'ărach** (Chaldee), *a´-rakh*; corresponding to 734; a *road*:—way.

736. אֹרְחָה, **'ôr^echâh,** *o-rekh-aw´*; feminine active participle of 732; a *caravan*:—(travelling) company.

737. אֲרֻחָה, **'ăruchâh,** *ar-oo-khaw´*; feminine passive participle of 732 (in the sense of *appointing*); a *ration* of food:—allowance, diet, dinner, victuals.

738. אֲרִי, **'ărîy,** *ar-ee´*; or (prolonged) אַרְיֵה, **'aryêh,** *ar-yay´*; from 717 (in the sense of *violence*); a *lion*:—(young) lion, + pierce [*from the margin*].

739. אֲרִיאֵל, **'ărîy'êl,** *ar-ee-ale´*; or אֲרִאֵל, **'ări'êl,** *ar-ee-ale´*; from 738 and 410; *lion of God*, i.e. *heroic*:—lionlike men.

740. אֲרִיאֵל, **'Ărîy'êl,** *ar-ee-ale´*; the same as 739; *Ariel*, a symbolical name for Jerusalem, also the name of an Israelite:—Ariel.

741. אֲרִאֵיל, **'ări'êyl,** *ar-ee-ale´*; either by transposition for 739 or, more probably, an orthographical variation for 2025; the *altar* of the Temple:—altar.

742. אֲרִידַי, **'Ărîyday,** *ar-ee-dah´-ee*; of Persian origin; *Aridai*, a son of Haman:—Aridai.

743. אֲרִידָתָא, **'Ărîydâthâ',** *ar-ee-daw-thaw´*; of Persian origin; *Aridatha*, a son of Haman:—Aridatha.

744. אַרְיֵה, **'aryêh** (Chaldee), *ar-yay´*; corresponding to 738:—lion.

745. אַרְיֵה, **'Aryêh,** *ar-yay´*; the same as 738; *lion; Arjeh*, an Israelite:—Arieh.

746. אַרְיוֹךְ, **'Aryôwk,** *ar-yoke´*; of foreign origin; *Arjok*, the name of two Babylonians:—Arioch.

747. אֲרִיסַי, **'Ărîysay,** *ar-ee-sah´-ee*; of Persian origin; *Arisai*, a son of Haman:—Arisai.

748. אָרַךְ, **'ârak,** *aw-rak´*; a primitive root; to *be* (causative *make*) *long* (literal or figurative):—defer, draw out, lengthen, (be, become, make, pro-) long, + (out-, over-) live, tarry (long).

A verb meaning to be long, prolong, draw out, or postpone. In most instances, it refers to the element of time. Most commonly, it bears the causative sense: to prolong one's days (Dt 5:16); to show continuance (Ex 20:12); tarry or stay long (Nu 9:19); to survive after (Jos 24:31); to postpone or defer anger (Isa 48:9); to draw out (1Ki 8:8). Used literally, it describes the growth of branches (Eze 31:5); and as a command, to lengthen one's cords (Isa 54:2).

749. אֲרַךְ, **'ărak** (Chaldee), *ar-ak´*; properly corresponding to 748, but used only in the sense of *reaching* to a given point; to *suit*:—be meet.

750. אָרֵךְ, **'ârêk,** *aw-rake´*; from 748; *long*:—long [-suffering, -winged], patient, slow [to anger].

An adjective meaning long, drawn out, or slow. This word primarily describes feelings pertaining to a person: either being slow of temper or patient. In wisdom literature, the person who is patient and does not anger quickly is extolled as a person of understanding (Pr 14:29; Ecc 7:8). When used to describe God, the Hebrew word means slow to anger and is immediately contrasted with God's great love, faithfulness, and power, demonstrating His true nature and His long-suffering (Ex 34:6). Also, this Hebrew word is used of an eagle's long pinions or feathers (Eze 17:3).

751. אֶרֶךְ, **'Erek,** *eh´-rek*; from 748; *length; Erek*, a place in Babylon:—Erech.

752. אָרֹךְ, **'ârôk,** *aw-roke´*; from 748; *long*:—long.

An adjective meaning long. It occurs only in the feminine singular tense and is used to modify exile (Jer 29:28); war (2Sa 3:1); and God's wisdom (Job 11:9). See the verb *'ârak* (748).

753. אֹרֶךְ, **'ôrek,** *o´-rek*; from 748; *length*:— + for ever, length, long.

A masculine noun meaning length, long. It is primarily used in describing physical measurements, for example, Noah's ark (Ge 6:15) and the land (Ge 13:17). It is also used for the qualities of patience (forbearance) in Pr 25:15 and limitless presence (forever) in Ps 23:6. In perhaps its most significant theological usage, it speaks of long life or "length of your days" (NASB), a desirable state of existence embodied in the Lord (Dt 30:20), given to those who walk in obedience (Ps 91:16; Pr 3:2) and wisdom (Pr 3:16). This kind of existence begins in the eternity of God and is granted to those He has chosen.

754. אַרְכָא, **'arkâ'** (Chaldee), *ar-kaw´*; or אַרְכָה, **'arkâh,** *ar-kaw´*; (Chaldee); from 749; *length*:—lengthening, prolonged.

An Aramaic feminine noun meaning lengthening, prolonging. It is used temporally (Da 4:27[24]; 7:12).

755. אַרְכֻבָה, **'arkubâh** (Chaldee), *ar-koo-baw´*; from an unused root corresponding to 7392 (in the sense of *bending* the knee); the *knee*:—knee.

756. אַרְכְוָי, **'Ark^evay** (Chaldee), *ar-kev-ah´ee*; patrial from 751; an *Arkevite* (collective) or native of Erek:—Archevite.

757. אַרְכִּי, **'Arkîy,** *ar-kee´*; patrial from another place (in Palestine) of similar name with 751; an *Arkite* or native of Erek:—Archi, Archite.

758. אֲרָם, **'Ărâm,** *arawm´*; from the same as 759; the *highland; Aram* or Syria, and its inhabitants; also the name of a son of Shem, a grandson of Nahor, and of an Israelite:—Aram, Mesopotamia, Syria, Syrians.

759. אַרְמוֹן, **'armôwn,** *ar-mone´*; from an unused root (meaning to *be elevated*); a *citadel* (from its *height*):—castle, palace. Compare 2038.

A masculine noun meaning fortress, citadel. Amos frequently equated God's judgment with the destruction of a fortress (Am 3:11). The word is used in parallel construction with strength (Am 3:11); siege tower (Isa 23:13); rampart (Ps 122:7; citadel, NIV; palace, NASB, NKJV, KJV); fortification (La 2:5; palace, NASB, NKJV, KJV, NIV).

760. אֲרַם צוֹבָה, **'Ăram Tsôwbâh,** *ar-am´ tso-baw´*; from 758 and 6678; *Aram of Tsoba* (or Coele-Syria):—Aram-zobah.

761. אֲרַמִּי, **'Ărammîy,** *ar-am-mee´*; patrial from 758; an *Aramite* or Aramæan:—Syrian, Aramitess.

762. אֲרָמִית, **'Ărâmîyth,** *ar-aw-meeth´*; feminine of 761; (only adverbial) *in Aramæan*:—in the Syrian language (tongue), in Syriack.

763. אֲרַם נַהֲרַיִם, **'Ăram Nahărayim,** *ar-am´ nah-har-ah´-yim*; from 758 and the dual of 5104; *Aram of* (the) *two rivers* (Euphrates and Tigris) or Mesopotamia:—Aham-naharaim, Mesopotamia.

764. אַרְמֹנִי, **'Armônîy,** *ar-mo-nee´*; from 759; *palatial; Armoni*, an Israelite:—Armoni.

765. אֲרָן, **'Ărân,** *ar-awn´*; from 7442; *stridulous; Aran*, an Edomite:—Aran.

766. אֹרֶן, **'ôren,** *o´-ren*; from the same as 765 (in the sense of *strength*); the *ash* tree (from its toughness):—ash.

767. אֹרֶן, **'Ôren,** *o´-ren*; the same as 766; *Oren*, an Israelite:—Oren.

768. אַרְנֶבֶת, **'arnebeth,** *ar-neh´-beth*; of uncertain derivation; the *hare*:—hare.

769. אַרְנוֹן, **'Arnôwn,** *ar-nohn´*; or אַרְנֹן, **'Arnôn,** *ar-nohn´*; from 7442; a *brauling* stream; the *Arnon*, a river east of the Jordan; also its territory:—Arnon.

770. אַרְנָן, **'Arnân,** *ar-nawn´*; probably from the same as 769; *noisy; Arnan*, an Israelite:—Arnan.

771. אָרְנָן, **'Ornân,** *or-nawn´*; probably from 766; *strong; Ornan*, a Jebusite:—Ornan. See 728.

772. אֲרַע, **'ăra'** (Chaldee), *ar-ah´*; corresponding to 776; the *earth*; by implication (figurative) *low*:—earth, interior.

An Aramaic, feminine noun meaning earth. Functioning as an adverb, it also carries the idea of downward, below, or toward the earth. This concept appears in Jer 10:11 in conjunction with the phrase "under the heavens" to say that the gods who did not make heaven and earth will perish. It is also used to mean the realm where humans live (Da 2:35). The word also occurs twice in Da 2:39; in the first instance, it means inferior or less than, and in the second occurrence, it means earth. See the equivalent Hebrew noun *'eres* (776).

773. אַרְעִי, **'ar'îy** (Chaldee), *arh-ee´*; feminine of 772; the *bottom*:—bottom.

774. אַרְפָּד, **'Arpâd,** *ar-pawd´*; from 7502; *spread* out; *Arpad*, a place in Syria:—Arpad, Arphad.

775. אַרְפַּכְשַׁד, **'Arpakshad,** *ar-pak-shad´*; probably of foreign origin; *Arpakshad*, a son of Noah; also the region settled by him:—Arphaxad.

776. אֶרֶץ, **'erets,** *eh´-rets*; from an unused root probably meaning to *be firm*; the *earth* (at large, or partitively a *land*):—× common, country, earth, field, ground, land, × nations, way, + wilderness, world.

A noun meaning the earth, land. It is used almost 2,500 times in the OT. It refers to the whole earth under God's dominion (Ge 1:1; 14:19; Ex 9:29; Ps 102:25[26]; Pr 8:31; Mic 4:13). Since the earth was God's possession, He promised to give the land of Canaan to Abraham's descendants (Ge 12:7; 15:7). The Promised Land was very important to Abraham's descendants and to the nation of Israel that possessed the land (Jos 1:2, 4). Israel's identity was tied to the land because it signified the fulfillment of God's promise to Abraham. If the Israelites were disobedient, however, they would be cursed by losing the land (Le 26:32–34, 36, 38, 39; Dt 28:63, 64; Jer 7:7).

777. אַרְצָא, **'artsâ',** *ar-tsaw´*; from 776; *earthiness; Artsa*, an Israelite:—Arza.

778. אֲרַק, **'âraq** (Chaldee), *ar-ak´*; by transmutation for 772; the *earth*:—earth.

An Aramaic, feminine noun meaning earth. Related to the Hebrew word *'eres* (776), it corresponds to the term planet. This Aramaic word occurs only once in the Hebrew Bible in Jer 10:11. The English word *earth* occurs twice in this verse, but it does not translate the same Aramaic word. The first is the Aramaic word being defined here; the second is the Aramaic noun *'ăra'* (772). Both of these words mean world.

779. אָרַר, **'ârar,** *aw-rar´*; a primitive root; to *execrate*:— × bitterly curse.

A verb generally denoting to inflict with a curse. There are at least five other Hebrew verbs with the same general meaning. This verb, in a more specific sense, means to bind (with a spell); to hem in with obstacles; to render powerless to resist. It is sometimes used as an antonym of *bârak* (1288). In Ge 3, God renders curses on the serpent, the woman, and the man for their sins in the Garden of Eden. To the serpent, God says, "Cursed are you more than all cattle, and more than every beast of the field" (Ge 3:14 NASB), meaning that the serpent would be the lowest of all animals. Then to the man, God says, "Cursed is the ground because of you," meaning that he would have difficulties in producing food from the soil. In Nu 22:6, King Balak of Moab asks Balaam to curse the Israelites. His desire is for the Israelites to be immobilized or rendered impotent so he can defeat them, his superior enemy.

780. אֲרָרַט, **'Ărâraṭ,** *ar-aw-rat´*; of foreign origin; *Ararat* (or rather Armenia):—Ararat, Armenia.

781. אָרַשׂ, **'âraś,** *aw-ras´*; a primitive root; to *engage* for matrimony:—betroth, espouse.

782. אֲרֶשֶׁת, **'ăresheth,** *ar-eh´-sheth*; from 781 (in the sense of *desiring* to possess); a *longing* for:—request.

783. אַרְתַּחְשַׁשְׁתָּא, **'Artachshashtâ',** *ar-takh-shash-taw´*; or אַרְתַּחְשַׁשְׂתְּא, **'Artachshasht',** *ar-takh-shasht´*; or by permutation אַרְתַּחְשַׁסְתְּא **'Artachshast',** *ar-takh-shast´*; of foreign origin; *Artachshasta* (or Artaxerxes), a title (rather than name) of several Persian kings:—Artaxerxes.

784. אֵשׁ, **'êsh,** *aysh*; a primitive word; *fire* (literal or figurative):—burning, fiery, fire, flaming, hot.

785. אֶשָּׁא, **'eshshâ'** (Chaldee), *esh-shaw´*; corresponding to 784:—flame.

786. אִשׁ, **'ish,** *eesh*; identical (in origin and formation) with 784; *entity*; used only adverbially, there *is* or *are*:—are there, none can. Compare 3426.

787. אֹשׁ, **'ôsh** (Chaldee), *ohsh*; corresponding (by transposition and abbreviation) to 803; a *foundation*:—foundation.

788. אַשְׁבֵּל, **'Ashbêl,** *ash-bale´*; probably from the same as 7640; *flowing; Ashbel*, an Israelite:—Ashbel.

789. אַשְׁבֵּלִי, **'Ashbêlîy,** *ash-bay-lee´*; patronymic from 788; an *Ashbelite* (collective) or descendants of Ashbel:—Ashbelites.

790. אֶשְׁבָּן, **'Eshbân,** *esh-bawn´*; probably from the same as 7644; *vigorous; Eshban*, an Idumæan:—Eshban.

791. אַשְׁבֵּעַ, **'Ashbêa',** *ash-bay´-ah*; from 7650; *adjurer; Asbeä*, an Israelite:—Ashbea.

792. אֶשְׁבַּעַל, **'Eshba'al,** *esh-bah´-al*; from 376 and 1168; *man of Baal; Eshbaal* (or Ishbosheth), a son of King Saul:—Eshbaal.

793. אֶשֶׁד, **'âshêd,** *awsh´-shade*; from an unused root meaning to *pour*; an *outpouring*:—stream.

794. אֲשֵׁדָה, **'ăshêdâh,** *ash-ay-daw´*; feminine of 793; a *ravine*:—springs.

795. אַשְׁדּוֹד, **'Ashdôwd,** *ash-dode´*; from 7703; *ravager; Ashdod*, a place in Palestine:—Ashdod.

796. אַשְׁדּוֹדִי, **'Ashdôwdîy,** *ash-do-dee´*; patrial from 795; an *Ashdodite* (often collective) or inhabitant of Ashdod:—Ashdodites, of Ashdod.

797. אַשְׁדּוֹדִית, **'Ashdôwdîyth,** *ash-do-deeth´*; feminine of 796; (only adverbial) *in the language of Ashdod*:—in the speech of Ashdod.

798. אַשְׁדּוֹת הַפִּסְגָּה, **'Ashdôwth hap-Pis-gâh,** *ash-doth´ hap-pis-gaw´*; from the plural of 794 and 6449 with the article interposed; *ravines of the Pisgah; Ashdoth-Pisgah*, a place east of the Jordan:—Ashdoth-pisgah.

799. אֶשְׁדָּת, **'êshdâth,** *aysh-dawth´*; from 784 and 1881; a *fire-law*:—fiery law.

800. אֶשָּׁה, **'eshshâh,** *esh-shaw´*; feminine of 784; *fire*:—fire.

801. אִשֶּׁה, **'ishsheh,** *ish-sheh´*; the same as 800, but used in a liturgical sense; properly a *burnt-offering*; but occasionally of any *sacrifice*:—(offering, sacrifice), (made) by fire.

A feminine noun meaning offering made by fire, fire offering. Its usage is highly religious and theological in a ritual context. The word describes how the various offerings were presented to the Lord; that is, they were offerings made by means of fire. This practice gave rise to referring to all the offerings the priests presented as fire offerings; hence, some consider this term a general term that applied to all the sacrifices of the Israelites (Dt 18:1; 1Sa 2:28). The fire was actually not offered. Instead, it was the means by which the various offerings were presented to God. The fire caused the offering to go up in smoke, a fact indicated by the causative form of the Hebrew verb, and that created a pleasant aroma to the Lord. The fire also purified what was offered. In this sense, the offerings could be called fire offerings or offerings made by fire. The other words for sacrifice in the OT are specific and describe a certain sacrifice, although *qorbân* (7133) is used in a general sense a few times. The word *'ishsheh* is slightly more specific.

The Levites were put in charge of all the offerings by fire to the Lord (Jos 13:14). Both animal sacrifices and nonanimal sacrifices were presented to the Lord by fire (Le 1:9; 2:10), as well as such items as the sacred bread and frankincense placed in the Holy Place (Le 24:7). These offerings by fire cover at least the burnt offering (Le 1:3–17; 6:8–13); the grain offering (Le 2:1–16; 6:14–23; 7:9, 10); the fellowship or peace offering (Le 3:9; 7:11–21, 28–34); the sin offering (Le 4:1–35; 5:1–13; 6:24–30); the guilt offering (Le 5:14–19; 7:1–10). All of these offerings were the Lord's (Nu 28:2), but the phrase "to the Lord" is explicitly stated most of the time (Ex 29:18; Le 2:11; Nu 28:13). As noted above, the offering by fire produced a pleasing or soothing aroma to the Lord as it ascended (cf. Le 1:9; Nu 15:13, 14; 29:13, 36), a phrase indicating that the Lord had accepted the sacrifice.

802. אִשָּׁה, **'ishshâh,** *ish-shaw´*; feminine of 376 or 582; irregular plural נָשִׁים, **nâshîym,** *naw-sheem´*; a *woman* (used in the same wide sense as 582):—[adulter]ess, each, every, female, × many, + none, one, + together, wife, woman. Often unexpressed in English.

A feminine noun meaning woman, wife, or female. The origin of this word has been recorded in Ge 2:23, where Adam said, "She shall be called Woman (*'ishshâh* [802]), because she was taken out of Man (*'iysh* [376]) (NASB)." While this word predominantly means woman or wife, it is further used in various ways: those able to bear children (Ge 18:11); a widow (Ru 4:5; 1Sa 27:3); an adulteress (Pr 6:26; 7:5); female children (Nu 31:18); or female animals (Ge 7:2).

803. אֲשׁיָה, **'ăshyâh,** *ash-yah´*; feminine passive participle from an unused root meaning to *found; foundation*:—foundation.

804. אַשּׁוּר, **'Ashshûwr,** *ash-shoor´*; or אַשֻּׁר, **'Ashshur,** *ash-shoor´*; apparently from 833 (in the sense of *successful*); *Ashshur*, the second son of Shem; also his descendants and the country occupied by them (i.e. Assyria), its region and its empire:—Asshur, Assur, Assyria, Assyrians. See 838.

805. אֲשׁוּרִי, **'Ăshûwrîy,** *ash-oo-ree´*; or אַשּׁוּרִי, **'Ash-shûwrîy,** *ash-shoo-ree´*; from a patrial word of the same form as 804; an

Ashurite (collective) or inhabitant of Ashur, a district in Palestine:—Asshurim, Ashurites.

806. אַשְׁחוּר, 'Ashchûwr, *ash-khoor´*; probably from 7835; *black; Ashchur*, an Israelite:—Ashur.

807. אֲשִׁימָא, 'Ăshîymâ', *ash-ee-maw´*; of foreign origin; *Ashima*, a deity of Hamath:—Ashima.

808. אָשִׁישׁ, 'âshîysh, *aw-sheesh´*; from the same as 784 (in the sense of *pressing* down firmly; compare 803); a (ruined) *foundation*:—foundation.

809. אֲשִׁישָׁה, 'ăshîyshâh, *ash-ee-shaw´*; feminine of 808; something closely *pressed* together, i.e. a *cake* of raisins or other comfits:—flagon.

810. אֶשֶׁךְ, 'eshek, *eh´-shek*; from an unused root (probably meaning to *bunch* together); a *testicle* (as a *lump*):—stone.

811. אֶשְׁכּוֹל, 'eshkôwl, *esh-kole´*; or אֶשְׁכֹּל, **'eshkôl,** *esh-kole´*; probably prolonged from 810; a *bunch of grapes* or other fruit:—cluster (of grapes).

812. אֶשְׁכֹּל, 'Eshkôl, *esh-kole´*; the same as 811; *Eshcol*, the name of an Amorite, also of a valley in Palestine:—Eshcol.

813. אַשְׁכְּנַז, 'Ashk^{e}naz, *ash-ken-az´*; of foreign origin; *Ashkenaz*, a Japhethite, also his descendants:—Ashkenaz.

814. אֶשְׁכָּר, 'eshkâr, *esh-cawr´*; for 7939; a *gratuity*:—gift, present.

815. אֵשֶׁל, 'êshel, *ay´-shel*; from a root of uncertain signification; a *tamarisk* tree; by extension a *grove* of any kind:—grove, tree.

A masculine noun meaning tamarisk tree. This tree has small leaves and survives well in the dry, hot climate of Israel. The word appears only three times in the OT: when Abraham planted a tamarisk tree near the well in Beersheba (Ge 21:33); the place where Saul and his men gathered (1Sa 22:6); and where Saul's bones were buried at Jabesh (1Sa 31:13).

816. אָשַׁם, 'âsham, *aw-sham´*; or אָשֵׁם, **'âshêm,** *aw-shame´*; a primitive root; to *be guilty*; by implication to *be punished* or *perish*:—× certainly, be (-come, made) desolate, destroy, × greatly, be (-come, found, hold) guilty, offend (acknowledge offence), trespass.

A verb meaning to be guilty or to do wrong. This word is most often used to describe the product of sin—that is, guilt before God. It may be used of individuals (Le 5:2–5; Nu 5:6, 7); congregations (Le 4:13); or nations (Eze 25:12; Hos 13:16[14:1]). Because of the close connection between guilt and sin, this word may be used as a synonym for sin (Hos 4:15; 13:1), while often the idea of punishment for a wrong done is implied (Hos 10:2; Zec 11:5). See the related nouns, *'âshâm* (817), meaning guilt, and *'ashmâh* (819), meaning guiltiness.

817. אָשָׁם, 'âshâm, *aw-shawm´*; from 816; *guilt*; by implication a *fault*; also a *sin-offering*:—guiltiness, (offering for) sin, trespass (offering).

A masculine noun used to express the concept of guilt or offence. It can connote the deeds which bring about guilt (Ps 68:21[22]). It can also express the condition of being guilty, that is, the results of the actions as shown in Ge 26:10 (NIV), "You would have brought guilt upon us." This word can also refer to the restitution that the guilty party was to make to the victim in the case of property damage (Nu 5:7). The biblical writer also uses this term to designate the guilt offering, the offering which is presented to the Lord in order to absolve the person guilty of an offence against God or man, which can be estimated and compensated (Le 5:6).

818. אָשֵׁם, 'âshêm, *aw-shame´*; from 816; *guilty*; hence *presenting a sin-offering*:—one which is faulty, guilty.

An adjective meaning guilty. This word comes from the verb *'âsham* (816), meaning to be guilty and is related to the nouns *'âshâm* (817), meaning guilt, and *'ashmâh* (819), referring to guiltiness. Thus, the adjective describes one who is in a guilty state. It describes Joseph's brothers, who declared, "Truly we are guilty concerning our brother" (Ge 42:21, NASB); David in not bringing back Absalom (2Sa 14:13); and priests who had married foreign wives (Ezr 10:19).

819. אַשְׁמָה, 'ashmâh, *ash-maw´*; feminine of 817; *guiltiness*, a *fault*, the *presentation of a sin-offering*:—offend, sin, (cause of) trespass (-ing, offering).

A feminine noun suggesting the concept of sin or guilt. It is similar in meaning to *'âshâm* (817). It can represent wrong actions (2Ch 24:18); the status of guilt which comes on a person by virtue of his or her wrong actions (Ezr 10:10); the guilt offering itself (Le 6:5[5:24]).

820. אַשְׁמָן, 'ashmân, *ash-mawn´*; probably from 8081; a *fat* field:—desolate place.

821. אַשְׁמֻרָה, 'ashmurâh, *ash-moo-raw´*; or אַשְׁמוּרָה, **'ashmûwrâh,** *ash-moo-raw´*; or אַשְׁמֹרֶת, **'ashmô-reth,** *ash-mo´-reth*; (feminine) from 8104; a night *watch*:—watch.

822. אֶשְׁנָב, 'eshnâb, *esh-nawb´*; apparently from an unused root (probably meaning to *leave interstices*); a latticed *window*:—casement, lattice.

823. אַשְׁנָה, 'Ashnâh, *ash-naw´*; probably a variation for 3466; *Ashnah*, the name of two places in Palestine:—Ashnah.

824. אֶשְׁעָן, 'Esh'ân, *esh-awn´*; from 8172; *support*; *Eshan*, a place in Palestine:—Eshean.

825. אַשָּׁף, 'ashshâph, *ash-shawf´*; from an unused root (probably meaning to *lisp*, i.e. *practise enchantment*); a *conjurer*:—astrologer.

A masculine noun meaning enchanters, conjurers of spirits, necromancers, or astrologers. Found only in the plural, this word is borrowed from the Aramaic language. It is found only in the book of Daniel in relation to wise men or diviners (Da 2:2; 5:11).

826. אַשָּׁף, 'ashshâph (Chaldee), *ash-shawf´*; corresponding to 825:—astrologer.

An Aramaic masculine noun which denotes a conjurer, enchanters, magicians. It is closely related to the Hebrew word *'ashshâph* (825). This designation, in both the Aramaic and the Hebrew forms, appears only in the book of Daniel. Since no etymology is apparent, its meaning must be determined by its context. The word always occurs in a list with one to three or four other words, whose meanings clearly refer to people with occult knowledge in the practice of divination (Da 2:10, 27; 4:7[4]; 5:7, 11, 15).

827. אַשְׁפָּה, 'ashpâh, *ash-paw´*; perhaps (feminine) from the same as 825 (in the sense of *covering*); a *quiver* or arrow case:—quiver.

828. אַשְׁפְּנַז, 'Ashp^{e}naz, *ash-pen-az´*; of foreign origin; *Ashpenaz*, a Babylonian eunuch:—Ashpenaz.

829. אֶשְׁפָּר, 'eshpâr, *esh-pawr´*; of uncertain derivation; a measured *portion*:—good piece (of flesh).

830. אַשְׁפֹּת, 'ashpôth, *ash-pohth´*; or אַשְׁפּוֹת, **'ashpôwth,** *ash-pohth´*; or (contracted) שְׁפֹת, **shephôth,** *shef-ohth´*; plural of a noun of the same form as 827, from 8192 (in the sense of *scraping*); a heap of *rubbish* or *filth*:—dung (hill).

831. אַשְׁקְלוֹן, 'Ashq^{e}lôwn, *ash-kel-one´*; probably from 8254 in the sense of *weighing*-place (i.e. *mart*); *Ashkelon*, a place in Palestine:—Ashkelon, Askalon.

832. אֶשְׁקְלוֹנִי, 'Eshq^{e}lôwnîy, *esh-kel-o-nee´*; patrial from 831; an *Ashkelonite* (collective) or inhabitant of Ashkelon:—Eshkalonites.

833. אָשַׁר, 'âshar, *aw-shar´*; or אָשֵׁר, **'âshêr,** *aw-share´*; a primitive root; to *be straight* (used in the widest sense, especially to *be level, right, happy*); (figurative) to *go forward, be honest, prosper*:—(call, be) bless (-ed, happy), go, guide, lead, relieve.

A verb meaning to go straight, to go on, to advance forward, to be called blessed, or to be made happy. Of blessing or happiness, this verb is primarily used causatively: to call one blessed (Ps 72:17); to pronounce happiness (Ge 30:13); to be made happy or blessed (Pr 3:18).

Used figuratively, it means to follow a straight path in understanding (Pr 9:6) or in one's heart (Pr 23:19). When it is used intensively, it means going straight or advancing (Pr 4:14).

834. אֲשֶׁר, 'ăsher, *ash-er´*; a primitive relative pronoun (of every gender and number); *who, which, what, that*; also (as adverb and conjunction) *when, where, how, because, in order that*, etc.:—× after, × alike, as (soon as), because, × every, for, + forasmuch, + from whence, + how (-soever), × if, (so) that ([thing] which, wherein), × though, + until, + whatsoever, when, where (+ -as, -in, -of, -on, -soever, -with), which, whilst, + whither (-soever), who (-m, -soever, -se). As it is indeclinable, it is often accompanied by the personal pronoun expletively, used to show the connection.

835. אֶשֶׁר, 'esher, *eh´-sher*; from 833; *happiness*; only in masculine plural construction as interjection, how *happy!*:—blessed, happy.

A masculine noun meaning a person's state of bliss. This Hebrew word is always used to refer to people and is never used of God. It is almost exclusively poetic and usually exclamatory, "O the bliss of . . ." In Proverbs, this blissfulness is frequently connected with wisdom (Pr 3:13; 8:32, 34). This term is also used to describe a person or nation who enjoys a relationship with God (Dt 33:29; Job 5:17; Ps 33:12; 146:5). In some contexts, the word does not seem to have any religious significance (1Ki 10:8; Pr 14:21; Ecc 10:17), and at least in one context, it has no religious significance (Ps 137:8, 9).

836. אָשֵׁר, 'Âshêr, *aw-share´*; from 833; *happy; Asher*, a son of Jacob, and the tribe descended from him, with its territory; also a place in Palestine:—Asher.

837. אֹשֶׁר, 'ôsher, *o´-sher*; from 833; *happiness*:—happy.

A masculine noun meaning happiness. The Hebrew word is found once in the Bible describing a feeling of joy (Ge 30:13).

838. אָשֻׁר, 'âshur, *aw-shoor´*; or אַשֻּׁר, **'ashshur**, *ash-shoor´*; from 833 in the sense of *going*; a *step*:—going, step.

839. אֲשֻׁר, 'ăshur, *ash-oor´*; contraction for 8391; the *cedar* tree or some other light elastic wood:—Ashurite.

840. אֲשַׂרְאֵל, 'Ăśar'êl, *as-ar-ale´*; by orthographical variation from 833 and 410; *right of God; Asarel*, an Israelite:—Asareel.

841. אֲשַׂרְאֵלָה, 'Ăśar'êlâh, *as-ar-ale´-aw*; from the same as 840; *right toward God; Asarelah*, an Israelite:—Asarelah. Compare 3480.

842. אֲשֵׁרָה, 'ăshêrâh, *ash-ay-raw´*; or אֲשֵׁירָה, **'ăshêy-râh**, *ash-ay-raw´*; from 833; *happy; Asherah* (or Astarte) a Phoenician goddess; also an *image* of the same:—grove. Compare 6253.

A feminine noun which signifies the Canaanite fertility goddess believed to be the consort of Baal. Because of this association, the worship of Baal and Asherah was often linked together (Jgs 3:7; 1Ki 18:19; 2Ki 23:4). The noun is most often used for a carved wooden image of the goddess instead of a proper name (Jgs 6:26; 1Ki 14:15). This image was frequently associated with high places and fresh (i.e. green) trees—the latter contributing to the misleading translations of the Septuagint and Vulgate that the word denoted "groves" (Dt 12:3; 1Ki 14:23; Jer 17:2). The Israelites were commanded by God to cut down and burn the images (Ex 34:13; Dt 12:3), and occasionally the Israelites took steps to eliminate them (1Ki 15:13; 2Ki 23:4, 6, 7). Nevertheless, throughout much of Israel's preexilic history, false worship was a problem, even to the extent that Asherah's image was erected in God's temple itself (2Ki 21:7; Isa 27:9).

843. אָשֵׁרִי, 'Âshêrîy, *aw-shay-ree´*; patronymic from 836; an *Asherite* (collective) or descendants of Asher:—Asherites.

844. אַשְׂרִיאֵל, 'Aśrîy'êl, *as-ree-ale´*; an orthographical variation for 840; *Asriel*, the name of two Israelites:—Ashriel, Asriel.

845. אַשְׂרִאֵלִי, 'Aśri'êlîy, *as-ree-ale-ee´*; patronymic from 844; an *Asrielite* (collective) or descendants of Asriel:—Asrielites.

846. אֻשַּׁרְנָא, 'ushsharnâ' (Chaldee), *oosh-ar-naw´*; from a root corresponding to 833; a *wall* (from its uprightness):—wall.

847. אֶשְׁתָּאֹל, 'Eshtâ'ôl, *esh-taw-ole´*; or אֶשְׁתָּאוֹל, **'Eshtâ'ôwl**, *esh-taw-ole´*; probably from 7592; *intreaty; Eshtaol*, a place in Palestine:—Eshtaol.

848. אֶשְׁתָּאֻלִי, 'Eshtâ'ulîy, *esh-taw-oo-lee´*; patrial from 847; an *Eshtaolite* (collectively) or inhabitant of Eshtaol:—Eshtaulites.

849. אֶשְׁתַּדּוּר, 'eshtaddûwr (Chaldee), *esh-tad-dure´*; from 7712 (in a bad sense); *rebellion*:—sedition.

850. אֶשְׁתּוֹן, 'Eshtôwn, *esh-tone´*; probably from the same as 7764; *restful; Eshton*, an Israelite:—Eshton.

851. אֶשְׁתְּמֹעַ, 'Eshtᵉmôaʻ, *esh-tem-o´-ah*; or אֶשְׁתְּמוֹעַ, **'Eshtemôwaʻ**, *esh-tem-o´-ah*; or אֶשְׁתְּמֹה, **'Eshtemôh**, *esh-tem-o´*; from 8085 (in the sense of *obedience*); *Eshtemoa* or *Eshtemoh*, a place in Palestine:—Eshtemoa, Eshtemoh.

852. אָת, 'âth (Chaldee), *awth*; corresponding to 226; a *portent*:—sign.

853. אֵת, 'êth, *ayth*; apparently contracted from 226 in the demonstrative sense of *entity*; properly *self* (but generally used to point out more definitely the object of a verb or preposition, *even* or *namely*):—[*as such unrepresented in English.*]

854. אֵת, 'êth, *ayth*; probably from 579; properly *nearness* (used only as a preposition or adverb), *near*; hence generally *with, by, at, among*, etc.:—against, among, before, by, for, from, in (-to), (out) of, with. Often with another preposition prefixed.

855. אֵת, 'êth, *ayth*; of uncertain derivation; a *hoe* or other digging implement:—coulter, plowshare.

856. אֶתְבַּעַל, 'Ethbaʻal, *eth-bah´-al*; from 854 and 1168; *with Baal; Ethbaal*, a Phoenician king:—Ethbaal.

857. אָתָה, 'âthâh, *aw-thaw´*; or אָתָא, **'âthâ'**, *aw-thaw´*; a primitive root [collaterally to 225 contraction]; to *arrive*:—(be-, things to) come (upon), bring.

858. אֲתָה, 'ăthâh, *ah-thaw´*; (Chaldee); or אֲתָא, **'ăthâ'**, *ah-thaw´*; corresponding to 857:—(be-) come, bring.

859. אַתָּה, 'attâh, *at-taw´*; or (shortened) אַתָּ, **'attâ**, *at-taw´*; or אַת, **'ath**, *ath*; feminine (irregular) sometimes אַתִּי, **'attîy**, *at-tee´*; plural masculine אַתֶּם, **'attem**, *at-tem´*; feminine אַתֶּן, **'atten**, *at-ten´*; or אַתֵּנָה, **'attênâh**, *at-tay´-naw*; or אַתֵּנָּה, **'attênnâh**, *at-tane´-naw*; a primitive pronoun of the secondary person; *thou* and *thee*, or (plural) *ye* and *you*:—thee, thou, ye, you.

860. אָתוֹן, 'âthôwn, *aw-thone´*; probably from the same as 386 (in the sense of *patience*); a female *ass* (from its docility):—(she) ass.

861. אַתּוּן, 'attûwn (Chaldee), *at-toon´*; probably from the corresponding to 784; probably a *fire-place*, i.e. *furnace*:—furnace.

862. אַתּוּק, 'attûwq, *at-tooke´*; or אַתִּיק, **'attîyq**, *at-teek´*; from 5423 in the sense of *decreasing*; a *ledge* or offset in a building:—gallery.

863. אִתַּי, 'Ittay, *it-tah´ee*; or אִיתַי, **'îythay**, *ee-thah´ee*; from 854; *near; Ittai* or *Ithai*, the name of a Gittite and of an Israelite:—Ithai, Ittai.

864. אֵתָם, 'Êthâm, *ay-thawm´*; of Egyptian derivation; *Etham*, a place in the Desert:—Etham.

865. אֶתְמוֹל, 'ethmôwl, *eth-mole´*; or אִתְמוֹל, **'ithmôwl**, *ith-mole´*; or אֶתְמוּל, **'ethmûwl**, *eth-mool´*; probably from 853 or 854 and 4136; *heretofore*; (definite) *yesterday*:— + before (that) time, + heretofore, of late (old), + times past, yester[day].

866. אֶתְנָה, 'ethnâh, *eth-naw´*; from 8566; a *present* (as the price of harlotry):—reward.

867. אֶתְנִי, ’Ethnîy, *eth-nee´*; perhaps from 866; munificence; Ethni, an Israelite:—Ethni.

868. אֶתְנַן, ’ethnan, *eth-nan´*; the same as 866; a *gift* (as the price of harlotry or idolatry):—hire, reward.

869. אֶתְנַן, ’Ethnan, *eth-nan´*; the same as 868 in the sense of 867; *Ethnan*, an Israelite:—Ethnan.

870. אֲתַר, ’ăthar (Chaldee), *ath-ar´*; from a root corresponding to that of 871; a *place*; (adverb) *after*:—after, place.

871. אֲתָרִים, ’Ăthârîym, *ath-aw-reem´*; plural from an unused root (probably meaning to *step*); *places; Atharim*, a place near Palestine:—spies.

872. בִּאָה, bi’âh, *bi-aw´*; from 935; an *entrance* to a building:—entry.

873. בִּאישׁ, bî’ysh, *beesh´*; (Chaldee); from 888; *wicked*:—bad.

874. בָּאַר, bâ’ar, *baw-ar´*; a primitive root; to *dig*; by analogy to *engrave*; (figurative) to *explain*:—declare, (make) plain (-ly).

875. בְּאֵר, beêr, *bĕ-ayr´*; from 874; a *pit*; especially a *well*:—pit, well.

876. בְּאֵר, Beêr, *bĕ-ayr´*; the same as 875; *Beër*, a place in the Desert, also one in Palestine:—Beer.

877. בֹּאר, bô’r, *bore*; from 874; a *cistern*:—cistern.

878. בְּאֵרָא, Beêrâ’, *bĕ-ay-raw´*; from 875; a *well; Beëra*, an Israelite:—Beera.

879. בְּאֵר אֵלִים, Beêr ’Êlîym, *bĕ-ayr´ ay-leem´*; from 875 and the plural of 410; *well of heroes; Beër-Elim*, a place in the Desert:—Beer-elim.

880. בְּאֵרָה, Beêrâh, *bĕ-ay-raw´*; the same as 878; *Beërah*, an Israelite:—Beerah.

881. בְּאֵרוֹת, Beêrôwth, *bĕ-ay-rohth´*; feminine plural of 875; *wells; Beëroth*, a place in Palestine:—Beeroth.

882. בְּאֵרִי, Beêrîy, *bĕ-ay-ree´*; from 875; *fountained; Beëri*, the name of a Hittite and of an Israelite:—Beeri.

883. בְּאֵר לַחַי רֹאִי, Beêr la-Chay Rô’îy, *bĕ-ayr´ lakh-ah´ee ro-ee´*; from 875 and 2416 (with prefix) and 7203; *well of a living* (One) *my Seer; Beër-Lachai-Roï*, a place in the Desert:—Beer-lahai-roi.

884. בְּאֵר שֶׁבַע, Beêr Sheba‘, *bĕ-ayr´ sheh´-bah*; from 875 and 7651 (in the sense of 7650); *well of an oath; Beër-Sheba*, a place in Palestine:—Beer-shebah.

885. בְּאֵרֹת בְּנֵי־יַעֲקָן, Beêrôth Benêy-Ya‘ăqan, *bĕ-ay-roth´ bĕ-nay´ yah-a-can´*; from the feminine plural of 875, and the plural contraction of 1121, and 3292; *wells of* (the) *sons of Jaakan; Beeroth-Bene-Jaakan*, a place in the Desert:—Beeroth of the children of Jaakan.

886. בְּאֵרֹתִי, Beêrôthîy, *bĕ-ay-ro-thee´*; patrial from 881; a *Beërothite* or inhabitant of Beëroth:—Beer-othite.

887. בָּאַשׁ, bâ’ash, *baw-ash´*; a primitive root; to *smell* bad; (figurative) to *be offensive* morally:—(make to) be abhorred (had in abomination, loathsome, odious), (cause a, make to) stink (-ing savour), × utterly.

A verb meaning to stink, to be offensive, to be repulsive. It denotes a bad physical smell, like the reeking odor of blood in the Nile River (Ex 7:21) or the odor of spoiled manna (Ex 16:20). In a figurative sense, it speaks of a person who becomes strongly revolting to another, a metaphorical "stench in the nostrils." Jacob worried that his sons' retributive murder of the Shechemites caused him to stink before the people of the land (Ge 34:30). The Israelites fretted that Moses' preaching caused them to be offensive to Pharaoh (Ex 5:21), thus risking their lives. The verb also negatively expresses the actions of the wicked (Pr 13:5); folly (Ecc 10:1); and the stinking of wounds resulting from God's reproof of sin (Ps 38:5[6]).

888. בְּאֵשׁ, beêsh, *bĕ-aysh´*; (Chaldee); corresponding to 887:—displease.

889. בְּאֹשׁ, beôsh, *bĕ-oshe´*; from 877; a *stench*:—stink.

890. בָּאְשָׁה, bo’shâh, *bosh-aw´*; feminine of 889; *stink-weed* or any other noxious or useless plant:—cockle.

891. בְּאֻשִׁים, beushîym, *bĕ-oo-sheem´*; plural of 889; *poison-berries*:—wild grapes.

892. בָּבָה, bâbâh, *baw-baw´*; feminine active participle of an unused root meaning to *hollow* out; something *hollowed* (as a *gate*), i.e. the *pupil* of the eye:—apple [of the eye].

893. בֵּבַי, Bêbay, *bay-bah´ee*; probably of foreign origin; *Bebai*, an Israelite:—Bebai.

894. בָּבֶל, Bâbel, *baw-bel´*; from 1101; *confusion; Babel* (i.e. Babylon), including Babylonia and the Babylonian empire:—Babel, Babylon.

895. בָּבֶל, Bâbel, *baw-bel´*; (Chaldee); corresponding to 894:—Babylon.

896. בַּבְלִי, Bablîy, *bab-lee´*; (Chaldee); patrial from 895; a *Babylonian*:—Babylonia.

897. בַּג, bag, *bag*; a Persian word; *food*:—spoil [*from the margin for* 957].

898. בָּגַד, bâgad, *baw-gad´*; a primitive root; to *cover* (with a garment); (figurative) to *act covertly*; (by implication) to *pillage*:—deal deceitfully (treacherously, unfaithfully), offend, transgress (-or), (depart), treacherous (dealer, -ly, man), unfaithful (-ly, man), × very.

A verb meaning to deal treacherously with, to be traitorous, to act unfaithfully, to betray. The verb connotes unfaithfulness in relationships like marriage (Ex 21:8; Jer 3:20; Mal 2:14); Israel's covenant with the Lord (Ps 78:57; 119:158); friendships (Job 6:15; Jer 3:20; Mal 2:10); leadership (Jgs 9:23).

899. בֶּגֶד, beged, *behg´-ed*; from 898; a *covering*, i.e. clothing; also *treachery* or *pillage*:—apparel, cloth (-es, -ing), garment, lap, rag, raiment, robe, × very [treacherously], vesture, wardrobe.

900. בֹּגְדוֹת, bôgedôwth, *bohg-ed-ōhth*; feminine plural active participle of 898; *treacheries*:—treacherous.

901. בָּגוֹד, bâgôwd, *baw-gode´*; from 898; *treacherous*:—treacherous.

902. בִּגְוַי, Bigvay, *big-vah´ee*; probably of foreign origin; *Bigvai*, an Israelite:—Bigvai.

903. בִּגְתָא, Bigthâ’, *big-thaw´*; of Persian derivation; *Bigtha*, a eunuch of Xerxes:—Bigtha.

904. בִּגְתָן, Bigthân, *big-thawn´*; or בִּגְתָנָא, **Bigthânâ’,** *big-thaw´-naw*; of similar derivation to 903; *Big-than* or *Bigthana*, a eunuch of Xerxes:—Bigthan, Bigthana.

905. בַּד, bad, *bad*; from 909; (properly) *separation*; (by implication) a *part* of the body, *branch* of a tree, *bar* for carrying; (figurative) *chief* of a city; especially (with prepositional prefix) as adverb, *apart, only, besides*:—alone, apart, bar, besides, branch, by self, of each alike, except, only, part, staff, strength.

906. בַּד, bad, *bad*; perhaps from 909 (in the sense of *divided* fibres); flaxen *thread* or yarn; hence a *linen* garment:—linen.

907. בַּד, bad, *bad*; from 908; a *brag* or *lie*; also a *liar*:—liar, lie.

908. בָּדָא, bâdâ’, *baw-daw´*; a primitive root; (figurative) to *invent*:—devise, feign.

909. בָּדַד, bâdad, *baw-dad´*; a primitive root; to *divide*, i.e. (reflexive) *be solitary*:—alone.

910. בָּדָד, bâdâd, *baw-dawd´*; from 909; *separate*; adverb *separately*:—alone, desolate, only, solitary.

911. בְּדַד, B^e^dad, *bed-ad´*; from 909; *separation; Bedad,* an Edomite:—Bedad.

912. בֵּדְיָה, Bêd^e^yâh, *bay-dĕ-yaw´*; probably shortened for 5662; *servant of Jehovah; Bedejah,* an Israelite:—Bedeiah.

913. בְּדִיל, b^e^dîyl, *bed-eel´*; from 914; *alloy* (because *removed* by smelting); (by analogy) *tin:*— + plummet, tin.

914. בָּדַל, bâdal, *baw-dal´*; a primitive root; to *divide* (in variation senses literal or figurative, *separate, distinguish, differ, select,* etc.):—(make, put) difference, divide (asunder), (make) separate (self, -ation), sever (out), × utterly.

A verb meaning to separate, to divide, to detach. This word is used most often of the various words that indicate these ideas. It is used both literally and figuratively in two different stems. The first stem is reflexive or passive in its function, and the second is causative. The reflexive sense of the word is used to express Israel's separation of themselves from intermarriage and the abominations and pollution of the nations around them (Ezr 6:21; 10:11) in order to dedicate themselves to the Lord and His Law (Ne 10:28[29]). Its passive usage indicates those being set apart for something (1Ch 23:13) or, in a negative sense, being excluded from something (e.g., from the community of Israel [Ezr 10:8]).

The verb is used most often in its active causative meanings that are the active counterparts to its passive reflexive meanings. Perhaps the most famous example of this is found in the creation story as God produces a separation between light and darkness (Ge 1:4). Just as significant is the distinction He makes between His people Israel and the peoples and nations surrounding them (Le 20:24). The fact that Moses set aside the Levites to administer and to carry out their holy duties is described by this word (Nu 8:14), as is the exclusion of a person from the Israelite community (Dt 29:21[20]). In the religious and ritualistic sphere, this word indicates a sharp division between the holy and unholy (profane) and the clean and unclean (Le 20:25). It also describes priests dividing sacrificial animals into pieces (Le 1:17).

The use of this word by the writer indicates that God desires to make discriminations between this people and the nations, among groups within His own people and within His larger creation, both animate and inanimate. These differences are important to God and are to be observed carefully, especially by His chosen nation.

915. בָּדָל, bâdâl, *baw-dawl´*; from 914; a *part:*—piece.

916. בְּדֹלַח, b^e^dôlach, *bed-o´-lakh*; probably from 914; something in *pieces,* i.e. *bdellium,* a (fragrant) gum (perhaps *amber*); others a *pearl:*—bdellium.

917. בְּדָן, B^e^dân, *bed-awn´*; probably shortened for 5658; *servile; Bedan,* the name of two Israelites:—Bedan.

918. בָּדַק, bâdaq, *baw-dak´*; a primitive root; to *gap* open; used only as a denominative from 919; to *mend* a breach:—repair.

919. בֶּדֶק, bedeq, *beh´-dek*; from 918; a *gap* or *leak* (in a building or a ship):—breach, + calker.

920. בִּדְקַר, Bidqar, *bid-car´*; probably from 1856 with prepostitional prefix; *by stabbing,* i.e. *assassin; Bidkar,* an Israelite:—Bidkar.

921. בְּדַר, b^e^dar, *bed-ar´*; (Chaldee); corresponding by transposition to 6504; to *scatter:*—scatter.

922. בֹּהוּ, bôhûw, *bo´-hoo*; from an unused root (meaning to *be empty*); a *vacuity,* i.e. (superficially) an undistinguishable *ruin:*—emptiness, void.

923. בַּהַט, bahaṭ, *bah´-hat*; from an unused root (probably meaning to *glisten*); white *marble* or perhaps *alabaster:*—red [marble].

924. בְּהִילוּ, b^e^hîylûw, *bĕ-hee-loo´*; (Chaldee); from 927; a *hurry;* only adverbial *hastily:*—in haste.

925. בָּהִיר, bâhîyr, *baw-here´*; from an unused root (meaning to *be bright*); *shining:*—bright.

926. בָּהַל, bâhal, *baw-hal´*; a primitive root; to *tremble* inwardly (or *palpitate*), i.e. (figurative) *be* (causative *make*) (suddenly) *alarmed* or *agitated*; by implication to *hasten* anxiously:—be (make) affrighted (afraid, amazed, dismayed, rash), (be, get, make) haste (-n, -y, -ily), (give) speedy (-ily), thrust out, trouble, vex.

A verb meaning to be dismayed or terrified. It is sometimes used when a sudden threat conveys great fear (Ex 15:15; 1Sa 28:21). This word can also mean hasten or to be in a hurry (2Ch 26:20; Ecc 8:3).

927. בְּהַל, b^e^hal, *bĕ-hal´*; (Chaldee); corresponding to 926; to *terrify, hasten:*—in haste, trouble.

An Aramaic verb meaning to be in a hurry; to be troubled, to be disturbed. It occurs only in the book of Daniel, where it is used of someone in a hurry (Da 2:25; 3:24; 6:19[20]) or someone who is terrified, frightened, or troubled (Da 4:5[2], 19[16]; 5:6, 9; 7:15, 28). In each of these cases, the people are terrified because of a dream or a vision from God.

928. בֶּהָלָה, behâlâh, *beh-haw-law´*; from 926; *panic, destruction:*—terror, trouble.

A feminine noun meaning dismay, sudden terror, or fright. One of the curses for not obeying the commands of the Lord is sudden terror (Le 26:16). When God makes the new heaven and earth, children will not be doomed to this terror (Isa 65:23). But the people in Jerusalem will be the object of such terror for not remaining faithful to God (Jer 15:8).

929. בְּהֵמָה, b^e^hêmâh, *bĕ-hay-maw´*; from an unused root (probably meaning to be *mute*); properly a *dumb* beast; especially any large quadruped or *animal* (often collective):—beast, cattle.

930. בְּהֵמוֹת, b^e^hêmôwth, *bĕ-hay-mōhth´*; in form a plural of 929, but really a singular of Egyptian derivation; a *water-ox,* i.e. the *hippopotamus* or Nile-horse:—Behemoth.

931. בֹּהֶן, bôhen, *bo´-hen*; from an unused root apparently meaning to *be thick*; the *thumb* of the hand or *great toe* of the foot:—thumb, great toe.

932. בֹּהַן, Bôhan, *bo´-han*; an orthographical variation of 931; *thumb; Bohan,* an Israelite:—Bohan.

933. בֹּהַק, bôhaq, *bo´-hak*; from an unused root meaning to *be pale*; white *scurf:*—freckled spot.

934. בֹּהֶרֶת, bahereth, *ba-heh´-reth*; feminine active participle of the same as 925; a *whitish* spot on the skin:—bright spot.

935. בּוֹא, bôw', *bo*; a primitive root; to *go* or *come* (in a wide variety of applications):—abide, apply, attain, × be, befall, + besiege, bring (forth, in, into, to pass), call, carry, × certainly, (cause, let, thing for) to come (against, in, out, upon, to pass), depart, × doubtless again, + eat, + employ, (cause to) enter (in, into, -tering, -trance, -try), be fallen, fetch, + follow, get, give, go (down, in, to war), grant, + have, × indeed, [in-]vade, lead, lift [up], mention, pull in, put, resort, run (down), send, set, × (well) stricken [in age], × surely, take (in), way.

936. בּוּז, bûwz, *booz*; a primitive root; to *disrespect:*—contemn, despise, × utterly.

937. בּוּז, bûwz, *booz*; from 936; *disrespect:*—contempt (-uously), despised, shamed.

938. בּוּז, Bûwz, *booz*; the same as 937; *Buz,* the name of a son of Nahor, and of an Israelite:—Buz.

939. בּוּזָה, bûwzâh, *boo-zaw´*; feminine passive participle of 936; something *scorned*; an object of *contempt:*—despised.

940. בּוּזִי, Bûwzîy, *boo-zee´*; patronymic from 938; a *Buzite* or descendant of Buz:—Buzite.

941. בּוּזִי, Bûwzîy, *boo-zee´*; the same as 940, *Buzi,* an Israelite:—Buzi.

942. בַּוַּי, **Bavvay,** *bav-vah´ee*; probably of Persian origin; *Bavvai*, an Israelite:—Bavai.

943. בּוּךְ, **bûwk,** *book*; a primitive root; to *involve* (literal or figurative):—be entangled (perplexed).

944. בּוּל, **bûwl,** *bool*; for 2981; *produce* (of the earth, etc.):—food, stock.

945. בּוּל, **Bûwl,** *bool*; the same as 944 (in the sense of *rain*); *Bul*, the eighth Hebrew month:—Bul.

946. בּוּנָה, **Bûwnâh,** *boo-naw´*; from 995; *discretion; Bunah*, an Israelite:—Bunah.

947. בּוּס, **bûws,** *boos*; a primitive root; to *trample* (literal or figurative):—loath, tread (down, under [foot]), be polluted.

A verb that signifies to tread down, to trample underfoot. This term generally has a negative connotation, implying a destructive action (Zec 10:5). God is often the subject of this verb, when He states that He will trample His enemies (Ps 60:12[14]); Isa 14:25; 63:6). It can also be used with people as the subject but with the understanding that they are only God's instruments (Ps 44:5[6]). This expression can also have a figurative meaning: to reject (Pr 27:7) and to desecrate (Isa 63:18).

948. בּוּץ, **bûwts,** *boots*; from an unused root (of the same form) meaning to *bleach*, i.e. (intransitive) *be white*; probably *cotton* (of some sort):—fine (white) linen.

949. בּוֹצֵץ, **Bôwtsêts,** *bo-tsates´*; from the same as 948; *shining; Botsets*, a rock near Michmash:—Bozez.

950. בּוּקָה, **bûwqâh,** *boo-kaw´*; feminine passive participle of an unused root (meaning to *be hollow*); *emptiness* (as adjective):—empty.

951. בּוֹקֵר, **bôwqêr,** *bo-kare´*; properly active participle from 1239 as denominative from 1241; a *cattletender*:—herdman.

952. בּוּר, **bûwr,** *boor*; a primitive root; to *bore*, i.e. (figurative) *examine*:—declare.

953. בּוֹר, **bôwr,** *bore*; from 952 (in the sense of 877); a pit *hole* (especially one used as a *cistern* or *prison*):—cistern, dungeon, fountain, pit, well.

A masculine noun meaning pit, cistern, well. The term can refer to rock-hewn reservoirs or man-made wells. When empty, such cisterns served as perfect prisons (i.e. Joseph [Ge 37:20, 22, 24, 28, 29] and Jeremiah [Jer 38:6, 7, 9–11, 13]). The semantic range extends to prisons in general. Joseph refers to Pharaoh's dungeon as *bôwr* (Ge 40:15). Figuratively, it carries positive and negative connotations. Positively, it can signify a man's wife (Pr 5:15), and Sarah is the cistern of Israel (Isa 51:1). Negatively, it represents death (Pr 28:17); Sheol (Ps 30:3[4]); exile (Zec 9:11).

954. בּוֹשׁ, **bôsh,** *bosh*; a primitive root; (properly) to *pale*, i.e. by implication to *be ashamed*; also (by implication) to *be disappointed*, or *delayed*:—(be, make, bring to, cause, put to, with, a-) shame (-d), be (put to) confounded (-fusion), become dry, delay, be long.

A verb meaning to be ashamed, to act shamefully, or to put to shame. It is both an external and a subjective experience, ranging from disgrace (Hos 10:6) to guilt (Ezr 9:6). In Ge 2:25, shame is related to the sexual nature of humans. Moreover, to act shamefully is equivalent to acting unwisely (Pr 10:5; 14:35). To be ashamed is to experience distress, as farmers with no harvest (Jer 14:4; Joel 1:11), but the blessing of God means that one will never be put to shame (Ps 25:20; Joel 2:26, 27).

955. בּוּשָׁה, **bûwshâh,** *boo-shaw´*; feminine participle passive of 954; *shame*:—shame.

A feminine noun meaning shame. Although this word is used only four times in the OT, its meaning is clear from an understanding of the verb *bôwsh* (954) meaning to be ashamed, to act shamefully, or to put to shame. This word refers to the shame that came on David during his distress (Ps 89:45[46]), as well as the shame associated with the destruction of an enemy (Mic 7:10); of Edom (Ob 1:10); and of the people in the land of Israel (Eze 7:18).

956. בִּית, **bîyth,** *beeth*; (Chaldee); apparently denominative from 1005; to *lodge* over night:—pass the night.

957. בַּז, **baz,** *baz*; from 962; *plunder*:—booty, prey, spoil (-ed).

958. בָּזָא, **bâzâ',** *baw-zaw´*; a primitive root; probably to *cleave*:—spoil.

959. בָּזָה, **bâzâh,** *baw-zaw´*; a primitive root; to *disesteem*:—despise, disdain, contemn (-ptible), + think to scorn, vile person.

960. בָּזֹה, **bâzôh,** *baw-zo´*; from 959; *scorned*:—despise.

961. בִּזָּה, **bizzâh,** *biz-zaw´*; feminine of 957; *booty*:—prey, spoil.

962. בָּזַז, **bâzaz,** *baw-zaz´*; a primitive root; to *plunder*:—catch, gather, (take) for a prey, rob (-ber), spoil, take (away, spoil), × utterly.

963. בִּזָּיוֹן, **bizzâyôwn,** *biz-zaw-yone´*; from 959:—*disesteem*:—contempt.

964. בִּזְיוֹתְיָה, **bizyôwth^e^yâh,** *biz-yo-thĕ-yaw´*; from 959 and 3050; *contempts of Jah; Bizjothjah*, a place in Palestine:—Bizjothjah.

965. בָּזָק, **bâzâq,** *baw-zawk´*; from an unused root meaning to *lighten*; a *flash* of lightning:—flash of lightning.

966. בֶּזֶק, **Bezeq,** *beh´-zek*; from 965; *lightning; Bezek*, a place in Palestine:—Bezek.

967. בָּזַר, **bâzar,** *baw-zar´*; a primitive root; to *disperse*:—scatter.

968. בִּזְּתָא, **Bizz^e^thâ',** *biz-ze-thaw´*; of Persian origin; *Biztha*, a eunuch of Xerxes:—Biztha.

969. בָּחוֹן, **bâchôwn,** *baw-khone´*; from 974; an *assayer* of metals:—tower.

970. בָּחוּר, **bâchûwr,** *baw-khoor´*; or בָּחֻר, **bâchur,** *baw-khoor´*; participle passive of 977; (properly) *selected*, i.e. a *youth* (often collective):—(choice) young (man), chosen, × hole.

971. בַּחִין, **bachîyn,** *bakh-een´*; another form of 975; a watch-*tower* of besiegers:—tower.

972. בָּחִיר, **bâchîyr,** *baw-kheer´*; from 977; *select*:—choose, chosen one, elect.

973. בָּחַל, **bâchal,** *baw-khal´*; a primitive root; to *loathe*:—abhor, get hastily [*from the margin for* 926].

A verb meaning to abhor or to obtain by greed. This word has two different, unrelated meanings. The first meaning is to abhor and comes from a Syriac word meaning to be nauseated by or to experience disgust with. It is used only in Zec 11:8 to refer to the flock who abhorred the shepherd. The second meaning, to obtain by greed, comes from an Arabic word with a similar meaning. This word only appears in Pr 20:21. However, a textual problem exists, and some people read the verse with the Hebrew word *bâhal* (926), meaning to be in haste.

974. בָּחַן, **bâchan,** *baw-khan´*; a primitive root; to *test* (especially metals); (general and figurative) to *investigate*:—examine, prove, tempt, try (trial).

A verb meaning to examine, to try, to prove. This verb can refer to any type of test. Joseph tested his brothers (Ge 42:15, 16); while Job and Elihu indicated that the ear tests words as the palate tastes food (Job 12:11; 34:3), thereby indicating that the hearer should be able to vindicate his or her assertions. However, it generally refers to God's testing of humanity. The psalmist acknowledges this fact (Ps 11:4, 5) and even requests it (Ps 139:23). The biblical writers sometimes compare God's testing to the refining of precious metals, like gold and silver (Job 23:10; Zec 13:9). There are also a few passages in which people test God, but these clearly state that this is not normal (Ps 95:9; Mal 3:10, 15).

975. בַּחַן, **bachan,** *bakh´-an*; from 974 (in the sense of keeping a *look-out*); a watch-*tower*:—tower.

976. בֹּחַן, **bôchan,** *bo´-khan*; from 974; *trial*:—tried.

A masculine noun meaning testing. This word is derived from the verb *bâhan* (974), meaning to examine, try, or prove. The idea is that the testing verifies or authenticates. In Eze 21:13[18], the strength of the sword is verified in its testing. In Isa 28:16, the stone is verified in that it has been tested and proved.

977. בָּחַר, **bâchar,** *baw-khar´*; a primitive root; properly to *try*, i.e. (by implication) *select*:—acceptable, appoint, choose (choice), excellent, join, be rather, require.

A verb whose meaning is to take a keen look at, to prove, to choose. It denotes a choice, which is based on a thorough examination of the situation and not an arbitrary whim. Although this word rarely means to prove, it does communicate that sense in Isa 48:10, where it describes the way God tested Israel in order to make a careful choice: "I have tested you in the furnace of affliction." In most contexts, the word suggests the concept to choose or to select. It can designate human choice (Ge 13:11; Dt 30:19; Jos 24:15; Jgs 10:14) or divine choice (Dt 7:7; 1Sa 2:28; Ne 9:7; Ps 135:4); however, in either case, it generally has theological overtones. This word can also have the connotations to desire, to like, or to delight in. A good example is Isa 1:29, where the word is in synonymous parallelism with *châmad* (2530), meaning to desire or take pleasure in.

978. בַּחֲרוּמִי, **Bachărûwmîy,** *bakh-ar-oo-mee´*; patrial from 980 (by transposition); a *Bacharumite* or inhabitant of Bachurim:—Baharumite.

979. בְּחֻרוֹת, **b^echurôwth,** *bekh-oo-rothe´*; or בְּחוּרוֹת, **bechûwrôwth,** *bekh-oo-roth´*; feminine plural of 970; also (masculine plural) בְּחֻרִים, **bechurîym,** *bekh-oo-reem´*; *youth* (collective and abstract):—young men, youth.

980. בַּחֻרִים, **Bachurîym,** *bakh-oo-reem´*; or בַּחוּרִים, **Bachûwrîym,** *bakh-oo-reem´*; masculine plural of 970; *young men; Bachurim*, a place in Palestine:—Bahurim.

981. בָּטָא, **bâṭâ',** *baw-taw´*; or בָּטָה, **bâṭâh,** *baw-taw´*; a primitive root; to *babble*; hence to *vociferate* angrily:—pronounce, speak (unadvisedly).

A verb meaning to speak rashly or thoughtlessly, to babble. It connotes a foolish utterance with an oath spoken thoughtlessly or flippantly (Le 5:4).

982. בָּטַח, **bâṭach,** *baw-takh´*; a primitive root; (properly) to *hie* for refuge [but not so *precipitately* as 2620]; (figurative) to *trust*, be *confident* or *sure*:—be bold (confident, secure, sure), careless (one, woman), put confidence, (make to) hope, (put, make to) trust.

A verb indicating to trust, to be confident. It expresses the feeling of safety and security that is felt when one can rely on someone or something else. It is used to show trust in God (2Ki 18:5; Ps 4:5[6]; Jer 49:11); in other people (Jgs 9:26; 20:36; Isa 36:5, 6, 9); or in things (Ps 44:6[7]; Jer 7:4; Hab 2:18). In addition, this expression can also relate to the state of being confident, secure, without fear (Jgs 18:7, 10, 27; Job 11:18; Pr 28:1).

983. בֶּטַח, **beṭach,** *beh´-takh*; from 982; (properly) a place of *refuge*; (abstract) *safety*, both the fact (*security*) and the feeling (*trust*); often (adverb with or without preposition) *safely*:—assurance, boldly, (without) care (-less), confidence, hope, safe (-ly, -ty), secure, surely.

A masculine noun or adjective meaning security. As a noun, it primarily means security or calm assurance (Ge 34:25; Isa 32:17). As an adjective, it means assurance or confidence. It is primarily a positive term: to dwell in safety because of God's protection (Le 25:18); to lie down safely or in security (Hos 2:18[20]); to walk securely or assuredly (Pr 10:9). In other instances, it is a negative term meaning to be too self-assured or careless (Eze 30:9; 39:6).

984. בֶּטַח, **Beṭach,** *beh´-takh*; the same as 983; *Betach*, a place in Syria:—Betah.

985. בִּטְחָה, **biṭchâh,** *bit-khaw´*; feminine of 984; *trust*:—confidence.

A feminine noun meaning trust, confidence. It is used only in Isa 30:15 where this trust was to characterize the people of God. Used as such, it explicates a key theme of Isaiah's theology: true belief in God should be exhibited by implicit trust (confidence) in Him (cf. Isa 26:3, 4). The people of God, even in their sinful failure, should glorify Him by quiet trust instead of reliance on self-stratagems and other powers (cf. Isa 7:4). This confident trust would bring divine strength and salvation. The failure to trust could only provoke judgment (cf. Isa 31:1). Such trust or confidence as indicative of belief is echoed throughout the OT, particularly in the Psalms.

986. בִּטָּחוֹן, **biṭṭâchôwn,** *bit-taw-khone´*; from 982; *trust*:—confidence, hope.

A masculine noun meaning trust or hope. It is used to signify Hezekiah's trust in God when Jerusalem was under siege (2Ki 18:19); or the hope that living people possess (Ecc 9:4).

987. בַּטֻּחוֹת, **baṭṭuchôwth,** *bat-too-khōth´*; feminine plural from 982; *security*:—secure.

A feminine plural noun meaning security, safety. Its only occurrence is Job 12:6.

988. בָּטַל, **bâṭal,** *baw-tal´*; a primitive root; to *desist* from labour:—cease.

989. בְּטֵל, **b^eṭêl,** *bet-ale´*; (Chaldee); corresponding to 988; to *stop*:—(cause, make to), cease, hinder.

990. בֶּטֶן, **beṭen,** *beh´-ten*; from an unused root probably meaning to *be hollow*; the *belly*, especially the *womb*; also the *bosom* or *body* of anything:—belly, body, + as they be born, + within, womb.

A feminine noun meaning belly, womb, inner body, rounded projection. With perhaps the general meaning of inside, *beṭen* often refers to the physical belly. It also frequently refers to the womb, where it is at times significantly linked with God's sovereign care, comfort, and the calling of His elect (Ps 22:9[10]; 139:13; Isa 44:2; 49:1; Jer 1:5). Defined as womb, the Hebrew word is sometimes used with the word *rechem*, also meaning womb (7358). First Kings 7:20 uses the word to refer to a rounded projection of a temple pillar. In a figurative sense, *beṭen* means the inner being of a person. Ancient wisdom literature pictured the belly, or inmost part, as the place where thoughts were treasured and the spiritual being expressed itself and was satisfied (Job 32:18; Pr 20:27).

991. בֶּטֶן, **Beṭen,** *beh´-ten*; the same as 990; *Beten*, a place in Palestine:—Beten.

992. בָּטְנָה, **boṭnâh,** *bot´-nah*; from 990; (only in plural) a *pistachio* nut (from its form):—nut.

993. בְּטֹנִים, **Beṭônîym,** *bet-o-neem´*; probably plural from 992; *hollows; Betonim*, a place in Palestine:—Betonim.

994. בִּי, **bîy,** *bee*; perhaps from 1158 (in the sense of *asking*); (properly) a *request*; used only adverbially (always with "my Lord"); *Oh that!; with leave*, or *if it please*:—alas, O, oh.

995. בִּין, **bîyn,** *bene*; a primitive root; to *separate* mentally (or *distinguish*), i.e. (general) *understand*:—attend, consider, be cunning, diligently, direct, discern, eloquent, feel, inform, instruct, have intelligence, know, look well to, mark, perceive, be prudent, regard, (can) skill (-ful), teach, think, (cause, make to, get, give, have) understand (-ing), view, (deal) wise (-ly, man).

A verb meaning to discern, to perceive, to observe, to pay attention to, to be intelligent, to be discreet, to understand; in the causative sense, to give understanding, to teach; in the reflexive sense, to consider diligently. People can perceive by means of their senses: eyes (Pr 7:7); ears (Pr 29:19); touch (Ps 58:9[10]); taste (Job 6:30). But actual discerning is not assured. Those who hear do not always understand (Da 12:8). In the final analysis, only God gives and conceals understanding (Isa 29:14).

996. בַּיִן**, bayin,** *ba-yin´*; (sometimes in the plural masculine or feminine); (properly) the constructive contraction form of an otherwise unused noun from 995; a *distinction*; but used only as a preposition, *between* (repeated before each noun, often with other particles); also as a conjunction, *either* … *or*:—among, asunder, at, between (-twixt … and), + from (the widest), × in, out of, whether (it be … or), within.

997. בֵּין**, bêyn,** *bane*; (Chaldee); corresponding to 996:—among, between.

998. בִּינָה**, bîynâh,** *bee-naw´*; from 995; *understanding*:—knowledge, meaning, × perfectly, understanding, wisdom.

A feminine noun meaning understanding, comprehension, discernment, righteous action. The word is found mainly in wisdom literature, the Psalms, in several of the major prophets, and 1 and 2 Chronicles. In nearly all the literary contexts in the Bible where it occurs with these basic meanings, it carries strong moral and religious connotations. In Job 28:28, the act of turning away from evil was said to be understanding and was based on a prior proper discernment of what was evil. A lack of this kind of understanding was morally culpable and resulted in sin and even drove away God's compassion for persons who did not have it (Isa 27:11). Happily, understanding as a moral or religious entity can be acquired (Pr 4:5, 7) and even increased (Isa 29:24) by seeking after it diligently. The understanding that God desires has a cognitive dimension, therefore, as further illustrated when the author of Proverbs spoke of words of "understanding" (Pr 1:2). The understanding and discernment that is the object of all knowing is the knowledge of the Holy One (Pr 9:10). Understanding is to mark God's people. It is not surprising, therefore, to learn that by means of understanding, God made all His created order (cf. Ps 136:5).

God has graciously endowed human beings with the ability of understanding and comprehension, but this faculty is not infallible, and, therefore, we are to ask God for guidance at all times (Pr 3:5). Our own ability of understanding should, however, function to give us discernment, for instance, in showing a proper attitude toward seeking the riches of this world (Pr 23:4). Our understanding is also the ability that enables us to understand languages (Isa 33:19), literature, visions, and dreams (Da 1:20). It is the ability that decodes the symbols of communication for us. The writer of Proverbs personifies understanding along with wisdom in the famous wisdom chapter of Proverbs (Pr 2:3; 8:14).

999. בִּינָה**, bîynâh,** *bee-naw´*; (Chaldee); corresponding to 998:—knowledge.

An Aramaic feminine noun meaning understanding. The Hebrew root for this word means to distinguish, to separate, to perceive. Therefore, this word carries the idea of discernment, as one separates the truth from lies (Da 2:21).

1000. בֵּיצָה**, bêytsâh,** *bay-tsaw´*; from the same as 948; an *egg* (from its whiteness):—egg.

1001. בִּירָה**, bîyrâh,** *bee-rah´*; (Chaldee); corresponding to 1002; a *palace*:—palace.

1002. בִּירָה**, bîyrâh,** *bee-raw´*; of foreign origin; a *castle* or *palace*:—palace.

1003. בִּירָנִיּוֹת**, bîyrânîyyoth,** *bee-raw-nee-yoth´*; from 1002; a *fortress*:—castle.

1004. בַּיִת**, bayith,** *bah´-yith*; probably from 1129 abbreviation; a *house* (in the greatest variation of applications, especially *family*, etc.):—court, daughter, door, + dungeon, family, + forth of, × great as would contain, hangings, home[born], [winter] house (-hold), inside (-ward), palace, place, + prison, + steward, + tablet, temple, web, + within (-out).

A noun meaning house, dwelling, family, temple, palace. It is used basically to denote a building in which a family lives (Dt 20:5) but can also refer to the family or household itself (Ge 15:2; Jos 7:14; 24:15). It often is used of a clan such as "house of Aaron" (Ps 115:10, 12; 118:3). Sometimes it means palace or dynasty when employed in the Hebrew phrase "house of the king" (Ge 12:15; 1Ki 4:6; Jer 39:8). When the OT speaks of the house of the Lord, it obviously refers to the Temple or tabernacle (Ex 23:19; Da 1:2). The word is also found in place names: Bethel, meaning "house of God" (Ge 12:8); Beth-shemesh, meaning "house of the sun" (Jos 15:10); and Bethlehem, meaning "house of bread" (Ge 35:19).

1005. בַּיִת**, bayith,** *bah-yith*; (Chaldee); corresponding to 1004:—house.

1006. בַּיִת**, Bayith,** *bah´-yith*; the same as 1004; *Bajith*, a place in Palestine:—Bajith.

1007. בֵּית אָוֶן**, Bêyth 'Âven,** *bayth aw´-ven*; from 1004 and 205; *house of vanity; Beth-Aven*, a place in Palestine:—Beth-aven.

1008. בֵּית־אֵל**, Bêyth-'Êl,** *bayth-ale´*; from 1004 and 410; *house of God; Beth-El*, a place in Palestine:—Beth-el.

1009. בֵּית אַרְבֵּאל**, Bêyth 'Arbê'l,** *bayth ar-bale´*; from 1004 and 695 and 410; *house of God's ambush; Beth-Arbel*, a place in Palestine:—Beth-Arbel.

1010. בֵּית בַּעַל מְעוֹן**, Bêyth Ba'al Me'ôwn,** *bayth bah´-al mĕ-own´*; from 1004 and 1168 and 4583; *house of Baal* of (the) *habitation of* [apparently by transposition]; or (shorter) בֵּית מְעוֹן, **Bêyth Me'ôwn,** *bayth mĕ-own´*; *house of habitation of* (Baal); *Beth-Baal-Meön*, a place in Palestine:—Beth-baal-meon. Compare 1136 and 1194.

1011. בֵּית בִּרְאִי**, Bêyth Bir'îy,** *bayth bir-ee´*; from 1004 and 1254; *house of a creative* one; *Beth-Biri*, a place in Palestine:—Beth-birei.

1012. בֵּית בָּרָה**, Bêyth Bârâh,** *bayth baw-raw´*; probably from 1004 and 5679; *house of* (the) *ford; Beth-Barah*, a place in Palestine:—Beth-barah.

1013. בֵּית־גָּדֵר**, Bêyth-Gâdêr,** *bayth-gaw-dare´*; from 1004 and 1447; *house of* (the) *wall; Beth-Gader*, a place in Palestine:—Beth-gader.

1014. בֵּית גָּמוּל**, Bêyth Gâmûwl,** *bayth gaw-mool´*; from 1004 and the passive participle of 1576; *house of* (the) *weaned; Beth-Gamul*, a place East of the Jordan:—Beth-gamul.

1015. בֵּית דִּבְלָתַיִם**, Bêyth Diblâthayim,** *bayth dib-law-thah´-yim*; from 1004 and the dual of 1690; *house of* (the) *two figcakes; Beth-Diblathajim*, a place East of the Jordan:—Beth-diblathaim.

1016. בֵּית־דָּגוֹן**, Bêyth-Dâgôwn,** *bayth-daw-gohn´*; from 1004 and 1712; *house of Dagon; Beth-Dagon*, the name of two places in Palestine:—Beth-dagon.

1017. בֵּית הָאֱלִי**, Bêyth hâ-'Ělîy,** *bayth haw-el-ee´*; patrial from 1008 with the article interposed; a *Beth-elite*, or inhabitant of Bethel:—Bethelite.

1018. בֵּית הָאֵצֶל**, Bêyth hâ'êtsel,** *bayth haw-ay´-tsel*; from 1004 and 681 with the article interposed; *house of the side; Beth-ha-Etsel*, a place in Palestine:—Beth-ezel.

1019. בֵּית הַגִּלְגָּל**, Bêyth hag-Gilgâl,** *bayth hag-gil-gawl´*; from 1004 and 1537 with the article interposed; *house of the Gilgal* (or *rolling*); *Beth-hag- Gilgal*, a place in Palestine:—Beth-gilgal.

1020. בֵּית הַיְשִׁימוֹת**, Bêyth ha-Yeshîymôwth,** *bayth hah-yesh-ee-mōth´*; from 1004 and the plural of 3451 with the article interposed; *house of the deserts; Beth-ha-Jeshimoth*, a town East of the Jordan:—Beth-jeshimoth.

1021. בֵּית הַכֶּרֶם**, Bêyth hak-Kerem,** *bayth hak-keh´-rem*; from 1004 and 3754 with the article interposed; *house of the vineyard; Beth-hak-Kerem*, a place in Palestine:—Beth-haccerem.

1022. בֵּית הַלַּחְמִי**, Bêyth hal-Lachmîy,** *bayth hal-lakh-mee´*; patrial from 1035 with the article inserted; a *Beth-lechemite*, or native of Bethlechem:— Bethlehemite.

1023. בֵּית הַמֶּרְחָק, **Bêyth ham-Merchâq,** *bayth ham-mer-khawk´*; from 1004 and 4801 with the article interposed; *house of the breadth; Beth-ham-Merchak,* a place in Palestine:—place that was far off.

1024. בֵּית הַמַּרְכָּבוֹת, **Bêyth ham-Markâbôwth,** *bayth ham-mar-kaw-both´*; or (shortened form) בֵּית מַרְכָּבוֹת, **Bêyth Markâbôwth,** *mar-kaw-both´*; from 1004 and the plural of 4818 (with or without the article interposed); *place of* (the) *chariots; Beth-ham-Markaboth* or *Beth-Markaboth,* a place in Palestine:—Beth-marcaboth.

1025. בֵּית הָעֵמֶק, **Bêyth hâ'Êmeq,** *bayth haw-Ay´-mek*; from 1004 and 6010 with the article interposed; *house of the valley; Beth-ha-Emek,* a place in Palestine:—Beth-emek.

1026. בֵּית הָעֲרָבָה, **Bêyth hâ-'Ărâbâh,** *bayth haw-ar-aw-baw´*; from 1004 and 6160 with the article interposed; *house of the Desert; Beth-ha-Arabah,* a place in Palestine:—Beth-arabah.

1027. בֵּית הָרָם, **Bêyth hâ-Râm,** *bayth haw-rawm´*; from 1004 and 7311 with the article interposed; *house of the height; Beth-ha-Ram,* a place East of the Jordan:—Beth-aram.

1028. בֵּית הָרָן, **Bêyth hâ-Rân,** *bayth haw-rawn´*; probably for 1027; *Beth-ha-Ran,* a place East of the Jordan:—Beth-haran.

1029. בֵּית הַשִּׁטָּה, **Bêyth hash-Shiṭṭâh,** *bayth hash-shit-taw´*; from 1004 and 7848 with the article interposed; *house of the acacia; Beth-hash-Shittah,* a place in Palestine:—Beth-shittah.

1030. בֵּית הַשִּׁמְשִׁי, **Bêyth hash-Shimshîy,** *bayth hash-shim-shee´*; patrial from 1053 with the article inserted; a *Beth-shimshite,* or inhabitant of Bethshe-mesh:—Bethshemite.

1031. בֵּית חָגְלָה, **Bêyth Choglâh,** *bayth chog-law´*; from 1004 and the same as 2295; *house of a partridge; Beth-Choglah,* a place in Palestine:—Beth-hoglah.

1032. בֵּית חוֹרוֹן, **Bêyth Chôwrôwn,** *bayth kho-rone´*; from 1004 and 2356; *house of hollowness; Beth-Choron,* the name of two adjoining places in Palestine:—Beth-horon.

1033. בֵּית כָּר, **Bêyth Kâr,** *bayth kawr*; from 1004 and 3733; *house of pasture; Beth-Car,* a place in Palestine:—Beth-car.

1034. בֵּית לְבָאוֹת, **Bêyth L^e^bâ'ôwth,** *bayth leb-aw-ōth´*; from 1004 and the plural of 3833; *house of lionesses; Beth-Lebaoth,* a place in Palestine:—Beth-lebaoth. Compare 3822.

1035. בֵּית לֶחֶם, **Bêyth Lechem,** *bayth leh´-khem*; from 1004 and 3899; *house of bread; Beth-Lechem,* a place in Palestine:—Beth-lehem.

1036. בֵּית לְעַפְרָה, **Bêyth l^e^Aphrâh,** *bayth lĕ-af-raw´*; from 1004 and the feminine of 6083 (with preposition interposed); *house to* (i.e. *of*) *dust; Beth-le-Aphrah,* a place in Palestine:—house of Aphrah.

1037. בֵּית מִלּוֹא, **Bêyth Millôw',** *bayth mil-lo*; or בֵּית מִלֹּא, **Bêyth Millô',** *bayth mil-lo´*; from 1004 and 4407; *house of* (the) *rampart; Beth-Millo,* the name of two citadels:—house of Millo.

1038. בֵּית מַעֲכָה, **Bêyth Ma'ăkâh,** *bayth mah-ak-aw´*; from 1004 and 4601; *house of Maakah; Beth-Maakah,* a place in Palestine:—Beth-maachah.

1039. בֵּית נִמְרָה, **Bêyth Nimrâh,** *bayth nim-raw´*; from 1004 and the feminine of 5246; *house of* (the) *leopard; Beth-Nimrah,* a place East of the Jordan:—Beth-nimrah. Compare 5247.

1040. בֵּית עֵדֶן, **Bêyth 'Êden,** *bayth ay´-den*; from 1004 and 5730; *house of pleasure; Beth-Eden,* a place in Syria:—Beth-eden.

1041. בֵּית עַזְמָוֶת, **Bêyth 'Azmâveth,** *bayth az-maw´-veth*; from 1004 and 5820; *house of Azmaveth,* a place in Palestine:—Beth-azmaveth. Compare 5820.

1042. בֵּית עֲנוֹת, **Bêyth 'Ănôwth,** *bayth an-ōth´*; from 1004 and a plural from 6030; *house of replies; Beth-Anoth,* a place in Palestine:—Beth-anoth.

1043. בֵּית עֲנָת, **Bêyth 'Ănâth,** *bayth an-awth´*; an orthographical variation for 1042; *Beth-Anath,* a place in Palestine:—Beth-anath.

1044. בֵּית עֵקֶד, **Bêyth 'Êqed,** *bayth ay´-ked*; from 1004 and a derivative of 6123; *house of* (the) *binding* (for sheep-shearing); *Beth-Eked,* a place in Palestine:—shearing house.

1045. בֵּית עַשְׁתָּרוֹת, **Bêyth 'Ashtârôwth,** *bayth ash-taw-rōth´*; from 1004 and 6252; *house of Ashtoreths; Beth-Ashtaroth,* a place in Palestine:—house of Ashtaroth. Compare 1203, 6252.

1046. בֵּית פֶּלֶט, **Bêyth Pelet,** *bayth peh´-let*; from 1004 and 6412; *house of escape; Beth-Palet,* a place in Palestine:—Beth-palet.

1047. בֵּית פְּעוֹר, **Bêyth P^e^'ôwr,** *bayth pĕ-ore´*; from 1004 and 6465; *house of Peor; Beth-Peor,* a place East of the Jordan:—Beth-peor.

1048. בֵּית פַּצֵּץ, **Bêyth Patstsêts,** *bayth pats-tsates´*; from 1004 and a derivative from 6327; *house of dispersion; Beth-Patstsets,* a place in Palestine:—Beth-pazzez.

1049. בֵּית צוּר, **Bêyth Tsûwr,** *bayth tsoor´*; from 1004 and 6697; *house of* (the) *rock; Beth-Tsur,* a place in Palestine:—Beth-zur.

1050. בֵּית רְחוֹב, **Bêyth R^e^chôwb,** *bayth rĕ-khobe´*; from 1004 and 7339; *house of* (the) *street; Beth-Rechob,* a place in Palestine:—Beth-rehob.

1051. בֵּית רָפָא, **Bêyth Râphâ',** *bayth raw-faw´*; from 1004 and 7497; *house of* (the) *giant; Beth-Rapha,* an Israelite:—Beth-rapha.

1052. בֵּית שְׁאָן, **Bêyth Sh^e^'ân,** *bayth shĕ-awn´*; or also בֵּית שָׁן, **Bêyth Shân,** *bayth shawn´*; from 1004 and 7599; *house of ease; Beth-Shean* or *Beth-Shan,* a place in Palestine:—Beth-shean, Beth-Shan.

1053. בֵּית שֶׁמֶשׁ, **Bêyth Shemesh,** *bayth sheh´-mesh*; from 1004 and 8121; *house of* (the) *sun; Beth-Shemesh,* a place in Palestine:—Beth-shemesh.

1054. בֵּית תַּפּוּחַ, **Bayth Tappûwach,** *bayth tap-poo´-akh*; from 1004 and 8598; *house of* (the) *apple; Beth-Tappuach,* a place in Palestine:—Beth-tappuah.

1055. בִּיתָן, **bîythân,** *bee-thawn´*; probably from 1004; a *palace* (i.e. *large house*):—palace.

1056. בָּכָא, **Bâkâ',** *baw-kaw´*; from 1058; *weeping; Baca,* a valley in Palestine:—Baca.

1057. בָּכָא, **bâkâ',** *baw-kaw´*; the same as 1056; the *weeping* tree (some gum-distilling tree, perhaps the *balsam*):—mulberry tree.

1058. בָּכָה, **bâkâh,** *baw-kaw´*; a primitive root; to *weep*; (generally) to *bemoan*:—× at all, bewail, complain, make lamentation, × more, mourn, × sore, × with tears, weep.

1059. בֶּכֶה, **bekeh,** *beh´-keh*; from 1058; a *weeping*:—× sore.

1060. בְּכוֹר, **b^e^kôwr,** *bek-ore´*; from 1069; *firstborn*; hence *chief*:—eldest (son), firstborn (-ling).

1061. בִּכּוּרִים, **bikkûwrîym,** *bik-koo-reem´*; from 1069; the *first-fruits* of the crop:—first fruit (-ripe [figurative]), hasty fruit.

1062. בְּכוֹרָה, **b^e^kôwrâh,** *bek-o-raw´*; or (shortened) בְּכֹרָה, **b^e^kôrâh,** *bek-o-raw´*; feminine of 1060; the *firstling* of man or beast; abstract *primogeniture*:—birthright, firstborn (-ling).

1063. בִּכּוּרָה, **bikkûwrâh,** *bik-koo-raw´*; feminine of 1061; (figurative) the *early*:—firstripe (fruit).

1064. בְּכוֹרַת, **B^e^kôwrath,** *bek-o-rath´*; feminine of 1062; *primogeniture; Bekorath,* an Israelite:—Bechorath.

1065. בְּכִי, **b**e**kîy,** *bek-ee´*; from 1058; a *weeping*; by analogy, a *dripping*:—overflowing, × sore, (continual) weeping, wept.

1066. בֹּכִים, **Bôkîym,** *bo-keem´*; plural active participle of 1058; (with the article) the *weepers; Bokim*, a place in Palestine:—Bochim.

1067. בְּכִירָה, **b**e**kîyrâh,** *bek-ee-raw´*; feminine from 1069; the *eldest* daughter:—firstborn.

1068. בְּכִית, **b**e**kîyth,** *bek-eeth´*; from 1058; a *weeping*:—mourning.

1069. בָּכַר, **bâkar,** *baw-kar´*; a primitive root; (properly) to *burst* the womb, i.e. (causative) *bear* or *make early fruit* (of woman or tree); also (as denominative from 1061) to *give the birthright*:—make firstborn, be firstling, bring forth first child (new fruit).

1070. בֶּכֶר, **bêker,** *bee´-ker*; from 1069 (in the sense of *youth*); a young *camel*:—dromedary.

1071. בֶּכֶר, **Beker,** *beh´-ker*; the same as 1070; *Beker*, the name of two Israelites:—Becher.

1072. בִּכְרָה, **bikrâh,** *bik-raw´*; feminine of 1070; a young *she-camel*:—dromedary. בְּכֹרָה, **b**e**kôrâh.** See 1062.

1073. בַּכֻּרָה, **bakkurâh,** *bak-koo-raw´*; by orthographical variation for 1063; a *first-ripe* fig:—first-ripe.

1074. בֹּכְרוּ, **Bôk**e**rûw,** *bo-ker-oo´*; from 1069; *first-born; Bokeru*, an Israelite:—Bocheru.

1075. בִּכְרִי, **Bikrîy,** *bik-ree´*; from 1069; *youthful; Bikri*, an Israelite:—Bichri.

1076. בַּכְרִי, **Bakrîy,** *bak-ree´*; patronymic from 1071; a *Bakrite* (collective) or descendants of Beker:—Bachrites.

1077. בַּל, **bal,** *bal*; from 1086; (properly) a *failure*; (by implication) *nothing*; usually (adverbial) *not* at all; also *lest*:—lest, neither, no, none (that …), not (any), nothing.

1078. בֵּל, **Bêl,** *bale*; by contraction for 1168; *Bel*, the Baal of the Babylonians:—Bel.

1079. בָּל, **bâl,** *bawl*; (Chaldee); from 1080; (properly) *anxiety*, i.e. (by implication) the *heart* (as its seat):—heart.

An Aramaic noun which means heart, mind. There is only one occurrence of this word in Scripture (Da 6:14[15], NKJV), where King Darius "set his heart on Daniel." The phrase expresses the concern the king had for Daniel.

1080. בְּלָא, **b**e**lâ',** *bel-aw´*; (Chaldee); corresponding to 1086 (but used only in a mental sense); to *afflict*:—wear out.

1081. בַּלְאֲדָן, **Bal'ădân,** *bal-ad-awn´*; from 1078 and 113 (contracted); *Bel* (is his) *lord; Baladan*, the name of a Babylonian prince:—Baladan.

1082. בָּלַג, **bâlag,** *baw-lag´*; a primitive root; to *break off* or *loose* (in a favourable or unfavourable sense), i.e. *desist* (from grief) or *invade* (with destruction):—comfort, (recover) strength (-en).

1083. בִּלְגָּה, **Bilgâh,** *bil-gaw´*; from 1082; *desistance; Bilgah*, the name of two Israelites:—Bilgah.

1084. בִּלְגַּי, **Bilgay,** *bil-gah´ee*; from 1082; *desistant; Bilgai*, an Israelite:—Bilgai.

1085. בִּלְדַּד, **Bildad,** *bil-dad´*; of uncertain derivation; *Bildad*, one of Job's friends:—Bildad.

1086. בָּלָה, **bâlâh,** *baw-law´*; a primitive root; to *fail*; (by implication) to *wear out, decay* (causative *consume, spend*):—consume, enjoy long, become (make, wax) old, spend, waste.

1087. בָּלֶה, **bâleh,** *baw-leh´*; from 1086; *worn out*:—old.

1088. בָּלָה, **Bâlâh,** *baw-law´*; feminine of 1087; *failure; Balah*, a place in Palestine:—Balah.

1089. בָּלַהּ, **bâlah,** *baw-lah*; a primitive root [rather by transposition for 926]; to *palpitate*; hence (causative) to *terrify*:—trouble.

1090. בִּלְהָה, **Bilhâh,** *bil-haw´*; from 1089; *timid; Bilhah*, the name of one of Jacob's concubines; also of a place in Palestine:—Bilhah.

1091. בַּלָּהָה, **ballâhâh,** *bal-law-haw´*; from 1089; *alarm*; hence *destruction*:—terror, trouble.

1092. בִּלְהָן, **Bilhân,** *bil-hawn´*; from 1089; *timid; Bilhan*, the name of an Edomite and of an Israelite:—Bilhan.

1093. בְּלוֹ, **b**e**lôw,** *bel-o´*; (Chaldee); from a root corresponding to 1086; *excise* (on articles consumed):—tribute.

1094. בְּלוֹא, **b**e**lôw',** *bel-o´*; or (fully) בְּלוֹי, **b**e**lôwy,** *bel-o´ee*; from 1086; (only in plural construct) *rags*:—old.

1095. בֵּלְטְשַׁאצַּר, **Bêlt**e**sha'tstsar,** *bale-tesh-ats-tsar´*; of foreign derivation; *Belteshatstsar*, the Babylonian name of Daniel:—Belteshazzar.

1096. בֵּלְטְשַׁאצַּר, **Bêlt**e**sha'tstsar,** *bale-tesh-ats-tsar´*; (Chaldee); corresponding to 1095:—Belteshazzar.

1097. בְּלִי, **b**e**lîy,** *bel-ee´*; from 1086; (properly) *failure*, i.e. *nothing* or *destruction*; usually (with preposition) *without, not yet, because not, as long as*, etc.:—corruption, ig[norantly], for lack of, where no … is, so that no, none, not, un[awares], without.

1098. בְּלִיל, **b**e**lîyl,** *bel-eel´*; from 1101; *mixed*, i.e. (specific) *feed* (for cattle):—corn, fodder, provender.

1099. בְּלִימָה, **b**e**lîymâh,** *bel-ee-mah´*; from 1097 and 4100; (as indefinite) *nothing whatever*:—nothing.

1100. בְּלִיַּעַל, **b**e**lîyya'al,** *bel-e-yah´-al*; from 1097 and 3276; *without profit, worthlessness*; (by extension) *destruction, wickedness* (often in connection with 376, 802, 1121, etc.):—Belial, evil, naughty, ungodly (men), wicked.

A masculine noun of unknown origin meaning worthlessness. Often a strong moral component in the context suggests the state of being good for nothing and therefore expresses the concept of wickedness (Job 34:18; Pr 6:12; Na 1:11). It is always used in reference to persons with only two exceptions, once for a disease and once for a nonspecific thing (Ps 41:8[9]; 101:3). The term is applied to the hard-hearted (Dt 15:9; 1Sa 30:22); perjurers (1Ki 21:13; Pr 19:28); and those promoting rebellion against a king's authority (2Sa 20:1; 2Ch 13:7) or God's authority (Dt 13:13[14]). This word was not treated as a proper name by the Septuagint translators of the OT, but it does appear in its Greek form as a name for the devil in the Dead Sea scrolls and in the NT (cf. 2Co 6:15).

1101. בָּלַל, **bâlal,** *baw-lal´*; a primitive root; to *overflow* (specifically with oil); (by implication) to *mix*; also (denominative from 1098) to *fodder*:—anoint, confound, × fade, mingle, mix (self), give provender, temper.

A verb meaning to mix, to mingle, to tangle, to confuse, to bewilder, to perplex, to anoint. The word is often used in a technical sense to signify the mixing of oil with the fine flour used to bake cakes without yeast that were then presented as grain offerings (Le 2:4; 14:21). Similarly, oil was mixed with fine wheat flour to bake wafers without yeast in a sacrificial setting (Ex 29:2). Sometimes oil was simply mingled with fine flour itself as part of a drink offering (Ex 29:40). While these food items readily combined with positive results, the verb can also indicate confusion, bewilderment, or perplexity. The language of the whole earth was confused by the Lord at the tower of Babel so that people could not understand each other (Ge 11:9).

Since the verb could mean to moisten or to dampen when used in the technical sacrificial examples noted above, it is a reasonable extension of that usage to the anointing of a person with oil. This usage is found (Ps 92:10[11]) where the psalmist rejoiced that he was anointed with fine oils.

The verb is used one time also to indicate the feeding of donkeys, (i.e. providing fodder for the animal to eat [Jgs 19:21]), but in this case, the verb is probably from a different original root.

1102. בָּלַם, **bâlam,** *baw-lam´*; a primitive root; to *muzzle*:—be held in.

1103. בָּלַס, **bâlas,** *baw-las´*; a primitive root; to *pinch* sycamore figs (a process necessary to ripen them):—gatherer.

1104. בָּלַע, **bâla',** *baw-lah´*; a primitive root; to *make away with* (specifically by *swallowing*); generally to *destroy*:—cover, destroy, devour, eat up, be at end, spend up, swallow down (up).

A verb meaning to swallow or engulf. The literal meaning of this word is to swallow, as a person swallows a fig (Isa 28:4) or as the great fish swallowed Jonah (Jnh 1:17[2:1]). It further describes how the earth consumed Pharaoh's army (Ex 15:12) and the rebellious Israelites (Nu 16:32); and a consuming destruction that comes on people (2Sa 17:16; Job 2:3; Ps 21:9[10]); cities (2Sa 20:19); or nations (La 2:5).

1105. בֶּלַע, **bela',** *beh´-lah*; from 1104; a *gulp*; (figurative) *destruction*:—devouring, that which he hath swallowed up.

A masculine noun meaning what is swallowed or devoured. This word is derived from the verb *bâla'* (1104), meaning to swallow or engulf. It is used only twice in the OT: In Ps 52:4[6], it speaks of "devouring words." In Jer 51:44, the word is used of the things the god Bel has swallowed. In both cases, the word connotes a destructive action.

1106. בֶּלַע, **Bela',** *beh´-lah*; the same as 1105; *Bela*, the name of a place, also an Edomite and of two Israelites:—Bela.

1107. בִּלְעֲדֵי, **bil'ădêy,** *bil-ad-ay´*; or בַּלְעֲדֵי, **bal'ă-dêy,** *bal-ad-ay´*; constructed plural from 1077 and 5703; *not till*, i.e. (as preposition or adverb) *except, without, besides*:—beside, not (in), save, without.

1108. בַּלְעִי, **Bal'îy,** *bel-ee´*; patronymic from 1106; a *Belaite* (collective) or descendants of Bela:—Belaites.

1109. בִּלְעָם, **Bil'âm,** *bil-awm´*; probably from 1077 and 5971; *not* (of the) *people*, i.e. *foreigner; Bilam*, a Mesopotamian prophet; also a place in Palestine:—Balaam, Bileam.

1110. בָּלַק, **bâlaq,** *baw-lak´*; a primitive root; to *annihilate*:—(make) waste.

1111. בָּלָק, **Bâlâq,** *baw-lawk´*; from 1110; *waster; Balak*, a Moabitish king:—Balak.

1112. בֵּלְשַׁאצַּר, **Bêlsha'tstsar,** *bale-shats-tsar´*; or בֵּלְאשַׁצַּר, **Bêl'shatsar,** *bale-shats-tsar´*; of foreign origin (compare 1095); *Belshatstsar*, a Babylonian king:—Belshazzar.

1113. בֵּלְשַׁאצַּר, **Bêlsha'tstsar,** *bale-shats-tsar´*; (Chaldee); corresponding to 1112:—Belshazzar.

1114. בִּלְשָׁן, **Bilshân,** *bil-shawn´*; of uncertain derivation; *Bilshan*, an Israelite:—Bilshan.

1115. בִּלְתִּי, **biltîy,** *bil-tee´*; constructed female of 1086 (equivalent to 1097); (properly) a *failure of*, i.e. (used only as a negative particle, usually with prepositional prefix) *not, except, without, unless, besides, because not, until*, etc.:—because un[satiable], beside, but, + continual, except, from, lest, neither, no more, none, not, nothing, save, that no, without.

1116. בָּמָה, **bâmâh,** *baw-maw´*; from an unused root (meaning to *be high*); an *elevation*:—height, high place, wave.

A feminine noun meaning high place. This word may refer to a physical high place, like a mountain (Ps 18:33[34]; Hab 3:19); or a place of worship. Although Samuel conducted sacrifices in these locations (1Sa 9:13), they were predominantly places of idol worship, which God hates (Ps 78:58). These high places became symbolic of the idolatry of the Israelites (2Ki 12:3[4]; 14:4; 15:4; Jer 19:5).

1117. בָּמָה, **Bâmâh,** *baw-maw´*; the same as 1116; *Bamah*, a place in Palestine:—Bamah. See also 1120.

1118. בִּמְהָל, **Bimhâl,** *bim-hawl´*; probably from 4107 with prepositional prefix; *with pruning; Bimhal*, an Israelite:—Bimhal.

1119. בְּמוֹ, **b^emôw,** *bem-o´*; prolonged for prepositional prefix; *in, with, by*, etc.:—for, in, into, through.

1120. בָּמוֹת, **Bâmôwth,** *baw-mōth´*; plural of 1116; *heights*; or (fully) בָּמוֹת בַּעַל, **Bâmôwth Ba'al,** *baw-mōth´ bah´-al*; from the same and 1168; *heights of Baal; Bamoth* or *Bamoth-Baal*, a place East of the Jordan:—Bamoth, Bamoth-baal.

1121. בֵּן, **bên,** *bane*; from 1129; a *son* (as a *builder* of the family name), in the widest sense (of literal and figurative relationship, including *grandson, subject, nation, quality* or *condition*, etc., [like 1, 251, etc.]):— + afflicted, age, [Ahoh-] [Ammon-] [Hachmon-] [Lev-]ite, [anoint-]ed one, appointed to, (+) arrow, [Assyr-] [Babylon-] [Egypt-] [Grec-]ian, one born, bough, branch, breed, + (young) bullock, + (young) calf, × came up in, child, colt, × common, × corn, daughter, × of first, + firstborn, foal, + very fruitful, + postage, × in, + kid, + lamb, (+) man, meet, + mighty, + nephew, old, (+) people, + rebel, + robber, × servant born, × soldier, son, + spark, + steward, + stranger, × surely, them of, + tumultuous one, + valiant[-est], whelp, worthy, young (one), youth.

A noun meaning son that occurs almost five thousand times in the OT. Although the most basic meaning and general translation is son, the direct male offspring of human parents (Ge 4:25; 27:32; Isa 49:15), it is more generally a relational term because of its variety of applications. This word can express an adopted child (Ex 2:10); children in general, male and female (Ge 3:16; 21:7; Ex 21:5); descendants, such as grandsons (Jos 22:24, 25, 27; 2Ki 10:30); relative age (Ge 5:32; 17:12; Pr 7:7; SS 2:3); the male offspring of animals (Le 22:28; Dt 22:6, 7; 1Sa 6:7, 10); a member of a guild, order, or class (1Ki 20:35; 1Ch 9:30; Ezr 4:1); a person with a certain quality or characteristic (1Sa 14:52; 2Sa 3:34; 2Ki 14:14). It may also have a gentilic sense and designate a person from a certain place (Ge 17:12; Ps 149:2; Eze 23:15, 17).

1122. בֵּן, **Bên,** *bane*; the same as 1121; *Ben*, an Israelite:—Ben.

1123. בֵּן, **bên,** *bane*; (Chaldee); corresponding to 1121:—child, son, young.

A masculine noun meaning son. This is the Aramaic equivalent of the Hebrew word *bên* (1121), meaning son. Thus, it is only used in the Aramaic sections of the OT (Ezr 4:8—6:18; 7:12–26; Da 2:4—7:28; Jer 10:11). Although it may refer to the offspring of animals (Ezr 6:9), it is used mostly of the sons of particular groups of people: of Israel (Ezr 6:16); of captives (Da 2:25; 5:13; 6:13[14]); of kings (Ezr 6:10; 7:23); of those who accused Daniel (Da 6:24[25]); of people in general (Da 2:38; 5:21).

1124. בְּנָא, **b^enâ',** *ben-aw´*; (Chaldee); or בְּנָה, **b^enâh,** *ben-aw´*; (Chaldee); corresponding to 1129; to *build*:—build, make.

1125. בֶּן־אֲבִינָדָב, **Ben-'Ăbîynâdâb,** *ben-ab-ee´-naw-dawb´*; from 1121 and 40; (the) *son of Abinadab; Ben-Abinadab*, an Israelite:—the son of Abinadab.

1126. בֶּן־אוֹנִי, **Ben-'Ôwnîy,** *ben-o-nee´*; from 1121 and 205; *son of my sorrow; Ben-Oni*, the original name of Benjamin:—Ben-oni.

1127. בֶּן־גֶּבֶר, **Ben-Geber,** *ben-gheh´-ber*; from 1121 and 1397; *son of* (the) *hero; Ben-Geber*, an Israelite:—the son of Geber.

1128. בֶּן־דֶּקֶר, **Ben-Deqer,** *ben-deh´-ker*; from 1121 and a derivative of 1856; *son of piercing* (or *of a lance*); *Ben-Deker*, an Israelite:—the son of Dekar.

1129. בָּנָה, **bânâh,** *baw-naw´*; a primitive root; to *build* (literal and figurative):—(begin to) build (-er), obtain children, make, repair, set (up), × surely.

1130. בֶּן־הֲדַד, **Ben-Hădad,** *ben-had-ad´*; from 1121 and 1908; *son of Hadad; Ben-Hadad*, the name of several Syrian kings:—Ben-hadad.

1131. בִּנּוּי**, Binnûwy,** *bin-noo´ee*; from 1129; *built* up; *Binnui*, an Israelite:—Binnui.

1132. בֶּן־זוֹחֵת**, Ben-Zôwchêth,** *ben-zo-khayth´*; from 1121 and 2105; *son of Zocheth; Ben-Zocheth*, an Israelite:—Ben-zoketh.

1133. בֶּן־חוּר**, Ben-Chûwr,** *ben-khoor´*; from 1121 and 2354; *son of Chur; Ben-Chur*, an Israelite:—the son of Hur.

1134. בֶּן־חַיִל**, Ben-Chayil,** *ben-khah´-yil*; from 1121 and 2428; *son of might; Ben-Chail*, an Israelite:—Ben-hail.

1135. בֶּן־חָנָן**, Ben-Chânân,** *ben-khaw-nawn´*; from 1121 and 2605; *son of Chanan; Ben-Chanan*, an Israelite:—Ben-hanan.

1136. בֶּן־חֶסֶד**, Ben-Chesed,** *ben-kheh´-sed*; from 1121 and 2617; *son of kindness; Ben-Chesed*, an Israelite:—the son of Hesed.

1137. בָּנִי**, Bânîy,** *baw-nee´*; from 1129; *built; Bani*, the name of five Israelites:—Bani.

1138. בֻּנִּי**, Bunnîy,** *boon-nee´*; or (fuller) בּוּנִי**, Bûw-nîy,** *boo-nee´*; from 1129; *built; Bunni* or *Buni*, an Israelite:—Bunni.

1139. בְּנֵי־בְרַק**, Bᵉnêy-Bᵉraq,** *ben-ay´-ber-ak´*; from the plural construct of 1121 and 1300; *sons of lightning, Bene-berak*, a place in Palestine:—Bene-barak.

1140. בִּנְיָה**, binyâh,** *bin-yaw´*; feminine from 1129; a *structure*:—building.

1141. בְּנָיָה**, Bᵉnâyâh,** *ben-aw-yaw´*; or (prolonged) בְּנָיָהוּ**, Bᵉnâyâhûw,** *ben-aw-yaw´-hoo*; from 1129 and 3050; *Jah has built; Benajah*, the name of twelve Israelites:—Benaiah.

1142. בְּנֵי יַעֲקָן**, Bᵉnêy Yaʻăqân,** *ben-ay´ yah-ak-awn´*; from the plural of 1121 and 3292; *sons of Yaakan; Bene-Jaakan*, a place in the Desert:—Bene-jaakan.

1143. בֵּנַיִם**, bênayim,** *bay-nah´-yim*; dual of 996; a *double interval*, i.e. the space between two armies:— + champion.

1144. בִּנְיָמִין**, Binyâmîyn,** *bin-yaw-mene´*; from 1121 and 3225; *son of* (the) *right hand; Binjamin*, youngest son of Jacob; also the tribe descended from him, and its territory:—Benjamin.

1145. בֶּן־יְמִינִי**, Ben-yᵉmîynîy,** *ben-yem-ee-nee´*; sometimes (with the article inserted) בֶּן־הַיְמִינִי**, Ben-hayyᵉmînîy,** *ben-hah-yem-ee-nee´*; with 376 inserted (1Sa 9:1) בֶּן־אִישׁ יְמִינִי**, Ben-'îysh Yᵉmîynîy,** *ben-eesh´ yem-ee-nee´*; *son of a man of Jemini*; or shortened (1Sa 9:4; Est 2:5) אִישׁ יְמִינִי **'Îysh Yᵉmîynîy,** *eesh yem-ee-nee´*; *a man of Jemini*; or (1Sa 20:1) simply יְמִינִי **Yᵉmîynîy,** *yem-ee-nee´*; *a Jeminite*; (plural בְּנֵי יְמִינִי **Bᵉnay Yᵉmîynîy,** *ben-ay´ yem-ee-nee´*;) patronymic from 1144; a *Benjaminite*, or descendant of Benjamin:—Benjamite, of Benjamin.

1146. בִּנְיָן**, binyân,** *bin-yawn´*; from 1129; an *edifice*:—building.

1147. בִּנְיָן**, binyân,** *bin-yawn´*; (Chaldee); corresponding to 1146:—building.

1148. בְּנִינוּ**, Bᵉnîynûw,** *ben-ee-noo´*; probably from 1121 with pronoun suffix; *our son; Beninu*, an Israelite:—Beninu.

1149. בְּנַס**, bᵉnas,** *ben-as´*; (Chaldee); of uncertain affinity: to *be enraged*:—be angry.

An Aramaic verb denoting to be angry. This verb is used often in the Aramaic translations but only once in the Hebrew Bible (Da 2:12), where Daniel states that Nebuchadnezzar was angry because his diviners could not reveal to him his dream and its interpretation. It is followed by the phrase *qĕtsaph* (7108) *śaggî'* (7690), meaning he was very angry.

1150. בִּנְעָא**, Binʻâ',** *bin-aw´*; or בִּנְעָה**, Binʻâh,** *bin-aw´*; of uncertain derivation; *Bina* or *Binah*, an Israelite:—Binea, Bineah.

1151. בֶּן־עַמִּי**, Ben-ʻAmmîy,** *ben-am-mee´*; from 1121 and 5971 with pronoun suffix; *son of my people; Ben-Ammi*, a son of Lot:—Ben-ammi.

1152. בְּסוֹדְיָה**, Bᵉsôwdᵉyâh,** *bes-o-deh-yaw´*; from 5475 and 3050 with prepositional prefix; *in* (the) *counsel of Jehovah; Besodejah*, an Israelite:—Besodeiah.

1153. בְּסַי**, Bêsay,** *bays-ah´-ee*; from 947; *domineering; Besai*, one of the Nethinim:—Besai.

1154. בֶּסֶר**, beser,** *beh´-ser*; from an unused root meaning to *be sour*; an *immature* grape:—unripe grape.

1155. בֹּסֶר**, bôser,** *bo´-ser*; from the same as 1154:—sour grape.

1156. בְּעָא**, bᵉʻâ',** *beh-aw´*; (Chaldee); or בְּעָה**, bᵉʻâh,** *beh-aw´*; (Chaldee); corresponding to 1158; to *seek* or *ask*:—ask, desire, make [petition], pray, request, seek.

A verb meaning to ask, seek, or request. An Aramaic word found only in Daniel, it connotes the idea to ask, request, or petition (Da 2:18). It also conveys the idea of praying to God or seeking out a person (Da 2:13); asking a person for something (Da 6:7[8]); making other inquiries (Da 7:16); or seeking out a fault (Da 6:4[5]).

1157. בְּעַד**, baʻad,** *ba-ad´*; from 5704 with prepositional prefix; *in up to* or *over against*; generally *at, beside, among, behind, for*, etc.:—about, at, by (means of), for, over, through, up (-on), within.

1158. בָּעָה**, bâʻâh,** *baw-aw*; a primitive root; to *gush* over, i.e. to *swell*; (figurative) to *desire* earnestly; (by implication) to *ask*:—cause, inquire, seek up, swell out.

A verb which means to cause to swell or boil up; to seek, to ask, to request. This verb describes a swelling of water (Isa 64:2[1]); or a rising of desire or interest (Isa 21:12). In the latter interpretation, the verb is also used in the passive form, to be searched (out), with the implication of being ransacked or plundered. This meaning is evident by the context and by the synonymous parallelism in the following verse, "But how Esau will be ransacked, his hidden treasures pillaged!" (Ob 1:6 NIV).

1159. בָּעוּ**, bâʻûw,** *baw-oo´*; (Chaldee); from 1156; a *request*:—petition.

A feminine noun meaning petition. An Aramaic term related to *beʻâ'* (1156), meaning to ask, seek, or request, this word occurs only twice in Scripture, both times in Daniel. It conveys the idea of petition (Da 6:7[8], 13[14]).

1160. בְּעוֹר**, Bᵉʻôwr,** *beh-ore´*; from 1197 (in the sense of *burning*); a *lamp; Beör*, the name of the father of an Edomitish king; also of that of Balaam:—Beor.

1161. בִּעוּתִים**, biʻûwthîym,** *be-oo-theme´*; masculine plural from 1204; *alarms*:—terrors.

1162. בֹּעַז**, Bôʻaz,** *bo´-az*; from an unused root of uncertain meaning; *Boaz*, the ancestor of David; also the name of a pillar in front of the temple:—Boaz.

1163. בָּעַט**, bâʻaṭ,** *baw-at´*; a primitive root; to *trample* down, i.e. (figurative) *despise*:—kick.

1164. בְּעִי**, bᵉʻiy,** *beh-ee´*; from 1158; a *prayer*:—grave.

A masculine noun meaning ruin (heap), against a ruin, entreaty; figuratively, a grave. In its only use in Job 30:24, it is probably best interpreted as an occurrence of the preposition *bᵉ* ("for" or "against") and *'iy* (5856, "ruin"), and should be translated as "against a ruin." However, some have interpreted this word as a derivative of *bâʻâh* (1158) and translated it as "entreaty" or "prayer," or in a derived meaning, "grave." Either translation would fit the context, for both communicate that the outstretched hand of God is present in the midst of destruction. This destroying hand has either brought a person (in this case, Job) to utter ruin or is the very thing against which there is no entreaty or prayer. Job is speaking from the shattered depths of utter personal ruin, where he perceives the hand of God as against him.

1165. בְּעִיר**, bᵉʻîyr,** *beh-ere´*; from 1197 (in the sense of *eating*); cattle:—beast, cattle.

1166. בָּעַל, bâʻal, *baw-al´*; a primitive root; to *be master*; hence (as denominative from 1167) to *marry*:—have dominion (over), be husband, marry (-ried, × wife).

A verb meaning to marry, have dominion, or to rule over. In relation to marriage, it refers to marrying a woman (Dt 24:1); or a woman to be married (Pr 30:23). Figuratively, it is used in connection with God's marriage to Israel (Jer 3:14), as well as Judah and Israel's marriage to the daughter of a foreign god (Mal 2:11). Other times, this verb means to have dominion over land (1Ch 4:22) or people (Isa 26:13). Used as a participle, it means to be married to (Ge 20:3).

1167. בַּעַל, baʻal, *bah´-al*; from 1166; a *master*; hence a *husband*, or (figurative) *owner* (often used with another noun in modifications of this latter sense):— + archer, + babbler, + bird, captain, chief man, + confederate, + have to do, + dreamer, those to whom it is due, + furious, those that are given to it, great, + hairy, he that hath it, have, + horseman, husband, lord, man, + married, master, person, + sworn, they of.

A masculine singular noun meaning lord, husband, owner, the title of a Canaanite deity (Baal). It can also denote rulers and leaders (Isa 16:8). Commonly, it refers to legally owning something such as an ox or bull (Ex 21:28); house (Ex 22:8[7]); or land (Job 31:38). The word can also describe possessing a quality, attribute, or characteristic like anger (Pr 22:24); wrath (Pr 29:22); hair (2Ki 1:8); appetite (Pr 23:2); wisdom (Ecc 7:12). When Joseph is called a dreamer, he is literally a possessor of dreams (Ge 37:19). Further, the word can connote husband as used of Abraham (Ge 20:3) and elsewhere (Ex 21:3; Dt 22:22). It often refers to the Canaanite deity, generally known as Baal in the OT and other local manifestations (Nu 25:3). Worship of this deity seems to have been common in the Northern Kingdom which is attested in the preponderance of the Baal theophoric element in many proper nouns. The Lord may also have been referred to with this generic term for "lord." But in light of the worship of Baal in the north, Hosea longed for a time when this usage would cease (Hos 2:16[18]).

1168. בַּעַל, Baʻal, *bah´-al*; the same as 1167; *Baal*, a Phoenician deity:—Baal, [*plural*] Baalim.

1169. בְּעֵל, beʻêl, *beh-ale´*; (Chaldee); corresponding to 1167:— + chancellor.

A masculine Aramaic noun meaning lord, master, overlord, owner. It is used in Ezr 4:8, 9, and 17 as an official title for Rehum, a Persian provincial officer, the "chancellor." It corresponds to the Hebrew word *baʻal* (1167), which also means lord or owner but is used with broader variations in meaning ranging from man, ruler, owner, and husband to the description of false gods.

1170. בַּעַל בְּרִית, Baʻal Berîyth, *bah´-al ber-eeth´*; from 1168 and 1285; *Baal of* (the) *covenant; Baal-Berith*, a special deity of the Shechemites:—Baal-berith.

1171. בַּעַל גָּד, Baʻal Gâd, *bah´-al gawd*; from 1168 and 1409; *Baal of Fortune; Baal-Gad*, a place in Syria:—Baal-gad.

1172. בַּעֲלָה, baʻălâh, *bah-al-aw´*; feminine of 1167; a *mistress*:—that hath, mistress.

A feminine singular noun meaning lady, owner, or possessor. It is the feminine form of *bâʻal* (1167). The word occurs three times in the Bible, and twice it refers to possessing occult abilities: possessor of ghosts (1Sa 28:7); and spells (Na 3:4).

1173. בַּעֲלָה, Baʻălâh, *bah-al-aw´*; the same as 1172; *Baalah*, the name of three places in Palestine:—Baalah.

1174. בַּעַל הָמוֹן, Baʻal Hâmôwn, *bah´-al haw-mone´*; from 1167 and 1995; *possessor of a multitude; Baal-Hamon*, a place in Palestine:—Baal-hamon.

1175. בְּעָלוֹת, Beʻâlôwth, *beh-aw-lōth´*; plural of 1172; *mistresses; Beäloth*, a place in Palestine:—Bealoth, in Aloth [*by mistake for a plural from* 5927 *with prepositional prefix*].

1176. בַּעַל זְבוּב, Baʻal Zebûwb, *bah´-al zeb-oob´*; from 1168 and 2070; *Baal of* (the) *Fly; Baal-Zebub*, a special deity of the Ekronites:—Baal-zebub.

1177. בַּעַל חָנָן, Baʻal Chânân, *bah´-al khaw-nawn´*; from 1167 and 2603; *possessor of grace; Baal-Chanan*, the name of an Edomite, also of an Israelite:—Baal-hanan.

1178. בַּעַל חָצוֹר, Baʻal Châtsôwr, *bah´-al khaw-tsore´*; from 1167 and a modification of 2691; *possessor of a village; Baal-Chatsor*, a place in Palestine:— Baal-hazor.

1179. בַּעַל חֶרְמוֹן, Baʻal Chermôwn, *bah´-al kher-mone´*; from 1167 and 2768; *possessor of Hermon; Baal-Chermon*, a place in Palestine:—Baal-hermon.

1180. בַּעֲלִי, Baʻălîy, *bah-al-ee´*; from 1167 with pronoun suffix; *my master; Baali*, a symbolical name for Jehovah:—Baali.

1181. בַּעֲלֵי בָמוֹת, Baʻălêy Bâmôwth, *bah-al-ay´ baw-mōth*; from the plural of 1168 and the plural of 1116; *Baals of* (the) *heights; Baale-Bamoth*, a place East of the Jordan:—lords of the high places.

1182. בְּעֶלְיָדָע, Beʻelyâdâʻ, *beh-el-yaw-daw´*; from 1168 and 3045; *Baal has known; Beëljada*, an Israelite:—Beeliada.

1183. בְּעַלְיָה, Beʻalyâh, *beh-al-yaw´*; from 1167 and 3050; *Jah* (is) *master; Bealjah*, an Israelite:—Bealiah.

1184. בַּעֲלֵי יְהוּדָה, Baʻălêy Yehûwdâh, *bah-al-ay´ yeh-hoo-daw´*; from the plural of 1167 and 3063; *masters of Judah; Baale-Jehudah*, a place in Palestine:—Baale of Judah.

1185. בַּעֲלִיס, Baʻălîys, *bah-al-ece´*; probably from a derivative of 5965 with prepositional prefix; *in exultation; Baalis*, an Ammonitish king:—Baalis.

1186. בַּעַל מְעוֹן, Baʻal Meʻôwn, *bah´-al meh-one´*; from 1168 and 4583; *Baal of* (the) *habitation* (of) [compare 1010]; *Baal-Meön*, a place East of the Jordan:—Baal-meon.

1187. בַּעַל פְּעוֹר, Baʻal Peʻôwr, *bah´-al peh-ore´*; from 1168 and 6465; *Baal of Peor; Baal-Peör*, a Moabitish deity:—Baal-peor.

1188. בַּעַל פְּרָצִים, Baʻal Perâtsîym, *bah´-al per-aw-tseem´*; from 1167 and the plural of 6556; *possessor of breaches; Baal-Peratsim*, a place in Palestine:—Baal-perazim.

1189. בַּעַל צְפוֹן, Baʻal Tsephôwn, *bah´-al tsef-one´*; from 1168 and 6828 (in the sense of *cold*) [according to others an Egyptian form of *Typhon*, the destroyer]; *Baal of winter; Baal-Tsephon*, a place in Egypt:—Baal-zephon.

1190. בַּעַל שָׁלִשָׁה, Baʻal Shâlishâh, *bah´-al shaw-lee-shaw´*; from 1168 and 8031; *Baal of Shalishah, Baal-Shalishah*, a place in Palestine:—Baal-shalisha.

1191. בַּעֲלָת, Baʻălâth, *bah-al-awth´*; a modification of 1172; *mistressship; Baalath*, a place in Palestine:—Baalath.

1192. בַּעֲלַת בְּאֵר, Baʻălath Beʼêr, *bah-al-ath´ beh-ayr´*; from 1172 and 875; *mistress of a well; Baalath-Beër*, a place in Palestine:—Baalath-beer.

1193. בַּעַל תָּמָר, Baʻal Tâmâr, *bah´-al taw-mawr´*; from 1167 and 8558; *possessor of* (the) *palm-tree; Baal-Tamar*, a place in Palestine:—Baal-tamar.

1194. בְּעֹן, Beʻôn, *beh-ohn´*; probably a contraction of 1010; *Beön*, a place East of the Jordan:—Beon.

1195. בַּעֲנָא, Baʻănâʼ, *bah-an-aw´*; the same as 1196; *Baana*, the name of four Israelites:—Baana, Baanah.

1196. בַּעֲנָה, Baʻănâh, *bah-an-aw´*; from a derivative of 6031 with prepositional prefix; *in affliction; Baanah*, the name of four Israelites:—Baanah.

1197. בָּעַר, bâʻar, *baw-ar´*; a primitive root; to *kindle*, i.e. *consume* (by fire or by eating); also (as denominative from 1198) to *be (-come) brutish*:—be brutish, bring (put, take) away, burn, (cause to) eat (up), feed, heat, kindle, set ([on fire]), waste.

1198. בַּעַר, **ba'ar,** *bah'-ar;* from 1197; (properly) *food* (as *consumed*); i.e. (by extension) of cattle *brutishness;* (concrete) *stupid:*—brutish (person), foolish.

1199. בַּעֲרָא, **Bâ'ărâ',** *bah-ar-aw';* from 1198; *brutish; Baara,* an Israelite woman:—Baara.

1200. בְּעֵרָה, **b**e**'êrâh,** *bĕ-ay-raw';* from 1197; a *burning:*—fire.

A feminine singular noun meaning burning. Its only occurrence is in Ex 22:6[5] where it connotes burning offerings.

1201. בַּעְשָׁא, **Ba'shâ',** *bah-shaw';* from an unused root meaning to *stink; offensiveness; Basha,* a king of Israel:—Baasha.

1202. בַּעֲשֵׂיָה, **Ba'ăsêyâh,** *bah-as-ay-yaw';* from 6213 and 3050 with prepositional prefix; *in* (the) *work of Jah; Baasejah,* an Israelite:—Baaseiah.

1203. בְּעֶשְׁתְּרָה, **B**e**'eshte**r**âh,** *beh-esh-ter-aw';* from 6251 (as singular of 6252) with prepositional prefix; *with Ashtoreth; Beështerah,* a place East of the Jordan:—Beeshterah.

1204. בָּעַת, **bâ'ath,** *baw-ath';* a primitive root; to *fear:*—affright, be (make) afraid, terrify, trouble.

A verb meaning to fear, to be or to make afraid, to startle. The basic ideas of this word can be summarized as an individual's realization that he or she is less powerful than someone or something else and can be overcome. An evil spirit tormented Saul (1Sa 16:14, 15), but God is also accused of making people afraid (Job 7:14; 9:34). It is used of humans, as when Haman was terrified (Est 7:6). This word can also mean to fall upon or to overwhelm (Job 3:5; Ps 18:4[5]).

1205. בְּעָתָה, **b**e**'âthâh,** *beh-aw-thaw';* from 1204; *fear:*—trouble.

1206. בֹּץ, **bôts,** *botse;* probably the same as 948; *mud* (as *whitish* clay):—mire.

1207. בִּצָּה, **bitstsâh,** *bits-tsaw';* intensive from 1206; a *swamp:*—fen, mire (-ry place).

1208. בָּצוּר, **bâtsûwr,** *baw-tsoor';* from 1219; *inaccessible,* i.e. *lofty:*—vintage [*by confusion with* 1210].

1209. בֵּצַי, **Bêtsay,** *bay-tsah'ee;* perhaps the same as 1153; *Betsai,* the name of two Israelites:—Bezai.

1210. בָּצִיר, **bâtsîyr,** *baw-tseer';* from 1219; *clipped,* i.e. the *grape crop:*—vintage.

1211. בָּצָל, **bâtsâl,** *baw'-tsawl;* from an unused root apparently meaning to *peel;* an *onion:*—onion.

1212. בְּצַלְאֵל, **B**e**tsal'êl,** *bets-al-ale';* probably from 6738 and 410 with prepositional prefix; *in* (the) *shadow* (i.e. protection) *of God; Betsalel;* the name of two Israelites:—Bezaleel.

1213. בַּצְלוּת, **Batslûwth,** *bats-looth';* or בַּצְלִית, **Batslîyth,** *bats-leeth';* from the same as 1211; a *peeling; Batsluth* or *Batslith;* an Israelite:—Bazlith, Bazluth.

1214. בָּצַע, **bâtsa',** *baw-tsah';* a primitive root to *break* off, i.e. (usually) *plunder;* (figurative) to *finish,* or (intrans.) *stop:*—(be) covet (-ous), cut (off), finish, fulfill, gain (greedily), get, be given to [covetousness], greedy, perform, be wounded.

A verb meaning to cut off, to gain by violence. Figuratively, it bears the sense of being destroyed or judged (Job 27:8; Isa 38:12; Jer 51:13). In some cases, it is used to express the dispensing of the Lord's judgment (Isa 10:12; La 2:17). The word also describes taking from someone out of greed (Pr 1:19; Jer 8:10; Eze 22:12).

1215. בֶּצַע, **betsa',** *beh'-tsah;* from 1214; *plunder;* (by extension) *gain* (usually unjust):—covetousness, (dishonest) gain, lucre, profit.

1216. בָּצֵק, **bâtsêq,** *baw-tsake';* a primitive root; perhaps to *swell* up, i.e. *blister:*—swell.

1217. בָּצֵק, **bâtsêq,** *baw-tsake';* from 1216; *dough* (as *swelling* by fermentation):—dough, flour.

1218. בָּצְקַת, **Botsqath,** *bots-cath';* from 1216; a *swell* of ground; *Botscath,* a place in Palestine:—Bozcath, Boskath.

1219. בָּצַר, **bâtsar,** *baw-tsar';* a primitive root; to *clip* off; specifically (as denominative from 1210) to *gather* grapes; also to *be isolated* (i.e. *inaccessible* by height or fortification):—cut off, (de-) fenced, fortify, (grape) gather (-er), mighty things, restrain, strong, wall (up), withhold.

1220. בֶּצֶר, **betser,** *beh'-tser;* from 1219; strictly a *clipping,* i.e. *gold* (as *dug* out):—gold defence.

1221. בֶּצֶר, **Betser,** *beh'-tser;* the same as 1220; an *inaccessible* spot; *Betser,* a place in Palestine; also an Israelite:—Bezer.

1222. בְּצַר, **b**e**tsar,** *bets-ar';* another form for 1220; *gold:*—gold.

1223. בָּצְרָה, **botsrâh,** *bots-raw';* feminine from 1219; an *enclosure,* i.e. *sheep-fold:*—Bozrah.

1224. בָּצְרָה, **Botsrâh,** *bots-raw';* the same as 1223; *Botsrah,* a place in Edom:—Bozrah.

1225. בִּצָּרוֹן, **bitstsârôwn,** *bits-tsaw-rone';* masculine intensive from 1219; a *fortress:*—stronghold.

1226. בַּצֹּרֶת, **batstsôreth,** *bats-tso'-reth;* feminine intensive from 1219; *restraint* (of rain), i.e. *drought:*—dearth, drought.

1227. בַּקְבּוּק, **Baqbûwq,** *bak-book';* the same as 1228; *Bakbuk,* one of the *Nethinim:*—Bakbuk.

1228. בַּקְבֻּק, **baqbuq,** *bak-book';* from 1238; a *bottle* (from the gurgling in *emptying*):—bottle, cruse.

1229. בַּקְבֻּקְיָה, **Baqbuqyâh,** *bak-book-yaw';* from 1228 and 3050; *emptying* (i.e. *wasting*) *of Jah; Bakbukjah,* an Israelite:—Bakbukiah.

1230. בַּקְבַּקַּר, **Baqbaqqar,** *bak-bak-kar';* reduplicated from 1239; *searcher; Bakbakkar,* an Israelite:—Bakbakkar.

1231. בֻּקִּי, **Buqqîy,** *book-kee';* from 1238; *wasteful; Bukki,* the name of two Israelites:—Bukki.

1232. בֻּקִּיָּה, **Buqqîyyâh,** *book-kee-yaw';* from 1238 and 3050; *wasting of Jah; Bukkijah,* an Israelite:—Bukkiah.

1233. בְּקִיעַ, **bâqîya',** *bawk-ee'-ah;* from 1234; a *fissure:*—breach, cleft.

1234. בָּקַע, **bâqa',** *baw-kah';* a primitive root; to *cleave;* (generally) to *rend, break, rip* or *open:*—make a breach, break forth (into, out, in pieces, through, up), be ready to burst, cleave (asunder), cut out, divide, hatch, rend (asunder), rip up, tear, win.

1235. בֶּקַע, **beqa',** *beh'-kah;* from 1234; a *section* (half) of a shekel, i.e. a *beka* (a weight and a coin):—bekah, half a shekel.

1236. בִּקְעָא, **biq'â',** *bik-aw';* (Chaldee); corresponding to 1237:—plain.

1237. בִּקְעָה, **biq'âh,** *bik-aw';* from 1234; (properly) a *split,* i.e. a wide level *valley* between mountains:—plain, valley.

1238. בָּקַק, **bâqaq,** *baw-kah';* a primitive root; to *pour* out, i.e. to *empty,* (figurative) to *depopulate;* (by analogy) to *spread* out (as a fruitful vine):—(make) empty (out), fail, × utterly, make void.

1239. בָּקַר, **bâqar,** *baw-kar';* a primitive root; (properly) to *plough,* or (generally) *break* forth, i.e. (figurative) to *inspect, admire, care for, consider:*—(make) inquire (-ry), (make) search, seek out.

1240. בְּקַר, **b**e**qar,** *bek-ar';* (Chaldee); corresponding to 1239:—inquire, make search.

1241. בָּקָר, **bâqâr,** *baw-kawr';* from 1239; a *beeve* or animal of the ox kind of either gender (as used for *ploughing*); (collectively) a *herd:*—beeve, bull (+ -ock), + calf, + cow, great [cattle], + heifer, herd, kine, ox.

1242. בֹּקֶר, bôqer, *bo´-ker*; from 1239; (properly) *dawn* (as the *break* of day); (generally) *morning*:—(+) day, early, morning, morrow.

1243. בַּקָּרָה, baqqârâh, *bak-kaw-raw´*; intensive from 1239; a *looking after*:—seek out.

1244. בִּקֹּרֶת, biqqôreth, *bik-ko´-reth*; from 1239; (properly) *examination*, i.e. (by implication) *punishment*:—scourged.

1245. בָּקַשׁ, bâqash, *baw-kash´*; a primitive root; to *search* out (by any method, specifically in worship or prayer); (by implication) to *strive after*:—ask, beg, beseech, desire, enquire, get, make inquisition, procure, (make) request, require, seek (for).

1246. בַּקָּשָׁה, baqqâshâh, *bak-kaw-shaw´*; from 1245; a *petition*:—request.

1247. בַּר, bar, *bar*; (Chaldee); corresponding to 1121; a *son, grandson*, etc.:—× old, son.

1248. בַּר, bar, *bar*; borrowed (as a title) from 1247; the *heir* (apparent to the throne):—son.

1249. בַּר, bar, *bar*; from 1305 (in its various senses); *beloved*; also *pure, empty*:—choice, clean, clear, pure.

An adjective meaning pure, clean, radiant. This term is extremely rare and occurs only in the poetic books. The word typically means purity or cleanness of heart (Ps 24:4; 73:1; cf. Job 11:4). This term also describes a clean feeding trough (Pr 14:4). Radiance is ascribed to both the commandments of the Lord and the Shulamite (Ps 19:8[9]; SS 6:10). The only other occurrence of this word also applies to the Shulamite and seems to indicate a select status, but this status is probably based on her purity (SS 6:9).

1250. בָּר, bâr, *bawr*; or בַּר, **bar,** *bar*; from 1305 (in the sense of *winnowing*); *grain* of any kind (even while standing in the field); (by extension) the open *country*:—corn, wheat.

1251. בַּר, bar, *bar*; (Chaldee); corresponding to 1250; a *field*:—field.

1252. בֹּר, bôr, *bore*; from 1305; *purity*:—cleanness, pureness.

A masculine noun indicating cleanness, purity. The connotation is a cleanness or pureness in the spiritual sense rather than the physical. Note the synonymous parallelism between this Hebrew word and *tsedeq* (6664), which means righteousness as the basis for divine reward or recompense (2Sa 22:21, 25; Ps 18:20[21], 24[25]). It occurs only once by itself (2Sa 22:25). It usually occurs with *yâd* (3027), meaning hand (2Sa 22:21; Ps 18:20[21], 24[25]), or *kaph* (3709), meaning palm (Job 9:30; 22:30).

1253. בֹּר, bôr, *bore*; the same as 1252; vegetable *lye* (from its *cleansing*); used as a *soap* for washing, or a *flux* for metals:—× never so, purely.

1254. בָּרָא, bârâ', *baw-raw´*; a primitive root; (absolute) to *create*; (qualified) to *cut* down (a wood), *select, feed* (as formative processes):—choose, create (creator), cut down, dispatch, do, make (fat).

A verb meaning to create. Only God is the subject of this verb. It is used for His creating: heaven and earth (Ge 1:1); humanity (Ge 1:27); the heavenly host (Isa 40:26); the ends of the earth (40:28); north and south (Ps 89:12[13]); righteousness; salvation (Isa 45:8); evil (Isa 45:7). David asked God to "create" in him a clean heart (Ps 51:10[12]). Isaiah promised that God will create a new heaven and earth (Isa 65:17).

There are other roots that are spelled the same, but have different meanings. These include: to make fat (1Sa 2:29); to clear timber (Jos 17:15, 18; Eze 23:47); and to choose (Eze 21:19[24], KJV).

1255. בְּרֹאדַךְ בַּלְאֲדָן, B^erô'dak Bal'ădân, *ber-o-dak´ bal-ad-awn´*; a variation of 4757; *Berodak-Baladan*, a Babylonian king:—Berodach-baladan.

1256. בְּרָאיָה, B^erâ'yâh, *ber-aw-yaw´*; from 1254 and 3050; *Jah has created; Berajah*, an Israelite:—Beraiah.

1257. בַּרְבֻּר, barbur, *bar-boor´*; by reduplication from 1250; a *fowl* (as fattened on *grain*):—fowl.

1258. בָּרַד, bârad, *baw-rad*; a primitive root, to *hail*:—hail.

1259. בָּרָד, bârâd, *baw-rawd´*; from 1258; *hail*:—hail ([stones]).

1260. בֶּרֶד, Bered, *beh´-red*; from 1258; *hail; Bered*, the name of a place south of Palestine, also of an Israelite:—Bered.

1261. בָּרֹד, bârôd, *baw-rode´*; from 1258; *spotted* (as if with *hail*):—grisled.

1262. בָּרָה, bârâh, *baw-raw´*; a primitive root; to *select*; also (as denominative from 1250) to *feed*; also (as equivalent to 1305) to *render clear* (Ecc 3:18):—choose, (cause to) eat, manifest, (give) meat.

1263. בָּרוּךְ, Bârûwk, *baw-rook´*; passive participle from 1288; *blessed; Baruk*, the name of three Israelites:—Baruch.

1264. בְּרֹמִים, b^erômîym, *ber-om-eem´*; probably of foreign origin; *damask* (stuff of variegated thread):—rich apparel.

1265. בְּרוֹשׁ, b^erôwsh, *ber-ōsh´*; of uncertain derivation; a *cypress* (?) tree; hence a *lance* or a *musical* instrument (as made of that wood):—fir (tree).

1266. בְּרוֹת, b^erôwth, *ber-ōth´*; a variation of 1265; the *cypress* (or some elastic tree):—fir.

1267. בָּרוּת, bârûwth, *baw-rooth´*; from 1262; *food*:—meat.

1268. בֵּרוֹתָה, Bêrôwthâh, *bay-ro-thaw´*; or בֵּרֹתַי, **Bêrôthay,** *bay-ro-thah´ee*; probably from 1266; *cypress* or *cypresslike; Berothah* or *Berothai*, a place north of Palestine:—Berothah, Berothai.

1269. בִּרְזָוִת, Birzâvith, *beer-zaw-vith´*; probably feminine plural from an unused root (apparently meaning to *pierce*); *holes; Birzoth*, an Israelite:—Birzavith [*from the margin*].

1270. בַּרְזֶל, barzel, *bar-zel´*; perhaps from the root of 1269; *iron* (as *cutting*); (by extension) an iron *implement*:—(ax) head, iron.

1271. בַּרְזִלַּי, Barzillay, *bar-zil-lah´ee*; from 1270; *iron* hearted; *Barzillai*, the name of three Israelites:—Barzillai.

1272. בָּרַח, bârach, *baw-rakh´*; a primitive root; to *bolt*, i.e. (figurative) to *flee* suddenly:—chase (away); drive away, fain, flee (away), put to flight, make haste, reach, run away, shoot.

1273. בַּרְחֻמִי, Barchumîy, *bar-khoo-mee´*; by transposition for 978; a *Barchumite*, or native of *Bachu-rim*:—Barhumite.

1274. בְּרִי, b^erîy, *ber-ee´*; from 1262; *fat*:—fat.

1275. בֵּרִי, Bêrîy, *bay-ree´*; probably by contraction from 882; *Beri*, an Israelite:—Beri.

1276. בֵּרִי, Bêrîy, *bay-ree´*; of uncertain derivation; (only in the plural and with the article) the *Berites*, a place in Palestine:—Berites.

1277. בָּרִיא, bârîy', *baw-ree´*; from 1254 (in the sense of 1262); *fatted* or *plump*:—fat ([fleshed], -ter), fed, firm, plenteous, rank.

1278. בְּרִיאָה, b^erîy'âh, *ber-ee-aw´*; feminine from 1254; a *creation*, i.e. a *novelty*:—new thing.

1279. בִּרְיָה, biryâh, *beer-yaw´*; feminine from 1262; *food*:—meat.

1280. בְּרִיחַ, b^erîyach, *ber-ee´-akh*; from 1272; a *bolt*:—bar, fugitive.

1281. בָּרִיחַ, bârîyach, *baw-ree´-akh*; or (shortened) בָּרִחַ, **bâriach,** *baw-ree´-akh*; from 1272; a *fugitive*, i.e. the *serpent* (as *fleeing*), and the constellation by that name:—crooked, noble, piercing.

1282. בָּרִיחַ, Bârîyach, *baw-ree´-akh*; the same as 1281; *Bariach*, an Israelite:—Bariah.

1283. בְּרִיעָה, **Beriy'âh**, *ber-ee'-aw*; apparently from the feminine of 7451 with prepositional prefix; *in trouble; Beriah*, the name of four Israelites:—Beriah.

1284. בְּרִיעִי, **Beriy'iy**, *ber-ee-ee'*; patronymic from 1283; a *Beriite* (collective) or descendants of Beriah:—Beerites.

1285. בְּרִית, **beriyth**, *ber-eeth'*; from 1262 (in the sense of *cutting* [like 1254]); a *compact* (because made by passing between *pieces* of flesh):—confederacy, [con-]feder[-ate], covenant, league.

A feminine noun meaning covenant, treaty, alliance, agreement. The word is used many times in the OT. Its basic uses are outlined here. It describes covenants, or agreements between and among human beings: between Abraham and the Amorites, Abraham and the Philistines, Jacob and Laban, etc. (Ge 14:13; 21:27, 32; 31:44). The nations were said to have made a covenant against Israel (Ps 83:5[6]). It is used figuratively to depict a covenant with death (Isa 28:15, 18) or with the stones of the field (Job 5:23).

It denotes an alliance, ordinance, or agreement between persons. References to covenants between people included Abraham's military treaty with the Ammorites (Ge 14:13); Jonathan and David's pledge of friendship (1Sa 18:3); David's covenant with Abner (2Sa 3:12); the covenant of marriage (Pr 2:17). The word *bĕriyth* is often preceded by the verb *karath* to express the technical idea of "cutting a covenant."

This word is used to describe God's making a covenant with humankind. It may be an alliance of friendship (Ps 25:14). The covenants made between God and humans defined the basis of God's character in the OT. They showed the strength of His divine promise from Adam all the way through to the exile and restoration. It is employed many times: God's covenant with Noah (Ge 9:11–13, 15–17; Isa 54:10) in the form of a promise; with Abraham, Isaac, and Jacob (Ge 15:18; 17:2, 4, 7, 9–11, 13, 14, 19, 21; Ex 2:24; Le 26:42) to increase their descendants, giving them Canaan and making them a blessing to the nations; with all Israel and Moses at Sinai (Ex 19:5; 24:7, 8; 34:10; Dt 29:1 [28:69]) with the stipulations of the Ten Commandments, including the guiding cases in the Book of the Covenant. The words of this covenant (*dibrêy habbĕriyth*) were kept in the ark in the Holy of Holies (Ex 34:28; 40:20). A covenant with Phinehas established an everlasting priesthood in Israel (Nu 25:12, 13). It is used to refer to the covenant established with David and his house (Ps 89:3[4], 28[29]; Jer 33:21), an eternal covenant establishing David and his descendants as the inheritors of an everlasting kingdom. Jeremiah refers to a new covenant (Jer 31:31) that God will establish in the future. The concept is personified in a person, a Servant who becomes the covenant of the people (Isa 42:6; 49:8).

In addition to the verb *kârath* mentioned above, the verb *qûm* is employed with *bĕriyth* meaning to establish a covenant (Ge 6:18; 9:9; Ex 6:4) or to confirm a covenant (Le 26:9; Dt 8:18). The word is used with *nâthan,* to give, meaning to give or make a covenant (Ge 17:2; Nu 25:12). Five other verbs are used in this way less often (Dt 29:12[11]; 2Sa 23:5; 2Ch 15:12; Ps 50:16; 111:9; Eze 16:8). A covenant could be transgressed or violated (Dt 17:2; Jgs 2:20), but the Lord never broke His covenants; He always remembered a covenant (Ge 9:15, 16; Ex 2:24; 6:5; Le 26:42).

1286. בְּרִית, **Beriyth**, *ber-eeth'*; the same as 1285; *Berith*, a Shechemitish deity:—Berith.

1287. בֹּרִית, **bôriyth**, *bo-reeth'*; feminine of 1253; vegetable *alkali*:—soap.

1288. בָּרַךְ, **bârak**, *baw-rak'*; a primitive root; to *kneel*; (by implication) to *bless* God (as an act of adoration), and (vice-versa) man (as a benefit); also (by euphemism) to *curse* (God or the king, as treason):— × abundantly, × altogether, × at all, blaspheme, bless, congratulate, curse, × greatly, × indeed, kneel (down), praise, salute, × still, thank.

A verb meaning to bless, kneel, salute, or greet. The verb derives from the noun knee and perhaps suggests the bending of the knee in blessing. Its derived meaning is to bless someone or something. The verb is used when blessing God (Ge 9:26) or people (Nu 24:9). God used this verb when He blessed Abraham in the Abrahamic covenant (Ge 12:3). The word is used intensively when God blesses people or people bless each other (Jos 17:14). When the word is used reflexively, it describes a person blessing or congratulating himself (Dt 29:19 [20]). Other meanings are to bend the knee (2Ch 6:13); and to greet someone with a salutation or friendliness (1Sa 25:14).

1289. בְּרַךְ, **berak**, *ber-ak'*; (Chaldee); corresponding to 1288:—bless, kneel.

1290. בֶּרֶךְ, **berek**, *beh'-rek*; from 1288; a *knee*:—knee.

1291. בְּרֵךְ, **berêk**, *beh'-rake*; (Chaldee); corresponding to 1290:—knee.

1292. בָּרַכְאֵל, **Barak'êl**, *baw-rak-ale'*; from 1288 and 410, *God has blessed; Barakel*, the father of one of Job's friends:—Barachel.

1293. בְּרָכָה, **Berâkâh**, *ber-aw-kaw'*; from 1288; *benediction*; (by implication) *prosperity*:—blessing, liberal, pool, present.

A feminine noun meaning blessing. The general idea of this word is one of good favour bestowed on another. This may be expressed in the giving of a tangible gift (Ge 33:11; 1Sa 25:27) or in the pronouncing of a verbal blessing (Ge 27:36; 49:28). Most often, however, this word speaks of God's favour on the righteous (Ge 12:2; Mal 3:10). It is related to the common verb *bârak* (1288), meaning to bless and is often used to contrast God's blessing and His curse.

1294. בְּרָכָה, **Berâkâh**, *ber-aw-kaw'*; the same as 1293; *Berakah*, the name of an Israelite, and also of a valley in Palestine:—Berachah.

1295. בְּרֵכָה, **berêkâh**, *ber-ay-kaw'*; from 1288; a *reservoir* (at which camels *kneel* as a resting place):—(fish-) pool.

1296. בֶּרֶכְיָה, **Berekyâh**, *beh-rek-yaw'*; or בֶּרֶכְיָהוּ, **Berekyâhûw**, *beh-rek-yaw'-hoo*; from 1290 and 3050; *knee* (i.e. *blessing*) of *Jah; Berekjah*, the name of six Israelites:—Berachiah, Berechiah.

1297. בְּרַם, **beram**, *ber-am'*; (Chaldee); perhaps from 7313 with prepositional prefix; (properly) *highly*, i.e. *surely*; but used adversatively, *however*:—but, nevertheless, yet.

1298. בֶּרַע, **Bera'**, *beh'-rah*; of uncertain derivation; *Bera*, a Sodomitish king:—Bera.

1299. בָּרַק, **bâraq**, *baw-rak'*; a primitive root; to *lighten* (lightning):—cast forth.

1300. בָּרָק, **bârâq**, *baw-rawk'*; from 1299; *lightning*; (by analogy) a *gleam*; (concrete) a *flashing* sword:—bright, glitter (-ing, sword), lightning.

1301. בָּרָק, **Bârâq**, *baw-rawk'*; the same as 1300; *Barak*, an Israelite:—Barak.

1302. בַּרְקוֹס, **Barqôws**, *bar-kose'*; of uncertain derivation; *Barkos*, one of the Nethimim:—Barkos.

1303. בַּרְקָן, **barqôn**, *bar-kon'*; from 1300; a *thorn* (perhaps as burning *brightly*):—brier.

1304. בָּרֶקֶת, **bâreqeth**, *baw-reh'-keth*; from 1300; a gem (as *flashing*), perhaps the *emerald*:—carbuncle.

1305. בָּרַר, **bârar**, *baw-rar'*; a primitive root; to *clarify* (i.e. *brighten*), *examine, select*:—make bright, choice, chosen, cleanse (be clean), clearly, polished, (shew self) pure (-ify), purge (out).

A verb signifying to purify, select. God declares that He will purge the rebels from Israel (Eze 20:38) and that He will give the people purified lips (Zep 3:9). The term can also mean to polish or make shine like polished arrows (Isa 49:2; Jer 51:11). Primarily used in the books of Chronicles, it points out that which was choice or select: men (1Ch 7:40); gatekeepers (1Ch 9:22); musicians (1Ch 16:41); sheep (Ne 5:18). It can also carry the connotation of testing or proving (Ecc 3:18).

1306. בִּרְשַׁע, **Birsha'**, *beer-shah'*; probably from 7562 with prepositional prefix; *with wickedness; Birsha*, a king of Gomorrah:—Birsha.

1307. בֵּרֹתִי, **Bêrôthiy**, *bay-ro-thee'*; patrial from 1268; a *Berothite*, or inhabitant of Berothai:—Berothite.

1308. בְּשׂוֹר**, Beˢôwr,** *bes-ore´*; from 1319; *cheerful; Besor,* a stream of Palestine:—Besor.

1309. בְּשׂוֹרָה**, beˢôwrâh,** *bes-o-raw´*; or (shortened) בְּשֹׂרָה**, beˢôrâh,** *bes-o-raw´*; feminine from 1319; glad *tidings*; (by implication) *reward for good news*:—reward for tidings.

1310. בָּשַׁל**, bâshal,** *baw-shal´*; a primitive root; (properly) to *boil* up; hence to *be done* in cooking; (figurative) to *ripen*:—bake, boil, bring forth, roast, seethe, sod (be sodden).

1311. בָּשֵׁל**, bâshêl,** *baw-shale´*; from 1310; *boiled*:— × at all, sodden.

1312. בִּשְׁלָם**, Bishlâm,** *bish-lawm´*; of foreign derivation; *Bishlam,* a Persian:—Bishlam.

1313. בָּשָׂם**, bâsâm,** *baw-sawm´*; from an unused root meaning to *be fragrant*; [compare 5561] the *balsam* plant:—spice.

1314. בֶּשֶׂם**, beśem,** *beh´-sem*; or בֹּשֶׂם**, bôsem,** *bo´-sem*; from the same as 1313; *fragrance*; (by implication) *spicery*; also the *balsam* plant:—smell, spice, sweet (odour).

1315. בָּשְׂמַת**, Bâsᵉmath,** *baw-se-math´*; feminine of 1314 (the second form); *fragrance; Bosmath,* the name of a wife of Esau, and of a daughter of Solomon:—Bashemath, Basmath.

1316. בָּשָׁן**, Bâshân,** *baw-shawn´*; of uncertain derivation; *Bashan* (often with the article), a region East of the Jordan:—Bashan.

1317. בָּשְׁנָה**, boshnâh,** *bosh-naw´*; feminine from 954; *shamefulness*:—shame.

1318. בָּשַׁס**, bâshas,** *baw-shas´*; a primitive root; to *trample* down:—tread.

1319. בָּשַׂר**, bâśar,** *baw-sar´*; a primitive root; (properly) to *be fresh,* i.e. *full, rosy;* (figurative) *cheerful*; to *announce* (glad news):—messenger, preach, publish, shew forth, (bear, bring, carry, preach, good, tell good) tidings.

A verb meaning to bring news or to bear tidings. The general idea of this word is that of a messenger announcing a message, which may either be bad news (1Sa 4:17, the death of Eli's sons) or good news (Jer 20:15, the birth of Jeremiah). It is often used within the military setting: a messenger coming from battle lines to report the news (2Sa 18:19, 20, 26) or victory (1Sa 31:9; 2Sa 1:20). When used of God's message, this word conveys the victorious salvation which God provides to His people (Ps 96:2; Isa 40:9; 52:7; 61:1).

1320. בָּשָׂר**, bâśâr,** *baw-sawr´*; from 1319; *flesh* (from its *freshness*); (by extension) *body, person*; also (by euphemism) the *pudenda* of a man:—body, [fat, lean] flesh [-ed], kin, [man-] kind, + nakedness, self, skin.

A masculine noun whose basic meaning is flesh. The basic meaning is frequently observed in the OT, especially in the literature concerning sacrificial practices (Le 7:17) and skin diseases (Le 13). It also is used of the animal body (Ge 41:2–4, 18, 19); the human body (Isa 10:18); the penis (Ge 17:11, 13, 14, 23–25); blood relations (Ge 2:23, 24; 29:14); and human frailty (Ge 6:3; Job 10:4). This word is further used in the phrase *kôl* (3605) *bâśâr,* meaning all flesh, to indicate all living beings (Ge 6:17, 19; 7:21); animals (Ge 7:15, 16; 8:17); humanity (Ge 6:12, 13).

1321. בְּשַׂר**, bᵉśar,** *bes-ar´*; (Chaldee); corresponding to 1320:—flesh.

A masculine noun meaning flesh. It is an Aramaic word found only in the book of Daniel. When used figuratively, it signifies all flesh or humankind (Da 2:11) and all creatures (Da 4:12[9]). It is also used in relation to the devouring of flesh in a literal sense (Da 7:5).

1322. בֹּשֶׁת**, bôsheth,** *bo´-sheth*; from 954; *shame* (the feeling and the condition, as well as its cause); (by implication, specifically) an *idol*:—ashamed, confusion, + greatly, (put to) shame (-ful thing).

1323. בַּת**, bath,** *bath*; from 1129 (as feminine of 1121); a *daughter* (used in the same wide sense as other terms of relationship, literal and figurative):—apple [of the eye], branch, company, daughter, × first, × old, + owl, town, village.

1324. בַּת**, bath,** *bath*; probably from the same as 1327; a *bath* or Hebrew measure (as a means of *division*) of liquids:—bath.

1325. בַּת**, bath,** *bath*; (Chaldee); corresponding to 1324:—bath.

1326. בָּתָה**, bâthâh,** *baw-thaw´*; probably an orthographical variation for 1327; *desolation*:—waste.

1327. בַּתָּה**, battâh,** *bat-taw´*; feminine from an unused root (meaning to *break* in pieces); *desolation*:—desolate.

1328. בְּתוּאֵל**, Bᵉthûw'êl,** *beth-oo-ale´*; apparently from the same as 1326 and 410; *destroyed of God; Bethuel,* the name of a nephew of Abraham, and of a place in Palestine:—Bethuel. Compare 1329.

1329. בְּתוּל**, Bᵉthûwl,** *beth-ool´*; for 1328; *Bethul* (i.e. *Bethuel*), a place in Palestine:—Bethuel.

1330. בְּתוּלָה**, bᵉthûwlâh,** *beth-oo-law´*; feminine passive participle of an unused root meaning to *separate*; a *virgin* (from her *privacy*); sometimes (by continuation) a *bride*; also (figurative) a *city* or *state*:—maid, virgin.

A feminine noun meaning virgin. Some scholars prefer to translate the term loosely as maiden or young woman. Yet in Ge 24:16, Rebekah is described as a beautiful woman and a *běthûlâh.* The text states that no man had known Rebekah—that is, had sexual relations with her. Also, Jgs 21:12 states that there were "four hundred young *běthûlâh,* that had known no man by lying with any male." In these verses, this Hebrew word certainly connotes virginity. But in Joel 1:8, the Lord describes the *běthûlâh* mourning for the husband of her youth. In this case, the word means young woman. Moreover, the word also refers to cities or countries that are personified as females (Isa 37:22; 47:1; Jer 18:13; 31:4, 21; Am 5:2). For further occurrences of this Hebrew word, see Dt 22:23, 28; Jgs 19:24; 2Sa 13:2, 18; 1Ki 1:2; Est 2:2; Zec 9:17.

1331. בְּתוּלִים**, bᵉthûwlîym,** *beth-oo-leem´*; masculine plural of the same as 1330; (collective and abstract) *virginity*; (by implication and concretely) the *tokens* of it:— × maid, virginity.

A feminine noun meaning virginity, virgin, or maiden. It is primarily used to describe the sexual purity or chastity of a young woman. Variations on this theme show it is used in contrast to a defiled or impure woman (Dt 22:14); to signify the virginal state of a woman to be married (Le 21:13); or to signify the virginal state of young women in general (Jgs 11:37).

1332. בִּתְיָה**, Bithyâh,** *bith-yaw´*; from 1323 and 3050; *daughter* (i.e. worshipper) *of Jah; Bithjah,* an Egyptian woman:—Bithiah.

1333. בָּתַק**, bâthaq,** *baw-thak´*; a primitive root; to *cut* in pieces:—thrust through.

1334. בָּתַר**, bâthar,** *baw-thar´*; a primitive root, to *chop* up:—divide.

1335. בֶּתֶר**, bether,** *beh´-ther*; from 1334; a *section*:—part, piece.

1336. בֶּתֶר**, Bether,** *beh´-ther*; the same as 1335; *Bether,* a (craggy) place in Palestine:—Bether.

1337. בַּת רַבִּים**, Bath Rabbîym,** *bath rab-beem´*; from 1323 and a masculine plural from 7227; the *daughter* (i.e. *city*) *of Rabbah*:—Bath-rabbim.

1338. בִּתְרוֹן**, Bithrôwn,** *bith-rone´*; from 1334; (with the article) the *craggy* spot; *Bithron,* a place East of the Jordan:—Bithron.

1339. בַּת־שֶׁבַע**, Bath-Sheba',** *bath-sheh´-bah*; from 1323 and 7651 (in the sense of 7650); *daughter of an oath; Bath-Sheba,* the mother of Solomon:—Bath-sheba.

1340. בַּת־שׁוּעַ, Bath-Shûwaʻ, *bath-shoo´-ah*; from 1323 and 7771; *daughter of wealth; Bath-shuä*, the same as 1339:—Bath-shua.

1341. גֵּא, gêʼ, *gay´*; for 1343; *haughty*:—proud.

1342. גָּאָה, gâʼâh, *gaw-aw´*; a primitive root; to *mount* up; hence in general to *rise*, (figurative) be *majestic*:—gloriously, grow up, increase, be risen, triumph.

A verb meaning to rise, to grow up, to exalt, to lift up. It is used physically of a stream in Eze 47:5, "The waters were risen"; and of plants in Job 8:11, "Can the rush grow up without mire?" In a figurative sense, it speaks of a lifting up or exaltation (specifically of God). The verb emphatically describes God's matchless power in Miriam's song (Ex 15:1, 21). This is the key usage of *gâʼâh*: The Lord only is highly exalted. The horse and rider He easily casts into the sea; He alone legitimately lifts up the head, as Job admits in Job 10:16. None can stand before Him. Some Hebrew words derived from this one express an important negative theme—that of lifting up of one's self in wrongful pride against the rightful place of God: *gêʼeh* (1343); *gaʼăwâh* (1346); and *gâʼôwn* (1347).

1343. גֵּאֶה, geʼeh, *gay-eh´*; from 1342; *lofty*; (figurative) *arrogant*:—proud.

1344. גֵּאָה, gêʼâh, *gay-aw´*; feminine from 1342; *arrogance*:—pride.

1345. גְּאוּאֵל, Geʼûwʼêl, *geh-oo-ale´*; from 1342 and 410; *majesty of God; Geüel*, an Israelite:—Geuel.

1346. גַּאֲוָה, gaʼăvâh, *gah-av-aw´*; from 1342; *arrogance* or *majesty*; (by implication and concretely) *ornament*:—excellency, haughtiness, highness, pride, proudly, swelling.

1347. גָּאוֹן, gâʼôwn, *gaw-ohn´*; from 1342; the same as 1346:—arrogancy, excellency (-lent), majesty, pomp, pride, proud, swelling.

1348. גֵּאוּת, gêʼûwth, *gay-ooth´*; from 1342; the same as 1346:—excellent things, lifting up, majesty, pride, proudly, raging.

1349. גַּאֲיוֹן, gaʼăyôwn, *gah-ăh-yone´*; from 1342; *haughty*:—proud.

1350. גָּאַל, gâʼal, *gaw-al´*; a primitive root, to *redeem* (according to the Oriental law of kinship), i.e. to *be the next of kin* (and as such to *buy back* a relative's property, *marry* his widow, etc.):—× in any wise, × at all, avenger, deliver, (do, perform the part of near, next) kinsfolk (-man), purchase, ransom, redeem (-er), revenger.

A verb meaning to redeem or act as a kinsman-redeemer. The word means to act as a redeemer for a deceased kinsman (Ru 3:13); to redeem or buy back from bondage (Le 25:48); to redeem or buy back a kinsman's possessions (Le 25:26); to avenge a kinsman's murder (Nu 35:19); to redeem an object through a payment (Le 27:13). Theologically, this word is used to convey God's redemption of individuals from spiritual death and His redemption of the nation of Israel from Egyptian bondage and also from exile (see Ex 6:6).

1351. גָּאַל, gâʼal, *gaw-al´*; a primitive root, [rather identical with 1350, through the idea of *freeing*, i.e. *repudiating*]; to *soil* or (figurative) *desecrate*:—defile, pollute, stain.

1352. גֹּאֶל, gôʼal, *go´-al*; from 1351; *profanation*:—defile.

1353. גְּאֻלָּה, geʼullâh, *geh-ool-law´*; feminine passive participle of 1350; *redemption* (including the right and the object); by implication *relationship*:—kindred, redeem, redemption, right.

A feminine singular noun meaning redemption. The term is typically used in legal texts denoting who can redeem (Le 25:24, 31, 32, 48); what they can redeem (Le 25:26); when (Le 25:26, 51, 52); and for how much (Le 25:26, 51, 52). Redemption was a means by which property remained in families or clans. The best picture of this custom in the Bible is Ru 4:6, 7.

1354. גַּב, gab, *gab*; from an unused root meaning to *hollow* or *curve*; the *back* (as *rounded* [compare 1460 and 1479]; by analogy the *top* or *rim*, a *boss*, a *vault, arch* of eye, *bulwarks*, etc.:—back, body, boss, eminent (higher) place, [eye] brows, nave, ring.

1355. גַּב, gab, *gab*; (Chaldee); corresponding to 1354:—back.

1356. גֵּב, gêb, *gabe*; from 1461; a *log* (as *cut* out); also *well* or *cistern* (as *dug*):—beam, ditch, pit.

1357. גֵּב, gêb, *gabe*; probably from 1461 [compare 1462]; a *locust* (from its *cutting*):—locust.

1358. גֹּב, gôb, *gobe*; (Chaldee); from a root corresponding to 1461; a *pit* (for wild animals) (as *cut* out):—den.

1359. גֹּב, Gôb, *gobe*; or (fully) גּוֹב, **Gôwb,** *gobe´*; from 1461; *pit; Gob*, a place in Palestine:—Gob.

1360. גֶּבֶא, gebeʼ, *geh´-beh*; from an unused root meaning probably to *collect*; a *reservoir*; by analogy a *marsh*:—marsh, pit.

1361. גָּבַהּ, gâbah, *gaw-bah´*; a primitive root; to *soar*, i.e. *be lofty*; (figurative) to *be haughty*:—exalt, be haughty, be (make) high (-er), lift up, mount up, be proud, raise up great height, upward.

1362. גָּבֹהַּ, gâbôah, *gaw-bo-ah´*; from 1361; *lofty* (literal or figurative):—high, proud.

1363. גֹּבַהּ, gôbah, *go´-bah*; from 1361; *elation, grandeur, arrogance*:—excellency, haughty, height, high, loftiness, pride.

1364. גָּבֹהַּ, gâbôah, *gaw-bo´-ah*; or (fully) גָּבוֹהַּ, **gâbôwah,** *gaw-bo´-ah*; from 1361; *elevated* (or *elated*), *powerful, arrogant*:—haughty, height, high (-er), lofty, proud, × exceeding proudly.

1365. גַּבְהוּת, gabhûwth, *gab-hooth´*; from 1361; *pride*:—loftiness, lofty.

1366. גְּבוּל, gebûwl, *geb-ool´*; or (shortened) גְּבֻל, **gebul,** *geb-ool´*; from 1379; (properly) a *cord* (as *twisted*), i.e. (by implication) a *boundary*; (by extension) the *territory* inclosed:—border, bound, coast, × great, landmark, limit, quarter, space.

1367. גְּבוּלָה, gebûwlâh, *geb-oo-law´*; or (shortened) גְּבֻלָה, **gebulâh,** *geb-oo-law´*; feminine of 1366; a *boundary, region*:—border, bound, coast, landmark, place.

1368. גִּבּוֹר, gibbôwr, *gib-bore´*; or (shortened) גִּבֹּר, **gibbôr,** *gib-bore´*; intensive from the same as 1397; *powerful*; (by implication) *warrior, tyrant*:—champion, chief, × excel, giant, man, mighty (man, one), strong (man), valiant man.

1369. גְּבוּרָה, gebûwrâh, *geb-oo-raw´*; feminine passive participle from the same as 1368; *force* (literal or figurative); (by implication) *valor, victory*:—force, mastery, might, mighty (act, power), power, strength.

1370. גְּבוּרָה, gebûwrâh, *geb-oo-raw´*; (Chaldee); corresponding to 1369; *power*:—might.

1371. גִּבֵּחַ, gibbêach, *gib-bay´-akh*; from an unused root meaning to *be high* (in the forehead); *bald* in the forehead:—forehead bald.

1372. גַּבַּחַת, gabbachath, *gab-bakh´-ath*; from the same as 1371; *baldness* in the forehead; (by analogy) a *bare spot* on the right side of cloth:—bald forehead, × without.

1373. גַּבַּי, Gabbay, *gab-bah´ee*; from the same as 1354; *collective*; *Gabbai*, an Israelite:—Gabbai.

1374. גֵּבִים, Gêbîym, *gay-beem´*; plural of 1356; *cisterns; Gebim*, a place in Palestine:—Gebim.

1375. גְּבִיעַ, gâbîyaʻ, *gawb-ee´-ah*; from an unused root (meaning to *be convex*); a *goblet*; (by analogy) the *calyx* of a flower:—house, cup, pot.

1376. גְּבִיר, gebîyr, *geb-eer´*; from 1396; a *master*:—lord.

1377. גְּבִירָה, gebîyrâh, *geb-ee-raw´*; feminine of 1376; a *mistress*:—queen.

1378. גָּבִישׁ, gâbîysh, *gaw-beesh´*; from an unused root (probably meaning to *freeze*); *crystal* (from its resemblance to *ice*):—pearl.

1379. גָּבַל, gâbal, *gaw-bal´*; a primitive root; (properly) to *twist* as a rope; only (as a denominative from 1366) to *bound* (as by a line):—be border, set (bounds about).

1380. גְּבַל, Gᵉbal, *geb-al´*; from 1379 (in the sense of a *chain* of hills); a *mountain; Gebal*, a place in Phoenicia:—Gebal.

1381. גְּבָל, Gᵉbâl, *geb-awl´*; the same as 1380; *Gebal*, a region in Idumæa:—Gebal.

1382. גִּבְלִי, Giblîy, *gib-lee´*; patrial from 1380; a *Gebalite*, or inhabitant of Gebal:—Giblites, stone-squarer.

1383. גַּבְלֻת, gabluth, *gab-looth´*; from 1379; a twisted *chain* or *lace*:—end.

1384. גִּבֵּן, gibbên, *gib-bane´*; from an unused root meaning to be *arched* or *contracted; hunch-backed*:—crookbackt.

1385. גְּבִנָה, gᵉbinâh, *geb-ee-naw´*; feminine from the same as 1384; *curdled* milk:—cheese.

1386. גַּבְנֹן, gabnôn, *gab-nohn´*; from the same as 1384; a *hump* or *peak* of hills:—high.

1387. גֶּבַע, Gebaʻ, *geh´-bah*; from the same as 1375; a *hillock; Geba*, a place in Palestine:—Gaba, Geba, Gibeah.

1388. גִּבְעָא, Gibʻâʼ, *gib-aw´*; by permutation for 1389; a *hill; Giba*, a place in Palestine:—Gibeah.

1389. גִּבְעָה, gibʻâh, *gib-aw´*; feminine from the same as 1387; a *hillock*:—hill, little hill.

1390. גִּבְעָה, Gibʻâh, *gib-aw´*; the same as 1389; *Gibah*; the name of three places in Palestine:—Gibeah, the hill.

1391. גִּבְעוֹן, Gibʻôwn, *gib-ohn´*; from the same as 1387; *hilly; Gibon*, a place in Palestine:—Gibeon.

1392. גִּבְעֹל, gibʻôl, *gib-ole´*; prolonged from 1375; the *calyx* of a flower:—bolled.

1393. גִּבְעֹנִי, Gibʻônîy, *gib-o-nee´*; patrial from 1391; a *Gibonite*, or inhabitant of Gibon:—Gibeonite.

1394. גִּבְעַת, Gibʻath, *gib-ath´*; from the same as 1375; *hilliness; Gibath*:—Gibeath.

1395. גִּבְעָתִי, Gibʻâthîy, *gib-aw-thee´*; patrial from 1390; a *Gibathite*, or inhabitant of Gibath:—Gibeathite.

1396. גָּבַר, gâbar, *gaw-bar´*; a primitive root; to *be strong*; (by implication) to *prevail, act insolently*:—exceed, confirm, be great, be mighty, prevail, put to more [strength], strengthen, be stronger, be valiant.

1397. גֶּבֶר, geber, *geh´-ber*; from 1396; (properly) a *valiant* man or *warrior*; (generally) a *person* simply:—every one, man, × mighty.

A masculine noun meaning man, mighty (virile) man, warrior. It is used of man but often contains more than just a reference to gender by referring to the nature of a man, usually with overtones of spiritual strength or masculinity, based on the verb *gâbar* (1396), meaning to be mighty. The word is used to contrast men with women and children (Ex 10:11) and to denote warrior ability (Jer 41:16). The fifteen occurrences of the word in Job are significant, presenting a vast contrast between the essence of man (even a good one) and God (Job 4:17; 22:2). This contrast only adds more force to the passage in Zec 13:7 where God calls Himself *geber*. This passage points to the coming of Jesus—the One who as God would take on sinful human nature. He is the Man (the Shepherd of the sheep).

1398. גֶּבֶר, Geber, *geh´-ber*; the same as 1397; *Geber*, the name of two Israelites:—Geber.

1399. גְּבַר, gᵉbar, *geb-ar´*; from 1396; the same as 1397; a person:—man.

A masculine noun meaning man. This is the construct of the Hebrew word *geber* (1397) and has the same meaning. It is found in the Psalms to describe a male who is upright before the Lord. He is described as a blameless man, literally, a man of no shame (Ps 18:25[26]).

1400. גְּבַר, gᵉbar, *geb-ar´*; (Chaldee); corresponding to 1399:—certain, man.

An Aramaic masculine singular noun meaning man. It occurs ten times. See the word *geber* (1397).

1401. גִּבָּר, gibbâr, *gib-bawr´*; (Chaldee); intensive of 1400; *valiant*, or *warrior*:—mighty.

An Aramaic masculine noun meaning mighty one, warrior, hero. This word is used only once in the Bible, where it is attached to another word meaning strength. It translates as "mighty one" or "strongest soldier" (Da 3:20).

1402. גִּבָּר, Gibbâr, *gib-bawr´*; intensive of 1399; *Gibbar*, an Israelite:—Gibbar.

1403. גַּבְרִיאֵל, Gabrîyʼêl, *gab-ree-ale´*; from 1397 and 410; *man of God; Gabriel*, an archangel:—Gabriel.

1404. גְּבֶרֶת, gᵉbereth, *geb-eh´-reth*; feminine of 1376; *mistress*:—lady, mistress.

A noun meaning lady, queen, mistress. In many cases, this word refers to either a woman who is a mistress or to the servant of a mistress (Ge 16:4, 8, 9; 2Ki 5:3; Pr 30:23). Also, it refers to a lady of a kingdom, that is, the queen (Isa 47:5, 7).

1405. גִּבְּתוֹן, Gibbᵉthôwn, *gib-beth-one´*; intensive from 1389; a *hilly* spot; *Gibbethon*, a place in Palestine:—Gibbethon.

1406. גָּג, gâg, *gawg*; probably by reduplication from 1342; a *roof*; (by analogy) the *top* of an altar:—roof (of the house), (house) top (of the house).

1407. גַּד, gad, *gad*; from 1413 (in the sense of *cutting*); *coriander* seed (from its furrows):—coriander.

1408. גַּד, Gad, *gad*; a variation of 1409; *Fortune*, a Babylonian deity:—that troop.

1409. גָּד, gâd, *gawd*; from 1464 (in the sense of *distributing*); *fortune*:—troop.

1410. גָּד, Gâd, *gawd*; from 1464; *Gad*, a son of Jacob, includ. his tribe and its territory; also a prophet:—Gad.

1411. גְּדָבַר, gᵉdâbar, *ged-aw-bar´*; (Chaldee); corresponding to 1489; a *treasurer*:—treasurer.

1412. גֻּדְגֹּדָה, Gudgôdâh, *gud-go´-daw*; by reduplication from 1413 (in the sense of *cutting*) *cleft; Gudgodah*, a place in the Desert:—Gudgodah.

1413. גָּדַד, gâdad, *gaw-dad´*; a primitive root [compare 1464]; to *crowd*; also to *gash* (as if by *pressing* into):—assemble (selves by troops), gather (selves together, self in troops), cut selves.

A verb meaning to cut, to crowd together. In some cases, this verb is used to describe cutting the skin in mourning (Jer 16:6; 41:5; 47:5) or in pagan religious practices (1Ki 18:28). God prohibited such pagan rites (Dt 14:1). This Hebrew verb also means to gather together, such as troops (Mic 5:1[4:14]) or a crowd (Jer 5:7).

1414. גְּדַד, gᵉdad, *ged-ad´*; (Chaldee); corresponding to 1413; to *cut* down:—hew down.

1415. גָּדָה, gâdâh, *gaw-daw´*; from an unused root (meaning to *cut* off); a *border* of a river (as *cut* into by the stream):—bank.

1416. גְּדוּד, gᵉdûwd, *ged-ood´*; from 1413; a *crowd* (especially of soldiers):—army, band (of men), company, troop (of robbers).

A masculine noun meaning a band, a troop. It is used to indicate a marauding band, a raiding party, or a group that makes inroads into enemy territory. It sometimes refers to Israel's military (2Sa 4:2; 2Ch

22:1), but more often, it refers to the marauding enemies of Israel (Ge 49:19; 1Sa 30:8, 15, 23; 1Ki 11:24; 2Ki 5:2; 6:23; 24:2). In some instances, these marauding bands operate independently and are thus labeled as troops of robbers (Hos 6:9; 7:1). By extension, the word sometimes refers to the actual raid itself (2Sa 3:22). On other occasions, it indicates the army in general (Job 29:25) or some division of troops within the army (1Ch 7:4; 2Ch 25:9, 10, 13; 26:11; Mic 5:1[4:14]). It is used figuratively for God's chastisements (Job 19:12) and His attacking forces (Job 25:3).

1417. גְּדוּד, **gᵉdûwd,** *ged-ood´*; or (feminine) גְּדֻדָה, **gedudâh,** *ged-oo-daw´*; from 1413; a *furrow* (as *cut*):—furrow.

1418. גְּדוּדָה, **gᵉdûwdâh,** *ged-oo-daw´*; feminine participle passive of 1413; an *incision*:—cutting.

1419. גָּדוֹל, **gâdôwl,** *gaw-dole´*; or (shortened) גָּדֹל, **gâdôl,** *gaw-dole´*; from 1431; *great* (in any sense); hence *older*; also *insolent*:— + aloud, elder (-est), + exceeding (-ly), + far, (man of) great (man, matter, thing, -er, -ness), high, long, loud, mighty, more, much, noble, proud thing, × sore, (×) very.

1420. גְּדוּלָה, **gᵉdûwlâh,** *ged-oo-law´*; or (shortened) גְּדֻלָּה, **gᵉdullâh,** *ged-ool-law´*; or (less accurately) גְּדוּלָּה, **gᵉdûwllâh,** *ged-ool-law´*; feminine of 1419; *greatness*; (concretely) *mighty acts*:—dignity, great things (-ness), majesty.

1421. גִּדּוּף, **giddûwph,** *gid-doof´*; or (shortened) גִּדֻּף, **gidduph,** *gid-doof´*; and (feminine) גִּדּוּפָה, **giddûwphâh,** *gid-doo-faw´*; or גִּדֻּפָה, **gidduphâh,** *gid-doo-faw´*; from 1422; *vilification*:—reproach, reviling.

1422. גְּדוּפָה, **gᵉdûwphâh,** *ged-oo-faw´*; feminine passive participle of 1442; a *revilement*:—taunt.

1423. גְּדִי, **gᵉdîy,** *ged-ee´*; from the same as 1415; a young *goat* (from *browsing*):—kid.

1424. גָּדִי, **Gâdîy,** *gaw-dee´*; from 1409; *fortunate; Gadi*, an Israelite:—Gadi.

1425. גָּדִי, **Gâdîy,** *gaw-dee´*; patronymic from 1410; a *Gadite* (collective) or descendants of Gad:—Gadites, children of Gad.

1426. גַּדִּי, **Gaddîy,** *gad-dee´*; intensive for 1424; *Gaddi*, an Israelite:—Gaddi.

1427. גַּדִּיאֵל, **Gaddîy'êl,** *gad-dee-ale´*; from 1409 and 410; *fortune of God; Gaddiel*, an Israelite:—Gaddiel.

1428. גִּדְיָה, **gidyâh,** *gid-yaw´*; or גַּדְיָה, **gadyâh,** *gad-yaw´*; the same as 1415; a river *brink*:—bank.

1429. גְּדִיָּה, **gᵉdîyyâh,** *ged-ee-yaw´*; feminine of 1423; a young female *goat*:—kid.

1430. גָּדִישׁ, **gâdîysh,** *gaw-deesh´*; from an unused root (meaning to *heap* up); a *stack* of sheaves; by analogy a *tomb*:—shock (stack) (of corn), tomb.

1431. גָּדַל, **gâdal,** *gaw-dal´*; a primitive root; (properly) to *twist* [compare 1434], i.e. to *be* (causative *make) large* (in various senses, as in body, mind, estate or honour, also in pride):—advance, boast, bring up, exceed, excellent, be (-come, do, give, make, wax), great (-er, come to … estate, + things), grow (up), increase, lift up, magnify (-ifical), be much set by, nourish (up), pass, promote, proudly [spoken], tower.

1432. גָּדֵל, **gâdêl,** *gaw-dale´*; from 1431; *large* (literal or figurative):—great, grew.

1433. גֹּדֶל, **gôdel,** *go´-del*; from 1431; *magnitude* (literal or figurative):—greatness, stout (-ness).

1434. גְּדִל, **gâdil,** *ged-eel´*; from 1431 (in the sense of *twisting*); *thread*, i.e. a *tassel* or *festoon*:—fringe, wreath.

1435. גִּדֵּל, **Giddêl,** *gid-dale´*; from 1431; *stout; Giddel*, the name of one of the Nethinim, also of one of "Solomon's servants":—Giddel.

1436. גְּדַלְיָה, **Gᵉdalyâh,** *ged-al-yaw´*; or (prolonged) גְּדַלְיָהוּ, **Gedalyâhûw,** *ged-al-yaw´-hoo*; from 1431 and 3050; *Jah has become great; Gedaljah*, the name of five Israelites:—Gedaliah.

1437. גִּדַּלְתִּי, **Giddaltîy,** *gid-dal´-tee*; from 1431; *I have made great; Giddalti*, an Israelite:—Giddalti.

1438. גָּדַע, **gâda',** *gaw-dah´*; a primitive root; to *fell* a tree; (generally) to *destroy* anything:—cut (asunder, in sunder, down, off), hew down.

1439. גִּדְעוֹן, **Gid'ôwn,** *gid-ohn´*; from 1438; *feller* (i.e. *warrior*); *Gidon*, an Israelite:—Gideon.

1440. גִּדְעֹם, **Gid'ôm,** *gid-ohm´*; from 1438; a *cutting* (i.e. *desolation*); *Gidom*, a place in Palestine:—Gidom.

1441. גִּדְעֹנִי, **Gid'ônîy,** *gid-o-nee´*; from 1438; *warlike* [compare 1439]; *Gidoni*, an Israelite:—Gideoni.

1442. גָּדַף, **gâdaph,** *gaw-daf´*; a primitive root; to *hack* (with words), i.e. *revile*:—blaspheme, reproach.

1443. גָּדַר, **gâdar,** *gaw-dar´*; a primitive root; to *wall* in or around:—close up, fence up, hedge, inclose, make up [a wall], mason, repairer.

1444. גֶּדֶר, **geder,** *geh´-der*; from 1443; a *circumvallation*:—wall.

1445. גֶּדֶר, **Geder,** *geh´-der*; the same as 1444; *Geder*, a place in Palestine:—Geder.

1446. גְּדֹר, **Gᵉdôr,** *ged-ore´*; or (fully) גְּדוֹר, **Gᵉdôwr,** *ged-ore´*; from 1443; *inclosure; Gedor*, a place in Palestine; also the name of three Israelites:—Gedor.

1447. גָּדֵר, **gâdêr,** *gaw-dare´*; from 1443; a *circumvallation*; (by implication) an *inclosure*:—fence, hedge, wall.

1448. גְּדֵרָה, **gᵉdêrâh,** *ged-ay-raw´*; feminine of 1447; *inclosure* (especially for flocks):—[sheep-] cote (fold) hedge, wall.

1449. גְּדֵרָה, **Gᵉdêrâh,** *ged-ay-raw´*; the same as 1448; (with the article) *Gederah*, a place in Palestine:—Gederah, hedges.

1450. גְּדֵרוֹת, **Gᵉdêrôwth,** *ged-ay-rohth´*; plural of 1448; *walls; Gederoth*, a place in Palestine:—Gederoth.

1451. גְּדֵרִי, **Gᵉdêrîy,** *ged-ay-ree´*; patrial from 1445; a *Gederite*, or inhabitant of Geder:—Gederite.

1452. גְּדֵרָתִי, **Gᵉdêrâthîy,** *ged-ay-raw-thee´*; patrial from 1449; a *Gederathite*, or inhabitant of Gederah:—Gederathite.

1453. גְּדֵרֹתַיִם, **Gᵉdêrôthayim,** *ged-ay-ro-thah´-yim*; dual of 1448; *double wall; Gederothajim*, a place in Palestine:—Gederothaim.

1454. גֵּה, **gêh,** *gay*; probably a clerical error for 2088; *this*:—this.

1455. גָּהָה, **gâhâh,** *gaw-haw´*; a primitive root; to *remove* (a bandage from a wound, i.e. *heal* it):—cure.

1456. גֵּהָה, **gêhâh,** *gay-haw´*; from 1455; a *cure*:—medicine.

1457. גָּהַר, **gâhar,** *gaw-har´*; a primitive root; to *prostrate* oneself:—cast self down, stretch self.

1458. גַּו, **gav,** *gav*; another form for 1460; the *back*:—back.

1459. גַּו, **gav,** *gav*; (Chaldee); corresponding to 1460; the *middle*:—midst, same, there- (where-) in.

1460. גֵּו, **gêv,** *gave*; from 1342 [corresponding to 1354]; the *back*; (by analogy) the *middle*:— + among, back, body.

I. A masculine noun meaning back. It depicts the back of a person's body. A fool's back is for lashes or a rod (Pr 10:13; 19:29; 26:3) so that he might learn wisdom. In a figure of speech, the Lord casts the sins of repentant persons behind His back (Isa 38:17). Walking on someone's back means to humiliate and denigrate him or her (Isa 51:23).

II. A masculine noun meaning midst, community. It indicates the fellowship or the midst of a community of persons (Job 30:5) from which the lowly in society are driven.

1461. **גּוּב, gûwb,** *goob*; a primitive root; to *dig*:—husbandman.

1462. **גּוֹב, gôwb,** *gobe*; from 1461; the *locust* (from its *grubbing* as a larve):—grasshopper, × great.

1463. **גּוֹג, Gôwg,** *gohg*; of uncertain derivation; *Gog*, the name of an Israelite, also of some northern nation:—Gog.

1464. **גּוּד, gûwd,** *goode*; a primitive root [akin to 1413]; to *crowd* upon, i.e. *attack*:—invade, overcome.

1465. **גֵּוָה, gêvâh,** *gay-vaw´*; feminine of 1460; the *back*, i.e. (by extension) the *person*:—body.

1466. **גֵּוָה, gêvâh,** *gay-vaw´*; the same as 1465; *exaltation*; (figurative) *arrogance*:—lifting up, pride.

1467. **גֵּוָה, gêvâh,** *gay-vaw´*; (Chaldee); corresponding to 1466:—pride.

1468. **גּוּז, gûwz,** *gooz*; a primitive root [compare 1494]; (properly) to *shear* off; but used only in the (figurative) sense of *passing* rapidly:—bring, cut off.

1469. **גּוֹזָל, gôwzzâl,** *goz-zawl´*; or (shortened) **גֹּזָל, gôzâl,** *go-zawl´*; from 1497; a *nestling* (as being comparatively *nude* of feathers):—young (pigeon).

1470. **גּוֹזָן, Gôwzân,** *go-zawn´*; probably from 1468; a *quarry* (as a place of *cutting* stones); *Gozan*, a province of Assyria:—Gozan.

1471. **גּוֹי, gôwy,** *go´ee*; rarely (shortened) **גֹּי, gôy,** *go´-ee*; apparently from the same root as 1465 (in the sense of *massing*); a foreign *nation*; hence a *Gentile*; also (figurative) a *troop* of animals, or a *flight* of locusts:—Gentile, heathen, nation, people.

A masculine noun meaning nation, people, Gentiles, country. The word is used to indicate a nation or nations in various contexts and settings: it especially indicates the offspring of Abraham that God made into a nation (Ge 12:2) and thereby set the stage for Israel's appearance in history as a nation (Ge 18:18; Ps 106:5). Israel was to be a holy nation (Ex 19:6). Even the descendants of Abraham that did not come from the seed of Isaac would develop into nations (Ge 21:13). God can create a nation, even a holy nation like Israel, through the descendants of the person whom He chooses, as He nearly does in the case of Moses when Israel rebels (Ex 32:10). Edom refers to Israel and Judah as two separate nations (Eze 35:10), but God planned for them to be united forever into one nation (Eze 37:22). Then they would become the head of the nations (Dt 28:12). In this overall literary, theological, and historical context, it is clear that Israel would share common ancestors, and would have a sufficient increase in numbers to be considered a nation. It would have a common place of habitation and a common origin, not only in flesh and blood, but in their religious heritage. It would share a common history, culture, society, religious worship, and purposes for the present and the future.

This noun is used to mean nations other than Israel as well; pagan, Gentile, or heathen nations (Ex 9:24; 34:10; Eze 5:6–8), for all the earth and all the nations belong to God (cf. Ex 19:5). Israel was to keep herself from the false religions, unclean practices, and views of these nations (Ezr 6:21). In the plural, the noun may indicate the generic humankind (Isa 42:6). In a few instances, the word refers to a group of people rather than to a nation (2Ki 6:18; Ps 43:1; Isa 26:2), although the exact translation is difficult in these cases.

The word is used in a figurative sense to refer to animals or insects, such as in Joel 1:6 where it depicts locusts.

1472. **גְּוִיָּה, gᵉvîyyâh,** *gev-ee-yaw´*; prolonged for 1465; a *body*, whether alive or dead:—(dead) body, carcase, corpse.

A feminine noun meaning body, corpse, carcass. Most often, this word is used to depict a dead body, either a human, such as Saul (1Sa 31:10), or an animal, such as Samson's lion (Jgs 14:8, 9). In the Bible, this word is used to describe the slaughter of a nation as dead bodies are scattered everywhere (Ps 110:6; Na 3:3). Sometimes the word refers to live bodies. But in these cases, the idea of defeat or humiliation is present (Ge 47:18; Ne 9:37). When the experience is visionary, however, the word depicts live beings with no humiliation implied (Eze 1:11, 23; Da 10:6).

1473. **גּוֹלָה, gôwlâh,** *go-law´*; or (shortened) **גֹּלָה, gôlâh,** *go-law´*; active participle feminine of 1540; *exile*; (concrete and collateral) *exiles*:—(carried away), captive (-ity), removing.

A feminine noun meaning captivity, exile, captives, exiles. This word is the feminine participle of *gâlâh* (1540). It most often refers to the Babylonian captivity and its captives (2Ki 24:16; Eze 1:1) but is also used of the Assyrian captivity (1Ch 5:22) and even of the exiles of foreign nations (Jer 48:7, 11; Am 1:15). The phrase, children of the captivity, occurs in Ezra and describes those who returned from the captivity in Babylon (Ezr 4:1; 6:19, 20; 10:7, 16).

1474. **גּוֹלָן, Gôwlân,** *go-lawn´*; from 1473; *captive; Golan*, a place east of the Jordan:—Golan.

1475. **גּוּמָּץ, gûwmmâts,** *goom-mawts´*; of uncertain derivation; a *pit*:—pit.

A masculine noun meaning pit. Although this word is used only once in the OT, its meaning is derived from a related Aramaic word, which means to dig. Thus, a pit is the result of digging. The meaning is clear when it is used in Ecc 10:8: "He that diggeth a pit shall fall into it" (KJV). Furthermore, this meaning is further verified in a similar passage found in Pr 26:27, in which a parallel word, *shachath* (7845), meaning pit, is used.

1476. **גּוּנִי, Gûwnîy,** *goo-nee´*; probably from 1598; *protected; Guni*, the name of two Israelites:—Guni.

1477. **גּוּנִי, Gûwnîy,** *goo-nee´*; patronymic from 1476; a *Gunite* (collective with article prefix) or descendants of Guni:—Gunites.

1478. **גָּוַע, gâvaʻ,** *gaw-vah´*; a primitive root; to *breathe* out, i.e. (by implication) *expire*:—die, be dead, give up the ghost, perish.

A verb meaning to expire, to die. The word is apparently from a root meaning to breathe out. This word is used to describe the death of humans and animals in the flood (Ge 6:17; 7:21). It is used in a repeated formula (along with *mûth* [4191], meaning to die) to describe the death of the patriarchs and Ishmael (Ge 25:8, 17; 35:29; 49:33). Sometimes the context of the word refers to the root meaning of breathing out (Job 34:14; Ps 104:29). In Zec 13:8, the word is used to predict the deaths of two-thirds of the nation of Israel.

1479. **גּוּף, gûwph,** *goof*; a primitive root; (properly) to *hollow* or *arch*, i.e. (figurative) *close*; to *shut*:—shut.

1480. **גּוּפָה, gûwphâh,** *goo-faw´*; from 1479; a *corpse* (as *closed* to sense):—body.

A feminine noun meaning dead body, corpse. This word appears only twice in the OT and in the same verse. First Chronicles 10:12 describes Saul and his son's dead bodies. The word has a similar meaning to *gĕwiyyâh* (1472), meaning body, as is demonstrated when that word is used in a parallel passage, 1Sa 31:12.

1481. **גּוּר, gûwr,** *goor*; a primitive root; properly to *turn* aside from the road (for a lodging or any other purpose), i.e. *sojourn* (as a guest); also to *shrink, fear* (as in a *strange* place); also to *gather* for hostility (as *afraid*):—abide, assemble, be afraid, dwell, fear, gather (together), inhabitant, remain, sojourn, stand in awe, (be) stranger, × surely.

A verb meaning to sojourn, to dwell as a foreigner; in the reflexive sense, to seek hospitality with. The term is commonly used of the patriarchs who sojourned in Canaan (Ge 26:3; 35:27); places outside Canaan (Ge 12:10; 20:1; 21:23; 32:4[5]; 47:4); Naomi and her family in Moab (Ru 1:1); the exiles in Babylonia (Jer 42:15). Metaphorically, the term is used of one who worships in God's temple (Ps 15:1; 61:4[5]). It is used reflexively with the meaning to seek hospitality with in 1Ki 17:20.

1482. **גּוּר, gûwr,** *goor*; or (shortened) **גֻּר, gur,** *goor*; perhaps from 1481; a *cub* (as still *abiding* in the lair), especially of the lion:—whelp, young one.

1483. **גּוּר, Gûwr,** *goor*; the same as 1482; *Gur*, a place in Palestine:—Gur.

1484. **גּוּר, gôwr,** *gore*; or (feminine) **גֹּרָה, gôrâh,** *go-raw´*; a variation of 1482:—whelp.

1485. **גּוּר־בַּעַל, Gûwr-Baʻal,** *goor-bah´-al*; from 1481 and 1168; *dwelling of Baal; Gur-Baal,* a place in Arabia:—Gur-baal.

1486. **גּוֹרָל, gôwrâl,** *go-rawl´*; or (shortened) **גֹּרָל, gôrâl,** *go-ral´*; from an unused root meaning to *be rough* (as stone); (properly) a *pebble,* i.e. a *lot* (small stones being used for that purpose); (figurative) a *portion* or *destiny* (as if determined by lot):—lot.

1487. **גּוּשׁ, gûwsh,** *goosh*; or rather (by permutation) **גִּישׁ, gîysh,** *geesh*; of uncertain derivation; a *mass* of earth:—clod.

1488. **גֵּז, gêz,** *gaze*; from 1494; a *fleece* (as *shorn*); also mown *grass*:—fleece, mowing, mown grass.

1489. **גִּזְבָּר, gizbâr,** *giz-bawr´*; of foreign derivation; *treasurer*:—treasurer.

1490. **גִּזְבָּר, gizbâr,** *giz-bawr´*; (Chaldee); corresponding to 1489:—treasurer.

1491. **גָּזָה, gâzâh,** *gaw-zaw´*; a primitive root [akin to 1468]; to *cut* off, i.e. *portion* out:—take.

1492. **גִּזָּה, gizzâh,** *giz-zaw´*; feminine from 1494; a *fleece*:—fleece.

1493. **גִּזוֹנִי, Gizôwnîy,** *gee-zo-nee´*; patrial from the unused name of a place apparently in Palestine; a *Gizonite* or inhabitant of Gizoh:—Gizonite.

1494. **גָּזַז, gâzaz,** *gaw-zaz´*; a primitive root [akin to 1468]; to *cut* off; specifically to *shear* a flock, or *shave* the hair; (figurative) to *destroy* an enemy:—cut off (down), poll, shave, ([sheep-]) shear (-er).

1495. **גָּזֵז, Gâzêz,** *gaw-zaze´*; from 1494; *shearer; Gazez,* the name of two Israelites:—Gazez.

1496. **גָּזִית, gâzîyth,** *gaw-zeeth´*; from 1491; something *cut,* i.e. *dressed* stone:—hewed, hewn stone, wrought.

1497. **גָּזַל, gâzal,** *gaw-zal´*; a primitive root; to *pluck* off; specifically to *flay, strip* or *rob*:—catch, consume, exercise [robbery], pluck (off), rob, spoil, take away (by force, violence), tear.

1498. **גָּזֵל, gâzêl,** *gaw-zale´*; from 1497; *robbery,* or (concrete) *plunder*:—robbery, thing taken away by violence.

1499. **גֵּזֶל, gêzel,** *ge´-zel*; from 1497; *plunder,* i.e. *violence*:—violence, violent perverting.

1500. **גְּזֵלָה, g**e**zêlâh,** *gez-ay-law´*; feminine of 1498 and meaning the same:—that (he had robbed) [which he took violently away], spoil, violence.

1501. **גָּזָם, gâzâm,** *gaw-zawm´*; from an unused root meaning to *devour*; a kind of *locust*:—palmer worm.

1502. **גַּזָּם, Gazzâm,** *gaz-zawm´*; from the same as 1501; *devourer; Gazzam,* one of the Nethinim:—Gazzam.

1503. **גֶּזַע, gezaʻ,** *geh´-zah*; from an unused root meaning to *cut* down (trees); the *trunk* or *stump* of a tree (as felled or as planted):—stem, stock.

1504. **גָּזַר, gâzar,** *gaw-zar´*; a primitive root; to *cut* down or off; (figurative) to *destroy, divide, exclude* or *decide*:—cut down (off), decree, divide, snatch.

A verb meaning to cut, to divide, to separate. The basic meaning of this word can be seen in Solomon's command to divide the baby in two pieces (1Ki 3:25, 26); in the act of cutting down trees (2Ki 6:4); or when God divided the Red Sea (Ps 136:13). The word also describes a person separated from God's temple (2Ch 26:21); from God's caring hand (Ps 88:5[6]); or from life itself (Isa 53:8). So great may be the separation that destruction may occur (La 3:54; Eze 37:11; Hab 3:17). In a few instances, this word means to decree (Est 2:1; Job 22:28). The meaning is related to the Hebrew idiom, to cut a covenant, which means to make a covenant. In that idiom, the synonym *kârath* (3772), meaning to cut, is used.

1505. **גְּזַר, g**e**zar,** *gez-ar´*; (Chaldee); corresponding to 1504; to *quarry; determine*:—cut out, soothsayer.

An Aramaic verb meaning to cut, to decide, to determine. The participle is used as a noun meaning soothsayer or astrologer. The verb occurs in Da 2:34 and 2:45 to describe a stone cut without hands—an image that symbolizes the kingdom of God. Apparently, the idea of future events being cut out led to the word being used to signify soothsayers or astrologers who could foretell the future (Da 2:27; 4:7[4]; 5:7, 11).

1506. **גֶּזֶר, gezer,** *geh´-zer*; from 1504; something *cut* off; a *portion*:—part, piece.

A masculine noun meaning part, portion, division, half. It is found only as a plural form. It refers to the halves of animals that Abraham prepared in the covenant ceremony of Ge 15:17 and the two halves of the Red Sea when God divided it (Ps 136:13).

1507. **גֶּזֶר, Gezer,** *geh´-zer*; the same as 1506; *Gezer,* a place in Palestine:—Gazer, Gezer.

1508. **גִּזְרָה, gizrâh,** *giz-raw´*; feminine of 1506; the *figure* or person (as if *cut* out); also an *inclosure* (as *separated*):—polishing, separate place.

1509. **גְּזֵרָה, g**e**zêrâh,** *gez-ay-raw´*; from 1504; a *desert* (as *separated*):—not inhabited.

1510. **גְּזֵרָה, g**e**zêrâh,** *gez-ay-raw´*; (Chaldee); from 1505 (as 1504); a *decree*:—decree.

1511. **גִּזְרִי, Gizrîy,** *giz-ree´*; (in the margin), patrial from 1507; a *Gezerite* (collective) or inhabitant of Gezer; but better (as in the text) by transpositon **גִּרְזִי, Girzîy,** *ger-zee´*; patrial of 1630; a *Girzite* (collective) or member of a native tribe in Palestine:—Gezrites.

1512. **גָּחוֹן, gâchôwn,** *gaw-khone´*; probably from 1518; the external *abdomen, belly* (as the *source* of the fetus [compare 1521]):—belly.

1513. **גֶּחֶל, gechel,** *ge´-khel*; or (feminine) **גַּחֶלֶת, gacheleth,** *gah-kheh´-leth*; from an unused root meaning to *glow* or *kindle*; an *ember*:—(burning) coal.

1514. **גַּחַם, Gacham,** *gah´-kham*; from an unused root meaning to *burn; flame; Gacham,* a son of Nahor:—Gaham.

1515. **גַּחַר, Gachar,** *gah´-khar*; from an unused root meaning to *hide; lurker; Gachar,* one of the Nethinim:—Gahar.

1516. **גַּיְא, gayʼ,** *gah´ee*; or (shortened) **גַּי, gay,** *gah´ee*; probably (by transcription) from the same root as 1466 (abbreviation); a *gorge* (from its *lofty* sides; hence narrow, but not a gully or winter-torrent):—valley.

1517. **גִּיד, gîyd,** *geed*; probably from 1464; a *thong* (as *compressing*); (by analogy) a *tendon*:—sinew.

1518. **גִּיחַ, gîyach,** *gee´-akh*; or (shortened) **גֹּחַ, gôach,** *go´-akh*; a primitive root; to *gush* forth (as water), generally to *issue*:—break forth, labour to bring forth, come forth, draw up, take out.

1519. **גִּיחַ, gîyach,** *gee´-akh*; (Chaldee); or (shortened) **גּוּחַ, gûwach,** *goo´-akh*; (Chaldee); corresponding to 1518; to *rush* forth:—strive.

1520. **גִּיחַ, Gîyach,** *gee´-akh*; from 1518; a *fountain; Giach,* a place in Palestine:—Giah.

1521. **גִּיחוֹן, Gîychôwn,** *gee-khone´*; or (shortened) **גִּחוֹן, Gichôwn,** *gee-khone´*; from 1518; *stream; Gichon,* a river of Paradise; also a valley (or pool) near Jerusalem:—Gihon.

1522. **גֵּיחֲזִי, Gêychăzîy,** *gay-khah-zee´*; or **גֵּחֲזִי, Gêchă-zîy,** *gay-khah-zee´*; apparently from 1516 and 2372; *valley of a visionary; Gechazi,* the servant of Elisha:—Gehazi.

1523. גִּיל, **gîyl,** *geel*; or (by permutation) גּוּל, **gûwl,** *gool*; a primitive root; (properly) to *spin* round (under the influence of any violent emotion), i.e. usually *rejoice*, or (as *cringing*) *fear*:—be glad, joy, be joyful, rejoice.

1524. גִּיל, **gîyl,** *geel*; from 1523; a *revolution* (of time, i.e. an *age*); also *joy*:— × exceedingly, gladness, × greatly, joy, rejoice (-ing), sort.

1525. גִּילָה, **gîylâh,** *gee-law´*; or גִּילַת, **gîylath,** *gee-lath´*; feminine of 1524; *joy*:—joy, rejoicing.

1526. גִּילֹנִי, **Gîylônîy,** *gee-lo-nee´*; patrial from 1542; a *Gilonite* or inhabitant of Giloh:—Gilonite.

1527. גִּינַת, **Gîynath,** *gee-nath´*; of uncertain derivation; *Ginath*, an Israelite:—Ginath.

1528. גִּיר, **gîyr,** *geer*; (Chaldee); corresponding to 1615; *lime*:—plaster.

1529. גֵּישָׁן, **Gêyshân,** *gay-shawn´*; from the same as 1487; *lumpish; Geshan*, an Israelite:—Geshan.

1530. גַּל, **gal,** *gal*; from 1556; something *rolled*, i.e. a *heap* of stone or dung (plural *ruins*), (by analogy) a *spring* of water (plural *waves*):—billow, heap, spring, wave.

1531. גֹּל, **gôl,** *gole*; from 1556; a *cup* for oil (as *round*):—bowl.

1532. גַּלָּב, **gallâb,** *gal-lawb´*; from an unused root meaning to *shave*; a *barber*:—barber.

1533. גִּלְבֹּעַ, **Gilbôaʻ,** *gil-bo´-ah*; from 1530 and 1158; *fountain of ebullition; Gilboa*, a mountain of Palestine:—Gilboa.

1534. גַּלְגַּל, **galgal,** *gal-gal´*; by reduplication from 1556; a *wheel*; (by analogy) a *whirlwind*; also *dust* (as *whirled*):—heaven, rolling thing, wheel.

A masculine noun meaning a wheel, a whirl, a whirlwind. This word primarily describes an object circling or rotating around and around. This can be seen in the related verb *gâlal* (1556), meaning to roll. This word is often used to describe wheels, like those on a chariot (Eze 23:24; 26:10); an instrument used to draw water from a cistern (Ecc 12:6); or the objects in Ezekiel's vision (Eze 10:2, 6, 13), which are similar to *'ôwph ân* (212), meaning wheels. In most passages, a sense of a whirling movement is found in swift wheels (Isa 5:28); rumbling, noisy wheels (Jer 47:3); swirling chaff (Isa 17:13); thunder in the swirling storm (Ps 77:18[19]).

1535. גַּלְגַּל, **galgal,** *gal-gal´*; (Chaldee); corresponding to 1534; a *wheel*:—wheel.

An Aramaic masculine noun meaning wheel. The word occurs only in Da 7:9, where it describes fiery wheels on the blazing throne of the Ancient of Days. It is thought that the throne is seen as connected to a chariot. The wheeled cherubim (cf. Eze 10:15, 20) may be related to the wheels of this throne (cf. 1Ch 28:18; Ps 99:1).

1536. גִּלְגָּל, **gilgâl,** *gil-gawl´*; a variation of 1534:—wheel.

A masculine noun meaning a cart wheel. It is the cart wheel used in the process of threshing or crushing grain (Isa 28:28). This word is a variation of the Hebrew word *galgal* (1534).

1537. גִּלְגָּל, **Gilgâl,** *gil-gawl´*; the same as 1536 (with the article as a proper noun); *Gilgal*, the name of three places in Palestine:—Gilgal. See also 1019.

1538. גֻּלְגֹּלֶת, **gulgôleth,** *gul-go´-leth*; by reduplication from 1556; a *skull* (as *round*); (by implication) a *head* (in enumeration of persons):—head, every man, poll, skull.

A feminine noun meaning skull, head, and thus a person. The author of Judges used this word when he described Abimelech's skull being cracked when a woman dropped a millstone on it (Jgs 9:53). When Jezebel was killed, her skull was one of the few remnants of her body when people buried her (2Ki 9:35). The Philistines hung up Saul's head in the temple of Dagon (1Ch 10:10). At other times, this word is used more generically to mean person, as when Moses instructed the Israelites to gather an omer of manna per person (Ex 16:16); a beka of silver per person for the tabernacle (Ex 38:26); or to redeem the Levites (Nu 3:47). It is also used in passages concerning the taking of a census (Nu 1:2, 18, 20, 22; 1Ch 23:3, 24). This word means the same as the Aramaic word *Golgotha*—the name of the place where Jesus was crucified (Lk 23:33).

1539. גֶּלֶד, **gêled,** *gay´-led*; from an unused root probably meaning to *polish*; the (human) *skin* (as *smooth*):—*skin*.

A masculine noun meaning skin. It is an archaic Hebrew word, since it is found only one time in the book of Job. The word is used when the text describes Job expressing his grief by sewing sackcloth over his skin (Job 16:15)—a common custom of mourning in ancient Israel.

1540. גָּלָה, **gâlâh,** *gaw-law´*; a primitive root; to *denude* (especially in a disgraceful sense); (by implication) to *exile* (captives being usually *stripped*); (figurative) to *reveal*:— + advertise, appear, bewray, bring, (carry, lead, go) captive (into captivity), depart, disclose, discover, exile, be gone, open, × plainly, publish, remove, reveal, × shamelessly, shew, × surely, tell, uncover.

A verb meaning to reveal, to be revealed, to uncover, to remove, to go into exile, to reveal oneself, to expose, to disclose. It is used with the words ear (1Sa 9:15; 20:2, 12, 13) and eyes (Nu 24:4), meaning to reveal. On occasion, it is used in the expression to uncover the nakedness of, which often implies sexual relations (Le 18:6).

1541. גְּלָה, **g^elâh,** *gel-aw´*; (Chaldee); or גְּלָא, **g^elâ',** *gel-aw´*; (Chaldee); corresponding to 1540:—bring over, carry away, reveal.

An Aramaic verb meaning to bring over, to take away (into exile), to reveal. This word is used of those who were deported to Babylonia (Ezr 4:10; 5:12). In the book of Daniel, the meaning is to uncover or to reveal. In the story of the dreams of Nebuchadnezzar, God is shown as the One who reveals hidden things, specifically the meanings of dreams (Da 2:22, 28, 29, 47).

1542. גִּלֹה, **Gilôh,** *gee-lo´*; or (fully) גִּילֹה, **Gîylôh,** *gee-lo´*; from 1540; *open; Giloh*, a place in Palestine:—Giloh.

1543. גֻּלָּה, **gullâh,** *gool-law´*; feminine from 1556; a *fountain*, *bowl* or *globe* (all as *round*):—bowl, pommel, spring.

1544. גִּלּוּל, **gillûwl,** *gil-lool´*; or (shortened) גִּלֻּל, **gillul,** *gil-lool´*; from 1556; (properly) a *log* (as *round*); (by implication) an *idol*:—idol.

A masculine noun meaning idols. The Hebrew word is always found in the plural form. The term is used thirty-eight times in Ezekiel and nine times in the rest of the OT. The people are told to destroy, abandon, and remove their idols. Dt 29:17[16] implies idols can be made of wood, stone, silver, or gold. Ezekiel longs for a day when Israel will no longer worship idols (Eze 37:23).

1545. גְּלוֹם, **g^elôwm,** *gel-ome´*; from 1563; *clothing* (as *wrapped*):—clothes.

1546. גָּלוּת, **gâlûwth,** *gaw-looth´*; feminine from 1540; *captivity*; (concrete) *exiles* (collective):—(they that are carried away) captives (-ity).

A feminine singular noun meaning exiles, captives, captivity. This word is used with the meaning of exiles in the prophetic messages concerning the prisoners of the king of Assyria (Isa 20:4); those exiles whom the Lord will free (Isa 45:13); and those whom God would protect (Jer 24:5; 28:4). It is also used to refer to Jehoiachin's captivity (2Ki 25:27; Eze 1:2), and the exile of the Israelites as a whole (Eze 33:21). The word comes from the Hebrew root *gâlâh* (1540).

1547. גָּלוּ, **gâlûw,** *gaw-loo´*; (Chaldee); corresponding to 1546:—captivity.

An Aramaic feminine singular noun meaning captivity, exile. It is the equivalent of the Hebrew word *gâlûth* (1546). In Aramaic, it is commonly used in the phrase, sons of captivity. In the book of Ezra, the word refers to the exiles who celebrated when the temple was rebuilt after King Darius's decree (Ezr 6:16). In the book of Daniel, it refers to Daniel's captivity (Da 2:25; 5:13; 6:13[14]).

1548. גָּלַח, **gâlach,** *gaw-lakh´*; a primitive root; (properly) to *be bald*, i.e. (causative) to *shave*; (figurative) to *lay waste*:—poll, shave (off).

1549. גִּלָּיוֹן, **gillâyôwn,** *gil-law-yone´*; or גִּלְיוֹן, **gilyôwn,** *gil-yone´*; from 1540; a *tablet* for writing (as *bare*); (by analogy) a *mirror* (as a *plate*):—glass, roll.

1550. גָּלִיל, **gâlîyl,** *gaw-leel´*; from 1556; a *valve* of a folding door (as *turning*); also a *ring* (as *round*):—folding, ring.

1551. גָּלִיל, **Gâlîyl,** *gaw-leel´*; or (prolonged) גָּלִילָה, **Gâlîylâh,** *gaw-lee-law´*; the same as 1550; a *circle* (with the article); *Galil* (as a special *circuit*) in the North of Palestine:—Galilee.

1552. גְּלִילָה, **geliylâh,** *gel-ee-law´*; feminine of 1550; a *circuit* or *region*:—border, coast, country.

1553. גְּלִילוֹת, **Gelîylôwth,** *gel-ee-lowth´*; plural of 1552; *circles; Geliloth*, a place in Palestine:—Geliloth.

1554. גַּלִּים, **Gallîym,** *gal-leem´*; plural of 1530; *springs; Gallim*, a place in Palestine:—Gallim.

1555. גָּלְיַת, **Golyath,** *gol-yath´*; perhaps from 1540; *exile; Goljath*, a Philistine:—Goliath.

1556. גָּלַל, **gâlal,** *gaw-lal´*; a primitive root; to *roll* (literal or figurative):—commit, remove, roll (away, down, together), run down, seek occasion, trust, wallow.

A verb meaning to roll, to remove, to commit, to trust. The root idea of the word is to roll. The Hebrew word often refers to rolling stones (Ge 29:8; Jos 10:18; Pr 26:27) as well as other concrete objects. It can also describe abstract concepts, such as reproach being rolled off (removed) from someone (Ps 119:22) or one's ways and works rolled onto (committed, entrusted) to someone (especially God) (Ps 37:5; Pr 16:3). This important root word is used to form many other names and words (cf. Gilgal in Jos 5:9).

1557. גָּלָל, **gâlâl,** *gaw-lawl´*; from 1556; *dung* (as in *balls*):—dung.

1558. גָּלָל, **gâlâl,** *gaw-lawl´*; from 1556; a *circumstance* (as *rolled* around); only used adverbially, on *account* of:—because of, for (sake).

1559. גָּלָל, **Gâlâl,** *gaw-lawl´*; from 1556, in the sense of 1560; *great; Galal*, the name of two Israelites:—Galal.

1560. גְּלָל, **gelâl,** *gel-awl´*; (Chaldee); from a root corresponding to 1556; *weight* or *size* (as if *rolled*):—great.

1561. גֵּלֶל, **gêlel,** *gay´-lel*; a variation of 1557; *dung* (plural *balls* of dung):—dung.

1562. גִּלֲלַי, **Gilălay,** *ge-lal-ah´ee*; from 1561; *dungy; Gilalai*, an Israelite:—Gilalai.

1563. גָּלַם, **gâlam,** *gaw-lam´*; a primitive root; to *fold*:—wrap together.

1564. גֹּלֶם, **gôlem,** *go´-lem*; from 1563; a *wrapped* (and unformed *mass*, i.e. as the *embryo*):—substance yet being unperfect.

1565. גַּלְמוּד, **galmûwd,** *gal-mood´*; probably by prolongation from 1563; *sterile* (as *wrapped* up too hard); (figurative) *desolate*:—desolate, solitary.

1566. גָּלַע, **gâla',** *gaw-lah´*; a primitive root; to *be obstinate*:—(inter-) meddle (with).

1567. גַּלְעֵד, **Galyêd,** *gal-ade´*; from 1530 and 5707; *heap of testimony; Galed*, a memorial cairn East of the Jordan:—Galeed.

1568. גִּלְעָד, **Gil'âd,** *gil-awd´*; probably from 1567; *Gilad*, a region East of the Jordan; also the name of three Israelites:—Gilead, Gileadite.

1569. גִּלְעָדִי, **Gil'âdîy,** *gil-aw-dee´*; patronymic from 1568; a *Giladite* or descendant of Gilad:—Gileadite.

1570. גָּלַשׁ, **gâlash,** *gaw-lash´*; a primitive root; probably to *caper* (as a goat):—appear.

1571. גַּם, **gam,** *gam*; by contraction from an unused root meaning to *gather*; (properly) *assemblage*; used only adverbially *also, even, yea, though*; often repeated as correlation *both … and*:—again, alike, also, (so much) as (soon), both (so) … and, but, either … or, even, for all, (in) likewise (manner), moreover, nay … neither, one, then (-refore), though, what, with, yea.

1572. גָּמָא, **gâmâ',** *gaw-maw´*; a primitive root (literal or figurative) to *absorb*:—swallow, drink.

1573. גֹּמֶא, **gôme',** *go´-meh*; from 1572; (properly) an *absorbent*, i.e. the *bulrush* (from its *porosity*); specifically the *papyrus*:—(bul-) rush.

1574. גֹּמֶד, **gômed,** *go´-med*; from an unused root apparently meaning to *grasp*; (properly) a *span*:—cubit.

1575. גַּמָּדִים, **gammâdîym,** *gam-maw-deem´*; from the same as 1574; a *warrior* (as *grasping* weapons):—Gammadims.

1576. גְּמוּל, **gemûwl,** *gem-ool´*; from 1580; *treatment*, i.e. an *act* (of good or ill); (by implication) *service* or *requital*:— + as hast served, benefit, desert, deserving, that which he hath given, recompense, reward.

1577. גָּמוּל, **gâmûwl,** *gaw-mool´*; passive participle of 1580; *rewarded; Gamul*, an Israelite:—Gamul. See also 1014.

1578. גְּמוּלָה, **gemûwlâh,** *gem-oo-law´*; feminine of 1576; meaning the same:—deed, recompense, such a reward.

1579. גִּמְזוֹ, **Gimzôw,** *gim-zo´*; of uncertain derivation; Gimzo, a place in Palestine:—Gimzo.

1580. גָּמַל, **gâmal,** *gaw-mal´*; a primitive root; to *treat* a person (well or ill), i.e. *benefit* or *requite*; by implication (of *toil*) to *ripen*, i.e. (specific) to *wean*:—bestow on, deal bountifully, do (good), recompense, requite, reward, ripen, + serve, mean, yield.

A verb meaning to recompense another, to bring to completion, to do good. This word has a broad spectrum of meanings. The predominant idea of this word is to recompense either with a benevolent reward (1Sa 24:17[18]; 2Sa 19:36[37]) or an evil recompense (Dt 32:6; 2Ch 20:11; Ps 137:8). The idea of bringing to an end is demonstrated in verses that describe a child who is weaned (Ge 21:8; 1Sa 1:22–24; Isa 11:8) or plants that have ripened (Nu 17:8[23]; Isa 18:5). At times this word is best translated to do good or to deal bountifully (Ps 119:17; Pr 11:17; Isa 63:7).

1581. גָּמָל, **gâmâl,** *gaw-mawl´*; apparently from 1580 (in the sense of *labour* or *burden-bearing*); a *camel*:—camel.

1582. גְּמַלִּי, **Gemallîy,** *gem-al-lee´*; probably from 1581; *camel-driver; Gemalli*, an Israelite:—Gemalli.

1583. גַּמְלִיאֵל, **Gamlîy'êl,** *gam-lee-ale´*; from 1580 and 410; *reward of God; Gamliel*, an Israelite:—Gamaliel.

1584. גָּמַר, **gâmar,** *gaw-mar´*; a primitive root; to *end* (in the sense of *completion* or *failure*):—cease, come to an end, fail, perfect, perform.

A verb meaning to complete, to perfect, to fail, to cease. The root idea of the word is to end. In three intransitive uses, the psalmist prayed for wickedness to end, cried out that the godly person fails, and asked if God's promise fails forever (Ps 7:9[10]; 12:1[2]; 77:8[9]). In two transitive uses, God is the subject. He will perfect that which concerns the psalmist and will complete (or perform) all things for him (Ps 57:2[3]; 138:8).

1585. גְּמַר, **gemar,** *gem-ar´*; (Chaldee); corresponding to 1584:—perfect.

A verb meaning to complete. This Aramaic word is used only once in the OT and is equivalent to the Hebrew word *gâmar* (1584), meaning to complete. It is found only in the introductory section of Artaxerxes' decree given to Ezra (Ezr 7:12). Although the exact meaning of this word is unclear, it is best to understand this word as an introductory comment similar to Ezr 5:7, where the Hebrew word *shĕlâm* (8001), meaning peace, is used.

1586. גֹּמֶר, Gômer, *go´-mer*; from 1584; *completion; Gomer*, the name of a son of Japheth and of his descendant; also of a Hebrewess:—Gomer.

1587. גְּמַרְיָה, G^eˢmaryâh, *gem-ar-yaw´*; or גְּמַרְיָהוּ, **G^eˢmaryâhûw,** *gem-ar-yaw´-hoo*; from 1584 and 3050; *Jah has perfected; Gemarjah*, the name of two Israelites:—Gemariah.

1588. גַּן, gan, *gan*; from 1598; a *garden* (as *fenced*):—garden.

1589. גָּנַב, gânab, *gaw-nab´*; a primitive root; to *thieve* (literal or figurative); (by implication) to *deceive*:—carry away, × indeed, secretly bring, steal (away), get by stealth.

1590. גַּנָּב, gannâb, *gan-nawb´*; from 1589; a *stealer*:—thief.

1591. גְּנֵבָה, g^eˢnêbâh, *gen-ay-baw´*; from 1589; *stealing*, i.e. (concrete) something *stolen*:—theft.

1592. גְּנֻבַת, G^eˢnubath, *gen-oo-bath´*; from 1589; *theft; Genubath*, an Edomitish prince:—Genubath.

1593. גַּנָּה, gannâh, *gan-naw´*; feminine of 1588; a *garden*:—garden.

1594. גִּנָּה, ginnâh, *gin-naw´*; another form for 1593:—garden.

1595. גֶּנֶז, genez, *geh´-nez*; from an unused root meaning to *store; treasure*; (by implication) a *coffer*:—chest, treasury.

1596. גְּנַז, g^eˢnaz, *gen-az´*; (Chaldee); corresponding to 1595; *treasure*:—treasure.

1597. גִּנְזַךְ, ganzak, *gan-zak´*; prolonged from 1595; a *treasury*:—treasury.

1598. גָּנַן, gânan, *gaw-nan´*; a primitive root; to *hedge* about, i.e. (generally) *protect*:—defend.

1599. גִּנְּתוֹן, Ginn^eˢthôwn, *gin-neth-ōne´*; or גִּנְּתוֹ, **Ginn^eˢthôw,** *gin-neth-o´*; from 1598; *gardener; Ginnethon* or *Ginnetho*, an Israelite:—Ginnetho, Ginnethon.

1600. גָּעָה, gâʻâh, *gaw-aw´*; a primitive root; to *bellow* (as cattle):—low.

1601. גֹּעָה, Gôʻâh, *go-aw´*; feminine active participle of 1600; *lowing; Goah*, a place near Jerusalem:—Goath.

1602. גָּעַל, gâʻal, *gaw-al´*; a primitive root; to *detest*; (by implication) to *reject*:—abhor, fail, lothe, vilely cast away.

A verb meaning to detest, to abhor. It is used in Le 26:15, 43 to warn Israel not to abhor God's commandments. He would otherwise abhor them (Le 26:30), yet not to such an extent that He would destroy them completely (Le 26:44). This word also describes Israel as an unfaithful wife who loathes her husband (God) and her children (Eze 16:45). A bull that is not able to mate with a cow or whose seed is miscarried is said, literally, to cause loathing (Job 21:10). In 2Sa 1:21, a shield that failed to protect its owner, Saul, was cast away as detested rather than being oiled.

1603. גַּעַל, Gaʻal, *gah´-al*; from 1602; *loathing; Gaal*, an Israelite:—Gaal.

1604. גֹּעַל, gôʻal, *go´-al*; from 1602; *abhorrence*:—loathing.

1605. גָּעַר, gâʻar, *gaw-ar´*; a primitive root; to *chide*:—corrupt, rebuke, reprove.

A verb meaning to rebuke. This word depicts the sharp criticism of one person to another: Jacob rebuked Joseph for telling his dream (Ge 37:10), and Boaz commanded his servants not to rebuke Ruth's gleaning activity (Ru 2:16). When depicting God's actions, this word is often used to describe the result of His righteous anger (Isa 54:9; Na 1:4) against those who rebel against Him, including wicked nations (Ps 9:5[6]; Isa 17:13); their offspring (Mal 2:3); the proud (Ps 119:21); and Satan (Zec 3:2). So authoritative is the Lord's rebuke that even nature obeys His voice (Ps 106:9; Na 1:4).

1606. גְּעָרָה, g^eˢʻârâh, *geh-aw-raw´*; from 1605; a *chiding*:—rebuke (-ing), reproof.

A feminine singular noun meaning rebuke. It occurs fifteen times in the Bible, always in poetic passages. Both God and humans are the subject of such rebukes (2Sa 22:16; Isa 50:2).

1607. גָּעַשׁ, gâʻash, *gaw-ash´*; a primitive root to *agitate* violently:—move, shake, toss, trouble.

1608. גַּעַשׁ, Gaʻash, *ga´-ash*; from 1607; a *quaking; Gaash*, a hill in Palestine:—Gaash.

1609. גַּעְתָּם, Gaʻtâm, *gah-tawm´*; of uncertain derivation; *Gatam*, an Edomite:—Gatam.

1610. גַּף, gaph, *gaf*; from an unused root meaning to *arch*; the *back*; (by extension) the *body* or self:— + highest places, himself.

1611. גַּף, gaph, *gaf*; (Chaldee); corresponding to 1610; a *wing*:—wing.

1612. גֶּפֶן, gephen, *geh´-fen*; from an unused root meaning to *bend*; a *vine* (as *twining*), especially the grape:—vine, tree.

1613. גֹּפֶר, gôpher, *go´-fer*; from an unused root, probably meaning to *house in*; a kind of tree or wood (as used for *building*), apparently the *cypress*:—gopher.

1614. גָּפְרִית, gophrîyth, *gof-reeth´*; probably feminine of 1613; (properly) cypress *resin*; (by analogy) *sulphur* (as equally inflammable):—brimstone.

1615. גִּר, gir, *geer*; perhaps from 3564; *lime* (from being *burned* in a kiln):—chalk [-stone].

1616. גֵּר, gêr, *gare*; or (fully) גֵּיר, **gêyr,** *gare*; from 1481; (properly) a *guest*; (by implication) a *foreigner*:—alien, sojourner, stranger.

A masculine noun meaning sojourner, alien, stranger. The word indicates in general anyone who is not native to a given land or among a given people (Ex 12:19). The word is used most often to describe strangers or sojourners in Israel who were not native-born Israelites and were temporary dwellers or newcomers. A person, family, or group might leave their homeland and people to go elsewhere because of war or immediate danger as Moses had done (Ex 2:22; cf. 2Sa 4:3); Naomi and her family were forced to travel to Moab to sojourn because of a famine in Israel (Ru 1:1). God's call to Abraham to leave his own land of Ur of the Chaldees and made him a sojourner and an alien in the land of Canaan (Ge 12:1). Israel's divinely orchestrated descent into Egypt resulted in their becoming an alien people in a foreign land for four hundred years (Ge 15:13). Abraham considered himself an alien, although he was in the land of Canaan, the land of promise, because he was living among the Hittites at Hebron (Ge 23:4).

This evidence indicates that strangers or aliens were those living in a strange land among strange people. Their stay was temporary or they did not identify with the group among whom they were living, no matter how long they stayed. The transitory nature of aliens' status is indicated in passages that describe them as seeking overnight lodging or accommodations (Job 31:32; Jer 14:8).

Sojourners or strangers in Israel were not to be oppressed but were to receive special consideration for several reasons: Israel knew about being aliens, for they had been aliens in Egypt (Ex 23:9); aliens had a right to rest and cessation from labour just as the native Israelites did (Ex 20:10); aliens were to be loved, for God loved them (Dt 10:18) just as He loved widows and orphans; aliens had a right to food to satisfy their needs just as orphans and widows did (Dt 14:29). In Ezekiel's vision of a new temple and temple area, the children of aliens and sojourners were given an allotment of land (Eze 47:22), for they were to be considered as native children of Israel. However, this shows that sojourners had to receive special concessions because they did not have all the rights of native Israelites. Aliens could eat the Lord's Passover only if they and their entire household submitted to circumcision (Ex 12:48, 49). They were then not allowed to eat anything with yeast in it during the celebration of the Passover, just like native Israelites (Ex 12:19, 20). However, major distinctions did exist between sojourners or aliens and native Israelites. Unclean food could be given to aliens to eat, but the Israelites were prohibited from eating the same food. To have done so would violate their holiness and consecration to the Lord God. Unfortunately, David himself laid forced labour on the shoulders of aliens in Israel to prepare to build the temple (1Ch 22:2; cf. 2Ch 8:7–9).

1617. גֵּרָא, **Gêrâ',** *gay-raw´*; perhaps from 1626; a *grain; Gera*, the name of six Israelites:—Gera.

1618. גָּרָב, **gârâb,** *gaw-rawb´*; from an unused root meaning to *scratch; scurf* (from *itching*):—scab, scurvy.

1619. גָּרֵב, **Gârêb,** *gaw-rabe´*; from the same as 1618; *scabby; Gareb*, the name of an Israelite, also of a hill near Jerusalem:—Gareb.

1620. גַּרְגַּר, **gargêr,** *gar-gayr´*; by reduplication from 1641; a *berry* (as if a pellet of *rumination*):—berry.

1621. גַּרְגְּרוֹת, **gargârôwth,** *gar-ghawr-owth´*; feminine plural from 1641; the *throat* (as used in *rumination*):—neck.

1622. גִּרְגָּשִׁי, **Girgâshîy,** *gir-gaw-shee´*; patrial from an unused name [of uncertain derivation]; a *Girgashite*, one of the native tribes of Canaan:—Girgashite, Girgasite.

1623. גָּרַד, **gârad,** *gaw-rad´*; a primitive root; to *abrade*:—scrape.

1624. גָּרָה, **gârâh,** *gaw-raw´*; a primitive root; (properly) to *grate*, i.e. (figurative) to *anger*:—contend, meddle, stir up, strive.

1625. גֵּרָה, **gêrâh,** *gay-raw´*; from 1641; the *cud* (as *scraping* the throat):—cud.

1626. גֵּרָה, **gêrâh,** *gay-raw´*; from 1641 (as in 1625); properly (like 1620) a *kernel* (round as if *scraped*), i.e. a *gerah* or small weight (and coin):—gerah.

1627. גָּרוֹן, **gârôwn,** *gaw-rone´*; or (shortened) גָּרֹן, **gârôn,** *gaw-rone´*; from 1641; the *throat* [compare 1621] (as *roughened* by swallowing):—× aloud, mouth, neck, throat.

1628. גֵּרוּת, **gêrûwth,** *gay-rooth´*; from 1481; a (temporary) *residence*:—habitation.

1629. גָּרַז, **gâraz,** *gaw-raz´*; a primitive root; to *cut* off:—cut off.

1630. גְּרִזִים, **G^e^rizîym,** *ger-ee-zeem´*; plural of an unused noun from 1629 [compare 1511], *cut* up (i.e. *rocky*); *Gerizim*, a mountain of Palestine:—Gerizim.

1631. גַּרְזֶן, **garzen,** *gar-zen´*; from 1629; an *ax*:—ax.

1632. גָּרֹל, **gârôl,** *gaw-role´*; from the same as 1486; *harsh*:—man of great [*as in the margin which reads* 1419].

1633. גָּרַם, **gâram,** *gaw-ram´*; a primitive root; to *be spare* or *skeleton-like*; used only as a denominative from 1634; (causative) to *bone*, i.e. *denude* (by extension) *crunch* the bones:—gnaw the bones, break.

1634. גֶּרֶם, **gerem,** *geh´-rem*; from 1633; a *bone* (as the *skeleton* of the body); hence *self*, i.e. (figurative) *very*:—bone, strong, top.

1635. גְּרַם, **g^e^ram,** *geh´-ram*; (Chaldee); corresponding to 1634; a *bone*:—bone.

1636. גַּרְמִי, **Garmîy,** *gar-mee´*; from 1634; *bony*, i.e. *strong*:—Garmite.

1637. גֹּרֶן, **gôren,** *go´-ren*; from an unused root meaning to *smooth*; a threshing-*floor* (as made *even*); (by analogy) any open *area*:—(barn, corn, threshing-) floor, (threshing-, void) place.

1638. גָּרַס, **gâras,** *gaw-ras´*; a primitive root; to *crush*; also (intransitive and figurative) to *dissolve*:—break.

1639. גָּרַע, **gâra',** *gaw-rah´*; a primitive root; to *scrape* off; (by implication) to *shave, remove, lessen* or *withhold*:—abate, clip, (di-) minish, do (take) away, keep back, restrain, make small, withdraw.

1640. גָּרַף, **gâraph,** *gaw-raf´*; a primitive root; to *bear* off violently:—sweep away.

1641. גָּרַר, **gârar,** *gaw-rar´*; a primitive root; to *drag* off roughly; (by implication) to *bring up* the cud (i.e. *ruminate*); (by analogy) to *saw*:—catch, chew, × continuing, destroy, saw.

A verb meaning to scrape, to drag, to ruminate, to saw. The idea of a noise made in the back of the throat seems to be the root idea so that the word is onomatopoetic like the English word gargle. The word is used once to signify rumination, an essential mark of a ceremonially clean animal (Le 11:7). It described hostile forces dragging people away (Pr 21:7) or catching them like fish in a net (Hab 1:15). The word also signifies sawing, as dragging a saw over wood (1Ki 7:9).

1642. גְּרָר, **G^e^râr,** *ger-awr´*; probably from 1641; a *rolling* country; *Gerar*, a Philistine city:—Gerar.

1643. גֶּרֶשׂ, **gereś,** *geh´-res*; from an unused root meaning to *husk*; a *kernel* (collective), i.e. *grain*:—beaten corn.

1644. גָּרַשׁ, **gârash,** *gaw-rash´*; a primitive root; to *drive* out from a possession; especially to *expatriate* or *divorce*:—cast up (out), divorced (woman), drive away (forth, out), expel, × surely put away, trouble, thrust out.

1645. גֶּרֶשׁ, **geresh,** *geh´-resh*; from 1644; *produce* (as if *expelled*):—put forth.

1646. גְּרֻשָׁה, **g^e^rushâh,** *ger-oo-shaw´*; feminine passive participle of 1644; (abstract) *dispossession*:—exaction.

1647. גֵּרְשֹׁם, **Gêr^e^shôm,** *gay-resh-ome´*; for 1648; *Gereshom*, the name of four Israelites:—Gershom.

1648. גֵּרְשׁוֹן, **Gêr^e^shôwn,** *gay-resh-one´*; or גֵּרְשׁוֹם, **Gêr^e^shôwm,** *gay-resh-ome´*; from 1644; a *refugee; Gereshon* or *Gereshom*, an Israelite:—Gershon, Gershom.

1649. גֵּרְשֻׁנִּי, **Gêr^e^shunnîy,** *gay-resh-oon-nee´*; patronymic from 1648; a *Gereshonite* or descendant of Gereshon:—Gershonite, sons of Gershon.

1650. גְּשׁוּר, **G^e^shûwr,** *gesh-oor´*; from an unused root (meaning to *join*); *bridge*; *Geshur*, a district of Syria:—Geshur, Geshurite.

1651. גְּשׁוּרִי, **G^e^shûwrîy,** *ge-shoo-ree´*; patrial from 1650; a *Geshurite* (also collective) or inhabitant of Geshur:—Geshuri, Geshurites.

1652. גָּשַׁם, **gâsham,** *gaw-sham´*; a primitive root; to *shower* violently:—(cause to) rain.

1653. גֶּשֶׁם, **geshem,** *geh´-shem*; from 1652; a *shower*:—rain, shower.

1654. גֶּשֶׁם, **Geshem,** *geh´-shem*; or (prolonged) גַּשְׁמוּ, **Gashmûw,** *gash-moo´*; the same as 1653; *Geshem* or *Gashmu*, an Arabian:—Geshem, Gashmu.

1655. גְּשֵׁם, **g^e^shêm,** *geh´-shame*; (Chaldee); apparently the same as 1653; used in a peculiar sense, the *body* (probably for the [figurative] idea of a *hard* rain):—body.

A masculine noun meaning body. This is an Aramaic term and is found only in the book of Daniel. When Shadrach, Meshach, and Abednego emerged from the fiery furnace, this word was used to describe their unscathed bodies (Da 3:27). This term was also used to describe the nature of Nebuchadnezzar's being when he was turned into a beast (Da 5:21).

1656. גֹּשֶׁם, **gôshem,** *go´-shem*; from 1652; equivalent to 1653:—rained upon.

1657. גֹּשֶׁן, **Gôshen,** *go´-shen*; probably of Egyptian origin; *Goshen*, the residence of the Israelites in Egypt; also a place in Palestine:—Goshen.

1658. גִּשְׁפָּא, **Gishpâ',** *gish-paw´*; of uncertain derivation; *Gishpa*, an Israelite:—Gispa.

1659. גָּשַׁשׁ, **gâshash,** *gaw-shash´*; a primitive root; apparently to *feel* about:—grope.

1660. גַּת, **gath,** *gath*; probably from 5059 (in the sense of *treading* out grapes); a wine-*press* (or vat for holding the grapes in pressing them):—(wine-) press (fat).

1661. גַּת, **Gath,** *gath*; the same as 1660; *Gath*, a Philistine city:—Gath.

1662. גַּת־הַחֵפֶר, **Gath-ha-Chêpher,** *gath-hah-khay´-fer*; or (abridged) גִּתָּה־חֵפֶר, **Gittâh-Chêpher,** *git-taw-khay´-fer*; from 1660 and 2658 with the article inserted; *wine-press of (the) well; Gath-Chepher*, a place in Palestine:—Gath-kephr, Gittah-kephr.

1663. גִּתִּי, **Gittîy,** *git-tee´*; patrial from 1661; a *Gittite* or inhabitant of Gath:—Gittite.

1664. גִּתַּיִם, **Gittayim,** *git-tah´-yim*; dual of 1660; *double wine-press; Gittajim*, a place in Palestine:—Gittaim.

1665. גִּתִּית, **Gittîyth,** *git-teeth´*; feminine of 1663; a *Gittite* harp:—Gittith.

1666. גֶּתֶר, **Gether,** *geh´-ther*; of uncertain derivation; *Gether*, a son of Aram, and the region settled by him:—Gether.

1667. גַּת־רִמּוֹן, **Gath-Rimmôwn,** *gath-rim-mone´*; from 1660 and 7416; *wine-press of* (the) *pomegranate; Gath-Rimmon*, a place in Palestine:—Gath-rimmon.

1668. דָּא, **dâ',** *daw*; (Chaldee); corresponding to 2088; *this*:—one … another, this.

1669. דָּאַב, **dâ'ab,** *daw-ab´*; a primitive root; to *pine*:—mourn, sorrow (-ful).

1670. דְּאָבָה, **d^e'âbâh,** *dĕh-aw-baw´*; from 1669; (properly) *pining*; (by analogy) *fear*:—sorrow.

1671. דְּאָבוֹן, **d^e'âbôwn,** *dĕh-aw-bone´*; from 1669; *pining*:—sorrow.

1672. דָּאַג, **dâ'ag,** *daw-ag´*; a primitive root; *be anxious*:—be afraid (careful, sorry), sorrow, take thought.

A verb meaning to be anxious, to fear. This word describes uneasiness of mind as a result of the circumstances of life. It denotes the anxiety of Saul's father when Saul was away from home (1Sa 9:5; 10:2); the anxiety of David which resulted from his sin (Ps 38:18[19]); and the fear of famine (Jer 42:16). On the other hand, Jeremiah described the righteous person as one who would not be anxious in drought (Jer 17:8). This word is also used as a synonym for the Hebrew word *yârê'* (3372), meaning to fear when speaking of the anxiety of King Zedekiah (Jer 38:19) or fear in general (Isa 57:11).

1673. דֹּאֵג, **Dô'êg,** *do-ayg´*; or (fully) דּוֹאֵג, **Dôw'êg,** *do-ayg´*; active participle of 1672; *anxious; Doëg*, an Edomite:—Doeg.

1674. דְּאָגָה, **d^e'âgâh,** *dĕh-aw-gaw´*; from 1672; *anxiety*:—care (-fulness), fear, heaviness, sorrow.

A feminine noun meaning anxiety, care. This word refers to apprehension because of approaching trouble. In Joshua 22:24, it refers to a concern that Israel might forget God and prompted the building of a memorial altar. Elsewhere, it refers to anxiety over running out of food or an anxiety caused by God's judgment (Eze 4:16; 12:18, 19). This anxiety was sometimes roused by bad news (Jer 49:23) and sometimes relieved by good words (Pr 12:25).

1675. דָּאָה, **dâ'âh,** *daw-aw´*; a primitive root; to *dart*, i.e. *fly* rapidly:—fly.

1676. דָּאָה, **dâ'âh,** *daw-aw´*; from 1675; the *kite* (from its rapid *flight*):—vulture. See 7201.

1677. דֹּב, **dôb,** *dobe*; or (fully) דּוֹב, **dôwb,** *dobe*; from 1680; the *bear* (as slow):—bear.

1678. דֹּב, **dôb,** *dobe*; (Chaldee); corresponding to 1677:—bear.

1679. דֹּבֶא, **dôbe',** *do´-beh*; from an unused root (compare 1680) (probably meaning to *be sluggish*, i.e. *restful*); *quiet*:—strength.

1680. דָּבַב, **dâbab,** *daw-bab´*; a primitive root (compare 1679); to *move* slowly, i.e. *glide*:—cause to speak.

A verb meaning to move slowly, to glide over. It is used in late Hebrew to mean to flow slowly or to drop. In the OT, it suggests something that causes one to speak. In the discourse of the Shulamite and the beloved, this word identifies the way wine gently or slowly moves over the taster's lips and teeth (SS 7:9[10]).

1681. דִּבָּה, **dibbâh,** *dib-baw´*; from 1680 (in the sense of *furtive* motion); *slander*:—defaming, evil report, infamy, slander.

1682. דְּבוֹרָה, **d^ebôwrâh,** *deb-o-raw´*; or (shortened) דְּבֹרָה, **d^ebôrâh,** *deb-o-raw´*; from 1696 (in the sense of *orderly* motion); the *bee* (from its *systematic* instincts):—bee.

1683. דְּבוֹרָה, **D^ebôwrâh,** *deb-o-raw´*; or (shortened) דְּבֹרָה, **D^ebôrâh,** *deb-o-raw´*; the same as 1682; *Deborah*, the name of two Hebrewesses:—Deborah.

1684. דְּבַח, **d^ebach,** *deb-akh´*; (Chaldee); corresponding to 2076; to *sacrifice* (an animal):—offer [sacrifice].

An Aramaic verb meaning to sacrifice, to offer sacrifices. When King Darius issued the decree permitting the rebuilding of the Temple, he specified that it would be a place to offer sacrifices (Ezr 6:3). This word is the equivalent of the Hebrew verb *zâbach* (2076).

1685. דְּבַח, **d^ebach,** *deb-akh´*; (Chaldee); from 1684; a *sacrifice*:—sacrifice.

A masculine noun meaning sacrifice. This word comes from the Aramaic and is derived from the verb *dĕbach* (1684), meaning to sacrifice. It is the term used when King Cyrus ordered a decree for the rebuilding of the Temple, describing it as the place where the Israelites offered sacrifices (Ezr 6:3).

1686. דִּבְיֹנִים, **dibyônîym,** *dib-yo-neem´*; in the margin for the textual reading חֲרְיוֹן, **cheryôwn,** *kher-yone´*; both (in the plural only and) of uncertain derivation; probably some cheap vegetable, perhaps a bulbous root:—dove's dung.

1687. דְּבִיר, **d^ebîyr,** *deb-eer´*; or (shortened) דְּבִר, **debir,** *deb-eer´*; from 1696 (apparently in the sense of *oracle*); the *shrine* or innermost part of the sanctuary:—oracle.

A masculine noun referring to the innermost part of Solomon's Temple, also called the Holy of Holies. This cubical room, which took up one-third of the space of the Temple, housed the Ark of the Covenant (1Ki 6:16, 19–23). The ark contained the original tablets of the Ten Commandments, was overarched by carved cherubim covered with gold, and was especially associated with God's presence. When it was first brought into the Holy of Holies, God's glory filled the Temple (1Ki 8:6; cf. 1Ki 8:10). In Ps 28:2, David spoke of lifting his hands to the *dĕbiyr*. Since the Temple had not yet been built, this likely referred to the heavenly reality that was the model for the Temple and earlier tabernacle (cf. Ps 18:6[7]; Heb 8:5; 9:3–5) or perhaps to the room in the tabernacle that housed the Ark of the Covenant.

1688. דְּבִיר, **D^ebîyr,** *deb-eer´*; or (shortened)דְּבִר, **D^ebir,** *deb-eer´*; (Jos 13:26 [but see 3810]), the same as 1687; *Debir*, the name of an Amoritish king and of two places in Palestine:—Debir.

1689. דִּבְלָה, **Diblâh,** *dib-law´*; probably an orthographical error for 7247; *Diblah*, a place in Syria:—Diblath.

1690. דְּבֵלָה, **d^ebêlâh,** *deb-ay-law´*; from an unused root (akin to 2082) probably meaning to *press* together; a *cake* of pressed figs:—cake (lump) of figs.

1691. דִּבְלַיִם, **Diblayim,** *dib-lah´-yim*; dual from the masculine of 1690; *two cakes; Diblajim*, a symbol. name:—Diblaim.

1692. דָּבַק, **dâbaq,** *daw-bak´*; a primitive root; (properly) to *impinge*, i.e. *cling* or *adhere*; (figurative) to *catch* by pursuit:—abide fast, cleave (fast together), follow close (hard after), be joined (together), keep (fast), overtake, pursue hard, stick, take.

1693. דְּבַק, **d^ebaq,** *deb-ak´*; (Chaldee); corresponding to 1692; to *stick* to:—cleave.

1694. דֶּבֶק, **debeq,** *deh´-bek*; from 1692; a *joint*; (by implication) *solder*:—joint, solder.

1695. דָּבֵק, **dâbêq,** *daw-bake´*; from 1692; *adhering*:—cleave, joining, stick closer.

1696. דָּבַר, **dâbar,** *daw-bar´*; a primitive root; (perhaps properly) to *arrange*; but used figuratively (of words) to *speak*; rarely (in a destructive sense) to *subdue*:—answer, appoint, bid, command, commune, declare, destroy, give, name, promise, pronounce, rehearse, say, speak, be spokesman, subdue, talk, teach, tell, think, use [entreaties], utter, × well, × work.

A verb meaning to speak, to say. God told Moses to tell Pharaoh what He said (Ex 6:29). It can mean to promise (Dt 1:11). When used with the word song, it can mean to sing or chant (Jgs 5:12). The word can also mean think, as when Solomon spoke in his heart (Ecc 2:15). In Jeremiah, it means to pronounce judgment (Jer 1:16). This verb also refers to speaking about or against someone (Mal 3:13) or someone speaking to someone else (Mal 3:16). It is closely related to the Hebrew noun *dâbâr* (1697).

1697. דָּבָר, **dâbâr,** *daw-bawr´*; from 1696; a *word*; (by implication) a *matter* (as *spoken* of) or *thing*; (adverbial) a *cause*:—act, advice, affair, answer, × any such (thing), + because of, book, business, care, case, cause, certain rate, + chronicles, commandment, × commune (-ication), + concern [-ing], + confer, counsel, + dearth, decree, deed, × disease, due, duty, effect, + eloquent, errand, [evil favoured-] ness, + glory, + harm, hurt, + iniquity, + judgment, language, + lying, manner, matter, message, [no] thing, oracle, × ought, × parts, + pertaining, + please, portion, + power, promise, provision, purpose, question, rate, reason, report, request, × (as hast) said, sake, saying, sentence, + sign, + so, some [uncleanness], somewhat to say, + song, speech, × spoken, talk, task, + that, × there done, thing (concerning), thought, + thus, tidings, what [-soever], + wherewith, which, word, work.

A masculine noun meaning word, speech, matter. This frequent word has a wide range of meanings associated with it. It signified spoken words or speech (Ge 11:1; Isa 36:5; Jer 51:64); a command or royal decree (Est 1:12, 19); a report or tidings (Ex 33:4); advice (Jgs 20:7); poetic writings of David (2Ch 29:30); business affairs (1Ch 26:32); a legal cause (Ex 18:16); the custom or manner of activity (Est 1:13); and something indefinite (thing, Ge 22:16). Most important was the use of this word to convey divine communication. Often the word of the Lord signified the revelation given to prophets (2Sa 7:4; Jer 25:3; Hos 1:1). Similarly, the Ten Commandments were literally called the ten words of the Lord (Ex 34:28; Dt 4:13).

1698. דֶּבֶר, **deber,** *deh´-ber*; from 1696 (in the sense of *destroying*); a *pestilence*:—murrain, pestilence, plague.

A noun meaning plague or pestilence. This plague is a dreaded disease similar to the bubonic plague in the Middle Ages. It was likely carried by rat fleas and produced tumors on the infected person. First Samuel 5—6 describes the plague on the Philistines as a punishment from God. The word is also used as the most dreaded threat of the Lord against His people (Le 26:25; Nu 14:12). The prophets use this word frequently to predict coming judgment and destruction as in the common phrase, sword, famine, and plague (Jer 21:9; 38:2; Eze 6:11, NIV).

1699. דֹּבֶר, **dôber,** *do´-ber*; from 1696 (in its original sense); a *pasture* (from its *arrangement* of the flock):—fold, manner. דִּבֵּר, **dibbêr,** *dib-bare´*, for 1697:—word.

1700. דִּבְרָה, **dibrâh,** *dib-raw´*; feminine of 1697; a *reason, suit* or *style*:—cause, end, estate, order, regard.

A feminine singular noun meaning cause, end, regard, manner. In the book of Job, Eliphaz used the word to describe how he was laying down his cause before God (Job 5:8). This word is also used in the Psalms when it describes the priest who would exercise his duties in the manner of Melchizedek (Ps 110:4). Sometimes, it is translated much more briefly than it reads in the original language, as the literal translation in Ecclesiastes would read, "concerning the situation of mankind," while the NIV translates it "as for men" (Ecc 3:18). It can also mean for this reason or because (Ecc 7:14; 8:2).

1701. דִּבְרָה, **dibrâh,** *dib-raw´*; (Chaldee); corresponding to 1700:—intent, sake.

An Aramaic feminine noun meaning purpose, end, cause. The word is similar to the Hebrew form of the same spelling (1700). The Aramaic form occurs in Da 2:30 and 4:17(14). In both places, it is used with other words to create a purpose clause which is translated in order that, for the purpose of, or for the sake of.

1702. דֹּבְרוֹת, **dôbᵉrôwth,** *do-ber-oth´*; feminine active participle of 1696 in the sense of *driving* [compare 1699]; a *raft*:—float.

1703. דַּבֶּרֶת, **dabbereth,** *dab-ber-eth´*; intensive from 1696; a *word*:—word.

A feminine noun meaning word. This word is found only once in the OT (Dt 33:3), where it is best translated words. In this context, it poetically describes the words God gave Moses to deliver to the people. It comes from the verb *dâbar* (1696), meaning to speak and is related to the much-used Hebrew noun *dâbâr* (1697).

1704. דִּבְרִי, **Dibrîy,** *dib-ree´*; from 1697; *wordy; Dibri*, an Israelite:—Dibri.

1705. דָּבְרַת, **Dâbᵉrath,** *daw-ber-ath´*; from 1697 (perhaps in the sense of 1699); *Daberath*, a place in Palestine:—Dabareh, Daberath.

1706. דְּבַשׁ, **dᵉbash,** *deb-ash´*; from an unused root meaning to *be gummy; honey* (from its *stickiness*); (by analogy) *syrup*:—honey ([-comb]).

1707. דַּבֶּשֶׁת, **dabbesheth,** *dab-beh´-sheth*; intensive from the same as 1706; a sticky *mass*, i.e. the *hump* of a camel:—hunch [of a camel].

1708. דַּבֶּשֶׁת, **Dabbesheth,** *dab-beh´-sheth*; the same as 1707; *Dabbesheth*, a place in Palestine:—Dabbesheth.

1709. דָּג, **dâg,** *dawg*; or (fully) דָּאג, **dâ'g,** *dawg*; (Ne 13:16), from 1711; a *fish* (as *prolific*); or perhaps rather from 1672 (as *timid*); but still better from 1672 (in the sense of *squirming*, i.e. moving by the vibratory action of the tail); a *fish* (often used collectively):—fish.

A masculine noun meaning fish. The word is derived from *dâgâh* (1711) based on the idea that fish multiply quickly. The word is used of fish in the sea, often occurring alongside birds of the heavens and beasts of the field (Ge 9:2; Ps 8:7[8], 8[9]; Eze 38:20). The word also signifies fish as food and thus gives the name fish gate to the gate where they were brought into Jerusalem to sell (2Ch 33:14; Ne 3:3; Zep 1:10). Further, it describes fish as an object of study (1Ki 4:33[5:13]); as a symbol of defenselessness (Hab 1:14); and as showing God's sovereign creative power (Job 12:8).

1710. דָּגָה, **dâgâh,** *daw-gaw´*; feminine of 1709, and meaning the same:—fish.

A feminine noun meaning fish. This word is identical in meaning to *dâg* (1709), which can be found in the book of Jonah, where the fish was called a *dâg* (Jnh 1:17[2:1]; 2:10[11]) but was called a *dâgâh* in Jnh 2:1[2]. In all other instances, this word was used in the collective sense to refer to the fish at creation (Ge 1:26, 28); the fish who died in the plague (Ex 7:18, 21; Ps 105:29); the fish eaten in Egypt (Nu 11:5); and the fish in the waters (Dt 4:18; Eze 29:4, 5; 47:9, 10).

1711. דָּגָה, **dâgâh,** *daw-gaw´*; a primitive root; to *move rapidly*; used only as a denominative from 1709; to *spawn*, i.e. *become numerous*:—grow.

A verb meaning to multiply, to grow. Its primary meaning is to cover. It is used only in Ge 48:16 where Jacob blessed Ephraim and Manasseh, the sons of Joseph. He desired that they multiply or grow into a multitude. Jacob prophesied that Ephraim, the younger brother, would be a multitude of nations, more populous than Manasseh (cf. Ge 48:17–19) but that both would be a model of blessedness (cf. Ge 48:20).

1712. דָּגוֹן**, Dâgôwn,** *daw-gohn´*; from 1709; the *fish-god; Dagon,* a Philistine deity:—Dagon.

1713. דָּגַל**, dâgal,** *daw-gal´*; a primitive root; to *flaunt,* i.e. *raise a flag;* (figurative) to *be conspicuous:*—(set up, with) banners, chiefest.

1714. דֶּגֶל**, degel,** *deh´-gel*; from 1713; a *flag:*—banner, standard.

1715. דָּגָן**, dâgân,** *daw-gawn´*; from 1711; (properly) *increase,* i.e. *grain:*—corn ([floor]), wheat.

1716. דָּגַר**, dâgar,** *daw-gar´*; a primitive root; to *brood* over eggs or young:—gather, sit.

1717. דַּד**, dad,** *dad*; apparently from the same as 1730; the *breast* (as the seat of *love,* or from its shape):—breast, teat.

1718. דָּדָה**, dâdâh,** *daw-daw´*; a doubtful root; to *walk gently:*—go (softly, with).

1719. דְּדָן**, Dᵉdân,** *ded-awn´*; or (prolonged) דְּדָנֶה**, Dedâneh,** *deh-daw´-neh*; (Eze 25:13), of uncertain derivation; *Dedan,* the name of two Cushites and of their territory:—Dedan.

1720. דְּדָנִים**, Dᵉdânîym,** *ded-aw-neem´*; plural of 1719 (as patrial); *Dedanites,* the descendant or inhabitant of Dedan:—Dedanim.

1721. דֹּדָנִים**, Dôdânîym,** *do-daw-neem´*; or (by orthographical error) רֹדָנִים**, Rôdânîym,** *ro-daw-neem´*; (1Ch 1:7), a plural of uncertain derivation; *Dodanites,* or descendant of a son of Javan:—Dodanim.

1722. דְּהַב**, dᵉhab,** *deh-hab´*; (Chaldee); corresponding to 2091; *gold:*—gold (-en).

1723. דַּהֲוָא**, Dehâvê',** *deh-hawv-ay´*; (Chaldee); of uncertain derivation; *Dahava,* a people colonized in Samaria:—Dehavites.

1724. דָּהַם**, dâham,** *daw-ham´*; a primitive root (compare 1740); to *be dumb,* i.e. (figurative) *dumbfounded:*—be astonished.

1725. דָּהַר**, dâhar,** *daw-har´*; a primitive root; to *curvet* or move irregularly:—pause.

1726. דַּהֲהַר**, dahăhar,** *dah-hah-har´*; by reduplication from 1725; a *gallop:*—pransing.

1727. דּוּב**, dûwb,** *doob*; a primitive root; to *mope,* i.e. (figurative) *pine:*—sorrow.

1728. דַּוָּג**, davvâg,** *dav-vawg´*; an orthographical variation of 1709 as a denominative [1771]; a *fisherman:*—fisher.

1729. דּוּגָה**, dûwgâh,** *doo-gaw´*; feminine from the same as 1728; (properly) *fishery,* i.e. a *hook* for fishing:—fish [hook].

1730. דּוֹד**, dôwd,** *dode*; or (shortened) דֹּד**, dôd,** *dode*; from an unused root meaning (properly) to *boil,* i.e. (figurative) to *love;* (by implication) a *love-token, lover, friend;* specifically an *uncle:*—(well-) beloved, father's brother, love, uncle.

A masculine noun meaning beloved, loved one, uncle. This word is used most often in the SS of Solomon and has three clear meanings: **(1)** the most frequent is an address to a lover, beloved (SS 5:4; 6:3; 7:9[10]); **(2)** love, used literally of an adulteress who seduced a naïve man (Pr 7:18), and of Solomon and his lover (SS 1:2, 4; 4:10) (This meaning of love is also used symbolically of Jerusalem reaching the age of love [Eze 16:8] and Jerusalem's adultery [bed of love] with the Babylonians [Eze 23:17]); and finally, **(3)** uncle (Le 10:4; 1Sa 10:14–16; Est 2:15).

1731. דּוּד**, dûwd,** *dood*; from the same as 1730; a *pot* (for *boiling*); also (by resemblance of shape) a *basket:*—basket, caldron, kettle, (seething) pot.

1732. דָּוִד**, Dâvid,** *daw-veed´*; rarely (fully) דָּוִיד**, Dâvîyd,** *daw-veed´*; from the same as 1730; *loving; David,* the youngest son of Jesse:—David.

1733. דּוֹדָה**, dôwdâh,** *do-daw´*; feminine of 1730; an *aunt:*—aunt, father's sister, uncle's wife.

1734. דּוֹדוֹ**, Dôwdôw,** *do-do´*; from 1730; *loving; Dodo,* the name of three Israelites:—Dodo.

1735. דּוֹדָוָהוּ**, Dôwdâvâhûw,** *do-daw-vaw´-hoo*; from 1730 and 3050; *love of Jah; Dodavah,* an Israelite:—Dodavah.

1736. דּוּדָאִים**, dûwdâ'îym,** *doo-daw´-eem*; from 1731; a *boiler* or *basket;* also the *mandrake* (as *aphrodisiac*):—basket, mandrake.

A masculine plural noun meaning mandrake. A fragrant plant (SS 7:13[14]), the mandrake was considered a potent aphrodisiac. This usage can be seen in Ge 30:14–16, where the text describes Leah using these plants to attract Jacob.

1737. דּוֹדַי**, Dôwday,** *do-dah´ee*; formed like 1736; *amatory; Dodai,* an Israelite:—Dodai.

1738. דָּוָה**, dâvâh,** *daw-vaw´*; a primitive root; to *be sick* (as if in menstruation):—infirmity.

1739. דָּוֶה**, dâveh,** *daw-veh´*; from 1738; *sick* (especially in menstruation):—faint, menstruous cloth, she that is sick, having sickness.

1740. דּוּחַ**, dûwach,** *doo´-akh*; a primitive root; to *thrust* away; (figurative) to *cleanse:*—cast out, purge, wash.

A verb meaning to rinse, to cleanse, to wash away. This word is used only four times in the OT. On two occasions, it is used within the sacrificial context to describe offerings that needed to be washed (2Ch 4:6; Eze 40:38). In other contexts, the word describes the washing away of the sins of those in Jerusalem (Isa 4:4) and Nebuchadnezzar's carrying away (or washing away) of Judah in the Babylonian exile (Jer 51:34).

1741. דְּוַי**, dᵉvay,** *dev-ah´ee*; from 1739; *sickness;* (figurative) *loathing:*—languishing, sorrowful.

1742. דַּוָּי**, davvây,** *dav-voy´*; from 1739; *sick;* (figurative) *troubled:*—faint.

1743. דּוּךְ**, dûwk,** *dook*; a primitive root; to *bruise* in a mortar:—beat.

1744. דּוּכִיפַת**, dûwkîyphath,** *doo-kee-fath´*; of uncertain derivation; the *hoopoe* or else the *grouse:*—lapwing.

1745. דּוּמָה**, dûwmâh,** *doo-maw´*; from an unused root meaning to *be dumb* (compare 1820); *silence;* (figurative) *death:*—silence.

1746. דּוּמָה**, Dûwmâh,** *doo-maw´*; the same as 1745; *Dumah,* a tribe and region of Arabia:—Dumah.

1747. דּוּמִיָּה**, dûwmîyyâh,** *doo-me-yaw´*; from 1820; *stillness;* (adverb) *silently;* (abstract) *quiet, trust:*—silence, silent, waiteth.

1748. דּוּמָם**, dûwmâm,** *doo-mawm´*; from 1826; *still;* (adverb) *silently:*—dumb, silent, quietly wait.

1749. דּוֹנַג**, dôwnag,** *do-nag´*; of uncertain derivation; *wax:*—wax.

1750. דּוּץ**, dûwts,** *doots*; a primitive root; to *leap:*—be turned.

1751. דְּקַק**, dᵉqaq,** *de-kak´*; (Chaldee); corresponding to 1854; to *crumble:*—be broken to pieces.

1752. דּוּר**, dûwr,** *dure*; a primitive root; (properly) to *gyrate* (or move in a circle), i.e. to *remain:*—dwell.

1753. דּוּר**, dûwr,** *dure*; (Chaldee); corresponding to 1752; to *reside:*—dwell.

1754. דּוּר**, dûwr,** *dure*; from 1752; a *circle, ball* or *pile:*—ball, turn, round about.

1755. דּוֹר**, dôwr,** *dore*; or (shortened) דֹּר**, dôr,** *dore*; from 1752; (properly) a *revolution* of time, i.e. an *age* or generation; also a *dwelling:*—age, × evermore, generation, [n-]ever, posterity.

A masculine noun meaning generation, period of time, posterity, age, time, setting of life. In general, the word indicates the time from birth to death; the time from one's birth to the birth of one's first child; the living adults of a certain time or place; a period as it is defined through major events, persons, behaviour, and the spirit of the age. It also marks a duration of time. There is no agreed on length of time which may stretch from twenty to one hundred years, but the word is also used figuratively to mean an indefinite or unending length of time in the past or future. These basic observations can be illustrated from various passages and contexts: the generation of Noah was characterized by wickedness and violence, yet he was a righteous man in his generation (Ge 7:1); Moses spoke of a crooked generation in his day and in the future (Dt 32:5); however, the psalmist spoke of a generation of righteous people (Ps 14:5) and a generation of people who seek the Lord (Ps 24:6). These generations will be blessed by God (Ps 112:2). Generations come and go without interruption (Ecc 1:4).

Time can be measured by the passing of generations, as when the great deeds of the Lord are passed on from generation to generation, in effect forever (Ps 145:4; Isa 34:17); God's throne lasts forever, from generation to generation (La 5:19). Likewise, God's judgments can endure forever (Jer 50:39). The closing of an era can be marked by the death of all the persons belonging to that generation (Ex 1:6; Jgs 2:10), but persons can be taken from their own proper age, dwellings, or circles of existence, as Hezekiah nearly was (Ps 102:24[25]; Isa 38:12), and a subgroup, such as fighting men, can pass away from an era (Dt 2:14). On the other hand, God's length of days spans all generations without end (Ps 102:24[25]).

The generation or generations mentioned may refer to the past, present, or future. Noah was perfect during the time of his contemporaries (Ge 6:9); the generations extended into the future when God established His covenant with Abraham and all future generations (Ge 17:7, 12; cf. Le 25:30) or when He gave His name as a memorial for all generations to come (Ex 3:15). The word often refers to past generations, such as the generation of the fathers (Ps 49:19[20]; Isa 51:9). God's constancy again stands out, for His days span all past eras as well as all future generations (Ps 102:24[25]). Israel was encouraged in Moses' song to remember the past generations of old (Dt 32:7) when God effected His foundational acts of deliverance for Israel and gave them the Law at Sinai. Present generations are to learn from past generations (Dt 32:7) and can affect future generations by declaring the Lord's power (Ps 71:18).

Certain generations were singled out for special note: the third and fourth generations of children are punished for the sins of their fathers (Ex 20:5; 34:7); the infamous generation that wandered in the wilderness for forty years experienced God's judgments until everyone in that generation died (Ps 95:10). Yet the love of God is not bound, for, in a figurative sense, it is passed on to thousands of generations (i.e. without limitation) forever and to every person (Ex 20:6; 34:7).

1756. דּוֹר, Dôwr, *dore*; or (by permuative) דּאר, **Dô'r,** *dore*; (Jos 17:11; 1Ki 4:11), from 1755; *dwelling; Dor,* a place in Palestine:—Dor.

1757. דּוּרָא, Dûwrâ', *doo-raw´*; (Chaldee); probably from 1753; *circle* or *dwelling; Dura,* a place in Babylon:—Dura.

1758. דּוּשׁ, dûwsh, *doosh*; or דּוֹשׁ, **dôwsh,** *dosh*; or דִּישׁ, **dîysh,** *deesh*; a primitive root; to *trample* or *thresh*:—break, tear, thresh, tread out (down), at grass [Jer 50:11, *by mistake for* 1877].

1759. דּוּשׁ, dûwsh, *doosh*; (Chaldee); corresponding to 1758; to *trample*:—tread down.

1760. דָּחָה, dâchâh, *daw-khaw´*; or דָּחַח, **dâchach,** *daw-khakh´*; (Jer 23:12), a primitive root; to *push* down:—chase, drive away (on), overthrow, outcast, × sore, thrust, totter.

1761. דַּחֲוָה, dachăvâh, *dakh-av-aw´*; (Chaldee); from the equivalent of 1760; probably a musical *instrument* (as being *struck*):—instrument of music.

1762. דְּחִי, d^echîy, *deh-khee´*; from 1760; a *push,* i.e. (by implication) a *fall*:—falling.

1763. דְּחַל, d^echal, *deh-khal´*; (Chaldee); corresponding to 2119; to *slink,* i.e. (by implication) to *fear,* or (causative) *be formidable*:—make afraid, dreadful, fear, terrible.

A verb meaning to fear, to slink. It comes from the Aramaic and corresponds to the Hebrew word *zâchal* (2119). The idea is one of slinking or crawling, such as a serpent or a worm; to back away or tremble in fear. People trembled before the greatness which God gave Nebuchadnezzar (Da 5:19). Darius turned this and focused on the Giver of the greatness, saying that people would tremble before God's awesome being (Da 6:26[27]).

1764. דֹּחַן, dôchan, *do´-khan*; of uncertain derivation; *millet*:—millet.

1765. דָּחַף, dâchaph, *daw-khaf´*; a primitive root; to *urge,* i.e. *hasten*:—(be) haste (-ned), pressed on.

1766. דָּחַק, dâchaq, *daw-khak´*; a primitive root; to *press,* i.e. *oppress*:—thrust, vex.

1767. דַּי, day, *dahee*; of uncertain derivation; *enough* (as noun or adverb), used chiefly with prepositional phrases:—able, according to, after (ability), among, as (oft as), (more than) enough, from, in, since, (much as is) sufficient (-ly), too much, very, when.

1768. דִּי, dîy, *dee*; (Chaldee); apparently for 1668; *that,* used as relative, conjunction, and especially (with preposition) in adverbial phrases; also as a preposition *of*:—× as, but, for (-asmuch), + now, of, seeing, than, that, therefore, until, + what (-soever), when, which, whom, whose.

1769. דִּיבוֹן, Dîybôwn, *dee-bone´*; or (shortened) דִּיבֹן, **Dîybôn,** *dee-bone´*; from 1727; *pining; Dibon,* the name of three places in Palestine:—Dibon. [*Also, with* 1410 *added,* Dibon-gad.]

1770. דִּיג, dîyg, *deeg*; denominative from 1709; to *fish*:—fish.

1771. דַּיָּג, dayyâg, *dah-yawg´*; from 1770; a *fisherman*:—fisher.

1772. דַּיָּה, dayyâh, *dah-yaw´*; intensive from 1675; a *falcon* (from its *rapid* flight):—vulture.

1773. דְּיוֹ, d^eyôw, *deh-yo´*; of uncertain derivation; *ink*:—ink.

1774. דִּי זָהָב, Dîy zâhâb, *dee zaw-hawb´*; as if from 1768 and 2091; *of gold; Dizahab,* a place in the Desert:—Dizahab.

1775. דִּימוֹן, Dîymôwn, *dee-mone´*; perhaps for 1769; *Dimon,* a place in Palestine:—Dimon.

1776. דִּימוֹנָה, Dîymôwnâh, *dee-mo-naw´*; feminine of 1775; *Dimonah,* a place in Palestine:—Dimonah.

1777. דִּין, dîyn, *deen*; or (Ge 6:3) דּוּן, **dûwn,** *doon*; a primitive root [compare 113]; to *rule*; (by implication) to *judge* (as umpire); also to *strive* (as at law):—contend, execute (judgment), judge, minister judgment, plead (the cause), at strife, strive.

A verb meaning to bring justice, to go to court, to pass sentence, to contend, to act as judge, to govern, to plead a cause, to be at strife, to quarrel. The verb regularly involves bringing justice or acting as judge; the Lord Himself is the chief judge over the whole earth and especially over those who oppose Him (1Sa 2:10). The tribe of Dan, whose name means "He provides justice" and is followed by this verb, will indeed provide justice for His people (Ge 30:6). The king of Israel was to deliver justice in righteousness (Ps 72:2). Israel's many sins included failure to obtain justice in the case of the orphan (Jer 5:28). The verb also signifies pleading a case: God's people often failed to plead the case of the orphan (Jer 5:28); this was a heinous sin for the house of David, for Judah was to administer justice every day for all those who needed it (Jer 21:12). Sometimes pleading a case resulted in vindication, as when God gave Rachel a son through her maidservant Bilhah, and Rachel in thanks named him Dan (Ge 30:6). At other times, it resulted in redress for evils done, as when God judges the nations in the day of His anger (Ps 110:6); Israel's plight because of their sin had become hopeless so they had no one to plead their cause (Jer 30:13).

The verb also signifies governance, contention, or going to law or court. It is hopeless for individuals to contend with persons who are far more powerful and advantaged than they are (Ecc 6:10). The high priest, Joshua, was given authority to govern, render justice, and judge the house of the Lord on the condition that he himself walked in the ways of the Lord (Zec 3:7).

In the passive-reflexive stem, the verb signifies to be at strife or to quarrel (2Sa 19:10).

1778. **דִּין, dîyn,** *deen*; (Chaldee); corresponding to 1777; to *judge*:—judge.

An Aramaic verb meaning to judge. It corresponds to the Hebrew word that is spelled the same or spelled as *diyn* (1777). The word occurs only in Ezr 7:25, where Artaxerxes commanded Ezra to appoint people to judge those beyond the river who knew God's laws.

1779. **דִּין, dîyn,** *deen*; or (Job 19:29) **דּוּן, dûwn,** *doon*; from 1777; *judgment* (the suit, justice, sentence or tribunal); (by implication) also *strife*:—cause, judgment, plea, strife.

A masculine noun meaning judgment, condemnation, plea, cause. This word carries a legal connotation and is found in poetic texts with most of its occurrences in the book of Job. The idea of judgment is often followed by justice (Job 36:17). Judah is called a wicked nation, one that does not plead the cause of the less fortunate (Jer 5:28). It also occurs in relation to strife in a legal case (Pr 22:10).

1780. **דִּין, dîyn,** *deen*; (Chaldee); corresponding to 1779:—judgment.

An Aramaic, masculine noun meaning justice, judgment. It is used to signify punishment (Ezr 7:26) or the justice of God (Da 4:37[34]). It is related to the Aramaic noun *dayyân* (1782) and the Aramaic verb *diyn* (1778). It is also similar to the Hebrew verb *diyn* (1777) and the Hebrew noun *diyn* (1779).

1781. **דַּיָּן, dayyân,** *dah-yawn´*; from 1777; a *judge* or *advocate*:—judge.

A masculine noun meaning judge, and more specifically, God as judge. David uses this word to refer to God as his judge (1Sa 24:15[16]). The psalmist uses this term to describe God as the defender or judge of the widows (Ps 68:5[6]).

1782. **דַּיָּן, dayyân,** *dah-yawn´*; (Chaldee); corresponding to 1781:—judge.

An Aramaic masculine noun meaning judge. It corresponds to the Hebrew word of the same spelling and meaning. This word is used only in Ezr 7:25 where it refers to judges that Ezra was to appoint over those who knew God's laws. The judges were to judge diligently and had power to imprison, execute, and banish people in addition to confiscating property (cf. Ezr 7:26).

1783. **דִּינָה, Dîynâh,** *dee-naw´*; feminine of 1779; *justice; Dinah*, the daughter of Jacob:—Dinah.

1784. **דִּינָיֵא, Dîynâyê',** *dee-naw´-yee*; (Chaldee); patrial from an uncertain primitive; a *Dinaite* or inhabitant of some unknown Assyrian province:—Dinaite.

1785. **דָּיֵק, dâyêq,** *daw-yake´*; from a root corresponding to 1751; a *battering*-tower:—fort.

1786. **דַּיִשׁ, dayish,** *dah´-yish*; from 1758; *threshing* time:—threshing.

1787. **דִּישׁוֹן, Dîyshôwn,** *dee-shone´*; **דִּשֹׁן, Dîyshôn,** *dee-shone´*; **דִּשׁוֹן, Dishôwn,** *dee-shone´*; or **דִּשֹׁן, Dishôn,** *dee-shone´*; the same as 1788; *Dishon*, the name of two Edomites:—Dishon.

1788. **דִּישֹׁן, dîyshôn,** *dee-shone´*; from 1758; the *leaper*, i.e. an *antelope*:—pygarg.

1789. **דִּישָׁן, Dîyshân,** *dee-shawn´*; another form of 1787; *Dishan*, an Edomite:—Dishan, Dishon.

1790. **דַּךְ, dak,** *dak*; from an unused root (compare 1794); *crushed*, i.e. (figurative) *injured*:—afflicted, oppressed.

1791. **דֵּךְ, dêk,** *dake*; (Chaldee); or **דָּךְ, dâk,** *dawk*; (Chaldee); prolonged from 1668; *this*:—the same, this.

1792. **דָּכָא, dâkâ',** *daw-kaw´*; a primitive root (compare 1794); to *crumble*; transposed to *bruise* (literal or figurative):—beat to pieces, break (in pieces), bruise, contrite, crush, destroy, humble, oppress, smite.

A verb meaning to crush, to beat down, to bruise, to oppress. The Hebrew word is often used in a poetic or figurative sense. Eliphaz spoke of those who lived in houses of clay, whose foundations were crushed easily (Job 4:19). The psalmist prayed that the king would crush an oppressor (Ps 72:4) and accused the wicked of crushing the Lord's people (Ps 94:5). The wise man exhorted others not to crush the needy in court (Pr 22:22). Isaiah said that it was the Lord's will to crush the Servant (Isa 53:10). Metaphorically, this word can also be used in the same way the English word *crushed* is used to mean dejected or sad (Isa 19:10).

1793. **דַּכָּא, dakkâ',** *dak-kaw´*; from 1792; *crushed*, (literal) *powder* or (figurative) *contrite*:—contrite, destruction.

An adjective meaning destruction, a crumbled substance, an object crushed into a powder, or pulverized dust. Thus, by extension, *dakkâ'* can mean humble or contrite. God is the healer and rescuer of one who is crushed in spirit (Ps 34:18[19]). He also lives with those whose spirits are contrite and humble (Isa 57:15). It comes from the Hebrew verb *dâkâ'* (1792), meaning to crush or to beat to pieces.

1794. **דָּכָה, dâkâh,** *daw-kaw´*; a primitive root (compare 1790, 1792); to *collapse* (physically or mentally):—break (sore), contrite, crouch.

1795. **דַּכָּה, dakkâh,** *dak-kaw´*; from 1794 like 1793; *mutilated*:—+ wounded.

1796. **דֳּכִי, dŏkîy,** *dok-ee´*; from 1794; a *dashing* of surf:—wave.

1797. **דִּכֵּן, dikkên,** *dik-kane´*; (Chaldee); prolonged from 1791; *this*:—same, that, this.

1798. **דְּכַר, d^{e}kar,** *dek-ar´*; (Chaldee); corresponding to 2145; (properly) a *male*, i.e. of sheep:—ram.

1799. **דִּכְרוֹן, dikrôwn,** *dik-rone´*; (Chaldee); or **דָּכְרָן, dokrân,** *dok-rawn´*; (Chaldee); corresponding to 2146; a *register*:—record.

1800. **דַּל, dal,** *dal*; from 1809; (properly) *dangling*, i.e. (by implication) *weak* or *thin*:—lean, needy, poor (man), weaker.

1801. **דָּלַג, dâlag,** *daw-lag´*; a primitive root; to *spring*:—leap.

1802. **דָּלָה, dâlâh,** *daw-law´*; a primitive root (compare 1809); (properly) to *dangle*, i.e. to *let down* a bucket (for *drawing* out water); (figurative) to *deliver*:—draw (out), × enough, lift up.

1803. **דַּלָּה, dallâh,** *dal-law´*; from 1802; (properly) something *dangling*, i.e. a loose *thread* or *hair*; (figurative) *indigent*:—hair, pining sickness, poor (-est sort).

1804. **דָּלַח, dâlach,** *daw-lakh´*; a primitive root; to *roil* water:—trouble.

1805. **דְּלִי, d^{e}lîy,** *del-ee´*; or **דֳּלִי, dŏlîy,** *dol-ee´*; from 1802; a *pail* or *jar* (for *drawing* water):—bucket.

1806. **דְּלָיָה, D^{e}lâyâh,** *del-aw-yaw´*; or (prolonged) **דְּלָיָהוּ, D^{e}lâyâhûw,** *del-aw-yaw´-hoo*; from 1802 and 3050; *Jah has delivered; Delajah*, the name of five Israelites:—Dalaiah, Delaiah.

1807. **דְּלִילָה, D^{e}lîylâh,** *del-ee-law´*; from 1809; *languishing; Delilah*, a Philistine woman:—Delilah.

1808. **דָּלִית, dâlîyth,** *daw-leeth´*; from 1802; something *dangling*, i.e. a *bough*:—branch.

1809. **דָּלַל, dâlal,** *daw-lal´*; a primitive root (compare 1802); to *slacken* or *be feeble*; (figurative) to *be oppressed*:—bring low, dry up, be emptied, be not equal, fail, be impoverished, be made thin.

1810. **דִּלְעָן, Dil'ân,** *dil-awn´*; of uncertain derivation; *Dilan*, a place in Palestine:—Dilean.

1811. **דָּלַף, dâlaph,** *daw-laf´*; a primitive root; to *drip*; (by implication) to *weep*:—drop through, melt, pour out.

1812. **דֶּלֶף, deleph,** *deh´-lef*; from 1811; a *dripping*:—dropping.

1813. דַּלְפוֹן, **Dalphôwn,** *dal-fone´*; from 1811; *dripping; Dalphon*, a son of Haman:—Dalphon.

1814. דָּלַק, **dâlaq,** *daw-lak´*; a primitive root; to *flame* (literal or figurative):—burning, chase, inflame, kindle, persecute (-or), pursue hotly.

1815. דְּלַק, **delaq,** *del-ak´*; (Chaldee); corresponding to 1814:—burn.

1816. דַּלֶּקֶת, **dalleqeth,** *dal-lek´-keth*; from 1814; a *burning* fever:—inflammation.

1817. דֶּלֶת, **deleth,** *deh´-leth*; from 1802 something *swinging*, i.e.. the *valve* of a door:—door (two-leaved), gate, leaf, lid. [In Ps 141:3, *dal*, irreg.]

1818. דָּם, **dâm,** *dawm*; from 1826 (compare 119); *blood* (as that which when shed causes *death*) of man or an animal; (by analogy) the *juice* of the grape; (figurative, especially in the plural) *bloodshed* (i.e. *drops* of blood):—blood (-y, -guiltiness, [-thirsty], + innocent.

A masculine singular noun meaning blood of either humans or animals. It is commonly used with the verb *shâphak* (8210) meaning to shed. Figuratively, it signifies violence and violent individuals: man of blood (2Sa 16:8); house of blood (2Sa 21:1); in wait for blood (Pr 1:11); shedder of blood (Eze 18:10). Blood also carries religious significance, having a major role in sacrificial rituals. The metaphor "blood of grapes" is used for wine (Ge 49:11).

1819. דָּמָה, **dâmâh,** *daw-maw´*; a primitive root; to *compare*; (by implication) to *resemble, liken, consider*:—compare, devise, (be) like (-n), mean, think, use similitudes.

1820. דָּמָה, **dâmâh,** *daw-maw´*; a primitive root; to *be dumb* or *silent*; hence to *fail* or *perish*; (transitive) to *destroy*:—cease, be cut down (off), destroy, be brought to silence, be undone, × utterly.

A verb meaning to cease, to cause to cease, to be silent, to destroy. It is used in reference to beasts that die (Ps 49:12[13]); a prophet who feels undone when he sees the Lord (Isa 6:5); Zion's destruction (Jer 6:2); eyes that weep without ceasing (La 3:49); the destruction of people who have no knowledge (Hos 4:6); the destruction of merchants (Zep 1:11); the destruction of the nation of Edom (Ob 1:5).

1821. דְּמָה, **demâh,** *dem-aw´*; (Chaldee); corresponding to 1819; to *resemble*:—be like.

1822. דֻּמָּה, **dumâh,** *doom-aw´*; from 1820; *desolation*; (concrete) *desolate*:—destroy.

A feminine noun of debated meaning. If it derives from *dâmâh* (1820), it would mean destroyed one; if from *dâmam* (1826), it would mean silent one. It is used only in Eze 27:32 where it describes the wealthy and beautiful seaport of Tyre as having sunk into the sea, a symbol of being overrun by foreign armies (cf. Eze 26:3–5). This judgment came on the people of Tyre because of their pride and because they rejoiced over the fall of Jerusalem (cf. Eze 26:2). The ruined city would be relatively silent (although fishermen would still spread their nets there), but in Eze 27:32 "destroyed one" seems to fit the context better.

1823. דְּמוּת, **demûwth,** *dem-ooth´*; from 1819; *resemblance*; (concrete) *model, shape*; (adverb) *like*:—fashion, like (-ness, as), manner, similitude.

A feminine noun meaning likeness. This word is often used to create a simile by comparing two unlike things, such as the wickedness of people and the venom of a snake (Ps 58:4[5]); the sound of God's gathering warriors and of many people (Isa 13:4); or the angelic messenger and a human being (Da 10:16). Additionally, this word is used in describing humans as being created in the image or likeness of God (Ge 1:26; 5:1); the likeness of Seth to Adam (Ge 5:3); the figures of oxen in the temple (2Ch 4:3); the pattern of the altar (2Ki 16:10). But most often, Ezekiel uses it as he describes his visions by comparing what he saw to something similar on earth (Eze 1:5, 16; 10:1).

1824. דְּמִי, **demîy,** *dem-ee´*; or דֳּמִי, **dŏmîy,** *dom-ee´*; from 1820; *quiet*:—cutting off, rest, silence.

1825. דִּמְיוֹן, **dimyôwn,** *dim-yone´*; from 1819; *resemblance*:—× like.

1826. דָּמַם, **dâmam,** *daw-mam´*; a primitive root [compare 1724, 1820]; to *be dumb*; (by implication) to *be astonished*, to *stop*; also to *perish*:—cease, be cut down (off), forbear, hold peace, quiet self, rest, be silent, keep (put to) silence, be (stand) still, tarry, wait.

1827. דְּמָמָה, **demâmâh,** *dem-aw-maw´*; feminine from 1826; *quiet*:—calm, silence, still.

1828. דֹּמֶן, **dômen,** *do´-men*; of uncertain derivation; *manure*:—dung.

1829. דִּמְנָה, **Dimnâh,** *dim-naw´*; feminine from the same as 1828; a *dung-heap; Dimnah*, a place in Palestine:—Dimnah.

1830. דָּמַע, **dâma',** *daw-mah´*; a primitive root; to *weep*:—× sore, weep.

1831. דֶּמַע, **dema',** *deh´-mah*; from 1830; a *tear*; (figurative) *juice*:—liquor.

1832. דִּמְעָה, **dim'âh,** *dim-aw´*; feminine of 1831; *weeping*:—tears.

1833. דְּמֶשֶׁק, **demesheq,** *dem-eh´-shek*; by orthographical variation from 1834; *damask* (as a fabric of Damascus):—in Damascus.

1834. דַּמֶּשֶׂק, **Dammeśeq,** *dam-meh´-sek*; or דּוּמֶּשֶׂק, **Dûwmeśeq,** *doo-meh´-sek*; or דַּרְמֶשֶׂק, **Darmeśeq,** *dar-meh´-sek*; of foreign origin; *Damascus*, a city of Syria:—Damascus.

1835. דָּן, **Dân,** *dawn*; from 1777; *judge; Dan*, one of the sons of Jacob; also the tribe descended from him, and its territory; likewise a place in Palestine colonized by them:—Dan.

1836. דְּנָה, **denâh,** *den-aw*; (Chaldee); an orthographical variation of 1791; *this*:—[afore-] time, + after this manner, here [-after], one ... another, such, there [-fore], these, this (matter), + thus, where [-fore], which.

1837. דַּנָּה, **Dannâh,** *dan-naw´*; of uncertain derivation; *Dannah*, a place in Palestine:—Dannah.

1838. דִּנְהָבָה, **Dinhâbâh,** *din-haw-baw´*; of uncertain derivation; *Dinhabah*, an Edomitish town:—Dinhabah.

1839. דָּנִי, **Dânîy,** *daw-nee´*; patronymic from 1835; a *Danite* (often collective) or descendant (or inhabitant) of Dan:—Danites, of Dan.

1840. דָּנִיֵּאל, **Dânîyyê'l,** *daw-nee-yale´*; in Ezekiel דָּנִאֵל, **Dânî'êl,** *daw-nee-ale´*; from 1835 and 410; *judge of God; Daniel* or *Danijel*, the name of two Israelites:—Daniel.

1841. דָּנִיֵּאל, **Dânîyyê'l,** *daw-nee-yale´*; (Chaldee); corresponding to 1840; *Danijel*, the Hebrew prophet:—Daniel.

1842. דָּן יַעַן, **Dân Ya'an,** *dawn yah´-an*; from 1835 and (apparently) 3282; *judge of purpose; Dan-Jaan*, a place in Palestine:—Dan-jaan.

1843. דֵּעַ, **dêa',** *day´-ah*; from 3045; *knowledge*:—knowledge, opinion.

A noun meaning knowledge. The word is possibly the masculine form of *dê'âh* (1844). It is used only by Elihu in the book of Job, where it refers to Elihu's opinion that he was about to make known to Job and his three friends (Job 32:6, 10, 17); knowledge as brought in from a distance, perhaps from heaven, since Elihu has just claimed to speak for God (Job 36:3); and God's perfect knowledge demonstrated in the clouds and lightning (37:16). The phrase "perfect in knowledge" occurs also in Job 36:4, apparently describing Elihu but using *dê'âh* (1844). It might be thought that Elihu was using a more modest word in describing his own knowledge. The word *dê'âh*, however, is also used to refer to God's knowledge (cf. 1Sa 2:3), and it is difficult to find any distinction of meaning between the two forms.

1844. דֵּעָה, **dêʻâh,** *day-aw´*; feminine of 1843; *knowledge:*—knowledge.

A feminine noun meaning knowledge. This word comes from the verb *yâdaʻ* (3045), meaning to know, and is equivalent in meaning to the much more common form of this noun, *daʻath* (1847), meaning knowledge. This particular word refers to the knowledge within God (1Sa 2:3; Ps 73:11). The word also describes the knowledge of God that was known throughout the land (Isa 11:9) or taught either by God or by His faithful shepherds (Jer 3:15).

1845. דְּעוּאֵל, **D^{e}ûwʼêl,** *deh-oo-ale´*; from 3045 and 410; *known of God; Deüel,* an Israelite:—Deuel.

1846. דָּעַךְ, **dâʻak,** *daw-ak´*; a primitive root; to *be extinguished;* (figurative) to *expire* or *be dried up:*—be extinct, consumed, put out, quenched.

1847. דַּעַת, **daʻath,** *dah´-ath*; from 3045; *knowledge:*—cunning, [ig-] norantly, know (-ledge), [un-] awares (wittingly).

A feminine noun meaning knowledge, knowing, learning, discernment, insight, and notion. The word occurs forty of its ninety-one times in Proverbs as one of the many words associated with the biblical concept of wisdom. The root meaning of the term is knowledge or knowing. In Pr 24:3, 4, it is the third word in a chain of three words describing the building of a house by wisdom, the establishment of that house by understanding, and finally, the filling of the rooms of the house by knowledge. The word describes God's gift of technical or specific knowledge along with wisdom and understanding to Bezalel so he could construct the tabernacle (Ex 31:3; 35:31; cf. Ps 94:10). It also describes the Israelites when they lacked the proper knowledge to please God (Isa 5:13; Hos 4:6). God holds both pagan unbelievers and Israelites responsible to know Him. On the other hand, a lack of knowledge also describes the absence of premeditation or intentionality. That lack of knowledge clears a person who has accidentally killed someone (Dt 4:42; Jos 20:3, 5).

The word is also used in the sense of knowing by experience, relationship, or encounter. For example, Balaam received knowledge from the Most High who met him in a vision (Nu 24:16); the knowledge gained by the suffering Servant of Isaiah justified many people (Isa 53:11); and to truly know the Holy God leads to real understanding (Pr 9:10). This moral, experiential knowledge of good and evil was forbidden to the human race in the Garden of Eden (Ge 2:9, 17). But the Messiah will have the Spirit of understanding in full measure as the Spirit of the Lord accompanied Him (Isa 11:2).

The term is also used to indicate insight or discernment. God imparted discernment to the psalmist when he trusted in God's commands (Ps 119:66). Job was guilty of speaking words without discernment (lit., words without knowledge, Job 34:35; 38:2).

God alone possesses all knowledge. No one can impart knowledge to God, for His knowledge, learning, and insight are perfect (Job 21:22); He alone has full knowledge about the guilt, innocence, or uprightness of a person (Job 10:7). God's knowledge of a human being is so profound and all-encompassing that the psalmist recognized that such knowledge is not attainable by people (Ps 139:6).

Some knowledge is empty and useless (Job 15:2), but God's people and a wise person are marked by true knowledge of life and the divine (Pr 2:5; 8:10; 10:14; 12:1). Knowledge affects behaviour, for persons who control their speech have true knowledge (Pr 17:27). While the preacher of Ecclesiastes admitted that knowledge may result in pain (Ecc 1:18), he also asserted that having knowledge is, in the end, better, for it protects the life of the one who has it (Ecc 7:12), and it is God's gift (Ecc 2:26).

1848. דֳּפִי, **dŏphîy,** *daf´-ee*; from an unused root (meaning to *push* over); a *stumbling*-block:—slanderest.

1849. דָּפַק, **dâphaq,** *daw-fak´*; a primitive root; to *knock;* (by analogy) to *press* severely:—beat, knock, overdrive.

1850. דָּפְקָה, **Dophqâh,** *dof-kaw´*; from 1849; a *knock; Dophkah,* a place in the Desert:—Dophkah.

1851. דַּק, **daq,** *dak*; from 1854; *crushed,* i.e. (by implication) *small* or *thin:*—dwarf, lean [-fleshed], very little thing, small, thin.

1852. דֹּק, **dôq,** *doke*; from 1854; something *crumbling,* i.e. *fine* (as a *thin* cloth):—curtain.

1853. דִּקְלָה, **Diqlâh,** *dik-law´*; of foreign origin; *Diklah,* a region of Arabia:—Diklah.

1854. דָּקַק, **dâqaq,** *daw-kak´*; a primitive root [compare 1915]; to *crush* (or intransitive) *crumble:*—beat in pieces (small), bruise, make dust, (into) × powder, (be, very) small, stamp (small).

1855. דְּקַק, **d^{e}qaq,** *dek-ak´*; (Chaldee); corresponding to 1854; to *crumble* or (transposed) *crush:*—break to pieces.

1856. דָּקַר, **dâqar,** *daw-kar´*; a primitive root; to *stab;* (by analogy) to *starve;* (figurative) to *revile:*—pierce, strike (thrust) through, wound.

1857. דֶּקֶר, **Deqer,** *deh´-ker*; from 1856; a *stab; Deker,* an Israelite:—Dekar.

1858. דַּר, **dar,** *dar*; apparently from the same as 1865; (properly) a *pearl* (from its sheen as rapidly *turned*); (by analogy) *pearl-stone,* i.e. mother-of-pearl or alabaster:— × white.

1859. דָּר, **dâr,** *dawr*; (Chaldee); corresponding to 1755; an *age:*—generation.

An Aramaic masculine noun meaning generation. This word is used only twice in the OT and is equivalent to the Hebrew word *dôwr* (1755), meaning generation. In both instances, the word is used in a phrase that is literally translated "with generation and generation," the idea referring to God's kingdom enduring from generation to generation (Da 4:3[3:33]; 4:34[31]).

1860. דְּרָאוֹן, **d^{e}râʼôwn,** *der-aw-one´*; or דֵּרָאוֹן, **dêrâʼ-ôwn,** *day-raw-one´*; from an unused root (meaning to *repulse*); an object of *aversion:*—abhorring, contempt.

A masculine noun meaning abhorrence. This word is related to an Arabic verb, which means to repel. Thus, the object of repulsion is an abhorrence. It is used only twice in the OT and in both cases speaks about the eternal abhorrence of those who rebelled against the Lord. The prophet Isaiah ended his message by declaring the abhorrence of wicked men in the eternal state (Isa 66:24). Daniel, likewise, spoke about the everlasting abhorrence of the wicked who were resurrected (Da 12:2).

1861. דָּרְבוֹן, **dorbôwn,** *dor-bone´*; [also *dorbawn´*]; of uncertain derivation; a *goad:*—goad.

1862. דַּרְדַּע, **Dardaʻ,** *dar-dah´*; apparently from 1858 and 1843; *pearl of knowledge; Darda,* an Israelite:—Darda.

1863. דַּרְדַּר, **dardar,** *dar-dar´*; of uncertain derivation; a *thorn:*—thistle.

1864. דָּרוֹם, **dârôwm,** *daw-rome´*; of uncertain derivation; the *south;* (poetic) the *south wind:*—south.

1865. דְּרוֹר, **d^{e}rôwr,** *der-ore´*; from an unused root (meaning to *move rapidly*); *freedom;* hence *spontaneity* of outflow, and so *clear:*—liberty, pure.

1866. דְּרוֹר, **d^{e}rôwr,** *der-ore´*; the same as 1865, applied to a bird; the *swift,* a kind of swallow:—swallow.

1867. דָּרְיָוֶשׁ, **Dâr^{e}yâvesh,** *daw-reh-yaw-vesh´*; of Persian origin; *Darejavesh,* a title (rather than name) of several Persian kings:—Darius.

1868. דָּרְיָוֶשׁ, **Dâr^{e}yâvesh,** *daw-reh-yaw-vesh´*; (Chaldee); corresponding to 1867:—Darius.

1869. דָּרַךְ, **dârak,** *daw-rak´*; a primitive root; to *tread;* (by implication) to *walk;* also to *string* a bow (by treading on it in bending):—archer, bend, come, draw, go (over), guide, lead (forth), thresh, tread (down), walk.

1870. דֶּרֶךְ, **derek**, *deh´-rek*; from 1869; a *road* (as *trodden*); (figurative) a *course* of life or *mode* of action, often adverbial:—along, away, because of, + by, conversation, custom, [east-] ward, journey, manner, passenger, through, toward, [high-] [path-] way [-side], whither [-soever].

A masculine noun meaning path, journey, way. This common word is derived from the Hebrew verb *dârak* (1869), meaning to walk or to tread, from which the basic idea of this word comes: the path that is traveled. The word may refer to a physical path or road (Ge 3:24; Nu 22:23; 1Ki 13:24) or to a journey along a road (Ge 30:36; Ex 5:3; 1Sa 15:18). However, this word is most often used metaphorically to refer to the pathways of one's life, suggesting the pattern of life (Pr 3:6); the obedient life (Dt 8:6); the righteous life (2Sa 22:22; Jer 5:4); the wicked life (1Ki 22:52[53]). The ways are described as ways of darkness (Pr 2:13); pleasant ways (Pr 3:17); and wise ways (Pr 6:6).

1871. דַּרְכְּמוֹן, **darkᵉmôwn**, *dar-kem-one´*; of Persian origin; a "*drachma*," or coin:—dram.

A noun meaning weight, monetary value. The word may refer to the Greek drachma that weighed 4.3 grams or to the Persian daric that weighed about twice as much. It occurs in Ezr 2:69 describing gold given toward Temple construction. In Ne 7:70–72 [69–71], it also refers to gold given toward the work of revitalizing Jerusalem. This word apparently has the same meaning as *'ădarkôn* (150) but may have a different origin.

1872. דְּרַע, **dᵉra'**, *der-aw´*; (Chaldee); corresponding to 2220; an *arm*:—arm.

1873. דָּרַע, **Dâra'**, *daw-rah´*; probably contracted from 1862; *Dara*, an Israelite:—Dara.

1874. דַּרְקוֹן, **Darqôwn**, *dar-kone´*; of uncertain derivation; *Darkon*, one of "Solomon's servants":—Darkon.

1875. דָּרַשׁ, **dârash**, *daw-rash´*; a primitive root; (properly) to *tread* or *frequent*; (usually) to *follow* (for pursuit or search); (by implication) to *seek* or *ask*; (specifically) to *worship*:—ask, × at all, care for, × diligently, inquire, make inquisition, [necro-] mancer, question, require, search, seek [for, out], × surely.

1876. דָּשָׁא, **dâshâ'**, *daw-shaw´*; a primitive root; to *sprout*:—bring forth, spring.

1877. דֶּשֶׁא, **deshe'**, *deh´-sheh*; from 1876; a *sprout*; (by analogy) *grass*:—(tender) grass, green, (tender) herb.

1878. דָּשֵׁן, **dâshên**, *daw-shane´*; a primitive root; to *be fat*; (transitive) to *fatten* (or regard as fat); (specifically) to *anoint*; (figurative) to *satisfy*; denominative (from 1880) to *remove* (fat) *ashes* (of sacrifices):—accept, anoint, take away the (receive) ashes (from), make (wax) fat.

A verb meaning to be fat, to grow fat, to fatten, or in a figurative sense, to anoint, to satisfy. In Proverbs, the word is used for one's bones growing fat (that is, one being in good health) after receiving good news (Pr 15:30). Conversely, when Israel came to the Promised Land, she grew fat with the food of the pagan culture and turned away to other gods (Dt 31:20). In Isaiah, the word is used to describe the ground being covered with the fat of animals (Isa 34:7).

1879. דָּשֵׁן, **dâshên**, *daw-shane´*; from 1878; *fat*; (figurative) *rich*, *fertile*:—fat.

1880. דֶּשֶׁן, **deshen**, *deh´-shen*; from 1878; the *fat*; (abstract) *fatness*, i.e. (figurative) *abundance*; (specifically) the (fatty) *ashes* of sacrifices:—ashes, fatness.

1881. דָּת, **dâth**, *dawth*; of uncertain (perhaps foreign) derivation; a royal *edict* or statute:—commandment, commission, decree, law, manner.

A feminine noun meaning law, edict. This word is used to describe either a permanent law that governed a nation or an edict sent out with the king's authority. The first meaning can be seen in Est 1:13, 15, where the king counseled with those who knew the law (cf. Est 3:8). The second meaning appears in the several occasions where King Ahasuerus (Xerxes) sent out a decree (Est 2:8; 3:14, 15). At times, it is difficult to distinguish between these two meanings (Est 1:8), for the edict of the king became a written law among the Persians (Est 1:19). With several exceptions, this word occurs only in the book of Esther (Ezr 8:36; cf. Dt 33:2).

1882. דָּת, **dâth**, *dawth*; (Chaldee); corresponding to 1881; decree, law.

An Aramaic noun meaning decree, law. It corresponds to the Hebrew word of the same spelling (1881). The decrees imposed on humans may agree more or less with God's Law, but God is always presented as controlling human laws. The word describes God's changeless Law in Ezr 7:12 and Da 6:5(6). Elsewhere, it signifies a king's decree made in anger (Da 2:9, 13). In the case of the Medes and Persians, a king could make the law at his own will but could not change it even if it were wrong (Da 6:8[9], 12[13], 15[16]). In Ezr 7:26, God's Law and the king's law coincide. In Da 7:25, a ruler was prophesied to speak against the Most High God and to set up laws in opposition to Him, but the ruler could only do so for a period of time set by God.

1883. דֶּתֶא, **dethe'**, *deh´-thay*; (Chaldee); corresponding to 1877:—tender grass.

1884. דְּתָבַר, **dᵉthâbar**, *deth-aw-bar´*; (Chaldee); of Persian origin; meaning one *skilled in law*; a *judge*:—counsellor.

1885. דָּתָן, **Dâthân**, *daw-thawn´*; of uncertain derivation; *Dathan*, an Israelite:—Dathan.

1886. דֹּתָן, **Dôthân**, *do´-thawn*; or (Chaldaizing dual) דֹּתַיִן, **Dôthayin**, *do-thah´-yin*; (Ge 37:17), of uncertain derivation; *Dothan*, a place in Palestine:—Dothan.

1887. הֵא, **hê'**, *hay*; a primitive particle; *lo!*:—behold, lo.

1888. הֵא, **hê'**, *hay*; (Chaldee); or הָא, **hâ'**, *haw*; (Chaldee); corresponding to 1887:—even, lo.

1889. הֶאָח, **he'âch**, *heh-awkh´*; from 1887 and 253; *aha!*:—ah, aha, ha.

1890. הַבְהָב, **habhab**, *hab-hab´*; by reduplication from 3051; *gift* (in sacrifice), i.e. *holocaust*:—offering.

A masculine noun meaning gift in the sense of sacrifice or offering. This type of sacrifice is not made by one person but always occurs with a plural subject. Israel (collectively) sacrificed animals to God as gift offerings—gifts God did not accept (Hos 8:13). This word comes from the verb *yâhab* (3051), meaning to give.

1891. הָבַל, **hâbal**, *haw-bal´*; a primitive root; to *be vain* in act, word, or expectation; (specifically) to *lead astray*:—be (become, make) vain.

1892. הֶבֶל, **hebel**, *heh´-bel*; or (rarely in the abstract) הֲבֵל, **hăbêl**, *hab-ale´*; from 1891; *emptiness* or *vanity*; (figurative) something *transitory* and *unsatisfactory*; often used as an adverb:— × altogether, vain, vanity.

1893. הֶבֶל, **Hebel**, *heh´-bel*; the same as 1892; *Hebel*, the son of Adam:—Abel.

1894. הָבְנִים, **hobnîym**, *hob´-neem*; only in plural, from an unused root meaning to *be hard; ebony*:—ebony.

1895. הָבַר, **hâbar**, *haw-bar´*; a primitive root of uncertain (perhaps foreign) derivation; to *be a horoscopist*:— + (astro-) loger.

1896. הֵגֵא, **Hêgê'**, *hay-gay´*; or (by permutation) הֵגַי, **Hêgay**, *hay-gah´ee*; probably of Persian origin; *Hege* or *Hegai*, a eunuch of Xerxes:—Hegai, Hege.

1897. הָגָה, **hâgâh**, *haw-gaw´*; a primitive root [compare 1901]; to *murmur* (in pleasure or anger); (by implication) to *ponder*:—imagine, meditate, mourn, mutter, roar, × sore, speak, study, talk, utter.

A verb meaning to growl, to groan, to sigh, to mutter, to speak; used figuratively: to meditate, to ponder. The Lord told Joshua to meditate on the Law day and night (Jos 1:8), and the Psalms proclaimed people blessed if they meditate on the Law (Ps 1:2). Job promised not to speak wickedness (Job 27:4). The Hebrew verb can also refer to the mutterings of mediums and wizards (Isa 8:19); the moans of grief (Isa 16:7); the growl of a lion (Isa 31:4); the coos of a dove (Isa 38:14).

1898. הָגָה, **hâgâh,** *haw-gaw´*; a primitive root; to *remove*:—stay, take away.

1899. הֶגֶה, **hegeh,** *heh´-geh*; from 1897; a *muttering* (in sighing, thought, or as thunder):—mourning, sound, tale.

A masculine noun meaning a muttering, rumbling, growling, moaning, or sighing sound. It generally describes a sound that comes from deep within the body. The Lord's voice is also described as making a rumbling sound associated with thunder (Job 37:2). The idea of moaning or sighing depicts the sound uttered in mourning, lamentation, woe (Eze 2:10), or in deep resignation (Ps 90:9).

1900. הָגוּת, **hâgûwth,** *haw-gooth´*; from 1897; *musing*:—meditation.

A feminine noun denoting meditation or musing. The psalmist describes the pondering of his heart as meditation (Ps 49:3[4]). This word is derived from the Hebrew word *hâgâh* (1897), which means to moan or to growl.

1901. הָגִיג, **hâgîyg,** *haw-gheeg´*; from an unused root akin to 1897; (properly) a *murmur*, i.e. *complaint*:—meditation, musing.

1902. הִגָּיוֹן, **higgâyôwn,** *hig-gaw-yone´*; intensive from 1897; a *murmuring* sound, i.e. a musical notation (probably similar to the modern *affettuoso* to indicate solemnity of movement); (by implication) a *machination*:—device, Higgaion, meditation, solemn sound.

1903. הָגִין, **hâgîyn,** *haw-gheen´*; of uncertain derivation; perhaps *suitable* or *turning*:—directly.

1904. הָגָר, **Hâgâr,** *haw-gawr´*; of uncertain (perhaps foreign) derivation; *Hagar*, the mother of Ishmael:—Hagar.

1905. הַגְרִי, **Hagrîy,** *hag-ree´*; or (prolonged) הַגְרִיא, **Hagrîy',** *hag-ree´*; perhaps patronymic from 1904; a *Hagrite* or member of a certain Arabian clan:—Hagarene, Hagarite, Haggeri.

1906. הֵד, **hêd,** *hade´*; for 1959; a *shout*:—sounding again.

1907. הַדָּבָר, **haddâbâr,** *had-daw-bawr´*; (Chaldee); probably of foreign origin; a *vizier*:—counsellor.

1908. הֲדַד, **Hădad,** *had-ad´*; probably of foreign origin [compare 111]; *Hadad*, the name of an idol, and of several kings of Edom:—Hadad.

1909. הֲדַדְעֶזֶר, **Hădad'ezer,** *had-ad-eh´-zer*; from 1908 and 5828; *Hadad* (is his) *help; Hadadezer*, a Syrian king:—Hadadezer. Compare 1928.

1910. הֲדַדְרִמּוֹן, **Hădadrimmôwn,** *had-ad-rim-mone´*; from 1908 and 7417; *Hadad-Rimmon*, a place in Palestine:—Hadad-rimmon.

1911. הָדָה, **hâdâh,** *haw-daw´*; a primitive root [compare 3034]; to *stretch forth* the hand:—put.

1912. הֹדּוּ, **Hôddûw,** *hod´-doo*; of foreign origin; *Hodu* (i.e. Hindustan):—India.

1913. הֲדוֹרָם, **Hădôwrâm,** *had-o-rawm´*; or הֲדֹרָם, **Hădôrâm,** *had-o-rawm´*; probably of foreign derivation; *Hadoram*, a son of Joktan, and the tribe descended from him:—Hadoram.

1914. הִדַּי, **Hidday,** *hid-dah´ee*; of uncertain derivation; *Hiddai*, an Israelite:—Hiddai.

1915. הָדַךְ, **hâdak,** *haw-dak´*; a primitive root [compare 1854]; to *crush* with the foot:—tread down.

1916. הֲדֹם, **hădôm,** *had-ome´*; from an unused root meaning to *stamp* upon; a foot-*stool*:—[foot-] stool.

1917. הַדָּם, **haddâm,** *had-dawm´*; (Chaldee); from a root corresponding to that of 1916; something *stamped* to pieces, i.e. a *bit*:—piece.

1918. הֲדַס, **hădas,** *had-as´*; of uncertain derivation; the *myrtle*:—myrtle (tree).

1919. הֲדַסָּה, **Hădassâh,** *had-as-saw´*; feminine of 1918; *Hadassah* (or Esther):—Hadassah.

1920. הָדַף, **hâdaph,** *haw-daf´*; a primitive root; to *push* away or down:—cast away (out), drive, expel, thrust (away).

1921. הָדַר, **hâdar,** *haw-dar´*; a primitive root; to *swell* up (literal or figurative, active or passive); (by implication) to *favour* or *honour, be high* or *proud*:—countenance, crooked place, glorious, honour, put forth.

A verb meaning to honour, to make glorious. The Israelites were commanded not to show unjust bias toward the poor (Ex 23:3) and to honour older people (Le 19:32). This did not always happen (La 5:12), but Solomon said that a person should not honour himself (Pr 25:6). Isaiah used this word when he prophesied that the Lord would come dressed in glory (Isa 63:1).

1922. הֲדַר, **hădar,** *had-ar´*; (Chaldee); corresponding to 1921; to *magnify* (figurative):—glorify, honour.

An Aramaic verb meaning to glorify, to magnify. Nebuchadnezzar built up Babylon to glorify himself until God took his power away and showed him who was sovereign. Then Nebuchadnezzar glorified God (Da 4:34[31], 37[34]). Unfortunately, King Belshazzar did not learn from his ancestor's mistake and also decided to honour himself instead of God (Da 5:23).

1923. הֲדַר, **hădar,** *had-ar´*; (Chaldee); from 1922; *magnificence*:—honour, majesty.

An Aramaic masculine noun meaning honour, majesty. In a meeting between Daniel and King Belshazzar, Daniel reminded Belshazzar that the Lord gave his father Nebuchadnezzar kingship, majesty, glory, and honour (Da 5:18).

1924. הֲדַר, **Hădar,** *had-ar´*; the same as 1926; *Hadar*, an Edomite:—Hadar.

1925. הֶדֶר, **heder,** *heh´-der*; from 1921; *honour*; used (figurative) for the *capital* city (Jerusalem):—glory.

A masculine noun meaning splendor, ornament. This word is used once in Daniel, where it speaks of the splendor of the kingdom (Da 11:20). This word is difficult to translate. It has been translated "the glory of the kingdom" (KJV), "royal splendor" (NIV), or a particular place, such as "the Jewel [the heart or gem] of his kingdom" (NASB).

1926. הָדָר, **hâdâr,** *haw-dawr´*; from 1921; *magnificence*, i.e. ornament or splendor:—beauty, comeliness, excellency, glorious, glory, goodly, honour, majesty.

A noun meaning glory, splendor, majesty. It describes the impressive character of God in 1Ch 16:27 and His thunderous voice in Ps 29:4. Isaiah describes sinners fleeing from the *hâdâr* of the Lord (Isa 2:10, 19). Often the Psalms use this word in conjunction with others to describe God's glory, splendor, and majesty (Ps 96:6; 145:5). It also refers to the majesty of kings (Ps 21:5[6]; 45:3[4]). Ps 8:5[6] expresses the splendor of God's creation of humans in comparison to the rest of creation. In Isaiah's prophetic description of the Suffering Servant, he uses *hâdâr* to say that the Servant will have no splendor to attract people to Him (Isa 53:2).

1927. הֲדָרָה, **hădârâh,** *had-aw-raw´*; feminine of 1926; *decoration*:—beauty, honour.

A feminine noun meaning adornment, glory. This word comes from the verb *hâdar* (1921), meaning to honour or to adorn and is related to the Hebrew noun *hâdâr* (1926), meaning majesty. In four of the five occurrences of this word, it occurs in the context of worshiping the Lord, "the beauty of holiness" (KJV) (1Ch 16:29; 2Ch 20:21; Ps 29:2; 96:9). In other instances, the word expresses the glory kings find in a multitude of people (Pr 14:28).

1928. הֲדַרְעֶזֶר, **Hădarʻezer,** *had-ar-eh´-zer*; from 1924 and 5828; *Hadar* (i.e. *Hadad*, 1908) is his *help; Hadarezer* (i.e. Hadadezer, 1909), a Syrian king:—Hadarezer.

1929. הָהּ, **hâh,** *haw*; a shortened form of 162; *ah!* expressing grief:—woe worth.

1930. הוֹ, **hôw,** *ho*; by permutation from 1929; *oh!*:—alas.

1931. הוּא, **hûwʼ,** *hoo*; of which the feminine (beyond the Pentateuch) is הִיא, **hîyʼ**, *he*; a primitive word, the third person pronoun singular, *he* (*she* or *it*); only expressed when emphatic or without a verb; also (intensive) *self*, or (especially with the article) the *same*; sometimes (as demonstrative) *this* or *that*; occasionally (instead of copula) *as* or *are*:—he, as for her, him (-self), it, the same, she (herself), such, that (… it), these, they, this, those, which (is), who.

1932. הוּא, **hûwʼ,** *hoo*; (Chaldee); or (feminine) הִיא, **hîyʼ**, *he*; (Chaldee); corresponding to 1931:—× are, it, this.

1933. הָוָא, **hâvâʼ,** *haw-vaw´*; or הָוָה, **hâvâh**, *haw-vaw´*; a primitive root [compare 183, 1961] supposed to mean (properly) to *breathe*; to *be* (in the sense of existence):—be, × have.

1934. הֲוָא, **hâvâʼ,** *hav-aw´*; (Chaldee); or הֲוָה, **hâvâh**, *hav-aw´*; (Chaldee); corresponding to 1933; to *exist*; used in a great variety of applications (especially in connection with other words):—be, become, + behold, + came (to pass), + cease, + cleave, + consider, + do, + give, + have, + judge, + keep, + labour, + mingle (self), + put, + see, + seek, + set, + slay, + take heed, tremble, + walk, + would.

1935. הוֹד, **hôwd,** *hode*; from an unused root; *grandeur* (i.e. an imposing form and appearance):—beauty, comeliness, excellency, glorious, glory, goodly, honour, majesty.

A masculine noun meaning vigour, authority, majesty. It refers to human physical vigour (Pr 5:9; Da 10:8); the fighting vigour of a horse in battle (Zec 10:3); and the growing vigour of an olive plant (Hos 14:6[7]). The word also implies authority, such as what Moses bestowed on Joshua (Nu 27:20); and royal majesty (1Ch 29:25; Jer 22:18). Thus, it is used to describe God's majesty (Job 37:22; Ps 145:5; Zec 6:13). The word often describes God's glory as displayed above the heavens (Ps 8:1[2]; 148:13; Hab 3:3; cf. Ps 96:6; 104:1, where the word is related to God's creation of the heavens).

1936. הוֹד, **Hôwd,** *hode*; the same as 1935; *Hod*, an Israelite:—Hod.

1937. הוֹדְוָה, **Hôwdᵉvâh,** *ho-dev-aw´*; a form of 1938; *Hodevah* (or Hodevjah), an Israelite:—Hodevah.

1938. הוֹדַוְיָה, **Hôwdavyâh,** *ho-dav-yaw´*; from 1935 and 3050; *majesty of Jah; Hodavjah*, the name of three Israelites:—Hodaviah.

1939. הוֹדַיְוָהוּ, **Hôwdayvâhûw,** *ho-dah-vaw´-hoo*; a form of 1938; *Hodajvah*, an Israelite:—Hodaiah.

1940. הוֹדִיָּה, **Hôwdîyyâh,** *ho-dee-yaw´*; a form for the feminine of 3064; a *Jewess*:—Hodiah.

1941. הוֹדִיָּה, **Hôwdîyyâh,** *ho-dee-yaw´*; a form of 1938; *Hodijah*, the name of three Israelites:—Hodijah.

1942. הַוָּה, **havvâh,** *hav-vaw´*; from 1933 (in the sense of eagerly *coveting* and *rushing* upon; by implication of *falling*); *desire*; also *ruin*:—calamity, iniquity, mischief, mischievous (thing), naughtiness, naughty, noisome, perverse thing, substance, very wickedness.

A feminine noun meaning destruction, desire. This word usually describes an event associated with calamity, evil, or destruction. It can speak of the wickedness of evildoers (Ps 5:9[10]); the devastation a foolish son could cause his father (Pr 19:13); the destruction intended by the tongue (Ps 38:12[13]; 52:2[4]); the calamities of life which require refuge in God for protection (Ps 57:1[2]). In several places, this word depicts the evil desires of the wicked that resulted in destruction: God would cast away the wicked person's desire (Pr 10:3); the evil desires of transgressors would be their downfall (Pr 11:6); and destruction awaited the ones who trust in their own desires (Ps 52:7[9]).

1943. הֹוָה, **hôvâh,** *ho-vaw´*; another form for 1942; *ruin*:—mischief.

A feminine noun meaning disaster. The root idea is a pit or chasm, a symbol of disaster. The word describes a disaster coming on Babylon that it will not be able to prevent with its occult practices (Isa 47:11). The only other occurrence of this word describes a series of disasters (literally, disaster upon disaster) prophesied to come on Israel because of idolatry (Eze 7:26). In this passage, there will be no escape although Israel will look for a prophetic vision.

1944. הוֹהָם, **Hôwhâm,** *ho-hawm´*; of uncertain derivation; *Hoham*, a Canaanitish king:—Hoham.

1945. הוֹי, **hôwy,** *hoh´ee*; a prolonged form of 1930 [akin to 188]; *oh!*:—ah, alas, ho, O, woe.

1946. הוּךְ, **hûwk,** *hook*; (Chaldee); corresponding to 1981; to *go*; (causative) to *bring*:—bring again, come, go (up).

1947. הוֹלֵלוֹת, **hôwlêlôwth,** *ho-lay-loth´*; feminine active participle of 1984; *folly*:—madness.

1948. הוֹלֵלוּת, **hôwlêlûwth,** *ho-lay-looth´*; from active participle of 1984; *folly*:—madness.

1949. הוּם, **hûwm,** *hoom*; a primitive root [compare 2000]; to *make an uproar*, or *agitate* greatly:—destroy, move, make a noise, put, ring again.

A verb meaning to rouse, to roar, to confuse. This verb describes a stirring or rousing, such as occurred in Bethlehem when Ruth and Naomi returned from Moab (Ru 1:19), or would occur in the nations when God would confuse them before their destruction (Dt 7:23). On several occasions, the audible effects of the rousing was emphasized, such as when Solomon was anointed king, the roar of the city could be heard (1Ki 1:45; cf. 1Sa 4:5; Mic 2:12). In the only other occurrence of this verb, David described himself as restless and roused (Ps 55:2[3]).

1950. הוֹמָם, **Hôwmâm,** *ho-mawm´*; from 2000; *raging; Homam*, an Edomitish chieftain:—Homam. Compare 1967.

1951. הוּן, **hûwn,** *hoon*; a primitive root; (properly) to *be naught*, i.e. (figurative) to *be* (causative *act*) *light*:—be ready.

1952. הוֹן, **hôwn,** *hone*; from the same as 1951 in the sense of 202; *wealth*; (by implication) *enough*:—enough, + for nought, riches, substance, wealth.

1953. הוֹשָׁמָע, **Hôwshâmâʻ,** *ho-shaw-maw´*; from 3068 and 8085; *Jehovah has heard; Hoshama*, an Israelite:—Hoshama.

1954. הוֹשֵׁעַ, **Hôwshêaʻ,** *ho-shay´-ah*; from 3467; *deliverer; Hosheä*, the name of five Israelites:—Hosea, Hoshea, Oshea.

1955. הוֹשַׁעְיָה, **Hôwshaʻyâh,** *ho-shah-yaw´*; from 3467 and 3050; *Jah has saved; Hoshajah*, the name of two Israelites:—Hoshaiah.

1956. הוֹתִיר, **Hôwthîyr,** *ho-theer´*; from 3498; *he has caused to remain; Hothir*, an Israelite:—Hothir.

1957. הָזָה, **hâzâh,** *haw-zaw´*; a primitive root [compare 2372]; to *dream*:—sleep.

1958. הִי, **hîy,** *he*; for 5092; *lamentation*:—woe.

1959. הֵידָד, **hêydâd,** *hay-dawd´*; from an unused root (meaning to *shout*); *acclamation*:—shout (-ing).

1960. הֻיְּדוֹת, **huyyᵉdôwth,** *hoo-yed-oth´*; from the same as 1959; (properly) an *acclaim*, i.e. a *choir* of singers:—thanksgiving.

1961. הָיָה, **hâyâh,** *haw-yaw´*; a primitive root [compare 1933]; to *exist*, i.e. *be* or *become, come to pass* (always emphatic, and not a mere copula or auxiliary):—beacon, × altogether, be (-come, accomplished, committed, like), break, cause, come (to pass), do, faint, fall, + follow, happen, × have, last, pertain, quit (one-) self, require, × use.

A verb meaning to exist, to be, to become, to happen, to come to pass, to be done. It is used over 3,500 times in the OT. In the simple stem, the verb often means to become, to take place, to happen. It indicates that something has occurred or come about, such as events that have turned out a certain way (1Sa 4:16); something has happened to someone, such as Moses (Ex 32:1, 23; 2Ki 7:20); or something has occurred just as God said it would (Ge 1:7, 9). Often a special Hebrew construction using the imperfect form of the verb asserts that something came to pass (cf. Ge 1:7, 9). Less often, the construction is used with the perfect form of the verb to refer to something coming to pass in the future (Isa 7:18, 21; Hos 2:16).

The verb is used to describe something that comes into being or arises. For instance, a great cry arose in Egypt when the firstborn were killed in the tenth plague (Ex 12:30; cf. Ge 9:16; Mic 7:4); and when God commanded light to appear, and it did (Ge 1:3). It is used to join the subject and verb as in Ge 1:2 where the earth was desolate and void, or to say Adam and Eve were naked (Ge 2:25). With certain prepositions, it can mean to follow or to be in favour of someone (Ps 124:1, 2). The verb is used with a variety of other words, normally prepositions, to express subtle differences in meaning, such as to be located somewhere (Ex 1:5); to serve or function as something (e.g., gods [Ex 20:3]); to become something or as something, as when a person becomes a living being (Ge 2:7); to be with or by someone (Dt 22:2); to be or come on someone or something (e.g., the fear of humans on the beasts [Ge 9:2]); to express the idea of better than or a comparison (Eze 15:2), as in the idea of too small (Ex 12:4).

1962. הַיָּה, hayyâh, *hah-yaw´*; another form for 1943; *ruin*:—calamity.

A feminine noun meaning destruction. This word occurs only once in the OT (Job 6:2) and is a slightly different form of *hawwâh* (1942), also meaning destruction.

1963. הֵיךְ, hêyk, *hake*; another form for 349; *how?*:—how.

1964. הֵיכָל, hêykâl, *hay-kawl´*; probably from 3201 (in the sense of *capacity*); a large public building, such as a *palace* or *temple*:—palace, temple.

A masculine noun meaning temple, palace. The word derives from the word *yâkôl* (3201), meaning to be able and comes from the idea of capacity. It refers to a king's palace or other royal buildings (1Ki 21:1; Isa 13:22) and, likely by extension, to the dwelling of God, whether on earth (Ps 79:1) or in heaven (Isa 6:1). The word is used of Solomon's Temple, the second Temple (Ezr 3:6; Ne 6:10) and also of the tabernacle. In reference to foreign buildings, it is sometimes difficult to say whether a palace or the temple of a false god is meant (2Ch 36:7; Joel 3:5[4:5]). A special usage of the word designates the holy place of the Temple as opposed to the Holy of Holies (1Ki 6:17; Eze 41:4, 15).

1965. הֵיכַל, hêykal, *hay-kal´*; (Chaldee); corresponding to 1964:—palace, temple.

A masculine noun meaning temple, palace. This is the Aramaic form of the Hebrew word *hêykâl* (1964). The word is used most often in relation to a king's palace (Ezr 4:14). When Belshazzar sees the handwriting on the wall of the palace, this is the word used (Da 5:5). It is also used in reference to the Temple of God in Jerusalem (Ezr 5:14, 15), as well as the temple in Babylon (Ezr 5:14).

1966. הֵילֵל, hêylêl, *hay-lale´*; from 1984 (in the sense of *brightness*); the *morning-star*:—lucifer.

1967. הֵימָם, Hêymâm, *hey-mawm´*; another form for 1950; *Hemam*, an Idumæan:—Hemam.

1968. הֵימָן, Hêymân, *hay-mawn´*; probably from 539; *faithful*; *Heman*, the name of at least two Israelites:—Heman.

1969. הִין, hîyn, *heen*; probably of Egypt origin; a *hin* or liquid measure:—hin.

1970. הָכַר, hâkar, *haw-kar´*; a primitive root; apparently to *injure*:—make self strange.

1971. הַכָּרָה, hakkârâh, *hak-kaw-raw´*; from 5234; *respect*, i.e. partiality:—shew.

1972. הָלָא, hâlâ', *haw-law´*; probably denominative from 1973; to *remove* or be *remote*:—cast far off.

1973. הָלְאָה, hâl^e'âh, *haw-leh-aw´*; from the primitive form of the article [הַל **hal**]; *to the distance*, i.e. *far away*; also (of time) *thus far*:—back, beyond, (hence-) forward, hitherto, thenceforth, yonder.

1974. הִלּוּל, hillûwl, *hil-lool´*; from 1984 (in the sense of *rejoicing*); a *celebration* of thanksgiving for harvest:—merry, praise.

1975. הַלָּז, hallâz, *hal-lawz´*; from 1976; *this* or *that*:—side, that, this.

1976. הַלָּזֶה, hallâzeh, *hal-law-zeh´*; from the article [see 1973] and 2088; *this very*:—this.

1977. הַלֵּזוּ, hallêzûw, *hal-lay-zoo´*; another form of 1976; *that*:—this.

1978. הָלִיךְ, hâlîyk, *haw-leek´*; from 1980; a *walk*, i.e. (by implication) a *step*:—step.

1979. הֲלִיכָה, hălîykâh, *hal-ee-kaw´*; feminine of 1978; a *walking*; (by implication) a *procession* or *march*, a *caravan*:—company, going, walk, way.

1980. הָלַךְ, hâlak, *haw-lak´*; akin to 3212; a primitive root; to *walk* (in a great variety of applications, literal and figurative):—(all) along, apace, behave (self), come, (on) continually, be conversant, depart, + be eased, enter, exercise (self), + follow, forth, forward, get, go (about, abroad, along, away, forward, on, out, up and down), + greater, grow, be wont to haunt, lead, march, × more and more, move (self), needs, on, pass (away), be at the point, quite, run (along), + send, speedily, spread, still, surely, + talebearer, + travel (-ler), walk (abroad, on, to and fro, up and down, to places), wander, wax, [way-] faring man, × be weak, whirl.

A verb meaning to go, to come, to walk. This common word carries with it the basic idea of movement: the flowing of a river (Ge 2:14); the descending of floods (Ge 8:3); the crawling of beasts (Le 11:27); the slithering of snakes (Le 11:42); the blowing of the wind (Ecc 1:6); the tossing of the sea (Jnh 1:13). Since it is usually a person who is moving, it is frequently translated "walk" (Ge 48:15; 2Sa 15:30). Like a similar verb *dârak* (1869), meaning to tread, this word is also used metaphorically to speak of the pathways (i.e. behaviour) of one's life. A son could walk in (i.e. follow after) the ways of his father (2Ch 17:3) or not (1Sa 8:3). Israel was commanded to walk in the ways of the Lord (Dt 28:9), but they often walked after other gods (2Ki 13:11).

1981. הֲלַךְ, hălak, *hal-ak´*; (Chaldee); corresponding to 1980 [compare 1946]; to *walk*:—walk.

1982. הֵלֶךְ, hêlek, *hay´-lek*; from 1980; (properly) a *journey*, i.e. (by implication) a *wayfarer*; also a *flowing*:— × dropped, traveller.

1983. הֲלָךְ, hălâk, *hal-awk´*; (Chaldee); from 1981; (properly) a *journey*, i.e. (by implication) *toll* on goods at a road:—custom.

1984. הָלַל, hâlal, *haw-lal´*; a primitive root; to *be clear* (origin of sound, but usually of colour); to *shine*; hence to *make a show*, to *boast*; and thus to *be* (clamorously) *foolish*; to *rave*; (causative) to *celebrate*; also to *stultify*:—(make) boast (self), celebrate, commend, (deal, make), fool (-ish, -ly), glory, give [light], be (make, feign self) mad (against), give in marriage, [sing, be worthy of] praise, rage, renowned, shine.

A verb meaning to praise, to commend, to boast, to shine. The root meaning may be to shine but could also be to shout. The word most often means praise and is associated with the ministry of the Levites who praised God morning and evening (1Ch 23:30). All creation, however, is urged to join in (Ps 148), and various instruments were used to increase the praise to God (Ps 150). The word hallelujah is a command to praise *Yah* (the Lord), derived from the word *hâlal* (Ps 105:45; 146:1). The reflexive form of the verb is often used to signify boasting, whether in a good object (Ps 34:2[3]) or a bad object (Ps

49:6[7]). Other forms of the word mean to act foolishly or to be mad (1Sa 21:13[14]; Ecc 7:7; Isa 44:25).

1985. הִלֵּל, Hillêl, *hil-layl´*; from 1984; *praising* (namely God); *Hillel*, an Israelite:—Hillel.

1986. הָלַם, hâlam, *haw-lam´*; a primitive root; to *strike* down; (by implication) to *hammer, stamp, conquer, disband*:—beat (down), break (down), overcome, smite (with the hammer).

A verb meaning to smite, to hammer, to strike down. It also carries the implication of conquering and disbanding. The author of Judges used this word to describe Jael hammering the tent peg through Sisera's head (Jgs 5:26). Isaiah employed this word figuratively to describe nations breaking down grapevines (Isa 16:8) and people overcome by wine (Isa 28:1).

1987. הֵלֶם, Helem, *hay´-lem*; from 1986; *smiter; Helem*, the name of two Israelites:—Helem.

1988. הֲלֹם, hălôm, *hal-ome´*; from the article [see 1973]; *hither*:—here, hither (-[to]), thither.

1989. הַלְמוּת, halmûwth, *hal-mooth´*; from 1986; a *hammer* (or *mallet*):—hammer.

1990. הָם, Hâm, *hawm*; of uncertain derivation; *Ham*, a region of Palestine:—Ham.

1991. הֵם, hêm, *haym*; from 1993; *abundance*, i.e. *wealth*:—any of theirs.

1992. הֵם, hêm, *haym*; or (prolonged) הֵמָּה, **hêmmâh,** *haym´-maw*; masculine plural from 1931; *they* (only used when emphatic):—it, like, × (how, so) many (soever, more as) they (be), (the) same, × so, × such, their, them, these, they, those, which, who, whom, withal, ye.

1993. הָמָה, hâmâh, *haw-maw´*; a primitive root [compare 1949]; to *make a loud sound* (like English "hum"); by implication to *be in great commotion* or *tumult*, to *rage, war, moan, clamour*:—clamorous, concourse, cry aloud, be disquieted, loud, mourn, be moved, make a noise, rage, roar, sound, be troubled, make in tumult, tumultuous, be in an uproar.

1994. הִמּוֹ, himmôw, *him-mo´*; (Chaldee); or (prolonged) הִמּוֹן **himmôwn,** *him-mone´*; (Chaldee); corresponding to 1992; *they*:—× are, them, those.

1995. הָמוֹן, hâmôwn, *haw-mone´*; or הָמֹן, **hâmôn,** *haw-mone´*; (Eze 5:7), from 1993; a *noise, tumult, crowd*; also *disquietude, wealth*:—abundance, company, many, multitude, multiply, noise, riches, rumbling, sounding, store, tumult.

1996. הֲמוֹן גּוֹג, Hămôwn Gôwg, *ham-one´ gohg*; from 1995 and 1463; the *multitude of Gog*; the fanciful name of an emblematic place in Palestine:—Hamon-gog.

1997. הֲמוֹנָה, Hămôwnâh, *ham-o-naw´*; feminine of 1995; *multitude; Hamonah*, the same as 1996:—Hamonah.

1998. הֶמְיָה, hemyâh, *hem-yaw´*; from 1993; *sound*:—noise.

1999. הֲמֻלָּה, hămulâh, *ham-ool-law´*; or (too fully) הֲמוּלָּה, **hămûwllâh,** *ham-ool-law´*; (Jer 11:16), feminine passive participle of an unused root meaning to *rush* (as rain with a windy roar); a *sound*:—speech, tumult.

A feminine noun meaning a rushing noise. The two occurrences of this word conjure up the sound of a great wind. The first is in the prophecy of Jeremiah, where Israel was called a strong olive tree, but the Lord would set the tree on fire with a great rushing sound as a sign of judgment (Jer 11:16). The word is also used in Ezekiel's vision, where the sound of the creatures' wings was like the roar of a rushing river (Eze 1:24).

2000. הָמַם, hâmam, *haw-mam´*; a primitive root [compare 1949, 1993]; (properly) to *put in commotion*; (by implication) to *disturb, drive, destroy*:—break, consume, crush, destroy, discomfit, trouble, vex.

A verb meaning to make a noise, to move noisily, to confuse, to put into commotion. When it means to move noisily, it often refers to the wheels of wagons or chariots (Isa 28:28). The idea of moving noisily or with commotion carries over into the idea of confusion: God confuses the Egyptians when they pursue Israel (Ex 14:24); and He sends confusion to the nations before the Israelites go into Canaan (Jos 10:10).

2001. הָמָן, Hâmân, *haw-mawn´*; of foreign derivation; *Haman*, a Persian vizier:—Haman.

2002. הַמְנִיךְ, hamnîyk, *ham-neek´*; (Chaldee); but the text is הַמוּנֵךְ, **hămûwnêk,** *ham-oo-nayk´*; of foreign origin; a *necklace*:—chain.

2003. הֲמָסִים, hămâsîym, *haw-maw-seem´*; from an unused root apparently meaning to *crackle*; a dry *twig* or *brushwood*:—melting.

2004. הֵן, hên, *hane*; feminine plural from 1931; *they* (only used when emphatic):—× in, such like, (with) them, thereby, therein, (more than) they, wherein, in which, whom, withal.

2005. הֵן, hên, *hane*; a primitive particle; *lo!*; also (as expressing surprise) *if*:—behold, if, lo, though.

2006. הֵן, hên, *hane*; (Chaldee); corresponding to 2005; *lo!* also *there* [-fore], [un-] *less, whether, but, if*:—(that) if, or, whether.

2007. הֵנָּה, hênnâh, *hane´-naw*; prolonged for 2004; *themselves* (often used emphatically for the copula, also in indirect relation):— × in, × such (and such things), their, (into) them, thence, therein, these, they (had), on this side, those, wherein.

2008. הֵנָּה, hênnâh, *hane´-naw*; from 2004; *hither* or *thither* (but used both of place and time):—here, hither [-to], now, on this (that) side, + since, this (that) way, thitherward, + thus far, to … fro, + yet.

2009. הִנֵּה, hinnêh, *hin-nay´*; prolonged for 2005; *lo!*:—behold, lo, see.

2010. הֲנָחָה, hănâchâh, *han-aw-khaw´*; from 5117; *permission* of rest, i.e. *quiet*:—release.

2011. הִנֹּם, Hinnôm, *hin-nome´*; probably of foreign origin; *Hinnom*, apparently a Jebusite:—Hinnom.

2012. הֵנַע, Hênaʻ, *hay-nah´*; probably of foreign derivation; *Hena*, a place apparently in Mesopotamia:—Hena.

2013. הָסָה, hâsâh, *haw-saw´*; a primitive root; to *hush*:—hold peace (tongue), (keep) silence, be silent, still.

2014. הֲפֻגָה, hăphugâh, *haf-oo-gaw´*; from 6313; *relaxation*:—intermission.

2015. הָפַךְ, hâphak, *haw-vak´*; a primitive root; to *turn* about or over; (by implication) to *change, overturn, return, pervert*:—× become, change, come, be converted, give, make [a bed], overthrow (-turn), perverse, retire, tumble, turn (again, aside, back, to the contrary, every way).

A verb meaning to turn around, to change, to throw down, to overturn, to pervert, to destroy, to be turned against, to turn here and there, to wander. The verb is used to describe the simple act of turning something over (2Ki 21:13; Hos 7:8) but also to indicate turning back from something (Ps 78:9). These turnings indicate that Jerusalem would lose all its inhabitants by being turned over as a dish is turned over after wiping it; "Ephraim has become a cake not turned," that is, overdone on one side, uncooked on the other, and not edible (Hos 7:8 NASB).

The verb becomes more figurative when it describes the act of overthrowing or destroying. Second Kings 21:13 is relevant here also, but Haggai speaks of God overthrowing the thrones of kingdoms (Persia) as well as chariots and riders (Hag 2:22). Even more violently, the verb describes the overthrow of the enemies of God and His people; Sodom and Gomorrah were especially singled out (Ge 19:21, 25; Dt 29:23[22]; cf. 2Sa 10:3). The word also indicates a change or is used to indicate defeat in battle when an army turned in flight (Jos 7:8) or simply the change in direction of something (1Ki 22:34). Metaphorically, the word comes to mean to change (by turning). For example, the Lord changed the curse of Balaam into a blessing (Dt 23:5[6]); He will change the mourning of His people into joy and gladness (Jer 31:13). The simple stem is also found in a reflexive sense; the men of Israel turned themselves about in battle against the Benjamites (Jgs 20:39, 41; cf. 2Ki 5:26; 2Ch 9:12).

The verb is used a few times in the reflexive stems to indicate turning oneself about: The Israelites are pictured as having turned themselves back against their enemies (Jos 8:20); and Pharaoh changed his heart in himself (Ex 14:5; Hos 11:8), thus changing his mind. The word is used in the sense of being overwhelmed or overcome by pain (1Sa 4:19); the clouds rolled about (Job. 37:12); the sword placed by the Lord to guard the Garden of Eden turned itself about (Ge 3:24); and the earth's surface was shaped and moved like clay being impressed under a seal (Job 38:14).

2016. הֶפֶךְ, hephek, *heh´-fek*; or הֵפֶךְ, **hêphek,** *hay´-fek*; from 2015; a *turn*, i.e. the *reverse*:—contrary.

2017. הֹפֶךְ, hôphek, *ho´-fek*; from 2015; an *upset*, i.e. (abstract) *perversity*:—turning of things upside down.

2018. הֲפֵכָה, hăphêkâh, *haf-ay-kaw´*; feminine of 2016; *destruction*:—overthrow.

2019. הֲפַכְפַּךְ, hăphakpak, *haf-ak-pak´*; by reduplication from 2015; *very perverse*:—froward.

2020. הַצָּלָה, hatstsâlâh, *hats-tsaw-loaw´*; from 5337; *rescue*:—deliverance.

2021. הֹצֶן, hôtsen, *ho´-tsen*; from an unused root meaning apparently to *be sharp* or *strong*; a *weapon* of war:—chariot.

2022. הַר, har, *har*; a shorter form of 2042; a *mountain* or *range* of hills (sometimes used figuratively):—hill (country), mount (-ain), × promotion.

2023. הֹר, Hôr, *hore*; another form for 2022; *mountain; Hor*, the name of a peak in Idumæa and of one in Syria:—Hor.

2024. הָרָא, Hârâ', *haw-raw´*; perhaps from 2022; *mountainousness; Hara*, a region of Media:—Hara.

2025. הַרְאֵל, har'êl, *har-ale´*; from 2022 and 410; *mount of God*; (figurative) the *altar* of burnt offering:—altar. Compare 739.

2026. הָרַג, hârag, *haw-rag´*; a primitive root; to *smite* with deadly intent:—destroy, out of hand, kill, murder (-er), put to [death], make [slaughter], slay (-er), × surely.

A verb meaning to kill, murder, slay. It carries a wide variety of usages. Its first use in the Bible is in the fratricide of Cain and Abel (Ge 4:8). The word is employed for war and slaughter (Jos 8:24; 1Ki 9:16; Est 8:11); God's killing in judgment (Ge 20:4; Ex 13:15; Am 2:3); humans killing animals (Le 20:15; Nu 22:29); animals killing humans (2Ki 17:25; Job 20:16).

2027. הֶרֶג, hereg, *heh´-reg*; from 2026; *slaughter*:—be slain, slaughter.

A masculine noun meaning slaughter. The Jews had a great victory and struck down all their enemies (Est 9:5), while the book of Proverbs advises that one should rescue those unwise people heading for the slaughter (Pr 24:11). Isaiah uses the "day of the great slaughter" to refer to the time of Israel's deliverance (Isa 30:25). In the prophecy against Tyre, Ezekiel warns of the day when a slaughter will take place there (Eze 26:15).

2028. הֲרֵגָה, hărêgâh, *har-ay-gaw´*; feminine of 2027; *slaughter*:—slaughter.

A noun meaning slaughter. It is the feminine form of *hereg* (2027) and is used only five times in the OT. Two of these are found in the phrase "valley of slaughter" (Jer 7:32; 19:6). In both of these occurrences, the Lord renames the Hinnom Valley because of the slaughter He will bring on the Israelites who have done horrifying deeds by sacrificing their children to other gods. Jeremiah also uses the word when he pleads with the Lord for the wicked to be taken away for the "day of slaughter" (Jer 12:3 NIV). Zechariah uses this word twice in a metaphor describing Israel as the "flock marked for slaughter" (Zec 11:4 NIV).

2029. הָרָה, hârâh, *haw-raw´*; a primitive root; to *be* (or *become*) *pregnant, conceive* (literal or figurative):—been, be with child, conceive, progenitor.

2030. הָרֶה, hâreh, *haw-reh´*; or הָרִי, **hârîy,** *haw-ree´*; (Hos 14:1), from 2029; *pregnant*:—(be, woman) with child, conceive, × great.

2031. הַרְהֹר, harhôr, *har-hor´*; (Chaldee); from a root corresponding to 2029; a mental *conception*:—thought.

2032. הֵרוֹן, hêrôwn, *hay-rone´*; or הֵרָיוֹן, **hêrâyôwn,** *hay-raw-yone´*; from 2029; *pregnancy*:—conception.

2033. הֲרוֹרִי, Hărôwrîy, *har-o-ree´*; another form for 2043; a *Harorite* or mountaineer:—Harorite.

2034. הֲרִיסָה, hărîysâh, *har-ee-saw´*; from 2040; something *demolished*:—ruin.

2035. הֲרִיסָה, hărîysâh, *har-ee-saw´*; from 2040; *demolition*:—destruction.

2036. הֹרָם, Hôrâm, *ho-rawm´*; from an unused root (meaning to *tower* up); *high; Horam*, a Canaanitish king:—Horam.

2037. הָרוּם, Hârûwm, *haw-room´*; passive participle of the same as 2036; *high; Harum*, an Israelite:—Harum.

2038. הַרְמוֹן, harmôwn, *har-mone´*; from the same as 2036; a *castle* (from its height):—palace.

2039. הָרָן, Hârân, *haw-rawn´*; perhaps from 2022; *mountaineer; Haran*, the name of two men:—Haran.

2040. הָרַס, hâras, *haw-ras´*; a primitive root; to *pull* down or in pieces, *break, destroy*:—beat down, break (down, through), destroy, overthrow, pluck down, pull down, ruin, throw down, × utterly.

A verb meaning to pull down, to break through, to overthrow, to destroy. In Miriam and Moses' song, God threw down His enemies (Ex 15:7). Elijah told God that the Israelites had pulled down God's altars (1Ki 19:10, 14). The psalmist wanted God to break out the teeth of the wicked (Ps 58:6[7]) and also said that God would tear down the wicked and not build them up again (Ps 28:5). The foolish woman tore down her own house (Pr 14:1). On Mount Sinai, God cautioned Moses to warn the people not to force their way through to see God and then perish (Ex 19:21). In Exodus, this word is used in an even stronger sense when God instructs the Israelites not to worship foreign gods but to utterly demolish them (Ex 23:24).

2041. הֶרֶס, heres, *heh´-res*; from 2040; *demolition*:—destruction.

2042. הָרָר, hârâr, *haw-rawr´*; from an unused root meaning to *loom* up; a *mountain*:—hill, mount (-ain).

2043. הֲרָרִי, Hărârîy, *hah-raw-ree´*; or הָרָרִי, **Hârârîy,** *haw-raw-ree´*; (2Sa 23:11), or הָאֲרָרִי, **Hâ'rârîy,** *haw-raw-ree´*; (2Sa 23:34, last clause), apparently from 2042; a *mountaineer*:—Hararite.

2044. הָשֵׁם, Hâshêm, *haw-shame´*; perhaps from the same as 2828; *wealthy; Hashem*, an Israelite:—Hashem.

2045. הַשְׁמָעוּת, hashmâ'ûwth, *hashmaw-ooth´*; from 8085; *announcement*:—to cause to hear.

2046. הִתּוּךְ, hittûwk, *hit-took´*; from 5413; a *melting*:—is melted.

2047. הֲתָךְ, Hăthâk, *hath-awk´*; probably of foreign origin; *Hathak*, a Persian eunuch:—Hatach.

2048. הָתַל, hâthal, *haw-thal´*; a primitive root; to *deride*; (by implication) to *cheat*:—deal deceitfully, deceive, mock.

2049. הֲתֻלִּים, hăthulîym, *haw-thoo-leem´*; from 2048 (only in plural collective); a *derision*:—mocker.

2050. הָתַת, hâthath, *haw-thath´*; a primitive root; (properly) to *break* in upon, i.e. to *assail*:—imagine mischief.

2051. וְדָן, Vᵉdân, *ved-awn´*; perhaps for 5730; *Vedan* (or Aden), a place in Arabia:—Dan also.

2052. וָהֵב, Vâhêb, *vaw-habe´*; of uncertain derivation; *Vaheb*, a place in Moab:—what he did.

2053. וָו, vâv, *vaw*; probably a *hook* (the name of the sixth Hebrew letter):—hook.

2054. וָזָר, vâzâr, *vaw-zawr´*; presumed to be from an unused root meaning to *bear* guilt; *crime*:— × strange.

A noun meaning guilty one. It occurs only once in the OT (Pr 21:8), where the immoral path of the guilty is contrasted to the pure behaviour of the innocent. The translators for the King James Version understood the word to be a combination of the word *and* with the adjective meaning strange. Therefore, they translated this Hebrew word, "The way of man is froward and strange." But modern translators translate this word "guilty."

2055. וַיְזָתָא, Vayzâthâ', *vah-zaw´-thaw*; of foreign origin; *Vajezatha*, a son of Haman:—Vajezatha.

2056. וָלָד, vâlâd, *vaw-lawd´*; for 3206; a *boy*:—child.

2057. וַנְיָה, Vanyâh, *van-yaw´*; perhaps for 6043; *Vanjah*, an Israelite:—Vaniah.

2058. וָפְסִי, Vophsîy, *vof-see´*; probably from 3254; *additional; Vophsi*, an Israelite:—Vophsi.

2059. וַשְׁנִי, Vashnîy, *vash-nee´*; probably from 3461; *weak; Vashni*, an Israelite:—Vashni.

2060. וַשְׁתִּי, Vashtîy, *vash-tee´*; of Persian origin; *Vashti*, the queen of Xerxes:—Vashti.

2061. זְאֵב, zᵉ'êb, *zeh-abe´*; from an unused root meaning to *be yellow*; a *wolf*:—wolf.

2062. זְאֵב, Zᵉ'êb, *zeh-abe´*; the same as 2061; *Zeëb*, a Midianitish prince:—Zeeb.

2063. זֹאת, zô'th, *zothe´*; irregular feminine of 2089; *this* (often used adverbially):—hereby (-in, -with), it, likewise, the one (other, same), she, so (much), such (deed), that, therefore, these, this (thing), thus.

2064. זָבַד, zâbad, *zaw-bad´*; a primitive root; to *confer*:—endure.

2065. זֶבֶד, zebed, *zeh´-bed*; from 2064; a *gift*:—dowry.

2066. זָבָד, Zâbâd, *zaw-bawd´*; from 2064; *giver; Zabad*, the name of seven Israelites:—Zabad.

2067. זַבְדִּי, Zabdîy, *zab-dee´*; from 2065; *giving; Zabdi*, the name of four Israelites:—Zabdi.

2068. זַבְדִּיאֵל, Zabdîy'êl, *zab-dee-ale´*; from 2065 and 410; *gift of God; Zabdiel*, the name of two Israelites:—Zabdiel.

2069. זְבַדְיָה, Zᵉbadyâh, *zeb-ad-yaw´*; or זְבַדְיָהוּ, **Zebadyâhûw,** *zeb-ad-yaw´-hoo*; from 2064 and 3050; *Jah has given; Zebadjah*, the name of nine Israelites:—Zebadiah.

2070. זְבוּב, zᵉbûwb, *zeb-oob´*; from an unused root (meaning to *flit*); a *fly* (especially one of a stinging nature):—fly.

2071. זָבוּד, Zâbûwd, *zaw-bood´*; from 2064; *given; Zabud*, an Israelite:—Zabud.

2072. זַבּוּד, Zabbûwd, *zab-bood´*; a form of 2071; *given; Zabbud*, an Israelite:—Zabbud.

2073. זְבוּל, zᵉbûwl, *ze-bool´*; or זְבֻל, **zebul,** *zeb-ool´*; from 2082; a *residence*:—dwell in, dwelling, habitation.

2074. זְבוּלוּן, Zᵉbûwlûwn, *zeb-oo-loon´*; or זְבֻלוּן, **Zebulûwn,** *zeb-oo-loon´*; or זְבוּלֻן, **Zebûwlun,** *zeb-oo-loon´*; from 2082; *habitation; Zebulon*, a son of Jacob; also his territory and tribe:—Zebulun.

2075. זְבוּלֹנִי, Zᵉbûwlônîy, *zeb-oo-lo-nee´*; patronymic from 2074; a *Zebulonite* or descendant of Zebulun:—Zebulonite.

2076. זָבַח, zâbach, *zaw-bakh´*; a primitive root; to *slaughter* an animal (usually in sacrifice):—kill, offer, (do) sacrifice, slay.

A verb meaning to slaughter, to kill, to offer, to sacrifice. The word is used in its broadest sense to indicate the slaughtering of various animals. It indicates the slaughter of animals for food (Dt 12:21; 1Sa 28:24) or for sacrifice with strong political implications (1Ki 1:9, 19); Elisha slaughtered his oxen to make his break with his past and establish his commitment to Elijah (1Ki 19:21). The word describes a sacrifice made to create communion or to seal a covenant. Jacob made a sacrificial meal to celebrate the peace between him and Laban (Ge 31:54); and the priests were to receive part of the bulls or sheep offered by the people (Dt 18:3). These slaughtered sacrificial animals were presented to gods or the true God; Jacob's sacrifice was to God (Ge 46:1) as were most of these sacrifices, but the nations sacrificed to other gods as well, such as Dagon (Jgs 16:23) or the gods of Damascus (2Ch 28:23).

Various kinds of sacrifices are given as the objects of this verb. For instance, sacrifices that open the womb (Ex 13:15); offerings of well-being, peace offerings, and burnt offerings (Ex 20:24); and animals of the flock and herd (Nu 22:40). Certain slaughtered sacrifices were prohibited, such as a sacrifice with blood and yeast in it (Ex 23:18; cf. Ex 12:15). In an exceptional setting, however, a prophet proclaimed the slaughter and sacrifice of the defiled priests who served at the forbidden high places (1Ki 13:2). God will exercise divine judgment on the enemies of His people, Gog and Magog, slaying and providing their carcasses as a great banquet for every kind of bird and animal (Eze 39:17, 19); Israel, in their rebellion, offered, although forbidden, their own sons as offerings (Eze 16:20).

2077. זֶבַח, zebach, *zeh´-bakh*; from 2076; (properly) a *slaughter*, i.e. the *flesh* of an animal; (by implication) a *sacrifice* (the victim or the act):—offer (-ing), sacrifice.

A masculine noun meaning sacrifice. This word refers to the kind of flesh sacrifice the offerer ate after it was given to God (parts of the flesh went to God and to the priests as well). This practice was ancient and did not solely apply to sacrifices to the true God of Israel (Ex 34:15; Nu 25:2). Other sacrifices of this type included the covenant between Jacob and Laban (Ge 31:54); the Passover Feast (Ex 34:25); the thank offering (Le 22:29); the annual sacrifice (1Sa 1:21); the sacrifice of a covenant with God (Ps 50:5). See the related Hebrew verb *zâbach* (2076).

2078. זֶבַח, Zebach, *zeh´-bakh*; the same as 2077; *sacrifice; Zebach*, a Midianitish prince:—Zebah.

2079. זַבַּי, Zabbay, *zab-bah´ee*; probably by orthographical error for 2140; *Zabbai* (or Zaccai), an Israelite:—Zabbai.

2080. זְבִידָה, Zᵉbîydâh, *zeb-ee-daw´*; feminine from 2064; *giving; Zebidah*, an Israelitess:—Zebudah.

2081. זְבִינָא, Zᵉbîynâ', *zeb-ee-naw´*; from an unused root (meaning to *purchase*); *gainfulness; Zebina*, an Israelite:—Zebina.

2082. זָבַל, zâbal, *zaw-bal´*; a primitive root; apparently (properly) to *inclose*, i.e. to *reside*:—dwell with.

2083. זְבֻל, Zᵉbul, *zeb-ool´*; the same as 2073; *dwelling; Zebul*, an Israelite:—Zebul. Compare 2073.

2084. זְבַן, zᵉban, *zeb-an´*; (Chaldee); corresponding to the root of 2081; to *acquire* by purchase:—gain.

2085. זָג, zâg, *zawg*; from an unused root probably meaning to *inclose*; the *skin* of a grape:—husk.

2086. זֵד, zêd, *zade´*; from 2102; *arrogant*:—presumptuous, proud.

An adjective meaning proud, arrogant. This word most often occurs in the Psalms where it is used in connection with sin (Ps 19:13[14]) or to describe the ungodly (Ps 86:14; 119:21, 85). Elsewhere in the OT, *zêd* describes the proud who will be judged (Isa 13:11; Mal 4:1[3:19]) and the disobedience of the proud (Jer 43:2).

2087. זָדוֹן, zâdôwn, *zaw-done´*; from 2102; *arrogance*:—presumptuously, pride, proud (man).

A noun meaning presumptuousness, pride. David's brothers accused him of being presumptuous when he wanted to challenge Goliath (1Sa 17:28). Ob 1:3 addresses the pride of the Edomites who fatally presumed that they had a safe place in the cliffs. Proverbs also describes the negative aspects of pride (Pr 11:2; 13:10; 21:24), while Ezekiel uses this word in his description of the day of judgment (Eze 7:10).

2088. זֶה, zeh, *zeh*; a primitive word; the masculine demonstrative pronoun, *this* or *that*:—he, × hence, × here, it (-self), × now, × of him, the one … the other, × than the other, (× out of) the (self) same, such (an one) that, these, this (hath, man), on this side … on that side, × thus, very, which. Compare 2063, 2090, 2097, 2098.

2089. זֶה, zeh, *zeh*; (1Sa 17:34), by permutation for 7716; a *sheep*:—lamb.

2090. זֹה, zôh, *zo*; for 2088; *this* or *that*:—as well as another, it, this, that, thus and thus.

2091. זָהָב, zâhâb, *zaw-hawb´*; from an unused root meaning to *shimmer; gold*; (figurative) something *gold-coloured* (i.e. *yellow*), as *oil*, a *clear sky*:—gold (-en), fair weather.

2092. זָהַם, zâham, *zaw-ham´*; a primitive root; to *be rancid*, i.e. (transposed) to *loathe*:—abhor.

2093. זַהַם, Zaham, *zah´-ham*; from 2092; *loathing; Zaham*, an Israelite:—Zaham.

2094. זָהַר, zâhar, *zaw-har´*; a primitive root; to *gleam*; (figurative) to *enlighten* (by caution):—admonish, shine, teach, (give) warn (-ing).

A verb meaning to teach, to warn, to shine. Ezekiel uses this verb more than any other OT writer. In chapter 3, he uses *zâhar* seven times consecutively when God commands him to warn the wicked and righteous about their sin (Eze 3:17–21). Similarly, Eze 33 uses this word eight times to describe coming judgment for sin (Eze 33:3–9). Other books also use *zâhar* to mean warn (2Ki 6:10; 2Ch 19:10) or admonish (Ecc 4:13; 12:12). Exodus uses this word to mean teach (Ex 18:20). Daniel is the only book which uses the future tense of the word (Da 12:3).

2095. זְהַר, zehar, *zeh-har´*; (Chaldee); corresponding to 2094; (passive) *be admonished*:—take heed.

An Aramaic verb meaning to take heed, to be admonished, to be cautious. The word *zĕhar* is used only once in Scripture. King Artaxerxes told his secretaries and other men under his command to be careful to obey his order (Ezr 4:22).

2096. זֹהַר, zôhar, *zo´-har*; from 2094; *brilliancy*:—brightness.

2097. זוֹ, zôw, *zo*; for 2088; *this* or *that*:—that, this.

2098. זוּ, zûw, *zoo*; for 2088; *this* or *that*:—that this, × wherein, which, whom.

2099. זִו, Ziv, *zeev´*; probably from an unused root meaning to *be prominent*; (properly) *brightness* [compare 2122], i.e. (figurative) the month of *flowers; Ziv* (corresponding to Ijar or May):—Zif.

2100. זוּב, zûwb, *zoob*; a primitive root; to *flow* freely (as water), i.e. (specifically) to *have a* (sexual) *flux*; (figurative) to *waste* away; also to *overflow*:—flow, gush out, have a (running) issue, pine away, run.

2101. זוֹב, zôwb, *zobe*; from 2100; a seminal or menstrual *flux*:—issue.

2102. זוּד, zûwd, *zood*; or (by permutation) **זִיד, zîyd,** *zeed*; a primitive root; to *seethe*; (figurative) to *be insolent*:—be proud, deal proudly, presume, (come) presumptuously, sod.

2103. זוּד, zûwd, *zood*; (Chaldee); corresponding to 2102; to *be proud*:—in pride.

2104. זוּזִים, Zûwzîym, *zoo-zeem´*; plural probably from the same as 2123; *prominent; Zuzites*, an aboriginal tribe of Palestine:—Zuzims.

2105. זוֹחֵת, Zôwchêth, *zo-khayth´*; of uncertain origin; *Zocheth*, an Israelite:—Zoheth.

2106. זָוִית, zâvîyth, *zaw-veeth´*; apparently from the same root as 2099 (in the sense of *prominence*); an *angle* (as *projecting*), i.e. (by implication) a *corner-column* (or *anta*):—corner (stone).

2107. זוּל, zûwl, *zool*; a primitive root [compare 2151]; probably to *shake* out, i.e. (by implication) to *scatter* profusely; (figurative) to *treat lightly*:—lavish, despise.

2108. זוּלָה, zûwlâh, *zoo-law´*; from 2107; (properly) *scattering*, i.e. *removal*; (used adverbially) *except*:—beside, but, only, save.

2109. זוּן, zûwn, *zoon*; a primitive root; perhaps (properly) to *be plump*, i.e. (transposed) to *nourish*:—feed.

2110. זוּן, zûwn, *zoon*; (Chaldee); corresponding to 2109:—feed.

2111. זוּעַ, zûwaʻ, *zoo´-ah*; a primitive root; (properly) to *shake* off, i.e. (figurative) to *agitate* (as with fear):—move, tremble, vex.

A verb meaning to tremble, to shake. Haman was angry when Mordecai did not tremble at his sight (Est 5:9). This word is also used to describe an old man (Ecc 12:3). In Habakkuk, it occurs in a causative sense, meaning to cause to tremble. This verse refers to the debtors of Israel (used figuratively for Babylon) who would make Israel tremble with fear (Hab 2:7). See the related Aramaic verb *zû'a* (2112).

2112. זוּעַ, zûwaʻ, *zoo´-ah*; (Chaldee); corresponding to 2111; to *shake* (with fear):—tremble.

An Aramaic verb meaning to tremble. This word is used only twice in the OT and is equivalent to the Hebrew word *zû'a* (2111), meaning to tremble or to shake. In Da 5:19, this word is used to describe the trembling fear of the people before the mighty Nebuchadnezzar. In Da 6:26[27], it describes the same trembling fear that people ought to have before the God of Daniel. In both instances, it is used synonymously with another Aramaic word meaning fear, *dĕchal* (1763).

2113. זְוָעָה, zevâʻâh, *zev-aw-aw´*; from 2111; *agitation, fear*:—be removed, trouble, vexation. Compare 2189.

2114. זוּר, zûwr, *zoor*; a primitive root; to *turn* aside (especially for lodging); hence to *be a foreigner, strange, profane*; specifically (active participle) to *commit adultery*:—(come from) another (man, place), fanner, go away, (e-) strange (-r, thing, woman).

A verb meaning to be a stranger. The basic meaning of this word is to turn aside (particularly for lodging); therefore, it refers to being strange or foreign. It can mean to go astray, to be wayward (Ps 58:3[4]). The participle is used frequently as an adjective, signifying something outside the law of God (Ex 30:9; Le 10:1); a person outside the family (Dt 25:5); the estranged way Job's guests and servants viewed him (Job 19:15); hallucinations from drunkenness (Pr 23:33). This word is used several times in Proverbs of the adulterous woman (Pr 2:16; 5:3, 20; 7:5; 22:14).

2115. זוּר, zûwr, *zoor*; a primitive root [compare 6695]; to *press* together, *tighten*:—close, crush, thrust together.

2116. זוּרֶה, zûwreh, *zoo-reh´*; from 2115; *trodden* on:—that which is crushed.

2117. זָזָא, zâzâʼ, *zaw-zaw*; probably from the root of 2123; *prominent; Zaza*, an Israelite:—Zaza.

2118. זָחַח, zâchach, *zaw-khakh´*; a primitive root; to *shove* or *displace*:—loose.

2119. זָחַל, zâchal, *zaw-khal´*; a primitive root; to *crawl*; (by implication) to *fear*:—be afraid, serpent, worm.

A verb meaning to crawl, to fear, and to be afraid. It can refer to the movement of a snake on the ground (Dt 32:24; Mic 7:17). It can also be a metaphor for an individual who is afraid or one who creeps forward slowly and cautiously (Job 32:6).

2120. זֹחֶלֶת, Zôcheleth, *zo-kheh´-leth*; feminine active participle of 2119; *crawling* (i.e. *serpent*); *Zoche-leth*, a boundary stone in Palestine:—Zoheleth.

2121. זֵידוֹן, zêydôwn, *zay-dohn´*; from 2102; *boiling* of water, i.e. *wave*:—proud.

2122. זִיו, zîyv, *zeev*; (Chaldee); corresponding to 2099; (figurative) *cheerfulness*:—brightness, countenance.

2123. זִיז, zîyz, *zeez*; from an unused root apparently meaning to *be conspicuous; fulness* of the breast; also a moving *creature*:—abundance, wild beast.

2124. זִיזָא, Zîyzâ', *zee-zaw´*; apparently from the same as 2123; *prominence; Ziza*, the name of two Israelites:—Ziza.

2125. זִיזָה, Zîyzâh, *zee-zaw´*; another form for 2124; *Zizah*, an Israelite:—Zizah.

2126. זִינָא, Zîynâ', *zee-naw´*; from 2109; well *fed*; or perhaps an orthographical error for 2124; *Zina*, an Israelite:—Zina.

2127. זִיעַ, Zîya', *zee´-ah*; from 2111; *agitation; Zia*, an Israelite:—Zia.

2128. זִיף, Zîyph, *zeef*; from the same as 2203; *flowing; Ziph*, the name of a place in Palestine; also of an Israelite:—Ziph.

2129. זִיפָה, Zîyphâh, *zee-faw´*; feminine of 2128; a *flowing; Ziphah*, an Israelite:—Ziphah.

2130. זִיפִי, Zîyphîy, *zee-fee´*; patrial from 2128; a *Ziphite* or inhabitant of Ziph:—Ziphim, Ziphite.

2131. זִיקָה, zîyqâh, *zee-kaw´*; (Isa 50:11), (feminine) and **זִק, ziq,** *zeek*; or **זֵק, zêq,** *zake*; from 2187; (properly) what *leaps* forth, i.e. *flash* of fire, or a burning *arrow*; also (from the original sense of the root) a *bond*:—chain, fetter, firebrand, spark.

2132. זַיִת, zayith, *zah´-yith*; probably from an unused root [akin to 2099]; an *olive* (as yielding *illuminating* oil), the tree, the branch or the berry:—olive (tree, -yard), Olivet.

2133. זֵיתָן, Zêythân, *zay-thawn´*; from 2132; *olive* grove; *Zethan*, an Israelite:—Zethan.

2134. זַךְ, zak, *zak*; from 2141; *clear*:—clean, pure.

An adjective meaning pure, clean. It is derived from the related verbs *zâkâh* (2135), meaning to be clear or pure, and *zâkak* (2141), meaning to be clean or pure. This word is used to describe objects used in the worship of God, such as pure oil (Ex 27:20; Le 24:2) and pure frankincense (Ex 30:34; Le 24:7). It also denotes the purity of the righteous, such as Job (Job 8:6; 33:9), in contrast with one living a crooked life (Pr 21:8). This word can also speak about all aspects of one's life: one's actions in general (Pr 16:2; 20:11); one's teaching (Job 11:4); or one's prayer (Job 16:17).

2135. זָכָה, zâkâh, *zaw-kaw´*; a primitive root [compare 2141]; to *be translucent*; (figurative) to *be innocent*:—be (make) clean, cleanse, be clear, count pure.

A verb meaning to clean, to be clean, to cleanse. Job's friends used this word twice, questioning how one born of a woman could be clean or righteous before God (Job 15:14; 25:4). It is also used to describe the state of the heart (Ps 73:13; Pr 20:9). In other uses, it carries the connotation of being pure or cleansed from sin (Ps 119:9; Isa 1:16; Mic 6:11).

2136. זָכוּ, zâkûw, *zaw-koo´*; (Chaldee); from a root corresponding to 2135; *purity*:—innocency.

2137. זְכוּכִית, z^ekûwkîyth, *zek-oo-keeth´*; from 2135; (properly) *transparency*, i.e. *glass*:—crystal.

2138. זְכוּר, z^ekûwr, *zeh-koor´*; (properly) passive participle of 2142, but used for 2145; a *male* (of man or animals):—males, men-children.

2139. זַכּוּר, Zakkûwr, *zak-koor´*; from 2142; *mindful; Zakkur*, the name of seven Israelites:—Zaccur, Zacchur.

2140. זַכַּי, Zakkay, *zak-kah´ee*; from 2141; *pure; Zakkai*, an Israelite:—Zaccai.

2141. זָכַךְ, zâkak, *zaw-kak´*; a primitive root [compare 2135]; to *be transparent* or *clean* (physical or moral):—be (make) clean, be pure (-r).

A verb meaning to be clean, to be pure. This word is used only four times in the OT. Job uses it to describe washing his hands to make them clean (Job 9:30). On two occasions, it speaks of the purity of the heavens (Job 15:15) and the stars (Job 25:5). The final usage of the word describes certain people as being purer than snow (La 4:7) in contrast with the blackness of soot (La 4:8). See the related verb, *zâkâh* (2135), meaning to be clear or pure, and the related noun, *zak* (2134), meaning pure.

2142. זָכַר, zâkar, *zaw-kar´*; a primitive root; (properly) to *mark* (so as to be recognized), i.e. to *remember*; (by implication) to *mention*; also (as denominative from 2145) to *be male*:—× burn [incense], × earnestly, be male, (make) mention (of), be mindful, recount, record (-er), remember, make to be remembered, bring (call, come, keep, put) to (in) remembrance, × still, think on, × well.

A verb meaning to remember, to mention, to recall, to think about, to think on, to be remembered, to recall, to acknowledge, to mention, to make known. The basic meaning indicates a process of mentioning or recalling either silently, verbally, or by means of a memorial sign or symbol. The verb often means to mention, to think about. The Lord warned the people and false prophets not to verbally mention the oracle of the Lord (Jer 23:36); the Lord thought about Ephraim in a good sense (Jer 31:20); and the psalmist thought or meditated on the Lord in his heart and mind without words (Ps 63:6[7]).

These meanings, of course, overlap with the primary translation of the verb, to remember. The psalmist remembered the Lord often, and 43 of the 165 uses of the simple stem are in the Book of Psalms. Remembering in ancient Israel was a major aspect of proper worship, as it is today.

Remembering involves many things, and various connotations are possible. God or people can be the subject that remembers. For example, because God had acted so often for His people, they were to remember Him and His acts on their behalf (Dt 5:15; 15:15; 24:18). They were to remember His covenant and commandments without fail (Ex 20:8; Mal 4:4[3:22]). Above all, they were to remember Him by His name. By remembering Him, they imitated the Lord, for He never forgot them (cf. Dt 4:29–31). He faithfully remembered His people (Ge 8:1), and they could beg Him to remember them, as Jeremiah did in his distress (Ne 13:31; Jer 15:15). The Lord especially remembered His covenant with the ancestors and fathers of Israel (Le 26:45; Dt 9:27; Jer 14:21) and with all humankind through Noah (Ge 9:15, 16).

In the passive stem, the word expresses similar meanings. For example, the psalmist prayed that the sins of his accuser's parents would be remembered against his accuser (Ps 109:14). Yet in an important passage on moral and religious responsibility before God, it was asserted that if righteous people abandoned their righteous ways and followed evil, their righteous deeds would not be remembered by the Lord. The opposite case is also true. None of the evil deeds people commit will be remembered against them if they turn to God (Eze 18:22), nor will the actions, good or evil, of their parents be held for or against them (Eze 18:22, 24). Righteous people will, in fact, be remembered throughout the ages (cf. Ps 112:6).

The causative stem indicates the act of bringing to memory or bringing to attention. It means to recall, as when the Lord challenged His people in Isaiah to recall their past in order to state their argument for their case (Ge 41:9; Isa 43:26). Eli, the high priest, recalled (i.e. mentioned) the ark and then died according to God's prophetic word (1Sa 4:18). The verb is used to indicate urging someone to remember something, such as sin (1Ki 17:18; Eze 21:23[28]; 29:16). It is also used to convey the idea of causing something to be acknowledged, as when the psalmist asserted that he would cause the Lord's righteousness to be acknowledged above all else (Ps 71:16). In the infinitive form, this word sometimes means petition, as found in the superscriptions of some Psalms (Ps 38:title[1], 70:title[1]). It may also mean performing an act of worship (Isa 66:3).

2143. זֵכֶר, zêker, *zay´-ker;* or זֶכֶר, **zeker,** *zeh´-ker;* from 2142; a *memento,* abstract *recollection* (rarely if ever); by implication *commemoration:*—memorial, memory, remembrance, scent.

A masculine noun meaning remembrance. This word comes from the verb *zâkar* (2142), meaning to remember. God has given His people many things as remembrances: Himself (Ps 102:12 [13]); His name (Ex 3:15; Hos 12:5[6]); His works (Ps 111:4); His goodness (Ps 145:7); His holiness (Ps 30:4[5]; 97:12); His deliverance of the Jews (Est 9:28). God also promises the remembrance of the righteous (Pr 10:7) but often cuts off the remembrance of the wicked (Job 18:17; Ps 34:16[17]; 109:15; Pr 10:7); wicked nations (Ex 17:14; Dt 25:19; 32:26); and the dead (Ecc 9:5; Isa 26:14). In several instances of this word, it is used synonymously with *shêm* (8034), meaning name, because one's name invokes the memory (Ex 3:15; Pr 10:7; Hos 12:5[6]).

2144. זֶכֶר, Zeker, *zeh´-ker;* the same as 2143; *Zeker,* an Israelite:—Zeker.

2145. זָכָר, zâkâr, *zaw-kawr´;* from 2142; (properly) *remembered,* i.e. a *male* (of man or animals, as being the most noteworthy sex):— × him, male, man (child, -kind).

2146. זִכָּרוֹן, zikkârôwn, *zik-ka-rone´;* from 2142; a *memento* (or memorable thing, day or writing):—memorial, record.

A masculine noun meaning memorial, remembrance, record, reminder. This word conveys the essential quality of remembering something in the past that has a particular significance (Ecc 1:11). It signifies stone monuments (Jos 4:7); the shoulder ornamentation of the ephod (Ex 28:12; 39:7); a sacrifice calling for explicit retrospection (Nu 5:15); the securing of a progeny (Isa 57:8); a written record (Ex 17:14; Est 6:1); a memorable adage or quote (Job 13:12); some proof of an historic claim (Ne 2:20); a festival memorializing a pivotal event (Ex 12:14; 13:9).

2147. זִכְרִי, Zikrîy, *zik-ree´;* from 2142; *memorable; Zicri,* the name of twelve Israelites:—Zichri.

2148. זְכַרְיָה, Z^e^karyâh, *zek-ar-yaw´;* or זְכַרְיָהוּ, **Z^e^karyâhûw,** *zek-ar-yaw´-hoo;* from 2142 and 3050; *Jah has remembered; Zecarjah,* the name of twenty-nine Israelites:—Zachariah, Zechariah.

2149. זֻלּוּת, zullûwth, *zool-looth´;* from 2151; (properly) a *shaking,* i.e. perhaps a *tempest:*—vilest.

2150. זַלְזַל, zalzal, *zal-zal´;* by reduplication from 2151; *tremulous,* i.e. a *twig:*—sprig.

2151. זָלַל, zâlal, *zaw-lal´;* a primitive root [compare 2107]; to *shake* (as in the wind), i.e. to *quake;* (figurative) to *be loose* morally, *worthless* or *prodigal:*—blow down, glutton, riotous (eater), vile.

2152. זַלְעָפָה, zal'âphâh, *zal-aw-faw´;* or זִלְעָפָה, **zil'âphâh,** *zil-aw-faw´;* from 2196; a *glow* (of wind or anger); also a *famine* (as *consuming*):—horrible, horror, terrible.

A feminine noun meaning burning heat. This word occurs only three times in the OT. In two of the locations, the literal usage of this word is implied. In La 5:10, Jeremiah explains the hunger pangs as the burning heat of famine. In Ps 11:6, David describes how God will pour out His wrath with this burning heat, along with fire and brimstone. In Ps 119:53, the psalmist speaks figuratively about his righteous, burning zeal on account of those who forsake God's law.

2153. זִלְפָּה, Zilpâh, *zil-paw;* from an unused root apparently meaning to *trickle,* as myrrh; fragrant *dropping; Zilpah,* Leah's maid:—Zilpah.

2154. זִמָּה, zimmâh, *zim-maw´;* or זַמָּה, **zammâh,** *zam-maw´;* from 2161; a *plan,* especially a bad one:—heinous crime, lewd (-ly, -ness), mischief, purpose, thought, wicked (device, mind, -ness).

A feminine noun meaning plan, purpose, counsel, wickedness, lewdness, sin. The word refers to the plans and purposes of the mind which give rise to one's actions. Yet the word rarely pertains to good intentions (Job 17:11). It is used in reference to the evil plotting of the wicked (Isa 32:7); the thoughts of foolish people (Pr 24:9); and mischievous motivations (Ps 119:150). Moreover, it relates to sexual sins that spring from lustful intentions, such as incest (Le 18:17); prostitution (Le 19:29); adultery (Job 31:11); and rape (Jgs 20:6). Figuratively, the word represents the wickedness of the people of Israel in their idolatry, calling to mind the connection with adultery (Jer 13:27; Eze 16:27).

2155. זִמָּה, Zimmâh, *zim-maw´;* the same as 2154; *Zimmah,* the name of two Israelites:—Zimmah.

2156. זְמוֹרָה, z^e^môwrâh, *zem-o-raw´;* or זְמֹרָה, **z^e^môrâh,** *zem-o-raw´* (feminine); and זְמֹר, **z^e^môr,** *zem-ore´* (masculine); from 2168; a *twig* (as *pruned*): —vine, branch, slip.

2157. זַמְזֻמִּים, Zamzummîym, *zam-zoom-meem´;* from 2161; *intriguing;* a *Zamzumite,* or native tribe of Palestine:—Zamzummim.

2158. זָמִיר, zâmîyr, *zaw-meer´;* or זָמִר, **zâmir,** *zaw-meer´;* and (feminine) זְמִרָה, **z^e^mirâh,** *zem-ee-raw´;* from 2167; a *song* to be accompanied with instrumental music:—psalm (-ist), singing, song.

2159. זָמִיר, zâmîyr, *zaw-meer´;* from 2168; a *twig* (as *pruned*):—branch.

2160. זְמִירָה, Z^e^mîyrâh, *zem-ee-raw´;* feminine of 2158; *song; Zemirah,* an Israelite:—Zemira.

2161. זָמַם, zâmam, *zaw-mam´;* a primitive root; to *plan,* usually in a bad sense:—consider, devise, imagine, plot, purpose, think (evil).

A verb meaning to consider, to purpose, to devise. This verb derives its meaning from the idea of talking to oneself in a low voice, as if arriving at some conclusion. It denotes the action of fixing thought on an object so as to acquire it (Pr 31:16); devising a plan or an agenda (La 2:17; Zec 8:15); conceiving an idea (Ge 11:6); and determining a course of action (Ps 17:3). In an adverse sense, it also denotes the plotting of evil against another (Ps 31:14; 37:12; Pr 30:32).

2162. זָמָם, zâmâm, *zaw-mawm´;* from 2161; a *plot:*—wicked device.

A masculine noun meaning plans. The Hebrew word occurs once in the OT. David uses this word as he pleads with the Lord to intercede in the plans of the wicked (Ps 140:8[9]).

2163. זָמַן, zâman, *zaw-man´;* a primitive root; to *fix* (a time):—appoint.

A verb meaning to fix, to appoint a time. In the book of Ezra, so many Israelites had violated the command not to marry foreign women that leaders had to set a fixed time for people to come by towns to repent (Ezr 10:14). In Nehemiah, the Levites, priests, and people worked out a time (by casting lots) for each family to contribute wood for the altar (Ne 10:34[35]). In the closing words of his book, Nehemiah reminded the Lord of his leadership in this matter (Ne 13:31). See the related Aramaic verb *zěman* (2164).

2164. זְמַן, z^e^man, *zem-an´;* (Chaldee); corresponding to 2163; to *agree* (on a time and place):—prepare.

An Aramaic verb meaning to agree together. Nebuchadnezzar believed that his wise men were conspiring together, which is why he insisted they tell him both his dream and its interpretation (Da 2:9). See the related Hebrew verb *zâman* (2163).

2165. זְמָן, z^e^mân, *zem-awn´;* from 2163; an *appointed* occasion:—season, time.

A masculine noun meaning appointed time, season. This word occurs only four times in the OT. Two of these are in the book of Esther, referring to the time set for the Feast of Purim (Est 9:27, 31). In the book of Nehemiah, it refers to an appointed time to return from a journey (Ne 2:6). In Ecclesiastes, it occurs in an often-quoted verse, "To every thing there is a season" (Ecc 3:1) to say that everything has a predestined time. The word translated time throughout Ecc 3 is *'êth* (6256). Thus, *zĕman* bears a different sense, emphasizing the specificity in time.

2166. זְמָן**, zᵉmân,** *zem-awn´*; (Chaldee); from 2165; the same as 2165:—season, time.

An Aramaic noun meaning a specific time, a time period. This word is used in Daniel indicating a duration of time or a period of time (Da 2:16; 7:12) and also in reference to the feast times (Da 7:25). See the Hebrew cognate 2165.

2167. זָמַר**, zâmar,** *zaw-mar´*; a primitive root [perhaps identical with 2168 through the idea of *striking* with the fingers]; (properly) to *touch* the strings or parts of a musical instrument, i.e. *play* upon it; to make *music*, accompanied by the voice; hence to *celebrate* in song and music:—give praise, sing forth praises, psalms.

A verb meaning to play an instrument, to sing with musical accompaniment. Stringed instruments are commonly specified in connection with this word, and the tambourine is also mentioned once (Ps 33:2; 71:22, 23; 149:3). The term occurs frequently in a call to praise—usually a summons to oneself (2Sa 22:50; 1Ch 16:9; Ps 66:4; Isa 12:5). In the Bible, the object of this praise is always the Lord, who is lauded for both His attributes and His actions (Jgs 5:3; Ps 101:1; 105:2). Besides the above references, this verb appears exclusively in the Book of Psalms, contributing to a note of praise in psalms of various types: hymns (Ps 104:33); psalms of thanksgiving (Ps 138:1); and even psalms of lament (Ps 144:9).

2168. זָמַר**, zâmar,** *zaw-mar´*; a primitive root [compare 2167, 5568, 6785]; to *trim* (a vine):—prune.

2169. זֶמֶר**, zemer,** *zeh´-mer*; apparently from 2167 or 2168; a *gazelle* (from its lightly *touching* the ground):—chamois.

2170. זְמָר**, zᵉmâr,** *zem-awr´*; (Chaldee); from a root corresponding to 2167; instrumental *music*:—musick.

2171. זַמָּר**, zammâr,** *zam-mawr´*; (Chaldee); from the same as 2170; an instrumental *musician*:—singer.

2172. זִמְרָה**, zimrâh,** *zim-raw´*; from 2167; a *musical* piece or *song* to be accompanied by an instrument:—melody, psalm.

2173. זִמְרָה**, zimrâh,** *zim-raw´*; from 2168, *pruned* (i.e. *choice*) fruit:—best fruit.

2174. זִמְרִי**, Zimrîy,** *zim-ree´*; from 2167; *musical; Zimri*, the name of five Israelites, and of an Arabian tribe:—Zimri.

2175. זִמְרָן**, Zimrân,** *zim-rawn´*; from 2167; *musical; Zimran*, a son of Abraham by Keturah:—Zimran.

2176. זִמְרָת**, zimrâth,** *zim-rawth´*; from 2167; instrumental *music*; (by implication) *praise*:—song.

2177. זַן**, zan,** *zan*; from 2109; (properly) *nourished* (or fully *developed*), i.e. a *form* or *sort*:—divers kinds, × all manner of store.

2178. זַן**, zan,** *zan*; (Chaldee); corresponding to 2177; *sort*:—kind.

2179. זָנַב**, zânab,** *zaw-nab´*; a primitive root meaning to *wag*; used only as a denominative from 2180; to *curtail*, i.e. *cut* off the rear:—smite the hindmost.

2180. זָנָב**, zânâb,** *zaw-nawb´*; from 2179 (in the original sense of *flapping*); the *tail* (literal or figurative):—tail.

2181. זָנָה**, zânâh,** *zaw-naw´*; a primitive root [highly *fed* and therefore *wanton*]; to *commit adultery* (usually of the female, and less often of simple fornication, rarely of involuntary ravishment); (figurative) to *commit idolatry* (the Jewish people being regarded as the spouse of Jehovah):—(cause to) commit fornication, × continually, × great, (be an, play the) harlot, (cause to be, play the) whore, (commit, fall to) whoredom, (cause to) go a-whoring, whorish.

A verb meaning to fornicate, to prostitute. It is typically used for women and only twice in reference to men (Nu 25:1). This verb occurs in connection with prostitution (Le 21:7; Pr 7:10); figuratively, Israel's improper relationships with other nations (Isa 23:17; Eze 23:30; Na 3:4); or other gods (Ex 34:15, 16; Dt 31:16; Eze 6:9; Hos 9:1). As a metaphor, it describes Israel's breach of the Lord's covenant relationship (Ex 34:16).

2182. זָנוֹחַ**, Zânôwach,** *zaw-no´-akh*; from 2186; *rejected; Zanoach*, the name of two places in Palestine:—Zanoah.

2183. זְנוּנִים**, zᵉnûwnîym,** *zeh-noo-neem´*; from 2181; *adultery*; (figurative) *idolatry*:—whoredom.

A masculine noun meaning fornication, prostitution, adultery, idolatry. Judah's daughter-in-law Tamar was accused of prostitution (Ge 38:24). This word can also be used to describe cities like Nineveh (Na 3:4). Most often, it is used in a religious sense to describe, for instance, the unfaithfulness of Israel. Jezebel practiced idolatry (2Ki 9:22); and Jerusalem's idolatry was portrayed in a story where she was the prostitute Aholibah (Eze 23:11, 29). God commanded Hosea to take an unfaithful wife (Hos 1:2), who was also a picture of Israel (Hos 2:2[4], 4[6]; 4:12; 5:4).

2184. זְנוּת**, zᵉnûwth,** *zen-ooth´*; from 2181; *adultery*, i.e. (figurative) *infidelity, idolatry*:—whoredom.

A feminine noun meaning fornication. In the literal sense, this word refers to sexual sin that violates the marriage covenant (Hos 4:11). Most often, however, this word is figuratively applied to God's nation Israel for their wickedness (Hos 6:10). This fornication is usually associated with the worship of other gods (Jer 3:2, 9; 13:27; Eze 23:27), but it can describe outright rebellion (Nu 14:33) or general iniquities (Eze 43:7, 9). This word comes from the common verb *zânâh* (2181), meaning to commit fornication.

2185. זֹנוֹת**, zônôwth,** *zo-noth´*; regarded by some as if from 2109 or an unused root, and applied to military *equipments*; but evidently the feminine plural active participle of 2181; *harlots*:—armour.

2186. זָנַח**, zânach,** *zaw-nakh´*; a primitive root meaning to *push* aside, i.e. *reject, forsake, fail*:—cast away (off), remove far away (off).

2187. זָנַק**, zânaq,** *zaw-nak´*; a primitive root; (properly) to *draw together* the feet (as an animal about to dart upon its prey), i.e. to *spring* forward:—leap.

2188. זֵעָה**, zêʻâh,** *zay-aw´*; from 2111 (in the sense of 3154); *perspiration*:—sweat.

2189. זַעֲוָה**, zaʻăvâh,** *zah-av-aw´*; by transposition for 2113; *agitation, maltreatment*:—× removed, trouble.

2190. זַעֲוָן**, Zaʻăvân,** *zah-av-awn´*; from 2111; *disquiet; Zaavan*, an Idumæan:—Zaavan.

2191. זְעֵיר**, zᵉʻêyr,** *zeh-ayr´*; from an unused root [akin (by permutation) to 6819], meaning to *dwindle; small*:—little.

2192. זְעֵיר**, zᵉʻêyr,** *zeh-ayr´*; (Chaldee); corresponding to 2191:—little.

2193. זָעַךְ**, zâʻak,** *zaw-ak´*; a primitive root; to *extinguish*:—be extinct.

2194. זָעַם**, zâʻam,** *zaw-am´*; a primitive root; (properly) to *foam* at the mouth, i.e. to *be enraged*:—abhor, abominable, (be) angry, defy, (have) indignation.

A verb meaning to be indignant, to be enraged. The root means literally to foam at the mouth, to be enraged. It is used to describe the fury of the king of the North against the holy covenant in Daniel's vision (Da 11:30). Because God is a righteous judge, He shows indignation against evil every day (Ps 7:11[12]). This theme is picked up again in Isaiah (Isa 66:14). God was angry with the towns of Judah (Zec 1:12), and Edom was under the wrath of the Lord (Mal 1:4). This anger can also show in one's face (Pr 25:23).

2195. זַעַם, za'am, *zah´-am*; from 2194; strictly *froth* at the mouth, i.e. (figurative) *fury* (especially of God's displeasure with sin):—angry, indignation, rage.

A masculine noun meaning intense anger, indignation, denunciation, curse. Although this noun can refer to a state of being or actions of a human being (Jer 15:17; Hos 7:16), it usually refers to those of the Lord (Isa 26:20; 30:27; Hab 3:12). This word is also used in parallel with other words with the connotation of anger: *'aph* (639) (Ps 69:24[25]; Isa 10:5, 25; 30:27; Zep 3:8); *'ebrâh* (5678) (Ps 78:49; Eze 21:31[36]; 22:31); and *qetseph* (7110) (Ps 102:10[11]; Jer 10:10).

2196. זָעַף, zâ'aph, *zaw-af´*; a primitive root; (properly) to *boil* up, i.e. (figurative) to *be peevish* or *angry*:—fret, sad, worse liking, be wroth.

A verb meaning to be dejected, to be enraged. The root idea of this word is to storm, which is seen in the use of the related noun *za'aph* (2197) to describe the raging sea in Jnh 1:15. The word describes an unsettled storm within a person that exhibits itself in either dejection or rage. The cupbearer and baker were dejected when they couldn't understand their dreams (Ge 40:6). The guard thought that Daniel and his friends would look downcast if denied the king's food (Da 1:10). King Uzziah was enraged when the priests attempted to remove him from the temple (2Ch 26:19).

2197. זַעַף, za'aph, *zah´-af*; from 2196; *anger*:—indignation, rage (-ing), wrath.

A noun meaning wrath, rage, indignation. This word is used to refer to the rage of kings (2Ch 28:9) or the stormy rage of the sea (Jnh 1:15).

2198. זָעֵף, zâ'êph, *zaw-afe´*; from 2196; *angry*:—displeased.

An adjective meaning dejected. This particular word is only used twice in the OT. In each instance, it describes the dejected attitude of King Ahab when the prophet told him bad news (1Ki 20:43) and when Naboth refused to sell his vineyard to Ahab (1Ki 21:4). See the related verb *zâ'aph* (2196), meaning to be dejected and the related noun *za'aph* (2197), meaning raging.

2199. זָעַק, zâ'aq, *zaw-ak´*; a primitive root; to *shriek* (from anguish or danger); by analogy (as a herald) to *announce* or *convene* publicly:—assemble, call (together), (make a) cry (out), come with such a company, gather (together), cause to be proclaimed.

A verb meaning to cry out, to exclaim, to call. The primary activity implied is that of crying out in pain or by reason of affliction (Ex 2:23; Job 35:9; Jer 25:34). The verb signifies the action of calling on the Lord in a time of need (Joel 1:14; Mic 3:4); uttering sounds of sorrow, distress, or alarm (2Sa 13:19; Isa 26:17; Eze 11:13); entreating for some favour (2Sa 19:28[29]); and issuing a summons for help (Jgs 12:2). By inference, it also implies assembling together as in response to a call (Jgs 6:34, 35; 1Sa 14:20); and the making of a proclamation by a herald (Jnh 3:7).

2200. זְעִק, z^{e}'iq, *zeh´-eek*; (Chaldee); corresponding to 2199; to *make an outcry*:—cry.

2201. זַעַק, za'aq, *zah´-ak*; and (feminine) זְעָקָה, **z^{e}'âqâh,** *zeh-aw-kaw´*; from 2199; a *shriek* or *outcry*:—cry (-ing).

2202. זִפְרֹן, Ziphrôn, *zi-fron´*; from an unused root (meaning to *be fragrant*); *Ziphron*, a place in Palestine:—Ziphron.

2203. זֶפֶת, zepheth, *zeh´-feth*; from an unused root (meaning to *liquify*); *asphalt* (from its tendency to *soften* in the sun):—pitch.

2204. זָקֵן, zâqên, *zaw-kane´*; a primitive root; to *be old*:—aged man, be (wax) old (man).

A verb meaning to be old, to become old. This word is related to the adjective *zâqên* (2205), meaning old, and the noun *zâqân* (2206), meaning beard. In Ps 37:25, David described himself as an aged person as opposed to a youth, *na'ar* (5288), "I have been young, and now am old" (KJV). Solomon also used the same words to demonstrate the contrast between a person when young and when old (Pr 22:6). This word is used of men (Ge 24:1; Jos 13:1; 1Sa 12:2); of women (Ge 18:13; Pr 23:22); or even a tree (Job 14:8). When used of older people, this word is often used to describe the last days of their lives (Ge 27:1, 2; 1Ki 1:1; 2Ch 24:15).

2205. זָקֵן, zâqên, *zaw-kane´*; from 2204; *old*:—aged, ancient (man), elder (-est), old (man, men and ... women), senator.

An adjective meaning elder, old, aged, old man, old woman (as a noun), leader(s). The word's basic meaning is old or aged. But from this basic meaning, several different meanings arise. The word means aged persons, but the ideas of dignity, rank, and privilege also became attached to this concept. The person referred to was usually an old man (Ge 19:4; Jgs 19:16, 17). One of the most famous was the old man in a robe (Samuel) that the witch of Endor saw (1Sa 28:14). Abraham and Sarah were both described as old in Genesis 18:11; the oldest servant in the master's house evidently had some prerogatives of seniority (Ge 24:2). Old men, women, and children were often spared in war and were given special care and protection (cf. Eze 9:6) but not in the corrupt city of Jerusalem at its fall.

The group of men called elders in Israel were a powerfully influential group. They represented the nation from the time of the wilderness period (Ex 19:7) and earlier (Ex 3:16; 4:29). Of the 180 times the phrase is found, it occurs thirty-four times in Exodus when Israel was being formed into a people. There were traditionally seventy elders, and they ate and drank before the Lord with Moses and Joshua on Mount Sinai (Ex 24:9, 11). The older priests held special respect among the priests (2Ki 19:2). The elders were equal to the judges in influence and regularly took part in making decisions (Dt 21:2, 19, 20). The elders of a city as a whole formed a major ruling group (Jos 20:4; Ru 4:2). For example, the elders of Jabesh tried to locate help and negotiated with the Ammonites who were besieging the city (1Sa 11:3). But the elders could lead in evil as well as good, for the picture Ezekiel painted of them was devastating and incriminating. The elders had become corrupt and helped lead the people astray. Their counsel would fail (Eze 7:26; 8:11, 12; 9:6).

2206. זָקָן, zâqân, *zaw-kawn´*; from 2204; the *beard* (as indicating *age*):—beard.

A feminine noun meaning beard. This word is usually used of the beards of men (1Ch 19:5; Isa 15:2) but once refers to the mane of a lion (1Sa 17:35). In biblical times, to have one's beard shaved was humbling. When shaved by another, it was an act of humiliation (2Sa 10:4, 5; Isa 7:20), but when pulled on (Ezr 9:3) or shaved by oneself, it was usually a sign of repentance (Jer 41:5; 48:37). The beard is mentioned in connection with infection (Le 13:29, 30) and was to be trimmed properly according to ceremonial requirements (Le 19:27; 21:5). Ezekiel shaved and divided up his beard as a sign against Jerusalem (Eze 5:1).

2207. זֹקֶן, zôqen, *zo´-ken*; from 2204; old *age*:—age.

A masculine noun meaning extreme old age. The word is used only once in the OT (Ge 48:10), describing Jacob at the time he blessed Ephriam above Manasseh. By this time, he was well-advanced in years, so much so that his sight was extremely poor.

2208. זְקֻנִים, z^{e}qunîym, *zaw-koon´*; (properly) passive participle of 2204 (used only in the plural as a noun); *old* age:—old age.

A passive participle, used only in the plural as a masculine noun, meaning old age. This word is used only four times in the OT, each time in the book of Genesis. It appears in reference to children born to parents late in life. Particularly, it is used of Isaac as the son of Abraham's old age (Ge 21:2, 7); and of Joseph (Ge 37:3) and Benjamin (Ge 44:20) as the sons of Jacob's old age.

2209. זִקְנָה, ziqnâh, *zik-naw´*; feminine of 2205; old *age*:—old (age).

A feminine noun meaning old, old age. This word is used most often to refer to people who are past their prime age. For example, it describes Sarah who is past the normal childbearing age (Ge 24:36). Ps 71 uses the word to ask the Lord not to turn away from the psalmist in his old age (Ps 71:9, 18). Isa 46:4 describes God's care for the aged, even though their bodies grow weak.

2210. זָקַף, zâqaph, *zaw-kaf´*; a primitive root; to *lift*, i.e. (figurative) *comfort*:—raise (up).

2211. **זְקַף, zᵉqaph,** *zek-af´*; (Chaldee); corresponding to 2210; to *hang,* i.e. *impale*:—set up.

2212. **זָקַק, zâqaq,** *zaw-kak´*; a primitive root; to *strain,* (figurative) *extract, clarify*:—fine, pour down, purge, purify, refine.

A verb meaning to refine, to purify. The literal meaning of this word is to strain or extract. It is used in reference to gold (1Ch 28:18); silver (1Ch 29:4; Ps 12:6[7]); water (Job 36:27); wine (Isa 25:6). It is also used of the purification of the Levites, comparing it to refining gold and silver (Mal 3:3).

2213. **זֵר, zêr,** *zare*; from 2237 (in the sense of *scattering*); a *chaplet* (as *spread* around the top), i.e. (specific) a border *moulding*:—crown.

2214. **זָרָא, zârâ',** *zaw-raw´*; from 2114 (in the sense of *estrangement*) [compare 2219]; *disgust*:—loathsome.

2215. **זָרַב, zârab,** *zaw-rab´*; a primitive root; to *flow* away:—wax warm.

2216. **זְרֻבָּבֶל, Zᵉrubbâbel,** *zer-oob-baw-bel´*; from 2215 and 894; *descended of* (i.e. from) *Babylon,* i.e. born there; *Zerubbabel,* an Israelite:—Zerubbabel.

2217. **זְרֻבָּבֶל, Zᵉrubbâbel,** *zer-oob-baw-bel´*; (Chaldee); corresponding to 2216:—Zerubbabel.

2218. **זֶרֶד, Zered,** *zeh´-red*; from an unused root meaning to *be exuberant* in growth; lined with *shrubbery; Zered,* a brook East of the Dead Sea:—Zared, Zered.

2219. **זָרָה, zârâh,** *zaw-raw´*; a primitive root [compare 2114; to *toss* about; (by implication) to *diffuse, winnow*:—cast away, compass, disperse, fan, scatter (away), spread, strew, winnow.

2220. **זְרוֹעַ, zᵉrôwa',** *zer-o´-ah*; or (shorter) **זְרֹעַ, zᵉrôa',** *zer-o´-ah*; and (feminine) **זְרוֹעָה, zᵉrôw'âh,** *zer-o-aw´*; or **זְרֹעָה, zᵉrô'âh,** *zer-o-aw´*; from 2232; the *arm* (as *stretched* out), or (of animals) the *foreleg*; (figurative) *force*:—arm, + help, mighty, power, shoulder, strength.

2221. **זֵרוּעַ, zêrûwa',** *zay-roo´-ah*; from 2232; something *sown,* i.e. a *plant*:—sowing, thing that is sown.

2222. **זַרְזִיף, zarzîyph,** *zar-zeef´*; by reduplication from an unused root meaning to *flow*; a *pouring rain*:—water.

2223. **זַרְזִיר, zarzîyr,** *zar-zeer´*; by reduplication from 2115; (properly) tightly *girt,* i.e. probably a *racer,* or some fleet animal (as being *slender* in the waist):— + greyhound.

2224. **זָרַח, zârach,** *zaw-rakh´*; a primitive root; (properly,) to *irradiate* (or shoot forth beams), i.e. to *rise* (as the sun); (specifically) to *appear* (as a symptom of leprosy):—arise, rise (up), as soon as it is up.

2225. **זֶרַח, zerach,** *zeh´-rakh*; from 2224; a *rising* of light:—rising.

2226. **זֶרַח, Zerach,** *zeh´-rakh*; the same as 2225; *Zerach,* the name of three Israelites, also of an Idumæan and an Ethiopian prince:—Zarah, Zerah.

2227. **זַרְחִי, Zarchîy,** *zar-khee´*; patronymic from 2226; a *Zarchite* or descendant of Zerach:—Zarchite.

2228. **זְרַחְיָה, Zᵉrachyâh,** *zer-akh-yaw´*; from 2225 and 3050; *Jah has risen; Zerachjah,* the name of two Israelites:—Zerahiah.

2229. **זָרַם, zâram,** *zaw-ram´*; a primitive root; to *gush* (as water):—carry away as with a flood, pour out.

2230. **זֶרֶם, zerem,** *zeh´-rem*; from 2229; a *gush* of water:—flood, overflowing, shower, storm, tempest.

2231. **זִרְמָה, zirmâh,** *zir-maw´*; feminine of 2230; a *gushing* of fluid (semen):—issue.

2232. **זָרַע, zâra',** *zaw-rah´*; a primitive root; to *sow*; (figurative) to *disseminate, plant, fructify*:—bear, conceive seed, set with, sow (-er), yield.

2233. **זֶרַע, zera',** *zeh´-rah*; from 2232; *seed*; (figurative) *fruit, plant, sowing-time, posterity*:— × carnally, child, fruitful, seed (-time), sowing-time.

A masculine noun meaning sowing, seed, descendants, offspring, children, and posterity. The literal use of the word indicates seed of the field (i.e. seed planted in the field). When Israel entered Egypt, Joseph instructed the Israelites to keep four-fifths of the crop as seed to plant in their fields and to serve as food for them (Ge 47:24); the season for planting seed was guaranteed by God to continue without fail (Ge 8:22); and successful, abundant harvests were promised right up until the sowing season if Israel followed the Lord's laws and commands (Le 26:5). God had created the seed of the field by decreeing that plants and trees would be self-perpetuating, producing their own seed (Ge 1:11) and that the seed-producing plants would be edible (Ge 1:29). Manna, the heavenly food, resembled coriander seed (Ex 16:31). Any seed could be rendered unclean and not usable if a dead body fell on it after the seed had been moistened (Le 11:38).

The noun is used to describe the seed (i.e. the offspring) of both people and animals. The seed of Judah and Israel would be united and planted peacefully in the land together with animals in a pleasant setting (Jer 31:27). Seed can be translated as son (i.e. seed as when God gives Hannah a promise of a son [1Sa 1:11]). The seed of a woman mentioned in Ge 3:15 is her offspring.

The offspring of humans is described many times by this word. Hannah was given additional children to replace Samuel, whom she gave to the Lord's service (1Sa 2:20). The most important seed that the author of Genesis describes is the seed of Abraham, the promised seed, referring to Isaac, Jacob, and his twelve sons (Ge 12:7; 15:3). The author of Genesis uses the word twenty-one times in this setting (Ex 32:13; Dt 1:8). The seed of the royal line of David was crucial to Israel's existence, and the term is used nine times to refer to David's offspring or descendants (2Sa 7:12). In a figurative sense, seed refers to King Zedekiah and perhaps to Israelites of royal lineage, whom Nebuchadnezzar established in Jerusalem (Eze 17:5). Royal lines or seed were found outside Israel, such as in Edom, where Hadad belonged to the royal line (1Ki 11:14), and in Judah, where the wicked Athaliah attempted to destroy the royal seed (2Ki 11:1; 25:25; Jer 41:1).

The seed or offspring of a particular nation can be characterized in moral and religious terms as well. Three verses stand out: The seed of Israel was called a holy seed (Ezr 9:2; Isa 6:13); and, in the case of Ezr 9:2, the seed corrupted itself by mixing with the peoples around them. The seed of Israel is a seed of God or a divine seed (Mal 2:15) through its union with God (cf. 2Pe 1:4). An offspring could be described as deceitful and wicked (Ps 37:28; Isa 57:4). It was important in Israel to prove that one's origin or seed stemmed from an Israelite ancestor, for some Israelites and Israelite priests who returned from exile could not show their origin (Ezr 2:59). The word also refers to the seed or posterity of the Messiah (Isa 53:10).

2234. **זְרַע, zᵉra',** *zer-ah´*; (Chaldee); corresponding to 2233; *posterity*:—seed.

An Aramaic noun meaning seed. This word is used only once in Da 2:43 in the idiomatic phrase "with the seed of men" (KJV). In this passage, Daniel interpreted King Nebuchadnezzar's dream about the gold, silver, bronze, iron, and clay statue. This mixing of people with the seed of men is a reference to other people groups joining a community or nation. Those who come afterward lack the national spirit to adhere to one another, just as iron does not mix with clay.

2235. **זֵרֹעַ, zêrôa',** *zay-ro´-ah*; or **זֵרָעֹן, zêrâ'ôn,** *zay-raw-ohn´*; from 2232; something *sown* (only in the plural), i.e. a *vegetable* (as food):—pulse.

2236. **זָרַק, zâraq,** *zaw-rak´*; a primitive root; to *sprinkle* (fluid or solid particles):—be here and there, scatter, sprinkle, strew.

A verb meaning to sprinkle, to scatter, to be sprinkled. This word is most often used to describe the actions of the priests performing the sacrificial rituals. They sprinkled the blood of the sacrifices (Le 1:5; 2Ki 16:13; 2Ch 29:22). It is also used of water (Nu 19:13; Eze 36:25). In a time of grief, Job's friends sprinkled dust on their heads (Job 2:12). King Josiah destroyed the false gods and scattered their pieces (powder, NASB) over the graves of those who had worshipped them (2Ch 34:4).

2237. זָרַר, zârar, *zaw-rar´*; a primitive root [compare 2114]; perhaps to *diffuse*, i.e. (specifically) to *sneeze*:—sneeze.

2238. זֶרֶשׁ, Zeresh, *zeh´-resh*; of Persian origin; *Zeresh*, Haman's wife:—Zeresh.

2239. זֶרֶת, zereth, *zeh´-reth*; from 2219; the *spread* of the fingers, i.e. a *span*:—span.

2240. זַתּוּא, Zattûw', *zat-too´*; of uncertain derivation; *Zattu*, an Israelite:—Zattu.

2241. זֵתָם, Zêthâm, *zay-thawm´*; apparently a variation for 2133; *Zetham*, an Israelite:—Zetham.

2242. זֵתַר, Zêthar, *zay-thar´*; of Persian origin; *Zethar*, a eunuch of Xerxes:—Zethar.

2243. חֹב, chôb, *khobe*; by contraction from 2245; (properly) a *cherisher*, i.e. the *bosom*:—bosom.

2244. חָבָא, châbâ', *khaw-baw´*; a primitive root [compare 2245]; to *secrete*:—× held, hide (self), do secretly.

2245. חָבַב, châbab, *khaw-bab´*; a primitive root [compare 2244, 2247]; (properly) to *hide* (as in the bosom), i.e. to *cherish* (with affection):—love.

A verb meaning to love. This word occurs only once in the OT, in which it describes God's love for the people of Israel (Dt 33:3). This verse is in a poetical section of Scripture, which helps to explain why this word is used only once. It is related to *chôb* (2243), meaning bosom, which is used only in Job 31:33. Thus, the love expressed here probably signifies an embracing, motherly affection.

2246. חֹבָב, Chôbâb, *kho-bawb´*; from 2245; *cherished; Chobab*, father-in-law of Moses:—Hobab.

2247. חָבָה, châbâh, *khaw-bah´*; a primitive root [compare 2245]; to *secrete*:—hide (self).

2248. חֲבוּלָה, chăbûwlâh, *khab-oo-law´*; (Chaldee); from 2255; (properly) *overthrown*, i.e. (moral) *crime*:—hurt.

2249. חָבוֹר, Châbôwr, *khaw-bore´*; from 2266; *united; Chabor*, a river of Assyria:—Habor.

2250. חַבּוּרָה, chabbûwrâh, *khab-boo-raw´*; or חַבֻּרָה, **chabburâh,** *khab-boo-raw´*; or חֲבֻרָה, **chăburâh,** *khab-oo-raw´*; from 2266; (properly) *bound* (with stripes), i.e. a *weal* (or black-and-blue mark itself):—blueness, bruise, hurt, stripe, wound.

2251. חָבַט, châbaṭ, *khaw-bat´*; a primitive root; to *knock* out or off:—beat (off, out), thresh.

2252. חֲבַיָּה, Chăbayyâh, *khab-ah-yaw´*; or חֲבָיָה, **Chăbâyâh,** *khab-aw-yaw´*; from 2247 and 3050; *Jah has hidden; Chabajah*, an Israelite:—Habaiah.

2253. חֶבְיוֹן, chebyôwn, *kheb-yone´*; from 2247; *concealment*:—hiding.

2254. חָבַל, châbal, *khaw-bal´*; a primitive root; to *wind* tightly (as a rope), i.e. to *bind*; specifically by a *pledge*; (figurative) to *pervert, destroy*; also to *writhe* in pain (especially of parturition):—× at all, band, bring forth, (deal) corrupt (-ly), destroy, offend, lay to (take a) pledge, spoil, travail, × very, withhold.

A verb meaning to take a pledge, to destroy. This verb is translated in a variety of ways. Most commonly, it means taking a pledge for such things as a loan (Ex 22:26[25]; Dt 24:6; Eze 18:16; Am 2:8). The word is used in Job in reference to debts (Job 22:6; 24:3, 9). It also describes the destruction of the wicked (Pr 13:13; Isa 32:7) or destruction of property (Isa 10:27; 13:5). This word can also mean to corrupt (Ne 1:7; Job 17:1). Zechariah used it in a metaphor describing the union between Israel and Judah (Zec 11:7, 14).

2255. חֲבַל, chăbal, *khab-al´*; (Chaldee); corresponding to 2254; to *ruin*:—destroy, hurt.

An Aramaic verb meaning to ruin, to hurt, to destroy. King Darius issued a decree that ended with a plea for God to overthrow anyone who tried to destroy the Temple (Ezr 6:12). The tree in Nebuchadnezzar's dream was cut down and destroyed (Da 4:23[20]). Because the angel shut the lions' mouths, they did not hurt Daniel (Da 6:22[23]). This word also refers to a kingdom that will never be destroyed. In the interpretation of one of Nebuchadnezzar's dreams, Daniel told of a kingdom that would never be destroyed (Da 2:44). King Darius praised God when Daniel was not eaten by lions, saying the kingdom of God would not be destroyed (Da 6:26[27]). Once again, Daniel saw a kingdom like this in his dream of the four beasts (Da 7:14).

2256. חֶבֶל, chebel, *kheh´-bel*; or חֵבֶל, **chêbel,** *khay´-bel*; from 2254; a *rope* (as *twisted*), especially a measuring *line*; (by implication) a *district* or *inheritance* (as *measured*); or a *noose* (as of *cords*); (figurative) a *company* (as if *tied* together); also a *throe* (especially of parturition); also *ruin*:—band, coast, company, cord, country, destruction, line, lot, pain, pang, portion, region, rope, snare, sorrow, tackling.

A masculine or feminine noun meaning cord, pangs, region, company. This word has many meanings, depending on the context. The most basic meaning is a rope or a cord, such as the rope the spies used to escape through Rahab's window (Jos 2:15) or the cords used to bind Jeremiah in the dungeon (Jer 38:11–13). Although these cords may be decorative (Est 1:6), they are usually used to bind and control objects, such as animals (Job 41:1[40:25]) or buildings (Isa 33:20). This word is also used symbolically to speak of the cords of sin and death (2Sa 22:6; Ps 18:4[5], 5[6]; Pr 5:22) or the pangs of childbirth (Isa 13:8; Jer 13:21; Hos 13:13). It can even be translated "destruction" (Job 21:17). This word is also used to describe a dividing line (2Sa 8:2; Am 7:17); a geographical region (Dt 3:13, 14; 1Ki 4:13; Zep 2:5, 6); or an allotment of an inheritance (Dt 32:9; Jos 17:5; Ps 105:11). In a few instances, this word describes a company of prophets (1Sa 10:5, 10).

2257. חֲבָל, chăbâl, *khab-awl´*; (Chaldee); from 2255; *harm* (personal or pecuniary):—damage, hurt.

2258. חֲבֹל, chăbôl, *khab-ole´*; or (feminine) חֲבֹלָה, **chăbôlâh,** *khab-o-law´*; from 2254; a *pawn* (as security for debt):—pledge.

A noun meaning pledge. This word is always used when speaking of those who do or do not return pledges, which were items taken to guarantee loans. These items were usually people's cloaks, and the Law stated that they were to be returned to the owners before the sun set because they were the only covering they had (cf. Ex 22:26[25], 27[26]). Righteous persons returned the pledges (Eze 18:7) or did not even require them (Eze 18:16), whereas wicked persons kept the items used for the pledge (Eze 18:12). But if they repented and returned them, they would live instead of die for the evil they did (Eze 33:15).

2259. חֹבֵל, chôbêl, *kho-bale´*; active participle from 2254 (in the sense of handling *ropes*); a *sailor*:—pilot, shipmaster.

2260. חִבֵּל, chibbêl, *khib-bale´*; from 2254 (in the sense of furnished with *ropes*); a *mast*:—mast.

2261. חֲבַצֶּלֶת, chăbatstseleth, *khab-ats-tseh´-leth*; of uncertain derivation; probably *meadow-saffron*:—rose.

2262. חֲבַצִּנְיָה, Chăbatstsinyâh, *khab-ats-tsin-yaw´*; of uncertain derivation; *Chabatstsanjah*, a Rechabite:—Habazaniah.

2263. חָבַק, châbaq, *khaw-bak´*; a primitive root; to *clasp* (the hands or in embrace):—embrace, fold.

2264. חִבֻּק, chibbuq, *khib-book´*; from 2263; a *clasping* of the hands (in idleness):—fold.

2265. חֲבַקּוּק, Chăbaqqûwq, *khab-ak-kook´*; by reduplication from 2263; *embrace; Chabakkuk*, the prophet:—Habakkuk.

2266. חָבַר, châbar, *khaw-bar´*; a primitive root; to *join* (literal or figurative); specifically (by means of spells) to *fascinate*:—charm (-er), be compact, couple (together), have fellowship with, heap up, join (self, together), league.

2267. חֶבֶר, **cheber,** *kheh´-ber*; from 2266; a *society*; also a *spell*:—+ charmer (-ing), company, enchantment, × wide.

A masculine noun meaning a company, an association, a spell. It is used to refer to a band of bad priests (Hos 6:9); a house of association, namely, a house shared with an antagonistic woman (Pr 21:9; 25:24); or a magical spell or incantation (Dt 18:11; Ps 58:5[6]; Isa 47:9, 12).

2268. חֶבֶר, **Cheber,** *kheh´-ber*; the same as 2267; *community; Cheber*, the name of a Kenite and of three Israelites:—Heber.

2269. חֲבַר, **chăbar,** *khab-ar´*; (Chaldee); from a root corresponding to 2266; an *associate*:—companion, fellow.

2270. חָבֵר, **châbêr,** *khaw-bare´*; from 2266; an *associate*:—companion, fellow, knit together.

2271. חַבָּר, **chabbâr,** *khab-bawr´*; from 2266; a *partner*:—companion.

2272. חֲבַרְבֻּרָה, **chăbarburâh,** *khab-ar-boo-raw´*; by reduplication from 2266; a *streak* (like a *line*), as on the tiger:—spot.

2273. חַבְרָה, **chabrâh,** *khab-raw´*; (Chaldee); feminine of 2269; an *associate*:—other.

2274. חֶבְרָה, **chebrâh,** *kheb-raw´*; feminine of 2267; *association*:—company.

2275. חֶבְרוֹן, **Chebrôwn,** *kheb-rone´*; from 2267; seat of *association; Chebron*, a place in Palestine, also the name of two Israelites:—Hebron.

2276. חֶבְרוֹנִי, **Chebrôwnîy,** *kheb-ro-nee´*; or חֶבְרֹנִי, **Chebrônîy,** *kheb-ro-nee´*; patronymic from 2275; *Chebronite* (collective), an inhabitant of Chebron:—Hebronites.

2277. חֶבְרִי, **Chebrîy,** *kheb-ree´*; patronymic from 2268; a *Chebrite* (collective) or descendants of Cheber:—Heberites.

2278. חֲבֶרֶת, **chăbereth,** *khab-eh´-reth*; feminine of 2270; a *consort*:—companion.

2279. חֹבֶרֶת, **chôbereth,** *kho-beh´-reth*; feminine active participle of 2266; a *joint*:—which coupleth, coupling.

2280. חָבַשׁ, **châbash,** *khaw-bash´*; a primitive root; to *wrap* firmly (especially a turban, compress, or *saddle*); (figurative) to *stop*, to *rule*:—bind (up), gird about, govern, healer, put, saddle, wrap about.

A verb meaning to bind. This word is used primarily to describe a binding or wrapping of one object with another. It is frequently used of saddling a donkey (Ge 22:3; Jgs 19:10; 1 Kgs 2:40) but can be used to describe the binding of caps on the priests' heads (Ex 29:9; Le 8:13); the tying of garments and carpets in a roll (Eze 27:24); the wrapping of weeds around Jonah's head (Jnh 2:5[6]); God stopping the floods (Job 28:11). This word is often used to describe binding wounds (both physical and spiritual) with the result that healing occurs (Isa 61:1; Eze 30:21; Hos 6:1). In a few cases, this binding may refer to one's ability to control (or rule) another (Job 34:17; 40:13).

2281. חֲבִתִּים, **chăbittîym,** *khaw-bit-teem´*; from an unused root probably meaning to *cook* [compare 4227]; something *fried*, probably a griddle-*cake*:—pan.

2282. חַג, **chag,** *khag*; or חָג, **châg,** *khawg*; from 2287; a *festival*, or a *victim* therefor:—(solemn) feast (day), sacrifice, solemnity.

A noun meaning a feast, a festival. This word is used numerous times throughout the OT referring to the feasts of the Hebrew religious calendar. It is used of the major feasts, including the Feast of Unleavened Bread and the Passover Feast (Ex 34:18, 25; Le 23:6; Dt 16:16; Ezr 6:22); the Feast of Weeks (Dt 16:16; 2Ch 8:13); and the Feast of Tabernacles (Le 23:34; Nu 29:12; Dt 31:10; Zech 14:16). It was used in the Temple dedication during Solomon's reign (1Ki 8:2, 65). Evil King Jeroboam held a festival described in 1Ki 12:32, 33. The prophets often used this word to describe the negligence of the people in keeping the feasts commanded by Mosaic Law (Isa 29:1; Am 5:21; Mal 2:3).

2283. חָגָּא, **châggâ',** *khawg-gaw´*; from an unused root meaning to *revolve* [compare 2287]; (properly) *vertigo*, i.e. (figurative) *fear*:—terror.

A feminine noun meaning terror. This word occurs only once in the OT in Isa 19:17 and speaks of the reeling terror that Judah would cause in Egypt.

2284. חָגָב, **châgâb,** *khaw-gawb´*; of uncertain derivation; a *locust*:—locust.

2285. חָגָב, **Châgâb,** *khaw-gawb´*; the same as 2284; *locust; Chagab*, one of the Nethinim:—Hagab.

2286. חֲגָבָא, **Chăgâbâ',** *khag-aw-baw´*; or חֲגָבָה, **Chăgâbâh,** *khag-aw-baw´*; feminine of 2285; *locust; Chagaba* or *Chagabah*, one of the Nethinim:—Hagaba, Hagabah.

2287. חָגַג, **châgag,** *khaw-gag´*; a primitive root [compare 2283, 2328]; (properly) to move in a *circle*, i.e. (specifically) to *march* in a sacred procession, to *observe* a festival; (by implication) to *be giddy*:—celebrate, dance, (keep, hold) a (solemn) feast (holiday), reel to and fro.

2288. חָגוּ, **châgûw,** *khaw-goo´*; from an unused root meaning to take *refuge*; a *rift* in rocks:—cleft.

2289. חָגוֹר, **chăgôwr,** *khaw-gore´*; from 2296; *belted*:—girded with.

2290. חֲגוֹר, **chăgôwr,** *khag-ore´*; or חֲגֹר **chăgôr,** *khag-ore´*; and (feminine) חֲגוֹרָה **chăgôwrâh,** *khag-o-raw´*; or חֲגֹרָה **chăgôrâh,** *khag-o-raw´*; from 2296; a *belt* (for the waist):—apron, armour, gird (-le).

2291. חַגִּי, **Chaggîy,** *khag-ghee´*; from 2287; *festive; Chaggi*, an Israelite; also (patronymic) a *Chaggite*, or descendant of the same:—Haggi, Haggites.

2292. חַגַּי, **Chaggay,** *khag-gah´ee*; from 2282; *festive; Chaggai*, a Hebrew prophet:—Haggai.

2293. חַגִּיָּה, **Chaggiyyâh,** *khag-ghee-yaw´*; from 2282 and 3050; *festival of Jah; Chaggijah*, an Israelite:—Haggiah.

2294. חַגִּית, **Chaggîyth,** *khag-gheeth´*; feminine of 2291; *festive; Chaggith*, a wife of David:—Haggith.

2295. חָגְלָה, **Choglâh,** *khog-law´*; of uncertain derivation; probably a *partridge; Choglah*, an Israelitess:—Hoglah. See also 1031.

2296. חָגַר, **châgar,** *khaw-gar´*; a primitive root; to *gird* on (as a belt, armour, etc.):—be able to put on, be afraid, appointed, gird, restrain, × on every side.

2297. חַד, **chad,** *khad*; abridged from 259; *one*:—one.

2298. חַד, **chad,** *khad*; (Chaldee); corresponding to 2297; (as cardinal) *one*; (as article) *single*; (as ordinal) *first*; (adverbial) *at once*:—a, first, one, together.

2299. חַד, **chad,** *khad*; from 2300; *sharp*:—sharp.

2300. חָדַד, **châdad,** *khaw-dad´*; a primitive root; to *be* (causative *make*) *sharp* or (figurative) *severe*:—be fierce, sharpen.

2301. חֲדַד, **Chădad,** *khad-ad´*; from 2300; *fierce; Chadad*, an Ishmaelite:—Hadad.

2302. חָדָה, **châdâh,** *khaw-daw´*; a primitive root; to *rejoice*:—make glad, be joined, rejoice.

2303. חַדּוּד, **chaddûwd,** *khad-dood´*; from 2300; a *point*:—sharp.

2304. חֶדְוָה, **chedvâh,** *khed-vaw´*; from 2302; *rejoicing*:—gladness, joy.

2305. חֶדְוָה, **chedvâh,** *khed-vaw´*; (Chaldee); corresponding to 2304:—joy.

2306. חֲדֵה, **chădêh,** *khad-ay´*; (Chaldee); corresponding to 2373; a *breast*:—breast.

2307. חָדִיד, Châdîyd, *khaw-deed´*; from 2300; a *peak; Chadid,* a place in Palestine:—Hadid.

2308. חָדַל, châdal, *khaw-dal´*; a primitive root; (properly) to *be flabby,* i.e. (by implication) *desist;* (figurative) *be lacking* or *idle:*—cease, end, fail, forbear, forsake, leave (off), let alone, rest, be unoccupied, want.

2309. חֶדֶל, chedel, *kheh´-del*; from 2308; *rest,* i.e. the state of the *dead:*—world.

A masculine noun meaning cessation, rest. This word occurs only in Isa 38:11 in the lamentation of Hezekiah. Despite the fact it is translated "world," it conveys the idea of a place of termination or repose. By considering the context in the OT, one comes to understand that the word refers to the grave, or more exactly, Sheol (cf. Isa 38:10).

2310. חָדֵל, châdêl, *khaw-dale´*; from 2308; *vacant,* i.e. *ceasing* or *destitute:*—he that forbeareth, frail, rejected.

2311. חַדְלַי, Chadlay, *khad-lah´ee*; from 2309; *idle; Chadlai,* an Israelite:—Hadlai.

2312. חֵדֶק, chêdeq, *khay´-dek*; from an unused root meaning to *sting;* a *prickly* plant:—brier, thorn.

2313. חִדֶּקֶל, Chiddeqel, *khid-deh´-kel*; probably of foreign origin; the *Chiddekel* (or Tigris) river:—Hiddekel.

2314. חָדַר, châdar, *khaw-dar´*; a primitive root; (properly) to *inclose* (as a room), i.e. (by analogy) to *beset* (as in a siege):—enter a privy chamber.

2315. חֶדֶר, cheder, *kheh´-der*; from 2314; an *apartment* (usually literal):—([bed] inner) chamber, innermost (-ward) part, parlour, + south, × within.

2316. חֲדַר, Chădar, *khad-ar´*; another form for 2315; *chamber; Chadar,* an Ishmaelite:—Hadar.

2317. חַדְרָךְ, Chadrâk, *khad-rawk´*; of uncertain derivation; *Chadrak,* a Syrian deity:—Hadrach.

2318. חָדַשׁ, châdash, *khaw-dash´*; a primitive root; to *be new;* (causative) to *rebuild:*—renew, repair.

2319. חָדָשׁ, châdâsh, *khaw-dawsh´*; from 2318; *new:*—fresh, new thing.

2320. חֹדֶשׁ, chôdesh, *kho´-desh*; from 2318; the *new* moon; (by implication) a *month:*—month (-ly), new moon.

2321. חֹדֶשׁ, Chôdesh, *kho´-desh*; the same as 2320; *Chodesh,* an Israelitess:—Hodesh.

2322. חֲדָשָׁה, Chădâshâh, *khad-aw-shaw´*; feminine of 2319; *new; Chadashah,* a place in Palestine:—Hadashah.

2323. חֲדַת, chădâth, *khad-ath´*; (Chaldee); corresponding to 2319; *new:*—new.

2324. חֲוָה, chăvâh, *khav-aw´*; (Chaldee); corresponding to 2331; to *show:*—shew.

2325. חוּב, chûwb, *khoob*; also חָיַב, **châyab,** *khaw-yab´*; a primitive root; (properly) perhaps to *tie,* i.e. (figurative and reflexive) to *owe,* or (by implication) to *forfeit:*—make endanger.

2326. חוֹב, chôwb, *khobe*; from 2325; *debt:*—debtor.

2327. חוֹבָה, chôwbâh, *kho-baw´*; feminine active participle of 2247; *hiding* place; *Chobah,* a place in Syria:—Hobah.

2328. חוּג, chûwg, *khoog*; a primitive root [compare 2287]; to describe a *circle:*—compass.

2329. חוּג, chûwg, *khoog*; from 2328; a *circle:*—circle, circuit, compass.

2330. חוּד, chûwd, *khood*; a primitive root; (properly) to *tie* a knot, i.e. (figurative) to *propound* a riddle:—put forth.

2331. חָוָה, châvâh, *khaw-vah´*; a primitive root; [compare 2324, 2421]; (properly) to *live;* (by implication) (intensive) to *declare* or *show:*—show.

2332. חַוָּה, Chavvâh, *khav-vaw´*; causative from 2331; *life-giver; Chavvah* (or Eve), the first woman:—Eve.

2333. חַוָּה, chavvâh, *khav-vaw´*; (properly) the same as 2332 (*life-giving,* i.e. *living-place*); (by implication) an encampment or *village:*—(small) town.

2334. חַוּוֹת יָאִיר, Chavvôth Yâ'îyr, *khav-vothe´ yaw-eer´*; from the plural of 2333 and a modification of 3265; *hamlets of Jair,* a region of Palestine:—[Bashan-] Havoth-jair.

2335. חוֹזַי, Chôwzay, *kho-zah´ee*; from 2374; *visionary; Chozai,* an Israelite:—the seers.

2336. חוֹחַ, chôwach, *kho´-akh*; from an unused root apparently meaning to *pierce;* a *thorn;* (by analogy) a *ring* for the nose:—bramble, thistle, thorn.

2337. חָוָח, châvâch, *khaw-vawkh´*; perhaps the same as 2336; a *dell* or *crevice* (as if *pierced* in the earth):—thicket.

2338. חוּט, chûwṭ, *khoot*; (Chaldee); corresponding to the root of 2339, perhaps as a denominative; to *string* together, i.e. (figurative) to *repair:*—join.

2339. חוּט, chûwṭ, *khoot*; from an unused root probably meaning to *sew;* a *string;* (by implication) a measuring *tape:*—cord, fillet, line, thread.

2340. חִוִּי, Chivvîy, *khiv-vee´*; perhaps from 2333; a *villager;* a *Chivvite,* one of the aboriginal tribes of Palestine:—Hivite.

2341. חֲוִילָה, Chăvîylâh, *khav-ee-law´*; probably from 2342; *circular; Chavilah,* the name of two or three eastern regions; also perhaps of two men:—Havilah.

2342. חוּל, chûwl, *khool*; or חִיל, **chîyl,** *kheel*; a primitive root; (properly) to *twist* or *whirl* (in a circular or spiral manner), i.e. (specific) to *dance,* to *writhe* in pain (especially of parturition) or fear; (figurative) to *wait,* to *pervert:*—bear, (make to) bring forth, (make to) calve, dance, drive away, fall grievously (with pain), fear, form, great, grieve, (be) grievous, hope, look, make, be in pain, be much (sore) pained, rest, shake, shapen, (be) sorrow (-ful), stay, tarry, travail (with pain), tremble, trust, wait carefully (patiently), be wounded.

A verb meaning to whirl, to shake, to fear, to dance, to writhe, to grieve. This word has many different meanings, most of which derive from two basic ideas: to whirl in motion and to writhe in pain. The first of these ideas may be seen in the shaking of the earth (Ps 29:8); the stirring of the waters (Ps 77:16[17]); or the trembling of the mountains (Hab 3:10). At times, this word is used in a context of shaking with fear (Dt 2:25; Jer 5:22); worshiping in trembling awe (1Ch 16:30; Ps 96:9); or anxiously waiting (Ge 8:10; Ps 37:7). It is also used to describe dancing women (Jgs 21:21, 23). The second idea of writhing in pain can be either physical, as when Saul was wounded in battle (1Sa 31:3), or emotional, as when Jeremiah grieved in anguish over Jerusalem's refusal to grieve (Jer 4:19). This word is often used to describe the labour pains of giving birth (Ps 29:9; Isa 26:17, 18; 51:2) but can also imply God's creating work (Dt 32:18; Job 15:7; Ps 90:2; Pr 8:24, 25).

2343. חוּל, Chûwl, *khool*; from 2342; a *circle; Chul,* a son of Aram; also the region settled by him:—Hul.

2344. חוֹל, chôwl, *khole*; from 2342; *sand* (as *round* or whirling particles):—sand.

2345. חוּם, chûwm, *khoom*; from an unused root meaning to *be warm,* i.e. (by implication) *sunburnt* or *swarthy* (blackish):—brown.

2346. חוֹמָה, chôwmâh, *kho-maw´*; feminine active participle of an unused root apparently meaning to *join;* a *wall* of protection:—wall, walled.

2347. **חוּס, chûws,** *khoos*; a primitive root; (properly) to *cover*, i.e. (figurative) to *compassionate*:—pity, regard, spare.

2348. **חוֹף, chôwph,** *khofe*; from an unused root meaning to *cover*; a *cove* (as a *sheltered* bay):—coast [of the sea], haven, shore, [sea-] side.

2349. **חוּפָם, Chûwphâm,** *khoo-fawm´*; from the same as 2348; *protection; Chupham*, an Israelite:—Hupham.

2350. **חוּפָמִי, Chûwphâmîy,** *khoo-faw-mee´*; patronymic from 2349; a *Chuphamite* or descendant of Chupham:—Huphamites.

2351. **חוּץ, chûwts,** *khoots*; or (shortened) **חֻץ, chuts,** *khoots*; (both forms feminine in the plural) from an unused root meaning to *sever*; (properly) *separate* by a wall, i.e. *outside, outdoors*:—abroad, field, forth, highway, more, out (-side, -ward), street, without.

2352. **חוּר, chûwr,** *khoor*; or (shortened) **חֻר, chur,** *khoor*; from an unused root probably meaning to *bore*; the *crevice* of a serpent; the *cell* of a prison:—hole.

2353. **חוּר, chûwr,** *khoor*; from 2357; *white* linen:—white.

2354. **חוּר, Chûwr,** *khoor*; the same as 2353 or 2352; *Chur*, the name of four Israelites and one Midianite:—Hur.

2355. **חוֹרָי, chôwrây,** *kho-raw-ee´*; the same as 2353; *white* linen:—network. Compare 2715.

2356. **חוֹר, chôwr,** *khore*; or (shortened) **חֹר, chôr,** *khore*; the same as 2352; a *cavity, socket, den*:—cave, hole.

2357. **חָוַר, châvar,** *khaw-var´*; a primitive root; to *blanch* (as with shame):—wax pale.

2358. **חִוָּר, chivvâr,** *khiv-vawr´*; (Chaldee); from a root corresponding to 2357; *white*:—white.

2359. **חוּרִי, Chûwrîy,** *khoo-ree´*; probably from 2353; *linen-worker; Churi*, an Israelite:—Huri.

2360. **חוּרַי, Chûwray,** *khoo-rah´ee*; probably an orthographical variation for 2359; *Churai*, an Israelite:—Hurai.

2361. **חוּרָם, Chûwrâm,** *khoo-rawm´*; probably from 2353; *whiteness*, i.e. noble; *Churam*, the name of an Israelite and two Syrians:—Huram. Compare 2438.

2362. **חַוְרָן, Chavrân,** *khav-rawn´*; apparently from 2357 (in the sense of 2352); *cavernous; Chavran*, a region East of the Jordan:—Hauran.

2363. **חוּשׁ, chûwsh,** *koosh*; a primitive root; to *hurry*; (figurative) to *be eager* with excitement or enjoyment:—(make) haste (-n), ready.

2364. **חוּשָׁה, Chûwshâh,** *khoo-shaw´*; from 2363; *haste; Chushah*, an Israelite:—Hushah.

2365. **חוּשַׁי, Chûwshay,** *khoo-shah´ee*; from 2363; *hasty; Chushai*, an Israelite:—Hushai.

2366. **חוּשִׁים, Chûwshîym,** *khoo-sheem´*; or **חֻשִׁים, Chushîym,** *khoo-sheem´*; or **חֻשִׁם, Chushim,** *khoo-sheem´*; plural from 2363; *hasters; Chushim*, the name of three Israelites:—Hushim.

2367. **חוּשָׁם, Chûwshâm,** *khoo-shawm´*; or **חֻשָׁם, Chushâm,** *khoo-shawm´*; from 2363; *hastily; Chu-sham*, an Idumæan:—Husham.

2368. **חוֹתָם, chôwthâm,** *kho-thawm´*; or **חֹתָם, chô-thâm,** *kho-thawm´*; from 2856; a *signature*-ring:—seal, signet.

2369. **חוֹתָם, Chôwthâm,** *kho-thawm´*; the same as 2368; *seal; Chotham*, the name of two Israelites:—Hotham, Hothan.

2370. **חֲזָא, chăzâ',** *khaz-aw´*; (Chaldee); or **חֲזָה, chăzâh,** *khaz-aw´*; (Chaldee); corresponding to 2372; to *gaze* upon; (mentally) to *dream, be usual* (i.e. *seem*):—behold, have [a dream], see, be wont.

An Aramaic verb meaning to see, to behold, to witness, to observe. This word appears only in the books of Ezra and Daniel. It signifies the literal sense of sight (Da 5:23); the observation of something with the eye (Da 3:25; 5:5); the witnessing of a king's dishonour (Ezr 4:14); beholding something in a dream (Da 2:41; 4:20[17]); and having a dream (Da 7:1). On one occasion, the verb is used to imply the usual condition or customary state of the furnace set to receive Shadrach, Meshach, and Abednego (Da 3:19). This use probably stresses the difference in the appearance of the furnace, which would be obvious to the observer.

2371. **חֲזָאֵל, Chăzâ'êl,** *khaz-aw-ale´*; or **חֲזָהאֵל, Chăzâh'êl,** *khaz-aw-ale´*; from 2372 and 410; *God has seen; Chazaël*, a king of Syria:—Hazael.

2372. **חָזָה, châzâh,** *khaw-zaw*; a primitive root; to *gaze* at; (mentally) to *perceive, contemplate* (with pleasure); specifically to *have a vision of*:—behold, look, prophesy, provide, see.

A verb meaning to see, to perceive. This term is more poetic than the common *râ'âh* (7200). It refers to seeing God (Ex 24:11; Job 19:26, 27; Ps 11:7; 17:15); astrological observations (Isa 47:13); prophetic vision and insight (Isa 1:1; La 2:14; Eze 12:27; Hab 1:1; Zec 10:2).

2373. **חָזֶה, châzeh,** *khaw-zeh´*; from 2372; the *breast* (as most *seen* in front):—breast.

2374. **חֹזֶה, chôzeh,** *kho-zeh´*; active participle of 2372; a *beholder* in vision; also a *compact* (as *looked upon* with approval):—agreement, prophet, see that, seer, [star-] gazer.

A masculine noun meaning a seer, a prophet. It is used only seventeen times in the OT, always in the present active participle. The word means one who sees or perceives; it is used in parallel with the participle of the verb that means literally to see, to perceive. In Isaiah a rebellious people sought to curb the functions of these seers (Isa 30:10). In 1Sa 9:9, the author parenthetically states that the word for prophet in his day, *nâbiy'* (5030), was formerly called a seer. However, for seer, he did not use *chôwzeh* but a present participle of the verb *râ'âh* (7200), meaning to see, to perceive. It appears that the participles of *chôwzeh* and of *râ'âh* function synonymously. But, terminology aside, a seer functioned the same as a prophet, who was moved by God and had divinely given insight. This Hebrew word is also used in parallel with the word prophet (2Ki 17:13; Am 7:12, 14); hence, its meaning overlaps with that term as well (cf. 2Ch 33:18; Isa 29:10). Seers sometimes served a specific person: Gad served as King David's seer and did not hesitate to declare the words the Lord gave him for the king (2Sa 24:11). David had more than one seer (cf. 1Ch 25:5; 2Ch 29:25).

The functions of a seer as indicated by this term included, besides receiving and reporting the word of the Lord, writing about David's reign (1Ch 29:29); receiving and writing down visions (2Ch 9:29); writing genealogical records under Rehoboam's reign (2Ch 12:15). In general, the Lord forewarned His people through His prophets and seers (2Ki 17:13; 2Ch 33:18). In many cases, these warnings were recorded in writing (2Ch 33:19).

2375. **חֲזוֹ, Chăzôw,** *khaz-o´*; from 2372; *seer; Chazo*, a nephew of Abraham:—Hazo.

2376. **חֵזוּ, chĕzûw,** *kheh´-zoo*; (Chaldee); from 2370; a *sight*:—look, vision.

An Aramaic masculine noun meaning a vision, a revelation. This word appears exclusively in the book of Daniel and draws attention to the nature of revelation. It denotes the nighttime dreams of Nebuchadnezzar (Da 2:19, 28; 4:5[2], 13[10]) and Daniel (Da 7:2, 7, 13) that have prophetic significance. There appears to be some connection with the ominous or troubling nature of these revelations (Da 7:15; cf. 2:1). Once the word pertains to the outward appearance of an object in the vision of the fourth beast (Da 7:20).

2377. **חָזוֹן, châzôwn,** *khaw-zone´*; from 2372; a *sight* (mentally), i.e. a *dream, revelation*, or *oracle*:—vision.

A masculine noun meaning a revelation by means of a vision, an oracle, a divine communication. The primary essence of this word is not so much the vision or dream itself as the message conveyed. It signifies the direct, specific communication between God and people through the prophetic office (1Sa 3:1; 1Ch 17:15; Ps 89:19[20]) or the collection of such messages (2Ch 32:32; Isa 1:1; Ob 1:1; Na 1:1; Hab 2:2, 3). Also, the word is used of the messages of false prophets (Jer 14:14; 23:16); a guiding communication from the Lord, often restricted when a people are under judgment (La 2:9; Eze 7:26; Mic 3:6); and the revelation of future events on a grand scale (Da 9:24; 10:14). People who disregard this divine communication face certain doom (Pr 29:18).

2378. חָזוֹת, châzôwth, *khaw-zooth´*; from 2372; a *revelation*:—vision.

A feminine noun meaning a vision, a revelation. This particular word is used only once in the description of a book of prophetic writings called the visions of Iddo (2Ch 9:29). See the related Hebrew verb *châzâh* (2372).

2379. חֲזוֹת, chăzôwth, *khaz-oth´*; (Chaldee); from 2370; a *view*:—sight.

2380. חָזוּת, châzûwth, *khaw-zooth´*; from 2372; a *look*; hence (figurative) striking *appearance, revelation*, or (by implication) *compact*:—agreement, notable (one), vision.

A feminine noun meaning a vision, a striking appearance. A difficult vision appeared to Isaiah (Isa 21:2); and another vision seemed to the Israelites to be words on a scroll (Isa 29:11). Daniel saw in his vision a goat with a visible (large) horn (Da 8:5). This word can also mean commitment or agreement, as in Isaiah's oracle against Ephraim (Isa 28:18). See the related Hebrew root *châzâh* (2372).

2381. חֲזִיאֵל, Chăzîy'êl, *khaz-ee-ale´*; from 2372 and 410; *seen of God; Chaziel*, a Levite:—Haziel.

2382. חֲזָיָה, Chăzâyâh, *khaz-aw-yaw´*; from 2372 and 3050; *Jah has seen; Chazajah*, an Israelite:—Hazaiah.

2383. חֶזְיוֹן, Chezyôwn, *khez-yone´*; from 2372; *vision; Chezjon*, a Syrian:—Hezion.

2384. חִזָּיוֹן, chizzâyôwn, *khiz-zaw-yone´*; from 2372; a *revelation*, especially by *dream*:—vision.

A masculine noun meaning a dream, a vision, a revelation. The primary stress of this word lies on the means and manner of divine revelation. It is used in reference to revelations that come in the night (2Sa 7:17; Job 4:13; 33:15); visions imparted (Zec 13:4); and dreams in a general sense (Job 7:14; 20:8). Metaphorically, Jerusalem is called the "valley of vision," alluding to the city as the center of prophetic activity (Isa 22:1, 5; cf. Lk 13:33).

2385. חֲזִיז, chăzîyz, *khaw-zeez´*; from an unused root meaning to *glare*; a *flash* of lightning:—bright cloud, lightning.

2386. חֲזִיר, chăzîyr, *khaz-eer´*; from an unused root probably meaning to *inclose*; a *hog* (perhaps as *penned*):—boar, swine.

2387. חֵזִיר, Chêzîyr, *khay-zeer´*; from the same as 2386; perhaps *protected; Chezir*, the name of two Israelites:—Hezir.

2388. חָזַק, châzaq, *khaw-zak´*; a primitive root; to *fasten* upon; hence to *seize, be strong* ([figurative] *courageous*, [causative] *strengthen, cure, help, repair, fortify*), *obstinate*; to *bind, restrain, conquer*:—aid, amend, × calker, catch, cleave, confirm, be constant, constrain, continue, be of good (take) courage (-ous, -ly), encourage (self), be established, fasten, force, fortify, make hard, harden, help, (lay) hold (fast), lean, maintain, play the man, mend, become (wax) mighty, prevail, be recovered, repair, retain, seize, be (wax) sore, strengthen (self), be stout, be (make, shew, wax) strong (-er), be sure, take (hold), be urgent, behave self valiantly, withstand.

A verb meaning to be strong, to strengthen, to be courageous, to overpower. This verb is widely used to express the strength of various phenomena, such as the severity of famine (2Ki 25:3; Jer 52:6); the strength of humans to overpower each other; the condition of Pharaoh's heart (Ex 7:13); David and Goliath (1Sa 17:50); Amnon and Tamar (2Sa 13:14); a battle situation (2Ch 8:3); Samson's strength for his last superhuman performance (Jgs 16:28). This word occurs in the commonly known charge, "Be strong and of good courage!" (Jos 1:9). Moses urges Joshua (Dt 31:6, 7) to be strong. The Lord also bids Joshua to be strong in taking the Promised Land (Dt 31:23; Jos 1:6, 7, 9), after which Joshua encourages the people in the same way (Jos 10:25).

2389. חָזָק, châzâq, *khaw-zawk´*; from 2388; *strong* (usually in a bad sense, *hard, bold, violent*):—harder, hottest, + impudent, loud, mighty, sore, stiff [-hearted], strong (-er).

A masculine adjective meaning firmness, strength. The feminine form of this word is *chăzâqâh*. It can refer to human strength or power (Nu 13:18; Jos 14:11); to human persistence or stubbornness (Eze 2:4; 3:8, 9); or to divine strength or power (Ex 3:19; Isa 40:10). In addition, it can refer to the strength of things, but it must be translated to fit the context: a *loud* trumpet blast (Ex 19:16); a *sore* war (1Sa 14:52); the *hottest* battle (2Sa 11:15); a *sore* sickness (1Ki 17:17); a *severe* famine (1Ki 18:2); a *strong* wind (Ex 10:19). This adjective can also be used as a substantive for a strong or mighty person (Job 5:15; Isa 40:10; Eze 34:16).

2390. חָזֵק, châzêq, *khaw-zake´*; from 2388; *powerful*:— × wax louder, stronger.

An adjective meaning stronger. This word is used only twice in Scripture. In Ex 19:19, it described the trumpet blast on Mount Sinai as the Lord's presence descended around Moses. In 2Sa 3:1, it described the strength of David's house over the house of Saul.

2391. חֵזֶק, chêzeq, *khay´-zek*; from 2388; *help*:—strength.

A masculine noun meaning strength. This particular word is used only once in the OT, where God is the strength of the psalmist (Ps 18:1[2]). See the related Hebrew root *châzaq* (2388) and the feminine form of this noun, *chezqâh* (2393).

2392. חֹזֶק, chôzeq, *kho´-zek*; from 2388; *power*:—strength.

A masculine noun meaning strength. This word is used to describe the Lord's strength in delivering Israel out of Egyptian bondage (Ex 13:3, 14, 16). It is also used to describe the military strength of Israel (Am 6:13) and of other kingdoms (Hag 2:22). Although this particular word is used only five times in the OT, its related verb, *châzaq* (2388), meaning to be strong, and its related adjective, *châzâq* (2389), meaning strong, are used many times.

2393. חֶזְקָה, chezqâh, *khez-kaw´*; feminine of 2391; prevailing *power*:—strength (-en self), (was) strong.

A feminine noun meaning strength, force. This word refers to the hand of the Lord on Isaiah as the Lord spoke to him (Isa 8:11). It is also used to describe the power of kings. When Rehoboam became strong and established his kingdom, he and his people abandoned the Law of the Lord (2Ch 12:1). When King Uzziah became strong, he became proud and went into the Temple to burn incense, even though that was the job of the priests (2Ch 26:16). In Daniel's vision, the fourth king gained power through his great wealth (Da 11:2). See the related Hebrew root *châzaq* (2388) and the masculine form of this noun *chêzeq* (2391).

2394. חָזְקָה, chozqâh, *khoz-kaw´*; feminine of 2392; *vehemence* (usually in a bad sense):—force, mightily, repair, sharply.

A feminine noun meaning strength, force. It always occurs with the preposition *b*ᵉ (with or by). It can be used to modify oppression (Jgs 4:3); rebuke (Jgs 8:1); capture (1Sa 2:16); ruling (Eze 34:4); crying to God (Jnh 3:8). Only the last of these references has a positive connotation. All the others connote a harsh, cruel, and self-serving connotation of the use of one's strength and power.

2395. חִזְקִי, Chizqîy, *khiz-kee´*; from 2388; *strong; Chizki*, an Israelite:—Hezeki.

2396. חִזְקִיָּה, Chizqîyyâh, *khiz-kee-yaw´*; or חִזְקִיָּהוּ, **Chizqîyyâhûw,** *khiz-kee-yaw´-hoo*; also יְחִזְקִיָּה, **Yᵉchizqîyyâh,** *yekh-iz-kee-yaw´*; or יְחִזְקִיָּהוּ, **Yᵉchiz-qîyyâhûw,** *yekh-iz-kee-yaw´-hoo*; from 2388 and 3050; *strengthened of Jah; Chizkijah*, a king of Judah, also the name of two other Israelites:—Hezekiah, Hizkiah, Hizkijah. Compare 3169.

2397. חָח, châch, *khawkh*; once (Eze 29:4) חָחִי, **châchîy,** *khakh-ee´*; from the same as 2336; a *ring* for the nose (or lips):—bracelet, chain, hook.

2398. חָטָא, **châṭâ'**, *khaw-taw'*; a primitive root; (properly) to *miss*; hence (figurative and general) to *sin*; (by inference) to *forfeit, lack, expiate, repent,* (causative) *lead astray, condemn*:—bear the blame, cleanse, commit [sin], by fault, harm he hath done, loss, miss, (make) offend (-er), offer for sin, purge, purify (self), make reconciliation, (cause, make) sin (-ful, -ness), trespass.

A verb meaning to miss the mark, to wrong, to sin, to lead into sin, to purify from sin, to free from sin. Four main Hebrew words express the idea of sin in the Hebrew Bible, with this word used most often. Its central meaning is to miss the mark or fail. It is used in a nonmoral or nonreligious sense to indicate the simple idea of missing or failing in any task or endeavour. In Jgs 20:16, it indicated the idea of a slinger missing his target. The verb also indicated the situation that arose when something was missing (Job 5:24); or it described a failure to reach a certain goal or age (Pr 19:2; Isa 65:20). These are minor uses of the verb. The word is used the most to describe human failure and sin. It indicates failure to do what is expected; the one who fails to find God in this life destroys himself (Pr 8:36). Many times the word indicates being at fault (Ge 20:9; Ex 10:16; 2Ki 18:14; Ne 6:13) as Pharaoh was toward Moses or to be guilty or responsible (Ge 43:9; 44:32). It regularly means to sin; Pharaoh sinned against God (Ex 10:16). People can also sin against other human beings (Ge 42:22; 1Sa 19:4, 5) or against their own souls (Pr 20:2). The verb is used to indicate sin with no object given, as when Pharaoh admitted flatly that he had sinned (Ex 9:27; Jgs 10:15) or when Israel was described as a "sinful nation" (Isa 1:4). Sometimes the writer used the noun from this same verbal root as the object of the verb for emphasis, such as in Ex 32:30, 31, where Moses asserted that Israel had sinned a great sin (Le 4:3; Nu 12:11). Sinning, unfortunately, is a universal experience, for there is no one who does not sin (Ecc 7:20). Persons may sin with various parts of their bodies or in certain ways or attitudes. They may sin with their tongues or lips (Job 2:10; Ps 39:1[2]). Persons may sin innocently or in such a way as to bring guilt on others (Le 4:2, 3; Nu 15:27).

Three other stems of this verb are used less often. The intensive stem is used to indicate people bearing their own material losses or failures (Ge 31:39); one freeing oneself from sin or purifying an object or person (Le 8:15; Ps 51:7[9]); and one bringing a sin offering (Le 6:26[19]; 2Ch 29:24). The causative stem, besides indicating failure to miss a literal target, means to lead into sin, to lead astray. Jeroboam was an infamous king who caused all Israel to walk in sin (1Ki 14:16; 15:26). The reflexive stem communicates the idea of freeing oneself from sin. The Levites purified themselves (i.e. set themselves apart from sin) so they could work at the sanctuary (Nu 8:21).

2399. חֵטְא, **chêṭ'**, *khate*; from 2398; a *crime* or its *penalty*:—fault, × grievously, offence, (punishment of) sin.

A masculine noun meaning sin, an offence, a fault. The word suggests the accumulated shortcomings that lead to punishment (Ge 41:9); errors or offences that cause the wrath of a supervisor (Ecc 10:4); and the charge against an individual for his or her actions contrary to the Law (Le 24:15; Nu 9:13; Dt 15:9; 23:21[22]). Isaiah uses the word to reinforce the tremendous sinfulness of Judah in contrast to the Messiah's redemptive suffering (Isa 53:12).

2400. חַטָּא, **chaṭṭâ'**, *khat-taw'*; intensive from 2398; a *criminal*, or one accounted *guilty*:—offender, sinful, sinner.

A masculine noun meaning sinners and an adjective meaning sinful. This word comes from the common verb *châṭâ'* (2398), meaning to sin, and is related to the common noun *chaṭṭâ'th* (2403), meaning sin or sin offering. As a noun, it is used to describe those who, by their actions, are under the wrath and judgment of God (Ps 1:5) and face ultimate destruction (Ge 13:13; Ps 104:35; Isa 1:28). The influence of these people is to be avoided (Ps 1:1; 26:9; Pr 1:10), but they are to be instructed in the way of righteousness (Ps 25:8; 51:13[15]). As an adjective, it describes the sinful people the tribes of Reuben and Gad were raising (Nu 32:14).

2401. חֲטָאָה, **chăṭâ'âh**, *khat-aw-aw'*; feminine of 2399; an *offence*, or a *sacrifice* for it:—sin (offering).

A feminine noun meaning sin, a sacrifice for sin. The word generally stands as a synonym for transgression (Ps 32:1). It is used to convey the evil committed by Abimelech in taking Sarah into his harem (Ge 20:9); the wickedness of idolatry committed by the Israelites at Sinai (Ex 32:21, 30, 31); and the perversion foisted on the Northern Kingdom by Jeroboam (2Ki 17:21). Conversely, the psalmist uses the Hebrew word once to mean a sin offering (Ps 40:6[7]).

2402. חַטָּאָה, **chaṭṭâ'âh**, *khat-taw-aw'*; (Chaldee); corresponding to 2401; an *offence*, and the *penalty* or *sacrifice* for it:—sin (offering).

A feminine noun meaning sin. This word is used only twice in the OT and is equivalent to the Hebrew word *chaṭṭâ'th* (2403), meaning sin. It is used in Ex 34:7 to speak of what God, in the greatness of His lovingkindness, will forgive. It is also used in Isa 5:18 to describe God's woe against those who sin greatly.

2403. חַטָּאָה, **chaṭṭâ'âh**, *khat-taw-aw'*; or חַטָּאת, **chaṭṭâ'th**, *khat-tawth'*; from 2398; an *offence* (sometimes habitual *sinfulness*), and its penalty, occasion, sacrifice, or expiation; also (concrete) an *offender*:—punishment (of sin), purifying (-fication for sin), sin (-ner, offering).

A feminine noun meaning sin, transgression, sin offering, punishment. The word denotes youthful indiscretions (Ps 25:7); evil committed against another (Ge 50:17); trespasses against God (2Ch 33:19; Ps 51:2[4]; Am 5:12); a general state of sinfulness (Isa 6:7); and the specific occasion of sin, particularly in reference to idolatry (Dt 9:21; Hos 10:8). It also implies an antidote to sin, including purification from ceremonial impurity (Nu 19:9, 17); the sacrificial offering for sin (Ex 29:14; Le 4:3); and the punishment for sin (La 4:6; Zec 14:19). In the story of Cain and Abel, sin appears as a creature, ready to pounce, lurking "at the door" of Cain's heart (Ge 4:7).

2404. חָטַב, **châṭab**, *khaw-tab'*; a primitive root; to *chop* or *carve* wood:—cut down, hew (-er), polish.

2405. חֲטֻבוֹת, **chăṭubôwth**, *khat-oo-both'*; feminine passive participle of 2404; (properly) a *carving*; hence a *tapestry* (as figured):—carved.

2406. חִטָּה, **chiṭṭâh**, *khit-taw'*; of uncertain derivation; *wheat*, whether the grain or the plant:—wheat (-en).

2407. חַטּוּשׁ, **Chaṭṭûwsh**, *khat-toosh'*; from an unused root of uncertain significance; *Chattush*, the name of four or five Israelites:—Hattush.

2408. חֲטִי, **chăṭây**, *khat-aw-ee'*; (Chaldee); from a root corresponding to 2398; an *offence*:—sin.

An Aramaic noun meaning sin. This word is used only once in the OT and is equivalent to the Hebrew word *chaṭṭâ'th* (2403), meaning sin or sin offering. Daniel advised King Nebuchadnezzar to turn from his sins (Da 4:27[24]).

2409. חַטָּיָא, **chaṭṭâyâ'**, *khat-taw-yaw'*; (Chaldee); from the same as 2408; an *expiation*:—sin offering.

A feminine noun meaning an offering for sin. This Aramaic word appears only in Ezr 6:17, where it indicates the particular sacrifice made at the dedication of the rebuilt Temple, following the return from exile. The text states that the "sin offering" consisted of twelve rams for the sins of the twelve tribes of Israel.

2410. חֲטִיטָא, **Chăṭîyṭâ'**, *khat-ee-taw'*; from an unused root apparently meaning to *dig* out; *explorer; Chatita*, a temple porter:—Hatita.

2411. חַטִּיל, **Chaṭṭîyl**, *khat-teel'*; from an unused root apparently meaning to *wave; fluctuating; Chattil*, one of "Solomon's servants":—Hattil.

2412. חֲטִיפָא, **Chăṭîyphâ'**, *khat-ee-faw'*; from 2414; *robber; Chatipha*, one of the Nethinim:—Hatipha.

2413. חָטַם, **châṭam**, *khaw-tam'*; a primitive root; to *stop*:—refrain.

2414. חָטַף, **châṭaph**, *khaw-taf'*; a primitive root; to *clutch*; hence to *seize* as a prisoner:—catch.

2415. חֹטֶר, **chôṭer**, *kho'-ter*; from an unused root of uncertain significance; a *twig*:—rod.

2416. **חַי**, **chay,** *khah´ee*; from 2421; *alive*; hence *raw* (flesh); *fresh* (plant, water, year), *strong*; also (as noun, especially in the feminine singular and masculine plural) *life* (or living thing), whether literal or figurative:— + age, alive, appetite, (wild) beast, company, congregation, life (-time), live (-ly), living (creature, thing), maintenance, + merry, multitude, + (be) old, quick, raw, running, springing, troop.

A feminine noun meaning a living thing, an animal, a beast, a living thing. The basic meaning is living things, but its most common translation is animals or beasts. The word refers to all kinds of animals and beasts of the field or earth (Ge 1:24, 25; 1Sa 17:46) and sometimes stands in parallel with birds of the air (Eze 29:5). The nations, such as Egypt, were referred to metaphorically as beasts (Ps 68:30[31]). Beasts were categorized in various ways: beasts of burden (Isa 46:1); land animals (Ge 1:28; 8:19); cattle (Nu 35:3); sea creatures (Ps 104:25); clean, edible creatures (Le 11:47; 14:4); unclean, nonedible creatures (Le 5:2); large and small creatures (Ps 104:25).

Two further categories of animals are noted: wild animals or animals of prey and animal or beastlike beings. God made the wild animals of the field. Sometimes the Lord used wild beasts as instruments of His judgments (Eze 14:15; 33:27), but on other occasions He protected His people from ravenous beasts (Ge 37:20; Le 26:6). At any rate, vicious beasts will not inhabit the land of the Lord's restored people (Isa 35:9). The bizarre living beings mentioned in Eze 1:5, 13, 22; 3:13 were like birds and animals but were composite beings. They could not be described adequately by human language, for they also had the forms of humans, each with faces of a man, lion, ox, and eagle. However, they did not resemble flesh and blood in their appearance (Eze 1:13) and were tied to the movement of the Spirit (Eze 1:20).

2417. **חַי**, **chay,** *khah´ee*; (Chaldee); from 2418; *alive*; also (as noun in plural) *life*:—life, that liveth, living.

An Aramaic adjective meaning living, alive. In the book of Daniel, it is used of people (Da 2:30; 4:17[14]); and King Darius used this word in his description of God (Da 6:20[21], 26[27]).

2418. **חֲיָא**, **chăyâ',** *khah-yaw´*; (Chaldee); or **חֲיָה**, **chăyâh,** *khah-yaw´*; (Chaldee); corresponding to 2421; to *live*:—live, keep alive.

An Aramaic verb meaning to live. The main usage of this word is the polite address for the king to live forever. The astrologers used this verb to address Nebuchadnezzar when they asked him to tell them his dream (Da 2:4) and again when they informed him that certain Jews were not bowing down to his golden image (Da 3:9). The queen used the verb to advise Belshazzar that Daniel could interpret the handwriting on the wall (Da 5:10). The king's advisors also used these words when they tricked King Darius into making a decree to worship only the king (Da 6:6[7]). Daniel also used this phrase when he explained to Darius that God saved him from the lions (Da 6:21[22]).

2419. **חִיאֵל**, **Chîy'êl,** *khee-ale´*; from 2416 and 410; *living of God; Chiel*, an Israelite:—Hiel.

2420. **חִידָה**, **chîydâh,** *khee-daw´*; from 2330; a *puzzle*; hence a *trick, conundrum*, sententious *maxim*:—dark saying (sentence, speech), hard question, proverb, riddle.

A feminine noun possibly meaning enigma. The Greek root of this English term is used in various contexts by the Septuagint (the Greek translation of the Hebrew OT) to translate the Hebrew word. Nearly half of this noun's occurrences refer to Samson's "riddle" when he tested the wits of the Philistines at his wedding feast (Jgs 14:12–19). The term is connected with several different words from the wisdom tradition, most notably the word frequently translated "proverb" (Ps 78:2; Pr 1:6; cf. 2Ch 9:1). The term is also associated with the prophetic tradition, where it was contrasted with clear speaking and compared with communication through more obscure means (Nu 12:8; Eze 17:2). Daniel prophesied of a future destructive king whose abilities include "understanding enigmas." A somewhat similar Aramaic expression is used of Daniel himself earlier in the book (cf. Da 5:12; 8:23).

2421. **חָיָה**, **châyâh,** *khaw-yaw´*; a primitive root [compare 2331, 2421]; to *live*, whether literal or figurative; (causative) to *revive*:—keep (leave, make) alive, × certainly, give (promise) life, (let, suffer to) live, nourish up, preserve (alive), quicken, recover, repair, restore (to life), revive, (× God) save (alive, life, lives), × surely, be whole.

A verb meaning to be alive, to live, to keep alive. This verb is used numerous times in Scripture. It is used in the sense of flourishing (Dt 8:1; 1Sa 10:24; Ps 22:26[27]); or to convey that an object is safe (Ge 12:13; Nu 14:38; Jos 6:17). It connotes reviving in Eze 37:5 and 1Ki 17:22 or healing in Joshua 5:8 and 2Ki 8:8. Genesis often uses the word when people are kept alive in danger (Ge 6:19, 20; 19:19; 47:25; 50:20). Also, the word is used in the genealogies of Genesis (Ge 5:3–30; 11:11–26). Ps 119 employs this word to say that God's Word preserves life (Ps 119:25, 37, 40, 88). Many verses instruct hearers to obey a command (either God's or a king's) in order to live (Ge 20:7; Pr 4:4; Jer 27:12).

2422. **חָיֶה**, **châyeh,** *khaw-yeh´*; from 2421; *vigorous*:—lively.

An adjective meaning strong, vigorous. It is found only in Ex 1:19, where the Egyptian midwives explained to Pharaoh that the Hebrew women were so vigorous in childbirth that they delivered before the midwives arrived.

2423. **חֵיוָא**, **chêyvâ',** *khay-vaw´*; (Chaldee); from 2418; an *animal*:—beast.

2424. **חַיּוּת**, **chayyûwth,** *khah-yooth´*; from 2421; *life*:— × living.

A feminine abstract noun meaning lifetime. This word occurs only in 2Sa 20:3, where it states that David provided for the ten concubines who were left to watch the palace in Jerusalem (2Sa 15:16) and were later violated by David's son, Absalom (2Sa 16:21, 22). Although David kept them and provided for their needs, he did not lie with them; consequently, they were like widows during the lifetime of their husband.

2425. **חָיַי**, **châyay,** *khaw-yah´ee*; a primitive root [compare 2421]; to *live*; (causative) to *revive*:—live, save life.

A verb meaning to live. This verb is often used in reference to the length of a person's life (Ge 5:5; 11:12, 14; 25:7). Ge 3:22 employs this word to describe eternal life represented by the tree of life. It is used in reference to life which is a result of seeing God (Ex 33:20; Dt 5:24[21]) or looking at the bronze serpent (Nu 21:8, 9). It is also used to refer to living by the Law (Le 18:5; Eze 20:11, 13, 21). Cities of refuge were established to which people could flee and live (Dt 4:42; 19:4, 5). This verb is identical in form and meaning to the verb *châyâh* (2421).

2426. **חֵיל**, **chêyl,** *khale*; or (shorter) **חֵל**, **chêl,** *khale*; a collateral form of 2428; an *army*; also (by analogy) an *intrenchment*:—army, bulwark, host, + poor, rampart, trench, wall.

A masculine noun meaning entrenchment, fortress, army, defense, fortified wall. The wall of Jezreel was the location where the dogs would gnaw on Jezebel's dead body (1Ki 21:23). The psalmist prayed for peace within the walls of Jerusalem (Ps 122:7). The Lord decided to tear down the wall around Israel (La 2:8). A surrounding river was the defense of Thebes (Na 3:8). See the related noun *chayil* (2428).

2427. **חִיל**, **chîyl,** *kheel*; and (feminine) **חִילָה**, **chîylâh,** *khee-law´*; from 2342; a *throe* (especially of childbirth):—pain, pang, sorrow.

2428. **חַיִל**, **chayil,** *khah´-yil*; from 2342; probably a *force*, whether of men, means or other resources; an *army, wealth, virtue, valor, strength*:—able, activity, (+) army, band of men (soldiers), company, (great) forces, goods, host, might, power, riches, strength, strong, substance, train, (+) valiant (-ly), valour, virtuous (-ly), war, worthy (-ily).

A masculine noun meaning strength, wealth, army. This word has the basic idea of strength and influence. It can be used to speak of the strength of people (1Sa 2:4; 9:1; 2Sa 22:40); of horses (Ps 33:17); or of nations (Est 1:3). God is often seen as the supplier of this strength (2Sa 22:33; Hab 3:19). When describing men, it can speak of those who are strong for war (Dt 3:18; 2Ki 24:16; Jer 48:14); able to judge (Ex 18:21, 25); or are righteous in behaviour (1Ki 1:52). When describing women, it speaks of virtuous character (Ru 3:11; Pr 12:4; 31:10). This idea of strength often is used to imply a financial influence (i.e. wealth) (Job 31:25; Ps 49:6[7]; Zec 14:14); a military influence (i.e. an army) (Ex 14:9; 2Ch 14:8[7], 9[8]; Isa 43:17); or a numerical influence (i.e. a great company) (1Ki 10:2; 2Ch 9:1).

2429. **חַיִל, chayil**, *khah´-yil*; (Chaldee); corresponding to 2428; an *army*, or *strength*:—aloud, army, × most [mighty], power.

An Aramaic masculine noun meaning strength, power, army. In the book of Ezra, Rehum and Shimshai forced the Jews to stop rebuilding the city (Ezr 4:23). It can mean a loud or powerful voice, such as Nebuchadnezzar's herald (Da 3:4); a messenger from heaven (Da 4:14[11]); and King Belshazzar to his enchanters (Da 5:7). Nebuchadnezzar had the most powerful soldiers bind up Shadrach, Meshach, and Abednego (Da 3:20). See the related Hebrew noun *chayil* (2428).

2430. **חֵילָה, chêylâh**, *khay-law´*; feminine of 2428; an *intrenchment*:—bulwark.

2431. **חֵילָם, Chêylâm**, *khay-lawm´*; or **חֵלְאָם, Chê-l'âm**, *khay-lawm´*; from 2428; *fortress; Chelam*, a place East of Palestine:—Helam.

2432. **חִילֵן, Chîylên**, *khee-lane*; from 2428; *fortress; Chilen*, a place in Palestine:—Hilen.

2433. **חִין, chîyn**, *kheen*; another form for 2580; *beauty*:—comely.

2434. **חַיִץ, chayits**, *khah´-yits*; another form for 2351; a *wall*:—wall.

2435. **חִיצוֹן, chîytsôwn**, *khee-tsone´*; from 2434; (properly) the (outer) *wall side*; hence *exterior*; (figurative) *secular* (as opposed to sacred):—outer, outward, utter, without.

2436. **חֵיק, chêyq**, *khake*; or **חֵק, chêq**, *khake*; and **חוֹק, chôwq**, *khoke*; from an unused root, apparently meaning to *inclose*; the *bosom* (literal or figurative):—bosom, bottom, lap, midst, within.

2437. **חִירָה, Chîyrâh**, *khee-raw´*; from 2357 in the sense of *splendor; Chirah*, an Adullamite:—Hirah.

2438. **חִירָם, Chîyrâm**, *khee-rawm´*; or **חִירוֹם, Chîy-rôwm**, *khee-rome´*; another form of 2361; *Chiram* or *Chirom*, the name of two Tyrians:—Hiram, Huram.

2439. **חִישׁ, chîysh**, *kheesh*; another form for 2363; to *hurry*:—make haste.

2440. **חִישׁ, chîysh**, *kheesh*; from 2439; (properly) a *hurry*; hence (adverb) *quickly*:—soon.

2441. **חֵךְ, chêk**, *khake*; probably from 2596 in the sense of *tasting*; (properly) the *palate* or inside of the mouth; hence the *mouth* itself (as the organ of speech, taste and kissing):—(roof of the) mouth, taste.

2442. **חָכָה, châkâh**, *khaw-kaw´*; a primitive root [apparently akin to 2707 through the idea of *piercing*]; (properly) to *adhere* to; hence to await:—long, tarry, wait.

2443. **חַכָּה, chakkâh**, *khak-kaw´*; probably from 2442; a *hook* (as *adhering*):—angle, hook.

2444. **חֲכִילָה, Chăkîylâh**, *khak-ee-law´*; from the same as 2447; *dark; Chakilah*, a hill in Palestine:—Hachilah.

2445. **חַכִּים, chakkîym**, *khak-keem´*; (Chaldee); from a root corresponding to 2449; *wise*, i.e. a *Magian*:—wise.

2446. **חֲכַלְיָה, Chăkalyâh**, *khak-al-yaw´*; from the base of 2447 and 3050; *darkness* of *Jah; Chakaljah*, an Israelite:—Hachaliah.

2447. **חַכְלִיל, chaklîyl**, *khak-leel´*; by reduplication from an unused root apparently meaning to *be dark*; darkly *flashing* (only of the eyes); in a good sense, *brilliant* (as stimulated by wine):—red.

2448. **חַכְלִלוּת, chaklilûwth**, *khak-lee-looth´*; from 2447; *flash* (of the eyes); in a bad sense, *blearedness*:—redness.

2449. **חָכַם, châkam**, *khaw-kam´*; a primitive root, to *be wise* (in mind, word or act):—× exceeding, teach wisdom, be (make self, shew self) wise, deal (never so) wisely, make wiser.

A verb meaning to be wise, to act according to wisdom, to make wise decisions, to manifest wisdom. This word is used to convey the act of instructing which if received brings wisdom (Job 35:11; Ps 105:22); the wise activity that derives from such instruction (Pr 6:6; 8:33); the way of conduct contrary to that of the wicked (Pr 23:19); the wisdom manifested in the animal kingdom (Pr 30:24). In the reflexive sense, the verb implies the tangible manifestation of wisdom (Ecc 2:19); the exaggerated perception of one's own wisdom (Ecc 7:16); and the cunning activities of the deceiver (Ex 1:10). The psalmist declares that the Lord delights in dispensing wisdom to the simpleminded (Ps 19:7[8]).

2450. **חָכָם, châkâm**, *khaw-kawm´*; from 2449; *wise*, (i.e. intelligent, skilful or artful):—cunning (man), subtil, ([un-]), wise ([hearted], man).

An adjective meaning wise. This word is used to describe one who is skilled or experienced. It was used in the physical arena to describe those men who were skilled as builders (Ex 31:6; 36:1, 2); as craftsmen of all sorts (1Ch 22:15); as precious metal workers (2Ch 2:7[6]); those women who could spin fabrics (Ex 35:25). This word was used in the social arena to express those who were the leaders of the day (Jer 51:57); who could interpret dreams (Ge 41:8; Ex 7:11); who were able to rule (Dt 1:13, 15); who knew the law (Est 1:13); who were counselors (Est 6:13; Jer 18:18). In the personal arena, this word denoted skill in living, which was embodied in Solomon like no other before or since (1Ki 3:12). The wise person is the one who learns (Pr 1:5; 9:9; 13:1); who heeds a rebuke (Pr 9:8; 15:31); and who speaks properly (Pr 14:3; 15:2; 16:23). See the verb *châkam* (2449), meaning to be wise, and the noun *chokmâh* (2451), meaning wisdom.

2451. **חָכְמָה, chokmâh**, *khok-maw´*; from 2449; *wisdom* (in a good sense):—skilful, wisdom, wisely, wit.

A feminine noun meaning wisdom, skill, experience, shrewdness. This is one of the wisdom words that cluster in Proverbs, Ecclesiastes, Job, and other wisdom literature scattered throughout the OT. The high point of this word and its concept is reached in Pr 8:1, 11, 12. In Pr 8:22–31, wisdom is personified. It is God's gracious creation and is thus inherent in the created order. God alone knows where wisdom dwells and where it originates (Job 28:12, 20); no other living being possesses this knowledge about wisdom (see Job 28:21). For humans, the beginning of wisdom and the supreme wisdom is to properly fear and reverence God (Job 28:28; Pr 1:7; cf. Pr 8:13); God is the master, creator, and giver of wisdom (see Job 28:27; Pr 8:22, 23). He employed wisdom as His master craftsman to create all things (Ps 104:24; Jer 10:12). Rulers govern wisely by means of wisdom provided by God (1Ki 3:28; cf. Pr 8:15, 16). Wisdom keeps company with all the other virtues: prudence, knowledge, and discretion (Pr 8:12). The portrayal of wisdom in Pr 8:22–24 lies behind Paul's magnificent picture of Christ in Colossians 1:15, 16, for all the treasures of wisdom are lodged in Christ (cf. Col 2:3).

Wisdom, ordained and created by God, manifests itself in many ways in the created universe. It is expressed as a technical capability (Ex 28:3; 31:3, 6; 1Ki 7:14). It becomes evident in experience and prudence as evidenced in a wise woman (2Sa 20:22) who fears the Lord (see Pr 31:30) or in a wise king (1Ki 2:6). Wisdom in general, and worldly wisdom in particular, was universal to humankind created in the image of God; Babylonians, men of the East, Egyptians, and Edomites could obtain it or be found with it (Isa 47:10; Jer 49:7). Wrongly used, however, for self-adulation or self-aggrandizement, this wisdom could be deadly. For unbelievers, wisdom led to piety, holiness, and devotion to the Lord and His will. The psalmist asked God to give him a wise heart (Ps 90:12). God imparted wisdom to His people by His Spirit (Ex 31:3), but His Anointed One, the Messiah, the Branch, would have His Spirit rest upon Him, the Spirit of wisdom (Isa 11:2), in abundance. Wisdom is also personified as a woman who seeks whoever will come and listen to her, thus receiving a blessing (Pr 1:20; 2:2; 3:13, 19). Wisdom ends its presentation in Pr 8 with the striking assertion that all who hate wisdom love death.

2452. **חָכְמָה, chokmâh**, *khok-maw´*; (Chaldee); corresponding to 2451; *wisdom*:—wisdom.

An Aramaic feminine noun meaning wisdom. This word is used only nine times in the OT and is equivalent to the Hebrew word *chokmâh* (2451), meaning wisdom. In these few instances, this word is used to speak of God's wisdom (Ezr 7:25; Da 2:20). It is God who gives this wisdom (Da 2:21, 23, 30) that was recognized by Belshazzar and the queen mother (Da 5:10, 11, 14).

2453. חַכְמוֹנִי, Chakmôwnîy, *khak-mo-nee´*; from 2449; *skilful; Chakmoni*, an Israelite:—Hachmoni, Hachmonite.

2454. חָכְמוֹת, chokmôwth, *khok-mōth´*; or **חַכְמוֹת, chakmôwth,** *khak-mōth´*; collateral forms of 2451; *wisdom*:—wisdom, every wise [woman].

A feminine noun meaning wisdom or that which is wise. Found exclusively in the wisdom literature of the OT, this word is a form of the Hebrew word *chokmâh* (2451). It denotes a wise woman (Pr 14:1); the feminine personification of wisdom (Pr 1:20; 9:1); and the wisdom that exceeds a fool's understanding (Pr 24:7); or wisdom that reveals deep understanding (Ps 49:3[4]).

2455. חֹל, chôl, *khole*; from 2490; (properly) *exposed*; hence *profane*:—common, profane (place), unholy.

A masculine noun meaning profane or common. This word comes from the verb *châlal* (2490), meaning to pollute or to profane and is always used in opposition to *qôdesh* (6944), meaning sacred or set apart. The priests were to make a distinction between the sacred and the common (Le 10:10). David discussed with the priest the difference between the common bread and the set–apart bread (1Sa 21:4[5], 5[6]). The priests would teach the difference between the sacred and the common (Eze 44:23)—a distinction the priests of Ezekiel's day failed to teach (Eze 22:26). The Temple, described by Ezekiel, had a wall separating the sacred and the common (Eze 42:20); there was to be a clear distinction between the land holy to the Lord and the common land (Eze 48:15).

2456. חָלָא, châlâ', *khaw-law´*; a primitive root [compare 2470]; to *be sick*:—be diseased.

2457. חֶלְאָה, chel'âh, *khel-aw´*; from 2456; (properly) *disease*; hence *rust*:—scum.

2458. חֶלְאָה, Chel'âh, *khel-aw´*; the same as 2457; *Chelah*, an Israelitess:—Helah.

2459. חֶלֶב, cheleb, *keh´-leb*; or **חֵלֶב, chêleb,** *khay´-leb*; from an unused root meaning to *be fat; fat*, whether literal or figurative.; hence the *richest* or *choice* part:— × best, fat (-ness), × finest, grease, marrow.

2460. חֵלֶב, Chêleb, *khay´-leb*; the same as 2459; *fatness; Cheleb*, an Israelite:—Heleb.

2461. חָלָב, châlâb, *khaw-lawb´*; from the same as 2459; *milk* (as the *richness* of kine):— + cheese, milk, sucking.

2462. חֶלְבָּה, Chelbâh, *khel-baw´*; feminine of 2459; *fertility; Chelbah*, a place in Palestine:—Helbah.

2463. חֶלְבּוֹן, Chelbôwn, *khel-bone´*; from 2459; *fruitful; Chelbon*, a place in Syria:—Helbon.

2464. חֶלְבְּנָה, chelbinâh, *khel-bin-aw´*; from 2459; *galbanam*, an odorous gum (as if *fatty*):—galbanum.

2465. חֶלֶד, cheled, *kheh´-led*; from an unused root apparently meaning to *glide* swiftly; *life* (as a *fleeting* portion of time); hence the *world* (as *transient*):—age, short time, world.

A masculine noun meaning age, duration of life, the world. The primary sense of the word is a duration or span of time. It signifies the world, that is, this present existence (Ps 17:14; 49:1[2]); life itself (Job 11:17); and the span of a person's life (Ps 39:5[6]).

2466. חֵלֶד, Chêled, *khay´-led*; the same as 2465; *Cheled*, an Israelite:—Heled.

2467. חֹלֶד, chôled, *kho´-led*; from the same as 2465; a *weasel* (from its *gliding* motion):—weasel.

2468. חֻלְדָּה, Chuldâh, *khool-daw´*; feminine of 2467; *Chuldah*, an Israelitess:—Huldah.

2469. חֶלְדַּי, Chelday, *khel-dah´-ee*; from 2466; *worldliness; Cheldai*, the name of two Israelites:—Heldai.

2470. חָלָה, châlâh, *khaw-law´*; a primitive root [compare 2342, 2470, 2490]; (properly) to *be rubbed* or *worn*; hence (figurative) to *be weak, sick, afflicted*; or (causative) to *grieve, make sick*; also to *stroke* (in flattering), *entreat*:—beseech, (be) diseased, (put to) grief, be grieved, (be) grievous; infirmity, intreat, lay to, put to pain, × pray, make prayer, be (fall, make) sick, sore, be sorry, make suit (× supplication), woman in travail, be (become) weak, be wounded.

2471. חַלָּה, challâh, *khal-law´*; from 2490; a *cake* (as usually *punctured*):—cake.

2472. חֲלוֹם, chălôwm, *khal-ome´*; or (shorter) **חֲלֹם, chălôm,** *khal-ome´*; from 2492; a *dream*:—dream (-er).

2473. חֹלוֹן, Chôlôwn, *kho-lone´*; or (shorter) **חֹלֹן, Chôlôn,** *kho-lone´*; probably from 2344; *sandy; Cholon*, the name of two places in Palestine:—Holon.

2474. חַלּוֹן, challôwn, *khal-lone´*; a *window* (as *perforated*):—window.

2475. חֲלוֹף, chălôwph, *khal-ofe´*; from 2498; (properly) *surviving*; (by implication and collective) *orphans*:— × destruction.

2476. חֲלוּשָׁה, chălûwshâh, *khal-oo-shaw´*; feminine passive participle of 2522; *defeat*:—being overcome.

2477. חֲלַח, Chălach, *khal-akh´*; probably of foreign origin; *Chalach*, a region of Assyria:—Halah.

2478. חַלְחוּל, Chalchûwl, *khal-khool´*; by reduplication from 2342; *contorted; Chalchul*, a place in Palestine:—Halhul.

2479. חַלְחָלָה, chalchâlâh, *khal-khaw-law´*; feminine from the same as 2478; *writhing* (in childbirth); (by implication) *terror*:—(great, much) pain.

2480. חָלַט, châlaṭ, *khaw-lat´*; a primitive root; to *snatch* at:—catch.

2481. חֲלִי, chălîy, *khal-ee´*; from 2470; a *trinket* (as *polished*):—jewel, ornament.

2482. חֲלִי, Chălîy, *khal-ee´*; the same as 2481; *Chali*, a place in Palestine:—Hali.

2483. חֳלִי, chŏlîy, *khol-ee´*; from 2470; *malady, anxiety, calamity*:—disease, grief, (is) sick (-ness).

2484. חֶלְיָה, chelyâh, *khel-yaw´*; feminine of 2481; a *trinket*:—jewel.

2485. חָלִיל, châlîyl, *khaw-leel´*; from 2490; a *flute* (as *perforated*):—pipe.

2486. חָלִילָה, châlîylâh, *khaw-lee´-law*; or **חָלִלָה, châlilâh,** *khaw-lee´-law*; a directive from 2490; (literal) *for a profaned* thing; used (interjectionally) *far be it!*:—be far, (× God) forbid.

2487. חֲלִיפָה, chălîyphâh, *khal-ee-faw´*; from 2498; *alternation*:—change, course.

2488. חֲלִיצָה, chălîytsâh, *khal-ee-tsaw´*; from 2503; *spoil*:—armour.

2489. חֵלְכָא, chêlkâ', *khayl-kaw´*; or **חֵלְכָה, chêlkâh,** *khayl-kaw´*; apparently from an unused root probably meaning to *be dark* or (figurative) *unhappy*; a *wretch*, i.e. unfortunate:—poor.

2490. חָלַל, châlal, *khaw-lal´*; a primitive root [compare 2470]; (properly) to *bore*, i.e. (by implication) to *wound*, to *dissolve*; (figurative) to *profane* (a person, place or thing), to *break* (one's word), to *begin* (as if by an "opening wedge"); denominative (from 2485) to *play* (the flute):—begin (× men began), defile, × break, defile, × eat (as common things), × first, × gather the grape thereof, × take inheritance, pipe, player on instruments, pollute, (cast as) profane (self), prostitute, slay (slain), sorrow, stain, wound.

A verb meaning to pierce, to play the pipe, to profane. This word has three distinct meanings. The first meaning is to pierce or wound, either physically unto death (Isa 53:5; Eze 32:26) or figuratively unto despair (Ps 109:22). The second meaning of this word is to play the pipe, which is used only twice in the OT (1Ki 1:40; Ps 87:7). The third meaning is to profane or to defile, which is used primarily of the ceremonial objects of worship (Ex 20:25; Eze 44:7; Da 11:31); of the Sabbath (Ex 31:14; Ne 13:17; Eze 23:38); of God's name (Le 18:21; Jer 34:16); of God's priests (Le 21:4, 6). However, it also refers to sexual defilement (Ge 49:4; Le 21:9); the breaking of a covenant (Ps 89:31[32], 34[35]; Mal 2:10); and making a vineyard common (Dt 20:6; 28:30). In the causative form of this verb, it means to begin (Ge 4:26; 2Ch 3:2).

2491. חָלָל**, châlâl,** *khaw-lawl´*; from 2490; *pierced* (especially to death); (figurative) *polluted*:—kill, profane, slain (man), × slew, (deadly) wounded.

A masculine noun or adjective meaning slain, pierced, mortally wounded, profaned. This word denotes the carnage of battle; the dead, generally as a result of warfare (Ge 34:27; Jer 14:18; Eze 21:29[34]); and those having sustained some fatal injury (Jgs 9:40; 1Sa 17:52). Also, by extension, the word is used twice to indicate a state of defilement or perversion. In the first instance, it denotes a woman whose virginity has been violated or, as it were, pierced (Le 21:7, 14). The other applies to a wicked regent of Israel destined for punishment, emphasizing that he is already, in a prophetic sense, mortally wounded (Eze 21:25[30]).

2492. חָלַם**, châlam,** *khaw-lam´*; a primitive root; (properly) to *bind* firmly, i.e. (by implication) to *be* (causative to *make*) *plump*; also (through the figurative sense of *dumbness*) to *dream*:—(cause to) dream (-er), be in good liking, recover.

2493. חֵלֶם**, chêlem,** *khay´-lem*; (Chaldee); from a root corresponding to 2492; a *dream*:—dream.

2494. חֵלֶם**, Chêlem,** *khay´-lem*; from 2492; a *dream; Chelem*, an Israelite:—Helem. Compare 2469.

2495. חַלָּמוּת**, challâmûwth,** *khal-law-mooth´*; from 2492 (in the sense of *insipidity*); probably *purslain*:—egg.

2496. חַלָּמִישׁ**, challâmîysh,** *khal-law-meesh´*; probably from 2492 (in the sense of *hardness*); *flint*:—flint (-y), rock.

2497. חֵלֹן**, Chêlôn,** *khay-lone´*; from 2428; *strong; Chelon*, an Israelite:—Helon.

2498. חָלַף**, châlaph,** *khaw-laf´*; a primitive root; (properly) to *slide* by, i.e. (by implication) to *hasten* away, *pass* on, *spring* up, *pierce* or *change*:—abolish, alter, change, cut off, go on forward, grow up, be over, pass (away, on, through), renew, sprout, strike through.

2499. חֲלַף**, chălaph,** *khal-af´*; (Chaldee); corresponding to 2498; to *pass* on (of time):—pass.

2500. חֵלֶף**, chêleph,** *khay´-lef*; from 2498; (properly) *exchange*; hence (as preposition) *instead* of:—× for.

2501. חֵלֶף**, Chêleph,** *khay´-lef*; the same as 2500; *change; Cheleph*, a place in Palestine:—Heleph.

2502. חָלַץ**, châlats,** *khaw-lats´*; a primitive root; to *pull* off; hence (intensive) to *strip*, (reflexive) to *depart*; (by implication) to *deliver, equip* (for fight); *present, strengthen*:—arm (self), (go, ready) armed (× man, soldier), deliver, draw out, make fat, loose, (ready) prepared, put off, take away, withdraw self.

A verb meaning to draw out, to prepare, to deliver, to equip for war. The primary meaning of the word is that of strengthening or fortifying (Isa 58:11). It is used to convey the activity of drawing out, such as occurs in breast-feeding (La 4:3); removing a shoe (Dt 25:9, 10; Isa 20:2); dispatching to another location (Le 14:40, 43); withdrawing from a crowd (Hos 5:6); removing or delivering from danger (2Sa 22:20; Ps 6:4[5]; 50:15). Significantly, this word conveys the notion of taking up arms for battle (Nu 31:3; 32:17) or preparing for a general state of military readiness (Jos 4:13; 2Ch 17:18).

2503. חֶלֶץ**, Chelets,** *kheh´-lets*; or חֵלֶץ**, Chêlets,** *khay´-lets*; from 2502; perhaps *strength; Chelets*, the name of two Israelites:—Helez.

2504. חֲלָצַיִם**, chălâtsayim,** *kha-law-tsa-yeem´*; from 2502 (in the sense of *strength*); only in the dual; the *loins* (as the seat of vigour):—loins, reins.

2505. חָלַק**, châlaq,** *khaw-lak´*; a primitive root; to *be smooth* (figurative); by implication (as smooth stones were used for *lots*) to *apportion* or *separate*:—deal, distribute, divide, flatter, give, (have, im-) part (-ner), take away a portion, receive, separate self, (be) smooth (-er).

2506. חֵלֶק**, chêleq,** *khay´-lek*; from 2505; (properly) *smoothness* (of the tongue); also an *allotment*:—flattery, inheritance, part, × partake, portion.

2507. חֵלֶק**, Chêleq,** *khay´-lek*; the same as 2506; *portion; Chelek*, an Israelite:—Helek.

2508. חֲלָק**, chălâq,** *khal-awk´*; (Chaldee); from a root corresponding to 2505; a *part*:—portion.

2509. חָלָק**, châlâq,** *khaw-lawk´*; from 2505; *smooth* (especially of tongue):—flattering, smooth.

2510. חָלָק**, Châlâq,** *khaw-lawk´*; the same as 2509; *bare; Chalak*, a mountain of Idumæa:—Halak.

2511. חַלָּק**, challâq,** *khal-lawk´*; from 2505; *smooth*:—smooth.

2512. חַלֻּק**, challuq,** *khal-look´*; from 2505; *smooth*:—smooth.

2513. חֶלְקָה**, chelqâh,** *khel-kaw´*; feminine of 2506; (properly) *smoothness*; (figurative) *flattery*; also an *allotment*:—field, flattering (-ry), ground, parcel, part, piece of land ([ground]), plat, portion, slippery place, smooth (thing).

2514. חֲלַקָּה**, chălaqqâh,** *kal-ak-kaw´*; feminine from 2505; *flattery*:—flattery.

2515. חֲלֻקָּה**, chăluqqâh,** *khal-ook-kaw*; feminine of 2512; a *distribution*:—division.

2516. חֶלְקִי**, Chelqây,** *khel-kaw-ee´*; patronymic from 2507; a *Chelkite* or descendant of Chelek:—Helkites.

2517. חֶלְקַי**, Chelqay,** *khel-kah´-ee*; from 2505; *apportioned; Chelkai*, an Israelite:—Helkai.

2518. חִלְקִיָּה**, Chilqîyyâh,** *khil-kee-yaw´*; or חִלְקִיָּהוּ**, Chilqîyyâhûw,** *khil-kee-yaw´-hoo*; from 2506 and 3050; *portion of Jah; Chilhijah*, the name of eight Israelites:—Hilkiah.

2519. חֲלַקְלַק**, chălaqlaq,** *khal-ak-lak´*; by reduplication from 2505; (properly) something *very smooth*; i.e. a *treacherous* spot; (figurative) *blandishment*:—flattery, slippery.

2520. חֶלְקַת**, Chelqath,** *khel-kath´*; a form of 2513; *smoothness; Chelkath*, a place in Palestine:—Helkath.

2521. חֶלְקַת הַצֻּרִים**, Chelqath hats-Tsurîym,** *khel-kath´ hats-tsoo-reem´*; from 2520 and the plural of 6697, with the article inserted; *smoothness of the rocks; Chelkath Hats-tsurim*, a place in Palestine:—Helkath-hazzurim.

2522. חָלַשׁ**, châlash,** *khaw-lash´*; a primitive root; to *prostrate*; (by implication) to *overthrow, decay*:—discomfit, waste away, weaken.

2523. חַלָּשׁ**, challâsh,** *khal-lawsh´*; from 2522; *frail*:—weak.

2524. חָם**, châm,** *khawm*; from the same as 2346; a *father-in-law* (as in *affinity*):—father in law.

2525. חָם**, châm,** *khawm*; from 2552; *hot*:—hot, warm.

2526. חָם**, Châm,** *khawm*; the same as 2525; *hot* (from the tropical habitat); *Cham*, a son of Noah; also (as a patronymic) his descendant or their country:—Ham.

2527. חֹם, **chôm,** *khome*; from 2552; *heat*:—heat, to be hot (warm).

2528. חֱמָא, **chĕmâ',** *khem-aw´*; (Chaldee); or חֲמָה, **chămâh,** *kham-aw´*; (Chaldee); corresponding to 2534; *anger*:—fury.

2529. חֶמְאָה, **chem'âh,** *khem-aw´*; or (shortened) חֵמָה, **chêmâh,** *khay-maw´*; from the same root as 2346; curdled *milk* or *cheese*:—butter.

2530. חָמַד, **châmad,** *khaw-mad´*; a primitive root; to *delight* in:—beauty, greatly beloved, covet, delectable thing, (× great) delight, desire, goodly, lust, (be) pleasant (thing), precious (thing).

A verb meaning to take pleasure in, to desire, to lust, to covet, to be desirable, to desire passionately. The verb can mean to desire intensely even in its simple stem: the tenth commandment prohibits desiring to the point of coveting, such as a neighbour's house, wife, or other assets (Ex 20:17; cf. Ex 34:24). Israel was not to covet silver or gold (Dt 7:25; Jos 7:21) or the fields and lands of others (Mic 2:2). The word can also express slight variations in its basic meaning: the mountains of Bashan, including Mt. Hermon, looked in envy on the chosen mountains of Zion (Ps 68:16[17]); the simple fool delighted in his naïve, senseless way of life (Pr 1:22); and a man was not to lust after the beauty of an adulterous woman (Pr 6:25).

The word expresses the idea of finding pleasure in something as when Israel took pleasure in committing spiritual fornication among its sacred oaks (Isa 1:29). The passive participle of the simple stem indicates someone beloved or endearing (Isa 53:2) but has a negative meaning in Job 20:20, indicating excessive desiring or craving (cf. Ps 39:11[12]).

The passive stem indicates something that is worthy of being desired, desirable; the fruit of the tree of the knowledge of good and evil appeared inviting to make a person wise (Ge 2:9; 3:6; Pr 21:20) but proved to be destructive. The plural of this verbal stem expresses satisfaction or reward for keeping God's Law (Ps 19:10[11]).

2531. חֶמֶד, **chemed,** *kheh´-med*; from 2530; *delight*:—desirable, pleasant.

2532. חֶמְדָּה, **chemdâh,** *khem-daw´*; feminine of 2531; *delight*:—desire, goodly, pleasant, precious.

2533. חֶמְדָּן, **Chemdân,** *khem-dawn´*; from 2531; *pleasant; Chemdan*, an Idumæan:—Hemdan.

2534. חֵמָה, **chêmâh,** *khay-maw´*; or (Da 11:44) חֵמָא, **chêmâ',** *khay-maw´*; from 3179; *heat*; (figurative) *anger, poison* (from its *fever*):—anger, bottles, hot displeasure, furious (-ly, -ry), heat, indignation, poison, rage, wrath (-ful). See 2529.

A noun meaning wrath, heat. The word is also synonymous with the feminine noun meaning heat or rage. Figuratively, it can signify anger, hot displeasure, indignation, poison, or rage. This noun describes the great fury that kings of the North executed in their utter destruction (Da 11:44); a person's burning anger (2Sa 11:20); and God's intense anger against Israel and those who practiced idolatry (2Ki 22:17).

2535. חַמָּה, **chammâh,** *kham-maw´*; from 2525; *heat*; (by implication) the *sun*:—heat, sun.

2536. חַמּוּאֵל, **Chammûw'êl,** *kham-moo-ale´*; from 2535 and 410; *anger of God; Chammuel*, an Israelite:—Hamuel.

2537. חֲמוּטַל, **Chămûwṭal,** *kham-oo-tal´*; or חֲמִיטַל, **Chămîyṭal,** *kham-ee-tal´*; from 2524 and 2919; *father-in-law of dew; Chamutal* or *Chamital*, an Israelitess:—Hamutal.

2538. חָמוּל, **Châmûwl,** *khaw-mool´*; from 2550; *pitied; Chamul*, an Israelite:—Hamul.

2539. חָמוּלִי, **Châmûwlîy,** *khaw-moo-lee´*; patronymic from 2538; a *Chamulite* (collective) or descendants of Chamul:—Hamulites.

2540. חַמּוֹן, **Chammôwn,** *kham-mone´*; from 2552; *warm* spring; *Chammon*, the name of two places in Palestine:—Hammon.

2541. חָמוֹץ, **châmôwts,** *khaw-motse´*; from 2556; (properly) *violent*; (by implication) a *robber*:—oppressed.

2542. חַמּוּק, **chammûwq,** *kham-mook´*; from 2559; a *wrapping*, i.e. *drawers*:—joints.

2543. חֲמוֹר, **chămôwr,** *kham-ore´*; or (shorter) חֲמֹר, **chămôr,** *kham-ore´*; from 2560; a male *ass* (from its dun *red*):—(he) ass.

2544. חֲמוֹר, **Chămôwr,** *kham-ore´*; the same as 2543; *ass; Chamor*, a Canaanite:—Hamor.

2545. חֲמוֹת, **chămôwth,** *kham-ōth´*; or (shorter) חֲמֹת, **chămôth,** *kham-ōth´*; feminine of 2524; a *mother-in-law*:—mother in law.

2546. חֹמֶט, **chômeṭ,** *kho´-met*; from an unused root probably meaning to *lie low*; a *lizard* (as *creeping*):—snail.

2547. חֻמְטָה, **Chumṭâh,** *khoom-taw´*; feminine of 2546; *low; Chumtah*, a place in Palestine:—Humtah.

2548. חָמִיץ, **châmîyts,** *khaw-meets´*; from 2556; *seasoned*, i.e. *salt* provender:—clean.

2549. חֲמִישִׁי, **chămîyshîy,** *kham-ee-shee´*; or חֲמִשִּׁי, **chămishshîy,** *kham-ish-shee´*; ordinal from 2568; *fifth*; also a *fifth*:—fifth (part).

2550. חָמַל, **châmal,** *khaw-mal´*; a primitive root; to *commiserate*; (by implication) to *spare*:—have compassion, (have) pity, spare.

2551. חֶמְלָה, **chemlâh,** *khem-law´*; from 2550; *commiseration*:—merciful, pity.

A feminine noun meaning compassion, mercy. It describes the act of the angelic beings who led Lot and his family out of Sodom (Ge 19:16). It is also used in Isa 63:9 when retelling God's deeds of the past. In light of His angel saving the people in Egypt, the text refers to God showing mercy on them. Therefore, in its two uses, it denotes God's compassion which spares one from destruction or similar dismal fates.

2552. חָמַם, **châmam,** *khaw-mam´*; a primitive root; to *be hot* (literal or figurative):—enflame self, get (have) heat, be (wax) hot, (be, wax) warm (self, at).

2553. חַמָּן, **chammân,** *kham-mawn´*; from 2535; a *sun*-pillar:—idol, image.

A masculine noun meaning sun pillar. It also means idol or pillar in general. This is a pillar used in idolatrous worship of the solar deities, similar to the images Asa and Josiah tore down as part of their religious reforms (2Ch 14:5[4]; 34:4). Isaiah also condemned the worship of these images (Isa 17:8; 27:9).

2554. חָמַס, **châmas,** *khaw-mas´*; a primitive root; to *be violent*; (by implication) to *maltreat*:—make bare, shake off, violate, do violence, take away violently, wrong, imagine wrongfully.

A verb meaning to be violent, to act violently, to act wrongly. The term can be used to describe one who treats people badly. The prophet Jeremiah condemned the wrong treatment of widows and orphans (Jer 22:3). The word can also denote unethical behaviour in a construction that takes *tôwrâh* (8451) as an object (Eze 22:26; Zep 3:4) (lit., "do violence to the law"). God did violence to His dwelling when Jerusalem was sacked (La 2:6). Job thought his accusers treated him wrongly (Job 21:27).

2555. חָמָס, **châmâs,** *khaw-mawce´*; from 2554; *violence*; (by implication) *wrong*; (by metonymy) unjust *gain*:—cruel (-ty), damage, false, injustice, × oppressor, unrighteous, violence (against, done), violent (dealing), wrong.

A masculine noun meaning violence, wrong. It implies cruelty, damage, and injustice. Abraham's cohabiting with Hagar is described as a wrong done to Sarah (Ge 16:5). In relation to physical violence, cruelty is implied (Jgs 9:24). When coupled with the term instrument or weapon, it becomes an attributive noun describing weapons or instruments of violence (Ps 58:2[3]). When it describes a person, it can mean an oppressor or a violent man (Pr 3:31).

2556. **חָמֵץ, châmêts,** *khaw-mates´*; a primitive root; to *be pungent*; i.e. in taste (*sour*, i.e. [literal] *fermented*, or [figurative] *harsh*), in colour (*dazzling*):—cruel (man), dyed, be grieved, leavened.

A verb meaning to be sour, to be leavened. The verb occurs four times in the Hebrew Bible. In connection with the Exodus from Egypt, the Israelites were told not to leaven the bread before their departure (Ex 12:34, 39). In Hos 7:4, the prophet used the image of a baker kneading dough until it was leavened. This verb was also used metaphorically to refer to the heart being soured or embittered (Ps 73:21).

Another root, spelled exactly the same, is listed under this entry by Strong. It occurs in Isa 63:1 and means to be stained red.

2557. **חָמֵץ, châmêts,** *khaw-mates´*; from 2556; *ferment*, (figurative) *extortion*:—leaven, leavened (bread).

A masculine noun meaning leaven. The Hebrew word refers particularly to yeast that causes bread to rise. Bread was made without leaven when Israel went out of Egypt because there was not enough time to leaven it. Thus, unleavened bread is known as "the bread of affliction" and is eaten the week after Passover as a celebration of the Exodus (Dt 16:3). Leaven was later used in offerings (Le 7:13; 23:17) but was not allowed to be burned (Le 2:11). In Am 4:5, leaven is associated with hypocrisy and insincerity, an association made more explicitly in the NT (Lk 12:1; 1Co 5:6–8).

2558. **חֹמֶץ, chômets,** *kho´-mets*; from 2556; *vinegar*:—vinegar.

2559. **חָמַק, châmaq,** *khaw-mak´*; a primitive root; (properly) to *enwrap*; hence to *depart* (i.e. turn about):—go about, withdraw self.

2560. **חָמַר, châmar,** *khaw-mar´*; a primitive root; (properly) to *boil* up; hence to *ferment* (with scum); to *glow* (with redness); as denominative (from 2564) to *smear* with pitch:—daub, befoul, be red, trouble.

2561. **חֶמֶר, chemer,** *kheh´-mer*; from 2560; *wine* (as *fermenting*):— × pure, red wine.

2562. **חֲמַר, chămar,** *kham-ar´*; (Chaldee); corresponding to 2561; *wine*:—wine.

2563. **חֹמֶר, chômer,** *kho´-mer*; from 2560; (properly) a *bubbling* up, i.e. of water, a *wave*; of earth, *mire* or *clay* (cement); also a *heap*; hence a *chomer* or dry measure:—clay, heap, homer, mire, motion.

2564. **חֵמָר, chêmâr,** *khay-mawr´*; from 2560; *bitumen* (as *rising* to the surface):—slime (-pit).

2565. **חֲמֹרָה, chămôrâh,** *kham-o-raw´*; from 2560 [compare 2563]; a *heap*:—heap.

2566. **חַמְרָן, Chamrân,** *kham-rawn´*; from 2560; *red; Chamran*, an Idumæan:—Amran.

2567. **חָמַשׁ, châmash,** *khaw-mash´*; a denominative from 2568; to *tax a fifth*:—take up the fifth part.

2568. **חָמֵשׁ, châmêsh,** *khaw-maysh´*; masculine **חֲמִשָּׁה, chămishshâh,** *kham-ish-shaw´*; a primitive numeral; *five*:—fif [-teen], fifth, five (× apiece).

2569. **חֹמֶשׁ, chômesh,** *kho´-mesh*; from 2567; a *fifth* tax:—fifth part.

2570. **חֹמֶשׁ, chômesh,** *kho´-mesh*; from an unused root probably meaning to *be stout*; the *abdomen* (as *obese*):—fifth [rib].

2571. **חָמֻשׁ, châmush,** *khaw-moosh´*; passive participle of the same as 2570; *staunch*, i.e. able-bodied *soldiers*:—armed (men), harnessed.

2572. **חֲמִשִּׁים, chămishshîym,** *kham-ish-sheem´*; multiple of 2568; *fifty*:—fifty.

2573. **חֵמֶת, chêmeth,** *khay´-meth*; from the same as 2346; a skin *bottle* (as *tied* up):—bottle.

2574. **חֲמָת, Chămâth,** *kham-awth´*; from the same as 2346; *walled; Chamath*, a place in Syria:—Hamath, Hemath.

2575. **חַמַּת, Chammath,** *kham-math´*; a variation for the first part of 2576; *hot* springs; *Chammath*, a place in Palestine:—Hammath.

2576. **חַמֹּת דֹּאר, Chammôth Dô'r,** *kham-moth´ dore*; from the plural of 2535 and 1756; *hot* springs *of Dor; Chammath-Dor*, a place in Palestine:—Hamath-Dor.

2577. **חֲמָתִי, Chămâthîy,** *kham-aw-thee´*; patrial from 2574; a *Chamathite* or native of *Chamath*:—Hamathite.

2578. **חֲמַת צוֹבָה, Chămath Tsôwbâh,** *kham-ath´ tso-baw´*; from 2574 and 6678; *Chamath of Tsobah; Chamath-Tsobah*; probably the same as 2574:—Hamath-Zobah.

2579. **חֲמַת רַבָּה, Chămath Rabbâh,** *kham-ath´ rab-baw´*; from 2574 and 7237; *Chamath of Rabbah; Chamath-Rabbah*, probably the same as 2574.

2580. **חֵן, chên,** *khane*; from 2603; *graciousness*, i.e. subjectively (*kindness, favour*) or objective (*beauty*):—favour, grace (-ious), pleasant, precious, [well-] favoured.

A masculine noun meaning favour, grace, acceptance. Ge 6:8 stands as the fundamental application of this word, meaning an unmerited favour or regard in God's sight. Beyond this, however, the word conveys a sense of acceptance or preference in a more general manner as well, such as the enticement of a woman (Pr 31:30; Na 3:4); elegant speech (Ecc 10:12); and some special standing or privilege with God or people (Nu 32:5; Est 5:2; Zec 12:10).

2581. **חֵן, Chên,** *khane*; the same as 2580; *grace; Chen*, a figurative name for an Israelite:—Hen.

2582. **חֵנָדָד, Chênâdâd,** *khay-naw-dawd´*; probably from 2580 and 1908; *favour of Hadad; Chenadad*, an Israelite:—Henadad.

2583. **חָנָה, chânâh,** *khaw-naw´*; a primitive root [compare 2603]; (properly) to *incline*; (by implication) to *decline* (of the slanting rays of evening); (specifically) to *pitch* a tent; (generally) to *encamp* (for abode or siege):—abide (in tents), camp, dwell, encamp, grow to an end, lie, pitch (tent), rest in tent.

2584. **חַנָּה, Channâh,** *khan-naw´*; from 2603; *favoured; Channah*, an Israelitess:—Hannah.

2585. **חֲנוֹךְ, Chănôwk,** *khan-oke´*; from 2596; *initiated; Chanok*, an antediluvian patriarch:—Enoch.

2586. **חָנוּן, Chânûwn,** *khaw-noon´*; from 2603; *favoured; Chanun*, the name of an Ammonite and of two Israelites:—Hanun.

2587. **חַנּוּן, channûwn,** *khan-noon´*; from 2603; *gracious*:—gracious.

An adjective meaning gracious, merciful. This word is used solely as a descriptive term of God. The Lord used this word when He revealed Himself to Moses (Ex 34:6), as One who is, above all else, merciful and abounding in compassion (Ps 86:15; 103:8). Elsewhere, it expresses the Lord's response to the cry of the oppressed (Ex 22:27[26]); His treatment of those that reverence Him (Ps 111:4; 112:4); His attitude toward those who repent (Joel 2:13); His mercy in the face of rebellion (Ne 9:17, 31; Jnh 4:2); and His leniency toward His people in the midst of judgment (2Ch 30:9).

2588. **חָנוּת, chânûwth,** *khaw-nooth´*; from 2583; (properly) a *vault* or *cell* (with an arch); (by implication) a *prison*:—cabin.

2589. **חַנּוֹת, channôwth,** *khan-nōth´*; from 2603 (in the sense of *prayer*); *supplication*:—be gracious, intreated.

2590. **חָנַט, chânaṭ,** *khaw-nat´*; a primitive root; to *spice*; (by implication) to *embalm*; also to *ripen*:—embalm, put forth.

2591. **חִנְטָא, chinṭâ',** *khint-taw´*; (Chaldee); corresponding to 2406; *wheat*:—wheat.

2592. **חַנִּיאֵל, Channîy'êl,** *khan-nee-ale´*; from 2603 and 410; *favour of God; Channiel*, the name of two Israelites:—Hanniel.

2593. **חָנִיךְ, chânîyk,** *kaw-neek´*; from 2596; *initiated;* i.e. *practised:*—trained.

2594. **חֲנִינָה, chănîynâh,** *khan-ee-naw´*; from 2603; *graciousness:*—favour.

2595. **חֲנִית, chănîyth,** *khan-eeth´*; from 2583; a *lance* (for *thrusting*, like *pitching* a tent):—javelin, spear.

2596. **חָנַךְ, chânak,** *khaw-nak´*; a primitive root; (properly) to *narrow* [compare 2614]; (figurative) to *initiate* or *discipline:*—dedicate, train up.

A verb meaning to train, to dedicate. It is used once for training a child (Pr 22:6). Its other use is related to the dedication of a house or temple (Dt 20:5; 1Ki 8:63; 2Ch 7:5).

2597. **חֲנֻכָּא, chănukkâ',** *khan-ook-kaw´*; (Chaldee); corresponding to 2598; *consecration:*—dedication.

An Aramaic feminine noun meaning dedication, consecration. The word is used in relation to the dedication of Nebuchadnezzar's image (Da 3:2); and the dedication of the new Temple of God (Ezr 6:16, 17).

2598. **חֲנֻכָּה, chănukkâh,** *khan-ook-kaw´*; from 2596; *initiation,* i.e. *consecration:*—dedicating (-tion).

A feminine noun meaning dedication, ceremony. It was used to show that something was officially in service. The word describes the dedication of the wall of Jerusalem after it was rebuilt under Nehemiah (Ne 12:27). It also refers to the dedication of David's house (Ps 30:title[1]; cf. Dt 20:5). The word refers to an altar dedication in 2Ch 7:9 and also in Nu 7 where it appears to refer particularly to the offerings offered on the altar (Nu 7:10, 11, 84, 88). The word is best known in reference to the altar rededication described in the apocryphal books of Maccabees, which has since been celebrated as the Jewish festival, Hanukkah.

2599. **חֲנֹכִי, Chănôkîy,** *khan-o-kee´*; patronymic from 2585; a *Chanokite* (collective) or descendants of Chanok:—Hanochites.

2600. **חִנָּם, chinnâm,** *khin-nawm´*; from 2580; *gratis,* i.e. devoid of cost, reason or advantage:—without a cause (cost, wages), causeless, to cost nothing, free (-ly), innocent, for nothing (nought), in vain.

An adverb meaning freely, undeservedly, without cause, for no purpose, in vain. The primary meaning of this Hebrew word is related to the English word *gratis.* It appears in connection with goods exchanged without monetary charge (2Sa 24:24); services rendered without pay (Jer 22:13); innocence, as having no offence (1Ki 2:31); food without restriction or limit (Nu 11:5); faith without rational justification (Job 1:9); hostility without provocation (Ps 69:4[5]); religious activities done in vain (Mal 1:10).

2601. **חֲנַמְאֵל, Chănam'êl,** *khan-am-ale´*; probably by orthographical variation for 2606; *Chanamel,* an Israelite:—Hanameel.

2602. **חֲנָמָל, chănâmâl,** *khan-aw-mawl´*; of uncertain derivation; perhaps the *aphis* or plant-louse:—frost.

2603. **חָנַן, chânan,** *khaw-nan´*; a primitive root [compare 2583]; (properly) to *bend* or stoop in kindness to an inferior; to *favour, bestow;* (causative) to *implore* (i.e. move to favour by petition):—beseech, × fair, (be, find, shew) favour (-able), be (deal, give, grant) gracious (-ly), intreat, (be) merciful, have (shew) mercy (on, upon), have pity upon, pray, make supplication, × very.

A verb meaning to be gracious toward, to favour, to have mercy on. In the wisdom literature, this verb is used primarily with human relations to denote gracious acts toward someone in need (Job 19:21; Pr 19:17). Though the wicked may pretend to act graciously, they do not do so; neither should it be done so toward them (Ps 37:21; Pr 21:10; 26:25; Isa 26:10). Outside of the wisdom literature, the agent of graciousness is most frequently God, including the often repeated cry, "Have mercy on me!" (Ex 33:19; Nu 6:25; Ps 26:11; 27:7; 119:58). A mixture of divine and human agencies occurs when God, in judgment, sends nations that will show no mercy to punish other nations through warfare (Dt 7:2; 28:50; Isa 27:11).

2604. **חֲנַן, chănan,** *khan-an´*; (Chaldee); corresponding to 2603; to *favour* or (causative) to *entreat:*—shew mercy, make supplication.

An Aramaic verb meaning to show mercy, to ask for mercy. It corresponds to the Hebrew word *chânan* (2603). It refers to showing mercy to the poor, an action that would help Nebuchadnezzar break away from his iniquities (Da 4:27[24]). Daniel was discovered asking God for mercy even though it was against the new law of the Medes and Persians to do so (Da 6:11[12]). Here the word occurs alongside *b*ᵉ*'â'* (1156), meaning to request.

2605. **חָנָן, Chânân,** *khaw-nawn´*; from 2603; *favour; Chanan,* the name of seven Israelites:—Canan.

2606. **חֲנַנְאֵל, Chănan'êl,** *khan-an-ale´*; from 2603 and 410; *God has favoured; Chananel,* probably an Israelite, from whom a tower of Jerusalem was named:—Hananeel.

2607. **חֲנָנִי, Chănânîy,** *khan-aw-nee´*; from 2603; *gracious; Chanani,* the name of six Israelites:—Hanani.

2608. **חֲנַנְיָה, Chănanyâh,** *khan-an-yaw´*; or **חֲנַנְיָהוּ, Chănanyâhûw,** *khan-an-yaw´-hoo*; from 2603 and 3050; *Jah has favoured; Chananjah,* the name of thirteen Israelites:—Hananiah.

2609. **חָנֵס, Chânês,** *khaw-nace´*; of Egyptian derivation; *Chanes,* a place in Egypt:—Hanes.

2610. **חָנֵף, chânêph,** *khaw-nafe´*; a primitive root; to *soil,* especially in a moral sense:—corrupt, defile, × greatly, pollute, profane.

A verb meaning to be defiled, to be profane, to pollute, to corrupt. This word most often appears in association with the defilement of the land, suggesting a tainting not by active commission but by passive contact with those committing sin. It denotes the pollution of the land through the shedding of blood (Nu 35:33); through divorce (Jer 3:1); and through breaking God's covenant (Isa 24:5). The prophets also used the term to define Zion's defilement by the Babylonians (Mic 4:11) and Israel by idolatry (Jer 3:9). Two notable exceptions to this linkage with the land further intensify the notion that the primary meaning is one of passive contamination. In Jeremiah, the Lord declared that the prophets and the priests were corrupted, seemingly by their association with the people's sin (Jer 23:11). Likewise, Daniel uses the word in reference to the corruption that comes from association with a deceiver (Da 11:32).

2611. **חָנֵף, chânêph,** *khaw-nafe´*; from 2610; *soiled* (i.e. with sin), *impious:*—hypocrite (-ical).

An adjective meaning profane, filthy, impious, godless. It is used as a substantive to refer to a person with such qualities. The root idea is to incline away (from God). The word refers to a person whose moral uncleanness separates him or her from God (Job 13:16). It commonly describes someone without hope after this life (Job 8:13; 20:5; 27:8), who can only expect anger from God (Job 36:13; Isa 33:14). Such people come into conflict with the righteous (Job 17:8; Pr 11:9) and are known by their cruelty to others (Ps 35:16; Pr 11:9).

2612. **חֹנֶף, chôneph,** *kho´-nef*; from 2610; moral *filth,* i.e. *wickedness:*—hypocrisy.

A masculine noun meaning hypocrisy, profaneness. This word is found only once in the Hebrew Bible. Isa 32:6 uses the word in reference to the ungodly practices of vile or foolish persons. Such individuals have little nobility as their hearts are inclined to ruthlessness and their mouths speak nonsense and error.

2613. **חֲנֻפָּה, chănuppâh,** *kha-noop-paw´*; feminine from 2610; *impiety:*—profaneness.

A feminine noun meaning filthiness, profaneness, godlessness. The word occurs only in Jer 23:15 where it describes the wickedness, including Baal worship, promoted by false prophets. The prophets' profaneness included substituting their own words for God's words. This led the people to hope for peace when they should have expected God's wrath.

2614. חָנַק, chânaq, *khaw-nak´*; a primitive root [compare 2596]; to *be narrow*; (by implication) to *throttle*, or (reflexive) to *choke* oneself to death (by a rope):—hang self, strangle.

2615. חַנָּתֹן, Channâthôn, *khan-naw-thone´*; probably from 2603; *favoured; Channathon*, a place in Palestine:—Hannathon.

2616. חָסַד, châsad, *khaw-sad´*; a primitive root; (properly) perhaps to *bow* (the neck only [compare 2603] in courtesy to an equal), i.e. to *be kind*; also (by euphemism [compare 1288], but rarely) to *reprove*:—shew self merciful, put to shame.

A verb which occurs twice in the Hebrew Bible with very different meanings. It is used reflexively as David sang to the Lord, meaning to show oneself as loyal or faithful to a covenant (2Sa 22:26; Ps 18:25[26]). This verb is related to the common noun *chesed* (2618). But in another context and in a different verbal stem, the same root carries the meaning to reproach or to bring shame upon (Pr 25:10).

2617. חֶסֶד, chêsêd, *kheh´-sed*; from 2616; *kindness*; by implication (toward God) *piety*; rarely (by opposition) *reproof*, or (subjective) *beauty*:—favour, good deed (-liness, -ness), kindly, (loving-) kindness, merciful (kindness), mercy, pity, reproach, wicked thing.

A masculine noun indicating kindness, lovingkindness, mercy, goodness, faithfulness, love, acts of kindness. This aspect of God is one of several important features of His character: truth; faithfulness; mercy; steadfastness; justice; righteousness; goodness. The classic text for understanding the significance of this word is Ps 136 where it is used twenty-six times to proclaim that God's kindness and love are eternal. The psalmist made it clear that God's kindness and faithfulness serves as the foundation for His actions and His character: it underlies His goodness (Ps 136:1); it supports His unchallenged position as God and Lord (Ps 136:2, 3); it is the basis for His great and wondrous acts in creation (Ps 136:4–9) and delivering and redeeming His people from Pharaoh and the Red Sea (Ps 136:10–15); the reason for His guidance in the desert (Ps 136:16); His gift of the land to Israel and defeat of their enemies (Ps 136:17–22); His ancient as well as His continuing deliverance of His people (Ps 136:23–25); His rulership in heaven (Ps 136:26). The entire span of creation to God's redemption, preservation, and permanent establishment is touched upon in this psalm. It all happened, is happening, and will continue to happen because of the Lord's covenant faithfulness and kindness.

The other more specific uses of the term develop the ideas contained in Ps 136 in greater detail. Because of His kindness, He meets the needs of His creation by delivering them from enemies and despair (Ge 19:19; Ex 15:13; Ps 109:26; Jer 31:3); He preserves their lives and redeems them from sin (Ps 51:1[3]; 86:13). As Ps 136 demonstrates, God's kindness is abundant, exceedingly great, without end, and good (Ex 34:6; Nu 14:19; Ps 103:8; 109:21; Jer 33:11). The plural of the noun indicates the many acts of God on behalf of His people (Ge 32:10[11]; Isa 63:7). He is the covenant-keeping God who maintains kindness and mercy (Dt 7:9) to those who love Him.

People are to imitate God. They are to display kindness and faithfulness toward each other (1Sa 20:15; Ps 141:5; Pr 19:22), especially toward the poor, weak, and needy (Job 6:14; Pr 20:28). Israel was to show kindness and faithfulness toward the Lord but often failed. In its youth, Israel showed faithfulness to God, but its devotion lagged later (Jer 2:2). It was not constant (Hos 6:4), appearing and leaving as the morning mist even though God desired this from His people more than sacrifices (Hos 6:6; cf. 1Sa 15:22). He looked for pious people (Isa 57:1) who would perform deeds of piety, faithfulness, and kindness (2Ch 32:32; 35:26; Ne 13:14); the Lord desired people who would maintain covenant loyalty and responsibility so that He could build His righteous community.

2618. חֶסֶד, Chesed, *kheh´-sed*; the same as 2617; *favour; Chesed*, an Israelite:—Hesed.

2619. חֲסַדְיָה, Chăsadyâh, *khas-ad-yaw´*; from 2617 and 3050; *Jah has favoured; Chasadjah*, an Israelite:—Hasadiah.

2620. חָסָה, châsâh, *khaw-saw´*; a primitive root; to *flee* for protection [compare 982]; (figurative) to *confide* in:—have hope, make refuge, (put) trust.

A verb meaning to seek, to take refuge. The word is used literally in reference to seeking a tree's shade (Jgs 9:15) and taking refuge in Zion (Isa 14:32). It is commonly used figuratively in relation to deities (Dt 32:37), particularly of Yahweh. He is a shield providing refuge (2Sa 22:31). Refuge is sought under His wings (Ru 2:12; Ps 36:7[8]; 57:1[2]; 61:4[5]; 91:4) and at the time of death (Pr 14:32).

2621. חֹסָה, Chôsâh, *kho-saw´*; from 2620; *hopeful; Chosah*, an Israelite; also a place in Palestine:—Hosah.

2622. חָסוּת, châsûwth, *khaw-sooth´*; from 2620; *confidence*:—trust.

A feminine noun meaning refuge, shelter, trust. It is not used frequently in the OT. Isaiah uses it to describe the false hope or trust that Israel put in Egypt (Isa 30:3). It comes from the Hebrew word *châsâh* (2620), meaning to take refuge.

2623. חָסִיד, châsîyd, *khaw-seed´*; from 2616; (properly) *kind*, i.e. (religiously) *pious* (a saint):—godly (man), good, holy (one), merciful, saint, [un-] godly.

An adjective meaning kind, benevolent, merciful, pious. The word carries the essential idea of the faithful kindness and piety that springs from mercy. It is used of the Lord twice: once to convey His holiness in the sense that His works are beyond reproach (Ps 145:17); and once to declare His tender mercy (Jer 3:12). Other occurrences of this word usually refer to those who reflect the character of God in their actions or personality. The word denotes those who share a personal relationship with the Lord (1Sa 2:9; Ps 4:3[4]; 97:10; 116:15); the state of one who fully trusts in God (Ps 86:2); and those who manifest the goodness or mercy of God in their conduct (2Sa 22:26; Ps 12:1, 2; Mic 7:2). More importantly, though, it signifies the nature of those who are specifically set apart by God to be the examples and mediators of His goodness and fidelity. Priests (Dt 33:8); prophets (Ps 89:19[20]); and the Messiah (Ps 16:10) all bear this "holy" mark and function.

2624. חֲסִידָה, chăsîydâh, *khas-ee-daw´*; feminine of 2623; the *kind* (maternal) bird, i.e. a *stork*:—× feather, stork.

2625. חָסִיל, châsîyl, *khaw-seel´*; from 2628; the *ravager*, i.e. a *locust*:—caterpillar.

2626. חֲסִין, chăsîyn, *khas-een´*; from 2630; (properly) *firm*, i.e. (by implcation) *mighty*:—strong.

2627. חַסִּיר, chassîyr, *khas-seer´*; (Chaldee); from a root corresponding to 2637; *deficient*:—wanting.

2628. חָסַל, châsal, *khaw-sal´*; a primitive root; to *eat* off:—consume.

2629. חָסַם, châsam, *khaw-sam´*; a primitive root; to *muzzle*; (by analogy) to *stop* the nose:—muzzle, stop.

2630. חָסַן, châsan, *khaw-san´*; a primitive root; (properly) to (be) *compact*; (by implication) to *hoard*:—lay up.

2631. חֲסַן, chăsan, *khas-an´*; (Chaldee); corresponding to 2630; to *hold* in occupancy:—possess.

2632. חֱסֵן, chěsên, *kheh´-sane*; (Chaldee); from 2631; *strength*:—power.

2633. חֹסֶן, chôsen, *kho´-sen*; from 2630; *wealth*:—riches, strength, treasure.

2634. חָסֹן, châsôn, *khaw-sone´*; from 2630; *powerful*:—strong.

2635. חֲסַף, chăsaph, *khas-af´*; (Chaldee); from a root corresponding to that of 2636; a *clod*:—clay.

2636. חַסְפַּס, chaspas, *khas-pas´*; reduplicated from an unused root meaning apparently to *peel*; a *shred* or *scale*:—round thing.

2637. חָסֵר, châsêr, *khaw-sare´*; a primitive root; to *lack*; (by implication) to *fail, want, lessen*:—be abated, bereave, decrease, (cause to) fail, (have) lack, make lower, want.

2638. חָסֵר, châsêr, *khaw-sare´*; from 2637; *lacking*; hence *without*:—destitute, fail, lack, have need, void, want.

2639. חֶסֶר, cheser, *kheh´-ser*; from 2637; *lack*; hence *destitution*:—poverty, want.

2640. חֹסֶר, chôser, *kho´-ser*; from 2637; *poverty*:—in want of.

2641. חַסְרָה, Chasrâh, *khas-raw´*; from 2637; *want; Chasrah*, an Israelite:—Hasrah.

2642. חֶסְרוֹן, chesrôwn, *khes-rone´*; from 2637; *deficiency*:—wanting.

2643. חַף, chaph, *khaf*; from 2653 (in the moral sense of *covered* from soil); *pure*:—innocent.

2644. חָפָא, châphâ', *khaw-faw´*; an orthographical variation of 2645; (properly) to *cover*, i.e. (in a sinister sense) to *act covertly*:—do secretly.

2645. חָפָה, châphâh, *khaw-faw´*; a primitive root [compare 2644, 2653]; to *cover*; (by implication) to *veil*, to *incase, protect*:—ceil, cover, overlay.

2646. חֻפָּה, chuppâh, *khoop-paw´*; from 2645; a *canopy*:—chamber, closet, defence.

2647. חֻפָּה, Chuppâh, *khoop-paw´*; the same as 2646; *Chuppah*, an Israelite:—Huppah.

2648. חָפַז, châphaz, *khaw-faz´*; a primitive root; (properly) to *start* up suddenly, i.e. (by implication) to *hasten* away, to *fear*:—(make) haste (away), tremble.

2649. חִפָּזוֹן, chippâzôwn, *khip-paw-zone´*; from 2648; *hasty flight*:—haste.

2650. חֻפִּים, Chuppîym, *khoop-peem´*; plural of 2646 [compare 2349]; *Chuppim*, an Israelite:—Huppim.

2651. חֹפֶן, chôphen, *kho´-fen*; from an unused root of uncertain significance; a *fist* (only in the dual):—fists, (both) hands, hand [-ful].

2652. חָפְנִי, Chophnîy, *khof-nee´*; from 2651; perhaps *pugilist; Chophni*, an Israelite:—Hophni.

2653. חָפַף, châphaph, *khaw-faf´*; a primitive root [compare 2645, 3182]; to *cover* (in protection):—cover.

2654. חָפֵץ, châphêts, *khaw-fates´*; a primitive root; (properly) to *incline* to; (by implication, literal but rarely) to *bend*; (figurative) to *be pleased* with, *desire*:— × any at all, (have, take) delight, desire, favour, like, move, be (well) pleased, have pleasure, will, would.

A verb meaning to delight in, to have pleasure, to have favour, to be pleased. Shechem took delight in Dinah (Ge 34:19); King Ahasuerus also took delight in Esther (Est 2:14). This word describes Solomon's pleasure in building the Temple (1Ki 9:1). The Lord is described as taking pleasure in His people Israel (Isa 62:4). He is also pleased with those who practice justice and righteousness (Jer 9:24[23]).

2655. חָפֵץ, châphêts, *khaw-fates´*; from 2654; *pleased* with:—delight in, desire, favour, please, have pleasure, whosoever would, willing, wish.

An adjective meaning having delight in, having pleasure in. It modifies both humans and God. A good example is Ps 35:27, which refers to people who delighted in the psalmist's vindication and the Lord who delighted in His servant's well-being. Ps 5:4[5] notes that God does not take pleasure in wickedness. It can also mean simply to want or to desire, as in the men who wanted to be priests of the high places (1Ki 13:33). See the related verb *châphêts* (2654) and noun *chêphets* (2656).

2656. חֵפֶץ, chêphets, *khay´-fets*; from 2654; *pleasure*; hence (abstract) *desire*; (concrete) a *valuable* thing; hence (by extension) a *matter* (as something in mind):—acceptable, delight (-some), desire, things desired, matter, pleasant (-ure), purpose, willingly.

A masculine noun meaning delight, pleasure, desire, matter. The root idea is to incline toward something. The word signifies delight in or (in an unrealized sense) a desire for earthly goods, such as Solomon's desire for timber (1Ki 9:11); a delight in fruitful land (Mal 3:12); or the delight of hands in their labour (Pr 31:13). The word also refers to people's delight in God's Law (Ps 1:2); His works (Ps 111:2); God's own delight in His works (Isa 46:10; 48:14); His lack of delight in foolish or disrespectful people (Ecc 5:4[3]; Mal 1:10). Three times the word is used to liken a person or nation to an undesirable vessel (Jer 22:28; 48:38; Hos 8:8). In addition, the word is used in Ecclesiastes to refer to a matter without respect to its delightfulness (Ecc 3:1, 17).

2657. חֶפְצִי־בָהּ, Chephtsîy-bâh, *khef-tsee´ bah*; from 2656 with suffixes; *my delight* (is) *in her; Cheptsi-bah*, a fanciful name for Palestine:—Hephzi-bah.

2658. חָפַר, châphar, *khaw-far´*; a primitive root; (properly) to *pry* into; (by implication) to *delve*, to *explore*:—dig, paw, search out, seek.

2659. חָפֵר, châphêr, *khaw-fare´*; a primitive root [perhaps rather the same as 2658 through the idea of *detection*]; to *blush*; (figurative) to *be ashamed, disappointed*; (causative) to *shame, reproach*:—be ashamed, be confounded, be brought to confusion (unto shame), come (be put to) shame, bring reproach.

2660. חֵפֶר, Chêpher, *khay´-fer*; from 2658 or 2659; a *pit* or *shame; Chepher*, a place in Palestine; also the name of three Israelites:—Hepher.

2661. חֲפֹר, chăphôr, *khaf-ore´*; from 2658; a *hole*; only in connection with 6512, which ought rather to be joined as one word, thus חֲפַרְפָּרָה, **chăpharpârâh,** *khaf-ar-pay-raw´*; by reduplication from 2658; a *burrower*, i.e. probably a *rat*:— + mole.

2662. חֶפְרִי, Chephrîy, *khef-ree´*; patronymic from 2660; a *Chephrite* (collective) or descendants of *Chepher*:—Hepherites.

2663. חֲפָרַיִם, Chăphârayim, *khaf-aw-rah´-yim*; dual of 2660; *double pit; Chapharajim*, a place in Palestine:—Haphraim.

2664. חָפַשׂ, châphaś, *khaw-fas´*; a primitive root; to *seek*; (causative) to *conceal* oneself (i.e. let be sought), or *mask*:—change, (make) diligent (search), disguise self, hide, search (for, out).

2665. חֵפֶשׂ, chêpheś, *khay´-fes*; from 2664; something *covert*, i.e. a *trick*:—search.

2666. חָפַשׁ, châphash, *khaw-fash´*; a primitive root; to *spread* loose, (figurative) to *manumit*:—be free.

2667. חֹפֶשׁ, Chôphesh, *kho´-fesh*; from 2666; something *spread* loosely, i.e. a *carpet*:—precious.

2668. חֻפְשָׁה, chuphshâh, *khoof-shaw´*; from 2666; *liberty* (from slavery):—freedom.

2669. חָפְשׁוּת, chophshûwth, *khof-shooth´*; and חָפְשִׁית, **chophshîyth,** *khof-sheeth´*; from 2666; *prostration* by sickness (with 1004, a *hospital*):—several.

2670. חָפְשִׁי, chophshîy, *khof-shee´*; from 2666; *exempt* (from bondage, tax or care):—free, liberty.

2671. חֵץ, chêts, *khayts*; from 2686; (properly) a *piercer*, i.e. an *arrow*; (by implication) a *wound*; (figurative, of God) *thunderbolt*; (by interchange for 6086) the *shaft* of a spear:— + archer, arrow, dart, shaft, staff, wound.

2672. חָצַב, châtsab, *khaw-tsab´*; or חָצֵב, **châtsêb,** *khaw-tsabe´*; a primitive root; to *cut* or carve (wood, stone or other material); (by implication) to *hew, split, square, quarry, engrave*:—cut, dig, divide, grave, hew (out, -er), make, mason.

2673. חָצָה, châtsâh, *khaw-tsaw´*; a primitive root [compare 2686]; to *cut* or *split* in two; to *halve*:—divide, × live out half, reach to the midst, part.

2674. חָצוֹר**, Châtsôwr,** *khaw-tsore´*; a collective form of 2691; *village; Chatsor,* the name (thus simply) of two places in Palestine and of one in Arabia:—Hazor.

2675. חָצוֹר חֲדַתָּה**, Châtsôwr Chădattâh,** *khaw-tsore´ khad-at-taw´*; from 2674 and a Chaldaizing form of the feminine of 2319 [compare 2323]; *new Chatsor,* a place in Palestine:—Hazor, Hadattah [*as if two places*].

2676. חֲצוֹת**, chătsôwth,** *kha-tsoth´*; from 2673; the *middle* (of the night):—mid [-night].

2677. חֲצִי**, chătsîy,** *kha-tsee´*; from 2673; the *half* or *middle*:—half, middle, mid [-night], midst, part, two parts.

2678. חִצִּי**, chitstsîy,** *khits-tsee´*; or חֵצִי**, chêtsîy,** *khay-tsee´*; prolonged from 2671; an *arrow*:—arrow.

2679. חֲצִי הַמְּנֻחוֹת**, Chătsîy ham-Mᵉnuchôwth,** *khat-tsee´ ham-men-oo-khoth´*; from 2677 and the plural of 4496, with the article interposed; *midst of the resting-places; Chatsi-ham-Menuchoth,* an Israelite:—half of the Manahethites.

2680. חֲצִי הַמְּנַחְתִּי**, Chătsîy ham-Mᵉnachtîy,** *khat-see´ ham-men-akh-tee´*; patronymic from 2679; a *Chatsi-ham-Menachtite* or descendant of Chatsi-ham-Menuchoth:—half of the Manahethites.

2681. חָצִיר**, châtsîyr,** *khaw-tseer´*; a collateral form of 2691; a *court* or *abode*:—court.

2682. חָצִיר**, châtsîyr,** *khaw-tseer´*; perhaps originally the same as 2681, from the *greenness* of a court-yard; *grass*; also a *leek* (collective):—grass, hay, herb, leek.

2683. חֵצֶן**, chêtsen,** *khay´-tsen*; from an unused root meaning to hold *firmly*; the *bosom* (as *comprised* between the arms):—bosom.

2684. חֹצֶן**, chôtsen,** *kho´-tsen*; a collateral form of 2683, and meaning the same:—arm, lap.

2685. חֲצַף**, chătsaph,** *khats-af´*; (Chaldee); a primitive root; (properly) to *shear* or cut close; (figurative) to *be severe*:—hasty, be urgent.

2686. חָצַץ**, châtsats,** *khaw-tsats´*; a primitive root [compare 2673]; (properly) to *chop* into, pierce or sever; hence to *curtail*, to *distribute* (into ranks); as denominative from 2671, to *shoot* an arrow:—archer, × bands, cut off in the midst.

2687. חָצָץ**, châtsâts,** *khaw-tsawts´*; from 2687; (properly) something *cutting*; hence *gravel* (as *grit*); also (like 2671) an *arrow*:—arrow, gravel (stone).

2688. חַצְצוֹן תָּמָר**, Chatstsôwn Tâmâr,** *khats-tsone´ taw-mawr´*; or חַצֲצֹן תָּמָר**, Chatsătsôn Tâmâr,** *khats-ats-one´ taw-mawr´*; from 2686 and 8558; *division* [i.e. perhaps *row*] *of* (the) *palm-tree; Chatsetson-tamar,* a place in Palestine:—Hazezon-tamar.

2689. חֲצֹצְרָה**, chătsôtsrâh,** *khats-ots-raw´*; by reduplication from 2690; a *trumpet* (from its *sundered* or quavering note):—trumpet (-er).

2690. חָצְצַר**, chatstsar,** *khawts-tsar´*; a primitive root; (properly) to *surround* with a stockade, and thus *separate* from the open country; but used only in the reduplicated form חֲצֹצֵר**, chătsôtsêr,** *khast-o-tsare´*; or (2Ch 5:12) חֲצֹרֵר**, chătsôrêr,** *khats-o-rare´*; as deminished from 2689; to *trumpet*, i.e. blow on that instrument:—blow, sound, trumpeter.

2691. חָצֵר**, châtsêr,** *khaw-tsare´*; (masculine and feminine); from 2690 in its original sense; a *yard* (as *inclosed* by a fence); also a *hamlet* (as similarly *surrounded* with walls):—court, tower, village.

2692. חֲצַר אַדָּר**, Chătsar 'Addâr,** *khats-ar´ ad-dawr´*; from 2691 and 146; (the) *village of Addar; Chatsar-Addar,* a place in Palestine:—Hazar-addar.

2693. חֲצַר גַּדָּה**, Chătsar Gaddâh,** *khats-ar´ gad-daw´*; from 2691 and a feminine of 1408; (the) *village of* (female) *Fortune; Chatsar-Gaddah,* a place in Palestine:—Hazar-gaddah.

2694. חֲצַר הַתִּיכוֹן**, Chătsar hat-Tîykôwn,** *khats-ar´ hat-tee-kone´*; from 2691 and 8484 with the article interposed; *village of the middle; Chatsar-hat-Tikon,* a place in Palestine:—Hazar-hatticon.

2695. חֶצְרוֹ**, Chetsrôw,** *khets-ro´*; by an orthographical variation for 2696; *inclosure; Chetsro,* an Israelite:—Hezro, Hezrai.

2696. חֶצְרוֹן**, Chetsrôwn,** *khets-rone´*; from 2691; *court-yard; Chetsron,* the name of a place in Palestine; also of two Israelites:—Hezron.

2697. חֶצְרוֹנִי**, Chetsrôwnîy,** *khets-ro-nee´*; patronymic from 2696; a *Chetsronite* or (collective) descendants of Chetsron:—Hezronites.

2698. חֲצֵרוֹת**, Chătsêrôwth,** *khats-ay-roth´*; feminine plural of 2691; *yards; Chatseroth,* a place in Palestine:—Hazeroth.

2699. חֲצֵרִים**, Chătsêrîym,** *khats-ay-reem´*; plural masculine of 2691; *yards; Chatserim,* a place in Palestine:—Hazerim.

2700. חֲצַרְמָוֶת**, Chătsarmâveth,** *khats-ar-maw´-veth*; from 2691 and 4194; *village of death; Chatsar-maveth,* a place in Arabia:—Hazarmaveth.

2701. חֲצַר סוּסָה**, Chătsar Sûwsâh,** *khats-ar´ soo-saw´*; from 2691 and 5484; *village of cavalry; Chatsar-Susah,* a place in Palestine:—Hazar-susah.

2702. חֲצַר סוּסִים**, Chătsar Sûwsîym,** *khats-ar´ soo-seem´*; from 2691 and the plural of 5483; *village of horses; Chatsar-Susim,* a place in Palestine:—Hazar-susim.

2703. חֲצַר עֵינוֹן**, Chătsar 'Êynôwn,** *khats-ar´ ay-nōne´*; from 2691 and a derivative of 5869; *village of springs; Chatsar-Enon,* a place in Palestine:—Hazar-enon.

2704. חֲצַר עֵינָן**, Chătsar 'Êynân,** *khats-ar´ ay-nawn´*; from 2691 and the same as 5881; *village of springs; Chatsar-Enan,* a place in Palestine:—Hazar-enan.

2705. חֲצַר שׁוּעָל**, Chătsar Shûw'âl,** *khats-ar´ shoo-awl´*; from 2691 and 7776; *village of* (the) *fox; Chatsar-Shual,* a place in Palestine:—Hazar-shual.

2706. חֹק**, chôq,** *khoke*; from 2710; an *enactment*; hence an *appointment* (of time, space, quantity, labour or usage):—appointed, bound, commandment, convenient, custom, decree (-d), due, law, measure, × necessary, ordinance (-nary), portion, set time, statute, task.

A masculine noun meaning regulation, law, ordinance, decree, custom. Primarily, this word represents an expectation or mandate prescribed by decree or custom. It is used to speak of the general decrees of God (Jer 5:22; Am 2:4); the statutes of God given to Moses (Ex 15:26; Nu 30:16[17]; Mal 4:4[3:22]); the lawful share deserved by virtue of status (Ge 47:22; Le 10:13, 14); the declared boundaries or limits of something (Job 14:5; 26:10); the prevailing cultural norm (Jgs 11:39); the binding legislation made by a ruler (Ge 47:26); and that which must be observed by strict ritual (Ex 12:24).

2707. חָקָה**, châqâh,** *khaw-kaw´*; a primitive root; to *carve*; (by implication) to *delineate*; also to *intrench*:—carved work, portrayed, set a print.

2708. חֻקָּה**, chuqqâh,** *khook-kaw´*; feminine of 2706, and meaning substantially the same:—appointed, custom, manner, ordinance, site, statute.

A noun meaning a statute, an ordinance, anything prescribed. It serves as the feminine of *chôq*. Since its basic meaning is not specific, the word takes on different connotations in each context. Its most common meaning is decrees, statutes, or a synonym of these words. The decrees of the Lord could be oral or written; they made God's will known and gave divine directions to His people. Abraham kept them, evidently, before they were written down (Ge 26:5). Moses and his assistants were to teach the statutes of the Lord to Israel (Ex 18:20; Le 10:11) so that the Israelites could discern between the clean and the unclean. The decrees of the Lord, along with His laws, regulations, and commandments, covered all areas of life. The Israelites were to follow His decrees so they would separate themselves from the practices of the pagan nations around them (Le 18:3, 4). Moses admonished the Israelites to keep God's decrees and statutes (Le 19:37; 20:22; 25:18). Blessing was the reward for keeping them (Le 26:3), but curses were promised for those who didn't obey them (Le 26:15, 43).

Throughout the passing of Israel's history, new decrees were added (Jos 24:25), and the people and leaders were judged with respect to their faithfulness in observing God's decrees, laws, statutes, and commandments. David was renowned for having observed them (2Sa 22:23). The Davidic covenant would be realized if later kings followed the Lord's decrees as David had (1Ki 6:12). However, most of the kings failed, including Solomon (1Ki 11:11; 2Ki 17:15, 34). Josiah renewed the covenant and exerted himself to follow the Lord's decrees (2Ki 23:3), but it was too late to save Judah from exile (see 2Ki 23:25–27).

The psalmist found great joy in the decrees, laws, commandments, precepts, ordinances, and instructions of the Lord; they were not burdensome (Ps 18:22[23]; 119:5). However, some leaders of Israel distorted God's decrees and established their own oppressive decrees on the people (see Isa 10:1).

God's issuance of a decree was effective and permanent: by His decree, He established the order of creation forever, the functions of the sun and the moon (Job 28:26; Jer 31:35). The prophets without fail condemned Israel and its leaders for not keeping the decrees of the Lord (Eze 11:12; 20:13; Am 2:4) but saw a future time when a redeemed people would follow them (Eze 36:27; 37:24).

2709. חֲקוּפָא, Chăqûwphâ', *khah-oo-faw´*; from an unused root probably meaning to *bend; crooked; Chakupha,* one of the Nethinim:—Hakupha.

2710. חָקַק, châqaq, *khaw-kak´*; a primitive root; (properly) to *hack,* i.e. *engrave* (Jgs 5:14, to *be a scribe* simply); (by implication) to *enact* (laws being *cut* in stone or metal tablets in primitive times) or (generally) *prescribe*:—appoint, decree, governor, grave, lawgiver, note, portray, print, set.

A verb meaning to cut, to inscribe, to engrave, to decree. The basic meaning, to cut, is used for cutting a tomb out of rock (Isa 22:16), but it is used more commonly of engraving or writing (Isa 30:8; Eze 4:1; 23:14). It is employed for decreeing (i.e. inscribing) a law (Isa 10:1); and the word statute (*chôq*[2706]) is derived from it. Figuratively, God is said to have inscribed a boundary over the deep at creation (Pr 8:27). It also expresses the idea of a commander of decrees (Dt 33:21; Jgs 5:9).

2711. חֵקֶק, chêqeq, *khay´-kek*; from 2710; an *enactment,* a *resolution*:—decree, thought.

A masculine noun meaning something prescribed, a decree, a thought. This word is the construct of *chôwq* (2706) and is only found twice in the OT. When Deborah and Barak sang a song to commemorate the victory over the Canaanites, they sang of the "great thoughts of the heart" (KJV), referring to the thoughts and statues within a person (Jgs 5:15). In the other occurrence, Isaiah declared that the judgment of God was on those who enacted wicked statutes (Isa 10:1).

2712. חֲקֹק, Chuqqôq, *khook-koke´*; or (fully) **חוּקֹק, Chûwqôq,** *khoo-koke´*; from 2710; *appointed; Chukkok* or *Chukok,* a place in Palestine:—Hukkok, Hukok.

2713. חָקַר, châqar, *khaw-kar´*; a primitive root; (properly) to *penetrate*; hence to *examine* intimately:—find out, (make) search (out), seek (out), sound, try.

2714. חֵקֶר, chêqer, *khay´-ker*; from 2713; *examination, enumeration, deliberation*:—finding out, number, [un-] search (-able, -ed out, -ing).

2715. חֹר, chôr, *khore*; or (fully) **חוֹר, chôwr,** *khore*; from 2787; (properly) *white* or *pure* (from the *cleansing* or *shining* power of fire [compare 2751]); hence (figurative) *noble* (in rank):—noble.

A masculine noun meaning noble. It occurs only in the plural form and apparently comes from a root, unused in the OT, which means free. The nobles were a social order having power over the lower classes of people, a power which they sometimes misused, exacting usury (Ne 5:7), even following a royal order to kill innocent Naboth (1Ki 21:8, 11). In Nehemiah's time, they maintained strong family connections (Ne 6:17). Ecc 10:17 indicates that nobility was inherited and could not be instantly attained by election or force; otherwise, all kings would be nobility by definition. Thus, nobles made the best kings (Ecc 10:17), apparently because they came from a background of involvement in civic affairs and were not suddenly vaulted to such a high position.

2716. חֶרֶא, chere', *kheh´-reh*; from an unused (and vulgar) root probably meaning to *evacuate* the bowels; *excrement*:—dung. Also **חֲרִי, chărîy,** *khar-ee´*.

2717. חָרַב, chârab, *khaw-rab´*; or **חָרֵב, chârêb,** *khaw-rabe´*; a primitive root; to *parch* (through drought), i.e. (by analogy) to *desolate, destroy, kill*:—decay, (be) desolate, destroy (-er), (be) dry (up), slay, × surely, (lay, lie, make) waste.

A verb meaning to be desolate, to be destroyed, to be dry, to dry up, to lay waste. Two related themes constitute the cardinal meaning of this word, devastation and drying up. Although each aspect is distinct from the other, both convey the notion of wasting away. The word is used to describe the drying of the earth after the flood (Ge 8:13); the drying of green vines (Jgs 16:7); the utter destruction of a physical structure (Eze 6:6); the devastation of war (Isa 37:18); the removal of human inhabitants (Eze 26:19); the slaughter of animals (Jer 50:27).

2718. חֲרַב, chărab, *khar-ab´*; (Chaldee); a root corresponding to 2717; to *demolish*:—destroy.

An Aramaic verb meaning to be utterly destroyed, to be laid waste. The only occurrence of this verb is preserved in a letter sent to Artaxerxes concerning the rebuilding of Jerusalem (Ezr 4:15). Certain antagonists of the Jewish people desired to hinder the rebuilding of the city and called to mind that it was due to wickedness that Jerusalem was destroyed by the Babylonians (cf. Jer 52:12–20). The result left the city in utter desolation and without defense (cf. Ne 2:17; Jer 9:11).

2719. חֶרֶב, chereb, *kheh´-reb*; from 2717; *drought*; also a *cutting* instrument (from its *destructive* effect), as a *knife, sword,* or other sharp implement:—axe, dagger, knife, mattock, sword, tool.

A feminine noun meaning a sword, a knife, a cutting tool. The word frequently pictures the sword, along with the bow and shield, as the standard fighting equipment of the times (Ge 48:22; Ps 76:3[4]; Hos 1:7). Warriors are referred to as those drawing the sword (Jgs 20; 1Ch 21:5). The sword may also stand for a larger unit of military power, sometimes pictured as coming on a people or land (Le 26:25; La 1:20; Eze 14:17). The cutting action of a sword is likened to eating, and its edges are literally referred to as mouths. Similarly, the mouths of people are likened to swords (Ps 59:7[8]; Pr 30:14; Isa 49:2). The sword is also a symbol of judgment executed by God (Ge 3:24; Dt 32:41; Jer 47:6); or His people (Ps 149:6). The word can refer to a knife (Jos 5:2, 3); or a tool for cutting stones (Ex 20:25).

2720. חָרֵב, chârêb, *khaw-rabe´*; from 2717; *parched* or *ruined*:—desolate, dry, waste.

An adjective meaning dry, desolate, wasted. Two connected ideas undergird the translation of this word. The first is the sense of dryness as opposed to wetness. In this line, it is used specifically of the grain offering (Le 7:10) or a morsel of food (Pr 17:1). The second is the sense of desolation. In this way, it is used to describe the wasted condition of Jerusalem after the Babylonian captivity (Ne 2:3); the emptiness of the land, which is comparable to the sparse population of the Garden of Eden (Eze 36:35); and the condition of the Temple in Haggai's day, as it still lay in ruins (Hag 1:4).

2721. חֹרֶב, chôreb, *kho´-reb*; a collateral form of 2719; *drought* or *desolation*:—desolation, drought, dry, heat, × utterly, waste.

2722. חֹרֵב, Chôrêb, *kho-rabe´*; from 2717; *desolate; Choreb*, a (generic) name for the Sinaitic mountains:—Horeb.

2723. חָרְבָּה, chorbâh, *khor-baw´*; feminine of 2721; (properly) *drought*, i.e. (by implication) a *desolation*:—decayed place, desolate (place, -tion), destruction, (laid) waste (place).

A feminine noun meaning ruin. The word almost always refers to an area ruined by the judgment of God. The destroyed area is usually a country or city but may also be individual property (Ps 109:10). Sometimes the ruins are referred to as being restored by God (Isa 51:3; 52:9; 58:12). The ruins of Job 3:14 may have been rebuilt by men; if so, the context makes clear that the rebuilding was unsuccessful. In Mal 1:4, God would not allow Edom to rebuild his ruins successfully; similarly, Ps 9:6[7] seems to refer to an eternal state of ruin. Eze 26:20 and Isa 58:12 refer to ancient ruins, but it is difficult to identify them definitely. The ruins of the latter passage would be restored by those who seek God sincerely with fasting.

2724. חָרָבָה, chârâbâh, *khaw-raw-baw´*; feminine of 2720; a *desert*:—dry (ground, land).

A feminine noun meaning dry land, dry ground. The central principle of this word is the lack of moisture. It is used to refer to the habitable ground inundated by the flood (Ge 7:22); dry waterbeds (Eze 30:12); and land in general (Hag 2:6). Three times the word describes the condition of a path made in the miraculous parting of water: for Moses and Israel (Ex 14:21); for Joshua and Israel (Jos 3:17); and for Elijah and Elisha (2Ki 2:8).

2725. חֲרָבוֹן, chărâbôwn, *khar-aw-bone´*; from 2717; parching *heat*:—drought.

2726. חַרְבוֹנָא, Charbôwnâʼ, *khar-bo-naw´*; or חַרְבוֹנָה, **Charbôwnâh,** *khar-bo-naw´*; of Persian origin; *Charbona* or *Charbonah*, a eunuch of Xerxes:—Harbona, Harbonah.

2727. חָרַג, chârag, *khaw-rag´*; a primitive root; (properly) to *leap* suddenly, i.e. (by implication) to *be dismayed*:—be afraid.

A verb meaning to be afraid, to quake. The word occurs only in Ps 18:45[46] where foreigners came quaking from their strongholds. The idea of foreigners coming out derives from the word *min* (4480), meaning from. However, a similar passage in Mic 7:17 (using a different verb but dependent on *min* for the idea of coming out) justifies the translation "to come quaking." The passage thus pictures foreigners surrendering their strongholds to David and coming out.

2728. חַרְגֹּל, chârgôl, *khar-gole´*; from 2727; the *leaping* insect, i.e. a *locust*:—beetle.

2729. חָרַד, chârad, *khaw-rad´*; a primitive root; to *shudder* with terror; hence to *fear*; also to *hasten* (with anxiety):—be (make) afraid, be careful, discomfit, fray (away), quake, tremble.

A verb meaning to tremble, to quake, to be terrified. The term is used in reference to mountains (Ex 19:18); islands (Isa 41:5); birds and beasts (Jer 7:33); and people (Eze 32:10). It can mark a disturbance, such as being startled from sleep (Ru 3:8); or terror brought on by a trumpet's sound (Am 3:6); or an act of God (1Sa 14:15). It is often connected with terrifying an enemy in battle. It is also used in the causative, meaning to terrify (Jgs 8:12; 2Sa 17:2; Zec 1:21[2:4]). See the word *chărâdâh* (2731).

2730. חָרֵד, chârêd, *khaw-rade´*; from 2729; *fearful*; also *reverential*:—afraid, trembling.

An adjective meaning trembling, reverential. God told Gideon to limit the number of warriors by telling those who were afraid or trembling to return to their camp at Gilead (Jgs 7:3). God honours and looks upon those who are contrite in spirit and tremble at His word (Isa 66:2). Those who tremble at God's words are also accounted as obedient (Ezr 9:4).

2731. חֲרָדָה, chărâdâh, *khar-aw-daw´*; feminine of 2730; *fear, anxiety*:—care, × exceedingly, fear, quaking, trembling.

A feminine noun meaning trembling, quaking, fear. This trembling is often brought on by acts of God. It is the terror of God that overcame the enemy (1Sa 14:15); and startled Daniel's friends in a vision (Da 10:7). Humans can also inspire fear (Pr 29:25). See the cognate verb *chârad* (2729).

2732. חֲרָדָה, Chărâdâh, *khar-aw-daw´*; the same as 2731; *Charadah*, a place in the Desert:—Haradah.

2733. חֲרֹדִי, Chărôdîy, *khar-o-dee´*; patrial from a derivative of 2729 [compare 5878]; a *Charodite*, or inhabitant of *Charod*:—Harodite.

2734. חָרָה, chârâh, *khaw-raw´*; a primitive root [compare 2787]; to *glow* or grow warm; figurative (usually) to *blaze* up, of anger, zeal, jealousy:—be angry, burn, be displeased, × earnestly, fret self, grieve, be (wax) hot, be incensed, kindle, × very, be wroth. See 8474.

A verb meaning to burn, to be kindled, to glow, to grow warm. Figuratively, it means to get angry or to become vexed. Anger can be between two people: Potiphar's anger was kindled against Joseph when his wife accused Joseph of rape (Ge 39:19). Anger can also be between God and a person: God's anger is against those who transgress His law (Jos 23:16). This word can also describe a future event of one becoming angry (Isa 41:11).

2735. חֹר הַגִּדְגָּד, Chôr hag-Gidgâd, *khore hag-ghid-gawd´*; from 2356 and a collateral (masculine) form of 1412, with the article interposed; *hole of the cleft; Chor-hag-Gidgad*, a place in the Desert:—Hor-hagidgad.

2736. חַרְהֲיָה, Charhăyâh, *khar-hah-yaw´*; from 2734 and 3050; *fearing Jah; Charhajah*, an Israelite:—Harhaiah.

2737. חָרוּז, chârûwz, *khaw-rooz´*; from an unused root meaning to *perforate*; (properly) *pierced*, i.e. a *bead* of pearl, gems or jewels (as strung):—chain.

2738. חָרוּל, chârûwl, *khaw-rool´*; or (shortened) חָרֻל, **chârul,** *khaw-rool´*; apparently passive participle of an unused root probably meaning to *be prickly*; (properly) *pointed*, i.e. a *bramble* or other thorny weed:—nettle.

2739. חֲרוּמַף, chărûwmaph, *khar-oo-maf´*; from passive participle of 2763 and 639; *snubnosed; Charumaph*, an Israelite:—Harumaph.

2740. חָרוֹן, chârôwn, *khaw-rone´*; or (shortened) חָרֹן, **chârôn,** *khaw-rone´*; from 2734; a *burning* of anger:—sore displeasure, fierce (-ness), fury, (fierce) wrath (-ful).

2741. חֲרוּפִי, Chărûwphîy, *khar-oo-fee´*; a patrial from (probably) a collateral form of 2756; a *Char-uphite* or inhabitant of Charuph (or Chariph):—Haruphite.

2742. חָרוּץ, chârûwts, *khaw-roots´*; or חָרֻץ, **châruts,** *khaw-roots´*; passive participle of 2782; (properly) *incised* or (active) *incisive*; hence (as noun masculine or feminine) a *trench* (as dug), *gold* (as mined), a *threshing-sledge* (having sharp teeth); (figurative) *determination*; also *eager*:—decision, diligent, (fine) gold, pointed things, sharp, threshing instrument, wall.

2743. חָרוּץ, Chârûwts, *khaw-roots´*; the same as 2742; *earnest; Charuts*, an Israelite:—Haruz.

2744. חַרְחוּר, Charchûwr, *khar-khoor´*; a fuller form of 2746; *inflammation; Charchur*, one of the Nethinim:—Harhur.

2745. חַרְחַס, Charchas, *khar-khas´*; from the same as 2775; perhaps *shining; Charchas*, an Israelite:—Harhas.

2746. חַרְחֻר, charchur, *khar-khoor´*; from 2787; *fever* (as *hot*):—extreme burning.

2747. חֶרֶט, cheret, *kheh´-ret*; from a primitive root meaning to *engrave*; a *chisel* or *graver*; also a *style* for writing:—graving tool, pen.

A masculine noun designating an engraving tool, a chisel. It is an instrument used by Aaron to "fashion" or "dress down" the golden calf

(Ex 32:4). Its use implicated Aaron further into the guilt of the Israelites. The word is also used in Isa 8:1 as a writing utensil.

2748. חַרְטֹם, **charṭôm,** *khar-tome´*; from the same as 2747; a *horoscopist* (as *drawing* magical lines or circles):—magician.

A masculine noun meaning engraver, a writer associated with the occult. These people seem to have had knowledge of astrology or divination and were commonly associated with the magicians of Egypt in Pharaoh's court. Pharaoh could not find any magicians to interpret his dream, so he called Joseph (Ge 41:24). Moses caused plagues to come upon Egypt which the magicians could not reverse (Ex 9:11).

2749. חַרְטֹם, **charṭôm,** *khar-tome´*; (Chaldee); the same as 2748:—magician.

An Aramaic noun meaning magician. It occurs only in the book of Daniel (Da 2:10, 27; 4:7[4], 9[6]; 5:11). These people, who practiced sorcery and other occult practices, were advisors and counselors of kings.

2750. חֳרִי, **chŏrîy,** *khor-ee´*; from 2734; a *burning* (i.e. intense) anger:—fierce, × great, heat.

A masculine noun meaning burning. It is used to describe anger. The word occurs with *'aph* (639) which primarily means nose, but in this case, it means anger as derived from the snorting of an angry person. The anger may be righteous anger, such as God's anger at Israel's unfaithfulness (Dt 29:24[23]; La 2:3); Moses' anger aroused by Pharaoh's stubbornness (Ex 11:8); and Jonathan's anger at Saul's outburst against David (1Sa 20:34). It may also be unrighteous anger, such as the anger of troops dismissed with pay because of God's word (2Ch 25:10); and the anger of the kings of Israel and Syria against Judah (Isa 7:4). In all cases, the heat of the anger is evident whether expressed by leaving the room or by attempting to put to death the object of anger (2Ch 25:10; cf. v. 13).

2751. חֹרִי, **chôrîy,** *kho-ree´*; from the same as 2353; *white* bread:—white.

2752. חֹרִי, **Chôrîy,** *kho-ree´*; from 2356; *cavedweller* or troglodyte; a *Chorite* or aboriginal Idumæan:—Horims, Horites.

2753. חֹרִי, **Chôrîy,** *kho-ree´*; or חוֹרִי, **Chôwrîy,** *kho-ree´*; the same as 2752; *Chori*, the name of two men:—Hori.

2754. חָרִיט, **chârîyṭ,** *khaw-reet´*; or חָרִט, **chârit,** *khaw-reet´*; from the same as 2747; (properly) *cut* out (or *hollow*), i.e. (by implication) a *pocket*:—bag, crisping pin.

2755. חֲרֵי־יוֹנִים, **chărêy-yôwnîym,** *khar-ay´-yo-neem´*; from the plural of 2716 and the plural of 3123; *excrements of doves* [or perhaps rather the plural of a single word חֲרָאיוֹן, **chărâ'yôwn,** *khar-aw-yone´*; of similar or uncertain derivation], probably a kind of vegetable:—doves' dung.

2756. חָרִיף, **Chârîyph,** *khaw-reef´*; from 2778; *autumnal; Chariph*, the name of two Israelites:—Hariph.

2757. חָרִיץ, **chârîyts,** *khaw-reets´*; or חָרִץ, **chârits,** *khaw-reets´*; from 2782; (properly) *incisure* or (passive) *incised* [compare 2742]; hence a *threshing-sledge* (with *sharp* teeth); also a *slice* (as cut):— + cheese, harrow.

2758. חָרִישׁ, **chârîysh,** *khaw-reesh´*; from 2790; *ploughing* or its season:—earing (time), ground.

2759. חֲרִישִׁי, **chărîyshîy,** *khar-ee-shee´*; from 2790 in the sense of *silence; quiet*, i.e. *sultry* (as noun feminine the *sirocco* or hot east wind):—vehement.

2760. חָרַךְ, **chârak,** *khaw-rak´*; a primitive root; to *braid* (i.e. to *entangle* or snare) or *catch* (game) in a net:—roast.

2761. חֲרַךְ, **chărak,** *khar-ak´*; (Chaldee); a root probably allied to the equivalent of 2787; to *scorch*:—singe.

2762. חֶרֶךְ, **chârâk,** *kheh´-rek*; from 2760; (properly) a *net*, i.e. (by analogy) *lattice*:—lattice.

2763. חָרַם, **châram,** *khaw-ram´*; a primitive root; to *seclude*; specifically (by a ban) to *devote* to religious uses (especially destruction); (physically and reflexively) to be *blunt* as to the nose:—make accursed, consecrate, (utterly) destroy, devote, forfeit, have a flat nose, utterly (slay, make away).

A verb meaning to destroy, to doom, to devote. This word is most commonly associated with the Israelites destroying the Canaanites upon their entry into the Promised Land (Dt 7:2; Jos 11:20). It indicates complete and utter destruction (Jgs 21:11; 1Sa 15:18); the severe judgment of God (Isa 11:15); the forfeiture of property (Ezr 10:8); being "accursed" or set apart for destruction (Jos 6:18). This latter application, being set apart, accounts for what appears to be a contradictory element in the verb. It is also used to mean devotion or consecration to the Lord (Le 27:28, 29; Mic 4:13). Just as something accursed is set apart for destruction, so something devoted to God is set apart for His use.

2764. חֵרֶם, **chêrem,** *khay´-rem*; or (Zec 14:11) חֶרֶם, **cherem,** *keh´-rem*; from 2763; physically (as *shutting in*) a *net* (either literal or figurative); usually a *doomed* object; (abstract) *extermination*:—(ac-) curse (-d, -d thing), dedicated thing, things which should have been utterly destroyed, (appointed to) utter destruction, devoted (thing), net.

A masculine noun meaning devoted things, devoted to destruction, devotion, things under ban, cursed. The basic meaning of the word, to be set aside or devoted, is qualified in several ways. Things, including persons, were set aside or devoted to a special function or an area of service by a declaration of God or His servants. The entire city of Jericho was a deadly threat to the formation of God's people and fell under a ban, except for Rahab and her family (Jos 6:17, 18), and was set aside for destruction. A person could be set aside for destruction (1Ki 20:42) as well as an entire people, such as Edom (Isa 34:5). The Lord set the Israelites apart for destruction when they turned to other gods (Dt 13:17[18]; Isa 43:28); the Israelites could not take idols of the conquered pagans into their houses, even when acquired in battle. These items were set aside for destruction only (Dt 7:26). This term was the last word in the text of the Prophets (Mal 4:6[3:24]) and expressed a potential curse on the entire restored exilic community of Israel. Happily, the Lord also announced a time when the ban for destruction would be lifted from Jerusalem forever (Zec 14:11).

Various items could become holy, that is, devoted to cultic or holy use, as in the case of a field given to the Lord (Le 27:21); or the spoils of war could be set aside for religious use only (Nu 18:14; Jos 6:18; 1Sa 15:21), including gold, silver, items of bronze or iron, and animals. These items, set aside exclusively to holy use, could not be used for everyday purposes, for to use such items in this way was a grave sin. Achan and others died for this offence (Jos 7:1, 12, 15; 22:20).

2765. חֳרֵם, **Chŏrêm,** *khor-ame´*; from 2763; *devoted; Chorem*, a place in Palestine:—Horem.

2766. חָרִם, **Chârim,** *khaw-reem´*; from 2763; *snub-nosed; Charim*, an Israelite:—Harim.

2767. חָרְמָה, **Chormâh,** *khor-maw´*; from 2763; *devoted; Chormah*, a place in Palestine:—Hormah.

2768. חֶרְמוֹן, **Chermôwn,** *kher-mone´*; from 2763; *abrupt; Chermon*, a mount of Palestine:—Hermon.

2769. חֶרְמוֹנִים, **Chermôwnîym,** *kher-mo-neem´*; plural of 2768; *Hermons*, i.e. its peaks:—the Hermonites.

2770. חֶרְמֵשׁ, **chermêsh,** *kher-mashe´*; from 2763; a *sickle* (as *cutting*):—sickle.

2771. חָרָן, **Chârân,** *khaw-rawn´*; from 2787; *parched; Charan*, the name of a man and also of a place:—Haran.

2772. חֹרֹנִי, **Chôrônîy,** *kho-ro-nee´*; patrial from 2773; a *Choronite* or inhabitant of Choronaim:—Horonite.

2773. חֹרֹנַיִם, **Chôrônayim,** *kho-ro-nah´-yim*; dual of a derivative from 2356; *double cave-town; Choro-najim*, a place in Moab:—Horonaim.

2774. חַרְנֶפֶר, **Charnepher,** *khar-neh´-fer*; of uncertain derivation; *Charnepher,* an Israelite:—Harnepher.

2775. חֶרֶס, **cheres,** *kheh´-res*; or (with a directive enclitic) חַרְסָה, **charsâh,** *khar´-saw*; from an unused root meaning to *scrape*; the *itch*; also [perhaps from the mediating idea of 2777] the *sun*:—itch, sun.

2776. חֶרֶס, **Cheres,** *kheh´-res*; the same as 2775; *shining; Cheres,* a mountain in Palestine:—Heres.

2777. חַרְסוּת, **charsûwth,** *khar-sooth´*; from 2775 (apparently in the sense of a red *tile* used for scraping); a *potsherd,* i.e. (by implication) a *pottery*; the name of a gate at Jerusalem:—east.

2778. חָרַף, **châraph,** *khaw-raf´*; a primitive root; to *pull* off, i.e. (by implication) to *expose* (as by *stripping*); specifically to *betroth* (as if a surrender); (figurative) to carp at, i.e. *defame*; (denominative [from 2779]) to spend the *winter*:—betroth, blaspheme, defy, jeopard, rail, reproach, upbraid.

2779. חֹרֶף, **chôreph,** *kho´-ref*; from 2778; (properly) the *crop* gathered, i.e. (by implication) the *autumn* (and winter) season; (figurative) *ripeness* of age:—cold, winter ([-house]), youth.

2780. חָרֵף, **Chârêph,** *khaw-rafe´*; from 2778; *reproachful; Chareph,* an Israelite:—Hareph.

2781. חֶרְפָּה, **cherpâh,** *kher-paw´*; from 2778; *contumely, disgrace,* the *pudenda*:—rebuke, reproach (-fully), shame.

A feminine noun meaning reproach, scorn, taunt. The term can be used for a taunt hurled at an enemy (1Sa 17:26; Ne 4:4 [3:36]) or for a state of shame that remains with an individual such as barrenness (Ge 30:23); uncircumcision (Ge 34:14); and widowhood (Isa 54:4).

2782. חָרַץ, **chârats,** *khaw-rats´*; a primitive root; (properly) to *point* sharply, i.e. (literal) to *wound*; (figurative) to *be alert,* to *decide*:—bestir self, decide, decree, determine, maim, move.

2783. חֲרַץ, **chărats,** *khar-ats´*; (Chaldee); from a root corresponding to 2782 in the sense of *vigour*; the *loin* (as the seat of strength):—loin.

2784. חַרְצֻבָּה, **chartsubbâh,** *khar-tsoob-baw´*; of uncertain derivation; a *fetter*; (figurative) a *pain*:—band.

2785. חַרְצַן, **chartsan,** *khar-tsan´*; from 2782; a *sour* grape (as *sharp* in taste):—kernel.

2786. חָרַק, **châraq,** *khaw-rak*; a primitive root; to *grate* the teeth:—gnash.

2787. חָרַר, **chârar,** *khaw-rar´*; a primitive root; to *glow,* i.e. literal (to *melt, burn, dry* up) or figurative (to *show* or *incite passion*):—be angry, burn, dry, kindle.

A verb meaning to be hot, to be scorched, to burn. Jerusalem is scorched under the figurative caldron that Ezekiel saw (Eze 24:11). It also describes the physical burning Job felt in his bones (Job 30:30). Figuratively, Jeremiah refers to Babylon as burning the bellows of Jerusalem (Jer 6:29). This word can also connote an angry person kindling strife (Pr 26:21).

2788. חָרֵר, **chârêr,** *khaw-rare´*; from 2787; *arid*:—parched place.

A noun meaning parched place, a scorched place. It occurs only in Jer 17:6 where it is plural and refers to places where lack of water keeps plants from prospering. This symbolizes the lives of those who trust in people rather than in God. In contrast, those who trust in God have enough water even in heat and drought (Jer 17:7, 8).

2789. חֶרֶשׂ, **chereś,** *kheh´-res*; a collateral form mediating between 2775 and 2791; a piece of *pottery*:—earth (-en), (pot-) sherd, + stone.

A masculine noun meaning earthenware, clay pottery, and potsherd. This word signifies any vessel made from clay (Le 15:12; Jer 19:1); the sharp fragments of broken pottery (Job 41:30[22]); and the larger potsherd useful to scoop burning coals from a fire (Isa 30:14); or to scrape boils (Job 2:8). Figuratively, David used the image of kiln-dried pottery to describe the depletion of his strength (Ps 22:15[16]).

2790. חָרַשׁ, **chârash,** *khaw-rash´*; a primitive root; to *scratch,* i.e. (by implication) to *engrave, plough*; hence (from the use of tools) to *fabricate* (of any material); (figurative) to *devise* (in a bad sense); hence (from the idea of secrecy) to be *silent,* to *let alone*; hence (by implication) to *be deaf* (as an accompaniment of dumbness):— × altogether, cease, conceal, be deaf, devise, ear, graven, imagine, leave off speaking, hold peace, plow (-er, -man), be quiet, rest, practise secretly, keep silence, be silent, speak not a word, be still, hold tongue, worker.

2791. חֶרֶשׁ, **cheresh,** *kheh´-resh*; from 2790; magical *craft*; also *silence*:—cunning, secretly.

2792. חֶרֶשׁ, **Cheresh,** *kheh´-resh*; the same as 2791; *Cheresh,* a Levite:—Heresh.

2793. חֹרֶשׁ, **chôresh,** *kho´-resh*; from 2790; a *forest* (perhaps as furnishing the material for fabric):—bough, forest, shroud, wood.

2794. חֹרֵשׁ, **chôrêsh,** *kho-rashe´*; active participle of 2790; a *fabricator* or mechanic:—artificer.

2795. חֵרֵשׁ, **chêrêsh,** *khay-rashe*; from 2790; *deaf* (whether literal or spiritual):—deaf.

2796. חָרָשׁ, **chârâsh,** *khaw-rawsh´*; from 2790; a *fabricator* of any material:—artificer, (+) carpenter, craftsman, engraver, maker, + mason, skilful, (+) smith, worker, workman, such as wrought.

A masculine noun meaning craftsman, artisan, and engraver. This Hebrew word denotes a craftsman who is skilled in a given medium. It appears in reference to one skilled in metalwork (1Ch 29:5; Hos 13:2); one skilled in woodwork (1Ch 14:1; Isa 40:20); and one skilled in stonework (Ex 28:11). More broadly, the term is applied to those who make their living by fashioning idols (Isa 45:16); or one highly skilled in his or her vocation (Eze 21:31[36]).

2797. חַרְשָׁא, **Charshâ',** *khar-shaw´*; from 2792; *magician; Charsha,* one of the Nethinim:—Harsha.

2798. חֲרָשִׁים, **Chărâshîym,** *khar-aw-sheem´*; plural of 2796; *mechanics,* the name of a valley in Jerusalem:—Charashim, craftsmen.

2799. חֲרֹשֶׁת, **chărôsheth,** *khar-o´-sheth*; from 2790; mechanical *work*:—carving, cutting.

2800. חֲרֹשֶׁת, **Chărôsheth,** *khar-o´-sheth*; the same as 2799; *Charosheth,* a place in Palestine:—Harosheth.

2801. חָרַת, **chârath,** *khaw-rath´*; a primitive root; to *engrave*:—graven.

2802. חֶרֶת, **Chereth,** *kheh´-reth*; from 2801 [but equivalent to 2793]; *forest; Chereth,* a thicket in Palestine:—Hereth.

2803. חָשַׁב, **châshab,** *khaw-shab´*; a primitive root; (properly) to *plait* or interpenetrate, i.e. (literal) to *weave* or (generally) to *fabricate*; (figurative) to *plot* or contrive (usually in a malicious sense); hence (from the mental effort) to *think, regard, value, compute*:—(make) account (of), conceive, consider, count, cunning (man, work, workman), devise, esteem, find out, forecast, hold, imagine, impute, invent, be like, mean, purpose, reckon (-ing be made), regard, think.

A verb meaning to think, to devise, to reckon, to regard, to invent, to consider, to be accounted, to consider, to reckon oneself. When the subject of this verb is God, the verb means to consider, to devise, to plan, to reckon. Job cried out to God and asked why God considered him His enemy (Job 13:24; 33:10); however, Job was falsely accusing his Creator. Through the evil actions of Joseph's brothers, God had intended good for all of them (Ge 50:20; Ps 40:17[18]). Against a wicked people, the Lord planned destruction (Jer 18:11; Mic 2:3). God also "reckoned" Abraham's faith as righteousness (Ge 15:6).

When humans are the subjects of this verb, the word has similar meanings: the king of Assyria thought he would destroy many nations (Isa 10:7); people devised or planned evil (Ge 50:20; Ps 35:4; Eze 38:10); Shimei begged David not to reckon his behaviour as sin against him (2Sa 19:19[20]; Ps 32:2). In addition, the word is used to mean to regard or to invent: the Medes did not esteem gold or silver as the Persians did (Isa 13:17); and the Servant of Isaiah's passage was not highly esteemed by men (Isa 53:3). God endowed people with the ability to invent new things, such as artistic and practical devices (Ex 31:4; 35:32, 35; 2Ch 2:14[13]); and instruments for music (Am 6:5).

When the verb is passive, the word expresses being valuable or being considered. Silver was not considered valuable in Solomon's reign (1Ki 10:21). In the time of Israel's wandering, the Emites were reckoned to be Rephaites or Moabites (Dt 2:11, 20).

This verb can also mean to plot, to think upon, to think out something. A person could think out his or her course of life (Pr 16:9; Hos 7:15); the evil person in Da 11:24 plotted the overthrow of all resistance to him; the boat that Jonah shipped out in came to the point of destruction in the storm (Jnh 1:4, lit., "it was thinking to be destroyed").

2804. חֲשַׁב, chăshab, *khash-ab´*; (Chaldee); corresponding to 2803; to *regard*:—repute.

2805. חֵשֶׁב, chêsheb, *khay´-sheb*; from 2803; a *belt* or strap (as being interlaced):—curious girdle.

2806. חַשְׁבַּדָּנָה, Chashbaddânâh, *khash-bad-daw´-naw*; from 2803 and 1777; *considerate judge; Chas-baddanah*, an Israelite:—Hasbadana.

2807. חֲשֻׁבָה, Chăshubâh, *khash-oo-baw´*; from 2803; *estimation; Chashubah*, an Israelite:—Hashubah.

2808. חֶשְׁבּוֹן, cheshbôwn, *khesh-bone´*; from 2803; (properly) *contrivance*; (by implication) *intelligence*:—account, device, reason.

2809. חֶשְׁבּוֹן, Cheshbôwn, *khesh-bone´*; the same as 2808; *Cheshbon*, a place East of the Jordan:—Heshbon.

2810. חִשָּׁבוֹן, chishshâbôwn, *khish-shaw-bone´*; from 2803; a *contrivance*, i.e. actual (a warlike *machine*) or mental (a *machination*):—engine, invention.

2811. חֲשַׁבְיָה, Chăshabyâh, *khash-ab-yaw´*; or חֲשַׁבְיָהוּ, **Chăshabyâhûw,** *khash-ab-yaw´-hoo*; from 2803 and 3050; *Jah has regarded; Chashabjah*, the name of nine Israelites:—Hashabiah.

2812. חֲשַׁבְנָה, Chăshabnâh, *khash-ab-naw´*; feminine of 2808; *inventiveness; Chashnah*, an Israelite:—Hashabnah.

2813. חֲשַׁבְנְיָה, Chăshabnᵉyâh, *khash-ab-neh-yaw´*; from 2808 and 3050; *thought of Jah; Chashabnejah*, the name of two Israelites:—Hashabniah.

2814. חָשָׁה, châshâh, *khaw-shaw´*; a primitive root; to *hush* or keep quiet:—hold peace, keep silence, be silent, (be) still.

2815. חַשּׁוּב, Chashshûwb, *khash-shoob´*; from 2803; *intelligent; Chashshub*, the name of two or three Israelites:—Hashub, Hasshub.

2816. חֲשׁוֹךְ, chăshôwk, *khash-oke´*; (Chaldee); from a root corresponding to 2821; the *dark*:—darkness.

2817. חֲשׂוּפָא, Chăśûwphâ', *khas-oo-faw´*; or חֲשֻׂפָא, **Chăśuphâ',** *khas-oo-faw´*; from 2834; *nakedness; Chasupha*, one of the Nethinim:—Hashupha, Hasupha.

2818. חֲשַׁח, chăshach, *khash-akh´*; (Chaldee); a collateral root to one corresponding to 2363 in the sense of *readiness*; to *be necessary* (from the idea of *convenience*) or (transitive) to *need*:—careful, have need of.

2819. חַשְׁחוּ, chashchûw, *khash-khoo´*; from a root corresponding to 2818; *necessity*:—be needful.

2820. חָשַׂךְ, châśak, *khaw-sak´*; a primitive root; to *restrain* or (reflexive) *refrain*; (by implication) to *refuse, spare, preserve*; also (by interch. with 2821) to *observe*:—assuage, × darken, forbear, hinder, hold back, keep (back), punish, refrain, reserve, spare, withhold.

2821. חָשַׁךְ, châshak, *khaw-shak´*; a primitive root; to *be dark* (as *withholding* light); (transitive) to *darken*:—be black, be (make) dark, darken, cause darkness, be dim, hide.

A verb meaning to be dark, to grow dim, to be black, to hide, to obscure. The primary meaning of the word is to darken. It is used to describe God's bringing about nightfall (Am 5:8); the deterioration of sight (La 5:17); the covering of the earth with insects so as to obscure the ground (Ex 10:15); the sullying of wisdom by foolishness (Job 38:2); the act of concealing from view (Ps 139:12). Poetically, the word denotes the change in one's countenance in response to abject fear or distress (Ecc 12:3).

2822. חֹשֶׁךְ, chôshek, *kho-shek´*; from 2821; the *dark*; hence (literal) *darkness*; (figurative) *misery, destruction, death, ignorance, sorrow, wickedness*:—dark (-ness), night, obscurity.

A masculine noun meaning darkness. As in English, the word has many symbolic uses. In its first occurrence, it is associated with disorder (Ge 1:2) and is distinguished and separated from light (Ge 1:4). In subsequent uses, whether used in a physical or a symbolic sense, it describes confusion and uncertainty (Job 12:25; 37:19); evil done in secret (Job 24:16; Pr 2:13; Eze 8:12); obscurity, vanity, things forgotten (Job 3:4; 10:21; Ecc 6:4); death (1Sa 2:9; Ps 88:12[13]). Although God created darkness (Isa 45:7) and uses it to judge His enemies (Ex 10:21, 22; figuratively, Ps 35:6), He enlightens the darkness of His people (Isa 9:2[1]); bringing them out of desperate situations (Ps 107:10, 14; Mic 7:8); observing secret actions (Job 34:22; Ps 139:11, 12); and giving insight and freedom (Isa 29:18; 42:7).

2823. חָשֹׁךְ, châshôk, *khaw-shoke´*; from 2821; *dark* (figurative i.e. *obscure*):—mean.

2824. חֶשְׁכָה, cheshkâh, *khesh-kaw´*; from 2821; *darkness*:—dark.

A feminine noun meaning dark or obscure. This Hebrew word is the construct form of the word *chăshêkâh* (2825). The psalmist alone uses this word in reference to the "dark waters" surrounding the Lord's pavilion (Ps 18:11[12]). The vivid picture is that of the murky darkness of extremely deep water. This imagery suggests the mystical, almost ethereal, gulf between the supernatural presence of the Holy One of Israel and the natural order.

2825. חֲשֵׁכָה, chăshêkâh, *khash-ay-kaw´*; or חֲשֵׁיכָה, **chăshêykâh,** *khash-ay-kaw´*; from 2821; *darkness*; (figurative) *misery*:—darkness.

A feminine noun meaning darkness. The word is similar in meaning to *chôshek* (2822). It refers to the experience of Abraham when God revealed to him the coming slavery of his descendants (Ge 15:12); to the failure of the wicked to see God's standards and that results in disorder for them (Ps 82:5; Isa 8:22); to the darkness sometimes surrounding persons that requires them to trust in God (Isa 50:10); He can see through darkness as well as light (Ps 139:12).

2826. חָשַׁל, châshal, *khaw-shal´*; a primitive root; to *make* (intransitive *be*) *unsteady*, i.e. *weak*:—feeble.

2827. חֲשַׁל, chăshal, *khash-al´*; (Chaldee); a root corresponding to 2826; to *weaken*, i.e. *crush*:—subdue.

2828. חָשֻׁם, Châshum, *khaw-shoom´*; from the same as 2831; *enriched; Chashum*, the name of two or three Israelites:—Hashum.

2829. חֶשְׁמוֹן, Cheshmôwn, *khesh-mone´*; the same as 2831; *opulent; Cheshmon*, a place in Palestine:—Heshmon.

2830. חַשְׁמַל, chashmal, *khash-mal´*; of uncertian derivation; probably *bronze* or polished spectrum metal:—amber.

2831. חַשְׁמַן, chashman, *khash-man´*; from an unused root (probably meaning *firm* or *capacious* in resources); apparently *wealthy*:—princes.

A noun which occurs in the plural in Ps 68:31[32]. It is translated "ambassador," but its meaning and derivation are unknown.

2832. חַשְׁמֹנָה, Chashmônâh, *khash-mo-naw´*; feminine of 2831; *fertile; Chasmonah*, a place in the Desert:—Hashmonah.

2833. חֹשֶׁן, chôshen, *kho´-shen*; from an unused root probably meaning to *contain* or *sparkle*; perhaps a *pocket* (as holding the Urim and Thummim), or *rich* (as containing gems), used only of the *gorget* of the highpriest:—breastplate.

2834. חָשַׂף, châśaph, *khaw-saf´*; a primitive root; to *strip* off, i.e. generally to *make naked* (for exertion or in disgrace), to *drain* away or *bail* up (a liquid):—make bare, clean, discover, draw out, take, uncover.

2835. חָשִׂף, châśiph, *khaw-seef´*; from 2834; (properly) *drawn off*, i.e. separated; hence a small *company* (as divided from the rest):—little flock.

2836. חָשַׁק, châshaq, *khaw-shak´*; a primitive root; to *cling*, i.e. *join*, (figurative) to *love, delight* in; elliptically (or by interchanging for 2820) to *deliver*:—have a delight, (have a) desire, fillet, long, set (in) love.

A verb meaning to be attached to, to love, to delight in, to bind. Laws in Deuteronomy described the procedure for taking a slave woman to whom one has become attached as a wife (Dt 21:11). Shechem's soul longed after and delighted in Dinah, who was an Israelite (Ge 34:8). God's binding love for Israel is described as unmerited love (Dt 7:7). Hezekiah describes the figurative way in which God's love for his soul delivered him by casting all his sins behind His back (Isa 38:17).

2837. חֵשֶׁק, chêsheq, *khay´-shek*; from 2836; *delight*:—desire, pleasure.

A noun meaning a desired thing. Three of its uses referred to Solomon's building projects. He was able to build the Temple and the other constructions that he desired (1Ki 9:1, 19; 2Ch 8:6). Isa 21:4 implied that the prophet desired Babylon's destruction, but the passage goes on to say that what he desired was so horrific that it terrified him.

2838. חָשֻׁק, châshuq, *khaw-shook´*; or **חָשׁוּק, châ-shûwq,** *khaw-shook´*; passive participle of 2836; *attached*, i.e. a fence-*rail* or rod connecting the posts or pillars:—fillet.

2839. חִשֻּׁק, chishshuq, *khish-shook´*; from 2836; *conjoined*, i.e. a wheel-*spoke* or rod connecting the hub with the rim:—felloe.

2840. חִשֻּׁר, chishshur, *khish-shoor´*; from an unused root meaning to *bind* together; *combined*, i.e. the *nave* or hub of a wheel (as holding the spokes together):—spoke.

2841. חַשְׁרָה, chashrâh, *khash-raw´*; from the same as 2840; (properly) a *combination* or gathering, i.e. of watery *clouds*:—dark.

2842. חָשַׁשׁ, châshash, *khaw-shash´*; by variation for 7179; dry *grass*:—chaff.

2843. חֻשָׁתִי, Chushâthîy, *khoo-shaw-thee´*; patronymic from 2364; a *Chushathite* or descendant of Chushah:—Hushathite.

2844. חַת, chath, *khath*; from 2865; (concrete) *crushed*; also *afraid*; (abstract) *terror*:—broken, dismayed, dread, fear.

2845. חֵת, Chêth, *khayth*; from 2865; *terror; Cheth*, an aboriginal Canaanite:—Heth.

2846. חָתָה, châthâh, *khaw-thaw´*; a primitive root; to lay *hold* of; especially to *pick* up fire:—heap, take (away).

2847. חִתָּה, chittâh, *khit-taw´*; from 2865; *fear*:—terror.

A feminine noun meaning terror, great fear. The Lord sent terror before Jacob into the land of Canaan as he returned from Mesopotamia so he and his family could pass through without being attacked by the native population (Ge 35:5).

2848. חִתּוּל, chittûwl, *khit-tool´*; from 2853; *swathed*, i.e. a *bandage*:—roller.

2849. חַתְחַת, chathchath, *khath-khath´*; from 2844; *terror*:—fear.

A noun meaning terror. It occurs in the plural in Ecc 12:5, referring to terrors on the road. It is part of a list of coming negative situations. The word is derived from the verbal root *châthath* (2865), meaning to be dismayed or to be shattered.

2850. חִתִּי, Chittîy, *khit-tee´*; patronymic from 2845; a *Chittite*, or descendant of Cheth:—Hittite, Hittites.

2851. חִתִּית, chittîyth, *khit-teeth´*; from 2865; *fear*:—terror.

A feminine noun meaning terror. This word is found exclusively in Ezekiel's writings where he described the reign of terror that powerful nations and cities brought on the Promised Land. For example, in Ezekiel's oracles to the nations, he described the terror that would come on Tyre when it was destroyed (Eze 26:17). When Assyria's slain army fell to the sword, they could no longer cause terror in the land (Eze 32:23).

2852. חָתַךְ, châthak, *khaw-thak´*; a primitive root; (properly) to *cut* off, i.e. (figurative) to *decree*:—determine.

2853. חָתַל, châthal, *khaw-thal´*; a primitive root; to *swathe*:—× at all, swaddle.

2854. חֲתֻלָּה, chăthullâh, *khath-ool-law´*; from 2853; a *swathing* cloth (figurative):—swaddling band.

2855. חֶתְלֹן, Chethlôn, *kheth-lone´*; from 2853; *enswathed; Chethlon*, a place in Palestine:—Hethlon.

2856. חָתַם, châtham, *khaw-tham´*; a primitive root; to *close* up; especially to *seal*:—make an end, mark, seal (up), stop.

2857. חֲתַם, chătham, *khath-am´*; (Chaldee); a root corresponding to 2856; to *seal*:—seal.

2858. חֹתֶמֶת, chôthemeth, *kho-the-meth*; feminine active participle of 2856; a *seal*:—signet.

2859. חָתַן, châthan, *khaw-than´*; a primitive root; to *give* (a daughter) *away* in marriage; hence (general) to *contract affinity* by marriage:—join in affinity, father in law, make marriages, mother in law, son in law.

2860. חָתָן, châthân, *khaw-thawn´*; from 2859; a *relative* by marriage (especially through the bride); (figurative) a *circumcised* child (as a species of religious espousal):—bridegroom, husband, son in law.

2861. חֲתֻנָּה, chăthunnâh, *khath-oon-naw´*; from 2859; a *wedding*:—espousal.

2862. חָתַף, châthaph, *khaw-thaf´*; a primitive root; to *clutch*:—take away.

2863. חֶתֶף, chetheph, *kheh´-thef*; from 2862; (properly) *rapine*; (figurative) *robbery*:—prey.

2864. חָתַר, châthar, *khaw-thar´*; a primitive root; to *force* a passage, as by burglary; figuratively with oars:—dig (through), row.

2865. חָתַת, châthath, *khaw-thath´*; a primitive root; (properly) to *prostrate*; hence to *break* down, either (literal) by violence, or (figurative) by confusion and fear:—abolish, affright, be (make) afraid, amaze, beat down, discourage, (cause to) dismay, go down, scare, terrify.

A verb meaning to be shattered, to be dismayed, to dismay, to shatter, to scare. The base meaning is probably breaking or shattering like a bow (Jer 51:56); or of the drought-cracked ground (Jer 14:4). Figuratively, it refers to nations shattered by God (Isa 7:8). It is also used with a intensive and causative meaning to scare, to terrify, or to dismay (Isa 30:31). Job said that God terrified him with dreams (Job 7:14). God's name can also cause dismay (Mal 2:5) where it is parallel to the word *yârê'* (3372).

2866. חֲתַת, chăthath, *khath-ath´*; from 2865; *dismay*:—casting down.

2867. חֲתַת, Chăthath, *khath-ath´*; the same as 2866; *Chathath*, an Israelite:—Hathath.

2868. טְאֵב, t^{e}'êb, *teh-abe´*; (Chaldee); a primitive root; to *rejoice*:—be glad.

2869. טָב, **ṭâb,** *tawb*; (Chaldee); from 2868; the same as 2896; *good*:—fine, good.

2870. טָבְאֵל, **ṭâbᵉʼêl,** *taw-beh-ale´*; from 2895 and 410; *pleasing* (to) *God; Tabeël*, the name of a Syrian and of a Persian:—Tabeal, Tabeel.

2871. טָבוּל, **ṭâbûwl,** *taw-bool´*; passive participle of 2881; (properly) *dyed*, i.e. a *turban* (probably as of *coloured* stuff):—dyed attire.

2872. טַבּוּר, **ṭabbûwr,** *tab-boor´*; from an unused root meaning to *pile* up; (properly) *accumulated*; i.e. (by implication) a *summit*:—middle, midst.

2873. טָבַח, **ṭâbach,** *taw-bakh´*; a primitive root; to *slaughter* (animals or men):—kill, (make) slaughter, slay.

A verb meaning to slaughter. It signifies the slaughter of livestock to prepare it for food (Ge 43:16; Ex 22:1[21:37]; 1Sa 25:11). The Hebrew word *zâbach* (2076), in contrast, signifies slaughtering livestock for sacrifice. Slaughter was used as a picture of destruction, whether attempted against righteous people (Ps 37:14; Jer 11:19) or brought on those being judged by God (La 2:21; Eze 21:10[15]). The slaughter of lambs, which do not comprehend or expect slaughter, symbolized an unexpected destruction (Jer 11:19). In Pr 9:2, the slaughtering of livestock symbolizes a feast prepared by wisdom.

2874. טֶבַח, **ṭebach,** *teh´-bakh*; from 2873; (properly) something *slaughtered*; hence a *beast* (or *meat*, as butchered); (abstract) *butchery* (or [concrete] a place of slaughter):—× beast, slaughter, × slay, × sore.

A masculine noun meaning slaughter. Originally, the term referred to the actual slaughtering of animals for food (Ge 43:16; Pr 9:2); however, this term has also been used metaphorically. It describes the condition of a man seduced by an adulteress (Pr 7:22), as well as the slaughter of the Suffering Servant (Isa 53:7). Furthermore, it characterizes the destinies of Edom (Isa 34:6); Moab (Jer 48:15); Babylon (Jer 50:27); and all those who forsake God (Isa 34:2; 65:12). A parallel term is *zebach* (2077), meaning slaughtering for a sacrifice.

2875. טֶבַח, **Ṭebach,** *teh´-bakh*; the same as 2874; *massacre; Tebach*, the name of a Mesopotamian and of an Israelite:—Tebah.

2876. טַבָּח, **ṭabbâch,** *tab-bawkh´*; from 2873; (properly) a *butcher*; hence a *lifeguardsman* (because acting as executioner); also a *cook* (as usually slaughtering the animal for food):—cook, guard.

2877. טַבָּח, **ṭabbâch,** *tab-bawkh´*; (Chaldee); the same as 2876; a *lifeguardsman*:—guard.

2878. טִבְחָה, **ṭibchâh,** *tib-khaw´*; feminine of 2874 and meaning the same:—flesh, slaughter.

A feminine noun meaning slaughtered meat, a slaughter. In 1Sa, Nabal questioned why he should give his food to David and his men (1Sa 25:11). But in Ps 44:22[23] and Jer 12:3, it is a generic term for slaughter. In both passages, it compared the punishment of people to the slaughtering of sheep. See the cognate verb *ṭâbach* (2873).

2879. טַבָּחָה, **ṭabbâchâh,** *tab-baw-khaw´*; feminine of 2876; a female *cook*:—cook.

2880. טִבְחַת, **Ṭibchath,** *tib-khath´*; from 2878; *slaughter; Tibchath*, a place in Syria:—Tibhath.

2881. טָבַל, **ṭâbal,** *taw-bal´*; a primitive root; to *dip*:—dip, plunge.

A verb meaning to dip. The term is often connected with ritual behaviour. The priest was to dip his fingers, a live bird, cedar wood, hyssop, and scarlet yarn into blood for various ceremonies (Le 4:6, 17; 9:9; 14:6, 51). The clean person was to dip hyssop in water and sprinkle it for purification on unclean persons or things (Nu 19:18). It is used intransitively with the preposition *bᵉ* when Naaman dipped himself in the Jordan to be healed of leprosy (2Ki 5:14).

2882. טְבַלְיָהוּ, **Ṭᵉbalyâhûw,** *teb-al-yaw´-hoo*; from 2881 and 3050; *Jah has dipped; Tebaljah*, an Israelite:—Tebaliah.

2883. טָבַע, **ṭâbaʻ,** *taw-bah´*; a primitive root; to *sink*:—drown, fasten, settle, sink.

2884. טַבָּעוֹת, **Ṭabbâʻôwth,** *tab-baw-othe´*; plural of 2885; *rings; Tabbaoth*, one of the Nethinim:—Tabbaoth.

2885. טַבַּעַת, **ṭabbaʻath,** *tab-bah´-ath*; from 2883; (properly) a *seal* (as *sunk* into the wax), i.e. *signet* (for sealing); hence (general) a *ring* of any kind:—ring.

2886. טַבְרִמּוֹן, **Ṭabrimmôwn,** *tab-rim-mone´*; from 2895 and 7417; *pleasing* (to) *Rimmon; Tabrimmon*, a Syrian:—Tabrimmon.

2887. טֵבֵת, **Ṭêbeth,** *tay´-beth*; probably of foreign derivation; *Tebeth*, the tenth Hebrew month:—Tebeth.

2888. טַבַּת, **Ṭabbath,** *tab-bath´*; of uncertain derivation; *Tabbath*, a place East of the Jordan:—Tabbath.

2889. טָהוֹר, **ṭâhôwr,** *haw-hore´*; or טָהֹר, **ṭâhôr,** *taw-hore´*; from 2891; *pure* (in a physical, chemical, ceremonial or moral sense):—clean, fair, pure (-ness).

An adjective meaning clean, pure, genuine. This word is used ninety times in the OT, primarily to distinguish things that were culturally pure, capable of being used in, or taking part in the religious rituals of Israel. The Lord decreed that Israel must mark off the clean from the unclean (Le 10:10; 11:47; Job 14:4). Persons could be ceremonially clean or unclean (Dt 12:15). A human corpse was especially defiling, and contact with it made a person unclean for seven days (Nu 19:11). When persons were clean, they could eat clean meat, but an unclean person could not (Le 7:19). Certain animals were considered ceremonially clean (Ge 7:2) and needed by Noah and his family for sacrifices after the flood (Ge 8:20). Ceremonially clean birds were used in various rituals (Le 14:4).

Clean things were considered normal; unclean things were considered polluted, but they could be restored to their state of purity (Le 11—15). Some things, however, were permanently unclean, such as unclean animals (Le 11:7, 26, 29–31). Other things were temporarily unclean. A woman in her period (Le 12:2) and a person with an infectious disease (Le 13:8) could be cleansed and be clean again (Le 12:4; 14:7); spring water could be considered as clean; even seed could be clean or unclean depending on whether a dead carcass had fallen on it while it was dry or wet (Le 11:36–38). Leprosy made a person unclean (Le 13:45, 46).

God expected His people to be morally pure and to imitate Him (Hab 1:13). This word served to express that state. Clean hands merited God's favour (Job 17:9), and pure words were pleasing to the Lord. God judged a sacrifice's value by the quality of the offerer's heart (Ps 51:10[12]); thus, David prayed for a pure heart.

The root meaning of the word shines through in its use to describe the quality of metals and other items. Pure gold was used in the construction of the Ark of the Covenant and many other items (Ex 25:11, 17; 28:14; 30:3); pure frankincense was prepared for use on the altar of incense (Ex 30:34, 35; 37:29). The fear of the Lord was proclaimed pure and therefore endured forever. It guided the psalmist to know God (Ps 19:9[10]).

2890. טְהוֹר, **ṭᵉhôwr,** *teh-hore´*; from 2891; *purity*:—pureness.

A masculine noun meaning cleanness. This word occurs only in Pr 22:11. As it is written in Hebrew, it is unpronounceable and appears to be a misspelling of the adjective *ṭâhôwr* (2889). However, the noun "cleanness," fits much better than the adjective "clean," both grammatically and contextually (cf. Pr 23:7, 8) and is the choice of the King James Version. Loving cleanness of heart (rather than "loving [the] clean of heart") results in graceful speech.

2891. טָהֵר, **ṭâhêr,** *taw-hare´*; a primitive root; (properly) to *be bright*; i.e. (by implication) to *be pure* ([physically] *sound, clear, unadulterated*; [Levitical] *uncontaminated*; [moral] *innocent* or *holy*):—be (make, make self, pronounce) clean, cleanse (self), purge, purify (-ier, self).

A verb meaning to be clean, to make clean, to be pure, to make pure. The term occurs most frequently in Leviticus where it was used for ritual cleansing of either things or persons (Le 14:48; 16:19; 22:7). The OT also speaks of ritual cleansing performed on persons within the sphere of false worship (Isa 66:17; Eze 22:24). Animals were not made clean (like people), for animals were either clean or unclean by nature; the concept did not apply to plants at all. Sometimes cleanness had a moral dimension that, of course, did not exclude the spiritual. One was not to think that persons made themselves clean nor that their cleanness exceeded that of their Maker (Job 4:17; Pr 20:9). Exilic and postexilic prophets prophesied of a future purification for God's people like the purifying of silver (Jer 33:8; Eze 36:25; Mal 3:3).

2892. **טֹהַר, ṭôhar,** *to´-har*; from 2891; (literal) *brightness*; (ceremonial) *purification*:—clearness, glory, purifying.

A masculine noun meaning purity, pureness, clarity, luster. This word is from a verb meaning to be pure or to be clean, both physically and ceremonially. It is used to denote the lustrous quality of a clear sky (Ex 24:10); the glory of an individual (Ps 89:44[45]); and the purification cycle after childbirth (Le 12:4, 6).

2893. **טָהֳרָה, ṭohŏrâh,** *toh-or-aw´*; feminine of 2892; (ceremonial) *purification*; (moral) *purity*:— × is cleansed, cleansing, purification (-fying).

A feminine noun meaning cleansing, purification. The word refers to a ceremonial cleansing pronounced by a priest on one formerly unclean (Le 13:7). The cleansing from such things as leprosy (Le 14:2, 23, 32); issues relating to genital organs (Le 15:13); touching a dead body (Nu 6:9); and childbirth (Le 12:4, 5) required additional procedures such as washing clothes and bathing. The birth of a child rendered a woman unclean, remaining in the blood of her purification (i.e. extra bleeding in the days following childbirth) for a set time after which she brought a sacrifice to the priest (cf. Lk 2:24). Cleansing from leprosy involved an extensive ceremony (Le 14:1–32). These ceremonies promoted good hygiene, but in the days of Hezekiah, God pardoned those who were seeking Him but failed to maintain ceremonial cleanness (2Ch 30:19).

2894. **טֵאטֵא, ṭêʼṭêʼ,** *tay-tay´*; a primitive root; to *sweep away*:—sweep.

2895. **טוֹב, ṭôwb,** *tobe*; a primitive root, to *be* (transitive *do* or *make*) *good* (or *well*) in the widest sense:—be (do) better, cheer, be (do, seem) good, (make) goodly, × please, (be, do, go, play) well.

A verb meaning to be happy, to please, to be loved, to be favoured, to seem good, to be acceptable, to endure, to be valuable, to do well, to do right. It means to be happy or glad, such as when Nabal, husband of Abigail, was joyous from drinking too much (1Sa 25:36; 2Sa 13:28; Est 1:10). The word naturally expresses the idea of being loved or enjoying the favour of someone. Samuel grew up in favour before the Lord and people (1Sa 2:26). It is used with the idiom "in the eyes of" to express the idea of seeming good or advisable; Abner informed David of everything that was good in the eyes of Israel (2Sa 3:19; 15:26). The word is used to express the meaning of good, as when the Israelites asserted they were better off in Egypt than in the wilderness (Nu 11:18; cf. Dt 5:29). The idea of being better or being valuable is expressed several times using this word: Jephthah asked the Ammonites whether they were better than Balak, son of Zippor (Jgs 11:25); while the psalmist asserted that it was good for him to have been afflicted, for thereby he learned the Lord's decrees (Ps 119:71).

The verb is used four times in the causative stem to mean to deal rightly or to deal justly. The Lord informed David that he had done well to plan to build a temple for God (2Ch 6:8) and informed Jehu that he had performed his assassination of Ahab's house well (2Ki 10:30).

2896. **טוֹב, ṭôwb,** *tobe*; from 2895; *good* (as an adjective) in the widest sense; used likewise as a noun, both in the masculine and the feminine, the singular and the plural (*good*, a *good* or *good* thing, a *good* man or woman; the *good, goods* or *good* things, *good* men or women), also as an adverb (*well*):—beautiful, best, better, bountiful, cheerful, at ease, × fair (word), (be in) favour, fine, glad, good (deed, -lier, -liest, -ly, -ness, -s), graciously, joyful, kindly, kindness, liketh (best), loving, merry, × most, pleasant, + pleaseth, pleasure, precious, prosperity, ready, sweet, wealth, welfare, (be) well ([-favoured]).

An adjective meaning good, well-pleasing, fruitful, morally correct, proper, convenient. This word is frequently encountered in the OT and is roughly equivalent to the English word *good* in terms of its function and scope of meaning. It describes that which is appealing and pleasant to the senses (Nu 14:7; Est 1:11; Ps 52:9[11]); is useful and profitable (Ge 2:18; Zec 11:12); is abundant and plentiful (Ge 41:22; Jgs 8:32); is kind and benevolent (1Sa 24:18[19]; 2Ch 5:13; Na 1:7); is good in a moral sense as opposed to evil (Ge 2:17; Le 27:14; Ps 37:27); is proper and becoming (Dt 1:14; 1Sa 1:23; Ps 92:1[2]); bears a general state of well-being or happiness (Dt 6:24; Ecc 2:24); is the better of two alternatives (Ge 29:19; Ex 14:12; Jnh 4:3). The creation narrative of Ge 1 best embodies all these various elements of meaning when the Lord declares each aspect of His handiwork to be "good."

2897. **טוֹב, Ṭôwb,** *tobe*; the same as 2896; *good; Tob*, a region apparently East of the Jordan:—Tob.

2898. **טוּב, ṭûwb,** *toob*; from 2895; *good* (as a noun), in the widest sense, especially *goodness* ([superlatively concrete] the *best*), *beauty, gladness, welfare*:—fair, gladness, good (-ness, thing, -s), joy, go well with.

A masculine noun meaning property, goods, goodness, fairness, and beauty. The root concept of this noun is that of desirability for enjoyment. It is used to identify the personal property of an individual (Ge 24:10); the plentiful harvest of the land (Ne 9:36; Jer 2:7); items of superior quality and desirability (2Ki 8:9); inward joy (Isa 65:14); the manifest goodness of the Lord (Ex 33:19; Ps 25:7). Notably, the psalmist employs the word to describe the state of spiritual blessing (Ps 31:19[20]; 65:4[5]).

2899. **טוֹב אֲדֹנִיָּהוּ, Ṭôwb ʼĂdônîyyâhûw,** *tobe ado-nee-yah´-hoo*; from 2896 and 138; *pleasing* (to) *Adonijah; Tob-Adonijah*, an Israelite:—Tob-adonijah.

2900. **טוֹבִיָּה, Ṭôwbîyyâh,** *to-bee-yaw´*; or **טוֹבִיָּהוּ, Ṭôwbîyyâhûw,** *to-bee-yaw´-hoo*; from 2896 and 3050; *goodness of Jehovah; Tobijah*, the name of three Israelites and of one Samaritan:—Tobiah, Tobijah.

2901. **טָוָה, ṭâvâh,** *taw-vaw´*; a primitive root; to *spin*:—spin.

2902. **טוּחַ, ṭûwach,** *too´-akh*; a primitive root; to *smear*, especially with lime:—daub, overlay, plaister, smut.

2903. **טוֹטָפוֹת, ṭôwṭâphôwth,** *to-taw-foth´*; from an unused root meaning to *go around* or *bind*; a *fillet* for the forehead:—frontlet.

2904. **טוּל, ṭûwl,** *tool*; a primitive root; to *pitch* over or *reel*; hence (transitive) to *cast* down or out:—carry away, (utterly) cast (down, forth, out), send out.

2905. **טוּר, ṭûwr,** *toor*; from an unused root meaning to *range* in a regular manner; a *row*; hence a *wall*:—row.

2906. **טוּר, ṭûwr,** *toor*; (Chaldee); corresponding to 6697; a *rock* or hill:—mountain.

2907. **טוּשׂ, ṭûwś,** *toos*; a primitive root; to *pounce* as a bird of prey:—haste.

2908. **טְוָת, ṭᵉvâth,** *tev-awth´*; (Chaldee); from a root corresponding to 2901; *hunger* (as *twisting*):—fasting.

2909. **טָחָה, ṭâchâh,** *taw-khaw´*; a primitive root; to *stretch* a bow, as an *archer*:—[bow-] shot.

2910. **טֻחוֹת, ṭuchôwth,** *too-khoth´*; from 2909 (or 2902) in the sense of *overlaying*; (in the plural only) the *kidneys* (as being *covered*); hence (figurative) the inmost *thought*:—inward parts.

2911. **טְחוֹן, ṭᵉchôwn,** *tekh-one´*; from 2912; a hand *mill*; hence a *millstone*:—to grind.

2912. טָחַן, ṭâchan, *taw-khan´*; a primitive root; to *grind* meal; hence to *be a concubine* (that being their employment):—grind (-er).

2913. טַחֲנָה, ṭachănâh, *takh-an-aw´*; from 2912; a hand *mill*; hence (figurative) *chewing*:—grinding.

2914. טְחֹר, tᵉchôr, *tekh-ore´*; from an unused root meaning to *burn*; a *boil* or ulcer (from the inflammation), especially a tumor in the anus or pudenda (the piles):—emerod.

2915. טִיחַ, ṭîyach, *tee´-akh*; from (the equivalent of) 2902; mortar or *plaster*:—daubing.

2916. טִיט, ṭîyṭ, *teet*; from an unused root meaning apparently to *be sticky* [rather perhaps a denominative from 2894, through the idea of dirt to be *swept* away]; *mud* or *clay*; (figurative) *calamity*:—clay, dirt, mire.

2917. טִין, ṭîyn, *teen*; (Chaldee); perhaps by interchange for a word corresponding to 2916; *clay*:—miry.

2918. טִירָה, ṭîyrâh, *tee-raw´*; feminine of (an equivalent to) 2905; a *wall*; hence a *fortress* or a *hamlet*:—(goodly) castle, habitation, palace, row.

2919. טַל, ṭal, *tal*; from 2926; *dew* (as *covering* vegetation):—dew.

2920. טַל, ṭal, *tal*; (Chaldee); the same as 2919:—dew.

2921. טָלָא, ṭâlâʾ, *taw-law´*; a primitive root; (properly) to *cover* with pieces; i.e. (by implication) to *spot* or *variegate* (as tapestry):—clouted, with divers colours, spotted.

2922. טְלָא, tᵉlâʾ, *tel-aw´*; apparently from 2921 in the (original) sense of *covering* (for protection); a *lamb* [compare 2924]:—lamb.

2923. טְלָאִים, Ṭᵉlâʾîym, *tel-aw-eem´*; from the plural of 2922; *lambs; Telaim*, a place in Palestine:—Telaim.

2924. טָלֶה, ṭâleh, *taw-leh´*; by variation for 2922; a *lamb*:—lamb.

2925. טַלְטֵלָה, ṭalṭêlâh, *tal-tay-law´*; from 2904; *overthrow* or *rejection*:—captivity.

2926. טָלַל, ṭâlal, *taw-lal´*; a primitive root; (properly) to *strew* over, i.e. (by implication) to *cover* in or *plate* (with beams):—cover.

2927. טְלַל, tᵉlal, *tel-al´*; (Chaldee); corresponding to 2926; to *cover* with shade:—have a shadow.

2928. טֶלֶם, Ṭelem, *teh´-lem*; from an unused root meaning to *break* up or treat violently; *oppression; Telem*, the name of a place in Idumæa, also of a temple doorkeeper:—Telem.

2929. טַלְמוֹן, Ṭalmôwn, *tal-mone´*; from the same as 2728; *oppressive; Talmon*, a temple doorkeeper:—Talmon.

2930. טָמֵא, ṭâmêʾ, *taw-may´*; a primitive root; to *be foul*, especially in a ceremonial or moral sense (*contaminated*):—defile (self), pollute (self), be (make, make self, pronounce) unclean, × utterly.

A verb meaning to be unclean, to desecrate, to defile, to make impure. The main idea of the action was that of contaminating or corrupting, especially in the sight of God. The Levitical Law often spoke in terms of sexual, religious, or ceremonial uncleanness. Any object or individual who was not clean could not be acceptable to the Holy God of Israel. Examples of actions that caused a state of impurity would include eating forbidden food (Hos 9:4); worshiping idols (Ps 106:39; Hos 5:3); committing adultery or engaging in sexual relations outside of marriage (Ge 34:5; Nu 5:13; Eze 18:6); touching unclean objects or individuals (Le 5:3; 18:24; 19:31); and any action that violated the sacredness of the Lord (Jer 32:34). It was the duty of the priesthood to discern matters of impurity (Le 13:3; Hag 2:13) and to see that the strict rituals of purification were followed.

2931. טָמֵא, ṭâmêʾ, *taw-may´*; from 2930; *foul* in a religious sense:—defiled, + infamous, polluted (-tion), unclean.

An adjective meaning unclean. It can denote impurity or defilement (Isa 6:5; Eze 22:5). It can also refer to ritually unclean items such as people, things, foods, and places. The land east of the Jordan (Jos 22:19) and foreign lands (Am 7:17) were unclean in contrast to the land of Israel.

2932. טֻמְאָה, ṭumʾâh, *toom-aw´*; from 2930; religious *impurity*:—filthiness, unclean (-ness).

A feminine noun meaning uncleanness, filthy. It refers to the sexual impurity of a woman during the menstrual cycle (Nu 5:19; La 1:9). It can also denote any unclean thing from which the temple needed to be purified (2Ch 29:16). Finally, both ethical and religious uncleanness were dealt with: in the laws referring to proper behaviour (Le 16:16); and in the heart, referring to an unclean spirit that causes one to lie (Eze 24:13).

2933. טָמָה, ṭâmâh, *taw-maw´*; a collateral form of 2930; to *be impure* in a religious sense:—be defiled, be reputed vile.

A verb which occurs once in the Hebrew Bible (Job 18:3). It is translated "stopped up," "stupid," or possibly "unclean."

2934. טָמַן, ṭâman, *taw-man´*; a primitive root; to *hide* (by *covering* over):—hide, lay privily, in secret.

2935. טֶנֶא, ṭeneʾ, *teh´-neh*; from an unused root probably meaning to *weave*; a *basket* (of interlaced osiers):—basket.

2936. טָנַף, ṭânaph, *taw-naf´*; a primitive root; to *soil*:—defile.

2937. טָעָה, ṭâʿâh, *taw-aw´*; a primitive root; to *wander*; (causative) to *lead astray*:—seduce.

2938. טָעַם, ṭâʿam, *taw-am´*; a primitive root; to *taste*; (figurative) to *perceive*:—× but, perceive, taste.

2939. טְעַם, tᵉʿam, *teh-am´*; (Chaldee); corresponding to 2938; to *taste*; (causative) to *feed*:—make to eat, feed.

2940. טַעַם, ṭaʿam, *tah´-am*; from 2938; (properly) a *taste*, i.e. (figurative) *perception*; (by implication) *intelligence*; (transitive) a *mandate*:—advice, behaviour, decree, discretion, judgment, reason, taste, understanding.

A masculine noun meaning taste, judgment, discernment, discretion. The word is used only thirteen times in the OT but is a key word when considering the concept of taste, perception, or decree. It is used to describe the experience of taste: it describes the physical taste of manna as something like wafers or cakes made with honey (Ex 16:31); or as something made with olive oil (Nu 11:8); it also refers to tasteless food needing salt in order to be eaten (Job 6:6). The word has several abstract meanings. It can mean mental or spiritual perception, discretion, or discernment. David thanked Abigail for her good discretion that kept him from killing Nabal and his men (1Sa 25:33). This Hebrew word is ranked along with knowledge as something the psalmist wanted from the Lord (i.e. good discernment or judgment [Ps 119:66]); and in a famous proverb, the beautiful woman without discretion is unfavourably compared to a gold ring in a pig's snout (Pr 11:22). The word can also mean an oral or written proclamation (i.e. a decree). It depicts the proclamation of the king of Nineveh (Jnh 3:7). Finally, its Aramaic equivalent *ṭaʿam* (2941) means decree or command.

2941. טַעַם, ṭaʿam, *tah´-am*; (Chaldee); from 2939; (properly) a *taste*, i.e. (as in 2940) a judicial *sentence*:—account, × to be commanded, commandment, matter.

An Aramaic noun meaning taste, judgment, command. It is closely related to the Hebrew word of the same spelling (*ṭaʿam* [2940]) and is equivalent to the Aramaic noun *ṭĕʿêm* (2942). In Ezr 6:14, the word refers to a command of God; and therefore some argue this vocalization is a theological scribal distinction to differentiate between it and *ṭĕʿêm*. The determined use of *ṭaʿĕmâʾ* in Ezr 5:5 could be declined from either *ṭaʿam* or *ṭĕʿêm*.

2942. טְעֵם, tᵉʿêm, *teh-ame´*; (Chaldee); from 2939, and equivalent to 2941; (properly) *flavor*; (figurative) *judgment* (both subjective and objective); hence *account* (both subjective and objective):— + chancellor, + command, commandment, decree, + regard, taste, wisdom.

An Aramaic masculine noun meaning taste, judgment, command, flavor. Belshazzar held a great feast and tasted wine from the consecrated vessels of God's Temple (Da 5:2). When used figuratively, the word has the meaning of judgment or discretion, such as Daniel's counsel and wisdom to Nebuchadnezzar's chief guard (Da 2:14). This word is also used in relaying a command of God, such as the rebuilding of the Temple (Ezr 6:14), or of a person, as in the decree to worship the golden image of Nebuchadnezzar (Da 3:10).

2943. טָעַן, ṭâ'an, *taw-an´*; a primitive root; to *load* a beast:—lade.

2944. טָעַן, ṭâ'an, *taw-an´*; a primitive root; to *stab*:—thrust through.

2945. טַף, ṭaph, *taf*; from 2952 (perhaps referring to the *tripping* gait of children); a *family* (mostly used collectively in the singular):—(little) children (ones), families.

A masculine singular noun meaning child, little one. Though the term is sometimes used in a parallel construction with *bâniym* (plural of 1121; Dt 1:39), elsewhere it often denotes younger children. It is distinguished from young men, virgins (Eze 9:6), and sons (2Ch 20:13, "children"). It is often used in the formulaic pattern "men, women, and children" (Dt 2:34; 3:6; 31:12; Jer 40:7; 43:6), meaning everyone.

2946. טָפַח, ṭâphach, *taw-fakh´*; a primitive root; to *flatten* out or *extend* (as a tent); (figurative) to *nurse* a child (as *promotive* of growth); or perhaps a denominative from 2947, from *dandling* on the palms:—span, swaddle.

2947. טֶפַח, ṭephach, *teh´-fakh*; from 2946; a *spread* of the hand, i.e. a *palm-breadth* (not "span" of the fingers); (architecture) a *corbel* (as a supporting palm):—coping, hand-breadth.

2948. טֹפַח, ṭôphach, *to´-fakh*; from 2946 (the same as 2947):—hand-breadth (broad).

2949. טִפֻּח, ṭippuch, *tip-pookh´*; from 2946; *nursing*:—span long.

2950. טָפַל, ṭâphal, *taw-fal´*; a primitive root; (properly) to *stick* on as a patch; (figurative) to *impute* falsely:—forge (-r), sew up.

2951. טִפְסַר, ṭiphsar, *tif-sar´*; of foreign derivation; a military *governor*:—captain.

A noun, probably masculine, meaning a military commander. In Jer 51:27, it appears to refer to the supreme commander of an army called to oppose Babylon. In the only other occurrence, Na 3:17, it is plural and has a slightly different spelling. Here it refers to commanders in the army of Nineveh, the capital of Assyria. Interestingly, in both passages, comparison is made between military power and different kinds of locusts.

2952. טָפַף, ṭâphaph, *taw-faf´*; a primitive root; apparently to *trip* (with short steps) coquettishly:—mince.

2953. טְפַר, ṭᵉphar, *tef-ar´*; (Chaldee); from a root corresponding to 6852, and meaning the same as 6856; a finger-*nail*; also a *hoof* or *claw*:—nail.

2954. טָפַשׁ, ṭâphash, *taw-fash´*; a primitive root; (properly) apparently to *be thick*; (figurative) to *be stupid*:—be fat.

2955. טָפַת, Ṭâphath, *taw-fath´*; probably from 5197; a *dropping* (of ointment); *Taphath*, an Israelitess:—Taphath.

2956. טָרַד, ṭârad, *taw-rad´*; a primitive root; to *drive* on; (figurative) to *follow* close:—continual.

2957. טְרַד, ṭᵉrad, *ter-ad´*; (Chaldee); corresponding to 2956; to *expel*:—drive.

2958. טְרוֹם, ṭᵉrôwm, *ter-ome´*; a variation of 2962; *not yet*:—before.

2959. טָרַח, ṭârach, *taw-rakh´*; a primitive root; to *overburden*:—weary.

2960. טֹרַח, ṭôrach, *to´-rakh*; from 2959; a *burden*:—cumbrance, trouble.

2961. טָרִי, ṭârîy, *taw-ree´*; from an unused root apparently meaning to *be moist*; (properly) *dripping*; hence *fresh* (i.e. recently made such):—new, putrefying.

2962. טֶרֶם, ṭerem, *teh´-rem*; from an unused root apparently meaning to *interrupt* or *suspend*; (properly) *non-occurrence*; (used adverbially) *not yet* or *before*:—before, ere, not yet.

2963. טָרַף, ṭâraph, *taw-raf´*; a primitive root; to *pluck* off or *pull* to pieces; (causative) to *supply* with food (as in morsels):—catch, × without doubt, feed, ravin, rend in pieces, × surely, tear (in pieces).

2964. טֶרֶף, ṭereph, *teh´-ref*; from 2963; something *torn*, i.e. a fragment, e.g., a *fresh* leaf, *prey, food*:—leaf, meat, prey, spoil.

2965. טָרָף, ṭârâph, *taw-rawf´*; from 2963; recently *torn* off, i.e. *fresh*:—plucked off.

2966. טְרֵפָה, ṭᵉrêphâh, *ter-ay-faw´*; feminine (collective) of 2964; *prey*, i.e. flocks devoured by animals:—ravin, (that which was) torn (of beasts, in pieces).

2967. טַרְפְּלַי, Ṭarpᵉlay, *tar-pel-ah´ee*; (Chaldee); from a name of foreign derivation; a *Tarpelite* (collective) or inhabitant of Tarpel, a place in Assyria:—Tarpelites.

2968. יָאַב, yâ'ab, *yaw-ab´*; a primitive root; to *desire*:—long.

2969. יָאָה, yâ'âh, *yaw-aw´*; a primitive root; to *be suitable*:—appertain.

2970. יַאֲזַנְיָה, Ya'ăzanyâh, *yah-az-an-yaw´*; or **יַאֲזַנְיָהוּ, Ya'ăzanyâhûw,** *yah-az-an-yaw´-hoo*; from 238 and 3050; *heard of Jah; Jaazanjah*, the name of four Israelites:—Jaazaniah. Compare 3153.

2971. יָאִיר, Yâ'îyr, *yaw-ere´*; from 215; *enlightener; Jair*, the name of four Israelites:—Jair.

2972. יָאִרִי, Yâ'irîy, *yaw-ee-ree´*; patronymic from 2971; a *Jaïrite* or descendant of Jair:—Jairite.

2973. יָאַל, yâ'al, *yaw-al´*; a primitive root; (properly) to *be slack*, i.e. (figurative) to *be foolish*:—dote, be (become, do) foolish (-ly).

2974. יָאַל, yâ'al, *yaw-al´*; a primitive root [probably rather the same as 2973 through the idea of mental *weakness*]; (properly) to *yield*, especially *assent*; hence (positively) to *undertake* as an act of volition:—assay, begin, be content, please, take upon, × willingly, would.

A verb meaning to choose to do something. The focus of this verb is on the decision to act. This concept is expressed on three levels. On the first level, the individual shows a willingness to act a certain way, to accept an invitation (Ex 2:21; Jos 7:7; Jgs 19:6). On the next level, the individual is more active and voluntarily decides to act a certain way (Ge 18:27; Dt 1:5). On the final level, the individual is even more active and voluntarily decides to act a certain way with determination and resolve (Jos 17:12; Jgs 1:27, 35; Hos 5:11). This verb provides strong support for the theological concept of human free will because humanity is permitted to decide to act a certain way. God, however, will hold humanity responsible for those decisions and actions.

2975. יְאֹר, yᵉ'ôr, *yeh-ore´*; of Egyptian origin; a *channel*, i.e. a fosse, canal, shaft; specifically the *Nile*, as the one river of Egypt, including its collateral trenches; also the *Tigris*, as the main river of Assyria:—brook, flood, river, stream.

2976. יָאַשׁ, yâ'ash, *yaw-ash´*; a primitive root; to *desist*, i.e. (figurative) to *despond*:—(cause to) despair, one that is desperate, be no hope.

A verb meaning to despair. The word refers to despair in the sense that one concludes that something desirable is out of reach and usually stops working toward it. In 1Sa 27:1, David hoped Saul would despair of finding him when he fled to the Philistines. The word may refer to loss of hope in God or a false god (Isa 57:10; Jer 2:25; 18:12). It may also refer, similarly, to a loss of meaning in life (Ecc 2:20; cf. Php 1:21, 22). In Job 6:26, the word describes an emotional state of despair without immediately focusing on the cause of despair. In three passages, the word occurs in a passive sense as a statement or exclamation meaning "it is hopeless" (Isa 57:10; Jer 2:25; 18:12).

2977. **יֹאשִׁיָּה, Yô'shîyyâh,** *yo-she-yaw´*; or **יֹאשִׁיָּהוּ, Yô'shîyyâhûw,** *yo-she-yaw´-hoo*; from the same root as 803 and 3050; *founded of Jah; Joshijah*, the name of two Israelites:—Josiah.

2978. **יִאתוֹן, yi'thôwn,** *yi-thone´*; from 857; an *entry*:—entrance.

2979. **יְאָתְרַי, y^{e}'âthray,** *yeh-awth-rah´ee*; from the same as 871; *stepping; Jeätherai*, an Israelite:—Jeaterai.

2980. **יָבַב, yâbab,** *yaw-bab*; a primitive root; to *bawl*:—cry out.

2981. **יְבוּל, y^{e}bûwl,** *yeb-ool´*; from 2986; *produce*, i.e. a *crop* or (figurative) *wealth*:—fruit, increase.

2982. **יְבוּס, Y^{e}bûws,** *yeb-oos´*; from 947; *trodden*, i.e. threshing-place; *Jebus*, the aboriginal name of Jerusalem:—Jebus.

2983. **יְבוּסִי, Y^{e}bûwsîy,** *yeb-oo-see´*; patrial from 2982; a *Jebusite* or inhabitant of Jebus:—Jebusite (-s).

2984. **יִבְחַר, Yibchar,** *yib-khar´*; from 977; *choice; Jibchar*, an Israelite:—Ibhar.

2985. **יָבִין, Yâbîyn,** *yaw-bene´*; from 995; *intelligent; Jabin*, the name of two Canaanitish kings:—Jabin.

2986. **יָבַל, yâbal,** *yaw-bal´*; a primitive root; (properly) to *flow*; (causative) to *bring* (especially with pomp):—bring (forth), carry, lead (forth).

2987. **יְבַל, y^{e}bal,** *yeb-al´*; (Chaldee); corresponding to 2986; to *bring*:—bring, carry.

2988. **יָבָל, yâbâl,** *yaw-bawl*; from 2986; a *stream*:—[water-] course, stream.

2989. **יָבָל, Yâbâl,** *yaw-bawl´*; the same as 2988; *Jabal*, an antediluvian:—Jabal.

2990. **יַבֶּלֶת, yabbeleth,** *yab-bel-eth´*; from 2986; having *running* sores:—wen.

2991. **יִבְלְעָם, Yibl^{e}'âm,** *yib-leh-awm´*; from 1104 and 5971; *devouring people; Jibleäm*, a place in Palestine:—Ibleam.

2992. **יָבַם, yâbam,** *yaw-bam´*; a primitive root of doubtful meaning; used only as a denominative from 2993; to *marry* a (deceased) brother's widow:—perform the duty of a husband's brother, marry.

2993. **יָבָם, yâbâm,** *yaw-bawm´*; from (the original of) 2992; a *brother-in-law*:—husband's brother.

2994. **יְבָמָה, y^{e}bâmâh,** *yeb-aw´-maw*; feminine participle of 2992; a *sister-in-law*:— brother's wife, sister in law.

2995. **יַבְנְאֵל, Yabn^{e}'êl,** *yab-neh-ale´*; from 1129 and 410; *built of God; Jabneël*, the name of two places in Palestine:—Jabneel.

2996. **יַבְנֶה, Yabneh,** *yab-neh´*; from 1129; a *building; Jabneh*, a place in Palestine:—Jabneh.

2997. **יִבְנְיָה, Yibn^{e}yâh,** *yib-neh-yaw´*; from 1129 and 3050; *built of Jah; Jibnejah*, an Israelite:—Ibneiah.

2998. **יִבְנִיָּה, Yibnîyyâh,** *yib-nee-yaw´*; from 1129 and 3050; *building of Jah; Jibnijah*, an Israelite:—Ibnijah.

2999. **יַבֹּק, Yabbôq,** *yab-boke´*; probably from 1238; *pouring forth; Jabbok*, a river East of the Jordan:—Jabbok.

3000. **יְבֶרֶכְיָהוּ, Y^{e}berekyâhûw,** *yeb-eh-rek-yaw´-hoo*; from 1288 and 3050; *blessed of Jah; Jeberekjah*, an Israelite:—Jeberechiah.

3001. **יָבֵשׁ, yâbêsh,** *yaw-bashe´*; a primitive root; to *be ashamed, confused* or *disappointed*; also (as failing) to *dry* up (as water) or *wither* (as herbage):—be ashamed, clean, be confounded, (make) dry (up), (do) shame (-fully), × utterly, wither (away).

A verb meaning to be dried up, to be dry, to be withered. This common intransitive verb refers to the drying up and withering of plants, trees, grass, crops, and the earth itself after the flood (Ge 8:14). It also occurs with an intensive and causative sense meaning to dry, to wither. *Yahweh* dried the waters, particularly the sea (Jos 2:10; Ps 74:15; Isa 42:15; Jer 51:36; Na 1:4). It is used figuratively to denote God destroying Babylon (Eze 17:24).

3002. **יָבֵשׁ, yâbêsh,** *yaw-bashe´*; from 3001; *dry*:—dried (away), dry.

An adjective meaning dry, dried. The Nazarite vow prohibited partaking of the fruit of the vine, including dried grapes (Nu 6:3). The Israelites complained in the desert because they had no food like they did in Egypt; all they had to eat was manna, and their souls were dried up (Nu 11:6). A second use of dry is when it refers to chaff that breaks in pieces. It is used figuratively of Job, who was weary and worn out (Job 13:25).

3003. **יָבֵשׁ, Yâbêsh,** *yaw-bashe´*; the same as 3002 (also **יָבֵישׁ, Yâbêysh,** *yaw-bashe´*; often with the addition of 1568, i.e. *Jabesh of Gilad*); *Jabesh*, the name of an Israelite and of a place in Palestine:—Jabesh ([-Gilead]).

3004. **יַבָּשָׁה, yabbâshâh,** *yab-baw-shaw´*; from 3001; *dry* ground:—dry (ground, land).

A feminine noun meaning dry land. This word can be an adjective as well. In all uses, it is contrasted with water. It often describes land formerly covered with water, such as the land appearing on the third day of creation; the land on which the people of Israel crossed the Red Sea (Ex 14:16, 22, 29; Ps 66:6); and the land on which they crossed the Jordan (Jos 4:22). It also describes land onto which water is poured both literally (Ex 4:9) and as a figure of the Holy Spirit being poured on the descendants of Jacob (Isa 44:3).

3005. **יִבְשָׂם, Yibsâm,** *yib-sawm´*; from the same as 1314; *fragrant; Jibsam*, an Israelite:—Jibsam.

3006. **יַבֶּשֶׁת, yabbesheth,** *yab-beh´-sheth*; a variation of 3004; *dry* ground:—dry land.

A feminine noun meaning dry land. It is apparently identical to *yabbâshâh* (3004). This word occurs only twice. In Ex 4:9, it refers to land upon which water had been poured and subsequently had turned to blood. In Ps 95:5, it refers to dry land (in contrast to the sea), which the Lord's hands formed.

3007. **יַבֶּשֶׁת, yabbesheth,** *yab-beh´-sheth*; (Chaldee); corresponding to 3006; *dry* land:—earth.

An Aramaic feminine noun meaning earth. This noun, appearing only in Da 2:10, suggests any patch of dry land on which a person can stand. Thus, the word is taken to imply the whole planet or the entire world.

3008. **יִגְאָל, Yig'âl,** *yig-awl´*; from 1350; *avenger; Jigal*, the name of three Israelites:—Igal, Igeal.

3009. **יָגַב, yâgab,** *yaw-gab´*; a primitive root; to *dig* or plough:—husbandman.

3010. **יָגֵב, yâgêb,** *yaw-gabe´*; from 3009; a ploughed *field*:—field.

3011. **יָגְבְּהָה, Yogb^{e}hâh,** *yog-beh-haw´*; feminine from 1361; *hillock; Jogbehah*, a place East of the Jordan:—Jogbehah.

3012. **יִגְדַּלְיָהוּ, Yigdalyâhûw,** *yig-dal-yaw´-hoo*; from 1431 and 3050; *magnified of Jah; Jigdaljah*, an Israelite:—Igdaliah.

3013. **יָגָה, yâgâh,** *yaw-gaw´*; a primitive root; to *grieve*:—afflict, cause grief, grieve, sorrowful, vex.

3014. **יָגָה, yâgâh,** *yaw-gaw´*; a primitive root [probably rather the same as 3013 through the common idea of *dissatisfaction*]; to *push* away:—be removed.

3015. **יָגוֹן, yâgôwn,** *yaw-gohn´*; from 3013; *affliction*:—grief, sorrow.

3016. **יָגוֹר, yâgôwr,** *yaw-gore´*; from 3025; *fearful*:—afraid, fearest.

3017. יָגוּר, **Yâgûwr,** *yaw-goor´*; probably from 1481; a *lodging; Jagur,* a place in Palestine:—Jagur.

3018. יְגִיעַ, **yᵉgîyaʻ,** *yeg-ee´-ah*; from 3021; *toil*; hence a *work, produce, property* (as the result of labour):—labour, work.

3019. יָגִיעַ, **yâgîyaʻ,** *haw-ghee´-ah*; from 3021; *tired*:—weary.

3020. יָגְלִי, **Yoglîy,** *yog-lee´*; from 1540; *exiled; Jogli,* an Israelite:—Jogli.

3021. יָגַע, **yâgaʻ,** *yaw-gah´*; a primitive root; (properly) to *gasp*; hence to *be exhausted,* to *tire,* to *toil*:—faint, (make to) labour, (be) weary.

3022. יָגָע, **yâgâʻ,** *yaw-gaw´*; from 3021; *earnings* (as the product of toil):—that which he laboured for.

3023. יָגֵעַ, **yâgêaʻ,** *yaw-gay´-ah*; from 3021; *tired*; hence (transposed) *tiresome*:—full of labour, weary.

3024. יְגִיעָה, **yᵉgîyʻâh,** *yeg-ee-aw´*; feminine of 3019; *fatigue*:—weariness.

3025. יָגֹר, **yâgôr,** *yaw-gore´*; a primitive root; to *fear*:—be afraid, fear.

A verb meaning to fear, to be afraid. In comparison to the more common verb for fear, *yârê'* (3372), which often refers to a general sense of vulnerability (cf. Ge 15:1), *yâgôr* refers to fear of specific occurrences such as catching a disease (Dt 28:60); being reproached or scorned (Ps 119:39); or being delivered into the power of specific people (Jer 39:17). It describes the fear of God in Dt 9:19 but focuses on the specific possibility of God destroying Israel.

3026. יְגַר שָׂהֲדוּתָא, **Yᵉgar Śahădûwthâ',** *yegar´ sah-had-oo-thaw´*; (Chaldee); from a word derived from an unused root (meaning to *gather*) and a derivative of a root corresponding to 7717; *heap of the testimony; Jegar-Sahadutha,* a cairn East of the Jordan:—Jegar-Sahadutha.

3027. יָד, **yâd,** *yawd*; a primitive word; a *hand* (the *open* one [indicating *power, means, direction,* etc.], in distinction from 3709, the *closed* one); used (as noun, adverb, etc.) in a great variety of applications, both literal and figurative, both proximate and remote [as follow]:— (+ be) able, × about, + armholes, at, axletree, because of, beside, border, × bounty, + broad, [broken-] handed, × by, charge, coast, + consecrate, + creditor, custody, debt, dominion, × enough, + fellowship, force, × from, hand [-staves, -y work], × he, himself, × in, labour, + large, ledge, [left-] handed, means, × mine, ministry, near, × of, × order, ordinance, × our, parts, pain, power, × presumptuously, service, side, sore, state, stay, draw with strength, stroke, + swear, terror, × thee, × by them, × themselves, × thine own, × thou, through, × throwing, + thumb, times, × to, × under, × us, × wait on, [way-] side, where, + wide, × with (him, me, you), work, + yield, × yourselves.

A feminine noun meaning hand, strength. This word frequently appears in the OT with literal, figurative, and technical uses. Literally, it implies the hand of a human being (Le 14:28; Jer 36:14) and occasionally the wrist (Ge 38:28). Metaphorically, it signifies strength or power (Dt 32:36; Isa 37:27); authority or right of possession (Ge 16:9; 2Ch 13:16); location or direction (Nu 24:24; Ps 141:6); the side of an object (1Sa 4:18); a fractional portion of the whole (Ge 47:24; Ne 11:1). In a technical sense, the word is used to identify the upright supports for the bronze laver (1Ki 7:35, 36); the tenons for the tabernacle (Ex 26:17); and an axle (1Ki 7:32, 33).

3028. יַד, **yad,** *yad*; (Chaldee); corresponding to 3027:—hand, power.

An Aramaic noun meaning hand, power, control, possession. The word corresponds to the Hebrew noun of the same spelling (3027) and refers to a literal hand (although not a human one) as writing (Da 5:5). From the ability of the hand to hold and manipulate objects, the word is used figuratively to describe control, power, or possession, such as Nebuchadnezzar's power over Israel (Ezr 5:12) and other people and animals (Da 2:38); God's power to do whatever He wishes (Da 4:35[32]); the lions' power to hurt a person (Da 6:27[28]; cf. 1Sa 17:37); the Jews' control over the rebuilding of the Temple (Ezr 5:8). The stone cut out without hands (Da 2:34) refers to a kingdom set up by God independently of human power (Da 2:45). In Ezr 6:12, the word refers to an attempt to gain power to change the edict of Darius.

3029. יְדָא, **yᵉdâ',** *yed-aw´*; (Chaldee); corresponding to 3034; to *praise*:—(give) thank (-s).

An Aramaic verb meaning to give thanks, to offer praise. Twice this word appears in the OT, both times in Daniel. It is solely directed to the Lord, signifying the thanks given to God for answered prayer (Da 2:23) and in reference to Daniel's daily devotional practice (Da 6:10[11]).

3030. יִדְאֲלָה, **Yid'ălâh,** *yid-al-aw´*; of uncertain derivation *Jidalah,* a place in Palestine:—Idalah.

3031. יִדְבָּשׁ, **Yidbâsh,** *yid-bawsh´*; from the same as 1706; perhaps *honeyed; Jidbash,* an Israelite:—Idbash.

3032. יָדַד, **yâdad,** *yaw-dad´*; a primitive root; (properly) to *handle* [compare 3034], i.e. to *throw,* e.g., lots:—cast.

3033. יְדִדוּת, **yᵉdidûwth,** *yed-ee-dooth´*; from 3039; (properly) *affection*; (concrete) a *darling* object:—dearly beloved.

A feminine noun meaning beloved, highly valued, dear one. It is derived from the word *yĕdiyd* (3039), which has a similar meaning. The word occurs only in Jer 12:7 where it describes Israel as beloved of God's soul but forsaken by Him and delivered to their enemies because they only pretended to return His love (Jer 12:1, 2).

3034. יָדָה, **yâdâh,** *yaw-daw´*; a primitive root; used only as denominative from 3027; (literal) to *use* (i.e. hold out) *the hand*; (physically) to *throw* (a stone, an arrow) at or away; especially to *revere* or *worship* (with extended hands); (intensive) to *bemoan* (by wringing the hands):—cast (out), (make) confess (-ion), praise, shoot, (give) thank (-ful, -s, -sgiving).

A verb meaning to acknowledge, to praise, to give thanks, to confess, to cast. The essential meaning is an act of acknowledging what is right about God in praise and thanksgiving (1Ch 16:34). It can also mean a right acknowledgment of self before God in confessing sin (Le 26:40) or of others in their God-given positions (Ge 49:8). It is often linked with the word *hâlal* (1984) in a hymnic liturgy of "thanking and praising" (1Ch 16:4; 23:30; Ezr 3:11; Ne 12:24, 46). This rightful, heavenward acknowledgment is structured in corporate worship (Ps 100:4; 107:1, 8, 15, 21, 31), yet is also part of personal lament and deliverance (Ps 88:11[10]). Several uses of *yâdâh* evidence an essence of motion or action (as something given), intensively referring twice to cast or to throw down (La 3:53; Zec 1:21 [2:4]), and once it means to shoot (as an arrow; Jer 50:14).

3035. יִדּוֹ, **Yiddôw,** *yid-do´*; from 3034; *praised; Jiddo,* an Israelite:—Iddo.

3036. יָדוֹן, **Yâdôwn,** *yaw-done´*; from 3034; *thankful; Jadon,* an Israelite:—Jadon.

3037. יַדּוּעַ, **Yaddûwaʻ,** *yad-doo´-ah*; from 3045; *knowing; Jadduä,* the name of two Israelites:—Jaddua.

3038. יְדוּתוּן, **Yᵉdûwthûwn,** *yed-oo-thoon´*; or יְדֻתוּן, **Yeduthûwn,** *yed-oo-thoon´*; or יְדִיתוּן, **Yedîythûwn,** *yed-ee-thoon´*; probably from 3034; *laudatory; Jedu-thun,* an Israelite:—Jeduthun.

3039. יְדִיד, **yâdîyd,** *yawd-eed´*; from the same as 1730; *loved*:—amiable, (well-) beloved, loves.

An adjective meaning beloved, well-loved. This word is often used in poetry. It is used mainly to describe a person who is beloved; for example, Moses called Benjamin the beloved of the Lord (Dt 33:12). Another use is to describe the loveliness of the tabernacle of the Lord (Ps 84:1[2]). A third use is its literal meaning, love. The psalmist calls his poem (Ps 45) a song of love.

3040. יְדִידָה, **Yᵉdîydâh,** *yed-ee-daw´*; feminine of 3039; *beloved; Jedidah,* an Israelitess:—Jedidah.

3041. יְדִידְיָה, **Yᵉdîydᵉyâh,** *yed-ee-deh-yaw´*; from 3039 and 3050; *beloved of Jah; Jedidejah,* a name of Solomon:—Jedidiah.

3042. **יְדָיָה, Yᵉdâyâh,** *yed-aw-yaw´*; from 3034 and 3050; *praised of Jah; Jedajah,* the name of two Israelites:—Jedaiah.

3043. **יְדִיעֲאֵל, Yᵉdîyʻăʼêl,** *yed-ee-ah-ale´*; from 3045 and 410; *knowing God; Jediaël,* the name of three Israelites:—Jediael.

3044. **יִדְלָף, Yidlâph,** *yid-lawf´*; from 1811; *tearful; Jidlaph,* a Mesopotamian:—Jidlaph.

3045. **יָדַע, yâdaʻ,** *yaw-dah´*; a primitive root; to *know* (properly to ascertain by *seeing*); used in a great variety of senses, figurative, literal, euphemism and inference (including *observation, care, recognition*; and causative *instruction, designation, punishment,* etc.) [as follow]:—acknowledge, acquaintance (-ted with), advise, answer, appoint, assuredly, be aware, [un-] awares, can [-not], certainly, for a certainty, comprehend, consider, × could they, cunning, declare, be diligent, (can, cause to) discern, discover, endued with, familiar friend, famous, feel, can have, be [ig-] norant, instruct, kinsfolk, kinsman, (cause to, let, make) know, (come to give, have, take) knowledge, have [knowledge], (be, make, make to be, make self) known, + be learned, + lie by man, mark, perceive, privy to, × prognosticator, regard, have respect, skilful, shew, can (man of) skill, be sure, of a surety, teach, (can) tell, understand, have [understanding], × will be, wist, wit, wot.

A verb meaning to know, to learn, to perceive, to discern, to experience, to confess, to consider, to know people relationally, to know how, to be skillful, to be made known, to make oneself known, to make to know.

The simple meaning, to know, is its most common translation out of the eight hundred or more uses. One of the primary uses means to know relationally and experientially: it refers to knowing or not knowing persons (Ge 29:5; Ex 1:8) personally or by reputation (Job 19:13). The word also refers to knowing a person sexually (Ge 4:1; 19:5; 1Ki 1:4). It may even describe knowing or not knowing God or foreign gods (Ex 5:2; Dt 11:28; Hos 2:20[22]; 8:2), but it especially signifies knowing what to do or think in general, especially with respect to God (Isa 1:3; 56:10). One of its most important uses is depicting God's knowledge of people: The Lord knows their hearts entirely (Ex 33:12; 2Sa 7:20; Ps 139:4; Jer 17:9; Hos 5:3); God knows the suffering of His people (Ex 2:25), and He cares.

The word also describes knowing various other things: when Adam and Eve sinned, knowing good and evil (Ge 3:22); knowing nothing (1Sa 20:39); and knowing the way of wisdom (Job 28:23). One could know by observation (1Sa 23:22, 23), as when Israel and Pharaoh came to know God through the plagues He brought on Egypt (Ex 10:2). People knew by experience (Jos 23:14) that God kept His promises; this kind of experience could lead to knowing by confession (Jer 3:13; 14:20). Persons could be charged to know what they were about to do (Jgs 18:14) or what the situation implied (1Ki 20:7) so they would be able to discriminate between right and wrong, good and bad, what was not proper or advantageous (Dt 1:39; 2Sa 19:35[36]).

The word describes different aspects of knowing in its other forms. In the passive forms, it describes making something or someone known. The most famous illustration is Ex 6:3 when God asserted to Moses that He did not make himself known to the fathers as Yahweh.

3046. **יְדַע, yᵉdaʻ,** *yed-ah´*; (Chaldee); corresponding to 3045:—certify, know, make known, teach.

An Aramaic verb meaning to know, to communicate, to inform, to cause to know. The word primarily refers to knowledge sharing or awareness and occurs often in the books of Ezra and Daniel. In Ezra, the men opposed to the rebuilding of Jerusalem wanted it to be known to Artaxerxes (Ezr 4:12, 13), and when opposing the Temple, they made it known to Darius (Ezr 5:8, 10). The book of Daniel presents a theological subtheme of true knowledge. In the desired and hidden meanings of life, only the God of Heaven truly knows the end from the beginning, and only He can ultimately reveal and wisely inform (Da 2:5, 21–23, 28–30; 4:9[6]; 5:8, 15, 16). Fearing Him is true knowing (Da 5:17, 21–23), a sovereign awareness that removes crippling human fear in circumstantial knowing (Da 3:18; 6:10[11]). *Yᵉdaʻ* compares with the Hebrew word *yâdaʻ* (3045), which is used with much broader variances of meaning in Scripture, ranging from cognitive to experiential to sexual relations.

3047. **יָדָע, Yâdâʻ,** *yaw-daw´*; from 3045; *knowing; Jada,* an Israelite:—Jada.

3048. **יְדַעְיָה, Yᵉdaʻyâh,** *yed-ah-yaw´*; from 3045 and 3050; *Jah has known; Jedajah,* the name of two Israelites:—Jedaiah.

3049. **יִדְּעֹנִי, yiddᵉʻônîy,** *yid-deh-o-nee´*; from 3045; (properly) a *knowing* one; (specifically) a *conjurer*; (by implication) a *ghost*:—wizard.

A masculine noun meaning a familiar spirit, a conjurer, and a wizard. In Levitical Law, this type of person was considered an abomination to the Lord (Dt 18:11). King Saul consulted such a medium when he desired to know the outcome of his war against the Philistines (1Sa 28:9). King Manasseh's evil deeds included the practice of consulting mediums and wizards (2Ki 21:6). Isaiah condemned the people of Israel for turning to the way of the Canaanites, who sought out mediums and wizards in order to hear from their dead (Isa 8:19).

3050. **יָהּ, Yâh,** *yaw*; contraction for 3068, and meaning the same; *Jah,* the sacred name:—Jah, the Lord, most vehement. Cp. names in "-iah," "-jah."

A neuter pronoun of God, a shortened form of Yahweh, often translated "LORD." This abbreviated noun for Yahweh is used in poetry, especially in the Psalms. The word is found first in Ex 15:2 and 17:16; in both cases, the LORD is exalted after He delivered His people from possible annihilation, first by Egypt and then by the Amalekites. These two poetic passages are then quoted later (Ps 118:14; Isa 12:2). In a poetic prayer, Hezekiah used the endearing term also (Isa 38:11). All other uses of the shortened name are found in Psalms (Ps 68:18[19]; 77:11 [12]; 130:3). Many times it is found in the phrase, "Hallelujah, praise be to Yah!" (Ps 104:35; 105:45; 106:1, 48).

3051. **יָהַב, yâhab,** *yaw-hab´*; a primitive root; to *give* (whether literal or figurative); generally to *put*; imperative (reflexive) *come*:—ascribe, bring, come on, give, go, set, take.

3052. **יְהַב, yᵉhab,** *yeh-hab´*; (Chaldee); corresponding to 3051:—deliver, give, lay, + prolong, pay, yield.

3053. **יְהָב, yᵉhâb,** *yeh-hawb´*; from 3051; (properly) what is *given* (by Providence), i.e. a *lot*:—burden.

3054. **יָהַד, yâhad,** *yaw-had´*; denominative from a form corresponding to 3061; to *Judaize,* i.e. become Jewish:—become Jews.

3055. **יְהֻד, Yᵉhud,** *yeh-hood´*; a briefer form of one corresponding to 3061; *Jehud,* a place in Palestine:—Jehud.

3056. **יֶהְדַּי, Yehday,** *yeh-dah´ee*; perhaps from a form corresponding to 3061; *Judaistic; Jehdai,* an Israelite:—Jehdai.

3057. **יְהֻדִיָּה, Yᵉhudîyyâh,** *yeh-hoo-dee-yaw´*; feminine of 3064; *Jehudijah,* a Jewess:—Jehudijah.

3058. **יֵהוּא, Yêhûwʼ,** *yay-hoo´*; from 3068 and 1931; *Jehovah* (is) *He; Jehu,* the name of five Israelites:—Jehu.

3059. **יְהוֹאָחָז, Yᵉhôwʼâchâz,** *yeh-ho-aw-khawz´*; from 3068 and 270; *Jehovah-seized; Jehoächaz,* the name of three Israelites:—Jehoahaz. Compare 3099.

3060. **יְהוֹאָשׁ, Yᵉhôwʼâsh,** *yeh-ho-awsh´*; from 3068 and (perhaps) 784; *Jehovah-fired; Jehoäsh,* the name of two Israelite kings:—Jehoash. Compare 3101.

3061. **יְהוּד, Yᵉhûwd,** *yeh-hood´*; (Chaldee); contracted from a form corresponding to 3063; (properly) *Judah,* hence *Judæa*:—Jewry, Judah, Judea.

3062. **יְהוּדָי, Yᵉhûwdây,** *yeh-hoo-daw-ee´*; (Chaldee); patrial from 3061; a *Jehudaïte* (or Judaite), i.e. Jew:—Jew.

3063. **יְהוּדָה, Yᵉhûwdâh,** *yeh-hoo-daw´*; from 3034; *celebrated; Jehudah* (or Judah), the name of five Israelites; also of the tribe descended from the first, and of its territory:—Judah.

3064. **יְהוּדִי, Yᵉhûwdîy,** *yeh-hoo-dee´*; patronymic from 3063; a *Jehudite* (i.e. Judaite or Jew), or descendant of Jehudah (i.e. Judah):—Jew.

3065. יְהוּדִי, **Yᵉhûwdîy,** *yeh-hoo-dee´*; the same as 3064; *Jehudi*, an Israelite:—Jehudi.

3066. יְהוּדִית, **Yᵉhûwdîyth,** *yeh-hoo-deeth´*; feminine of 3064; the *Jewish* (used adverbially) language:—in the Jews' language.

3067. יְהוּדִית, **Yᵉhûwdîyth,** *yeh-hoo-deeth´*; the same as 3066; *Jewess; Jehudith*, a Canaanitess:—Judith.

3068. יְהוָֹה, **Yᵉhôvâh,** *yeh-ho-vaw´*; from 1961; (the) self-*Existent* or Eternal; *Jehovah*, Jewish national name of God:—Jehovah, the Lord. Compare 3050, 3069.

A noun meaning God. The word refers to the proper name of the God of Israel, particularly the name by which He revealed Himself to Moses (Ex 6:2, 3). The divine name has traditionally not been pronounced, primarily out of respect for its sacredness (cf. Ex 20:7; Dt 28:58). Until the Renaissance, it was written without vowels in the Hebrew text of the OT, being rendered as YHWH. However, since that time, the vowels of another word, *'ădônây* (136), have been supplied in hopes of reconstructing the pronunciation. Although the exact derivation of the name is uncertain, most scholars agree that its primary meaning should be understood in the context of God's existence, namely, that He is the "I AM THAT I AM" (Ex 3:14), the One who was, who is, and who always will be (cf. Rev 11:17). Older translations of the Bible and many newer ones employ the practice of rendering the divine name in capital letters, so as to distinguish it from other Hebrew words. It is most often rendered as LORD (Ge 4:1; Dt 6:18; Ps 18:31[32]; Jer 33:2; Jnh 1:9) but also as GOD (Ge 6:5; 2Sa 12:22) or JEHOVAH (Ps 83:18[19]; Isa 26:4). The frequent appearance of this name in relation to God's redemptive work underscores its tremendous importance (Le 26:45; Ps 19:14[15]). Also, it is sometimes compounded with another word to describe the character of the Lord in greater detail (see Ge 22:14; Ex 17:15; Jgs 6:24).

3069. יְהוִֹה, **Yᵉhôvih,** *yeh-ho-vee´*; a variation of 3068 [used after 136, and pronounced by Jews as 430, in order to prevent the repetition of the same sound, since they elsewhere pronounce 3068 as 136]:—God.

3070. יְהוָֹה יִרְאֶה, **Yᵉhôvâh yir'eh,** *yeh-ho-vaw´ yir-eh´*; from 3068 and 7200; *Jehovah will see* (to it); *Jehovah-Jireh*, a symbolical name for Mt. Moriah:—Jehovah-jireh.

3071. יְהוָֹה נִסִּי, **Yᵉhôvâh Nissîy,** *yeh-ho-vaw´ nis-see´*; from 3068 and 5251 with pronoun suffix; *Jehovah* (is) *my banner; Jehovah-Nissi*, a symbolical name of an altar in the Desert:—Jehovah-nissi.

3072. יְהוָֹה צִדְקֵנוּ, **Yᵉhôvâh Tsidqênûw,** *yeh-ho-vaw´ tsid-kay´-noo*; from 3068 and 6664 with pronoun suffix; *Jehovah* (is) *our right; Jehovah-Tsidkenu*, a symbolical epithet of the Messiah and of Jerusalem:—the Lord our righteousness.

3073. יְהוָֹה שָׁלוֹם, **Yᵉhôvâh shâlôwm,** *yeh-ho-vaw´ shaw-lome´*; from 3068 and 7965; *Jehovah* (is) *peace; Jehovah-Shalom*, a symbolical name of an altar in Palestine:—Jehovah-shalom.

3074. יְהוָֹה שָׁמָּה, **Yᵉhôvâh shâmmâh,** *yeh-ho-vaw´ shawm´-maw*; from 3068 and 8033 with directive enclitic; *Jehovah* (is) *thither; Jehovah-Shammah*, a symbolic title of Jerusalem:—Jehovah-shammah.

3075. יְהוֹזָבָד, **Yᵉhôwzâbâd,** *yeh-ho-zaw-bawd´*; from 3068 and 2064; *Jehovah-endowed; Jehozabad*, the name of three Israelites:—Jehozabad. Compare 3107.

3076. יְהוֹחָנָן, **Yᵉhôwchânân,** *yeh-ho-khaw-nawn´*; from 3068 and 2603; *Jehovah-favoured; Jehochanan*, the name of eight Israelites:—Jehohanan, Johanan. Compare 3110.

3077. יְהוֹיָדָע, **Yᵉhôwyâdâ',** *yeh-ho-yaw-daw´*; from 3068 and 3045; *Jehovah-known; Jehojada*, the name of three Israelites:—Jehoiada. Compare 3111.

3078. יְהוֹיָכִין, **Yᵉhôwyâkîyn,** *yeh-ho-yaw-keen´*; from 3068 and 3559; *Jehovah will establish; Jehojakin*, a Jewish king:—Jehoiachin. Compare 3112.

3079. יְהוֹיָקִים, **Yᵉhôwyâqîym,** *yeh-ho-yaw-keem´*; from 3068 abbreviation and 6965; *Jehovah will raise; Jehojakim*, a Jewish king:—Jehoiakim. Compare 3113.

3080. יְהוֹיָרִיב, **Yᵉhôwyârîyb,** *yeh-ho-yaw-reeb´*; from 3068 and 7378; *Jehovah will contend; Jehojarib*, the name of two Israelites:—Jehoiarib. Compare 3114.

3081. יְהוּכַל, **Yᵉhûwkal,** *yeh-hoo-kal´*; from 3201; *potent; Jehukal*, an Israelite:—Jehucal. Compare 3116.

3082. יְהוֹנָדָב, **Yᵉhôwnâdâb,** *yeh-ho-naw-dawb´*; from 3068 and 5068; *Jehovah-largessed; Jehonadab*, the name of an Israelite and of an Arab:—Jehonadab, Jonadab. Compare 3122.

3083. יְהוֹנָתָן, **Yᵉhôwnâthân,** *yeh-ho-naw-thawn´*; from 3068 and 5414; *Jehovah-given; Jehonathan*, the name of four Israelites:—Jonathan. Compare 3129.

3084. יְהוֹסֵף, **Yᵉhôwsêph,** *yeh-ho-safe´*; a fuller form of 3130; *Jehoseph* (i.e. Joseph), a son of Jacob:—Joseph.

3085. יְהוֹעַדָּה, **Yᵉhôw'addâh,** *yeh-ho-ad-daw´*; from 3068 and 5710; *Jehovah-adorned; Jehoäddah*, an Israelite:—Jehoada.

3086. יְהוֹעַדִּין, **Yᵉhôw'addîyn,** *yeh-ho-ad-deen´*; or יְהוֹעַדָּן, **Yᵉhôw'addân,** *yeh-ho-ad-dawn´*; from 3068 and 5727; *Jehovah-pleased; Jehoäddin* or *Jehoäddan*, an Israelitess:—Jehoaddan.

3087. יְהוֹצָדָק, **Yᵉhôwtsâdâq,** *yeh-ho-tsaw-dawk´*; from 3068 and 6663; *Jehovah-righted; Jehotsadak*, an Israelite:—Jehozadek, Josedech. Compare 3136.

3088. יְהוֹרָם, **Yᵉhôwrâm,** *yeh-ho-rawm´*; from 3068 and 7311; *Jehovah-raised; Jehoram*, the name of a Syrian and of three Israelites:—Jehoram, Joram. Compare 3141.

3089. יְהוֹשֶׁבַע, **Yᵉhôwsheba',** *yeh-ho-sheh´-bah*; from 3068 and 7650; *Jehovah-sworn; Jehosheba*, an Israelitess:—Jehosheba. Compare 3090.

3090. יְהוֹשַׁבְעַת, **Yᵉhôwshab'ath,** *yeh-ho-shab-ath´*; a form of 3089; *Jehoshabath*, an Israelitess:—Jehoshabeath.

3091. יְהוֹשׁוּעַ, **Yᵉhôwshûwa',** *yeh-ho-shoo´-ah*; or יְהוֹשֻׁעַ, **Yᵉhôwshua',** *yeh-ho-shoo´-ah*; from 3068 and 3467; *Jehovah-saved; Jehoshuä* (i.e. Joshua), the Jewish leader:—Jehoshua, Jehoshuah, Joshua. Compare 1954, 3442.

3092. יְהוֹשָׁפָט, **Yᵉhôwshâphâṭ,** *yeh-ho-shaw-fawt´*; from 3068 and 8199; *Jehovah-judged; Jehoshaphat*, the name of six Israelites; also of a valley near Jerusalem:—Jehoshaphat. Compare 3146.

3093. יָהִיר, **yâhîyr,** *yaw-here´*; probably from the same as 2022; *elated*; hence *arrogant*:—haughty, proud.

3094. יְהַלֶּלְאֵל, **Yᵉhallel'êl,** *yeh-hal-lel-ale´*; from 1984 and 410; *praising God; Jehallelel*, the name of two Israelites:—Jehaleleel, Jehalelel.

3095. יַהֲלֹם, **yahălôm,** *yah-hal-ome´*; from 1986 (in the sense of *hardness*); a precious stone, probably *onyx*:—diamond.

3096. יַהַץ, **Yahats,** *yah´-hats*; or יַהְצָה, **Yahtsâh,** *yah´-tsaw*; or (feminine) יַהְצָה, **Yahtsâh,** *yah-tsaw´*; from an unused root meaning to *stamp*; perhaps *threshing*-floor; *Jahats* or *Jahtsah*, a place East of the Jordan:—Jahaz, Jahazah, Jahzah.

3097. יוֹאָב, **Yôw'âb,** *yo-awb´*; from 3068 and 1; *Jehovah-fathered; Joäb*, the name of three Israelites:—Joab.

3098. יוֹאָח, **Yôw'âch,** *yo-awkh´*; from 3068 and 251; *Jehovah-brothered; Joach*, the name of four Israelites:—Joah.

3099. יוֹאָחָז, **Yôw'âchâz,** *yo-aw-khawz´*; a form of 3059; *Joächaz*, the name of two Israelites:—Jehoahaz, Joahaz.

3100. יוֹאֵל, **Yôw'êl,** *yo-ale´*; from 3068 and 410; *Jehovah* (is his) *God; Joël*, the name of twelve Israelites:—Joel.

3101. יוֹאָשׁ, Yôw'âsh, *yo-awsh´*; or **יֹאָשׁ, Yô'âsh,** *yo-awsh´*; (2Ch 24:1), a form of 3060; *Joäsh*, the name of six Israelites:—Joash.

3102. יוֹב, Yôwb, *yobe*; perhaps a form of 3103, but more probably by erroneous transcription for 3437; *Job*, an Israelite:—Job.

3103. יוֹבָב, Yôwbâb, *yo-bawb´*; from 2980; *howler; Jobab*, the name of two Israelites and of three foreigners:—Jobab.

3104. יוֹבֵל, yôwbêl, *yo-bale´*; or **יֹבֵל, yôbêl,** *yo-bale´*; apparently from 2986; the *blast* of a horn (from its *continuous* sound); specifically the *signal* of the silver trumpets; hence the instrument itself and the festival thus introduced:—jubile, ram's horn, trumpet.

3105. יוּבַל, yûwbal, *yoo-bal´*; from 2986; a *stream:*—river.

3106. יוּבָל, Yûwbâl, *yoo-bawl´*; from 2986; *stream; Jubal*, an antediluvian:—Jubal.

3107. יוֹזָבָד, Yôwzâbâd, *yo-zaw-bawd´*; a form of 3075; *Jozabad*, the name of ten Israelites:—Josabad, Jozabad.

3108. יוֹזָכָר, Yôwzâkâr, *yo-zaw-kawr´*; from 3068 and 2142; *Jehovah-remembered; Jozacar*, an Israelite:—Jozachar.

3109. יוֹחָא, Yôwchâ', *yo-khaw´*; probably from 3068 and a variation of 2421; *Jehovah-revived; Jocha*, the name of two Israelites:—Joha.

3110. יוֹחָנָן, Yôwchânân, *yo-khaw-nawn´*; a form of 3076; *Jochanan*, the name of nine Israelites:—Johanan.

3111. יוֹיָדָע, Yôwyâdâ', *yo-yaw-daw´*; a form of 3077; *Jojada*, the name of two Israelites:—Jehoiada, Joiada.

3112. יוֹיָכִין, Yôwyâkîyn, *yo-yaw-keen´*; a form of 3078; *Jojakin*, an Israelite king:—Jehoiachin.

3113. יוֹיָקִים, Yôwyâqîym, *yo-yaw-keem´*; a form of 3079; *Jojakim*, an Israelite:—Joiakim. Compare 3137.

3114. יוֹיָרִיב, Yôwyârîyb, *yo-yaw-reeb´*; a form of 3080; *Jojarib*, the name of four Israelites:—Joiarib.

3115. יוֹכֶבֶד, Yôwkebed, *yo-keh´-bed*; from 3068 contracted and 3513; *Jehovah-gloried; Jokebed*, the mother of Moses:—Jochebed.

3116. יוּכַל, Yûwkal, *yoo-kal´*; a form of 3081; *Jukal*, an Israelite:—Jucal.

3117. יוֹם, yôwm, *yome*; from an unused root meaning to *be hot*; a *day* (as the *warm* hours), whether literal (from sunrise to sunset, or from one sunset to the next), or figurative (a space of time defined by an associated term), [often used adverbially]:—age, + always, + chronicles, continually (-ance), daily, ([birth-], each, to) day, (now a, two) days (agone), + elder, × end, + evening, + (for) ever (-lasting, -more), × full, life, as (so) long as (… live), (even) now, + old, + outlived, + perpetually, presently, + remaineth, × required, season, × since, space, then, (process of) time, + as at other times, + in trouble, weather, (as) when, (a, the, within a) while (that), × whole (+ age), (full) year (-ly), + younger.

A masculine noun meaning day, time, year. This word stands as the most basic conception of time in the OT. It designates such wide-ranging elements as the daylight hours from sunrise to sunset (Ge 1:5; 1Ki 19:4); a literal twenty-four hour cycle (Dt 16:8; 2Ki 25:30); a generic span of time (Ge 26:8; Nu 20:15); a given point in time (Ge 2:17; 47:29; Eze 33:12). In the plural, the word may also mean the span of life (Ps 102:3 [4]) or a year (Le 25:29; 1 Sam 27:7). The prophets often infuse the word with end–times meanings or connotations, using it in connection with a future period of consequential events, such as the "day of the LORD" (Jer 46:10; Zec 14:1) or simply, "that day" (Isa 19:23; Zec 14:20, 21).

3118. יוֹם, yôwm, *yome*; (Chaldee); corresponding to 3117; a *day:*—day (by day), time.

A masculine Aramaic noun meaning day. The word corresponds to the Hebrew noun of the same spelling and meaning. It refers to a twenty-four hour period (in which Daniel prays three times) (Da 6:10[11], 13[14]. In the plural, it describes a time period marked by a particular state of affairs as, for example, the days of Nebuchadnezzar's madness (Da 4:34[31]) or the days of Belshazzar's father (Da 5:11). The number of days may be specified; in the book of Daniel, only King Darius could legally be worshipped for thirty days (Da 6:7[8], 12[13]). The word is used to refer to God as the Ancient of Days, emphasizing in human terms God's eternal existence (Da 7:9, 13, 22).

3119. יוֹמָם, yôwmâm, *yo-mawm´*; from 3117; *daily:*—daily, (by, in the) day (-time).

An adverb meaning in daytime, by day. It is used to mean during the day, such as the cloud of the Lord that led the Israelites by day in the wilderness (Nu 10:34; Ne 9:19). It is often also used in parallel to something occurring by night, such as the sun by day and the moon by night (Jer 31:35). It comes from the Hebrew word *yôwm* (3117).

3120. יָוָן, Yâvân, *yaw-vawn´*; probably from the same as 3196; *effervescing* (i.e. hot and active); *Javan*, the name of a son of Joktan, and of the race (*Ionians*, i.e. Greeks) descended from him, with their territory; also of a place in Arabia:—Javan.

3121. יָוֵן, yâvên, *yaw-ven´*; from the same as 3196; (properly) *dregs* (as *effervescing*); hence *mud:*—mire, miry.

3122. יוֹנָדָב, Yôwnâdâb, *yo-naw-dawb´*; a form of 3082; *Jonadab*, the name of an Israelite and of a Rechabite:—Jonadab.

3123. יוֹנָה, yôwnâh, *yo-naw´*; probably from the same as 3196; a *dove* (apparently from the *warmth* of their mating):—dove, pigeon.

3124. יוֹנָה, Yôwnâh, *yo-naw´*; the same as 3123; *Jonah*, an Israelite:—Jonah.

3125. יְוָנִי, Yevânîy, *yev-aw-nee´*; patronymic from 3121; a *Jevanite*, or descendant of Javan:—Grecian.

3126. יוֹנֵק, yôwnêq, *yo-nake´*; active participle of 3243; a *sucker*; hence a *twig* (of a tree felled and sprouting):—tender plant.

3127. יוֹנֶקֶת, yôwneqeth, *yo-neh´-keth*; feminine of 3126; a *sprout:*—(tender) branch, young twig.

3128. יוֹנַת אֵלֶם רְחֹקִים, yôwnath 'êlem rechôqîym, *yo-nath´ ay´-lem rekh-o-keem´*; from 3123 and 482 and the plural of 7350; *dove of* (the) *silence* (i.e. *dumb* Israel) *of* (i.e. among) *distances* (i.e. strangers); the title of a ditty (used for a name of its melody):—Jonath-elem-rechokim.

3129. יוֹנָתָן, Yôwnâthân, *yo-naw-thawn´*; a form of 3083; *Jonathan*, the name of ten Israelites:—Jonathan.

3130. יוֹסֵף, Yôwsêph, *yo-safe´*; future of 3254; *let him add* (or perhaps simply active participle *adding*); *Joseph*, the name of seven Israelites:—Joseph. Compare 3084.

3131. יוֹסִפְיָה, Yôwsiphyâh, *yo-sif-yaw´*; from active participle of 3254 and 3050; *Jah* (is) *adding; Josiph-jah*, an Israelite:—Josiphiah.

3132. יוֹעֵאלָה, Yôw'ê'lâh, *yo-ay-law´*; perhaps feminine active participle of 3276; *furthermore; Joelah*, an Israelite:—Joelah.

3133. יוֹעֵד, Yôw'êd, *yo-ade´*; apparently active participle of 3259; *appointer; Joed*, an Israelite:—Joed.

3134. יוֹעֶזֶר, Yôw'ezer, *yo-eh´-zer*; from 3068 and 5828; *Jehovah* (is his) *help; Joezer*, an Israelite:—Joezer.

3135. יוֹעָשׁ, Yôw'âsh, *yo-awsh´*; from 3068 and 5789; *Jehovah-hastened; Joash*, the name of two Israelites:—Joash.

3136. יוֹצָדָק, Yôwtsâdâq, *yo-tsaw-dawk´*; a form of 3087; *Jotsadak*, an Israelite:—Jozadak.

3137. יוֹקִים, Yôwqîym, *yo-keem´*; a form of 3113; *Jokim*, an Israelite:—Jokim.

3138. יוֹרֶה, yôwreh, *yo-reh´*; active participle of 3384; *sprinkling*; hence a *sprinkling* (or autumnal showers):—first rain, former [rain].

3139. יוֹרָה, Yôwrâh, *yo-raw´*; from 3384; *rainy; Jorah*, an Israelite:—Jorah.

3140. יוֹרַי, Yôwray, *yo-rah´-ee*; from 3384; *rainy; Jorai*, an Israelite:—Jorai.

3141. יוֹרָם, Yôwrâm, *yo-rawm´*; a form of 3088; *Joram*, the name of three Israelites and one Syrian:—Joram.

3142. יוּשַׁב חֶסֶד, Yûwshab Chesed, *yoo-shab´ kheh´-sed*; from 7725 and 2617; *kindness will be returned; Jushab-Chesed*, an Israelite:—Jushab-hesed.

3143. יוֹשִׁבְיָה, Yôwshibyâh, *yo-shib-yaw´*; from 3427 and 3050; *Jehovah will cause to dwell; Joshibjah*, an Israelite:—Josibiah.

3144. יוֹשָׁה, Yôwshâh, *yo-shaw´*; probably a form of 3145; *Joshah*, an Israelite:—Joshah.

3145. יוֹשַׁוְיָה, Yôwshavyâh, *yo-shav-yaw´*; from 3068 and 7737; *Jehovah-set; Joshavjah*, an Israelite:—Joshaviah. Compare 3144.

3146. יוֹשָׁפָט, Yôwshâphâṭ, *yo-shaw-fawt´*; a form of 3092; *Joshaphat*, an Israelite:—Joshaphat.

3147. יוֹתָם, Yôwthâm, *yo-thawm´*; from 3068 and 8535; *Jehovah* (is) *perfect; Jotham*, the name of three Israelites:—Jotham.

3148. יוֹתֵר, yôwthêr, *yo-thare´*; active participle of 3498; (properly) *redundant*; hence *over and above*, as adjective, noun, adverb or conjunction [as follows]:—better, more (-over), over, profit.

3149. יְזִיאֵל, Y^e^zîy'êl, *yez-ee-ale´*; from an unused root (meaning to *sprinkle*) and 410; *sprinkled of God; Jezavel*, an Israelite:—Jeziel [*from the margin*].

3150. יִזִּיָּה, Yizzîyyâh, *yiz-zee-yaw´*; from the same as the first part of 3149 and 3050; *sprinkled of Jah; Jizzijah*, an Israelite:—Jeziah.

3151. יָזִיז, Yâzîyz, *yaw-zeez´*; from the same as 2123; *he will make prominent; Jaziz*, an Israelite:—Jaziz.

3152. יִזְלִיאָה, Yizlîy'âh, *yiz-lee-aw´*; perhaps from an unused root (meaning to *draw up*); *he will draw out; Jizliah*, an Israelite:—Jezliah.

3153. יְזַנְיָה, Y^e^zanyâh, *yez-an-yaw´*; or יְזַנְיָהוּ, **Y^e^zanyâhûw,** *yez-an-yaw´-hoo*; probably for 2970; *Jezanjah*, an Israelite:—Jezaniah.

3154. יֶזַע, yezaʻ, *yeh´-zah*; from an unused root meaning to *ooze; sweat*, i.e. (by implication) a *sweating* dress:—any thing that causeth sweat.

3155. יִזְרָח, Yizrâch, *yiz-rawkh´*; a variation for 250; a *Jizrach* (i.e. Ezrachite or Zarchite) or descendant of Zerach:—Izrahite.

3156. יִזְרַחְיָה, Yizrachyâh, *yiz-rakh-yaw´*; from 2224 and 3050; *Jah will shine; Jizrachjah*, the name of two Israelites:—Izrahiah, Jezrahiah.

3157. יִזְרְעֶאל, Yizr^e^ʻe'l, *yiz-reh-ell´*; from 2232 and 410; *God will sow; Jizreël*, the name of two places in Palestine and of two Israelites:—Jezreel.

3158. יִזְרְעֵאלִי, Yizr^e^ʻê'lîy, *yiz-reh-ay-lee´*; patronymic from 3157; a *Jizreëlite* or native of Jizreel:—Jezreelite.

3159. יִזְרְעֵאלִית, Yizr^e^ʻê'lîyth, *yiz-reh-ay-leeth´*; feminine of 3158; a *Jezreëlitess*:—Jezreelitess.

3160. יְחֻבָּה, Y^e^chubbâh, *yekh-oob-baw´*; from 2247; *hidden; Jechubbah*, an Israelite:—Jehubbah.

3161. יָחַד, yâchad, *yaw-khad´*; a primitive root; to *be* (or become) *one*:—join, unite.

3162. יַחַד, yachad, *yakh´-ad*; from 3161; (properly) a *unit*, i.e. (adverb) *unitedly*:—alike, at all (once), both, likewise, only, (al-) together, withal.

3163. יַחְדּוֹ, Yachdôw, *yakh-doe´*; from 3162 with pronoun suffix; *his unity*, i.e. (adverb) *together; Jachdo*, an Israelite:—Jahdo.

3164. יַחְדִּיאֵל, Yachdîy'êl, *yakh-dee-ale´*; from 3162 and 410; *unity of God; Jachdiel*, an Israelite:—Jahdiel.

3165. יֶחְדְּיָהוּ, Yechd^e^yâhûw, *yekh-deh-yaw´-hoo*; from 3162 and 3050; *unity of Jah; Jechdijah*, the name of two Israelites:—Jehdeiah.

3166. יַחֲזִיאֵל, Yachăzîy'êl, *yakh-az-ee-ale´*; from 2372 and 410; *beheld of God; Jachaziël*, the name of five Israelites:—Jahaziel, Jahziel.

3167. יַחְזְיָה, Yachz^e^yâh, *yakh-zeh-yaw´*; from 2372 and 3050; *Jah will behold; Jachzejah*, an Israelite:—Jahaziah.

3168. יְחֶזְקֵאל, Y^e^chezqê'l, *yekh-ez-kale´*; from 2388 and 410; *God will strengthen; Jechezkel*, the name of two Israelites:—Ezekiel, Jehezekel.

3169. יְחִזְקִיָּה, Y^e^chizqîyyâh, *yekh-iz-kee-yaw´*; or יְחִזְקִיָּהוּ, **Y^e^chizqîyyâhûw,** *yekh-iz-kee-yaw´-hoo*; from 3388 and 3050; *strengthened of Jah; Jechizkijah*, the name of five Israelites:—Hezekiah, Jehizkiah. Compare 2396.

3170. יַחְזֵרָה, Yachzêrâh, *yakh-zay-raw´*; from the same as 2386; perhaps *protection; Jachzerah*, an Israelite:—Jahzerah.

3171. יְחִיאֵל, Y^e^chîy'êl, *yekh-ee-ale´*; or (2Ch 29:14) יְחַוְאֵל, **Y^e^chav'êl,** *yekh-av-ale´*; from 2421 and 410; *God will live; Jechiël* (or *Jechavel*), the name of eight Israelites:—Jehiel.

3172. יְחִיאֵלִי, Y^e^chîy'êlîy, *yekh-ee-ay-lee´*; patronymic from 3171; a *Jechiëlite* or descendant of Jechiel:—Jehieli.

3173. יָחִיד, yâchîyd, *yaw-kheed´*; from 3161; (properly) *united*, i.e. *sole*; (by implication) *beloved*; also *lonely*; (feminine) the *life* (as not to be replaced):—darling, desolate, only (child, son), solitary.

An adjective meaning sole, only, solitary. This word is frequently used to refer to an only child. Isaac was Abraham's only son by Sarah (Ge 22:2, 12, 16). Jepthah's daughter was his only child, who came running out to greet him after his vow to sacrifice the first thing to come out of his door (Jgs 11:34). The father of an only child began teaching him wisdom when he was very young (Pr 4:3). Mourning an only child was considered an especially grievous sorrow (Jer 6:26; Am 8:10; Zec 12:10). The feminine form is used parallel to life or soul, portraying the precious, only life we are given (Ps 22:20[21]; 35:17). It is also used to mean lonely or alone (Ps 25:16; 68:6[7]). See the related Hebrew root *yâchad* (3161).

3174. יְחִיָּה, Y^e^chîyyâh, *yekh-ee-yaw´*; from 2421 and 3050; *Jah will live; Jechijah*, an Israelite:—Jehiah.

3175. יָחִיל, yâchîyl, *yaw-kheel´*; from 3176; *expectant*:—should hope.

This word occurs only in La 3:26, and its exact meaning is difficult to determine. It could be derived from *yâchal* (3176) and be an adjective meaning hopeful. Or it could also be a verb derived from *chûl* (2342) and thus refer to waiting (cf. Ps 37:7). In this case, the word might imply painful waiting as in childbirth, which would harmonize with the next verse. Whether hopefully or in pain (or both), the verse says it is good to wait in silence for the salvation of the Lord.

3176. יָחַל, yâchal, *yaw-chal´*; a primitive root; to *wait*; by implication to *be patient, hope*:—(cause to, have, make to) hope, be pained, stay, tarry, trust, wait.

A verb meaning to wait, to hope, to tarry. It is used of Noah (Ge 8:12); Saul (1Sa 10:8; 13:8); Joab (2Sa 18:14); the king of Aram (2Ki 6:33); Job (Job 6:11; 13:15; 14:14); Elihu (Job 32:11, 16). In the Psalms, it frequently means to wait with hope (Ps 31:24[25]; 33:18, 22; 38:15[16]); 42:5[6], 11[12]). This meaning also occurs in Isaiah (Isa 42:4; 51:5); Lamentations (La 3:21, 24); Ezekiel (Eze 19:5); and Micah (Mic 7:7).

3177. יַחְלְאֵל, Yachlᵉʾêl, *yakh-leh-ale´*; from 3176 and 410; *expectant of God; Jachleël*, an Israelite:—Jahleel.

3178. יַחְלְאֵלִי, Yachlᵉʾêlîy, *yakh-leh-ay-lee´*; patronymic from 3177; a *Jachleëlite* or descendant of Jachleel:—Jahleelites.

3179. יָחַם, yâcham, *yaw-kham´*; a primitive root; probably to *be hot*; (figurative) to *conceive*:—get heat, be hot, conceive, be warm.

3180. יַחְמוּר, yachmûwr, *yakh-moor´*; from 2560; a kind of *deer* (from the colour; compare 2543):—fallow deer.

3181. יַחְמַי, Yachmay, *yakh-mah´-ee*; probably from 3179; *hot; Jachmai*, an Israelite:—Jahmai.

3182. יָחֵף, yâchêph, *yaw-khafe´*; from an unused root meaning to *take off the shoes; unsandalled*:—barefoot, being unshod.

3183. יַחְצְאֵל, Yachtsᵉʾêl, *yakh-tseh-ale´*; from 2673 and 410; *God will allot; Jachtseël*, an Israelite:—Jahzeel. Compare 3185.

3184. יַחְצְאֵלִי, Yachtsᵉʾêlîy, *yakh-tseh-ay-lee´*; patronymic from 3183; a *Jachtseëlite* (collective) or descendants of Jachtseel:—Jahzeelites.

3185. יַחְצִיאֵל, Yachtsîyʾêl, *yakh-tsee-ale´*; from 2673 and 410; *allotted of God; Jachtsiël*, an Israelite:—Jahziel. Compare 3183.

3186. יָחַר, yâchar, *yaw-khar´*; a primitive root; to *delay*:—tarry longer.

3187. יָחַשׂ, yâchaś, *yaw-khas´*; a primitive root; to *sprout*; used only as denominative from 3188; to *enroll* by pedigree:—(number after, number throughout the) genealogy (to be reckoned), be reckoned by genealogies.

3188. יַחַשׂ, yachaś, *yakh´-as*; from 3187; a *pedigree* or family list (as *growing* spontaneously):—genealogy.

3189. יַחַת, Yachath, *yakh´-ath*; from 3161; *unity; Jachath*, the name of four Israelites:—Jahath.

3190. יָטַב, yâṭab, *yaw-tab´*; a primitive root; to *be* (causative) *make well*, literal (*sound, beautiful*) or figurative (*happy, successful, right*):—be accepted, amend, use aright, benefit, be (make) better, seem best, make cheerful, be comely, + be content, diligent (-ly), dress, earnestly, find favour, give, be glad, do (be, make) good ([-ness]), be (make) merry, please (+ well), shew more [kindness], skilfully, × very small, surely, make sweet, thoroughly, tire, trim, very, be (can, deal, entreat, go, have) well [said, seen].

A verb meaning to be good, to be well, to be pleasing. In the causative stem, it means to do good, to do well, to please, to make pleasing. It is often used in idiomatic expressions with heart (*lêb* [3820]), meaning to be pleased or to be happy (Jgs 18:20; 19:6, 9; Ru 3:7); and with eyes, to be pleasing to someone else (i.e. pleasing or good in their eyes [Ge 34:18; 1Sa 18:5]). The term does not necessarily carry a moral weight but can be translated adverbially as "well." For instance, see Mic 7:3 where their hands do evil well (cf. 1Sa 16:17; Pr 30:29; Isa 23:16). The word can also imply morality (Ps 36:3[4]; 119:68).

3191. יְטַב, yᵉṭab, *yet-ab´*; (Chaldee); corresponding to 3190:—seem good.

3192. יָטְבָה, Yoṭbâh, *yot-baw´*; from 3190; *pleasantness; Jotbah*, a place in Palestine:—Jotbah.

3193. יָטְבָתָה, Yoṭbâthâh, *yot-baw´-thaw*; from 3192; *Jotbathah*, a place in the Desert:—Jotbath, Jotbathah.

3194. יֻטָּה, Yuṭṭâh, *yoot-taw´*; or יוּטָּה, **Yûwṭṭâh,** *yoo-taw´*; from 5186; *extended; Juttah* (or *Jutah*), a place in Palestine:—Juttah.

3195. יְטוּר, Yᵉṭûwr, *yet-oor´*; probably from the same as 2905; *encircled* (i.e. inclosed); *Jetur*, a son of Ishmael:—Jetur.

3196. יַיִן, yayin, *yah´-yin*; from an unused root meaning to *effervesce; wine* (as fermented); (by implication) *intoxication*:—banqueting, wine, wine [-bibber].

3197. יַךְ, yak, *yak*; by erroneous transcription for 3027; a *hand* or *side*:—[way-] side.

3198. יָכַח, yâkach, *yaw-kakh´*; a primitive root; to *be right* (i.e. correct); (reciprocal) to *argue*; (causative) to *decide, justify* or *convict*:—appoint, argue, chasten, convince, correct (-ion), daysman, dispute, judge, maintain, plead, reason (together), rebuke, reprove (-r), surely, in any wise.

A verb meaning to argue, to convince, to convict, to judge, to reprove. The word usually refers to the clarification of people's moral standing, which may involve arguments being made for them (Job 13:15; Isa 11:4) or against them (Job 19:5; Ps 50:21). The word may refer to the judgment of a case between people (Ge 31:37, 42) or even (in the days before Christ) to someone desired to mediate between God and humankind (Job 9:33). The word may also refer to physical circumstances being used to reprove sin (2Sa 7:14; Hab 1:12). Reproving sin, whether done by God (Pr 3:12) or persons (Le 19:17), was pictured as a demonstration of love, but some people were too rebellious or scornful to be reproved (Pr 9:7; 15:12; Eze 3:26). In Genesis 24:14, 44, the word referred to God's appointment (or judgment) of Rebekah as the one to be married to Isaac.

3199. יָכִין, Yâkîyn, *yaw-keen´*; from 3559; *he* (or *it*) *will establish; Jakin*, the name of three Israelites and of a temple pillar:—Jachin.

3200. יָכִינִי, Yâkîynîy, *yaw-kee-nee´*; patronymic from 3199; a *Jakinite* (collective) or descendants of Jakin:—Jachinites.

3201. יָכֹל, yâkôl, *yaw-kole´*; or (fuller) יָכוֹל, **yâkôwl,** *yaw-kole´*; a primitive root; to *be able*, literal (*can, could*) or moral (*may, might*):—be able, any at all (ways), attain, can (away with, [-not]), could, endure, might, overcome, have power, prevail, still, suffer.

3202. יְכֵל, yᵉkil, *yek-ill´*; (Chaldee); or יְכִיל, **yᵉkîyl,** *yek-eel´*; (Chaldee); corresponding to 3201:—be able, can, couldest, prevail.

3203. יְכָלְיָה, Yᵉkolyâh, *yek-ol-yaw´*; and יְכָלְיָהוּ, **Yᵉkolyâhûw,** *yek-ol-yaw´-hoo*; or (2Ch 26:3) יְכִילְיָה, **Yᵉkîylᵉyâh,** *yek-ee-leh-yaw´*; from 3201 and 3050; *Jah will enable; Jekoljah* or *Jekiljah*, an Israelitess:—Jecholiah, Jecoliah.

3204. יְכָנְיָה, Yᵉkonyâh, *yek-on-yaw´(-hoo)*; and יְכָנְיָהוּ, **Yᵉkonyâhûw,** *yek-on-yaw´-hoo*; or (Jer 27:20) יְכוֹנְיָה, **Yᵉkôwnᵉyâh,** *yek-o-neh-yaw´*; from 3559 and 3050; *Jah will establish; Jekonjah*, a Jewish king:—Jeconiah. Compare 3659.

3205. יָלַד, yâlad, *yaw-lad´*; a primitive root; to *bear* young; (causative) to *beget*; to *act as midwife*; specifically to *show lineage*:—bear, beget, birth ([-day]), born, (make to) bring forth (children, young), bring up, calve, child, come, be delivered (of a child), time of delivery, gender, hatch, labour, (do the office of a) midwife, declare pedigrees, be the son of, (woman in, woman that) travail (-eth, -ing woman).

3206. יֶלֶד, yeled, *yeh´-led*; from 3205; something *born*, i.e. a *lad* or *offspring*:—boy, child, fruit, son, young man (one).

3207. יַלְדָּה, yaldâh, *yal-daw´*; feminine of 3206; a *lass*:—damsel, girl.

3208. יַלְדוּת, yaldûwth, *yal-dooth´*; abstracted from 3206; *boyhood* (or *girlhood*):—childhood, youth.

3209. יִלּוֹד, yillôwd, *yil-lode´*; passive from 3205; *born*:—born.

3210. יָלוֹן, Yâlôwn, *yaw-lone´*; from 3885; *lodging; Jalon*, an Israelite:—Jalon.

3211. **יָלִיד, yâlîyd,** *yaw-leed´*; from 3205; *born*:—([home-]) born, child, son.

3212. **יָלַךְ, yâlak,** *yaw-lak´*; a primitive root [compare 1980]; to *walk* (literal or figurative); (causative) to *carry* (in various senses):— × again, away, bear, bring, carry (away), come (away), depart, flow, + follow (-ing), get (away, hence, him), (cause to, make) go (away, -ing, -ne, one's way, out), grow, lead (forth), let down, march, prosper, + pursue, cause to run, spread, take away ([-journey]), vanish, (cause to) walk (-ing), wax, × be weak.

3213. **יָלַל, yâlal,** *yaw-lal´*; a primitive root; to *howl* (with a wailing tone) or *yell* (with a boisterous one):—(make to) howl, be howling.

3214. **יְלֵל, yᵉlêl,** *yel-ale´*; from 3213; a *howl*:—howling.

3215. **יְלָלָה, yᵉlâlâh,** *yel-aw-law´*; feminine of 3214; a *howling*:—howling.

3216. **יָלַע, yâlaʻ,** *yaw-lah´*; a primitive root; to *blurt* or utter inconsiderately:—devour.

3217. **יַלֶּפֶת, yallepheth,** *yal-leh´-feth*; from an unused root apparently meaning to *stick* or *scrape; scurf* or *tetter*:—scabbed.

3218. **יֶלֶק, yeleq,** *yeh´-lek*; from an unused root meaning to *lick* up; a *devourer*; specifically the young *locust*:—cankerworm, caterpillar.

3219. **יַלְקוּט, yalqûwṭ,** *yal-koot´*; from 3950; a travelling *pouch* (as if for gleanings):—scrip.

3220. **יָם, yâm,** *yawm*; from an unused root meaning to *roar*; a *sea* (as breaking in *noisy* surf) or large body of water; specifically (with the article) the *Mediter-ranean*; sometimes a large *river*, or an artificial *basin*; locally, the *west*, or (rarely) the *south*:—sea (× -faring man, [-shore]), south, west (-ern, side, -ward).

3221. **יָם, yam,** *yam*; (Chaldee); corresponding to 3220:—sea.

3222. **יֵם, yêm,** *yame*; from the same as 3117; a *warm* spring:—mule.

3223. **יְמוּאֵל, Yᵉmûwʼêl,** *yem-oo-ale´*; from 3117 and 410; *day of God; Jemuel*, an Israelite:—Jemuel.

3224. **יְמִימָה, Yᵉmîymâh,** *yem-ee-maw´*; perhaps from the same as 3117; (properly) *warm*, i.e. *affectionate*; hence *dove* [compare 3123]; *Jemimah*, one of Job's daughters:—Jemimah.

3225. **יָמִין, yâmîyn,** *yaw-meen´*; from 3231; the *right* hand or side (leg, eye) of a person or other object (as the *stronger* and more dexterous); locally, the *south*:— + left-handed, right (hand, side), south.

3226. **יָמִין, Yâmîyn,** *yaw-meen´*; the same as 3225; *Jamin*, the name of three Israelites:—Jamin. See also 1144.

3227. **יְמִינִי, yᵉmîynîy,** *yem-ee-nee´*; for 3225; *right*:—(on the) right (hand).

3228. **יְמִינִי, Yᵉmîynîy,** *yem-ee-nee´*; patronymic from 3226; a *Jeminite* (collective) or descendants of Jamin:—Jaminites. See also 1145.

3229. **יִמְלָא, Yimlâʼ,** *yeem-law´*; or **יִמְלָה, Yimlâh,** *yim-law´*; from 4390; *full; Jimla* or *Jimlah*, an Israelite:—Imla, Imlah.

3230. **יַמְלֵךְ, Yamlêk,** *yam-lake´*; from 4427; *he will make king; Jamlek*, an Israelite:—Jamlech.

3231. **יָמַן, yâman,** *yaw-man´*; a primitive root; to *be* (physical) *right* (i.e. firm); but used only as denominative from 3225 and transitive, to *be right-handed* or *take the right-hand* side:—go (turn) to (on, use) the right hand.

3232. **יִמְנָה, Yimnâh,** *yim-naw´*; from 3231; *prosperity* (as betokened by the *right* hand); *Jimnah*, the name of two Israelites; also (with the article) of the posterity of one of them:—Imna, Imnah, Jimnah, Jimnites.

3233. **יְמָנִי, yᵉmânîy,** *yem-aw-nee´*; from 3231; *right* (i.e. at the right hand):—(on the) right (hand).

3234. **יִמְנָע, Yimnâʻ,** *yim-naw´*; from 4513; *he will restrain; Jimna*, an Israelite:—Imna.

3235. **יָמַר, yâmar,** *yaw-mar´*; a primitive root; to *exchange*; (by implication) to *change places*:—boast selves, change.

3236. **יִמְרָה, Yimrâh,** *yim-raw´*; probably from 3235; *interchange; Jimrah*, an Israelite:—Imrah.

3237. **יָמַשׁ, yâmash,** *yaw-mash´*; a primitive root; to *touch*:—feel.

3238. **יָנָה, yânâh,** *yaw-naw´*; a primitive root; to *rage* or *be violent*; (by implication) to *suppress*, to *maltreat*:—destroy, (thrust out by) oppress (-ing, -ion, -or), proud, vex, do violence.

A verb meaning to oppress, to treat violently. The term is used in Ex 22:21[20], Le 25:14, 17, and Dt 23:16 [17] to refer to improper treatment of strangers and the poor. The participle functions as a noun meaning oppressor (Jer 25:38; 46:16; 50:16). In the Prophets, the term is typically used of foreign oppressors.

3239. **יָנוֹחַ, Yânôwach,** *yaw-no´-akh*; or (with enclitic) **יָנוֹחָה, Yânôwchâh,** *yaw-no´-khaw*; from 3240; *quiet; Janoäch* or *Janochah*, a place in Palestine:—Janoah, Janohah.

3240. **יָנַח, yânach,** *yaw-nakh´*; a primitive root; to *deposit*; (by implication) to *allow to stay*:—bestow, cast down, lay (down, up), leave (off), let alone (remain), pacify, place, put, set (down), suffer, withdraw, withhold. (The Hiphil forms with the *dagesh* are here referred to, in accordance with the older grammarians; but if any distinction of the kind is to be made, these should rather be referred to 5117, and the others here.)

3241. **יָנִים, Yânîym,** *yaw-neem´*; from 5123; *asleep; Janim*, a place in Palestine:—Janum [*from the margin*].

3242. **יְנִיקָה, yᵉnîyqâh,** *yen-ee-kaw´*; from 3243; a *sucker* or sapling:—young twig.

3243. **יָנַק, yânaq,** *yaw-nak´*; a primitive root; to *suck*; (causative) to *give milk*:—milch, nurse (-ing mother), (give, make to) suck (-ing child, -ling).

3244. **יַנְשׁוּף, yanshûwph,** *yan-shoof´*; or **יַנְשׁוֹף, yanshôwph,** *yan-shofe´*; apparently from 5398; an unclean (aquatic) bird; probably the *heron* (perhaps from its *blowing* cry, or because the *night*-heron is meant [compare 5399]):—(great) owl.

3245. **יָסַד, yâsad,** *yaw-sad´*; a primitive root; to *set* (literal or figurative); (intensive) to *found*; (reflexive) to *sit* down together, i.e. *settle, consult*:—appoint, take counsel, establish, (lay the, lay for a) found (-ation), instruct, lay, ordain, set, × sure.

A verb meaning to establish, to found, to fix. In a literal sense, this term can refer to laying the foundation of a building, primarily the Temple (1Ki 5:17[31]; 6:37; Ezr 3:11; Isa 44:28); or to laying the foundation of a city like Jericho (Jos 6:26; 1Ki 16:34); or Zion (Isa 14:32). In a metaphorical sense, it can allude to the founding of Egypt (Ex 9:18); the earth (Isa 48:13). This word can also connote the appointment or ordination of an individual(s) to a task or position (1Ch 9:22; Est 1:8). Probably one of the most noteworthy occurrences of this word is in Isa 28:16, where God declares that He will "lay in Zion for a foundation a stone, a tried stone, a precious corner stone, a sure foundation: he that believeth shall not make haste" (KJV). The NT writers announce that that stone is Jesus Christ (Ro 9:33; 1Pe 2:6).

3246. **יְסֻד, yᵉsud,** *yes-ood´*; from 3245; a *foundation* (figuratively) *beginning*:— × began.

3247. **יְסוֹד, yᵉsôwd,** *yes-ode´*; from 3245; a *foundation* (literal or figurative):—bottom, foundation, repairing.

A noun meaning foundation. The word refers to a base on which people build structures. It is used several times to refer to the base of the sacrificial altar, where the blood of sacrifices was poured (Ex 29:12;

Le 4:7, 18, 25, 30, 34). The Gate of the Foundation, mentioned in 2Ch 23:5, may have been named from its proximity to the altar. In reference to larger buildings, the word is usually used to express the extent of destruction which sometimes included razing a city down to its foundation (Ps 137:7; Mic 1:6) and sometimes even the destruction of the foundation itself (La 4:11; Eze 30:4). Egypt's foundations appear to symbolize its dependence on other nations (Eze 30:4, 5). Symbolically, the word refers to principles on which people build their lives, whether they be faulty (Job 4:19; 22:16) or sound (Pr 10:25; cf. Mt 7:24–27).

3248. יְסוּדָה, ye**sûwdâh,** *yes-oo-daw´*; feminine of 3246; a *foundation*:—foundation.

A feminine noun meaning foundation. This word occurs only in Ps 87:1. The words in Zec 4:9, 8:9, and 12:1, are forms of the verb *yâsad* (3245); the words in Isa 28:16, although difficult to analyze, also do not appear to belong under this reference. In Ps 87:1, the word refers to Jerusalem as God's foundation or base in the holy mountain. The psalm enlarges on this, saying that Jerusalem will be the place of His particular dwelling, the home of a large number of His people, and a source of blessing.

3249. יָסוּר, yâsûwr, *yaw-soor´*; from 5493; *departing*:—they that depart.

3250. יִסּוֹר, yissôwr, *yis-sore´*; from 3256; a *reprover*:—instruct.

A masculine singular noun meaning one who reproves. The word comes from the verb *yâsar* (3256). Its only occurrence is in Job 40:2.

3251. יָסַךְ, yâsak, *yaw-sak´*; a primitive root; to *pour* (intransitive):—be poured.

3252. יִסְכָּה, Yiskâh, *yis-kaw´*; from an unused root meaning to *watch; observant; Jiskah*, sister of Lot:—Iscah.

3253. יִסְמַכְיָהוּ, Yismakyâhûw, *yis-mak-yaw-hoo´*; from 5564 and 3050; *Jah will sustain; Jismakjah*, an Israelite:—Ismachiah.

3254. יָסַף, yâsaph, *yaw-saf´*; a primitive root; to *add* or *augment* (often adverbial) to *continue* to do a thing:—add, × again, × any more, × cease, × come more, + conceive again, continue, exceed, × further, × gather together, get more, give moreover, × henceforth, increase (more and more), join, × longer (bring, do, make, much, put), × (the, much, yet) more (and more), proceed (further), prolong, put, be [strong-] er, × yet, yield.

3255. יְסַף, ye**saph,** *yes-af´*; (Chaldee); corresponding to 3254:—add.

3256. יָסַר, yâsar, *yaw-sar´*; a primitive root; to *chastise*, literal (with blows) or figurative (with words); hence to *instruct*:—bind, chasten, chastise, correct, instruct, punish, reform, reprove, sore, teach.

A verb meaning to discipline, to chasten, to instruct, to teach, to punish. It is used with two general poles of meaning (chastening or instructing) that at times merge. Both aspects are presented in Scripture in terms of God and humans. Others can instruct and teach (Job 4:3), as can the conscience (Ps 16:7). Still others can discipline, but God is the ultimate source of true instruction and chastening. He often chides toward an instructive end, especially for His covenant people (Le 26:18, 23; Jer 46:28); wisdom presents the disciplined one as blessed, even though the process is painful (Ps 94:12; 118:18). However, chastisement is not always presented as positive or instructive, for Rehoboam promised an evil chastening that eventually split the united kingdom (1Ki 12:11, 14); and God's just, unremitted punishment would bring desolation (Jer 6:8; 10:24).

3257. יָע, yâ', *yaw*; from 3261; a *shovel*:—shovel.

3258. יַעְבֵּץ, Ya'bêts, *yah-bates´*; from an unused root probably meaning to *grieve; sorrowful; Jabets*, the name of an Israelite, and also of a place in Palestine:—Jabez.

3259. יָעַד, yâ'ad, *yaw-ad´*; a primitive root; to *fix* upon (by agreement or appointment); (by implication) to *meet* (at a stated time), to *summon* (to trial), to *direct* (in a certain quarter or position), to *engage* (for marriage):—agree, (make an) appoint (-ment, a time), assemble (selves), betroth, gather (selves, together), meet (together), set (a time).

A verb meaning to appoint, to summon, to engage, to agree, to assemble. It also means allotted or appointed time, such as the amount of time David appointed to Amasa to assemble the men of Judah (2Sa 20:5). This word can also take the meaning of appointing or designating someone to be married (Ex 21:8, 9). Another meaning is to meet someone at an appointed time. Amos asked the question, How can two walk together unless they appoint a time at which to meet (Am 3:3)?

3260. יֶעְדִּי, Ye**'dîy,** *yed-ee´*; from 3259; *appointed; Jedi*, an Israelite:—Iddo [*from the margin*]. See 3035.

3261. יָעָה, yâ'âh, *yaw-aw´*; a primitive root; apparently to *brush* aside:—sweep away.

3262. יְעוּאֵל, Ye**'ûw'êl,** *yeh-oo-ale´*; from 3261 and 410; *carried away of God; Jeüel*, the name of four Israelites:—Jehiel, Jeiel, Jeuel. Compare 3273.

3263. יְעוּץ, Ye**'ûwts,** *yeh-oots´*; from 5779; *counsellor; Jeüts*, an Israelite:—Jeuz.

3264. יְעוֹרִים, ye**'ôwrîym,** *yeh-ow-reem´*; a variation of 3293; a *forest*:—wood.

3265. יָעוּר, Yâ'ûwr, *yaw-oor´*; apparently passive participle of the same as 3293; *wooded; Jaür*, an Israelite:—Jair [*from the margin*].

3266. יְעוּשׁ, Ye**'ûwsh,** *yeh-oosh´*; from 5789; *hasty; Jeüsh*, the name of an Edomite and of four Israelites:—Jehush, Jeush. Compare 3274.

3267. יָעַז, yâ'az, *yaw-az´*; a primitive root; to be *bold* or *obstinate*:—fierce.

3268. יַעֲזִיאֵל, Ya'ăzîy'êl, *yah-az-ee-ale´*; from 3267 and 410; *emboldened of God; Jaaziël*, an Israelite:—Jaaziel.

3269. יַעֲזִיָּהוּ, Ya'ăzîyyâhûw, *yah-az-ee-yaw´-hoo*; from 3267 and 3050; *emboldened of Jah; Jaazijah*, an Israelite:—Jaaziah.

3270. יַעֲזֵיר, Ya'ăzêyr, *yah-az-ayr´*; or **יַעְזֵר, Ya'zêr,** *yah-zare´*; from 5826; *helpful; Jaazer* or *Jazer*, a place East of the Jordan:—Jaazer, Jazer.

3271. יָעַט, yâ'aṭ, *yaw-at´*; a primitive root; to *clothe*:—cover.

3272. יְעַט, ye**'aṭ,** *yeh-at´*; (Chaldee); corresponding to 3289; to *counsel*; (reflexive) to *consult*:—counsellor, consult together.

3273. יְעִיאֵל, Ye**'îy'êl,** *yeh-ee-ale´*; from 3261 and 410; *carried away of God; Jeïel*, the name of six Israelites:—Jeiel, Jehiel. Compare 3262.

3274. יְעִישׁ, Ye**'îysh,** *yeh-eesh´*; from 5789; *hasty; Jeïsh*, the name of an Edomite and of an Israelite:—Jeush [*from the margin*]. Compare 3266.

3275. יַעְכָּן, Ya'kân, *yah-kawn´*; from the same as 5912; *troublesome; Jakan*, an Israelite:—Jachan.

3276. יָעַל, ya'al, *yaw-al´*; a primitive root; (properly) to *ascend*; (figurative) to *be valuable* ([objective] *useful*, [subjective] *benefited*):— × at all, set forward, can do good, (be, have) profit (-able).

3277. יָעֵל, yâ'êl, *yaw-ale´*; from 3276; an *ibex* (as *climbing*):—wild goat.

3278. יָעֵל, Yâ'êl, *yaw-ale´*; the same as 3277; *Jaël*, a Canaanite:—Jael.

3279. יַעֲלָא, Ya'ălâ', *yah-al-aw´*; or **יַעֲלָה, Ya'ălâh,** *yah-al-aw´*; the same as 3280 or direct from 3276; *Jaala* or *Jaalah*, one of the Nethinim:—Jaala, Jaalah.

3280. יַעֲלָה, ya'ălâh, *yah-al-aw´*; feminine of 3277; wild goat:—roe.

3281. **יַעְלָם, Ya'lâm,** *yah-lawm´*; from 5956; *occult; Jalam,* an Edomite:—Jalam.

3282. **יַעַן, ya'an,** *yah´-an*; from an unused root meaning to *pay attention*; (properly) *heed*; (by implication) *purpose* (sake or account); used adverbially to indicate the *reason* or cause:—because (that), forasmuch (+ as), seeing then, + that, + whereas, + why.

3283. **יָעֵן, yâ'ên,** *yaw-ane´*; from the same as 3282; the *ostrich* (probably from its *answering* cry:—ostrich.

3284. **יַעֲנָה, ya'ănâh,** *yah-an-aw´*; feminine of 3283, and meaning the same:— + owl.

3285. **יַעְנַי, Ya'nay,** *yah-nah´ee*; from the same as 3283; *responsive; Jaanai,* an Israelite:—Jaanai.

3286. **יָעַף, yâ'aph,** *yaw-af´*; a primitive root; to *tire* (as if from wearisome *flight*):—faint, cause to fly, (be) weary (self).

3287. **יָעֵף, yâ'êph,** *yaw-afe´*; from 3286; *fatigued*; (figurative) *exhausted*:—faint, weary.

3288. **יְעָף, yᵉ'âph,** *yeh-awf´*; from 3286; *fatigue* (adverbial) utterly *exhausted*:—swiftly.

3289. **יָעַץ, yâ'ats,** *yaw-ats´*; a primitive root; to *advise*; (reflexive) to *deliberate* or *resolve*:—advertise, take advice, advise (well), consult, (give, take) counsel (-lor), determine, devise, guide, purpose.

A verb meaning to advise, to consult, to counsel, to be advised, to deliberate, to conspire, to take counsel. Jethro, Moses' father-in-law, advised Moses about how to judge the people of Israel (Ex 18:19); and wise men, such as Hushai and Ahithophel, served as counselors to kings and other important people (2Sa 17:15; 1Ki 12:9); as did prophets (Jer 38:15). Many counselors help ensure that plans will succeed (Pr 15:22); God counseled His servants (Ps 16:7); the coming ruler of Israel will be the "Wonderful Counselor" (Isa 9:6[5]). The verb also means to decide, to make plans or decisions. These plans can be for or against someone or something with God or a human as a subject of the sentence (Isa 7:5; 14:24; Jer 49:20; Hab 2:10), but God's plans will never fail (Isa 14:24).

In the passive, this verb means to permit oneself to be counseled—wisdom is gained by a person who acts in this manner (Pr 13:10; cf. 1:5). More often, this stem expresses a reciprocal sense: Rehoboam consulted together with the elders (1Ki 12:6); and the enemies of the psalmist conspired against him (Ps 71:10). In the reflexive stem, it means to take counsel against as when the Lord's enemies conspired against His people (Ps 83:3[4]).

3290. **יַעֲקֹב, Ya'ăqôb,** *yah-ak-obe´*; from 6117; *heel*-catcher (i.e. supplanter); *Jaakob,* the Israelite patriarch:—Jacob.

3291. **יַעֲקֹבָה, Ya'ăqôbâh,** *yah-ak-o´-baw*; from 3290; *Jaakobah,* an Israelite:—Jaakobah.

3292. **יַעֲקָן, Ya'ăqân,** *yah-ak-awn´*; from the same as 6130; *Jaakan,* an Idumæan:—Jaakan. Compare 1142.

3293. **יַעַר, ya'ar,** *yah´-ar*; from an unused root probably meaning to *thicken* with verdure; a *copse* of bushes; hence a *forest*; hence *honey* in the *comb* (as hived in trees):—[honey-] comb, forest, wood.

3294. **יַעְרָה, Ya'râh,** *yah-raw´*; a form of 3295; *Jarah,* an Israelite:—Jarah.

3295. **יַעֲרָה, ya'ărâh,** *yah-ar-aw´*; feminine of 3293, and meaning the same:—[honey-] comb, forest.

3296. **יַעֲרֵי אֹרְגִים, Ya'ărêy 'Ôrᵉgîym,** *yah-ar-ay´ o-reg-eem´*; from the plural of 3293 and the masculine plural participle active of 707; *woods of weavers; Jaare-Oregim,* an Israelite:—Jaare-oregim.

3297. **יְעָרִים, Yᵉ'ârîym,** *yeh-aw-reem´*; plural of 3293; *forests; Jeärim,* a place in Palestine:—Jearim. Compare 7157.

3298. **יַעֲרֶשְׁיָה, Ya'ăreshyâh,** *yah-ar-esh-yaw´*; from an unused root of uncertain significance and 3050; *Jaareshjah,* an Israelite:—Jaresiah.

3299. **יַעֲשׂוּ, Ya'ăsâv,** *yah-as-awv´*; from 6213; *they will do; Jaasu,* an Israelite:—Jaasau.

3300. **יַעֲשִׂיאֵל, Ya'ăsîy'êl,** *yah-as-ee-ale´*; from 6213 and 410; *made of God; Jaasiel,* an Israelite:—Jaasiel, Jasiel.

3301. **יִפְדְיָה, Yiphdᵉyâh,** *yif-deh-yaw´*; from 6299 and 3050; *Jah will liberate; Jiphdejah,* an Israelite:—Iphedeiah.

3302. **יָפָה, yâphâh,** *yaw-faw´*; a primitive root; (properly) to *be bright,* i.e. (by implication) *beautiful*:—be beautiful, be (make self) fair (-r), deck.

3303. **יָפֶה, yâpheh,** *yaw-feh´*; from 3302; *beautiful* (literal or figurative):— + beautiful, beauty, comely, fair (-est, one), + goodly, pleasant, well.

3304. **יְפֵה־פִיָּה, yᵉphêh-phîyyâh,** *yef-eh´ fee-yaw´*; from 3302 by reduplication; *very beautiful*:—very fair.

3305. **יָפוֹ, Yâphôw,** *yaw-fo´*; or **יָפוֹא, Yâphôw',** *yaw-fo´*; (Ezr 3:7), from 3302; *beautiful; Japho,* a place in Palestine:—Japha, Joppa.

3306. **יָפַח, yâphach,** *yaw-fakh´*; a primitive root; (properly) to *breathe* hard, i.e. (by implication) to *sigh*:—bewail self.

3307. **יָפֵחַ, yâphêach,** *yaw-fay´-akh*; from 3306; (properly) *puffing,* i.e. (figurative) *meditating*:—such as breathe out.

3308. **יֳפִי, yŏphîy,** *yof-ee´*; from 3302; *beauty*:—beauty.

3309. **יָפִיעַ, Yâphîya',** *yaw-fee´-ah*; from 3313; *bright; Japhia,* the name of a Canaanite, an Israelite, and a place in Palestine:—Japhia.

3310. **יַפְלֵט, Yaphlêt,** *yaf-late´*; from 6403; *he will deliver; Japhlet,* an Israelite:—Japhlet.

3311. **יַפְלֵטִי, Yaphlêtîy,** *yaf-lay-tee´*; patronymic from 3310; a *Japhletite* or descendant of Japhlet:—Japhleti.

3312. **יְפֻנֶּה, Yᵉphunneh,** *yef-oon-neh´*; from 6437; *he will be prepared; Jephunneh,* the name of two Israelites:—Jephunneh.

3313. **יָפַע, yâpha',** *yaw-fah´*; a primitive root; to *shine*:—be light, shew self, (cause to) shine (forth).

3314. **יִפְעָה, yiph'âh,** *yif-aw´*; from 3313; *splendor* or (figurative) *beauty*:—brightness.

3315. **יֶפֶת, Yepheth,** *yeh´-feth*; from 6601; *expansion; Jepheth,* a son of Noah; also his posterity:—Japheth.

3316. **יִפְתָּח, Yiphtâch,** *yif-tawkh´*; from 6605; *he will open; Jiphtach,* an Israelite; also a place in Palestine:—Jephthah, Jiphtah.

3317. **יִפְתַּח־אֵל, Yiphtach-'êl,** *yif-tach-ale´*; from 6605 and 410; *God will open; Jiphtach-el,* a place in Palestine:—Jiphthah-el.

3318. **יָצָא, yâtsâ',** *yaw-tsaw´*; a primitive root; to *go* (causatively, *bring*) *out,* in a great variety of applications, literal and figurative, direct and proximate:— × after, appear, × assuredly, bear out, × begotten, break out, bring forth (out, up), carry out, come (abroad, out, thereat, without), + be condemned, depart (-ing, -ure), draw forth, in the end, escape, exact, fail, fall (out), fetch forth (out), get away (forth, hence, out), (able to, cause to, let) go abroad (forth, on, out), going out, grow, have forth (out), issue out, lay (lie) out, lead out, pluck out, proceed, pull out, put away, be risen, × scarce, send with commandment, shoot forth, spread, spring out, stand out, × still, × surely, take forth (out), at any time, × to [and fro], utter.

3319. **יְצָא, yᵉtsa',** *yets-ah´*; (Chaldee); corresponding to 3318:—finish.

3320. יָצַב, yâtsab, *yaw-tsab´*; a primitive root; to *place* (any thing so as to stay); (reflexive) to *station, offer, continue*:—present selves, remaining, resort, set (selves), (be able to, can, with-) stand (fast, forth, -ing, still, up).

3321. יְצַב, y^e^tsab, *yets-ab´*; (Chaldee); corresponding to 3320; to *be firm*; hence to *speak surely*:—truth.

An Aramaic verb meaning to take, to make a stand, to gain certainty, to know the truth. It is used only once in the entire OT, in Da 7:19, where Daniel desired to know the truth of the fourth beast's identity. This corresponds with the Hebrew word *yâtsab* (3320), meaning to make one's stand, to take one's stand, or to present oneself.

3322. יָצַג, yâtsag, *yaw-tsag´*; a primitive root; to *place* permanently:—establish, leave, make, present, put, set, stay.

3323. יִצְהָר, yitshâr, *yits-hawr´*; from 6671; *oil* (as producing *light*); (figurative) *anointing*:— + anointed, oil.

A masculine noun meaning fresh oil, anointing oil. It most commonly refers to fresh oil produced from the land, most likely from olive trees (2Ki 18:32). This oil could be in an unprocessed state (Dt 7:13). Concerning religious uses, people gave this oil to the Levites and priests as a means of support (2Ch 31:5). The Hebrew word is also used once for the purpose of anointing (Zec 4:14).

3324. יִצְהָר, Yitshâr, *yits-hawr´*; the same as 3323; *Jitshar*, an Israelite:—Izhar.

3325. יִצְהָרִי, Yitshârîy, *yits-haw-ree´*; patronymic from 3324; a *Jitsharite* or descendant of Jitshar:—Izeharites, Izharites.

3326. יָצוּעַ, yâtsûwa', *yaw-tsoo´-ah*; passive participle of 3331; *spread*, i.e. a *bed*; (architecturally) an *extension*, i.e. *wing* or *lean-to* (a single story or collectively):—bed, chamber, couch.

3327. יִצְחָק, Yitschâq, *yits-khawk´*; from 6711; *laughter* (i.e. *mockery*); *Jitschak* (or Isaac), son of Abraham:—Isaac. Compare 3446.

3328. יִצְחַר, Yitschar, *yits-khar´*; from the same as 6713; *he will shine; Jitschar*, an Israelite:—and Zehoar [*from the margin*].

3329. יָצִיא, yâtsîy', *yaw-tsee´*; from 3318; *issue*, i.e. offspring:—those that came forth.

3330. יַצִּיב, yatstsîyb, *yats-tseeb´*; (Chaldee); from 3321; *fixed, sure*; (concrete) *certainty*:—certain (-ty), true, truth.

3331. יַצַע, yatsa', *yaw-tsah´*; a primitive root; to *strew* as a surface:—make [one's] bed, × lie, spread.

3332. יָצַק, yâtsaq, *yaw-tsak´*; a primitive root; (properly) to *pour* out (transitive or intransitive); (by implication) to *melt* or *cast* as metal; (by extension) to *place* firmly, to *stiffen* or grow hard:—cast, cleave fast, be (as) firm, grow, be hard, lay out, molten, overflow, pour (out), run out, set down, steadfast.

3333. יְצֻקָה, y^e^tsuqâh, *yets-oo-kaw´*; passive participle feminine of 3332; *poured* out, i.e. *run* into a mould:—when it was cast.

3334. יָצַר, yâtsar, *yaw-tsar´*; a primitive root; to *press* (intrans.), i.e. *be narrow*; (figurative) *be in distress*:—be distressed, be narrow, be straitened (in straits), be vexed.

3335. יָצַר, yâtsar, *yaw-tsar´*; probably identical with 3334 (through the *squeezing* into shape); ([compare 3331]); to *mould* into a form; especially as a *potter*; (figurative) to *determine* (i.e. form a resolution):—× earthen, fashion, form, frame, make (-r), potter, purpose.

A verb meaning to form, to fashion, to shape, to devise. The primary meaning of the word is derived from the idea of cutting or framing. It is used of God's fashioning man from the dust of the ground (Ge 2:7); God's creative works in nature (Ps 95:5; Am 4:13); and in the womb (Ps 139:16; Jer 1:5; cf. Zec 12:1); the molding of clay (Isa 29:16; 45:9); the framing of seasons (Ps 74:17); the forging of metal (Isa 44:12); the crafting of weapons (Isa 54:17); the making of plans (Ps 94:20; Isa 46:11; Jer 18:11). It also signifies a potter (Ps 2:9; Isa 41:25); a sculptor (Isa 44:9); or the Creator (Isa 43:1; 44:2, 24). By extension, the word conveys the notion of predestination and election (2Ki 19:25; Isa 49:5).

3336. יֵצֶר, yêtser, *yay´-tser*; from 3335; a *form*; (figurative) *conception* (i.e. purpose):—frame, thing framed, imagination, mind, work.

A masculine noun meaning form, framing, purpose, imagination. One use of this word was to refer to a pottery vessel formed by a potter (i.e. that which was formed [Isa 29:16]). Another example of a formed object was a graven image (Hab 2:18). The psalmist said that man was formed from the dust (Ps 103:14). This word also carries the connotation of something thought of in the mind, such as wickedness in people's hearts (Ge 6:5); or something treasured or stored in the heart (1Ch 29:18).

3337. יֵצֶר, Yêtser, *yay´-tser*; the same as 3336; *Jetser*, an Israelite:—Jezer.

3338. יָצֻר, yâtsur, *yaw-tsoor´*; passive participle of 3335; *structure*, i.e. limb or part:—member.

3339. יִצְרִי, Yitsrîy, *yits-ree´*; from 3335; *formative; Jitsri*, an Israelite:—Isri.

3340. יִצְרִי, Yitsrîy, *yits-ree´*; patron. from 3337; a *Jitsrite* (collectively) or descendant of Jetser:—Jezerites.

3341. יָצַת, yâtsath, *yaw-tsath´*; a primitive root; to *burn* or *set on fire*; (figurative) to *desolate*:—burn (up), be desolate, set (on) fire ([fire]), kindle.

3342. יֶקֶב, yeqeb, *yeh´-keb*; from an unused root meaning to *excavate*; a *trough* (as dug out); specifically a wine-*vat* (whether the lower one, into which the juice drains; or the upper, in which the grapes are crushed):—fats, presses, press-fat, wine (-press).

3343. יְקַבְצְאֵל, Y^e^qabts^e'^êl, *yek-ab-tseh-ale´*; from 6908 and 410; *God will gather; Jekabtseël*, a place in Palestine:—Jekabzeel. Compare 6909.

3344. יָקַד, yâqad, *yaw-kad´*; a primitive root; to *burn*:—(be) burn (-ing), × from the hearth, kindle.

3345. יְקַד, y^e^qad, *yek-ad´*; (Chaldee); corresponding to 3344:—burning.

3346. יְקֵדָה, y^e^qêdâh, *yek-ay-daw´*; (Chaldee); from 3345; a *conflagration*:—burning.

3347. יָקְדְעָם, Yoqd^e'^âm, *yok-deh-awm´*; from 3344 and 5971; *burning of* (the) *people; Jokdeäm*, a place in Palestine:—Jokdeam.

3348. יָקֶה, Yâqeh, *yaw-keh´*; from an unused root probably meaning to *obey; obedient; Jakeh*, a symbolical name (for Solomon):—Jakeh.

3349. יְקָהָה, y^e^qâhâh, *yek-aw-haw´*; from the same as 3348; *obedience*:—gathering, to obey.

A feminine noun meaning obedience. In Jacob's prophecy to Judah, he said that the kingship would not depart from Judah's descendants until one came who would have the obedience of the nations (Ge 49:10). This verse is considered by many to be prophetic of Jesus Christ. In the sayings of Agur, the disobedient child should have his eyes pecked out by ravens and vultures (Pr 30:17).

3350. יְקוֹד, y^e^qôwd, *yek-ode´*; from 3344; a *burning*:—burning.

3351. יְקוּם, y^e^qûwm, *yek-oom´*; from 6965; (properly) *standing* (extant), i.e. (by implication) a *living thing*:—(living) substance.

3352. יָקוֹשׁ, yâqôwsh, *yaw-koshe´*; from 3369; (properly) *entangling*; hence a *snarer*:—fowler.

3353. יָקוּשׁ, yâqûwsh, *yaw-koosh´*; passive participle of 3369; (properly) *entangled*, i.e. (by implication) (intransitive) a *snare*, or (transitive) a *snarer*:—fowler, snare.

3354. יְקוּתִיאֵל, Yᵉqûwthîy'êl, *yek-ooth-ee´-ale*; from the same as 3348 and 410; *obedience of God; Jekuthiël*, an Israelite:—Jekuthiel.

3355. יָקְטָן, Yoqtân, *yok-tawn´*; from 6994; *he will be made little; Joktan*, an Arabian patriarch:—Joktan.

3356. יָקִים, Yâqîym, *yaw-keem´*; from 6965; *he will raise; Jakim*, the name of two Israelites:—Jakim. Compare 3079.

3357. יַקִּיר, yaqqîyr, *yak-keer´*; from 3365; *precious*:—dear.

3358. יַקִּיר, yaqqîyr, *yak-keer´*; (Chaldee); corresponding to 3357:—noble, rare.

3359. יְקַמְיָה, Yᵉqamyâh, *yek-am-yaw´*; from 6965 and 3050; *Jah will rise; Jekamjah*, the name of two Israelites:—Jekamiah. Compare 3079.

3360. יְקַמְעָם, Yᵉqamʻâm, *yek-am´-awm*; from 6965 and 5971; (the) *people will rise; Jekamam*, an Israelite:—Jekameam. Compare 3079, 3361.

3361. יָקְמְעָם, Yoqmᵉʻâm, *yok-meh-awm´*; from 6965 and 5971; (the) *people will be raised; Jokmeäm*, a place in Palestine:—Jokmeam. Compare 3360, 3362.

3362. יָקְנְעָם, Yoqnᵉʻâm, *yok-neh-awm´*; from 6969 and 5971; (the) *people will be lamented; Jokneäm*, a place in Palestine:—Jokneam.

3363. יָקַע, yâqaʻ, *yaw-kah´*; a primitive root; (properly) to *sever* oneself, i.e. (by implication) to *be dislocated*; (figurative) to *abandon*; (causative) to *impale* (and thus allow to drop to pieces by *rotting*):—be alienated, depart, hang (up), be out of joint.

3364. יָקַץ, yâqats, *yaw-kats´*; a primitive root; to *awake* (intransitive):—(be) awake (-d).

3365. יָקַר, yâqar, *yaw-kar´*; a primitive root; (properly) apparently to *be heavy*, i.e. (figurative) *valuable*; (causative) to *make rare*; (figurative) to *inhibit*:—be (make) precious, be prized, be set by, withdraw.

3366. יְקָר, yᵉqâr, *yek-awr´*; from 3365; *value*, i.e. (concrete) *wealth*; (abstract) *costliness, dignity*:—honour, precious (things), price.

3367. יְקָר, yᵉqâr, *yek-awr´*; (Chaldee); corresponding to 3366:—glory, honour.

3368. יָקָר, yâqâr, *yaw-kawr´*; from 3365; *valuable* (objective or subjective):—brightness, clear, costly, excellent, fat, honourable women, precious, reputation.

3369. יָקֹשׁ, yâqôsh, *yaw-koshe´*; a primitive root; to *ensnare* (literal or figurative):—fowler (lay a) snare.

A verb meaning to snare. The word refers primarily to the snaring of animals, especially birds (Ps 124:7; Ecc 9:12). However, this word always refers figuratively to the catching of a person or people in an undesirable situation. The bait of these snares is people's desire for other gods (Dt 7:25; Ps 141:9, cf. Ps 141:4). Pride makes persons susceptible to snares (Jer 50:24[cf. Jer 50:31, 32]) while humility (Pr 6:2) and the help of God may deliver them. In two similar passages in Isaiah, Israel is snared by their rejection of God's word (Isa 8:15; 28:13).

3370. יָקְשָׁן, Yoqshân, *yok-shawn´*; from 3369; *insidious; Jokshan*, an Arabian patriarch:—Jokshan.

3371. יָקְתְאֵל, Yoqthᵉʼêl, *yok-theh-ale´*; probably from the same as 3348 and 410; *veneration of God* [compare 3354]; *Joktheël*, the name of a place in Palestine, and of one in Idumæa:—Joktheel.

3372. יָרֵא, yârê', *yaw-ray´*; a primitive root; to *fear*; (moral) to *revere*; (causative) to *frighten*:—affright, be (make) afraid, dread (-ful), (put in) fear (-ful, -fully, -ing), (be had in) reverence (-end), × see, terrible (act, -ness, thing).

A verb meaning to fear, to respect, to reverence, to be afraid, to be awesome, to be feared, to make afraid, to frighten. The most common translations are to be afraid, to fear, to fear God. "The fear of the LORD is the beginning of knowledge" is a famous use of the noun (Pr 1:7 NIV); the famous narrative of the near sacrifice of Isaac proved to God that Abraham feared Him above all (Ge 22:12); people who feared God were considered faithful and trustworthy for such fear constrained them to believe and act morally (Ex 18:21). The midwives of Pharaoh feared God and did not kill the newborn Hebrew males (Ex 1:17, 21). The fear of the Lord was closely tied to keeping God's decrees and laws (Dt 6:2); people who fear God delight in hearing of His deeds for His people (Ps 66:16). The God of Israel was an object of respectful fear (Le 19:30; 26:2) for Obadiah and Hezekiah (1Ki 18:3, 12; Jer 26:19). In addition, because Israel feared and worshipped other gods, they were destroyed by Assyria (Jgs 6:10; 2Ki 17:7, 35). They were to worship and fear only the Lord their God (Jos 24:14). Israel had an unnecessary and unhealthy fear of the nations of Canaan (Dt 7:19). The verb describes the fear of men: Jacob feared Esau, his brother (Ge 32:7[8]); and the official in charge of Daniel feared the king (Da 1:10). In the sense of respectful fear, each person was to honour his mother and father (Le 19:3). As a stative verb, it describes a state of being or attitude, such as being afraid or fearful: a man afraid of war was to remove himself from the army of Israel (Dt 20:3, 8; Jgs 7:3); as a result of rebellion, Adam and Eve were afraid before the Lord (Ge 3:10).

In the passive form, the word expresses the idea of being feared, held in esteem: God was feared and awesome (Ex 15:11; Ps 130:4); His deeds were awe-inspiring (Dt 10:21; 2Sa 7:23); the Cushites were an aggressive people feared by many (Isa 18:2); even the threatening desert area was considered fearful or dreadful (Dt 8:15).

The factitive or intensive form means to frighten or to impart fear: the wise woman of Tekoa was frightened by the people (2Sa 14:15); and the governor of Samaria, Sanballat, attempted to frighten Nehemiah so that he would not rebuild the wall of Jerusalem (Ne 6:9).

3373. יָרֵא, yârê', *yaw-ray´*; from 3372; *fearing*; moral *reverent*:—afraid, fear (-ful).

An adjective meaning fearing, afraid. The Hebrew word is used when the author of Genesis speaks of Abraham fearing God because he did not hold back his only son (Ge 22:12). Jacob asked God to save him from Esau, because he was afraid that Esau would attack him (Ge 32:11[12]). Jethro told Moses to select as judges men who feared God (Ex 18:21). Proverbs says that a woman who fears the Lord is to be praised (Pr 31:30). Jeremiah told the Israelite army that God said not to fear the king of Babylon (Jer 42:11). See the primary verb *yârê'* (3372).

3374. יִרְאָה, yir'âh, *yir-aw´*; feminine of 3373; *fear* (also used as infinitive); moral *reverence*:— × dreadful, × exceedingly, fear (-fulness).

A feminine noun meaning fear. The word usually refers to the fear of God and is viewed as a positive quality. This fear acknowledges God's good intentions (Ex 20:20). It will motivate and delight even the Messiah (Isa 11:2, 3). This fear is produced by God's Word (Ps 119:38; Pr 2:5) and makes a person receptive to wisdom and knowledge (Pr 1:7; 9:10). It is even identified with wisdom (Job 28:28; Pr 15:33). The fear of the Lord may be lost by despair of one's own situation (Job 6:14) or envy of a sinner's (Pr 23:17). This fear restrains people from sin (Ge 20:11; Ex 20:20; Ne 5:9); gives confidence (Job 4:6; Pr 14:26); helps rulers and causes judges to act justly (2Sa 23:3; 2Ch 19:9; Ne 5:15); results in good sleep (Pr 19:23); with humility, leads to riches, honour, and life (Pr 22:4). The word also refers to the fear of briers and thorns (Isa 7:25); and the fear of Israel that would fall on other nations (Dt 2:25).

3375. יִרְאוֹן, Yir'ôwn, *yir-ohn´*; from 3372; *fearfulness; Jiron*, a place in Palestine:—Iron.

3376. יִרְאִיָּיה, Yir'îyyâyh, *yir-ee-yaw´*; from 3373 and 3050; *fearful of Jah; Jirijah*, an Israelite:—Irijah.

3377. יָרֵב, Yârêb, *yaw-rabe´*; from 7378; *he will contend; Jareb*, a symbolical name for Assyria:—Jareb. Compare 3402.

3378. יְרֻבַּעַל, Yᵉrubbaʻal, *yer-oob-bah´-al*; from 7378 and 1168; *Baal will contend; Jerubbaal*, a symbolical name of Gideon:—Jerubbaal.

3379. יָרָבְעָם, Yârob'âm, *yaw-rob-awm´*; from 7378 and 5971; (the) *people will contend; Jarobam*, the name of two Israelites kings:—Jeroboam.

3380. יְרֻבֶּשֶׁת, Yᵉrubbesheth, *yer-oob-beh´-sheth*; from 7378 and 1322; *shame* (i.e. the idol) *will contend; Jerubbesheth*, a symbolical name for Gideon:—Jerubbesheth.

3381. יָרַד, yârad, *yaw-rad´*; a primitive root; to *descend* (literally) to *go downwards*; or conventionally to a lower region, as the shore, a boundary, the enemy, etc.; (figuratively) to *fall*; (causative) to *bring down* (in all the above applications):—× abundantly, bring down, carry down, cast down, (cause to) come (-ing) down, fall (down), get down, go (-ing) down (-ward), hang down, × indeed, let down, light (down), put down (off), (cause to, let) run down, sink, subdue, take down.

3382. יֶרֶד, Yered, *yeh´-red*; from 3381; a *descent; Jered*, the name of an antediluvian, and of an Israelite:—Jared.

3383. יַרְדֵּן, Yardên, *yar-dane´*; from 3381; a *descender; Jarden*, the principal river of Palestine:—Jordan.

3384. יָרָה, yârâh, *yaw-raw´*; or (2Ch 26:15) יָרָא, **yârâ',** *yaw-raw´*; a primitive root; (properly) to *flow* as water (i.e. to *rain*); (transitive) to *lay* or *throw* (especially an arrow, i.e. to *shoot*); (figurative) to *point* out (as if by *aiming* the finger), to *teach*:—(+) archer, cast, direct, inform, instruct, lay, shew, shoot, teach (-er, -ing), through.

A verb meaning to shoot, to throw, to pour. God hurled Pharaoh's army into the sea (Ex 15:4); Joshua cast lots (Jos 18:6); and God asked Job who laid the cornerstone of the earth (Job 38:6). This word is used often in reference to shooting with arrows, as Jonathan (1Sa 20:36); and those who killed some of David's men (2Sa 11:24). King Uzziah made machines that shot arrows (2Ch 26:15); and the wicked shot arrows at the upright of heart (Ps 11:2; 64:4[5]). In the sense of throwing, people were overthrown (Nu 21:30); and Job said that God had thrown him in the mud (Job 30:19).

3385. יְרוּאֵל, Yᵉrûw'êl, *yer-oo-ale´*; from 3384 and 410; *founded of God; Jeruel*, a place in Palestine:—Jeruel.

3386. יָרוֹחַ, Yârôwach, *yaw-ro´-akh*; perhaps denominative from 3394; (born at the) new *moon; Jaroäch*, an Israelite:—Jaroah.

3387. יָרוֹק, yârôwq, *yaw-roke´*; from 3417; *green*, i.e. an herb:—green thing.

3388. יְרוּשָׁא, Yᵉrûwshâ', *yer-oo-shaw´*; or יְרוּשָׁה, **Yᵉrûwshâh,** *yer-oo-shaw´*; feminine passive participle of 3423; *possessed; Jerusha* or *Jerushàh*, an Israelitess:—Jerusha, Jerushah.

3389. יְרוּשָׁלַםִ, Yᵉrûwshâlaim, *yer-oo-shaw-lah´-im*; rarely יְרוּשָׁלַיִם, **Yᵉrûwshâlayim,** *yer-oo-shaw-lah´-yim*; a dual (in allusion to its two main hills [the true pointing, at least of the former reading, seems to be that of 3390]); probably from (the passive participle of) 3384 and 7999; *founded peaceful; Jerushalaïm* or *Jerushalem*, the capital city of Palestine:—Jerusalem.

3390. יְרוּשְׁלֶם, Yᵉrûwshâlem, *yer-oo-shaw-lem´*; (Chaldee); corresponding to 3389:—Jerusalem.

3391. יֶרַח, yerach, *yeh´-rakh*; from an unused root of uncertain significance; a *lunation*, i.e. *month*:—month, moon.

3392. יֶרַח, Yerach, *yeh´-rakh*; the same as 3391; *Jerach*, an Arabian patriarch:—Jerah.

3393. יְרַח, yᵉrach, *yeh-rakh´*; (Chaldee); corresponding to 3391; a *month*:—month.

3394. יָרֵחַ, yârêach, *yaw-ray´-akh*; from the same as 3391; the *moon*:—moon.

3395. יְרֹחָם, Yᵉrôchâm, *yer-o-khawm´*; from 7355; *compassionate; Jerocham*, the name of seven or eight Israelites:—Jeroham.

3396. יְרַחְמְאֵל, Yᵉrachmᵉ'êl, *yer-akh-meh-ale´*; from 7355 and 410; *God will compassionate; Jerachmeël*, the name of three Israelites:—Jerahmeel.

3397. יְרַחְמְאֵלִי, Yᵉrachmᵉ'êlîy, *yer-akh-meh-ay-lee´*; patronymic from 3396; a *Jerachmeëlite* or descendant of Jerachmeel:—Jerahmeelites.

3398. יַרְחָע, Yarchâ', *yar-khaw´*; probably of Egyptian origin; *Jarcha*, an Egyptian:—Jarha.

3399. יָרַט, yâraṭ, *yaw-rat´*; a primitive root; to *precipitate* or *hurl* (*rush*) headlong; (intransitive) to *be rash*:—be perverse, turn over.

3400. יְרִיאֵל, Yᵉrîy'êl, *yer-ee-ale´*; from 3384 and 410; *thrown of God; Jeriël*, an Israelite:—Jeriel. Compare 3385.

3401. יָרִיב, yârîyb, *yaw-rebe´*; from 7378; (literally) *he will contend*; proper adjective *contentious*; used as noun, an *adversary*:—that contend (-eth), that strive.

3402. יָרִיב, Yârîyb, *yaw-rebe´*; the same as 3401; *Jarib*, the name of three Israelites:—Jarib.

3403. יְרִיבַי, Yᵉrîybay, *yer-eeb-ah´ee*; from 3401; *contentious; Jeribai*, an Israelite:—Jeribai.

3404. יְרִיָּה, Yᵉrîyyâh, *yer-ee-yaw´*; or יְרִיָּהוּ, **Yᵉrîy-yâhûw,** *yer-ee-yaw´-hoo*; from 3384 and 3050; *Jah will throw; Jerijah*, an Israelite:—Jeriah, Jerijah.

3405. יְרִיחוֹ, Yᵉrîychôw, *yer-ee-kho´*; or יְרֵחוֹ, **Yᵉrêchôw,** *yer-ay-kho´*; or variation (1Ki 16:34) יְרִיחֹה, **Yᵉrîychôh,** *yer-ee-kho´*; perhaps from 3394; *its month*; or else from 7306; *fragrant; Jericho* or *Jerecho*, a place in Palestine:—Jericho.

3406. יְרִימוֹת, Yᵉrîymôwth, *yer-ee-mohth´*; or יְרֵימוֹת, **Yᵉrêymôwth,** *yer-ay-mohth´*; or יְרֵמוֹת, **Yᵉrêmôwth,** *yer-ay-mohth´*; feminine plural from 7311; *elevations; Jerimoth* or *Jeremoth*, the name of twelve Israelites:—Jeremoth, Jerimoth, and Ramoth [*from the margin*].

3407. יְרִיעָה, yᵉrîy'âh, *yer-ee-aw´*; from 3415; a *hanging* (as *tremulous*):—curtain.

3408. יְרִיעוֹת, Yᵉrîy'ôwth, *yer-ee-ohth´*; plural of 3407; *curtains; Jerioth*, an Israelitess:—Jerioth.

3409. יָרֵךְ, yârêk, *yaw-rake´*; from an unused root meaning to *be soft*; the *thigh* (from its fleshy *softness*); (by euphemism) the *generative parts*; (figurative) a *shank, flank, side*:—× body, loins, shaft, side, thigh.

A feminine singular noun meaning a thigh, a side, a base. The word is used of Jacob's thigh in the story of his wrestling with God (Ge 32:25[26], 32[33]) and is most likely used euphemistically of genitals (Ge 46:26; Ex 1:5; Jgs 8:30). It is best translated side in the cultic language of Le 1:11 and Nu 3:29, 35. The Pentateuch also employs it with the meaning of a base (Ex 25:31).

3410. יַרְכָה, yarkâh, *yar-ka´*; (Chaldee); corresponding to 3411; a *thigh*:—thigh.

3411. יְרֵכָה, yᵉrêkâh, *yer-ay-kaw´*; feminine of 3409; (properly) the *flank*; but used only figuratively, the *rear* or *recess*:—border, coast, part, quarter, side.

3412. יַרְמוּת, Yarmûwth, *yar-mooth´*; from 7311; *elevation; Jarmuth*, the name of two places in Palestine:—Jarmuth.

3413. יְרֵמַי, Yᵉrêmay, *yer-ay-mah´ee*; from 7311; *elevated; Jeremai*, an Israelite:—Jeremai.

3414. יִרְמְיָה, Yirmᵉyâh, *yir-meh-yaw´*; or יִרְמְיָהוּ, **Yirmᵉyâhûw,** *yir-meh-yaw´-hoo*; from 7311 and 3050; *Jah will rise; Jirmejah*, the name of eight or nine Israelites:—Jeremiah.

3415. יָרַע**, yâra‘,** *yaw-rah´*; a primitive root; (properly) to *be broken* up (with any violent action), i.e. (figurative) to *fear*:—be grievous [*only Isa 15:4; the rest belong* to 7489].

A verb meaning to tremble. It occurs only in Isa 15:4. As the result of the sudden devastation of Moab, his (i.e. Moab's or possibly an individual soldier's) life (or soul) trembles. The sentence could refer to inner turmoil: his soul trembles within him; or it could refer to an objective sense that his prospects of surviving are shaky; his life trembles before him (cf. Dt 28:66). Of course, both meanings could be true; both could even be implied.

3416. יִרְפְּאֵל**, Yirp^{e}'êl,** *yir-peh-ale´*; from 7495 and 410; *God will heal; Jirpeël*, a place in Palestine:—Irpeel.

3417. יָרַק**, yâraq,** *yaw-rak´*; a primitive root; to *spit*:— × but, spit.

3418. יֶרֶק**, yereq,** *yeh´-rek*; from 3417 (in the sense of *vacuity* of colour); (properly) *pallor*, i.e. hence the yellowish *green* of young and sickly vegetation; (concrete) *verdure*, i.e. grass or vegetation:—grass, green (thing).

3419. יָרָק**, yârâq,** *yaw-rawk´*; from the same as 3418; (properly) *green*; (concrete) a *vegetable*:—green, herbs.

3420. יֵרָקוֹן**, yêrâqôwn,** *yay-raw-kone´*; from 3418; *paleness*, whether of persons (from fright), or of plants (from drought):—greenish, yellow.

3421. יָרְקְעָם**, Yorqŏ‘âm,** *yor-ko-awm´*; from 7324 and 5971; *people will be poured forth; Jorkeäm*, a place in Palestine:—Jorkeam.

3422. יְרַקְרַק**, y^{e}raqraq,** *yer-ak-rak´*; from the same as 3418; *yellowishness*:—greenish, yellow.

3423. יָרַשׁ**, yârash,** *yaw-rash´*; or יָרֵשׁ**, yârêsh,** *yaw-raysh´*; a primitive root; to *occupy* (by *driving* out previous tenants, and *possessing* in their place); (by implication) to *seize*, to *rob*, to *inherit*; also to *expel*, to *impoverish*, to *ruin*:—cast out, consume, destroy, disinherit, dispossess, drive (-ing) out, enjoy, expel, × without fail, (give to, leave for) inherit (-ance, -or), + magistrate, be (make) poor, come to poverty, (give to, make to) possess, get (have) in (take) possession, seize upon, succeed, × utterly.

A verb meaning to take possession, to inherit, to dispossess, to drive out. This term is sometimes used in the generic sense of inheriting possessions (Ge 15:3, 4). But the word is used usually in connection with the idea of conquering a land. This verb is a theme of Deuteronomy in particular where God's promise of covenantal relationship is directly related to Israelite possession (and thereby foreign dispossession) of the land of Israel. This theme continued throughout Israel's history and prophetic message. Possession of the land was directly connected to a person's relationship with the Lord; breaking the covenantal relationship led to dispossession. But even in exile, Israelites awaited the day when they would repossess the land (Jer 30:3).

3424. יְרֵשָׁה**, y^{e}rêshâh,** *yer-ay-shaw´*; from 3423; *occupancy*:—possession.

A feminine noun meaning possession, property. It refers to a nation and is used only once in the Hebrew Bible. In Nu 24:18, Edom and Seir would become the possession of someone else (i.e. they would be defeated). This word comes from the root word *yârêsh* (3423).

3425. יְרֻשָּׁה**, y^{e}rushshâh,** *yer-oosh-shaw´*; from 3423; something *occupied*; a *conquest*; also a *patrimony*:—heritage, inheritance, possession.

A feminine noun meaning possession, inheritance. The word refers to an inheritance given, to a possession taken by force, or both. The word describes the land God gave to the Edomites, Moabites, and Ammonites (Dt 2:5, 9, 19). The Edomites and Ammonites, however, seized land from other tribes (Dt 2:12, 19). The Israelites, likewise, had to fight to gain their inheritance (Dt 3:20; Jos 12:6, 7). However, God later protected Israel's inheritance against the unjust claims of discontent Edomites, Moabites, and Ammonites (2Ch 20:11). The word is also used to refer to the possession of wives (Jgs 21:17) and land (Jer 32:8), both of which still waited to be claimed (sinfully in the former passage). In Ps 61:5[6], the word refers to God's presence as the inheritance of those who fear God.

3426. יֵשׁ**, yêsh,** *yaysh*; perhaps from an unused root meaning to *stand* out, or *exist; entity*; used adverbially or as a copula for the substantive verb (1961); there *is* or *are* (or any other form of the verb to *be*, as may suit the connection):—(there) are, (he, it, shall, there, there may, there shall, there should) be, thou do, had, hast, (which) hath, (I, shalt, that) have, (he, it, there) is, substance, it (there) was, (there) were, ye will, thou wilt, wouldest.

3427. יָשַׁב**, yâshab,** *yaw-shab´*; a primitive root; (properly) to *sit* down (specifically as judge, in ambush, in quiet); (by implication) to *dwell*, to *remain*; (causative) to *settle*, to *marry*:—(make to) abide (-ing), continue, (cause to, make to) dwell (-ing), ease self, endure, establish, × fail, habitation, haunt, (make to) inhabit (-ant), make to keep [house], lurking, × marry (-ing), (bring again to) place, remain, return, seat, set (-tle), (down-) sit (-down, still, -ting down, -ting [place] -uate), take, tarry.

A verb meaning to sit, to dwell, to inhabit, to endure, to stay. Apparently, to sit is the root idea, and other meanings are derived from this. The subject of the verb may be God, human, animal (Jer 50:39), or inanimate matter. The word sometimes emphasizes the location of persons, whether they were sitting under a tree (Jgs 6:11; 1Ki 19:4) or in a house (2Ki 6:32). It could also reflect a person's position: one sat as a judge (Pr 20:8; Isa 28:6); as a widow (Ge 38:11); or on a throne as king (Ex 12:29; 2Ki 13:13). Sometimes it indicated one's companions; one sits with scoffers (Ps 1:1); or with the elders of the land (Pr 31:23). The word may signify "to dwell," either temporarily (Le 23:42) or in a permanent dwelling (Ge 4:16; Zep 2:15). Sometimes the word means that an object or person stays in a limited area (Ex 16:29); or abides for a period of time (Le 12:4, 5; 2Sa 6:11); or for eternity (Ps 9:7[8]; 102:12[13]; 125:1). The years are even said to sit, that is, to pass (1Ki 22:1).

3428. יֶשֶׁבְאָב**, Yesheb'âb,** *yeh-sheb-awb´*; from 3427 and 1; *seat of* (his) *father; Jeshebab*, an Israelite:—Jeshebeab.

3429. יֹשֵׁב בַּשֶּׁבֶת**, Yôshêb bash-Shebeth,** *yo-shabe´ bash-sheh´-beth*; from the active participle of 3427 and 7674, with a preposition and the article interposed; *sitting in the seat; Josheb-bash-Shebeth*, an Israelite:—that sat in the seat.

3430. יִשְׁבִּי בְנֹב**, Yishbîy b^{e}-Nôb,** *yish-bee´ beh-nobe´*; from 3427 and 5011, with a pronoun suffix and a preposition interposed; *his dwelling* (is) *in Nob; Jishbo-be-Nob*, a Philistine:—Ishbi-benob [*from the margin*].

3431. יִשְׁבַּח**, Yishbach,** *yish-bakh´*; from 7623; *he will praise; Jishbach*, an Israelite:—Ishbah.

3432. יָשֻׁבִי**, Yâshubîy,** *yaw-shoo-bee´*; patronymic from 3437; a *Jashubite*, or descendant of Jashub:—Jashubites.

3433. יָשֻׁבִי לֶחֶם**, Yâshubîy Lechem,** *yaw-shoo´-bee leh´-khem*; from 7725 and 3899; *returner of bread; Jashubi-Lechem*, an Israelite:—Jashubi-lehem. [Probably the text should be pointed יֹשְׁבֵי לֶחֶם**, Yôshbêy Lechem,** *yosh-bay´ leh´-khem*, and rendered "(they were) inhabitants of Lechem," i.e. of Bethlehem (by contraction). Compare 3902].

3434. יָשָׁבְעָם**, Yâshob‘âm,** *yaw-shob-awm´*; from 7725 and 5971; *people will return; Jashobam*, the name of two or three Israelites:—Jashobeam.

3435. יִשְׁבָּק**, Yishbâq,** *yish-bawk´*; from an unused root corresponding to 7662; *he will leave; Jishbak*, a son of Abraham:—Ishbak.

3436. יָשְׁבְּקָשָׁה**, Yoshb^{e}qâshâh,** *yosh-bek-aw-shaw´*; from 3427 and 7186; a *hard seat; Joshbekashah*, an Israelite:—Joshbekashah.

3437. יָשׁוּב**, Yâshûwb,** *yaw-shoob´*; or יָשִׁיב**, Yâshîyb,** *yaw-sheeb´*; from 7725; *he will return; Jashub*, the name of two Israelites:—Jashub.

3438. **יִשְׁוָה, Yishvâh,** *yish-vaw´*; from 7737; *he will level; Jishvah,* an Israelite:—Ishvah, Isvah.

3439. **יְשׁוֹחָיָה, Yeshôwchâyâh,** *yesh-o-khaw-yaw´*; from the same as 3445 and 3050; *Jah will empty; Jeshochajah,* an Israelite:—Jeshoaiah.

3440. **יִשְׁוִי, Yishvîy,** *yish-vee´*; from 7737; *level; Jishvi,* the name of two Israelites:—Ishuai, Ishvi, Isui, Jesui.

3441. **יִשְׁוִי, Yishvîy,** *yish-vee´*; patronymic from 3440; a *Jishvite* (collective) or descendants of Jishvi:—Jesuites.

3442. **יֵשׁוּעַ, Yêshûwa',** *yah-shoo´-ah*; for 3091; *he will save; Jeshua,* the name of ten Israelites, also of a place in Palestine:—Jeshua.

3443. **יֵשׁוּעַ, Yêshûwa',** *yah-shoo´-ah*; (Chaldee); corresponding to 3442:—Jeshua.

3444. **יְשׁוּעָה, yeshûw'âh,** *yesh-oo´-aw*; feminine passive participle of 3467; something *saved,* i.e. (abstract) *deliverance*; hence *aid, victory, prosperity*:—deliverance, health, help (-ing), salvation, save, saving (health), welfare.

A feminine noun meaning salvation, deliverance, help, victory, prosperity. The primary meaning is to rescue from distress or danger. It is used to signify help given by other human beings (1Sa 14:45; 2Sa 10:11); help or security offered by fortified walls, delivering in the sense of preventing what would have happened if the walls were not there (Isa 26:1); one's welfare and safety (Job 30:15); salvation by God, with reference to being rescued by Him from physical harm (Ex 14:13; 2Ch 20:17); being rescued from the punishment due for sin (Ps 70:4[5]; Isa 33:6; 49:6; 52:7). Used in the plural, it signifies works of help (Ps 44:4[5]; 74:12); and God's salvation (2Sa 22:51; Ps 42:5[6]; 116:13).

3445. **יֶשַׁח, yeshach,** *yeh´-shakh*; from an unused root meaning to *gape* (as the empty stomach); *hunger*:—casting down.

3446. **יִשְׂחָק, Yisçhâq,** *yis-khawk´*; from 7831; *he will laugh; Jischak,* the heir of Abraham:—Isaac. Compare 3327.

3447. **יָשַׁט, yâshaṭ,** *yaw-shat´*; a primitive root; to *extend*:—hold out.

3448. **יִשַׁי, Yîshay,** *yee-shah´ee*; by Chaldee אִישַׁי, **'îyshay,** *ee-shah´ee*; from the same as 3426; *extant; Jishai,* David's father:—Jesse.

3449. **יִשִּׁיָּה, Yishshîyyâh,** *yish-shee-yaw´*; or יִשִּׁיָּהוּ, **Yishshîyyâhûw,** *yish-shee-yaw´-hoo*; from 5383 and 3050; *Jah will lend; Jishshijah,* the name of five Israelites:—Ishiah, Isshiah, Ishijah, Jesiah.

3450. **יְשִׂימָאֵל, Yesîymi'êl,** *yes-eem-aw-ale´*; from 7760 and 410; *God will place; Jesimaël,* an Israelite:—Jesimael.

3451. **יְשִׁימָה, yeshîymâh,** *yesh-ee-maw´*; from 3456; *desolation*:—let death seize [*from the margin*].

A feminine noun meaning desolation. It occurs in Ps 55:15[16] in an imprecatory sense, where desolation was to be the ultimate end of a wicked and false person. As such, it links with the developed wisdom theme of wickedness as consummating in nothingness. Here the word invoked the result of falsity and idolatry that the true believer would escape by steadfast loyalty to God (cf. Ps 55:16, 17, 22). Ezekiel used the verb from which this word is derived (*yâsham,* 3456) several times in describing the habitation of Israel due to idolatry and unbelief (Eze 6:6; 12:19; 19:7). The one who would falsely break the covenant (Ps 55:20[21], 21[22]) could expect desolation–a message Ezekiel preached to the people of the covenant.

3452. **יְשִׁימוֹן, yeshîymôwn,** *yesh-ee-mone´*; from 3456; a *desolation*:—desert, Jeshimon, solitary, wilderness.

3453. **יָשִׁישׁ, yâshîysh,** *yaw-sheesh´*; from 3486; an *old* man:—(very) aged (man), ancient, very old.

An adjective meaning aged. This word is found only in Job and referred to people who had gray hair; they were considered old or aged (Job 15:10; 32:6). It referred to a class of people, such as modern-day senior citizens (Job 12:12; 29:8).

3454. **יְשִׁישַׁי, Yeshîyshay,** *yesh-ee-shah´ee*; from 3453; *aged; Jeshishai,* an Israelite:—Jeshishai.

3455. **יָשַׂם, yâśam,** *yaw-sam´*; a primitive root; to *place*; (intransitive) to *be placed*:—be put (set).

3456. **יָשַׁם, yâsham,** *yaw-sham´*; a primitive root; to *lie waste*:—be desolate.

A verb meaning to be desolate, to lie waste. In most cases, the people affected were afraid famine would cause the land to lie waste. During the famine, the Egyptians asked Joseph to buy them and their land so they would not die and their land become desolate (Ge 47:19). The Israelites were commanded to tell the people of Canaan that they were to soon experience the fear and trembling of the Lord that would cause them to leave their land (Eze 12:19).

3457. **יִשְׁמָא, Yishmâ',** *yish-maw´*; from 3456; *desolate; Jishma,* an Israelite:—Ishma.

3458. **יִשְׁמָעֵאל, Yishmâ'ê'l,** *yish-maw-ale´*; from 8085 and 410; *God will hear; Jishmaël,* the name of Abraham's oldest son, and of five Israelites:—Ishmael.

3459. **יִשְׁמְעֵאלִי, Yishme'ê'lîy,** *yish-meh-ay-lee´*; patronymic from 3458; a *Jishmaëlite* or descendant of Jishmael:—Ishmaelite.

3460. **יִשְׁמַעְיָה, Yishma'yâh,** *yish-mah-yaw´*; or יִשְׁמַעְיָהוּ, **Yishma'yâhûw,** *yish-mah-yaw´-hoo*; from 8085 and 3050; *Jah will hear; Jishmajah,* the name of two Israelites:—Ishmaiah.

3461. **יִשְׁמְרַי, Yishmeray,** *yish-mer-ah´ee*; from 8104; *preservative; Jishmerai,* an Israelite:—Ishmerai.

3462. **יָשֵׁן, yâshên,** *yaw-shane´*; a primitive root; (properly) to *be slack* or *languid,* i.e. (by implication) to *sleep;* (figurative) to *die*; also to *grow old, stale* or *inveterate*:—old (store), remain long, (make to) sleep.

3463. **יָשֵׁן, yâshên,** *yaw-shane´*; from 3462; *sleepy*:—asleep, (one out of) sleep (-eth, -ing), slept.

3464. **יָשֵׁן, Yâshên,** *yaw-shane´*; the same as 3463; *Jashen,* an Israelite:—Jashen.

3465. **יָשָׁן, yâshân,** *yaw-shawn´*; from 3462; *old*:—old.

3466. **יְשָׁנָה, Yeshânâh,** *yesh-aw-naw´*; feminine of 3465; *Jeshanah,* a place in Palestine:—Jeshanah.

3467. **יָשַׁע, yâsha',** *yaw-shah´*; a primitive root; (properly) to *be open, wide* or *free,* i.e. (by implication) to *be safe*; (causative) to *free* or *succor*:— × at all, avenging, defend, deliver (-er), help, preserve, rescue, be safe, bring (having) salvation, save (-iour), get victory.

A verb meaning to save, to help, to deliver, to defend. The underlying idea of this verb is bringing to a place of safety or broad pasture as opposed to a narrow strait, symbolic of distress and danger. The word conveys the notion of deliverance from tribulation (Jgs 10:13, 14); deliverance from certain death (Ps 22:21[22]); rescue from one's enemies (Dt 28:31; Jgs 6:14); victory in time of war (1Sa 14:6); the protective duty of a shepherd (Eze 34:22; cf. Jgs 10:1); avenging wrongs (1Sa 25:33); compassionate aid in a time of need (2Ki 6:26, 27; Ps 12:1[2]); the salvation that only comes from God (Isa 33:22; Zep 3:17).

3468. **יֶשַׁע, yesha',** *yeh´-shah*; or יֵשַׁע, **yêsha',** *yay´-shah*; from 3467; *liberty, deliverance, prosperity*:—safety, salvation, saving.

A masculine noun meaning deliverance, rescue, liberty, welfare, salvation. David used the word salvation to describe the hope and welfare he had in the midst of strife due to his covenant with God (2Sa 23:5). God saves communities, as when He promised relief to Jerusalem (Isa 62:11) as well as individuals (see Mic 7:7).

3469. **יִשְׁעִי, Yish'îy,** *yish-ee´*; from 3467; *saving; Jishi,* the name of four Israelites:—Ishi.

3470. יְשַׁעְיָה**, Yᵉshaʻyâh,** *yesh-ah-yaw´*; or יְשַׁעְיָהוּ, **Yᵉshaʻyâhûw,** *yesh-ah-yaw´-hoo*; from 3467 and 3050; *Jah has saved; Jeshajah*, the name of seven Israelites:—Isaiah, Jesaiah, Jeshaiah.

3471. יָשְׁפֵה**, yâshᵉphêh,** *yaw-shef-ay´*; from an unused root meaning to *polish*; a gem supposed to be *jasper* (from the resemblance in name):—jasper.

3472. יִשְׁפָּה**, Yishpâh,** *yish-paw´*; perhaps from 8192; *he will scratch; Jishpah*, an Israelite:—Ispah.

3473. יִשְׁפָּן**, Yishpân,** *yish-pawn´*; probably from the same as 8227; *he will hide; Jishpan*, an Israelite:—Ishpan.

3474. יָשַׁר**, yâshar,** *yaw-shar´*; a primitive root; to *be straight* or *even*; (figurative) to *be* (causative, to *make*) *right, pleasant, prosperous*:—direct, fit, seem good (meet), + please (well), be (esteem, go) right (on), bring (look, make, take the) straight (way), be upright (-ly).

A verb meaning to be straight, to be upright, to be smooth, to be pleasing. When it means straight, it applies in a physical and an ethical sense as in straightforward. Therefore, this word can be used to refer to a path (1Sa 6:12); water (2Ch 32:30); the commands of God (Ps 119:128); or of a person (Hab 2:4). This word is also used to mean pleasing, as Samson found a Philistine woman pleasing to him (Jgs 14:7); but the cities that Solomon gave to Hiram were not pleasing (1Ki 9:12). It can also mean to make (or be) smooth or even, as with gold (1Ki 6:35); or a level road (Isa 40:3).

3475. יֵשֶׁר**, Yêsher,** *yay´-sher*; from 3474; the *right; Jesher*, an Israelite:—Jesher.

3476. יֹשֶׁר**, yôsher,** *yo´-sher*; from 3474; the *right*:—equity, meet, right, upright (-ness).

A masculine noun meaning straightness or uprightness, equity. The OT often talks of two paths in life and warns people to stay on the straight path and not to stray onto the crooked path (Pr 2:13). David was praised for walking in an upright manner before the Lord (1Ki 9:4). Uprightness was also praised as a good quality to possess (Pr 17:26). The word can also designate virtuous words that one speaks (Job 6:25). Another meaning less common is related to equity: one should give to another what is due to him or her (Pr 11:24).

3477. יָשָׁר**, yâshâr,** *yaw-shawr´*; from 3474; *straight* (literal or figurative):—convenient, equity, Jasher, just, meet (-est), + pleased well right (-eous), straight, (most) upright (-ly, -ness).

An adjective meaning straight, just, right. This word can refer to something physical, such as a path (Ps 107:7; Isa 26:7), but it more often means right in an ethical or an emotional sense, as agreeable or pleasing. Examples of this include what is right in God's eyes (Ex 15:26; 1Ki 11:33, 38; 2Ki 10:30); or in the eyes of people (Pr 12:15; Jer 40:5). It also means upright, such as God (Ps 25:8); and His ways (Hos 14:9[10]). Some people were considered upright, such as David (1Sa 29:6); and Job (Job 1:1). An ancient history book was called the book of Jashar or the book of the Upright (Jos 10:13; 2Sa 1:18). See the Hebrew root *yâshar* (3474).

3478. יִשְׂרָאֵל**, Yiśrâ'êl,** *yis-raw-ale´*; from 8280 and 410; *he will rule* as *God; Jisraël*, a symbolical name of Jacob; also (typically) of his posterity:—Israel.

3479. יִשְׂרָאֵל**, Yiśrâ'êl,** *yis-raw-ale´*; (Chaldee); corresponding to 3478:—Israel.

3480. יְשַׂרְאֵלָה**, Yᵉśar'êlâh,** *yes-ar-ale´-aw*; by variation from 3477 and 410 with directive enclitic; *right toward God; Jesarelah*, an Israelite:—Jesharelah. Compare 841.

3481. יִשְׂרְאֵלִי**, Yiśrᵉ'êlîy,** *yish-reh-ay-lee´*; patronymic from 3478; a *Jisreëlite* or descendant of Jisrael:—of Israel, Israelite.

3482. יִשְׂרְאֵלִית**, Yiśrᵉ'êlîyth,** *yis-reh-ay-leeth´*; feminine of 3481; a *Jisreëlitess* or female descendant of Jisrael:—Israelite.

3483. יִשְׁרָה**, yishrâh,** *yish-raw´*; feminine of 3477; *rectitude*:—uprightness.

A feminine noun meaning uprightness. The word is derived from *yâshar* (3474). It occurs only in 1Ki 3:6 where Solomon's prayer referred to the uprightness of David's heart that was rewarded with lovingkindness, especially the lovingkindness of having his son reign after him. David's life ruled out any meaning of sinlessness and pointed to repentance, faith, and knowledge of God as central to his uprightness (cf. Ro 4:6–8).

3484. יְשֻׁרוּן**, Yᵉshurûwn,** *yesh-oo-roon´*; from 3474; *upright; Jeshurun*, a symbolical name for Israel:—Jeshurun.

3485. יִשָּׂכָר**, Yiśśâkâr,** *yis-saw-kawr´*; (strictly יִשָּׂשכָר, **Yiśśâśkâr,** *yis-saws-kawr´*), from 5375 and 7939; *he will bring a reward; Jissaskar*, a son of Jacob:—Issachar.

3486. יָשֵׁשׁ**, yâshêsh,** *yaw-shaysh´*; from an unused root meaning to *blanch; gray*-haired, i.e. an *aged* man:—stoop for age.

An adjective meaning aged or decrepit. It is used only with the word *zâqên* (2204). When King Zedekiah rebelled, the Lord caused the king of the Chaldeans to destroy Jerusalem and all the people in it. The Chaldean king showed no mercy for any of the people, including the aged or old (2Ch 36:17).

3487. יַת**, yâth,** *yawth*; (Chaldee); corresponding to 853; a sign of the object of a verb:— + whom.

3488. יְתִב**, yᵉthib,** *yeth-eeb´*; (Chaldee); corresponding to 3427; to *sit* or *dwell*:—dwell, (be) set, sit.

3489. יָתֵד**, yâthêd,** *yaw-thade´*; from an unused root meaning to *pin* through or fast; a *peg*:—nail, paddle, pin, stake.

3490. יָתוֹם**, yâthôwm,** *yaw-thome´*; from an unused root meaning to *be lonely*; a *bereaved* person:—fatherless (child), orphan.

3491. יְתוּר**, yᵉthûwr,** *yeh-thoor´*; passive participle of 3498; (properly) what is *left*, i.e. (by implication) a *gleaning*:—range.

3492. יַתִּיר**, Yattîyr,** *yat-teer´*; from 3498; *redundant; Jattir*, a place in Palestine:—Jattir.

3493. יַתִּיר**, yattîyr,** *yat-teer´*; (Chaldee); corresponding to 3492; *preeminent*; (adverb) *very*:—exceeding (-ly), excellent.

3494. יִתְלָה**, Yithlâh,** *yith-law´*; probably from 8518; it *will hang*, i.e. be high; *Jithlah*, a place in Palestine:—Jethlah.

3495. יִתְמָה**, Yithmâh,** *yith-maw´*; from the same as 3490; *orphanage; Jithmah*, an Israelite:—Ithmah.

3496. יַתְנִיאֵל**, Yathnîy'êl,** *yath-nee-ale´*; from an unused root meaning to *endure*, and 410; *continued of God; Jathniël*, an Israelite:—Jathniel.

3497. יִתְנָן**, Yithnân,** *yith-nawn´*; from the same as 8577; *extensive; Jithnan*, a place in Palestine:—Ithnan.

3498. יָתַר**, yâthar,** *yaw-thar´*; a primitive root; to *jut* over or *exceed*; (by implication) to *excel*; (intransitive) to *remain* or *be left*; (causative) to *leave, cause to abound, preserve*:—excel, leave (a remnant), left behind, too much, make plenteous, preserve, (be, let) remain (-der, -ing, -nant), reserve, residue, rest.

A verb meaning to be left over, to remain. Jacob was left alone after he sent his family across the river (Ge 32:24[25]); nothing remained after the locusts came (Ex 10:15); Absalom was thought to have killed all the king's sons with not one remaining (2Sa 13:30); Isaiah prophesied to Hezekiah that nothing would be left of his kingdom (2Ki 20:17); God said that when He destroyed Judah, He would leave a remnant (Eze 6:8).

3499. יֶתֶר**, yether,** *yeh´-ther*; from 3498; (properly) an *overhanging*, i.e. (by implication) an *excess, superiority, remainder*; also a small *rope* (as hanging free):— + abundant, cord, exceeding, excellency (-ent), what they leave, that hath left, plentifully, remnant, residue, rest, string, with.

A masculine noun meaning remainder, the rest, abundance, excellence, a cord. The word refers to that which is left over: the produce of a field not used by people (and left for beasts) (Ex 23:11); the years of a life span not yet finished (Isa 38:10); temple vessels besides the ones specifically mentioned (Jer 27:19). The word also signifies abundance as what was left beyond the necessities of life (Job 22:20; Ps 17:14). In Genesis 49:3, the word means excellence, referring to the extra honour and power accorded to the firstborn. The word may refer to the cord of a tent or to a bowstring (Job 30:11; Ps 11:2), both apparently derived from the idea of a string hanging over something, being extra. The word may be used adverbially to mean abundantly or exceedingly (Da 8:9).

3500. יֶתֶר, Yether, *yeh´-ther*; the same as 3499; *Jether*, the name of five or six Israelites and of one Midianite:—Jether, Jethro. Compare 3503.

3501. יִתְרָא, Yithrâ', *yith-raw´*; by variation for 3502; *Jithra*, an Israelite (or Ishmaelite):—Ithra.

3502. יִתְרָה, yithrâh, *yith-raw´*; feminine of 3499; (properly) *excellence*, i.e. (by implication) *wealth*:—abundance, riches.

3503. יִתְרוֹ, Yithrôw, *yith-ro´*; from 3499 with pronoun suffix; *his excellence; Jethro*, Moses' father-in-law:—Jethro. Compare 3500.

3504. יִתְרוֹן, yithrôwn, *yith-rone´*; from 3498; *preeminence, gain*:—better, excellency (-leth), profit (-able).

3505. יִתְרִי, Yithrîy, *yith-ree´*; patronymic from 3500; a *Jithrite* or descendant of Jether:—Ithrite.

3506. יִתְרָן, Yithrân, *yith-rawn´*; from 3498; *excellent; Jithran*, the name of an Edomite and of an Israelite:—Ithran.

3507. יִתְרְעָם, Yithr^e'âm, *yith-reh-awm´*; from 3499 and 5971; *excellence of people; Jithreäm*, a son of David:—Ithream.

3508. יֹתֶרֶת, yôthereth, *yo-theh´-reth*; feminine active participle of 3498; the *lobe* or *flap* of the liver (as if redundant or outhanging):—caul.

3509. יְתֵת, Y^ethêth, *yeh-thayth´*; of uncertain derivation; *Jetheth*, an Edomite:—Jetheth.

3510. כָּאַב, kâ'ab, *kaw-ab´*; a primitive root; (properly) to feel *pain*; (by implication) to *grieve*; (figuratively) to *spoil*:—grieving, mar, have pain, make sad (sore), (be) sorrowful.

3511. כְּאֵב, k^e'êb, *keh-abe´*; from 3510; *suffering* (physical or mental), *adversity*:—grief, pain, sorrow.

3512. כָּאָה, kâ'âh, *kaw-aw´*; a primitive root; to *despond*; (causative) to *deject*:—broken, be grieved, make sad.

3513. כָּבַד, kâbad, *kaw-bad*; or כָּבֵד, **kâbêd,** *kaw-bade´*; a primitive root; to *be heavy*, i.e. in a bad sense (*burdensome, severe, dull*) or in a good sense (*numerous, rich, honourable*); (causative) to *make weighty* (in the same two senses):—abounding with, more grievously afflict, boast, be chargeable, × be dim, glorify, be (make) glorious (things), glory, (very) great, be grievous, harden, be (make) heavy, be heavier, lay heavily, (bring to, come to, do, get, be had in) honour (self), (be) honourable (man), lade, × more be laid, make self many, nobles, prevail, promote (to honour), be rich, be (go) sore, stop.

A verb meaning to weigh heavily, to be heavy, to be honoured, to be made heavy, to get honour, to make dull, to let weigh down, to harden, to multiply.

In the simple form, the verb means to be heavy, to weigh heavily, to be honoured. The hands of both humans and God were described metaphorically as heavy, that is, powerful. The heavy hand of Joseph dispossessed the Amorites of their land, and the Lord's hand was heavy against the city of Ashdod (i.e. He brought devastation upon it [1Sa 5:6]). The Hebrew word refers to mere physical weight as well; the description of Absalom's hair is a celebrated example of this use (2Sa 14:26). The labour of the Israelites in Egypt became burdensome (Ex 5:9). The word's metaphorical use extended to the description of failing senses, such as Jacob's eyes (Israel's) in old age (Ge 48:10; Isa 59:1). This is one of three words describing the dulling or hardening of Pharaoh's heart in the plagues. Pharaoh's heart became dull, obstinate, heavy (Ex 9:7) to the Lord's warnings. Yet the word also describes honour being bestowed on someone (Job 14:21; Isa 66:5).

In the passive form, the word expresses the idea of enjoying honour or glory. It describes the smug self-glorification of Amaziah (2Sa 6:22; 2Ki 14:10); God's honouring Himself through the defeat of Pharaoh is also expressed by this stem (Ex 14:4, 17, 18; Isa 26:15). In the factitive or intensive stem, the verb expresses the idea of causing or making something unfeeling (1Sa 6:6) but also the act of honouring people or God (Jgs 9:9; Ps 22:23[24]). God's people also honour some things: the Sabbath (Isa 58:13); Jerusalem; God's sanctuary (Isa 60:13); wisdom (Pr 4:8). The causative form carries the ideas of making something heavy (1Ki 12:10; Isa 47:6); or dull and heavy, especially Pharaoh's heart (Ex 8:15[11], 32[28]; 9:34). In two places, the word means to make into many or multiply (Jer 30:19); as when God's people multiplied (cf. 2Ch 25:19). It is used once in the reflexive form meaning to act deceptively (i.e. to pretend something [Pr 12:9]).

3514. כֹּבֶד, kôbed, *ko´-bed*; from 3513; *weight, multitude, vehemence*:—grievousness, heavy, great number.

3515. כָּבֵד, kâbêd, *kaw-bade´*; from 3513; *heavy*; (figurative) in a good sense (*numerous*) or in a bad sense (*severe, difficult, stupid*):—(so) great, grievous, hard (-ened), (too) heavy (-ier), laden, much, slow, sore, thick.

3516. כָּבֵד, kâbêd, *kaw-bade´*; the same as 3515; the *liver* (as the *heaviest* of the viscera):—liver.

3517. כְּבֵדֻת, k^ebêduth, *keb-ay-dooth´*; feminine of 3515; *difficulty*:— × heavily.

3518. כָּבָה, kâbâh, *kaw-baw´*; a primitive root; to *expire* or (causative) to *extinguish* (fire, light, anger):—go (put) out, quench.

3519. כָּבוֹד, kâbôwd, *kaw-bode´*; rarely כָּבֹד, **kâbôd,** *kaw-bode´*; from 3513; (properly) *weight*; but only figurative in a good sense, *splendor* or *copiousness*:—glorious (-ly), glory, honour (-able).

A masculine singular noun meaning honour, glory, majesty, wealth. This term is commonly used of God (Ex 33:18; Ps 72:19; Isa 3:8; Eze 1:28); humans (Ge 45:13; Job 19:9; Ps 8:5[6]; 21:5[6]); and objects (1Sa 2:8; Est 1:4; Isa 10:18), particularly of the Ark of the Covenant (1Sa 4:21, 22).

3520. כְּבוּדָּה, k^ebûwddâh, *keb-ood-daw´*; irregular feminine passive participle of 3513; *weightiness*, i.e. *magnificence, wealth*:—carriage, all glorious, stately.

3521. כָּבוּל, Kâbûwl, *kaw-bool´*; from the same as 3525 in the sense of *limitation; sterile; Cabul*, the name of two places in Palestine:—Cabul.

3522. כַּבּוֹן, Kabbôwn, *kab-bone´*; from an unused root meaning to *heap* up; *hilly; Cabbon*, a place in Palestine:—Cabbon.

3523. כְּבִיר, kâbîyr, *kawb-eer*; from 3527 in the original sense of *plaiting*; a *matrass* (of intertwined materials):—pillow.

3524. כַּבִּיר, kabbîyr, *kab-beer´*; from 3527; *vast*, whether in extent (figurative of power, *mighty*; of time, *aged*), or in number, *many*:— + feeble, mighty, most, much, strong, valiant.

3525. כֶּבֶל, kebel, *keh´-bel*; from an unused root meaning to *twine* or braid together; a *fetter*:—fetter.

3526. כָּבַס, kâbas, *kaw-bas´*; a primitive root; to *trample*; hence to *wash* (properly, by stamping with the feet), whether literal (including the *fulling* process) or figurative:—fuller, wash (-ing).

A verb meaning to wash. The root meaning of the verb is to trample, which was the means of washing clothes. The word most often refers to washing clothes (Ge 49:11; 2Sa 19:24[25]), especially ceremonially (Ex 19:10; Le 15; Nu 19). As a participle, the word means fuller, one who left clothes to dry in the fuller's field (2Ki 18:17; Isa 7:3; 36:2). An intensive form of the verb is used of the fuller in Mal 3:2, whose soap is a symbol of Christ's demand for purity. In Jer 2:22, the word may refer literally to ceremonial washings but also implies mere human effort used in an external attempt to overcome sin. In Ps 51:2[4], 7[9], the word refers to God's internal cleansing of the heart, making it as white as snow. Jer 4:14, however, showed that God's people must work to cleanse their hearts and avoid temporal destruction.

3527. כָּבַר**, kâbar,** *kaw-bar´*; a primitive root; (properly) to *plait* together, i.e. (figurative) to *augment* (especially in number or quantity, to *accumulate*):—in abundance, multiply.

3528. כְּבָר**, kᵉbâr,** *keb-awr´*; from 3527; (properly) *extent* of time, i.e. a *great while*; hence *long ago, formerly, hitherto*:—already, (seeing that which), now.

3529. כְּבָר**, Kᵉbâr,** *keb-awr´*; the same as 3528; *length; Kebar*, a river of Mesopotamia:—Chebar. Compare 2249.

3530. כִּבְרָה**, kibrâh,** *kib-raw´*; feminine of 3528; (properly) *length*, i.e. a *measure* (of uncertain dimension):— × little.

3531. כְּבָרָה**, kᵉbârâh,** *keb-aw-raw´*; from 3527 in its original sense; a *sieve* (as netted):—sieve.

3532. כֶּבֶשׂ**, kebeś,** *keh-bes´*; from an unused root meaning to *dominate*; a *ram* (just old enough to *butt*):—lamb, sheep.

3533. כָּבַשׁ**, kâbash,** *kaw-bash´*; a primitive root; to *tread* down; hence negative to *disregard*; positive to *conquer, subjugate, violate*:—bring into bondage, force, keep under, subdue, bring into subjection.

3534. כֶּבֶשׁ**, kebesh,** *keh´-besh*; from 3533; a *footstool* (as trodden upon):—footstool.

3535. כִּבְשָׂה**, kibśâh,** *kib-saw´*; or כַּבְשָׂה**, kabśâh,** *kab-saw´*; feminine of 3532; a *ewe*:—(ewe) lamb.

3536. כִּבְשָׁן**, kibshân,** *kib-shawn´*; from 3533; a smelting *furnace* (as *reducing* metals):—furnace.

3537. כַּד**, kad,** *kad*; from an unused root meaning to *deepen*; (properly) a *pail*; but generically of earthenware; a *jar* for domestic purposes:—barrel, pitcher.

3538. כְּדַב**, kᵉdab,** *ked-ab´*; (Chaldee); from a root corresponding to 3576; *false*:—lying.

3539. כַּדְכֹּד**, kadkôd,** *kad-kode´*; from the same as 3537 in the sense of *striking fire* from a metal forged; a *sparkling* gem, probably the ruby:—agate.

3540. כְּדָרְלָעֹמֶר**, Kᵉdorlâʻômer,** *ked-or-law-o´-mer*; of foreign origin; *Kedorlaomer*, an early Persian king:—Chedorlaomer.

3541. כֹּה**, kôh,** *ko*; from the prefix *k* and 1931; (properly) *like this*, i.e. (by implication, of manner) *thus* (or *so*); also (of place) *here* (or *hither*); or (of time) *now*:—also, here, + hitherto, like, on the other side, so (and much), such, on that manner, (on) this (manner, side, way, way and that way), + meanwhile, yonder.

3542. כָּה**, kâh,** *kaw*; (Chaldee); corresponding to 3541:—hitherto.

3543. כָּהָה**, kâhâh,** *kaw-haw´*; a primitive root; to *be weak*, i.e. (figurative) to *despond* (causative, to *rebuke*), or (of light, the eye) to *grow dull*:—darken, be dim, fail, faint, restrain, × utterly.

3544. כֵּהֶה**, kêheh,** *kay-heh´*; from 3543; *feeble, obscure*:—somewhat dark, darkish, wax dim, heaviness, smoking.

3545. כֵּהָה**, kêhâh,** *kay-haw´*; feminine of 3544; (properly) a *weakening*; (figurative) *alleviation*, i.e. cure:—healing.

3546. כְּהַל**, kᵉhal,** *ke-hal´*; (Chaldee); a root corresponding to 3201 and 3557; to *be able*:—be able, could.

3547. כָּהַן**, kâhan,** *kaw-han´*; a primitive root, apparently meaning to *mediate* in religious services; but used only as denominative from 3548; to *officiate* as a priest; (figurative) to *put on regalia*:—deck, be (do the office of a, execute the, minister in the) priest ('s office).

A verb meaning to act, to serve as a priest. This is a denominative verb from the noun *kôhên* (3548). The verb occurs twenty-three times in the Hebrew Bible, and twelve of them occur in Exodus. The most unusual usage is Isa 61:10 where it seems to refer to dressing in a priestly (i.e. ornate) manner.

3548. כֹּהֵן**, kôhên,** *ko-hane´*; active participle of 3547; literally one *officiating*, a *priest*; also (by courtesy) an *acting priest* (although a layman):—chief ruler, × own, priest, prince, principal officer.

A masculine noun meaning priest. The word is used to designate the various classes of priests in Israel. These people performed the function of mediators between God and His people. God called the nation of Israel to be a kingdom of priests (Ex 19:6), but God also appointed a priesthood to function within the nation. All the priests were to come from the tribe of Levi (Dt 17:9, 18). The Lord set up a high priest who was over all the priestly services. The high priest was literally the great priest or head priest: Jehoiada was described as a high or great priest (2Ki 12:10[11]). Joshua is called the high priest over the community that returned from the Babylonian exile (Hag 1:12; 2:2). God appointed Aaron to serve as high priest and his sons as priests when the entire priestly order was established (Le 21:10; Nu 35:25). The high point of the religious year was the atonement ritual the high priest performed on the Day of Atonement (Le 16). Aaron's family line produced the Aaronic priests or priesthood. Zadok became the ancestor of the legitimate priests from the time of Solomon's reign (1Ki 1:8, 38, 44); and the prophet Ezekiel approved of this line of priests from among the Levites (Eze 40:46; 43:19). The priests were in charge of all the holy things in Israel: they bore the ark (Jos 3:13, 14) and trumpets (Nu 10:8). They even counseled kings (1Sa 22:21; 1Ki 1:38, 44). However, there arose priests who were not appointed by the Lord and who functioned illegitimately, such as Micah's priests during the time of the judges (Jgs 17:5, 10, 12) or Jeroboam's priests who did not come from the sons of Levi (1Ki 12:31).

Some priests who functioned in other religions or nations are mentioned in Scripture. The most famous was Melchizedek, who was also a king in Canaan (Ge 14:18). His priesthood became the model for Christ's eternal priesthood (Heb 6:20). Jethro, Moses' father-in-law, was a priest among the Midianites (Ex 2:16; 3:1). Joseph married Asenath, the daughter of an Egyptian priest (Ge 41:45). There were priests of the Philistines (1Sa 6:2); and priests who served the false gods, the Baals, and the Asherim (2Ch 34:5) of the heathen nations.

3549. כָּהֵן**, kâhên,** *kaw-hane´*; (Chaldee); corresponding to 3548:—priest.

3550. כְּהֻנָּה**, kᵉhunnâh,** *keh-hoon-naw´*; from 3547; *priesthood*:—priesthood, priest's office.

A feminine noun meaning priesthood, the priest's office. The priest's office belonged to Aaron and his sons and involved making sacrifices and entering the Holy of Holies (Nu 18:7), work from which the other Levites were excluded (Nu 18:1, 7). Because of the holiness of the priesthood, those without right who presumed to act in it (Nu 16:10), as well as priests who misused the office, faced severe judgments. Levites outside of Aaron's descendants were permitted to do other service in the tabernacle; and, thus, the priesthood was referred to as their inheritance in place of land (Jos 18:7). The ordination of priests was described in Ex 29 and included the use of anointing oil, special clothes, and sacrifices.

3551. כַּוָּה**, kavvâh,** *kav-vaw´*; (Chaldee); from a root corresponding to 3854 in the sense of *piercing*; a *window* (as a perforation):—window.

3552. כּוּב**, Kûwb,** *koob*; of foreign derivation; *Kub*, a country near Egypt:—Chub.

3553. כּוֹבַע**, kôwbaʻ,** *ko´-bah*; from an unused root meaning to be *high* or *rounded*; a *helmet* (as *arched*):—helmet. Compare 6959.

3554. כָּוָה**, kâvâh,** *kaw-vaw´*; a primitive root; (properly) to *prick* or *penetrate*; hence to *blister* (as smarting or eating into):—burn.

3555. כְּוִיָּה**, kᵉvîyyâh,** *kev-ee-yaw´*; from 3554; a *branding*:—burning.

3556. כּוֹכָב, kôwkâb, *ko-kawb´*; probably from the same as 3522 (in the sense of *rolling*) or 3554 (in the sense of *blazing*); a *star* (as *round* or as *shining*); (figurative) a *prince*:—star ([-gazer]).

3557. כּוּל, kûwl, *kool*; a primitive root; (properly) to *keep in*; hence to *measure*; (figurative) to *maintain* (in various senses):—(be able to, can) abide, bear, comprehend, contain, feed, forbearing, guide, hold (-ing in), nourish (-er), be present, make provision, receive, sustain, provide sustenance (victuals).

3558. כּוּמָז, kûwmâz, *koo-mawz´*; from an unused root meaning to *store* away; a *jewel* (probably gold beads):—tablet.

3559. כּוּן, kûwn, *koon*; a primitive root; (properly) to *be erect* (i.e. stand perpendicular); hence (causative) to *set up*, in a great variety of applications, whether literal (*establish, fix, prepare, apply*), or figurative (*appoint, render sure, proper* or *prosperous*):—certain (-ty), confirm, direct, faithfulness, fashion, fasten, firm, be fitted, be fixed, frame, be meet, ordain, order, perfect, (make) preparation, prepare (self), provide, make provision, (be, make) ready, right, set (aright, fast, forth), be stable, (e-) stablish, stand, tarry, × very deed.

A verb meaning to set up, to make firm, to establish, to prepare. The primary action of this verb is to cause to stand in an upright position, and thus the word also means fixed or steadfast. It signifies the action of setting in place or erecting an object (Isa 40:20; Mic 4:1); establishing a royal dynasty (2Sa 7:13; 1Ch 17:12); founding a city (Hab 2:12); creating the natural order (Dt 32:6; Ps 8:3[4]; Pr 8:27); fashioning a people for oneself (2Sa 7:24); adjusting weapons for targets (Ps 7:12[13]; 11:2); appointing to an office (Jos 4:4); confirming a position (1Ki 2:12); making ready or preparing for use (2Ch 31:11; Ps 103:19; Zep 1:7); attaining certainty (Dt 13:14[15]; 1Sa 23:23).

3560. כּוּן, Kûwn, *koon*; probably from 3559; *established; Kun*, a place in Syria:—Chun.

3561. כַּוָּן, kavvân, *kav-vawn´*; from 3559; something *prepared*, i.e. a sacrificial *wafer*:—cake.

3562. כּוֹנַנְיָהוּ, Kôwnanyâhûw, *ko-nan-yaw´-hoo*; from 3559 and 3050; *Jah has sustained; Conanjah*, the name of two Israelites:—Conaniah, Cononiah. Compare 3663.

3563. כּוֹס, kôws, *koce*; from an unused root meaning to *hold* together; a *cup* (as a container); (often figurative) a *lot* (as if a potion); also some unclean bird, probably an *owl* (perhaps from the cup-like cavity of its eye):—cup, (small) owl. Compare 3599.

3564. כּוּר, kûwr, *koor*; from an unused root meaning properly to *dig* through; a *pot* or *furnace* (as if excavated):—furnace. Compare 3600.

3565. כּוֹר עָשָׁן, Kôwr ʿÂshân, *kore aw-shawn´*; from 3564 and 6227; *furnace of smoke; Cor-Ashan*, a place in Palestine:—Chorashan.

3566. כּוֹרֶשׁ, Kôwresh, *ko´-resh*; or (Ezr 1:1 [last time], 2) כֹּרֶשׁ, **Kôresh,** *ko´-resh*; from the Persian; *Koresh* (or Cyrus), the Persian king:—Cyrus.

3567. כּוֹרֶשׁ, Kôwresh, *ko´-resh*; (Chaldee); corresponding to 3566:—Cyrus.

3568. כּוּשׁ, Kûwsh, *koosh*; probably of foreign origin; *Cush* (or Ethiopia), the name of a son of Ham, and of his territory; also of an Israelite:—Chush, Cush, Ethiopia.

3569. כּוּשִׁי, Kûwshîy, *koo-shee´*; patronymic from 3568; a *Cushite*, or descendant of Cush:—Cushi, Cushite, Ethiopian (-s).

3570. כּוּשִׁי, Kûwshîy, *koo-shee´*; the same as 3569; *Cushi*, the name of two Israelites:—Cushi.

3571. כּוּשִׁית, Kûwshîyth, *koo-sheeth´*; feminine of 3569; a *Cushite woman*:—Ethiopian.

3572. כּוּשָׁן, Kûwshân, *koo-shawn´*; perhaps from 3568; *Cushan*, a region of Arabia:—Cushan.

3573. כּוּשַׁן רִשְׁעָתַיִם, Kûwshan Rishʿâthayim, *koo-shan´ rish-aw-thah´-yim*; apparently from 3572 and the dual of 7564; *Cushan of double wickedness; Cushan-Rishathajim*, a Mesopotamian king:—Chushan-rishathayim.

3574. כּוֹשָׁרָה, kôwshârâh, *ko-shaw-raw´*; from 3787; *prosperity*; in plural *freedom*:—× chain.

3575. כּוּת, Kûwth, *kooth*; or (feminine) כּוּתָה, **Kûwthâh,** *koo-thaw´*; of foreign origin; *Cuth* or *Cuthah*, a province of Assyria:—Cuth.

3576. כָּזַב, kâzab, *kaw-zab´*; a primitive root; to *lie* (i.e. *deceive*), literal or figurative:—fail, (be found a, make a) liar, lie, lying, be in vain.

A verb meaning to lie, to be a liar, to declare a liar, to make a liar of someone. This verb occurs sixteen times and refers to false witnesses (Pr 14:5); worshippers (Pr 30:6); and figuratively of water (Isa 58:11). The book of Job, filled with courtroom rhetoric, debating the trustworthiness of the speakers' accounts, uses the verb four times (Job 6:28; 24:25; 34:6; 41:9[1]).

3577. כָּזָב, kâzâb, *kaw-zawb´*; from 3576; *falsehood*; literal (*untruth*) or figurative (*idol*):—deceitful, false, leasing, + liar, lie, lying.

A masculine noun meaning a lie, a deception, a falsehood. Indeed, the idea of nontruth is unequivocally presented as antithetical to God. He destroys liars (Ps 5:6[7]; 62:4[5]) and calls them an abomination (Pr 6:19). Lies and deceptions place one against God and guarantee His punishment (Pr 19:5, 9). Isaiah graphically depicted one taking shelter in lying and falsehood as equivalent to making a covenant with death and an agreement with hell—a contract that cannot save on Judgment Day (28:15, 17). Freedom from falsehood is both the character and heritage of God's children (Ps 40:4[5]; Zep 3:13). The verb *kâzab* (3576) also develops the anti-God theme of lying: God cannot lie (Nu 23:19); and His word will never deceive (Ps 89:35[36]), unlike false prophets and humans.

3578. כֹּזֵבָא, Kôzêbâʾ, *ko-zeeb-aw´*; from 3576; *fallacious; Cozeba*, a place in Palestine:—Choseba.

3579. כָּזְבִּי, Kozbîy, *koz-bee´*; from 3576; *false; Cozbi*, a Midianitess:—Cozbi.

3580. כְּזִיב, Kezîyb, *kez-eeb´*; from 3576; *falsified; Kezib*, a place in Palestine:—Chezib.

3581. כֹּחַ, kôach, *ko´-akh*; or (Da 11:6) כּוֹחַ, **kôwach,** *ko´-akh*; from an unused root meaning to *be firm; vigour*, literal (*force*, in a good or a bad sense) or figurative (*capacity, means, produce*); also (from its hardiness) a large *lizard*:—ability, able, chameleon, force, fruits, might, power (-ful), strength, substance, wealth.

3582. כָּחַד, kâchad, *kaw-khad´*; a primitive root; to *secrete*, by act or word; hence (intensive) to *destroy*:—conceal, cut down (off), desolate, hide.

3583. כָּחַל, kâchal, *kaw-khal´*; a primitive root; to *paint* (with stibium):—paint.

3584. כָּחַשׁ, kâchash, *kaw-khash´*; a primitive root; to *be untrue*, in word (to *lie, feign, disown*) or deed (to *disappoint, fail, cringe*):—deceive, deny, dissemble, fail, deal falsely, be found liars, (be-) lie, lying, submit selves.

3585. כַּחַשׁ, kachash, *kakh´-ash*; from 3584; (literal) a *failure* of flesh, i.e. *emaciation*; (figurative) *hypocrisy*:—leanness, lies, lying.

3586. כֶּחָשׁ, kechâsh, *kekh-awsh´*; from 3584; *faithless*:—lying.

An adjective meaning deceptive, false, lying. This word occurs only in Isa 30:9. The reference is to the deceitfulness of Israel. Their rebellious activities included urging prophets to prophesy falsely and to subvert the authority of the Lord (Isa 30:10, 11).

3587. כִּי, kîy, *kee*; from 3554; a *brand* or *scar*:—burning.

3588. כִּי, **kîy,** *kee;* a primitive particle [the full form of the prepositional prefix] indicating *causal* relations of all kinds, antecedent or consequent; (by implication) very widely used as a relative conjuction or adverb [as below]; often largely modified by other particles annexed:—and, + (forasmuch, inasmuch, where-) as, assured [-ly], + but, certainly, doubtless, + else, even, + except, for, how, (because, in, so, than) that, + nevertheless, now, rightly, seeing, since, surely, then, therefore, + (al-) though, + till, truly, + until, when, whether, while, whom, yea, yet.

3589. כִּיד, **kîyd,** *keed;* from a primitive root meaning to *strike;* a *crushing;* (figurative) *calamity:*—destruction.

A masculine noun of uncertain meaning. It comes from a primitive root word and most likely means a crushing, a calamity, or a misfortune. Job responded to Zophar and lamented about the wicked. Job wished that the wicked would see God's wrath and their own destruction (Job 21:20).

3590. כִּידוֹד, **kîydôwd,** *kee-dode´;* from the same as 3589 [compare 3539]; (properly) something *struck* off, i.e. a *spark* (as struck):—spark.

3591. כִּידוֹן, **kîydôwn,** *kee-dohn´;* from the same as 3589; (properly) something to *strike* with, i.e. a *dart* (perhaps smaller than 2595):—lance, shield, spear, target.

3592. כִּידֹן, **Kîydôn,** *kee-dohn´;* the same as 3591; *Kidon,* a place in Palestine:—Chidon.

3593. כִּידוֹר, **kîydôwr,** *kee-dore´;* of uncertain derivation; perhaps *tumult:*—battle.

3594. כִּיּוּן, **Kîyyûwn,** *kee-yoon´;* from 3559; (properly) a *statue,* i.e. idol; but used (by euphemism) for some heathen deity (perhaps corresponding to Priapus or Baal-peor):—Chiun.

3595. כִּיּוֹר, **kîyyôwr,** *kee-yore´;* or כִּיֹּר, **kîyyôr,** *kee-yore´;* from the same as 3564; (properly) something *round* (as *excavated* or *bored*), i.e. a chafing-*dish* for coals or a *caldron* for cooking; hence (from similarity of form) a *washbowl;* also (for the same reason) a *pulpit* or platform:—hearth, laver, pan, scaffold.

3596. כִּילַי, **kîylay,** *kee-lah´ee;* or כֵּלַי, **kêlay,** *kay-lah´ee;* from 3557 in the sense of *withholding; niggardly:*—churl.

3597. כֵּילַף, **kêylaph,** *kay-laf´;* from an unused root meaning to *clap* or strike with noise; a *club* or sledge-hammer:—hammer.

3598. כִּימָה, **Kîymâh,** *kee-maw´;* from the same as 3558; a *cluster* of stars, i.e. the *Pleiades:*—Pleiades, seven stars.

3599. כִּיס, **kîys,** *keece;* a form for 3563; a *cup;* also a *bag* for money or weights:—bag, cup, purse.

3600. כִּיר, **kîyr,** *keer;* a form for 3564 (only in the dual); a cooking *range* (consisting of two parallel stones, across which the boiler is set):—ranges for pots.

3601. כִּישׁוֹר, **kîyshôwr,** *kee-shore´;* from 3787; (literal) a *director,* i.e. the *spindle* or shank of a distaff (6418), by which it is twirled:—spindle.

3602. כָּכָה, **kâkâh,** *kaw´-kaw;* from 3541; *just so,* referring to the previous or following context:—after that (this) manner, this matter, (even) so, in such a case, thus.

3603. כִּכָּר, **kikâr,** *kik-kawr´;* from 3769; a *circle,* i.e. (by implication) a circumjacent *tract* or region, especially the *Ghor* or valley of the Jordan; also a (round) *loaf;* also a *talent* (or large [round] coin):—loaf, morsel, piece, plain, talent.

3604. כַּכַּר, **kakkar,** *kak-kar´;* (Chaldee); corresponding to 3603; a *talent:*—talent.

3605. כֹּל, **kôl,** *kole;* or (Jer 33:8) כּוֹל, **kôwl,** *kole;* from 3634; (properly) the *whole;* hence *all, any* or *every* (in the singular only, but often in a plural sense):—(in) all (manner, [ye]), altogether, any (manner), enough, every (one, place, thing), howsoever, as many as, [no-] thing, ought, whatsoever, (the) whole, whoso (-ever).

3606. כֹּל, **kôl,** *kole;* (Chaldee); corresponding to 3605:—all, any, + (forasmuch) as, + be- (for this) cause, every, + no (manner, -ne), + there (where) -fore, + though, what (where, who) -soever, (the) whole.

3607. כָּלָא, **kâlâ',** *kaw-law´;* a primitive root; to *restrict,* by act (*hold* back or in) or word (*prohibit*):—finish, forbid, keep (back), refrain, restrain, retain, shut up, be stayed, withhold.

3608. כֶּלֶא, **kele',** *keh´-leh;* from 3607; a *prison:*—prison. Compare 3610, 3628.

3609. כִּלְאָב, **Kil'âb,** *kil-awb´;* apparently from 3607 and 1; *restraint of* (his) *father; Kilab,* an Israelite:—Chileab.

3610. כִּלְאַיִם, **kil'ayim,** *kil-ah´-yim;* dual of 3608 in the original sense of *separation; two heterogeneities:*—divers seeds (-e kinds), mingled (seed).

3611. כֶּלֶב, **keleb,** *keh´-leb;* from an unused root meaning to *yelp,* or else to *attack;* a *dog;* hence (by euphemism) a male *prostitute:*—dog.

3612. כָּלֵב, **Kâlêb,** *kaw-labe´;* perhaps a form of 3611, or else from the same root in the sense of *forcible; Caleb,* the name of three Israelites:—Caleb.

3613. כָּלֵב אֶפְרָתָה, **Kâlêb 'Ephrâthâh,** *kaw-labe´ ef-raw´-thaw;* from 3612 and 672; *Caleb-Ephrathah,* a place in Egypt (if the text is correct):—Caleb-ephrathah.

3614. כָּלִבּוֹ, **Kâlibbôw,** *kaw-lib-bo´;* probably by erroneous transcription for כָּלֵבִּי, **Kâlêbîy,** *kaw-lay-bee´;* patronymic from 3612; a *Calebite* or descendant of Caleb:—of the house of Caleb.

3615. כָּלָה, **kâlâh,** *kaw-law´;* a primitive root; to *end,* whether intransitive (to *cease, be finished, perish*) or transitive (to *complete, prepare, consume*):—accomplish, cease, consume (away), determine, destroy (utterly), be (when ... were) done, (be an) end (of), expire, (cause to) fail, faint, finish, fulfil, × fully, × have, leave (off), long, bring to pass, wholly reap, make clean riddance, spend, quite take away, waste.

A verb meaning to complete, to accomplish, to end, to finish, to fail, to exhaust. Its primary meaning is to consummate or to bring to completion. This occasionally occurs in a positive sense as in the awesome goodness of God's perfected and finished creation (Ge 2:1, 2). It also represents the favourable conclusion of meaningful human labour as in building the tabernacle (Ex 39:32); or preparing tithes (Dt 26:12). However, *kâlâh* is more often used with a negative connotation. God threatened to consume human unbelief (as in completing the life span), a promise terribly fulfilled at Korah's rebellion (Nu 16:21). Also, Israel was to be God's vehicle in consuming or finishing the heathen nations in the land (Dt 7:22), thus completing the ban. The verb also describes the transitory reality of fallen human nature. We finish our years like a sigh (Ps 90:9), passing away like an exhausted cloud (Job 7:9).

3616. כָּלֶה, **kâleh,** *kaw-leh´;* from 3615; *pining:*—fail.

3617. כָּלָה, **kâlâh,** *kaw-law´;* from 3615; a *completion;* adverb *completely;* also *destruction:*—altogether, (be, utterly) consume (-d), consummation (-ption), was determined, (full, utter) end, riddance.

A feminine noun meaning completion, complete destruction, annihilation. In the sense of completion, God told Moses that Pharaoh would let the Israelites go by driving them completely out of Egypt (Ex 11:1). Complete destruction or annihilation was most often attributed to God. Isaiah prophesied that the Lord would make a determined end to Israel (Isa 10:23); Nahum spoke of God's judgment by which He made an utter end of His enemies (Na 1:8). Destruction of such massive quantity is attributed to humans in Daniel's prophecy of Greece (Da 11:16).

3618. **כַּלָּה, kallâh,** *kal-law´*; from 3634; a *bride* (as if *perfect*); hence a *son's wife*:—bride, daughter-in-law, spouse.

3619. **כְּלוּב, k^elûwb,** *kel-oob´*; from the same as 3611; a bird-*trap* (as furnished with a *clap*-stick or treadle to spring it); hence a *basket* (as resembling a wicker cage):—basket, cage.

3620. **כְּלוּב, K^elûwb,** *kel-oob´*; the same as 3619; *Kelub,* the name of two Israelites:—Chelub.

3621. **כְּלוּבָי, K^elûwbây,** *kel-oo-baw´ee*; a form of 3612; *Kelubai,* an Israelite:—Chelubai.

3622. **כְּלֻהִי, K^eluhîy,** *kel-oo-hee´*; from 3615; *completed;* an Israelite:—Chelluh.

3623. **כְּלוּלָה, k^elûwlâh,** *kel-oo-law´*; denominative passive participle from 3618; *bridehood* (only in the plural):—espousal.

3624. **כֶּלַח, kelach,** *keh´-lakh*; from an unused root meaning to *be complete; maturity*:—full (old) age.

3625. **כֶּלַח, Kelach,** *keh´-lakh*; the same as 3624; *Kelach,* a place in Assyria:—Calah.

3626. **כָּל־חֹזֶה, Kol-Chôzeh,** *kol-kho-zeh´*; from 3605 and 2374; *every seer; Col-Chozeh,* an Israelite:—Col-hozeh.

3627. **כְּלִי, k^elîy,** *kel-ee´*; from 3615; something *prepared,* i.e. any *apparatus* (as an implement, utensil, dress, vessel or weapon):—armour ([-bearer]), artillery, bag, carriage, + furnish, furniture, instrument, jewel, that is made of, × one from another, that which pertaineth, pot, + psaltery, sack, stuff, thing, tool, vessel, ware, weapon, + whatsoever.

3628. **כְּלִיא, k^elîy',** *kel-ee´*; or **כְּלוּא, k^elûw',** *kel-oo´*; from 3607 [compare 3608]; a *prison*:—prison.

3629. **כִּלְיָה, kilyâh,** *kil-yaw´*; feminine of 3627 (only in the plural); a *kidney* (as an essential *organ*); (figurative) the *mind* (as the interior self):—kidneys, reins.

3630. **כִּלְיוֹן, Kilyôwn,** *kil-yone´*; a form of 3631; *Kiljon,* an Israelite:—Chilion.

3631. **כִּלָּיוֹן, killâyôwn,** *kil-law-yone´*; from 3615; *pining, destruction*:—consumption, failing.

3632. **כָּלִיל, kâlîyl,** *kaw-leel´*; from 3634; *complete*; as noun, the *whole* (specifically a sacrifice *entirely consumed*); as adverb *fully*:—all, every whit, flame, perfect (-ion), utterly, whole burnt offering (sacrifice), wholly.

An adjective meaning whole, entire, perfect, complete. This word can refer to an offering that was entirely consumed (Dt 33:10; 1Sa 7:9); figuratively, it refers to burning a whole town that worshipped other gods (Dt 13:16 [17]). The ephod had to be all purple (Ex 28:31; 39:22); Isaiah prophesied of a day when idols would completely disappear (Isa 2:18). This word also referred to Jerusalem's complete beauty (La 2:15; Eze 16:14); or Tyre's (Eze 27:3; 28:12). See the Hebrew root *kâlal* (3634).

3633. **כַּלְכֹּל, Kalkôl,** *kal-kole´*; from 3557; *sustenance; Calcol,* an Israelite:—Calcol, Chalcol.

3634. **כָּלַל, kâlal,** *kaw-lal´*; a primitive root; to *complete*:—(make) perfect.

A verb meaning to complete, to make perfect. Ezekiel lamented over Tyre's pride concerning her perfected beauty (Eze 27:4). Builders as well as war bounty came from all over the Near East to the port city of Tyre and added to the perfect beauty of the city (Eze 27:11).

3635. **כְּלַל, k^elal,** *kel-al´*; (Chaldee); corresponding to 3634; to *complete*:—finish, make (set) up.

An Aramaic verb meaning to complete. This word described the completed Temple (Ezr 5:11). It also carries the meaning of to restore (Ezr 4:12, 13, 16; 5:3, 9). See the related Hebrew root *kâlal* (3634) and the related Hebrew adjective *kâliyl* (3632).

3636. **כְּלָל, K^elâl,** *kel-awl´*; from 3634; *complete; Kelal,* an Israelite:—Chelal.

3637. **כָּלַם, kâlam,** *kaw-lawm´*; a primitive root; (properly) to *wound*; but only figurative, to *taunt* or *insult*:—be (make) ashamed, blush, be confounded, be put to confusion, hurt, reproach, (do, put to) shame.

3638. **כִּלְמַד, Kilmad,** *kil-mad´*; of foreign derivation; *Kilmad,* a place apparently in the Assyrian empire:—Chilmad.

3639. **כְּלִמָּה, k^elimmâh,** *kel-im-maw´*; from 3637; *disgrace*:—confusion, dishonour, reproach, shame.

3640. **כְּלִמּוּת, k^elimmûwth,** *kel-im-mooth´*; from 3639; *disgrace*:—shame.

3641. **כַּלְנֶה, Kalneh,** *kal-neh´*; or **כַּלְנֵה, Kalnêh,** *kal-nay´*; also **כַּלְנוֹ, Kalnôw,** *kal-no´*; of foreign derivation; *Calneh* or *Calno,* a place in the Assyrian empire:—Calneh, Calno. Compare 3656.

3642. **כָּמַהּ, kâmah,** *kaw-mah´*; a primitive root; to *pine* after:—long.

3643. **כִּמְהָם, Kimhâm,** *kim-hawm´*; from 3642; *pining; Kimham,* an Israelite:—Chimham.

3644. **כְּמוֹ, k^emôw,** *kem-o´*; or **כָּמוֹ, kâmôw,** *kaw-mo´*; a form of the prefix *k*, but used separately [compare 3651]; *as, thus, so*:—according to, (such) as (it were, well as), in comparison of, like (as, to, unto), thus, when, worth.

3645. **כְּמוֹשׁ, K^emôwsh,** *kem-oshe´*; or (Jer 48:7) **כְּמִישׁ, K^emîysh,** *kem-eesh´*; from an unused root meaning to *subdue*; the *powerful; Kemosh,* the god of the Moabites:—Chemosh.

3646. **כַּמֹּן, kammôn,** *kam-mone´*; from an unused root meaning to *store* up or *preserve*; "*cummin*" (from its use as a *condiment*):—cummin.

3647. **כָּמַס, kâmas,** *kaw-mas´*; a primitive root; to *store* away, i.e. (figurative) in the memory:—lay up in store.

3648. **כָּמַר, kâmar,** *kaw-mar´*; a primitive root; (properly) to *intertwine* or *contract*, i.e. (by implication) to *shrivel* (as with heat); (figurative) to *be* deeply *affected* with passion (love or pity):—be black, be kindled, yearn.

3649. **כֹּמֶר, kômer,** *kow-mer´*; from 3648; (properly) an *ascetic* (as if *shrunk* with self-maceration), i.e. an idolatrous *priest* (only in plural):—Chemarims, (idolatrous) priests.

A masculine noun meaning a (pagan) priest. In the OT, this word occurs three times. In 2Ki 23:5, Josiah's reformation got rid of priests who burned incense in the idolatrous high places. In Hos 10:5, Hosea prophesied that priests would mourn over the calf statue they worshipped when it was carried off to Assyrian captivity. In Zep 1:4, God promised to cut off the names of unfaithful priests, along with His own priests (cf. Zep 1:5, 6).

3650. **כִּמְרִיר, kimrîyr,** *kim-reer´*; reduplication from 3648; *obscuration* (as if from *shrinkage* of light; i.e. an *eclipse* (only in plural):—blackness.

3651. **כֵּן, kên,** *kane*; from 3559; (properly) *set* upright; hence (figurative as adjective) *just*; but usually (as adverb or conjunction) *rightly* or *so* (in various applications to manner, time and relation; often with other particles):— + after that (this, -ward, -wards), as … as, + [for-] asmuch as yet, + be (for which) cause, + following, howbeit, in (the) like (manner, -wise), × the more, right, (even) so, state, straightway, such (thing), surely, + there (where) -fore, this, thus, true, well, × you.

A word that is used either as an adverb or adjective, depending on the context of the sentence. The word is derived from the verb meaning to stand upright or to establish. As an adjective, it means correct, according to an established standard (Nu 27:7); upright and honest (Ge 42:11); it is used as a statement of general agreement (Ge 44:10; Jos 2:21). As an adverb, it is usually translated as "thus" or "so" but conveys quality (Est 4:16; Job 9:35; Na 1:12); quantity (Jgs 21:14); cause and effect (Jgs 10:13; Isa 5:24); or time (Ne 2:16).

3652. כֵּן, **kên,** *kane*; (Chaldee); corresponding to 3651; *so*:—thus.

3653. כֵּן, **kên,** *kane*; the same as 3651, used as a noun; a *stand*, i.e. pedestal or station:—base, estate, foot, office, place, well.

3654. כֵּן, **kên,** *kane*; from 3661, in the sense of *fastening*; a *gnat* (from infixing its sting; used only in plural [and irregular in Ex 8:17, 18; Hebrew 8:13, 14]):—lice, × manner.

3655. כָּנָה, **kânâh,** *kaw-naw´*; a primitive root; to *address* by an additional name; hence, to *eulogize*:—give flattering titles, surname (himself).

3656. כַּנֶּה, **Kanneh,** *kan-neh´*; for 3641; *Canneh*, a place in Assyria:—Canneh.

3657. כַּנָּה, **kannâh,** *kan-naw´*; from 3661; a *plant* (as *set*):—× vineyard.

3658. כִּנּוֹר, **kinnôwr,** *kin-nore´*; from an unused root meaning to *twang*; a *harp*:—harp.

3659. כָּנְיָהוּ, **Konyâhûw,** *kon-yaw´-hoo*; for 3204; *Conjah*, an Israelite king:—Coniah.

3660. כְּנֵמָא, **k**^{e}**nêmâ',** *ken-ay-maw´*; (Chaldee); corresponding to 3644; *so* or *thus*:—so, (in) this manner (sort), thus.

3661. כָּנַן, **kânan,** *kaw-nan´*; a primitive root; to *set* out, i.e. *plant*:—× vineyard.

3662. כְּנָנִי, **K**^{e}**nânîy,** *ken-aw-nee´*; from 3661; *planted; Kenani*, an Israelite:—Chenani.

3663. כְּנַנְיָה, **K**^{e}**nanyâh,** *ken-an-yaw´*; or כְּנַנְיָהוּ, **K**^{e}**nanyâhûw,** *ken-an-yaw´-hoo*; from 3661 and 3050; *Jah has planted; Kenanjah*, an Israelite:—Chenaniah.

3664. כָּנַס, **kânas,** *kaw-nas´*; a primitive root; to *collect*; hence, to *enfold*:—gather (together), heap up, wrap self.

A verb meaning to gather, to collect. David assembled foreigners to be stonecutters (1Ch 22:2). Esther instructed Mordecai to gather the Jews and fast (Est 4:16). The Lord gathered the waters (Ps 33:7). The writer of Ecclesiastes collected silver and gold for himself (Ecc 2:8); there is a time to gather stones (Ecc 3:5). The Lord told Ezekiel that He would gather Jerusalem together for punishment (Eze 22:21).

3665. כָּנַע, **kâna‛,** *kaw-nah´*; a primitive root; (properly) to *bend* the knee; hence to *humiliate, vanquish*:—bring down (low), into subjection, under, humble (self), subdue.

3666. כִּנְעָה, **kin‛âh,** *kin-aw´*; from 3665 in the sense of *folding* [compare 3664]; a *package*:—wares.

3667. כְּנַעַן, **K**^{e}**na‛an,** *ken-ah´-an*; from 3665; *humiliated; Kenaan*, a son of Ham; also the country inhabited by him:—Canaan, merchant, traffick.

3668. כְּנַעֲנָה, **K**^{e}**na‛ănâh,** *ken-ah-an-aw´*; feminine of 3667; *Kenaanah*, the name of two Israelites:—Chenaanah.

3669. כְּנַעֲנִי, **K**^{e}**na‛ănîy,** *ken-ah-an-ee´*; patrial from 3667; a *Kenaanite* or inhabitant of Kenaan; (by implication) a *pedlar* (the Canaanites standing for their neighbours the Ishmaelites, who conducted mercantile caravans):—Canaanite, merchant, trafficker.

3670. כָּנַף, **kânaph,** *kaw-naf´*; a primitive root; (properly) to *project* laterally, i.e. probably (reflexive) to *withdraw*:—be removed.

3671. כָּנָף, **kânâph,** *kaw-nawf´*; from 3670; an *edge* or *extremity*; specifically (of a bird or army) a *wing*, (of a garment or bed-clothing) a *flap*, (of the earth) a *quarter*, (of a building) a *pinnacle*:— + bird, border, corner, end, feather [-ed], × flying, + (one an-) other, overspreading, × quarters, skirt, × sort, uttermost part, wing ([-ed]).

3672. כִּנְּרוֹת, **Kinn**^{e}**rôwth,** *kin-ner-ōth´*; or כִּנֶּרֶת, **Kinnereth,** *kin-neh´-reth*; respectively plural and singular feminine from the same as 3658; perhaps *harp*-shaped; *Kinneroth* or *Kinnereth*, a place in Palestine:—Chinnereth, Chinneroth, Cinneroth.

3673. כְּנַשׁ, **k**^{e}**nash,** *keh-nash´*; (Chaldee); corresponding to 3664; to *assemble*:—gather together.

An Aramaic verb meaning to assemble, to be assembled. It corresponds to the Hebrew word *kânas* (3664) and occurs only in Da 3:2, 3, and 27. It referred to the assembling of Babylonian officials, initiated by Nebuchadnezzar, to dedicate and worship an image. The assembly was apparently a formal occasion with high officials standing before the image, a herald proclaiming the purpose of the assembly, and musicians playing various instruments. Those assembled saw the Hebrews who refused to obey sentenced to the fiery furnace and subsequently delivered from it.

3674. כְּנָת, **k**^{e}**nâth,** *ken-awth´*; from 3655; a *colleague* (as having the same title):—companion.

3675. כְּנָת, **k**^{e}**nâth,** *ken-awth´*; (Chaldee); corresponding to 3674:—companion.

3676. כֵּס, **kês,** *kace*; apparently a contraction for 3678, but probably by erroneous transcription for 5251:—sworn.

3677. כֶּסֶא, **kese',** *keh´-seh*; or כֶּסֶה, **keseh,** *keh´-seh*; apparently from 3680; (properly) *fulness* or the *full moon*, i.e. its festival:—(time) appointed.

3678. כִּסֵּא, **kissê',** *kis-say´*; or כִּסֵּה, **kissêh,** *kis-say´*; from 3680; (properly) *covered*, i.e. a *throne* (as *canopied*):—seat, stool, throne.

A masculine noun meaning throne, a place of honour. Pharaoh put Joseph over everything in his kingdom except his throne (Ge 41:40). Other references to leaders on the throne include Pharaoh (Ex 11:5; 12:29); Solomon and Bathsheba (1Ki 2:19); King Ahasuerus (Est 5:1); departed kings (Isa 14:9); the princes of the coast (Eze 26:16); the prophetic one who will build the temple of the Lord (Zec 6:13). Scripture also depicts God as sitting on a throne (Isa 6:1; Eze 1:26). The throne can also be a symbol of a kingdom or power (2Sa 7:16; 14:9; Isa 16:5).

3679. כַּסְדַּי, **Kasdây,** *kas-daw´ee*; for 3778:—Chaldean.

3680. כָּסָה, **kâsâh,** *kaw-saw´*; a primitive root; (properly) to *plump*, i.e. *fill up* hollows; (by implication) to *cover* (for clothing or secrecy):—clad self, close, clothe, conceal, cover (self), (flee to) hide, overwhelm. Compare 3780.

A verb meaning to cover, to clothe, to conceal. The active meaning of this verb is to cover, to cover up. It is used in a literal sense to indicate that something is covering something else, as when the waters of the Red Sea covered the Egyptians or the cloud of God's glory covered Mount Sinai or the tabernacle (Ex 15:5; 24:15). In a metaphorical sense, the word describes shame covering the guilty (Ps 69:7[8]; Jer 3:25; Hab 2:17); the Israelites' covering the altar with tears (Mal 2:13); and the concealing of Joseph's blood to hide his brothers' guilt and sin (Ge 37:26). On the other hand, the psalmist found reconciliation with God by not concealing his sin but confessing it (Ps 32:5; Pr 10:11). The word sometimes means to cover oneself with clothing or sackcloth, to clothe oneself with something (Eze 16:18; Jnh 3:6).

The passive form of the verb means to be covered, such as when the mountains were covered by the waters of the great flood (Ge 7:19; Ps 80:10[11]). The reflexive form is used to mean to cover oneself; for example, when the people of Nineveh covered themselves in repentance at Jonah's preaching (Jnh 3:8). The word in Ecc 6:4 describes the name of a stillborn child covering itself in darkness.

3681. כָּסוּי, **kâsûwy,** *kaw-soo´ee*; passive participle of 3680; (properly) *covered*, i.e. (as noun) a *covering*:—covering.

3682. כְּסוּת, **k**^{e}**sûwth,** *kes-ooth´*; from 3680; a *cover* (garment); (figurative) a *veiling*:—covering, raiment, vesture.

3683. כָּסַח, **kâsach,** *kaw-sakh´*; a primitive root; to *cut off*:—cut down (up).

3684. **כְּסִיל, k^e^sîyl,** *kes-eel´*; from 3688; (properly) *fat*, i.e. (figurative) stupid or *silly*:—fool (-ish).

3685. **כְּסִיל, K^e^sîyl,** *kes-eel´*; the same as 3684; any notable *constellation*; specifically *Orion* (as if a *burly* one):—constellation, Orion.

3686. **כְּסִיל, K^e^sîyl,** *kes-eel´*; the same as 3684; *Kesil*, a place in Palestine:—Chesil.

3687. **כְּסִילוּת, k^e^sîylûwth,** *kes-eel-ooth´*; from 3684; *silliness*:—foolish.

A feminine noun meaning foolishness, stupidity. This abstract noun is derived from the adjective *kĕsiyl* (3684), which means fat and, thus, (in a negative sense) stupid, foolish (or as a substantive, a foolish one). *Kĕsiylûth* occurs only in Pr 9:13, naming the woman of folly, a symbolic character who appealed to the evil desires of naive people in order to cause them to stray from right paths into paths that lead to death.

3688. **כָּסַל, kâsal,** *kaw-sal´*; a primitive root; (properly) to *be fat*, i.e. (figurative) *silly*:—be foolish.

A verb meaning to be stupid, to become stupid. It occurs once as a verb in Jer 10:8, referring to those taught by idols.

3689. **כֶּסֶל, kesel,** *keh´-sel*; from 3688; (properly) *fatness*, i.e. by implication (literal) the *loin* (as the seat of the leaf *fat*) or (generic) the *viscera*; also (figurative) *silliness* or (in a good sense) *trust*:—confidence, flank, folly, hope, loin.

A masculine noun meaning loins, confidence, stupidity. The first use can actually mean the waist area, the kidneys, etc. (Le 3:4, 10, 15; 4:9; 7:4; Job 15:27). The second use is more ambiguous, meaning that in which one puts trust or confidence (Job 8:14; 31:24; Ps 78:7; Pr 3:26). The final usage is a false self-trust or stupidity (Ps 49:13[14]; Ecc 7:25). See the related Hebrew verb *kâsal* (3688) and Hebrew noun *kislâh* (3690).

3690. **כִּסְלָה, kislâh,** *kis-law´*; feminine of 3689; in a good sense, *trust*; in a bad one, *silliness*:—confidence, folly.

A feminine noun meaning foolishness, stupidity, confidence. The root idea of fatness (see *kâsal* [3688]) may have two implications. In Job 4:6, *kĕsilâh* means the confidence of one who is fat and firm. Eliphaz cast doubt on Job's righteousness by asking why he was confused if he really feared God. In Ps 85:8[9], on the other hand, God warned His restored people not to return to their former folly. In that verse, the word refers to sluggish foolishness that is no longer alive to the fear of God.

3691. **כִּסְלֵו, Kislêv,** *kis-lave´*; probably of foreign origin; *Kisleu*, the 9th Hebrew month:—Chisleu.

3692. **כִּסְלוֹן, Kislôwn,** *kis-lone´*; from 3688; *hopeful; Kislon*, an Israelite:—Chislon.

3693. **כְּסָלוֹן, K^e^sâlôwn,** *kes-aw-lone´*; from 3688; *fertile; Kesalon*, a place in Palestine:—Chesalon.

3694. **כְּסוּלּוֹת, K^e^sûwllôwth,** *kes-ool-lōth´*; feminine plural of assive participle of 3688; *fattened, Kesul-loth*, a place in Palestine:—Chesulloth.

5. **כַּסְלֻחִים, Kasluchîym,** *kas-loo´-kheem*; a plural probably reign derivation; *Casluchim*, a people cognate to the Egypt--Casluhim.

כִּסְלֹת תָּבֹר, Kislôth Tâbôr, *kis-lōth´ taw-bore´*; from the e plural of 3689 and 8396; *flanks of Tabor; Kisloth-Tabor*, n Palestine:—Chisloth-tabor.

כָּ, kâsam, *kaw-sam´*; a primitive root; to *shear*:—l. Compare 3765.

kussemeth, *koos-seh´-meth*; from 3697; *spelt* (from as if just *shorn*):—fitches, rie.

sas, *kaw-sas´*; a primitive root; to *estimate*:—make

3700. **כָּסַף, kâsaph,** *kaw-saf´*; a primitive root; (properly) to become *pale*, i.e. (by implication) to *pine* after; also to *fear*:—[have] desire, be greedy, long, sore.

3701. **כֶּסֶף, keseph,** *keh´-sef*; from 3700; *silver* (from its *pale* colour); (by implication) *money*:—money, price, silver (-ling).

3702. **כְּסַף, k^e^saph,** *kes-af´*; (Chaldee); corresponding to 3701:—money, silver.

3703. **כָּסִפְיָא, Kâsiphyâ',** *kaw-sif-yaw´*; perhaps from 3701; *silvery; Casiphja*, a place in Babylon:—Casiphia.

3704. **כֶּסֶת, keseth,** *keh´-seth*; from 3680; a *cushion* or pillow (as *covering* a seat or bed):—pillow.

3705. **כְּעַן, k^e^'an,** *keh-an´*; (Chaldee); probably from 3652; *now*:—now.

3706. **כְּעֶנֶת, k^e^'eneth,** *keh-eh´-neth*; (Chaldee); or **כְּעֶת, k^e^'eth,** *keh-eth´*; (Chaldee); feminine of 3705; *thus* (only in the formula "and *so forth*"):—at such a time.

3707. **כָּעַס, kâ'as,** *kaw-as´*; a primitive root; to *trouble*; (by implication) to *grieve, rage, be indignant*:—be angry, be grieved, take indignation, provoke (to anger, unto wrath), have sorrow, vex, be wroth.

A verb meaning to be angry, to provoke to anger. The causative sense of the verb occurs most often and frequently signifies idolatry provoking God to anger (cf. 1Ki 14:9; Ps 106:29; Eze 8:17). The result of provocation may be expressed as *'aph*, anger (639) (Dt 9:18; 2Ki 23:26; Jer 7:20). In a noncausative sense, the verb means to be angry; people were warned not to become angry hastily (Ecc 7:9); God says that after He punishes, He will not be angry (Eze 16:42). Three times it refers to the people's anger directed toward righteousness (2Ch 16:10; Ne 4:1[3:33]; Ps 112:10).

3708. **כַּעַס, ka'as,** *kah´-as*; or (in Job) **כַּעַשׂ, ka'aś,** *kah´-as*; from 3707; *vexation*:—anger, angry, grief, indignation, provocation, provoking, × sore, sorrow, spite, wrath.

A masculine singular noun meaning anger, provocation, vexation. The alternate spelling of the word occurs only in Job. The majority of occurrences are in poetic literature. Human sinfulness and idolatry (1Ki 15:30; Eze 20:28) cause God's anger, while fools, sons, wives, and rival wives can also cause vexation (1Sa 1:6; Pr 27:3; 17:25; 21:19, respectively).

3709. **כַּף, kaph,** *kaf*; from 3721; the hollow *hand* or palm (so of the *paw* of an animal, of the *sole*, and even of the *bowl* of a dish or sling, the *handle* of a bolt, the *leaves* of a palm-tree); (figurative) *power*:—branch, + foot, hand ([-ful], -dle, [-led]), hollow, middle, palm, paw, power, sole, spoon.

A feminine noun meaning hand, the flat of the hand, the flat of the foot, hollow, bent. The principal meaning is hollow, often used of the hollow of the physical hand or foot. It also relates to cupped or bent objects such as spoons (Nu 7:80). In metaphysical overtones, Job declared his cleanness of hand (Job 9:30); and David linked clean hands with a pure heart (Ps 24:4). The righteous correctly lift up their hands in God's name (Ps 63:4[5]; 141:2), but the wicked are snared by their own hands' work (Ps 9:16). At wicked Jezebel's death, dogs devoured her but refused the palms of her hands (2Ki 9:35). The Israelites inherited every place on which their soles treaded in the Promised Land (Dt 11:24); the returning exiles were delivered from the hand of the enemy (Ezr 8:31). Ultimately, God is the skillful Shepherd, securely holding His own with a sovereign hand (Ps 139:5).

3710. **כֵּף, kêph,** *kafe*; from 3721; a hollow *rock*:—rock.

3711. **כָּפָה, kâphâh,** *kaw-faw´*; a primitive root; (properly) to *bend*, i.e. (figurative) to *tame* or subdue:—pacify.

3712. **כִּפָּה, kippâh,** *kip-paw´*; feminine of 3709; a *leaf* of a palm-tree:—branch.

3713. **כְּפוֹר, k^e^phôwr,** *kef-ore´*; from 3722; (properly) a *cover*, i.e. (by implication) a *tankard* (or *covered* goblet); also white *frost* (as *covering* the ground):—bason, hoar (-y) frost.

3714. כָּפִּיס, kâphîys, *kaw-fece´*; from an unused root meaning to *connect*; a *girder*:—beam.

3715. כְּפִיר, kᵉphîyr, *kef-eer´*; from 3722; a *village* (as *covered* in by walls); also a young *lion* (perhaps as *covered* with a mane):—(young) lion, village. Compare 3723.

3716. כְּפִירָה, Kᵉphîyrâh, *kef-ee-raw´*; feminine of 3715; the *village* (always with the article); *Kephirah*, a place in Palestine:—Chephirah.

3717. כָּפַל, kâphal, *kaw-fal´*; a primitive root; to *fold* together; (figurative) to *repeat*:—double.

3718. כֶּפֶל, kephel, *keh´-fel*; from 3717; a *duplicate*:—double.

3719. כָּפַן, kâphan, *kaw-fan´*; a primitive root; to *bend*:—bend.

3720. כָּפָן, kâphân, *kaw-fawn´*; from 3719; *hunger* (as making to *stoop* with emptiness and pain):—famine.

3721. כָּפַף, kâphaph, *kaw-faf´*; a primitive root; to *curve*:—bow down (self).

3722. כָּפַר, kâphar, *kaw-far´*; a primitive root; to *cover* (specifically with bitumen); (figurative) to *expiate* or *condone*, to *placate* or *cancel*:—appease, make (an) atonement, cleanse, disannul, forgive, be merciful, pacify, pardon, purge (away), put off, (make) reconcile (-liation).

A verb meaning to cover, to forgive, to expiate, to reconcile. This word is of supreme theological importance in the OT as it is central to an OT understanding of the remission of sin. At its most basic level, the word conveys the notion of covering but not in the sense of merely concealing. Rather, it suggests the imposing of something to change its appearance or nature. It is therefore employed to signify the cancellation or "writing over" of a contract (Isa 28:18); the appeasing of anger (Ge 32:20[21]; Pr 16:14); and the overlaying of wood with pitch so as to make it waterproof (Ge 6:14). The word also communicates God's covering of sin. Persons made reconciliation with God for their sins by imposing something that would appease the offended party (in this case the Lord) and cover the sinners with righteousness (Ex 32:30; Eze 45:17; cf. Da 9:24). In the OT, the blood of sacrifices was most notably imposed (Ex 30:10). By this imposition, sin was purged (Ps 79:9; Isa 6:7) and forgiven (Ps 78:38). The offences were removed, leaving the sinners clothed in righteousness (cf. Zec 3:3, 4). Of course, the imposition of the blood of bulls and of goats could never fully cover our sin (see Heb 10:4), but with the coming of Christ and the imposition of His shed blood, a perfect atonement was made (Ro 5:9–11).

3723. כָּפָר, kâphâr, *kaw-fawr´*; from 3722; a *village* (as *protected* by walls):—village. Compare 3715.

3724. כֹּפֶר, kôpher, *ko´-fer*; from 3722; (properly) a *cover*, i.e. (literal) a *village* (as *covered* in); (specific) *bitumen* (as used for *coating*), and the *henna* plant (as used for *dyeing*); (figurative) a *redemption*-price:—bribe, camphire, pitch, ransom, satisfaction, sum of money, village.

A masculine noun meaning a ransom, a bribe, a half-shekel. The most common translation of the word is ransom. It refers to the price demanded in order to redeem or rescue a person. The irresponsible owner of a bull that killed someone and was known to have gored people previously could be redeemed by the ransom that would be placed on him (Ex 21:30). When a census of people was taken in Israel, adult males had to pay a half-shekel ransom to keep the Lord's plague from striking them (Ex 30:12). A murderer could not be redeemed by a ransom (Nu 35:31). Yet money, without God's explicit approval, could not serve as a ransom for a human being (Ps 49:7[8]). On the other hand, money could serve as a ransom to buy off a person's human enemies (Pr 13:8). God sometimes used a wicked person as a ransom to redeem a righteous person (Pr 21:18); God ransomed Israel from Babylonian captivity for the ransom price of three nations (Isa 43:3): Egypt, Seba, and Cush.

The meaning of the word becomes a bribe when used in certain circumstances. For example, Samuel declared that he had never taken a bribe (1Sa 12:3); and Amos castigated the leaders of Israel for taking bribes (Am 5:12). Pr 6:35 describes a jealous husband whose fury would not allow him to take a bribe to lessen his anger.

3725. כִּפֻּר, kippur, *kip-poor´*; from 3722; *expiation* (only in plural):—atonement.

A masculine plural noun meaning atonement, the act of reconciliation, the Day of Atonement. It is used five times to indicate the act or process of reconciliation: a young bull was sacrificed each day for seven days during the ordination ceremony of Aaron and his sons to make atonement (Ex 29:36). Once a year, the blood of a sin offering was used to make atonement on the horns of the altar of incense located in front of the Holy of Holies (Ex 30:10). Ransom money of a half-shekel was used to effect atonement or reconciliation for male Israelites who were at least twenty years old (Ex 30:16). The money was then used to service the Tent of Meeting.

When a person had wronged the Lord or another person, a ram was presented to the priest, along with proper restitution (Nu 5:8); a sin offering for atonement was presented yearly on the Day of Atonement (Nu 29:11). Three times the noun is used to indicate the Day of Atonement itself (Le 23:27, 28; 25:9).

3726. כְּפַר הָעַמֹּנִי, Kᵉphar hâʻAmmôwnîy, *kef-ar´ haw-am-mo-nee´*; from 3723 and 5984, with the article interposed; *village of the Ammonite; Kefar-ha-Ammoni*, a place in Palestine:—Chefar-haamonai.

3727. כַּפֹּרֶת, kappôreth, *kap-po´-reth*; from 3722; a *lid* (used only of the *cover* of the sacred Ark):—mercy seat.

A noun meaning a lid, propitiation. This word refers to the lid that covered the ark of the testimony. It was made of gold and was decorated with two cherubim. God resided above this mercy seat (Ex 25:17–22). Only at specific times could the high priest come before the mercy seat (Le 16:2). On the Day of Atonement, the high priest made atonement for himself, the tabernacle, and the people by a sin offering, which included sprinkling blood on this lid (Le 16:13–15).

3728. כָּפַשׁ, kâphash, *kaw-fash´*; a primitive root; to *tread* down; (figurative) to *humiliate*:—cover.

A verb meaning to bend, to trample down, to humiliate, to cover over. This word is a primary root, but it is used only once in the Hebrew Bible. There the writer of Lamentations felt like he was trampled in the dust (La 3:16).

3729. כְּפַת, kᵉphath, *kef-ath´*; (Chaldee); a root of uncertain correspondence; to *fetter*:—bind.

3730. כַּפְתֹּר, kaphtôr, *kaf-tore´*; or (Am 9:1) כַּפְתּוֹר, **kaphtôwr,** *kaf-tore´*; probably from an unused root meaning to *encircle*; a *chaplet*; but used only in an architectonic sense, i.e. the *capital* of a column, or a wreath-like *button* or *disk* on the candelabrum:—knop, (upper) lintel.

3731. כַּפְתֹּר, Kaphtôr, *kaf-tore´*; or (Am 9:7) כַּפְתּוֹר, **Kaphtôwr,** *kaf-tore´*; apparently the same as 3730; *Caphtor* (i.e. a *wreath*-shaped island), the original seat of the Philistines:—Caphtor.

3732. כַּפְתֹּרִי, Kaphtôrîy, *kaf-to-ree´*; patrial from 3731; a *Caphtorite* (collective) or native of Caphtor:—Caphthorim, Caphtorim (-s).

3733. כַּר, kar, *kar*; from 3769 in the sense of *plumpness*; a *ram* (as *full-grown* and *fat*), including a *battering-ram* (as *butting*); hence a *meadow* (as *for sheep*); also a *pad* or camel's saddle (as *puffed out*):—captain, furniture, lamb, (large) pasture, ram. See also 1033, 3746.

A masculine noun meaning pasture, a male lamb, and a batterin ram. When used to mean pasture, it describes a bountiful restoratio for the Israelites. Like sheep, they would have large pastures in whic to graze (Isa 30:23). In reference to sheep, it means a male lamb compared to ewes, lambs, or fatlings (1Sa 15:9). Tribute often came the form of both ewes and rams, such as Mesha, king of Moab, paid the king of Israel (2Ki 3:4). This word also connotes a battering r such as those used in siege warfare (Eze 4:2). It is also interpreted saddle (Ge 31:34).

3734. כֹּר, kôr, *kore*; from the same as 3564; (properly) a deep round *vessel*, i.e. (specific) a *cor* or measure for things dry:—cor, measure. Chaldee the same.

3735. כְּרָא, kᵉrâʼ, *keh-raw´*; (Chaldee); probably corresponding to 3738 in the sense of *piercing* (figurative); to *grieve*:—be grieved.

3736. כַּרְבֵּל, karbêl, *kar-bale´*; from the same as 3525; to *gird* or *clothe*:—clothed.

3737. כַּרְבְּלָה, karbᵉlâh, *kar-bel-aw´*; (Chaldee); from a verb corresponding to that of 3736; a *mantle*:—hat.

3738. כָּרָה, kârâh, *kaw-raw´*; a primitive root; (properly) to *dig*; (figurative) to *plot*; (generally) to *bore* or open:—dig, × make (a banquet), open.

3739. כָּרָה, kârâh, *kaw-raw´*; usually assigned as a primitive root, but probably only a special application of 3738 (through the common idea of *planning* implied in a bargain); to *purchase*:—buy, prepare.

3740. כֵּרָה, kêrâh, *kay-raw´*; from 3739; a *purchase*:—provision.

3741. כָּרָה, kârâh, *kaw-raw´*; feminine of 3733; a *meadow*:—cottage.

3742. כְּרוּב, kᵉrûwb, *ker-oob´*; of uncertain derivation; a *cherub* or imaginary figure:—cherub, [*plural*] cherubims.

A masculine noun of uncertain derivation meaning an angelic being. It is commonly translated as cherub (plural, cherubim). The Bible provides scant details concerning the likeness of these winged creatures, except for the apocalyptic visions of Ezekiel in Eze 10. However, current pictures of cherubim as chubby infants with wings or as feminine creatures find no scriptural basis. The Bible portrays cherubim as the guardians of the Garden of Eden (Ge 3:24) and seemingly the glory of the Lord (cf. Eze 10:3, 4, 18–20); as flanking the throne of God (Ps 99:1; cf. Isa 37:16; though these may be poetic references to the mercy seat in the tabernacle [Nu 7:89]); as embroidered images on the tapestry of the tabernacle (Ex 26:1, 31); and as sculpted images arching above the mercy seat on the Ark of the Covenant (Ex 25:18–20, 22; 1Ki 6:23–28; 2Ch 3:10–13). Figuratively, the word is used to describe God's winged transport (2Sa 22:11; Ps 18:10[11]). Interestingly, Satan is described as being the anointed cherub (Eze 28:14) before he was cast out of heaven.

3743. כְּרוּב, Kᵉrûwb, *ker-oob´*; the same as 3742; *Kerub*, a place in Babylon:—Cherub.

3744. כָּרוֹז, kârôwz, *kaw-roze´*; (Chaldee); from 3745; a *herald*:—herald.

3745. כְּרַז, kᵉraz, *ker-az´*; (Chaldee); probably of Greek origin; to *proclaim*:—make a proclamation.

3746. כָּרִי, kârîy, *kaw-ree´*; perhaps an abridged plural of 3733 in the sense of *leader* (of the flock); a *life-guardsman*:—captains, Cherethites [*from the margin*].

A noun meaning a military order, the Kerethites or Cherethites. Under Benaiah (2Sa 20:23), the Kerethites or Cherethites, along with the Pelethites, remained loyal to David and Solomon when Adonijah attempted to become king. Joab, the commander of David's army, however, supported Adonijah (cf. 1Ki 1:18, 19).

The Karites or Carites again supported a king against treachery when they helped overthrow Athaliah and installed Joash as king (2Ki 11:19). It is possible that the Pelethites in 2Ki were a different group of Pelethites because the spelling of the Hebrew word is slightly different than in other references. What is clear is this term designates a special military unit.

3747. כְּרִית, Kᵉrîyth, *ker-eeth´*; from 3772; a *cut; Kerith*, a brook of Palestine:—Cherith.

3748. כְּרִיתוּת, kᵉrîythûwth, *ker-ee-thooth´*; from 3772; a *cutting* (of the matrimonial bond), i.e. *divorce*:—divorce (-ment).

A feminine noun meaning divorce. If a man was to find that his wife was unfaithful or any uncleanness in her, he was able to write a certificate of divorce that resulted in her expulsion from his house (Dt 24:1). Metaphorically, the Lord asked where Israel's certificate of divorce was. She should have had one to act so loosely (i.e. following other gods [Isa 50:1; Jer 3:8]).

3749. כַּרְכֹּב, karkôb, *kar-kobe´*; expanded from the same as 3522; a *rim* or top margin:—compass.

3750. כַּרְכֹּם, karkôm, *kar-kome´*; probably of foreign origin; the *crocus*:—saffron.

3751. כַּרְכְּמִישׁ, Karkᵉmîysh, *kar-kem-eesh´*; of foreign derivation; *Karkemish*, a place in Syria:—Carchemish.

3752. כַּרְכַּס, Karkas, *kar-kas´*; of Persian origin; *Karkas*, a eunuch of Xerxes:—Carcas.

3753. כִּרְכָּרָה, kirkârâh, *kir-kaw-raw´*; from 3769; a *dromedary* (from its *rapid* motion as if dancing):—swift beast.

3754. כֶּרֶם, kerem, *keh´-rem*; from an unused root of uncertain meaning; a *garden* or *vineyard*:—vines, (increase of the) vineyard (-s), vintage. See also 1021.

3755. כֹּרֵם, kôrêm, *ko-rame*; active participle of an imaginary denominative from 3754; a *vinedresser*:—vine dresser [*as one or two words*].

3756. כַּרְמִי, Karmîy, *kar-mee´*; from 3754; *gardener; Karmi*, the name of three Israelites:—Carmi.

3757. כַּרְמִי, Karmîy, *kar-mee´*; patronymic from 3756; a *Karmite* or descendant of *Karmi*:—Carmites.

3758. כַּרְמִיל, karmîyl, *kar-mele´*; probably of foreign origin; *carmine*, a deep red:—crimson.

3759. כַּרְמֶל, karmel, *kar-mel´*; from 3754; a planted *field* (garden, orchard, vineyard or park); (by implication) garden *produce*:—full (green) ears (of corn), fruitful field (place), plentiful (field).

3760. כַּרְמֶל, Karmel, *kar-mel´*; the same as 3759; *Karmel*, the name of a hill and of a town in Palestine:—Carmel, fruitful (plentiful) field, (place).

3761. כַּרְמְלִי, Karmᵉlîy, *kar-mel-ee´*; patronymic from 3760; a *Karmelite* or inhabitant of Karmel (the town):—Carmelite.

3762. כַּרְמְלִית, Karmᵉlîyth, *kar-mel-eeth´*; feminine of 3761; a *Karmelitess* or female inhabitant of Karmel:—Carmelitess.

3763. כְּרָן, Kᵉrân, *ker-awn´*; of uncertain derivation; *Keran*, an aboriginal Idumæan:—Cheran.

3764. כָּרְסֵא, korsêʼ, *kor-say´*; (Chaldee); corresponding to 3678; a *throne*:—throne.

An Aramaic masculine noun meaning throne. Daniel reminded Belshazzer that Nebuchadnezzar had been deposed from his throne because of pride (Da 5:20). Daniel had a dream about a throne that belonged to the Ancient of Days (Da 7:9). See the related Hebrew nouns *kissêʼ* and *kissêh* (3678).

3765. כִּרְסֵם, kirsêm, *kir-same´*; from 3697; to *lay waste*:—waste.

3766. כָּרַע, kâraʽ, *kaw-rah´*; a primitive root; to *bend* the knee; (by implication) to *sink*, to *prostrate*:—bow (down, self), bring down (low), cast down, couch, fall, feeble, kneeling, sink, smite (stoop) down, subdue, × very.

A verb meaning to bow. The word signifies the crouching of a lion before going to sleep (Ge 49:9; Nu 24:9); the bowing of an animal (Job 39:3); or a woman in order to give birth (1Sa 4:19); the bowing down of a man over a woman in sexual intercourse (adulterous, in this case) (Job 31:10); the yielding of knees from weakness, sometimes after one has been wounded (Jgs 5:27; 2Ki 9:24); the bowing of knees under a heavy burden (Isa 10:4; 46:2); the bowing of knees in submission or subjugation (Est 3:2, 5; Isa 45:23); bowing in repentance (Ezr 9:5); to worship a false god (1Ki 19:18); or the true God (2Ch 29:29; Ps 95:6).

3767. כְּרַע, kᵉrâʽ, *keh-raw´*; from 3766; the *leg* (from the knee to the ankle) of men or locusts (only in the dual):—leg.

3768. כַּרְפַּס, **karpas,** *kar-pas´*; of foreign origin; *byssus* or fine vegetable wool:—green.

3769. כָּרַר, **kârar,** *kaw-rar´*; a primitive root; to *dance* (i.e. *whirl*):—dance (-ing).

3770. כָּרֵשׂ, **kârêś,** *kaw-race´*; by variation from 7164; the *paunch* or belly (as *swelling* out):—belly.

3771. כַּרְשְׁנָא, **Karsh**e**nâ',** *kar-shen-aw´*; of foreign origin; *Karshena*, a courtier of Xerxes:—Carshena.

3772. כָּרַת, **kârath,** *kaw-rath´*; a primitive root; to *cut* (off, down or asunder); (by implication) to *destroy* or *consume*; specifically to *covenant* (i.e. make an alliance or bargain, originally by cutting flesh and passing between the pieces):—be chewed, be con-[feder-] ate, covenant, cut (down, off), destroy, fail, feller, be freed, hew (down), make a league ([covenant]), × lose, perish, × utterly, × want.

A verb meaning to cut off, to cut down, to make a covenant. This word can mean literally to cut something down or off, as grapes (Nu 13:23, 24); or branches (Jgs 9:48, 49). It can also be used figuratively, as with people (Jer 11:19; 50:16). Another important use of this word is to make a covenant (lit., to cut a covenant), perhaps deriving from the practice of cutting an animal in two in the covenant ceremony. God made a covenant with Abraham (Ge 15:18); Abraham made one with Abimelech (Ge 21:27). Finally, this word can also mean to destroy, as in Micah's prophecy (Mic 5:10).

3773. כָּרֻתוֹת, **k**e**ruthôwth,** *keh-rooth-oth´*; passive participle feminine of 3772; something *cut*, i.e. a hewn *timber*:—beam.

3774. כְּרֵתִי, **K**e**rêthîy,** *ker-ay-thee´*; probably from 3772 in the sense of *executioner*; a *Kerethite* or *life-guardsman* [compare 2876] (only collective in the singular as plural):—Cherethims, Cherethites.

3775. כֶּשֶׂב, **keśeb,** *keh´-seb*; apparently by transposition for 3532; a young *sheep*:—lamb.

3776. כִּשְׂבָּה, **kiśbâh,** *kis-baw´*; feminine of 3775; a young *ewe*:—lamb.

3777. כֶּשֶׂד, **Keśed,** *keh´-sed*; from an unused root of uncertain meaning; *Kesed*, a relative of Abraham:—Chesed.

3778. כַּשְׂדִּים, **Kaśdîym,** *kas-deem´*; (occasionally with enclitic כַּשְׂדִּימָה, **Kaśdîymâh**, *kas-dee´-maw; toward* the *Kasdites*:—into Chaldea), patronymic from 3777 (only in the plural); a *Kasdite*, or descendant of Kesed; (by implication) a *Chaldæan* (as if so descended); also an *astrologer* (as if proverbial of that people):—Chaldeans, Chaldees, inhabitants of Chaldea.

3779. כַּשְׂדַּי, **Kaśdây,** *kas-daw´ee*; (Chaldee); corresponding to 3778; a *Chaldæan* or inhabitant of Chaldæa; by implication a *Magian* or professional astrologer:—Chaldean.

3780. כָּשָׂה, **kâśâh,** *kaw-saw´*; a primitive root; to *grow fat* (i.e. be *covered* with flesh):—be covered. Compare 3680.

3781. כַּשִּׁיל, **kashshîyl,** *kash-sheel´*; from 3782; (properly) a *feller*, i.e. an *ax*:—ax.

3782. כָּשַׁל, **kâshal,** *kaw-shal´*; a primitive root; to *totter* or *waver* (through weakness of the legs, especially the ankle); (by implication) to *falter, stumble*, faint or fall:—bereave [*from the margin*], cast down, be decayed, (cause to) fail, (cause, make to) fall (down, -ing), feeble, be (the) ruin (-ed, of), (be) overthrown, (cause to) stumble, × utterly, be weak.

A verb meaning to stumble, to stagger, to totter, to cause to stumble, to overthrow, to make weak. This word is used literally of individuals falling or figuratively of cities and nations falling (Isa 3:8; Hos 14:1[2]). People can fall by the sword (Da 11:33); or because of evil (Pr 24:16); wickedness (Eze 33:12); and iniquity (Hos 5:5).

3783. כִּשָּׁלוֹן, **kishshâlôwn,** *kish-shaw-lone´*; from 3782; (properly) a *tottering*, i.e. *ruin*:—fall.

3784. כָּשַׁף, **kâshaph,** *kaw-shaf´*; a primitive root; (properly) to *whisper* a spell, i.e. to *inchant* or practise magic:—sorcerer, (use) witch (-craft).

A verb meaning to practice magic, to practice sorcery. It occurs with words of similar meaning in Dt 18:10 and 2Ch 33:6. While the exact meaning of the word is obscure, it involved the use of supernatural powers that hardened hearts against the truth (Ex 7:11). Those in Israel who used such powers were to be executed (Ex 22:18[17]). King Manasseh's involvement in sorcery to the point of making his children pass through fire, helped lead Judah to the breaking point of God's patience (2Ch 33:6; cf. 2Ki 24:3, 4). Judgment is promised against sorcerers when the Messiah returns (Mal 3:5). However, in a pagan country, where sorcery was practiced with greater ignorance, Daniel acted to save magicians from death while demonstrating that God's power exceeded that of the sorcerers (Da 2:2).

3785. כֶּשֶׁף, **kesheph,** *keh´-shef*; from 3784; *magic*:—sorcery, witchcraft.

A masculine noun meaning occult magic, sorcery. While specific practices included under this term cannot be established, the word occurs along with other similar terms such as enchantments and soothsaying, thus providing clues through association (Isa 47:9, 12; Mic 5:12[11]). This word always appears in a plural form, and half the time, it is modified by the word "numerous" (2Ki 9:22; Isa 47:9, 12). The plurals may indicate different manifestations, or they may represent plurals of intensification. Twice this term is linked with metaphorical harlotry (2Ki 9:22; Na 3:4). In the OT, magic was connected with several nations: Babylon, Nineveh, the Northern Kingdom and the Southern Kingdom (2Ki 9:22; Isa 47:9–12; Mic 5:12[11]; Na 3:4).

3786. כַּשָּׁף, **kashshâph,** *kash-shawf´*; from 3784; a *magician*:—sorcerer.

A masculine singular noun meaning sorcerer. It occurs once in the Hebrew Bible in Jer 27:9.

3787. כָּשֵׁר, **kâshêr,** *kaw-share´*; a primitive root; (properly) to be *straight* or *right*; (by implication) to *be acceptable*; also to *succeed* or prosper:—direct, be right, prosper.

A verb meaning to be successful, to cause to succeed. In Ecc 10:10, the word refers to success as the result of wisdom that enables one to go through difficult situations like a sharp ax through wood. In Ecc 11:6, the word refers to the success of seeds in growing, a matter beyond complete human control. Like other human ventures, successful farming calls for diligence and diversification. In Est 8:5, the word is used to confirm the king's opinion of Esther's proposal, whether in his view it would work smoothly.

3788. כִּשְׁרוֹן, **kishrôwn,** *kish-rone´*; from 3787; *success, advantage*:—equity, good, right.

A noun meaning profit, productivity. It occurs three times and refers to increase which brings no lasting satisfaction. In Ecc 2:21, it refers to the profit from labour which, at an owner's death, is given to one who did not labour for it. In Ecc 4:4, the word refers to the profit produced by hard work which is caused by or results in competition with and is the envy of one's neighbours. In Ecc 5:11[10], the word refers to the (lack of) profit in producing more than one can use.

3789. כָּתַב, **kâthab,** *kaw-thab´*; a primitive root; to *grave*; (by implication) to *write* (describe, inscribe, prescribe, subscribe):—describe, record, prescribe, subscribe, write (-ing, -ten).

3790. כְּתַב, **k**e**thab,** *keth-ab´*; (Chaldee); corresponding to 3789:—write (-ten).

3791. כְּתָב, **k**e**thâb,** *keh-thawb´*; from 3789; something *written*, i.e. a *writing, record* or *book*:—register, Scripture, writing.

3792. כְּתָב, **k**e**thâb,** *keth-awb´*; (Chaldee); corresponding to 3791:—prescribing, writing (-ten).

3793. כְּתֹבֶת, **k**e**thôbeth,** *keth-o´-beth*; from 3789; a *letter* or other *mark* branded on the skin:— × any [mark].

3794. כִּתִּי, **Kittîy,** *kit-tee´*; or כִּתִּיִּי, **Kittîyyîy,** *kit-tee-ee´*; patrial from an unused name denoting Cyprus (only in the plural); a

Kittite or Cypriote; hence an *islander* in general, i.e. the Greeks or Romans on the shores opposite Palestine:—Chittim, Kittim.

3795. כָּתִית, kâthîyth, *kaw-theeth´*; from 3807; *beaten,* i.e. pure (oil):—beaten.

3796. כֹּתֶל, kôthel, *ko´-thel*; from an unused root meaning to *compact*; a *wall* (as *gathering* inmates):—wall.

3797. כְּתַל, kᵉthal, *keth-al´*; (Chaldee); corresponding to 3796:—wall.

3798. כִּתְלִישׁ, Kithlîysh, *kith-leesh´*; from 3796 and 376; *wall of a man; Kithlish,* a place in Palestine:—Kithlish.

3799. כָּתַם, kâtham, *kaw-tham´*; a primitive root; (properly) to *carve* or *engrave,* i.e. (by implication) to *inscribe* indelibly:—mark.

3800. כֶּתֶם, kethem, *keh´-them*; from 3799; (properly) something *carved* out, i.e. *ore*; hence *gold* (pure as originally mined):—([most] fine, pure) gold (-en wedge).

3801. כְּתֹנֶת, kuttôneth, *koot-to´-neth*; from an unused root meaning to *cover* [compare 3802]; a *shirt*:—coat, garment, robe.

3802. כָּתֵף, kâthêph, *kaw-thafe´*; from an unused root meaning to *clothe*; the *shoulder* (properly, i.e. upper end of the arm; as being the spot where the garments hang); (figurative) *side-piece* or lateral projection of anything:—arm, corner, shoulder (-piece), side, undersetter.

3803. כָּתַר, kâthar, *kaw-thar´*; a primitive root; to *enclose*; hence (in a friendly sense) to *crown,* (in a hostile one) to *besiege*; also to *wait* (as restraining oneself):—beset round, compass about, be crowned, inclose round, suffer.

3804. כֶּתֶר, kether, *keh´-ther*; from 3803; (properly) a *circlet,* i.e. a *diadem*:—crown.

3805. כֹּתֶרֶת, kôthereth, *ko-theh´-reth*; feminine active participle of 3803; the *capital* of a column:—chapiter.

3806. כָּתַשׁ, kâthash, *kaw-thash´*; a primitive root; to *butt* or *pound*:—bray.

3807. כָּתַת, kâthath, *kaw-thath´*; a primitive root; to *bruise* or violently *strike*:—beat (down, to pieces), break in pieces, crushed, destroy, discomfit, smite, stamp.

A verb meaning to beat, to crush, to hammer. This term is used in reference to the destruction of the golden calf (Dt 9:21); and in the eschatological hope of hammering swords into plowshares (Isa 2:4; Mic 4:3). It can also be used figuratively for destroying an enemy (Dt 1:44).

3808. לֹא, lô', *lo*; or לוֹא, **lôw',** *lo*; or לֹה, **lôh,** *lo*; (Dt 3:11), a primitive particle; *not* (the simple or abstract negation); (by implication) *no*; often used with other particles (as follows):—× before, + or else, ere, + except, ig [-norant], much, less, nay, neither, never, no ([-ne], -r, [-thing]), (× as though …, [can-], for) not (out of), of nought, otherwise, out of, + surely, + as truly as, + of a truth, + verily, for want, + whether, without.

An adverb meaning no, not. The term is primarily utilized as an ordinary negation, as in Ge 3:4: "You will not surely die" (NIV cf. Jgs 14:4; Ps 16:10). Often it is used to express an unconditional prohibition, thus having the force of an imperative: "You shall not (= do not ever) steal" (Ex 20:15 NIV; cf. Jgs 13:5). Frequently, it functions as an absolute in answer to a question (Job 23:6; Zec 4:5). The word is also employed in questions to denote that an affirmative answer is expected (2Ki 5:26; Jnh 4:11). When it is prefixed to a noun or adjective, it negates that word, making it have an opposite or contrary meaning (e.g., god becomes non-god; strong becomes weak; cf. Dt 32:21; Pr 30:25). When prefixed by the preposition *bᵉ*, meaning in or by, the combined term carries the temporal meaning of beyond or before (Le 15:25); the meaning without is also not uncommon for this combination (Job 8:11). A prefixed preposition *lᵉ*, meaning to or for, gives the term the meaning of without (2Ch 15:3) or as though not (Job 39:16). Occasionally, the word suggests the meaning not only, on account of the context (Dt 5:3).

3809. לָא, lâ', *law*; (Chaldee); or לָה, **lâh,** *law*; (Chaldee) (Da 4:32), corresponding to 3808:—or even, neither, no (-ne, -r), ([can-]) not, as nothing, without.

3810. לֹא דְבַר, Lô' Dᵉbar, *lo deb-ar´*; or לוֹ דְבַר, **Lôw Dᵉbar,** *lo deb-ar´*; (2Sa 9:44, 5), or לִדְבִר, **Lidbir,** *lid-beer´*; (Jos 13:26), [probably rather לֹדְבַר, **Lôdᵉbar,** *lo-deb-ar´*; from 3808 and 1699; *pastureless; Lo-Debar,* a place in Palestine:—Debir, Lodebar.

3811. לָאָה, lâ'âh, *law-aw´*; a primitive root; to *tire*; (figurative) to *be* (or *make*) *disgusted*:—faint, grieve, lothe, (be, make) weary (selves).

3812. לֵאָה, Lê'âh, *lay-aw´*; from 3811; *weary; Leah,* a wife of Jacob:—Leah.

3813. לָאַט, lâ'at, *law-at´*; a primitive root; to *muffle*:—cover.

3814. לָאט, lâ't, *lawt*; from 3813 (or perhaps for active participle of 3874); (properly) *muffled,* i.e. *silently*:—softly.

3815. לָאֵל, Lâ'êl, *law-ale´*; from the prepositional prefix and 410; (belonging) *to God; Laël,* an Israelite:—Lael.

3816. לְאֹם, lᵉ'ôm, *leh-ome´*; or לְאוֹם, **lᵉ'ôwm,** *leh-ome´*; from an unused root meaning to *gather*; a *community*:—nation, people.

A masculine singular noun meaning people. This poetic term is used often as a synonym for people (*'am* [5971]) or nation (*gôwy* [1471]). It can refer to Israel or to humanity in general. A well-known passage (Ge 25:23) uses this term in regard to the two peoples in Rebekah's womb—Israel and Edom.

3817. לְאֻמִּים, Lᵉ'ummîym, *leh-oom-meem´*; plural of 3816; *communities; Leümmim,* an Arabian:—Leummim.

3818. לֹא עַמִּי, Lô' 'Ammîy, *lo am-mee´*; from 3808 and 5971 with pronoun suffix; *not my people; Lo-Ammi,* the symbolical name of a son of Hosea:—Lo-ammi.

3819. לֹא רֻחָמָה, Lô' Ruchâmâh, *lo roo-khaw-maw´*; from 3808 and 7355; *not pitied; Lo-Ruchamah,* the symbolical name of a son of Hosea:—Lo-ruhamah.

3820. לֵב, lêb, *labe*; a form of 3824; the *heart*; also used (figurative) very widely for the feelings, the will and even the intellect; likewise for the *centre* of anything:— + care for, comfortably, consent, × considered, courag [-eous], friend [-ly], ([broken-], [hard-], [merry-], [stiff-], [stout-], double) heart ([-ed]), × heed, × I, kindly, midst, mind (-ed), × regard ([-ed]), × themselves, × unawares, understanding, × well, willingly, wisdom.

A masculine noun usually rendered as heart but whose range of meaning is extensive. It can denote the heart as a human physical organ (Ex 28:29; 1Sa 25:37; 2Ki 9:24); or an animal (Job 41:24[16]). However, it usually refers to some aspect of the immaterial inner self or being since the heart is considered to be the seat of one's inner nature as well as one of its components. It can be used in a general sense (1Ki 8:23; Ps 84:2[3]; Jer 3:10); or it can be used of a specific aspect of personality: the mind (Ge 6:5; Dt 29:4[3]; Ne 6:8); the will (Ex 35:5; 2Ch 12:14; Job 11:13); the emotions (Ge 6:6[Note that God is the subject]; 1Sa 24:5[6]; 25:31). In addition, the word can also allude to the inside or middle (Ex 15:8; Dt 4:11).

3821. לֵב, lêb, *labe*; (Chaldee); corresponding to 3820:—heart.

An Aramaic masculine singular noun meaning heart. In this form, its only occurrence in the Hebrew Bible is in Da 7:28.

3822. לְבָאוֹת, Lᵉbâ'ôwth, *leb-aw-ōth´*; plural of 3833; *lionesses; Lebaoth,* a place in Palestine:—Lebaoth. See also 1034.

3823. לָבַב, lâbab, *law-bab´*; a primitive root; (properly) to *be enclosed* (as if with *fat*); (by implication, as denominative from 3824) to *unheart,* i.e. (in a good sense) *transport* (with love), or (in a bad sense) *stultify*; also (as denominative from 3834) to *make cakes*:—make cakes, ravish, be wise.

A verb meaning to stir the heart, to make cakes. This word is related to the common Hebrew nouns *lêb* (3820) and *lêbâb* (3824), which both mean heart, mind, or inner being. Solomon used this word twice in the same verse to express the stirring of his heart with affection for his lover (SS 4:9); Zophar used it to describe the mind of an idiot being made intelligent (Job 11:12). In the only other instances of this word, it describes the making of bread or a cake that was kneaded and baked (2Sa 13:6, 8).

3824. לֵבָב, lêbâb, *lay-bawb´*; from 3823; the *heart* (as the most interior organ); used also like 3820:— + bethink themselves, breast, comfortably, courage, ([faint], [tender-] heart [-ed]), midst, mind, × unawares, understanding.

A masculine noun meaning heart, mind, inner person. The primary usage of this word describes the entire disposition of the inner person that God can discern (1Sa 16:7); be devoted to the Lord (1Ki 15:3); seek the Lord (2Ch 11:16); turn against people (Ex 14:5); be uncircumcised (Le 26:41); be hardened (1Sa 6:6); be totally committed to the Lord (Dt 6:5; 2Ch 15:15). It is also used to describe the place where the rational, thinking process occurs that allows a person to know God's blessings (Jos 23:14); to plan for the future (1Ki 8:18); to communicate (2Ch 9:1); and to understand God's message (Isa 6:10). Like our English usage, it often refers to the seat of emotions, whether it refers to joy (Dt 28:47); discouragement (Jos 2:11); comfort (Jgs 19:8); grief (1Sa 1:8); sorrow (Ps 13:2[3]); or gladness (Isa 30:29).

3825. לְבַב, l^ebab, *leb-ab´*; (Chaldee); corresponding to 3824:—heart.

An Aramaic masculine noun meaning heart, mind, the inner person. This word is equivalent to the Hebrew word *lêbâb* (3824). It is used to describe the entire disposition of the inner person, which God can change (Da 4:16[13]; 5:21; 7:4). This inner person can be lifted up in pride (Da 5:20) or made low in humility (Da 5:22). The rational, thinking process is demonstrated when Daniel described the thoughts of the king's mind (Da 2:30).

3826. לִבָּה, libbâh, *lib-baw´*; feminine of 3820; the *heart*:—heart.

A feminine noun meaning heart. A variant of the word *lêb* (3820), it suggests the seat of emotions or the will (Eze 16:30).

3827. לַבָּה, labbâh, *lab-baw´*; for 3852; *flame*:—flame.

3828. לְבוֹנָה, l^ebôwnâh, *leb-o-naw´*; or לְבֹנָה, **lebô-nâh,** *leb-o-naw´*; from 3836; *frankincense* (from its *whiteness* or perhaps that of its smoke):—(frank-) incense.

3829. לְבוֹנָה, L^ebôwnâh, *leb-o-naw´*; the same as 3828; *Lebonah*, a place in Palestine:—Lebonah.

3830. לְבוּשׁ, l^ebûwsh, *leb-oosh´*; or לְבֻשׁ, **l^ebush,** *leb-oosh´*; from 3847; a *garment* (literal or figurative); by implication (euphemistic) a *wife*:—apparel, clothed with, clothing, garment, raiment, vestment, vesture.

3831. לְבוּשׁ, l^ebûwsh, *leb-oosh´*; (Chaldee); corresponding to 3830:—garment.

3832. לָבַט, lâbaṭ, *law-bat´*; a primitive root; to *overthrow*; (intransitive) to *fall*:—fall.

3833. לָבִיא, lâbîy', *law-bee´*; or (Eze 19:2) לְבִיָּא, **l^ebîyyâ',** *leb-ee-yaw´*; irregular masculine plural לְבָאִים, **l^ebâ'îym,** *leb-aw-eem´*; irregular feminine plural לְבָאוֹת, **l^ebâ'ôwth,** *leb-aw-oth´*; from an unused root meaning to *roar*; a *lion* (properly, a *lioness* as the fiercer [although not a *roarer*; compare 738]):—(great, old, stout) lion, lioness, young [lion].

3834. לָבִיבָה, lâbîybâh, *law-bee-baw´*; or rather לְבִבָה, **l^ebibâh,** *leb-ee-baw´*; from 3823 in its original sense of *fatness* (or perhaps of *folding*); a *cake* (either as *fried* or *turned*):—cake.

3835. לָבַן, lâban, *law-ban´*; a primitive root; to *be* (or *become*) *white*; also (as denominative from 3843) to *make bricks*:—make brick, be (made, make) white (-r).

3836. לָבָן, lâbân, *law-bawn´*; or (Ge 49:12) לָבֵן, **lâbên,** *law-bane´*; from 3835; *white*:—white.

3837. לָבָן, Lâbân, *law-bawn´*; the same as 3836; *Laban*, a Mesopotamian; also a place in the Desert:—Laban.

3838. לְבָנָא, L^ebânâ', *leb-aw-naw´*; or לְבָנָה, **Lebânâh,** *leb-aw-naw´*; the same as 3842; *Lebana* or *Lebanah*, one of the Nethinim:—Lebana, Lebanah.

3839. לִבְנֶה, libneh, *lib-neh´*; from 3835; some sort of *whitish* tree, perhaps the *storax*:—poplar.

3840. לִבְנָה, libnâh, *lib-naw´*; from 3835; (properly) *whiteness*, i.e. (by implication) *transparency*:—paved.

3841. לִבְנָה, Libnâh, *lib-naw´*; the same as 3839; *Libnah*, a place in the Desert and one in Palestine:—Libnah.

3842. לְבָנָה, l^ebânâh, *leb-aw-naw´*; from 3835; properly (the) *white*, i.e. the *moon*:—moon. See also 3838.

3843. לְבֵנָה, l^ebênâh, *leb-ay-naw´*; from 3835; a *brick* (from the *whiteness* of the clay):—(altar of) brick, tile.

3844. לְבָנוֹן, L^ebânôwn, *leb-aw-nohn´*; from 3825; (the) *white* mountain (from its snow); *Lebanon*, a mountain range in Palestine:—Lebanon.

3845. לִבְנִי, Libnîy, *lib-nee´*; from 3835; *white; Libni*, an Israelite:—Libni.

3846. לִבְנִי, Libnîy, *lib-nee´*; patronymic from 3845; a *Libnite* or descendant of Libni (collective):—Libnites.

3847. לָבַשׁ, lâbash, *law-bash´*; or לָבֵשׁ, **lâbêsh,** *law-bashe´*; a primitive root; (properly) *wrap* around, i.e. (by implication) to *put on* a garment or *clothe* (oneself, or another), literal or figurative:—(in) apparel, arm, array (self), clothe (self), come upon, put (on, upon), wear.

3848. לְבַשׁ, l^ebash, *leb-ash´*; (Chaldee); corresponding to 3847:—clothe.

3849. לֹג, lôg, *lohg*; from an unused root apparently meaning to *deepen* or *hollow* [like 3537]; a *log* or measure for liquids:—log [of oil].

3850. לֹד, Lôd, *lode*; from an unused root of uncertain significance; *Lod*, a place in Palestine:—Lod.

3851. לַהַב, lahab, *lah´-hab*; from an unused root meaning to *gleam*; a *flash*; (figurative) a sharply polished *blade* or *point* of a weapon:—blade, bright, flame, glittering.

3852. לֶהָבָה, lehâbâh, *leh-aw-baw´*; or לַהֶבֶת, **lahebeth,** *lah-eh´-beth*; feminine of 3851, and meaning the same:—flame (-ming), head [of a spear].

3853. לְהָבִים, L^ehâbîym, *leh-haw-beem´*; plural of 3851; *flames; Lehabim*, a son of Mizrain, and his descendants:—Lehabim.

3854. לַהַג, lahag, *lah´-hag*; from an unused root meaning to *be eager*; intense mental *application*:—study.

3855. לַהַד, Lâhad, *law´-had*; from an unused root meaning to *glow* [compare 3851] or else to *be earnest* [compare 3854]; *Lahad*, an Israelite:—Lahad.

3856. לָהַהּ, lâhah, *law-hah´*; a primitive root meaning properly to *burn*, i.e. (by implication) to *be rabid;* (figurative) *insane;* also (from the *exhaustion* of frenzy) to *languish*:—faint, mad.

3857. לָהַט, lâhaṭ, *law-hat´*; a primitive root; (properly) to *lick*, i.e. (by implication) to *blaze*:—burn (up), set on fire, flaming, kindle.

3858. לַהַט, lahaṭ, *lah´-hat*; from 3857; a *blaze*; also (from the idea of *enwrapping*) *magic* (as *covert*):—flaming, enchantment.

A masculine noun meaning flame. This word is used only once in the OT. It describes the "flaming sword" of the cherubim stationed at the east side of the Garden of Eden (Ge 3:24). This word comes from the verb, *lâhaṭ* (3857), meaning to flame or to set on fire.

3859. לָהַם, lâham, *law-ham´*; a primitive root; (properly) to *burn* in, i.e. (figurative) to *rankle*:—wound.

3860. לָהֵן, lâhên, *law-hane´*; from the prefix preposition meaning *to* or *for* and 2005; (properly) *for if*; hence *therefore*:—for them [*by mistake for prepositional suffix*].

3861. לָהֵן, lâhên, *law-hane´*; (Chaldee); corresponding to 3860; *therefore*; also *except*:—but, except, save, therefore, wherefore.

3862. לַהֲקָה, lahăqâh, *lah-hak-aw´*; probably from an unused root meaning to *gather*; an *assembly*:—company.

3863. לוּא, lûw', *loo*; or **לֻא, lu',** *loo*; or **לוּ, lûw,** *loo*; a conditional particle; *if*; by implication (interjection as a wish) *would that!*:—if (haply), peradventure, I pray thee, though, I would, would God (that).

3864. לוּבִי, Lûwbîy, *loo-bee´*; or **לֻבִּי, Lubbîy,** *loob-bee´*; (Da 11:43), patrial from a name probably derived from an unused root meaning to *thirst*, i.e. a *dry* region; apparently a *Libyan* or inhabitant of interior Africa (only in plural):—Lubim (-s), Libyans.

3865. לוּד, Lûwd, *lood*; probably of foreign derivation; *Lud*, the name of two nations:—Lud, Lydia.

3866. לוּדִי, Lûwdîy, *loo-dee´*; or **לוּדִיִּי, Lûwdîyyîy,** *loo-dee-ee´*; patrial from 3865; a *Ludite* or inhabitant of Lud (only in plural):—Ludim, Lydians.

3867. לָוָה, lâvâh, *law-vaw´*; a primitive root; (properly) to *twine*, i.e. (by implication) to *unite*, to *remain*; also to *borrow* (as a form of *obligation*) or (causative) to *lend*:—abide with, borrow (-er), cleave, join (self), lend (-er).

3868. לוּז, lûwz, *looz*; a primitive root; to *turn* aside [compare 3867, 3874 and 3885], i.e. (literal) to *depart*, (figurative) *be perverse*:—depart, froward, perverse (-ness).

3869. לוּז, lûwz, *looz*; probably of foreign origin; some kind of *nut*-tree, perhaps the *almond*:—hazel.

3870. לוּז, Lûwz, *looz*; probably from 3869 (as growing there); *Luz*, the name of two places in Palestine:—Luz.

3871. לוּחַ, lûwach, *loo´-akh*; or **לֻחַ, luach,** *loo´-akh*; from a primitive root; probably meaning to *glisten*; a *tablet* (as *polished*), of stone, wood or metal:—board, plate, table.

3872. לוּחִית, Lûwchîyth, *loo-kheeth´*; or **לֻחוֹת, Luchôwth,** *loo-khoth´*; (Jer 48:5), from the same as 3871; *floored; Luchith*, a place East of the Jordan:—Luhith.

3873. לוֹחֵשׁ, Lôwchêsh, *lo-khashe´*; active participle of 3907; (the) *enchanter; Lochesh*, an Israelite:—Hallohesh, Haloshesh [*including the art*].

3874. לוּט, lûwṭ, *loot*; a primitive root; to *wrap* up:—cast, wrap.

3875. לוֹט, lôwṭ, *lote*; from 3874; a *veil*:—covering.

3876. לוֹט, Lôwṭ, *lote*; the same as 3875; *Lot*, Abraham's nephew:—Lot.

3877. לוֹטָן, Lôwṭân, *lo-tawn´*; from 3875; *covering; Lotan*, an Idumæan:—Lotan.

3878. לֵוִי, Lêvîy, *lay-vee´*; from 3867; *attached; Levi*, a son of Jacob:—Levi. See also 3879, 3881.

3879. לֵוָי, Lêvây, *lay-vaw´*; (Chaldee); corresponding to 3880:—Levite.

3880. לִוְיָה, livyâh, *liv-yaw´*; from 3867; something *attached*, i.e. a *wreath*:—ornament.

3881. לֵוִיִּי, Lêvîyyîy, *lay-vee-ee´*; or **לֵוִי, Lêvîy,** *lay-vee´*; patronymic from 3878; a *Leviite* or descendant of Levi:—Levite.

3882. לִוְיָתָן, livyâthân, *liv-yaw-thawn´*; from 3867; a *wreathed* animal, i.e. a *serpent* (especially the *crocodile* or some other large sea-monster); (figurative) the constellation of the *dragon*; also as a symbol of *Babylon*:—leviathan, mourning.

3883. לוּל, lûwl, *lool*; from an unused root meaning to *fold* back; a *spiral* step:—winding stair. Compare 3924.

3884. לוּלֵא, lûwlê', *loo-lay´*; or **לוּלֵי, lûwlêy,** *loo-lay´*; from 3863 and 3808; *if not*:—except, had not, if (… not), unless, were it not that.

3885. לוּן, lûwn, *loon*; or **לִין, lîyn,** *leen*; a primitive root; to *stop* (usually over night); (by implication) to *stay* permanently; hence (in a bad sense) to be *obstinate* (especially in words, to *complain*):—abide (all night), continue, dwell, endure, grudge, be left, lie all night, (cause to) lodge (all night, in, -ing, this night), (make to) murmur, remain, tarry (all night, that night).

3886. לָעַע, lâ'a', *law´-ah*; a primitive root; to *gulp*; (figurative) to *be rash*:—swallow down (up).

3887. לוּץ, lûwts, *loots*; a primitive root; (properly) to *make mouths* at, i.e. to *scoff*; hence (from the effort to pronounce a foreign language) to *interpret*, or (generic) *intercede*:—ambassador, have in derision, interpreter, make a mock, mocker, scorn (-er, -ful), teacher.

A verb meaning to boast, to scorn, to mock, to deride, or to imitate. This Hebrew verb is frequently found in the book of Proverbs (Pr 9:7, 8; 13:1; 20:1), and means to deride or to boast so as to express utter contempt. The activity of the scornful is condemned as an abomination to people (Pr 24:9) and contrary to the Law of the Lord (Ps 1:1). Both Job (Job 16:20) and the psalmist (Ps 119:51) expressed the pain inflicted by the scornful, but in the end, the scorner will reap what he has sown (Pr 3:34). By extension the word is used to signify ambassadors (2Ch 32:31); interpreters (Ge 42:23); and spokesmen (Isa 43:27). These meanings arise from the sense of speaking indirectly implied in the root word. Some grammarians view the participle of this verb as a separate noun. For a list of these references, see the division in the concordance.

3888. לוּשׁ, lûwsh, *loosh*; a primitive root; to *knead*:—knead.

3889. לוּשׁ, Lûwsh, *loosh*; from 3888; *kneading; Lush*, a place in Palestine:—Laish [*from the margin*]. Compare 3919.

3890. לְוָת, l^evâth, *lev-awth´*; (Chaldee); from a root corresponding to 3867; (properly) *adhesion*, i.e. (as prephaps) *with*:—× thee.

3891. לְזוּת, lâzûwth, *lawz-ooth´*; from 3868; *perverseness*:—perverse.

3892. לַח, lach, *lakh*; from an unused root meaning to *be new; fresh*, i.e. unused or undried:—green, moist.

3893. לֵחַ, lêach, *lay´-akh*; from the same as 3892; *freshness*, i.e. vigour:—natural force.

3894. לְחוּם, l^echûwm, *leh-khoom´*; or **לָחֻם, lâchum,** *law-khoom´*; passive participle of 3898; (properly) *eaten*, i.e. *food*; also *flesh*, i.e. *body*:—while … is eating, flesh.

A masculine noun meaning bowels, intestines. This word is of uncertain meaning, owing to its rare use in Scripture, but it is generally understood to mean the intestines or inward parts of the body. It is a derivative of the Hebrew word *lâcham* (3898), meaning to fight. Occurring only in Job 20:23 and Zep 1:17, the context is the outpouring of the Lord's wrath. In the latter text, the apocalyptic image is a most graphic picture of battle: "Their blood will be poured out like dust and their flesh [*lâchûm*, inner parts] like dung" (NASB).

3895. לְחִי, l^echîy, *lekh-ee´*; from an unused root meaning to *be soft*; the *cheek* (from its *fleshiness*); hence the *jaw*-bone:—cheek (bone), jaw (bone).

3896. לְחִי, Lechîy, *lekh´-ee*; a form of 3895; *Lechi*, a place in Palestine:—Lehi. Compare also 7437.

3897. לָחַךְ, **lâchak,** *law-khak´*; a primitive root; to *lick*:—lick (up).

3898. לָחַם, **lâcham,** *law-kham´*; a primitive root; to *feed* on; (figurative) to *consume*; (by implication) to *battle* (as *destruction*):—devour, eat, × ever, fight (-ing), overcome, prevail, (make) war (-ring).

3899. לֶחֶם, **lechem,** *lekh´-em*; from 3898; *food* (for man or beast), especially *bread*, or *grain* (for making it):—([shew-]) bread, × eat, food, fruit, loaf, meat, victuals. See also 1036.

3900. לְחֶם, **l^echem,** *lekh-em´*; (Chaldee); corresponding to 3899:—feast.

3901. לָחֶם, **lâchem,** *law-khem´*; from 3898, *battle*:—war.

3902. לַחְמִי, **Lachmîy,** *lakh-mee´*; from 3899; *foodful; Lachmi*, an Israelite; or rather probably a brief form (or perhaps erroneous transcription) for 1022:—Lahmi. See also 3433.

3903. לַחְמָס, **Lachmâs,** *lakh-maws´*; probably by erroneous transcription for לַחְמָם, **Lachmâm,** *lakh-mawm´*; from 3899; *food-like; Lachmam* or *Lachmas*, a place in Palestine:—Lahmam.

3904. לְחֵנָה, **l^echênâh,** *lekh-ay-naw´*; (Chaldee); from an unused root of uncertain meaning; a *concubine*:—concubine.

3905. לָחַץ, **lâchats,** *law-khats´*; a primitive root; (properly) to *press*, i.e. (figurative) to *distress*:—afflict, crush, force, hold fast, oppress (-or), thrust self.

3906. לַחַץ, **lachats,** *lakh´-ats*; from 3905; *distress*:—affliction, oppression.

3907. לָחַשׁ, **lâchash,** *law-khash´*; a primitive root; to *whisper*; (by implication) to *mumble* a spell (as a magician):—charmer, whisper (together).

A verb meaning to whisper, to charm. This word is used only three times in the OT. In two of these cases, this word is best translated as whisper to describe the quiet talk of David's servants at the death of his child (2Sa 12:19); and the secretive talk of David's enemies (Ps 41:7[8]). The other instance of this word described the snake charmers (Ps 58:5[6]). See also the related noun, *lachash* (3908), meaning whispering or charming.

3908. לַחַשׁ, **lachash,** *lakh´-ash*; from 3907; (properly) a *whisper*, i.e. by implication (in a good sense) a private *prayer*, (in a bad one) an *incantation*; (concrete) an *amulet*:—charmed, earring, enchantment, orator, prayer.

A masculine noun meaning whispering, enchantment, and charm. The action of whispering, with the connotations of casting a spell, is the basis for this word. It is used in the Hebrew to signify charms or amulets worn by women (Isa 3:20); the charming of a snake (Ecc 10:11; Jer 8:17); one who crafts clever words so as to enchant (Isa 3:3); a prayer whispered in a time of sudden distress (Isa 26:16).

3909. לָט, **lâṭ,** *lawt*; a form of 3814 or else participle from 3874; (properly) *covered*, i.e. *secret*; (by implication) *incantation*; also *secrecy* or (adverbial) *covertly*:—enchantment, privily, secretly, softly.

A masculine noun meaning secrecy, enchantment, mystery, privacy. A form of the Hebrew word *lâ'ṭ* (3814), this word conveys the sense of a secret known to only a select group or to something done in secrecy. Three times the word is used in reference to the enchantments of the Egyptian sorcerers in Pharaoh's court (Ex 7:22; 8:7[13], 18[14]). The other occurrences in the OT signify an action done without another party's notice (Ru 3:7) or in private (1Sa 18:22).

3910. לֹט, **lôṭ,** *lote*; probably from 3874; a gum (from its *sticky* nature), probably *ladanum*:—myrrh.

3911. לְטָאָה, **l^eṭâ'âh,** *let-aw-aw´*; from an unused root meaning to *hide*; a kind of *lizard* (from its *covert* habits):—lizard.

3912. לְטוּשִׁם, **L^eṭûwshim,** *let-oo-sheem´*; masculine plural of passive participle of 3913; *hammered* (i.e. *oppressed*) ones; *Letushim*, an Arabian tribe:—Letushim.

3913. לָטַשׁ, **lâṭash,** *law-tash´*; a primitive root; (properly) to *hammer* out (an edge), i.e. to *sharpen*:—instructer, sharp (-en), whet.

3914. לֹיָה, **lôyâh,** *lo-yaw´*; a form of 3880; a *wreath*:—addition.

3915. לַיִל, **layil,** *lah´-yil*; or (Isa 21:11) לֵיל, **lêyl,** *lale*; also לַיְלָה, **lay^elâh,** *lah´-yel-aw*; from the same as 3883; (properly) a *twist* (away of the light), i.e. *night*; (figurative) *adversity*:—([mid-]) night (season).

A masculine noun meaning night, midnight. This Hebrew word primarily describes the portion of day between sunset and sunrise (Ge 1:5; cf. Ps 136:9). Figuratively, it signifies the gloom or despair that sometimes engulfs the human heart from an absence of divine guidance (Mic 3:6); calamity (Job 36:20); or affliction (Job 30:17). Nevertheless, even in the dark night of the soul, the Lord gives His people a song of joy (Job 35:10; Ps 42:8[9]).

3916. לֵילְיָא, **lêyl^eyâ',** *lay-leh-yaw´*; (Chaldee); corresponding to 3915:—night.

An Aramaic masculine noun meaning night. All the undisputed instances occur in the book of Daniel. Most often, the term is utilized to declare the time in which several of Daniel's visions took place (Da 2:19; 7:2, 7, 13). However, it functions once to indicate when the assassination of the Babylonian king, Belshazzar, transpired (Da 5:30). The word closely corresponds with the Hebrew noun *layil* or *layĕlâh* (3915).

3917. לִילִית, **lîylîyth,** *lee-leeth´*; from 3915; a *night* spectre:—screech owl.

3918. לַיִשׁ, **layish,** *lah´-yish*; from 3888 in the sense of *crushing*; a lion (from his destructive *blows*):—(old) lion.

3919. לַיִשׁ, **Layish,** *lah´-yish*; the same as 3918; *Laïsh*, the name of two places in Palestine:—Laish. Compare 3889.

3920. לָכַד, **lâkad,** *law-kad´*; a primitive root; to *catch* (in a net, trap or pit); (generally) to *capture* or occupy; also to *choose* (by lot); (figurative) to *cohere*:— × at all, catch (self), be frozen, be holden, stick together, take.

3921. לֶכֶד, **leked,** *leh´-ked*; from 3920; something to *capture* with, i.e. a *noose*:—being taken.

3922. לֵכָה, **lêkâh,** *lay-kaw´*; from 3212; a *journey; Lekah*, a place in Palestine:—Lecah.

3923. לָכִישׁ, **Lâkîysh,** *law-keesh´*; from an unused root of uncertain meaning; *Lakish*, a place in Palestine:—Lachish.

3924. לֻלָאוֹת, **lulâ'ôwth,** *loo-law-oth´*; from the same as 3883; a *loop*:—loop.

3925. לָמַד, **lâmad,** *law-mad´*; a primitive root; (properly) to *goad*, i.e. (by implication) to *teach* (the rod being an Oriental *incentive*):—[un-] accustomed, × diligently, expert, instruct, learn, skilful, teach (-er, -ing).

A verb meaning to learn, to study, to teach, to be taught, to be learned. The verb describes learning war, training for war, the lack of training (Isa 2:4; Mic 4:3), or the acquisition of instruction (Isa 29:24). God's people were warned not to learn the ways of the nations, that is, to acquire their corrupt and false practices and standards (Jer 10:2) but to learn the ways of God instead (Jer 12:16). The verb is sometimes used with an infinitive following it suggesting the meaning to learn to do something. Israel was not to learn to do the abominations of surrounding nations (Dt 18:9); it describes metaphorically the actions of Jehoahaz against his countrymen as he tore them as a lion would tear its prey (Eze 19:3).

In the intensive or factitive form, the root takes on the meaning of imparting learning (i.e. teaching). The verb simply means to teach (2Ch 17:7, 9) or to teach people or things; the Lord taught His people (Jer 31:34) His decrees and laws (Dt 4:1). The participle of this form often means teacher (Ps 119:99).

The passive forms of this verb mean to be teachable or to be knowledgeable or well-trained by the Lord (Jer 31:18) or people (Isa 29:13).

3926. לְמוֹ, **lᵉmôw,** *lem-o´*; a prolonged and separable form of the prefix preposition; *to* or *for*:—at, for, to, upon.

3927. לְמוּאֵל, **Lᵉmûw'êl,** *lem-oo-ale´*; or לְמוֹאֵל, **Lᵉmôw'êl,** *lem-o-ale´*; from 3926 and 410; (belonging) *to God; Lemuël* or *Lemoël*, a symbolical name of Solomon:—Lemuel.

3928. לִמּוּד, **limmûwd,** *lim-mood´*; or לִמֻּד, **limmud,** *lim-mood´*; from 3925; *instructed*:—accustomed, disciple, learned, taught, used.

A masculine adjective meaning accustomed, used to something, learned, practiced, an expert, one taught, a follower, a disciple. It was used to describe those who habitually practice evil (Jer 13:23). It was also employed to help portray Israel as a wild donkey in heat that was accustomed to life in the rugged wilderness (Jer 2:24). The Lord gave the Suffering Servant a "tongue of the learned," that is, the gift of inspirational and instructive speech and an ear that listens like those being taught (Isa 50:4). Isaiah says that the children of the desolate woman or widow will be taught by the Lord Himself (Isa 54:13). The word is also used once to denote Isaiah's disciples (Isa 8:16). It is derived from the verb *lâmad* (3925).

3929. לֶמֶךְ, **Lemek,** *leh´-mek*; from an unused root of uncertain meaning; *Lemek*, the name of two antediluvian patriarchs:—Lamech.

3930. לֹעַ, **lôaʻ,** *lo´ah*; from 3886; the *gullet*:—throat.

3931. לָעַב, **lâʻab,** *law-ab´*; a primitive root; to *deride*:—mock.

3932. לָעַג, **lâʻag,** *law-ag´*; a primitive root; to *deride*; by implication (as if imitating a foreigner) to *speak unintelligibly*:—have in derision, laugh (to scorn), mock (on), stammering.

3933. לַעַג, **laʻag,** *lah´-ag*; from 3932; *derision, scoffing*:—derision, scorn (-ing).

3934. לָעֵג, **lâʻêg,** *law-ayg´*; from 3932; a *buffoon*; also a *foreigner*:—mocker, stammering.

3935. לַעְדָּה, **Laʻdâh,** *lah-daw´*; from an unused root of uncertain meaning; *Ladah*, an Israelite:—Laadah.

3936. לַעְדָּן, **Laʻdân,** *lah-dawn´*; from the same as 3935; *Ladan*, the name of two Israelites:—Laadan.

3937. לָעַז, **lâʻaz,** *law-az´*; a primitive root; to *speak in a foreign tongue*:—strange language.

A verb meaning to speak in an incomprehensible foreign language. The term is used in a participial form to describe the Egyptians among whom the Hebrews lived for 430 years, a people who spoke a much different language (Ps 114:1). See the verb *lâʻag* (3932) that appears to semantically overlap with this word.

3938. לָעַט, **lâʻaṭ,** *law-at´*; a primitive root; to *swallow* greedily; (causative) to *feed*:—feed.

3939. לַעֲנָה, **laʻănâh,** *lah-an-aw´*; from an unused root supposed to mean to *curse; wormwood* (regarded as *poisonous*, and therefore *accursed*):—hemlock, wormwood.

3940. לַפִּיד, **lappîyd,** *lap-peed´*; or לַפִּד, **lappid,** *lap-peed´*; from an unused root probably meaning to *shine*; a *flambeau, lamp* or *flame*:—(fire-) brand, (burning) lamp, lightning, torch.

3941. לַפִּידוֹת, **Lappîydôwth,** *lap-pee-dōth´*; feminine plural of 3940; *Lappidoth*, the husband of Deborah:—Lappidoth.

3942. לִפְנָי, **liphnây,** *lif-naw´ee*; from the prefix preposition (*to* or *for*) and 6440; *anterior*:—before.

3943. לָפַת, **lâphath,** *law-fath´*; a primitive root; (properly) to *bend*, i.e. (by implication) to *clasp*; also (reflexive) to *turn* around or aside:—take hold, turn aside (self).

3944. לָצוֹן, **lâtsôwn,** *law-tsone´*; from 3887; *derision*:—scornful (-ning).

3945. לָצַץ, **lâtsats,** *law-tsats´*; a primitive root; to *deride*:—scorn.

3946. לַקּוּם, **Laqûwm,** *lak-koom´*; from an unused root thought to mean to *stop* up by a barricade; perhaps *fortification; Lakkum*, a place in Palestine:—Lakum.

3947. לָקַח, **lâqach,** *law-kakh´*; a primitive root; to *take* (in the widest variety of applications):—accept, bring, buy, carry away, drawn, fetch, get, infold, × many, mingle, place, receive (-ing), reserve, seize, send for, take (away, -ing, up), use, win.

3948. לֶקַח, **leqach,** *leh´-kakh*; from 3947; properly something *received*, i.e. (mentally) *instruction* (whether on the part of the teacher or hearer); also (in an active and sinister sense) *inveiglement*:—doctrine, learning, fair speech.

A masculine noun meaning something received, instruction. Having this basal sense, the word's usage can be divided further into three categories, each with its own distinctive variation of meaning. First, the word can signify the learning, insight, or understanding that a person receives, perceives, or learns through an instructor or some other means (Pr 1:5; 9:9; Isa 29:24). The second variation is similar to the first, yet only slightly different in that it arises from the perspective of the one dispensing the knowledge (i.e. a teacher or instructor), rather than that of the learner. It describes that which is being communicated to others, therefore giving the sense of teaching, instruction, or discourse (Dt 32:2; Pr 4:2). Finally, the term seems to have the force of persuasive speech, whether for a positive or a deceitful intent (Pr 7:21; 16:21). This noun derives from the verb *lâqach* (3947).

3949. לִקְחִי, **Liqchîy,** *lik-khee´*; from 3947; *learned; Likchi*, an Israelite:—Likhi.

3950. לָקַט, **lâqaṭ,** *law-kat´*; a primitive root; (properly) to *pick* up, i.e. (general) to *gather*; (specifically) to *glean*:—gather (up), glean.

A verb meaning to pick up, to gather. This word occurs with various objects such as manna, lilies, firewood, and people (Ex 16:4, 5; Jgs 11:3; SS 6:2; Jer 7:18); however, by far it is used most often with food, including once with grapes (Le 19:10; Isa 17:5). Even animals are able to gather the food God graciously provides (Ps 104:28). About half of the occurrences of this term relate to the provision of the Mosaic Law to take care of the needy by allowing them to glean the fields, a provision featured prominently in the story of Ruth (Le 19:9, 10; 23:22; Ru 2:2, 3, 7, 8, 15–19, 23). Isaiah used this term in both a picture of judgment and of restoration for the nation of Israel (Isa 17:5; 27:12).

3951. לֶקֶט, **leqeṭ,** *leh´-ket*; from 3950; the *gleaning*:—gleaning.

3952. לָקַק, **lâqaq,** *law-kak´*; a primitive root; to *lick* or *lap*:—lap, lick.

3953. לָקַשׁ, **lâqash,** *law-kash´*; a primitive root; to *gather* the *after* crop:—gather.

A verb of uncertain meaning, translated as to despoil, to take everything, to glean. Its only occurrence is in Job 24:6. It is most likely the denominative verb of the noun *leqesh* (3954), meaning spring crop or aftergrowth.

3954. לֶקֶשׁ, **leqesh,** *leh´-kesh*; from 3953; the *after crop*:—latter growth.

3955. לְשַׁד, **lâshâd,** *lawsh-awd´*; from an unused root of uncertain meaning; apparently *juice*, i.e. (figurative) *vigour*; also a sweet or fat *cake*:—fresh, moisture.

3956. לָשׁוֹן, **lâshôwn,** *law-shone´*; or לָשֹׁן, **lâshôn,** *law-shone´*; also (in plural) feminine לְשֹׁנָה, **lᵉshônâh,** *lesh-o-naw´*; from 3960; the *tongue* (of man or animals), used literal (as the instrument of licking, eating, or speech), and figurative (speech, an ingot, a fork of flame, a cove of water):— + babbler, bay, + evil speaker, language, talker, tongue, wedge.

3957. לִשְׁכָּה, **lishkâh,** *lish-kaw´*; from an unused root of uncertain meaning; a *room* in a building (whether for storage, eating, or lodging):—chamber, parlour. Compare 5393.

3958. לֶשֶׁם, **leshem,** *leh´-shem*; from an unused root of uncertain meaning; a *gem*, perhaps the *jacinth*:—ligure.

3959. לֶשֶׁם, **Leshem,** *leh´-shem*; the same as 3958; *Leshem*, a place in Palestine:—Leshem.

3960. לָשַׁן, **lâshan,** *law-shan´*; a primitive root; (properly) to *lick*; but used only as a denominative from 3956; to *wag the tongue*, i.e. to *calumniate*:—accuse, slander.

3961. לִשָּׁן, **lishshân,** *lish-shawn´*; (Chaldee); corresponding to 3956; *speech*, i.e. a *nation*:—language.

3962. לֶשַׁע, **Lesha',** *leh´-shah*; from an unused root thought to mean to *break* through; a boiling *spring; Lesha*, a place probably East of the Jordan:—Lasha.

3963. לֶתֶךְ, **lethek,** *leh´-thek*; from an unused root of uncertain meaning; a *measure* for things dry:—half homer.

3964. מָא, **mâ',** *maw*; (Chaldee); corresponding to 4100; (as indefinite) *that*:— + what.

3965. מַאֲבוּס, **ma'ăbûws,** *mah-ab-ooce´*; from 75; a *granary*:—storehouse.

3966. מְאֹד, **me'ôd,** *meh-ode´*; from the same as 181; (properly) *vehemence*, i.e. (with or without preposition) *vehemently*; (by implication) *wholly, speedily*, etc. (often with other words as an intensive or superlative; especially when repeated):—diligently, especially, exceeding (-ly), far, fast, good, great (-ly), × louder and louder, might (-ily, -y), (so) much, quickly, (so) sore, utterly, very (+ much, sore), well.

3967. מֵאָה, **mê'âh,** *may-aw´*; or מֵאיָה, **mê'yâh,** *may-yaw´*; probably a primitive numeral; a *hundred*; also as a multiplicative and a fraction:—hundred ([-fold], -th), + sixscore.

3968. מֵאָה, **Mê'âh,** *may-aw´*; the same as 3967; *Meäh*, a tower in Jerusalem:—Meah.

3969. מְאָה, **me'âh,** *meh-aw´*; (Chaldee); corresponding to 3967:—hundred.

3970. מַאֲוַיִּים, **ma'ăvayyîym,** *mah-av-ah´ee*; from 183; a *desire*:—desire.

3971. מאוּם, **m'ûwm,** *moom*; usually מוּם, **mûwm,** *moom*; as if passive participle from an unused root probably meaning to *stain*; a *blemish* (physical or moral):—blemish, blot, spot.

A masculine noun meaning blemish, defect. This word usually describes a physical characteristic that is deemed to be bad. A man with any sort of blemish could not be a priest (Le 21:17, 18, 21, 23) nor could an animal which had a blemish be sacrificed (Le 22:20, 21; Nu 19:2; Dt 17:1). The word is also used to describe an injury caused by another (Le 24:19, 20). On the other hand, the absence of any blemish was a sign of beauty (2Sa 14:25; SS 4:7) or potential (Da 1:4). In a figurative sense, the word is used to describe the effect of sin (Dt 32:5; Job 11:15; 31:7) or insult (Pr 9:7).

3972. מְאוּמָה, **me'ûwmâh,** *meh-oo´-maw*; apparently a form of 3971; (properly) a *speck* or *point*, i.e. (by implication) *something*; (with negative) *nothing*:—fault, + no (-ught), ought, somewhat, any ([no-]) thing.

3973. מָאוֹס, **mâ'ôws,** *maw-oce´*; from 3988; *refuse*:—refuse.

3974. מָאוֹר, **mâ'ôwr,** *maw-ore´*; or מָאֹר, **mâ'ôr,** *maw-ore´*; also (in plural) feminine מְאוֹרָה, **me'ôwrâh,** *meh-o-raw´*; or מְאֹרָה, **me'ôrâh,** *meh-o-raw´*; from 215; (properly) a *luminous* body or *luminary*, i.e. (abstract) *light* (as an element); (figurative) *brightness*, i.e. *cheerfulness*; (specifically) a *chandelier*:—bright, light.

A masculine singular noun meaning luminary, a light. This noun is employed in connection with the lamp in the tabernacle (Ex 35:14; Le 24:2; Nu 4:16). It is also used to describe the heavenly lights in the creation story of Ge 1:15, 16.

3975. מְאוּרָה, **me'ûwrâh,** *meh-oo-raw´*; feminine passive participle of 215; something *lighted*, i.e. an *aperture*; (by implication) a *crevice* or *hole* of a serpent):—den.

3976. מֹאזְנַיִם, **mô'zenayim,** *mo-ze-nah´-yim*; from 239; (only in the dual) a pair of *scales*:—balances.

3977. מֹאזְנֵא, **mô'zenê',** *mo-zeh-nay´*; (Chaldee); corresponding to 3976:—balances.

3978. מַאֲכָל, **ma'ăkâl,** *mah-ak-awl´*; from 398; an *eatable* (including provender, flesh and fruit):—food, fruit, ([bake-]) meat (-s), victual.

3979. מַאֲכֶלֶת, **ma'ăkeleth,** *mah-ak-eh´-leth*; from 398; something to *eat* with, i.e. a *knife*:—knife.

3980. מַאֲכֹלֶת, **ma'ăkôleth,** *mah-ak-o´-leth*; from 398; something *eaten* (by fire), i.e. *fuel*:—fuel.

3981. מַאֲמָץ, **ma'ămâts,** *mah-am-awts´*; from 553; *strength*, i.e. (plural) *resources*:—force.

3982. מַאֲמַר, **ma'ămar,** *mah-am-ar´*; from 559; something (authoritatively) *said*, i.e. an *edict*:—commandment, decree.

A masculine noun meaning word or command. In all three of its instances in the OT, this word is best translated, command (i.e. that which is spoken with authority). It referred to the command of King Ahasuerus that Queen Vashti ignored (Est 1:15). It described Mordecai's instructions to Esther to keep quiet about her nationality (Est 2:20). Finally, it referred to Esther's edict about the establishment of the days of Purim (Est 9:32). This word comes from the common verb *'âmar* (559), meaning to say, which can be translated to command, depending on the context (2Ch 31:11; Est 1:10).

3983. מֵאמַר, **mê'mar,** *may-mar´*; (Chaldee); corresponding to 3982:—appointment, word.

An Aramaic masculine noun meaning word, command. This word is used only twice in the OT and is equivalent to the Hebrew word *ma'ămar* (3982). It describes the words the priests spoke to request supplies for rebuilding the temple (Ezr 6:9); and it also refers to the words of the holy ones that issued the edict in Nebuchadnezzar's dream (Da 4:17[14]). This word comes from the common Aramaic verb, *'ămar* (560), meaning to say.

3984. מָאן, **mâ'n,** *mawn*; (Chaldee); probably from a root corresponding to 579 in the sense of an *inclosure* by sides; a *utensil*:—vessel.

3985. מָאֵן, **mâ'an,** *maw-an´*; a primitive root; to *refuse*:—refuse, × utterly.

A verb meaning to refuse. The basic idea of this word is a refusal or rejection of an offer. It is used to describe the refusal to obey God (Ex 16:28; Ne 9:17; Isa 1:20; Jer 9:6[5]); His messengers, (1Sa 8:19); or other men (Est 1:12). Jacob refused comfort when he thought Joseph had died (Ge 37:35); Joseph refused Potiphar's wife's offer to sin (Ge 39:8); Pharaoh refused to let Israel go (Ex 4:23; 7:14); Balaam refused Balak's offer to curse Israel (Nu 22:13, 14); both Saul and Ammon refused to eat food offered to them (1Sa 28:23; 2Sa 13:9).

3986. מָאֵן, **mâ'ên,** *maw-ane´*; from 3985; *unwilling*:—refuse.

An adjective meaning refusing, disobeying. This word is found in the context of disobedience to a command. A prime example was that of the Israelites in bondage. God said that if Pharaoh refused to let His people go, He would bring various plagues on Egypt (Ex 8:2[7:27]; 9:2). King Zedekiah was warned that he would be captured by Babylon if he refused to surrender to the Lord (Jer 38:21).

3987. מֵאֵן, **mê'ên,** *may-ane´*; from 3985; *refractory*:—refuse.

An adjective meaning refusing. This word is used only once in the OT and comes from the verb *mâ'ên* (3985), meaning to refuse. In Jer 13:10, it described the people of Judah as those refusing to listen to God's words.

3988. מָאַס, **mâ'as,** *maw-as´*; a primitive root; to *spurn*; also (intransitive) to *disappear*:—abhor, cast away (off), contemn, despise, disdain, (become) loathe (-some), melt away, refuse, reject, reprobate, × utterly, vile person.

A verb meaning to reject, to despise, to abhor, to refuse. The primary meaning of this word is to reject or treat as loathsome. It designates people's actions in refusing to heed God or accept His authority (1Sa 10:19; Jer 8:9); esteeming God's commands lightly (Le 26:15; Isa 30:12); and despising one's spiritual condition in an act of repentance (Job 42:6). Scripture also speaks of the Lord rejecting His people (Hos 4:6) and their worship (Am 5:21) because of their rejection of Him. A secondary and more rare meaning of the word is to run or flow. This use appears in Ps 58:7[8] as David prayed for the wicked to melt away like a flowing river.

3989. מַאֲפֶה, ma'ăpheh, *mah-af-eh´*; from 644; something *baked*, i.e. a *batch*:—baken.

3990. מַאֲפֵל, ma'ăphêl, *mah-af-ale´*; from the same as 651; something *opaque*:—darkness.

3991. מַאְפֵלְיָה, ma'pêlyâh, *mah-pel-yaw´*; prolonged feminine of 3990; *opaqueness*:—darkness.

3992. מָאַר, mâ'ar, *maw-ar´*; a primitive root; to *be bitter* or (causative) to *embitter*, i.e. *be painful*:—fretting, picking.

3993. מַאֲרָב, ma'ărâb, *mah-ar-awb´*; from 693; an *ambuscade*:—lie in ambush, ambushment, lurking place, lying in wait.

3994. מְאֵרָה, m^e'êrâh, *meh-ay-raw´*; from 779; an *execration*:—curse.

3995. מִבְדָּלָה, mibdâlâh, *mib-daw-law´*; from 914; a *separation*, i.e. (concrete) a *separate* place:—separate.

3996. מָבוֹא, mâbôw', *maw-bo´*; from 935; an *entrance* (the place or the act); specifically (with or without 8121) *sunset* or the *west*; also (adverb with preposition) *toward*:—by which came, as cometh, in coming, as men enter into, entering, entrance into, entry, where goeth, going down, + westward. Compare 4126.

3997. מְבוֹאָה, m^ebôw'âh, *meb-o-aw´*; feminine of 3996; a *haven*:—entry.

3998. מְבוּכָה, m^ebûwkâh, *meb-oo-kaw´*; from 943; *perplexity*:—perplexity.

3999. מַבּוּל, mabbûwl, *mab-bool´*; from 2986 in the sense of *flowing*; a *deluge*:—flood.

4000. מְבוּנִים, m^ebûwnîym, *meh-boo-neem´*; from 995; *instructing*:—taught.

4001. מְבוּסָה, m^ebûwsâh, *meb-oo-saw´*; from 947; a *trampling*:—treading (trodden) down (under foot).

4002. מַבּוּעַ, mabbûwa', *mab-boo´-ah*; from 5042; a *fountain*:—fountain, spring.

4003. מְבוּקָה, m^ebûwqâh, *meb-oo-kah´*; from the same as 950; *emptiness*:—void.

4004. מִבְחוֹר, mibchôwr, *mib-khore´*; from 977; *select*, i.e. well fortified:—choice.

4005. מִבְחָר, mibchâr, *mib-khawr´*; from 977; *select*, i.e. best:—choice (-st), chosen.

4006. מִבְחָר, Mibchâr, *mib-khawr´*; the same as 4005; *Mibchar*, an Israelite:—Mibhar.

4007. מַבָּט, mabbâṭ, *mab-bawt´*; or מֶבָּט, **mebbâṭ,** *meb-bawt´*; from 5027; something *expected*, i.e. (abstract) *expectation*:—expectation.

4008. מִבְטָא, mibṭâ', *mib-taw´*; from 981; a rash *utterance* (hasty vow):—(that which ...) uttered (out of).

4009. מִבְטָח, mibṭâch, *mib-tawkh´*; from 982; (properly) a *refuge*, i.e. (objective) *security*, or (subjective) *assurance*:—confidence, hope, sure, trust.

4010. מַבְלִיגִית, mablîygîyth, *mab-leeg-eeth´*; from 1082; *desistance* (or rather *desolation*):—comfort self.

4011. מִבְנֶה, mibneh, *mib-neh´*; from 1129; a *building*:—frame.

4012. מְבֻנַּי, M^ebunnay, *meb-oon-nah´ee*; from 1129; *built* up; *Mebunnai*, an Israelite:—Mebunnai.

4013. מִבְצָר, mibtsâr, *mib-tsawr´*; also (in plural) feminine (Da 11:15) מִבְצָרָה, **mibtsârâh,** *mib-tsaw-raw´*; from 1219; a *fortification, castle*, or *fortified* city; (figurative) a *defender*:—(de-, most) fenced, fortress, (most) strong (hold).

4014. מִבְצָר, Mibtsâr, *mib-tsawr´*; the same as 4013; *Mibtsar*, an Idumæan:—Mibzar.

4015. מִבְרָח, mibrâch, *mib-rawkh´*; from 1272; a *refugee*:—fugitive.

4016. מְבוּשִׁים, m^ebûwshîym, *meh-boo-sheem´*; from 954; (plural) the (male) *pudenda*:—secrets.

4017. מִבְשָׂם, Mibśâm, *mib-sawm´*; from the same as 1314; *fragrant; Mibsam*, the name of an Ishmaelite and of an Israelite:—Mibsam.

4018. מְבַשְּׁלוֹת, m^ebashsh^elôwth, *meb-ash-shel-oth´*; from 1310; a cooking *hearth*:—boiling-place.

4019. מַגְבִּישׁ, Magbîysh, *mag-beesh´*; from the same as 1378; *stiffening; Magbish*, an Israelite, or a place in Palestine:—Magbish.

4020. מִגְבָּלוֹת, migbâlôwth, *mig-bawl-oth´*; from 1379; a *border*:—end.

4021. מִגְבָּעָה, migbâ'âh, *mig-baw-aw´*; from the same as 1389; a *cap* (as *hemispherical*):—bonnet.

4022. מֶגֶד, meged, *meh´-ghed*; from an unused root (properly) meaning to *be eminent*; properly a *distinguished* thing; hence something *valuable*, as a product or fruit:—pleasant, precious fruit (thing).

4023. מְגִדּוֹן, M^egiddôwn, *meg-id-dōne´*; (Zec 12:11), or מְגִדּוֹ, **Megiddôw,** *meg-id-do´*; from 1413; *rendezvous; Megiddon* or *Megiddo*, a place in Palestine:—Megiddo, Megiddon.

4024. מִגְדּוֹל, Migdôwl, *mig-dole´*; or מִגְדֹּל, **Migdôl,** *mig-dole´*; probably of Egyptian origin; *Migdol*, a place in Egypt:—Migdol, tower.

4025. מַגְדִּיאֵל, Magdîy'êl, *mag-dee-ale´*; from 4022 and 410; *preciousness of God; Magdiël*, an Idumæan:—Magdiel.

4026. מִגְדָּל, migdâl, *mig-dawl´*; also (in plural) feminine מִגְדָּלָה, **migdâlâh,** *mig-daw-law´*; from 1431; a *tower* (from its size or height); (by analogy) a *rostrum*; (figurative) a (pyramidal) *bed* of flowers:—castle, flower, tower. Compare the names following.

4027. מִגְדַּל־אֵל, Migdal-'Êl, *mig-dal-ale´*; from 4026 and 410; *tower of God; Migdal-El*, a place in Palestine:—Migdal-el.

4028. מִגְדַּל־גָּד, Migdal-Gâd, *mig-dal-gawd´*; from 4026 and 1408; *tower of Fortune; Migdal-Gad*, a place in Palestine:—Migdal-gad.

4029. מִגְדַּל־עֵדֶר, Migdal-'Êder, *mig-dal´-ay´-der*; from 4026 and 5739; *tower of a flock; Migdal-Eder*, a place in Palestine:—Migdal-eder, tower of the flock.

4030. מִגְדָּנָה, migdânâh, *mig-daw-naw´*; from the same as 4022; *preciousness*, i.e. a *gem*:—precious thing, present.

4031. מָגוֹג, Mâgôwg, *maw-gogue´*; from 1463; *Magog*, a son of Japheth; also a barbarous northern region:—Magog.

4032. מָגוֹר, mâgôwr, *maw-gore´*; or (La 2:22) מָגוּר, **mâgûwr,** *maw-goor´*; from 1481 in the sense of *fearing*; a *fright* (objective or subjective):—fear, terror. Compare 4036.

A masculine noun meaning fear, terror. The fundamental concept underlying this word is a sense of impending doom. It is used to signify the fear that surrounds one whose life is being plotted against (Ps 31:13[14]); the fear that causes a soldier to retreat in the face of an invincible foe (Isa 31:9; Jer 6:25); and the horrors that befall those facing God's judgment (La 2:22). Of interest is the prophecy of Jeremiah concerning Pashur after he had Jeremiah placed in the stocks for prophesying against the idolatry of Jerusalem (cf. Jer 20:1–6). The Lord would no longer call Pashur by his name. He gave him a new one, Magormissabib or Magor-Missabib ("fear on every side"), because the Lord would make him, as it were, afraid of his own shadow (Jer 20:4).

4033. מָגוֹר**, mâgôwr,** *maw-gor´*; or מָגֻר**, mâgur,** *maw-goor´*; from 1481 in the sense of *lodging*; a temporary *abode*; (by extension) a permanent *residence*:—dwelling, pilgrimage, where sojourn, be a stranger. Compare 4032.

A masculine noun meaning sojourning or a dwelling place. This word comes from the verb, *gûr* (1481), meaning to sojourn. Most often, this word is used to describe Israel as a sojourning people, who will inherit the land of Canaan, where they sojourned (Ge 17:8; 37:1; Ex 6:4). The psalmist described the preciousness of God's statutes in his sojourning (Ps 119:54). The wicked are described as having evil in their dwelling places (Ps 55:15[16]), which will result with God removing them from their dwelling places (Eze 20:38). As a result, the wicked will have no offspring in their dwelling places (Job 18:19).

4034. מְגוֹרָה**, m^egôwrâh,** *meg-o-raw´*; feminine of 4032; *affright*:—fear.

A feminine noun meaning fear, terror. The feminine form of *mâgôwr* (4032), this word occurs only once in the Bible. Pr 10:24 contrasts the fate of the wicked with that of the righteous. The ones serving the Lord will get their hearts' desires, but the wicked will get their worst nightmares—judgment.

4035. מְגוּרָה**, m^egûwrâh,** *meg-oo-raw´*; feminine of 4032 or of 4033; a *fright*; also a *granary*:—barn, fear.

A feminine noun meaning fear, terror. The use of this word for fear tends to imply the haunting apprehensions that one holds deep within. The Lord's judgments bring people's worst fears to reality (Isa 66:4), while His love frees us from them (Ps 34:4[5]; cf. 1Jn 4:18). Haggai, however, uses this word to signify a storage place or a barn (Hag 2:19). The link between the divergent ideas comes from the root word *gûr* (1481), which carries the connotation of dwelling as well as fear.

4036. מָגוֹר מִסָּבִיב**, Mâgôwr mis-Sâbîyb,** *maw-gore´ mis-saw-beeb´*; from 4032 and 5439 with the preposition inserted; *affright from around; Magor-mis-Sabib*, a symbolical name of Pashur:—Magor-missabib.

4037. מַגְזֵרָה**, magzêrâh,** *mag-zay-raw´*; from 1504; a *cutting* implement, i.e. a *blade*:—axe.

4038. מַגָּל**, maggâl,** *mag-gawl´*; from an unused root meaning to *reap*; a *sickle*:—sickle.

4039. מְגִלָּה**, m^egillâh,** *meg-il-law´*; from 1556; a *roll*:—roll, volume.

A feminine noun meaning roll, volume, writing, scroll. This Hebrew word is approximately equivalent to the English word "book." In ancient Israel, instead of pages bound into a cover, "books" were written on scrolls of leather or other durable material and rolled together. All but one appearance of this word (Ps 40:7[8]) occurs in Jer 36. The importance of this word is found in its reference to the sacred volume recording God's own words (cf. Jer 36:2).

4040. מְגִלָּה**, m^egillâh,** *meg-il-law´*; (Chaldee); corresponding to 4039:—roll.

An Aramaic noun meaning roll, scroll. The term is used to describe the object upon which was written an official record of King Cyrus' decree concerning the rebuilding of the Temple at Jerusalem (Ezr 6:2).

4041. מְגַמָּה**, m^egammâh,** *meg-am-maw´*; from the same as 1571; (properly) *accumulation*, i.e. *impulse* or *direction*:—sup up.

4042. מָגַן**, mâgan,** *maw-gan´*; a denominative from 4043; (properly) to *shield; encompass* with; (figurative) to *rescue*, to *hand* safely *over* (i.e. *surrender*):—deliver.

4043. מָגֵן**, mâgên,** *maw-gane´*; also (in plural) feminine מְגִנָּה**, m^eginnâh,** *meg-in-naw´*; from 1598; a *shield* (i.e. the small one or *buckler*); (figurative) a *protector*; also the scaly *hide* of the crocodile:— × armed, buckler, defence, ruler, + scale, shield.

4044. מְגִנָּה**, m^eginnâh,** *meg-in-naw´*; from 4042; a *covering* (in a bad sense), i.e. *blindness* or obduracy:—sorrow. See also 4043.

4045. מִגְעֶרֶת**, mig'ereth,** *mig-eh´-reth*; from 1605; *reproof* (i.e. curse):—rebuke.

4046. מַגֵּפָה**, maggêphâh,** *mag-gay-faw´*; from 5062; a *pestilence*; (by analogy) *defeat*:—(× be) plague (-d), slaughter, stroke.

4047. מַגְפִּיעָשׁ**, Magpîy'âsh,** *mag-pee-awsh´*; apparently from 1479 or 5062 and 6211; *exterminator of* (the) *moth; Magpiash*, an Israelite:—Magpiash.

4048. מָגַר**, mâgar,** *maw-gar´*; a primitive root; to *yield up*; (intensive) to *precipitate*:—cast down, terror.

A verb meaning to cast before, to deliver over, to yield up. In a participial form, the term is used once to describe the people and princes of Israel who were being thrown to the sword because they stubbornly refused to heed God's discipline (Eze 21:12[17]). When used in its intensive form, the verb conveys the idea to cast down or to overthrow, as witnessed in Ps 89:44[45]: "You have made his splendor to cease and cast his throne to the ground" (NASB). See the verb *nâgar* (5064).

4049. מְגַר**, m^egar,** *meg-ar´*; (Chaldee); corresponding to 4048; to *overthrow*:—destroy.

An Aramaic verb meaning to overthrow, to cast down. In an edict decreed by King Darius, this verb describes what Darius hoped the God of heaven would do to any king or people who altered his edict or tried to destroy the Temple in Jerusalem (Ezr 6:12). The term is closely related to the Hebrew verb *mâgar* (4048).

4050. מְגֵרָה**, m^egêrâh,** *meg-ay-raw´*; from 1641; a *saw*:—axe, saw.

4051. מִגְרוֹן**, Migrôwn,** *mig-rone´*; from 4048; *preci-pice; Migron*, a place in Palestine:—Migron.

4052. מִגְרָעָה**, migrâ'âh,** *mig-raw-aw´*; from 1639; a *ledge* or offset:—narrowed rest.

4053. מִגְרָף**, migrâph,** *mig-rawf´*; from 1640; something *thrown off* (by the spade), i.e. a *clod*:—clod.

4054. מִגְרָשׁ**, migrâsh,** *mig-rawsh´*; also (in plural) feminine (Eze 27:28) מִגְרָשָׁה**, migrâshâh,** *mig-raw-shaw´*; from 1644; a *suburb* (i.e. open country whither flocks are *driven* for pasture); hence the *area* around a building, or the *margin* of the sea:—cast out, suburb.

4055. מַד**, mad,** *mad*; or מֵד**, mêd,** *made*; from 4058; (properly) *extent*, i.e. *height*; also a *measure*; (by implication) a *vesture* (as measured); also a *carpet*:—armour, clothes, garment, judgment, measure, raiment, stature.

4056. מַדְבַּח**, madbach,** *mad-bakh´*; (Chaldee); from 1684; a sacrificial *altar*:—altar.

4057. מִדְבָּר**, midbâr,** *mid-bawr´*; from 1696 in the sense of *driving*; a *pasture* (i.e. open field, whither cattle are driven); (by implication) a *desert*; also *speech* (including its organs):—desert, south, speech, wilderness.

4058. מָדַד**, mâdad,** *maw-dad´*; a primitive root; (properly) to *stretch*; (by implication) to *measure* (as if by *stretching* a line); (figurative) to *be extended*:—measure, mete, stretch self.

4059. מִדַּד**, middad,** *mid-dad´*; from 5074; *flight*:—be gone.

4060. מִדָּה**, middâh,** *mid-daw´*; feminine of 4055; (properly) *extension*, i.e. height or breadth; also a *measure* (including its standard); hence a *portion* (as measured) or a *vestment*; specifically *tribute* (as measured):—garment, measure (-ing, meteyard, piece, size, (great) stature, tribute, wide.

4061. מִדָּה**, middâh,** *mid-daw´*; (Chaldee); or מִנְדָּה**, mindâh,** *min-daw´*; (Chaldee); corresponding to 4060; *tribute* in money:—toll, tribute.

4062. מַדְהֵבָה**, madhêbâh,** *mad-hay-baw´*; perhaps from the equivalent of 1722; *gold-making*, i.e. *exactress*:—golden city.

4063. **מָדוּ, mâdûw,** *maw´-doo*; from an unused root meaning to *stretch*; (properly) *extent*, i.e. *measure*; (by implication) a *dress* (as measured):—garment.

4064. **מַדְוֶה, madveh,** *mad-veh´*; from 1738; *sickness*:—disease.

4065. **מַדּוּחַ, maddûwach,** *mad-doo´-akh*; from 5080; *seduction*:—cause of banishment.

4066. **מָדוֹן, mâdôwn,** *maw-dohn´*; from 1777; a *contest* or quarrel:—brawling, contention (-ous), discord, strife. Compare 4079, 4090.

4067. **מָדוֹן, mâdôwn,** *maw-dohn´*; from the same as 4063; *extensiveness*, i.e. height:—stature.

4068. **מָדוֹן, Mâdôwn,** *maw-dohn´*; the same as 4067; *Madon*, a place in Palestine:—Madon.

4069. **מַדּוּעַ, maddûwaʻ,** *mad-doo´-ah*; or **מַדֻּעַ, madduaʻ,** *mad-doo´-ah*; from 4100 and the passive participle of 3045; *what* (is) *known*; i.e. (by implication) (adverb) *why*:—how, wherefore, why.

4070. **מְדוֹר, mᵉdôwr,** *med-ore´*; (Chaldee); or **מְדֹר, mᵉdôr,** *med-ore´*; (Chaldee); or **מְדָר, mᵉdâr,** *med-awr´*; (Chaldee); from 1753; a *dwelling*:—dwelling.

4071. **מְדוּרָה, mᵉdûwrâh,** *med-oo-raw´*; or **מְדֻרָה, medurâh,** *med-oo-raw´*; from 1752 in the sense of *accumulation*; a *pile* of fuel:—pile (for fire).

4072. **מִדְחֶה, midcheh,** *mid-kheh´*; from 1760; *overthrow*:—ruin.

4073. **מְדַחְפָה, madchêphâh,** *mad-khay-faw´*; from 1765; a *push*, i.e. ruin:—overthrow.

4074. **מָדַי, Mâday,** *maw-dah´ee*; of foreign derivation; *Madai*, a country of central Asia:—Madai, Medes, Media.

4075. **מָדִי, Mâdîy,** *maw-dee´*; patrial from 4074; a *Madian* or native of Madai:—Mede.

4076. **מָדַי, Mâday,** *maw-dah´ee*; (Chaldee); corresponding to 4074:—Mede (-s).

4077. **מָדָיָא, Mâdâyʼâ,** *maw-daw´-aw*; (Chaldee); corresponding to 4075:—Median.

4078. **מַדַּי, madday,** *mad-dah´ee*; from 4100 and 1767; *what* (is) *enough*, i.e. *sufficiently*:—sufficiently.

4079. **מִדְיָנִים, midyânîym,** *mid-yaw-neem´*; a variation for 4066:—brawling, contention (-ous).

4080. **מִדְיָן, Midyân,** *mid-yawn´*; the same as 4079; *Midjan*, a son of Abraham; also his country and (collective) his descendants:—Midian, Midianite.

4081. **מִדִּין, Middîyn,** *mid-deen´*; a variation for 4080:—Middin.

4082. **מְדִינָה, mᵉdîynâh,** *med-ee-naw´*; from 1777; (properly) a *judgeship*, i.e. *jurisdiction*; (by implication) a *district* (as ruled by a judge); (generally) a *region*:—(× every) province.

4083. **מְדִינָה, mᵉdîynâh,** *med-ee-naw´*; (Chaldee); corresponding to 4082:—province.

4084. **מִדְיָנִי, Midyânîy,** *mid-yaw-nee´*; patronymic or patrial from 4080; a *Midjanite* or descendant (native) of Midjan:—Midianite. Compare 4092.

4085. **מְדֹכָה, mᵉdôkâh,** *med-o-kaw´*; from 1743; a *mortar*:—mortar.

4086. **מַדְמֵן, Madmên,** *mad-mane´*; from the same as 1828; *dunghill; Madmen*, a place in Palestine:—Madmen.

4087. **מַדְמֵנָה, madmênâh,** *mad-may-naw´*; feminine from the same as 1828; a *dunghill*:—dunghill.

4088. **מַדְמֵנָה, Madmênâh,** *mad-may-naw´*; the same as 4087; *Madmenah*, a place in Palestine:—Madmenah.

4089. **מַדְמַנָּה, Madmannâh,** *mad-man-naw´*; a variation for 4087; *Madmannah*, a place in Palestine:—Madmannah.

4090. **מְדָנִים, mᵉdânîym,** *med-aw-neem´*; a form of 4066:—discord, strife.

4091. **מְדָן, Mᵉdân,** *med-awn´*; the same as 4090; *Medan*, a son of Abraham:—Medan.

4092. **מְדָנִי, Mᵉdânîy,** *med-aw-nee´*; a variation of 4084:—Midianite.

4093. **מַדָּע, maddâʻ,** *mad-daw´*; or **מַדַּע, maddaʻ,** *mad-dah´*; from 3045; *intelligence* or *consciousness*:—knowledge, science, thought.

4094. **מַדְקֵרָה, madqêrâh,** *mad-kay-raw´*; from 1856; a *wound*:—piercing.

4095. **מַדְרֵגָה, madrêgâh,** *mad-ray-gaw´*; from an unused root meaning to *step*; (properly) a *step*; (by implication) a *steep* or inaccessible place:—stair, steep place.

4096. **מִדְרָךְ, midrâk,** *mid-rawk´*; from 1869; a *treading*, i.e. a place for stepping on:—[foot-] breadth.

4097. **מִדְרָשׁ, midrâsh,** *mid-rawsh´*; from 1875; (properly) an *investigation*, i.e. (by implication) a *treatise* or elaborate compilation:—story.

4098. **מְדֻשָׁה, mᵉdushâh,** *meh-doo-shaw´*; from 1758; a *threshing*, i.e. (concrete and figurative) *down-trodden* people:—threshing.

4099. **מְדָתָא, Mᵉdâthâʼ,** *med-aw-thaw´*; of Persian origin; *Medatha*, the father of Haman:—Hammedatha [*including the art.*].

4100. **מָה, mâh,** *maw*; or **מַה, mah,** *mah*; or **מָ־, mâ,** *maw*; or **מַ־, ma,** *mah*; also **מֶה, meh,** *meh*; a primitive particle; (properly) interrogative *what* (including *how why when*); but also exclamation *what!* (including *how!*), or indefinite *what* (including *whatever*, and even relative *that which*); often used with prefixes in various adverb or conjunction senses:—how (long, oft, [-soever]), [no-] thing, what (end, good, purpose, thing), whereby (-fore, -in, -to, -with), (for) why.

4101. **מָה, mâh,** *maw*; (Chaldee); corresponding to 4100:—how great (mighty), that which, what (-soever), why.

4102. **מָהַהּ, mâhah,** *maw-hah´*; apparently a denominative from 4100; (properly) to *question* or hesitate, i.e. (by implication) to *be reluctant*:—delay, linger, stay selves, tarry.

4103. **מְהוּמָה, mᵉhûwmâh,** *meh-hoo-maw´*; from 1949; *confusion* or uproar:—destruction, discomfiture, trouble, tumult, vexation, vexed.

A feminine noun meaning confusion, panic, tumult, disturbance. If the Israelites diligently observed God's covenant stipulations, He would throw the nations occupying Canaan into a great panic and give them over into the Israelites' hands (Dt 7:23). If, however, the Israelites did not obey and thus forsook the Lord their God, this same panic would be sent upon them instead (Dt 28:20). After the Philistines captured the ark of God and brought it to Gath (one of their five main cities), the Lord struck the people of that city with a great panic and severe tumors (1Sa 5:9, 11). Isaiah the prophet warned Jerusalem that a day of tumult, trampling, and confusion was at hand for it (Isa 22:5). The term also functions to describe daily life in certain geographical locations during troubled periods of time: Jerusalem (Eze 22:5); Israel and the surrounding lands (2Ch 15:5); and the mountains of Samaria (Am 3:9). Once the word describes the trouble wealth brings to a household that does not fear the Lord (Pr 15:16). The term derives from the verb *hûm* (1949).

4104. **מְהוּמָן, Mᵉhûwmân,** *meh-hoo-mawn´*; of Persian origin; *Mehuman*, a eunuch of Xerxes:—Mehuman.

4105. מְהֵיטַבְאֵל, **Mᵉhêyṭab'êl,** *meh-hay-tab-ale´*; from 3190 (augmented) and 410; *bettered of God; Mehetabel,* the name of an Edomitish man and woman:—Mehetabeel, Mehetabel.

4106. מָהִיר, **mâhîyr,** *maw-here´*; or מָהִר, **mâhir,** *maw-here´*; from 4116; *quick*; hence *skilful*:—diligent, hasty, ready.

4107. מָהַל, **mâhal,** *maw-hal´*; a primitive root; (properly) to *cut down* or *reduce,* i.e. (by implication) to *adulterate*:—mixed.

4108. מַהְלְכִים, **mahlᵉkîym,** *mah-leh-keem´*; from 1980; a *walking* (plural collective), i.e. *access*:—place to walk.

4109. מַהֲלָךְ, **mahălâk,** *mah-hal-awk´*; from 1980; a *walk,* i.e. a *passage* or a *distance*:—journey, walk.

4110. מַהֲלָל, **mahălâl,** *mah-hal-awl´*; from 1984; *fame*:—praise.

4111. מַהֲלַלְאֵל, **Mahălal'êl,** *mah-hal-al-ale´*; from 4110 and 410; *praise of God; Mahalalel,* the name of an antediluvian patriarch and of an Israelite:—Mahalaleel.

4112. מַהֲלֻמוֹת, **mahălumôwth,** *mah-hal-oo-moth´*; from 1986; a *blow*:—stripe, stroke.

4113. מַהֲמֹר, **mahămôr,** *mah-ha-mor´*; from an unused root of uncertain meaning; perhaps an *abyss*:—deep pit.

4114. מַהְפֵּכָה, **mahpêkâh,** *mah-pay-kaw´*; from 2015; a *destruction*:—when … overthrew, overthrow (-n).

4115. מַהְפֶּכֶת, **mahpeketh,** *mah-peh´-keth*; from 2015; a *wrench,* i.e. the *stocks*:—prison, stocks.

4116. מָהַר, **mâhar,** *maw-har´*; a primitive root; (properly) to *be liquid* or *flow* easily, i.e. (by implication); to *hurry* (in a good or a bad sense); often used (with another verb) adverb *promptly*:—be carried headlong, fearful, (cause to make, in, make) haste (-n, -ily), (be) hasty, (fetch, make ready) × quickly, rash, × shortly, (be so) × soon, make speed, × speedily, × straightway, × suddenly, swift.

4117. מָהַר, **mâhar,** *maw-har´*; a primitive root (perhaps rather the same as 4116 through the idea of *readiness* in assent); to *bargain* (for a wife), i.e. to *wed*:—endow, × surely.

4118. מַהֵר, **mahêr,** *mah-hare´*; from 4116; (properly) *hurrying*; hence (adverb) *in a hurry*:—hasteth, hastily, at once, quickly, soon, speedily, suddenly.

4119. מֹהַר, **môhar,** *mo´-har*; from 4117; a *price* (for a wife):—dowry.

4120. מְהֵרָה, **mᵉhêrâh,** *meh-hay-raw´*; feminine of 4118; (properly) a *hurry*; hence (adverb) *promptly*:—hastily, quickly, shortly, soon, make (with) speed (-ily), swiftly.

4121. מַהֲרַי, **Mahăray,** *mah-har-ah´ee*; from 4116; *hasty; Maharai,* an Israelite:—Maharai.

4122. מַהֵר שָׁלָל חָשׁ בַּז, **Mahêr Shâlâl Châsh Baz,** *mah-hare´ shaw-lawl´ khawsh baz*; from 4118 and 7998 and 2363 and 957; *hasting* (is he [the enemy] to the) *booty, swift* (to the) *prey; Maher-Shalal-Chash-Baz*; the symbolic name of the son of Isaiah:—Maher-shalal-hash-baz.

4123. מַהֲתַלָּה, **mahăthallâh,** *mah-hath-al-law´*; from 2048; a *delusion*:—deceit.

4124. מוֹאָב, **Môw'âb,** *mo-awb*; from a prolonged form of the prepositional prefix *m-* and 1; *from* (her [the mother's]) *father; Moäb,* an incestuous son of Lot; also his territory and descendant:—Moab.

4125. מוֹאָבִי, **Môw'âbîy,** *mo-aw-bee´*; feminine מוֹאָבִיָּה, **Môw'âbîyyâh,** *mo-aw-bee-yaw´*; or מוֹאָבִית, **Môw'âbîyth,** *mo-aw-beeth´*; patronymic from 4124; a *Moäbite* or *Moäbitess,* i.e. a descendant from Moab:—(woman) of Moab, Moabite (-ish, -ss).

4126. מוֹבָא, **môwbâ',** *mo-baw´*; by transposition for 3996; an *entrance*:—coming.

4127. מוּג, **mûwg,** *moog*; a primitive root; to *melt,* i.e. literal (to *soften,* flow down, *disappear*), or figurative (to *fear, faint*):—consume, dissolve, (be) faint (-hearted), melt (away), make soft.

4128. מוּד, **môwd,** *mowd*; a primitive root; to *shake*:—measure.

4129. מוֹדַע, **môwda',** *mo-dah´*; or rather מֹדָע, **môdâ',** *mo-daw´*; from 3045; an *acquaintance*:—kinswoman.

4130. מוֹדַעַת, **môwda'ath,** *mo-dah´-ath*; from 3045; *acquaintance*:—kindred.

4131. מוֹט, **môwṭ,** *mote´*; a primitive root; to *waver*; (by implication) to *slip, shake, fall*:—be carried, cast, be out of course, be fallen in decay, × exceedingly, fall (-ing down), be (re-) moved, be ready, shake, slide, slip.

4132. מוֹט, **môwṭ,** *mote´*; from 4131; a *wavering,* i.e. *fall*; (by implication) a *pole* (as shaking); hence a *yoke* (as essentially a bent pole):—bar, be moved, staff, yoke.

4133. מוֹטָה, **môwṭâh,** *mo-taw´*; feminine of 4132; a *pole*; (by implication) an ox-*bow*; hence a *yoke* (either literal or figurative):—bands, heavy, staves, yoke.

4134. מוּךְ, **mûwk,** *mook*; a primitive root; to *become thin,* i.e. (figurative) *be impoverished*:—be (waxen) poor (-er).

4135. מוּל, **mûwl,** *mool*; a primitive root; to *cut* short, i.e. *curtail* (specifically the prepuce, i.e. to *circumcise*); (by implication) to *blunt*; (figurative) to *destroy*:—circumcise (-ing, selves), cut down (in pieces), destroy, × must needs.

A verb meaning to cut short, to cut off, to circumcise. Abraham was commanded to circumcise both himself and his offspring as a sign of the covenant made between him and God (Ge 17:10–14). As a result, Abraham had his son Ishmael, all the male slaves in his house, and himself circumcised that same day (Ge 17:23–27). Later, when Isaac was born, Abraham circumcised him as well (Ge 21:4). Moses commanded the Israelites to circumcise their hearts, that is, to remove the hardness and to love God (Dt 10:16; cf. 30:6; Jer 4:4). When used in its intensive form, the verb carries the meaning to cut down, as seen in Ps 90:6: "In the morning it [the grass] flourisheth, and groweth up; in the evening it is cut down, and withereth" (KJV). Used in the causative sense, the verb gives the meaning to cut off, to destroy (Ps 118:10–12; lit., "I will cause them to be cut off"). See also the related verbs *mâhal* (4107), *mâlal* (4448), and *nâmal* (5243).

4136. מוּל, **mûwl,** *mool*; or מוֹל, **môwl,** *mole*; (Dt 1:1), or מוֹאל, **môw'l,** *mole*; (Ne 12:38), or מֻל, **mul,** *mool*; (Nu 22:5), from 4135; (properly) *abrupt,* i.e. a *precipice*; (by implication) the *front*; used only adverb (with prepositional prefix) *opposite*:—(over) against, before, [fore-] front, from, [God-] ward, toward, with.

4137. מוֹלָדָה, **Môwlâdâh,** *mo-law-daw´*; from 3205; *birth; Moladah,* a place in Palestine:—Moladah.

4138. מוֹלֶדֶת, **môwledeth,** *mo-leh´-deth*; from 3205; *nativity* (plural *birth-place*); (by implication) *lineage, native country*; also *offspring, family*:—begotten, born, issue, kindred, native (-ity).

4139. מוּלָה, **mûwlâh,** *moo-law´*; from 4135; *circumcision*:—circumcision.

A feminine noun meaning circumcision. Derived from the verb *mûl* (4135), the only undisputed occurrence of the term is found at the end of Ex 4:26.

4140. מוֹלִיד, **Môwlîyd,** *mo-leed*; from 3205; *genitor; Molid,* an Israelite:—Molid.

4141. מוּסָב, **mûwsâb,** *moo-sawb´*; from 5437; a *turn,* i.e. *circuit* (of a building):—winding about.

4142. מוּסַבָּה, **mûwsabbâh,** *moo-sab-baw´*; or מֻסַבָּה, **musabbâh,** *moo-sab-baw´*; feminine of 4141; a *reversal,* i.e. the *backside* (of a gem), *fold* (of a double-leaved door), *transmutation* (of a name):—being changed, inclosed, be set, turning.

4143. מוּסָד**, mûwsâd,** *moo-sawd´*; from 3245; a *foundation*:—foundation.

A masculine singular noun meaning foundation, foundation laying. Its only occurrences are in Isa 28:16 and 2Ch 8:16 that refer to the foundations of Zion and the Temple, respectively.

4144. מוֹסָד**, môwsâd,** *mo-sawd´*; from 3245; a *foundation*:—foundation.

4145. מוּסָדָה**, mûwsâdâh,** *moo-saw-daw´*; feminine of 4143; a *foundation*; (figurative) an *appointment*:—foundation, grounded. Compare 4328.

A feminine noun meaning foundation or appointment. This word is used only twice in the OT and comes from the verb *yâsad* (3245), meaning to establish. Ezekiel used this word to describe the foundation of the Temple in his vision (Eze 41:8). Isaiah used it to describe the appointed rod of punishment by which the Lord would smite Assyria (Isa 30:32).

4146. מוֹסָדָה**, môwsâdâh,** *mo-saw-daw´*; or מֹסָדָה**, môsâdâh,** *mo-saw-daw´*; feminine of 4144; a *foundation*:—foundation.

A feminine singular noun meaning foundation. It always occurs in the plural. It often refers to the foundation of the world (2Sa 22:16; Ps 18:15[16]) or to the base of a man-made construction, such as a building or wall (Jer 51:26).

4147. מוֹסֵר**, môwsêr,** *mo-sare´*; also (in plural) feminine מוֹסֵרָה**, môwsêrâh,** *mo-say-raw´*; or מֹסְרָה**, môs^e^râh,** *mo-ser-aw´*; from 3256; (properly) *chastisement*, i.e. (by implication) a *halter*; (figurative) *restraint*:—band, bond.

4148. מוּסָר**, mûwsâr,** *moo-sawr´*; from 3256; (properly) *chastisement*; (figurative) *reproof*, *warning* or *instruction*; also *restraint*:—bond, chastening ([-eth]), chastisement, check, correction, discipline, doctrine, instruction, rebuke.

A masculine noun meaning instruction, discipline. It occurs almost exclusively in the poetic and prophetic literature. In Proverbs, instruction and discipline come primarily through the father (or a father figure such as a teacher) and usually are conveyed orally but may come via the rod (Pr 1:8; 13:1, 24). Those who are wise receive instruction, but fools reject it (Pr 1:7; 8:33; 13:1; 15:5). The reception of instruction brings life, wisdom, and the favour of the Lord (Pr 4:13; 8:33); however, rejection brings death, poverty, and shame (Pr 5:23; 13:18). Apart from Proverbs, this noun is always associated with God—with two exceptions (Job 20:3; Jer 10:8). When God's instruction is rejected, it results in punishments of various kinds (Job 36:10; Jer 7:28; 17:23; 32:33; Zep 3:2). The discipline of the Lord is not to be despised, for it is a demonstration of His love for His children (Job 5:17; Pr 3:11; cf. Heb 12:5, 6). The supreme demonstration of God's love came when Jesus Christ bore the "chastisement of our peace" (Isa 53:5).

4149. מוֹסֵרָה**, Môwsêrâh,** *mo-say-raw´*; or (plural) מֹסְרוֹת**, Môs^e^rôwth,** *mo-ser-othe´*; feminine of 4147; *correction* or *corrections; Moserah* or *Moseroth*, a place in the Desert:—Mosera, Moseroth.

4150. מוֹעֵד**, môw'êd,** *mo-ade´*; or מֹעֵד**, mô'êd,** *mo-ade´*; or (feminine) מוֹעָדָה**, môw'âdâh,** *mo-aw-daw´*; (2Ch 8:13), from 3259; (properly) an *appointment*, i.e. a fixed *time* or season; (specifically) a *festival*; conventionally a *year*; (by implication) an *assembly* (as convened for a definite purpose); (technically) the *congregation*; (by extension) the *place of meeting*; also a *signal* (as appointed beforehand):—appointed (sign, time), (place of, solemn) assembly, congregation, (set, solemn) feast, (appointed, due) season, solemn (-ity), synagogue, (set) time (appointed).

A masculine noun meaning an appointed time or place. It can signify an appointed meeting time in general (Ge 18:14; Ex 13:10); a specific appointed time, usually for a sacred feast or festival (Hos 9:5; 12:9[10]); the time of the birds' migration (Jer 8:7); the time of wine (Hos 2:9[11]); the same time next year (Ge 17:21). In addition to the concept of time, this word can also signify an appointed meeting place: "The mount of the congregation" identifies the meeting place of God or the gods (Isa 14:13), and "the house appointed for all living" identifies the meeting place of the dead—that is, the netherworld (Job 30:23). Moreover, the term is used to distinguish those places where God's people were to focus on God and their relationship with Him, which would include: the tent of meeting (Ex 33:7); the Temple (La 2:6); the synagogue (Ps 74:8).

4151. מוֹעָד**, môw'âd,** *mo-awd´*; from 3259; (properly) an *assembly* [as in 4150]; (figurative) a *troop*:—appointed time.

A masculine noun meaning appointed place. This word is used only once in the OT and comes from the verb *yâ'ad* (3259), meaning to appoint. It describes the appointed places for soldiers, often translated as ranks (Isa 14:31).

4152. מוּעָדָה**, mûw'âdâh,** *moo-aw-daw´*; from 3259; an *appointed* place, i.e. *asylum*:—appointed.

4153. מוֹעַדְיָה**, Môw'adyâh,** *mo-ad-yaw´*; from 4151 and 3050; *assembly of Jah; Moädjah*, an Israelite:—Moadiah. Compare 4573.

4154. מוּעֶדֶת**, mûw'edeth,** *moo-eh´-deth*; feminine passive participle of 4571; (properly) *made to slip*, i.e. *dislocated*:—out of joint.

4155. מוּעָף**, mûw'âph,** *moo-awf´*; from 5774; (properly) *covered*, i.e. *dark*; (abstract) *obscurity*, i.e. *distress*:—dimness.

4156. מוֹעֵצָה**, môw'êtsâh,** *mo-ay-tsaw´*; from 3289; a *purpose*:—counsel, device.

4157. מוּעָקָה**, mûw'âqâh,** *moo-aw-kaw´*; from 5781; *pressure*, i.e. (figurative) *distress*:—affliction.

4158. מוֹפַעַת**, Môwpha'ath,** *mo-fah´-ath*; (Jer 48:21), or מֵיפַעַת**, Mêypha'ath,** *may-fah´-ath*; or מֵפַעַת**, Mêpha'ath,** *may-fah´-ath*; from 3313; *illuminative; Mophaath* or *Mephaath*, a place in Palestine:—Mephaath.

4159. מוֹפֵת**, môwphêth,** *mo-faith´*; or מֹפֵת**, mô-phêth,** *mo-faith´*; from 3302 in the sense of *conspicuousness*; a *miracle*; (by implication) a *token* or *omen*:—miracle, sign, wonder (-ed at).

A masculine noun meaning a wonder, a sign, a portent, a token. It is often a phenomenon displaying God's power, used to describe some of the plagues God placed on Egypt (Ex 7:3; 11:9) directly or through Moses and Aaron (Ex 4:21; 11:10); the psalmists sang of these wonders (Ps 105:5); false prophets could work counterfeit wonders (Dt 13:1[2], 2[3]); God worked these signs in the heavens sometimes (Joel 2:30[3:3]). Even people can become signs and tokens. Both Isaiah and his children served as signs to Israel (Isa 8:18), as did Ezekiel (12:6, 11; Zec 3:8). The curses that God described in the Law would be signs and wonders to cause His people to see His activity in judging them if they broke His covenant (Dt 28:46).

4160. מִיץ**, mêts,** *mayts*; a primitive root; to *press*, i.e. (figurative) to *oppress*:—extortioner.

4161. מוֹצָא**, môwtsâ',** *mo-tsaw´*; or מֹצָא**, môtsâ',** *mo-tsaw´*; from 3318; a *going forth*, i.e. (the act) an *egress*, or (the place) an *exit*; hence a *source* or *product*; specifically *dawn*, the *rising* of the sun (the *East*), *exportation, utterance*, a *gate*, a *fountain*, a *mine*, a *meadow* (as producing grass):—brought out, bud, that which came out, east, going forth, goings out, that which (thing that) is gone out, outgoing, proceeded out, spring, vein, [water-] course [springs].

4162. מוֹצָא**, môwtsâ',** *mo-tsaw´*; the same as 4161; *Motsa*, the name of two Israelites:—Moza.

4163. מוֹצָאָה**, môwtsâ'âh,** *mo-tsaw-aw´*; feminine of 4161; a family *descent*; also a *sewer* [margin; compare 6675]:—draught house; going forth.

4164. מוּצַק**, mûwtsaq,** *moo-tsak´*; or מוּצָק**, mûwtsâq,** *moo-tsawk´*; from 3332; *narrowness*; (figurative) *distress*:—anguish, is straitened, straitness.

4165. מוּצָק, **mûwtsâq,** *moo-tsawk´*; from 5694; (properly) *fusion*, i.e. (literal) a *casting* (of metal); (figurative) a *mass* (of clay):—casting, hardness.

4166. מוּצָקָה, **mûwtsâqâh,** *moo-tsaw-kaw´*; or מֻצָקָה, **mutsâqâh,** *moo-tsaw-kaw´*; from 3332; (properly) something *poured* out, i.e. a *casting* (of metal); (by implication) a *tube* (as cast):—when it was cast, pipe.

4167. מוּק, **mûwq,** *mook*; a primitive root; to *jeer*, i.e. (intensive) *blaspheme*:—be corrupt.

A verb meaning to mock, to deride. This word is used only once in the OT. In Ps 73:8, it describes the proud, mocking speech of the wicked.

4168. מוֹקֵד, **môwqêd,** *mo-kade´*; from 3344; a *fire* or *fuel*; (abstract) a *conflagration*:—burning, hearth.

4169. מוֹקְדָה, **môwqᵉdâh,** *mo-ked-aw´*; feminine of 4168; *fuel*:—burning.

4170. מוֹקֵשׁ, **môwqêsh,** *mo-kashe´*; or מֹקֵשׁ, **môqêsh,** *mo-kashe´*; from 3369; a *noose* (for catching animals) (literal or figurative); (by implication) a *hook* (for the nose):—be ensnared, gin, (is) snare (-d), trap.

A masculine noun meaning a snare, a trap, bait. The proper understanding of this Hebrew word is the lure or bait placed in a hunter's trap. From this sense comes the primary use of the term to mean the snare itself. It is used to signify a trap by which birds or beasts are captured (Am 3:5); a moral pitfall (Pr 18:7; 20:25); and anything that lures one to ruin and disaster (Jgs 2:3; Pr 29:6).

4171. מוּר, **mûwr,** *moor*; a primitive root; to *alter*; (by implication) to *barter*, to *dispose of*:— × at all, (ex-) change, remove.

4172. מוֹרָא, **môwrâ',** *mo-raw´*; or מֹרָא, **môrâ',** *mo-raw´*; or מוֹרָה, **môwrâh,** *mo-raw´*; (Ps 9:20), from 3372; *fear*; (by implication) a *fearful* thing or deed:—dread, (that ought to be) fear (-ed), terribleness, terror.

A masculine noun meaning fear, terror, reverence. The primary concept underlying the meaning of this word is a sense of fear or awe that causes separation or brings respect. It is used to denote the fear animals have for humans (Ge 9:2); terror on the Canaanites as Israel entered the Promised Land (Dt 11:25); the reverence due those in authority (Mal 1:6); an object of reverence, which for Israel was to be God, *yĕhôwâh* (3068), alone (Isa 8:12, 13); a spectacle or event that inspires awe or horror (Dt 4:34; 34:12; Jer 32:21).

4173. מוֹרַג, **môwrag,** *mo-rag´*; or מֹרַג, **môrag,** *mo-rag´*; from an unused root meaning to *triturate*; a threshing *sledge*:—threshing instrument.

4174. מוֹרָד, **môwrâd,** *mo-rawd´*; from 3381; a *descent*; (architecturally) an ornamental *appendage*, perhaps a *festoon*:—going down, steep place, thin work.

4175. מוֹרֶה, **môwreh,** *mo-reh´*; from 3384; an *archer*; also *teacher* or *teaching*; also the *early rain* [see 3138]:—(early) rain.

4176. מוֹרֶה, **Môwreh,** *mo-reh´*; or מֹרֶה, **Môreh,** *mo-reh´*; the same as 4175; *Moreh*, a Canaanite; also a hill (perhaps named from him):—Moreh.

4177. מוֹרָה, **môwrâh,** *mo-raw´*; from 4171 in the sense of *shearing*; a *razor*:—razor.

4178. מוֹרָט, **môwrâṭ,** *mo-rawt´*; from 3399; *obstinate*, i.e. independent:—peeled.

4179. מוֹרִיָּה, **Môwrîyyâh,** *mo-ree-yaw´*; or מֹרִיָּה, **Môrîyyâh,** *mo-ree-yaw´*; from 7200 and 3050; *seen of Jah; Morijah*, a hill in Palestine:—Moriah.

4180. מוֹרָשׁ, **môwrâsh,** *mo-rawsh´*; from 3423; a *possession*; (figurative) *delight*:—possession, thought.

4181. מוֹרָשָׁה, **môwrâshâh,** *mo-raw-shaw´*; feminine of 4180; a *possession*:—heritage, inheritance, possession.

A feminine noun meaning a possession, an inheritance. This word comes from the verb *yârash* (3423), meaning to take possession of, to inherit. This word is used to refer to God giving land to Israel as an inheritance (Ex 6:8; Eze 11:15; 33:24), but it also refers to God giving the land to other nations to possess (Eze 25:10). In one instance, the Edomites took land as a possession for themselves (Eze 36:5). In its other instances, God gave the Law as a possession (Dt 33:4); God delivered the people of Israel over to other nations for a possession (Eze 25:4; 36:3); and the people took the high places as possessions (Eze 36:2).

4182. מוֹרֶשֶׁת גַּת, **Môwresheth Gath,** *mo-reh´-sheth gath*; from 3423 and 1661; *possession of Gath; Moresheth-Gath*, a place in Palestine:—Moresheth-gath.

4183. מוֹרַשְׁתִּי, **Môwrashtîy,** *mo-rash-tee´*; patrial from 4182; a *Morashtite* or inhabitant of Moresheth-Gath:—Morashthite.

4184. מוּשׁ, **mûwsh,** *moosh*; a primitive root; to *touch*:—feel, handle.

4185. מוּשׁ, **mûwsh,** *moosh*; a primitive root [perhaps rather the same as 4184 through the idea of receding by *contact*]; to *withdraw* (both literal and figurative, whether intrans. or trans.):—cease, depart, go back, remove, take away.

4186. מוֹשָׁב, **môwshâb,** *mo-shawb´*; or מֹשָׁב, **môshâb,** *mo-shawb´*; from 3427; a *seat*; (figurative) a *site*; (abstract) a *session*; (by extension) an *abode* (the place or the time); (by implication) *population*:—assembly, dwell in, dwelling (-place), wherein (that) dwelt (in), inhabited place, seat, sitting, situation, sojourning.

A masculine noun meaning a seat, a habitation, a dwelling place, inhabitants. The primary notion giving rise to this word is that of remaining or abiding in a given location. It signifies a place to be seated (1Sa 20:18; Job 29:7); the sitting of an assembly (Ps 107:32); the location or situation of a city (2Ki 2:19); a place of habitation (Ge 27:39; Nu 24:21); the inhabitants of a particular residence (2Sa 9:12). The psalmist stated that the Lord Himself chose Zion as His dwelling place (Ps 132:13).

4187. מוּשִׁי, **Mûwshîy,** *moo-shee´*; or מֻשִּׁי, **Mushshîy,** *mush-shee´*; from 4184; *sensitive; Mushi*, a Levite:—Mushi.

4188. מוּשִׁי, **Mûwshîy,** *moo-shee´*; patronymic from 4187; a *Mushite* (collective) or descendants of Mushi:—Mushites.

4189. מוֹשְׁכָה, **môwshᵉkâh,** *mo-shek-aw´*; active participle feminine of 4900; something *drawing*, i.e. (figurative) a *cord*:—band.

4190. מוֹשָׁעָה, **môwshâ'âh,** *mo-shaw-aw´*; from 3467; *deliverance*:—salvation.

A feminine noun meaning salvation, deliverance. This word appears only once in the Bible, signifying the saving acts of the Lord (Ps 68:20[21]).

4191. מוּת, **mûwth,** *mooth*; a primitive root; to *die* (literal or figurative); (causative) to *kill*:— × at all, × crying, (be) dead (body, man, one), (put to, worthy of) death, destroy (-er), (cause to, be like to, must) die, kill, necro [-mancer], × must needs, slay, × surely, × very suddenly, × in [no] wise.

A verb meaning to die, to kill, to put to death, to execute. It occurs in the simple stem of the verb in 600 of its 809 occurrences, meaning to be dead or to die. It indicates a natural death in peace at an old age, as in the case of Abraham (Ge 25:8; Jgs 8:32). Dying, however, was not intended to be a natural aspect of being human. It came about through unbelief and rebellion against God (Ge 3:4) so that Adam and Eve died. The word describes dying because of failure to pursue a moral life (Pr 5:23; 10:21). It describes various kinds of death: at the hand of God—the Lord smote Nabal, and he died (1Sa 25:37); the execution of the offender in capital offence cases (Ge 2:17; 20:7); the sons of Job from the violence of a mighty storm (Job 1:19); a murderer could be handed over to die at the hand of the avenger of blood (Dt 19:12). The prophets declared that many people would die by the hand of the Lord when He would bring the sword, famine, and plagues upon them (Jer 11:22; cf. 14:12). The present participle of this form may indicate someone who is dying (Ge 20:3); dead or a corpse

(Dt 25:5; Isa 22:2). People could also be put to death by legal or human authority (Ge 42:20; Ex 10:28).

The word indicates the dying of various nonhuman, nonanimal entities. A nation could die, such as Moab, Ephraim, or Israel (Eze 18:31; Hos 13:1; Am 2:2). A more powerful use of the verb is its description of the death of wisdom (Job 12:2) or courage (1Sa 25:37).

4192. מוּת, **Mûwth,** *mooth*; (Ps 48:14), or מוּת לַבֵּן, **Mûwth Labbên,** *mooth lab-bane´*; from 4191 and 1121 with the preposition and article interposed; "*To die for the son,*" probably the title of a popular song:—death, Muth-labben.

A phrase found only in the superscription at the top of Ps 9. It is part of the musical directions for the singing of this psalm, yet the meaning is ambiguous. Various renderings have been offered by interpreters, the most likely options being that the phrase is either a title of a tune to which the psalm was to be sung or that the phrase means "death to the son" or "to die for the son." Also possible is the combination of these two options, namely, that the phrase is a title of a tune called "Death to the Son"/"To die for the Son" to which Ps 9 was to be sung.

4193. מוֹת, **môwth,** *mohth*; (Chaldee); corresponding to 4194; *death*:—death.

An Aramaic masculine noun meaning death. In writing a letter to Ezra the scribe, King Artaxerxes of Persia used this term to designate execution as one of the viable means of punishment available to Ezra in dealing with those who refused to obey the Law of God and the law of the king in the newly resettled land of Israel (Ezr 7:26). The term is the equivalent of the Hebrew noun *mâweth* (4194).

4194. מָוֶת, **mâveth,** *maw´-veth*; from 4191; *death* (natural or violent); (concrete) the *dead*, their place or state (*hades*); (figurative) *pestilence, ruin*:—(be) dead ([-ly]), death, die (-d).

A masculine noun meaning death. The term signifies death occurring by both natural and violent means (natural: Ge 27:7, 10; Nu 16:29; violent: Le 16:1; Jgs 16:30). In other texts, it designates the place where the dead dwell known as Sheol (*shᵉ'ôwl* [7585]; Job 28:22; Ps 9:13[14]; Pr 7:27). Because death and disease are so intimately related and due to the context, the word suggests the intended meaning of deadly disease, plague, epidemic, or pestilence (Job 27:15; Jer 15:2, 18:21, 43:11). Figuratively, the term expresses the idea of ruin and destruction, especially when contrasted with the desirable notions of life, prosperity, and happiness (Pr 11:19; 12:28; cf. Ex 10:17). This noun is derived from the verb *mûth* (4191).

4195. מוֹתָר, **môwthâr,** *mo-thar´*; from 3498; (literal) *gain*; (figurative) *superiority*:—plenteousness, preeminence, profit.

4196. מִזְבֵּחַ, **mizbêach,** *miz-bay´-akh*; from 2076; an *altar*:—altar.

A masculine noun meaning the altar, the place of sacrifice. It is a noun formed from the verb *zâbach* (2076), which means to slaughter an animal, usually for a sacrifice. The sacrificial system was at the focal point of the pre-Israelite and Israelite systems of worship since the sacrifice and subsequent meal were used to solemnize a covenant or treaty and to symbolize a positive relationship between the two parties. Noah built an altar and offered sacrifices on exiting the ark (Ge 8:20); the patriarchs built altars and sacrificed at various points along their journeys: Abram (Ge 12:7, 8; 22:9); Isaac (Ge 26:25); Jacob (Ge 35:7); Moses (Ex 24:4). At Mount Sinai, God commanded that the Israelites build the tabernacle and include two altars: a bronze altar in the courtyard for the sacrificing of animals (Ex 27:1–8; 38:1–7) and a golden altar inside the tabernacle for the burning of incense (Ex 30:1–10; 37:25–29). Solomon (1Ki 6:20, 22; 8:64) and Ezekiel (Eze 41:22; 43:13–17) followed a similar pattern. God also commanded that the altar for burnt offerings be made of earth or undressed stones because human working of the stones would defile it. Moreover, God commanded that the altar should have no steps so that human nakedness would not be exposed on it (Ex 20:24–26).

4197. מֶזֶג, **mezeg,** *meh´-zeg*; from an unused root meaning to *mingle* (water with wine); *tempered* wine:—liquor.

4198. מָזֶה, **mâzeh,** *maw-zeh´*; from an unused root meaning to *suck* out; *exhausted*:—burnt.

4199. מִזָּה, **Mizzâh,** *miz-zaw´*; probably from an unused root meaning to *faint* with fear; *terror; Mizzah*, an Edomite:—Mizzah.

4200. מָזוּ, **mâzûw,** *maw´-zoo*; probably from an unused root meaning to *gather* in; a *granary*:—garner.

4201. מְזוּזָה, **mᵉzûwzâh,** *mez-oo-zaw´*; or מְזֻזָה, **mᵉzu-zâh,** *mez-oo-zaw´*; from the same as 2123; a *door-post* (as *prominent*):—(door, side) post.

4202. מָזוֹן, **mâzôwn,** *maw-zone´*; from 2109; *food*:—meat, victual.

4203. מָזוֹן, **mâzôwn,** *maw-zone´*; (Chaldee); corresponding to 4202:—meat.

4204. מָזוֹר, **mâzôwr,** *maw-zore´*; from 2114 in the sense of *turning aside* from truth; *treachery*, i.e. a *plot*:—wound.

4205. מָזוֹר, **mâzôwr,** *maw-zore´*; or מָזֹר, **mâzôr,** *maw-zore´*; from 2115 in the sense of *binding* up; a *bandage*, i.e. remedy; hence a *sore* (as needing a compress):—bound up, wound.

4206. מָזִיחַ, **mâzîyach,** *maw-zee´-akh*; or מֵזַח, **mê-zach,** *may-zakh´*; from 2118; a *belt* (as movable):—girdle, strength.

4207. מַזְלֵג, **mazlêg,** *maz-layg´*; or (feminine) מִזְלָגָה, **mizlâgâh,** *miz-law-gaw´*; from an unused root meaning to *draw* up; a *fork*:—fleshhook.

4208. מַזָּלָה, **mazzâlâh,** *maz-zaw-law´*; apparently from 5140 in the sense of *raining*; a *constellation*, i.e. Zodiacal sign (perhaps as affecting the weather):—planet. Compare 4216.

4209. מְזִמָּה, **mᵉzimmâh,** *mez-im-maw´*; from 2161; a *plan*, usually evil (*machination*), sometimes good (*sagacity*):—(wicked) device, discretion, intent, witty invention, lewdness, mischievous (device), thought, wickedly.

A feminine noun meaning a plan, a thought. Most often the term denotes the evil plans, schemes, or plots humanity devises that are contrary to God's righteous decrees. The Lord declared to Jeremiah that in carrying out their evil, idolatrous plans, His people forfeited their right to enter His house (i.e. the Temple, Jer 11:15). The psalmist prayed that the wicked might be ensnared by the very schemes they had planned to unleash on the poor (Ps 10:2). The cunning plans that God's enemies intend to execute against Him never succeed (Ps 21:11[12]; cf. Ps 37:7). Moreover, those who plot evil are condemned and hated by Him (Pr 12:2, 14:17). Often, the wicked are so blinded by pride that their only thought about God is that He doesn't exist (Ps 10:4). Another significant use of this word occurs when it describes an intention of God and so conveys the idea of purpose or plan. After the Lord confronted Job in the whirlwind, Job was deeply humbled and acknowledged that no purpose of the Lord's can be thwarted (Job 42:2). The Lord's anger so burned on account of the false prophets of Jeremiah's day that it would not be turned back until He had executed and accomplished the purpose of His heart against them (Jer 23:20; cf. Jer 30:24). The Lord's purpose for Babylon was to utterly destroy it for all the evil they had committed against Jerusalem and the Temple (Jer 51:11). In Proverbs, the word often conveys the sense of prudence, discretion, and wisdom. In his prologue to the book of Proverbs, Solomon expressed that one reason he was writing the work was to impart discretion to young men (Pr 1:4; cf. Pr 5:2). Solomon urged them to hold on to wisdom and not let it out of their sight once they acquired it (Pr 3:21). Wisdom and prudence go hand in hand (Pr 8:12). This noun derives from the verb *zâmam* (2161).

4210. מִזְמוֹר, **mizmôwr,** *miz-more´*; from 2167; (properly) instrumental *music*; (by implication) a *poem* set to notes:—psalm.

4211. מַזְמֵרָה, **mazmêrâh,** *maz-may-raw´*; from 2168; a *pruning-knife*:—pruning-hook.

4212. מְזַמֶּרֶת, **mᵉzammereth,** *mez-am-mer-eth´*; from 2168; a *tweezer* (only in the plural):—snuffers.

4213. מִזְעָר, **miz'âr,** *miz-awr´*; from the same as 2191; *fewness*; (by implication) as superlative *diminutiveness*:—few, × very.

4214. מִזְרֶה, **mizreh,** *miz-reh´*; from 2219; a winnowing *shovel* (as scattering the chaff):—fan.

4215. מְזָרֶה, **m^e^zâreh,** *mez-aw-reh´*; apparently from 2219; (properly) a *scatterer,* i.e. the north *wind* (as dispersing clouds; only in plural):—north.

4216. מַזָּרָה, **mazzârâh,** *maz-zaw-raw´*; apparently from 5144 in the sense of *distinction*; some noted *constellation* (only in the plural), (perhaps collectively) the *zodiac*:—Mazzoroth. Compare 4208.

4217. מִזְרָח, **mizrâch,** *miz-rawkh´*; from 2224; *sunrise,* i.e. the *east*:—east (side, -ward), (sun-) rising (of the sun).

4218. מִזְרָע, **mizrâ',** *miz-raw´*; from 2232; a planted *field*:—thing sown.

4219. מִזְרָק, **mizrâq,** *miz-rawk´*; from 2236; a *bowl* (as if for sprinkling):—bason, bowl.

4220. מֵחַ, **mêach,** *may´-akh*; from 4229 in the sense of *greasing; fat*; (figurative) *rich*:—fatling (one).

4221. מֹחַ, **môach,** *mo´-akh*; from the same as 4220; *fat,* i.e. marrow:—marrow.

4222. מָחָא, **mâchâ',** *maw-khaw´*; a primitive root; to *rub* or *strike* the hands together (in exultation):—clap.

4223. מְחָא, **m^e^châ',** *mekh-aw´*; (Chaldee); corresponding to 4222; to *strike* in pieces; also to *arrest*; specifically to *impale*:—hang, smite, stay.

An Aramaic verb meaning to smite, to strike. The term corresponds closely with the Hebrew verbs *mâkâh* (4229) and *nâkâh* (5221). When combined with the prepositional phrase *bĕyad* (3027) meaning on the hand, the term attains the idiomatic sense to restrain, to hinder, to prevent, or to stay (Da 4:35[32]). On one occasion, the word vividly described the penalty of impalement (on a beam) which awaited any individual who dared to alter King Darius' edict concerning the rebuilding of the Temple in Jerusalem (Ezr 6:11).

4224. מַחֲבֵא, **machăbê',** *makh-ab-ay´*; or מַחֲבֹא, **machăbô',** *makh-ab-o´*; from 2244; a *refuge*:—hiding (lurking) place.

4225. מַחְבֶּרֶת, **machbereth,** *makh-beh´-reth*; from 2266; a *junction,* i.e. seam or sewed piece:—coupling.

4226. מְחַבְּרָה, **m^e^chabb^e^râh,** *mekh-ab-ber-aw´*; from 2266; a *joiner,* i.e. brace or cramp:—coupling, joining.

4227. מַחֲבַת, **machăbath,** *makh-ab-ath´*; from the same as 2281; a *pan* for baking in:—pan.

4228. מַחֲגֹרֶת, **machăgôreth,** *makh-ag-o´-reth*; from 2296; a *girdle*:—girding.

4229. מָחָה, **mâchâh,** *maw-khaw´*; a primitive root; (properly) to *stroke* or *rub*; (by implication) to *erase*; also to *smooth* (as if with oil), i.e. *grease* or make fat; also to *touch,* i.e. reach to:—abolish, blot out, destroy, full of marrow, put out, reach unto, × utterly, wipe (away, out).

A verb meaning to wipe, to wipe out. This term is often connected with divine judgment. It is used of God wiping out all life in the flood (Ge 7:23); destroying Jerusalem (2Ki 21:13); and threatening to wipe out Israel's name (Dt 9:14). God also wipes out sin (Ps 51:1[3]; Isa 43:25); and wipes away tears (Isa 25:8). Humans also act as the subject of this verb; the Israelites nearly wiped out the Benjamites (Jgs 21:17); and a prostitute wipes her mouth after eating (Pr 30:20).

4230. מְחוּגָה, **m^e^chûwgâh,** *mekh-oo-gaw´*; from 2328; an instrument for marking a circle, i.e. *compasses*:—compass.

4231. מָחוֹז, **mâchôwz,** *maw-khoze´*; from an unused root meaning to *enclose*; a *harbor* (as *shut* in by the shore):—haven.

4232. מְחוּיָאֵל, **M^e^chûwyâ'êl,** *mekh-oo-yaw-ale´*; or מְחִיָּיאֵל, **M^e^chîyyây'êl,** *mekh-ee-yaw-ale´*; from 4229 and 410; *smitten of God; Mechujael* or *Mechijael,* an antediluvian patriarch:—Mehujael.

4233. מַחֲוִים, **Machăvîym,** *makh-av-eem´*; apparently a patrial, but from an unknown place (in the plural only for a singular); a *Machavite* or inhabitant of some place named Machaveh:—Mahavite.

4234. מָחוֹל, **mâchôwl,** *maw-khole´*; from 2342; a (round) *dance*:—dance (-cing).

4235. מָחוֹל, **Mâchôwl,** *maw-khole´*; the same as 4234; *dancing; Machol,* an Israelite:—Mahol.

4236. מַחֲזֶה, **machăzeh,** *makh-az-eh´*; from 2372; a *vision*:—vision.

A masculine noun meaning vision. This word is used only four times in the OT and comes from the verb *châzâh* (2372), meaning to see. God came to Abram in a vision (Ge 15:1); Balaam could rightly prophesy because he saw a vision of the Almighty (Nu 24:4, 16). However, false prophets saw a false vision and thus prophesied falsely (Eze 13:7).

4237. מֶחֱזָה, **mechĕzâh,** *mekh-ez-aw´*; from 2372; a *window*:—light.

4238. מַחֲזִיאוֹת, **Machăzîy'ôwth,** *makh-az-ee-oth´*; feminine plural from 2372; *visions; Machazioth,* an Israelite:—Mahazioth.

4239. מְחִי, **m^e^chîy,** *mekh-ee´*; from 4229; a *stroke,* i.e. battering-*ram*:—engines.

4240. מְחִידָא, **M^e^chîydâ',** *mekh-ee-daw´*; from 2330; *junction; Mechida,* one of the Nethinim:—Mehida.

4241. מִחְיָה, **michyâh,** *mikh-yaw´*; from 2421; *preservation of life*; hence *sustenance*; also the live flesh, i.e. the *quick*:—preserve life, quick, recover selves, reviving, sustenance, victuals.

A feminine singular noun meaning preservation of life, sustenance, raw flesh. Joseph said he was sent to Egypt for the preservation of life (Ge 45:5). The term is also used to mean food or sustenance (Jgs 6:4; 17:10). The Levitical Law used the term to refer to raw flesh because of a skin disease (Le 13:10, 24).

4242. מְחִיר, **m^e^chîyr,** *mekh-eer´*; from an unused root meaning to *buy; price, payment, wages*:—gain, hire, price, sold, worth.

4243. מְחִיר, **M^e^chîyr,** *mekh-eer´*; the same as 4242; *price; Mechir,* an Israelite:—Mehir.

4244. מַחְלָה, **Machlâh,** *makh-law´*; from 2470; *sickness; Machlah,* the name apparently of two Israelitesses:—Mahlah.

4245. מַחֲלֶה, **machăleh,** *makh-al-eh´*; or (feminine) מַחֲלָה, **machălâh,** *makh-al-aw´*; from 2470; *sickness*:—disease, infirmity, sickness.

4246. מְחֹלָה, **m^e^chôlâh,** *mekh-o-law´*; feminine of 4234; a *dance*:—company, dances (-cing).

4247. מְחִלָּה, **m^e^chillâh,** *mekh-il-law´*; from 2490; a *cavern* (as if excavated):—cave.

4248. מַחְלוֹן, **Machlôwn,** *makh-lone´*; from 2470; *sick; Machlon,* an Israelite:—Mahlon.

4249. מַחְלִי, **Machlîy,** *makh-lee´*; from 2470; *sick; Machli,* the name of two Israelites:—Mahli.

4250. מַחְלִי, **Machlîy,** *makh-lee´*; patronymic from 4249; a *Machlite* or (collective) descendants of Machli:—Mahlites.

4251. מַחֲלֻיִים, **machăluyîym,** *makh-ah-loo-yeem´*; from 2470; a *disease*:—disease.

4252. מַחֲלָף, **machălâph,** *makh-al-awf´*; from 2498; a (sacrificial) *knife* (as *gliding* through the flesh):—knife.

4253. מַחְלָפָה, **machlâphâh,** *makh-law-faw´*; from 2498; a *ringlet* of hair (as *gliding* over each other):—lock.

4254. מַחֲלָצָה, machălâtsâh, *makh-al-aw-tsaw´*; from 2502; a *mantle* (as easily *drawn off*):—changeable suit of apparel, change of raiment.

4255. מַחְלְקָה, machl^eqâh, *makh-lek-aw´*; (Chaldee); corresponding to 4256; a *section* (of the Levites):—course.

4256. מַחֲלֹקֶת, machălôqeth, *makh-al-o´-keth*; from 2505; a *section* (of Levites, people or soldiers):—company, course, division, portion. See also 5555.

4257. מָחֲלַת, mâchălath, *mawkh-al-ath´*; from 2470; *sickness; Machalath*, probably the title (initial word) of a popular song:—Mahalath.

4258. מָחֲלַת, Mâchălath, *mawkh-al-ath´*; the same as 4257; *sickness; Machalath*, the name of an Ishmaelitess and of an Israelitess:—Mahalath.

4259. מְחֹלָתִי, M^echôlâthîy, *mekh-o-law-thee´*; patrial from 65; a *Meholathite* or inhabitant of Abel-Meholah:—Meholathite.

4260. מַחְמָאֹת, machmâ'ôth, *makh-maw-oth´*; a denominative from 2529; something *buttery* (i.e. unctuous and pleasant), as (figurative) *flattery*:— × than butter.

4261. מַחְמָד, machmâd, *makh-mawd´*; from 2530; *delightful*; hence a *delight*, i.e. object of affection or desire:—beloved, desire, goodly, lovely, pleasant (thing).

4262. מַחְמֹד, machmôd, *makh-mode´*; from 2530; *desired*; hence a *valuable*:—pleasant thing.

4263. מַחְמָל, machmâl, *makh-mawl´*; from 2550; (properly) *sympathy*; (by paronomasia with 4261) *delight*:—pitieth.

A masculine noun meaning an object of mercy. This word occurs only once in the OT and comes from the verb *châmal* (2550), meaning to spare. In Eze 24:21, this word is used to describe the compassion and delight that the Temple was to the Israelites. In this section of Scripture, Ezekiel's desire and delight for his wife is compared to Israel's desire and delight for the Temple (Eze 24:15–27).

4264. מַחֲנֶה, machăneh, *makh-an-eh´*; from 2583; an *encampment* (of travellers or troops); hence an *army*, whether literal (of soldiers) or figurative (of dancers, angels, cattle, locusts, stars; or even the sacred courts):—army, band, battle, camp, company, drove, host, tents.

A masculine noun meaning a camp, an army, and a company. This word comes from the verb *chânâh* (2583), meaning to encamp. The basic idea of this word is that of a multitude of people who have gathered together (Eze 1:24). This word is often used within the context of travel, like the wandering Israelites (Ex 14:19, 20; Nu 4:5); or within the context of war (1Sa 17:1; 2Ki 6:24; 19:35). This word is most often used of Israel but is also used to describe foreign nations (Jos 10:5; Jgs 7:8–11, 13–15; 1Sa 29:1); or even God's encampment (Ge 32:2[3]; 1Ch 12:22[23]).

4265. מַחֲנֵה־דָן, Machănêh-Dân, *makh-an-ay´-dawn*; from 4264 and 1835; *camp of Dan; Machaneh-Dan*, a place in Palestine:—Mahaneh-dan.

4266. מַחֲנַיִם, Machănayim, *makh-an-ah´-yim*; dual of 4264; *double camp; Machanajim*, a place in Palestine:—Mahanaim.

4267. מַחֲנָק, machănaq, *makh-an-ak´*; from 2614; *choking*:—strangling.

4268. מַחֲסֶה, machseh, *makh-as-eh´*; or מַחְסֶה, **machseh,** *makh-seh´*; from 2620; a *shelter* (literal or figurative):—hope, (place of) refuge, shelter, trust.

4269. מַחְסוֹם, machsôwm, *makh-sohm´*; from 2629; a *muzzle*:—bridle.

4270. מַחְסוֹר, machsôwr, *makh-sore´*; or מַחְסֹר, **machsôr,** *makh-sore´*; from 2637; *deficiency*; hence *impoverishment*:—lack, need, penury, poor, poverty, want.

4271. מַחְסֵיָה, Machsêyâh, *makh-say-yaw´*; from 4268 and 3050; *refuge of* (i.e. *in*) *Jah; Machsejah*, an Israelite:—Maaseiah.

4272. מָחַץ, mâchats, *maw-khats´*; a primitive root; to *dash* asunder; (by implication) to *crush, smash* or violently *plunge*; (figurative) to *subdue* or *destroy*:—dip, pierce (through), smite (through), strike through, wound.

A verb meaning to wound severely, to pierce through, and to shatter. This word describes bodily destruction and is best illustrated in Jgs 5:26, where Jael pierced through Sisera's head from temple to temple with a tent peg. David used this word to describe some of his victories in which those wounded were not able to rise again (2Sa 22:39; Ps 18:38[39]). In all other instances of this word, God is in complete control (Dt 32:39; Job 5:18) and completely shatters His enemies (Ps 68:21[22]; 110:5, 6; Hab 3:13). This word occurs only in the poetical passages of the OT, which highlights the intensity of this word.

4273. מַחַץ, machats, *makh´-ats*; from 4272; a *contusion*:—stroke.

A masculine singular noun meaning a severe wound. It occurs only once in the Hebrew Bible (Isa 30:26), referring to God healing His wounded people.

4274. מַחְצֵב, machtsêb, *makh-tsabe´*; from 2672; (properly) a *hewing*; (concrete) a *quarry*:—hewed (-n).

4275. מֶחֱצָה, mechětsâh, *mekh-ets-aw´*; from 2673; a *halving*:—half.

4276. מַחֲצִית, machătsiyth, *makh-ats-eeth´*; from 2673; a *halving* or the *middle*:—half (so much), mid [-day].

4277. מָחַק, mâchaq, *maw-khak´*; a primitive root; to *crush*:—smite off.

A verb meaning to utterly destroy. This word is used only once in the OT, where it is used as a near synonym with *mâchats* (4272), meaning to wound severely, to pierce through, or to shatter. It describes Jael's actions in destroying Sisera by driving a tent peg between his temples (Jgs 5:26).

4278. מֶחְקָר, mechqâr, *mekh-kawr´*; from 2713; (properly) *scrutinized*, i.e. (by implication) a *recess*:—deep place.

4279. מָחָר, mâchâr, *maw-khar´*; probably from 309; (properly) *deferred*, i.e. the *morrow*; usually (adverb) *tomorrow*; (indefinite) *hereafter*:—time to come, tomorrow.

4280. מַחֲרָאָה, machărâ'âh, *makh-ar-aw-aw´*; from the same as 2716; a *sink*:—draught house.

4281. מַחֲרֵשָׁה, machărêshâh, *makh-ar-ay-shaw´*; from 2790; probably a *pick*-axe:—mattock.

4282. מַחֲרֶשֶׁת, machăresheth, *makh-ar-eh´-sheth*; from 2790; probably a *hoe*:—share.

4283. מָחֳרָת, mochŏrâth, *mokh-or-awth´*; or מָחֳרָתָם, **mochŏrâthâm,** *mokh-or-aw-thawm´*; (1Sa 30:17), feminine from the same as 4279; the *morrow* or (adverb) *tomorrow*:—morrow, next day.

4284. מַחֲשָׁבָה, machăshâbâh, *makh-ash-aw-baw´*; or מַחֲשֶׁבֶת, **machăshebeth,** *makh-ash-eh´-beth*; from 2803; a *contrivance*, i.e. (concrete) a *texture, machine*, or (abstract) *intention, plan* (whether bad, a *plot*; or good, *advice*):—cunning (work), curious work, device (-sed), imagination, invented, means, purpose, thought.

A feminine noun meaning a thought, a purpose, a device, an intention. Largely poetic in its use, this Hebrew word means thought or the inventions that spring from such thoughts. It denotes the thoughts of the mind, either belonging to people (1Ch 28:9; Ps 94:11); or God (Jer 29:11; Mic 4:12); the plans or intentions that arise from these thoughts (Pr 15:22; 19:21); the schemes of a wicked heart (La 3:60); skillful inventions coming from the mind of an artist (Ex 31:4; 2Ch 26:15).

4285. מַחְשָׁךְ, machshâk, *makh-shawk´*; from 2821; *darkness*; (concrete) a *dark place*:—dark (-ness, place).

A masculine noun meaning a dark place, a hiding place, secrecy. The primary meaning of this word is darkness that is both blinding and confining. Poetically, it is used to draw an image of the darkness and inescapability of the grave (Ps 88:6[7]; La 3:6). The range of meaning also extends to the unknown things the Lord makes plain (Isa 42:16); and the back alleys where deviant behaviour abounds (Ps 74:20).

4286. מַחְשֹׂף, **machśôph**, *makh-sofe´*; from 2834; a *peeling*:—made appear.

4287. מַחַת, **Machath**, *makh´-ath*; probably from 4229; *erasure; Machath*, the name of two Israelites:—Mahath.

4288. מְחִתָּה, **m^echittâh**, *mekh-it-taw´*; from 2846; (properly) a *dissolution*; (concrete) a *ruin*, or (abstract) *consternation*:—destruction, dismaying, ruin, terror.

A feminine noun meaning destruction, ruin, terror. This word comes from the verb *châthath* (2865), meaning to be broken or afraid. It is used most often in a figurative sense in Proverbs to describe the ruin of the foolish (Pr 10:14; 13:3; 18:7); and the workers of iniquity (Pr 10:29; 21:15). It also describes the result of poverty (Pr 10:15); and the failure to support a prince (Pr 14:28). Elsewhere, this word depicted the power of God bringing destruction (Ps 89:40[41]), which resulted in an object lesson to all around (Jer 48:39). It is the blessing of God that people live without this terror (Isa 54:14; Jer 17:17).

4289. מַחְתָּה, **machtâh**, *makh-taw´*; the same as 4288 in the sense of *removal*; a *pan* for live coals:—censer, firepan, snuffdish.

4290. מַחְתֶּרֶת, **machtereth**, *makh-teh´-reth*; from 2864; a *burglary*; (figurative) *unexpected examination*:—breaking up, secret search.

4291. מְטָא, **m^etâ'**, *met-aw´*; (Chaldee); or מְטָה, **m^etâh**, *met-aw´*; (Chaldee); apparently corresponding to 4672 in the intransitive sense of being found *present*; to *arrive, extend* or *happen*:—come, reach.

4292. מַטְאֲטֵא, **maṭ'ăṭê'**, *mat-at-ay´*; apparently a denominative from 2916; a *broom* (as removing *dirt* [compare English "to dust," i.e. remove dust]):—besom.

4293. מַטְבֵּחַ, **maṭbêach**, *mat-bay´-akh*; from 2873; *slaughter*:—slaughter.

4294. מַטֶּה, **maṭṭeh**, *mat-teh´*; or (feminine) מַטָּה, **maṭṭâh**, *mat-taw´*; from 5186; a *branch* (as *extending*); (figurative) a *tribe*; also a *rod*, whether for chastising (figurative, *correction*), ruling (a *sceptre*), throwing (a *lance*), or walking (a *staff*; [figurative] a *support* of life, e.g., bread):—rod, staff, tribe.

A masculine noun meaning a rod, a staff, a branch, a tribe. This word signifies, variously, a walking stick (Ex 4:2); a branch of a tree (Eze 19:11ff.); a spear used in battle (Hab 3:14); an instrument of chastisement (Isa 10:24); an instrument used in the threshing process (Isa 28:27). Metaphorically, the image of a staff symbolizes the supply of food (Le 26:26); strength (Isa 14:5); and authority (Ps 110:2). Uniquely, the word also signifies a tribe, such as one of the twelve tribes of Israel (Nu 36:3, 4; Jos 13:29). The origin of this use derives from the image of the leader of the tribe going before the company with his staff in hand (cf. Nu 17:2[17]).

4295. מַטָּה, **maṭṭâh**, *mat´-taw*; from 5786 with directive enclitic appended; *downward, below* or *beneath*; often adverbial with or without prefixes:—beneath, down (-ward), less, very low, under (-neath).

4296. מִטָּה, **miṭṭâh**, *mit-taw´*; from 5186; a *bed* (as *extended*) for sleeping or eating; (by analogy) a *sofa, litter* or *bier*:—bed ([-chamber]), bier.

4297. מֻטֶּה, **muṭṭeh**, *moot-teh´*; from 5186; a *stretching*, i.e. *distortion;* (figurative) *iniquity*:—perverseness.

A masculine noun meaning something perverted, twisted, warped. Occurring only in Eze 9:9, this word derives its meaning from a primitive root meaning to stretch, to incline, or to bend (5186). It was used by the Lord to describe the perverseness of Judah in distorting His Law and justice.

4298. מֻטָּה, **muṭṭâh**, *moot-taw´*; from 5186; *expansion*:—stretching out.

4299. מַטְוֶה, **maṭveh**, *mat-veh´*; from 2901; something *spun*:—spun.

4300. מָטִיל, **mâṭîyl**, *mawt-eel´*; from 2904 in the sense of *hammering* out; an iron *bar* (as *forged*):—bar.

4301. מַטְמוֹן, **maṭmôwn**, *mat-mone´*; or מַטְמֹן, **maṭ-môn**, *mat-mone´*; or מַטְמֻן, **maṭmun**, *mat-moon´*; from 2934; a *secret* storehouse; hence a *secreted* valuable (buried); generally *money*:—hidden riches, (hid) treasure (-s).

4302. מַטָּע, **maṭṭâ'**, *mat-taw´*; from 5193; something *planted*, i.e. the place (a *garden* or vineyard), or the thing (a *plant*, figurative of men); (by implication) the act, *planting*:—plant (-ation, -ing).

4303. מַטְעָם, **maṭ'am**, *mat-am´*; or (feminine) מַטְעַמָּה, **maṭ'ammâh**, *mat-am-maw´*; from 2938; a *delicacy*:—dainty (meat), savoury meat.

4304. מִטְפַּחַת, **miṭpachath**, *mit-pakh´-ath*; from 2946; a wide *cloak* (for a woman):—vail, wimple.

4305. מָטַר, **mâṭar**, *maw-tar´*; a primitive root; to *rain*:—(cause to) rain (upon).

4306. מָטָר, **mâṭâr**, *maw-tawr´*; from 4305; *rain*:—rain.

4307. מַטָּרָא, **maṭṭârâ'**, *mat-taw-raw´*; or מַטָּרָה, **maṭṭârâh**, *mat-taw-raw´*; from 5201; a *jail* (as a *guard*-house); also an *aim* (as being closely *watched*):—mark, prison.

4308. מַטְרֵד, **Maṭrêd**, *mat-rade´*; from 2956; *propulsive; Matred*, an Edomitess:—Matred.

4309. מַטְרִי, **Maṭrîy**, *mat-ree´*; from 4305; *rainy; Matri*, an Israelite:—Matri.

4310. מִי, **mîy**, *me*; an interrogative pronoun of persons, as 4100 is of things, *who* (occasionally, by a peculiar idiom, of things); also (indefinite) *whoever*; often used in oblique construction with prefix or suffix:—any (man), × he, × him, + O that! what, which, who (-m, -se, -soever), + would to God.

4311. מֵידְבָא, **Mêyd^ebâ'**, *may-deb-aw´*; from 4325 and 1679; *water of quiet; Medeba*, a place in Palestine:—Medeba.

4312. מֵידָד, **Mêydâd**, *may-dawd´*; from 3032 in the sense of *loving; affectionate; Medad*, an Israelite:—Medad.

4313. מֵי הַיַּרְקוֹן, **Mêy hay-Yarqôwn**, *may hah´-ee-yar-kone´*; from 4325 and 3420 with the article interposed; *water of the yellowness; Me-haj-Jarkon*, a place in Palestine:—Me-jarkon.

4314. מֵי זָהָב, **Mêy Zâhâb**, *may zaw-hawb´*; from 4325 and 2091, *water of gold; Me-Zahab*, an Edomite:—Mezahab.

4315. מֵיטָב, **mêyṭâb**, *may-tawb´*; from 3190; the *best* part:—best.

4316. מִיכָא, **Mîykâ'**, *mee-kaw´*; a variation for 4318; *Mica*, the name of two Israelites:—Micha.

4317. מִיכָאֵל, **Mîykâ'êl**, *me-kaw-ale´*; from 4310 and (the prefixed derivative from) 3588 and 410; *who* (is) *like God; Mikael*, the name of an archangel and of nine Israelites:—Michael.

4318. מִיכָה, **Mîykâh**, *mee-kaw´*; an abbreviation of 4320; *Micah*, the name of seven Israelites:—Micah, Micaiah, Michah.

4319. מִיכָהוּ, **Mîykâhûw**, *me-kaw´-hoo*; a contraction for 4321 *Mikehu*, an Israelite prophet:—Micaiah (2Ch 18:8).

4320. מִיכָיָה, **Mîykâyâh**, *me-kaw-yaw´*; from 4310 and (the prefixed derivative from) 3588 and 3050; *who* (is) *like Jah; Micajah*, the name of two Israelites:—Micah, Michaiah. Compare 4318.

4321. מִיכָיְהוּ, **Mîykây^ehûw**, *me-kaw-yeh-hoo´*; or מִכָיְהוּ, **Mikây^ehûw**, *me-kaw-yeh-hoo´*; (Jer 36:11), abbreviation for 4322; *Mikajah*, the name of three Israelites:—Micah, Micaiah, Michaiah.

4322. מִיכָיָהוּ, **Mîykâyâhûw,** *me-kaw-yaw´-hoo;* for 4320; *Mikajah,* the name of an Israelite and an Israelitess:—Michaiah.

4323. מִיכָל, **mîykâl,** *me-kawl´;* from 3201; (properly) a *container,* i.e. a *streamlet:*—brook.

4324. מִיכַל, **Mîykal,** *me-kal´;* apparently the same as 4323; *rivulet; Mikal,* Saul's daughter:—Michal.

4325. מַיִם, **mayim,** *mah´-yim;* dual of a primitive noun (but used in a singular sense); *water;* (figurative) *juice;* (by euphemism) *urine, semen:*— + piss, wasting, water (-ing, [-course, -flood, -spring]).

4326. מִיָּמִן, **Mîyyâmin,** *me-yaw-meem´;* a form for 4509; *Mijamin,* the name of three Israelites:—Miamin, Mijamin.

4327. מִין, **mîyn,** *meen;* from an unused root meaning to *portion* out; a *sort,* i.e. *species:*—kind. Compare 4480.

4328. מְיֻסָּדָה, **m^eyussâdâh,** *meh-yoos-saw-daw´;* properly feminine passive participle of 3245; something *founded,* i.e. a *foundation:*—foundation.

4329. מוּסָךְ, **mûwsâk,** *moo-sawk´;* from 5526; a *portico* (as *covered):*—covert.

4330. מִיץ, **mîyts,** *meets;* from 4160; *pressure:*—churning, forcing, wringing.

4331. מֵישָׁא, **Mêyshâ',** *may-shaw´;* from 4185; *departure; Mesha,* a place in Arabia; also an Israelite:—Mesha.

4332. מִישָׁאֵל, **Mîyshâ'êl,** *mee-shaw-ale;* from 4310 and 410 with the abbreviation inseparable relative [see 834] interposed; *who* (is) *what God* (is); *Mishaël,* the name of three Israelites:—Mishael.

4333. מִישָׁאֵל, **Mîyshâ'êl,** *mee-shaw-ale´;* (Chaldee); corresponding to 4332; *Mishaël,* an Israelite:—Mishael.

4334. מִישׁוֹר, **mîyshôwr,** *mee-shore´;* or מִישֹׁר, **mîyshôr,** *mee-shore´;* from 3474; a *level,* i.e. a *plain* (often used [with the article prefixed] as a proper name of certain districts); (figurative) *concord;* also *straightness,* i.e. (figurative) *justice;* (sometimes adverbial) *justly:*—equity, even place, plain, right (-eously), (made) straight, uprightness.

A masculine noun meaning plain, evenness, straightness, righteousness, equity. Evenness is the fundamental sense of this word. It denotes straight, as opposed to crooked (Isa 40:4; 42:16); level land, such as a plain (Dt 3:10; 1Ki 20:23); and a safe, unobstructed path (Ps 27:11). By analogy, it is likewise used to imply a righteous lifestyle (Ps 143:10); and equitable leadership (Ps 45:6[7]; Isa 11:4).

4335. מֵישַׁךְ, **Mêyshak,** *may-shak´;* borrowed from 4336; *Meshak,* an Israelite:—Meshak.

4336. מֵישַׁךְ, **Mêyshak,** *may-shak´;* (Chaldee); of foreign origin and doubtful signification; *Meshak,* the Babylonian name of 4333:—Meshak.

4337. מֵישַׁע, **Mêyshâ',** *may-shah´;* from 3467; *safety; Mesha,* an Israelite:—Mesha.

4338. מֵישַׁע, **Mêysha',** *may-shaw´;* a variation for 4337; *safety; Mesha,* a Moabite:—Mesha.

4339. מֵישָׁר, **mêyshâr,** *may-shawr´;* from 3474; *evenness,* i.e. (figurative) *prosperity* or *concord;* also *straightness,* i.e. (figurative) *rectitude* (only in plural with singular sense; often adverbial):—agreement, aright, that are equal, equity, (things that are) right (-eously, things), sweetly, upright (-ly, -ness).

4340. מֵיתָר, **mêythâr,** *may-thawr´;* from 3498; a *cord* (of a tent) [compare 3499] or the *string* (of a bow):—cord, string.

4341. מַכְאֹב, **mak'ôb,** *mak-obe´;* sometimes מַכְאוֹב, **mak'ôwb,** *mak-obe´;* also (feminine Isa 53:3) מַכְאֹבָה, **mak'ôbâh,** *mak-o-baw´;* from 3510; *anguish* or (figurative) *affliction:*—grief, pain, sorrow.

4342. מַכְבִּיר, **makbîyr,** *mak-beer´;* transposed participle of 3527; *plenty:*—abundance.

4343. מַכְבֵּנָא, **Makbênâ',** *mak-bay-naw´;* from the same as 3522; *knoll; Macbena,* a place in Palestine settled by him:—Machbenah.

4344. מַכְבַּנַּי, **Makbannay,** *mak-ban-nah´ee;* patrial from 4343; a *Macbannite* or native of Macbena:—Machbanai.

4345. מִכְבָּר, **mikbâr,** *mik-bawr;* from 3527 in the sense of *covering* [compare 3531]; a *grate:*—grate.

4346. מִכְבֵּר, **mikbêr,** *mak-bare´;* from 3527 in the sense of *covering;* a cloth (as *netted* [compare 4345]):—thick cloth.

4347. מַכָּה, **makkâh,** *mak-kaw´;* or (masculine) מַכֶּה, **makkeh,** *mak-keh´;* (plural only) from 5221 a *blow* (in 2Ch 2:10, of the flail); (by implication) a *wound;* (figurative) *carnage,* also *pestilence:*—beaten, blow, plague, slaughter, smote, × sore, stripe, stroke, wound ([-ed]).

A feminine noun meaning a blow, a stroke. When the word carries this literal sense, often a weapon (sword, rod, whip) functions as the instrument by which the blow is delivered. The individual judged to be in the wrong in a legal case could receive as punishment a beating of up to forty blows or lashes (Dt 25:3). In accordance with the royal edict decreed in the name of Xerxes, King of Persia, the Jews struck down their enemies with the blow of the sword (Est 9:5). The Lord declared to Israel and Judah that He had dealt them their blows because their guilt was so great (Jer 30:14). Elsewhere, the term signifies the result of a blow: a wound. King Joram rested in Jezreel to recover from wounds incurred in battle against the Arameans (2Ki 9:15). In another battle, King Ahab died of a wound, having been pierced by an arrow (1Ki 22:35; cf. Isa 1:6; Jer 6:7; 30:17; Mic 1:9). In other passages, the word described calamities inflicted by God: affliction, misery, and plague. The Lord solemnly warned Israel that failing to diligently obey His commands would result in His overwhelming them with severe and lasting afflictions (Dt 28:59, 61). The Philistines remembered that the "gods" of the Hebrews struck the Egyptians with all kinds of miseries (1Sa 4:8; cf. Jer 10:19, 49:17). Finally, the term can convey the sense of defeat or slaughter. Joshua and his fighting men handed the Amorites a great defeat at Gibeon (Jos 10:10; cf. Jos 10:20). Samson took revenge on the Philistines, killing many in a terrible slaughter because they had burned his wife and father-in-law (Jgs 15:8; cf. Jgs 11:33; 1Sa 4:10; 14:14). This noun is related to the verb *nâkâh* (5221).

4348. מִכְוָה, **mikvâh,** *mik-vaw´;* from 3554; a *burn:*—that burneth, burning.

4349. מָכוֹן, **mâkôwn,** *maw-kone´;* from 3559; (properly) a *fixture,* i.e. a *basis;* (generically) a *place,* especially as an *abode:*—foundation, habitation, (dwelling-, settled) place.

4350. מְכוֹנָה, **m^ekôwnâh,** *mek-o-naw´;* or מְכֹנָה, **m^ekônâh,** *mek-o-naw´;* feminine of 4349; a *pedestal,* also a *spot:*—base.

4351. מְכוּרָה, **m^ekûwrâh,** *mek-oo-raw´;* or מְכֹרָה, **m^ekôrâh,** *mek-o-raw´;* from the same as 3564 in the sense of *digging; origin* (as if a mine):—birth, habitation, nativity.

4352. מָכִי, **Mâkîy,** *maw-kee´;* probably from 4134; *pining; Maki,* an Israelite:—Machi.

4353. מָכִיר, **Mâkîyr,** *maw-keer´;* from 4376; *salesman; Makir,* an Israelite:—Machir.

4354. מָכִירִי, **Mâkîyrîy,** *maw-kee-ree´;* patronymic from 4353; a *Makirite* or descendant of Makir:—of Machir.

4355. מָכַךְ, **mâkak,** *maw-kak´;* a primitive root; to *tumble* (in ruins); (figurative) to *perish:*—be brought low, decay.

4356. מִכְלָאָה, **miklâ'âh,** *mik-law-aw´;* or מִכְלָה, **miklâh,** *mik-law´;* from 3607; a *pen* (for flocks):—([sheep-]) fold. Compare 4357.

4357. מִכְלָה, **miklâh,** *mik-law´*; from 3615; *completion;* (in plural concrete adverb) *wholly:*—perfect. Compare 4356.

4358. מִכְלוֹל, **miklôwl,** *mik-lole´*; from 3634; *perfection,* i.e. (concrete adverb) *splendidly:*—most gorgeously, all sorts.

4359. מִכְלָל, **miklâl,** *mik-lawl´*; from 3634; *perfection* (of beauty):—perfection.

4360. מַכְלוּל, **maklûl,** *mak-lool´*; from 3634; something *perfect,* i.e. a splendid *garment:*—all sorts.

4361. מַכֹּלֶת, **makkôleth,** *mak-ko´-leth*; from 398; *nourishment:*—food.

4362. מִכְמַן, **mikman,** *mik-man´*; from the same as 3646 in the sense of *hiding; treasure* (as *hidden*):—treasure.

4363. מִכְמָס, **Mikmâs,** *mik-maws´*; (Ezr 2:27; Ne 7:31), or מִכְמָשׂ, **Mikmâsh,** *mik-mawsh´*; or מִכְמַשׂ, **Mikmash,** *mik-mash´*; (Ne 11:31), from 3647; *hidden; Mikmas* or *Mikmash,* a place in Palestine:—Mikmas, Mikmash.

4364. מַכְמֹר, **makmôr,** *mak-mor´*; or מִכְמָר, **mikmâr,** *mik-mawr´*; from 3648 in the sense of *blackening* by heat; a (hunter's) *net* (as *dark* from concealment):—net.

4365. מִכְמֶרֶת, **mikmereth,** *mik-meh´-reth*; or מִכְמֹרֶת, **mikmôreth,** *mik-mo´-reth*; feminine of 4364; a (fisher's) *net:*—drag, net.

4366. מִכְמְתָת, **Mikmethâth,** *mik-meth-awth´*; apparently from an unused root meaning to *hide; concealment; Mikmethath,* a place in Palestine:— Michmethath.

4367. מַכְנַדְבַי, **Maknadbay,** *mak-nad-bah´ee*; from 4100 and 5068 with a particle interposed; *what* (is) *like* (a) *liberal* (man); *Maknadbai,* an Israelite:—Machnadebai.

4368. מְכֹנָה, **Mekônâh,** *mek-o-naw´*; the same as 4350; a *base; Mekonah,* a place in Palestine:—Mekonah.

4369. מְכֻנָה, **mekunâh,** *mek-oo-naw´*; the same as 4350; a *spot:*—base.

4370. מִכְנָס, **miknâs,** *mik-nawce´*; from 3647 in the sense of *hiding*; (only in dual) *drawers* (from *concealing* the private parts):—breeches.

4371. מֶכֶס, **mekes,** *meh´-kes*; probably from an unused root meaning to *enumerate*; an *assessment* (as based upon a *census*):—tribute.

4372. מִכְסֶה, **mikseh,** *mik-seh´*; from 3680; a *covering,* i.e. weather-*boarding:*—covering.

4373. מִכְסָה, **miksâh,** *mik-saw´*; feminine of 4371; an *enumeration;* (by implication) a *valuation:*—number, worth.

4374. מְכַסֶּה, **mekasseh,** *mek-as-seh´*; from 3680; a *covering,* i.e. *garment*; (specifically) a *coverlet* (for a bed), an *awning* (from the sun); also the *omentum* (as covering the intestines):—clothing, to cover, that which covereth.

4375. מַכְפֵּלָה, **Makpêlâh,** *mak-pay-law´*; from 3717; a *fold; Makpelah,* a place in Palestine:—Machpelah.

4376. מָכַר, **mâkar,** *maw-kar´*; a primitive root; to *sell,* literal (as merchandise, a daughter in marriage, into slavery), or figurative (to *surrender*):— × at all, sell (away, -er, self).

4377. מֶכֶר, **mekker,** *meh´-ker*; from 4376; *merchandise*; also *value:*—pay, price, ware.

4378. מַכָּר, **makkâr,** *mak-kawr´*; from 5234; an *acquaintance:*—acquaintance.

4379. מִכְרֶה, **mikreh,** *mik-reh´*; from 3738; a *pit* (for salt):—[salt-] pit.

4380. מְכֵרָה, **mekêrâh,** *mek-ay-raw´*; probably from the same as 3564 in the sense of *stabbing*; a *sword:*—habitation.

4381. מִכְרִי, **Mikrîy,** *mik-ree´*; from 4376; *salesman; Mikri,* an Israelite:—Michri.

4382. מְכֵרָתִי, **Mekêrâthîy,** *mek-ay-raw-thee´*; patrial from an unused name (the same as 4380) of a place in Palestine; a *Mekerathite,* or inhabitant of Mekerah:—Mecherathite.

4383. מִכְשׁוֹל, **mikshôwl,** *mik-shole´*; or מִכְשֹׁל, **mikshôl,** *mikshole´*; masculine from 3782; a *stumbling-block,* literal or figurative (*obstacle, enticement* [specifically an idol], *scruple*):—caused to fall, offence, × [no-] thing offered, ruin, stumbling-block.

A masculine noun meaning a stumbling block, an obstacle. Sometimes the term refers to something an individual can literally stumble over. For instance, the Lord commanded the people of Israel not to put a stumbling block before the blind (Le 19:14). More often, however, it is used in a figurative sense. The Lord Himself will become the obstacle over which both houses of Israel will stumble (Isa 8:14). Much later in Isaiah, it is written that the Lord will demand that the obstacle be removed from His people's way (Isa 57:14). In other places, the word refers to that which causes people to stumble morally, that is, to sin: gold and silver (Eze 7:19); idols (Eze 14:3); the Levites (Eze 44:12). In other places, the term describes something that causes people to fall to their ruin. Because of Israel's persistent rejection of God's Law, He laid a stumbling block before them so they would trip and perish (Jer 6:21; cf. Ps 119:165; Eze 3:20; 18:30). This term is derived from the verb *kâshal* (3782).

4384. מַכְשֵׁלָה, **makshêlâh,** *mak-shay-law´*; feminine from 3782; a *stumbling-block,* but only figurative (*fall, enticement* [idol]):—ruin, stumbling-block.

A feminine noun meaning a heap of rubble, ruins. Isaiah prophesied to the people of Judah that because of their rebellion against the Lord, He was going to desolate their land so thoroughly that they would soon search for leaders to care for them and for the ruins of what remained, yet find none (Isa 3:6). This noun stems from the verb *kâshal* (3782).

4385. מִכְתָּב, **miktâb,** *mik-tawb´*; from 3789; a thing *written,* the *characters,* or a *document* (letter, copy, edict, poem):—writing.

4386. מְכִתָּה, **mekittâh,** *mek-it-taw´*; from 3807; a *fracture:*—bursting.

4387. מִכְתָּם, **miktâm,** *mik-tawm´*; from 3799; an *engraving,* i.e. (technical) a *poem:*—Michtam.

4388. מַכְתֵּשׁ, **maktêsh,** *mak-taysh´*; from 3806; a *mortar*; (by analogy) a *socket* (of a tooth):—hollow place, mortar.

4389. מַכְתֵּשׁ, **Maktêsh,** *mak-taysh´*; the same as 4388; *dell*; the *Maktesh,* a place in Jerusalem:—Maktesh.

4390. מָלֵא, **mâlê',** *maw-lay´*; or מָלָא, **mâlâ',** *maw-law´*; (Est 7:5), a primitive root, to *fill* or (intransitive) *be full* of, in a wide application (literal and figurative):—accomplish, confirm, + consecrate, be at an end, be expired, be fenced, fill, fulfil, (be, become, × draw, give in, go) full (-ly, -ly set, tale), [over-] flow, fulness, furnish, gather (selves, together), presume, replenish, satisfy, set, space, take a [hand-] full, + have wholly.

A verb meaning to fill, to be full, to be complete, to fulfill, to finish, to satisfy. This word occurs 251 times in the OT and functions both in a spatial and temporal sense. Spatially, the term pictures the act of making that which was empty of a particular content no longer so. It can also express that state of being in which a certain container is holding to capacity a particular object or objects. God commanded the water creatures to fill the seas (Ge 1:22); and humanity to fill the earth (Ge 1:28). Elijah directed the people to fill four water jars; the trench was also filled (1Ki 18:34, 35). The word can also function in an abstract way: Judah filled the land with violence (Eze 8:17; cf. Le 19:29; Jer 51:5). Theologically, the glory of the Lord filled the Temple (1Ki 8:10, 11; cf. Isa 6:1); and Jeremiah declared that God fills heaven and earth (Jer 23:24). Temporally, the term refers to the completion of a specified segment of time. According to the Law, a woman who had given birth to a boy could not enter the sanctuary until the thirty-three days of her blood purification were completed (Le 12:4). The Lord promised to establish King David's kingdom after his days were fulfilled (i.e. he died: 2Sa 7:12; cf. La 4:18).

A final important use of the word entails the keeping of a vow or promise. The Lord fulfilled His promise to David that his son would build a house for His name (2Ch 6:4, 15; cf. 2Sa 7:12; 1Ki 2:27; 2Ch 36:21).

4391. מְלָא**, mᵉlâʼ,** *mel-aw´*; (Chaldee); corresponding to 4390; to *fill*:—fill, be full.

4392. מָלֵא**, mâlêʼ,** *maw-lay´*; from 4390; *full* (literal or figurative) or *filling* (literal); also (concrete) *fulness*; (adverb) *fully*:— × she that was with child, fill (-ed, -ed with), full (-ly), multitude, as is worth.

4393. מְלֹא**, mᵉlôʼ,** *mel-o´*; rarely מְלוֹא, **mᵉlôwʼ**, *mel-o´*; or מְלוֹ, **mᵉlôw**, *mel-o´*; (Eze 41:8), from 4390; *fulness* (literal or figurative):— × all along, × all that is (there-) in, fill, (× that whereof … was) full, fulness, [hand-] full, multitude.

4394. מִלֻּא**, milluʼ,** *mil-loo´*; from 4390; a *fulfilling* (only in plural), i.e. (literal) a *setting* (of gems), or (technical) *consecration;* (also concrete) a dedicatory *sacrifice*:—consecration, be set.

4395. מְלֵאָה**, mᵉlêʼâh,** *mel-ay-aw´*; feminine of 4392; something *fulfilled*, i.e. *abundance* (of produce):—(first of ripe) fruit, fulness.

4396. מִלֻּאָה**, milluʼâh,** *mil-loo-aw´*; feminine of 4394; a *filling*, i.e. *setting* (of gems):—inclosing, setting.

4397. מַלְאָךְ**, malʼâk,** *mal-awk´*; from an unused root meaning to *despatch* as a deputy; a *messenger*; specifically of God, i.e. an *angel* (also a prophet, priest or teacher):—ambassador, angel, king, messenger.

A masculine noun meaning a messenger, an angel. The term often denotes one sent on business or diplomacy by another (human) personage. Jacob sent messengers on ahead to his brother Esau in the hope of finding favour in his eyes (Ge 32:3[4], 6[7]). The elders of Jabesh sent messengers throughout Israel in a desperate attempt to locate someone who could rescue their town from the dire threat of the Ammonites (1Sa 11:3, 4, 9; cf. 2Sa 11:19; 1Ki 19:2; 2Ki 5:10). Very often, the term referred to messengers sent from God. Sometimes these were human messengers, whether prophets (Isa 44:26; Hag 1:13; Mal 3:1); priests (Ecc 5:6[5]; Mal 2:7); or the whole nation of Israel (Isa 42:19). More often, however, the term referred to heavenly beings who often assumed human form (Ge 19:1; Jgs 13:6, 15, 16) and appeared to people as bearers of the Lord's commands and tidings (Jgs 6:11, 12; 13:3). They were often responsible for aiding, protecting, and fighting for those who trusted in the Lord (Ge 24:7; Ex 23:20; 33:2; 1Ki 19:5; Ps 34:7[8]; 91:11). They also acted as instruments of divine judgment, meting out punishment on the rebellious and the guilty (2Sa 24:16, 17; Ps 35:5, 6; 78:49; Isa 37:36). Sometimes the angel of the Lord and his message are so closely identified with the Lord Himself that the text simply refers to the angel as "the Lord" or "God" (Ge 16:7; 22:11; 31:11; Ex 3:2; Jgs 13:18; cf. Ge 16:13; 22:12; 31:13, 16; Ex 3:4; Jgs 6:22; 13:22).

4398. מַלְאַךְ**, malʼak,** *mal-ak´*; (Chaldee); corresponding to 4397; an *angel*:—angel.

An Aramaic noun meaning angel (Da 3:28; 6:22 [23]). The word is a cognate of the Hebrew noun *malʼâk* (4397).

4399. מְלָאכָה**, mᵉlâʼkâh,** *mel-aw-kaw´*; from the same as 4397; (properly) *deputyship*, i.e. ministry; (generally) *employment* (never servile) or work (abstract or concrete); also *property* (as the result of *labour*):—business, + cattle, + industrious, occupation, (+ -pied), + officer, thing (made), use, (manner of) work ([-man], -manship).

A feminine singular noun meaning work, occupation, business, something made, property, workmanship. This word is used for God's creative work (Ge 2:2, 3); as well as for human labour (Ex 20:9, 10); skilled craftsmanship (Le 13:48); and agricultural tasks (1Ch 27:26). It is used for livestock (Ge 33:14); property (Ex 22:8[7]); public and religious business. For instance, Ezr 10:13 employs the term in reference to the divorce of foreign wives.

4400. מַלְאָכוּת**, malʼâkûwth,** *mal-awk-ooth´*; from the same as 4397; a *message*:—message.

A feminine noun meaning message. This word is used only once in the OT, where it described Haggai's message from the Lord (Hag 1:13). This word is related to the common noun *malʼâk* (4397), meaning messenger, which is also used in Hag 1:13.

4401. מַלְאָכִי**, Malʼâkîy,** *mal-aw-kee´*; from the same as 4397; *ministrative; Malaki*, a prophet:—Malachi.

4402. מִלֵּאת**, millêʼth,** *mil-layth´*; from 4390; *fulness*, i.e. (concrete) a *plump* socket (of the eye):— × fitly.

4403. מַלְבּוּשׁ**, malbûwsh,** *mal-boosh´*; or מַלְבֻּשׁ, **malbush**, *mal-boosh´*; from 3847; a *garment*, or (collective) *clothing*:—apparel, raiment, vestment.

4404. מַלְבֵּן**, malbên,** *mal-bane´*; from 3835 (denominative); a *brick-kiln*:—brick kiln.

4405. מִלָּה**, millâh,** *mil-law´*; from 4448 (plural masculine as if from מִלֶּה, **milleh**, *mil-leh´*); a *word*; (collective) a *discourse*; (figurative) a *topic*:— + answer, byword, matter, any thing (what) to say, to speak (-ing), speak, talking, word.

A feminine singular noun meaning word, speech, utterance. It is the poetic equivalent of *dâbâr* (1697), carrying the same range of meaning (2Sa 23:2; Ps 19:4[5]; 139:4; Pr 23:9). Of its thirty-eight uses in the Hebrew portion of the OT, Job contains thirty-four (see concordance for references).

4406. מִלָּה**, millâh,** *mil-law´*; (Chaldee); corresponding to 4405; a *word, command, discourse*, or *subject*:—commandment, matter, thing, word.

An Aramaic feminine noun meaning word, command, matter. This word, used only in Daniel, is equivalent to the Hebrew word *millâh* (4405), meaning word or speech, and comes from the Hebrew verb *mâlal* (4448), meaning to speak or say. This word is used to describe words that were spoken (Da 4:31[28]; 7:11, 25), which, depending on the context, can be translated as command (Da 2:5; 3:22; 5:10). Often this word described an entire series of circumstances or matters (Da 2:9–11; 4:33[30]; 7:1).

4407. מִלּוֹא**, millôwʼ,** *mil-lo´*; or מִלֹּא, **millôʼ**, *mil-lo´*; (2Ki 12:20), from 4390; a *rampart* (as *filled* in), i.e. the *citadel*:—Millo. See also 1037.

4408. מַלּוּחַ**, mallûwach,** *mal-loo´-akh*; from 4414; *sea-purslain* (from its *saltness*):—mallows.

4409. מַלּוּךְ**, Mallûwk,** *mal-luke*; or מַלּוּכִי, **Malûw-kîy**, *mal-loo-kee´*; (Ne 12:14), from 4427; *regnant; Malluk*, the name of five Israelites:—Malluch, Melichu [*from the margin*].

4410. מְלוּכָה**, mᵉlûwkâh,** *mel-oo-kaw´*; feminine passive participle of 4427; something *ruled*, i.e. a *realm*:—kingdom, king's, × royal.

4411. מָלוֹן**, mâlôwn,** *maw-lone´*; from 3885; a *lodgment*, i.e. *caravanserai* or *encampment*:—inn, place where … lodge, lodging (place).

4412. מְלוּנָה**, mᵉlûwnâh,** *mel-oo-naw´*; feminine from 3885; a *hut*, a *hammock*:—cottage, lodge.

4413. מַלּוֹתִי**, Mallôwthîy,** *mal-lo´-thee*; apparently from 4448; *I have talked* (i.e. *loquacious*):—*Mallothi*, an Israelite:—Mallothi.

4414. מָלַח**, mâlach,** *maw-lakh´*; a primitive root; (properly) to *rub* to pieces or pulverize; (intransitive) to *disappear* as dust; also (as denominative from 4417) to *salt* whether internal (to *season* with salt) or external (to *rub* with salt):— × at all, salt, season, temper together, vanish away.

4415. מְלַח**, mᵉlach,** *mel-akh´*; (Chaldee); corresponding to 4414; to *eat* salt, i.e. (general) *subsist*:— + have maintenance.

4416. מְלַח, m^e^lach, *mel-akh´*; (Chaldee); from 4415; *salt*:—+ maintenance, salt.

4417. מֶלַח, melach, *meh´-lakh*; from 4414; (properly) *powder*, i.e. (specific) *salt* (as easily pulverized and dissolved):—salt ([-pit]).

4418. מֶלָח, melâch, *meh-lakh´*; from 4414 in its original sense; a *rag* or old garment:—rotten rag.

4419. מַלָּח, mallâch, *mal-lawkh´*; from 4414 in its secondary sense; a *sailor* (as following "the salt"):—mariner.

4420. מְלֵחָה, m^e^lêchâh, *mel-ay-khaw´*; from 4414 (in its denominative sense); (properly) *salted* (i.e. land [776 being understood]), i.e. a *desert*:—barren land (-ness), salt [land].

4421. מִלְחָמָה, milchâmâh, *mil-khaw-maw´*; from 3898 (in the sense of *fighting*); a *battle* (i.e. the *engagement*); generally *war* (i.e. *warfare*):—battle, fight, (-ing), war ([-rior]).

4422. מָלַט, mâlaṭ, *maw-lat´*; a primitive root; (properly) to *be smooth*, i.e. (by implication) to *escape* (as if by *slipperiness*); (causative) to *release* or *rescue*; (specifically) to *bring forth* young, *emit* sparks:—deliver (self), escape, lay, leap out, let alone, let go, preserve, save, × speedily, × surely.

A verb meaning to escape. The picture of escape is as sparks leaping out of the fire (Job 41:19[11]); or like a bird escaping the fowlers (Ps 124:7). This word is usually used within the context of fleeing for one's life as Lot was urged to do (Ge 19:17, 19, 20, 22); as David did from the hands of Saul (1Sa 19:10–12; 27:1); or as Zedekiah could not do when facing the Chaldeans (Jer 32:4; 34:3). It is also used to describe rescue from death (Est 4:13; Ps 89:48[49]; Am 2:14, 15); calamity (Job 1:15–17, 19); or punishment (Pr 11:21; 19:5; 28:26). In a few instances, the word is used to describe protection (Ecc 9:15; Isa 31:5); in one instance, it means to give birth to a child (Isa 66:7).

4423. מֶלֶט, meleṭ, *meh´-let*; from 4422, *cement* (from its plastic *smoothness*):—clay.

4424. מְלַטְיָה, M^e^laṭyâh, *mel-at-yaw´*; from 4423 and 3050; (whom) *Jah has delivered; Melatjah*, a Gibeonite:—Melatiah.

4425. מְלִילָה, m^e^lîylâh, *mel-ee-law´*; from 4449 (in the sense of *cropping* [compare 4135]; a *head* of grain (as *cut* off):—ear.

4426. מְלִיצָה, m^e^lîytsâh, *mel-ee-tsaw´*; from 3887; an *aphorism*; also a *satire*:—interpretation, taunting.

4427. מָלַךְ, mâlak, *maw-lak´*; a primitive root; to *reign*; (inceptive) to *ascend the throne*; (causative) to *induct* into royalty; hence (by implication) to *take counsel*:—consult, × indeed, be (make, set a, set up) king, be (make) queen, (begin to, make to) reign (-ing), rule, × surely.

A verb meaning to rule, to be king, to make king. The verb is used approximately three hundred times in its simple form to mean to rule, to be king, to have sway, power, and dominion over people and nations. God is King and will rule over the whole earth in the day when He judges the earth and establishes Mount Zion (Isa 24:23). Israel rejected God from ruling over them during the time of Samuel (1Sa 8:7; cf. Eze 20:33); the verb is used to proclaim the rulership of a king when he is installed, as when Adonijah prematurely attempted to usurp the throne of his father David (1Ki 1:11). The Lord reigns as the Lord Almighty over both earthly and divine subjects (Isa 24:23; Mic 4:7).

The verb also describes the rulership of human kings—the establishment of rulership and the process itself (Ge 36:31; Jgs 9:8; Pr 30:22). It describes the rule of Athaliah the queen over Judah for six years (2Ki 11:3). In the causative form, it depicts the installation of a king. It describes God's establishment of Saul as the first king over Israel (1Sa 15:35). Hos 8:4 indicates that the Israelites had set up kings without the Lord's approval.

4428. מֶלֶךְ, melek, *meh´-lek*; from 4427; a *king*:—king, royal.

A masculine noun meaning king. The feminine form is *malkâh* (4436), meaning queen, though the concept is more of a king's consort than a monarchical ruler. The word *melek* appears over 2,500 times in the OT. In many biblical contexts, this term is simply a general term, denoting an individual with power and authority. It is parallel with and conceptually related to a number of other Hebrew words that are usually translated as lord, captain, prince, chief, or ruler. It is used in reference to men and often with a genitive of people or place (Ge 14:1; Ex 1:15; 2Sa 2:4); the Lord who demonstrates His power and authority over Israel (Isa 41:21; 44:6); and over each individual (Ps 5:2[3]; 44:4[5]). In pagan worship, the worshippers of idols attribute this term with its connotations to their idols (Isa 8:21; Am 5:26).

4429. מֶלֶךְ, Melek, *meh´-lek*; the same as 4428; *king; Melek*, the name of two Israelites:—Melech, Hammelech [*by including the article*].

4430. מֶלֶךְ, melek, *meh´-lek*; (Chaldee); corresponding to 4428; a *king*:—king, royal.

An Aramaic masculine noun meaning king. This very common word is equivalent to the Hebrew word *melek* (4428), meaning king. It is used to speak of the top government official. It is used to speak of the following kings: Artaxerxes (Ezr 4:8 ff.); Darius (Ezr 5:6ff; Da 6:2[3] ff.); Cyrus (Ezr 5:13 ff.); Nebuchadnezzar (Da 2:4 ff.); Belshazzar (Da 5:1 ff.); kings that will arise on the earth (Da 7:17, 24).

4431. מְלַךְ, m^e^lak, *mel-ak´*; (Chaldee); from a root corresponding to 4427 in the sense of *consultation; advice*:—counsel.

4432. מֹלֶךְ, Môlek, *mo´-lek*; from 4427; *Molek* (i.e. king), the chief deity of the Ammonites:—Molech. Compare 4445.

4433. מַלְכָּה, malkâh, *mal-kaw´*; (Chaldee); corresponding to 4436; a *queen*:—queen.

An Aramaic feminine noun meaning queen. This word, equivalent to the Hebrew word *malkâh* (4436), is used twice in Da 5:10. It designated the proper title of the wife of the king. Scholars disagree as to whether she was the wife or the mother of the last king of the neo-Babylonian Empire, Belshazzar.

4434. מַלְכֹּדֶת, malkôdeth, *mal-ko´-deth*; from 3920; a *snare*:—trap.

A feminine noun meaning a trap, a snare, a noose. This word is found only in Job 18:10. In his disputation with Job, Bildad the Shuhite used the word to describe the pitfalls that lay before the wicked.

4435. מִלְכָּה, Milkâh, *mil-kaw´*; a form of 4436; *queen; Milcah*, the name of a Hebrewess and of an Israelite:—Milcah.

4436. מַלְכָּה, malkâh, *mal-kaw´*; feminine of 4428; a *queen*:—queen.

A feminine noun meaning queen. The noun means queen exclusively, but the queen stands in several possible social positions. The queen is often merely the wife of the king; she was, for example, subordinate to the king, and was expected to do his bidding (Est 1:11, 12, 16, 17). She also had much court authority herself (Est 1:9). The only time the word is used to apply to Israelite women is in the plural, and they were part of Solomon's harem (SS 6:8, 9).

The term means queen without stressing the spousal relationship to the king, but it is not used in this way of any Israelite woman in the time of the monarchy. The queen of Sheba, from southwest Arabia, was a powerful monarch in her own right, traveled extensively (1Ki 10:1, 10), and was considered a wise woman and ruler (2Ch 9:1). Esther became queen in Persia because of her beauty but won over the king by gaining his approval and favour (see Est 2:17, 18).

4437. מַלְכוּ, malkûw, *mal-koo´*; (Chaldee); corresponding to 4438; *dominion* (abstract or concrete):—kingdom, kingly, realm, reign.

An Aramaic feminine noun meaning royalty, reign, kingdom, kingly authority. This word, corresponding to the word *malkûth* (4438), distinguishes the propriety of royalty from all else (e.g., Da 5:20). It is used to denote the reign of a particular sovereign (Da 6:28[29]); the extent of a king's authority (Ezr 7:13); the territorial or administrative dominion of a monarch (Da 6:3[4]); the nation or kingdom in a general sense (Da 5:31[6:1]).

4438. מַלְכוּת, malkûwth, *mal-kooth´*; or מַלְכֻת, **malkuth,** *mal-kooth´*; or (in plural) מַלְכֻיָּה, **mal-kuyyâh,** *mal-koo-yaw´*; from

4427; a *rule*; (concrete) a *dominion*:—empire, kingdom, realm, reign, royal.

A feminine noun meaning royalty, reign, dominion, kingdom. This term chiefly describes that which pertains to royalty or the natural outflow of power from the royal station. The book of Esther especially illustrates how this word is used to distinguish the royal from the ordinary, speaking of royal wine (Est 1:7); a royal command (Est 1:19); and royal clothing (Est 5:1). It is specifically used to signify the reign of a monarch (2Ch 15:10; Da 1:1); and the kingdom or territorial realm under the authority of a particular sovereign (1Ch 12:23 [24]; 2Ch 11:17; Da 10:13).

4439. מַלְכִּיאֵל, **Malkîy'êl,** *mal-kee-ale´*; from 4428 and 410; *king of* (i.e. appointed by) *God; Malkiël*, an Israelite:—Malchiel.

4440. מַלְכִּיאֵלִי, **Malkîy'êlîy,** *mal-kee-ay-lee´*; patronymic from 4439; a *Malkiëlite* or descendant of Malkiel:—Malchielite.

4441. מַלְכִּיָּה, **Malkîyyâh,** *mal-kee-yaw´*; or מַלְכִּיָּהוּ, **Malkiyâhûw,** *mal-kee-yaw´-hoo*; (Jer 38:6), from 4428 and 3050; *king of* (i.e. appointed by) *Jah; Malkijah*, the name of ten Israelites:—Malchiah, Malchijah.

4442. מַלְכִּי־צֶדֶק, **Malkîy-Tsedeq,** *mal-kee-tseh´-dek*; from 4428 and 6664; *king of right; Malki-Tsedek*, an early king in Palestine:—Melchizedek.

4443. מַלְכִּירָם, **Malkîyrâm,** *mal-kee-rawm´*; from 4428 and 7311; *king of a high* one (i.e. of exaltation); *Malkiram*, an Israelite:—Malchiram.

4444. מַלְכִּישׁוּעַ, **Malkîyshûwa',** *mal-kee-shoo´-ah*; from 4428 and 7769; *king of wealth; Malkishua*, an Israelite:—Malchishua.

4445. מַלְכָּם, **Malkâm,** *mal-kawm´*; or מִלְכֹּם, **Mil-kôm,** *mil-kome´*; from 4428 for 4432; *Malcam* or *Milcom*, the national idol of the Ammonites:—Malcham, Milcom.

4446. מְלֶכֶת, **m^{e}leketh,** *mel-eh´-keth*; from 4427; a *queen*:—queen.

A feminine noun meaning queen. Rather than being just another term for a female regent, this word's significance is found in the chronicle of Judah's idolatry. It is used solely to designate a fertility goddess worshipped in Jeremiah's day, the queen of the heavens (*mĕleketh hashshâmayim* [8064]). Although the references are cryptic, it is believed that this queen of the heavens was either the goddess Ashtoreth, symbolized by the moon, or Astarte, symbolized by the planet Venus. Women baked cakes to offer to this goddess (Jer 7:18) and burned incense (Jer 44:17–19) in hopes of securing the blessings of fertility. However, the judgment of the Lord on this practice made it counterproductive (cf. Jer 44:25ff.).

4447. מֹלֶכֶת, **Môleketh,** *mo-leh´-keth*; feminine active participle of 4427; *queen; Moleketh*, an Israelitess:—Hammoleketh [*including the article*].

4448. מָלַל, **mâlal,** *maw-lal´*; a primitive root; to *speak* (mostly poetical) or *say*:—say, speak, utter.

A verb meaning to speak, to say, to declare, to utter. Except for an occurance found in Pr 6:13 (a wicked man "speaks"[that is, gives a sign] with his feet), the verb is utilized mostly with the intensive stem. Sarah said, "Who would have said to Abraham that Sarah would nurse children?" (Ge 21:7). Elihu stated that his lips would utter upright knowledge to Job (Job 33:3; cf. Job 8:2). The psalmist exclaimed that no one can declare the mighty acts of God (Ps 106:2). The term compares closely in meaning with the Hebrew verb *dâbar* (1696).

4449. מְלַל, **m^{e}lal,** *mel-al´*; (Chaldee); corresponding to 4448; to *speak*:—say, speak (-ing).

An Aramaic verb meaning to speak. All undisputed instances of this term occur in the Aramaic sections of the book of Daniel. In Daniel's vision of the four beasts, the fourth beast had a little horn upon which was a mouth speaking arrogantly (Da 7:8, 11, 20). This horn (symbolic of a king) spoke words against the Most High (Da 7:25). This term is closely related to the Hebrew verb *mâlal* (4448).

4450. מִלֲלַי, **Milălay,** *mee-lal-ah´ee*; from 4448; *talkative; Milalai*, an Israelite:—Milalai.

4451. מַלְמָד, **malmâd,** *mal-mawd´*; from 3925; a *goad* for oxen:—goad.

4452. מָלַץ, **mâlats,** *maw-lats´*; a primitive root; to *be smooth*, i.e. (figurative) *pleasant*:—be sweet.

4453. מֶלְצַר, **meltsâr,** *mel-tsawr´*; of Persian derivation; the *butler* or other officer in the Babylonian court:—Melzar.

4454. מָלַק, **mâlaq,** *maw-lak´*; a primitive root; to *crack* a joint; (by implication) to *wring* the neck of a fowl (without separating it):—wring off.

4455. מַלְקוֹחַ, **malqôwach,** *mal-ko´-akh*; from 3947; transposed (in dual) the *jaws* (as taking food); (intransitive) *spoil* [and captives] (as taken):—booty, jaws, prey.

4456. מַלְקוֹשׁ, **malqôwsh,** *mal-koshe´*; from 3953; the spring *rain* (compare 3954); (figurative) *eloquence*:—latter rain.

4457. מֶלְקָחַיִם, **melqâchayim,** *mel-kaw-kha-yim´*; from 3947; (only in dual) *tweezers*:—snuffers, tongs.

4458. מֶלְתָּחָה, **meltâchâh,** *mel-taw-khaw´*; from an unused root meaning to *spread* out; a *wardrobe* (i.e. room where clothing is *spread*):—vestry.

4459. מַלְתָּעוֹת, **maltâ'ôwth,** *mal-taw-oth´*; transposed for 4973; a *grinder*, i.e. back *tooth*:—great tooth.

4460. מַמְּגֻרָה, **mamm^{e}gûwrâh,** *mam-meg-oo-raw´*; from 4048 (in the sense of *depositing*); a *granary*:—barn.

4461. מֵמַד, **mêmad,** *may-mad´*; from 4058; a *measure*:—measure.

4462. מְמוּכָן, **M^{e}mûwkân,** *mem-oo-kawn´*; or (transposed) מוֹמֻכָן, **Môwmukân,** *mo-moo-kawn´*; (Est 1:16), of Persian derivation; *Memucan* or *Momucan*, a Persian satrap:—Memucan.

4463. מָמוֹת, **mâmôwth,** *maw-mothe´*; from 4191; a mortal *disease*; (concrete) a *corpse*:—death.

4464. מַמְזֵר, **mamzêr,** *mam-zare´*; from an unused root meaning to *alienate*; a *mongrel*, i.e. born of a Jewish father and a heathen mother:—bastard.

4465. מִמְכָּר, **mimkâr,** *mim-kawr´*; from 4376; *merchandise*; (abstract) a *selling*:—× ought, (that which cometh of) sale, that which … sold, ware.

4466. מִמְכֶּרֶת, **mimkereth,** *mim-keh´-reth*; feminine of 4465; a *sale*:— + sold as.

4467. מַמְלָכָה, **mamlâkâh,** *mam-law-kaw´*; from 4427; *dominion*, i.e. (abstract) the estate (*rule*) or (concrete) the country (*realm*):—kingdom, king's, reign, royal.

A feminine noun meaning kingdom. Often the term refers to the royal power an individual in sovereign authority possesses. Because Solomon did not keep the Lord's covenant and commandments, his kingdom (that is, his power to rule) was torn from his son (1Ki 11:11; cf. 1Sa 28:17; 1Ki 14:8). In many other places, however, the word is utilized concretely to denote a people under a king (that is, a realm). The kingdom (or realm) of King Sihon of the Amorites and the kingdom (realm) of King Og of Bashan were given to the Gadites, Reubenites, and the half-tribe of Manasseh (Nu 32:33; cf. Ex 19:6; Dt 28:25; 1Sa 24:20[21]). In some passages, the word functions as an adjective, meaning royal (e.g., city of the kingdom = royal city; Jos 10:2; 1Sa 27:5; cf. 2Ki 11:1; 2Ch 23:20; Am 7:13). This noun derives from the verb *mâlak* (4427), as does its synonym, *malkûth* (4438).

4468. מַמְלָכוּת, **mamlâkûwth,** *mam-law-kooth´*; a form of 4467 and equivalent to it:—kingdom, reign.

A feminine noun meaning kingdom, royal power. It is equivalent in meaning with the term *mamlâkâh* (4467) and occurs only in the construct form. Samuel told Saul that the Lord had torn the kingdom of Israel from him and given it to another better than he (1Sa 15:28).

The Lord declared to Hosea that He was going to put an end to the kingdom of Israel (Hos 1:4; cf. Jos 13:12; 2Sa 16:3; Jer 26:1). This noun is derived from the verb *mâlak* (4427).

4469. מִמְסָךְ, mimsâk, *mim-sawk´*; from 4537; *mixture*, i.e. (specific) wine *mixed* (with water or spices):—drink-offering, mixed wine.

4470. מֶמֶר, memer, *meh´-mer*; from an unused root meaning to *grieve; sorrow*:—bitterness.

4471. מַמְרֵא, Mamrê', *mam-ray´*; from 4754 (in the sense of *vigour*); *lusty; Mamre*, an Amorite:—Mamre.

4472. מַמְרֹר, mamrôr, *mam-rore´*; from 4843; a *bitterness*, i.e. (figurative) calamity:—bitterness.

4473. מִמְשַׁח, mimshach, *mim-shakh´*; from 4886, in the sense of *expansion; outspread* (i.e. with outstretched wings):—anointed.

A masculine noun possibly meaning expansion, extension. The word occurs only in Eze 28:14 and would, with this meaning, read "cherub of extension" (that is, a cherub with wings outstretched). However, this definition is now seriously questioned, largely because the term derives from the verb *mâshach* (4886), meaning to anoint. The term more likely expresses the sense of anointment or anointing. Taking the word this way, the phrase conveys the more satisfying expression "cherub of anointing," that is, the anointed cherub.

4474. מִמְשָׁל, mimshâl, *mim-shawl´*; from 4910; a *ruler* or (abstract) *rule*:—dominion, that ruled.

A masculine noun meaning dominion, sovereign authority, ruling power. One in human form spoke with Daniel, telling him about a warrior king and an officer who would soon rule their respective kingdoms with great authority (Da 11:3, 5). In 1Ch 26:6, the word describes the sons of Shemaiah as those who exercised ruling authority in their ancestral homes because of their great capabilities. The term stems from the verb *mâshal* (4910).

4475. מֶמְשָׁלָה, memshâlâh, *mem-shaw-law´*; feminine of 4474; *rule*; also (concrete in plural) a *realm* or a *ruler*:—dominion, government, power, to rule.

A feminine noun meaning dominion, rule, authority, province, realm. Often this term denotes the ruling power which one in authority exercises over his domain or kingdom. God made the sun to have authority over the day and the moon to have authority over the night (Ge 1:16; Ps 136:8). The Lord sent the prophet Isaiah to announce to Shebna that He was going to forcibly remove him from office and give his authority to Eliakim instead (Isa 22:21). In other places, the word refers to the territory over which one rules or governs. Hezekiah showed his whole realm to the king of Babylon's messengers (2Ki 20:13; cf. Ps 103:22; 114:2). Once it refers collectively to an envoy of powerful ambassadors, such as rulers, princes, or chief officers (2Ch 32:9). This term is derived from the verb *mâshal* (4910; see also the related word *mimshâl* [4474]).

4476. מִמְשָׁק, mimshâq, *mim-shawk´*; from the same as 4943; a *possession*:—breeding.

4477. מַמְתַקִּים, mamtaqqîym, *mam-tak-keem´*; from 4985; something *sweet* (literal or figurative):—(most) sweet.

4478. מָן, man, *man*; from 4100; (literal) a *whatness* (so to speak), i.e. *manna* (so called from the question about it):—manna.

A masculine noun meaning manna, who, or what. This is the reaction that the Israelites had to the substance that the Lord gave them to eat (Ex 16:15). They asked "What is it?" which translates into *mân*. This substance is described as wafers made with honey and like white coriander seeds in shape (Ex 16:31). The manna could be ground into grain and cooked into cakes (see Nu 11:7, 8). When the Israelites entered the Promised Land, God caused the manna to cease (Jos 5:12).

4479. מָן, man, *man*; (Chaldee); from 4101; *who* or *what* (properly interrogative, hence also indefinite and relative):—what, who (-msoever, + -so).

4480. מִן, min, *min*; or מִנִּי, **minnîy,** *min-nee´*; or מִנֵּי, **minnêy,** *min-nay´*; (constructive plural); (Isa 30:11), for 4482; (properly) a *part* of; hence (prepositional), *from* or *out of* in many senses (as follows):—above, after, among, at, because of, by (reason of), from (among), in, × neither, × nor, (out) of, over, since, × then, through, × whether, with.

4481. מִן, min, *min*; (Chaldee); corresponding to 4480:—according, after, + because, + before, by, for, from, × him, × more than, (out) of, part, since, × these, to, upon, + when.

4482. מֵן, mên, *mane*; from an unused root meaning to *apportion*; a *part*; hence a musical *chord* (as parted into strings):—in [the same] (Ps 68:23), stringed instrument (Ps 150:4), whereby (Ps 45:8 *[defective plural]*).

4483. מְנָא, m^enâ', *men-aw´*; (Chaldee); or מְנָה, **m^enâh,** *men-aw´*; (Chaldee); corresponding to 4487; to *count, appoint*:—number, ordain, set.

4484. מְנֵא, m^enê', *men-ay´*; (Chaldee); passive participle of 4483; *numbered*:—Mene.

4485. מַנְגִּינָה, mangîynâh, *man-ghee-naw´*; from 5059; a *satire*:—music.

4486. מַנְדַּע, manda', *man-dah´*; (Chaldee); corresponding to 4093; *wisdom* or *intelligence*:—knowledge, reason, understanding.

An Aramaic masculine noun meaning knowledge, reason, intelligence, power of knowing. This word is found only in Daniel. When King Nebuchadnezzar was turned into an animal, he was said to have lost his reason and understanding. Upon his restoration to his human body, his mind was also restored (Da 4:36[33]). Daniel himself was described as a man of understanding and knowledge with an excellent spirit (Da 5:12).

4487. מָנָה, mânâh, *maw-naw´*; a primitive root; (properly) to *weigh* out; (by implication) to *allot* or constitute officially; also to *enumerate* or enroll:—appoint, count, number, prepare, set, tell.

4488. מָנֶה, mâneh, *maw-neh´*; from 4487; (properly) a fixed *weight* or measured amount, i.e. (technical) a *maneh* or mina:—maneh, pound.

4489. מֹנֶה, môneh, *mo-neh´*; from 4487; (properly) something *weighed* out, i.e. (figurative) a *portion* of time, i.e. an *instance*:—time.

4490. מָנָה, mânâh, *maw-naw´*; from 4487; (properly) something *weighed* out, i.e. (general) a *division*; specifically (of food) a *ration*; also a *lot*:—such things as belonged, part, portion.

4491. מִנְהָג, minhâg, *min-hawg´*; from 5090; the *driving* (of a chariot):—driving.

4492. מִנְהָרָה, minhârâh, *min-haw-raw´*; from 5102; (properly) a *channel* or fissure, i.e. (by implication) a *cavern*:—den.

4493. מָנוֹד, mânôwd, *maw-node´*; from 5110; a *nodding* or *toss* (of the head in derision):—shaking.

4494. מָנוֹחַ, mânôwach, *maw-no´-akh*; from 5117; *quiet*, i.e. (concrete) a *settled spot*, or (figurative) a *home*:—(place of) rest.

4495. מָנוֹחַ, Mânôwach, *maw-no´-akh*; the same as 4494; *rest; Manoäch*, an Israelite:—Manoah.

4496. מְנוּחָה, m^enûwchâh, *men-oo-khaw´*; or מְנֻחָה, **m^enuchâh,** *men-oo-khaw´*; feminine of 4495; *repose* or (adverb) *peacefully*; (figurative) *consolation* (specifically) *matrimony*; hence (concrete) an *abode*:—comfortable, ease, quiet, rest (-ing place), still.

4497. מָנוֹן, mânôwn, *maw-nohn´*; from 5125; a *continuator*, i.e. *heir*:—son.

4498. **מָנוֹס, mânôws,** *maw-noce´*; from 5127; a *retreat* (literal or figurative); (abstract) a *fleeing*:— × apace, escape, way to flee, flight, refuge.

4499. **מְנוּסָה, m^e^nûwsâh,** *men-oo-saw´*; or **מְנֻסָה, m^e^nusâh,** *men-oo-saw´*; feminine of 4498; *retreat*:—fleeing, flight.

4500. **מָנוֹר, mânôwr,** *maw-nore´*; from 5214; a *yoke* (properly, for *ploughing*), i.e. the *frame* of a loom:—beam.

4501. **מְנוֹרָה, m^e^nôwrâh,** *men-o-raw´*; or **מְנֹרָה, m^e^nôrâh,** *men-o-raw´*; feminine of 4500 (in the original sense of 5216); a *chandelier*:—candlestick.

4502. **מִנְּזָר, minn^e^zâr,** *min-ez-awr´*; from 5144; a *prince*:—crowned.

4503. **מִנְחָה, minchâh,** *min-khaw´*; from an unused root meaning to *apportion*, i.e. *bestow*; a *donation*; (euphemism) *tribute*; specifically a sacrificial *offering* (usually bloodless and voluntary):—gift, oblation, (meat) offering, present, sacrifice.

A feminine noun meaning a gift, a tribute, an offering. This word is used to signify a gift as in the peace gifts that Jacob presented to Esau (Ge 32:13[14]). Secondly, it signifies a tribute. An example of the use of this word is Jgs 3:15, where Ehud was sent from Israel to Moab on the pretense of bringing a tribute. Perhaps the most frequent use of this word is to denote a grain offering. Grain offerings were brought on pans, suggesting cakes (Le 2:5) and mixed with oil and other substances (Nu 6:15).

4504. **מִנְחָה, minchâh,** *min-khaw´*; (Chaldee); corresponding to 4503; a sacrificial *offering*:—oblation, meat offering.

An Aramaic feminine noun meaning a gift, a sacrificial offering, an oblation, a meat offering. When Daniel was promoted to chief administrator of Babylon, the celebration included the presentation of an offering signified by this Aramaic word (Da 2:46). King Artaxerxes also used this Aramaic word to command Ezra to offer sacrificial gifts on the altar of God when he arrived in Jerusalem (Ezr 7:17). This word corresponds directly to *minchâh* (4503).

4505. **מְנַחֵם, M^e^nachêm,** *men-akh-ame´*; from 5162; *comforter; Menachem*, an Israelite:—Menahem.

4506. **מָנַחַת, Mânachath,** *maw-nakh´-ath*; from 5117; *rest; Manachath*, the name of an Edomite and of a place in Moab:—Manahath.

4507. **מְנִי, M^e^nîy,** *men-ee´*; from 4487; the *Appor-tioner*, i.e. Fate (as an idol):—number.

4508. **מִנִּי, Minnîy,** *min-nee´*; of foreign derivation; *Minni*, an Armenian province:—Minni.

4509. **מִנְיָמִין, Minyâmîyn,** *min-yaw-meen´*; from 4480 and 3225; *from* (the) *right hand; Minjamin*, the name of two Israelites:—Miniamin. Compare 4326.

4510. **מִנְיָן, minyân,** *min-yawn´*; (Chaldee); from 4483; *enumeration*:—number.

4511. **מִנִּית, Minnîyth,** *min-neeth´*; from the same as 4482; *enumeration; Minnith*, a place East of the Jordan:—Minnith.

4512. **מִנְלֶה, minleh,** *min-leh´*; from 5239; *completion*, i.e. (in produce) *wealth*:—perfection.

4513. **מָנַע, mâna‛,** *maw-nah´*; a primitive root; to *debar* (negative or positive) from benefit or injury:—deny, keep (back), refrain, restrain, withhold.

4514. **מַנְעוּל, man‛ûwl,** *man-ool´*; or **מַנְעֻל, man‛ul,** *man-ool´*; from 5274; a *bolt*:—lock.

4515. **מִנְעָל, min‛âl,** *min-awl´*; from 5274; a *bolt*:—shoe.

4516. **מַנְעַמִּים, man‛ammîym,** *man-am-meem´*; from 5276; a *delicacy*:—dainty.

4517. **מְנַעַנְעִים, m^e^na‛an‛îym,** *men-ah-ah-neem´*; from 5128; a *sistrum* (so called from its *rattling* sound):—cornet.

4518. **מְנַקִּית, m^e^naqqîyth,** *men-ak-keeth´*; from 5352; a *sacrificial basin* (for holding blood):—bowl.

4519. **מְנַשֶּׁה, M^e^nashsheh,** *men-ash-sheh´*; from 5382; *causing to forget; Menashsheh*, a grandson of Jacob, also the tribe descendant from him, and its territory:—Manasseh.

4520. **מְנַשִּׁי, M^e^nashshîy,** *men-ash-shee´*; from 4519; a *Menashshite* or descendant of Menashsheh:—of Manasseh, Manassites.

4521. **מְנָת, m^e^nâth,** *men-awth´*; from 4487; an *allotment* (by courtesy, law or providence):—portion.

4522. **מַס, mas,** *mas*; or **מִס, mis,** *mees*; from 4549; (properly) a *burden* (as causing to *faint*), i.e. a *tax* in the form of forced *labour*:—discomfited, levy, task [-master], tribute (-tary).

4523. **מָס, mâs,** *mawce*; from 4549; *fainting*, i.e. (figurative) *disconsolate*:—is afflicted.

4524. **מֵסַב, mêsab,** *may-sab´*; plural masculine **מְסִבִּים, mesibbîym,** *mes-ib-beem´*; or feminine **מְסִבּוֹת, mesibbôwth,** *mes-ib-bohth´*; from 5437; a *divan* (as *enclosing* the room); abstract (adverb) *around*:—that compass about, (place) round about, at table.

4525. **מַסְגֵּר, masgêr,** *mas-gare´*; from 5462; a *fastener*, i.e. (of a person) a *smith*, (of a thing) a *prison*:—prison, smith.

4526. **מִסְגֶּרֶת, misgereth,** *mis-gheh´-reth*; from 5462; something *enclosing*, i.e. a *margin* (of a region, of a panel); (concrete) a *stronghold*:—border, close place, hole.

4527. **מַסַּד, massad,** *mas-sad´*; from 3245; a *foundation*:—foundation.

4528. **מִסְדְּרוֹן, misd^e^rôwn,** *mis-der-ohn´*; from the same as 5468; a *colonnade* or internal portico (from its *rows* of pillars):—porch.

4529. **מָסָה, mâsâh,** *maw-saw´*; a primitive root; to *dissolve*:—make to consume away, (make to) melt, water.

4530. **מִסָּה, missâh,** *mis-saw´*; from 4549 (in the sense of *flowing*); *abundance*, i.e. (adverb) *liberally*:—tribute.

4531. **מַסָּה, massâh,** *mas-saw´*; from 5254; a *testing*, of men (judicial) or of God (querulous):—temptation, trial.

A feminine noun meaning despair, a test, a trial, proving. The Hebrew word is actually two homographs—words that are spelled the same yet have distinct origins and meanings. The first homograph is derived from the verb *mâsas* (4549), meaning to dissolve or melt, and it means despair. This word occurs only in Job 9:23. The second homograph is derived from the verb *nâsâh* (5254), meaning to test or try, and denotes a test, a trial, or proving. It is used in reference to the manifestations of God's power and handiwork before the Egyptians at the Exodus (Dt 4:34; 7:19; 29:3[2]. Furthermore, this term has become a proper noun, *massâh* (4532), to designate the place where the Israelites tested God (Ex 17:7; Dt 6:16; 9:22; Ps 95:8); and where Levi was tested (Dt 33:8).

4532. **מַסָּה, Massâh,** *mas-saw´*; the same as 4531; *Massah*, a place in the Desert:—Massah.

4533. **מַסְוֶה, masveh,** *mas-veh´*; apparently from an unused root meaning to *cover*; a *veil*:—vail.

4534. **מְסוּכָה, m^e^sûwkâh,** *mes-oo-kaw´*; for 4881; a *hedge*:—thorn hedge.

4535. **מַסָּח, massâch,** *mas-sawkh´*; from 5255 in the sense of *staving* off; a *cordon*, (adverb) or (as a) military *barrier*:—broken down.

4536. **מִסְחָר, mischâr,** *mis-khawr´*; from 5503; *trade*:—traffic.

4537. **מָסַךְ, mâsak,** *maw-sak´*; a primitive root; to *mix*, especially wine (with spices):—mingle.

4538. **מֶסֶךְ, mesek,** *meh´-sek*; from 4537; a *mixture*, i.e. of wine with spices:—mixture.

4539. מָסָךְ, **mâsâk**, *maw-sawk*; from 5526; a *cover*, i.e. *veil*:—covering, curtain, hanging.

4540. מְסֻכָּה, **mᵉsukkâh**, *mes-ook-kaw´*; from 5526; a *covering*, i.e. garniture:—covering.

4541. מַסֵּכָה, **massêkâh**, *mas-say-kaw´*; from 5258; (properly) a *pouring* over, i.e. *fusion* of metal (especially a *cast* image); (by implication) a *libation*, i.e. league; (concrete) a *coverlet* (as if *poured* out):—covering, molten (image), vail.

A feminine noun meaning an image, molten metal, covering, an alliance. When the word means a libation or drink offering, it is associated with sacrifices that seal a covenant relationship (Isa 25:7; 28:20; 30:1); however, the word usually signifies an image or molten metal. In those cases, the word identifies an idol, which has been formed from molten metal and has been poured into a cast. The worship of such images is clearly prohibited by God (Ex 34:17; Le 19:4; Dt 27:15). The Israelites were commanded to destroy any idols they discovered in Canaan (Nu 33:52). The prophets proclaimed the futility of all idols, including those described as *massêkâh* (Isa 42:17); and God would punish those who worshipped them (Hos 13:2, 3; Na 1:14; Hab 2:18). In spite of all this, the Israelites formed and worshipped idols, including molten idols like Aaron's golden calf (Ex 32:4, 8; Dt 9:16; Ne 9:18); Micah's idols (Jgs 17:3, 4; 18:17, 18); and Jeroboam's idols (1Ki 14:9; cf. 1Ki 12:28–30).

4542. מִסְכֵּן, **miskên**, *mis-kane´*; from 5531; *indigent*:—poor (man).

4543. מִסְכְּנוֹת, **miskᵉnôwth**, *mis-ken-oth´*; by transposition from 3664; a *magazine*:—store (-house), treasure.

4544. מִסְכֵּנֻת, **miskênuth**, *mis-kay-nooth´*; from 4542; *indigence*:—scarceness.

4545. מַסֶּכֶת, **masseketh**, *mas-seh´-keth*; from 5259 in the sense of *spreading* out; something *expanded*, i.e. the *warp* in a loom (as *stretched* out to receive the woof):—web.

4546. מְסִלָּה, **mᵉsillâh**, *mes-il-law´*; from 5549; a *thoroughfare* (as *turnpiked*), literal or figurative; specifically a *viaduct*, a *staircase*:—causeway, course, highway, path, terrace.

4547. מַסְלוּל, **maslûwl**, *mas-lool´*; from 5549; a *thoroughfare* (as turnpiked):—highway.

4548. מַסְמֵר, **masmêr**, *mas-mare´*; or מִסְמֵר, **mismêr**, *mis-mare´*; also (feminine) מַסְמְרָה, **masmᵉrâh**, *mas-mer-aw´*; or מִסְמְרָה, **mismᵉrâh**, *mis-mer-aw´*; or even מַשְׂמְרָה **maśmᵉrâh**, *mas-mer-aw´*; (Ecc 12:11), from 5568; a *peg* (as *bristling* from the surface):—nail.

4549. מָסַס, **mâsas**, *maw-sas´*; a primitive root; to *liquefy*; (figurative) to *waste* (with disease), to *faint* (with fatigue, fear or grief):—discourage, faint, be loosed, melt (away), refuse, × utterly.

4550. מַסַּע, **massaʻ**, *mas-sah*; from 5265; a *departure* (from *striking* the tents), i.e. march (not necessarily a single day's travel); (by implication) a *station* (or point of *departure*):—journey (-ing).

4551. מַסָּע, **massâʻ**, *mas-saw´*; from 5265 in the sense of *projecting*; a *missile* (spear or arrow); also a *quarry* (whence stones are, as it were, *ejected*):—before it was brought, dart.

4552. מִסְעָד, **misʻâd**, *mis-awd´*; from 5582; a *balus-trade* (for stairs):—pillar.

4553. מִסְפֵּד, **mispêd**, *mis-pade´*; from 5594; a *lamentation*:—lamentation, one mourneth, mourning, wailing.

4554. מִסְפּוֹא, **mispôwʼ**, *mis-po´*; from an unused root meaning to *collect; fodder*:—provender.

4555. מִסְפָּחָה, **mispâchâh**, *mis-paw-khaw´*; from 5596; a *veil* (as *spread* out):—kerchief.

4556. מִסְפַּחַת, **mispachath**, *mis-pakh´-ath*; from 5596; *scurf* (as *spreading* over the surface):—scab.

4557. מִסְפָּר, **mispâr**, *mis-pawr´*; from 5608; a *number*, definite (arithmetical) or indefinite (large, *innumerable*; small, a *few*); also (abstract) *narration*:— + abundance, account, × all, × few, [in-] finite, (certain) number (-ed), tale, telling, + time.

4558. מִסְפָּר, **Mispâr**, *mis-pawr´*; the same as 4457; *number; Mispar*, an Israelite:—Mizpar. Compare 4559.

4559. מִסְפֶּרֶת, **Mispereth**, *mis-peh´-reth*; feminine of 4457; *enumeration; Mispereth*, an Israelite:—Mispereth. Compare 4458.

4560. מָסַר, **mâsar**, *maw-sar´*; a primitive root; to *sunder*, i.e. (transitive) *set apart*, or (reflexive) *apostatize*:—commit, deliver.

4561. מֹסָר, **môsâr**, *mo-sawr´*; from 3256; *admonition*:—instruction.

4562. מָסֹרֶת, **mâsôreth**, *maw-so´-reth*; from 631; a *band*:—bond.

4563. מִסְתּוֹר, **mistôwr**, *mis-tore´*; from 5641; a *refuge*:—covert.

4564. מַסְתֵּר, **mastêr**, *mas-tare´*; from 5641; (properly) a *hider*, i.e. (abstract) a hiding, i.e. *aversion*:—hid.

4565. מִסְתָּר, **mistâr**, *mis-tawr´*; from 5641; (properly) a *concealer*, i.e. a *covert*:—secret (-ly, place).

4566. מַעְבָּד, **maʻăbâd**, *mah-ah-bawd´*; from 5647; an *act*:—work.

4567. מַעְבָד, **maʻăbâd**, *mah-ah-bawd´*; (Chaldee); corresponding to 4566; an *act*:—work.

4568. מַעֲבֶה, **maʻăbeh**, *mah-ab-eh´*; from 5666; (properly) *compact* (part of soil), i.e. *loam*:—clay.

4569. מַעֲבָר, **maʻăbâr**, *mah-ab-awr´*; or feminine מַעְבָּרָה, **maʻbârâh**, *mah-baw-raw´*; from 5674; a *crossing*-place (of a river, a *ford*; of a mountain, a *pass*); (abstract) a *transit*, i.e. (figurative) *overwhelming*:—ford, place where … pass, passage.

4570. מַעְגָּל, **maʻgâl**, *mah-gawl´*; or feminine מַעְגָּלָה, **maʻgâlâh**, *mah-gaw-law´*; from the same as 5696; a *track* (literal or figurative); also a *rampart* (as *circular*):—going, path, trench, way ([-side]).

4571. מָעַד, **mâʻad**, *maw-ad´*; a primitive root; to *waver*:—make to shake, slide, slip.

4572. מַעֲדַי, **Maʻăday**, *mah-ad-ah´ee*; from 5710; *ornamental; Maadai*, an Israelite:—Maadai.

4573. מַעַדְיָה, **Maʻadyâh**, *mah-ad-yaw´*; from 5710 and 3050; *ornament of Jah; Maadjah*, an Israelite:—Maadiah. Compare 4153.

4574. מַעֲדָן, **maʻădân**, *mah-ad-awn´*; or (feminine) מַעֲדַנָּה, **maʻădannâh**, *mah-ad-an-naw´*; from 5727; a *delicacy* or (abstract) *pleasure* (adverb *cheerfully*):—dainty, delicately, delight.

4575. מַעֲדַנּוֹת, **maʻădannôwth**, *mah-ad-an-noth´*; by transposition from 6029; a *bond*, i.e. *group*:—influence.

4576. מַעְדֵּר, **maʻdêr**, *mah-dare´*; from 5737; a (weeding) *hoe*:—mattock.

4577. מְעֵה, **mᵉʻêh**, *meh-ay´*; (Chaldee); or מְעָא, **mᵉʻâʼ**, *meh-aw´*; (Chaldee); corresponding to 4578; only in plural the *bowels*:—belly.

4578. מֵעֶה, **mêʻeh**, *may-aw´*; from an unused root probably meaning to *be soft*; used only in plural the *intestines*, or (collective) the *abdomen*, (figurative) *sympathy*; (by implication) a *vest*; (by extension) the *stomach*, the *uterus* (or of men, the seat of generation), the *heart* (figurative):—belly, bowels, × heart, womb.

A masculine noun meaning internal organs, intestines, belly, womb, sexual organs, sympathy. It refers to internal organs. When Joab stabbed Amasa, his entrails fell onto the ground (2Sa 20:10); the digestive tract; when a woman was suspected of infidelity, she was made to take an oath cursing the water that entered her stomach (Nu 5:22); and the sexual organs; God promised Abram that he would bear a son from his own loins (Ge 15:4). It can also be used figuratively to mean the seat of emotions or heart (Isa 16:11).

4579. **מֵעָה, mâ'âh,** *maw-aw´*; feminine of 4578; the *belly,* i.e.(figurative) interior:—gravel.

4580. **מָעוֹג, mâ'ôwg,** *maw-ogue´*; from 5746; a *cake* of bread (with 3934 a *table-buffoon,* i.e. *parasite*):—cake, feast.

4581. **מָעוֹז, mâ'ôwz,** *maw-oze´*; (also **מָעוּז, mâ'ûwz,** *maw-ooz´*; or **מָעֹז, mâ'ôz,** *maw-oze´* (also **מָעֻז, mâ'uz,** *maw-ooz´*; from 5810; a *fortified* place; (figurative) a *defence*:—force, fort (-ress), rock, strength (-en), (× most) strong (hold).

4582. **מָעוֹךְ, Mâ'ôwk,** *maw-oke´*; from 4600; *oppressed; Maok,* a Philistine:—Maoch.

4583. **מָעוֹן, mâ'ôwn,** *maw-ohn´*; or **מָעִין, mâ'îyn,** *maw-een´*; (1Ch 4:41), from the same as 5772; an *abode,* of God (the tabernacle or the Temple), men (their home) or animals (their lair); hence a *retreat* (asylum):—den, dwelling ([-] place), habitation.

4584. **מָעוֹן, Mâ'ôwn,** *maw-ohn´*; the same as 4583; a *residence; Maon,* the name of an Israelite and of a place in Palestine:—Maon, Maonites. Compare 1010, 4586.

4585. **מְעוֹנָה, me'ôwnâh,** *meh-o-naw´*; or **מְעֹנָה, me'ônâh,** *meh-o-naw´*; feminine of 4583, and meaning the same:—den, habitation, (dwelling) place, refuge.

4586. **מְעוּנִי, Me'ûwnîy,** *meh-oo-nee´*; or **מְעִינִי, Me'îy-nîy,** *meh-ee-nee´*; probably patrial from 4584; a *Meünite,* or inhabitant of Maon (only in plural):—Mehunim (-s), Meunim.

4587. **מְעוֹנֹתַי, Me'ônôwthay,** *meh-o-no-thah´ee*; plural of 4585; *habitative; Meonothai,* an Israelite:—Meonothai.

4588. **מָעוּף, mâ'ûwph,** *maw-oof´*; from 5774 in the sense of *covering* with shade [compare 4155]; *darkness*:—dimness.

4589. **מָעוֹר, mâ'ôwr,** *maw-ore´*; from 5783; *nakedness,* i.e. (in plural) the *pudenda*:—nakedness.

4590. **מַעַזְיָה, Ma'azyâh,** *mah-az-yaw´*; or **מַעַזְיָהוּ, Ma'azyâhûw,** *mah-az-yaw´-hoo*; probably from 5756 (in the sense of *protection*) and 3050; *rescue of Jah; Maazjah,* the name of two Israelites:—Maaziah.

4591. **מָעַט, mâ'aṭ,** *maw-at´*; a primitive root; (properly) to *pare* off, i.e. *lessen*; (intransitive) to *be* (causative, to *make*) *small* or *few;* (figurative) *ineffective*:—suffer to decrease, diminish, (be, × borrow a, give, make) few (in number, -ness), gather least (little), be (seem) little, (× give the) less, be minished, bring to nothing.

4592. **מְעַט, me'aṭ,** *meh-at´*; or **מְעָט, me'âṭ,** *meh-awt´*; from 4591; a *little* or *few* (often adverbial or comparative):—almost, (some, very) few (-er, -est), lightly, little (while), (very) small (matter, thing), some, soon, × very.

4593. **מְעֻטָּה, me'uṭṭâh,** *maw-ote´*; passive adjective of 4591; *thinned* (as to the edge), i.e. *sharp*:—wrapped up.

4594. **מַעֲטֶה, ma'ăṭeh,** *mah-at-eh´*; from 5844; a *vestment*:—garment.

4595. **מַעֲטֶפֶת, ma'ăṭepheth,** *mah-at-aw-faw´*; from 5848; a *cloak*:—mantle.

4596. **מְעִי, me'îy,** *meh-ee´*; from 5753; a *pile* of rubbish (as *contorted*), i.e. a *ruin* (compare 5856):—heap.

4597. **מָעַי, Mâ'ay,** *maw-ah´ee*; probably from 4578; *sympathetic; Maai,* an Israelite:—Maai.

4598. **מְעִיל, me'îyl,** *meh-eel´*; from 4603 in the sense of *covering*; a *robe* (i.e. upper and outer *garment*):—cloke, coat, mantle, robe.

4599. **מַעְיָן, ma'yân,** *mah-yawn´*; or **מַעְיְנוֹ, ma'yenôw,** *mah-yen-o´*; (Ps 114:8), or (feminine) **מַעְיָנָה, ma'yânâh,** *mah-yaw-naw´*; from 5869 (as a denominative in the sense of a *spring*); a *fountain* (also collective), (figurative) a *source* (of satisfaction):—fountain, spring, well.

4600. **מָעַךְ, mâ'ak,** *maw-ak´*; a primitive root; to *press,* i.e. to *pierce, emasculate, handle*:—bruised, stuck, be pressed.

4601. **מַעֲכָה, Ma'ăkâh,** *mah-ak-aw´*; or **מַעֲכָת, Ma'ă-kâth,** *mah-ak-awth´*; (Jos 13:13), from 4600; *depression; Maakah* (or *Maakath*), the name of a place in Syria, also of a Mesopotamian, of three Israelites, and of four Israelitesses and one Syrian woman:—Maachah, Maachathites. See also 1038.

4602. **מַעֲכָתִי, Ma'ăkâthîy,** *mah-ak-aw-thee´*; patrial from 4601; a *Maakathite,* or inhabitant of Maakah:—Maachathite.

4603. **מָעַל, mâ'al,** *maw-al´*; a primitive root; (properly) to *cover* up; (used only figurative) to *act covertly,* i.e. *treacherously*:—transgress, (commit, do a) trespass (-ing).

A verb meaning to violate one's duty. The term is used often as a synonym for sin; however, this word almost always denotes a willing act (Nu 5:6; Eze 14:13). It occurs principally in the later books of the OT and is almost exclusively a religious term. There are only two secular uses: one for a wife's unfaithfulness to her husband and the other for a king's unfaithfulness in judgment (Nu 5:12, 27; Pr 16:10). Although the offence is usually against God Himself, three times the unfaithfulness is directed against something under divine ban and not directly against God (Jos 22:20; 1Ch 10:13; Eze 18:24). The writer of 1 and 2 Chronicles often connected national unfaithfulness with God's sending of punitive wars; ultimately, the outcome meant deportation for the Northern Kingdom and destruction and exile for the Southern Kingdom (1Ch 5:25; 2Ch 12:2; 28:19, 22; 36:14).

4604. **מַעַל, ma'al,** *mah´-al*; from 4603; *treachery,* i.e. sin:—falsehood, grievously, sore, transgression, trespass, × very.

A masculine noun meaning an unfaithful act, a treacherous act. Of its twenty-nine occurrences, it appears twenty times as a cognate accusative to the verb *mâ'al* (4603), meaning to act unfaithfully or treacherously. It can apply to actions against another person, such as a wife against her husband (Nu 5:12, 27); Job by his "comforters" (Job 21:34). However, it usually applies to actions against God, whether those actions be committed by an individual (Le 5:15; 6:2[5:21]; Jos 7:1; 22:20); or by the nation of Israel collectively (Jos 22:22; 1Ch 9:1; Ezr 9:2, 4; 10:6; Eze 39:26).

4605. **מַעַל, ma'al,** *mah´-al*; from 5927; (properly) the *upper* part, used only adverb with prefix *upward, above, overhead, from the top,* etc.:—above, exceeding (-ly), forward, on (× very) high, over, up (-on, -ward), very.

4606. **מֵעָל, me'âl,** *meh-awl´*; (Chaldee); from 5954; (only in plural as singular) the *setting* (of the sun):—going down.

4607. **מֹעַל, mô'al,** *mo´-al*; from 5927; a *raising* (of the hands):—lifting up.

4608. **מַעֲלֶה, ma'ăleh,** *mah-al-eh´*; from 5927; an *elevation,* i.e. (concrete) *acclivity* or *platform*; abstract (the relation or state) a *rise* or (figurative) *priority*:—ascent, before, chiefest, cliff, that goeth up, going up, hill, mounting up, stairs.

4609. **מַעֲלָה, ma'ălâh,** *mah-al-aw´*; feminine of 4608; *elevation,* i.e. the act; (literal) a *journey* to a higher place; (figurative) a *thought* arising; (concrete) the condition (literal) a *step* or *grade*-mark; (figurative) a *superiority* of station; (specifically) a climactic *progression* (in certain Psalms):—things that come up, (high) degree, deal, go up, stair, step, story.

4610. **מַעֲלֵה עַקְרַבִּים, Ma'ălêh 'Aqrabbîym,** *mah-al-ay´ ak-rab-beem´*; from 4608 and (the plural of) 6137; *Steep of Scorpions,* a place in the Desert:—Maaleh-accrabim, the ascent (going up) of Akrabbim.

4611. **מַעֲלָל, ma'ălâl,** *mah-al-awl´*; from 5953; an *act* (good or bad):—doing, endeavour, invention, work.

4612. מַעֲמָד, **maʻămâd,** *mah-am-awd´*; from 5975; (figurative) a *position*:—attendance, office, place, state.

4613. מָעֳמָד, **moʻŏmâd,** *moh-om-awd´*; from 5975; (literal) a *foothold*:—standing.

4614. מַעֲמָסָה, **maʻămâsâh,** *mah-am-aw-saw´*; from 6006; *burdensomeness*:—burdensome.

4615. מַעֲמַקִּים, **maʻămaqqîym,** *mah-am-ak-keem´*; from 6009; a *deep*:—deep, depth.

4616. מַעַן, **maʻan,** *mah´-an*; from 6030; (properly) *heed*, i.e. *purpose*; (used only adverbially) *on account of* (as a motive or an aim); (teleologically) *in order that*:—because of, to the end (intent) that, for (to, … 's sake), + lest, that, to.

4617. מַעֲנֶה, **maʻăneh,** *mah-an-eh´*; from 6030; a *reply* (favourable or contradictory):—answer, × himself.

4618. מַעֲנָה, **maʻănâh,** *mah-an-aw´*; from 6031, in the sense of *depression* or *tilling*; a *furrow*:— + acre, furrow.

4619. מַעַץ, **Maʻats,** *mah´-ats*; from 6095; *closure; Maats*, an Israelite:—Maaz.

4620. מַעֲצֵבָה, **maʻătsêbâh,** *mah-ats-ay-baw´*; from 6087; *anguish*:—sorrow.

4621. מַעֲצָד, **maʻătsâd,** *mah-ats-awd´*; from an unused root meaning to *hew*; an *ax*:—ax, tongs.

4622. מַעְצוֹר, **maʻtsôwr,** *mah-tsore´*; from 6113; (objective) a *hindrance*:—restraint.

A masculine noun meaning a restraint, a hindrance. This noun is derived from the verb *ʻâtsar* (6113), meaning to restrain or to retain. It occurs only one time, where Jonathan tells his armourbearer that "there is no restraint to the LORD to save by many or by few" (1Sa 14:6, KJV).

4623. מַעְצָר, **maʻtsâr,** *mah-tsawr´*; from 6113; (subjective) *control*:—rule.

A masculine noun meaning a restraint, a control. This noun is derived from the verb *ʻâtsar* (6113), meaning to restrain or retain. Its only occurrence is to characterize a person as one who is without self-control. This person is also compared to a ruined city without walls (Pr 25:28).

4624. מַעֲקֶה, **maʻăqeh,** *mah-ak-eh´*; from an unused root meaning to *repress*; a *parapet*:—battlement.

4625. מַעֲקַשִּׁים, **maʻăqâshshîym,** *mah-ak-ash-sheem´*; from 6140; a *crook* (in a road):—crooked thing.

4626. מַעַר, **maʻar,** *mah´-ar*; from 6168; a *nude* place, i.e. (literal) the *pudenda*, or (figurative) a vacant *space*:—nakedness, proportion.

4627. מַעֲרָב, **maʻărâb,** *mah-ar-awb´*; from 6148, in the sense of *trading; traffic*; (by implication) mercantile *goods*:—market, merchandise.

4628. מַעֲרָב, **maʻărâb,** *mah-ar-awb´*; or (feminine) מַעֲרָבָה, **maʻărâbâh,** *mah-ar-aw-baw´*; from 6150, in the sense of *shading*; the *west* (as the region of the *evening* sun):—west.

4629. מַעֲרֶה, **maʻăreh,** *mah-ar-eh´*; from 6168; a *nude* place, i.e. a *common*:—meadows.

4630. מַעֲרָה, **maʻărâh,** *mah-ar-aw´*; feminine of 4629; an *open* spot:—army [*from the margin*].

4631. מְעָרָה, **m^eʻârâh,** *meh-aw-raw´*; from 5783; a *cavern* (as dark):—cave, den, hole.

4632. מְעָרָה, **M^eʻârâh,** *meh-aw-raw´*; the same as 4631; *cave; Meärah*, a place in Palestine:—Mearah.

4633. מַעֲרָךְ, **maʻărâk,** *mah-ar-awk´*; from 6186; an *arrangement*, i.e. (figurative) mental *disposition*:—preparation.

4634. מַעֲרָכָה, **maʻărâkâh,** *mah-ar-aw-kaw´*; feminine of 4633; an *arrangement*; (concrete) a *pile*; (specifically) a military *array*:—army, fight, be set in order, ordered place, rank, row.

4635. מַעֲרֶכֶת, **maʻăreketh,** *mah-ar-eh´-keth*; from 6186; an *arrangement*, i.e. (concrete) a *pile* (of loaves):—row, shewbread.

A feminine noun meaning a row, a line. This word comes from the verb *ʻârak* (6186), meaning to arrange or to line up. The first time this word appears is in Le 24:6, 7, where it describes the arrangement of the showbread: two rows of bread with six pieces in a row. In the other seven instances of this word, it is best translated "showbread" (i.e. the bread that was lined up in a row) (1Ch 9:32; 23:29; 28:16; 2Ch 2:4; 13:11; 29:18; Ne 10:33[34]).

4636. מַעֲרֹם, **maʻărôm,** *mah-ar-ome´*; from 6191, in the sense of *stripping; bare*:—naked.

4637. מַעֲרָצָה, **maʻărâtsâh,** *mah-ar-aw-tsaw´*; from 6206; *violence*:—terror.

4638. מַעֲרָת, **Maʻărâth,** *mah-ar-awth´*; a form of 4630; *waste; Maarath*, a place in Palestine:—Maarath.

4639. מַעֲשֶׂה, **maʻăseh,** *mah-as-eh´*; from 6213; an *action* (good or bad); (generally) a *transaction*; (abstract) *activity*; (by implication) a *product* (specifically) a *poem*; or (generic) *property*:—act, art, + bakemeat, business, deed, do (-ing), labour, thing made, ware of making, occupation, thing offered, operation, possession, × well, ([handy-, needle-, net-]) work (-ing, -manship), wrought.

4640. מַעֲשַׂי, **Maʻăśay,** *mah-as-ah´ee*; from 6213; *operative; Maasai*, an Israelite:—Maasiai.

4641. מַעֲשֵׂיָה, **Maʻăśêyâh,** *mah-as-ay-yaw´*; or מַעֲשֵׂיָהוּ, **Maʻăśêyâhûw,** *mah-as-ay-yaw´-hoo*; from 4639 and 3050; *work of Jah; Maasejah*, the name of sixteen Israelites:—Maaseiah.

4642. מַעֲשַׁקּוֹת, **maʻăshaqqôth,** *mah-ash-ak-koth´*; from 6231; *oppression*:—oppression, × oppressor.

4643. מַעֲשֵׂר, **maʻăśêr,** *mah-as-ayr´*; or מַעֲשַׂר, **maʻăśar,** *mah-as-ar´*; and (in plural) feminine מַעַשְׂרָה, **maʻaśrâh,** *mah-as-raw´*; from 6240; a *tenth*; especially a *tithe*:—tenth (part), tithe (-ing).

A masculine noun meaning tithe, tenth. This word is related to *ʻeśer* (6235), meaning ten, and often means tenth (Ge 14:20; Eze 45:11, 14). In the Levitical system of the OT, this word refers to the tenth part, which came to be known as the tithe. Israelites were to tithe from their land, herds, flocks, and other sources (Le 27:30–32). Such tithes were intended to support the Levites in their priestly duties (Nu 18:21, 24, 26, 28); as well as strangers, orphans, and widows (Dt 26:12). When Israel failed to give the tithe, it was a demonstration of their disobedience (Mal 3:8, 10); when they reinstituted the tithe, it was a sign of reform, as in Hezekiah's (2Ch 31:5, 6, 12) and Nehemiah's times (Ne 10:37[38], 38[39]; 12:44).

4644. מֹף, **Môph,** *mofe*; of Egyptian origin; *Moph*, the capital of Lower Egypt:—Memphis. Compare 5297.

4645. מִפְגָּע, **miphgâʻ,** *mif-gaw´*; from 6293; an *object of attack*:—mark.

4646. מַפָּח, **mappâch,** *map-pawkh´*; from 5301; a *breathing out* (of life), i.e. expiring:—giving up.

A masculine noun meaning breathing out. This word comes from the verb *nâphach* (5301), meaning to breathe or to blow, and occurs only once in the OT. In Job 11:20, this word describes the soul that expires.

4647. מַפֻּחַ, **mappuach,** *map-poo´-akh*; from 5301; the *bellows* (i.e. *blower*) of a forge:—bellows.

4648. מְפִיבֹשֶׁת, **M^ephîybôsheth,** *mef-ee-bo´-sheth*; or מְפִבֹשֶׁת, **Mephibôsheth,** *mef-ee-bo´-sheth*; probably from 6284 and 1322; *dispeller of shame* (i.e. of Baal); *Mephibosheth*, the name of two Israelites:—Mephibosheth.

4649. מֻפִּים, **Muppîym,** *moop-peem´*; a plural apparently from 5130; *wavings; Muppim*, an Israelite:—Muppim. Compare 8206.

4650. מֵפִיץ, mêphîyts, *may-feets´*; from 6327; a *breaker*, i.e. mallet:—maul.

4651. מַפָּל, mappâl, *map-pawl´*; from 5307; a *falling* off, i.e. chaff; also something *pendulous*, i.e. a flap:—flake, refuse.

4652. מִפְלָאָה, miphlâ'âh, *mif-law-aw´*; from 6381; a *miracle*:—wondrous work.

4653. מִפְלַגָּה, miphlaggâh, *mif-lag-gaw´*; from 6385; a *classification*:—division.

A feminine noun meaning division. This word comes from the verb *pâlâh* (6395), meaning to separate, and occurs only once in the OT. In 2Ch 35:12, this word is used to describe the household divisions among the Levites.

4654. מַפָּלָה, mappâlâh, *map-paw-law´*; or מַפֵּלָה, **mappêlâh,** *map-pay-law´*; from 5307; something *fallen*, i.e. a *ruin*:—ruin (-ous).

4655. מִפְלָט, miphlâṭ, *mif-lawt´*; from 6403; an *escape*:—escape.

4656. מִפְלֶצֶת, miphletseth, *mif-leh´-tseth*; from 6426; a *terror*, i.e. an idol:—idol.

A feminine noun meaning horrid thing. This word comes from the verb *pâlats* (6426), meaning to shudder, and described something so horrible that one would shudder. It was used only to describe an image (perhaps some sort of idol) that Maacah had made as an object of worship (1Ki 15:13; 2Ch 15:16).

4657. מִפְלָשׂ, miphlâś, *mif-lawce´*; from an unused root meaning to *balance*; a *poising*:—balancing.

4658. מַפֶּלֶת, mappeleth, *map-peh´-leth*; from 5307; *fall*, i.e. *decadence*; (concrete) a *ruin*; (specifically) a *carcase*:—carcase, fall, ruin.

A feminine noun meaning a carcass, a ruin, overthrow. This word comes from the verb *nâphal* (5307), meaning to fall. It described the physical carcass of a dead animal (Jgs 14:8); and the practical ruin of the wicked (Pr 29:16). It also described the overthrow of two nations: Tyre (Eze 26:15, 18; 27:27); and Egypt (Eze 31:13, 16; 32:10).

4659. מִפְעַל, miph'âl, *mif-awl´*; or (feminine) מִפְעָלָה, **miph'âlâh,** *mif-aw-law´*; from 6466; a *performance*:—work.

4660. מַפָּץ, mappâts, *map-pawts´*; from 5310; a *smiting* to pieces:—slaughter.

A masculine noun meaning a smashing, a shattering. This word is used in this form only once and refers to a dangerous weapon for smashing (Eze 9:2). See the related Hebrew root *nâphats* (5310), as well as the Hebrew words *nephets* (5311) and *maphphêts* (4661).

4661. מַפֵּץ, mappêts, *map-pates´*; from 5310; a *smiter*, i.e. a war *club*:—battle ax.

4662. מִפְקָד, miphqâd, *mif-kawd´*; from 6485; an *appointment*, i.e. *mandate*; (concrete) a designated *spot*; (specifically) a *census*:—appointed place, commandment, number.

A masculine noun meaning a mandate, an appointment, a counting, a census; an appointed place. Ten men became assistant overseers for the management of offerings in the house of the Lord by the appointment of King Hezekiah (2Ch 31:13). King David ordered Joab to take a census of the number of people under his rule (2Sa 24:9; 1Ch 21:5). Twice the word functions to designate a location. In Eze 43:21, the bull of the sin offering was to be burnt in the appointed place of the Temple precincts. In Ne 3:31, the word was utilized (possibly as a proper name) to identify a particular gate in the city of Jerusalem. This term stems from the verb *pâqad* (6485).

4663. מִפְקָד, Miphqâd, *mif-kawd´*; the same as 4662; *assignment*; *Miphkad*, the name of a gate in Jerusalem:—Miphkad.

4664. מִפְרָץ, miphrâts, *mif-rawts´*; from 6555; a *break* (in the shore), i.e. a *haven*:—breach.

4665. מַפְרֶקֶת, maphreqeth, *maf-reh´-keth*; from 6561; (properly) a *fracture*, i.e. *joint* (*vertebra*) of the neck:—neck.

4666. מִפְרָשׂ, miphrâś, *mif-rawce´*; from 6566; an *expansion*:—that which … spreadest forth, spreading.

4667. מִפְשָׂעָה, miphśâ'âh, *mif-saw-aw´*; from 6585; a *stride*, i.e. (by euphemism) the *crotch*:—buttocks.

4668. מַפְתֵּחַ, maphtêach, *maf-tay´-akh*; from 6605; an *opener*, i.e. a *key*:—key.

4669. מִפְתָּח, miphtâch, *mif-tawkh´*; from 6605; an *aperture*, i.e. (figurative) *utterance*:—opening.

4670. מִפְתָּן, miphtân, *mif-tawn´*; from the same as 6620; a *stretcher*, i.e. a *sill*:—threshold.

4671. מֹץ, môts, *motes*; or מוֹץ, **môwts,** *motes*; (Zep 2:2), from 4160; *chaff* (as *pressed* out, i.e. *winnowed* or [rather] threshed loose):—chaff.

4672. מָצָא, mâtsâ', *maw-tsaw´*; a primitive root; (properly) to *come* forth to, i.e. *appear* or *exist*; transposed to *attain*, i.e. *find* or *acquire*; (figurative) to *occur, meet* or *be present*:— + be able, befall, being, catch, × certainly, (cause to) come (on, to, to hand), deliver, be enough (cause to) find (-ing, occasion, out), get (hold upon), × have (here), be here, hit, be left, light (up-) on, meet (with), × occasion serve, (be) present, ready, speed, suffice, take hold on.

4673. מַצָּב, matstsâb, *mats-tsawb´*; from 5324; a fixed *spot*; (figurative) an *office*, a military *post*:—garrison, station, place where … stood.

4674. מֻצָּב, mutstsâb, *moots-tsawb´*; from 5324; a *station*, i.e. military *post*:—mount.

4675. מַצָּבָה, matstsâbâh, *mats-tsaw-baw´*; or מִצָּבָה, **mitstsâbâh,** *mits-tsaw-baw´*; feminine of 4673; a military *guard*:—army, garrison.

4676. מַצֵּבָה, matstsêbâh, *mats-tsay-baw´*; feminine (causative) participle of 5324; something *stationed*, i.e. a *column* or (memorial *stone*); (by analogy) an *idol*:—garrison, (standing) image, pillar.

A feminine noun meaning something set upright. The word most often refers to a standing, unhewn block of stone utilized for religious and memorial purposes. After a powerful experience of the Lord in a dream, Jacob set up as a pillar the stone on which he had laid his head, in commemoration of the event (Ge 28:18, 22; cf. Ge 31:45; 35:20). Moses set up an altar and also twelve pillars at the base of Mount Sinai to represent the twelve tribes of Israel (Ex 24:4). These pillars were erected as monuments to God (Hos 3:4); or, more commonly, to pagan deities (1Ki 14:23, Mic 5:13[12]). Many times in 2Ki, the term refers to a sacred pillar that aided people in their worship of pagan gods, especially the Canaanite god Baal. In most of these passages, the sacred columns were used by Israelites, contrary to the Lord's prohibition concerning the worship of any other god (2Ki 3:2; 10:26, 27; 18:4; 23:14; cf. Hos 10:1, 2; Mic 5:13[12]). This noun stems from the verb *nâtsab* (5324).

4677. מְצֹבָיָה, M^e^tsôbyâh, *meh-tsob-yaw´*; apparently from 4672 and 3050; *found of Jah; Metsobajah*, a place in Palestine:—Mesobaite.

4678. מַצֶּבֶת, matstsebeth, *mats-tseh´-beth*; from 5324; something *stationary*, i.e. a monumental *stone*; also the *stock* of a tree:—pillar, substance.

A feminine noun meaning a pillar, a stump, a standing stone. A monument could be set up to commemorate a divine appearance, such as the pillar of stone Jacob set up at Bethel (Ge 35:14). The word can also refer to a pillar or monument set up to honour oneself, such as the one Absalom set up for himself in order that his name would be remembered (2Sa 18:18).

4679. מְצַד, m^e^tsad, *mets-ad´*; or מְצָד, **metsâd,** *mets-awd´*; or (feminine) מְצָדָה, **metsâdâh,** *mets-aw-daw´*; from 6679; a *fastness* (as a *covert* of ambush):—castle, fort, (strong) hold, munition.

4680. מָצָה, **mâtsâh,** *maw-tsaw´*; a primitive root; to *suck* out; (by implication) to *drain*, to *squeeze* out:—suck, wring (out).

4681. מֹצָה, **Môtsâh,** *mo-tsaw´*; active participle feminine of 4680; *drained; Motsah*, a place in Palestine:—Mozah.

4682. מַצָּה, **matstsâh,** *mats-tsaw´*; from 4711 in the sense of *greedily* devouring for sweetness; (properly) *sweetness*; (concrete) *sweet* (i.e. not soured or bittered with yeast); (specifically) an *unfermented cake* or loaf, or (elliptically) the festival of *Passover* (because no leaven was then used):—unleavened (bread, cake), without leaven.

A feminine noun meaning unleavened bread or cakes. This food was a staple in Israelite diets and could be prepared in a hurry for a meal (Ge 19:3, 1Sa 28:24). One of the three Israelite national feasts was the Feast of Unleavened Bread where the people ate flat bread for seven days to commemorate their deliverance from Egypt (Ex 23:15). Unleavened bread or cakes could also be anointed with oil and presented to the priests as a sacrifice (Ex 29:2).

4683. מַצָּה, **matstsâh,** *mats-tsaw´*; from 5327; a *quarrel*:—contention, debate, strife.

4684. מַצְהָלוֹת, **matshâlôwth,** *mats-haw-loth´*; from 6670; a *whinnying* (through impatience for battle or lust):—neighing.

4685. מָצוֹד, **mâtsôwd,** *maw-tsode´*; or (feminine) מְצוֹדָה, **m^{e}tsôwdâh,** *mets-o-daw´*; or מְצֹדָה, **m^{e}tsô-dâh,** *mets-o-daw´*; from 6679; a *net* (for *capturing* animals or fishes); also (by interch. for 4679) a *fastness* or (besieging) *tower*:—bulwark, hold, munition, net, snare.

A masculine noun meaning a net, a hunting implement, a siege tower. Job claimed that God had surrounded him with a net (Job 19:6). Used figuratively, a wicked person delighted in catching other evil ones (Pr 12:12); the seductress threw out nets to capture men (Ecc 7:26). Siegeworks or bulwarks described the method of attack against a city (Ecc 9:14).

4686. מָצוּד, **mâtsûwd,** *maw-tsood´*; or (feminine) מְצוּדָה, **m^{e}tsûwdâh,** *mets-oo-daw´*; or מְצֻדָה, **m^{e}tsudâh,** *mets-oo-daw´*; for 4685; a *net*, or (abstract) *capture*; also a *fastness*:—castle, defence, fort (-ress), (strong) hold, be hunted, net, snare, strong place.

4687. מִצְוָה, **mitsvâh,** *mits-vaw´*; from 6680; a *command*, whether human or divine; (collective) the *Law*:—(which was) commanded (-ment), law, ordinance, precept.

A feminine noun meaning a commandment. It can apply to the edicts issued by a human being, most likely the king (1Ki 2:43; Est 3:3; Pr 6:20; Isa 36:21; Jer 35:18). It can also relate to a general corpus of human precepts (Isa 29:13); or a body of teachings (Pr 2:1; 3:1). On the other hand, this expression can reference God's commands. In the Pentateuch, this is its only usage. It does not refer to human commandments. In the singular, it may distinguish a certain commandment (1Ki 13:21); yet it appears most frequently in the plural to designate the entire corpus of divine law and instruction (Ge 26:5; Ex 16:28; Dt 6:2; 1Ki 2:3). It is also important to note that, in the plural, this word often appears in synonymous parallelism with such words as *chuqqîm* (2706); *mishpâṭîm* (4941); *'êdôth* (5715); *tôwrôwth* (8451).

4688. מְצוֹלָה, **m^{e}tsôwlâh,** *mets-o-law´*; or מְצֹלָה, **m^{e}tsôlâh,** *mets-o-law´*; also מְצוּלָה, **m^{e}tsûwlâh,** *mets-oo-law´*; or מְצֻלָה, **m^{e}tsulâh,** *mets-oo-law´*; from the same as 6683; a *deep* place (of water or mud):—bottom, deep, depth.

4689. מָצוֹק, **mâtsôwq,** *maw-tsoke´*; from 6693; a *narrow* place, i.e. (abstract and figurative) *confinement* or *disability*:—anguish, distress, straitness.

4690. מָצוּק, **mâtsûwq,** *maw-tsook´*; or מָצֻק, **mâtsuq,** *maw-tsook´*; from 6693; something *narrow*, i.e. a *column* or *hill*-top:—pillar, situate.

4691. מְצוּקָה, **m^{e}tsûwqâh,** *mets-oo-kaw´*; or מְצֻקָה, **m^{e}tsuqâh,** *mets-oo-kaw´*; feminine of 4690; *narrowness*, i.e. (figurative) *trouble*:—anguish, distress.

4692. מָצוֹר, **mâtsôwr,** *maw-tsore´*; or מָצוּר, **mâtsûwr,** *maw-tsoor´*; from 6696; something *hemming* in, i.e. (objective) a *mound* (of besiegers), (abstract) a *siege*, (figurative) *distress*; or (subjective) a *fastness*:—besieged, bulwark, defence, fenced, fortress, siege, strong (hold), tower.

4693. מָצוֹר, **mâtsôwr,** *maw-tsore´*; the same as 4692 in the sense of a *limit; Egypt* (as the *border* of Palestine):—besieged places, defence, fortified.

4694. מְצוּרָה, **m^{e}tsûwrâh,** *mets-oo-raw´*; or מְצֻרָה, **m^{e}tsurâh,** *mets-oo-raw´*; feminine of 4692; a *hemming* in, i.e. (objective) a *mound* (of siege), or (subjective) a *rampart* (of protection), (abstract) *fortification*:—fenced (city), fort, munition, strong hold.

4695. מַצּוּת, **matstsûwth,** *mats-tsooth´*; from 5327; a *quarrel*:—that contended.

4696. מֵצַח, **mêtsach,** *may´-tsakh*; from an unused root meaning to be *clear*, i.e. *conspicuous*; the *forehead* (as *open* and *prominent*):—brow, forehead, + impudent.

4697. מִצְחָה, **mitschâh,** *mits-khaw´*; from the same as 4696; a *shin-piece* of armour (as *prominent*), only plural:—greaves.

4698. מְצִלָּה, **m^{e}tsillâh,** *mets-il-law´*; from 6750; a *tinkler*, i.e. a *bell*:—bell.

4699. מְצֻלָה, **m^{e}tsulâh,** *mets-oo-law´*; from 6751; *shade*:—bottom.

4700. מְצִלְתַּיִם, **m^{e}tsiltayim,** *mets-il´-ta-yeem*; from 6750; (only dual) double *tinklers*, i.e. cymbals:—cymbals.

4701. מִצְנֶפֶת, **mitsnepheth,** *mits-neh´-feth´*; from 6801; a *tiara*, i.e. official *turban* (of a king or high priest):—diadem, mitre.

4702. מַצָּע, **matstsâ',** *mats-tsaw´*; from 3331; a *couch*:—bed.

4703. מִצְעָד, **mits'âd,** *mits-awd´*; from 6805; a *step*; (figurative) *companionship*:—going, step.

4704. מִצְּעִירָה, **mitsts^e'îyrâh,** *mits-tseh-ee-raw´*; feminine of 4705; (properly) *littleness*; (concrete) *diminutive*:—little.

4705. מִצְעָר, **mits'âr,** *mits-awr´*; from 6819; *petty* (in size or number); (adverbial) a *short* (time):—little one (while), small.

4706. מִצְעָר, **Mits'âr,** *mits-awr´*; the same as 4705; *Mitsar*, a peak of Lebanon:—Mizar.

4707. מִצְפֶּה, **mitspeh,** *mits-peh´*; from 6822; an *observatory*, especially for military purposes:—watch tower.

4708. מִצְפֶּה, **Mitspeh,** *mits-peh´*; the same as 4707; *Mitspeh*, the name of five places in Palestine:—Mizpeh, watch tower. Compare 4709.

4709. מִצְפָּה, **Mitspâh,** *mits-paw´*; feminine of 4708; *Mitspah*, the name of two places in Palestine:—Mitspah. [This seems rather to be only an orthographical variation of 4708 when "in pause".]

4710. מִצְפֻּן, **matspôwn,** *mits-pone´*; from 6845; a *secret* (place or thing, perhaps *treasure*):—hidden thing.

4711. מָצַץ, **mâtsats,** *maw-tsats´*; a primitive root; to *suck*:—milk.

4712. מֵצַר, **mêtsar,** *may-tsar´*; from 6896; something *tight*, i.e. (figurative) *trouble*:—distress, pain, strait.

4713. מִצְרִי, **Mitsrîy,** *mits-ree´*; from 4714; a *Mitsrite*, or inhabitant of Mitsrajim:—Egyptian, of Egypt.

4714. מִצְרַיִם, **Mitsrayim,** *mits-rah´-yim*; dual of 4693; *Mitsrajim*, i.e. Upper and Lower Egypt:—Egypt, Egyptians, Mizraim.

4715. מִצְרֵף, **matsrêph,** *mats-rafe´*; from 6884; a *crucible*:—refining pot.

4716. מַק, **maq,** *mak*; from 4743; (properly) a *melting*, i.e. *putridity*:—rottenness, stink.

4717. מַקֶּבֶת, maqqebeth, *mak-keh-beth´*; from 5344; (properly) a *perforatrix*, i.e. a *hammer* (as *piercing*):—hammer.

4718. מַקֶּבֶת, maqqebeth, *mak-keh´-beth*; from 5344; (properly) a *perforator*, i.e. a *hammer* (as *piercing*); also (intransitive) a *perforation*, i.e. a *quarry*:—hammer, hole.

4719. מַקֵּדָה, Maqqêdâh, *mak-kay-daw´*; from the same as 5348 in the denominative sense of *herding* (compare 5349); *fold; Makkedah*, a place in Palestine:—Makkedah.

4720. מִקְדָּשׁ, miqdâsh, *mik-dawsh´*; or מִקְּדָשׁ, **miq-qᵉdâsh,** *mik-ked-awsh´*; (Ex 15:17), from 6942; a *consecrated* thing or place, especially a *palace, sanctuary* (whether of Jehovah or of idols) or *asylum*:—chapel, hallowed part, holy place, sanctuary.

A masculine noun meaning a holy or sacred place, a sanctuary. As a nominal form from the verb *qâdash* (6942), meaning to be set apart or to be consecrated, this noun designates that which has been sanctified or set apart as sacred and holy as opposed to the secular, common, or profane. It is a general term for anything sacred and holy, such as the articles of the tabernacle that were devoted for use during worship (Nu 10:21); or the best portion of the offerings given to the Lord (Nu 18:29). Most often, it connotes a sanctuary, the physical place of worship. In this sense, the word encompasses a variety of these concepts: the old Israelite sanctuaries (Jos 24:26); the tabernacle (Ex 25:8; Le 12:4; 21:12); the Temple (1Ch 22:19; 2Ch 29:21; Da 11:31); the sanctuaries dedicated to false worship (Le 26:31; Isa 16:12; Am 7:9). It can also denote a place of refuge or asylum because this status was accorded to sacred places among the Hebrews (Isa 8:14; Eze 11:16; cf. 1Ki 1:50; 2:28).

4721. מַקְהֵל, maqhêl, *mak-hale´*; or (feminine) מַקְהֵלָה, **maqhêlâh,** *mak-hay-law´*; from 6950; an *assembly*:—congregation.

4722. מַקְהֵלֹת, Maqhêlôth, *mak-hay-loth´*; plural of 4721 (feminine); *assemblies; Makheloth*, a place in the Desert:—Makheloth.

4723. מִקְוֶה, miqveh, *mik-veh´*; or מִקְוֵה, **miqvêh,** *mik-vay´*; (1Ki 10:28), or מִקְוֵא, **miqvê',** *mik-vay´*; (2Ch 1:16), from 6960; something *waited* for, i.e. *confidence* (object or subject); also a *collection*, i.e. (of water) a *pond*, or (of men and horses) a *caravan* or *drove*:—abiding, gathering together, hope, linen yarn, plenty [of water], pool.

A masculine noun meaning hope. The word is used four times and is highly significant theologically. It is used twice as a designation for the Lord. King David, shortly before he died, asserted that as for humans, their days were without any hope in this life (1Ch 29:15). But Jeremiah answered this challenge in the midst of drought, famine, and sword. Jeremiah cried out to the Lord, calling Him the Hope of Israel in parallel with Saviour (Jer 14:8). He also viewed the day of the Lord prophetically at a time when there was no positive outlook for Judah. Jeremiah asserted that the Lord was the only hope Judah had; to turn from Him would result in shame (Jer 17:13).

Those who returned from exile and established the community found themselves near the brink of rejection, but one brave soul was moved to assert that there was still some hope for Israel to be spared (Ezr 10:2). The word has within its root meaning the thought of waiting for the Lord to act.

4724. מִקְוָה, miqvâh, *mik-vaw´*; feminine of 4723; a *collection*, i.e. (of water) a *reservoir*:—ditch.

4725. מָקוֹם, mâqôwm, *maw-kome´*; or מָקֹם, **mâqôm,** *maw-kome´*; also (feminine) מְקוֹמָה, **mᵉqôwmâh,** *mek-o-mah´*; or מְקֹמָה, **mᵉqômâh,** *mek-o-mah´*; from 6965; (properly) a *standing*, i.e. a *spot*; but used widely of a *locality* (general or specific); also (figurative) of a *condition* (of body or mind):—country, × home, × open, place, room, space, × whither [-soever].

4726. מָקוֹר, mâqôwr, *maw-kore´*; or מָקֹר, **mâqôr,** *maw-kore´*; from 6979; (properly) something *dug*, i.e. a (general) *source* (of water, even when naturally flowing; also of tears, blood [by euphemism of the female *pudenda*]; figurative of happiness, wisdom, progeny):—fountain, issue, spring, well (-spring).

4727. מִקָּח, miqqâch, *mik-kawkh´*; from 3947; *reception*:—taking.

4728. מַקָּחוֹת, maqqâchôwth, *mak-kaw-khoth´*; from 3947; something *received*, i.e. *merchandise* (purchased):—ware.

4729. מִקְטָר, miqtâr, *mik-tawr´*; from 6999; something to *fume* (incense) on, i.e. a *hearth* place:—to burn … upon.

4730. מִקְטֶרֶת, miqtereth, *mik-teh´-reth*; feminine of 4729; something to *fume* (incense) in, i.e. a *coal-pan*:—censer.

4731. מַקֵּל, maqqêl, *mak-kale´*; or (feminine) מַקְּלָה, **maqqᵉlâh,** *mak-kel-aw´*; from an unused root meaning apparently to *germinate*; a *shoot*, i.e. *stick* (with leaves on, or for walking, striking, guiding, divining):—rod, ([hand-]) staff.

4732. מִקְלוֹת, Miqlôwth, *mik-lohth´*; (or perhaps *mik-kel-ohth´*); plural of (feminine) 4731; *rods; Mikloth*, a place in the Desert:—Mikloth.

4733. מִקְלָט, miqlât, *mik-lawt´*; from 7038 in the sense of *taking* in; an *asylum* (as a *receptacle*):—refuge.

4734. מִקְלַעַת, miqla'ath, *mik-lah´-ath*; from 7049; a *sculpture* (probably in bass-relief):—carved (figure), carving, graving.

4735. מִקְנֶה, miqneh, *mik-neh´*; from 7069; something *bought*, i.e. *property*, but only live *stock*; (abstract) *acquisition*:—cattle, flock, herd, possession, purchase, substance.

4736. מִקְנָה, miqnâh, *mik-naw´*; feminine of 4735; (properly) a *buying*, i.e. *acquisition*; (concrete) a piece of *property* (land or living); also the *sum* paid:—(he that is) bought, possession, piece, purchase.

4737. מִקְנֵיָהוּ, Miqnêyâhûw, *mik-nay-yaw´-hoo*; from 4735 and 3050; *possession of Jah; Miknejah*, an Israelite:—Mikneiah.

4738. מִקְסָם, miqsâm, *mik-sawm´*; from 7080; an *augury*:—divination.

4739. מָקַץ, Mâqats, *maw-kats´*; from 7112; *end; Makats*, a place in Palestine:—Makaz.

4740. מִקְצוֹעַ, miqtsôwa', *mik-tso´-ah*; or מִקְצֹעַ, **miqtsôa',** *mik-tso´-ah*; or (feminine) מַקְצֹעָה, **maqtsô'âh,** *mak-tso-aw´*; from 7106 in the denominative sense of *bending*; an *angle* or recess:—corner, turning.

4741. מַקְצֻעָה, maqtsu'âh, *mak-tsoo-aw´*; from 7106; a *scraper*, i.e. a carving *chisel*:—plane.

4742. מְקֻצְעָה, mᵉquts'âh, *mek-oots-aw´*; from 7106 in the denominative sense of *bending*; an *angle*:—corner.

4743. מָקַק, mâqaq, *maw-kak´*; a primitive root; to *melt*; (figurative) to *flow, dwindle, vanish*:—consume away, be corrupt, dissolve, pine away.

4744. מִקְרָא, miqrâ', *mik-raw´*; from 7121; something *called* out, i.e. a public *meeting* (the act, the persons, or the place); also a *rehearsal*:—assembly, calling, convocation, reading.

A masculine noun meaning a convocation, reading, a public meeting, and an assembly. This word usually refers to an assembly for religious purposes. The Passover included a holy convocation on the first and seventh days (Ex 12:16); other festivals also included the gathering of the people (Nu 28:18, 25, 26; 29:1, 7, 12). This word can also mean reading in the sense of a public reading or that which is read in such a meeting. For example, Ezra read the Law of God to a gathering of the Israelites, explaining so the people could understand (Ne 8:8).

4745. מִקְרֶה, miqreh, *mik-reh´*; from 7136; something *met* with, i.e. an *accident* or *fortune*:—something befallen, befalleth, chance, event, hap (-peneth).

4746. מְקָרֶה, mᵉqâreh, *mek-aw-reh´*; from 7136; (properly) something *meeting*, i.e. a *frame* (of timbers):—building.

4747. מְקֵרָה, mᵉqêrâh, *mek-ay-raw´*; from the same as 7119; a *cooling* off:— × summer.

4748. מִקְשֶׁה, miqsheh, *mik-sheh´*; from 7185 in the sense of *knotting* up round and hard; something *turned* (rounded), i.e. a *curl* (of tresses):— × well [set] hair.

4749. מִקְשָׁה, miqshâh, *mik-shaw´*; feminine of 4748; *rounded* work, i.e. moulded by *hammering* (*repoussé*):—beaten (out of one piece, work), upright, whole piece.

4750. מִקְשָׁה, miqshâh, *mik-shaw´*; denominative from 7180; (literal) a *cucumbered* field, i.e. a *cucumber* patch:—garden of cucumbers.

4751. מַר, mar, *mar*; or (feminine) **מָרָה, mârâh,** *maw-raw´*; from 4843; *bitter* (literal or figurative); also (as noun) *bitterness*, or (adverb) *bitterly*:— + angry, bitter (-ly, -ness), chafed, discontented, × great, heavy.

A masculine adjective meaning bitter. The feminine form is *mârâh*. As is common with Hebrew adjectives, it can modify another noun (Ex 15:23), or it can be a substantive, functioning alone as the noun bitterness (Isa 38:15, 17). This word can also operate as an adverb, meaning bitterly (Isa 33:7; Eze 27:30). Used literally, it may modify water (Ex 15:23) and food (Pr 27:7). The Hebrew word can also be used to describe the results of continued fighting (2Sa 2:26). It can be used metaphorically to modify a cry or mourning (Ge 27:34; Est 4:1; Eze 27:30); to represent a characteristic of death (1Sa 15:32); or to describe a person as hot-tempered (Jgs 18:25); discontented (1Sa 22:2); provoked (2Sa 17:8); anguished (Eze 27:31); or ruthless (Hab 1:6). One instance of this word that deserves special attention is the "bitter water," that determined the legal status of a woman accused of infidelity (Nu 5:18, 19, 23, 24, 27). This was holy water that was combined with dust from the tabernacle floor and ink (see Nu 5:17, 23) and then was ingested by the accused. This water was literally "bitter" and would produce "bitterness" or punishment if the woman were guilty.

4752. מַר, mar, *mar*; from 4843 in its original sense of *distillation*; a *drop*:—drop.

4753. מֹר, môr, *more*; or **מוֹר, môwr,** *more*; from 4843; *myrrh* (as *distilling* in drops, and also as *bitter*):—myrrh.

4754. מָרָא, mârâ', *maw-raw´*; a primitive root; to *rebel*; hence (through the idea of *maltreating*) to *whip*, i.e. *lash* (self with wings, as the ostrich in running):—be filthy, lift up self.

4755. מָרָא, Mârâ', *maw-raw´*; for 4751 feminine; *bitter; Mara*, a symbolical name of Naomi:—Mara.

4756. מָרֵא, mârê', *maw-ray´*; (Chaldee); from a root corresponding to 4754 in the sense of *domineering*; a *master*:—lord, Lord.

An Aramaic noun meaning lord or king. It appears only four times, and all occurrences are found in the book of Daniel. It is applied to King Nebuchadnezzar (Da 4:19[16], 24[21]) and to God (Da 2:47; 5:23). This term appears in parallel with *melek* (4430), meaning king (Da 2:47; 4:24[21]) in two of the occurrences. It appears in reference to a human king (and in virtual parallelism with *melek* [4430]) in another occurrence (Da 4:19[16]). In the final occurrence (Da 5:23), it appears in the phrase, *mârê' shĕmayyâ'* (8065), "the Lord of heaven," which is a reference to the divine monarch. Therefore, it is clear that this is a term that represents an individual with much power, authority, and respect.

4757. מְרֹדַךְ בַּלְאֲדָן, Mᵉrôdak Bal'ădân, *mer-o-dak´ bal-ah-dawn´*; of foreign derivation; *Merodak-Baladan*, a Babylonian king:—Merodach-baladan. Compare 4781.

4758. מַרְאֶה, mar'eh, *mar-eh´*; from 7200; a *view* (the act of seeing); also an *appearance* (the thing seen), whether (real) a *shape* (especially if handsome, *comeliness*; often plural the *looks*), or (mental) a *vision*:— × apparently, appearance (-reth), × as soon as beautiful (-ly), countenance, fair, favoured, form, goodly, to look (up) on (to), look [-eth], pattern, to see, seem, sight, visage, vision.

A masculine noun meaning a sight, an appearance, a vision. Derived from the verb *râ'âh* (7200), meaning to see, this noun bears many of the same shades of meaning as the verb. It can represent the act of seeing (Ge 2:9; Le 13:12); the appearance of the object (Le 13:3; Da 1:13); the object which is seen (Ex 3:3); the face, being that part of the person which is visible (SS 2:14; 5:15); a supernatural vision (Eze 8:4; 11:24; Da 8:16, 27); the ability to see (Ecc 6:9);the shining light of a fire (Nu 9:15) or of lightning (Da 10:6).

4759. מַרְאָה, mar'âh, *mar-aw´*; feminine of 4758; a *vision*; also (causative) a *mirror*:—looking glass, vision.

A feminine noun meaning a supernatural vision, a mirror. This noun is derived from the verb *râ'âh* (7200), meaning to see. As a supernatural vision, it is a means of divine revelation (Nu 12:6). This term can stand by itself (1Sa 3:15); or it can function as a cognate accusative (Da 10:7, 8). The word is sometimes used in the expression *mar'ôth halaylâh* (3915), meaning visions of the night (Ge 46:2); and *mar'ôwth 'ĕlôhiym* (430), meaning visions of God (Eze 1:1; 8:3; 40:2). The word is only used once in the Hebrew Bible to signify a mirror or a polished metal plate (Ex 38:8).

4760. מֻרְאָה, mur'âh, *moor-aw´*; apparently feminine passive causative participle of 7200; something *conspicuous*, i.e. the *craw* of a bird (from its *prominence*):—crop.

4761. מַרְאָשׁוֹת, mar'âshôth, *mar-aw-shoth´*; denominative from 7218; (properly) *headship*, i.e. (plural for collective) *dominion*:—principality.

4762. מַרְאֵשָׁה, Mârê'shâh, *mawr-ay-shaw´*; or **מָרֵשָׁה, Mârêshâh,** *mawr-ay-shaw´*; formed like 4761; *summit; Mareshah*, the name of two Israelites and of a place in Palestine:—Mareshah.

4763. מְרַאֲשָׁה, mᵉra'ăshâh, *mer-ah-ash-aw´*; formed like 4761; (properly) a *headpiece*, i.e. (plural for adverb) *at* (or *as*) the *head-rest* (or pillow):—bolster, head, pillow. Compare 4772.

4764. מֵרַב, Mêrab, *may-rab´*; from 7231; *increase; Merab*, a daughter of Saul:—Merab.

4765. מַרְבַד, marbad, *mar-bad´*; from 7234; a *coverlet*:—covering of tapestry.

4766. מַרְבֶּה, marbeh, *mar-beh´*; from 7235; (properly) *increasing*; as noun, *greatness*, or (adverb) *greatly*:—great, increase.

4767. מִרְבָּה, mirbâh, *meer-baw´*; from 7235; *abundance*, i.e. a great quantity:—much.

4768. מַרְבִּית, marbîyth, *mar-beeth´*; from 7235; a *multitude*; also *offspring*; (specifically) *interest* (on capital):—greatest part, greatness, increase, multitude.

4769. מַרְבֵּץ, marbêts, *mar-bates´*; from 7257; a *reclining* place, i.e. *fold* (for flocks):—couching place, place to lie down.

4770. מַרְבֵּק, marbêq, *mar-bake´*; from an unused root meaning to *tie* up; a *stall* (for cattle):— × fat (-ted), stall.

4771. מַרְגּוֹעַ, margôwa', *mar-go´-ah*; from 7280; a *resting* place:—rest.

4772. מַרְגְּלוֹת, margᵉlôwth, *mar-ghel-oth´*; denominative from 7272; (plural for collective) a *footpiece*, i.e. (adverb) *at the foot*, or (directive) the *foot* itself:—feet. Compare 4763.

4773. מַרְגֵּמָה, margêmâh, *mar-gay-maw´*; from 7275; a *stone-heap*:—sling.

4774. מַרְגֵּעָה, margê'âh, *mar-gay-aw´*; from 7280; *rest*:—refreshing.

4775. מָרַד, mârad, *maw-rad´*; a primitive root; to *rebel*:—rebel (-lious).

A verb meaning to rebel. This word usually described the activity of resisting authority, whether against the Lord (Nu 14:9; Da 9:9) or against human kings (Ge 14:4; Ne 2:19). In one instance, it is used to describe those who rebel against the light (i.e. God's truth [Job 24:13]). This word is also used to describe a general, rebellious character of a nation (Eze 2:3; 20:38); as well as a specific act of rebellion, such as Hezekiah's rebellion against Sennacherib (2Ki 18:7, 20; Isa 36:5); or Zedekiah's rebellion against Nebuchadnezzar (2Ki 24:20; Jer 52:3; Eze 17:15).

4776. מְרַד, mᵉrad, *mer-ad´*; (Chaldee); from a root corresponding to 4775; *rebellion*:—rebellion.

An Aramaic masculine noun meaning rebellion. This word is used only once in the OT and is related to the Hebrew word *mârad* (4775), meaning to rebel. In Ezr 4:19, this word described Jerusalem's past rebellion.

4777. מֶרֶד, **mered,** *meh´-red*; from 4775; *rebellion*:—rebellion.

A masculine noun meaning rebellion. This word comes from the verb *mârad* (4775), meaning to rebel, and occurs only once in the OT. In Jos 22:22, it was used to describe the act of building another altar on the east of the Jordan River as rebellious.

4778. מֶרֶד, **Mered,** *meh´-red*; the same as 4777; *Mered*, an Israelite:—Mered.

4779. מָרָד, **mârâd,** *maw-rawd´*; (Chaldee); from the same as 4776; *rebellious*:—rebellious.

An Aramaic adjective meaning rebellious. This word is used only twice in the OT and is related to the Hebrew word *mârad* (4775), meaning to rebel. In Ezr 4:12, 15, it described the historically rebellious character of Jerusalem.

4780. מַרְדּוּת, **mardûwth,** *mar-dooth´*; from 4775; *rebelliousness*:— × rebellious.

A feminine noun meaning rebelliousness. This word comes from the verb *mârad* (4775), meaning to rebel, and occurs only once in the OT. In 1Sa 20:30, Saul used it in his anger against Jonathan as a derogatory word to describe Jonathan's mother.

4781. מְרֹדָךְ, **Mᵉrôdâk,** *mer-o-dawk´*; of foreign derivation; *Merodak*, a Babylonian idol:—Merodach. Compare 4757.

4782. מָרְדְּכַי, **Mordᵉkay,** *mor-dek-ah´ee*; of foreign derivation; *Mordecai*, an Israelite:—Mordecai.

4783. מֻרְדָּף, **murdâph,** *moor-dawf´*; from 7291; *persecuted*:—persecuted.

4784. מָרָה, **mârâh,** *maw-raw´*; a primitive root; to *be* (causative, *make*) *bitter* (or unpleasant); (figurative) to *rebel* or *resist*; (causative) to *provoke*:—bitter, change, be disobedient, disobey, grievously, provocation, provoke (-ing), (be) rebel (against, -lious).

A verb meaning to be rebellious. In one instance, this word spoke of a son's rebellion against his parents (Dt 21:18, 20). In all other instances, this word was used of rebellion against God, which provoked Him to action. This word is usually used as an indictment against a nation's rebellion, whether Israel's (Dt 9:23, 24; Ps 78:8; Jer 5:23); Samaria's (Hos 13:16[14:1]); or David's enemies (Ps 5:10[11]). In a few instances, it is used to indict specific people, as Moses (Nu 20:24; 27:14), or a man of God who disobeyed (1Ki 13:21, 26).

4785. מָרָה, **Mârâh,** *maw-raw´*; the same as 4751 feminine; *bitter; Marah*, a place in the Desert:—Marah.

4786. מֹרָה, **môrâh,** *mo-raw´*; from 4843; *bitterness*, i.e. (figurative) *trouble*:—grief.

4787. מָרָה, **môrâh,** *mo-raw´*; from 4786; *trouble*:—bitterness.

4788. מָרוּד, **mârûwd,** *maw-rood´*; from 7300 in the sense of *maltreatment*; an *outcast*; (abstract) *destitution*:—cast out, misery.

4789. מֵרוֹז, **Mêrôwz,** *may-roze´*; of uncertain derivation; *Meroz*, a place in Palestine:—Meroz.

4790. מְרוֹחַ, **mârôwach,** *mawr-o-akh´*; from 4799; *bruised*, i.e. *emasculated*:—broken.

4791. מָרוֹם, **mârôwm,** *maw-rome´*; from 7311; *altitude*, i.e. concrete (an *elevated place*), abstract (*elevation*), figurative (*elation*), or adverb (*aloft*):—(far) above, dignity, haughty, height, (most, on) high (one, place), loftily, upward.

4792. מֵרוֹם, **Mêrôwm,** *may-rome´*; formed like 4791; *height; Merom*, a lake in Palestine:—Merom.

4793. מֵרוֹץ, **mêrôwts,** *may-rotes´*; from 7323; a *run* (the trial of speed):—race.

4794. מְרוּצָה, **mᵉrûwtsâh,** *mer-oo-tsaw´*; or מְרֻצָה, **mᵉrutsâh,** *mer-oo-tsaw´*; feminine of 4793; a *race* (the act), whether the manner or the progress:—course, running. Compare 4835.

4795. מָרוּק, **mârûwq,** *maw-rook´*; from 4838; (properly) *rubbed*; but used abstractly, a *rubbing* (with perfumery):—purification.

A masculine noun meaning rubbing, purification. The one occurrence of this word is in the book of Esther and mentions the treatments the women underwent for a year prior to meeting King Ahasuerus. This entailed being cleansed and perfumed with various oils (Est 2:12). See the related Hebrew root *mâraq* (4838).

4796. מָרוֹת, **Mârôwth,** *maw-rohth´*; plural of 4751 feminine; *bitter* springs; *Maroth*, a place in Palestine:—Maroth.

4797. מִרְזַח, **mirzach,** *meer-zakh´*; from an unused root meaning to *scream*; a *cry*, i.e. (of joy), a *revel*:—banquet.

4798. מַרְזֵחַ, **marzêach,** *mar-zay´-akh*; formed like 4797; a *cry*, i.e. (of grief) a *lamentation*:—mourning.

4799. מָרַח, **mârach,** *maw-rakh´*; a primitive root; (properly) to *soften* by rubbing or pressure; hence (medicinally) to *apply* as an emollient:—lay for a plaister.

4800. מֶרְחָב, **merchâb,** *mer-khawb´*; from 7337; *enlargement*, either literal (an *open space*, usually in a good sense), or figurative (*liberty*):—breadth, large place (room).

4801. מֶרְחָק, **merchâq,** *mer-khawk´*; from 7368; *remoteness*, i.e. (concrete) a *distant* place; often (adverb) *from afar*:—(a-, dwell in, very) far (country, off). See also 1023.

4802. מַרְחֶשֶׁת, **marchesheth,** *mar-kheh´-sheth*; from 7370; a *stew*-pan:—frying pan.

4803. מָרַט, **mâraṭ,** *maw-rat´*; a primitive root; to *polish*; (by implication) to *make bald* (the head), to *gall* (the shoulder); also, to *sharpen*:—bright, furbish, (have his) hair (be) fallen off, peeled, pluck off (hair).

4804. מְרַט, **mᵉraṭ,** *mer-at´*; (Chaldee); corresponding to 4803; to *pull* off:—be plucked.

4805. מְרִי, **mᵉrîy,** *mer-ee´*; from 4784; *bitterness*, i.e. (figurative) *rebellion*; (concrete) *bitter*, or *rebellious*:—bitter, (most) rebel (-lion, -lious).

A masculine noun meaning obstinacy, stubbornness, rebelliousness. The term consistently stays within this tight semantic range and most often describes the Israelites' determined refusal to obey the precepts laid down by the Lord in His Law or Torah. This characteristic attitude was a visible manifestation of their hard hearts. Moses had the Book of the Law placed beside the Ark of the Covenant to remain there as a witness against the Israelites' rebelliousness after he died (Dt 31:27; Nu 17:10[25]). The Lord rejected Saul as king over Israel because of his rebellion against the command the Lord had earlier given him (1Sa 15:23). Continually in Ezekiel, the Lord refers to Israel as the "house of rebelliousness" (= rebellious people; Eze 2:5–8; 3:9, 26, 27; 12:2, 3, 9). This noun is derived from the verb *mârâh* (4784).

4806. מְרִיא, **mᵉrîy',** *mer-ee´*; from 4754 in the sense of *grossness*, through the idea of *domineering* (compare 4756); *stall-fed*; often (as noun) a *beeve*:—fat (fed) beast (cattle, -ling).

4807. מְרִיב בַּעַל, **Mᵉrîyb Baʻal,** *mer-eeb´ bah´-al*; from 7378 and 1168; *quarreller of Baal; Merib-Baal*, an epithet of Gideon:—Merib-baal. Compare 4810.

4808. מְרִיבָה, **mᵉrîybâh,** *mer-ee-baw´*; from 7378; *quarrel*:—provocation, strife.

4809. מְרִיבָה, **Mᵉrîybâh,** *mer-ee-baw´*; the same as 4808; *Meribah*, the name of two places in the Desert:—Meribah.

4810. מְרִי בַעַל, **Mᵉrîy Baʻal,** *mer-ee´ bah´-al*; from 4805 and 1168; *rebellion of* (i.e. *against*) *Baal; Meri-Baal*, an epithet of Gideon:—Meri-baal. Compare 4807.

4811. מְרָיָה, **M^erâyâh**, *mer-aw-yaw´*; from 4784; *rebellion; Merajah*, an Israelite:—Meraiah. Compare 3236.

4812. מְרָיוֹת, **M^erâyôwth**, *mer-aw-yohth´*; plural of 4811; *rebellious; Merajoth*, the name of two Israelites:—Meraioth.

4813. מִרְיָם, **Miryâm**, *meer-yawm´*; from 4805; *rebelliously; Mirjam*, the name of two Israelitesses:—Miriam.

4814. מְרִירוּת, **m^erîyrûwth**, *mer-ee-rooth´*; from 4843; *bitterness*, i.e. (figurative) *grief*:—bitterness.

4815. מְרִירִי, **m^erîyrîy**, *mer-ee-ree´*; from 4843; *bitter*, i.e. *poisonous*:—bitter.

4816. מֹרֶךְ, **môrek**, *mo´-rek*; perhaps from 7401; *softness*, i.e. (figurative) *fear*:—faintness.

4817. מֶרְכָּב, **merkâb**, *mer-kawb´*; from 7392; a *chariot*; also a *seat* (in a vehicle):—chariot, covering, saddle.

4818. מֶרְכָּבָה, **merkâbâh**, *mer-kaw-baw´*; feminine of 4817; a *chariot*:—chariot. See also 1024.

4819. מַרְכֹּלֶת, **markôleth**, *mar-ko´-leth*; from 7402; a *mart*:—merchandise.

4820. מִרְמָה, **mirmâh**, *meer-maw´*; from 7411 in the sense of *deceiving; fraud*:—craft, deceit (-ful, -fully), false, feigned, guile, subtilly, treachery.

A feminine noun meaning fraud, deceit. The term signifies the intentional misleading of someone else through distorting or withholding the truth. Jacob stole Esau's blessing through deceit (Ge 27:35; cf. Ge 34:13). Deceit fills the heart of those who plan evil (Pr 12:20; cf. Ps 36:3[4]; Pr 12:5, 17; 14:8). David exhorted his children to keep their tongues from evil and their lips from words of deceit (Ps 34:13[14]). The Lord cannot tolerate deceitful weights (Mic 6:11); and a false balance is an abomination to Him (Pr 11:1).

4821. מִרְמָה, **Mirmâh**, *meer-maw´*; the same as 4820; *Mirmah*, an Israelite:—Mirma.

4822. מְרֵמוֹת, **M^erêmôwth**, *mer-ay-mohth´*; plural from 7311; *heights; Meremoth*, the name of two Israelites:—Meremoth.

4823. מִרְמָס, **mirmâs**, *meer-mawce´*; from 7429; *abasement* (the act or the thing):—tread (down) -ing, (to be) trodden (down) under foot.

4824. מֵרֹנֹתִי, **Mêrônôthîy**, *may-ro-no-thee´*; patrial from an unused noun; a *Meronothite*, or inhabitant of some (otherwise unknown) Meronoth:—Meronothite.

4825. מֶרֶס, **Meres**, *meh´-res*; of foreign derivation; *Meres*, a Persian:—Meres.

4826. מַרְסְנָא, **Mars^enâ'**, *mar-sen-aw´*; of foreign derivation; *Marsena*, a Persian:—Marsena.

4827. מֵרַע, **mêra'**, *may-rah´*; from 7489; used as (abstract) noun, *wickedness*:—do mischief.

4828. מֵרֵעַ, **mêrêa'**, *may-ray´-ah*; from 7462 in the sense of *companionship*; a *friend*:—companion, friend.

4829. מִרְעֶה, **mir'eh**, *meer-eh´*; from 7462 in the sense of *feeding; pasture* (the place or the act); also the *haunt* of wild animals:—feeding place, pasture.

4830. מַרְעִית, **mar'îyth**, *mar-eeth´*; from 7462 in the sense of *feeding; pasturage*; (concrete) a *flock*:—flock, pasture.

4831. מַרְעֲלָה, **Mar'âlâh**, *mar-al-aw´*; from 7477; perhaps *earthquake; Maralah*, a place in Palestine:—Maralah.

4832. מַרְפֵּא, **marpê'**, *mar-pay´*; from 7495; (properly) *curative*, i.e. literal (concrete) a *medicine*, or (abstract) a *cure*; figurative (concrete) *deliverance*, or (abstract) *placidity*:—([in-]) cure (-able), healing (-lth), remedy, sound, wholesome, yielding.

4833. מִרְפָּשׂ, **mirpâs**, *meer-paws´*; from 7515; *muddled* water:—that which … have fouled.

4834. מָרַץ, **mârats**, *maw-rats´*; a primitive root; (properly) to *press*, i.e. (figurative) to be *pungent* or vehement; to *irritate*:—embolden, be forcible, grievous, sore.

4835. מְרוּצָה, **m^erûwtsâh**, *mer-oo-tsaw´*; from 7533; *oppression*:—violence. See also 4794.

4836. מַרְצֵעַ, **martsêa'**, *mar-tsay´-ah*; from 7527; an *awl*:—aul.

4837. מַרְצֶפֶת, **martsepheth**, *mar-tseh´-feth*; from 7528; a *pavement*:—pavement.

4838. מָרַק, **mâraq**, *maw-rak´*; a primitive root; to *polish*; (by implication) to *sharpen*; also to *rinse*:—bright, furbish, scour.

4839. מָרָק, **mâraq**, *maw-rak´*; from 4838; *soup* (as if a *rinsing*):—broth. See also 6564.

4840. מֶרְקָח, **merqâch**, *mer-kawkh´*; from 7543; a *spicy* herb:—× sweet.

4841. מֶרְקָחָה, **merqâchâh**, *mer-kaw-khaw´*; feminine of 4840; (abstract) a *seasoning* (with spicery); (concrete) an *unguent-kettle* (for preparing spiced oil):—pot of ointment, × well.

4842. מִרְקַחַת, **mirqachath**, *meer-kakh´-ath*; from 7543; an aromatic *unguent*; also an *unguent-pot*:—prepared by the apothecaries' art, compound, ointment.

4843. מָרַר, **mârar**, *maw-rar´*; a primitive root; (properly) to *trickle* [see 4752]; but used only as a denominative from 4751; to *be* (causative, *make*) *bitter* (literal or figurative):—(be, be in, deal, have, make) bitter (-ly, -ness), be moved with choler, (be, have sorely, it) grieved (-eth), provoke, vex.

4844. מְרֹר, **mârôr**, *mawr-ore´*; or מָרוֹר, **mârôwr**, *mawr-ore´*; from 4843; a *bitter* herb:—bitter (-ness).

4845. מְרֵרָה, **m^erêrâh**, *mer-ay-raw´*; from 4843; *bile* (from its bitterness):—gall.

4846. מְרֹרָה, **m^erôrâh**, *mer-o-raw´*; or מְרוֹרָה, **m^erôwrâh**, *mer-o-raw´*; from 4843; (properly) *bitterness*; (concrete) a *bitter thing*; (specifically) *bile*; also *venom* (of a serpent):—bitter (thing), gall.

4847. מְרָרִי, **M^erârîy**, *mer-aw-ree´*; from 4843; *bitter; Merari*, an Israelite:—Merari. See also 4848.

4848. מְרָרִי, **M^erârîy**, *mer-aw-ree´*; from 4847; a *Merarite* (collective), or descendants of Merari:—Merarites.

4849. מִרְשַׁעַת, **mirsha'ath**, *meer-shah´-ath*; from 7561; a female *wicked doer*:—wicked woman.

4850. מְרָתַיִם, **M^erâthayim**, *mer-aw-thah´-yim*; dual of 4751 feminine; *double bitterness; Merathajim*, an epithet of Babylon:—Merathaim.

4851. מַשׁ, **Mash**, *mash*; of foreign derivation; *Mash*, a son of Aram, and the people descendant from him:—Mash.

4852. מֵשָׁא, **Mêshâ'**, *may-shaw´*; of foreign derivation; *Mesha*, a place in Arabia:—Mesha.

4853. מַשָּׂא, **maśśâ'**, *mas-saw´*; from 5375; a *burden*; (specifically) *tribute*, or (abstract) *porterage*; (figurative) an *utterance*, chiefly a *doom*, especially *singing*; mental, *desire*:—burden, carry away, prophecy, × they set, song, tribute.

A masculine noun meaning a burden or load; by extension, a burden in the form of a prophetic utterance or oracle. It is derived from the verb *nâśâ'* (5375) meaning to lift, to bear, to carry. When used to express a burden or load, it is commonly used to describe that which is placed on the backs of pack animals, like donkeys (Ex 23:5); mules (2Ki 5:17); or camels (2Ki 8:9). Another common usage is in designating what parts of the tabernacle the sons of Kohath, Gershon, and Merari were to carry (Nu 4:15, 19, 24, 27, 31, 32, 47, 49). In Eze 24:25, it is interesting that the lifting of one's soul, *maśśâ'naphshâm* (5315), is used to mean the desires of the heart and that to which persons lift up their souls. By extension, this term is also applied to certain divine oracles that were negative proclamations. Isaiah used this formula to pronounce judgments against the nations of Babylon (Isa 13:1); Philistia (Isa 14:28); Moab (Isa 15:1); Damascus (Isa 17:1); Egypt (Isa 19:1); the desert of the sea (Isa 21:1); Dumah (Isa 21:11); Arabia (Isa 21:13); the Valley of Vision (Isa 22:1); Tyre (Isa 23:1). Other prophets used the same formula to pronounce judgments on Nineveh (Na 1:1); Judah (Hab 1:1); Damascus (Zec 9:1); Jerusalem (Zec 12:1); Israel (Mal 1:1). This formula was also employed to prophesy threats or judgments on individuals (2Ki 9:25; 2Ch 24:27; Pr 30:1; 31:1).

4854. מַשָּׂא**, Maśśâ',** *mas-saw´*; the same as 4853; *burden; Massa*, a son of Ishmael:—Massa.

4855. מַשָּׁא**, mashshâ',** *mash-shaw´*; from 5383; a *loan*; (by implication) *interest* on a debt:—exaction, usury.

4856. מַשֹּׂא**, maśśô',** *mas-so´*; from 5375; *partiality* (as a *lifting* up):—respect.

4857. מַשְׁאָב**, mash'âb,** *mash-awb´*; from 7579; a *trough* for cattle to drink from:—place of drawing water.

4858. מַשָּׂאָה**, maśśâ'âh,** *mas-saw-aw´*; from 5375; a *conflagration* (from the *rising* of smoke):—burden.

4859. מַשָּׁאָה**, mashshâ'âh,** *mash-shaw-aw´*; feminine of 4855; a *loan*:— × any [-thing], debt.

4860. מַשָּׁאוֹן**, mashshâ'ôwn,** *mash-shaw-ohn´*; from 5377; *dissimulation*:—deceit.

4861. מִשְׁאָל**, Mish'âl,** *mish-awl´*; from 7592; *request; Mishal*, a place in Palestine:—Mishal, Misheal. Compare 4913.

4862. מִשְׁאָלָה**, mish'âlâh,** *mish-aw-law´*; from 7592; a *request*:—desire, petition.

4863. מִשְׁאֶרֶת**, mish'ereth,** *mish-eh´-reth*; from 7604 in the original sense of *swelling*; a *kneading-trough* (in which the dough *rises*):—kneading trough, store.

4864. מַשְׂאֵת**, maś'êth,** *mas-ayth´*; from 5375; properly (abstract) a *raising* (as of the hands in prayer), or *rising* (of flame); (figurative) an *utterance*; (concrete) a *beacon* (as *raised*); a *present* (as taken), *mess*, or *tribute*; (figurative) a *reproach* (as a burden):—burden, collection, sign of fire, (great) flame, gift, lifting up, mess, oblation, reward.

A feminine noun meaning an uprising, an utterance, a burden, a portion, a tribute, a reward. The main use connotes something that rises or is lifted up, such as smoke in a smoke signal (Jgs 20:38); or hands in a sacrifice of praise (Ps 141:2). Figuratively, a reproach could be lifted up as a burden (Zep 3:18). This word can also depict a portion or a gift that is carried to someone, often from the table of nobility. For example, David sent a gift of food to Uriah's house (2Sa 11:8); as part of the feast honouring Queen Esther, the king sent gifts to his subjects (Est 2:18).

4865. מִשְׁבְּצוֹת**, mishbᵉtsôwth,** *mish-bets-oth´*; from 7660; a *brocade*; (by analogy) a reticulated *setting* of a gem:—ouch, wrought.

4866. מִשְׁבֵּר**, mashbêr,** *mish-bare´*; from 7665; the *orifice* of the womb (from which the fetus *breaks* forth):—birth, breaking forth.

4867. מִשְׁבָּר**, mishbâr,** *mish-bawr´*; from 7665; a *breaker* (of the sea):—billow, wave.

4868. מִשְׁבָּת**, mishbâth,** *mish-bawth´*; from 7673; *cessation*, i.e. destruction, downfall:—sabbaths (KJV).

4869. מִשְׂגָּב**, miśgâb,** *mis-gawb´*; from 7682; (properly) a *cliff* (or other *lofty* or *inaccessible* place); (abstract) *altitude*; (figurative) a *refuge*:—defence, high fort (tower), refuge. 4869; *Misgab*, a place in Moab:—Misgab.

4870. מִשְׁגֶּה**, mishgeh,** *mish-gay´*, from 7686; an *error*:—oversight.

4871. מָשָׁה**, mâshâh,** *maw-shaw´*; a primitive root; to *pull* out (literal or figurative):—draw (out).

4872. מֹשֶׁה**, Môsheh,** *mo-sheh´*; from 4871; *drawing* out (of the water), i.e. *rescued; Mosheh*, the Israelite lawgiver:—Moses.

4873. מֹשֶׁה**, Môsheh,** *mo-sheh´*; (Chaldee); corresponding to 4872:—Moses.

4874. מַשֶּׁה**, mashsheh,** *mash-sheh´*; from 5383; a *debt*:— + creditor.

4875. מְשׁוֹאָה**, mᵉshôw'âh,** *mesh-o-aw´*; or מְשֹׁאָה**, mᵉshô'âh,** *mesh-o-aw´*; from the same as 7722; (a) *ruin*, abstract (the act) or concrete (the wreck):—desolation, waste.

4876. מַשּׁוּאָה**, mashshûw'âh,** *mash-shoo-aw´*; or מַשֻּׁאָה**, mashshu'âh,** *mash-shoo-aw´*; for 4875; *ruin*:—desolation, destruction.

A plural feminine noun meaning deceptions, destructions, and desolations. The psalmist took solace in the fact that God would cause the destruction of the wicked (Ps 73:18). He also called on God to remember the righteous who had been in the depths of desolation (Ps 74:3).

4877. מְשׁוֹבָב**, Mᵉshôwbâb,** *mesh-o-bawb´*; from 7725; *returned; Meshobab*, an Israelite:—Meshobab.

4878. מְשׁוּבָה**, mᵉshûwbâh,** *mesh-oo-baw´*; or מְשֻׁבָה**, meshubâh,** *mesh-oo-baw´*; from 7725; *apostasy*:—backsliding, turning away.

4879. מְשׁוּגָה**, mᵉshûwgâh,** *mesh-oo-gaw´*; from an unused root meaning to *stray; mistake*:—error.

4880. מָשׁוֹט**, mâshôwṭ,** *maw-shote´*; or מִשּׁוֹט**, mish-shôwṭ,** *mish-shote´*; from 7751; an *oar*:—oar.

4881. מְשׂוּכָּה**, mᵉśûwkkâh,** *mes-ook-kaw´*; or מְשֻׂכָה**, mᵉśukkâh,** *mes-oo-kaw´*; from 7753; a *hedge*:—hedge.

4882. מְשׁוּסָה**, mᵉshûwsâh,** *mesh-oo-saw´*; from an unused root meaning to *plunder; spoliation*:—spoil.

4883. מַשּׂוֹר**, maśśôwr,** *mas-sore´*; from an unused root meaning to *rasp*; a *saw*:—saw.

4884. מְשׂוּרָה**, mᵉśûwrâh,** *mes-oo-raw´*; from an unused root meaning apparently to *divide*; a *measure* (for liquids):—measure.

4885. מָשׂוֹשׂ**, mâśôwś,** *maw-soce´*; from 7797; *delight*, concrete (the cause or object) or abstract (the feeling):—joy, mirth, rejoice.

4886. מָשַׁח**, mâshach,** *maw-shakh´*; a primitive root; to *rub* with oil, i.e. to *anoint*; (by implication) to *consecrate*; also to *paint*:—anoint, paint.

A verb meaning to smear, to anoint. In its common usage, this verb can refer to the rubbing of a shield with oil (Isa 21:5); the painting of a house (Jer 22:14); the anointing of an individual with ointments or lotions (Am 6:6); the spreading of oil on wafers (Ex 29:2). If the verb is used in association with a religious ceremony, it connotes the sanctification of things or people for divine service. Once the tabernacle was erected, it and all its furnishings were anointed with oil to consecrate them (Ex 40:9–11). The most common usage of this verb is the ritual of divine installation of individuals into positions of leadership by the pouring oil on their heads. Most frequently, people were anointed for kingship: Saul (1Sa 10:1); David (1Sa 16:13); and Solomon (1Ki 1:34). The word is also used of people anointed as priests (Ex 28:41; Nu 35:25); and prophets (1Ki 19:16; Isa 61:1).

4887. מְשַׁח**, mᵉshach,** *mesh-akh´*; (Chaldee); from a root corresponding to 4886; *oil*:—oil.

An Aramaic noun meaning olive oil. This word appears only in two passages (Ezr 6:9; 7:22). These passages cite the provisions, including silver, livestock, wheat, salt, wine, and oil, that kings Darius and Artaxerxes supplied to the restoration priests at the Temple in Jerusalem.

4888. מִשְׁחָה, **mishchâh,** *meesh-khaw´*; or מָשְׁחָה, **moshchâh,** *mosh-khaw´*; from 4886; *unction* (the act); (by implication) a consecratory *gift*:—(to be) anointed (-ing), ointment.

A feminine noun meaning anointing, a priestly portion. When used in reference to the anointing, *mishchâh* is always used to modify *shemen* (8081), meaning olive oil (Ex 37:29). At times, this phrase is further qualified by the addition of another modifier, like *qôdesh* (6944), meaning holy (Ex 30:31); *yĕhôwâh* (3068), the proper name of the God of Israel (Le 10:7); or *'ĕlôhym* (430), meaning his God (Le 21:12). This "oil of anointing" was made from a combination of olive oil and spices (Ex 30:25; 35:8, 28). It was then used to anoint someone or something and to consecrate the individual or item to God, such as the Aaronic priests (Ex 29:7, 21; Le 8:2, 12, 30; 21:10); and the tabernacle (Ex 40:9; Le 8:10). It was also used in the customary ministrations of the tabernacle (Ex 31:11; 35:15; Nu 4:16). In addition, this term identified the portion of the sacrifices presented to God, then given to the priests (Le 7:35).

4889. מַשְׁחִית, **mashchîyth,** *mash-kheeth´*; from 7843; *destructive*, i.e. (as noun) *destruction*, literal (specifically a *snare*) or figurative (*corruption*):—corruption, (to) destroy (-ing), destruction, trap, × utterly.

A feminine noun meaning destruction, corruption (Ex 12:13; 2Ki 23:13; 2Ch 20:23; 22:4; Pr 18:9; 28:24; Isa 54:16; Jer 5:26; 22:7; 51:1; Eze 9:6; 21:31[36]; 25:15; Da 10:8.). See also 7843.

4890. מִשְׂחָק, **miśchâq,** *mis-khawk´*; from 7831; a *laughing-stock*:—scorn.

4891. מִשְׁחָר, **mishchâr,** *mish-khawr´*; from 7836 in the sense of day *breaking; dawn*:—morning.

4892. מַשְׁחֵת, **mashchêth,** *mash-khayth´*; for 4889; *destruction*:—destroying.

4893. מִשְׁחָת, **mishchâth,** *mish-khawth´*; or מָשְׁחָת, **moshchâth,** *mosh-khawth´*; from 7843; *disfigurement*:—corruption, marred.

4894. מִשְׁטוֹחַ, **mishṭôwach,** *mish-to´-akh*; or מִשְׁטַח, **mishṭach,** *mish-takh´*; from 7849; a *spreading*-place:—(to) spread (forth, -ing, upon).

4895. מַשְׂטֵמָה, **maśṭêmâh,** *mas-tay-maw´*; from the same as 7850; *enmity*:—hatred.

4896. מִשְׁטָר, **mishṭâr,** *mish-tawr´*; from 7860; *jurisdiction*:—dominion.

4897. מֶשִׁי, **meshîy,** *meh´-shee*; from 4871; *silk* (as *drawn* from the cocoon):—silk.

4898. מְשֵׁיזַבְאֵל, **M**ᵉ**shêyzab'êl,** *mesh-ay-zab-ale´*; from an equivalent to 7804 and 410; *delivered of God; Meshezabel*, an Israelite:—Meshezabeel.

4899. מָשִׁיחַ, **mâshîyach,** *maw-shee´-akh*; from 4886; *anointed*; usually a *consecrated* person (as a king, priest, or saint); specifically the *Messiah*:—anointed, Messiah.

A masculine noun meaning anointed one. Although this word is a noun, it can function both as a substantive (1Sa 24:6[7], 10[11]); or an adjective (Le 4:3, 5, 16). Since it refers to an individual who has been anointed by divine command (2Sa 1:14, 16), it can reference the high priest of Israel (Le 4:3, 5, 16; 6:22[15]); however, it is usually reserved as a marker for kingship, primarily the kings of Israel (1Sa 26:9, 11, 16, 23). In this way, the patriarchs were regarded as God's anointed kings (1Ch 16:22; Ps 105:15). One unique instance of this term is in reference to Cyrus the Persian, a non-Israelite who was regarded as God's anointed (Isa 45:1); therefore, one is forced to understand this characterization, not as a statement of the individual's inherent goodness and perfection, since Cyrus was a worshipper of pagan deities like Marduk. On the contrary, it is a statement of God's appointing or choosing an individual for a task. Furthermore, the concept of the *mâshiyach*, meaning Messiah, as a Saviour is not fully developed in the OT. The closest that one comes to this in the OT is Da 9:25, 26. This concept is developed later, during the NT period and fits better with the parallel Greek word *christos*.

4900. מָשַׁךְ, **mâshak,** *maw-shak´*; a primitive root; to *draw*, used in a great variety of applications (including to *sow*, to *sound*, to *prolong*, to *develop*, to *march*, to *remove*, to *delay*, to *be tall*, etc.):—draw (along, out), continue, defer, extend, forbear, × give, handle, make (pro-, sound) long, × sow, scatter, stretch out.

4901. מֶשֶׁךְ, **meshek,** *meh´-shek*; from 4900; a *sowing*; also a *possession*:—precious, price.

4902. מֶשֶׁךְ, **Meshek,** *meh´-shek*; the same in form as 4901, but probably of foreign derivation; *Meshek*, a son of Japheth, and the people descendant from him:—Mesech, Meshech.

4903. מִשְׁכַּב, **mishkab,** *mish-kab´*; (Chaldee); corresponding to 4904; a *bed*:—bed.

4904. מִשְׁכָּב, **mishkâb,** *mish-kawb´*; from 7901; a *bed;* (figurative) a *bier*; (abstract) *sleep*; (by euphemism) carnal *intercourse*:—bed ([-chamber]), couch, lieth (lying) with.

4905. מַשְׂכִּיל, **maśkîyl,** *mas-keel´*; from 7919; *instructive*, i.e. a *didactic* poem:—Maschil.

4906. מַשְׂכִּית, **maśkîyth,** *mas-keeth´*; from the same as 7906; a *figure* (carved on stone, the wall, or any object); (figurative) *imagination*:—conceit, image (-ry), picture, × wish.

A feminine noun meaning an image, the imagination. It is usually used of a carved image or sculpture, often idolatrous, whether of stone (Le 26:1); silver (Pr 25:11); or of unspecified material (Nu 33:52; Eze 8:12). It is also utilized as a metaphor for one's imagination or conceit (Ps 73:7 *maśkiyyôwthlêbâb* [3824], meaning images of the heart; cf. Pr 18:11).

4907. מִשְׁכַּן, **mishkan,** *mish-kan´*; (Chaldee); corresponding to 4908; *residence*:—habitation.

4908. מִשְׁכָּן, **mishkân,** *mish-kawn´*; from 7931; a *residence* (including a shepherd's *hut*, the *lair* of animals); (figurative) the *grave*; also the *Temple*; (specifically) the *tabernacle* (properly, its wooden walls):—dwelleth, dwelling (place), habitation, tabernacle, tent.

A masculine noun meaning dwelling, tabernacle, or sanctuary. The most significant meaning of the word indicates the dwelling place of the Lord, the tabernacle. The word is often used in Exodus to indicate the temporary lodging of God and His glory among His people, the tabernacle (Le 26:11; Ps 26:8). It is used parallel to the word meaning sanctuary or holy place in the preceding verse (Ex 25:9, cf. v. 8). The noun is formed from the verbal root *shâkan* (7931), which indicates temporary lodging (Ex 25:9; 26:1, 6; 2Sa 7:6). This noun is also often found in parallel with or described by the Hebrew word for tent (Ex 26:35; Jer 30:18).

The tabernacle was called the Tent of Meeting (1Ch 6:32[17]; see Ex 28:43; 30:20; 40:32), for there the Lord met with His people. It was also called the Tent of Testimony (Ex 38:21; Nu 9:15; cf. Nu 17:22, 23; 18:2), since the covenantal documents, the Ten Commandments, were lodged in the Holy of Holies. The Hebrew noun is used with the definite article in 74 of 130 times, indicating that the author expected the reader to know what tabernacle he meant. God gave Moses the pattern of the structure for the tabernacle (Ex 25:9; 26:30). The Lord had His tabernacle set up at Shiloh in Canaan, but it was later abandoned (Ps 78:60). The word is hardly ever used regarding the later Temple of Solomon, of Ezekiel's visionary Temple (2Ch 29:6; Ps 26:8; 46:4[5]; Eze 37:27); or the Lord's dwelling place in Zion (Ps 132:5, 7). The word used most often to describe Solomon's Temple and the postexilic Temple is *bayith* (1004), meaning house.

The word also indicates the dwelling places of the Israelites and other peoples; it describes Korah's dwelling place (Nu 16:24, 27); Israel's dwelling place (Nu 24:5; Isa 32:18; Jer 30:18). Twice the word indicates the dwelling of the dead, i.e. the grave Jerusalem made for herself, and the abode of all classes of men (Ps 49:11[12]; Isa 22:16).

4909. מַשְׂכֹּרֶת, **maśkôreth,** *mas-koh´-reth*; from 7936; *wages* or a *reward*:—reward, wages.

4910. מָשַׁל, **mâshal,** *maw-shal´*; a primitive root; to *rule*:—(have, make to have) dominion, governor, × indeed, reign, (bear, cause to, have) rule (-ing, -r), have power.

A verb denoting to rule, to reign, or to have dominion over. Although its general tone communicates leadership and authority, its specific nuance and connotation are derived from the context in which it appears. In the creation narratives on the fourth day, God created the great luminaries. The greater luminary was to rule the day, and the lesser was to rule the night (Ge 1:18). It is also applied to people who rule: a servant over his master's household (Ge 24:2); a king over his country (Jos 12:5); or his people (Jgs 8:22, 23); a people over another people (Jgs 14:4). God is also said to rule over His people (Jgs 8:23); not over His adversaries (Isa 63:19); over the nations (2Ch 20:6; Ps 22:28[29]); over Jacob (Ps 59:13[14]); over all things (1Ch 29:12).

4911. מָשַׁל, **mâshal,** *maw-shal´*; denominative from 4912; to *liken*, i.e. (transposed) to use figurative language (an allegory, adage, song or the like); (intransitive) to *resemble*:—be (-come) like, compare, use (as a) proverb, speak (in proverbs), utter.

4912. מָשָׁל, **mâshâl,** *maw-shawl´*; apparently from 4910 in some original sense of *superiority* in mental action; (properly) a pithy *maxim*, usually of a metaphorical nature; hence a *simile* (as an adage, poem, discourse):—byword, like, parable, proverb.

4913. מָשָׁל, **Mâshâl,** *maw-shawl´*; for 4861; *Mashal*, a place in Palestine:—Mashal.

4914. מְשֹׁל, **mᵉshôl,** *mesh-ol´*; from 4911; a *satire*:—byword.

4915. מֹשֶׁל, **môshel,** *mo´-shel*; **(1)** from 4910; *empire*; **(2)** from 4911; a *parallel*:—dominion, like.

A masculine noun meaning likeness, dominion. This number in Strong's is associated with two words. The first comes from the verb *mâshal* (4911), meaning to represent or to be like, and is found only in Job 41:33[25], where it is translated "likeness." The second comes from the verb *mâshal* (4910), meaning to rule or to govern. This word is found in Da 11:4 and Zec 9:10, where it describes the dominion of Alexander and the coming Messiah.

4916. מִשְׁלוֹחַ, **mishlôwach,** *mish-lo´-akh*; or מִשְׁלֹחַ, **mishlôach,** *mish-lo´-akh*; also מִשְׁלָח, **mishlâch,** *mish-lawkh´*; from 7971; a *sending* out, i.e. (abstract) *presentation* (favourable), or *seizure* (unfavourable); also (concrete) a place of *dismissal*, or a *business* to be discharged:—to lay, to put, sending (forth), to set.

4917. מִשְׁלַחַת, **mishlachath,** *mish-lakh´-ath*; feminine of 4916; a *mission*, i.e. (abstract and favourable) *release*, or (concrete and unfavourable) an *army*:—discharge, sending.

4918. מְשֻׁלָּם, **Mᵉshullâm,** *mesh-ool-lawm´*; from 7999; *allied; Meshullam*, the name of seventeen Israelites:—Meshullam.

4919. מְשִׁלֵּמוֹת, **Mᵉshillêmôwth,** *mesh-il-lay-mohth´*; plural from 7999; *reconciliations:—Meshillemoth*, an Israelite:—Meshillemoth. Compare 4921.

4920. מְשֶׁלֶמְיָה, **Mᵉshelemyâh,** *mesh-eh-lem-yaw´*; or מְשֶׁלֶמְיָהוּ, **Mᵉshelemyâhûw,** *mesh-eh-lem-yaw´-hoo*; from 7999 and 3050; *ally of Jah; Meshelemjah*, an Israelite:—Meshelemiah.

4921. מְשִׁלֵּמִית, **Mᵉshillêmîyth,** *mesh-il-lay-meeth´*; from 7999; *reconciliation; Meshillemith*, an Israelite:—Meshillemith. Compare 4919.

4922. מְשֻׁלֶּמֶת, **Mᵉshullemeth,** *mesh-ool-leh´-meth*; feminine of 4918; *Meshullemeth*, an Israelitess:—Meshullemeth.

4923. מְשַׁמָּה, **mᵉshammâh,** *mesh-am-maw´*; from 8074; a *waste* or *amazement*:—astonishment, desolate.

4924. מַשְׁמָן, **mishmân,** *mish-mawn´*; from 8080; *fat*, i.e. (literal and abstract) *fatness*; but usually (figurative and concrete) a *rich* dish, a *fertile* field, a *robust* man:—fat (one, -ness, -test, -test place).

4925. מַשְׁמַנָּה, **Mishmannâh,** *mish-man-naw´*; from 8080; *fatness; Mashmannah*, an Israelite:—Mishmannah.

4926. מִשְׁמָע, **mishmâʻ,** *mish-maw´*; from 8085; a *report*:—hearing.

4927. מִשְׁמָע, **Mishmâʻ,** *mish-maw´*; the same as 4926; *Mishma*, the name of a son of Ishmael, and of an Israelite:—Mishma.

4928. מִשְׁמַעַת, **mishmaʻath,** *mish-mah´-ath*; feminine of 4926; *audience*, i.e. the royal *court*; also *obedience*, i.e. (concrete) a *subject*:—bidding, guard, obey.

A feminine noun meaning obedient subjects. This word comes from the verb *shâmaʻ* (8085), meaning to hear and obey, and describes a group of people who are bound to obey. In several instances of this word, it describes a king's personal guard (1Sa 22:14; 2Sa 23:23; 1Ch 11:25). In the only other instance, it depicts a conquered people who are bound to obey (Isa 11:14).

4929. מִשְׁמָר, **mishmâr,** *mish-mawr´*; from 8104; a *guard* (the man, the post, or the *prison*); (figurative) a *deposit*; also (as observed) a *usage* (abstract), or an *example* (concrete):—diligence, guard, office, prison, ward, watch.

4930. מַשְׂמְרָה, **maśmêrâh,** *mas-mayr-aw´*; for 4548 feminine; a *peg*:—nail.

4931. מִשְׁמֶרֶת, **mishmereth,** *mish-meh´-reth*; feminine of 4929; *watch*, i.e. the act (*custody*) or (concrete) the *sentry*, the *post*; (objective) *preservation*, or (concrete) *safe*; (figurative) *observance*, i.e. (abstract) *duty*, or (objective) a *usage* or *party*:—charge, keep, to be kept, office, ordinance, safeguard, ward, watch.

A feminine noun meaning guard, charge, duty. This word comes from the verb *shâmar* (8104), meaning to watch, to keep, to protect, or to guard, and has a multiplicity of usages. In its most basic sense, it describes a guarded place (Nu 17:10[25]; 1Sa 22:23); keeping for later use (Ex 12:6; 16:32–34); or protection against enemies (2Ki 11:5–7). In several instances, it is used of a guard post (Isa 21:8; Hab 2:1). The idea of obedience (i.e. keeping the commandments) is often depicted, which leads to a translation of charge (Ge 26:5; Dt 11:1; Zec 3:7) or duty (Nu 3:7; 9:23; 2Ch 8:14).

4932. מִשְׁנֶה, **mishneh,** *mish-neh´*; from 8138; (properly) a *repetition*, i.e. a *duplicate* (*copy* of a document), or a *double* (in amount); (by implication) a *second* (in order, rank, age, quality or location):—college, copy, double, fatlings, next, second (ordinal), twice as much.

4933. מְשִׁסָּה, **mᵉshissâh,** *mesh-is-saw´*; from 8155; *plunder*:—booty, spoil.

4934. מִשְׁעוֹל, **mishʻôwl,** *mish-ole´*; from the same as 8168; a *hollow*, i.e. a narrow passage:—path.

4935. מִשְׁעִי, **mishʻîy,** *mish-ee´*; probably from 8159; *inspection*:—to supple.

4936. מִשְׁעָם, **Mishʻâm,** *mish-awm´*; apparently from 8159; *inspection; Misham*, an Israelite:—Misham.

4937. מַשְׁעֵן, **mashʻên,** *mash-ane´*; or מִשְׁעָן, **mishʻân,** *mish-awn´*; from 8172; a *support* (concrete), i.e. (figurative) a *protector* or *sustenance*:—stay.

4938. מַשְׁעֵנָה, **mashʻênâh,** *mash-ay-naw´*; or מִשְׁעֶנֶת, **mishʻeneth,** *mish-eh´-neth*; feminine of 4937; *support* (abstract), i.e. (figurative) *sustenance* or (concrete) a *walking-stick*:—staff.

4939. מִשְׂפָּח, **miśpâch,** *mis-pawkh´*; from 5596; *slaughter*:—oppression.

4940. מִשְׁפָּחָה, **mishpâchâh,** *mish-paw-khaw´*; from 8192 [compare 8198]; a *family*, i.e. circle of relatives; (figurative) a *class* (of persons), a *species* (of animals) or *sort* (of things); (by extension) a *tribe* or *people*:—family, kind (-red).

A feminine noun meaning an extended family, a tribe, a clan. It is a group in which there is a close blood relationship. In a technical sense, a *mishpâchâh* is the middle of the subdivisions of the Israelite peoples. The inhabitants of an individual household were identified as a *bayith* (1004), meaning house. Several households together constituted a *mishpâchâh* (Ge 10:31, 32; Ex 6:14, 15, 19, 25). Several families or clans together constituted a *shêbeṭ* (7626) or *maṭṭeh* (4294), meaning tribe. This noun is also used in a less technical sense to indicate an entire people or nation (Eze 20:32; Mic 2:3); an ethnic or racial group (Ge 10:5; 12:3); a tribe (Jos 7:17; Jgs 13:2; 18:2, 11). It occurs in the sense of a guild of scribes in one verse (1Ch 2:55) because the scribal profession was originally a hereditary position. It can also represent a species or kind of animal (Ge 8:19); or a divine plague (Jer 15:3).

4941. מִשְׁפָּט, **mishpâṭ,** *mish-pawt´*; from 8199; (properly) a *verdict* (favourable or unfavourable) pronounced judicially, especially a *sentence* or formal decree (human or [participle] divine *law*, individual or collective), including the act, the place, the suit, the crime, and the penalty; (abstract) *justice*, including a participle *right*, or *privilege* (statutory or customary), or even a *style*:— + adversary, ceremony, charge, × crime, custom, desert, determination, discretion, disposing, due, fashion, form, to be judged, judgment, just (-ice, -ly), (manner of) law (-ful), manner, measure, (due) order, ordinance, right, sentence, usest, × worth, + wrong.

A masculine noun meaning a judgment, a legal decision, a legal case, a claim, proper, rectitude. The word connotes several variations in meanings depending on the context. It is used to describe a legal decision or judgment rendered: it describes a legal decision given by God to be followed by the people (Isa 58:2; Zep 2:3; Mal 2:17). These decisions could come through the use of the Urim and Thummim (Nu 27:21). The high priest wore a pouch called the breastpiece of justice, containing the Urim and Thummim by which decisions were obtained from the Lord (Ex 28:30). Doing what was right and just in the Lord's eyes was far more important than presenting sacrifices to Him (Ge 18:19; Pr 21:3, 15). God was declared to be the Judge of the whole earth who rendered justice faithfully (Ge 18:25; Isa 30:18). In the plural form, the word describes legal judgments, cases, examples, laws, and specifications.

The word describes the legal case or cause presented by someone. The Servant spoken of by Isaiah asked who brought his case of justice against him (Isa 50:8); Job brought his case to vindicate himself (Job 13:18; 23:4). The legal claim or control in a situation is also described by the word. Samuel warned the people of the civil and legal demands a king would place on them (1Sa 8:9); Moses gave legislation to protect the rightful claim of daughters (Ex 21:9). The Hebrew word also described the legal right to property (Jer 32:8). Not surprisingly, the place where judgments were rendered was also described by this word; disputes were to be taken to the place of judgment (Dt 25:1). Solomon built a hall of justice where he served as judge (1Ki 7:7).

The word also describes plans or instructions: it describes the building plans for the tabernacle (Ex 35—40); and the specifications for the Temple (1Ki 6:38); the instructions the angelic messenger gave to Samson's parents about how he was to be brought up (Jgs 13:12). In a more abstract sense, it depicts the manner of life a people followed, such as the Sidonians (Jgs 18:7; 1Sa 2:13).

The word means simple justice in some contexts, often in parallel with synonymous words, such as *chôq* (2706) or *tsedeq* (6664), meaning ordinance or righteousness. It describes justice as one thing Jerusalem was to be filled with along with righteousness (Isa 1:21). Justice and righteousness characterize the Lord's throne (Ps 89:14[15]); and these were coupled with love and faithfulness (cf. Ps 101:1; 111:7). Executing or doing justice was the central goal that Yahweh had for His people (Jer 7:5; Eze 18:8), for that equaled righteousness (Eze 18:9).

4942. מִשְׁפְּתַיִם, **mishpᵉthayim,** *mish-peh-tha-yeem´*; from 8192; a *stall* for cattle (only dual):—burden, sheepfold.

4943. מֶשֶׁק, **mesheq,** *meh´-shek*; from an unused root meaning to *hold; possession*:— + steward.

4944. מַשָּׁק, **mashshâq,** *mash-shawk´*; from 8264; a *traversing*, i.e. rapid *motion*:—running to and fro.

4945. מַשְׁקֶה, **mashqeh,** *mash-keh´*; from 8248; (properly) *causing to drink*, i.e. a *butler*; by implication (intransitive) *drink* (itself); (figurative) a *well-watered* region:—butler (-ship), cupbearer, drink (-ing), fat pasture, watered.

4946. מִשְׁקוֹל, **mishqôwl,** *mish-kole´*; from 8254; *weight*:—weight.

4947. מַשְׁקוֹף, **mashqôwph,** *mash-kofe´*; from 8259 in its original sense of *overhanging*; a *lintel*:—lintel.

4948. מִשְׁקָל, **mishqâl,** *mish-kawl´*; from 8254; *weight* (numerically estimated); hence, *weighing* (the act):—(full) weight.

4949. מִשְׁקֶלֶת, **mishqeleth,** *mish-keh´-leth*; or מִשְׁקֹלֶת, **mishqôleth,** *mish-ko´-leth*; feminine of 4948 or 4947; a *weight*, i.e. a *plummet* (with line attached):—plummet.

4950. מִשְׁקָע, **mishqâʻ,** *mish-kaw´*; from 8257; a *settling* place (of water), i.e. a pond:—deep.

4951. מִשְׂרָה, **miśrâh,** *mis-raw´*; from 8280; *empire*:—government.

4952. מִשְׁרָה, **mishrâh,** *mish-raw´*; from 8281 in the sense of *loosening; maceration*, i.e. steeped *juice*:—liquor.

4953. מַשְׁרוֹקִי, **mashrôwqîy,** *mash-ro-kee´*; (Chaldee); from a root corresponding to 8319; a (musical) *pipe* (from its *whistling* sound):—flute.

4954. מִשְׁרָעִי, **Mishrâʻîy,** *mish-raw-ee´*; patrial from an unused noun from an unused root; probably meaning to *stretch* out; *extension*; a *Mishraite*, or inhabitant (collective) of Mishra:—Mishraites.

4955. מִשְׂרָפָה, **miśrâphâh,** *mis-raw-faw´*; from 8313; *combustion*, i.e. *cremation* (of a corpse), or *calcination* (of lime):—burning.

4956. מִשְׂרְפוֹת מַיִם, **Miśrᵉphôwth mayim,** *mis-ref-ohth´ mah´-yim*; from the plural of 4955 and 4325; *burnings of water; Misrephoth-Majim*, a place in Palestine:—Misrephoth-mayim.

4957. מַשְׂרֵקָה, **Maśrêqâh,** *mas-ray-kaw´*; a form for 7796 used denominatively; *vineyard; Masrekah*, a place in Idumæa:—Masrekah.

4958. מַשְׂרֵת, **maśrêth,** *mas-rayth´*; apparently from an unused root meaning to *perforate*, i.e. hollow out; a *pan*:—pan.

4959. מָשַׁשׁ, **mâshash,** *maw-shash´*; a primitive root; to *feel* of; (by implication) to *grope*:—feel, grope, search.

4960. מִשְׁתֶּה, **mishteh,** *mish-teh´*; from 8354; *drink*; (by implication) *drinking* (the act); also (by implication), a *banquet* or (general) feast:—banquet, drank, drink, feast ([-ed], -ing).

A masculine noun meaning a drink, a feast. This word comes from the verb *shâthâh* (8354), meaning to drink. In a few instances, this word referred specifically to drinks (Ezr 3:7; Da 1:5, 8, 10, 16), but it usually referred to feasts prepared for special occasions: hospitality (Ge 19:3); the weaning of a child (Ge 21:8); making peace (Ge 26:30; 2Sa 3:20); a wedding (Ge 29:22; Jgs 14:10, 12, 17; Est 2:18); merriment (Est 1:3; 9:17–19; Job 1:4, 5; Ecc 7:2). A feast was indicative of blessing (Pr 15:15; Isa 25:6).

4961. מִשְׁתֵּא, **mishtêʼ,** *mish-tay´*; (Chaldee); corresponding to 4960; a *banquet*:—banquet.

4962. מַת, **math,** *math*; from the same as 4970; (properly) an *adult* (as of full length); (by implication) a *man* (only in the plural):— + few, × friends, men, persons, × small.

4963. מַתְבֵּן, **mathbên,** *math-bane´*; denominative from 8401; *straw* in the heap:—straw.

4964. מֶתֶג, **metheg,** *meh´-theg*; from an unused root meaning to *curb*; a *bit*:—bit, bridle.

4965. מֶתֶג הָאַמָּה, **Metheg hâʼAmmâh,** *meh´-theg haw-am-maw´*; from 4964 and 520 with the article interposed; *bit of the metropolis; Metheg-ha-Ammah*, an epithet of Gath:—Metheg-ammah.

4966. מָתוֹק, **mâthôwq,** *maw-thoke´*; or מָתוּק, **mâ-thûwq,** *maw-thook´*; from 4985; *sweet*:—sweet (-er, -ness).

4967. מְתוּשָׁאֵל, **M^e^thûwshâ'êl,** *meth-oo-shaw-ale´*; from 4962 and 410, with the relative interposed; *man who* (is) *of God; Methushaël*, an antediluvian patriarch:—Methusael.

4968. מְתוּשֶׁלַח, **M^e^thûwshelach,** *meth-oo-sheh´-lakh*; from 4962 and 7973; *man of a dart; Methushelach*, an antediluvian patriarch:—Methuselah.

4969. מָתַח, **mâthach,** *maw-thakh´*; a primitive root; to *stretch* out:—spread out.

4970. מָתַי, **mâthay,** *maw-thah´ee*; from an unused root meaning to *extend*; (properly) *extent* (of time); but used only adverb (especially with other particles prefixed), *when* (either relative or interrogitive):—long, when.

4971. מַתְכֹּנֶת, **mathkôneth,** *math-ko´-neth*; or מַתְכֻּנֶת, **mathkuneth,** *math-koo´-neth*; from 8505 in the transferred sense of *measuring; proportion* (in size, number or ingredients):—composition, measure, state, tale.

4972. מַתְּלָאָה, **matt^e^lâ'âh,** *mat-tel-aw-aw´*; from 4100 and 8513; *what a trouble!*:—what a weariness.

4973. מְתַלְּעוֹת, **m^e^thall^e^'ôwth,** *meth-al-leh-oth´*; contraction from 3216; (properly) a *biter*, i.e. a *tooth*:—cheek (jaw) tooth, jaw.

4974. מְתֹם, **m^e^thôm,** *meth-ohm´*; from 8552; *wholesomeness*; also (adverb) *completely*:—men [*by reading* 4962], soundness.

4975. מָתְנַיִם, **mothnayim,** *moth´-na-yim*; from an unused root meaning to *be slender*; (properly) the *waist* or small of the back; only in plural the *loins*:— + greyhound, loins, side.

4976. מַתָּן, **mattân,** *mat-tawn´*; from 5414; a *present*:—gift, to give, reward.

4977. מַתָּן, **Mattân,** *mat-tawn´*; the same as 4976; *Mattan*, the name of a priest of Baal, and of an Israelite:—Mattan.

4978. מַתְּנָא, **matt^e^nâ',** *mat-ten-aw´*; (Chaldee); corresponding to 4979:—gift.

4979. מַתָּנָה, **mattânâh,** *mat-taw-naw´*; feminine of 4976; a *present*; specifically (in a good sense) a sacrificial *offering*, (in a bad sense) a *bribe*:—gift.

4980. מַתָּנָה, **Mattânâh,** *mat-taw-naw´*; the same as 4979; *Mattanah*, a place in the Desert:—Mattanah.

4981. מִתְנִי, **Mithnîy,** *mith-nee´*; probably patrial from an unused noun meaning *slenderness*; a *Mith-nite*, or inhabitant of Methen:—Mithnite.

4982. מַתְּנַי, **Matt^e^nay,** *mat-ten-ah´ee*; from 4976; *liberal; Mattenai*, the name of three Israelites:—Mattenai.

4983. מַתַּנְיָה, **Mattanyâh,** *mat-tan-yaw´*; or מַתַּנְיָהוּ, **Mattanyâhûw,** *mat-tan-yaw´-hoo*; from 4976 and 3050; *gift of Jah; Mattanjah*, the name of ten Israelites:—Mattaniah.

4984. מִתְנַשֵּׂא, **mithnaśśê',** *mith-nas-say´*; from 5375; (used as abstract) supreme *exaltation*:—exalted.

4985. מָתַק, **mâthaq,** *maw-thak´*; a primitive root; to *suck*; (by implication) to *relish*, or (intransitive) *be sweet*:—be (made, × take) sweet.

4986. מֶתֶק, **metheq,** *meh´-thek*; from 4985; (figurative) *pleasantness* (of discourse):—sweetness.

4987. מֹתֶק, **môtheq,** *mo´-thek*; from 4985; *sweetness*:—sweetness.

4988. מָתָק, **mâthâq,** *maw-thawk´*; from 4985; a *dainty*, i.e. (general) *food*:—feed sweetly.

4989. מִתְקָה, **Mithqâh,** *mith-kaw´*; feminine of 4987; *sweetness; Mithkah*, a place in the Desert:—Mithcah.

4990. מִתְרְדָת, **Mithr^e^dâth,** *mith-red-awth´*; of Persian origin; *Mithredath*, the name of two Persians:—Mithredath.

4991. מַתָּת, **mattâth,** *mat-tawth´*; feminine of 4976 abbreviation; a *present*:—gift.

4992. מַתַּתָּה, **Mattattâh,** *mat-tat-taw´*; for 4993; *gift of Jah; Mattattah*, an Israelite:—Mattathah.

4993. מַתִּתְיָה, **Mattithyâh,** *mat-tith-yaw´*; or מַתִּתְיָהוּ, **Mattithyâhûw,** *mat-tith-yaw´-hoo*; from 4991 and 3050; *gift of Jah; Mattithjah*, the name of four Israelites:—Mattithiah.

4994. נָא, **nâ',** *naw*; a primitive particle of incitement and entreaty, which may usually be rendered *I pray, now* or *then*; added mostly to verbs (in the imperative or future), or to interject, occasionally to an adverb or conjuction:—I beseech (pray) thee (you), go to, now, oh.

A participle meaning please, now. The most common use of this word is similar to the antiquated use of pray as in pray tell. Since it was frequently used as a polite form of asking for something, it was often left untranslated in many English versions of the Bible. Abraham used this word when he asked Sarah to say she was his sister (Ge 12:13); Moses used the word when he asked the people to listen to him (Nu 20:10). It was often used to ask permission (Nu 20:17).

4995. נָא, **nâ',** *naw*; apparently from 5106 in the sense of *harshness* from refusal; (properly) *tough*, i.e. *uncooked* (flesh):—raw.

4996. נֹא, **Nô',** *no*; of Egyptian origin; *No* (i.e. *Thebes*), the capital of Upper Egypt:—No. Compare 528.

4997. נֹאד, **nô'd,** *node*; or נוֹאד, **nôw'd,** *node*; also (feminine) נֹאדָה, **nô'dâh,** *no-daw´*; from an unused root of uncertain significance; a (skin or leather) *bag* (for fluids):—bottle.

4998. נָאָה, **nâ'âh,** *naw-aw´*; a primitive root; (properly) to *be at home*, i.e. (by implication) to be *pleasant* (or *suitable*), i.e. *beautiful*:—be beautiful, become, be comely.

4999. נָאָה, **nâ'âh,** *naw-aw´*; from 4998; a *home*; (figurative) a *pasture*:—habitation, house, pasture, pleasant place.

A feminine noun meaning a dwelling, an abode, a residence, a habitation, a pasture, a meadow. This word describes a place where humans permanently settle and live; or to an area where flocks and herds graze, reside, lie down, and rest. In His fierce anger for their iniquities, the Lord vented His wrath on Israel, destroying without mercy the dwellings found within its borders (La 2:2; cf. Jer 25:37). The Lord roars from Zion, and the pastures of the shepherds wither (Am 1:2). Painting a picture of abundant provisions, the psalmist praises God for the overflowing pastures of the wilderness (Ps 65:12[13]; cf. the description of wilderness pastures in Jer 9:10[9]). The most famous use of the term comes in Ps 23, where in vivid imagery the Lord is depicted as the great Shepherd who causes His sheep to lie down in green pastures (Ps 23:2). Once it is used in conjunction with the term used for God, forming the phrase pastures of God. In the context, the phrase refers to the land of Israel and recalls the idea of the people of Israel as God's flock (Ps 83:12[13]). This term stems from the verb *nâ'âh* (4998).

5000. נָאוֶה, **nâ'veh,** *naw-veh´*; from 4998 or 5116; *suitable*, or *beautiful*:—becometh, comely, seemly.

5001. נָאַם, **nâ'am,** *naw-am´*; a primitive root; (properly) to *whisper*, i.e. (by implication) to *utter* as an oracle:—say.

A verb meaning to murmur, to mutter, to whisper, to utter. The term is used once to describe the occupation which the false prophets of Jeremiah's day habitually practiced. They uttered false prophecies and claimed they were from the Lord, thus leading many people astray (Jer 23:31).

5002. נְאֻם, **n^e^'um,** *nah-oom´*; from 5001; an *oracle*:—(hath) said, saith.

5003. נָאַף, **nâ'aph,** *naw-af´*; a primitive root; to *commit adultery*; (figurative) to *apostatize*:—adulterer (-ess), commit (-ing) adultery, woman that breaketh wedlock.

5004. נִאֻף, **ni'uph,** *nee-oof´*; from 5003; *adultery*:—adultery.

5005. נַאֲפוּף, na'ăphûwph, *nah-af-oof´*; from 5003; *adultery*:—adultery.

5006. נָאַץ, nâ'ats, *naw-ats´*; a primitive root; to *scorn*; or (Ecc 12:5) by interchange for 5132, to *bloom*:—abhor, (give occasion to) blaspheme, contemn, despise, flourish, × great, provoke.

A verb meaning to revile, to scorn, to reject. It is related to *nâtsats* (5340), meaning to scorn or to blaspheme. This word often refers to rejecting the counsel of a wise person. This scornful attitude results in an unhappy life: people live in affliction because they reject God's counsel (Ps 107:11). Another example of a passage that uses this word is Pr 1:30, where wisdom laments that people scorn her reproof. In another instance of this word, the Israelites were chastised because they had rejected God's Law (Isa 5:24).

5007. נְאָצָה, ne**'âtsâh**, *neh-aw-tsaw´*; or נֶאָצָה, **ne'âtsâh**, *neh-aw-tsaw´*; from 5006; *scorn*:—blasphemy.

5008. נָאַק, nâ'aq, *naw-ak´*; a primitive root; to *groan*:—groan.

5009. נְאָקָה, ne**'âqâh**, *neh-aw-kaw´*; from 5008; a *groan*:—groaning.

5010. נָאַר, nâ'ar, *naw-ar´*; a primitive root; to *reject*:—abhor, make void.

5011. נֹב, Nôb, *nobe*; the same as 5108; *fruit; Nob*, a place in Palestine:—Nob.

5012. נָבָא, nâbâ', *naw-baw´*; a primitive root; to *prophesy*, i.e. speak (or sing) by inspiration (in prediction or simple discourse):—prophesy (-ing), make self a prophet.

A verb meaning to prophesy, to speak by inspiration, to predict. This most commonly refers to the way in which the word of the Lord came to the people (Jer 19:14; Eze 11:13). There were various means in which people came to prophesy. Eldad and Medad became ecstatic when they prophesied (Nu 11:25–27); whereas the sons of Asaph used songs and instruments when they prophesied (1Ch 25:1). False prophets were also known to prophesy (Zec 13:3).

5013. נְבָא, ne**bâ'**, *neb-aw´*; (Chaldee); corresponding to 5012:—prophesy.

An Aramaic verb meaning to prophesy. This word corresponds to the Hebrew word *nâbâ'* (5012). It is possible that this word takes on the meaning of being carried away through prophecy. Only found once in the OT, this word is used to describe the means by which Haggai and Zechariah prophesied to the people of Israel (Ezr 5:1).

5014. נָבַב, nâbab, *naw-bab´*; a primitive root; to *pierce*; to *be hollow*, or (figurative) *foolish*:—hollow, vain.

5015. נְבוֹ, Ne**bôw**, *neb-o´*; probably of foreign derivation; *Nebo*, the name of a Babylonian deity, also of a mountain in Moab, and of a place in Palestine:—Nebo.

5016. נְבוּאָה, ne**bûw'âh**, *neb-oo-aw´*; from 5012; a *prediction* (spoken or written):—prophecy.

A feminine noun meaning prophecy, a prophetic word. Shemaiah gave a false prophecy to Nehemiah in order to cause him to sin and to saddle him with a bad name (Ne 6:12). The prophecy of Azariah, son of Oded, encouraged King Asa of Judah to implement religious reform in the country, bringing the people back to the Lord their God (2Ch 15:8). Once the word refers to a written prophecy by a prophet named Ahijah (2Ch 9:29). This word stems from the verb *nâbâ'* (5012).

5017. נְבוּאָה, ne**bûw'âh**, *neb-oo-aw´*; (Chaldee); corresponding to 5016; inspired *teaching*:—prophesying.

An Aramaic feminine noun meaning prophesying. It refers to the role and functions of a prophet and appears only once in the OT, where it is recorded that the elders prospered through the prophesying of Haggai the prophet and Zechariah the son of Iddo (Ezr 6:14). It is probably closely related to the Hebrew word *nĕbû'âh* (5016).

5018. נְבוּזַרְאֲדָן, Ne**bûwzar'ădân**, *neb-oo-zar-ad-awn´*; of foreign origin; *Nebuzaradan*, a Babylonian general:—Nebuzaradan.

5019. נְבוּכַדְנֶאצַּר, Ne**bûwkadne'tstsar**, *neb-oo-kad-nets-tsar´*; or נְבֻכַדְנֶאצַּר, **N**e**bukadne'tstsar**, *neb-oo-kad-nets-tsar´*; or נְבֻכַדְנֶצַּר, **N**e**bukadnetstsar**, *neb-oo-kad-nets-tsar´*; or נְבוּכַדְנֶאצַּר, **N**e**bûwkad Ne'tstsar**, *neb-oo-kad nets-tsar´*, (Jer 28:3); or נְבוּכַד נֶצַּר, **N**e**bûwkad Netstsar**, *neb-oo-kad nets-tsar´*; or נְבוּכַדְרֶאצּוֹר, **Nebûwkadre'tsôwr**, *neb-oo-kad-tsore*, (Jer 49:8); or נְבוּכַדְרֶאצַּר, **Nebûwkadre'tstsar**, *neb-oo-kad-rets-tsar´*; of foreign derivation; *Nebukadnetstsar* (or *-retstsar*, or *-retstsor*), king of Babylon:—Nebuchadnezzar, Nebuchadrezzar.

5020. נְבוּכַדְנֶצַּר, Ne**bûwkadnetstsar**, *neb-oo-kad-nets-tsar´*; (Chaldee); corresponding to 5019:—Nebuchadnezzar.

5021. נְבוּשַׁזְבָּן, Ne**bûwshazbân**, *neb-oo-shaz-bawn´*; of foreign derivation; *Nebushazban*, Nebuchadnezzar's chief eunuch:—Nebushazban.

5022. נָבוֹת, Nâbôwth, *naw-both´*; feminine plural from the same as 5011; *fruits; Naboth*, an Israelite:—Naboth.

5023. נְבִזְבָּה, ne**bizbâh**, *neb-iz-baw´*; (Chaldee); of uncertain derivation; a *largess*:—reward.

5024. נָבַח, nâbach, *naw-bakh*; a primitive root; to *bark* (as a dog):—bark.

5025. נֹבַח, Nôbach, *no´-bach*; from 5024; a *bark; Nobach*, the name of an Israelite, and of a place East of the Jordan:—Nobah.

5026. נִבְחַז, Nibchaz, *nib-khaz´*; of foreign origin; *Nibchaz*, a deity of the Avites:—Nibhaz.

5027. נָבַט, nâbaṭ, *naw-bat´*; a primitive root; to *scan*, i.e. look intently at; (by implication) to *regard* with pleasure, favour or care:—(cause to) behold, consider, look (down), regard, have respect, see.

5028. נְבָט, Ne**bâṭ**, *neb-awt´*; from 5027; *regard; Nebat*, the father of Jeroboam I:—Nebat.

5029. נְבִיא, ne**bîy'**, *neb-ee´*; (Chaldee); corresponding to 5030; a *prophet*:—prophet.

An Aramaic masculine noun meaning prophet. It refers to an individual that fulfilled the role and functions of a prophet (Ezr 5:1, 2; 6:14). The word is probably closely related to the biblical Hebrew word (if not the same word), *nâbiy'* (5030); as such, it would share similar, if not the same, variations in meaning.

5030. נָבִיא, nâbîy', *naw-bee´*; from 5012; a *prophet* or (general) *inspired* man:—prophecy, that prophesy, prophet.

A masculine noun meaning a prophet, a spokesman. The meaning is consistently one of prophet and inspired spokesman. Moses was the greatest prophet of the OT (Dt 34:10) and the example for all later prophets. He displayed every aspect of a true prophet, both in his call, his work, his faithfulness, and, at times, his doubts. Only Abraham is called a prophet before Moses (Ge 20:7).

Moses received a call from God to speak His words and perform a specific task (see Ex 3:4, 10; 4:17, 29; 5:1) with the promise that the Lord would be with him and help him accomplish it (see Ex 3:12, 20; 4:12, 14–16). He responded, though reluctantly (see Ex 3:11, 13; 4:1), and God did what He had said He would do (see Ex 6:1; 14:30, 31; 40:34, 38). Moses' prophetic voice spoke to Israel of the past (see Dt 1—3), the present (see Dt 4:1; 26:18), and the future (see Dt 31:20–22), as would every major prophet after him. This pattern, or much of it, is found in the case of every true prophet (see Isa 6; Jer 1; Eze 1—3; Hos 1:2; Am 7:14, 15; Jnh 1:1). All the true prophets stood in the counsel of God to receive their messages (see 1Ki 22:19; Jer 23:22; Am 3:7).

This word describes one who was raised up by God and, as such, could only proclaim that which the Lord gave him to say. A prophet could not contradict the Law of the Lord or speak from his own mind or heart. To do so was to be a false prophet (Jer 14:14; 23:16, 26, 30). What a prophet declared had to come true, or he was false (Dt 18:22; Jer 23:9).

The noun is found parallel to two other words meaning a seer, a prophet (*chôzeh*[2374], *rô'eh*[1Sa 9:9; 2Sa 24:11]), which tends to stress the visionary or perceptive aspects of a prophet's experiences. There were "sons of the prophets," a phrase indicating bands or companies of prophets, "son" in this case meaning a member (1Ki 20:35; 2Ki 2:3,

5; 4:1). Kings sometimes had a group of prophets around them (1Ki 22:22; 2Ch 18:21, 22). Prophets were designated from Israel (Eze 13:2, 4); Samaria (Jer 23:13); and Jerusalem (Zep 3:4). In an unusual development, David set aside some of the sons of Asaph, Heman, and Jeduthun to serve as prophets. Their prophesying was accompanied with musical instruments and possibly was brought on and aided by these instruments. This phenomenon is described mainly in the book of 2 Chronicles (see 2Ch 20:14; 29:30). Evidently, Zechariah, the priest, also prophesied in that era. But Moses himself desired that all God's people have the Spirit of God on them, as did the prophets (Nu 11:29).

5031. נְבִיאָה, nᵉbîyʼâh, *neb-ee-yaw´*; feminine of 5030; a *prophetess* or (generally) *inspired* woman; (by implication) a *poetess*; (by association) a *prophet's wife*:—prophetess.

A feminine noun meaning prophetess. It is the feminine form of the Hebrew *nâbîʼ* (5030), meaning a spokesman, a speaker, or a prophet. The ancient concept of a prophetess was a woman who had the gift of song, like Miriam (Ex 15:20) or Deborah (Jgs 4:4; cf. 5:1). The later concept of a prophetess, being more in line with the concept of a prophet, was one who was consulted in order to receive a word from the Lord, like Huldah (2Ki 22:14; 2Ch 34:22). It also described a false prophetess, Noadiah (Ne 6:14). A unique usage may be its reference to the wife of Isaiah as a prophetess (Isa 8:3). Is this because of her own position and work or because of her relationship with Isaiah, a prophet? It has been interpreted both ways.

5032. נְבָיוֹת, Nᵉbâyôwth, *neb-aw-yoth´*; or **נְבָיֹת, Nebâyôth,** *neb-aw-yoth´*; feminine plural from 5107; *fruitfulnesses; Nebajoth*, a son of Ishmael, and the country settled by him:—Nebaioth, Nebajoth.

5033. נֵבֶךְ, nêbek, *nay´-bek*; from an unused root meaning to *burst* forth; a *fountain*:—spring.

5034. נָבֵל, nâbêl, *naw-bale´*; a primitive root; to *wilt*; (generally) to *fall* away, *fail, faint*; (figurative) to *be foolish* or (moral) *wicked*; (causative) to *despise, disgrace*:—disgrace, dishonour, lightly esteem, fade (away, -ing), fall (down, -ling, off), do foolishly, come to nought, × surely, make vile, wither.

5035. נֶבֶל, nebel, *neh´-bel*; or **נֵבֶל, nêbel,** *nay´-bel*; from 5034; a skin-*bag* for liquids (from *collapsing* when empty); hence, a *vase* (as similar in shape when full); also a *lyre* (as having a body of like form):—bottle, pitcher, psaltery vessel, viol.

5036. נָבָל, nâbâl, *naw-bawl´*; from 5034; *stupid; wicked* (especially *impious*):—fool (-ish, -ish man, -ish woman), vile person.

5037. נָבָל, Nâbâl, *naw-bawl´*; the same as 5036; *dolt; Nabal*, an Israelite:—Nabal.

5038. נְבֵלָה, nᵉbêlâh, *neb-ay-law´*; from 5034; a *flabby* thing, i.e. a *carcase* or *carrion* (human or bestial, often collective); (figurative) an *idol*:—(dead) body, (dead) carcase, dead of itself, which died, (beast) that (which) dieth of itself.

A feminine noun meaning a carcass, a corpse. It describes a body devoid of life, whether human (Jos 8:29; Isa 5:25) or animal (Dt 14:8). The Law clearly stated that contact with the carcass of a dead animal (Le 5:2) or with the body of a dead person (cf. Nu 19:11) would render an individual unclean. Also, it was possible for the land to be defiled by the presence of an unburied corpse (Dt 21:23). Hence, Jeremiah used the word *nĕbêlâh* for idols. Pagan idols were devoid of life just like corpses and were a source of defilement for the people, priests, and land.

5039. נְבָלָה, nᵉbâlâh, *neb-aw-law´*; feminine of 5036; *foolishness*, i.e. (moral) *wickedness*; (concrete) a *crime*; (by extension) *punishment*:—folly, vile, villany.

5040. נַבְלוּת, nablûwth, *nab-looth´*; from 5036; (properly) *disgrace*, i.e. the (female) *pudenda*:—lewdness.

5041. נְבַלָּט, Nᵉballâṭ, *neb-al-lawt´*; apparently from 5036 and 3909; *foolish secrecy; Neballat*, a place in Palestine:—Neballat.

5042. נָבַע, nâbaʻ, *naw-bah´*; a primitive root; to *gush* forth; (figurative) to *utter* (good or bad words); (specifically) to *emit* (a foul odor):—belch out, flowing, pour out, send forth, utter (abundantly).

5043. נֶבְרְשָׁא, nebrᵉshâʼ, *neb-reh-shaw´*; (Chaldee); from an unused root meaning to *shine*; a *light*; plural (collective) a *chandelier*:—candlestick.

5044. נִבְשָׁן, Nibshân, *nib-shawn´*; of uncertain derivation; *Nibshan*, a place in Palestine:—Nibshan.

5045. נֶגֶב, negeb, *neh´-gheb*; from an unused root meaning to *be parched*; the *south* (from its drought); (specifically) the *Negeb* or southern district of Judah, occasionally, *Egypt* (as south to Palestine):—south (country, side, -ward).

5046. נָגַד, nâgad, *naw-gad´*; a primitive root; (properly) to *front*, i.e. stand boldly out opposite; by implication (causative), to *manifest*; (figurative) to *announce* (always by word of mouth to one present); (specifically) to *expose, predict, explain, praise*:—bewray, × certainly, certify, declare (-ing), denounce, expound, × fully, messenger, plainly, profess, rehearse, report, shew (forth), speak, × surely, tell, utter.

A verb meaning to tell, to report, to make known, to explain, to be reported. The root idea of the word and the causative form in which it is used is to declare something. The manner and context in which this is done creates the various shades of meaning of the verb. Its simplest use is to announce, to report, to share. Samuel, when a child, was afraid to report the vision he had to Eli (1Sa 3:15, 18; 1Ki 1:23). In some cases, it means to solve or explain, to make known. God asked Adam who had made him know he was naked (Ge 3:11; 12:18); it indicated the resolution of a riddle (Jgs 14:12, 15); or dream (Job 11:6; Da 2:2). Close to this is its meaning to share with or to inform someone of something, to speak out. People were responsible to speak out when they knew something relevant to a case (Le 5:1; Jos 2:14; Pr 29:24). It is used to proclaim or announce something, often proclaiming the character and attributes of the Lord. The psalmist proclaimed the great deeds of the Lord (Ps 9:11[12]); the posterity of the righteous psalmist would declare God's righteousness (Ps 22:31[32]); the Lord's love was regularly proclaimed (Ps 92:2[3]). The participle of the verb may indicate a messenger (Jer 51:31).

The passive use of the verb means to be told, to be announced. If an Israelite turned and followed false gods, this act of rebellion was to be brought to the attention of the leaders (Dt 17:4); anything that needed to be reported could be covered by this verb (Jgs 9:25; 2Sa 10:17). The Queen of Sheba used this verb when she declared that not even half the splendor of Solomon's wisdom and wealth had been told her (1Ki 10:7; Isa 21:2).

5047. נְגַד, nᵉgad, *neg-ad´*; (Chaldee); corresponding to 5046; to *flow* (through the idea of *clearing* the way):—issue.

5048. נֶגֶד, neged, *neh´-ghed*; from 5046; a *front*, i.e. part opposite; (specifically) a *counterpart*, or mate; usually (adverb, especially with preposition) *over against* or *before*:—about, (over) against, × aloof, × far (off), × from, over, presence, × other side, sight, × to view.

5049. נֶגֶד, neged, *neh´-ghed*; (Chaldee); corresponding to 5048; *opposite*:—toward.

5050. נָגַהּ, nâgah, *naw-găh´*; a primitive root; to *glitter*; (causative) to *illuminate*:—(en-) lighten, (cause to) shine.

5051. נֹגַהּ, nôgah, *no´-găh*; from 5050; *brilliancy* (literal or figurative):—bright (-ness), light, (clear) shining.

5052. נֹגַהּ, Nôgah, *no´-găh*; the same as 5051; *Nogah*, a son of David:—Nogah.

5053. נֹגַהּ, nôgah, *no´-găh*; (Chaldee); corresponding to 5051; *dawn*:—morning.

5054. נְגֹהָה, nᵉgôhâh, *neg-o-haw´*; feminine of 5051; *splendor*:—brightness.

5055. נָגַח, nâgach, *naw-gakh´*; a primitive root; to *but* with the horns; (figurative) to *war* against:—gore, push (down, -ing).

5056. נַגָּח**, naggâch**, *nag-gawkh´*; from 5055; *butting*, i.e. *vicious*:—used (wont) to push.

5057. נָגִיד**, nâgîyd**, *naw-gheed´*; or נָגִד**, nâgid**, *naw-gheed´*; from 5046; a *commander* (as occupying the *front*), civil, military or religious; generally (abstract plural), *honourable* themes:—captain, chief, excellent thing, (chief) governor, leader, noble, prince, (chief) ruler.

A masculine noun meaning a leader, a ruler, a prince. This term has a broad range of applications. At the top, it could allude to the king of Israel (1Sa 9:16; 13:14; 1Ki 1:35); a ruler from a foreign land like Tyre (Eze 28:2); or Assyria (2Ch 32:21). It could also be used regarding cultic leaders and officials from the high priest down (1Ch 9:11, 20; 2Ch 31:12, 13; 35:8; Jer 20:1). It could also be a label for various other lesser positions of leadership (1Ch 27:16; 2Ch 11:11, 22; 19:11; Job 29:10). The word is also used in an abstract sense to convey that which is princely, noble, and honourable (Pr 8:6).

5058. נְגִינָה**, nᵉgîynâh**, *neg-ee-naw´*; or נְגִינַת**, nᵉgîynath**, *neg-ee-nath´*; (Ps 611:title), from 5059; (properly) instrumental *music*; (by implication) a stringed *instrument*; (by extension) a *poem* set to music; (specifically) an *epigram*:—stringed instrument, musick, Neginoth [*plural*], song.

5059. נָגַן**, nâgan**, *naw-gan´*; a primitive root; (properly) to *thrum*, i.e. *beat* a tune with the fingers; especially to *play* on a stringed instrument; hence (general) to *make music*:—player on instruments, sing to the stringed instruments, melody, minstrel, play (-er, -ing).

5060. נָגַע**, nâgaʿ**, *naw-gah´*; a primitive root; (properly) to *touch*, i.e. *lay the hand upon* (for any purpose); (euphemism) to *lie with* a woman; (by implication) to *reach;* (figurative) to *arrive, acquire*; violently, to *strike* (punish, defeat, destroy, etc.):—beat, (× be able to) bring (down), cast, come (nigh), draw near (nigh), get up, happen, join, near, plague, reach (up), smite, strike, touch.

A verb meaning to touch, to reach, to strike. The basic import of this verb is physical contact from one person to another. Since interpersonal contact can come in one (or more) of many varieties, this verb carries a range of semantic possibilities. Its use could represent mere physical contact (Ge 3:3; 1Ki 6:27; Est 5:2). On a deeper level, it could designate striking (Job 1:19; Isa 53:4; Eze 17:10). Along these lines is the figurative use to identify God's judgment (1Sa 6:9; Job 1:11; 19:21). On an even deeper level, it indicates doing actual harm (Ge 26:11; Jos 9:19; 2Sa 14:10). In a metaphorical sense, this verb can also portray the concept to reach or extend (Isa 16:8; Jer 51:9; Jnh 3:6). In the passive form, it denotes the idea to allow oneself to be beaten in a military context (Jos 8:15). In the intensive form, this verb means to afflict or to be afflicted (Ge 12:17; 2Ki 15:5; Ps 73:5).

5061. נֶגַע**, negaʿ**, *neh´-gah*; from 5060; a *blow;* (figurative) *infliction;* also (by implication) a *spot;* (concrete) a *leprous* person or dress:—plague, sore, stricken, stripe, stroke, wound.

A masculine noun meaning a blemish, a mark, a stroke, a plague. This word comes from the verb *nâgaʿ* (5060), meaning to touch or to strike, and is best understood as a blemish that has been created by touching or striking. In the majority of instances, it described a blemish inflicted by leprosy or a skin disease that the priest was to discern (used over sixty times in Le 13—14). It also referred to a physical injury inflicted by another person (Dt 17:8; 21:5; Isa 53:8); or by God Himself (Ps 89:32[33]). When describing land or property, it is best translated plague (Ge 12:17; Ex 11:1; 1Ki 8:37). At times, this word described a nonphysical blemish (1Ki 8:38; 2Ch 6:29; Pr 6:33).

5062. נָגַף**, nâgaph**, *naw-gaf´*; a primitive root; to *push, gore, defeat, stub* (the toe), *inflict* (a disease):—beat, dash, hurt, plague, slay, smite (down), strike, stumble, × surely, put to the worse.

A verb meaning to strike, to smite. This word is most often used within the context of warring nations when one nation struck another (Le 26:17; Nu 14:42; Dt 28:7, 25). At times, this was followed by the death of many (Jgs 20:35; 1Sa 4:10; 2Sa 18:7); at others, it merely signified defeat in war, with no mention of death (1Ki 8:33; 2Ki 14:12). God is often the One who smote, which led to incurable illness (2Ch 21:18; Zec 14:12, 18); or even death (1Sa 25:38; 2Sa 12:15). This word is also used to describe the stumbling of the foot (Pr 3:23; Jer 13:16); the causing of injury to another person (Ex 21:22); or to an animal (Ex 21:35).

5063. נֶגֶף**, negeph**, *neh´-ghef*; from 5062; a *trip* (of the foot); (figurative) an *infliction* (of disease):—plague, stumbling.

A masculine noun meaning a plague, stumbling. This word comes from the verb *nâgaph* (5062), meaning to strike or to smite, and described the effect of being struck or smitten. It usually described a plague that God sent on a disobedient people (Ex 12:13; 30:12; Nu 8:19; Jos 22:17). In one instance, it described the stone of stumbling (Isa 8:14).

5064. נָגַר**, nâgar**, *naw-gar´*; a primitive root; to *flow*; (figurative) to *stretch* out; (causative) to *pour* out or down; (figurative) to *deliver* over:—fall, flow away, pour down (out), run, shed, spilt, trickle down.

5065. נָגַשׂ**, nâgaś**, *naw-gas´*; a primitive root; to *drive* (an animal, a workman, a debtor, an army); (by implication) to *tax, harass, tyrannize*:—distress, driver, exact (-or), oppress (-or), × raiser of taxes, taskmaster.

5066. נָגַשׁ**, nâgash**, *naw-gash´*; a primitive root; to *be* or *come* (causative, *bring*) *near* (for any purpose); (euphemism) to *lie with* a woman; as an enemy, to *attack*; (religious) to *worship*; (causative) to *present*; (figurative) to *adduce* an argument; (by reversal) to *stand back*:—(make to) approach (nigh), bring (forth, hither, near), (cause to) come (hither, near, nigh), give place, go hard (up), (be, draw, go) near (nigh), offer, overtake, present, put, stand.

A verb meaning to come near, to approach, to draw near, to bring near, to be brought near. In the simple form of the verb, it indicates coming near, as when Jacob went near to Isaac his father who reached out and touched him (Ge 27:22); it simply describes approaching a person for whatever reason (Ge 43:19; Ex 19:15). It is used of priests approaching the Lord (Eze 44:13); or the altar to carry out their priestly duties (Ex 28:43; 30:20); and of armies drawing near for engagement in battle (Jgs 20:23; 2Sa 10:13). The word asserts close proximity in all these cases and can even describe the closeness of the scales of a crocodile (Job 41:16[8]).

In the reflexive form, it describes coming near. Dt 25:9 prescribed the action of a widow toward her brother-in-law who would not perform his Levitical duty toward her: She was to approach him, take off one of his sandals, and spit in his face (cf. Isa 45:20).

In the causative form, the verb means to bring near: a slave who decided to remain with his master perpetually was brought to the judges and to the doorpost so his ear could be bored with an awl (Ex 21:6; 1Sa 15:32); sacrifices were brought near as well (1Sa 13:9; 14:34). In a metaphorical sense, the word is used to call for the presentation of legal argumentation (Isa 41:21). The passive use of this form describes what is offered or presented, once to indicate that Abner's feet were not brought near, that is, they were not placed in chains (2Sa 3:34); and once to describe incense and pure offerings brought in the Lord's name (Mal 1:11).

5067. נֵד**, nêd**, *nade*; from 5110 in the sense of *piling* up; a *mound*, i.e. *wave*:—heap.

5068. נָדַב**, nâdab**, *naw-dab´*; a primitive root; to *impel*; hence to *volunteer* (as a soldier), to *present* spontaneously:—offer freely, be (give, make, offer self) willing (-ly).

A verb meaning to incite willingly. This word described the free, voluntary desire of the heart to give of oneself or of one's resources to the service of the Lord. It was used to describe the willing contributions that the people of Israel made to build the tabernacle (Ex 25:2; 35:21, 29); Solomon's Temple (1Ch 29:5, 6, 9, 14, 17); and Zerubbabel's Temple (Ezr 1:6; 2:68; 3:5). In a few other instances, it spoke of the willing sacrifice of service that Amaziah made (2Ch 17:16); the returning exiles made (Ne 11:2); and Deborah commended (Jgs 5:2, 9). See the related noun *nĕdâbâh* (5071), meaning freewill offering.

5069. נְדַב**, nᵉdab,** *ned-ab´*; (Chaldee); corresponding to 5068; *be* (or *give*) *liberal* (*-ly*):—(be minded of … own) freewill (offering), offer freely (willingly).

An Aramaic verb meaning to offer willingly, to make a freewill offering. This word is used exclusively in the book of Ezra and refers to those who could leave Babylon freely (Ezr 7:13). It also indicates the gifts given freely by a king (Ezr 7:15); and the Israelites (Ezr 7:16). See the related Hebrew verbs *nâdab* (5068) and *nĕdâbâh* (5071).

5070. נָדָב**, Nâdâb,** *naw-dawb´*; from 5068; *liberal; Nadab*, the name of four Israelites:—Nadab.

5071. נְדָבָה**, nᵉdâbâh,** *ned-aw-baw´*; from 5068; properly (abstract) *spontaneity*, or (adjective) *spontaneous*; also (concrete) a *spontaneous* or (by inference, in plural) *abundant* gift:—free (-will) offering, freely, plentiful, voluntary (-ily, offering), willing (-ly, offering).

A feminine noun meaning willingness, a freewill offering, a voluntary gift. As an adverb, it means willingly, freely, spontaneously, voluntarily. This term can denote that state of being which allows a person to offer a gift or a favour to someone else without any thought of return or payback. The favour is not given out of any obligation owed by the giver; rather, it is the result of an overflow from an abundance within the heart. The Lord declares that He loves Israel freely because His anger has turned away from them (Hos 14:4[5]). The Hebrews were commanded to diligently perform the vows they freely uttered to the Lord (Dt 23:23[24]). Most often, however, the term is utilized to signify an offering, a gift, or a sacrifice given voluntarily, as opposed to one offered in dutiful fulfillment of an obligation or vow (Le 22:23). Many from the congregation of Israel whose hearts were willing gave of their possessions as freewill offerings for the building of the Tent of Meeting and its services (Ex 35:29; 36:3; cf. Le 7:16; Ezr 1:4; 3:5; 8:28; Eze 46:12; Am 4:5). Once the word possibly functions to convey an abundance, that is, of rain (Ps 68:9[10]). This term is derived from the verb *nâdab* (5068).

5072. נְדַבְיָה**, Nᵉdabyâh,** *ned-ab-yaw´*; from 5068 and 3050; *largess of Jah; Nedabjah*, an Israelite:—Nedabiah.

5073. נִדְבָּךְ**, nidbâk,** *nid-bawk´*; (Chaldee); from a root meaning to *stick*; a *layer* (of building materials):—row.

5074. נָדַד**, nâdad,** *naw-dad´*; a primitive root; (properly) to *wave* to and fro (rarely, to *flap* up and down); (figurative) to *rove, flee*, or (causative) to *drive* away:—chase (away), × could not, depart, flee (× apace, away), (re-) move, thrust away, wander (abroad, -er, -ing).

5075. נְדַד**, nᵉdad,** *ned-ad´*; (Chaldee); corresponding to 5074; to *depart*:—go from.

5076. נְדֻדִים**, nᵉdudîym,** *ned-oo-deem´*; passive participle of 5074; (properly) *tossed*; (abstract) a *rolling* (on the bed):—tossing to and fro.

5077. נָדָה**, nâdâh,** *naw-daw´*; or נָדָא**, nâdâ'**, *naw-daw´*; (2Ki 17:21), a primitive root; (properly) to *toss*; (figurative) to *exclude*, i.e. banish, postpone, prohibit:—cast out, drive, put far away.

5078. נֵדֶה**, nêdeh,** *nay´-deh*; from 5077 in the sense of freely *flinging* money; a *bounty* (for prostitution):—gifts.

5079. נִדָּה**, niddâh,** *nid-daw´*; from 5074; (properly) *rejection*; (by implication) *impurity*, especially personal (menstruation) or moral (idolatry, incest):— × far, filthiness, × flowers, menstruous (woman), put apart, × removed (woman), separation, set apart, unclean (-ness, thing, with filthiness).

5080. נָדַח**, nâdach,** *naw-dakh´*; a primitive root; to *push* off; used in a great variety of applications, literal and figurative (to expel, mislead, strike, inflict, etc.):—banish, bring, cast down (out), chase, compel, draw away, drive (away, out, quite), fetch a stroke, force, go away, outcast, thrust away (out), withdraw.

5081. נָדִיב**, nâdîyb,** *naw-deeb´*; from 5068; (properly) *voluntary*, i.e. generous; hence, *magnanimous*; as noun, a *grandee* (sometimes a *tyrant*):—free, liberal (things), noble, prince, willing ([hearted]).

An adjective meaning willing, generous, noble; as a noun, those of noble birth. The word often denotes an attitude of heart which consents or agrees (often readily and cheerfully) to a course of action. The Hebrews who were of willing hearts gave as offerings to the Lord jewelry and gold for the construction of the tabernacle and its accessories (Ex 35:5, 22; cf. 2Ch 29:31; Ps 51:12[14]). In many other places, the term describes an individual as one of excellent moral character. Proverbs states that to punish the noble for their integrity is wrong (Pr 17:26; cf. Pr 17:7; Isa 32:5, 8). At other times, the word signifies those born into lineages of nobility. The Lord lifts the needy from the ash heap and causes them to sit with princes (1Sa 2:8; cf. Nu 21:18; Job 12:21; 34:18; Ps 47:9[10]; 107:40; 113:8; 118:9; Pr 25:7; Isa 13:2). This term is closely related to the verb *nâdab* (5068).

5082. נְדִיבָה**, nᵉdîybâh,** *ned-ee-baw´*; feminine of 5081; (properly) *nobility*, i.e. reputation:—soul.

5083. נָדָן**, nâdân,** *naw-dawn´*; probably from an unused root meaning to *give*; a *present* (for prostitution):—gift.

5084. נָדָן**, nâdân,** *naw-dawn´*; of uncertain derivation; a *sheath* (of a sword):—sheath.

5085. נִדְנֶה**, nidneh,** *nid-neh´*; (Chaldee); from the same as 5084; a *sheath*; (figurative) the *body* (as the receptacle of the soul):—body.

An Aramaic masculine noun meaning sheath for a sword. It is used only in the book of Daniel, where it figuratively described the relationship between Daniel's spirit and body. His spirit was within his body in the same way as a sword fits into its sheath (Da 7:15). The Hebrew counterpart of this word is *nâdân* (5084).

5086. נָדַף**, nâdaph,** *naw-daf´*; a primitive root; to *shove* asunder, i.e. *disperse*:—drive (away, to and fro), thrust down, shaken, tossed to and fro.

5087. נָדַר**, nâdar,** *naw-dar´*; a primitive root; to *promise* (positively, to do or give something to God):—(make a) vow.

A verb meaning to vow. The verbal concept denotes the making of an oral, voluntary promise to give or do something as an expression of consecration or devotion to the service of God. Jacob vowed to return a tenth of all that God bestowed on him if God would protect and preserve him on his journey (Ge 28:20). Le 27:8 discusses the special vow offerings to the Lord and the cost of redeeming someone or something which had been dedicated to the Lord. King David also made a vow that he would deny himself the pleasures of his house and his bed until the time came when he had established a resting place and a habitation for the Lord (Ps 132:2). The sailors, unable to save themselves and having cast Jonah into the sea with the resulting calm, greatly feared the Lord, offered sacrifices, and made vows to Him (Jnh 1:16).

5088. נֶדֶר**, neder,** *neh´-der*; or נֵדֶר**, nêder,** *nay´-der*; from 5087; a *promise* (to God); also (concrete) a thing *promised*:—vow ([-ed]).

A masculine noun meaning vow. The word is found twenty-five times in the OT and basically means a solemn promise to God or the thing promised. Several times, the word refers to the specific words given in a vow. Jacob vowed that the Lord would be his God and he would give Him a tenth of everything the Lord gave him (Ge 28:20; 31:13; Nu 21:2; Jgs 11:30). The word is used to describe the object or intent of vows: a Nazirite vow (Nu 6:2, 5, 21); a vow made by a wife (Nu 30:9[10]); or by people in a difficult situation who made a promise before the Lord (Jnh 1:16). The object of the vow can be a sacrifice (Le 7:16; 22:21); or a person dedicated to the Lord (Le 27:2). Neither money earned by prostitution nor deformed animals could be used as part of a vow (Le 22:23; Dt 23:18[19]). Once made, a vow had to be paid by the one who made it, for if he or she did not pay, it was considered a sin (Dt 23:21[22]; 2Sa 15:7; Ps 56:12[13]). Pr 20:25 warned against making a vow before carefully considering the wisdom of doing so. Jephthah made a rash vow without considering its implications and suffered greatly for it (Jgs 11:30, 39). The word also describes the vow of some of the Israelites and their wives to burn incense and give libation offerings to the Queen of Heaven in the time of Jeremiah (Jer 44:25).

5089. נֹהַּ, **nôah,** *no´-ăh*; from an unused root meaning to *lament; lamentation*:—wailing.

5090. נָהַג, **nâhag,** *naw-hag´*; a primitive root; to *drive* forth (a person, an animal or chariot), i.e. *lead, carry away*; (reflexive) to *proceed* (i.e. impel or guide oneself); also (from the *panting* induced by effort), to *sigh*:—acquaint, bring (away), carry away, drive (away), lead (away, forth), (be) guide, lead (away, forth).

5091. נָהָה, **nâhâh,** *naw-haw´*; a primitive root; to *groan*, i.e. *bewail*; hence (through the idea of *crying* aloud) to *assemble* (as if on proclamation):—lament, wail.

5092. נְהִי, **n**e**hîy,** *neh-hee´*; from 5091; an *elegy*:—lamentation, wailing.

5093. נִהְיָה, **nihyâh,** *nih-yaw´*; feminine of 5092; *lamentation*:—doleful.

5094. נְהִיר, **n**e**hîyr,** *neh-heere´*; (Chaldee); or נַהִירוּ, **nahîyrûw,** *nah-hee-roo´*; (Chaldee); from the same as 5105; *illumination*, i.e. (figurative) wisdom:—light.

An Aramaic feminine noun meaning illumination, wisdom, or insight. This word is found only in Daniel. The story of the handwriting on the wall in Belshazzar's banquet hall established the fact that Daniel was able to discern things people found baffling. Belshazzar described Daniel's wisdom as light and understanding coming from the Spirit of God within him (Da 5:11, 14).

5095. נָהַל, **nâhal,** *naw-hal´*; a primitive root; (properly) to run with a *sparkle*, i.e. *flow*; hence (transitive) to *conduct*, and (by inference) to *protect, sustain*:—carry, feed, guide, lead (gently, on).

5096. נַהֲלָל, **Nahălâl,** *năh-hal-awl´*; or נַהֲלֹל, **Nahălôl,** *năh-hal-ole´*; the same as 5097; *Nahalal* or *Nahalol*, a place in Palestine:—Nahalal, Nahallal, Nahalol.

5097. נַהֲלֹל, **nahălôl,** *năh-hal-ole´*; from 5095; *pasture*:—bush.

5098. נָהַם, **nâham,** *naw-ham´*; a primitive root; to *growl*:—mourn, roar (-ing).

5099. נַהַם, **naham,** *năh´-ham*; from 5098; a *snarl*:—roaring.

5100. נְהָמָה, **n**e**hâmâh,** *neh-haw-maw´*; feminine of 5099; *snarling*:—disquietness, roaring.

5101. נָהַק, **nâhaq,** *naw-hak´*; a primitive root; to *bray* (as an ass), *scream* (from hunger):—bray.

5102. נָהַר, **nâhar,** *naw-har´*; a primitive root; to *sparkle*, i.e. (figurative) *be cheerful*; hence (from the *sheen* of a running stream) to *flow*, i.e. (figurative) *assemble*:—flow (together), be lightened.

5103. נְהַר, **n**e**har,** *neh-har´*; (Chaldee); from a root corresponding to 5102; a *river*, especially the Euphrates:—river, stream.

5104. נָהָר, **nâhâr,** *naw-hawr´*; from 5102; a *stream* (including the *sea*; especially the Nile, Euphrates, etc.); (figurative) *prosperity*:—flood, river.

5105. נְהָרָה, **n**e**hârâh,** *neh-haw-raw´*; from 5102 in its original sense; *daylight*:—light.

5106. נוּא, **nûw',** *noo*; a primitive root; to *refuse, forbid, dissuade*, or *neutralise*:—break, disallow, discourage, make of no effect.

5107. נוּב, **nûwb,** *noob*; a primitive root; to *germinate*, i.e. (figurative) to (causative, *make*) *flourish*; also (of words), to *utter*:—bring forth (fruit), make cheerful, increase.

5108. נוֹב, **nôwb,** *nobe*; or נִיב, **nîyb,** *neeb*; from 5107; *produce*, literal or figurative:—fruit.

5109. נוֹבַי, **Nôwbay,** *no-bah´ee*; from 5108; *fruitful; Nobai*, an Israelite:—Nebai [*from the margin*].

5110. נוּד, **nûwd,** *nood*; a primitive root; to *nod*, i.e. waver; (figurative) to *wander, flee, disappear*; also (from *shaking* the head in sympathy), to *console, deplore*, or (from *tossing* the head in scorn) *taunt*:—bemoan, flee, get, mourn, make to move, take pity, remove, shake, skip for joy, be sorry, vagabond, way, wandering.

5111. נוּד, **nûwd,** *nood*; (Chaldee); corresponding to 5116; to *flee*:—get away.

5112. נוֹד, **nôwd,** *node*; [only defective נֹד, **nôd,** *node*]; from 5110; *exile*:—wandering.

5113. נוֹד, **Nôwd,** *node*; the same as 5112; *vagrancy; Nod*, the land of Cain:—Nod.

5114. נוֹדָב, **Nôwdâb,** *no-dawb´*; from 5068; *noble; Nodab*, an Arab tribe:—Nodab.

5115. נָוָה, **nâvâh,** *naw-vaw´*; a primitive root; to *rest* (as at home); causative (through the implied idea of *beauty* [compare 5116], to *celebrate* (with praises):—keep at home, prepare an habitation.

5116. נָוֶה, **nâveh,** *naw-veh´*; or (feminine) נָוָה, **nâvâh,** *naw-vaw´*; from 5115; (adjective) *at home*; hence (by implication of satisfaction) *lovely*; also (noun) a *home*, of God (temple), men (residence), flocks (pasture), or wild animals (*den*):—comely, dwelling (place), fold, habitation, pleasant place, sheepcote, stable, tarried.

5117. נוּחַ, **nûwach,** *noo´-akh*; a primitive root; to *rest*, i.e. *settle* down; used in a great variety of applications, literal and figurative, intransivitive, transitive and causative (to *dwell, stay, let fall, place, let alone, withdraw, give comfort*, etc.):—cease, be confederate, lay, let down, (be) quiet, remain, (cause to, be at, give, have, make to) rest, set down. Compare 3241.

5118. נוּחַ, **nûwach,** *noo´-akh*; or נֹחַ, **nôwach,** *no´-akh*; from 5117; *quiet*:—rest (-ed, -ing place).

5119. נוֹחָה, **Nôwchâh,** *no-khaw´*; feminine of 5118; *quietude; Nochah*, an Israelite:—Nohah.

5120. נוּט, **nûwṭ,** *noot*; to *quake*:—be moved.

5121. נָוִית, **Nâwôwth,** *naw-vowth´*; but in the Qere it is נָיוֹת, **Nâyôwth,** *naw-yoth´*; from 5115; *residence;* a place in Palestine:—Naioth [*from the margin*].

5122. נְוָלוּ, **n**e**vâlûw,** *nev-aw-loo´*; (Chaldee); or נְוָלִי, **n**e**vâlîy,** *nev-aw-lee´*; (Chaldee); from an unused root probably meaning to be *foul*; a *sink*:—dunghill.

5123. נוּם, **nûwm,** *noom*; a primitive root; to *slumber* (from drowsiness):—sleep, slumber.

5124. נוּמָה, **nûwmâh,** *noo-maw´*; from 5123; *sleepiness*:—drowsiness.

5125. נוּן, **nûwn,** *noon*; a primitive root; to *resprout*, i.e. propagate by shoots; (figurative) to *be perpetual*:—be continued.

5126. נוּן, **Nûwn,** *noon*; or נוֹן, **Nôwn,** *nohn*; (1Ch 7:27), from 5125; *perpetuity; Nun* or *Non*, the father of Joshua:—Non, Nun.

5127. נוּס, **nûws,** *noos*; a primitive root; to *flit*, i.e. *vanish* away (subside, escape); (causative) chase, impel, deliver:— × abate, away, be displayed, (make to) flee (away, -ing), put to flight, × hide, lift up a standard.

5128. נוּעַ, **nûwa',** *noo´-ah*; a primitive root; to *waver*, in a great variety of applications, literal and figurative (as subjoined):—continually, fugitive, × make to [go] up and down, be gone away, (be) move (-able, -d), be promoted, reel, remove, scatter, set, shake, sift, stagger, to and fro, be vagabond, wag, (make) wander (up and down).

5129. נוֹעַדְיָה, **Nôw'adyâh,** *no-ad-yaw´*; from 3259 and 3050; *convened of Jah; Noädjah*, the name of an Israelite, and a false prophetess:—Noadiah.

5130. נוּף, **nûwph,** *noof*; a primitive root; to *quiver* (i.e. *vibrate* up and down, or *rock* to and fro); used in a great variety of applications (including sprinkling, beckoning, rubbing, bastinadoing, sawing, waving, etc.):—lift up, move, offer, perfume, send, shake, sift, strike, wave.

A verb meaning to move back and forth, to sprinkle. This verb only occurs in the basic verbal form once, where it refers to sprinkling a bed with myrrh (Pr 7:17). Most often, it occurs in the causative form, where it can carry a similar semantic idea, namely making rain fall (Ps 68:9[10]). However, it usually carries the idea of moving back and forth or waving. It could be used to represent the reciprocating motion of a tool, like a sword (Ex 20:25); a sickle (Dt 23:25[26]); a tool for dressing stone (Dt 27:5); or a saw (Isa 10:15). It could also be used of the motion of one's hand as a healing ritual (2Ki 5:11); as retribution (Isa 11:15; 19:16); or as a signal (Isa 13:2). In a cultic context, this verb is a technical term that referenced the actions of the priest as he offered a sacrifice to God by waving it before the altar (Ex 29:24; Le 23:11; Nu 5:25).

5131. נוֹף, **nôwph,** *nofe*; from 5130; *elevation*:—situation. Compare 5297.

5132. נוּץ, **nûwts,** *noots*; a primitive root; (properly) to *flash*; hence, to *blossom* (from the brilliancy of colour); also, to *fly away* (from the quickness of motion):—flee away, bud (forth).

5133. נוֹצָה, **nôwtsâh,** *no-tsaw´*; or נֹצָה, **nôtsâh,** *no-tsaw´*; feminine active participle of 5327 in the sense of *flying*; a *pinion* (or wing feather); often (collective) *plumage*:—feather (-s), ostrich.

5134. נוּק, **nûwq,** *nook*; a primitive root; to *suckle*:—nurse.

5135. נוּר, **nûwr,** *noor*; (Chaldee); from an unused root (corresponding to that of 5216) meaning to *shine; fire*:—fiery, fire.

5136. נוּשׁ, **nûwsh,** *noosh*; a primitive root; to *be sick*, i.e. (figurative) *distressed*:—be full of heaviness.

5137. נָזָה, **nâzâh,** *naw-zaw´*; a primitive root; to *spirt*, i.e. *besprinkle* (especially in expiation):—sprinkle.

A verb meaning to spurt, to spatter, to sprinkle, to spring, to leap. This verb appears only a few times in the basic verbal form and carries the connotation of blood spurting or spattering (Le 6:27[20]; 2Ki 9:33; Isa 63:3). In the causative form, the verb connotes the sprinkling of a liquid as part of a ritual cleansing. The sprinkled liquid could be blood (Le 5:9; 14:7); oil (Le 8:11); water (Nu 19:18, 19); blood and oil (Ex 29:21); or blood and water (Le 14:51). Also in the causative form, this verb could signify to leap or to spring, especially with the connotation of surprise or joy (Isa 52:15).

5138. נָזִיד, **nâzîyd,** *naw-zeed´*; from 2102; something *boiled*, i.e. *soup*:—pottage.

5139. נָזִיר, **nâzîyr,** *naw-zeer´*; or נָזִר, **nâzir,** *naw-zeer´*; from 5144; *separate*, i.e. consecrated (as *prince*, a *Nazirite*); hence (figurative from the latter) an *unpruned* vine (like an unshorn Nazirite):—Nazarite [*by a false alliteration with Nazareth*], separate (-d), vine undressed.

A masculine noun meaning one consecrated, separated, devoted, a Nazarite. The term Nazarite means one who is consecrated to God. The Nazarite vow included abstinence from strong drink or the cutting of his hair, and no contact with dead bodies (Jgs 13:4–7). Samuel, as well as Samson, was dedicated before birth by his mother to be a Nazarite (cf. 1Sa 1:11). Less common is the meaning of a prince or ruler being consecrated, as was the case with Joseph, who was separated from his brothers (Ge 49:26). A third meaning of this word depicts an untrimmed vine (Le 25:5).

5140. נָזַל, **nâzal,** *naw-zal´*; a primitive root; to *drip*, or *shed* by trickling:—distil, drop, flood, (cause to) flow (-ing), gush out, melt, pour (down), running water, stream.

5141. נֶזֶם, **nezem,** *neh´-zem*; from an unused root of uncertain meaning; a nose-*ring*:—earring, jewel.

5142. נְזַק, **nᵉzaq,** *nez-ak´*; (Chaldee); corresponding to the root of 5143; to *suffer* (causative, *inflict*) *loss*:—have (en-) damage, hurt (-ful).

5143. נֵזֶק, **nêzeq,** *nay´-zek*; from an unused root meaning to *injure; loss*:—damage.

5144. נָזַר, **nâzar,** *naw-zar´*; a primitive root; to *hold aloof*, i.e. (intransitive) *abstain* (from food and drink, from impurity, and even from divine worship [i.e. *apostatize*]); (specifically) to *set apart* (to sacred purposes), i.e. *devote*:—consecrate, separate (-ing, self).

A verb meaning to dedicate, to consecrate. In the passive or reflexive form, it can signify a dedication to (Hos 9:10) or a separation from a deity (Eze 14:7). It can also indicate considering something as sacred and consecrated (Le 22:2). This verb also expresses the idea of consecrating oneself by fasting (Zec 7:3). In the causative form, it can denote to separate or to refrain from something (Le 15:31); or to take on the obligations of a Nazirite, a *nâziyr* (5139) (Nu 6:2, 5, 12).

5145. נֶזֶר, **nezer,** *neh´-zer*; or נֵזֶר, **nêzer,** *nay´-zer*; from 5144; (properly) something *set apart*, i.e. (abstract) *dedication* (of a priest or Nazirite); hence (concrete) unshorn *locks*; also (by implication) a *chaplet* (especially of royalty):—consecration, crown, hair, separation.

A masculine noun meaning a consecration, an ordination. This could be the consecration of the high priest (Le 21:12); or of a person taking a vow as a Nazirite (Nu 6:5, 7, 9, 12). This term is also used to identify a crown as the symbol of the wearer's consecration. This could be the king's crown (2Sa 1:10; 2Ki 11:12); or the golden crown of the high priest (Ex 29:6; 39:30). Jeremiah also used this term to refer to the hair of the personified Jerusalem (Jer 7:29). The basis of this extension could be the connection between the Nazirite and his long, uncut hair as his symbol of consecration (Nu 6:5); or to the idea that a woman's long hair itself is her "crown of consecration." This would be similar to Paul's teaching in the NT (cf. 1Co 11:15).

5146. נֹחַ, **Nôach,** *no´-akh*; the same as 5118; *rest; Noäch*, the patriarch of the flood:—Noah.

5147. נַחְבִּי, **Nachbîy,** *nakh-bee´*; from 2247; *occult; Nachbi*, an Israelite:—Nakbi.

5148. נָחָה, **nâchâh,** *naw-khaw´*; a primitive root; to *guide*; (by implication) to *transport* (into exile, or as colonists):—bestow, bring, govern, guide, lead (forth), put, straiten.

A verb meaning to lead, to guide, usually in the right direction or on the proper path. The verb sometimes occurs with a human subject (Ex 32:34; Ps 60:9[11]; 108:10[11]); however, it usually appears with the Lord as the subject (Ge 24:27; Ex 13:17; 15:13). This term is also used metaphorically to represent spiritual guidance in righteousness (Ps 5:8[9]; 27:11; 139:24). This term also carries a connotation of treating kindly (Job 31:18); blessing (Ps 23:3); deliverance (Ps 31:3[4]); protection (Ps 61:2[3]); or wisdom (Ps 73:24).

5149. נְחוּם, **Nᵉchûwm,** *neh-khoom´*; from 5162; *comforted; Nechum*, an Israelite:—Nehum.

5150. נִחוּם, **nichûwm,** *nee-khoom´*; or נִחֻם, **nichum,** *nee-khoom´*; from 5162; (properly) *consoled*; (abstract) *solace*:—comfort (-able), repenting.

5151. נַחוּם, **Nachûwm,** *nakh-oom´*; from 5162; *comfortable; Nachum*, an Israelite prophet:—Nahum.

5152. נָחוֹר, **Nâchôwr,** *naw-khore´*; from the same as 5170; *snorer; Nachor*, the name of the grandfather and a brother of Abraham:—Nahor.

5153. נָחוּשׁ, **nâchûwsh,** *naw-khoosh´*; apparently passive participle of 5172 (perhaps in the sense of *ringing*, i.e. bell-metal; or from the *red* colour of the throat of a serpent [5175, as denominative] when hissing); *coppery*, i.e. (figurative) hard:—of brass.

5154. נְחוּשָׁה, **nᵉchûwshâh,** *nekh-oo-shaw´*; or נְחֻשָׁה, **nᵉchushâh,** *nekh-oo-shaw´*; feminine of 5153; *copper*:—brass, steel. Compare 5176.

5155. נְחִילָה, **nᵉchîylâh,** *nekh-ee-law´*; probably denominative from 2485; a *flute*:—[*plural*] Nehiloth.

5156. נָחִיר, nâchîyr, *nawkh-eer´*; from the same as 5170; a *nostril*:—[*dual*] nostrils.

5157. נָחַל, nâchal, *naw-khal´*; a primitive root; to *inherit* (as a [figurative] mode of descent), or (generally) to *occupy*; (causative) to *bequeath*, or (generally) *distribute, instate*:—divide, have ([inheritance]), take as an heritage, (cause to, give to, make to) inherit, (distribute for, divide [for, for an, by], give for, have, leave for, take [for]) inheritance, (have in, cause to, be made to) possess (-ion).

A verb meaning to receive, to take property as a permanent possession. The verb was formed from the noun *nachălâh* (5159) which refers to a possession or inheritance. It can refer to the actual taking of the Promised Land, whether it was the entire land of Canaan as a gift from God (Ex 23:30; 32:13); a tribal allotment (Jos 16:4); or a familial portion (Jos 17:6). In addition to the taking of Canaan, God declared that Israel's remnant would possess the lands of Moab and Edom (Zep 2:9). It can also refer to the division and distribution of the land of Canaan to the tribal units (Jos 14:1). This verb is further used of God acquiring possession of Israel (Ex 34:9; Zec 2:12[16]); and the nations as His own private property (Ps 82:8). In the causative form, the verb denotes the giving of a possession (Dt 1:38; 3:28); or inheritance (Dt 21:16). This term is used figuratively to indicate the acquiring of things other than real property, like testimonies (Ps 119:111); glory (Pr 3:35); good things (Pr 28:10); lies (Jer 16:19); wind (Pr 11:29); simplicity (Pr 14:18); blessings (Zec 8:12).

5158. נַחַל, nachal, *nakh´-al*; or (feminine) נַחְלָה, **nachlâh,** *nakh´-law*; (Ps 124:4), or נַחֲלָה, **nachălâh,** *nakh-al-aw´*; (Eze 47:19; 48:28), from 5157 in its original sense; a *stream*, especially a winter *torrent*; (by implication) a (narrow) *valley* (in which a brook runs); also a *shaft* (of a mine):—brook, flood, river, stream, valley.

5159. נַחֲלָה, nachălâh, *nakh-al-aw´*; from 5157 (in its usual sense); (properly) something *inherited*, i.e. (abstract) *occupancy*, or (concrete) an *heirloom*; (generally) an *estate, patrimony* or *portion*:—heritage, to inherit, inheritance, possession. Compare 5158.

A feminine noun meaning possession, property, inheritance. This word implied property that was given by means of a will or as a heritage. It denoted the land of Canaan given to Israel and distributed among the tribes (Nu 26:53–56; Eze 48:29); a portion or state of blessing assigned by God to His people (Isa 54:17), or any possession presented by a father (Nu 27:8, 9; Job 42:15). The Lord Himself was declared to be the portion and inheritance of the Levites who served Him (Nu 18:20).

5160. נַחֲלִיאֵל, Nachălîy'êl, *nakh-al-ee-ale´*; from 5158 and 410; *valley of God; Nachaliël*, a place in the Desert:—Nahaliel.

5161. נֶחֱלָמִי, Nechělâmîy, *nekh-el-aw-mee´*; apparently a patronymic from an unused name (apparently passive participle of 2492); *dreamed*; a *Nechelamite*, or descend. of Nechlam:—Nehelamite.

5162. נָחַם, nâcham, *naw-kham´*; a primitive root; (properly) to *sigh*, i.e. *breathe* strongly; (by implication) to *be sorry*, i.e. (in a favourable sense) to *pity, console* or (reflexive) *rue*; or (unfavourably) to *avenge* (oneself):—comfort (self), ease [one's self], repent (-er, -ing, self).

A verb meaning to be sorry, to pity, to comfort, to avenge. The verb often means to be sorry or to regret: the Lord was sorry that He had made people (Ge 6:6); He led Israel in a direction to avoid war when they left Egypt, lest they became so sorry and grieved that they would turn back (Ex 13:17). The Lord had compassion on His people (i.e. He became sorry for them because of the oppression their enemies placed on them [Jgs 2:18]). While the Lord could be grieved, He did not grieve or become sorry so that He changed His mind as a human does (1Sa 15:29). The word also means to comfort or console oneself. Isaac was comforted after Sarah, his mother, died (Ge 24:67).

The verb always means to console or comfort. Jacob refused to be comforted when he believed that Joseph had been killed (Ge 37:35). To console is synonymous with showing kindness to someone, as when David consoled Hanun, king of the Ammonites, over the death of his father (2Sa 10:2). God refused to be consoled over the destruction of His people (Isa 22:4; 40:1); yet He comforts those who need it (Ps 119:82; Isa 12:1). The passive form of the word means to be comforted: the afflicted city of Zion would be comforted by the Lord (Isa 54:11; 66:13). In the reflexive stem, it can mean to get revenge for oneself (Ge 27:42; Eze 5:13); to let oneself be sorry or have compassion (Nu 23:19; Dt 32:36); and to let oneself be comforted (Ge 37:35; Ps 119:52).

5163. נַחַם, Nacham, *nakh´-am*; from 5162; *consolation; Nacham*, an Israelite:—Naham.

5164. נֹחַם, nôcham, *no´-kham*; from 5162; *ruefulness*, i.e. desistance:—repentance.

A masculine noun meaning sorrow, repentance, compassion. This word comes from the verb *nâcham* (5162), meaning to be sorry or to repent, and occurs only once in the OT. In Hos 13:14, it described the compassion that God would not have toward sinful Ephraim.

5165. נֶחָמָה, nechâmâh, *nekh-aw-maw´*; from 5162; *consolation*:—comfort.

A feminine noun meaning compassion, consolation. This word comes from the verb *nâcham* (5162), meaning to be sorry or to repent, and occurs twice in the OT. In Job 6:10, Job was comforted that in the midst of his trials, he did not deny the Holy One; the psalmist declared that his comfort in his affliction was God's Word, which revived him (Ps 119:50).

5166. נְחֶמְיָה, Neᵉchemyâh, *nekh-em-yaw´*; from 5162 and 3050; *consolation of Jah; Nechemjah*, the name of three Israelites:—Nehemiah.

5167. נַחֲמָנִי, Nachămânîy, *nakh-am-aw-nee´*; from 5162; *consolatory; Nachamani*, an Israelite:—Nahamani.

5168. נַחְנוּ, nachnûw, *nakh-noo´*; for 587; *we*:—we.

5169. נָחַץ, nâchats, *naw-khats´*; a primitive root; to *be urgent*:—require haste.

5170. נַחַר, nachar, *nakh´-ar*; and (feminine) נַחֲרָה, **nachărâh,** *nakh-ar-aw´*; from an unused root meaning to *snort* or *snore*; a *snorting*:—nostrils, snorting.

5171. נַחֲרַי, Nachăray, *nakh-ar-ah´ee*; or נַחְרַי, **Nach-ray,** *nakh-rah´ee*; from the same as 5170; *snorer; Nacharai* or *Nachrai*, an Israelite:—Naharai, Nahari.

5172. נָחַשׁ, nâchash, *naw-khash´*; a primitive root; (properly) to *hiss*, i.e. *whisper* a (magic) spell; (generally) to *prognosticate*:—× certainly, divine, enchanter, (use) × enchantment, learn by experience, × indeed, diligently observe.

A verb meaning to practice divination, to observe omens. This verb described the pagan practice of seeking knowledge through divination, which was expressly forbidden in the Law of Moses (Le 19:26; Dt 18:10); and was used as an indication that the kings of Israel and Judah were wicked (2Ki 17:17; 21:6; 2Ch 33:6). In its other usages, Laban used divination to confirm that Jacob was a blessing to him (Ge 30:27); Joseph claimed that a cup helped him practice divination (Ge 44:5, 15); and the Arameans took Ahab's words as an omen (1Ki 20:33).

5173. נַחַשׁ, nachash, *nakh´-ash*; from 5172; an *incantation* or *augury*:—enchantment.

A masculine noun meaning divination, omen. This word comes from the verb *nâchash* (5172), meaning to practice divination or to observe omens, and is used only twice in the OT. In both instances of this word, it is used within the context of Balaam and his prophecies. In one discourse, Balaam declared that there was no omen against Jacob (Nu 23:23); and in preparing for another discourse, he did not seek omens (Nu 24:1).

5174. נְחָשׁ, nᵉchâsh, *nekh-awsh´*; (Chaldee); corresponding to 5154; *copper*:—brass.

5175. נָחָשׁ, nâchâsh, *naw-khawsh´*; from 5172; a *snake* (from its *hiss*):—serpent.

A masculine noun meaning snake. It is used to refer to an actual serpent (Ex 4:3; Nu 21:6; Dt 8:15; Ecc 10:8; Am 5:19); or an image of one (Nu 21:9), but it is also used figuratively. Some of these symbolic uses include the tempter (Ge 3:1, 2, 4, 13, 14); the tribe of Dan (Ge 49:17); wicked rulers (Ps 58:4[5]); and enemies (Isa 14:29; Jer 8:17; 46:22).

5176. נָחָשׁ, **Nâchâsh**, *naw-khawsh´*; the same as 5175; *Nachash*, the name of two persons apparently non-Israelite:—Nahash.

5177. נַחְשׁוֹן, **Nachshôwn**, *nakh-shone´*; from 5172; *enchanter; Nachshon*, an Israelite:—Naashon, Nahshon.

5178. נְחֹשֶׁת, **nᵉchôsheth**, *nekh-o´-sheth*; for 5154; *copper*; hence, something made of that metal, i.e. *coin*, a *fetter*; (figurative) *base* (as compared with gold or silver):—brasen, brass, chain, copper, fetter (of brass), filthiness, steel.

5179. נְחֻשְׁתָּא, **Nᵉchushtâ'**, *nekh-oosh-taw´*; from 5178; *copper; Nechushta*, an Israelitess:—Nehushta.

5180. נְחֻשְׁתָּן, **Nᵉchushtân**, *nekh-oosh-tawn´*; from 5178; something made *of copper*, i.e. the copper *serpent* of the Desert:—Nehushtan.

5181. נָחַת, **nâchath**, *naw-khath´*; a primitive root; to *sink*, i.e. *descend*; (causative) to *press* or *lead* down:—be broken, (cause to) come down, enter, go down, press sore, settle, stick fast.

5182. נְחַת, **nᵉchath**, *nekh-ath´*; (Chaldee); corresponding to 5181; to *descend*; (causative) to *bring away, deposit, depose*:—carry, come down, depose, lay up, place.

5183. נַחַת, **nachath**, *nakh´-ath*; from 5182; a *descent*, i.e. imposition, unfavourable (*punishment*) or favourable (*food*); also (intransitive; perhaps from 5117), *restfulness*:—lighting down, quiet (-ness), to rest, be set on.

5184. נַחַת, **Nachath**, *nakh´-ath*; the same as 5183; *quiet; Nachath*, the name of an Edomite and of two Israelites:—Nahath.

5185. נָחֵת, **nâchêth**, *naw-khayth´*; from 5181; *descending*:—come down.

5186. נָטָה, **nâṭâh**, *naw-taw´*; a primitive root; to *stretch* or spread out; (by implication) to *bend* away (including moral deflection); used in a great variety of applications (as follows):— + afternoon, apply, bow (down, -ing), carry aside, decline, deliver, extend, go down, be gone, incline, intend, lay, let down, offer, outstretched, overthrown, pervert, pitch, prolong, put away, shew, spread (out), stretch (forth, out), take (aside), turn (aside, away), wrest, cause to yield.

5187. נְטִיל, **nâṭîyl**, *nawt-eel´*; from 5190; *laden*:—that bear.

5188. נְטִיפָה, **nᵉṭîyphâh**, *net-ee-faw´*; from 5197; a *pendant* for the ears (especially of pearls):—chain, collar.

5189. נְטִישָׁה, **nᵉṭîyshâh**, *net-ee-shaw´*; from 5203; a *tendril* (as an offshoot):—battlement, branch, plant.

5190. נָטַל, **nâṭal**, *naw-tal´*; a primitive root; to *lift*; (by implication) to *impose*:—bear, offer, take up.

5191. נְטַל, **nᵉṭal**, *net-al´*; (Chaldee); corresponding to 5190; to *raise*:—take up.

5192. נֵטֶל, **nêṭel**, *nay´-tel*; from 5190; a *burden*:—weighty.

5193. נָטַע, **nâṭaʻ**, *naw-tah´*; a primitive root; (properly) to *strike* in, i.e. *fix*; (specifically) to *plant* (literal or figurative):—fastened, plant (-er).

5194. נֶטַע, **neṭaʻ**, *neh´-tah*; from 5193; a *plant*; (collective) a *plantation*; (abstract) a *planting*:—plant.

5195. נָטִיעַ, **nâṭîyaʻ**, *naw-tee´-ah*; from 5193; a *plant*:—plant.

5196. נְטָעִים, **Nᵉṭâʻîym**, *net-aw-eem´*; plural of 5194; *Netaïm*, a place in Palestine:—plants.

5197. נָטַף, **nâṭaph**, *naw-taf´*; a primitive root; to *ooze*, i.e. *distil* gradually; (by implication) to *fall in drops*; (figurative) to *speak* by inspiration:—drop (-ping), prophesy (-et).

A verb meaning to drip, to drop, to flow. It is used to describe rain (Jgs 5:4; Ps 68:8[9]); and words which are like rain (Job 29:22). Lips may drip with honey (Pr 5:3); and hands may drip with myrrh (SS 5:5). This word can also be taken figuratively, meaning to prophesy (Eze 21:2[7]; Am 7:16). It is sometimes used to refer to false prophets (Mic 2:6).

5198. נָטָף, **nâṭâph**, *naw-tawf´*; from 5197; a *drop*; specifically, an aromatic *gum* (probably *stacte*):—drop, stacte.

5199. נְטֹפָה, **Nᵉṭôphâh**, *net-o-faw´*; from 5197; *distillation; Netophah*, a place in Palestine:—Netophah.

5200. נְטֹפָתִי, **Nᵉṭôphâthîy**, *net-o-faw-thee´*; patronymic from 5199; a *Netophathite*, or inhabitant of Netophah:—Netophathite.

5201. נָטַר, **nâṭar**, *naw-tar´*; a primitive root; to *guard*; (figurative) to *cherish* (anger):—bear grudge, keep (-er), reserve.

5202. נְטַר, **nᵉṭar**, *net-ar´*; (Chaldee); corresponding to 5201; to *retain*:—keep.

5203. נָטַשׁ, **nâṭash**, *naw-tash´*; a primitive root; (properly) to *pound*, i.e. *smite*; by implication (as if beating out, and thus expanding) to *disperse*; also, to *thrust* off, down, out or upon (including *reject, let alone, permit, remit*, etc.):—cast off, drawn, let fall, forsake, join [battle], leave (off), lie still, loose, spread (self) abroad, stretch out, suffer.

A verb meaning to forsake, to leave alone. The word occurs in relation to the land that should be unused ("forsaken") in the seventh year (Ex 23:11); the Israelites who abandoned God (Dt 32:15); Saul's father who forgot about the donkeys and began to worry about him (1Sa 10:2); David who left his flock with a shepherd (1Sa 17:20); the psalmist who pleaded with God not to turn from him (Ps 27:9). This word is used once to mean to not permit when Laban was not allowed to kiss his grandchildren good-bye (Ge 31:28).

5204. נִי, **nîy**, *nee*; a doubtful word; apparently from 5091; *lamentation*:—wailing.

5205. נִיד, **nîyd**, *need*; from 5110; *motion* (of the lips in speech):—moving.

5206. נִידָה, **nîydâh**, *nee-daw´*; feminine of 5205; *removal*, i.e. exile:—removed.

5207. נִיחוֹחַ, **nîychôwach**, *nee-kho´-akh*; or נִיחֹחַ, **nîychôach**, *nee-kho´-akh*; from 5117; (properly) *restful*, i.e. *pleasant*; (abstract) *delight*:—sweet (odour).

5208. נִיחוֹחַ, **nîychôwach**, *nee-kho´-akh*; (Chaldee); or (shorter) נִיחֹחַ, **nîychôach**, *nee-kho´-akh*; (Chaldee); corresponding to 5207; *pleasure*:—sweet odour (savour).

5209. נִין, **nîyn**, *neen*; from 5125; *progeny*:—son.

5210. נִינְוֵה, **Nîynᵉvêh**, *nee-nev-ay´*; of foreign origin; *Nineveh*, the capital of Assyria:—Nineveh.

5211. נִיס, **nîys**, *neece*; from 5127; *fugitive*:—that fleeth.

5212. נִיסָן, **Nîysân**, *nee-sawn´*; probably of foreign origin; *Nisan*, the first month of the Jewish sacred year:—Nisan.

5213. נִיצוֹץ, **nîytsôwts**, *nee-tsotes´*; from 5340; a *spark*:—spark.

5214. נִיר, **nîyr**, *neer*; a root probably identical with that of 5216, through the idea of the *gleam* of a fresh furrow; to *till* the soil:—break up.

5215. נִיר, **nîyr**, *neer*; or נִר, **nir**, *neer*; from 5214; (properly) *ploughing*, i.e. (concrete) freshly *ploughed* land:—fallow ground, ploughing, tillage.

5216. נִיר, **nîyr**, *neer*; or נִר, **nir**, *neer*; also נֵיר, **nêyr**, *nare*; or נֵר, **nêr**, *nare*; or (feminine) נֵרָה, **nêrâh**, *nay-raw´*; from a primitive root [see 5214; 5135] properly meaning to *glisten*; a *lamp* (i.e. the burner) or *light* (literal or figurative):—candle, lamp, light.

A masculine noun meaning lamp, light. This word referred to the lamps of the tabernacle (Ex 27:20); the lamp in the Temple with Samuel (1Sa 3:3); the Word of God that lights the way (Ps 119:105); and the noble wife that does not let her lamp go out at night (Pr 31:18). The lamp can be used figuratively, as when God promised that David would always have a lamp before Him in Jerusalem (1Ki 11:36; 2Ch 21:7). This word corresponds to the Aramaic noun *nûr* (5135), which can be masculine or feminine and means fire or flame. See the book of Daniel, where the fire does not harm the three Hebrews (see Da 3:27); and where fire describes the Ancient of Days (see Da 7:9, 10).

5217. נָכָא, nâkâ', *naw-kaw´*; a primitive root; to *smite*, i.e. *drive* away:—be viler.

5218. נָכֵא, nâkê', *naw-kay´*; or **נָכָא, nâkâ'**, *naw-kaw´*; from 5217; *smitten*, i.e. (figurative) *afflicted*:—broken, stricken, wounded.

5219. נְכֹאת, nᵉk'ôth, *nek-ohth´*; from 5218; (properly) a *smiting*, i.e. (concrete) an aromatic *gum* [perhaps *styrax*] (as *powdered*):—spicery (-ces).

5220. נֶכֶד, neked, *neh´-ked*; from an unused root meaning to *propagate; offspring*:—nephew, son's son.

5221. נָכָה, nâkâh, *naw-kaw´*; a primitive root; to *strike* (lightly or severely, literal or figurative):—beat, cast forth, clap, give [wounds], × go forward, × indeed, kill, make [slaughter], murderer, punish, slaughter, slay (-er, -ing), smite (-r, -ing), strike, be stricken, (give) stripes, × surely, wound.

A verb meaning to beat, to strike, to wound. There are many instances of striking physically (Ex 21:15, 19; Job 16:10; Ps 3:7[8]; SS 5:7). This word is also used in a different sense, as when the men of Sodom and Gomorrah were stricken blind by the two angels (Ge 19:11); when a priest stuck a fork into the kettle (1Sa 2:14); when people clapped their hands (2Ki 11:12); or when people verbally abused Jeremiah (Jer 18:18). God struck the Egyptians with plagues (Ex 3:20); and struck people down in judgment (Isa 5:25).

5222. נֵכֶה, nêkeh, *nay-keh´*; from 5221; a *smiter*, i.e. (figurative) *traducer*:—abject.

5223. נָכֶה, nâkeh, *naw-keh´*; *smitten*, i.e. (literal) maimed, or (figurative) dejected:—contrite, lame.

5224. נְכוֹ, Nᵉkôw, *nek-o´*; probably of Egyptian origin; *Neko* an Egyptian king:—Necho. Compare 6549.

5225. נָכוֹן, Nâkôwn, *naw-kone´*; from 3559; *prepared; Nakon*, probably an Israelite:—Nachon.

5226. נֵכַח, nêkach, *nay´-kakh*; from an unused root meaning to *be straightforward*; (properly) the *fore* part; (used adverbially) *opposite*:—before, over against.

5227. נֹכַח, nôkach, *no´-kakh*; from the same as 5226; (properly,) the *front* part; (used adverbially, especially with a preposition) *opposite, in front of, forward, in behalf of*:—(over) against, before, direct [-ly], for, right (on).

5228. נָכֹחַ, nâkôach, *naw-ko´-akh*; from the same as 5226; *straightforward*, i.e. (figurative) *equitable, correct*, or (abstract) *integrity*:—plain, right, uprightness.

An adjective meaning straightforward, honest. In 2Sa 15:3, it is used to describe a legal case as straightforward, obviously deserving amends. In Pr 8:9, it describes wisdom's words as straightforward, not perverted, to the one who has the right attitude to receive them. In Pr 24:26, the adjective describes words spoken honestly, without partiality (cf. Pr 24:23–25); lips speaking this way kiss the hearer. The word occurs as a noun in Isa 57:2 and means straightforwardness or honesty. For the feminine form of the word, see *nĕkôchâh* (5229).

5229. נְכֹחָה, nᵉkôchâh, *nek-o-khaw´*; feminine of 5228; (properly) *straightforwardness*, i.e. (figurative) *integrity*, or (concrete) *a truth*:—equity, right (thing), uprightness.

5230. נָכַל, nâkal, *naw-kal´*; a primitive root; to *defraud*, i.e. *act treacherously*:—beguile, conspire, deceiver, deal subtilly.

5231. נֵכֶל, nêkel, *nay´-kel*; from 5230; *deceit*:—wile.

5232. נְכַס, nᵉkas, *nek-as´*; (Chaldee); corresponding to 5233:—goods.

5233. נֶכֶס, nekes, *neh´-kes*; from an unused root meaning to *accumulate; treasure*:—riches, wealth.

5234. נָכַר, nâkar, *naw-kar´*; a primitive root; (properly) to *scrutinize*, i.e. look intently at; hence (with *recognition* implied), to *acknowledge, be acquainted with, care for, respect, revere*, or (with *suspicion* implied), to *disregard, ignore, be strange* toward, *reject, resign, dissimulate* (as if ignorant or disowning):—acknowledge, × could, deliver, discern, dissemble, estrange, feign self to be another, know, take knowledge (notice), perceive, regard, (have) respect, behave (make) self strange (-ly).

A verb meaning to pretend, to consider carefully, to investigate, to acknowledge, to recognize, to make unrecognizable. This verb is used mainly in the causative stem to indicate the process of investigation, knowing something, or knowing how to do something. Jacob told Laban to investigate to see if he could recognize his gods in any of Jacob's tents (Ge 31:32); Tamar challenged Judah to investigate the seal and cord she had to see if he could recognize them (Ge 38:25, 26). The Hebrew word is also used to indicate someone already known previously (1Ki 18:7; 20:41). The word is found metaphorically meaning to acknowledge, to follow, or to refuse to do so: evildoers refused to acknowledge the light (God's laws) and did not walk according to God's laws (Job 24:13). When the word is used with an infinitive, it means to know how to do something or to know something so that a person acts in a certain way. Judeans, who had intermarried with foreigners, had children who did not know how to speak the language of Judah, which was Hebrew (Ne 13:24).

Finally, in the reflexive stem, the word means to present oneself in such a way as to fool others (1Ki 14:5, 6); or to hide one's identity, as Joseph hid his identity from his brothers (Ge 42:7). In the case of children, they reflected their characters by their actions, revealing their essential dispositions (Pr 20:11).

5235. נֶכֶר, neker, *neh´-ker*; or **נֹכֶר, nôker**, *no´-ker*; from 5234; something *strange*, i.e. unexpected *calamity*:—strange.

A masculine noun meaning disaster, calamity. The meaning derives from the idea of strangeness (cf. *nêkâr* [5236]); a calamity interrupts the normal flow of life. The word occurs in Job 31:3 where it refers to calamity as the punishment of iniquity. In Ob 1:12, the word occurs along with several words of similar meaning (cf. Ob 1:13, 14), describing a time in which Judah met with calamity.

5236. נֵכָר, nêkâr, *nay-kawr´*; from 5234; *foreign*, or (concrete) a *foreigner*, or (abstract) *heathendom*:—alien, strange (+ -er).

A masculine noun meaning foreign. The word comes from a root meaning to scrutinize, perhaps drawing on the idea that people look closely at something foreign or strange (see *nâkar*[5234]). The word modifies other nouns to signify a foreigner or a foreign god. Foreigners with their false gods posed a threat to Israel's service to the Lord (Dt 32:12; Jgs 10:16; Mal 2:11); sometimes even infiltrating the Temple service (Ne 13:30; Eze 44:9). They also posed a physical threat at times (Ps 144:7; Isa 62:8; Jer 5:19). However, foreigners sometimes turned to Israel's God (Isa 56:3, 6). The word also refers (with other words) to foreign land (Ps 137:4; Jer 5:19); and a foreign power (Ps 144:7).

5237. נָכְרִי, nokrîy, *nok-ree´*; from 5235 (second form); *strange*, in a variety of degrees and applications (*foreign, non-relative, adulterous, different, wonderful*):—alien, foreigner, outlandish, strange (-r, woman).

An adjective meaning strange, foreign, stranger, foreigner. It refers to someone who was not part of the family (Ge 31:15; cf. Ge 31:14; Ps 69:8[9]), especially the extended family of Israel (Dt 17:15). Under the Law, strangers were not allowed to rule in Israel (Dt 17:15); they were not released from their debts every seven years as Hebrews were (Dt 15:3); and could be sold certain ceremonially unclean food (Dt 14:21). Strangers were regarded as unholy (Dt 14:21); and were often looked down on (Ru 2:10; Job 19:15). Some hope for the conversion of foreigners was offered (Ru 2:10; 1Ki 8:41, 43); but with this word, more emphasis was placed on avoiding the defilement of foreign women (1Ki 11:1; Ezr 10:2, 10, 11, 14, 17, 18, 44; Pr 6:24); and foreign ways (Isa 2:6; Jer 2:21; Zep 1:8). The word *gêr* (1616), meaning sojourner, focuses more sympathetically on foreigners in Israel.

5238. **נְכֹת, nᵉkôth,** *nek-ōth´*; probably for 5219; *spicery*, i.e. (generally) *valuables*:—precious things.

5239. **נָלָה, nâlâh,** *naw-law´*; apparently a primitive root; to *complete*:—make an end.

5240. **נְמִבְזָה, nᵉmibzâh,** *nem-ib-zaw´*; from 959; *despised*:—vile.

5241. **נְמוּאֵל, Nᵉmûw'êl,** *nem-oo-ale´*; apparently for 3223; *Nemuel*, the name of two Israelites:—Nemuel.

5242. **נְמוּאֵלִי, Nᵉmûw'êlîy,** *nem-oo-ay-lee´*; from 5241; a *Nemuelite*, or descendant of Nemuel:—Nemuelite.

5243. **נָמַל, nâmal,** *naw-mal´*; a primitive root; to *become clipped* or (specific) *circumcised*:—(branch to) be cut down (off), circumcise.

A noun assumed to be the root for the Hebrew word *nᵉmâlâh* (5244), meaning ant (see Pr 6:6; 30:25). The actual word does not exist in Scripture. Scholars assume that the word means cut or circumcised (Ge 17:11; Job 14:2; 18:16; 24:24; Ps 37:2).

5244. **נְמָלָה, nᵉmâlâh,** *nem-aw-law´*; feminine from 5243; an *ant* (probably from its almost *bisected* form):—ant.

5245. **נְמַר, nᵉmar,** *nem-ar´*; (Chaldee); corresponding to 5246:—leopard.

5246. **נָמֵר, nâmêr,** *naw-mare´*; from an unused root meaning properly to *filtrate*, i.e. *be limpid* [compare 5247 and 5249]; and thus to *spot* or *stain* as if by dripping; a *leopard* (from its stripes):—leopard.

5247. **נִמְרָה, Nimrâh,** *nim-raw´*; from the same as 5246; *clear* water; *Nimrah*, a place East of the Jordan:—Nimrah. See also 1039, 5249.

5248. **נִמְרוֹד, Nimrôwd,** *nim-rode´*; or **נִמְרֹד, Nimrôd,** *nim-rode´*; probably of foreign origin; *Nimrod*, a son of Cush:—Nimrod.

5249. **נִמְרִים, Nimrîym,** *nim-reem´*; plural of a masculine corresponding to 5247; *clear* waters; *Nimrim*, a place East of the Jordan:—Nimrim. Compare 1039.

5250. **נִמְשִׁי, Nimshîy,** *nim-shee´*; probably from 4871; *extricated; Nimshi*, the (grand-) father of Jehu:—Nimshi.

5251. **נֵס, nês,** *nace*; from 5264; a *flag*; also a *sail*; (by implication) a *flagstaff*; (generally) a *signal*; (figurative) a *token*:—banner, pole, sail, (en-) sign, standard.

5252. **נְסִבָּה, nᵉsibbâh,** *nes-ib-baw´*; feminine participle passive of 5437; (properly) an *environment*, i.e. *circumstance* or *turn* of affairs:—cause.

5253. **נָסַג, nâsag,** *naw-sag´*; a primitive root; to *retreat*:—departing away, remove, take (hold), turn away.

5254. **נָסָה, nâsâh,** *naw-saw´*; a primitive root; to *test*; (by implication) to *attempt*:—adventure, assay, prove, tempt, try.

A verb meaning to test, to try, to prove. Appearing nearly forty times in the OT, this term often refers to God testing the faith and faithfulness of human beings, including Abraham (Ge 22:1); the nation of Israel (Ex 15:25; 16:4; 20:20; Dt 8:2, 16; 13:3[4]; Jgs 2:22; 3:1, 4); Hezekiah (2Ch 32:31); David (Ps 26:2). Although people were forbidden from putting God to the test, they often did so (Ex 17:2, 7; Nu 14:22; Dt 6:16; 33:8; Ps 78:18, 41, 56; 95:9; 106:14; Isa 7:12). Testing, however, does not always suggest tempting or enticing someone to sin, as when the Queen of Sheba tested Solomon's wisdom (1Ki 10:1; 2Ch 9:1); and Daniel's physical appearance was tested after a ten-day vegetarian diet (Da 1:12, 14). Finally, this term can refer to the testing of equipment, such as swords or armour (1Sa 17:39).

5255. **נָסַח, nâsach,** *naw-sakh´*; a primitive root; to *tear* away:—destroy, pluck, root.

A verb meaning to tear down, to tear out. In the Hebrew OT, this verb almost always occurs in poetical literature and always occurs in contexts of judgment. For example, as the result of disobedience to God's covenant, He promised to remove Israel from the land. According to the psalmist, God would snatch the unrighteous from the comforts of their homes for putting trust in material wealth rather than in Him (Ps 52:5[7]). Similarly, Pr 2:22 indicates that the righteous would remain in the land while the unrighteous would be removed from it. Finally, the Lord promised to tear down or destroy the house of the proud person (Pr 15:25).

5256. **נְסַח, nᵉsach,** *nes-akh´*; (Chaldee); corresponding to 5255:—pull down.

An Aramaic verb meaning to be pulled out. Found only once in the OT, this word refers to the removal of a beam of wood from the house of any person who altered the decree of King Cyrus. As punishment for disregarding the decree, the offending party would be hung or impaled on the wooden beam (Ezr 6:11).

5257. **נְסִיךְ, nᵉsîyk,** *nes-eek´*; from 5258; (properly) something *poured* out, i.e. a *libation*; also a molten *image*; (by implication) a *prince* (as *anointed*):—drink offering, duke, prince (-ipal).

A masculine noun meaning a drink offering, a molten image. Derived from a verb meaning to pour out, this term refers to the pouring out of a drink offering or libation (Dt 32:38). Here God mockingly inquires about the whereabouts of the gods that drank the drink offerings of wine offered by their pagan worshippers. In Da 11:8, this term refers to metal idols or images brought home by the Egyptian ruler Ptolemy after defeating the Syrian army.

5258. **נָסַךְ, nâsak,** *naw-sak´*; a primitive root; to *pour* out, especially a libation, or to *cast* (metal); (by analogy) to *anoint* a king:—cover, melt, offer, (cause to) pour (out), set (up).

A verb meaning to pour out. Frequently, this term refers to pouring out drink offerings or libations. These offerings usually employed wine (Hos 9:4); or another fermented drink (Nu 28:7). But David offered water as a drink offering to the Lord (2Sa 23:16; 1Ch 11:18). In the books of Moses (Nu 28:7), God clearly outlined instructions for making proper sacrifices. For example, He prohibited pouring a drink offering on the altar of incense (Ex 30:9). Scripture clearly condemned the practice of making drink offerings to false gods (Jer 19:13; 44:17–19, 25); a practice that angered God and incurred His judgment (Jer 7:18; 32:29; Eze 20:28). Infrequently, this Hebrew term referred to the casting of idols from metal (Isa 40:19; 44:10); and in one instance, to a deep sleep that the Lord poured over the inhabitants of Jerusalem (Isa 29:10).

5259. **נָסַךְ, nâsak,** *naw-sak´*; a primitive root [probably identical with 5258 through the idea of fusion]; to *interweave*, i.e. (figurative) to *overspread*:—that is spread.

5260. **נְסַךְ, nᵉsak,** *nes-ak´*; (Chaldee); corresponding to 5258; to *pour* out a libation:—offer.

5261. **נְסַךְ, nᵉsak,** *nes-ak´*; (Chaldee); corresponding to 5262; a *libation*:—drink offering.

An Aramaic masculine singular noun meaning drink offering, libation. Its only occurrence in the Hebrew Bible is in Ezr 7:17 where Artaxerxes provided offerings and sacrifices to be delivered for the Temple in Jerusalem. This term is related to the verb *nĕsak* (5260), meaning to pour out. For the Hebrew cognate of this noun, see *nesek* (5262).

5262. **נֶסֶךְ, nesek,** *neh´-sek*; or **נֵסֶךְ, nêsek,** *nay´-sek*; from 5258; a *libation*; also a *cast idol*:—cover, drink offering, molten image.

A masculine singular noun meaning drink offering, libation, molten image. The most common usage of the term referred to a liquid offering that was poured out (*nâsak* [5258]) (Ge 35:14; Le 23:37; Nu 15:5, 7, 10, 24). It is employed both for offerings made to *Yahweh* as well as to foreign deities (2Ki 16:13; Isa 57:6). In four passages, the term is used for a molten image (i.e. a "poured out" thing) (Isa 41:29; 48:5; Jer 10:14).

5263. **נָסַס, nâsas,** *naw-sas´*; a primitive root; to *wane,* i.e. *be sick:*—faint.

5264. **נָסַס, nâsas,** *naw-sas´*; a primitive root; to *gleam* from afar, i.e. to *be conspicuous* as a signal; or rather perhaps a denominative from 5251 [and identical with 5263, through the idea of a flag as *fluttering* in the wind]; to *raise a beacon:*—lift up as an ensign.

5265. **נָסַע, nâsaʻ,** *naw-sah´*; a primitive root; (properly) to *pull* up, especially the tent-pins, i.e. *start* on a journey:—cause to blow, bring, get, (make to) go (away, forth, forward, onward, out), (take) journey, march, remove, set aside (forward), × still, be on his (go their) way.

5266. **נָסַק, nâsaq,** *naw-sak´*; a primitive root; to *go* up:—ascend.

5267. **נְסַק, nᵉsaq,** *nes-ak´*; (Chaldee); corresponding to 5266:—take up.

5268. **נִסְרֹךְ, Nisrôk,** *nis-roke´*; of foreign origin; *Nisrok,* a Babylonian idol:—Nisroch.

5269. **נֵעָה, Nêʻâh,** *nay-aw´*; from 5128; *motion; Neäh,* a place in Palestine:—Neah.

5270. **נֹעָה, Nôʻâh,** *no-aw´*; from 5128; *movement; Noäh,* an Israelitess:—Noah.

5271. **נְעוּרִים, nᵉʻûwrîym,** *neh-oo-reem´*; properly passive participle from 5288 as denominative; (only in plural collective or emphatical) *youth,* the state (*juvenility*) or the persons (*young* people):—childhood, youth.

5272. **נְעִיאֵל, Nᵉʻîyʼêl,** *neh-ee-ale´*; from 5128 and 410; *moved of God; Neïel,* a place in Palestine:—Neiel.

5273. **נָעִים, nâʻîym,** *naw-eem´*; from 5276; *delightful* (objective or subjective, literal or figurative):—pleasant (-ure), sweet.

5274. **נָעַל, nâʻal,** *naw-al´*; a primitive root; (properly) to *fasten* up, i.e. with a bar or cord; hence (denominative from 5275), to *sandal,* i.e. furnish with slippers:—bolt, inclose, lock, shoe, shut up.

5275. **נַעַל, naʻal,** *nah´-al*; or (feminine) **נַעֲלָה, naʻălâh,** *nah-al-aw´*; from 5274; (properly) a sandal *tongue*; (by extension) a *sandal* or slipper (sometimes as a symbol of occupancy, a refusal to marry, or of something valueless):—dryshod, (pair of) shoe ([-latchet], -s).

5276. **נָעֵם, nâʻêm,** *naw-ame´*; a primitive root; to *be agreeable* (literal or figurative):—pass in beauty, be delight, be pleasant, be sweet.

5277. **נַעַם, Naʻam,** *nah´-am*; from 5276; *pleasure; Naam,* an Israelite:—Naam.

5278. **נֹעַם, nôʻam,** *no´-am*; from 5276; *agreeableness,* i.e. *delight, suitableness, splendor* or *grace:*—beauty, pleasant (-ness).

5279. **נַעֲמָה, Naʻămâh,** *nah-am-aw´*; feminine of 5277; *pleasantness; Naamah,* the name of an antediluvian woman, of an Ammonitess, and of a place in Palestine:—Naamah.

5280. **נַעֲמִי, Naʻămîy,** *nah-am-ee´*; patronymic from 5283; a *Naamanite,* or descendant of Naaman (collective):—Naamites.

5281. **נָעֳמִי, Noʻŏmîy,** *nŏ-om-ee´*; from 5278; *pleasant; Noömi,* an Israelitess:—Naomi.

5282. **נַעֲמָן, naʻămân,** *nah-am-awn´*; from 5276; *pleasantness* (plural as concrete):—pleasant.

5283. **נַעֲמָן, Naʻămân,** *nah-am-awn´*; the same as 5282; *Naaman,* the name of an Israelite and of a Damascene:—Naaman.

5284. **נַעֲמָתִי, Naʻămâthîy,** *nah-am-aw-thee´*; patrial from a place corresponding in name (but not identical) with 5279; a *Naamathite,* or inhabitant of Naamah:—Naamathite.

5285. **נַעֲצוּץ, naʻătsûwts,** *nah-ats-oots´*; from an unused root meaning to *prick*; probably a *brier*; (by implication) a *thicket* of thorny bushes:—thorn.

5286. **נָעַר, nâʻar,** *naw-ar´*; a primitive root; to *growl:*—yell.

5287. **נָעַר, nâʻar,** *naw-ar´*; a primitive root [probably identical with 5286, through the idea of the *rustling* of mane, which usually accompanies the lion's roar]; to *tumble* about:—shake (off, out, self), overthrow, toss up and down.

5288. **נַעַר, naʻar,** *nah´-ar*; from 5287; (concrete) a *boy* (as active), from the age of infancy to adolescence; (by implication) a *servant*; also (by interchange of sex), a *girl* (of similar latitude in age):—babe, boy, child, damsel [*from the margin*], lad, servant, young (man).

5289. **נַעַר, naʻar,** *nah´-ar*; from 5287 in its derivative sense of *tossing* about; a *wanderer:*—young one.

5290. **נֹעַר, nôʻar,** *no´-ar*; from 5287; (abstract) *boyhood* [compare 5288]:—child, youth.

5291. **נַעֲרָה, naʻărâh,** *nah-ar-aw´*; feminine of 5288; a *girl* (from infancy to adolescence):—damsel, maid (-en), young (woman).

5292. **נַעֲרָה, Naʻărâh,** *nah-ar-aw´*; the same as 5291; *Naarah,* the name of an Israelitess, and of a place in Palestine:—Naarah, Naarath.

5293. **נַעֲרַי, Naʻăray,** *nah-ar-ah´ee*; from 5288; *youthful; Naarai,* an Israelite:—Naarai.

5294. **נְעַרְיָה, Nᵉʻaryâh,** *neh-ar-yaw´*; from 5288 and 3050; *servant of Jah; Neärjah,* the name of two Israelites:—Neariah.

5295. **נַעֲרָן, Naʻărân,** *nah-ar-awn´*; from 5288; *juvenile; Naaran,* a place in Palestine:—Naaran.

5296. **נְעֹרֶת, nᵉʻôreth,** *neh-o´-reth*; from 5287; something *shaken* out, i.e. *tow* (as the refuse of flax):—tow.

5297. **נֹף, Nôph,** *nofe*; a variation of 4644; *Noph,* the capital of Upper Egypt:—Noph.

5298. **נֶפֶג, Nepheg,** *neh´-feg*; from an unused root probably meaning to *spring* forth; a *sprout; Nepheg,* the name of two Israelites:—Nepheg.

5299. **נָפָה, nâphâh,** *naw-faw´*; from 5130 in the sense of *lifting*; a *height*; also a *sieve:*—border, coast, region, sieve.

5300. **נְפוּשְׁסִים, Nᵉphûwshᵉsîym,** *nef-oo-shes-eem´*; for 5304; *Nephushesim,* a Temple-servant:—Nephisesim [*from the margin*].

5301. **נָפַח, nâphach,** *naw-fakh´*; a primitive root; to *puff,* in various applications; (literal) to *inflate, blow* hard, *scatter, kindle, expire*; (figurative) to *disesteem:*—blow, breath, give up, cause to lose [life], seething, snuff.

5302. **נֹפַח, Nôphach,** *no´-fach*; from 5301; a *gust; Nophach,* a place in Moab:—Nophah.

5303. **נְפִילִים, nᵉphîylîym,** *nef-eel-eem´*; from 5307; (properly) a *feller,* i.e. a *bully* or *tyrant:*—giant.

A masculine noun used only in the plural meaning giants. The celebrated, puzzling passage where this term is first used is Ge 6:4 which merely transliterates the Hebrew word into English as Nephilim. These beings evidently appeared on the earth in the ancient past when divine beings cohabited with woman, and Nephilim, the mighty men or warriors of great fame, were the offspring. This huge race of Nephilim struck fear into the Israelite spies who had gone up to survey the land of Canaan (see Nu 13:31–33). The sons of Anak, a tall race of people, came from the Nephilim (Nu 13:33; cf. Dt 2:10, 11; 9:2; Jos 15:14). Eze 32:21, 27 may have the Nephilim in mind, possibly equating them with the mighty men or mighty warriors in the passage. These beings were not divine but only at best great, powerful men.

5304. נְפִיסִים, Nᵉphîysîym, *nef-ee-seem´*; plural from an unused root meaning to *scatter; expansions; Nephism*, a Temple-servant:—Nephusim [*from the margin*].

5305. נָפִישׁ, Nâphîysh, *naw-feesh´*; from 5314; *refreshed; Naphish*, a son of Ishmael, and his posterity:—Naphish.

5306. נֹפֶךְ, nôphek, *no´-fek*; from an unused root meaning to *glisten; shining*; a gem, probably the *garnet*:—emerald.

5307. נָפַל, nâphal, *naw-fal´*; a primitive root; to *fall*, in a great variety of applications (intransitive or causative, literal or figurative):—be accepted, cast (down, self, [lots], out), cease, die, divide (by lot), (let) fail, (cause to, let, make, ready to) fall (away, down, -en, -ing), fell (-ing), fugitive, have [inheritance], inferior, be judged [*by mistake for* 6419], lay (along), (cause to) lie down, light (down), be (× hast) lost, lying, overthrow, overwhelm, perish, present (-ed, -ing), (make to) rot, slay, smite out, × surely, throw down.

A verb meaning to fall, to lie, to prostrate oneself, to overthrow. This common Hebrew verb carries many possible variations in meaning, much like the English verb to fall. For instance, it can be used literally of someone or something falling down (Ge 14:10; 1Sa 4:18; 17:49; 2Ki 6:5); or into a pit (Ex 21:33; Dt 22:4). It is employed for inanimate objects like walls, towers, trees, and hailstones (1Ki 20:30; Ecc 11:3). It is used idiomatically for a violent death, especially in battle (Jgs 5:27; 1Sa 4:10; Am 7:17); and for the overthrow of a city (Jer 51:8). The word also describes those who fall prostrate before God or those in authority (Ge 50:18; 2Ch 20:18). With the preposition *'al* (5921), meaning upon, it carries the meaning to attack (literally, to fall upon) (Job 1:19); to desert (to fall away) (2Ki 25:11; Jer 21:9); to be overcome by sleep or emotion (to fall into) (Ge 4:5; 15:12; Jos 2:9; 1Sa 17:32; Ne 6:16). It is used to express the idea of being bedridden or debilitated (Ex 21:18); to be overtaken (lit., to fall into the hands of) (Jgs 15:18; La 1:7); and to be born (Isa 26:18). In its causative usage, it also takes the meaning to cast lots (Ne 10:34[35]; Isa 34:17).

5308. נְפַל, nᵉphal, *nef-al´*; (Chaldee); corresponding to 5307:—fall (down), have occasion.

An Aramaic verb meaning to fall, to prostrate oneself, to die. The verb is commonly used in reference to paying homage to a human being (Da 2:46); or to an image (Da 3:5–7). It is also used to denote a violent death (Da 7:20). It carries the meaning of responsibility in Ezr 7:20, where it referred to taking responsibility for carrying out the king's order. See the Hebrew word *nâphal* (5307).

5309. נֶפֶל, nephel, *neh´-fel*; or **נֵפֶל, nêphel,** *nay´-fel*; from 5307; something *fallen*, i.e. an *abortion*:—untimely birth.

A masculine noun meaning an untimely birth, a miscarriage. This word is taken from the Hebrew root *nâphal* (5307), meaning to fall. Job thought it might have been better to have been stillborn than to be born and live with his trouble (Job 3:16). The psalmist hoped the wicked would be put away like a miscarried infant (Ps 58:8[9]). The teacher in Ecclesiastes thought it would have been better for people to never be born than not to be able to enjoy their riches and have proper burials (Ecc 6:3).

5310. נָפַץ, nâphats, *naw-fats´*; a primitive root; to *dash* to pieces, or *scatter*:—be beaten in sunder, break (in pieces), broken, dash (in pieces), cause to be discharged, dispersed, be overspread, scatter.

5311. נֶפֶץ, nephets, *neh´-fets*; from 5310; a *storm* (as dispersing):—scattering.

5312. נְפַק, nᵉphaq, *nef-ak´*; (Chaldee); a primitive root; to *issue*; (causative) to *bring out*:—come (go, take) forth (out).

5313. נִפְקָה, niphqâh, *nif-kaw´*; (Chaldee); from 5312; an *outgo*, i.e. expense:—expense.

5314. נָפַשׁ, nâphash, *naw-fash´*; a primitive root; to *breathe*; (passive) to *be breathed* upon, i.e. (figurative) *refreshed* (as if by a current of air):—(be) refresh selves (-ed).

5315. נֶפֶשׁ, nephesh, *neh´-fesh*; from 5314; (properly) a *breathing* creature, i.e. *animal* or (abstract) *vitality*; used very widely in a literal, accommodated or figurative sense (bodily or mental):—any, appetite, beast, body, breath, creature, × dead (-ly), desire, × [dis-] contented, × fish, ghost, + greedy, he, heart (-y), (hath, × jeopardy of) life (× in jeopardy), lust, man, me, mind, mortally, one, own, person, pleasure, (her-, him-, my-, thy-) self, them (your) -selves, + slay, soul, + tablet, they, thing, (× she) will, × would have it.

A feminine noun meaning breath, the inner being with its thoughts and emotions. It is used 753 times in the OT and has a broad range of meanings. Most of its uses fall into these categories: breath, literally or figuratively (Jer 15:9); the inner being with its thoughts and emotions (Jgs 10:16; Pr 14:10; Eze 25:6); and by extension, the whole person (Ge 12:5; Le 4:2; Eze 18:4). Moreover, the term can cover the animating force of a person or his or her dead body (Le 21:11; Nu 6:6; Jer 2:34). It is even applied to animals in a number of the above senses: the breath (Job 41:21[13]); the inner being (Jer 2:24); the whole creature (Ge 1:20); and the animating force (Le 17:11). When this word is applied to a person, it doesn't refer to a specific part of a human being. The Scriptures view a person as a composite whole, fully relating to God and not divided in any way (Dt 6:5; cf. 1Th 5:23).

5316. נֶפֶת, nepheth, *neh´-feth*; for 5299; a *height*:—country.

5317. נֹפֶת, nôpheth, *no´-feth*; from 5130 in the sense of *shaking* to pieces; a *dripping* i.e. of *honey* (from the comb):—honeycomb.

5318. נֶפְתּוֹחַ, Nephtôwach, *nef-to´-akh*; from 6605; *opened*, i.e. a *spring; Nephtoäch*, a place in Palestine:—Neptoah.

5319. נַפְתּוּלִים, naphtûwlîym, *naf-too-leem´*; from 6617; (properly) *wrestled*; but used (in the plural) transposed, a *struggle*:—wrestling.

5320. נַפְתֻּחִים, Naphtuchîym, *naf-too-kheem´*; plural of foreign origin; *Naphtuchim*, an Egyptian tribe:—Naptuhim.

5321. נַפְתָּלִי, Naphtâlîy, *naf-taw-lee´*; from 6617; *my wrestling; Naphtali*, a son of Jacob, with the tribe descended from him, and its territory:—Naphtali.

5322. נֵץ, nêts, *nayts*; from 5340; a *flower* (from its *brilliancy*); also a *hawk* (from its *flashing* speed):—blossom, hawk.

5323. נָצָא, nâtsâ', *naw-tsaw´*; a primitive root; to *go away*:—flee.

5324. נָצַב, nâtsab, *naw-tsab´*; a primitive root; to *station*, in various applications (literal or figurative):—appointed, deputy, erect, establish, × Huzzah [*by mistake for a proper name*], lay, officer, pillar, present, rear up, set (over, up) settle, sharpen, stablish, (make to) stand (-ing, still, up, upright), best state.

A verb meaning to station, to appoint, to erect, to take a stand. Abraham's servant stationed himself beside the well to find a wife for Isaac (Ge 24:13); Jacob set up a stone pillar (Ge 35:14, 20); the people stood up when Moses went out to the tent to meet God (Ex 33:8); God established the boundaries for Israel (Dt 32:8); Boaz asked the work supervisor (the one who stands over) about Ruth (Ru 2:5, 6). See the related Hebrew noun *nitstsâb* (5325) and the Aramaic noun *nitsbâh* (5326).

5325. נִצָּב, nitstsâb, *nits-tsawb´*; passive participle of 5324; *fixed*, i.e. a *handle*:—haft.

5326. נִצְבָּה, nitsbâh, *nits-baw´*; (Chaldee); from a root corresponding to 5324; *fixedness*, i.e. *firmness*:—strength.

5327. נָצָה, nâtsâh, *naw-tsaw´*; a primitive root; (properly) to *go forth*, i.e. (by implication) to *be expelled*, and (consequently) *desolate*; (causative) to *lay waste*; also (specific), to *quarrel*:—be laid waste, ruinous, strive (together).

5328. נִצָּה, nitstsâh, *nits-tsaw´*; feminine of 5322; a *blossom*:—flower.

5329. נָצַח, **nâtsach,** *naw-tsakh´*; a primitive root; (properly) to *glitter* from afar, i.e. to be *eminent* (as a superintendent, especially of the Temple services and its music); also (as denominative from 5331), to *be permanent*:—excel, chief musician (singer), oversee (-r), set forward.

5330. נְצַח, **n^e^tsach,** *nets-akh´*; (Chaldee); corresponding to 5329; to *become chief*:—be preferred.

5331. נֶצַח, **netsach,** *neh´-tsakh*; or נֵצַח, **nêtsach,** *nay´-tsakh*; from 5329; (properly) a *goal*, i.e. the bright object at a distance travelled toward; hence (figurative), *splendor*, or (subjective) *truthfulness*, or (objective) *confidence*; but usually (adverb), *continually* (i.e. to the most distant point of view):—alway (-s), constantly, end, (+ n-) ever (more), perpetual, strength, victory.

A noun meaning ever, always, perpetual. The word is used especially in prayers to ask whether God has forgotten His people forever (Ps 13:1[2]; 77:8[9]; Jer 15:18); and to affirm that He has not (Ps 9:18[19]; 103:9). With a negative, the word may be translated never (Ps 10:11; Isa 13:20; Am 8:7). The word also describes as perpetual (or appearing so to the writer) such things as ruins (Ps 74:3); and pain (Jer 15:18). In some passages, the word points to God's eternal nature (Ps 68:16[17]; Isa 25:8); and in 1Ch 29:11, *nêtsach* is among those attributes ascribed to God, namely, the kingdom, power, and glory. God even refers to Himself as the *nêtsach* of Israel (1Sa 15:29), a usage that may indicate His glory (see *nâtsach*[5329]). It also points to His eternal, truthful nature that is contrary to lying or changing.

5332. נֵצַח, **nêtsach,** *nay´-tsakh*; probably identical with 5331, through the idea of *brilliancy* of colour; *juice* of the grape (as blood red):—blood, strength.

A masculine noun meaning grape juice. The word occurs only in Isa 63:3, 6. In this passage, God's treading of grapes is a picture of His judgment of Israel's enemies, particularly Edom (cf. Isa 63:1). Grape juice, as elsewhere in the OT (cf. Dt 32:14) and the NT, is a symbol of blood. In Isa 63, God returned from judgment with His garments stained with blood like the garments of a grape treader are stained with juice.

5333. נְצִיב, **n^e^tsîyb,** *nets-eeb´*; or נְצִב, **n^e^tsib,** *nets-eeb´*; from 5324; something *stationary*, i.e. a *prefect*, a military *post*, a *statue*:—garrison, officer, pillar.

5334. נְצִיב, **N^e^tsîyb,** *nets-eeb´*; the same as 5333; *station; Netsib*, a place in Palestine:—Nezib.

5335. נְצִיחַ, **n^e^tsîyach,** *nets-ee´-akh*; from 5329; *conspicuous; Netsiach*, a Temple-servant:—Neziah.

5336. נָצִיר, **nâtsîyr,** *naw-tsere´*; from 5341; (properly) *conservative*; but used passively, *delivered*:—preserved.

5337. נָצַל, **nâtsal,** *naw-tsal´*; a primitive root; to *snatch* away, whether in a good or a bad sense:— × at all, defend, deliver (self), escape, × without fail, part, pluck, preserve, recover, rescue, rid, save, spoil, strip, × surely, take (out).

A verb meaning to deliver. Deliverance often indicated the power of one entity overcoming the power of another. It was frequently expressed as deliverance from the hand (i.e. power) of another (Ge 32:11[12]; Hos 2:10[12]). Thus, idols (1Sa 12:21) and mere human might (Ps 33:16) were belittled as unable to deliver. God was frequently honoured as delivering His people, whether from earthly enemies (2Sa 22:1; Jer 1:8); or from more abstract things like transgressions (Ps 39:8[9]); and death (Ps 33:19; 56:13[14]). The word also refers to the taking of objects from another's power and is thus translated to recover (Jgs 11:26; 1Sa 30:8); to strip (2Ch 20:25); or to spoil (Ex 3:22; 12:36). In a special usage, the word signifies warriors delivering one's eyes, that is, escaping from sight (2Sa 20:6). In 2Sa 14:6, a participle referred to one who would separate two men fighting each other. In Ps 119:43, the psalmist asked God not to take (or deliver) His word out of his mouth.

5338. נְצַל, **n^e^tsal,** *nets-al´*; (Chaldee); corresponding to 5337; to *extricate*:—deliver, rescue.

An Aramaic verb meaning to deliver. The word corresponds to the Hebrew word *nâtsal* (5337)and occurs three times in the OT. In Da 3:29, it referred to God's deliverance of the three Hebrews from the fiery furnace, an action Nebuchadnezzar recognized as beyond any other so-called god. In Da 6:14[15], the word referred to Daniel's deliverance from the lions' den, a feat that Darius unsuccessfully attempted. Da 6:27[28] referred to God's successful deliverance of Daniel from the hand (i.e. power) of the lions. As with the Hebrew form, this word acknowledges God as the deliverer of those who trust in Him.

5339. נִצָּן, **nitstsân,** *nits-tsawn´*; from 5322; a *blossom*:—flower.

5340. נָצַץ, **nâtsats,** *naw-tsats´*; a primitive root; to *glare*, i.e. *be bright*-coloured:—sparkle.

5341. נָצַר, **nâtsar,** *naw-tsar´*; a primitive root; to *guard*, in a good sense (to *protect, maintain, obey*, etc.) or a bad one (to *conceal*, etc.):—besieged, hidden thing, keep (-er, -ing), monument, observe, preserve (-r), subtil, watcher (-man).

A verb meaning to guard, to keep, to observe, to preserve, to hide. The word refers to people's maintaining things entrusted to them, especially to keeping the truths of God in both actions and mind (Ps 119:100, 115). God's Word is to be kept with our whole hearts (Ps 119:69); our hearts, in turn, ought to be maintained in a right state (Pr 4:23). The word also refers to keeping speech under control (Ps 34:13 [14]; 141:3); the maintenance of a tree (Pr 27:18); the work of God's character (Ps 40:11[12]); its reflection in humans as preserving them (Ps 25:21; Pr 2:11). Sometimes the word refers directly to God's preservation and maintenance of His people (Pr 24:12; Isa 49:8). The passive participle form of the verb describes an adulteress' heart as guarded or kept secret (Pr 7:10). It also describes a city as guarded or besieged (Isa 1:8). The active participle is used to signify a watchman (2Ki 17:9; Jer 31:6).

5342. נֵצֶר, **nêtser,** *nay´-tser*; from 5341 in the sense of *greenness* as a striking colour; a *shoot*; (figurative) a *descendant*:—branch.

5343. נְקֵא, **n^e^qê',** *nek-ay´*; (Chaldee); from a root corresponding to 5352; *clean*:—pure.

5344. נָקַב, **nâqab,** *naw-kab´*; a primitive root; to *puncture*, literal (to *perforate*, with more or less violence) or figurative (to *specify, designate, libel*):—appoint, blaspheme, bore, curse, express, with holes, name, pierce, strike through.

A verb meaning to pierce, to designate, to curse. The word signifies the piercing of an animal's head, jaw, or nose with a spear (Job 40:24; 41:2[40:26]; Hab 3:14). It also signifies the piercing of a person's hand by a reed, symbolic of pain. Egypt was charged with bringing such pain on its allies (2Ki 18:21; Isa 36:6). In Hag 1:6, the passive participle described a bag as being pierced. This word can also refer to wages being paid (Ge 30:28); and to men being singled out for some task or distinction (2Ch 28:15; Am 6:1). The meaning to curse may also be derived from a different root, *qâbab* (6895). It signified the cursing or blaspheming of God's name (Le 24:11, 16); the speaking of a negative spiritual sentence on people (Nu 23:8; Pr 11:26; 24:24); or things associated with people (Job 3:8; 5:3).

5345. נֶקֶב, **neqeb,** *nek´-keb*; a *bezel* (for a gem):—pipe.

5346. נֶקֶב, **Neqeb,** *nek´-keb*; the same as 5345; *dell; Nekeb*, a place in Palestine:—Nekeb.

5347. נְקֵבָה, **n^e^qêbâh,** *nek-ay-baw´*; from 5344; *female* (from the sexual form):—female.

A feminine noun meaning female. It can refer either to a woman (Ge 1:27; 5:2; Le 12:5, 7; 15:33; 27:4, 5, 6, 7; Nu 5:3; 31:15; Jer 31:22); or a female animal (Ge 6:19; 7:3, 9, 16; Le 3:1, 6; 4:28, 32; 5:6).

5348. נָקֹד, **nâqôd,** *naw-kode´*; from an unused root meaning to *mark* (by *puncturing* or *branding*); *spotted*:—speckled.

5349. נֹקֵד, **nôqêd,** *no-kade´*; active participle from the same as 5348; a *spotter* (of sheep or cattle), i.e. the owner or tender (who thus marks them):—herdman, sheepmaster.

5350. נִקֻּדִים, niqqudîym, *nik-koo-deem´*; from the same as 5348; a *crumb* (as *broken* to spots); also a *biscuit* (as *pricked*):—cracknel, mouldy.

5351. נְקֻדָּה, neqquddâh, *nek-ood-daw´*; feminine of 5348; a *boss*:—stud.

5352. נָקָה, nâqâh, *naw-kaw´*; a primitive root; to *be* (or *make*) *clean* (literal or figurative); by implication (in an adverse sense) to *be bare*, i.e. *extirpated*:—acquit × at all, × altogether, be blameless, cleanse, (be) clear (-ing), cut off, be desolate, be free, be (hold) guiltless, be (hold) innocent, × by no means, be quit, be (leave) unpunished, × utterly, × wholly.

A verb meaning to be free, to be clean, to be pure. Originally, this verb meant to be emptied; therefore, its most basic sentiment is to be poured out and can have a negative or positive connotation. In the negative sense, it refers to a city which has been deserted, emptied of people (Isa 3:26). In the positive sense, it is used to connote freedom from the obligations of an oath (Ge 24:8, 41); from guilt (Nu 5:31; Jgs 15:3; Jer 2:35); and from punishment (Ex 21:19; Nu 5:28; 1Sa 26:9). Regardless of whether the connotation is positive or negative, most occurrences of this verb have a moral or ethical implication. Aside from the passive or stative form, this verb also has a factitive form. (The factitive concept is to make something a certain state, in this instance, to make something clean or pure.) The factitive form has two aspects: **(1)** acquittal, the declaration of someone as innocent (Job 9:28; 10:14; Ps 19:12[13]); **(2)** leaving someone unpunished (Ex 20:7; 34:7; Jer 30:11).

5353. נְקוֹדָא, Neqôwdâ', *nek-o-daw´*; feminine of 5348 (in the figurative sense of *marked*); *distinction; Nekoda*, a Temple-servant:—Nekoda.

5354. נָקַט, nâqaṭ, *naw-kat´*; a primitive root; to *loathe*:—weary.

5355. נָקִי, nâqîy, *naw-kee´*; or **נָקִיא, nâqîy',** *naw-kee´*; (Joel 4:19; Jnh 1:14), from 5352; *innocent*:—blameless, clean, clear, exempted, free, guiltless, innocent, quit.

An adjective meaning clean, free from, exempt. This term frequently refers to innocent blood, that is, the shed blood of an innocent individual (Dt 19:10, 13; 21:8, 9; 1Sa 19:5; 2Ki 21:16; 24:4; Ps 94:21; 106:38; Pr 6:17; Isa 59:7; Jer 7:6; 22:3, 17). It also refers to a person who is innocent (Job 4:7; 17:8; 22:19, 30; 27:17; Ps 10:8; 15:5; Pr 1:11). According to Ps 24:4, it is a necessary quality for those who will stand in the presence of the Lord. It also refers to those who are free from blame (Ge 44:10); free from liability or punishment (Ex 21:28; 2Sa 14:9); released from an oath (Ge 24:41; Jos 2:17, 19, 20); exempt from various obligations (Nu 32:22); or free from the obligation of military service (Dt 24:5).

5356. נִקָּיוֹן, niqqâyôwn, *nik-kaw-yone´*; or **נִקָּיֹן, niqqâyôn,** *nik-kaw-yone´*; from 5352; *clearness* (literal or figurative):—cleanness, innocency.

A masculine noun meaning cleanness, whiteness, innocence. The Hebrew word generally implies innocence or freedom from guilt applied in the realm of sexual morality (Ge 20:5); and ritual purification or personal conduct as it relates to worship (Ps 26:6; 73:13). Choosing to embrace idolatry rather than innocence in their worship, Israel faced God's judgment (Hos 8:5). In Am 4:6, this term appears in a phrase that literally means cleanness of teeth, which is an idiomatic expression implying empty stomachs or nothing to eat.

5357. נָקִיק, nâqîyq, *naw-keek´*; from an unused root meaning to *bore*; a *cleft*:—hole.

5358. נָקַם, nâqam, *naw-kam´*; a primitive root; to *grudge*, i.e. *avenge* or *punish*:—avenge (-r, self), punish, revenge (self), × surely, take vengeance.

A verb meaning to avenge, to take revenge, to be avenged, to suffer vengeance, to take one's revenge. In actual usage, the following ideas come out: in the simple, intensive, and reflexive stems, the word can mean to take vengeance, to avenge. The Lord instructed His people not to seek revenge against each other, for to do so was unworthy of them (Le 19:18); the Lord took vengeance on His enemies and the enemies of His people (Na 1:2); but He would also take vengeance on His own people if necessary (Le 26:25); and He would avenge the death of His servants, the prophets (2Ki 9:7); and His city, Jerusalem (Jer 51:36). The reflexive idea of taking one's vengeance is found in the Lord's avenging Himself on Judah (Jer 5:9).

5359. נָקָם, nâqâm, *naw-kawm´*; from 5358; *revenge*:— + avenged, quarrel, vengeance.

A masculine noun meaning revenge or vengeance. This term is employed to signify human vengeance. For example, Samson sought revenge against the Philistines for gouging out his eyes (Jgs 16:28). According to Proverbs, a jealous husband will show no mercy when he exacts vengeance on his wife's adulterous lover (Pr 6:34). More often, however, this Hebrew term refers to divine repayment (Le 26:25; Dt 32:35, 41, 43; Eze 24:8; Mic 5:15[14]). For example, the psalmist encouraged the righteous with the hope that someday they will be avenged, and God will redress the wrongs committed against them (Ps 58:10[11]). In fact, He will judge those who have acted with vengeance toward His people (Eze 25:12, 15). Ultimately, the judgment of God's enemies will mean redemption for His people (Isa 34:8; 35:4; 47:3; 59:17; 63:4).

5360. נְקָמָה, neqâmâh, *nek-aw-maw´*; feminine of 5359; *avengement*, whether the act or the passion:— + avenge, revenge (-ing), vengeance.

A feminine singular noun meaning vengeance. Jeremiah employed this word most frequently, referring to the vengeance of God (Jer 11:20; 46:10; 50:15, 28; 51:6, 11, 36). The worship of false gods, improper sacrifices, and a plot against Jeremiah himself all stirred up the vengeance of God. But it is also used with Israel as the subject (Nu 31:2; Ps 149:7); and object (La 3:60; Eze 25:15). Even when Israel took vengeance on an enemy, it was God's vengeance that they delivered (Nu 31:2, 3).

5361. נָקַע, nâqa', *naw-kah´*; a primitive root; to *feel aversion*:—be alienated.

5362. נָקַף, nâqaph, *naw-kaf´*; a primitive root; to *strike* with more or less violence (*beat, fell, corrode*); by implication (of attack) to *knock together*, i.e. *surround* or *circulate*:—compass (about, -ing), cut down, destroy, go round (about), inclose, round.

A verb meaning to strike off, to strip away. It occurs twice in the Hebrew Bible. It is used passively in Isa 10:34 where it referred to the stripping away the forest thicket, describing God's destruction of Lebanon with an ax. In Job 19:26, the word is employed figuratively to describe the effects of his disease on his skin.

5363. נֹקֶף, nôqeph, *no´-kef*; from 5362; a *threshing* (of olives):—shaking.

5364. נִקְפָּה, niqpâh, *nik-paw´*; from 5362; probably a *rope* (as *encircling*):—rent.

5365. נָקַר, nâqar, *naw-kar´*; a primitive root; to *bore* (*penetrate, quarry*):—dig pick out, pierce, put (thrust) out.

5366. נְקָרָה, neqârâh, *nek-aw-raw´*; from 5365; a *fissure*:—cleft, clift.

5367. נָקַשׁ, nâqash, *naw-kash´*; a primitive root; to *entrap* (with a noose), literal or figurative:—catch, (lay a) snare.

A verb meaning to strike, to strike down, to knock, to bring down. This word is associated with hunting birds, and therefore it is often translated to ensnare. It occurs four times in the Hebrew Bible and is used with the connotation of a subject attempting to destroy the object. For instance, the witch of Endor asked why Saul was entrapping her (1Sa 28:9). Dt 12:30 warned of being ensnared by the worship of other gods. According to Ps 109:11, a creditor could also strike down one's estate.

5368. נְקַשׁ, neqash, *nek-ash´*; (Chaldee); corresponding to 5367; but used in the sense of 5362; to *knock*:—smote.

An Aramaic verb meaning to knock. It occurs only once in the Hebrew Bible. Da 5:6 employed the idiomatic phase knocking knees to express Belshazzar's fear when he saw a finger mysteriously writing on the wall. See the Hebrew word *nâqash* (5367).

5369. נֵר, **Nêr,** *nare;* the same as 5216; *lamp; Ner,* an Israelite:—Ner.

5370. נֵרְגַל, **Nêr^{e}gal,** *nay-re-gal´;* of foreign origin; *Nergal,* a Cuthite deity:—Nergal.

5371. נֵרְגַל שַׁרְאֶצֶר, **Nêr^{e}gal Shar'etser,** *nay-re-gal´ shar-eh´-tser;* from 5370 and 8272; *Nergal-Sharetser,* the name of two Babylonians:—Nergal-sharezer.

5372. נִרְגָּן, **nirgân,** *neer-gawn´;* from an unused root meaning to *roll* to pieces; a *slanderer:*—talebearer, whisperer.

5373. נֵרְדְּ, **nêrd,** *nayrd;* of foreign origin; *nard,* an aromatic:—spikenard.

5374. נֵרִיָּה, **Nêrîyyâh,** *nay-ree-yaw´;* or נֵרִיָּהוּ, **Nêrîyyâhûw,** *nay-ree-yaw´-hoo;* from 5216 and 3050; *light of Jah; Nerijah,* an Israelite:—Neriah.

5375. נָשָׂא, **nâśâ',** *naw-saw´;* or נָסָה, **nâsâh,** *naw-saw´;* (Ps 4:6 [7]), a primitive root; to *lift,* in a great variety of applications, literal and figurative, absolutely and relatively (as follows):—accept, advance, arise, (able to, [armour], suffer to) bear (-er, up), bring (forth), burn, carry (away), cast, contain, desire, ease, exact, exalt (self), extol, fetch, forgive, furnish, further, give, go on, help, high, hold up, honourable (+ man), lade, lay, lift (self) up, lofty, marry, magnify, × needs, obtain, pardon, raise (up), receive, regard, respect, set (up), spare, stir up, + swear, take (away, up), × utterly, wear, yield.

A verb meaning to lift, to carry, to take away. This verb is used almost six hundred times in the Hebrew Bible and covers three distinct semantic ranges. The first range is to lift, which occurs in both literal (Ge 7:17; 29:1; Eze 10:16) and figurative statements: to lift the hand in taking an oath (Dt 32:40); in combat (2Sa 18:28); as a sign (Isa 49:22); in retribution (Ps 10:12). Other figurative statements include the lifting of: the head (Ge 40:13); the face (2Sa 2:22); the eyes (Ge 13:10); the voice (1Sa 30:4). It is also important to note that a person can take up or induce iniquity by a number of actions (Ex 28:43; Le 19:17; 22:9; Nu 18:32). The second semantic category is to bear or to carry and is used especially in reference to the bearing of guilt or punishment of sin (Ge 4:13; Le 5:1). This flows easily then into the concept of the representative or substitutionary bearing of one person's guilt by another (Le 10:17; 16:22). The final category is to take away. It can be used in the simple sense of taking something (Ge 27:3); to take a wife or to get married (Ru 1:4); to take away guilt or to forgive (Ge 50:17); to take away or to destroy (Job 32:22).

5376. נְשָׂא, **n^{e}śâ',** *nes-aw´;* (Chaldee); corresponding to 5375:—carry away, make insurrection, take.

5377. נָשָׁא, **nâshâ',** *naw-shaw´;* a primitive root; to *lead astray,* i.e. (mentally) to *delude,* or (morally) to *seduce:*—beguile, deceive, × greatly, × utterly.

5378. נָשָׁא, **nâshâ',** *naw-shaw´;* a primitive root [perhaps identical with 5377, through the idea of *imposition*]; to *lend* on interest; (by implication) to *dun* for debt:— × debt, exact, giver of usury.

5379. נִשֵּׂאת, **niśśê'th,** *nis-sayth´;* passive participle feminine of 5375; something *taken,* i.e. a *present:*—gift.

5380. נָשַׁב, **nâshab,** *naw-shab´;* a primitive root; to *blow;* (by implication) to *disperse:*—(cause to) blow, drive away.

5381. נָשַׂג, **nâśag,** *naw-sag´;* a primitive root; to *reach* (literal or figurative):—ability, be able, attain (unto), (be able to, can) get, lay at, put, reach, remove, wax rich, × surely, (over-) take (hold of, on, upon).

5382. נָשָׁה, **nâshâh,** *naw-shaw´;* a primitive root; to *forget;* (figurative) to *neglect;* (causative) to *remit, remove:*—forget, deprive, exact.

5383. נָשָׁה, **nâshâh,** *naw-shaw´;* a primitive root [rather identical with 5382, in the sense of 5378]; to *lend* or (by reciprocity) *borrow* on security or interest:—creditor, exact, extortioner, lend, usurer, lend on (taker of) usury.

5384. נָשֶׁה, **nâsheh,** *naw-sheh´;* from 5382, in the sense of *failure; rheumatic* or *crippled* (from the incident to Jacob):—which shrank.

5385. נְשׂוּאָה, **n^{e}śûw'âh,** *nes-oo-aw´;* or rather נְשֻׂאָה, **n^{e}śu'âh,** *nes-oo-aw´;* feminine passive participle of 5375; something *borne,* i.e. a *load:*—carriage.

5386. נְשִׁי, **n^{e}shîy,** *nesh-ee´;* from 5383; a *debt:*—debt.

5387. נָשִׂיא, **nâśîy',** *naw-see´;* or נָשִׂא, **nâśi',** *naw-see´;* from 5375; (properly) an *exalted* one, i.e. a *king* or *sheik;* also a rising *mist:*—captain, chief, cloud, governor, prince, ruler, vapour.

A noun meaning something that is lifted up, a prince, a mist. The Hebrew word is formed from the verb *nâśâ'* (5375), meaning to lift. It refers to a leader of the people (Ge 23:6; Ex 16:22; 22:28[27]). Although rare, it can refer to the king (1Ki 11:34); or to a non-Israelite leader (Ge 34:2; Nu 25:18; Jos 13:21). Some scholars have proposed that the term refers to elected officials, contending that these were common people who were elevated or lifted up. They often buttress their argument with Nu 1:16, which talks of these leaders as the ones called, chosen, or appointed from the congregation. In a few instances, this word also indicates mist or vapors that rise from the earth to form clouds and herald the coming of rain (Ps 135:7; Pr 25:14; Jer 10:13; 51:16).

5388. נְשִׁיָּה, **n^{e}shîyyâh,** *nesh-ee-yaw´;* from 5382; *oblivion:*—forgetfulness.

5389. נָשִׁין, **n^{e}shîyn,** *neh-sheen´;* (Chaldee); irregular plural feminine of 606:—women.

5390. נְשִׁיקָה, **n^{e}shîyqâh,** *nesh-ee-kaw´;* from 5401; a *kiss:*—kiss.

5391. נָשַׁךְ, **nâshak,** *naw-shak´;* a primitive root; to *strike* with a sting (as a serpent); (figurative) to *oppress* with interest on a loan:—bite, lend upon usury.

5392. נֶשֶׁךְ, **neshek,** *neh´-shek;* from 5391; *interest* on a debt:—usury.

5393. נִשְׁכָּה, **nishkâh,** *nish-kaw´;* for 3957; a *cell:*—chamber.

5394. נָשַׁל, **nâshal,** *naw-shal´;* a primitive root; to *pluck* off, i.e. *divest, eject,* or *drop:*—cast (out), drive, loose, put off (out), slip.

5395. נָשַׁם, **nâsham,** *naw-sham´;* a primitive root; (properly) to *blow* away, i.e. *destroy:*—destroy.

A verb meaning to breathe heavily, to pant. This particular form of the word is used only once in the Bible and describes the deep breathing and gasping of a woman in labour. God said that although He had been silent, He would cry out like a woman about to give birth (Isa 42:14). See the related Aramaic noun *nishmâ'* (5396) and Hebrew noun *nĕshâmâh* (5397).

5396. נִשְׁמָה, **nishmâh,** *nish-maw´;* (Chaldee); corresponding to 5397; vital *breath:*—breath.

5397. נְשָׁמָה, **n^{e}shâmâh,** *nesh-aw-maw´;* from 5395; a *puff,* i.e. *wind,* angry or vital *breath,* divine *inspiration, intellect,* or (concrete) an *animal:*—blast, (that) breath (-eth), inspiration, soul, spirit.

A feminine noun meaning breath, wind, spirit. Its meaning is parallel to *nephesh* (5315) and *rûach* (7307). It refers to the breath of God as a destructive wind that kills and clears the foundations of the earth (2Sa 22:16; Job 4:9); a stream of brimstone that kindles a fire (Isa 30:33); a freezing wind that produces frost (Job 37:10); the source of life that vitalizes humanity (Job 33:4). The breath of humans is recognized as the source and center of life (1Ki 17:17; Job 27:3). It is also understood that such breath originates with God, and He can withhold it, thereby withholding life from humanity (Ge 2:7; Job 34:14; Isa 42:5). Therefore, people's breath is a symbol of their weakness and frailty (Isa 2:22). Since breath is the source of life, by extension, this word is also used to represent life and anything that is alive (Dt 20:16; Jos 10:40; 11:11, 14; Isa 57:16). Like *nephesh* (5315), this word also connotes the human mind or intellect (Pr 20:27).

5398. **נָשַׁף, nâshaph,** *naw-shaf´*; a primitive root; to *breeze*, i.e. *blow* up fresh (as the wind):—blow.

5399. **נֶשֶׁף, nesheph,** *neh´-shef*; from 5398; (properly) a *breeze*, i.e. (by implication) *dusk* (when the evening breeze prevails):—dark, dawning of the day (morning), night, twilight.

5400. **נָשַׂק, nâśaq,** *naw-sak´*; a primitive root; to *catch* fire:—burn, kindle.

5401. **נָשַׁק, nâshaq,** *naw-shak´*; a primitive root [identical with 5400, through the idea of *fastening* up; compare 2388, 2836]; to *kiss*, literal or figurative (*touch*); also (as a mode of *attachment*), to *equip* with weapons:—armed (men), rule, kiss, that touched.

A verb meaning to kiss, to touch lightly. The word rarely has romantic implications (Pr 7:13; SS 1:2). Often, along with tears and embraces, kisses expressed the dearness of relationships between friends and family, especially at a farewell (Ru 1:9, 14; 1Sa 20:41; 1Ki 19:20); or a reunion (Ge 45:15, cf. Ro 16:16; 1Pe 5:14). Kisses also expressed acceptance of a person (Ge 45:15; 2Sa 14:33); and even the mutual acceptance or harmony of moral qualities (Ps 85:10[11]). They also were associated with giving blessings (Ge 27:27; 2Sa 19:39[40]). Kisses sometimes expressed the worship of idols (1Ki 19:18; Hos 13:2); and the worship of the Messiah (Ps 2:12; cf. Ps 2:7; Heb 1:5). Some kisses, however, were deceitful (2Sa 20:9). The meaning of lightly touching occurs in Eze 3:13.

5402. **נֶשֶׁק, nesheq,** *neh´-shek*; or נֵשֶׁק, **nêsheq,** *nay´-shek*; from 5401; military *equipment*, i.e. (collective) *arms* (offensive or defensive), or (concrete) an *arsenal*:—armed men, armour (-y), battle, harness, weapon.

A noun meaning weapons, battle, armoury. The word refers to a variety of weapons, both offensive (bows, arrows, spears, and clubs) and defensive (shields). Weapons were sometimes given as gifts (1Ki 10:25; 2Ch 9:24); and were kept in the palace Solomon built (Isa 22:8); thus, they probably involved a high level of craftsmanship and were sometimes made of precious metals (cf. 1Ki 10:16, 17, shields of gold); as well as iron and bronze (Job 20:24). In Ne 3:19, the word means armoury, a place where weapons were kept. The word also referred to a battle (Job 39:21; Ps 140:7[8]) as a place where horses charged, weapons flew, and one's head needed God's protection.

5403. **נְשַׁר, n^e^shar,** *nesh-ar´*; (Chaldee); corresponding to 5404; an *eagle*:—eagle.

5404. **נֶשֶׁר, nesher,** *neh´-sher*; from an unused root meaning to *lacerate*; the *eagle* (or other large bird of prey):—eagle.

5405. **נָשַׁת, nâshath,** *naw-shath´*; a primitive root; (properly) to *eliminate*, i.e. (intransitive) to *dry* up:—fail.

5406. **נִשְׁתְּוָן, nisht^e^vân,** *nish-tev-awn´*; probably of Persian origin; an *epistle*:—letter.

5407. **נִשְׁתְּוָן, nisht^e^vân,** *nish-tev-awn´*; (Chaldee); corresponding to 5406:—letter.

5408. **נָתַח, nâthach,** *naw-thakh´*; a primitive root; to *dismember*:—cut (in pieces), divide, hew in pieces.

5409. **נֵתַח, nêthach,** *nay´-thakh*; from 5408; a *fragment*:—part, piece.

5410. **נָתִיב, nâthîyb,** *naw-theeb´*; or (feminine) נְתִיבָה, **n^e^thîybâh,** *neth-ee-baw´*; or נְתִבָה, **n^e^thibâh,** *neth-ee-baw´* (Jer 6:16), from an unused root meaning to *tramp*; a (beaten) *track*:—path ([-way]), × travel [-ler], way.

5411. **נָתִין, Nâthîyn,** *naw-theen´*; or נָתוּן, **Nâthûwn,** *naw-thoon´*; (Ezr 8:17), (the proper form, as passive participle), from 5414; one *given*, i.e. (in the plural only) the *Nethinim*, or Temple-servants (as *given* up to that duty):—Nethinims.

5412. **נְתִין, N^e^thîyn,** *neth-een´*; (Chaldee); corresponding to 5411:—Nethinims.

5413. **נָתַךְ, nâthak,** *naw-thak´*; a primitive root; to *flow* forth (literal or figurative); (by implication) to *liquefy*:—drop, gather (together), melt, pour (forth, out).

5414. **נָתַן, nâthan,** *naw-than´*; a primitive root; to *give*, used with great latitude of application (*put, make*, etc.):—add, apply, appoint, ascribe, assign, × avenge, × be ([healed]), bestow, bring (forth, hither), cast, cause, charge, come, commit, consider, count, + cry, deliver (up), direct, distribute, do, × doubtless, × without fail, fasten, frame, × get, give (forth, over, up), grant, hang (up), × have, × indeed, lay (unto charge, up), (give) leave, lend, let (out), + lie, lift up, make, + O that, occupy, offer, ordain, pay, perform, place, pour, print, × pull, put (forth), recompense, render, requite, restore, send (out), set (forth), shew, shoot forth (up), + sing, + slander, strike, [sub-] mit, suffer, × surely, × take, thrust, trade, turn, utter, + weep, × willingly, + withdraw, + would (to) God, yield.

A verb meaning to give, to place. This verb is used approximately two thousand times in the OT; therefore, it is understandable that it should have a broad semantic range. However, it is possible to identify three general categories of semantic variation: **(1)** to give, whether it be the exchange of tangible property (Ge 3:6; Ex 5:18); the production of fruit (Ps 1:3); the presentation of an offering to the Lord (Ex 30:14); the passing on of knowledge and instruction (Pr 9:9); the granting of permission (Ge 20:6). Often, God provides either preservation (Le 26:4; Dt 11:14, 15; Jer 45:5); or plague (Ex 9:23). **(2)** This Hebrew word also means to put, to place, or something literally placed: the luminaries in the sky (Ge 1:17); God's bow in the clouds (Ge 9:13); the ark on a cart (1Sa 6:8); the abomination in the temple. It could also be something figuratively placed: an obstacle (Eze 3:20); God's Spirit (Isa 42:1); reproach (Jer 23:40); curses (Dt 30:7). **(3)** The word can also mean to make or to constitute, such as the prohibition against making incisions in one's flesh (Le 19:28); God making Abraham into a father of many nations (Ge 17:5); or Solomon making silver as stones (1Ki 10:27).

5415. **נְתַן, n^e^than,** *neth-an´*; (Chaldee); corresponding to 5414; *give*:—bestow, give, pay.

5416. **נָתָן, Nâthân,** *naw-thawn´*; from 5414; *given; Nathan*, the name of five Israelites:—Nathan.

5417. **נְתַנְאֵל, N^e^than'êl,** *neth-an-ale´*; from 5414 and 410; *given of God; Nethanel*, the name of ten Israelites:—Nethaneel.

5418. **נְתַנְיָה, N^e^thanyâh,** *neth-an-yaw´*; or נְתַנְיָהוּ, **N^e^thanyâhûw,** *neth-an-yaw´-hoo*; from 5414 and 3050; *given of Jah; Nethanjah*, the name of four Israelites:—Nethaniah.

5419. **נְתַן־מֶלֶךְ, N^e^than-Melek,** *neth-an´ meh´-lek*; from 5414 and 4428; *given of* (the) *king; Nethan-Melek*, an Israelite:—Nathan-melech.

5420. **נָתַס, nâthas,** *naw-thas´*; a primitive root; to *tear* up:—mar.

5421. **נָתַע, nâtha',** *naw-thah´*; for 5422; to *tear* out:—break.

5422. **נָתַץ, nâthats,** *naw-thats´*; a primitive root; to *tear* down:—beat down, break down (out), cast down, destroy, overthrow, pull down, throw down.

A verb meaning to tear down, to destroy. The idea is the breaking down of a structure so that it can no longer support its own weight. Most often the word signified the destruction of idolatrous religious structures such as the altars that Israel was commanded to tear down on entering the Promised Land (Dt 7:5; 12:3; Jgs 2:2; 2Ch 31:1). The word also signified the destruction of buildings: a tower (Jgs 8:9, 17; Eze 26:9); a leprous house (Le 14:45); or an entire city (Jgs 9:45). In a spiritual sense, the word signified the tearing down of an individual (Ps 52:5[7]); or a nation (Jer 18:7). In Ps 58:6[7], the word signified breaking the teeth of fierce lions.

5423. **נָתַק, nâthaq,** *naw-thak´*; a primitive root; to *tear* off:—break (off), burst, draw (away), lift up, pluck (away, off), pull (out), root out.

5424. **נֶתֶק, netheq,** *neh´-thek*; from 5423; *scurf*:—(dry) scall.

5425. נָתַר, **nâthar,** *naw-thar´*; a primitive root; to *jump*, i.e. *be* violently *agitated*; (causative) to *terrify, shake* off, *untie*:—drive asunder, leap, (let) loose, × make, move, undo.

5426. נְתַר, **nᵉthar,** *neth-ar´*; (Chaldee); corresponding to 5425:—shake off.

5427. נֶתֶר, **nether,** *neh´-ther*; from 5425; mineral *potash* (so called from *effervescing* with acid):—nitre.

5428. נָתַשׁ, **nâthash,** *naw-thash´*; a primitive root; to *tear* away:—destroy, forsake, pluck (out, up, by the roots), pull up, root out (up), × utterly.

5429. סְאָה, **sᵉʾâh,** *seh-aw´*; from an unused root meaning to *define*; a *seäh*, or certain measure (as *determinative*) for grain:—measure.

5430. סְאוֹן, **sᵉʾôwn,** *seh-own´*; from 5431; perhaps a military *boot* (as a protection from *mud*):—battle.

5431. סָאַן, **sâʾan,** *saw-an´*; a primitive root; to *be miry*; used only as denominative from 5430; to *shoe*, i.e. (active participle) a *soldier* shod:—warrior.

5432. סַאסְּאָה, **saʾssᵉʾâh,** *sahs-seh-aw´*; from 5429; *measurement*, i.e. *moderation*:—measure.

5433. סָבָא, **sâbâʾ,** *saw-baw´*; a primitive root; to *quaff* to satiety, i.e. *become tipsy*:—drunkard, fill self, Sabean, [wine-] bibber.

5434. סְבָא, **Sᵉbâʾ,** *seb-aw´*; of foreign origin; *Seba*, a son of Cush, and the country settled by him:—Seba.

5435. סֹבֶא, **sôbeʾ,** *so´-beh*; from 5433; *potation*, concrete (*wine*), or abstract (*carousal*):—drink, drunken, wine.

5436. סְבָאִי, **Sᵉbâʾîy,** *seb-aw-ee´*; patrial from 5434; a *Sebaite*, or inhabitant of Seba:—Sabean.

5437. סָבַב, **sâbab,** *saw-bab´*; a primitive root; to *revolve, surround* or *border*; used in various applications, literal and figurative (as follows):—bring, cast, fetch, lead, make, walk, × whirl, × round about, be about on every side, apply, avoid, beset (about), besiege, bring again, carry (about), change, cause to come about, × circuit, (fetch a) compass (about, round), drive, environ, × on every side, beset (close, come, compass, go, stand) round about, inclose, remove, return, set, sit down, turn (self) (about, aside, away, back).

5438. סִבָּה, **sibbâh,** *sib-baw´*; from 5437; a (providential) *turn* (of affairs):—cause.

5439. סָבִיב, **sâbîyb,** *saw-beeb´*; or (feminine) סְבִיבָה, **sebîybâh,** *seb-ee-baw´*; from 5437; (as noun) a *circle, neighbour*, or *environs*; but chiefly (as adverb, with or without preposition) *around*:—(place, round) about, circuit, compass, on every side.

5440. סָבַךְ, **sâbak,** *saw-bak´*; a primitive root; to *entwine*:—fold together, wrap.

5441. סְבֹךְ, **sᵉbôk,** *seh´-bok*; from 5440; a *copse*:—thicket.

5442. סְבָךְ, **sᵉbak,** *seb-ak´*; or סְבַךְ, **sᵉbâk,** *seb-awk´*; from 5440; a *copse*:—thick (-et).

5443. סַבְּכָא, **sabbᵉkâʾ,** *sab-bek-aw´*; (Chaldee); or שַׂבְּכָא, **śabbᵉkâʾ**, *sab-bek-aw´*; (Chaldee); from a root corresponding to 5440; a *lyre*:—sackbut.

5444. סִבְּכַי, **Sibbᵉkay,** *sib-bek-ah´ee*; from 5440; *corpse-like; Sibbecai*, an Israelite:—Sibbecai, Sibbechai.

5445. סָבַל, **sâbal,** *saw-bal´*; a primitive root; to *carry* (literal or figurative), or (reflexive) *be burdensome*; (specifically) to *be gravid*:—bear, be a burden, carry, strong to labour.

5446. סְבַל, **sᵉbal,** *seb-al´*; (Chaldee); corresponding to 5445; to *erect*:—strongly laid.

5447. סֵבֶל, **sêbel,** *say´-bel*; from 5445; a *load* (literal or figurative):—burden, charge.

5448. סֹבֶל, **sôbel,** *so´-bel*; [only in the form סֻבָּל, **subbâl,** *soob-bawl´*; from 5445; a *load* (figurative):—burden.

5449. סַבָּל, **sabbâl,** *sab-bawl´*; from 5445; a *porter*:—(to bear, bearer of) burden (-s).

5450. סְבָלָה, **sᵉbâlâh,** *seb-aw-law´*; from 5447; *porterage*:—burden.

5451. סִבֹּלֶת, **sibbôleth,** *sib-bo´-leth*; for 7641; an *ear* of grain:—Sibboleth.

5452. סְבַר, **sᵉbar,** *seb-ar´*; (Chaldee); a primitive root; to *bear in mind*, i.e. *hope*:—think.

5453. סִבְרַיִם, **Sibrayim,** *sib-rah´-yim*; dual from a root corresponding to 5452; *double hope; Sibrajim*, a place in Syria:—Sibraim.

5454. סַבְתָּא, **Sabtâʾ,** *sab-taw´*; or סַבְתָּה, **Sabtâh,** *sab-taw´*; probably of foreign derivative; *Sabta* or *Sabtah*, the name of a son of Cush, and the country occupied by his posterity:—Sabta, Sabtah.

5455. סַבְתְּכָא, **Sabtᵉkâʾ,** *sab-tek-aw´*; probably of foreign derivation; *Sabteca*, the name of a son of Cush, and the region settled by him:—Sabtecha, Sabtechah.

5456. סָגַד, **sâgad,** *saw-gad´*; a primitive root; to *prostrate* oneself (in homage):—fall down.

A verb meaning to fall down, to bow down, to lie down in worship. The word occurs four times, only in Isaiah (Isa 44:15, 17, 19; 46:6). It refers to bowing or lying flat before a wooden or golden idol to worship, to pray, or to seek deliverance from it (Isa 44:17). Isaiah satirized those who lowered themselves in this way before an idol and did not recognize that an idol is only the work of human hands.

5457. סְגִד, **sᵉgid,** *seg-eed´*; (Chaldee); corresponding to 5456:—worship.

An Aramaic verb meaning to worship, to bow, to lie in worship. The word corresponds to the Hebrew word *sâgad* (5456). It occurs in Da 2:46, referring to King Nebuchadnezzar's prostration before Daniel and his command that an offering and incense be offered to Daniel for interpreting his dream. The only other occurrences are the eleven uses in Da 3, referring to the worship of the gold image Nebuchadnezzar made. All these occurrences are accompanied by the words to fall (5308) or to serve (6399). The three Hebrew officials appointed by Nebuchadnezzar at Daniel's recommendation refused to fall and worship this foreign gods. Instead, they yielded their own bodies to God in the fiery furnace (Da 3:28; cf. Ro 12:1).

5458. סְגוֹר, **sᵉgôwr,** *seg-ore´*; from 5462; (properly) *shut up*, i.e. the *breast* (as inclosing the heart); also *gold* (as generally *shut* up safely):—caul, gold.

5459. סְגֻלָּה, **sᵉgullâh,** *seg-ool-law´*; feminine passive participle of an unused root meaning to *shut* up; *wealth* (as closely *shut* up):—jewel, peculiar (treasure), proper good, special.

A feminine noun meaning a personal possession, a special possession, property. This noun is used only six times, but it gives one of the most memorable depictions of the Lord's relationship to His people and the place established for them.

The primary meaning of the word theologically is its designation "unique possession." God has made Israel His own unique possession (Ex 19:5). Israel holds a special position among the nations of the world, although all nations belong to the Lord. Israel's position, function, character, responsibility, and calling create its uniqueness (Dt 7:6; 14:2; 26:18; Ps 135:4). Israel is to be a priestly community that honours and fears the Lord, to be His alone (Mal 3:17). In the NT, 1 Peter 2:9 quotes Ex 19:5, applying it to the church.

The word is used in a secular sense to indicate personal possessions, such as when David gave his own gold and silver to the Lord (1Ch 29:3; Ecc 2:8).

5460. סְגַן, **s**e**gan**, *seg-an´*; (Chaldee); corresponding to 5461:—governor.

An Aramaic masculine noun meaning prefect, governor. King Nebuchadnezzar positioned Daniel to be the head of all the governors of Babylon (Da 2:48). Da 3:2 lists the various officers of the neo-Babylonian Empire, one of which was the office signified by this term. Later, King Nebuchadnezzar summoned these and other officials to the dedication of the golden image he had erected. At this dedication, all the officials were expected to fall down and worship the image. Later, Darius the Mede issued a similar edict (Da 6:7[8]). However, in both instances, some refused, including Daniel.

5461. סָגָן, **sâgân**, *saw-gawn´*; from an unused root meaning to *superintend*; a *præfect* of a province:—prince, ruler.

A masculine noun meaning prefect or ruler. Sometimes this term refers to an official of the Assyrian or Babylonian Empire (Isa 41:25; Jer 51:23, 28, 57; Eze 23:6, 12, 23). It can also refer to the head of a Jewish community (Ezr 9:2); as well as lesser officials of Judah (Ne 2:16; 4:14[8], 19[13]; 5:7, 17; 7:5; 12:40; 13:11).

5462. סָגַר, **sâgar**, *saw-gar´*; a primitive root; to *shut* up; (figurative) to *surrender*:—close up, deliver (up), give over (up), inclose, × pure, repair, shut (in, self, out, up, up together), stop, × straitly.

5463. סְגַר, **s**e**gar**, *seg-ar´*; (Chaldee); corresponding to 5462:—shut up.

5464. סַגְרִיר, **sagrîyr**, *sag-reer´*; probably from 5462 in the sense of *sweeping* away; a pouring rain:—very rainy.

5465. סַד, **sad**, *sad*; from an unused root meaning to *estop*; the *stocks*:—stocks.

5466. סָדִין, **sâdîyn**, *saw-deen´*; from an unused root meaning to *envelop*; a *wrapper*, i.e. *shirt*:—fine linen, sheet.

5467. סְדֹם, **S**e**dôm**, *sed-ome´*; from an unused root meaning to *scorch; burnt* (i.e. *volcanic* or *bituminous*) district; *Sedom*, a place near the Dead Sea:—Sodom.

5468. סֶדֶר, **seder**, *seh´-der*; from an unused root meaning to *arrange; order*:—order.

5469. סַהַר, **sahar**, *sah´-har*; from an unused root meaning to *be round; roundness*:—round.

5470. סֹהַר, **sôhar**, *so´-har*; from the same as 5469; a *dungeon* (as *surrounded* by walls):—prison.

5471. סוֹא, **Sôw'**, *so*; of foreign derivation; *So*, an Egyptian king:—So.

5472. סוּג, **sûwg**, *soog*; a primitive root; properly to *flinch*, i.e. (by implication) to *go back;* (literal) to *retreat*; (figurative) to *apostatize*:—backslider, drive, go back, turn (away, back).

5473. סוּג, **sûwg**, *soog*; a primitive root [probably rather identical with 5472 through the idea of *shrinking* from a hedge; compare 7735]; to *hem* in, i.e. *bind*:—set about.

5474. סוּגַר, **sûwgar**, *soo-gar´*; from 5462; an *inclosure*, i.e. *cage* (for an animal):—ward.

5475. סוֹד, **sôwd**, *sode*; from 3245; a *session*, i.e. *company* of persons (in close deliberation); (by implication) *intimacy, consultation*, a *secret*:—assembly, counsel, inward, secret (counsel).

A masculine noun meaning counsel. Confidentiality is at the heart of this term. According to Pr 25:9, information shared in confidence should remain confidential. Yet gossip makes it difficult to do this (Pr 11:13; 20:19). Elsewhere, this term reflects a more general meaning of counsel, which is viewed as essential to successful planning (Pr 15:22). When it means counsel, this term suggests the idea of intimacy. For example, Job used this term to refer to his close friendship with God (Job 29:4); and with individuals he thought of as his close friends (Job 19:19). David used this term to describe one of his close friendships (Ps 55:14[15]). God establishes a close, intimate relationship with those who revere Him and walk uprightly (Ps 25:14; Pr 3:32). Sometimes, however, human relationships involve less than ideal associations (Ge 49:6). Used in a negative sense, this term can denote evil plotting (Ps 64:2[3]; 83:3[4]).

5476. סוֹדִי, **Sôwdîy**, *so-dee´*; from 5475; a *confidant; Sodi*, an Israelite:—Sodi.

5477. סוּחַ, **Sûwach**, *soo´-akh*; from an unused root meaning to *wipe* away; *sweeping; Suäch*, an Israelite:—Suah.

5478. סוּחָה, **sûwchâh**, *soo-kahw´*; from the same as 5477; something *swept* away, i.e. *filth*:—torn.

5479. סוֹטַי, **Sôwṭay**, *so-tah´ee*; from 7750; *roving; Sotai*, one of the Nethinim:—Sotai.

5480. סוּךְ, **sûwk**, *sook*; a primitive root; (properly) to *smear* over (with oil), i.e. *anoint*:—anoint (self), × at all.

A verb meaning to anoint, to pour upon. Oil is frequently the substance used for anointing (Dt 28:40; 2Sa 14:2; Eze 16:9; Mic 6:15). This procedure could be performed on oneself (2Sa 12:20; Ru 3:3; Da 10:3) as well as on another person (2Ch 28:15; Eze 16:9). In several instances, the absence of anointing oil among God's people is an indication of divine judgment (Dt 28:40; Mic 6:15).

5481. סוּמְפּוֹנְיָה, **sûwmpôwn**e**yâh**, *soom-po-neh-yaw´*; (Chaldee); or סוּמְפֹּנְיָה, **sûwmpôn**e**yâh**, *soom-po-neh-yaw´*; (Chaldee); or סִיפֹנְיָא, **sîyphôn**e**yâ'**, *see-fo-neh-yaw´*; (Da 3:10) (Chaldee), of Greek origin a *bagpipe* (with a double pipe):—dulcimer.

5482. סְוֵנֵה, **S**e**vênêh**, *sev-ay-nay´*; [rather to be written סְוֵנָה, **S**e**vênâh**, *sev-ay´-naw*; for סְוֵן, **S**e**vên**, *sev-ane´*; i.e. *to Seven*]; of Egyptian derivation; *Seven*, a place in Upper Egypt:—Syene.

5483. סוּס, **sûws**, *soos*; or סֻס, **sus**, *soos*; from an unused root meaning to *skip* (properly for joy); a *horse* (as leaping); also a *swallow* (from its rapid *flight*):—crane, horse ([-back, -hoof]). Compare 6571.

5484. סוּסָה, **sûwsâh**, *soo-saw´*; feminine of 5483; a *mare*:—company of horses.

5485. סוּסִי, **Sûwsîy**, *soo-see´*; from 5483; *horselike; Susi*, an Israelite:—Susi.

5486. סוּף, **sûwph**, *soof*; a primitive root; to *snatch* away, i.e. *terminate*:—consume, have an end, perish, × be utterly.

A verb meaning to come to an end, to cease, to terminate. The OT describes Purim as an annual observance whose celebration should not cease (Est 9:28). The psalmist used the term to describe how quickly the prosperity enjoyed by the wicked is brought to an end (Ps 73:19). Elsewhere, it is a general term that refers to the end of something as a result of God's judgment (Isa 66:17; Jer 8:13; Zep 1:2, 3).

5487. סוּף, **sûwph**, *soof*; (Chaldee); corresponding to 5486; to *come to an end*:—consume, fulfil.

An Aramaic verb meaning to be fulfilled, to be ended, to end. The word is used in Da 2:44 in connection with the divinely established kingdom that will never be destroyed and will bring all other kingdoms to an end. In Da 4:33[30], it referred to King Nebuchadnezzar, who finished speaking as God began to address him.

5488. סוּף, **sûwph**, *soof*; probably of Egyptian origin; a *reed*, especially the *papyrus*:—flag, Red [sea], weed. Compare 5489.

5489. סוּף, **Sûwph**, *soof*; for 5488 (by ellipsis of 3220); the *Reed* (*Sea*):—Red sea.

5490. סוֹף, **sôwph**, *sofe*; from 5486; a *termination*:—conclusion, end, hinder part.

5491. סוֹף, **sôwph**, *sofe*; (Chaldee); corresponding to 5490:—end.

5492. סוּפָה, **sûwphâh**, *soo-faw´*; from 5486; a *hurricane*:—Red Sea, storm, tempest, whirlwind, Red sea.

5493. סוּר, **sûwr**, *soor*; or שׂוּר, **śûwr**, *soor*; (Hos 9:12), a primitive root; to *turn* off (literal or figurative):—be [-head], bring, call back, decline, depart, eschew, get [you], go (aside), × grievous, lay away (by), leave undone, be past, pluck away, put (away, down), rebel, remove (to and fro), revolt, × be sour, take (away, off), turn (aside, away, in), withdraw, be without.

A verb meaning to turn away, to go away, to desert, to quit, to keep far away, to stop, to take away, to remove, to be removed, to make depart. The word is used equally in the simple and causative stems. The basic meaning of the root, to turn away, takes on various connotations in the simple stem according to context. In the simple stem, the verb means to turn aside, as Moses turned aside to see why the bush was not being consumed by the fire (Ex 3:3, 4); it is used metaphorically to describe turning away from the Lord because of a rebellious heart (Jer 5:23); or taking time to turn aside and seek someone's welfare (Jer 15:5). The word describes leaving or going away literally (Ex 8:31[27]); or figuratively, the scepter would not leave Judah (Ge 49:10); but Samson's strength left him (Jgs 16:19). Its meaning extends further to indicate falling away, as when one is enticed to fall away from following the Lord to pursue other gods (Dt 11:16; 1Sa 12:20; Ps 14:3). It means to stop something; for example, the banqueting and carousing of Israel would cease at the time of exile (Hos 4:18; Am 6:7). It also indicates the act of keeping away from something, such as evil (Isa 59:15); or when the Lord kept Himself from His people (Hos 9:12). Wise teaching helps keep a person far from the dangers of death (Pr 13:14, 19).

The causative stem adds the idea of making something move, go away, turn away, or simply to put aside. The priests would set aside burnt offerings to be offered up (2Ch 35:12); and clothing was put aside as Tamar removed her widow's clothes to deceive Judah (Ge 38:14; 1Sa 17:39; 1Ki 20:41). God removed Israel from His presence because He was angry with them (2Ki 17:18, 23; 23:27); Jacob charged his entire clan to get rid of their strange gods (Ge 35:2; Jos 24:14, 23).

When the verb is passive, it means to be removed, such as when the fat of offerings was removed by the priests (Le 4:31, 35). In Da 12:11, the word expresses the idea that the daily sacrifice was removed.

5494. סוּר, **sûwr,** *soor*; probably passive participle of 5493; *turned* off, i.e. *deteriorated*:—degenerate.

5495. סוּר, **Sûwr,** *soor*; the same as 5494; *Sur*, a gate of the Temple:—Sur.

5496. סוּת, **sûwth,** *sooth*; perhaps denominative from 7898; (properly) to *prick*, i.e. (figurative) stimulate; (by implication) to *seduce*:—entice, move, persuade, provoke, remove, set on, stir up, take away.

5497. סוּת, **sûwth,** *sooth*; probably from the same root as 4533; *covering*, i.e. *clothing*:—clothes.

5498. סָחַב, **sâchab,** *saw-khab´*; a primitive root; to *trail* along:—draw (out), tear.

5499. סְחָבָה, **s^e^châbâh,** *seh-khaw-baw´*; from 5498; a *rag*:—cast clout.

5500. סָחָה, **sâchâh,** *saw-khaw´*; a primitive root; to *sweep* away:—scrape.

5501. סְחִי, **s^e^chîy,** *seh-khee´*; from 5500; *refuse* (as *swept* off):—offscouring.

5502. סָחַף, **sâchaph,** *saw-khaf´*; a primitive root; to *scrape* off:—sweep (away).

5503. סָחַר, **sâchar,** *saw-khar´*; a primitive root; to *travel* round (specifically as a *pedlar*); (intensive) to *palpitate*:—go about, merchant (-man), occupy with, pant, trade, traffick.

5504. סַחַר, **sachar,** *sakh´-ar*; from 5503; *profit* (from trade):—merchandise.

5505. סָחַר, **sachar,** *sah-khar´*; from 5503; an *emporium*; (abstract) *profit* (from trade):—mart, merchandise.

5506. סְחֹרָה, **s^e^chôrâh,** *sekh-o-raw´*; from 5503; *traffic*:—merchandise.

5507. סֹחֵרָה, **sôchêrâh,** *so-khay-raw´*; properly active participle feminine of 5503; something *surrounding* the person, i.e. a *shield*:—buckler.

5508. סֹחֶרֶת, **sôchereth,** *so-kheh´-reth*; similar to 5507; probably a (black) *tile* (or *tessara*) for laying borders with:—black marble.

5509. סִיג, **sîyg,** *seeg*; or סוּג, **sûwg,** *soog*; (Eze 22:18), from 5472 in the sense of *refuse; scoria*:—dross.

5510. סִיוָן, **Sîyvân,** *see-vawn´*; probably of Persian origin; *Sivan*, the third Hebrew month:—Sivan.

5511. סִיחוֹן, **Sîychôwn,** *see-khone´*; or סִיחֹן, **Sîychôn,** *see-khone´*; from the same as 5477; *tempestuous; Sichon*, an Amoritish king:—Sihon.

5512. סִין, **Sîyn,** *seen*; of uncertain derivation; *Sin*, the name of an Egyptian town and (probably) desert adjoining:—Sin.

5513. סִינִי, **Sîynîy,** *see-nee´*; from an otherwise unknown name of a man; a *Sinite*, or descendant of one of the sons of Canaan:—Sinite.

5514. סִינַי, **Sîynay,** *see-nah´ee*; of uncertain derivation; *Sinai*, a mountain of Arabia:—Sinai.

5515. סִינִים, **Sîynîym,** *see-neem´*; plural of an otherwise unknown name; *Sinim*, a distant Oriental region:—Sinim.

5516. סִיסְרָא, **Sîys^e^râ',** *see-ser-aw´*; of uncertain derivation; *Sisera*, the name of a Canaanitish king and of one of the Nethinim:—Sisera.

5517. סִיעָא, **Sîy'â',** *see-ah´*; or סִיעֲהָא, **Sîy'ăhâ',** *see-ah-haw´*; from an unused root meaning to *converse; congregation; Sia*, or *Siaha*, one of the Nethinim:—Sia, Siaha.

5518. סִיר, **sîyr,** *seer*; or (feminine) סִירָה, **sîyrâh,** *see-raw´*; or סִרָה, **sirâh,** *see-raw´*; (Jer 52:18), from a primitive root meaning to *boil* up; a *pot*; also a *thorn* (as springing up rapidly); (by implication) a *hook*:—caldron, fishhook, pan, ([wash-]) pot, thorn.

5519. סָךְ, **sâk,** *sawk*; from 5526; (properly) a *thicket* of men, i.e. a *crowd*:—multitude.

5520. סֹךְ, **sôk,** *soke*; from 5526; a *hut* (as of *entwined* boughs); also a *lair*:—covert, den, pavilion, tabernacle.

5521. סֻכָּה, **sukkâh,** *sook-kaw´*; feminine of 5520; a *hut* or *lair*:—booth, cottage, covert, pavilion, tabernacle, tent.

A feminine singular noun meaning a booth, a thicket. This term is used for temporary shelters used to cover animals (Ge 33:17); warriors (2Sa 11:11); and the prophet Jonah (Jnh 4:5). It is used poetically to refer to the clouds (Job 36:29; Ps 18:11[12]). A specialized usage is employed for booths constructed for the fall harvest festival (Le 23:42, 43). The festival was known as the *chag hassukkôwth* (2282), the Feast of Booths (Dt 16:13, 16). This was to remind the Israelites that they lived in booths when the Lord brought them up from Egypt (Le 23:43).

5522. סִכּוּת, **sikkûwth,** *sik-kooth´*; feminine of 5519; an (idolatrous) *booth*:—tabernacle.

An obscure masculine singular noun that occurs only in Am 5:26 and may mean tabernacle. This passage clearly describes the Israelites' false and improper worship. The question is how detailed the prophet's charge was. Some have translated the phrase as booth or shrine, while the Septuagint (Greek OT) reads "shrine of Molech." Some have suggested that both terms represent Akkadian astral deities, Sakkut and Kaiwan.

5523. סֻכּוֹת, **Sukkôwth,** *sook-kohth´*; or סֻכֹּת, **Sukkôth,** *sook-kohth´*; plural of 5521; *booths; Succoth*, the name of a place in Egypt and of three in Palestine:—Succoth.

5524. סֻכּוֹת בְּנוֹת, **Sukkôwth b^e^nôwth,** *sook-kohth´ ben-ohth´*; from 5523 and the (irregular) plural of 1323; *booths of* (*the*) *daughters; brothels*, i.e. idolatrous *tents* for impure purposes:—Succoth-benoth.

5525. סֻכִּי, **Sukkîy,** *sook-kee´*; patrial from an unknown name (perhaps 5520); a *Sukkite*, or inhabitant of some place near Egypt (i.e. *hut-dwellers*):— Sukkiims.

5526. **סָכַךְ, sâkak,** *saw-kak´*; or **שָׂכַךְ, śâkak,** *saw-kak´*; (Ex 33:22), a primitive root; (properly) to *entwine* as a screen; (by implication) to *fence* in, *cover* over, (figurative) *protect*:—cover, defence, defend, hedge in, join together, set, shut up.

5527. **סְכָכָה, Sᵉkâkâh,** *sek-aw-kaw´*; from 5526; *inclosure; Secacah*, a place in Palestine:—Secacah.

5528. **סָכַל, sâkal,** *saw-kal´*; for 3688; to *be silly*:—do (make, play the, turn into) fool (-ish, -ishly, -ishness).

5529. **סֶכֶל, sekel,** *seh´-kel*; from 5528; *silliness*; (concrete and collective) *dolts*:—folly.

5530. **סָכָל, sâkâl,** *saw-kawl´*; from 5528; *silly*:—fool (-ish), sottish.

5531. **סִכְלוּת, siklûwth,** *sik-looth´*; or **שִׂכְלוּת, śiklûwth,** *sik-looth´*; (Ecc 1:17), from 5528; *silliness*:—folly, foolishness.

5532. **סָכַן, sâkan,** *saw-kan´*; a primitive root; to *be familiar* with; (by implication) to *minister* to, *be serviceable* to, *be customary*:—acquaint (self), be advantage, × ever, (be, [un-]) profit (-able), treasurer, be wont.

5533. **סָכַן, sâkan,** *saw-kan´*; probably a denominative from 7915; (properly) *to cut*, i.e. *damage*; also to *grow* (causative, *make*) *poor*:—endanger, impoverish.

5534. **סָכַר, sâkar,** *saw-kar´*; a primitive root; to *shut* up; (by implication) to *surrender*:—stop, give over. See also 5462; 7936.

5535. **סָכַת, sâkath,** *saw-kath´*; a primitive root; to *be silent*; (by implication) to *observe* quietly:—take heed.

5536. **סַל, sal,** *sal*; from 5549; (properly) a willow *twig* (as *pendulous*), i.e. an *osier*; but only as woven into a *basket*:—basket.

5537. **סָלָא, sâlâʼ,** *saw-law´*; a primitive root; to *suspend* in a balance, i.e. *weigh*:—compare.

5538. **סִלָּא, Sillâʼ,** *sil-law´*; from 5549; an *embankment; Silla*, a place in Jerusalem:—Silla.

5539. **סָלַד, sâlad,** *saw-lad´*; a primitive root; probably to *leap* (with joy), i.e. *exult*:—harden self.

5540. **סֶלֶד, Seled,** *seh´-led*; from 5539; *exultation; Seled*, an Israelite:—Seled.

5541. **סָלָה, sâlâh,** *saw-law´*; a primitive root; to *hang* up, i.e. *weigh*, or (figurative) *contemn*:—tread down (under foot), value.

5542. **סֶלָה, selâh,** *seh´-law*; from 5541; *suspension* (of music), i.e. *pause*:—Selah.

5543. **סַלּוּ, Sallûw,** *sal-loo´*; or **סַלּוּא, Sallûwʼ,** *sal-loo´*; or **סָלוּא, Sâlûwʼ,** *saw-loo´*; or **סַלֻּא, Salluʼ,** *sal-loo´*; from 5541; *weighed; Sallu* or *Sallai*, the name of two Israelites:—Sallai, Sallu, Salu.

5544. **סִלּוֹן, sillôwn,** *sil-lone´*; or **סַלּוֹן, sallôwn,** *sal-lone´*; from 5541; a *prickle* (as if *pendulous*):—brier, thorn.

5545. **סָלַח, sâlach,** *saw-lakh´*; a primitive root; to *forgive*:—forgive, pardon, spare.

A verb meaning to forgive, to pardon, to spare, to be forgiven. The verb's subject is always God: He forgave the people of Israel after Moses interceded for them in the desert (Nu 14:20; Isa 55:7); Solomon prayed that the Lord would always hear and forgive His people (1Ki 8:30, 39; Da 9:19; Am 7:2). Some sins of Israel, however, were not forgiven. Jehoiachin had shed so much innocent blood that the Lord was not willing to forgive him (2Ki 24:4; La 3:42). The verb means to free from or release from something: the word describes the Lord pardoning or releasing a young woman from her vows in some instances (Nu 30:5[6], 8[9]); the Lord will not forgive an Israelite who in his heart approves of his own rebellious actions and continues in them (Dt 29:20[19]). The Lord forgives wickedness if it is repented of (Ex 34:9; Nu 14:19).

In the passive stem, the Hebrew word means to be forgiven; the people are forgiven (Le 4:20, 26; 5:10; 19:22) for their unintentional sins (Nu 15:25, 28) by turning away from them.

5546. **סַלָּח, sallâch,** *sal-lawkh´*; from 5545; *placable*:—ready to forgive.

An adjective meaning forgiving. This particular word is used only once in the Bible in a verse that describes the love and mercy of God (Ps 86:5). See the related Hebrew root *sâlach* (5545) and noun *sĕlîychâh* (5547).

5547. **סְלִיחָה, sᵉlîychâh,** *sel-ee-khaw´*; from 5545; *pardon*:—forgiveness, pardon.

A feminine noun meaning forgiveness. God is a forgiving God (Ne 9:17). He does not keep a record of sin, but with Him there is forgiveness (Ps 130:4). Daniel also proclaimed that God is forgiving, even though the Hebrews had sinned greatly against Him (Da 9:9). See the related Hebrew root *sâlach* (5545) and the related Hebrew adjective *sallâch* (5546).

5548. **סַלְכָה, Salkâh,** *sal-kaw´*; from an unused root meaning to *walk; walking; Salcah*, a place East of the Jordan:—Salcah, Salchah.

5549. **סָלַל, sâlal,** *saw-lal´*; a primitive root; to *mound* up (especially a turnpike); (figurative) to *exalt*; reflex, to *oppose* (as by a dam):—cast up, exalt (self), extol, make plain, raise up.

5550. **סֹלְלָה, sôlᵉlâh,** *so-lel-aw´*; or **סוֹלְלָה, sôwlᵉlâh,** *so-lel-aw´*; active participle feminine of 5549, but used passively; a military *mound*, i.e. *rampart* of besiegers:—bank, mount.

5551. **סֻלָּם, sullâm,** *sool-lawm´*; from 5549; a *stair-case*:—ladder.

5552. **סַלְסִלָּה, salsillâh,** *sal-sil-law´*; from 5541; a *twig* (as *pendulous*):—basket.

5553. **סֶלַע, selaʻ,** *seh´-lah*; from an unused root meaning to be *lofty*; a craggy *rock*, literal or figurative (a *fortress*):—(ragged) rock, stone (-ny), strong hold.

5554. **סֶלַע, Selaʻ,** *seh´-lah*; the same as 5553; *Sela*, the rock-city of Idumæa:—rock, Sela (-h).

5555. **סֶלַע הַמַּחְלְקוֹת, Selaʻ ham-machlᵉqôwth,** *seh´-lah ham-makh-lek-ōth´*; from 5553 and the plural of 4256 with the article interposed; *rock of the divisions; Sela-ham-Machlekoth*, a place in Palestine:—Sela-hammalekoth.

5556. **סָלְעָם, solʻâm,** *sol-awm´*; apparently from the same as 5553 in the sense of *crushing* as with a rock, i.e. consuming; a kind of *locust* (from its *destructiveness*):—bald locust.

5557. **סָלַף, sâlaph,** *saw-laf´*; a primitive root; properly to *wrench*, i.e. (figurative) to *subvert*:—overthrow, pervert.

5558. **סֶלֶף, seleph,** *seh´-lef*; from 5557; *distortion*, i.e. (figurative) *viciousness*:—perverseness.

5559. **סְלִק, sᵉliq,** *sel-eek´*; (Chaldee); a primitive root; to *ascend*:—come (up).

5560. **סֹלֶת, sôleth,** *so´-leth*; from an unused root meaning to *strip; flour* (as *chipped* off):—(fine) flour, meal.

5561. **סַם, sam,** *sam*; from an unused root meaning to *smell* sweet; an *aroma*:—sweet (spice).

5562. **סַמְגַּר נְבוֹ, Samgar Nᵉbôw,** *sam-gar´ neb-o´*; of foreign origin; *Samgar-Nebo*, a Babylonian general:—Samgar-nebo.

5563. **סְמָדַר, sᵉmâdar,** *sem-aw-dar´*; of uncertain derivation; a vine *blossom*; used also adverbially *abloom*:—tender grape.

5564. **סָמַךְ, sâmak,** *saw-mak´*; a primitive root; to *prop* (literal or figurative); (reflexive) to *lean* upon or *take hold* of (in a favourable or unfavourable sense):—bear up, establish, (up-) hold, lay, lean, lie hard, put, rest self, set self, stand fast, stay (self), sustain.

5565. סְמַכְיָהוּ, Sᵉmakyâhûw, *sem-ak-yaw´-hoo*; from 5564 and 3050; *supported of Jah; Semakjah*, an Israelite:—Semachiah.

5566. סֶמֶל, semel, *seh´-mel*; or סֵמֶל, **sêmel,** *say´-mel*; from an unused root meaning to *resemble*; a *likeness*:—figure, idol, image.

A masculine noun meaning statue, image, idol. Moses instructed the people to keep careful watch on themselves, lest they make an idol and worship it (Dt 4:16). Manasseh put a carved image in God's Temple but later humbled himself before God and removed it (2Ch 33:7, 15). In a vision, Ezekiel saw an idol of jealousy—an idol in the north gate that was standing near the glory of the God of Israel (Eze 8:3, 5).

5567. סָמַן, sâman, *saw-man´*; a primitive root; to *designate*:—appointed.

5568. סָמַר, sâmar, *saw-mar´*; a primitive root; to *be erect*, i.e. *bristle* as hair:—stand up, tremble.

5569. סָמָר, sâmâr, *saw-mawr´*; from 5568; *bristling*, i.e. *shaggy*:—rough.

5570. סְנָאָה, Sᵉnâ'âh, *sen-aw-aw´*; from an unused root meaning to *prick; thorny; Senaah*, a place in Palestine:—Senaah, Hassenaah [*with the article*].

5571. סַנְבַלַּט, Sanballaṭ, *san-bal-lat´*; of foreign origin; *Sanballat*, a Persian satrap of Samaria:—Sanballat.

5572. סְנֶה, sᵉneh, *sen-eh´*; from an unused root meaning to *prick*; a *bramble*:—bush.

5573. סֶנֶּה, Senneh, *sehn´-neh*; the same as 5572; *thorn; Seneh*, a crag in Palestine:—Seneh.

5574. סְנוּאָה, Sᵉnûw'âh, *sen-oo-aw´*; or סְנֻאָה, **Sᵉnu'âh,** *sen-oo-aw´*; from the same as 5570; *pointed*; (used with the article as a proper name) *Senuah*, the name of two Israelites:—Hasenuah [*including the article*], Senuah.

5575. סַנְוֵרִים, sanvêrîym, *san-vay-reem´*; of uncertain derivation; (in plural) *blindness*:—blindness.

5576. סַנְחֵרִיב, Sanchêrîyb, *san-khay-reeb´*; of foreign origin; *Sancherib*, an Assyrian king:—Sennacherib.

5577. סַנְסִנָּה, sansinnâh, *san-seen-aw´*; from an unused root meaning to be *pointed*; a *twig* (as *tapering*):—bough.

5578. סַנְסַנָּה, Sansannâh, *san-san-naw´*; feminine of a form of 5577; a *bough; Sansannah*, a place in Palestine:—Sansannah.

5579. סְנַפִּיר, sᵉnappîyr, *sen-ap-peer´*; of uncertain derivation; a *fin* (collective):—fins.

5580. סָס, sâs, *sawce*; from the same as 5483; a *moth* (from the *agility* of the fly):—moth.

5581. סִסְמַי, Sismay, *sis-mah´ee*; of uncertain derivation; *Sismai*, an Israelite:—Sisamai.

5582. סָעַד, sâ'ad, *saw-ad´*; a primitive root; to *support* (mostly figurative):—comfort, establish, hold up, refresh self, strengthen, be upholden.

5583. סְעַד, sᵉ'ad, *seh-ad´*; (Chaldee); corresponding to 5582; to *aid*:—helping.

5584. סָעָה, sâ'âh, *saw-aw´*; a primitive root; to *rush*:—storm.

5585. סָעִיף, sâ'îyph, *saw-eef´*; from 5586; a *fissure* (of rocks); also a *bough* (as *subdivided*):—(outmost) branch, clift, top.

5586. סָעַף, sâ'aph, *saw-af´*; a primitive root; (properly) to *divide* up; but used only as denominative from 5585, to *disbranch* (a tree):—top.

5587. סְעִפִּים, sᵉ'ippîym, *seh-ip-peem´*; from 5586; *divided* (in mind), i.e. (abstract) a *sentiment*:—opinion.

A noun meaning a division, an opinion, a belief. The word comes from a root meaning to divide. It occurs only in 1Ki 18:21, where Elijah asked the Israelites how long they would halt between two opinions. In context, the word refers to belief, whether in the Lord or in Baal.

5588. סֵעֵף, sê'êph, *say-afe´*; from 5586; *divided* (in mind), i.e. (concrete) a *skeptic*:—thought.

5589. סְעַפָּה, sᵉ'appâh, *seh-ap-paw´*; feminine of 5585; a *twig*:—bough, branch. Compare 5634.

5590. סָעַר, sâ'ar, *saw-ar´*; a primitive root; to *rush* upon; (by implication) to *toss* (transitive or intransitive, literal or figurative):—be (toss with) tempest (-uous), be sore troubled, come out as a (drive with the, scatter with a) whirlwind.

5591. סַעַר, sa'ar, *sah´-ar*; or (feminine) סְעָרָה, **sᵉ'ârâh,** *seh-aw-raw´*; from 5590; a *hurricane*:—storm (-y), tempest, whirlwind.

5592. סַף, saph, *saf*; from 5605, in its original sense of *containing*; a *vestibule* (as a *limit*); also a *dish* (for holding blood or wine):—bason, bowl, cup, door (post), gate, post, threshold.

5593. סַף, Saph, *saf*; the same as 5592; *Saph*, a Philistine:—Saph. Compare 5598.

5594. סָפַד, sâphad, *saw-fad´*; a primitive root; (properly) to *tear* the hair and *beat* the breasts (as Orientals do in grief); (generally) to *lament*; (by implication) to *wail*:—lament, mourn (-er), wail.

5595. סָפָה, sâphâh, *saw-faw´*; a primitive root; properly to *scrape* (literally, to *shave*; but usually figurative) together (i.e. to *accumulate* or *increase*) or away (i.e. to *scatter, remove* or *ruin*; [intransitive] to *perish*):—add, augment, consume, destroy, heap, join, perish, put.

A verb meaning to scrape or sweep away, to destroy, to perish, to be captured. The word refers to the destruction or sweeping away of people (Ps 40:14[15]); or a city (Ge 18:23, 24); especially as the judgment of God. In Dt 29:19[18], the word refers to complete destruction: the destruction of the saturated with the dry. In Isa 13:15, it means captured as if swept up into another's possession. It is also used of the scraping away (i.e. shaving) of a beard (Isa 7:20).

5596. סָפַח, sâphach, *saw-fakh´*; or שָׂפַח, **śâphach,** *saw-fakh´*; (Isa 3:17), a primitive root; (properly) to *scrape* out, but in certain peculiar senses (of *removal* or *association*):—abiding, gather together, cleave, smite with the scab.

A verb meaning to join, to be gathered together, to be joined, to cleave, to join oneself, to abide in. The word refers to putting a priest into office, that is, joining him to the office (1Sa 2:36). It refers to David remaining in Israel's inheritance in spite of death threats from Saul (1Sa 26:19); similarly, it refers to the Gentiles being joined to Israel (Isa 14:1). In Job 30:7, it refers to the gathering of foolish poor people for protection under a plant. It appears to refer to the joining of heat (that is, poison) to a drink meant to make someone drunk; but the word here may be a copyist's error for *saph* (5592), meaning goblet (Hab 2:15). In Isa 3:17, the word means to smite with a scab, but here it is spelled *śippach.* and may belong to another root of similar spelling.

5597. סַפַּחַת, sappachath, *sap-pakh´-ath*; from 5596; the *mange* (as making the hair fall off):—scab.

5598. סִפַּי, Sippay, *sip-pah´ee*; from 5592; *bason-like; Sippai*, a Philistine:—Sippai. Compare 5593.

5599. סָפִיחַ, sâphîyach, *saw-fee´-akh*; from 5596; something (spontaneously) *falling* off, i.e. a *self-sown* crop; (figurative) a *freshet*:—(such) things as (which) grow (of themselves), which groweth of its own accord (itself).

5600. סְפִינָה, sᵉphîynâh, *sef-ee-naw´*; from 5603; a (sea-going) *vessel* (as *ceiled* with a deck):—ship.

5601. סַפִּיר, sappîyr, *sap-peer´*; from 5608; a *gem* (perhaps as used for *scratching* other substances), probably the *sapphire*:—sapphire.

5602. סֵפֶל, sêphel, *say´-fel*; from an unused root meaning to *depress*; a *basin* (as *deepened* out):—bowl, dish.

5603. **סָפַן, sâphan,** *saw-fan'*; a primitive root; to *hide* by covering; (specifically) to *roof* (passive participle as noun, a *roof*) or *wainscot*; (figurative) to *reserve*:—cieled, cover, seated.

5604. **סִפֻּן, sippun,** *sip-poon'*; from 5603; a *wainscot*:—cieling.

5605. **סָפַף, sâphaph,** *saw-faf'*; a primitive root; (properly) to *snatch* away, i.e. *terminate*; but used only as denominative from 5592 (in the sense of a *vestibule*), to *wait at* the *threshold*:—be a doorkeeper.

5606. **סָפַק, sâphaq,** *saw-fak'*; or **שָׂפַק, śâphaq,** *saw-fak'*; (1Ki 20:10; Job 27:23; Isa 2:6), a primitive root; to *clap* the hands (in token of compact, derision, grief, indignation or punishment); (by implication of satisfaction) to *be enough*; (by implication of excess) to *vomit*:—clap, smite, strike, suffice, wallow.

A verb meaning to clap, to strike, to smite. It signifies the clapping of hands in derision or disrespect, sometimes accompanied by hissing (Job 27:23; 34:37; La 2:15); the clapping of the hand on the thigh as a sign of grief or shame (Jer 31:19; Eze 21:12[17]); or the clapping of the hands in anger (Nu 24:10). The word is used to refer to God's striking of people in public rebuke for backsliding (Job 34:26); and the wallowing or splashing of Moab in its vomit (Jer 48:26). In Isa 2:6, the word referred to the striking of hands, that is, making deals with foreigners. The meaning, "suffice," found in 1Ki 20:10, appears to belong under another root, and this may also be true of Isa 2:6 (both passages spell the word with *ś* instead of *s*).

5607. **סֵפֶק, sêpheq,** *say'-fek*; or **שֶׂפֶק, śepheq,** *seh'-fek*; (Job 20:22; 36:18), from 5606; *chastisement*; also *satiety*:—stroke, sufficiency.

5608. **סָפַר, sâphar,** *saw-far'*; a primitive root; (properly) to *score* with a mark as a tally or record, i.e. (by implication) to *inscribe*, and also to *enumerate*; (intensive) to *recount*, i.e. *celebrate*:—commune, (ac-) count, declare, number, + penknife, reckon, scribe, shew forth, speak, talk, tell (out), writer.

A verb meaning to number, to recount, to relate, to declare. It is used to signify the numbering or counting of objects (Ge 15:5; Ps 48:12[13]); and people, as in a census (1Ch 21:2; 2Ch 2:17[16]). It also refers to a quantity that is too great to number (Ge 16:10; Jer 33:22). God's numbering of one's steps is a sign of His care (Job 14:16; cf. Mt 10:30). The word also means to relate or to recount and is used often to refer to the communication of important information and truths to those who have not heard them, especially to foreign nations (Ex 9:16; 1Ch 16:24; Ps 96:3); or to the children in Israel (Ps 73:15; 78:4, 6; 79:13). The matter communicated included dreams (Ge 40:9; 41:8, 12; Jgs 7:13); God's works (Ex 18:8; Ps 73:28; Jer 51:10); and recounting one's own ways to God (Ps 119:26). The word also signifies the silent witness of the creation to its Creator and His wisdom and glory (Job 12:8; 28:27; Ps 19:1[2]).

The participle form of the word *sôphêr*, means scribe and occurs about fifty times in the OT. Scribes such as Ezra studied, practiced, and taught the Law (Ezr 7:11). Scribes also served kings, writing and sometimes carrying messages to and from court (2Ki 18:18; 19:2; Est 3:12; 8:9). In 2Ki 22:10, a scribe read the recovered scroll of the Law to King Josiah, bringing about a personal revival. Scribes, as people who could read and count, also acted militarily, gathering the troops (2Ki 25:19; Jer 52:25). The occupation of scribe could belong to a family (1Ch 2:55). Also, some Levites occupied the position as part of their job (2Ch 34:13).

5609. **סְפַר, sᵉphar,** *sef-ar'*; (Chaldee); from a root corresponding to 5608; a *book*:—book, roll.

An Aramaic masculine noun meaning a book, a scroll. The word refers to the book of Moses, the first five books of the Bible, that were used to instruct the priests and Levites in their duties (Ezr 6:18). It refers to books of national records that rulers in Babylon could check regarding Israeli-Babylonian relations (Ezr 4:15). It also refers to books that the Ancient of Days will use to judge in favour of His saints against the boastful little horn (Da 7:10, cf. Da 7:21ff.). The word is used to signify a library or archive, as a house of books in Ezr 6:1.

5610. **סְפָר, sᵉphâr,** *sef-awr'*; from 5608; a *census*:—numbering.

5611. **סְפָר, Sᵉphâr,** *sef-awr'*; the same as 5610; *Sephar*, a place in Arabia:—Sephar.

5612. **סֵפֶר, sêpher,** *say'-fer*; or (feminine) **סִפְרָה, siphrâh,** *sif-raw'*; (Ps 56:8 [99]), from 5608; (properly) *writing* (the art or a document); (by implication) a *book*:—bill, book, evidence, × learn [-ed] (-ing), letter, register, scroll.

A masculine noun meaning a document, a writing, a book, a scroll. Borrowed from an Assyrian word meaning missive or message, this word can refer to a letter (2Sa 11:14, 15; 1Ki 21:8, 9, 11; 2Ki 10:1, 2, 6, 7; Jer 29:1); a divorce decree (Dt 24:1, 3; Isa 50:1; Jer 3:8); a proof of purchase deed (Jer 32:10–12, 14, 16); a book in which things were written for a need in the future (Ex 17:14; 1Sa 10:25; Isa 30:8); a book of laws (Ex 24:7; Dt 30:10; Jos 1:8; Ne 8:1, 3; 13:1); a genealogical record (Ge 5:1; Ne 7:5); writing and language (Da 1:4, 17).

5613. **סָפַר, sâphar,** *saw-fare'*; (Chaldee); from the same as 5609; a *scribe* (secular or sacred):—scribe.

An Aramaic masculine noun meaning a clerk, a secretary, a scribe. This term can refer to someone who had the ability to read and write documents, but it can also refer to someone who held a special government office. A Persian official named Shimshai was identified as a scribe, whose duties probably included copying documents as well as translating documents from and into Aramaic (Ezr 4:8, 9, 17, 23). In the official Persian office of scribe, Ezra was especially qualified to interpret and teach the Law of God (Ezr 7:12, 21).

5614. **סְפָרָד, Sᵉphârâd,** *sef-aw-rawd'*; of foreign derivation; *Sepharad*, a region of Assyria:—Sepharad.

5615. **סְפֹרָה, sᵉphôrâh,** *sef-o-raw'*; from 5608; a *numeration*:—number.

5616. **סְפַרְוִי, Sᵉpharvîy,** *sef-ar-vee'*; patrial from 5617; a *Sepharvite* or inhabitant of Sepharvain:—Sepharvite.

5617. **סְפַרְוַיִם, Sᵉpharvayim,** *sef-ar-vah'-yim*; (dual) or **סְפָרִים, Sᵉphârîym,** *sef-aw-reem'*; (plural), of foreign derivation; *Sepharvajim* or *Sepharim*, a place in Assyria:—Sepharvaim.

5618. **סֹפֶרֶת, Sôphereth,** *so-feh'-reth*; feminine active participle of 5608; a *scribe* (properly female); *Sophereth*, a temple servant:—Sophereth.

5619. **סָקַל, sâqal,** *saw-kal'*; a primitive root; (properly) to *be weighty*; but used only in the sense of *lapidation* or its contrary (as if a *de*lapidation):—(cast, gather out, throw) stone (-s), × surely.

5620. **סַר, sar,** *sar*; from 5637 contraction; *peevish*:—heavy, sad.

5621. **סָרָב, sârâb,** *saw-rawb'*; from an unused root meaning to *sting*; a thistle:—brier.

5622. **סַרְבַּל, sarbal,** *sar-bal'*; (Chaldee); of uncertain derivation; a *cloak*:—coat.

5623. **סַרְגּוֹן, Sargôwn,** *sar-gōne'*; of foreign derivation; *Sargon*, an Assian king:—Sargon.

5624. **סֶרֶד, Sered,** *seh'-red*; from a primitive root meaning to *tremble; trembling; Sered*, an Israelite:—Sered.

5625. **סַרְדִּי, Sardîy,** *sar-dee'*; patronymic from 5624; a *Seredite* (collective) or descendants of Sered:—Sardites.

5626. **סִרָה, Sirâh,** *see-raw'*; from 5493; *departure; Sirah*, a cistern so-called:—Sirah. See also 5518.

5627. **סָרָה, sârâh,** *saw-raw'*; from 5493; *apostasy, crime*; (figurative) *remission*:— × continual, rebellion, revolt ([-ed]), turn away, wrong.

A feminine noun meaning a defection, a revolt, an apostasy. Derived from a verb that means to turn aside, this term refers to God's people turning away from Him to follow false gods (Dt 13:5[6]). Frequently, it describes those who chose to rebel against God (Isa 1:5; 31:6; 59:13; Jer 28:16; 29:32). Although some translations of this term in Dt 19:16 suggest it simply means a general offence, its use elsewhere in Deuteronomy and the rest of the OT indicates that this word refers to apostasy.

5628. סָרַח, **sârach,** *saw-rakh´*; a primitive root; to *extend* (even to *excess*):—exceeding, hand, spread, stretch self, banish.

5629. סֶרַח, **serach,** *seh´-rakh*; from 5628; a *redundancy*:—remnant.

A masculine noun meaning excess. Derived from a verbal form that means to hang over or overrun, this noun form occurs only once in the OT. In Ex 26:12, it refers to the remaining or excess material of the curtains in the tabernacle.

5630. סִרְיֹן, **siryôn,** *sir-yone´*; for 8302; a coat of *mail*:—brigandine.

5631. סָרִיס, **sârîys,** *saw-reece´*; or סָרִס, **sâris,** *saw-reece´*; from an unused root meaning to *castrate*; a *eunuch*; (by implication) *valet* (especially of the female apartments), and thus a *minister* of state:—chamberlain, eunuch, officer. Compare 7249.

A masculine noun meaning a court official, a eunuch. Derived from an Assyrian phrase meaning one who is the head or chief, this word can refer to someone with a high-ranking military or political status (Ge 40:2, 7; 1Sa 8:15). Potiphar held an official post called the captain of the guard while working in the court of an Egyptian pharaoh (Ge 37:36; 39:1). The term eunuch comes from the custom of placing castrated males in certain key government positions (2Ki 20:18; Est 2:3, 14, 15, 21; 4:4, 5; Isa 39:7). According to Mosaic Law, males who had defective genital organs would have been excluded from the worshiping community of Israel (cf. Le 21:20; Dt 23:1). In 2Ki 18:17, the term appears in a phrase that probably does not denote a eunuch but simply means an important government official (Jer 39:3, 13).

5632. סָרַךְ, **sârak,** *saw-rak´*; (Chaldee); of foreign origin; an *emir*:—president.

An Aramaic masculine noun meaning an official, a president. A loanword from Persian for head or chief, this term appears in the OT only in Daniel. It is a title given to three high-ranking government officials, one of whom was Daniel (Da 6:2–4[3–5], 6[7], 7[8]). Appointed by Darius the Mede, the three officials oversaw the work of 120 satraps, whose function may have been to collect taxes for the king from throughout the empire.

5633. סֶרֶן, **seren,** *seh´-ren*; from an unused root of uncertain meaning; an *axle*; (figurative) a *peer*:—lord, plate.

A masculine singular noun meaning a lord, a tyrant. This term is a Philistine loan word and was applied only to Philistine rulers. Five rulers reigned in the five main cities of the Philistines: Ashdod, Gaza, Ashkelon, Gath, and Ekron (1Sa 6:16, 18). In one passage, the word is translated axle of brass, based on the Septuagint rendering (1Ki 7:30), but the etymology is unknown. David and his men were sent away by the *seren* and not allowed to fight for the Philistines (1Ch 12:19[20]).

5634. סַרְעַפָּה, **sar'appâh,** *sar-ap-paw´*; for 5589; a *twig*:—bough.

5635. סָרַף, **sâraph,** *saw-raf´*; a primitive root; to *cremate*, i.e. to *be* (near) *of kin* (such being privileged to kindle the pyre):—burn.

5636. סִרְפָּד, **sirpâd,** *sir-pawd´*; from 5635; a *nettle* (as stinging like a *burn*):—brier.

5637. סָרַר, **sârar,** *saw-rar´*; a primitive root; to *turn* away, i.e. (moral) *be refractory*:—× away, backsliding, rebellious, revolter (-ing), slide back, stubborn, withdrew.

A verb meaning to be stubborn, to be rebellious. Israel was said to be stubborn for forming an alliance with Egypt against God's ordained plan (Isa 30:1); performing improper sacrifices, eating unclean things, and worshiping ancestors (Isa 65:2). They were even compared to a stubborn heifer (Hos 4:16). They stubbornly turned their backs (lit., shoulders) on God and His words (Ne 9:29; Zec 7:11). The son who rebelled against his parents could be severely disciplined and was eventually stoned (Dt 21:18, 21). The term is also used of an immoral woman (Pr 7:11).

5638. סְתָו, **s^e^thâv,** *seth-awv´*; from an unused root meaning to *hide; winter* (as the dark season):—winter.

5639. סְתוּר, **S^e^thûwr,** *seth-oor´*; from 5641; *hidden; Sethur*, an Israelite:—Sethur.

5640. סָתַם, **sâtham,** *saw-tham´*; or שָׂתַם, **śâtham,** *saw-tham´*; (Nu 24:15), a primitive root; to *stop* up; (by implication) to *repair*; (figurative) to *keep secret*:—closed up, hidden, secret, shut out (up), stop.

5641. סָתַר, **sâthar,** *saw-thar´*; a primitive root; to *hide* (by covering), literal or figurative:—be absent, keep close, conceal, hide (self), (keep) secret, × surely.

5642. סְתַר, **s^e^thar,** *seth-ar´*; (Chaldee); corresponding to 5641; to *conceal*; (figurative) to *demolish*:—destroy, secret thing.

An Aramaic verb derived from two separate roots. One of these means to hide. It occurs as a passive participle in Da 2:22 where it refers to hidden things that God reveals to the wise. See the Hebrew word *sâthar* (5641). The second means to destroy. Its one usage describes the actions of Nebuchadnezzar, the Chaldean, who destroyed God's Temple in Jerusalem (Ezr 5:12). It is possibly related to the Hebrew root *śâthar* (8368).

5643. סֵתֶר, **sêther,** *say´-ther*; or (feminine) סִתְרָה, **sithrâh,** *sith-raw´*; (Dt 32:38), from 5641; a *cover* (in a good or a bad, a literal or a figurative sense):—backbiting, covering, covert, × disguise [-th], hiding place, privily, protection, secret (-ly, place).

5644. סִתְרִי, **Sithrîy,** *sith-ree´*; from 5643; *protective; Sithri*, an Israelite:—Zithri.

5645. עָב, **'âb,** *awb*; (masculine and feminine), from 5743; (properly) an *envelope*, i.e. *darkness* (or *density*, 2Ch 4:17); (specifically) a (scud) *cloud*; also a *copse*:—clay, (thick) cloud, × thick, thicket. Compare 5672.

5646. עָב, **'âb,** *awb*; or עֹב, **'ôb,** *obe*; from an unused root meaning to *cover*; properly equivalent to 5645; but used only as an architectural term, an *architrave* (as *shading* the pillars):—thick (beam, plant).

5647. עָבַד, **'âbad,** *aw-bad´*; a primitive root; to *work* (in any sense); (by implication) to *serve, till*, (causative) *enslave*, etc.:—× be, keep in bondage, be bondmen, bond-service, compel, do, dress, ear, execute, + husbandman, keep, labour (-ing man), bring to pass, (cause to, make to) serve (-ing, self), (be, become) servant (-s), do (use) service, till (-er), transgress [*from margin*], (set a) work, be wrought, worshipper.

A verb meaning to work, to serve. This labour may be focused on things, other people, or God. When it is used in reference to things, that item is usually expressed: to till the ground (Ge 2:5; 3:23; 4:2); to work in a garden (Ge 2:15); or to dress a vineyard (Dt 28:39). Similarly, this term is also applied to artisans and craftsmen, like workers in fine flax (Isa 19:9); and labourers of the city (Eze 48:19). When the focus of the labour is another person, that person is usually expressed: Jacob's service to Laban (Ge 29:15); the Israelites' service for the Egyptians (Ex 1:14); and a people's service to the king (Jgs 9:28; 1Sa 11:1). When the focus of the labour is the Lord, it is a religious service to worship Him. Moreover, in these cases, the word does not have connotations of toilsome labour but instead of a joyful experience of liberation (Ex 3:12; 4:23; 7:16; Jos 24:15, 18). Unfortunately, this worship service was often given to false gods (Dt 7:16; 2Ki 10:18, 19, 21–23).

5648. עֲבַד, **'ăbad,** *ab-ad´*; (Chaldee); corresponding to 5647; to *do, make, prepare, keep*, etc.:—× cut, do, execute, go on, make, move, work.

5649. עֲבַד, **'ăbad,** *ab-ad´*; (Chaldee); from 5648; a *servant*:—servant.

An Aramaic masculine singular noun meaning a slave, a servant. It is used for servants of God or of human beings. King Nebuchadnezzar refers to Shadrach, Meshach, and Abednego as servants of the Most High God (Da 3:26). Darius calls Daniel the servant of the living God (Da 6:20[21]). One could also be known as a servant of the king (Da 2:7). This noun is derived from the verb *'ăbad* (5648), meaning to do or make. See the Hebrew cognate *'ebed* (5650).

5650. עֶבֶד, **‘ebed,** *eh´-bed*; from 5647; a *servant*:— × bondage, bondman, [bond-] servant, (man-) servant.

A masculine noun meaning a servant, a slave. Although the most basic concept of this term is that of a slave, slavery in the Bible was not the same as the slavery of modern times. The period of slavery was limited to six years (Ex 21:2). Slaves had rights and protection under the Law (Ex 21:20). It was also possible for slaves to attain positions of power and honour (Ge 24:2; 41:12). In addition, the people under the king were called his servants (Ge 21:25); as well as his officers (1Sa 19:1); officials (2Ki 22:12); ambassadors (Nu 22:18); vassal kings (2Sa 10:19); tributary nations (1Ch 18:2, 6, 13). This word is also a humble way of referring to one's self when speaking with another of equal or superior rank (Ge 33:5). The term is also applied to those who worship God (Ne 1:10); and to those who minister or serve Him (Isa 49:5, 6). The phrase, the servant of the Lord, is the most outstanding reference to the Messiah in the OT, and its teachings are concentrated at the end of Isaiah (Isa 42:1, 19; 43:10; 49:3, 5–7; 52:13; 53:11).

5651. עֶבֶד, **‘Ebed,** *eh´-bed*; the same as 5650; *Ebed*, the name of two Israelites:—Ebed.

5652. עֲבָד, **‘âbâd,** *ab-awd´*; from 5647; a *deed*:—work.

5653. עַבְדָּא, **‘Abdâ',** *ab-daw´*; from 5647; *work; Abda*, the name of two Israelites:—Abda.

5654. עֹבֵד אֱדוֹם, **‘Ôbêd 'Ĕdôwm,** *o-bade´ ed-ome´*; from the active participle of 5647 and 123; *worker of Edom; Obed-Edom*, the name of five Israelites:—Obed-edom.

5655. עַבְדְאֵל, **‘Abdᵉ'êl,** *ab-deh-ale´*; from 5647 and 410; *serving God; Abdeël*, an Israelite:—Abdeel. Compare 5661.

5656. עֲבֹדָה, **‘ăbôdâh,** *ab-o-daw´*; or עֲבוֹדָה, **‘ăbôwdâh,** *ab-o-daw´*; from 5647; *work* of any kind:—act, bondage, + bondservant, effect, labour, ministering (-try), office, service (-ile, -itude), tillage, use, work, × wrought.

A feminine noun meaning service, work. This word encompasses the wide variations of meaning of the English word "work"—from delicate artistry to forced labour. The Egyptians made the Israelites do slave labour (Ex 1:14); for certain feast days, the Israelites were not allowed to do any work (Le 23:7ff.); different parts of the tabernacle were considered to be in its service (Nu 4:26, 32); the descendants of Judah included workers of linen (1Ch 4:21). God handed the Israelites into the hand of Shishak so they would learn the difference between serving Him and serving other kings (2Ch 12:8). See the related Hebrew root *‘âbad* (5647).

5657. עֲבֻדָּה, **‘ăbuddâh,** *ab-ood-daw´*; passive participle of 5647; something *wrought*, i.e. (concrete) *service*:—household, store of servants.

A feminine noun meaning service, servants. This word usually refers to an entire household of servants. The Philistines were jealous of Isaac because of his wealth, including his livestock and servants (Ge 26:14). Job was considered the wealthiest man of the East because of all his possessions, including his multitude of servants (Job 1:3). See the related Hebrew root *‘âbad* (5647), Aramaic root *‘ăbad* (5648), Aramaic noun *‘ăbêd* (5649), and Hebrew noun *‘ebed* (5650).

5658. עַבְדּוֹן, **‘Abdôwn,** *ab-dohn´*; from 5647; *servitude; Abdon*, the name of a place in Palestine and of four Israelites:—Abdon. Compare 5683.

5659. עַבְדוּת, **‘abdûwth,** *ab-dooth´*; from 5647; *servitude*:—bondage.

A feminine noun meaning bondage, slavery. This word is derived from the word *‘âbad* (5647), meaning to serve. It occurs three times in the Hebrew Bible. In Ezr 9:8, 9, it refers twice to the bondage of the Hebrews under Babylon, a bondage where God revived them a little by allowing them to rebuild the wall and temple. In Ne 9:17, it refers to severe bondage in Egypt (see Ne 9:9), to which some rebellious Hebrews wanted to return.

5660. עַבְדִּי, **‘Abdîy,** *ab-dee´*; from 5647; *serviceable; Abdi*, the name of two Israelites:—Abdi.

5661. עַבְדִיאֵל, **‘Abdîy'êl,** *ab-dee-ale´*; from 5650 and 410; *servant of God; Abdiël*, an Israelite:—Abdiel. Compare 5655.

5662. עֹבַדְיָה, **‘Ôbadyâh,** *o-bad-yaw´*; or עֹבַדְיָהוּ, **‘Ôbadyâhûw,** *o-bad-yaw´-hoo*; active participle of 5647 and 3050; *serving Jah; Obadjah*, the name of thirteen Israelites:—Obadiah.

5663. עֶבֶד מֶלֶךְ, **‘Ebed Melek,** *eh´-bed meh´-lek*; from 5650 and 4428; *servant of a king; Ebed-Melek*, a eunuch of king Zedekeah:—Ebed-melech.

5664. עֲבֵד נְגוֹ, **‘Ăbêd Nᵉgôw,** *ab-ade´ neg-o´*; the same as 5665; *Abed-Nego*, the Babylonian name of one of Daniel's companions:—Abed-nego.

5665. עֲבֵד נְגוֹא, **‘Ăbêd Nᵉgôw',** *ab-ade´ neg-o´*; (Chaldee); of foreign origin; *Abed-Nego*, the name of Azariah:—Abed-nego.

5666. עָבָה, **‘âbâh,** *aw-baw´*; a primitive root; to *be dense*:—be (grow) thick (-er).

5667. עֲבוֹט, **‘ăbôwṭ,** *ab-ote´*; or עֲבֹט, **‘ăbôṭ,** *ab-ote´*; from 5670; a *pawn*:—pledge.

5668. עָבוּר, **‘âbûwr,** *aw-boor´*; or עָבֻר, **‘âbur,** *aw-boor´*; passive participle of 5674; (properly) *crossed*, i.e. (abstract) *transit*; used only adverbially on *account* of, in *order* that:—because of, for (… 's sake), (intent) that, to.

5669. עָבוּר, **‘âbûwr,** *a-boor´*; the same as 5668; *passed*, i.e. *kept* over; used only of *stored* grain:—old corn.

5670. עָבַט, **‘âbaṭ,** *aw-bat´*; a primitive root; to *pawn*; (causative) to *lend* (on security); (figurative) to *entangle*:—borrow, break [*ranks*], fetch [*a pledge*], lend, × surely.

5671. עַבְטִיט, **‘abṭîyṭ,** *ab-teet´*; from 5670; something *pledged*, i.e. (collective) *pawned* goods:—thick clay [*by a false etymology*].

5672. עֲבִי, **‘ăbîy,** *ab-ee´*; or עֳבִי, **‘ŏbîy,** *ob-ee´*; from 5666; *density*, i.e. *depth* or *width*:—thick (-ness). Compare 5645.

5673. עֲבִידָה, **‘ăbîydâh,** *ab-ee-daw´*; (Chaldee); from 5648; *labour* or *business*:—affairs, service, work.

5674. עָבַר, **‘âbar,** *aw-bar´*; a primitive root; to *cross* over; used very widely of any *transition* (literal or figurative; transitive, intransitive, intensive or causative); specifically to *cover* (in copulation):—alienate, alter, × at all, beyond, bring (over, through), carry over, (over-) come (on, over), conduct (over), convey over, current, deliver, do away, enter, escape, fail, gender, get over, (make) go (away, beyond, by, forth, his way, in, on, over, through), have away (more), lay, meddle, overrun, make partition, (cause to, give, make to, over) pass (-age, along, away, beyond, by, -enger, on, out, over, through), (cause to, make) + proclaim (-amation), perish, provoke to anger, put away, rage, + raiser of taxes, remove, send over, set apart, + shave, cause to (make) sound, × speedily, × sweet smelling, take (away), (make to) transgress (-or), translate, turn away, [way-] faring man, be wrath.

A verb meaning to pass through or over, to cover, to go beyond, to go along, to be crossed over, to make to cross over, to go through, to go away. This verb indicates the physical act of crossing or passing over and takes on a figurative usage that exhibits many variations in meaning. Two figurative meanings are of primary importance theologically; the verb means going beyond, overstepping a covenant or a command of God or man. Moses uses the word when charging the people with disobeying and overstepping the Lord's commands (Nu 14:41; Jos 7:11, 15). Esther 3:3 depicts Mordecai's transgressing of the king's command. The word is used of God's passing over His people's rebellion (Mic 7:18); but also of His decision not to pass over or spare them any longer (Am 7:8; 8:2). The verb relates to the placement of a yoke of punishment on the neck of Ephraim, God's rebellious nation (Hos 10:11; cf. Job 13:13).

The word indicates the literal movement of material subjects and objects in time and space in various contexts: a stream or river is passed over (Jos 3:14); as are boundaries (Nu 20:17). An attacking army passes through its enemies' territories, conquering them like a flood (cf. Jos 18:9; Isa 8:8; Da 11:10, 40); and as the literal flood waters of Noah's day covered the earth (Ps 42:7[8]; 88:16[17]; Isa 54:9). In a figurative sense, the word describes the feeling of jealousy that can come over a suspecting or jealous husband (Nu 5:14, 30); or the movement of God's Spirit (1Ki 22:24; 2Ch 18:23; Jer 5:28). The location of an event could move or pass on, as when the Israelites routed the Philistines, and the battle, both in location and progress, passed by Beth Aven (1Sa 14:23; 2Sa 16:1; Jer 5:22).

The word indicates passing away or leaving (emigrating) from a certain territory (Mic 1:11). It indicates dying or perishing, as when the Lord described the perishing of Assyria's allies (Na 1:12); or the disappearance of Job's safety (Job 30:15; 33:18); it describes the passing of a law's validity or its passing out of use (Est 1:19; 9:27).

The causative stem adds the aspect of making these things happen as described in the simple stem. Jacob caused his family to cross over the Jabbok River (Ge 32:23[24]). The word is used of the heinous act of devoting children to pagan gods (Jer 32:35; Eze 23:37). A proclamation or the sound of the shofar can pass through the land (Ex 36:6; Le 25:9).

The word means to cause something to pass away. Many things could be noted: God caused Saul's kingdom to pass over to David (2Sa 3:10); evil could be put away, as when Asa, king of Judah, put away male prostitutes from the religions of Israel (1Ki 15:12); or holy persons turned away their eyes from vain things (Ps 119:37).

The word is used one time in the passive stem to indicate a river that cannot be crossed (Eze 47:5); and in the factitive or intensive stem to describe Solomon's stringing gold chains across the front area inside the Holy Place in the Temple (1Ki 6:21).

5675. **עֲבַר, 'ăbar,** *ab-ar´*; (Chaldee); corresponding to 5676:—beyond, this side.

5676. **עֵבֶר, 'êber,** *ay´-ber*; from 5674; (properly) a region *across*; but used only adverbially (with or without a preposition) on the *opposite* side (especially of the Jordan; usually meaning the *east*):— × against, beyond, by, × from, over, passage, quarter, (other, this) side, straight.

5677. **עֵבֶר, 'Êber,** *ay´-ber*; the same as 5676; *Eber*, the name of two patriarchs and four Israelites:—Eber, Heber.

5678. **עֶבְרָה, 'ebrâh,** *eb-raw´*; feminine of 5676; an *outburst* of passion:—anger, rage, wrath.

A feminine noun meaning wrath, fury. The word is derived from the word *'âbar* (5674) and thus implies an overflowing anger. When the word is used of people, it usually describes a fault of character, a cruel anger (Ge 49:7; Am 1:11); associated with pride (Pr 21:24; Isa 16:6). The wrath of a king toward shameful servants, however, is justifiable, representing God's anger (Pr 14:35, cf. Pr 14:34; Ro 13:4). The word most often signifies God's wrath, an attribute people generally fail to properly appreciate (Ps 90:11). God's wrath disregards a person's wealth (Pr 11:4); and brings fiery judgment, purging the sin of His people (Eze 22:21, cf. Eze 22:22); and ultimately bringing wickedness and wicked people to an end on earth (Zep 1:15, 18). The instrument of wrath is sometimes pictured as a rod (Pr 22:8; La 3:1).

5679. **עֲבָרָה, 'ăbârâh,** *ab-aw-raw´*; from 5674; a *crossing*-place:—ferry, plain [*from the margin*].

5680. **עִבְרִי, 'Ibrîy,** *ib-ree´*; patronymic from 5677; an *Eberite* (i.e. Hebrew) or descendant of Eber:—Hebrew (-ess, woman).

5681. **עִבְרִי, 'Ibrîy,** *ib-ree´*; the same as 5680; *Ibri*, an Israelite:—Ibri.

5682. **עֲבָרִים, 'Ăbârîym,** *ab-aw-reem´*; plural of 5676; regions *beyond; Abarim*, a place in Palestine:—Abarim, passages.

5683. **עֶבְרֹן, 'Ebrôn,** *eb-rone´*; from 5676; *transitional; Ebron*, a place in Palestine:—Hebron. Perhaps a clerical error for 5658.

5684. **עַבְרֹנָה, 'Abrônâh,** *ab-roe-naw´*; or **עֶבְרֹנָה, 'Ebrônâh,** *eb-roe-naw´*; feminine of 5683; *Ebronah*, a place in the Desert:—Ebronah.

5685. **עָבַשׁ, 'âbash,** *aw-bash´*; a primitive root; to *dry* up:—be rotten.

5686. **עָבַת, 'âbath,** *aw-bath´*; a primitive root; to *interlace*, i.e. (figurative) to *pervert*:—wrap up.

5687. **עָבֹת, 'âbôth,** *aw-both´*; or **עָבוֹת, 'âbôwth,** *aw-both´*; from 5686; *intwined*, i.e. *dense*:—thick.

5688. **עֲבֹת, 'ăbôth,** *ab-oth´*; or **עֲבוֹת, 'ăbôwth,** *ab-oth´*; or (feminine) **עֲבֹתָה, 'ăbôthâh,** *ab-oth-aw´*; the same as 5687; something *intwined*, i.e. a *string, wreath* or *foliage*:—band, cord, rope, thick bough (branch), wreathen (chain).

5689. **עָגַב, 'âgab,** *aw-gab´*; a primitive root; to *breathe* after, i.e. to *love* (sensually):—dote, lover.

A verb meaning to lust after. The word occurs in Eze 23 six times where it refers to the desire of Jerusalem and Samaria for foreign ways under the figure of two sisters who lust after foreigners. Ezekiel warned that, just as Assyria, the object of Samaria's lust, had destroyed them, so sensual Babylon would destroy Jerusalem. The word also occurs as a participle in Jer 4:30 and means lovers. Again, the word is used figuratively in a warning that Jerusalem's foreign lovers would despise and destroy them.

5690. **עֲגָבִים, 'âgâbîym,** *ag-aw-beem´*; from 5689; *love* (concrete), i.e. *amative* words:—much love, very lovely.

5691. **עֲגָבָה, 'ăgâbâh,** *ag-aw-baw´*; from 5689; *love* (abstract), i.e. *amorousness*:—inordinate love.

5692. **עֻגָה, 'ugâh,** *oo-gaw´*; from 5746; an *ashcake* (as *round*):—cake (upon the hearth).

5693. **עָגוּר, 'âgûwr,** *aw-goor´*; passive participle [but with active sense] of an unused root meaning to *twitter*; probably the *swallow*:—swallow.

5694. **עָגִיל, 'âgîyl,** *aw-gheel´*; from the same as 5696; something *round*, i.e. a *ring* (for the ears):—earring.

5695. **עֵגֶל, 'êgel,** *ay´-ghel*; from the same as 5696; a (male) *calf* (as *frisking* round), especially one nearly grown (i.e. a *steer*):—bullock, calf.

5696. **עָגֹל, 'âgôl,** *aw-gole´*; or **עָגוֹל, 'âgôwl,** *aw-gole´*; from an unused root meaning to *revolve, circular*:—round.

5697. **עֶגְלָה, 'eglâh,** *eg-law´*; feminine of 5695; a (female) *calf*, especially one nearly grown (i.e. a *heifer*):—calf, cow, heifer.

5698. **עֶגְלָה, 'Eglâh,** *eg-law´*; the same as 5697; *Eglah*, a wife of David:—Eglah.

5699. **עֲגָלָה, 'ăgâlâh,** *ag-aw-law´*; from the same as 5696; something *revolving*, i.e. a wheeled *vehicle*:—cart, chariot, wagon.

5700. **עֶגְלוֹן, 'Eglôwn,** *eg-lawn´*; from 5695; *vituline; Eglon*, the name of a place in Palestine and of a Moabitish king:—Eglon.

5701. **עָגַם, 'âgam,** *aw-gam´*; a primitive root; to *be sad*:—grieve.

5702. **עָגַן, 'âgan,** *aw-gan´*; a primitive root; to *debar*, i.e. from marriage:—stay.

5703. **עַד, 'ad,** *ad*; from 5710; properly a (peremptory) *terminus*, i.e. (by implication) *duration*, in the sense of *advance* or *perpetuity* (substantially as a noun, either with or without a preposition):—eternity, ever (-lasting, -more), old, perpetually, + world without end.

A noun meaning eternity. The word signifies God's dwelling place (Isa 57:15). It also refers to the continuance of a king on the throne (Ex 15:18; 1Ch 28:9; Ps 132:12; Pr 29:14). The word can indicate continual joy (Ps 61:8[9]; Isa 65:18); or continual anger (Mic 7:18; Am 1:11). The word's references to mountains that would be shattered (Hab 3:6); the sun and the moon (Ps 148:6) may show that the word sometimes means less than eternity or only an apparent eternity. The word occurs with the word *'ôwlâm* (5769) (Ps 10:16; 45:6[7]; Da 12:3) and sometimes with the word *netsach* (5331) (Ps 9:18[19]; Am 1:11).

5704. עַד, ʻad, *ad*; properly the same as 5703 (used as a preposition, adverb or conjunction; especially with a preposition); *as far* (or *long*, or *much*) *as*, whether of space (*even unto*) or time (*during, while, until*) or degree (*equally with*):—against, and, as, at, before, by (that), even (to), for (-asmuch as), [hither-] to, + how long, into, as long (much) as, (so) that, till, toward, until, when, while, (+ as) yet.

5705. עַד, ʻad, *ad*; (Chaldee); corresponding to 5704:— × and, at, for, [hither-] to, on, till (un-) to, until, within.

5706. עַד, ʻad, *ad*; the same as 5703 in the sense of the *aim* of an attack; *booty*:—prey.

5707. עֵד, ʻêd, *ayd*; from 5749 contraction; (concrete) *a witness*; (abstract) *testimony*; (specifically) a *recorder*, i.e. *prince*:—witness.

5708. עֵד, ʻêd, *ayd*; from an unused root meaning to *set* a period [compare 5710, 5749]; the *menstrual* flux (as periodical); by implication (in plural) *soiling*:—filthy.

5709. עֲדָה, ʻădâh, *ad-aw´*; (Chaldee); corresponding to 5710:—alter, depart, pass (away), remove, take (away).

5710. עָדָה, ʻâdâh, *aw-daw´*; a primitive root; to *advance*, i.e. *pass* on or *continue*; (causative) to *remove*; (specifically) to *bedeck* (i.e. bring an ornament upon):—adorn, deck (self), pass by, take away.

5711. עָדָה, ʻÂdâh, *aw-daw´*; from 5710; *ornament; Adah*, the name of two women:—Adah.

5712. עֵדָה, ʻêdâh, *ay-daw´*; feminine of 5707 in the original sense of *fixture*; a stated *assemblage* (specifically, a *concourse*; or generically, a *family* or *crowd*):—assembly, company, congregation, multitude, people, swarm. Compare 5713.

A feminine noun meaning a congregation, an assembly, a band, an entourage, a pack. The word is modified to indicate various kinds of groups or communities. It is used to describe a congregation of heavenly or human beings; an assembly of divine beings over which God presides (Ps 82:1); a gathering of nations (Ps 7:7[8]); a community of the righteous (Ps 1:5); a group of evildoers (Nu 26:9; Ps 22:16[17]); ruthless people (Ps 86:14). It describes an entire circle of families and friends (Job 16:7).

Most often the word refers to Israel as a group in many settings. It describes all Israel gathered before Solomon (1Ki 8:5; 12:20); or as a total community in general (Hos 7:12); it refers to the community of Israel at the Exodus in phrases like the congregation of the Lord (Nu 27:17; 31:16; Jos 22:16); the community of Israel (Ex 12:3, 6; Nu 16:9); or the community of the sons of Israel (Ex 16:1, 2; 17:1). At times leaders in Israel were described as the leaders or elders of the congregation (Ex 16:22; Le 4:15; Nu 4:34).

The word is used to describe a swarm of bees (Jgs 14:8); and figuratively describes the people in Ps 68:30[31] as bulls, evidently supporters of foreign nations.

5713. עֵדָה, ʻêdâh, *ay-daw´*; feminine of 5707 in its technical sense; *testimony*:—testimony, witness. Compare 5712.

A feminine noun meaning a testimony, a witness. Derived from a word that denotes permanence, this term refers to the act of testifying to a fact or an event. For example, by accepting Abraham's gift of ewe lambs, Abimelech acknowledged the truth of Abraham's statement about the ownership of the well at Beersheba (Ge 21:30). Likewise, a heap of stones became a witness to the boundary agreement reached between Jacob and Laban (Ge 31:52). Within the context of a covenant renewal ceremony, Joshua placed a single large stone to function as a witness of the covenant established between the Lord and His people (Jos 24:27).

5714. עִדּוֹ, ʻIddôw, *id-do´*; or **עִדּוֹא, ʻIddôw,** *id-do´*; from 5710; *timely; Iddo* (or *Iddi*), the name of five Israelites:—Iddo. Compare 3035, 3260.

5715. עֵדוּת, ʻêdûwth, *ay-dooth´*; feminine of 5707; *testimony*:—testimony, witness.

A feminine noun meaning testimony, precept, warning sign. It is always used in connection with the testimony of God and most frequently in association with the tabernacle (Ex 38:21; Nu 1:50, 53). The stone tablets containing the Ten Commandments are identified as God's testimony (Ex 25:16; 31:18; 32:15). Because the Ten Commandments represent the covenant that God made with Israel (see Ex 34:27, 28), they are also called the "tables of the covenant" (see Dt 9:9; 11:15); and they were preeminent in the tabernacle. As a result, the tabernacle is sometimes called the tabernacle of the testimony (Ex 38:21; Nu 1:50, 53); and the ark is sometimes called the ark of the testimony (Ex 25:22; 26:33, 34; 30:6, 26). This term is also used alone to represent the ark (Ex 16:34; 27:21; 30:36; Le 16:13). In time, this term came to stand for the laws or precepts that God had delivered to humanity (Ps 19:7[8]; 119:88; 122:4).

5716. עֲדִי, ʻădîy, *ad-ee´*; from 5710 in the sense of *trappings*; *finery*; (generically) an *outfit*; (specifically) a *headstall*:— × excellent, mouth, ornament.

5717. עֲדִיאֵל, ʻĂdîyʼêl, *ad-ee-ale´*; from 5716 and 410; *ornament of God; Adiël*, the name of three Israelites:—Adiel.

5718. עֲדָיָה, ʻĂdâyâh, *ad-aw-yaw´*; or **עֲדָיָהוּ, ʻĂdâ-yâhûw,** *ad-aw-yaw´-hoo*; from 5710 and 3050; *Jah has adorned; Adajah*, the name of eight Israelites:—Adaiah.

5719. עָדִין, ʻâdîyn, *aw-deen´*; from 5727; *voluptuous*:—given to pleasures.

5720. עָדִין, ʻÂdîyn, *aw-deen´*; the same as 5719; *Adin*, the name of two Israelites:—Adin.

5721. עֲדִינָא, ʻĂdîynâʼ, *ad-ee-naw´*; from 5719; *effeminacy; Adina*, an Israelite:—Adina.

5722. עֲדִינוֹ, ʻădîynôw, *ad-ee-no´*; probably from 5719 in the original sense of *slender* (i.e. a *spear*); *his spear*:—Adino.

5723. עֲדִיתַיִם, ʻĂdîythayim, *ad-ee-thah´-yim*; dual of a feminine of 5706; *double prey; Adithajim*, a place in Palestine:—Adithaim.

5724. עַדְלַי, ʻAdlay, *ad-lah´ee*; probably from an unused root of uncertain meaning; *Adlai*, an Israelite:—Adlai.

5725. עֲדֻלָּם, ʻĂdullâm, *ad-ool-lawm´*; probably from the passive participle of the same as 5724; *Adullam*, a place in Palestine:—Adullam.

5726. עֲדֻלָּמִי, ʻĂdullâmîy, *ad-ool-law-mee´*; patrial from 5725; an *Adullamite* or native of Adullam:—Adullamite.

5727. עָדַן, ʻâdan, *aw-dan´*; a primitive root; to be *soft* or *pleasant*; (figurative and reflexive) to *live voluptuously*:—delight self.

5728. עֲדֶן, ʻăden, *ad-en´*; or **עֲדֶנָּה, ʻădennâh,** *ad-en´-naw*; from 5704 and 2004; *till now*:—yet.

5729. עֶדֶן, ʻEden, *eh´-den*; from 5727; *pleasure; Eden*, a place in Mesopotamia:—Eden.

5730. עֵדֶן, ʻêden, *ay´-den*; or (feminine) **עֶדְנָה, ʻednâh,** *ed-naw´*; from 5727; *pleasure*:—delicate, delight, pleasure. See also 1040.

5731. עֵדֶן, ʻÊden, *ay´-den*; the same as 5730 (masculine); *Eden*, the region of Adam's home:—Eden.

5732. עִדָּן, ʻiddân, *id-dawn´*; (Chaldee); from a root corresponding to that of 5708; a set *time*; (technical) a *year*:—time.

5733. עַדְנָא, ʻAdnâʼ, *ad-naw´*; from 5727; *pleasure; Adna*, the name of two Israelites:—Adna.

5734. עַדְנָה, ʻAdnâh, *ad-naw´*; from 5727; *pleasure; Adnah*, the name of two Israelites:—Adnah.

5735. עֲדְעָדָה, ʻAdʻâdâh, *ad-aw-daw´*; from 5712; *festival; Adadah*, a place in Palestine:—Adadah.

5736. עָדַף, ʻâdaph, *aw-daf´*; a primitive root; to *be* (causative, *have*) *redundant*:—be more, odd number, be (have) over (and above), overplus, remain.

5737. עָדַר**, ʻâdar,** *aw-dar´*; a primitive root; to *arrange*, as a battle, a vineyard (to *hoe*); hence to *muster*, and so to *miss* (or find *wanting*):—dig, fail, keep (rank), lack.

5738. עֶדֶר**, ʻEder,** *eh´-der*; from 5737; an *arrangement* (i.e. drove); *Eder*, an Israelite:—Ader.

5739. עֵדֶר**, ʻêder,** *ay´-der*; from 5737; an *arrangement*, i.e. *muster* (of animals):—drove, flock, herd.

5740. עֵדֶר**, ʻÊder,** *ay´-der*; the same as 5739; *Eder*, the name of an Israelite and of two places in Palestine:—Edar, Eder.

5741. עַדְרִיאֵל**, ʻAdrîyʼêl,** *ad-ree-ale´*; from 5739 and 410; *flock of God; Adriel*, an Israelite:—Adriel.

5742. עֲדָשָׁה**, ʻădâshâh,** *ah-daw-shaw´*; from an unused root of uncertain meaning; a *lentil*:—lentile.

5743. עוּב**, ʻûwb,** *oob*; a primitive root; to be *dense* or *dark*, i.e. to *becloud*:—cover with a cloud.

5744. עוֹבֵד**, ʻÔwbêd,** *o-bade´*; active participle of 5647; *serving; Obed*, the name of five Israelites:—Obed.

5745. עוֹבָל**, ʻÔwbâl,** *o-bawl´*; of foreign derivation; *Obal*, a son of Joktan:—Obal.

5746. עוּג**, ʻûwg,** *oog*; a primitive root; (properly) to *gyrate*; but used only as denominative from 5692, to *bake* (round cakes on the hearth):—bake.

5747. עוֹג**, ʻÔwg,** *ogue*; probably from 5746; *round; Og*, a king of Bashan:—Og.

5748. עוּגָב**, ʻûwgâb,** *oo-gawb´*; or עֻגָּב**, ʻuggâb,** *oog-gawb´*; from 5689 in the original sense of *breathing*; a *reed*-instrument of music:—organ.

5749. עוּד**, ʻûwd,** *ood*; a primitive root; to *duplicate* or *repeat*; (by implication) to *protest, testify* (as by reiteration); (intensive) to *encompass, restore* (as a sort of reduplication):—admonish, charge, earnestly, lift up, protest, call (take) to record, relieve, rob, solemnly, stand upright, testify, give warning, (bear, call to, give, take to) witness.

A verb meaning to bear witness, to testify. Specifically, it can signify either to serve as a witness or to testify against someone, albeit falsely (1Ki 21:10, 13); or in favour of someone (Job 29:11). It can also mean either to admonish someone (Ge 43:3; Ne 9:26, 30); or to warn solemnly (Ge 43:3; Ex 19:21; Dt 32:46; 1Sa 8:9; 1Ki 2:42; 2Ch 24:19; Ne 9:29; 13:15, 21; Jer 42:19; Am 3:13). Such warnings frequently came from the Lord (2Ki 17:13, 15; Jer 11:7); but they were also mediated through His prophets (2Ch 24:19; Jer 42:19). In the causative form, it can mean to call to witness, to take as a witness (Dt 4:26; Isa 8:2); or to obtain witnesses, that is, authentication (Jer 32:10, 25, 44).

5750. עוֹד**, ʻôwd,** *ode*; or עֹד**, ʻôd,** *ode*; from 5749; (properly) *iteration* or *continuance*; used only adverb (with or without preposition), *again, repeatedly, still, more*:—again, × all life long, at all, besides, but, else, further (-more), henceforth, (any) longer, (any) more (-over), × once, since, (be) still, when, (good, the) while (having being), (as, because, whether, while) yet (within).

5751. עוֹד**, ʻôwd,** *ode*; (Chaldee); corresponding to 5750:—while.

5752. עוֹדֵד**, ʻÔwdêd,** *o-dade´*; or עֹדֵד**, ʻÔdêd,** *o-dade´*; from 5749; *reiteration; Oded*, the name of two Israelites:—Oded.

5753. עָוָה**, ʻâvâh,** *aw-vaw´*; a primitive root; to *crook*, literal or figurative (as follows):—do amiss, bow down, make crooked, commit iniquity, pervert, (do) perverse (-ly), trouble, × turn, do wickedly, do wrong.

A verb meaning to bend, to twist. In its various uses, the word means to do wrong, to commit iniquity (Est 1:16; Da 9:5); or to be physically or emotionally distressed (Isa 21:3). It is used with reference to a person with a disturbed mind (Pr 12:8). In the intensive form, it can mean to distort something, such as the face of the earth (Isa 24:1); or the path that one walks (La 3:9). In its causative form, it refers to perverting right behaviour (Job 33:27; Jer 3:21); or simply doing that which is wrong (2Sa 7:14; 19:19[20]; Jer 9:5[4]); referring to behaviour acknowledged as wrong by the psalmist (Ps 106:6); by David (2Sa 24:17); and by Solomon (1Ki 8:47; 2Ch 6:37).

5754. עַוָּה**, ʻavvâh,** *av-vaw´*; intensive from 5753 abbreviation; *overthrow*:— × overturn.

5755. עִוָּה**, ʻIvvâh,** *iv-vaw´*; or עַוָּא**, ʻAvvâʼ,** *av-vaw´*; (2Ki 17:24), for 5754; *Ivvah* or *Avva*, a region of Assyria:—Ava, Ivah.

5756. עוּז**, ʻûwz,** *ooz*; a primitive root; to *be strong*; (causative) to *strengthen*, i.e. (figurative) to *save* (by flight):—gather (self, self to flee), retire.

5757. עַוִּי**, ʻAvviy,** *av-vee´*; patrial from 5755; an *Avvite* or native of Avvah (only plural):—Avims, Avites.

5758. עִוְיָה**, ʻăvâyâh,** *ah-vaw-yaw´*; (Chaldee); from a root corresponding to 5753; *perverseness*:—iniquity.

An Aramaic feminine noun meaning offence, iniquity. Related to a Hebrew word whose root meaning is iniquity or guilt, this Aramaic term is found only once in the OT, in Daniel's interpretation of one of King Nebuchadnezzar's dreams (Da 4:27[24]). In his interpretation, Daniel warned the king that unless he repented of his sins and iniquities and began to act righteously and show mercy, judgment would fall on him.

5759. עֲוִיל**, ʻăvîyl,** *av-eel´*; from 5764; a *babe*:—young child, little one.

5760. עֲוִיל**, ʻăvîyl,** *av-eel´*; from 5765; *perverse* (moral):—ungodly.

A masculine noun meaning an unjust one, an evil one. Derived from a verb meaning to act wrongfully, this term appears once in the OT, where it has the sense of ungodly or evil people (Job 16:11). Job used the term to describe Bildad, Zophar, and Eliphaz, his accusers, whom he sarcastically referred to as his friends (cf. Job 16:20).

5761. עַוִּים**, ʻAvviym,** *av-veem´*; plural of 5757; *Avvim* (as inhabited by Avvites), a place in Palestine (with the article prefixed):—Avim.

5762. עֲוִית**, ʻĂvîyth,** *av-veeth´*; or [perhaps עַיּוֹת**, ʻAyyôwth,** *ah-yoth´*, as if plural of 5857] עַיּוּת**, ʻAyûwth,** *ah-yooth´*; from 5753; *ruin; Avvith* (or *Avvoth*), a place in Palestine:—Avith.

5763. עוּל**, ʻûwl,** *ool*; a primitive root; to *suckle*, i.e. *give milk*:—milch, (ewe great) with young.

5764. עוּל**, ʻûwl,** *ool*; from 5763; a *babe*:—sucking child, infant.

5765. עָוַל**, ʻâval,** *aw-val´*; a primitive root; to *distort* (moral):—deal unjustly, unrighteous.

A verb meaning to act wrongfully, to act unjustly, to deviate from the moral standard. The word is derived from the noun meaning injustice or iniquity. It occurs in Isa 26:10, where the prophet bemoaned the fact that despite God's showing grace to the wicked, they continued to act wrongfully. The verb occurs as a substantive participle where the psalmist prayed for deliverance from the clutches of the unrighteous (Ps 71:4). See the noun *ʻâwel* (5766).

5766. עֶוֶל**, ʻevel,** *eh´-vel*; or עָוֶל**, ʻâvel,** *aw´-vel*; and (feminine) עַוְלָה**, ʻavlâh,** *av-law´*; or עוֹלָה**, ʻôwlâh,** *o-law´*; or עֹלָה**, ʻôlâh,** *o-law´*; from 5765; (moral) *evil*:—iniquity, perverseness, unjust (-ly), unrighteousness (-ly), wicked (-ness).

A masculine singular noun meaning injustice, unrighteousness. The word refers to anything that deviates from the right way of doing things. It is often the direct object of *ʻâśâh* (6213), meaning to do (Le 19:15; Dt 25:16; Ps 7:3[4]; Eze 3:20; 33:13); and is in direct contrast to words like righteous (Pr 29:27); upright (Ps 107:42); and justice (Dt 32:4). God has no part with injustice (Dt 32:4; 2Ch 19:7; Job 34:10; Jer 2:5). See the verb *ʻâwal* (5765).

5767. עַוָּל**, ʻavvâl,** *av-vawl´*; intensive from 5765; *evil* (moral):—unjust, unrighteous, wicked.

A masculine singular noun meaning an unjust person, an unrighteous person. This word occurs five times in the Hebrew Bible with four of them occurring in the Book of Job. Job said that an *ʻawwâl* deserved God's punishment (Job 31:3). But he countered the implications of his friends by stating adamantly that he was not such a person (Job 29:17). Likewise, Zephaniah argued that God is righteous and not an *ʻawwâl*, contrary to the corrupted leaders of Jerusalem (Zep 3:5).

5768. עוֹלֵל, **ʻôwlêl,** *o-lale´*; or עֹלָל, **ʻôlâl,** *o-lawl´*; from 5763; a *suckling*:—babe, (young) child, infant, little one.

5769. עוֹלָם, **ʻôwlâm,** *o-lawm´*; or עֹלָם, **ʻôlâm,** *o-lawm´*; from 5956; (properly) *concealed*, i.e. the *vanishing* point; (generally) time *out of mind* (past or future), i.e. (practical) *eternity*; frequent adverb (especially with prepositional prefix) *always*:—alway (-s), ancient (time), any more, continuance, eternal, (for, [n-]) ever (-lasting, -more, of old), lasting, long (time), (of) old (time), perpetual, at any time, (beginning of the) world (+ without end). Compare 5331, 5703.

A masculine noun meaning a very long time. The word usually refers to looking forward but many times expresses the idea of looking backward. It may cover a given person's lifetime (Ex 21:6; 1Sa 1:22); a period of many generations (Jos 24:2; Pr 22:28); the time of the present created order (Dt 33:15; Ps 73:12); time beyond this temporal sphere, especially when used regarding God (Ge 21:33; Ps 90:2; Da 12:2, 7). The term also applies to many things associated with God, such as His decrees, His covenants, and the Messiah (Ge 9:16; Ex 12:14; Mic 5:2[1]). This word describes the span of time in which God is to be obeyed and praised (1Ch 16:36; Ps 89:1[2]; 119:112). In the age to come, there will be no need for sun or moon, for God Himself will be the everlasting light (Isa 60:19, 20; cf. Rev 22:5).

5770. עָוַן, **ʻâvan,** *aw-van´*; denominative from 5869; to *watch* (with jealousy):—eye.

5771. עָוֹן, **ʻâvôwn,** *aw-vone´*; or עָווֹן, **ʻâvôwn,** *aw-vone´*; (2Ki 7:9; Ps 51:5 [77]), from 5753; *perversity*, i.e. (moral) *evil*:—fault, iniquity, mischief, punishment (of iniquity), sin.

A masculine noun meaning iniquity, evil, guilt, punishment. This is one of the four main words indicating sin in the OT. This word indicates sin that is particularly evil, since it strongly conveys the idea of twisting or perverting deliberately. The noun carries along with it the idea of guilt from conscious wrongdoing (Ge 44:16; Jer 2:22). The punishment that goes with this deliberate act as a consequence is indicated by the word also (Ge 4:13; Isa 53:11).

The Hebrew word means sin or transgression in a conscious sense, as when David kept (consciously) from transgression or sin (2Sa 22:24); Israel by choice returned to the sins their ancestors had committed (Jer 11:10; 13:22).

This word for sin can also indicate the guilt that results from the act of sin: Moses prayed that the Lord would forgive the guilt and sin of rebellious Israel (Nu 14:19); the guilt of the Amorites was not yet full in the time of Abraham (Ge 15:16); God would remove the guilt of His people when they returned from exile (Jer 50:20); the guilt of the fathers was a recurring phrase in the OT (Ex 20:5; 34:7).

The word also indicates in some contexts the punishment that results from sin and guilt; Cain's punishment was unbearable for him (Ge 4:13; Jer 51:6). Edom was condemned for not helping Israel in the time of Israel's punishment (Eze 35:5); and the Levites had to bear their punishment because they strayed from following the Lord (Ps 31:10[11]; Eze 44:10, 12).

5772. עוֹנָה, **ʻôwnâh,** *o-naw´*; from an unused root apparently meaning to *dwell* together; (sexual) *cohabitation*:—duty of marriage.

5773. עִוְעִים, **ʻivʻîym,** *iv-eem´*; from 5753; *perversity*:—× perverse.

5774. עוּף, **ʻûwph,** *oof*; a primitive root; to *cover* (with wings or obscurity); hence (as denominative from 5775) to *fly*; also (by implication of dimness) to *faint* (from the darkness of swooning):—brandish, be (wax) faint, flee away, fly (away), × set, shine forth, weary.

5775. עוֹף, **ʻôwph,** *ofe*; from 5774; a *bird* (as *covered* with feathers, or rather as *covering* with wings), often collective:—bird, that flieth, flying, fowl.

5776. עוֹף, **ʻôwph,** *ofe*; (Chaldee); corresponding to 5775:—fowl.

5777. עוֹפֶרֶת, **ʻôwphereth,** *o-feh´-reth*; or עֹפֶרֶת, **ʻôphereth,** *o-feh´-reth*; feminine participle active of 6080; *lead* (from its *dusty* colour):—lead.

5778. עֵיפַי, **ʻÊyphay,** *ay-fah´-ee*; from 5775; *birdlike; Ephai*, an Israelite:—Ephai [*from margin*].

5779. עוּץ, **ʻûwts,** *oots*; a primitive root; to *consult*:—take advice ([counsel] together).

5780. עוּץ, **ʻÛwts,** *oots*; apparently from 5779; *consultation; Uts*, a son of Aram, also a Seirite, and the regions settled by them:—Uz.

5781. עוּק, **ʻûwq,** *ook*; a primitive root; to *pack*:—be pressed.

5782. עוּר, **ʻûwr,** *oor*; a primitive root [rather identical with 5783 through the idea of *opening* the eyes]; to *wake* (literal or figurative):—(a-) wake (-n, up), lift up (self), × master, raise (up), stir up (self).

5783. עוּר, **ʻûwr,** *oor*; a primitive root; to (*be*) *bare*:—be made naked.

5784. עוּר, **ʻûwr,** *oor*; (Chaldee); *chaff* (as the *naked* husk):—chaff.

5785. עוֹר, **ʻôwr,** *ore*; from 5783; *skin* (as *naked*); (by implication) *hide, leather*:—hide, leather, skin.

A masculine singular noun meaning skin. It is used literally of human skin, such as Moses' shining face (Ex 34:29); or in connection with regulations regarding leprosy or skin diseases (Le 13:2). It is employed figuratively in the expression, skin of my teeth (Job 19:20). It can also denote skins of animals, typically already skinned (with the exception of Job 41:7[40:31]). Skins were used for the garments that God made for Adam and Eve (Ge 3:21); and for coverings of items like the tabernacle (Ex 25:5); and the ark (Nu 4:6).

5786. עָוַר, **ʻâvar,** *aw-var´*; a primitive root [rather denominative from 5785 through the idea of a *film* over the eyes]; to *blind*:—blind, put out. See also 5895.

5787. עִוֵּר, **ʻivvêr,** *iv-vare´*; intensive from 5786; *blind* (literal or figurative):—blind (men, people).

5788. עִוָּרוֹן, **ʻivvârôwn,** *iv-vaw-rone´*; and (feminine) עַוֶּרֶת, **ʻavvereth,** *av-veh´-reth*; from 5787; *blindness*:—blind (-ness).

5789. עוּשׁ, **ʻûwsh,** *oosh*; a primitive root; to *hasten*:—assemble self.

A verb which occurs once in the Hebrew Bible (Joel 3:11[4:11]). Recent translations have abandoned the former translation, to lend aid, to come to help, for a different Arabic cognate, meaning to hurry. Joel used the word with the verb to come to summon all the nations to prepare for battle in the Valley of Jehoshaphat. At that location, God will judge them, trampling them like grapes in a winepress.

5790. עוּת, **ʻûwth,** *ooth*; for 5789; to *hasten*, i.e. *succor*:—speak in season.

A verb which occurs once in the Hebrew Bible (Isa 50:4). It is traditionally translated to help but the meaning is uncertain. In this context, Isaiah proclaimed that the Lord gave him a tongue to help the weary.

5791. עָוַת, **ʻâvath,** *aw-vath´*; a primitive root; to *wrest*:—bow self, (make) crooked, falsifying, overthrow, deal perversely, pervert, subvert, turn upside down.

A verb meaning to be bent, to be crooked. It is always used in the intensive stems with the meaning to bend, to subvert, or to pervert. Except for Ecc 12:3, where it refers to the strong men bending themselves (that is, bowing down), it is used figuratively of bending or perverting justice and righteousness. Bildad and Elihu told Job that

God does not pervert justice (Job 8:3; 34:12); but Job thought God had been crooked with him (Job 19:6).

5792. עַוָּתָה, ʻavvâthâh, *av-vaw-thaw´*; from 5791; *oppression*:—wrong.

A feminine singular noun meaning a subversion, a perversion. It is used only in La 3:59 where the poet declared that God had seen the perversion of justice done to Jerusalem (that is, its destruction). This passage is interesting because the writer saw God's judgment as severe. See the verb *ʻâwath* (5791).

5793. עוּתַי, ʻÛwthay, *oo-thah´-ee*; from 5790; *succoring; Uthai*, the name of two Israelites:—Uthai.

5794. עַז, ʻaz, *az*; from 5810; *strong, vehement, harsh*:—fierce, + greedy, mighty, power, roughly, strong.

5795. עֵז, ʻêz, *aze*; from 5810; a she-*goat* (as *strong*), but masculine in plural (which also is used elliptically for *goats' hair*):—(she) goat, kid.

5796. עֵז, ʻêz, *aze*; (Chaldee); corresponding to 5795:—goat.

5797. עֹז, ʻôz, *oze*; or (fully) עוֹז, **ʻôwz,** *oze*; from 5810; *strength* in various applications (*force, security, majesty, praise*):—boldness, loud, might, power, strength, strong.

5798. עֻזָּא, ʻUzzâʼ, *ooz-zaw´*; or עֻזָּה, **ʻUzzâh,** *ooz-zaw´*; feminine of 5797; *strength; Uzza* or *Uzzah*, the name of five Israelites:—Uzza, Uzzah.

5799. עֲזָאזֵל, ʻăzâʼzêl, *az-aw-zale´*; from 5795 and 235; *goat of departure*; the *scapegoat*:—scapegoat.

5800. עָזַב, ʻâzab, *aw-zab´*; a primitive root; to *loosen*, i.e. *relinquish, permit*, etc.:—commit self, fail, forsake, fortify, help, leave (destitute, off), refuse, × surely.

A verb derived from two separate roots. The more common in the Hebrew Bible is *ʻâzab* I, meaning to leave, to abandon, to forsake, to loose. It can be used to designate going away to a new locale (2Ki 8:6); or to separate oneself from another person (Ge 44:22; Ru 1:16). When Zipporah's father found her without Moses, he asked, "Why did you leave him?" (Ex 2:20). A man is to leave his parents to marry (Ge 2:24). To leave in the hand of is an idiomatic expression meaning to entrust (Ge 39:6). The word can also carry a much more negative connotation. Israelites abandoned their towns after the army fled (1Sa 31:7); the ultimate sign of defeat (and often God's judgment) were abandoned cities (Isa 17:9; Jer 4:29; Zep 2:4). The Israelites often were warned and accused of forsaking God by sacrificing to other gods (Dt 28:20; Jgs 10:10; Jer 1:16). The prophets called on them to forsake idols and sin instead (Isa 55:7; Eze 20:8; 23:8). While the psalmist said that God would not abandon his soul (Ps 16:10), God does on occasion abandon humans because of their sin (Dt 31:17; Eze 8:12). But despite the psalmist's cry which Jesus quoted from the cross (Ps 22:1[2]), most Biblical writers took heart because God would not abandon them (Ezr 9:9; Isa 42:16).The word *ʻâzab* can also mean to restore or repair. It occurs only in Ne 3:8 in reference to the walls of Jerusalem.

5801. עִזָּבוֹן, ʻizzâbôwn, *iz-zaw-bone´*; from 5800 in the sense of *letting go* (for a price, i.e. *selling*); *trade*, i.e. the place (*mart*) or the payment (*revenue*):—fair, ware.

5802. עַזְבּוּק, ʻAzbûwq, *az-book´*; from 5794 and the root of 950; *stern depopulator; Azbuk*, an Israelite:—Azbuk.

5803. עַזְגָּד, ʻAzgâd, *az-gawd´*; from 5794 and 1409; *stern troop; Azgad*, an Israelite:—Azgad.

5804. עַזָּה, ʻAzzâh, *az-zaw´*; feminine of 5794; *strong; Azzah*, a place in Palestine:—Azzah, Gaza.

5805. עֲזוּבָה, ʻăzûwbâh, *az-oo-baw´*; feminine passive participle of 5800; *desertion* (of inhabitants):—forsaking.

5806. עֲזוּבָה, ʻĂzûwbâh, *az-oo-baw´*; the same as 5805; *Azubah*, the name of two Israelitesses:—Azubah.

5807. עֱזוּז, ʻĕzûwz, *ez-ooz´*; from 5810; *forcibleness*:—might, strength.

5808. עִזּוּז, ʻizzûwz, *iz-zooz´*; from 5810; *forcible*; (collective and concrete) an *army*:—power, strong.

5809. עַזּוּר, ʻAzzûwr, *az-zoor´*; or עַזֻּר, **ʻAzzur,** *az-zoor´*; from 5826; *helpful; Azzur*, the name of three Israelites:—Azur, Azzur.

5810. עָזַז, ʻâzaz, *aw-zaz´*; a primitive root; to *be stout* (literal or figurative):—harden, impudent, prevail, strengthen (self), be strong.

5811. עָזָז, ʻÂzâz, *aw-zawz´*; from 5810; *strong; Azaz*, an Israelite:—Azaz.

5812. עֲזַזְיָהוּ, ʻĂzazyâhûw, *az-az-yaw´-hoo*; from 5810 and 3050; *Jah has strengthened; Azazjah*, the name of three Israelites:—Azaziah.

5813. עֻזִּי, ʻUzzîy, *ooz-zee´*; from 5810; *forceful; Uzzi*, the name of six Israelites:—Uzzi.

5814. עֻזִּיָּה, ʻUzzîyyâh, *ooz-zee-yaw´*; or עֻזִּיָּא, **ʻUzîyyâʼ,** *oo-zee-yaw´*; perhaps for 5818; *Uzzija*, an Israelite:—Uzzia.

5815. עֲזִיאֵל, ʻĂzîyʼêl, *az-ee-ale´*; from 5756 and 410; *strengthened of God; Aziël*, an Israelite:—Aziel. Compare 3268.

5816. עֻזִּיאֵל, ʻUzzîyʼêl, *ooz-zee-ale´*; from 5797 and 410; *strength of God; Uzziël*, the name of six Israelites:—Uzziel.

5817. עָזִּיאֵלִי, ʻOzzîyʼêlîy, *oz-zee-ay-lee´*; patronymic from 5816; an *Uzziëlite* (collective) or descendants of Uzziel:—Uzzielites.

5818. עֻזִּיָּה, ʻUzzîyyâh, *ooz-zee-yaw´*; or עֻזִּיָּהוּ, **ʻUz-zîyyâhûw,** *ooz-zee-yaw´-hoo*; from 5797 and 3050; *strength of Jah; Uzzijah*, the name of five Israelites:—Uzziah.

5819. עֲזִיזָא, ʻĂzîyzâʼ, *az-ee-zaw´*; from 5756; *strengthfulness; Aziza*, an Israelite:—Aziza.

5820. עַזְמָוֶת, ʻAzmâveth, *az-maw´-veth*; from 5794 and 4194; *strong* one *of death; Azmaveth*, the name of three Israelites and of a place in Palestine:—Azmaveth. See also 1041.

5821. עַזָּן, ʻAzzân, *az-zawn´*; from 5794; *strong* one; *Azzan*, an Israelite:—Azzan.

5822. עָזְנִיָּה, ʻoznîyyâh, *oz-nee-yaw´*; probably feminine of 5797; probably the *sea-eagle* (from its *strength*):—ospray.

5823. עָזַק, ʻâzaq, *aw-zak´*; a primitive root; to *grub* over:—fence about.

5824. עִזְקָא, ʻizqâʼ, *iz-kaw´*; (Chaldee); from a root corresponding to 5823; a *signet*-ring (as engraved):—signet.

5825. עֲזֵקָה, ʻĂzêqâh, *az-ay-kaw´*; from 5823; *tilled; Azekah*, a place in Palestine:—Azekah.

5826. עָזַר, ʻâzar, *aw-zar´*; a primitive root; to *surround*, i.e. *protect* or *aid*:—help, succour.

5827. עֶזֶר, ʻEzer, *eh´-zer*; from 5826; *help; Ezer*, the name of two Israelites:—Ezer. Compare 5829.

5828. עֵזֶר, ʻêzer, *ay´-zer*; from 5826; *aid*:—help.

5829. עֵזֶר, ʻÊzer, *ay´-zer*; the same as 5828; *Ezer*, the name of four Israelites:—Ezer. Compare 5827.

5830. עֶזְרָא, ʻEzrâʼ, *ez-raw´*; a variation of 5833; *Ezra*, an Israelite:—Ezra.

5831. עֶזְרָא, ʻEzrâʼ, *ez-raw´*; (Chaldee); corresponding to 5830; *Ezra*, an Israelite:—Ezra.

5832. עֲזַרְאֵל, ʻĂzarʼêl, *az-ar-ale´*; from 5826 and 410; *God has helped; Azarel*, the name of five Israelites:—Azarael, Azareel.

5833. עֶזְרָה, ʻezrâh, *ez-raw´*; or עֶזְרָת, **ʻezrâth,** *ez-rawth´*; (Ps 60:11 [13]; 108:12 [133]), feminine of 5828; *aid*:—help (-ed, -er).

5834. עֶזְרָה, ʻEzrâh, *ez-raw´*; the same as 5833; *Ezrah*, an Israelite:—Ezrah.

5835. עֲזָרָה, **'ăzârâh,** *az-aw-raw´*; from 5826 in its original meaning of *surrounding*; an *inclosure*; also a *border*:—court, settle.

5836. עֶזְרִי, **'Ezrîy,** *ez-ree´*; from 5828; *helpful; Ezri*, an Israelite:—Ezri.

5837. עַזְרִיאֵל, **'Azrîy'êl,** *az-ree-ale´*; from 5828 and 410; *help of God; Azriël*, the name of three Israelites:—Azriel.

5838. עֲזַרְיָה, **'Ăzaryâh,** *az-ar-yaw´*; or עֲזַרְיָהוּ, **'Ăzar-yâhûw,** *az-ar-yaw´-hoo*; from 5826 and 3050; *Jah has helped; Azarjah*, the name of nineteen Israelites:—Azariah.

5839. עֲזַרְיָה, **'Ăzaryâh,** *az-ar-yaw´*; (Chaldee); corresponding to 5838; *Azarjah*, one of Daniel's companions:—Azariah.

5840. עַזְרִיקָם, **'Azrîyqâm,** *az-ree-kawm´*; from 5828 and active participle of 6965; *help of an enemy; Azrikam*, the name of four Israelites:—Azrikam.

5841. עַזָּתִי, **'Azzâthîy,** *az-zaw-thee´*; patrial from 5804; an *Azzathite* or inhabitant of Azzah:—Gazathite, Gazite.

5842. עֵט, **'êṭ,** *ate*; from 5860 (contraction) in the sense of *swooping*, i.e. *side-long stroke*; a *stylus* or marking stick:—pen.

5843. עֵטָה, **'êṭâh,** *ay-taw´*; (Chaldee); from 3272; *prudence*:—counsel.

5844. עָטָה, **'âṭâh,** *aw-taw´*; a primitive root; to *wrap*, i.e. *cover, veil, clothe* or *roll*:—array self, be clad, (put a) cover (-ing, self), fill, put on, × surely, turn aside.

5845. עֲטִין, **'ăṭîyn,** *at-een´*; from an unused root meaning apparently to *contain*; a *receptacle* (for milk, i.e. *pail*; [figurative] *breast*):—breast.

5846. עֲטִישָׁה, **'ăṭîyshâh,** *at-ee-shaw´*; from an unused root meaning to *sneeze; sneezing*:—sneezing.

5847. עֲטַלֵּף, **'ăṭallêph,** *at-al-lafe´*; of uncertain derivation; a *bat*:—bat.

5848. עָטַף, **'âṭaph,** *aw-taf´*; a primitive root; to *shroud*, i.e. *clothe* (whether transitive or reflexive); hence (from the idea of *darkness*) to *languish*:—cover (over), fail, faint, feebler, hide self, be overwhelmed, swoon.

5849. עָטַר, **'âṭar,** *aw-tar´*; a primitive root; to *encircle* (for attack or protection); especially to *crown* (literal or figurative):—compass, crown.

5850. עֲטָרָה, **'ăṭârâh,** *at-aw-raw´*; from 5849; a *crown*:—crown.

5851. עֲטָרָה, **'Ăṭârâh,** *at-aw-raw´*; the same as 5850; *Atarah*, an Israelitess:—Atarah.

5852. עֲטָרוֹת, **'Ăṭârôwth,** *at-aw-rōth´*; or עֲטָרֹת, **'Ăṭârôth,** *at-aw-rōth´*; plural of 5850; *Ataroth*, the name (thus simply) of two places in Palestine:—Ataroth.

5853. עַטְרוֹת אַדָּר, **'Aṭrôwth 'Addâr,** *at-rōth´ ad-dawr´*; from the same as 5852 and 146; *crowns of Addar; Atroth-Addar*, a place in Palestine:—Ataroth-adar (-addar).

5854. עַטְרוֹת בֵּית יוֹאָב, **'Aṭrôth bêyth Yôw'âb,** *at-rōth´ bayth yo-awb´*; from the same as 5852 and 1004 and 3097; *crowns of the house of Joäb; Atroth-beth-Joäb*, a place in Palestine:—Ataroth the house of Joab.

5855. עַטְרוֹת שׁוֹפָן, **'Aṭrôwth Shôwphân,** *at-rōth´ sho-fawn´*; from the same as 5852 and a name otherwise unused [being from the same as 8226] meaning *hidden; crowns of Shophan; Atroth-Shophan*, a place in Palestine:—Atroth, Shophan [*as if two places*].

5856. עִי, **'îy,** *ee*; from 5753; a *ruin* (as if overturned):—heap.

5857. עַי, **'Ay,** *ah´ee*; or (feminine) עַיָּא, **'Ayyâ',** *ah-yaw´*; (Ne 11:31), or עַיָּת, **'Ayyâth,** *ah-yawth´*; (Isa 10:28), for 5856; *Ai, Aja* or *Ajath*, a place in Palestine:—Ai, Aija, Aijath, Hai.

5858. עֵיבָל, **'Êybâl,** *ay-bawl´*; perhaps from an unused root probably meaning to be *bald; bare; Ebal*, a mountain of Palestine:—Ebal.

5859. עִיּוֹן, **'Iyyôwn,** *ee-yone´*; from 5856; *ruin; Ijon*, a place in Palestine:—Ijon.

5860. עִיט, **'îyṭ,** *eet*; a primitive root; to *swoop* down upon (literal or figurative):—fly, rail.

5861. עַיִט, **'ayiṭ,** *ah´-yit*; from 5860; a *hawk* or other bird of prey:—bird, fowl, ravenous (bird).

5862. עֵיטָם, **'Êyṭâm,** *ay-tawm´*; from 5861; *hawk-ground; Etam*, a place in Palestine:—Etam.

5863. עִיֵּי הָעֲבָרִים, **'Îyyêy hâ'Ăbârîym,** *ee-yay´ haw-ab-aw-reem´*; from the plural of 5856 and the plural of the active participle of 5674 with the article interposed; *ruins of the passers; Ije-ha-Abarim*, a place near Palestine:—Ije-abarim.

5864. עִיִּים, **'Îyyîym,** *ee-yeem´*; plural of 5856; *ruins; Ijim*, a place in the Desert:—Iim.

5865. עֵילוֹם, **'êylôwm,** *ay-lome´*; for 5769:—ever.

5866. עִילַי, **'Îylay,** *ee-lah´ee*; from 5927; *elevated; Ilai*, an Israelite:—Ilai.

5867. עֵילָם, **'Êylâm,** *ay-lawm´*; or עוֹלָם, **'Ôwlâm,** *o-lawm´*; (Ezr 10:2; Jer 49:36), probably from 5956; *hidden*, i.e. *distant; Elam*, a son of Shem, and his descendant, with their country; also of six Israelites:—Elam.

5868. עֲיָם, **'ăyâm,** *ah-yawm´*; of doubtful origin and authenticity; probably meaning *strength*:—mighty.

5869. עַיִן, **'ayin,** *ah´-yin*; probably a primitive word; an *eye* (literal or figurative); (by analogy) a *fountain* (as the *eye* of the landscape):—affliction, outward appearance, + before, + think best, colour, conceit, + be content, countenance, + displease, eye ([brow], [-d], -sight), face, + favour, fountain, furrow [*from the margin*], × him, + humble, knowledge, look, (+ well), × me, open (-ly), + (not) please, presence, + regard, resemblance, sight, × thee, × them, + think, × us, well, × you (-rselves).

A feminine noun meaning an eye, a spring, a fountain. This Hebrew word is used to refer to either an aperture or a source. It is used to signify the physical organ of sight (Pr 20:12); the providential oversight of the Lord (Ps 33:18); and a water well (Ge 16:7; Ex 15:27). By extension, it refers to being in the presence of another (Jer 32:12); the visible surface of the earth (Nu 22:5); the human face (1Ki 20:38; 2Ki 9:30); and the general appearance of something (1Sa 16:7; Eze 1:4). In a figurative sense, the eye was seen as the avenue of temptation (Job 31:7); the scope of personal judgment or opinion (Jgs 17:6); and the source of self-assessment (Pr 26:5).

5870. עַיִן, **'ayin,** *ah´-yin*; (Chaldee); corresponding to 5869; an *eye*:—eye.

5871. עַיִן, **'Ayin,** *ah´-yin*; the same as 5869; *fountain; Ajin*, the name (thus simply) of two places in Palestine:—Ain.

5872. עֵין גֶּדִי, **'Êyn Gedîy,** *ane geh´-dee*; from 5869 and 1423; *fountain of a kid; En-Gedi*, a place in Palestine:—En-gedi.

5873. עֵין גַּנִּים, **'Êyn Gannîym,** *ane gan-neem´*; from 5869 and the plural of 1588; *fountain of gardens; En-Gannim*, a place in Palestine:—En-gannim.

5874. עֵין־דֹּאר, **'Êyn-D'ôr,** *ane-dore´*; or עֵין דּוֹר, **'Êyn Dôwr,** *ane dore*; or עֵין־דֹּר, **'Êyn-Dôr,** *ane-dore´*; from 5869 and 1755; *fountain of dwelling; En-Dor*, a place in Palestine:—En-dor.

5875. עֵין הַקּוֹרֵא, **'Êyn haqQôwrê',** *ane hak-ko-ray´*; from 5869 and the active participle of 7121; *fountain of One calling; En-hak-Korè*, a place near Palestine:—En-hakhore.

5876. עֵין חַדָּה, **'Êyn Chaddâh,** *ane khad-daw´*; from 5869 and the feminine of a derivative from 2300; *fountain of sharpness; En-Chaddah*, a place in Palestine:—En-haddah.

5877. עֵין חָצוֹר, **'Êyn Châtsôwr,** *ane khaw-tsore´*; from 5869 and the same as 2674; *fountain of a village; En-Chatsor*, a place in Palestine:—En-hazor.

5878. עֵין חֲרֹד, **'Êyn Chărôd,** *ane khar-ode´*; from 5869 and a derivative of 2729; *fountain of trembling; En-Charod*, a place in Palestine:—well of Harod.

5879. עֵינַיִם, **'Êynayim,** *ay-nah´-yim*; or עֵינָם, **'Êynâm,** *ay-nawm´*; dual of 5869 *double fountain; Enajim* or *Enam*, a place in Palestine:—Enaim, openly (Ge 38:21).

5880. עֵין מִשְׁפָּט, **'Êyn Mishpâṭ,** *ayn mish-pawt´*; from 5869 and 4941; *fountain of judgment; En-Mishpat*, a place near Palestine:—En-mishpat.

5881. עֵינָן, **'Êynân,** *ay-nawn´*; from 5869; *having eyes; Enan*, an Israelite:—Enan. Compare 2704.

5882. עֵין עֶגְלַיִם, **'Êyn 'Eglayim,** *ayn eg-lah´-yim*; from 5869 and the dual of 5695; *fountain of two calves; En-Eglajim*, a place in Palestine:—En-eglaim.

5883. עֵין רֹגֵל, **'Êyn Rôgêl,** *ayn ro-gale´*; from 5869 and the active participle of 7270; *fountain of a traveller; En-Rogel*, a place near Jerusalem:—En-rogel.

5884. עֵין רִמּוֹן, **'Êyn Rimmôwn,** *ayn rim-mone´*; from 5869 and 7416; *fountain of a pomegranate; En-Rimmon*, a place in Palestine:—En-rimmon.

5885. עֵין שֶׁמֶשׁ, **'Êyn Shemesh,** *ayn sheh´-mesh*; from 5869 and 8121; *fountain of* the *sun; En-Shemesh*, a place in Palestine:—En-shemesh.

5886. עֵין הַתַּנִּים, **'Êyn hattannîym,** *ayn hat-tan-neem´*; from 5869 and the plural of 8565; *fountain of jackals; En-Tannim*, a pool near Jerusalem:—dragon well.

5887. עֵין תַּפּוּחַ, **'Êyn Tappûwach,** *ayn tap-poo´-akh*; from 5869 and 8598; *fountain of an apple*-tree; *En-Tappuäch*, a place in Palestine:—En-tappuah.

5888. עָיֵף, **'âyêph,** *aw-yafe´*; a primitive root; to *languish*:—be wearied.

5889. עָיֵף, **'âyêph,** *aw-yafe´*; from 5888; *languid*:—faint, thirsty, weary.

5890. עֵיפָה, **'êyphâh,** *ay-faw´*; feminine from 5774; *obscurity* (as if from *covering*):—darkness.

A feminine noun meaning darkness. This word appears only twice in the OT in Job 10:22 and Am 4:13. In both instances, the word implies the darkness of night as opposed to the light of day. In Job, the word is used in parallel to the word *'ôphel* (652), meaning spiritual gloom or despair.

5891. עֵיפָה, **'Êyphâh,** *ay-faw´*; the same as 5890; *Ephah*, the name of a son of Midian, and of the region settled by him; also of an Israelite and of an Israelitess:—Ephah.

5892. עִיר, **'îyr,** *eer*; or (in the plural) עָר, **'âr,** *awr*; or עָיַר, **'âyar,** *aw-yar´*; (Jgs 10:4), from 5782 a *city* (a place guarded by *waking* or a watch) in the widest sense (even of a mere *encampment* or *post*):—Ai [*from margin*], city, court [*from margin*], town.

5893. עִיר, **'Îyr,** *eer*; the same as 5892; *Ir*, an Israelite:—Ir.

5894. עִיר, **'îyr,** *eer*; (Chaldee); from a root corresponding to 5782; a *watcher*, i.e. an *angel* (as guardian):—watcher.

5895. עַיִר, **'ayir,** *ah´-yeer*; from 5782 in the sense of *raising* (i.e. *bearing* a burden); (properly) a young *ass* (as just broken to a load); hence an ass-*colt*:—(ass) colt, foal, young ass.

5896. עִירָא, **'Îyrâ',** *ee-raw´*; from 5782; *wakefulness; Ira*, the name of three Israelites:—Ira.

5897. עִירָד, **'Îyrâd,** *ee-rawd´*; from the same as 6166; *fugitive; Irad*, an antediluvian:—Irad.

5898. עִיר הַמֶּלַח, **'Îyr hamMelach,** *eer ham-meh´-lakh*; from 5892 and 4417 with the article of substance interpretation; *city of* (*the*) *salt; Ir-ham-Melach*, a place near Palestine:—the city of salt.

5899. עִיר הַתְּמָרִים, **'Îyr hatTᵉmârîym,** *err hat-tem-aw-reem´*; from 5892 and the plural of 8558 with the article interposed; *city of the palmtrees; Ir-hat-Temarim*, a place in Palestine:—the city of palmtrees.

5900. עִירוּ, **'Îyrûw,** *ee-roo´*; from 5892; a *citizen; Iru*, an Israelite:—Iru.

5901. עִירִי, **'Îyrîy,** *ee-ree´*; from 5892; *urbane; Iri*, an Israelite:—Iri.

5902. עִירָם, **'Îyrâm,** *ee-rawm´*; from 5892; *city-wise; Iram*, an Idumæan:—Iram.

5903. עֵירֹם, **'êyrôm,** *ay-rome´*; or עֵרֹם, **'êrôm,** *ay-rome´*; from 6191; *nudity*:—naked (-ness).

5904. עִיר נָחָשׁ, **'Îyr Nâchâsh,** *eer naw-khawsh´*; from 5892 and 5175; *city of a serpent; Ir-Nachash*, a place in Palestine:—Ir-nahash.

5905. עִיר שֶׁמֶשׁ, **'Îyr Shemesh,** *err sheh´-mesh*; from 5892 and 8121; *city of* the *sun; Ir-Shemesh*, a place in Palestine:—Ir-shemesh.

5906. עַיִשׁ, **'Ayish,** *ah´-yish*; or עָשׁ, **'Âsh,** *awsh*; from 5789; the constellation of the Great *Bear* (perhaps from its *migration* through the heavens):—Arcturus.

5907. עַכְבּוֹר, **'Akbôwr,** *ak-bore´*; probably for 5909; *Akbor*, the name of an Idumæan and two Israelites:—Achbor.

5908. עַכָּבִישׁ, **'akkâbîysh,** *ak-kaw-beesh´*; probably from an unused root in the literal sense of *entangling*; a *spider* (as *weaving* a network):—spider.

5909. עַכְבָּר, **'akbâr,** *ak-bawr´*; probably from the same as 5908 in the secondary sense of *attacking*; a *mouse* (as *nibbling*):—mouse.

5910. עַכּוֹ, **'Akkôw,** *ak-ko´*; apparently from an unused root meaning to *hem* in; *Akko* (from its situation on a *bay*):—Accho.

5911. עָכוֹר, **'Âkôwr,** *aw-kore´*; from 5916; *troubled; Akor*, the name of a place in Palestine:—Achor.

5912. עָכָן, **'Âkân,** *aw-kawn´*; from an unused root meaning to *trouble; troublesome; Akan*, an Israelite:—Achan. Compare 5917.

5913. עָכַס, **'âkas,** *aw-kas´*; a primitive root; (properly) to *tie*, specifically with fetters; but used only as denominative from 5914; to *put on anklets*:—make a tinkling ornament.

5914. עֶכֶס, **'ekes,** *eh´-kes*; from 5913; a *fetter*; hence an *anklet*:—stocks, tinkling ornament.

5915. עַכְסָה, **'Aksâh,** *ak-saw´*; feminine of 5914; *anklet; Aksah*, an Israelitess:—Achsah.

5916. עָכַר, **'âkar,** *aw-kar´*; a primitive root; (properly) to *roil* water; (figurative) to *disturb* or *afflict*:—trouble, stir.

5917. עָכָר, **'Âkâr,** *aw-kawr´*; from 5916; *troublesome; Akar*, an Israelite:—Achar. Compare 5912.

5918. עָכְרָן, **'Okrân,** *ok-rawn´*; from 5916; *muddler; Okran*, an Israelite:—Ocran.

5919. עַכְשׁוּב, **'akshûwb,** *ak-shoob´*; probably from an unused root meaning to *coil*; an *asp* (from lurking *coiled* up):—adder.

5920. עַל**, 'al,** *al*; from 5927; (properly) the *top*; (specifically) the *Highest* (i.e. *God*); also (adverb) *aloft, to Jehovah*:—above, high, most High.

5921. עַל**, 'al,** *al*; properly the same as 5920 used as a preposition (in the singular or plural, often with prefix, or as conjunction with a particle following); *above, over, upon,* or *against* (yet always in this last relation with a downward aspect) in a great variety of applications (as follow):—above, according to (-ly), after, (as) against, among, and, × as, at, because of, beside (the rest of), between, beyond the time, × both and, by (reason of), × had the charge of, concerning for, in (that), (forth, out) of, (from) (off), (up-) on, over, than, through (-out), to touching, × with.

5922. עַל**, 'al,** *al*; (Chaldee); corresponding to 5921:—about, against, concerning, for, [there-] fore, from, in, × more, of, (there-, up-) on, (in-) to, + why, with.

5923. עֹל**, 'ôl,** *ole*; or עוֹל**, 'ôwl,** *ole*; from 5953; a *yoke* (as *imposed* on the neck), literal or figurative:—yoke.

5924. עֵלָּא**, 'êllâ',** *ale-law´*; (Chaldee); from 5922; *above*:—over.

5925. עֻלָּא**, 'Ullâ',** *ool-law´*; feminine of 5923; *burden; Ulla*, an Israelite:—Ulla.

5926. עִלֵּג**, 'illêg,** *il-layg´*; from an unused root meaning to *stutter; stuttering*:—stammerer.

5927. עָלָה**, 'âlâh,** *aw-law´*; a primitive root; to *ascend*, intransitive (*be high*) or active (*mount*); used in a great variety of senses, primary and secondary, literal and figurative (as follow):—arise (up), (cause to) ascend up, at once, break [*the day*] (up), bring (up), (cause to) burn, carry up, cast up, + shew, climb (up), (cause to, make to) come (up), cut off, dawn, depart, exalt, excel, fall, fetch up, get up, (make to) go (away, up), grow (over), increase, lay, leap, levy, lift (self) up, light, [make] up, × mention, mount up, offer, make to pay, + perfect, prefer, put (on), raise, recover, restore, (make to) rise (up), scale, set (up), shoot forth (up), (begin to) spring (up), stir up, take away (up), work.

A verb meaning to go up, to ascend, to take away, to lift, to offer. This Hebrew word carries with it the connotation of an upward motion. It is used generically to denote an ascension to a higher place (Nu 13:17); a departure in a northerly direction (Ge 45:25); the flight of a bird (Isa 40:31); the springing up of plants (Isa 34:13); the preference of one thing above another (Ps 137:6); and the offering of a sacrifice (Jgs 6:28; 2Ki 3:20). Theologically significant is the fact that this verb is used in relationship to a person's appearance before God. One must go up to stand before the Lord (Ex 34:24; see also Ge 35:1).

5928. עֲלָה**, 'ălâh,** *al-aw´*; (Chaldee); corresponding to 5930; a *holocaust*:—burnt offering.

An Aramaic feminine noun meaning a burnt offering, a holocaust. This word parallels the Hebrew word *'ôlâh* (5930). It is used only by Ezra in reference to the daily burnt sacrifices required under the Law (Ezr 6:9).

5929. עָלֶה**, 'âleh,** *aw-leh´*; from 5927; a *leaf* (as *coming up* on a tree); (collective) *foliage*:—branch, leaf.

5930. עֹלָה**, 'ôlâh,** *o-law´*; or עוֹלָה**, 'ôwlâh,** *o-law´*; feminine active participle of 5927; a *step* or (collective) *stairs*, as *ascending*; usually a *holocaust* (as *going up* in smoke):—ascent, burnt offering (sacrifice), go up to. See also 5766.

A feminine noun meaning a whole burnt offering, that which goes up. The primary discussion of this offering is found in Le 1; 6:9[2], 10[3], 12[5]). The noun is a feminine participial form of the verb meaning to go up, to ascend. The offering was voluntary. The Israelites understood the animal or fowl that was being sacrificed as a gift to God and thus ascending to God as smoke from the altar (Le 1:9), hence its name. The sacrifice was a pleasing odor acceptable to the Lord (Le 1:9). Those presenting the animal laid hands on the sacrifice—possibly to indicate ownership or to indicate that the animal was a substitute for themselves (Le 1:4). The blood of the sacrifice was sprinkled against the altar (Le 1:6). The offering and its ritual properly carried out atoned for the offerers, and they became acceptable before the Lord.

The total burning of the sacrifice indicates the total consecration of the presenter to the Lord. The animals that could be offered were bulls, sheep, rams, or male birds (Le 1:3, 10, 14). The ashes of the offering remained on the altar overnight. The priest removed them and deposited them in an approved location (Le 6:9[2], 10[3]).

The burnt offerings were presented often in conjunction with the peace and grain offerings (Jos 8:31; Jgs 6:26; 1Ki 3:4; 8:64). The burnt offerings, along with other offerings, were employed in the various feasts, festivals, and celebrations recorded in the prophetic books. Often, however, the burnt offerings were condemned as useless because the Israelites didn't have their hearts right before God (Jer 6:20; 7:21). Ezekiel foresaw renewed burnt offerings in a new Temple (Eze 40:38, 39). When Israel returned from exile, burnt offerings, along with others, were once again presented to the Lord (Ezr 3:2; 8:35). David's observation was correct and to the point, for he noted that whole burnt offerings did not satisfy or delight the Lord. Only an offering of a broken spirit and humble heart could do that (Ps 51:16[18]). Only then could acceptable sacrifices be given to the Lord (Ps 51:19[21]; 66:13).

5931. עִלָּה**, 'illâh,** *il-law´*; (Chaldee); feminine from a root corresponding to 5927; a *pretext* (as *arising* artificially):—occasion.

5932. עַלְוָה**, 'alvâh,** *al-vaw´*; for 5766; moral *perverseness*:—iniquity.

A feminine noun meaning injustice, unrighteousness, iniquity. Hos 10:9 is the sole occurrence of this word in the Bible. It is used to denote the supreme wickedness and depravity of Israel. The prophet relates the current situation to an episode at Gibeah during the time of the judges (cf. Jgs 19:1—20:28).

5933. עַלְוָה**, 'Alvâh,** *al-vaw´*; or עַלְיָה**, 'Alyâh,** *al-yaw´*; the same as 5932; *Alvah* or *Aljah*, an Idumæan:—Aliah, Alvah.

5934. עֲלוּמִים**, 'ălûwmîym,** *aw-loom-eem´*; passive participle of 5956 in the denominative sense of 5958; (only in plural as abstract) *adolescence*; (figurative) *vigour*:—youth.

5935. עַלְוָן**, 'Alvân,** *al-vawn´*; or עַלְיָן**, 'Alyân,** *al-yawn´*; from 5927; *lofty; Alvan* or *Aljan*, an Idumæan:—Alian, Alvan.

5936. עֲלוּקָה**, 'ălûwqâh,** *al-oo-kaw´*; feminine passive participle of an unused root meaning to *suck*; the *leech*:—horse-leech.

5937. עָלַז**, 'âlaz,** *aw-laz´*; a primitive root; to *jump* for joy, i.e. *exult*:—be joyful, rejoice, triumph.

5938. עָלֵז**, 'âlêz,** *aw-laze´*; from 5937; *exultant*:—that rejoiceth.

5939. עֲלָטָה**, 'ălâṭâh,** *al-aw-taw´*; feminine from an unused root meaning to *cover; dusk*:—dark, twilight.

5940. עֱלִי**, 'ĕlîy,** *el-ee´*; from 5927; a *pestle* (as *lifted*):—pestle.

5941. עֵלִי**, 'Êlîy,** *ay-lee´*; from 5927; *lofty; Eli*, an Israelite high-priest:—Eli.

5942. עִלִּי**, 'illîy,** *il-lee´*; from 5927; *high*, i.e. compare:—upper.

5943. עִלַּי**, 'illay,** *il-lah´ee*; (Chaldee); corresponding to 5942; *supreme* (i.e. *God*):—(most) high.

An Aramaic masculine adjective meaning highest. This adjective always refers to God and shows the supremacy of God over humanity and other gods. It can occur as an adjective to modify *'ĕlâh* (426), meaning God. Nebuchadnezzar used this term of God to indicate His supremacy in general (Da 4:2 [3:32]). Daniel also used this term of God (Da 5:18, 21) to reveal the difference between God and Belshazzar, who had lifted up [himself] against the Lord of heaven (see Da 5:23). This term can also occur as a noun to represent God, especially in His role as the supreme Ruler of the kingdoms of humanity (Da 4:17[14], 24[21], 25[22], 32[29], 34[31]).

5944. עֲלִיָּה**, 'ălîyyâh,** *al-ee-yaw´*; feminine from 5927; something *lofty*, i.e. a *stair-way*; also a *second-story* room (or even one on the roof); (figurative) the *sky*:—ascent, (upper) chamber, going up, loft, parlour.

5945. עֶלְיוֹן, **'elyôwn,** *el-yone´*; from 5927; an *elevation*, i.e. (adjective) *lofty* (comparative); as title, the *Supreme*:—(Most, on) high (-er, -est), upper (-most).

A masculine noun meaning Most High, the Highest. The word serves as an epithet for God and is used thirty-one times in the OT. The most celebrated use of this word is in Genesis 14:18—20: Melchizedek was priest of God Most High (*'êl 'elyôwn*), so the term in context defines the God whom he served. But in this same passage, Abraham equated the God Most High with the Lord his God, the Creator of heaven and earth (Ge 14:20). In Nu 24:16, this epithet stands in parallel to the epithet God and Shaddai; it depicts the God who gave Balaam his knowledge and visions. The term also stands in parallel with other names of God, such as the LORD (Dt 32:8; 2Sa 22:14; Ps 18:13[14]); and God (Ps 46:4[5]; 50:14).

5946. עֶלְיוֹן, **'elyôwn,** *el-yone´*; (Chaldee); corresponding to 5945; the *Supreme*:—Most high.

An Aramaic masculine adjective meaning Most High God. This term always appears in the plural of majesty, comparable to the Hebrew word *'ĕlôhiym* (430). Furthermore, it always occurs in the construct with *qaddiysh* (6922), meaning the holy ones or saints of the Most High God, and in the context of Daniel's interpretation of Nebuchadnezzar's dream of the four beasts, where four kingdoms were represented (Da 7:18, 22, 25, 27).

5947. עַלִּיז, **'allîyz,** *al-leez´*; from 5937; *exultant*:—joyous, (that) rejoice (-ing).

5948. עֲלִיל, **'ălîyl,** *al-eel´*; from 5953 in the sense of *completing*; probably a *crucible* (as *working* over the metal):—furnace.

5949. עֲלִילָה, **'ălîylâh,** *al-ee-law´*; or עֲלִלָה, **'ălilâh,** *al-ee-law´*; from 5953 in the sense of *effecting*; an *exploit* (of God), or a *performance* (of man, often in a bad sense); (by implication) an *opportunity*:—act (-ion), deed, doing, invention, occasion, work.

5950. עֲלִילִיָּה, **'ălîylîyyâh,** *al-ee-lee-yaw´*; for 5949; (miraculous) *execution*:—work.

5951. עֲלִיצוּת, **'ălîytsûwth,** *al-ee-tsooth´*; from 5970; *exultation*:—rejoicing.

5952. עִלִּי, **'illîy,** *il-lee´*; from 5927; a *second-story* room:—chamber. Compare 5944.

5953. עָלַל, **'âlal,** *aw-lal´*; a primitive root; to *effect* thoroughly; specifically to *glean* (also figurative); by implication (in a bad sense) to *overdo*, i.e. maltreat, be saucy to, pain, impose (also literal):—abuse, affect, × child, defile, do, glean, mock, practise, thoroughly, work (wonderfully).

5954. עֲלַל, **'ălal,** *al-al´*; (Chaldee); corresponding to 5953 (in the sense of *thrusting* oneself in), to *enter*; (causative) to *introduce*:—bring in, come in, go in.

5955. עֹלֵלוֹת, **'ôlêlôwth,** *o-lay-loth´*; feminine active participle of 5953; only in plural *gleanings*; (by extension) *gleaning-time*:—(gleaning) (of the) grapes, grapegleanings.

5956. עָלַם, **'âlam,** *aw-lam´*; a primitive root; to *veil* from sight, i.e. *conceal* (literal or figurative):— × any ways, blind, dissembler, hide (self), secret (thing).

5957. עָלַם, **'âlam,** *aw-lam´*; (Chaldee); corresponding to 5769; *remote* time, i.e. the *future* or *past* indefinitely; often adverbial *forever*:—for ([n-]) ever (lasting), old.

An Aramaic masculine noun meaning perpetuity, antiquity. This word is related to the Hebrew word *'ôwlâm* (5769). It can mean a perpetual period in the future (Da 4:3[3:33]; 7:27); or a period of distant antiquity (Ezr 4:15, 19). It can also represent a period of time with no limits, either past or present (Da 4:34[31]). It can stand alone (Da 4:3[3:33]) or with the following prepositions, where it acts more like an adverb: *min* (4481) (Da 2:20); and *'ad* (5705) (Da 2:20; 7:18).

5958. עֶלֶם, **'elem,** *eh´-lem*; from 5956; (properly) something *kept out of sight* [compare 5959], i.e. a *lad*:—young man, stripling.

A masculine noun meaning a young man. Its feminine counterpart is found in the word *'almâh* (5959). The focus of this term is probably sexual maturity. It connotes an individual who has gone through puberty and is therefore sexually mature. Thus, *'elem* is the picture of an individual who has crossed (or is crossing) the threshold from boyhood or girlhood to manhood or womanhood, and, as such, is of marriageable age. Saul applied this term to David after he killed Goliath (1Sa 17:56); and Jonathan used it to refer to his armourbearer (1Sa 20:22).

5959. עַלְמָה, **'almâh,** *al-maw´*; feminine of 5958; a *lass* (as *veiled* or private):—damsel, maid, virgin.

A feminine noun meaning a maiden, a young woman, a girl, and a virgin. The word describes young women in different categories: Rebekah was understood to be a marriageable young woman by Abraham's servant (Ge 24:43); as was the maiden described in Pr 30:19, for in this case, the man was wooing her as a possible wife. Moses' sister was probably in this category (Ex 2:8). Sometimes it is unclear how old or mature these young maidens were (Ps 68:25[26]). The most famous passage where this term is used is Isa 7:14, where it asserts an *'almâh* will give birth to a son. The author of Matthew 1:23 understood this woman to be a virgin.

5960. עַלְמוֹן, **'Almôwn,** *al-mone´*; from 5956; *hidden; Almon*, a place in Palestine:—Almon. See also 5963.

5961. עֲלָמוֹת, **'Ălâmôwth,** *al-aw-mōth´*; plural of 5959; (properly) *girls*, i.e. the *soprano* or female voice, perhaps *falsetto*:—Alamoth.

5962. עֵלְמָי, **'Êlmây,** *ayl-maw´ee*; (Chaldee); patrial from a name corresponding to 5867 contraction; an *Elamite* or inhabitant of Elam:—Elamite.

5963. עַלְמֹן דִּבְלָתָיְמָה, **'Almôn Diblâthây^{e}mâh,** *al-mone´ dib-law-thaw´-yem-aw*; from the same as 5960 and the dual of 1690 [compare 1015] with enclitic of direction; *Almon toward Diblathajim; Almon-Diblathajemah*, a place in Moab:—Almon-dilathaim.

5964. עָלֶמֶת, **'Âlemeth,** *aw-leh´-meth*; from 5956; a *covering; Alemeth*, the name of a place in Palestine and of two Israelites:—Alameth, Alemeth.

5965. עָלַס, **'âlas,** *aw-las´*; a primitive root; to *leap* for joy, i.e. *exult, wave* joyously:— × peacock, rejoice, solace self.

5966. עָלַע, **'âla',** *aw-lah´*; a primitive root; to *sip* up:—suck up.

5967. עֲלַע, **'âla',** *al-ah´*; (Chaldee); corresponding to 6763; a *rib*:—rib.

5968. עָלַף, **'âlaph,** *aw-laf´*; a primitive root; to *veil* or *cover*; (figurative) to *be languid*:—faint, overlaid, wrap self.

5969. עֻלְפֶּה, **'ulpeh,** *ool-peh´*; from 5968; an *envelope*, i.e. (figurative) *mourning*:—fainted.

5970. עָלַץ, **'âlats,** *aw-lats´*; a primitive root; to *jump* for joy, i.e. *exult*:—be joyful, rejoice, triumph.

5971. עַם, **'am,** *am*; from 6004; a *people* (as a congregated *unit*); (specifically) a *tribe* (as those of Israel); hence (collective) *troops* or *attendants*; (figurative) a *flock*:—folk, men, nation, people.

A masculine noun meaning a people, peoples, people of the land, citizens. The word is used over nineteen hundred times to indicate groups of people that can be categorized in various ways. The largest group of people is the one comprising the whole earth (see Ge 11:1); it constituted one people (Ge 11:6); who shared a common language (Ge 11:6; Eze 3:5); a common location (see Ge 11:2); and a common purpose and goal (see Ge 11:4). However, the Lord scattered the group and brought about multiple languages, thereby producing many groups who would then develop into new peoples united around common languages, including common ancestors, religious beliefs, traditions, and ongoing blood relationships.

The word is used to describe various groups that developed. The people of the sons of Israel (Ex 1:9; Ezr 9:1), was a term referring to all Israel. The people of Judah were a subgroup of Israel (2Sa 19:40[41]), as was northern Israel (2Ki 9:6). The people of Israel as a whole could be described in religious or moral terms as a holy, special people (Dt 7:6; 14:2; Da 8:24); or the Lord's inheritance (Dt 4:20). Above all, they were to be the Lord's people (Jgs 5:11; 1Sa 2:24); and the people of God (2Sa 14:13). They were the Lord's own people because He had rescued them from slavery to Pharaoh and his gods (Ex 6:7). But the Lord Himself characterized His people as stiff-necked (Ex 32:9; 33:3; 34:9; Dt 9:13). To be a member of the Lord's people was to have the Lord as one's God (Ru 1:16); if God's people rejected the Lord, they ceased to be His people. Therefore, it is clear that God's presence and ownership of His people gave them their identity (Ex 33:13, 16; Hos 1:9; cf. Dt 32:21).

In the plural form, the word refers to many peoples or nations. Jerusalem, destroyed and lamenting, called for the people of the world to look on it and its guilt (La 1:18). Israel was chosen from among all the peoples of the earth (Ex 19:5, 7; Dt 14:2). The Lord is in control of all the plans of the nations and peoples (Ps 33:10). The word is used in parallel with *gôwyim* (1471). Isaac prayed for Jacob's offspring to become a community of peoples that would include the twelve tribes of Israel (Ge 28:3).

The word described people in general—that is, nonethnic or national groups. It refers to all the people as individuals in the world (Isa 42:5). When persons died, they were gathered to their people (Ge 25:8, 17). It also referred to people from a particular city (Ru 4:9; 2Ch 32:18); or people from a specific land (e.g., Canaan [Zep 1:11]). Centuries earlier, Pharaoh referred to the Hebrews living in Egypt under slavery as the people of the land (Ex 5:5). This phrase could refer to the population at large in Solomon's time and later (2Ki 11:14, 18; 15:5); or to the population of Canaan in Abraham's time (Ge 23:7).

The term also depicted foreign peoples and nations. The Moabites were the people of the god Chemosh (Nu 21:29). The word designated foreigners in general as strange or alien people (Ex 21:8); the people of Egypt were considered the people of Pharaoh (Ex 1:9, 22).

The word is even used to describe a gathering of ants (Pr 30:25); or rock badgers (Pr 30:26).

5972. עַם, **'am,** *am*; (Chaldee); corresponding to 5971:—people.

An Aramaic masculine noun meaning people. It was not used in reference to a disparate group of individuals or to a specific ethnic group. This is seen especially in its parallel usage with *'ûmmâh* (524), meaning nation, and *lishshân* (3961), meaning tongue (Da 3:4, 7, 29). The specific ethnic group being identified could be either the Israelites (Ezr 5:12; Da 7:27); or the Gentiles (Ezr 6:12; Da 2:44).

5973. עִם, **'im,** *eem*; from 6004; adverb or preposition, *with* (i.e. in *conjunction* with), in varied applications; (specifically) *equally with*; often with prepositional prefix (and then usually unrepresented in English):—accompanying, against, and, as (× long as), before, beside, by (reason of), for all, from (among, between), in, like, more than, of, (un-) to, with (-al).

5974. עִם, **'im,** *eem*; (Chaldee); corresponding to 5973:—by, from, like, to (-ward), with.

5975. עָמַד, **'âmad,** *aw-mad´*; a primitive root; to *stand*, in various relations (literal and figurative, intransitive and transitive):—abide (behind), appoint, arise, cease, confirm, continue, dwell, be employed, endure, establish, leave, make, ordain, be [over], place, (be) present (self), raise up, remain, repair, + serve, set (forth, over, -tle, up), (make to, make to be at a, with-) stand (by, fast, firm, still, up), (be at a) stay (up), tarry.

5976. עָמַד, **'âmad,** *aw-mad´*; for 4571; to *shake*:—be at a stand.

5977. עֹמֶד, **'ômed,** *o´-med*; from 5975; a *spot* (as being *fixed*):—place, (+ where) stood, upright.

5978. עִמָּד, **'immâd,** *im-mawd´*; prolonged for 5973; along *with*:—against, by, from, in, + me, + mine, of, + that I take, unto, upon, with (-in).

5979. עֶמְדָּה, **'emdâh,** *em-daw´*; from 5975; a *station*, i.e. domicile:—standing.

5980. עֻמָּה, **'ummâh,** *oom-maw´*; from 6004; *conjunction*, i.e. *society*; mostly adverb or preposition (with prepositional prefix), *near, beside, along with*:—(over) against, at, beside, hard by, in points.

5981. עֻמָּה, **'Ummâh,** *oom-maw´*; the same as 5980; *association; Ummah*, a place in Palestine:—Ummah.

5982. עַמּוּד, **'ammûwd,** *am-mood´*; or עַמֻּד, **'ammud,** *am-mood´*; from 5975; a *column* (as *standing*); also a *stand*, i.e. platform:—× apiece, pillar.

5983. עַמּוֹן, **'Ammôwn,** *am-mone´*; from 5971; *tribal*, i.e. *inbred; Ammon*, a son of Lot; also his posterity and their country:—Ammon, Ammonites.

5984. עַמּוֹנִי, **'Ammôwnîy,** *am-mo-nee´*; patronymic from 5983; an *Ammonite* or (adjective) *Ammoni-tish*:—Ammonite (-s).

5985. עַמּוֹנִית, **'Ammôwnîyth,** *am-mo-neeth´*; feminine of 5984; an *Ammonitess*:—Ammonite (-ss).

5986. עָמוֹס, **'Âmôws,** *aw-moce´*; from 6006; *burdensome; Amos*, an Israelite prophet:—Amos.

5987. עָמוֹק, **'Âmôwq,** *aw-moke´*; from 6009; *deep; Amok*, an Israelite:—Amok.

5988. עַמִּיאֵל, **'Ammîy'êl,** *am-mee-ale´*; from 5971 and 410; *people of God; Ammiël*, the name of three or four Israelites:—Ammiel.

5989. עַמִּיהוּד, **'Ammîyhûwd,** *am-mee-hood´*; from 5971 and 1935; *people of splendor; Ammihud*, the name of three Israelites:—Ammihud.

5990. עַמִּיזָבָד, **'Ammîyzâbâd,** *am-mee-zaw-bawd´*; from 5971 and 2064; *people of endowment; Ammi-zabad*, an Israelite:—Ammizabad.

5991. עַמִּיחוּר, **'Ammîychûwr,** *am-mee-khoor´*; from 5971 and 2353; *people of nobility; Ammichur*, a Syrian prince:—Ammihud [*from the margin*].

5992. עַמִּינָדָב, **'Ammîynâdâb,** *am-mee-naw-dawb´*; from 5971 and 5068; *people of liberality; Ammi-nadab*, the name of four Israelites:—Amminadab.

5993. עַמִּי נָדִיב, **'Ammîy Nâdîyb,** *am-mee´ naw-deeb´*; from 5971 and 5081; *my people* (is) *liberal; Ammi-Nadib*, probably an Israelite:—Amminadib.

5994. עֲמִיק, **'ămîyq,** *am-eek´*; (Chaldee); corresponding to 6012; *profound*, i.e. unsearchable:—deep.

5995. עָמִיר, **'âmîyr,** *aw-meer´*; from 6014; a *bunch* of grain:—handful, sheaf.

5996. עַמִּישַׁדַּי, **'Ammîyshadday,** *am-mee-shad-dah´ee*; from 5971 and 7706; *people of* (the) *Almighty; Ammishaddai*, an Israelite:—Ammishaddai.

5997. עָמִית, **'âmîyth,** *aw-meeth´*; from a primitive root meaning to *associate; companionship*; hence (concrete) a *comrade* or kindred man:—another, fellow, neighbour.

5998. עָמַל, **'âmal,** *aw-mal´*; a primitive root; to *toil*, i.e. *work severely* and with irksomeness:—[take] labour (in).

5999. עָמָל, **'âmâl,** *aw-mawl´*; from 5998; *toil*, i.e. *wearing effort*; hence *worry*, whether of body or mind:—grievance (-vousness), iniquity, labour, mischief, miserable (-sery), pain (-ful), perverseness, sorrow, toil, travail, trouble, wearisome, wickedness.

A masculine singular noun meaning trouble, labour, toil. This word can be used for the general difficulties and hardships of life, which can be seen by its use in conjunction with sorrow (Jer 20:18); affliction (Dt 26:7; Ps 25:18); and futility (Job 7:3). It can also refer to trouble or mischief directed at another person. The evil person talks of causing trouble (Pr 24:2); and God cannot look at the trouble caused by sin (Hab 1:3, 13). Its usage in Ecclesiastes and Ps 105:44 and 107:12 is best rendered labour. The Teacher in Ecclesiastes repeatedly asked what benefit toil was (Ecc 2:10, 11).

6000. עָמָל, 'Âmâl, *aw-mawl´*; the same as 5999; *Amal*, an Israelite:—Amal.

6001. עָמֵל, 'âmêl, *aw-male´*; from 5998; *toiling*; (concrete) a *labourer*; (figurative) *sorrowful*:—that laboureth, that is a misery, had taken [labour], wicked, workman.

A verbal adjective meaning toiling. This form is used exclusively in Ecclesiastes (Ecc 2:18, 22; 3:9; 4:8; 9:9) and always as a predicate adjective. The overall use of the word is to stress the meaninglessness of human efforts. Toiling under the sun appears to the writer to have no lasting value. One must leave the rewards to those who come afterward (Ecc 2:18). This working results in nothing more than pain and grief (Ecc 2:22). See the word *'âmâl* (5999).

6002. עֲמָלֵק, 'Ămâlêq, *am-aw-lake´*; probably of foreign origin; *Amalek*, a descendant of Esau; also his posterity and their country:—Amalek.

6003. עֲמָלֵקִי, 'Ămâlêqîy, *am-aw-lay-kee´*; patronymic from 6002; an *Amalekite* (collective, the *Amalekites*) or descendant of Amalek:—Amalekite (-s).

6004. עָמַם, 'âmam, *aw-mam´*; a primitive root; to *associate*; (by implication) to *overshadow* (by *huddling* together):—become dim, hide.

6005. עִמָּנוּאֵל, 'Immânûw'êl, *im-maw-noo-ale´*; from 5973 and 410 with suffix pronoun inserted; *with us* (is) *God; Immanuel*, a typical name of Isaiah's son:—Immanuel.

6006. עָמַס, 'âmas, *aw-mas´*; or עָמַשׂ, **'âmaś,** *aw-mas´*; a primitive root; to *load*, i.e. *impose* a burden; (figurative) *infliction*:—be borne, (heavy) burden (self), lade, load, put.

6007. עֲמַסְיָה, 'Ămasyâh, *am-as-yaw´*; from 6006 and 3050; *Jah has loaded; Amasjah*, an Israelite:—Amasiah.

6008. עַמְעָד, 'Am'âd, *am-awd´*; from 5971 and 5703; *people of time; Amad*, a place in Palestine:—Amad.

6009. עָמַק, 'âmaq, *aw-mak´*; a primitive root; to *be* (causative, *make*) *deep* (literal or figurative):—(be, have, make, seek) deep (-ly), depth, be profound.

6010. עֵמֶק, 'êmeq, *ay´-mek*; from 6009; a *vale* (i.e. broad *depression*):—dale, vale, valley [*often used as a part of proper names*]. See also 1025.

6011. עֹמֶק, 'ômeq, *o´-mek*; from 6009; *depth*:—depth.

6012. עָמֵק, 'âmêq, *aw-make´*; from 6009; *deep* (literal or figurative):—deeper, depth, strange.

An adjective meaning deep, unfathomable. Both times it is used to describe the speech of foreign peoples as unintelligible. Isaiah spoke of the return from Babylon, telling the people that they would no longer hear the unintelligible speech of foreigners (Isa 33:19). When God called Ezekiel, He told him that he was to speak to the house of Israel, not to people of unintelligible speech (Eze 3:5, 6).

6013. עָמֹק, 'âmôq, *aw-moke´*; from 6009; *deep* (literal or figurative):—(× exceeding) deep (thing).

6014. עָמַר, 'âmar, *aw-mar´*; a primitive root; (properly) apparently to *heap*; (figurative) to *chastise* (as if *piling* blows); specifically (as denominative from 6016) to *gather* grain:—bind sheaves, make merchandise of.

6015. עֲמַר, 'ămar, *am-ar´*; (Chaldee); corresponding to 6785; *wool*:—wool.

6016. עֹמֶר, 'ômer, *o´-mer*; from 6014; (properly) a *heap*, i.e. a *sheaf*; also an *omer*, as a dry measure:—omer, sheaf.

6017. עֲמֹרָה, 'Ămôrâh, *am-o-raw´*; from 6014; a (ruined) *heap; Amorah*, a place in Palestine:—Gomorrah.

6018. עָמְרִי, 'Omrîy, *om-ree´*; from 6014; *heaping; Omri*, an Israelite:—Omri.

6019. עַמְרָם, 'Amrâm, *am-rawm´*; probably from 5971 and 7311; *high people; Amram*, the name of two Israelites:—Amram.

6020. עַמְרָמִי, 'Amrâmîy, *am-raw-mee´*; patronymic from 6019; an *Amramite* or descendant of Amram:—Amramite.

6021. עֲמָשָׂא, 'Ămâśâ', *am-aw-saw´*; from 6006; *burden; Amasa*, the name of two Israelites:—Amasa.

6022. עֲמָשַׂי, 'Ămâśay, *am-aw-sah´ee*; from 6006; *burdensome; Amasai*, the name of three Israelites:—Amasai.

6023. עֲמַשְׁסַי, 'Ămashsay, *am-ash-sah´ee*; probably from 6006; *burdensome; Amashsay*, an Israelite:—Amashai.

6024. עֲנָב, 'Ănâb, *an-awb´*; from the same as 6025; *fruit; Anab*, a place in Palestine:—Anab.

6025. עֵנָב, 'ênâb, *ay-nawb´*; from an unused root probably meaning to *bear* fruit; a *grape*:—(ripe) grape, wine.

6026. עָנַג, 'ânag, *aw-nag´*; a primitive root; to be *soft* or pliable, i.e. (figurative) *effeminate* or luxurious:—delicate (-ness), (have) delight (self), sport self.

6027. עֹנֶג, 'ôneg, *o´-neg*; from 6026; *luxury*:—delight, pleasant.

6028. עָנֹג, 'ânôg, *aw-nogue´*; from 6026; *luxurious*:—delicate.

6029. עָנַד, 'ânad, *aw-nad´*; a primitive root; to *lace* fast:—bind, tie.

6030. עָנָה, 'ânâh, *aw-naw´*; a primitive root; (properly) to *eye* or (general) to *heed*, i.e. *pay attention*; (by implication) to *respond*; (by extension) to *begin* to speak; (specifically) to *sing, shout, testify, announce*:—give account, afflict [*by mistake for* 6031], (cause to, give) answer, bring low [*by mistake for* 6031], cry, hear, Leannoth, lift up, say, × scholar, (give a) shout, sing (together by course), speak, testify, utter, (bear) witness. See also 1042, 1043.

6031. עָנָה, 'ânâh, *aw-naw´*; a primitive root [possibly rather identical with 6030 through the idea of *looking* down or *browbeating*]; to *depress* (literal or figurative, transitive or intransitive, in various applications, as follow):—abase self, afflict (-ion, self), answer [*by mistake for* 6030], chasten self, deal hardly with, defile, exercise, force, gentleness, humble (self), hurt, ravish, sing [*by mistake for* 6030], speak [*by mistake for* 6030], submit self, weaken, × in any wise.

6032. עֲנָה, 'ănâh, *an-aw´*; (Chaldee); corresponding to 6030:—answer, speak.

6033. עֲנָה, 'ănâh, *an-aw´*; (Chaldee); corresponding to 6031:—poor.

6034. עֲנָה, 'Ănâh, *an-aw´*; probably from 6030; an *answer; Anah*, the name of two Edomites and one Edomitess:—Anah.

6035. עָנָו, 'ânâv, *aw-nawv´*; or [by intermixture with 6041] עָנָיו, **'ânâyv,** *aw-nawv´*; from 6031; *depressed* (figurative), in mind (*gentle*) or circumstances (*needy*, especially *saintly*):—humble, lowly, meek, poor. Compare 6041.

6036. עָנוּב, 'Ânûwb, *aw-noob´*; passive participle from the same as 6025; *borne* (as fruit); *Anub*, an Israelite:—Anub.

6037. עַנְוָה, 'anvâh, *an-vaw´*; feminine of 6035; *mildness* (royal); also (concrete) *oppressed*:—gentleness, meekness.

6038. עֲנָוָה, 'ănâvâh, *an-aw-vaw´*; from 6035; *condescension*, human and subjective (*modesty*), or divine and objective (*clemency*):—gentleness, humility, meekness.

6039. עֱנוּת, 'ĕnûwth, *en-ooth´*; from 6031; *affliction*:—affliction.

6040. עֳנִי, 'ŏnîy, *on-ee´*; from 6031; *depression*, i.e. misery:—afflicted (-ion), trouble.

6041. עָנִי, 'ânîy, *aw-nee´*; from 6031; *depressed*, in mind or circumstances [practically the same as 6035, although the margin constantly disputes this, making 6035 subjective and 6041 objective]:—afflicted, humble, lowly, needy, poor.

6042. עֻנִּי, ‘Unnîy, *oon-nee´*; from 6031; *afflicted; Unni*, the name of two Israelites:—Unni.

6043. עֲנָיָה, ‘Ănâyâh, *an-aw-yaw´*; from 6030; *Jah has answered; Anajah*, the name of two Israelites:—Anaiah.

6044. עָנִים, ‘Ânîym, *aw-neem´*; for plural of 5869; *fountains; Anim*, a place in Palestine:—Anim.

6045. עִנְיָן, ‘inyân, *in-yawn´*; from 6031; *ado*, i.e. (general) *employment* or (specific) an *affair*:—business, travail.

6046. עָנֵם, ‘Ânêm, *aw-name´*; from the dual of 5869; *two fountains; Anem*, a place in Palestine:—Anem.

6047. עֲנָמִים, ‘Ănâmîym, *an-aw-meem´*; as if plural of some Egyptian word; *Anamim*, a son of Mizraim and his descendant, with their country:—Anamim.

6048. עֲנַמֶּלֶךְ, ‘Ănammelek, *an-am-meh´-lek*; of foreign origin; *Anammelek*, an Assyrian deity:—Anammelech.

6049. עָנַן, ‘ânan, *aw-nan´*; a primitive root; to *cover*; used only as denominative from 6051, to *cloud* over; (figurative) to *act covertly*, i.e. practise magic:— × bring, enchanter, Meonemin, observe (-r of) times, soothsayer, sorcerer.

A verb meaning to practice soothsaying, fortune-telling, divining, magic. While it is clear from the contexts and the versions that this term is used for some type of magic or witchcraft, its etymology is unclear. Therefore, the specifics of the practice it connotes are equally unclear. However, it is clear that it was strictly forbidden, and the one who practiced this act was detestable to God (Dt 18:10, 12). Isaiah appears to use the term figuratively to demean the idolatrous Israelites (Isa 57:3).

6050. עֲנַן, ‘ănan, *an-an´*; (Chaldee); corresponding to 6051:—cloud.

A masculine singular Aramaic noun meaning cloud. It occurs only in Da 7:13 in the phrase, clouds of heaven. In a night vision, Daniel saw the Son of Man coming with the clouds of heaven. This use of clouds in apocalyptic language is familiar to the writer of Revelation who echoes the same phrase, "Look, he is coming with the clouds" (Rev 1:7, NIV). See the Hebrew cognate *‘ânân* (6051).

6051. עָנָן, ‘ânân, *aw-nawn´*; from 6049; a *cloud* (as *covering* the sky), i.e. the *nimbus* or thundercloud:—cloud (-y).

A masculine singular noun meaning cloud. In the ancient world, clouds were often seen as the pedestal or shroud of the divine presence. This imagery is also present in the Hebrew Bible. God preceded the Israelites through the wilderness in a pillar of cloud (Ex 13:21, 22); and the same cloud rested over the tabernacle (Ex 33:10). The cloud was over Mount Sinai (Ex 19:9); and entered the Temple in Jerusalem (1Ki 8:10, 11). Clouds are typical of the apocalyptic language of the Day of God (Eze 30:3; Joel 2:2; Zep 1:15). Other poetic uses of cloud describe God's shelter (Isa 4:5); Israel's evaporating love (Hos 6:4); the transient nature of life (Job 7:9); and the breadth of a great army (Eze 38:9). See the Aramaic *‘ănân* (6050).

6052. עָנָן, ‘Ânân, *aw-nawn´*; the same as 6051; *cloud; Anan*, an Israelite:—Anan.

6053. עֲנָנָה, ‘ănânâh, *an-aw-naw´*; feminine of 6051; *cloudiness*:—cloud.

6054. עֲנָנִי, ‘Ănânîy, *an-aw-nee´*; from 6051; *cloudy; Anani*, an Israelite:—Anani.

6055. עֲנַנְיָה, ‘Ănanᵉyâh, *a-naw-ne-yaw´*; from 6049 and 3050; *Jah has covered; Ananjah*, the name of an Israelite and of a place in Palestine:—Ananiah.

6056. עֲנַף, ‘ănaph, *an-af´*; (Chaldee); or עֶנֶף, **‘eneph,** *eh´-nef*; (Chaldee); corresponding to 6057:—bough, branch.

6057. עָנָף, ‘ânâph, *aw-nawf´*; from an unused root meaning to *cover*; a *twig* (as *covering* the limbs):—bough, branch.

6058. עָנֵף, ‘ânêph, *aw-nafe´*; from the same as 6057; *branching*:—full of branches.

6059. עָנַק, ‘ânaq, *aw-nak´*; a primitive root; (properly) to *choke*; used only as denominative from 6060, to *collar*, i.e. adorn with a necklace; (figurative) to *fit out* with supplies:—compass about as a chain, furnish, liberally.

6060. עֲנָק, ‘ănâq, *ah-nawk´*; from 6059; a *necklace* (as if *strangling*):—chain.

6061. עֲנָק, ‘Ânâq, *aw-nawk´*; the same as 6060; *Anak*, a Canaanite:—Anak.

6062. עֲנָקִי, ‘Ănâqîy, *an-aw-kee´*; patronymic from 6061; an *Anakite* or descendant of Anak:—Anakim.

6063. עָנֵר, ‘Ânêr, *aw-nare´*; probably for 5288; *Aner*, an Amorite, also a place in Palestine:—Aner.

6064. עָנַשׁ, ‘ânash, *aw-nash´*; a primitive root; (properly) to *urge*; (by implication) to *inflict* a penalty, (specifically) to *fine*:—amerce, condemn, punish, × surely.

A verb meaning to fine, to penalize with a fine. The primary meaning is the monetary assessment for a crime and is clearly seen in Dt 22:19 (see also Ex 21:22). Similarly, Amos used the word to denote the condemnation that rests on those under punishment (Am 2:8). In a practical sense, the writer of wisdom extolled the educational benefits of applying such a fine to the wicked (Pr 21:11); but he expressly warned against punishing the righteous (Pr 17:26).

6065. עֲנָשׁ, ‘ănash, *an-ash´*; (Chaldee); corresponding to 6066; a *mulct*:—confiscation.

An Aramaic masculine noun meaning confiscation, repossession. This word appears only once in Ezr 7:26 and simply refers to the seizure of goods as a legal penalty for crimes.

6066. עֹנֶשׁ, ‘ônesh, *o´-nesh*; from 6064; a *fine*:—punishment, tribute.

A masculine noun meaning a fine, a penalty, an indemnity. The basic meaning of the word is a monetary obligation placed on one who violated the Law or was under subjugation to a higher authority. It was used to refer to the tribute forced on Jehoahaz by the Egyptian pharaoh (2Ki 23:33); and the punishment facing unrestrained anger (Pr 19:19).

6067. עֲנָת, ‘Ănâth, *an-awth´*; from 6030; *answer; Anath*, an Israelite:—Anath.

6068. עֲנָתוֹת, ‘Ănâthôwth, *an-aw-thōth´*; plural of 6067; *Anathoth*, the name of two Israelites, also of a place in Palestine:—Anathoth.

6069. עַנְתֹתִי, ‘Anthôthîy, *an-tho-thee´*; or עַנְּתוֹתִי, **‘Annᵉthôwthîy,** *an-ne-tho-thee´*; patrial from 6068; an *Antothite* or inhabitant of Anathoth:—of Anathoth, Anethothite, Anetothite, Antothite.

6070. עַנְתֹתִיָּה, ‘Anthôthîyyâh, *an-tho-thee-yaw´*; from the same as 6068 and 3050; *answers of Jah; Anthothijah*, an Israelite:—Antothijah.

6071. עָסִיס, ‘âsîys, *aw-sees´*; from 6072; *must* or fresh grape juice (as just *trodden* out):—juice, new (sweet) wine.

6072. עָסַס, ‘âsas, *aw-sas´*; a primitive root; to *squeeze* out juice; (figurative) to *trample*:—tread down.

6073. עֳפָאִים, ‘ŏphâ’îym, *of-aw-yim´*; from an unused root meaning to *cover*; a *bough* (as covering the tree):—branch.

6074. עֳפִי, ‘ŏphîy, *of-ee´*; (Chaldee); corresponding to 6073; a *twig*; bough, i.e. (collective) *foliage*:—leaves.

6075. עָפַל, ‘âphal, *aw-fal´*; a primitive root; to *swell*; (figurative) to *be elated*:—be lifted up, presume.

6076. עֹפֶל, ‘ôphel, *o´-fel*; from 6075; a *tumor*; also a *mound*, i.e. fortress:—emerod, fort, strong hold, tower.

I. A masculine noun meaning hill, fort, citadel (2Ki 5:24; Isa 32:14; Mic 4:8).

II. A masculine noun meaning tumor (Dt 28:27; 1Sa 5:6, 9, 12; 6:4, 5).

6077. עֹפֶל, **'Ôphel,** *o´-fel*; the same as 6076; *Ophel*, a ridge in Jerusalem:—Ophel.

6078. עָפְנִי, **'Ophnîy,** *of-nee´*; from an unused noun [denoting a place in Palestine; from an unused root of uncertain meaning]; an *Ophnite* (collective) or inhabitant of Ophen:—Ophni.

6079. עַפְעַף, **'aph'aph,** *af-af´*; from 5774; an *eyelash* (as *fluttering*); (figurative) morning *ray*:—dawning, eyelid.

6080. עָפַר, **'âphar,** *aw-far´*; a primitive root; meaning either to *be gray* or perhaps rather to *pulverize*; used only as denominative from 6083, to *be dust*:—cast [dust].

A verb meaning to powder, to dust. This word literally means to sprinkle dust or dirt and conveys the image of a dusty garment whose appearance is gray. It was used to describe the scornful action of Shimei as he threw dirt on David and his procession (2Sa 16:13).

6081. עֵפֶר, **'Êpher,** *ay´-fer*; probably a variation of 6082; *gazelle; Epher*, the name of an Arabian and of two Israelites:—Epher.

6082. עֹפֶר, **'ôpher,** *o´-fer*; from 6080; a *fawn* (from the *dusty* colour):—young roe [hart].

6083. עָפָר, **'âphâr,** *aw-fawr´*; from 6080; *dust* (as *powdered* or *gray*); hence *clay, earth, mud*:—ashes, dust, earth, ground, morter, powder, rubbish.

A masculine noun meaning dust, dry earth, loose dirt. The primary meaning of this word is the dry, loose dirt or dust that covers the ground (Am 2:7; Mic 1:10). It is used to imply earth or soil (Job 5:6; 28:2); the original material used to form the first man (Ge 2:7); the material used to plaster walls (Le 14:42); the remains of a destroyed city (Eze 26:4); and anything pulverized into powder (Dt 9:21). Figuratively, it signifies abundance (Ge 13:16); utter defeat (2Ki 13:7); and humiliation (Job 16:15).

6084. עָפְרָה, **'Ophrâh,** *of-raw´*; feminine of 6082; *female fawn; Ophrah*, the name of an Israelite and of two places in Palestine:—Ophrah.

6085. עֶפְרוֹן, **'Ephrôwn,** *ef-rone´*; from the same as 6081; *fawn-like; Ephron*, the name of a Canaanite and of two places in Palestine:—Ephron, Ephrain [*from the margin*].

6086. עֵץ, **'êts,** *ates*; from 6095; a *tree* (from its *firmness*); hence *wood* (plural *sticks*):—+ carpenter, gallows, helve, + pine, plank, staff, stalk, stick, stock, timber, tree, wood.

6087. עָצַב, **'âtsab,** *aw-tsab´*; a primitive root; (properly) to *carve*, i.e. *fabricate* or *fashion*; hence (in a bad sense) to *worry, pain* or *anger*:—displease, grieve, hurt, make, be sorry, vex, worship, wrest.

A verb meaning to hurt, to pain, to grieve, to shape, to fashion. This word has two separate meanings. The first meaning deals with physical pain (Ecc 10:9); emotional pain (1Sa 20:34); or some combination of physical and emotional pain (1Ch 4:10). The word is also used of David's inaction when Adonijah attempted to usurp the throne (1Ki 1:6). The second meaning generally refers to creative activity, such as the kind God exercised when He created human bodies (Job 10:8); or the creative activity of people (Jer 44:19). In both these instances, the word occurs in parallel with the word *'âśâh* (6213), which means to make or to do.

6088. עֲצִיב, **'ătsîyb,** *ats-eeb´*; (Chaldee); corresponding to 6087; to *afflict*:—lamentable.

An Aramaic verb meaning to pain, to grieve. It is similar to the Hebrew word *'âtsab* (6087). It appears only one time in the form of a passive participle and is used as an adjective to modify *qôwl* (6963), meaning voice. In this instance, King Darius called into the lion's den for Daniel with a pained voice to see if God had preserved Daniel and kept him safe from harm (Da 6:20[21]).

6089. עֶצֶב, **'etseb,** *eh´-tseb*; from 6087; an earthen *vessel*; usually (painful) *toil*; also a *pang* (whether of body or mind):—grievous, idol, labour, sorrow.

A masculine noun meaning pain, hurt, toil. Since, like the noun *'ôtseb* (6090), it is derived from the verb *'âtsab* (6087), this noun carries the same variations of meaning. The word is used of physical pain, such as a woman's pain in childbirth (Ge 3:16); or of emotional pain, such as that caused by inappropriate words (Pr 15:1). The word can also express both meanings (cf. Pr 10:22); and can also refer to hard work or toil (Ps 127:2; Pr 5:10; 14:23).

6090. עֹצֶב, **'ôtseb,** *o´-tseb*; a variation of 6089; an *idol* (as fashioned); also *pain* (bodily or mental):—idol, sorrow, × wicked.

A masculine noun meaning pain, image, idol. Like the noun *'etseb* (6089), this word is derived from the verb *'âtsab* (6087). It can be used to depict the physical pain of childbirth (1Ch 4:9); a painful way, meaning a harmful habit like idolatry (Ps 139:24); and the sorrow and hardship of the Babylonian exile (Isa 14:3). In the final passage, this word is in parallel with *rôgez* (7267), meaning disquiet or turmoil.

6091. עָצָב, **'âtsâb,** *aw-tsawb´*; from 6087; an (idolatrous) *image*:—idol, image.

A masculine noun used to identify an idol. This term always appears in the plural. It is derived from the second meaning of the verb *'âtsab* (6087), meaning to form or fashion, and thereby highlights the fact that these idols ("gods") were formed by human hands. This term can allude to idols in general (Hos 4:17); idols of silver (Hos 13:2); or idols of gold and silver (Hos 8:4). It appears in parallel with *massêkâh* (4541), meaning a molten image (Hos 13:2); and *gillûl* (1544), meaning idols (Jer 50:2).

6092. עָצֵב, **'âtsêb,** *aw-tsabe´*; from 6087; a (hired) *workman*:—labour.

A masculine noun meaning a labourer, a worker. This noun is derived from the verb *'âtsab* (6087), which conveys the idea of physical or emotional pain and suffering. This noun occurs only in Isa 58:3, where God condemned the people of Israel for not properly fasting because they sacrificed nothing personally while exploiting their labourers or workers.

6093. עִצָּבוֹן, **'itstsâbôwn,** *its-tsaw-bone´*; from 6087; *worrisomeness*, i.e. *labour* or *pain*:—sorrow, toil.

A masculine noun meaning pain, toil. This noun is derived from the verb *'âtsab* (6087) and occurs three times in Genesis, relating to the curse that God placed on fallen humanity. To the woman, God stated that she would have pain and toil during childbirth (Ge 3:16). To the man, God stated that he would have pain and toil in working the ground to produce food (Ge 3:17; 5:29).

6094. עַצֶּבֶת, **'atstsebeth,** *ats-tseh´-beth*; from 6087; an *idol*; also a *pain* or *wound*:—sorrow, wound.

A feminine noun meaning hurt, injury, pain. This noun is derived from the verb *'âtsab* (6087). This noun is used only in Hebrew poetry and refers to the grief or sorrow that causes fear of discipline (Job 9:28); the grief caused by idolatry (Ps 16:4); the grief that comes with being brokenhearted (Ps 147:3); the grief caused by one who winks with the eye (Pr 10:10); or grief that causes the spirit to be broken (Pr 15:13). Although sometimes portrayed in physical terms (Ps 147:3), this term clearly refers to emotional suffering and not physical pain or injury.

6095. עָצָה, **'âtsâh,** *aw-tsaw´*; a primitive root; (properly) to *fasten* (or *make firm*), i.e. to *close* (the eyes):—shut.

6096. עָצֶה, **'âtseh,** *aw-tseh´*; from 6095; the *spine* (as giving *firmness* to the body):—back bone.

6097. עֵצָה, **'êtsâh,** *ay-tsaw´*; feminine of 6086; *timber*:—trees.

6098. עֵצָה, **'êtsâh,** *ay-tsaw´*; from 3289; *advice*; (by implication) *plan*; also *prudence*:—advice, advisement, counsel ([-lor]), purpose.

A feminine noun meaning advice, a plan. It sometimes may suggest the idea of a plot (Ne 4:15[4:9]; Pr 21:30); of a judgment or decision (Jgs 20:7; 2Sa 16:20; Ezr 10:3, 8). The term occurs in a positive sense in association with wisdom and understanding (Job 12:13; Pr 8:14; 12:15). Thus, the meaning of advice came from the sages of Israel and the astrologers of Babylon who were viewed as wise in their communities (Isa 47:13; Jer 18:18). Kings and would-be kings sought out advice but did not always have the discernment to choose the good (2Sa 17:7, 14, 23; 1Ki 12:8, 13, 14). This term is used quite often as a possession of God and the promised Messiah (Pr 19:21; Isa 5:19; 11:2; Jer 32:19).

6099. עָצוּם, **'âtsûwm,** *aw-tsoom´*; or עָצֻם, **'âtsum,** *aw-tsoom´*; passive participle of 6105; *powerful* (specifically, a *paw*); (by implication) *numerous*:— + feeble, great, mighty, must, strong.

6100. עֶצְיוֹן גֶּבֶר, **'Etsyôwn Geber,** *ets-yone´ gheh´-ber*; (shorter עֶצְיֹן גֶּבֶר, **'Etsyôn Geber,** *ets-yone´ gheh´-ber*; Ezion-gaber, a place on the Red Sea:—Ezion-geber.

6101. עָצַל, **'âtsal,** *aw-tsal´*; a primitive root; to *lean* idly, i.e. to be *indolent* or *slack*:—be slothful.

6102. עָצֵל, **'âtsêl,** *aw-tsale*; from 6101; *indolent*:—slothful, sluggard.

6103. עַצְלָה, **'atslâh,** *ats-law´*; feminine of 6102; (as abstract) *indolence*:—slothfulness.

6104. עַצְלוּת, **'atslûwth,** *ats-looth´*; from 6101; *indolence*:—idleness.

6105. עָצַם, **'âtsam,** *aw-tsam´*; a primitive root; to *bind* fast, i.e. *close* (the eyes); (intransitive) to *be* (causative, *make*) *powerful* or *numerous*; denominative (from 6106) to *crunch* the bones:—break the bones, close, be great, be increased, be (wax) mighty (-ier), be more, shut, be (-come, make) strong (-er).

6106. עֶצֶם, **'etsem,** *eh´-tsem*; from 6105; a *bone* (as *strong*); (by extension) the *body*; (figurative) the *substance*, i.e. (as pronoun) *selfsame*:—body, bone, × life, (self-) same, strength, × very.

A feminine singular noun meaning bone, substance, self. The first use of the term in the Bible is in Genesis when Adam proclaimed Eve was bone of his bones (Ge 2:23). This phrase is echoed later as an idiom of close relationship (Jgs 9:2; 2Sa 19:13[14]). The word can also be employed for animal bones (Ex 12:46; Nu 9:12; Job 40:18). Speaking figuratively, Jeremiah said that the Word of God was like fire shut in his bones (Jer 20:9). *'Etsem* can also denote identity, as in the phrase *b^{e}'etsem hayyôwm hazzeh,* (in this very day; Ex 12:17). A similar construction is seen in Ex 24:10 (the sky itself).

6107. עֶצֶם, **'Etsem,** *eh´-tsem*; the same as 6106; *bone*; *Etsem*, a place in Palestine:—Azem, Ezem.

6108. עֹצֶם, **'ôtsem,** *o´-tsem*; from 6105; *power*; hence *body*:—might, strong, substance.

6109. עָצְמָה, **'otsmâh,** *ots-maw´*; feminine of 6108; *powerfulness*; (by extension) *numerousness*:—abundance, strength.

6110. עֲצֻמוֹת, **'ătsumôwth,** *ah-tsoo-moth´*; feminine of 6099; a *bulwark*, i.e. (figurative) *argument*:—strong.

6111. עַצְמוֹן, **'Atsmôwn,** *ats-mone´*; or עַצְמֹן, **'Ats-môn,** *ats-mone´*; from 6107; *bone-like; Atsmon*, a place near Palestine:—Azmon.

6112. עֵצֶן, **'êtsen,** *ay´-tsen*; from an unused root meaning to *be sharp* or *strong*; a *spear*:—Eznite [*from the margin*].

6113. עָצַר, **'âtsar,** *aw-tsar´*; a primitive root; to *inclose*; (by analogy) to *hold back*; also to *maintain, rule, assemble*:— × be able, close up, detain, fast, keep (self close, still), prevail, recover, refrain, × reign, restrain, retain, shut (up), slack, stay, stop, withhold (self).

6114. עֶצֶר, **'etser,** *eh´-tser*; from 6113; *restraint*:— + magistrate.

6115. עֹצֶר, **'ôtser,** *o´-tser*; from 6113; *closure*; also *constraint*:— × barren, oppression, × prison.

6116. עֲצָרָה, **'ătsârâh,** *ats-aw-raw´*; or עֲצֶרֶת, **'ătsereth,** *ats-eh´-reth*; from 6113; an *assembly*, especially on a *festival* or *holiday*:—(solemn) assembly (meeting).

A feminine singular noun meaning assembly. This use of assembly usually has some religious or cultic connection; thus, it is often translated solemn assembly. These assemblies may be according to God's Law, such as the Feast of Passover (Dt 16:8); or the all-day gathering at the end of the Feast of Booths in Ne 8:18. But other assemblies were for the worship of other gods (2Ki 10:20); or were detestable to God because of Israel's wickedness (Isa 1:13; Am 5:21).

6117. עָקַב, **'âqab,** *aw-kab´*; a primitive root; (properly) to *swell* out or up; used only as denominative from 6119, to *seize by the heel*; (figurative) to *circumvent* (as if *tripping* up the heels); also to *restrain* (as if holding by the heel):—take by the heel, stay, supplant, × utterly.

A verb meaning to grasp at the heel, to supplant, to deceive. This verb is derived from the noun meaning heel (*'âqêb* [6119]) and is connected etymologically to the name Jacob (*ya'ăqôb*). The first occurrence sets the backdrop for the other uses. After Jacob tricked his brother Esau out of Isaac's blessing, Esau says, "He is rightly called 'Jacob'—for he has tricked (*Jacobed*) me twice" (Ge 27:36). In Jer 9:4[3], reflecting on the Jacob story, the prophet said every brother deceives. Hosea used the term in its more literal meaning when he recalled that Jacob grasped the heel of his brother in the womb (Hos 12:3[4]).

6118. עֵקֶב, **'êqeb,** *ay´-keb*; from 6117 in the sense of 6119; a *heel*, i.e. (figurative) the *last* of anything (used adverb *for ever*); also *result*, i.e. *compensation*; and so (adverb with preposition or relative) on *account* of:— × because, by, end, for, if, reward.

6119. עָקֵב, **'âqêb,** *aw-kabe´*; or (feminine) עִקְּבָה, **'iqq^{e}bâh,** *ik-keb-aw´*; from 6117; a *heel* (as *protuberant*); hence a *track*; (figurative) the *rear* (of an army):—heel, [horse-] hoof, last, lier in wait [*by mistake for* 6120], (foot-) step.

A masculine singular noun meaning a heel, footprints, a back, a rear. The basic meaning of the word is heel and is seen in the passage where the serpent was told that he would strike at the heel of Eve's offspring (Ge 3:15). Jacob grasped Esau's heel in the womb (Ge 25:26). But the term can also be used to refer to the mark left by the heel (that is, a footprint) (Ps 56:6[7]; 77:19[20]; SS 1:8). It is also used in a military context to mean rear, that is, at the heels (Ge 49:19; Jos 8:13).

6120. עָקֵב, **'âqêb,** *aw-kabe´*; from 6117 in its denominative sense; a *lier in wait*:—heel [*by mistake for* 6119].

6121. עָקֹב, **'âqôb,** *aw-kobe´*; from 6117; in the original sense, a *knoll* (as *swelling* up); in the denominative sense (transitive) *fraudulent* or (intransitive) *tracked*:—crooked, deceitful, polluted.

This form actually represents two adjectives. The first means deceitful, insidious, "footprinted." It is from the verb *'âqab* (6117) and the noun *'âqêb* (6119). As Jeremiah proclaimed God's efforts with sinful humanity, he also declared that the heart is more deceitful than anything (Jer 17:9). The other usage is related to the word for footprint. To describe the wickedness of Gilead, the prophet called it a town of bloody footprints (Hos 6:8). The second adjective means steep, hilly. Isaiah spoke of making a path for the exiles to return, making the hilly places like a plain (Isa 40:4). This famous passage is appropriated in the Gospels to describe John the Baptist's preparation for Jesus' ministry.

6122. עָקְבָה, **'oqbâh,** *ok-baw´*; feminine of an unused form from 6117 meaning a *trick*; *trickery*:—subtilty.

6123. עָקַד, **'âqad,** *aw-kad´*; a primitive root; to *tie* with thongs:—bind.

6124. עָקֹד, **'âqôd,** *aw-kode´*; from 6123; *striped* (with *bands*):—ring straked.

6125. עָקָה, **'âqâh,** *aw-kaw´*; from 5781; *constraint*:—oppression.

6126. עַקּוּב, **'Aqqûwb,** *ak-koob´*; from 6117; *insidious; Akkub*, the name of five Israelites:—Akkub.

6127. עָקַל, **'âqal,** *aw-kal´*; a primitive root; to *wrest*:—wrong.

6128. עֲקַלְקַל, **ʽăqalqal,** *ak-al-kal´*; from 6127; *winding*:—by [-way], crooked way.

6129. עֲקַלָּתוֹן, **ʽăqallâthôwn,** *ak-al-law-thone´*; from 6127; *tortuous*:—crooked.

6130. עָקָן, **ʽÂqân,** *ah-kawn´*; from an unused root meaning to *twist; tortuous; Akan,* an Idumæan:—Akan. Compare 3292.

6131. עָקַר, **ʽâqar,** *aw-kar´*; a primitive root; to *pluck* up (especially by the roots); (specifically) to *hamstring*; (figurative) to *exterminate*:—dig down, hough, pluck up, root up.

6132. עֲקַר, **ʽăqar,** *ak-ar´*; (Chaldee); corresponding to 6131:—pluck up by the roots.

6133. עֵקֶר, **ʽêqer,** *ay´-ker*; from 6131; (figurative) a *transplanted* person, i.e. naturalized citizen:—stock.

6134. עֵקֶר, **ʽÊqer,** *ay´-ker*; the same as 6133; *Eker,* an Israelite:—Eker.

6135. עָקָר, **ʽâqâr,** *aw-kawr´*; from 6131; *sterile* (as if *extirpated* in the generative organs):—(× male or female) barren (woman).

6136. עִקַּר, **ʽiqqar,** *ik-kar´*; (Chaldee); from 6132; a *stock*:—stump.

6137. עַקְרָב, **ʽaqrâb,** *ak-rawb´*; of uncertain derivation; a *scorpion*; (figurative) a *scourge* or knotted whip:—scorpion.

6138. עֶקְרוֹן, **ʽEqrôwn,** *ek-rone´*; from 6131; *eradication; Ekron,* a place in Palestine:—Ekron.

6139. עֶקְרוֹנִי, **ʽEqrôwnîy,** *ek-ro-nee´*; or עֶקְרֹנִי, **ʽEqrônîy,** *ek-ro-nee´*; patrial from 6138; an *Ekronite* or inhabitant of Ekron:—Ekronite.

6140. עָקַשׁ, **ʽâqash,** *aw-kash´*; a primitive root; to *knot* or *distort*; (figurative) to *pervert* (act or declare perverse):—make crooked, (prove, that is) perverse (-rt).

6141. עִקֵּשׁ, **ʽiqqêsh,** *ik-kashe´*; from 6140; *distorted*; hence *false*:—crooked, froward, perverse.

6142. עִקֵּשׁ, **ʽIqqêsh,** *ik-kashe´*; the same as 6141; *perverse; Ikkesh,* an Israelite:—Ikkesh.

6143. עִקְּשׁוּת, **ʽiqqᵉshûwth,** *ik-kesh-ooth´*; from 6141; *perversity*:— × froward.

6144. עָר, **ʽÂr,** *awr*; the same as 5892; a *city; Ar,* a place in Moab:—Ar.

6145. עָר, **ʽâr,** *awr*; from 5782; a *foe* (as *watchful* for mischief):—enemy.

6146. עָר, **ʽâr,** *awr*; (Chaldee); corresponding to 6145:—enemy.

6147. עֵר, **ʽÊr,** *ayr*; from 5782; *watchful; Er,* the name of two Israelites:—Er.

6148. עָרַב, **ʽârab,** *aw-rab´*; a primitive root; to *braid,* i.e. *intermix*; (technical) to *traffic* (as if by barter); also to *give* or *be security* (as a kind of exchange):—engage, (inter-) meddle (with), mingle (self), mortgage, occupy, give pledges, be (-come, put in) surety, undertake.

A verb meaning to exchange, to take as a pledge, to give as a pledge. This word denotes the action of giving a pledge or a guarantee (Ge 43:9); a pledge given in exchange for the delivery of material goods (2Ki 18:23); the action of taking possession of exchanged material (Eze 27:9); and the mortgage of property (Ne 5:3). By extension, it was used in reference to the scattering of the Jews among the nations (Ps 106:35); and implied sharing or association at a meaningful level (Pr 14:10; 20:19). In Jer 30:21, it conveyed the idea of purposing or engaging to meet with the Lord.

6149. עָרֵב, **ʽârab,** *aw-rab´*; a primitive root [rather identical with 6148 through the idea of close *association*]; to be *agreeable*:—be pleasant (-ing), take pleasure in, be sweet.

6150. עָרַב, **ʽârab,** *aw-rab´*; a primitive root [rather identical with 6148 through the idea of *covering* with a texture]; to *grow dusky* at sundown:—be darkened, (toward) evening.

6151. עֲרַב, **ʽărab,** *ar-ab´*; (Chaldee); corresponding to 6148; to *commingle*:—mingle (self), mix.

An Aramaic verb meaning to mix, to mingle, to join together. Daniel used this word to describe the feet of the image Nebuchadnezzar saw in his dream (Da 2:41, 43). They were a curious mixture of clay and iron. Thus, the word implies an amalgamation of two uncomplementary materials, which is at best unstable.

6152. עֲרָב, **ʽĂrâb,** *ar-ab´*; or עֲרַב, **ʽĂrab,** *ar-awb´*; from 6150 in the figurative sense of *sterility; Arab* (i.e. *Arabia*), a country East of Palestine:—Arabia.

6153. עֶרֶב, **ʽereb,** *eh´-reb*; from 6150; *dusk*:— + day, even (-ing, tide), night.

6154. עֵרֶב, **ʽêreb,** *ay´-reb*; or עֶרֶב, **ʽereb,** *eh´-reb*; (1Ki 10:15), (with the article prefixed), from 6148; the *web* (or transverse threads of cloth); also a *mixture,* (or *mongrel* race):—Arabia, mingled people, mixed (multitude), woof.

A masculine noun meaning a mixture, a mixed company, interwoven. The primary meaning is a grouping of people from various ethnic and cultural backgrounds. It was used of any heterogeneous band associated with the nation of Israel as it departed Egypt (Ex 12:38); the tribes not aligned with any specific culture (Jer 25:24); and the mingled people resulting from the Babylonian captivity (Jer 50:37). By extension, the word was also used of interwoven material of varying fibers (Le 13:48).

6155. עֲרָבָה, **ʽărâbâh,** *ah-raw-baw´*; from 6148; a *willow* (from the use of osiers as wattles):—willow.

6156. עָרֵב, **ʽârêb,** *aw-rabe´*; from 6149; *pleasant*:—sweet.

6157. עָרֹב, **ʽârôb,** *aw-robe´*; from 6148; a *mosquito* (from its *swarming*):—divers sorts of flies, swarm.

6158. עֹרֵב, **ʽôrêb,** *o-rabe´*; or עוֹרֵב, **ʽôwrêb,** *o-rabe´*; from 6150; a *raven* (from its *dusky* hue):—raven.

6159. עֹרֵב, **ʽÔrêb,** *o-rabe´*; or עוֹרֵב, **ʽÔwrêb,** *o-rabe´*; the same as 6158; *Oreb,* the name of a Midianite and of a cliff near the Jordan:—Oreb.

6160. עֲרָבָה, **ʽărâbâh,** *ar-aw-baw´*; from 6150 (in the sense of *sterility*); a *desert*; especially (with the article prefixed) the (general) sterile valley of the Jordan and its continuation to the Red Sea:—Arabah, champaign, desert, evening, heaven, plain, wilderness. See also 1026.

A feminine noun meaning a desert plain, a steppe, a wilderness. This word designates a prominent geographic feature of the Middle East. It is used to designate the arid plateau in south Judah (Isa 51:3; see also 1Sa 23:24); various portions of the Jordan River valley and the adjacent plains (Jos 12:1; 2Sa 2:29); the desert area in northern Arabia (Dt 1:1); and any generic land formation similar to these arid plateaus (Dt 1:7; Isa 40:3). There is some uncertainty as to the use of this word in Ps 68:4[5]. Most translations render the word as heavens or clouds, rather than the more literal meaning, desert.

6161. עֲרֻבָּה, **ʽărubbâh,** *ar-oob-baw´*; feminine passive participle of 6048 in the sense of a *bargain* or *exchange*; something given as *security,* i.e. (literal) a *token* (of safety) or (metaphorical) a *bondsman*:—pledge, surety.

A feminine noun meaning a pledge, a guarantee, a token. Occurring only twice in the Hebrew Bible, this word implies a tangible sign of a current or soon-expected reality. It was used specifically in reference to an assurance of well-being brought from the battlefield (1Sa 17:18); and a collateral exchanged at the making of a pledge (Pr 17:18).

6162. עֵרָבוֹן, **ʽêrâbôwn,** *ay-raw-bone´*; from 6148 (in the sense of *exchange*); a *pawn* (given as security):—pledge.

A masculine noun meaning pledge. It is a deposit given as evidence and proof that something else will be done. When the act is accomplished, the pledge is returned. Judah gave his seal and staff to Tamar, whom he believed was a temple prostitute, as a guarantee that he would return the next day so he might give her a young goat as payment for her services and then reacquire his seal and staff (Ge 38:17, 18, 20). It is also probable that this word is what is meant in Job's reply to Eliphaz (see Job 17:3).

6163. עֲרָבִי, **'Ărâbîy,** *ar-aw-bee'*; or עַרְבִי, **'Arbîy,** *ar-bee'*; patrial from 6152; an *Arabian* or inhabitant of Arab (i.e. Arabia):—Arabian.

6164. עַרְבָתִי, **'Arbâthîy,** *ar-baw-thee'*; patrial from 1026; an *Arbathite* or inhabitant of (Beth-) Arabah:—Arbathite.

6165. עָרַג, **'ârag,** *aw-rag'*; a primitive root; to *long* for:—cry, pant.

6166. עֲרָד, **'Ărâd,** *ar-awd'*; from an unused root meaning to *sequester* itself; *fugitive; Arad,* the name of a place near Palestine, also of a Canaanite and an Israelite:—Arad.

6167. עֲרָד, **'ărâd,** *ar-awd'*; (Chaldee); corresponding to 6171; an *onager*:—wild ass.

6168. עֵרָבוֹן, **'êrâbôwn,** *ay-raw-bone'*; a primitive root; to *be* (causative, *make*) *bare*; hence to *empty, pour* out, *demolish*:—leave destitute, discover, empty, make naked, pour (out), rase, spread self, uncover.

6169. עָרָה, **'ârâh,** *aw-raw'*; feminine from 6168; a *naked* (i.e. level) plot:—paper reed.

6170. עֲרוּגָה, **'ărûwgâh,** *ar-oo-gaw'*; or עֲרֻגָה, **'ăru-gâh,** *ar-oo-gaw'*; feminine passive participle of 6165; something *piled* up (as if [figurative] *raised* by mental aspiration), i.e. a *parterre*:—bed, furrow.

6171. עָרוֹד, **'ârôwd,** *aw-rode'*; from the same as 6166; an *onager* (from his *lonesome* habits):—wild ass.

6172. עֶרְוָה, **'ervâh,** *er-vaw'*; from 6168; *nudity,* literal (especially the *pudenda*) or figurative (*disgrace, blemish*):—nakedness, shame, unclean (-ness).

A feminine noun expressing nakedness. This word can pertain to physical nakedness for either a man or a woman (Ge 9:22, 23; Ex 20:26); however, it is more often used in a figurative sense. When used with the verbs *gâlâh* (1540), meaning to uncover or remove, and *râ'âh* (7200), meaning to see, one finds a common euphemism for sexual relations—to uncover one's nakedness (Le 18:6; 20:17). On the other hand, when combined with the verb *kâsâh* (3680), meaning to cover, one finds a common idiom for entering into a marriage contract (Eze 16:8). Nakedness is also a symbol of the shame and disgrace of Egypt (Isa 20:4); Babylonia (Isa 47:3); and Jerusalem (Eze 16:37). Furthermore, when in construct with *dâbâr* (1697), meaning a word, matter, or thing, this term forms an idiom for indecent or improper behaviour (Dt 23:14[15]; 24:1). When in construct with the word *'erets* (776), it can refer to exposed or undefended areas (Ge 42:9, 12).

6173. עַרְוָה, **'arvâh,** *ar-vaw'*; (Chaldee); corresponding to 6172; *nakedness,* i.e. (figurative) *impoverishment*:—dishonour.

6174. עָרוֹם, **'ârôwm,** *aw-rome'*; or עָרֹם, **'ârôm,** *aw-rome'*; from 6191 (in its orig. sense); *nude,* either partially or totally:—naked.

An adjective meaning naked. It can allude to physical nakedness (Ge 2:25; 1Sa 19:24; Isa 20:2–4). It can also be used figuratively to relate to one who has no possessions (Job 1:21; Ecc 5:15 [14]). Moreover, Sheol is described as being naked before God, a statement of its openness and vulnerability to God and His power (Job 26:6).

6175. עָרוּם, **'ârûwm,** *aw-room'*; passive participle of 6191; *cunning* (usually in a bad sense):—crafty, prudent, subtil.

An adjective meaning crafty, shrewd, sensible. This adjective can have either a positive or negative connotation. In a positive connotation, it is understood as being prudent. As such, a prudent individual takes no offence at an insult (Pr 12:16); does not flaunt his knowledge (Pr 12:23); takes careful thought of his ways (Pr 14:8); takes careful thought before action (Pr 14:15); is crowned with knowledge (Pr 14:18); and sees and avoids danger (Pr 22:3; 27:12). When the word has a negative meaning, it means being crafty (Job 5:12; 15:5). This word is used when the Bible describes the serpent in the Garden of Eden. The serpent was more subtle [crafty] than any beast of the field (Ge 3:1). This description is presented in stark contrast to the situation of Adam and Eve. They sought to be crafty like the serpent, but they only realized that they were *'êyrôm* (5903), meaning naked.

6176. עֲרוֹעֵר, **'ărôw'êr,** *ar-o-ayr'*; or עַרְעָר, **'ar'âr,** *ar-awr'*; from 6209 reduplication; a *juniper* (from its *nudity* of situation):—heath.

6177. עֲרוֹעֵר, **'Ărôw'êr,** *ar-o-ayr'*; or עֲרֹעֵר, **'Ărô'êr,** *ar-o-ayr'*; or עַרְעוֹר, **'Ar'ôwr,** *ar-ore'*; the same as 6176; *nudity* of situation; *Aroër,* the name of three places in or near Palestine:—Aroer.

6178. עָרוּץ, **'ârûwts,** *aw-roots'*; passive participle of 6206; *feared,* i.e. (concrete) a *horrible* place or *chasm*:—cliffs.

6179. עֵרִי, **'Êrîy,** *ay-ree'*; from 5782; *watchful; Eri,* an Israelite:—Eri.

6180. עֵרִי, **'Êrîy,** *ay-ree'*; patronymic of 6179; an *Erite* (collective) or descendants of Eri:—Erites.

6181. עֶרְיָה, **'eryâh,** *er-yaw'*; for 6172; *nudity*:—bare, naked, × quite.

A feminine noun meaning nakedness. This term is only used figuratively. It can function as a metaphor for shame and disgrace. In the allegory of unfaithful Jerusalem, God stated that Jerusalem was naked and bare, *'êrôm* (5903) *wĕ'eryâh* (Eze 16:7). The inhabitants of Shaphir were considered to be in the nakedness of shame, *'eryâh bôsheth* (1322) (Mic 1:11). It is also used to indicate the outpouring of God's wrath on the earth by the allusion to God's bow being naked or uncovered, meaning that it was taken from its storage place and put to use (Hab 3:9).

6182. עֲרִיסָה, **'ărîysâh,** *ar-ee-saw'*; from an unused root meaning to *comminute; meal*:—dough.

6183. עָרִיפִים, **'ârîyphîym,** *aw-reef-eem'*; from 6201; the *sky* (as *drooping* at the horizon):—heaven.

A masculine noun meaning cloud. Isaiah used this word when he pronounced God's judgments on Israel by means of foreign nations. He stated that the judgment would be so severe that there would be only darkness and distress; there would be no light, as when storm clouds block out the light (Isa 5:30).

6184. עָרִיץ, **'ârîyts,** *aw-reets'*; from 6206; *fearful,* i.e. *powerful* or *tyrannical*:—mighty, oppressor, in great power, strong, terrible, violent.

6185. עֲרִירִי, **'ărîyrîy,** *ar-ee-ree'*; from 6209; *bare,* i.e. destitute (of children):—childless.

6186. עָרַךְ, **'ârak,** *aw-rak'*; a primitive root; to set in a *row,* i.e. *arrange,* put in *order* (in a very wide variety of applications):—put (set) (the battle, self) in array, compare, direct, equal, esteem, estimate, expert [in war], furnish, handle, join [battle], ordain, (lay, put, reckon up, set) (in) order, prepare, tax, value.

6187. עֵרֶךְ, **'êrek,** *eh'-rek*; from 6186; a *pile, equipment, estimate*:—equal, estimation, (things that are set in) order, price, proportion, × set at, suit, taxation, × valuest.

6188. עָרֵל, **'ârêl,** *aw-rale'*; a primitive root; (properly) to *strip*; but used only as denominative from 6189; to *expose* or *remove* the *prepuce,* whether literal (to *go naked*) or figurative (to *refrain* from using):—count uncircumcised, foreskin to be uncovered.

6189. עָרֵל, **'ârêl,** *aw-rale'*; from 6188; (properly) *exposed,* i.e. projecting loose (as to the prepuce); (used only technically) *uncircumcised* (i.e. still having the prepuce uncurtailed):—uncircumcised (person).

A masculine adjective meaning uncircumcised. In the literal sense, it was used to designate a specific individual (Ge 17:14; Ex 12:48); a group (Jos 5:7); or a nation, especially the Philistines (1Sa 14:6; Isa 52:1). In addition to the simple statement of physical condition, the term could also convey an attitude of derision since the object was considered unclean and impure (Jgs 14:3; 15:18). Furthermore, the term could be used metaphorically to describe the corrupted nature of certain body parts: uncircumcised lips denoted an inability to speak effectively (Ex 6:12, 30; cf. Isa 6:5); uncircumcised in heart represented a flawed character and precluded entrance to the Temple (Eze 44:7, 9); and uncircumcised in the ear signified an inability to hear (Jer 6:10). Also, the fruit of newly planted trees was considered uncircumcised (unclean) for the first three years (Le 19:23).

6190. עָרְלָה, **'orlâh,** *or-law´*; feminine of 6189; the *prepuce*:—foreskin, + uncircumcised.

A feminine noun meaning foreskin. The word could represent just the foreskin (Ge 17:11; 1Sa 18:25, 27); the state of being uncircumcised (having a foreskin [Ge 34:14]); or the act of circumcision (cutting off the foreskin [Ex 4:25]). Like the word *'ârêl* (6189), this term could be used figuratively to represent the impure nature of fruit trees (Le 19:23); or the human heart (Dt 10:16; Jer 4:4).

6191. עָרַם, **'âram,** *aw-ram´*; a primitive root; (properly) to *be* (or *make*) *bare*; but used only in the derivative sense (through the idea perhaps of *smoothness*) to *be cunning* (usually in a bad sense):—× very, beware, take crafty [counsel], be prudent, deal subtilly.

A verb meaning to be shrewd, to be subtle. This verb has a neutral tone but can assume either a negative tone: crafty and tricky (1Sa 23:22; Ps 83:3[4]); or a positive tone: prudent and wise (Pr 15:5; 19:25).

6192. עָרַם, **'âram,** *aw-ram´*; a primitive root; to *pile* up:—gather together.

A verb meaning to be heaped up. This verb occurs once in the Hebrew Bible in Ex 15:8. In Moses' song at the sea, he describes God's miraculous act by singing about how the waters were heaped up.

6193. עֹרֶם, **'ôrem,** *o´-rem*; from 6191; a *stratagem*:—craftiness.

A masculine singular noun meaning craftiness. Its only use in the Hebrew Bible is in the book of Job. Eliphaz told Job that God catches the wise in their craftiness. He cannot be fooled (Job 5:13). See the verb *'âram* (6191).

6194. עָרֵם, **'ârêm,** *aw-rame´*; (Jer 50:26), or (feminine) עֲרֵמָה, **'ărêmâh,** *ar-ay-maw´*; from 6192; a *heap*; (specifically) a *sheaf*:—heap (of corn), sheaf.

6195. עָרְמָה, **'ormâh,** *or-maw´*; feminine of 6193; *trickery*; or (in a good sense) *discretion*:—guile, prudence, subtilty, wilily, wisdom.

A feminine singular noun meaning craftiness, prudence. Ex 21:14 employs it adverbially (schemes craftily) as does Jos 9:4, where the foreign kings tricked Joshua into making a treaty. In Proverbs, the word has a different connotation. Both in the instruction for a son (Pr 1:4) and in describing Lady Wisdom who has *'ormâh* with her (Pr 8:5, 12), the term is best translated prudence. See the verb *'âram* (6191).

6196. עַרְמוֹן, **'armôwn,** *ar-mone´*; probably from 6191; the *plane* tree (from its *smooth* and shed bark):—chestnut tree.

6197. עֵרָן, **'Êrân,** *ay-rawn´*; probably from 5782; *watchful; Eran*, an Israelite:—Eran.

6198. עֵרָנִי, **'Êrânîy,** *ay-raw-nee´*; patronymic from 6197; an *Eranite* or descendants (collective) of Eran:—Eranites.

6199. עַרְעָר, **'ar'âr,** *ar-awr´*; from 6209; *naked*, i.e. (figurative) *poor*:—destitute. See also 6176.

6200. עֲרֹעֵרִי, **'Ărô'êrîy,** *ar-o-ay-ree´*; patronymic from 6177; an *Aroërite* or inhabitant of Aroër:—Aroerite.

6201. עָרַף, **'âraph,** *aw-raf´*; a primitive root; to *droop*; hence to *drip*:—drop (down).

A verb translated to drip, to drop. In Moses' final blessing of Israel, he says they would experience God's security and bounty where His heavens drop dew (Dt 33:28). In Moses' final song, he prayed that his teaching would drop like rain on his listeners (Dt 32:2). See the nominal form of this root, *'ărâphel* (6205), which means cloud.

6202. עָרַף, **'âraph,** *aw-raf´*; a primitive root [rather identical with 6201 through the idea of *sloping*]; (properly) to *bend* downward; but used only as a denominative from 6203, to *break the neck*; hence (figurative) to *destroy*:—that is beheaded, break down, break (cut off, strike off) neck.

6203. עֹרֶף, **'ôreph,** *o-ref´*; from 6202; the *nape* or back of the neck (as *declining*); hence the *back* generally (whether literal or figurative):—back ([stiff-]) neck ([-ed]).

6204. עָרְפָּה, **'Orpâh,** *or-paw´*; feminine of 6203; *mane; Orpah*, a Moabitess:—Orpah.

6205. עֲרָפֶל, **'ărâphel,** *ar-aw-fel´*; probably from 6201; *gloom* (as of a *lowering* sky):—(gross, thick) dark (cloud, -ness).

A masculine singular noun meaning cloud. A cloud enshrouded God (Ex 20:21; Job 22:13); and also served as His pedestal (2Sa 22:10; Ps 18:9[10]). The term is used figuratively to depict a stormy sea that has clouds for a garment (Job 38:9). Prophetic pictures of God's judgment are filled with clouds, darkening the ominous Day of the Lord (Jer 13:16; Eze 34:12; Joel 2:2; Zep 1:15).

6206. עָרַץ, **'ârats,** *aw-rats´*; a primitive root; to *awe* or (intrans.) to *dread*; hence to *harass*:—be affrighted (afraid, dread, feared, terrified), break, dread, fear, oppress, prevail, shake terribly.

A verb which means to tremble, to cause to tremble, to strike with awe, to strike with dread. The Lord's splendor can make the earth tremble (Isa 2:19, 21). Job wondered why God must overwhelm humans who are nothing more than driven leaves (Job 13:25). God and His leaders continually reminded the Israelites before battle not to be terrified by the enemy because God who would fight for them (Dt 1:29; 7:21; 20:3; 31:6; Jos 1:9). If God is with us, we have no need to dread humans and their conspiracies and plots (Isa 8:12).

6207. עָרַק, **'âraq,** *aw-rak´*; a primitive root; to *gnaw*, i.e. (figurative) *eat* (by hyperbole); also (participle) a *pain*:—fleeing, sinew.

6208. עַרְקִי, **'Arqîy,** *ar-kee´*; patrial from an unused name meaning a *tush*; an *Arkite* or inhabitant of Erek:—Arkite.

6209. עָרַר, **'ârar,** *aw-rar´*; a primitive root; to *bare*; (figurative) to *demolish*:—make bare, break, raise up [*perhaps by clerical error for* RAZE], × utterly.

6210. עֶרֶשׂ, **'eres,** *eh´-res*; from an unused root meaning perhaps to *arch*; a *couch* (properly with a *canopy*):—bed (-stead), couch.

6211. עָשׁ, **'âsh,** *awsh*; from 6244; a *moth*:—moth. See also 5906. NOTE: Strong's has two words numbered 6211; the second definition follows: עֲשַׂב, **'ăśab,** *as-ab´*, (Chaldee); 6212:—grass.

6212. עֵשֶׂב, **'eśeb,** *eh´-seb*; from an unused root meaning to *glisten* (or *be green*); *grass* (or any tender shoot):—grass, herb.

6213. עָשָׂה, **'âśâh,** *aw-saw´*; a primitive root; to *do* or *make*, in the broadest sense and widest application (as follows):—accomplish, advance, appoint, apt, be at, become, bear, bestow, bring forth, bruise, be busy, × certainly, have the charge of, commit, deal (with), deck, + displease, do, (ready) dress (-ed), (put in) execute (-ion), exercise, fashion, + feast, [fight-] ing man, + finish, fit, fly, follow, fulfil, furnish, gather, get, go about, govern, grant, great, + hinder, hold ([a feast]), × indeed, + be industrious, + journey, keep, labour, maintain, make, be meet, observe, be occupied, offer, + officer, pare, bring (come) to pass, perform, practise, prepare, procure, provide, put, requite, × sacrifice, serve, set, shew, × sin, spend, × surely, take, × throughly, trim, × very, + vex, be [warr-] ior, work (-man), yield, use.

A verb meaning to do, to make, to accomplish, to complete. This frequently used Hebrew verb conveys the central notion of performing an activity with a distinct purpose, a moral obligation, or a goal in view (cf. Ge 11:6). Particularly, it was used in conjunction with God's commands (Dt 16:12). It described the process of construction (Ge 13:4; Job 9:9; Pr 8:26); engaging in warfare (Jos 11:18); the yielding of grain (Hos 8:7); observing a religious ceremony (Ex 31:16; Nu 9:4); and the completion of something (Ezr 10:3; Isa 46:10). Provocatively, the word appears twice in Ezekiel to imply the intimate action of caressing or fondling the female breast (Eze 23:3, 8).

6214. **עֲשָׂהאֵל, 'Ăśâh'êl,** *as-aw-ale´*; from 6213 and 410; *God has made; Asahel,* the name of four Israelites:—Asahel.

6215. **עֵשָׂו, 'Êśâv,** *ay-sawv´*; apparently a form of the passive participle of 6213 in the original sense of *handling; rough* (i.e. sensibly *felt*); *Esav,* a son of Isaac, including his posterity:—Esau.

6216. **עָשׁוֹק, 'âshôwq,** *aw-shoke´*; from 6231; *oppressive* (as noun, a *tyrant*):—oppressor.

6217. **עֲשׁוּקִים, 'ăshûwqîym,** *aw-shoo-keem´*; passive participle of 6231; used in plural masculine as abstract *tyranny*:—oppressed (-ion). [*Doubtful.*]

6218. **עָשׂוֹר, 'âśôwr,** *aw-sore´*; or **עָשֹׂר, 'âśôr,** *aw-sore´*; from 6235; *ten*; by abbreviation ten *strings,* and so a *decachord*:—(instrument of) ten (strings, -th).

6219. **עָשׁוֹת, 'âshôwth,** *aw-shōth´*; from 6245; *shining,* i.e. polished:—bright.

6220. **עַשְׁוָת, 'Ashvâth,** *ash-vawth´*; for 6219; *bright; Ashvath,* an Israelite:—Ashvath.

6221. **עֲשִׂיאֵל, 'Ăśîy'êl,** *as-ee-ale´*; from 6213 and 410; *made of God; Asiel,* an Israelite:—Asiel.

6222. **עֲשָׂיָה, 'Ăśâyâh,** *aw-saw-yaw´*; from 6213 and 3050; *Jah has made; Asajah,* the name of three or four Israelites:—Asaiah.

6223. **עָשִׁיר, 'âshîyr,** *aw-sheer´*; from 6238; *rich,* whether literal or figurative (*noble*):—rich (man).

6224. **עֲשִׂירִי, 'ăśîyrîy,** *as-ee-ree´*; from 6235; *tenth*; (by abbreviation) *tenth month* or (feminine) *part*:—tenth (part).

6225. **עָשַׁן, 'âshan,** *aw-shan´*; a primitive root; to *smoke,* whether literal or figurative:—be angry (be on a) smoke.

A verb meaning to smoke, to be angry, to be furious. The literal meaning of this Hebrew word is to smolder or smoke (Ex 19:18; Ps 144:5). Metaphorically, it was used by the psalmist to convey the idea of fuming anger (Ps 74:1; 80:4[5]).

6226. **עָשֵׁן, 'âshên,** *aw-shane´*; from 6225; *smoky*:—smoking.

6227. **עָשָׁן, 'âshân,** *aw-shawn´*; from 6225; *smoke,* literal or figurative (*vapor, dust, anger*):—smoke (-ing).

6228. **עָשָׁן, 'Âshân,** *aw-shawn´*; the same as 6227; *Ashan,* a place in Palestine:—Ashan.

6229. **עָשַׂק, 'âśaq,** *aw-sak´*; a primitive root (identical with 6231); to *press upon,* i.e. *quarrel*:—strive with.

6230. **עֵשֶׂק, 'êśeq,** *ay´-sek*; from 6229; *strife*:—Esek.

6231. **עָשַׁק, 'âshaq,** *aw-shak´*; a primitive root (compare 6229); to *press* upon, i.e. *oppress, defraud, violate, overflow*:—get deceitfully, deceive, defraud, drink up, (use) oppress ([-ion], -or), do violence (wrong).

6232. **עֵשֶׁק, 'Êsheq,** *ay-shek´*; from 6231; *oppression; Eshek,* an Israelite:—Eshek.

6233. **עֹשֶׁק, 'ôsheq,** *o´-shek*; from 6231; *injury, fraud,* (subjective) *distress,* (concrete) *unjust gain*:—cruelly, extortion, oppression, thing [deceitfully gotten].

6234. **עָשְׁקָה, 'oshqâh,** *osh-kaw´*; feminine of 6233; *anguish*:—oppressed.

6235. **עֶשֶׂר, 'eśer,** *eh´-ser*; masculine **עֲשָׂרָה, 'ăśârâh,** *as-aw-raw´*; from 6237; *ten* (as an *accumulation* to the extent of the digits):—ten, [fif-, seven-] teen.

6236. **עֲשַׂר, 'ăśar,** *as-ar´*; (Chaldee); masculine **עַשְׂרָה, 'aśrâh,** *as-raw´*; (Chaldee); corresponding to 6235; *ten*:—ten, + twelve.

6237. **עָשַׂר, 'âśar,** *aw-sar´*; a primitive root (identical with 6238); to *accumulate*; but used only as denominative from 6235; to *tithe,* i.e. take or give a tenth:—× surely, give (take) the tenth, (have, take) tithe (-ing, -s), × truly.

A verb meaning to give a tenth part, to take a tenth part, to give the tithe, to receive the tithe. This pivotal Hebrew word first appears in reference to a vow made by Jacob (Ge 28:22). He promised to return one-tenth of his possessions to the Lord if the Lord would go with him. Under the Law given by Moses, this tithe was made mandatory on all increase (Dt 14:22; see also Dt 26:12). It was the duty of the priest to receive these tithes (Ne 10:37[38], 38[39]). Samuel also used this word to describe the taxes imposed by a king (1Sa 8:15, 17).

6238. **עָשַׁר, 'âshar,** *aw-shar´*; a primitive root; (properly) to *accumulate*; chiefly (specific) to *grow* (causative, *make*) *rich*:—be (-come, en-, make, make self, wax) rich, make [1Ki 22:48 *margin*]. See 6240.

6239. **עֹשֶׁר, 'ôsher,** *o´-sher*; from 6238; *wealth*:— × far [richer], riches.

6240. **עָשָׂר, 'âśâr,** *aw-sawr´*; for 6235; *ten* (only in combination), i.e. *-teen*; also (ordinal) *-teenth*:—[eigh-, fif-, four-, nine-, seven-, six-, thir-] teen (-th), + eleven (-th), + sixscore thousand, + twelve (-th).

6241. **עִשָּׂרוֹן, 'iśśârôwn,** *is-saw-rone´*; or **עִשָּׂרֹן, 'iśśârôn,** *is-saw-rone´*; from 6235; (fractional) a *tenth* part:—tenth deal.

6242. **עֶשְׂרִים, 'esrîym,** *es-reem´*; from 6235; *twenty*; also (ordinal) *twentieth*:—[six-] score, twenty (-ieth).

6243. **עֶשְׂרִין, 'eśrîyn,** *es-reen´*; (Chaldee); corresponding to 6242:—twenty.

6244. **עָשֵׁשׁ, 'âshêsh,** *aw-shaysh´*; a primitive root; probably to *shrink,* i.e. *fail*:—be consumed.

6245. **עָשַׁת, 'âshath,** *aw-shath´*; a primitive root; probably to be *sleek,* i.e. *glossy*; hence (through the idea of *polishing*) to *excogitate* (as if *forming* in the mind):—shine, think.

6246. **עֲשִׁת, 'ăshith,** *ash-eeth´*; (Chaldee); corresponding to 6245; to *purpose*:—think.

6247. **עֶשֶׁת, 'esheth,** *eh´-sheth*; from 6245; a *fabric*:—bright.

6248. **עַשְׁתּוּת, 'ashtûwth,** *ash-tooth´*; from 6245; *cogitation*:—thought.

6249. **עַשְׁתֵּי, 'ashtêy,** *ash-tay´*; apparently masculine plural construction of 6247 in the sense of an *afterthought*; (used only in connection with 6240 in lieu of 259) *eleven* or (ordinal) *eleventh*:— + eleven (-th).

6250. **עֶשְׁתֹּנָה, 'eshtônâh,** *esh-to-naw´*; from 6245; *thinking*:—thought.

6251. **עַשְׁתְּרֶת, 'ashtereth,** *ash-ter-eth´*; probably from 6238; *increase*:—flock.

6252. **עַשְׁתָּרוֹת, 'Ashtârôwth,** *ash-taw-rōth´*; or **עַשְׁתָּרֹת, 'Ashtârôth,** *ash-taw-rōth´*; plural of 6251; *Ashtaroth,* the name of a Sidonian deity, and of a place East of the Jordan:—Ashtaroth, Astaroth. See also 1045, 6253, 6255.

6253. **עַשְׁתֹּרֶת, 'Ashtôreth,** *ash-to´-reth*; probably for 6251; *Ashtoreth,* the Phoenician goddess of love (and *increase*):—Ashtoreth.

6254. **עַשְׁתְּרָתִי, 'Ashtᵉrâthîy,** *ash-ter-aw-thee´*; patrial from 6252; an *Ashterathite* or inhabitant of Ashtaroth:—Ashterathite.

6255. **עַשְׁתְּרֹת קַרְנַיִם, 'Ashtᵉrôth Qarnayim,** *ash-ter-ōth´ kar-nah´-yim*; from 6252 and the dual of 7161; *Ashtaroth of* (the) *double horns* (a symbol of the deity); *Ashteroth-Karnaïm,* a place East of the Jordan:—Ashtoreth Karnaim.

6256. **עֵת, 'êth,** *ayth*; from 5703; *time,* especially (adverb with preposition) *now, when,* etc.:— + after, [al-] ways, × certain, + continually, + evening, long, (due) season, so [long] as, [even-, evening-, noon-] tide, ([meal-], what) time, when.

A masculine or feminine noun meaning time. The word basically means time. But in context, it expresses many aspects of time and kinds of time. It is used most often to express the time of the occurrence of some event. The word means at that time in a general sense, as when Abimelech and Phicol spoke to Abraham during the days when Ishmael was growing up (Ge 21:22; 38:1). The time described can be more specific, such as when Moses refers to the time of crisis in the wilderness when the people wanted meat to eat (Dt 1:9). It may refer to a specific date (Ex 9:18; 1Sa 9:16); or a part of a day, as when the dove returned to Noah in the evening (Ge 8:11; 24:11). The word can refer to a duration of time, as for all time (Ex 18:22; Pr 8:30); or for any time in general (Le 16:2). The time referred to may be past, present, or future (Nu 23:23; Jgs 13:23; Isa 9:1[8:23]). The word can describe times of the Lord's anger (Ps 21:9[10]); or times of trouble (Ps 9:9[10]). In fact, this word can be made to refer to about any kind of time or duration of time by its modifying words and context.

It is used to describe the time when certain appropriate things took place in general. For example, kings customarily went forth to war in the spring (2Sa 11:1; 1Ch 20:1). It can depict times that are fitting or suitable for certain reasons, such as rain falling on the land in its season (Dt 11:14; Jer 5:24); and fruit trees bearing fruit at the proper time (Ps 1:3). The author of Pr 15:23 spoke of a proper time for fitting words. Ecc 3 described all of life as a grand mosaic of times and seasons; there is a time to do everything—to be born, to die, to plant, to uproot, to kill, to heal, to love, to hate (Ecc 3:1–3, 8). This word occurs nineteen times in these verses (Ecc 3:1–8), along with a synonym of this word, *zĕmân* (2165), to make twenty references to time.

The Hebrew word can be used to designate a time even more accurately. When the exiles returned, it was time for the house of the Lord to be rebuilt (Hag 1:2). The word designated the set time of marriage (1Sa 18:19). It pinpointed the time of God's judgments (Isa 13:22; Eze 7:7, 12); but also the many times in the past when He delivered them (Ne 9:28). The Lord stands in readiness to judge every nation when its time comes (Jer 27:7). There will be a time of the end for all the nations as well (Da 8:17; 11:35; 12:4, 9). In contrast, the word in context can be combined with chance to indicate uncertain time (Ecc 9:11); and, appropriately, it describes life in general and its content, whether good or bad (Ps 31:15[16]; Isa 33:6).

6257. עָתַד, 'âthad, *aw-thad´*; a primitive root; to *prepare*:—make fit, be ready to become.

6258. עַתָּה, 'attâh, *at-taw´*; from 6256; at *this time*, whether adverb, conjunction or expletive:—henceforth, now, straightway, this time, whereas.

6259. עָתוּד, 'âthûwd, *aw-thood´*; passive participle of 6257; *prepared*:—ready.

6260. עַתּוּד, 'attûwd, *at-tood´*; or עַתֻּד, **'attud,** *at-tood´*; from 6257; *prepared*, i.e. *full grown*; spoken only (in plural) of *he-goats*, or (figurative) *leaders* of the people:—chief one, (he) goat, ram.

6261. עִתִּי, 'ittîy, *it-tee´*; from 6256; *timely*:—fit.

6262. עַתַּי, 'Attay, *at-tah´ee*; for 6261; *Attai*, the name of three Israelites:—Attai.

6263. עֲתִיד, 'ăthîyd, *ath-eed´*; (Chaldee); corresponding to 6264; *prepared*:—ready.

6264. עָתִיד, 'âthîyd, *aw-theed´*; from 6257; *prepared*; (by implication) *skilful*; feminine plural the *future*; also *treasure*:—things that shall come, ready, treasures.

6265. עֲתָיָה, 'Ăthâyâh, *ath-aw-yaw´*; from 5790 and 3050; *Jah has helped; Athajah*, an Israelite:—Athaiah.

6266. עָתִיק, 'âthîyq, *aw-theek´*; from 6275; (properly) *antique*, i.e. *venerable* or *splendid*:—durable.

6267. עַתִּיק, 'attîyq, *at-teek´*; from 6275; *removed*, i.e. *weaned*; also *antique*:—ancient, drawn.

6268. עַתִּיק, 'attîyq, *at-teek´*; (Chaldee); corresponding to 6267; *venerable*:—ancient.

6269. עֲתָךְ, 'Ăthâk, *ath-awk´*; from an unused root meaning to *sojourn; lodging; Athak*, a place in Palestine:—Athach.

6270. עַתְלַי, 'Athlay, *ath-lah´ee*; from an unused root meaning to *compress; constringent; Athlai*, an Israelite:—Athlai.

6271. עֲתַלְיָה, 'Ăthalyâh, *ath-al-yaw´*; or עֲתַלְיָהוּ, **'Ăthalyâhûw,** *ath-al-yaw´-hoo*; from the same as 6270 and 3050; *Jah has constrained; Athaljah*, the name of an Israelitess and two Israelites:—Athaliah.

6272. עָתַם, 'âtham, *aw-tham´*; a primitive root; probably to *glow*, i.e. (figurative) *be desolated*:—be darkened.

6273. עָתְנִי, 'Othnîy, *oth-nee´*; from an unused root meaning to *force; forcible; Othni*, an Israelite:—Othni.

6274. עָתְנִיאֵל, 'Othnîy'êl, *oth-nee-ale´*; from the same as 6273 and 410; *force of God; Othniël*, an Israelite:—Othniel.

6275. עָתַק, 'âthaq, *aw-thak´*; a primitive root; to *remove* (intransitive or transitive); (figurative) to *grow old*; (specifically) to *transcribe*:—copy out, leave off, become (wax) old, remove.

6276. עָתֵק, 'âthêq, *aw-thake´*; from 6275; *antique*, i.e. *valued*:—durable.

6277. עָתָק, 'âthâq, *aw-thawk´*; from 6275 in the sense of *license; impudent*:—arrogancy, grievous (hard) things, stiff.

6278. עֵת קָצִין, 'Êth Qâtsîyn, *ayth kaw-tseen´*; from 6256 and 7011; *time of a judge; Eth-Katsin*, a place in Palestine:—Ittah-kazin [*by including directive enclitic*].

6279. עָתַר, 'âthar, *aw-thar´*; a primitive root [rather denominative from 6281]; to burn *incense* in worship, i.e. *intercede* (reciprocal, *listen* to prayer):—intreat, (make) pray (-er).

A verb meaning to pray, to entreat, to supplicate. The fundamental meaning of this word is that of a cry to the Lord for deliverance. It was used in Isaac's prayer concerning his wife's barrenness (Ge 25:21); and the prayers of Moses to stop the plagues in Egypt (Ex 8:8[4]). Scripture says that the Lord is faithful to hear such prayers (Job 33:26).

6280. עָתַר, 'âthar, *aw-thar´*; a primitive root; to *be* (causative, *make*) *abundant*:—deceitful, multiply.

6281. עֶתֶר, 'Ether, *eh´-ther*; from 6280; *abundance; Ether*, a place in Palestine:—Ether.

6282. עָתָר, 'âthâr, *aw-thawr´*; from 6280; *incense* (as increasing to a *volume* of smoke); hence (from 6279) a *worshipper*:—suppliant, thick.

6283. עֲתֶרֶת, 'ăthereth, *ath-eh´-reth*; from 6280; *copiousness*:—abundance.

6284. פָּאָה, pâ'âh, *paw-aw´*; a primitive root; to *puff*, i.e. *blow* away:—scatter into corners.

6285. פֵּאָה, pê'âh, *pay-aw´*; feminine of 6311; (properly) *mouth* in a figurative sense, i.e. *direction, region, extremity*:—corner, end, quarter, side.

6286. פָּאַר, pâ'ar, *paw-ar´*; a primitive root; to *gleam*, (causative) *embellish*; (figurative) to *boast*; also to *explain* (i.e. make clear) oneself; denominative from 6288, to *shake* a tree:—beautify, boast self, go over the boughs, glorify (self), glory, vaunt self.

A verb meaning to beautify, to glorify. In the factitive form, God brings beauty and glory to His chosen people (Ps 149:4; Isa 55:5; 60:9); and to His Temple (Ezr 7:27; Isa 60:7). In the reflexive form, one beautifies and glorifies one's self and not others. Gideon is instructed to reduce the number of men in his army so the Israelites could not give themselves the glory for the victory that was to come (Jgs 7:2). In God's judgment against Assyria—a country that was merely an instrument in God's hand—Isaiah rhetorically asked whether the ax and the saw could take credit for the work accomplished through them (Isa 10:15). Obviously, the answer is no. In the same way, people should not take glory in what God is doing through their lives. In several passages, Isaiah also states that God brings glory to Himself by His actions through His people (Isa 44:23; 49:3; 60:21; 61:3).

6287. פְּאֵר, p^e'êr, *peh-ayr´*; from 6286; an *embellishment,* i.e. fancy *head-dress:*—beauty, bonnet, goodly, ornament, tire.

6288. פְּאֹרָה, p^e'ôrâh, *peh-o-raw´*; or **פֹּרָאה, pôrâ'h,** *po-raw´*; or **פֻּארָה, pu'râh,** *poo-raw´*; from 6286; (properly) *ornamentation,* i.e. (plural) *foliage* (including the limbs) as *bright* green:—bough, branch, sprig.

6289. פָּארוּר, pâ'rûwr, *paw-roor´*; from 6286; (properly) *illuminated,* i.e. a *glow*; as noun, a *flush* (of anxiety):—blackness.

A masculine noun whose meaning is assumed to be in dread or fear; however, the meaning of this word is uncertain. It occurs two times, each with the verb *qâbats* (6908), meaning to gather. From the context, it is clear that the term is a negative one. In Joel 2:6, the context is a warning against the Day of the Lord, when an imposing army will invade, and people will be struck with great fear. In Na 2:10[11], the context is a prophecy of judgment against and the impending doom of Nineveh, which was like a lion's den, a place of safety and sanctuary (yet no fear) but would soon be a place of destruction and devastation.

6290. פָּארָן, Pâ'rân, *paw-rawn´*; from 6286; *ornamental; Paran,* a desert of Arabia:—Paran.

6291. פַּג, pag, *pag*; from an unused root meaning to *be torpid,* i.e. *crude*; an *unripe* fig:—green fig.

6292. פִּגּוּל, piggûwl, *pig-gool´*; or **פִּגֻּל, piggul,** *pig-gool´*; from an unused root meaning to *stink*; (properly) *fetid,* i.e. (figurative) *unclean* (ceremonially):—abominable (-tion, thing).

A masculine noun meaning a foul thing, refuse. It is a technical term for a part of a sacrifice that has become or been rendered unclean. This was applied to the fellowship offering that was to be eaten the same day it was offered or the next day. If it remained until the third day, it was considered unclean (Le 7:18; 19:7). Isaiah recorded the prophecy of God where He defined the activities of people that rendered them unclean, including contact with the deceased and eating unclean food, namely pork (Isa 65:4). Ezekiel protested God's instruction to him because he had never eaten any unclean meat; however, he failed to define what unclean meat was (Eze 4:14).

6293. פָּגַע, pâga', *paw-gah´*; a primitive root; to *impinge,* by accident or violence, or (figurative) by importunity:—come (betwixt), cause to entreat, fall (upon), make intercession, intercessor, intreat, lay, light [upon], meet (together), pray, reach, run.

A verb meaning to meet, to encounter, to reach. It could simply mean to meet (Ex 5:20; 1Sa 10:5). It could also signify to meet someone with hostility, where it is usually rendered to fall upon (Jos 2:16; Jgs 8:21; Ru 2:22). In addition, it could convey the concept of meeting with a request or entreaty and is usually rendered as intercession (Jer 7:16). This verb is used to designate the establishment of a boundary, probably with the idea of extending the boundary to reach a certain point (Jos 16:7; 19:11, 22, 26, 27, 34).

6294. פֶּגַע, pega', *peh´-gah*; from 6293; *impact* (casual):—chance, occurrent.

6295. פַּגְעִיאֵל, Pag'îy'êl, *pag-ee-ale´*; from 6294 and 410; *accident of God; Pagiël,* an Israelite:—Pagiel.

6296. פָּגַר, pâgar, *paw-gar´*; a primitive root; to *relax,* i.e. become *exhausted:*—be faint.

6297. פֶּגֶר, peger, *peh´-gher*; from 6296; a *carcase* (as *limp*), whether of man or beast; (figurative) an idolatrous *image:*—carcase, corpse, dead body.

A masculine noun meaning a corpse, a carcass. It can refer to the carcasses of animals (Ge 15:11); however, it is usually used in connection with human corpses. Though this term can refer to a single body (Isa 14:19), it is usually found in the plural (Isa 34:3; Jer 31:40; Eze 6:5). In several instances, the singular is used as a collective (1Sa 17:46; Am 8:3; Na 3:3). One occurrence of this word is a metaphor for the lifelessness of idols (Le 26:30).

6298. פָּגַשׁ, pâgash, *paw-gash´*; a primitive root; to *come in contact with,* whether by accident or violence; (figurative) to *concur:*—meet (with, together).

6299. פָּדָה, pâdâh, *paw-daw´*; a primitive root; to *sever,* i.e. *ransom*; (generally) to *release, preserve:*— × at all, deliver, × by any means, ransom, (that are to be, let be) redeem (-ed), rescue, × surely.

A verb meaning to ransom, to redeem, and to deliver. The word is used to depict God's act of redeeming; He redeemed His people with a mighty hand from Pharaoh and the slavery they were under in Egypt (Dt 7:8; Mic 6:4). Egypt was literally the house of slavery and became the symbol of slavery and oppression from which Israel was delivered (Dt 9:26; 24:18). After Israel was in exile in Babylon, the Lord redeemed them from their strong enemies (Jer 31:11). He had longed to redeem them from their apostasy before He gave them over to judgment, but they would not respond to His call (Hos 7:13; 13:14).

The Lord also redeemed individuals in the sense of rescuing them. He delivered David (2Sa 4:9; 1Ki 1:29); Abraham (Isa 29:22); Jeremiah (Jer 15:21); and the psalmist (Ps 26:11; 31:5[6]).

The word often describes the process of ransoming persons in the cultic setting of ancient Israel. The firstborn was ransomed or redeemed (Ex 13:13, 15; Nu 18:15); animals were redeemed by payment of a half-shekel of ransom money (Le 27:27; Nu 18:15). The firstborn of an ox, sheep, or goat could not be redeemed (Nu 18:17). The word described the action of both the community and friends to redeem individuals (1Sa 14:45; Job 6:23).

In the passive stem, the word means to be redeemed. The word is used to describe a female slave who has not been ransomed (Le 19:20). A person under the ban for destruction could not be ransomed either (Le 27:29). Zion would be redeemed through justice (Isa 1:27); one person could not be redeemed by the life of another (Ps 49:7[8]).

In the causative stem, it means to bring about deliverance or redemption; the master who did not accept his slave girl had to cause her to be redeemed (Ex 21:8); the firstborn male of unclean animals and humans had to be redeemed as well (Nu 18:15, 16).

6300. פְּדַהְאֵל, P^edah'êl, *ped-ah-ale´*; from 6299 and 410; *God has ransomed; Pedahel,* an Israelite:—Pedahel.

6301. פְּדָהצוּר, P^edâhtsûwr, *ped-aw-tsoor´*; from 6299 and 6697; a *rock* (i.e. God) *has ransomed; Pedahtsur,* an Israelite:—Pedahzur.

6302. פְּדוּיִם, p^edûwyim, *pe-doo´-yim*; passive participle of 6299; *ransomed* (and so occurring under 6299); as abstract (in plural masculine) a *ransom:*—(that are) to be (that were) redeemed.

A masculine noun meaning ransom. Like the word *pidyôwm* (6306), it is an abstract form of the basic passive participle derived from the verb *pâdâh* (6299), meaning to ransom. As such, it occurs three times in the context of Israel's ransoming their firstborn males. In this context, this term is parallel with the silver that was used to redeem firstborn males and then given to Aaron and his sons (Nu 3:46, 48; 51).

6303. פָּדוֹן, Pâdôwn, *paw-done´*; from 6299; *ransom; Padon,* one of the Nethinim:—Padon.

6304. פְּדוּת, p^edûwth, *ped-ooth´*; or **פְּדֻת, p^eduth,** *ped-ooth´*; from 6929; *distinction*; also *deliverance:*—division, redeem, redemption.

A feminine noun meaning ransom, redemption. It is used four times in the OT and could refer to redemption in general (Ps 111:9); redemption from sins (Ps 130:7); or redemption from exile (Isa 50:2). The meaning of the fourth occurrence of this word (Ex 8:23[19]) is difficult to ascertain. The Septuagint renders the Hebrew with *diastole* (1293, NT), meaning a division or distinction, and English translations follow suit.

6305. פְּדָיָה, P^edâyâh, *ped-aw-yaw´*; or **פְּדָיָהוּ, P^edâ-yâhûw,** *ped-aw-yaw´-hoo*; from 6299 and 3050; *Jah has ransomed; Pedajah,* the name of six Israelites:—Pedaiah.

6306. פִּדְיוֹם, pidyôwm, *pid-yome´*; or **פִּדְיֹם, pidyôm,** *pid-yome´*; also **פִּדְיוֹן, pidyôwn,** *pid-yone´*; or **פִּדְיֹן, pidyôn,** *pid-yone´*; from 6299; a *ransom:*—ransom, that were redeemed, redemption.

A masculine noun meaning ransom, ransom money. Like the word *pâdûy* (6302), *pidyôwm* is an abstract form of the basic passive participle derived from the verb *pâdâh* (6299), meaning to ransom. As such, it occurs in the same context as *pâdûy*, referring to the ransoming of the Israelite firstborn males (Nu 3:49, 51).

Pidyôwn is a masculine noun meaning ransom money. The word is closely related to *pidyôwm* (see above paragraph) and *pâdûy* (6302); yet it is a substantive noun and not an abstract noun. It refers to the money exchanged as a ransom, not simply to the concept of ransoming. In addition, this term always occurs in connection with the term *nephesh* (5315), meaning life (Ex 21:30; Ps 49:8[9]).

6307. פַּדָּן, Paddân, *pad-dawn´*; from an unused root meaning to *extend*; a *plateau*; or פַּדַּן אֲרָם, **Paddan 'Ărâm,** *pad-dan´ ar-awm´*; from the same as 758; the *table-land of Aram; Paddan* or *Paddan-Aram*, a region of Syria:—Padan, Padan-aram.

6308. פָּדַע, pâdaʻ, *paw-dah´*; a primitive root; to *retrieve*:—deliver.

A verb derived from an unknown root. It occurs only in Job 33:24, and the context requires that it carry a meaning like to deliver, to rescue. The verse talks of delivering one from going down to the pit.

6309. פֶּדֶר, peder, *peh´-der*; from an unused root meaning to *be greasy; suet*:—fat.

6310. פֶּה, peh, *peh*; from 6284; the *mouth* (as the means of *blowing*), whether literal or figurative (particularly *speech*); (specifically) *edge, portion* or *side*; (adverbially, with preposition) *according to*:—accord (-ing as, -ing to), after, appointment, assent, collar, command (-ment), × eat, edge, end, entry, + file, hole, × in, mind, mouth, part, portion, × (should) say (-ing), sentence, skirt, sound, speech, × spoken, talk, tenor, × to, + two-edged, wish, word.

A masculine singular noun meaning mouth. Besides the literal meaning, this term is used as the instrument of speech and figuratively for speech itself. When Moses claimed to be an ineffective speaker, he was heavy of mouth (Ex 4:10); the psalmist also uses *peh* to mean speech (Ps 49:13[14]; Ecc 10:13; Isa 29:13). The word is rendered edge in the expression the mouth of the sword (Jgs 4:16; Pr 5:4); or in some measurements from edge to edge or end to end (2Ki 10:21; 21:16; Ezr 9:11). It is also used for other openings like those in caves, gates, wells, or sacks. In land and inheritance references, it is translated as share or portion (Dt 21:17; 2Ki 2:9; Zec 13:8). With the preposition *lᵉ*, it means in proportion to or according to.

6311. פֹּה, pôh, *po*; or פֹּא, **pô',** *po*; (Job 38:11), or פּוֹ, **pôw,** *po*; probably from a primitive inseparable particle פּ **p** (of demonstrative force) and 1931; *this place* (French *ici*), i.e. *here* or *hence*:—here, hither, the one (other, this, that) side.

6312. פּוּאָה, Pûw'âh, *poo-aw´*; or פֻּוָּה, **Puvvâh,** *poov-vaw´*; from 6284; a *blast; Puäh* or *Puvvah*, the name of two Israelites:—Phuvah, Pua, Puah.

6313. פּוּג, pûwg, *poog*; a primitive root; to *be sluggish*:—cease, be feeble, faint, be slacked.

6314. פּוּגָה, pûwgâh, *poo-gaw´*; from 6313; *intermission*:—rest.

6315. פּוּחַ, pûwach, *poo´-akh*; a primitive root; to *puff*, i.e. blow with the breath or air; hence to *fan* (as a breeze), to *utter*, to *kindle* (a fire), to *scoff*:—blow (upon), break, puff, bring into a snare, speak, utter.

A verb translated to breathe, to blow. The word is only used in poetic contexts in the Hebrew Bible. In the Song of Songs, the expression until the day breathes refers to the early morning when shadows flee (SS 2:17; 4:6); and the north wind is told to blow on the garden (SS 4:16). But just as often, the word implies a negative connotation, such as to snort at an enemy (Ps 10:5); to incite a city (Pr 29:8); or the Lord to blow out His anger (Eze 21:31[36]). In a unique usage, Proverbs uses the verb to refer to speaking lies (Pr 6:19; 14:5, 25; 19:5, 9); but once for speaking truth (Pr 12:17).

6316. פּוּט, Pûwt, *poot*; of foreign origin; *Put*, a son of Ham, also the name of his descendants or their region, and of a Persian tribe:—Phut, Put.

6317. פּוּטִיאֵל, Pûwṭîy'êl, *poo-tee-ale´*; from an unused root (probably meaning to *disparage*) and 410; *contempt of God; Putiël*, an Israelite:—Putiel.

6318. פּוֹטִיפַר, Pôwṭîyphar, *po-tee-far´*; of Egyptian derivation; *Potiphar*, an Egyptian:—Potiphar.

6319. פּוֹטִי פֶרַע, Pôwṭîy Pheraʻ, *po´-tee feh´-rah*; of Egyptian derivation; *Poti-Phera*, an Egyptian:—Poti-pherah.

6320. פּוּךְ, pûwk, *pook*; from an unused root meaning to *paint; dye* (specifically *stibium* for the eyes):—fair colours, glistering, paint [-ed] (-ing).

6321. פּוֹל, pôwl, *pole*; from an unused root meaning to *be thick*; a *bean* (as *plump*):—beans.

6322. פּוּל, Pûwl, *pool*; of foreign origin; *Pul*, the name of an Assyrian king and of an Ethiopian tribe:—Pul.

6323. פּוּן, pûwn, *poon*; a primitive root meaning to *turn*, i.e. *be perplexed*:—be distracted.

6324. פּוּנִי, Pûwnîy, *poo-nee´*; patronymic from an unused name meaning a *turn*; a *Punite* (collective) or descendants of an unknown Pun:—Punites.

6325. פּוּנֹן, Pûwnôn, *poo-none´*; from 6323; *perplexity; Punon*, a place in the Desert:—Punon.

6326. פּוּעָה, Pûwʻâh, *poo-aw´*; from an unused root meaning to *glitter; brilliancy; Puäh*, an Israelitess:—Puah.

6327. פּוּץ, pûwts, *poots*; a primitive root; to *dash* in pieces, literal or figurative (especially to *disperse*):—break (dash, shake) in (to) pieces, cast (abroad), disperse (selves), drive, retire, scatter (abroad), spread abroad.

6328. פּוּק, pûwq, *pook*; a primitive root; to *waver*:—stumble, move.

6329. פּוּק, pûwq, *pook*; a primitive root [rather identical with 6328 through the idea of *dropping* out; compare 5312]; to *issue*, i.e. *furnish*; (causative) to *secure*; (figurative) to *succeed*:—afford, draw out, further, get, obtain.

6330. פּוּקָה, pûwqâh, *poo-kaw´*; from 6328; a *stumbling-block*:—grief.

6331. פּוּר, pûwr, *poor*; a primitive root; to *crush*:—break, bring to nought, × utterly take.

6332. פּוּר, Pûwr, *poor*; also (plural) פּוּרִים, **Pûwrîym,** *poo-reem´*; or פֻּרִים, **Purîym,** *poo-reem´*; from 6331; a *lot* (as by means of a *broken* piece):—Pur, Purim.

6333. פּוּרָה, pûwrâh, *poo-raw´*; from 6331; a *wine-press* (as *crushing* the grapes):—winepress.

6334. פּוֹרָתָא, Pôwrâthâh, *po-raw-thaw´*; of Persian origin; *Poratha*, a son of Haman:—Poratha.

6335. פּוּשׁ, pûwsh, *poosh*; a primitive root; to *spread*; (figurative) to *act proudly*:—grow up, be grown fat, spread selves, be scattered.

6336. פּוּתִי, Pûwthîy, *poo-thee´*; patronymic from an unused name meaning a *hinge*; a *Puthite* (collective) or descendant of an unknown Puth:—Puhites [*as if from* 6312].

6337. פָּז, pâz, *pawz*; from 6388; *pure* (gold); hence *gold* itself (as refined):—fine (pure) gold.

6338. פָּזַז, pâzaz, *paw-zaz´*; a primitive root; to *refine* (gold):—best [gold].

6339. **פָּזַז, pâzaz,** *paw-zaz´*; a primitive root [rather identical with 6338]; to *solidify* (as if by *refining*); also to *spring* (as if *separating* the limbs):—leap, be made strong.

6340. **פָּזַר, pâzar,** *paw-zar´*; a primitive root; to *scatter*, whether in enmity or bounty:—disperse, scatter (abroad).

6341. **פַּח, pach,** *pakh*; from 6351; a (metallic) *sheet* (as *pounded* thin); also a spring *net* (as spread out like a *lamina*):—gin, (thin) plate, snare.

A masculine singular noun translated bird trap. It is used in its literal sense in Am 3:5, Pr 7:23, and Ecc 9:12. But more often it is used figuratively for a human ensnarement. Jeremiah prophesied that a snare awaited Moab (Jer 48:43); while Proverbs said that snares were set for the wicked (Pr 22:5). Eliphaz told Job that snares surrounded him (Job 22:10). The psalmist's path was filled with the snares of his enemies (Ps 140:5[6]; 142:3[4]). But retribution was envisioned as the enemies' tables turned into a snare (Ps 69:22[23]).

6342. **פָּחַד, pâchad,** *paw-khad´*; a primitive root; to *be startled* (by a sudden alarm); hence to *fear* in general:—be afraid, stand in awe, (be in) fear, make to shake.

A verb meaning to dread, to be in dread, to be in awe. This verb occurs in poetry. Those who worship and trust God have no need to dread, but those who break the Law (Dt 28:66); sinners in Zion (Isa 33:14); and worshippers of idols (Isa 44:11) have reason to fear. It often takes a cognate accusative. For a positive use, in the eschatological perspective of Isa 60:5, the term is best translated to be awed.

6343. **פַּחַד, pachad,** *pakh´-ad*; from 6342; a (sudden) *alarm* (properly, the object feared; by implication, the feeling):—dread (-ful), fear, (thing) great [fear, -ly feared], terror.

A masculine singular noun translated dread, terror. This dread was often caused by the Lord (1Sa 11:7; Job 13:11; Isa 2:10, 19, 21). The dread could cause trembling (Job 13:11; Ps 119:120). The noun often occurs in a cognate accusative construction (see *pâchad* [6342]) (Dt 28:67; Job 3:25; Ps 14:5). A unique use of the term is found in Genesis 31:42, often translated the Dread or Fear of Isaac, parallel to the God of Abraham.

6344. **פַּחַד, pachad,** *pakh´-ad*; the same as 6343; a *testicle* (as a cause of *shame* akin to fear):—stone.

6345. **פַּחְדָּה, pachdâh,** *pakh-daw´*; feminine of 6343; *alarm* (i.e. *awe*):—fear.

A feminine noun meaning fear, religious awe. This Hebrew word appears only in Jer 2:19, where it refers to the proper respect and reverence due to the Lord, which is lacking when one forsakes God and His commands.

6346. **פֶּחָה, pechâh,** *peh-khaw´*; of foreign origin; a *prefect* (of a city or small district):—captain, deputy, governor.

A masculine noun meaning a governor, a captain. The primary meaning of this word is that of a lord over a given district or territory. It signified an office that is appointed and not received by virtue of birth or other right. It was generally used of the leader of the Jewish nation after the exile (Ne 12:26; Hag 1:14; Mal 1:8); but in other places it was used of a deputy bureaucrat in any given location (Est 8:9; Jer 51:23); or a military leader (1Ki 20:24).

6347. **פֶּחָה, pechâh,** *peh-khaw´*; (Chaldee); corresponding to 6346:—captain, governor.

An Aramaic masculine noun meaning a governor, a satrap, a captain. Corresponding to the Hebrew word *pechâh* (6346), this word means a governor or other similarly appointed authority. It was used particularly of a provincial governor in the Persian Empire (Ezr 5:6); the postexilic leader of the Jewish nation (Ezr 6:7); and various similar officers involved in the political structure (Da 6:7[8]).

6348. **פָּחַז, pâchaz,** *paw-khaz´*; a primitive root; to *bubble* up or *froth* (as boiling water), i.e. (figurative) to *be unimportant*:—light.

6349. **פַּחַז, pachaz,** *pakh´-az*; from 6348; *ebullition*, i.e. froth (figurative) *lust*:—unstable.

6350. **פַּחֲזוּת, pachăzûwth,** *pakh-az-ooth´*; from 6348; *frivolity*:—lightness.

6351. **פָּחַח, pâchach,** *paw-khakh´*; a primitive root; to *batter* out; but used only as denominative from 6341, to *spread a net*:—be snared.

6352. **פֶּחָם, pechâm,** *peh-khawm´*; perhaps from an unused root probably meaning to *be black*; a *coal*, whether charred or live:—coals.

6353. **פֶּחָר, pechâr,** *peh-khawr´*; (Chaldee); from an unused root probably meaning to *fashion*; a *potter*:—potter.

6354. **פַּחַת, pachath,** *pakh´-ath*; probably from an unused root apparently meaning to *dig*; a *pit*, especially for catching animals:—hole, pit, snare.

A masculine singular noun meaning a pit, a cave. Within the prophecies of Isaiah and Jeremiah, the term is used in judgment as a trap for the wicked enemies of the Lord and Israel (Isa 24:17, 18; Jer 48:28, 43, 44). In Lamentations, it was a place for sinful Jerusalem (La 3:47). The term is used for the cave where David and his men were hiding (2Sa 17:9); and for the pit in which Absalom's body was thrown (2Sa 18:17).

6355. **פַּחַת מוֹאָב, Pachath Môw'âb,** *pakh´-ath mo-awb´*; from 6354 and 4124; *pit of Moäb; Pachath-Moäb*, an Israelite:—Pahath-moab.

6356. **פְּחֶתֶת, pchetheth,** *pekh-eh´-theth*; from the same as 6354; a *hole* (by mildew in a garment):—fret inward.

A feminine noun meaning bored out, eaten away. This word is used once to denote the condition of a decaying leprous garment (Le 13:55). The image underlying the word is similar to that of a wormhole or spot eaten away by a moth.

6357. **פִּטְדָה, piṭdâh,** *pit-daw´*; of foreign derivation; a *gem*, probably the *topaz*:—topaz.

6358. **פָּטוּר, pâṭûwr,** *paw-toor´*; passive participle of 6362; *opened*, i.e. (as noun) a *bud*:—open.

6359. **פָּטִיר, pâṭîyr,** *paw-teer´*; from 6362; *open*, i.e. *unoccupied*:—free.

6360. **פַּטִּישׁ, paṭṭîysh,** *pat-teesh´*; intensive from an unused root meaning to *pound*; a *hammer*:—hammer.

6361. **פַּטִּישׁ, paṭṭîysh,** *pat-teesh´*; (Chaldee); from a root corresponding to that of 6360; a *gown* (as if *hammered* out wide):—hose.

6362. **פָּטַר, pâṭar,** *paw-tar´*; a primitive root; to *cleave* or burst through, i.e. (causative) to *emit*, whether literal or figurative (*gape*):—dismiss, free, let (shoot) out, slip away.

6363. **פֶּטֶר, peṭer,** *peh´-ter*; or **פִּטְרָה, piṭrâh,** *pit-raw´*; from 6362; a *fissure*, i.e. (concrete) *firstling* (as *opening* the matrix):—firstling, openeth, such as open.

6364. **פִּי־בֶסֶת, Pîy-Beseth,** *pee beh´-seth*; of Egyptian origin; *Pi-Beseth*, a place in Egypt:—Pi-beseth.

6365. **פִּיד, pîyd,** *peed*; from an unused root probably meaning to *pierce*; (figurative) *misfortune*:—destruction, ruin.

A masculine noun meaning a ruin, a disaster. It is used of divine judgment (Job 30:24; 31:29), as when the father encouraged his son to avoid the wicked and focus on God because God's judgment will eventually come on the wicked (Pr 24:22).

6366. **פֵּיוֹת, pêyôwth,** *pay-oth´*; feminine of 6310; an *edge*:—(two-) edge (-d).

6367. **פִּי הַחִרֹת, Pîy ha-Chirôth,** *pee hah-khee-rōth´*; from 6310 and the feminine plural of a noun (from the same root as 2356, with the article internal; *mouth of the gorges; Pi-ha-Chiroth*, a place in Egypt:—Pi-hahiroth. [In Nu 14:19 without Pi-.]

6368. פִּיחַ, pîyach, *pee´-akh*; from 6315; a *powder* (as easily *puffed* away), i.e. *ashes* or *dust*:—ashes.

6369. פִּיכֹל, Pîykôl, *pee-kole´*; apparently from 6310 and 3605; *mouth of all; Picol*, a Philistine:—Phichol.

6370. פִּילֶגֶשׁ, pîylegesh, *pee-leh´-ghesh*; or **פִּלֶגֶשׁ, pilegesh,** *pee-leh´-ghesh*; of uncertain derivation; a *concubine*; also (masculine) a *paramour*:—concubine, paramour.

A feminine noun meaning a concubine. A concubine was a legitimate wife; however, she was of secondary rank. This is evident by the references to the concubine as having a husband (Jgs 19:2); and that this man and her father are considered to be son-in-law (cf. Jgs 19:5) and father-in-law (cf. Jgs 19:4), respectively. But concubines were presented opposite the wives of higher rank (1Ki 11:3; SS 6:8). The ability to have and to keep concubines was a sign of wealth, status, and often of royalty (1Ki 11:3; Est 2:14; SS 6:8). To sleep with a king's concubine would have indicated plans to usurp the throne (2Sa 3:7; 16:21, 22; cf. 1Ki 2:21–24).

6371. פִּימָה, pîymâh, *pee-maw´*; probably from an unused root meaning to *be plump; obesity*:—collops.

6372. פִּינְחָס, Pîynᵉchâs, *pee-nekh-aws´*; apparently from 6310 and a variation of 5175; *mouth of a serpent; Pinechas*, the name of three Israelites:—Phinehas.

6373. פִּינֹן, pîynôn, *pee-none´*; probably the same as 6325; *Pinon*, an Idumæan:—Pinon.

6374. פִּיפִיּוֹת, pîyphîyyôwth, *pee-fee-yoth´*; for 6366; an *edge* or *tooth*:—tooth, × two-edged.

6375. פִּיק, pîyq, *peek*; from 6329; a *tottering*:—smite together.

A masculine noun meaning tottering. This noun only occurs in one passage, where the devastation of Nineveh is portrayed: "She is empty, and void, and waste: and the heart melteth, and the knees smite together, and much pain is in all loins, and the faces of them all gather blackness" (Na 2:10[11] KJV).

6376. פִּישׁוֹן, Pîyshôwn, *pee-shone´*; from 6335; *dispersive; Pishon*, a river of Eden:—Pison.

6377. פִּיתוֹן, Pîythôwn, *pee-thone´*; probably from the same as 6596; *expansive; Pithon*, an Israelite:—Pithon.

6378. פַּךְ, pak, *pak*; from 6379; a *flask* (from which a liquid may *flow*):—box, vial.

6379. פָּכָה, pâkâh, *paw-kaw´*; a primitive root; to *pour*:—run out.

6380. פֹּכֶרֶת הַצְּבָיִים, Pôkereth hats-Tsᵉbâyîym, *po-keh´-reth hats-tseb-aw-yeem´*; from the active participle (of the same form as the first word) feminine of an unused root (meaning to *entrap*) and plural of 6643; *trap of gazelles; Pokereth-Tsebajim*, one of the "servants of Solomon":—Pochereth of Zebaim.

6381. פָּלָא, pâlâʼ, *paw-law´*; a primitive root; (properly) perhaps to *separate*, i.e. *distinguish* (literal or figurative); (by implication) to *be* (causative, *make*) *great, difficult, wonderful*:—accomplish, (arise … too, be too) hard, hidden, things too high, (be, do, do a, shew) marvelous (-ly, -els, things, work), miracles, perform, separate, make singular, (be, great, make) wonderful (-ers, -ly, things, works), wondrous (things, works, -ly).

A verb meaning to do something wonderful, to do something extraordinary, or difficult. It frequently signifies the wondrous works of God, especially His deliverance and judgments (Ex 3:20; Ps 106:22; 136:4; Mic 7:15). Because God's extraordinary deeds inspire thanksgiving and praise, this Hebrew word occurs often in the hymnic literature of the Bible and of the Dead Sea Scrolls (Ps 9:1[2]; 107:8; 145:5). While nothing is too extraordinary for God, various things are said to be beyond the abilities of some individuals to do or comprehend (Dt 17:8; Pr 30:18; Jer 32:17); however, obeying God's commandments is not too difficult a task (Dt 30:11). A rare use of this Hebrew word expresses the performance of a special vow beyond the ordinary commitment (Le 27:2; Nu 6:2; 15:3, 8).

6382. פֶּלֶא, peleʼ, *peh´-leh*; from 6381; a *miracle*:—marvelous thing, wonder (-ful, -fully).

A masculine noun meaning a wonder, a miracle, a marvel. This word is used to represent something unusual or extraordinary. Except for La 1:9, this term always appears in the context of God's words or deeds. It is used of God's actions among His people (Isa 29:14); the Law of God (Ps 119:129); God's acts of judgment and deliverance (Ex 15:11; Ps 78:12; Isa 25:1); and the child to be born as the Messiah (Isa 9:6[5]). These things then become the focus of people's worship of God (Ps 77:11[12], 14[15]). This word is also used as an adverb to reveal how astounding, significant, and extreme was the fall of the city of Jerusalem (La 1:9).

6383. פִּלְאִי, pilʼîy, *pil-ee´*; or **פֶּלְאִי, pelʼîy,** *pel-ee´*; from 6381; *remarkable*:—secret, wonderful.

A masculine adjective meaning wonderful, incomprehensible. The feminine form of this adjective is *pĕliʼâyh* or *pilʼiyyâh*. It was used as a description of the name of the angel of the Lord (Jgs 13:18); and as a description of the knowledge of the Lord (Ps 139:6).

6384. פַּלֻּאִי, Palluʼîy, *pal-loo-ee´*; patronymic from 6396; a *Palluïte* (collective) or descendants of Pallu:—Palluites.

6385. פָּלַג, pâlag, *paw-lag´*; a primitive root; to *split* (literal or figurative):—divide.

A verb meaning to split, to divide. It is used in the passive form to refer to the earth being divided (Ge 10:25). In the factitive form, it refers to making or dividing a watercourse or cleaving a channel (Job 38:25). The factitive form is also used metaphorically of the Lord to cause dissension, that is, dividing their tongues (Ps 55:9[10]).

6386. פְּלַג, pᵉlag, *pel-ag´*; (Chaldee); corresponding to 6385:—divided.

An Aramaic verb meaning to split, to divide. This word is the equivalent of the Hebrew verb *pâlag* (6385). It is used only once when Daniel was interpreting Nebuchadnezzar's dream. The feet of the statue in the dream were composed partly of clay and partly of iron, representing the idea that the kingdom would be divided (Da 2:41).

6387. פְּלַג, pᵉlag, *pel-ag´*; (Chaldee); from 6386; a *half*:—dividing.

An Aramaic masculine noun meaning half. Like the word *pĕluggâh* (6392), this noun is derived from the verb *pĕlag* (6386), meaning to divide, and represented the results of that action, the production of parts or divisions. Unlike the word *pĕluggâh*, this term seems to assume a single division into two equal parts or halves. This term is used only once in the famous passage stating that the saints will be delivered for a time, times and a half time (Da 7:25).

6388. פֶּלֶג, peleg, *peh´-leg*; from 6385; a *rill* (i.e. small *channel* of water, as in irrigation):—river, stream.

6389. פֶּלֶג, Peleg, *peh´-leg*; the same as 6388; *earthquake; Peleg*, a son of Shem:—Peleg.

6390. פְּלַגָּה, pᵉlaggâh, *pel-ag-gaw´*; from 6385; a *runlet*, i.e. *gully*:—division, river.

A feminine noun meaning a stream, a division. This noun is derived from the verb *pâlag* (6385), whose basic idea is to divide and which, in the extensive-factitive form, can refer to making a watercourse. It can also denote a stream (Job 20:17). See the words *nâhâr* (5104), meaning river, and *nachal* (6391), meaning a torrent or wadi.

6391. פְּלֻגָּה, pᵉluggâh, *pel-oog-gaw´*; from 6385; a *section*:—division.

A feminine noun meaning division. It can only be found in 2Ch 35:5, where Josiah instructed the people of Israel to stand in the holy place by their family divisions.

6392. פְּלֻגָּה, pᵉluggâh, *pel-oog-gaw´*; (Chaldee); corresponding to 6391:—division.

An Aramaic feminine noun meaning division. Like the word *pĕlag* (6387), this noun is derived from the verb *pĕlag* (6386), meaning to divide, and represented the results of that action: the production of parts or divisions. Unlike *pĕlag* (6387), this term seems to assume multiple divisions yielding several equal parts. It is only used once to refer to the apportionment of priests into the divisions that would share the responsibility for the restored Temple (Ezr 6:18).

6393. פְּלָדָה, pᵉlâdâh, *pel-aw-daw´*; from an unused root meaning to *divide*; a *cleaver*, i.e. iron *armature* (of a chariot):—torch.

6394. פִּלְדָּשׁ, Pildâsh, *pil-dawsh´*; of uncertain derivation; *Pildash*, a relative of Abraham:—Pildash.

6395. פָּלָה, pâlâh, *paw-law´*; a primitive root; to *distinguish* (literal or figurative):—put a difference, show marvelous, separate, set apart, sever, make wonderfully.

6396. פַּלּוּא, Pallûw', *pal-loo´*; from 6395; *distinguished; Pallu*, an Israelite:—Pallu, Phallu.

6397. פְּלוֹנִי, Pᵉlôwnîy, *pel-o-nee´*; patronymic from an unused name (from 6395) meaning *separate*; a *Pelonite* or inhabitant of an unknown Palon:—Pelonite.

6398. פָּלַח, pâlach, *paw-lakh´*; a primitive root; to *slice*, i.e. *break* open or *pierce*:—bring forth, cleave, cut, shred, strike through.

6399. פְּלַח, pᵉlach, *pel-akh´*; (Chaldee); corresponding to 6398; to *serve* or worship:—minister, serve.

An Aramaic verb meaning to serve, to revere, to worship. King Nebuchadnezzar was amazed when Daniel's three friends were not harmed in the furnace; he recognized their God for rescuing them because they would not serve any other (Da 3:28). King Darius referred to God as the One Daniel served continually (Da 6:16[17], 20[21]). Later, Daniel wrote of his vision of the Ancient of Days and how all nations worshipped Him (Da 7:14). This thought is echoed later in the same passage (Da 7:27). This word was also used to denote servants of the Temple (Ezr 7:24).

6400. פֶּלַח, pelach, *peh´-lakh*; from 6398; a *slice*:—piece.

6401. פִּלְחָא, Pilchâ', *pil-khaw´*; from 6400; *slicing; Pilcha*, an Israelite:—Pilcha.

6402. פָּלְחָן, polchân, *pol-khawn´*; (Chaldee); from 6399; *worship*:—service.

6403. פָּלַט, pâlaṭ, *paw-lat´*; a primitive root; to *slip* out, i.e. *escape*; (causative) to *deliver*:—calve, carry away safe, deliver, (cause to) escape.

6404. פֶּלֶט, Peleṭ, *peh´-let*; from 6403; *escape; Pelet*, the name of two Israelites:—Pelet. See also 1046.

6405. פַּלֵּט, pallêṭ, *pal-late´*; from 6403; *escape*:—deliverance, escape.

6406. פַּלְטִי, Palṭîy, *pal-tee´*; from 6403; *delivered; Palti*, the name of two Israelites:—Palti, Phalti.

6407. פַּלְטִי, Palṭîy, *pal-tee´*; patronymic from 6406; a *Paltite* or descendant of Palti:—Paltite.

6408. פִּלְטַי, Pilṭay, *pil-tah´ee*; for 6407; *Piltai*, an Israelite:—Piltai.

6409. פַּלְטִיאֵל, Palṭîy'êl, *pal-tee-ale´*; from the same as 6404 and 410; *deliverance of God; Paltiël*, the name of two Israelites:—Paltiel, Phaltiel.

6410. פְּלַטְיָה, Pᵉlaṭyâh, *pel-at-yaw´*; or פְּלַטְיָהוּ, **Pᵉlaṭyâhûw,** *pel-at-yaw´-hoo*; from 6403 and 3050; *Jah has delivered; Pelatjah*, the name of four Israelites:—Pelatiah.

6411. פְּלָיָה, Pᵉlâyâh, *pel-aw-yaw´*; or פְּלָאיָה, **Pᵉlâ'yâh,** *pel-aw-yaw´*; from 6381 and 3050; *Jah has distinguished; Pelajah*, the name of three Israelites:—Pelaiah.

6412. פָּלִיט, pâlîyṭ, *paw-leet´*; or פָּלֵיט, **pâlêyṭ,** *paw-late´*; or פָּלֵט, **pâlêṭ,** *paw-late´*; from 6403; a *refugee*:—(that have) escape (-d, -th), fugitive.

6413. פְּלֵיטָה, pᵉlêyṭâh, *pel-ay-taw´*; or פְּלֵטָה, **pᵉlêṭâh,** *pel-ay-taw´*; feminine of 6412; *deliverance*; (concrete) an *escaped* portion:—deliverance, (that is) escape (-d), remnant.

A feminine noun meaning deliverance, something delivered, a remnant. Jacob split his group into two camps so that if Esau attacked one, the other could escape (Ge 32:8[9]). Joseph told his brothers that God used what they meant for evil to be deliverance for them (Ge 45:7). Moses told Pharaoh that the locusts would eat whatever was left from the hail (Ex 10:5). The Israelites looked for wives for the Benjamites who were left (Jgs 21:17). David had everyone flee, or no one would be safe from Absalom (2Sa 15:14).

6414. פָּלִיל, pâlîyl, *paw-leel´*; from 6419; a *magistrate*:—judge.

A masculine noun meaning judge. This word is only used in the plural in the Hebrew OT. The song of Moses said that even the enemies of Israel judged the Israelite God to be different from other gods (Dt 32:31). As Job listed all the sins he had not committed, he mentioned that it would be shameful to be judged by those sins (Job 31:11). See the related Hebrew root *pâlal* (6419).

6415. פְּלִילָה, pᵉlîylâh, *pel-ee-law´*; feminine of 6414; *justice*:—judgment.

A feminine noun meaning a settlement, a judgment. This form of the word is used only once in the Hebrew OT in the book of Isaiah. In the oracle against Moab, the women cried out for a judgment or settlement to be made for them (Isa 16:3). See the masculine form of this word *pâliyl* (6414) and the related Hebrew root *pâlal* (6419).

6416. פְּלִילִי, pᵉlîylîy, *pel-ee-lee´*; from 6414; *judicial*:—judge.

6417. פְּלִילִיָּה, pᵉlîylîyyâh, *pel-ee-lee-yaw´*; feminine of 6416; *judicature*:—judgment.

6418. פֶּלֶךְ, pelek, *peh´-lek*; from an unused root meaning to *be round*; a *circuit* (i.e. *district*); also a *spindle* (as *whirled*); hence a *crutch*:—(di-) staff, part.

6419. פָּלַל, pâlal, *paw-lal´*; a primitive root; to *judge* (officially or mentally); (by extension) to *intercede, pray*:—intreat, judge (-ment), (make) pray (-er, -ing), make supplication.

A verb meaning to pray, to intercede. This is the most common Hebrew word used to describe the general act of prayer (Jer 29:7). It was often used to describe prayer offered in a time of distress, such as Hannah's prayer for a son (1Sa 1:10, 12); Elisha's prayer for the dead boy (2Ki 4:33); Hezekiah's prayer for protection and health (2Ki 19:15; 20:2); and Jonah's prayer from the fish (Jnh 2:1[2]). In some contexts, this word described a specific intercession of one person praying to the Lord for another, such as Abraham for Abimelech (Ge 20:7, 17); Moses and Samuel for Israel (Nu 11:2; 21:7; 1Sa 7:5); the man of God for the king (1Ki 13:6); or Ezra and Daniel for Israel's sins (Ezr 10:1; Da 9:4, 20). This prayer of intercession could also be made to a false god (Isa 44:17; 45:14).

6420. פָּלָל, Pâlâl, *paw-lawl´*; from 6419; *judge; Palal*, an Israelite:—Palal.

6421. פְּלַלְיָה, Pᵉlalyâh, *pel-al-yaw´*; from 6419 and 3050; *Jah has judged; Pelajah*, an Israelite:—Pelaliah.

6422. פַּלְמוֹנִי, palmôwnîy, *pal-mo-nee´*; probably for 6423; a *certain* one, i.e. so-and-so:—certain.

6423. פְּלֹנִי, pᵉlônîy, *pel-o-nee´*; from 6395; *such* a one, i.e. a specified *person*:—such.

6424. פָּלַס, pâlas, *paw-las´*; a primitive root; (properly) to *roll* flat, i.e. *prepare* (a road); also to *revolve*, i.e. *weigh* (mentally):—make, ponder, weigh.

6425. פֶּלֶס, peles, *peh´-les*; from 6424; a *balance*:—scales, weight.

6426. פָּלַץ, pâlats, *paw-lats´*; a primitive root; (properly, perhaps) to *rend*, i.e. (by implication) to *quiver*:—tremble.

6427. פַּלָּצוּת, pallâtsûwth, *pal-law-tsooth´*; from 6426; *affright*:—fearfulness, horror, trembling.

A feminine noun meaning shuddering. This word describes the physical reaction of the body in response to fear. Job shuddered at the fate of the wicked (Job 21:6); David shuddered in fear of his enemy (Ps 55:5[6]); Isaiah shuddered because of God's judgment (Isa 21:4); and those about to be judged by God will shudder (Eze 7:18). See the word *miphletseth* (4656).

6428. פָּלַשׁ, pâlash, *paw-lash´*; a primitive root; to *roll* (in dust):—roll (wallow) self.

6429. פְּלֶשֶׁת, Pᵉlesheth, *pel-eh´-sheth*; from 6428; *rolling*, i.e. *migratory; Pelesheth*, a region of Syria:—Palestina, Palestine, Philistia, Philistines.

6430. פְּלִשְׁתִּי, Pᵉlishtîy, *pel-ish-tee´*; patrial from 6429; a *Pelishtite* or inhabitant of Pelesheth:—Philistine.

6431. פֶּלֶת, Peleth, *peh´-leth*; from an unused root meaning to *flee; swiftness; Peleth*, the name of two Israelites:—Peleth.

6432. פְּלֵתִי, Pᵉlêthîy, *pel-ay-thee´*; from the same form as 6431; a *courier* (collective) or official *messenger*:—Pelethites.

6433. פֻּם, pum, *poom*; (Chaldee); probably for 6310; the *mouth* (literal or figurative):—mouth.

6434. פֵּן, pên, *pane*; from an unused root meaning to *turn*; an *angle* (of a street or wall):—corner.

6435. פֵּן, pen, *pen*; from 6437; (properly) *removal*; used only (in the construct) adverb as conjunction *lest*:—(lest) (peradventure), that … not.

6436. פַּנַּג, pannag, *pan-nag´*; of uncertain derivation; probably *pastry*:—Pannag.

6437. פָּנָה, pânâh, *paw-naw´*; a primitive root; to *turn*; (by implication) to *face*, i.e. *appear, look*, etc.:—appear, at [even-] tide, behold, cast out, come on, × corner, dawning, empty, go away, lie, look, mark, pass away, prepare, regard, (have) respect (to), (re-) turn (aside, away, back, face, self), × right [early].

6438. פִּנָּה, pinnâh, *pin-naw´*; feminine of 6434; an *angle*; (by implication) a *pinnacle*; (figurative) a *chieftain*:—bulwark, chief, corner, stay, tower.

6439. פְּנוּאֵל, Pᵉnûwʼêl, *pen-oo-ale´*; or (more properly) פְּנִיאֵל, **Pᵉnîyʼêl**, *pen-ee-ale´*; from 6437 and 410; *face of God; Penuël* or *Peniël*, a place East of Jordan; also (as Penuel) the name of two Israelites:—Peniel, Penuel.

6440. פָּנִים, pânîym, *paw-neem´*; plural (but always as singular) of an unused noun [פָּנֶה **pâneh**, *paw-neh´*; from 6437]; the *face* (as the part that *turns*); used in a great variety of applications (literal and figurative); also (with prepositional prefix) as a preposition (*before*, etc.):— + accept, a- (be-) fore (-time), against, anger, × as (long as), at, + battle, + because (of), + beseech, countenance, edge, + employ, endure, + enquire, face, favour, fear of, for, forefront (-part), form (-er time, -ward), from, front, heaviness, × him (-self), + honourable, + impudent, + in, it, look [-eth] (-s), × me, + meet, × more than, mouth, of, off, (of) old (time), × on, open, + out of, over against, the partial, person, + please, presence, propect, was purposed, by reason, of, + regard, right forth, + serve, × shewbread, sight, state, straight, + street, × thee, × them (-selves), through (+ -out), till, time (-s) past, (un-) to (-ward), + upon, upside (+ down), with (-in, + -stand), × ye, × you.

A masculine plural noun meaning a face. Although the literal meaning of face is possible (Ge 43:31; Le 13:41; 1Ki 19:13), most of the time this word occurs in a figurative, idiomatic phrase. Face can be a substitute for the entire person (Ex 33:14, 15); or it can be a reflection of the person's mood or attitude: defiant (Jer 5:3); ruthless (Dt 28:50); joyful (Job 29:24); humiliated (2Sa 19:5[6]); terrified (Isa 13:8); displeased (Ge 4:5). It is also used to indicate direction (Ge 31:21); or purpose (Jer 42:15, 17). This noun also designates the top or surface of something: the ground (Ge 2:6; 4:14); a field (Isa 28:25); or water (Ge 1:2). It also connotes the front of something, like a pot (Jer 1:13); or an army (Joel 2:20). With various prepositions, *pânîm* takes on the nature of a particle and expresses such concepts as upon (Ex 23:17; Le 14:53); before a place (Nu 8:22); before a time (Eze 42:12; Am 1:1); in the presence of (Est 1:10).

6441. פְּנִימָה, pᵉnîymâh, *pen-ee´-maw*; from 6440 with directive enclitic; *faceward*, i.e. *indoors*:—(with-) in (-ner part, -ward).

6442. פְּנִימִי, pᵉnîymîy, *pen-ee-mee´*; from 6440; *interior*:—(with-) in (-ner, -ward).

6443. פְּנִינִים, pᵉnîyniym, *pe-nee-neem´*; or פָּנִי, **pânîy**, *paw-nee´*; from the same as 6434; probably a *pearl* (as *round*):—ruby.

6444. פְּנִנָּה, Pᵉninnâh, *pen-in-naw´*; probably feminine from 6443 contracted; *Peninnah*, an Israelitess:—Peninnah.

6445. פָּנַק, pânaq, *paw-nak´*; a primitive root; to *enervate*:—bring up.

6446. פַּס, pas, *pas*; from 6461; (properly) the *palm* (of the hand) or *sole* (of the foot) [compare 6447]; by implication (plural) a *long and sleeved* tunic (perhaps simply a *wide* one; from the original sense of the root, i.e. of *many breadths*):—(divers) colours.

6447. פַּס, pas, *pas*; (Chaldee); from a root corresponding to 6461; the *palm* (of the hand, as being *spread* out):—part.

6448. פָּסַג, pâsag, *paw-sag´*; a primitive root; to *cut up*, i.e. (figurative) *contemplate*:—consider.

6449. פִּסְגָּה, Pisgâh, *pis-gaw´*; from 6448; a *cleft; Pisgah*, a mountain East of Jordan:—Pisgah.

6450. פַּס דַּמִּים, Pas Dammîym, *pas dam-meem´*; from 6446 and the plural of 1818; *palm* (i.e. *dell*) *of bloodshed; Pas-Dammim*, a place in Palestine:—Pas-dammim. Compare 658.

6451. פִּסָּה, pissâh, *pis-saw´*; from 6461; *expansion*, i.e. *abundance*:—handful.

6452. פָּסַח, pâsach, *paw-sakh´*; a primitive root; to *hop*, i.e. (figurative) *skip* over (or *spare*); (by implication) to *hesitate*; also (literal) to *limp*, to *dance*:—halt, become lame, leap, pass over.

A verb meaning to leap, to pass over, to halt, to limp, to be lame. The first occurrence of this verb is in Exodus, where God states that He will preserve the Israelites by passing over their homes when He goes through Egypt to kill the firstborn (Ex 12:13, 23, 27). This sentiment is echoed by the prophet Isaiah (Isa 31:5). In 2Sa 4:4, the word is used of Saul's grandson who became lame. Before Elijah confronted the prophets of Baal, he confronted the Israelites for their syncretism. He asked them how long they would bounce back and forth between the Lord and Baal (1Ki 18:21). Then during Elijah's confrontation, the prophets of Baal began to dance on the altar that they had constructed (1Ki 18:26). This was probably some sort of cultic dance performed as part of the sacrifice ritual.

6453. פֶּסַח, pesach, *peh´-sakh*; from 6452; a *pretermission*, i.e. *exemption*; used only technically of the Jewish *Passover* (the festival or the victim):—passover (offering).

A masculine noun meaning Passover, a Passover animal, a sacrifice. The word is used forty-nine times, usually referring to the Passover festival or celebration. It is first used to describe the Passover ritual while Israel was still in Egypt (Ex 12:11, 27, 43, 48; 34:25). The first Passover ideally was constituted as follows: on the human level, the Israelites killed the Passover sacrifice on the evening of the fourteenth day of the first month, Abib or Nisan (March or April). They then took some of the blood of the slain Passover animal (Dt 16:2, 5) and smeared it on the sides and tops of the doorframes of their houses (cf. Ex 12:7). The Passover ritual and the Passover animal were directed to and belonged to the Lord (Ex 12:11, 48; Dt 16:1). They then roasted the animal (lamb, kid, young ram, goat—a one-year-old without any defect) and ate it with their sandals on their feet and their staffs in their hands ready to move out in haste at any time. The angel of death passed through Egypt and passed over the Israelites' houses with the blood of the lambs on the doorposts, but the angel struck the firstborn of all the Egyptian households (cf. Ex 12:12, 13, 29). Later Passovers were held in commemoration of the historical event of Israel's deliverance from Egyptian bondage.

The animals eaten were also called the *pesach*, the Passover sacrifice (Ex 12:21; 2Ch 30:15; 35:1). The Passover was celebrated throughout Israel's history before and after the exile (Nu 9:4; Jos 5:10; 2Ki 23:22; Ezr 6:19, 20).

6454. פָּסֵחַ, Pâsêach, *paw-say´-akh*; from 6452; *limping; Paseäch,* the name of two Israelites:—Paseah, Phaseah.

6455. פִּסֵּחַ, pissêach, *pis-say´-akh*; from 6452; *lame*:—lame.

6456. פָּסִיל, pâsîyl, *paws-eel´*; from 6458; an *idol*:—carved (graven) image, quarry.

A masculine noun meaning idol. This word comes from the verb *pâsal* (6458), meaning to hew or to cut, which was done to create a carved image. In the Law of the OT, it was clear that such idols should be burned (Dt 7:5, 25); and cut down (Dt 12:3); for they provoked God to anger (Ps 78:58; Jer 8:19); and incited Him to judgment (Jer 51:47, 52; Mic 1:7; 5:13[12]). The presence of these idols were indicative of the sin and rebellion of the people (2Ch 33:19, 22; Hos 11:2); while the removal of such idols was a sign of repentance (2Ch 34:3, 4, 7; Isa 30:22).

6457. פָּסַךְ, Pâsak, *paw-sak´*; from an unused root meaning to *divide; divider; Pasak,* an Israelite:—Pasach.

6458. פָּסַל, pâsal, *paw-sal´*; a primitive root; to *carve,* whether wood or stone:—grave, hew.

A verb meaning to hew, to cut. This word is used most often in the context of cutting stone. Moses cut two stone tablets so God could record His words on them (Ex 34:1, 4; Dt 10:1, 3); the builders cut stones in building the Temple (1Ki 5:18[32]); and an idol maker cut the material to create an idol (Hab 2:18). See the related nouns *pĕsiyl* (6456) and *pesel* (6459), meaning idol.

6459. פֶּסֶל, pesel, *peh´-sel*; from 6458; an *idol*:—carved (graven) image.

A noun meaning idol, a graven image. This word comes from the verb *pâsal* (6458), meaning to hew or to cut, which was done to create an idol. In the Law of the OT, the Lord forbade Israel to create such images (Ex 20:4; Le 26:1; Dt 5:8); for they were an abomination to Him (Dt 27:15). Those who served idols would be ashamed in the judgment (Ps 97:7; Isa 42:17); and the Lord would cut them off from Him (Na 1:14). The presence of these idols were indicative of the sin and rebellion of the people (Dt 4:16, 23, 25; 2Ch 33:7). The prophets often demonstrated the folly of these idols: they were profitable for nothing (Isa 44:10; Hab 2:18); they could easily be burned (Isa 44:15); they had no breath (Jer 10:14); and they could not save (Isa 45:20). Idols could be made of metal (Jgs 17:3, 4; Isa 40:19); wood (Isa 40:20; 44:15, 17); or possibly stone (Hab 2:18; cf. Hab 2:19).

6460. פְּסַנְטֵרִין, pᵉsanṭêrîyn, *pes-an-tay-reen´*; (Chaldee); or **פְּסַנְתֵּרִין, pᵉsantêrîyn,** *pes-an-tay-reen´*; a transliteration of the Greek *psalterion*; a *lyre*:—psaltery.

6461. פָּסַס, pâsas, *paw-sas´*; a primitive root; probably to *disperse,* i.e. (intrans.) *disappear*:—cease.

6462. פִּסְפָּה, Pispâh, *pis-paw´*; perhaps from 6461; *dispersion; Pispah,* an Israelite:—Pispah.

6463. פָּעָה, pâ'âh, *paw-aw´*; a primitive root; to *scream*:—cry.

6464. פָּעוּ, Pâ'ûw, *paw-oo´*; or **פָּעִי, Pâ'îy,** *paw-ee´*; from 6463; *screaming; Paü* or *Paï,* a place in Edom:—Pai, Pau.

6465. פְּעוֹר, Pᵉ'ôwr, *peh-ore´*; from 6473; a *gap; Peör,* a mountain East of Jordan; also (for 1187) a deity worshipped there:—Peor. See also 1047.

6466. פָּעַל, pâ'al, *paw-al´*; a primitive root; to *do* or *make* (systematically and habitually), especially to *practise*:—commit, [evil-] do (-er), make (-r), ordain, work (-er).

6467. פֹּעַל, pô'al, *po´-al*; from 6466; an *act* or *work* (concrete):—act, deed, do, getting, maker, work.

6468. פְּעֻלָּה, pᵉ'ullâh, *peh-ool-law´*; feminine passive participle of 6466; (abstract) *work*:—labour, reward, wages, work.

6469. פְּעֻלְּתַי, Pᵉ'ullᵉthay, *peh-ool-leh-thah´ee*; from 6468; *laborious; Peüllethai,* an Israelite:—Peulthai.

6470. פָּעַם, pâ'am, *paw-am´*; a primitive root; to *tap,* i.e. beat regularly; hence (general) to *impel* or *agitate*:—move, trouble.

6471. פַּעַם, pa'am, *pah´-am*; or (feminine) **פַּעֲמָה, pa'ămâh,** *pah-am-aw´*; from 6470; a *stroke,* literal or figurative (in various applications, as follow):—anvil, corner, foot (-step), going, [hundred-] fold, × now, (this) + once, order, rank, step, + thrice, ([often-], second, this, two) time (-s), twice, wheel.

6472. פַּעֲמֹן, pa'ămôn, *pah-am-one´*; from 6471; a *bell* (as *struck*):—bell.

6473. פָּעַר, pâ'ar, *paw-ar´*; a primitive root; to *yawn,* i.e. *open* wide (literal or figurative):—gape, open (wide).

6474. פַּעֲרַי, Pa'ăray, *pah-ar-ah´ee*; from 6473; *yawning; Paarai,* an Israelite:—Paarai.

6475. פָּצָה, pâtsâh, *paw-tsaw´*; a primitive root; to *rend,* i.e. *open* (especially the mouth):—deliver, gape, open, rid, utter.

6476. פָּצַח, pâtsach, *paw-tsakh´*; a primitive root; to *break* out (in joyful sound):—break (forth, forth into joy), make a loud noise.

6477. פְּצִירָה, pᵉtsîyrâh, *pets-ee-raw´*; from 6484; *bluntness*:—+ file.

6478. פָּצַל, pâtsal, *paw-tsal´*; a primitive root; to *peel*:—pill.

6479. פְּצָלָה, pᵉtsâlâh, *pets-aw-law´*; from 6478; a *peeling*:—strake.

6480. פָּצַם, pâtsam, *paw-tsam´*; a primitive root; to *rend* (by earthquake):—break.

6481. פָּצַע, pâtsa', *paw-tsah´*; a primitive root; to *split,* i.e. *wound*:—wound.

6482. פֶּצַע, petsa', *peh´-tsah*; from 6481; a *wound*:—wound (-ing).

6483. פִּצֵּץ, Pitstsêts, *pits-tsates´*; from an unused root meaning to *dissever; dispersive; Pitstsets,* a priest:—Apses [*including the article*].

6484. פָּצַר, pâtsar, *paw-tsar´*; a primitive root; to *peck* at, i.e. (figurative) *stun* or *dull*:—press, urge, stubbornness.

6485. פָּקַד, pâqad, *paw-kad´*; a primitive root; to *visit* (with friendly or hostile intent); (by analogy) to *oversee, muster, charge, care for, miss, deposit,* etc.:—appoint, × at all, avenge, bestow, (appoint to have the, give a) charge, commit, count, deliver to keep, be empty, enjoin, go see, hurt, do judgment, lack, lay up, look, make, × by any means, miss, number, officer, (make) overseer, have (the) oversight, punish, reckon, (call to) remember (-brance), set (over), sum, × surely, visit, want.

A verb meaning to attend, to visit, and to search out. The word refers to someone (usually God) paying attention to persons, either to do them good (Ge 50:24, 25; Ex 3:16; 1Sa 2:21; Jer 23:2); or to bring punishment or harm (Ex 20:5; Isa 10:12; Jer 23:2). The word also means, usually in a causative form, to appoint over or to commit to, that is, to cause people to attend to something placed under their care (Ge 39:4, 5; Jos 10:18; Isa 62:6). The passive causative form means to deposit, that is, to cause something to be attended to (Le 6:4[5:23]). The word also means to number or to be numbered, which is an activity requiring attention. This meaning occurs over ninety times in the book of Numbers. The word can also mean (usually in a passive form) lacking or missing, as if a quantity was numbered less than an original amount (Jgs 21:3; 1Sa 20:18; 1Ki 20:39).

6486. פְּקֻדָּה, pᵉquddâh, *pek-ood-daw´*; feminine passive participle of 6485; *visitation* (in many senses, chiefly official):—account, (that have the) charge, custody, that which … laid up, numbers, office (-r), ordering, oversight, + prison, reckoning, visitation.

A feminine noun meaning an arrangement, an office, an officer, accounting. The root idea is something that is attended to or set in order. The word signifies the arrangement of fighting men under an officer (2Ch 17:14), of priests or Levites in an order (1Ch 23:11; 24:19); or the arrangement of the tabernacle and its contents (Nu 4:16[2x]). It signifies the office of one in charge of something (Ps

109:8); and the officers themselves (2Ki 11:18; Isa 60:17). Most often, the word means accounting and refers to a time of accounting when God attended to people's actions, usually to call them to account for their sins (Nu 16:29; Jer 48:44). In Job 10:12, however, God's attention was for Job's good.

6487. **פִּקָּדוֹן, piqqâdôwn,** *pik-kaw-done´*; from 6485; a *deposit*:—that which was delivered (to keep), store.

A masculine noun meaning deposit. The root idea is that something is left under someone's care or attention. The word occurs three times in the OT. In Genesis 41:36, the word referred to a store of food that Joseph advised Pharaoh to store up for the coming famine. In Le 6:2[5:21], 4[5:23], the word signified any deposit left in someone's care. If the keeper of this deposit dealt dishonestly with it, he had to pay a 20 percent penalty in addition to the deposit.

6488. **פְּקִדֻת, pᵉqiduth,** *pek-ee-dooth´*; from 6496; *supervision*:—ward.

A feminine noun meaning supervision, oversight. It occurs only in Jer 37:13, where it refers with the word *ba'al* (1167), meaning master, to an official or policeman as a master of supervision. In this passage, the officer was stationed at the Gate of Benjamin where financial transactions took place (cf. Dt 21:19; Ru 4:1ff.); and where the king sometimes officiated (cf. Jer 38:7). The office gave its bearer the legal power to arrest Jeremiah (Jer 37:13).

6489. **פְּקוֹד, Pᵉqôwd,** *pek-ode´*; from 6485; *punishment; Pekod*, a symbolical name for Babylon:—Pekod.

6490. **פִּקּוּד, piqqûwd,** *pik-kood´*; or **פִּקֻּד, piqqud,** *pik-kood´*; from 6485; (properly) *appointed*, i.e. a *mandate* (of God; plural only, collective for the *Law*):—commandment, precept, statute.

A masculine noun meaning precept, instruction. The root expresses the idea that God is paying attention to how He wants things ordered (see *pâqad* [6485]). God's precepts strike those who love Him as right and delightful (Ps 19:8[9]). This word is always plural and is only found in the Psalms, mostly in Ps 119 (twenty-one times). This psalm talked of seeking (Ps 119:40, 45, 94); keeping (Ps 119:63, 69, 134); and not forgetting God's instructions (Ps 119:87, 93, 141); even when opposed by the proud (Ps 119:69, 78). The psalmist's diligence in obeying God's precepts was rewarded with understanding and the hatred of evil (Ps 119:100, 104); liberty (Ps 119:45); confidence in asking God's help (Ps 119:94, 173); and spiritual life (Ps 119:93).

6491. **פָּקַח, pâqach,** *paw-kakh´*; a primitive root; to *open* (the senses, especially the eyes); (figurative) to *be observant*:—open.

6492. **פֶּקַח, Peqach,** *peh´-kakh*; from 6491; *watch; Pekach*, an Israelite king:—Pekah.

6493. **פִּקֵּחַ, piqqêach,** *pik-kay´-akh*; from 6491; *clear-sighted*; (figurative) *intelligent*:—seeing, wise.

A masculine adjective meaning seeing, sight. This noun is derived from the verb *pâqach* (6491), meaning to open the eyes and ears. In a literal sense, it occurs in Ex 4:11 when God answered Moses' objections for leading the people out of Egypt. In a metaphorical sense, this term represented those who could see clearly but could be blinded by a gift (Ex 23:8).

6494. **פְּקַחְיָה, Pᵉqachyâh,** *pek-akh-yaw´*; from 6491 and 3050; *Jah has observed; Pekachjah*, an Israelite king:—Pekahiah.

6495. **פְּקַח־קוֹחַ, pᵉqach-qôwach,** *pek-akh-ko´-akh*; from 6491 redoubled; *opening* (of a dungeon), i.e. *jail-delivery;* (figurative) *salvation* from sin:—opening of the prison.

6496. **פָּקִיד, pâqîyd,** *paw-keed´*; from 6485; a *superintendent* (civil, military or religious):—which had the charge, governor, office, overseer, [that] was set.

A masculine noun meaning a commissioner, a deputy, and an overseer. Depending on the context, this term has a broad range of possible meanings. It could apply to government representatives whose positions are temporary, like the officers appointed by Pharaoh to collect grain during the seven plentiful years (Ge 41:34). It could also represent a permanent position of leadership for a king (Jgs 9:28); a high priest (2Ch 24:11); or a Levite (2Ch 31:13). It could further signify a general leader of men, such as a military officer (2Ki 25:19); a tribal leader (Ne 11:9); or a priestly leader (Ne 11:14).

6497. **פְּקָעִים, peqâ'îym,** *peh´-kah-eem*; from an unused root meaning to *burst*; only used as an architectural term of an ornament similar to 6498, a *semi-globe*:—knop.

6498. **פַּקֻּעָה, paqqu'âh,** *pak-koo-aw´*; from the same as 6497; the *wild cucumber* (from *splitting* open to shed its seeds):—gourd.

6499. **פַּר, par,** *par*; or **פָּר, pâr,** *pawr*; from 6565; a *bullock* (apparently as *breaking* forth in wild strength, or perhaps as *dividing* the hoof):—(+ young) bull (-ock), calf, ox.

6500. **פָּרָא, pârâ',** *paw-raw´*; a primitive root; to *bear fruit*:—be fruitful.

6501. **פֶּרֶא, pere',** *peh´-reh*; or **פֶּרֶה, pereh,** *peh´-reh*; (Jer 2:24), from 6500 in the secondary sense of *running* wild; the *onager*:—wild (ass).

6502. **פִּרְאָם, Pir'âm,** *pir-awm´*; from 6501; *wildly; Piram*, a Canaanite:—Piram.

6503. **פַּרְבָּר, Parbâr,** *par-bawr´*; or **פַּרְוָר, Parvâr,** *par-vawr´*; of foreign origin; *Parbar* or *Parvar*, a quarter of Jerusalem:—Parbar, suburb.

6504. **פָּרַד, pârad,** *paw-rad´*; a primitive root; to *break* through, i.e. *spread* or *separate* (oneself):—disperse, divide, be out of joint, part, scatter (abroad), separate (self), sever self, stretch, sunder.

6505. **פֶּרֶד, pered,** *peh´-red*; from 6504; a *mule* (perhaps from his *lonely* habits):—mule.

6506. **פִּרְדָּה, pᵉrudâh,** *per-oo-daw´*; feminine of 6505; a *she-mule*:—mule.

6507. **פְּרֻדוֹת, pᵉrudôth,** *per-oo-doth´*; feminine passive participle of 6504; something *separated*, i.e. a *kernel*:—seed.

6508. **פַּרְדֵּס, pardês,** *par-dace´*; of foreign origin; a *park*:—forest, orchard.

6509. **פָּרָה, pârâh,** *paw-raw´*; a primitive root; to *bear fruit* (literal or figurative):—bear, bring forth (fruit), (be, cause to be, make) fruitful, grow, increase.

6510. **פָּרָה, pârâh,** *paw-raw´*; feminine of 6499; a *heifer*:—cow, heifer, kine.

6511. **פָּרָה, Pârâh,** *paw-raw´*; the same as 6510; *Parah*, a place in Palestine:—Parah.

6512. **פֵּרָה, pêrâh,** *pay-raw´*; from 6331; a *hole* (as *broken*, i.e. dug):— + mole. Compare 2661.

6513. **פֻּרָה, Purâh,** *poo-raw´*; for 6288; *foliage; Purah*, an Israelite:—Phurah.

6514. **פְּרוּדָא, Pᵉrûwdâ',** *per-oo-daw´*; or **פְּרִידָא, Pᵉrîydâ',** *per-ee-daw´*; from 6504; *dispersion; Peruda* or *Perida*, one of "Solomon's servants":—Perida, Peruda.

6515. **פָּרוּחַ, Pârûwach,** *paw-roo´-akh*; passive participle of 6524; *blossomed; Paruäh*, an Israelite:—Paruah.

6516. **פַּרְוַיִם, Parvayim,** *par-vah´-yim*; of foreign origin; *Parvajim*, an Oriental region:—Parvaim.

6517. **פָּרוּר, pârûwr,** *paw-roor´*; passive participle of 6565 in the sense of *spreading* out [compare 6524]; a *skillet* (as *flat* or *deep*):—pan, pot.

6518. **פָּרָז, pâraz,** *paw-rawz´*; from an unused root meaning to *separate*, i.e. *decide*; a *chieftain*:—village.

6519. **פְּרָזָה, pᵉrâzâh,** *per-aw-zaw´*; from the same as 6518; an *open* country:—(unwalled) town (without walls), unwalled village.

6520. **פְּרָזוֹן, p^e^râzôwn,** *per-aw-zone'*; from the same as 6518; *magistracy,* i.e. *leadership* (also [concrete] *chieftains*):—village.

6521. **פְּרָזִי, p^e^râzîy,** *per-aw-zee*; or **פְּרוֹזִי, p^e^rôwzîy,** *per-o-zee'*; from 6519; a *rustic:*—village.

6522. **פְּרִזִּי, P^e^rizzîy,** *per-iz-zee'*; for 6521; inhabitant *of the open country*; a *Perizzite,* one of the Canaanitish tribes:—Perizzite.

6523. **פַּרְזֶל, parzel,** *par-zel'*; (Chaldee); corresponding to 1270; *iron:*—iron.

6524. **פָּרַח, pârach,** *paw-rakh'*; a primitive root; to *break* forth as a bud, i.e. *bloom*; (generally) to *spread*; (specifically) to *fly* (as extending the wings); (figurative) to *flourish:*— × abroad, × abundantly, blossom, break forth (out), bud, flourish, make fly, grow, spread, spring (up).

6525. **פֶּרַח, perach,** *peh'-rakh*; from 6524; a *calyx* (native or artificial); (general) *bloom:*—blossom, bud, flower.

6526. **פִּרְחַח, pirchach,** *pir-khakh'*; from 6524; *progeny,* i.e. a *brood:*—youth.

6527. **פָּרַט, pâraṭ,** *paw-rat'*; a primitive root; to *scatter* words, i.e. *prate* (or *hum*):—chant.

6528. **פֶּרֶט, pereṭ,** *peh'-ret*; from 6527; a *stray* or *single* berry:—grape.

6529. **פְּרִי, p^e^rîy,** *per-ee'*; from 6509; *fruit* (literal or figurative):—bough, ([first-]) fruit ([-full]), reward.

6530. **פָּרִיץ, pârîyts,** *pawr-eets'*; from 6555; *violent,* i.e. a *tyrant:*—destroyer, ravenous, robber.

A masculine noun meaning a violent individual. The term was usually applied to a person or people. David claimed to have refrained from the ways of the violent (Ps 17:4). God asked if the Temple had become the dwelling place of the violent (Jer 7:11). God proclaimed through the prophet Ezekiel that the end would come when the violent desecrate God's treasured place (Eze 7:22); they would be punished (Eze 18:10). The prophet Isaiah also applied this term to wild animals like the lion (Isa 35:9).

6531. **פֶּרֶךְ, perek,** *peh'-rek*; from an unused root meaning to *break* apart; *fracture,* i.e. *severity:*—cruelty, rigour.

6532. **פָּרֹכֶת, pârôketh,** *paw-roh'-keth*; feminine active participle of the same as 6531; a *separatrix,* i.e. (the sacred) *screen:*—vail.

6533. **פָּרַם, pâram,** *paw-ram'*; a primitive root; to *tear:*—rend.

6534. **פַּרְמַשְׁתָּא, Parmashtâ',** *par-mash-taw'*; of Persian origin; *Parmashta,* a son of Haman:—Parmasta.

6535. **פַּרְנָךְ, Parnak,** *par-nak'*; of uncertain derivation; *Parnak,* an Israelite:—Parnach.

6536. **פָּרַס, pâras,** *paw-ras'*; a primitive root; to *break* in pieces, i.e. (usually without violence) to *split, distribute:*—deal, divide, have hoofs, part, tear.

6537. **פְּרַס, p^e^ras,** *per-as'*; (Chaldee); corresponding to 6536; to *split* up:—divide, [U-] pharsin.

6538. **פֶּרֶס, peres,** *peh'-res*; from 6536; a *claw*; also a kind of *eagle:*—claw, ossifrage.

6539. **פָּרַס, Pâras,** *paw-ras'*; of foreign origin; *Paras* (i.e. *Persia*), an Eastern country, including its inhabitants:—Persia, Persians.

6540. **פָּרַס, Pâras,** *paw-ras'*; (Chaldee); corresponding to 6539:—Persia, Persians.

6541. **פַּרְסָה, parsâh,** *par-saw'*; feminine of 6538; a *claw* or split *hoof:*—claw, [cloven-] footed, hoof.

6542. **פַּרְסִי, Parsîy,** *par-see'*; patrial from 6539; a *Parsite* (i.e. *Persian*), or inhabitant of Peres:—Persian.

6543. **פַּרְסָי, Parsây,** *par-saw'ee*; (Chaldee); corresponding to 6542:—Persian.

6544. **פָּרַע, pâra',** *paw-rah'*; a primitive root; to *loosen*; (by implication) to *expose, dismiss*; (figurative) to *absolve, begin:*—avenge, avoid, bare, go back, let, (make) naked, set at nought, perish, refuse, uncover.

A verb meaning to let go, to let loose, to unbind. Moses saw that Aaron had let the Israelites get out of hand when Moses was up on the mountain (Ex 32:25[2x]). This word can also apply to hair, as with those who were commanded not to let their hair down from their turbans. This warning was given to Aaron concerning mourning (Le 10:6); and to high priests in general (Le 21:10). However, lepers were to let their hair down to call attention to their condition (Le 13:45). A possible unfaithful wife had her hair loosened by the priest in connection with the drinking of bitter water to see if she was guilty (Nu 5:18). This word can also mean to ignore (Pr 1:25); to avoid (Pr 4:15); or to lead (Jgs 5:2).

6545. **פֶּרַע, pera',** *peh'-rah*; from 6544; the *hair* (as *dishevelled*):—locks.

6546. **פֶּרַע, pera',** *peh'-rah*; feminine of 6545 (in the sense of *beginning*); *leadership* (plural [concrete] *leaders*):— + avenging, revenge.

A feminine noun meaning leaders. This specific form of the word is not used in the Hebrew Bible, but the plural form is used. In the song of Moses, the Lord proclaimed that He would overcome the enemy leaders (Dt 32:42). See the Hebrew root *pâra'* (6544).

6547. **פַּרְעֹה, Par'ôh,** *par-o'*; of Egyptian derivation; *Paroh,* a generic title of Egyptian kings:—Pharaoh.

6548. **פַּרְעֹה חָפְרַע, Par'ôh Chophra',** *par-o' khof-rah'*; of Egyptian derivation; *Paroh-Chophra,* an Egyptian king:—Pharaoh-hophra.

6549. **פַּרְעֹה נְכֹה, Par'ôh N^e^kôh,** *par-o' nek-o'*; or **פַּרְעֹה נְכוֹ, Par'ôh N^e^kôw,** *par-o' nek-o'*; of Egyptian derivation; *Paroh-Nekoh* (or *-Neko*), an Egyptian king:—Pharaoh-necho, Pharaoh-nechoh.

6550. **פַּרְעֹשׁ, par'ôsh,** *par-oshe'*; probably from 6544 and 6211; a *flea* (as the *isolated insect*):—flea.

6551. **פַּרְעֹשׁ, Par'ôsh,** *par-oshe'*; the same as 6550; *Parosh,* the name of four Israelites:—Parosh, Pharosh.

6552. **פִּרְעָתוֹן, Pir'âthôwn,** *pir-aw-thone'*; from 6546; *chieftaincy; Pirathon,* a place in Palestine:—Pirathon.

6553. **פִּרְעָתוֹנִי, Pir'âthôwnîy,** *pir-aw-tho-nee'*; or **פִּרְעָתֹנִי, Pir'âthônîy,** *pir-aw-tho-nee'*; patrial from 6552; a *Pirathonite* or inhabitant of Pirathon:—Pirathonite.

6554. **פַּרְפַּר, Parpar,** *par-par'*; probably from 6565 in the sense of *rushing; rapid; Parpar,* a river of Syria:—Pharpar.

6555. **פָּרַץ, pârats,** *paw-rats'*; a primitive root; to *break* out (in many applications, direct and indirect, literal and figurative):— × abroad, (make a) breach, break (away, down, -er, forth, in, up), burst out, come (spread) abroad, compel, disperse, grow, increase, open, press, scatter, urge.

6556. **פֶּרֶץ, perets,** *peh'-rets*; from 6555; a *break* (literal or figurative):—breach, breaking forth (in), × forth, gap.

6557. **פֶּרֶץ, Perets,** *peh'-rets*; the same as 6556; *Perets,* the name of two Israelites:—Perez, Pharez.

6558. **פַּרְצִי, Partsîy,** *par-tsee'*; patronymic from 6557; a *Partsite* (collective) or descendants of Perets:—Pharzites.

6559. **פְּרָצִים, p^e^râtsîym,** *per-aw-tseem'*; plural of 6556; *breaks; Peratsim,* a mountain in Palestine:—Perazim.

6560. **פֶּרֶץ עֻזָּא, Perets 'Uzzâ',** *peh'-rets ooz-zaw'*; from 6556 and 5798; *break of Uzza; Perets-Uzza,* a place in Palestine:—Perez-uzza.

6561. **פָּרַק, pâraq,** *paw-rak´*; a primitive root; to *break* off or *crunch*; (figurative) to *deliver*:—break (off), deliver, redeem, rend (in pieces), tear in pieces.

6562. **פְּרַק, perak,** *per-ak´*; (Chaldee); corresponding to 6561; to *discontinue*:—break off.

6563. **פֶּרֶק, pereq,** *peh´-rek*; from 6561; *rapine*; also a *fork* (in roads):—crossway, robbery.

6564. **פָּרָק, pârâq,** *paw-rawk´*; from 6561; *soup* (as full of *crumbed* meat):—broth. See also 4832.

6565. **פָּרַר, pârar,** *paw-rar´*; a primitive root; to *break* up (usually figurative, i.e. to *violate, frustrate*):— × any ways, break (asunder), cast off, cause to cease, × clean, defeat, disannul, disappoint, dissolve, divide, make of no effect, fail, frustrate, bring (come) to nought, × utterly, make void.

A verb meaning to break, to divide, to frustrate. This word is often used in conjunction with a covenant or agreement. The Lord warned the Israelites what would happen if they broke the covenant with Him (Le 26:15); and pledged to them that He would not break it (Le 26:44). Asa, king of Judah, asked the king of Aram to break a covenant Aram had made with Israel (1Ki 15:19). This word is also used to refer to the frustration of plans, as the enemies of Israel did to the Israelites trying to rebuild the Temple (Ezr 4:5). However, the Lord's purposes cannot be frustrated (Isa 14:27).

6566. **פָּרַשׂ, pâraś,** *paw-ras´*; a primitive root; to *break* apart, *disperse*, etc.:—break, chop in pieces, lay open, scatter, spread (abroad, forth, selves, out), stretch (forth, out).

6567. **פָּרַשׁ, pârash,** *paw-rash´*; a primitive root; to *separate*, literal (to *disperse*) or figurative (to *specify*); also (by implication) to *wound*:—scatter, declare, distinctly, shew, sting.

6568. **פְּרַשׁ, perash,** *per-ash´*; (Chaldee); corresponding to 6567; to *specify*:—distinctly.

6569. **פֶּרֶשׁ, peresh,** *peh´-resh*; from 6567; *excrement* (as *eliminated*):—dung.

6570. **פֶּרֶשׁ, Peresh,** *peh´-resh*; the same as 6569; *Peresh*, an Israelite:—Peresh.

6571. **פָּרָשׁ, pârâsh,** *paw-rawsh´*; from 6567; a *steed* (as *stretched* out to a vehicle, not single nor for mounting [compare 5483]); also (by implication) a *driver* (in a chariot), i.e. (collective) cavalry:—horseman.

6572. **פַּרְשֶׁגֶן, parshegen,** *par-sheh´-ghen*; or **פַּתְשֶׁגֶן, pathshegen,** *path-sheh´-gen*; of foreign origin; a *transcript*:—copy.

6573. **פַּרְשֶׁגֶן, parshegen,** *par-sheh´-ghen*; (Chaldee); corresponding to 6572:—copy.

6574. **פַּרְשְׁדֹן, parshedôn,** *par-shed-one´*; perhaps by compounding 6567 and 6504 (in the sense of *straddling*) [compare 6576]; the *crotch* (or *anus*):—dirt.

6575. **פָּרָשָׁה, pârâshâh,** *paw-raw-shaw´*; from 6567; *exposition*:—declaration, sum.

6576. **פַּרְשֵׁז, parshêz,** *par-shaze´*; a root apparently formed by compounding 6567 and that of 6518 [compare 6574]; to *expand*:—spread.

6577. **פַּרְשַׁנְדָּתָא, Parshandâthâ',** *par-shan-daw-thaw´*; of Persian origin; *Parshandatha*, a son of Haman:—Parshandatha.

6578. **פְּרָת, Perâth,** *per-awth´*; from an unused root meaning to *break* forth; *rushing*; *Perath* (i.e. *Euphrates*), a river of the East:—Euphrates.

6579. **פַּרְתְּמִים, partemîym,** *par-teh-meem´*; of Persian origin; a *grandee*:—(most) noble, prince.

A noun meaning a prince, a noble. This word is only used in the plural form in the Hebrew OT. The most important people in the kingdom were invited to King Xerxes' banquet (Est 1:3). Haman suggested to the king that the appropriate way to honour someone was to have a nobleman lead him around the kingdom in the king's robe and on the king's horse (Est 6:9). When Babylon captured Jerusalem, the young Israelite nobility were taken into Nebuchadnezzar's service (Da 1:3). Shadrach, Meshach, Abednego, and Daniel were part of this group.

6580. **פַּשׁ, pash,** *pash*; probably from an unused root meaning to *disintegrate; stupidity* (as a result of *grossness* or of *degeneracy*):—extremity.

6581. **פָּשָׂה, pâśâh,** *paw-saw´*; a primitive root; to *spread*:—spread.

6582. **פָּשַׁח, pâshach,** *paw-shakh´*; a primitive root; to *tear* in pieces:—pull in pieces.

6583. **פַּשְׁחוּר, Pashchûwr,** *pash-khoor´*; probably from 6582; *liberation; Pashchur*, the name of four Israelites:—Pashur.

6584. **פָּשַׁט, pâshaṭ,** *paw-shat´*; a primitive root; to *spread* out (i.e. *deploy* in hostile array); (by analogy) to *strip* (i.e. *unclothe, plunder, flay*, etc.):—fall upon, flay, invade, make an invasion, pull off, put off, make a road, run upon, rush, set, spoil, spread selves (abroad), strip (off, self).

6585. **פָּשַׂע, pâśa',** *paw-sah´*; a primitive root; to *stride* (from *spreading* the legs), i.e. *rush* upon:—go.

6586. **פָּשַׁע, pâsha',** *paw-shah´*; a primitive root [rather identical with 6585 through the idea of *expansion*]; to *break* away (from just authority), i.e. *trespass, apostatize, quarrel*:—offend, rebel, revolt, transgress (-ion, -or).

A verb meaning to rebel, to transgress, to revolt, to sin. This verb is used about forty times in the simple stem of the verb. It means to sin, but the sin involved is one of revolt or rebellion in nearly every case. It indicates rebellion against various parties; the people of Israel rebelled against their God (Isa 1:2; 66:24; Jer 2:29; 3:13); especially their leaders (Jer 2:8). Nations and peoples revolted or broke with one another: Israel broke from and rebelled against Judah (1Ki 12:19); Moab rebelled against Israel (2Ki 1:1; 3:5); and Edom revolted against Judah (2Ki 8:20). Revolt and rebellion against the Lord, Isaiah said, was a part of the character of Israel from its birth and throughout its history (Isa 48:8; 59:13). Amos described Israel's insistence to worship at the unapproved sanctuaries at Bethel and Gilgal as revolt and rebellion (Am 4:4). The postexilic community rebelled through intermarriages with pagans (Ezr 10:13). God asserted that He would restore His people, forgiving their sins of rebellion (Jer 33:8). Unrestrained rebellion seems to be a mark of the end times as noted by Da 8:23.

6587. **פֶּשַׂע, peśa',** *peh´-sah*; from 6585; a *stride*:—step.

6588. **פֶּשַׁע, pesha',** *peh´-shah*; from 6586; a *revolt* (national, moral or religious):—rebellion, sin, transgression, trespass.

A masculine noun meaning transgression, rebellion. Though it can be a transgression of one individual against another (Ge 31:36; 50:17; Ex 22:9[8]); or of one nation against another (Am 1:3, 6, 9, 11, 13; 2:1); this word primarily expresses a rebellion against God and His laws (Isa 58:1; 59:12; Am 5:12). Since it is possible for humanity to recognize this transgression (Ps 32:5; 51:3[5]), God's first step in dealing with it is to reveal it and call His people to accountability (Job 36:9; Mic 3:8). He then punishes the guilty (Isa 53:5, 8; Am 2:4, 6) in the hope of restoring the relationship and forgiving the transgressors who repent (Eze 18:30, 31). In addition to the act of transgression itself, this term can also be used to convey the guilt that comes from the transgression (Job 33:9; 34:6; Ps 59:3[4]); the punishment for the transgression (Da 8:12, 13; 9:24); or the offering that is presented to atone for the transgression (Mic 6:7).

6589. **פָּשַׂק, pâśaq,** *paw-sak´*; a primitive root; to *dispart* (the feet or lips), i.e. *become licentious*:—open (wide).

6590. **פְּשַׁר, peshar,** *pesh-ar´*; (Chaldee); corresponding to 6622; to *interpret*:—make [interpretations], interpreting.

6591. **פְּשַׁר, peshar,** *pesh-ar´*; (Chaldee); from 6590; an *interpretation*:—interpretation.

6592. **פְּשַׁר, pêsher,** *pay´-sher;* corresponding to 6591:—interpretation.

6593. **פֵּשֶׁת, pêsheth,** *pay-sheth´;* from the same as 6580 as in the sense of *comminuting; linen* (i.e. the thread, as *carded*):—flax, linen.

6594. **פִּשְׁתָּה, pishtâh,** *pish-taw´;* feminine of 6593; *flax;* (by implication) a *wick:*—flax, tow.

6595. **פַּת, path,** *path;* from 6626; a *bit:*—meat, morsel, piece.

6596. **פֹּת, pôth,** *pohth;* or **פֹּתָה, pôthâh,** *po-thaw´;* (Eze 13:19), from an unused root meaning to *open;* a *hole,* i.e. *hinge* or the female *pudenda:*—hinge, secret part.

6597. **פִּתְאוֹם, pith'ôwm,** *pith-ome´;* or **פִּתְאֹם, pith'ôm,** *pith-ome´;* from 6621; *instantly:*—straightway, sudden (-ly).

6598. **פַּתְבַּג, pathbag,** *path-bag´;* of Persian origin; a *dainty:*—portion (provision) of meat.

6599. **פִּתְגָּם, pithgâm,** *pith-gawm´;* of Persian origin; a (judicial) *sentence:*—decree, sentence.

A masculine noun meaning an edict, a decree. This word is used only twice in the OT. In Est 1:20, it describes a king's authoritative edict (or law) that could not be repealed (cf. Est 1:19). In Ecc 8:11, it refers to a court sentence (or judgment) that should be executed against evil.

6600. **פִּתְגָם, pithgâm,** *pith-gawm´;* (Chaldee); corresponding to 6599; a *word, answer, letter* or *decree:*—answer, letter, matter, word.

An Aramaic masculine noun meaning a written word, an affair. This word is related to the Hebrew word *pithgâm* (6599) and was used in Ezra to describe the written communication that was used between the kings, the Israelites, and their adversaries (Ezr 4:17; 5:7, 11; 6:11). In Daniel, this word described the affair surrounding the unwillingness of Shadrach, Meshach, and Abednego to bow to the golden image (Da 3:16); in addition to the matters contained in Nebuchadnezzar's dream (Da 4:17[14]).

6601. **פָּתָה, pâthâh,** *paw-thaw´;* a primitive root; to *open,* i.e. *be* (causative, *make*) *roomy;* usually figurative (in a mental or moral sense) to *be* (causative, *make*) *simple* or (in a sinister way) *delude:*—allure, deceive, enlarge, entice, flatter, persuade, silly (one).

6602. **פְּתוּאֵל, Pᵉthûw'êl,** *peth-oo-ale´;* from 6601 and 410; *enlarged of God; Pethuël,* an Israelite:—Pethuel.

6603. **פִּתּוּחַ, pittûwach,** *pit-too´-akh;* or **פִּתֻּחַ, pittuach,** *pit-too´-akh;* passive participle of 6605; *sculpture* (in low or high relief or even intaglio):—carved (work) (are, en-) grave (-ing, -n).

6604. **פְּתוֹר, Pᵉthôwr,** *peth-ore´;* of foreign origin; *Pethor,* a place in Mesopotamia:—Pethor.

6605. **פָּתַח, pâthach,** *paw-thakh´;* a primitive root; to *open* wide (literal or figurative); (specifically) to *loosen, begin, plough, carve:*—appear, break forth, draw (out), let go free, (en-) grave (-n), loose (self), (be, be set) open (-ing), put off, ungird, unstop, have vent.

6606. **פְּתַח, pᵉthach,** *peth-akh´;* (Chaldee); corresponding to 6605; to *open:*—open.

6607. **פֶּתַח, pethach,** *peh´-thakh;* from 6605; an *opening* (literal), i.e. *door* (*gate*) or *entrance* way:—door, entering (in), entrance (-ry), gate, opening, place.

6608. **פֵּתַח, pêthach,** *pah´-thakh;* from 6605; *opening* (figurative) i.e. *disclosure:*—entrance.

6609. **פְּתִיחָה, pᵉthîychâh,** *peth-ee-khaw´;* from 6605; something *opened,* i.e. a *drawn* sword:—drawn sword.

6610. **פִּתְחוֹן, pithchôwn,** *pith-khone´;* from 6605; *opening* (the act):—open (-ing).

6611. **פְּתַחְיָה, Pᵉthachyâh,** *peth-akh-yaw´;* from 6605 and 3050; *Jah has opened; Pethachjah,* the name of four Israelites:—Pethakiah.

6612. **פְּתִי, pᵉthîy,** *peth-ee´;* or **פֶּתִי, pethîy,** *peh´-thee;* or **פְּתָאִי, pᵉthâ'îy,** *peth-aw-ee´;* from 6601; *silly* (i.e. *seducible*):—foolish, simple (-icity, one).

6613. **פְּתַי, pᵉthây,** *peth-aw´ee;* (Chaldee); from a root corresponding to 6601; *open,* i.e. (as noun) *width:*—breadth.

6614. **פְּתִיגִיל, pᵉthîygîyl,** *peth-eeg-eel´;* of uncertain derivation; probably a figured *mantle* for holidays:—stomacher.

6615. **פְּתַיּוּת, pᵉthayyûwth,** *peth-ah-yooth´;* from 6612; *silliness* (i.e. *seducibility*):—simple.

6616. **פָּתִיל, pâthîyl,** *paw-theel´;* from 6617; *twine:*—bound, bracelet, lace, line, ribband, thread, wire.

6617. **פָּתַל, pâthal,** *paw-thal´;* a primitive root; to *twine,* i.e. (literal) to *struggle* or (figurative) *be* (moral) *tortuous:*—(shew self) froward, shew self unsavoury, wrestle.

6618. **פְּתַלְתֹּל, pᵉthaltôl,** *peth-al-tole´;* from 6617; *tortuous* (i.e. crafty):—crooked.

6619. **פִּתֹם, Pithôm,** *pee-thome´;* of Egyptian derivation; *Pithom,* a place in Egypt:—Pithom.

6620. **פֶּתֶן, pethen,** *peh´-then;* from an unused root meaning to *twist;* an *asp* (from its *contortions*):—adder.

6621. **פֶּתַע, petha',** *peh´-thah;* from an unused root meaning to *open* (the eyes); a *wink,* i.e. *moment* [compare 6597] (used only [with or without preposition] adverbially *quickly* or *unexpectedly*):—at an instant, suddenly, × very.

6622. **פָּתַר, pâthar,** *paw-thar´;* a primitive root; to *open* up, i.e. (figurative) *interpret* (a dream):—interpret (-ation, -er).

6623. **פִּתְרוֹן, pithrôwn,** *pith-rone´;* or **פִּתְרֹן, pithrôn,** *pith-rone´;* from 6622; *interpretation* (of a dream):—interpretation.

6624. **פַּתְרוֹס, Pathrôws,** *path-roce´;* of Egyptian derivation; *Pathros,* a part of Egypt:—Pathros.

6625. **פַּתְרֻסִי, Pathrusîy,** *path-roo-see´;* patrial from 6624; a *Pathrusite,* or inhabitant of Pathros:—Pathrusim.

6626. **פָּתַת, pâthath,** *paw-thath´;* a primitive root; to *open,* i.e. *break:*—part.

6627. **צָאָה, tsê'âh,** *tsay-aw´;* from 3318; *issue,* i.e. (human) *excrement:*—that (which) cometh from (out).

6628. **צֶאֱלִים, tse'ĕlîym,** *tseh´-el-eem;* from an unused root meaning to *be slender;* the *lotus* tree:—shady tree.

6629. **צֹאן, tsô'n,** *tsone;* or **צאוֹן, tsᵉ'ôwn,** *tseh-one´;* (Ps 144:13), from an unused root meaning to *migrate;* a collective name for a *flock* (of sheep or goats); also figurative (of men):—(small) cattle, flock (+ -s), lamb (+ -s), sheep ([-cote, -fold, -shearer, -herds]).

6630. **צַאֲנָן, Tsa'ănân,** *tsah-an-awn´;* from the same as 6629 used denominative; *sheep* pasture; *Zaanan,* a place in Palestine:—Zaanan.

6631. **צֶאֱצָא, tse'ĕtsâ',** *tseh-ets-aw´;* from 3318; *issue,* i.e. *produce, children:*—that which cometh forth (out), offspring.

6632. **צָב, tsâb,** *tsawb;* from an unused root meaning to *establish;* a *palanquin* or *canopy* (as a *fixture*); also a species of *lizard* (probably as clinging *fast*):—covered, litter, tortoise.

6633. **צָבָא, tsâbâ',** *tsaw-baw´;* a primitive root; to *mass* (an army or servants):—assemble, fight, perform, muster, wait upon, war.

A verb meaning to wage war, to muster into service, to serve. This word is primarily used to describe a gathering of people waging war against another city or country (Nu 31:7, 42; Isa 29:7, 8; Zec 14:12).

In one instance, it was used to depict the Lord waging war (Isa 31:4). In several contexts, this word referred to the mustering of people into service (2Ki 25:19; Jer 52:25). Finally, this word described the religious service in the tabernacle (Ex 38:8; Nu 4:23; 8:24; 1Sa 2:22).

6634. צְבָא, tsᵉbâʼ, *tseb-aw´*; (Chaldee); corresponding to 6633 in the figurative sense of *summoning* one's wishes; to *please*:—will, would.

6635. צָבָא, tsâbâʼ, *tsaw-baw´*; or (feminine) צְבָאָה, **tsebâʼâh,** *tseb-aw-aw´*; from 6633; a *mass* of persons (or figurative things), especially reg. organized for war (an *army*); (by implication) a *campaign*, literal or figurative (specifically *hardship, worship*):—appointed time, (+) army, (+) battle, company, host, service, soldiers, waiting upon, war (-fare).

A masculine noun meaning service, servants. It may apply to military service (Nu 1:3; 1Sa 17:55); hard, difficult service (Job 7:1; Isa 40:2); or divine service (Nu 4:3; 8:24, 25; Ps 68:11[12]). The angels and the heavens alike are in divine service and therefore come under this term (Ge 2:1; 1Ki 22:19; Jer 33:22; cf. Lk 2:13). Over half of its nearly five hundred uses come in the phrase, the Lord [or God] of hosts. The phrase is absent from the first five books of the Bible. But frequently in the Prophets, the phrase introduces a divine declaration. At least once the hosts (always plural) in this expression are identified as human armies, but elsewhere they most likely refer to angelic forces (Jos 5:13–15; 1Sa 17:55; Ps 103:21; Isa 1:9). The title the LORD of hosts was often translated in the Septuagint as the LORD of powers or the LORD Almighty (Ps 24:10; Zec 4:6). On other occasions, the Hebrew word for hosts was transliterated into Greek (1Sa 1:3, 11). This Greek form of the Hebrew word shows up twice in the NT, once in a quotation from Isaiah (cf. Ro 9:29; Jas 5:4).

6636. צְבֹאִים, Tsᵉbôʼîym, *tseb-o-eem´*; or (more correctly) צְבֹיִּים, **Tsᵉbôʼyîm,** *tse-bo-yeem´*; or צְבִיִּם, **Tsᵉbôyîm,** *tse-bo-yeem´*; plural of 6643; *gazelles; Tseboïm* or *Tsebijim*, a place in Palestine:—Zeboiim, Zeboim.

6637. צֹבֵבָה, Tsôbêbâh, *tso-bay-baw´*; feminine active participle of the same as 6632; the *canopier* (with the article); *Tsobebah*, an Israelitess:—Zobebah.

6638. צָבָה, tsâbâh, *tsaw-baw´*; a primitive root; to *amass*, i.e. *grow turgid*; (specifically) to *array* an army against:—fight, swell.

6639. צָבֶה, tsâbeh, *tsaw-beh´*; from 6638; *turgid*:—swell.

6640. צְבוּ, tsᵉbûw, *tseb-oo´*; (Chaldee); from 6634; (properly) *will*; (concrete) an *affair* (as a matter of *determination*):—purpose.

6641. צָבוּעַ, tsâbûwaʻ, *tsaw-boo´-ah*; passive participle of the same as 6648; *dyed* (in stripes), i.e. the *hyena*:—speckled.

6642. צָבַט, tsâbaṭ, *tsaw-bat´*; a primitive root; to *grasp*, i.e. *hand* out:—reach.

6643. צְבִי, tsᵉbîy, *tseb-ee´*; from 6638 in the sense of *prominence; splendor* (as *conspicuous*); also a *gazelle* (as *beautiful*):—beautiful (-ty), glorious (-ry), goodly, pleasant, roe (-buck).

A masculine noun meaning beauty, glory, a gazelle. This word has essentially two meanings. The first meaning describes something that is beautiful or glorious, such as the glorious land which God gave Israel that flowed with milk and honey (Eze 20:6, 15); or the beautiful flower of Ephraim (Isa 28:1). This word was normally used to depict the glory of a nation: Israel (2Sa 1:19); Babylon (Isa 13:19); Tyre (Isa 23:9); Ephraim (Isa 28:1, 4); a city (Eze 25:9); a mountain (Da 11:45); or a land in general (Da 8:9; 11:16, 41). In a few instances, it speaks of the Lord Himself (Isa 4:2; Isa 28:5). The second meaning of this word is a gazelle, which is described in the dietary laws of the OT (Dt 12:15, 22); used to describe the speed of a runner (2Sa 2:18; 1Ch 12:8[9]; Pr 6:5); and compared to a lover (SS 2:9, 17; 8:14).

6644. צִבְיָא, Tsibyâʼ, *tsib-yaw´*; for 6645; *Tsibja*, an Israelite:—Zibia.

6645. צִבְיָה, Tsibyâh, *tsib-yaw´*; for 6646; *Tsibjah*, an Israelitess:—Zibiah.

6646. צְבִיָּה, tsᵉbîyyâh, *tseb-ee-yaw´*; feminine of 6643; a *female* gazelle:—roe.

6647. צְבַע, tsᵉbaʻ, *tseb-ah´*; (Chaldee); a root corresponding to that of 6648; to *dip*:—wet.

6648. צֶבַע, tsebaʻ, *tseh´-bah*; from an unused root meaning to *dip* (into colouring fluid); a *dye*:—divers, colours.

6649. צִבְעוֹן, Tsibʻôwn, *tsib-one´*; from the same as 6648; *variegated; Tsibon*, an Idumæan:—Zibeon.

6650. צְבֹעִים, Tsᵉbôʻîym, *tseb-o-eem´*; plural of 6641; *hyenas; Tseboïm*, a place in Palestine:—Zeboim.

6651. צָבַר, tsâbar, *tsaw-bar´*; a primitive root; to *aggregate*:—gather (together), heap (up), lay up.

6652. צִבֻּר, tsibbur, *tsib-boor´*; from 6551; a *pile*:—heap.

6653. צֶבֶת, tsebeth, *tseh´-beth*; from an unused root apparently meaning to *grip*; a *lock* of stalks:—handful.

6654. צַד, tsad, *tsad*; contracted from an unused root meaning to *sidle* off; a *side*; (figurative) an *adversary*:—(be-) side.

6655. צַד, tsad, *tsad*; (Chaldee); corresponding to 6654; used adverbially (with preposition) at or upon the *side* of:—against, concerning.

6656. צְדָא, tsᵉdâʼ, *tsed-aw´*; (Chaldee); from an unused root corresponding to 6658 in the sense of *intentness*; a (sinister) *design*:—true.

An Aramaic masculine noun meaning purpose. The word refers to doing something with malicious intent and is found once in the OT in the form of a question. Nebuchadnezzar approached Shadrach, Meshach, and Abednego, asking them if their intent was to defy him by not serving his gods or the golden image (Da 3:14).

6657. צְדָד, Tsᵉdâd, *tsed-awd´*; from the same as 6654; a *siding; Tsedad*, a place near Palestine:—Zedad.

6658. צָדָה, tsâdâh, *tsaw-daw´*; a primitive root; to *chase*; (by implication) to *desolate*:—destroy, hunt, lie in wait.

A verb meaning to hunt, to lie in wait. The word occurs only twice in the OT. In Ex 21:13, it signified deliberation and planning before a murder; those who were lying in wait were to be executed. Those, however, who committed a murder without lying in wait could flee to a city of refuge and be protected within its borders (cf. Nu 35:9–34). In 1Sa 24:11[12], the word signified Saul's attempt to hunt down David and kill him.

6659. צָדוֹק, Tsâdôwq, *tsaw-doke´*; from 6663; *just; Tsadok*, the name of eight or nine Israelites:—Zadok.

6660. צְדִיָּה, tsᵉdîyyâh, *tsed-ee-yaw´*; from 6658; *design* [compare 6656]:—lying in wait.

6661. צִדִּים, Tsiddîym, *tsid-deem´*; plural of 6654; *sides; Tsiddim* (with the article), a place in Palestine:—Ziddim.

6662. צַדִּיק, tsaddîyq, *tsad-deek´*; from 6663; *just*:—just, lawful, righteous (man).

An adjective meaning just, righteous. The term bears primarily a moral or ethical significance. Someone or something is considered to be just or righteous because of conformity to a given standard. It could be used to describe people or actions in a legal context, indicating they were in accordance with the legal standards (2Ki 10:9); or in a religious context, that they were in accordance with God's standards (Ge 6:9). It is used of human beings, such as the Davidic king (2Sa 23:3); judges and rulers (Pr 29:2; Eze 23:45); and individuals (Ge 6:9). It is also often applied to God, who is the ultimate standard used to define justice and righteousness (Ex 9:27; Ezr 9:15; Ps 7:11[12]). As a substantive, the righteous is used to convey the ideal concept of those who follow God's standards (Mal 3:18). In this way, it is often in antithetic parallelism with the wicked, *râshâʻ* (7563), the epitome of those who reject God and His standards (Pr 29:7).

6663. **צָדַק, tsâdaq,** *tsaw-dak´*; a primitive root; to *be* (causative, *make*) *right* (in a moral or forensic sense):—cleanse, clear self, (be, do) just (-ice, -ify, -ify self), (be, turn to) righteous (-ness).

A verb meaning to be right, to be righteous, to be just, to be innocent, to be put right, to justify, to declare right, to prove oneself innocent. The word is used twenty out of forty times in the simple stem. In this stem, it basically means to be right or just. God challenged His own people to show they were right in their claims (Isa 43:26). The verb can also connote being innocent, for God's people, through the Lord, will be found innocent (Ps 51:4[6]; Isa 45:25). Job argued his case effectively, proving himself right and vindicated (Job 11:2; 40:8). The ordinances of God were declared right by the psalmist (Ps 19:9[10]).

In the passive stem, it means to be put right. The verb refers to the altar in the second Temple being put right after its defilement (Da 8:14). In the intensive stem, the verb means to make or to declare righteous. Judah, because of her sin, made Samaria, her wicked sister, seem righteous (Eze 16:51, 52); the Lord asserted that northern Israel had been more just than Judah (Jer 3:11; cf. Job 32:2).

In the causative stem, the verb takes on the meaning of bringing about justice: Absalom began his conspiracy against David by declaring that he would administer justice for everyone (2Sa 15:4). The Lord vindicates His servant (Isa 50:8); every person of God is to declare the rights of the poor or oppressed (Ps 82:3). In Isa 53:11, it has the sense of the Servant helping other persons obtain their rights. Once in the reflexive stem, it means to justify oneself, as when Judah was at a loss as to how he and his brothers could possibly justify themselves before Pharaoh (Ge 44:16).

6664. **צֶדֶק, tsedeq,** *tseh´-dek*; from 6663; the *right* (natural, moral or legal); also (abstract) *equity* or (figurative) *prosperity*:—× even, (× that which is altogether) just (-ice), ([un-]) right (-eous) (cause, -ly, -ness).

A masculine noun meaning a right relation to an ethical or legal standard. The Hebrew word occurs most often in the Psalms and Isaiah. The word is frequently connected with the term justice (Ps 119:106; Isa 58:2). Kings, judges, and other leaders were to execute their duties based on righteous standards (Dt 1:16; Pr 8:15; Isa 32:1). God Himself acts in righteousness both in judgment and deliverance (Ps 119:75, 160; Isa 51:5; 62:1). Furthermore, God can be credited for generating human righteousness (Ps 4:1[2]; Jer 23:6). The concept of righteousness was so important in the OT period that the community that housed the Dead Sea scrolls called their most prominent leader the "Teacher of Righteousness," a person whom many regard as the founder of the sect.

6665. **צִדְקָה, tsidqâh,** *tsid-kaw´*; (Chaldee); corresponding to 6666; *beneficence*:—righteousness.

An Aramaic feminine noun meaning righteousness. The word occurs only in Da 4:27[24] where it signifies righteousness as positive action by which a person breaks off from sin. The Hebrew word in that verse is parallel to a Hebrew word meaning to show mercy. Daniel warned Nebuchadnezzar that he would go insane because of his arrogance (see Da 4:25) but that righteousness might prolong his prosperous state. For the corresponding Hebrew noun, see *tsĕdâqâh* (6666).

6666. **צְדָקָה, tsᵉdâqâh,** *tsed-aw-kaw´*; from 6663; *rightness* (abstract), subjective (*rectitude*), objective (*justice*), moral (*virtue*) or figurative (*prosperity*):—justice, moderately, right (-eous) (act, -ly, -ness).

A feminine noun meaning righteousness, blameless conduct, and integrity. The noun describes justice, right actions, and right attitudes, as expected from both God and people when they judge. God came speaking justice and righteousness as the divine Judge (Isa 63:1; Jer 9:24[23]; Mic 7:9); the Lord's holiness was made known by His righteousness in judgments (Isa 5:16; 10:22). Human judges were to imitate the divine Judge in righteousness and justice (Ge 18:19; 2Sa 8:15; Ps 72:3; Isa 56:1).

The word describes the attitude and actions God had and expected His people to maintain. He is unequivocally righteous; righteousness is entirely His prerogative. His people are to sow righteousness, and they will receive the same in return (Hos 10:12). He dealt with His people according to their righteousness and blamelessness (2Sa 22:21; Eze 3:20). Faith in God was counted as righteousness to Abraham (Ge 15:6); and obedience to the Lord's Law was further evidence of faith that God considered as righteousness (Dt 6:25). Returning a poor man's cloak was an act of obedience that was considered righteous and just before the Lord (Dt 24:13). Jacob declared that his integrity (honesty, righteousness) would speak for him in the future to Laban (Ge 30:33). The lives of people are to reflect righteousness and integrity (Pr 8:20; 15:9); even old age may be attained by living a life of righteousness (Pr 16:31).

The noun describes the justice of God or His will: persons are to act according to God's righteousness toward other persons (Dt 33:21; Isa 48:1). The word is also synonymous with truth or integrity. God declares His words are based on His own truthfulness (Isa 45:23). The word depicts God's salvation or deliverance, such as when Isaiah spoke of the Lord bringing near His righteousness as equal to bringing near His salvation (Isa 46:13; 51:6; 56:1).

The word may indicate a just claim before the king (2Sa 19:28[29]); or the righteous claim for vindication God gives to His people (Ne 2:20; Isa 54:17). A person who was denied justice but was righteous was, in fact, innocent (Isa 5:23). In the plural, the word referred to the righteous acts that God performed for His people (1Sa 12:7); or, in the plural used in an abstract sense, it depicted people living righteously (Isa 33:15). The word was used to mean legitimate and blameless, referring to the Lord's righteous Branch (Jer 23:5; 33:15) who will act justly and righteously in the restored land.

6667. **צִדְקִיָּה, Tsidqîyyâh,** *tsid-kee-yaw´*; or **צִדְקִיָּהוּ, Tsidqîyâhûw,** *tsid-kee-yaw´-hoo*; from 6664 and 3050; *right of Jah*; *Tsidkijah*, the name of six Israelites:—Zedekiah, Zidkijah.

6668. **צָהַב, tsâhab,** *tsaw-hab´*; a primitive root; to *glitter*, i.e. *be golden* in colour:—× fine.

6669. **צָהֹב, tsâhôb,** *tsaw-obe´*; from 6668; *golden* in colour:—yellow.

6670. **צָהַל, tsâhal,** *tsaw-hal´*; a primitive root; to *gleam*, i.e. (figurative) *be cheerful*; (by transformation) to *sound* clear (of various animal or human expressions):—bellow, cry aloud (out), lift up, neigh, rejoice, make to shine, shout.

6671. **צָהַר, tsâhar,** *tsaw-har´*; a primitive root; to *glisten*; used only as denominative from 3323, to *press* out *oil*:—make oil.

6672. **צֹהַר, tsôhar,** *tso´-har*; from 6671; a *light* (i.e. *window*); dual *double light*, i.e. *noon*:—midday, noon (-day, -tide), window.

6673. **צַו, tsav,** *tsav*; or **צָו, tsâv,** *tsawv*; from 6680; an *injunction*:—commandment, precept.

6674. **צוֹא, tsôw',** *tso*; or **צֹא, tsô',** *tso*; from an unused root meaning to *issue; soiled* (as if *excrementitious*):—filthy.

6675. **צוֹאָה, tsôw'âh,** *tso-aw´*; or **צֹאָה, tsô'âh,** *tso-aw´*; feminine of 6674; *excrement*; (generic) *dirt*; (figurative) *pollution*:—dung, filth (-iness). Margin for 2716.

6676. **צַוַּאר, tsavva'r,** *tsav-var´*; (Chaldee); corresponding to 6677:—neck.

6677. **צַוָּאר, tsavvâ'r,** *tsav-vawr´*; or **צַוָּר, tsavvâr,** *-vawr´*; (Ne 3:5), or **צַוָּרֹן, tsavvârôn,** *-vaw-rone´*; (SS 4:9), or (feminine) **צַוָּארָה, tsavvâ'râh,** *-vaw-raw*; (Mic 2:3), intensive from 6696 in the sense of *binding*; the back of the *neck* (as that on which burdens are *bound*):—neck.

6678. **צוֹבָא, Tsôwbâ',** *tso-baw´*; or **צוֹבָה, Tsôwbâh,** *tso-baw´*; or **צֹבָה, Tsôbâh,** *tso-baw´*; from an unused root meaning to *station*; a *station; Zoba* or *Zobah*, a region of Syria:—Zoba, Zobah.

6679. **צוּד, tsûwd,** *tsood*; a primitive root; to *lie* alongside (i.e. in wait); (by implication) to *catch* an animal (figurative, men); (denominative from 6718) to *victual* (for a journey):—chase, hunt, sore, take (provision).

6680. **צָוָה, tsâvâh,** *tsaw-vaw´*; a primitive root; (intensive) to *constitute, enjoin*:—appoint, (for-) bid, (give a) charge, (give a, give in, send with) command (-er, -ment), send a messenger, put, (set) in order.

A verb meaning to order, to direct, to appoint, to command, to charge, to be ordered, to be commanded. The word means to give an order or to command, to direct someone; it indicates commands given to people in various situations. The Lord commanded Adam and Eve to eat from certain trees but to refrain from eating from the tree of the knowledge of good and evil (Ge 2:16; 3:17). He ordered Moses hundreds of times to do or say certain things as He established Israel's worship, feasts, festivals, and rituals (Ex 7:2; 16:34; Nu 15:23). Israel was to keep all the directives the Lord gave them (Dt 4:2; 1Ki 11:10). The Lord commanded His prophets to speak (Am 6:11; Na 1:14; Zec 1:6). People gave orders to others as well, as when Pharaoh ordered that all newborn Hebrew males should be drowned in the Nile River (Ex 1:22). Deborah ordered Barak to defeat Sisera (Jgs 4:6). Abraham ordered his family to follow the ways of the Lord (Ge 18:19). Kings commanded their people (1Ki 5:17[31]; Jer 36:26). Priests in Israel gave directives to the people about what to do under certain circumstances (Le 9:6; cf. Le 13:58). A person who was chosen for a task or position was commanded concerning his responsibilities by the priestly authorities (Nu 27:19, 23). The word may mean to give directives or to set in order as when the Lord told Hezekiah to order—that is, to set things in order, in his household, for he was about to die (2Ki 20:1).

God commands not only people but creation: He created all things by His command (Ps 33:9; 148:5); He commanded the clouds not to send their rain on a disobedient vineyard (i.e. Israel [Ps 78:23; Isa 5:6]); He commands the entire heavenly realms (Isa 45:12). God commands historical processes; He will ultimately set up David, His ruler, as the one who commands (Isa 55:4).

6681. צָוַח**, tsâvach,** *tsaw-vakh´*; a primitive root; to *screech* (exultingly):—shout.

6682. צְוָחָה**, ts^e^vâchâh,** *tsev-aw-khaw´*; from 6681; a *screech* (of anguish):—cry (-ing).

6683. צוּלָה**, tsûwlâh,** *tsoo-law´*; from an unused root meaning to *sink*; an *abyss* (of the sea):—deep.

6684. צוּם**, tsûwm,** *tsoom*; a primitive root; to *cover* over (the mouth), i.e. to *fast*:— × at all, fast.

6685. צוֹם**, tsôwm,** *tsome*; or צֹם**, tsôm,** *tsome*; from 6684; a *fast*:—fast (-ing).

6686. צוּעָר**, Tsûw'âr,** *tsoo-awr´*; from 6819; *small; Tsuär*, an Israelite:—Zuar.

6687. צוּף**, tsûwph,** *tsoof*; a primitive root; to *overflow*:—(make to over-) flow, swim.

6688. צוּף**, tsûwph,** *tsoof*; from 6687; *comb* of honey (from *dripping*):—honeycomb.

6689. צוּף**, Tsûwph,** *tsoof*; or צוֹפַי**, Tsôwphay,** *tso-fah´ee*; or צִיף**, Tsîyph,** *tseef*; from 6688; *honey-comb; Tsuph* or *Tsophai* or *Tsiph*, the name of an Israelite and of a place in Palestine:—Zophai, Zuph.

6690. צוֹפַח**, Tsôwphach,** *tso-fakh´*; from an unused root meaning to *expand, breadth; Tsophach*, an Israelite:—Zophah.

6691. צוֹפַר**, Tsôwphar,** *tso-far´*; from 6852; *departing; Tsophar*, a friend of Job:—Zophar.

6692. צוּץ**, tsûwts,** *tsoots*; a primitive root; to *twinkle*, i.e. *glance*; (by analogy) to *blossom* (figurative) to *flourish*:—bloom, blossom, flourish, shew self.

6693. צוּק**, tsûwq,** *tsook*; a primitive root; to *compress*, i.e. (figurative) *oppress, distress*:—constrain, distress, lie sore, (op-) press (-or), straiten.

6694. צוּק**, tsûwq,** *tsook*; a primitive root [rather identical with 6693 through the idea of *narrowness* (of orifice)]; to *pour* out, i.e. (figurative) *smelt, utter*:—be molten, pour.

6695. צוֹק**, tsôwq,** *tsoke*; or (feminine) צוּקָה**, tsûw-qâh,** *tsoo-kaw´*; from 6693; a *strait*, i.e. (figurative) *distress*:—anguish, × troublous.

6696. צוּר**, tsûwr,** *tsoor*; a primitive root; to *cramp*, i.e. *confine* (in many applications, literal and figurative, formative or hostile):—adversary, assault, beset, besiege, bind (up), cast, distress, fashion, fortify, inclose, lay siege, put up in bags.

6697. צוּר**, tsûwr,** *tsoor*; or צֻר**, tsur,** *tsoor*; from 6696; (properly) a *cliff* (or sharp rock, as *compressed*); (generally) a *rock* or *boulder*; (figurative) a *refuge*; also an *edge* (as *precipitous*):—edge, × (mighty) God (one), rock, × sharp, stone, × strength, × strong. See also 1049.

6698. צוּר**, Tsûwr,** *tsoor*; the same as 6697; *rock; Tsur*, the name of a Midianite and of an Israelite:—Zur.

6699. צוּרָה**, tsûwrâh,** *tsoo-raw´*; feminine of 6697 a *rock* (Job 28:10); also a *form* (as if *pressed* out):—form, rock.

6700. צוּרִיאֵל**, Tsûwrîy'êl,** *tsoo-ree-ale´*; from 6697 and 410; *rock of God; Tsuriël*, an Israelite:—Zuriel.

6701. צוּרִישַׁדַּי**, Tsûwrîyshadday,** *tsoo-ree-shad-dah´ee*; from 6697 and 7706; *rock of* (the) *Almighty; Tsurishaddai*, an Israelite:—Zurishaddai.

6702. צוּת**, tsûwth,** *tsooth*; a primitive root; to *blaze*:—burn.

6703. צַח**, tsach,** *tsakh*; from 6705; *dazzling*, i.e. *sunny, bright*, (figurative) *evident*:—clear, dry, plainly, white.

6704. צִחֶה**, tsicheh,** *tsee-kheh´*; from an unused root meaning to *glow; parched*:—dried up.

6705. צָחַח**, tsâchach,** *tsaw-khakh´*; a primitive root; to *glare*, i.e. *be dazzling* white:—be whiter.

6706. צְחִיחַ**, ts^e^chîyach,** *tsekh-ee´-akh*; from 6705; *glaring*, i.e. *exposed* to the bright sun:—higher place, top.

6707. צְחִיחָה**, ts^e^chîychâh,** *tsekh-ee-khaw´*; feminine of 6706; a *parched* region, i.e. the *desert*:—dry land.

6708. צְחִיחִי**, ts^e^chîychîy,** *tsekh-ee-khee´*; from 6706; *bare* spot, i.e. in the *glaring* sun:—higher place.

6709. צַחֲנָה**, tsachănâh,** *tsakh-an-aw´*; from an unused root meaning to *putrefy; stench*:—ill savour.

6710. צַחְצָחָה**, tsachtsâchâh,** *tsakh-tsaw-khaw´*; from 6705; a *dry* place, i.e. *desert*:—drought.

6711. צָחַק**, tsâchaq,** *tsaw-khak´*; a primitive root; to *laugh* outright (in merriment or scorn); (by implication) to *sport*:—laugh, mock, play, make sport.

6712. צְחֹק**, ts^e^chôq,** *tsekh-oke´*; from 6711; *laughter* (in pleasure or derision):—laugh (-ed to scorn).

6713. צַחַר**, tsachar,** *tsakh´-ar*; from an unused root meaning to *dazzle; sheen*, i.e. *whiteness*:—white.

6714. צֹחַר**, Tsôchar,** *tso´-khar*; from the same as 6713; *whiteness; Tsochar*, the name of a Hittite and of an Israelite:—Zohar. Compare 3328.

6715. צָחֹר**, tsâchôr,** *tsaw-khore´*; from the same as 6713; *white*:—white.

6716. צִי**, tsîy,** *tsee*; from 6680; a *ship* (as a *fixture*):—ship.

6717. צִיבָא**, Tsîybâ',** *tsee-baw´*; from the same as 6678; *station; Tsiba*, an Israelite:—Ziba.

6718. צַיִד**, tsayid,** *tsah´-yid*; from a form of 6679 and meaning the same; the *chase*; also *game* (thus taken); (general) *lunch* (especially for a journey):— × catcheth, food, × hunter, (that which he took in) hunting, venison, victuals.

6719. צַיָּד, tsayyâd, *tsah´-yawd*; from the same as 6718; a *huntsman*:—hunter.

6720. צֵידָה, tsêydâh, *tsay-daw´*; or **צֵדָה, tsêdâh,** *tsay-daw´*; feminine of 6718; *food*:—meat, provision, venison, victuals.

6721. צִידוֹן, Tsîydôwn, *tsee-done´*; or **צִידֹן, Tsîydôn,** *tsee-done´*; from 6679 in the sense of *catching* fish; *fishery; Tsidon*, the name of a son of Canaan, and of a place in Palestine:—Sidon, Zidon.

6722. צִידֹנִי, Tsîydônîy, *tsee-do-nee´*; patrial from 6721; a *Tsidonian* or inhabitant of Tsidon:—Sidonian, of Sidon, Zidonian.

6723. צִיָּה, tsîyyâh, *tsee-yaw´*; from an unused root meaning to *parch; aridity*; (concrete) a *desert*:—barren, drought, dry (land, place), solitary place, wilderness.

6724. צָיוֹן, tsâyôwn, *tsaw-yone´*; from the same as 6723; a *desert*:—dry place.

6725. צִיּוּן, tsîyyûwn, *tsee-yoon´*; from the same as 6723 in the sense of *conspicuousness* [compare 5329]; a monumental or guiding *pillar*:—sign, title, waymark.

6726. צִיּוֹן, Tsîyyôwn, *tsee-yone´*; the same (regular) as 6725; *Tsijon* (as a permanent *capital*), a mountain of Jerusalem:—Zion.

6727. צִיחָא, Tsîychâ', *tsee-kahw´*; or **צִחָא, Tsichâ',** *tsee-khaw´*; as if feminine of 6704; *drought; Tsicha*, the name of two Nethinim:—Ziha.

6728. צִיִּים, tsîyyîym, *tsee-eem´*; from the same as 6723; a *desert-dweller*, i.e. *nomad* or wild *beast*:—wild beast of the desert, that dwell in (inhabiting) the wilderness.

6729. צִינֹק, tsîynôq, *tsee-noke´*; from an unused root meaning to *confine*; the *pillory*:—stocks.

6730. צִיעֹר, Tsîy'ôr, *tsee-ore´*; from 6819; *small; Tsior*, a place in Palestine:—Zior.

6731. צִיץ, tsîyts, *tseets*; or **צִץ, tsits,** *tseets*; from 6692; (properly) *glistening*, i.e. a burnished *plate*; also a *flower* (as *bright* coloured); a *wing* (as *gleaming* in the air):—blossom, flower, plate, wing.

6732. צִיץ, Tsîyts, *tseets*; the same as 6731; *bloom; Tsits*, a place in Palestine:—Ziz.

6733. צִיצָה, tsîytsâh, *tsee-tsaw´*; feminine of 6731; a *flower*:—flower.

6734. צִיצִת, tsîytsith, *tsee-tseeth´*; feminine of 6731; a *floral* or *wing*-like projection, i.e. a *fore-lock* of hair, a *tassel*:—fringe, lock.

6735. צִיר, tsîyr, *tseer*; from 6696; a *hinge* (as *pressed* in turning); also a *throe* (as a physical or mental *pressure*); also a *herald* or errand-doer (as *constrained* by the principal):—ambassador, hinge, messenger, pain, pang, sorrow. Compare 6736.

6736. צִיר, tsîyr, *tseer*; the same as 6735; a *form* (of beauty; as if *pressed* out, i.e. carved); hence an (idolatrous) *image*:—beauty, idol.

A masculine noun meaning a form, an image. This noun focuses on the physical appearance of an item. That form and structure could be of the human body: the psalmist records how dead bodies decay in the grave (Ps 49:14[15]). That form and structure could also be that of an idol: Isaiah states that those who formed idols would be ashamed and confounded (Isa 45:16).

6737. צָיַר, tsâyar, *tsaw-yar´*; a denominative from 6735 in the sense of *ambassador*; to *make an errand*, i.e. *betake* oneself:—make as if … had been ambassador.

6738. צֵל, tsêl, *tsale*; from 6751; *shade*, whether literal or figurative:—defence, shade (-ow).

A masculine noun meaning a shade, a shadow. This word is frequently used as a symbol for protection or refuge. This can be seen in the allegory of the trees (Jgs 9:15); and of the vine (Ps 80:10[11]). God protects in the shadow of His wings (Ps 17:8; 36:7[8]; 57:1[2]). The Lord is portrayed as the shade (Ps 121:5); and hid His servant in the shadow of His hand (Isa 49:2). The writer of Ecclesiastes taught that money and wisdom are both forms of protection, but wisdom could save one's life (Ecc 7:12).

6739. צְלָא, tsᵉlâ', *tsel-aw´*; (Chaldee); probably corresponding to 6760 in the sense of *bowing; pray*:—pray.

An Aramaic verb meaning to pray. Daniel was praying to God when the royal administrators caught him after King Darius' edict petitions should only be made of the king (Da 6:10[11]). King Darius instructed his governors to give to the Israelites whatever they needed to rebuild the Temple so they could offer sacrifices to God and continue praying for him (Ezr 6:10).

6740. צָלָה, tsâlâh, *tsaw-law´*; a primitive root; to *roast*:—roast.

6741. צִלָּה, Tsillâh, *tsil-law´*; feminine of 6738; *Tsillah*, an antediluvian woman:—Zillah.

6742. צְלוּל, tsᵉlûwl, *tsel-ool´*; from 6749 in the sense of *rolling*; a (round or flattened) *cake*:—cake.

6743. צָלַח, tsâlach, *tsaw-lakh´*; or **צָלֵחַ, tsâlêach,** *tsaw-lay´-akh*; a primitive root; to *push* forward, in various senses (literal or figurative, transitive or intransitive):—break out, come (mightily), go over, be good, be meet, be profitable, (cause to, effect, make to, send) prosper (-ity, -ous, -ously).

6744. צְלַח, tsᵉlach, *tsel-akh´*; (Chaldee); corresponding to 6743; to *advance* (transitive or intransitive):—promote, prosper.

6745. צֵלָחָה, tsêlâchâh, *tsay-law-khaw´*; from 6743; something *protracted* or flattened out, i.e. a *platter*:—pan.

6746. צְלֹחִית, tsᵉlôchîyth, *tsel-o-kheeth´*; from 6743; something *prolonged* or tall, i.e. a *vial* or salt-*cellar*:—cruse.

6747. צַלַּחַת, tsallachath, *tsal-lakh´-ath*; from 6743; something *advanced* or deep, i.e. a *bowl*; (figurative) the *bosom*:—bosom, dish.

6748. צָלִי, tsâlîy, *tsaw-lee´*; passive participle of 6740; *roasted*:—roast.

6749. צָלַל, tsâlal, *tsaw-lal´*; a primitive root; (properly) to *tumble* down, i.e. *settle* by a waving motion:—sink. Compare 6750, 6751.

6750. צָלַל, tsâlal, *tsaw-lal´*; a primitive root [rather identical with 6749 through the idea of *vibration*]; to *tinkle*, i.e. *rattle* together (as the ears in *reddening* with shame, or the teeth in *chattering* with fear):—quiver, tingle.

6751. צָלַל, tsâlal, *tsaw-lal´*; a primitive root [rather identical with 6749 through the idea of *hovering* over (compare 6754)]; to *shade*, as twilight or an opaque object:—begin to be dark, shadowing.

A Hebrew verb meaning to be dark, to grow dim. This word is used only twice in the Hebrew OT. Nehemiah spoke of the gates of Jerusalem growing dim (in other words, evening came, and it grew dark) (Ne 13:19). Assyria was compared to a Lebanese cedar that had such long, thick branches that it darkened the forest (Eze 31:3).

6752. צֵלֶל, tsêlel, *tsay´-lel*; from 6751; *shade*:—shadow.

A masculine noun meaning shadow. This word occurs only four times in the OT. In Job it described the shade of trees (Job 40:22). In the other instances, it depicted the time of day when the shadows fled (SS 2:17; 4:6) or lengthened (Jer 6:4).

6753. צְלֶלְפּוֹנִי, Tsᵉlelpôwnîy, *tsel-el-po-nee´*; from 6752 and the active participle of 6437; *shade-facing; Tselelponi*, an Israelitess:—Hazelelponi [*including the article*].

6754. צֶלֶם, tselem, *tseh´-lem*; from an unused root meaning to *shade*; a *phantom*, i.e. (figurative) *illusion, resemblance*; hence a representative *figure*, especially an *idol*:—image, vain shew.

A masculine noun meaning an image, a likeness, a statue, a model, a drawing, a shadow. The word means image or likeness; its most celebrated theological and anthropological use was to depict human beings as made in God's own image (Ge 1:26, 27; 5:3). People continue to be in His image even after the Fall, although the image is marred (Ge 9:6), and still serves as the basis of the prohibition not to kill human beings.

It is used metaphorically to depict persons as shadows, phantoms, or unknowing, senseless, fleeting beings carrying out the motions of life (Ps 39:6[7]); unless they have hope in God (see Ps 39:7[8]). In a similar vein, the wicked before the Lord are considered as mere dreams or fantasies (Ps 73:20).

The word is also used in a concrete sense to depict images cut out of or molded from various materials. The word describes the images or idols of foreign or strange gods (2Ki 11:18; Am 5:26). The people of Israel produced images used as idols from their own jewelry (Eze 7:20; 16:17). Israel was, on its entrance into Canaan, to destroy all the molten images of the heathen (Nu 33:52). In Ezekiel 23:14, this word refers to pictures of Babylonians that enticed the people of Israel into apostasy when they saw them (Eze 23:14).

6755. צְלֵם**, tselem,** *tseh´-lem*; (Chaldee); or צְלֵם**, tsᵉlêm,** *tsel-ame´*; (Chaldee); corresponding to 6754; an idolatrous *figure:*—form, image.

An Aramaic masculine noun meaning a statue, an image. This word is related to the Hebrew word *tselem* (6754), meaning image. It was used to describe the statue in Nebuchadnezzar's dream (Da 2:31, 32, 34, 35); the image that Nebuchadnezzar built (Da 3:1–3, 5, 7); and the distortion of Nebuchadnezzar's face in anger when he heard the response of Shadrach, Meshach, and Abednego (Da 3:19).

6756. צַלְמוֹן**, Tsalmôwn,** *tsal-mone´*; from 6754; *shady; Tsalmon,* the name of a place in Palestine and of an Israelite:—Zalmon.

6757. צַלְמָוֶת**, tsalmâveth,** *tsal-maw´-veth*; from 6738 and 4194; *shade of death,* i.e. the *grave;* (figurative) *calamity:*—shadow of death.

A masculine noun meaning a death shadow, a deep shadow. This word is made up of two Hebrew words, *tsêl* (6738) or *tsêlel* (6752), meaning shadow, and *mâweth* (4194), meaning death, which gives rise to the translation of shadow of death (Ps 23:4). In some contexts, this word was used to describe death (Job 38:17); or those close to death (Ps 107:10, 14). In other contexts, it was used to describe a physical darkness (Job 24:17; Am 5:8); a spiritual darkness (Isa 9:2[1]); a darkness of understanding (Job 12:22); a gloomy countenance (Job 16:16); or a dangerous land (Jer 2:6). Occasionally, both elements of death and darkness are present in the context (Job 3:5; 10:21, 22).

6758. צַלְמֹנָה**, Tsalmônâh,** *tsal-mo-naw´*; feminine of 6757; *shadiness; Tsalmonah,* a place in the Desert:—Zalmonah.

6759. צַלְמֻנָּע**, Tsalmunnâʻ,** *tsal-moon-naw´*; from 6738 and 4513; *shade has been denied; Tsalmunna,* a Midianite:—Zalmunna.

6760. צָלַע**, tsâlaʻ,** *tsaw-lah´*; a primitive root; probably to *curve;* used only as denominative from 6763, to *limp* (as if *one-sided*):—halt.

6761. צֶלַע**, tselaʻ,** *tseh´-lah*; from 6760; a *limping* or *fall* (figurative):—adversity, halt (-ing).

6762. צֶלַע**, Tsêlaʻ,** *tsay´-lah*; the same as 6761; *Tsela,* a place in Palestine:—Zelah.

6763. צֵלָע**, tsêlâʻ,** *tsay-law´*; or (feminine) צַלְעָה**, tsalʻâh,** *tsal-aw´*; from 6760; a *rib* (as *curved*), literal (of the body), or figurative (of a door, i.e. *leaf*); hence a *side,* literal (of a person) or figurative (of an object or the sky, i.e. *quarter*); architecturally a (especially floor or ceiling) *timber* or *plank* (single or collective, i.e. a *flooring*):—beam, board, chamber, corner, leaf, plank, rib, side (chamber).

6764. צָלָף**, Tsâlâph,** *tsaw-lawf´*; from an unused root of unknown meaning; *Tsalaph,* an Israelite:—Zalaph.

6765. צְלָפְחָד**, Tsᵉlophchâd,** *tsel-of-khawd´*; from the same as 6764 and 259; *Tselopchad,* an Israelite:—Zelophehad.

6766. צֶלְצַח**, Tseltsach,** *tsel-tsakh´*; from 6738 and 6703; *clear shade; Tseltsach,* a place in Palestine:—Zelzah.

6767. צְלָצַל**, tsᵉlâtsal,** *tsel-aw-tsal´*; from 6750 reduplication; a *clatter,* i.e. (abstract) *whirring* (of wings); (concrete) a *cricket;* also a *harpoon* (as *rattling*), a *cymbal* (as *clanging*):—cymbal, locust, shadowing, spear.

6768. צֶלֶק**, Tseleq,** *tseh´-lek*; from an unused root meaning to *split; fissure; Tselek,* an Israelite:—Zelek.

6769. צִלְּתַי**, Tsillᵉthay,** *tsil-leth-ah´ee*; from the feminine of 6738; *shady; Tsillethai,* the name of two Israelites:—Zilthai.

6770. צָמֵא**, tsâmêʼ,** *tsaw-may´*; a primitive root; to *thirst* (literal or figurative):—(be a-, suffer) thirst (-y).

6771. צָמֵא**, tsâmêʼ,** *tsaw-may´*; from 6770; *thirsty* (literal or figurative):—(that) thirst (-eth, -y).

6772. צָמָא**, tsâmâʼ,** *tsaw-maw´*; from 6770; *thirst* (literal or figurative):—thirst (-y).

6773. צִמְאָה**, tsimʼâh,** *tsim-aw´*; feminine of 6772; *thirst;* (figurative) *libidinousnes:*—thirst.

6774. צִמָּאוֹן**, tsimmâʼôwn,** *tsim-maw-one´*; from 6771; a *thirsty* place, i.e. *desert:*—drought, dry ground, thirsty land.

6775. צָמַד**, tsâmad,** *tsaw-mad´*; a primitive root; to *link,* i.e. *gird;* (figurative) to *serve,* (mentally) *contrive:*—fasten, frame, join (self).

6776. צֶמֶד**, tsemed,** *tseh´-med*; a *yoke* or *team* (i.e. pair); hence an *acre* (i.e. day's task for a yoke of cattle to plough):—acre, couple, × together, two [asses], yoke (of oxen).

6777. צַמָּה**, tsammâh,** *tsam-maw´*; from an unused root meaning to *fasten* on; a *veil:*—locks.

6778. צִמּוּקִים**, tsimmûwqîym,** *tsim-moo-keem´*; from 6784; a cake of *dried* grapes:—bunch (cluster) of raisins.

6779. צָמַח**, tsâmach,** *tsaw-makh´*; a primitive root; to *sprout* (transitive or intransitive, literal or figurative):—bear, bring forth, (cause to, make to) bud (forth), (cause to, make to) grow (again, up), (cause to) spring (forth, up).

6780. צֶמַח**, tsemach,** *tseh´-makh*; from 6779; a *sprout* (usually concrete), literal or figurative:—branch, bud, that which (where) grew (upon), spring (-ing).

6781. צָמִיד**, tsâmîyd,** *tsaw-meed´*; or צָמִד**, tsâmid,** *tsaw-meed´*; from 6775; a *bracelet* or *arm-clasp*; (generally) a *lid:*—bracelet, covering.

6782. צַמִּים**, tsammîym,** *tsam-meem´*; from the same as 6777; a *noose* (as *fastening*); (figurative) *destruction:*—robber.

6783. צְמִיתֻת**, tsᵉmîythuth,** *tsem-ee-thooth´*; or צְמִתֻת**, tsᵉmithuth,** *tsem-ee-thooth´*; from 6789; *excision,* i.e. *destruction;* used only (adverb) with prepositional prefix *to extinction,* i.e. *perpetually:*—ever.

A feminine noun meaning completion, finality. This word is used only twice in the OT and comes from the verb *tsâmath* (6789), meaning to put to an end. It was used in the Levitical Law to describe the duration of property ownership (Le 25:23, 30).

6784. צָמַק**, tsâmaq,** *tsaw-mak´*; a primitive root; to *dry* up:—dry.

6785. צֶמֶר**, tsemer,** *tseh´-mer*; from an unused root probably meaning to *be shaggy; wool:*—wool (-len).

6786. צְמָרִי**, Tsᵉmârîy,** *tsem-aw-ree´*; patrial from an unused name of a place in Palestine; a *Tsemarite* or branch of the Canaanites:—Zemarite.

6787. צְמָרַיִם**, Tsᵉmârayim,** *tsem-aw-rah´-yim*; dual of 6785; *double fleece; Tsemarajim,* a place in Palestine:—Zemaraim.

6788. צַמֶּרֶת**, tsammereth,** *tsam-meh´-reth*; from the same as 6785; *fleeciness,* i.e. *foliage:*—highest branch, top.

6789. צָמַת, tsâmath, *tsaw-math´*; a primitive root; to *extirpate* (literal or figurative):—consume, cut off, destroy, vanish.

A verb meaning to put to an end. This word appears most often in the imprecatory psalms—that is, the psalms that call down curses on one's enemies. The word occurs within the context of putting an end to the wicked (Ps 73:27; 101:8); or to one's enemies (2Sa 22:41; Ps 54:5[7]; 143:12). In both of these cases, this word alludes to the physical death of these people. But in other instances, this word describes the process of rendering powerless by putting persons in prison (La 3:53); the drying up of riverbeds (Job 6:17); or the wearying of the psalmist (Ps 119:139).

6790. צִן, Tsin, *tseen*; from an unused root meaning to *prick*; a *crag; Tsin*, a part of the Desert:—Zin.

6791. צֵן, tsên, *tsane*; from an unused root meaning to *be prickly*; a *thorn*; hence a cactus-*hedge*:—thorn.

6792. צֹנֵא, tsônê, *tso-nay´*; or צֹנֶה, **tsôneh,** *tso-neh´*; for 6629; a *flock*:—sheep.

6793. צִנָּה, tsinnâh, *tsin-naw´*; feminine of 6791; a *hook* (as *pointed*); also a (large) *shield* (as if guarding by *prickliness*); also *cold* (as *piercing*):—buckler, cold, hook, shield, target.

6794. צִנּוֹר, tsinnôwr, *tsin-nor´*; from an unused root perhaps meaning to *be hollow*; a *culvert*:—gutter, water-spout.

6795. צָנַח, tsânach, *tsaw-nakh´*; a primitive root; to *alight*; (transitive) to *cause to descend*, i.e. *drive* down:—fasten, light [from off].

6796. צָנִין, tsânîyn, *tsaw-neen´*; or צָנִן, **tsânin,** *tsaw-neen*; from the same as 6791; a *thorn*:—thorn.

6797. צָנִיף, tsânîyph, *tsaw-neef´*; or צָנוֹף, **tsânôwph,** *tsaw-nofe´*; or (feminine) צָנִיפָה, **tsânîyphâh,** *tsaw-nee-faw´*; from 6801; a *head-dress* (i.e. piece of cloth *wrapped* around):—diadem, hood, mitre.

6798. צָנַם, tsânam, *tsaw-nam´*; a primitive root; to *blast* or *shrink*:—withered.

6799. צְנָן, Tsᵉnân, *tsen-awn´*; probably for 6630; *Tsenan*, a place near Palestine:—Zenan.

6800. צָנַע, tsânaʻ, *tsaw-nah´*; a primitive root; to *humiliate*:—humbly, lowly.

6801. צָנַף, tsânaph, *tsaw-naf´*; a primitive root; to *wrap*, i.e. *roll* or *dress*:—be attired, × surely, violently turn.

6802. צְנֵפָה, tsᵉnêphâh, *tsen-ay-faw´*; from 6801; a *ball*:—× toss.

6803. צִנְצֶנֶת, tsintseneth, *tsin-tseh´-neth*; from the same as 6791; a *vase* (probably a vial *tapering* at the top):—pot.

6804. צַנְתְּרוֹת, tsantᵉrôwth, *tsan-teh-rowth´*; probably from the same as 6794; a *tube*:—pipe.

6805. צָעַד, tsâʻad, *tsaw-ad´*; a primitive root; to *pace*, i.e. *step* regularly; (upward) to *mount*; (along) to *march*; (down and causative) to *hurl*:—bring, go, march (through), run over.

6806. צַעַד, tsaʻad, *tsah´-ad*; from 6804; a *pace* or regular *step*:—pace, step.

6807. צְעָדָה, tsᵉʻâdâh, *tseh-aw-daw´*; feminine of 6806; a *march*; (concrete) an (ornamental) *ankle-chain*:—going, ornament of the legs.

6808. צָעָה, tsâʻâh, *tsaw-aw´*; a primitive root; to *tip* over (for the purpose of *spilling* or *pouring* out), i.e. (figurative) *depopulate*; (by implication) to *imprison* or *conquer*; (reflexive) to *lie down* (for coition):—captive exile, travelling, (cause to) wander (-er).

6809. צָעִיף, tsâʻîyph, *tsaw-eef´*; from an unused root meaning to *wrap* over; a *veil*:—vail.

6810. צָעִיר, tsâʻîyr, *tsaw-eer´*; or צָעוֹר, **tsâʻôwr,** *tsaw-ore´*; from 6819; *little*; (in number) *few*; (in age) *young*, (in value) *ignoble*:—least, little (one), small (one), + young (-er, -est).

6811. צָעִיר, Tsâʻîyr, *tsaw-eer´*; the same as 6810; *Tsaïr*, a place in Idumæa:—Zair.

6812. צְעִירָה, tsᵉʻîyrâh, *tseh-ee-raw´*; feminine of 6810; *smallness* (of age), i.e. *juvenility*:—youth.

6813. צָעַן, tsâʻan, *tsaw-an´*; a primitive root; to *load* up (beasts), i.e. to *migrate*:—be taken down.

6814. צֹעַן, Tsôʻan, *tso´-an*; of Egyptian derivation; *Tsoän*, a place in Egypt:—Zoan.

6815. צַעֲנַנִּים, Tsaʻănannîym, *tsah-an-an-neem´*; or (dual) צַעֲנַיִם, **Tsaʻănayim,** *tsah-an-ah´-yim*; plural from 6813; *removals; Tsaanannim* or *Tsaanajim*, a place in Palestine:—Zaannannim, Zaanaim.

6816. צַעֲצֻעִים, tsaʻătsuʻîym, *tsah-ah-tsoo´-eem*; from an unused root meaning to *bestrew* with carvings; *sculpture*:—image [work].

6817. צָעַק, tsâʻaq, *tsaw-ak´*; a primitive root; to *shriek*; (by implication) to *proclaim* (an assembly):— × at all, call together, cry (out), gather (selves) (together).

6818. צְעָקָה, tsᵉʻâqâh, *tseh-awk-aw´*; from 6817; a *shriek*:—cry (-ing).

6819. צָעַר, tsâʻar, *tsaw-ar´*; a primitive root; to *be small*, i.e. (figurative) *ignoble*:—be brought low, little one, be small.

6820. צֹעַר, Tsôʻar, *tso´-ar*; from 6819; *little; Tsoär*, a place East of the Jordan:—Zoar.

6821. צָפַד, tsâphad, *tsaw-fad´*; a primitive root; to *adhere*:—cleave.

6822. צָפָה, tsâphâh, *tsaw-faw´*; a primitive root; (properly) to *lean* forward, i.e. to *peer* into the distance; (by implication) to *observe, await*:—behold, espy, look up (well), wait for, (keep the) watch (-man).

6823. צָפָה, tsâphâh, *tsaw-faw´*; a primitive root [probably rather identical with 6822 through the idea of *expansion* in outlook transferred to act]; to *sheet* over (especially with metal):—cover, overlay.

6824. צָפָה, tsâphâh, *tsaw-faw´*; from 6823; an *inundation* (as *covering*):— × swimmest (KJV).

6825. צְפוֹ, Tsᵉphôw, *tsef-o´*; or צְפִי, **Tsᵉphîy,** *tsef-ee´*; from 6822; *observant; Tsepho* or *Tsephi*, an Idumæan:—Zephi, Zepho.

6826. צִפּוּי, tsippûwy, *tsip-poo´ee*; from 6823; *encasement* (with metal):—covering, overlaying.

6827. צְפוֹן, Tsᵉphôwn, *tsef-one´*; probably for 6837; *Tsephon*, an Israelite:—Zephon.

6828. צָפוֹן, tsâphôwn, *tsaw-fone´*; or צָפֹן, **tsâphôn,** *tsaw-fone´*; from 6845; (properly) *hidden*, i.e. *dark*; used only of the *north* as a quarter (*gloomy* and *unknown*):—north (-ern, side, -ward, wind).

6829. צָפוֹן, Tsâphôwn, *tsaw-fone´*; the same as 6828; *boreal; Tsaphon*, a place in Palestine:—Zaphon.

6830. צְפוֹנִי, tsᵉphôwnîy, *tsef-o-nee´*; from 6828; *northern*:—northern.

6831. צְפוֹנִי, Tsᵉphôwnîy, *tsef-o-nee´*; patronymic from 6827; a *Tsephonite*, or (collective) descendants of Tsephon:—Zephonites.

6832. צְפִיעַ, tsâphîyaʻ, *tsaw-fee´-ah*; from the same as 6848; *excrement* (as *protruded*):—dung.

6833. צִפּוֹר**, tsippôwr,** *tsip-pore´*; or צִפֹּר**, tsippôr,** *tsip-pore´*; from 6852; a little *bird* (as *hopping*):—bird, fowl, sparrow.

6834. צִפּוֹר**, Tsippôwr,** *tsip-pore´*; the same as 6833; *Tsippor*, a Moabite:—Zippor.

6835. צַפַּחַת**, tsappachath,** *tsap-pakh´-ath*; from an unused root meaning to *expand*; a *saucer* (as *flat*):—cruse.

6836. צְפִיָּה**, tsᵉphîyyâh,** *tsef-ee-yaw´*; from 6822; *watchfulness*:—watching.

6837. צִפְיוֹן**, Tsiphyôwn,** *tsif-yone´*; from 6822; *watch*-tower; *Tsiphjon*, an Israelite:—Ziphion. Compare 6827.

6838. צַפִּיחִת**, tsappîychith,** *tsap-pee-kheeth´*; from the same as 6835; a flat thin *cake*:—wafer.

6839. צֹפִים**, Tsôphîym,** *tso-feem´*; plural of active participle of 6822; *watchers; Tsophim*, a place East of the Jordan:—Zophim.

6840. צָפִין**, tsâphîyn,** *tsaw-feen´*; from 6845; a *treasure* (as *hidden*):—hid.

6841. צְפִיר**, tsᵉphîyr,** *tsef-eer´*; (Chaldee); corresponding to 6842; a he-*goat*:—he [goat].

6842. צָפִיר**, tsâphîyr,** *tsaw-feer´*; from 6852; a male *goat* (as *prancing*):—(he) goat.

6843. צְפִירָה**, tsᵉphîyrâh,** *tsef-ee-raw´*; feminine formed like 6842; a *crown* (as *encircling* the head); also a *turn* of affairs (i.e. *mishap*):—diadem, morning.

6844. צָפִית**, tsâphîyth,** *tsaw-feeth´*; from 6822; a *sentry*:—watchtower.

6845. צָפַן**, tsâphan,** *tsaw-fan´*; a primitive root; to *hide* (by *covering* over); (by implication) to *hoard* or *reserve*; (figurative) to *deny*; specifically (favourably) to *protect*, (unfavourably) to *lurk*:—esteem, hide (-den one, self), lay up, lurk (be set) privily, (keep) secret (-ly, place).

6846. צְפַנְיָה**, Tsᵉphanyâh,** *tsef-an-yaw´*; or צְפַנְיָהוּ**, Tsᵉphanyâhûw,** *tsef-an-yaw´-hoo*; from 6845 and 3050; *Jah has secreted; Tsephanjah*, the name of four Israelites:—Zephaniah.

6847. צָפְנַת פַּעְנֵחַ**, Tsâphnath Paʻnêach,** *tsof-nath´ pah-nay´-akh*; of Egyptian derivation; *Tsophnath-Paneäh*, Joseph's Egyptian name:—Zaphnath-paaneah.

6848. צֶפַע**, tsephaʻ,** *tseh´-fah*; or צִפְעֹנִי**, tsiphʻônîy,** *tsif-o-nee´*; from an unused root meaning to *extrude*; a *viper* (as *thrusting* out the tongue, i.e. *hissing*):—adder, cockatrice.

6849. צְפִעָה**, tsᵉphiʻâh,** *tsef-ee-aw´*; feminine from the same as 6848; an *outcast* thing:—issue.

6850. צָפַף**, tsâphaph,** *tsaw-faf´*; a primitive root; to *coo* or *chirp* (as a bird):—chatter, peep, whisper.

6851. צַפְצָפָה**, tsaphtsâphâh,** *tsaf-tsaw-faw´*; from 6687; a *willow* (as growing in *overflowed* places):—willow tree.

6852. צָפַר**, tsâphar,** *tsaw-far´*; a primitive root; to *skip* about, i.e. *return*:—depart early.

6853. צְפַר**, tsippar,** *tsip-par´*; (Chaldee); corresponding to 6833; a *bird*:—bird.

6854. צְפַרְדֵּעַ**, tsᵉphardêaʻ,** *tsef-ar-day´-ah*; from 6852 and a word elsewhere unused meaning a *swamp*; a *marsh-leaper*, i.e. *frog*:—frog.

6855. צִפֹּרָה**, Tsippôrâh,** *tsip-po-raw´*; feminine of 6833; *bird; Tsipporah*, Moses' wife:—Zipporah.

6856. צִפֹּרֶן**, tsippôren,** *tsip-po´-ren*; from 6852 (in the denominative sense [from 6833] of *scratching*); (properly) a *claw*, i.e. (human) *nail*; also the *point* of a style (or pen, tipped with adamant):—nail, point.

6857. צְפַת**, Tsᵉphath,** *tsef-ath´*; from 6822; *watch*-tower; *Tsephath*, a place in Palestine:—Zephath.

6858. צֶפֶת**, tsepheth,** *tseh´-feth*; from an unused root meaning to *encircle*; a *capital* of a column:—chapiter.

6859. צְפָתָה**, Tsᵉphâthâh,** *tsef-aw´-thaw*; the same as 6857; *Tsephathah*, a place in Palestine:—Zephathah.

6860. צִקְלַג**, Tsiqlag,** *tsik-lag´*; or צִיקְלַג**, Tsîyqᵉlag,** *tsee-kel-ag´*; (1Ch 12:1, 20), of uncertain derivation; *Tsiklag* or *Tsikelag*, a place in Palestine:—Ziklag.

6861. צִקְלוֹן**, tsiqqâlôwn,** *tsik-ka-lone´*; from an unused root meaning to *wind*; a *sack* (as *tied* at the mouth):—husk.

6862. צַר**, tsar,** *tsar*; or צָר**, tsâr,** *tsawr*; from 6887; *narrow*; (as a noun) a *tight* place (usually figurative, i.e. *trouble*); also a *pebble* (as in 6864); (transitive) an *opponent* (as *crowding*):—adversary, afflicted (-tion), anguish, close, distress, enemy, flint, foe, narrow, small, sorrow, strait, tribulation, trouble.

6863. צֵר**, Tsêr,** *tsare*; from 6887; *rock; Tser*, a place in Palestine:—Zer.

6864. צֹר**, tsôr,** *tsore*; from 6696; a *stone* (as if *pressed* hard or to a point); (by implication of use) a *knife*:—flint, sharp stone.

6865. צֹר**, Tsôr,** *tsore*; or צוֹר**, Tsôwr,** *tsore*; the same as 6864; a *rock; Tsor*, a place in Palestine:—Tyre, Tyrus.

6866. צָרַב**, tsârab,** *tsaw-rab´*; a primitive root; to *burn*:—burn.

6867. צָרֶבֶת**, tsârebeth,** *tsaw-reh´-beth*; from 6686; *conflagration* (of fire or disease):—burning, inflammation.

6868. צְרֵדָה**, Tsᵉrêdâh,** *tser-ay-daw´*; or צְרֵדָתָה**, Tsᵉrêdâthâh,** *tser-ay-daw´-thaw*; apparently from an unused root meaning to *pierce; puncture; Tseredah*, a place in Palestine:—Zereda, Zeredathah.

6869. צָרָה**, tsârâh,** *tsaw-raw´*; feminine of 6862; *tightness* (i.e. [figurative] *trouble*); (transitive) a female *rival*:—adversary, adversity, affliction, anguish, distress, tribulation, trouble.

6870. צְרוּיָה**, Tsᵉrûwyâh,** *tser-oo-yaw´*; feminine participle passive from the same as 6875; *wounded; Tserujah*, an Israelitess:—Zeruiah.

6871. צְרוּעָה**, Tsᵉrûwʻâh,** *tser-oo-aw´*; feminine passive participle of 6879; *leprous; Tseruäh*, an Israelitess:—Zeruah.

6872. צְרוֹר**, tsᵉrôwr,** *tser-ore´*; or (shorter) צְרֹר**, tsᵉrôr,** *tser-ore´*; from 6887; a *parcel* (as *packed* up); also a *kernel* or *particle* (as if a *package*):—bag, × bendeth, bundle, least grain, small stone.

6873. צָרַח**, tsârach,** *tsaw-rakh´*; a primitive root; to *be clear* (in tone, i.e. *shrill*), i.e. to *whoop*:—cry, roar.

6874. צְרִי**, Tsᵉrîy,** *tser-ee´*; the same as 6875; *Tseri*, an Israelite:—Zeri. Compare 3340.

6875. צְרִי**, tsᵉrîy,** *tser-ee´*; or צֳרִי**, tsŏrîy,** *tsor-ee´*; from an unused root meaning to *crack* [as by *pressure*], hence to *leak; distillation*, i.e. *balsam*:—balm.

6876. צֹרִי**, Tsôrîy,** *tso-ree´*; patrial from 6865; a *Tsorite* or inhabitant of Tsor (i.e. *Syrian*):—(man) of Tyre.

6877. צְרִיחַ**, tsᵉrîyach,** *tser-ee´-akh*; from 6873 in the sense of *clearness* of vision; a *citadel*:—high place, hold.

6878. צֹרֶךְ**, tsôrek,** *tso´-rek*; from an unused root meaning to *need; need*:—need.

6879. צָרַע**, tsâraʻ,** *tsaw-rah´*; a primitive root; to *scourge*, i.e. (intransitive and figurative) to *be stricken with leprosy*:—leper, leprous.

6880. צִרְעָה**, tsirʻâh,** *tsir-aw´*; from 6879; a *wasp* (as *stinging*):—hornet.

6881. צָרְעָה, Tsor'âh, *tsor-aw´*; apparently another form for 6880; *Tsorah*, a place in Palestine:—Zareah, Zorah, Zoreah.

6882. צָרְעִי, Tsor'iy, *tsor-ee´*; or **צָרְעָתִי, Tsor'âthîy,** *tsor-aw-thee´*; patrial from 6881; a *Tsorite* or *Tsorathite*, i.e. inhabitant of Tsorah:—Zorites, Zareathites, Zorathites.

6883. צָרַעַת, tsâra'ath, *tsaw-rah´-ath*; from 6879; *leprosy*:—leprosy.

6884. צָרַף, tsâraph, *tsaw-raf´*; a primitive root; to *fuse* (metal), i.e. *refine* (literal or figurative):—cast, (re-) fine (-er), founder, goldsmith, melt, pure, purge away, try.

A verb meaning to refine, to test. This word describes the purifying process of a refiner, who heats metal, takes away the dross, and is left with a pure substance (Pr 25:4). As a participle, this word refers to a tradesman (i.e. a goldsmith or silversmith) who does the refining work (Jgs 17:4; Ne 3:8; Isa 41:7). This word is also used to speak of the Word of God that is described as pure and refined (2Sa 22:31; Ps 12:6[7]; Pr 30:5). When applied to people, this word refers to the purifying effects of external trials (Ps 66:10; 105:19; Isa 48:10) that God often uses to purify His people from sin (Isa 1:25; Zec 13:9); or to remove the wicked from His people (Jer 6:29; Mal 3:2, 3).

6885. צֹרְפִי, Tsôrephîy, *tso-ref-ee´*; from 6884; *refiner*; *Tsorephi* (with the article), an Israelite:—goldsmith's.

6886. צָרְפַת, Tsârephath, *tsaw-ref-ath´*; from 6884; *refinement; Tsarephath*, a place in Palestine:—Zarephath.

6887. צָרַר, tsârar, *tsaw-rar´*; a primitive root; to *cramp*, literal or figurative, transitive or intransitive (as follows):—adversary, (be in) afflict (-ion), besiege, bind (up), (be in, bring) distress, enemy, narrower, oppress, pangs, shut up, be in a strait (trouble), vex.

6888. צְרֵרָה, Tserêrâh, *tser-ay-raw´*; apparently by erroneous transcription for 6868; *Tsererah* for *Tseredah*:—Zererath.

6889. צֶרֶת, Tsereth, *tseh´-reth*; perhaps from 6671; *splendor; Tsereth*, an Israelite:—Zereth.

6890. צֶרֶת הַשַּׁחַר, Tsereth hash-Shachar, *tseh´-reth hash-shakh´-ar*; from the same as 6889 and 7837 with the article interposed; *splendor of the dawn; Tsereth-hash-Shachar*, a place in Palestine:—Zareth-shahar.

6891. צָרְתָן, Tsârethân, *tsaw-reth-awn´*; perhaps for 6868; *Tsarethan*, a place in Palestine:—Zarthan.

6892. קֵא, qê', *kay*; or **קִיא, qîy',** *kee*; from 6958; *vomit*:—vomit.

6893. קָאַת, qâ'ath, *kaw-ath´*; from 6958; probably the *pelican* (from *vomiting*):—cormorant.

6894. קַב, qab, *kab*; from 6895; a *hollow*, i.e. vessel used as a (dry) *measure*:—cab.

6895. קָבַב, qâbab, *kaw-bab´*; a primitive root; to *scoop* out, i.e. (figurative) to *malign* or *execrate* (i.e. *stab* with words):—× at all, curse.

A verb meaning to curse. The general idea of this word is a pronouncement of bad fortune or ill favour bestowed on another. This word is used often in the story of Balaam and Balak, where Balak repeatedly requested that Balaam pronounce a curse on Israel (Nu 22:11; 23:13, 27). Rather than a curse, Balaam pronounced a blessing on them (Nu 23:8; 24:10). In other instances of this word, it describes cursing the Lord (Le 24:11); cursing the day of one's birth (Job 3:8); or cursing the home of the foolish (Job 5:3). It is used twice in the Proverbs in a general way (Pr 11:26; 24:24) as an opposite to the word *bĕrâkâh* (1293), meaning blessing, and similar to the much more frequent word *qâlal* (7043), meaning to curse.

6896. קֵבָה, qêbâh, *kay-baw´*; from 6895; the *paunch* (as a *cavity*) or first stomach of ruminants:—maw.

6897. קֹבָה, qôbâh, *ko´-baw*; from 6895; the *abdomen* (as a cavity):—belly.

6898. קֻבָּה, qubbâh, *koob-baw´*; from 6895; a *pavilion* (as a domed *cavity*):—tent.

A feminine noun meaning a large tent, a domed cavity, a pavilion. This word is not found often in the OT, but where it does appear, it refers to some sort of habitation. Phinehas chased a man and woman who were idolaters into one of these large tents and thrust them through with a javelin, thus ending a plague on Israel (Nu 25:8).

6899. קִבּוּץ, qibbûwts, *kib-boots´*; from 6908; a *throng*:—company.

6900. קְבוּרָה, qebûwrâh, *keb-oo-raw´*; or **קְבֻרָה, qeburâh,** *keb-oo-raw´*; feminine passive participle of 6912; *sepulture*; (concrete) a *sepulchre*:—burial, burying place, grave, sepulchre.

A feminine noun meaning a grave, a burial place. It is the passive participle of *qâbar* (6912), meaning to bury. The word can signify various types of graves: the dignified grave of a king (2Ki 21:26; 23:30); the unknown burial place of Moses (Dt 34:6); and the burial place of a donkey where Jehoiakim would be buried (Jer 22:19). Burial was important to the Hebrews of the OT; the lack of a grave was considered a tragedy, the sign of an unwanted life that was best forgotten (Ecc 6:3; Isa 14:20). The meaning is similar to the word *qeber* (6913).

6901. קָבַל, qâbal, *kaw-bal´*; a primitive root; to *admit*, i.e. *take* (literal or figurative):—choose, (take) hold, receive, (under-) take.

6902. קְבַל, qebal, *keb-al´*; (Chaldee); corresponding to 6901; to *acquire*:—receive, take.

6903. קְבֵל, qebêl, *keb-ale´*; (Chaldee); or **קֳבֵל, qŏbêl,** *kob-ale´*; (Chaldee); corresponding to 6905; (adverb) *in front of*; usually (with other particles) *on account of, so* as, *since, hence*:— + according to, + as, + because, before, + for this cause, + forasmuch as, + by this means, over against, by reason of, + that, + therefore, + though, + wherefore.

6904. קֹבֶל, qôbel, *ko´-bel*; from 6901 in the sense of *confronting* (as standing *opposite* in order to receive); a *battering* ram:—war.

6905. קָבָל, qâbâl, *kaw-bawl´*; from 6901 in the sense of *opposite* [see 6904]; the *presence*, i.e. (adverb) *in front of*:—before.

6906. קָבַע, qâba', *kaw-bah´*; a primitive root; to *cover*, i.e. (figurative) *defraud*:—rob, spoil.

6907. קֻבַּעַת, qubba'ath, *koob-bah´-ath*; from 6906; a *goblet* (as deep like a *cover*):—dregs.

6908. קָבַץ, qâbats, *kaw-bats´*; a primitive root; to *grasp*, i.e. *collect*:—assemble (selves), gather (bring) (together, selves together, up), heap, resort, × surely, take up.

A verb meaning to gather, to collect, to assemble. The passive form is used to signify the gathering or assembling of people, especially for battle (Jos 9:2; Ne 4:20[14]; Jer 49:14); and for religious and national purposes (1Ch 11:1; Ezr 10:1, 7). The word in an active form often signifies the gathering of materials: food into storehouses (Ge 41:35); sheaves (Mic 4:12); money and wealth (2Ch 24:5; Pr 28:8); lambs by a shepherd (Isa 13:14; 40:11; Jer 23:3). The word also refers to God's gathering of nations for judgment in the end times (Isa 43:9; 66:18; Joel 3:2[4:2]); and especially to the gathering of His scattered people, Israel (Ps 106:47; Jer 29:14; 31:10; Hos 1:11[2:2]).

6909. קַבְצְאֵל, Qabtse'êl, *keb-tseh-ale´*; from 6908 and 410; *God has gathered; Kabtseël*, a place in Palestine:—Kabzeel. Compare 3343.

6910. קְבֻצָה, qebutsâh, *keb-oo-tsaw´*; feminine passive participle of 6908; a *hoard*:— × gather.

A feminine noun meaning gathering. This word is the feminine passive participle of *qâbats* (6908), meaning to gather. It occurs only in Eze 22:20 where it signifies the gathering of metals into a furnace, which is a picture of God gathering Israel to pour out His burning anger on them.

6911. קִבְצַיִם, Qibtsayim, *kib-tsah´-yim*; dual from 6908; a *double heap; Kibtsajim*, a place in Palestine:—Kibzaim.

6912. קָבַר, **qâbar,** *kaw-bar´*; a primitive root; to *inter*:—× in any wise, bury (-ier).

A verb meaning to bury, to entomb, to be buried. The word often refers to the placing of a body in a cave or a stone sepulchre rather than directly into the ground (Ge 23:4; 50:13; 2Sa 21:14; 1Ki 13:31; cf. Isa 22:16). Abraham stated that one goal of burial was to get the dead out of sight (Ge 23:4). Dead bodies were seen as polluting the land until they were buried (Eze 39:11–14). It was also a reproach to the dead to be buried in a foreign place or not to be buried at all (Ge 47:29, 30; 50:5; cf. 50:24–26; Jer 20:6). Bones were sometimes specifically mentioned as the object of burial (Jos 24:32; 1Sa 31:13; 1Ki 13:31). Buried persons were said to sleep or be buried with their fathers, and they were often placed in the same tomb (Ge 47:30; 50:13; Jgs 16:31; 2Sa 2:32; 17:23).

6913. קֶבֶר, **qeber,** *keh´-ber*; or (feminine) קִבְרָה, **qibrâh,** *kib-raw´*; from 6912; a *sepulchre*:—burying place, grave, sepulchre.

A masculine noun meaning a grave, a sepulchre. The grave was a place of grief (2Sa 3:32; Ps 88:11[12]); the end of life in contrast to the womb (Job 10:19; Jer 20:17). The dead were laid to rest, often with previously deceased relatives (2Sa 19:37[38]). In the OT, graves were associated with uncleanness: one who touched a grave (or a bone, cf. 2Ch 34:5) had to be ceremonially cleansed (Nu 19:16–19). Josiah sprinkled the dust of crushed idolatrous paraphernalia on graves of idol worshippers to defile the idols (2Ki 23:6; 2Ch 34:4). In a figurative sense, Isaiah prophesied against his self-righteous countrymen as living among graves and eating the flesh of swine (Isa 65:4; cf. Mt 23:27, 28). Ezekiel prophesied that God would revive the Israelites from their graves, that is, from their exile and defilement among idolatrous nations (Eze 37:12, 13).

6914. קִבְרוֹת הַתַּאֲוָה, **Qibrôwth hat-Ta'ăvâh,** *kib-rōth´ hat-tah-av-aw´*; from the feminine plural of 6913 and 8378 with the article interposed; *graves of the longing; Kibroth-hat-Taavh*, a place in the Desert:—Kibroth-hattaavah.

6915. קָדַד, **qâdad,** *kaw-dad´*; a primitive root; to *shrivel* up, i.e. *contract* or *bend* the body (or neck) in deference:—bow (down) (the) head, stoop.

6916. קִדָּה, **qiddâh,** *kid-daw´*; from 6915; *cassia* bark (as in *shrivelled* rolls):—cassia.

6917. קְדוּמִים, **q^edûwmîym,** *keh-doo-meem´*; passive participle of 6923; a *pristine* hero:—ancient.

6918. קָדוֹשׁ, **qâdôwsh,** *kaw-doshe´*; or קָדֹשׁ, **qâdôsh,** *kaw-doshe´*; from 6942; *sacred* (ceremonially or morally); (as noun) *God* (by eminence), an *angel*, a *saint*, a *sanctuary*:—holy (One), saint.

An adjective meaning sacred, holy. It is used to denote someone or something that is inherently sacred or has been designated as sacred by divine rite or cultic ceremony. It designates that which is the opposite of common or profane. It could be said the *qâdôwsh* is a positive term regarding the character of its referent, where common is a neutral term and profane a very negative term. This word is often used to refer to God as being inherently holy, sacred, and set apart (Ps 22:3[4]; Isa 6:3; 57:15); and as being free from the attributes of fallen humanity (Hos 11:9). Therefore, in the OT, God is accorded the title "The Holy One of Israel" (2Ki 19:22; Ps 78:41; Isa 17:7; Jer 50:29). As such, God instructed that humanity should be holy because He is holy (Le 11:44, 45; 19:2). In addition to its divine references, this word can also modify places, like the court of the tabernacle (Ex 29:31); the camp of Israel (Dt 23:14[15]); Jerusalem (Ecc 8:10); heaven (Isa 57:15); people, like the priests (Le 21:7, 8); a Nazirite (Nu 6:5, 8); the prophet Elisha (2Ki 4:9); Levites (2Ch 35:3); saints [angels] (Job 5:1; 15:15; Da 8:13); water (Nu 5:17); time (Ne 8:9–11; Isa 58:13).

6919. קָדַח, **qâdach,** *kaw-dakh´*; a primitive root; to *inflame*:—burn, kindle.

6920. קַדַּחַת, **qaddachath,** *kad-dakh´-ath*; from 6919; *inflammation*, i.e. febrile disease:—burning ague, fever.

6921. קָדִים, **qâdîym,** *kaw-deem´*; or קָדִם, **qâdim,** *kaw-deem´*; from 6923; the *fore* or front part; hence (by orientation) the *East* ([often adverbial] *eastward*; [for brevity] the *east wind*):—east (-ward, wind).

6922. קַדִּישׁ, **qaddîysh,** *kad-deesh´*; (Chaldee); corresponding to 6918:—holy (One), saint.

An Aramaic masculine adjective meaning holy. It is the Aramaic equivalent of the Hebrew word *qâdôwsh* (6918). This term can modify the word *'ĕlâh* (426), meaning God or gods (Da 4:8[5], 9[6], 18[15]; 5:11). As a substantive, it could stand for angel(s), the supernatural holy one(s) (Da 4:13[10], 17[14], 23[20]). It could also refer to God's people, human holy ones, or saints (Da 7:18, 21, 22, 25, 27).

6923. קָדַם, **qâdam,** *kaw-dam´*; a primitive root; to *project* (one self), i.e. *precede*; hence to *anticipate, hasten, meet* (usually for help):—come (go, [flee]) before, + disappoint, meet, prevent.

6924. קֶדֶם, **qedem,** *keh´-dem*; or קֵדְמָה, **qêdmâh,** *kayd´-maw*; from 6923; the *front*, of place ([absolute] the *fore part*; [relative] the *East*) or time (*antiquity*); often used adverbially (*before, anciently, eastward*):—aforetime, ancient (time), before, east (end, part, side, -ward), eternal, × ever (-lasting), forward, old, past. Compare 6926.

A masculine noun meaning the east, earlier, formerly, long ago. The word is used regularly to mean east or eastern. The Lord planted the Garden of Eden in the east (Ge 2:8; 3:24); Abraham traveled toward the eastern hills (Ge 12:8; 13:11). The word describes the East as a place known for its wise men (Ge 29:1; Jgs 6:3; 1Ki 4:30 [5:10]); Job was the greatest among these people (Job 1:3). Isaiah, however, called the East a place of superstitions (Isa 2:6). One of Jeremiah's oracles was directed against the people of the East (Jer 49:28); but not, according to Ezekiel, until the Lord gave Judah to one of the peoples of the East—Babylon (Eze 25:4, 10). The famous movement of the whole earth's population to the east to build the Tower of Babel in the plain of Shinar is toward the area of Babylon (Ge 11:2).

The word is also used to refer to former times, times of old. It describes the works of God before the world was created (Pr 8:22, 23). The psalmist implored the Lord to remember the people He purchased long before (Ps 74:2; 77:11[12]; 143:5); for He was the psalmist's King from old (Ps 74:12). The psalmist of Ps 78:2 uttered wisdom and parables as a wise man from ancient times. God planned the fall of Assryia long before it happened (Isa 37:26; La 2:17). The word also refers to Tyre, describing it as an old, ancient city (Isa 23:7). In an important passage, Mic 5:2[1] describes the Lord's coming Ruler from Bethlehem whose origins were from eternity or from ancient days. This word describes the mountains and the heavens as old, of long ago (Dt 33:15; Ps 68:33[34]; Isa 46:10).

A few times the word means front or in front. The Lord knows His people before and behind—thus, altogether (Ps 139:5). The Lord spurred Rezin's foes against him (i.e. from the front) to confront him (Isa 9:12[11]).

6925. קֳדָם, **qŏdâm,** *kod-awm´*; (Chaldee); or קְדָם, **q^edâm,** *ked-awm´*; (Chaldee) (Da 7:13), corresponding to 6924; *before*:—before, × from, × I (thought), × me, + of, × it pleased, presence.

6926. קִדְמָה, **qidmâh,** *kid-maw´*; feminine of 6924; the *forward* part (or relative) *East* (often adverbial *on the east* or *in front*):—east (-ward).

6927. קַדְמָה, **qadmâh,** *kad-maw´*; from 6923; *priority* (in time); also used adverbially (*before*):—afore, antiquity, former (old) estate.

A feminine noun meaning a beginning, a former time. In the oracle concerning Tyre, it was called the city of old (Isa 23:7). The Lord promised to restore Sodom, Samaria, and Jerusalem to what they were before in order to bring shame on Jerusalem (Eze 16:55). A prophecy to the mountains of Israel said that they would be populated as they were in the past (Eze 36:11). See the Hebrew noun *qedem* (6924) and Aramaic noun *qadmâh* (6928).

6928. קַדְמָה, **qadmâh,** *kad-maw´*; (Chaldee); corresponding to 6927; *former* time:—afore [-time], ago.

An Aramaic feminine noun meaning a former time. When the elders of Judah were questioned about rebuilding the Temple, they answered that they were restoring something built long ago (Ezr 5:11). Even after the edict from King Darius, Daniel continued to pray as he had done before (Da 6:10[11]). See the Hebrew noun *qadmâh* (6927).

6929. קֵדְמָה, **Qêdᵉmâh,** *kayd´-maw*; from 6923; *precedence; Kedemah*, a son of Ishmael:—Kedemah.

6930. קַדְמוֹן, **qadmôwn,** *kad-mone´*; from 6923; *eastern*:—east.

6931. קַדְמוֹנִי, **qadmôwnîy,** *kad-mo-nee´*; or קַדְמֹנִי, **qadmônîy,** *kad-mo-nee´*; from 6930; (of time) *anterior* or (of place) *oriental*:—ancient, they that went before, east, (thing of) old.

6932. קְדֵמוֹת, **Qᵉdêmôwth,** *ked-ay-mothe´*; from 6923; *beginnings; Kedemoth*, a place in eastern Palestine:—Kedemoth.

6933. קַדְמַי, **qadmây,** *kad-maw´ee*; (Chaldee); from a root corresponding to 6923; *first*:—first.

6934. קַדְמִיאֵל, **Qadmîy'êl,** *kad-mee-ale´*; from 6924 and 410; *presence of God; Kadmiël*, the name of three Israelites:—Kadmiel.

6935. קַדְמֹנִי, **Qadmônîy,** *kad-mo-nee´*; the same as 6931; *ancient*, i.e. aboriginal; *Kadmonite* (collective), the name of a tribe in Palestine:—Kadmonites.

6936. קָדְקֹד, **qodqôd,** *kod-kode´*; from 6915; the *crown* of the head (as the part most *bowed*):—crown (of the head), pate, scalp, top of the head.

6937. קָדַר, **qâdar,** *kaw-dar´*; a primitive root; to *be ashy*, i.e. *dark*-coloured; (by implication) to *mourn* (in sackcloth or sordid garments):—be black (-ish), be (make) dark (-en), × heavily, (cause to) mourn.

A verb meaning to be dark. This word can also mean to mourn in the sense of being dark with sadness or gloom (Job 5:11; Ps 35:14; Jer 8:21). Sometimes the sky grew dark due to an actual storm (1Ki 18:45). Other times, it was not a literal darkness, as when the prophet Ezekiel prophesied against Pharaoh, saying that the heavens would be darkened when God acted against him (Eze 32:7, 8). Another example of symbolism was when Micah warned the false prophets that dark days were coming for them due to a lack of revelation (Mic 3:6).

6938. קֵדָר, **Qêdâr,** *kay-dawr´*; from 6937; *dusky* (of the skin or the tent); *Kedar*, a son of Ishmael; also (collective) *bedawin* (as his descendants or representatives):—Kedar.

6939. קִדְרוֹן, **Qidrôwn,** *kid-rone´*; from 6937; *dusky* place; *Kidron*, a brook near Jerusalem:—Kidron.

6940. קַדְרוּת, **qadrûwth,** *kad-rooth´*; from 6937; *duskiness*:—blackness.

A feminine noun meaning blackness. This word is used only once in the OT and comes from the verb *qâdar* (6937), meaning to be dark. In Isa 50:3, this word described the ability of God to clothe the heavens with blackness (that is, make them dark).

6941. קְדֹרַנִּית, **qᵉdôranniyth,** *ked-o-ran-neeth´*; adverb from 6937; *blackish ones* (i.e. *in sackcloth*); used adverbially in *mourning* weeds:—mournfully.

An adverb meaning mournfully. This word is used only once in the OT and comes from the verb *qâdar* (6937), meaning to be dark. In Mal 3:14, this word describes those who acted as mourners (i.e. those who were gloomy in their countenances).

6942. קָדַשׁ, **qâdash,** *kaw-dash´*; a primitive root; to *be* (causative, *make, pronounce* or *observe* as) *clean* (ceremonially or morally):—appoint, bid, consecrate, dedicate, defile, hallow, (be, keep) holy (-er, place), keep, prepare, proclaim, purify, sanctify (-ied one, self), × wholly.

A verb meaning to be set apart, to be holy, to show oneself holy, to be treated as holy, to consecrate, to treat as holy, to dedicate, to be made holy, to declare holy or consecrated, to behave, to act holy, to dedicate oneself. The verb, in the simple stem, declares the act of setting apart, being holy (i.e. withdrawing someone or something from profane or ordinary use). The Lord set aside Aaron and his sons, consecrated them, and made them holy for the priesthood (Ex 29:21). The altar was made holy, and anything coming into contact with it became holy (Ex 29:37). The tabernacle, the ark, the table of showbread, the altar of burnt offering, and all the smaller accessories and utensils used in the cult of Israel were anointed with a special anointing oil so they became holy. Whatever came in contact with them became holy (Ex 30:26–29). The men accompanying David as his military were declared holy (1Sa 21:5[6]).

The word is used most often in the intensive stem, meaning to pronounce or to make holy, to consecrate. The Lord pronounced the Sabbath day holy (Ge 2:3; Ex 20:8). Places could be dedicated as holy, such as a part of the courtyard of the Temple (1Ki 8:64); or Mount Sinai itself (Ex 19:23). The Year of Jubilee, the fiftieth year, was declared holy (Le 25:10). Persons could be consecrated to holy duties: Aaron and his sons were consecrated to serve as priests of the Lord (Ex 28:3, 41; 1Sa 7:1); the firstborn males of people or animals were consecrated to the Lord (Ex 13:2). Holy times were designated using this word in the factitive stem: Jehu deceitfully proclaimed a holy assembly to Baal (2Ki 10:20); a holy fast could be consecrated as Joel did (Joel 1:14). With the Lord as the subject, the word describes establishing something as holy. The Lord Himself consecrated or made holy His people (Ex 31:13; Le 20:8; 21:8); through His judgments on Israel and the nations, God proved the holiness of His name (Eze 36:23). The priests' holy garments serving in Ezekiel's restored Temple will make those who touch them holy (Eze 44:19; 46:20).

In the causative stem, the meanings overlap with the meanings in the intensive stem. It indicates designating something as consecrated or holy; Jeremiah was declared holy (Jer 1:5); as was the Temple (1Ki 9:3). The word means to treat as holy or dedicated. Gifts, fields, or money could be treated as holy (Le 27:16; 2Sa 8:11; 2Ki 12:18[19]). God declared things holy to Himself (1Ki 9:7); God Himself is to be treated as holy (Nu 20:12; 27:14; Isa 29:23).

In the passive stems, the word means to be consecrated, to be treated as holy, or to show oneself as holy. Ezekiel described the Zadokite priests as consecrated for service at a future Temple (Eze 48:11); Ezr 3:5 described the established holy feasts of the Lord in the return from exile. The entrance at the tabernacle was to be treated as consecrated and holy through the Lord's glory (Ex 29:43). The Lord showed Himself as holy (Le 10:3; 22:32; Eze 20:41).

In the reflexive stem, the verb means to show oneself holy or consecrated: the priests had to properly consecrate themselves before coming before the Lord (Ex 19:22; Le 11:44); the Lord would prove Himself holy before the nations and Israel (Eze 38:23). The word indicates putting oneself or another into a state of holiness to the Lord (Nu 11:18; Jos 3:5; 1Sa 16:5; 2Ch 31:18).

6943. קֶדֶשׁ, **Qedesh,** *keh´-desh*; from 6942; a *sanctum; Kedesh*, the name of four places in Palestine:—Kedesh.

6944. קֹדֶשׁ, **qôdesh,** *ko´-desh*; from 6942; a *sacred* place or thing; (rarely abstract) *sanctity*:—consecrated (thing), dedicated (thing), hallowed (thing), holiness, (× most) holy (× day, portion, thing), saint, sanctuary.

A masculine noun meaning a holy thing, holiness, and sacredness. The word indicates something consecrated and set aside for sacred use only; it was not to be put into common use, for if it was, it became profaned and common (*chôwl*), not holy. This noun described holy offerings or things used in Israel's cult; it described the holy offerings which only the priest or his family could eat (Le 22:10). Some of the offerings of the Lord were described as Most Holy (Le 2:3, 10; Nu 18:9); various things could be consecrated as holy: warriors (1Sa 21:6); food (Ex 29:33); and the places where the holy ark had been located (2Ch 8:11). Only holy priests could go into the Temple (2Ch 23:6). Many vessels and items used in the tabernacle or Temple areas were holy (Ezr 8:28; Ex 30:32, 35). The Sabbath was, of course, holy (Ex 31:14).

This word also designates divine holiness: the Lord alone can swear by His own holiness (Ps 89:35[36]; Am 4:2); and His ways are holy (Ps 77:13[14]). In fact, God is marvelous in holiness (Ex 15:11).

Since the Lord is holy, He expected Israel to be holy. This word described the essence of the Israelites: They were His holy people (Ex 22:31[30]; 28:36).

The word describes holiness when it relates to various things: holiness adhered to the Lord's house and beautified it (Ps 93:5). The Lord's name is holy (Le 20:3; 22:2; Eze 39:7, 25; Am 2:7). The Lord will establish His holy mountain when all the earth will know Him (Isa 11:9; 56:7). Zion is God's holy hill (Da 9:20; Joel 3:17[4:17]).

The word is also used when referring to holy places. God's presence is what makes any place, anything, or anyone holy (Ex 3:5). The Holy Place in the tabernacle (Ex 26:33; 28:29) was separated from the Most Holy Place by a curtain (Ex 26:33); it refers to the Most Holy Place in the Temple as well (1Ki 6:16). This word with the definite article refers to the entire tabernacle (Ex 36:1, 3, 4; 38:27) and later the Temple Solomon built (1Ki 8:8); literally, the Holy Place (Ps 60:6[8]; 63:2[3]).

6945. קָדֵשׁ, qâdêsh, *kaw-dashe´*; from 6942; a (quasi) *sacred* person, i.e. (technical) a (male) *devotee* (by prostitution) to licentious idolatry:—sodomite, unclean.

A masculine noun meaning male temple prostitute. The feminine form of this word is *qĕdêshâh* (6948). Although the term denotes one who was holy or sacred, the question must be asked, "Holy for what?" In the context of a pagan temple cult, which was the proper context for this word, it connotes a man who was set apart for pagan temple service, namely, male prostitution (Dt 23:17[18]; 1Ki 14:24; 15:12; 22:46 [47]). This term is sometimes translated as sodomite, which is an excellent expression of the likelihood that these were homosexual or at least bisexual prostitutes.

6946. קָדֵשׁ, Qâdêsh, *kaw-dashe´*; the same as 6945; *sanctuary; Kadesh*, a place in the Desert:—Kadesh. Compare 6947.

6947. קָדֵשׁ בַּרְנֵעַ, Qâdêsh Barnêaʻ, *kaw-dashe´ bar-nay´-ah*; from the same as 6946 and an otherwise unused word (apparently compounded of a correspondent to 1251 and a derivitive of 5128) meaning *desert of a fugitive; Kadesh of* (the) *Wilderness of Wandering; Kadesh-Barneä*, a place in the Desert:—Kadesh-barnea.

6948. קְדֵשָׁה, qᵉdêshâh, *ked-ay-shaw´*; feminine of 6945; a female *devotee* (i.e. *prostitute*):—harlot, whore.

A feminine noun meaning a female temple prostitute. The masculine form of this word is *qâdêsh* (6945). Although the term refers to a person that was holy or sacred, it is necessary to know what they were holy to. When referring to a pagan temple cult, it connotes a woman set apart for pagan temple service, namely, female prostitution (Dt 23:17[18]; Hos 4:14). It is also possible that this term was used as a general term for prostitution (Ge 38:21, 22) because of its parallel usage with *zânâh* (2181) (see Ge 38:15). However, it is at the same time possible that *zânâh* was merely the more general term for a prostitute, while *qĕdêshâh* was the exclusive term for a shrine prostitute.

6949. קָהָה, qâhâh, *kaw-haw´*; a primitive root; to be *dull*:—be set on edge, be blunt.

6950. קָהַל, qâhal, *kaw-hal´*; a primitive root; to *convoke*:—assemble (selves) (together), gather (selves) (together).

A verb meaning to gather, to assemble. The meaning of this verb is closely connected with that of *qâhâl* (6951), a Hebrew noun meaning a convocation, a congregation, or an assembly. It indicates an assembling together for a convocation or as a congregation, often for religious purposes. The word is used in reference to the act of congregating to fulfill a chiefly religious end (Jos 18:1); of assembling for battle (Jgs 20:1; 2Sa 20:14); and of summoning to an appointed religious assembly (Dt 31:28).

6951. קָהָל, qâhâl, *kaw-hawl*; from 6950; *assemblage* (usually concrete):—assembly, company, congregation, multitude.

A masculine noun meaning an assembly, a community, a congregation, a crowd, a company, a throng, a mob. The word describes various gatherings and assemblies called together. It can describe a gathering called for evil purposes—such as the deceitful assembly of the brothers Simeon and Levi to plan violence against the city of Shechem (Ge 49:6; Eze 23:47). The man of God abhors the gathering of evildoers (Ps 26:5); but he should proclaim the Lord's name in the worshiping congregation (Ps 22:22[23]). An assembly for war or a group of soldiers was common in the OT (Nu 22:4; Jgs 20:2; 1Sa 17:47); the various groups of exiles that traveled from Babylon to Jerusalem were a renewed community (Ezr 2:64; Ne 7:66; Jer 31:8). Many assemblies were convened for holy religious purposes: the congregation of Israel gathered at Sinai to hear the Lord's words (Dt 9:10); many feasts and holy convocations called for worship and fasting as noted by the author of Chronicles (2Ch 20:5; 30:25).

The word describes Israel as a congregation, an organized community. Israel was the Lord's community (Nu 16:3; 20:4). The word also describes the gathering of Israel before King Solomon when he dedicated the Temple (1Ki 8:14); the high priest atoned for the whole community of Israel on the Day of Atonement (Le 16:17; Dt 31:30). The word designates the community restored in Jerusalem after the Babylonian exile (Ezr 10:8, 12, 14); the gathering of the congregation of Israel when they killed the Passover lambs (Ex 12:6).

The word refers to gatherings of any assembled multitude: an assembly of nations (Ge 35:11); or of peoples (Ge 28:3), such as Abraham's descendants were to comprise. It refers to a great mass of people as mentioned by Balak, king of Moab (Nu 22:4).

6952. קְהִלָּה, qᵉhillâh, *keh-hil-law´*; from 6950; an *assemblage*:—assembly, congregation.

A feminine noun meaning an assembly, a congregation. This word expresses the gathering of a collection of people, such as the congregation of Jacob referred to by Moses in his blessing of the tribes (Dt 33:4). This word can also describe the gathering of people for legal action (Ne 5:7).

6953. קֹהֶלֶת, qôheleth, *ko-heh´-leth*; feminine of active participle from 6950; a (female) *assembler* (i.e. lecturer); (abstract) *preaching* (used as a "nom de plume," *Koheleth*):—preacher.

A noun meaning a collector of wisdom, a preacher. This word is the active feminine participle of the word *qâhal* (6950), meaning to gather or to assemble. Thus, the root meaning appears to indicate a person who gathered wisdom. The word has a feminine form because it referred to an office or position, but it was usually used with masculine verbs and always referred to a man. *Qôheleth* only occurs in Ecclesiastes: three times at the beginning and end of the book and once in the middle (Ecc 7:27). It is also the Hebrew name of the book. The word Ecclesiastes is a translation of this Hebrew word into Greek and referred to someone who addressed a public assembly. This is another meaning of the word based on the fact that the preacher had gathered knowledge to speak about life. Solomon used the word to describe himself as one who gathered wisdom (Ecc 12:9, 10; cf. 1Ki 4:32–34[5:12–14]); and as one who spoke to people about wisdom (Ecc 12:9; cf. 2Ch 9:23).

6954. קְהֵלָתָה, Qᵉhêlâthâh, *keh-hay-law´-thaw*; from 6950; *convocation; Kehelathah*, a place in the Desert:—Kehelathah.

6955. קְהָת, Qᵉhâth, *keh-hawth´*; from an unused root meaning to *ally* oneself; *allied; Kehath*, an Israelite:—Kohath.

6956. קֳהָתִי, Qŏhâthîy, *ko-haw-thee´*; patronymic from 6955; a *Kohathite* (collective) or descendants of Kehath:—Kohathites.

6957. קַו, qav, *kav*; or קָו, **qâv,** *kawv*; from 6960 [compare 6961]; a *cord* (as *connecting*), especially for measuring; (figurative) a *rule*; also a *rim*, a musical *string* or *accord*:—line. Compare 6978.

6958. קָיָא, qâyaʼ, *kaw-yah´*; (Jer 25:27), a primitive root; to *vomit*:—spue (out), vomit (out, up, up again).

6959. קוֹבַע, qôwbaʻ, *ko´-bah*; a form collateral to 3553; a *helmet*:—helmet.

6960. קָוָה, qâvâh, *kaw-vaw´*; a primitive root; to *bind* together (perhaps by *twisting*), i.e. *collect*; (figurative) to *expect*:—gather (together), look, patiently, tarry, wait (for, on, upon).

A verb meaning to wait for, to look for, to hope for. The root meaning is that of twisting or winding a strand of cord or rope, but it is uncertain how that root meaning relates to the idea of hope. The word is used to signify depending on and ordering activities around a future event (Job 7:2; Mic 5:7[6]). The hopes of someone can remain unfulfilled, especially when a person or a nation is sinning (Job 3:9; Ps 69:20[21]; Isa 5:2, 4, 7). Hoping, however, for what God has promised will not ultimately be disappointed, although it may not appear to succeed in the short run (Job 30:26; Isa 59:11; cf. Isa 59:15–21). The Lord will give strength to those who hope in Him (Ps 27:14[2x]; Isa 40:31). Because He is all-powerful (Jer 14:22), He will eventually bring His promises to pass (La 3:25). These promises include the establishing of His kingdom on earth (Ps 37:9, 34; Isa 25:9[2x]). The word also means to be gathered and refers to the gathering of waters (Ge 1:9) and of people (Jer 3:17).

6961. קָוֶה**, qâveh,** *kaw-veh´*; from 6960; a (measuring) *cord* (as if for *binding*):—line.

6962. קוּט**, qûwṭ,** *koot*; a primitive root; (properly) to *cut off*, i.e. (figurative) *detest*:—be grieved, lothe self.

6963. קוֹל**, qôwl,** *kole*; or קֹל**, qôl,** *kole*; from an unused root meaning to *call* aloud; a *voice* or *sound*:— + aloud, bleating, crackling, cry (+ out), fame, lightness, lowing, noise, + hold peace, [pro-] claim, proclamation, + sing, sound, + spark, thunder (-ing), voice, + yell.

6964. קוֹלָיָה**, Qôwlâyâh,** *ko-law-yaw´*; from 6963 and 3050; *voice of Jah; Kolajah*, the name of two Israelites:—Kolaiah.

6965. קוּם**, qûwm,** *koom*; a primitive root; to *rise* (in various applications, literal, figurative, intensive and causative):—abide, accomplish, × be clearer, confirm, continue, decree, × be dim, endure, × enemy, enjoin, get up, make good, help, hold, (help to) lift up (again), make, × but newly, ordain, perform, pitch, raise (up), rear (up), remain, (a-) rise (up) (again, against), rouse up, set (up), (e-) stablish, (make to) stand (up), stir up, strengthen, succeed, (as-, make) sure (-ly), (be) up (-hold, -rising).

A verb meaning to arise, to stand, to stand up. The basic meaning of this word is the physical action of rising up (Ge 19:33, 35; Ru 3:14); or the resultant end of that action, standing (Jos 7:12, 13). However, a myriad of derived and figurative meanings for this term have developed. It can designate the following attributes: to show honour and respect (Ge 27:19; Ex 33:10; Nu 23:18); to move (Ex 10:23); to recover (Ex 21:19); to belong (Le 25:30); to cost (Le 27:14, 17); to be valid (Nu 30:5); to appear (Dt 13:1[2]); to follow (Dt 29:22[21]); to be hostile (Jgs 9:18); to endure (1Sa 13:14); to replace (1Ki 8:20). The word can also mean to ratify (Ru 4:7); to obligate (Est 9:21, 27, 31); to establish or strengthen (Ps 119:28); to fulfill (Eze 13:6). In the causative form, it means to provide (Ge 38:8; 2Sa 12:11); to rouse (Ge 49:9); to perform (Dt 9:5); to revive (Ru 4:5, 10); to keep one's word (1Sa 3:12); to erect (1Ki 7:21); to appoint (1Ki 11:14); to be victorious (Ps 89:43[44]); to bring to silence (Ps 107:29).

6966. קוּם**, qûwm,** *koom*; (Chaldee); corresponding to 6965:—appoint, establish, make, raise up self, (a-) rise (up), (make to) stand, set (up).

6967. קוֹמָה**, qôwmâh,** *ko-maw´*; from 6965; *height*:— × along, height, high, stature, tall.

6968. קוֹמְמִיּוּת**, qôwmᵉmîyyûwth,** *ko-mem-ee-yooth´*; from 6965; *elevation*, i.e. (adverb) *erectly* (figurative):—upright.

6969. קוּן**, qûwn,** *koon*; a primitive root; to *strike* a musical note, i.e. *chant* or *wail* (at a funeral):—lament, mourning woman.

6970. קוֹעַ**, Qôwaʻ,** *ko´-ah*; probably from 6972 in the original sense of *cutting* off; *curtailment; Koä*, a region of Babylon:—Koa.

6971. קוֹף**, qôwph,** *kofe*; or קֹף**, qôph,** *kofe*; probably of foreign origin; a *monkey*:—ape.

6972. קוּץ**, qûwts,** *koots*; a primitive root; to *clip* off; used only as denominative from 7019; to *spend the harvest* season:—summer.

6973. קוּץ**, qûwts,** *koots*; a primitive root [rather identical with 6972 through the idea of *severing* oneself from (compare 6962)]; to be (causative, *make*) *disgusted* or *anxious*:—abhor, be distressed, be grieved, loathe, vex, be weary.

A verb meaning to loathe, to be disgusted, to be sick of. The word signifies God's revulsion toward pagan practices (Le 20:23); by Israel toward manna (ungratefully and wrongly) after eating it for years (Nu 21:5; cf. Ps 78:22–25); by Rebekah toward her Hittite daughters-in-law (Ge 27:46); and by Solomon's son toward the Lord's rebuke (Pr 3:11). It also signified the loathing felt by enemies toward Israel's prosperity (Ex 1:12; Nu 22:3). In Isa 7:6, the causative sense means to vex. By taking over, the enemies planned to cause Judah to abhor them.

6974. קוּץ**, qûwts,** *koots*; a primitive root [rather identical with 6972 through the idea of *abruptness* in starting up from sleep (compare 3364)]; to *awake* (literal or figurative):—arise, (be) (a-) wake, watch.

6975. קוֹץ**, qôwts,** *kotse*; or קֹץ**, qôts,** *kotse*; from 6972 (in the sense of *pricking*); a *thorn*:—thorn.

6976. קוֹץ**, Qôwts,** *kotse*; the same as 6975; *Kots*, the name of two Israelites:—Koz, Hakkoz [*including the article*].

6977. קְוֻצָּה**, qᵉvutstsâh,** *kev-oots-tsaw´*; feminine passive participle of 6972 in its original sense; a *forelock* (as *shorn*):—lock.

6978. קַו־קַו**, qav-qav,** *kav-kav´*; from 6957 (in the sense of a *fastening*); *stalwart*:— × meted out.

6979. קוּר**, qûwr,** *koor*; a primitive root; to *trench*; (by implication) to *throw forth*; also (denominative from 7023) to *wall up*, whether literal (to *build* a wall) or figurative (to *estop*):—break down, cast out, destroy, dig.

6980. קוּר**, qûwr,** *koor*; from 6979; (only plural) *trenches*, i.e. a *web* (as if so formed):—web.

6981. קוֹרֵא**, Qôwrêʼ,** *ko-ray´*; or קֹרֵא**, Qôrêʼ,** *ko-ray´*; (1Ch 26:1), active participle of 7121; *crier; Korè*, the name of two Israelites:—Kore.

6982. קוֹרָה**, qôwrâh,** *ko-raw´*; or קֹרָה**, qôrâh,** *ko-raw´*; from 6979; a *rafter* (forming *trenches* as it were); (by implication) a *roof*:—beam, roof.

6983. קוֹשׁ**, qûwsh,** *kooshe*; a primitive root; to *bend*; used only as denominative for 3369, to *set a trap*:—lay a snare.

A verb meaning to set a trap, to lay a snare. The root idea may be that of bending, as the energy stored in bent wood powers a snare. *Qôwsh* occurs only in Isa 29:21 where it figuratively refers to the laying of a snare to cause trouble and to silence the person who judges justly and thwarts the wicked.

6984. קוּשָׁיָהוּ**, qûwshâyâhûw,** *koo-shaw-yaw´-hoo*; from the passive participle of 6983 and 3050; *entrapped of Jah; Kushajah*, an Israelite:—Kushaiah.

6985. קַט**, qaṭ,** *kat´*; from 6990 in the sense of *abbreviation*; a *little*, i.e. (adverb) *merely*:—very.

6986. קֶטֶב**, qeṭeb,** *keh´-teb*; from an unused root meaning to *cut* off; *ruin*:—destroying, destruction.

A masculine noun meaning destruction. It is closely associated with the word *qôṭeb* (6987). God is always connected with this concept of destruction. It seems ironic that in two passages, God was the source of the destruction (Dt 32:24; Isa 28:2), while in another passage, He was the salvation from the destruction (Ps 91:6). On further reflection, though, it becomes evident that God is the source of this destruction, which was a means of divine retribution. The difference is that in Deuteronomy and Isaiah, God was brought His judgment on the wicked, but in Psalms, God preserved the righteous in the midst of His judgment on the wicked. The specific nature of the destruction is flexible. In each of the passages, it is set in a different context and is parallel with a different word: *reshep* (7566), meaning fire (Dt 32:24); *deber* (1698), meaning plague or pestilence (Ps 91:6); and *mayim* (4325), meaning water (Isa 28:2).

6987. קֹטֶב**, qôṭeb,** *ko´-teb*; from the same as 6986; *extermination*:—destruction.

A masculine noun meaning destruction. It is closely associated with the word *qeṭeb* (6986). It occurs only once where it refers to the judgment that God was going to bring against Samaria for its wickedness (Hos 13:14). See the word *deber* (1698), meaning plague or pestilence, as in Ps 91:6. Even though this word appears in the context of God's impending judgment for wickedness, the specific verse in which it appears is actually a vision of hope for a coming restoration. God is going to allow judgment for a time, but then He will remove it because, without His permission, death and Sheol have no power.

6988. קְטוֹרָה**, qᵉṭôwrâh,** *ket-o-raw´*; from 6999; *perfume*:—incense.

6989. קְטוּרָה**, Qᵉṭûwrâh,** *ket-oo-raw´*; feminine passive participle of 6999; *perfumed; Keturah*, a wife of Abraham:—Keturah.

6990. קָטַט**, qâṭaṭ,** *kaw-tat´*; a primitive root; to *clip* off, i.e. (figurative) *destroy*:—be cut off.

6991. קָטַל**, qâṭal,** *kaw-tal´*; a primitive root; (properly) to *cut* off, i.e. (figurative) *put to death*:—kill, slay.

6992. קְטַל**, qᵉṭal,** *ket-al´*; (Chaldee); corresponding to 6991; to *kill*:—slay.

6993. קֶטֶל**, qeṭel,** *keh´-tel*; from 6991; a violent *death*:—slaughter.

6994. קָטֹן**, qâṭôn,** *kaw-tone´*; a primitive root [rather denominative from 6996]; to *diminish*, i.e. *be* (causative, *make*) *diminutive* or (figurative) *of no account*:—be a (make) small (thing), be not worthy.

6995. קֹטֶן**, qôṭen,** *ko´-ten*; from 6994; a *pettiness*, i.e. the *little finger*:—little finger.

6996. קָטָן**, qâṭân,** *kaw-tawn´*; or קָטֹן**, qâṭôn,** *kaw-tone´*; from 6962; *abbreviated*, i.e. *diminutive*, literal (in quantity, size or number) or figurative (in age or importance):—least, less (-ser), little (one), small (-est, one, quantity, thing), young (-er, -est).

6997. קָטָן**, Qâṭân,** *kaw-tawn´*; the same as 6996; *small; Katan*, an Israelite:—Hakkatan [*including the article*].

6998. קָטַף**, qâṭaph,** *kaw-taf´*; a primitive root; to *strip* off:—crop off, cut down (up), pluck.

6999. קָטַר**, qâṭar,** *kaw-tar´*; a primitive root [rather identical with 7000 through the idea of fumigation in a *close* place and perhaps thus *driving* out the occupants]; to *smoke*, i.e. turn into fragrance by fire (especially as an act of worship):—burn (incense, sacrifice) (upon), (altar for) incense, kindle, offer (incense, a sacrifice).

A verb meaning to produce smoke. Often smoke is made by burning incense, but every major offering may also be associated with this word (Ex 30:7; Le 1:9; 2:2; 3:5; 4:10; 7:5). One unusual use of this term describes Solomon's carriage as perfumed with myrrh and incense (SS 3:6). Many times this verb is used of improper worship directed either to the true God or to false gods (1Ki 12:33; 2Ch 26:16, 18, 19; Jer 48:35). In the OT, the burning of incense was restricted to the Aaronic priesthood (Nu 16:40[17:5]; 2Ch 26:16, 18, 19). In the NT, Zacharias, a priest and the father of John the Baptist, burned incense; and prayers of saints are compared to burning incense (cf. Lk 1:10, 11; Rev 5:8; 8:3, 4).

7000. קָטַר**, qâṭar,** *kaw-tar´*; a primitive root; to *inclose*:—join.

7001. קְטַר**, qᵉṭar,** *ket-ar´*; (Chaldee); from a root corresponding to 7000; a *knot* (as *tied* up), i.e. (figurative) a *riddle*; also a *vertebra* (as if a knot):—doubt, joint.

7002. קִטֵּר**, qiṭṭêr,** *kit-tare´*; from 6999; *perfume*:—incense.

7003. קִטְרוֹן**, Qiṭrôwn,** *kit-rone´*; from 6999; *fumigative; Kitron*, a place in Palestine:—Kitron.

7004. קְטֹרֶת**, qᵉṭôreth,** *ket-o´-reth*; from 6999; a *fumigation*:—(sweet) incense, perfume.

A feminine noun meaning smoke, incense, the smell of a burning sacrifice. Incense was one of the valid gifts Moses was to ask from the people (Ex 25:6); and it played an important role in Aaron's atonement for the sin of his sons (Le 16:13). David's plans for the Temple included an altar for incense (1Ch 28:18); and David prayed that his prayers would be like incense to the Lord (Ps 141:2). God told Judah that the smell of worthless sacrifices was detestable (Isa 1:13). See the related Hebrew verb *qâṭar* (6999).

7005. קַטָּת**, Qaṭṭâth,** *kat-tawth´*; from 6996; *littleness, Kattath*, a place in Palestine:—Kattath.

7006. קָיָה**, qâyâh,** *kaw-yaw´*; a primitive root; to *vomit*:—spue.

7007. קַיִט**, qayiṭ,** *kah´-yit*; (Chaldee); corresponding to 7019; *harvest*:—summer.

7008. קִיטוֹר**, qîyṭôwr,** *kee-tore´*; or קִיטֹר**, qîyṭôr,** *kee-tore´*; from 6999; a *fume*, i.e. *cloud*:—smoke, vapour.

7009. קִים**, qîym,** *keem*; from 6965; an *opponent* (as *rising* against one), i.e. (collective) enemies:—substance.

7010. קְיָם**, qᵉyâm,** *keh-yawm´*; (Chaldee); from 6966; an *edict* (as *arising* in law):—decree, statute.

An Aramaic masculine noun meaning a decree, a statute. A form of this word is only used twice in the Hebrew OT, both times in the book of Daniel. When King Darius' advisors wanted to get rid of Daniel, they persuaded Darius to make a law that forbade worship of anyone but himself (Da 6:7[8]). When Daniel broke this law, the advisors compelled Darius to enforce the punishment because the edict he issued could not be revoked (Da 6:15[16]).

7011. קַיָּם**, qayyâm,** *kah-yawm´*; (Chaldee); from 6966; *permanent* (as *rising* firmly):—steadfast, sure.

7012. קִימָה**, qîymâh,** *kee-maw´*; from 6965; an *arising*:—rising up.

7013. קַיִן**, qayin,** *kah´-yin*; from 6969 in the original sense of *fixity*; a *lance* (as *striking fast*):—spear.

7014. קַיִן**, Qayin,** *kah´-yin*; the same as 7013 (with a play upon the affinity to 7069); *Kajin*, the name of the first child, also of a place in Palestine, and of an Oriental tribe:—Cain, Kenite (-s).

7015. קִינָה**, qîynâh,** *kee-naw´*; from 6969; a *dirge* (as accompanied by *beating* the breasts or on instruments):—lamentation.

7016. קִינָה**, Qîynâh,** *kee-naw´*; the same as 7015; *Kinah*, a place in Palestine:—Kinah.

7017. קֵינִי**, Qêynîy,** *kay-nee´*; or קִינִי**, Qîynîy,** *kee-nee´*; (1Ch 2:55), patronymic from 7014; a *Kenite* or member of the tribe of Kajin:—Kenite.

7018. קֵינָן**, Qêynân,** *kay-nawn´*; from the same as 7064; *fixed; Kenan*, an antediluvian:—Cainan, Kenan.

7019. קַיִץ**, qayits,** *kah´-yits*; from 6972; *harvest* (as the *crop*), whether the product (grain or fruit) or the (dry) season:—summer (fruit, house).

7020. קִיצוֹן**, qîytsôwn,** *kee-tsone´*; from 6972; *terminal*:—out- (utter-) most.

7021. קִיקָיוֹן**, qîyqâyôwn,** *kee-kaw-yone´*; perhaps from 7006; the *gourd* (as *nauseous*):—gourd.

7022. קִיקָלוֹן**, qîyqâlôwn,** *kee-kaw-lone´*; from 7036; intense *disgrace*:—shameful spewing.

7023. קִיר**, qîyr,** *keer*; or קִר**, qir,** *keer*; (Isa 22:5), or (feminine) קִירָה**, qîyrâh,** *kee-raw´*; from 6979; a *wall* (as built in a *trench*):— + mason, side, town, × very, wall.

A masculine noun meaning wall. Balaam's donkey, afraid of the angel, pressed against a wall and crushed Balaam's foot (Nu 22:25). Saul wanted to pin David to a wall with his spear (1Sa 18:11). This word also was used to describe a place one thought was safe (Am 5:19). Solomon lined the interior walls of the Temple with cedar (1Ki 6:15); and Jezebel's blood splattered on a wall (2Ki 9:33). The Hebrew phrase, walls of one's heart, means something like the depths of one's soul in Jer 4:19. The King James Version translates that Hebrew phrase as, my very heart. In Ezekiel's vision of the new Temple, the walls were six cubits thick (Eze 41:5).

7024. קִיר**, Qîyr,** *keer*; the same as 7023; *fortress; Kir*, a place in Assyria; also one in Moab:—Kir. Compare 7025.

7025. קִיר חֶרֶשׂ**, Qîyr Chereś,** *(keer) kheh´-res*; or (feminine of the latter word) קִיר חֲרֶשֶׂת**, Qîyr Chăreśeth,** *khar-eh´-seth*; from 7023 and 2789; *fortress of earthenware; Kir-Cheres* or *Kir-Chareseth*, a place in Moab:—Kir-haraseth, Kir-hareseth, Kir-haresh, Kir-heres.

7026. קֵירֹס**, Qêyrôs,** *kay-roce´*; or קֵרֹס**, Qêrôs,** *kay-roce´*; from the same as 7166; *ankled; Keros*, one of the Nethinim:—Keros.

7027. **קִישׁ, Qîysh,** *keesh*; from 6983; a *bow; Kish*, the name of five Israelites:—Kish.

7028. **קִישׁוֹן, Qîyshôwn,** *kee-shone´*; from 6983; *winding; Kishon*, a river of Palestine:—Kishon, Kison.

7029. **קִישִׁי, Qîyshîy,** *kee-shee´*; from 6983; *bowed; Kishi*, an Israelite:—Kishi.

7030. **קִיתָרֹס, qîythârôs,** *kee-thaw-roce´*; (Chaldee); of Greek origin; a *lyre*:—harp.

7031. **קַל, qal,** *kal*; contracted from 7043; *light*; (by implication) *rapid* (also adverb):—light, swift (-ly).

7032. **קָל, qâl,** *kawl*; (Chaldee); corresponding to 6963:—sound, voice.

7033. **קָלָה, qâlâh,** *kaw-law´*; a primitive root [rather identical with 7034 through the idea of *shrinkage* by heat]; to *toast*, i.e. *scorch* partially or slowly:—dried, loathsome, parch, roast.

7034. **קָלָה, qâlâh,** *kaw-law´*; a primitive root; to *be light* (as implied in *rapid* motion), but figurative only (*be* [causative *hold*] *in contempt*):—base, contemn, despise, lightly esteem, set light, seem vile.

7035. **קָלַה, qâlah,** *kaw-lah´*; for 6950; to *assemble*:—gather together.

A verb meaning to assemble. This word is used only once in the OT. It occurs in 2Sa 20:14 where Joab gathered the people together.

7036. **קָלוֹן, qâlôwn,** *kaw-lone´*; from 7034; *disgrace*; (by implication) the *pudenda*:—confusion, dishonour, ignominy, reproach, shame.

7037. **קַלַּחַת, qallachath,** *kal-lakh´-ath*; apparently but a form for 6747; a *kettle*:—caldron.

7038. **קָלַט, qâlaṭ,** *kaw-lat´*; a primitive root; to *maim*:—lacking in his parts.

7039. **קָלִי, qâlîy,** *kaw-lee´*; or **קָלִיא, qâlîy',** *kaw-lee´*; from 7033; *roasted* ears of grain:—parched corn.

7040. **קַלַּי, Qallay,** *kal-lah´ee*; from 7043; *frivolous; Kallai*, an Israelite:—Kallai.

7041. **קֵלָיָה, Qêlâyâh,** *kay-law-yaw´*; from 7034; *insignificance; Kelajah*, an Israelite:—Kelaiah.

7042. **קְלִיטָא, Q^e^lîytâ',** *kel-ee-taw´*; from 7038; *maiming; Kelita*, the name of three Israelites:—Kelita.

7043. **קָלַל, qâlal,** *kaw-lal´*; a primitive root; to *be* (causative, *make*) *light*, literal (*swift, small, sharp*, etc.) or figurative (*easy, trifling, vile*, etc.):—abate, make bright, bring into contempt, (ac-) curse, despise, (be) ease (-y, -ier), (be a, make, make somewhat, move, seem a, set) light (-en, -er, -ly, -ly afflict, -ly esteem, thing), × slight [-ly], be swift (-er), (be, be more, make, re-) vile, whet.

A verb meaning to be slight, to be trivial, to be swift. This word is used in many different ways, but most uses trace back to the basic idea of this word, which is lightness. In its most simple meaning, it referred to the easing of a burden (Ex 18:22); lightening judgment (1Sa 6:5); lessening labour (1Ki 12:9, 10; 2Ch 10:9, 10); or the lightening of a ship (Jnh 1:5). This idea leads to its usage to describe people who were swifter than eagles (2Sa 1:23); swift animals (Hab 1:8); or days that pass quickly (Job 7:6; 9:25). When describing an event or a circumstance, it means trivial (1Sa 18:23; 1Ki 16:31; Isa 49:6). In many instances, it is used to describe speaking lightly of another or cursing another: a person cursing another person (Ex 21:17; 2Sa 16:9–11; Ne 13:2); people cursing God (Le 24:11); or God cursing people (Ge 12:3; 1Sa 2:30; Ps 37:22).

7044. **קָלָל, qâlâl,** *kaw-lawl´*; from 7043; *brightened* (as if *sharpened*):—burnished, polished.

7045. **קְלָלָה, q^e^lâlâh,** *kel-aw-law´*; from 7043; *vilification*:—(ac-) curse (-d, -ing).

A feminine noun meaning curse. This word comes from the verb *qâlal* (7043), meaning to curse. This noun describes the general speaking of ill-will against another (2Sa 16:12; Ps 109:17, 18); as well as the official pronouncement on a person, as Jacob feared he would receive from Isaac (Ge 27:12, 13); or on a nation, as Balaam gave to Moab (Dt 23:5[6]; Ne 13:2). God's curse is on the disobedient (Dt 11:28; 28:15; Jer 44:8); while His blessing, *bĕrâkâh* (1293), is on the righteous (Dt 11:26; 30:19). Jeremiah used several other words in close connection with this one to describe the undesirable nature of this word: reproach, proverb, taunt, curse, hissing, desolation, and imprecation (Jer 24:9; 25:18; 42:18).

7046. **קָלַס, qâlas,** *kaw-las´*; a primitive root; to *disparage*, i.e. ridicule:—mock, scoff, scorn.

7047. **קֶלֶס, qeles,** *keh´-les*; from 7046; a *laughingstock*:—derision.

7048. **קַלָּסָה, qallâsâh,** *kal-law-saw´*; intensive from 7046; *ridicule*:—mocking.

7049. **קָלַע, qâla‘,** *kaw-lah´*; a primitive root; to *sling*; also to *carve* (as if a *circular* motion, or into *light* forms):—carve, sling (out).

7050. **קֶלַע, qela‘,** *kah´-lah*; from 7049; a *sling*; also a (door) *screen* (as if *slung* across), or the *valve* (of the door) itself:—hanging, leaf, sling.

7051. **קַלָּע, qallâ‘,** *kal-law´*; intensive from 7049; a *slinger*:—slinger.

7052. **קְלֹקֵל, q^e^lôqêl,** *kel-o-kale´*; from 7043; *insubstantial*:—light.

7053. **קִלְּשׁוֹן, qill^e^shôwn,** *kil-lesh-one´*; from an unused root meaning to *prick*; a *prong*, i.e. hay-fork:—fork.

7054. **קָמָה, qâmâh,** *kaw-maw´*; feminine of active participle of 6965; something that *rises*, i.e. a *stalk* of grain:—(standing) corn, grown up, stalk.

7055. **קְמוּאֵל, Q^e^mûw'êl,** *kem-oo-ale´*; from 6965 and 410; *raised of God; Kemuël*, the name of a relative of Abraham, and of two Israelites:—Kemuel.

7056. **קָמוֹן, Qâmôwn,** *kaw-mone´*; from 6965; an *elevation; Kamon*, a place East of the Jordan:—Camon.

7057. **קִמּוֹשׂ, qimmôwś,** *kim-mos´*; from an unused root meaning to *sting*; a *prickly* plant:—nettle. Compare 7063.

7058. **קֶמַח, qemach,** *keh´-makh*; from an unused root probably meaning to *grind; flour*:—flour, meal.

7059. **קָמַט, qâmaṭ,** *kaw-mat´*; a primitive root; to *pluck*, i.e. destroy:—cut down, fill with wrinkles.

7060. **קָמַל, qâmal,** *kaw-mal´*; a primitive root; to *wither*:—hew down, wither.

7061. **קָמַץ, qâmats,** *kaw-mats´*; a primitive root; to *grasp* with the hand:—take an handful.

7062. **קֹמֶץ, qômets,** *ko´-mets*; from 7061; a *grasp*, i.e. *handful*:—handful.

7063. **קִמָּשׁוֹן, qimmâśôwn,** *kim-maw-sone´*; from the same as 7057; a *prickly* plant:—thorn.

7064. **קֵן, qên,** *kane*; contracted from 7077; a *nest* (as *fixed*), sometimes including the *nestlings*; (figurative) a *chamber* or *dwelling*:—nest, room.

7065. **קָנָא, qânâ',** *kaw-naw´*; a primitive root; to *be* (causative, *make*) *zealous*, i.e. (in a bad sense) *jealous* or *envious*:—(be) envy (-ious), be (move to, provoke to) jealous (-y), × very, (be) zeal (-ous).

A verb meaning to be jealous, to be envious, to be zealous. This is a verb derived from a noun, and, as such, occurs in the extensive and causative forms only. The point of the verb is to express a strong emotion in which the subject is desirous of some aspect or possession of the object. It can express jealousy, where persons are zealous for their own property or positions for fear they might lose them (Nu 5:14, 30;

Isa 11:13); or envy, where persons are zealous for the property or positions of others, hoping they might gain them (Ge 26:14; 30:1; 37:11). Furthermore, it can indicate someone being zealous on behalf of another (Nu 11:29; 2Sa 21:2); on behalf of God (Nu 25:13; 1Ki 19:10, 14); as well as God being zealous (Eze 39:25; Joel 2:18; Zec 1:14; 8:2). It is also used to denote the arousing of one's jealousy or zeal (Dt 32:16, 21; 1Ki 14:22; Ps 78:58).

7066. קְנָא**, qᵉnâʼ,** *ken-aw´*; (Chaldee); corresponding to 7069; to *purchase*:—buy.

7067. קַנָּא**, qannâʼ,** *kan-naw´*; from 7065; *jealous*:—jealous. Compare 7072.

An adjective meaning jealous. This word comes from the verb *qânâʼ* (7065), meaning to be jealous or zealous. In every instance of this word, it is used to describe the character of the Lord. He is a jealous God who will not tolerate the worship of other gods (Ex 20:5; Dt 5:9). This word is always used to describe God's attitude toward the worship of false gods, which arouses His jealousy and anger in judgment against the idol worshippers (Dt 4:24; 6:15). So closely is this characteristic associated with God that His name is Jealous (Ex 34:14).

7068. קִנְאָה**, qinʼâh,** *kin-aw´*; from 7065; *jealousy* or *envy*:—envy (-ied), jealousy, × sake, zeal.

A feminine noun meaning zeal, jealousy. This word comes from the verb *qânâʼ* (7065), meaning to be jealous or zealous, and describes an intense fervor, passion, and emotion that is greater than a person's wrath and anger (Pr 27:4). It can be either good or bad: Phinehas was commended for taking up the Lord's jealousy (Nu 25:11); but such passion can also be rottenness to the bones (Pr 14:30). It is used to describe a spirit of jealousy, which comes on a man for his wife (Nu 5:14, 15, 29). Most often, however, this word describes God's zeal, which will accomplish His purpose (2Ki 19:31; Isa 9:7[6]; 37:32); and will be the instrument of His wrath in judgment (Ps 79:5; Eze 36:5, 6; Zep 3:8).

7069. קָנָה**, qânâh,** *kaw-naw´*; a primitive root; to *erect*, i.e. *create*; (by extension) to *procure*, especially by purchase (causative, *sell*); (by implication) to *own*:—attain, buy (-er), teach to keep cattle, get, provoke to jealousy, possess (-or), purchase, recover, redeem, × surely, × verily.

7070. קָנֶה**, qâneh,** *kaw-neh´*; from 7069; a *reed* (as *erect*); (by resemblance) a *rod* (especially for measuring), *shaft, tube, stem*, the *radius* (of the arm), *beam* (of a steelyard):—balance, bone, branch, calamus, cane, reed, × spearman, stalk.

7071. קָנָה**, Qânâh,** *kaw-naw´*; feminine of 7070; *reediness; Kanah*, the name of a stream and of a place in Palestine:—Kanah.

7072. קַנּוֹא**, qannôwʼ,** *kan-no´*; for 7067; *jealous* or *angry*:—jealous.

7073. קְנַז**, Qᵉnaz,** *ken-az´*; probably from an unused root meaning to *hunt; hunter; Kenaz*, the name of an Edomite and of two Israelites:—Kenaz.

7074. קְנִזִּי**, Qᵉnizzîy,** *ken-iz-zee´*; patronymic from 7073, a *Kenizzite* or descendants of Kenaz:—Kenezite, Kenizzites.

7075. קִנְיָן**, qinyân,** *kin-yawn´*; from 7069; *creation*, i.e. (concrete) *creatures*; also *acquisition, purchase, wealth*:—getting, goods, × with money, riches, substance.

7076. קִנָּמוֹן**, qinnâmôwn,** *kin-naw-mone´*; from an unused root (meaning to *erect*); *cinnamon* bark (as in *upright* rolls):—cinnamon.

7077. קָנַן**, qânan,** *kaw-nan´*; a primitive root; to *erect*; but used only as denominative from 7064; to *nestle*, i.e. *build* or *occupy* as a nest:—make … nest.

7078. קֶנֶץ**, qenets,** *keh´-nets*; from an unused root probably meaning to *wrench; perversion*:—end.

7079. קְנָת**, Qᵉnâth,** *ken-awth´*; from 7069; *possession; Kenath*, a place East of the Jordan:—Kenath.

7080. קָסַם**, qâsam,** *kaw-sam´*; a primitive root; (properly) to *distribute*, i.e. *determine* by lot or magical scroll; (by implication) to *divine*:—divine (-r, -ation), prudent, soothsayer, use [divination].

A verb meaning to practice divination. It occurs most frequently in the prophetic books as God's prophets proclaimed the judgment this practice brings (Isa 3:2; Mic 3:6, 7). God had earlier established that He would guide His people through true prophets, not through diviners (Dt 18:10, 14). Thus, the falsity of divination is repeatedly pointed out by the prophets (Jer 29:8; Eze 13:9; 22:28; Zec 10:2). Nevertheless, divination was a problem for Israel as well as for other nations (1Sa 6:2; 28:8; 2Ki 17:17). This Hebrew term is broad enough to encompass necromancy, augury, and visions (1Sa 28:8; Eze 21:21–29; Mic 3:6, 7). Divination was quite profitable for some even in NT times (cf. Ac 16:16–18).

7081. קֶסֶם**, qesem,** *keh´-sem*; from 7080; a *lot*; also *divination* (including its *fee*), *oracle*:—(reward of) divination, divine sentence, witchcraft.

A masculine noun meaning divination. This word described the cultic practice of foreign nations that was prohibited in Israel (Dt 18:10); and considered a great sin (1Sa 15:23; 2Ki 17:17). False prophets used divination to prophesy in God's name, but God identified them as false (Jer 14:14; Eze 13:6); and pledged to remove such practices from Israel (Eze 13:23). Several verses give some insight into what this actual practice looked like: it was compared to a kingly sentence (Pr 16:10); and was used to discern between two choices (Eze 21:21[26], 22[27]).

7082. קָסַס**, qâsas,** *kaw-sas´*; a primitive root; to *lop* off:—cut off.

7083. קֶסֶת**, qeseth,** *keh´-seth*; from the same as 3563 (or as 7185); (properly) a *cup*, i.e. an *ink-stand*:—inkhorn.

7084. קְעִילָה**, Qᵉʻîylâh,** *keh-ee-law´*; perhaps from 7049 in the sense of *inclosing; citadel; Keïlah*, a place in Palestine:—Keilah.

7085. קַעֲקַע**, qaʻăqaʻ,** *kah-ak-ah´*; from the same as 6970; an *incision* or gash:— + mark.

7086. קְעָרָה**, qᵉʻârâh,** *keh-aw-raw´*; probably from 7167; a *bowl* (as *cut* out hollow):—charger, dish.

7087. קָפָא**, qâphâʼ,** *kaw-faw´*; a primitive root; to *shrink*, i.e. *thicken* (as unracked wine, curdled milk, clouded sky, frozen water):—congeal, curdle, dark, settle.

7088. קָפַד**, qâphad,** *kaw-fad´*; a primitive root; to *contract*, i.e. roll together:—cut off.

7089. קְפָדָה**, qᵉphâdâh,** *kef-aw-daw´*; from 7088; *shrinking*, i.e. terror:—destruction.

A feminine noun meaning horror, terror. Early Jewish interpreters translated the word as destruction; however, terror follows better from the root, which means to roll up, to contract (*qâphad* [7088]). The word occurs only in Eze 7:25 where it refers to the fear that would come on Israel, causing them to seek peace they would not find. Ezekiel was prophesying of the coming Babylonian invasion, which led to the fall of Jerusalem in 586 B.C.

7090. קִפּוֹד**, qippôwd,** *kip-pode´*; or קִפֹּד**, qippôd,** *kip-pode´*; from 7088; a species of bird, perhaps the *bittern* (from its *contracted* form):—bittern.

7091. קִפּוֹז**, qippôwz,** *kip-poze´*; from an unused root meaning to *contract*, i.e. *spring* forward; an *arrow-snake* (as *darting* on its prey):—great owl.

7092. קָפַץ**, qâphats,** *kaw-fats´*; a primitive root; to *draw together*, i.e. close; (by implication) to *leap* (by *contracting* the limbs); specifically to *die* (from *gathering* up the feet):—shut (up), skip, stop, take out of the way.

7093. קֵץ**, qêts,** *kates*; contracted from 7112; an *extremity*; adverb (with prepositional prefix) *after*:— + after, (utmost) border, end, [in-] finite, × process.

7094. קָצַב**, qâtsab,** *kaw-tsab´*; a primitive root; to *clip*, or (general) *chop*:—cut down, shorn.

7095. קֶצֶב, **qetseb,** *keh´-tseb*; from 7094; *shape* (as if *cut* out); *base* (as if there *cut* off):—bottom, size.

7096. קָצָה, **qâtsâh,** *kaw-tsaw´*; a primitive root; to *cut* off; (figurative) to *destroy*; (partial) to *scrape* off:—cut off, cut short, scrape (off).

7097. קָצֶה, **qâtseh,** *kaw-tseh´*; or (negative only) קֵצֶה, **qêtseh,** *kay-tseh´*; from 7096; an *extremity* (used in a great variety of applications and idioms; compare 7093):— × after, border, brim, brink, edge, end, [in-] finite, frontier, outmost coast, quarter, shore, (out-) side, × some, ut (-ter) most (part).

7098. קָצָה, **qâtsâh,** *kaw-tsaw´*; feminine of 7097; a *termination* (used like 7097):—coast, corner, (selv-) edge, lowest, (uttermost) part.

7099. קָצוּ, **qâtsûw,** *kaw´-tsoo*; and (feminine) קִצְוָה, **qitsvâh,** *kits-vaw´*; from 7096; a *limit* (used like 7097, but with less variety):—end, edge, uttermost part.

7100. קֶצַח, **qetsach,** *keh´-tsakh*; from an unused root apparently meaning to *incise; fennel-flower* (from its *pungency*):—fitches.

7101. קָצִין, **qâtsîyn,** *kaw-tseen´*; from 7096 in the sense of *determining*; a *magistrate* (as *deciding*) or other *leader*:—captain, guide, prince, ruler. Compare 6278.

A masculine noun meaning a captain, a ruler. The root meaning is one who decides. Sometimes the word indicates military leadership (Jos 10:24; Jgs 11:6, 11; cf. Jgs 11:9; Da 11:18), but it can signify a nonmilitary authority (Isa 3:6, 7). A captain could be chosen by men (Jgs 11:6; Isa 3:6); but he was ultimately appointed by God (Jgs 11:11; cf. Jgs 2:16, 18; 11:29). Captains were sometimes subordinate to a higher human authority (Jos 10:24; Da 11:18); but not always (Jgs 11:6, 11; cf. Jgs 12:7, 8). They had responsibility before God for the moral state of their followers (Isa 1:10; Mic 3:1, 9); but their subordinates also had responsibility to influence their rulers positively (Pr 25:15).

7102. קְצִיעָה, **q^etsiy'âh,** *kets-ee-aw´*; from 7106; *cassia* (as *peeled*; plural, the *bark*):—cassia.

7103. קְצִיעָה, **Q^etsîy'âh,** *kets-ee-aw´*; the same as 7102; *Ketsiah*, a daughter of Job:—Kezia.

7104. קְצִיץ, **Q^etsîyts,** *kets-eets´*; from 7112; *abrupt; Keziz*, a valley in Palestine:—Keziz.

7105. קָצִיר, **qâtsîyr,** *kaw-tseer´*; from 7114; *severed*, i.e. *harvest* (as *reaped*), the crop, the time, the reaper, or figurative; also a *limb* (of a tree, or simply *foliage*):—bough, branch, harvest (man).

7106. קָצַע, **qâtsa',** *kaw-tsah´*; a primitive root; to *strip* off, i.e. (partial) *scrape*; (by implication) to *segregate* (as an angle):—cause to scrape, corner.

7107. קָצַף, **qâtsaph,** *kaw-tsaf´*; a primitive root; to *crack* off, i.e. (figurative) *burst* out in rage:—(be) anger (-ry), displease, fret self, (provoke to) wrath (come), be wroth.

A verb meaning to be angry, to provoke to anger. The word refers to anger that arose because people failed to perform their duties properly. Pharaoh was angry with his baker and butcher (Ge 40:2; 41:10); while Moses was angry with the people for hoarding manna (Ex 16:20); Aaron's sons' apparent failure to follow rules of sacrifice (Le 10:16); and the captains' failure to finish off the enemy (Nu 31:14). King Ahasuerus was also angry with Vashti for failing to show off her beauty when summoned (Est 1:12). The word often expressed an authority being angry with a subject but not always (2Ki 13:19; Est 2:21). Sometimes the anger was not justified (2Ki 5:11; Jer 37:15). The word could also refer to God being angry or provoked (Dt 9:7, 8, 22; Zec 1:2; 8:14); an anger that could be aroused by a corporate failure to keep troublemakers in line (Nu 16:22; Jos 22:18). Isa 8:21 contains a reflexive form of the word, as if the anger was unable to find a reasonable object and thus caused the occult practitioners to fret themselves.

7108. קְצַף, **q^etsaph,** *kets-af´*; (Chaldee); corresponding to 7107; to *become enraged*:—be furious.

An Aramaic verb meaning to be angry. It corresponds to the Hebrew word *qâtsaph* (7107) and refers to anger aroused by someone's failure to fulfill a duty properly. It occurs only in Da 2:12 where Nebuchadnezzar became angry over the failure of the Babylonian wise men to tell him his dream with its interpretation.

7109. קְצַף, **q^etsaph,** *kets-af´*; (Chaldee); from 7108; *rage*:—wrath.

An Aramaic masculine noun meaning anger. Like the word *qĕtsaph* (7108), this word refers to anger aroused by someone's failure to fulfill a duty properly. The word occurs only in Ezr 7:23 where Artaxerxes commanded that work necessary for the second Temple was to be done diligently, lest God's wrath fall on Persia. Artaxerxes understood that his responsibility was to see that his subjects did their duties.

7110. קֶצֶף, **qetseph,** *keh´-tsef*; from 7107; a *splinter* (as *chipped* off); (figurative) *rage* or *strife*:—foam, indignation, × sore, wrath.

A masculine noun meaning wrath. The word refers to anger aroused by someone's failure to do a duty. For example, a wife in Persia who showed contempt for her husband by not doing her duties would arouse his wrath (Est 1:18). This word usually refers to God's wrath aroused by people failing to do their duties (Dt 29:28[27]; Ps 38:1[2]; Isa 34:2). In some cases, this wrath was directed against sinful Gentile nations (Isa 34:2; Zec 1:15; cf. Ro 1:18). In Israel's case, this duty was expressed in the Law of Moses (2Ch 19:10; Zec 7:12; cf. Ro 4:15). Atonement performed by priests turned away God's wrath when laws were broken (Nu 16:46 [17:11]; 2Ch 29:8; 27:24; 2Ch 29:8).

7111. קְצָפָה, **q^etsâphâh,** *kets-aw-faw´*; from 7107; a *fragment*:—bark [-ed].

7112. קָצַץ, **qâtsats,** *kaw-tsats´*; a primitive root; to *chop* off (literal or figurative):—cut (asunder, in pieces, in sunder, off), × utmost.

7113. קְצַץ, **q^etsats,** *kets-ats´*; (Chaldee); corresponding to 7112:—cut off.

7114. קָצַר, **qâtsar,** *kaw-tsar´*; a primitive root; to *dock* off, i.e. *curtail* (transitive or intransitive, literal or figurative); especially to *harvest* (grass or grain):— × at all, cut down, much discouraged, grieve, harvestman, lothe, mourn, reap (-er), (be, wax) short (-en, -er), straiten, trouble, vex.

7115. קֹצֶר, **qôtser,** *ko´-tser*; from 7114; *shortness* (of spirit), i.e. impatience:—anguish.

7116. קָצֵר, **qâtsêr,** *kaw-tsare´*; from 7114; *short* (whether in size, number, life, strength or temper):—few, hasty, small, soon.

7117. קְצָת, **q^etsâth,** *kets-awth´*; from 7096; a *termination* (literal or figurative); also (by implication) a *portion*; adverb (with prepositional prefix) *after*:—end, part, × some.

7118. קְצָת, **q^etsâth,** *kets-awth´*; (Chaldee); corresponding to 7117:—end, partly.

7119. קַר, **qar,** *kar*; contracted from an unused root meaning to *chill; cool*; (figurative) *quiet*:—cold, excellent [*from the margin*].

7120. קֹר, **qôr,** *kore*; from the same as 7119; *cold*:—cold.

7121. קָרָא, **qârâ',** *kaw-raw´*; a primitive root [rather identical with 7122 through the idea of *accosting* a person met]; to *call* out to (i.e. [properly] *address* by name, but used in a wide variety of applications):—bewray [self], that are bidden, call (for, forth, self, upon), cry (unto), (be) famous, guest, invite, mention, (give) name, preach, (make) proclaim (-ation), pronounce, publish, read, renowned, say.

A verb meaning to call, to declare, to summon, to invite, to read, to be called, to be invoked, to be named. The verb means to call or to summon, but its context and surrounding grammatical setting determine the various shades of meaning given to the word. Abraham called on the name of the Lord (Ge 4:26; 12:8); the Lord called to Adam (Ge 3:9; Ex 3:4). With the Hebrew preposition meaning to, the verb means to name. Adam named all the animals and birds (Ge 2:20;

3:20); and God named the light day (Ge 1:5). The word may introduce a long message, as in Ex 34:6, that gives the moral and ethical definition of God. It can also mean to summon, such as when God summoned Bezalel to build the tabernacle (Ex 31:2).

In certain contexts, the verb has the sense of proclaiming or announcing. Jezebel urged Ahab to proclaim a holy day of fasting so Naboth could be killed (1Ki 21:9); the Servant of Isaiah proclaimed freedom for the captives and prisoners (Isa 61:1). The word may mean simply to call out or cry out, as Potiphar's wife said she did (Ge 39:15; 1Ki 18:27, 28).

The word means to read aloud from a scroll or a book: the king of Israel was to read aloud from a copy of the Law (Dt 17:19); just as Moses read the Book of the Covenant to all Israel at Sinai (Ex 24:7). Baruch read the scroll of Jeremiah to the people (Jer 36:6, 8).

In the passive stem, the word means to be called or summoned: Esther was called by name (Est 2:14); in the book of Esther, the secretaries who were to carry out the king's orders were summoned (Est 3:12; Isa 31:4). News that was delivered was called out or reported (Jer 4:20). In Nehemiah's reform, the Book of Moses was read aloud in the audience of the people (Ne 13:1). Also, Eve was called, that is, named, woman (Ge 2:23). The word takes on the nuance of to be reckoned or called. Genesis 21:12 describes how Abraham's seed would be reckoned by the Lord through Isaac.

7122. קָרָא, **qârâ',** *kaw-raw´*; a primitive root; to *encounter*, whether accidentally or in a hostile manner:—befall, (by) chance, (cause to) come (upon), fall out, happen, meet.

7123. קְרָא, **qᵉrâ',** *ker-aw´*; (Chaldee); corresponding to 7121:—call, cry, read.

7124. קֹרֵא, **qôrê',** *ko-ray´*; properly active participle of 7121; a *caller*, i.e. *partridge* (from its *cry*):—partridge. See also 6981.

7125. קִרְאָה, **qir'âh,** *keer-aw´*; from 7122; an *encountering*, accidental, friendly or hostile (also adverb *opposite*):— × against (he come), help, meet, seek, × to, × in the way.

7126. קָרַב, **qârab,** *kaw-rab´*; a primitive root; to *approach* (causative, *bring near*) for whatever purpose:—(cause to) approach, (cause to) bring (forth, near), (cause to) come (near, nigh), (cause to) draw near (nigh), go (near), be at hand, join, be near, offer, present, produce, make ready, stand, take.

A verb meaning to come near, to approach. The basic concept is a close, spatial proximity of the subject and the object (Ge 37:18; Dt 4:11); although it is also possible for this word to introduce actual contact (Eze 37:7; cf. Ex 14:20; Jgs 19:13). This verb is also used in a temporal context to indicate the imminence of some event (Ge 27:41). This usage is common to communicate the impending doom of God's judgment, like Moses' day of calamity and the prophet's day of the Lord (La 4:18). This term has also developed several technical meanings. It can refer to armed conflict. Sometimes it is clarified by modifiers, such as to fight or unto battle (Dt 20:10). Other times, this word alone carries the full verbal idea of entering into battle. Some of these instances are clear by context (Dt 25:11; Jos 8:5); however, there are others where this meaning may be missed (Dt 2:37; Ps 27:2; 91:10; 119:150; cf. Dt 2:19). Another technical meaning refers to sexual relations (Ge 20:4; Dt 22:14; Isa 8:3). One other technical meaning refers to the protocol for presenting an offering to God (Ex 29:4; Le 1:5, 13, 14; Nu 16:9).

7127. קְרֵב, **qᵉrêb,** *ker-abe´*; (Chaldee); corresponding to 7126:—approach, come (near, nigh), draw near.

7128. קְרָב, **qᵉrâb,** *ker-awb´*; from 7126; hostile *encounter*:—battle, war.

7129. קְרָב, **qᵉrâb,** *ker-awb´*; (Chaldee); corresponding to 7128:—war.

7130. קֶרֶב, **qereb,** *keh´-reb*; from 7126; (properly) the *nearest* part, i.e. the *centre*, whether literal, figurative or adverbial (especially with preposition):— × among, × before, bowels, × unto charge, + eat (up), × heart, × him, × in, inward (× -ly, part, -s, thought), midst, + out of, purtenance, × therein, × through, × within self.

A masculine noun meaning midst, middle, interior, inner part, inner organs, bowels, inner being. The term occurs 222 times in the OT and denotes the center or inner part of anything, e.g., the middle of a battle (1Ki 20:39); middle of the streets (Isa 5:25); but especially the inner organs of the body. In the ceremony to ordain Aaron and his sons as priests for ministry to the Lord, all the fat that covered the inner organs of the sacrifices was to be burned on the altar (Ex 29:13, 22; see also Le 1:13, 9:14). On many other occasions, however, the word is utilized abstractly to describe the inner being of a person. This place was regarded as the home of the heart from which the emotions spring (Ps 39:3[4]; 55:4[5]; La 1:20). It was also viewed as the source of thoughts (Ge 18:12; Ps 62:4[5]; Jer 9:8[7]), which are often deceitful, wicked, and full of cursing. Yet wisdom from God can reside there also (1Ki 3:28). This inner being is also the seat of one's moral disposition and thus one's affections and desires. David, grieved over his sin with Bathsheba, pleaded with God to place a right or steadfast spirit within him (lit., in [his] inner being), so that he might always desire to stay close to God and obey His laws (Ps 51:10[12]). The Lord promised to place His Law in the inner beings of His people Israel (Jer 31:33; see also Eze 11:19, 36:26, 27).

7131. קָרֵב, **qârêb,** *kaw-rabe´*; from 7126; *near*:—approach, come (near, nigh), draw near.

7132. קְרָבָה, **qirbâh,** *kir-baw´*; from 7126; *approach*:—approaching, draw near.

7133. קָרְבָּן, **qorbân,** *kor-bawn´*; or קֻרְבָּן, **qurbân,** *koor-bawn´*; from 7126; something *brought near* the altar, i.e. a sacrificial *present*:—oblation, that is offered, offering.

A masculine noun meaning an offering, a gift. This is the most general term, used eighty times in the OT, for offerings and gifts of all kinds. The word is found in Leviticus referring to animal offerings of all permissible types (Le 1:2, 3); grain offerings of fine flour (Le 2:1, 5); gifts or votive offerings of gold vessels. It is found in Numbers referring to silver vessels and rings (Nu 7:13; 31:50) and jewelry (Nu 31:50).

Ezekiel uses the word to designate an offering. Israel corrupted the land by presenting their offerings at every high hill, leafy tree, and high place (Eze 20:28). Happily, the second use in Ezekiel depicts the table where the flesh offering would be properly presented within the restored Temple (Eze 40:43).

7134. קַרְדֹּם, **qardôm,** *kar-dome´*; perhaps from 6923 in the sense of *striking* upon; an *axe*:—ax.

7135. קָרָה, **qârâh,** *kaw-raw´*; feminine of 7119; *coolness*:—cold.

7136. קָרָה, **qârâh,** *kaw-raw´*; a primitive root; to *light upon* (chiefly by accident); (causative) to *bring about*; (specifically) to *impose* timbers (for roof or floor):—appoint, lay (make) beams, befall, bring, come (to pass unto), floor, [hap] was, happen (unto), meet, send good speed.

7137. קָרֶה, **qâreh,** *kaw-reh´*; from 7136; an (unfortunate) *occurrence*, i.e. some accidental (ceremonial) *disqualification*:—uncleanness that chanceth.

7138. קָרוֹב, **qârôwb,** *kaw-robe´*; or קָרֹב, **qârôb,** *kaw-robe´*; from 7126; *near* (in place, kindred or time):—allied, approach, at hand, + any of kin, kinsfolk (-sman), (that is) near (of kin), neighbour, (that is) next, (them that come) nigh (at hand), more ready, short (-ly).

7139. קָרַח, **qârach,** *kaw-rakh´*; a primitive root; to *depilate*:—make (self) bald.

7140. קֶרַח, **qerach,** *keh´-rakh*; or קֹרַח, **qôrach,** *ko´-rakh*; from 7139; *ice* (as if bald, i.e. *smooth*); hence, *hail*; (by resemblance) rock *crystal*:—crystal, frost, ice.

7141. קֹרַח, **Qôrach,** *ko´-rakh*; from 7139; *ice; Korach*, the name of two Edomites and three Israelites:—Korah.

7142. קֵרֵחַ, **qêrêach,** *kay-ray´-akh*; from 7139; *bald* (on the back of the head):—bald (head).

7143. קָרֵחַ, **Qârêach,** *kaw-ray´-akh*; from 7139; *bald; Kareäch*, an Israelite:—Careah, Kareah.

7144. קָרְחָה, **qorchâh,** *kor-khaw´*; or קָרְחָא, **qorchâ',** *kor-khaw´*; (Eze 27:31), from 7139; *baldness:*—bald (-ness), × utterly.

7145. קָרְחִי, **Qorchîy,** *kor-khee´*; patronymic from 7141; a *Korchite* (collective) or descendants of Korach:—Korahite, Korathite, sons of Kore, Korhite.

7146. קָרַחַת, **qârachath,** *kaw-rakh´-ath*; from 7139; a *bald* spot (on the back of the head); (figurative) a *threadbare* spot (on the back side of the cloth):—bald head, bare within.

7147. קְרִי, **qᵉrîy,** *ker-ee´*; from 7136; hostile *encounter:*—contrary.

7148. קָרִיא, **qârîy',** *kaw-ree´*; from 7121; *called,* i.e. *select:*—famous, renowned.

7149. קִרְיָא, **qiryâ',** *keer-yaw´*; (Chaldee); or קִרְיָה, **qiryâh,** *keer-yaw´*; (Chaldee); corresponding to 7151:—city.

7150. קְרִיאָה, **qᵉrîy'âh,** *ker-ee-aw´*; from 7121; a *proclamation:*—preaching.

7151. קִרְיָה, **qiryâh,** *kir-yaw´*; from 7136 in the sense of *flooring,* i.e. building; a *city:*—city.

7152. קְרִיּוֹת, **Qᵉrîyyôwth,** *ker-ee-yōth´*; plural of 7151; *buildings; Kerioth,* the name of two places in Palestine:—Kerioth, Kirioth.

7153. קִרְיַת אַרְבַּע, **Qiryath 'Arba',** *(keer-yath´) ar-bah´*; or (with the article interposed) קִרְיַת הָאַרְבַּע, **Qiryath Hâ'arba',** *haw-ar-bah´*; (Ne 11:25), from 7151 and 704 or 702; *city of Arba,* or *city of the four* (giants); *Kirjath-Arba* or *Kirjath-ha-Arba,* a place in Palestine:—Kirjath-arba.

7154. קִרְיַת בַּעַל, **Qiryath Ba'al,** *keer-yath´ bah´-al*; from 7151 and 1168; *city of Baal; Kirjath-Baal,* a place in Palestine:—Kirjath-baal.

7155. קִרְיַת חֻצוֹת, **Qiryath Chutsôwth,** *keer-yath´ khoo-tsōth´*; from 7151 and the feminine plural of 2351; *city of streets; Kirjath-Chutsoth,* a place in Moab:—Kirjath-huzoth.

7156. קִרְיָתַיִם, **Qiryâthayim,** *keer-yaw-thah´-yim*; dual of 7151; *double city; Kirjathaïm,* the name of two places in Palestine:—Kiriathaim, Kirjathaim.

7157. קִרְיַת יְעָרִים, **Qiryath Yᵉ'ârîym,** *(keer-yath´) yeh-aw-reem´*; or (Jer 26:20) with the article interposed; or (Jos 18:28) simply the former part of the word; or קִרְיַת עָרִים, **Qiryath 'Ârîym,** *aw-reem´*; from 7151 and the plural of 3293 or 5892; *city of forests,* or *city of towns; Kirjath-Jeärim* or *Kirjath-Arim,* a place in Palestine:—Kirjath, Kirjath-jearim, Kirjath-arim.

7158. קִרְיַת סַנָּה, **Qiryath Sannâh,** *keer-yath´ san-naw´*; or קִרְיַת סֵפֶר, **Qiryath Sêpher,** *keer-yath´ say´-fer*; from 7151 and a simpler feminine from the same as 5577, or (for the latter name) 5612; *city of branches,* or *of a book; Kirjath-Sannah* or *Kirjath-Sepher,* a place in Palestine:—Kirjath-sannah, Kirjath-sepher.

7159. קָרַם, **qâram,** *kaw-ram´*; a primitive root; to *cover:*—cover.

7160. קָרַן, **qâran,** *kaw-ran´*; a primitive root; to *push* or gore; used only as denominative from 7161, to *shoot out horns;* (figurative) *rays:*—have horns, shine.

7161. קֶרֶן, **qeren,** *keh´-ren*; from 7160; a *horn* (as *projecting*); (by implication) a *flask, cornet;* (by resemblance) an elephant's *tooth* (i.e. *ivory*), a *corner* (of the altar), a *peak* (of a mountain), a *ray* (of light); (figurative) *power:*— × hill, horn.

7162. קֶרֶן, **qeren,** *keh´-ren*; (Chaldee); corresponding to 7161; a *horn* (literal or for sound):—horn, cornet.

7163. קֶרֶן הַפּוּךְ, **qeren happûwk,** *keh´-ren hap-pook´*; from 7161 and 6320; *horn of cosmetic; Keren-hap-Puk,* one of Job's daughters:—Keren-happuch.

7164. קָרַס, **qâras,** *kaw-ras´*; a primitive root; (properly) to *protrude;* used only as denominative from 7165 (for alliteration with 7167), to *hunch,* i.e. be humpbacked:—stoop.

7165. קֶרֶס, **qeres,** *keh´-res*; from 7164; a *knob* or belaying-pin (from its swelling form):—tache.

7166. קַרְסֹל, **qarsôl,** *kar-sole´*; from 7164; an *ankle* (as a *protuberance* or joint):—foot.

7167. קָרַע, **qâra',** *kaw-rah´*; a primitive root; to *rend,* literal or figurative (*revile, paint* the eyes, as if enlarging them):—cut out, rend, × surely, tear.

7168. קֶרַע, **qera',** *keh´-rah*; from 7167; a *rag:*—piece, rag.

7169. קָרַץ, **qârats,** *kaw-rats´*; a primitive root; to *pinch,* i.e. (partial) to *bite* the lips, *blink* the eyes (as a gesture of malice), or (fully) to *squeeze* off (a piece of clay in order to mould a vessel from it):—form, move, wink.

7170. קְרַץ, **qᵉrats,** *ker-ats´*; (Chaldee); corresponding to 7171 in the sense of a *bit* (to "eat the *morsels* of" any one, i.e. *chew* him up [figurative] by *slander*):— + accuse.

7171. קֶרֶץ, **qerets,** *keh´-rets*; from 7169; *extirpation* (as if by *constriction*):—destruction.

A masculine noun possibly meaning destruction. It is found only in Jer 46:20. Due to the immediate context of the passage, however, the more probable meaning is biter (i.e. a biting fly, such as a gadfly, a horsefly, or a mosquito). Egypt was described as a beautiful heifer, but a biting fly from the north (i.e. Babylon) was being sent to punish her. This noun is derived from the verb *qârats* (7169).

7172. קַרְקַע, **qarqa',** *kar-kah´*; from 7167; *floor* (as if a pavement of pieces or *tessaræ*), of a building or the sea:—bottom, (× one side of the) floor.

7173. קַרְקַע, **Qarqa',** *kar-kah´*; the same as 7172; *ground-floor; Karka* (with the article prefixed), a place in Palestine:—Karkaa.

7174. קַרְקֹר, **Qarqôr,** *kar-kore´*; from 6979; *foundation; Karkor,* a place East of the Jordan:—Karkor.

7175. קֶרֶשׁ, **qeresh,** *keh´-resh*; from an unused root meaning to *split* off; a *slab* or plank; (by implication) a *deck* of a ship:—bench, board.

7176. קֶרֶת, **qereth,** *keh´-reth*; from 7136 in the sense of building; a *city:*—city.

7177. קַרְתָּה, **Qartâh,** *kar-taw´*; from 7176; *city; Kartah,* a place in Palestine:—Kartah.

7178. קַרְתָּן, **Qartân,** *kar-tawn´*; from 7176; *city-plot; Kartan,* a place in Palestine:—Kartan.

7179. קַשׁ, **qash,** *kash*; from 7197; *straw* (as *dry*):—stubble.

7180. קִשֻּׁאָה, **qishshu'âh,** *kish-shoo´-aw*; from an unused root (meaning to be *hard*); a *cucumber* (from the difficulty of *digestion*):—cucumber.

7181. קָשַׁב, **qâshab,** *kaw-shab´*; a primitive root; to *prick up* the ears, i.e. *hearken:*—attend, (cause to) hear (-ken), give heed, incline, mark (well), regard.

A verb meaning to listen carefully, to pay attention, to give heed, to obey. The basic significance of the term is to denote the activity of paying close attention to something, usually another person's words or sometimes to something that can be seen (e.g., Isa 21:7). Job pleaded for his three friends to listen to his words (Job 13:6; see also Isa 32:3; Jer 23:18). Often the term functioned as an appeal to God to hear and respond to an urgent prayer (Ps 17:1; 61:1[2]; 66:19; cf. Ps 5:2[3]). At other times, it denoted the obedience that was expected after the hearing of the Lord's requirements (1Sa 15:22; Ne 9:34; Isa 48:18). Israel's history, however, was characterized by a life of hard-heartedness and rebellion. Jeremiah declared that this was due to the fact that Israel's ears were uncircumcised; therefore, they could not listen so they were able to obey (Jer 6:10).

7182. קֶשֶׁב, **qesheb,** *keh´-sheb*; from 7181; a *hearkening*:— × diligently, hearing, much heed, that regarded.

7183. קַשָּׁב, **qashshâb,** *kash-shawb´*; or קַשֻּׁב, **qash-shub,** *kash-shoob´*; from 7181; *hearkening*:—attent (-ive).

7184. קָשָׂה, **qâsâh,** *kaw-saw´*; or קַשְׂוָה, **qaśvâh,** *kas-vaw´*; from an unused root meaning to be *round*; a *jug* (from its shape):—cover, cup.

7185. קָשָׁה, **qâshâh,** *kaw-shaw´*; a primitive root; (properly) to *be dense*, i.e. tough or *severe* (in various applications):—be cruel, be fiercer, make grievous, be ([ask a], be in, have, seem, would) hard (-en, [labour], -ly, thing), be sore, (be, make) stiff (-en, [-necked]).

7186. קָשֶׁה, **qâsheh,** *kaw-sheh´*; from 7185; *severe* (in various applications):—churlish, cruel, grievous, hard ([-hearted], thing), heavy, + impudent, obstinate, prevailed, rough (-ly), sore, sorrowful, stiff ([-necked]), stubborn, + in trouble.

An adjective meaning hard, harsh, cruel, severe, strong, violent, fierce. This term's basic function is to describe something as hard. The word modifies a variety of different subjects and encompasses a fairly broad range of meanings. The labour the Egyptians imposed on the Hebrews was described as hard (i.e. harsh, Ex 1:14; 6:9). Joseph spoke hard words to his brothers at first (Ge 42:7, 30; cf. 1Sa 20:10). A Calebite named Nabal was labeled as being hard, i.e. cruel and evil (1Sa 25:3). The Israelites were often characterized as being hard or stiff of neck, i.e. stubborn, rebellious, obstinate (Ex 32:9, 33:3, 5; Dt 9:6, 13; cf. Eze 3:7). An experience could be hard, i.e. painful (Ps 60:3[5]); as could a vision or revelation (Isa 21:2). Hannah was hard of spirit, that is, deeply troubled (1Sa 1:15). Both battles and winds could be hard, i.e. fierce (2Sa 2:17; Isa 27:8). Moses chose capable men from all Israel to serve as judges; they judged minor cases while Moses himself judged the difficult ones (Ex 18:26).

7187. קְשׁוֹט, **qᵉshôwt,** *kesh-ote´*; (Chaldee); or קְשֹׁט, **qᵉshôṭ,** *kesh-ote´*; (Chaldee); corresponding to 7189; *fidelity*:—truth.

An Aramaic masculine noun meaning truth. The term is utilized twice, with both occurrences embedded within the book of Daniel. After being deeply humbled by the Lord, Nebuchadnezzar praised God and acknowledged that all His works were truth (Da 4:37[34]). Prior to this humbling, King Nebuchadnezzar had declared Daniel's God in truth to be the God of gods, i.e. truly (Da 2:47). Nevertheless, this knowledge failed to penetrate his proud heart, because in the very next section of text, Nebuchadnezzar built a monumental golden idol. This word is equivalent to the Hebrew term *qôsheṭ* (7189).

7188. קָשַׁח, **qâshach,** *kaw-shakh´*; a primitive root; to *be* (causative, *make*) *unfeeling*:—harden.

A verb meaning to make hard, to treat roughly. Used twice in the OT, this word implies a hardening similar to the formation of a callous. It signifies the hardening of a mother's heart toward her offspring (Job 39:16); and is used by Isaiah to connote the spiritual dullness of the people toward God (Isa 63:17).

7189. קֹשֶׁט, **qosheṭ,** *ko´-shet*; or קֹשְׁט, **qoshṭ,** *kosht*; from an unused root meaning to *balance; equity* (as evenly *weighed*), i.e. *reality*:—truth.

A masculine noun meaning truth, certainty. This word comes from an unused root meaning to balance, as in a scale. It appears twice in the Wisdom Literature, meaning the vindication of a true assessment by reality (Ps 60:4[6]); and the realization of a person's truthfulness by an intimate knowledge of the individual (Pr 22:21).

7190. קְשִׁי, **qᵉshîy,** *kesh-ee´*; from 7185; *obstinacy*:—stubbornness.

7191. קִשְׁיוֹן, **Qishyôwn,** *kish-yone´*; from 7190; *hard ground; Kishjon*, a place in Palestine:—Kishion, Keshon.

7192. קְשִׂיטָה, **qᵉśîyṭâh,** *kes-ee-taw´*; from an unused root (probably meaning to *weigh* out); an *ingot* (as definitely *estimated* and stamped for a coin):—piece of money (silver).

7193. קַשְׂקֶשֶׂת, **qaśqeśeth,** *kas-keh´-seth;* by reduplication from an unused root meaning to *shale* off as bark; a *scale* (of a fish); hence a coat of *mail* (as composed of or covered with jointed *plates* of metal):—mail, scale.

7194. קָשַׁר, **qâshar,** *kaw-shar´*; a primitive root; to *tie*, physical (*gird, confine, compact*) or mentally (in *love, league*):—bind (up), (make a) conspire (-acy, -ator), join together, knit, stronger, work [treason].

7195. קֶשֶׁר, **qesher,** *keh´-sher*; from 7194; an (unlawful) *alliance*:—confederacy, conspiracy, treason.

7196. קִשֻּׁרִים, **qishshurîym,** *kish-shoor-eem´*; from 7194; an (ornamental) *girdle* (for women):—attire, headband.

7197. קָשַׁשׁ, **qâshash,** *kaw-shash´*; a primitive root; to *become sapless* through drought; used only as denominative from 7179; to *forage* for straw, stubble or wood; (figurative) to *assemble*:—gather (selves) (together).

7198. קֶשֶׁת, **qesheth,** *keh´-sheth*; from 7185 in the original sense (of 6983) of *bending*; a *bow*, for *shooting* (hence [figurative] *strength*) or the *iris*:— × arch (-er), + arrow, bow ([-man, -shot]).

7199. קַשָּׁת, **qashshâth,** *kash-shawth´*; intensive (as denominative) from 7198; a *bowman*:— × archer.

7200. רָאָה, **râ'âh,** *raw-aw´*; a primitive root; to *see*, literal or figurative (in numerous applications, direct and implied, transitive, intransitive and causative):—advise self, appear, approve, behold, × certainly, consider, discern, (make to) enjoy, have experience, gaze, take heed, × indeed, × joyfully, lo, look (on, one another, one on another, one upon another, out, up, upon), mark, meet, × be near, perceive, present, provide, regard, (have) respect, (fore-, cause to, let) see (-r, -m, one another), shew (self), × sight of others, (e-) spy, stare, × surely, × think, view, visions.

A verb meaning to see. Its basic denotation is to see with the eyes (Ge 27:1). It can also have the following derived meanings, all of which require the individual to see physically outside of himself or herself: to see so that one can learn to know, whether it be another person (Dt 33:9) or God (Dt 1:31; 11:2); to experience (Jer 5:12; 14:13; 20:18; 42:14); to perceive (Ge 1:4, 10, 12, 18, 21, 25, 31; Ex 3:4); to see by volition (Ge 9:22, 23; 42:9, 12); to look after or to visit (Ge 37:14; 1Sa 20:29); to watch (1Sa 6:9); to find (1Sa 16:17); to select (2Ki 10:3); to be concerned with (Ge 39:23). It is also possible for this verb to require the individual to make a mental observation. As an imperative, it can function as an exclamation similar to *hinnêh* (2009), which means to behold (Ge 27:27; 31:50). Further, it can denote to give attention to (Jer 2:31); to look into or inquire (1Sa 24:15[16]); to take heed (Ex 10:10); to discern (Ecc 1:16; 3:13); to distinguish (Mal 3:18); to consider or reflect on (Ecc 7:14). It can also connote a spiritual observation and comprehension by means of seeing visions (Ge 41:22; Isa 30:10).

7201. רָאָה, **râ'âh,** *raw-aw´*; from 7200; a *bird* of prey (probably the *vulture*, from its sharp *sight*):—glede. Compare 1676.

7202. רָאֶה, **râ'eh,** *raw-eh´*; from 7200; *seeing*, i.e. experiencing:—see.

An adjective meaning seeing. This word appears in Job 10:15 in an idiomatic use, meaning to be drenched or utterly covered with affliction. The connection with the root meaning stems from the visible signs of being afflicted.

7203. רֹאֶה, **rô'eh,** *ro-eh´*; active participle of 7200; a *seer* (as often rendered); but also (abstract) a *vision*:—vision.

A masculine noun meaning a seer, prophetic vision. The word is the active participle of *râ'âh* (7200), which signifies a prophet (see 1Ch 9:22, Isa 30:10). It refers to the vision or insight that the prophet receives (Isa 28:7).

7204. רֹאֵה, **Rô'êh,** *ro-ay´*; for 7203; *prophet; Roëh*, an Israelite:—Haroeh [*including the article*].

7205. רְאוּבֵן, **Rᵉ'ûwbên,** *reh-oo-bane´*; from the imperative of 7200 and 1121; *see* ye a *son; Reüben*, a son of Jacob:—Reuben.

7206. רְאוּבֵנִי, **R**e**'ûwbênîy,** *reh-oo-bay-nee´*; patronymic from 7205; a *Reübenite* or descendant of Reüben:—children of Reuben, Reubenites.

7207. רַאֲוָה, **ra'ăvâh,** *rah-av-aw´*; from 7200; *sight,* i.e. satisfaction:—behold.

A verb infinitive meaning to behold, to see. Appearing only once in the OT, the word alludes to looking on the outward appearance and fondly admiring an object (Ecc 5:11[10]).

7208. רְאוּמָה, **R**e**'ûwmâh,** *reh-oo-maw´*; feminine passive participle of 7213; *raised; Reümah,* a Syrian woman:—Reumah.

7209. רְאִי, **r**e**'îy,** *reh-ee´*; from 7200; a *mirror* (as *seen*):—looking glass.

A masculine noun meaning mirror . The primary meaning is that of a looking glass used to see one's own reflection. Job uses the word metaphorically to refer to the sky (Job 37:18).

7210. רֳאִי, **rŏ'îy,** *ro-ee´*; from 7200; *sight,* whether abstract (*vision*) or concrete (a *spectacle*):—gazingstock, look to, (that) see (-th).

A masculine noun meaning sight, an appearance, a spectacle. The basic force of this word is that of a visible appearance. It is used in reference to God's ability to see (Ge 16:13); the outward look of an individual (1Sa 16:12); and a visual spectacle that drew attention to itself (Na 3:6).

7211. רְאָיָה, **R**e**'âyâh,** *reh-aw-yaw´*; from 7200 and 3050; *Jah has seen; Reäjah,* the name of three Israelites:—Reaia, Reaiah.

7212. רְאִית, **r**e**'îyth,** *reh-eeth´*; from 7200; *sight*:—beholding.

A feminine noun meaning look, sight. The word is derived from the verb *râ'âh* (7200) and is used to denote a looking on of goods by their owner. The author of Ecclesiastes rhetorically inquired as to the good of increasing wealth and goods, if only for the owner merely to look on them (Ecc 5:11[10]).

7213. רָאַם, **râ'am,** *raw-am´*; a primitive root; to *rise*:—be lifted up.

7214. רְאֵם, **r**e**'êm,** *reh-ame´*; or רְאֵים, **r**e**'êym,** *reh-ame´*; or רֵים, **rêym,** *rame*; or רֵם, **rêm,** *rame*; from 7213; a wild *bull* (from its *conspicuousness*):—unicorn.

7215. רָאמוֹת, **râ'môwth,** *raw-moth´*; from 7213; something *high* in value, i.e. perhaps *coral*:—coral.

7216. רָאמוֹת, **Râ'môwth,** *raw-mōth´*; or רָאמֹת, **Râ'môth,** *raw-mōth´*; plural of 7215; *heights; Ramoth,* the name of two places in Palestine:—Ramoth.

7217. רֵאשׁ, **rê'sh,** *raysh*; (Chaldee); corresponding to 7218; the *head*; (figurative) the *sum*:—chief, head, sum.

An Aramaic masculine noun meaning head. The word is used to indicate the head of a man (Da 3:27); of an image constructed by Nebuchadnezzar (Da 2:32, 38); and a beast in Daniel's vision (Da 7:6, 20). This word is also used to denote a receptacle for dreams and visions (i.e. the head [Da 7:1]), and in the same verse it represents the sum total (i.e. essential matter). Ezra used this noun to indicate those people who served in the capacity of leaders (Ezr 5:10).

7218. רֹאשׁ, **rô'sh,** *roshe*; from an unused root apparently meaning to *shake*; the *head* (as most easily *shaken*), whether literal or figurative (in many applications, of place, time, rank, etc.):—band, beginning, captain, chapiter, chief (-est place, man, things), company, end, × every [man], excellent, first, forefront, ([be-]) head, height, (on) high (-est part, [priest]), × lead, × poor, principal, ruler, sum, top.

A masculine noun meaning a head, hair, a person, a point, the top, the beginning, the best, a chief, a leader. It is clear from the multitude of legitimate translations of this word that it has many metaphorical meanings. In Scripture, the word is used to refer to a human head (Ge 40:16); it also refers to animal heads as well, such as the serpent's head (Ge 3:15); a dog; an ass; a living being (2Sa 3:8; 2Ki 6:25; Eze 1:22). It regularly indicates the heads of animals being sacrificed (Ex 12:9; 29:15, 19).

This word is used in several Hebrew idioms: to bring something down on someone's head is to get vengeance (Eze 9:10); and to sprinkle dust on one's head is to mourn and show despair (Jos 7:6; Eze 27:30).

The word can designate an individual person: It refers to Joseph's head as representative of his whole tribe (Ge 49:26; Dt 33:16). It refers to the top or peak of things and indicates the tops of mountains (Ge 8:5); such as the top of Mount Olives in 2Sa 15:32 or even the top of a bed (Ge 47:31).

This Hebrew word commonly designates the beginning of something: It refers to the head or beginning of the year (Eze 40:1); or month (Ex 12:2). Its use extends to describing the best of something. The best spices or myrrh were depicted by this word (Ex 30:23), as were the most influential persons: commanders (Dt 20:9; Eze 10:11); the heads or leaders of families and chiefs (1Ki 8:1; 1Ch 24:31); the chief priest of Israel (1Ch 27:5). It is used with a superlative connotation to describe the chief cornerstone (Ps 118:22); or the most lofty stars (Job 22:12).

In some places, the word is best translated to indicate the entire or complete amount of something: the Lord made the chief part of the dust of the earth, i.e. all of it (Pr 8:26). It also meant to take (or lift up) the total number of people, i.e. take a census (Ex 30:12). The psalmist asserted that the sum total of God's words are righteous forever (Ps 119:160).

It also indicates the source of a river or branch as its head (Ge 2:10). When combined with the noun dog, it expresses a major insult. Abner used the term of himself, a dog's head, as a term of disgust (2Sa 3:8).

7219. רֹאשׁ, **rô'sh,** *roshe*; or רוֹשׁ, **rôwsh,** *roshe*; (Dt 32:32), apparently the same as 7218; a poisonous *plant,* probably the *poppy* (from its conspicuous *head*); (generally) *poison* (even of serpents):—gall, hemlock, poison, venom.

7220. רֹאשׁ, **Rô'sh,** *roshe*; probably the same as 7218; *Rosh,* the name of an Israelite and of a foreign nation:—Rosh.

7221. רִאשָׁה, **ri'shâh,** *ree-shaw´*; from the same as 7218; a *beginning*:—beginning.

A feminine noun meaning a beginning. Ezekiel used the word to denote an earlier time (Eze 36:11). He spoke figuratively, saying that the Lord would make the mountains of Israel more prosperous than before. The Lord would also increase the number of people and animals, who would in turn be fruitful and multiply.

7222. רֹאשָׁה, **rô'shâh,** *ro-shaw´*; feminine of 7218; the *head*:—head [-stone].

An adjective meaning head, chief. It occurs only in Zec 4:7 where it describes a stone. The adjective sometimes indicates that the stone is the cornerstone, the first stone laid (see *rô'sh* [7218]). However, it often refers to the top stone as being at a prominent place on the Temple structure (cf. Mt 4:5), like the head is atop the body. The latter makes better sense in context because the foundation was already laid at the time of the prophecies that use this word (cf. Ezr 5; Zec 1:1; 4:9). The stone may be the same stone mentioned in Zec 3:9 and 4:10, which is clearly a symbol of Christ (cf. Zec 4:10; Rev 5:6). It would make sense for Jesus, the Alpha and the Omega (Rev 1:8), to be both the first stone (cf. Isa 28:16; 1Pe 2:4–8) and the last stone laid in the Temple.

7223. רִאשׁוֹן, **ri'shôwn,** *ree-shone´*; or רִאשֹׁן, **ri'shôn,** *ree-shone´*; from 7221; *first,* in place, time or rank (as adjective or noun):—ancestor, (that were) before (-time), beginning, eldest, first, fore [-father] (-most), former (thing), of old time, past.

An adjective meaning first, former, foremost, earlier, head, chief. This term occurs 182 times and denotes that which comes first among given items, whether in place, rank, or order (Ge 25:25, 32:17[18]; 2Ki 1:14) or (more frequently) in time. Moses had the tabernacle set up in the first month, just as the Lord commanded (Ex 40:2, 17; cf. Nu 9:5; Ezr 7:9; Eze 45:18, 21). Zechariah warned the exiles who returned to the Promised Land from the Babylonian captivity not to be like their ancestors who refused to listen to the former prophets (Zec 1:4, 7:7, 12). The Lord declares Himself to be the first and the last, the Eternal One (Isa 44:6, 48:12). In later Hebrew, the word came to signify the highest in rank or authority (i.e. chief, head). The archangel Michael is portrayed as holding the rank of chief prince (Da 10:13; cf. 1Ch 18:17; Est 1:14). This word is derived from the noun *rô'sh* (7218).

7224. רִאשֹׁנִי, **ri'shônîy,** *ree-sho-nee´*; from 7223; *first*:—first.

An adjective meaning first. The word is derived from the noun *rô'sh* (7218) and corresponds closely in meaning to the adjective *ri'shôwn* (7223). It occurs only in Jer 25:1. The word of the Lord concerning all the people of Judah came to Jeremiah in the first year of King Nebuchadnezzar's reign over all Babylon.

7225. רֵאשִׁית, **rê'shîyth,** *ray-sheeth´*; from the same as 7218; the *first*, in place, time, order or rank (specifically a *firstfruit*):—beginning, chief (-est), first (-fruits, part, time), principal thing.

A noun meaning the beginning, the first, the chief, the best, the firstfruits. Occurring fifty-one times in the OT, this term holds the honour of being the first word written in the entire Bible (Ge 1:1). Often, the term denotes the point in time or space at which something started, except when it specifies the point when time and space themselves were started (Isa 46:10). It conveys the beginning of strife (Pr 17:14); of a ruler's reign (Jer 26:1, 27:1; 28:1; 49:34); of a sin (Mic 1:13); of a kingdom (Ge 10:10); or of wisdom and knowledge (Ps 111:10; Pr 1:7). On other occasions, the term signifies the highest of anything, i.e. the best or most excellent, such as the choicest parts of offerings (1Sa 2:29); the best of the spoil (1Sa 15:21); or the finest in oils (Am 6:6). Elsewhere, the word designates the earliest or first products or results of something. It refers many times to the first products of a harvest (Le 23:10; Dt 18:4; Ne 12:44); and sometimes to the first product, i.e. the firstborn of a father (Ge 49:3; Dt 21:17). Both this term and the noun *rô'sh* (7218) are derived from the same unused verbal root.

7226. רַאֲשֹׁת, **ra'ăshôth,** *rah-ash-ōth´*; from 7218; a *pillow* (being for the *head*):—bolster.

7227. רַב, **rab,** *rab*; by contraction from 7231; *abundant* (in quantity, size, age, number, rank, quality):—(in) abound (-undance, -ant, -antly), captain, elder, enough, exceedingly, full, great (-ly, man, one), increase, long (enough, [time]), (do, have) many (-ifold, things, a time), ([ship-]) master, mighty, more, (too, very) much, multiply (-tude), officer, often [-times], plenteous, populous, prince, process [of time], suffice (-ient).

7228. רַב, **rab,** *rab*; by contraction from 7232; an *archer* [or perhaps the same as 7227]:—archer.

7229. רַב, **rab,** *rab*; (Chaldee); corresponding to 7227:—captain, chief, great, lord, master, stout.

7230. רֹב, **rôb,** *robe*; from 7231; *abundance* (in any respect):—abundance (-antly), all, × common [sort], excellent, great (-ly, -ness, number), huge, be increased, long, many, more in number, most, much, multitude, plenty (-ifully), × very [age].

7231. רָבַב, **râbab,** *raw-bab´*; a primitive root; (properly) to *cast* together [compare 7241], i.e. *increase*, especially in number; also (as denominative from 7233) to *multiply by the myriad*:—increase, be many (-ifold), be more, multiply, ten thousands.

7232. רָבַב, **râbab,** *raw-bab´*; a primitive root [rather identical with 7231 through the idea of *projection*]; to *shoot* an arrow:—shoot.

7233. רְבָבָה, **rᵉbâbâh,** *reb-aw-baw*; from 7231; *abundance* (in number), i.e. (specific) a *myriad* (whether defensive or indefensive):—many, million, × multiply, ten thousand.

7234. רָבַד, **râbad,** *raw-bad´*; a primitive root; to *spread*:—deck.

7235. רָבָה, **râbâh,** *raw-baw´*; a primitive root; to *increase* (in whatever respect):—[bring in] abundance (× -antly), + archer [*by mistake for* 7232], be in authority, bring up, × continue, enlarge, excel, exceeding (-ly), be full of, (be, make) great (-er, -ly, × -ness), grow up, heap, increase, be long, (be, give, have, make, use) many (a time), (any, be, give, give the, have) more (in number), (as, be, be so, gather, over, take, yield) much (greater, more), (make to) multiply, nourish, plenty (-eous), × process [of time], sore, store, thoroughly, very.

7236. רְבָה, **rᵉbâh,** *reb-aw´*; (Chaldee); corresponding to 7235:—make a great man, grow.

7237. רַבָּה, **Rabbâh,** *rab-baw´*; feminine of 7227; *great; Rabbah*, the name of two places in Palestine, East and West:—Rabbah, Rabbath.

7238. רְבוּ, **rᵉbûw,** *reb-oo´*; (Chaldee); from a root corresponding to 7235; *increase* (of dignity):—greatness, majesty.

7239. רִבּוֹ, **ribbôw,** *rib-bo´*; from 7231; or רִבּוֹא, **ribbôw',** *rib-bo´*; from 7231; a *myriad*, i.e. indefensive *large number*:—great things, ten ([eight] -een, [for] -ty, + sixscore, + threescore, × twenty, [twen] -ty) thousand.

7240. רִבּוֹ, **ribbôw,** *rib-bo´*; (Chaldee); corresponding to 7239:—× ten thousand times ten thousand.

7241. רָבִיב, **râbîyb,** *raw-beeb´*; from 7231; a *rain* (as an *accumulation* of drops):—shower.

7242. רָבִיד, **râbîyd,** *raw-beed´*; from 7234; a *collar* (as *spread* around the neck):—chain.

7243. רְבִיעִי, **rᵉbîy'îy,** *reb-ee-ee´*; or רְבִעִי, **rebi'îy,** *reb-ee-ee´*; from 7251; *fourth*; also (fractional) a *fourth*:—four-square, fourth (part).

7244. רְבִיעַי, **rᵉbîy'îy,** *reb-ee-ee´*; (Chaldee); corresponding to 7243:—fourth.

7245. רַבִּית, **Rabbîyth,** *rab-beeth´*; from 7231; *multitude; Rabbith*, a place in Palestine:—Rabbith.

7246. רָבַךְ, **râbak,** *raw-bak´*; a primitive root; to *soak* (bread in oil):—baken, (that which is) fried.

7247. רִבְלָה, **Riblâh,** *rib-law´*; from an unused root meaning to *be fruitful; fertile; Riblah*, a place in Syria:—Riblah.

7248. רַב־מָג, **Rab-Mâg,** *rab-mawg´*; from 7227 and a foreign word for a Magian; *chief Magian; Rab-Mag*, a Babylonian official:—Rab-mag.

7249. רַב־סָרִיס, **Rab-Sârîys,** *rab-saw-reece´*; from 7227 and a foreign word for a eunuch; *chief chamberlain; Rab-Saris*, a Babylonian official:—Rab-saris.

7250. רָבַע, **râba',** *raw-bah´*; a primitive root; to *squat* or *lie* out flat, i.e. (specific) in copulation:—let gender, lie down.

7251. רָבַע, **râba',** *raw-bah´*; a primitive root [rather identical with 7250 through the idea of *sprawling* "at all fours" (or possibly the reverse is the order of derivation); compare 702]; (properly) to *be four* (sided); used only as denominative of 7253; to *be quadrate*:—(four-) square (-d).

7252. רֶבַע, **reba',** *reh´-bah*; from 7250; *prostration* (for sleep):—lying down.

7253. רֶבַע, **reba',** *reh´-bah*; from 7251; a *fourth* (part or side):—fourth part, side, square.

7254. רֶבַע, **Reba',** *reh´-bah*; the same as 7253; *Reba*, a Midianite:—Reba.

7255. רֹבַע, **rôba',** *ro´-bah*; from 7251; a *quarter*:—fourth part.

7256. רִבֵּעַ, **ribbêa',** *rib-bay´-ah*; from 7251; a descendant of the *fourth* generation, i.e. *great great grandchild*:—fourth.

7257. רָבַץ, **râbats,** *raw-bats´*; a primitive root; to *crouch* (on all four legs folded, like a recumbent animal); (by implication) to *recline, repose, brood, lurk, imbed*:—crouch (down), fall down, make a fold, lay, (cause to, make to) lie (down), make to rest, sit.

7258. רֵבֶץ, **rêbets,** *reh´-bets*; from 7257; a *couch* or place of repose:—where each lay, lie down in, resting place.

7259. רִבְקָה, **Ribqâh,** *rib-kaw´*; from an unused root probably meaning to *clog* by tying up the fetlock; *fettering* (by beauty); *Ribkah*, the wife of Isaac:—Rebekah.

7260. רַבְרַב, **rabrab,** *rab-rab´*; (Chaldee); from 7229; *huge* (in size); *domineering* (in character):—(very) great (things).

7261. **רַבְרְבָן, rabr^e^bân,** *rab-reb-awn´*; (Chaldee); from 7260; a *magnate*:—lord, prince.

An Aramaic masculine noun meaning a noble, a lord. The term occurs only in the plural and is found only in the book of Daniel. Nebuchadnezzar and Belshazzar, both kings of Babylon at one point, were served and sought by a great host of these important officials (Da 4:36[33]; 5:1–3, 9, 10, 23; 6:17[18]).

7262. **רַבְשָׁקֵה, Rabshâqêh,** *rab-shaw-kay´*; from 7227 and 8248; *chief butler; Rabshakeh*, a Babylonian official:—Rabshakeh.

7263. **רֶגֶב, regeb,** *reh´-gheb*; from an unused root meaning to *pile* together; a *lump* of clay:—clod.

7264. **רָגַז, râgaz,** *raw-gaz´*; a primitive root; to *quiver* (with any violent emotion, especially anger or fear):—be afraid, stand in awe, disquiet, fall out, fret, move, provoke, quake, rage, shake, tremble, trouble, be wroth.

A verb meaning to shake, to tremble, to agitate, to disturb, to rouse up, to rage, to provoke. This term occurs forty-one times in the OT and is utilized most often to express the idea of the physical moving or shaking of someone or something. Lands (1Sa 14:15; Am 8:8); mountains (Ps 18:7[8]; Isa 5:25); the heavens (2Sa 22:8); kingdoms (Isa 23:11); and even the whole earth (Joel 2:10) are described as being shaken in this way, with the Lord's anger often given as the basis for the quaking. Often people, whether groups or individuals, would shake, i.e. were moved or stirred by deep emotions in response to specific circumstances. They trembled in fear (Ex 15:14; Dt 2:25; Isa 64:2[1]; Joel 2:1; Mic 7:17); or shook in agitation or anger (Pr 29:9; Eze 16:43); and even grief (2Sa 18:33[19:1]). Sometimes the word signifies the disturbing or rousing up of someone (1Sa 28:15; 2Sa 7:10; 1Ch 17:9). Occasionally, it conveys the act of rebelling or raging against another, literally, to shake oneself against someone (cf. 2Ki 19:27, 28; Isa 37:28, 29). This verb is related to the verbs *râga'* and *râgash* (7283). The noun *rôgez* (7267) is directly derived from it.

7265. **רְגַז, r^e^gaz,** *reg-az´*; (Chaldee); corresponding to 7264:—provoke unto wrath.

An Aramaic verb meaning to provoke, to anger. The term occurs only once in the entire OT. In a report written to King Darius, the elders of the Jews were quoted as conceding to the fact that the Babylonian exile and destruction of Solomon's Temple (ca. 586 B.C.) took place because their ancestors had angered the God of heaven (Ezr 5:12). This verb corresponds to the Hebrew verb *râgaz* (7264).

7266. **רְגַז, r^e^gaz,** *reg-az´*; (Chaldee); from 7265; violent *anger*:—rage.

An Aramaic masculine noun meaning violent anger, rage. The term occurs only once in the entire OT. When King Nebuchadnezzar heard that three Jews—Shadrach, Meshach, and Abednego—refused to worship the image of gold that he had erected, he flew into a rage (Da 3:13). This term is derived from the Aramaic verb *rĕgaz* (7265) and is related to the Hebrew noun *rôgez* (7267).

7267. **רֹגֶז, rôgez,** *ro´-ghez*; from 7264; *commotion, restlessness* (of a horse), *crash* (of thunder), *disquiet, anger*:—fear, noise, rage, trouble (-ing), wrath.

A masculine noun meaning commotion, raging, excitement. The primary meaning of this word is a state of agitation or uproar. It denotes the tumult that comes from fear (Isa 14:3); the fury of the Lord's judgment (Hab 3:2); a general state of upheaval (Job 3:26); and the chaos of ordinary life in this world (Job 14:1).

7268. **רַגָּז, raggâz,** *rag-gawz´*; intensive from 7264; *timid*:—trembling.

An adjective meaning trembling, shaking. Deuteronomy 28:65 records the sole occurrence of this word. It describes a fainting heart that is full of unease.

7269. **רָגְזָה, rogzâh,** *rog-zaw´*; feminine of 7267; *trepidation*:—trembling.

A feminine noun meaning a trembling, a quaking. In Eze 12:18, this word is used to imply a trembling or quivering hand. The suggestion is that of tremendous worry or unsteadiness even during routine activities.

7270. **רָגַל, râgal,** *raw-gal´*; a primitive root; to *walk* along; but only in specific applications, to *reconnoitre*, to *be a tale-bearer* (i.e. slander); also (as denominative from 7272) to *lead about*:—backbite, search, slander, (e-) spy (out), teach to go, view.

7271. **רְגַל, r^e^gal,** *reg-al´*; (Chaldee); corresponding to 7272:—foot.

7272. **רֶגֶל, regel,** *reh´-gel*; from 7270; a *foot* (as used in *walking*); (by implication) a *step*; (by euphemism) the *pudenda*:— × be able to endure, × according as, × after, × coming, × follow, ([broken-]) foot ([-ed, -stool]), × great toe, × haunt, × journey, leg, + piss, + possession, time.

7273. **רַגְלִי, raglîy,** *rag-lee´*; from 7272; a *footman* (soldier):—(on) foot (-man).

7274. **רֹגְלִים, Rôg^e^lîym,** *ro-gel-eem´*; plural of active participle of 7270; *fullers* (as *tramping* the cloth in washing); *Rogelim*, a place East of the Jordan:—Rogelim.

7275. **רָגַם, râgam,** *raw-gam´*; a primitive root [compare 7263, 7321, 7551]; to *cast* together (stones), i.e. to *lapidate*:— × certainly, stone.

7276. **רֶגֶם, Regem,** *reh´-gem*; from 7275; stone-*heap; Regem*, an Israelite:—Regem.

7277. **רִגְמָה, rigmâh,** *rig-maw´*; feminine of the same as 7276; a *pile* (of stones), i.e. (figurative) a *throng*:—council.

7278. **רֶגֶם מֶלֶךְ, Regem Melek,** *reh´-gem meh´-lek*; from 7276 and 4428; *king's heap; Regem-Melek*, an Israelite:—Regem-melech.

7279. **רָגַן, râgan,** *raw-gan´*; a primitive root; to *grumble*, i.e. *rebel*:—murmur.

7280. **רָגַע, râga',** *raw-gah´*; a primitive root; (properly) to *toss* violently and suddenly (the sea with waves, the skin with boils); figurative (in a favourable manner) to *settle*, i.e. quiet; (specifically) to *wink* (from the motion of the eyelids):—break, divide, find ease, be a moment, (cause, give, make to) rest, make suddenly.

7281. **רֶגַע, rega',** *reh´-gah*; from 7280; a *wink* (of the eyes), i.e. a very *short space* of time:—instant, moment, space, suddenly.

7282. **רָגֵעַ, râgêa',** *raw-gay´-ah*; from 7280; *restful*, i.e. peaceable:—that are quiet.

7283. **רָגַשׁ, râgash,** *raw-gash´*; a primitive root; to *be tumultuous*:—rage.

A verb meaning to be in commotion, to rage against. This word appears only in Ps 2:1 where it denotes the uproar and plotting of the wicked against the righteous. The image of a gathering lynch mob conveys well the action suggested here.

7284. **רְגַשׁ, r^e^gash,** *reg-ash´*; (Chaldee); corresponding to 7283; to *gather* tumultuously:—assemble (together).

An Aramaic verb meaning to assemble in a throng, to be turbulent, to be in tumult. Occurring only in Daniel, this word describes the gathering of the men who conspired against the prophet (Da 6:6[7], 11[12], 15[16]).

7285. **רֶגֶשׁ, regesh,** *reh´-ghesh*; or (feminine) **רִגְשָׁה, rigshâh,** *rig-shaw´*; from 7283; a tumultuous *crowd*:—company, insurrection.

A noun meaning a crowd, a company, an insurrection. The basic meaning of this word is that of a thronging mass of people. The word refers to worshippers going to the Temple in a large group (Ps 55:14 [15]); and the riotous scheming that could result from a large gathering of people whose minds were not directed toward God (Ps 64:2[3]).

7286. **רָדַד, râdad,** *raw-dad´*; a primitive root; to *tread* in pieces, i.e. (figurative) to *conquer*, or (specific) to *overlay*:—spend, spread, subdue.

7287. **רָדָה, râdâh,** *raw-daw´*; a primitive root; to *tread* down, i.e. *subjugate*; (specifically) to *crumble* off:—(come to, make to) have dominion, prevail against, reign, (bear, make to) rule (-r, over), take.

A verb meaning to rule, to have dominion, to subjugate. This Hebrew word conveys the notion of exercising domain, whether legitimate or not, over those who are powerless or otherwise under one's control. It is related as the exercise of authority by the priesthood (Jer 5:31); by slave owners over their slaves (Le 25:43); by supervisors over their workers (1Ki 9:23); and by a king over his kingdom (1Ki 4:24[5:4]). Theologically significant is the use of this word to identify people's God-ordained relationship to the created world around them (Ge 1:26, 28).

7288. רַדַּי**, Radday,** *rad-dah´ee*; intensive from 7287; *domineering; Raddai*, an Israelite:—Raddai.

7289. רָדִיד**, râdîyd,** *raw-deed´*; from 7286 in the sense of *spreading*; a *veil* (as expanded):—vail, veil.

7290. רָדַם**, râdam,** *raw-dam´*; a primitive root; to *stun*, i.e. *stupefy* (with sleep or death):—(be fast a-, be in a deep, cast into a dead, that) sleep (-er, -eth).

7291. רָדַף**, râdaph,** *raw-daf´*; a primitive root; to *run after* (usually with hostile intent; figurative [of time] *gone by*):—chase, put to flight, follow (after, on), hunt, (be under) persecute (-ion, -or), pursue (-r).

7292. רָהַב**, râhab,** *raw-hab´*; a primitive root; to *urge* severely, i.e. (figurative) *importune, embolden, capture, act insolently*:—overcome, behave self proudly, make sure, strengthen.

7293. רַהַב**, rahab,** *rah´-hab*; from 7292; *bluster* (-*er*):—proud, strength.

7294. רַהַב**, Rahab,** *rah´-hab*; the same as 7293; *Rahab* (i.e. *boaster*), an epithet of Egypt:—Rahab.

7295. רָהָב**, râhâb,** *raw-hawb´*; from 7292; *insolent*:—proud.

7296. רֹהַב**, rôhab,** *ro´-hab*; from 7292; *pride*:—strength.

7297. רָהָה**, râhâh,** *raw-haw´*; a primitive root; to *fear*:—be afraid.

A verb meaning to be afraid, to fear. Occurring only in Isa 44:8, this word implies a fear that stems from uncertainty or a sense of being utterly alone. In the text, the Lord offered His assurance that He was still living and was in control of all situations.

7298. רַהַט**, rahaṭ,** *rah´-hat*; from an unused root apparently meaning to *hollow out*; a *channel* or watering-box; by resemblance a *ringlet* of hair (as forming parallel lines):—gallery, gutter, trough.

7299. רֵו**, rêv,** *rave*; (Chaldee); from a root corresponding to 7200; *aspect*:—form.

7300. רוּד**, rûwd,** *rood*; a primitive root; to *tramp* about, i.e. *ramble* (free or disconsolate):—have the dominion, be lord, mourn, rule.

A verb meaning to wander restlessly, to roam. Hosea uses the verb figuratively to refer to Judah's restlessness, that is, their lack of obedience to God (Hos 11:12[12:1]). The Lord uses the verb in Jeremiah to ask why His people felt they were free to roam (Jer 2:31). Esau, after Jacob deceived Isaac, was doomed to live by the sword and serve his brother. However, there would come a time when he would become restless and throw off his yoke (Ge 27:40).

7301. רָוָה**, râvâh,** *raw-vaw´*; a primitive root; to *slake* the thirst (occasionally of other appetites):—bathe, make drunk, (take the) fill, satiate, (abundantly) satisfy, soak, water (abundantly).

7302. רָוֶה**, râveh,** *raw-veh´*; from 7301; *sated* (with drink):—drunkenness, watered.

7303. רוֹהֲגָה**, Rôwhăgâh,** *ro-hag-aw´*; from an unused root probably meaning to *cry* out; *outcry; Rohagah*, an Israelite:—Rohgah.

7304. רָוַח**, râvach,** *raw-vakh´*; a primitive root [rather identical with 7306]; (properly) to *breathe* freely, i.e. *revive*; (by implication) to *have ample room*:—be refreshed, large.

A verb meaning to breathe freely, to be spacious, to smell. The primary meaning is to breathe freely by means of being spacious or revived. This word is used to indicate a relief that comes to a troubled mind or spirit (1Sa 16:23; Job 32:20). Shallem, son of Josiah, stated that he would build a great palace with spacious upper rooms (Jer 22:14). *Râwah* was also used to dictate the smelling of aromas of both the burnt offering and incense (see Ge 8:21; Ex 30:38). In Genesis, the burnt offerings had a pleasing aroma to God, which in turn prompted Him to state His covenant. In Exodus, the people were warned against making the special mixture of incense (meant only for the use of an incense offering to God) simply to enjoy its aroma. The punishment for disobeying this command was to be cut off from one's own people.

7305. רֶוַח**, revach,** *reh´-vakh*; from 7304; *room*, literal (an *interval*) or figurative (*deliverance*):—enlargement, space.

A masculine noun meaning a space, an interval, a respite, a relief, a liberation. In Genesis, the word is used in Jacob's command to keep a space between the herds that were given as gifts to his brother Esau (Ge 32:16[17]). This space gave Jacob more time to prepare, looked more impressive to the receiver (i.e. controlled herds), and gave a better impression of the size or amount of the gift. In Esther, Mordecai indicated that if Esther kept silent, then relief for the Jews would arise from another place, and she and her father's family would die (Est 4:14).

7306. רוּחַ**, rûwach,** *roo´-akh*; a primitive root; (properly) to *blow*, i.e. *breathe*; only (literal) to *smell*;(by implication) to *perceive;* (figurative) to *anticipate, enjoy*:—accept, smell, × touch, make of quick understanding.

A verb meaning to feel relief, to be spacious, to smell. This verb is used rarely in the Hebrew Bible. In the simple stem, it occurs twice meaning to gain or feel relief. When David played the harp, Saul found relief (1Sa 16:23); the verbose Elihu had to speak in order to get relief from his anxiety (Job 32:20). In its single use in the passive intensive stem, it means roomy or spacious. The vain King Shallum proposed to build himself a palace with spacious, roomy, upper chambers (Jer 22:14).

The verb is used most often in the causative stem to mean to smell. Gods of wood cannot smell (Dt 4:28); nor can idols of gold or silver (Ps 115:6). Isaac smelled the clothes that Jacob wore to deceive him (Ge 27:27). In 1Sa 26:19, however, the verb refers to God being pleased by the aroma of an offering (Ge 8:21; Le 26:31). The verb evidently means to be burned with in Jgs 16:9, for the ropes holding Samson snapped as when they sensed (i.e. were burned) with fire. The Shoot of Jesse, the Branch, will respond (i.e. be sensitive) to the fear of the Lord (Isa 11:1, 2).

7307. רוּחַ**, rûwach,** *roo´-akh*; from 7306; *wind*; (by resemblance) *breath*, i.e. a sensible (or even violent) exhalation; (figurative) *life, anger, unsubstantiality*; (by extension) a *region* of the sky; (by resemblance) *spirit*, but only of a rational being (including its expression and functions):—air, anger, blast, breath, × cool, courage, mind, × quarter, × side, spirit ([-ual]), tempest, × vain, ([whirl-]) wind (-y).

A feminine noun meaning spirit, wind, breath. The word is used to refer to the Spirit of God or the Lord. The Spirit of the Lord inspired prophets to utter their prophecies (Nu 11:17, 25; 1Sa 10:6; 19:20); the Spirit of the Lord moved the prophets in time and space, as in the case of Elijah (1Ki 18:12; Eze 2:2). The word could be modified by an adjective to refer to an evil spirit from the Lord (1Sa 16:15, 16; 1Ki 22:22, 23). The Spirit of God is properly referred to as the Holy Spirit (Ps 51:11[13]; 106:33; Isa 63:10, 11). The Spirit produced and controlled the message of the prophets, even of a Mesopotamian prophet like Balaam (Nu 24:2). David was inspired to speak as a prophet by the Spirit (2Sa 23:2). The Spirit was present among the returned exiles in Jerusalem (Hag 2:5; Zec 4:6); and will be poured out in the latter days on all flesh, imparting prophecy, dreams, and visions (Joel 2:28[3:1]). The Spirit of God was grieved by the rebellion of God's people (Isa 63:10).

The Lord's Spirit imparted other gifts: giving Bezalel skill and ability in all kinds of work (Ex 31:3; 35:31); including the skill to teach others (see Ex 35:34); the Spirit gave understanding as well (Job 32:8). The Spirit of the Lord had a part in creating the universe; the Spirit hovered over the deep and imparted life to persons (Ge 1:2; Job 33:4); and even revived the dead (Eze 37:5, 10; 39:29).

The human spirit and the Spirit of God are closely linked with moral character and moral attributes. God will give His people a new spirit so they will follow His decrees and laws (Eze 11:19; 36:26). God's Spirit will rest on His people, transforming them (Isa 59:21). The Lord preserves those who have heavy spirits and broken hearts (Ps 34:18[19]; Isa 65:14).

The human spirit is sometimes depicted as the seat of emotion, the mind, and the will. In a song of praise, Isaiah asserted that the spirit desires the Lord (Isa 26:9; Job 7:11). The spirit imparts wisdom for understanding (Ex 28:3; Dt 34:9); and carrying out one's responsibilities. David prayed for a willing spirit to aid him (Ex 35:21; Ps 51:10[12]).

The spirit made flesh alive and is the life force of living humans and animals. The Lord makes the spirits of people that give them life (Zec 12:1). This spirit is from God and leaves at death (Ge 6:3; Ps 78:39; Ecc 3:21). The spirit is pictured as giving animation, agitation, or liveliness; the Queen of Sheba was overcome in her spirit when she saw the splendors of Solomon's world (1Ki 10:5). Not to have any spirit is to lose all courage; the Amorite kings had no spirit in them when they learned how Israel had crossed the Jordan. To be short of spirit is to be despondent or impatient (Ecc 6:9).

The word also describes the breath of a human being or the natural wind that blows. The idols of the goldsmith have no breath in them; they are inanimate (Jer 10:14; 51:17). Human speech is sometimes only words of wind that mean nothing (Job 16:3). By the gust of his nostrils, the Lord piled up the waters of the Red Sea (Ex 15:8). Often, the word refers to wind or a synonym of wind. The Lord sent a wind over the earth to dry up the floodwaters (Ge 8:1; Ex 15:10; Nu 11:31). Jeremiah spoke of the four winds, referring to the entire earth (Jer 49:36; Eze 37:9). The word is also used to mean wind in the sense of nothing (Ecc 1:14; 2:11; Isa 26:18). The wind, like the Spirit, cannot be caught, tamed, or found (Ecc 2:11).

7308. רוּחַ, rûwach, *roo´-akh*; (Chaldee); corresponding to 7307:—mind, spirit, wind.

An Aramaic noun meaning wind; spirit of a person, mind; spirit divine. All occurrences of the word are located in the book of Daniel. For the Hebrew mind, the term at its heart encapsulated the experience of any mysterious, invisible, awesome, living power. This included such forces as the wind (Da 2:35; 7:2); the active inner being of a person where attitudes, feelings, and intellect resided (Da 5:12, 20; 6:3[4]; 7:15); the divine Spirit that could come down from God and indwell individuals, often giving them supernatural abilities, such as Daniel's ability to interpret dreams (Da 4:8[5], 9[6], 18[15]; 5:11, 14). This term is identical in form and meaning to the Hebrew noun *rûah* (7307).

7309. רְוָחָה, r^evâchâh, *rev-aw-khaw´*; feminine of 7305; *relief*:—breathing, respite.

A feminine noun meaning breathing space, relief, respite. The term occurs only twice in the entire OT and is derived from the verb *râwah* (7304), meaning to breathe, to have breathing room, or to feel relief. In its first occurrence, the word denotes the alleviation that resulted from God's act of terminating the plague of frogs in Egypt (Ex 8:15[11]). The second use of the term involves a desperate cry to the Lord for deliverance and rest from merciless enemies (La 3:56).

7310. רְוָיָה, r^evâyâh, *rev-aw-yaw´*; from 7301; *satisfaction*:—runneth over, wealthy.

7311. רוּם, rûwm, *room*; a primitive root; to *be high;* (active) to *rise* or *raise* (in various applications, literal or figurative):—bring up, exalt (self), extol, give, go up, haughty; heave (up), (be, lift up on, make on, set up on, too) high (-er, one), hold up, levy, lift (-er) up, (be) lofty, (× a-) loud, mount up, offer (up), + presumptuously, (be) promote (-ion), proud, set up, tall (-er), take (away, off, up), breed worms.

7312. רוּם, rûwm, *room*; or **רֻם, rum,** *room*; from 7311; (literal) *elevation* or (figurative) *elation*:—haughtiness, height, × high.

7313. רוּם, rûwm, *room*; (Chaldee); corresponding to 7311; (figurative only):—extol, lift up (self), set up.

7314. רוּם, rûwm, *room*; (Chaldee); from 7313; (literal) *altitude*:—height.

7315. רוֹם, rôwm, *rome*; from 7311; *elevation*, i.e. (adverb) *aloft*:—on high.

7316. רוּמָה, Rûwmâh, *roo-maw´*; from 7311; *height; Rumah*, a place in Palestine:—Rumah.

7317. רוֹמָה, rôwmâh, *ro-maw´*; feminine of 7315; *elation*, i.e. (adverb) *proudly*:—haughtily.

7318. רוֹמָם, rôwmam, *ro-mam´*; from 7426; *exaltation*, i.e. (figurative and specific) *praise*:—be extolled.

7319. רוֹמְמָה, rôwm^emâh, *ro-mem-aw´*; feminine active participle of 7426; *exaltation*, i.e. *praise*:—high.

7320. רוֹמַמְתִּי עֶזֶר, Rôwmamtîy ʽEzer (or **רֹמַמְתִּי Rômamtîy**), *ro-mam´-tee eh´-zer*; from 7311 and 5828; *I have raised* up a *help; Romamti-Ezer*, an Israelite:—Romamti-ezer.

7321. רוּעַ, rûwaʽ, *roo-ah´*; a primitive root; to *mar* (especially by breaking); (figurative) to *split* the ears (with sound), i.e. *shout* (for alarm or joy):—blow an alarm, cry (alarm, aloud, out), destroy, make a joyful noise, smart, shout (for joy), sound an alarm, triumph.

A verb meaning to shout, to sound a blast. The term occurs thirty-three times in the OT and was utilized fundamentally to convey the action of shouting or the making of a loud noise. Shouting often took place just before a people or army rushed into battle against opposition; sometimes the war cry became the very signal used to commence engagement with the enemy (Jos 6:10, 16, 20; Jgs 15:14; 1Sa 4:5; 17:20; 2Ch 13:15). Many times the shout was a cry of joy, often in response to the Lord's creating or delivering activity on behalf of His people (Job 38:7; Ps 47:1[2]; 95:1, 2; Isa 44:23; Zep 3:14; Zec 9:9). In several other instances, the shout expressed triumph and victory over a foe (Ps 41:11[12]; 60:8[10]; 108:9[10]); and occasionally mourning (Isa 15:4; Mic 4:9). A few times, the term denotes the shout of a trumpet (i.e. the blast), usually as a signal to begin battle (Nu 10:9; 2Ch 13:12; cf. Hos 5:8; Joel 2:1).

7322. רוּף, rûwph, *roof*; a primitive root; (properly) to *triturate* (in a mortar), i.e. (figurative) to *agitate* (by concussion):—tremble.

7323. רוּץ, rûwts, *roots*; a primitive root; to *run* (for whatever reason, especially to *rush*):—break down, divide speedily, footman, guard, bring hastily, (make) run (away, through), post.

7324. רוּק, rûwq, *rook*; a primitive root; to *pour* out (literal or figurative), i.e. *empty*:— × arm, cast out, draw (out), (make) empty, pour forth (out).

7325. רוּר, rûwr, *roor*; a primitive root; to *slaver* (with spittle), i.e. (by analogy) to *emit* a fluid (ulcerous or natural):—run.

7326. רוּשׁ, rûwsh, *roosh*; a primitive root; to *be destitute*:—lack, needy, (make self) poor (man).

7327. רוּת, Rûwth, *rooth*; probably for 7468; *friend; Ruth*, a Moabitess:—Ruth.

7328. רָז, râz, *rawz*; (Chaldee); from an unused root probably meaning to *attenuate*, i.e. (figurative) *hide*; a *mystery*:—secret.

7329. רָזָה, râzâh, *raw-zaw´*; a primitive root; to *emaciate*, i.e. *make* (*become*) *thin* (literal or figurative):—famish, wax lean.

7330. רָזֶה, râzeh, *raw-zeh*; from 7329; *thin*:—lean.

7331. רְזוֹן, R^ezôwn, *rez-one´*; from 7336; *prince; Rezon*, a Syrian:—Rezon.

7332. רָזוֹן, râzôwn, *raw-zone´*; from 7329; *thinness*:—leanness, × scant.

7333. רָזוֹן, râzôwn, *raw-zone´*; from 7336; a *dignitary*:—prince.

A masculine noun meaning a dignitary, a ruler, a prince. The term occurs once in the entire OT in Pr 14:28 and is synonymous with the noun *melek* (4428), meaning king. The proverb states that what makes or breaks a prince is whether or not he has a multitude of subjects to rule over. The term is derived from the verb *râzan* (7336).

7334. רָזִי, **râzîy,** *raw-zee´*; from 7329; *thinness*:—leanness.

7335. רָזַם, **râzam,** *raw-zam´*; a primitive root; to *twinkle* the eye (in mockery):—wink.

7336. רָזַן, **râzan,** *raw-zan´*; a primitive root; probably to be *heavy*, i.e. (figurative) *honourable*:—prince, ruler.

A verb meaning to be heavy, to be weighty, to be honoured, to be mighty. The term also occurs six times as a noun, meaning rulers. Five times the word is used in conjunction with the Hebrew word for king (*melek* [4428]; Jgs 5:3; Ps 2:2; Pr 8:15; 31:4; Hab 1:10); and once with judge (a participle of the verb *shâphat*[8199]; Isa 40:23). Rulers were summoned to listen to Deborah's victory song (Jgs 5:3); warned to not conspire against the Lord and His anointed one (Ps 2:2); enabled by wisdom to decree just laws (Pr 8:15); abstained from strong drink (Pr 31:4); and were made as nothing by the Lord (Isa 40:23). The noun *râzôwn* (7333) is derived from this verb; also see the verb *kâbêd* (3513).

7337. רָחַב, **râchab,** *raw-khab´*; a primitive root; to *broaden* (intransitive or transitive, literal or figurative):—be an en-(make) large (-ing), make room, make (open) wide.

7338. רַחַב, **rachab,** *rakh´-ab*; from 7337; a *width*:—breadth, broad place.

7339. רְחֹב, **rᵉchôb,** *rekh-obe´*; or רְחוֹב, **rᵉchôwb,** *rekh-obe´*; from 7337; a *width*, i.e. (concrete) *avenue* or *area*:—broad place (way), street. See also 1050.

7340. רְחֹב, **Rᵉchôb,** *rekh-obe´*; or רְחוֹב, **Rᵉchôwb,** *rekh-obe´*; the same as 7339; *Rechob*, the name of a place in Syria, also of a Syrian and an Israelite:—Rehob.

7341. רֹחַב, **rôchab,** *ro´-khab*; from 7337; *width* (literal or figurative):—breadth, broad, largeness, thickness, wideness.

7342. רָחָב, **râchâb,** *raw-khawb´*; from 7337; *roomy*, in any (or every) direction, literal or figurative:—broad, large, at liberty, proud, wide.

7343. רָחָב, **Râchâb,** *raw-khawb´*; the same as 7342; *proud; Rachab*, a Canaanitess:—Rahab.

7344. רְחֹבוֹת, **Rᵉchôbôwth,** *rekh-o-bōth´*; or רְחֹבֹת, **Rechôbôth,** *rekh-o-bōth´*; plural of 7339; *streets; Rechoboth*, a place in Assyria and one in Palestine:—Rehoboth.

7345. רְחַבְיָה, **Rᵉchabyâh,** *rekh-ab-yaw´*; or רְחַבְיָהוּ, **Rechabyâhûw,** *rekh-ab-yaw´-hoo*; from 7337 and 3050; *Jah has enlarged; Rechabjah*, an Israelite:—Rehabiah.

7346. רְחַבְעָם, **Rᵉchab'âm,** *rekh-ab-awm´*; from 7337 and 5971; *a people has enlarged; Rechabam*, an Israelite king:—Rehoboam.

7347. רֵחֶה, **rêcheh,** *ray-kheh´*; from an unused root meaning to *pulverize*; a *mill*-stone:—mill (stone).

7348. רְחוּם, **Rᵉchûwm,** *rekh-oom´*; a form of 7349; *Rechum*, the name of a Persian and of three Israelites:—Rehum.

7349. רַחוּם, **rachûwm,** *rakh-oom´*; from 7355; *compassionate*:—full of compassion, merciful.

7350. רָחוֹק, **râchôwq,** *raw-khoke´*; or רָחֹק, **râchôq,** *raw-khoke´*; from 7368; *remote*, literal or figurative, of place or time; (specifically) *precious*; often used adverb (with preposition):—(a-) far (abroad, off), long ago, of old, space, great while to come.

7351. רְחִיט, **râchîyṭ,** *rekh-eet´*; from the same as 7298; a *panel* (as resembling a *trough*):—rafter.

7352. רַחִיק, **rachîyq,** *rakh-eek´*; (Chaldee); corresponding to 7350:—far.

7353. רָחֵל, **râchêl,** *raw-khale´*; from an unused root meaning to *journey*; a *ewe* [the *females* being the predominant element of a flock] (as a good *traveller*):—ewe, sheep.

7354. רָחֵל, **Râchêl,** *raw-khale´*; the same as 7353; *Rachel*, a wife of Jacob:—Rachel.

7355. רָחַם, **râcham,** *raw-kham´*; a primitive root; to *fondle*; (by implication) to *love*, especially to *compassionate*:—have compassion (on, upon), love, (find, have, obtain, shew) mercy (-iful, on, upon), (have) pity, Ruhamah, × surely.

A verb meaning to have compassion, to have mercy, to find mercy. The word pictures a deep, kindly sympathy and sorrow felt for another who has been struck with affliction or misfortune, accompanied with a desire to relieve the suffering. The word occurs forty-seven times in the OT, with God being by far the most common subject and His afflicted people the object (Dt 13:17[18]; 2Ki 13:23; Isa 14:1; 30:18; 60:10; Jer 12:15; 31:20; La 3:32). Though the Lord showed compassion, it was not because of any meritorious work the recipient had done; it was solely due to God's sovereign freedom to bestow it on whom He chose (Ex 33:19; cf. Ro 9:14–16). Two types of people God has sovereignly chosen to have mercy on include those who fear Him (Ps 103:13); and those who confess and forsake their sin (Pr 28:13).

7356. רַחַם, **racham,** *rakh´-am*; from 7355; *compassion* (in the plural); (by extension) the *womb* (as *cherishing* the fetus); (by implication) a *maiden*:—bowels, compassion, damsel, tender love, (great, tender) mercy, pity, womb.

A feminine noun meaning womb, compassion, mercy, affection, maiden. The singular form of this word always signified the physical womb of a woman and was commonly used in this way (Ge 49:25). Yet when the plural form was used, the author had in mind the idea of compassion, tenderness, or mercy. The OT authors thought of the womb or bowels as the seat of warm and tender emotions. For example, when Joseph saw his brother Benjamin, he became overwhelmed with tender affection (lit., wombs [Ge 43:30]). Through the prophet Zechariah, the Lord commanded His people to show compassion to one another (Zec 7:9; cf. Dt 13:17 [18]; Ps 25:6; 103:4; Isa 47:6).

7357. רַחַם, **Racham,** *rakh´-am*; the same as 7356; *pity; Racham*, an Israelite:—Raham.

7358. רֶחֶם, **rechem,** *rekh´-em*; from 7355; the *womb* [compare 7356]:—matrix, womb.

7359. רַחֲמִין, **rachămîyn,** *ra-kha-meen´*; (Chaldee); corresponding to 7356; (plural) *pity*:—mercy.

7360. רָחָם, **râchâm,** *raw-khawm´*; or (feminine) רָחָמָה, **râchâmâh,** *raw-khaw-maw´*; from 7355; a kind of *vulture* (supposed to be *tender* toward its young):—gier-eagle.

7361. רַחֲמָה, **rachămâh,** *rakh-am-aw´*; feminine of 7356; a *maiden*:—damsel.

7362. רַחְמָנִי, **rachmânîy,** *rakh-maw-nee´*; from 7355; *compassionate*:—pitiful.

7363. רָחַף, **râchaph,** *raw-khaf´*; a primitive root; to *brood*; (by implication) to *be relaxed*:—flutter, move, shake.

7364. רָחַץ, **râchats,** *raw-khats´*; a primitive root; to *lave* (the whole or a part of a thing):—bathe (self), wash (self).

A verb meaning to wash off, to wash away, to bathe. This Hebrew word carries the connotation of washing with water in order to make clean. It describes the action involved in washing the hands or feet (Ex 30:19); the face (Ge 43:31); the body (2Sa 11:2); clothes (Le 14:9); or the parts of a sacrificial offering (Le 1:9). Symbolically, such a washing was declarative of innocence (Dt 21:6); and was figurative of cleansing from sin (Pr 30:12; Isa 4:4).

7365. רְחַץ, **rᵉchats,** *rekh-ats´*; (Chaldee); corresponding to 7364 [probably through the accessory idea of *ministering* as a servant at the bath]; to *attend* upon:—trust.

7366. רַחַץ, **rachats,** *rakh´-ats*; from 7364; a *bath*:—wash[-pot].

A masculine noun meaning washing. This word appears twice where it refers to a washing pot (Ps 60:8[10]; 108:9[10]). In both instances, it was a term of derision and was meant to convey a sense of utter contempt.

7367. רַחְצָה, **rachtsâh,** *rakh-tsaw´*; feminine of 7366; a *bathing* place:—washing.

A feminine noun meaning washing. The primary meaning of this word is found in its two uses in the SS of Solomon. Both times it referred to the bathing of sheep in water that caused them to be clean and white (SS 4:2; 6:6).

7368. רָחַק, **râchaq,** *raw-khak´*; a primitive root; to *widen* (in any direction), i.e. (intransitive) *recede* or (transitive) *remove* (literal or figurative, of place or relation):—(a-, be, cast, drive, get, go, keep [self], put, remove, be too, [wander], withdraw) far (away, off), loose, × refrain, very, (be) a good way (off).

7369. רָחֵק, **râchêq,** *raw-khake´*; from 7368; *remote*:—that are far.

7370. רָחַשׁ, **râchash,** *raw-khash´*; a primitive root; to *gush*:—indite.

7371. רַחַת, **rachath,** *rakh´-ath*; from 7306; a *winnowing*-fork (as *blowing* the chaff away):—shovel.

7372. רָטַב, **râṭab,** *raw-tab´*; a primitive root; to *be moist*:—be wet.

7373. רָטֹב, **râṭôb,** *raw-tobe´*; from 7372; *moist* (with sap):—green.

7374. רֶטֶט, **reṭeṭ,** *reh´-tet*; from an unused root meaning to *tremble; terror*:—fear.

A masculine noun meaning fear, trembling, panic. From an unused root meaning to tremble, this word is found only in Jer 49:24. It denoted fear or hysteria in the face of impending attack.

7375. רֻטֲפַשׁ, **ruṭăphash,** *roo-taf-ash´*; a root compounded from 7373 and 2954; to *be rejuvenated*:—be fresh.

7376. רָטַשׁ, **râṭash,** *raw-tash´*; a primitive root; to *dash* down:—dash (in pieces).

7377. רִי, **rîy,** *ree*; from 7301; *irrigation*, i.e. a shower:—watering.

7378. רִיב, **rîyb,** *reeb*; or רוּב, **rûwb,** *roob*; a primitive root; (properly) to *toss*, i.e. *grapple*; (mostly figurative) to *wrangle*, i.e. *hold a controversy*; (by implication) to *defend*:—adversary, chide, complain, contend, debate, × ever, × lay wait, plead, rebuke, strive, × thoroughly.

A verb meaning to strive, to contend, to dispute, and to conduct a lawsuit. The verb means to conduct a lawsuit or legal case and all that it involves. The Lord conducts His case against the leaders of His people (Isa 3:13). He relents in His case from accusing humankind, knowing how weak they are (Isa 57:16). David pleaded with the Lord to give him vindication in his case (1Sa 24:15[16]); as did Israel when God contended for them (Mic 7:9).

The word means to contend or to strive for some reason in a nonlegal setting as well. The servants of Isaac and Abimelech contended over wells they had dug or claimed to own (Ge 26:21). Two men could quarrel and come to blows (Ex 21:18; Jgs 11:25). Jacob and Laban disputed with one another (Ge 31:36). The people of Israel complained bitterly against the Lord at Meribah (Nu 20:13).

The word means to raise complaints or accusations against others. The tribes of Israel complained because some of their women were taken and given as wives to the Benjamites (Jgs 21:22). An arrogant Israel would dare to bring charges against the Lord (Isa 45:9; Jer 2:29; 12:1). The tribe of Levi contended with the Lord at Meribah as well (Dt 33:8; cf. Nu 20:13).

The causative stem of this verb means to bring a case against (i.e. to oppose). The Lord will judge those who oppose Him (1Sa 2:10).

7379. רִיב, **rîyb,** *reeb*; or רִב, **rib,** *reeb*; from 7378; a *contest* (personal or legal):— + adversary, cause, chiding, contend (-tion), controversy, multitude [*from the margin*], pleading, strife, strive (-ing), suit.

A masculine noun meaning a strife, a controversy, a contention. The primary idea of this noun is that of a quarrel or dispute. It appears in reference to an argument over land-use rights (Ge 13:7); the logical dispute the Lord has with sinners (Jer 25:31); any general state of contention between individuals (Pr 20:3); the clamouring of people for station or possessions (2Sa 22:44); and open hostilities with an enemy (Jgs 12:2). Israel is commanded not to pervert justice in a lawsuit (Ex 23:2). Similarly, the word is used in a legal sense to refer to an argument or case made in one's defense (Dt 21:5; Pr 18:17; Mic 7:9).

7380. רִיבַי, **Rîybay,** *ree-bah´ee*; from 7378; *contentious; Ribai*, an Israelite:—Ribai.

7381. רֵיחַ, **rêyach,** *ray´-akh*; from 7306; *odor* (as if *blown*):—savour, scent, smell.

7382. רֵיחַ, **rêyach,** *ray´-akh*; (Chaldee); corresponding to 7381:—smell.

7383. רִיפָה, **rîyphâh,** *ree-faw´*; or רִפָה, **riphâh,** *ree-faw´*; from 7322; (only plural), *grits* (as *pounded*):—ground corn, wheat.

7384. רִיפַת, **Rîyphath,** *ree-fath´*; or (probably by orthographic error) דִּיפַת, **Dîyphath,** *dee-fath´*; of foreign origin; *Riphath*, a grandson of Japheth and his descendant:—Riphath.

7385. רִיק, **rîyq,** *reek*; from 7324; *emptiness*; (figurative) a *worthless* thing; (adverbial) *in vain*:—empty, to no purpose, (in) vain (thing), vanity.

7386. רֵיק, **rêyq,** *rake*; or (shorter) רֵק, **rêq,** *rake*; from 7324; *empty*; (figurative) *worthless*:—emptied (-ty), vain (fellow, man).

7387. רֵיקָם, **rêyqâm,** *ray-kawm´*; from 7386; *emptily*; figurative (objective) *ineffectually*, (subjective) *undeservedly*:—without cause, empty, in vain, void.

7388. רִיר, **rîyr,** *reer*; from 7325; *saliva*; (by resemblance) *broth*:—spittle, white [of an egg].

7389. רֵישׁ, **rêysh,** *raysh*; or רֵאשׁ, **rê'sh,** *raysh*; or רִישׁ, **rîysh,** *reesh*; from 7326; *poverty*:—poverty.

7390. רַךְ, **rak,** *rak*; from 7401; *tender* (literal or figurative); (by implication) *weak*:—faint [-hearted], soft, tender ([-hearted], one), weak.

7391. רֹךְ, **rôk,** *roke*; from 7401; *softness* (figurative):—tenderness.

7392. רָכַב, **râkab,** *raw-kab´*; a primitive root; to *ride* (on an animal or in a vehicle); (causative) to *place upon* (for riding or general), to *despatch*:—bring (on [horse-] back), carry, get [oneself] up, on [horse-] back, put, (cause to, make to) ride (in a chariot, on, -r), set.

7393. רֶכֶב, **rekeb,** *reh´-keb*; from 7392; a *vehicle*; (by implication) a *team*; (by extension) *cavalry*; (by analogy) a *rider*, i.e. the upper millstone:—chariot, (upper) millstone, multitude [*from the margin*], wagon.

7394. רֵכָב, **Rêkâb,** *ray-kawb´*; from 7392; *rider; Rekab*, the name of two Arabs and of two Israelites:—Rechab.

7395. רַכָּב, **rakkâb,** *rak-kawb´*; from 7392; a *charioteer*:—chariot man, driver of a chariot, horseman.

7396. רִכְבָּה, **rikbâh,** *rik-baw´*; feminine of 7393; a *chariot* (collective):—chariots.

7397. רֵכָה, **Rêkâh,** *ray-kaw´*; probably feminine from 7401; *softness; Rekah*, a place in Palestine:—Rechah.

7398. רְכוּב, **r^{e}kûwb,** *rek-oob´*; from passive participle of 7392; a *vehicle* (as *ridden* on):—chariot.

7399. רְכוּשׁ, **r^e^kûwsh,** *rek-oosh´*; or רְכֻשׁ, **r^e^kush,** *rek-oosh´*; from passive participle of 7408; *property* (as *gathered*):—good, riches, substance.

7400. רָכִיל, **râkîyl,** *raw-keel´*; from 7402; a *scandal-monger* (as *travelling* about):—slander, carry tales, talebearer.

7401. רָכַךְ, **râkak,** *raw-kak´*; a primitive root; to *soften* (intransitive or transitive), used figuratively:—(be) faint ([-hearted]), mollify, (be, make) soft (-er), be tender.

7402. רָכַל, **râkal,** *raw-kal´*; a primitive root; to *travel* for trading:—(spice) merchant.

7403. רָכָל, **Râkâl,** *raw-kawl´*; from 7402; *merchant; Rakal,* a place in Palestine:—Rachal.

7404. רְכֻלָּה, **r^e^kullâh,** *rek-ool-law´*; feminine passive participle of 7402; *trade* (as *peddled*):—merchandise, traffic.

7405. רָכַס, **râkas,** *raw-kas´*; a primitive root; to *tie*:—bind.

7406. רֶכֶס, **rekes,** *reh´-kes*; from 7405; a mountain *ridge* (as of *tied* summits):—rough place.

7407. רֹכֶס, **rôkes,** *ro´-kes*; from 7405; a *snare* (as of *tied* meshes):—pride.

7408. רָכַשׁ, **râkash,** *raw-kash´*; a primitive root; to *lay up*, i.e. collect:—gather, get.

7409. רֶכֶשׁ, **rekesh,** *reh´-kesh*; from 7408; a *relay* of animals on a post-route (as *stored* up for that purpose); (by implication) a *courser*:—dromedary, mule, swift beast.

7410. רָם, **Râm,** *rawm*; active participle of 7311; *high; Ram,* the name of an Arabian and of an Israelite:—Ram. See also 1027.

7411. רָמָה, **râmâh,** *raw-maw´*; a primitive root; to *hurl*; (specifically) to *shoot*; (figurative) to *delude* or *betray* (as if causing to fall):—beguile, betray, [bow-] man, carry, deceive, throw.

7412. רְמָה, **r^e^mâh,** *rem-aw´*; (Chaldee); corresponding to 7411; to *throw, set,* (figurative) *assess*:—cast (down), impose.

7413. רָמָה, **râmâh,** *raw-maw´*; feminine active participle of 7311; a *height* (as a seat of idolatry):—high place.

7414. רָמָה, **Râmâh,** *raw-maw´*; the same as 7413; *Ramah,* the name of four places in Palestine:—Ramah.

7415. רִמָּה, **rimmâh,** *rim-maw´*; from 7426 in the sense of *breeding* [compare 7311]; a *maggot* (as rapidly *bred*), literal or figurative:—worm.

7416. רִמּוֹן, **rimmôwn,** *rim-mone´*; or רִמֹּן, **rimmôn,** *rim-mone´*; from 7426; a *pomegranate,* the tree (from its *upright* growth) or the fruit (also an artificial ornament):—pomegranate.

7417. רִמּוֹן, **Rimmôwn,** *rim-mone´*; or (shorter) רִמֹּן, **Rimmôn,** *rim-mone´*; or רִמּוֹנוֹ, **Rimmôwnôw,** *rim-mo-no´*; (1Ch 6:62 [777]), the same as 7416 *Rimmon,* the name of a Syrian deity, also of five places in Palestine:—Remmon, Rimmon. The addition "-methoar" (Jos 19:13) is הַמְּתֹאָר **ham-m^e^thô'âr,** *ham-meth-o-awr´*; passive participle of 8388 with the article; *the* (one) *marked off,* i.e. *which pertains*; mistaken for part of the name.

7418. רָמוֹת־נֶגֶב, **Râmôwth-Negeb,** *raw-mōth-neh´-gheb*; or נֶגֶב רָמַת, **Râmath Negeb,** *raw´-math neh´-gheb*; from the plural or construct of 7413 and 5045; *heights* (or *height*) *of* the *South; Ramoth-Negeb* or *Ramath-Negeb,* a place in Palestine:—south Ramoth, Ramath of the south.

7419. רָמוּת, **râmûwth,** *raw-mooth´*; from 7311; a *heap* (of carcases):—height.

7420. רֹמַח, **rômach,** *ro´-makh*; from an unused root meaning to *hurl*; a *lance* (as *thrown*); especially the iron *point*:—buckler, javelin, lancet, spear.

7421. רַמִּי, **rammîy,** *ram-mee´*; for 761; a *Ramite,* i.e. Aramæan:—Syrian.

7422. רַמְיָה, **Ramyâh,** *ram-yaw´*; from 7311 and 3050; *Jah has raised; Ramjah,* an Israelite:—Ramiah.

7423. רְמִיָּה, **r^e^mîyyâh,** *rem-ee-yaw´*; from 7411; *remissness, treachery*:—deceit (-ful, -fully), false, guile, idle, slack, slothful.

7424. רַמָּךְ, **rammâk,** *ram-mawk´*; of foreign origin; a brood *mare*:—dromedary.

7425. רְמַלְיָהוּ, **R^e^malyâhûw,** *rem-al-yaw´-hoo*; from an unused root and 3050 (perhaps meaning to *deck*); *Jah has bedecked; Remaljah,* an Israelite:—Remaliah.

7426. רָמַם, **râmam,** *raw-mam´*; a primitive root; to *rise* (literal or figurative):—exalt, get [oneself] up, lift up (self), mount up.

7427. רֹמֵמֻת, **rômêmuth,** *ro-may-mooth´*; from the active participle of 7426; *exaltation*:—lifting up of self.

7428. רִמֹּן פֶּרֶץ, **Rimmôn Perets,** *rim-mone´ peh´-rets*; from 7416 and 6556; *pomegranate of* the *breach; Rimmon-Perets,* a place in the Desert:—Rimmon-parez.

7429. רָמַס, **râmas,** *raw-mas´*; a primitive root; to *tread* upon (as a potter, in walking or abusively):—oppressor, stamp upon, trample (under feet), tread (down, upon).

7430. רָמַשׂ, **râmaś,** *raw-mas´*; a primitive root; (properly) to *glide* swiftly, i.e. to *crawl* or *move* with short steps; (by analogy) to *swarm*:—creep, move.

7431. רֶמֶשׂ, **remeś,** *reh´-mes*; from 7430; a *reptile* or any other rapidly moving animal:—that creepeth, creeping (moving) thing.

7432. רֶמֶת, **Remeth,** *reh´-meth*; from 7411; *height; Remeth,* a place in Palestine:—Remeth.

7433. רָמֹת (or רָמוֹת **Râmôwth**) גִּלְעָד **Râmôth Gil'âd** (2Ch 22:5), *raw-mōth´ gil-awd´*; from the plural of 7413 and 1568; *heights of Gilad; Ramoth-Gilad,* a place East of the Jordan:—Ramoth-gilead, Ramoth in Gilead. See also 7216.

7434. רָמַת הַמִּצְפֶּה, **Râmath ham-Mitspeh,** *raw-math´ ham-mits-peh´*; from 7413 and 4707 with the article interposed; *height of the watch*-tower; *Ramath-ham-Mitspeh,* a place in Palestine:—Ramath-mizpeh.

7435. רָמָתִי, **Râmâthîy,** *raw-maw-thee´*; patronymic of 7414; a *Ramathite* or inhabitant of Ramah:—Ramathite.

7436. רָמָתַיִם צוֹפִים, **Râmâthayim Tsôwphîym,** *raw-maw-thah´-yim tso-feem´*; from the dual of 7413 and the plural of the active participle of 6822; *double height of watchers; Ramathajim-Tsophim,* a place in Palestine:—Ramathaim-zophim.

7437. רָמַת לֶחִי, **Râmath Lechîy,** *raw´-math lekh´-ee*; from 7413 and 3895; *height of* a *jaw-bone; Ramath-Lechi,* a place in Palestine:—Ramath-lehi.

7438. רֹן, **rôn,** *rone*; from 7442; a *shout* (of deliverance):—song.

7439. רָנָה, **rânâh,** *raw-naw´*; a primitive root; to *whiz*:—rattle.

7440. רִנָּה, **rinnâh,** *rin-naw´*; from 7442; (properly) a *creaking* (or shrill sound), i.e. *shout* (of joy or grief):—cry, gladness, joy, proclamation, rejoicing, shouting, sing (-ing), triumph.

7441. רִנָּה, **Rinnâh,** *rin-naw´*; the same as 7440; *Rinnah,* an Israelite:—Rinnah.

7442. רָנַן, **rânan,** *raw-nan´*; a primitive root; (properly) to *creak* (or emit a stridulous sound), i.e. to *shout* (usually for joy):—aloud for joy, cry out, be joyful, (greatly, make to) rejoice, (cause to) shout (for joy), (cause to) sing (aloud, for joy, out), triumph.

7443. רֶנֶן, **renen,** *reh´-nen*; from 7442; an *ostrich* (from its *wail*):—× goodly.

7444. **רַנֵּן, rannên,** *ran-nane´*; intensive from 7442; *shouting* (for joy):—singing.

7445. **רְנָנָה, rᵉnânâh,** *ren-aw-naw´*; from 7442; a *shout* (for joy):—joyful (voice), singing, triumphing.

7446. **רִסָּה, Rissâh,** *ris-saw´*; from 7450; a *ruin* (as *dripping* to pieces); *Rissah*, a place in the Desert:—Rissah.

7447. **רָסִיס, râsîys,** *raw-sees´*; from 7450; (properly) *dripping* to pieces, i.e. a *ruin* also a dew-*drop*:—breach, drop.

7448. **רֶסֶן, resen,** *reh´-sen*; from an unused root meaning to *curb*; a *halter* (as *restraining*); (by implication) the *jaw*:—bridle.

7449. **רֶסֶן, Resen,** *reh´-sen*; the same as 7448; *Resen*, a place in Assyria:—Resen.

7450. **רָסַס, râsas,** *raw-sas´*; a primitive root; to *comminute*; used only as denominative from 7447, to *moisten* (with drops):—temper.

7451. **רַע, raʻ,** *rah*; from 7489; *bad* or (as noun) *evil* (natural or moral):—adversity, affliction, bad, calamity, + displease (-ure), distress, evil ([-favouredness], man, thing), + exceedingly, × great, grief (-vous), harm, heavy, hurt (-ful), ill (favoured), + mark, mischief (-vous), misery, naught (-ty), noisome, + not please, sad (-ly), sore, sorrow, trouble, vex, wicked (-ly, -ness, one), worse (-st), wretchedness, wrong. [Including feminine **רָעָה, râʻâh,** *raw-aw´*; as adjective or noun.]

An adjective meaning bad, evil. The basic meaning of this word displays ten or more various shades of the meaning of evil according to its contextual usage. It means bad in a moral and ethical sense and is used to describe, along with good, the entire spectrum of good and evil; hence, it depicts evil in an absolute, negative sense, as when it describes the tree of the knowledge of good and evil (Ge 2:9; 3:5, 22). It was necessary for a wise king to be able to discern the evil or the good in the actions of his people (Ecc 12:14); men and women are characterized as evil (1Sa 30:22; Est 7:6; Jer 2:33). The human heart is evil all day long (Ge 6:5) from childhood (Ge 8:21); yet the people of God are to purge evil from among them (Dt 17:7). The Lord is the final arbiter of whether something was good or evil; if something was evil in the eyes of the Lord, there is no further court of appeals (Dt 9:18; 1Ki 14:22). The day of the Lord's judgment is called an evil day, a day of reckoning and condemnation (Am 6:3). Jacob would have undergone grave evil (i.e. pain, misery, and ultimate disaster) if he had lost Benjamin (Ge 44:34). The word can refer to circumstances as evil, as when the Israelite foremen were placed in a grave situation (Ex 5:19; 2Ki 14:10).

The word takes on the aspect of something disagreeable, unwholesome, or harmful. Jacob evaluated his life as evil and destructive (Ge 47:9; Nu 20:5); and the Israelites considered the wilderness as a threatening, terrifying place. The Canaanite women were evil in the eyes of Isaac (i.e. displeasing [Ge 28:8]). The rabble's cry within Israel for meat was displeasing in the eyes of Moses (Nu 11:10). This word describes the vicious animal that killed Joseph, so Jacob thought (Ge 37:33). The despondent countenances of persons can be described by this word; the baker's and the butler's faces were downcast because of their dreams (Ge 40:7). It can also describe one who is heavy in heart (Pr 25:20).

In a literal sense, the word depicts something that is of poor quality or even ugly in appearance. The weak, lean cows of Pharaoh's dream were decrepit, ugly-looking (Ge 41:3, 20, 27); poisonous drinking water was described as bad (2Ki 2:19; 4:41). From these observations, it is clear that the word can be used to attribute a negative aspect to nearly anything.

Used as a noun, the word indicates realities that are inherently evil, wicked, or bad; the psalmist feared no evil (Ps 23:4). The noun also depicts people of wickedness, that is, wicked people. Aaron characterized the people of Israel as inherently wicked in order to clear himself (Ex 32:22). Calamities, failures, and miseries are all connotations of this word when it is used as a noun.

7452. **רֵעַ, rêaʻ,** *rah´-ah*; from 7321; a *crash* (of thunder), *noise* (of war), *shout* (of joy):—× aloud, noise, shouted.

7453. **רֵעַ, rêaʻ,** *ray´-ah*; or **רֵיעַ, rêyaʻ,** *ray´-ah*; from 7462; an *associate* (more or less close):—brother, companion, fellow, friend, husband, lover, neighbour, × (an-) other.

A masculine noun meaning another person. Most frequently, this term is used to refer to the second party in a personal interaction without indicating any particular relationship (Ge 11:7; Jgs 7:13, 14; Ru 3:14). It is extremely broad, covering everyone from a lover (Hos 3:1); a close friend (Job 2:11); an acquaintance (Pr 6:1); an adversary in court (Ex 18:16); an enemy in combat (2Sa 2:16). Thus, this word is well-suited for its widely inclusive use in the Ten Commandments (see Ex 20:16, 17; Dt 5:20, 21; cf. Lk 10:29–37).

7454. **רֵעַ, rêaʻ,** *ray´-ah*; from 7462; a *thought* (as *association* of ideas):—thought.

7455. **רֹעַ, rôaʻ,** *ro´-ah*; from 7489; *badness* (as *marring*), physical or moral:—× be so bad, badness, (× be so) evil, naughtiness, sadness, sorrow, wickedness.

A masculine noun meaning badness, evil. This word is used to depict the quality of meat and produce (Ge 41:19, Jer 24:2, 3, 8). In Genesis, the word is used to describe cows, while in Jeremiah it describes figs. Eliab, David's oldest brother, describes David as conceited with a wicked heart, for he claims that David left the sheep only to come and watch the battle (1Sa 17:28). *Rôaʻ* is also used as a reason for punishment or for the wrath of God (i.e. for evil that had been done [Dt 28:20; Isa 1:16; Jer 4:4; 21:12]). This word is also used to denote sadness or sorrow (Ecc 7:3). In Ecclesiastes, the author states that sorrow is better than laughter, for a sad face is good for the heart.

7456. **רָעֵב, râʻêb,** *raw-abe´*; a primitive root; to *hunger*:—(suffer to) famish, (be, have, suffer, suffer to) hunger (-ry).

7457. **רָעֵב, râʻêb,** *raw-abe´*; from 7456; *hungry* (more or less intensely):—hunger bitten, hungry.

7458. **רָעָב, râʻâb,** *raw-awb´*; from 7456; *hunger* (more or less extensive):—dearth, famine, + famished, hunger.

7459. **רְעָבוֹן, rᵉʻâbôwn,** *reh-aw-bone´*; from 7456; *famine*:—famine.

7460. **רָעַד, râʻad,** *raw-ad´*; a primitive root; to *shudder* (more or less violently):—tremble.

A verb meaning to tremble, to quake. The psalmist uses the word in a description of the holiness, majesty, and power of God, where the earth is depicted as trembling at the mere gaze of the Lord (Ps 104:32). Daniel trembled in fear and reverence at the sight and presence of the vision before he heard the words that the messenger had been sent to deliver (Da 10:11).

7461. **רַעַד, raʻad,** *rah´-ad*; or (feminine) **רְעָדָה, rᵉʻâdâh,** *reh-aw-daw´*; from 7460; a *shudder*:—trembling.

A masculine noun meaning trembling. In the song of Moses and Miriam, the leaders of Moab were described as being seized with trembling before the power of the Lord (Ex 15:15). In a cry to God, the psalmist uses the word to state that fear and trembling had bent him (Ps 55:5[6]). He cried out for God to come to his rescue and deliver him from his enemies.

7462. **רָעָה, râʻâh,** *raw-aw´*; a primitive root; to *tend* a flock, i.e. *pasture* it; (intransitive) to *graze* (literal or figurative); (generally) to *rule*; (by extension) to *associate* with (as a friend):—× break, companion, keep company with, devour, eat up, evil entreat, feed, use as a friend, make friendship with, herdman, keep [sheep] (-er), pastor, + shearing house, shepherd, wander, waste.

7463. **רֵעֶה, rêʻeh,** *ray-eh´*; from 7462; a (male) *companion*:—friend.

7464. **רֵעָה, rêʻâh,** *ray´-aw*; feminine of 7453; a female *associate*:—companion, fellow.

7465. **רֹעָה, rôʻâh,** *ro-aw´*; for 7455; *breakage*:—broken, utterly.

7466. **רְעוּ, Rᵉʻûw,** *reh-oo´*; for 7471 in the sense of 7453; *friend*; *Reü*, a postdiluvian patriarch:—Reu.

7467. רְעוּאֵל**, Reʻûwʼêl,** *reh-oo-ale´*; from the same as 7466 and 410; *friend of God; Reüel,* the name of Moses' father-in-law, also of an Edomite and an Israelite:—Raguel, Reuel.

7468. רְעוּת**, reʻûwth,** *reh-ooth´*; from 7462 in the sense of 7453; a female *associate*; (generally) an *additional* one:— + another, mate, neighbour.

A feminine noun meaning a fellow woman, an associate. In Jeremiah, the women were to teach one another (i.e. their associates or companions) a lament (Jer 19:20[19]). Isaiah used the word to denote the mates of falcons or birds of prey (Isa 34:15, 16). In a figurative use, Zechariah used the word to denote that the people who remained would be left to eat one another's flesh (Zec 11:9). In Esther, King Xerxes was advised to make a decree stating that Vashti was never again to enter his presence and that her position was to be given to one of her associates that was better than she was (Est 1:19).

7469. רְעוּת**, reʻûwth,** *reh-ooth´*; probably from 7462; a *feeding* upon, i.e. grasping after:—vexation.

7470. רְעוּ**, reʻûw,** *reh-oo´*; (Chaldee); corresponding to 7469; *desire*:—pleasure, will.

7471. רְעִי**, reʻîy,** *reh-ee´*; from 7462; *pasture*:—pasture.

7472. רֵעִי**, Rêʻîy,** *ray-ee´*; from 7453; *social; Reï,* an Israelite:—Rei.

7473. רֹעִי**, rôʻîy,** *ro-ee´*; from active participle of 7462; *pastoral*; as noun, a *shepherd*:—shepherd.

7474. רַעְיָה**, raʻyâh,** *rah-yaw´*; feminine of 7453; a female *associate*:—fellow, love.

7475. רַעְיוֹן**, raʻyôwn,** *rah-yone´*; from 7462 in the sense of 7469; *desire*:—vexation.

7476. רַעְיוֹן**, raʻyôwn,** *rah-yone´*; (Chaldee); corresponding to 7475; a *grasp,* i.e. (figurative) mental *conception*:—cogitation, thought.

7477. רָעַל**, râʻal,** *raw-al´*; a primitive root; to *reel,* i.e. (figurative) to *brandish*:—terribly shake.

7478. רַעַל**, raʻal,** *rah´-al*; from 7477; a *reeling* (from intoxication):—trembling.

7479. רְעָלָה**, reʻâlâh,** *reh-aw-law´*; feminine of 7478; a long *veil* (as *fluttering*):—muffler.

7480. רְעֵלָיָה**, Reʻêlâyâh,** *reh-ay-law-yaw´*; from 7477 and 3050; *made to tremble* (i.e. *fearful*) *of Jah; Reëlajah,* an Israelite:—Reeliah.

7481. רָעַם**, râʻam,** *raw-am´*; a primitive root; to *tumble,* i.e. *be* violently *agitated*; (specifically) to *crash* (of thunder); (figurative) to *irritate* (with anger):—make to fret, roar, thunder, trouble.

7482. רַעַם**, raʻam,** *rah´-am*; from 7481; a *peal* of thunder:—thunder.

7483. רַעְמָה**, raʻmâh,** *rah-maw´*; feminine of 7482; the *mane* of a horse (as *quivering* in the wind):—thunder.

7484. רַעְמָה**, Raʻmâh,** *rah-maw´*; the same as 7483; *Ramah,* the name of a grandson of Ham, and of a place (perhaps founded by him):—Raamah.

7485. רַעַמְיָה**, Raʻamyâh,** *rah-am-yaw´*; from 7481 and 3050; *Jah has shaken; Ramjah,* an Israelite:—Raamiah.

7486. רַעְמְסֵס**, Raʻmesês,** *rah-mes-ace´*; or רַעַמְסֵס**, Raʻamsês,** *rah-am-sace´*; of Egyptian origin; *Rameses* or *Raamses,* a place in Egypt:—Raamses, Rameses.

7487. רַעֲנַן**, raʻănan,** *rah-aw-nan´*; (Chaldee); corresponding to 7488; *green,* i.e. (figurative) *prosperous*:—flourishing.

7488. רַעֲנָן**, raʻănân,** *rah-an-awn´*; from an unused root meaning to *be green; verdant*; (by analogy) *new*; (figurative) *prosperous*:—green, flourishing.

7489. רָעַע**, râʻaʻ,** *raw-ah´*; a primitive root; (properly) to *spoil* (literally, by *breaking* to pieces); (figurative) to *make* (or *be*) *good for nothing,* i.e. *bad* (physically, socially or morally):—afflict, associate selves [*by mistake for* 7462], break (down, in pieces), + displease, (be, bring, do) evil (doer, entreat, man), show self friendly [*by mistake for* 7462], do harm, (do) hurt, (behave self, deal) ill, × indeed, do mischief, punish, still, vex, (do) wicked (doer, -ly), be (deal, do) worse.

A verb meaning to be bad, to do wrong. The root of the word indicates breaking, in contrast to the word *tâmam* (8552), which means to be whole. For example, tree branches that break are bad (Jer 11:16). The word also refers to moral evil: an eye could be evil, that is, covetous (Dt 15:9); or a person could do evil (Ge 44:5; Pr 4:16; Jer 4:22). The word also refers to physical evil: God harmed or punished those who provoked Him (Zec 8:14); and Laban would have hurt Jacob without God's prevention (Ge 31:7). In addition, the word expresses sadness and describes the face or heart as being bad (1Sa 1:8; Ne 2:3). The causative participle signifies an evildoer (Ps 37:1; Isa 9:17[16]). The idiomatic phrase, to be evil in someone's eyes, means to displease (Ge 48:17; 2Sa 11:25; Jnh 4:1).

7490. רְעַע**, reʻaʻ,** *reh-ah´*; (Chaldee); corresponding to 7489:—break, bruise.

An Aramaic verb meaning to break in pieces, to shatter, to crush. The term occurs only twice in the OT; both are located within the same passage in the book of Daniel. In interpreting King Nebuchadnezzar's dream, Daniel declared that the fourth kingdom, represented by the legs of iron and feet of iron mixed with clay of the statue, would be as strong as iron and would break the previously mentioned kingdoms into pieces (Da 2:40). This term is closely related to the Hebrew verb *râʻaʻ* (7489).

7491. רָעַף**, râʻaph,** *raw-af´*; a primitive root; to *drip*:—distil, drop (down).

7492. רָעַץ**, râʻats,** *raw-ats´*; a primitive root; to *break* in pieces; (figurative) *harass*:—dash in pieces, vex.

7493. רָעַשׁ**, râʻash,** *raw-ash*; a primitive root; to *undulate* (as the earth, the sky, etc.; also a field of grain), particularly through fear; (specifically) to *spring* (as a locust):—make afraid, (re-) move, quake, (make to) shake, (make to) tremble.

A verb meaning to quake, to tremble, to shake, to leap, to be abundant. The word occurs thirty times in the OT and most often refers to the physical, forceful (often violent), quick, back-and-forth movement of a physical body by an outside force. Frequently, the trembling or shaking takes place as nature's response to God's presence or to His activity of rendering divine judgment. Things shaken included the walls of a city (Eze 26:10); the thresholds of doors (Am 9:1); the heavens (Joel 2:10, 3:16[4:16]; Hag 2:6); the mountains (Jer 4:24; Na 1:5); coastlands or islands (Eze 26:15); kingdoms (Isa 14:16); the earth or lands (Jgs 5:4; 2Sa 22:8; Ps 60:2[4]; 68:8[9]; 77:18[19]; Isa 13:13; Jer 8:16; 10:10; 49:21); Gentile nations (Eze 31:16; Hag 2:7); and every living creature of creation (Eze 38:20). Twice the term conveys a much different action than the one related above. In the first rare usage, the verb portrays the leaping ability of a warhorse (Job 39:20). The second unique use expresses the psalmist's desire that there be an abundance of grain in the land (Ps 72:16).

7494. רַעַשׁ**, raʻash,** *rah´-ash*; from 7493; *vibration, bounding, uproar*:—commotion, confused noise, earthquake, fierceness, quaking, rattling, rushing, shaking.

7495. רָפָא**, râphâʼ,** *raw-faw´*; or רָפָה**, râphâh,** *raw-faw´*; a primitive root; (properly) to *mend* (by stitching), i.e. (figurative) to *cure*:—cure, (cause to) heal, physician, repair, × thoroughly, make whole. See 7503.

7496. רָפָא**, râphâʼ,** *raw-faw´*; from 7495 in the sense of 7503; (properly) *lax*; i.e. (figurative) a *ghost* (as *dead*; in plural only):—dead, deceased.

A masculine noun meaning shades, departed spirits, deceased ones, dead ones. The term always occurs in the plural form (*rĕphâ'iym*) and consistently denotes those who died and entered into a shadowy existence within *shĕ'ôwl* (7585) (Job 26:5; Pr 9:18; Isa 14:9). Three times the word is employed in direct parallelism with the Hebrew term for dead ones (*mêthiym,* from *mûth* [4191], to die) (Ps 88:10[11]; Isa 26:14, 19). "Shades" or deceased ones do not rise (Isa 26:14). They reside in a place of darkness and oblivion (Ps 88:10[11]). They cannot praise God (Ps 88:10 [11]). The smooth words of the adulteress bring her victims down to death, to the place of the shades, never to return (Pr 21:16; cf. Pr 2:16–19; 9:13–18). Yet even in the OT, a confident resurrection hope was gloriously and joyously held out to those in Sheol who obeyed God while alive (Isa 26:19).

7497. רָפָא, **râphâ',** *raw-faw´*; or רָפָה, **râphâh,** *raw-faw´*; from 7495 in the sense of *invigorating*; a *giant*:—giant, Rapha, Rephaim (-s). See also 1051.

A masculine noun meaning a giant, Rephaim (an ethnic people group), Valley of Rephaim. Frequently, the term (only with the plural form) designated a Canaanite tribe that inhabited the Promised Land prior to the Hebrew conquest and who were known for their unusually large size (Ge 14:5; 15:20; Dt 2:11, 20; 3:11, 13; Jos 12:4; 13:12; 17:15). In two accounts, the singular form was utilized to refer to a particular giant, perhaps an ancestor of the tribe of the Rephaim (2Sa 21:16, 18, 20, 22; 1Ch 20:6, 8). In a different vein, the word (also only in the plural form) acted as the proper name of a valley located southwest of Jerusalem (Jos 15:8; 18:16; 2Sa 5:18, 22; 23:13; 1Ch 11:15; 14:9; Isa 17:5).

7498. רָפָא, **Râphâ',** *raw-faw´*; or רָפָה, **Râphâh,** *raw-faw´*; probably the same as 7497; *giant; Rapha* or *Raphah*, the name of two Israelites:—Rapha.

7499. רְפוּאָה, **rᵉphûw'âh,** *ref-oo-aw´*; feminine passive participle of 7495; a *medicament*:—heal [-ed], medicine.

7500. רִפְאוּת, **riph'ûwth,** *rif-ooth´*; from 7495; a *cure*:—health.

7501. רְפָאֵל, **Rᵉphâ'êl,** *ref-aw-ale´*; from 7495 and 410; *God has cured; Rephaël*, an Israelite:—Rephael.

7502. רָפַד, **râphad,** *raw-fad´*; a primitive root; to *spread* (a bed); (by implication) to *refresh*:—comfort, make [a bed], spread.

7503. רָפָה, **râphâh,** *raw-faw´*; a primitive root; to *slacken* (in many applications, literal or figurative):—abate, cease, consume, draw [toward evening], fail, (be) faint, be (wax) feeble, forsake, idle, leave, let alone (go, down), (be) slack, stay, be still, be slothful, (be) weak (-en). See 7495.

A verb meaning to become slack, to relax, to cease, to desist, to become discouraged, to become disheartened, to become weak, to become feeble, to let drop, to discourage, to leave alone, to let go, to forsake, to abandon, to be lazy. The word occurs forty-five times, often with the word *yâd* (3027), meaning hand, forming an idiomatic phrase that requires careful translation within the context of a particular passage. For example, when Ish-Bosheth, Saul's son, heard that Abner had died, his hands became feeble, i.e. his courage failed him (2Sa 4:1; cf. 2Ch 15:7; Isa 13:7; Jer 6:24, 50:43; Eze 7:17; 21:7[12]). The term was also employed to signify the act of ceasing from something (Jgs 8:3; 2Sa 24:16; Ne 6:9; Ps 37:8); of leaving someone alone (Ex 4:26; Dt 9:14; Jgs 11:37; Job 7:19); of letting go (Job 27:6; Pr 4:13; SS 3:4); and of abandoning or forsaking someone (Dt 4:31; 31:6, 8; Jos 1:5; 10:6; Ps 138:8). On rare occasions, the term conveyed a state of laziness or complacency (Ex 5:8, 17; Jos 18:3; Pr 18:9).

7504. רָפֶה, **râpheh,** *raw-feh´*; from 7503; *slack* (in body or mind):—weak.

7505. רָפוּא, **Râphûw',** *raw-foo´*; passive participle of 7495; *cured; Raphu*, an Israelite:—Raphu.

7506. רֶפַח, **Rephach,** *reh´-fakh*; from an unused root apparently meaning to *sustain; support; Rephach*, an Israelite:—Rephah.

7507. רְפִידָה, **rᵉphîydâh,** *ref-ee-daw´*; from 7502; a *railing* (as *spread* along):—bottom.

7508. רְפִידִים, **Rᵉphîydîym,** *ref-ee-deem´*; plural of the masculine of the same as 7507; *ballusters; Rephidim*, a place in the Desert:—Rephidim.

7509. רְפָיָה, **Rᵉphâyâh,** *ref-aw-yaw´*; from 7495 and 3050; *Jah has cured; Rephajah*, the name of five Israelites:—Rephaiah.

7510. רִפְיוֹן, **riphyôwn,** *rif-yone´*; from 7503; *slackness*:—feebleness.

7511. רָפַס, **râphas,** *raw-fas´*; a primitive root; to *trample*, i.e. *prostrate*:—humble self, submit self.

7512. רְפַס, **rᵉphas,** *ref-as´*; (Chaldee); corresponding to 7511:—stamp.

7513. רַפְסֹדָה, **raphsôdâh,** *raf-so-daw´*; from 7511; a *raft* (as *flat* on the water):—flote.

7514. רָפַק, **râphaq,** *raw-fak´*; a primitive root; to *recline*:—lean.

7515. רָפַשׂ, **râphaś,** *raw-fas´*; a primitive root; to *trample*, i.e. *roil* water:—foul, trouble.

7516. רֶפֶשׁ, **rephesh,** *reh´-fesh*; from 7515; *mud* (as *roiled*):—mire.

7517. רֶפֶת, **repheth,** *reh´-feth*; probably from 7503; a *stall* for cattle (from their *resting* there):—stall.

7518. רַץ, **rats,** *rats*; contracted from 7533; a *fragment*:—piece.

7519. רָצָא, **râtsâ',** *raw-tsaw´*; a primitive root; to *run*; also to *delight* in:—accept, run.

7520. רָצַד, **râtsad,** *raw-tsad´*; a primitive root; probably to *look askant*, i.e. (figurative) *be jealous*:—leap.

7521. רָצָה, **râtsâh,** *raw-tsaw´*; a primitive root; to *be pleased with*; (specifically) to *satisfy* a debt:—(be) accept (-able), accomplish, set affection, approve, consent with, delight (self), enjoy, (be, have a) favour (-able), like, observe, pardon, (be, have, take) please (-ure), reconcile self.

A verb meaning to delight, to take pleasure, to treat favourably, to favour, to accept, to pay off, to pay for, to make up for. Both humans (cf. Ge 33:10; Dt 33:24; 1Ch 29:3; Ps 50:18; Pr 3:12); and the Lord can be found as the subjects (1Ch 28:4; Ps 51:16[18]; 147:10; Mic 6:7; Hag 1:8). The Lord takes pleasure in uprightness (1Ch 29:17); in those who fear Him (Ps 147:11); and in His Servant (Isa 42:1). The word is also utilized within texts concerning sacrifices, offerings, and worship, denoting that which was acceptable or unacceptable to the Lord (Le 1:4; 7:18; Ps 119:108; Jer 14:12; Hos 8:13; Am 5:22; Mal 1:8). Less common is the employment of the term to communicate the satisfying of a debt (e.g., when the land must pay off or make up for the Sabbath years that it owes [Le 26:34; cf. Le 26:41, 43; 2Ch 36:21; Isa 40:2]).

7522. רָצוֹן, **râtsôwn,** *raw-tsone´*; or רָצֹן, **râtsôn,** *raw-tsone´*; from 7521; *delight* (especially as shown):—(be) acceptable (-ance, -ed), delight, desire, favour, (good) pleasure, (own, self, voluntary) will, as ... (what) would.

A masculine noun meaning pleasure, delight, desire, will, favour, acceptance. This term is ascribed both to human agents and to God. For humans, the word often described what the heart was set on having or doing, whether for good or evil (Ge 49:6; 2Ch 15:15; Ne 9:24, 37; Est 1:8; Ps 145:16, 19; Da 8:4; 11:3). When attributed to God, the term expresses the divine goodwill which He extends to humanity as He sees fit (Dt 33:16, 23; Ps 5:12[13]; 69:13[14]; 106:4; Pr 12:2; 18:22; Isa 49:8; 60:10; 61:2). In passages pertaining to the offering of sacrifices, offerings, or fasting in worship, the word designates the favourable reception of the worshippers (and thus their worship) by the Lord (Ex 28:38; Le 1:3; 19:5; 22:19–21, 29; 23:11; Isa 56:7; 58:5; 60:7; Jer 6:20). On a few occasions, the word denotes anything that is pleasing to God (i.e. His will [lit., His pleasure]; Ps 40:8[9]; 103:21; 143:10). This noun is derived from the verb *râsâh* (7521).

7523. רָצַח, **râtsach,** *raw-tsakh´*; a primitive root; (properly) to *dash* in pieces, i.e. *kill* (a human being), (especially) to *murder*:—put to death, kill, (man-) slay (-er), murder (-er).

A verb meaning to murder, to slay, to kill. The taking of a human life is the primary concept behind this word. It is used to indicate a premeditated murder (Dt 5:17; 1Ki 21:19; Jer 7:9); an accidental killing (Nu 35:11; Jos 20:3); the ultimate act of revenge (Nu 35:27); and death by means of an animal attack (Pr 22:13). Provocatively, Hosea refers to the lewdness of the priests that led people astray as being equal to murder (Hos 6:9).

7524. רֶצַח, retsach, *reh´-tsakh*; from 7523; a *crushing*; (specifically) a *murder*-cry:—slaughter, sword.

7525. רִצְיָא, Ritsyâʼ, *rits-yaw´*; from 7521; *delight; Ritsjah*, an Israelite:—Rezia.

7526. רְצִין, Re**tsîyn,** *rets-een´*; probably for 7522; *Retsin*, the name of a Syrian and of an Israelite:—Rezin.

7527. רָצַע, râtsaʻ, *raw-tsah´*; a primitive root; to *pierce*:—bore.

7528. רָצַף, râtsaph, *raw-tsaf´*; a denominative from 7529; to *tessellate*, i.e. embroider (as if with bright stones):—pave.

7529. רֶצֶף, retseph, *reh´-tsef*; for 7565; a red-hot *stone* (for baking):—coal.

7530. רֶצֶף, Retseph, *reh´-tsef*; the same as 7529; *Retseph*, a place in Assyria:—Rezeph.

7531. רִצְפָּה, ritspâh, *rits-paw´*; feminine of 7529; a hot *stone*; also a tessellated *pavement*:—live coal, pavement.

7532. רִצְפָּה, Ritspâh, *rits-paw´*; the same as 7531; *Ritspah*, an Israelitess:—Rizpah.

7533. רָצַץ, râtsats, *raw-tsats´*; a primitive root; to *crack* in pieces, literal or figurative:—break, bruise, crush, discourage, oppress, struggle together.

7534. רַק, raq, *rak*; from 7556 in its orig. sense; *emaciated* (as if *flattened* out):—lean ([-fleshed]), thin.

7535. רַק, raq, *rak*; the same as 7534 as a noun; (properly) *leanness*, i.e. (figurative) limitation; (only adverbial) *merely*, or (conjunctive) *although*:—but, even, except, howbeit, howsoever, at the least, nevertheless, nothing but, notwithstanding, only, save, so [that], surely, yet (so), in any wise.

7536. רֹק, rôq, *roke*; from 7556; *spittle*:—spit (-ting, -tle).

7537. רָקַב, râqab, *raw-kab´*; a primitive root; to *decay* (as by worm-eating):—rot.

7538. רָקָב, râqâb, *raw-kawb´*; from 7537; *decay* (by *caries*):—rottenness (thing).

7539. רִקָּבוֹן, riqqâbôwn, *rik-kaw-bone´*; from 7538; *decay* (by *caries*):—rotten.

7540. רָקַד, râqad, *raw-kad´*; a primitive root; (properly) to *stamp*, i.e. to *spring* about (wildly or for joy):—dance, jump, leap, skip.

7541. רַקָּה, raqqâh, *rak-kaw´*; feminine of 7534; (properly) *thinness*, i.e. the *side* of the head:—temple.

7542. רַקּוֹן, Raqqôwn, *rak-kone´*; from 7534; *thinness; Rakkon*, a place in Palestine:—Rakkon.

7543. רָקַח, râqach, *raw-kakh´*; a primitive root; to *perfume*:—apothecary, compound, make [ointment], prepare, spice.

7544. רֶקַח, reqach, *reh´-kakh*; from 7543; (properly) *perfumery*, i.e. (by implication) *spicery* (for flavor):—spiced.

7545. רֹקַח, rôqach, *ro´-kakh*; from 7542; an *aromatic*:—confection, ointment.

7546. רַקָּח, raqqâch, *rak-kawkh´*; from 7543; a male *perfumer*:—apothecary.

7547. רִקֻּחַ, riqquach, *rik-koo´-akh*; from 7543; a *scented* substance:—perfume.

7548. רַקָּחָה, raqqâchâh, *rak-kaw-khaw´*; feminine of 7547; a female *perfumer*:—confectioner.

7549. רָקִיעַ, râqîyaʻ, *raw-kee´-ah*; from 7554; (properly) an *expanse*, i.e. the *firmament* or (apparently) visible arch of the sky:—firmament.

A masculine noun meaning an expanse, the firmament, an extended surface. Literally, this word refers to a great expanse and, in particular, the vault of the heavens above the earth. It denotes the literal sky that stretches from horizon to horizon (Ge 1:6–8); the heavens above that contain the sun, moon, and stars (Ge 1:14); or any vaulted ceiling or expanse that stands above (Eze 10:1). By extension, the psalmist uses the word to refer to the infinite and sweeping power of the Lord (Ps 150:1).

7550. רָקִיק, râqîyq, *raw-keek´*; from 7556 in its original sense; a thin *cake*:—cake, wafer.

7551. רָקַם, râqam, *raw-kam´*; a primitive root; to *variegate* colour, i.e. *embroider*; (by implication) to *fabricate*:—embroiderer, needlework, curiously work.

7552. רֶקֶם, Reqem, *reh´-kem*; from 7551; *versicolor; Rekem*, the name of a place in Palestine, also of a Midianite and an Israelite:—Rekem.

7553. רִקְמָה, riqmâh, *rik-maw´*; from 7551; *variegation* of colour; (specifically) *embroidery*:—broidered (work), divers colours, (raiment of) needlework (on both sides).

7554. רָקַע, râqaʻ, *raw-kah´*; a primitive root; to *pound* the earth (as a sign of passion); (by analogy) to *expand* (by hammering); (by implication) to *overlay* (with thin sheets of metal):—beat, make broad, spread abroad (forth, over, out, into plates), stamp, stretch.

A verb meaning to beat, to stamp, to stretch out. The fundamental picture is that of a smith pounding a piece of metal that in turn causes the metal to spread out as it flattens. This word conveys the action of flattening metal for some specific use (Ex 39:3); stamping one's foot on the ground as a symbol of displeasure (Eze 6:11); the laying out of the earth in creation (Isa 42:5); and the flattening of an enemy (2Sa 22:43).

7555. רִקֻּעַ, riqquaʻ, *rik-koo´-ah*; from 7554; *beaten* out, i.e. a (metallic) *plate*:—broad.

A masculine noun meaning expansion, broad. Signifying the stretching effect produced when metal is beaten, this word appears only in reference to the plates covering the altar of the tabernacle (Nu 16:38[17:3]).

7556. רָקַק, râqaq, *raw-kak´*; a primitive root; to *spit*:—spit.

7557. רַקַּת, Raqqath, *rak-kath´*; from 7556 in its original sense of *diffusing*; a *beach* (as *expanded* shingle); *Rakkath*, a place in Palestine:—Rakkath.

7558. רִשְׁיוֹן, rishyôwn, *rish-yone´*; from an unused root meaning to *have leave*; a *permit*:—grant.

7559. רָשַׁם, râsham, *raw-sham´*; a primitive root; to *record*:—note.

7560. רְשַׁם, re**sham,** *resh-am´*; (Chaldee); corresponding to 7559:—sign, write.

7561. רָשַׁע, râshaʻ, *raw-shah´*; a primitive root; to *be* (causative, *do* or *declare*) *wrong*; (by implication) to *disturb, violate*:—condemn, make trouble, vex, be (commit, deal, depart, do) wicked (-ly, -ness).

A verb meaning to be in the wrong, to be guilty, to be wicked, to do wickedly, to condemn. In the simple stem, this verb means to be or to become guilty, to act wickedly. When God's people confessed that they acted wickedly, then the Lord forgave them (1Ki 8:47; Ecc 7:17; Da 9:15); to depart from the Lord is an act of wickedness (2Sa 22:22; Ps 18:21[22]).

In the causative stem, the word carries the idea of condemning others or doing wickedness; the people confessed that they had done wickedness (Ne 9:33; Ps 106:6; Da 12:10). The verb also means to condemn. God declares who is guilty in cases of illegal possession (Ex 22:9[8]; Dt 25:1); when a moral or ethical offence has occurred, the Lord will judge in order to declare the guilty (1Ki 8:32; Job 9:20).

7562. רֶשַׁע, **resha‘**, *reh´-shah*; from 7561; a *wrong* (especially moral):—iniquity, wicked (-ness).

A masculine noun meaning wickedness, injustice, and unrighteousness. It embodies that character which is opposite the character of God (Job 34:10; Ps 5:4[5]; 84:10[11]). It is also placed in opposition to justice and righteousness, *tsedeq* (6664), which is often used to describe God's character (Ps 45:7[8]). This word is presented as the bad and evil actions that are done by humanity (Job 34:8); and, as such, these actions became the object of God's judgment (see Job 34:26). It describes those actions that are violent. In Pr 4:17, this word is a parallel to *châmâs* (2555), meaning violence. In addition, the Hebrew word means violations of civil law, especially fraud and deceit (Pr 8:7; note the word's opposition to *'emeth*[571], which means truth; cf. Mic 6:10, 11). It can also denote the actions of enemy nations (Ps 125:3; note its opposition to *tsaddiyq* (6662), which means just or righteous; cf. Eze 31:11). In a general sense, it may represent wrongful deeds (Dt 9:27; note the parallel with *chaṭṭâ'th* (2403), which means sin).

7563. רָשָׁע, **râshâ‘**, *raw-shaw´*; from 7561; moral *wrong*; (concrete) an (actively) *bad* person:— + condemned, guilty, ungodly, wicked (man), that did wrong.

An adjective meaning wicked, guilty, in the wrong, criminal, transgressor. This adjective is used 264 times, many more times than the verb formed from it. It means essentially someone guilty or in the wrong and is an antonym to the Hebrew word *tsaddiyq* (6662), meaning righteous, in the right. Moses accused the Hebrew man who was in the wrong and was fighting with another Hebrew (Ex 2:13); no one was to aid wicked persons in their wickedness (Ex 23:1). A murderer worthy of death could not be ransomed (Nu 35:31); guilty, wicked persons accept bribes (Pr 17:23; 18:5). The word may describe wicked people as murderers (2Sa 4:11).

The word indicates people who are enemies of God and His people: the psalmist prayed to be rescued from the wicked (Ps 17:13). Those described by this word are evil and do not learn righteousness. Instead, they pursue their wicked ways among the righteous (Isa 26:10); but the Lord will eventually slay the wicked (Isa 11:4). Pharaoh admitted he was in the wrong in his attitude and actions against Moses, the Lord, and His people (Ex 9:27; Isa 14:5).

The word indicates the guilt engendered by sinning against others, including God. The Lord moved to destroy the leaders and the wicked people who revolted against Him in the desert (Nu 16:26); the wicked are those who do not serve God and are as a result wicked and guilty before Him (Mal 3:18). If wicked people continue in their ways toward God or others, they will die in their sins (Eze 3:18); but the righteous do not die with the wicked (Ge 18:23, 25). The counsel of the wicked is avoided by the persons blessed by God (Job 10:3; 21:16; Ps 1:1). Several phrases became idiomatic when talking about the wicked described by this word: the counsel of the wicked (Ps 1:1); the way of the wicked (Pr 15:9); the path of the wicked (Mic 6:10); the tent of the wicked (Job 8:22); the life (literally, candle) of the wicked (Job 21:7). All these terms describe things, people, and locations that God's people are to avoid so He will not destroy them in the end.

7564. רִשְׁעָה, **rish‘âh**, *rish-aw´*; feminine of 7562; *wrong* (especially moral):—fault, wickedly (-ness).

A feminine noun meaning wickedness, guilt. This word for immorality refers to a wide range of evil. It indicates a crime worthy of punishment (Dt 25:2); the unrestrained evil that lurks in the human heart (Isa 9:18[17]); the vileness of surrounding enemies (Mal 1:4); the breach of a religious expectation (Mal 4:1[3:19]); or an unlawful act in general (Eze 33:19).

7565. רֶשֶׁף, **resheph**, *reh´-shef*; from 8313; a live *coal*; (by analogy) *lightning*; (figurative) an *arrow* (as *flashing* through the air); (specifically) *fever*:—arrow, (burning) coal, burning heat, + spark, hot thunderbolt.

7566. רֶשֶׁף, **Resheph**, *reh´-shef*; the same as 7565; *Resheph*, an Israelite:—Resheph.

7567. רָשַׁשׁ, **râshash**, *raw-shash´*; a primitive root; to *demolish*:—impoverish.

7568. רֶשֶׁת, **resheth**, *reh´-sheth*; from 3423; a *net* (as *catching* animals):—net [-work].

7569. רַתּוֹק, **rattôwq**, *rat-toke´*; from 7576; a *chain*:—chain.

7570. רָתַח, **râthach**, *raw-thakh´*; a primitive root; to *boil*:—boil.

7571. רֶתַח, **rethach**, *reh´-thakh*; from 7570; a *boiling*:— × [boil] well.

7572. רַתִּיקָה, **rattîyqâh**, *rat-tee-kaw´*; from 7576; a *chain*:—chain.

7573. רָתַם, **râtham**, *raw-tham´*; a primitive root; to *yoke* up (to the pole of a vehicle):—bind.

7574. רֶתֶם, **rethem**, *reh´-them*; or רֹתֶם, **rôthem**, *ro´-them*; from 7573; the Spanish *broom* (from its pole-like stems):—juniper (tree).

7575. רִתְמָה, **Rithmâh**, *rith-maw´*; feminine of 7574; *Rithmah*, a place in the Desert:—Rithmah.

7576. רָתַק, **râthaq**, *raw-thak´*; a primitive root; to *fasten*:—bind.

7577. רְתוּקָה, **r^ethûwqâh**, *reth-oo-kaw´*; feminine passive participle of 7576; something *fastened*, i.e. a *chain*:—chain.

7578. רְתֵת, **r^ethêth**, *reth-ayth´*; for 7374; *terror*:—trembling.

7579. שָׁאַב, **shâ'ab**, *shaw-ab´*; a primitive root; to *bale* up water:—(woman to) draw (-er, water).

7580. שָׁאַג, **shâ'ag**, *shaw-ag´*; a primitive root; to *rumble* or *moan*:— × mightily, roar.

7581. שְׁאָגָה, **sh^e'âgâh**, *sheh-aw-gaw´*; from 7580; a *rumbling* or *moan*:—roaring.

7582. שָׁאָה, **shâ'âh**, *shaw-aw´*; a primitive root; to *rush*; (by implication) to *desolate*:—be desolate, (make a) rush (-ing), (lay) waste.

7583. שָׁאָה, **shâ'âh**, *shaw-aw´*; a primitive root [rather identical with 7582 through the idea of *whirling* to giddiness]; to *stun*, i.e. (intransitive) *be astonished*:—wonder.

7584. שַׁאֲוָה, **sha'ăvâh**, *shah-av-aw´*; from 7582; a *tempest* (as *rushing*):—desolation.

A feminine noun meaning a storm, a tempest. This type of storm is used to describe the aftermath of rejecting Lady Wisdom's advice on how to live wisely (Pr 1:27).

7585. שְׁאוֹל, **sh^e'ôwl**, *sheh-ole´*; or שְׁאֹל, **sh^e'ôl**, *sheh-ole´*; from 7592; *hades* or the world of the dead (as if a subterranean *retreat*), including its accessories and inmates:—grave, hell, pit.

A noun meaning the world of the dead, Sheol, the grave, death, the depths. The word describes the underworld but usually in the sense of the grave and is most often translated as grave. Jacob described himself as going to the grave upon Joseph's supposed death (Ge 37:35; 42:38); Korah, Dathan, and Abiram went down into the ground, which becomes their grave, when God judges them (Nu 16:30, 33; 1Sa 2:6). David described his brush with death at the hands of Saul as feeling the ropes or bands of the grave clutching him (2Sa 22:6). The Lord declares that He will ransom His people from the grave or Sheol (Hos 13:14). Habakkuk declared that the grave's desire for more victims is never satiated (Hab 2:5).

The word means depths or Sheol. Job called the ways of the Almighty higher than heaven and lower than Sheol or the depths of the earth (Job 11:8). The psalmist could not escape the Lord even in the lowest depths of the earth, in contrast to the high heavens (Ps 139:8; Am 9:2). It means the deepest valley or depths of the earth in Isa 7:11.

In a few cases, Sheol seems to mean death or a similar concept; that Abaddon (destruction) lies uncovered seems to be matched with Sheol's meaning of death (Job 26:6). It means death or the grave, for neither is ever satisfied (Pr 7:27; cf. Isa 38:10) The word is best translated as death or the depths in Dt 32:22.

Sheol or the grave is the place of the wicked (Ps 9:17[18]; 31:17[18]); Ezekiel pictured it as the place of the uncircumcised (Eze 31:15; 32:21, 27). Israel's search for more wickedness and apostasy took them to the depths of Sheol (Isa 57:9). On the other hand, the righteous were not made for the grave or Sheol; it was not their proper abode. They were not left in the grave or Sheol (Ps 16:10) but were rescued from that place (Ps 49:15[16]). Adulterers and fornicators were, metaphorically, described as in the lower parts of Sheol or the grave (Pr 9:18). Sheol and Abaddon (destruction) are as open to the eyes of God as are the hearts and thoughts of humankind; there is nothing mysterious about them to Him (Pr 15:11).

7586. שָׁאוּל, Shâ'ûwl, *shaw-ool´*; passive participle of 7592; *asked; Shaül,* the name of an Edomite and two Israelites:—Saul, Shaul.

7587. שָׁאוּלִי, Shâ'ûwlîy, *shaw-oo-lee´*; patronymic from 7856; a *Shaülite* or descendant of Shaul:—Shaulites.

7588. שָׁאוֹן, shâ'ôwn, *shaw-one´*; from 7582; *uproar* (as of *rushing*); (by implication) *destruction*:— × horrible, noise, pomp, rushing, tumult (× -uous).

A masculine noun meaning a roar, a din, a crash. This term is found mostly in the prophets and generally refers to the din of battle (Hos 10:14; Am 2:2); or the crash of waves (Isa 17:12). A less frequent use of the word describes the merriment or uproar of revelers (Isa 24:8).

7589. שְׁאָט, sh^e'âṭ, *sheh-awt´*; from an unused root meaning to *push* aside; *contempt*:—despite (-ful).

7590. שָׁאט, shâ'ṭ, *shawt*; for active participle of 7750 [compare 7589]; one *contemning*:—that (which) despise (-d).

7591. שְׁאִיָּה, sh^e'îyyâh, *sheh-ee-yaw´*; from 7582; *desolation*:—destruction.

A feminine noun meaning ruin. This word is used only once in the OT and comes from the verb *shâ'âh* (7582), meaning to crash into ruins. In Isa 24:12, it describes the destroyed gate of the city that had been battered into ruins.

7592. שָׁאַל, shâ'al, *shaw-al´*; or **שָׁאֵל, shâ'êl,** *shaw-ale´*; a primitive root; to *inquire*; (by implication) to *request*; (by extension) to *demand*:—ask (counsel, on), beg, borrow, lay to charge, consult, demand, desire, × earnestly, enquire, + greet, obtain leave, lend, pray, request, require, + salute, × straitly, × surely, wish.

A verb meaning to ask. One could ask another person or even God for something (1Sa 23:2; Ps 122:6; 137:3; Ecc 7:10). People sometimes sought information by asking Urim and Thummim (Nu 27:21), or an occult wooden object (Eze 21:21[26]; Hos 4:12). Asking could be done as a begging request or a stern demand (1Ki 2:16; Job 38:3; Ps 109:10; Mic 7:3). The Hebrew expression of asking about someone's peace is similar to the English expression, "How are you?" (Ge 43:27; Jgs 18:15; Jer 15:5). Very rarely, the term could refer to borrowing or lending. But this is certainly not the meaning when the people of Israel asked goods from the Egyptians they plundered (Ex 3:22; 22:14[13]; 1Sa 1:28; 2:20; 2Ki 4:3; 6:5).

7593. שְׁאֵל, sh^e'êl, *sheh-ale´*; (Chaldee); corresponding to 7592:—ask, demand, require.

An Aramaic verb meaning to ask, to demand, to require. The word is closely related to the Hebrew verb *shâ'al* (7592), meaning to ask. Tattenai, the governor of the province beyond the river, asked the elders of the returned Jews for their names and for the name of the one who authorized their rebuilding of the Temple in Jerusalem (Ezr 5:9, 10). Later on, King Artaxerxes decreed that the treasurers in that same province had to provide whatever Ezra asked of them so that the priestly ministry at the newly rebuilt Temple could be maintained (Ezr 7:21; cf. Da 2:10, 11, 27).

7594. שְׁאָל, Sh^e'âl, *sheh-awl´*; from 7592; *request; Sheäl,* an Israelite:—Sheal.

7595. שְׁאֵלָה, sh^e'êlâh, *sheh-ay-law´*; (Chaldee); from 7593; (properly) a *question* (at law), i.e. judicial *decision* or mandate:—demand.

An Aramaic feminine noun meaning a decision, a verdict, a decree. The word occurs only in Da 4:17 (4:14) and is derived from the verbal root *shĕ'êl* (7593). It is also related to the Hebrew noun *shĕ'êlâh* (7596). The word denotes a question at law (i.e. a judicial decision or edict). In Nebuchadnezzar's second dream, he witnessed an angelic watchman crying out and announcing the verdict concerning the greatest tree in all the earth. Daniel later interpreted the dream, declaring that the great tree represented Nebuchadnezzar himself (cf. Da 4:4–27).

7596. שְׁאֵלָה, sh^e'êlâh, *sheh-ay-law´*; or **שֵׁלָה, shêlâh,** *shay-law´*; (1Sa 1:17), from 7592; a *petition*; (by implication) a *loan*:—loan, petition, request.

A feminine noun meaning a request, a petition. The term is derived from the verb *shâ'al* (7592) and signifies what a person or group asks for from another party. The request can be made of another human: Gideon, for gold earrings from the Ishmaelites (Jgs 8:24); Adonijah, for Abishag the Shunammite from Solomon with Bathsheba as intermediary (1Ki 2:16, 20); Esther, for the king's presence at her banquet; also for the sparing of the Jews' and her own life (Est 5:6–8; 7:2, 3; 9:12); or of God: Hannah, for a son (1Sa 1:17, 27; 2:20); Job, for death (Job 6:8); the Israelites, for delicious food (Ps 106:15[cf. Nu 11:4–6, 31–35]).

7597. שְׁאַלְתִּיאֵל, Sh^e'altîy'êl, *sheh-al-tee-ale´*; or **שַׁלְתִּיאֵל, Shaltîy'êl,** *shal-tee-ale´*; from 7592 and 410; *I have asked God; Sheältiël,* an Israelite:—Shalthiel, Shealtiel.

7598. שְׁאַלְתִּיאֵל, Sh^e'altîy'êl, *sheh-al-tee-ale´*; (Chaldee); corresponding to 7597:—Shealtiel.

7599. שָׁאַן, shâ'an, *shaw-an´*; a primitive root; to *loll*, i.e. *be peaceful*:—be at ease, be quiet, rest. See also 1052.

7600. שַׁאֲנָן, sha'ănân, *shah-an-awn´*; from 7599; *secure*; in a bad sense, *haughty*:—that is at ease, quiet, tumult. Compare 7946.

7601. שָׁאַס, shâ'as, *shaw-as´*; a primitive root; to *plunder*:—spoil.

7602. שָׁאַף, shâ'aph, *shaw-af´*; a primitive root; to *inhale* eagerly; (figurative) to *covet*; (by implication) to *be angry*; also to *hasten*:—desire (earnestly), devour, haste, pant, snuff up, swallow up.

7603. שְׂאֹר, ś^e'ôr, *seh-ore´*; from 7604; *barm* or yeast-cake (as *swelling* by fermentation):—leaven.

7604. שָׁאַר, shâ'ar, *shaw-ar´*; a primitive root; (properly) to *swell* up, i.e. *be* (causative, *make*) *redundant*:—leave, (be) left, let, remain, remnant, reserve, the rest.

A verb meaning to remain, to be left over; to leave, to let remain, to spare. The term maintains a narrow semantic range throughout OT literature. The verb and the nouns that derive from it (see *shĕ'âr*[7605] and *shĕ 'êriyth*[7611]) play a key role in the development of the remnant theme that unfolds and evolves over the course of OT history. From the early beginnings of salvation history in Genesis and all the way through to the end of the OT and beyond, God has sovereignly acted to preserve for Himself a remnant of people who will worship Him alone (cf. Ge 7:23; 32:8[9]; 1Ki 19:18; Ezr 9:8; Isa 4:3; 11:11, 16; 37:31; Eze 9:8; Zep 3:12; see also Ro 11:5). Nevertheless, though this usage became the most significant function of the term, the verb was also employed in a variety of other contexts. For instance, the Egyptians came to Joseph for help because they had no remaining money to buy food (Ge 47:18). After the Israelites crossed the Red Sea, the waters caved in on Pharaoh's army. Not one person remained (Ex 14:28). The blood that remained from the sin offering was to be drained out at the base of the altar (Le 5:9).

7605. שְׁאָר, sh^e'âr, *sheh-awr´*; from 7604; a *remainder*:— × other, remnant, residue, rest.

A masculine noun meaning a remnant, a remainder, the rest. The term plays an important role in the development of the remnant theme concerning God's people. This theme is interwoven throughout Scripture, and a variety of words were employed to convey the idea (cf. Isa 10:20, 21, 22; 11:11, 16). However, this term is not limited to the designation of the remnant of God's people. For instance, it was also employed to denote the remnant of other nations: Assyria (Isa 10:19); Babylon (Isa 14:22); Moab (Isa 16:14); Aram (Isa 17:3); Kedar (Isa 21:17). Moreover, the word was always utilized as a collective, never referring to a single individual (cf. 1Ch 16:41; Ezr 3:8; 4:3, 7; Est 9:16; Zep 1:4). See also the verb *shâ'ar* (7604), from which this noun is derived, and its corresponding feminine cognate *shĕ'êriyth* (7611).

7606. שְׁאָר, **sh^e'âr,** *sheh-awr´*; (Chaldee); corresponding to 7605:— × whatsoever more, residue, rest.

An Aramaic masculine noun meaning the remainder, the rest. The word closely corresponds with the Hebrew noun *shĕ'âr* (7605). It signifies that which was left over after the removal of everything else. The fourth beast in Daniel's vision devoured, broke things in pieces, and stamped the remainder with its feet (Da 7:7, 19; cf. Da 2:18; 7:12). The people of Israel, the priests, the Levites, and the rest of the returned exiles joyfully celebrated the dedication of the newly rebuilt Temple (Ezr 6:16; cf. Ezr 4:9, 10, 17; 7:18, 20).

7607. שְׁאֵר, **sh^e'êr,** *sheh-ayr´*; from 7604; *flesh* (as *swelling* out), as living or for food; (generally) *food* of any kind; (figurative) *kindred* by blood:—body, flesh, food, (near) kin (-sman, -swoman), near (nigh) [of kin].

A masculine noun meaning flesh, food, meat, body, self, blood relative, blood kindred. The word is roughly synonymous with the noun *bâśâr* (1320), meaning flesh. The term connotes the meaty part of an animal which can be eaten: quail (Ps 78:20, 27; cf. Nu 11:31); or food in general (Ex 21:10). Frequently, on account of context, the term strongly implies the idea of close (blood) relative or kindred (Le 18:6, 12, 13, 17; 20:19; 21:2; 25:49; Nu 27:11). In two contexts, the word suggests the notion of physical strength (Ps 73:26; Pr 5:11); and in Mic 3:2, 3, it refers to the actual physical flesh of a human body.

7608. שַׁאֲרָה, **sha'ărâh,** *shah-ar-aw´*; feminine of 7607; female *kindred* by blood:—near kinswomen.

7609. שֶׁאֱרָה, **She'ĕrâh,** *sheh-er-aw´*; the same as 7608; *Sheërah*, an Israelitess:—Sherah.

7610. שְׁאָר יָשׁוּב, **Sh^e'âr Yâshûwb,** *sheh-awr´ yaw-shoob´*; from 7605 and 7725; a *remnant will return; Sheär-Jashub*, the symbolical name of one of Isaiah's sons:—Shear-jashub.

7611. שְׁאֵרִית, **sh^e'êrîyth,** *sheh-ay-reeth´*; from 7604; a *remainder* or residual (surviving, final) portion:—that had escaped, be left, posterity, remain (-der), remnant, residue, rest.

A feminine noun meaning a remnant, a residue, the remainder. The primary meaning conveyed by this word is that which is left over or remains. It was used with reference to scrap pieces of wood (Isa 44:17); undesignated territory (Isa 15:9); and any group of people that remained (Jer 15:9; Am 1:8). Most significant was the technical use of this word by the prophets to denote the few among Israel or Judah that remained faithful to God (Isa 37:32; Mic 5:7[6], 8[7]); or those who survived the calamity of the exile (Zec 8:11). Joseph declared that the purpose of his captivity was to preserve a remnant of Jacob's lineage (Ge 45:7).

7612. שֵׁאת, **shê'th,** *shayth*; from 7582; *devastation*:—desolation.

7613. שְׂאֵת, **ś^e'êth,** *seh-ayth´*; from 5375; an *elevation* or leprous scab; (figurative) *elation* or cheerfulness; *exaltation* in rank or character:—be accepted, dignity, excellency, highness, raise up self, rising.

7614. שְׁבָא, **Sh^{e}bâ',** *sheb-aw´*; of foreign origin; *Sheba*, the name of three early progenitors of tribes and of an Ethiopian district:—Sheba, Sabeans.

7615. שְׁבָאִי, **Sh^{e}bâ'îy,** *sheb-aw-ee´*; patronymic from 7614; a *Shebaïte* or descendant of Sheba:—Sabean.

7616. שְׁבָבִים, **sh^{e}bâbîym,** *she-baw-beem´*; from an unused root meaning to *break* up; a *fragment*, i.e. *ruin*:—broken in pieces.

7617. שָׁבָה, **shâbâh,** *shaw-baw´*; a primitive root; to *transport* into captivity:—(bring away, carry, carry away, lead, lead away, take) captive (-s), drive (take) away.

A verb meaning to take captive, to lead into captivity. The main idea behind this word is that of being taken prisoner as a spoil of war or other military raid. It signified the fate that befell Lot at the hands of Chedorlaomer and his compatriots (Ge 14:14); the threat that hung over the heads of any rebellious people (1Ki 8:46); and forced enslavement by a foreign military power (2Ki 5:2).

7618. שְׁבוֹ, **sh^{e}bôw,** *sheb-oh´*; from an unused root (probably identical with that of 7617 through the idea of *subdivision* into flashes or streamers [compare 7632] meaning to *flame*; a *gem* (from its sparkle), probably the *agate*:—agate.

7619. שְׁבוּאֵל, **Sh^{e}bûw'êl,** *sheb-oo-ale´*; or שׁוּבָאֵל, **Shûwbâ'êl,** *shoo-baw-ale´*; from 7617 (abbreviated) or 7725 and 410; *captive* (or *returned*) *of God; Shebuël*, the name of two Israelites:—Shebuel, Shubael.

7620. שָׁבוּעַ, **shâbûwa',** *shaw-boo´-ah*; or שָׁבֻעַ, **shâbua',** *shaw-boo´-ah*; also (feminine) שְׁבֻעָה, **shebu'âh,** *sheb-oo-aw´*; properly passive participle of 7650 as a denominative of 7651; (literal) *sevened*, i.e. a *week* (specifically of years):—seven, week.

7621. שְׁבוּעָה, **sh^{e}bûw'âh,** *sheb-oo-aw´*; feminine passive participle of 7650; (properly something *sworn*, i.e. an *oath*:—curse, oath, × sworn.

A feminine noun meaning oath. An oath is a sacred promise attesting to what one has done or will do. God swore an oath to Abraham, Isaac, and Jacob that He would fulfill His covenant with them (Ge 26:3; Dt 7:8; 1Ch 16:16). An oath could also be sworn by a person to declare innocence (Ex 22:11[10]; Nu 5:21); to proclaim friendship (2Sa 21:7); to affirm a promise (Le 5:4; 1Ki 2:43); to ratify a peace treaty (Jos 9:20); to pledge loyalty to God (2Ch 15:15); or to another person (Ne 6:18). An oath was considered to be an unbreakable contract; however, in two instances, the Bible presents well-defined possibilities in which an oath could be nullified and the obligated party could be acquitted. Abraham provided for his servant to be released from his obligation to find a bride for Isaac if the woman refused to follow (Ge 24:8); and the spies provided for their own release from their oath to Rahab if she did not display the scarlet cord and stay in her house or if she revealed the intentions of the Israelites (Jos 2:17, 20).

7622. שְׁבוּת, **sh^{e}bûwth,** *sheb-ooth´*; or שְׁבִית, **sh^{e}bîyth,** *sheb-eeth´*; from 7617; *exile*; (concrete) *prisoners*; (figurative) a *former state* of prosperity:—captive (-ity).

A feminine noun meaning captivity, captives. This word conveys either a state of exile, such as being taken for a spoil of war, or the subjects of such captivity. The chief use was in declaring the liberating power of the Lord in releasing His people from such banishment (Dt 30:3; Jer 33:7; Hos 6:11). Interestingly, when Job's fortunes were restored, he was said to have been freed from captivity (Job 42:10).

7623. שָׁבַח, **shâbach,** *shaw-bakh´*; a primitive root; (properly) to *address* in a loud tone, i.e. (specifically) *loud*; (figurative) to *pacify* (as if by words):—commend, glory, keep in, praise, still, triumph.

A verb meaning to soothe, to stroke, to praise. The primary meaning of this word is to calm or still. It was used particularly in reference to the calming of the sea (Ps 65:7[8]). A secondary current of meaning associated with this word is that of praise. In this sense, it was employed to denote either the exaltation of God (Ps 63:3[4]); or the holding of something in higher esteem (Ecc 4:2). The connection between the two may stem from the soothing effect of praise on the ego.

7624. שְׁבַח, **sh^{e}bach,** *sheb-akh´*; (Chaldee); corresponding to 7623; to *adulate*, i.e. *adore*:—praise.

An Aramaic verb meaning to praise, to adore. This word occurs five times in the book of Daniel. It denotes Daniel's praise of the Lord (Da 2:23); the praise of the Lord by a humbled Nebuchadnezzar (Da 4:37[34]); and the praise given to idols during Belshazzar's debaucherous feast (Da 5:4, 23).

7625. שְׁבַט, **sh^{e}baṭ,** *sheb-at´*; (Chaldee); corresponding to 7626; a *clan*:—tribe.

An Aramaic masculine noun meaning a clan, a tribe. This word occurs only in Ezr 6:17 and is used in reference to the tribal divisions of Israel (cf. Ge 49:28).

7626. שֵׁבֶט, **shêbeṭ,** *shay´-bet*; from an unused root probably meaning to *branch* off; a *scion*, i.e. (literal) a *stick* (for punishing, writing, fighting, ruling, walking, etc.) or (figurative) a *clan*:— × correction, dart, rod, sceptre, staff, tribe.

A masculine noun meaning a rod, a scepter, and a tribe. It is presented in parallel with the word *maṭṭeh* (4294) that designates a rod or a tribe (Isa 10:15). As a rod, it represents a common tool used as a shepherd's staff (Le 27:32; Eze 20:37); a crude weapon (2Sa 23:21); or for beating out cumin (Isa 28:27). It also refers to the shaft of a spear (2Sa 18:14). The rod was also used in meting out discipline, both literally for a slave (Ex 21:20); a fool (Pr 10:13; 26:3); and a son (Pr 13:24; 22:15; 29:15); and figuratively of God against Solomon (2Sa 7:14); of God against Israel through Assyria (Isa 10:24); against Philistia (Isa 14:29); and of God against Assyria (Isa 30:31). Because of the association between smiting and ruling, the rod became a symbol of the authority of the one bearing it; thus, this word can also mean a scepter (Ge 49:10; Jgs 5:14; Isa 14:5). Also, the connotation of tribe is based on the connection between this term and the concept of rulership. It can connote the tribes of Israel collectively (Ge 49:16; Dt 33:5); or individually (Jos 7:16; Jgs 18:1). It can also represent a portion of one of the tribes (Nu 4:18; Jgs 20:12; 1Sa 9:21). Eventually, the term was used in the singular to denote Israel as a whole (Ps 74:2; Jer 10:16; 51:19). It is also interesting to note that this word was never used in reference to the tribes of other nations.

7627. שְׁבָט, **Shᵉbâṭ**, *sheb-awt´*; of foreign origin; *Shebat*, a Jewish month:—Sebat.

7628. שְׁבִי, **shᵉbîy**, *sheb-ee´*; from 7618; *exiled; captured*; as noun, *exile* (abstract or concrete and collective); (by extension) *booty*:—captive (-ity), prisoners, × take away, that was taken.

A masculine noun meaning captivity, captives. This word comes from the verb *shâbâh* (7617), meaning to take captive, and was normally used to describe those captured in war and taken back to the conquering country (Nu 21:1; Ezr 3:8; Ne 1:2). It could describe anything captured, such as booty (Nu 31:26); or horses (Am 4:10). The word could also be used to describe prisoners in a dungeon (Ex 12:29).

7629. שֹׁבִי, **Shôbîy**, *sho-bee´*; from 7617; *captor; Shobi*, an Ammonite:—Shobi.

7630. שֹׁבַי, **Shôbay**, *sho-bah´ee*; for 7629; *Shobai*, an Israelite:—Shobai.

7631. שְׁבִיב, **shᵉbîyb**, *sheb-eeb´*; (Chaldee); corresponding to 7632:—flame.

7632. שָׁבִיב, **shâbîyb**, *shaw-beeb´*; from the same as 7616; *flame* (as *split* into tongues):—spark.

7633. שִׁבְיָה, **shibyâh**, *shib-yaw´*; feminine of 7628; *exile* (abstract or concrete and collective):—captives (-ity).

A feminine noun meaning captives. This word comes from the verb *shâbâh* (7617), meaning to take captive. It always describes those who had been defeated in war and were taken captive into a foreign land. It was also used to describe the captives taken in victory by Israel (Dt 21:11); as well as those taken in defeat from Israel by a foreign nation (2Ch 28:11, 13–15; Ne 4:4[3:36]).

7634. שָׁבְיָה, **Shobyâh**, *shob-yaw´*; feminine of the same as 7629; *captivation; Shobjah*, an Israelite:—Shachia [*from the margin*].

7635. שְׁבִיל, **shᵉbîyl**, *she-beel´*; from the same as 7640; a *track* or passageway (as if *flowing* along):—path.

7636. שָׁבִיס, **shâbîys**, *shaw-beece´*; from an unused root meaning to *interweave*; a *netting* for the hair:—caul.

7637. שְׁבִיעִי, **shᵉbîyʻîy**, *sheb-ee-ee´*; or שְׁבִעִי, **shebiʻîy**, *sheb-ee-ee´*; ordinal from 7657; *seventh*:—seventh (time).

An adjective meaning seventh. This word is normally used in relation to time: the seventh day (Le 13:5, 6; Jos 6:4; Est 1:10); the seventh week (Le 23:16); the seventh month (Le 23:27; Jer 28:17; Hag 2:1); and the seventh year (Le 25:4; 2Ki 11:4; 2Ch 23:1). When this word refers to the seventh day, it can refer to the Sabbath (Ge 2:2; Ex 20:10, 11; Dt 16:8). In other usages, this word describes the seventh of a series of events (Jos 6:16; 1Ki 18:44); the seventh lot (Jos 19:40; 1Ch 24:10); the seventh son (1Ch 2:15; 26:3); the seventh mighty man (1Ch 12:11[12]); and the seventh commander (1Ch 27:10).

7638. שָׂבָךְ, **śâbâk**, *saw-bawk´*; from an unused root meaning to *intwine*; a *netting* (ornament to the capital of a column):—net.

7639. שְׂבָכָה, **śᵉbâkâh**, *seb-aw-kaw´*; feminine of 7638; a *network*, i.e. (in hunting) a *snare*, (in architecture) a *ballustrade*; also a *reticulated* ornament to a pillar:—checker, lattice, network, snare, wreath (-enwork).

7640. שֹׁבֶל, **shôbel**, *show´-bel*; from an unused root meaning to *flow*; a lady's *train* (as *trailing* after her):—leg.

7641. שִׁבֹּל, **shibbôl**, *shib-bole´*; or (feminine) שִׁבֹּלֶת, **shibbôleth**, *shib-bo´-leth*; from the same as 7640; a *stream* (as *flowing*); also an *ear* of grain (as *growing* out); (by analogy) a *branch*:—branch, channel, ear (of corn), ([water-]) flood, Shibboleth. Compare 5451.

7642. שַׁבְלוּל, **shablûwl**, *shab-lool´*; from the same as 7640; a *snail* (as if *floating* in its own slime):—snail.

7643. שְׂבָם, **Śᵉbâm**, *seb-awm´*; or (feminine) שִׂבְמָה, **Śibmâh**, *sib-maw´*; probably from 1313; *spice; Sebam* or *Sibmah*, a place in Moab:—Shebam, Shibmah, Sibmah.

7644. שֶׁבְנָא, **Shebnâʼ**, *sheb-naw´*; or שֶׁבְנָה, **Shebnâh**, *sheb-naw´*; from an unused root meaning to *grow; growth; Shebna* or *Shebnah*, an Israelite:—Shebna, Shebnah.

7645. שְׁבַנְיָה, **Shᵉbanyâh**, *sheb-an-yaw´*; or שְׁבַנְיָהוּ, **Shebanyâhûw**, *sheb-an-yaw´-hoo*; from the same as 7644 and 3050; *Jah has grown* (i.e. *prospered*); *Shebanjah*, the name of three or four Israelites:—Shebaniah.

7646. שָׂבַע, **śâbaʻ**, *saw-bah´*; or שָׂבֵעַ, **śâbêaʻ**, *saw-bay´-ah*; a primitive root; to *sate*, i.e. *fill* to satisfaction (literal or figurative):—have enough, fill (full, self, with), be (to the) full (of), have plenty of, be satiate, satisfy (with), suffice, be weary of.

7647. שָׂבָע, **śâbâʻ**, *saw-baw´*; from 7646; *copiousness*:—abundance, plenteous (-ness, -ly).

7648. שֹׂבַע, **śôbaʻ**, *so´-bah*; from 7646; *satisfaction* (of food or [figurative] joy):—fill, full (-ness), satisfying, be satisfied.

7649. שָׂבֵעַ, **śâbêaʻ**, *saw-bay´-ah*; from 7646; *satiated* (in a pleasant or disagreeable sense):—full (of), satisfied (with).

7650. שָׁבַע, **shâbaʻ**, *shaw-bah´*; a primitive root; (properly) to *be complete*, but used only as a denominative from 7651; to *seven* oneself, i.e. *swear* (as if by repeating a declaration seven times):—adjure, charge (by an oath, with an oath), feed to the full [*by mistake for* 7646], take an oath, × straitly, (cause to, make to) swear.

A verb meaning to swear, to take an oath, to make to swear an oath. In the passive reflexive stem, the verb means to swear, to take an oath; Abimelech and Phicol asked Abraham to swear his kindness and integrity to them and their descendants (Ge 21:23; Jgs 21:1; 2Sa 21:2). The Lord swears by Himself, since there is nothing greater to swear by. God swore to multiply and bless Abraham's descendants (Ge 22:16; Jer 22:5). God also swore an oath to Abraham personally (Ge 24:7; Ex 13:11). God swore by His holiness to lead Israel into captivity (Am 4:2).

In the causative stem, the verb means to make, to cause someone to take an oath: Abraham made his servant swear an oath to get Isaac a wife from Abraham's own people (Ge 24:37). A wife suspected of adultery was forced to take an oath affirming the proposed curse on her if she were found guilty (Nu 5:21). Saul had ordered the people to take an oath not to eat honey or food while they were engaged in battle with the Philistines (1Sa 14:27; 1Ki 18:10). In this stem, the word can mean to charge someone or to adjure that person. David's men adjured him not to go into battle with them again (2Sa 21:17; 1Ki 22:16). The land of Canaan became the Promised Land the Lord gave to His people based on His oath. He brought them into the land as He had promised by oath to their fathers (Ex 13:5; Dt 1:8, 35; 6:10; Jos 1:6; Jgs 2:1; Jer 11:5).

7651. **שֶׁבַע, sheba'**, *sheh´-bah*; or (masculine) **שִׁבְעָה, shib'âh**, *shib-aw´*; from 7650; a primitive cardinal number; *seven* (as the sacred *full* one); also (adverb) *seven times*; (by implication) a *week*; (by extension) an *indefinite* number:—(+ by) seven ([-fold], -s, [-teen, -teenth], -th, times). Compare 7658.

7652. **שֶׁבַע, sheba'**, *sheh´-bah*; the same as 7651; *seven; Sheba*, the name of a place in Palestine, and of two Israelites:—Sheba.

7653. **שִׂבְעָה, śib'âh**, *sib-aw´*; feminine of 7647; *satiety*:—fulness.

7654. **שָׂבְעָה, śob'âh**, *sob-aw´*; feminine of 7648; *satiety*:—(to have) enough, × till … be full, [un-] satiable, satisfy, × sufficiently.

7655. **שִׁבְעָה, shib'âh**, *shib-aw´*; (Chaldee); corresponding to 7651:—seven (times).

7656. **שִׁבְעָה, Shib'âh**, *shib-aw´*; masculine of 7651; *seven (-th)*; *Shebah*, a well in Palestine:—Shebah.

7657. **שִׁבְעִים, shib'îym**, *shib-eem´*; multiple of 7651; *seventy*:—seventy, threescore and ten (+ -teen).

7658. **שִׁבְעָנָה, shib'ânâh**, *shib-aw-naw´*; prolonged for the masculine of 7651; *seven*:—seven.

7659. **שִׁבְעָתַיִם, shib'âthayim**, *shib-aw-thah´-yim*; dual (adverb) of 7651; *seven-times*:—seven (-fold, times).

7660. **שָׁבַץ, shâbats**, *shaw-bats´*; a primitive root; to *interweave* (coloured) threads in squares; by implication (*of reticulation*) to *enchase* gems in gold:—embroider, set.

7661. **שָׁבָץ, shâbâts**, *shaw-bawts´*; from 7660; *intanglement*, i.e. (figurative) *perplexity*:—anguish.

7662. **שְׁבַק, sh^ebaq**, *sheb-ak´*; (Chaldee); corresponding to the root of 7733; to *quit*, i.e. allow to remain:—leave, let alone.

7663. **שָׂבַר, śâbar**, *saw-bar´*; erroneously **שָׁבַר, shâbar**, *shaw-bar´*; (Ne 2:13, 15), a primitive root; to *scrutinize*; by implication (of *watching*) to *expect* (with hope and patience):—hope, tarry, view, wait.

A verb meaning to scrutinize, to expect with hope and patience, to hope, to tarry, to view, to wait. Nehemiah used this word to express an examination of the broken walls of Jerusalem before the returning exiles began rebuilding (Ne 2:13–15). In this context, the verb did not only refer to Nehemiah's viewing of simply a broken wall but also a metaphorical viewing of Israel's brokenness and need for the return of the presence of God to Jerusalem.

7664. **שֵׂבֶר, śêber**, *say´-ber*; from 7663; *expectation*:—hope.

7665. **שָׁבַר, shâbar**, *shaw-bar´*; a primitive root; to *burst* (literal or figurative):—break (down, off, in pieces, up), broken ([-hearted]), bring to the birth, crush, destroy, hurt, quench, × quite, tear, view [*by mistake for* 7663].

A verb meaning to break, to burst, to break in pieces, to break down, to break up, to smash, to shatter, to bring to birth. The word is most often used to express bursting or breaking. Other meanings include God's actions against stubborn pride (Le 26:19); or a metaphor for deliverance expressed figuratively by the breaking of a yoke (Jer 28:2). In a figurative sense, the word describes the breaking of Pharaoh's arms (Eze 30:21, 22). It also depicts the literal smashing or shattering of the tablets of the commandments (Ex 32:19). Further expressions of the word can mean to bring to the moment of birth (Isa 66:9); to break down or destroy a people (Isa 14:25); to break objects of material quality (Ge 19:9; Le 6:28[21]; Jer 49:35).

7666. **שָׁבַר, shâbar**, *shaw-bar´*; denominative from 7668; to *deal* in grain:—buy, sell.

7667. **שֶׁבֶר, sheber**, *sheh´-ber*; or **שֵׁבֶר, shêber**, *shay´-ber*; from 7665; a *fracture*, (figurative) *ruin*; (specifically) a *solution* (of a dream):—affliction, breach, breaking, broken [-footed, -handed], bruise, crashing, destruction, hurt, interpretation, vexation.

A masculine noun meaning destruction, ruin, affliction, fracture, solution of a dream, breach. This noun can be used to express the result from the breaking of a dream (i.e. its interpretation [Jgs 7:15]). Isaiah used this noun to express the possible result of sin by speaking metaphorically of the shattering of a wall (Isa 30:13). In Leviticus, this noun is used to designate a fracture of the foot or hand, indicating a cripple (Le 21:19). The noun can also be used to indicate the primary reason for suffering due to disobedience to God.

7668. **שֶׁבֶר, sheber**, *sheh´-ber*; the same as 7667; *grain* (as if *broken* into kernels):—corn, victuals.

A masculine noun meaning grain, i.e. that which is broken into kernels, corn, or food stuff. The word is used nine times in the OT as a general term for grain, with seven being used in the Joseph narratives of Genesis. This noun can connote grain that is for sale (Ge 42:1); especially that which is eaten during a famine (Ge 42:19). This word is the food stuff eaten when people are less particular about what they eat. In Nehemiah, it describes the food brought in by neighboring countries to sell on the Sabbath. The remnant that had returned promised God they would not buy it (Ne 10:31[32]). The noun is also used in reference to Israel's greed and disobedience when they were waiting impatiently for the end of the Sabbath that they might once again sell grain (Am 8:5).

7669. **שֶׁבֶר, Sheber**, *sheh´-ber*; the same as 7667; *Sheber*, an Israelite:—Sheber.

7670. **שִׁבְרוֹן, shibrôwn**, *shib-rone´*; from 7665; *rupture*, i.e. a *pang*; (figurative) *ruin*:—breaking, destruction.

A masculine noun meaning rupture (i.e. a pang). It is used figuratively for ruin, breaking, and destruction. This noun was used figuratively in Jeremiah to describe emotional distress by way of broken loins (Jer 17:18). It was used in reference to the coming exile, in which it would seem as if Israel had been cut off from the covenant of God, although God, being faithful and true, would provide a remnant or a branch of David. It was also used in Ezekiel as the reason for distress and sorrow (Eze 21:6[11]). This reference was also for the coming exile of Israel, in which God would give the Israelites over to those they hated.

7671. **שְׁבָרִים, Sh^ebârîym**, *sheb-aw-reem´*; plural of 7667; *ruins; Shebarim*, a place in Palestine:—Shebarim.

7672. **שְׁבַשׁ, sh^ebash**, *sheb-ash´*; (Chaldee); corresponding to 7660; to *intangle*, i.e. *perplex*:—be astonished.

7673. **שָׁבַת, shâbath**, *shaw-bath´*; a primitive root; to *repose*, i.e. *desist* from exertion; used in many implication relations (causative, figurative or specific):—(cause to, let, make to) cease, celebrate, cause (make) to fail, keep (sabbath), suffer to be lacking, leave, put away (down), (make to) rest, rid, still, take away.

A verb meaning to repose, to rest, to rid of, to still, to put away, to leave. Most often, the word expresses the idea of resting (i.e. abstaining from labour), especially on the seventh day (see Ex 20:8–11). It is from this root that the noun for *Sabbath* originates, a word designating the time to be set aside for rest. The verb is used of God to describe His resting after the completion of creation (Ge 2:2). This example of rest by God at creation set the requirement of rest that He desires for His people in order that they may live lives pleasing to Him, full of worship and adoration (Ex 31:17). In Joshua, the verb expresses a cessation of the provision of manna by God to the Israelites (Jos 5:12). The land was also depicted as enjoying a rest from the Israelite farmers while they were in exile (Le 26:34, 35).

Daniel uses this verb to indicate a ceasing of ritual sacrifice and offerings (Da 9:27). In that passage, Daniel was speaking of the Messiah's coming and the establishment of the New Covenant, when there would be no more need for ritual sacrifices. In another context, the verb can mean to exterminate or destroy a certain object, such as in Am 8:4 in which Amos addresses those who trampled the needy and did away with the poor. The verb means to cause, to desist from, as in God's declaration of action against the shepherds (Eze 34:10). The word suggests a removing of people or other objects (Ex 12:15; Eze 23:27, 48; Isa 30:11). In still other contexts, the causative stem means to fail or to leave lacking. In Ru 4:14, God was praised because He did not leave Naomi without a kinsman-redeemer.

7674. שֶׁבֶת**, shebeth,** *sheh´-beth*; from 7673; *rest, interruption, cessation*:—cease, sit, still, loss of time.

7675. שֶׁבֶת**, shebeth,** *sheh´-beth*; infinitive of 3427; (properly) *session*; but used also concretely an *abode* or *locality*:—place, seat. Compare 3429.

7676. שַׁבָּת**, shabbâth,** *shab-bawth´*; intensive from 7673; *intermission*, i.e. (specific) the *Sabbath*:—(+ every) sabbath.

A noun meaning Sabbath, Day of Atonement, Sabbath week or year, weeks. The word can be translated as Sabbath in practically every instance. The seventh day was set aside at creation, but the holy Sabbath was first given to Israel and first mentioned in the biblical text in Ex 16:23 as a gift to God's people (Ex 16:25, 26, 29). The word describes the day as it was officially established in the Ten Commandments at Sinai. It was the seventh day, and it was to be kept holy, set apart to the Lord (Ex 20:8, 10). That day was blessed by the Lord (Ex 20:11); and was to be observed by Israel forever (Ex 31:13–16; Eze 20:12). Not even a fire could be lit in any house on the Sabbath (Ex 35:3; Le 23:32; Ne 10:31[32]; Isa 58:13; Jer 17:22); nor could work, even on the tabernacle, be performed (Ex 35:2). Special offerings were presented on the Sabbath in addition to the regular daily burnt offerings, properly termed Sabbath offerings (Nu 28:9, 10). The purpose for the Sabbath was rest for all God's people; its basis was found in God's cessation from work at Creation (Ex 20:11; cf. Ex 31:17); and Israel's historic experience of forced labour in Egypt (Dt 5:15). Unfortunately, God's people chose to utterly desecrate the Lord's Sabbaths (Eze 20:13, 16, 20).

The high point of the religious year for Israel was the Day of Atonement which the author described as a Sabbath of Sabbaths (Le 16:31; 23:32), a Sabbath of rest. Every seventh year was described as a Sabbath to the Lord or, using the same term employed for the Day of Atonement, a Sabbath of Sabbaths (Le 25:4). During this time, the land was to remain unplowed; thus, the land itself was to enjoy its Sabbaths (Le 25:6; 26:34). When Israel was in exile, God remembered the land, giving it rest, so that it was refreshed by lying fallow for seventy years (Le 26:34, 35, 43); enjoying its Sabbaths that Israel had not observed (2Ch 36:21). Seven Sabbaths or seven weeks of years were equal to forty-nine years (Le 25:8). The produce of the land that grew of itself during the Sabbath year is described as the Sabbath (produce) of the land (Le 25:6).

7677. שַׁבָּתוֹן**, shabbâthôn,** *shab-baw-thone´*; from 7676; a *sabbatism* or special holiday:—rest, sabbath.

A masculine noun meaning a time to rest, a special holiday, a day of rest, a Sabbath feast. The meaning most often denoted from this word is that of the day of rest (Ex 31:15). In Leviticus, this noun is used to refer to the Day of Atonement (Le 16:31); the sabbatical year (Le 25:4); the Feast of Trumpets (Le 23:24); and the first and eighth days of the Feast of Tabernacles (Le 23:39).

During the sabbatical year, the land was not to be plowed but to be given a Sabbath rest, a time of refreshing to the Lord. This word was also used to describe the requirements of rest on the first and eighth days of the Feast of Tabernacles. In any context, however, the meaning of this noun is still one of a requirement for God's people to rest on the seventh day or any other holy day as directed.

7678. שַׁבְּתַי**, Shabb^ethay,** *shab-beth-ah´ee*; from 7676; *restful; Shabbethai*, the name of three Israelites:—Shabbethai.

7679. שָׂגָא**, sâgâ',** *saw-gaw´*; a primitive root; to *grow*, i.e. (causative) to *enlarge*, (figurative) *laud*:—increase, magnify.

7680. שְׂגָא**, s^egâ',** *seg-aw´*; (Chaldee); corresponding to 7679; to *increase*:—grow, be multiplied.

7681. שָׁגֵא**, Shâgê',** *shaw-gay´*; probably from 7686; *erring; Shagè*, an Israelite:—Shage.

7682. שָׂגַב**, sâgab,** *saw-gab´*; a primitive root; to *be* (causative, *make*) *lofty*, especially *inaccessible*; (by implication) *safe, strong*; used literal and figurative:—defend, exalt, be excellent, (be, set on) high, lofty, be safe, set up (on high), be too strong.

7683. שָׁגַג**, shâgag,** *shaw-gag´*; a primitive root; to *stray*, i.e. (figurative) *sin* (with more or less apology):— × also for that, deceived, err, go astray, sin ignorantly.

A verb meaning to stray, to be deceived, to err, to go astray, to sin ignorantly. The primary meaning of this word is to commit an error, to sin inadvertently. In Leviticus, this word referred to the unintentional sin atoned for by the sacrifice of a ram, referred to as a guilt offering (Le 5:18). In addition to Leviticus, Nu 15:28 also described the priestly function in atonement for one's unintentional sin. Recognition of sin may result from a realization or awareness of covenant violations due to the work of the human consciousness. The psalmist used this word to describe an action before he was afflicted (i.e. he went astray [Ps 119:67]). This verb was also used to designate erring mentally on the part of self or another person (i.e. being the deceived or the deceiver [Job 12:16]).

7684. שְׁגָגָה**, sh^egâgâh,** *sheg-aw-gaw´*; from 7683; a *mistake* or inadvertent *transgression*:—error, ignorance, at unawares, unwittingly.

A feminine noun meaning mistake, inadvertent transgression, error, ignorance. The primary meaning is an inadvertent error performed in the daily routine of life that ranged from a slip of the tongue (Ecc 5:6[5]); to accidental manslaughter (Nu 35:11, 15; Jos 20:3, 9). When used with the word *chậtâ'* (2398), it describes a procedure or policy used by priests for the guilt offering that atones for inadvertent sin (Le 4:2, 22, 27; 5:15, 18). Unatoned sin breaks the order and peace between God and people, even if unintentional, and an atonement has to be made. The noun also describes acts in which the sinner is conscious, yet the sinfulness of those acts becomes known after the act takes place.

7685. שָׂגָה**, sâgâh,** *saw-gaw´*; a primitive root; to *enlarge* (especially upward, also figurative):—grow (up), increase.

7686. שָׁגָה**, shâgâh,** *shaw-gaw´*; a primitive root; to *stray* (causative, *mislead*), usually (figurative) to *mistake*, especially (moral) to *transgress*; by extension (through the idea of intoxication) to *reel*, (figurative) *be enraptured*:—(cause to) go astray, deceive, err, be ravished, sin through ignorance, (let, make to) wander.

A verb meaning to stray, to go astray, to err, to deceive, to wander, to make a mistake, to reel. It is primarily used to express the idea of straying or wandering. It is used frequently to describe a wandering or aimless flock, both figuratively and literally (Eze 34:6). Isaiah used this verb to suggest swerving, meandering, or reeling in drunkenness (Isa 28:7). At times, it could define intoxication, not only from wine or beer but also from love (Pr 5:19, 20). This verb also depicts moral corruption (Pr 5:23). Dt 27:18 describes it as a reason for being cursed (i.e. leading a blind man astray). Le 4:13 indicates a sin of ignorance of which the person is still guilty and must provide an atonement when knowledge of the sin is known. The word also expresses a misleading mentally (i.e. being a deceiver or the deceived). The idea of atonement for sin, even of that which is an inadvertent or unintentional sin, is a prevalent thought found in Scripture (Eze 45:20).

7687. שְׂגוּב**, S^egûwb,** *seg-oob´*; from 7682; *aloft; Segub*, the name of two Israelites:—Segub.

7688. שָׁגַח**, shâgach,** *shaw-gakh´*; a primitive root; to *peep*, i.e. *glance* sharply at:—look (narrowly).

7689. שַׂגִּיא**, śaggîy',** *sag-ghee´*; from 7679; (superlative) *mighty*:—excellent, great.

7690. שַׂגִּיא**, śaggîy',** *sag-ghee´*; (Chaldee); corresponding to 7689; *large* (in size, quantity or number, also adverbial):—exceeding, great (-ly), many, much, sore, very.

7691. שְׁגִיאָה**, sh^egîy'âh,** *sheg-ee-aw´*; from 7686; a moral *mistake*:—error.

A feminine noun meaning a moral mistake, an error. As written in Ps 19:12[13], the noun signifies an error or lapse that is hidden from the sight of others. The inclusion of this noun in the verse seems to indicate that only God can see or discern this type of error or moral mistake. In its plural absolute form, this noun indicates a willful sin (Ps 19:13).

7692. שִׁגָּיוֹן, shiggâyôwn, *shig-gaw-yone´*; or שִׁגְיֹנָה, **shiggâyônâh,** *shig-gaw-yo-naw´*; from 7686; (properly) *aberration*, i.e. (technical) a *dithyramb* or rambling poem:—Shiggaion, Shigionoth.

7693. שָׁגַל, shâgal, *shaw-gal´*; a primitive root; to *copulate* with:—lie with, ravish.

7694. שֵׁגָל, shêgal, *shay-gal´*; from 7693; a *queen* (from cohabitation):—queen.

A feminine noun meaning a queen, a concubine, a harem favourite, a consort. The primary meaning of this noun is queen. This noun was used by Nehemiah to describe the queen who sat beside the king (Ne 2:6). In the book of Psalms, the psalmist used this noun to designate the queen who sat at the right hand of the king (Ps 45:9[10]). Concubine, harem favourite, and consort are also possible definitions due to the close connection of this word with *shâgal* (7693), which can mean to sleep or to have sexual intercourse with.

7695. שֵׁגַל, shêgal, *shay-gal´*; (Chaldee); corresponding to 7694; a (legitimate) *queen*:—wife.

7696. שָׁגַע, shâga‘, *shaw-gah´*; a primitive root; to *rave* through insanity:—(be, play the) mad (man).

7697. שִׁגָּעוֹן, shiggâ‘ôwn, *shig-gaw-yone´*; from 7696; *craziness*:—furiously, madness.

7698. שֶׁגֶר, sheger, *sheh´-ger*; from an unused root probably meaning to *eject*; the *fetus* (as finally *expelled*):—that cometh of, increase.

7699. שַׁד, shad, *shad*; or שֹׁד, **shôd,** *shode*; probably from 7736 (in its original sense) contraction; the *breast* of a woman or animal (as *bulging*):—breast, pap, teat.

7700. שֵׁד, shêd, *shade*; from 7736; a *demon* (as *malignant*):—devil.

A masculine noun meaning a demon, a devil. The primary or typical translation of this noun is demon or demons. This noun was used to describe the recipient of a sacrifice (i.e. a sacrifice that was not directed or given to God [Dt 32:17]). Certain sacrifices in which sons and daughters were sacrificed were also directed toward demons (Ps 106:37). This word is also used to designate the recipients of forbidden sacrifices.

7701. שֹׁד, shôd, *shode*; or שׁוֹד, **shôwd,** *shode*; (Job 5:21), from 7736; *violence, ravage*:—desolation, destruction, oppression, robbery, spoil (-ed, -er, -ing), wasting.

A masculine noun meaning violence, destruction, desolation, robbery, spoil, wasting. The primary meaning of this word is violence or destruction. In Job, the noun is used to describe an object or idea of which not to fear (Job 5:21). The word is also used in Psalms to designate a reason for God's arising to protect the weak (Ps 12:5[6]). Isaiah used the noun to depict the reason that God weeps bitterly (i.e. the destruction of His people due to their sin [Isa 22:4]). This word was also used by Jeremiah and Amos to describe violence and havoc as social sins (Jer 6:7; Am 3:10). The primary meaning of destruction was used by Hosea to express God's reason for the coming destruction of a nation (Hos 7:13).

7702. שָׂדַד, śâdad, *saw-dad´*; a primitive root; to *abrade*, i.e. *harrow* a field:—break clods, harrow.

7703. שָׁדַד, shâdad, *shaw-dad´*; a primitive root; (properly) to *be burly*, i.e. (figurative) *powerful* (passive, *impregnable*); (by implication) to *ravage*:—dead, destroy (-er), oppress, robber, spoil (-er), × utterly, (lay) waste.

A verb meaning to be burly, to ravage, to destroy, to oppress, to assault, to spoil, to lay waste, to devastate. The primary meaning of the verb is to devastate or to destroy. This word is used to describe the destruction of the unfaithful, an action taken due to their duplicity (Pr 11:3). The verb is also used in Isaiah's prophecy against Moab to describe the action that would result on its cities (Isa 15:1). The actions of an outlaw or thief are depicted by the verb concerning a righteous person's house (Pr 24:15). The word expresses God's judgment on Egypt and the overthrowing of its hordes (Eze 32:12). The verb is also used to describe the actions of subjects such as a lion, a wolf, or a leopard in the figurative sense as a response to the rebellions and backsliding of Jerusalem (Jer 5:6). Jeremiah uses the word to describe the destruction of the tabernacle and the barrenness when everything was taken away (Jer 10:20).

7704. שָׂדֶה, śâdeh, *saw-deh´*; or שָׂדַי, **śâday,** *saw-dah´ee*; from an unused root meaning to *spread* out; a *field* (as *flat*):—country, field, ground, land, soil, × wild.

A masculine noun meaning open country, a field, a domain, a plot (of land). The primary meaning of the word is a field, oftentimes defined more descriptively as an open field. The noun is used to describe pastureland in which flocks of sheep were fed (Ge 29:2). The word is also used to describe a field or a plot of land that was normally unfrequented and in which one could meditate without being disturbed (Ge 24:63, 65). Another meaning of the word is a field in which a slain man was found (Dt 21:1). The word is also used as a place opposite of the Tent of Meeting in which the Israelites had made sacrifices but were to no longer (Le 17:5). In Numbers, the noun is used to indicate a land or territory that belonged to a nation or tribe (Nu 21:20).

7705. שִׁדָּה, shiddâh, *shid-dah´*; from 7703; a *wife* (as *mistress* of the house):— × all sorts, musical instrument.

7706. שַׁדַּי, Shadday, *shad-dah´ee*; from 7703; the *Almighty*:—Almighty.

A masculine noun and name for God meaning Shaddai, Almighty. The word occurs only forty-eight times in the Hebrew Bible, thirty-one times in the book of Job. This is a name for the Lord—the OT people of faith referring to Him as El Shaddai, God Almighty. The term is found in the passages that report God's promises of fertility, land, and abundance to them, indicating that He, the Almighty, could fulfill His promises (Ge 17:1; 28:3; 35:11). The Lord appeared to Abraham when he was ninety-nine years old and identified himself as El Shaddai, God Almighty (Ge 17:1). All three patriarchs knew Him by this name (Ge 28:1–3; 35:11); as did Joseph (Ge 48:3; cf. Ex 6:3); Ezekiel the prophet knew the tradition of Shaddai as well (Eze 10:5). Balaam, Naomi, the psalmist, Joel, and Isaiah employed the term Shaddai, Almighty (Nu 24:4; Ru 1:20; Ps 68:14[15]; Isa 13:6; Joel 1:15). But it is especially Job who uses the term appropriately as a non-Israelite (Job 5:17; 13:3; 24:1; 37:23), since it is a universal term for God. It is always found in poetic sections of material. The book of Job also uses the name the LORD, Yahweh, twenty-seven times, and it is found all but five times in the prose sections (Job 1—2; 42:7–17; see concordance for specific references).

7707. שְׁדֵיאוּר, Sheđêy'ûwr, *shed-ay-oor´*; from the same as 7704 and 217; *spreader of light; Shedejur*, an Israelite:—Shedeur.

7708. שִׂדִּים, Śiddîym, *sid-deem´*; plural from the same as 7704; *flats; Siddim*, a valley in Palestine:—Siddim.

7709. שְׁדֵמָה, sheđêmâh, *shed-ay-maw´*; apparently from 7704; a cultivated *field*:—blasted, field.

7710. שָׁדַף, shâdaph, *shaw-daf´*; a primitive root; to *scorch*:—blast.

7711. שְׁדֵפָה, sheđêphâh, *shed-ay-faw´*; or שִׁדָּפוֹן, **shiddâphôwn,** *shid-daw-fone´*; from 7710; *blight*:—blasted (-ing).

7712. שְׁדַר, sheđar, *shed-ar´*; (Chaldee); a primitive root; to *endeavour*:—labour.

7713. שְׂדֵרָה, śeđêrâh, *sed-ay-raw´*; from an unused root meaning to *regulate*; a *row*, i.e. *rank* (of soldiers), *story* (of rooms):—board, range.

7714. שַׁדְרַךְ, Shadrak, *shad-rak´*; probably of foreign origin; *Shadrak*, the Babylonian name of one of Daniel's companions:—Shadrach.

7715. שַׁדְרַךְ, Shadrak, *shad-rak´*; (Chaldee); the same as 7714:—Shadrach.

7716. שֶׂה, **śeh**, *seh*; or שֵׂי, **śêy**, *say*; probably from 7582 through the idea of *pushing* out to graze; a member of a flock, i.e. a *sheep* or *goat*:—(lesser, small) cattle, ewe, goat, lamb, sheep. Compare 2089.

7717. שָׂהֵד, **śâhêd**, *saw-hade´*; from an unused root meaning to *testify*; a *witness*:—record.

7718. שֹׁהַם, **shôham**, *sho´-ham*; from an unused root probably meaning to *blanch*; a gem, probably the *beryl* (from its *pale* green colour):—onyx.

7719. שֹׁהַם, **Shôham**, *sho´-ham*; the same as 7718; *Shoham*, an Israelite:—Shoham.

7720. שַׂהֲרֹן, **śahărôn**, *sah-har-one´*; from the same as 5469; a round *pendant* for the neck:—ornament, round tire like the moon.

7721. שׂוֹא, **śôw'**, *so*; from an unused root (akin to 5375 and 7722) meaning to *rise*; a *rising*:—arise.

7722. שׁוֹא, **shôw'**, *sho*; or (feminine) שׁוֹאָה, **shôw'âh**, *sho-aw´*; or שֹׁאָה, **shô'âh**, *sho-aw´*; from an unused root meaning to *rush* over; a *tempest*; (by implication) *devastation*:—desolate (-ion), destroy, destruction, storm, wasteness.

A masculine noun meaning ravage. When used in the feminine form *shô'âh*, the noun means devastation, ruin, desolation, or noise. The primary meaning of the word is devastation. Often this word carries with it a sense of something sudden or unexpected like that of a devastating storm (Eze 38:9). In Isaiah, the word describes a coming disaster on the day of reckoning (Isa 10:3). The noun is used to depict a wasteland or a desert (Job 30:3; 38:27). Ps 35:17 uses the masculine form of the word to indicate the ravages that held the psalmist down.

7723. שָׁוְא, **shâv'**, *shawv*; or שַׁו, **shav**, *shav*; from the same as 7722 in the sense of *desolating; evil* (as *destructive*), literal (*ruin*) or moral (especially *guile*); (figurative) *idolatry* (as false, subjective), *uselessness* (as deceptive, objective; also adverb in *vain*):—false (-ly), lie, lying, vain, vanity.

A masculine noun meaning emptiness, vanity, evil, ruin, uselessness, deception, worthless, without result, fraud, deceit. The primary meaning of the word is deceit, lie, or falsehood. God used the word to indicate that He punished Judah in vain. The word is used by the psalmist to state that all activities such as labouring, guarding, rising early, staying up late, and toiling for food were useless without God's assistance (Ps 127:1, 2). In the Ten Commandments, the word is used to describe what is prohibited (Dt 5:20). The word is used in Proverbs to indicate that which the author desires to be kept away from him: in this case, falsehood and lies (Pr 30:8). Idols were declared worthless with the usage of the noun in Jeremiah (Jer 18:15). These idols were those that led the people of God to forget Him.

7724. שְׁוָא, **Sheᵉvâ'**, *shev-aw´*; from the same as 7723; *false; Sheva*, an Israelite:—Sheva.

7725. שׁוּב, **shûwb**, *shoob*; a primitive root; to *turn* back (hence, away) transitive or intransitive, literal or figurative (not necessarily with the idea of *return* to the starting point); (generally) to *retreat*; (often adverbial) *again*:—([break, build, circumcise, dig, do anything, do evil, feed, lay down, lie down, lodge, make, rejoice, send, take, weep]) × again, (cause to) answer (+ again), × in any case (wise), × at all, averse, bring (again, back, home again), call [to mind], carry again (back), cease, × certainly, come again (back) × consider, + continually, convert, deliver (again), + deny, draw back, fetch home again, × fro, get [oneself] (back) again, × give (again), go again (back, home), [go] out, hinder, let, [see] more, × needs, be past, × pay, pervert, pull in again, put (again, up again), recall, recompense, recover, refresh, relieve, render (again), requite, rescue, restore, retrieve, (cause to, make to) return, reverse, reward, + say nay, send back, set again, slide back, still, × surely, take back (off), (cause to, make to) turn (again, self again, away, back, back again, backward, from, off), withdraw.

A verb meaning to turn, to return, to go back, to do again, to change, to withdraw, to bring back, to reestablish, to be returned, to bring back, to take, to restore, to recompense, to answer, to hinder. The verb is used over one thousand times and has various shades of meaning in its four stems. In the simple stem, it is used to describe divine and human reactions, attitudes, and feelings. The verb describes the possibility that Israel might change (turn) their minds and return to Egypt (Ex 13:17). Josiah the king turned back to the Lord with all his heart, soul, and strength (2Ki 23:25; Jer 34:15). Nevertheless, the Lord did not turn from the anger He held toward Judah (2Ki 23:26; Jer 4:28). Job pleaded with his miserable comforters to relent (i.e. turn away) from him (Job 6:29). God's people will return (repent) and seek Him in the last days (Dt 30:2; Isa 59:20; Hos 3:5) instead of turning away from Him as they are now; to return to Egypt (Isa 6:10; Hos 11:5). God's call was persistently for His people to return to Him (1Ki 8:33; Jer 4:1). Any nation can repent and turn to God for forgiveness (Jer 18:8).

The word is used metaphorically to describe things returning: God's Word will not be revoked (returned) once it has been uttered (Isa 45:23; 55:11); Jacob stayed with Laban until Esau's anger cooled off (turned back) (Ge 27:44, 45); blood guilt could return on one's own head (1Ki 2:33; Ps 7:16[17]). This word also describes the sword of Saul that did not return without success from the battlefield (2Sa 1:22).

The verb also indicates to returning to or to change into. For example, human beings return to the dust of the earth (Ge 3:19; Ecc 12:7); but a person cannot naturally return to life (2Sa 12:23); unless God's Spirit brings it about (1Ki 13:6). A land of great natural fertility can be reduced (turned into) to a farmer's cropland (Isa 29:17).

In its simplest sense, the word means to return, to restore, to go back. Abraham's descendants in their fourth generation would return to Canaan (Ge 15:16); God returned to visit His people (Ge 8:9; 18:10). It is also used to describe turning chariots about when needed (1Ki 22:33; Mic 2:8).

This verb is used with other verbs of motion, all in their infinitive or participial forms, to describe a back and forth motion; the ravens Noah sent out went back and forth (Ge 8:7). Used with another verb in general, *shûb* is either not translated or means to do again whatever action is indicated by the other verb, such as when Isaac dug again the wells his father had previously dug (Ge 26:18). A similar meaning is to take back or recapture when this verb is used with the Hebrew verb *lâqach* (3947), meaning to take or to receive (2Ki 13:25; Mic 7:19). Finally, if this verb is used with a following infinitive of another verb, it means to do over and over or more and more; Israel angered the Lord more and more than they had already angered Him by performing pagan rituals (Eze 8:17).

7726. שׁוֹבָב, **shôwbâb**, *sho-bawb´*; from 7725; *apostate*, i.e. idolatrous:—backsliding, frowardly, turn away [*from margin*].

7727. שׁוֹבָב, **Shôwbâb**, *sho-bawb´*; the same as 7726; *rebellious; Shobab*, the name of two Israelites:—Shobab.

7728. שׁוֹבֵב, **shôwbêb**, *sho-babe´*; from 7725; *apostate*, i.e. heathenish or (actually) heathen:—backsliding.

7729. שׁוּבָה, **shûwbâh**, *shoo-baw´*; from 7725; a *return*:—returning.

7730. שׂוֹבֶךְ, **śôwbek**, *so´-bek*; for 5441; a *thicket*, i.e. interlaced branches:—thick boughs.

7731. שׁוֹבָךְ, **Shôwbâk**, *sho-bawk´*; perhaps for 7730; *Shobak*, a Syrian:—Shobach.

7732. שׁוֹבָל, **Shôwbâl**, *sho-bawl´*; from the same as 7640; *overflowing; Shobal*, the name of an Edomite and two Israelites:—Shobal.

7733. שׁוֹבֵק, **Shôwbêq**, *sho-bake´*; active participle from a primitive root meaning to *leave* (compare 7662); *forsaking; Shobek*, an Israelite:—Shobek.

7734. שׂוּג, **śûwg**, *soog*; a primitive root; to *retreat*:—turn back.

7735. שׂוּג, **śûwg**, *soog*; a primitive root; to *hedge* in:—make to grow.

7736. שׁוּד, **shûwd**, *shood*; a primitive root; (properly to) *swell* up, i.e. figurative (by implication of *insolence*) to *devastate*:—waste.

7737. שָׁוָה, **shâvâh**, *shaw-vaw´*; a primitive root; (properly) to *level*, i.e. *equalize*; (figurative) to *resemble*; (by implication) to *adjust* (i.e. counterbalance, be suitable, compose, place, yield, etc.):—avail, behave, bring forth, compare, countervail, (be, make) equal, lay, be (make, a-) like, make plain, profit, reckon.

7738. שָׁוָה, **shâvâh**, *shaw-vaw´*; a primitive root; to *destroy*:—× substance [*from the margin*].

7739. שְׁוָה, **shᵉvâh**, *shev-aw´*; (Chaldee); corresponding to 7737; to *resemble*:—make like.

7740. שָׁוֵה, **Shâvêh**, *shaw-vay´*; from 7737; *plain; Shaveh*, a place in Palestine:—Shaveh.

7741. שָׁוֵה קִרְיָתַיִם, **Shâvêh Qiryâthayim**, *shaw-vay´ kir-yaw-thah´-yim*; from the same as 7740 and the dual of 7151; *plain of a double city; Shaveh-Kirjathajim*, a place East of the Jordan:—Shaveh Kiriathaim.

7742. שׂוּחַ, **śûwach**, *soo´-akh*; a primitive root; to *muse* pensively:—meditate.

7743. שׁוּחַ, **shûwach**, *shoo´-akh*; a primitive root; to *sink*, literal or figurative:—bow down, incline, humble.

7744. שׁוּחַ, **Shûwach**, *shoo´-akh*; from 7743; *dell; Shuäch*, a son of Abraham:—Shuah.

7745. שׁוּחָה, **shûwchâh**, *shoo-khaw´*; from 7743; a *chasm*:—ditch, pit.

A feminine noun meaning a ditch, a pit, a chasm. The primary meaning of the word is pit. The verb is used primarily to describe figuratively a trap that leads to ruin. Proverbs uses this word in a figurative sense to describe a prostitute as a deep pit in comparison to a wayward wife as a narrow well (Pr 23:27). This word could also be used to describe plots against someone, as where Jeremiah stated that his accusers had dug pits for him (Jer 18:20). The word also describes the mouth of an adulteress (i.e. a deep pit [Pr 22:14]). Out of the six times that it is used in the OT, only one is used in its literal sense, describing a rift through which God led His people (Jer 2:6).

7746. שׁוּחָה, **Shûwchâh**, *shoo-khaw´*; the same as 7745; *Shuchah*, an Israelite:—Shuah.

7747. שׁוּחִי, **Shûwchîy**, *shoo-khee´*; patronymic from 7744; a *Shuchite* or descendant of Shuach:—Shuhite.

7748. שׁוּחָם, **Shûwchâm**, *shoo-khawm´*; from 7743; *humbly; Shucham*, an Israelite:—Shuham.

7749. שׁוּחָמִי, **Shûwchâmîy**, *shoo-khaw-mee´*; patronymic from 7748; a *Shuchamite* (collective):—Shuhamites.

7750. שׂוּט, **śûwṭ**, *soot*; or (by permutation) סוּט, **sûwṭ**, *soot*; a primitive root; to *detrude*, i.e. (intransitive and figurative) *become derelict* (wrongly practise; namely, idolatry):—turn aside to.

7751. שׁוּט, **shûwṭ**, *shoot*; a primitive root; (properly) to *push* forth; (but used only figurative) to *lash*, i.e. (the sea with oars) to *row*; (by implication) to *travel*:—go (about, through, to and fro), mariner, rower, run to and fro.

7752. שׁוֹט, **shôwṭ**, *shote*; from 7751; a *lash* (literal or figurative):—scourge, whip.

7753. שׂוּךְ, **śûwk**, *sook*; a primitive root; to *entwine*, i.e. *shut* in (for formation, protection or restraint):—fence, (make an) hedge (up).

7754. שׂוֹךְ, **śôwk**, *soke*; or (feminine) שׂוֹכָה, **śôwkâh**, *so-kaw´*; from 7753; a *branch* (as *interleaved*):—bough.

7755. שׂוֹכֹה, **Śôwkôh**, *so-ko´*; or שֹׂכֹה, **Śôkôh**, *so-ko´*; or שׂוֹכוֹ, **Śôwkôw**, *so-ko´*; from 7753; *Sokoh* or *Soko*, the name of two places in Palestine:—Shocho, Shochoh, Sochoh, Soco, Socoh.

7756. שׂוּכָתִי, **Śûwkâthîy**, *soo-kaw-thee´*; probably patronymic from a name corresponding to 7754 (feminine); a *Sukathite* or descendant of an unknown Israelite named Sukah:—Suchathite.

7757. שׁוּל, **shûwl**, *shool*; from an unused root meaning to *hang* down; a *skirt*; (by implication) a bottom *edge*:—hem, skirt, train.

7758. שׁוֹלָל, **shôwlâl**, *sho-lawl´*; or שֵׁילָל, **shêylâl**, *shay-lawl´*; (Mic 1:8), from 7997; *nude* (especially barefoot); (by implication) *captive*:—spoiled, stripped.

7759. שׁוּלַמִּית, **Shûwlammîyth**, *shoo-lam-meeth´*; from 7999; *peaceful* (with the article always prefixed, making it a pet name); the *Shulammith*, an epithet of Solomon's queen:—Shulamite.

7760. שׂוּם, **śûwm**, *soom*; or שִׂים, **śîym**, *seem*; a primitive root; to *put* (used in a great variety of applications, literal, figurative, inference and ellipsis):— × any wise, appoint, bring, call [a name], care, cast in, change, charge, commit, consider, convey, determine, + disguise, dispose, do, get, give, heap up, hold, impute, lay (down, up), leave, look, make (out), mark, + name, × on, ordain, order, + paint, place, preserve, purpose, put (on), + regard, rehearse, reward, (cause to) set (on, up), shew, + steadfastly, take, × tell, + tread down, ([over-]) turn, × wholly, work.

A verb meaning to appoint, to bring, to call, to put, to change, to charge, to commit, to consider, to convey, to determine. The primary meaning of the verb is to put, to set, or to place. The verb indicates that which God put on the earth, as noted in Genesis where God put the man and woman that He formed in the Garden of Eden (Ge 2:8). The usage of the verb in this sense indicates God's sovereignty over all creation, especially that of humankind. The verb is also used to describe Samuel's action concerning the stone he named Ebenezer (1Sa 7:12). This stone was set up between Mizpah and Shen to remember God's deliverance of the Israelites from the Philistines. The verb is used to describe a committing of one's cause before God (Job 5:8). The word is used in Exodus in response to an interaction between Moses and God, in which God gave a new decree and law to the Israelites (Ex 15:25). In this setting, the verb again emphasizes God's sovereignty, His ability to establish the order of things, and His ability to control the elements of nature and disease. In Deuteronomy, *śûm* is used to describe God's appointing of leaders over the different tribes of Israel, for their numbers were too great for Moses alone (Dt 1:13). The word is also used to indicate a charging of someone, as where a man charged his wife with premarital sex (Dt 22:14).

7761. שׂוּם, **śûwm**, *soom*; (Chaldee); corresponding to 7760:—+ command, give, lay, make, + name, + regard, set.

7762. שׁוּם, **shûwm**, *shoom*; from an unused root meaning to *exhale; garlic* (from its rank *odor*):—garlic.

7763. שׁוֹמֵר, **Shôwmêr**, *sho-mare´*; or שֹׁמֵר, **Shômêr**, *sho-mare´*; active participle of 8104; *keeper; Shomer*, the name of two Israelites:—Shomer.

7764. שׁוּנִי, **Shûwnîy**, *shoo-nee´*; from an unused root meaning to *rest; quiet; Shuni*, an Israelite:—Shuni.

7765. שׁוּנִי, **Shûwnîy**, *shoo-nee´*; patronymic from 7764; a *Shunite* (collective) or descendants of Shuni:—Shunites.

7766. שׁוּנֵם, **Shûwnêm**, *shoo-name´*; probably from the same as 7764; *quietly; Shunem*, a place in Palestine:—Shunem.

7767. שׁוּנַמִּית, **Shûwnammîyth**, *shoo-nam-meeth´*; patrial from 7766; a *Shunammitess*, or female inhabitant of Shunem:—Shunamite.

7768. שָׁוַע, **shâva‘**, *shaw-vah´*; a primitive root; (properly) to *be free*; but used only causative and reflexive to *halloo* (for help, i.e. *freedom* from some trouble):—cry (aloud, out), shout.

7769. שׁוּעַ, **shûwa‘**, *shoo´-ah*; from 7768; a *halloo*:—cry, riches.

7770. שׁוּעַ, **Shûwa‘**, *shoo´-ah*; the same as 7769; *Shuä*, a Canaanite:—Shua, Shuah.

7771. שׁוֹעַ**, shôwa'**, *sho´-ah*; from 7768 in the original sense of *freedom*; a *noble*, i.e. *liberal, opulent*; also (as noun in the derived sense) a *halloo*:—bountiful, crying, rich.

7772. שׁוֹעַ**, Shôwa'**, *sho´-ah*; the same as 7771; *rich; Shoä*, an Oriental people:—Shoa.

7773. שֶׁוַע**, sheva'**, *sheh´-vah*; from 7768; a *halloo*:—cry.

7774. שׁוּעָא**, Shûw'â'**, *shoo-aw´*; from 7768; *wealth; Shuä*, an Israelitess:—Shua.

7775. שַׁוְעָה**, shav'âh**, *shav-aw´*; feminine of 7773; a *hallooing*:—crying.

7776. שׁוּעָל**, shûw'âl**, *shoo-awl´*; or שֻׁעָל**, shu'âl**, *shoo-awl´*; from the same as 8168; a *jackal* (as a *burrower*):—fox.

7777. שׁוּעָל**, Shûw'âl**, *shoo-awl´*; the same as 7776; *Shuäl*, the name of an Israelite and of a place in Palestine:—Shual.

7778. שׁוֹעֵר**, shôw'êr**, *sho-are´*; or שֹׁעֵר**, shô'êr**, *sho-are´*; active participle of 8176 (as denominative from 8179); a *janitor*:—door-keeper, porter.

7779. שׁוּף**, shûwph**, *shoof*; a primitive root; (properly) to *gape*, i.e. *snap* at; (figurative) to *overwhelm*:—break, bruise, cover.

7780. שׁוֹפָךְ**, Shôwphâk**, *sho-fawk´*; from 8210; *poured; Shophak*, a Syrian:—Shophach.

7781. שׁוּפָמִי**, Shûwphâmîy**, *shoo-faw-mee´*; patronymic from 8197; a *Shuphamite* (collective) or descendants of Shephupham:—Shuphamite.

7782. שׁוֹפָר**, shôwphâr**, *sho-far´*; or שֹׁפָר**, shôphâr**, *sho-far´*; from 8231 in the original sense of *incising*; a *cornet* (as giving a *clear* sound) or curved horn:—cornet, trumpet.

7783. שׁוּק**, shûwq**, *shook*; a primitive root; to *run* after or over, i.e. *overflow*:—overflow, water.

7784. שׁוּק**, shûwq**, *shook*; from 7783; a *street* (as *run* over):—street.

7785. שׁוֹק**, shôwq**, *shoke*; from 7783; the (lower) *leg* (as a *runner*):—hip, leg, shoulder, thigh.

7786. שׂוּר**, śûwr**, *soor*; a primitive root; (properly) to *vanquish*; (by implication) to *rule* (causative, *crown*):—make princes, have power, reign. See 5493.

A verb meaning to vanquish, to rule, to have power. The primary meaning of this word is to rule or to have power over. In Hosea, the verb denotes what will happen to the parents of children (i.e. they will be vanquished and bereaved of their children) when God turns away from them (see Hos 9:12).

The word is also used to describe Abimelech's ruling of Israel for three years (Jgs 9:22). God sent an evil spirit between Abimelech and the people of Shechem, and they acted treacherously against Abimelech. This was done so that the shedding of the blood of Jerub-Baal's seventy sons might be avenged on their brother Abimelech and the citizens of Shechem who helped him. The verb also denotes one of the reasons for Israel's upcoming punishment. Not only did they choose princes without Yahweh's approval, but Israel also made and worshipped idols in blatant disregard for the rulership and dominion of Yahweh over them (Hos 8:4).

7787. שׂוּר**, śûwr**, *soor*; a primitive root [rather identical with 7786 through the idea of *reducing* to pieces; compare 4883]; to *saw*:—cut.

7788. שׁוּר**, shûwr**, *shoor*; a primitive root; (properly) to *turn*, i.e. *travel* about (as a harlot or a merchant):—go, singular See also 7891.

7789. שׁוּר**, shûwr**, *shoor*; a primitive root [rather identical with 7788 through the idea of *going round* for inspection]; to *spy* out, i.e. (general) *survey*, (for evil) *lurk for*, (for good) *care for*:—behold, lay wait, look, observe, perceive, regard, see.

7790. שׁוּר**, shûwr**, *shoor*; from 7889; a *foe* (as *lying in wait*):—enemy.

7791. שׁוּר**, shûwr**, *shoor*; from 7788; a *wall* (as *going about*):—wall.

7792. שׁוּר**, shûwr**, *shoor*; (Chaldee); corresponding to 7791:—wall.

7793. שׁוּר**, Shûwr**, *shoor*; the same as 7791; *Shur*, a region of the Desert:—Shur.

7794. שׁוֹר**, shôwr**, *shore*; from 7788; a *bullock* (as a *traveller*):—bull (-ock), cow, ox, wall [*by mistake for* 7791].

7795. שׂוֹרָה**, śôwrâh**, *so-raw´*; from 7786 in the primitive sense of 5493; (properly) a *ring*, i.e. (by analogy) a *row* (adverb):—principal.

7796. שׂוֹרֵק**, Sôwrêq**, *so-rake´*; the same as 8321; a *vine; Sorek*, a valley in Palestine:—Sorek.

7797. שׂוּשׂ**, śûwś**, *soos*; or שִׂישׂ**, śîyś**, *sece*; a primitive root; to *be bright*, i.e. *cheerful*:—be glad, × greatly, joy, make mirth, rejoice.

7798. שַׁוְשָׁא**, Shavshâ'**, *shav-shaw´*; from 7797; *joyful; Shavsha*, an Israelite:—Shavsha.

7799. שׁוּשַׁן**, shûwshan**, *shoo-shan´*; or שׁוֹשָׁן**, shôwshân**, *sho-shawn´*; or שֹׁשָׁן**, shôshân**, *sho-shawn´*; and (feminine) שׁוֹשַׁנָּה**, shôwshannâh**, *sho-shan-naw´*; from 7797; a *lily* (from its *whiteness*), as a flower or architectural ornament; also a (straight) *trumpet* (from the *tubular* shape):—lily, Shoshannim.

7800. שׁוּשַׁן**, Shûwshan**, *shoo-shan´*; the same as 7799; *Shushan*, a place in Persia:—Shushan.

7801. שׁוּשַׁנְכִי**, Shûwshankîy**, *shoo-shan-kee´*; (Chaldee); of foreign origin; a *Shushankite* (collective) or inhabitant of some unknown place in Assyria:—Susanchites.

7802. שׁוּשַׁן עֵדוּת**, Shûwshan 'Êdûwth**, *shoo-shan´ ay-dooth´*; or (plural of former) שׁוֹשַׁנִּים עֵדוּת**, Shôwshannîym 'Êdûwth**, *sho-shan-neem´ ay-dooth´*; from 7799 and 5715; *lily* (or *trumpet*) *of assemblage; Shushan-Eduth* or *Shoshannim-Eduth*, the title of a popular song:—Shoshannim-Eduth, Shushan-eduth.

7803. שׁוּתֶלַח**, Shûwthelach**, *shoo-theh´-lakh*; probably from 7582 and the same as 8520; *crash of breakage; Shuthelach*, the name of two Israelites:—Shuthelah.

7804. שְׁזַב**, sh^ezab**, *shez-ab´*; (Chaldee); corresponding to 5800; to *leave*, i.e. (causative) *free*:—deliver.

7805. שָׁזַף**, shâzaph**, *shaw-zaf´*; a primitive root; to *tan* (by sunburning); figurative (as if by a piercing ray) to *scan*:—look up, see.

7806. שָׁזַר**, shâzar**, *shaw-zar´*; a primitive root; to *twist* (a thread of straw):—twine.

7807. שַׁח**, shach**, *shakh*; from 7817; *sunk*, i.e. *downcast*:— + humble.

7808. שֵׂחַ**, śêach**, *say´-akh*; for 7879; *communion*, i.e. (reflexive) *meditation*:—thought.

7809. שָׁחַד**, shâchad**, *shaw-khad´*; a primitive root; to *donate*, i.e. *bribe*:—hire, give a reward.

7810. שַׁחַד**, shôchad**, *shokh´-ad*; from 7809; a *donation* (venal or redemptive):—bribe (-ry), gift, present, reward.

7811. שָׂחָה**, śâchâh**, *saw-khaw´*; a primitive root; to *swim*; (causative) to *inundate*:—(make to) swim.

7812. שָׁחָה**, shâchâh**, *shaw-khaw´*; a primitive root; to *depress*, i.e. *prostrate* (especially reflexive in homage to royalty or God):—bow (self) down, crouch, fall down (flat), humbly beseech, do (make) obeisance, do reverence, make to stoop, worship.

A verb meaning to bow down, to prostrate oneself, to crouch, to fall down, to humbly beseech, to do reverence, to worship. The primary meaning of the word is to bow down. This verb is used to indicate bowing before a monarch or a superior and paying homage to him or her (Ge 43:28). In contexts such as Genesis 24:26, *shâchâh* is used to indicate bowing down in worship to Yahweh. The psalmists used this word to describe all the earth bowing down in worship to God as a response to His great power (Ps 66:4); or bowing down in worship and kneeling before the Lord (Ps 95:6). This act of worship is given to God because He deserves it and because those that are speaking are people of His pasture.

The word is also used of Joseph when he described the sheaves of his brothers and parents bowing down to his sheaf after it stood upright in a dream that he had (Ge 37:7). Gideon also interacted with a dream through which God spoke. When he overheard a man telling his friend a dream that the man had and its interpretation, he worshipped God (Jgs 7:15).

Joshua instructed the people of Israel not to associate with the nations remaining around them and not to bow down to or serve any of their gods. He instructed Israel to hold fast to the true God, Yahweh (Jos 23:7). In Zephaniah, the word is also used for worship. When Yahweh destroys all the gods of the land, the nations on every shore will worship Him (Zep 2:11).

7813. שָׂחוּ, **sâchûw**, *saw´-khoo*; from 7811; a *pond* (for *swimming*):—to swim in.

7814. שְׂחוֹק, **s^e^chôwq**, *sekh-oke´*; or שְׂחֹק, **s^e^chôq**, *sekh-oke´*; from 7832; *laughter* (in merriment or defiance):—derision, laughter (-ed to scorn, -ing), mocked, sport.

7815. שְׁחוֹר, **sh^e^chôwr**, *shekh-ore´*; from 7835; *dinginess*, i.e. perhaps *soot*:—coal.

A masculine noun meaning dinginess, blackness. This word is used to describe a punishment of Israel, i.e. they were blacker than soot, and their skin had shriveled on their bones (La 4:8). The people of different nations told the Israelites that they must leave for they were seen as unclean. This is similar to the descriptions of the results of the Day of the Lord, which will be a day of blackness (see Joel 2:2). This blackness figuratively represents an army of locusts with which Yahweh will punish those who live in the land for their sin. For this reason, the prophet declared that all who live in the land should and will tremble in fear.

7816. שְׁחוּת, **sh^e^chûwth**, *shekh-ooth´*; from 7812; *pit*:—pit.

A feminine noun meaning pit. Metaphorically speaking, it is a trap that is created as one leads the upright along the path of evil (Pr 28:10). This trap or pit will eventually ensnare its builder. As the wicked plot and scheme against the righteous, in the end, they will only succeed in being caught in their own traps.

7817. שָׁחַח, **shâchach**, *shaw-khakh´*; a primitive root; to *sink* or *depress* (reflexive or causative):—bend, bow (down), bring (cast) down, couch, humble self, be (bring) low, stoop.

7818. שָׂחַט, **sâchaṭ**, *saw-khat´*; a primitive root; to *tread* out, i.e. *squeeze* (grapes):—press.

7819. שָׁחַט, **shâchaṭ**, *shaw-khat´*; a primitive root; to *slaughter* (in sacrifice or massacre):—kill, offer, shoot out, slay, slaughter.

A verb meaning to slaughter, to kill, to offer, to shoot out, to slay. The primary meaning of the verb is to slaughter. In Leviticus, the word is used to indicate that the one who brings the sacrifice is the person who will slaughter the animal (Le 1:5). After the slaughtering, the priests brought the blood and other parts of the animal to the altar. In contrast to Leviticus, 2 Chronicles indicates that the worshippers could not slaughter their sacrifices because they did not consecrate themselves and were ceremonially unclean. In this case, the Levites (i.e. priests) had to slaughter the lambs for all who were ceremonially unclean (cf. 2Ch 30:17). This verb is also used to indicate an ineffective sacrifice where the offerers were only going through the motions of worship (Isa 66:3). Even though the object of their worship appears to be God, their hearts were still bent toward evil. This failure is the reason for their upcoming judgment. Another usage of the verb depicts Saul's army pouncing on the plunder, butchering sheep, cattle, and calves, and eating the meat together with the blood, which was forbidden in the Law (1Sa 14:32). This makes the actions of Saul's army in direct disobedience of God's Law.

The verb is also used to describe the process of a human sacrifice to Yahweh (i.e. the process used to test Abraham with his son Isaac [Ge 22:10]). Since He does not desire human sacrifices, God stopped Abraham from sacrificing his son Isaac. When used in the context of a human sacrifice to false gods, the verb describes the actual process being carried out rather than the anticipated process such as that found with Abraham (Isa 57:5; Eze 16:21; 23:39).

7820. שָׁחַט, **shâchaṭ**, *shaw-khat´*; a primitive root [rather identical with 7819 through the idea of *striking*]; to *hammer out*:—beat.

7821. שְׁחִיטָה, **sh^e^chîyṭâh**, *shekh-ee-taw´*; from 7819; *slaughter*:—killing.

7822. שְׁחִין, **sh^e^chîyn**, *shekh-een´*; from an unused root probably meaning to *burn; inflammation*, i.e. an *ulcer*:—boil, botch.

7823. שָׁחִיס, **shâchîys**, *shaw-khece´*; or סָחִישׁ, **sâchîysh**, *saw-kheesh´*; from an unused root apparently meaning to *sprout; after-growth*:—(that) which springeth of the same.

7824. שָׂחִיף, **sâchîyph**, *shaw-kheef´*; from the same as 7828; a *board* (as *chipped* thin):—cieled with.

7825. שְׁחִית, **sh^e^chîyth**, *shekh-eeth´*; from 7812; a *pit*-fall (literal or figurative):—destruction, pit.

A feminine noun meaning a pit, destruction, and pitfall. In La 4:20, the Lord's anointed, King Zedekiah, was caught in the trap of the Babylonians. In Psalms, the noun is used to indicate the crisis from which Yahweh saves those who cry out to Him in their troubles (Ps 107:20). By simply a mere utterance and sending forth His word, God heals and rescues from destruction those who cry out to Him. The proper response of those rescued is to give thank offerings and tell of His works through songs of joy.

7826. שַׁחַל, **shachal**, *shakh´-al*; from an unused root probably meaning to *roar*; a *lion* (from his characteristic *roar*):—(fierce) lion.

7827. שְׁחֵלֶת, **sh^e^chêleth**, *shekh-ay´-leth*; apparently from the same as 7826 through some obscure idea, perhaps that of *peeling* off by concussion of sound; a *scale* or shell, i.e. the aromatic *mussel*:—onycha.

7828. שַׁחַף, **shachaph**, *shakh´-af*; from an unused root meaning to *peel*, i.e. *emaciate*; the *gull* (as *thin*):—cuckoo.

7829. שַׁחֶפֶת, **shachepheth**, *shakh-eh´-feth*; from the same as 7828; *emaciation*:—consumption.

7830. שַׁחַץ, **shachats**, *shakh´-ats*; from an unused root apparently meaning to *strut; haughtiness* (as evinced by the attitude):—× lion, pride.

7831. שַׁחֲצוֹם, **Shachătsôwm**, *shakh-ats-ome´*; from the same as 7830; *proudly; Shachatsom*, a place in Palestine:—Shahazimah [*from the margin*].

7832. שָׂחַק, **sâchaq**, *saw-khak´*; a primitive root; to *laugh* (in pleasure or detraction); (by implication) to *play*:—deride, have in derision, laugh, make merry, mock (-er), play, rejoice, (laugh to) scorn, be in (make) sport.

7833. שָׁחַק, **shâchaq**, *shaw-khak´*; a primitive root; to *comminate* (by trituration or attrition):—beat, wear.

A verb meaning to beat, to wear, to rub away, to beat fine, to pulverize. The primary usage of the verb is to beat fine or to rub away. In Job, the word is used to describe water wearing away stones in conjunction with torrents washing away the soil. This definition was used as a simile for Job's accusation that Yahweh was destroying a person's hope (Job 14:19). Yahweh uses the verb to dictate to Moses how a blend of incense was to be made (Ex 30:36). This formula, which was placed in front of the Testimony in the Tent of Meeting, was to be regarded as holy and only meant for the Lord. Anyone who used it in another context would be cut off from his people. In a figurative sense, *shâchaq* is used to describe David's victory over his enemies in which he beat them down like fine dust (2Sa 22:43, Ps 18:42[Ps 18:43]).

7834. שַׁחַק, shachaq, *shakh´-ak*; from 7833; a *powder* (as *beaten* small); (by analogy) a thin *vapor*; (by extension) the *firmament*:—cloud, small dust, heaven, sky.

A masculine noun meaning dust, a fine cloud, a thin cloud. The primary usage of the word denotes a cloud. Often this word is used to depict a cloud or clouds (in the plural) in the sky (Job 35:5, Pr 8:28). In Psalms, this word is used to describe the heavens (Ps 36:5[Ps 36:6]). In a metaphorical sense, Moses described God as riding on the heavens and clouds in His majesty to help His people (Dt 33:26). Used in this sense, it denotes Yahweh as Ruler over the heavens and all that is in them. This word is used to depict dark rain clouds which form a canopy around Him (2Sa 22:12). The word can also be used to denote nations as fine dust (Isa 40:15).

7835. שָׁחַר, shâchar, *shaw-khar´*; a primitive root [rather identical with 7836 through the idea of the *duskiness* of early dawn]; to be *dim* or dark (in colour):—be black.

7836. שָׁחַר, shâchar, *shaw-khar´*; a primitive root; (properly) to *dawn*, i.e. (figurative) *be* (up) *early* at any task (with the implication of earnestness); (by extension) to *search* for (with painstaking):—[do something] betimes, enquire early, rise (seek) betimes, seek diligently (early, in the morning).

7837. שַׁחַר, shachar, *shakh´-ar*; from 7836; *dawn* (literal, figurative or adverb):—day (-spring), early, light, morning, whence riseth.

7838. שָׁחֹר, shâchôr, *shaw-khore´*; or שָׁחוֹר, **shâ-chôwr,** *shaw-khore´*; from 7835; (properly) *dusky*, but also (absolute) *jetty*:—black.

7839. שַׁחֲרוּת, shachărûwth, *shakh-ar-ooth´*; from 7836; a *dawning*, i.e. (figurative) *juvenescence*:—youth.

7840. שְׁחַרְחֹר, sheharchôr, *shekh-ar-khor´*; from 7835; *swarthy*:—black.

7841. שְׁחַרְיָה, Shecharyâh, *shekh-ar-yaw´*; from 7836 and 3050; *Jah has sought; Shecharjah*, an Israelite:—Shehariah.

7842. שַׁחֲרַיִם, Shachărayim, *shakh-ar-ah´-yim*; dual of 7837; *double dawn; Shacharajim*, an Israelite:—Shaharaim.

7843. שָׁחַת, shâchath, *shaw-khath´*; a primitive root; to *decay*, i.e. (causative) *ruin* (literal or figurative):—batter, cast off, corrupt (-er, thing), destroy (-er, -uction), lose, mar, perish, spill, spoiler, × utterly, waste (-r).

A verb meaning to spoil, to ruin, to destroy, to pervert, to corrupt, to become corrupt, to wipe out. The verb is used to denote the action(s) of the world (i.e. it is corrupt) and ultimately the reason for God's flooding it (Ge 6:11, 12). However, even in total destruction meant to punish the evil of humans, God was sure to save a remnant and therefore keep His part of the covenant. This idea of a saved remnant is predominant throughout the rest of the OT.

Another usage of the verb depicts disobedience to God's command to be fruitful and multiply by spoiling or wasting semen on the ground (Ge 38:9). In this case, Onan's disobedience led to his death, for what he did was wicked in the eyes of Yahweh. The verb is also used to describe violating the covenant in terms of being corrupt (Mal 2:8). As Lot looked over the valley of the Jordan, this word was used to depict what would happen to Sodom and Gomorrah in a future time because of their wickedness (Ge 13:10). In the context of the plagues, the smearing of blood on the lintels and doorposts protected Israel from the destruction of their firstborn (Ex 12:23). When the destroyer came, he would pass by those who had blood on the lintels and doorposts of their houses.

Jerusalem was saved from destruction in 2 Samuel when the Lord was grieved due to the calamity of His people (2Sa 24:16). This verb is used to denote the destruction of a slave's eye that allowed him to go free (Ex 21:26). In Deuteronomy, God prohibited the destruction of fruit trees, for their fruit could be eaten (Dt 20:19–20). He commanded this, for the trees were for the benefit of humans. He also prohibited the shaving (i.e. in terms of spoiling, destroying) of one's beard (Le 19:27).

7844. שְׁחַת, shechath, *shekh-ath´*; (Chaldee); corresponding to 7843:—corrupt, fault.

An Aramaic verb meaning to corrupt. This word can also function as a noun, in which it designates fault. The verb is used in Daniel to depict what the astrologers did to their words in an effort to gain more time from the king (Da 2:9). The inability of the astrologers and other wise men to interpret Nebuchadnezzar's dream set the stage for Daniel.

In Da 6:5, the word is used as a noun and designated the charge against Daniel. Since no fault could be found, the administrators and satraps persuaded King Darius to issue and enforce the decree that no one could pray to anyone or anything but him for a period of thirty days or be thrown into the lions' den.

7845. שַׁחַת, shachath, *shakh´-ath*; from 7743; a *pit* (especially as a trap); (figurative) *destruction*:—corruption, destruction, ditch, grave, pit.

A feminine noun denoting a pit, a ditch, a grave, a hollow place. Its prominent usage is pit. The word is used to describe the pit of destruction from which the Lord's love saves (Isa 38:17). The psalmist uses the word figuratively to designate a type of trap that those who are seeking his life have dug for him (Ps 35:7). The occurrence of the word in Ezekiel metaphorically denotes a pit in which lions are caught (Eze 19:4). The term lion is used to represent Israel's Prince Jehoahaz and is a metaphorical representation of his policies. He learned to tear prey and devour people. The noun is also used to denote Sheol (Job 33:24; Eze 28:8). Job uses the word in a rhetorical sense to describe a situation in which there is no hope (Job 17:14). He stated that if he allowed himself to call corruption his father and the worm his mother and sister, where would his hope lie?

7846. שֵׂט, sêṭ, *sayte*; or סֵט, **sêṭ,** *sayt*; from 7750; a *departure* from right, i.e. *sin*:—revolter, that turn aside.

7847. שָׂטָה, sâṭâh, *saw-taw´*; a primitive root; to *deviate* from duty:—decline, go aside, turn.

7848. שִׁטָּה, shiṭṭâh, *shit-taw´*; feminine of a derivative [only in the plural שִׁטִּים, **shiṭṭîym,** *shit-teem´*, meaning the *sticks* of wood] from the same as 7850; the *acacia* (from its *scourging* thorns):—shittah, shittim. See also 1029.

7849. שָׁטַח, shâṭach, *shaw-takh´*; a primitive root; to *expand*:—all abroad, enlarge, spread, stretch out.

7850. שֹׁטֵט, shôṭêṭ, *sho-tate´*; active participle of an otherwise unused root meaning (properly, to *pierce*; but only as denominative from 7752) to *flog*; a *goad*:—scourge.

7851. שִׁטִּים, Shiṭṭîym, *shit-teem´*; the same as the plural of 7848; *acacia* trees; *Shittim*, a place East of the Jordan:—Shittim.

7852. שָׂטַם, sâṭam, *saw-tam´*; a primitive root; (properly) to *lurk* for, i.e. *persecute*:—hate, oppose self against.

7853. שָׂטַן, sâṭan, *saw-tan´*; a primitive root; to *attack*, (figurative) *accuse*:—(be an) adversary, resist.

A verb meaning to accuse, to slander, and to harbor animosity toward. The verb is used only six times and presents a negative attitude or bias against something. The psalmist complained about those who attacked or slandered him when he pursued what was good (Ps 38:20[21]); even accusing or attacking him in spite of his positive attitude toward them (Ps 109:4). The psalmist asked for his accusers to be destroyed by shame (Ps 71:13; 109:20, 29). Satan stood ready to accuse or to persecute Joshua, the high priest, in the postexilic community (Zec 3:1). Also, see the noun *śâṭân* (7854).

7854. שָׂטָן, sâṭân, *saw-tawn´*; from 7853; an *opponent*; especially (with the article prefixed) *Satan*, the arch-enemy of good:—adversary, Satan, withstand.

A masculine noun meaning an adversary, Satan, an accuser. This noun is used twenty-seven times. In Job it is found fourteen times meaning (the) Satan, the accuser. Satan presented himself among the sons of God and roundly accused Job of not loving or serving God with integrity (Job 1:6, 7; 2:1, 2, 4, 7); all of these uses are in the prologue of the book (Job 1—2). In Zechariah, this noun is used three times with the verb to accuse (*śâṭan* [7853]). Satan stood ready to accuse the high priest Joshua (Zec 3:1, 2). In 1Ch 21:1, Satan was depicted as the one who motivated David insolently to take a census of Israel's army (cf. 2Sa 24:1).

The noun is used in a general sense to indicate any adversary or someone who hinders or opposes. The angel of the Lord opposed Balaam and his donkey on their way to curse Israel, acting in opposition (Nu 22:22, 32); the Philistines feared that David might act in opposition to them in battle (1Sa 29:4; 2Sa 19:22[23]). In Solomon's day, the Lord had given him rest all around him (cf. 1Ki 4:24[5:4]); except for Rezon who reigned in Aram (1Ki 11:14, 23, 25). The psalmist's enemies appointed an accuser to attack him, a person who was wicked (Ps 109:6).

7855. **שִׂטְנָה, śiṭnâh,** *sit-naw´*; from 7853; *opposition* (by letter):—accusation.

A feminine noun meaning accusation, opposition, hostility. Its primary meaning of the word is accusation. In Ezra, the word is used to depict the accusation which those who opposed the rebuilding of the Temple in Jerusalem brought before the king (Ezr 4:6). This accusation stated that the Jews were a rebellious people and that if the completion of the Temple were allowed, they would not submit to the authority of Artaxerxes, king of Persia. This accusation resulted in stopping the building process until the second year of the reign of Darius.

7856. **שִׂטְנָה, Śiṭnâh,** *sit-naw´*; the same as 7855; *Sitnah*, the name of a well in Palestine:—Sitnah.

7857. **שָׁטַף, shâṭaph,** *shaw-taf´*; a primitive root; to *gush*; (by implication) to *inundate, cleanse*; (by analogy) to *gallop, conquer*:—drown, (over-) flow (-whelm), rinse, run, rush, (thoroughly) wash (away).

A verb meaning to gush, to cleanse, to conquer, to drown, to overflow, to overwhelm, to rinse, to run, to rush, to wash away. In its prominent meaning, the word means to wash away. *Šâṭaph* is used to depict what the Lord will do to a hiding place, that is, He will overflow it (Isa 28:17). This word is used to describe God's power as a flooding downpour (Isa 28:2). It also describes a medium through which God delivers punishment (Jer 47:2). The Lord declared that the time had come to destroy the Philistines, and He would do so, metaphorically speaking, by raising up the waters into an overflowing torrent. If a man with a discharge touched another without rinsing his hands, the person touched had to wash the infected clothing and take a bath with water; he or she would be unclean until evening (Le 15:11). Ezekiel used *shâṭaph* metaphorically to describe the Lord cleansing His bride (Eze 16:9). The Song of Songs uses this word to depict what cannot be done to love, that is, waters cannot flood or quench it. True love withstands all tests (SS 8:7). The psalmist made use of *shâṭaph* to indicate a weariness of life and its trials, speaking metaphorically of sinking into the miry depths in which there is no foothold (Ps 69:2[3]). In Ps 124:4, the psalmist used the word to indicate a physical or material tragedy that is avoided with God on his side. Isaiah used the verb to indicate divine judgment against Judah (Isa 8:8); and Ephraim (Isa 28:2, 15, 17, 18). The usage of this word can also indicate a flooding over or utter destruction at the hands of another nation, sometimes dictated by God and at other times simply by the nature of people (Jer 47:2; Da 11:10, 22, 40).

7858. **שֶׁטֶף, sheṭeph,** *sheh´-tef*; or **שֵׁטֶף, shêṭeph,** *shay´-tef*; from 7857; a *deluge* (literal or figurative):—flood, outrageous, overflowing.

A masculine noun meaning a flood, mighty waters, a torrent. Its primary usage is flood. The noun is used figuratively to indicate coming judgment (Da 9:26; Na 1:8). In Job, the Lord is depicted as being able to cut channels for torrents of rain (Job 38:25). The psalmist indicates that through prayer, one can avoid the mighty waters (Ps 32:6). The word is also used figuratively to depict the intensity of anger (Pr 27:4).

7859. **שְׁטַר, sheṭar,** *shet-ar´*; (Chaldee); of uncertain derivation; a *side*:—side.

7860. **שֹׁטֵר, shôṭêr,** *sho-tare´*; active participle of an otherwise unused root probably meaning to *write*; (properly) a *scribe*, i.e. (by analogy or implication) an official *superintendent* or *magistrate*:—officer, overseer, ruler.

A masculine noun meaning a scribe, an official, a magistrate, a record keeper, and an officer. The word is used primarily to denote an officer or overseer. Proverbs contrasts the ant with the sluggard. While the ant has no overseer or ruler, it stores up in the summer and gathers at harvest in contrast to the sluggard who does not (Pr 6:7). The word is also used to denote an officer in the military (2Ch 26:11). In Joshua, the word denoted the person that was responsible for organizing the camp for departure (Jos 1:10; 3:2). In addition, *shôṭêr* denoted those that organized the army and appointed its officers (Dt 20:5, 8, 9). In Exodus, the slave drivers appointed Israelite foremen over the other workers (Ex 5:14). The word is used to denote the officials appointed over Israel (Nu 11:16); and the designation of the Levites as officials (2Ch 19:11).

7861. **שִׁטְרַי, Shiṭray,** *shit-rah´ee*; from the same as 7860; *magisterial; Shitrai*, an Israelite:—Shitrai.

7862. **שַׁי, shay,** *shah´ee*; probably from 7737; a *gift* (as *available*):—present.

7863. **שִׂיא, śîy',** *see*; from the same as 7721 by permutation; *elevation*:—excellency.

7864. **שְׁיָא, Sheyâ',** *sheh-yaw´*; for 7724; *Sheja*, an Israelite:—Sheva [*from the margin*].

7865. **שִׂיאֹן, Śîy'ôn,** *see-ohn´*; from 7863; *peak; Sion*, the summit of Mount Hermon:—Sion.

7866. **שִׁיאֹן, Shîy'ôn,** *shee-ohn´*; from the same as 7722; *ruin; Shijon*, a place in Palestine:—Shihon.

7867. **שִׂיב, śîyb,** *seeb*; a primitive root; (properly) to *become aged*, i.e. (by implication) to *grow gray*:—(be) grayheaded.

A verb meaning to grow gray. In Samuel's farewell speech, he stated that it was time for him to step down, for he was old and gray (1Sa 12:2). Eliphaz used the word in Job to designate those that have grown gray-haired and aged, in his somewhat skewed argument to Job. These people are denoted as having wisdom above anyone else of a younger age (Job 15:10).

7868. **שִׂיב, śîyb,** *seeb*; (Chaldee); corresponding to 7867:—elder.

An Aramaic verb meaning to become aged, to grow gray. The word is used in Ezra to denote those appointed as leaders over Israel (Ezr 5:5). It is again used in Ezra to depict the elders of the Jews, in whom the responsibility for rebuilding the Temple lay, according to Darius (Ezr 6:7, 8, 14).

7869. **שֵׂיב, śêyb,** *sabe*; from 7867; old *age*:—age.

A masculine noun meaning old age. In 1Ki, Ahijah is described as being aged, and his eyesight has failed (1Ki 14:4). The usage of this word for Ahijah designates his wisdom. To have a head of gray hair is to have a crown of wisdom.

7870. **שִׁיבָה, shîybâh,** *shee-baw´*; by permutation from 7725; a *return* (of property):—captivity.

7871. **שִׁיבָה, shîybâh,** *shee-baw´*; from 3427; *residence*:—while … lay.

7872. **שֵׂיבָה, śêybâh,** *say-baw´*; feminine of 7869; old *age*:—(be) gray (grey, hoar, -y) hairs (head, -ed), old age.

A feminine noun meaning old age or gray hair. The word is used to denote that Joseph's brothers would bring to the grave the gray head of their father (Ge 44:31). Hosea uses the word figuratively to depict Ephraim being old before its natural time, that is, its hair was sprinkled with gray (Hos 7:9). In Proverbs, gray hair is a crown of splendor (Pr 16:31); while 1Ki denotes the gray head, not as wise, but simply old (1Ki 2:6, 9). The psalmist uses the word to depict a point in life in which he could not perform the same deeds as before. On account of this, the psalmist asked God not to forsake him until he was able to declare God's glory to the coming generation (Ps 71:18). Genesis uses the word to denote the time Abraham will be buried, that is, a good old age (Ge 15:15; 25:8). Naomi's friends predicted that her grandson Obed would renew her life and sustain her in her old age (Ru 4:15).

7873. שִׂיג, **śîyg,** *seeg*; from 7734; a *withdrawal* (into a private place):—pursuing.

7874. שִׂיד, **śîyd,** *seed*; a primitive root probably meaning to *boil* up (compare 7736); used only as denominative from 7875; to *plaster*:—plaister.

7875. שִׂיד, **śîyd,** *seed*; from 7874; *lime* (as *boiling* when slacked):—lime, plaister.

7876. שָׁיָה, **shâyâh,** *shaw-yaw´*; a primitive root; to *keep* in memory:—be unmindful. [Render Dt 32:18, "A Rock bore thee, *thou must recollect*; and (yet) thou hast forgotten," etc.]

7877. שִׁיזָא, **Shîyzâʼ,** *shee-zaw´*; of unknown derivation; *Shiza*, an Israelite:—Shiza.

7878. שִׂיחַ, **śîyach,** *see´-akh*; a primitive root; to *ponder*, i.e. (by implication) *converse* (with oneself, and hence aloud) or (transitive) *utter*:—commune, complain, declare, meditate, muse, pray, speak, talk (with).

A verb meaning to ponder, to converse, to utter, to complain, to meditate, to pray, to speak. Its primary use is to complain. In Job, the word denotes the action that Job took against the bitterness in his soul, that is, his complaints (Job 7:11). God's people were instructed to sing praises to Him (1Ch 16:9; Ps 105:2). This singing tells of all His wondrous acts. The word is used in Job to denote speaking to the earth (Job 12:8); while Isaiah used it to depict Christ's dying without children, that is, descendants (Isa 53:8). Isaiah's rhetorical question denoted that an absence of descendants was normally a shameful thing in the culture.

7879. שִׂיחַ, **śîyach,** *see´-akh*; from 7878; a *contemplation*; (by implication) an *utterance*:—babbling, communication, complaint, meditation, prayer, talk.

A masculine noun meaning contemplation, meditation, prayer, talk, utterance, babbling. The primary meaning of the word is a complaint. In Job's narrative, he stated that even his couch would not ease his complaint (Job 7:13); that even if he were to forget his complaint, he would still dread all of his sufferings (Job 9:27); and because he loathed his very life, he would give free reign to his complaint (Job 10:1). Elijah mocked the prophets of Baal, telling them to cry louder because their god might be deep in thought (1Ki 18:27). The word is also used to denote Hannah's prayer containing words of great anguish (1Sa 1:16). The psalmist used the word to depict meditation that he hoped would be pleasing to the Lord (Ps 104:34).

7880. שִׂיחַ, **śîyach,** *see´-akh*; from 7878; a *shoot* (as if *uttered* or put forth), i.e. (general) *shrubbery*:—bush, plant, shrub.

A masculine noun meaning a shoot, brush, a plant, a shrub. The most common usage of this word is a shrub or brush. It is used to denote that when the Lord made the heavens and earth, no shrub of the field had yet appeared nor had any plant sprung up (Ge 2:5). *Śiyach* designates the bushes under which Hagar placed Ishmael to die (Ge 21:15). The two were dying due to lack of water, and therefore Hagar placed Ishmael underneath bushes, walked out of sight, still in hearing distance, and sat down. She did not want to watch her son die. In his discourse, Job designated the brush as the place where fathers of the sons who mocked him gathered salt herbs (Job 30:4). The bushes were also the place in which these fathers brayed (Job 30:7).

7881. שִׂיחָה, **śîychâh,** *see-khaw´*; feminine of 7879; *reflection*; (by extension) *devotion*:—meditation, prayer.

A feminine noun meaning meditation, reflection, concern of one's thoughts, musing, reflection. The word is primarily used to indicate meditation. The psalmist indicated the proper procedure for an individual's response to God's Law. Because of his love for God's Law, the psalmist was prompted to meditate on it all day long. Due to his practice of meditation, the psalmist received more understanding than his elders (Ps 119:97, 99). As Job expressed his feelings and frustrations, Eliphaz responded condemningly, stating that what Job was feeling and saying was hindering devotion to God (Job 15:4). Eliphaz's response was that of an ignorant man who did not realize the true nature of devotion to God.

7882. שִׁיחָה, **shîychâh,** *shee-khaw´*; for 7745; a *pit*-fall:—pit.

A feminine noun meaning a pit. Jeremiah used a metaphorical rendering of the word to describe his enemies' actions against him, they had dug a pit to capture him (Jer 18:22). The psalmist also used a similar rendering of the word to describe what his enemies had done. They had dug a pit for him but had fallen into it themselves (Ps 57:6[7]). In Ps 119:85, the word was used to indicate attempts on the part of the arrogant to cause the psalmist to act contrary to God's Law. However, the psalmist's firm grounding in the laws and precepts of *Yahweh* kept him from falling into their traps.

7883. שִׁיחוֹר, **Shîychôwr,** *shee-khore´*; or שִׁחוֹר, **Shi-chôwr,** *shee-khore´*; or שִׁחֹר, **Shichôr,** *shee-khore´*; probably from 7835; *dark*, i.e. *turbid; Shichor*, a stream of Egypt:—Shihor, Sihor.

7884. שִׁיחוֹר לִבְנָת, **Shîychôwr Libenâth,** *shee-khore´ lib-nawth´*; from the same as 7883 and 3835; *darkish whiteness; Shichor-Libnath*, a stream of Palestine:—Shihor-libnath.

7885. שַׁיִט, **shayiṭ,** *shah´-yit*; from 7751; an *oar*; also (compare 7752) a *scourge* (figurative):—oar, scourge.

7886. שִׁילֹה, **Shîylôh,** *shee-lo´*; from 7951; *tranquil; Shiloh*, an epithet of the Messiah:—Shiloh.

7887. שִׁילֹה, **Shîylôh,** *shee-lo´*; or שִׁלֹה, **Shilôh,** *shee-lo´*; or שִׁילוֹ, **Shîylôw,** *shee-lo´*; or שִׁלוֹ, **Shilôw,** *shee-lo´*; from the same as 7886; *Shiloh*, a place in Palestine:—Shiloh.

7888. שִׁילוֹנִי, **Shîylôwnîy,** *shee-lo-nee´*; or שִׁילֹנִי, **Shîylônîy,** *shee-lo-nee´*; or שִׁלֹנִי, **Shilônîy,** *shee-lo-nee´*; from 7887; a *Shilonite* or inhabitant of Shiloh:—Shilonite.

7889. שִׁימוֹן, **Shîymôwn,** *shee-mone´*; apparently for 3452; *desert; Shimon*, an Israelite:—Shimon.

7890. שַׁיִן, **shayin,** *shah´-yin*; from an unused root meaning to *urinate; urine*:—piss.

7891. שִׁיר, **shîyr,** *sheer*; or (the original form) שׁוּר, **shûwr,** *shoor*; (1Sa 18:6), a primitive root [rather identical with 7788 through the idea of *strolling* minstrelsy]; to *sing*:—behold [*by mistake for* 7789], sing (-er, -ing man, -ing woman).

A verb meaning to sing. This word occurs often in a call to praise the Lord; the call may be directed toward oneself or others (Ps 27:6; 96:1, 2; 101:1; Jer 20:13). This term is frequently associated with the Levitical worship established by David and emphasized by postexilic writers (1Ch 15:16; Ezr 2:41; Ne 7:1). Although the Levitical singers were all men, women also were singers in ancient Israel both in religious and secular settings (Ex 15:21; Jgs 5:1–3; Ecc 2:8). Secular occasions for singing included celebration of victory in battle (1Sa 18:6); mourning over death (2Ch 35:25); entertainment (2Sa 19:35[36]); and an expression of love (Isa 5:1). The Bible once mentions the singing of birds (Zep 2:14).

7892. שִׁיר, **shîyr,** *sheer*; or feminine שִׁירָה, **shîyrâh,** *shee-raw´*; from 7891; a *song*; (abstract) *singing*:—musical (-ick), × sing (-er, -ing), song.

A masculine noun meaning a song. This word is used to indicate a type of lyrical song, a religious song, or a specific song of Levitical choirs. In Amos, God uses the word to indicate that He will turn their joyful singing into mourning because of their unfaithfulness to Him (Am 8:10). This time of mourning will be like that of mourning for an only son, and it will end in a bitter day. In a similar usage, Laban asks Jacob why he ran off secretly without telling Laban. If Jacob would have stated he wanted to leave, Laban would have sent him off with joy and singing (Ge 31:27). Isaiah uses the word to indicate the type of songs that will no longer be sung when the Lord lays waste the earth (Isa 24:9). The type of drunken revels associated with drinking wine and beer will no longer be heard.

This word is also used in Nehemiah to denote songs of praise (Ne 12:46). In this particular context, Nehemiah indicates that the music directors in the days of David and Asaph led songs of praise. The noun is also used to indicate specific songs of Levitical choirs accompanied by musical instruments. When David and the Israelites brought the ark of the Lord from Baalah of Judah (Kiriath Jearim), they celebrated with songs (1Ch 13:8). Amos uses the word to denote complacency and apathy. Many Israelites lay on ivory couches and strummed their musical instruments while dining on fattened calves and choice lambs. These people were so caught up in themselves that they did not even give thought to the threat of destruction by the Lord.

7893. שַׁיִשׁ, **shayish,** *shah´-yish*; from an unused root meaning to *bleach*, i.e. *whiten; white*, i.e. *marble*:—marble. See 8336.

7894. שִׁישָׁא, **Shîyshâ',** *shee-shaw´*; from the same as 7893; *whiteness; Shisha*, an Israelite:—Shisha.

7895. שִׁישַׁק, **Shîyshaq,** *shee-shak´*; or שׁוּשַׁק, **Shûw-shaq,** *shoo-shak´*; of Egyptian derivation; *Shishak*, an Egyptian king:—Shishak.

7896. שִׁית, **shîyth,** *sheeth*; a primitive root; to *place* (in a very wide application):—apply, appoint, array, bring, consider, lay (up), let alone, × look, make, mark, put (on), + regard, set, shew, be stayed, × take.

7897. שִׁית, **shîyth,** *sheeth*; from 7896; a *dress* (as *put* on):—attire.

7898. שַׁיִת, **shayith,** *shah´-yith*; from 7896; *scrub* or *trash*, i.e. wild *growth* of weeds or briers (as if *put* on the field):—thorns.

7899. שֵׂךְ, **sêk,** *sake*; from 5526 in the sense of 7753; a *brier* (as of a hedge):—prick.

7900. שֹׂךְ, **sôk,** *soke*; from 5526 in the sense of 7753; a *booth* (as *interlaced*):—tabernacle.

7901. שָׁכַב, **shâkab,** *shaw-kab´*; a primitive root; to *lie* down (for rest, sexual connection, decease or any other purpose):— × at all, cast down, ([over-]) lay (self) (down), (make to) lie (down, down to sleep, still, with), lodge, ravish, take rest, sleep, stay.

7902. שְׁכָבָה, **shᵉkâbâh,** *shek-aw-baw´*; from 7901; a *lying* down (of dew, or for the sexual act):— × carnally, copulation, × lay, seed.

7903. שְׁכֹבֶת, **shᵉkôbeth,** *shek-o´-beth*; from 7901; a (sexual) *lying* with:— × lie.

7904. שָׁכָה, **shâkâh,** *shaw-kaw´*; a primitive root; to *roam* (through lust):—in the morning [*by mistake for* 7925].

7905. שֻׂכָּה, **śukkâh,** *sook-kaw´*; feminine of 7900 in the sense of 7899; a *dart* (as pointed like a *thorn*):—barbed iron.

7906. שֵׂכוּ, **Śêkûw,** *say´-koo*; from an unused root apparently meaning to *surmount*; an *observatory* (with the article); *Seku*, a place in Palestine:—Sechu.

7907. שֶׂכְוִי, **śekvîy,** *sek-vee´*; from the same as 7906; *observant*, i.e. (concrete) the *mind*:—heart.

A masculine noun meaning a celestial appearance or phenomenon, the mind. This word is used in Job to denote the mind that has been given understanding (Job 38:36). In a rhetorical question, the Lord indicated His sovereignty over all, including the lives of His servants. The exact meaning of this word is unclear.

7908. שְׁכוֹל, **shᵉkôwl,** *shek-ole´*; infinitive of 7921; *bereavement*:—loss of children, spoiling.

A masculine noun meaning bereavement. This word primarily indicates a loss of children. In Isaiah's oracle against Babylon, he stated that the woman who thought of herself as lasting forever would become a widow and suffer the loss of her children. The Virgin Daughter of Babylon, who once thought that there was none like her, would suffer the fate of a common person (Isa 47:8). The word is also used to denote how the soul is left after a ruthless witness repays evil for good (Ps 35:12).

7909. שַׁכּוּל, **shakkûwl,** *shak-kool´*; or שַׁכֻּל, **shakkul,** *shak-kool´*; from 7921; *bereaved*:—barren, bereaved (robbed) of children (whelps).

An adjective meaning bereaved. The word is used figuratively to describe the fierceness of David and his men by comparing them to a wild bear robbed of her cubs (2Sa 17:8). In another analogy, the intensity of God's punishment is described as a bear robbed of her cubs. God would attack the Israelites for their sins and rip them open (Hos 13:8). Proverbs used the same figurative language, stating that it is better to meet a bear robbed of her cubs than a fool in his folly (Pr 17:12). In a different sense, Jeremiah used this word to describe a punishment in which wives would be made childless and widows (Jer 18:21).

7910. שִׁכּוֹר, **shikkôwr,** *shik-kore´*; or שִׁכֹּר, **shikkôr,** *shik-kore´*; from 7937; *intoxicated*, as a state or a habit:—drunk (-ard, -en, -en man).

7911. שָׁכַח, **shâkach,** *shaw-kakh´*; or שָׁכֵחַ, **shâkêach,** *shaw-kay´-akh*; a primitive root; to *mislay*, i.e. to *be oblivious* of, from want of memory or attention:— × at all, (cause to) forget.

7912. שְׁכַח, **shᵉkach,** *shek-akh´*; (Chaldee); corresponding to 7911 through the idea of disclosure of a *covered* or *forgotten* thing; to *discover* (literal or figurative):—find.

7913. שָׁכֵחַ, **shâkêach,** *shaw-kay´-akh*; from 7911; *oblivious*:—forget.

7914. שְׂכִיָּה, **śᵉkîyyâh,** *sek-ee-yaw´*; feminine from the same as 7906; a *conspicuous* object:—picture.

7915. שַׂכִּין, **śakkîyn,** *sak-keen´*; intensive perhaps from the same as 7906 in the sense of 7753; a *knife* (as *pointed* or edged):—knife.

7916. שָׂכִיר, **śâkîyr,** *saw-keer´*; from 7936; a man *at wages* by the day or year:—hired (man, servant), hireling.

7917. שְׂכִירָה, **śᵉkîyrâh,** *sek-ee-raw´*; feminine of 7916; a *hiring*:—that is hired.

7918. שָׁכַךְ, **shâkak,** *shaw-kak´*; a primitive root; to *weave* (i.e. *lay*) a trap; figurative (through the idea of *secreting*) to *allay* (passions; [physical] *abate* a flood):—appease, assuage, make to cease, pacify, set.

7919. שָׂכַל, **śâkal,** *saw-kal´*; a primitive root; to *be* (causative, *make* or *act*) *circumspect* and hence *intelligent*:—consider, expert, instruct, prosper, (deal) prudent (-ly), (give) skill (-ful), have good success, teach, (have, make to) understand (-ing), wisdom, (be, behave self, consider, make) wise (-ly), guide wittingly.

A verb meaning to act with insight, to be prudent, to give insight, to teach, to prosper, to consider, to ponder, to understand, to act prudently, to act with devotion. The primary meaning of the word is to be prudent. The word is used in Isaiah to denote what was hoped and expected of Israel, i.e. that they would consider and understand that the hand of the Lord had acted (Isa 41:20). The word is also used in Deuteronomy to denote a lack of understanding on the part of the people. If they were wise and would understand, they would know what their end would be (Dt 32:29). Jeremiah used this word to denote wisdom in terms of insight and comprehension (Jer 9:24[23]). In a similar usage of the word, fools are to take heed and become wise (Ps 94:8). The wisdom of comprehension will open their eyes to the Lord, who sees and punishes wrong actions. In a confession of sins, the Holy Spirit is remembered as having been sent to instruct (Ne 9:20); the prudent person keeps quiet in evil times (Am 5:13); those who meditate on the Book of the Law day and night, being careful to do everything in it, will be prosperous and successful (Jos 1:8). In the causative form, *śâkal* denoted God's actions to Solomon if he observed what the Lord required and walked in His ways. If this pattern were followed, the Lord would prosper Solomon (1Ki 2:3).

7920. שְׂכַל, **śᵉkal,** *sek-al´*; (Chaldee); corresponding to 7919:—consider.

An Aramaic verb meaning to consider. The reflexive form of the word is used in Daniel to depict the state of mind that Daniel was in while he was shown the vision. While Daniel was contemplating the horns that he had previously seen, a smaller horn appeared and brought his attention back to the vision itself (Da 7:8).

7921. **שָׁכֹל**, **shâkôl**, *shaw-kole´*; a primitive root; (properly) to *miscarry*, i.e. *suffer abortion*; (by analogy) to *bereave* (literal or figurative):—bereave (of children), barren, cast calf (fruit, young), be (make) childless, deprive, destroy, × expect, lose children, miscarry, rob of children, spoil.

7922. **שֶׂכֶל**, **śekel**, *seh´-kel*; or **שֵׂכֶל**, **śêkel**, *say´-kel*; from 7919; *intelligence*; (by implication) *success*:—discretion, knowledge, policy, prudence, sense, understanding, wisdom, wise.

A masculine noun meaning intelligence, good sense. This intelligence is more than just mere book knowledge or learning about a particular subject. It has a greater significance and means insight or understanding. This insight is a gift from God (1Ch 22:12); and God holds the freedom to give it or to take it away whenever He chooses (Job 17:4). The results from having this intelligence and insight is that it gives a person patience (Pr 19:11); and wins praise from others (Pr 12:8). Only fools despise this intelligence (Pr 23:9). This noun is used once with a negative connotation in Da 8:25 where it stands for cunning, requiring much intelligence.

7923. **שִׁכֻּלִים**, **shikkulîym**, *shik-koo-leem´*; plural from 7921; *childlessness* (by continued bereavements):—to have after loss of others.

7924. **שָׂכְלְתָנוּ**, **śoklᵉthânûw**, *sok-leth-aw-noo´*; (Chaldee); from 7920; *intelligence*:—understanding.

An Aramaic feminine noun meaning wisdom, insight. It is used in Da 5:11, 12, and 14. In this context, it described Daniel's wisdom and insight into the interpretation of dreams. It was obvious to the people around Daniel that his wisdom was not merely human wisdom, for they said he had the spirit of the gods living in him and that he was like the gods. Thus, this wisdom cannot be gained by mere human training. It comes as a gift from God. The pagan culture did not attribute it to the one true God but to their gods.

7925. **שָׁכַם**, **shâkam**, *shaw-kam´*; a primitive root; (properly) to *incline* (the shoulder to a burden); but used only as denominative from 7926; (literal) to *load up* (on the back of man or beast), i.e. to *start early* in the morning:—(arise, be up, get [oneself] up, rise up) early (betimes), morning.

7926. **שְׁכֶם**, **shᵉkem**, *shek-em´*; from 7925; the *neck* (between the shoulders) as the place of burdens; (figurative) the *spur* of a hill:—back, × consent, portion, shoulder.

7927. **שְׁכֶם**, **Shᵉkem**, *shek-em´*; the same as 7926; *ridge; Shekem*, a place in Palestine:—Shechem.

7928. **שֶׁכֶם**, **Shekem**, *sheh´-kem*; for 7926; *Shekem*, the name of a Hivite and two Israelites:—Shechem.

7929. **שִׁכְמָה**, **shikmâh**, *shik-maw´*; feminine of 7926; the *shoulder*-bone:—shoulder blade.

7930. **שִׁכְמִי**, **Shikmîy**, *shik-mee´*; patronymic from 7928; a *Shikmite* (collective), or descendants of Shekem:—Shichemites.

7931. **שָׁכַן**, **shâkan**, *shaw-kan´*; a primitive root [apparently akin (by transmission) to 7901 through the idea of *lodging*; compare 5531, 7925]; to *reside* or permanently stay (literal or figurative):—abide, continue, (cause to, make to) dwell (-er), have habitation, inhabit, lay, place, (cause to) remain, rest, set (up).

A verb meaning to settle down, to dwell. In its most simple form, three slight variations of meaning are found for this verb. First, it simply means to settle down (Ex 24:16; Nu 24:2; Ps 102:28[29]). Second, it can mean to lie down or rest. When used this way, it can refer to objects (Nu 9:17; Job 3:5); animals (Isa 13:21); and people (Jer 23:6; 33:16). When people are the object of the verb, it means that they are resting in peace and security. Third, it may mean to dwell or abide. Again, this can have several referents such as people (Ps 37:27; Pr 2:21); the dead (Job 26:5); God (1Ki 8:12; Isa 8:18); or objects such as the tabernacle (Jos 22:19). In the intensive form, it means to establish. The word is used in this way in Dt 12:11 and Ps 78:60 to describe how God set up a dwelling place for His name, establishing Himself in Israel. Finally, the causative form means to lay, to place, to set (Ge 3:24; Jos 18:1); or to cause to dwell (Job 11:14; Ps 78:55).

7932. **שְׁכַן**, **shᵉkan**, *shek-an´*; (Chaldee); corresponding to 7931:—cause to dwell, have habitation.

7933. **שֶׁכֶן**, **sheken**, *sheh´-ken*; from 7931; a *residence*:—habitation.

7934. **שָׁכֵן**, **shâkên**, *shaw-kane´*; from 7931; a *resident*; (by extension) a fellow-*citizen*:—inhabitant, neighbour, nigh.

An adjective meaning inhabitant. This word usually refers to an inhabitant of a city (Isa 33:24; Hos 10:5). It can also have the more specific meaning of neighbour. These neighbours can either be people who are friends or enemies (Ex 3:22; Ru 4:17); or nations (Dt 1:7). Neighbours can also be extremely influential (Eze 16:26). Israel was said to have engaged in prostitution with her neighbour Egypt, meaning that she followed the gods and religions of Egypt rather than following the one true God.

7935. **שְׁכַנְיָה**, **Shᵉkanyâh**, *shek-an-yaw´*; or (prolonged) **שְׁכַנְיָהוּ**, **Shᵉkanyâhûw**, *shek-an-yaw´-hoo*; from 7931 and 3050; *Jah has dwelt; Shekanjah*, the name of nine Israelites:—Shecaniah, Shechaniah.

7936. **שָׂכַר**, **śâkar**, *saw-kar´*; or (by permutation) **סָכַר**, **sâkar**, *saw-kar´*; (Ezr 4:5), a primitive root [apparently akin (by prosthesis) to 3739 through the idea of temporary *purchase*; compare 7937]; to *hire*:—earn wages, hire (out self), reward, × surely.

7937. **שָׁכַר**, **shâkar**, *shaw-kar´*; a primitive root; to *become tipsy*; in a qualified sense, to *satiate* with a stimulating drink or (figurative) influence:—(be filled with) drink (abundantly), (be, make) drunk (-en), be merry. [Superlative of 8248.]

7938. **שֶׂכֶר**, **śeker**, *seh´-ker*; from 7936; *wages*:—reward, sluices.

7939. **שָׂכָר**, **śâkâr**, *saw-kawr´*; from 7936; *payment* of contract; (concrete) *salary, fare, maintenance*; (by implication) *compensation, benefit*:—hire, price, reward [-ed], wages, worth.

7940. **שָׂכָר**, **Śâkâr**, *saw-kawr´*; the same as 7939; *recompense; Sakar*, the name of two Israelites:—Sacar.

7941. **שֵׁכָר**, **shêkâr**, *shay-kawr´*; from 7937; an *intoxicant*, i.e. intensely alcoholic *liquor*:—strong drink, + drunkard, strong wine.

7942. **שִׁכְּרוֹן**, **Shikkᵉrôwn**, *shik-ker-one´*; for 7943; *drunkenness; Shikkeron*, a place in Palestine:—Shicron.

7943. **שִׁכָּרוֹן**, **shikkârôwn**, *shik-kaw-rone´*; from 7937; *intoxication*:—(be) drunken (-ness).

7944. **שַׁל**, **shal**, *shal*; from 7952 abbreviated; a *fault*:—error.

A masculine noun meaning a sin, an error. It comes from the verb *shâlâh* (7952), meaning to sin. This noun is used only once in the OT in 2Sa 6:7, but from this usage, we can gain the insight that the error described by this word is a great one. The context is that of Uzzah, whom God struck down because he touched the ark: this error cost him his life. This word has strong connotations of a great sin or error deserving of death.

7945. **שֶׁל**, **shel**, *shel*; for the relative 834; used with prepositional prefix, and often followed by some pronoun affixed; on *account* of, *what*soever, *which*soever:—cause, sake.

7946. **שַׁלְאֲנָן**, **shal'ănân**, *shal-an-awn´*; for 7600; *tranquil*:—being at ease.

7947. **שָׁלַב**, **shâlab**, *shaw-lab´*; a primitive root; to *space* off; intensive (*evenly*) to *make equidistant*:—equally distant, set in order.

7948. **שָׁלָב**, **shâlâb**, *shaw-lawb´*; from 7947; a *spacer* or raised *interval*, i.e. the *stile* in a frame or panel:—ledge.

7949. **שָׁלַג**, **shâlag**, *shaw-lag´*; a primitive root; (properly) meaning to be *white*; used only as denominative from 7950; to be *snow-white* (with the linen clothing of the slain):—be as snow.

7950. שֶׁלֶג, **sheleg,** *sheh´-leg;* from 7949; *snow* (probably from its *whiteness*):—snow (-y).

7951. שָׁלָה, **shâlâh,** *shaw-law´;* or שָׁלַו, **shâlav,** *shaw-lav´;* (Job 3:26), a primitive root; to be *tranquil,* i.e. *secure* or *successful*:—be happy, prosper, be in safety.

7952. שָׁלָה, **shâlâh,** *shaw-law´;* a primitive root [probably rather identical with 7953 through the idea of *educing*]; to *mislead*:—deceive, be negligent.

A verb meaning to be careless, to be thoughtless, to sin. The sin described by this verb does not seem to be a deliberate sin but rather one that is committed by ignorance or inadvertence. The verb is used only in the passive and causative forms. In the passive form, it holds the meaning of being negligent or being careless of duties (2Ch 29:11). The causative form means to lead astray or to deceive. It is used in 2Ki 4:28 when the Shunammite woman felt deceived that she had been promised a son who later died. Although the sins described by this verb were not intentional, they were still deserving of punishment in God's sight.

7953. שָׁלָה, **shâlâh,** *shaw-law´;* a primitive root [rather cognate (by contrete) to the base of 5394, 7997 and their congeners through the idea of *extracting*]; to *draw* out or off, i.e. *remove* (the soul by death):—take away.

7954. שְׁלֵה, **sh^{e}lêh,** *shel-ay´;* (Chaldee); corresponding to 7951; to *be secure*:—at rest.

7955. שָׁלֻה, **shâluh,** *shaw-loo´;* (Chaldee); from a root corresponding to 7952; a *wrong*:—thing amiss.

7956. שֵׁלָה, **Shêlâh,** *shay-law´;* the same as 7596 (shortened); *request; Shelah,* the name of a postdiluvian patriarch and of an Israelite:—Shelah.

7957. שַׁלְהֶבֶת, **shalhebeth,** *shal-heh´-beth;* from the same as 3851 with sibilant prefix; a *flare* of fire:—(flaming) flame.

7958. שְׂלָו, **ś^{e}lâv,** *sel-awv´;* or שְׂלָיו, **ś^{e}lâyv,** *sel-awv´;* by orthographic variation from 7951 through the idea of *sluggishness;* the *quail* collective (as *slow* in flight from its weight):—quails.

7959. שָׁלוּ, **shâlûw,** *shaw´-loo;* from 7951; *security*:—prosperity.

7960. שָׁלוּ, **shâlûw,** *shaw-loo´;* (Chaldee); or שָׁלוּת, **shâlûwth,** *shaw-looth´;* (Chaldee); from the same as 7955; a *fault*:—error, × fail, thing amiss.

7961. שָׁלֵו, **shâlêv,** *shaw-lave´;* or שָׁלֵיו, **shâlêyv,** *shaw-lave´;* feminine שְׁלֵוָה, **sh^{e}lêvâh,** *shel-ay-vaw´;* from 7951; *tranquil;* (in a bad sense) *careless;* (abstract) *security*:—(being) at ease, peaceable, (in) prosper (-ity), quiet (-ness), wealthy.

7962. שַׁלְוָה, **shalvâh,** *shal-vaw´;* from 7951; *security* (genuine or false):—abundance, peace (-ably), prosperity, quietness.

7963. שְׁלֵוָה, **sh^{e}lêvâh,** *shel-ay-vaw´;* (Chaldee); corresponding to 7962; *safety*:—tranquillity. See also 7961.

7964. שִׁלּוּחִים, **shillûwchîym,** *shil-loo´-kheem;* or שִׁלֻּחִים, **shilluchîym,** *shil-loo´-kheem;* from 7971; (only in plural) a *dismissal,* i.e. (of a wife) *divorce* (especially the document); also (of a daughter) *dower*:—presents, have sent back.

7965. שָׁלוֹם, **shâlôwm,** *shaw-lome´;* or שָׁלֹם, **shâlôm,** *shaw-lome´;* from 7999; *safe,* i.e. (figurative) *well, happy, friendly;* also (abstract) *welfare,* i.e. health, prosperity, peace:— × do, familiar, × fare, favour, + friend, × great, (good) health, (× perfect, such as be at) peace (-able, -ably), prosper (-ity, -ous), rest, safe (-ty), salute, welfare, (× all is, be) well, × wholly.

A masculine noun meaning peace or tranquility. This Hebrew term is used 237 times in the OT and is used to greet someone (Jgs 19:20; 1Ch 12:18[19]; Da 10:19). It is common in Hebrew to ask how one's peace is (Ge 43:27; Ex 18:7; Jgs 18:15), which is equivalent to asking "How are you?" Moreover, this word was often used to describe someone's manner of coming or going; sometimes this took the form of a blessing: Go in peace (Jgs 8:9; 1Sa 1:17; Mal 2:6). Another common expression involved dying or being buried in peace (Ge 15:15; 2Ch 34:28; Jer 34:5) Peace is present with the wise but absent from the wicked (Pr 3:2, 17; Isa 57:21; 59:8). It is often pictured as coming from God; Gideon built an altar and called the altar *Yahweh-shalom* (the Lord Is Peace; Nu 6:26; Jgs 6:24; Isa 26:3).

7966. שִׁלּוּם, **shillûwm,** *shil-loom´;* or שִׁלֻּם, **shillum,** *shil-loom´;* from 7999; a *requital,* i.e. (secure) *retribution,* (venal) a *fee*:—recompense, reward.

A masculine noun meaning a requital, a retribution. It is derived from the verb *shâlam* (7999). In context, this noun is used as God's punishment of Israel for their repeated disobedience (Isa 34:8; Hos 9:7). It is not something given on a whim but is deserved. This noun can also mean a reward, or more accurately, a bribe (Mic 7:3). Only the corrupt accept these bribes, which are used to distort justice. Such people have no care for what is right or wrong but only in what they will receive. Ultimately, they will receive their retribution from God for their wrongdoings.

7967. שַׁלּוּם, **Shallûwm,** *shal-loom´;* or (shorter) שַׁלֻּם, **Shallum,** *shal-loom´;* the same as 7966; *Shallum,* the name of fourteen Israelites:—Shallum.

7968. שַׁלּוּן, **Shalûwn,** *shal-loon´;* probably for 7967; *Shallun,* an Israelite:—Shallum.

7969. שָׁלוֹשׁ, **shâlôwsh,** *shaw-loshe´;* or שָׁלֹשׁ, **shâ-lôsh,** *shaw-loshe´;* masculine שְׁלוֹשָׁה, **sh^{e}lôwshâh,** *shel-o-shaw´;* or שְׁלֹשָׁה, **sh^{e}lôshâh,** *shel-o-shaw´;* a primitive number; *three;* occasionally (ordinal) *third,* or (multiple) *thrice*:— + fork, + often [-times], third, thir [-teen, -teenth], three, + thrice. Compare 7991.

7970. שְׁלוֹשִׁים, **sh^{e}lôwshîym,** *shel-o-sheem´;* or שְׁלֹשִׁים, **sh^{e}lôshîym,** *shel-o-sheem´;* multiple of 7969; *thirty;* or (ordinal) *thirtieth*:—thirty, thirtieth. Compare 7991.

7971. שָׁלַח, **shâlach,** *shaw-lakh´;* a primitive root; to *send* away, for, or out (in a great variety of applications):— × any wise, appoint, bring (on the way), cast (away, out), conduct, × earnestly, forsake, give (up), grow long, lay, leave, let depart (down, go, loose), push away, put (away, forth, in, out), reach forth, send (away, forth, out), set, shoot (forth, out), sow, spread, stretch forth (out).

7972. שְׁלַח, **sh^{e}lach,** *shel-akh´;* (Chaldee); corresponding to 7971:—put, send.

7973. שֶׁלַח, **shelach,** *sheh´-lakh;* from 7971; a *missile* of attack, i.e. *spear;* also (figurative) a *shoot* of growth, i.e. *branch*:—dart, plant, × put off, sword, weapon.

7974. שֶׁלַח, **Shelach,** *sheh´-lakh;* the same as 7973; *Shelach,* a postdiluvian patriarch:—Salah, Shelah. Compare 7975.

7975. שִׁלֹּחַ, **Shilôach,** *shee-lo´-akh;* or (in imitation of 7974 שֶׁלַח, **Shelach,** *sheh´-lakh;* (Ne 3:15), from 7971; *rill;* Shiloäch, a fountain of Jerusalem:—Shiloah, Siloah.

7976. שִׁלֻּחָה, **shilluchâh,** *shil-loo-kahw´;* feminine of 7964; a *shoot*:—branch.

7977. שִׁלְחִי, **Shilchîy,** *shil-khee´;* from 7973; *missive,* i.e. *armed; Shilchi,* an Israelite:—Shilhi.

7978. שִׁלְחִים, **Shilchîym,** *shil-kheem´;* plural of 7973; *javelins* or *sprouts; Shilchim,* a place in Palestine:—Shilhim.

7979. שֻׁלְחָן, **shulchân,** *shool-khawn´;* from 7971; a *table* (as *spread* out); (by implication) a *meal*:—table.

7980. שָׁלַט, **shâlaṭ,** *shaw-lat´;* a primitive root; to *dominate,* i.e. *govern;* by implication to *permit*:—(bear, have) rule, have dominion, give (have) power.

A verb meaning to domineer, to be master of. In the simple form, it takes the connotation of ruling. This can be ruling over people (Ne 5:15; Ecc 8:9); or possessions which one has been given control of (Ecc 2:19). It can also mean to obtain power or to get mastery over something. Examples of this would be how sin can have power over a person (Ps 119:133); or people can have power over each other (Est 9:1). This verb is also used in the causative form, meaning to give power (Ecc 5:19[18]; 6:2). In these contexts, God gives people power over their lives, possessions, honour, and wealth. God is the only legitimate source of power, and all power flows from Him.

7981. שְׁלֵט, **shᵉlêṭ,** *shel-ate´*; (Chaldee); corresponding to 7980:—have the mastery, have power, bear rule, be (make) ruler.

An Aramaic verb meaning to have power, to rule over. It is found in the intensive and causative forms only. In the causative form, it means to make rule or to cause to rule, referring to someone in power who gives that power to another (Da 2:38, 48). In the intensive form, it may mean merely to have power in the sense of controlling other people (Da 3:27, 6:24[25]), or to rule or be a ruler. In this sense, it is used in the context of King Belshazzar, who promised that whoever could interpret his dream would become a ruler (Da 5:7, 16).

7982. שֶׁלֶט, **sheleṭ,** *sheh´-let*; from 7980; probably a *shield* (as *controlling*, i.e. protecting the person):—shield.

A masculine noun meaning a shield. Most commonly, this word is used to refer to shields used for protection in battle. In Eze 27:11, they were hung on walls; in Jer 51:11, they were to be taken up as warriors prepared to defend themselves. Another context in which this word is used is in describing the gold shields that King David took from people he defeated (2Sa 8:7). They were then kept in the Temple and used when Jehoida presented Joash as king (2Ki 11:10).

7983. שִׁלְטוֹן, **shilṭôwn,** *shil-tone´*; from 7980; a *potentate*:—power.

A masculine noun meaning mastery. It can be used to mean powerful, as in the words of a king that are described as being supreme (Ecc 8:4). It can also mean having power over. It is used in Ecc 8:8 to say that no one has power over the day of his or her death. This word carries the connotation of legitimate authority, not just power that persons claim they have or have taken from others. A king's words had legitimate authority, for he was the ruler of his people; and no one except God has legitimate authority over death.

7984. שִׁלְטוֹן, **shilṭôwn,** *shil-tone´*; (Chaldee); or שִׁלְטֹן, **shilṭôn,** *shil-tone´*; corresponding to 7983:—ruler.

An Aramaic noun meaning a lord, a magistrate, an official. This noun is used only once in Da 3:2, where it is found at the end of a long list of officials whom King Nebuchadnezzar called together before him. This noun is the last word used and seems to be a catchall phrase to account for any official who was missed in the specific titles given before. Due to the lack of specificity, it would appear that this is a general noun used to name anyone who holds a position of authority.

7985. שָׁלְטָן, **sholṭân,** *shol-tawn´*; (Chaldee); from 7981; *empire* (abstract or concrete):—dominion.

An Aramaic masculine noun meaning dominion, sovereignty. Most frequently, this noun is used in conjunction with God, showing that He has dominion over everything that exists (Da 4:3[3:33]; 4:34[31]). His dominion is greater than that of a person's many ways, one being that it is an everlasting dominion that can never be destroyed (Da 7:14). This noun can also be used of kings (Da 4:22[19]). It was used in Daniel's dream of the four beasts to describe the dominion they have (Da 7:6, 12, 26). God both gives and takes away the dominion of all human rulers. Much less frequently, this word can be used in the concrete sense of a physical kingdom (Da 6:26[27]).

7986. שַׁלֶּטֶת, **shalleṭeth,** *shal-leh´-teth*; feminine from 7980; a *vixen*:—imperious.

7987. שְׁלִי, **shᵉlîy,** *shel-ee´*; from 7951; *privacy*:— + quietly.

7988. שִׁלְיָה, **shilyâh,** *shil-yaw´*; feminine from 7953; a *fetus* or *babe* (as *extruded* in birth):—young one.

7989. שַׁלִּיט, **shallîyṭ,** *shal-leet´*; from 7980; *potent*; (concrete) a *prince* or *warrior*:—governor, mighty, that hath power, ruler.

An adjective meaning mastery, power. This could be used to describe power over anything, but it is used in a limited context in the OT. With this meaning, it is only found in Ecc 8:8, where people are said to have no power over the wind. It can also be used as a noun meaning a ruler or one who has mastery (Ge 42:6). Rulers can also be a cause of evil (Ecc 10:5).

7990. שַׁלִּיט, **shallîyṭ,** *shal-leet´*; (Chaldee); corresponding to 7989; *mighty*; (abstract) *permission*; (concrete) a *premier*:—captain, be lawful, rule (-r).

An Aramaic masculine adjective meaning mastery. It is commonly used of God and His sovereignty that gives Him mastery over everything. There is nothing that is not under His authority, including the kingdoms of people (Da 4:17[14]; 5:21). God's mastery covers everything that exists. This adjective can also be used in describing the power that kings have (Ezr 4:20); and the authority they can exercise (Ezr 7:24). This word can also be used as a noun meaning captain or one who has authority and mastery over others (Da 2:15).

7991. שָׁלִישׁ, **shâlîysh,** *shaw-leesh´*; or שָׁלוֹשׁ, **shâ-lôwsh,** *shaw-loshe´*; (1Ch 11:11; 12:18), or שָׁלֹשׁ, **shâlôsh,** *shaw-loshe´*; (2Sa 23:13), from 7969; a *triple*, i.e. (as a musical instrument) a *triangle* (or perhaps rather *three*-stringed lute); also (as an indefinite great quantity) a *three*-fold measure (perhaps a *treble* ephah); also (as an officer) a general of the *third* rank (upward, i.e. the highest):—captain, instrument of musick, (great) lord, (great) measure, prince, three [*from the margin*].

A masculine noun carrying many different meanings associated with the number three. First of all, it can be used to signify a measure, perhaps originally a third or an ephah. From the contexts in which it is used, it is clear the word stands for a large measure (Ps 80:5[6]; Isa 40:12). It is also used once as a noun for a type of musical instrument—perhaps a three-cornered one with strings, such as a lute. This instrument was played with songs of celebration (1Sa 18:6). Finally, this word can signify a particular type of high–ranking officer or the third man in a chariot during battle (Ex 14:7; 2Sa 23:8; 2Ki 9:25).

7992. שְׁלִישִׁי, **shᵉlîyshîy,** *shel-ee-shee´*; ordinal from 7969; *third*; feminine a *third* (part); (by extension) a *third* (day, year or time); (specifically) a *third*-story cell:—third (part, rank, time), three (years old).

7993. שָׁלַךְ, **shâlak,** *shaw-lak´*; a primitive root; to *throw* out, down or away (literal or figurative):—adventure, cast (away, down, forth, off, out), hurl, pluck, throw.

A verb meaning to throw, to cast. In the causative form, several different variations of meaning are associated with this verb. The basic meaning to cast or throw is found in Ge 21:15 and Nu 35:20. It can also mean to cast away in the sense of getting rid of something that hinders, such as sin (Eze 18:31); or fetters (Ps 2:3). This verb is also used to describe God's rejection of someone (2Ki 17:20; 24:20). In a good sense, God will sustain those who cast their cares on Him (Ps 55:22[23]). In the passive causative form, this verb means to be cast, to be thrown or to be cast out. Usually, this is used in a negative sense, as when someone was cast out of his or her burial site (Isa 14:19; Jer 36:30); or when people were cast away because of their disobedience to God (Jer 14:16). Yet it can also be used in a good sense. In Ps 22:10[11], the writer says that from birth he had been cast on God. So this verb can have either positive or negative connotations.

7994. שָׁלָךְ, **shâlâk,** *shaw-lawk´*; from 7993; *bird of prey*, usually thought to be the *pelican* (from *casting* itself into the sea):—cormorant.

7995. שַׁלֶּכֶת, **shalleketh,** *shal-leh´-keth*; from 7993; a *felling* (of trees):—when cast.

7996. שַׁלֶּכֶת, **Shalleketh,** *shal-leh´-keth*; the same as 7995; *Shalleketh*, a gate in Jerusalem:—Shalleketh.

7997. שָׁלַל, **shâlal,** *shaw-lal´*; a primitive root; to *drop* or *strip*; (by implication) to *plunder*:—let fall, make self a prey, × of purpose, (make a, [take]) spoil.

7998. שָׁלָל, **shâlâl,** *shaw-lawl´*; from 7997; *booty*:—prey, spoil.

7999. שָׁלַם, **shâlam,** *shaw-lam´*; a primitive root; to *be safe* (in mind, body or estate); (figurative) to *be* (causative, *make*) *completed*; (by implication) to *be friendly*; (by extension) to *reciprocate* (in various applications):—make amends, (make an) end, finish, full, give again, make good, (re-) pay (again), (make) (to) (be at) peace (-able), that is perfect, perform, (make) prosper (-ous), recompense, render, requite, make restitution, restore, reward, × surely.

A verb meaning to be safe, to be completed. The primary meaning is to be safe or uninjured in mind or body (Job 8:6; 9:4). This word is normally used when God is keeping His people safe. In its simple form, this verb also means to be completed or to be finished. This could refer to something concrete such as a building (1Ki 7:51); or things more abstract, such as plans (Job 23:14). Other meanings of this verb include to be at peace with another person (Ps 7:4[5]); to make a treaty of peace (Jos 11:19; Job 5:23); to pay, to give a reward (Ps 62:12[13]); to restore, repay, or make retribution (Ex 21:36; Ps 37:21).

8000. **שְׁלַם, sh^elam,** *shel-am´*; (Chaldee); corresponding to 7999; to *complete*, to *restore*:—deliver, finish.

An Aramaic verb meaning to complete, to finish. This word corresponds to the Hebrew verb *shâlam* (7999). It refers to work being done, such as rebuilding the Temple in Jerusalem (Ezr 5:16). Closely related to this meaning is the secondary meaning, to make an end. In Da 5:26, this word is used to say that God would bring the days of Belshazzar's reign to an end. This word could also mean to restore in the sense of delivering something from captivity and returning it to the rightful owner. It was used when discussing the restoration of the temple furnishings in Jerusalem (Ezr 7:19).

8001. **שְׁלָם, sh^elâm,** *shel-awm´*; (Chaldee); corresponding to 7965; *prosperity*:—peace.

A masculine singular noun meaning peace. This word is most frequently used in the context of a greeting and may be used in both the singular and plural forms with the same meaning. As a greeting, these words signified a wish for peace, prosperity, and general good welfare to those who were being greeted. This seems to have been a common way to begin letters in ancient biblical times. In Nebuchadnezzar's letter to his subjects, he started by wishing prosperity to all his subjects (Da 4:1[3:31]); and in the letter which Tatnai sent to King Darius, he used this word as a greeting of well-wishing (Ezr 5:7).

8002. **שֶׁלֶם, shelem,** *sheh´-lem*; from 7999; (properly) *requital*, i.e. a (voluntary) sacrifice in *thanks*:—peace offering.

A noun meaning thanksgiving offerings, also called peace offerings. These offerings were voluntary, given to God in thanks or in praise to Him. These offerings were first described in the book of Leviticus, and the word is used many times after that, especially in the remaining sections of the Law dealing with sacrifices (Le 3:1, 7:11; Nu 7:17). This noun is also used in the plural form, which has a wider significance (Am 5:22). In this context, the thanksgiving offerings were offered in great distress, not out of thankful hearts. They were offered to try to gain God's favour, but God rejected them because they were not given out of love and thankfulness to Him.

8003. **שָׁלֵם, shâlêm,** *shaw-lame´*; from 7999; *complete* (literal or figurative); especially *friendly*:—full, just, made ready, peaceable, perfect (-ed), quiet, Shalem [*by mistake for a name*], whole.

An adjective meaning full, complete, safe, whole, peaceful. This adjective has several uses when it means complete, safe, unharmed, natural. Moses instructed the Israelites to build the altar on Mount Ebal of natural, unhewn or whole stones (Dt 27:6; Jos 8:31). Stones that were whole, finished, and from a rock quarry could be used to build the Temple (1Ki 6:7). The word describes the work on the Lord's Temple as finished, complete (2Ch 8:16). The word describes weights that had to be solid, accurate, and fair for use in the marketplace (Dt 25:15; Pr 11:1); it described wages paid as full, complete, rich (Ru 2:12). It described Jacob traveling safely to the city of Shechem (Ge 33:18). When referring to groups of people, it means entire or whole, such as whole communities taken captive in Amos's day (Am 1:6, 9). Something could be described as not yet complete or full; the sin of the Amorites was not yet complete (Ge 15:16).

The word connotes the idea of whole or undivided; the hearts of the Israelites were to be wholly centered on the Lord and His decrees (1Ki 8:61), but Solomon's heart was not so committed (1Ki 11:4; 2Ki 20:3; Isa 38:3).

The word means peaceful or peaceable when used of persons in certain relationships; the people of Shechem believed the Israelites intended to live in a peaceful relationship with them (Ge 34:21).

8004. **שָׁלֵם, Shâlêm,** *shaw-lame´*; the same as 8003; *peaceful*; *Shalem*, an early name of Jerusalem:—Salem.

8005. **שִׁלֵּם, shillêm,** *shil-lame´*; from 7999; *requital*:—recompense.

A masculine singular noun meaning retribution, requital, recompense. It is used when speaking of a deserved punishment, in the sense of a repayment for whatever wrong was done by a person (Dt 32:35). In addition, it can also signify rewards for good that has been done. The idea behind this word is that it is a reward or punishment that is deserved and is in conjunction with what was done beforehand. Ultimately, only God has the power of retribution. It is His right only to avenge wrongdoers and give those persons what they deserve or to reward those who have done right.

8006. **שִׁלֵּם, Shillêm,** *shil-lame´*; the same as 8005; *Shillem*, an Israelite:—Shillem.

8007. **שַׂלְמָא, Śalmâ',** *sal-maw´*; probably for 8008; *clothing*; *Salma*, the name of two Israelites:—Salma.

8008. **שַׂלְמָה, śalmâh,** *sal-maw´*; transposed for 8071; a *dress*:—clothes, garment, raiment.

8009. **שַׂלְמָה, Śalmâh,** *sal-maw´*; the same as 8008; *clothing*; *Salmah*, an Israelite:—Salmon. Compare 8012.

8010. **שְׁלֹמֹה, Sh^elômôh,** *shel-o-mo´*; from 7965; *peaceful*; *Shelomoh*, David's successor:—Solomon.

8011. **שִׁלֻּמָה, shillumâh,** *shil-loo-maw´*; feminine of 7966; *retribution*:—recompense.

A feminine singular noun meaning retribution, punishment, penalty. This word has negative meanings when it is used in Scripture, for example, persons were punished or repaid for whatever evil they did. The word does not seem to have anything to do with repayment in the sense of receiving rewards for doing what is right, but this could be because of its limited use in the OT. The righteous remained safe in God's protection, but the wicked received their punishment before the eyes of the righteous (Ps 91:8). God Himself is the giver of this retribution.

8012. **שַׂלְמוֹן, Śalmôwn,** *sal-mone´*; from 8008; *investiture*; *Salmon*, an Israelite:—Salmon. Compare 8009.

8013. **שְׁלֹמוֹת, Sh^elômôwth,** *shel-o-mōth´*; feminine plural of 7965; *pacifications*; *Shelomoth*, the name of two Israelites:—Shelomith [*from the margin*], Shelomoth. Compare 8019.

8014. **שַׂלְמַי, Śalmay,** *sal-mah´ee*; from 8008; *clothed*; *Salmai*, an Israelite:—Shalmai.

8015. **שְׁלֹמִי, Sh^elômîy,** *shel-o-mee´*; from 7965; *peaceable*; *Shelomi*, an Israelite:—Shelomi.

8016. **שִׁלֵּמִי, Shillêmîy,** *shil-lay-mee*; patronymic from 8006; a *Shilemite* (collective) or descendants of Shillem:—Shillemites.

8017. **שְׁלֻמִיאֵל, Sh^elumîy'êl,** *shel-oo-mee-ale´*; from 7965 and 410; *peace of God*; *Shelumiël*, an Israelite:—Shelumiel.

8018. **שֶׁלֶמְיָה, Shelemyâh,** *shel-em-yaw´*; or **שֶׁלֶמְיָהוּ, Shelemyâhûw,** *shel-em-yaw´-hoo*; from 8002 and 3050; *thank-offering of Jah*; *Shelemjah*, the name of nine Israelites:—Shelemiah.

8019. **שְׁלֹמִית, Sh^elômîyth,** *shel-o-meeth´*; or **שְׁלוֹמִית, Sh^elôwmîyth,** *shel-o-meeth´*; (Ezr 8:10), from 7965; *peaceableness*; *Shelomith*, the name of five Israelites and three Israelitesses:—Shelomith.

8020. **שַׁלְמַן, Shalman,** *shal-man´*; of foreign derivation; *Shalman*, a king apparently of Assyria:—Shalman. Compare 8022.

8021. **שַׁלְמֹן, shalmôn,** *shal-mone´*; from 7999; a *bribe*:—reward.

A masculine noun meaning a gift. It is used only in its plural form of *shalmôniym*. This word is not used to describe simple gifts given out of goodwill but gifts given as bribes to try to sway persons in authority to do what the giver wants them to do (Isa 1:23). These bribes are accepted only by corrupt people and end up corrupting people even further. Those who are totally corrupt even seek out bribes. Along with these bribes went the idea of a lack of justice and righteousness as a result of God's will not being done in those matters.

8022. **שַׁלְמַנְאֶסֶר, Shalman'eser,** *shal-man-eh´-ser*; of foreign derivation; *Shalmaneser*, an Assyrian king:—Shalmaneser. Compare 8020.

8023. **שִׁלֹנִי, Shilônîy,** *shee-lo-nee´*; the same as 7888; *Shiloni*, an Israelite:—Shiloni.

8024. **שֵׁלָנִי, Shêlânîy,** *shay-law-nee´*; from 7956; a *Shelanite* (collective), or descendants of Shelah:—Shelanites.

8025. **שָׁלַף, shâlaph,** *shaw-laf´*; a primitive root; to *pull* out, up or off:—draw (off), grow up, pluck off.

8026. **שֶׁלֶף, sheleph,** *sheh´-lef*; from 8025; *extract; Sheleph*, a son of Jokthan:—Sheleph.

8027. **שָׁלַשׁ, shâlash,** *shaw-lash´*; a primitive root perhaps originally to *intensify*, i.e. *treble*; but apparently used only as denominative from 7969, to *be* (causative, *make*) *triplicate* (by restoration, in portions, strands, days or years):—do the third time, (divide into, stay) three (days, -fold, parts, years old).

8028. **שֶׁלֶשׁ, Shêlesh,** *shay´-lesh*; from 8027; *triplet; Shelesh*, an Israelite:—Shelesh.

8029. **שִׁלֵּשׁ, shillêsh,** *shil-laysh´*; from 8027; a descendant of the *third* degree, i.e. *great grandchild*:—third [generation].

8030. **שִׁלְשָׁה, Shilshâh,** *shil-shaw´*; feminine from the same as 8028; *triplication; Shilshah*, an Israelite:—Shilshah.

8031. **שָׁלִשָׁה, Shâlishâh,** *shaw-lee-shaw´*; feminine from 8027; *trebled* land; *Shalishah*, a place in Palestine:—Shalisha.

8032. **שִׁלְשׁוֹם, shilshôwm,** *shil-shome´*; or **שִׁלְשֹׁם, shilshôm,** *shil-shome´*; from the same as 8028; *trebly*, i.e. (in time) *day before yesterday*:— + before (that time, -time), excellent things [*from the margin*], + heretofore, three days, + time past.

8033. **שָׁם, shâm,** *shawm*; a primitive particle [rather from the relative 834]; *there* (transferred to time) *then*; often *thither*, or *thence*:—in it, + thence, there (-in, + of, + out), + thither, + whither.

8034. **שֵׁם, shêm,** *shame*; a primitive word [perhaps rather from 7760 through the idea of definite and conspicuous *position*; compare 8064]; an *appellation*, as a mark or memorial of individuality; (by implication) *honour, authority, character*:— + base, [in-] fame [-ous], name (-d), renown, report.

8035. **שֵׁם, Shêm,** *shame*; the same as 8034; *name; Shem*, a son of Noah (often including his posterity):—Sem, Shem.

8036. **שֻׁם, shum,** *shoom*; (Chaldee); corresponding to 8034:—name.

8037. **שַׁמָּא, Shammâ',** *sham-maw´*; from 8074; *desolation; Shamma*, an Israelite:—Shamma.

8038. **שֶׁמְאֵבֶר, Shem'êber,** *shem-ay´-ber*; apparently from 8034 and 83; *name of pinion*, i.e. *illustrious; Shemeber*, a king of Zeboim:—Shemeber.

8039. **שִׁמְאָה, Shim'âh,** *shim-aw´*; perhaps for 8093; *Shimah*, an Israelite:—Shimah. Compare 8043.

8040. **שְׂמֹאול, s̓ᵉmô'l,** *sem-ole´*; or **שְׂמֹאל, s̓ᵉm'ôl,** *sem-ole´*; a primitive word [rather perhaps from the same as 8071 (by insertion of aleph) through the idea of *wrapping* up]; (properly) *dark* (as *enveloped*), i.e. the *north*; hence (by orientation) the *left* hand:—left (hand, side).

8041. **שָׂמַאל, s̓ᵉmô'l,** *seh-mol´*; a primitive root [rather denominative from 8040]; to use the *left* hand or pass in that direction):—(go, turn) (on the, to the) left.

8042. **שְׂמָאלִי, s̓ᵉmâ'lîy,** *sem-aw-lee´*; from 8040; situated on the *left* side:—left.

8043. **שִׁמְאָם, Shim'âm,** *shim-awm´*; for 8039 [compare 38]; *Shimam*, an Israelite:—Shimeam.

8044. **שַׁמְגַּר, Shamgar,** *sham-gar´*; of uncertain derivation; *Shamgar*, an Israelite judge:—Shamgar.

8045. **שָׁמַד, shâmad,** *shaw-mad´*; a primitive root; to *desolate*:—destroy (-uction), bring to nought, overthrow, perish, pluck down, × utterly.

A verb meaning to be destroyed. This verb is not used in its simple form and is only used in the passive and causative stems of the verb. The primary passive meaning is to be destroyed, to be exterminated, or to be annihilated, referring to individual people, households, or nations (Ge 34:30; Pr 14:11; Eze 32:12). It can also signify the devastation of land and places (Hos 10:8). The causative forms have the same root meanings as the passive forms. It can mean to annihilate, to exterminate people (Dt 1:27, 2:22); or to destroy objects such as cities, fortresses, or idols (Isa 23:11; Mic 5:14[13]). The difference between these two verb forms lies in who is destroying and who is being destroyed.

8046. **שְׁמַד, shᵉmad,** *shem-ad´*; (Chaldee); corresponding to 8045:—consume.

An Aramaic verb meaning to destroy. The word corresponds to the Hebrew verb *shâmad* (8045). It signifies more than simply ruining or destroying something but described a destruction that could not be reversed or fixed. Its connotations go far beyond mere destruction to mean to consume, to destroy completely without hope of restoration. In Da 7:26, this verb was used to signify a total destruction of a ruler's power. This verb is used only to describe a final destruction. God is the power behind this ultimate destruction.

8047. **שַׁמָּה, shammâh,** *sham-maw´*; from 8074; *ruin*; (by implication) *consternation*:—astonishment, desolate (-ion), waste, wonderful thing.

A feminine singular noun meaning ruin, astonishment. The primary meaning is that of ruin and wasting. This noun can be used to refer to evil people and their households who deserved to be destroyed because of their sins (Ps 73:19; Isa 5:9); also of land, towns, and buildings that were destroyed as a result of the evil people who lived there (Jer 2:15). A second meaning of astonishment, dismay, and horror is not clearly related to the primary meaning, but it is used to describe feelings toward Israel and its cities in their times of disobedience. Israel is seen as a horror, an object of scorn to all who saw her (Dt 28:37; Jer 19:8). It is also used to describe the extreme dismay people can feel at seeing destruction, a horror that fills persons (Jer 8:21).

8048. **שַׁמָּה, Shammâh,** *sham-maw´*; the same as 8047; *Shammah*, the name of an Edomite and four Israelites:—Shammah.

8049. **שַׁמְהוּת, Shamhûwth,** *sham-hooth´*; for 8048; *desolation; Shamhuth*, an Israelite:—Shamhuth.

8050. **שְׁמוּאֵל, Shᵉmûw'êl,** *shem-oo-ale´*; from the passive participle of 8085 and 410; *heard of God; Shemuël*, the name of three Israelites:—Samuel, Shemuel.

8051. **שַׁמּוּעַ, Shammûwa',** *sham-moo´-ah*; from 8074; *renowned; Shammua*, the name of four Israelites:—Shammua, Shammuah.

8052. **שְׁמוּעָה, shᵉmûw'âh,** *shem-oo-aw´*; feminine passive participle of 8074; something *heard*, i.e. an *announcement*:—bruit, doctrine, fame, mentioned, news, report, rumor, tidings.

8053. **שָׁמוּר, Shâmûwr,** *shaw-moor´*; passive participle of 8103; *observed; Shamur*, an Israelite:—Shamir [*from the margin*].

8054. **שַׁמּוֹת, Shammôwth,** *sham-mōth´*; plural of 8047; *ruins; Shammoth*, an Israelite:—Shamoth.

8055. שָׂמַח, śâmach, *saw-makh´*; a primitive root; probably to *brighten* up, i.e. (figurative) *be* (causative, make) *blithe* or *gleesome*:—cheer up, be (make) glad, (have, make) joy (-ful), be (make) merry, (cause to, make to) rejoice, × very.

8056. שָׂמֵחַ, śâmêach, *saw-may´-akh*; from 8055; *blithe* or *gleeful*:—(be) glad, joyful, (making) merry ([-hearted], -ily), rejoice (-ing).

8057. שִׂמְחָה, śimchâh, *sim-khaw´*; from 8056; *blithesomeness* or *glee*, (religious or festival):— × exceeding (-ly), gladness, joy (-fulness), mirth, pleasure, rejoice (-ing).

8058. שָׁמַט, shâmaṭ, *shaw-mat´*; a primitive root; to *fling* down; (incipiently) to *jostle*; (figurative) to *let alone, desist, remit*:—discontinue, overthrow, release, let rest, shake, stumble, throw down.

8059. שְׁמִטָּה, sh^{e}miṭṭâh, *shem-it-taw´*; from 8058; *remission* (of debt) or *suspension* (of labour):—release.

A feminine noun meaning a remission, a release, a suspension. This word signifies the cancellation of a debt that was owed to another person. This was a debt which a person would, under ordinary circumstances, be obligated to pay back. In Israel, at the end of every seven years, the people were to release and forgive their fellow people from debts owed to them. This word was used in this context of the seventh year to show that the debtor was released from any obligation to pay back what had been loaned to him before that time (Dt 15:1, 2, 9; 31:10). In the OT, this noun was used only in the context of forgiving debts at the end of every seven years.

8060. שַׁמַּי, Shammay, *sham-mah´ee*; from 8073; *destructive*; *Shammai*, the name of three Israelites:—Shammai.

8061. שְׁמִידָע, Sh^{e}mîydâ', *shem-ee-daw´*; apparently from 8034 and 3045; *name of knowing; Shemida*, an Israelite:—Shemida, Shemidah.

8062. שְׁמִידָעִי, Sh^{e}mîydâ'îy, *shem-ee-daw-ee´*; patronymic from 8061; a *Shemidaïte* (collective) or descendants of Shemida:—Shemidaites.

8063. שְׂמִיכָה, ś^{e}mîykâh, *sem-ee-kaw´*; from 5564; a *rug* (as *sustaining* the Oriental sitter):—mantle.

8064. שָׁמַיִם, shâmayim, *shaw-mah´-yim*; dual of an unused singular שָׁמֶה, **shâmeh,** *shaw-meh´*; from an unused root meaning to *be lofty*; the *sky* (as *aloft*; the dual perhaps alluding to the visible arch in which the clouds move, as well as to the higher ether where the celestial bodies revolve):—air, × astrologer, heaven (-s).

A masculine noun meaning sky, heaven, abode, firmament, air, stars. Although the word is plural or dual in form, it can be translated into English as singular or plural depending on the context. The word describes everything God made besides the earth: God made the heavens of the universe (Ge 1:1; 14:19); the firmament or expanse which He created around the earth was named sky or heaven as well (Ge 1:8). He stretched out the heavens (Isa 40:22); creating them (Isa 42:5; 45:18).

The heavens that humans observe with their senses are indicated by this word. The stars are part of the heavens (Ge 15:5) and are personified in some cases (Jgs 5:20); the sun and the moon, along with the stars, make up a major part of the hosts of heaven (Dt 4:19). Unfortunately, these things were worshipped as gods by even the Israelites (Jer 8:2). The heavens became a source of knowing the future and life in general, for scanners of the heavens and astrologers searched the heavens for signs (Isa 47:13). A favourite pagan deity was the Queen of Heaven whom the people worshipped (Jer 7:18; 44:17). God created waters above and below the heavens (Ge 1:8, 9). The clouds are a feature of the sky (Ge 8:2; Jgs 5:4; 1Ki 18:45; Job 26:13). The word indicates the total inhabited earth when it speaks of from under heaven, as when the Amalekites were to be destroyed from under heaven (Ge 6:17; Ex 17:14). The teacher of Ecclesiastes spoke of examining everything under heaven, i.e. everything done in the world in which humans live (Ecc 1:13; 2:3; 3:1); birds and other fowl fly in the sky (Ge 1:20). In God's new world, there will be a new heaven and a new earth (Isa 65:17; 66:22).

The invisible heavens are the abode of God. Heaven is the Lord's throne, the earth is the resting place of His feet—a beautiful metaphor of God's sovereignty over the universe (Isa 66:1). He extends the heavens as the tent roof of the universe (Isa 40:22); He dwells in heaven (1Ki 8:30, 32); yet He is not contained in even the heaven of heavens, the most exclusive part of the heavens (1Ki 8:27).

Heaven describes the place from which God operates: He calls to people from heaven (Ge 21:17; 22:11). The Ten Commandments were spoken from heaven (Ex 20:22; Ne 9:13). He sent down manna from heaven for His people in the desert (Ex 16:4). He is not merely a dweller in heaven, but He is the God of heaven (Ge 24:3; 2Ch 36:23; Ezr 1:2). The heavens grow old and pass away, but God is eternal (Job 14:12; Isa 13:10; 65:17). Satan aspired to usurp God's reign in heaven and was cast out (Isa 14:12, 13). Elijah the prophet, because he faithfully followed the Lord, was taken up into heaven in a whirlwind (2Ki 2:1, 11).

8065. שְׁמַיִן, sh^{e}mayin, *sheh-mah´-yin*; (Chaldee); corresponding to 8064:—heaven.

An Aramaic noun meaning sky, heavens. This word has several different connotations, but the basic meaning is that of the sky (Da 4:11[8]; 7:2). Reaching beyond the simple meaning of sky, this word also referred to heaven, the dwelling place of God that is much higher than any other place (Da 2:28; 4:34[31]). The heavens are great not because of what they are but because of who lives there. Not only does God dwell in heaven, but His messengers, the angels, also dwell there and are sent down to earth to do His work (Da 4:13[10]). This word also signifies the whole universe where God showed His mighty signs and made His works known to all (Da 6:27[28]). It is combined to form phrases such as the God of heaven (Ezr 5:11, 12; Da 2:18, 19, 28, 37, 44); birds of the sky (Da 2:38); winds of heaven (Da 7:2, 13). This noun corresponds to the Hebrew noun *shâmayim* (8064), that is very similar in meaning.

8066. שְׁמִינִי, sh^{e}mîynîy, *shem-ee-nee´*; from 8083; *eight*:—eight.

8067. שְׁמִינִית, sh^{e}mîynîyth, *shem-ee-neeth´*; feminine of 8066; probably an *eight*-stringed lyre:—Sheminith.

8068. שָׁמִיר, shâmîyr, *shaw-meer´*; from 8104 in the original sense of *pricking*; a *thorn*; also (from its *keenness* for scratching) a gem, probably the *diamond*:—adamant (stone), brier, diamond.

8069. שָׁמִיר, Shâmîyr, *shaw-meer´*; the same as 8068; *Shamir*, the name of two places in Palestine:—Shamir. Compare 8053.

8070. שְׁמִירָמוֹת, Sh^{e}mîyrâmôwth, *shem-ee-raw-mōth´*; or שְׁמָרִימוֹת, **Sh^{e}mârîymôwth,** *shem-aw-ree-mōth´*; probably from 8034 and plural of 7413; *name of heights; Shemiramoth*, the name of two Israelites:—Shemiramoth.

8071. שִׂמְלָה, śimlâh, *sim-law´*; perhaps by permutation for the feminine of 5566 (through the idea of a *cover* assuming the shape of the object beneath); a *dress*, especially a *mantle*:—apparel, cloth (-es, -ing), garment, raiment. Compare 8008.

8072. שַׂמְלָה, Śamlâh, *sam-law´*; probably for the same as 8071; *Samlah*, an Edomite:—Samlah.

8073. שַׁמְלַי, Shamlay, *sham-lah´ee*; for 8014; *Shamlai*, one of the Nethinim:—Shalmai [*from the margin*].

8074. שָׁמֵם, shâmêm, *shaw-mame´*; a primitive root; to *stun* (or [intransitive] *grow numb*), i.e. *devastate* or (figurative) *stupefy* (both usually in a passive sense):—make amazed, be astonied, (be an) astonish (-ment), (be, bring into, unto, lay, lie, make) desolate (-ion, places), be destitute, destroy (self), (lay, lie, make) waste, wonder.

A verb meaning to be desolated, to be destroyed. The desolation or destruction that this verb refers to can be used of both people (2Sa 13:20; La 1:13, 16); and places (Le 26:31, 32; Isa 61:4; Eze 35:12) and is used in both its simple and causative forms. A second meaning of this verb, which is extremely common, is to be appalled or astonished and is used in the simple, passive, and passive causative stems (Job

18:20; Isa 52:14; Jer 18:16). The connection between these two meanings is not entirely clear; yet they are both used with great frequency. When this verb is used in the second meaning, it often describes a person's reaction on seeing desolation and destruction. For example, in 1Ki 9:8, the reaction of people to a destroyed land was described with this verb. A much less common use of this verb is in the reflexive stem. Here it meant to be disheartened or dismayed (Ps 143:4).

8075. שְׁמַם, **shᵉmam,** *shem-am´*; (Chaldee); corresponding to 8074:—be astonied.

8076. שָׁמֵם, **shâmêm,** *shaw-mame´*; from 8074; *ruined*:—desolate.

A masculine adjective meaning ruined, wasted, desolate. This adjective corresponds to the verb *shâmêm* (8074). This adjective can be used to describe both land and objects that have been destroyed. The connotations here are of an extreme destruction that has lasting effects and causes all people to stand up and take notice of what has happened. When Jerusalem fell, the Temple was torn apart and utterly destroyed, and this adjective was used to describe the condition of the Temple (Da 9:17). In Jer 12:11, it is also used to prophesy what the land would be like after the fall of Jerusalem. This adjective paints a picture of harsh destruction. In these contexts, this destruction is indicative of God's judgment on His people.

8077. שְׁמָמָה, **shᵉmâmâh,** *shem-aw-maw´*; feminine of 8076; *devastation*; (figurative) *astonishment*:—(laid, × most) desolate (-ion), waste.

A feminine singular noun meaning desolation, waste. This noun can be used to refer to many things such as land, cities, or houses (Ex 23:29; Le 26:33; Isa 1:7). Most often it is used in conjunction with a passage describing what did happen to the land of Israel after God judged His people and sent them into exile. This shows the totality of the destruction that Israel endured. Nothing was to be saved from this destruction. Fields and vineyards were turned into wastelands and desolate fields after God's judgment (Jer 12:10). God allowed such desolation as a punishment for the sins of His people because they refused to repent. This punishment could even fall on people of other nations, such as the Edomites (Eze 33:28, 29; 35:3).

8078. שִׁמָּמוֹן, **shimmâmôwn,** *shim-maw-mone´*; from 8074; *stupefaction*:—astonishment.

8079. שְׂמָמִית, **śᵉmâmîyth,** *sem-aw-meeth´*; probably from 8074 (in the sense of *poisoning*); a *lizard* (from the superstition of its *noxiousness*):—spider.

8080. שָׁמַן, **shâman,** *shaw-man´*; a primitive root; to *shine*, i.e. (by analogy) *be* (causative. *make*) *oily* or *gross*:—become (make, wax) fat.

8081. שֶׁמֶן, **shemen,** *sheh´-men*; from 8080; *grease*, especially liquid (as from the olive, often perfumed); (figurative) *richness*:—anointing, × fat (things), × fruitful, oil ([-ed]), ointment, olive, + pine.

A masculine noun meaning fat, oil. This word has a wide range of figurative meanings relating to richness and plenty. Most simply, it is used of food, relating to feasts of good, rich food (Isa 25:6). It is also used frequently of oil. This can be oil used for food and cooking (Dt 8:8; 32:13); for oil which was used to anoint holy objects or kings (Ex 30:25; 1Sa 10:1); or for oil used as an ointment to soothe and cleanse, leading to healing (Ps 133:2; Isa 1:6). The figurative meanings are also important. This word can be used to signify strength, such as in Isa 10:27 where growing fat meant growing strong. It also frequently relates to fruitfulness and fertile places where good things grew (Isa 5:1; 28:1). The overall picture one gets from this word is that of richness, strength, and fertility.

8082. שָׁמֵן, **shâmên,** *shaw-mane´*; from 8080; *greasy*, i.e. *gross*; (figurative) *rich*:—fat, lusty, plenteous.

8083. שְׁמֹנֶה, **shᵉmôneh,** *shem-o-neh´*; or שְׁמוֹנֶה, **shᵉmôwneh,** *shem-o-neh´*; feminine שְׁמֹנָה, **shᵉmô-nâh,** *shem-o-naw´*; or שְׁמוֹנָה, **shᵉmôwnâh,** *shem-o-naw´*; apparently from 8082 through the idea of *plumpness*; a cardinal number, *eight* (as if a *surplus* above the "perfect" seven); also (as ordinal) *eighth*:—eight ([-een, -eenth]), eighth.

8084. שְׁמֹנִים, **shᵉmônîym,** *shem-o-neem´*; or שְׁמוֹנִים, **shᵉmôwnîym,** *shem-o-neem´*; mult. from 8083; *eighty*; also *eightieth*:—eighty (-ieth), fourscore.

8085. שָׁמַע, **shâma‘,** *shaw-mah´*; a primitive root; to *hear* intelligently (often with implication of attention, obedience, etc.; [causative] to *tell*, etc.):— × attentively, call (gather) together, × carefully, × certainly, consent, consider, be content, declare, × diligently, discern, give ear, (cause to, let, make to) hear (-ken, tell), × indeed, listen, make (a) noise, (be) obedient, obey, perceive, (make a) proclaim (-ation), publish, regard, report, shew (forth), (make a) sound, × surely, tell, understand, whosoever [heareth], witness.

A verb meaning to hear, to obey, to listen, to be heard of, to be regarded, to cause to hear, to proclaim, to sound aloud. The verb basically means to hear and in context expresses various connotations of this. The most famous use of this word is to introduce the Shema, "Hear, O, Israel," followed by the content of what the Israelites are to understand about the Lord their God and how they are to respond to Him (Dt 6:4). In a parallel usage, the heavens are commanded to "Hear, Oh heavens!" to the prophet's message about Israel (Isa 1:2). The word calls attention to hear various things: It means to hear another person speaking (Ge 27:6); the Lord's voice (Ge 3:10); or anything that can be perceived by the ear. Used with or without the preposition *'el* (413) following, the word means to listen to someone. The house of Israel was not willing to listen to Ezekiel (Eze 3:7); the Lord was not willing to listen to the beautiful worship services of God's people, for they were not following justice (Ge 27:5; Am 5:23).

The word takes on the connotation of obedience in certain contexts and with certain Hebrew constructions: It can mean to heed a request or command, such as Abraham's request concerning Ishmael (Ge 17:20). The Lord listened to Hagar's prayer and gave her a son (Ge 16:11; 30:6). It means to obey in certain contexts (Ge 3:17; 22:18; Ex 24:7; 2Ki 14:11).

The word is used to connote the idea of understanding. God confused the speech of the people at the Tower of Babel so they could not understand each other (Ge 11:7; Isa 33:19). Solomon wanted a heart of discernment and understanding (hearing) to govern his people (Dt 1:16; 1Ki 3:9); to be able to decide between good and evil (2Sa 14:17).

In the passive stem, the word means to be heard. Pharaoh heard the news that Joseph's brothers had arrived in Egypt (Ge 45:16). No sound of a tool was heard as the Temple was being built (Dt 4:32; 1Ki 6:7). It also meant to be obedient to King David (2Sa 22:45); or to make hear, to call, or to summon as when Saul summoned his soldiers (1Sa 15:4; 23:8).

The word is used often in the causative stem to mean to cause to listen, to proclaim, to announce. When Israel assembled at Mount Horeb (Sinai), the Lord caused them to hear His words (Dt 4:10; Jos 6:10). It also means to proclaim, to summon; Isaiah spoke of those who proclaim peace (1Ki 15:22; Isa 52:7); and the psalmist proclaimed the praise of the Lord (Ps 26:7).

8086. שְׁמַע, **shᵉma‘,** *shem-ah´*; (Chaldee); corresponding to 8085:—hear, obey.

An Aramaic verb meaning to hear. This verb is used only in the book of Daniel and is used when speaking of words that have been heard from another person (Da 5:14, 16); or when hearing sounds, such as the sounds of music from many instruments (Da 3:5, 7, 10). In a broader perspective, it can also mean to have a sense of hearing as opposed to being deaf (Da 5:23). This verb can also be used in the reflexive form and means that one shows one's obedience to what has been heard (Da 7:27).

8087. שֶׁמַע, **Shema‘,** *sheh´-mah*; for the same as 8088; *Shema*, the name of a place in Palestine and of four Israelites:—Shema.

8088. שֵׁמַע, **shêma‘,** *shay´-mah*; from 8085; something *heard*, i.e. a *sound, rumor, announcement*; (abstract) *audience*:—bruit, fame, hear (-ing), loud, report, speech, tidings.

A masculine noun meaning hearing. This word can mean hearing as opposed to or in addition to seeing (Job 42:5; Ps 18:44[45]). This word can also be used to represent a rumor, a report, or an announcement, as these are things that have been announced and heard by others. These reports may be good news to be greeted joyously, such as a report of fame and good deeds (Ge 29:13; 1Ki 10:1); bad news to be concerned about (Isa 23:5); or even lies and malicious rumors causing others to suffer (Ex 23:1).

8089. שֹׁמַע, shôma', *sho´-mah*; from 8085; a *report*:—fame.

8090. שְׁמָע, Shemâ', *shem-aw´*; for 8087; *Shema*, a place in Palestine:—Shema.

8091. שָׁמָע, Shâmâ', *shaw-maw´*; from 8085; *obedient; Shama*, an Israelite:—Shama.

8092. שִׁמְעָא, Shim'â', *shim-aw´*; for 8093; *Shima*, the name of four Israelites:—Shimea, Shimei, Shamma.

8093. שִׁמְעָה, Shim'âh, *shim-aw´*; feminine of 8088; *annunciation; Shimah*, an Israelite:—Shimeah.

8094. שְׁמָעָה, Shemâ'âh, *shem-aw-aw´*; for 8093; *Shemaah*, an Israelite:—Shemaah.

8095. שִׁמְעוֹן, Shim'ôwn, *shim-ōne´*; from 8085; *hearing; Shimon*, one of Jacob's sons, also the tribe descendants from him:—Simeon.

8096. שִׁמְעִי, Shim'iy, *shim-ee´*; from 8088; *famous; Shimi*, the name of twenty Israelites:—Shimeah [*from the margin*], Shimei, Shimhi, Shimi.

8097. שִׁמְעִי, Shim'îy, *shim-ee´*; patronymic from 8096; a *Shimite* (collective) or descendants of Shimi:—of Shimi, Shimites.

8098. שְׁמַעְיָה, Shema'yâh, *shem-aw-yaw´*; or שְׁמַעְיָהוּ, **Shema'yâhûw**, *shem-aw-yaw´-hoo*; from 8085 and 3050; *Jah has heard; Shemajah*, the name of twenty-five Israelites:—Shemaiah.

8099. שִׁמְעֹנִי, Shim'ônîy, *shim-o-nee´*; patronymic from 8095; a *Shimonite* (collective) or descendants of Shimon:—tribe of Simeon, Simeonites.

8100. שִׁמְעָת, Shim'âth, *shim-awth´*; feminine of 8088; *annunciation; Shimath*, an Ammonitess:—Shimath.

8101. שִׁמְעָתִי, Shim'âthîy, *shim-aw-thee´*; patronymic from 8093; a *Shimathite* (collective) or descendants of Shimah:—Shimeathites.

8102. שֶׁמֶץ, shemets, *sheh´-mets*; from an unused root meaning to *emit* a sound; an *inkling*:—a little.

8103. שִׁמְצָה, shimtsâh, *shim-tsaw´*; feminine of 8102; scornful *whispering* (of hostile spectators):—shame.

8104. שָׁמַר, shâmar, *shaw-mar´*; a primitive root; (properly) to *hedge* about (as with thorns), i.e. *guard*; (generally) to *protect, attend to*, etc.:—beware, be circumspect, take heed (to self), keep (-er, self), mark, look narrowly, observe, preserve, regard, reserve, save (self), sure, (that lay) wait (for), watch (-man).

A verb meaning to watch, to keep, to preserve, to guard, to be careful, to watch over, to watch carefully over, to be on one's guard. The verb means to watch, to guard, to care for. Adam and Eve were to watch over and care for the Garden of Eden where the Lord had placed them (Ge 2:15); cultic and holy things were to be taken care of dutifully by priests (2Ki 22:14). The word can suggest the idea of protecting: David gave orders to keep Absalom safe (1Sa 26:15; 2Sa 18:12); the Lord keeps those who look to Him (Ps 121:7). The word can mean to simply save or to preserve certain items; objects could be delivered to another person for safekeeping (Ge 41:35; Ex 22:7[6]). The word also means to pay close attention to: Eli the priest continued to observe Hannah's lips closely as she prayed (1Sa 1:12; Isa 42:20). Closely related to this meaning is the connotation to continue to do something, as when Joab maintained his siege of the city of Rabbah (2Sa 11:16). The verb also indicates caring for sheep (1Sa 17:20).

The Hebrew word means to maintain or to observe something for a purpose and is followed by another verb indicating the purpose or manner, as in the following examples: Israel was to observe the laws of the Lord, so as to do them (Dt 4:6; 5:1); Balaam had to observe accurately what he had been charged with (Nu 23:12); and Israel was responsible to keep the way of the Lord and walk in it (Ge 17:9; 18:19).

The word naturally means to watch over some physical object, to keep an eye on it. In its participial form, the word means human guards, those who watch for people or over designated objects (Jgs 1:24; Ne 12:25). The Lord, as the moral Governor of the world, watches over the moral and spiritual behaviour of people (Job 10:14).

In the passive reflexive stem, it means to be taken care of. To take care in the passive aspect, the verb was used to assert that Israel was watched over (Hos 12:13[14]). Most often it means to take care, as when the Lord instructed Laban to take care not to harm Jacob (Ge 31:29). Amasa did not guard himself carefully and was killed by Joab (2Sa 20:10). Pharaoh warned Moses to take care not to come into his presence again or he would die (Ex 10:28; cf. Ge 24:6; 2Ki 6:10; Jer 17:21).

The word in its intensive stem means to pay regard to or attach oneself to. In the participial form of this verb, it means those who give heed to useless vanities (Jnh 2:8[9]). In the reflexive stem, it means to keep oneself. David declared he was blameless since he had kept himself from sin (2Sa 22:24; Ps 18:23[24]).

8105. שֶׁמֶר, shemer, *sheh´-mer*; from 8104; something *preserved*, i.e. the *settlings* (plural only) of wine:—dregs, (wines on the) lees.

8106. שֶׁמֶר, Shemer, *sheh´-mer*; the same as 8105; *Shemer*, the name of three Israelites:—Shamer, Shemer.

8107. שִׁמֻּר, shimmur, *shim-moor´*; from 8104; an *observance*:—× be (much) observed.

8108. שָׁמְרָה, shomrâh, *shom-raw´*; feminine of an unused noun from 8104 meaning a *guard; watchfulness*:—watch.

8109. שְׁמֻרָה, shemurâh, *shem-oo-raw´*; feminine of passive participle of 8104; something *guarded*, i.e. an *eye-lid*:—waking.

8110. שִׁמְרוֹן, Shimrôwn, *shim-rone´*; from 8105 in its original sense; *guardianship; Shimron*, the name of an Israelite and of a place in Palestine:—Shimron.

8111. שֹׁמְרוֹן, Shômerôwn, *sho-mer-ōne´*; from the active participle of 8104; *watch-station; Shomeron*, a place in Palestine:—Samaria.

8112. שִׁמְרוֹן מְראוֹן, Shimrôwn Merô'ôwn, *shim-rone´ mer-oh-one´*; from 8110 and a derivative of 4754; *guard of lashing; Shimron-Meron*, a place in Palestine:—Shimon-meron.

8113. שִׁמְרִי, Shimrîy, *shim-ree´*; from 8105 in its original sense; *watchful; Shimri*, the name of four Israelites:—Shimri.

8114. שְׁמַרְיָה, Shemaryâh, *shem-ar-yaw´*; or שְׁמַרְיָהוּ, **Shemaryâhûw**, *shem-ar-yaw´-hoo*; from 8104 and 3050; *Jah has guarded; Shemarjah*, the name of four Israelites:—Shamariah, Shemariah.

8115. שָׁמְרַיִן, Shâmerayin, *shaw-meh-rah´-yin*; (Chaldee); corresponding to 8111; *Shomraïn*, a place in Palestine:—Samaria.

8116. שִׁמְרִית, Shimrîyth, *shim-reeth´*; feminine of 8113; *female guard; Shimrith*, a Moabitess:—Shimrith.

8117. שִׁמְרֹנִי, Shimrônîy, *shim-ro-nee´*; patronymic from 8110; a *Shimronite* (collective) or descendants of Shimron:—Shimronites.

8118. שֹׁמְרֹנִי, Shômerônîy, *sho-mer-o-nee´*; patrial from 8111; a *Shomeronite* (collective) or inhabitant of Shomeron:—Samaritans.

8119. שִׁמְרָת, Shimrâth, *shim-rawth´*; from 8104; *guardship; Shimrath*, an Israelite:—Shimrath.

8120. שְׁמַשׁ, shᵉmash, *shem-ash´*; (Chaldee); corresponding to the root of 8121 through the idea of *activity* implied in daylight; to *serve*:—minister.

An Aramaic verb meaning to serve, to minister to, and to attend to. This word is used only in Da 7:10 in a stunning vision of God, the Ancient of Days, on His throne. Thousands attend God, serving Him only. In this limited context, we get the idea that this verb is one that signifies much more than just serving or attending someone as a paid servant or a slave would do out of necessity. The connotation here seems to be that of having absolute devotion to the person, just as all who serve God must be wholeheartedly devoted to Him. This serving is voluntary for those who love God.

8121. שֶׁמֶשׁ, shemesh, *sheh´-mesh*; from an unused root meaning to be *brilliant*; the *sun*; (by implication) the *east*; (figurative) a *ray*, i.e. (architectural) a notched *battlement*:— + east side (-ward), sun ([rising]), + west (-ward), window. See also 1053.

8122. שֶׁמֶשׁ, shemesh, *sheh´-mesh*; (Chaldee); corresponding to 8121; the *sun*:—sun.

8123. שִׁמְשׁוֹן, Shimshôwn, *shim-shone´*; from 8121; *sunlight; Shimshon*, an Israelite:—Samson.

8124. שִׁמְשַׁי, Shimshay, *shim-shah´ee*; (Chaldee); from 8122; *sunny; Shimshai*, a Samaritan:—Shimshai.

8125. שַׁמְשְׁרַי, Shamshᵉray, *sham-sher-ah´ee*; apparently from 8121; *sunlike; Shamsherai*, an Israelite:—Shamsherai.

8126. שֻׁמָתִי, Shumâthîy, *shoo-maw-thee´*; patronymic from an unused name from 7762 probably meaning *garlic*-smell; a *Shumathite* (collective) or descendants of Shumah:—Shumathites.

8127. שֵׁן, shên, *shane´*; from 8150; a *tooth* (as *sharp*); specifically (for 8143) *ivory*; (figurative) a *cliff*:—crag, × forefront, ivory, × sharp, tooth.

8128. שֵׁן, shên, *shane*; (Chaldee); corresponding to 8127; a *tooth*:—tooth.

8129. שֵׁן, Shên, *shane*; the same as 8127; *crag; Shen*, a place in Palestine:—Shen.

8130. שָׂנֵא, śânê', *saw-nay´*; a primitive root; to *hate* (personal):—enemy, foe, (be) hate (-ful, -r), odious, × utterly.

A verb meaning to hate, to be unwilling, to be hated. This verb is the antonym of the Hebrew verb *'âhab* (157), meaning to love. The verb means to hate God or persons; God punishes children for the sins of their fathers to the third and fourth generation of those who hate Him, but He shows kindness instead of punishment to those who love (*'âhab*) Him (Ex 20:5). God hates as His enemies those who love cruelty and wickedness (Ps 11:5); they do not keep His covenant and are not loyal to Him (Ex 20:5). God's people were not to become allied to those who hated the Lord (2Ch 19:2; Ps 139:21). God or persons can be the subject of the verb; God came to hate the palaces of Jacob (Am 6:8; Hos 9:15); and even the religious services of His own people because they were false (Am 5:21). In fact, God hates all who do evil (Ps 5:5[6]); and wickedness (Ps 45:7[8]); thus, to fear God means to hate evil (Pr 8:13).

God is different from all other so-called gods, so much so that He hates the corrupt things the heathen do when they worship these gods (Dt 12:31). The word describes the haters or enemies of persons. David's enemies were those whom his soul hated (2Sa 5:8); the enemies of Rebekah would be those who might hate her descendants (Ge 24:60). The lack of hatred toward a person cleared someone who accidentally killed another person without planning to do so and did not previously hate the person (Dt 4:42). Absalom, on the other hand, hated his brother Ammon for humiliating his sister and planned his death because he hated him (2Sa 13:22). The negative rendition of love your neighbour as yourself asserted that you should not hate your brother in your heart (Le 19:17).

The word means to dislike, to be hostile to, or to loathe someone or something in some contexts: Isaac accused Abimelech of rejecting him or acting hostile toward him when he asked Isaac to move away from him (Ge 26:27; Jgs 11:7); Joseph's brothers became bitter and hostile toward him and his dreams (Ge 37:5); Malachi asserted that God hated Esau but loved Jacob to explain how God had dealt with their descendants (Mal 1:3); God cared for Esau and gave him offspring. A similar use of this word is found concerning Jacob's love for Rachel and the hyperbolic statement that he hated Leah (Ge 29:31, 33; Dt 21:16, 17); Jethro instructed Moses to choose faithful men who despised increasing their wealth in dishonest ways (Ex 18:21). In the passive stem of the verb, it is used once to refer to the poor who are despised by their friends or neighbours in contrast to the rich who have many friends (Pr 14:20).

In the intensive stem, the word means one who radiates hatred (i.e. an enemy); Moses prayed for the Lord to strike the enemies of Levi (Dt 33:11; 2Sa 22:41). The word described the enemies of the Lord (Nu 10:35; Dt 32:41). The word also described the person who hates wisdom; such a person loves death (Pr 8:36).

8131. שְׂנֵא, śᵉnê', *sen-ay´*; (Chaldee); corresponding to 8130:—hate.

An Aramaic verb meaning an enemy. This word only occurs once in the Hebrew Bible and refers to those who hate a person. In Da 4:19[16], this word is used when Daniel is speaking to King Nebuchadnezzar about the interpretation of his dream. The interpretation is so unfavourable that Daniel says he wishes it were for the king's enemies instead of being for the king himself.

8132. שָׁנָא, shânâ', *shaw-naw´*; a primitive root; to *alter*:—change.

8133. שְׁנָא, shᵉnâ', *shen-aw´*; (Chaldee); corresponding to 8132:—alter, change, (be) diverse.

8134. שִׁנְאָב, Shin'âb, *shin-awb´*; probably from 8132 and 1; a *father has turned; Shinab*, a Canaanite:—Shinab.

8135. שִׂנְאָה, śin'âh, *sin-aw´*; from 8130; *hate*:— + exceedingly, hate (-ful, -red).

A feminine noun meaning hating, hatred. The word is derived from the verb *śânê'* (8130) and signifies a strong feeling of hatred. It is most commonly used to describe hatred that one human feels toward another. This hate can be so strong that it leads to murder (Nu 35:20); or it can be a hate that causes unrest and dissension between people, yet not necessarily leading to violence (Pr 10:12; 15:17). In one place, this noun is even used to describe sexual revulsion and is indicative of a strong hate (2Sa 13:15). This word can be used as a verb at times, such as in Dt 1:27 and 9:28. Here God is the subject, and the people were complaining that He hated them, although this was not true. The connotations the people had with this word showed through because they felt that God hated them so much that He would hand them over to be killed by their enemies.

8136. שִׁנְאָן, shin'ân, *shin-awn´*; from 8132; *change*, i.e. *repetition*:— × angels.

A masculine noun meaning repeating, repetition. This word is used only once in the OT, in Ps 68:17[18], where it is preceded by the word that means a thousand. Therefore, it means a thousand in repetition or thousands of thousands. Here it is in reference to the chariots of God, which shows how mighty and powerful God is because He is the ruler over so much. Chariots were also a sign of wealth; and since God had so many chariots, it showed that all the wealth in the world belongs to Him alone.

8137. שֶׁנְאַצַּר, Shen'atstsar, *shen-ats-tsar´*; apparently of Babylonian origin; *Shenatstsar*, an Israelite:—Senazar.

8138. שָׁנָה, shânâh, *shaw-naw´*; a primitive root; to *fold*, i.e. *duplicate* (literal or figurative); (by implication) to *transmute* (transitive or intransitive):—do (speak, strike) again, alter, double, (be given to) change, disguise, (be) diverse, pervert, prefer, repeat, return, do the second time.

8139. שְׁנָה, shᵉnâh, *shen-aw´*; (Chaldee); corresponding to 8142:—sleep.

8140. שְׁנָה, shᵉnâh, *shen-aw´*; (Chaldee); corresponding to 8141:—year.

8141. **שָׁנָה, shânâh,** *shaw-naw´*; from 8138; a *year* (as a *revolution* of time):— + whole age, × long, + old, year (× -ly).

8142. **שֵׁנָה, shênâh,** *shay-naw´*; or **שֵׁנָא, shênâ',** *shay-naw´*; (Ps 127:2), from 3462; *sleep*:—sleep.

8143. **שֶׁנְהַבִּים, shenhabbîym,** *shen-hab-beem´*; from 8127 and the plural apparently of a foreign word; probably *tooth of elephants*, i.e. *ivory tusk*:—ivory.

8144. **שָׁנִי, shânîy,** *shaw-nee´*; of uncertain derivation; *crimson*, (properly) the insect or its colour, also stuff dyed with it:—crimson, scarlet (thread).

8145. **שֵׁנִי, shênîy,** *shay-nee´*; from 8138; (properly) *double*, i.e. *second*; (also adverb) *again*:—again, either [of them], (an-) other, second (time).

8146. **שָׂנִיא, śânîy',** *saw-nee´*; from 8130; *hated*:—hated.

A feminine adjective meaning one who is hated or held in aversion. It is used in Dt 21:15 contrasting a wife who is loved with a wife who is hated. There does not seem to be a connotation of extreme hate here but rather of dislike, preferring one wife to the other. The terms are used as opposites, but the strength of opposition cannot be determined accurately. In this limited context, it is difficult to tell how strong of a connotation the word really holds, but here it seems to connote more dislike or neglect than strong hate that would lead to overtly hateful actions toward that person.

8147. **שְׁנַיִם, sh^enayim,** *shen-ah´-yim*; dual of 8145; feminine **שְׁתַּיִם, sh^ettayim,** *shet-tah´-yim*; *two*; also (as ordinal) *twofold*:—both, couple, double, second, twain, + twelfth, + twelve, + twenty (sixscore) thousand, twice, two.

8148. **שְׁנִינָה, sh^enîynâh,** *shen-ee-naw´*; from 8150; something *pointed*, i.e. a *gibe*:—byword, taunt.

8149. **שְׁנִיר, Sh^enîyr,** *shen-eer´*; or **סְנִיר, Ś^enîyr,** *sen-eer´*; from an unused root meaning to *be pointed; peak; Shenir* or *Senir*, a summit of Lebanon:—Senir, Shenir.

8150. **שָׁנַן, shânan,** *shaw-nan´*; a primitive root; to *point* (transitive or intransitive); (intensive) to *pierce*; (figurative) to *inculcate*:—prick, sharp (-en), teach diligently, whet.

A verb meaning to whet, to sharpen. This word is used in three of the basic stems. In its simple meaning of sharpen, it can be used to refer to the sharpening of a sword. In context it refers to God sharpening His sword of judgment (Dt 32:41). Also, it can be used in reference to sharp arrows (Ps 45:5[6]; Isa 5:28). Figuratively, this verb can be used to signify sharp words that a person says in order to hurt someone else (Ps 64:3[4]; 140:3[4]). In the intensive form of the verb, it means to teach incisively (Dt 6:7). The idea here is that just as words are cut into a stone tablet with a sharp object, so the Law should be impressed on the hearts of the children of every generation. Finally, in the reflexive stem, this verb means to be pierced by grief or envy or to be wounded (Ps 73:21).

8151. **שָׁנַס, shânas,** *shaw-nas´*; a primitive root; to *compress* (with a belt):—gird up.

8152. **שִׁנְעָר, Shin'âr,** *shin-awr´*; probably of foreign derivation; *Shinar*, a plain in Babylon:—Shinar.

8153. **שְׁנָת, sh^enâth,** *shen-awth´*; from 3462; *sleep*:—sleep.

8154. **שָׁסָה, shâsâh,** *shaw-saw´*; or **שָׂשָׂה, shâśâh,** *shaw-saw´*; (Isa 10:13), a primitive root; to *plunder*:—destroyer, rob, spoil (-er).

A verb that means to spoil, to plunder. This verb is used only in the simple stem and in the participle form. It can refer to the plundering of both land and objects (Jgs 2:14; 1Sa 14:48; Hos 13:15). In almost every reference where this word is found, enemies were plundering the land and the people of Israel. God allowed this in judgment on the sins of the Israelites after they had been warned and refused to repent or as a warning to call them to repentance. The participle form of this verb refers to people who do the plundering (Isa 10:13; 42:22). Ultimately, God allowed any persons to be plunderers. But if they overstepped their boundaries, they too would be plundered as the punishment for their sins.

8155. **שָׁסַס, shâsas,** *shaw-sas´*; a primitive root; to *plunder*:—rifle, spoil.

8156. **שָׁסַע, shâsa',** *shaw-sah´*; a primitive root; to *split* or *tear*; (figurative) to *upbraid*:—cleave, (be) cloven ([footed]), rend, stay.

8157. **שֶׁסַע, shesa',** *sheh´-sah*; from 8156; a *fissure*:—cleft, cloven-footed.

8158. **שָׁסַף, shâsaph,** *shaw-saf´*; a primitive root; to *cut* in pieces, i.e. slaughter:—hew in pieces.

8159. **שָׁעָה, shâ'âh,** *shaw-aw´*; a primitive root; to *gaze* at or about (properly, for help); (by implication) to *inspect, consider, compassionate, be nonplussed* (as looking around in amazement) or *bewildered*:—depart, be dim, be dismayed, look (away), regard, have respect, spare, turn.

8160. **שָׁעָה, shâ'âh,** *shaw-aw´*; (Chaldee); from a root corresponding to 8159; (properly) a *look*, i.e. a *moment*:—hour.

8161. **שַׁעֲטָה, sha'ătâh,** *shah´-at-aw*; feminine from an unused root meaning to *stamp*; a *clatter* (of hoofs):—stamping.

8162. **שַׁעַטְנֵז, sha'atnêz,** *shah-at-naze´*; probably of foreign derivative; *linsey-woolsey*, i.e. cloth of linen and wool carded and spun together:—garment of divers sorts, linen and woollen.

8163. **שָׂעִיר, śâ'îyr,** *saw-eer´*; or **שָׂעִר, śâ'ir,** *saw-eer´*; from 8175; *shaggy*; as noun, a *he-goat*; (by analogy) a *faun*:—devil, goat, hairy, kid, rough, satyr.

A masculine noun meaning a male goat, a buck. Occasionally, the word can be used figuratively to mean a hairy one. Under the Israelite sacrificial system, a male goat was an acceptable sin offering. This noun is used many times in conjunction with the sin offering, in which a male goat without any defects was offered by the priest to atone for the sins of himself and the people (Le 9:15; 2Ch 29:23; Eze 43:25). On the negative side, the Israelites worshipped the goat as an idol in times of rebellion against God; the same noun is used in these references (Le 17:7; 2Ch 11:15).

8164. **שָׂעִיר, śâ'îyr,** *saw-eer´*; formed the same as 8163; a *shower* (as *tempestuous*):—small rain.

8165. **שֵׂעִיר, Śê'îyr,** *say-eer´*; formed like 8163; *rough; Seïr*, a mountain of Idumæa and its aboriginal occupants, also one in Palestine:—Seir.

8166. **שְׂעִירָה, ś^e'îyrâh,** *seh-ee-raw´*; feminine of 8163; a *she-goat*:—kid.

8167. **שְׂעִירָה, Ś^e'îyrâh,** *seh-ee-raw´*; formed as 8166; *roughness; Seïrah*, a place in Palestine:—Seirath.

8168. **שֹׁעַל, shô'al,** *sho´-al*; from an unused root meaning to *hollow* out; the *palm*; (by extension) a *handful*:—handful, hollow of the hand.

8169. **שַׁעַלְבִים, Sha'albîym,** *shah-al-beem´*; or **שַׁעֲלַבִּין, Sha'ălabbîyn,** *shah-al-ab-been´*; plural from 7776; *fox-holes; Shaalbim* or *Shaalabbin*, a place in Palestine:—Shaalabbin, Shaalbim.

8170. **שַׁעַלְבֹנִי, Sha'albônîy,** *shah-al-bo-nee´*; patrial from 8169; a *Shaalbonite* or inhabitant of Shaalbin:—Shaalbonite.

8171. **שַׁעֲלִים, Sha'alîym,** *shah-al-eem´*; plural of 7776; *foxes; Shaalim*, a place in Palestine:—Shalim.

8172. **שָׁעַן, shâ'an,** *shaw-an´*; a primitive root; to *support* one's self:—lean, lie, rely, rest (on, self), stay.

A verb meaning to lean, to rely, to support oneself. This verb is found only in the passive form, but it is active in meaning. In its simplest meaning, it refers to leaning on things for support, such as trees (Ge 18:4) and pillars (Jgs 16:26). The idea conveyed here is simply that of resting one's weight against something to give it support, but not all things leaned on will actually support (Job 8:15). This verb is also used in the sense of a king leaning or relying on his closest friends and advisors. This may mean literally leaning on someone's arm or trusting in his or her counsel (2Ki 5:18; 7:2, 17). Leaning on can also mean trusting in persons, whether it be God (Mic 3:11); other people (Eze 29:7); or oneself (Pr 3:5). Ultimately, God should be trusted and leaned on, for He will never fail.

8173. שָׁעַע, **shâʻaʻ,** *shaw-ah´*; a primitive root; (in a good acceptation) to *look* upon (with complacency), i.e. *fondle, please* or *amuse* (self); (in a bad one) to *look* about (in dismay), i.e. *stare*:—cry (out) *[by confusion with 7768]*, dandle, delight (self), play, shut.

8174. שַׁעַף, **Shaʻaph,** *shah´-af*; from 5586; *fluctuation; Shaaph*, the name of two Israelites:—Shaaph.

8175. שָׂעַר, **śâʻar,** *saw-ar´*; a primitive root; to *storm*; (by implication) to *shiver*, i.e. *fear*:—be (horribly) afraid, fear, hurl as a storm, be tempestuous, come like (take away as with) a whirlwind.

A verb meaning to sweep away, to whirl away. The image brought to mind when this verb is used is that of a stormy wind sweeping things away that cannot stand against its power. It appears in the simple, passive, intensive, and reflexive stems of the verb, but the meanings in each stem are all comparable. This verb is often used to describe the fate of evil persons (Job 27:21; Ps 58:9[10]). Their punishment from God is that they will be swept away suddenly, just as a stormy wind arises suddenly to sweep things away. Another use of this word is to describe God in all His power and glory, the Ruler of the universe (Ps 50:3); and it can also be used to describe a battle where one ruler storms out against another (Da 11:40).

8176. שָׁעַר, **shâʻar,** *shaw-ar´*; a primitive root; to *split* or *open*, i.e. (literal, but only as denominative from 8179) to *act as gatekeeper* (see 7778); (figurative) to *estimate*:—think.

A verb possibly meaning to cleave, to divide, but it took on the meaning of to calculate, to estimate, to set a price on. The meaning was transferred to the sense of judging something, thereby setting a price to it. There are no references to the verb meaning to cleave in the OT, but in Pr 23:7, this verb is used to mean to calculate or to set a price on. The context here is that of misers who count the cost of everything that their guests eat or drink. They find no enjoyment in their guests but only worry about the cost of it all.

8177. שְׂעַר, **śᵉʻar,** *seh-ar´*; (Chaldee); corresponding to 8181; *hair*:—hair.

8178. שַׂעַר, **śaʻar,** *sah´-ar*; from 8175; a *tempest*; also a *terror*:—affrighted, × horribly, × sore, storm. See 8181.

A masculine noun meaning horror. The horror described by the use of this noun is what people feel when witnessing the destruction that God allows to happen to evil people of this world. In Job 18:20, it is said that people were seized with horror at the fate of an evil person. In Eze 27:35 and 32:10, this word is used in the context of laments composed for the land of Tyre and Pharaoh of Egypt, who were both destroyed. When people see the destruction wrought on them, they are filled with horror at their fate. A less common use of this word holds the meaning of storm (Isa 28:2).

8179. שַׁעַר, **shaʻar,** *shah´-ar*; from 8176 in its original sense; an *opening*, i.e. *door* or *gate*:—city, door, gate, port (× -er).

8180. שַׁעַר, **shaʻar,** *shah´-ar*; from 8176; a *measure* (as a *section*):—[hundred-] fold.

8181. שֵׂעָר, **śêʻâr,** *say-awr´*; or שַׂעַר, **śaʻar,** *sah´-ar*; (Isa 7:20), from 8175 in the sense of *dishevelling; hair* (as if *tossed* or *bristling*):—hair (-y), × rough.

8182. שֹׁעָר, **shôʻâr,** *sho-awr´*; from 8176; *harsh* or *horrid*, i.e. *offensive*:—vile.

An adjective meaning horrid, bad, disagreeable. This word is used only once in the OT in Jer 29:17 when describing figs that are so bad they cannot be eaten. There is absolutely no use for them but to be thrown away. This is used to explain what would become of the Israelites who remained in their land instead of going into exile. God would send the sword, famine, and plague against them so that in the end they too would be as worthless as bad figs. They would not be slightly disagreeable but would be so ruined and so horrid that they would simply be destroyed.

8183. שְׂעָרָה, **śᵉʻârâh,** *seh-aw-raw´*; feminine of 8178; a *hurricane*:—storm, tempest.

8184. שְׂעֹרָה, **śᵉʻôrâh,** *seh-o-raw´*; or שְׂעוֹרָה, **śᵉʻôwrâh,** *seh-o-raw´*; (feminine meaning the *plant*); and (masculine meaning the *grain*); also שְׂעֹר, **śᵉʻôr,** *seh-ore´*; or שְׂעוֹר, **śᵉʻôwr,** *seh-ore´*; from 8175 in the sense of *roughness; barley* (as *villose*):—barley.

8185. שַׂעֲרָה, **śaʻărâh,** *sah-ar-aw´*; feminine of 8181; *hairiness*:—hair.

8186. שַׁעֲרוּרָה, **shaʻărûwrâh,** *shah-ar-oo-raw´*; or שַׁעֲרִירִיָּה, **shaʻărîyrîyyâh,** *shah-ar-ee-ree-yaw´*; or שַׁעֲרֻרִת, **shaʻărurith,** *shah-ar-oo-reeth´*; feminine from 8176 in the sense of 8175; something *fearful*:—horrible thing.

A feminine noun meaning horror, a horrible thing. It is used to describe how bad the apostasy and apathy of the Israelites was. What they did in worshiping idols and prophesying falsely were truly horrible things in the eyes of God and the prophets who denounced them (Jer 5:30; 23:14). There are two variant spellings of this word. One, *shaʻărûriy-yâh*, is found in Hos 6:10 and another, *shaʻărurith*, is found in Jer 18:13. The uses of these variant spellings are exactly the same as the most common spelling. In every instance of the use of this word, it refers to the horror of the things that Israel was doing and the sins they were committing against the Lord.

8187. שְׁעַרְיָה, **Shᵉʻaryâh,** *sheh-ar-yaw´*; from 8176 and 3050; *Jah has stormed; Sheärjah*, an Israelite:—Sheariah.

8188. שְׂעֹרִים, **Śᵉʻôrîym,** *seh-o-reem´*; masculine plural of 8184; *barley* grains; *Seörim*, an Israelite:—Seorim.

8189. שַׁעֲרַיִם, **Shaʻărayim,** *shah-ar-ah´-yim*; dual of 8179; *double gates; Shaarajim*, a place in Palestine:—Shaaraim.

8190. שַׁעַשְׁגַז, **Shaʻashgaz,** *shah-ash-gaz´*; of Persian derivation; *Shaashgaz*, a eunuch of Xerxes:—Shaashgaz.

8191. שַׁעֲשֻׁעִים, **shaʻăshuʻîym,** *sha-ah-shoo´-eem*; from 8173; *enjoyment*:—delight, pleasure.

8192. שָׁפָה, **shâphâh,** *shaw-faw´*; a primitive root; to *abrade*, i.e. *bare*:—high, stick out.

8193. שָׂפָה, **śâphâh,** *saw-faw´*; or (in dual and plural) שֶׂפֶת, **śepheth,** *sef-eth´*; probably from 5595 or 8192 through the idea of *termination* (compare 5490); the *lip* (as a natural boundary); (by implication) *language*; (by analogy) a *margin* (of a vessel, water, cloth, etc.):—band, bank, binding, border, brim, brink, edge, language, lip, prating, ([sea-]) shore, side, speech, talk, [vain] words.

A feminine noun meaning a lip, a language, an edge, a border. The most common use of this word is that of lip. It can be used merely to describe the organ of speech (Ex 6:12, 30; Ps 63:5[6]); and the place from where laughter comes (Job 8:21). Yet it can also be used as a feature of beauty in descriptions of a beautiful person (SS 4:3, 11). Finally, it can refer to the place from where divine speech comes, from the lips of God (Job 23:12; Ps 17:4). A more general meaning is that of language that originates from the lips (Ge 11:6, 7; Ps 81:5[6]; Isa 33:19). When an edge or a border is the meaning of this word, it can refer to a wide variety of things such as the shore of a sea (Ge 22:17); the edge or brim of a variety of objects (1Ki 7:23; Eze 43:13); or the boundary between geographical sites (Jgs 7:22).

8194. שָׁפָה, **shâphâh,** *shaw-faw´*; from 8192 in the sense of *clarifying*; a *cheese* (as *strained* from the whey):—cheese.

8195. שְׁפוֹ, **Shᵉphôw,** *shef-o´*; or שְׁפִי, **Shᵉphîy,** *shef-ee´*; from 8192; *baldness* [compare 8205]; *Shepho* or *Shephi*, an Idumæan:—Shephi, Shepho.

8196. שְׁפוֹט, **shᵉphôwṭ,** *shef-ote´*; or שְׁפוּט, **shᵉphûwṭ,** *shef-oot´*; from 8199; a judicial *sentence*, i.e. *punishment*:—judgment.

8197. **שְׁפוּפָם, Sh^e^phûwphâm,** *shef-oo-fawm´*; or **שְׁפוּפָן, Sh^e^phûwphân,** *shef-oo-fawn´*; from the same as 8207; *serpent-like; Shephupham* or *Shephuphan*, an Israelite:—Shephuphan, Shupham.

8198. **שִׁפְחָה, shiphchâh,** *shif-khaw´*; feminine from an unused root meaning to *spread* out (as a *family*; see 4940); a *female slave* (as a member of the *household*):—(bond-, hand-) maid (-en, -servant), wench, bondwoman, womanservant.

8199. **שָׁפַט, shâphaṭ,** *shaw-fat´*; a primitive root; to *judge*, i.e. pronounce *sentence* (for or against); (by implication) to *vindicate* or *punish*; (by extension) to *govern*; (passive) to *litigate* (literal or figurative):— + avenge, × that condemn, contend, defend, execute (judgment), (be a) judge (-ment), × needs, plead, reason, rule.

A verb meaning to judge, to govern. This word, though often translated as judge, is much more inclusive than the modern concept of judging and encompasses all the facets and functions of government: executive, legislative, and judicial. Consequently, this term can be understood in any one of the following ways. It could designate, in its broadest sense, to function as ruler or governor. This function could be fulfilled by individual judges (Jgs 16:31; 1Sa 7:16); the king (1Ki 3:9); or even God Himself (Ps 50:6; 75:7[8]); since He is the source of authority (cf. Ro 13:1) and will eventually conduct all judgments (Ps 96:13). In a judicial sense, the word could also indicate, because of the exalted status of the ruler, the arbitration of civil, domestic, and religious disputes (Dt 25:1). As before, this function could be fulfilled by the congregation of Israel (Nu 35:24); individual judges (Ex 18:16; Dt 1:16); the king (1Sa 8:5, 6, 20); or even God Himself (Ge 16:5; 1Sa 24:12[13], 15[16]). In the executive sense, it could denote to execute judgment, to bring about what had been decided. This could be in the form of a vindication (Ps 10:18; Isa 1:17, 23); or a condemnation and punishment (Eze 7:3, 8; 23:45).

8200. **שְׁפַט, sh^e^phaṭ,** *shef-at´*; (Chaldee); corresponding to 8199; to *judge*:—magistrate.

An Aramaic verb meaning to judge, to govern. This word is used only once in the OT and is related to the Hebrew word *shâphaṭ* (8199), meaning to judge or to govern. In Ezr 7:25, this word is used to describe one of the governing rulers that Ezra was to appoint. These rulers were to perform similar functions as the *dayyân* (1782) or judges that Ezra was also to appoint.

8201. **שֶׁפֶט, shepheṭ,** *sheh´-fet*; from 8199; a *sentence*, i.e. *infliction*:—judgment.

A masculine noun meaning judgment. This word comes from the verb *shâphaṭ* (8199), meaning to judge, and usually describes the active role of God in punishing. In several instances, such judgment is described as the sword, famine, wild beasts, plagues, stoning, and burning (Eze 14:21; 16:41). The plagues that God inflicted on Egypt are described as judgments (Ex 6:6; 7:4; 12:12; Nu 33:4). This word describes both the defeat of Israel (2Ch 24:24; Eze 5:10, 15); as well as the defeat of other nations (Eze 25:11; 28:22, 26). In one instance, this word speaks more generally, not of specific nations, but of unruly scoffers who will receive physical chastisement (Pr 19:29).

8202. **שָׁפָט, Shâphâṭ,** *shaw-fawt´*; from 8199; *judge; Shaphat*, the name of four Israelites:—Shaphat.

8203. **שְׁפַטְיָה, Sh^e^phaṭyâh,** *shef-at-yaw´*; or **שְׁפַטְיָהוּ, Sh^e^phaṭyâhûw,** *shef-at-yaw´-hoo*; from 8199 and 3050; *Jah has judged; Shephatjah*, the name of ten Israelites:—Shephatiah.

8204. **שִׁפְטָן, Shiphṭân,** *shif-tawn´*; from 8199; *judge-like; Shiphtan*, an Israelite:—Shiphtan.

8205. **שְׁפִי, sh^e^phîy,** *shef-ee´*; from 8192; *bareness*; (concrete) a *bare* hill or plain:—high place, stick out.

A masculine noun meaning bare. This word carries the idea of a barren or smooth place and is used to describe dry places where God will open rivers (Isa 41:18); and infertile places where God will create pastures (Isa 49:9). The donkeys could not find grass in such places (Jer 14:6). The barren place was where Balaam went to meet God (Nu 23:3); and where Israel was to lament their destruction (Jer 7:29). At times, it could describe the bare hills (Jer 3:2, 21) from which the dry winds originated in the barren wilderness (Jer 4:11; 12:12).

8206. **שֻׁפִּים, Shuppîym,** *shoop-peem´*; plural of an unused noun from the same as 8207 and meaning the same; *serpents; Shuppim*, an Israelite:—Shuppim.

8207. **שְׁפִיפֹן, sh^e^phîyphôn,** *shef-ee-fone´*; from an unused root meaning the same as 7779; a kind of *serpent* (as *snapping*), probably the *cerastes* or horned adder:—adder.

8208. **שָׁפִיר, Shâphîyr,** *shaf-eer´*; from 8231; *beautiful; Shaphir*, a place in Palestine:—Saphir.

8209. **שַׁפִּיר, shappîyr,** *shap-peer´*; (Chaldee); intensive of a form corresponding to 8208; *beautiful*:—fair.

8210. **שָׁפַךְ, shâphak,** *shaw-fak´*; a primitive root; to *spill* forth (blood, a libation, liquid metal; or even a solid, i.e. to *mound* up); also (figurative) to *expend* (life, soul, complaint, money, etc.); (intensive) to *sprawl* out:—cast (up), gush out, pour (out), shed (-der, out), slip.

A verb meaning to pour out. In its most basic sense, this word refers to the pouring out of something, for example, fluid on the ground (Ex 4:9; Dt 12:16; 1Sa 7:6); or blood on an altar (Ex 29:12; Le 4:7; Dt 12:27). In several instances, it describes the casting up of a mound against a city to form a siege ramp for attacking it (2Sa 20:15; Eze 4:2; Da 11:15). This word is also used idiomatically to refer to the shedding of blood (Ge 9:6; 1Ki 2:31); especially of innocent blood (2Ki 21:16; Pr 6:17). A dependent prayer is described as the pouring out of one's soul (1Sa 1:15; Ps 42:4[5]); one's heart (Ps 62:8[9]; La 2:19); or one's inner parts before the Lord (La 2:11). God poured out both His wrath (Ps 69:24[25]; Isa 42:25; Jer 6:11; Hos 5:10); and His grace (Joel 2:28[3:1], 29[3:2]; Zec 12:10) from heaven on people.

8211. **שֶׁפֶךְ, shephek,** *sheh´-fek*; from 8210; an *emptying* place, e.g., an ash-*heap*:—are poured out.

A masculine noun meaning a place of pouring, a place of emptying. It comes from the word *shâphak* (8210), meaning to spill forth, and is used in Leviticus to describe the place where the priest was to burn the remains of the bull sacrifice, i.e. next to the place where the ashes were poured out (Le 4:12).

8212. **שָׁפְכָה, shophkâh,** *shof-kaw´*; feminine of a derivative from 8210; a *pipe* (for *pouring* forth, e.g., wine), i.e. the *penis*:—privy member.

8213. **שָׁפֵל, shâphêl,** *shaw-fale´*; a primitive root; to *depress* or *sink* (especially figurative, to *humiliate*, intransitive or trans.):—abase, bring (cast, put) down, debase, humble (self), be (bring, lay, make, put) low (-er).

8214. **שְׁפַל, sh^e^phal,** *shef-al´*; (Chaldee); corresponding to 8213:—abase, humble, put down, subdue.

8215. **שְׁפַל, sh^e^phal,** *shef-al´*; (Chaldee); from 8214; *low*:—basest.

8216. **שֵׁפֶל, shêphel,** *shay´-fel*; from 8213; an *humble* rank:—low estate (place).

8217. **שָׁפָל, shâphâl,** *shaw-fawl´*; from 8213; *depressed*, literal or figurative:—base (-st), humble, low (-er, -ly).

8218. **שִׁפְלָה, shiphlâh,** *shif-law´*; feminine of 8216; *depression*:—low place.

8219. **שְׁפֵלָה, sh^e^phêlâh,** *shef-ay-law´*; from 8213; *Lowland*, i.e. (with the article) the maritime slope of Palestine:—low country, (low) plain, vale (-ley).

8220. **שִׁפְלוּת, shiphlûwth,** *shif-looth´*; from 8213; *remissness*:—idleness.

8221. **שְׁפָם, Sh^e^phâm,** *shef-awm´*; probably from 8192; *bare* spot; *Shepham*, a place in or near Palestine:—Shepham.

8222. **שָׂפָם, śâphâm,** *saw-fawm´*; from 8193; the *beard* (as a *lip-piece*):—beard, (upper) lip.

A masculine noun meaning a mustache, a beard. The most basic understanding of this word is evident in 2Sa 19:24 [25], where the text refers to the proper grooming of one's mustache or beard. By extension, this word is also used to imply the upper lip where a mustache grows (Le 13:45); and the mouth in general (Eze 24:17; Mic 3:7).

8223. שָׁפָם, **Shâphâm,** *shaw-fawm´*; formed like 8221; *baldly; Shapham*, an Israelite:—Shapham.

8224. שִׂפְמוֹת, **Śiphmôwth,** *sif-mōth´*; feminine plural of 8221; *Siphmoth*, a place in Palestine:—Siphmoth.

8225. שִׁפְמִי, **Shiphmîy,** *shif-mee´*; patrial from 8221; a *Shiphmite* or inhabitant of Shepham:—Shiphmite.

8226. שָׂפַן, **śâphan,** *saw-fan´*; a primitive root; to *conceal* (as a valuable):—treasure.

8227. שָׁפָן, **shâphân,** *shaw-fawn´*; from 8226; a species of *rock-rabbit* (from its *hiding*), i.e. probably the *hyrax*:—coney.

8228. שֶׁפַע, **shephaʻ,** *sheh´-fah*; from an unused root meaning to *abound; resources*:—abundance.

8229. שִׁפְעָה, **shiphʻâh,** *shif-aw´*; feminine of 8228; *copiousness*:—abundance, company, multitude.

8230. שִׁפְעִי, **Shiphʻîy,** *shif-ee´*; from 8228; *copious; Shiphi*, an Israelite:—Shiphi.

8231. שָׁפַר, **shâphar,** *shaw-far´*; a primitive root; to *glisten*, i.e. (figurative) *be* (causative, *make*) *fair*:— × goodly.

8232. שְׁפַר, **sh^ephar,** *shef-ar´*; (Chaldee); corresponding to 8231; to *be beautiful*:—be acceptable, please, + think good.

8233. שֶׁפֶר, **shepher,** *sheh´-fer*; from 8231; *beauty*:— × goodly.

8234. שֶׁפֶר, **Shepher,** *sheh´-fer*; the same as 8233; *Shepher*, a place in the Desert:—Shapper.

8235. שִׁפְרָה, **shiphrâh,** *shif-raw´*; from 8231; *brightness*:—garnish.

8236. שִׁפְרָה, **Shiphrâh,** *shif-raw´*; the same as 8235; *Shiphrah*, an Israelitess:—Shiphrah.

8237. שַׁפְרִיר, **shaphrîyr,** *shaf-reer´*; from 8231; *splendid*, i.e. a *tapestry* or *canopy*:—royal pavilion.

8238. שְׁפַרְפָּר, **sh^epharpâr,** *shef-ar-pawr´*; (Chaldee); from 8231; the *dawn* (as *brilliant* with aurora):— × very early in the morning.

8239. שָׁפַת, **shâphath,** *shaw-fath´*; a primitive root; to *locate*, i.e. (general) *hang* on or (figurative) *establish, reduce*:—bring, ordain, set on.

8240. שְׁפַתַּיִם, **sh^ephatayim,** *shef-ah-tah´-yeem*; from 8239; a (double) *stall* (for cattle); also a (two-pronged) *hook* (for flaying animals on):—hook, pot.

8241. שֶׁצֶף, **shetseph,** *sheh´-tsef*; from 7857 (for alliteration with 7110); an *outburst* (of anger):—little.

8242. שַׂק, **śaq,** *sak*; from 8264; (properly) a *mesh* (as allowing a liquid to *run* through), i.e. coarse loose cloth or *sacking* (used in mourning and for bagging); hence a *bag* (for grain, etc.):—sack (-cloth, -clothes).

8243. שָׁק, **shâq,** *shawk*; (Chaldee); corresponding to 7785; the *leg*:—leg.

8244. שָׂקַד, **śâqad,** *saw-kad´*; a primitive root; to *fasten*:—bind.

8245. שָׁקַד, **shâqad,** *shaw-kad´*; a primitive root; to *be alert*, i.e. *sleepless*; hence to *be on the lookout* (whether for good or ill):—hasten, remain, wake, watch (for).

8246. שָׁקַד, **shâqad,** *shaw-kad´*; a denominative from 8247; to *be* (intensive, *make*) *almond-shaped*:—make like (unto, after the fashion of) almonds.

8247. שָׁקֵד, **shâqêd,** *shaw-kade´*; from 8245; the *almond* (tree or nut; as being the *earliest* in bloom):—almond (tree).

8248. שָׁקָה, **shâqâh,** *shaw-kaw´*; a primitive root; to *quaff*, i.e. (causative) to *irrigate* or *furnish a potion* to:—cause to (give, give to, let, make to) drink, drown, moisten, water. See 7937, 8354.

8249. שִׁקֻּו, **shiqquv,** *shik-koov´*; from 8248; (plural collective) a *draught*:—drink.

8250. שִׁקּוּי, **shiqqûwy,** *shik-koo´ee*; from 8248; a *beverage; moisture*, i.e. (figurative) *refreshment*:—drink, marrow.

8251. שִׁקּוּץ, **shiqqûwts,** *shik-koots´*; or שִׁקֻּץ, **shiq-quts,** *shik-koots´*; from 8262; *disgusting*, i.e. *filthy*; especially *idolatrous* or (concrete) an *idol*:—abominable filth (idol, -ation), detestable (thing).

A masculine noun meaning a detestable thing, an abomination, and an idol. This Hebrew word identifies an object that is abhorrent or blasphemous. It is used to denote filth (Na 3:6); forbidden food (Zec 9:7); and a blasphemous activity (Da 9:27). Most often, it is used as a synonym for an idol or idolatry (Jer 7:30; Hos 9:10).

8252. שָׁקַט, **shâqaṭ,** *shaw-kat´*; a primitive root; to *repose* (usually figurative):—appease, idleness, (at, be at, be in, give) quiet (-ness), (be at, be in, give, have, take) rest, settle, be still.

A verb meaning to be still, to be quiet, to be undisturbed. The primary meaning of this verb is the state or condition of tranquility (cf. Job 37:17). It signifies the condition during the absence of war (Jgs 3:30; 2Ch 20:30); a sense of safety and security (Eze 38:11); inactivity or passivity (Ps 83:1[2]; Isa 18:4); keeping silent (Ru 3:18; Isa 62:1); and an inner confidence or peace (Isa 7:4). Scripture declares that righteousness brings true security and tranquility (Isa 32:17); but also warns of the false security that comes to the unrighteous (Eze 16:49).

8253. שֶׁקֶט, **sheqeṭ,** *sheh´-ket*; from 8252; *tranquillity*:—quietness.

A masculine noun meaning quietness, tranquility. The only occurrence of this word is found in 1Ch 22:9 and is parallel to the Hebrew word for peace (*shâlôwm*, 7965). It is used to describe the state of tranquility during the reign of Solomon when all enemies were defeated and the united kingdom was at its height.

8254. שָׁקַל, **shâqal,** *shaw-kal´*; a primitive root; to *suspend* or *poise* (especially in trade):—pay, receive (-r), spend, × thoroughly, weigh.

8255. שֶׁקֶל, **sheqel,** *sheh´-kel*; from 8254; probably a *weight*; used as a commercial standard:—shekel.

8256. שָׁקָם, **shâqâm,** *shaw-kawm´*; or (feminine) שִׁקְמָה, **shiqmâh,** *shik-maw´*; of uncertain derivation; a *sycamore* (usually the tree):—sycamore (fruit, tree).

8257. שָׁקַע, **shâqaʻ,** *shaw-kah´*; (abbreviated in Am 8:8), a primitive root; to *subside*; (by implication) to *be overflowed, cease*; (causative) to *abate, subdue*:—make deep, let down, drown, quench, sink.

8258. שְׁקַעֲרוּרָה, **sh^eqaʻărûwrâh,** *she-kah-ah-roo-raw´*; from 8257; a *depression*:—hollow strake.

8259. שָׁקַף, **shâqaph,** *shaw-kaf´*; a primitive root; (properly) to *lean out* (of a window), i.e. (by implication) *peep* or *gaze* (passive *be a spectacle*):—appear, look (down, forth, out).

8260. שֶׁקֶף, **sheqeph,** *sheh´-kef*; from 8259; a *loophole* (for *looking out*), to admit light and air:—window.

8261. שָׁקֻף, **shâquph,** *shaw-koof´*; passive participle of 8259; an *embrasure* or opening [compare 8260] with bevelled jam:—light, window.

8262. שָׁקַץ, **shâqats,** *shaw-kats´*; a primitive root; to *be filthy*, i.e. (intensive) to *loathe, pollute*:—abhor, make abominable, have in abomination, detest, × utterly.

A verb meaning to detest, to make abominable. The primary meaning of this word is to make or to consider something odious. It is used to describe the attitude the Israelites were to have toward a graven image or idol (Dt 7:26); and certain nonkosher foods (Le 11:11, 13). If the Israelites failed to observe this command by partaking of unclean food, they would become detestable to the Lord (Le 20:25). On the other hand, the psalmist stated that this was never the Lord's attitude toward the cries of the afflicted (Ps 22:24[25]).

8263. שֶׁקֶץ, **sheqets,** *sheh´-kets*; from 8262; *filth*, i.e. (figurative and specific) an *idolatrous* object:—abominable (-tion).

A masculine noun meaning a detestation, an abomination, and a detestable thing. Chiefly, this Hebrew word marks those things that were ceremonially unclean and forbidden (Le 7:21). It is used of certain sea creatures (Le 11:10); birds of prey (Le 11:13ff.); and various creeping things (Le 11:20, 23, 41, 42).

8264. שָׁקַק, **shâqaq,** *shaw-kak´*; a primitive root; to *course* (like a beast of prey); by implication to *seek* greedily:—have appetite, justle one against another, long, range, run (to and fro).

8265. שָׂקַר, **śâqar,** *saw-kar´*; a primitive root; to *ogle*, i.e. *blink* coquettishly:—wanton.

8266. שָׁקַר, **shâqar,** *shaw-kar´*; a primitive root; to *cheat*, i.e. *be untrue* (usually in words):—fail, deal falsely, lie.

A verb meaning to engage in deceit, to deal falsely. The notion of a treacherous or deceptive activity forms the fundamental meaning of this word. It is used to describe an agreement entered into with deceitful intentions (Ge 21:23); outright lying (Le 19:11); and the violation of a covenant (Ps 44:17[18]). Scripture states clearly that such activity is the domain of humans, not of God (1Sa 15:29).

8267. שֶׁקֶר, **sheqer,** *sheh´-ker*; from 8266; an *untruth*; (by implication) a *sham* (often adverbial):—without a cause, deceit (-ful), false (-hood, -ly), feignedly, liar, + lie, lying, vain (thing), wrongfully.

A noun meaning a lie, vanity, without cause. This word is used of a lying witness (Dt 19:18); of false prophets (Jer 5:31; 20:6; 29:9); of telling lies (Le 19:12; Jer 37:14); and of a liar (Pr 17:4). In other cases, it describes something done in vain (1Sa 25:21; Ps 33:17); or an action without cause (Ps 38:19[20]; 119:78, 86).

8268. שֹׁקֶת, **shôqeth,** *sho´-keth*; from 8248; a *trough* (for *watering*):—trough.

8269. שַׂר, **śar,** *sar*; from 8323; a *head* person (of any rank or class):—captain (that had rule), chief (captain), general, governor, keeper, lord, ([-task-]) master, prince (-ipal), ruler, steward.

A masculine noun meaning a chieftain, a chief, a ruler, an official, a captain, a prince. The primary usage is official in the sense that this individual has immediate authority as the leader. While he was at Gath, David became the leader for those who were in distress, in debt, or were discontented (1Sa 22:2). The word describes the powers of a magistrate when a man posed a sarcastic question to Moses (Ex 2:14). In Genesis, the noun refers to Phicol as the commander of Abimelech's forces (Ge 21:22). In a similar usage of the word, Joshua was met by the commander of the Lord's army. This commander was so entrusted by God that Joshua had to take off his shoes due to the glory of God surrounding the man (Jos 5:14).

In terms of priesthood, *śar* designates a leading priest, i.e. a priest that is above the others (Ezr 8:24, 29). In this situation with Ezra, the leading priest was entrusted with the articles of the Temple and had to guard them with his life. The noun depicts Michael as one of the chief princes who came to Daniel's aid (Da 10:13). In Da 8:11, the word is used to denote the little horn setting itself up to be as great as the Prince of the host. This horn would set itself up, take away the daily sacrifice, and desecrate the Temple of God.

8270. שֹׁר, **shôr,** *shore*; from 8324; a *string* (as *twisted* [compare 8306]), i.e. (specific) the umbilical cord (also figurative as the centre of strength):—navel.

8271. שְׁרֵא, **shᵉrêʼ,** *sher-ay´*; (Chaldee); a root corresponding to that of 8293; to *free, separate*; (figurative) to *unravel, commence*; by implication (of unloading beasts) to *reside*:—begin dissolve, dwell, loose.

8272. שַׁרְאֶצֶר, **Sharʼetser,** *shar-eh´-tser*; of foreign derivation; *Sharetser*, the name of an Assyrian and an Israelite:—Sharezer.

8273. שָׁרָב, **shârâb,** *shaw-rawb´*; from an unused root meaning to *glare*; quivering *glow* (of the air), especially the *mirage*:—heat, parched ground.

8274. שֵׁרֵבְיָה, **Shêrêbyâh,** *shay-rayb-yaw´*; from 8273 and 3050; *Jah has brought heat; Sherebjah*, the name of two Israelites:—Sherebiah.

8275. שַׁרְבִיט, **sharbîyt,** *shar-beet´*; for 7626; a *rod* of empire:—sceptre.

A masculine noun meaning a scepter. This word is only found in the book of Esther. In Esther's response to Mordecai, she stated that anyone who went to see the king without being summoned would die unless the king extended the gold scepter in a symbolic act that saved the life of the individual (Est 4:11). In Est 5:2, Esther went before the king, touched the scepter that was extended to her, then stated her request that Haman come to a feast that she had provided for him and the king. Finally, Esther went again before the king and fell at his feet weeping and begging that he would stop Haman's evil plan. King Xerxes again extended the scepter to Esther, who in turn stood and restated her request (Est 8:4).

8276. שָׂרַג, **śârag,** *saw-rag´*; a primitive root; to *intwine*:—wrap together, wreath.

8277. שָׂרַד, **śârad,** *saw-rad´*; a primitive root; (properly) to *puncture* [compare 8279], i.e. (figurative, through the idea of *slipping* out) to *escape* or survive:—remain.

8278. שְׂרָד, **śᵉrâd,** *ser-awd´*; from 8277; *stitching* (as *pierced* with a needle):—service.

8279. שֶׂרֶד, **śered,** *seh´-red*; from 8277; a (carpenter's) *scribing-awl* (for *pricking* or scratching measurements):—line.

8280. שָׂרָה, **śârâh,** *saw-raw´*; a primitive root; to *prevail*:—have power (as a prince).

A verb meaning to persist, to exert oneself, to persevere. The primary meaning is to exert oneself. In Genesis, the word depicts Jacob, who had struggled with God and persons and prevailed. This achievement resulted in a name change to Israel (Ge 32:28[29]). The word is used figuratively in Hosea, recollecting on the memory of Jacob's struggle with God at Peniel to describe a reason for Ephraim's punishment (Hos 12:4[5]). This comparison relates Ephraim back to Jacob, the father of their tribe, as a call to repentance.

8281. שָׁרָה, **shârâh,** *shaw-raw´*; a primitive root; to *free*:—direct.

A verb meaning to let loose. This word occurs in the OT only once. In Job 37:3, it describes God's loosing of thunder and lightning.

8282. שָׂרָה, **śârâh,** *saw-raw´*; feminine of 8269; a *mistress*, i.e. female noble:—lady, princess, queen.

A feminine noun meaning a princess, a royal lady. This word comes from the verb *śârar* (8323), meaning to rule or to act as prince, and is the feminine form of the word *śar* (8269), meaning prince, captain, or ruler. This word always refers to women who had access to the royal court. It is used of the particular princesses who associated with Deborah, Solomon, and the nation of Persia (Jgs 5:29; 1Ki 11:3; Est 1:18). It is also used in a general sense to describe princesses who were humbled to become nurses and servants (Isa 49:23; La 1:1).

8283. שָׂרָה, **Śârâh,** *saw-raw´*; the same as 8282; *Sarah*, Abraham's wife:—Sarah.

8284. שָׁרָה, **shârâh,** *shaw-raw´*; probably feminine of 7791; a *fortification* (literal or figurative):—sing [*by mistake for* 7891], wall.

8285. שֵׁרָה, **shêrâh,** *shay-raw´*; from 8324 in its original sense of *pressing*; a wrist-*band* (as *compact* or *clasping*):—bracelet.

8286. שְׂרוּג, **Śᵉrûwg,** *ser-oog´*; from 8276; *tendril; Serug*, a postdiluvian patriarch:—Serug.

8287. שָׁרוּחֶן, **Shârûwchen,** *shaw-roo-khen´*; probably from 8281 (in the sense of *dwelling* [compare 8271] and 2580; *abode of pleasure; Sharuchen*, a place in Palestine:—Sharuhen.

8288. שְׂרוֹךְ, **śᵉrôwk,** *ser-oke´*; from 8308; a *thong* (as *laced* or *tied*):—([shoe-]) latchet.

8289. שָׁרוֹן, **Shârôwn,** *shaw-rone´*; probably abridged from 3474; *plain; Sharon*, the name of a place in Palestine:—Lasharon, Sharon.

8290. שָׁרוֹנִי, **Shârôwnîy,** *shaw-ro-nee´*; patrial from 8289; a *Sharonite* or inhabitant of Sharon:—Sharonite.

8291. שַׂרֻק, **śârôq,** *sar-ook´*; passive participle from the same as 8321; a *grapevine*:—principal plant. See 8320, 8321.

8292. שְׁרוּקָה, **shᵉrûwqâh,** *sher-oo-kaw´*; or (by permutation) שְׁרִיקָה, **shᵉrîyqâh,** *sher-ee-kaw´*; feminine passive participle of 8319; a *whistling* (in scorn); (by analogy) a *piping*:—bleating, hissing.

8293. שֵׁרוּת, **shêrûwth,** *shay-rooth´*; from 8281 abbreviated; *freedom*:—remnant.

A feminine noun meaning a beginning. This word is another form of the word *shârâh* (8281). In Jer 15:11, this word refers to God setting Jeremiah free.

8294. שֶׂרַח, **Śerach,** *seh´-rakh*; (by permutation) for 5629; *superfluity; Serach*, an Israelitess:—Sarah, Serah.

8295. שָׂרַט, **śâraṭ,** *saw-rat´*; a primitive root; to *gash*:—cut in pieces, make [cuttings] pieces.

8296. שֶׂרֶט, **śereṭ,** *seh´-ret*; and שָׂרֶטֶת, **śâreṭeth,** *saw-reh´-teth*; from 8295; an *incision*:—cutting.

8297. שָׂרַי, **Śâray,** *saw-rah´ee*; from 8269; *dominative; Sarai*, the wife of Abraham:—Sarai.

8298. שָׁרַי, **Shâray,** *shaw-rah´ee*; probably from 8324; *hostile; Sharay*, an Israelite:—Sharai.

8299. שָׂרִיג, **śârîyg,** *saw-reeg´*; from 8276; a *tendril* (as *intwining*):—branch.

8300. שָׂרִיד, **śârîyd,** *saw-reed´*; from 8277; a *survivor*:—× alive, left, remain (-ing), remnant, rest.

A masculine noun meaning a survivor. This word comes from the verb *śârad* (8277), meaning an escape. In one instance of this word, it is used to describe physical things that had not been devoured (Job 20:21). In all other instances, it is used to describe people who had survived the onslaught of an enemy (Nu 24:19; Jos 10:20; Jer 31:2). It is often used with the negative to describe total desolation, i.e. there were no survivors (Nu 21:35; Jos 10:28; Jer 42:17).

8301. שָׂרִיד, **Śârîyd,** *saw-reed´*; the same as 8300; *Sarid*, a place in Palestine:—Sarid.

8302. שִׁרְיוֹן, **shiryôwn,** *shir-yone´*; or שִׁרְיֹן, **shiryôn,** *shir-yone´*; and שִׁרְיָן, **shiryân,** *shir-yawn´*; also (feminine) שִׁרְיָה, **shiryâh,** *shir-yaw´*; and שִׁרְיֹנָה, **shir-yônâh,** *shir-yo-naw´*; from 8281 in the orig. sense of *turning*; a *corslet* (as if *twisted*):—breastplate, coat of mail, habergeon, harness. See 5630.

8303. שִׁרְיוֹן, **Shiryôwn,** *shir-yone´*; and שִׂרְיֹן, **Śiryôn,** *sir-yone´*; the same as 8304 (i.e. *sheeted* with snow); *Shirjon* or *Sirjon*, a peak of the Lebanon:—Sirion.

8304. שְׂרָיָה, **Śᵉrâyâh,** *ser-aw-yaw´*; or שְׂרָיָהוּ, **Śᵉrâ-yâhûw,** *ser-aw-yaw´-hoo*; from 8280 and 3050; *Jah has prevailed; Serajah*, the name of nine Israelites:—Seraiah.

8305. שָׂרִיק, **śârîyq,** *saw-reek´*; from the same as 8321 in the original sense of *piercing; hetchelling* (or combing flax), i.e. (concrete) *tow;* (by extension) *linen* cloth:—fine.

8306. שָׁרִיר, **shârîyr,** *shaw-reer´*; from 8324 in the original sense as in 8270 (compare 8326); a *cord*, i.e. (by analogy) *sinew*:—navel.

8307. שְׁרִירוּת, **shᵉrîyrûwth,** *sher-ee-rooth´*; from 8324 in the sense of *twisted*, i.e. *firm; obstinacy*:—imagination, lust.

A feminine noun meaning hardness, stubbornness. This word has the basic idea of firmness or hardness, but in its ten usages in the OT, it is always used in conjunction with the word *lêb* (3820), meaning heart, to describe disobedient Israel. Thus, it is best to translate this word stubbornness. It is used to describe those who did evil (Jer 16:12); who walked after their own plans (Jer 18:12); who refused to listen to God's words (Jer 13:10); who did not obey God's counsel (Jer 7:24; 9:14[13]; 11:8); and who were deluded to think they were at peace (Dt 29:19[18]; Jer 23:17). God gave such people over to their own devices (Ps 81:12[13]).

8308. שָׂרַךְ, **śârak,** *saw-rak´*; a primitive root; to *interlace*:—traverse.

8309. שְׁרֵמָה, **shᵉrêmâh,** *sher-ay-maw´*; probably by orthographic error for 7709; a *common*:—field.

8310. שַׂרְסְכִים, **Śarsᵉkîym,** *sar-seh-keem´*; of foreign derivation; *Sarsekim*, a Babylonian general:—Sarsechim.

8311. שָׂרַע, **śâraʻ,** *saw-rah´*; a primitive root; to *prolong*, i.e. (reflexive) *be deformed* by excess of members:—stretch out self, (have any) superfluous thing.

8312. שַׂרְעַפִּים, **śarʻappîym,** *sar-ap-peem´*; for 5587; *cogitation*:—thought.

A masculine noun meaning a disquieting thought, an anxious feeling. The psalmist rejoiced that the Lord calmed his inner anxieties (Ps 94:19). This is the same word used by the psalmist when he asked God to search him and know his anxieties (Ps 139:23).

8313. שָׂרַף, **śâraph,** *saw-raf´*; a primitive root; to *be* (causative, *set*) *on fire*:—(cause to, make a) burn ([-ing], up), kindle, × utterly.

A verb meaning to burn. Most often, this word is used to mean to burn with intent, to destroy, or to consume. It is normally used to refer to sacrifices. Many sacrificial laws prescribed specific ways for offerings to be burnt (Ex 29:14). Burning could also be a form of punishment, as in the story of Achan (Jos 7:25). Buildings and cities were other common objects of burning: Men of Ephraim threatened to burn down Jephthah's house with fire (Jgs 12:1). Less frequently, this word refers to the process of firing bricks (Ge 11:3).

8314. שָׂרָף, **śârâph,** *saw-rawf´*; from 8313; *burning*, i.e. (figurative) *poisonous* (serpent); (specifically) a *saraph* or symbolic creature (from their copper colour):—fiery (serpent), seraph.

A masculine noun meaning a serpent. This word generally refers to a poisonous snake, deriving its origin from the burning sensation of the serpent's bite (see Dt 8:15). It is used specifically of the fiery serpents that were sent as judgment. The likeness of a serpent was made of brass at the Lord's command (Nu 21:8). The word is used twice by Isaiah to apparently denote a dragon (Isa 14:29; 30:6).

8315. שָׂרָף, **Śârâph,** *saw-rawf´*; the same as 8314; *Saraph*, an Israelite:—Saraph.

8316. שְׂרֵפָה, **śᵉrêphâh,** *ser-ay-faw´*; from 8313; *cremation*:—burning.

A feminine noun meaning burning, thoroughly burnt. The connotation of this word is that of being thoroughly consumed with fire. It is used to refer to kiln-firing brick (Ge 11:3); a destructive flame (Am 4:11); an inactive volcano (Jer 51:25); divine judgment (Le 10:6); and the burning of the red heifer (Nu 19:6). This word vividly portrays the state of the Temple during the Babylonian captivity (Isa 64:11[10]).

8317. שָׁרַץ, **shârats,** *shaw-rats´*; a primitive root; to *wriggle*, i.e. (by implication) *swarm* or *abound*:—breed (bring forth, increase) abundantly (in abundance), creep, move.

8318. שֶׁרֶץ, **sherets,** *sheh´-rets*; from 8317; a *swarm*, i.e. active mass of minute animals:—creep (-ing thing), move (-ing creature).

8319. שָׁרַק, **shâraq,** *shaw-rak´*; a primitive root; (properly) to *be shrill*, i.e. to whistle or *hiss* (as a call or in scorn):—hiss.

8320. שָׂרֹק**, śârôq,** *saw-rok´*; from 8319; *bright red* (as *piercing* to the sight), i.e. *bay*:—speckled. See 8291.

8321. שֹׂרֵק**, śôrêq,** *so-rake´*; or שׂוֹרֵק**, śôwrêq,** *so-rake´*; and (feminine) שֹׂרֵקָה, **śôrêqâh,** *so-ray-kaw´*; from 8319 in the sense of *redness* (compare 8320); a *vine* stock (properly, one yielding *purple* grapes, the richest variety):—choice (-st, noble) wine. Compare 8291.

8322. שְׁרֵקָה**, sheréqâh,** *sher-ay-kaw´*; from 8319; a *derision*:—hissing.

8323. שָׂרַר**, śârar,** *saw-rar´*; a primitive root; to *have* (transitive, *exercise*; reflexive, *get*) *dominion*:— × altogether, make self a prince, (bear) rule.

A verb meaning to reign as a prince, to be a prince, to rule. This Hebrew word means literally to rule or to govern as a prince, as is evident in Isa 32:1. This word also may imply an unwelcome exercise of authority over another, as the protest against Moses in Nu 16:13 suggests.

8324. שָׁרַר**, shârar,** *shaw-rar´*; a primitive root; to *be hostile* (only active participle, an *opponent*):—enemy.

8325. שָׁרָר**, Shârâr,** *shaw-rawr´*; from 8324; *hostile; Sharar*, an Israelite:—Sharar.

8326. שֹׁרֶר**, shôrer,** *sho´-rer*; from 8324 in the sense of *twisting* (compare 8270); the umbilical *cord*, i.e. (by extension) a *bodice*:—navel.

8327. שָׁרַשׁ**, shârash,** *shaw-rash´*; a primitive root; to *root*, i.e. strike into the soil, or (by implication) to pluck from it:—(take, cause to take) root (out).

8328. שֶׁרֶשׁ**, sheresh,** *sheh´-resh*; from 8327; a *root* (literal or figurative):—bottom, deep, heel, root.

8329. שֶׁרֶשׁ**, Sheresh,** *sheh´-resh*; the same as 8328; *Sheresh*, an Israelite:—Sharesh.

8330. שֹׁרֶשׁ**, shôresh,** *sho´-resh*; (Chaldee); corresponding to 8328:—root.

8331. שַׁרְשָׁה**, sharshâh,** *shar-shaw´*; from 8327; a *chain* (as *rooted*, i.e. *linked*):—chain. Compare 8333.

8332. שְׁרֹשׁוּ**, sherôshûw,** *sher-o-shoo´*; (Chaldee); from a root corresponding to 8327; *eradication*, i.e. (figurative) *exile*:—banishment.

8333. שַׁרְשְׁרָה**, sharsherâh,** *shar-sher-aw´*; from 8327 [compare 8331]; a *chain*; (architecture) probably a *garland*:—chain.

8334. שָׁרַת**, shârath,** *shaw-rath´*; a primitive root; to *attend* as a menial or worshipper; (figurative) to *contribute* to:—minister (unto), (do) serve (-ant, -ice, -itor), wait on.

A verb meaning to minister, to serve. This Hebrew word was utilized in a generic sense to describe various activities, including that of a domestic servant serving a ranking official (Ge 39:4; 2Sa 13:17, 18); a chief assistant to an authority figure, such as Joshua was to Moses (Ex 24:13); the angelic host to God (Ps 103:21); and assistants to kings (Isa 60:10). More particularly, the word is used in the context of religious service before the Lord, such as that required of the priests (Ex 28:35; 1Ki 8:11); or Levites (Nu 3:6).

8335. שָׁרֵת**, shârêth,** *shaw-rayth´*; infinitive of 8334; *service* (in the Temple):—minister (-ry).

A masculine noun meaning religious ministry, service. Service in the place of worship underlies the primary meaning of this word. It is used twice in reference to the instruments used by those ministering in the tabernacle (Nu 4:12); and the vessels used for ritual in the Temple (2Ch 24:14). The stress was upon the connection to the functions of the priestly office.

8336. שֵׁשׁ**, shêsh,** *shaysh*; or (for alliteration with 4897) שְׁשִׁי, **sheshîy,** *shesh-ee´*; for 7893; *bleached* stuff, i.e. *white* linen or (by analogy) marble:— × blue, fine ([twined]) linen, marble, silk.

8337. שֵׁשׁ**, shêsh,** *shaysh*; masculine שִׁשָּׁה**, shishshâh,** *shish-shaw´*; a primitive number; *six* (as an overplus [see 7797] beyond five or the fingers of the hand); as ordinal *sixth*:—six ([-teen, -teenth]), sixth.

8338. שָׁשָׁא**, shâshâ',** *shaw-shaw´*; a primitive root; apparently to *annihilate*:—leave but the sixth part [*by confusion with* 8341].

8339. שֵׁשְׁבַּצַּר**, Shêshbatstsar,** *shaysh-bats-tsar´*; of foreign derivation; *Sheshbatstsar*, Zerubbabel's Persian name:—Sheshbazzar.

8340. שֵׁשְׁבַּצַּר**, Shêshbatstsar,** *shaysh-bats-tsar´*; (Chaldee); corresponding to 8339:—Sheshbazzar.

8341. שָׁשָׁה**, shâshâh,** *shaw-shaw´*; a denominative from 8337; to *sixth* or divide into sixths:—give the sixth part.

8342. שָׂשׂוֹן**, śâśôwn,** *saw-sone´*; or שָׂשֹׂן**, śâśôn,** *saw-sone´*; from 7797; *cheerfulness*; (specifically) *welcome*:—gladness, joy, mirth, rejoicing.

8343. שָׁשַׁי**, Shâshay,** *shaw-shah´ee*; perhaps from 8336; *whitish; Shashai*, an Israelite:—Shashai.

8344. שֵׁשַׁי**, Shêshay,** *shay-shah´ee*; probably for 8343; *Sheshai*, a Canaanite:—Sheshai.

8345. שִׁשִּׁי**, shishshîy,** *shish-shee´*; from 8337; *sixth*, ordinal or (feminine) fractional:—sixth (part).

8346. שִׁשִּׁים**, shishshîym,** *shish-sheem´*; multiple of 8337; *sixty*:—sixty, three score.

8347. שֵׁשַׁךְ**, Shêshak,** *shay-shak´*; of foreign derivation; *Sheshak*, a symbolic name of Babylon:—Sheshach.

8348. שֵׁשָׁן**, Shêshân,** *shay-shawn´*; perhaps for 7799; *lily; Sheshan*, an Israelite:—Sheshan.

8349. שָׁשָׁק**, Shâshâq,** *shaw-shawk´*; probably from the base of 7785; *pedestrian; Shashak*, an Israelite:—Shashak.

8350. שָׁשַׁר**, shâshar,** *shaw-shar´*; perhaps from the base of 8324 in the sense of that of 8320; *red* ochre (from its *piercing* colour):—vermillion.

8351. שֵׁת**, shêth,** *shayth*; (Nu 24:17), from 7582; *tumult*:—Sheth.

8352. שֵׁת**, Shêth,** *shayth*; from 7896; *put*, i.e. *substituted; Sheth*, third son of Adam:—Seth, Sheth.

8353. שֵׁת**, shêth,** *shayth*; (Chaldee); or שִׁת**, shith,** *sheeth*; (Chaldee); corresponding to 8337:—six (-th).

8354. שָׁתָה**, shâthâh,** *shaw-thaw´*; a primitive root; to *imbibe* (literal or figurative):— × assuredly, banquet, × certainly, drink (-er, -ing), drunk (× -ard), surely. [Properly intensive of 8248.]

8355. שְׁתָה**, shethâh,** *sheth-aw´*; (Chaldee); corresponding to 8354:—drink.

8356. שָׁתָה**, shâthâh,** *shaw-thaw´*; from 7896; a *basis*, i.e. (figurative) political or moral *support*:—foundation, purpose.

8357. שֵׁתָה**, shêthâh,** *shay-thaw´*; from 7896; the *seat* (of the person):—buttock.

8358. שְׁתִי**, shethîy,** *sheth-ee´*; from 8354; *intoxication*:—drunkenness.

8359. שְׁתִי**, shethîy,** *sheth-ee´*; from 7896; a *fixture*, i.e. the *warp* in weaving:—warp.

8360. שְׁתִיָּה**, shethîyyâh,** *sheth-ee-yaw´*; feminine of 8358; *potation*:—drinking.

8361. שִׁתִּין**, shittîyn,** *shit-teen´*; (Chaldee); corresponding to 8346 [compare 8353]; *sixty*:—threescore.

8362. שָׁתַל**, shâthal,** *shaw-thal´*; a primitive root; to *transplant*:—plant.

8363. **שְׁתִיל, shᵉthîyl,** *sheth-eel´*; from 8362; a *sprig* (as if *transplanted*), i.e. *sucker*:—plant.

8364. **שֻׁתַלְחִי, Shuthalchîy,** *shoo-thal-khee´*; patronymic from 7803; a *Shuthalchite* (collective) or descendants of Shuthelach:—Shuthalhites.

8365. **שָׁתַם, shâtham,** *shaw-tham´*; a primitive root; to *unveil* (figurative):—be open.

8366. **שָׁתַן, shâthan,** *shaw-than´*; a primitive root; (causative) to *make water*, i.e. *urinate*:—piss.

8367. **שָׁתַק, shâthaq,** *shaw-thak´*; a primitive root; to *subside*:—be calm, cease, be quiet.

8368. **שָׂתַר, sâthar,** *saw-thar´*; a primitive root; to *break* out (as an eruption):—have in [one's] secret parts.

8369. **שֵׁתָר, Shêthâr,** *shay-thawr´*; of foreign derivation; *Shethar*, a Persian satrap:—Shethar.

8370. **שְׁתַר בּוֹזְנַי, Shᵉthar Bôwzᵉnay,** *sheth-ar´ bo-zen-ah´ee*; of foreign derivation; *Shethar-Bozenai*, a Persian officer:—Shethar-boznai.

8371. **שָׁתַת, shâthath,** *shaw-thath´*; a primitive root; to *place*, i.e. *array*; (reflexive) to *lie*:—be laid, set.

8372. **תָּא, tâʼ,** *taw*; and (feminine) **תָּאָה, tâʼâh,** *taw-aw´*; (Eze 40:12), from (the base of) 8376; a *room* (as *circumscribed*):—(little) chamber.

8373. **תָּאַב, tâʼab,** *taw-ab´*; a primitive root; to *desire*:—long.

8374. **תָּאַב, tâʼab,** *taw-ab´*; a primitive root [probably rather identical with 8373 through the idea of *puffing* disdainfully at; compare 340]; to *loathe* (moral):—abhor.

A verb meaning to loathe, to abhor. This unquestionably strong term of detest is used only in Am 6:8. The Lord employed it to convey His utter contempt for the pride of the people of Jacob.

8375. **תַּאֲבָה, taʼăbâh,** *tah-ab-aw´*; from 8374 [compare 15]; *desire*:—longing.

8376. **תָּאָה, tâʼâh,** *taw-aw´*; a primitive root; to *mark* off, i.e. (intensive) *designate*:—point out.

8377. **תְּאוֹ, tᵉʼôw,** *teh-o´*; and **תּוֹא, tôwʼ,** *toh*; (the original form), from 8376; a species of *antelope* (probably from the white *stripe* on the cheek):—wild bull (ox).

8378. **תַּאֲוָה, taʼăvâh,** *tah-av-aw´*; from 183 (abbreviated); a *longing*; (by implication) a *delight* (subjective, *satisfaction*; objective, a *charm*):—dainty, desire, × exceedingly, × greedily, lust (-ing), pleasant. See also 6914.

8379. **תַּאֲוָה, taʼăvâh,** *tah-av-aw´*; from 8376; a *limit*, i.e. full extent:—utmost bound.

8380. **תָּאוֹם, tâʼôwm,** *taw-ome´*; or **תָּאֹם, tâʼôm,** *taw-ome´*; from 8382; a *twin* (in plural only), literal or figurative:—twins.

8381. **תַּאֲלָה, taʼălâh,** *tah-al-aw´*; from 422; an *imprecation*:—curse.

8382. **תָּאַם, tâʼam,** *taw-am´*; a primitive root; to *be complete*; but used only as denominative from 8380, to *be* (causative, *make*) *twinned*, i.e. (figurative) *duplicate* or (architecture) *jointed*:—coupled (together), bear twins.

A verb meaning to be double, to couple, to be joined. The primary thrust of this word is that of joining in a matched pair. It is used only in two contexts: to describe the action of linking two corners of a curtain together (Ex 26:24; 36:29); and poetically, to describe the birthing of twins (SS 4:2; 6:6).

8383. **תְּאֻן, tᵉʼun,** *teh-oon´*; from 205; *naughtiness*, i.e. *toil*:—lie.

8384. **תְּאֵן, tᵉʼên,** *teh-ane´*; or (in the singular, feminine) **תְּאֵנָה, tᵉʼênâh,** *teh-ay-naw´*; perhaps of foreign derivation; the *fig* (tree or fruit):—fig (tree).

8385. **תַּאֲנָה, taʼănâh,** *tah-an-aw´*; or **תֹּאֲנָה, tôʼănâh,** *to-an-aw´*; from 579; an *opportunity* or (subjective) *purpose*:—occasion.

8386. **תַּאֲנִיָּה, taʼănîyyâh,** *tah-an-ee-yaw´*; from 578; *lamentation*:—heaviness, mourning.

8387. **תַּאֲנַת שִׁלֹה, Taʼănath Shilôh,** *tah-an-ath´ shee-lo´*; from 8385 and 7887; *approach of Shiloh; Taanath-Shiloh*, a place in Palestine:—Taanath-shiloh.

8388. **תָּאַר, tâʼar,** *taw-ar´*; a primitive root; to *delineate*; (reflexive) to *extend*:—be drawn, mark out, [Rimmon-] methoar [*by union with* 7417].

8389. **תֹּאַר, tôʼar,** *to´-ar*; from 8388; *outline*, i.e. *figure* or *appearance*:— + beautiful, × comely, countenance, + fair, × favoured, form, × goodly, × resemble, visage.

8390. **תַּאֲרֵעַ, Taʼărêaʻ,** *tah-ar-ay´-ah*; perhaps from 772; *Taareä*, an Israelite:—Tarea. See 8475.

8391. **תְּאַשּׁוּר, tᵉʼashshûwr,** *teh-ash-shoor´*; from 833; a species of *cedar* (from its *erectness*):—box (tree).

8392. **תֵּבָה, têbâh,** *tay-baw´*; perhaps of foreign derivation; a *box*:—ark.

8393. **תְּבוּאָה, tᵉbûwʼâh,** *teb-oo-aw´*; from 935; *income*, i.e. *produce* (literal or figurative):—fruit, gain, increase, revenue.

8394. **תָּבוּן, tâbûwn,** *taw-boon´*; and (feminine) **תְּבוּנָה, tebûwnâh,** *teb-oo-naw´*; or **תּוֹבֻנָה, tôwbunâh,** *to-boo-naw´*; from 995; *intelligence*; (by implication) an *argument*; (by extension) *caprice*:—discretion, reason, skilfulness, understanding, wisdom.

A feminine noun meaning understanding, insight. It occurs primarily in the Wisdom Literature and is associated with both wisdom and knowledge (Ex 35:31; Pr 8:1; 21:30); and is contrasted with foolishness (Pr 15:21; 18:2). A person of understanding is slow to wrath and walks uprightly (Pr 14:29; 15:21). God has understanding and gives it (Job 12:13; Ps 147:5; Pr 2:6; Isa 40:28). On the other hand, idolaters, who fashion idols by their own understanding, have no understanding at all (Isa 44:19; Hos 13:2).

8395. **תְּבוּסָה, tᵉbûwsâh,** *teb-oo-saw´*; from 947; a *treading down*, i.e. *ruin*:—destruction.

A feminine noun meaning ruin, downfall. The word is used in 2 Chronicles to depict God's judgment on Ahaziah and more generally the house of Ahab (2Ch 22:7). Jehu, God's chosen instrument, killed Ahaziah and Joram, the princes of Judah, in addition to the sons of Ahaziah's relatives.

8396. **תָּבוֹר, Tâbôwr,** *taw-bore´*; from a root corresponding to 8406; *broken* region; *Tabor*, a mountain in Palestine, also a city adjacent:—Tabor.

8397. **תֶּבֶל, tebel,** *teh´-bel*; apparently from 1101; *mixture*, i.e. *unnatural* bestiality:—confusion.

8398. **תֵּבֵל, têbêl,** *tay-bale´*; from 2986; the *earth* (as *moist* and therefore inhabited); (by extension) the *globe*; (by implication) its *inhabitants*; (specifically) a particular *land*, as Babylonia, Palestine:—habitable part, world.

A feminine noun meaning world, earth. The word is used in a description of the clouds responding to the command of God, i.e. they swirled over the face of the whole earth (Job 37:12). In Proverbs, the created world was a reason for rejoicing (Pr 8:31). This word is also used to indicate the foundations of the earth, as in 2 Samuel where the foundations of the earth were laid bare at the rebuke of the Lord (2Sa 22:16). *Têbêl* is also used to denote what was firmly established, i.e. the world (Ps 93:1; 96:10); something that would be punished for its evil (Isa 13:11); and what will be filled by Israel upon their blossoming (Isa 27:6). In Nahum, the world and all who live in it will tremble at the presence of the Lord (Na 1:5).

8399. **תַּבְלִית, tablîyth,** *tab-leeth´*; from 1086; *consumption*:—destruction.

A feminine noun meaning destruction. In Isaiah, the word is used to denote the end result of the direction of the wrath of the Lord, i.e.

the destruction of the Assyrians (Isa 10:25). Even though disobedient, Israel was still loved and protected by the Lord, who maintained a remnant.

8400. תְּבַלֻּל, t^{e}ballul, *teb-al-lool´*; from 1101 in the original sense of *flowing*; a *cataract* (in the eye):—blemish.

A masculine noun meaning confusion, obscurity. This word comes from the verb *bâlal* (1101), meaning to mix or to confuse, and is used only once in the OT. In Le 21:20, it is used to describe an obscurity or some sort of defect in the eye that would prohibit a man from being a priest.

8401. תֶּבֶן, teben, *teh´-ben*; probably from 1129; (properly) *material*, i.e. (specific) refuse *haum* or stalks of grain (as *chopped* in threshing and used for fodder):—chaff, straw, stubble.

8402. תִּבְנִי, Tibnîy, *tib-nee´*; from 8401; *strawy*; *Tibni*, an Israelite:—Tibni.

8403. תַּבְנִית, tabnîyth, *tab-neeth´*; from 1129; *structure*; (by implication) a *model, resemblance*:—figure, form, likeness, pattern, similitude.

A feminine noun meaning a plan, a pattern, a form. This noun comes from the verb *bânâh* (1129), meaning to build, and refers to the plans of a building or an object, such as the pattern of the tabernacle and its contents (Ex 25:9, 40); an altar (Jos 22:28; 2Ki 16:10); and the Temple and its contents (1Ch 28:11, 12, 18, 19). However, in other contexts, it refers to an image that was patterned after something else, such as a graven image of a god (Dt 4:16–18); the calf at Horeb (Ps 106:20); pillars (Ps 144:12); or a person (Isa 44:13). In a few contexts, it refers to something in the form of an animal (Eze 8:10); or a hand (Eze 8:3; 10:8). Synonyms for this word are *temûnâh* (8544), meaning likeness or form, and *demût* (1823), meaning likeness.

8404. תַּבְעֵרָה, Tab'êrâh, *tab-ay-raw´*; from 1197; *burning*; *Taberah*, a place in the Desert:—Taberah.

8405. תֵּבֵץ, Têbêts, *tay-bates´*; from the same as 948; *whiteness*; *Tebets*, a place in Palestine:—Thebez.

8406. תְּבַר, t^{e}bar, *teb-ar´*; (Chaldee); corresponding to 7665; to *be fragile* (figurative):—broken.

8407. תִּגְלַת פִּלְאֶסֶר, Tiglath Pil'eser, *tig-lath´ pil-eh´-ser*; or **תִּגְלַת פְּלֶסֶר Tiglath P^{e}leser,** *tig-lath pel-eh-ser*; or **תִּלְגַת פִּלְנְאֶסֶר Tilgath Piln^{e}eser,** *til-gath´ pil-neh-eh´-ser*; **תִּלְגַת פִּלְנֶסֶר Tilgath Pilneser,** *til-gath´ pil-neh´-ser*; of foreign derivation; *Tiglath-Pileser* or *Tilgath-pilneser*, an Assyrian king:—Tiglath-pileser, Tilgath-pilneser.

8408. תַּגְמוּל, tagmûwl, *tag-mool´*; from 1580; a *bestowment*:—benefit.

8409. תִּגְרָה, tigrâh, *tig-raw´*; from 1624; *strife*, i.e. *infliction*:—blow.

8410. תִּדְהָר, tidhâr, *tid-hawr´*; apparently from 1725; *enduring*; a species of hardwood or *lasting* tree (perhaps *oak*):—pine (tree).

8411. תְּדִירָא, t^{e}dîyrâ', *ted-ee-raw´*; (Chaldee); from 1753 in the original sense of *enduring; permanence*, i.e. (adverb) *constantly*:—continually.

8412. תַּדְמֹר, Tadmôr, *tad-more´*; or **תַּמֹּר, Tammôr,** *tam-more´*; (1Ki 9:18), apparently from 8558; *palm*-city; *Tadmor*, a place near Palestine:—Tadmor.

8413. תִּדְעָל, Tid'âl, *tid-awl´*; perhaps from 1763; *fearfulness; Tidal*, a Canaanite:—Tidal.

8414. תֹּהוּ, tôhûw, *to´-hoo*; from an unused root meaning to lie *waste*; a *desolation* (of surface), i.e. *desert*; (figurative) a *worthless* thing; (adverbial) in *vain*:—confusion, empty place, without form, nothing, (thing of) nought, vain, vanity, waste, wilderness.

A masculine noun meaning formlessness, confusion. The exact meaning of this term is difficult at best since its study is limited to its relatively few OT occurrences. It is used to describe primeval earth before the seven creative days (Ge 1:2); a land reduced to primeval chaos and formlessness (Isa 34:11; 45:18; Jer 4:23); a destroyed city (Isa 24:10); nothingness or empty space (Job 26:7); a barren wasteland (Dt 32:10; Job 6:18; 12:24; Ps 107:40); that which is vain and futile (1Sa 12:21; Isa 45:19; 49:4); like idolatry (Isa 41:29; 44:9); unfounded allegations (Isa 29:21; 59:4); the nations compared to God (Isa 40:17); or human rulers (Isa 40:23). Although it is impossible to grasp the full import of this word, it is obvious that it has a negative and disparaging tone. It represents chaos, confusion, and disorder, all things that are opposed to the organization, direction, and order that God has demonstrated.

8415. תְּהוֹם, t^{e}hôwm, *teh-home´*; or **תְּהֹם, t^{e}hôm,** *teh-home´*; (usually feminine) from 1949; an *abyss* (as a *surging* mass of water), especially the *deep* (the *main* sea or the subterranean *water-supply*):—deep (place), depth.

8416. תְּהִלָּה, t^{e}hillâh, *teh-hil-law´*; from 1984; *laudation*; specifically (concrete) a *hymn*:—praise.

A feminine noun meaning praise, a song of praise. This word is a noun derived from the verb *hâlal* (1984), which connotes genuine appreciation for the great actions or the character of its object. It is used especially of the adoration and thanksgiving that humanity renders to God (Ps 34:1[2]). By extension, it also represents the character of God that deserves praise (Ps 111:10); and the specific divine acts that elicit human veneration (Ex 15:11). It can also refer to the condition of fame and renown that comes with receiving this sort of praise and, as such, was applied to God (Dt 10:21; Hab 3:3); Israel (Dt 26:19; Jer 13:11); Jerusalem (Isa 62:7; Zep 3:19, 20); Damascus (Jer 49:25); Moab (Jer 48:2); Babylon (Jer 51:41). In late Hebrew, this term became a technical term for a psalm of praise. In this capacity, it is used in the title of Ps 145 to designate it as David's Psalm of Praise. It has also become the Hebrew title for the entire book of Psalms.

8417. תָּהֳלָה, tohŏlâh, *to-hol-aw´*; feminine of an unused noun (apparently from 1984) meaning *bluster; braggadocio*, i.e. (by implication) *fatuity*:—folly.

8418. תַּהֲלֻכָה, tahălukâh, *tah-hal-oo-kaw´*; from 1980; a *procession*:—× went.

8419. תַּהְפֻּכָה, tahpukâh, *tah-poo-kaw´*; from 2015; a *perversity* or *fraud*:—(very) froward (-ness, thing), perverse thing.

8420. תָּו, tâv, *tawv*; from 8427; a *mark*; (by implication) a *signature*:—desire, mark.

8421. תּוּב, tûwb, *toob*; (Chaldee); corresponding to 7725; to *come back*; specifically (transitive and ellipsis) to *reply*:—answer, restore, return (an answer).

8422. תּוּבַל, Tûwbal, *too-bal´*; or **תֻּבַל, Tubal,** *too-bal´*; probably of foreign derivation; *Tubal*, a postdiluvian patriarch and his posterity:—Tubal.

8423. תּוּבַל קַיִן, Tûwbal Qayin, *too-bal´ kah´-yin*; apparently from 2986 (compare 2981) and 7014; *offspring of Cain; Tubal-Kajin*, an antediluvian patriarch:—Tubal-cain.

8424. תּוּגָה, tûwgâh, *too-gaw´*; from 3013; *depression* (of spirits); (concrete) a *grief*:—heaviness, sorrow.

8425. תּוֹגַרְמָה, Tôwgarmâh, *to-gar-maw´*; or **תֹּגַרְמָה, Tôgarmâh,** *to-gar-maw´*; probably of foreign derivation; *Togarmah*, a son of Gomer and his posterity:—Togarmah.

8426. תּוֹדָה, tôwdâh, *to-daw´*; from 3034; (properly) an *extension* of the hand, i.e. (by implication) *avowal*, or (usually) *adoration*; specifically a *choir* of worshippers:—confession, (sacrifice of) praise, thanks (-giving, offering).

A feminine noun meaning praise, thanksgiving. The word describes an offering of thanks or a sacrifice of thanksgiving, It is a subcategory of the fellowship offering or the offering of well-being; the fellowship offering could be presented as a thank offering (Le 7:12, 13, 15; 22:29; 2Ch 29:31; Am 4:5). The word depicts worship by the presentation of songs of thanksgiving and praise that extolled the mighty wonders of the Lord (Ne 12:27; Ps 26:7; Isa 51:3). It refers to shouts of jubilation and thanksgiving (Ps 42:4[5]; Jnh 2:9[10]). It describes the purpose of the choirs used by Nehemiah, i.e. they were choirs of praise (Ne 12:31, 38). The goodness and praise of God were to be on the lips of even an enemy of the Lord, such as Achan, in the sense of proclaiming the glory of God while confessing and abandoning sin (Jos 7:19).

8427. **תָּוָה, tâvâh,** *taw-vaw´*; a primitive root; to *mark* out, i.e. (primitive) *scratch* or (defensive) *imprint*:—scrabble, set [a mark].

8428. **תָּוָה, tâvâh,** *taw-vaw´*; a primitive root [or perhaps identical with 8427 through a similar idea from *scraping* to pieces]; to *grieve*:—limit [*by confusion with* 8427].

8429. **תְּוַהּ, t^e^vah,** *tev-ah´*; (Chaldee); corresponding to 8539 or perhaps to 7582 through the idea of *sweeping* to ruin [compare 8428]; to *amaze*, i.e. (reflexive by implication) *take alarm*:—be astonied.

8430. **תּוֹחַ, Tôwach,** *to´-akh*; from an unused root meaning to *depress; humble; Toäch*, an Israelite:—Toah.

8431. **תּוֹחֶלֶת, tôwcheleth,** *to-kheh´-leth*; from 3176; *expectation*:—hope.

A feminine noun meaning hope. This word is found most often in the Wisdom Literature of Proverbs. Hope is associated with the prosperity of the righteous (Pr 10:28; 11:7); and is seen as the spring from which the desire for life flows (Pr 13:12). Jeremiah lamented that his soul was destitute because his hope in the Lord had perished (La 3:18).

8432. **תָּוֶךְ, tâvek,** *taw´-vek*; from an unused root meaning to *sever*; a *bisection*, i.e. (by implication) the *centre*:—among (-st), × between, half, × (there-, where-) in (-to), middle, mid [-night], midst (among), × out (of), × through, × with (-in).

A substantive meaning in the midst, in the middle, at the heart. The word can have the implication of something being surrounded on all sides, as when God made a firmament in the midst of the waters (Ge 1:6). It can also refer to something in the middle of a line: Samson destroyed the Temple by pushing over two middle pillars that supported it (Jgs 16:29). In relation to people, it can mean dwelling among (1 Sam 10:10); or taken from among a group (Nu 3:12).

8433. **תּוֹכֵחָה, tôwkêchâh,** *to-kay-khaw´*; and **תּוֹכַחַת, tôwkachath,** *to-kakh´-ath*; from 3198; *chastisement*; figurative (by words) *correction, refutation, proof* (even in defence):—argument, × chastened, correction, reasoning, rebuke, reproof, × be (often) reproved.

A feminine noun meaning a rebuke, a correction, a reproof, an argument. The primary thrust of this word is that of correcting some wrong. It is employed to express the concept of rebuking (Pr 15:10); judgment (Hos 5:9); reckoning (2Ki 19:3); or the argument of a claim (Job 13:6; Hab 2:1).

8434. **תּוֹלָד, Tôwlâd,** *to-lawd´*; from 3205; *posterity; Tolad*, a place in Palestine:—Tolad. Compare 513.

8435. **תּוֹלְדוֹת, tôwlêdôwth,** *to-lay-doth´*; from 3205; (plural only) *descent*, i.e. *family*; (figurative) *history*:—birth, generations.

A feminine noun meaning a generation. This key Hebrew word carries with it the notion of everything entailed in a person's life and that of his or her progeny (Ge 5:1; 6:9). In the plural, it is used to denote the chronological procession of history as humans shape it. It refers to the successive generations in one family (Ge 10:32); or a broader division by lineage (Nu 1:20ff.). In Ge 2:4, the word accounts for the history of the created world.

8436. **תִּילוֹן, Tîylôwn,** *tee-lone´*; from 8524; *suspension; Tulon*, an Israelite:—Tilon [*from the margin*].

8437. **תּוֹלָל, tôwlâl,** *to-lawl´*; from 3213; *causing to howl*, i.e. an *oppressor*:—that wasted.

8438. **תּוֹלָע, tôwlâ',** *to-law´*; and (feminine) **תּוֹלֵעָה, tôwlê'âh,** *to-lay-aw´*; or **תּוֹלַעַת, tôwla'ath,** *to-lah´-ath*; or **תֹּלַעַת, tôla'ath,** *to-lah´-ath*; from 3216; a *maggot* (as *voracious*); specifically (often with ellipsis of 8144) the crimson-*grub*, but used only (in this connection) of the colour from it, and cloths dyed therewith:—crimson, scarlet, worm.

8439. **תּוֹלָע, Tôwlâ',** *to-law´*; the same as 8438; *worm; Tola*, the name of two Israelites:—Tola.

8440. **תּוֹלָעִי, Tôwlâ'iy,** *to-law-ee´*; patronymic from 8439; a *Tolaïte* (collective) or descendants of Tola:—Tolaites.

8441. **תּוֹעֵבָה, tôw'êbah,** *to-ay-baw´*; or **תֹּעֵבָה, tô'ê-bah,** *to-ay-baw´*; feminine active participle of 8581; (properly) something *disgusting* (moral), i.e. (as noun) an *abhorrence*; especially *idolatry* or (concrete) an *idol*:—abominable (custom, thing), abomination.

A feminine noun meaning an abomination. This word is primarily understood in the context of the Law. It identifies unclean food (Dt 14:3); the activity of the idolater (Isa 41:24); the practice of child sacrifice (Dt 12:31); intermarriage by the Israelites (Mal 2:11); the religious activities of the wicked (Pr 21:27); and homosexual behaviour (Le 18:22). In a broader sense, the word is used to identify anything offensive (Pr 8:7).

8442. **תּוֹעָה, tôw'âh,** *to-aw´*; feminine active participle of 8582; *mistake*, i.e. (moral) *impiety*, or (political) *injury*:—error, hinder.

8443. **תּוֹעָפָה, tôw'âphâh,** *to-aw-faw´*; from 3286; (only in plural collective) *weariness*, i.e. (by implication) *toil* (*treasure* so obtained) or *speed*:—plenty, strength.

8444. **תּוֹצָאָה, tôwtsâ'âh,** *to-tsaw-aw´*; or **תֹּצָאָה, tôtsâ'âh,** *to-tsaw-aw´*; from 3318; (only in plural collective) *exit*, i.e. (geographical) *boundary*, or (figurative) *deliverance*, (active) *source*:—border (-s), going (-s) forth (out), issues, outgoings.

8445. **תּוֹקְהַת, Tôwqahath,** *to-kah´-ath*; from the same as 3349; *obedience; Tokahath*, an Israelite:—Tikvath [*by correction for* 8616].

8446. **תּוּר, tûwr,** *toor*; a primitive root; to *meander* (causative, *guide*) about, especially for trade or reconnoitring:—chap [-man], sent to descry, be excellent, merchant [-man], search (out), seek, (e-) spy (out).

8447. **תּוֹר, tôwr,** *tore*; or **תֹּר, tôr,** *tore*; from 8446; a *succession*, i.e. a *string* or (abstract) *order*:—border, row, turn.

8448. **תּוֹר, tôwr,** *tore*; probably the same as 8447; a *manner* (as a sort of *turn*):—estate.

8449. **תּוֹר, tôwr,** *tore*; or **תֹּר, tôr,** *tore*; probably the same as 8447; a *ring*-dove, often (figurative) as a term of endearment:—(turtle) dove.

8450. **תּוֹר, tôwr,** *tore*; (Chaldee); corresponding (by permutation) to 7794; a *bull*:—bullock, ox.

8451. **תּוֹרָה, tôwrâh,** *to-raw´*; or **תֹּרָה, tôrâh,** *to-raw´*; from 3384; a *precept* or *statute*, especially the *Decalogue* or *Pentateuch*:—law.

A feminine noun meaning instruction, direction, law, Torah, the whole Law. This noun comes from the verb *yârâh* (3384), which has, as one of its major meanings, to teach, to instruct. The noun means instruction in a general way from God; for example, Eliphaz uttered truth when he encouraged Job and his readers to be willing to receive instruction from God, the Almighty (Job 22:22). In Israel, a father and mother were sources of instruction for life (Pr 1:8; 6:20); along with wise persons (Pr 13:14; 28:4). In contrast, rebellious people were not willing to accept God's instructions in any manner (Isa 30:8, 9); the scribes handled the instructions of the Lord deceitfully and falsely (Jer 8:8). Various words are found in synonyms parallel with this term: It is paralleled by the sayings of the Holy One (Isa 5:24); the word of the Lord (Isa 1:10); and the testimony or witness (Isa 8:20). It is used regularly to depict priestly instructions in general or as a whole. The Lord rejected the priests of Israel for they had disregarded (lit., forgotten) the Law (Jer 2:8; Hos 4:6). They had been charged to carry out and teach all the instructions of the Lord (Dt 17:11).

The term takes on the meaning of law in certain settings, although it is still currently debated about how to translate the various words that describe the laws, ordinances, commands, decrees, and requirements of the Lord. This word *tôwrâh* is used as a summary term of various bodies of legal, cultic, or civil instructions. The word refers to the entire book of Deuteronomy and Moses' exposition of the Torah found in it (Dt 1:5). By implication, the word here also refers to the laws given in Exodus, Leviticus, and Numbers. Numerous times this word refers to the whole Law of Moses, the Book of the Law of Moses, the Book of the Law of God, the Law of the Lord, and the Law of God given at Sinai (in order of titles listed, 1Ki 2:3; Ne 8:1; Jos 24:26; Ps 1:2; Ne 10:28[29], 29[30]). The kings of Israel were held to the standard of the Law of Moses (1Ki 2:3; 2Ki 10:31; 14:6; 23:25). The word can also refer to a single law, for example, the law of the burnt offering (Le 6:9[2]; 7:7; Ne 12:44).

It is used of special laws for the Feast of Unleavened Bread (Ex 13:9); the Passover (Ex 12:49); of decisions by Moses (Ex 18:16, 20); for the content of the Book of the Covenant (Ex 24:12). The Law or Torah of God is pursued diligently by the psalmist; this word is found twenty-five times in Ps 119 in parallel with various near synonyms. The word means the usual way, custom, or manner of God as David addressed his surprise to the Lord about the way He had dealt with him (2Sa 7:19).

8452. תּוֹרָה**, tôwrâh,** *to-raw´*; probably feminine of 8448; a *custom*:—manner.

8453. תּוֹשָׁב**, tôwshâb,** *to-shawb´*; or תֹּשָׁב**, tôshâb,** *to-shawb´*; (1Ki 17:1), from 3427; a *dweller* (but not outlandish [5237]); especially (as distinguished from a native citizen [active participle of 3427] and a temporary inmate [1616] or mere lodger [3885]) resident *alien*:—foreigner, inhabitant, sojourner, stranger.

A masculine noun meaning a sojourner, a foreigner. This word implies temporary visitors who were dependent in some way on the nation in which they were residing. It denotes a sojourner who received shelter from a priest (Le 22:10); foreigners who were closely linked to the economy of the people (Le 25:40, 47); and a wanderer with close ties to the land occupied by another people (Ge 23:4). David proclaimed himself to be such a sojourner with the Lord (Ps 39:12[13]).

8454. תּוּשִׁיָּה**, tûwshîyyâh,** *too-shee-yaw´*; or תֻּשִׁיָּה**, tushîyyâh,** *too-shee-yaw´*; from an unused root probably meaning to *substantiate; support* or (by implication) *ability*, i.e. (direct) *help*, (in purpose) an *undertaking*, (intellectual) *understanding*:—enterprise, that which (thing as it) is, substance, (sound) wisdom, working.

A feminine noun meaning sound wisdom, continuing success. The primary meaning of this Hebrew word is wisdom or ability that brings continued advancement. Used in the Wisdom Literature of the OT, it describes the wisdom of the Lord that keeps a person on the right path (Pr 3:21; Isa 28:29); the wisdom that recognizes the things of God (Mic 6:9); and the success that comes from heeding wise counsel (Job 5:12; 6:13).

8455. תּוֹתָח**, tôwthâch,** *to-thawkh´*; from an unused root meaning to *smite*; a *club*:—darts.

8456. תָּזַז**, tâzaz,** *taw-zaz´*; a primitive root; to *lop* off:—cut down.

8457. תַּזְנוּת**, taznûwth,** *taz-nooth´*; or תַּזְנֻת**, taznuth,** *taz-nooth´*; from 2181; *harlotry*, i.e. (figurative) *idolatry*:—fornication, whoredom.

A noun meaning whoredom, prostitution. This word is found only in Eze 16 and 23. Chapter sixteen is an allegorical story about Jerusalem's faithlessness to the Lord (Eze 16:26). In this chapter, the Lord indicts Jerusalem for acting like a prostitute, throwing herself to the gods of foreign nations (Eze 16:15, 20, 33, 36). Chapter twenty-three is a similar story about Judah and Israel portrayed as two sisters in whoredom with the foreign nations (Eze 23:7, 14, 18, 35). These passages expose the vileness of the Israelites' sin.

8458. תַּחְבֻּלָה**, tachbulâh,** *takh-boo-law´*; or תַּחְבּוּלָה**, tachbûwlâh,** *takh-boo-law´*; from 2254 as denominative from 2256; (only in plural) properly *steerage* (as a management of *ropes*), i.e. (figurative) *guidance* or (by implication) a *plan*:—good advice, (wise) counsels.

8459. תֹּחוּ**, Tôchûw,** *to´-khoo*; from an unused root meaning to *depress; abasement; Tochu*, an Israelite:—Tohu.

8460. תְּחוֹת**, t^echôwth,** *tekh-ōth´*; (Chaldee); or תְּחֹת**, t^echôth,** *tekh-ōth´*; (Chaldee); corresponding to 8478; *beneath*:—under.

8461. תַּחְכְּמֹנִי**, Tachk^emônîy,** *takh-kem-o-nee´*; probably for 2453; *sagacious; Tachkemoni*, an Israelite:—Tachmonite.

8462. תְּחִלָּה**, t^echillâh,** *tekh-il-law´*; from 2490 in the sense of *opening*; a *commencement*; (relative) *original;* (adverb) *originally*:—begin (-ning), first (time).

8463. תַּחֲלוּא**, tachălûw',** *takh-al-oo´*; or תַּחֲלֻא**, tachălu',** *takh-al-oo´*; from 2456; a *malady*:—disease, × grievous, (that are) sick (-ness).

8464. תַּחְמָס**, tachmâs,** *takh-mawce´*; from 2554; a species of unclean bird (from its *violence*), perhaps an *owl*:—night hawk.

8465. תַּחַן**, Tachan,** *takh´-an*; probably from 2583; *station; Tachan*, the name of two Israelites:—Tahan.

8466. תַּחֲנָה**, tachănâh,** *takh-an-aw´*; from 2583; (only plural collateral) an *encampment*:—camp.

8467. תְּחִנָּה**, t^echinnâh,** *tekh-in-naw´*; from 2603; *graciousness*; (causative) *entreaty*:—favour, grace, supplication.

A feminine noun meaning a request for favour. The request for favour is always directed toward God—with two exceptions when the request is made to the king (Jer 37:20; 38:26). This seldom-used term occurred predominately in connection with Solomon's dedication of the Temple (1Ki 8:28, 30, 38, 45, 49, 52, 54; 2Ch 6:14–42). In these passages, the request was often connected with prayer and associated with a distinct relationship to God. On two occasions, the word was used to refer to favour itself (Jos 11:20; Ezr 9:8).

8468. תְּחִנָּה**, T^echinnâh,** *tekh-in-naw´*; the same as 8467; *Techinnah*, an Israelite:—Tehinnah.

8469. תַּחֲנוּן**, tachănûwn,** *takh-an-oon´*; or (feminine) תַּחֲנוּנָה**, tachănûwnâh,** *takh-an-oo-naw´*; from 2603; earnest *prayer*:—intreaty, supplication.

A masculine noun meaning supplication. The word refers to asking for favour and is used in a comparison of a rich man with a poor man. The rich man answers harshly, while the poor man pleads for mercy (Pr 18:23). Daniel used the word to indicate how he turned to the Lord in a prayer of petition, i.e. he pleaded with Him in prayers of petition with fasting and in sackcloth and ashes (Da 9:3). He also called to God to hear the prayers and petitions of His servant (Da 9:17). The noun was also used by the psalmist, who made a plea to God to hear his cry for mercy (Ps 28:2; 31:22[23]; 86:6). In Jeremiah, a cry was heard on the barren heights, along with weeping and pleading by the people of Israel (Jer 3:21). The word was also used to inform Daniel that as soon as he began his prayer or petition, an answer would be given to him (Da 9:23).

8470. תַּחֲנִי**, Tachănîy,** *takh-an-ee´*; patronymic from 8465; a *Tachanite* (collective) or descendants of Tachan:—Tahanites.

8471. תַּחְפַּנְחֵס**, Tachpanchês,** *takh-pan-khace´*; or תְּחַפְנְחֵס**, T^echaphn^echês,** *tekh-af-nekh-ace´*; (Eze 30:18), or תַּחְפְּנֵס**, Tachp^enês,** *takh-pen-ace´*; (Jer 2:16), of Egyptian deriative; *Tachpanches, Techaph-neches* or *Tachpenes*, a place in Egypt:—Tahapanes, Tahpanhes, Tehaphnehes.

8472. תַּחְפְּנֵיס**, Tachp^enêys,** *takh-pen-ace´*; of Egyptian derivation; *Tachpenes*, an Egyptian woman:—Tahpenes.

8473. תַּחֲרָא**, tachărâ',** *takh-ar-aw´*; from 2734 in the original sense of 2352 or 2353; a linen *corslet* (as *white* or *hollow*):—habergeon.

8474. תַּחָרָה**, tachârâh,** *takh-aw-raw´*; a factitious root from 2734 through the idea of the *heat* of jealousy; to *vie* with a rival:—close, contend.

8475. תַּחְרֵעַ**, Tachrêaʻ**, *takh-ray´-ah*; for 8390; *Tachreä*, an Israelite:—Tahrea.

8476. תַּחַשׁ**, tachash**, *takh´-ash*; probably of foreign derivation; a (clean) animal with fur, probably a species of *antelope*:—badger.

8477. תַּחַשׁ**, Tachash**, *takh´-ash*; the same as 8476; *Tachash*, a relative of Abraham:—Thahash.

8478. תַּחַת**, tachath**, *takh´-ath*; from the same as 8430; the *bottom* (as *depressed*); (only adverb) *below* (often with prepositional prefix *underneath*), in *lieu of*, etc.:—as, beneath, × flat, in (-stead), (same) place (where … is), room, for … sake, stead of, under, × unto, × when … was mine, whereas, [where-] fore, with.

8479. תַּחַת**, tachath**, *takh´-ath*; (Chaldee); corresponding to 8478:—under.

8480. תַּחַת**, Tachath**, *takh´-ath*; the same as 8478; *Tachath*, the name of a place in the Desert, also of three Israelites:—Tahath.

8481. תַּחְתּוֹן**, tachtôwn**, *takh-tone´*; or תַּחְתֹּן**, tach-tôn**, *takh-tone´*; from 8478; *bottommost*:—lower (-est), nether (-most).

8482. תַּחְתִּי**, tachtîy**, *takh-tee´*; from 8478; *lowermost*; as noun (feminine plural) the *depths* (figurative, a *pit*, the *womb*):—low (parts, -er, -er parts, -est), nether (part).

8483. תַּחְתִּים חָדְשִׁי**, Tachtîym Chodshîy**, *takh-teem´ khod-shee´*; apparently from the plural masculine of 8482 or 8478 and 2320; *lower* (ones) *monthly; Tachtim-Chodshi*, a place in Palestine:—Tahtim-hodshi.

8484. תִּיכוֹן**, tîykôwn**, *tee-kone´*; or תִּיכֹן**, tîykôn**, *tee-kone´*; from 8432; *central*:—middle (-most), midst.

8485. תֵּימָא**, Têymâʼ**, *tay-maw´*; or תֵּמָא**, Têmâʼ**, *tay-maw´*; probably of foreign derivation; *Tema*, a son of Ishmael, and the region settled by him:—Tema.

8486. תֵּימָן**, têymân**, *tay-mawn´*; or תֵּמָן**, têmân**, *tay-mawn´*; denominative from 3225; the *south* (as being on the *right* hand of a person facing the east):—south (side, -ward, wind).

8487. תֵּימָן**, Têymân**, *tay-mawn´*; or תֵּמָן**, Têmân**, *tay-mawn´*; the same as 8486; *Teman*, the name of two Edomites, and of the region and descendant of one of them:—south, Teman.

8488. תֵּימְנִי**, Têymᵉnîy**, *tay-men-ee´*; probably for 8489; *Temeni*, an Israelite:—Temeni.

8489. תֵּימָנִי**, Têymânîy**, *tay-maw-nee´*; patronymic from 8487; a *Temanite* or descendant of Teman:—Temani, Temanite.

8490. תִּימָרָה**, tîymârâh**, *tee-maw-raw´*; or תִּמָרָה**, timârâh**, *tee-maw-raw´*; from the same as 8558; a *column*, i.e. cloud:—pillar.

8491. תִּיצִי**, Tîytsîy**, *tee-tsee´*; patrial or patronymic from an unused noun of uncertain meaning; a *Titsite* or descendant or inhabitant of an unknown Tits:—Tizite.

8492. תִּירוֹשׁ**, tîyrôwsh**, *tee-roshe´*; or תִּירשׁ**, tîyrôsh**, *tee-roshe´*; from 3423 in the sense of *expulsion; must* or fresh grape juice (as just *squeezed* out); by implication (rarely) fermented *wine*:—(new, sweet) wine.

8493. תִּירְיָא**, Tîyrᵉyâʼ**, *tee-reh-yaw´*; probably from 3372; *fearful; Tirja*, an Israelite:—Tiria.

8494. תִּירָס**, Tîyrâs**, *tee-rawce´*; probably of foreign derivative; *Tiras*, a son of Japheth:—Tiras.

8495. תַּיִשׁ**, tayish**, *tah´-yeesh*; from an unused root meaning to *butt*; a *buck* or he-goat (as given to *butting*):—he goat.

8496. תֹּךְ**, tôk**, *toke*; or תּוֹךְ**, tôwk**, *toke*; (Ps 72:14), from the same base as 8432 (in the sense of *cutting* to pieces); *oppression*:—deceit, fraud.

8497. תָּכָה**, tâkâh**, *taw-kaw´*; a primitive root; to *strew*, i.e. *encamp*:—sit down.

8498. תְּכוּנָה**, tᵉkûwnâh**, *tek-oo-naw´*; feminine passive participle of 8505; *adjustment*, i.e. *structure*; (by implication) *equipage*:—fashion, store.

8499. תְּכוּנָה**, tᵉkûwnâh**, *tek-oo-naw´*; from 3559; or probably identical with 8498; something *arranged* or *fixed*, i.e. a *place*:—seat.

8500. תֻּכִּיִּים**, tukkîyyîym**, *took-kee-yeem´*; or תּוּכִּיִּים**, tûwkkîyîym**, *took-kee-eem´*; probably of foreign derivation; some imported creature, probably a *peacock*:—peacock.

8501. תָּכָךְ**, tâkâk**, *taw-kawk´*; from an unused root meaning to *dissever*, i.e. *crush*:—deceitful.

8502. תִּכְלָה**, tiklâh**, *tik-law´*; from 3615; *completeness*:—perfection.

8503. תַּכְלִית**, taklîyth**, *tak-leeth´*; from 3615; *completion*; (by implication) an *extremity*:—end, perfect (-ion).

8504. תְּכֵלֶת**, tᵉkêleth**, *tek-ay´-leth*; probably for 7827; the cerulean *mussel*, i.e. the colour (*violet*) obtained therefrom or stuff dyed therewith:—blue.

8505. תָּכַן**, tâkan**, *taw-kan´*; a primitive root; to *balance*, i.e. *measure* out (by weight or dimension); (figurative) to *arrange, equalize*, through the idea of *levelling* (mentally *estimate, test*):—bear up, direct, be ([un-]) equal, mete, ponder, tell, weigh.

8506. תֹּכֶן**, tôken**, *to´-ken*; from 8505; a fixed *quantity*:—measure, tale.

8507. תֹּכֶן**, Tôken**, *to´-ken*; the same as 8506; *Token*, a place in Palestine:—Tochen.

8508. תָּכְנִית**, toknîyth**, *tok-neeth´*; from 8506; *admeasurement*, i.e. *consummation*:—pattern, sum.

8509. תַּכְרִיךְ**, takrîyk**, *tak-reek´*; apparently from an unused root meaning to *encompass*; a *wrapper* or robe:—garment.

8510. תֵּל**, têl**, *tale*; (by contraction) from 8524; a *mound*:—heap, × strength.

8511. תָּלָא**, tâlâʼ**, *taw-law´*; a primitive root; to *suspend*; figurative (through *hesitation*) to *be uncertain*; by implication (of mental *dependence*) to *habituate*:—be bent, hang (in doubt).

8512. תֵּל אָבִיב**, Têl ʼÂbîyb**, *tale aw-beeb´*; from 8510 and 24; *mound* of *green* growth; *Tel-Abib*, a place in Chaldæa:—Tel-abib.

8513. תְּלָאָה**, tᵉlâʼâh**, *tel-aw-aw´*; from 3811; *distress*:—travail, travel, trouble.

8514. תַּלְאוּבָה**, talʼûwbâh**, *tal-oo-baw´*; from 3851; *desiccation*:—great drought.

8515. תְּלַאשָּׂר**, Tᵉlaʼśśâr**, *tel-as-sawr´*; or תְּלַשָּׂר**, Tᵉlaś-śâr**, *tel-as-sawr´*; of foreign derivation; *Telassar*, a region of Assyria:—Telassar.

8516. תַּלְבֹּשֶׁת**, tilbôsheth**, *til-bo´-sheth*; from 3847; a *garment*:—clothing.

8517. תְּלַג**, tᵉlag**, *tel-ag´*; (Chaldee); corresponding to 7950; *snow*:—snow.

8518. תָּלָה**, tâlâh**, *taw-law´*; a primitive root; to *suspend* (especially to *gibbet*):—hang (up).

8519. תְּלוּנָּה**, tᵉlûwnâh**, *tel-oo-naw´*; or תְּלֻנָּה**, tᵉlunnâh**, *tel-oon-naw´*; from 3885 in the sense of *obstinacy*; a *grumbling*:—murmuring.

8520. תֶּלַח**, Telach**, *teh´-lakh*; probably from an unused root meaning to *dissever; breach; Telach*, an Israelite:—Telah.

8521. תֵּל חַרְשָׁא, Têl Charshâ', *tale khar-shaw´*; from 8510 and the feminine of 2798; *mound of workmanship; Tel-Charsha*, a place in Babylon:—Tel-haresha, Tel-harsa.

8522. תְּלִי, tᵉlîy, *tel-ee´*; probably from 8518; a *quiver* (as *slung*):—quiver.

8523. תְּלִיתַי, tᵉlîythây, *tel-ee-thaw´ee*; (Chaldee); or **תַּלְתִּי, taltîy,** *tal-tee´*; (Chaldee); ordinal from 8532; *third*:—third.

8524. תָּלוּל, tâlûwl, *taw-lool´*; a primitive root; to *pile* up, i.e. *elevate*:—eminent. Compare 2048.

8525. תֶּלֶם, telem, *teh´-lem*; from an unused root meaning to *accumulate*; a *bank* or *terrace*:—furrow, ridge.

8526. תַּלְמַי, Talmay, *tal-mah´ee*; from 8525; *ridged; Talmai*, the name of a Canaanite and a Syrian:—Talmai.

8527. תַּלְמִיד, talmîyd, *tal-meed´*; from 3925; a *pupil*:—scholar.

8528. תֵּל מֶלַח, Têl Melach, *tale meh´-lakh*; from 8510 and 4417; *mound of salt; Tel-Melach*, a place in Babylon:—Tel-melah.

8529. תָּלַע, tâla', *taw-law´*; a denominative from 8438; to *crimson*, i.e. dye that colour:— × scarlet.

8530. תַּלְפִּיּוֹת, talpîyyôwth, *tal-pee-yoth´*; feminine from an unused root meaning to *tower*; something *tall*, i.e. (plural collective) *slenderness*:—armoury.

8531. תְּלַת, tᵉlath, *tel-ath´*; (Chaldee); from 8532; a *tertiary* rank:—third.

8532. תְּלָת, tᵉlâth, *tel-awth´*; (Chaldee); masculine **תְּלָתָה, tᵉlâthâh,** *tel-aw-thaw´*; (Chaldee); or **תְּלָתָא, tᵉlâthâ',** *tel-aw-thaw´*; (Chaldee); corresponding to 7969; *three* or *third*:—third, three.

8533. תְּלָתִין, tᵉlâthîyn, *tel-aw-theen´*; (Chaldee); multiple of 8532; *ten times three*:—thirty.

8534. תַּלְתַּל, taltal, *tal-tal´*; by reduplication from 8524 through the idea of *vibration*; a trailing *bough* (as *pendulous*):—bushy.

8535. תָּם, tâm, *tawm*; from 8552; *complete*; usually (moral) *pious*; (specifically) *gentle, dear*:—coupled together, perfect, plain, undefiled, upright.

An adjective meaning integrity, completeness. This is a rare, almost exclusively poetic term often translated perfect but not carrying the sense of totally free from fault, for it was used of quite flawed people. It describes the mild manner of Jacob in contrast to his brother Esau, who was characterized by shedding blood (Ge 25:27; see also Pr 29:10). The term often carries a rather strong moral component in certain contexts (Job 1:1; 9:20–22; Ps 37:37; 64:4[5]). This word appears among a list of glowing terms describing the admirable qualities of the Shulamite lover (SS 5:2; 6:9).

8536. תָּם, tâm, *tawm*; (Chaldee); corresponding to 8033; *there*:— × thence, there, × where.

8537. תֹּם, tôm, *tome*; from 8552; *completeness*; (figurative) *prosperity*; usually (moral) *innocence*:—full, integrity, perfect (-ion), simplicity, upright (-ly, -ness), at a venture. See 8550.

A masculine noun meaning completeness, integrity. This word is used in Job to describe how a man could die, i.e. in complete security (Job 21:23). When Absalom invited two hundred men from Jerusalem to his party, the word denoted that the men did not have any idea of what was about to happen (2Sa 15:11). In Genesis, Abimelech acted with a clear conscience after Abraham stated that Sarah was his sister (Ge 20:5, 6). In a statement of wisdom, Proverbs uses the word to indicate that righteousness guards the person of integrity (Pr 13:6); while the psalmist asks that his integrity and uprightness protect him because his hope is in the Lord (Ps 25:21).

8538. תֻּמָּה, tummâh, *toom-maw´*; feminine of 8537; *innocence*:—integrity.

A feminine noun meaning integrity. This comes from the verb *tâmam* (8552), meaning to be complete, and is the feminine equivalent of the word *tôm* (8537), meaning completeness or integrity. This word is used only five times in the OT and is only found in the Wisdom Literature of Job and the Psalms. In four of these instances, it is used by God, Job, and Job's wife to refer to Job's integrity (Job 2:3, 9; 27:5; 31:6). In Pr 11:3, integrity guides the upright person. See the related adjective *tâm* (8535), meaning complete.

8539. תָּמַהּ, tâmah, *taw-mah´*; a primitive root; to *be in consternation*:—be amazed, be astonished, marvel (-lously), wonder.

8540. תְּמַהּ, tᵉmah, *tem-ah´*; (Chaldee); from a root corresponding to 8539; a *miracle*:—wonder.

An Aramaic masculine noun meaning wonder. This word is related to the Hebrew verb *tâmah* (8539), meaning to be astonished. In its only three instances, this word speaks of the wondrous and perhaps miraculous deeds of God (Da 4:2[3:32], 3[3:33]; 6:27[28]). In every instance, it is used in close connection with *'âth* (852), meaning signs.

8541. תִּמָּהוֹן, timmâhôwn, *tim-maw-hone´*; from 8539; *consternation*:—astonishment.

8542. תַּמּוּז, Tammûwz, *tam-mooz´*; of uncertain derivation; *Tammuz*, a Phoenician deity:—Tammuz.

8543. תְּמוֹל, tᵉmôwl, *tem-ole´*; or **תְּמֹל, tᵉmôl,** *tem-ole´*; probably for 865; (properly) *ago*, i.e. a (short or long) *time since*; especially *yesterday*, or (with 8032) *day before* yesterday: + before (-time), + these [three] days, + heretofore, + time past, yesterday.

8544. תְּמוּנָה, tᵉmûwnâh, *tem-oo-naw´*; or **תְּמֻנָה, tᵉmunâh,** *tem-oo-naw´*; from 4327; *something portioned* (i.e. *fashioned*) out, as a *shape*, i.e. (indefinite) *phantom*, or (specific) *embodiment*, or (figurative) *manifestation* (of favour):—image, likeness, similitude.

A feminine noun meaning a likeness or a form. This word is related to the noun *miyn* (4327), meaning kind or species. The main idea of this word is one of likeness or similarity. It is normally used to describe God's ban on creating images of anything that would attempt to resemble (or be like) Him (Ex 20:4; Dt 4:15, 16; 5:8). This word can also describe the form or likeness of a visible image (Job 4:16; Ps 17:15). Synonyms for this word are *tabniyt* (8403) meaning plan, pattern, or form, and *demût* (1823), meaning likeness.

8545. תְּמוּרָה, tᵉmûwrâh, *tem-oo-raw´*; from 4171; *barter, compensation*:—(ex-) change (-ing), recompense, restitution.

A feminine noun meaning an exchange. This word comes from the verb *mûr* (4171), meaning to change or to exchange. The word usually refers to the exchanging of one item for another. In Leviticus, it is used to give rules for the exchange of animals and land that were dedicated to the Lord (Le 27:10, 33). In Ruth, the word indicates the Israelite custom of exchanging items to confirm a vow (Ru 4:7). In Job, this word describes financial transactions (Job 20:18; 28:17). This word may be translated recompense in Job 15:31, where it describes the natural result of a life trusting in vanity.

8546. תְּמוּתָה, tᵉmûwthâh, *tem-oo-thaw´*; from 4191; *execution* (as a doom):—death, die.

A feminine noun meaning death. This word comes from the verb *mûth* (4191), meaning to die. In its only two occurrences in the OT, it is used to describe those who were appointed to and deserving of death. More literally, it was those who were appointed to death (Ps 79:11; 102:20[21]).

8547. תֶּמַח, Temach, *teh´-makh*; of uncertain derivation; *Temach*, one of the Nethinim:—Tamah, Thamah.

8548. תָּמִיד, tâmîyd, *taw-meed´*; from an unused root meaning to *stretch*; (properly) *continuance* (as indefinite *extension*); but used only (attributively as adjective) *constant* (or adverb *constantly*); elliptically the *regular* (daily) sacrifice:—alway (-s), continual (employment, -ly), daily, ([n-]) ever (-more), perpetual.

A masculine noun meaning continuity. This word commonly refers to actions concerning religious rituals: God commanded that the Israelites always set showbread on a table in the tabernacle (Ex 25:30). Similarly, special bread was to be set on the table continually every Sabbath (Le 24:8). Mealtime could also be seen as following a set pattern: David commanded that Mephibosheth always eat with him (2Sa 9:7). In another light, the psalmist referred to God as One he could continually turn to in times of need (Ps 71:3).

8549. תָּמִים, **tâmîym,** *taw-meem´*; from 8552; *entire* (literal, figurative or moral); also (as noun) *integrity, truth*:—without blemish, complete, full, perfect, sincerely (-ity), sound, without spot, undefiled, upright (-ly), whole.

An adjective meaning blameless, complete. In over half of its occurrences, it describes an animal to be sacrificed to the Lord, whether a ram, a bull, or a lamb (Ex 29:1; Le 4:3; 14:10). With respect to time, the term is used to refer to a complete day, a complete seven Sabbaths (weeks), and a complete year (Le 23:15; 25:30; Jos 10:13). When used in a moral sense, this word is linked with truth, virtue, uprightness, and righteousness (Jos 24:14; Ps 18:23[24]; Pr 2:21; 11:5). The term is used of one's relationship with another person (Jgs 9:19; Pr 28:18; Am 5:10); and of one's relationship with God (Ge 17:1; Dt 18:13; 2Sa 22:24, 26). Moreover, this word described the blamelessness of God's way, knowledge, and Law (2Sa 22:31; Job 37:16; Ps 19:7[8]).

8550. תֻּמִּים, **Tummîym,** *toom-meem´*; plural of 8537; *perfections*, i.e. (technical) one of the epithets of the objects in the high-priest's breastplate as an emblem of *complete* Truth:—Thummim.

8551. תָּמַךְ, **tâmak,** *taw-mak´*; a primitive root; to *sustain*; (by implication) to *obtain, keep fast*; (figurative) to *help, follow close*:—(take, up-) hold (up), maintain, retain, stay (up).

8552. תָּמַם, **tâmam,** *taw-mam´*; a primitive root; to *complete*, in a good or a bad sense, literal or figurative, transitive or intransitive (as follows):—accomplish, cease, be clean [pass-] ed, consume, have done, (come to an, have an, make an) end, fail, come to the full, be all gone, × be all here, be (make) perfect, be spent, sum, be (shew self) upright, be wasted, whole.

A verb meaning to be complete, to finish, to conclude. At its root, this word carries the connotation of finishing or bringing closure. It is used to signify the concluding of an oration (Dt 31:30); the completing of a building project (1Ki 6:22); the exhausting of resources (Ge 47:15; Le 26:20); the utter destruction of something (Nu 14:33); and the fulfilling of an established period of time (Dt 34:8).

8553. תִּמְנָה, **Timnâh,** *tim-naw´*; from 4487; a *portion* assigned; *Timnah*, the name of two places in Palestine:—Timnah, Timnath, Thimnathah.

8554. תִּמְנִי, **Timnîy,** *tim-nee´*; patrial from 8553; a *Timnite* or inhabitant of Timnah:—Timnite.

8555. תִּמְנָע, **Timnâʿ,** *tim-naw´*; from 4513; *restraint; Timna*, the name of two Edomites:—Timna, Timnah.

8556. תִּמְנַת חֶרֶס, **Timnath Cheres,** *tim-nath kheh´-res*; or תִּמְנַת סֶרַח, **Timnath Serach,** *tim-nath seh´-rakh*; from 8553 and 2775; *portion of* (the) *sun; Timnath-Cheres*, a place in Palestine:—Timnath-heres, Timnath-serah.

8557. תֶּמֶס, **temes,** *teh´-mes*; from 4529; *liquefaction*, i.e. *disappearance*:—melt.

8558. תָּמָר, **tâmâr,** *taw-mawr´*; from an unused root meaning to *be erect*; a *palm* tree:—palm (tree).

8559. תָּמָר, **Tâmâr,** *taw-mawr´*; the same as 8558; *Tamar*, the name of three women and a place:—Tamar.

8560. תֹּמֶר, **tômer,** *to´-mer*; from the same root as 8558; a *palm* trunk:—palm tree.

8561. תִּמֹּר, **timmôr,** *tim-more´*; (plural only) or (feminine) תִּמֹּרָה, **timmôrâh,** *tim-mo-raw´*; (singular and plural), from the same root as 8558; (architecture) a *palm*-like pilaster (i.e. umbellate):—palm tree.

8562. תַּמְרוּק, **tamrûwq,** *tam-rook´*; or תַּמְרֻק, **tamruq,** *tam-rook´*; or תַּמְרִיק, **tamrîyq,** *tam-reek´*; from 4838; (properly) a *scouring*, i.e. *soap* or *perfumery* for the bath; (figurative) a *detergent*:—× cleanse, (thing for) purification (-fying).

A masculine noun meaning scraping, rubbing, purifying. This Hebrew word carries the connotation of scraping away that which is impure or harmful. This word appears three times in reference to ritual purification following menstruation (Est 2:3, 9, 12). Figuratively, it is used to imply a remedy for an illness (Pr 20:30).

8563. תַּמְרוּר, **tamrûwr,** *tam-roor´*; from 4843; *bitterness* (plural as collective):—× most bitter (-ly).

8564. תַּמְרוּר, **tamrûwr,** *tam-roor´*; from the same root as 8558; an *erection*, i.e. *pillar* (probably for a guide-board):—high heap.

8565. תַּן, **tan,** *tan*; from an unused root probably meaning to *elongate*; a *monster* (as preternaturally formed), i.e. a *sea-serpent* (or other huge marine animal); also a *jackal* (or other hideous land animal):—dragon, whale. Compare 8577.

8566. תָּנָה, **tânâh,** *taw-naw´*; a primitive root; to *present* (a mercenary inducement), i.e. *bargain* with (a harlot):—hire.

8567. תָּנָה, **tânâh,** *taw-naw´*; a primitive root [rather identical with 8566 through the idea of *attributing* honour]; to *ascribe* (praise), i.e. *celebrate, commemorate*:—lament, rehearse.

8568. תַּנָּה, **tannâh,** *tan-naw´*; probably feminine of 8565; a female *jackal*:—dragon.

8569. תְּנוּאָה, **t^{e}nûw'âh,** *ten-oo-aw´*; from 5106; *alienation*; (by implication) *enmity*:—breach of promise, occasion.

8570. תְּנוּבָה, **t^{e}nûwbâh,** *ten-oo-baw´*; from 5107; *produce*:—fruit, increase.

8571. תְּנוּךְ, **t^{e}nûwk,** *ten-ook´*; perhaps from the same as 594 through the idea of *protraction*; a *pinnacle*, i.e. *extremity*:—tip.

8572. תְּנוּמָה, **t^{e}nûwmâh,** *ten-oo-maw´*; from 5123; *drowsiness*, i.e. *sleep*:—slumber (-ing).

8573. תְּנוּפָה, **t^{e}nûwphâh,** *ten-oo-faw´*; from 5130; a *brandishing* (in threat); (by implication) *tumult*; specifically the official *undulation* of sacrificial offerings:—offering, shaking, wave (offering).

A feminine noun meaning swinging, waving, a wave offering, an offering. In a general sense, this word implies the side to side motion involved in waving. It is used specifically as a technical term for the wave offering (Ex 29:24; Le 8:27). Twice the word is taken to mean an offering in general (Ex 38:24, 29).

8574. תַּנּוּר, **tannûwr,** *tan-noor´*; from 5216; a *fire-pot*:—furnace, oven.

8575. תַּנְחוּם, **tanchûwm,** *tan-khoom´*; or תַּנְחֻם, **tanchum,** *tan-khoom´*; and (feminine) תַּנְחוּמָה, **tanchûwmâh,** *tan-khoo-maw´*; from 5162; *compassion, solace*:—comfort, consolation.

8576. תַּנְחֻמֶת, **Tanchumeth,** *tan-khoo´-meth*; for 8575 (feminine); *Tanchumeth*, an Israelite:—Tanhumeth.

8577. תַּנִּין, **tannîyn,** *tan-neen´*; or תַּנִּים, **tannîym,** *tan-neem´*; (Eze 29:3), intensive from the same as 8565; a marine or land *monster*, i.e. *sea-serpent* or *jackal*:—dragon, sea-monster, serpent, whale.

A masculine noun meaning a serpent, a dragon, and a sea monster. It can connote a creature living in the water (Ge 1:21; Job 7:12; Ps 148:7). When the word is used this way, it is also used figuratively to represent the crocodile, which was the symbol of Pharaoh and Egypt (Ps 74:13; Isa 27:1; 51:9; Eze 29:3). This imagery may help us better understand the confrontation between Moses and Pharaoh, when Aaron's staff became a serpent and then swallowed the staff-serpents of Pharaoh's magicians (Ex 7:9, 10, 12). God was providing a graphic sign of what was to come. It can also connote a creature that lives on the land (Dt 32:33; Ps 91:13; Jer 51:34). There is one other occurrence of this term in the OT where it is used as a descriptor or part of a proper name for a well or a spring (Ne 2:13). In all its occurrences, this term has either a neutral (Ge 1:21; Ps 148:7); or a negative meaning (Isa 27:1; 51:9; Jer 51:34). In a few instances, the negative meaning is somewhat lessened, as when God provides a serpent to save His people (Ex 7:9, 10, 12); or when a serpent was divinely restrained (Ps 91:13).

8578. תִּנְיָן, tinyân, *tin-yawn´*; (Chaldee); corresponding to 8147; *second*:—second.

8579. תִּנְיָנוּת, tinyânûwth, *tin-yaw-nooth´*; (Chaldee); from 8578; a *second time*:—again.

8580. תִּנְשֶׁמֶת, tinshemeth, *tan-sheh´-meth*; from 5395; (properly) a hard *breather*, i.e. the name of two unclean creatures, a lizard and a bird (both perhaps from changing colour through their *irascibility*), probably the *tree-toad* and the *water-hen*:—mole, swan.

8581. תָּעַב, tâ'ab, *taw-ab´*; a primitive root; to *loathe*, i.e. (moral) *detest*:—(make to be) abhor (-red), (be, commit more, do) abominable (-y), × utterly.

A verb meaning to abhor, to be abhorrent, to do abominably. This word expresses a strongly detestable activity or the logical response to such an activity. It is associated with a severe sense of loathing (Dt 23:7[8]; 1Ch 21:6); the condition of sinful people (Job 15:16); the activity of idol worship (1Ki 21:26); and the Lord's opposition to sin (Ps 5:6[7]).

8582. תָּעָה, tâ'âh, *taw-aw´*; a primitive root; to *vacillate*, i.e. *reel* or *stray* (literal or figurative); also causative of both:—(cause to) go astray, deceive, dissemble, (cause to, make to) err, pant, seduce, (make to) stagger, (cause to) wander, be out of the way.

A verb meaning to err, to wander, and to go astray. The meaning of this Hebrew word primarily rests in the notion of wandering about (Ex 23:4; Job 38:41). Figuratively, it is used in reference to one who is intoxicated (Isa 28:7). Most often, however, it refers to erring or being misled in a moral or religious sense (Isa 53:6; Eze 44:10[2x]; Hos 4:12).

8583. תֹּעוּ, Tô'ûw, *to´-oo*; or **תֹּעִי, Tô'îy,** *to´-ee*; from 8582; *error*; *Toü* or *Toï*, a Syrian king:—Toi, Tou.

8584. תְּעוּדָה, tᵉ'ûwdâh, *teh-oo-daw´*; from 5749; *attestation*, i.e. a *precept, usage*:—testimony.

A noun meaning a testimony, a custom. This noun is used in Isa 8:16, 20 in combination with the word law. In these verses, the testimony was the law of God's people that instructed them on how to live. In Ru 4:7, this word refers to the common custom of sealing a legal agreement.

8585. תְּעָלָה, tᵉ'âlâh, *teh-aw-law´*; from 5927; a *channel* (into which water is *raised* for irrigation); also a *bandage* or *plaster* (as placed *upon* a wound):—conduit, cured, healing, little river, trench, watercourse.

8586. תַּעֲלוּלִים, ta'ălûwlîym, *tah-al-ool-eem´*; from 5953; *caprice* (as a fit *coming on*), i.e. *vexation*; (concrete) a *tyrant*:—babe, delusion.

8587. תַּעֲלֻמָּה, ta'ălumâh, *tah-al-oo-maw´*; from 5956; a *secret*:—thing that is hid, secret.

8588. תַּעֲנוּג, ta'ănûwg, *tah-an-oog´*; or **תַּעֲנֻג, ta'ănug,** *tah-an-oog´*; and (feminine) **תַּעֲנֻגָה, ta'ănugâh,** *tah-an-oog-aw´*; from 6026; *luxury*:—delicate, delight, pleasant.

8589. תַּעֲנִית, ta'ănîyth, *tah-an-eeth´*; from 6031; *affliction* (of self), i.e. *fasting*:—heaviness.

8590. תַּעֲנָךְ, Ta'ănâk, *tah-an-awk´*; or **תַּעְנָךְ, Ta'nâk,** *tah-nawk´*; of uncertain derivation; *Taanak* or *Tanak*, a place in Palestine:—Taanach, Tanach.

8591. תָּעַע, tâ'a', *taw-ah´*; a primitive root; to *cheat*; (by analogy) to *maltreat*:—deceive, misuse.

8592. תַּעֲצֻמָה, ta'ătsumâh, *tah-ats-oo-maw´*; from 6105; *might* (plural collective):—power.

8593. תַּעַר, ta'ar, *tah´-ar*; from 6168; a *knife* or *razor* (as *making* bare); also a *scabbard* (as *being bare*, i.e. empty):—[pen-] knife, rasor, scabbard, shave, sheath.

8594. תַּעֲרֻבָה, ta'ărubâh, *tah-ar-oo-baw´*; from 6148; *suretyship*, i.e. (concrete) a *pledge*:— + hostage.

8595. תַּעְתֻּעִים, ta'tu'îym, *tah-too´-eem*; from 8591; a *fraud*:—error.

A masculine plural noun meaning mockings, errors. Jeremiah used this word twice when he ridiculed the idols of the Israelites (Jer 10:15; 51:18). These two verses are identical and are found in identical passages. Jeremiah assaulted the idols, saying how worthless they were and that they were works of mockery whose end will be judgment.

8596. תֹּף, tôph, *tofe*; from 8608 contraction; a *tambourine*:—tabret, timbrel.

8597. תִּפְאָרָה, tiph'ârâh, *tif-aw-raw´*; or **תִּפְאֶרֶת, tiph'ereth,** *tif-eh´-reth*; from 6286; *ornament* (abstract or concrete, literal or figurative):—beauty (-iful), bravery, comely, fair, glory (-ious), honour, majesty.

A feminine noun meaning beauty, glory. Isaiah used the word to denote the so-called beauty of finery that would be snatched away by the Lord (Isa 3:18). The word was used in a similar manner in Ezekiel to denote that which the people trusted in other than God, in addition to what would be stripped away (Eze 16:17; 23:26). The making of priestly garments and other apparel brought glory to Aaron and his sons, giving them dignity and honour (Ex 28:2, 40). Wisdom was portrayed as giving a garland of grace and a crown of splendor in Proverbs (Pr 4:9); Zion was told that it will be a crown of splendor in the Lord's hand (Isa 62:3); and in the book of Jeremiah, the king and queen were told that the crowns would fall from their heads (Jer 13:18). The word was used in Deuteronomy to describe how God would recognize His people (Dt 26:19). In Lamentations, it was used in an opposite manner to describe the splendor of Israel that was thrown down from heaven to earth in the Lord's anger (La 2:1). Deborah used the word to describe the honour or glory of a warrior which would not be Barak's because he handled the situation wrongly (Jgs 4:9).

8598. תַּפּוּחַ, tappûwach, *tap-poo´-akh*; from 5301; an *apple* (from its *fragrance*), i.e. the fruit or the tree (probably including others of the *pome* order, as the quince, the orange, etc.):—apple (tree). See also 1054.

8599. תַּפּוּחַ, Tappûwach, *tap-poo´-akh*; the same as 8598; *Tappuäch*, the name of two places in Palestine, also of an Israelite:—Tappuah.

8600. תְּפוֹצָה, tᵉphôwtsâh, *tef-o-tsaw´*; from 6327; a *dispersal*:—dispersion.

8601. תֻּפִינִים, tuppîynîym, *toop-peen-eem´*; from 644; *cookery*, i.e. (concrete) a *cake*:—baked piece.

8602. תָּפֵל, tâphêl, *taw-fale´*; from an unused root meaning to *smear; plaster* (as *gummy*) or *slime*; (figurative) *frivolity*:—foolish things, unsavoury, untempered.

8603. תֹּפֶל, Tôphel, *to´-fel*; from the same as 8602; *quagmire*; *Tophel*, a place near the Desert:—Tophel.

8604. תִּפְלָה, tiphlâh, *tif-law´*; from the same as 8602; *frivolity*:—folly, foolishly.

8605. תְּפִלָּה, tᵉphillâh, *tef-il-law´*; from 6419; *intercession, supplication*; (by implication) a *hymn*:—prayer.

A feminine noun meaning prayer. The word is used to describe a prayer that was similar to a plea (1Ki 8:38; 2Ch 6:29). In Samuel, David is described as having the courage to offer his prayer to God (2Sa 7:27). King Hezekiah was instructed to pray for the remnant that still survived (2Ki 19:4); and in Jeremiah, the word is used to denote what not to do, i.e. do not pray with any plea or petition (Jer 7:16). The word is used by the psalmist as he cried to God to hear his prayer (Ps 4:1[2]). He asked God not to be deaf to his weeping but to take heed to the turmoil His servant was in. In a similar manner, the psalmist again uses the word in a plea to God to hear his prayer and to know that it did not come from deceitful lips (Ps 17:1[2]). The word is also used in Habakkuk as an introduction to the rest of the chapter, indicating that what followed was his prayer (Hab 3:1).

8606. תִּפְלֶצֶת, **tiphletseth,** *tif-leh´-tseth*; from 6426; *fearfulness*:—terrible.

8607. תִּפְסַח, **Tiphsach,** *tif-sakh´*; from 6452; *ford; Tiphsach*, a place in Mesopotamia:—Tipsah.

8608. תָּפַף, **tâphaph,** *taw-faf´*; a primitive root; to *drum*, i.e. play (as) on the tambourine:—taber, play with timbrels.

8609. תָּפַר, **tâphar,** *taw-far´*; a primitive root; to *sew*:—(women that) sew (together).

8610. תָּפַשׂ, **tâphaś,** *taw-fas´*; a primitive root; to *manipulate*, i.e. *seize*; (chiefly) to *capture, wield*; (specifically) to *overlay*; (figurative) to *use* unwarrantably:—catch, handle, (lay, take) hold (on, over), stop, × surely, surprise, take.

8611. תֹּפֶת, **tôpheth,** *to´-feth*; from the base of 8608; a *smiting*, i.e. (figurative) *contempt*:—tabret.

8612. תֹּפֶת, **Tôpheth,** *to´-feth*; the same as 8611; *Topheth*, a place near Jerusalem:—Tophet, Topheth.

8613. תָּפְתֶּה, **Tophteh,** *tof-teh´*; probably a form of 8612; *Tophteh*, a place of cremation:—Tophet.

8614. תִּפְתָּי, **tiphtây,** *tif-taw´ee*; (Chaldee); perhaps from 8199; *judicial*, i.e. a *lawyer*:—sheriff.

8615. תִּקְוָה, **tiqvâh,** *tik-vaw´*; from 6960; (literal) a *cord* (as an *attachment* [compare 6961]); (figurative) *expectancy*:—expectation ([-ted]), hope, live, thing that I long for.

8616. תִּקְוָה, **Tiqvâh,** *tik-vaw´*; the same as 8615; *Tikvah*, the name of two Israelites:—Tikvah.

8617. תְּקוּמָה, **t^eqûwmâh,** *tek-oo-maw´*; from 6965; *resistfulness*:—power to stand.

8618. תְּקוֹמֵם, **t^eqôwmêm,** *tek-o-mame´*; from 6965; an *opponent*:—rise up against.

8619. תָּקוֹעַ, **tâqôwa‘,** *taw-ko´-ah*; from 8628 (in the musical sense); a *trumpet*:—trumpet.

8620. תְּקוֹעַ, **T^eqôwa‘,** *tek-o´-ah*; a form of 8619; *Tekoä*, a place in Palestine:—Tekoa, Tekoah.

8621. תְּקוֹעִי, **T^eqôw‘iy,** *tek-o-ee´*; or תְּקֹעִי, **T^eqô‘iy,** *tek-o-ee´*; patronymic from 8620; a *Tekoïte* or inhabitant of Tekoah:—Tekoite.

8622. תְּקוּפָה, **t^eqûwphâh,** *tek-oo-faw´*; or תְּקֻפָה, **t^equphâh,** *tek-oo-faw´*; from 5362; a *revolution*, i.e. (of the sun) *course*, (of time) *lapse*:—circuit, come about, end.

8623. תַּקִּיף, **taqqîyph,** *tak-keef´*; from 8630; *powerful*:—mightier.

8624. תַּקִּיף, **taqqîyph,** *tak-keef´*; (Chaldee); corresponding to 8623:—mighty, strong.

8625. תְּקַל, **t^eqal,** *tek-al´*; (Chaldee); corresponding to 8254; to *balance*:—Tekel, be weighed.

8626. תָּקַן, **tâqan,** *taw-kan´*; a primitive root; to *equalize*, i.e. *straighten* (intransitive or transitive); (figurative) to *compose*:—set in order, make straight.

8627. תְּקַן, **t^eqan,** *tek-an´*; (Chaldee); corresponding to 8626; to *straighten* up, i.e. *confirm*:—establish.

8628. תָּקַע, **tâqa‘,** *taw-kah´*; a primitive root; to *clatter*, i.e. *slap* (the hands together), *clang* (an instrument); (by analogy) to *drive* (a nail or tent-pin, a dart, etc.); (by implication) to *become bondsman* (by hand-clasping):—blow ([a trumpet]), cast, clap, fasten, pitch [tent], smite, sound, strike, × suretiship, thrust.

A verb meaning to thrust, to fasten, to clap, to blow. The basic idea of this word is a thrust or a burst, such as the wind blowing away locusts (Ex 10:19); the thrusting of a spear through a body (2Sa 18:14); or the driving of a nail into the ground to secure an object, such as a tent (Ge 31:25; Jgs 4:21; Jer 6:3). At times, this word has the connotation of fastening as a pin fastens hair (Jgs 16:14); a nail fastens to a secure place (Isa 22:23, 25); or the fastening of Saul's body to the wall of a pagan temple (1Sa 31:10; 1Ch 10:10). When describing hands, it can denote the clapping of hands in victory (Ps 47:1[2]; Na 3:19); or the clasping of hands in an agreement (Job 17:3; Pr 11:15; 17:18). In the majority of usages, it refers to the blowing of trumpets (Nu 10:3–8; Jos 6:8, 9; Jgs 7:18–20; Joel 2:15).

8629. תֵּקַע, **têqa‘,** *tay-kah´*; from 8628; a *blast* of a trumpet:—sound.

8630. תָּקַף, **tâqaph,** *taw-kaf´*; a primitive root; to *overpower*:—prevail (against).

8631. תְּקֵף, **t^eqêph,** *tek-afe´*; (Chaldee); corresponding to 8630; to *become* (causative, *make*) *mighty* or (figurative) *obstinate*:—make firm, harden, be (-come) strong.

An Aramaic verb meaning to be strong, to grow strong. This word is related to the Hebrew verb *tâqaêph* (8630), meaning to prevail over. It describes the growing strength of the tree in Nebuchadnezzar's dream (Da 4:11[8], 20[17]) that referred to the growing strength of the king (Da 4:22[19]). It was also used to describe the growing arrogance of Belshazzar (Da 5:20). In its only other instance, it describes a strong enforcement of an edict (Da 6:7[8]).

8632. תְּקֹף, **t^eqôph,** *tek-ofe´*; (Chaldee); corresponding to 8633; *power*:—might, strength.

8633. תֹּקֶף, **tôqeph,** *to´-kef*; from 8630; *might* or (figurative) *positiveness*:—authority, power, strength.

8634. תַּרְאֲלָה, **Tar'ălâh,** *tar-al-aw´*; probably for 8653; a *reeling*; *Taralah*, a place in Palestine:—Taralah.

8635. תַּרְבּוּת, **tarbûwth,** *tar-booth´*; from 7235; *multiplication*, i.e. *progeny*:—increase.

8636. תַּרְבִּית, **tarbîyth,** *tar-beeth´*; from 7235; *multiplication*, i.e. *percentage* or *bonus* in addition to principal:—increase, unjust gain.

8637. תִּרְגַּל, **tirgal,** *teer-gal´*; a denominative from 7270; to *cause to walk*:—teach to go.

8638. תִּרְגַּם, **tirgam,** *teer-gam´*; a denominative from 7275 in the sense of *throwing* over; to *transfer*, i.e. *translate*:—interpret.

8639. תַּרְדֵּמָה, **tardêmâh,** *tar-day-maw´*; from 7290; a *lethargy* or (by implication) *trance*:—deep sleep.

8640. תִּרְהָקָה, **Tirhâqâh,** *teer-haw´-kaw*; of foreign derivation; *Tirhakah*, a king of Kush:—Tirhakah.

8641. תְּרוּמָה, **t^erûwmâh,** *ter-oo-maw´*; or תְּרֻמָה, **t^erumâh,** *ter-oo-maw´*; (Dt 12:11), from 7311; a *present* (as offered *up*), especially in *sacrifice* or as *tribute*:—gift, heave offering ([shoulder]), oblation, offered (-ing).

A feminine noun meaning offering. This word comes from the verb *rûm* (7311), meaning to be high or to lift up. The basic idea of this Hebrew noun is something being lifted up, i.e. an offering. It is normally used to describe a variety of offerings: a contribution of materials for building (Ex 25:2; 35:5); an offering of an animal for sacrifice (Ex 29:27; Nu 6:20); a financial offering for the priests (Nu 31:52); an allotment of land for the priests (Eze 45:6, 7); or even the materials for an idol (Isa 40:20). In one instance, this word is used to describe a ruler who received bribes (Pr 29:4).

8642. תְּרוּמִיָּה, **t^erûwmîyyâh,** *ter-oo-mee-yaw´*; formed as 8641; a sacrificial *offering*:—oblation.

A feminine noun meaning an offering, an allotment. This word occurs only once in the OT and is a slightly different form of the word *tĕrûmâh* (8641), meaning offering. In Eze 48:12, it describes the allotment (*tĕrû-miyyâh*) of the allotment of land (*tĕrûmâh*) that will be given to the Levites.

8643. תְּרוּעָה**, tᵉrûwʻâh,** *ter-oo-aw´*; from 7321; *clamour*, i.e. *acclamation* of joy or a *battle-cry*; especially *clangor* of trumpets, as an *alarum*:—alarm, blow (-ing) (of, the) (trumpets), joy, jubile, loud noise, rejoicing, shout (-ing), (high, joyful) sound (-ing).

8644. תְּרוּפָה**, tᵉrûwphâh,** *ter-oo-faw´*; from 7322 in the sense of its congener 7495; a *remedy*:—medicine.

8645. תִּרְזָה**, tirzâh,** *teer-zaw´*; probably from 7329; a species of tree (apparently from its *slenderness*), perhaps the *cypress*:—cypress.

8646. תֶּרַח**, Terach,** *teh´-rakh*; of uncertain derivation; *Terach*, the father of Abraham; also a place in the Desert:—Tarah, Terah.

8647. תִּרְחֲנָה**, Tirchănâh,** *teer-khan-aw´*; of uncertain derivation; *Tirchanah*, an Israelite:—Tirhanah.

8648. תְּרֵין**, tᵉrêyn,** *ter-ane´*; (Chaldee); feminine תַּרְתֵּין**, tartêyn,** *tar-tane´*; corresponding to 8147; *two*:—second, + twelve, two.

8649. תָּרְמָה**, tormâh,** *tor-maw´*; and תַּרְמוּת**, tarmûwth,** *tar-mooth´*; or תַּרְמִית**, tarmîyth,** *tar-meeth´*; from 7411; *fraud*:—deceit (-ful), privily.

8650. תֹּרֶן**, tôren,** *to´-ren*; probably for 766; a *pole* (as a mast or flag-staff):—beacon, mast.

8651. תְּרַע**, tᵉraʻ,** *ter-ah´*; (Chaldee); corresponding to 8179; a *door*; (by implication) a *palace*:—gate mouth.

8652. תָּרָע**, târâʻ,** *taw-raw´*; (Chaldee); from 8651; a *door-keeper*:—porter.

8653. תַּרְעֵלָה**, tarʻêlâh,** *tar-ay-law´*; from 7477; *reeling*:—astonishment, trembling.

8654. תִּרְעָתִי**, Tirʻâthîy,** *teer-aw-thee´*; patrial from an unused name meaning *gate*; a *Tirathite* or inhabitant of an unknown Tirah:—Tirathite.

8655. תְּרָפִים**, tᵉrâphîym,** *ter-aw-feme´*; plural person from 7495; a *healer; Teraphim* (singular or plural) a family idol:—idols (-atry), images, teraphim.

A masculine plural noun meaning household gods, cultic objects, teraphim. This word refers to a kind of idols or objects of worship whose ownership was possibly tied to inheritance rights. They were employed in divination. Rachel stole these objects from her father Laban for some reason not entirely clear to us now, but they were probably not tied to ancestor worship (Ge 31:19, 34). These objects seemed to have had the shape of persons. But in one case, the word refers to something larger than the objects Rachel stole from Laban (1Sa 19:13, 16). Some have suggested that the teraphim used here were old pieces of cloth. The word refers to idols owned by Micah during the time of the judges (Jgs 17:5).

These objects are more strongly condemned in other passages: the wickedness of consulting teraphim is asserted in 1Sa 15:23 (see Eze 21:21[26]; Zec 10:2). Josiah cast them out when he got rid of the mediums and spiritists, literally, the ghosts and familiar spirits (2Ki 23:24).

8656. תִּרְצָה**, Tirtsâh,** *teer-tsaw´*; from 7521; *delightsomeness; Tirtsah*, a place in Palestine; also an Israelitess:—Tirzah.

8657. תֶּרֶשׁ**, Teresh,** *teh´-resh*; of foreign derivation; *Teresh*, a eunuch of Xerxes:—Teresh.

8658. תַּרְשִׁישׁ**, tarshîysh,** *tar-sheesh´*; probably of foreign derivation [compare 8659]; a gem, perhaps the *topaz*:—beryl.

8659. תַּרְשִׁישׁ**, Tarshîysh,** *tar-sheesh´*; probably the same as 8658 (as the region of the stone, or the reverse); *Tarshish*, a place on the Mediterranean, hence the epithet of a *merchant* vessel (as if for or from that port); also the name of a Persian and of an Israelite:—Tarshish, Tharshish.

8660. תִּרְשָׁתָא**, Tirshâthâʼ,** *teer-shaw-thaw´*; of foreign derivation; the title of a Persian deputy or *governor*:—Tirshatha.

8661. תַּרְתָּן**, Tartân,** *tar-tawn´*; of foreign derivation; *Tartan*, an Assyrian:—Tartan.

8662. תַּרְתָּק**, Tartâq,** *tar-tawk´*; of foreign derivation; *Tartak*, a deity of the Avvites:—Tartak.

8663. תְּשֻׁאָה**, tᵉshuʼâh,** *tesh-oo-aw´*; from 7722; a *crashing* or loud *clamour*:—crying, noise, shouting, stir.

8664. תִּשְׁבִּי**, Tishbîy,** *tish-bee´*; patrial from an unused name meaning *recourse*; a *Tishbite* or inhabitant of Tishbeh (in Gilead):—Tishbite.

8665. תַּשְׁבֵּץ**, tashbêts,** *tash-bates´*; from 7660; *checkered* stuff (as *reticulated*):—broidered.

8666. תְּשׁוּבָה**, tᵉshûwbâh,** *tesh-oo-baw´*; or תְּשֻׁבָה**, teshubâh,** *tesh-oo-baw´*; from 7725; a *recurrence* (of time or place); a *reply* (as *returned*):—answer, be expired, return.

8667. תְּשׂוּמֶת**, tᵉśûwmeth,** *tes-oo-meth´*; from 7760; a *deposit*, i.e. *pledging*:— + fellowship.

8668. תְּשׁוּעָה**, tᵉshûwʻâh,** *tesh-oo-aw´*; or תְּשֻׁעָה**, tᵉshuʻâh,** *tesh-oo-aw´*; from 7768 in the sense of 3467; *rescue* (literal or figurative, person, national or spirit):—deliverance, help, safety, salvation, victory.

A feminine noun meaning a deliverance, a victory, safety. Typically, the term is used in the context of military conflict (Jgs 15:18; 1Sa 11:13; 1Ch 11:14). While victory was usually not obtained through human means (Ps 33:17; 108:12[13]; 146:3; Pr 21:31), safety came through a multitude of counselors (Pr 11:14; 24:6). Principally, however, deliverance was to be found only in God (2Ch 6:41; Ps 119:81; 144:10). The deliverance of the Lord was on the minds of both Isaiah and Jeremiah during the troubled times in which they lived (Isa 45:17; 46:13; Jer 3:23; La 3:26).

8669. תְּשׁוּקָה**, tᵉshûwqâh,** *tesh-oo-kaw´*; from 7783 in the original sense of *stretching* out after; a *longing*:—desire.

A feminine noun meaning longing. It was used to describe the strong feelings of desire that one person had for another, but it was not always a healthy desire. As part of the judgment after Adam and Eve's sin, God said that a woman would long for her husband (Ge 3:16). People are not the only thing that can long: God told Cain that sin was lying at his door, desiring to enter (Ge 4:7).

8670. תְּשׁוּרָה**, tᵉshûwrâh,** *tesh-oo-raw´*; from 7788 in the sense of *arrival*; a *gift*:—present.

8671. תְּשִׁיעִי**, tᵉshîyʻîy,** *tesh-ee-ee´*; ordinal from 8672; *ninth*:—ninth.

8672. תֵּשַׁע**, têshaʻ,** *tay´-shah*; or (masculine) תִּשְׁעָה**, tishʻâh,** *tish-aw´*; perhaps from 8159 through the idea of a *turn* to the next or full number ten; *nine* or (ordinal) *ninth*:—nine (+ -teen, + -teenth, -th).

8673. תִּשְׁעִים**, tishʻîym,** *tish-eem´*; multiple from 8672; *ninety*:—ninety.

8674. תַּתְּנַי**, Tattᵉnay,** *tat-ten-ah´ee*; of foreign derivation; *Tattenai*, a Persian:—Tatnai.

AMG's Annotated Strong's Greek Dictionary Of the New Testament

Transliteration of Greek Alphabet

Capital Letter	Lowercase Letter	Greek Name	Trans– literation	Phonetic Sound	Example
Α	α	alpha	a	a	as in father
Β	β	bēta	b	v	as in victory
Γ	γ	gamma	g	y	as in yell (soft gutteral)
Δ	δ	delta	d	th	as in there
Ε	ϵ	epsilon	e	e	as in met
Ζ	ζ	zēta	z	z	as in zebra
Η	η	ēta	ē	ee	as in see
Θ	θ	thēta	th	th	as in thin
Ι	ι	iōta	i	i	as in machine
Κ	κ	kappa	k	k	as in kill (soft accent)
Λ	λ	lambda	l	l	as in land
Μ	μ	mē	m	m	as in mother
Ν	ν	nē	n	n	as in now
Ξ	ξ	xi	x	x	as in wax
Ο	ο	omicron	o	o	as in obey
Π	π	pi	p	p	as in pet (soft accent)
Ρ	ρ	ro	r	r	as in courage
Σ	σ, ς*	sigma	s	s	as in sit
Τ	τ	tau	t	t	as in tell (soft accent)
ϒ	υ	ēpsilon	u	ee	as in see
Φ	ϕ	phi	ph	ph	as in graphic
Χ	χ	chi	ch	h	as in heel
Ψ	ψ	psi	ps	ps	as in ships
Ω	ω	omega	ō	o	as in obey

*At the end of words

Combinations of Consonants

Letters	Name	Transliteration	Phonetic Sound	Example
γγ	gamma + gamma	gg	g	as in go
γκ	gamma + kappa	gk	g	as in go
γχ	gamma + chi	gch	gh	as in ghost

Transliteration of Greek Alphabet

μπ	mē + pi	mp	b	as in boy
ντ	nē + tau	nt	d	as in dog
τζ	tau + zēta	tz	g	as in gym

Diphthongs (double vowels)

αι	alpha + iōta	ai	ai	as in hair
αυ	alpha + ēpsilon	au	af, av	as in waft or lava
ει	epsilon + iōta	ei	ee	as in see
ευ	epsilon + ēpsilon	eu	ef, ev	as in effort or every
ηυ	ēta + ēpsilon	ēu	eef, eev	as in reef or sleeve
οι	omicron + iōta	oi	ee	as in see
ου	omicron + ēpsilon	ou	ou	as in group
υι	ēpsilon + iōta	ui	ee	as in see

Breathing Marks

The smooth breathing mark (ʼ) is not transliterated or pronounced. When words begin with vowels, it may occur at the beginning of words with every vowel or double vowel (diphthong). **ἔργον**—*ergon*, work; **εὐχή**—*euchē*, vow.

The rough breathing mark (ʽ) is represented by an "h" in the transliteration. When words begin with vowels, it may occur at the beginning of words with every vowel or double vowel (diphthong). In modern Greek there is no distinction in pronunciation from the smooth breathing.

When rho or ēpsilon begin a word, they always have the rough breathing. There they are transliterated rh, hu, respectively. **ῥέω**—*rheō*, flow; **ὑπομονή**—*hupomonē*, patience.

Special Symbols

:— (*colon and one-em dash*) are used within each entry to mark the end of the discussion of syntax and meaning of the word under consideration, and to mark the beginning of the list of word(s) used to render it in translation.

() (*parentheses*) denote, in the translation renderings only, a word or syllable given in connection with the principal word it follows.

+ (*addition symbol*) denotes a rendering in translation of one or more Hebrew words in connection with the one under consideration.

× (*multiplication symbol*) denotes a rendering within translation that results from an idiom peculiar to the Greek.

1. Α, α, *al´-fah*; of Hebrew origin; the first letter of the alphabet; figurative only (from its use as a numeral) the *first*:—Alpha. Often used (usually **ἀν *an***, before a vowel) also in composition (as a contraction from 427) in the sense of *privation*; so in many words beginning with this letter; occasionally in the sense of *union* (as a contraction of 260).

2. Ἀαρών, Aarōn, *ah-ar-ohn´*; of Hebrew origin [175]; *Aaron*, the brother of Moses:—Aaron.

3. Ἀβαδδών, Abaddōn, *ab-ad-dohn´*; of Hebrew origin [11]; a destroying *angel*:—Abaddon.

4. ἀβαρής, abarēs, *ab-ar-ace´*; from 1 (as a negative particle) and 922; *weightless*, i.e. (figurative) *not burdensome*:—from being burdensome.

5. Ἀββᾶ, Abba, *ab-bah´*; of Chaldee origin [2]; *father* (as a vocative):—Abba.

6. Ἄβελ, Abel, *ab´-el*; of Hebrew origin [1893]; *Abel*, the son of Adam:—Abel.

7. Ἀβιά, Abia, *ab-ee-ah´*; of Hebrew origin [29]; *Abijah*, the name of two Israelites:—Abia.

8. Ἀβιάθαρ, Abiathar, *ab-ee-ath´-ar*; of Hebrew origin [54]; *Abiathar*, an Israelite:—Abiathar.

9. Ἀβιληνή, Abilēnē, *ab-ee-lay-nay´*; of foreign origin [compare 58]; *Abilene*, a region of Syria:—Abilene.

10. Ἀβιούδ, Abioud, *ab-ee-ood´*; of Hebrew origin [31]; *Abihud*, an Israelite:—Abiud.

11. Ἀβραάμ, Abraam, *ab-rah-am´*; of Hebrew origin [85; *Abraham*, the Hebrew patriarch:—Abraham. [In Ac 7:16 the text should probably read *Jacob*.]

12. ἄβυσσος, abussos, *ab´-us-sos*; from 1 (as a negative particle) and a variation of 1037; *depthless*, i.e. (special) (infernal) "*abyss*":—deep, (bottomless) pit.

13. Ἄγαβος, Agabos, *ag´-ab-os*; of Hebrew origin [compare 2285]; *Agabus*, an Israelite:—Agabus.

14. ἀγαθοεργέω, agathoergeō, *ag-ath-er-gheh´-o*; from 18 and 2041; to *work good*:—do good.

From *agathoergós* (n.f.), doing good, which is from *agathós* (18), benevolent, and *érgon* (2041), work. To do good to others, to work good, i.e. to act for someone's advantage or benefit. (Mk 3:4; Lk 6:9, 35; Ac 6:33; 14:7); also to do well, to act virtuously (1Pe 2:15, 20; 3:6, 17; 3Jn 11).

In Ac 14:17, the UBS text has *agathourgṓn* instead of *agathopoiṓn* as in the TR.

Syn.: *sumphérō* (4851), to cause things to be brought together for the glory of God and the benefit of oneself and others; *kalopoiéō* (2569), to do well and thus show one's good nature; *euergetéō* (2109), to do acts of benevolence instead of just having a benevolent attitude.

15. ἀγαθοποιέω, agathopoieō, *ag-ath-op-oy-eh´-o*; from 17; to *be a well-doer* (as a favour or a duty):—(when) do good (well).

From *agathós* (18), benevolent, and *poiéō* (4160), to make or do. To do good to others (Mk 3:4; Lk 6:9, 33, 35; Ac 14:17; 1Pe 2:15, 20; 3:6, 17).

Deriv.: *agathopoiḯa* (16), benevolence; *agathapoiós* (17), one that does well.

Syn.: *agathoergéō* (14), to do good works; *kalopoiéō* (2569), to do well or show one's good nature by doing good; *euergetéō* (2109), to do an act of benevolence; *sumphérō* (4851), to cause things to be brought together for the glory of God and the benefit of oneself and others.

16. ἀγαθοποιΐα, agathopoiia, *ag-ath-op-oy-ee´-ah*; from 17; *well-doing*, i.e. *virtue*:—well-doing.

17. ἀγαθοποιός, agathopoios, *ag-ath-op-oy-os´*; from 18 and 4160; a *well-doer*, i.e. *virtuous*:—them that do well.

18. ἀγαθός, agathos, *ag-ath-os´*; a primary word; "*good*" (in any sense, often as noun):—benefit, good (-s, things), well. Compare 2570.

Adjective meaning good and benevolent, profitable, useful.

(I) Good, excellent, distinguished, best, of persons (Mt 19:16, 17; Mk 10:17, 18; Lk 18:18, 19; Sept.: 1Sa 9:2); of things (Lk 10:42; Jn 1:46; 2Th 2:16; Sept.: Ezr 8:27).

(II) Good, i.e. of good character, disposition, quality.

(A) Of persons: upright, virtuous (Mt 5:45; 12:35; 25:21, 23; Lk 6:45; 19:17; 23:50; Jn 7:12; Ac 11:24; Sept.: 2Ch 21:13; Pr 13:2, where *agathós* is used as opposed to *paránomos*, unlawful; Pr 15:3; Isa 63:7, a benevolent judge). Of their external conditions, appearance, dress (Mt 22:10).

(B) Of things: **(1)** in a physical sense, e.g., a tree (Mt 7:17, 18); ground (Lk 8:8; Sept.: Ex 3:8). **(2)** in a moral sense, good, upright, virtuous; e.g., heart (Lk 8:15); commandment (Ro 7:12); word (2Th 2:17); will of God (Ro 12:2); the Spirit (Sept.: Ne 9:20; Ps 143:10); good conscience, i.e. conscious of integrity (Ac 23:1; 1Ti 1:5, 19; 1Pe 3:16, 21); good works, deeds, virtue, rectitude (Ro 2:7; 13:3; Eph 2:10; Col 1:10; 2Ti 2:21; 3:17; Tit 1:16; 3:1; Heb 13:21; Sept.: 1Sa 19:4).

(C) Of abstract things: *agathón* (sing.) and *agathá* (pl.), meaning virtue, rectitude, love of virtue (Mt 12:34, 35; 19:16; Lk 6:45; Jn 5:29; Ro 2:10; 3:8; 7:18, 19; 9:11; 12:9; 13:3; 16:19; 2Co 5:10; 1Pe 3:11, 13; 3Jn 11). In Ro 7:13 *tó agathón* means that which is in itself good; Ro 14:16, the good cause, the gospel of Christ; Sept.: Ps 34:14; 53:1, 3.

(III) Good, in respect to operation or influence on others, i.e. useful, beneficial, profitable.

(A) Of persons: benevolent, beneficent (Mt 20:15; Ro 5:7; 1Th 3:6; Tit 2:5; 1Pe 2:18; Sept.: 2Ch 30:19; Ps 73:1).

(B) Of things: e.g., *dómata* (1390), gifts (Mt 7:11; Lk 11:13); *dósis* (1394), gift (Jas 1:17); work (Php 1:6); conduct (1Pe 3:16); fruit (Jas 3:17); fidelity (Tit 2:10); benevolent way (Sept.: 1Sa 12:23); benevolent commandments (Sept.: Ne 9:13). Benevolent treasure or treasure of good things (Mt 12:35; Lk 6:45); good deeds, benefits (Ac 9:36; 2Co 9:8; 1Ti 2:10; 5:10). With the meaning of suitable or adapted to (Ro 15:2; Eph 4:29, word suitable for education).

(C) Of abstract things: *tó agathón*, something useful and profitable, beneficial (Ro 8:28; 12:21; 13:4; Gal 6:10; Eph 4:28; 6:8; 1Th 5:15; Phm 6, 14). In the plural *tá agathá*, things good and useful, benefits, blessings (Mt 7:11; Lk 1:53; 16:25; Gal 6:6; Heb 9:11; 10:1). With the meaning of goods, wealth (Lk 12:18, 19; Sept.: Ge 24:10; 45:18, 20; Dt 6:11).

(IV) Good in respect to the feelings, excited, i.e. pleasant, joyful, happy (1Pe 3:10; Ro 10:15, blessed times; Sept.: Ps 34:12; Zec 8:19).

Deriv.: *agathopoiéo* (15), to do good to others; *agathōsúnē* (19), goodness; *philágathos* (5358), love of good men.

Syn.: *kalós* (2570), constitutionally good but not necessarily benefiting others; *chrēstós* (5543), useful, kind.

19. ἀγαθωσύνη, agathōsunē, *ag-ath-o-soo´-nay*; from 18; *goodness*, i.e. *virtue* or *beneficence*:—goodness.

Noun from *agathós* (18), benevolent. Active goodness.

(I) Of disposition and character, virtue (Ro 15:14; Eph 5:9; 2Th 1:11; Sept.: 2Ch 24:16).

(II) Beneficence, in Gal 5:22 referred to as goodness.

Syn.: *euergesía* (2108), good deed; *cháris* (5485), grace, benefit; *tó agathón* (from *agathós* [18], benevolent), the good action or deed, benefit; *eúnoia* (2133), that which is owed to someone; *eupoiḯa* (2140), the good deeds done; *philanthrōpía* (5363), love for human beings, philanthropy.

20. ἀγαλλίασις, agalliasis, *ag-al-lee´-as-is*; from 21; *exultation*; specially *welcome*:—gladness, (exceeding) joy.

Noun from *agalliáō* (21), to exult. Exultation, exuberant joy. Not found in Gr. writers but often meaning joy, exultation (Sept.: Ps 30:5; 45:15; 65:12, rejoicing with song, dancing. See Ps 126:2, 6); great joy (Ps 45:7; 51:8, 12). In the NT, joy, gladness, rejoicing (Lk 1:14, 44; Ac 2:46; Heb 1:9 from Ps 45:7, oil of gladness with which guests were anointed at feasts, where used as an emblem of the highest honours [cf. Jude 24]).

Syn.: *chará* (5479), joy, delight, the feeling experienced in one's heart, especially a result of God's grace (*cháris* [5485]), whereas *agallíasis* is the demonstration of that joy; *euphrosúnē* (2167), good cheer, joy.

21. ἀγαλλιάω, agalliaō, *ag-al-lee-ah´-o*; from **ἄγαν**, ***agan*** (*much*) and 242; properly to *jump for joy*, i.e. *exult*:—be (exceeding) glad, with exceeding joy, rejoice (greatly).

From *ágan* (n.f.), much, and *hállomai* (242), to leap. To exult, leap for joy, to show one's joy by leaping and skipping denoting excessive or ecstatic joy and delight. Hence in the NT to rejoice, exult. Often spoken of rejoicing with song and dance (Sept.: Ps 2:11; 20:5; 40:16; 68:3). Usually found in the middle deponent *agalliáomai*.

(I) Used in an absolute sense (Ac 2:26, "my tongue was glad," meaning I rejoiced in words, sang aloud; Lk 10:21; Ac 16:34). It is sometimes put after *chaírō* (5463), to rejoice, which is of less intense significance, and produces an expression meaning to rejoice exceedingly (Mt 5:12; 1Pe 4:13; Rev 19:7; see Ps 40:16; 90:14).

(II) With a noun of the same significance in an adverb sense (1 Pet 1:8 with *chará* [5479], joy, "rejoice with joy unspeakable").

(III) Followed by *hína* (2443), so that, with the subjunctive (Jn 8:56, "he rejoiced that he should see my day" [a.t.]).

(IV) Followed by *epí* (1909), upon, with the dat. (Lk 1:47).

(V) Followed by *en* (1722), in, with the dat. where a simple dat. might stand (Jn 5:35; Ac 16:34; 1Pe 1:16; Sept.: Ps 13:5; 89:16).

Deriv.: *agallíasis* (20), exultation.

Syn.: *euphraínō* (2165), to cheer, gladden; *chaírō* (5463), to rejoice; *kaucháomai* (2744), to boast, glory, rejoice; *katakaucháomai* (2620), to glory against.

22. ἄγαμος, agamos, *ag´-am-os*; from 1 (as a negative particle) and 1062; *unmarried*:—unmarried.

23. ἀγανακτέω, aganakteō, *ag-an-ak-teh´-o*; from **ἄγαν**, ***agan*** (*much*) and **ἄχθος**, ***achthŏs*** (*grief*; akin to the base of 43); to *be greatly afflicted*, i.e. (figurative) *indignant*:—be much (sore) displeased, have (be moved with, with) indignation.

24. ἀγανάκτησις, aganaktēsis, *ag-an-ak´-tay-sis*; from 23; *indignation*:—indignation.

25. ἀγαπάω, agapaō, *ag-ap-ah´-o*; perhaps from **ἄγαν**, ***agan*** (*much*) [or compare 5689]; to *love* (in a social or moral sense):—(be-) love (-ed). Compare 5368.

To love. It differs from *philéō* (5368), to love, indicating feelings, warm affection, the kind of love expressed by a kiss (*phílēma* [5370]).

(I) To love, to regard with strong affection (Lk 7:42; Jn 3:35; 8:42; 21:15; 2Co 9:7; Rev 3:9; Sept.: Ge 24:67; Ru 4:15). With the accusative of the corresponding noun, "his great love wherewith he loved us" (Eph 2:4 [cf. 2Sa 13:15]). Perf. pass. part. *ēgapēménos*, beloved (Eph 1:6; Col 3:12).

(II) As referring to superiors and including the idea of duty, respect, veneration, meaning to love and serve with fidelity (Mt 6:24; 22:37; Mk 12:30, 33; Lk 16:13; Ro 8:28; Sept.: 1Sa 18:16). The present act. part. used substantively of those loving the Lord, meaning faithful disciples or followers of the Lord (Eph 6:24; Jas 1:12; 2:5; Sept.: Ex 20:6; Dt 5:10).

(III) To love, i.e. to regard with favour, goodwill, benevolence (Mk 10:21; Lk 7:5; Jn 10:17). In other passages the effects of benevolence are expressed as to wish well to or do good to. To love one's neighbour, one's enemies (Mt 5:43; 19:19; 22:39; Lk 6:32). The fut. imper., *agapḗseis*, especially in regard to one's enemies, should not necessarily be taken to mean doing that which will please them, but choosing to show them favour and goodwill (Mt 5:43, 44). In 2Co 12:15 it means, "even if, having conferred greater benefits on you, I receive less from you" (a.t.).

(IV) Spoken of things: to love, i.e. to delight in (Lk 11:43; Jn 3:19; Heb 1:9; 1Jn 2:15). The expression "not to love" means to neglect, disregard, condemn (Rev 12:11, meaning they condemned their lives even unto death, i.e. they willingly exposed themselves to death).

Deriv.: *agápē* (26), love; *agapētós* (27), beloved, dear.

Syn.: *philéō* (5368), to befriend, love.

26. ἀγάπη, agapē, *ag-ah´-pay*; from 25; *love*, i.e. *affection* or *benevolence*; specially (plural) a *love-feast*:—(feast of) charity ([-ably]), dear, love.

Noun from *agapáō* (25), to love. Love, affectionate regard, goodwill, benevolence.

(I) Generally, love as in 1Co 4:21, "Shall I come unto you with a rod, or in love," meaning full of love, all love; Col 1:13, "the kingdom of his dear Son [the Son of His love]," is the same as *ho agapētós*, beloved son. Spoken especially of goodwill toward others, the love of our neighbour, brotherly affection, which the Lord Jesus commands and inspires (Jn 15:13; 17:26; Ro 13:10; 1Co 13:1; 2Co 2:4, 8; 2Th 1:3; Heb 6:10; 1Pe 4:8; 1Jn 4:7). In 2Co 13:11, "the God of love" means the author and source of love, who Himself is love. In Ro 15:30, "the love of the Spirit" means that love which the Spirit inspires.

(II) Specifically "the love of God" or "of Christ":

(A) Subj. or act., means the love which God or Christ exercises toward Christians. The love that is derived from God (Ro 5:5; Eph 2:4; 2Th 3:5). Followed by *eis* (1519), unto someone (Ro 5:8), and by *en* (1722), in someone (1Jn 4:9, 16). The love of Christ means the love which is derived from Christ (2Co 5:14).

(B) Obj. or pass., that love of which God or Christ is the object in the hearts of Christians. Of God (Lk 11:42; Jn 5:42; 1Jn 2:5). Also used in an absolute sense (1Jn 4:16, 18; 2Jn 6; 3Jn 6). Of Christ (Jn 15:10; Ro 8:35).

(III) Metaphorically, the effect or proof of love, benevolence, benefit conferred (Eph 1:15; 3:19; 1Jn 3:1; 2Th 2:10, "the love of the truth," meaning the true love, the true and real benefits conferred by God through Christ).

(IV) In the plural, *agápai*, love feasts, public banquets of a frugal kind instituted by the early Christian church and connected with the celebration of the Lord's Supper. The provisions were contributed by the more wealthy individuals and were made common to all Christians, whether rich or poor, who chose to partake. Portions were also sent to the sick and absent members. These love feasts were intended as an exhibition of that mutual love which is required by the Christian faith, but as they became subject to abuses, they were discontinued.

Syn.: *philía* (5373), friendship based on common interests; *philanthrōpía* (5363), love for man, philanthropy; *agápai heortḗ* (1859), a feast or festival; *deípnon* (1173), the chief meal of the day, dinner; *dochḗ* (1403), a reception, feast, banquet.

27. ἀγαπητός, agapētos, *ag-ap-ay-tos´*; from 25; *beloved*:—(dearly, well) beloved, dear.

Adjective from *agapáō* (25), to love. Beloved, dear.

(I) Spoken of Christians as united with God or with each other in the bonds of holy love. *Agapētoí*, the plural (Ac 15:25; Ro 12:19; 2Co 7:1; 12:19; Col 1:7; 4:14; 1Th 2:8; 1Ti 6:2; Heb 6:9; 1Pe 2:11; 4:12; 2Pe 3:1, 8, 14, 15, 17; 1Jn 3:2, 21; 4:1, 7, 11; 2Jn 1, 2, 5, 11; Jude 3, 17, 20), meaning conjoined in the bonds of faith and love. In 1Co 15:58, "beloved brethren," i.e. Christians. See Eph 6:21; Php 4:1; Col 4:7, 9; Phm 1, 2, 16; Jas 1:16, 19; 2:5. *Agapētoí Theoú*, beloved of God, means chosen by Him to salvation (Ro 1:7; 11:28; Eph 5:1). *Agapētoí sou*, your beloved, refers to the worshippers of God (Sept.: Ps 60:5; 108:6; 127:2). Paul seems to apply the term particularly to those converted under his ministry when he speaks of *Epaíneton tón agapētón mou* in Ro 16:5. Also see Ro 16:8, 9, 12, "Timotheus, who is my beloved son . . . in the Lord" (cf. 1Co 4:17; 2Ti 1:2). Spoken also of a whole church gathered by Paul (1Co 4:14, "My beloved sons"). See 1Co 10:14; Php 2:12.

(II) The phrase *huiós agapētós* (*huiós* [5207], son; *agapētós*, inherently beloved) means the only son as being the object of peculiar love. In the NT, spoken only of Christ, the Son beloved of God (Mt 3:17; 12:18; 17:5; Mk 1:11; 9:7; Lk 3:22; 9:35; 2Pe 1:17). In Mk 12:6, "one son, his well-beloved," meaning his only son. See Lk 20:13; Sept.: Ge 22:2, 12. The phrase *pénthos agapētoú* (*pénthos* [3997], mourning; *agapētoú*, of a beloved one) e.g., mourning for an only son, i.e. deep sorrow (Jer 6:26; Am 8:10; Zec 12:10).

28. Ἄγαρ, Agar, *ag´-ar*; of Hebrew origin [1904]; *Hagar*, the concubine of Abraham:—Hagar.

29. ἀγγαρεύω, aggareuō, *ang-ar-yew´-o*; of foreign origin [compare 104]; properly to *be a courier*, i.e. (by implication) to *press* into public service:—compel (to go).

To press into service, to send off an *ággaros* or public courier. This word is of Persian origin, and after being received into the Gr. language, passed also into use among the Jews and Romans. The *ággaroi*, couriers, had authority to press into their service men, horses, ships or anything which came in their way and which might serve to hasten their journey. Afterwards *aggareúō* came to mean to press into service for a journey in the manner of an *ággaros*. In the NT, to compel, to press, to accompany one (Mt 5:41; 27:32; Mk 15:21).

Syn.: *anagkázō* (315), to constrain, whether by threat, entreaty, force or persuasion.

30. ἀγγεῖον, aggeion, *ang-eye´-on*; from **ἄγκάλη**, ***aggŏs*** (a *pail*, perhaps as *bent*; compare the base of 43); a *receptacle*:—vessel.

31. ἀγγελία, aggelia, *ang-el-ee´-ah*; from 32; an *announcement*, i.e. (by implication) *precept*:—message.

Noun from *ággelos* (32), messenger. Message (1Jn 3:11; Sept.: Pr 12:25).

Syn.: *akoḗ* (189), the thing heard; *kḗrugma* (2782), proclamation, preaching.

32. ἄγγελος, aggelos, *ang´-el-os*; from **ἀγγέλλω**, ***aggellō***; [probable derivative from 71; compare 34] (to *bring tidings*); a *messenger*; especially an "*angel*"; (by implication) a *pastor*:—angel, messenger.

A noun meaning messenger, one sent to announce or proclaim.

(I) A messenger, one who is sent in order to announce, teach, perform, or explore something (Mt 11:10; Lk 7:24; 9:52; Gal 4:14; Jas 2:25; Sept.: Jos 6:17; Mal 2:7). In 1Co 11:10, *aggélous*, accusative plural, is interpreted variably as spies or angels, good or evil, even demons. The angels of the seven churches are probably the bishops or pastors of those churches, who were the delegates or messengers of the churches to God in the offering of prayer, etc. Others refer this to guardian angels (Rev 1:20; 2:1, 8, 12, 18; 3:1, 7, 14).

(II) An angel, a celestial messenger, a being superior to man. God is represented as surrounded by a host of beings of a higher order than man. These He uses as His messengers and agents in administering the affairs of the world and in promoting the welfare of humans (Mt 1:20; 18:10; 22:30; Ac 7:30). As to the numbers of the angels, see Heb 12:22; Rev 5:11. See *archággelos* (743), archangel. In 2Pe 2:4; Jude 6, some of the angels that sinned are said to have been cast down to hell. They are called the angels of the devil or Satan (Mt 25:41; 2Co 12:7; Rev 12:9). In Rev 9:11, the angel of the bottomless pit is the destroying angel *Abaddṓn* (3), Abaddon.

Deriv.: *aggelía* (31), message; *archággelos* (743), archangel; *isággelos* (2465), like or equal to an angel.

Syn.: *apóstolos* (652), apostle, messenger.

33. ἄγε, age, *ag´-eh*; imperative of 71; properly *lead*, i.e. *come on*:—go to.

34. ἀγέλη, agelē, *ag-el´-ay*; from 71 [compare 32]; a *drove*:—herd.

35. ἀγενεαλόγητος, agenealogētos, *ag-en-eh-al-og´-ay-tos*; from 1 (as negative particle) and 1075; *unregistered* as to birth:—without descent.

Adjective from the priv. *a* (1), without, and *genealogéō* (1075), to trace a genealogy. Without a genealogy or pedigree. Melchizedec was said to be without genealogy (Heb 7:3) because, being a Canaanite, and not standing in the public genealogical registers as belonging to the family of Aaron, he was a priest not by right of sacerdotal descent, but by the grace of God (cf. Ex 40:15; Nu 3:10).

Syn.: *amḗtōr* (282), without the record of a mother; *apátōr* (540), without the record of a father.

36. ἀγενής, agenēs, *ag-en-ace´*; from 1 (as negative particle) and 1085; properly *without kin*, i.e. (of unknown descent, and by implication) *ignoble*:—base things.

37. ἁγιάζω, hagiazō, *hag-ee-ad´-zo*; from 40; to *make holy*, i.e. (ceremony) *purify* or *consecrate*; (mentally) to *venerate*:—hallow, be holy, sanctify.

From *hágios* (40), holy. To make holy, sanctify.

(I) To make clean, render pure.

(A) Particularly in Heb 9:13.

(B) Metaphorically, to render clean in a moral sense, to purify, sanctify (Ro 15:16, "being sanctified by the Holy Ghost," meaning by the sanctifying influences of the Holy Spirit on the heart. See 1Co 6:11; Eph 5:26; 1Th 5:23; 1Ti 4:5; Heb 2:11; 10:10, 14, 29; 13:12; Rev 22:11). *Hoi hēgiasménoi*, those who are sanctified, is a reference to Christians in general (Ac 20:32; 26:18; 1Co 1:2; Jude 1). In 1Co 7:14, the perf. tense *hēgíastai*, has been sanctified, refers to an unbelieving husband or wife who is sanctified by a believing spouse and is to be regarded, not as unclean or as an idolater, but as belonging to the Christian community.

(II) To consecrate, devote, set apart from a common to a sacred use since in the Jewish ritual, this was one great object of the purifications:

(A) Spoken of things (Mt 23:17; 23:19; 2Ti 2:21; Sept.: Le 8:10f., 30).

(B) Spoken of persons: to consecrate as being set apart of God and sent by Him for the performance of His will (Jn 10:36, "whom the father hath sanctified, and sent into the world"; 17:17, "Sanctify them through [or in the promulgation of] thy truth" [cf. Jn 17:18, 19]).

(III) To regard and venerate as holy, to hallow (Mt 6:9; Lk 11:2; 1Pe 3:15; Sept.: Isa 8:13; 10:17; 29:23). Thus the verb *hagiázō*, to sanctify, when its object is something that is filthy or common, can only be accomplished by separation (*aphorízō* [873]) or withdrawal. It also refers to the withdrawal from fellowship with the world and selfishness by gaining fellowship with God.

Deriv.: *hagiasmós* (38), sanctification.

38. ἁγιασμός, hagiasmos, *hag-ee-as-mos´*; from 37; properly *purification*, i.e. (the state) *purity*; concrete (by Hebrew) a *purifier*:—holiness, sanctification.

Noun from *hagiázō* (37), to sanctify. Sanctification, translated "holiness" (Ro 6:19, 22; 1Th 4:7; 1Ti 2:15; Heb 12:14). Separation unto God (in 1Co 1:30, cause or author of sanctification; 2Th 2:13, "sanctification of the Spirit," meaning produced by the Holy Spirit; 1Pe 1:2). The resultant state, the behaviour befitting those so separated (1Th 4:3, 4, resulting in abstention from fornication). There are two other Gr. words which are translated "holiness" but they must be distinguished from *hagiasmós*, sanctification. They are *hagiótēs* (41), the attribute of holiness, and *hagiōsúnē* (42), the state of being sanctified, i.e. sanctification not as a process but as the result of a process. *Hagiasmós* is similar to *dikaíōsis* (1347), justification, which denotes not only the act of God's free grace in justifying sinners, but also the result of that justification upon the sinner in making him just and equipping him to recognize the rights of God on his life. *Hagiasmós* refers not only to the activity of the Holy Spirit in setting man apart unto salvation and transferring him into the ranks of the redeemed, but also to enabling him to be holy even as God is holy (2Th 2:13).

Syn.: *hosiótēs* (3742), the quality of ceremonial conformity; *eusébeia* (2150), piety, godliness; *eilikríneia* (1505), sincerity.

39. ἅγιον, hagion, *hag´-ee-on*; neuter of 40; a *sacred* thing (i.e. spot):—holiest (of all), holy place, sanctuary.

Neuter of the adj. *hágios* (40), holy. Used of those structures set apart for God:

(I) Generally (Ac 6:13; 21:28; Heb 9:1).

(II) Specifically, the sanctuary of the temple of Jerusalem, either terrestrial (Heb 9:2), or heavenly (Heb 9:8, 12, 24; 10:19). Also, *tá hágia hagíōn*, the holy of holies, the inner sanctuary (Heb 9:3).

Syn.: *naós* (3485), the inner part of the temple in Jerusalem; *hierón* (2411), a sacred place, the entire area of the temple.

40. ἅγιος, hagios, *hag´-ee-os*; from **ἅγος**, ***hagos*** (an *awful* thing) [compare 53, 2282]; *sacred* (physical *pure*, moral *blameless* or *religious*, ceremony *consecrated*):—(most) holy (one, thing), saint.

Adjective from *hágos* (n.f.), any matter of religious awe, expiation, sacrifice. Primarily, pure, clean, including the notion of respect and veneration. Holy.

(I) Pure, clean, i.e. ceremonially or morally clean, including the idea of deserved respect, reverence:

(A) Particularly, perfect, without blemish (Ro 12:1).

(**B**) Metaphorically, morally pure, upright, blameless in heart and life, virtuous, holy: (**1**) Generally (Mk 6:20; Ro 7:12; 1Co 7:34; Eph 1:4; 5:27; 1Pe 1:16; Sept.: Le 11:44). (**2**) Spoken of those who are purified and sanctified by the influences of the Spirit, a saint. This is assumed of all who profess the Christian name, hence *hágios*, saint, *hágioi*, saints, Christians (Ac 9:13, 14, 32, 41; 26:10; Ro 1:7; 8:27; 1Th 3:13). Spoken of those who are to be in any way included in the Christian community (1Co 7:14).

(**II**) Consecrated, devoted, sacred, holy, i.e. set apart from a common to a sacred use; spoken of places, temples, cities, the priesthood, men (Mt 4:5; 7:6; 24:15; 27:53; Ac 6:13; 7:33; 1Pe 2:5); of persons (Lk 2:23; Ro 11:16); of apostles (Eph 3:5); of prophets (Lk 1:70; Ac 3:21; 2Pe 1:21); of angels (Mt 25:31).

(**III**) Holy, hallowed, worthy of reverence and veneration. Spoken of God (Jn 17:11; Rev 4:8; 6:10; Sept.: Isa 5:16; 6:3); of His Name (Lk 1:49; Sept.: Le 22:2); of the Holy Spirit (Mt 1:18); of holy covenant (Lk 1:72); of the Holy Scriptures (Ro 1:2; Sept.: Da 11:28, 30).

Deriv.: *hagiázō* (37), to sanctify; *hagiótēs* (41), holiness; *hagiōsúnē* (42), holiness, the quality of sanctification.

Syn.: *hieroprepḗs* (2412), a fitting sanctity; *eusebḗs* (2152), godly, pious; *hósios* (3741), pure from evil contact, ceremonially pure; *áspilos* (784), without spot; *hierós* (2413), sacred, outwardly associated with God; *eilikrinḗs* (1506), sincere, pure.

41. ἁγιότης, hagiotes, *hag-ee-ot´-ace*; from 40; *sanctity* (i.e. properly the state):—holiness.

Noun from *hágios* (40), holy. Holiness. In the NT, used figuratively: sanctity of living, virtue, holiness. Only in Heb 12:10.

Syn.: *hagiōsúnē* (42), the attribute of holiness.

42. ἁγιωσύνη, hagiōsunē, *hag-ee-o-soo´-nay*; from 40; *sacredness* (i.e. properly the quality):—holiness.

Noun from *hágios* (40), holy. Sanctity, virtue (2Co 7:1; 1Th 3:13); the state of him who is deserving of veneration and worship, i.e. sanctity, majesty (Ro 1:4, speaking of Christ's spiritual state of exultation and majesty as Messiah, in contrast to *sárka* [*sárx* {4561} flesh] in the preceding verse).

Syn.: *hagiasmós* (38), sanctification; *hosiótēs* (41), the quality of ceremonial compliance; *eusébeia* (2150), piety, godliness.

43. ἀγκάλη, agkalē, *ang-kal´-ay*; from **ἄγκος, *agkos*** (a *bend*, "ache"); an *arm* (as *curved*):—arm.

44. ἄγκιστρον, agkistron, *ang´-kis-tron*; from the same as 43; a *hook* (as *bent*):—hook.

45. ἄγκυρα, agkura, *ang´-koo-rah*; from the same as 43; an "*anchor*" (as *crooked*):—anchor.

46. ἄγναφος, agnaphos, *ag´-naf-os*; from 1 (as a negative particle) and the same as 1102; properly *unfulled*, i.e. (by implication) *new* (cloth):—new.

47. ἁγνεία, hagneia, *hag-ni´-ah*; from 53; *cleanliness* (the quality), i.e. (special) *chastity*:—purity.

Noun from *hagnós* (53), pure from defilement, not contaminated. Purity, referring to chastity. Used only in 1Ti 4:12; 5:2.

Syn.: *katharótēs* (2514), the state of remaining clean; *katharismós* (2512), the act or process of cleansing, corresponding to *hagnismós* (49), ceremonial purification.

48. ἁγνίζω, hagnizō, *hag-nid´-zo*; from 53; to *make clean*, i.e. (figurative) *sanctify* (ceremony or moral):—purify (self).

From *hagnós* (53), pure. To make clean, purify.

(**I**) To consecrate, purify (Jn 11:55, to prepare one's self by purification for the sacred festivals, which was done by visiting the temple, offering up prayers, abstaining from certain kinds of food, washing the clothes, bathing, shaving the head, etc. [cf. Sept.: Ex 19:10, 14ff.; 2Ch 29:16, 18]).

(**II**) It is used in the middle, *hagnízomai*, perf. and aor. pass. *hḗgnismai, hēgnísthēn* with middle meaning to live as one under a vow of abstinence, i.e. like a Nazarite (Ac 21:24, 26; 24:18). The Jews were accustomed, when under a vow of this kind, to abstain for a certain time from the better kinds of food, to let their hair grow, to keep themselves from all pollution, and so forth. When this time had expired, they were freed from the obligation of their vow by a particular sacrifice (Nu 6:2–21).

(**III**) Metaphorically, to render pure in a moral sense, to reform (Jas 4:8; 1Pe 1:22; 1Jn 3:3).

Deriv.: *hagnismós* (49), ceremonial purification.

Syn.: *katharízō* (2511), to cleanse; *kathaírō* (2508), to cleanse, purge; *ekkathaírō* (1571), to cleanse out, purge from; *diakatharízō* (1245), to cleanse thoroughly.

49. ἁγνισμός, hagnismos, *hag-nis-mos´*; from 48; a *cleansing* (the act), i.e. (ceremony) *lustration*:—purification.

Noun from *hagnízō* (48), to consecrate. Act of consecration, purification of the Levites (Nu 8:7; 31:23; see 6:9–13). In the NT, religious abstinence in consequence of a vow. Only in Ac 21:26.

Syn.: *katharismós* (2512), the act of cleansing; *katharótēs* (2514), the result or state of cleansing.

50. ἀγνοέω, agnoeō, *ag-no-eh´-o*; from 1 (as a negative particle) and 3539; *not to know* (through lack of information or intelligence); (by implication) to *ignore* (through disinclination):—(be) ignorant (-ly), not know, not understand, unknown.

From the priv. *a* (1), not, and *noéō* (3539), to perceive, understand. Not to recognize or know.

(**I**) To be ignorant of, unacquainted with (Ac 17:23; Ro 6:3; 7:1; 10:3; 11:25; 2Co 2:11; Gal 1:22); spoken of voluntary ignorance (1Co 14:38), where others prefer the meaning "to act foolishly," as in Sept.: Nu 12:11; not to understand or comprehend (Mk 9:32; Lk 9:45; Ro 2:4; 10:3); not to acknowledge or receive, i.e. to reject (Ac 13:27; 17:23), pass. unknown, i.e. rejected (2Co 6:9).

(**II**) To sin, to do wrong, originally with the idea of its being done ignorantly and involuntarily, but in the NT this idea no longer remains (Heb 5:2, those who commit sin; 2Pe 2:12, things they know not).

Deriv.: *agnóēma* (51), mistake, oversight, sin resulting from ignorance; *ágnoia* (52), ignorance.

Syn.: *lanthánō* (2990), to be hidden, concealed, unknown.

51. ἀγνόημα, agnoēma, *ag-no´-ay-mah*; from 50; a thing *ignored*, i.e. *shortcoming*:—error.

Noun from *agnoéō* (50) not to know, ignore. Error, ignorance, involuntary error (Sept.: Ge 43:12). In the NT, sin, error. Only in Heb 9:7.

Syn.: *hamartía* (266), sin.

52. ἄγνοια, agnoia, *ag´-noy-ah*; from 50; *ignorance* (properly the quality):—ignorance.

Noun from *agnoéō* (50), not to know. Want of knowledge, ignorance (Ac 3:17). Spoken of ignorance of God and divine things (Ac 17:30; Eph 4:18; 1Pe 1:14).

53. ἁγνός, hagnos, *hag-nos´*; from the same as 40; properly *clean*, i.e. (figurative) *innocent, modest, perfect*:—chaste, clean, pure.

Adjective. Akin to *hágios* (40), holy. Pure, clean. In the NT, used figuratively:

(**I**) Pure, perfect, holy. Of God (1Jn 3:3); of His wisdom (Jas 3:17; Sept.: Ps 12:1; 19:11).

(**II**) Innocent, blameless (2Co 7:11; Php 4:8; 1Ti 5:22).

(**III**) Modest, chaste (2Co 11:2; Tit 2:5; 1Pe 3:2).

Deriv.: *hagneía* (47), purity, cleanliness; *hagnízō* (48), to make clean, purify; *hagnótēs* (54), cleanness, pureness; *hagnṓs* (55), purely, sincerely.

Syn.: *alēthinós* (228), true; *gnḗsios* (1103), genuine; *apseudḗs* (893), true; *ádolos* (97), unadulterated; *katharós* (2513), clean; *amíantos* (283), undefiled; *áspilos* (784), unspotted; *haploús* (573), single, clear; *eilikrinḗs* (1506), sincere; *akéraios* (185), harmless, innocent; *ádolos* (97), without deceit.

54. ἁγνότης, hagnotēs, *hag-not´-ace*; from 53; *cleanness* (the state), i.e. (figurative) *blamelessness*:—pureness.

Noun from *hagnós* (53), pure. Purity, sincerity (2Co 6:6). In 2Co 11:3 UBS *hagnótēs* occurs with *haplótēs* (572), sincerity, simpleness, the opposite of duplicity, whereas the TR has only *haplótēs*. *Haplótēs* refers to sincerity, *eilikríneia* (1505), as part of the character of a person and not necessarily its influence on others.

Syn.: *hagneía* (47), purity; *katharótēs* (2514), cleanness, purification.

55. ἁγνῶς, hagnōs, *hag-noce´*; adverb from 53; *purely*, i.e. *honestly*:—sincerely.

Adverb from *hagnós* (53), chaste. Purely, sincerely. In Php 1:16, it refers to the simplicity of spirit with the absence of selfish motives. Therefore, *hagnō̃s* can really mean without duplicity.

Syn.: *haplō̃s* (5740, simply, without duplicity).

56. ἀγνωσία, agnōsia, *ag-no-see´-ah*; from 1 (as negative particle) and 1108; *ignorance* (properly the state):—ignorance, not the knowledge.

Noun from the priv. *a* (1), without, and *gnō̃sis* (1108), knowledge. Ignorance. In Class. Gr., it meant not being acquainted with something. In the NT, used figuratively: willful ignorance, blindness (1Co 15:34, contempt of God [cf. Eph 2:12; 1Pe 2:15; Sept.: Job 35:16]).

Syn.: *ágnoia* (52), ignorance.

57. ἄγνωστος, agnōstos, *ag´-noce-tos*; from 1 (as negative particle) and 1110; *unknown*:—unknown.

Adjective from the priv. *a* (1), not, and *gnōstós* (1110), known. Unknown (Ac 17:23).

Syn.: *apókruphos* (614), hidden, kept secret; *kruptós* (2927), private, concealed secret; *ádēlos* (82), indistinct, uncertain; *aphanḗs* (852), unapparent; *árrētos* (731), unsaid, unspeakable, inexpressible.

58. ἀγορά, agora, *ag-or-ah´*; from **ἀγείρω**, *ageiro* (to *gather*; probably akin to 1453); properly the *town-square* (as a place of public resort); (by implication) a *market* or *thoroughfare*:—market (-place), street.

Noun from *ageírō* (n.f.), to collect, gather. A place in which the people assemble, assembly.

(I) The place of meeting, a public place, a broad street, and so forth (Mt 11:16; 20:3; 23:7; Mk 6:56; 12:38; Lk 7:32; 11:43; 20:46; see Sept.: Ecc 12:4, 5).

(II) A forum, a marketplace where things were exposed for sale and where assemblies and public trials were held (Mk 7:4; Ac 16:19; 17:17).

Deriv.: *agorázō* (59), to buy; *agoraíos* (60), relating to the marketplace, a vulgar person.

Syn.: *plateía* (4113), broadway, square; *ámphodon* (296), an open place where two streets meet, the open street.

59. ἀγοράζω, agorazō, *ag-or-ad´-zo*; from 58; properly to *go to market*, i.e. (by implication) to *purchase*; specially to *redeem*:—buy, redeem.

From *agorá* (58), marketplace. To buy, to purchase:

(I) Particularly (Mt 13:44, 46; 14:15; 25:9, 10; 27:7; Mk 6:36, 37; 15:46; 16:1; Lk 9:13; 14:18, 19; 22:36; Jn 4:8; 6:5; Sept.: Ge 41:57; Isa 24:2).

(II) Metaphorically, to redeem, to acquire for one's self by a ransom or price paid; in the NT, spoken of those whom Christ has redeemed by his blood from the bondage of sin and death (1Co 6:20; 7:23; 2Pe 2:1; Rev 14:3, 4).

Deriv.: *exagorázō* (1805), to buy out, especially to purchase a slave for his freedom.

Syn.: *ōnéomai* (5608), to buy; *emporeúomai* (1710), to trade, both buying and selling; *ktáomai* (2932), to obtain; *peripoiéō* (4046), to gain, possess, purchase; *lutróō* (3084), to release on receipt of ransom, redeem.

60. ἀγοραῖος, agoraios, *ag-or-ah´-yos*; from 58; *relating to the market-place*, i.e. *forensic* (times); (by implication) *vulgar*:—baser sort, low.

61. ἄγρα, agra, *ag´-rah*; from 71; (abstract) a *catching* (of fish); also (concrete) a *haul* (of fish):—draught.

62. ἀγράμματος, agrammatos, *ag-ram-mat-os*; from 1 (as negative particle) and 1121; *unlettered*, i.e. *illiterate*:—unlearned.

63. ἀγραυλέω, agrauleō, *ag-row-leh´-o*; from 68 and 832 (in the sense of 833); to *camp out*:—abide in the field.

64. ἀγρεύω, agreuō, *ag-rew-´o*; from 61; to *hunt*, i.e. (figurative) to *entrap*:—catch.

65. ἀγριέλαιος, agrielaios, *ag-ree-el´-ah-yos*; from 66 and 1636; an *oleaster*:—olive tree (which is) wild.

66. ἄγριος, agrios, *ag´-ree-os*; from 68; *wild* (as pertaining to the *country*), literal (*natural*) or figurative (*fierce*):—wild, raging.

67. Ἀγρίππας, Agrippas, *ag-rip´-pas*; apparently from 66 and 2462; *wild-horse* tamer; *Agrippas*, one of the Herods:—Agrippa.

68. ἀγρός, agros, *ag-ros´*; from 71; a *field* (as a *drive* for cattle); generically the *country*; specially a *farm*, i.e. *hamlet*:—country, farm, piece of ground, land.

69. ἀγρυπνέω, agrupneō, *ag-roop-neh´-o*; ultimately from 1 (as negative particle) and 5258; to *be sleepless*, i.e. *keep awake*:—watch.

70. ἀγρυπνία, agrupnia, *ag-roop-nee´-ah*; from 69; *sleeplessness*, i.e. a *keeping awake*:—watch.

71. ἄγω, agō, *ag´-o*; a primary verb; properly to *lead*; (by implication) to *bring, drive,* (reflexive) *go*, (special) *pass* (time), or (figurative) *induce*:—be, bring (forth), carry, (let) go, keep, lead away, be open.

To lead, lead along, bring, carry, remove.

(I) Transitively or in an absolute sense, to lead, conduct, bring:

(A) Used in a variety of modifications which are determined by adjuncts. **(1)** *Ágō éxō* (1854) out, to lead out, bring forth (Jn 19:4, 13). **(2)** Followed by *héōs* (2193), until (Lk 4:29; Ac 17:15). **(3)** Used with *epí* (1909), upon, with the accusative of person or place, to lead or conduct, bring before (Mt 10:18; Lk 21:12; 23:1; Ac 17:19; 18:12; Sept.: Ex 22:13; Jer 25:9; Eze 43:1). See in Ac 8:32, *epí sphagḗn* (*sphagḗn* [4967], slaughter), for the purpose of slaughtering, in fulfillment of Isa 53:7. **(4)** Followed by *hō̃de* (5602), hither, to bring hither (Lk 19:27; Sept.: Jgs 18:3). **(5)** To lead or bring to anyone, followed by *prós* (4314), toward (Lk 4:40; 18:40; 19:35; Jn 1:42; 8:3; 9:13; Ac 9:27; 23:18; Sept.: Ge 2:19, 22). Used in the same sense with the dat. in Mt 21:2, *agageté moi*, bring to me. The verb is also used by itself in the same sense as to bring (Mt 21:7; Mk 11:2, 7; Lk 19:30; Jn 7:45; 10:16; Ac 5:21, 26, 27; 19:37; 20:12; 25:6, 17, 23). **(6)** To bring with one (Ac 21:16, "brought with them one Mnason of Cyprus"; 1Th 4:14, "will God bring with him" meaning into heaven, see 1Th 4:17; 2Ti 4:11, "bring him with thee"). **(7)** To lead out or away; either simply (Mk 13:11; Lk 22:54; 23:32); or followed by *eis* (1519), unto, with the accusative of place, and so forth, lead away to, conduct to (Lk 4:1, 9; 10:34; Jn 18:28; Ac 6:12; 9:2; 11:26; 21:34; 22:5; 23:10, 31). In Ac 17:5, "to bring them out to the people"; Heb 2:10, "unto glory." Followed by *epí* (1909), upon, unto (Ac 9:21, "bring them bound unto the chief priests"). **(8)** Similar to the Hebrew *bō* (935, OT), to bring forth, i.e. to cause to come, cause to arise as in Ac 13:23 UBS, "raised unto Israel a Saviour, Jesus," instead of *égeire*, the aor. of *egeírō* (1453), to raise, as in the TR. Also Sept.: Isa 46:11; Zec 3:8.

(B) Metaphorically, to lead, induce, incite, guide (Ro 2:4, "to repentance"; 1Co 12:2, "even as ye were led," meaning to idolatry, the figure being drawn from pastoral life [cf. Ex 3:1; Isa 11:6]). Also, to be led by the Spirit of God (Ro 8:14; Gal 5:18); by lusts (2Ti 3:6).

(II) Transitively spoken of time:

(A) To pass, to spend. Lk 24:21, "today is the third day," where *ágei* is either impersonal or the word *chrónos* (5550), time, is implied.

(B) To celebrate, hold, e.g., a birthday (Mt 14:6); judicial days (Ac 19:38), which were held in the marketplace; see Sept.: Est 9:18, 19, 21, 22.

(III) Intransitively or reflexively, to go, depart, with *hēmás heautoús* implied meaning "Let us go" (Mk 14:42 [cf. Mt 26:46; Jn 11:16]). Followed by *enteúthen* (1782), hence, from here (Jn 14:31); followed by *eis* (1519), unto (Mk 1:38; Jn 11:7); followed by *prós* (4314), toward (Jn 11:15).

Deriv.: *agélē* (34), a herd; *agōgḗ* (72), course of life, manner of leading or spending it; *anágō* (321), to bring, lead, carry, or take up; *áxios* (514), to estimate or value; *apágō* (520), to lead, carry or take away; *diágō* (1236), to lead one's life, to live; *doulagōgéō* (1396), to bring into subjection; *eiságō* (1521), to bring in, introduce; *exágō* (1806), to lead forth or bring out; *epágō* (1863), to bring upon; *hēgéomai* (2233), to lead, consider; *katágō* (2609), to bring down; *metágō* (3329), to turn about; *parágō* (3855), to depart, pass away; *periágō* (4013), to lead about; *proágō* (4254), to go before, lead, precede; *proságō* (4317), to bring or come to, to bring; *stratēgós* (4755), the leader, commander of an army; *sulagōgéō* (4812), to lead off as prey; *sunágō* (4863), to bring together, assemble; *hupágō* (5217), to depart, go away; *chalinagōgéō* (5468), to bridle; *cheiragōgós* (5497), one who leads another by the hand.

Syn.: *phérō* (5342), to carry, bear, lead; *hodēgéō* (3594), to lead the way, guide; *komízō* (2865), to receive, bring in; *aírō* (142), to take away; *anaphérō* (399), to offer up; *eisphérō* (1533), to carry or bring in.

72. ἀγωγή, agōgē, *ag-o-gay´*; reduplication from 71; a *bringing* up, i.e. *mode of living*:—manner of life.

73. ἀγών, agōn, *ag-one´*; from 71; properly a place of *assembly* (as if *led*), i.e. (by implication) a *contest* (held there); (figurative) an *effort* or *anxiety*:—conflict, contention, fight, race.

A noun meaning place of assembly, where games were often celebrated; a stadium, course, place of contest. In the NT:

(I) Metaphorically, a stadium, a place of contest, used to mean a course of life full of toil and conflict (Heb 12:1).

(II) A contest, combat; particularly a conflict in the public games. In the NT, metaphorically, spoken of unwearied zeal in promoting the spread of the gospel; generally (1Ti 6:12; 2Ti 4:7), and with the accessory idea of peril, toil, affliction (Php 1:30; Col 2:1; 1Th 2:2 [cf. Mt 26:37, 38; Jn 12:27]).

Deriv.: *agōnía* (74), agony; verb: *agōnízomai* (75), to contend.

Syn.: *áthlēsis* (119), combat, contest of athletes, a struggle or fight; *pólemos* (4171), war; *máchē* (3163), a fight, strife; *pálē* (3823), wrestling; *kópos* (2873), labour, weariness; *móchthos* (3449), painfulness, travail; *talaipōría* (5004), misery.

74. ἀγωνία, agōnia, *ag-o-nee´-ah*; from 73; a *struggle* (properly the state), i.e. (figurative) *anguish*:—agony.

Noun from *agṓn* (73), contest. In the NT, used metaphorically for anguish, agony, or perturbation of mind (Lk 22:44).

Syn.: *stenochōría* (4730), anguish, distress; *sunochḗ* (4928), anxiety, anguish; *phóbos* (5401), fear; *tarachḗ* (5016), disturbance, trouble; *súgchusis* (4799), riotous disturbance, confusion; *thórubos* (2351), disturbance, uproar; *anágkē* (318), distress.

75. ἀγωνίζομαι, agōnizomai, *ag-o-nid´-zom-ahee*; from 73; to *struggle*, literally (to *compete* for a prize), figurativ (to *contend* with an adversary), or genitive (to *endeavour* to accomplish something):—fight, labour fervently, strive.

From *agṓn* (73), conflict. To be a combatant in the public games (1Co 9:25); to fight, to contend with an adversary (Jn 18:36); to exert oneself, to strive earnestly (Lk 13:24; Col 1:29; 4:12); also used metaphorically, with the idea of labour and toil in behalf of the cause of Christ (1Ti 6:12; 2Ti 4:7).

Deriv.: *antagōnízomai* (464), to antagonize, strive against; *epagōnízomai* (1864), to contend; *katagōnízomai* (2610), to subdue; *sunagōnízomai* (4865), to struggle in company with, strive together with.

Syn.: *epilambánomai* (1949), to lay hold upon, take hold of, help; *kópiáō* (2872), to toil, feel fatigue; *ergázomai* (2038), to work; *kóptomai* (2875), to beat the breast in grief, lament; *máchomai* (3164), to fight, strive; *poleméō* (4170), to carry on a war, fight; *athléō* (118), to contend in competitive games, strive; *strateúomai* (4754), to contend, be a soldier, go to war; *hoplízomai* (3695), to equip with weapons, arm oneself.

76. Ἀδάμ, Adam, *ad-am´*; of Hebrew origin [121]; *Adam*, the first man; typical (of Jesus) *man* (as his representative):—Adam.

77. ἀδάπανος, adapanos, *ad-ap´-an-os*; from 1 (as negative particle) and 1160; *costless*, i.e. *gratuitous*:—without expense.

78. Ἀδδί, Addi, *ad-dee´*; probably of Hebrew origin [compare 5716]; *Addi*, an Israelite:—Addi.

79. ἀδελφή, adelphē, *ad-el-fay´*; feminine of 80; a *sister* (native or ecclesiastical):—sister.

80. ἀδελφός, adelphos, *ad-el-fos´*; from 1 (as a connective particle) and **δελφύς**, ***delphus*** (the *womb*); a *brother* (literal or figurative) near or remote [much like 1]:—brother.

Noun from the collative *a* (1), denoting unity, and *delphús* (n.f.), a womb.

(I) A brother, whether derived from the same father (Mt 1:2; Lk 3:1, 19) or also born of the same mother (Lk 6:14).

(II) Metaphorically, one who is connected with another in any kind of intimacy or fellowship:

(A) A near relative, a kinsman by blood, cousin (Mt 12:46; Jn 7:3; Ac 1:14; Gal 1:19; Sept.: Ge 13:8; 14:16).

(B) One born in the same country, descended from the same stock; a fellow countryman (Mt 5:47; Ac 3:22; Heb 7:5; Sept.: Ex 2:11; 4:18).

(C) One of equal rank and dignity (Mt 23:8; cf. Sept.: Pr 18:9).

(D) Spoken of disciples, followers, etc. (Mt 25:40; Heb 2:11, 12).

(E) One of the same faith, a fellow Christian (Ac 9:30; 1Co 5:11).

(F) An associate, colleague, in office or dignity (1Co 1:1; 2Co 1:1; 2:12; Sept.: Ezr 3:2).

(G) One of the same nature, fellow man (Mt 5:22–24; 7:5; Heb 2:17; 8:11; Sept.: Ge 13:11; 26:31).

(H) By implication, one beloved as a brother (Ac 2:29; 6:3; 1Th 5:1).

Deriv.: *adelphótēs* (81), brotherhood; *philádelphos* (5361), one who loves his brother; *pseudádelphos* (5569), false brother.

Syn.: *súntrophos* (4939), companion; *suggenḗs* (4773), relative.

81. ἀδελφότης, adelphotēs, *ad-el-fot´-ace*; from 80; *brotherhood* (properly the feeling of *brotherliness*), i.e. the (Christian) *fraternity*:—brethren, brotherhood.

Noun from *adelphós* (80), brother. Brotherly affection. In the NT, a fraternity, the Christian brotherhood (1Pe 2:17; 5:9).

82. ἄδηλος, adēlos, *ad´-ay-los*; from 1 (as a negative particle) and 1212; *hidden*, (figurative) *indistinct*:—appear not, uncertain.

83. ἀδηλότης, adēlotēs, *ad-ay-lot´-ace*; from 82; *uncertainty*:—× uncertain.

84. ἀδήλως, adēlōs, *ad-ay´-loce*; adverb from 82; *uncertainly*:—uncertainly.

85. ἀδημονέω, adēmoneō, *ad-ay-mon-eh´-o*; from a derivative of **ἀδέω**, ***adeō*** (to be *sated* to loathing); to *be in distress* (of mind):—be full of heaviness, be very heavy.

86. ᾅδης, haidēs, *hah´-dace*; from 1 (as a negative particle) and 1492; properly *unseen*, i.e. "*Hades*" or the place (state) of departed souls:—grave, hell.

Noun from the priv. *a* (1), not, and *idein*, the inf. of the 2d aor. *eidō* (1492), to see. What is in darkness; hence in Class. Gr., orcus, the infernal regions. Used very frequently in the Sept. to translate the Heb šeʾôl ([7585, OT] e.g., Sept.: Isa 14:9). So also in the NT, the abode or world of the dead, hades, orcus. According to the notions of the Hebrews, hades was a vast subterranean receptacle where the souls of the dead existed in a separate state until the resurrection of their bodies. The region of the blessed during this interval, the inferior paradise, they supposed to be in the upper part of this receptacle; while beneath was the abyss or Gehenna, Tartarus, in which the souls of the wicked were subjected to punishment.

(I) Generally (Ac 2:27, 31; Rev 1:18). In this sense *hádēs* is personified (1Co 15:55; Rev 6:8; 20:13, 14). In a metaphorical sense, to be cast down to the very lowest place (Mt 11:23; Lk 10:15).

(II) By metonymy of the whole for a part, the abyss of hades, place of punishment (Lk 16:23).

Syn.: *Géenna* (1067), the final destiny of the wicked, hell; *tartaróō* (5020), the prison of the fallen angels or evil spirits; *ábussos* (12), abyss, the place where the dragon (*drákōn* [1404]), i.e. Satan, is bound during the millennial reign (cf. Lk 8:31; Rev 9:11); *límnē* (3041) and *toú purós* (4442), lake of fire, the place into which the beast and the false prophet are cast after their defeat by Christ. An additional statement in Rev 21:8 describes those who have their part in the lake of fire, compare the description of those who are outside the city (Rev 22:15).

87. ἀδιάκριτος, adiakritos, *ad-ee-ak´-ree-tos*; from 1 (as a negative particle) and a derivative of 1252; properly *undistinguished*, i.e. (active) *impartial*:—without partiality.

Adjective from *a* (1), without, and *diakrínō* (1252), to separate, distinguish, judge. Indistinguishable. In the NT, used metaphorically: not open to distinction or doubt, unambiguous. Only in Jas 3:17, translated "without partiality."

Syn.: *díkaios* (1342), just.

88. ἀδιάλειπτος, adialeiptos, *ad-ee-al´-ipe-tos*; from 1 (as a negative particle) and a derivative of a compound of 1223 and 3007; *unintermitted*, i.e. *permanent*:—without ceasing, continual.

89. ἀδιαλείπτως, adialeiptōs, *ad-ee-al-ipe´-toce*; adverb from 88; *uninterruptedly*, i.e. *without omission* (on an appropriate occasion):—without ceasing.

90. ἀδιαφθορία, adiaphthoria, *ad-ee-af-thor-ee´-ah*; from a derivative of a compound of 1 (as a negative particle) and a derivative of 1311; *incorruptibleness*, i.e. (figurative) *purity* (of doctrine):—uncorruptness.

91. ἀδικέω, adikeō, *ad-ee-keh´-o*; from 94; to *be unjust*, i.e. (active) *do wrong* (moral, socially or physical):—hurt, injure, be an offender, be unjust, (do, suffer, take) wrong.

From *ádikos* (94), unjust. To do wrong, to act unjustly; to hurt, damage, harm.

(I) To do wrong:

(A) In respect to law, to break the law, to transgress (Ac 25:10, 11; 2Co 7:12; Col 3:25; Rev 22:11; Sept.: 1Ki 8:47; 2Ch 26:16; Ps 106:6; Jer 37:18).

(B) In respect to others, to wrong, to injure (Mt 20:13; Ac 7:26, 27; 1Co 6:8; 2Co 7:2; Gal 4:12; Phm 18). In a pass. sense, to be wronged, to suffer wrong or injury (Ac 7:24; 2Co 7:12). In the middle voice, to suffer one's self to be wronged (1Co 6:7).

(II) By metonymy, to hurt, damage, harm (Lk 10:19; Rev 2:11; 6:6; 7:2, 3; 9:4, 10, 19; 11:5; Sept.: Le 6:2; Isa 3:15; 10:20; 51:23).

Deriv.: *adíkēma* (92), a misdeed, an injury.

Syn.: *bláptō* (984), to injure, damage; *kakóō* (2559), to harm; *kakouchéō* (2558), to mistreat; *parabaínō* (3845), to transgress; *paranoméō* (3891), to act contrary to law; *zēmióō* (2210), to suffer loss; *lumaínomai* (3705), to cause havoc; *páschō* (3958), to suffer.

92. ἀδίκημα, adikēma, *ad-eek´-ay-mah*; from 91; a *wrong* done:—evil doing, iniquity, matter of wrong.

Noun from *adikéō* (91), to act unjustly. Wrong, transgression, iniquity (Ac 18:14; 24:20; Rev 18:5; Sept.: 1Sa 20:1; 26:18; 2Sa 22:49; Isa 59:12).

Syn.: *adikía* (93), wrong, the act of injustice; *húbris* (5196), injurious treatment, hurt; *tó kakón* (the neuter of *kakós* [2556] with the article), an evil thing, harm; *anomía* (458), violation of law.

93. ἀδικία, adikia, *ad-ee-kee´-ah*; from 94; (legal) *injustice* (properly, the quality; by implication, the act); moral *wrongfulness* (of character, life or act):—iniquity, unjust, unrighteousness, wrong.

Noun from *ádikos* (94), unjust. Injustice.

(I) Wrong, injustice, unrighteousness: generally (Lk 18:6; Ro 9:14); as done to others, wrong, injury (2Co 12:13; Sept.: Ps 7:3; Mic 3:10).

(II) As related to *dikaiosúnē* (1343), righteousness, which is often used to describe character of life, *adikía* takes by antithesis the sense of impropriety, iniquity, unrighteousness, wickedness (Lk 13:27; Ac 1:18; Ro 1:29; 3:5; 6:13; 2Ti 2:19; Heb 8:12; Jas 3:6; 2Pe 2:13; 1Jn 1:9; 5:17). This wickedness or unrighteousness is seen more particularly in the neglect of the true God and His laws and in an adherence to the world or to idolatry; hence, *adikía* may mean impiety, ungodliness, contempt of God, as opposed to *alḗtheia* ([225], truth), piety toward God. In Ro 1:18, those "who hold the truth in unrighteousness," are those who impede the worship of the true God by their obstinate adherence to worldliness or to idolatry (Ro 2:8; 2Th 2:10, 12; 2Pe 2:15).

(III) In the sense of fraud, deceit, guile (Jn 7:18); a dishonest steward (Lk 16:8); wealth fraudulently acquired (Lk 16:9).

Syn.: *hamartía* (266), sin, missing the mark, *ponēría* (4189), wickedness; *kríma* (2917), condemnation, judgement; *égklēma* (1462), crime; *anomía* (458), lawlessness; *paranomía* (3892), transgression, iniquity.

94. ἄδικος, adikos, *ad´-ee-kos*; from 1 (as a negative particle) and 1349; *unjust*; by extension *wicked*; (by implication) *treacherous*; specially *heathen*:—unjust, unrighteous.

Adjective from the priv. *a* (1), without, and *díkē* (1349), justice. Unjust.

(I) Unjust toward others (Lk 18:11; Ro 3:5; Heb 6:10)

(II) As a characteristic of life, wicked, impious, ungodly (Mt 5:45; Ac 24:15; 1Co 6:9; 1Pe 3:18; 2Pe 2:9). So also an unbeliever, a pagan (1Co 6:1).

(III) Fraudulent, false, deceitful (Lk 16:10, 11; Sept.: Dt 19:18; Jer 5:31; 29:9).

Deriv.: *adikéō* (91), to act unjustly; *adikía* (93), injustice; *adíkōs* (95), unjustly.

Syn.: *athémitos* (111), unlawful; *skoliós* (4646), warped; *dólios* (1386), deceitful; *ponērós* (4190), evil; *kakós* (2556), bad; *phaúlos* (5337), foul, trivial; *hamartōlós* (268), sinful.

95. ἀδίκως, adikōs, *ad-ee´-koce*; adverb from 94; *unjustly*:—wrongfully.

96. ἀδόκιμος, adokimos, *ad-ok´-ee-mos*; from 1 (as a negative particle) and 1384; *unapproved*, i.e. *rejected*; (by implication) *worthless* (literal or moral):—castaway, rejected, reprobate.

Adjective from the priv. *a* (1), without, and *dókimos* (1384), acceptable. Not approved, rejected. Spoken of metals (Sept.: Pr 25:4; Isa 1:22). In the NT, used metaphorically: worthy of condemnation, reprobate (Ro 1:28; 1Co 9:27; 2Co 13:5–7; 2Ti 3:8); by implication, useless, worthless (Tit 1:16; Heb 6:8).

Syn.: *anáxios* (370), unworthy; *dólios* (1386), deceitful; *pseudḗs* (5571), false; *ásēmos* (767), mean, ignoble, one not bearing the mark; *koinós* (2839), common; *eleeinós* (1652), pitiable, miserable; *apóblētos* (579), cast away, rejected one; *achreíos* (888), useless; *áchrēstos* (890), inefficient.

97. ἄδολος, adolos, *ad´-ol-os*; from 1 (as a negative particle) and 1388; *undeceitful*, i.e. (figurative) *unadulterated*:—sincere.

Adjective from the priv. *a* (1), without, and *dólos* (1388), guile. Without deceit, sincere. In the NT, used only of milk in 1Pe 2:2, meaning unadulterated, pure, genuine, metaphorically for pure doctrine.

Syn.: *alēthinós* (228), true; *apseudḗs* (893), veracious, incapable of lying; *haploús* (573), single, without duplicity; *ákakos* (172), constitutionally harmless; *akéraios* (185), without admixture; *gnḗsios* (1103), true, genuine; *eilikrinḗs* (1506), sincere; *hagnós* (53), pure, undefiled.

98. Ἀδραμυττηνός, Adramuttēnos, *ad-ram-oot-tay-nos´*; from **Ἀδραμύττειον**, ***Adramutteion*** (a place in Asia Minor); *Adramyttene* or belonging to Adramyttium:—of Adramyttium.

99. Ἀδρίας, Adrias, *ad-ree´-as*; from **Ἀδρία**, ***Adria*** (a place near its shore); the *Adriatic* sea (including the Ionian):—Adria.

100. ἁδρότης, hadrotēs, *had-rot´-ace*; from **ἁδρός**, ***hadros*** (*stout*); *plumpness*, i.e. (figurative) *liberality*:—abundance.

Noun from *hadrós* (n.f.), full-grown, ripe. Maturity, fullness. In the NT, abundance, copiousness (2Co 8:20).

Syn.: *perisseía* (4050), overflowing, and *perísseuma* (4051), abundance; *huperbolḗ* (5236), exceeding greatness; *eulogía* (2129), a blessing; *haplótēs* (572), bountifulness, liberality.

101. ἀδυνατέω, adunateō, *ad-oo-nat-eh´-o*; from 102; to *be unable*, i.e. (passive) *impossible*:—be impossible.

102. ἀδύνατος, adunatos, *ad-oo´-nat-os*; from 1 (as a negative particle) and 1415; *unable*, i.e. *weak* (literal or figurative); passive *impossible*:—could not do, impossible, impotent, not possible, weak.

103. ᾄδω, aidō, *ad´-o*; a primary verb; to *sing*:—sing.

104. ἀεί, aei, *ah-eye´*; from an obsolete primary noun (apparently meaning continued *duration*); "*ever*;" by qualification *regularly*; (by implication) *earnestly*:—always, ever.

105. ἀετός, aetos, *ah-et-os´*; from the same as 109; an *eagle* (from its *wind*-like flight):—eagle.

106. ἄζυμος, azumos, *ad´-zoo-mos*; from 1 (as a negative particle) and 2219; *unleavened*, i.e. (figurative) *uncorrupted*; (in the neuter plural) specially (by implication) the *Passover* week:—unleavened (bread).

Adjective from the priv. *a* (1), without, and *zúmē* (2219), leaven. Unleavened.

(I) Spoken of bread: unleavened cakes or bread; hence the "feast of unleavened bread" or "day of unleavened bread," indicating the festival day or days in which the Jews were to eat unleavened bread in commemoration of their departure from Egypt, i.e. the Passover (Mt 26:17; Mk 14:1, 12; Lk 22:1, 7; Ac 12:3; 20:6).

(II) Metaphorically, unmixed, unadulterated, uncorrupted (1Co 5:7, 8).

Syn.: *alēthinós* (228), true; *gnḗsios* (1103), genuine; *apseudḗs*, (893), without falsehood; *ádolos* (97), without deceit.

107. Ἀζώρ, Azōr, *ad-zore´*; of Hebrew origin [compare 5809]; *Azor*, an Israelite:—Azor.

108. Ἄζωτος, Azōtos, *ad´-zo-tos*; of Hebrew origin [795]; *Azotus* (i.e. Ashdod), a place in Palestine:—Azotus.

109. ἀήρ, aēr, *ah-ayr´*; from **ἄημι**, ***aēmi*** (to *breathe* unconsciously, i.e. *respire*; by analogy to *blow*); "*air*" (as naturally *circumambient*):—air. Compare 5594.

110. ἀθανασία, athanasia, *ath-an-as-ee´-ah*; from a compound of 1 (as a negative particle) and 2288; *deathlessness*:—immortality.

Noun from *athánatos* (n.f.), immortal, which is from the priv. *a* (1), without, and *thánatos* (2288), death. Immortality (1Co 15:53, 54; 1Ti 6:16).

Syn.: *aphtharsía* (861) incorruptibility.

111. ἀθέμιτος, athemitos, *ath-em´-ee-tos*; from 1 (as a negative particle) and a derivative of **θέμις**, ***themis*** (*statute*; from the base of 5087); *illegal*; (by implication) *flagitious*:—abominable, unlawful thing.

Adjective from the priv. *a* (1), not, and *themitós* (n.f.), lawful. Unlawful, forbidden (Ac 10:28; 1Pe 4:3).

Syn.: *ánomos* (459), lawless; *áthesmos* (113), lawless; *bdeluktós* (947), abominable; *ádikos* (94), unjust; *ponē-rós* (4190), evil; *kakós* (2556), bad; *phaúlos* (5337), foul.

112. ἄθεος, atheos, *ath´-eh-os*; from 1 (as a negative particle) and 2316; *godless*:—without God.

Adjective from the priv. *a* (1), without, and *Theós* (2316), God. Godless, impious. In the NT, estranged from the knowledge and worship of the true God. Only in Eph 2:12.

Syn.: *asebḗs* (765), impious, ungodly; *anósios* (462), unholy, profane.

113. ἄθεσμος, athesmos, *ath´-es-mos*; from 1 (as a negative particle) and a derivative of 5087 (in the sense of *enacting*); *lawless*, i.e. (by implication) *criminal*:—wicked.

114. ἀθετέω, atheteō, *ath-et-eh´-o*; from a compound of 1 (as a negative particle) and a derivative of 5087; to *set aside*, i.e. (by implication) to *disesteem, neutralize* or *violate*:—cast off, despise, disannul, frustrate, bring to nought, reject.

115. ἀθέτησις, athetēsis, *ath-et´-ay-sis*; from 114; *cancellation* (literal or figurative):—disannulling, put away.

116. Ἀθῆναι, Athēnai, *ath-ay´-nahee*; plural of **Ἀθήνη**, ***Athēnē*** (the goddess of wisdom, who was reputed to have founded the city); *Athenæ*, the capital of Greece:—Athens.

117. Ἀθηναῖος, Athēnaios, *ath-ay-nah´-yos*; from 116; an *Athenæan* or inhabitant of Athenæ:—Athenian.

118. ἀθλέω, athleō, *ath-leh´-o*; from **ἆθλος**, ***athlos*** (a *contest* in the public lists); to *contend* in the competitive games:—strive.

119. ἄθλησις, athlēsis, *ath´-lay-sis*; from 118; a *struggle* (figurative):—fight.

120. ἀθυμέω, athumeō, *ath-oo-meh´-o*; from a compound of 1 (as a negative particle) and 2372; to *be spiritless*, i.e. *disheartened*:—be dismayed.

121. ἄθωος, athōos, *ath´-o-os*; from 1 (as a negative particle) and a probable derivative of 5087 (meaning a *penalty*); *not guilty*:—innocent.

122. αἴγειος, aigeios, *ah´ee-ghi-os*; from **αἴξ**, ***aix*** (a *goat*); belonging to a *goat*:—goat.

123. αἰγιαλός, aigialos, *ahee-ghee-al-os´*; from **ἀΐσσω**, ***aïssō*** (to *rush*) and 251 (in the sense of the *sea*); a *beach* (on which the *waves dash*):—shore.

124. Αἰγύπτιος, Aiguptios, *ahee-goop´-tee-os*; from 125; an *Ægyptian* or inhabitant of Ægyptus:—Egyptian.

125. Αἴγυπτος, Aiguptos, *ah´ee-goop-tos*; of uncertain derivative; *Ægyptus*, the land of the Nile:—Egypt.

126. ἀΐδιος, aïdios, *ah-id´-ee-os*; from 104; *everduring* (forward and backward, or forward only):—eternal, everlasting.

Adjective from *aeí* (104), ever, always. Always existing, eternal, everlasting (Ro 1:20; Jude 6).

Syn.: *aiṓnios* (166), eternal, primarily without end but possibly with a beginning such as eternal life.

127. αἰδώς, aidōs, *ahee-doce´*; perhaps from 1 (as a negative particle) and 1492 (through the idea of *downcast* eyes); *bashfulness*, i.e. (toward men), *modesty* or (toward God) *awe*:—reverence, shamefacedness.

A noun meaning modesty (1Ti 2:9); reverence, veneration (Heb 12:28).

Syn.: *entropḗ* (1791), withdrawal into oneself, recoiling; *aischúnē* (152) is subjective confusion, a feeling of shame felt by oneself or by others; *eulábeia* (2124), reverence.

128. Αἰθίοψ, Aithiops, *ahee-thee´-ops*; from **αἴθω**, ***Aithō*** (to *scorch*) and **ὤψ**, ***Ōps*** (the *face*, from 3700); an *Æthiopian* (as a *blackamoor*):—Ethiopian.

129. αἷμα, aima, *hah´ee-mah*; of uncertain derivative; *blood*, literal (of men or animals), figurative (the *juice* of grapes) or special (the atoning *blood* of Christ); (by implication) *bloodshed*, also *kindred*:—blood.

A noun meaning blood, bloodshed, blood-guiltiness, blood-relationship, kindred.

(I) Blood, either human or animal:

(A) Generally (Mk 5:25, 29; Lk 8:43, 44; 13:1).

(B) Figuratively, something may be said to be or become blood, or as blood, from its dark colour (Ac 2:19; Rev 8:7, 8; 11:6).

(II) Spoken of blood which has been shed:

(A) Of victims and other slaughtered animals (Heb 9:7, 12, 13, 18–25; 10:4; 11:28; 13:11). The Jews regarded the blood as the seat and principle of life; hence they were to offer it in sacrifice to God, but were forbidden to eat it (Le 17:10–14; Dt 12:23); so James charged early Gentile believers living among the Jews (Ac 15:20, 29; 21:25).

(B) Of men: generally (Lk 13:1; Jn 19:34; Rev 14:20); of the innocent, of martyrs (Mt 23:35; 27:4; Rev 17:6).

(C) Of the blood of Christ shed on the cross: in relation to the sacred supper (Mt 26:28; Mk 14:24; Lk 22:20; 1Co 10:16; 11:25, 27; 1Jn 6:53–58), in relation to his church (Ac 20:28; Col 1:20; Eph 2:13); to the atonement made by his death (Ro 3:25; 5:9; Eph 1:7; Heb 9:12, 14; 1Pe 1:2, 19; Rev 5:9), and to the new covenant (Heb 10:29; 12:24; 13:20).

(D) In conjunction with *sárx* ([4561], flesh), flesh and blood, i.e. the human body, mortal man (Mt 16:17; 1Co 15:50; Gal 1:16; Eph 6:12; Heb 2:14).

(E) With the verb *ekchéō* ([1632], spill, pour forth), to shed blood, i.e. to kill, put to death (Lk 11:50; Ac 22:20; Ro 3:15; Rev 16:6).

(III) By metonymy, bloodshed, i.e. death, violent death, slaughter, murder (Mt 23:30; 27:6, 8, 24; Ac 1:19; Rev 6:10; 18:24; 19:2).

(IV) From the Hebrew, blood-guiltiness, i.e. the guilt and punishment of shedding blood (Mt 23:35; 27:25; Ac 5:28; 18:6; 20:26; Sept.: Nu 35:27; Jos 2:19; Eze 9:9; 33:4; 2Sa 1:16).

(V) Figuratively, blood-relationship, kindred, lineage, progeny, seed (Jn 1:13; Ac 17:26).

Deriv.: *haimatekchusía* (130), shedding of blood; *haimorroéō* (131), to hemorrhage.

130. αἱματεκχυσία, aihmatekchusia, *hahee-mat-ek-khoo-see´-ah*; from 129 and a derivative of 1632; an *effusion of blood*:—shedding of blood.

Noun from *haíma* (129), blood, and *ekchéō* (1632), to pour out. Shedding of blood. Only in Heb 9:22.

131. αἱμοῤῥέω, aihmorrheō, *hahee-mor-hreh´-o*; from 129 and 4482; to *flow blood,* i.e. *have a hæmorrhage*:—diseased with an issue of blood.

132. Αἰνέας, Aineas, *ahee-neh´-as*; of uncertain derivative; *Æneas,* an Israelite:—Æneas.

133. αἴνεσις, ainesis, *ah´ee-nes-is*; from 134; a *praising* (the act), i.e. (special) a *thank* (-offering):—praise.

Noun from *ainéō* (134), to praise. The act of praise (Heb 13:15).

Syn.: *húmnos* (5215), hymn; *psalmós* (5568), a sacred ode or poem, music accompanied with the voice, harp, or other instrument; *ōdḗ* (5603), a religious metrical composition, a song; *eulogía* (2129), blessing, praise.

134. αἰνέω, aineō, *ahee-neh´-o*; from 136; to *praise* (God):—praise.

To praise, to celebrate. Spoken in the NT only of God (Lk 2:13, 20; 19:37; 24:53; Ac 2:47; 3:8, 9; Ro 15:11; Rev 19:5; Sept.: Ge 49:8; 1Ch 16:4, 10; Ps 100:4).

Deriv.: *aínesis* (133), the act of praise; *aínos* (136), a tale or narration which came to denote praise; *epainéō* (1867), to commend; *parainéō* (3867), to exhort, admonish.

Syn.: *humnéō* (5214), to laud, to sing a hymn; *psállō* (5567), to twitch or twang as a bowstring, to play a stringed instrument with the fingers; *eulogéō* (2127), to speak well of, praise.

135. αἴνιγμα, ainigma, *ah´ee-nig-ma*; from a derivative of 136 (in its primary sense); an *obscure* saying ("enigma"), i.e. (abstract) *obscureness*:—× darkly.

136. αἶνος, ainos, *ah´ee-nos*; apparently a primary word; properly a *story,* but used in the sense of 1868; *praise* (of God):—praise.

Noun from *ainéō* (134), to praise. Praise (Mt 21:16; Lk 18:43; Sept.: Ps 8:3).

Deriv.: *épainos* (1868), approval, commendation.

137. Αἰνών, Ainōn, *ahee-nohn´*; of Hebrew origin [a derivative of 5869, *place of springs*]; *Ænon,* a place in Palestine:—Ænon.

138. αἱρέομαι, aihreomai, *hahee-reh´-om-ahee*; probably akin to 142; to *take for oneself,* i.e. to *prefer*:—choose. Some of the forms are borrowed from a cognate **ἕλλομαι, *hellomai,*** *hel´-lom-ahee*; which is otherwise obsolete.

To take. In the NT, only in the middle: to take for oneself, i.e. to choose, elect, prefer (Php 1:22; 2Th 2:13; Heb 11:25; Sept.: 2Sa 15:15; Job 34:42).

Deriv.: *haíresis* (139), heresy; *hairetízō* (140), to choose, akin to *hairetós,* that which may be taken; *hairetikós* (141), heretic; *anairéō* (337), to take up or away, abolish; *authaíretos* (830), of one's own accord; *aphairéō* (851), to take away; *diairéō* (1244), to separate, divide, distribute; *exairéō* (1807), to tear out, to select, to release, deliver, pluck out, rescue; *kathairéō* (2507), to take down; *periairéō* (4014), to take away that which surrounds; *proairéomai* (4255), prefer, propose, intend, purpose.

Syn.: *eklégomai* (1586), to choose out, elect; *epilégomai* (1951), to be called or named.

139. αἵρεσις, hairesis, *hah´ee-res-is*; from 138; properly a *choice,* i.e. (special) a *party* or (abstract) *disunion*:—heresy [*which is the Greek word itself*], sect.

Noun from *hairéō* (138), to choose, select. In the NT, a chosen way of life: a sect, school, party (Ac 5:17; 15:5; 24:5, 14; 26:5; 28:22); by implication, discord, dissension (1Co 11:19; Gal 5:20; 2Pe 2:1).

140. αἱρετίζω, aihretizō, *hahee-ret-id´-zo*; from a derivative of 138; to *make a choice*:—choose.

From *hairéō* (138), to take. To choose. In the NT, to prefer, to love. Only in Mt 12:18.

Syn.: *chōrízō* (5563), to separate; *anadeíknumi* (322), to indicate, appoint; *egkrínō* (1469), to accept as approved; *eklégomai* (1586), to choose because of love; *epilégomai* (1951), to select; *hairéomai* (138), to take for oneself, prefer; *aírō* (142), to take up or away.

141. αἱρετικός, aihretikos, *hahee-ret-ee-kos´*; from the same as 140; a *schismatic*:—heretic [*the Greek word itself*].

Noun from *hairéō* (138), to take. One who creates dissension, introduces errors, etc. a factious person. Only in Tit 3:10.

Syn.: *ápistos* (571), unfaithful.

142. αἴρω, airō, *ah´ee-ro*; a primary verb; to *lift*; (by implication) to *take up* or *away*; (figurative) to *raise* (the voice), *keep in suspense* (the mind); specially to *sail* away (i.e. *weigh anchor*); by Hebrew [compare 5375] to *expiate* sin:—away with, bear (up), carry, lift up, loose, make to doubt, put away, remove, take (away, up).

To take up, carry, remove.

(I) To take up, to lift up, to raise:

(A) Particularly, as stones from the ground (Jn 8:59); serpents (Mk 16:18); anchors (Ac 27:13); the hand (Rev 10:5); see also Sept.: Dt 32:40; Isa 49:22. Pass. *árthēti* (Mt 21:21).

(B) Figuratively, to raise, elevate; the eyes (Jn 11:41; see also Sept.: Ps 121:1; 123:1); the voice, meaning, to cry out, to sing (Lk 17:13; Ac 4:24; see also Sept.: Jgs 21:2; 1Sa 11:4). To hold the mind or soul of someone suspended, i.e. in suspense or doubt (Jn 10:24).

(II) To take up and place on oneself, to take up and bear, meaning to bear, carry (Mt 4:6; Sept.: Ps 91:12); my yoke (Mt 11:29; see also Sept.: La 3:27); the cross (Mt 16:24; 27:32; Mk 15:21); to take or carry with one (Mk 6:8; Lk 9:3; Sept.: Ge 44:1; 2Ki 7:8).

(III) To take up and carry away, meaning to take away, to remove by carrying: spoken of a bed (Mt 9:6; Jn 5:8); a dead body, a person, etc. (Mt 14:12; 22:13; Ac 20:9); bread, with the idea of laying up, making use of (Mt 14:20; 15:37; Mk 8:8, 19, 20). Generally (Mt 17:27; Ac 21:11). In a metaphorical sense, to take away sin, meaning the imputation or punishment of sin (Jn 1:29; 1Jn 3:5; 1Sa 15:25); to bear the punishment of sin (Le 5:17; Nu 5:31; 14:33); to take away by taking upon oneself (Mt 8:17; 1Pe 2:24).

(IV) To take away, remove, lift away from, usually with the idea of violence and authority:

(A) Particularly (Lk 6:29, 30; 11:22); of branches, meaning to cut off, prune (Jn 15:2); spoken of persons: to take away or remove from a church, excommunicate (1Co 5:2, in some MSS *exarthḗ* [1808]). To take away or remove out of the world by death (Mt 24:39; Ac 8:33; Isa 53:8; 57:1, 2). In the imper., "away with!" meaning put out of the way, kill (Lk 23:18; Jn 19:15; Ac 21:36; 22:22).

(B) Figuratively, to destroy (Jn 11:48); to deprive of, as the kingdom of heaven (Mt 21:43), the word of God (Mk 4:15; Lk 8:12, 18), gifts (Mk 4:25), joy (Jn 16:22; see also Sept.: Isa 16:10). Spoken of vices: to put away (Eph 4:31); of a law: to abrogate (Col 2:14).

Deriv.: *apaírō* (522), to lift off; *exaírō* (1808), to put away from the midst; *epaírō* (1869), to lift up, as in the eyes, the head, the hands or the heel; *sunaírō* (4868), to take up together, to reckon; *huperaírō* (5229), to be exalted above measure.

Syn.: *bastázō* (941), to bear; *phérō* (5342), to bring, carry; *methístēmi* (3179), to remove; *lambánō* (2983), to take, lay hold of; *piázō* (4084), to lay hold of forcefully; *airéō* (138), to take; *komízō* (2865), to bring.

143. αἰσθάνομαι, aisthanomai, *ahee-sthan´-om-ahee*; of uncertain derivative; to *apprehend* (properly, by the senses):—perceive.

From *aíō* (n.f.), to perceive. To perceive, primarily with the external senses. In the NT, used metaphorically of spiritual perception: to understand (Lk 9:45; Sept.: Job 23:5; Pr 24:14).

Deriv.: *aísthēsis* (144), perception, discernment; *aisthētḗrion* (145), organ of perception.

Syn.: *krínō* (2919), to judge, conclude; *suníēmi* (4920), to comprehend; *sōphronéō* (4993), to exercise a sound mind; *diakrínō* (1252), to discern.

144. αἴσθησις, aisthēsis, *ah´ee-sthay-sis*; from 143; *perception,* i.e. (figurative) *discernment*:—judgement.

Noun from *aisthánomai* (143), to perceive with the external senses. Perception by the external senses. In the NT, used metaphorically: understanding, the power of discerning (Php 1:9; Sept.: Pr 1:4, 22; Ex 28:3).

Syn.: *krísis* (2920), decision, judgement, evaluation; *gnṓmē* (1106), opinion, purpose.

145. αἰσθητήριον, aisthētērion, *ahee-sthay-tay´-ree-on*; from a derivative of 143; properly an *organ of perception*, i.e. (figurative) *judgement*:—senses.

Noun from *aisthánomai* (143), to perceive with the external senses. The seat of the senses. In the NT, used metaphorically: internal sense, faculty of perception. Only in Heb 5:14.

146. αἰσχροκερδής, aischrokerdēs, *ahee-skhrok-er-dace´*; from 150 and **κέρδος**, ***kerdos*** (*gain*); *sordid*:—given to (greedy of) filthy lucre.

147. αἰσχροκερδῶς, aischrokerdōs, *ahee-skhrok-er-doce´*; adverb from 146; *sordidly*:—for filthy lucre's sake.

148. αἰσχρολογία, aischrologia, *ahee-skhrol-og-ee´-ah*; from 150 and 3056; *vile conversation*:—filthy communication.

149. αἰσχρόν, aischron, *ahee-skhron´*; neuter of 150; a *shameful* thing, i.e. *indecorum*:—shame.

150. αἰσχρός, aischros, *ahee-skhros´*; from the same as 153; *shameful*, i.e. *base* (specially *venal*):—filthy.

151. αἰσχρότης, aischrotēs, *ahee-skhrot´-ace*; from 150; *shamefulness*, i.e. *obscenity*:—filthiness.

152. αἰσχύνη, aischunē, *ahee-skhoo´-nay*; from 153; *shame* or *disgrace* (abstract or concrete):—dishonesty, shame.

Noun from *aíschos* (n.f.), shame. Disgrace, shame.

(I) Subjectively: a sense of shame, fear of disgrace (Lk 14:9).

(II) Objectively: disgrace, reproach (Heb 12:2; Sept.: Job 8:22; Ps 69:20; Isa 50:6).

(III) Cause of shame, i.e. a shameful thing or action, disgraceful conduct. (2Co 4:2; Php 3:19; Heb 12:2; Jude 13; Rev 3:18; Sept.: 1Sa 20:30).

Syn.: *atimía* (819), dishonour; *entropḗ* (1791), hidden shame; *aschēmosúnē* (808), unseemliness; *aidṓs* (127), shame arising from conviction of others.

153. αἰσχύνομαι, aischunomai, *ahee-skhoo´-nom-ahee*; from **αἶσχος**, ***aischos*** (*disfigurement*, i.e. *disgrace*); to *feel shame* (for oneself):—be ashamed.

154. αἰτέω, aiteō, *ahee-teh´-o*; of uncertain derivative; to *ask* (in general):—ask, beg, call for, crave, desire, require. Compare 4441.

To ask, request, beg.

(I) Generally (Mt 5:42; 7:9, 10; Mk 6:22–25; Lk 11:9–13; 1Jn 5:14–16; Sept.: Jos 15:18; 19:50). Spoken in respect to God, to supplicate, to pray for (Mt 6:8; 7:7, 8, 11; 18:19; Col 1:9; Jas 1:5, 6; Sept.: Isa 7:11, 12).

(II) To ask or call for, require, demand (Lk 1:63; 12:48; 23:23; Ac 3:14; 25:15; 1Pe 3:15; Sept.: Job 6:22; Da 2:49).

(III) By Hebraism, to desire (Ac 7:46; Sept.: 1Ki 19:4; Ecc 2:10; Dt 14:26).

Deriv.: *aítēma* (155), request, petition; *aitía* (156), an accusation; *apaitéō* (523), to require; *exaitéomai* (1809), to ask to have; *epaitéō* (1871), to beg; *paraitéomai* (3868), to refuse, give up; *prosaitéō* (4319), to ask earnestly.

Syn.: *punthánomai* (4441), to ask by way of inquiry; *zētéō* (2212), to seek; *parakaléō* (3870), to beseech; *déomai* (1189), to make a specific request; *epithuméō* (1937), desire, long for; *epizētéō* (1934), to demand; *diṓkō* (1377), to pursue; *erōtáō* (2065), to ask.

155. αἴτημα, aitēma, *ah´ee-tay-mah*; from 154; a *thing asked* or (abstract) an *asking*:—petition, request, required.

Noun from *aitéō* (154), to ask. Thing asked for, object sought, request (Lk 23:24; 1Jn 5:15). From the Hebrew, desire (Php 4:6).

Syn.: *déēsis* (1162), supplication or prayer for particular benefits; *énteuxis* (1783), intercession; *eucharistía* (2169), thanksgiving; *hiketēría* (2428), entreaty, supplication; *boúlēma* (1013), will, purpose; *boulḗ* (1012) will; *epithumía* (1939), a longing; *thélēma* (2307), volition, determination; *paráklēsis* (3874), request.

156. αἰτία, aitia, *ahee-tee´-a*; from the same as 154; a *cause* (as if *asked* for), i.e. (logical) *reason* (motive, matter), (legal) *crime* (alleged or proved):—accusation, case, cause, crime, fault, [wh-]ere [-fore].

Noun from *aitéō* (154), to ask or require. Efficient cause, motive, reason, ground (Mt 19:3; Lk 8:47; Ac 22:24; 28:20; 2Ti 1:6, 12; Tit 1:13; Heb 2:11). Also in the sense of affair, matter, case (Mt 19:10; Ac 10:21; 23:28). In a forensic sense, an accusation of crime, charge (Mt 27:37; Mk 15:26; Ac 25:18, 27); fault, guilt, crime (Jn 18:38; 19:4, 6; Ac 13:28; 28:18; Sept.: Ge 4:13; Pr 28:17).

Deriv.: *anaítios* (338), innocent.

Syn.: *katēgoría* (2724), an accusation; *lógos* (3056), reason.

157. αἰτίαμα, aitiama, *ahee-tee´-am-ah*; from a derivative of 156; a *thing charged*:—complaint.

158. αἴτιον, aition, *ah´ee-tee-on*; neuter of 159; a *reason* or *crime* [like 156]:—cause, fault.

159. αἴτιος, aitios, *ah´ee-tee-os*; from the same as 154; *causative*, i.e. (concrete) a *causer*:—author.

160. αἰφνίδιος, aiphnidios, *aheef-nid´-ee-os*; from a compound of 1 (as a negative particle) and 5316 [compare 1810] (meaning *non-apparent*); *unexpected*, i.e. (adverb) *suddenly*:—sudden, unawares.

161. αἰχμαλωσία, aichmalōsia, *aheekh-mal-o-see´-ah*; from 164; *captivity*:—captivity.

162. αἰχμαλωτεύω, aichmalōteuō, *aheekh-mal-o-tew´-o*; from 164; to *capture* [like 163]:—lead captive.

163. αἰχμαλωτίζω, aichmalōtizō, *aheekh-mal-o-tid´-zo*; from 164; to *make captive*:—lead away captive, bring into captivity.

164. αἰχμαλωτός, aichmalōtos, *aheekh-mal-o-tos´*; from **αἰχμή**, ***aichmē*** (a *spear*) and a derivative of the same as 259; properly a *prisoner of war*, i.e. (generally) a *captive*:—captive.

165. αἰών, aiōn, *ahee-ohn´*; from the same as 104; properly an *age*; by extension *perpetuity* (also past); (by implication) the *world*; specially (Jewish) a Messianic period (present or future):—age, course, eternal, (for) ever (-more), [n-]ever, (beginning of the, while the) world (began, without end). Compare 5550.

A noun meaning age, the world.

(I) Age, an indefinitely long period or lapse of time, perpetuity, ever, forever, eternity:

(A) Spoken of time future in the following phrases: **(1)** *Eis tón aiṓna*, lit. "unto the age," i.e. forever, without end, to the remotest time (Mk 11:14; Lk 1:55; Jn 6:51, 58; 8:35; 12:34; 13:8; 14:16; 1Co 8:13; Heb 5:6, 21; 1Pe 1:25; 2Jn 2); spoken of Christ (Heb 6:20; 7:17; 7:24, 28); spoken of the blessedness of the righteous (Jn 6:51, 58; 2Co 9:9; 1Jn 2:17; 2Pe 2:17); of the punishment of the wicked (Jude 13). With a neg., meaning never (Mt 21:19; Mk 3:29; Jn 4:14; 8:51, 52; 10:28; 11:26; Sept.: Dt 29:29; Isa 28:28; 40:8; 51:6, 8; Jer 50:39). **(2)** *Eis toús aiṓnas*, lit. "unto the ages," i.e. ever, forever, to all eternity (Mt 6:13; Lk 1:33; Ro 16:27; Heb 13:8); spoken of God (Ro 1:25; 9:5; 11:36; 2Co 11:31); of Christ (Lk 1:33; Heb 13:8; Sept.: Ps 77:8). **(3)** *Eis toús aiṓnas tṓn aiṓnōn*, lit. "unto the ages of the ages," an intensive form meaning forever and ever (2Ti 4:18; Heb 13:21; 1Pe 4:11; Rev 1:6; 5:13; 7:12; 19:3; 22:5); spoken of God (Gal 1:5; Php 4:20; 1Ti 1:17; 1Pe 5:11). Also in the expression *eis pásas tás geneás toú aiṓnos tṓn aiṓnōn*, lit. "unto all generations of the age of the ages," meaning throughout all ages (see *pás* [3956], every, all; *geneá* [1074], generation), spoken of Christ (2Pe 3:18; Rev 1:18; 5:13; 11:15); of the blessedness of the saints (Rev 22:5); of the punishment of the wicked (Rev 14:11; 19:3; 20:10).

(B) Spoken of time past in the following phrases: **(1)** *Ap' aiṓnos*, lit. "from the age" (see *apó* [575], from), often translated of old, from ancient times, from the beginning of the world (Lk 1:70; Ac 3:21; 15:18). **(2)** *Apó tṓn aiṓnōn*, lit. "from the ages" (Eph 3:9; Col 1:26). **(3)** *Ek toú aiṓnos ou*, lit. "from the ages not" (see *ek* [1537], from; *ou* [3756], not), i.e. never (Jn 9:32). **(4)** *Pró tṓn aiṓnōn*, lit. "from the ages" (*pró* [4253], before), translated before the ages, before the world (1Co 2:7).

(II) The world, i.e. this present world or the world to come, understood either in the sense of the time after the destruction of the present world and resurrection of the dead, or as the earthly reign of the Messiah, awaited by the Jews. In the NT, *aiṓn* is used of the future world chiefly in the first of these senses.

(A) This world and the next: **(1)** As implying duration (Mt 12:32, "neither in this world nor the next" [a.t.], meaning never; Mk 10:30; Lk 18:30). **(2)** The present world, with its cares, temptations, and desires; the idea of evil, both moral and physical, being everywhere implied (Mt 13:22; Lk 16:8; 20:34; Ro 12:2; 1Co 1:20; 2:6, 8; 2Ti 4:10; Tit 2:12). Hence this world is called *aiṓn ponērós*, "evil world" (Gal 1:4; see *ponērós*, [4190], evil). Satan is called the "god of this world" (2Co 4:4; Sept.: Ecc 3:11). **(3)** By metonymy, the men of this world, wicked generation, etc. (Eph 2:2). *Huioí toú aiṓnos toútou*, translated "the children of this world," is literally rendered "the sons of this age" (Lk 16:8; 20:34; see *huioí*, the plural of *huiós* [5207], son). **(4)** By metonymy, the world itself as an object of creation and existence (Mt 13:40; 24:3; 1Ti 1:17; Heb 1:2; 11:3).

(B) Spoken in reference to the advent of the Messiah, meaning age: **(1)** The age or world before the Messiah, the Jewish dispensation (1Co 10:11, "the ends of the world"). **(2)** The age or world after the Messiah, the gospel dispensation, the kingdom of the Messiah (Eph 2:7; Heb 6:5; see also Heb 2:5).

Deriv.: *aiṓnios* (166), eternal.

Syn.: *geneá* (1074), generation, the people of a certain period of time; *hēméra* (2250), day or period of time.

166. αἰώνιος, aiōnios, *ahee-o´-nee-os*; from 165; *perpetual* (also used of past time, or past and future as well):—eternal, for ever, everlasting, world (began).

Adjective from *aiṓn* (165), age. Eternal, perpetual, denoting those things which are not transitory.

(I) Spoken chiefly of future time:

(A) Of God (Ro 16:26; 1Ti 6:16; Sept.: Ge 21:33; Isa 40:28).

(B) Of the blessedness of the righteous (Mt 19:29; 25:46; Mk 10:30; Jn 3:15, 16, 36; Ro 2:7; 2Co 4:17). In some passages this *zōḗ aiṓnios*, lit. "life eternal" (see *zōḗ* [2222], life), is equivalent to entrance into the kingdom of God (Mt 19:16; Jn 3:3, 5, 15; Ac 13:46).

(C) Of the punishment of the wicked (Mt 18:8; 25:41, 46; Mk 3:29; 2Th 1:9; Heb 6:2; Jude 7; Sept.: Da 12:2).

(D) Generally (2Co 4:18; 5:1; Heb 9:14; 13:20; 1Jn 1:2; Rev 14:6). In the Sept.: *diathḗkē aiṓnios*, "eternal covenant" (Ge 9:16; 17:7; see *diathḗkē* [1242], testament, covenant).

(II) Spoken of time past (Ro 16:25), *chrónois aiōníois*, meaning times eternal, ancient ages, of old (2Ti 1:9; Tit 1:2; see *chrónos* [5550], time).

Syn.: *aḯdios* (126), having no beginning and no ending, everlasting.

167. ἀκαθαρσία, akatharsia, *ak-ath-ar-see´-ah*; from 169; *impurity* (the quality), physical or moral:—uncleanness.

Noun from *akáthartos* (169), unclean. Uncleanness, impurity, filth in a physical sense (Mt 23:27; Sept.: 2Sa 11:4). Moral uncleanness, lewdness, pollution, as opposed to chastity (Ro 1:24; 6:19; 2Co 12:21; Eph 4:19; 5:3; 1Th 2:3; 4:7; Sept.: Eze 22:15; 36:25).

Syn.: *miasmós* (3394), a defilement; *rhúpos* (4509), dirt, filth; *aischrótēs* (151), obscenity, impurity; *rhuparía* (4507), moral defilement; *molusmós* (3436), a soiling, defilement; *asélgeia* (766), lasciviousness, wantonness; *miasmós* (3394), contamination, uncleanness; *míasma* (3393), foulness, pollution; *spílos* (4696), stain, blemish defect, spot; *stígma* (4742), stigma, mark, scar.

168. ἀκαθάρτης, akathartēs, *ak-ath-ar´-tace*; from 169; *impurity* (the state moral:—filthiness.

Noun from the priv. *a* (1), without, and *katharótēs* (2514), cleanness. Uncleanness, filthiness, i.e. lewdness; used figuratively of idolatry, only in Rev 17:4.

Syn.: *akatharsía* (167), uncleanness.

169. ἀκάθαρτος, akathartos, *ak-ath´-ar-tos*; from 1 (as a negative particle) and a presumed derivative of 2508 (meaning *cleansed*); *impure* (ceremonial, moral [*lewd*] or special [*dæmonic*]):—foul, unclean.

Adjective from the priv. *a* (1), without, and *kathaírō* (2508), to cleanse. Unclean, impure.

(I) In the Levitical sense, i.e. ceremonially unclean (Ac 10:14, 28; 11:8; Rev 18:2 [cf. Le 5:2; 11:4, 25; 13:45; Dt 14:7]); so of persons who are not Jews, or who do not belong to the Christian community (Ac 10:28; 1Co 7:14; 2Co 6:17; Sept.: Isa 52:1; Am 7:17).

(II) In the sense of lewd, lascivious (Eph 5:5); spoken figuratively of idolatry (Rev 17:4); in this sense, partly, the devils or demons are called *pneúmata akátharta*, unclean spirits (Mt 10:1; 12:43; Mk 1:23, 26; Lk 4:33; 9:42; Ac 5:16; 8:7; Rev 16:13; 18:2; see also *pneúma* [4151], spirit). They are also probably so called as being impious, wicked (Mt 12:45; Ac 19:13, 15).

Deriv.: *akatharsía* (167), uncleanness.

Syn.: *bébēlos* (952), profane; *rhuparós* (4508), vile; *ponērós* (4190), evil, but sometimes used as unclean; *koinós* (2839), common, defiled.

170. ἀκαιρέομαι, akairēomai, *ak-ahee-reh´-om-ahee*; from a compound of 1 (as a negative particle) and 2540 (meaning *unseasonable*); to *be inopportune* (for oneself), i.e. to *fail of a proper occasion*:—lack opportunity.

171. ἀκαίρως, akairōs, *ak-ah´ee-roce*; adverb from the same as 170; *inopportunely*:—out of season.

172. ἄκακος, akakos, *ak´-ak-os*; from 1 (as a negative particle) and 2556; *not bad*, i.e. (objective) *innocent* or (subjective) *unsuspecting*:—harmless, simple.

Adjective from the priv. *a* (1), without, and *kakós* (2556), constitutionally bad. Harmless, well disposed, blameless (Heb 7:26); also in the sense of simple-hearted, confiding (Ro 16:18).

Syn.: *haploús* (573), single or without duplicity; *ádolos* (97), without guile; *akéraios* (185), without any foreign matter or without admixture; *athṓos* (121), unpunished, innocent; *kalós* (2570), good; *agathós* (18), benevolent; *chrēstós* (5543), gentle, mellow.

173. ἄκανθα, akantha, *ak´-an-thah*; probably from the same as 188; a *thorn*:—thorn.

174. ἀκάνθινος, akanthinos, *ak-an´-thee-nos*; from 173; *thorny*:—of thorns.

175. ἄκαρπος, akarpos, *ak´-ar-pos*; from 1 (as a negative particle) and 2590; *barren* (literal or figurative):—without fruit, unfruitful.

176. ἀκατάγνωστος, akatagnōstos, *ak-at-ag´-noce-tos*; from 1 (as a negative particle) and a derivative of 2607; *unblameable*:—that cannot be condemned.

Adjective from the priv. *a* (1), without, and *kataginṓskō* (2607), condemn. Irreprehensible, not worthy of condemnation, not to be condemned or blamed (Tit 2:8).

177. ἀκατακάλυπτος, akatakaluptos, *ak-at-ak-al´-oop-tos*; from 1 (as a negative particle) and a derivative of a compound of 2596 and 2572; *unveiled*:—uncovered.

178. ἀκατάκριτος, akatakritos, *ak-at-ak´-ree-tos*; from 1 (as a negative particle) and a derivative of 2632; *without* (legal) *trial*:—uncondemned.

179. ἀκατάλυτος, akatalutos, *ak-at-al´-oo-tos*; from 1 (as a negative particle) and a derivative of 2647; *indissoluble*, i.e. (figurative) *permanent*:—endless.

180. ἀκατάπαυστος, akatapaustos, *ak-at-ap´-ow-stos*; from 1 (as a negative particle) and a derivative of 2664; *unrefraining*:—that cannot cease.

181. ἀκαταστασία, akatastasia, *ak-at-as-tah-see´-ah*; from 182; *instability*, i.e. *disorder*:—commotion, confusion, tumult.

Noun from *akatástatos* (182), unstable. Commotion, tumult (Lk 21:9; 1Co 14:33; 2Co 6:5, "uncertainty of residence" [a.t.], i.e. exile ["tumults"]; 2Co 12:20; Jas 3:16; Sept.: Pr 26:28).

Syn.: *súgchusis* (4799), confusion; *thórubos* (2351), noise, tumult; *tarachḗ* (5016), disturbance.

182. ἀκατάστατος, akatastatos, *ak-at-as´-tat-os*; from 1 (as a negative particle) and a derivative of 2525; *inconstant*:—unstable.

Adjective from the priv. *a* (1), not, and *kathístēmi* (2525), to settle. Unsettled, unsteady, unstable (Jas 1:8).

Deriv.: *akatastasía* (181), instability.

Syn.: *akatáschetos* (183), one that cannot be restrained; *astḗriktos* (793), unstable; *átaktos* (813), insubordinate, unruly.

183. ἀκατάσχετος, akataschetos, *ak-at-as´-khet-os*; from 1 (as a negative particle) and a derivative of 2722; *unrestrainable*:—unruly.

184. Ἀκελδαμά, Akeldama, *ak-el-dam-ah´*; of Chaldee origin [meaning *field of blood*; corresponding to 2506 and 1818]; *Akeldama*, a place near Jerus.:—Aceldama.

185. ἀκέραιος, akeraios, *ak-er´-ah-yos*; from 1 (as a negative particle) and a presumed derivative of 2767: *unmixed*, i.e. (figurative) *innocent*:—harmless, simple.

Adjective from the priv. *a* (1), without, and *keránnumi* (2767), to mix. Unmixed. In the NT, used metaphorically: without guile, cunning, or deceit; blameless (Mt 10:16; Ro 16:19; Php 2:15).

Syn.: *euschḗmōn* (2158), comely, honourable; *téleios* (185), perfect, one who has reached the goal; *ártios* (739), complete; *holóklēros* (3648), entire, whole; *plḗrēs* (4134), complete, full; *tímios* (5093), honest; *éntimos* (1784), reputable, honourable; *euthús* (2117), straight; *chrēstós* (5543), of good and useful morals; *áxios* (514), worthy; *ákakos* (172), not bad, innocent; *ádolos* (97), without guile; *haploús* (573), without wrinkles or duplicity, single or simple.

186. ἀκλινής, aklinēs, *ak-lee-nace´*; from 1 (as a negative particle) and 2827; *not leaning*, i.e. (figurative) *firm*:—without wavering.

187. ἀκμάζω, akmazō, *ak-mad´-zo*; from the same as 188; to *make a point*, i.e. (figurative) *mature*:—be fully ripe.

188. ἀκμήν, akmēn, *ak-mane´*; accusative of a noun ("*acme*") akin to **ἀκή**, ***akē*** (a *point*) and meaning the same; adverb *just* now, i.e. *still*:—yet.

189. ἀκοή, akoē, *ak-o-ay´*; from 191; *hearing* (the act, the sense or the thing heard):—audience, ear, fame, which ye heard, hearing, preached, report, rumoural.

Noun from *akoúō* (191), to hear. Hearing, as the sense of hearing, or referring to that which is heard.

(I) The sense of hearing (1Co 12:17); also spoken of the organ or instrument of hearing, the ear (Mk 7:35; Ac 17:20; 2Ti 4:3, 4). Thus the expression *akoḗ akoúein*, "to hear with the ears" (with *akoúō* [191], to hear), meaning to listen attentively (Mt 13:14; Ac 28:26).

(II) That which is or may be heard: a thing announced, instruction, teaching (Jn 12:38; Ro 10:16, 17; Gal 3:2, 5; 1Th 2:13; Heb 4:2; 2Pe 2:8); a rumour, report (Mt 4:24; 14:1; 24:6; Mk 1:28; 13:7).

Syn.: *oús* (3775), ear; *ōtíon* (5621), a diminutive of *oús*, ear; *phḗmē* (5346), fame, report; *lógos* (3056), a word, report, account; *ḗchos* (2279), noise, sound, rumour, echo; *aggelía* (31), a message, proclamation, news; *presbeía* (4242), embassy, a message, messengers; *kḗrugma* (2782), proclamation, preaching; *marturía* (3141), witness, report; *diágnōsis* (1233), diagnosis, hearing for the purpose of discerning; *akroatḗrion* (201), a place of hearing.

190. ἀκολουθέω, akoloutheō, *ak-ol-oo-theh´-o*; from 1 (as a particle of union) and **κέλευθος**, ***keleuthos*** (a *road*); properly to *be in the same way with*, i.e. to *accompany* (specially as a disciple):—follow, reach.

From *akólouthos* (n.f.), attendant, follower, which is from the coll. *a* (1), together, and *kéleuthos* (n.f.), a way. To accompany, to go with, to follow.

(I) Generally (Mt 8:1; 9:19, 27; Mk 5:24; 10:32; Lk 22:54; Jn 11:31; 1Co 10:4; Sept.: Ru 1:14; 1Sa 25:42).

(II) Specifically, to follow a teacher, i.e. to be or become the disciple of someone:

(A) To accompany him personally, as was usual with the followers of Jewish doctors and Greek philosophers (Mt 4:20, 22, 25; 9:9; 19:27, 28; 27:55; Mk 1:18; 9:38; Jn 1:41; 12:26; Lk 9:49; Sept.: 1Ki 19:20, 21; Isa 45:14).

(B) To be or become the disciple of anyone as to faith and practice, to follow his teaching, etc. (Mt 10:38; 16:24; Mk 8:34; Lk 9:23; Jn 8:12; 12:26).

(III) Of time, to follow in succession, to succeed (Rev 14:8, 9).

(IV) Spoken of things, or actions: to accompany, follow (Rev 14:13).

Deriv.: *exakolouthéō* (1811), to follow up, to continue to the end; *epakolouthéō* (1872), to follow after, close upon; *katakolouthéō* (2628), to follow behind or intently after; *parakolouthéō* (3877), to follow close up or side by side, hence to accompany, conform to, follow intending to practice; *sunakolouthéō* (4870), to follow along with, to accompany a leader.

Syn.: *hupakoúō* (5219), to obey; *diṓkō* (1377), to pursue without hostility, to follow; *miméomai* (3401), to imitate; *epioúsios* (1967), the following.

191. ἀκούω, akouō, *ak-oo´-o*; a primary verb; to *hear* (in various senses):—give (in the) audience (of), come (to the ears), ([shall]) hear (-er, -ken), be noised, be reported, understand.

To hear, also to learn by hearing, be informed.

(I) To hear, to perceive with the ears:

(A) Generally (Mt 2:3, 9, 18; 9:12; 10:27; 11:5; 12:19; Mk 7:25; 10:41; 14:64; Lk 7:3, 9; Jn 3:8; Sept.: Ge 3:8, 10).

(B) To hear with attention, to give ear to, listen to (Mk 4:3; 7:14; 12:29, 37; Lk 5:1; 10:39; 11:31; Ac 2:22; 15:7); in respect to a teacher (Mk 6:20; Lk 15:1; 19:48), hence *hoi akoúontes*, hearers, i.e. disciples.

(C) By implication, to give heed to, to obey (Mt 10:14; Lk 10:16; 16:29, 31 [cf. Jn 5:24; 8:47; 18:37; Ac 3:22, 23; 4:19; 1Jn 4:5, 6]; Sept.: Ge 3:17; Ex 16:20; Dt 11:27; 2Ch 20:14; Isa 48:18). Here belongs the phrase "he who hath ears, let him hear," i.e. give heed, obey (Mt 11:15; 13:9, 13; Rev 2:7, 11, 17, 29). In the writings of John as spoken of God: to heed, regard, i.e. to hear and answer prayer (Jn 9:31; 11:41, 42; 1Jn 5:15).

(II) To hear, i.e. to learn by hearing, be informed, know:

(A) Generally (Mt 2:3, 22; 4:12; 5:21, 27; 11:2; Mk 5:27; 6:14; Ac 14:14; 15:24); spoken of instruction, doctrines (Jn 8:40; 15:15; Ac 1:4; 4:20; Ro 10:14, 18; Heb 2:1; 1Jn 2:7, 24). Pass. meaning, to be heard of, to be reported (Mt 28:14; Mk 2:1; Lk 12:3; Ac 11:22; 1Co 5:1; Sept.: 2Ch 26:15).

(B) In a forensic sense, to hear as a judge or magistrate, i.e. to try, examine judicially (Ac 25:22; Jn 7:51).

(C) In the sense of to understand, comprehend (Mk 4:33; Jn 6:60; 1Co 14:2; Gal 4:21; Sept.: Ge 11:7; 42:23).

Deriv.: *akoḗ* (189), hearing; *diakoúō* (1251), to hear through, hear fully; *eisakoúō* (1522), to listen to, to hear and obey; *epakoúō* (1873), to listen to, hear with favour on an occasion; *parakoúō* (3878), to overhear or hear amiss; *proakoúō* (4257), to hear before; *hupakoúō* (5219), to obey.

Syn.: *epakroáomai* (1874), to listen attentively to; *enōtízomai* (1801), to give ear to, to listen; *peitharchéō* (3980), to obey one in authority, be obedient; *peíthomai* (3982), to be persuaded.

192. ἀκρασία, akrasia, *ak-ras-ee´-a*; from 193; *want of self-restraint*:—excess, incontinency.

193. ἀκράτης, akratēs, *ak-rat´-ace*; from 1 (as a negative particle) and 2904; *powerless*, i.e. *without self-control*:—incontinent.

194. ἄκρατος, akratos, *ak´-rat-os*; from 1 (as a negative particle) and a presumed derivative of 2767; *undiluted*:—without mixture.

195. ἀκρίβεια, akribeia, *ak-ree´-bi-ah*; from the same as 196; *exactness*:—perfect manner.

196. ἀκριβέστατος, akribestatos, *ak-ree-bes´-ta-tos*; superlative of **ἀκριβης**, ***akribēs*** (a derivative of the same as 206); *most exact*:—most straitest.

197. ἀκριβέστερον, akribesteron, *ak-ree-bes´-ter-on*; neuter of the comparative of the same as 196; (adverb) *more exactly*:—more perfect (-ly).

198. ἀκριβόω, akriboō, *ak-ree-bo´-o*; from the same as 196; to *be exact*, i.e. *ascertain*:—enquire diligently.

199. ἀκριβῶς, akribōs, *ak-ree-boce´*; adverb from the same as 196; *exactly*:—circumspectly, diligently, perfect (-ly).

200. ἀκρίς, akris, *ak-rece´*; apparently from the same as 206; a *locust* (as *pointed*, or as *lighting* on the *top* of vegetation):—locust.

201. ἀκροατήριον, akroaterion, *ak-ro-at-ay´-ree-on*; from 202; an *audience-room*:—place of hearing.

202. ἀκροατής, akroatēs, *ak-ro-at-ace´*; from **ἀκροάομαι,** ***akroaomai*** (to *listen*; apparently an intensive of 191); a *hearer* (merely):—hearer.

203. ἀκροβυστία, akrobustia, *ak-rob-oos-tee´-ah*; from 206 and probably a modified form of **πόσθη,** ***posthē*** (the *penis* or male sexual organ); the *prepuce*; (by implication) an *uncircumcised* (i.e. *Gentile*; figurative, *unregenerate*) state or person:—not circumcised, uncircumcised [*with* 2192], uncircumcision.

Noun from *ákron* (206), the extreme, and *búō* (n.f.), to cover. The foreskin. In Ac 11:3, "uncircumcised men" is lit. *ándras akrobustían échontas*, "men having foreskins" (*ándras* [*anḗr* {435}, man] *échontas* [*échō* {2192}, to have]), thus the term may be translated as uncircumcision (Ro 2:25, 26; 1Co 7:18, 19; Gal 5:6; 6:15; Col 2:13). By metonymy, uncircumcised refers to Gentiles or pagans, as opposed to the circumcision (*peritomḗ* [4061]), i.e. the Jews (Ro 2:26, 27; 3:30; 4:9–12; Gal 2:7; Eph 2:11; Col 3:11). The Jews in scorn called all other nations "uncircumcised" (Jgs 14:3; 15:18; Isa 52:1).

Syn.: *aperítmētos* (564), uncircumcised; verb: *epispáomai* (1986), to draw over, to become uncircumcised, as if to efface Judaism.

204. ἀκρογωνιαῖος, akrogōniaios, *ak-rog-o-nee-ah´-yos*; from 206 and 1137; belonging to the extreme *corner*:—chief corner.

205. ἀκροθίνιον, akrothinion, *ak-roth-in´-ee-on*; from 206 and **θίς,** *this* (a *heap*); properly (in the plural) the *top of the heap*, i.e. (by implication) *best of the booty*:—spoils.

206. ἄκρον, akron, *ak´-ron*; neuter of an adjective probably akin to the base of 188; the *extremity*:—one end … other, tip, top, uttermost part.

207. Ἀκύλας, Akulas, *ak-oo´-las*; probably for Latin *aquila* (an *eagle*); *Akulas*, an Israelite:—Aquila.

208. ἀκυρόω, akuroō, *ak-oo-ro´-o*; from 1 (as a negative particle) and 2964; to *invalidate*:—disannul, make of no effect.

209. ἀκωλύτως, akōlutōs, *ak-o-loo´-toce*; adverb from a compound of 1 (as a negative particle) and a derivative of 2967; in *an unhindered manner*, i.e. *freely*:—no man forbidding him.

210. ἄκων, akōn, *ak´-ohn*; from 1 (as a negative particle) and 1635; *unwilling*:—against the will.

From the priv. *a* (1), without, and *hekṓn* (1635), willing. Unwillingly, against one's will, forced. Occurs only in 1Co 9:17.

Syn.: *akousíōs*, unwillingly, often used in the Sept., but not in the NT; *anagkastṓs* (317), by compulsion.

211. ἀλάβαστρον, alabastron, *al-ab´-as-tron*; neuter of **ἀλάβαστρος,** ***alabastros*** (of uncertain derivative), the name of a stone; properly an "*alabaster*" box, i.e. (by extension) a perfume *vase* (of any material):—(alabaster) box.

212. ἀλαζονεία, alazoneia, *al-ad-zon-i´-a*; from 213; *braggadocio*, i.e. (by implication) *self-confidence*:—boasting, pride.

213. ἀλαζών, alazōn, *al-ad-zone´*; from **ἄλη,** ***alē*** (*vagrancy*); *braggart*:—boaster.

Masculine noun from *álē* (n.f.), a wandering about. A boaster, braggart (Ro 1:30; 2Ti 3:2; Sept.: Hab 2:5).

Deriv.: *alazoneía* (212), vaunting in those things one does not possess.

Syn.: *huperḗphanos* (5244), proud, one who shows himself above his fellows; *hubristḗs* (5197), insolent wrongdoer to others for the pleasure which the affliction imparts.

214. ἀλαλάζω, alalazō, *al-al-ad´-zo*; from **ἀλαλή,** ***alalē*** (a *shout*, "*halloo*"); to *vociferate*, i.e. (by implication) to *wail*; (figurative) to *clang*:—tinkle, wail.

215. ἀλάλητος, alalētos, *al-al´-ay-tos*; from 1 (as a negative particle) and a derivative of 2980; *unspeakable*:—unutterable, which cannot be uttered.

216. ἄλαλος, alalos, *al´-al-os*; from 1 (as a negative particle) and 2980; *mute*:—dumb.

217. ἅλας, halas, *hal´-as*; from 251; *salt*; (figurative) *prudence*:—salt.

218. ἀλείφω, aleiphō, *al-i´-fo*; from 1 (as particle of union) and the base of 3045; to *oil* (with perfume):—anoint.

To rub, to cover over, besmear. In the NT: to anoint (Mt 6:17; Mk 6:13; 16:1; Lk 7:38, 46; Jn 11:2; 12:3; Jas 5:14; Sept.: Ge 31:13; Eze 13:10–12). The Jews were accustomed not only to anoint the head at their feasts in token of joy, but also both the head and the feet of those whom they wished to distinguish by special honour. In the case of sick persons and also of the dead, they anointed the whole body (see Ge 50:2; Ps 23:5; 45:7; 104:15; Ecc 9:8; Lk 7:37, 38; Jn 19:40).

Deriv.: *exaleíphō* (1813), to blot out, wipe away.

Syn.: *chríō* (5548), more limited in its use of sacred and symbolical anointing; *murízō* (3642), to anoint the body for burial.

219. ἀλεκτοροφωνία, alektorophōnia, *al-ek-tor-of-o-nee´-ah*; from 220 and 5456; *cock-crow*, i.e. the third night-watch:—cockcrowing.

220. ἀλέκτωρ, alektōr, *al-ek´-tore*; from **ἀλέκω,** ***alekō*** (to *ward* off); a *cock* or male fowl:—cock.

221. Ἀλεξανδρεύς, Alexandreus, *al-ex-and-reuce´*; from **Ἀλεξάνδρεια,** ***Alexandreia*** (the city so called); an *Alexandreian* or inhabitant of Alexandria:—of Alexandria, Alexandrian.

222. Ἀλεξανδρῖνος, Alexandrinos, *al-ex-an-dree´-nos*; from the same as 221; *Alexandrine*, or belonging to Alexandria:—of Alexandria.

223. Ἀλέξανδρος, Alexandros, *al-ex´-an-dros*; from the same as (the first part of) 220 and 435; *mandefender*; *Alexander*, the name of three Israelites and one other man:—Alexander.

224. ἄλευρον, aleuron, *al´-yoo-ron*; from **ἀλέω,** ***aleō*** (to *grind*); *flour*:—meal.

225. ἀλήθεια, alētheia, *al-ay´-thi-a*; from 227; *truth*:—true, × truly, truth, verity.

Noun from *alēthḗs* (227), true. What is not concealed, but open and known; hence truth.

(I) Truth, verity, reality, conformity to the nature and reality of things:

(A) As evidenced in relation to facts (Mk 5:33; Jn 5:33; 16:7; Ac 26:25; Ro 9:1; 2Co 6:7; 12:6; Eph 4:25; 1Ti 2:7; Sept.: 1Ki 22:16; 2Ch 18:15). Prefixed by *epí* (1909), upon, *epí alētheías*, of a truth, as the fact or event shows (Lk 4:25; 22:59; Ac 4:27; 10:34; Sept.: Job 9:2; Isa 37:18).

(B) Spoken of what is true in itself, purity from all error or falsehood (Mk 12:32; Ac 26:25; Ro 2:20; 2Co 7:14; 12:6; Col 1:6; 2Ti 2:18; 3:7, 8; 4:4). "The truth of the gospel" (Gal 2:5), "the word of truth," the true doctrine (Eph 1:13; Col 1:5; 2Ti 2:15; Jas 1:18).

(II) Truth, i.e. love of truth, both in words and conduct, sincerity, veracity (Mt 22:16; Mk 12:14; Lk 20:21; Jn 4:23, 24; Jn 8:44; Eph 4:24; 5:9; 6:14; Php 1:18; 1Jn 1:6, 8; 2:4; 3:18, 19; 5:6; 2Jn 3; 3Jn 3; Sept.: Jos 2:14; 1Sa 12:24; 2Sa 2:6; 1Ki 2:4; 3:6; 2Ch 19:9; Ps 35:6).

(III) In the NT especially, divine truth or the faith and practice of the true religion is called "truth" either as being true in itself and derived from the true God, or as declaring the existence and will of the one true God, in opposition to the worship of false idols. Hence *alḗtheia* comes to mean divine truth, gospel truth, as opposed to heathen and Jewish fables (Jn 1:14, 17; 8:32, 40; 16:13; 18:37; Ro 1:18, 25; 2Co 4:2; 13:8; Gal 3:1; 5:7; 2Th 2:10; 1Ti 2:4; 3:15; 2Ti 2:25; Tit 1:1, 14; Heb 10:26; Jas 1:18; 3:14; 1Pe 1:22; 2Pe 1:12; 2:2; 1Jn 2:21; 2Jn 2, 4; 3Jn 8). Hence the Lord Jesus is called "the truth," i.e. truth incarnate, the teacher of divine truth (Jn 14:6). So also "the Spirit of truth," who declares or reveals divine truth (Jn 14:17; 15:26; 16:13).

(IV) Conduct conformed to the truth, integrity, probity, virtue, a life conformed to the precepts of the gospel. In Jn 3:21, *ho poiṓn tḗn alḗtheian*, lit. "he who does truth" (see *poiéō* [4160], to make or to do), meaning someone who lives uprightly. See also Jn 8:44; Ro 2:8; 1Co 13:6; Eph 4:21; 1Ti 6:5; Jas 5:19; 3Jn 3, 4, 12; Sept.: Ps 119:30; Pr 28:6; Isa 26:10.

Syn.: *hupóstasis* (5287), substance; *bebaíōsis* (951), confirmation; *plḗrōma* (4138), fulfillment.

226. ἀληθεύω, alētheuō, *al-ayth-yoo´-o*; from 227; to *be true* (in doctrine and profession):—speak (tell) the truth.

From *alēthḗs* (227), real, actual, not counterfeit. To act truly, speak the truth, be sincere (Eph 4:15; Gal 4:16; Sept.: Ge 42:16; Pr 21:3).

Syn.: *bebaióō* (950), to confirm; *plēróō* (4137), to accomplish.

227. ἀληθής, alēthēs, *al-ay-thace´*; from 1 (as a negative particle) and 2990; *true* (as *not concealing*):—true, truly, truth.

Adjective from the priv. *a* (1), without, and *lḗthō*, an older form of *lanthánō* (2990), to be hid, unawares. Unconcealed, open; hence true.

(I) True, real, conformed to the nature and reality of things (Jn 8:16; 19:35; Ac 12:9; Sept.: Pr 22:21). Also, true as shown by the result or event (Jn 10:41; Tit 1:13, 2Pe 2:22), thus credible, not to be rejected as a witness (Jn 5:31, 32; 8:13, 14, 17; 21:24; a teacher [2Co 6:8]; grace [1Pe 5:12]; 1Jn 2:27; 3Jn 12; Sept.: Job 42:7, 8; Da 8:26).

(II) True, loving truth, sincere, veracious (Mt 22:16; Mk 12:14; Jn 3:33; 8:26; Ro 3:4).

(III) True in conduct, sincere, upright, honest, just (Jn 7:18; Php 4:8; Sept.: Isa 41:26).

Deriv.: *alḗtheia* (225), truth; *alētheúō* (226), to deal faithfully or truly; *alēthinós* (228), real, ideal, genuine (*alēthḗs* denotes the reality of the thing while *alēthinós* defines the relation of the concept to the corresponding thing, genuine); *alēthṓs* (230), truly, surely, indeed.

228. ἀληθινός, alēthinos, *al-ay-thee-nos´*; from 227; *truthful*:—true.

From *alēthḗs* (227), true. Real, genuine.

(I) True, conformed to truth (Jn 4:37; 19:35). In the sense of real, unfeigned, not fictitious (Jn 17:3; 1Th 1:9; 1Jn 5:20; Rev 3:7; Sept.: 2Ch 15:3; Isa 65:16). Spoken of what is true in itself, genuine, real, as opposed to that which is false or pretended (Jn 1:9; 4:23; 1Jn 2:8); of the vine (Jn 15:1; Sept.: Jer 2:21); of Jerusalem (Sept.: Zec 8:3); of the bread coming down from heaven (Jn 6:32, of which the manna was the type); so in Heb 8:2, *skēnḗ alēthinḗ*, the true tabernacle (*skēnḗ* [4633], tabernacle), i.e. the heavenly temple, after the model of which the Jews regarded the temple of Jerusalem as built; also *tá alēthiná hágia*, the true holy place alluded to in Heb 9:24 (*hágion* [39], holy place, sanctuary), as opposed to the earthly copy. See Rev 11:19; 15:5.

(II) True, i.e. loving truth, veracious and hence worthy of credit (Jn 7:28; Rev 3:14; 19:9, 11; 21:5; 22:6; Sept.: Pr 12:19).

(III) True, i.e. sincere, upright of the heart (Heb 10:22; Sept.: Job 2:3; 8:6; 27:17; Isa 38:3); of a judge or judgement, meaning upright, just (Rev 6:10; 15:3; 16:7; 19:2; Sept.: Dt 25:15; Isa 25:1; 59:4).

Syn.: *gnḗsios* (1103), true, genuine, sincere; *pistós* (4103), faithful, true; *ádolos* (97), sincere, without guile; *apseudḗs* (893), veracious, one who cannot lie; *eilikrinḗs* (1506), sincere, tested as genuine.

229. ἀλήθω, alēthō, *al-ay´-tho*; from the same as 224; to *grind*:—grind.

230. ἀληθῶς, alēthōs, *al-ay-thoce´*; adverb from 227; *truly*:—indeed, surely, of a surety, truly, of a (in) truth, verily, very.

231. ἁλιεύς, halieus, *hal-ee-yoos´*; from 251; a *sailor* (as engaged on the *salt* water), i.e. (by implication) a *fisher*:—fisher (-man).

232. ἁλιεύω, halieuō, *hal-ee-yoo´-o*; from 231; to *be a fisher*, i.e. (by implication) to *fish*:—go a fishing.

233. ἁλίζω, halizō, *hal-id´-zo*; from 251; to *salt*:—salt.

234. ἀλίσγεμα, alisgema, *al-is´-ghem-ah*; from **ἀλισγέω, alisgeō** (to *soil*); (ceremonial) *defilement*:—pollution.

235. ἀλλά, alla, *al-lah´*; neuter plural of 243; properly *other* things, i.e. (adverb) *contrariwise* (in many relations):—and, but (even), howbeit, indeed, nay, nevertheless, no, notwithstanding, save, therefore, yea, yet.

236. ἀλλάσσω, allassō, *al-las´-so*; from 243; to *make different*:—change.

From *állos* (243), other, another. To change.

(I) To change the form or nature of a thing, to transform the voice or tone (Gal 4:20). To change for the better, in the pass. (1Co 15:51, 52; Sept.: Jer 13:23). To change for the worse, to corrupt, cause to decay, e.g., the heavens (Heb 1:10–12 [cf. Ps 102:26; Isa 51:6]). In Ac 6:14, to "change the customs," i.e. do away with them (Sept.: Ezr 6:11, 12).

(II) To change one thing for another, to exchange (Ro 1:23; Sept.: Ge 41:14, of garments; Le 27:10, 33; 2Sa 12:20; Ps 106:20).

Deriv.: *apallássō* (525), to change, to free from, release, deliver; *diallássō* (1259), to reconcile in cases of mutual hostility yielding to mutual concession; *katallássō* (2644), to reconcile to God in His relationship to sinful man; *metallássō* (3337), exchange one thing for another or into another.

Syn.: *metabállō* (3328), change; *metastréphō* (3344), to turn about; *katargéō* (2673), to abolish; *rhúomai* (4506), to rescue from; *antibállō* (474), to exchange, spoken usually of words that can be exchanged one with another.

237. ἀλλαχόθεν, allachothen, *al-lakh-oth´-en*; from 243; *from elsewhere*:—some other way.

238. ἀλληγορέω, allēgoreo, *al-lay-gor-eh´-o*; from 243 and **ἀγορέω, agoreō** (to *harangue* [compare 58]); to *allegorize*:—be an allegory [*the Greek word itself*].

From *állos* (243), another, and *agoreúō* (n.f.), to speak in a place of assembly, which is from *agorá* (58), marketplace. To allegorize, to speak allegorically where the thing spoken of is emblematic or representative. Only in Gal 4:24.

Syn.: *túpos* (5179), type; *múthos* (3454), a fable; *analogía* (356), analogy; *mustḗrion* (3466), mystery. All these may be classified as allegorical or figurative, insofar as they point to a meaning different from that contained in the word or words used.

239. ἀλληλούϊα, allēlouïa, *al-lay-loo´-ee-ah*; of Hebrew origin [imperative of 1984 and 3050]; *praise ye Jah!*, an adoring exclamation:—alleluiah.

240. ἀλλήλων, allēlōn, *al-lay´-lone*; Genitive plural from 243 reduplication; *one another*:—each other, mutual, one another, (the other), (them-, your-) selves, (selves) together [*sometimes with* 3326 *or* 4314].

Form of the reciprocal pron. *allḗlous*, one another, from *állos* (243), another. One another (Mt 24:10; Jn 15:12, 17).

241. ἀλλογενής, allogenēs, *al-log-en-ace´*; from 243 and 1085; *foreign*, i.e. not a Jew:—stranger.

Adjective from *állos* (243), other, and *génos* (1085), a nation, race. Used as a substantive, one of another nation, a stranger, foreigner, i.e. not a Jew (Lk 17:18, see Lk 17:16; Sept.: Ex 12:43; 29:33; Job 15:19; Isa 56:3, 6).

Syn.: *allóphulos* (246), one of another race, nation; *xénos* (3581), stranger, foreigner; *allótrios* (245), stranger; *pároikos* (3941), a pilgrim; *héteros* (2087), another of a different kind, a stranger; *parepídēmos* (3927), pilgrim or sojourner.

242. ἅλλομαι, hallomai, *hal´-lom-ahee*; middle of apparently a primary verb; to *jump*; (figurative) to *gush*:—leap, spring up.

243. ἄλλος, allos, *al´-los*; a primary word; "*else*," i.e. *different* (in many applications):—more, one (another), (an-, some an-) other (-s, -wise).

Adjective. Another, but of the same kind; another numerically; in contrast to *éteros* (2087), another qualitatively, another of a different kind.

(I) Without the article: other, another, some other:

(A) Simply (Mt 2:12; 13:33; 26:71; 27:42; Gal 1:7); another of the same kind (Mk 7:4, 8; Jn 21:25); another besides (Mt 25:16, 17; Mk 12:32; 15:41; Jn 6:22; 14:16); marking succession, i.e. in the second or third place (Mk 12:4, 5; Jn 20:30; Rev 12:3; 13:11).

(B) Distributively, when repeated or joined with other pronouns, e.g., *hoútos—állos*, meaning this or that, one or another (Mt 8:9; see *hoútos* [3778], this one); *hoi mén—álloi dé*, some or others (Mt 16:14; see *mén—dé* [3303, 1161], on the one hand or on the other); *álloi—álloi*, some or others (Mt 13:5–8; Mk 4:7, 8; 6:15; 8:28; 1Co 12:8–10); *állos prós állon*, one to another (Ac 2:12; see *prós* [4314], to); *álloi mén oún állo ti ékrazon*, "Some therefore cried one thing, and some another" (Ac 19:32; see *oún* [3767] therefore; *ti* [5100], something; *krázō* [2896], to cry).

(II) With the article, *ho állos*, the other (Mt 5:39; 10:23; 12:13; Jn 18:16; Rev 17:10). *Hoi álloi*, the others, the rest (Jn 21:8; 1Co 14:29).

Deriv.: *allá* (235), but; *allássō* / *alláttō* (236), to change; *allachóthen* (237), from another place; *allēgoréō* (238), to allegorize; *allḗlōn* (240), of one another; *allogenḗs* (241), one of another nation; *allótrios* (245), another's; *allóphulos* (246), one of another race or nation; *állōs* (247), an adverb meaning otherwise.

Syn.: *diáphoros* (1313), different.

244. ἀλλοτριεπίσκοπος, allotriepiskopos, *al-lot-ree-ep-is´-kop-os*; from 245 and 1985; *overseeing others*' affairs, i.e. a *meddler* (specially in Gentile customs):—busybody in other men's matters.

Noun from *allótrios* (245), another's, and *epískopos* (1985), superintendent, overseer, bishop. An inspector of foreign or strange things, one who busies himself with what does not concern him, a busybody. Found only in the NT, 1Pe 4:15.

245. ἀλλότριος, allotrios, *al-lot´-ree-os*; from 243; *another's*, i.e. not one's own; by extension *foreign, not akin, hostile*:—alien, (an-) other (man's, men's), strange (-r).

From *állos* (243), other. Another's, belonging to another, different (Lk 16:12; Ro 14:4; 15:20; 2Co 10:15, 16; 1Ti 5:22; Heb 9:25). Spoken of a country, strange, foreign (Ac 7:6; Heb 11:9); of persons, strangers, not belonging to one's own family (Mt 17:25, 26). By implication, hostile, an enemy; in the NT with the idea of impiety, i.e. heathen enemy, Gentile (Heb 11:34; Sept.: Ps 54:3; 1Ki 8:41; Ezr 10:2).

Deriv.: *allotrioepískopos* (244), busybody.

Syn.: Distinguished from *allóphulos* (246), one of another race or nation; *allogenḗs* (241), one of another nation, not a Jew, a stranger, foreigner (Lk 17:18); *héteros* (2087), another of a different kind; *xénos* (3581), alien, foreign, foreigner; *parádoxos* (3861), contrary to prevailing opinion or custom.

246. ἀλλόφυλος, allophulos, *al-lof´-oo-los*; from 243 and 5443; *foreign*, i.e. (special) *Gentile*:—one of another nation.

Adjective from *állos* (243), other, and *phulḗ* (5443), a tribe or race. Not a Jew, one of another race or nation (Ac 10:28; Sept.: 2Ki 8:28; Isa 2:6; 61:5).

Syn.: *éthnos* (1484), nation, not Jewish; *ethnikós* (1482), Gentile, non-Jewish; *allogenḗs* (241), of another nation or race; *allótrios* (245), belonging to another.

247. ἄλλως, allōs, *al´-loce*; adverb from 243; *differently*:—otherwise.

Adverb from *állos* (243), other. Otherwise. Only in 1Ti 5:25, also Sept.: Job 11:12; Est 1:19; 9:27.

Syn.: *hetérōs* (2088), otherwise, of a different frame of mind; *ei dé mḗge* (1490), not indeed, otherwise.

248. ἀλοάω, aloaō, *al-o-ah´-o*; from the same as 257; to *tread* out grain:—thresh, tread out the corn.

249. ἄλογος, alogos, *al´-og-os*; from 1 (as a negative particle) and 3056; *irrational*:—brute, unreasonable.

250. ἀλοή, aloē, *al´-o-ay´*; of foreign origin [compare 174]; *aloes* (the gum):—aloes.

251. ἅλς, hals, *halce*; a primary word; "*salt*":—salt.

252. ἁλυκός, halukos, *hal-oo-kos´*; from 251; *briny*:—salt.

253. ἀλυπότερος, alupoteros, *al-oo-pot´-er-os*; comparative of a compound of 1 (as a negative particle) and 3077; *more without grief*:—less sorrowful.

254. ἅλυσις, halusis, *hal´-oo-sis*; of uncertain derivative; a *fetter* or *manacle*:—bonds, chain.

255. ἀλυσιτελής, alusitelēs, *al-oo-sit-el-ace´*; from 1 (as a negative particle) and the base of 3081; *gainless*, i.e. (by implication) *pernicious*:—unprofitable.

256. Ἀλφαῖος, Alphaios, *al-fah´-yos*; of Hebrew origin [compare 2501]; *Alphæus*, an Israelite:—Alpheus.

257. ἅλων, halōn, *hal´-ohn*; probably from the base of 1507; a threshing-*floor* (as *rolled* hard), i.e. (figurative) the *grain* (and chaff, as just threshed):—floor.

258. ἀλώπηξ, alōpex, *al-o´-pakes*; of uncertain derivative; a *fox*, i.e. (figurative) a *cunning* person:—fox.

259. ἅλωσις, halōsis, *hal´-o-sis*; from a collateral form of 138; *capture*:—be taken.

260. ἅμα, hama, *ham´-ah*; a primary particle; properly *at the "same" time*, but freely used as a preposition or adverb denoting close association:—also, and, together, with (-al).

261. ἀμαθής, amathēs, *am-ath-ace´*; from 1 (as a negative particle) and 3129; *ignorant*:—unlearned.

262. ἀμαράντινος, amarantinos, *am-ar-an´-tee-nos*; from 263; "*amaranthine*," i.e. (by implication) *fadeless*:—that fadeth not away.

Adjective corresponding to *amárantos* (263), unfading; hence, enduring. Only in 1Pe 5:4.

Syn.: *amárantos* (263), unfading; *áphthartos* (862), incorruptible; *amíantos* (283), unsoiled, undefiled.

263. ἀμάραντος, amarantos, *am-ar´-an-tos*; from 1 (as a negative particle) and a presumed derivative of 3133; *unfading*, i.e. (by implication) *perpetual*:—that fadeth not away.

Adjective from the priv. *a* (1), without, and *maraínō* (3133), to fade. Unfading; hence, enduring. Only in 1Pe 1:4.

264. ἁμαρτάνω, hamartanō, *ham-ar-tan´-o*; perhaps from 1 (as a negative particle) and the base of 3313; properly to *miss* the mark (and so *not share* in the prize), i.e. (figurative) to *err*, especially (moral) to *sin*:—for your faults, offend, sin, trespass.

To miss the mark, swerve from the way. In the NT, used metaphorically:

(I) To err, swerve from the truth, go wrong; speaking of errors of doctrine or faith (1Co 15:34; Tit 3:11).

(II) To err in action, in respect to a prescribed law, i.e. to commit errors, to do wrong, sin:

(A) Generally, to sin, spoken of any sin, used in an absolute sense (Mt 27:4; Jn 5:14; 8:11; 9:2, 3; Ro 2:12; 3:23; 5:12, 14, 16; 6:15; 1Co 7:28, 36; Eph 4:26; 1Ti 5:20; Heb 3:17; 10:26; 1Pe 2:20; 2Pe 2:4; 1Jn 1:10; 2:1; 3:6, 8, 9; 5:16, 18; Sept.: Ex 32:30; Le 4:14, 23, 28).

(B) With the prep. *eis* (1519), unto, to sin against anyone, to offend, wrong (Mt 18:15, 21; Lk 15:18, 21; 17:3, 4; Ac 25:8; 1Co 6:18; 8:12; Sept.: Ge 20:6, 9; 43:9; 1Sa 2:25).

(C) The Hebraism *hamartánein enṓpion*, lit. "to sin in the face of [someone]" (see *enṓpion* [1799], in the face of), is usually translated "to do evil in the sight of someone," i.e. to sin against, to wrong, as above (Lk 15:21; Sept.: Ge 39:9; Dt 1:41; 20:18; 1Sa 7:6; 12:23; 14:33, 34).

Deriv.: *amártēma* (265), sin; *hamartía* (266), sin, sinful; *hamartōlós* (268), a sinner; *anamártētos* (361), without sin; *proamartánō* (4258), to sin previously.

Syn.: *ptaíō* (4417), to stumble, offend; *adikéō* (91), to do wrong; *skandalízō* (4624), to offend, be a stumbling block to someone, trip someone; *astochéō* (795), to miss the goal; *parabaínō* (3845), to transgress; *píptō* (4098), to fall; *parapíptō* (3895), to fall away; *paranoméō* (3891), to go contrary to law; *peripíptō* (4045), to fall by the side; *planáomai* (4105), to go astray.

265. ἁμάρτημα, hamartēma, *ham-ar´-tay-mah*; from 264; a *sin* (properly concrete):—sin.

Noun from *hamartánō* (264), to sin. A mistake, miss; in the NT, used metaphorically: an error, transgression, sin (Mk 3:28; 4:12; Ro 3:25; 1Co 6:18; Sept.: Ge 31:36; Isa 58:1).

Syn.: *paráptōma* (3900), the deed of trespassing, a trespass; *adíkēma* (92), a wrong, an iniquity perpetrated; *agnóēma* (51), shortcoming, error, a thing ignored; *opheílēma* (3783), that which one owes, a debt; *hḗttēma* (2275), a loss, defeat, defect; *plánē* (4106), deceit, delusion.

266. ἁμαρτία, hamartia, *ham-ar-tee´-ah*; from 264; *sin* (properly abstract):—offence, sin (-ful).

Noun from *hamartánō* (264), to sin. Miss, failure; in the NT, used metaphorically:

(I) Aberration from the truth, error (Jn 8:46; 16:8, 9).

(II) Sin, i.e. aberration from a prescribed law or rule of duty, whether in general or of particular sins:

(A) Generally (Mt 3:6; 9:2, 5, 6; Mk 1:4, 5; Jn 9:34; Ro 7:5; 1Co 15:3; 2Co 11:7; Heb 4:15; 10:26; Jas 2:9; 1Pe 2:22; Sept.: Ge 15:16; 18:20; Isa 53:5).

(B) Spoken of particular sins, which are to be gathered from the context; e.g., of unbelief (Jn 8:21, 24); of lewdness (2Pe 2:14); of defection from the gospel of Christ (Heb 11:25; 12:1).

(C) By metonymy of abstract for concrete, *hamartía* for *hamartōlós* ([268], sinner), meaning sinful, i.e. either as causing sin (Ro 7:7, i.e. "Is the law the cause of sin?"), or as committing sin (2Co 5:21, i.e. "He has been treated as if He were a sinner").

(D) By metonymy, the practice of sinning, habit of sin (Ro 3:9; 5:12, 20, 21; Gal 3:22).

(E) By metonymy, proneness to sin, sinful desire or propensity (Jn 8:34; Ro 6:1, 2, 6, 12, 14; 7:7ff.; Heb 3:13).

(III) From the Hebrew, the imputation or consequences of sin, the guilt and punishment of sin as in the phrase "to take away [or bear] sin," i.e. the imputation of it (Jn 1:29; Ro 11:27; Heb 9:26; 10:11; 1Pe 2:24; 1Jn 3:5). So also to remit (*aphíēmi* [863]) sins and the remission (*áphesis* [859]) of sins means to remove the guilt, punishment, and power of sin (Mt 9:2, 5, 6; 26:28; Lk 7:47–49; Jn 20:23; Heb 10:4); thus in Jn 9:41, "your sin remaineth" means your guilt and exposure to punishment remain (cf. Jn 15:22, 24; 1Jn 1:9). The same may be said of 1Co 15:17, where "ye are yet in your sins" indicates one is still under the guilt and power of sin (Heb 9:26, 28; Sept.: Le 22:9; Nu 9:13; Pr 10:16; Isa 5:18; 53:6, 11; La 3:39; Eze 3:20; Zec 14:19).

Syn.: *agnóēma* (51), a sin of ignorance; *opheílēma* ([3783] akin to *opheilḗ* [3782], a debt), that which is legally due; *adikía* (93), unrighteousness; *adíkēma* (92), a wrong, an injury; *ponēría* (4189), wickedness; *paranomía* (3892), law-breaking; *anomía* (458), lawlessness; *parábasis* (3847), violation, transgression; *kríma* (2917), condemnation; *égklēma* (1462), crime which is tried in court; *sunōmosía* (4945), a plot, conspiracy; *asébeia* (763), impiety, ungodliness; *parakoḗ* (3876), disobedience; *apeítheia* (543), obstinate rejection of God's will; *paráptōma* (3900), a false step, a blunder; *ptṓsis* (4431), a fall; *apostasía* (646), a standing away from, although not necessarily a departure from a position in which one stood; *aitía* (156) and *aítion* (158), a crime, a legal ground for punishment, fault; *hḗttēma* (2275), a loss, defeat, defect; *hamártēma* (265), an act of sin or disobedience to divine requirement and expectation.

267. ἀμάρτυρος, amarturos, *am-ar´-too-ros*; from 1 (as a negative particle) and a form of 3144; *unattested*:—without witness.

268. ἁμαρτωλός, hamartōlos, *ham-ar-to-los´*; from 264; *sinful*, i.e. a *sinner*:—sinful, sinner.

Adjective from *hamartánō* (264), to deviate, miss the mark, sin. Erring from the way or mark. In the NT, used metaphorically:

(I) As adj.: erring from the divine law, sinful, wicked, impious:

(A) Generally: a sinful generation (Mk 8:38); a sinful man, a sinner (Lk 5:8; 19:7; 24:7; Jn 9:16, 24); a sinful woman (Lk 7:37, 39; Sept.: Nu 32:14; Isa 1:4); "more wicked than all others" (a.t.; Lk 13:2); a sinner (Lk 18:13; Ro 3:7); sinful, sinners (Ro 5:8; Gal 2:17; Jas 4:8).

(B) Oblivious to the consequences of sin, guilty and exposed to punishment (Ro 5:19; 7:13; Gal 2:15; Jude 15).

(II) As substantive, a sinner, transgressor, impious person:

(A) Generally (Mt 9:10, 11, 13; 11:19; Mk 2:15–17; Lk 5:30, 32; 6:32–34; 7:34; 15:1, 2, 7, 10; Jn 9:25, 31; 1Ti 1:9, 15; Heb 7:26; 12:3; Jas 5:20; 1Pe 4:18; Sept.: Ps 1:1, 5; 37:12, 20; Isa 13:9; Eze 33:8, 19; Am 9:8).

(B) Sinners, despisers of God; used by the Jews to refer to the Gentiles, heathen or pagan nations (Mt 26:45 [cf. Mt 20:19; Mk 10:33; Lk 18:32; Sept.: Isa 14:5]).

Syn.: *asebḗs* (765), impious, ungodly; *ápistos* (571), an unbeliever; *opheilétēs* (3781), a debtor; *énochos* (177), guilty of something; *aítios* (159), one to be blamed; *ádikos* (94), unjust.

269. ἄμαχος, amachos, *am´-akh-os*; from 1 (as a negative particle) and 3163; *peaceable*:—not a brawler.

270. ἀμάω, amaō, *am-ah´-o*; from 260; properly to *collect*, i.e. (by implication) *reap*:—reap down.

271. ἀμέθυστος, amethustos, *am-eth´-oos-tos*; from 1 (as a negative particle) and a derivative of 3184; the "*amethyst*" (supposed to *prevent intoxication*):—amethyst.

272. ἀμελέω, ameleo, *am-el-eh´-o*; from 1 (as a negative particle) and 3199; to *be careless* of:—make light of, neglect, be negligent, not regard.

273. ἄμεμπτος, amemptos, *am´-emp-tos*; from 1 (as a negative particle) and a derivative of 3201; *irreproachable*:—blameless, faultless, unblameable.

Adjective from the priv. *a* (1), without, and *mémphomai* (3201), to find fault. Blameless (Lk 1:6; Php 2:15; 3:6; 1Th 3:13; Heb 8:7).

Deriv.: *amémptōs* (274), unblamably.

Syn.: *ámōmos* (299), unblemished, unspotted. The *ámōmos*, the unblemished, may be *ámemptos*, unblamed; *áspilos* (784), without spot; *anégklētos* (410), legally irreproachable; *anepílēptos* (423), irreprehensible, one who cannot be caught and accused; *anaítios* (338), guiltless, blameless; *ádolos* (97), without guile; *ákakos* (172), without being bad in oneself; *akéraios* (185), without foreign mixture, sincere, harmless; *haploús* (573), single, without duplicity; *amṓmētos* (298), without blemish.

274. ἀμέμπτως, amemptōs, *am-emp´-toce*; adverb from 273; *faultlessly*:—blameless, unblamably.

275. ἀμέριμνος, amerimnos, *am-er´-im-nos*; from 1 (as a negative particle) and 3308; *not anxious*:—without care (-fulness), secure.

276. ἀμετάθετος, ametathetos, *am-et-ath´-et-os*; from 1 (as a negative particle) and a derivative of 3346; *unchangeable*, or (neuter as abstract) *unchangeability*:—immutable (-ility).

277. ἀμετακίνητος, ametakinētos, *am-et-ak-in´-ay-tos*; from 1 (as a negative particle) and a derivative of 3334; *immovable*:—unmovable.

278. ἀμεταμέλητος, ametamelētos, *am-et-am-el´-ay-tos*; from 1 (as a negative particle) and a presumed derivative of 3338; *irrevocable*:—without repentance, not to be repented of.

279. ἀμετανόητος, ametanoētos, *am-et-an-o´-ay-tos*; from 1 (as negative particle) and a presumed derivative of 3340; *unrepentant*:—impenitent.

Adjective from the priv. *a* (1), without, and *metanoéō* (3340), to repent or change one's mind. Inflexible, impenitent (Ro 2:5).

Syn.: *ametamélētos* (278), not to be concerned after an act has been committed (Ro 11:29; 2Co 7:10).

280. ἄμετρος, ametros, *am´-et-ros*; from 1 (as a negative particle) and 3358; *immoderate*:—(thing) without measure.

281. ἀμήν, amēn, *am-ane´*; of Hebrew origin [543]; properly *firm*, i.e. (figurative) *trustworthy*; adverb *surely* (often as interjection *so be it*):—amen, verily.

282. ἀμήτωρ, amētōr, *am-ay´-tore*; from 1 (as a negative particle) and 3384; *motherless*, i.e. *of unknown maternity*:—without mother.

283. ἀμίαντος, amiantos, *am-ee´-an-tos*; from 1 (as a negative particle) and a derivative of 3392; *unsoiled*, i.e. (figurative) *pure*:—undefiled.

Adjective from the priv. *a* (1), not or without, and *miaínō* (3392), to defile. That which has nothing in it that defiles; unpolluted, unstained, unsoiled, undefiled by sin (Heb 7:26); of marriage (Heb 13:4), chaste; of the worship of God (Jas 1:27), pure, sincere; of the heavenly inheritance (1Pe 1:4), inviolate.

Syn.: *hagnós* (53), pure from defilement; *katharós* (2513), cleansed; *eilikrinḗs* (1506), sincere, unalloyed; *hágios* (40), holy as being free from admixture of evil; *hósios* (3741), one who observes duties toward God, Godlike; *tímios* (5093), honourable; *hierós* (2413), sacred, outwardly associated with God.

284. Ἀμιναδάβ, Aminadab, *am-ee-nad-ab´*; of Hebrew origin [5992]; *Aminadab*, an Israelite:—Aminadab.

285. ἄμμος, ammos, *am´-mos*; perhaps from 260; *sand* (as *heaped* on the beach):—sand.

286. ἀμνός, amnos, *am-nos´*; apparently a primary word; a *lamb*:—lamb.

A noun meaning lamb. In the NT, used metaphorically of Christ delivered over to death as a lamb to the sacrifice (Jn 1:29, 36; Ac 8:32; 1Pe 1:19; Sept.: Ex 12:5; Le 14:10, 12, 13; Isa 16:1).

287. ἀμοιβή, amoibē, *am-oy-bay´*; from **ἀμείβω,** ***ameibō*** (to *exchange*); *requital*:—requite.

288. ἄμπελος, ampelos, *am´-pel-os*; probably from the base of 297 and that of 257; a *vine* (as *coiling about* a support):—vine.

289. ἀμπελουργός, ampelourgos, *am-pel-oor-gos´*; from 288 and 2041; a *vine-worker*, i.e. *pruner*:—vine-dresser.

290. ἀμπελών, ampelōn, *am-pel-ohn´*; from 288; a *vineyard*:—vineyard.

291. Ἀμπλίας, Amplias, *am-plee´-as*; contracted from Latin *ampliatus* [*enlarged*]; *Amplias*, a Roman Christian:—Amplias.

292. ἀμύνομαι, amunomai, *am-oo´-nom-ahee*; middle of a primary verb; to *ward off* (for oneself), i.e. *protect*:—defend.

293. ἀμφίβληστρον, amphiblēstron, *am-fib´-lace-tron*; from a compound of the base of 297 and 906; a (fishing) *net* (as *thrown about* the fish):—net.

Noun from *amphibállō* (n.f.), to throw around, which is from the prefix *amphí*, round about, and *bállō* (906), to throw. In the NT, a fish net, a casting net (Mt 4:18; Mk 1:16; Sept.: Ps 141:10; Ecc 9:12; Hab 1:15–17).

Syn.: *díktuon* (1350), a general term for net; *sagḗnē* (4522), a dragnet; *ágkistron* (44), a hook.

294. ἀμφιέννυμι, amphiennumi, *am-fee-en´-noo-mee*; from the base of 297 and **ἕννυμι,** ***hennumi*** (to *invest*); to *enrobe*:—clothe.

295. Ἀμφίπολις, Amphipolis, *am-fip´-ol-is*; from the base of 297 and 4172; a *city surrounded* by a river; *Amphipolis*, a place in Macedonia:—Amphipolis.

296. ἄμφοδον, amphodon, *am´-fod-on*; from the base of 297 and 3598; a *fork* in the road:—where two ways meet.

297. ἀμφότερος, amphoteros, *am-fot´-er-os*; comparative of **ἀμφί,** ***amphi*** (*around*); (in plural) *both*:—both.

298. ἀμώμητος, amōmētos, *am-o´-may-tos*; from 1 (as a negative particle) and a derivative of 3469; *unblameable*:—blameless.

299. ἄμωμος, amōmos, *am´-o-mos*; from 1 (as a negative particle) and 3470; *unblemished* (literal or figurative):—without blame (blemish, fault, spot), faultless, unblameable.

Adjective from the priv. *a* (1), without, and *mṓmos* (3470), spot, blemish. Spotless, without blemish. In the NT, spoken metaphorically of Christ, a lamb without blemish, as was required by Levitical law in regard to all victims (Heb 9:14; 1Pe 1:19; see Le 1:10; 22:19–22); also generally, blameless (Eph 1:4; 5:27; Col 1:22; Heb 9:14; Jude 24; Rev 14:5)

Syn.: *ámemptos* (273), unblameable, related to *mémphomai* (3201), to blame, find fault; *anaítios* (338), guiltless; *anepílēptos* (423), irreproachable; *anégklētos* (410), not chargeable in court; *díkaios* (1342), just; *euthús* (2117), straight; *orthós* (3717), straight, upright; *akatákritos* (178), uncondemned; *anepaíschuntos* (422), irreprehensible.

300. Ἀμών, Amōn, *am-one´*; of Hebrew origin [526]; *Amon*, an Israelite:—Amon.

301. Ἀμώς, Amōs, *am-oce´*; of Hebrew origin [531]; *Amos*, an Israelite:—Amos.

302. ἄν, an, *an*; a primary particle, denoting a *supposition, wish, possibility* or *uncertainty*:—[what-, where-, whither-, who-] soever. Usually unexpressed except by the subjunctive or potential mood. Also contracted from 1437.

Particle, sometimes properly rendered by "perhaps"; more commonly not translated in Eng. by any corresponding particle, but only giving to a proposition or sentence a stamp of uncertainty and mere possibility, and indicating a dependence on circumstances.

(I) Indicating that a supposition or possibility will be realized, under the circumstances implied by *án*:

(A) In vows or wishes, as in Ac 26:29, where it gives the sense of "I could pray to God, and under the circumstances do pray to Him."

(B) Where the thing inquired about is possible, or certain, but the inquirer is uncertain when or how it is to take place. Lk 1:62, "how he might wish him to be called" (a.t.), i.e. since he was to have a name, what that name should be. See also Lk 9:46; Jn 13:24; Ac 2:12; 5:24; 17:18; 21:33.

(II) Used with relative words, rendering them more general and indicating mere possibility:

(A) With relative pronouns or particles, *án* implies some condition or uncertainty whether or where the thing will take place; equivalent to -ever, -soever. Thus in conjunction with *hós* [(3739), rel. pron; he who], for example, *hós án* becomes translated whoever, whosoever (Mt 5:21, 31, 32; 10:11; 12:32; Mk 3:29; Jn 1:33; Sept.: Da 3:5, 6). Again, combined with a word like *hópou* ([3699], where, at whichever spot), i.e. *hópou án*, the expression is translated wheresoever (Mk 9:18; 14:9; Lk 9:57; Rev 14:4).

(B) With particles of time, *án* indicates an element of uncertainty, not to the occurrence of an event, but to the time that event will occur. For example, in Mt 2:13, *án* appears with *héōs* ([2193], until); "be thou there until (*héōs án*) I bring thee word." The uncertainty lies not in whether or not they will be informed, but in the time of that occurrence (see also Mt 2:13; 5:18, 26; 10:11, 23; Mk 6:10; Lk 20:43; Ac 2:35). In the same way, combined with *hṓs* ([5613], as), in 1Co 11:34, *án* conveys the meaning when, as soon as: "And the rest will I set in order when (*hṓs án*) I come." Paul will come; the time of his coming, however, is uncertain.

(C) Used with the particle *hópōs* [(3704), that, in order that], *án* again brings the idea of indefiniteness. Ac 15:16, 17 says, for example, "After this I will return, and will build again the tabernacle of David, … that (*hópōs án*) the residue of men might seek after the Lord." The resulting seeking that occurs after the Lord's return will certainly take place; the time, however, is indefinite, as is the duration of this seeking. So *hópōs án* carries the sense of "at some time or another" or "sooner or later." By contrast, *hópōs* occurs by itself in Mt 6:16, "for they disfigure their faces, that (*hópōs*) they may appear unto men to fast." Here, the effect is much more immediate and definite. Other occurrences of *hópōs án* are in Lk 2:35; Ac 3:19; Ro 3:4.

(III) With the indic. in the historical tenses (but not in the primary ones), *án* is used in the apodosis (the result) of a conditional sentence in which *ei* ([1487], if) precedes and indicates that the thing in question would have taken place, if that contingency which is the subject of the protasis (the proposition) had also taken place; but that in fact neither the one nor the other has taken place. In Mt 11:21, it means that if these miracles had been done in Tyre, they would have repented; but the miracles were not done, and they did not repent (see also Lk 10:13; Jn 4:10; 9:41; Heb 4:8; Jn 8:42, where the meaning is, if God were your Father, you would love me; however, neither is true [similarly in Mt 11:23; 12:7; 23:30; 24:22, 43; Mk 13:20; Jn 11:21; Ro 9:29; 1Co 2:8; 11:31; Gal 1:10; 1Jn 2:19]).

(IV) When, in relative clauses, a relative pron. with *án* is followed by the indic., Class. Gr. writers employed the subjunctive or optative. This occurs in the NT when a thing is spoken of as actually taking place, not at a definite time or in a definite manner, but as often as opportunity arises. It is thus found only with a preterite, a verb tense that indicates action in the past without reference to duration, continuance, or repetition. Used in Mk 6:56, meaning, "as many as" or "however many"; Ac 2:45; 4:35; 1Co 12:2, meaning led away to idol worship, just as he happened to be led, i.e. I do not say by whom or how; see also Sept.: Ge 2:19; Le 5:3. Once with the present indic. in Mk 11:24, where some MSS have the indic. verb *aiteísthe* in the subjunctive (*aitḗsthe*, from *aitéomai* [154], to ask, beg). See also Lk 8:18; 10:8.

(V) As an adverb or in a false construction, meaning perhaps, possibly. Thus the translation in 2Co 10:9, "as if I would terrify you." In 1Co 7:5, the idea is "except perhaps by consent."

303. ἀνά, ana, *an-ah´*; a primary preposition and adverb; properly *up*; but (by extension) used (distributively) *severally*, or (locally) *at* (etc.):—and, apiece, by, each, every (man), in, through. In compounds (as a prefix) it often means (by implication) *repetition, intensity, reversal*, etc.

Preposition meaning on, upon, in.

(**I**) In the NT, used with other words, it forms a periphrase (a longer phrasing in place of a possible shorter and plainer form of expression) for an adverb; e.g., *aná méros* ([3313], part), by turns, alternately (1Co 14:27); *aná méson* ([3319], midst, middle), in the midst of, through the midst of, between. So with this use spoken of place (Mt 13:25; Mk 7:31; Rev 7:17; Sept.: Isa 57:5; 2Ki 16:14); spoken of persons (1Co 6:5). In Mt 20:9, 10 *aná dēnárion* (*aná* [303], to each, *dēnárion* [1220], dinar), "to each a dinar" (a.t.).

(**II**) With numerical words it marks distribution, e.g., "and sent them two and two (*aná dúo*) before his face" (Lk 10:1; see also Mk 6:40; Lk 9:3, 14; Jn 2:6; Rev 4:8; 21:21; Sept.: Isa 6:2).

In composition, *aná* denotes: (**a**) up or upward, as *anabaínō* (305), I go up; (**b**) back or again, equal to the Eng. prefix re-, implying repetition, increase, intensity, as *anakainízō* (340), to renew; *anachōréō* (402), to depart; *anaginṓskō* (314), to know again, to read.

304. ἀναβαθμός, anabathmos, *an-ab-ath-mos´*; from 305 [compare 898]; a *stairway*:—stairs.

305. ἀναβαίνω, anabainō, *an-ab-ah´ee-no*; from 303 and the base of 939; to *go up* (literal or figurative):—arise, ascend (up), climb (go, grow, rise, spring) up, come (up).

From *aná* (303), up, and *baínō* (n.f.), to go. To go or come up, to ascend, cause to ascend from a lower to a higher place.

(**I**) Spoken of persons, animals: to go or come up (Mt 5:1; Mk 3:13; Lk 5:19; Sept.: Ge 49:4). Specifically, to climb (Lk 19:4); to enter into a boat, to embark (Mk 6:51); climbing up or entering some other way (Jn 10:1); to get up into a chariot (Ac 8:31); from the water (Mt 3:16); out of the water, from the water, upon the land (Ac 8:39; see Ac 8:38); of those who go from a lower to a higher region of country, e.g., from Galilee or Caesarea to Judea (Lk 2:4; Ac 18:22) and especially to Jerusalem (Mt 20:17, 18; Jn 7:8, 10; 12:20); of those who ascend into heaven or to the heights, either to have communion with God or to dwell there (Jn 3:13; 6:62; 20:17; Ro 10:6; Eph 4:8–10; Rev 4:1; 11:12); spoken of angels who are said to ascend and descend upon the Son of man (Jn 1:51).

(**II**) Spoken of inanimate things which are said to go up, ascend, rise, e.g., smoke (Rev 8:4; 9:2; 14:11; 19:3; Sept.: Ex 19:18; Isa 34:10); of plants, fruit: to spring up, grow (Mt 13:7; Mk 4:8, 32; Sept.: Isa 5:24; 32:13; 55:13); of a rumour (Ac 21:31, lit. "word was brought up to the chief captain"); of thoughts, actions, which come up into one's mind: to spring up, arise in the heart (Lk 24:38); upon the heart (Ac 7:23; 1Co 2:9); of prayers (Ac 10:4). See also Isa 65:17; Jer 3:16; 32:35; 44:21.

Deriv.: *anabathmós* (304), the act of ascending; *prosanabaínō* (4320), to go up higher; *sunanabaínō* (4872), to come up with.

Syn.: *anatéllō* (393), to arise, spring up; *érchomai* (2064), to come or go; *hḗkō* (2240), to come or be present; *katantáō* (2658), to come to; *anérchomai* (424), to go up; *phúō* (5453), to germinate, spring up, sprout; *blastánō* (985), to sprout.

306. ἀναβάλλομαι, anaballomai, *an-ab-al´-lom-ahee*; middle from 303 and 906; to *put off* (for oneself):—defer.

307. ἀναβιβάζω, anabibazō, *an-ab-ee-bad´-zo*; from 303 and a derivative of the base of 939; to *cause to go up*, i.e. *haul* (a net):—draw.

308. ἀναβλέπω, anablepō, *an-ab-lep´-o*; from 303 and 991; to *look up*; (by implication) to *recover sight*:—look (up), see, receive sight.

309. ἀνάβλεψις, anablepsis, *an-ab´-lep-sis*; from 308; *restoration of sight*:—recovering of sight.

310. ἀναβοάω, anaboaō, *an-ab-o-ah´-o*; from 303 and 994; to *halloo*:—cry (aloud, out).

311. ἀναβολή, anabolē, *an-ab-ol-ay´*; from 306; a *putting off*:—delay.

312. ἀναγγέλλω, anaggellō, *an-ang-el´-lo*; from 303 and the base of 32; to *announce* (in detail):—declare, rehearse, report, show, speak, tell.

From *aná* (303), on, upon, and *aggéllō* (n.f., see below), to tell, declare, which is from *ággelos* (32), messenger. To announce, make known, declare, tell of things done (Mk 5:14, 19; Ac 14:27; 15:4; 16:38; 2Co 7:7). To bring word, inform (Jn 5:15); of things fut., to show beforehand, foretell (Jn 16:13; Sept.: Isa 41:22, 23; 46:10); of the Christian doctrine, to declare, show forth, teach (Jn 4:25; 16:14, 15, 25; Ac 20:20, 27; Ro 15:21; 1Pe 1:12; 1Jn 1:5; Sept.: Dt 8:3; 26:3; Da 2:9); of evil deeds, meaning to declare, confess (Ac 19:18; Sept.: Job 33:23; Ps 38:18; Isa 3:8).

Deriv. of *angéllō* (n.f.): *apaggéllō* (518), to announce; *diaggéllō* (1229), to declare; *exaggéllō* (1804), to publish, show forth; *epaggéllō* (1861), to proclaim; *kataggéllō* (2605), to declare plainly, *paraggéllō* (3853), charge, command.

Syn.: *diēgéomai* (1334), to relate in full; *ekdiēgéomai* (1555), to narrate in full; *exēgéomai* (1834), to make known, explain, declare; *dēlóō* (1213), to make plain; *phrázō* (5419), to explain, declare; *gnōrízō* (1107), to make known; *emphanízō* (1718), to declare plainly; *phaneróō* (5319), to manifest; *anatíthēmi* (394), to make known, to place before, declare to someone; *marturéō* (3140), to testify; *diaphēmízō* (1310), to spread abroad; *mēnúō* (3377), to disclose, make known; *légō* (3004), to tell; *laléō* (2980), to speak; *apophthéggomai* (669), to speak forth, give utterance; *prosphōnéō* (4377), to address, call to; *eréō* (2046), to speak; *dialégomai* (1256), to discuss, reason, speak; *chrēmatízō* (5537), to warn, instruct as if through an oracle; *apologéomai* (626), to make a defence; *eklaléō* (1583), to speak out; *diasaphéō* (1285), to make clear.

313. ἀναγεννάω, anagennaō, *an-ag-en-nah´-o*; from 303 and 1080; to *beget* or (by extension) *bear* (again):—beget, (bear) × again.

From *aná* (303), again, and *gennáō* (1080), to beget. To beget again. In the NT, used metaphorically for a change of carnal nature to a Christian life; to regenerate. In the pass. *anagennáomai*, to be begotten again, regenerated (1Pe 1:3, 23). It is equivalent to being a child of God (Gal 3:26), being born of God (Jn 1:12, 13; 1Jn 3:9), being born from above (*ánōthen* [509], Jn 3:3), or becoming a new (*kainós* [2537]) creation or creature (*ktísis* [2937]), as in 2Co 5:17.

Syn.: *apokuéō* (616), to give birth to; *tíktō* (5088), to bring forth.

314. ἀναγινώσκω, anaginōskō, *an-ag-in-oce´-ko*; from 303 and 1097; to *know again*, i.e. (by extension) to *read*:—read.

From *aná* (303), an emphatic, and *ginṓskō* (1097), to know. To know accurately, to distinguish. In the NT, to know by reading, to read:

(**I**) To read for oneself, to learn by reading (Mt 12:3, 5; 21:16, 42; 22:31; 24:15; Mk 2:25; 13:14; Lk 6:3; 10:26; Jn 19:20; Ac 8:28, 30, 32; 15:31; 23:34; 2Co 1:13; Eph 3:4; Rev 1:3; 5:4; Sept.: Dt 17:19; 2Ki 5:7; Isa 29:11, 12). Metaphorically in 2Co 3:2, "our epistle … read of all men," i.e. open, manifest.

(**II**) To read aloud before others (Lk 4:16; Ac 13:27; 15:21; 2Co 3:15; Col 4:16; 1Th 5:27; Sept.: Dt 31:11; 2Ki 22:11; Ne 13:1).

Deriv.: *anágnōsis* (320), reading.

315. ἀναγκάζω, anagkazō, *an-ang-kad´-zo*; from 318; to *necessitate*; compel, constrain.

To necessitate, to compel, to constrain. To compel by force, threats, circumstances, etc. (Ac 26:11; 28:19; 2Co 12:11; Gal 2:3, 14).To constrain by entreaty, invitations, etc.; to persuade (Mt 14:22; Mk 6:45; Lk 14:23; Gal 6:12).

Syn.: *aggareúō* (29), to press into service; *parabiázomai* (3849), to employ force contrary to nature and right, to compel by using force; *sunéchō* (4912), to constrain.

316. ἀναγκαῖος, anagkaios, *an-ang-kah´-yos*; from 318; *necessary*; (by implication) *close* (of kin):—near, necessary, necessity, needful.

Adjective from *anágkē* (318), necessity. Compulsive, compelled. In the NT, necessary. Used of things required by nature (1Co 12:22; Tit 3:14); necessary from natural ties of relationship or affinity (Ac 10:24); and necessary from a moral or spiritual standpoint, i.e. right, proper (Ac 13:46; 2Co 9:5; Php 1:24; 2:25; Heb 8:3).

Syn.: *epitḗdeios* (2006), suitable, convenient, necessary; *eúkairos*

(2121), timely, seasonable; *chrḗsimos* (5539), useful; *eúchrēstos* (2173), serviceable; *ōphélimos* (5624), profitable.

317. ἀναγκαστῶς, anagkastōs, *an-ang-kas-toce´*; adverb from a derivative of 315; *compulsorily*:—by constraint.

318. ἀναγκή, anagkē, *an-ang-kay´*; from 303 and the base of 43; *constraint* (literal or figurative); (by implication) *distress*:—distress, must needs, (of) necessity (-sary), needeth, needful.

(I) Spoken of as arising from the influence of other persons: constraint, compulsion (1Co 7:37; 2Co 9:7; Phm 14); as arising from the good or bad disposition of a person or persons, or from the nature and circumstances of the case (Mt 18:7; Heb 7:12, 27; 9:16, 23); spoken of the obligation of duty: to be right, proper, just; I must (Ro 13:5; 1Co 9:16; Jude 3).

(II) Unavoidable distress, calamity (Lk 21:23; 1Co 7:26; 2Co 6:4; 12:10; 1Th 3:7; Sept.: Ps 25:17; 107:6; 109:143; Job 27:9).

Deriv.: *anagkázō* (315), to force; *anagkaíos* (316), needful; *anagkastṓs* (317), of necessity, by constraint; *epánagkes* (1876), of necessity.

Syn.: *stenochōría* (4730), narrowness of place, distress; *thlípsis* (2347), affliction; *sunochḗ* (4928), a compressing together, distress, anguish; *chreía* (5532), a need, necessity; *deí* (1163), it is necessary; *déon*, from *déomai* (1189), to petition, related to *deí* (1163), it is necessary, used as a noun meaning that which is needful, due, proper; *prépō* (4241), I must; *epitagḗ* (2003), an injunction, decree, commandment.

319. ἀναγνωρίζομαι, anagnōrizomai, *an-ag-no-rid´-zom-ahee*; middle from 303 and 1107; to *make* (oneself) *known*:—be made known.

From *aná* (303), again, and *gnōrízō* (1107), to know. To know again, to recognize. Pass.: *anagnōrízomai*, to be made known again (Ac 7:13; Sept.: Ge 45:1); *anegnōrísthēn*, aor. pass. with reflexive meaning, to make oneself known.

Syn.: the phrase *phanerós gínomai* (*phanerós* [5318], manifest; *gínomai* [1096], become), to become manifest; *epiginṓskō* (1921), to fully know; *epístamai* (1987), to understand; *manthánō* (3129), to learn; *homologéō* (3670), to acknowledge, confess; *paradéchomai* (3858), to admit; *apodéchomai* (588), approve, accept; *egkrínō* (1469), approve; *sumphōnéō* (4856), to agree with.

320. ἀνάγνωσις, anagnōsis, *an-ag´-no-sis*; from 314; (the act of) *reading*:—reading.

Noun from *anaginṓskō* (314), to know accurately, to read. Reading, whether public or private (Ac 13:15; 2Co 3:14; 1Ti 4:13; Sept.: Ne 8:3).

321. ἀνάγω, anagō, *an-ag´-o*; from 303 and 71; to *lead up*; by extension to *bring out*; specially to *sail* away:—bring (again, forth, up again), depart, launch (forth), lead (up), loose, offer, sail, set forth, take up.

322. ἀναδείκνυμι, anadeiknumi, *an-ad-ike´-noo-mee*; from 303 and 1166; to *exhibit*, i.e. (by implication) to *indicate, appoint*:—appoint, shew.

323. ἀνάδειξις, anadeixis, *an-ad´-ike-sis*; from 322; (the act of) *exhibition*:—shewing.

324. ἀναδέχομαι, anadechomai, *an-ad-ekh´-om-ahee*; from 303 and 1209; to *entertain* (as a guest):—receive.

From *aná* (303), an emphatic, and *déchomai* (1209), to receive. To take upon oneself. In the NT, to receive, in the sense of to embrace, trust in (Heb 10:17); also, to receive a guest, i.e. to entertain (Ac 28:7).

Syn.: *lambánō* (2983), to receive; *analambánō* (353), to take to oneself, receive; *apolambánō* (618), to receive from another; *hupolambánō* (5274), to receive.

325. ἀναδίδωμι, anadidōmi, *an-ad-eed´-om-ee*; from 303 and 1325; to *hand over*:—deliver.

326. ἀναζάω, anazaō, *an-ad-zah´-o*; from 303 and 2198; to *recover life* (literal or figurative):—(be a-) live again, revive.

327. ἀναζητέω, anazēteō, *an-ad-zay-teh´-o*; from 303 and 2212; to *search* out:—seek.

328. ἀναζώννυμι, anazōnnumi, *an-ad-zone´-noo-mee*; from 303 and 2224; to *gird afresh*:—gird up.

329. ἀναζωπυρέω, anazōpureō, *an-ad-zo-poor-eh´-o*; from 303 and a compound of the base of 2226 and 4442; to *re-enkindle*:—stir up.

330. ἀναθάλλω, anathallō, *an-ath-al´-lo*; from 303 and **θάλλω,** ***thallō*** (to *flourish*); to *revive*:—flourish again.

331. ἀνάθεμα, anathema, *an-ath´-em-ah*; from 394; a (religious) *ban* or (concrete) *excommunicated* (thing or person):—accused, anathema, curse, × great.

Noun from *anatíthēmi* (394), to place, lay up. Anything laid up or suspended as an offering in the temple of a god, anything consecrated to God. In the Sept., *anáthema* is used to translate the Heb *ḥērem* (2764, OT), which is spoken in like manner of animals, persons, etc. (Le 27:28). Because every living thing thus consecrated to God could not be redeemed, but was to be put to death (Le 27:29), both *ḥērem* and Sept. *anáthema* are used to denote anything irrevocably devoted to death, destruction, etc., or anything on which a curse is laid, as cities and their inhabitants (Jos 6:17, 18; 7:1), and therefore anything abominable and detestable (Dt 7:26).

In the NT, *anáthema* is used to indicate an accursed thing, or, spoken of persons, one accursed; someone excluded from the favour of God and devoted to destruction (1Co 12:13; 16:22; Gal 1:8, 9; Ac 23:14; Ro 9:3).

Deriv.: *anathematízō* (332), to declare anathema, to curse; *katanáthema* (2652), an accursed thing.

Syn.: *ará* (685), a malediction, cursing; *katára* (2671), a curse.

332. ἀναθεματίζω, anathematizō, *an-ath-em-at-id´-zo*; from 331; to *declare* or *vow* under penalty of execration:—(bind under a) curse, bind with an oath.

From *anáthema* (331), a curse. To declare one to be accursed, to curse, to bind by a curse (Mk 14:71; Ac 23:12, 14, 21).

Deriv.: *katanathematízō* (2653), to utterly curse.

Syn.: *kataráomai* (2672), to pray or wish evil against a person or thing; *kakologéō* (2551), to speak evil.

333. ἀναθεωρέω, anatheōreō, *an-ath-eh-o-reh´-o*; from 303 and 2334; to *look again* (i.e. *attentively*) at (literal or figurative):—behold, consider.

334. ἀνάθημα, anathēma, *an-ath´-ay-mah*; from 394 [like 331, but in a good sense]; a *votive* offering:—gift.

From *anatíthēmi* (394), to separate, lay up. Anything consecrated to God and laid up or suspended in the temple; a gift, an offering (Lk 21:5). Votive offerings, such as shields, chaplets, golden chains, candlesticks, etc. were common in the temples of the heathen; the same custom was imitated in the Jewish temple.

Syn.: *dṓron* (1435), a gift; *dōreá* (1431), a gift emphasizing the freeness of the gift; *dṓrēma* (1434), that which is given as a gift, boon; *dóma* (1390), a gift as such without any benefit necessarily derived from it; *dósis* (1394), the act of giving; *chárisma* (5486), the gift resulting from grace or *cháris* (5485); *prosphorá* (4376), an offering; *holokaútōma* (3646), a burnt offering.

335. ἀναίδεια, anaideia, *an-ah´ee-die-ah´*; from a compound of 1 (as a negative particle [compare 427]) and 127; *impudence*, i.e. (by implication) *importunity*:—importunity.

Noun from *anaidḗs* (n.f.), impudent, which is from the priv. *a* (1), without, and *aidṓs* (127), shame. Want of modesty, shamelessness, insolence. Recklessness or disregard of consideration by the one making the request (Lk 11:8).

Syn.: *atimía* (819), shame, disgrace, dishonour; *aschēmosúnē* (808), unseemliness, shame.

336. ἀναίρεσις, anairesis, *an-ah´ee-res-is*; from 337; (the act of) *killing*:—death.

337. ἀναιρέω, anaireō, *an-ahee-reh´-o*; from 303 and (the active of) 138; to *take up*, i.e. *adopt*; (by implication) to *take away* (violently), i.e. *abolish, murder*:—put to death, kill, slay, take away, take up.

338. ἀναίτιος, anaitios, *an-ah´ee-tee-os;* from 1 (as a negative particle) and 159 (in the sense of 156); *innocent:*—blameless, guiltless.

339. ἀνακαθίζω, anakathizō, *an-ak-ath-id´-zo;* from 303 and 2523; properly to *set up,* i.e. (reflex.) to *sit up:*—sit up.

340. ἀνακαινίζω, anakainizō, *an-ak-ahee-nid´-zo;* from 303 and a derivative of 2537; to *restore:*—renew.

From *aná* (303), again, and *kainízō* (n.f.), to renew, which is from *kainós* (2537), qualitatively new. To renew, to restore to its former state. In the NT, used metaphorically, spoken of those who have fallen from the true faith: to bring back to repentance and former faith (Heb 6:6; Sept.: Ps 103:5).

Syn.: *ananeóō* (365), to renew in the sense of making young or replacing numerically. See both *néos* (3501), new, either numerically or one coming later, and *kainós* (2537), qualitatively new.

341. ἀνακαινόω, anakainoō, *an-ak-ahee-no´-o;* from 303 and a derivative of 2537; to *renovate:*—renew.

From *aná* (303), again, and *kainóō* (n.f.), to make new, which is from *kainós* (2537), qualitatively new. In the NT, found only in the writings of Paul: to renew; to renovate, in the sense of to change from a carnal to a Christian life; to increase in faith, hope, virtue, etc. (2Co 4:16; Col 3:10, cf. Eph 4:23).

Deriv.: *anakaínōsis* (342), renewal.

Syn.: *ananeóō* (365), to reform, renew with the same kind of experience as in the past; *neótēs* (3503), youth with reference simply to age and not quality of life.

342. ἀνακαίνωσις, anakainōsis, *an-ak-ah´ee-no-sis;* from 341; *renovation:*—renewing.

From *anakainóō* (341), to renew qualitatively. Therefore, a renewing or a renovation which makes a person different than in the past. Occurs in Ro 12:2; Tit 3:5 (cf. Jn 3:5). See also *anakainízō* (340), to renew qualitatively.

Syn.: *paliggenesía* (3824), rebirth, renewal.

343. ἀνακαλύπτω, anakaluptō, *an-ak-al-oop´-to;* from 303 (in the sense of *reversal*) and 2572; to *unveil:*—open, ([un-]) taken away.

344. ἀνακάμπτω, anakamptō, *an-ak-amp´-to;* from 303 and 2578; to *turn back:*—(re-) turn.

345. ἀνακεῖμαι, anakeimai, *an-ak-i´-mahee;* from 303 and 2749; to *recline* (as a corpse or at a meal):—guest, lean, lie, sit (down, at meat), at the table.

346. ἀνακεφαλαίομαι, anakephalaiomai, *an-ak-ef-al-ah´ee-om-ahee;* from 303 and 2775 (in its original sense); to *sum up:*—briefly comprehend, gather together in one.

From *aná* (303), an emphatic meaning again, and *kephalaióō* (2775), to sum up, recapitulate. To sum up, as an orator at the close of his discourse. In the NT, to comprehend several things under one, to reduce under one head (Ro 13:9; Eph 1:10; 2:14, 15).

347. ἀνακλίνω, anaklinō, *an-ak-lee´-no;* from 303 and 2827; to *lean back:*—lay, (make) sit down.

348. ἀνακόπτω, anakoptō, *an-ak-op´-to;* from 303 and 2875; to *beat back,* i.e. *check:*—hinder.

349. ἀνακράζω, anakrazō, *an-ak-rad´-zo;* from 303 and 2896; to *scream up* (aloud):—cry out.

350. ἀνακρίνω, anakrinō, *an-ak-ree´-no;* from 303 and 2919; properly to *scrutinize,* i.e. (by implication) *investigate, interrogate, determine:*—ask, question, discern, examine, judge, search.

351. ἀνάκρισις, anakrisis, *an-ak´-ree-sis;* from 350; a (judicial) *investigation:*—examination.

352. ἀνακύπτω, anakuptō, *an-ak-oop´-to;* from 303 (in the sense of *reversal*) and 2955; to *unbend,* i.e. *rise;* (figurative) *be elated:*—lift up, look up.

353. ἀναλαμβάνω, analambanō, *an-al-am-ban´-o;* from 303 and 2983; to *take up:*—receive up, take (in, unto, up).

354. ἀνάληψις, analēpsis, *an-al´-ape-sis;* from 353; *ascension:*—taking up.

355. ἀναλίσκω, analiskō, *an-al-is´-ko;* from 303 and a form of the alternate of 138; properly to *use up,* i.e. *destroy:*—consume.

356. ἀναλογία, analogia, *an-al-og-ee´-ah;* from a compound of 303 and 3056; *proportion:*—proportion.

Noun from *aná* (303), denoting distribution, and *lógos* (3056), account. Proportion, ratio. Only in Ro 12:6.

Syn.: *métron* (3358), measure.

357. ἀναλογίζομαι, analogizomai, *an-al-og-id´-zom-ahee;* middle from 356; to *estimate,* i.e. (figurative) *contemplate:*—consider.

358. ἄναλος, analos, *an´-al-os;* from 1 (as a negative particle) and 251; *saltless,* i.e. *insipid:*—× lose saltness.

359. ἀνάλυσις, analusis, *an-al´-oo-sis;* from 360; *departure:*—departure.

360. ἀναλύω, analuō, *an-al-oo´-o;* from 303 and 3089; to *break up,* i.e. *depart* (literal or figurative):—depart, return.

361. ἀναμάρτητος, anamartētos, *an-am-ar´-tay-tos;* from 1 (as a negative particle) and a presumed derivative of 264; *sinless:*—that is without sin.

Adjective from the priv. *a* (1), without, and *hamartánō* (264), to sin, miss the mark. Without sin, sinless, faultless. Occurs only in Jn 8:7.

Syn.: *ámemptos* (273), unblameable; *athō̃os* (121), innocent; *anaítios* (338), blameless, guiltless; *anepílēmptos* or *anepílēptos* (423), irreproachable; *hágios* (40), saint, holy; *díkaios* (1342), righteous.

362. ἀναμένω, anamenō, *an-am-en´-o;* from 303 and 3306; to *await:*—wait for.

363. ἀναμιμνήσκω, anamimnēskō, *an-am-im-nace´-ko;* from 303 and 3403; to *remind;* reflexive to *recollect:*—call to mind, (bring to, call to, put in) remember (-brance).

364. ἀνάμνησις, anamnēsis, *an-am´-nay-sis;* from 363; *recollection:*—*remembrance* (again).

Noun from *anamimnḗskō* (363), to remind. Remembrance (Lk 22:19; 1Co 11:24, 25; Heb 10:3).

365. ἀνανεόω, ananeōō, *an-an-neh-o´-o;* from 303 and a derivative of 3501; to *renovate,* i.e. *reform:*—renew.

From *aná* (303), again, and *neóō,* to renew (n.f.), which is from *néos* (3501), new, another. In the NT, to renew oneself; to be renewed in spirit, i.e. changed from a carnal to a Christian life. Only in Eph 4:3.

Syn.: *anakainízō* (340) and *anakainóō* (341), to make qualitatively new; *kainós* (2537), qualitatively new.

366. ἀνανήφω, ananēphō, *an-an-ay´-fo;* from 303 and 3525; to become *sober again,* i.e. (figurative) *regain* (one's) *senses:*—recover self.

367. Ἀνανίας, Ananias, *an-an-ee´-as;* of Hebrew origin [2608]; *Ananias,* the name of three Israelites:—Ananias.

368. ἀναντίρρητος, anantirrhētos, *an-an-tir´-hray-tos;* from 1 (as a negative particle) and a presumed derivative of a compound of 473 and 4483; *indisputable:*—cannot be spoken against.

369. ἀναντιῤῥήτως, anantirrhētōs, *an-an-tir-hray´-toce;* adverb from 368; *promptly:*—without gainsaying.

370. ἀνάξιος, anaxios, *an-ax´-ee-os;* from 1 (as a negative particle) and 514; *unfit:*—unworthy.

371. ἀναξίως, anaxiōs, *an-ax-ee´-oce;* adverb from 370; *irreverently:*—unworthily.

372. ἀνάπαυσις, anapausis, *an-ap´-ow-sis;* from 373; *intermission;* (by implication) *recreation:*—rest.

Noun from *anapaúō* (373), act., to give rest. Rest, quiet, from occupation, oppression, or torment (Mt 11:29; Rev 4:8; 14:11; Sept.: Ex 16:23; Le 25:8; Jer 14:3). By metonymy: place of rest, fixed habitation (Mt 12:43; Lk 11:24; Sept.: Ge 8:9; Ru 3:1; 1Ch 28:2).

Syn.: *anápsuxis* (403), recovery of breath; *ánesis* (425) relief; *katápausis* (2663), rest, cessation of labour; *sabbatismós* (4520), a sabbath keeping, sabbath rest; *koímēsis* (2838), a resting, reclining; *eirḗnē* (1515), peace.

373. ἀναπαύω, anapauō, *an-ap-ow´-o*; from 303 and 3973; (reflexive) to *repose* (literal or figurative [*be exempt*], *remain*); (by implication) to *refresh*:—take ease, refresh, (give, take) rest.

374. ἀναπείθω, anapeithō, *an-ap-i´-tho*; from 303 and 3982; to *incite*:—persuade.

375. ἀναπέμπω, anapempō, *an-ap-em´-po*; from 303 and 3992; to *send up* or *back*:—send (again).

376. ἀνάπηρος, anapēros, *an-ap´-ay-ros*; from 303 (in the sense of *intensity*) and **πῆρος, pēros** (*maimed*); *crippled*:—maimed.

377. ἀναπίπτω, anapipto, *an-ap-ip´-to*; from 303 and 4098; to *fall back*, i.e. *lie down, lean back*:—lean, sit down (to meat).

378. ἀναπληρόω, anaplēroō, *an-ap-lay-ro´-o*; from 303 and 4137; to *complete*; (by implication) to *occupy, supply*; (figurative) to *accomplish* (by coincidence or obedience):—fill up, fulfil, occupy, supply.

From *aná* (303), up, or as an emphatic, and *plēróō* (4137), to fill. To fill up, to fulfill, to complete. Spoken of measure: to fill up (Mt 23:32; 1Th 2:16); spoken of prophecy: to fulfill (Mt 13:14); spoken of a work or duty: to fulfill, to perform (Gal 6:2); spoken of persons: to fill the place of someone, i.e. to sustain his character (1Co 14:16).

Deriv.: *antanaplēróō* (466), to fill up, supplement; *prosanaplēróō* (4322), to supply abundantly.

Syn.: *pímplēmi* (4130), to fill; *empíplēmi* (1705), to fill full; *gemízō* (1072), to fill or load full; *korénnumi* (2880), to fill or to satisfy; *mestóō* (3325), to fill full; *teléō* (5055), to fulfill, to bring to its intended end; *sunteléō* (4931), to complete; *teleióō* (5048), to bring to an end.

379. ἀναπολόγητος, anapologētos, *an-ap-ol-og´-ay-tos*; from 1 (as a negative particle) and a presumed derivative of 626; *indefensible*:—without excuse, inexcusable.

380. ἀναπτύσσω, anaptussō, *an-ap-toos´-so*; from 303 (in the sense of *reversal*) and 4428; to *unroll* (a scroll or volume):—open.

381. ἀνάπτω, anaptō, *an-ap´-to*; from 303 and 681; to *enkindle*:—kindle, light.

382. ἀναρίθμητος, anarithmētos, *an-ar-ith´-may-tos*; from 1 (as a negative particle) and a derivative of 705; *unnumbered*, i.e. *without number*:—innumerable.

383. ἀνασείω, anaseiō, *an-as-i´-o*; from 303 and 4579; (figurative) to *excite*:—move, stir up.

384. ἀνασκευάζω, anaskeuazō, *an-ask-yoo-ad´-zo*; from 303 (in the sense of *reversal*) and a derivative of 4632; properly to *pack up* (baggage), i.e. (by implication and figurative) to *upset*:—subvert.

385. ἀνασπάω, anaspaō, *an-as-pah´-o*; from 303 and 4685; to *take up* or *extricate*:—draw up, pull out.

386. ἀνάστασις, anastasis, *an-as´-tas-is*; from 450; a *standing up* again, i.e. (literal) a *resurrection* from death (individual, genitive or by implication [its author]), or (figurative) a (moral) *recovery* (of spiritual truth):—raised to life again, resurrection, rise from the dead, that should rise, rising again.

Noun from *anístēmi* (450), to stand up. A rising up:

(I) A rising up as opposed to falling. By metonymy, the author or cause of rising up; so metaphorically, the author of a better state, of higher prosperity, of eternal happiness (Lk 2:34).

(II) Resurrection of the body from death, return to life:

(A) Spoken of individuals who have returned to life (Heb 11:35; Sept.: 1Ki 17:17f.; 2Ki 4:20f.); of the resurrection of Jesus (Ac 1:22; 2:31; 4:33; 17:18; Ro 1:4; 6:5; Php 3:10; 1Pe 1:3; 3:21).

(B) Spoken of the future and general resurrection at the end of all things (Jn 11:24; Ac 17:32; 24:15, 21; 26:23; 1Co 15:12, 13, 21, 42; Heb 6:2); of both the resurrection of life (*anástasin zōḗs*, form *zōḗ* [2222], life), and the resurrection of damnation (*anástasin kríseōs*, from *krísis* [2920], judgement, condemnation) in Jn 5:29. This general resurrection was denied by the Sadducees (Mt 22:23, 28, 30, 31; Mk 12:18, 23; Lk 20:27, 33; Ac 23:8), and also certain Christians (2Ti 2:18).

(C) Spoken of the resurrection of the righteous (Mt 22:30; Lk 14:14; 20:35, 36), also called the first resurrection (Rev 20:5, 6, cf. 1Co 15:23, 24; 1Th 4:16).

(D) By metonymy, the author of resurrection (Jn 11:25).

Syn.: *égersis* (1454), a rousing, resurrection (Mt 27:53).

387. ἀναστατόω, anastatoō, *an-as-tat-o´-o*; from a derivative of 450 (in the sense of *removal*); properly to *drive out* of home, i.e. (by implication) to *disturb* (literal or figurative):—trouble, turn upside down, make an uproar.

From *anástatos* (n.f.), made to rise up and depart, which is from *anístēmi* (450), to stand up. To disturb, agitate, put in commotion. Spoken of cities (Ac 17:6; 21:38); of the minds of Christians (Gal 5:12).

Syn.: *epegeírō* (1892), to stir up; *diegeírō* (1326), to arouse or stir up; *anaseíō* (383), to shake out, move to and fro, stir up; *saleúō* (4531), to shake, stir up; *paroxúnō* (3947), to provoke; *erethízō* (2042), to stir up, provoke; *tarássō* (5015), to trouble; *diatarássō* (1298), to agitate greatly, and *ektarássō* (1613), to throw into great trouble; *enochléō* (1776), to disturb, vex; *parenochléō* (3926), to annoy, trouble; *skúllō* (4660), to annoy; *thorubéō* (2350), to make noise or an uproar; *throéō* (2360), to make an outcry; *thorubéō* (2350), to disturb, trouble, or *turbázō* (5182), to trouble.

388. ἀνασταυρόω, anastauroō, *an-as-tow-ro´-o*; from 303 and 4717; to *recrucify* (figurative):—crucify afresh.

From *aná* (303), again or up, and *stauróō* (4717), to crucify. To crucify again or afresh (Heb 6:6).

389. ἀναστενάζω, anastenazō, *an-as-ten-ad´-zo*; from 303 and 4727; to *sigh deeply*:—sigh deeply.

390. ἀναστρέφω, anastrepho, *an-as-tref´-o*; from 303 and 4762; to *overturn*; also to *return*; (by implication) to *busy* oneself, i.e. *remain, live*:—abide, behave self, have conversation, live, overthrow, pass, return, be used.

391. ἀναστροφή, anastrophē, *an-as-trof-ay´*; from 390; *behaviour*:—conversation.

392. ἀνατάσσομαι, anatassomai, *an-at-as´-som-ahee*; from 303 and the middle of 5021; to *arrange*:—set in order.

From *aná* (303), an intensive, and *tássō* (5021), to place in one's proper category. To set in order, to arrange. Only in Lk 1:1.

Syn.: *horízō* (3724), to determine, define; *títhēmi* (5087), to place; *paratíthēmi* (3908), to place alongside; *apokathístēmi* (600), to restore.

393. ἀνατέλλω, anatellō, *an-at-el´-lo*; from 303 and the base of 5056; to (*cause to*) *arise*:—(a-, make to) rise, at the rising of, spring (up), be up.

394. ἀνατίθεμαι, anatithemai, *an-at-ith´-em-ahee*; from 303 and the middle of 5087; to *set forth* (for oneself), i.e. *propound*:—communicate, declare.

395. ἀνατολή, anatolē, *an-at-ol-ay´*; from 393; a *rising* of light, i.e. *dawn* (figurative); (by implication) the *east* (also in plural):—dayspring, east, rising.

396. ἀνατρέπω, anatrepō, *an-at-rep´-o*; from 303 and the base of 5157; to *overturn* (figurative):—overthrow, subvert.

397. ἀνατρέφω, anatrephō, *an-at-ref´-o*; from 303 and 5142; to *rear* (physical or mental):—bring up, nourish (up).

398. ἀναφαίνω, anaphainō, *an-af-ah´ee-no*; from 303 and 5316; to *show*, i.e. (reflexive) *appear*, or (passive) *have pointed out*:—(should) appear, discover.

399. ἀναφέρω, anapherō, *an-af-er´-o*; from 303 and 5342; to *take up* (literal or figurative):—bear, bring (carry, lead) up, offer (up).

400. ἀναφωνέω, anaphōneō, *an-af-o-neh´-o*; from 303 and 5455; to *exclaim*:—speak out.

401. ἀνάχυσις, anachusis, *an-akh´-oo-sis*; from a compound of 303 and **χέω**, *cheō* (to *pour*); properly *effusion*, i.e. (figurative) *license*:—excess.

402. ἀναχωρέω, anachōreō, *an-akh-o-reh´-o*; from 303 and 5562; to *retire*:—depart, give place, go (turn) aside, withdraw self.

403. ἀνάψυξις, anapsuxis, *an-aps´-ook-sis*; from 404; properly a *recovery of breath*, i.e. (figurative) *revival*:—revival.

404. ἀναψύχω, anapsuchō, *an-aps-oo´-kho*; from 303 and 5594; properly to *cool off*, i.e. (figurative) *relieve*:—refresh.

From *aná* (303), again, and *psúchō* (5594), to breathe, to cool. To draw breath again, to take breath, i.e. to revive, be refreshed. In the NT, to refresh, recreate. Only in 2Ti 1:16.

Deriv.: *anápsuxis* (403), refreshing.

Syn.: *anapaúō* (373), to give inner rest; *sunanapaúonai* (4875), to rest with; *katapaúō* (2664), to cause to rest by ceasing from labour; *hēsucházō* (2270), to be still, rest from labour; *epanapaúomai* (1879), to rest upon; *aníēmi* (447), to refresh.

405. ἀνδραποδιστής, andrapodistēs, *an-drap-od-is-tace´*; from a derivative of a compound of 435 and 4228; an *enslaver* (as bringing *men* to his *feet*):—menstealer.

406. Ἀνδρέας, Andreas, *an-dreh´-as*; from 435; *manly; Andreas*, an Israelite:—Andrew.

407. ἀνδρίζομαι, andrizomai, *an-drid´-zom-ahee*; middle from 435; to *act manly*:—quit like men.

408. Ἀνδρόνικος, Andronikos, *an-dron´-ee-kos*; from 435 and 3534; *man of victory; Andronicos*, an Israelite:—Andronicus.

409. ἀνδροφόνος, androphonos, *an-drof-on´-os*; from 435 and 5408; a *murderer*:—manslayer.

410. ἀνέγκλητος, anegklētos, *an-eng´-klay-tos*; from 1 (as a negative particle) and a derivative of 1458; *unaccused*, i.e. (by implication) *irreproachable*:—blameless.

Adjective from the priv. *a* (1), without, and *egkaléō* (1458), to accuse in court. Not arraignable; hence in the NT, unblameable, irreprehensible (1Co 1:8; Col 1:22; 1Ti 3:10; Tit 1:6, 7).

Syn.: *ámemptos* (273), unblameable; *ámōmos* (299), unblemished; *anepílēptos* (423), irreproachable; *áspilos* (784), unspotted; *amṓmētos* (298), without blemish; *anaítios* (338), guiltless.

411. ἀνεκδιήγητος, anekdiēgētos, *an-ek-dee-ay´-gay-tos*; from 1 (as a negative particle) and a presumed derivative of 1555; *not expounded* in full, i.e. *indescribable*:—unspeakable.

412. ἀνεκλάλητος, aneklalētos, *an-ek-lal´-ay-tos*; from 1 (as a negative particle) and a presumed derivative of 1583; *not spoken out*, i.e. (by implication) *unutterable*:—unspeakable.

413. ἀνέκλειπτος, anekleiptos, *an-ek´-lipe-tos*; from 1 (as a negative particle) and a presumed derivative of 1587; *not left out*, i.e. (by implication) *inexhaustible*:—that faileth not.

414. ἀνεκτότερος, anektoteros, *an-ek-tot´-er-os*; comparative of a derivative of 430; *more endurable*:—more tolerable.

415. ἀνελεήμων, aneleēmōn, *an-eleh-ay´-mone*; from 1 (as a negative particle) and 1655; *merciless*:—unmerciful.

Adjective from the priv. *a* (1), without, and *eleḗmōn* (1655), merciful. Unmerciful, cruel, not compassionate (Ro 1:31; Sept.: Pr 5:9).

Syn.: *aníleōs* (448), unmerciful, merciless.

416. ἀνεμίζω, anemizō, *an-em-id´-zo*; from 417; to *toss with the wind*:—drive with the wind.

417. ἄνεμος, anemos, *an´-em-os*; from the base of 109; *wind*; (plural) by implication (the four) *quarters* (of the earth):—wind.

A noun meaning wind, i.e. air in motion:

(I) Spoken particularly of wind (Mt 11:7; Mk 4:41; Lk 7:24; Rev 7:1); of violent, stormy winds (Mt 7:25, 27; Mk 4:37, 39; Lk 8:23, 24; Ac 28:4, 7, 14, 15; Jas 3:4); of the four cardinal winds (Rev 7:1; Sept.: Jer 49:36).

(II) By metonymy, the four quarters of the earth or heavens, whence the cardinal winds blow (Mt 24:31; Mk 13:27, cf. Lk 13:29; Sept.: 1Ch 9:24; Da 11:4).

(III) Metaphorically, "wind of doctrine," i.e. empty doctrine, unstable opinion (Eph 4:14).

Deriv.: *anemízō* (416), to toss or drive with the wind.

Syn.: *pnoḗ* (4157), breath, used of the rushing wind at Pentecost (Ac 2:2); *pneúma* (4151), spirit (Jn 3:8); *thúella* (2366), tempest; *laílaps* (2978), whirlwind.

418. ἀνένδεκτος, anendektos, *an-en´-dek-tos*; from 1 (as a negative particle) and a derivative of the same as 1735; *unadmitted*, i.e. (by implication) *not supposable*:—impossible.

419. ἀνεξερεύνητος, anexereunētos, *an-ex-er-yoo´-nay-tos*; from 1 (as a negative particle) and a presumed derivative of 1830; *not searched out*, i.e. (by implication) *inscrutable*:—unsearchable.

420. ἀνεξίκακος, anexikakos, *an-ex-ik´-ak-os*; from 430 and 2556; *enduring of ill*, i.e. *forbearing*:—patient.

Adjective from *anéchō* (430), to bear, and *kakós* (2556), bad. Patient under evils and injuries. Only in 2Ti 2:24.

Syn.: *epieikḗs* (1933), tolerant. This stresses the positive attitude in contrast to *anexíkakos*, which stresses the negative attitude of being patient regarding wrong; *anektóteros* (414), more tolerable.

421. ἀνεξιχνίαστος, anexichniastos, *an-ex-ikh-nee´-as-tos*; from 1 (as a negative particle) and a presumed derivative of a compound of 1537 and a derivative of 2487; *not tracked out*, i.e. (by implication) *untraceable*:—past finding out, unsearchable.

422. ἀνεπαίσχυντος, anepaischuntos, *an-ep-ah´ee-skhoon-tos*; from 1 (as a negative particle) and a presumed derivative of a compound of 1909 and 153; *not ashamed*, i.e. (by implication) *irreprehensible*:—that needeth not to be ashamed.

423. ἀνεπίληπτος, anepilēptos, *an-ep-eel´-ape-tos*; from 1 (as a negative particle) and a derivative of 1949; *not arrested*, i.e. (by implication) *inculpable*:—blameless, unrebukeable.

Adjective from the priv. *a* (1), without, and *epilambánō* (1949), to seize. Not to be apprehended. In the NT, used metaphorically: irreprehensible, unblameable (1Ti 3:2 [cf. Tit 1:7, *anégklētos* {410}]; 5:7; 6:14).

Syn.: *anégklētos* (410), legally unaccused. *Anepílēptos* demonstrates a higher morality on which no blame can be found to base an accusation, while *anégklētos* indicates that one cannot be legally charged; *ámōmos* (299), without blemish; *amṓmētos* (298), unblameable; *ámemptos* (273), one in whom no fault can be found; *eúphēmos* (2163), of good report; *anaítios* (338), guiltless; *akatákritos* (178), uncondemned; *áspilos* (784), unspotted; *dókimos* (1384), approved; *áxios* (514), worthy.

424. ἀνέρχομαι, anerchomai, *an-erkh´-om-ahee*; from 303 and 2064; to *ascend*:—go up.

425. ἄνεσις, anesis, *an´-es-is*; from 447; *relaxation* or (figurative) *relief*:—eased, liberty, rest.

Noun from *aníēmi* (447), to loose. A letting loose, remission, relaxation: from bonds, imprisonment (Ac 24:23; Sept.: 2Ch 23:15); from active exertion, labour (2Co 8:13); figuratively, remission, rest, quiet, either internal (2Co 2:12) or external (2Th 1:7).

Syn.: *anápausis* (372), inward rest while labouring, whereas *ánesis* indicates a relaxation brought about by a source other than oneself; *chará* (5479), joy; *agallíasis* (20), exuberance; *euphrosúnē* (2167), rejoicing; *áphesis* (859), release, liberty, forgiveness; *eleuthería* (1657), freedom; *katápausis* (2663), rest by ceasing to work.

426. ἀνετάζω, anetazō, *an-et-ad´-zo*; from 303 and **ἐτάζω,** ***etazō*** (to *test*); to *investigate* (judicially):—(should have) examine (-d).

427. ἄνευ, aneu, *an´-yoo*; a primary particle; *without*:—without. Compare 1.

428. ἀνεύθετος, aneuthetos, *an-yoo´-the-tos*; from 1 (as a negative particle) and 2111; *not well set*, i.e. *inconvenient*:—not commodious.

429. ἀνευρίσκω, aneuriskō, *an-yoo-ris´-ko*; from 303 and 2147; to *find out*:—find.

430. ἀνέχομαι, anechomai, *an-ekh´-om-ahee*; middle from 303 and 2192; to *hold oneself up* against, i.e. (figurative) *put up* with:—bear with, endure, forbear, suffer.

From *aná* (303), in, and *échō* (2192), to have. To hold up or back from falling, to hold in or back, restrain, stop. In the NT, to hold oneself upright, to bear up, hold out, endure:

(I) Spoken of things: to endure, bear patiently, as afflictions (2Th 1:4). See Sept.: Isa 42:14. Used in an absolute sense (1Co 4:12; 2Co 11:20).

(II) Spoken of persons: to bear with, have patience with in regard to the errors or weaknesses of anyone (Mt 17:17; Mk 9:19; Lk 9:41; 2Co 11:1, 19; Eph 4:2; Col 3:13; Sept.: Isa 46:4; 63:15).

(III) By implication, to admit, receive, i.e. to listen to, spoken of persons (Ac 18:14); of doctrine (2Co 11:4, see 2Ti 4:3; Heb 13:22).

Deriv.: *anektóteros* (414), more tolerable; *anexíkakos* (420), forbearing; *anochḗ* (463), forbearance, tolerance.

Syn.: *bastázō* (941), to support, carry, take up; *phérō* (5342), to bring or bear; *hupophérō* (5297), to bear up under, endure; *phoréō* (5409), to bear or endure habitually; *tropophoréō* (5159), to bear as a matter of permanent attitude; *stégō* (4722), to bear up against; *metriopathéō* (3356), to treat with mildness or moderation, bear gently with; *karteréō* (2594), to be steadfast, patient (Heb 11:27); *kakopathéō* (2553), to suffer evil; *páschō* (3958), to suffer; *hupéchō* (5254), to hold under; *hupoménō* (5278), to endure as far as things or circumstances are concerned; *maktrothuméō* (3114), enduring or being longsuffering toward people.

431. ἀνέψιος, anepsios, *an-eps´-ee-os*; from 1 (as a particle of union) and an obsolete **νέπος,** ***nepos*** (a *brood*); properly *akin*, i.e. (special) a *cousin*:—sister's son.

432. ἄνηθον, anēthon, *an´-ay-thon*; probably of foreign origin; *dill*:—anise.

433. ἀνήκω, anēkō, *an-ay´-ko*; from 303 and 2240; to *attain to*, i.e. (figurative) *be proper*:—convenient, be fit.

434. ἀνήμερος, anēmeros, *an-ay´-mer-os*; from 1 (as a negative particle) and **ἥμερος,** ***hēmeros*** (*lame*); *savage*:—fierce.

435. ἀνήρ, anēr, *an´-ayr*; a primary word [compare 444]; a *man* (properly as an individual male):—fellow, husband, man, sir.

(I) A man, i.e. an adult male person:

(A) Males as distinguished from females (Mt 14:21; 15:38; Lk 1:34). Spoken of men in various relations and circumstances where the context determines the proper meaning; e.g., husband (Mt 1:16; Mk 10:2, 12; Lk 2:36; Ro 7:2, 3; 1Co 7:2–4, ff.; 2Co 11:2; Gal 4:27; Eph 5:22–25, 28, 33; Col 3:18, 19; 1Ti 2:8, 12; 3:2, 12; 5:9; Tit 1:6; 2:5; 1Pe 3:1, 5, 7; Sept.: Ge 2:23; 3:6); a bridegroom betrothed (Mt 1:19; Rev 21:2; Sept.: Dt 22:23); a soldier (Lk 22:63). In a direct address, *ándres*, men!, sirs! (Ac 14:15; 19:25; 27:10, 21, 25); in this sense, it also expresses respect and deference, and so implies a man of importance (Lk 24:19; Jn 1:30; Jas 2:2).

(B) Joined with an adj. or noun, it forms a periphrasis for a subst., e.g., *anḗr hamartōlós* ([268], sinner), a sinner (Lk 5:8, cf. Mt 7:24, 26); *anḗr phoneús* ([5406], murderer), a murderer (Ac 3:14); *anḗr Ioudaíos* ([2453], Jewish), a Jew (Ac 10:28; see Mt 12:41; Ac 8:27; 11:20; 16:9). With other adj. in a direct address, *ándres Athēnaíoi*, men of Athens, i.e. Athenians (Ac 17:22); Ephesians (Ac 19:35); Israelites (Ac 2:22; 3:12; 5:35; 13:16; 21:28); Galileans (Ac 1:11); brethren (Ac 1:16).

(C) Figuratively, a man of mature understanding, as opposed to a child (1Co 13:11). So in Eph 4:13 the progress of a Christian is likened to the growth of a child into a "perfect man," i.e. in understanding and true wisdom.

(II) Indefinitely, a man, one of the human race, a person (Mk 6:44; Lk 5:12, 18; 8:27; 9:38; 11:29, 31; Ac 6:11; Jas 1:8, 20, 23; 3:2; Sept.: Pr 16:27–29; Ne 4:18).

Deriv.: *andrízō* (407), to act manly; *androphónos* (409), murderer; *húpandros* (5220), one under the authority of a man.

Syn.: *árrēn* (730), male; *téleios* (5046), perfect, one of mature or ripe age; *súzugos* (4805), a yokefellow, hence a husband or wife.

436. ἀνθίστημι, anthistēmi, *anth-is´-tay-mee*; from 473 and 2476; to *stand against*, i.e. *oppose*:—resist, withstand.

437. ἀνθομολογέομαι, anthomologeomai, *anth-om-ol-og-eh´-om-ahee*; from 473 and the middle of 3670; to *confess in turn*, i.e. *respond* in praise:—give thanks.

438. ἄνθος, anthos, *anth´-os*; a primary word; a *blossom*:—flower.

439. ἀνθρακιά, anthrakia, *anth-rak-ee-ah´*; from 440; a bed of burning *coals*:—fire of coals.

440. ἄνθραξ, anthrax, *anth´-rax*; of uncertain derivative; a live *coal*:—coal of fire.

441. ἀνθρωπάρεσκος, anthrōpareskos, *anth-ro-par´-es-kos*; from 444 and 700; *man-courting*, i.e. *fawning*:—men-pleaser.

Adjective from *ánthrōpos* (444), man, and *aréskō* (700), to please. Desirous to please men, without regard to God (Eph 6:6; Col 3:22).

442. ἀνθρώπινος, anthrōpinos, *anth-ro´-pee-nos*; from 444; *human*:—human, common to man, man [-kind], [man-]kind, men's, after the manner of men.

443. ἀνθρωποκτόνος, anthrōpoktonos, *anth-ro-pok-ton´-os*; from 444 and **κτείνω,** ***kteinē*** (to *kill*); a *manslayer*:—murderer. Compare 5406.

Adjective from *ánthrōpos* (444), man and *kteinō* (n.f.), to kill. A murderer; spoken of Satan as the author of sin and death (Jn 8:44); a murderer in heart, in purpose (1Jn 3:15).

Syn.: *phoneús* (5406), murderer, a more general word; *sikários* (4607), an assassin; *patrolṓas* (3964), a murderer of one's father; *mētralṓas* (3389), a murderer of one's mother.

444. ἄνθρωπος, anthrōpos, *anth´-ro-pos*; from 435 and **ὤψ,** ***ōps*** (the *countenance*; from 3700); *man-faced*, i.e. a *human* being:—certain, man.

A noun meaning man, i.e. an individual of the human race, a man or woman, a person:

(I) Generally and universally (Mt 4:19; 12:12; Mk 7:21; Lk 2:52; 5:10; Jn 1:4; 1Co 4:9). In a direct address, "O man" (*ṓ ánthrōpe*) implies an inferior or common person (Lk 5:20; 12:14; 22:58, 60; Ro 2:1, 3; 9:20; Jas 2:20; Sept.: Isa 2:9; 5:15). *Hoi ánthrōpoi*, men, i.e. the living, are those with whom we live, people (Mt 5:13, 16, 19; 6:1; 8:27; 13:25; Mk 8:24, 27; Rev 9:10, 15, 18, 20); men of this world or generation, i.e. wicked men (Mt 10:17; 17:22; Lk 6:22, 26).

(A) Spoken in reference to his human nature, a man, i.e. a human being, a mortal: **(1)** With the idea of human infirmity and imperfection, especially when spoken in contrast to God and divine things (1Co 1:25; 3:21; Gal 1:11, 12; Php 2:7; 1Ti 2:5; Jas 5:17; Rev 4:7; 9:7). Used with this sense in the expression "to speak after the manner of men," i.e. in accordance with human views, and so forth, to illustrate by human example or institutions, to use a popular manner of speaking (Ro 3:5; 1Co 9:8; Gal 3:15). **(2)** Metaphorically, used of the internal man, meaning the mind, soul, the rational man (Ro 7:22; Eph 3:16); "the hidden man of the heart," (1Pe 3:4) to which is opposed the outward or external, visible man (2Co 4:16). So the old man (*ho palaiós* [3820]) or heart, and the new man (*kainós*, 2537), the disposition which is created and cherished by the new nature that Jesus Christ gives to the believer (Ro 6:6; Eph 2:15; 4:22, 24; Col 3:9).

(B) Spoken with reference to the character and condition of a person and applied in various senses according to the context: **(1)** A man, a male person of maturity and ripe age (Mt 8:9; 11:8; 25:24; Mk 3:3; Lk 19:21; Jn 1:6; 3:1; Ac 4:13). The expression "man of God" (*ánthrōpos toú Theoú*), i.e. a minister or messenger of God, one devoted to His service

(1Ti 6:11; 2Ti 3:17; 2Pe 1:21; Sept.: 1Ki 13:1; 2Ki 1:9–13; 4:7, 9, 21). The "man of sin," i.e. the Antichrist (2Th 2:3; so named in 1Jn 2:18, 22; 4:3; 2Jn 7). **(2)** A husband as contrasted to a wife (Mt 19:3, 10; 1Co 7:1; Sept.: Dt 22:30). **(3)** A son as contrasted to a father (Mt 10:35), or a male child generally (Jn 7:23; 16:21). **(4)** A master as contrasted to servants (Mt 10:36). **(5)** A servant (Lk 12:36; Rev 18:13; Sept.: Eze 27:13).

(II) Used with *tis* (5100), an enclitic indefinite pron. meaning any man, a certain man, i.e. one, someone, anyone:

(A) Generally *ánthrōpós tis*, a certain man (Lk 10:30; 12:16; 14:2; Jn 5:5); *heís ánthrōpos*, "one man" (*heís* [1520], one), meaning a man, anyone out of a number (Jn 11:50; 18:14). In Ro 3:28, "a man is justified by faith" means anyone who has faith, irrespective of who he is (see also 1Co 11:28).

(B) Joined with an adj. or noun, it forms a periphrase for a substantive, e.g., *anthrṓpō basileí* (*basileús* [935]), king (Mt 18:23); *ánthrōpos oikodespótēs* (*oikodespótēs* [3617]), householder (Mt 21:33); *hoi ánthrōpoi hoi poiménes* (*poimḗn* [4166]), shepherds (Lk 2:15).

(III) *Ho ánthrōpos* with the article, meaning this or that man, he (Mt 12:13, 45; 26:72), this man of whom you speak (Mk 14:71. See Mk 3:3, 5; 14:21; Lk 6:10; 23:4, 6; Jn 4:50; 19:5; Sept.: Ge 24:29, 30, 32). Sometimes *ekeínos* (1565), that one, is added, as in Mt 26:24, *ho ánthrōpos ekeínos* (Mk 14:21; Jas 1:7).

(IV) *Huiós* (5207) *toú anthrṓpou*, son of man, from the Hebrew:

(A) Equivalent to *ánthrōpos*, a man; so "sons of men" are simply men (Mt 12:31; Mk 3:28; Heb 2:6; Rev 1:13).

(B) As a proper name for the Messiah, with the article, *ho huiós toú anthrṓpou*, drawn from Da 7:13, where the phrase appears in the Sept. for the Aram. *bar 'enāš* (*bar* [1247, OT], son; *'enāš* [606, OT], man). It is used by Jesus of Himself, but is applied to Him by no other person except Stephen (Ac 7:56). It would seem to refer not so much to His human nature as to the fact of His being the Messiah, who is described as coming from heaven in human form (Da 7:13; 10:16; Rev 1:13; 14:14). Often, the names "Son of Man," "Son of God," and "Christ" are used interchangeably (Mt 16:13, 16, 20; Lk 22:69, 70; Jn 12:34); by using this name of Himself before His judges, Jesus openly professed Himself to be the Messiah, and was so understood by all present (Mt 26:64; Mk 14:62; Lk 22:69, 70).

Deriv.: *anthrōpáreskos* (441), man-pleaser; *anthrṓpinos* (442), human; *anthrōpoktónos* (443), murderer.

445. ἀνθυπατεύω, anthupateuō, *anth-oo-pat-yoo´-o*; from 446; to *act as proconsul*:—be the deputy.

446. ἀνθύπατος, anthupatos, *anth-oo´-pat-os*; from 473 and a superlative of 5228; *instead* of the *highest* officer, i.e. (special) a Roman *proconsul*:—deputy.

447. ἀνίημι, aniēmi, *an-ee´-ay-mee*; from 303 and **ἵημι,** ***hiēmi*** (*to send*); to *let up*, i.e. (literal) *slacken*, or (figurative) *desert*, *desist* from:—forbear, leave, loose.

448. ἀνίλεως, anileōs, *an-ee´-leh-oce*; from 1 (as a negative particle) and 2436; *inexorable*:—without mercy.

Adjective from *a* (1), not, and *híleōs* (2436), merciful. Unmerciful, uncompassionate, stern. Only in Jas 2:13.

Syn.: *aneleḗmōn* (415), without mercy.

449. ἄνιπτος, aniptos, *an´-ip-tos*; from 1 (as a negative particle) and a presumed derivative of 3538; *without ablution*:—unwashen.

450. ἀνίστημι, anistēmi, *an-is´-tay-mee*; from 303 and 2476; to *stand up* (literal or figurative, transitive or intransitive):—arise, lift up, raise up (again), rise (again), stand up (-right).

From *aná* (303), again, and *hístēmi* (2476), to stand. To stand again. This verb may have a transitive or an intransitive meaning, as *hístēmi* (2476):

(I) Transitively, meaning to cause to rise up, to raise up, cause to stand:

(A) Spoken of those lying down (Ac 9:41; Sept.: Le 26:1; Nu 7:1); of the dead, meaning to raise up, recall to life (Jn 6:39, 40, 44, 54; Ac 2:32; 13:33); *ek nekrṓn* (*ek* [1537], out of; *nekrṓn* [3498], of the dead [pl.]) as in Ac 13:34; 17:31.

(B) Metaphorically, to raise up, to cause to exist, cause to appear (Mt 22:24 [cf. Ge 38:8]; Ac 2:30; 3:22, 26; 7:37; Sept.: Dt 18:18).

(II) Intransitively, to rise up, arise:

(A) Particularly spoken of those who are sitting or lying down (Mt 26:62; Mk 5:42; 9:27; 14:60; Lk 4:16; 5:25; 6:8; 22:45); rising up from prayer, i.e. from a kneeling or recumbent posture (Lk 17:19); rising from bed or from sleep (Lk 11:7, 8; 22:46); arising from the dead, returning to life (Mt 17:9; Mk 9:9, 10; Lk 16:31; Jn 20:9; Ac 17:3); without *ek nekrṓn* from among the dead (Mt 20:19; Mk 8:31; 9:31; 10:34; Lk 9:8, 19; 18:33; 1Th 4:14, 16). Metaphorically in Eph 5:14, to arise from the death of sin and put on the new man in Christ.

(B) Metaphorically, to arise, come into existence, to be (Ac 7:18; 20:30; Sept.: Ex 1:8; Da 8:22; 11:2).

(C) Meaning to stand forth, come forward, appear (Mt 12:41; Mk 14:57; Lk 10:25; 11:32; Ac 5:36, 37; 6:9; Sept.: 2Ch 20:5). Followed by *epí* ([1909], upon), meaning to rise up against any one, assault (Mk 3:26; Sept.: Ge 4:8; 2Ch 24:13).

(D) Followed by verbs of going or doing (Mt 9:9, "he arose, and followed him"; Mk 1:35; 2:14; 7:24; 10:1, 50; Lk 1:39; 5:28; 15:18, 20; Ac 8:26, 27; 9:6, 11; Sept.: 1Sa 24:5; 2Sa 13:31. See Ro 15:12 [cf. Isa 11:10]; 1Co 10:7 [cf. Ex 32:6]).

Deriv.: *anástasis* (386), resurrection; *exanístēmi* (1817), to rise out of or from among; *epanístamai* (1881), to rise up or against, to arise.

Syn.: *egeírō* (1453), to raise; *anatéllō* (393), to arise; *aírō* (142), to raise, take up, lift; *epaírō* (1869), to lift up, raise; *hupsóō* (5312), to lift or raise up; *anorthóō* (461), to set upright; *anakúptō* (352), to lift oneself up; *exegeírō* (1825), to raise up from; *sunegeírō* (4891), to raise together; *epegeírō* (1892), to rouse up, excite; *stḗkō* (4739), to stand fast.

451. Ἄννα, Anna, *an´-nah*; of Hebrew origin [2584]; *Anna*, an Israelitess:—Anna.

452. Ἄννας, Annas, *an´-nas*; of Hebrew origin [2608]; *Annas* (i.e. 367), an Israelite:—Annas.

453. ἀνόητος, anoētos, *an-o´-ay-tos*; from 1 (as a negative particle) and a derivative of 3539; *unintelligent*; (by implication) *sensual*:—fool (-ish), unwise.

Adjective from the priv. *a* (1), without, and *noéō* (3539), to comprehend. Lacking intelligence, unwise; spoken of those who are slow to understand and receive moral and religious truth (Lk 24:25; Ro 1:14; Gal 3:1, 3; Tit 3:3). Spoken of lusts: imprudent, brutal (1Ti 6:9; Sept.: Dt 32:31; Ps 49:13; Pr 15:21; 17:28).

Syn.: *áphrōn* (878), without reason; *mōrós* (3474), foolish; *asúnetos* (801), without discernment; *ásophos* (781), unwise.

454. ἄνοια, anoia, *an´-oy-ah*; from a compound of 1 (as a negative particle) and 3563; *stupidity*; (by implication) *rage*:—folly, madness.

Noun from *ánous* (n.f.), mad, foolish, from the priv. *a* (1), without, and *noús* (3563), mind, understanding. Want of understanding, folly. In the NT, spoken of rage, malignity (Lk 6:11; 2Ti 3:9).

Syn.: *mōría* (3472), foolishness; *aphrosúnē* (877), senselessness; *manía* (3130), madness, mania; *paraphronía* (3913), mind aberration.

455. ἀνοίγω, anoigō, *an-oy´-go*; from 303 and **οἴγω,** ***oigō*** (to *open*); to *open up* (literal or figurative, in various applications):—open.

456. ἀνοικοδομέω, anoikodomeō, *an-oy-kod-om-eh´-o*; from 303 and 3618; to *rebuild*:—build again.

457. ἄνοιξις, anoixis, *an´-oix-is*; from 455; *opening* (throat):—× open.

458. ἀνομία, anomia, *an-om-ee´-ah*; from 459; *illegality*, i.e. *violation of law* or (genitive) *wickedness*:—iniquity, × transgress (-ion of) the law, unrighteousness.

From *ánomos* (459), lawless. Lawlessness, violation of law, transgression. In the NT, spoken chiefly of the divine law:

(I) Particularly, in 1Jn 3:4, where lawlessness is joined with sin: "Whosoever committeth sin transgresseth also the law [*anomían*]: for sin is the [*anomía*] transgression of the law."

(II) By implication, therefore, *anomía* is used of sin, iniquity, unrighteousness (Mt 23:28; 24:12; Ro 4:7; 6:19; 2Co 6:14; Tit 2:14); hence *ho poiṓn anomían*, a "worker of iniquity" (*poiéō* [4160], to make, to do), i.e. wicked, impious (Mt 7:23; 13:41; Sept.: Job 31:3; Ps

5:6). Also spoken of defection from Christianity to idolatry, apostasy (2Th 2:7).

Syn.: *paranomía* (3892), transgression; *hamártēma* (265), individual sin; *hamartía* (266), sin; *kríma* (2917), condemnation; *opheílēma* (3783), debt; *égklēma* (1462), indictable crime; *athétēsis* (115), acting contrary to accepted custom; *adikía* (93), unrighteousness *adíkēma* (92), a wrong, injury, misdeed; *ponēría* (4189), wickedness, *ho ponērós* (4190) one of the designations of the devil; *parábasis* (3847), an overstepping, transgression; *paráptōma* (3900), sidestepping; *plánē* (4106), a wandering or forsaking of the right path; *agnóēma* (51), a sin of ignorance; *hamártēma* (265), evil deed; *asébeia* (763), impiety; *parábasis* (3847), transgression.

459. ἄνομος, anomos, *an´-om-os*; from 1 (as a negative particle) and 3551; *lawless*, i.e. (negative) *not subject to* (the Jewish) *law*; (by implication, a *Gentile*), or (positive) *wicked*:—without law, lawless, transgressor, unlawful, wicked.

Adjective from the priv. *a* (1), without, and *nómos* (3551), law. Lawless. Without law, not subject to the law of Moses (1Co 9:21); hence put for Gentile, pagan (Ac 2:23). By implication, a violator of the divine law, a transgressor, impious, wicked (Mk 15:28; Lk 22:37; Ac 2:23; 2Th 2:8; 1Ti 1:9; 2Pe 2:8; Sept.: Isa 53:12; 55:7; Eze 18:24; 33:8, 12).

Deriv.: *anomía* (458), lawlessness; *anómōs* (460), lawlessly.

Syn.: *ékthetos* (1570), exposed to perish, cast out; *ádikos* (94), unjust; *athémitos* (111), contrary to accepted customs; *anósios* (462), wicked, unholy, the strongest term denoting presumptuous and wicked self-assertion.

460. ἀνόμως, anomōs, *an-om´-oce*; adverb from 459; *lawlessly*, i.e. (special) *not amenable to* (the Jewish) *law*:—without law.

461. ἀνορθόω, anorthoō, *an-orth-o´-o*; from 303 and a derivative of the base of 3717; to *straighten up*:—lift (set) up, make straight.

From *aná* (303), again or up, and *orthóō* (n.f.), to erect, which is from *orthós* (3717), right, upright, erect. To make straight or upright again, to stand erect (Lk 13:13; Sept.: Ps 20:8). In the sense of to confirm, strengthen, establish (Heb 12:12 quoted from Isa 35:3; Sept.: 2Sa 7:13, 16; Ps 145:14; 146:8; Jer 33:2). To erect again, to rebuild (Ac 15:16).

Syn.: *egeírō* (1453), to raise up; *stḗkō* (4739), to stand fast, persevere; *exanístēmi* (1817), to raise or rise up; *exegeírō* (1825), to raise up; *aírō* (142), to raise or take up, lift; *epaírō* (1869), to raise, used of lifting up the eyes; *hupsóō* (5312), to lift or raise up; *anístēmi* (450), to lift or raise up; *anakúptō* (352), to lift oneself up.

462. ἀνόσιος, anosios, *an-os´-ee-os*; from 1 (as a negative particle) and 3741; *wicked*:—unholy.

463. ἀνοχή, anochē, *an-okh-ay´*; from 430; *self-restraint*, i.e. *tolerance*:—forbearance.

From *anéchō* (430), to bear with, suffer. Forbearance, a holding back, delay. In the NT, self-restraint, forbearance, patience (Ro 2:4; 3:25).

Syn.: *epieíkeia* (1932), clemency; *hupomonḗ* (5281), patience; *makrothumía* (3115), longsuffering toward people.

464. ἀνταγωνίζομαι, antagōnizomai, *an-tag-o-nid´-zom-ahee*; from 473 and 75; to *struggle against* (figurative) ["antagonize"]:—strive against.

From *antí* (473), against, and *agōnízomai* (75), to fight against a person. To be an antagonist, to contend with, strive against. Only in Heb 12:4.

Syn.: *pukteúō* (4438), to box, fight; *máchomai* (3164), to fight, strive; *poleméō* (4170), to war; *diamáchomai* (1264), to struggle against; *erízō* (2051), to wrangle, strive; *athléō* (118), to contend in games, wrestle.

465. ἀντάλλαγμα, antallagma, *an-tal´-ag-mah*; from a compound of 473 and 236; an *equivalent* or *ransom*:—in exchange.

Noun from *antallássō* (n.f.), to exchange, barter, which is from *antí* (473), against or instead of, and *allássō* (236), to change, make other than it is. That which is exchanged for anything, compensation, equivalent, generally the price paid for something (Mt 16:26; Mk 8:37; Sept.: Ru 4:7; Jer 15:13; Job 28:15).

Syn.: *antapódosis* (469), reward.

466. ἀνταναπληρόω, antanaplēroō, *an-tan-ap-lay-ro´-o*; from 473 and 378; to *supplement*:—fill up.

467. ἀνταποδίδωμι, antapodidōmi, *an-tap-od-ee´-do-mee*; from 473 and 591; to *requite* (good or evil):—recompense, render, repay.

468. ἀνταπόδομα, antapodoma, *an-tap-od´-om-ah*; from 467; a *requital* (properly the thing):—recompense.

469. ἀνταπόδοσις, antapodosis, *an-tap-od´-os-is*; from 467; *requital* (properly the act):—reward.

470. ἀνταποκρίνομαι, antapokrinomai, *an-tap-ok-ree´-nom-ahee*; from 473 and 611; to *contradict* or *dispute*:—answer again, reply against.

From *antí* (473), against, and *apokrínomai* (611), to answer. To answer again, to reply against (Lk 14:6; Ro 9:20; Sept.: Jgs 5:29; Job 16:8; 32:12).

Syn.: *apologéomai* (626), to apologize, to speak for oneself; *antilégō* (483), to speak against.

471. ἀντέπω, antepō, *an-tep´-o*; from 473 and 2036; to *refute* or *deny*:—gainsay, say against.

472. ἀντέχομαι, antechomai, *an-tekh´-om-ahee*; from 473 and the middle of 2192; to *hold* oneself *opposite* to, i.e. (by implication) *adhere to*; by extension to *care for*:—hold fast, hold to, support.

From *antí* (473), against or to, and *échō* (2192), have. In the NT, to hold fast to, cleave to, i.e. to be faithfully attached to any person or thing (Mt 6:24; Lk 16:13; Tit 1:9); faithfully to care for (1Th 5:14; Sept.: Pr 3:18; 4:6; Isa 56:2, 4, 6; Jer 2:8; 8:2; Zep 1:6).

Syn.: *kratéō* (2902), to take hold of, keep, retain; *epilambánomai* (1949), to take hold of; *antilambánomai* (482), to help, support; *tēréō* (5083), to keep, give heed to, observe; *phulássō* (5442), to guard, hold.

473. ἀντί, anti, *an-tee´*; a primary particle; *opposite*, i.e. *instead* or *because* of (rarely *in addition* to):—for, in the room of. Often used in composition to denote *contrast, requital, substitution, correspondence*, etc.

Preposition with the general meaning of over against, in the presence of, in lieu of. Spoken metaphorically either in a hostile sense, meaning against, or by way of comparison, where it implies something of equivalent value, and denotes substitution, exchange, requital. In the NT used in the following:

(I) By way of substitution, in place of, instead of (Lk 11:11; 1Co 11:15; Jas 4:15). As implying succession (Mt 2:22); so Jn 1:16, "and grace for grace," meaning grace upon grace, most abundant grace, one favour after another.

(II) By way of exchange, requital, equivalent, meaning in consideration of, on account of: spoken of price: for (Heb 12:16; Sept.: Nu 18:21, 31); of persons: for whom or for the sake of whom, in behalf of (Mt 17:27; 20:28; Mk 10:45); of retribution: for (Mt 5:38; Ro 12:17; 1Th 5:15; 1Pe 3:9); of the cause, motive, occasion: on account of, because of (Lk 12:3; Eph 5:31; Heb 12:2. See also Sept. for Jer 11:17). In composition *antí* denotes: **(a)** over against, as *antitássomai* (498), to resist, oppose; **(b)** contrary to, as *antilégō* (483), to gainsay or speak against; **(c)** reciprocity, as *antapodídōmi* (467), to recompense or requite; **(d)** Substitution, as *anthúpatos* (446), a deputy, proconsul; **(e)** Similarity or correspondence, as *antíthesis* (477), opposition.

Deriv.: *antikrú* (481), opposite to, over against.

474. ἀντιβάλλω, antiballō, *an-tee-bal´-lo*; from 473 and 906; to *bandy*:—have.

475. ἀντιδιατίθεμαι, antidiatithemai, *an-tee-dee-at-eeth´-em-ahee*; from 473 and 1303; to *set oneself opposite*, i.e. *be disputatious*:—that oppose themselves.

476. ἀντίδικος, antidikos, *an-tid´-ee-kos*; from 473 and 1349; an *opponent* (in a lawsuit); specially *Satan* (as the arch-enemy):—adversary.

Noun from *antí* (473), against, and *díkē* (1349), a cause or suit at law. An opponent, accuser, e.g., the plaintiff in a suit at law (Mt 5:25; Lk 12:58). Hence generally, an adversary, enemy (Lk 18:3); also alluding to the Jewish notion that Satan is the accuser of men before God (1Pe 5:8 [cf. Job 1:6; Zec 3:1; Rev 12:10]; Sept.: 1Sa 2:10; Isa 41:11; Jer 50:34; 51:36).

Syn.: *hupenantíos* (5227), one who is contrary to; *ho antikeímenos* (480), the one lying in opposition, the adversary; *diábolos*, the devil, the false accuser; *Satanás* (4567), the adversary, Satan; *ho ponērós* (4190), the wicked one, the devil.

477. ἀντίθεσις, antithesis, *an-tith´-es-is*; from a compound of 473 and 5087; *opposition*, i.e. a *conflict* (of theories):—opposition.

478. ἀντικαθίστημι, antikathistēmi, *an-tee-kath-is´-tay-mee*; from 473 and 2525; to *set down* (troops) *against*, i.e. *withstand*:—resist.

479. ἀντικαλέω, antikaleō, *an-tee-kal-eh´-o*; from 473 and 2564; to *invite in return*:—bid again.

480. ἀντίκειμαι, antikeimai, *an-tik´-i-mahee*; from 473 and 2749; to *lie opposite*, i.e. *be adverse* (figurative, *repugnant*) to:—adversary, be contrary, oppose.

481. ἀντικρύ, antikru, *an-tee-kroo´*; prolonged from 473; *opposite*:—over against.

482. ἀντιλαμβάνομαι, antilambanomai, *an-tee-lam-ban´-om-ahee*; from 473 and the middle of 2983; to *take* hold of *in turn*, i.e. *succor*; also to *participate*:—help, partaker, support.

From *antí* (473), mutually or against, and *lambánō* (2983), to take, to hold. In the NT, to take hold of in one's turn, to take part in, to interest one's self for. Spoken of things (1Ti 6:2, "partakers of the benefit"); of persons: to aid, protect, relieve (Lk 1:54; Ac 20:35).

Deriv.: *antílēpsis* (484), a help, assistance; *sunantilambánō* (4878), to help.

Syn.: *sunantilambánomai* (4878), to take hold of; *boēthéō* (997), aid, help, succor; *sumbállō* (4820), to throw together, helping or benefiting; *sunupourgéō* (4943), to help together, to serve with anyone; *sunergéō* (4903), to help in work, cooperate; *parístēmi* (3936), to stand by for help; *antéchomai* (472), to support, hold.

483. ἀντίλεγω, antilegō, *an-til´-eg-o*; from 473 and 3004; to *dispute, refuse*:—answer again, contradict, deny, gainsay (-er), speak against.

484. ἀντίληψις, antilēpsis, *an-til´-ape-sis*; from 482; *relief*:—help.

Noun from *antilambánō* (482), help, relief. In the NT, by metonymy of abstract for concrete: a helper, reliever. Only in 1Co 12:28, where it refers to those appointed to take care of the poor and sick.

Syn.: *boḗtheia* (996), help; *epikouría* (1947), help or assistance; *ōphéleia* (5622), usefulness; *euergesía* (2108), well-doing; *eupoiḯa* (2140), benefiting others; *chrēstótes* (5544), usefulness, kindness; *sumphéron* (4851), benefit.

485. ἀντιλογία, antilogia, *an-tee-log-ee´-ah*; from a derivative of 483; *dispute, disobedience*:—contradiction, gainsaying, strife.

486. ἀντιλοιδορέω, antiloidoreō, *an-tee-loy-dor-eh´-o*; from 473 and 3058; to *rail in reply*:—revile again.

487. ἀντίλυτρον, antilutron, *an-til´-oo-tron*; from 473 and 3083; a *redemption-price*:—ransom.

Noun from *antí* (473), in return, or correspondence, and *lútron* (3083), a ransom. A ransom, a price of redemption (Mt 20:28; 1Ti 2:6).

Syn.: *eleuthería* (1657), freedom; *sōtería* (4991), salvation; *sōtḗrion* (4992), means of salvation.

488. ἀντιμετρέω, antimetreō, *an-tee-met-reh´-o*; from 473 and 3354; to *mete in return*:—measure again.

489. ἀντιμισθία, antimisthia, *an-tee-mis-thee´-ah*; from a compound of 473 and 3408; *requital, correspondence*:—recompense.

490. Ἀντιόχεια, Antiocheia, *an-tee-okh´-i-ah*; from **Ἀντίοχος**, ***Antiochos*** (a Syrian king); *Antiochia*, a place in Syria:—Antioch.

491. Ἀντιοχεύς, Antiocheus, *an-tee-okh-yoos´*; from 490; an *Antiochian* or inhabitant of Antiochia:—of Antioch.

492. ἀντιπαρέρχομαι, antiparerchomai, *an-tee-par-er´-khom-ahee*; from 473 and 3928; to *go along opposite*:—pass by on the other side.

493. Ἀντίπας, Antipas, *an-tee´-pas*; contracted from a compound of 473 and a derivative of 3962; *Antipas*, a Christian:—Antipas.

494. Ἀντιπατρίς, Antipatris, *an-tip-at-rece´*; from the same as 493; *Antipatris*, a place in Palestine:—Antipatris.

495. ἀντιπέραν, antiperan, *an-tee-per´-an*; from 473 and 4008; *on the opposite side*:—over against.

496. ἀντιπίπτω, antipiptō, *an-tee-pip´-to*; from 473 and 4098 (including its alternate); to *oppose*:—resist.

497. ἀντιστρατεύομαι, antistrateuomai, *an-tee-strat-yoo´-om-ahee*; from 473 and 4754; (figurative) to *attack*, i.e. (by implication) *destroy*:—war against.

498. ἀντιτάσσομαι, antitassomai, *an-tee-tas´-som-ahee*; from 473 and the middle of 5021; to *range oneself against*, i.e. *oppose*:—oppose themselves, resist.

499. ἀντίτυπον, antitupon, *an-teet´-oo-pon*; neuter of a compound of 473 and 5179; *correspond-ing* ["antitype"], i.e. a *representative, counterpart*:—(like) figure (whereunto).

The neuter of the adj. *antítupos* (n.f.), from *antí* (473), against, instead of, corresponding to, and *túpos* (5179), a type, model, figure, form, impression, print. In the NT, *antí* (473) in composition implies resemblance, correspondence; hence, formed after a type or model, like unto, corresponding. Used as a substantive meaning antitype, that which corresponds to a type (Heb 9:24; 1Pe 3:21).

Syn.: *parabolḗ* (3850), a parable; *hupódeigma* (5262), a pattern that is placed under for tracing; *homoíōma* (3667), something which is made to resemble something else; *eikṓn* (1504), an image representing something which has reality; *deígma* (1164), sample, example; *homoíōsis* (3669), making something to look like something else; *homoiótēs* (3665), likeness.

500. ἀντίχριστος, antichristos, *an-tee´-khris-tos*; from 473 and 5547; an *opponent of the Messiah*:—antichrist.

Noun from *antí* (473), instead of or against, and *Christós* (5547), Christ, anointed. Antichrist, literally an opposer of Christ. Found only in John's epistles, and there defined to be, collectively, all who deny that Jesus is the Messiah and that the Messiah is come in the flesh (1Jn 2:18, 22; 4:3; 2Jn 7). What class of persons the apostle had in mind is unknown; probably Jewish adversaries.

Syn.: *pseudóchristos* (5580), a false christ.

501. ἀντλέω, antleō, *ant-leh´-o*; from **ἄντλος**, ***antlos*** (the *hold* of a ship); to *bale* up (properly bilge water), i.e. *dip* water (with a bucket, pitcher, etc.):—draw (out).

502. ἄντλημα, antlēma, *ant´-lay-mah*; from 501; a *baling-vessel*:—thing to draw with.

503. ἀντοφθαλμέω, antophthalmeō, *ant-of-thal-meh´-o*; from a compound of 473 and 3788; to *face*:—bear up into.

504. ἄνυδρος, anudros, *an´-oo-dros*; from 1 (as a negative particle) and 5204; *waterless*, i.e. *dry*:—dry, without water.

505. ἀνυπόκριτος, anupokritos, *an-oo-pok´-ree-tos*; from 1 (as a negative particle) and a presumed derivative of 5271; *undissembled*, i.e. *sincere*:—without dissimulation (hypocrisy), unfeigned.

Adjective from the priv. *a* (1), without, and *hupokrínomai* (5271), to pretend, simulate.Unfeigned, genuine, real, true, sincere (Ro 12:9; 2Co 6:6; 1Ti 1:5; 2Ti 1:5; Jas 3:17; 1Pe 1:22).

Syn.: *ádolos* (97), pure, sincere; *gnḗsios* (1103), genuine; *eilikrinḗs* (1506), pure, sincere; *hagnós* (53), pure, chaste.

506. ἀνυπότακτος, anupotaktos, *an-oo-pot´-ak-tos*; from 1 (as a negative particle) and a presumed derivative of 5293; *unsubdued*, i.e. *insubordinate* (in fact or temper):—disobedient, that is not put under, unruly.

From the priv. *a* (1), without, and *hupotássō* (5293), to subject, sit under in an orderly manner. Spoken of things: not subject (Heb 2:8); spoken of persons: disobedient to authority, disorderly (1Ti 1:9; Tit 1:6, 10).

Syn.: *apeithḗs* (545), unwilling to be persuaded, disobedient.

507. ἄνω, anō, *an´-o*; adverb from 473; *upward* or *on the top*:—above, brim, high, up.

Adverb meaning above, in a higher place (Ac 2:19; Rev 5:3, Majority Text); With the article, what is above, upper, referred to heaven, and therefore heavenly, celestial (Gal 4:26; Php 3:14). So for heaven (Jn 8:23 [cf. 3:13, 31; 6:38]); and things above, heavenly or divine things (Col 3:1, 2). Also, motion to a higher place, upwards (Jn 11:41; Heb 12:15; Sept.: 1Ch 22:5; Ecc 3:21; Isa 8:21; 37:21).

Deriv.: *anṓgeon* (508), an upper room or chamber; *ánōthen* (509), from above, from the beginning, again; *epánō* (1883), above, more than; *huperáno* (5231), high above.

Syn.: *hupsēlós* (5308), high, lofty; *húpsistos* (5310), most high; *mégas* (3173), great, high; *húpsos* (5311), height; *húpsōma* (5313), high thing or height.

508. ἀνώγεον, anōgeon, *an-ogue´-eh-on*; from 507 and 1093; *above* the *ground*, i.e. (properly) the *second floor* of a building; used for a *dome* or a *balcony* on the upper story:—upper room.

509. ἄνωθεν, anōthen, *an´-o-then*; from 507; *from above*; (by analogy) *from the first*; (by implication) *anew*:—from above, again, from the beginning (very first), the top.

Adverb from *ánō* (507), above, and the suffix *-then* denoting from. From above:

(I) Of place: from above, from a higher place (Mt 27:51; Mk 15:38; Jn 19:23). Hence spoken of whatever is heavenly or from heaven, and since God dwells in heaven, it signifies from God, in a divine manner (Jn 3:31; 19:11; Jas 1:17; 3:17).

(II) Of time, meaning from the first, from the beginning (Lk 1:3; Ac 26:5; Gal 4:9). Also, again, another time, as in Jn 3:3, 7, *gennēthḗ ánōthen*, translated "be born again" (*gennáō* [1080], to bear, be born). This could also be translated "to be born from above," doubtless equal to being "born of God" in Jn 1:13. In Jn 3:4, however, Nicodemus clearly takes it as synonymous with *deúteron* (1208), a second time.

Syn.: *dís* (1364), twice; *pálin* (3825), again; *próteron* (4386), before, first; *prṓtos* (4413), first; *prṓton* (4412), firstly, of time; *en archḗ* (*en* [1722], in; *archḗ* [746], beginning) from the beginning; *ap' archḗs* (*apó* [575], from, *archḗs* [n.f.], beginning), from the beginning.

510. ἀνωτερικός, anōterikos, *an-o-ter-ee-kos´*; from 511; *superior*, i.e. (locally) *more remote*:—upper.

511. ἀνώτερος, anōteros, *an-o´-ter-os*; comparative degree of 507; *upper*, i.e. (neuter as adverb) to a *more conspicuous* place, in a *former* part of the book:—above, higher.

512. ἀνωφέλες, anōpheles, *an-o-fel´-ace*; from 1 (as a negative particle) and the base of 5624; *useless* or (neuter) *inutility*:—unprofitable (-ness).

513. ἀξίνη, axinē, *ax-ee´-nay*; probably from **ἄγνυμι,** ***agnumi*** (to *break*; compare 4486); an *axe*:—axe.

514. ἄξιος, axios, *ax´-ee-os*; probably from 71; *deserving, comparable* or *suitable* (as if *drawing* praise):—due reward, meet, [un-] worthy.

515. ἀξιόω, axioō, *ax-ee-o´-o*; from 514; to *deem entitled* or *fit*:—desire, think good, count (think) worthy.

516. ἀξίως, axiōs, *ax-ee´-oce*; adverb from 514; *appropriately*:—as becometh, after a godly sort, worthily (-thy).

517. ἀόρατος, aoratos, *ah-or´-at-os*; from 1 (as a negative particle) and 3707; *invisible*:—invisible (thing).

518. ἀπαγγέλλω, apaggellō, *ap-ang-el´-lo*; from 575 and the base of 32; to *announce*:—bring word (again), declare, report, shew (again), tell.

From *apó* (575), from, and *aggéllō* (n.f., see *anaggéllō* [312]), to tell, declare. To announce:

(I) To bring a message from any person or place:

(A) To relate, inform, tell what has occurred (Mt 8:33; 14:12; Mk 6:30; 16:10, 13; Lk 8:20, 36; Jn 4:51; 20:18; Ac 11:13; Ac 4:23; 1Th 1:9; Sept.: Jgs 13:10).

(B) To announce, make known, declare, tell what is done or to be done (Mt 12:18; Ac 5:25; 15:27; 16:36; 28:21; Heb 2:12; 1Jn 1:2, 3; Sept.: Ge 24:49; 29:15; Jos 2:2; Jgs 13:6; Ps 78:4, 6 quoted from 22:23). To praise, celebrate (Sept.: Ps 89:1; 105:1). By implication, to confess (Lk 8:47; 1Co 14:25; Sept.: Ge 12:18).

(II) To bring back word from anyone, report (Mt 2:8; 11:4; Lk 7:22; 14:21; Ac 22:26; Sept.: Ge 27:42; 29:12).

Syn.: *diēgéomai* (1334), to narrate, relate; *ekdiēgéomai* (1555), to narrate in full; *exēgéomai* (1834), to lead out, make known, rehearse; *dēlóō* (1213), to declare; *phrázō* (5419), to express, declare; *gnōrízō* (1107), to make known; *marturéō* (3140), to testify; *diaphēmízō* (1310), to report to the public; *phaneróō* (5319), to make manifest; *légō* (3004), to tell; *laléō* (2980), to speak; *eklaléō* (1583), to speak out; *eréō* (2046), to say; *diasaphéō* (1285), to make clear; *mēnúō* (3377), to show or make known.

519. ἀπάγχομαι, apagchomai, *ap-ang´-khom-ahee*; from 575 and **ἄγχω,** ***agchō*** (to *choke*; akin to the base of 43); to *strangle oneself off* (i.e. to death):—hang himself.

520. ἀπάγω, apagō, *ap-ag´-o*; from 575 and 71; to *take off* (in various senses):—bring, carry away, lead (away), put to death, take away.

521. ἀπαίδευτος, apaideutos, *ap-ah´ee-dyoo-tos*; from 1 (as a negative particle) and a derivative of 3811; *uninstructed*, i.e. (figurative) *stupid*:—unlearned.

Adjective from the priv. *a* (1), without, and *paideúō* (3811), to instruct, chastise, correct. Unlearned, untaught, ignorant, stupid, foolish. Of persons (Sept.: Pr 8:5; 15:15; 17:21). In the NT, nonsensical, i.e. inept, trifling, absurd disputations. Only in 2Ti 2:23.

Syn.: *agrámmatos* (62), unlettered, unlearned; *amathḗs* (261), unlearned, ignorant; *idiṓtēs* (2399), a private citizen, an ignorant person; *áphrōn* (878), without reason; *anóētos* (453), without understanding; *mōrós* (3474), dull, sluggish in understanding; *asúnetos* (801), without discernment; *agoraíos* (60), one relating to the marketplace, a commoner.

522. ἀπαίρω, apairō, *ap-ah´ee-ro*; from 575 and 142; to *lift off*, i.e. *remove*:—take (away).

523. ἀπαιτέω, apaiteō, *ap-ah´ee-teh-o*; from 575 and 154; to *demand back*:—ask again, require.

From *apó* (575), again, and *aitéō* (154), to ask. To recall, demand back what is one's own, require (Lk 6:30; 12:20).

Syn.: *zētéō* (2212), to seek, inquire, desire; *epizētéō* (1934), to seek after or for; *ekzētéō* (1567), to seek out.

524. ἀπαλγέω, apalgeō, *ap-alg-eh´-o*; from 575 and **ἀλγέω,** ***algeō*** (to *smart*); to *grieve out*, i.e. *become apathetic*:—be past feeling.

525. ἀπαλλάσσω, apallassō, *ap-al-las´-so*; from 575 and 236; to *change away*, i.e. *release*, (reflexive) *remove*:—deliver, depart.

From *apó* (575), from, and *allássō* (236), to change. To remove from. In the NT: to remove one's self from, to depart, to leave (Ac 19:12; Sept.: Ex 19:22). By implication, to set free, to dismiss; to be set free (Lk 12:58); used metaphorically in Heb 2:15.

Syn.: *eleutheróō* (1659), to set free, deliver; *apolúō* (630), to loose from; *aphíēmi* (863), to remit, forgive; *lutróō* (3084), to ransom, redeem; *apolúō* (630), to release.

526. ἀπαλλοτριόω, apallotrioō, *ap-al-lot-ree-o´-o*; from 575 and a derivative of 245; to *estrange away*, i.e. (passive and figurative) to *be non-participant*:—alienate, be alien.

From *apó* (575), from, and *allotrióō* (n.f.), to alienate. To estrange, to be alienated from, to be a stranger (Eph 2:12; 4:18; Col 1:21). It denotes the state prior to man's reconciliation to God. See Sept.: Job 21:29; Ps 58:3; Eze 14:5.

527. ἁπαλός, apalos, *ap-al-os´*; of uncertain derivative; *soft*:—tender.

528. ἀπαντάω, apantaō, *ap-an-tah´-o*; from 575 and a derivative of 473; to *meet away*, i.e. *encounter*:—meet.

529. ἀπάντησις, apantēsis, *ap-an´-tay-sis*; from 528; a (friendly) *encounter*:—meet.

530. ἅπαξ, hapax, *hap´-ax*; probably from 537; *one* (or a *single*) *time* (numerically or conclusively):—once.

531. ἀπαράβατος, aparabatos, *ap-ar-ab´-at-os*; from 1 (as a negative particle) and a derivative of 3845; *not passing away*, i.e. *untransferable* (perpetual):—unchangeable.

Adjective from the priv. *a* (1), without, and *parabaínō* (3845), to go beyond, transgress. Not passing over, i.e. not transgressing; in the pass., not violated, inviolate. In the NT, spoken of Christ's priesthood as not transient, perpetual or immutable, unchanging, only in Heb 7:24.

Syn.: *hedraíos* (1476) and *ametakínētos* (277), immovable; *ametáthetos* (276), unchangeable; *stereós* (4731), solid, stable, steadfast; *bébaios* (949), firm.

532. ἀπαρασκεύαστος, aparaskeuastos, *ap-ar-ask-yoo´-as-tos*; from 1 (as a negative particle) and a derivative of 3903; *unready*:—unprepared.

533. ἀπαρνέομαι, aparneomai, *ap-ar-neh´-om-ahee*; from 575 and 720; to *deny utterly*, i.e. *disown, abstain*:—deny.

From *apó* (575), from, and *arnéomai* (720), to deny, refuse. Spoken of persons, to deny, disown, abjure:

(I) Of Christ and his religion (Mt 26:34, 35, 75; Mk 14:30, 31, 72; Lk 22:34 [TR], 61; Jn 13:38 [TR]); of persons denied by Christ (Lk 12:9).

(II) Followed by *heautón* (1438), oneself: to deny oneself, i.e. to disown and renounce self, to disregard all personal interests and enjoyments (Mt 16:24; Mk 8:34).

Syn.: *antilégō* (483), to speak against, contradict; *paraitéomai* (3868), to avoid, reject; *apodokimázō* (513), to reject, disapprove; *athetéō* (114), to make void, nullify, disallow; *anthístēmi* (436), to set against; *antikathístēmi* (478), to stand firm against; *antitássō* (498), to set oneself against, oppose; *antipíptō* (496), to strive against, resist.

534. ἀπάρτι, aparti, *ap-ar´-tee*; from 575 and 737; *from now*, i.e. *henceforth* (*already*):—from henceforth.

535. ἀπαρτισμός, apartismos, *ap-ar-tis-mos´*; from a derivative of 534; *completion*:—finishing.

536. ἀπαρχή, aparchē, *ap-ar-khay´*; from a compound of 575 and 756; a *beginning* of sacrifice, i.e. the (Jewish) *first-fruit* (figurative):—first-fruits.

Noun from *apárchomai* (n.f.), from *apó* (575), from, and *árchomai* (756), to begin. An offering of firstfruits; then, an offering generally. In the NT, the firstfruits, which were usually consecrated to God:

(I) The first part of something. In Ro 11:16, the firstfruits, the first portion, metaphorically spoken of the patriarchs and ancestors of the Jewish nation. Used figuratively in Ro 8:23, "the firstfruits of the Spirit," i.e. the first gifts of the Spirit, the earnest, the pledge of future and still higher gifts.

(II) Spoken of persons: first in time, the first of whom any particular thing may be predicated (Ro 16:5; 1Co 15:20, 23; 16:15; Jas 1:18; Rev 14:4).

Syn.: *prṓtos* (4413), beginning, first.

537. ἅπας, hapas, *hap´-as*; from 1 (as a particle of union) and 3956; absolutely *all* or (singular) *every* one:—all (things), every (one), whole.

538. ἀπατάω, apataō, *ap-at-ah´-o*; of uncertain derivative; to *cheat*, i.e. *delude*:—deceive.

539. ἀπάτη, apatē, *ap-at´-ay*; from 538; *delusion*:—deceit (-ful, -fulness), deceivableness (-ving).

540. ἀπάτωρ, apatōr, *ap-at´-ore*; from 1 (as a negative particle) and 3962; *fatherless*, i.e. *of unrecorded paternity*:—without father.

541. ἀπαύγασμα, apaugasma, *ap-ow´-gas-mah*; from a compound of 575 and 826; an *off-flash*, i.e. *effulgence*:—brightness.

Noun from *apaugázō* (n.f.), to emit light or splendour, which is from *apó* (575), from, and *augázō* (826), to shine. Reflected splendour or brightness. Only in Heb 1:3, used figuratively, meaning in whom the divine majesty is conspicuous.

Syn.: *phṓs* (5457), light; *phéggos* (5338), brightness, lustre.

542. ἀπείδω, apeidō, *ap-i´-do*; from 575 and the same as 1492; to *see* fully:—see.

543. ἀπείθεια, apeitheia, *ap-i´-thi-ah*; from 545; *disbelief* (obstinate and rebellious):—disobedience, unbelief.

Noun from *apeithḗs* (545), disobedient. Disobedience, unwillingness to be persuaded, willful unbelief, obstinacy (Ro 11:30, 32; Eph 2:2; 5:6; Heb 4:6, 11); by Hebraism, *huioí tḗs apaitheías*, "children of disobedience" (*huiós* [5207], son, child), i.e. heathen, pagans (Col 3:6 [TR]).

Syn.: *parakoḗ* (3876), hearing amiss, hence disobedience; *apistía* (570), unbelief; *parábasis* (3847), transgression; *paranomía* (3892), law-breaking.

544. ἀπειθέω, apeitheō, *ap-i-theh´-o*; from 545; to *disbelieve* (wilfully and perversely):—not believe, disobedient, obey not, unbelieving.

From *apeithḗs* (545), disobedient. Not to allow oneself to be persuaded or believe, to disbelieve, be disobedient:

(I) Spoken of disbelievers in Christ (Ac 14:2; 17:5; 19:9; Ro 15:31; 1Pe 2:8); of those who are disobedient to God (Ro 10:21; 11:31; Heb 3:18; 1Pe 3:20; Sept.: Dt 9:7; Isa 50:5; 63:10; 65:2). In Heb 11:31 *hoi apeithḗsantes*, those who did disobey, unbelievers, heathen. See Sept.: Isa 66:14.

(II) Of those disobedient to the Son (Jn 3:36); to God (Ro 11:30; Sept.: Nu 14:43); to the truth (Ro 2:8); to the Word (1Pe 2:8; 3:1); to the gospel (1Pe 4:17 [cf. Dt 1:26; 9:23; 32:51]).

Syn.: *apistéō* (569), to disbelieve; *parakoúō* (3878), to hear imperfectly and thus to disobey; *parabaínō* (3845), to transgress; *anthístēmi* (436), to stand against; *exanístēmi* (1817), to object; *epanístamai* (1881), to rise up against; *aphístēmi* (868), to stand afar, desist; *ataktéō* (812), to behave in a disorderly manner.

545. ἀπειθής, apeithēs, *ap-i-thace´*; from 1 (as a negative particle) and 3982; *unpersuadable*, i.e. *contumacious*:—disobedient.

Adjective from the priv. *a* (1), without, and *peíthō* (3982), to persuade. Unwilling to be persuaded, unbelieving, disobedient (Lk 1:17; Ac 26:19; Ro 1:30; 2Ti 3:2; Tit 1:16; 3:3).

Deriv.: *apeítheia* (543), disobedience; *apeithéō* (544), to be disobedient.

Syn.: *anupótaktos* (506), disobedient; *átaktos* (313), unruly; *sklērós* (4642), hard, not pliable.

546. ἀπειλέω, apeileō, *ap-i-leh´-o*; of uncertain derivative; to *menace*; (by implication) to *forbid*:—threaten.

547. ἀπειλή, apeilē, *ap-i-lay´*; from 546; a *menace*:—× straitly, threatening.

548. ἄπειμι, apeimi, *ap´-i-mee*; from 575 and 1510; to *be away*:—be absent. Compare 549.

From *apó* (575), from, and *eimí* (1510), to be. To be absent (1Co 5:3; 2Co 10:1, 11; 13:2, 10; Php 1:27; Col 2:5).

Deriv.: *apousía* (666), absence.

Syn.: *aphístēmi* (868), to stand away from, desist; *ekdēméō* (1553), to vacate, exit, be absent; *analúō* (360), to depart; *chōrízomai* (5563), to separate oneself.

549. ἄπειμι, apeimi, *ap´-i-mee*; from 575 and **εἶμι**, ***eimi*** (to *go*); to *go away*:—go. Compare 548.

550. ἀπειπόμην, apeipomēn, *ap-i-pom´-ane*; reflexive past of a compound of 575 and 2036; to *say off* for oneself, i.e. *disown*:—renounce.

551. ἀπείραστος, apeirastos, *ap-i´-ras-tos*; from 1 (as a negative particle) and a presumed derivative of 3987; *untried*, i.e. *not temptable*:—not to be tempted.

Adjective from the priv. *a* (1), without, and *peirázō* (3985), to tempt or test. Untried, untempted, i.e. incapable of being tempted. Only in Jas 1:13.

552. ἄπειρος, apeiros, *ap´-i-ros*; from 1 (as a negative particle) and 3984; *inexperienced*, i.e. *ignorant*:—unskilful.

553. ἀπεκδέχομαι, apekdechomai, *ap-ek-dekh´-om-ahee*; from 575 and 1551; to *expect fully*:—look (wait) for.

From *apó* (575), an intensive, and *ekdéchomai* (1551), to expect, look for. To wait out, i.e. to wait long for, to await ardently, to expect (Ro 8:19, 23, 25; 1Co 1:7; Gal 5:5; Php 3:20; Heb 9:28 [cf. 1Pe 3:20]).

Syn.: *prosdokáō* (4328), to await, expect; *prosdéchomai* (4327), to expect, look for; *anaménō* (362), to wait for with patience and confident expectancy; *periménō* (4037), to wait around for the fulfillment of an event; *proskarteréō* (4342), to wait around looking forward to the fulfillment of something one expects to take place; *elpízō* (1679), to hope; *prosménō* (4357), to tarry, wait with patience and steadfastness; *apoblépō* (578), to look away from all else at one object, to look steadfastly.

554. ἀπεκδύομαι, apekduomai, *ap-ek-doo´-om-ahee*; middle from 575 and 1562; to *divest wholly* oneself, or (for oneself) *despoil*:—put off, spoil.

555. ἀπέκδυσις, apekdusis, *ap-ek´-doo-sis*; from 554; *divestment*:—putting off.

556. ἀπελαύνω, apelaunō, *ap-el-ow´-no*; from 575 and 1643; to *dismiss*:—drive.

557. ἀπελεγμός, apelegmos, *ap-el-eg-mos´*; from a compound of 575 and 1651; *refutation*, i.e. (by implication) *contempt*:—nought.

558. ἀπελεύθερος, apeleutheros, *ap-el-yoo´-ther-os*; from 575 and 1658; one *freed away*, i.e. a *freedman*:—freeman.

Noun from *apó* (575), from, and *eleútheros* (1658), free. A freedman. Only in 1Co 7:22.

559. Ἀπελλῆς, Apellēs, *ap-el-lace´*; of Latin origin; *Apelles*, a Christian:—Apelles.

560. ἀπελπίζω, apelpizō, *ap-el-pid´-zo*; from 575 and 1679; to *hope out*, i.e. *fully expect*:—hope for again.

From *apó* (575), from, and *elpízō* (1679), to hope.

Syn.: *exaporéō* (1820), to be wholly without resource, to despair utterly; *aporéō* (639), despair or be perplexed. To have done hoping, to despair. Only in Lk 6:35, cf. 6:34.

561. ἀπέναντι, apenanti, *ap-en´-an-tee*; from 575 and 1725; *from in front*, i.e. *opposite, before* or *against*:—before, contrary, over against, in the presence of.

562. ἀπέραντος, aperantos, *ap-er´-an-tos*; from 1 (as a negative particle) and a secondary derivative of 4008; *unfinished*, i.e. (by implication) *interminable*:—endless.

563. ἀπερισπάστως, aperispastōs, *ap-er-is-pas´-toce*; adverb from a compound of 1 (as a negative particle) and a presumed derivative of 4049; *undistractedly*, i.e. *free from* (domestic) *solicitude*:—without distraction.

564. ἀπερίτμητος, aperitmētos, *ap-er-eet´-may-tos*; from 1 (as a negative particle) and a presumed derivative of 4059; *uncircumcised* (figurative):—uncircumcised.

Adjective from the priv. *a* (1), without, and *peritémnō* (4059), to circumcise. Uncircumcised. In the NT, used metaphorically in Ac 7:51, "uncircumcised in heart and ears," those who do not listen or obey the divine precepts. See Sept.: Ge 17:14; Ex 12:48; Le 26:41; Jer 6:10; 9:26; Eze 44:7, 9.

565. ἀπέρχομαι, aperchomai, *ap-erkh´-om-ahee*; from 575 and 2064; to *go off* (i.e. *depart*), *aside* (i.e. *apart*) or *behind* (i.e. *follow*), literal or figurative:—come, depart, go (aside, away, back, out, … ways), pass away, be past.

566. ἀπέχει, apechei, *ap-ekh´-i*; third person singular present indicative active of 568 used impersonally; *it is sufficient*:—it is enough.

Used impersonally, from the verb *apéchō* (568), to have, receive. Literally, "to have off or out," meaning to have all that is one's due so as to cease from demanding or having any more. Thus, used in this manner, *apéchei* means it is enough as in Mk 14:41, meaning you have slept enough.

567. ἀπέχομαι, apechomai, *ap-ekh´-om-ahee*; middle (reflexive) of 568; to *hold oneself off*, i.e. *refrain*:—abstain.

The middle voice of *apéchō* (568), to keep oneself from. To abstain or refrain (Ac 15:20, 29; 1Th 4:3; 5:22; 1Ti 4:3; 1Pe 2:11; Sept.: Job 1:1, 8; Pr 23:4).

Syn.: *egkrateúomai* (1467), to exercise self-restraint; *nḗphō* (3525), to be sober; *sōphronéō* (4993), to exercise soundness of mind, to think soberly, use self-control.

568. ἀπέχω, apechō, *ap-ekh´-o*; from 575 and 2192; (active) to *have out*, i.e. *receive in full*; (intransitive) to *keep* (oneself) *away*, i.e. *be distant* (literal or figurative):—be, have, receive.

From *apó* (575), from, and *échō* (2192), to have, be. To hold off from, as a ship from the shore; to be distant from, absent (Lk 7:6; 15:20; 24:13; Sept.: Isa 55:9); used figuratively, of the heart (Mt 15:8; Mk 7:6). Also, to have all that is one's due, to have received in full, spoken of reward, or wages (Mt 6:2, 15, 16; Lk 6:24; Php 4:18); spoken of a person: to have for good and all (Phm 15).

Deriv.: *apéchei* (566), it is enough.

Syn.: *aphístēmi* (868), to desist, stand off; *apotrépomai* (665), to turn away from.

569. ἀπιστέω, apisteō, *ap-is-teh´-o*; from 571; to *be unbelieving*, i.e. (transitive) *disbelieve*, or (by implication) *disobey*:—believe not.

From *ápistos* (571), untrustworthy. To withhold belief, to doubt, to distrust (Mk 16:11; Lk 24:11; Ac 28:24). Hence, to disbelieve, to be unbelieving, i.e. without faith in God and Christ (Mk 16:16; Ro 3:3); to break one's faith, to prove false (2Ti 2:13).

Syn.: *apeithéō* (544), to refuse to be persuaded or believe.

570. ἀπιστία, apistia, *ap-is-tee´-ah*; from 571; *faithlessness*, i.e. (negative) *disbelief* (*want of* Christian *faith*), or (positive) *unfaithfulness* (*disobedience*):—unbelief.

Noun from *ápistos* (571), untrustworthy. Faithlessness or uncertainty, distrust, unbelief. In respect to declarations, doctrines, promises, etc. (Mt 13:58; 17:20; Mk 9:24; Ro 3:3; 11; 20, 23). A state of unbelief, before embracing the gospel (1Ti 1:13). A violation of faith, apostasy (Heb 3:12, 19).

Syn.: *apeítheia* (543), disobedience; *parakoḗ* (3876), hearing amiss, an act of disobedience.

571. ἄπιστος, apistos, *ap´-is-tos*; from 1 (as a negative particle) and 4103; (active) *disbelieving*, i.e. *without* Christian *faith* (specially a *heathen*); (passive) *untrustworthy* (person), or *incredible* (thing):—that believeth not, faithless, incredible thing, infidel, unbeliever (-ing).

Adjective from *a* (1), without, and *pistós* (4103), believing, faithful. Not worthy of confidence, untrustworthy. Spoken of things: incredible, unbelievable (Ac 26:8); spoken of persons: withholding belief, incredulous, distrustful (Mt 17:17; Mk 9:19; Lk 9:41; Jn 20:27; 2Co 4:4). By implication, heathen, pagan, i.e. those who have not believed on Christ (1Co 6:6; 7:12, 13, 14; 14:22). So with the idea of impiety (2Co 6:14, 15; 1Ti 5:8; Tit 1:15).

Deriv.: *apistéō* (569), to disbelieve; *apistía* (570), unbelief.

Syn.: *apeithḗs* (545), spurning belief, disobedient; *anupótaktos* (506), insubordinate, disobedient.

572. ἁπλότης, haplotēs, *hap-lot´-ace*; from 573; *singleness*, i.e. (subjective) *sincerity* (*without dissimulation* or *self-seeking*), or (objective) *generosity* (*copious bestowal*):—bountifulness, liberal (-ity), simplicity, singleness.

Noun from *haplóos* contracted *haploús* (573), simplicity. Generally, sincerity, candor (2Co 1:12; Sept.: 2Sa 15:11; Pr 19:1); simplicity of heart (Eph 6:5; Col 3:22; Sept.: 1Ch 29:17). Specifically spoken of Christian simplicity, frankness, integrity, fidelity, etc. (Ro 12:8; 2Co 8:2; 9:11, 13; 11:3).

Syn.: *aphelótēs* (858), simplicity, singleness; *eulogía* (2129), a blessing, indicating abundance; *cháris* (5485), grace, with the meaning of bounty; *hadrótēs* (100), fatness, indicating abundance; *perisseía* (4050), an exceeding measure; *huperbolḗ* (5236), beyond measure.

573. ἁπλοῦς, haplous, *hap-looce´*; probably from 1 (as a particle of union) and the base of 4120; properly *folded together*, i.e. *single* (figurative, *clear*):—single.

Simple, sound, perfect (Mt 6:22; Lk 11:34).

Deriv.: *haplótēs* (572), singleness; *haplṓs* (574), bountifully.

Syn.: *ákakos* (172), harmless, unwilling to do harm; *akéraios* (185), harmless; *ádolos* (97), without guile; *gnḗsios* (1103), sincere, genuine; *eilikrinḗs* (1506), pure, sincere; *agathós* (18), benevolent; *kalós* (2570), good; *chrēstós* (5443), kindly.

574. ἁπλῶς, haplōs, *hap-loce´*; adverb from 573 (in the objective sense of 572); *bountifully*:—liberally.

575. ἀπό, apo, *apo´*; a primary particle; "*off*," i.e. *away* (from something near), in various senses (of place, time, or relation; literal or figurative):—(× here-) after, ago, at, because of, before, by (the space of), for (-th), from, in, (out) of, off, (up-) on (-ce), since, with. In composition (as a prefix) it usually denotes *separation, departure, cessation, completion, reversal*, etc.

576. ἀποβαίνω, apobainō, *ap-ob-ah´ee-no*; from 575 and the base of 939; literal to *disembark*; (figurative) to *eventuate*:—become, go out, turn.

577. ἀποβάλλω, apoballō, *ap-ob-al´-lo*; from 575 and 906; to *throw off*; (figurative) to *lose*:—cast away.

578. ἀποβλέπω, apoblepō, *ap-ob-lep´-o*; from 575 and 991; to *look away* from everything else, i.e. (figurative) intently *regard*:—have respect.

579. ἀπόβλητος, apoblētos, *ap-ob´-lay-tos*; from 577; *cast off*, i.e. (figurative) such as to *be rejected*:—be refused.

580. ἀποβολή, apobolē, *ap-ob-ol-ay´*; from 577; *rejection*; (figurative) *loss*:—casting away, loss.

581. ἀπογενόμενος, apogenomenos, *ap-og-en-om´-en-os*; past participle of a compound of 575 and 1096; *absent*, i.e. *deceased* (figurative, *renounced*):—being dead.

Second aor. middle part. of *apogínomai* (n.f.), from *apó* (575), from, and *gínomai* (1096), to become. To be absent from, to depart, i.e. to die. In the NT, used metaphorically: to die to something, i.e. to renounce. Only in 1Pe 2:24.

Syn.: *thnḗskō* (2348), to die; *apothnḗskō* (599), to die off; *teleutáō* (5053), to end one's life; *ekleípō* (1587), to cease, die; *suntríbō* (4937), to break in pieces; *sbénnumi* (4570), to extinguish; *apóllumi* (622), to destroy, die, lose; *leípō* (3007), to be wanting, lacking; *apoleípō* (620), to leave behind; *phtheírō* (5351), to corrupt, destroy.

582. ἀπογραφή, apographē, *ap-og-raf-ay´*; from 583; an *enrollment*; (by implication) an *assessment*:—taxing.

583. ἀπογράφω, apographō, *ap-og-raf´-o*; from 575 and 1125; to *write off* (a copy or list), i.e. *enroll*:—tax, write.

584. ἀποδείκνυμι, apodeiknumi, *ap-od-ike´-noo-mee*; from 575 and 1166; to *show off*, i.e. *exhibit*; (figurative) to *demonstrate*, i.e. *accredit*:—(ap-) prove, set forth, shew.

585. ἀπόδειξις, apodeixis, *ap-od´-ike-sis*; from 584; *manifestation*:—demonstration.

586. ἀποδεκατόω, apodekatoō, *ap-od-ek-at-o´-o*; from 575 and 1183; to *tithe* (as debtor or creditor):—(give, pay, take) tithe.

587. ἀπόδεκτος, apodektos, *ap-od´-ek-tos*; from 588; *accepted*, i.e. *agreeable*:—acceptable.

Adjective from *apodéchomai* (588), to welcome. Acceptable (1Ti 2:3; 5:4).

Syn.: *euárestos* (2101), well-pleasing; *euprósdektos* (2144), acceptable, favourable; *dókimos* (1384), approved, acceptable.

588. ἀποδέχομαι, apodechomai, *ap-od-ekh´-om-ahee*; from 575 and 1209; to *take fully*, i.e. *welcome* (persons), *approve* (things):—accept, receive (gladly).

From *apó* (575), an intensive, and *déchomai* (1209), to take from another for oneself, to receive. Spoken of persons, to receive as a friend or guest, to bid welcome (Lk 8:40; Ac 15:4; 28:30). Figuratively, of doctrine: to admit, to embrace (Ac 2:41). To accept with joy, to welcome, and by implication, to applaud, extol (Ac 24:3).

Deriv.: *apodektós* (587), acceptable; *apodochḗ* (594), a receiving back.

Syn.: *lambánō* (2983), to receive without necessarily indicating a favourable reception; *paralambánō* (3880), to receive from another; *apolambánō* (618), to receive from another as one's due; *proslambánō* (4355), to take to oneself; *eudokéō* (2106), to approve; *sugkatatíthemai* (4784), to consent; *euarestéō* (2100), to please or be pleased; *paradéchomai* (3858), to accept with delight, receive; *prosdéchomai* (4327), to accept, to look for; *egkrínō* (1469), to reckon on, approve; *homologéō* (3670), to assent, confess, accept, accept together.

589. ἀποδημέω, apodēmeō, *ap-od-ay-meh´-o*; from 590; to *go abroad*, i.e. *visit a foreign land*:—go (travel) into a far country, journey.

590. ἀπόδημος, apodēmos, *ap-od´-ay-mos*; from 575 and 1218; *absent from* one's own *people*, i.e. a *foreign traveller*:—taking a far journey.

591. ἀποδίδωμι, apodidōmi, *ap-od-eed´-o-mee*; from 575 and 1325; to *give away*, i.e. *up, over, back*, etc. (in various applications):—deliver (again), give (again), (re-) pay (-ment be made), perform, recompense, render, requite, restore, reward, sell, yield.

592. ἀποδιορίζω, apodiorizō, *ap-od-ee-or-id´-zo*; from 575 and a compound of 1223 and 3724; to *disjoin* (by a boundary, figuratively, a party):—separate.

From *apó* (575), from, and *diorízō* (n.f.), to divide, separate. To set bounds. In the NT, used metaphorically: to divide off, separate. Only in Jude 19.

Syn.: *aphorízō* (873), to mark off by bounds; *chōrízō* (5563), to separate.

593. ἀποδοκιμάζω, apodokimazō, *ap-od-ok-ee-mad´-zo*; from 575 and 1381; to *disapprove*, i.e. (by implication) to *repudiate*:—disallow, reject.

From *apó* (575), from, and *dokimázō* (1381), to prove. To disapprove, to reject. Spoken of a stone rejected or worthless (Mt 21:42; Mk 12:10; Lk 20:17; 1Pe 4:7; Sept.: Jer 6:30); of Jesus rejected as the Messiah by the Jews (Mk 8:31; Lk 9:22; 17:25); of Esau (Heb 12:17; Sept.: Jer 6:30; 7:28; 14:19; 31:36).

Syn.: *athetéō* (114), to make void, nullify, reject; *ekptúō* (1609), to spit out, spurn; *paraitéomai* (3868), to refuse; *akuróō* (208), to disannul, render of no effect; *aporríptō* (641), to reject.

594. ἀποδοχή, apodochē, *ap-od-okh-ay´*; from 588; *acceptance*:—acceptation.

Noun from *apodéchomai* (588), to receive from. Reception, particularly of a guest. In the NT, used metaphorically: assent, approbation, praise. Only in 1Ti 1:15; 4:9.

Syn.: *sugkatáthesis* (4783), agreement; *eudokía* (2107), good pleasure; *homología* (3671), acknowledgement, confession; *bebaíōsis* (951), confirmation; *anochḗ* (463), forbearance.

595. ἀπόθεσις, apothesis, *ap-oth´-es-is*; from 659; a *laying aside* (literal or figurative):—putting away (off).

596. ἀποθήκη, apothēkē, *ap-oth-ay´-kay*; from 659; a *repository*, i.e. *granary*:—barn, garner.

597. ἀποθησαυρίζω, apothēsaurizō, *ap-oth-ay-sow-rid´-zo*; from 575 and 2343; to *treasure away*:—lay up in store.

598. ἀποθλίβω, apothlibō, *ap-oth-lee´-bo*; from 575 and 2346; to *crowd* from (every side):—press.

599. ἀποθνήσκω, apothnēskō, *ap-oth-nace´-ko*; from 575 and 2348; to *die* off (literal or figurative):—be dead, death, die, lie a-dying, be slain (× with).

From *apó* (575) an intensive, and *thnḗskō* (2348), to die. To die; through the force of *apó*, to die out, to become quite dead. Hence it is stronger than *thnḗskō*, though generally used synonymously with it and instead of it:

(I) Spoken of persons (Mt 9:24; Mk 5:35, 39; Lk 8:42; Jn 21:23; Ac 9:37; Ro 6:10; 7:2, 3; 14:7, 8; Heb 11:4; Rev 14:13). Spoken of a violent death: to be put to death, to be killed, to perish (Mt 26:35; Ac 21:13; Ro 5:6–8; Rev 8:9, 11). So of animals, to perish (Mt 8:32; Rev 16:3); spoken of the punishment of death (Jn 19:7; Heb 10:28).

(II) Of vegetable life: to rot (Jn 12:24; 1Co 15:36); of trees: to wither, to die (Jude 12, figuratively).

(III) In an inchoative sense: to be dying, to be near death (Lk 8:42); to be exposed to death, to be in danger of death (1Co 15:31; 2Co 6:9). Also, to be subject to death, to be mortal (Ro 5:15; 1Co 15:22; Heb 7:8).

(IV) Metaphorically, referring to religious faith, works, etc.: to be ready to expire, become extinct (Rev 3:2). Also, to die to or from something, i.e. to renounce, to forsake (Ro 6:2; Gal 2:19; Col 2:20).

(V) Figuratively, to die forever, to come under condemnation of eternal death, i.e. exclusion from the Messiah's kingdom, and subjection to eternal punishment for sin (Jn 6:50; 8:21, 24; Ro 7:10; 8:13).

Deriv.: *sunapothnḗskō* (4880), to die with.

Syn.: *teleutáō* (5053), to end one's life; *koimáō* (2837), to fall asleep, figuratively, to die; *apogínomai* (581), to be away from, to die; *apóllumi* (622), to destroy, die.

600. ἀποκαθίστημι, apokathistēmi, *ap-ok-ath-is´-tay-mee*; from 575 and 2525; to *reconstitute* (in health, home or organization):—restore (again).

From *apó* (575), back again, and *kathístēmi* (2525), to constitute. To put back into a former state, to restore. Spoken of restoration to health (Mt 12:13; Mk 3:5; 8:25; Lk 6:10; Sept.: Ex 4:7; Le 13:16); of the Jewish kingdom and government, which the Messiah was expected to restore and enlarge (Mt 17:11; Mk 9:12 [cf. Mal 4:6; Lk 1:16, 17]); of restoration of one's friends and country, e.g., from prison (Heb 13:19; Sept.: Jer 16:15; 24:6).

Deriv.: *apokatástasis* (605), restitution of a thing to its former condition.

Syn.: *epistréphō* (1994) and *epanágō* (1877), to return; *epanérchomai* (1880), to come again; *therapeúō* (2323), to cure, restore health.

601. ἀποκαλύπτω, apokaluptō, *ap-ok-al-oop´-to*; from 575 and 2572; to take *off the cover*, i.e. *disclose*:—reveal.

From *apó* (575), from, and *kalúptō* (2572), to cover, conceal. To uncover. In the NT, used metaphorically: to reveal, to disclose, to bring to light:

(I) Generally (Mt 10:26; Lk 12:2). In the pass., of things which become known by their effects (Lk 2:35; Jn 12:38; Ro 1:17, 18; 1Pe 5:1).

(II) Spoken of things revealed from God, i.e. taught, communicated, made known, by his Spirit and influences (Mt 11:25; 16:17; Lk 10:21; 1Co 2:10; 14:30; Eph 3:5; Php 3:15; 1Pe 1:12). Spoken of things revealed from God through Christ (Mt 11:27; Lk 10:22); through Paul (Gal 1:16).

(III) Spoken of persons, in the pass.: to be revealed, to appear; spoken of Christ's appearing from heaven (Lk 17:30); spoken of Antichrist (2Th 2:3, 6, 8).

Deriv.: *apokálupsis* (602), disclosure, revelation.

Syn.: *chrēmatízō* (5537), to give divine instruction; *apostegázō* (648), to unroof, uncover; *anakalúptō* (343), to unveil, discover, open up; *emphanízō* (1718), to manifest; *anaptússō* (380), to unroll, open up.

602. ἀποκάλυψις, apokalupsis, *ap-ok-al´-oop-sis*; from 601; *disclosure*:—appearing, coming, lighten, manifestation, be revealed, revelation.

Noun from *apokalúptō* (601), to reveal. An uncovering, nakedness (Sept.: 1Sa 20:30). In the NT, used metaphorically:

(I) Of the removal of the veil of ignorance and darkness by the communication of light and knowledge; illumination, instruction (Lk 2:32).

(II) In the sense of revelation, disclosure, manifestation (Ro 2:5; 8:19). So of that which before was unknown and concealed, especially the divine mysteries, purposes, doctrines, etc. (Ro 16:25; 1Co 14:6, 26); of revelations from God or Christ (2Co 12:1, 7; Gal 1:12; 2:2; Eph 3:3). Spoken of future events in Rev 1:1, where it makes part of the title of the book.

(III) In the sense of appearance, and spoken of Christ's appearance from heaven (2Th 1:7; 1Co 1:7; 1Pe 1:7, 13; 4:13).

Syn.: *gumnótēs* (1132), nakedness; *phanérōsis* (5321), manifestation; *éleusis* (1660), coming (Ac 7:32).

603. ἀποκαραδοκία, apokaradokia, *ap-ok-ar-ad-ok-ee´-ah*; from a compound of 575 and a compound of **κάρα**, ***kara*** (the *head*) and 1380 (in the sense of *watching*); *intense anticipation*:—earnest expectation.

Noun from *apokaradokéō* (n.f.), to expect earnestly. Earnest expectation (Ro 8:19; Php 1:20, where it is *karadokía* in some MSS; Sept.: Ps 37:7).

Syn.: *prosdokía* (4329), expectation; *ekdochḗ* (1561), the looking for, expectation.

604. ἀποκαταλλάσσω, apokatallassō, *ap-ok-at-al-las´-so*; from 575 and 2644; to *reconcile fully*:—reconcile.

From *apó* (575), from, indicating the state to be left behind, and *katallássō* (2644), to reconcile. To change from one state of feeling to another, i.e. to reconcile (Eph 2:16; Col 1:20, 21).

Syn.: *diallássō* (1259), to reconcile in cases of mutual hostility; *eirēnopoiéō* (1517), to make peace; *sumbibázō* (4822), to drive together.

605. ἀποκατάστασις, apokatastasis, *ap-ok-at-as´-tas-is*; from 600; *reconstitution*:—restitution.

Noun from *apokathístēmi* (600), to restore. A restoration of a thing to its former state. Only in Ac 3:21, "the times of restitution of all things," i.e. the Messiah's future kingdom.

606. ἀπόκειμαι, apokeimai, *ap-ok´-i-mahee*; from 575 and 2749; to *be reserved*; (figurative) to *await*:—be appointed, (be) laid up.

607. ἀποκεφαλίζω, apokephalizō, *ap-ok-ef-al-id´-zo*; from 575 and 2776; to *decapitate*:—behead.

608. ἀποκλείω, apokleiō, *ap-ok-li´-o*; from 575 and 2808; to *close fully*:—shut up.

609. ἀποκόπτω, apokoptō, *ap-ok-op´-to*; from 575 and 2875; to *amputate*; reflexive (by irony) to *mutilate* (the privy parts):—cut off. Compare 2699.

610. ἀπόκριμα, apokrima, *ap-ok´-ree-mah*; from 611 (in its original sense of *judging*); a judicial *decision*:—sentence.

Noun from *apokrínomai* (611), to answer. An answer, judicial response, sentence. In the NT, sentence of death (1Co 1:9), i.e. constant exposure to death, despair of life.

Syn.: *chrēmatismós* (5538), a divine response through an oracle; *apología:* (627), a verbal defence; *eperṓtēma* (1906), a legal questioning or appeal; *katadíkē* (UBS) or *díkē* (TR) (1349), a judicial sentence, condemnation; *katákrisis* (2633), sentencing adversely.

611. ἀποκρίνομαι, apokrinomai, *ap-ok-ree´-nom-ahee*; from 575 and **κρινω**, ***krino***; to *conclude for oneself*, i.e. (by implication) to *respond*; by Hebrew [compare 6030] to *begin to speak* (where an address is expected):—answer.

From *apó* (575), from, and *krínō* (2919), to separate, discern, judge. To give a judicial answer. Generally, to answer, to respond:

(I) Particularly, to a question (Mt 11:4; 13:11; 19:4; Mk 12:34); to a judicial interrogation or accusation (Mt 26:62; 27:12, 14; Mk 14:61); to an entreaty, exhortation, proposition (Mt 4:4; Lk 22:68); by way of contradiction or denial (Mt 3:15; 12:48; Mk 7:28; Jn 2:18; Ac 25:4).

(II) By way of Hebraism, to proceed to speak, either to continue the discourse (Mt 11:25; 22:1; Mk 9:19; 10:24), or more frequently, to begin to speak, probably with reference to what another had already said (Mt 17:4, 17; Mk 9:5; 10:51; Ac 3:12). So of an interrogation (Mt 27:21; Rev 7:13).

Deriv.: *antapokrínomai* (470), to answer in contradiction, to answer back; *apókrima* (610), answer or judicial sentence; *apókrisis* (612), the act of answering.

Syn.: *hupolambánō* (5274), to catch up in speech, to answer; *apologéomai* (626), to speak back, to answer in making a defence for oneself; *antilégō* (483), to speak or answer against; *proslaléō* (4354), to speak to; *phthéggomai* (5350), to utter a sound or voice; *apophthéggomai* (669), to speak forth; *chrēmatízō* (5537), to utter an oracle.

612. ἀπόκρισις, apokrisis, *ap-ok´-ree-sis*; from 611; a *response*:—answer.

Noun from *apokrínomai* (611), answer. An answer, a reply (Lk 2:47; 20:26; Jn 1:22; 19:9; Sept.: Dt 1:22; Job 32:5; Ps 15:1). For syn. and ant. see *apókrima* (610), answer, sentence. The distinction between *apókrisis* and *apókrima* is that the first is the act of answering and the second is the answer itself.

613. ἀποκρύπτω, apokruptō, *ap-ok-roop´-to*; from 575 and 2928; to *conceal away* (i.e. *fully*); (figurative) to *keep secret*:—hide.

614. ἀπόκρυφος, apokruphos, *ap-ok´-roo-fos*; from 613; *secret*; (by implication) *treasured*:—hid, kept secret.

615. ἀποκτείνω, apokteinō, *ap-ok-ti´-no*; from 575 and **κτείνω**, ***kteinō*** (to *slay*); to *kill* outright; (figurative) to *destroy*:—put to death, kill, slay.

616. ἀποκυέω, apokueō, *ap-ok-oo-eh´o*; from 575 and the base of 2949; to *breed forth*, i.e. (by transfer) to *generate* (figurative):—beget, produce.

From *apó* (575), from, and *kuéō* (n.f.), to swell, be pregnant. To beget, bear. In the NT, used metaphorically (Jas 1:15, 18 [cf. 1Co 4:15; 1Pe 1:3, 23]).

Deriv.: of *kúō*, to swell (n.f.): *égkuos* (1471), pregnant; *kúma* (2949), a wave.

Syn.: *tíktō* (5088), to bring forth; *gennáō* (1080), to beget, give birth.

617. ἀποκυλίω, apokuliō, *ap-ok-oo-lee´-o*; from 575 and 2947; to *roll away*:—roll away (back).

618. ἀπολαμβάνω, apolambanō, *ap-ol-am-ban´-o*; from 575 and 2983; to *receive* (specially in *full*, or as a host); also to *take aside*:—receive, take.

619. ἀπόλαυσις, apolausis, *ap-ol´-ow-sis*; from a compound of 575 and **λαύω**, ***lauō*** (to *enjoy*); full *enjoyment*:—enjoy (-ment).

620. ἀπολείπω, apoleipō, *ap-ol-ipe´-o*; from 575 and 3007; to *leave* behind (passive *remain*); (by implication) to *forsake*:—leave, remain.

621. ἀπολείχω, apoleichō, *ap-ol-i´-kho*; from 575 and **λείχω**, ***leichō*** (to "*lick*"); to *lick* clean:—lick.

622. ἀπόλλυμι, apollumi, *ap-ol´-loo-mee*; from 575 and the base of 3639; to *destroy* fully (reflexive to *perish*, or *lose*), literal or figurative:—destroy, die, lose, mar, perish.

From *apó* (575) an intensive, the middle *óllumi* (n.f.), to destroy. The force of *apó* here is away or wholly; therefore, the verb is stronger than the simple *óllumi*. To destroy, middle be destroyed, perish. Also from *óllumi* (n.f.): *ólethros* (3639), rain, destruction.

(I) To destroy, cause to perish, transitively:

(A) Spoken of things figuratively (1Co 1:19, meaning to bring to naught, render void the wisdom of the wise, quoted from Isa 29:14).

(B) Of persons, to destroy, put to death, cause to perish: **(1)** Spoken of physical death (Mt 2:13; 12:14; 21:41; 22:7; Mk 3:6; 9:22; 11:18; 12:9; Lk 6:9 [TR]; 17:27, 29; 19:47; 20:16; Jn 10:10; Jude 5; Sept.: Ge 20:4; Dt 11:4; Est 4:9; 9:16). In a judicial sense, to sentence to death (Mt 27:20; Jas 4:12). **(2)** Spoken of eternal death, i.e. future punishment, exclusion from the Messiah's kingdom. In this sense it has the same meaning as *apothnḗskō* (599), to die (Mt 10:28; Mk 1:24; Lk 4:34; 9:56). This eternal death is called the second death (Rev 20:14). In Lk 9:25, to "destroy himself" (a.t.) means to subject himself to eternal death.

(II) To lose, be deprived of, transitively of such things as reward (Mk 9:41); a sheep (Lk 15:4); a drachma or coin (Lk 15:8, 9). See Jn 6:39; 2Jn 8; Sept.: Pr 29:3. To lose one's life or soul (Mt 10:39; 16:25; Mk 8:35; Lk 9:24; 17:33; Jn 12:25).

(III) In the middle and pass. forms, to be destroyed, perish; spoken of:

(A) Things (Mt 5:29, 30; 9:17; Mk 2:22; Lk 5:37; Jn 6:27; Heb 1:11; Jas 1:11; 1Pe 1:7).

(B) Persons, to be put to death, to die, perish, relating to physical death (Mt 8:25; 26:52; Mk 4:38; Lk 8:24; 11:51; 13:33; 15:17; Jn 18:14; Ac 5:37; 1Co 10:9, 10; 2Co 4:9; 2Pe 3:6; Jude 11; Sept.: Le 23:30; Est 9:12). Spoken of eternal death (see I, B, 2), to perish eternally, i.e. to be deprived of eternal life (Lk 13:3, 5; Jn 3:15, 16; 10:28; 17:12; Ro 2:12; 1Co 15:18; 2Pe 3:9).

(C) To be lost to the owner (Lk 21:18; Jn 6:12). Spoken of those who wander away and are lost, e.g., the prodigal son (Lk 15:24); sheep straying in the desert (Lk 15:4, 6). Metaphorically (Mt 10:6; 15:24; Sept.: Ps 119:176; Jer 50:6; Eze 34:4).

Deriv.: *Apollúōn* (623), destroyer; *apṓleia* (684), destruction; *sunapóllumi* (4881), to destroy with.

Syn.: *katargéō* (2673), abolish; *kathairéō* (2507), to cast down; *lúō* (3089), to loose; *katalúō* (2647), to destroy utterly; *olothreúō* (2645), to destroy; *exolothreúō* (1842), to destroy utterly; *phtheírō* (5351), to corrupt; *porthéō* (4199), to ruin by laying waste, to make havoc; *thnḗskō* (2348), to die; *apothnḗskō* (599), to die off or out; *teleutáō* (5053), to end, to die; *apogínomai* (581), to die, to become something else.

623. Ἀπολλύων, Apolluōn, *ap-ol-loo´-ohn*; active participle of 622; a *destroyer* (i.e. *Satan*):—Apollyon.

Masculine part. from *apóllumi* (622), to destroy, corrupt. The destroyer (Rev 9:11). A Greek name for the demon of the abyss (*ábussos* [12]). The Hebrew name is transliterated *Abaddṓn* (3).

Syn.: *olothreutḗs* (3644), a destroyer.

624. Ἀπολλωνία, Apollōnia, *ap-ol-lo-nee´-ah*; from the pagan deity **Ἀπόλλων**, ***Apollōn*** (i.e. the *sun*; from 622); *Apollonia*, a place in Macedonia:—Apollonia.

625. Ἀπολλώς, Apollōs, *ap-ol-loce´*; probably from the same as 624; *Apollos*, an Israelite:—Apollos.

626. ἀπολογέομαι, apologeomai, *ap-ol-og-eh´-om-ahee*; middle from a compound of 575 and 3056; to give an *account* (legal *plea*) of oneself, i.e. *exculpate* (self):—answer (for self), make defence, excuse (self), speak for self.

627. ἀπολογία, apologia, *ap-ol-og-ee´-ah*; from the same as 626; a *plea* ("apology"):—answer (for self), clearing of self, defence.

628. ἀπολούω, apolouō, *ap-ol-oo´-o*; from 575 and 3068; to *wash* fully, i.e. (figurative) *have remitted* (reflexive):—wash (away).

From *apó* (575), from, and *loúō* (3068), to wash, bathe. In the NT, used in the middle voice: to wash oneself clean from, i.e. to wash away; metaphorically, to be freed from the consequences of sin (Ac 22:16; 1Co 6:11; Sept.: Job 9:30; cf. Ps 51:4; Isa 1:16; Jer 4:14).

Syn.: *níptō* (3538), to wash part of the body; *aponíptō* (633), to wash off; *plúnō* (4150), to wash inanimate objects; *apoplúnō* (637) used of garments and figuratively; *rhantízō* (4472), to sprinkle; *bréchō* (1026), to wet; *baptízō* (907), to baptize.

629. ἀπολύτρωσις, apolutrōsis, *ap-ol-oo´-tro-sis*; from a compound of 575 and 3083; (the act) *ransom* in full, i.e. (figurative) *riddance*, or (specifically) Christian *salvation*:—deliverance, redemption.

Noun from *apolutróō* (n.f.), to let go free for a ransom. Redemption:

(I) Deliverance on account of the ransom paid; spoken of the deliverance from the power and consequences of sin which Christ procured by laying down His life as a ransom (*lútron* [3083]) for those who believe (Ro 3:24; 1Co 1:30; Eph 1:7, 14; Col 1:14; Heb 9:15 [cf. Mt 20:28; Ac 20:28]).

(II) Deliverance without the idea of ransom, i.e. from calamities and death (Lk 21:28; Heb 11:35). So also of the soul from the body as its prison (Ro 8:23 at the coming of the Lord; Eph 4:30 [cf. Ro 7:24]).

Syn.: *áphesis* (859), remission, forgiveness; *hilasmós* (2434), propitiation; *katallagḗ* (2643), reconciliation, atonement.

630. ἀπολύω, apoluō, *ap-ol-oo´-o*; from 575 and 3089; to *free* fully, i.e. (literal) *relieve, release, dismiss* (reflexive *depart*), or (figurative) *let die, pardon,* or (specifically) *divorce*:—(let) depart, dismiss, divorce, forgive, let go, loose, put (send) away, release, set at liberty.

From *apó* (575), from, and *lúō* (3089), to loose. To let loose from, to loose or unbind a person or thing:

(I) To free or relieve from sickness (Lk 13:12).

(II) To release, let go free, set at liberty, such as a debtor (Mt 18:27) or persons accused or imprisoned (Mt 27:15; Mk 15:6; Lk 22:68; Jn 19:10; Ac 4:21; 26:32; 28:18). Metaphorically: to overlook, forgive (Lk 6:37).

(III) Spoken of a wife, to let go free, put away, divorce (Mt 1:19; 5:31, 32; 19:3). So also of a husband (Mk 10:12).

(IV) To dismiss, i.e. simply to let go, send away, transitively (Mt 14:15, 22, 23; 15:32, 39; Lk 8:38; 9:12; 14:4; Ac 13:3; 15:30; 19:41; 23:22). Middle *apolúomai*, to depart, go away (Ac 15:33; 28:25; Sept.: Ex 33:11).

(V) To dismiss from life, let depart, die (Lk 2:29; Sept.: Nu 20:29).

Syn.: *chōrízō* (5563), to put apart, separate; *apochōrízō* (673), to separate off; *diachōrízomai* (1316), to be separated through or completely; *analúō* (360), to depart, unloose; *aphístēmi* (868), to cause to depart; *aphíēmi* (863), to send away; *ápeimi* (548), to go away; *aníēmi* (447), to let up, forbear.

631. ἀπομάσσομαι, apomassomai, *ap-om-as´-som-ahee*; middle from 575 and **μάσσω,** ***massō*** (to *squeeze, knead, smear*); to *scrape away*:—wipe off.

632. ἀπονέμω, aponemō, *ap-on-em´-o*; from 575 and the base of 3551; to *apportion,* i.e. *bestow*:—give.

633. ἀπονίπτω, aponiptō, *ap-on-ip´-to*; from 575 and 3538; to *wash off* (reflexive one's own hands symbolically):—wash.

634. ἀποπίπτω, apopiptō, *ap-op-ip´-to*; from 575 and 4098; to *fall off*:—fall.

635. ἀποπλανάω, apoplanaō, *ap-op-lan-ah´-o*; from 575 and 4105; to *lead astray* (figurative) passive to *stray* (from truth):—err, seduce.

636. ἀποπλέω, apopleō, *ap-op-leh´-o*; from 575 and 4126; to *set sail*:—sail away.

637. ἀποπλύνω, apoplunō, *ap-op-loo´-no*; from 575 and 4150; to *rinse off*:—wash.

638. ἀποπνίγω, apopnigō, *ap-op-nee´-go*; from 575 and 4155; to *stifle* (by drowning or overgrowth):—choke.

639. ἀπορέω, aporeō, *ap-or-eh´-o*; from a compound of 1 (as a negative particle) and the base of 4198; to *have no way* out, i.e. *be at a loss* (mentally):—(stand in) doubt, be perplexed.

640. ἀπορία, aporia, *ap-or-ee´-a*; from the same as 639; a (state of) *quandary*:—perplexity.

641. ἀποῤῥίπτω, aporrhiptō, *ap-or-hrip´-to*; from 575 and 4496; to *hurl off,* i.e. *precipitate* (oneself):—cast.

642. ἀπορφανίζω, aporphanizō, *ap-or-fan-id´-zo*; from 575 and a derivative of 3737; to *bereave wholly,* i.e. (figurative) *separate* (from intercourse):—take.

643. ἀποσκευάζω, aposkeuazō, *ap-osk-yoo-ad´-zo*; from 575 and a derivative of 4632; to *pack up* (one's) *baggage*:—take up … carriages.

644. ἀποσκίασμα, aposkiasma, *ap-os-kee´-as-mah*; from a compound of 575 and a derivative of 4639; a *shading off,* i.e. *obscuration*:—shadow.

645. ἀποσπάω, apospaō, *ap-os-pah´-o*; from 575 and 4685; to *drag forth,* i.e. (lit.) *unsheathe* (a sword), or relative (with a degree of force implied) *retire* (person or factiously):—(with-) draw (away), after we were gotten from.

646. ἀποστασία, apostasia, *ap-os-tas-ee´-ah*; feminine of the same as 647; *defection* from truth (properly the state) ["apostasy"]:—falling away, forsake.

Noun from *aphístēmi* (868), to depart. Defection, apostasy. Occurs in Ac 21:21 translated "forsake" and in 2Th 2:3, "a falling away"; Sept.: 2Ch 29:19; Jer 29:32.

647. ἀποστάσιον, apostasion, *ap-os-tas´-ee-on*; neuter of a (presumed) adjective from a derivative of 868; properly something *separative,* i.e. (special) *divorce*:—(writing of) divorcement.

648. ἀποστεγάζω, apostegazō, *ap-os-teg-ad´-zo*; from 575 and a derivative of 4721; to *unroof*:—uncover.

649. ἀποστέλλω, apostellō, *ap-os-tel´-lo*; from 575 and 4724; *set apart,* i.e. (by implication) to *send out* (properly on a mission) literal or figurative:—put in, send (away, forth, out), set [at liberty].

From *apó* (575), from, and *stéllō* (4724), to withdraw from, avoid. To send off, forth, out:

(I) Spoken of persons sent as agents, messengers, etc. (Mt 10:5, 16; 21:1; Mk 6:7; Lk 14:32); of prophets, messengers, teachers, angels, sent from God (Mt 10:40; 15:24; Lk 1:26; Jn 1:6; 3:17; Ac 3:26; Heb 1:14; Rev 1:1). Also in the sense of to expel, to drive away (Mk 5:10; 12:3, 4).

(II) Figuratively, spoken of things: to send forth, i.e. to proclaim, to bestow (Lk 24:49; Ac 10:36; 13:26; 28:28); so of physical things (Mk 4:29; Ac 11:30).

(III) In the sense of to dismiss, to let go (Mk 8:26; Lk 4:18).

Deriv.: *apostolḗ* (651), dispatching or sending forth; *apóstolos* (652), one sent, apostle, ambassador; *exapostéllō* (1821), to send away, forth; *sunapostéllō* (4882), to send along with.

Syn.: *ekbállō* (1544), to send out; *apotássomai* (657), to send forth; *ekpémpō* (1599), to send forth; *pémpō* (3992), to send.

650. ἀποστερέω, apostereō, *ap-os-ter-eh´-o*; from 575 and **στερέω,** ***stereō*** (to *deprive*); to *despoil*:—defraud, destitute, kept back by fraud.

651. ἀποστολή, apostolē, *ap-os-tol-ay´*; from 649; *commission,* i.e. (special) *apostolate*:—apostleship.

Noun from *apostéllō* (649), to send. Dispatching or sending forth, also that which is sent, e.g., a present. In the NT, apostleship (Ac 1:25; Ro 1:5; 1Co 9:2; Gal 2:8).

Syn.: *presbeía* (4242), persons sent as ambassadors.

652. ἀπόστολος, apostolos, *ap-os´-tol-os*; from 649; a *delegate*; specially an *ambassador* of the gospel; officially a *commissioner* of Christ ["*apostle*"] (with miraculous powers):—apostle, messenger, he that is sent.

Noun from *apostéllō* (649), to send. Used as a substantive, one sent, apostle, ambassador:

(I) Generally, a messenger (Jn 13:16; Php 2:25).

(II) Spoken of messengers or ambassadors sent from God (Lk 11:49; Eph 3:15; Rev 2:2; 28:20).

(III) Of the twelve apostles of Christ (Mt 10:2; Lk 6:13; Ac 1:26; Jude 17; Rev 21:14), so of Paul, reckoned as the "apostle of the gentiles" (1Ti 2:17; 2Ti 1:11). Also, in a wider sense, spoken of the helpers and companions of the twelve, as aiding to gather churches (2Co 8:23); so of Paul and Barnabas (Ac 14:4, 14); and of Andronicus and Junias (Ro 16:7).

Deriv.: *pseudapóstolos* (5570), a false apostle.

Syn.: *ággelos* (32), a messenger, an angel.

653. ἀποστοματίζω, apostomatizō, *ap-os-tom-at-id´-zo*; from 575 and a (presumed) derivative of 4750; to *speak off-hand* (properly *dictate*), i.e. to *catechize* (in an invidious manner):—provoke to speak.

654. ἀποστρέφω, apostrephō, *ap-os-tref´-o*; from 575 and 4762; to *turn away* or *back* (literal or figurative):—bring again, pervert, turn away (from).

From *apó* (575), from or back again, and *stréphō* (4762), to turn. To turn away from, to turn aside, to avert:

(I) Particularly, turning aside ears from the truth (2Ti 4:4); turning away from iniquities (Ac 3:26); "preverteth the people," i.e. turning aside the people, inciting rebellion (Lk 23:14). In the sense of to put away from, to remove (Ro 11:26).

(II) In the middle, to turn oneself away from, i.e. either to forsake, to desert (2Ti 1:15), or to refuse, reject (Mt 5:42; Tit 1:14; Heb 12:25).

(III) To turn back, i.e. to return, to restore (Mt 27:3; Sept.: Ge 24:5, 6). Spoken of a sword: to put back, to replace (Mt 26:52).

Syn.: *apotíthēmi* (659), to put away; *apōthéō* (683), to thrust away; *apobaínō* (576), to turn out, to go; *metatíthēmi* (3346), to change, remove; *ektrépō* (1624), to cause to turn aside; *apotrépō* (665), to cause to turn away; *ekklínō* (1578), to turn aside; *anachōréō* (402), to withdraw; *apéchomai* (567), to hold oneself off, refrain; *bdelússomai* (948), to detest, abhor.

655. ἀποστυγέω, apostugeō, *ap-os-toog-eh´-o*; from 575 and the base of 4767; to *detest* utterly:—abhor.

From *apó* (575), from, or an intensive, and *stugéō* (n.f., see below), to hate. To hate, abhor, detest (Ro 12:9).

Deriv. of *stugéō* (n.f.): *theostugḗs* (2319), haters of God; *stugētós* (4767) hateful, detestable.

Syn.: *apostréphomai* (654), to turn away from; *apotrépō* (665), to deflect; *apophérō* (667), to bear off; *apéchomai* (567), to hold oneself off, refrain; *bdelússomai* (948), to abhor, detest; *phríssō* (5425), to shudder; *apōthéomai* (683), to push off.

656. ἀποσυνάγωγος, aposunagōgos, *ap-os-oon-ag´-o-gos*; from 575 and 4864; *excommunicated*:—(put) out of the synagogue (-s).

Adjective from *apó* (575), from, and *sunagōgḗ* (4864), synagogue. Excluded from the synagogue, excommunicated (John 9:22; 12:42; 16:2). There were three degrees of excommunication or banishment among the Jews. The first continued for one month, and prohibited a person from bathing, from shaving his head, or from approaching any person nearer than four cubits; but if he submitted to this, he was not debarred the privilege of attending the sacred rites. The second involved an exclusion from the sacred assemblies, was accompanied with heavy maledictions, and prohibited all communication with the person subjected to it. The last was a perpetual exclusion from all the rights and privileges of the Jewish people, both civil and religious.

Syn.: *apóblētos* (579), a rejected or cast off one.

657. ἀποτάσσομαι, apotassomai, *ap-ot-as´-som-ahee*; middle from 575 and 5021; literal to *say adieu* (by departing or dismissing); (figurative) to *renounce*:—bid farewell, forsake, take leave, send away.

From *apó* (575), from, and *tássō* (5021), to place in order. To assign to different places, to separate. In the NT, only in the middle meaning to take leave of, bid farewell; to dismiss, forsake, or renounce (Lk 9:61; Ac 18:18, 21; 2Co 2:13). In the sense of to dismiss, send away (Mk 6:46, cf. Mt 14:23). Used figuratively: to renounce, to forsake (Lk 14:33).

Syn.: *kataleípō* (2641), to leave behind; *egkataleípō* (1459), to abandon, leave; *aphíēmi* (863), to leave, forsake; *aníēmi* (447), to let go, to go up; *apoleípō* (620), to leave behind; *apaspázomai* in Ac 21:6 (UBS) and *aspázomai* (782 [TR]) to enfold in the arms, embrace, take leave.

658. ἀποτελέω, apoteleō, *ap-ot-el-eh´-o*; from 575 and 5055; to *complete entirely*, i.e. *consummate*:—finish.

659. ἀποτίθημι, apotithēmi, *ap-ot-eeth´-ay-mee*; from 575 and 5087; to *put away* (literal or figurative):—cast off, lay apart (aside, down), put away (off).

660. ἀποτινάσσω, apotinassō, *ap-ot-in-as´-so*; from 575 and **τινάσσω,** ***tinassō*** (to *jostle*); to *brush off*:—shake off.

661. ἀποτίνω, apotinō, *ap-ot-ee´-no*; from 575 and 5099; to *pay* in full:—repay.

662. ἀποτολμάω, apotōlmaō, *ap-ot-ol-mah´-o*; from 575 and 5111; to *venture* plainly:—be very bold.

663. ἀποτομία, apotomia, *ap-ot-om-ee´-ah*; from the base of 664; (figurative) *decisiveness*, i.e. *rigour*:—severity.

664. ἀποτόμως, apotomōs, *ap-ot-om´-oce*; adverb from a derivative of a compound of 575 and **τέμνω,** ***temnō*** (to *cut*); *abruptly*, i.e. *peremptorily*:—sharply (-ness).

665. ἀποτρέπω, apotrepō, *ap-ot-rep´-o*; from 575 and the base of 5157; to *deflect*, i.e. (reflexive) *avoid*:—turn away.

666. ἀπουσία, apousia, *ap-oo-see´-ah*; from the participle of 548; a *being away*:—absence.

667. ἀποφέρω, apopherō, *ap-of-er´-o*; from 575 and 5342; to *bear off* (literal or relative):—bring, carry (away).

668. ἀποφεύγω, apopheugō, *ap-of-yoo´-go*; from 575 and 5343; (figurative) to *escape*:—escape.

669. ἀποφθέγγομαι, apophtheggomai, *ap-of-theng´-om-ahee*; from 575 and 5350; to *enunciate* plainly, i.e. *declare*:—say, speak forth, utterance.

670. ἀποφορτίζομαι, apophortizomai, *ap-of-or-tid´-zom-ahee*; from 575 and the middle of 5412; to *unload*:—unlade.

671. ἀπόχρησις, apochrēsis, *ap-okh´-ray-sis*; from a compound of 575 and 5530; the act of *using up*, i.e. *consumption*:—using.

672. ἀποχωρέω, apochōreō, *ap-okh-o-reh´-o*; from 575 and 5562; to *go away*:—depart.

673. ἀποχωρίζω, apochōrizō, *ap-okh-o-rid´-zo*; from 575 and 5563; to *rend apart*; reflexive to *separate*:—depart (asunder).

674. ἀποψύχω, apopsuchō, *ap-ops-oo´-kho*; from 575 and 5594; to *breathe out*, i.e. *faint*:—hearts failing.

From *apó* (575) denoting privation, and *psúchō* (5594), to breathe, wax cold. In the NT, to be faint of heart due to fear or terror. Only in Lk 21:26 (cf. Mt 28:4).

Syn.: *kámnō* (2577), to faint or be weary as a result of continuous labour.

675. Ἄππιος, Appios, *ap´-pee-os*; of Latin origin; (in the genitive, i.e. possessive case) *of Appius*, the name of a Roman:—Appii.

676. ἀπρόσιτος, aprositos, *ap-ros´-ee-tos*; from 1 (as a negative particle) and a derivative of a compound of 4314 and **εἶμι,** ***eimi*** (to *go*); *inaccessible*:—which no man can approach.

677. ἀπρόσκοπος, aproskopos, *ap-ros´-kop-os*; from 1 (as a negative particle) and a presumed derivative of 4350; act. *inoffensive*, i.e. *not leading into sin*; passive *faultless*, i.e. *not led into sin*:—none (void of, without) offence.

Adjective from the priv. *a* (1), not, and *proskóptō* (4350), to strike at, to trip. Not stumbling, i.e. not causing to stumble. In the NT, used metaphorically: giving no offence, not causing to sin (1Co 10:32). Also, not stumbling, i.e. not falling into sin, pure (Ac 24:16).

Syn.: *áptaistos* (679), not stumbling; *eleútheros* (1658), free, at liberty.

678. ἀπροσωπολήπτως, aprosōpolēptōs, *ap-ros-o-pol-ape´-toce*; adverb from a compound of 1 (as a negative particle) and a presumed derivative of a presumed compound of 4383 and 2983 [compare 4381]; in a way *not accepting* the *person*, i.e. *impartially*:—without respect of persons.

679. ἄπταιστος, aptaistos, *ap-tah´ee-stos*; from 1 (as a negative particle) and a derivative of 4417; *not stumbling*, i.e. (figurative) *without sin*:—from falling.

680. ἅπτομαι, haptomai, *hap´-tom-ahee*; reflexive of 681; properly to *attach* oneself to, i.e. to *touch* (in many implied relations):—touch.

From *háptō* (681), to connect, bind. To apply oneself to, to touch; generally (Mt 8:3, 15; 9:20; Mk 1:41; Lk 7:14); in the Levitical sense (2Co 6:17; Col 2:21); figuratively, to have sexual intercourse (1Co 7:1); by implication, to harm, to injure (1Jn 5:18).

Syn.: *prospsaúō* (4379), to touch upon, touch slightly (Lk 11:46); *eggízō* (1448), to come near; *piázō* (4084), to lay hand on; *kolláō* (2853), to glue; *proseggízō* (4331), to approach.

681. ἅπτω, haptō, *hap´-to*; a primary verb; properly to *fasten* to, i.e. (special) to *set* on fire:—kindle, light.

To put one thing to another, to adjoin, to apply. In the NT, spoken of fire as applied to things: to set fire to, kindle, light (Lk 8:16; 11:33; 15:8; 22:55).

Deriv.: *anáptō* (381), to light up, kindle; *háptomai* (680), to touch; *aphḗ* (860), a joint; *katháptō* (2510), to bind, fasten.

Syn.: with the meaning of to light: *phōtízō* (5461), to shine, give light; *epiphaúō* (2017), to shine forth; *lámpō* (2989), to give forth the light of a torch; *epiphaínō* (2014), to show forth; *kaíō* (2545), to burn, a light. With the meaning to touch: *thiggánō* (2345), to touch.

682. Ἀπφία, Apphia, *ap-fee´-a*; probably of foreign origin; *Apphia*, a woman of Colossæ:—Apphia.

683. ἀπωθέομαι, apōtheomai, *ap-o-theh´-om-ahee*; or **ἀπώομαι**, *apōthomai, ap-o´-thom-ahee*; from 575 and the middle of **ὠθέω**, *ōtheō*; or **ὤθω**, *ōthō* (to *shove*); to *push off*, (figurative) to *reject*:—cast away, put away (from), thrust away (from).

684. ἀπώλεια, apōleia, *ap-o´-li-a*; from a presumed derivative of 622; *ruin* or *loss* (physical, spiritual or eternal):—damnable (-nation), destruction, die, perdition, × perish, pernicious ways, waste.

Noun from *apóllumi* (622), to destroy fully. Loss, destruction. Spoken of things: waste (Mt 26:8; Mk 14:4). Spoken of persons: destruction, death (Ac 25:16); the second death, perdition, i.e. exclusion from the Messiah's kingdom (Mt 7:13; Ac 8:20; Ro 9:22; Php 1:28; 1Ti 6:9; Heb 10:39; 2Pe 2:1, 3; 3:7, 16; Rev 17:8, 11).

Syn.: *phthorá* (5356), destruction that comes with corruption, consumption by using up; *súntrimma* (4938), a breaking in pieces; *thánatos* (2288), death; *anaíresis* (336), a taking up or off, usually used in regard to life; *teleutḗ* (5054), an end of life, death; *zēmía* (2209), loss; *apobolḗ* (580), a casting away; *hḗttēma* (2275), defeat, loss, defect; *kathaíresis* (2506), a taking or pulling down, hence destruction; *ólethros* (3639), an eschatological destruction surprising people like labour pains coming upon a pregnant woman.

685. ἀρά, ara, *ar-ah´*; probably from 142; properly *prayer* (as *lifted* to Heaven), i.e. (by implication) *imprecation*:—curse.

In the NT, implication, curse. Only in Ro 3:14.

Deriv.: *katára* (2671), a curse.

Syn.: *anáthema* (331), a curse, disfavour of God; *katanáthema* (2652), an accursed thing.

686. ἄρα, ara, *ar´-ah*; probably from 142 (through the idea of *drawing* a conclusion); a particle denoting an *inference* more or less decisive (as follows):—haply, (what) manner (of man), no doubt, perhaps, so be, then, therefore, truly, wherefore. Often used in connection with other particles, especially 1065 or 3767 (after) or 1487 (before). Compare also 687.

687. ἆρα, ara, *ar´-ah*; a form of 686, denoting an *interrogation* to which a negative answer is presumed:—therefore.

688. Ἀραβία, Arabia, *ar-ab-ee´-ah*; of Hebrew origin [6152]; *Arabia*, a region of Asia:—Arabia.

689. Ἀράμ, Aram, *ar-am´*; of Hebrew origin [7410]; *Aram* (i.e. *Ram*), an Israelite:—Aram.

690. Ἄραψ, Araps, *ar´-aps*; from 688; an *Arab* or native of Arabia:—Arabian.

691. ἀργέω, argeō, *arg-eh´-o*; from 692; to *be idle*, i.e. (figurative) to *delay*:—linger.

From *argós* (692), idle. In the NT, to be inactive, idle; metaphorically, to be still, to linger. Only in 2Pe 2:3.

Deriv.: *katargéō* (2673), entirely idle, abolish, cease.

Syn.: *scholázō* (4980), to be at leisure.

692. ἀργός, argos, *ar-gos´*; from 1 (as a negative particle) and 2041; *inactive*, i.e. *unemployed*; (by implication) *lazy, useless*:—barren, idle, slow.

Adjective from the priv. *a* (1), without, and *érgon* (2041), work. Not at work, idle, not employed, inactive (Mt 20:3, 6); with the idea of choice (1Ti 5:13). By implication: indolent, slothful, slow (2Pe 1:8); *gastéres argaí*, lit. "slow bellies" (see *gastḗr* [1064], stomach), i.e. lazy gluttons (Tit 1:12). Also by implication: idle, insincere, false, unprofitable (Mt 12:36, cf. 2Pe 1:8).

Deriv.: *argéō* (691), to be idle.

Syn.: *bradús* (1021), slow; *oknērós* (3636), indolent, slothful.

693. ἀργύρεος, argureos, *ar-goo´-reh-os*; from 696; made *of silver*:—(of) silver.

694. ἀργύριον, argurion, *ar-goo´-ree-on*; neuter of a presumed derivative of 696; *silvery*, i.e. (by implication) *cash*; specially a *silverling* (i.e. *drachma* or *shekel*):—money, (piece of) silver (piece).

695. ἀργυροκόπος, argurokopos, *ar-goo-rok-op´-os*; from 696 and 2875; a *beater* (i.e. *worker*) *of silver*:—silversmith.

696. ἄργυρος, arguros, *ar´-goo-ros*; from **ἀργός**, *argos* (*shining*); *silver* (the metal, in the articles or coin):—silver.

697. Ἄρειος Πάγος, Areios Pagos, *ar´-i-os pag´-os*; from **Ἄρης**, *Arēs* (the name of the Greek deity of war) and a derivative of 4078; *rock of Ares*, a place in Athens:—Areopagus, Mars' Hill.

698. Ἀρεοπαγίτης, Areopagitēs, *ar-eh-op-ag-ee´-tace*; from 697; an *Areopagite* or member of the court held on Mars' Hill:—Areopagite.

699. ἀρέσκεια, areskeia, *ar-es´-ki-ah*; from a derivative of 700; *complaisance*:—pleasing.

Noun from *aréskō* (700), to please. Desire of pleasing. Only in Col 1:10.

Syn.: *hēdonḗ* (2237), pleasure; *eudokía* (2107), good pleasure; *thélēma* (2307), will, pleasure, favour; *euphrosúnē* (2167), joyfulness, gladness; *chará* (5479), joy; *apólausis* (619), enjoyment; *agallíasis* (20), exuberance.

700. ἀρέσκω, areskō, *ar-es´-ko*; probably from 142 (through the idea of *exciting* emotion); to *be agreeable* (or, by implication, to seek to be so):—please.

From *árō* (n.f., see *podḗrēs* [4158]), to fit, adapt. To please. In the sense of to be pleasing, acceptable to (Mt 14:6; Mk 6:22; Ro 8:8; 1Co 7:33, 34; Gal 1:10; 1Th 2:15; 2Ti 2:4). In the sense of to seek to please or gratify, to accommodate oneself to (Ro 15:1–3; 1Co 10:33; Gal 1:10; 1Th 2:4).

Deriv.: *anthrōpáreskos* (441), one who endeavours to please men; *aréskeia* (699), the endeavour to please; *arestós* (701), dear, pleasant, well-pleasing; *euárestos* (2101), pleasing, agreeable.

Syn.: *eudokéō* (2106), to think well of; *thélō* (2309), to wish, desire; *dokimázō* (1381), to approve; *eucharistéō* (2168), to express gratitude, give thanks; *apolambánō* (618), to receive; *entrupháō* (1792), to revel in; *euphraínō* (2165), to rejoice, make glad.

701. ἀρεστός, arestos, *ar-es-tos´*; from 700; *agreeable*; (by implication) *fit*:—(things that) please (-ing), reason.

Adjective from *aréskō* (700), to please or to be content with. Pleasing, acceptable, grateful (Jn 8:29; Ac 12:3; 1Jn 3:22).

Syn.: *eúthetos* (2111), fit, proper; *kalós* (2570), good; *sumpathḗs* (4835), sympathetic; *euprósdektos* (2144), well-received, approved, favourable; *glukús* (1099), sweet; *dektós* (1184), approved, referring to relationship. *Arestós* presupposes man's relationship with God, but it also tells about God's judgement to man's conduct.

702. Ἀρέτας, Aretas, *ar-et´-as*; of foreign origin; *Aretas*, an Arabian:—Aretas.

703. ἀρέτη, aretē, *ar-et´-ay*; from the same as 730; properly *manliness* (*valor*), i.e. *excellence* (intrinsic or attributed):—praise, virtue.

A noun meaning virtue, i.e. good quality, excellence of any kind. In the NT, spoken of the divine power (2Pe 1:3); of goodness of action, virtuous deeds (Php 4:8; 2Pe 1:5). Spoken of God: wondrous deeds, as displays of divine power and goodness (1Pe 2:9; Sept.: Isa 42:12; 63:7; Hab 3:3).

Syn.: *huperbolḗ* (5236), a throwing beyond, surpassing, an excellence; *huperochḗ* (5247), the act of overhanging, hence superiority, preeminence, excellency; *aínos* (136), praise; *épainos* (1868), approbation, commendation; *dóxa* (1391), glory; *dúnamis* (1411), power; *chárisma* (5486), gift; *ōphéleia* (5622), usefulness, benefit.

704. ἀρήν, arēn, *ar-ane´*; perhaps the same as 730; a *lamb* (as a *male*):—lamb.

705. ἀριθμέω, arithmeō, *ar-ith-meh´-o*; from 706; to *enumerate* or *count*:—number.

706. ἀριθμός, arithmos, *ar-ith-mos´*; from 142; a *number* (as reckoned *up*):—number.

707. Ἀριμαθαία, Arimathaia, *ar-ee-math-ah´ee-ah*; of Hebrew origin [7414]; *Arimathæa* (or *Ramah*), a place in Palestine:—Arimathæa.

708. Ἀρίσταρχος, Aristarchos, *ar-is´-tar-khos*; from the same as 712 and 757; *best ruling; Aristar-chus*, a Macedonian:—Aristarchus.

709. ἀριστάω, aristaō, *ar-is-tah´-o*; from 712; to *take the principal meal*:—dine.

710. ἀριστερός, aristēros, *ar-is-ter-os´*; apparently a compound of the same as 712; the *left* hand (as *second-best*):—left [hand].

711. Ἀριστόβουλος, Aristoboulos, *ar-is-tob´-oo-los*; from the same as 712 and 1012; *best counseling; Aristoboulus*, a Christian:—Aristobulus.

712. ἄριστον, ariston, *ar´-is-ton*; apparently neuter of a superlative from the same as 730; the *best* meal [or *breakfast*; perhaps from **ἦρι**, *ēri* ("*early*")], i.e. *luncheon*:—dinner.

713. ἀρκετός, arketos, *ar-ket-os´*; from 714; *satisfactory*:—enough, suffice (-ient).

714. ἀρκέω, arkeō, *ar-keh´-o*; apparently a primary verb [but probably akin to 142 through the idea of *raising* a barrier]; properly to *ward off*, i.e. (by implication) to *avail* (figurative, *be satisfactory*):—be content, be enough, suffice, be sufficient.

715. ἄρκτος, arktos, *ark´-tos*; probably from 714; a *bear* (as *obstructing* by ferocity):—bear.

716. ἅρμα, harma, *har´-mah*; probably from 142 [perhaps with 1 (as a particle of union) prefixed]; a *chariot* (as *raised* or fitted *together* [compare 719]):—chariot.

717. Ἀρμαγεδδών, Armageddōn, *ar-mag-ed-dohn´*; of Hebrew origin [2022 and 4023]; *Armageddon* (or *Har-Megiddon*), a symbolical name:—Armageddon.

718. ἁρμόζω, harmozō, *har-mod´-zo*; from 719; to *joint*, i.e. (figurative) to *woo* (reflexive to *betroth*):—espouse.

719. ἁρμός, harmos, *har-mos´*; from the same as 716; an *articulation* (of the body):—joint.

720. ἀρνέομαι, arneomai, *ar-neh´-om-ahee*; perhaps from 1 (as a negative particle) and the middle of 4483; to *contradict*, i.e. *disavow, reject, abnegate*:—deny, refuse.

Deponent verb meaning to deny:

(I) To contradict, to affirm not to be (Mt 26:70, 72; Mk 14:68, 70; Jn 1:20; 18:25, 27; Lk 8:45; 22:57; Ac 4:16; Tit 1:16; 1Jn 2:22, 23). To refuse (Heb 9:24).

(II) To renounce, to reject, e.g., to reject Christ (Mt 10:33; Lk 12:9; Ac 3:13, 14; 2Ti 2:12; 2Pe 2:1; Jude 4); to desert the Christian faith, to apostatize (1Ti 5:8; Rev 2:13; 3:8); spoken of Christ as rejecting men (Mt 10:33; 2Ti 2:13). Used figuratively: to deny onself, i.e. disregard personal interests and enjoyments (Lk 9:23); to deny oneself, i.e. to renounce one's own character, to be inconsistent with oneself (2Ti 2:13). Also figuratively in Tit 2:12; 2Ti 3:5.

Deriv.: *aparnéomai* (533), to deny.

Syn.: *antitássomai* (498), to place oneself against, oppose, resist; *aporríptō* (641), to hurl off, reject; *aposteréō* (650), to despoil, keep back; *periphronéō* (4065), to despise, depreciate; *apōthéomai* (683), to reject, push away; *apotrépō* (665), to deflect, avoid, turn away; *apophérō* (667), to bear off, carry away; *aparnéomai* (533), to deny completely; *apotássomai* (657), to renounce; *paraitéomai* (3868), to avoid, reject; *apodokimázō* (593), to disapprove; *athetéō* (114), to break faith with, reject; *ekptúō* (1609), to spit out.

721. ἀρνίον, arnion, *ar-nee´-on*; diminutive from 704; a *lambkin*:—lamb.

A noun meaning lamb. In the NT, used figuratively for the followers of Christ (Jn 21:15), and of Christ Himself (Rev 5:6, 8, 12, 13; 6:1, 16; 7:9, 10, 14, 17; 12:11; 13:8; 14:1, 4, 10; 15:3; 17:14; 19:7, 9; 21:9, 14, 22, 23, 27; 22:1, 3).

722. ἀροτριόω, arotrioō, *ar-ot-ree-o´-o*; from 723; to *plough*:—plow.

723. ἄροτρον, arotron, *ar´-ot-ron*; from **ἀρόω**, ***aroō*** (to *till*); a *plough*:—plow.

724. ἁρπαγή, harpagē, *har-pag-ay´*; from 726; *pillage* (properly abstract):—extortion, ravening, spoiling.

From *harpázō* (726), to seize upon with force. Plundering, pillage, i.e. the act of spoiling (Heb 10:34). Used metaphorically of a disposition to plunder, ravening (Mt 23:25; Lk 11:39).

Syn.: *pleonexía* (4124), covetousness, extortion; *skúlon* (4661), in the plural meaning spoils, arms stripped from an enemy; *akrothínion* (205), the top of a heap, the choicest spoils in war.

725. ἁρπαγμός, harpagmos, *har-pag-mos´*; from 726; *plunder* (properly concrete):—robbery.

Noun from *harpázō* (726), to seize upon with force. Robbery. In the NT, used figuratively of the object of plunder, something to be eagerly coveted. Only in Php 2:6.

Syn.: *klopḗ* (2829), theft; *klémma* (2809), a thing stolen.

726. ἁρπάζω, harpazō, *har-pad´-zo*; from a derivative of 138; to *seize* (in various applications):—catch (away, up), pluck, pull, take (by force).

A verb meaning to seize upon, spoil, snatch away:

(I) Spoken of beasts of prey (Jn 10:12; Sept.: Ge 37:33; Eze 22:25, 27). Used metaphorically: to seize with eagerness or greed (Mt 11:12, cf. Lk 16:16).

(II) Spoken of what is snatched suddenly away (Mt 13:19; Jude 23); in the sense of to rob, plunder (Jn 10:28, 29).

(III) To carry away, to hurry off; spoken of persons (Jn 6:15; Ac 8:39; 23:10; 2Co 12:2, 4; 1Th 4:17; Rev 12:5).

Deriv.: *harpagḗ* (724), robbery, plundering; *harpagmós* (725), robbery; *hárpax* (727), a rapacious person; *diarpázō* (1282), to seize, plunder; *sunarpázō* (4884), to seize or grasp with great violence.

Syn.: *paralambánō* (3880), to receive; *proslambánō* (4355), to receive unto; *apospáō* (645), to draw away; *aphairéō* (851), to remove; *exaírō* (1808), to take away; *exairéō* (1807), to pluck out, deliver, rescue; *aníēmi* (447), to let go; *apotássō* (657), to take away from and place in proper order.

727. ἅρπαξ, harpax, *har´-pax*; from 726; *rapacious*:—extortion, ravening.

728. ἀῤῥαβών, arrhabōn, *ar-hrab-ohn´*; of Hebrew origin [6162]; a *pledge*, i.e. part of the purchase money or property given in advance as *security* for the rest:—earnest.

Noun transliterated from the Hebrew *'arabōn* (6162, OT). Earnest money, a pledge given to ratify a contract (Sept.: Ge 38:17, 18, 20). In the NT, used metaphorically, spoken of the privileges of Christians in this life, especially the gift of the Holy Spirit, as being an earnest, a pledge of future bliss in the Messiah's kingdom (2Co 1:22; 5:5; Eph 1:14).

Syn.: *aparchḗ* (536), translated "firstfruits"; *parakatathḗkē* (3872), a deposit.

729. ἄῤῥαφος, arrhaphos, *ar´-hraf-os*; from 1 (as a negative particle) and a presumed derivative of the same as 4476; *unsewed*, i.e. of a single piece:—without seam.

730. ἄῤῥην, arrhēn, *ar´-hrane*; or **αρσην, arsēn;** *ar´-sane*; probably from 142; *male* (as stronger for *lifting*):—male, man.

731. ἄῤῥητος, arrhētos, *ar´-hray-tos*; from 1 (as a negative particle) and the same as 4490; *unsaid*, i.e. (by implication) *inexpressible*:—unspeakable.

732. ἄῤῥωστος, arrhōstos, *ar´-hroce-tos*; from 1 (as a negative particle) and a presumed derivative of 4517; *infirm*:—sick (folk, -ly).

Adjective from *a* (1), without, and *rhṓnnumi* (4517), to strengthen. Infirm, feeble, sick, invalid (Mt 14:14; Mk 6:5, 13; 16:18; 1Co 11:30; Sept.: Mal 1:8).

Syn.: *asthenḗs* (772), without strength, feeble, hence sick.

733. ἀρσενοκοίτης, arsenokoitēs, *ar-sen-ok-oy´-tace*; from 730 and 2845; a *sodomite*:—abuser of (that defile) self with mankind.

734. Ἀρτεμᾶς, Artemas, *ar-tem-as´*; contracted from a compound of 735 and 1435; *gift of Artemis; Artemas* (or *Artemidorus*), a Christian:—Artemas.

735. Ἄρτεμις, Artemis, *ar´-tem-is*; probably from the same as 736; *prompt; Artemis*, the name of a Grecian goddess borrowed by certain Asian peoples for one of their deities:—Diana.

736. ἀρτέμων, artemōn, *ar-tem´-ohn*; from a derivative of 737; properly something *ready* [or else more remotely from 142 (compare 740); something *hung* up], i.e. (special) the *topsail* (rather *foresail* or *jib*) of a vessel:—mainsail.

737. ἄρτι, arti, *ar´-tee*; adverb from a derivative of 142 (compare 740) through the idea of *suspension*; just *now*:—this day (hour), hence [-forth], here [-after], hither [-to], (even) now, (this) present.

738. ἀρτιγέννητος, artigennētos, *ar-teeg-en´-nay-tos*; from 737 and 1084; *just born*, i.e. (figurative) a *young convert*:—newborn.

Adjective from *árti* (737), now, lately, and *gennētós* (1084), born. Lately born, newborn. In the NT, used metaphorically of those who have just embraced the Christian faith. Only in 1Pe 2:2.

Syn.: *neossós* (3502), a youngling, used only of birds.

739. ἄρτιος, artios, *ar´-tee-os*; from 737; *fresh*, i.e. (by implication) *complete*:—perfect.

Adjective from *árti* (737), now, exactly. Complete, perfect. Spoken of a religious teacher, who should be wanting in nothing. Only in 2Ti 3:17.

Syn.: *téleios* (5046), perfect, complete; *pantelḗs* (3838), entire, complete; *akéraios* (185), unmixed, blameless, without guile; *plḗrēs* (4134), complete; *ámemptos* (273), faultless, blameless; *áptaistos* (679), not stumbling, without sin; *holotelḗs* (3651), complete to the end.

740. ἄρτος, artos, *ar´-tos*; from 142; *bread* (as *raised*) or a *loaf*:—(shew-) bread, loaf.

741. ἀρτύω, artuō, *ar-too´-o*; from a presumed derivative of 142; to *prepare*, i.e. *spice* (with *stimulating* condiments):—season.

742. Ἀρφαξάδ, Arphaxad, *ar-fax-ad´*; of Hebrew origin [775]; *Arphaxad*, a post-diluvian patriarch:—Arphaxad.

743. ἀρχάγγελος, archaggelos, *ar-khang´-el-os*; from 757 and 32; a *chief angel*:—archangel.

Noun from *árchōn* (758), chief, and *ággelos* (32), angel or messenger. An archangel, i.e. a chief angel (1Th 4:16; Jude 9). Of these there are said to be seven, who stand immediately before the throne of God (Lk 1:19; Rev 8:2), who have authority over other angels (Rev 12:7), and are the patrons of particular nations (Da 10:13; 12:1). The names of only two are found in Scripture: Michael, the patron of the Jewish nation (Da 10:13; 12:1; Jude 9; Rev 12:7), and Gabriel (Da 8:16; 9:21; Lk 1:19, 26).

744. ἀρχαῖος, archaios, *ar-khah´-yos*; from 746; *original* or *primeval*:—(them of) old (time).

Adjective from *archḗ* (746), beginning. Ancient, of former days, of old time (Mt 5:21, 27, 33; Lk 9:8, 19; Ac 15:7, 21; 2Co 5:17; 2Pe 2:5; Rev 12:9).

Syn.: *proginomai* (4266), to be already or to have previously come to exist; *patroparádotos* (3970), traditional; *patrṓos* (3971), hereditary.

745. Ἀρχέλαος, Archelaos, *ar-khel´-ah-os*; from 757 and 2994; *people-ruling; Archelaus*, a Jewish king:—Archelaus.

746. ἀρχή, archē, *ar-khay´*; from 756; (properly abstract) a *commencement*, or (concrete) *chief* (in various applications of order, time, place or rank):—beginning, corner, (at the, the) first (estate), magistrate, power, principality, principle, rule.

A noun meaning beginning:

(I) Spoken of time: the beginning, commencement (Mt 24:8; Mk 1:1; 13:9; Jn 2:11; Heb 3:14; 7:3). Used in conjunction with various prepositions:

(A) *Ap' archḗs*, from the beginning (see *apó* [575]); of all things (Mt 19:4, 8; Jn 8:44; 1Jn 3:8); of any particular thing, e.g., of the gospel dispensation, or of the Christian experience (Lk 1:2; Jn 15:27; 2Th 2:13; 1Jn 1:1; 2:7); of life (Ac 26:4).

(B) *En archḗ*, in the beginning (see *en* [1722]); of all things, of the world (Jn 1:1, 2); of any particular thing, e.g., of the gospel dispensation, or of the Christian experience (Ac 11:15; Php 4:15).

(C) *Ex archḗs*, from the beginning, from the first (see *ek* [1537]), e.g., of Christ's ministry (Jn 6:64; 16:4).

(D) *Kat' archás*, at the beginning, i.e. of old (Heb 1:10); see *katá* (2596).

(E) The accusative form, *tḗn archḗn* may be used adverbially, meaning at the beginning, at first; hence in the NT: from the very beginning on, throughout, wholly (Jn 8:25).

(II) By metonymy of abstract for concrete, spoken of persons: the first (Col 1:18). So the expression *archḗ kaí télos*, the first and the last (see *télos* [5056], last), i.e. the beginning and the end (Rev 1:8 [TR]; 21:6; 22:13).

(III) Spoken of place: the extremity; corner, e.g., of a sheet (Ac 10:11; 11:5).

(IV) Spoken of dignity, meaning the first place, power, dominion (Lk 20:20; Sept.: Ge 1:16; Jer 34:1; Mic 4:8); in the sense of preeminence, precedence, princedom (Jude 6). By metonymy of abstract for concrete: rulers, magistrates, princes, i.e. persons of influence and authority (Lk 12:11; Tit 3:1); spoken of the princes or chiefs among angels (Eph 1:21; 3:10; Col 2:10); among demons (1Co 15:24; Eph 6:12; Col 2:15); the powers of the other world (Ro 8:38; Col 1:16 [cf. *exousía* {1849}, authority]).

Deriv.: *archaíos* (744), of old, original; *archēgós* (747), a leader; *árchō* (757), to be first or to rule; *patriárchēs* (3966), patriarch, progenitor.

Syn.: *gōnía* (1137), corner; *prṓtos* (4413), first, preeminent; *dúnamis* (1411), ruling power; *exousía* (1849), authority; *krátos* (2904), dominion; *hēgemṓn* (2232), a leader, ruler; *megistán* (3175), used usually in the plural *megistánes* meaning, great ones, magnates, chiefs; *kanṓn* (2583), a rule; with the meaning of ruler: *kosmokrátōr* (2888), a ruler of this world; *pantokrátōr* (3841), universal ruler or ruler of all things, sovereign; *politárchēs* (4173), a ruler of a city; *architríklinos* (755), a superintendent of a banquet.

747. ἀρχηγός, archēgos, *ar-khay-gos´*; from 746 and 71; a *chief leader*:—author, captain, prince.

Noun from *archḗ* (746), beginning or rule, and *ágō* (71), to lead. One who makes a beginning, i.e. the author, source, cause of anything (Ac 3:15; Heb 2:10; 12:2; Sept.: Mic 1:13). Also, a leader, chief, prince, etc. (Ac 5:31 [cf. Ac 2:36; Eph 1:20]; Sept.: Jgs 5:15; 2Ch 23:14; Isa 30:4).

Syn.: *aítios* (159), he who causes something, the author; *chiliarchos* (5506), commander of a thousand soldiers; *stratēgós* (4755), commander of an army; *stratopedárchēs* (4759), camp commander; *árchōn* (758), he who rules but may not be a ruler per se, *hēgemṓn* (2232), a leader, ruler; *megistánes* (3175), the great ones, princes, lords.

748. ἀρχιερατικός, archieratikos, *ar-khee-er-at-ee-kos´*; from 746 and a derivative of 2413; *high-priestly*:—of the high-priest.

749. ἀρχιερεύς, archiereus, *ar-khee-er-yuce´*; from 746 and 2409; the *high-priest* (literal of the Jews, typical Christ); by extension a *chief priest*:—chief (high) priest, chief of the priests.

Noun from *archí-*, denoting rank or degree, and *hiereús* (2409), a priest. A high priest, chief priest (Sept.: Le 4:3); more usually called the great priest (Sept.: Le 21:10; Nu 35:25).

(I) The high priest of the Jews (Mt 26:3, 62, 63, 65; Mk 2:26; Lk 22:50). By the original divine appointment he was to be of the family of Aaron (Ex 29:9), but by the time of the Roman Empire, the office had become venal and was given even to foreign Jews. It was also no longer for life, so that there were often several persons living at one time who had borne the office, and still retained the title of high priest. There appears also to have been a *sāgān* (5461, OT), i.e. vicar or substitute for the high priest, to perform his duties on various occasions. Such a substitute is not expressly mentioned in the Scriptures, though such a person seems to be implied by the title "second priest" in 2Ki 25:18 and Jer 52:24. In one of these senses Annas is called high priest (Lk 3:2; Jn 18:13; Ac 4:6).

(II) A chief priest, as spoken of those who were at the head of the twenty-four classes of priests mentioned in 1Ch 24, and who are there called "the chief[s] of the fathers of the priests and Levites" (1Ch 24:6 [cf. Mt 2:4; 26:3; Mk 14:1; Lk 22:2]). These were members of the Sanhedrin, and indeed the expressions "chief priests and scribes" (Mt 2:4) and "chief priests and Pharisees" (Jn 7:32, 45) seem to be put by way of circumlocution for "the Sanhedrin," and in some instances the word *archiereús* appears to be used by itself in a general sense to denote the same council (Jn 12:10, cf. 11:47).

(III) In the epistle to the Hebrews (e.g., Heb 2:17; 3:1; 4:14; 5:5; 6:20), Christ is called *archiereús* and compared to the high priest of the Jews, as having offered Himself as a sacrifice for sin (cf. Heb 9:7, 11, 12).

Deriv.: *archieratikós* (748), high-priestly.

750. ἀρχιποίμην, archipoimēn, *ar-khee-poy´-mane*; from 746 and 4166; a *head shepherd*:—chief shepherd.

Noun from *archí-*, denoting rank or degree, and *poimḗn* (4166), a shepherd. Chief shepherd, applied to Christ (1Pe 5:4; cf. Heb 13:20).

Syn.: *archiereús* (749), chief priest; *árchōn* (758), a ruler; *archisunágōgos* (752), a ruler of a synagogue.

751. Ἄρχιππος, Archippos, *ar´-khip-pos*; from 746 and 2462; *horse-ruler; Archippus*, a Christian:—Archippus.

752. ἀρχισυνάγωγος, archisunagōgos, *ar-khee-soon-ag´-o-gos*; from 746 and 4864; *director of* the *synagogue* services:—(chief) ruler of the synagogue.

753. ἀρχιτέκτων, architektōn, *ar-khee-tek´-tone*; from 746 and 5045; a *chief constructor*, i.e. "*architect*":—masterbuilder.

754. ἀρχιτελώνης, architelōnēs, *ar-khee-tel-o´-nace*; from 746 and 5057; a *principal tax-gatherer*:—chief among the publicans.

755. ἀρχιτρίκλινος, architriklinos, *ar-khee-tree´-klee-nos*; from 746 and a compound of 5140 and 2827 (a *dinner-bed*, because composed of three couches); *director of* the *entertainment*:—governor (ruler) of the feast.

756. ἄρχομαι, archomai, *ar´-khom-ahee*; middle of 757 (through the implication of *precedence*); to *commence* (in order of time):—(rehearse from the) begin (-ning).

757. ἄρχω, archō, *ar´-kho*; a primary verb; to be *first* (in political rank or power):—reign (rule) over.

From *archḗ* (746), beginning, first. To begin, to be first:

(I) To be first in rank, dignity, etc., i.e. to rule, to reign (Mk 10:42; Ro 15:12; Sept.: Ge 1:18; Dt 15:6).

(II) Used in the middle voice, *árchomai*, to begin. Generally (Mt 4:17; 11:7, 20; Mk 1:45; Lk 4:21; Ac 1:1); by Hebraism, used emphatically implying difficulty: to attempt, to undertake, to venture (Mk 10:28, 32; Lk 3:8).

(III) As a participle, *arxámenos*, beginning from, expressing the point of departure in a narration, transaction, etc. (Mt 20:8; Lk 23:5; 24:27; Jn 8:9; Ac 1:22; 8:35; 10:37).

Deriv.: *árchomai* (756), beginning; *Asiárchēs* (775), a ruler of Asia; *ethnárchēs* (1481), the governor of a district; *hekatontárchēs* (1543), centurion; *politárchēs* (4173), ruler of the city; *stratopedárchēs* (4759), captain of the guard; *tetrárchēs* (5076), tetrarch; *hupárchō* (5225), to behave, live; *chilíarchos* (5506), captain.

Syn.: *basileúō* (936), to reign; *hēgemoneúō* (2230), to act as a ruler; *hēgéomai* (2233), to lead; *oikodespotéō* (3616), to rule a house; *proḯstēmi* (4291), to stand before, to rule; *poimaínō* (4165), to act as a shepherd; *exousiázō* (1850), to exercise authority upon; *katexousiázō* (2715), to exercise full authority; *kurieúō* (2961), to exercise lordship over; *katakurieúō* (2634), to lord it over completely; *prōteúō* (4409), to be first.

758. ἄρχων, archōn, *ar´-khone*; present participle of 757; a *first* (in rank or power):—chief (ruler), magistrate, prince, ruler.

Masculine part. of *árchō* (757), to rule. One first in power, authority, dominion; hence a ruler, lord, prince, a chief person. Generally (Mt 20:25; Ac 4:26; Ro 13:3; 1Co 2:6, 8; Sept.: Ge 49:20; Nu 23:21; 2Ch 8:9). Spoken of the Messiah as King of kings (Rev 1:5); of Moses as a ruler and leader of Israel (Ac 7:27, 35); of magistrates of any kind such as the high priest (Ac 23:5); of civil judges (Lk 12:58; Ac 16:19); of persons of weight and influence among the Pharisees and other sects at Jerusalem who also were members of the Sanhedrin (Lk 14:1; 18:18; 23:13, 35; 24:20; Jn 3:1 [cf. 7:45, 50; Jn 7:26, 48; 12:42; Ac 3:17; 4:5, 8; 13:27; 14:5]); of magnates (Sept.: Ne 5:7); of the chief of the fallen angels, Satan, "the prince of devils" (Mt 9:34; 12:24; Mk 3:22; Lk 11:15), called also "the ruler of this world," as ruling in the hearts of worldly and wicked men (Jn 12:31; 14:30; 16:11), also "the prince of the power of the air" (Eph 2:2).

Deriv.: *archággelos* (743), archangel.

Syn.: *stratēgós* (4755), captain, magistrate; *megistán* (3175), a great man; *kosmokrátōr* (2888), a ruler of the world; *pantokrátōr* (3841), almighty; *politárchēs* (4173), a ruler of a city; *architríklinos* (755), superintendent of a banquet; *hēgemṓn* (2232), a leader.

759. ἄρωμα, arōma, *ar´-o-mah*; from 142 (in the sense of *sending* off scent); an *aromatic*:—(sweet) spice.

760. Ἀσά, Asa, *as-ah´*; of Hebrew origin [609]; *Asa*, an Israelite:—Asa.

761. ἀσάλευτος, asaleutos, *as-al´-yoo-tos*; from 1 (as a negative particle) and a derivative of 4531; *unshaken*, i.e. (by implication) *immovable* (figurative):—which cannot be moved, unmovable.

762. ἄσβεστος, asbestos, *as´-bes-tos*; from 1 (as a negative particle) and a derivative of 4570; *not extinguished*, i.e. (by implication) *perpetual*:—not to be quenched, unquenchable.

763. ἀσέβεια, asebeia, *as-eb´-i-ah*; from 765; *impiety*, i.e. (by implication) *wickedness*:—ungodly (-liness).

Noun from *asebḗs* (765), impious, ungodly, wicked. Impiety toward God, ungodliness, either in thought or action (Ro 1:18; 11:26; 2Ti 2:16; Tit 2:12; Jude 15, 18; Sept.: Pr 4:17; Ecc 8:8; Jer 5:6; Eze 16:58; 21:24).

Syn.: *adikía* (93), injustice, unrighteousness, iniquity; *anomía* (458), illegality, violation of law, wickedness; *hamartía* (266), sin; *ponēría* (4189), wickedness, malevolence; *kakía* (2549), wickedness, badness; *paranomía* (3892), law breaking; *anaídeia* (335), impudence, insolence; *kakoḗtheia* (2550), mischievousness, depravity of heart.

764. ἀσεβέω, asebeō, *as-eb-eh´-o*; from 765; to *be* (by implication, *act*) *impious* or *wicked*:—commit (live, that after should live) ungodly.

From *asebḗs* (765), impious, ungodly, wicked. To be ungodly, to live impiously (2Pe 2:6; Jude 15).

Syn.: *adikéō* (91), to be unjust, to do wrong; *hamartánō* (264), to sin, offend; *kataphronéō* (2706), to despise; *periphronéō* (4065), to depreciate, not to give due respect.

765. ἀσεβής, asebēs, *as-eb-ace´*; from 1 (as a negative particle) and a presumed derivative of 4576; *irreverent*, i.e. (by extension) *impious* or *wicked*:—ungodly (man).

Adjective from the priv. *a* (1), without, and *sébomai* (4576), to worship, venerate. Impious, ungodly, wicked (1Ti 1:9; 2Pe 2:5; 3:7; Jude 4, 15). Also implying exposure to punishment (Ro 4:5; 5:6).

Deriv.: *asébeia* (763), impiety; *asebéō* (764), to act impiously.

Syn.: *hamartōlós* (268), sinful, sinner; *anósios* (462), wicked, unholy; *bébēlos* (952), wicked, profane; *theostugḗs* (2319), impious, hater of God; *hubristḗs* (5197), an insulter.

766. ἀσέλγεια, aselgeia, *as-elg´-i-a*; from a compound of 1 (as a negative particle) and a presumed **σελγής, selgēs** (of uncertain derivative, but apparently meaning *continent*); *licentiousness* (sometimes including other vices):—filthy, lasciviousness, wantonness.

Noun, from *aselgḗs* (n.f.), licentious, brutal. Excess, immoderation, intemperance in anything, e.g.: in language, speech: arrogance, insolence (Mk 7:22); in general conduct: licentiousness, madness (2Pe 2:2); particularly: wantonness, lasciviousness (Ro 13:13; 2Co 12:21; Gal 5:19; 2Pe 2:7, 18); in a wider sense: debauchery, perversion in general (Eph 4:19; 1Pe 4:3; Jude 4).

Syn.: *asōtía* (810), wastefulness and riotous excess; *epithumía* (1939), lust; *aischrótēs* (151), impropriety, all that is contrary to purity; *rhuparía* (4507), filth; *molusmós* (3436), defilement; *strḗnos* (4764), insolent luxury; *porneía* (4202), fornication; *akrasía* (192), lack of self-restraint, incontinency; *hēdonḗ* (2237), lust, pleasure; *kraipálē* (2897), debauchery, glut, drunkenness.

767. ἄσημος, asēmos, *as´-ay-mos*; from 1 (as a negative particle) and the base of 4591; *unmarked*, i.e. (figurative) *ignoble*:—mean.

768. Ἀσήρ, Asēr, *as-ayr´*; of Hebrew origin [836]; *Aser* (i.e. *Asher*), an Israelite tribe:—Aser.

769. ἀσθένεια, astheneia, *as-then´-i-ah*; from 772; *feebleness* (of body or mind); (by implication) *malady*; moral *frailty*:—disease, infirmity, sickness, weakness.

Noun from *asthenḗs* (772), weak, sick. Want of strength, infirmity, weakness:

(I) Generally (Ro 6:19; 1Co 15:43; 2Co 11:30; 12:5, 9, 10); spoken of the general weakness and infirmity of human nature (2Co 13:4; Heb 4:15; 5:2; 7:28).

(II) Specifically, infirmity of the body, i.e. disease, sickness (Mt 8:17; Lk 5:15; 9:2; 13:12; Jn 5:5; 11:4; Ac 28:9; 1Ti 5:23; Heb 11:34).

(III) Figuratively, of the mind: feebleness, depression, want of energy (1Co 2:3); by implication: sorrow, affliction, distress producing depression and perplexity of mind (Ro 8:26; Gal 4:13; Sept.: Ps 16:4).

Syn.: *árrōstos* (732), infirm, without robustness; *Malakía* (3119), weakness, softness; *nósos* (3554), disease, malady.

770. ἀσθενέω, astheneō, *as-then-eh´-o*; from 772; to *be feeble* (in any sense):—be diseased, impotent folk (man), (be) sick, (be, be made) weak.

From *asthenḗs* (772), without strength, powerless, sick. To lack strength, be infirm, weak, feeble:

(I) To be weak (Ro 8:3; 2Co 13:3, 4, 9; Sept.: 1Sa 2:5; 2Sa 3:1; La 2:8).

(II) Specifically, to be infirm in the body, i.e. to be sick, to suffer from disease or the consequences thereof (Mt 10:8; 25:36; Mk 6:56; Lk 4:40; 7:10; Jn 4:46; Ac 9:37; Php 2:26; Jas 5:14).

(III) Figuratively, of the mind: to be feebleminded, faint-hearted, timid (2Co 11:21). By Hebraism, implying a want of firmness and decision of mind: to be weak-minded, to hesitate, to vacillate, spoken of those whose minds are easily disturbed (Ro 14:2, 21; 1Co 8:9, 11, 12). Also, to be weak, not settled in the faith (Ro 4:19), or in opinion (Ro 14:1).

(IV) By implication: to be afflicted, to be distressed by want, oppression, calamity, etc. (Ac 20:35; 2Co 11:29; Sept.: Job 4:4).

Deriv.: *asthénēma* (771), infirmity.

Syn.: *noséō* (3552), to be sick; *échō kakṓs* (*échō* [2192], to have; *kakṓs* [2560], badly), to have it badly, to be ill; *páschō* (3958), to suffer; *hupophérō* (5297), to endure, to bear from underneath; *basanízō* (928), to suffer pain; *phtheírō* (5351), to pine or waste away, to corrupt in the sense of degeneration; *sunéchō* (4912), to be sick, confined.

771. ἀσθένημα, asthenēma, *as-then´-ay-mah*; from 770; a *scruple* of conscience:—infirmity.

Noun from *asthenéō* (770), to be weak or powerless. Infirmity. Used metaphorically: doubt, hesitation, scruple. Only in Ro 15:1.

772. ἀσθενής, asthenēs, *as-then-ace´*; from 1 (as a negative particle) and the base of 4599; *strengthless* (in various applications, literal, figurative and moral):—more feeble, impotent, sick, without strength, weak (-er, -ness, thing).

Adjective from the priv. *a* (1), without, and *sthénos* (n.f.), strength. Without strength, infirm, weak, feeble:

(I) Generally (Mt 26:41; Mk 14:38; 1Pe 3:7; Sept.: Nu 13:19; Job 4:3; Eze 17:14). Including the idea of imperfection (1Co 12:22; Gal 4:9; Heb 7:18).

(II) Infirm in body; sick, sickly, diseased (Mt 25:39, 43, 44; Lk 10:9; Ac 4:9; 5:15, 16; 1Co 11:30).

(III) Figuratively, of the mind: faint-hearted, timid (2Co 10:10 [cf. 11:21; 1Co 2:3]). Implying a want of decision and firmness of mind: weak-minded, i.e. doubting, hesitating, vacillating, in opinion or faith (1Co 8:7, 10; 9:22; 1Th 5:14).

(IV) By implication: afflicted, distressed by oppression, calamity, etc. (1Co 4:10). In a moral sense: wretched, diseased, i.e. in a state of sin and wretchedness (Ro 5:6).

Deriv.: *asthéneia* (769), lack of strength, powerlessness, weakness; *asthenéō* (770), to be weak or powerless, sick.

Syn.: *árrōstos* (732), sick, without strength or robustness; *adúnatos* (102), weak, without strength.

773. Ἀσία, Asia, *as-ee´-ah*; of uncertain derivative; *Asia*, i.e. *Asia Minor*, or (usually) only its western shore:—Asia.

774. Ἀσιανός, Asianos, *as-ee-an-os´*; from 773; an *Asian* (i.e. *Asiatic*) or inhabitant of Asia:—of Asia.

775. Ἀσιάρχης, Asiarchēs, *as-ee-ar´-khace*; from 773 and 746; an *Asiarch* or president of the public festivities in a city of Asia Minor:—chief of Asia.

776. ἀσιτία, asitia, *as-ee-tee´-ah*; from 777; *fasting* (the state):—abstinence.

777. ἄσιτος, asitos, *as´-ee-tos*; from 1 (as a negative particle) and 4621; *without* (taking) *food*:—fasting.

778. ἀσκέω, askeō, *as-keh´-o*; probably from the same as 4632; to *elaborate*, i.e. (figurative) *train* (by implication, *strive*):—exercise.

779. ἀσκός, askos, *as-kos´*; from the same as 778; a leathern (or skin) *bag* used as a bottle:—bottle.

780. ἀσμένως, asmenōs, *as-men´-oce*; adverb from a derivative of the base of 2237; *with pleasure*:—gladly.

781. ἄσοφος, asophos, *as´-of-os*; from 1 (as a negative particle) and 4680; *unwise*:—fool.

782. ἀσπάζομαι, aspazomai, *as-pad´-zom-ahee*; from 1 (as a particle of union) and a presumed form of 4685; to *enfold* in the arms, i.e. (by implication) to *salute*, (figurative) to *welcome*:—embrace, greet, salute, take leave.

783. ἀσπασμός, aspasmos, *as-pas-mos´*; from 782; a *greeting* (in person or by letter):—greeting, salutation.

784. ἄσπιλος, aspilos, *as´-pee-los*; from 1 (as a negative particle) and 4695; *unblemished* (physical or moral):—without spot, unspotted.

Adjective from the priv. *a* (1), without, and *spílos* (4696), spot. Without blemish or spot, free from spot, unblemished, pure. Spoken of Christ in 1Pe 1:19; of doctrine in 1Ti 6:14; of moral conduct in Jas 1:27; 2Pe 3:14.

Syn.: *katharós* (2513), clean, pure; *amíantos* (283), pure, undefiled; *hagnós* (53), clean, chaste; *kalós* (2570), good; *chrēstós* (5543), useful, kind, gracious; *hierós* (2413), sacred, holy; *hágios* (40), holy, blameless; *hósios* (3741), consecrated, holy; *tímios* (5093), valuable, honored, of good reputation.

785. ἀσπίς, aspis, *as-pece´*; of uncertain derivative; a *buckler* (or *round* shield); used of a serpent (as *coiling* itself), probably the "*asp*":—asp.

786. ἄσπονδος, aspondos, *as´-pon-dos*; from 1 (as a negative particle) and a derivative of 4689; literal *without libation* (which usually accompanied a treaty), i.e. (by implication) *truceless*:—implacable, truce-breaker.

Adjective from the priv. *a* (1), without, and *spondḗ* (n.f.), libation or drink offering. In the NT, averse to any compact, i.e. implacable (Ro 1:31; 2Ti 3:3).

Syn.: *asúmphōnos* (800), one not agreeing; *philóneikos* (5380), quarrelsome, born of strife.

787. ἀσσάριον, assarion, *as-sar´-ee-on*; of Latin origin; an *assarius* or *as*, a Roman coin:—farthing.

788. ἆσσον, asson, *as´-son*; neuter comparative of the base of 1451; *more nearly*, i.e. *very near*:—close.

789. Ἄσσος, Assos, *as´-sos*; probably of foreign origin; *Assus*, a city of Asia Minor:—Assos.

790. ἀστατέω, astateō, *as-tat-eh´-o*; from 1 (as a negative particle) and a derivative of 2476; to *be non-stationary*, i.e. (figurative) *homeless*:—have no certain dwelling-place.

From *ástatos* (n.f.), unstable, which is from the priv. *a* (1), not, and *hístēmi* (2476), to stand, be fixed. To be unsettled, have no certain or fixed abode (1Co 4:11).

Syn.: *kinéō* (2795), to move; *metakinéō* (3334), to remove.

791. ἀστεῖος, asteios, *as-ti´-os*; from **ἄστυ,** ***astu*** (a *city*); *urbane*, i.e. (by implication) *handsome*:—fair.

Adjective from *ástu* (n.f.), a city. Urbane, polished. In the NT, elegant, and spoken of external form: fair, beautiful (Heb 11:23). By Hebraism, the phrase *asteíos tṓ theṓ*, lit. "beautiful to God" (see *theós* [2316]), translated "exceeding fair" (Ac 7:20).

Syn.: *hōraíos* (5611), beautiful; *kalós* (2570), good, beautiful.

792. ἀστήρ, astēr, *as-tare´*; probably from the base of 4766; a *star* (as *strown* over the sky), literal or figurative:—star.

793. ἀστήρικτος, astēriktos, *as-tay´-rik-tos*; from 1 (as a negative particle) and a presumed derivative of 4741; *unfixed*, i.e. (figurative) *vacillating*:—unstable.

794. ἄστοργος, astorgos, *as´-tor-gos*; from 1 (as a negative particle) and a presumed derivative of **στέργω,** ***stergō*** (to *cherish* affectionately); *hard-hearted* toward kindred:—without natural affection.

Adjective from the priv. *a* (1), without, and the noun *storgḗ* (n.f.), family love. Without natural affection; inhuman (Ro 1:31; 2Ti 3:3).

Syn.: *aphilágathos* (865), hostile to benevolence; *stugnētós* (4767), odious, hateful.

795. ἀστοχέω, astocheō, *as-tokh-eh´-o*; from a compound of 1 (as a negative particle) and **στόιχος,** ***stoichos*** (an *aim*); to *miss* the mark, i.e. (figurative) *deviate* from truth:—err, swerve.

796. ἀστραπή, astrapē, *as-trap-ay´*; from 797; *lightning*; (by analogy) *glare*:—lightning, bright shining.

797. ἀστράπτω, astraptō, *as-trap´-to*; probably from 792; to *flash* as lightning:—lighten, shine.

798. ἄστρον, astron, *as´-tron*; neuter from 792; properly a *constellation*; put for a single *star* (natural or artificial):—star.

799. Ἀσύγκριτος, Asugkritos, *as-oong´-kree-tos*; from 1 (as a negative particle) and a derivative of 4793; *incomparable*; *Asyncritus*, a Christian:—Asyncritus.

800. ἀσύμφωνος, asumphōnos, *as-oom´-fo-nos*; from 1 (as a negative particle) and 4859; *inharmonious* (figurative):—agree not.

801. ἀσύνετος, asunetos, *as-oon´-ay-tos*; from 1 (as a negative particle) and 4908; *unintelligent*; (by implication) *wicked*:—foolish, without understanding.

Adjective from the priv. *a* (1), without, and *sunetós* (4908), discerning. Void of understanding, dull of apprehension, foolish (Mt 15:16; Mk 7:18; Sept.: Ps 92:7). From the Hebrew, with the accessory idea of impiety: ungodly, as neglecting the true wisdom and continuing in sin, heathenism, etc. (Ro 1:21, 31; 10:19; Sept.: Dt 32:1 [cf. Job 2:10; Ps 14:1]).

Syn.: *áphrōn* (878), without reason, mental insanity; *mátaios* (3152), vain; *anóētos* (453), thinking incorrectly; *mōrós* (3474), stupid, morally worthless, sluggish.

802. ἀσύνθετος, asunthetos, *as-oon´-thet-os*; from 1 (as a negative particle) and a derivative of 4934; properly *not agreed*, i.e. *treacherous* to compacts:—covenant-breaker.

Adjective from the priv. *a* (1), not, and the pass. of *suntithēmi* (4934), to consent, make agreement. Not put together nor made up of several parts. In the NT, a breaker of a covenant or agreement, faithless, treacherous (Ro 1:31; Sept.: Jer 3:7, 8, 10, 11).

Syn.: *áspondos* (786), implacable (although *asúnthetos* presupposes a state of peace or an agreement interrupted by the unrighteous, while *áspondos* presupposes a broken treaty and a state of war involving a refusal to terminate the hostilities); *asúnetos* (801), foolish, without insight.

803. ἀσφάλεια, asphaleia, *as-fal´-i-ah*; from 804; *security* (literal or figurative):—certainty, safety.

804. ἀσφαλής, asphalēs, *as-fal-ace´*; from 1 (as a negative particle) and **σφάλλω,** ***sphallō*** (to "*fail*"); *secure* (literal or figurative):—certain (-ty), safe, sure.

805. ἀσφαλίζω, asphalizō, *as-fal-id´-zo*; from 804; to *render secure*:—make fast (sure).

806. ἀσφαλῶς, asphalōs, *as-fal-oce´*; adverb from 804; *securely* (literal or figurative):—assuredly, safely.

807. ἀσχημονέω, aschēmoneō, *as-kay-mon-eh´-o*; from 809; to *be* (i.e. *act*) *unbecoming*:—behave self uncomely (unseemly).

808. ἀσχημοσύνη, aschēmosunē, *as-kay-mos-oo´-nay*; from 809; an *indecency*; (by implication) the *pudenda*:—shame, that which is unseemly.

809. ἀσχήμων, aschēmōn, *as-kay´-mone*; from 1 (as a negative particle) and a presumed derivative of 2192 (in the sense of its congener 4976); properly *shapeless*, i.e. (figurative) *inelegant*:—uncomely.

810. ἀσωτία, asōtia, *as-o-tee´-ah*; from a compound of 1 (as a negative particle) and a presumed derivative of 4982; properly *unsavedness*, i.e. (by implication) *profligacy*:—excess, riot.

Noun from *ásōtos* (n.f.), not saveable, incorrigible, dissolute, past hope; which is from the priv. *a* (1), and *sṓzō* (4982), to save. Dissoluteness, debauchery, revelry (Eph 5:18; Tit 1:6; 1Pe 4:4; Sept.: Pr 28:7).

Syn.: *akrasía* (192), lack of self-restraint; *hēdonḗ* (2237), lust, pleasure; *kraipálē* (2897), drunkenness, debauchery; *dapánē* (1160), expense, prodigality.

811. ἀσώτως, asōtōs, *as-o´-toce*; adverb from the same as 810; *dissolutely*:—riotous.

812. ἀτακτέω, atakteō, *at-ak-teh´-o*; from 813; to *be* (i.e. *act*) *irregular*:—behave self disorderly.

From *átaktos* (813), one out of order. To break the ranks (as of soldiers), to behave irregularly or in a disorderly manner, to neglect one's duties (2Th 3:7).

Syn.: *apeithéō* (544), to disbelieve, be disobedient; *anthístēmi* (436), to oppose, resist; *parabaínō* (3845), to transgress; *epanístamai* (1881), to rise up against; *parakoúō* (3878), to disobey, neglect to hear.

813. ἄτακτος, ataktos, *at´-ak-tos*; from 1 (as a negative particle) and a derivative of 5021; *unarranged*, i.e. (by implication) *insubordinate* (religiously):—unruly.

Adjective from the priv. *a* (1), and *tássō* (5021), to set in order. Disorderly, irregular, neglectful of duties. Only in 1Th 5:14.

Deriv.: *ataktéō* (812), to behave irregularly; *atáktōs* (814), irregularly and in a disorderly fashion.

Syn.: *akatástatos* (182), inconstant, unstable; *apeithḗs* (545), disobedient; *anupótaktos* (506), insubordinate.

814. ἀτάκτως, ataktōs, *at-ak´-toce*; adverb from 813; *irregularly* (moral):—disorderly.

815. ἄτεκνος, ateknos, *at´-ek-nos*; from 1 (as a negative particle) and 5043; *childless*:—childless, without children.

816. ἀτενίζω, atenizō, *at-en-id´-zo*; from a compound of 1 (as a particle of union) and **τείνω, *teinō*** (to *stretch*); to *gaze* intently:—behold earnestly (steadfastly), fasten (eyes), look (earnestly, steadfastly, up steadfastly), set eyes.

From *atenḗs* (n.f.), strained, intent, which is from the intensive *a* (1), and *teínō* (n.f.), stretch, strain. To look fixedly, gaze intently (Lk 4:20; 22:56; Ac 1:10; 3:4, 12; 6:15; 7:55; 10:4; 11:6; 13:9; 14:9; 23:1; 2Co 3:7, 13).

Syn.: *horáō* (3708), to perceive, see; *blépō* (991), to look, see,; *emblépō* (1689), to look earnestly; *theōréō* (2334), to carefully observe; *theáomai* (2300), to look with wonder; *elpízō* (1679), to hope; *prosdokáō* (4328), to expect, look for; *apekdéchomai* (553), to expect fully, look for; *anaménō* (362), to wait for; *skopéō* (4648), to look at, take heed.

817. ἄτερ, ater, *at´-er*; a particle probably akin to 427; *aloof*, i.e. *apart* from (literal or figurative):—in the absence of, without.

818. ἀτιμάζω, atimazō, *at-im-ad´-zo*; from 820; to *render infamous*, i.e. (by implication) *contemn* or *maltreat*:—despise, dishonour, suffer shame, entreat shamefully.

819. ἀτιμία, atimia, *at-ee-mee´-ah*; from 820; *infamy*, i.e. (subjective) comparative *indignity*, (objective) *disgrace*:—dishonour, reproach, shame, vile.

820. ἄτιμος, atimos, *at´-ee-mos*; from 1 (as a negative particle) and 5092; (negative) *unhonoured* or (positive) *dishonoured*:—despised, without honour, less honourable [*comparative degree*].

821. ἀτιμόω, atimoō, *at-ee-mo´-o*; from 820; used like 818, to *maltreat*:—handle shamefully.

822. ἀτμίς, atmis, *at-mece´*; from the same as 109; *mist*:—vapour.

823. ἄτομος, atomos, *at´-om-os*; from 1 (as a negative particle) and the base of 5114; *uncut*, i.e. (by implication) *indivisible* [an "*atom*" of time]:—moment.

824. ἄτοπος, atopos, *at´-op-os*; from 1 (as a negative particle) and 5117; *out of place*, i.e. (figurative) *improper, injurious, wicked*:—amiss, harm, unreasonable.

825. Ἀττάλεια, Attaleia, *at-tal´-i-ah*; from **Ἄτταλος, *Attalos*** (a king of Pergamus); *Attaleia*, a place in Pamphylia:—Attalia.

826. αὐγάζω, augazō, *ow-gad´-zo*; from 827; to *beam* forth (figurative):—shine.

From *augḗ* (827), dawn. Used transitively: to illuminate; intransitively: to shine (2Co 4:4; irradiate, beam, shine forth; Sept.: Le 13:24–26, 28).

Deriv.: *diaugázō* (1306), to shine through.

Syn.: *phaínō* (5316), to cause to appear, to shine; *epiphaínō* (2014), to shine upon, give light; *lámpō* (2989), to shine as a torch; *eklámpō* (1584), to shine forth; *astráptō* (797), to flash as lightning; *periastráptō* (4015), to flash around; *epiphaúskō* or *epiphaúō* (2017), to shine forth; *phōtízō* (5461), to illuminate; *anáptō* (381), to kindle, light.

827. αὐγή, augē, *owg-ay´*; of uncertain derivative; a *ray* of light, i.e. (by implication) *radiance, dawn*:—break of day.

A noun meaning brightness, light; spoken of the light of day, the sun, etc. (Ac 20:11; Sept.: Isa 59:9).

Deriv.: *augázō* (826), to shine.

Syn.: *órthros* (3722), dawn.

828. Αὔγουστος, Augoustos, *ow´-goos-tos*; from Latin ["august"]; *Augustus*, a title of the Roman emperor:—Augustus.

829. αὐθάδης, authadēs, *ow-thad´-ace*; from 846 and the base of 2237; *self-pleasing*, i.e. *arrogant*:—self-willed.

Adjective from *autós* (846), himself, and *hḗdomai* (n.f.), to please. Self-complacent; by implication: assuming, arrogant, imperious (Tit 1:7; 2Pe 2:10; Sept.: Ge 49:3, 7; Pr 21:24). Also from *hḗdomai* (n.f.): *asménōs* (780): gladly, with joy.

Syn.: *phílautos* (5367), loving self, selfish; *propetḗs* (4312), precipitous, headlong, heady, rash; *hubristḗs* (5197), an insulter.

830. αὐθαίρετος, authairetos, *ow-thah´ee-ret-os*; from 846 and the same as 140; *self-chosen*, i.e. (by implication) *voluntary*:—of own accord, willing of self.

831. αὐθεντέω, authenteō, *ow-then-teh´-o*; from a compound of 846 and an obsolete **ἕντης, *hentēs*** (a *worker*); to *act of oneself*, i.e. (figurative) *dominate*:—usurp authority over.

832. αὐλέω, auleō, *ow-leh´-o*; from 836; to play the *flute*:—pipe.

833. αὐλή, aulē, *ow-lay´*; from the same as 109; a *yard* (as open to the *wind*); (by implication) a *mansion*:—court, ([sheep-]) fold, hall, palace.

834. αὐλητής, aulētēs, *ow-lay-tace´*; from 832; a *flute-player*:—minstrel, piper.

835. αὐλίζομαι, aulizomai, *ow-lid´-zom-ahee*; middle from 833; to *pass the night* (properly in the open air):—abide, lodge.

836. αὐλός, aulos, *ow-los´*; from the same as 109, a *flute* (as *blown*):—pipe.

837. αὐξάνω, auxanō, *owx-an´-o*; a prolonged form of a primary verb; to *grow* ("*wax*"), i.e. *enlarge* (literal or figurative, active or passive):—grow (up), (give the) increase.

838. αὔξησις, auxēsis, *owx´-ay-sis*; from 837; *growth*:—increase.

839. αὔριον, aurion, *ow´-ree-on*; from a derivative of the same as 109 (meaning a *breeze*, i.e. the morning *air*); properly *fresh*, i.e. (adverb with ellipsis of 2250) *to-morrow*:—(to-) morrow, next day.

840. αὐστηρός, austēros, *ow-stay-ros´*; from a (presumed) derivative of the same as 109 (meaning *blown*); *rough* (properly as a *gale*), i.e. (figurative) *severe*:—austere.

Adjective meaning austere, exacting (Lk 19:21, 22).

Syn.: *chalepós* (5467), difficult, furious, perilous; *oxús* (3691), sharp; *pikrós* (4089), bitter.

841. αὐτάρκεια, autarkeia, *ow-tar´-ki-ah*; from 842; *self-satisfaction*, i.e. (abstract) *contentedness*, or (concrete) a *competence*:—contentment, sufficiency.

842. αὐτάρκης, autarkēs, *ow-tar´-kace*; from 846 and 714; *self-complacent*, i.e. *contented*:—content.

843. αὐτοκατάκριτος, autokatakritos, *ow-tok-at-ak´-ree-tos*; from 846 and a derivative of 2632; *self-condemned*:—condemned of self.

Adjective from *autós* (846), himself, and *katakrínō* (2632), to condemn. Self-condemned, condemned by one's own decision (Tit 3:11).

844. αὐτόματος, automatos, *ow-tom´-at-os*; from 846 and the same as 3155; *self-moved* ["automatic"], i.e. *spontaneous*:—of own accord, of self.

845. αὐτόπτης, autoptēs, *ow-top´-tace*; from 846 and 3700; *self-seeing*, i.e. an *eyewitness*:—eyewitness.

846. αὐτός, autos, *ow-tos´*; from the particle **αὖ, *au***; [perhaps akin to the base of 109 through the idea of a *baffling* wind] (*backward*); the reflexive pronoun *self*, used (alone or in the compound 1438) of the third person, and (with the properly personal pronoun) of the other persons:—her, it (-self), one, the other, (mine) own, said, ([self-], the) same, ([him-, my-, thy-]) self, [your-] selves, she, that, their (-s), them ([-selves]), there [-at, -by, -in, -into, -of, -on, -with], they, (these) things, this (man), those, together, very, which. Compare 848.

847. αὐτοῦ, autou, *ow-too´*; genitive (i.e. possessive) of 846, used as an adverb of location; properly belonging to the *same* spot, i.e. *in this* (or *that*) *place*:—(t-) here.

848. αὑτοῦ, hautou, *how-too´*; contracted from 1438; *self* (in some oblique case or reflexive relation):—her (own), (of) him (-self), his (own), of it, thee, their (own), them (-selves), they.

849. αὐτόχειρ, autocheir, *ow-tokh´-ire*; from 846 and 5495; *self-handed*, i.e. doing *personally*:—with … own hands.

850. αὐχμηρός, auchmēros, *owkh-may-ros´*; from **αὐχμός, *auchmos***; [probably from a base akin to that of 109] (*dust*, as *dried* by wind); properly *dirty*, i.e. (by implication) *obscure*:—dark.

851. ἀφαιρέω, aphaireō, *af-ahee-reh´-o*; from 575 and 138; to *remove* (literal or figurative):—cut (smite) off, take away.

852. ἀφανής, aphanēs, *af-an-ace´*; from 1 (as a negative particle) and 5316; *non-apparent*:—that is not manifest.

853. ἀφανίζω, aphanizō, *af-an-id´-zo*; from 852; to *render unapparent*, i.e. (active) *consume* (*becloud*), or (passive) *disappear* (*be destroyed*):—corrupt, disfigure, perish, vanish away.

854. ἀφανισμός, aphanismos, *af-an-is-mos´*; from 853; *disappearance*, i.e. (figurative) *abrogation*:—vanish away.

855. ἄφαντος, aphantos, *af´-an-tos*; from 1 (as a negative particle) and a derivative of 5316; *non-manifested*, i.e. *invisible*:—vanished out of sight.

856. ἀφεδρών, aphedrōn, *af-ed-rone´*; from a compound of 575 and the base of 1476; a place of *sitting apart*, i.e. a *privy*:—draught.

857. ἀφειδία, apheidia, *af-i-dee´-ah*; from a compound of 1 (as a negative particle) and 5339; *unsparingness*, i.e. *austerity* (*ascetism*):—neglecting.

858. ἀφελότης, aphelotēs, *af-el-ot´-ace*; from a compound of 1 (as a negative particle) and **φέλλος, *phellos*** (in the sense of a *stone* as *stubbing* the foot); *smoothness*, i.e. (figurative) *simplicity*:—singleness.

859. ἄφεσις, aphesis, *af´-es-is*; from 863; *freedom*; (figurative) *pardon*:—deliverance, forgiveness, liberty, remission.

Noun from *aphíēmi* (863), to cause to stand away, to release one's sins from the sinner. Dismission, i.e. deliverance from service, captivity, etc. (Lk 4:18; Sept.: Isa 63:6; Le 25:10). Also remission, i.e. forgiveness, pardon of sins (Mk 1:4; 3:29; Lk 1:77; 3:3; 4:18; 24:47; Ac 2:38; 5:31; 10:43; 13:38; 26:18; Eph 1:7; Col 1:14; Heb 9:22; 10:18; Sept.: Le 25:11; Dt 15:3; Est 2:18; Isa 61:1).

Syn.: *apolútrōsis* (629), redemption; *ánesis* (425), a relaxing, letting loose; *aníēmi* (441), to stand up or to provide liberty or rest; *eleuthería* (1657), freedom, which is the resultant effect of forgiveness or *áphesis*; *hilasmós* (2434), atonement, propitiation; *cháris* (5485), grace (indicating the disposition of the one forgiving, while *áphesis* expresses the result of the acceptance of that grace); *sōtēría* (4991), salvation, deliverance; *dikaíōsis* (1347), justification, being more than acquittal since it also renders a person just.

860. ἀφή, haphē, *haf-ay´*; from 680; probably a *ligament* (as *fastening*):—joint.

861. ἀφθαρσία, aphtharsia, *af-thar-see´-ah*; from 862; *incorruptibility*; genitive *unending existence*; (figurative) *genuineness*:—immortality, incorruption, sincerity.

862. ἄφθαρτος, aphthartos, *af´-thar-tos*; from 1 (as a negative particle) and a derivative of 5351; *undecaying* (in essence or continuance):—not (in-, un-) corruptible, immortal.

Adjective from the priv. *a* (1), not, and *phthartós* (n.f.), corruptible, which is from *phtheírō* (5351), to corrupt. Incorruptible, i.e. spoken of persons: immortal, as God (Ro 1:23; 1Ti 1:17); the future bodies of saints (1Co 15:52). Spoken also of things: imperishable, enduring (1Co 9:25; 1Pe 1:4, 23; 3:4).

Deriv.: *aphtharsía* (861), incorruptibility.

Syn.: *akatálutos* (179), indissoluble, permanent, endless; *aiṓnios* (166), eternal, perpetual; *akéraios* (185), unmixed, unaffected.

863. ἀφίημι, aphiēmi, *af-ee´-ay-mee*; from 575 and **ἵημι, *hiēmi*** (to *send*; an intensive form of **εἶμι, *eimi***; to *go*); to *send forth*, in various applications (as follow):—cry, forgive, forsake, lay aside, leave, let (alone, be, go, have), omit, put (send) away, remit, suffer, yield up.

From *apó* (575), from, and *hiēmi* (n.f., see *iós* [2447]), to send. To send forth or away, let go from oneself:

(I) To dismiss, e.g., the multitudes (Mt 13:36); to give up or let go (Mt 27:50; Mk 15:37); of a wife: to put her away (1Co 7:11–13).

(II) To let go from one's power, possession, to let go free, let escape (Mt 24:40, 41; Lk 17:34–36; Sept.: Pr 4:13). Metaphorically: to let go from obligation toward oneself, to remit, e.g., a debt, offence (Mt 18:27, 32, 35; Mk 11:25; Sept.: Dt 15:2). Of sins: to remit the penalty of sins, i.e. to pardon, forgive, e.g., *opheilḗmata* (3783), debts, faults (Mt 6:12); *hamartías* (266), sins (Mt 9:2, 5, 6; 12:31; Mk 2:5, 7, 9, 10); *blasphēmían* (988), blasphemy, evil speaking (Mt 12:31, 32); *paraptṓmata* (3900), trespasses, offenses (Mt 6:14, 15; Mk 11:25); *hamartḗmata* (265), individual sins (Mk 3:28; 4:12); *anomías* (458), iniquities, acts of lawlessness (Ro 4:7). Also Sept.: Ge 50:17; Ex 32:32; Le 4:20; 5:10, 13; Ps 25:18; 32:5; Isa 22:14; 55:7.

(III) To let go from one's further notice, care, attendance, occupancy, i.e. to leave or let alone:

(A) Spoken of persons: to quit, forsake or abandon (Mt 4:11; 8:15; 15:14; 26:44, 56; Mk 4:36; Jn 10:12). Of things: to leave, abandon, e.g., the nets (Mt 4:20); the house (Mk 13:34); Judea (Jn 4:3); all things (Mt 19:27, 29). See also Sept.: 1Sa 17:20, 28; Jer 12:7. To leave in any place or state, let remain (Mt 5:24; 18:12; Mk 1:20; Lk 10:30; Jn 4:28; 8:29; 14:18, 27; 16:32; Ac 14:17; Sept.: Ge 42:33; Ex 9:21; 2Sa 15:16; 1Ki 19:3; 1Ch 16:21). To leave to anyone, i.e. to let him have or take (Mt 5:40). To leave behind, as at death (Mt 22:25; Mk 12:19–22; Sept.: Ps 17:14; Ecc 2:18). To leave remaining, and in the pass., to be left, remain (Mt 23:38; 24:2; Mk 13:2; Lk 13:35; 19:44; 21:6; Heb 2:8; Sept.: Jgs 2:23; 3:1).

(B) Metaphorically, in various senses: to leave, desert, quit (Ro 1:27, "the natural use"; Rev 2:4). To omit, pass by (Heb 6:1, leaving the word of the beginning). To neglect, to omit (Mt 23:23; Mk 7:8; Lk 11:42; Sept.: Ecc 11:6).

(IV) To let go, i.e. to let pass, permit (Mt 8:22; 13:30; 19:14; Mk 1:34; 5:37). Followed by *hína* (2443), so that, after verbs of command (Mk 11:16). The imper. *áphes* (sing.) and *áphete* (pl.) are followed by the subjunctive without *hína*, e.g., *áphes ídōmen* (first person plural 2d aor. subjunctive of *horáō* [3708], to see, let us see, suffer us to see [Mt 27:49; Mk 15:36]); Mt 7:4, "Let me pull out"; Lk 6:42.

Deriv.: *áphesis* (859), remission, forgiveness.

Syn.: *paúō* (3973), to stop, quit; *katapaúō* (2664), to cease; *katargéō* (2673), to render inactive; *charízomai* (5483), to bestow a favour, to forgive; *apolúō* (630), to release, dismiss; *kataleípō* (2641), to leave behind; *egkataleípō* (1459), to forsake, abandon; *apotássō* (657), to place in order away from oneself; *apotíthēmi* (659), to put off from oneself; *apoleípō* (620), to remain; *perileípō* (4035), to leave around; *eáō* (1439), to let, permit; *hupolimpánō* (5277), a late form of *leípō* (3007), to leave; *epitrépō* (2010), to permit; *apotíthēmi* (659), to put away; *chōrízō* (5563), to separate; *apostréphō* (654), to turn away; *apōthéomai* (683), to thrust away; *lúō* (3089), to loose; *pémpō* (3992), to send.

864. ἀφικνέομαι, aphikneomai, *af-ik-neh´-om-ahee*; from 575 and the base of 2425; to *go* (i.e. *spread*) *forth* (by rumour):—come abroad.

865. ἀφιλάγαθος, aphilagathos, *af-il-ag´-ath-os*; from 1 (as a negative particle) and 5358; *hostile to virtue*:—despiser of those that are good.

Adjective from the priv. *a* (1), and *philágathos* (5358), a lover of being good. Unfriendly, hostile to good men. Only in 2Ti 3:3.

Syn.: *kakós* (2556), bad; *phaúlos* (5337), foul, trivial; *aischrós* (150), shameful; *átimos* (820), without honour; *achreíos* (888), useless, unprofitable; *kataphronētḗs* (2707), a despiser.

866. ἀφιλάργυρος, aphilarguros, *af-il-ar´-goo-ros*; from 1 (as a negative particle) and 5366; *unavaricious*:—without covetousness, not greedy of filthy lucre.

867. ἄφιξις, aphixis, *af´-ix-is*; from 864; properly *arrival*, i.e. (by implication) *departure*:—departing.

868. ἀφίστημι, aphistēmi, *af-is´-tay-mee*; from 575 and 2476; to *remove*, i.e. (active) *instigate* to revolt; usually (reflexive) to *desist, desert*, etc.:—depart, draw (fall) away, refrain, withdraw self.

From *apó*, from, and *hístēmi* (2476), to stand, to place:

(I) Transitively: to place away from, to separate, i.e. to remove, to cause to depart. In the NT, to lead away, to seduce, as a people from their allegiance (Ac 5:37).

(II) Intransitively: to separate oneself, to depart:

(A) Generally: to go away from, to leave (Lk 2:37; 4:13; Ac 12:10; 19:9). In the sense of to forsake, to desert (Ac 15:38). In the sense of to withdraw from, to avoid (1Ti 6:5; 2Ti 2:19).

(B) Metaphorically: to desist from, to refrain from, to let alone (Ac 5:38; 22:29; 2Co 12:8; Sept.: Job 7:16; 1Sa 6:3).

(C) To make defection from, to revolt, to apostatize (Lk 8:13; 1Ti 4:1; Heb 3:12).

Deriv.: *apostasía* (646), apostasy, staying away from; *apostásion* (647), separative, divorce.

Syn.: *apolúō* (630), to depart, dismiss; *apospáō* (645), to draw away; *apochōrízō* (673), to separate, depart from; *apochōréō* (672), to depart from; *hupágō* (5217), to depart, go; *apérchomai* (565), to depart; *apopíptō* (634), to fall from.

869. ἄφνω, aphnō, *af´-no*; adverb from 852 (contraction); *unawares*, i.e. *unexpectedly*:—suddenly.

870. ἀφόβως, aphobōs, *af-ob´-oce*; adverb from a compound of 1 (as a negative particle) and 5401; *fearlessly*:—without fear.

871. ἀφομοιόω, aphomoioō, *af-om-oy-o´-o*; from 575 and 3666; to *assimilate* closely:—make like.

872. ἀφοράω, aphoraō, *af-or-ah´-o*; from 575 and 3708; to *consider* attentively:—look.

873. ἀφορίζω, aphorizō, *af-or-id´-zo*; from 575 and 3724; to *set off* by boundary, i.e. (figurative) *limit, exclude, appoint*, etc.:—divide, separate, sever.

From *apó* (575), from, and *horízō* (3724), to define. To set off by bounds. In the NT, to set off apart, to separate (Mt 13:49; 25:32 [cf. Ac 19:9]; 2Co 6:17; Gal 2:12; Sept.: Le 20:25; Isa 56:3); to set apart for something, to select, to choose (Ac 13:2; Ro 1:1; Gal 1:15). In the sense of to excommunicate (Lk 6:22).

Syn.: *diakrínō* (1252), to separate; *chōrízō* (5563), to separate; *apodiorízō* (592), to mark off, separate; *katargéō* (2673), to reduce to inactivity; *diachōrízō* (1316), to remove completely; *arnéomai* (720), to disavow; *ántitássō* (498), to oppose; *aporríptō* (641), to reject; *periphronéō* (4065), despise; *apōthéomai* (683), to push off, reject; *periphronéō* (4065), to depreciate, despise; *apotrépō* (665), to avoid, turn away; *apophérō* (667), to bear off; *aparnéomai* (533), to deny utterly, disown; *apotássomai* (657), to put in one's proper category away from self.

874. ἀφορμή, aphormē, *af-or-may´*; from a compound of 575 and 3729; a *starting*-point, i.e. (figurative) an *opportunity*:—occasion.

875. ἀφρίζω, aphrizō, *af-rid´-zo*; from 876; to *froth* at the mouth (in epilepsy):—foam.

876. ἀφρός, aphros, *af-ros´*; apparently a primary word; *froth*, i.e. *slaver*:—foaming.

877. ἀφροσύνη, aphrosunē, *af-ros-oo´-nay*; from 878; *senselessness*, i.e. (euphemistic) *egotism*; (moral) *recklessness*:—folly, foolishly (-ness).

878. ἄφρων, aphrōn, *af´-rone*; from 1 (as a negative particle) and 5424; properly *mindless*, i.e. *stupid*, (by implication) *ignorant*, (special) *egotistic*, (practically) *rash*, or (moral) *unbelieving*:—fool (-ish), unwise.

879. ἀφυπνόω, aphupnoō, *af-oop-no´-o*; from a compound of 575 and 5258; properly to *become awake*, i.e. (by implication) to *drop* (off) in slumber:—fall asleep.

880. ἄφωνος, aphōnos, *af´-o-nos*; from 1 (as a negative particle) and 5456; *voiceless*, i.e. *mute* (by nature or choice); (figurative) *unmeaning*:—dumb, without signification.

881. Ἀχάζ, Achaz, *akh-adz´*; of Hebrew origin [271]; *Achaz*, an Israelite:—Achaz.

882. Ἀχαΐα, Achaïa, *ach-ah-ee´-ah*; of uncertain derivative; *Achaïa* (i.e. *Greece*), a country of Europe:—Achaia.

883. Ἀχαϊκός, Achaïkos, *ach-ah-ee-kos´*; from 882; an *Achaïan*; *Achaïus*, a Christian:—Achaicus.

884. ἀχάριστος, acharistos, *ach-ar´-is-tos*; from 1 (as a negative particle) and a presumed derivative of 5483; *thankless*, i.e. *ungrateful*:—unthankful.

885. Ἀχείμ, Acheim, *akh-ime´*; probably of Hebrew origin [compare 3137]; *Achim*, an Israelite:—Achim.

886. ἀχειροποίητος, acheiropoiētos, *akh-i-rop-oy´-ay-tos*; from 1 (as a negative particle) and 5499; *unmanufactured*, i.e. *inartificial*:—made without (not made with) hands.

887. ἀχλύς, achlus, *akh-looce´*; of uncertain derivative; *dimness* of sight, i.e. (probably) a *cataract*:—mist.

A noun meaning thick mist, cloud, darkness, which shrouds objects from view. In the NT, spoken of the eyes: a mist before the eyes (Ac 13:11).

Syn.: *skótos* (4655), darkness; *gnóphos* (1105), a thick dark cloud; *zóphos* (2217), thick darkness resulting from foggy weather or smoke; *néphos* (3509), cloud; *nephélē* (3507), a definitely shaped cloud.

888. ἀχρεῖος, achreios, *akh-ri´-os*; from 1 (as a negative particle) and a derivative of 5534 [compare 5532]; *useless*, i.e. (euphemism) *unmeritorious*:—unprofitable.

Adjective from the priv. *a* (1), without, and *chreía* (5532), utility, usefulness. Unprofitable, useless. In the NT, by implication: slothful, wicked (Mt 25:30 [cf. Mt 25:26]); spoken in humility: humble, of little value (Lk 17:10, humble, of little value; Sept.: 2Sa 6:22).

Deriv.: *achreióō* (889), to render useless, to become unprofitable.

Syn.: *áchrēstos* (890), unprofitable, useless; *alusitelḗs* (255), not advantageous, not useful; *anōphelḗs* (512), not serviceable, unprofitable, useless; *kenós* (2756), empty, vain; *mátaios* (3152), vain, empty, profitless; *adókimos* (96), unapproved, unfit; *alusitelḗs* (255), unprofitable, useless.

889. ἀχρειόω, achreioō, *akh-ri-o´-o*; from 888; to *render useless*, i.e. *spoil*:—become unprofitable.

890. ἄχρηστος, achrēstos, *akh´-race-tos*; from 1 (as a negative particle) and 5543; *inefficient*, i.e. (by implication) *detrimental*:—unprofitable.

Adjective from the priv. *a* (1), without, and *chrēstós* (5543), profitable. Unprofitable, useless. In the NT, metaphorically and by implication: worse than useless, wicked, detrimental (Phm 11 [see Phm 18]).

Syn.: *achreíos* (888), unprofitable.

891. ἄχρι, achri, *akh´-ree*; or **ἄχρις, *achris*,** *akh´-rece*; akin to 206 (through the idea of a *terminus*); (of time) *until* or (of place) *up to*:—as far as, for, in (-to), till, (even, un-) to, until, while. Compare 3360.

892. ἄχυρον, achuron, *akh´-oo-ron*; perhaps remotely from **χέω, *cheō*** (to *shed* forth); *chaff* (as *diffusive*):—chaff.

893. ἀψευδής, apseudēs, *aps-yoo-dace´*; from 1 (as a negative particle) and 5579; *veracious*:—that cannot lie.

894. ἄψινθος, apsinthos, *ap´-sin-thos*; of uncertain derivative; *wormwood* (as a type of *bitterness*, i.e. [figurative] *calamity*):—wormwood.

895. ἄψυχος, apsuchos, *ap´-soo-khos*; from 1 (as a negative particle) and 5590; *lifeless*, i.e. *inanimate* (mechanical):—without life.

Adjective from the priv. *a* (1), without, and *psuchḗ* (5590), soul or the breath of life. Lifeless, inanimate, void of sense and life (1Co 14:7).

Syn.: *adúnatos* (102), weak; *asthenḗs* (772), without strength, sick; *nekrós* (3498), dead.

896. Βάαλ, Baal, *bah´-al*; of Hebrew origin [1168]; *Baal*, a Phoenician deity (used as a symbol of idolatry):—Baal.

897. Βαβυλών, Babulōn, *bab-oo-lone´*; of Hebrew origin [894]; *Babylon*, the capital of Chaldæa (literal or figurative [as a type of tyranny]):—Babylon.

898. βαθμός, bathmos, *bath-mos´*; from the same as 899; a *step*, i.e. (figurative) *grade* (of dignity):—degree.

899. βάθος, bathos, *bath´-os*; from the same as 901; *profundity*, i.e. (by implication) *extent*; (figurative) *mystery*:—deep (-ness, things), depth.

900. βαθύνω, bathunō, *bath-oo´-no*; from 901; to *deepen*:—deep.

901. βαθύς, bathus, *bath-oos´*; from the base of 939; *profound* (as *going* down), literal or figurative:—deep, very early.

902. βαΐον, baïon, *bah-ee´-on*; a diminutive of a derivative probably of the base of 939; a palm *twig* (as *going* out far):—branch.

903. Βαλαάμ, Balaam, *bal-ah-am´*; of Hebrew origin [1109]; *Balaam*, a Mesopotamian (symbolic of a false teacher):—Balaam.

904. Βαλάκ, Balak, *bal-ak´*; of Hebrew origin [1111]; *Balak*, a Moabite:—Balac.

905. βαλάντιον, balantion, *bal-an´-tee-on*; probably remotely from 906 (as a *depository*); a *pouch* (for money):—bag, purse.

906. βάλλω, ballō, *bal´-lo*; a primary verb; to *throw* (in various applications, more or less violent or intense):—arise, cast (out), × dung, lay, lie, pour, put (up), send, strike, throw (down), thrust. Compare 4496.

To cast, throw:

(I) To cast lots (Mt 27:35; Mk 15:24; Lk 23:25; Sept.: 1Sa 14:42; Ne 10:34; 11:1). Spoken of a tree: to cast its fruit (Rev 6:13). To cast oneself, and with *kátō* (2736), down, to cast oneself down (Mt 4:6; Lk 4:9). Followed by the dat. as in Mt 15:26; Mk 7:27, to cast to or before anyone; Mt 25:27, to put out or place out money with the brokers. When used with different prep. and particles, the meaning is altered accordingly, but with the idea of throwing always maintained:

(A) Followed by *apó* (575), from: to throw from one, cast away (Mt 5:29; 18:8, 9).

(B) Followed by *ek* (1537), out of: to cast out of the mouth, to vomit (Rev 12:15, 16).

(C) Followed by *éxō* (1854), away, forth, out, out of: to cast out or throw away, reject (Mt 5:13; 13:48; Lk 14:35; Jn 15:6).

(D) Followed by *eis* (1519), into: to cast into, i.e. a bed (Rev 2:22); the fire (Mt 3:10; 5:29; 6:30; 13:42; Mk 9:22, 45; Sept.: Da 3:21, 24); the sea (Mt 21:21; Mk 11:23; Rev 18:21); of nets: to cast into or let down into the sea (Mt 4:18; 13:47; Sept.: Isa 19:8); to cast into prison (Mt 18:30; Lk 12:58; Ac 16:37); to cast contributions of money into a treasury (Mk 12:41, 43; Lk 21:1, 4); to deposit (Mt 27:6); of a sword: to thrust into the sheath, to put away (Jn 18:11); of a sickle (Rev 14:19); of the finger, hand: to thrust into, put into (Mk 7:33; Jn 20:27 [cf. Sept.: Job 28:9]; Da 11:42 [*ekteínō* {1614}, to stretch forth]); to put or place bits in horses' mouths (Jas 3:3). Spoken of liquids as wine and water where we can only translate by saying to put or pour into (Mt 9:17; Mk 2:22; Lk 5:37; Jn 13:5; Sept.: Jgs 6:19). Metaphorically: to put into one's heart, suggest to one's mind (Jn 13:2).

(E) Followed by *émprosthen* (1715), in front of, or *enṓpion* (1799), before, meaning to cast before anyone or anything (Mt 7:6; Rev 2:14; 4:10).

(F) Followed by *epí* (1909), upon: to cast upon, as the seed upon the earth, to sow, scatter seed (Mk 4:26; Sept.: Ps 126:6); to cast stones at anyone (Jn 8:7, 59; Sept.: Ecc 3:5; Isa 37:33; Eze 21:22); to send peace upon the earth (Mt 10:34); to put upon, impose (Rev 2:24). Spoken of a sickle: to thrust in (Rev 14:16). Spoken of liquids: to pour (Mt 26:12 [see also Mt 26:7]).

(II) Perf. and pluperf. pass., *béblēmai*, to be cast, meaning to be laid down, to lie, equivalent to *keímai* (2749), to lie outstretched (Mt 8:6, a paralytic was lying in the house [see Mt 8:14]); laid on a bed (Mt 9:2; Mk 7:30) laid at a gate (Lk 16:20).

(III) With the accusative of person, to throw at anyone (Mk 14:65, "they threw at him with blows" [a.t.], means they gave him blows). See Sept.: 2Ch 26:15; Ps 78:9.

(IV) Intransitively or with *heautón* [(1438), himself] implied: to cast oneself, to rush forward; as spoken of a wind: to blow (Ac 27:14).

Deriv.: *anabállō* (306), to defer, put off; *antibállō* (474), to have; *apobállō* (577), to throw off from, lay aside; *bélos* (956), a missile; *blētéos* (992), that which one must put out; *bolḗ* (1000), a throw; *bolís* (1002), dart; *diabállō* (1225), to throw in between; *ekbállō* (1544), to cast out of or from; *embállō* (1685), to cast into; *epibállō* (1911), to cast upon; *katabállō* (2598), to cast down or around; *lithoboléō* (3036), to cast stones; *metabállō* (3328), to throw over, change mind; *parabállō* (3846), to arrive, compare; *peribállō* (4016), to cast about; *probállō* (4261), to put forward; *sumbállō* (4820), to confer, encounter; *huperbállō* (5235), to excel, pass; *hupobállō* (5260), to suborn.

Syn.: With the meaning of to cast: *rhíptō* (4496), to throw with a certain motion; *apōthéō* (683), to thrust away; *apotíthēmi* (659), to put off; *ektíthēmi* (1620), to expose, cast out; *kathairéō* (2507), to cast down, demolish. With the meaning of to lay down: *títhēmi* (5087), to put or place, set; *anaklínō* (347), to lay down; *keímai* (2749), to lie; *apókeimai* (606), to be laid away or up, as money in a box or purse; *katákeimai* (2621), to lie down; *epíkeimai* (1945), to lie upon; *epipíptō* (1968), to fall upon; *anákeimai* (345), to be laid up, to lie. With the meaning of to pour as liquids: *katachéō* (2708), to pour down upon; *ekchéō* (1632), to pour out of; *ekchúnō* (1632), to pour out, shed; *epichéō* (2022), to pour upon. With the meaning of to put: *títhēmi* (5087), to place, lay, set; *apolúō* (630), to let go, dismiss; *aphíēmi* (863), to send away; *periairéō* (4014), to take away; *exaírō* (1808), to put away from; *apekdúō* (554), to strip off clothes or arms; *methístēmi* (3179), to remove; *anágō* (321), to lead or bring up; *endúō* (1746), to put on oneself; *embibázō* (1688), to put in; *probibázō* (4264), to put forward; *apostréphō* (654), to turn away, remove; *ekteínō* (1614), to stretch forth; *lúō* (3089), to loose. With the meaning of to send: *apostéllō* (649), to send forth; *pémpō* (3992), to send; *apotássomai* (657), to place in a proper order away from oneself. With the meaning of thrust: *katatoxeúō* (2700), to strike down with an arrow; *exōthéō* (1856), to drive out.

907. βαπτίζω, baptizō, *bap-tid´-zo*; from a derivative of 911; to *make whelmed* (i.e. *fully wet*); used only (in the NT) of ceremonial *ablution*, especially (technical) of the ordinance of Christian *baptism*:—baptist, baptize, wash.

From *báptō* (911), to dip. Immerse, submerge for a religious purpose, to overwhelm, saturate, baptize:

(I) To wash, to cleanse by washing; in the middle, to wash oneself, to bathe, to perform ablution (Mk 7:4 [cf. v. 3, where the phrase "wash their hands" is the translation of *níptō* (3538), to wash part of the body]).

(II) To baptize, to administer the rite of baptism, either that of John or Christ. Pass. and middle: to be baptized or to cause oneself to be baptized. In the early churches, where, according to oriental habits, bathing was to them what washing is to us, the rite appears to have been ordinarily, though not necessarily, performed by immersion.

(A) Spoken of simply (Mt 3:6, 11; Mk 1:4, 5, 8, 9; Lk 3:7, 12, 16, 21; 7:30; Jn 1:25, 28; 3:22, 23, 26; 4:1, 2; 10:40; Ac 2:38, 41; 8:12, 13, 36, 38; 9:18; 10:47; 16:15, 33; 18:8; 22:16; 1Co 1:14, 16, 17).

(B) With adjuncts marking the object and effect of baptism: especially *eis* (1519), into, unto: to baptize or to be baptized into anything, meaning into the belief, profession, or observance of anything (Mt 3:11, "unto repentance"; Ac 2:38; 19:3; Ro 6:3; 1Co 12:13). Spoken of persons, it means to baptize or be baptized into a profession of faith or into anyone, in sincere obedience to him. Also in 1Co 10:2, "unto Moses"; Gal 3:27, "unto Christ"; also "into the name of someone" means to be identified with what the name of that one stands for (Mt 28:19; Ac 8:16; 19:5; 1Co 1:13, 15). The same sense is understood when the prep. *epí* [(1909), upon], or *en* [(1722), in], followed by *onómati* [(3686), name], is used (Ac 2:38, *epí*; 10:48, *en*). With *hupér* (5228), on behalf of or for (1Co 15:29, those being "baptized for [or on account of] the dead," i.e. on a belief of the resurrection of the dead).

(III) Metaphorically and in direct allusion to the practice of water baptism: to baptize in or with the Holy Spirit and in or with fire, the baptism in the Holy Spirit being the spiritual counterpart of the water baptism (Mt 3:11; Mk 1:8; Lk 3:16; Jn 1:33; Ac 1:5; 11:16).

(IV) Metaphorically, in connection with calamities: to baptize with calamities, i.e. to be overwhelmed with sufferings (Mt 20:22, 23; Mk 10:38, 39). In 1Co 15:29, "What shall those being baptized for the dead do? Why therefore are they baptized on their behalf?" (a.t.) means if the dead do not rise, why expose ourselves to so much danger and suffering in the hope of a resurrection?

Deriv.: *báptisma* (908), baptism, the result of baptizing; *baptismós* (909), the ceremonial washing of articles; *baptistḗs* (910), baptist, used of John to qualify him as one baptizing.

Syn.: *buthízō* (1036), to sink, but not necessarily to drown; *katapontízō* (2670), to plunge down, submerge; *embáptō* (1686), to dip.

908. βάπτισμα, baptisma, *bap´-tis-mah*; from 907; *baptism* (technical or figurative):—baptism.

Noun from *báptō* (911), to dip. Something immersed. In the NT, baptism, spoken of the rite, e.g., of John's baptism (Mt 3:7; 21:25; Mk 1:4; 11:30; Lk 3:3; 7:29; 20:4; Ac 1:22; 10:37; 13:24; 18:25; 19:3, 4); of the baptism instituted by Jesus (Ro 6:4; Eph 4:5; Col 2:12; 1Pe 3:21). Metaphorically: baptism into calamity, i.e. afflictions with which one is oppressed or overwhelmed (Mt 20:22, 23; Mk 10:38, 39; Lk 12:50).

909. βαπτισμός, baptismos, *bap-tis-mos´*; from 907; *ablution* (ceremony or Christian):—baptism, washing.

Noun from *baptízō* (907), to baptize. Washing, ablution of vessels, etc. (Mk 7:4, 8; Heb 6:2; Sept.: Le 11:32). Baptism, i.e. the Christian rite (Heb 6:2).

Syn.: *loutrón* (3067), a bath, metaphorically meaning the Word of God which, when believed, brings spiritual cleansing.

910. Βαπτιστής, Baptistēs, *bap-tis-tace´*; from 907; a *baptizer*, as an epithet of Christ's forerunner:—Baptist.

Noun from *baptízō* (907), to baptize. A baptizer or baptist, referring to John the Baptist (Mt 3:1; 11:11, 12; 14:2, 8; 16:14; 17:13; Mk 6:24, 25; 8:28; Lk 7:20, 28, 33; 9:19).

911. βάπτω, baptō, *bap´-to*; a primary verb; to *whelm*, i.e. cover wholly with a fluid; in the NT only in a qualified or special sense, i.e. (literal) to *moisten* (a part of one's person), or (by implication) to *stain* (as with dye):—dip.

To immerse, dip, transitively (Lk 16:24 of the thing touched; Jn 13:26). To dye by dipping (Rev 19:13, to tinge, dye). As a compound with the prep. *en*, in, *embáptō* (1686), to dip in (Mt 26:23; Mk 14:20; Sept.: Le 4:6; 14:6; Nu 19:18; Ru 2:14; 2Ki 8:15; Job 9:31).

Deriv.: *baptízō* (907), to baptize; *embáptō* (1686), to dip in.

912. Βαραββᾶς, Barabbas, *bar-ab-bas´*; of Chaldee origin [1347 and 5]; *son of Abba; Bar-abbas*, an Israelite:—Barabbas.

913. Βαράκ, Barak, *bar-ak´*; of Hebrew origin [1301]; *Barak*, an Israelite:—Barak.

914. Βαραχίας, Barachias, *bar-akh-ee´-as*; of Hebrew origin [1296]; *Barachias* (i.e. *Berechijah*), an Israelite:—Barachias.

915. βάρβαρος, barbaros, *bar´-bar-os*; of uncertain derivative; a *foreigner* (i.e. *non-Greek*):—barbarian (-rous).

916. βαρέω, bareō, *bar-eh´-o*; from 926; to *weigh* down (figurative):—burden, charge, heavy, press.

917. βαρέως, bareōs, *bar-eh´-oce*; adverb from 926; *heavily* (figurative):—dull.

918. Βαρθολομαῖος, Bartholomaios, *bar-thol-om-ah´-yos*; of Chaldee origin [1247 and 8526]; *son of Tolmai; Bar-tholomæus*, a Christian apostle:—Bartholomeus.

919. βαριησοῦς, Bariēsous, *bar-ee-ay-sooce´*; of Chaldee origin [1247 and 3091]; *son of Jesus* (or *Joshua*); *Bar-jesus*, an Israelite:—Barjesus.

920. Βαριωνᾶς, Bariōnas, *bar-ee-oo-nas´*; of Chaldee origin [1247 and 3124]; *son of Jonas* (or *Jonah*); *Bar-jonas*, an Israelite:—Bar-jona.

921. Βαρνάβας, Barnabas, *bar-nab´-as*; of Chaldee origin [1247 and 5029]; *son of Nabas* (i.e. *prophecy*); *Barnabas*, an Israelite:—Barnabas.

922. βάρος, baros, *bar´-os*; probably from the same as 939 (through the notion of *going* down; compare 899); *weight*; in the NT only figurative, a *load, abundance, authority*:—burden (-some), weight.

923. Βαρσαβᾶς, Barsabas, *bar-sab-as´*; of Chaldee origin [1247 and probably 6634]; *son of Sabas* (or *Tsaba*); *Bar-sabas*, the name of two Israelites:—Barsabas.

924. Βαρτιμαῖος, Bartimaios, *bar-tim-ah´-yos*; of Chaldee origin [1247 and 2931]; *son of Timæus* (or the *unclean*); *Bartimæus*, an Israelite:—Bartimæus.

925. βαρύνω, barunō, *bar-oo´-no*; from 926; to *burden* (figurative):—overcharge.

926. βαρύς, barus, *bar-ooce´*; from the same as 922; *weighty*, i.e. (figurative) *burdensome, grave*:—grievous, heavy, weightier.

927. βαρύτιμος, barutimos, *bar-oo´-tim-os*; from 926 and 5092; highly *valuable*:—very precious.

928. βασανίζω, basanizō, *bas-an-id´-zo*; from 931; to *torture*:—pain, toil, torment, toss, vex.

929. βασανισμός, basanismos, *bas-an-is-mos´*; from 928; *torture*:—torment.

930. βασανιστής, basanistēs, *bas-an-is-tace´*; from 928; a *torturer*:—tormentor.

931. βάσανος, basanos, *bas´-an-os*; perhaps remotely from the same as 939 (through the notion of *going* to the bottom); a *touch-stone*, i.e. (by analogy) *torture*:—torment.

932. βασιλεία, basileia, *bas-il-i´-ah*; from 935; properly *royalty*, i.e. (abstract) *rule*, or (concrete) a *realm* (literal or figurative):—kingdom, + reign.

(I) Dominion, reign, the exercise of kingly power (Mt 6:13; Lk 1:33; 19:12, 15; Heb 1:8; Rev 17:12, 17, 18; Sept.: 1Sa 10:16, 25; 13:13; 28:17). In Rev 1:6, the TR has *basileís* (935), kings.

(II) Dominions, realm, i.e. a people in a territory under kingly rule (Mt 4:8; 12:25, 26; 24:7; Mk 3:24; 6:23; 13:8; Lk 4:5; 11:17, 18; 21:10; Heb 11:33; Rev 11:15; 16:10; Sept.: Ge 10:10; Nu 32:33; Jos 11:10; Est 2:3).

(III) The phrases *hē basileía toú Theoú* (2316), "the kingdom of God" (Mt 6:33; Mk 1:15; Lk 4:43; 6:20; Jn 3:5); "his kingdom," referring to Christ (Mt 13:41 [cf. 20:21]); "the kingdom of our father David" (Mk 11:10); "the kingdom of Christ and of God" (Eph 5:5); "the kingdom ... of Jesus Christ" (Rev 1:9); "heavenly kingdom" (2Ti 4:18); and *he basileía*, "the kingdom" (Mt 8:12; 9:35) are all syn. in the NT and mean the divine spiritual kingdom, the glorious reign of the Messiah. The idea of the kingdom has its basis in the prophecies of the OT where the coming of the Messiah and His triumphs are foretold (e.g., Ps 2; 110; Isa 2:1–4; 11:1ff.; Jer 23:5ff.; 31:31ff.; 32:37ff.; 33:14ff.; Eze 34:23ff.; 37:24ff.; Mic 4:1ff., and especially Da 2:44; 7:14, 27; 9:25ff.). His reign is described as a golden age when true righteousness will be established, and with it the theocracy will be established bringing peace and happiness. Prior to the visible manifestation of this kingdom and its extension to the material and natural realms of the world, it exists spiritually in the hearts of men, and thus it was understood by Zacharias (Lk 1:67ff.); Simeon (Lk 2:25ff.); Anna (Lk 2:36ff.); Joseph (Lk 23:50, 51).

The Jews, however, generally gave to these prophecies a temporal meaning and expected a Messiah who should come in the clouds of heaven. As king of the Jewish people, He was expected to restore the ancient Jewish religion and worship, reform the corrupt morals of the people, make expiation for their sins, give freedom from the yoke of foreign dominion, and at length reign over the whole earth in peace and glory.

The concept of the kingdom in the OT is partly fulfilled in the NT. First we have the Christian dispensation. The kingdom of heaven or God on earth, consisting of the community of those who receive Jesus as their Saviour, and who, through the Holy Spirit, form His Church with Him as its head. This spiritual kingdom has both an internal and external form. As internal, it already exists and rules in the hearts of all Christians and is therefore present. As external, it is either embodied both in the visible and invisible Church, and thus is present and progressive; or it is to be perfected in the coming of the Son of Man to judge and reign in bliss and glory. This is the further realization of the kingdom of God in the future.

However, these different aspects are not always distinguished. The expression often embraces both the internal and external kingdom and refers both to its commencement in this world and its completion in the world to come. Hence, in the NT we find it spoken about in the Jewish temporal sense by Jews and the apostles before the day of Pentecost (Mt 18:1; 20:21; Lk 17:20; 19:11; Ac 1:6); in the Christian sense as announced by John, where perhaps something of the Jewish view was intermingled (Mt 3:2 [cf. Lk 23:51]); as announced by Jesus and others (Mt 4:17, 23; 9:35; 10:7; Mk 1:14, 15; Lk 10:9, 11; Ac 28:31); in the internal spiritual sense (Mt 6:33; Mk 10:15; Lk 17:21; 18:17; Jn 3:3, 5; Ro 14:17; 1Co 4:20); in the external sense, i.e. as embodied in the visible church and the universal spread of the gospel (Mt 6:10; 12:28; 13:24, 31, 33, 44, 47; 16:28; Mk 4:30; 11:10; Lk 13:18, 20; Ac 19:8); as perfected in the future world (Mt 13:43; 16:19; 26:29; Mk 14:25; Lk 22:29, 30; 2Pe 1:11; Rev 12:10). In this latter view it denotes especially the bliss of heaven which is to be enjoyed in the Redeemer's kingdom, i.e. eternal life (Mt 8:11; 25:34; Mk 9:47; Lk 13:28, 29; Ac 14:22; 1Co 6:9, 10; 15:50; Gal 5:21; Eph 5:5; 2Th 1:5; 2Ti 4:18; Heb 12:28; Jas 2:5). The kingdom spoken of generally (Mt 5:19). In Mt 8:12, "the sons of the kingdom" (a.t.) means the Jews who thought that the Messiah's reign was destined only for them and that by ancestry alone, which claimed belief in the God of Abraham, they had the right to be called the sons of the kingdom (Jn 8:33, 37, 39). However, "the children of the kingdom" in Mt 13:38 are the true citizens of the kingdom of God. See also Mt 11:11, 12; 13:11, 19, 44, 45, 52; 18:4, 23; 19:12, 24; 20:1. Spoken also generally of the privileges and rewards of the divine kingdom, both here and hereafter (Mt 5:3, 10, 20; 7:21; 18:3; Col 1:13; 1Th 2:12).

Syn.: *hēgemonía* (2231), reign; *thrónos* (2362), throne, and by implication the power that the throne represents, kingdom; *aulḗ* (833), palace, as standing for kingdom; *krátos* (2904), dominion; *archḗ* (746), rule; *exousía* (1849), authority.

933. βασίλειον, basileion, *bas-il´-i-on*; neuter of 934; a *palace*:—king's court.

934. βασίλειος, basileios, *bas-il´-i-os*; from 935; *kingly* (in nature):—royal.

Adjective meaning royal, regal. Particularly (1Pe 2:9, "a royal priesthood," consecrated to God as kings and priests, i.e. in a distinguished manner). As a subst.: a royal mansion, palace (Lk 7:25).

Syn.: *baslikós* (937), royal.

935. βασιλεύς, basileus, *bas-il-yooce´*; probably from 939 (through the notion of a *foundation* of power); a *sovereign* (abstract, relative or figurative):—king.

Masculine noun meaning king, monarch, i.e. one who exercises royal authority and sovereignty:

(I) Of David (Mt 1:6; Ac 13:22); of Pharaoh (Ac 7:10, 18; Heb 11:23, 27); of the Roman emperor (Jn 19:15); of ancient Jewish kings (Lk 10:24); of Jesus as the Messiah who is often called King, King of Israel or of the Jews (Mt 2:2; 21:5; 25:34, 40; Lk 19:38; Jn 1:49; 12:13, 15; Sept.: Ps 2:6); spoken of God (1Ti 1:17; 6:15; Rev 15:3; 17:14, "King of kings" by way of emphasis; Sept.: Ps 5:2; 29:10; 47:2; 95:3). "The city of the great King" (Mt 5:35) means of God, Jerusalem as the seat of His worship (Ps 47:2).

(II) In a more general and lower sense, as a title of distinguished honour, e.g., viceroy, prince, leader, chief. Herod the Great and his successors had the title of king, but were dependent for the name and power on the Romans (Mt 2:1, 3, 9; Lk 1:5; Ac 12:1; 25:13ff.; 26:2ff.), and Herod Antipas was in fact only a tetrarch, meaning ruler of only a fourth of the kingdom (Mt 14:1; Lk 3:1, 19; 9:7), though he is called "king" in Mt 14:9; Mk 6:14. See also Aretas, king of Arabia, Petraea (2Co 11:32). Also used when joined with *hēgemónes* (2232), leaders, rulers (Mt 10:18; Mk 13:9; Lk 21:12; Sept.: Ps 2:2; 102:15). Generally (Mt 17:25; 18:23; Ac 9:15; 2Ti 2:2; 1Pe 2:13, 17; Rev 9:11). Figuratively spoken of Christians as about to reign with the Messiah over the nations (Rev 1:6 [{TR} cf. 5:10; 20:6]).

Deriv.: *basileía* (932), kingdom; *basíleios* (934), royal, kingly in nature; *basileúō* (936), to reign; *basilikós* (937), belonging to a king, such as a courtier or something kingly; *basílissa* (938), queen.

Syn.: *árchōn* (758), ruler; *politárchēs* (4173), ruler of a city; *despótēs* (1203), despot, an absolute ruler; *kúrios* (2962), lord; *pantokrátōr* (3841), the all-ruling, almighty, omnipotent; *hēgemṓn* (2232), a leader, ruler, governor; *Kaísar* (2541), Caesar, a title of the Roman emperor; *dunástēs* (1413), mighty potentate.

936. βασιλεύω, basileuō, *bas-il-yoo´-o*; from 935; to *rule* (literal or figurative):—king, reign.

From *basileús* (935), a king. To reign, rule, be king:

(I) To reign over (Lk 19:4, 17; 1Ti 6:15). Spoken of Archelaus, who for a time had the title of king (Mt 2:22; Sept.: Jgs 9:8, 10; 1Sa 8:9, 11). Spoken of the Messiah (Lk 1:33; 1Co 15:25; Rev 11:15).

(II) Absolutely: to reign, i.e. to possess and to exercise dominion; spoken of God as vindicating to himself his regal power (Rev 11:17; 19:6). Figuratively, spoken of Christians who are to reign with Christ, i.e. enjoy the high privileges, honours, and felicity of the Messiah's kingdom (Ro 5:17; Rev 5:10; 20:4, 6; 22:5). So of Christians on earth: to enjoy the honour and prosperity of kings (1Co 4:8). Figuratively: to have dominion, to prevail, to be predominant, e.g., death (Ro 5:14, 17); sin and grace (Ro 5:21; 6:12).

Deriv.: *sumbasileúō* (4821), to reign with someone.

Syn.: *huperéchō* (5242), to hold oneself above, be superior; *proéchō* (4284), to excel; *diakrínomai* (1252), to distinguish oneself as superior; *prōteúō* (4409), to have preeminence; *kurieúō* (2961), to exercise lordship, have dominion over; *árchō* (757), to reign, rule over; *sumbasileúō* (4821), to reign together; *hēgéomai* (2233), to rule over; *hēgemoneúō* (2230), to act as a ruler.

937. βασιλικός, basilikos, *bas-il-ee-kos´*; from 935; *regal* (in relation), i.e. (literal) belonging to (or befitting) the sovereign (as land, dress, or a *courtier*), or (figurative) *preeminent*:—king's, nobleman, royal.

Adjective from *basileús* (935), king. Kingly, royal, i.e. belonging to a king (Ac 12:20, a territory; Jn 4:46, 49, a nobleman, a person attached to a court; Sept.: Nu 20:17; 21:22; 2Sa 14:26; Est 8:15). Befitting a king, of kingly dignity (Ac 12:21, a robe; Jas 2:8, noble, excellent, preeminent, referring to law).

Syn.: *basíleios* (934), royal.

938. βασίλισσα, basilissa, *bas-il´-is-sah*; feminine from 936; a *queen*:—queen.

939. βάσις, basis, *bas´-ece*; from **βαίνω**, *bainō* (to *walk*); a *pace* ("base"), i.e. (by implication) the *foot*:—foot.

940. βασκαίνω, baskainō, *bas-kah´ee-no*; akin to 5335; to *malign*, i.e. (by extension) to *fascinate* (by false representations):—bewitch.

941. βαστάζω, bastazō, *bas-tad´-zo*; perhaps remotely derivative from the base of 939 (through the idea of *removal*); to *lift*, literal or figurative (*endure, declare, sustain, receive*, etc.):—bear, carry, take up.

942. βάτος, batos, *bat´-os*; of uncertain derivative; a *brier* shrub:—bramble, bush.

943. βάτος, batos, *bat´-os*; of Hebrew origin [1324]; a *bath*, or measure for liquids:—measure.

944. βάτραχος, batrachos, *bat´-rakh-os*; of uncertain derivative; a *frog*:—frog.

945. βαττολογέω, battologeō, *bat-tol-og-eh´-o*; from **Βάττος**, ***Battos*** (a proverbial stammerer) and 3056; to *stutter*, i.e. (by implication) to *prate* tediously:—use vain repetitions.

From *báttos* (n.f.), a proverbial stammerer, and *lógos* (3056), word. To speak foolishly, babble, chatter (see Le 5:4; Job 11:2, 3; Isa 16:6; 44:25). Not to be confused with *battarízō*, to stutter. Characterizes *polulogía* (4180), wordiness. Much talk without content, repeating the same thing over and over again (Mt 6:7), useless speaking without distinct expression of purpose as contrasted to succinct, knowledgeable speech, thus foolish speaking.

Syn.: *phluaréō* (5396), to be a babbler; *phlúaros* (5397), to be a tattler or one who talks unnecessarily and too much; *mōrología* (3473), foolish talking.

946. βδέλυγμα, bdelugma, *bdel´-oog-mah*; from 948; a *detestation*, i.e. (special) *idolatry*:—abomination.

Noun from *bdelússō* (948), to emit a foul odour, to turn away through loathing or disgust, abhor. An abomination, i.e. something abominable, detestable.

(I) Generally: that which is detestable to God (Lk 16:15; Sept.: Pr 11:1; 15:8, 9; 20:23; 21:27).

(II) That which was unclean in the Jewish tradition, and especially of impure idol worship; hence idolatry, licentiousness, abominable impurity (Rev 17:4, 5; 21:27; Sept.: 2Ki 16:3; 21:2 [cf. Le 18:22; also Le 11:10, 12, 13; Jer 11:15]).

(III) In connection with (II) is the expression "the abomination of desolation" (*to bdélugma tēs erēmṓseōs* [2050], robbery, desolation, emptying out). This expression is found in the Olivet Discourse of our Lord (Mt 24:15; Mk 13:14), and applied to what was to take place at the destruction of Jerusalem by the Romans (cf. Lk 21:20). It is probably to be referred to the pollution of the temple by idol worship or the setting up of images, though express historical testimony is lacking (cf. Mt 24:15; 2Th 2:4; Sept.: 1Ki 11:5; 21:26; Isa 17:8).

947. βδελυκτός, bdeluktos, *bdel-ook-tos´*; from 948; *detestable*, i.e. (special) *idolatrous*:—abominable.

Adjective from *bdelússō* (948), to abominate. Abominable, detestable (Tit 1:16; Sept.: Pr 17:15).

Syn.: *anósios* (462), unholy; *bébēlos* (952), wicked, profane; *theostugḗs* (2319), impious, hater of God; *stugnētós* (4767), odious.

948. βδελύσσω, bdelussō, *bdel-oos´-so*; from a (presumed) derivative of **βδέω, *bdeō*** (to *stink*); to *be disgusted*, i.e. (by implication) *detest* (especially of idolatry):—abhor, abominable.

From *bdéō* (n.f.), to stink. To emit a stench, to excite disgust. In the NT, used in the middle: to feel disgust, to abhor (Ro 2:22; Rev 21:8; Sept.: Le 26:11; Dt 23:7; Am 5:10). In the perf. pass. part. *ebdelugménos*: abominable, detestable, i.e. polluted with crimes (Sept.: Le 18:30; Job 15:16; Pr 8:7; Isa 14:19; Hos 9:10).

Deriv.: *bdélugma* (946), an abomination; *bdeluktós* (947), abominable.

Syn.: *apostréphō* (654), to turn away.

949. βέβαιος, bebaios, *beb´-ah-yos*; from the base of 939 (through the idea of *basality*); *stable* (literal or figurative):—firm, of force, steadfast, sure.

Adjective from *bainō* (n.f.), to go. Fixed, firm, sure, certain, steadfast (see Ro 4:16; 2Co 1:7; Heb 2:2; 3:6, 14; 9:17; 2Pe 1:10, 19). In the NT, of objects (Heb 6:19), that which does not fail or waver, immovable, and on which one may rely.

Deriv.: *bebaióō* (950), to establish.

Syn.: *alēthḗs* (227), true; *asphalḗs* (804), safe, sure; *pistós* (4103), faithful, trustworthy; *hedraíos* (1476), steadfast, equivalent to *stereós* (4731), fast, firm, hard.

950. βεβαιόω, bebaioō, *beb-ah-yo´-o*; from 949; to *stabilitate* (figurative):—confirm, (e-) stablish.

From *bébaios* (949), sure, fixed. To make firm or steadfast, to confirm; spoken of persons (1Co 1:8; 2Co 1:21; Col 2:7; Heb 13:9; Sept.: Ps 41:13; 119:28); spoken of things: to corroborate, to ratify, to establish by arguments, proofs, etc. (Mk 16:20; Ro 15:8; 1Co 1:6; Heb 2:3).

Deriv.: *bebaíōsis* (951), confirmation; *diabebaióomai* (1226), to make firm.

Syn.: *stērízō* (4741), to set steadfastly; *epistērízō* (1991), to strengthen; *kuróō* (2964), to make valid, ratify; *stereóō* (4732), to make firm; *marturéō* (3140), to testify; *dēlóō* (1213), to declare; *apodeíknumi* (584), to prove.

951. βεβαίωσις, bebaiōsis, *beb-ah´-yo-sis*; from 950; *stabiliment*:—confirmation.

Noun from *bebaióō* (950), to establish. Ratification, confirmation, corroboration, firm establishment (Php 1:7; Heb 6:16).

Syn.: *stērigmós* (4740), stability; *aspháleia* (803), certainty, safety; *pepoíthēsis* (4006), confidence, trust; *apódeixis* (585), manifestation; *plērophoría* (4136), entire confidence, assurance.

952. βέβηλος, bebēlos, *beb´-ay-los*; from the base of 939 and **βηλός, *bēlos*** (a *threshold*); *accessible* (as by *crossing the door-way*), i.e. (by implication, of Jewish notions) *heathenish, wicked*:—profane (person).

Adjective from *bainō* (n.f.), to go, and *bḗlos* (n.f.), a threshold. Particularly, of place: accessible to all; hence, common, profane, in opposition to *hágios* (40), holy. In the NT, spoken of persons: profane, i.e. impious, a scoffer (2Ti 1:9; Heb 12:16; Sept.: Eze 21:25); spoken of things, as disputes, etc.: common, unholy, unsanctified (1Ti 4:7; 6:20; 2Ti 2:16).

Deriv.: *bebēlóō* (953), to profane, pollute.

Syn.: *anósios* (462), unholy; *theostugḗs* (2319), hateful to God, impious.

953. βεβηλόω, bebēloō, *beb-ay-lo´-o*; from 952; to *desecrate*:—profane.

From *bébēlos* (952), profane. To profane, to cross the threshold (Mt 12:5; Ac 24:6; Sept.: Ex 31:14; Le 19:8, 12; Eze 43:7, 8).

Syn.: *miaínō* (3392), to taint, contaminate, defile; *molúnō* (3435), to soil; *asebéō* (764), to act impiously; *hierosuléō* (2416), to be a temple-robber, commit sacrilege; *blasphēméō* (987), to blaspheme, revile, speak evil; *koinóō* (2840), to defile, pollute; *spilóō* (4695), to stain, soil, spot.

954. Βεελζεβούλ, Beelzeboul, *beh-el-zeb-ool´*; of Chaldee origin [by parody upon 1176]; *dung-god; Beelzebul*, a name of Satan:—Beelzebub.

955. Βελίαλ, Belial, *bel-ee´-al*; of Hebrew origin [1100], *worthlessness; Belial*, as an epithet of Satan:—Belial.

956. βέλος, belos, *bel´-os*; from 906; a *missile*, i.e. *spear* or *arrow*:—dart.

957. βελτίον, beltion, *bel-tee´-on*; neuter of a compound of a derivative of 906 (used for the comparative of 18); *better*:—very well.

958. Βενιαμίν, Beniamin, *ben-ee-am-een´*; of Hebrew origin [1144]; *Benjamin*, an Israelite:—Benjamin.

959. Βερνίκη, Bernikē, *ber-nee´-kay*; from a provincial form of 5342 and 3529; *victorious; Bernicè*, a member of the Herodian family:—Bernice.

960. Βέροια, Beroia, *ber´-oy-ah*; perhaps a provincial from a derivative of 4008 [*Peræa*, i.e. the region *beyond* the coastline]; *Beroea*, a place in Macedonia:—Berea.

961. Βεροιαῖος, Beroiaios, *ber-oy-ah´-yos*; from 960; a *Beroeæan* or native of Berœea:—of Berea.

962. Βηθαβαρά, Bēthabara, *bay-thab-ar-ah´*; of Hebrew origin [1004 and 5679]; *ferry-house; Beth-abara* (i.e. *Bethabarah*), a place on the Jordan:—Bethabara.

963. Βηθανία, Bēthania, *bay-than-ee´-ah*; of Chaldee origin; *date-house; Beth-any*, a place in Palestine:—Bethany.

964. Βηθεσδά, Bēthesda, *bay-thes-dah´*; of Chaldee origin [compare 1004 and 2617]; *house of kindness; Beth-esda*, a pool in Jerusalem:—Bethesda.

965. Βηθλεέμ, Bēthleem, *bayth-leh-em´*; of Hebrew origin [1036]; *Bethleem* (i.e. *Beth-lechem*), a place in Palestine:—Bethlehem.

966. Βηθσαϊδά, Bēthsaïda, *bayth-sahee-dah´*; of Chaldee origin [compare 1004 and 6719]; *fishing-house; Bethsaïda*, a place in Palestine:—Bethsaida.

967. Βηθφαγή, Bethphagē, *bayth-fag-ay´*; of Chaldee origin [compare 1004 and 6291]; *fig-house; Bethphagè*, a place in Palestine:—Bethphage.

968. βῆμα, bēma, *bay´-ma*; from the base of 939; a *step*, i.e. *foot-breath*; (by implication) a *rostrum*, i.e. *tribunal*:—judgement seat, set [foot] on, throne.

969. βήρυλλος, bērullos, *bay´-rool-los*; of uncertain derivative; a "*beryl*":—beryl.

970. βία, bia, *bee´-ah*; probably akin to 979 (through the idea of *vital* activity); *force*:—violence.

971. βιάζω, biazō, *bee-ad´-zo*; from 970; to *force*, i.e. (reflex.) to *crowd oneself* (into), or (passive) to *be seized*:—press, suffer violence.

From *bía* (970), violence. To force, to urge. In the NT, used in the middle: to use force, to force, to press (Lk 16:16); in the pass.: to suffer violence, be taken by force (Mt 11:12). Both of these occurrences imply the eagerness with which the gospel was received in the agitated state of men's minds.

Deriv.: *biastḗs* (973), a person who is violent; *parabiázomai* (3849), to coerce, persuade.

Syn.: *hormáō* (3729), to rush.

972. βίαιος, biaios, *bee´-ah-yos*; from 970; *violent*:—mighty.

973. βιαστής, biastēs, *bee-as-tace´*; from 971; a *forcer*, i.e. (figurative) *energetic*:—violent.

974. βιβλιαρίδιον, bibliaridion, *bib-lee-ar-id´-ee-on*; a diminutive of 975; a *booklet*:—little book.

975. βιβλίον, biblion, *bib-lee´-on*; a diminutive of 976; a *roll*:—bill, book, scroll, writing.

976. βίβλος, biblos, *bib´-los*; properly the inner *bark* of the papyrus plant, i.e. (by implication) a *sheet* or *scroll* of writing:—book.

A noun meaning inner rind of the papyrus, anciently used for writing. In the NT, a roll, volume, scroll, i.e. a book (Mk 12:26, "in the book of Moses" meaning the Law; Lk 3:4; 20:42; Ac 1:20; 7:42; 19:19; Sept.: Jos 1:8; 1Sa 10:25; Ezr 6:18). Spoken of a genealogical table or catalog (Mt 1:1; Sept.: Ge 5:1). The phrase, "the book of life [*biblos tḗs zōḗs* {2222}, life]" is equal in the Sept. to the book of the living ones (Ps 69:28 [cf. Ex 32:32, 33]), where God is shown as having the names of the righteous who are to inherit eternal life inscribed in a book. See also Php 4:3; Rev 3:5; 20:15. This is the same phrase as *tó biblíon* (975), a diminutive of *bíblos* (Rev 17:8; 20:12; 21:27; Sept.: Da 12:1). Different from this is the book in which God has from eternity inscribed the destinies of men (Ps 139:16 [cf. Job 14:5]). The plural and the diminutive *biblía* are twice mentioned in Rev 20:12 referring to the books of judgement in which the actions of men are recorded (see Da 7:10).

Deriv.: *bibliarídion* (974), a little scroll; *biblíon* (975), a roll, scroll.

977. βιβρώσκω, bibrōskō, *bib-ro´-sko*; a reduplicated and prolonged form of an obsolete primary verb [perhaps causative of 1006]; to *eat*:—eat.

978. Βιθυνία, Bithunia, *bee-thoo-nee´-ah*; of uncertain derivative; *Bithynia*, a region of Asia:—Bithynia.

979. βίος, bios, *bee´-os*; a primary word; *life*, i.e. (literal) the present state of existence; (by implication) the means of *livelihood*:—good life, living.

A noun meaning life. Particularly, the present life (Lk 8:14; 1Th 2:2; 2Ti 2:4; 1Pe 4:3). Used figuratively: means of life, living, sustenance (Mk 12:44; Lk 8:43; 15:12, 30; 21:4).

Deriv.: *bióō* (980), to live, to pass one's life without reference to its quality.

Syn.: with the meaning of goods, wealth: *húparxis* (5223), subsistence, goods, and also as a plural part. noun, *tá hupárchonta*; *skeúos* (4632), primarily a vessel, but also goods; *psuchḗ* (5590), with the meaning of natural life, breath of life, the seat of personality; *agōgḗ* (72), a manner of life, conduct; *anastrophḗ* (391), behaviour, conduct.

980. βιόω, bioō, *bee-o´-o*; from 979; to *spend* existence:—live.

981. Βίωσις, Biōsis, *bee´-o-sis*; from 980; *living* (properly, the act; by implication, the mode):—manner of life.

982. βιωτικός, biōtikos, *bee-o-tee-kos´*; from a derivative of 980; *relating to* the present *existence*:—of (pertaining to, things that pertain to) this life.

983. βλαβερός, blaberos, *blab-er-os´*; from 984; *injurious*:—hurtful.

984. βλάπτω, blaptō, *blap´-to*; a primary verb; properly to *hinder*, i.e. (by implication) to *injure*:—hurt.

985. βλαστάνω, blastanō, *blas-tan´-o*; from **βλαστός, blastos** (a *sprout*); to *germinate*; (by implication) to *yield* fruit:—bring forth, bud, spring (up).

986. Βλάστος, Blastos, *blas´-tos*; perhaps the same as the base of 985; *Blastus*, an officer of Herod Agrippa:—Blastus.

987. βλασφημέω, blasphēmeō, *blas-fay-meh´-o*; from 989; to *vilify*; specially to *speak impiously*:—(speak) blaspheme (-er, -mously, -my), defame, rail on, revile, speak evil.

From *blásphēmos* (989), blasphemous or a blasphemer. To blaspheme, revile:

(I) Generally, spoken of men and things: to speak evil of, to slander, to defame, to revile (Mk 3:28; 15:29; Lk 23:39; Jn 10:36; Ac 18:6; 19:37; 26:11 [cf. Ac 26:9]; Ro 3:8; 14:16; 1Co 4:13; 10:30; 1Ti 1:20; 6:1; Tit 3:2; Jas 2:7; 1Pe 4:4, 14; 2Pe 2:2, 10, 12; Jude 8, 10; Sept.: 2Ki 19:6, 23).

(II) Spoken of God and his spirit, or of divine things: to revile, to treat with irreverence and scornful insolence (Mt 9:3; 26:65; Ac 13:45; Ro 2:24; Tit 2:5; Rev 16:9, 11, 21). In the NT generally syn. with *oneidízō* (3679), revile, and *loidoréō* (3058), to reproach (Mt 27:39; Mk 15:29; Lk 22:65; 23:39; Ro 3:8; 14:16; 1Co 4:13; Tit 3:2; 2Pe 2:10; Jude 8); especially to revile God and divine things (Rev 13:6).

Syn.: *hēttáō* (2274), to make inferior; *hubrízō* (5195), to insult; *kataráomai* (2672), to curse; *anathematízō* (332), to curse with an oath; *asebéō* (764), to be impious, disrespectful; *hierosuléō* (2416), to commit sacrilege.

988. βλασφημία, blasphēmia, *blas-fay-me´-ah*; from 989; *vilification* (especially against God):—blasphemy, evil speaking, railing.

From *blásphēmos* (989), blasphemous or a blasphemer. Blasphemy: Generally, spoken of men and things: evil speakings, slander, reviling (Mt 12:31; 15:19; Mk 3:28; 7:22; Eph 4:31; Col 3:8; 1Ti 6:4; Rev 2:9). Spoken of God and His Spirit, or divine things: reviling, impious irreverence (Mt 12:31; Mk 2:7; 14:64; Lk 5:21; Jn 10:33; Rev 13:5, 6); against the Holy Spirit (Mt 12:31; Mk 3:28; Lk 12:10).

Syn.: *katalalía* (2636), evil speaking, backbiting; *loidoría* (3059), abuse, railing, reviling; *apistía* (570), unbelief; *asébeia* (763), impiety; *húbris* (5196), insult, hurt, reproach; *dusphēmía* (1426), defamation.

989. βλάσφημος, blasphēmos, *blas´-fay-mos*; from a derivative of 984 and 5345; *scurrilous*, i.e. *calumnious* (against man), or (special) *impious* (against God):—blasphemer (-mous), railing.

Adjective from *bláx* (n.f.), sluggish, slow, stupid, and *phḗmē* (5345), rumour, fame. Blasphemous, spoken of words uttered against God and divine things (Ac 6:11, 13). So of words against men: slanderous, haughtily contemptuous, insulting (2Pe 2:11). Used as a substantive, in respect to God: a blasphemer (1Ti 1:13); in respect to men: a slanderer, reviler (2Ti 3:2).

Deriv.: *blasphēméō* (987), to blaspheme; *blasphēmía* (988), blaspheming abuse against someone.

Syn.: *loídoros* (3060), reviling, railing, or a railer; *hubristḗs* (5197), an insulter; *empaíktēs* (1703), a derider, mocker.

990. βλέμμα, blemma, *blem´-mah*; from 991; *vision* (properly, concrete; by implication, abstract):—seeing.

991. βλέπω, blepō, *blep´-o*; a primary verb; to *look* at (literal or figurative):—behold, beware, lie, look (on, to), perceive, regard, see, sight, take heed. Compare 3700.

(I) To be able to see, i.e. to have the faculty of sight, and as spoken of the blind, to recover sight (Mt 12:22). In Ac 9:9, "without sight" means blind. See Rev 3:18; 9:20; Sept.: Ex 4:11; 23:8; 1Sa 3:2; Ps 69:23. The present inf. with the neuter article *tó blépein*, used as a substantive means sight, the faculty of seeing (Lk 7:21). Used figuratively in Jn 9:39: "that they which see not might see; and that they which see might be made blind" or may not see (cf. Jn 9:41). So by Hebraism, with a part. of the same verb for emphasis, e.g., "seeing ye shall see" in (Mt 13:14; Mk 4:12; Ac 28:26 [cf. Isa 6:9]).

(II) To perceive as with the eyes, meaning to discern, to understand (Mt 7:3; 11:4; 14:30; 24:2; Mk 8:24; Lk 11:33; Jn 1:29; 21:9; Sept.: 2Ki 9:17; Am 8:1). In Rev 1:12, "to see the voice," means to see where it came from. By implication: to have before the eyes, spoken of what is present (Ro 8:24, cf. v. 25]). Hence, the part. *blepómenos*, seen, may mean present (Ro 8:24). So *tá blepómena*, things seen, meaning present things; and *tá mḗ blepómena*, things not seen, meaning future things (2Co 4:18; Heb 11:1, 7). Spoken of a vision: to see in vision (Rev 1:11; 6:1, 3, 5, 7 [TR], where other texts read *íde*, the imper. of *eídō* [1492], to see).

(III) Metaphorically: to perceive with the mind, be aware of, observe (Ro 7:23; 2Co 7:8; Heb 3:19; 10:25; Jas 2:22; Sept.: Ne 2:17).

(IV) To look, i.e. to look at or upon, to direct the eyes upon, to behold:

(A) Spoken of persons (Mt 5:28; Rev 5:3, 4; Sept.: Hag 2:4). In Mt 18:10, "their angels do always behold the face of my Father," i.e. in accordance with the customs of oriental monarchs, they have constant access to him, are admitted to his privacy as his friends. See 2Ki 25:19; Est 1:14; Jer 52:25. Followed by *eis* [(1519), unto], meaning to look upon, behold (Ac 3:4). In Jn 13:22; Lk 9:62, *eis* [(1519), unto] *tá opísō* [(3694), behind], to look back (Sept.: Ge 19:17). Spoken of a place: to look, i.e. to be situated (Ac 27:12; Sept.: 2Ch 4:4; Eze 40:6, 21–23, 46; 46:1, 13, 20).

(B) Metaphorically: to look to, direct the mind upon, consider, take heed (Mt 22:16; 1Co 1:26; 10:18; Php 3:2; Col 2:5; Sept.: Ge 39:23; Ps 37:37; Isa 22:11). Spoken by way of caution, in the imper. *blepétō* or *blépete*: look to it, take heed, be on the watch, beware (Mk 13:23, 33; Mk 13:9; 2Jn 8). Also *blépete mḗ* [(3361), not], meaning watch out, take heed lest (Lk 21:8; Ac 13:40; 1Co 10:12; Gal 5:15).

Deriv.: *anablépō* (308), to look up, and when spoken of the blind, to receive their sight; *apoblépō* (578), to look away from all else and toward one object, to look steadfastly; *blémma* (990), a look, glance, sight; *diablépō* (1227), to see clearly or to see through; *emblépō* (1689), to look earnestly, with the object of learning lessons of faith from, e.g., the birds; *epiblépō* (1914), to look upon or with favour; *periblépō* (4017), to look around; *problépō* (4265), to foresee, provide.

Syn.: *atenízō* (816), to gaze upon, behold earnestly; *katoptrízō* (2734), to look in a mirror; *aphoráō* (872), to look away from one thing so as to see another; *kathoráō* (2529), to look down upon, discern clearly. With the meaning of to heed: *proséchō* (4337), to pay attention to, beware; *phulássō* (5442), to guard, watch; *epéchō* (1907), to give attention to; *skopéō* (4648), to take heed; *muōpázō* (3467), to be shortsighted; *phaínō* (5316), to cause to appear.

992. βλητέος, blēteos, *blay-teh´-os*; from 906; fit *to be cast* (i.e. *applied*):—must be put.

993. Βοανεργές, Boanerges, *bo-an-erg-es´*; of Chaldee origin [1123 and 7266]; *sons of commotion; Boänerges*, an epithet of two of the apostles:—Boanerges.

994. βοάω, boaō, *bo-ah´-o*; apparently a prolonged form of a primary verb; to *halloo*, i.e. *shout* (for help or in a tumultuous way):—cry.

995. βοή, boē, *bo-ay´*; from 994; a *halloo*, i.e. *call* (for aid, etc.):—cry.

996. βοήθεια, boētheia, *bo-ay´-thi-ah*; from 998; *aid*; specially a rope or chain for *frapping* a vessel:—help.

997. βοηθέω, boētheō, *bo-ay-theh´-o*; from 998; to *aid* or *relieve*:—help, succour.

998. βοηθός, boēthos, *bo-ay-thos´*; from 995 and **θέω, *theō*** (to *run*); a *succourer*:—helper.

999. βόθυνος, bothunos, *both´-oo-nos*; akin to 900; a *hole* (in the ground); specially a *cistern*:—ditch, pit.

1000. βολή, bolē, *bol-ay´*; from 906; a *throw* (as a measure of distance):—cast.

1001. βολίζω, bolizō, *bol-id´-zo*; from 1002; to *heave* the lead:—sound.

1002. βολίς, bolis, *bol-ece´*; from 906; a *missile*, i.e. *javelin*:—dart.

1003. Βοόζ, Booz, *bo-oz´*; of Hebrew origin [1162]; *Boöz* (i.e. *Boäz*), an Israelite:—Booz.

1004. βόρβορος, borboros, *bor´-bor-os*; of uncertain derivative; *mud*:—mire.

1005. βοῤῥᾶς, borrhas, *bor-hras´*; of uncertain derivative; the *north* (properly wind):—north.

1006. βόσκω, boskō, *bos´-ko*; a prolonged form of a primary verb [compare 977, 1016]; to *pasture*; by extension to *fodder*; reflexive to *graze*:—feed, keep.

To feed sheep, to pasture or tend while grazing. Middle *bóskomai*, to feed, i.e. to be feeding or grazing (Mt 8:30, 33; Mk 5:11, 14; Lk 8:32, 34; 15:15; Sept.: Ge 29:7, 9; 37:12, 16). Used metaphorically of a Christian teacher: to instruct (Jn 21:15, 17; Sept.: Eze 34:2, 3, 8, 10).

Deriv.: *botánē* (1008), herbage, plants.

Syn.: *poimaínō* (4165), to shepherd, to act as shepherd, tend, involving much more than feeding

1007. Βοσόρ, Bosor, *bos-or´*; of Hebrew origin [1160]; *Bosor* (i.e. *Beör*), a Moabite:—Bosor.

1008. βοτάνη, botanē, *bot-an´-ay*; from 1006; *herbage* (as if for *grazing*):—herb.

1009. βότρυς, botrus, *bot´-rooce*; of uncertain derivative; a *bunch* (of grapes):—(vine) cluster (of the vine).

1010. βουλευτής, bouleutēs, *bool-yoo-tace´*; from 1011; an *adviser*, i.e. (special) a *councillor* or member of the Jewish Sanhedrin:—counsellor.

1011. βουλεύω, bouleuō, *bool-yoo´-o*; from 1012; to *advise*, i.e. (reflexive) *deliberate*, or (by implication) *resolve*:—consult, take counsel, determine, be minded, purpose.

1012. βουλή, boulē, *boo-lay´*; from 1014; *volition*, i.e. (object) *advice*, or (by implication) *purpose*:— + advise, counsel, will.

A noun meaning counsel, senate. In the NT, counsel, i.e. determination, decision, decree; spoken of God (Lk 7:30; Ac 2:23; 13:36; 20:27; Eph 1:11; Heb 6:17); of men (Lk 23:51; Ac 27:12; Sept.: Pr 19:21; Isa 5:19; Jer 49:20, 30). By implication: purpose, plan, etc. (Ac 4:28; 5:38; 27:42; Sept.: Ezr 4:5; Ne 4:15); spoken of secret thoughts, purpose (1Co 4:5; Sept.: Job 5:12; Isa 55:7, 8 [cf. Ezr 6:22]).

Deriv.: *bouleúō* (1011), to take counsel; *epiboulḗ* (1917), a plot, conspiracy; *súmboulos* (4825), a councilman, council member.

Syn.: *gnṓmē* (1106), the faculty of knowledge, reason, opinion, resolve, purpose; *krísis* (2920), judgement, decision; *kritḗrion* (2922), a tribunal or the place or assembly where a judgement or decision is made; *phrónēma* (5427), thought or the object of thought; *phrónēsis* (5428), the ability to make a decision, prudence; *próthesis* (4286), purpose.

1013. βούλημα, boulēma, *boo´-lay-mah*; from 1014; a *resolve*:—purpose, will.

Noun from *boúlomai* (1014), to will. That which is willed, i.e. will (Ac 27:43; Ro 9:19).

1014. βούλομαι, boulomai, *boo´-lom-ahee*; middle of a primary verb; to "*will*," i.e. (reflexive) *be willing*:—be disposed, minded, intend, list, (be, of own) will (-ing). Compare 2309.

To will, be willing, wish, desire. *Boúlomai* expresses a merely passive desire, propensity, willingness, while *thélō* (2309) expresses an active volition and purpose. *Boúlomai* expresses also the inward predisposition and bent from which active volition proceeds. In speaking of the gods, Homer uses *boúlomai* in the sense of *thélō* (2309).

(I) As spoken of men: to be willing, inclined, disposed (Mk 15:15; Ac 17:20; 18:27; 19:30; 22:30; 23:28; 25:22; 27:43; 28:18; Phm 13; 3Jn 10; Sept.: Le 26:21; Dt 25:7, 8; Job 9:3; 39:9); to intend, purpose, have in mind (Mt 1:19; Ac 5:28; 12:4; 2Co 1:15; Sept.: Ezr 4:5). Also in a stronger sense: to desire, to aim at (1Ti 6:9; Jas 4:4). With the meaning of to choose, prefer, decide (Jn 18:39; Ac 18:15; 25:20; Jas 3:4; 2Jn 12). As implying command or direction: to will, that is, to direct (Php 1:12,

"It is my will" [a.t.]; 1Ti 2:8; 5:14; Tit 3:8; Jude 5, "I will that ye call to mind" [a.t.]).

(II) Spoken of God: equivalent to *thélō* (2309), to will, that is, to please, appoint, decree (Lk 22:42; Heb 6:17; Jas 1:18; 2Pe 3:9); of Jesus as the Son of God (Mt 11:27; Lk 10:22); of the Spirit (1Co 12:11).

Deriv.: *boúlēma* (1013), purpose, will.

Syn.: *axióō* (515), to desire worthily; *epithuméō* (1937), to desire earnestly stressing an inward impulse rather than an object desired, equivalent to covet; *orégomai* (3713), to long after something; *epizētéō* (1934), to seek earnestly; *epipothéō* (1971), to long after, usually in a bad sense meaning to lust; *parakaléō* (3870), to beseech; *bouleúō* (1011), to take counsel; *eúchomai* (2172), to wish.

1015. βουνός, bounos, *boo-nos´*; probably of foreign origin; a *hillock*:—hill.

1016. βοῦς, bous, *booce*; probably from the base of 1006; an *ox* (as *grazing*), i.e. an animal of that species ("beef"):—ox.

1017. βραβεῖον, brabeion, *brab-i´-on*; from **βραβεύς, brabeus** (an *umpire*; of uncertain derivative); an *award* (of arbitration), i.e. (special) a *prize* in the public games:—prize.

1018. βραβεύω, brabeuō, *brab-yoo´-o*; from the same as 1017; to *arbitrate*, i.e. (genitive) to *govern* (figurative, *prevail*):—rule.

1019. βραδύνω, bradunō, *brad-oo´-no*; from 1021; to *delay*:—be slack, tarry.

1020. βραδυπλοέω, braduploeō, *brad-oo-plo-eh´-o*; from 1021 and a prolonged form of 4126; to *sail slowly*:—sail slowly.

1021. βραδύς, bradus, *brad-ooce´*; of uncertain affinity; *slow*; (figurative) *dull*:—slow.

Adjective meaning slow, i.e. not hasty (Jas 1:19). Metaphorically: "slow of understanding," heavy, stupid (Lk 24:25).

Deriv.: *bradúnō* (1019), to be slow, delay; *braduploéō* (1020), to sail slowly; *bradútēs* (1022), slackness.

Syn.: *nōthrós* (3576), sluggish; *argós* (692), inactive; *oknērós* (3636), shrinking, irksome.

1022. βραδύτης, bradutēs, *brad-oo´-tace*; from 1021; *tardiness*:—slackness.

1023. βραχίων, brachiōn, *brakh-ee´-own*; properly, comparative of 1024, but apparently in the sense of **βράσσω, brassō** (to *wield*); the *arm*, i.e. (figurative) *strength*:—arm.

1024. βραχύς, brachus, *brakh-ooce´*; of uncertain affinity; *short* (of time, place, quantity, or number):—few words, little (space, while).

1025. βρέφος, brephos, *bref´-os*; of uncertain affinity; an *infant* (properly unborn) literal or figurative:—babe, (young) child, infant.

A noun meaning child. Spoken of a child yet unborn, a fetus (Lk 1:41, 44); usually an infant, babe, suckling (Lk 2:12, 16; 18:15; Ac 7:19; 2Ti 3:15). Used metaphorically of those who have just embraced the Christian religion (1Pe 2:2 [cf. 1Co 3:2; Heb 5:12, 13]).

Syn.: *nḗpios* (3516), a little child; *teknı́on* (5040), a little child; *téknon* (5043), child; *paidíon* (3813), a little or young child, an infant just born; *paîs* (3816), child; *paidárion* (3808), a little boy or girl; *korásion* (2877), a little girl, damsel; *paidískē* (3814), a little girl.

1026. βρέχω, brechō, *brekh´-o*; a primary verb; to *moisten* (especially by a shower):—(send) rain, wash.

1027. βροντή, brontē, *bron-tay´*; akin to **βρέμω, bremō** (to *roar*); *thunder*:—thunder (-ing).

1028. βροχή, brochē, *brokh-ay´*; from 1026; *rain*:—rain.

1029. βρόχος, brochos, *brokh´-os*; of uncertain derivative; a *noose*:—snare.

1030. βρυγμός, brugmos, *broog-mos´*; from 1031; a *grating* (of the teeth):—gnashing.

1031. βρύχω, bruchō, *broo´-kho*; a primary verb; to *grate* the teeth (in pain or rage):—gnash.

1032. βρύω, bruō, *broo´-o*; a primary verb; to *swell* out, i.e. (by implication) to *gush*:—send forth.

1033. βρῶμα, brōma, *bro´-mah*; from the base of 977; *food* (literal or figurative), especially (ceremonial) articles allowed or forbidden by the Jewish law:—meat, victuals.

1034. βρώσιμος, brōsimos, *bro´-sim-os*; from 1035; *eatable*:—meat.

1035. βρῶσις, brōsis, *bro´-sis*; from the base of 977; (abstract) *eating* (literal or figurative); by extension (concrete) *food* (literal or figurative):—eating, food, meat.

1036. βυθίζω, buthizō, *boo-thid´-zo*; from 1037; to *sink*; (by implication) to *drown*:—begin to sink, drown.

1037. βυθός, buthos, *boo-thos´*; a variation of 899; *depth*, i.e. (by implication) the *sea*:—deep.

1038. βυρσεύς, burseus, *boorce-yooce´*; from **βύρσα, bursa** (a *hide*); a *tanner*:—tanner.

1039. βύσσινος, bussinos, *boos´-see-nos*; from 1040; made of *linen* (neuter a linen *cloth*):—fine linen.

1040. βύσσος, bussos, *boos´-sos*; of Hebrew origin [948]; white *linen*:—fine linen.

1041. βῶμος, bōmos, *bo´-mos*; from the base of 939; properly a *stand*, i.e. (specifcally) an *altar*:—altar.

Noun from *baínō* (n.f.), to go, step. A step, base, pedestal. In the NT, it is used of idolatrous altars (Ac 17:23; Sept.: Ex 34:13; Nu 23:1). Contrast *thusiastḗrion* (2379), an altar of the true God.

1042. γαββαθά, gabbatha, *gab-bath-ah´*; of Chaldee origin [compare 1355]; *the knoll; gabbatha*, a vernacular term for the Roman tribunal in Jerusalem:—Gabbatha.

1043. Γαβριήλ, Gabriēl, *gab-ree-ale´*; of Hebrew origin [1403]; *Gabriel*, an archangel:—Gabriel.

1044. γάγγραινα, gaggraina, *gang´-grahee-nah*; from **γραίνω, grainō** (to *gnaw*); an *ulcer* ("gangrene"):—canker.

1045. Γάδ, Gad, *gad*; of Hebrew origin [1410]; *Gad*, a tribe of Israel:—Gad.

1046. Γαδαρηνός, Gadarēnos, *gad-ar-ay-nos´*; from **Γαδαρά, Gadara** (a town East of the Jordan); a *Gadarene* or inhabitant of Gadara:—Gadarene.

1047. γάζα, gaza, *gad´-zah*; of foreign origin; a *treasure*:—treasure.

1048. Γάζα, Gaza, *gad´-zah*; of Hebrew origin [5804]; *Gazah* (i.e. *Azzah*), a place in Palestine:—Gaza.

1049. γαζοφυλάκιον, gazophulakion, *gad-zof-oo-lak´-ee-on*; from 1047 and 5438; a *treasure-house*, i.e. a court in the temple for the collection-boxes:—treasury.

1050. Γάϊος, Gaïos, *gah´-ee-os*; of Latin origin; *Gaïus* (i.e. *Caius*), a Christian:—Gaius.

1051. γάλα, gala, *gal´-ah*; of uncertain affinity; *milk* (figurative):—milk.

A noun meaning milk (1Co 9:7; Sept.: Ge 18:8; 49:12). Used figuratively for the first elements of Christian instruction (1Co 3:2; Heb 5:12, 13). In 1Pe 2:2, milk is put as the emblem of pure spiritual nourishment, or of Christian instruction in general.

1052. Γαλάτης, Galatēs, *gal-at´-ace*; from 1053; a *Galatian* or inhabitant of Galatia:—Galatian.

1053. Γαλατία, Galatia, *gal-at-ee´-ah*; of foreign origin; *Galatia*, a region of Asia:—Galatia.

1054. Γαλατικός, Galatikos, *gal-at-ee-kos´*; from 1053; *Galatic* or relating to Galatia:—of Galatia.

1055. γαλήνη, galēnē, *gal-ay´-nay*; of uncertain derivative; *tranquillity*:—calm.

1056. Γαλιλαία, Galilaia, *gal-il-ah-yah*; of Hebrew origin [1551]; *Galilæa* (i.e. the heathen *circle*), a region of Palestine:—Galilee.

1057. Γαλιλαῖος, Galilaios, *gal-ee-lah´-yos*; from 1056; *Galilæan* or belonging to Galilæa:—Galilæan, of Galilee.

1058. Γαλλίων, Galliōn, *gal-lee´-own*; of Latin origin; *Gallion* (i.e. *Gallio*), a Roman officer:—Gallio.

1059. Γαμαλιήλ, Gamaliēl, *gam-al-ee-ale´*; of Hebrew origin [1583]; *Gamaliel* (i.e. *Gamliel*), an Israelite:—Gamaliel.

1060. γαμέω, gameō, *gam-eh´-o*; from 1062; to *wed* (of either sex):—marry (a wife).

1061. γαμίσκω, gamiskō, *gam-is´-ko*; from 1062; to *espouse* (a daughter to a husband):—give in marriage.

1062. γάμος, gamos, *gam´-os*; of uncertain affinity; *nuptials*:—marriage, wedding.

A noun meaning wedding, nuptials, i.e. the nuptial solemnities, etc.:

(I) Spoken particularly of a wedding garment (Mt 22:11, 12); a nuptial banquet (Mt 22:10–12; Lk 14:8; Jn 2:1, 2; Rev 19:9). The happiness of the Messiah's kingdom is represented under the figure of a nuptial feast (Rev 19:7, 9, cf. Mt 25:1). Also, by metonymy, the place or hall where the nuptial feast is held (Mt 22:10).

(II) In common parlance, any festive banquet (Lk 12:36; 14:8; Sept.: Est 9:22).

(III) By metonymy: marriage, i.e. the marriage state (Heb 13:4).

Deriv.: *ágamos* (22), unmarried; *gaméō* (1060), to marry; *gamískō* (1061), to give in marriage.

1063. γάρ, gar, *gar*; a primary particle; properly assigning a *reason* (used in argument, explanation or intensification; often with other particles):—and, as, because (that), but, even, for, indeed, no doubt, seeing, then, therefore, verily, what, why, yet.

1064. γαστήρ, gastēr, *gas-tare´*; of uncertain derivative; the *stomach*; (by analogy) the *matrix*; (figurative) a *gourmand*:—belly, + with child, womb.

1065. γέ, ge, *gheh*; a primary particle of *emphasis* or *qualification* (often used with other particles prefixed):—and besides, doubtless, at least, yet.

1066. Γεδεών, Gedeōn, *ghed-eh-own´*; of Hebrew origin [1439]; *Gedeon* (i.e. *Gid[e]on*), an Israelite:—Gedeon.

1067. γέεννα, geenna, *gheh´-en-nah*; of Hebrew origin [1516 and 2011]; *valley of* (the son of) *Hinnom; gehenna* (or *Ge-Hinnom*), a valley of Jerusalem, used (figurative) as a name for the place (or state) of everlasting punishment:—hell.

A noun meaning Gehenna, i.e. the place of punishment in hades or the world of the dead, equivalent to *Tártaros* (2Pe 2:4, where it appears as the verb *tartaróō* [5020], to cast into hell), the lake of fire (Rev 20:14, 15), the everlasting fire (Mt 25:41; Jude 7). So simply for hell (Mt 5:29, 30; 10:28; Lk 12:5; Jas 3:6); with *púr* (4442, fire): hell-fire, the fire of hell (Mt 5:22; 18:9; Mk 9:47); spoken of as *tó púr tó ásbeston* (*ásbestos* [762], unquenchable), the unquenchable fire, the fire that never shall be quenched (Mk 9:43, 45, cf. vv. 44, 46, 48). So the expression *huión géennēs*, son of Gehenna, son of hell (*huiós* [5207], son), i.e. worthy of punishment in hell (Mt 23:15); also *krísis tḗs génnēs* (*krísis* [2920], condemnation, judgement), condemnation to Gehenna (Mt 23:33. cf. Jude 7). It is therefore a place of eternal fire, and of thick darkness (cf. Jude 6, 13).

The name Gehenna is the Hebrew *gēy' hinnōm* (1516/2011, OT), valley of Hinnom (Jos 15:8), the narrow valley skirting Jerusalem on the south, running westward from the valley of Jehoshaphat under Mount Zion. Here the ancient Israelites established the idolatrous worship of Moloch, to whom they burned infants in sacrifice (1Ki 11:7; 2Ki 16:3; Jer 7:31; 32:35). This worship was broken up and the place desecrated by Josiah (2Ki 23:10, 14), after which it seems to have become the receptacle for all the filth of the city, and also for the carcasses of animals and the dead bodies of malefactors left unburied, to consume which fires would appear to have been from time to time kept up. It was also called Tophet (8612, OT [Jer 7:31]), i.e. abomination, place to be spit upon, from *tûp* (n.f., to spit), or more probably, since it had this name among idolaters, from *tāpeteh* (8613, OT), a place of burning, cremation. By an easy metaphor the Jews transferred the name to the place of punishment in the other world, the abode of demons and the souls of wicked men.

1068. Γεθσημανῆ, Gethsēmanē, *gheth-say-man-ay´*; of Chaldee origin [compare 1660 and 8081]; *oil-press*; *Gethsemane*, a garden near Jerusalem:—Gethsemane.

1069. γείτων, geitōn, *ghi´-tone*; from 1093; a *neighbour* (as adjoining one's *ground*); (by implication) a *friend*:—neighbour.

1070. γελάω, gelaō, *ghel-ah´-o*; of uncertain affinity; to *laugh* (as a sign of joy or satisfaction):—laugh.

1071. γέλως, gelōs, *ghel´-oce*; from 1070; *laughter* (as a mark of gratification):—laughter.

1072. γεμίζω, gemizō, *ghem-id´-zo*; transitive from 1073; to *fill* entirely:—fill (be) full.

1073. γέμω, gemō, *ghem´-o*; a primary verb; to *swell* out, i.e. *be full*:—be full.

1074. γενεά, genea, *ghen-eh-ah´*; from (a presumed derivative of) 1085; a *generation*; by implication an *age* (the period or the persons):—age, generation, nation, time.

Collective noun from *gínomai* (1096), to become. Birth. In the NT: generation, in the following senses:

(I) Offspring, progeny; generally and figuratively (Ac 8:33, quoted from Isa 53:8; Sept.: Ge 17:12; Nu 13:22; Est 9:28).

(II) A descent, a degree in a genealogical line of ancestors or descendants. Generation (Mt 1:17; Sept.: Ge 15:16; 25:13; Dt 23:3).

(III) Spoken of the period of time from one descendant to another, i.e. the average duration of human life, reckoned apparently by the ancient Jews at one hundred years (cf. Ge 15:16 with Ex 12:40, 41); by the Greeks at three generations for every one hundred years, that is, thirty-three and a half years each. Hence, in the NT of a less definite period: an age, time, period, day, as ancient generations, i.e. times of old (Lk 1:50 [cf. Rev 1:6; Ac 14:16; 15:21; Eph 3:5, 21; Col 1:26. See Sept.: Ge 9:12; Ps 72:5; Pr 27:24; Isa 34:17; Joel 3:20]). In Lk 16:8, "in their very own generation" (a.t.), means they are wiser in their day, so far as it concerns this life.

(IV) Metaphorically, spoken of the people of any generation or age, those living in any one period, a race or class, e.g., "this generation," meaning the present generation (Mt 11:16; 12:39, 41, 42, 45; 16:4; 17:17; 23:36; 24:34; Mk 8:12, 38; 9:19; 13:30; Lk 7:31; 9:41; 11:29–32, 50, 51; 17:25; 21:32; Ac 2:40; Php 2:15). Spoken of a former generation (Ac 13:36; Heb 3:10); of the future (Lk 1:48; Sept.: Dt 32:5, 20; Ps 12:8; 14:5; 24:6; 78:6, 8).

Deriv.: *genealogéō* (1075), to reckon by generations; *genetḗ* (1079), from his birth or the beginning of his life.

Syn.: *génos* (1085), kind, family, generation; *génnēma* (1081), generation, but with the idea of having had birth from; *éthnos* (1484), nation or people of the same kind; *aiṓn* (165), an age, era.

1075. γενεαλογέω, genealogeō, *ghen-eh-al-og-eh´-o*; from 1074 and 3056; to *reckon by generations*, i.e. *trace in genealogy*:—count by descent.

From *geneá* (1074), generation, and *légō* (3004), to reckon. In the NT in the middle/pass., *genealogéomai* or *genealogoúmai*, fut. *genealogḗsomai*: to be traced or inscribed in a genealogy, to be reckoned by descent (Heb 7:6, to trace one's descent or to derive one's origin; Sept.: 1Ch 5:1; 9:1; Ezr 2:61).

Deriv.: *agenealógētos* (35), one without recorded pedigree or genealogy; *genealogía* (1076), genealogy.

1076. γενεαλογία, genealogia, *ghen-eh-al-og-ee´-ah*; from the same as 1075; *tracing by generations*, i.e. "*genealogy*":—genealogy.

Noun from *genealogéō* (1075), to make a genealogical register. Genealogy, genealogical table of ancestors, etc. (1Ti 1:4; Tit 1:10; 3:9; Sept.: 1Ch 7:5, 7; 9:22).

1077. γενέσια, genesia, *ghen-es´-ee-ah*; neuter plural of a derivative of 1078; *birthday* ceremonies:—birthday.

1078. γένεσις, genesis, *ghen´-es-is*; from the same as 1074; *nativity*; (figurative) *nature*:—generation, nature (-ral).

Noun from *gínomai* (1096), to form. In the NT, birth, nativity:

(I) Particularly (Mt 1:18; Lk 1:14; Jas 1:23). Used figuratively in Jas 3:6, *tróchos tḗs genéseōs*, lit. "the wheel of birth" (*tróchos* [5164], wheel), set in motion at birth and rolls on through life, i.e. course of life.

(II) In the sense of descent, lineage, and *bíblos genéseōs*, book of descent (*bíblos* [976], book), i.e. genealogy, genealogical table (Mt 1:1).

Deriv.: *genésia* (1077), birthday; *paliggenesía* (3824), regeneration.

1079. γενετή, genetē, *ghen-et-ay´*; feminine of a presumed derivative of the base of 1074; *birth*:—birth.

1080. γεννάω, gennaō, *ghen-nah´-o*; from a variation of 1085; to *procreate* (properly of the father, but by extension of the mother); (figurative) to *regenerate*:—bear, beget, be born, bring forth, conceive, be delivered of, gender, make, spring.

From *génos* (1085), generation, kind, offspring. To beget as spoken of men; to bear as spoken of women; pass., to be begotten or be born:

(I) In the act. sense:

(A) Spoken of men, to beget (Mt 1:2–16; Ac 7:8, 29; Sept.: Ge 5:3ff.). Metaphorically, to generate, to occasion, e.g., strifes (2Ti 2:23).

(B) Spoken in the Jewish manner of the relation between a teacher and his disciples, to beget in a spiritual sense, to be the spiritual father of someone, i.e. the instrument of his conversion to a new spiritual life (1Co 4:15; Phm 10).

(C) Spoken of God begetting in a spiritual sense which consists in regenerating, sanctifying, quickening anew, and ennobling the powers of the natural man by imparting to him a new life and a new spirit in Christ (1Jn 5:1). Hence, Christians are said to be born of God and to be the sons of God (Ro 8:14; Gal 3:26; 4:6). Spoken of the relationship between God and the Messiah, called His Son (Ac 13:33; Ro 1:4; Heb 1:5; 5:5; Sept.: Ps 2:6–8 [cf. *huiós* {5207}, son]).

(D) Spoken of women, to bear, bring forth (Lk 1:13, 57; 23:29; Jn 16:21; figuratively Gal 4:24; Sept.: Ge 46:15; Ex 6:20; Ezr 10:44).

(II) In the pass. sense *gennáomai*, contracted *gennṓmai*:

(A) To be begotten (Mt 1:20, "that which is conceived in her" or begotten, i.e. in her womb, the fetus; Heb 11:12).

(B) To be born as used generally (Mt 2:1, 4; 19:12; 26:24; Mk 14:21; Jn 3:4, blind; 9:2, 19, 20, 32; 16:21, "into the world"; Ac 7:20; 22:28, I have been born a Roman; Ro 9:11; Heb 11:23; Gal 4:23, 29, "after the flesh," in the course of nature). With *eis* (1510), unto, denoting finality, destination (Jn 18:37; 2Pe 2:12). In Mt 1:16, "of whom [fem. gen.]" meaning of the mother. See Lk 1:35. In Jn 3:6, with *ek* (1537), "out of the flesh" (a.t.), indicating the source. See also Jn 8:41. With *en* (1722), in, and the dat. of place (Ac 22:3). With the dat. of state or condition (Jn 9:34, in the state of sinfulness or sins). In Ac 2:8, "wherein we were born," meaning the dialect, the native tongue. Metaphorically, *ek* (1537), out of God or of the Spirit, only in the writings of John, meaning to be born of God or of the Spirit, in a spiritual sense, to have received from God a new spiritual life. See also Jn 1:13; 3:5, 6, 8; 1Jn 2:29; 3:9; 4:7; 5:1, 4, 18, and to be "born again" or from above which is equivalent to be born of God (Jn 3:3, 7); also *ánōthen* (509), from above.

Deriv.: *anagennáō* (313), to give new birth; *génnēma* (1081), offspring; *génnēsis* (1083), birth; *gennētós* (1084), born.

Syn.: *apokuéō* (616), to give birth to, bring forth. Used in a spiritual sense: *tíktō* (5088), to bring forth, give birth to a child, also used metaphorically in regard to sin in Jas 1:15.

1081. γέννημα, gennēma, *ghen´-nay-mah*; from 1080; *offspring*; (by analogy) *produce* (literal or figurative):—fruit, generation.

1082. Γεννησαρέτ, Gennēsaret, *ghen-nay-sar-et´*; of Hebrew origin [compare 3672]; *Gennesaret* (i.e. *Kinnereth*), a lake and plain in Palestine:—Gennesaret.

1083. γέννησις, gennēsis, *ghen´-nay-sis*; from 1080; *nativity*:—birth.

1084. γεννητός, gennētos, *ghen-nay-tos´*; from 1080; *born*:—they that are born.

1085. γένος, genos, *ghen´-os*; from 1096; "*kin*" (abstract or concrete, literal or figurative, individual or collective):—born, country (-man), diversity, generation, kind (-red), nation, offspring, stock.

1086. Γεργεσηνός, Gergesēnos, *gher-ghes-ay-nos´*; of Hebrew origin [1622]; a *Gergesene* (i.e. *Girgashite*) or one of the aborigines of Palestine:—Gergesene.

1087. γερουσία, gerousia, *gher-oo-see´-ah*; from 1088; the *eldership*, i.e. (collective) the Jewish *Sanhedrin*:—senate.

1088. γέρων, gerōn, *gher´-own*; of uncertain affinity [compare 1094]; *aged*:—old.

1089. γεύομαι, geuomai, *ghyoo´-om-ahee*; a primary verb; to *taste*; (by implication) to *eat*; (figurative) to *experience* (good or ill):—eat, taste.

To cause to taste, to let taste (Sept.: Ge 25:30). With the meaning of to eat, partake (Lk 14:24; Ac 10:10; 20:11; 23:14; Sept.: 1Sa 14:24 of bread; 2Sa 3:35). Metaphorically: to experience, prove, partake of (Mt 16:28; Mk 9:1; Lk 9:27; Jn 8:52; Heb 2:9; 6:5).

Syn.: With the meaning of to eat: *esthíō* (2068), to eat; *phágō* (5315), to eat, devour, consume; *trṓgō* (5176), to chew, eat; *bibrṓskō* (977), to eat, devour.

1090. γεωργέω, geōrgeō, *gheh-ore-gheh´-o*; from 1092; to *till* (the soil):—dress.

1091. γεώργιον, geōrgion, *gheh-ore´-ghee-on*; neuter of a (presumed) derivative of 1092; *cultivable*, i.e. a *farm*:—husbandry.

1092. γεωργός, geōrgos, *gheh-ore-gos´*; from 1093 and the base of 2041; a *land-worker*, i.e. *farmer*:—husbandman.

1093. γῆ, gē, *ghay*; contrete from a primary word; *soil*; by extension a *region*, or the solid part or the whole of the *terrene* globe (including the occupants in each application):—country, earth (-ly), ground, land, world.

(I) In reference to its vegetative power: earth, soil (Mt 13:5, 8, 23; Mk 4:5, 8, 20; Lk 14:35; Jn 12:24; Ge 1:11, 12; 3:14, 19; Sept.: Ge 4:2, 3).

(II) As that on which we tread, the ground (Mt 10:29; 15:35; Lk 6:49; 22:44; 24:5; Jn 8:6, 8; Ac 9:4, 8; Sept.: Ex 3:5; 9:33; 1Sa 26:7, 8; 2Sa 17:12).

(III) In distinction from the sea or a lake: the land, solid ground (Mk 4:1; 6:47; Jn 6:21; Ac 27:39, 43, 44; Sept.: Ge 8:7, 9; Jnh 1:13).

(IV) Of a country, region, territory, as the land of Israel (Mt 2:20, 21); Canaan (Ac 13:19); Egypt (Ac 7:11, 36, 40; 13:17); Judah (Mt 2:6); Zebulon (Mt 4:15); Gennesareth (Mt 14:34; Mk 6:53). Of the country adjacent to any place or city (Mt 9:26, 31). With a gen. of person, one's native land (Ac 7:3). Spoken particularly of and used in an absolute sense of the land of the Jews, Palestine (Mt 23:35; 27:45; Mk 15:33; Lk 4:25; 21:23; Ro 9:28; Jas 5:17; Isa 10:23). Also in the expression to "inherit the earth" (Mt 5:5 quoted from Ps 37:11; see Ps 37:9, 22, 29; 25:13; Isa 60:21 [cf. Le 20:24; Dt 16:20]). Figuratively used for the inhabitants of a country (Mt 10:15; 11:24).

(V) The earth, in distinction from *ho ouranós* (3772), heaven (Mt 5:18, 35; 6:10, 19; Lk 2:14; Ac 2:19; 7:49; Sept.: Ge 1:1, 2; 2:4; 4:11; 7:4; 1Ch 16:30); hence, "all things … that are in heaven, and that are in earth" means the universe (Col 1:16, 20). "A new earth" (2Pe 3:13; Rev 21:1) means qualitatively new (*kainḗ* [2537]), not just another earth.

(VI) Spoken of the habitable earth (*hē oikouménē* [3625]) (Lk 11:31; 21:35; Ac 10:12; 11:6; 17:26; Heb 11:13; Rev 3:10; Sept.: Ge 6:1, 5, 7, 11, 12; Isa 24:1), hence the expression *tá epí tḗs gḗs* (*tá epí* [1909], those upon; *tḗs gḗs*, of the earth), upon earthly things or pertaining to this life (Col 3:2); "all the earth" (Ro 9:17; 10:18); "upon the earth" (Col 3:5); the inhabitants of the earth, men (Rev 6:8; 11:6; 13:3; 19:2; Sept.: Ge 9:19; 11:1; 19:31). Also where things are said to be done or take place on earth, which have reference chiefly to men (Mt 5:13; 6:10; 10:34; Lk 12:49; Jn 17:4). In Jn 3:31, "he being of the earth" (a.t.), means he who is of human birth and speaks only of worldly things.

Deriv.: *geōrgós* (1092); a farmer; *epígeios* (1919), of this earth, earthly.

Syn.: *agrós* (68), a field; *patrís* (3968), native country or one's fatherland; *chṓra* (5561), country, land; *períchōros* (4066), country round about; *oikouménē* (3625), the inhabited earth; *katachthónios* (2709), under the earth; *choïkós* (5517), of the soil or earthy; *édaphos* (1475), the ground; *chōríon* (5564), a piece of land; *kósmos* (2889), the earth, but primarily the people who dwell on the earth.

1094. γῆρας, gēras, *ghay´-ras*; akin to 1088; *senil-ity*:—old age.

1095. γηράσκω, gēraskō, *ghay-ras´-ko*; from 1094; to *be senescent*:—be (wax) old.

1096. γίνομαι, ginomai, *ghin´-om-ahee*; a prolonged and middle form of a primary verb; to *cause to be* ("*gen*"-*erate*), i.e. (reflexive) to *become* (*come into being*), used with great latitude (literal, figurative, intensive, etc.):—arise, be assembled, be (-come, -fall, -have self), be brought (to pass), (be) come (to pass), continue, be divided, draw, be ended, fall, be finished, follow, be found, be fulfilled, + God forbid, grow, happen, have, be kept, be made, be married, be ordained to be, partake, pass, be performed, be published, require, seem, be showed, × soon as it was, sound, be taken, be turned, use, wax, will, would, be wrought.

To begin to be, that is, to come into existence or into any state; and in the aor. and 2d perf. to have come into existence or simply to be:

(I) To begin to be, to come into existence, as implying origin (either from natural causes or through special agencies), result, change of state, place, and so forth:

(A) As implying origin in the ordinary course of nature: **(1)** Spoken of persons, to be born (Jn 8:58; Jas 3:9), to be born of, descended from (Ro 1:3; Gal 4:4; 1Pe 3:6; Sept.: Ge 21:3, 5). **(2)** Of plants and fruits: to be produced, grow (Mt 21:19; 1Co 15:37). **(3)** Of the phenomena, occurrences of nature: to arise, to come on, occur, e.g., *seismós* (4578), earthquake (Mt 8:24); *laílaps* (2978), storm, tempest (Mk 4:37); *galḗnē* (1055), tranquillity (Mt 8:26; Mk 4:39); *skótos* (4655), darkness (Mt 27:45; Mk 15:33); *nephélē* (3507), cloudiness (Mk 9:7; Lk 9:34); *brontḗ* (1027), thunder (Jn 12:29). So also of a voice or cry, tumult as *phōnḗ* (5456), voice (Jn 12:30); *kraugḗ* (2906), clamor, cry (Mt 25:6); *thórubos* (2351), disturbance, uproar (Mt 26:5; 27:24); *stásis* (4714), an uprising (Lk 23:19); *schísma* (4978), division (Jn 7:43); *zḗtēsis* (2214), questioning (Jn 3:25); *sigḗ* (4602), silence (Ac 21:40; Rev 8:1). Also of emotions as *thlípsis* (2347), tribulation, affliction (Mt 13:21; see also Lk 15:10; 22:24; 1Ti 6:4). **(4)** Spoken of time such as day, night, evening: to come or come on, approach (Mt 8:16; 14:15, 23; 27:1; Mk 6:2; 11:19; 15:33; Lk 22:14; Jn 6:16; 21:4; Ac 27:27).

(II) As implying origin through an agency specially exerted: to be made, created, equal to *poioúmai*, the middle pass. of *poiéō* (4160), to make or to do:

(A) Spoken of the works of creation (Jn 1:3, 10; 1Co 15:45; Heb 4:3; 11:3; Sept.: Ge 2:4; Isa 48:7).

(B) Of works of art (Ac 19:26, "with hands").

(C) Of miracles and the like: to be wrought, performed (Mt 11:20; Ac 4:22; 8:13); with *diá*, through or with (Mk 6:2; Ac 2:43; 4:16); with *hupó* (5259), by (Lk 9:7; 13:17).

(D) Of a promise, plot: to be made (Ac 26:6; 20:3); of waste, *apṓleia* (684), loss, waste (Mk 14:4).

(E) Of the will or desire of someone: to be done, fulfilled (Mt 6:10; 26:42; Lk 11:2; 23:24; Ac 21:14).

(F) Of a meal: to be prepared, made ready (Jn 13:2); of a judicial investigation: to be made, initiated (Ac 25:26); so also of a change of law (Heb 7:12, 18).

(G) Of particular days, festivals to be held or celebrated (Mt 26:2; Jn 2:1; 10:22; Sept.: 2Ki 23:22).

(H) Of persons advanced to any station or office: to be made, constituted, appointed (1Co 1:30; Col 1:23, 25; Heb 5:5; 6:20); so also with *epánō* (1883), upon (Lk 19:19).

(I) Of customs, institutes: to be appointed, instituted (Mk 2:27, the Sabbath; Gal 3:17, the existing law).

(J) Of what is done to or in someone (Lk 23:31; Gal 3:13).

(III) As implying a result, event to take place or come to pass: occur, be done:

(A) Generally (Mt 1:22, "And all this took place" [a.t.]; Mk 5:14; Lk 1:20, "until these things take place" [a.t.]; 2:15; Jn 3:9; Ac 4:21; 5:24; 1Co 15:54; 1Th 3:4; Rev 1:19). In Heb 9:15, "death having taken place" (a.t.), that is, through His death. See also Mt 18:31; Lk 8:34; Jas 3:10; 2Pe 1:20. So also in the phrase *mḗ génoito* (*mḗ* [3361], not; *génoito* [1096], it be): let it not happen, God forbid, an exclamation of aversion (Lk 20:16; Ro 3:4, 6, 31; 6:2, 15; 7:7 [cf. Sept.: Ge 44:7, 17; Jos 22:29; 1Ki 21:3]).

(B) Of persons: to happen to someone (Mk 9:21; Lk 14:12; Jn 5:14; 1Pe 4:12). With the inf. as subj. (Ac 20:16; Gal 6:14; Sept.: Ge 44:7, 17). With an adverb of manner (Mk 5:16; Eph 6:3).

(C) With a prep. in the same sense as *eis* (1519), unto, followed by *tiná*, someone (Ac 28:6). In Mk 5:33, *epí* (1909), upon, with the dat. *tiní*, someone.

(D) With an inf. and accusative expressed or implied: to come to pass that (Mt 18:13, "if it comes to pass that he find it" [a.t.]; Mk 2:23; Ac 27:44, "it came to pass, that they escaped"; 28:8).

(IV) As implying a change of state, condition, or the passing from one state to another: to become, to enter upon any state, condition:

(A) Spoken of persons or things which receive any new character or form: **(1)** Where the predicate is a noun (Mt 4:3, "that these stones become bread" [a.t.]; 5:45, "that ye may become the sons of the father" [a.t.]; 13:32, "becomes a tree" [a.t.]; Mk 1:17, "that you may become fishers of men" [a.t.]; Lk 4:3; 6:16; 23:12; Jn 1:12, 14; 2:9; Ac 12:18, "what was become of Peter"; 26:28; Ro 4:18; Heb 2:17; Rev 8:8). **(2)** Construed with *eis* (1519), unto something as the predicate (Mt 21:42, He "became unto a cornerstone" [a.t.] or "He became a cornerstone" [a.t.]; Mk 12:10; Lk 13:19; Jn 16:20; Ac 5:36; Sept.: Ge 2:7; 1Sa 30:25). **(3)** When the predicate is an adj. (Mt 6:16, "do not … become of a sad countenance" [a.t.], do not put on or affect sadness; 10:16, "therefore become prudent" [a.t.]; 12:45, "last … shall be worse" [a.t.]; 13:22, "becomes fruitless" [a.t.]; 23:26; 24:32, 44, become ready, prepare yourselves; Jn 9:39; Ac 7:32; 10:4; Ro 3:19). With a particle of manner (Mt 10:25, "so that he become as his teachers" [a.t.]; 18:3; 28:4, "they became as if they were dead" [a.t.]). In 1Co 9:20, 22, with the dat. of person, for or in respect to whom. **(4)** With the gen. of possession or relation (Lk 20:14, "that the inheritance become ours" [a.t.]; 20:33; Rev 11:15). **(5)** With the dat. of person as possessor (Ro 7:3, 4, to become married to another man; Sept.: Le 22:12; Jer 3:1).

(B) Construed with prep. or adverb implying motion, it denotes change or transition to another place, to come. **(1)** With the prep. *eis* (1519), unto: to come to or into, to arrive at (Ac 20:16; 21:17; 25:15). Figuratively: the voice (Lk 1:44); the blessing (Gal 3:14); the gospel (1Th 1:5); sore or ulcer (Rev 16:2). **(2)** With *ek* (1537), out of: to come from a place, as the voice (Mk 1:11; Lk 3:22; 9:35), but *ek mésou* [(3319), from the midst] with *gínomai*: to be put out of the way (2Th 2:7). **(3)** With *en* (1722), in, used metaphorically (Ac 12:11, "being come to himself" [a.t. {cf. Lk 15:17}]). **(4)** With *epí* (1909), upon: to come upon, arrive at (Lk 22:40; Jn 6:21; Ac 21:35). With the accusative (Lk 1:65, fear; 4:36; 24:22; Ac 8:1); of an oracle (Lk 3:2). **(5)** With *katá* (2596), upon: to come throughout (Ac 10:37); to come to (Lk 10:32; Ac 27:7). **(6)** With *prós* (4314), toward: to come to (2Jn 12); of oracles (Ac 7:31; 10:13; Sept.: Ge 15:1, 4; Jer 1:2, 4). **(7)** With the adverb *eggús* (1451), near: to come or draw near (Jn 6:19; metaphorically Eph 2:13); *hṓde* (5602), hither (Jn 6:25); *ekeí* (1563), thither (Ac 19:21).

(V) In the aor. and perf.: to have begun to be, to have come into existence, meaning simply to be, to exist.

(A) Generally: to be, to exist (Jn 1:6, "there came to be a man" [a.t.]; Ro 11:5; 1Jn 2:18). With *en* (1722), in (2Pe 2:1); *émprosthen* (1715), before someone (Jn 1:15, 30); *epí* (1909), upon the earth (Rev 16:18).

(B) As a copula connecting a subj. and predicate: **(1)** Of quality, with the nom. (Lk 1:2, those who "from the beginning became eyewitnesses … of the word" [a.t.]; 2:2; Jn 14:22; Ac 4:4; 1Co 4:16; 2Co 1:18, 19; 1Th 2:8; Tit 3:7). With the dat. of advantage: to be anything to, for, or in behalf of (Ac 1:16; Lk 11:30; Col 4:11; 1Th 1:7). With an adverb (1Th 2:10). With a gen. of age (Lk 2:42; 1Ti 5:9). **(2)** Implying propriety (Mt 11:26; Lk 10:21, "such was thy good pleasure" [a.t.]). **(3)** Joined with the part. of another verb, it forms patterns like *eínai* (1511), to be, a periphrasis for a finite tense of that verb (Mk 1:4, literally, "it came to be John baptizing," which really stands for the verb "was baptizing"; see also 9:3, 7; Heb 5:12; Rev 16:10; Sept.: Ne 1:4.

(C) Joined with a prep. it implies locality or state, disposition of mind: **(1)** With *en* (1722), in, spoken of place: to be in a place (Mt 26:6, "when Jesus was in Bethany"; Mk 9:33, "in the house"; Ac 13:5; 2Ti 1:17; Rev 1:9). Spoken of condition or state: to be in any state (Lk 22:44, "when he came to be in agony" [a.t.]; Ac 22:17, "in ecstasy" [a.t.]; Ro 16:7, "in Christ," i.e. to be in the number of Christ's followers, Christians; Php 2:7, "having become the likeness" [a.t.], equal to "having likened himself" [a.t.]; 1Ti 2:14, "having placed herself in the state of the transgression" [a.t.]; Rev 1:10; 4:2). **(2)** With *metá* (3326), with, followed by the gen. of person: to be with someone (Ac 9:19; 20:18). In Mk 16:10, "those who had been with him" (a.t.), means His friends, companions. **(3)** Followed by *prós* (4314), to or toward, with an accusative: to be toward, that is, disposed toward someone (1Co 2:3; 16:10). **(4)** Followed by *sún* (4862), with: to be with (Lk 2:13).

Deriv.: *geneá* (1074), age, generation, nation; *génesis* (1078), generation, nature; *génos* (1085), generation, kind, offspring; *goneús* (1118), a parent; *diagínomai* (1230), to intervene, to elapse, pass; *epigínomai* (1920), to spring up, blow; *paragínomai* (3854), to be present; *progínomai* (4266), to happen before.

Syn.: *érchomai* (2064), to come; *apérchomai* (565), to come away from; *hḗkō* (2240), to come, be present; *aphiknéomai* (864), to arrive at a place; *enístēmi* (1764), to stand in, be present; *ephístēmi* (2186), to stand by or over; *katantáō* (2658), to come to, over against; *parístēmi* (3936), to stand by or near; *phérō* (5342), to come, to bring; *phthánō* (5348), to come upon, arrive at; *proseggízō* (4331), to come near; *diateléō* (1300), to bring through to an end; *ménō* (3306), to abide; *epioúsa* (1966), the next day, used as a verb meaning to come, arrive; *auxánō* (837), to grow or increase, to become something that one was not; *phúō* (5453), to produce, grow; *hupárchō* (5225), to exist, to continue to be what one was before; *eimí* (1510), to be; *diérchomai* (1330), to pass through or over; *apérchomai* (5656), to go away; *diabaínō* (1224), to step across or over; *metabaínō* (3327), to pass over from one place to another; *parágō* (3855), to pass by or away; *diaperáō* (1276), to pass over; *diodeúō* (1353), to travel through or along; *chōráō* (5562), to pass, retire; *katargéō* (2673), to do away with, abolish; *paroíchomai* (3944), to have passed by, be gone; *anachōréō* (402), to withdraw; *chōréō* (5562), to have place; *phthánō* (5348), to arrive, catch up; *parístēmi* (3936), to be pressed, arrive; *sumbaínō* (4819), to come to pass; *prokóptō* (4298), to advance from within.

1097. γινώσκω, ginōskō, *ghin-oce´-ko*; a prolonged form of a primary verb; to "*know*" (absolute), in a great variety of applications and with many implication (as follows, with others not thus clearly expressed):—allow, be aware (of), feel, (have) know (-ledge), perceive, be resolved, can speak, be sure, understand.

To know, in a beginning or a completed sense:

(I) To know, in a beginning sense: that is, to come to know, to gain or receive a knowledge of:

(A) Generally (Mt 12:7; Mk 6:38; Lk 12:47; Jn 7:26; 8:32, 52; Ac 1:7; Ro 1:21; 1Co 4:19; 13:9; 2Co 2:9; Jas 2:20; 1Jn 3:16, 19, 24; 4:13). In the pass.: to be known or distinguished (1Co 14:7).

(B) In a judicial sense: to know by trial, to inquire into or examine the reason or cause (Jn 7:51; Ac 23:28).

(C) In the sense of to know from others, learn, find out. In the pass.: to be made known, disclosed (Mt 10:26; Mk 5:43; Ac 9:24; 21:34; Col 4:8; Mt 9:30; Lk 9:11; Sept.: 1Sa 21:2).

(D) In the sense of to perceive, observe, be aware of (Mt 16:8; 22:18; 26:10; Mk 5:29; Ac 23:6; Sept.: Ru 3:4).

(E) In the sense of to understand or comprehend (Mt 13:11; Mk 4:13; Lk 18:34; Jn 3:10; 7:49; 1Co 2:8, 14; Jn 10:6; 12:16; 13:12; Ac 8:30; Ro 11:34; Sept.: 1Sa 20:39; Pr 1:2).

(F) By euphemism: to lie with a person of another sex as spoken of a man or men (Mt 1:25; Sept.: Ge 4:1, 17; 24:16); of a woman or women (Lk 1:34; Sept.: Ge 19:8; Nu 31:17, 35).

(II) To know in a completed sense, that is, to have the knowledge of:

(A) Generally (Mt 6:3; 24:43; Lk 2:43; 7:39; 16:15; Jn 2:25; Ac 19:35; Ro 2:18; 10:19; 2Co 5:21; Eph 5:5; 1Jn 3:20). With persons: to know as by sight or person (Jn 1:48; 2Co 5:16); to know one's character (Jn 1:10; 2:24; 14:7, 9; 16:3; Ac 19:15; Sept.: Dt 34:10; Ps 87:4; 139:1).

(B) In the sense of to know, as being what one is or professes to be, to acknowledge (Mt 7:23). Passive tense (1Co 8:3; Gal 4:9; Sept.: Isa 33:13; 61:9; 63:16).

(C) With the idea of volition or goodwill: to know and approve or love, to care for, spoken of persons (Jn 10:14, 15, 27; 1Ti 2:18; Sept.: Ps 144:3; Am 3:2; Na 1:7); of things (Ro 7:15; Sept.: Ps 1:6).

Deriv.: *anaginṓskō* (314), to read; *gnṓmē* (1106), cognition; *gnṓsis* (1108), knowledge; *gnṓstēs* (1109), a knower, expert; *gnōstós* (1110), well-known, acquaintance; *diaginṓskō* (1231), to know thoroughly; *epiginṓskō* (1921), to observe, fully perceive, notice attentively, discern; *kardiognṓstēs* (2589), heart-knower; *kataginṓskō* (2607), to blame condemn; *proginṓskō* (4267), to know beforehand.

Syn.: *epístamai* (1987), to know or acquire knowledge; *sunoída* (4894), to know together, be conscious of; *theōréō* (2334), to be a spectator and thus to understand or perceive; *aisthánomai* (143), to perceive with the senses, while *ginṓskō* is to perceive through the mind; *noéō* (3539), to perceive with the mind, to understand; *katanoéō* (2657), to understand more fully; *katalambánō* (2638), to lay hold of, apprehend, perceive; *blépō* (991), to see and perceive; *suníēmi* (4920), to mentally put it together, to perceive, understand; *punthánomai* (4441), to inquire in order to know; *parakolouthéō* (3877), to follow, observe, understand; *gnōrízō* (1107), to come to know, know; *diagnōrízō* (1232), to make known widely; *gnōstós* (1110), known; *ágnōstos* (57), unknown; *agnōsía* (56), ignorance; *kardiognṓstēs* (2589), one who knows the heart; *anagnōrízō* (319), to recognize, to make oneself known; *diagnōrízō* (1232), to make known; *diaginṓskō* (1231), to determine by thorough examination; *gnōrízō* (1107), to make known, understand.

1098. γλεῦκος, gleukos, *glyoo´-kos*; akin to 1099; *sweet* wine, i.e. (properly) *must* (fresh juice), but used of the more saccharine (and therefore highly inebriating) fermented *wine*:—new wine.

Noun from *glukús* (1099), sweet. Musk; new or sweet wine (Ac 2:13; Sept.: Job 32:19).

1099. γλυκύς, glukus, *gloo-koos´*; of uncertain affinity; *sweet* (i.e. not bitter nor salt):—sweet, fresh.

1100. γλῶσσα, glōssa, *gloce´-sah*; of uncertain affinity; the *tongue*; (by implication) a *language* (specially one naturally unacquired):—tongue.

A noun meaning tongue:

(I) An organ of the body (Rev 16:10); as of taste (Lk 16:24); of speech (Mk 7:33, 35; Lk 1:64; 1Co 14:9; Jas 3:5, 6); personified (Ro 14:11; Php 2:11, "every tongue" means every person [cf. Ac 2:26; Sept.: Isa 45:23 {see also Ps 16:9}). To bridle the tongue (Jas 1:26; 3:8; 1Pe 3:10; Sept.: Jgs 7:5; Job 29:10; 33:2).

(II) Metaphorically, speech or language:

(A) Generally (1Jn 3:18; Sept.: Pr 25:15; 31:26).

(B) Of a particular language or dialect as spoken by a particular people (Ac 2:11; 1Co 13:1; Sept.: Ge 10:5, 20; Da 1:4). Used for the people who speak a particular language, e.g., tribes, people, and tongues (Rev 5:9; 7:9; 10:11; 11:9; 13:7; 14:6; 17:15; Sept.: Isa 66:18; Da 3:4, 7, 30, 32).

(C) In the phrases *glṓssais hetérais* (2083), different tongues (Ac 2:4); *glṓssais kainaís* (2537), new tongues (Mk 16:17); *glṓssais laleín* (2980), to speak in tongues (Ac 10:46; 19:6; 1Co 12:30; 14:2, 4–6, 13, 18, 23, 27, 39); *proseuchésthai glṓssē* (4336), to pray in a tongue (1Co 14:14); *lógoi en glṓssē* (3056), discourse in a tongue (1Co 14:19); or simply *glṓssai*, tongues (1Co 12:10, 28; 13:8; 14:22, 26). Here, according to the two passages in Mark and Acts, the sense would seem to be to speak in other living languages. But if the passages in 1 Corinthians are taken as the basis, these phrases would seem to mean to speak another kind of language, i.e. referring perhaps to a state of high spiritual excitement or ecstasy from inspiration, unconscious of external things and wholly absorbed in adoring communication with God, breaking forth into abrupt expressions of praise and devotion which are not coherent and therefore not always intelligible to others (cf. 1Co 14:2, 4, 6, 7). Most interpreters have adopted the first meaning; some prefer the latter. Others suppose there is a reference to two distinct gifts.

(III) Figuratively, for anything resembling a tongue in shape (Ac 2:3).

Deriv.: *glōssókomon* (1101), a bag, case; *heteróglōssos* (2084), a person speaking a tongue other than one's native tongue.

Syn.: *diálektos* (1258), dialect, an ethnic language.

1101. γλωσσόκομον, glōssokomon, *gloce-sok´-om-on*; from 1100 and the base of 2889; properly a *case* (to keep mouthpieces of wind-instruments in), i.e. (by extension) a *casket* or (special) *purse*:—bag.

1102. γναφεύς, gnapheus, *gnaf-yuce´*; by variation for a derivative from **κνάπτω,** ***knaptō*** (to *tease* cloth); a cloth-*dresser*:—fuller.

1103. γνήσιος, gnēsios, *gnay´-see-os*; from the same as 1077; *legitimate* (of birth), i.e. *genuine*:—own, sincerity, true.

1104. γνησίως, gnēsiōs, *gnay-see´-oce*; adverb from 1103; *genuinely*, i.e. *really*:—naturally.

1105. γνόφος, gnophos, *gnof´-os*; akin to 3509; *gloom* (as of a storm):—blackness.

Noun from *néphos* (3509), a cloud. A thick dark cloud (Heb 12:18; Sept.: Ex 20:21; Dt 4:11; 5:22; 2Sa 22:10).

Syn.: *skótos* (4655), darkness; *zóphos* (2217), darkness, foggy weather, smoke which is used to imply infernal darkness; *achlús* (887), a thick mist or a fog.

1106. γνώμη, gnōmē, *gno´-may*; from 1097; *cognition*, i.e. (subject) *opinion*, or (object) *resolve* (*counsel, consent*, etc.):—advice, + agree, judgement, mind, purpose, will.

Noun from *ginṓskō* (1097), to discern, know. Generally it means capacity of judgement, faculty of discernment as far as conduct is determined:

(I) As implying will: in the sense of accord, consent (Phm 14). In the sense of purpose, counsel, determination (Ac 20:3; Rev 17:17); in the sense of bent, inclination, desire (1Co 1:10; Rev 17:13).

(II) As implying opinion: judgement, in reference to oneself (1Co 7:40, "according to my opinion" [a.t.]); in reference to others: advice (1Co 7:25; 2Co 8:10).

Syn.: *boulḗ* (1012), a piece of advice, counsel; *krísis* (2920), legal decision, judgement; *kríma* (2917), condemnatory judgement; *aísthēsis* (144), perception resulting from the senses; *phrónēma* (5427), thought; *phrónēsis* (5428), the thought process, understanding; *boúlēma* (1013), deliberate intention or purpose; *thélēma* (2307), a desire expressive of the will; *próthesis* (4286), purpose; *thélēsis* (2308), the act of willing or wishing; *eudokía* (2107), good pleasure or will; *eúnoia* (2133), goodwill; *diánoia* (1271), intelligence, understanding; *dianóēma* (1270), something thought through, a thought, consideration.

1107. γνωρίζω, gnōrizō, *gno-rid´-zo*; from a derivative of 1097; to *make known*; subject to *know*:—certify, declare, make known, give to understand, do to wit, wot.

(I) To others:

(A) Generally to make known, declare, reveal (Ro 9:22, 23); with the dat. (Lk 2:15; Ac 2:28 quoted from Ps 16:11; Eph 3:3, 5, 10; Col 1:27; Gal 1:11); with the prep. *pros* (4314), to (Php 4:6; Sept.: 1Sa 16:3; 1Ch 16:8; Ps 25:4).

(B) In the sense of to narrate, tell, inform (Eph 6:21; Col 4:7, 9; 2Co 8:1).

(C) Spoken of a teacher who unfolds divine things, to announce, declare, proclaim (Jn 15:15; 17:26; Ro 16:26; Eph 1:9; 6:19; 2Pe 1:16; Sept.: Eze 20:11).

(D) In the sense of to put in mind of, impress upon, confirm (1Co 12:3; 15:1).

(II) To make known to oneself, to ascertain, find out (Php 1:22; Sept.: Job 34:25).

Deriv.: *anagnōrízomai* (319), to make known; *diagnōrízō* (1232), to tell abroad.

Syn.: *epístamai* (1987), to know, understand; *apokalúptō* (601), to reveal.

1108. γνῶσις, gnōsis, *gno´-sis*; from 1097; *knowing* (the act), i.e. (by implication) *knowledge*:—knowledge, science.

(I) The power of knowing, intelligence, comprehension (Ro 8:35; 1Co 12:31; 13:2; Eph 3:19).

(II) Subjectively spoken of what one knows: knowledge (Lk 1:77; Ro 11:33; Php 3:8; Sept.: Ps 73:11; 139:6; Hos 4:6); of the knowledge of Christianity generally (Ro 15:14; 1Co 1:5; 8:1; 2Pe 3:18); of a deeper and better Christian knowledge, both theoretical and experimental (1Co 8:7, 10, 11; 2Co 11:6). Spoken of practical knowledge, discretion, prudence (2Co 6:6; 1Pe 3:7; 2Pe 1:5, 6; Sept.: Pr 13:16).

(III) Objectively spoken of what is known: the object of knowledge, generally knowledge, doctrine, science (2Co 2:14; 4:6; Col 2:3; Sept.: Da 1:4; Mal 2:7); of religious knowledge, i.e. doctrine, science as spoken of Jewish teachers (Lk 11:52; Ro 2:20; 1Ti 6:20); of a deeper Christian knowledge, Christian doctrine (1Co 12:8; 1Co 13:2, 8; 14:6; 2Co 8:7). Hence in 2Co 10:5, "against the true doctrine of God" (a.t.), i.e. against the Christian religion. From *gnṓsis* is derived "gnosticism," a cult of pre-Christian and early Christian centuries distinguished by the conviction that matter is evil and that emancipation comes through *gnṓsis*, knowledge.

Deriv.: *agnōsía* (56), without knowledge.

1109. γνώστης, gnōstēs, *gnoce´-tace*; from 1097; a *knower*:—expert.

Noun from *ginṓskō* (1097), to know. One who knows. Only in Ac 26:3.

1110. γνωστός, gnōstos, *gnoce-tos´*; from 1097; well *known*:—acquaintance, (which may be) known, notable.

Adjective from *ginṓskō* (1097), to know. Known:

(I) Generally (Jn 18:15, 16; Ac 1:19; 9:42; 15:18; 19:17; 28:22). *Gnōstón éstō* (present imper. of *eimí* [1510], to be), be it known (Ac 2:14; 4:10; 13:38; 28:28; Sept.: Eze 36:32; Ezr 4:12, 13). In the sense of knowable, *tó gnōstón toú Theoú*, what may be known of God or the knowledge of God, equal to *gnṓsis* (1108) as in Ro 1:19. God is knowable or known by man because of the demonstration of His power in His creation. Here reference is made not to the knowledge possessed by God, but to man's knowledge of God (Sept.: Ge 2:9). In an emphatic sense, known of all, i.e. notable, incontrovertible (Ac 4:16).

(II) As a substantive with the article *ho gnōstós*, it means an acquaintance (Lk 2:44; 23:49; Sept.: 2Ki 10:11; Ps 88:8, 18).

Deriv.: *ágnōstos* (57), unknown.

Syn.: *phanerós* (5318), visible, manifest, known.

1111. γογγύζω, gogguzō, *gong-good´-zo*; of uncertain derivative; to *grumble*:—murmur.

1112. γογγυσμός, goggusmos, *gong-goos-mos´*; from 1111; a *grumbling*:—grudging, murmuring.

1113. γογγυστής, goggustēs, *gong-goos-tace´*; from 1111; a *grumbler*:—murmurer.

1114. γόης, goēs, *go´-ace*; from **γοάω**, *goaō* (to *wail*); properly a *wizard* (as *muttering* spells), i.e. (by implication) an *imposter*:—seducer.

1115. Γολγοθᾶ, Golgotha, *gol-goth-ah´*; of Chaldee origin [compare 1538]; *the skull; Golgotha*, a knoll near Jerusalem:—Golgotha.

1116. Γόμορρα, Gomorrha, *gom´-or-hrhah*; of Hebrew origin [6017]; *Gomorrha* (i.e. *Amorah*), a place near the Dead Sea:—Gomorrha.

1117. γόμος, gomos, *gom´-os*; from 1073; a *load* (as *filling*), i.e. (special) a *cargo*, or (by extension) *wares*:—burden, merchandise.

1118. γονεύς, goneus, *gon-yooce´*; from the base of 1096; a *parent*:—parent.

1119. γονύ, gonu, *gon-oo´*; of uncertain affinity; the "*knee*":—knee (× -l).

1120. γονυπετέω, gonupeteō, *gon-oo-pet-eh´-o*; from a compound of 1119 and the alternative of 4098; to *fall* on the *knee*:—bow the knee, kneel down.

1121. γράμμα, gramma, *gram´-mah*; from 1125; a *writing*, i.e. a *letter, note, epistle, book*, etc.; plural *learning*:—bill, learning, letter, Scripture, writing, written.

Noun from *gráphō* (1125), to write. In the NT, lit. "the written," i.e, something written or cut in with the stylus, in the ancient manner of writing. Used of a letter of the alphabet (Lk 23:38; Gal 6:11); a letter, epistle (Ac 28:21; Gal 6:11); a bill, bond, note (Lk 16:6, 7); writings, a book, etc., e.g., of Moses (Jn 5:47); of the OT, i.e. the Scriptures (2Ti 3:15), so Jn 7:15, since the Jews had no other literature; used figuratively: the writing, the letter, i.e. the literal or verbal meaning, in antithesis to the spirit, spoken of the Mosaic Law (Ro 2:27, 29; 7:6; 2Co 3:6, 7). Also used of letters, learning, as contained in books (Ac 26:24).

Deriv.: *agrámmatos* (62), unlearned.

Syn.: *biblíon* (975), a small book, any scroll or sheet on which something is written; *didaskalía* (1319), teaching instruction, doctrine; *epistolḗ* (1992), epistle, letter; *pinakídion* (4093), a tablet on which one can write.

1122. γραμματεύς, grammateus, *gram-mat-yooce´*; from 1121; a *writer*, i.e. (professionally) *scribe* or *secretary*:—scribe, town-clerk.

Noun from *gráphō* (1125), to write. A scribe or writer:

(I) In the Greek sense, a public officer in the cities of Asia Minor, whose duty it seems to have been to preside in the senate, to enroll and have charge of the laws and decrees, and to read what was to be made known to the people; a public clerk, secretary (Ac 19:35). The office varied much in different places.

(II) In the Jewish sense, in the Sept. like the Hebrew *sōpēr* (from 5608, OT), the king's scribe, secretary of state (2Sa 8:17; 20:25); military clerk (2Ki 25:19; 2Ch 26:11). Later, in Sept. and in NT: a scribe, i.e. one skilled in the Jewish law, an interpreter of the Scriptures, a lawyer. The scribes had the charge of transcribing the sacred books, of interpreting difficult passages, and of deciding in cases which grew out of the ceremonial law. Their influence was of course great; and since many of them were members of the Sanhedrin, we often find them mentioned with the elders and the chief priests (Mt 2:4; 5:20; 7:29; 12:38; 20:18; 21:15). They are also called *nomikoí* (3544), experts in the law, lawyers, and *nomodidáskaloi* (3547), a teacher of the law (cf. Mk 12:28 with Mt 22:35). Hence, the term is used also of one instructed, a scholar, a learned teacher of religion (Mt 13:52; 23:34; 1Co 1:20).

Syn.: *nomikós* (3544), lawyer; *nomodidáskalos* (3547), teacher of the law.

1123. γραπτός, graptos, *grap-tos´*; from 1125; *inscribed* (figurative):—written.

1124. γραφή, graphē, *graf-ay´*; from 1125; a *document*, i.e. holy *Writ* (or its contents or a statement in it):—Scripture.

Noun from *gráphō* (1125), to write. In the NT: Scripture, the Scriptures, i.e. of the Jews. The Old Testament (Mt 21:42; Jn 5:39; Ac 8:32; Ro 1:2; 9:17); Holy Scriptures (Ro 1:2; Sept.: Ezr 6:18). Put for the contents of Scripture, i.e. scriptural declaration, promise, etc. (Mt 22:29; Mk 12:24; Jn 10:35; Ac 1:16; Jas 2:23), scriptural prophecy (Mt 26:54, 56; Lk 4:21; Ro 16:26). In 2Pe 3:16, some think the writings of Paul and other apostles are meant.

1125. γράφω, graphō, *graf´-o*; a primary verb; to "*grave*," especially to *write*; (figurative) to *describe*:—describe, write (-ing, -ten).

To engrave or cut in, to insculp (Sept.: 1Ki 6:28). To sketch, picture. In the NT, to write:

(I) Particularly, to form letters with a stylus, in the ancient manner, so that the letters were cut in or graven upon the material (Jn 8:6, 8; 2Th 3:17). In the sense of to write upon, i.e. to fill with writing (Rev 5:1).

(II) To commit to writing, to express by writing (Lk 1:63; 16:6, 7; Jn 19:21, 22; 20:30, 31; 21:24, 25; Ro 16:22; Rev 1:11; 10:4). Spoken of what is written or contained in the Scriptures (Mk 1:2; Lk 3:4; Jn 8:17); so the expression "it is written" as a formula of citation (Mt 4:4, 6, 7, 10; Lk 4:4, 8, 10; Ro 1:17; 2:24). In the sense of to write about, to describe (Jn 1:46; Ro 10:5).

(III) To compose or prepare in writing (Mk 10:4; Lk 23:38; Ac 23:25; 2Pe 3:1).

(IV) To write to someone, i.e. to make known by writing (Ro 15:15; 2Co 1:13; 2:4; Php 3:1; 1Jn 2:12–14; Rev 2:1). So of written directions, instructions, information, etc. (Ac 15:23; 18:27; 1Co 5:9; 7:1; 2Co 9:1). Hence used in the expression "to write a command, precept" (Mk 10:5; 12:19; Lk 20:28; 1Jn 2:7).

(V) To inscribe, e.g., one's name in a book, register, etc. (Lk 10:20; Rev 13:8; 17:8).

Deriv.: *apográphō* (583), to write, tax; *grámma* (1121), bill, letter, Scripture; *grammateús* (1122), scribe, town clerk; *graptós* (1123), written; *graphḗ* (1124), Scripture; *eggráphō* (1449), engrave; *epigráphō* (1924), to inscribe; *prográphō* (4270), to write previously, before ordain; *cheirógraphon* (5498), handwriting.

1126. γραώδης, graōdēs, *grah-o´-dace*; from **γραῦς, graus** (an *old woman*) and 1491; *crone-like*, i.e. *silly*:—old wives'.

1127. γρηγορεύω, grēgoreuō, *gray-gor-yoo´-o*; from 1453; to *keep awake*, i.e. *watch* (literal or figurative):—be vigilant, wake, (be) watch (-ful).

From *egeírō* (1453) to arise, arouse. To wake, to keep awake, to watch. Particularly (Mt 24:43; 26:38, 40, 41; Mk 13:34; 14:34, 37, 38; Lk 12:37, 39). Used figuratively: to watch, i.e. be vigilant, attentive (Mt 24:42; 25:13; Mk 13:35, 37; Ac 20:31; 1Co 16:13; 1Pe 5:8; Rev 3:2, 3); also to wake, i.e. to live (1Th 5:10, where *katheúdō* [2518], to sleep, is referred to death).

Deriv.: *diagrēgoréō* (1235), to be awake.

Syn.: *agrupnéō* (69), keep awake; *blépō* (991), to take heed, beware; *horáō* (3708), behold, take heed; *proséchō* (4337), turn one's attention to, take heed; *epéchō* (1907), to give attention to, give heed; *skopéō* (4648), to watch, look, take heed; *phulássō* (5442), to guard.

1128. γυμνάζω, gumnazō, *goom-nad´-zo*; from 1131; to *practise naked* (in the games), i.e. *train* (figurative):—exercise.

1129. γυμνασία, gumnasia, *goom-nas-ee´-ah*; from 1128; *training*, i.e. (figurative) *asceticism*:—exercise.

1130. γυμνητεύω, gumnēteuō, *goom-nayt-yoo´-o*; from a derivative of 1131; to *strip*, i.e. (reflexive) *go poorly clad*:—be naked.

1131. γυμνός, gumnos, *goom-nos´*; of uncertain affinity; *nude* (absolute or relative, literal or figurative):—naked.

(I) In respect to the body: wholly nude, without any clothing (perhaps Mk 14:51, 52; figuratively, Rev 16:15; 17:16); also spoken of one who has no outer garment and is clad only in a tunic, which is fitted close to the body (Jn 21:7; Ac 19:16; probably Mk 14:51; Sept.: 1Sa 19:24; Isa 20:2). As in Eng., half-naked, i.e. poorly clad, destitute as to clothing, implying poverty and want (Mt 25:36, 38, 43, 44; Jas 2:15; Sept.: Job 31:19; 24:7; Isa 58:7). Figuratively: destitute of spiritual goods (Rev 3:17).

(II) Figuratively spoken of the soul as disencumbered of the body in which it had been clothed (2Co 5:3, cf. v. 4 and 15:51).

(III) Spoken of any thing as taken alone, abstractly, separate from everything else: naked, mere, bare (1Co 15:37).

(IV) Metaphorically: uncovered, open, manifest (Heb 4:13).

Deriv.: *gumnázō* (1128), to exercise; *gumnēteúō* (1130), to be naked or scantily clothed; *gumnótēs* (1132), nakedness, lack of sufficient clothing, metaphorically lack of spirituality.

1132. γυμνότης, gumnotēs, *goom-not´-ace*; from 1131; *nudity* (absolute or comparative):—nakedness.

Noun from *gumnós* (1131), naked. Nakedness, i.e. spoken of the state of one who is poorly clad (Ro 8:35; 2Co 11:27; Sept.: Dt 28:48); by euphemism, for the parts of shame (figuratively, Rev 3:18; Sept.: Ge 9:22, 23).

Syn.: *apobolḗ* (580), a casting off; *apékdusis* (555), a divestment, putting off.

1133. γυναικάριον, gunaikarion, *goo-nahee-kar´-ee-on*; a diminutive from 1135; a *little* (i.e. *foolish*) *woman*:—silly woman.

1134. γυναικεῖος, gunaikeios, *goo-nahee-ki´-os*; from 1135; *feminine*:—wife.

1135. γυνή, gunē, *goo-nay´*; probably from the base of 1096; a *woman*; specially a *wife*:—wife, woman.

1136. Γώγ, Gōg, *gogue*; of Hebrew origin [1463]; *Gog*, a symbolical name for some future Antichrist:—Gog.

1137. γωνία, gōnia, *go-nee´-ah*; probably akin to 1119; an *angle*:—corner, quarter.

1138. Δαβίδ, Dabid, *dab-eed´*; of Hebrew origin [1732]; *Dabid* (i.e. *David*), the Israelites king:—David.

1139. δαιμονίζομαι, daimonizomai, *dahee-mon-id´-zom-ahee*; middle from 1142; to *be exercised by a dæmon*:—have a (be vexed with, be possessed with) devil (-s).

From *daímōn* (1142), demon. To be afflicted, vexed, possessed, with an evil spirit; to be a demoniac (Mt 8:16, 28, 33; 9:32; 12:22; 15:22; Mk 1:32; 5:15, 16, 18; Lk 8:36; Jn 10:21, see Jn 10:20). It is much disputed whether the writers of the NT used this word to denote the actual presence of evil spirits in the persons affected, or whether they employed it only in compliance with popular usage and belief, just as we now use the word "lunatic" without assenting to the old opinion of the influence of the moon. A serious difficulty in the way of this latter supposition is that the demoniacs everywhere at once address Jesus as the Messiah (e.g., Mt 8:29; Mk 1:24; Lk 4:34; 8:28).

1140. δαιμόνιον, daimonion, *dahee-mon´-ee-on*; neuter of a derivative of 1142; a *dæmonic being*; by extension a *deity*:—devil, god.

1141. δαιμονιώδης, daimoniōdēs, *dahee-mon-ee-o´-dace*; from 1140 and 1142; *dæmon-like*:—devilish.

1142. δαίμων, daimōn, *dah´ee-mown*; from **δαίω, *daiō*** (to *distribute* fortunes); a *dæmon* or supernatural spirit (of a bad nature):—devil.

A noun meaning demon, an evil spirit (Mt 8:31; Mk 5:12; Lk 8:29; Rev 16:14 [TR]; 18:2 [TR]).

Deriv.: *daimonizomai* (1139), to be possessed of a demon; *daimónion* (1140), a little demon.

1143. δάκνω, daknō, *dak´-no*; a prolonged form of a primary root; to *bite*, i.e. (figurative) *thwart*:—bite.

1144. δάκρυ, dakru, *dak´-roo*; or **δάκρυον, *dakruon,*** *dak´-roo-on*; of uncertain affinity; a *tear*:—tear.

1145. δακρύω, dakruō, *dak-roo´-o*; from 1144; to *shed tears*:—weep. Compare 2799.

1146. δακτύλιος, daktulios, *dak-too´-lee-os*; from 1147; a *finger*-ring:—ring.

1147. δάκτυλος, daktulos, *dak´-too-los*; probably from 1176; a *finger*:—finger.

1148. Δαλμανουθά, Dalmanoutha, *dal-man-oo-thah´*; probably of Chaldee origin; *Dalmanutha*, a place in Palestine:—Dalmanutha.

1149. Δαλματία, Dalmatia, *dal-mat-ee´-ah*; probably of foreign derivative; *Dalmatia*, a region of Europe:—Dalmatia.

1150. δαμάζω, damazō, *dam-ad´-zo*; a variation of an obsolete primary of the same meaning; to *tame*:—tame.

1151. δάμαλις, damalis, *dam´-al-is*; probably from the base of 1150; a *heifer* (as *tame*):—heifer.

1152. Δάμαρις, Damaris, *dam´-ar-is*; probably from the base of 1150; perhaps *gentle; Damaris*, an Athenian woman:—Damaris.

1153. Δαμασκηνός, Damaskēnos, *dam-as-kay-nos´*; from 1154; a *Damascene* or inhabitant of Damascus:—Damascene.

1154. Δαμασκός, Damaskos, *dam-as-kos´*; of Hebrew origin [1834]; *Damascus*, a city of Syria:—Damascus.

1155. δανείζω, daneizō, *dan-ide´-zo*; from 1156; to *loan* on interest; reflexive to *borrow*:—borrow, lend.

1156. δάνειον, daneion, *dan´-i-on*; from **δάνος, *danos*** (a *gift*); probably akin to the base of 1325; a *loan*:—debt.

1157. δανειστής, daneistēs, *dan-ice-tace´*; from 1155; a *lender*:—creditor.

1158. Δανιήλ, Daniēl, *dan-ee-ale´*; of Hebrew origin [1840]; *Daniel*, an Israelite:—Daniel.

1159. δαπανάω, dapanaō, *dap-an-ah´-o*; from 1160; to *expend*, i.e. (in a good sense) to *incur cost*, or (in a bad one) to *waste*:—be at charges, consume, spend.

1160. δαπάνη, dapanē, *dap-an´-ay*; from **δάπτω, *daptō*** (to *devour*); *expense* (as *consuming*):—cost.

1161. δέ, de, *deh*; a primary particle (adversative or continuative); *but, and*, etc.:—also, and, but, moreover, now [*often unexpressed in English*].

1162. δέησις, deēsis, *deh´-ay-sis*; from 1189; a *petition*:—prayer, request, supplication.

Noun from *déomai* (1189), to make known one's particular need. Want, need. In the NT: prayer, as the expression of need, desire, etc.; supplication, petition for oneself (Lk 1:13; Php 4:6; Heb 5:7; 1Pe 3:12; Sept.: Job 27:9; Ps 39:12; 40:2; 1Ki 8:28, 30); in behalf of others (Php 1:19; Jas 5:16); with *hupér* (5228), on behalf of (Ro 10:1; 2Co 1:11; 9:14; Php 1:4; 2Ti 2:1); with *peri* (4012), concerning (Eph 6:18). Generally, spoken of any prayer (Lk 2:37; 5:33; Ac 1:14; Eph 6:18; Php 1:4; 2Ti 5:5; 2Ti 1:3; Sept.: 1Ki 8:45; 2Ch 6:40).

Syn.: *proseuchḗ* (4335), a more general word for prayer to God in particular which is a more sacred word than *déēsis*; *euchḗ* (2171), translated "prayer," but in reality meaning a vow or wish; *énteuxis* (1783), intercession, a petition to a superior; *aítēma* (155), something asked for; *hiketēría* (2428), originally an olive branch carried by a suppliant.

1163. δεῖ, dei, *die*; third person singular active present of 1210; also **δεόν, *deon,*** *deh-on´*; neuter active participle of the same; both used impersonal; *it is* (*was*, etc.) *necessary* (as *binding*):—behoved, be meet, must (needs), (be) need (-ful), ought, should.

In the NT: it needs, it is necessary:

(I) Particularly, from the nature of the case, from a sense of duty, etc.: one must (Mt 16:21; 26:35; Mk 14:31; Lk 2:49; 4:43; Jn 3:7, 30; 1Co 11:19; Heb 9:26). So spoken of what is made necessary by divine appointment (Jn 3:14; 20:9; Ac 4:2). Of things unavoidable (Mt 24:6; Mk 13:7; Ac 1:16; Ro 1:27; 2Co 11:30).

(II) Spoken of what is right and proper in itself, or prescribed by law, duty, custom, etc.: it is right or proper, one must, it ought, it should (Mt 18:33; 25:27; Mk 13:14; Lk 13:14, 16; Jn 4:20; Ac 5:29; 2Ti 2:6; Sept.: Job 15:3). Also that which prudence would dictate (Ac 27:21).

Syn.: *opheílō* (3784), morally obliged or personally obliged; *chrḗzō* (5535), to need; *chrē* (5534), if needs be; *opheilḗ* (3782), obligation, duty; *áxios* (514), worthy, fit; *hikanós* (2425), sufficient, competent, fit; *kalós* (2570), proper, meet; *eúthetos* (2111), correct, well-placed; *díkaios* (1342), just, meet; *anagkaíos* (316), necessary; *anágkē* (318), a necessity; *epánagkes* (1876), of necessity; *chreía* (5532), a need; *kathḗkon*, that which is necessary, becoming; *kathḗkō* (2520), to reach down to do what is right and necessary.

1164. δεῖγμα, deigma, *digh´-mah*; from the base of 1166; a *specimen* (as *shown*):—example.

1165. δειγματίζω, deigmatizō, *digh-mat-id´-zo*; from 1164; to *exhibit*:—make a shew.

1166. δεικνύω, deiknuō, *dike-noo´-o*; a prolonged form of an obstract primary of the same meaning; to *show* (literal or figurative):—shew.

1167. δειλία, deilia, *di-lee´-ah*; from 1169; *timid-ity*:—fear.

Noun from *deilós* (1169), fearful, timid. Cowardice, timidity, reticence, fearfulness (2Ti 1:7; Sept.: Ps 54:5).

Syn.: *Deilía* is always in a bad sense as contrasted with *phóbos* (5401), fear.

1168. δειλιάω, deiliaō, *di-lee-ah´-o*; from 1167; to *be timid*:—be afraid.

1169. δειλός, deilos, *di-los´*; from **δέος, *deos*** (*dread*); *timid*, i.e. (by implication) *faithless*:—fearful.

1170. δεῖνα, deina, *di´-nah*; probably from the same as 1171 (through the idea of forgetting the name as *fearful*, i.e. *strange*); *so and so* (when the person is not specified):—such a man.

1171. δεινῶς, deinōs, *di-noce´*; adverb from a derivative of the same as 1169; *terribly*, i.e. *exces-sively*:—grievously, vehemently.

1172. δειπνέω, deipneō, *dipe-neh´-o*; from 1173; to *dine*, i.e. take the principal (or evening) meal:—sup (×-per).

1173. δεῖπνον, deipnon, *dipe´-non*; from the same as 1160; *dinner*, i.e. the chief meal (usually in the evening):—feast, supper.

1174. δεισιδαιμονέστερος, deisidaimonesteros, *dice-ee-dahee-mon-es´-ter-os*; the compound of a derivative of the base of 1169 and 1142; *more religious* than others:—too superstitious.

The comparative of *deisidaímōn* (n.f.), fearing the gods. Fearing the gods, i.e. in a good sense: religiously disposed; in a bad sense: superstitious. In the NT, in the first sense, spoken of the Athenians (Ac 17:22).

1175. δεισιδαιμονία, deisidaimonia, *dice-ee-dahee-mon-ee´-ah*; from the same as 1174; *religion*:—superstition.

Noun from *deisidaímōn* (n.f.), fearing the gods. Fear of the gods, i.e. religiousness, i.e. religious (Ac 25:19).

Syn.: *thrēskeía* (2356), religion in its external aspect, religious worship, especially the ceremonial service of religion; *theosébeia* (2317), reverential worship of God; *eusébeia* (2150), piety; *eulábeia* (2124), the devotion arising from godly fear.

1176. δέκα, deka, *dek´-ah*; a primary number; *ten*:—[eight-] een, ten.

1177. δεκαδύο, dekaduo, *dek-ad-oo´-o*; from 1176 and 1417; *two* and *ten*, i.e. *twelve*:—twelve.

1178. δεκαπέντε, dekapente, *dek-ap-en´-teh*; from 1176 and 4002; *ten* and *five*, i.e. *fifteen*:—fifteen.

1179. Δεκάπολις, Dekapolis, *dek-ap´-ol-is*; from 1176 and 4172; the *ten-city* region; the *Decapolis*, a district in Syria:—Decapolis.

1180. δεκατέσσαρες, dekatessares, *dek-at-es´-sar-es*; from 1176 and 5064; *ten* and *four*, i.e. *fourteen*:—fourteen.

1181. δεκάτη, dekatē, *dek-at´-ay*; feminine of 1182; a *tenth*, i.e. as a percentage or (technical) *tithe*:—tenth (part), tithe.

1182. δέκατος, dekatos, *dek´-at-os*; ordinal from 1176; *tenth*:—tenth.

1183. δεκατόω, dekatoō, *dek-at-o´-o*; from 1181; to *tithe*, i.e. to *give* or *take a tenth*:—pay (receive) tithes.

1184. δεκτός, dektos, *dek-tos´*; from 1209; *approved*; (figurative) *propitious*:—accepted (-table).

Verbal adj. from *déchomai* (1209), to accept, decide fabourably. Accepted, i.e. metaphorically: acceptable, approved (Lk 4:24; Ac 10:35; Php 4:18). By implication: favourable, gracious; spoken of a time, i.e. a time of favour (Lk 4:19; 2Co 4:2, cf. Isa 49:8).

Syn.: *euárestos* (2101), well-pleasing, acceptable.

1185. δελεάζω, deleazō, *del-eh-ad´-zo*; from the base of 1388; to *entrap*, i.e. (figurative) *delude*:—allure, beguile, entice.

1186. δένδρον, dendron, *den´-dron*; probably from **δρύς, *drus*** (an *oak*); a *tree*:—tree.

1187. δεξιολάβος, dexiolabos, *dex-ee-ol-ab´-os*; from 1188 and 2983; a *guardsman* (as if *taking the right*) or light-armed soldier:—spearman.

1188. δεξιός, dexios, *dex-ee-os´*; from 1209; the *right* side or (feminine) hand (as that which usually *takes*):—right (hand, side).

Adjective meaning right as opposed to left, right hand or side:

(I) With a substantive expressed, e.g., hand (Mt 5:30; Lk 6:6; Ac 3:7; Rev 1:16, 17); foot (Rev 10:2); eye (Mt 5:29); ear (Lk 22:50; Jn 18:10); cheek (Mt 5:39); the right side (Jn 21:6).

(II) Without a substantive expressed:

(A) Meaning "right hand" (Mt 6:3; 27:29; Rev 1:20; 2:1; 5:1, 7). The "right hand" of fellowship (Gal 3:9). Put for the right hand or side in general: the right (Heb 1:3; 8:1; 12:2); so the "right hand of God" (Ac 2:33; 5:31; Ro 8:34; Eph 1:20; Col 3:1; Heb 10:12; 1Pe 3:22).

(B) Meaning "the right parts," i.e. the right in general, e.g., "on the right" (Mt 27:38; Mk 15:27; Lk 23:33); so in the expression to sit or stand on the right of the Messiah or God, i.e. to be next in rank and power, to have the highest seat of honour and distinction (Mt 20:21, 23; 22:44; Mk 10:37, 40; 12:36; Lk 20:42; Ac 2:34; 7:55, 56; Heb 1:13); also "to be at one's right hand," i.e. to be one's helper, protector (Ac 2:25).

Deriv.: *dexiolábos* (1187), spearman, bodyguard.

1189. δέομαι, deomai, *deh´-om-ahee*; middle of 1210; to *beg* (as *binding oneself*), i.e. *petition*:—beseech, pray (to), make request. Compare 4441.

To lack for oneself, to need. Hence in the NT: to make one's need known, to beseech, ask. *Déēsis* (1162), prayer for a particular need, supplication. Used with the gen. of the person (Lk 8:38; 9:40 [cf. Ac 26:3; 2Co 10:2]). With the accusative (2Co 8:4). Followed by *hópōs* (3704), so that (Mt 9:38; Lk 10:2 [cf. Ac 8:24]). Followed by *hína* (2443), in order (Lk 9:40 [cf. Lk 21:36; 22:32]). Followed by *mḗ* (3378), an interrogative neg. meaning never, not (Lk 8:28). Spoken of prayer to God in general (Ac 8:22, with the gen. of God, "I beseech of God" [a.t.]; 10:2). With the prep. *prós* (4314), and the accusative *tón Kúrion* ([3588], [2962]), the Lord (Ac 8:24). Used in an absolute sense in Lk 21:36; 22:32; Ac 4:31; 1Th 3:10; Sept.: Da 6:11; Job 8:5; Ps 30:8; Isa 37:4. Used generally and in an absolute sense in Ro 1:10, "making request"; 2Co 5:20. Followed by the gen. of person (Lk 5:12; 9:38, 40; Ac 8:34, "I pray thee"; 21:39; 26:3; Gal 4:12; Sept.: Dt 3:23; 2Ki 1:13; Pr 26:25). Followed by the accusative of thing or inf. for accusative (2Co 8:4; 10:2). While *proseuchḗ* (4335) refers to prayer in general, *déēsis* refers to a particular need for which one prays. Thus *déomai* is related to *aitéō* (154), to make a request, ask as an inferior of a superior.

Deriv.: *déēsis* (1162), prayer, request; *prosdéomai* (4326), to require additionally.

Syn.: *chrḗzō* (5535), to have need; *parakaléō* (3870), literally to call to one's side, hence to call to one's aid, being the most commonly used word with this sense; *erōtáō* (2065), to beseech, to ask; *eúchomai* (2172), translated "pray," but in reality it means to wish.

1190. Δερβαῖος, Derbaios, *der-bah´ee-os*; from 1191; a *Derbæan* or inhabitant of Derbe:—of Derbe.

1191. Δέρβη, Derbē, *der´-bay*; of foreign origin; *Derbè*, a place in Asia Minor:—Derbe.

1192. δέρμα, derma, *der´-mah*; from 1194; a *hide*:—skin.

1193. δερμάτινος, dermatinos, *der-mat´-ee-nos*; from 1192; made of *hide*:—leathern, of a skin.

1194. δέρω, derō, *der´-o*; a primary verb; properly to *flay*, i.e. (by implication) to *scourge*, or (by analogy) to *thrash*:—beat, smite.

1195. δεσμεύω, desmeuō, *des-myoo´-o*; from a (presumed) derivative of 1196; to *be a binder* (*captor*), i.e. to *enchain* (a prisoner), to *tie on* (a load):—bind.

1196. δεσμέω, desmeō, *des-meh´-o*; from 1199; to *tie*, i.e. *shackle*:—bind.

1197. δεσμή, desmē, *des-may´*; from 1196; a *bundle*:—bundle.

1198. δέσμιος, desmios, *des´-mee-os*; from 1199; a *captive* (as *bound*):—in bonds, prisoner.

1199. δεσμόν, desmon, *des-mon´*; or **δεσμός, *desmos,*** *des-mos´*; neuter and masculine respectively from 1210; a *band*, i.e. *ligament* (of the body) or *shackle* (of a prisoner); (figurative) an *impediment* or *disability*:—band, bond, chain, string.

1200. δεσμοφύλαξ, desmophulax, *des-mof-oo´-lax*; from 1199 and 5441; a *jailer* (as *guarding* the *prisoners*):—jailor, keeper of the prison.

1201. δεσμωτήριον, desmōtērion, *des-mo-tay´-ree-on*; from a derivative of 1199 (equivalent to 1196); a *place of bondage*, i.e. a *dungeon*:—prison.

1202. δεσμώτης, desmōtēs, *des-mo´-tace*; from the same as 1201; (passive) a *captive*:—prisoner.

1203. δεσπότης, despotēs, *des-pot´-ace*; perhaps from 1210 and **πόσις, *posis*** (a *husband*); an absolute *ruler* ("despot"):—Lord, master.

A noun meaning master, as opposed to servant; the head of a family (1Ti 6:1, 2; 2Ti 2:21; Tit 2:9; 1Pe 2:18). By implication, as denoting supreme authority: Lord; spoken of God (Lk 2:29; Ac 4:24; Rev 6:10); of Christ (2Pe 2:1; Jude 4).

Deriv.: *oikodespótēs* (3617), householder, master of the house.

Syn.: *megistán* (3175), great, denoting chief men, nobles; *hēgemṓn* (2232), a chief person, ruler; *prōtótokos* (4416), in the sense of being the first over, supreme, in which case it is equivalent to *prōteúōn* (4409), having the preeminence; *árchōn* (758), chief ruler, prince; *kubernḗtēs* (2942), captain, master of a ship; *dunástēs* (1413), a ruler or officer, potentate, one who possesses great power (*dúnamis* [1411]). *Kúrios* (2962), lord, master. *Despótēs* wields unlimited authority, while *kúrios* exercises morally restricted authority for good. Jesus is predominantly called *Kúrios*, Lord, because of His omnipotent concern. God is *Kúrios*, Lord, because He is *despótēs* of all things (cf. Job 5:8ff.).

1204. δεῦρο, deuro, *dyoo´-ro*; of uncertain affinity; *here*; used also imperative *hither!*; and of time, *hitherto*:—come (hither), hither [-to].

1205. δεῦτε, deute, *dyoo´-teh*; from 1204 and an imperative form of **εἶμι, *eimi*** (to *go*); *come hither!*:—come, × follow.

1206. δευτεραῖος, deuteraios, *dyoo-ter-ah´-yos*; from 1208; *secondary*, i.e. (special) on the *second* day:—next day.

1207. δευτερόπρωτος, deuteroprōtos, *dyoo-ter-op´-ro-tos*; from 1208 and 4413; *second-first*, i.e. (special) a designation of the Sabbath immediately after the Paschal week (being the *second* after Passover day, and the *first* of the seven Sabbaths intervening before Pentecost):—second … after the first.

1208. δεύτερος, deuteros, *dyoo´-ter-os*; as the comparative of 1417; (ordinal) *second* (in time, place or rank; also adverbial):—afterward, again, second (-arily, time).

1209. δέχομαι, dechomai, *dekh´-om-ahee*; middle of a primary verb; to *receive* (in various applications, literal or figurative):—accept, receive, take. Compare 2983.

To take to oneself what is presented or brought by another, to receive:

(I) Of things:

(A) To take, receive, receive into one's hands (Lk 2:28; Lk 16:6, 7; Lk 22:17; Eph 6:17; Sept.: 2Ch 29:16, 22).

(B) Generally: to receive, accept, e.g., letters (Ac 22:5; 28:21); the grace or the collection (2Co 8:4); whatever was sent from the Philippians (Php 4:18). See Sept.: Ge 33:10; Ex 29:25; 32:4.

(C) Metaphorically: to receive the kingdom of God (Mk 10:15; Lk 18:17); living words (Ac 7:38); the grace of God (2Co 6:1; Sept.: Jer 9:20; 17:23). Also of what is received by the ear: to hear of, learn, as the gospel (2Co 11:4). To receive, admit with the mind and heart, i.e. by implication: to approve, embrace, follow (Mt 11:14; Lk 8:13; Ac 8:14; 11:1; 17:11; 1Th 1:6; 2:13; Jas 1:21); the things of the Spirit (1Co 2:14); the exhortation or teaching (2Co 8:17); the love of the truth (2Th 2:10). Also Sept.: Pr 10:8; Zep 3:7.

(II) Of persons: to receive, admit, accept. To receive kindly, welcome as a teacher, friend, or guest into the house (Lk 16:4); into the eternal habitations or heaven (Lk 16:9; Ac 7:59). In the sense of to admit to one's presence, to the house where one is, as the multitudes (Lk 9:11). By implication in 2Co 11:16, to bear with.

Deriv.: *anadéchomai* (324), to entertain anyone hospitality; *apodéchomai* (588), to receive heartily, welcome; *dektós* (1184), accepted, acceptable, agreeable; *diadéchomai* (1237), to come after; *dókimos* (1384), to prove, try; *dochḗ* (1403), a feast, acceptance, reception; *eisdéchomai* (1523), to receive into; *ekdéchomai* (1551), to take or receive from, to await, expect; *endéchomai* (1735), to accept; *epidéchomai* (1926), to receive; *paradéchomai* (3858), to receive, to admit; *prosdéchomai* (4327), to take, accept, receive, expect; *hupodéchomai* (5264), to entertain hospitably.

Syn.: *lambánō* (2983) to receive; *apéchō* (568), to have in full, to have received all that is due; *chōréō* (5562), to make room for, receive with the mind; *lagchánō* (2975), to obtain by lot.

1210. δέω, deō, *deh´-o*; a primary verb; to *bind* (in various applications, literal or figurative):—bind, be in bonds, knit, tie, wind. See also 1163, 1189.

To bind:

(I) Of things: to bind together or to anything, to bind around, fasten (Mt 13:30; 21:2; Mk 11:2, 4; Lk 19:30; Ac 10:11; Sept.: Jos 2:21; Jgs 15:4). Spoken of dead bodies which are bound or wound around with graveclothes (Jn 11:44; 19:40). Here also belong Mt 16:19; 18:18, where the allusion is to the ancient manner of binding together the doors of houses with a chain to which a padlock was sometimes suspended. Others here translate to interdict, to prohibit, i.e. to exclude, like Aram. *'āsar* (631, OT), decree (Da 8, 9, 13, 15).

(II) Of persons: to bind the hands, feet, etc.; to put in bonds, i.e. to deprive of liberty. Generally (Mt 12:29; 14:3; 22:13; Mk 3:27; 15:1; Jn 18:12; Ac 9:14; 21:11; Rev 20:2). Pass.: to be bound, to be in bonds, in prison, etc. (Mk 15:7; Jn 18:24; Ac 9:2, 21; 21:13; 24:27; Col 4:3; Rev 9:14). Figuratively in Lk 13:16, "whom Satan hath bound," i.e. deprived of the use of her limbs (v. 11); Satan being here represented as the author of physical evil. Also in 2Ti 2:9, i.e. the preaching of the word is not hindered because I am in bonds.

(III) Perf. pass.: to be bound, metaphorically spoken of the conjugal bond: to be bound to someone (Ro 7:2; 1Co 7:27, 39). Also used metaphorically in the expression "bound in spirit" (Ac 20:22), i.e. impelled in mind, compelled (cf. 18:5).

Deriv.: *désmē* (1197), a bundle; *desmós* (1199), a band, bond, fetter; *katadéō* (2611), to bind or tie down; *peridéō* (4019), to bind around; *sundéō* (4887), to bind together; *hupodéō* (5265), to bind underneath, used of binding of sandals.

Syn.: *sunistáō* or *sunístēmi* (4921), to set or hold together; *suntássō* (4929), to arrange jointly; *katartízō* (2675), to fit, join together; *sunéchō* (4912), to hold together.

1211. δή, dē, *day*; probably akin to 1161; a particle of emphasis or explicitness; *now, then*, etc.:—also, and, doubtless, now, therefore.

1212. δῆλος, dēlos, *day´-los*; of uncertain derivative; *clear*:—+ bewray, certain, evident, manifest.

1213. δηλόω, dēloō, *day-lo´-o*; from 1212; to *make plain* (by words):—declare, shew, signify.

1214. Δημᾶς, Dēmas, *day-mas´*; probably for 1216; *Demas*, a Christian:—Demas.

1215. δημηγορέω, dēmēgoreō, *day-may-gor-eh´-o*; from a compound of 1218 and 58; to *be a people-gatherer*, i.e. to *address* a public assembly:—make an oration.

1216. Δημήτριος, Dēmētrios, *day-may´-tree-os*; from **Δημήτηρ, *Dēmētēr*** (*Ceres*); *Demetrius*, the name of an Ephesian and of a Christian:—Demetrius.

1217. δημιουργός, dēmiourgos, *day-me-oor-gos´*; from 1218 and 2041; a *worker* for the *people*, i.e. *mechanic* (spoken of the *Creator*):—maker.

Adjective from *dḗmos* (1218), a people, and *érgon* (2041), work. Used as a substantive to denote one who works for the public or performs public works such as an architect. Hence generally and in the NT: an artist or artificer, maker, author. Only in Heb 11:10.

Syn.: *ktístēs* (2939), founder of a city, creator; *poiētḗs* (4162), a poet (Ac 17:28), a maker, doer (Ro 2:13; Jas 1:22, 23, 25; 4:11); *plástēs* (n.f.), a molder, an artist who works in clay or wax (see *plássō* [4111]).

1218. δῆμος, dēmos, *day´-mos*; from 1210; the *public* (as *bound* together socially):—people.

Noun from *déō* (1210), to bind. The people, populus (Ac 12:22; 17:5; 19:30, 33). From this word is derived "democracy" where the people or the public rules.

Deriv.: *apódēmos* (590), taking a far journey; *dēmēgoréō* (1215), to make an oration; *dēmiourgós* (1217), maker; *dēmósios* (1219), public, common.

Syn.: *laós* (2992), people; *óchlos* (3793), a crowd, throng; *éthnos* (1484), a nation; *kósmos* (2889), world, people; *koinōnía* (2842), partnership, communion, fellowship.

1219. δημόσιος, dēmosios, *day-mos´-ee-os*; from 1218; *public*; (feminine singular dative as adverb) *in public*:—common, openly, publickly.

1220. δηνάριον, dēnarion, *day-nar´-ee-on*; of Latin origin; a *denarius* (or *ten asses*):—pence, penny [-worth].

1221. δήποτε, dēpote, *day´-pot-eh*; from 1211 and 4218; a particle of generalization; *indeed, at any time*:—(what-) soever.

1222. δήπου, dēpou, *day´-poo*; from 1211 and 4225; a particle of asseveration; *indeed doubtless*:—verily.

1223. διά, dia, *dee-ah´*; a primary preposition denoting the *channel* of an act; *through* (in very wide applications, local, causal or occasional):—after, always, among, at, to avoid, because of (that), briefly, by, for (cause) … fore, from, in, by occasion of, of, by reason of, for sake, that, thereby, therefore, × though, through (-out), to, wherefore, with (-in). In composition it retains the same general import.

1224. διαβαίνω, diabainō, *dee-ab-ah´ee-no*; from 1223 and the base of 939; to *cross*:—come over, pass (through).

1225. διαβάλλω, diaballō, *dee-ab-al´-lo*; from 1223 and 906; (figurative) to *traduce*:—accuse.

From *diá* (1223), through, and *bállō* (906), to cast, throw. To accuse falsely. Hence metaphorically and in the NT: to carry or deliver over to someone in words, i.e. to report or inform against, to disgrace, to accuse. Used only in Lk 16:1.

Deriv.: *diábolos* (1228), false accuser.

Syn.: *egkaléō* (1458), to bring a charge against, usually in court; *epēreázō* (1908), to insult, misuse, treat despitefully; *katēgoréō* (2723), to accuse; *sukophantéō* (4811), to accuse wrongfully; *proaitiáomai* (4256), to bring a previous charge against; *katalaléō* (2635), to speak against; *kakologéō* (2551), to speak evil.

1226. διαβεβαιόομαι, diabebaioomai, *dee-ab-eb-ahee-o´-om-ahee*; middle of a compound of 1223 and 950; to *confirm thoroughly* (by words), i.e. *asseverate*:—affirm constantly.

Deponent from *diá* (1223), an intensive, and *bebaióō* (950), to confirm. To assure firmly, affirm, make firm (1Ti 1:7; Tit 3:8).

Syn.: *diïschurízomai* (1340), to assert vehemently; *pháskō* (5335), to show or make known one's thoughts, to affirm by way of alleging or professing.

1227. διαβλέπω, diablepō, *dee-ab-lep´-o*; from 1223 and 991; to *look through*, i.e. *recover* full *vision*:—see clearly.

1228. διάβολος, diabolos, *dee-ab´-ol-os*; from 1225; a *traducer*; specially *Satan* [compare 7854]:—false accuser, devil, slanderer.

Noun from *diabállō* (1225), to accuse. A false accuser, slanderer:

(I) Generally (1Ti 3:11; 2Ti 3:3; Tit 2:3; Sept.: Est 7:4; 8:1).

(II) With the article *ho diábolos*, the devil, i.e. the accuser; the same as Hebrew *śāṭān* (adversary; 7854, OT) with the article, i.e. the adversary, Satan. According to the later Hebrews, he acts as the accuser and calumniator of men before God (Job 1:7, 12; Zec 3:1, 2, cf. Rev 12:9, 10), seduces them to sin (1Ch 21:1), and is the author of evil, both physical and moral, by which the human race is afflicted. In the NT, *ho diábolos* appears as the constant enemy of God, of Christ, of the divine kingdom, of the followers of Christ, and of all truth; full of falsehood and malice, and seducing to evil in every possible way (Mt 4:1, 5, 8, 11; 25:41; Lk 4:2, 3, 5, 6, 13; 8:12; Jn 13:2; Ac 10:38; Eph 4:27; 6:11; 1Ti 3:6, 7; 2Ti 2:26; Heb 2:14; Jas 4:7; 1Pe 5:8; Jude 9; Rev 2:10; 20:2, 10). Hence the expression "child of the devil" (Jn 8:44; Ac 13:10, cf. Jn 6:70).

Syn.: *ho katḗgoros* (2725), the accuser; *Satanás* (4567), Satan or adversary; *apollúōn* (623), the destroyer.

1229. διαγγέλλω, diaggellō, *de-ang-gel´-lo*; from 1223 and the base of 32; to *herald thoroughly*:—declare, preach, signify.

From *diá* (1223), through, and *aggéllō* (n.f., see *anaggéllō* [312]), to tell, declare. To announce throughout, to publish, to proclaim (Lk 9:60; Ro 9:17, pass.; Sept.: Ex 9:16; Ps 2:7). Implying completeness: to declare plainly, fully, exactly (Ac 21:26; Sept.: Jos 6:10).

Syn.: *diēgéomai* (1334), to conduct a narration through to the end; *ekdiēgéomai* (1555), to narrate in full; *exēgéomai* (1834), to lead out, make known, declare; *dēlóō* (1213), to make plain, declare plainly; *phrázō* (5419), to declare by making it clear; *gnōrízō* (1107), to make known; *emphanízō* (1718), to declare plainly; *phaneróō* (5319), to manifest; *kērússō* (2784), to preach; *parrēsiázomai* (3955), to be bold in speech, to preach boldly; *laléō* (2980), to speak; *dialégomai* (1256), to give a reasoned discourse or to discuss.

1230. διαγίνομαι, diaginomai, *dee-ag-in´-om-ahee*; from 1223 and 1096; to *elapse meanwhile*:— × after, be past, be spent.

1231. διαγινώσκω, diaginōskō, *dee-ag-in-o´-sko*; from 1223 and 1097; to *know thoroughly*, i.e. *ascertain exactly*:—(would) enquire, know the uttermost.

From *diá* (1223), denoting separation or emphasis, and *ginṓskō* (1097), to know experientially. To know throughout, i.e. accurately; to distinguish (Sept.: Dt 2:7). In the NT: to inquire fully into, to examine, to investigate (Ac 23:15; 24:22).

Deriv.: *diágnōsis* (1233), discernment.

Syn.: *oída* (1492), to know intuitively, to perceive; *epístamai* (1987), to understand; *suniēmi* (4920), to bring or set together, to put it together, understand; *noéō* (3539), to perceive with the mind; *punthánomai* (4441), to inquire, to understand; *gnōrízō* (1107), to make known; *manthánō* (3129), to learn; *phronéō* (5426), to mind, understand; *parakolouthéō* (3877), to follow up, to trace, have understanding; *plērophoréō* (4135), used in the pass., to be fully assured; *anagnōrízō* (319), to recognize; *diagnōrízō* (1232), to make known; *krínō* (2919), to be of an opinion, to determine; *horízō* (3724) to declare, determine, specify; *epilúō* (1956), to solve.

1232. διαγνωρίζω, diagnōrizō, *dee-ag-no-rid´-zo*; from 1123 and 1107; to *tell abroad*:—make known.

From *diá* (1223), denoting separation, and *gnōrízō* (1107), to know. To make known throughout, i.e. everywhere; to tell abroad, to publish. Only in Lk 2:17.

Syn.: *plērophoréō* (4135), to make fully known; *diaggéllō* (1229), to declare fully; *exaggéllō* (1804), to tell out, proclaim abroad; *diēgéomai* (1334), to relate in full; *anaggéllō* (312), to report, declare; *phaneróō* (5319), to manifest; *dēlóō* (1213), to make plain; *apaggéllō* (518), to announce, declare.

1233. διάγνωσις, diagnōsis, *dee-ag´-no-sis*; from 1231; (magisterial) *examination* ("diagnosis"):—hearing.

Noun from *diaginṓskō* (1231), to know thoroughly. Exact knowledge. In the NT, in a judicial sense: examination, trial, hearing. Only in Ac 25:21.

Syn.: *diákrisis* (1253), a distinguishing, a decision, discerning.

1234. διαγογγύζω, diagogguzō, *dee-ag-ong-good´-zo*; from 1223 and 1111; to *complain throughout* a crowd:—murmur.

1235. διαγρηγορέω, diagrēgoreō, *dee-ag-ray-gor-eh´-o*; from 1223 and 1127; to *waken thoroughly*:—be awake.

1236. διάγω, diagō, *dee-ag´-o*; from 1223 and 71; to *pass* time or life:—lead life, living.

1237. διαδέχομαι, diadechomai, *dee-ad-ekh´-om-ahee*; from 1223 and 1209; to *receive in turn*, i.e. (figurative) *succeed to*:—come after.

From *diá* (1223), denoting transition, and *déchomai* (1209), to receive. To receive by succession from another or former possessor. Only in Ac 7:45.

Deriv.: *diádochos* (1240), a successor.

Syn.: *akolouthéō* (190), to follow, come after.

1238. διάδημα, diadēma, *dee-ad´-ay-mah*; from a compound of 1223 and 1210; a "*diadem*" (as *bound about* the head):—crown. Compare 4735.

Noun from *diadéō* (n.f.), to bind around, which is from the prep. *diá* (1223), around, and *déō* (1210), to bind. A diadem, the symbol of royal dignity. (Rev 12:3; 13:1; 19:12; Sept.: Est 1:11; 2:17; Isa 62:3).

Syn.: *stéphanos* (4735), crown.

1239. διαδίδωμι, diadidōmi, *dee-ad-id´-o-mee*; from 1223 and 1325; to *give throughout* a crowd, i.e. *deal out*; also to *deliver* over (as to a successor):—(make) distribute (-ion), divide, give.

1240. διάδοχος, diadochos, *dee-ad´-okh-os*; from 1237; a *successor* in office:—room.

Noun from *diadéchomai* (1237), to succeed, follow after. A successor. Only in Ac 24:27.

Syn.: *hústeros* (5306), latter; *opísō* (3694), one who follows.

1241. διαζώννυμι, diazōnnumi, *dee-az-own´-noo-mee*; from 1223 and 2224; to *gird tightly*:—gird.

1242. διαθήκη, diathēkē, *dee-ath-ay´-kay*; from 1303; properly a *disposition*, i.e. (special) a *contract* (especially a devisory *will*):—covenant, testament.

Noun from *diatíthēmi* (1303), to set out in order, to dispose in a certain order. A disposition, arrangement:

(I) Spoken of a testamentary disposition: a testament, a will (Heb 9:16, 17).

(II) A covenant, i.e. a mutual agreement or mutual promises on mutual conditions (Gal 3:15; Sept.: 1Sa 18:3; 23; 18). In the NT, spoken of God's covenants with men, i.e. the divine promises conditioned on obedience:

(A) Of the Abrahamic covenant, confirmed also to the other patriarchs, of which circumcision was the sign (Ge 15:1–18; 17:1–19). So Lk 1:72; Ac 3:25; Gal 3:17).

(B) Of the Mosaic covenant, entered into at Mount Sinai, with sacrifice and blood of victims (Ex 24:3–12; Dt 5:2; Heb 8:9; 9:20); also called "the first covenant," i.e. the Old or Jewish dispensation, in reference to the gospel (Heb 9:15). So also in Heb 9:4, "the ark of the covenant," and "the tables of the covenant," i.e. the Ark that was the symbol of God's presence under the Mosaic covenant, and the tables of the Law which the people had covenanted to obey (Rev 11:19, cf. Heb 8:5). The Mosaic covenant was strictly the renewal of the Abrahamic; hence Paul uses the plural in Ro 9:4 and Eph 2:12. Since the ancient covenant is contained in the Mosaic books, *diathḗkē* is used by metonymy for the book of the covenant, the Mosaic writings, i.e. the Law (2Co 3:14).

(C) Of the new covenant promised of old and sanctioned by the blood of Christ: the gospel dispensation (Ro 11:27; Heb 8:10; 10:16, 29); also called the "new covenant" (with *néos* [3501], Heb 12:24; with *kainós* [2537], Lk 22:20; 1Co 11:25; 2Co 3:6; Heb 9:15), "better testament" (Heb 7:22; 8:6; see *kreittōn* [2909], better), and "everlasting covenant" (Heb 13:20; see *aiṓnios* [166], everlasting).

1243. διαίρεσις, diairesis, *dee-ah´ee-res-is*; from 1244; a *distinction* or (concrete) *variety*:—difference, diversity.

Noun from *diairéō* (1244), to divide. Division, act of dividing. Used only in 1Co 12:4–6, speaking of diversities, differences, classes of gifts.

Syn.: *diastolḗ* (1293), a setting asunder, distinction; *merismós* (3311), division, partition, distribution.

1244. διαιρέω, diaireō, *dee-ahee-reh´-o*; from 1223 and 138; to *separate*, i.e. *distribute*:—divide.

From *diá* (1223), through or denoting separation, and *hairéō* (138), to take, grasp, seize. To take from, divide, partition, apportion, assign. In the NT, it means to distribute among (Lk 15:12; 1Co 12:11; Sept.: Jos 18:5; 1Ch 23:6).

Deriv.: *diaíresis* (1243), diversity.

Syn.: *aphorízō* (873), to mark off by boundaries, separate, divide; *apodiorízō* (592), to mark off, make separations or divisions; *diadídōmi* (1239), to deal out, distribute; *diakrínō* (1252), to separate, discriminate; *merízō* (3307), to divide into; *diamerízō* (1266), to divide up; *kataklērodotéō* (2624), to distribute lots; *chōrízō* (5563), to separate; *apochōrízō* (673), to separate, tear apart; *schízō* (4977), to split or sever.

1245. διακαθαρίζω, diakatharizō, *dee-ak-ath-ar-id´-zo*; from 1223 and 2511; to *cleanse perfectly*, i.e. (special) *winnow*:—thoroughly purge.

1246. διακατελέγχομαι, diakatelegchomai, *dee-ak-at-el-eng´-khom-ahee*; middle from 1223 and a compound of 2596 and 1651; to *prove downright*, i.e. *confute*:—convince.

1247. διακονέω, diakoneō, *dee-ak-on-eh´-o*; from 1249; to *be an attendant*, i.e. *wait upon* (menially or as a host, friend or [figurative] teacher); techn. to *act as a* Christian *deacon*:—(ad-) minister (unto), serve, use the office of a deacon.

From *diákonos* (1249), servant, deacon. To serve, wait upon, minister to:

(I) To serve at a table, to wait upon (Mt 8:15; 20:28; 27:55; Mk 1:31; 10:45; 15:41; Lk 4:39; 10:40; 12:37; 17:8; 22:26, 27; Jn 12:2). In Ac 6:2, to serve over money tables, i.e. have charge of the alms and other pecuniary matters.

(II) To minister to the wants of someone, to supply someone's needs (Mt 4:11; 25:44; Mk 1:13; Lk 8:3).

(III) Used also of the alms collected by the churches, the distribution of alms (Ro 15:25; Heb 6:10; 1Pe 4:11).

(IV) To be an attendant or assistant to someone, as Timothy and Erastos were said to be ministering to Paul (Ac 19:22). Spoken of service in the early church: to fill the office of a deacon, i.e. to have charge over the poor and sick (1Ti 3:10, 13).

(V) Of things: to administer, provide something for someone. Spoken of prophets who minister, i.e. announce, deliver the divine will (1Pe 1:12). Also to minister something to someone; to administer, provide (2Co 3:3; 2Ti 1:18). By implication: to minister to one's wants (1Pe 4:10).

Syn.: *leitourgéō* (3008), to render public service; *hupēretéō* (5256), to toil, render service; *therapeúō* (2323), to wait upon menially, relieve, cure; *hierourgéō* (2418), to minister in priestly service; *ergázomai* (2038), to work; *prosedreúō* (4332), to attend as a servant; *proskarteréō* (4342), to serve in a close personal relationship.

1248. διακονία, diakonia, *dee-ak-on-ee´-ah*; from 1249; *attendance* (as a servant, etc.); figurative (eleemosynary) *aid*, (official) *service* (especially of the Christian teacher, or technical of the *diaconate*):—(ad-) minister (-ing, -tration, -try), office, relief, service (-ing).

Noun from *diákonos* (1249), deacon, servant. Service, attendance, ministry:

(I) Service toward a master or guest, at table or in hospitality (Lk 10:40; 1Co 16:15).

(II) Ministry, ministration, i.e. the office of ministering in divine things, spoken chiefly of apostles and teachers (Ac 1:17, 25; 6:4; 20:24; 21:19; Ro 11:13; 1Co 12:5; 2Co 3:7–9; 4:1; 5:18; 6:3; Eph 4:12; Col 4:17; 1Ti 1:12; 2Ti 4:5, 11). Used once of the office of a *diákonos* (1249), deacon (Ro 12:7). Some, however, take this to have a wider sense as above.

(III) In the sense of aid or relief as spoken of alms, contributions (Ac 11:29; Ro 15:31 [see Ro 15:26]; 2Co 8:4; 9:1, 13; 11:8; Rev 2:19). Spoken of the distribution or ministration of alms collected (Ac 6:1; 12:25, see 11:30; 2Co 9:12).

Syn.: *ōphéleia* (5622), advantage, profit; *euergesía* (2108), benevolence; *chrēstótēs* (5544), usefulness, kindness; *sumphéron* (4851), profit, expedience; *therapeía* (2322), attendance, service or healing with tenderness; *leitourgía* (3009), a sacred or priestly ministration; *latreía* (2999), primarily hired service; *episkopḗ* (1984), inspection, the office of a bishop, visitation; *episústasis* (1999), responsibility for oversight based upon authority; *prónoia* (4307), forethought, provision, providence; *epiméleia* (1958), kind attention, care.

1249. διάκονος, diakonos, *dee-ak´-on-os*; probably from an obsolete **διάκω, diakō** (to *run* on errands; compare 1377); an *attendant*, i.e. (genitive) a *waiter* (at table or in other menial duties); specially a Christian *teacher* and *pastor* (technically a *deacon* or *deaconess*):—deacon, minister, servant.

A noun meaning minister, servant, attendant:

(I) Spoken of those who wait at table (Jn 2:5, 9); of the servants or attendants of a king (Mt 22:13; Ro 13:4); of an attendant, disciple (Jn 12:26); of ministers, teachers of divine things who act for God (1Co 3:5; 2Co 3:6; 11:23; Eph 6:21; 1Th 3:2).

(II) As an officer in the early church: one who has charge of the alms and money of the church, an overseer of the poor and sick (Php 1:1; 1Ti 3:8, 12; 4:6; see Ac 6:1–6); also of a female who had charge of the female poor and sick (Ro 16:1). Hence the Eng. word "deacon," but in a different sense.

Deriv.: *diakonéō* (1247), to minister, adjust, regulate, set in order; *diakonía* (1248), ministry, service.

Syn.: *doúlos* (1401), a slave; *therápōn* (2324), attendant; *hupērétēs* (5257), servant; *leitourgós* (3011), a public servant, usually one serving at the temple or one who performs religious public duties; *místhios* (3407) and *misthōtós* (3411), a hired servant; *oikétēs* (3610), a household servant; *país* (3816), basically a child, but is also an attendant; *epískopos* (1985), a bishop, supervisor, one who serves as a leader in a church.

1250. διακόσιοι, diakosioi, *dee-ak-os´-ee-oy*; from 1364 and 1540; *two hundred*:—two hundred.

1251. διακούομαι, diakouomai, *dee-ak-oo´-om-ahee*; middle from 1223 and 191; to *hear throughout*, i.e. *patiently listen* (to a prisoner's plea):—hear.

1252. διακρίνω, diakrinō, *dee-ak-ree´-no*; from 1223 and 2919; to *separate thoroughly* i.e. (literal and reflexive) to *withdraw* from, or (by implication) *oppose*; (figurative) to *discriminate*, (by implication) *decide*, or (reflexive) *hesitate*:—contend, make (to) differ (-ence), discern, doubt, judge, be partial, stagger, waver.

From *diá* (1223), denoting separation, and *krínō* (2919), to distinguish, decide, judge. To separate throughout, completely. In the middle, to separate oneself:

(I) Particularly, spoken of physical separation in Jude 22: "And on some [i.e. those not Christians] have compassion, making a difference," i.e. separating yourselves from them. (TR only; for NASB, see IV, B, below.)

(II) By implication: to distinguish, make a distinction, cause to differ (Ac 15:9; 1Co 11:29); with the idea of preference or prerogative (1Co 4:7). In the middle, to make a distinction within a group, to be partial (Jas 2:4). Figuratively it means to distinguish, discern clearly, note accurately (Mt 16:3; 1Co 11:31; 14:29; 1Jn 4:1; Sept.: Job 12:11).

(III) To consider accurately, judge, decide (1Co 6:5; Sept.: Ex 18:16; 1Ki 3:9; Ps 50:4; Pr 31:9).

(IV) In the middle *diakrínomai*, to separate oneself from, i.e. to contend with. In the NT used metaphorically:

(A) To contend or strive with, dispute with (Ac 11:2; Jude 9; Sept.: Jer 15:10; Eze 20:35).

(B) To be in strife with oneself, i.e. to doubt, hesitate, waver (Mt 21:21; Mk 11:23; Ro 4:20; 14:23; Jas 1:6; Jude 22 [NASB only, following the syntax of the UBS text; for TR, see I, above]).

Deriv.: *adiákritos* (87), undistinguished, without partiality; *diákrisis* (1253), a distinguishing.

Syn.: *epagōnízomai* (1864), to contend; *diaginṓskō* (1231), to distinguish, judge; *diaphérō* (1308), to be different from or superior to; *dokimázō* (1381), to test, prove; *aporéō* (639), to be in doubt, perplexity; *diaporéomai* (1280), to be in utter perplexity; *distázō* (1365), to hesitate, to stand at a crossroad with uncertainty as to which way to take; *meteōrízō* (3349), make doubtful; *apostréphomai* (654), to withdraw; *apōthéomai* (683), to thrust oneself away.

1253. διάκρισις, diakrisis, *dee-ak´-ree-sis*; from 1252; judicial *estimation*:—discern (-ing), disputation.

Noun from *diakrínō* (1252), to distinguish, decide, judge. A distinguishing, discerning clearly, i.e. spoken of the act or power (1Co 12:10; Heb 5:14). By implication Ro 14:1, literally meaning not for scrutinizing of thoughts, i.e. not with searching out and pronouncing judgement on their opinions (cf. Ro 14:5, 13). This also could be rendered as doubts, scruples.

Syn.: *diágnōsis* (1233), diagnosis, judgement, thorough understanding; *gnṓmē* (1106), opinion.

1254. διακωλύω, diakōluō, *dee-ak-o-loo´-o*; from 1223 and 2967; to *hinder altogether*, i.e. *utterly prohibit*:—forbid.

1255. διαλαλέω, dialaleō, *dee-al-al-eh´-o*; from 1223 and 2980; to *talk throughout* a company, i.e. *converse* or (genitive) *publish*:—commune, noise abroad.

1256. διαλέγομαι, dialegomai, *dee-al-eg´-om-ahee*; middle from 1223 and 3004; to *say thoroughly*, i.e. *discuss* (in argument or exhortation):—dispute, preach (unto), reason (with), speak.

1257. διαλείπω, dialeipō, *dee-al-i´-po*; from 1223 and 3007; to *leave off in the middle*, i.e. *intermit*:—cease.

From *diá* (1223), between, and *leípō* (3007), to leave. To intermit, desist, cease; to leave an interval of space or time between (Lk 7:45; Sept.: Jer 17:8; 44:18).

Deriv.: *adiáleiptos* (88), unceasing, continual.

Syn.: *paúō* (3973), to stop, make an end, rest; *hēsucházō* (2270), to be quiet, still, at rest; *kopázō* (2869), to stop raging; *aphíēmi* (863), to let go; *katapaúō* (2664), to rest, cease.

1258. διάλεκτος, dialektos, *dee-al´-ek-tos*; from 1256; a (mode of) *discourse*, i.e. "*dialect*":—language, tongue.

1259. διαλλάσσω, diallassō, *dee-al-las´-so*; from 1223 and 236; to *change thoroughly*, i.e. (mental) to *conciliate*:—reconcile.

From *diá* (1223), denoting transition, and *allássō* (236), to change. To change one's own feelings toward, to reconcile oneself, become reconciled. In the middle voice, *diallássomai* or *dialáttomai*, to be reconciled, only in Mt 5:24.

Syn.: *eirēnopoiéō* (1517), to cause a state of peace or reconciliation between two persons.

1260. διαλογίζομαι, dialogizomai, *dee-al-og-id´-zom-ahee*; from 1223 and 3049; to *reckon thoroughly*, i.e. (genitive) to *deliberate* (by reflection or discussion):—cast in mind, consider, dispute, muse, reason, think.

From *diá* (1223), an intensive, and *logízomai* (3049), to reckon, reason. To reckon through, to settle an account. In the NT: to consider, reflect, ponder (Mt 21:25; Mk 2:6, 8; Lk 1:29; 3:15; 5:21, 22; 12:17; see Sept.: Ps 77:6; 119:59). Also, to consider together, deliberate, debate (Mt 16:7, 8; Mk 8:16, 17; Lk 20:14).

Deriv.: *dialogismós* (1261), word, account, reasoning.

Syn.: *noéō* (3539), to perceive; *katanoéō* (2657), to perceive clearly, consider carefully; *analogízomai* (357), to consider; *skopéō* (4648), to mark, consider, focus; *suníēmi* (4920), understand, put things together; *suzētéō* (4802), to discuss, examine together; *sullogízomai* (4817), to reason, compute; *dokéō* (1380), to think; *hēgéomai* (2233), to account, consider; *huponoéō* (5282), to surmise; *nomízō* (3543), to suppose; *phronéō* (5426), to think; *sōphronéō* (4993), to exercise sound mind or judgement; *krínō* (2919), to reckon, judge.

1261. διαλογισμός, dialogismos, *dee-al-og-is-mos´*; from 1260; *discussion*, i.e. (internal) *consideration* (by implication, *purpose*), or (external) *debate*:—dispute, doubtful (-ing), imagination, reasoning, thought.

Noun from *dialogízomai* (1260), to reason. Reflection, thought:

(I) Used generally (Lk 2:35; 5:22; 6:8; 9:47; Jas 2:4; Sept.: Ps 92:6; Isa 59:7; Da 2:29, 30). Reasoning, opinion (Ro 1:21; 1Co 3:20; Ro 14:1; Sept.: Ps 94:11). Mind, purpose, intention (Lk 6:8). Especially evil thoughts, purposes (Mt 15:19; Mk 7:21; Sept.: Ps 56:6, evil; Isa 59:7), doubts (Lk 24:38, doubtful thoughts, suspense).

(II) In the sense of dispute, debate, contention (Mk 9:33, 34; Lk 9:46; Php 2:14; 1Ti 2:8).

Syn.: *suzḗtēsis* (4803), a dispute, questioning; *antilogía* (485), contradiction, gainsaying; *logismós* (3053), a thought suggestive of evil intent, imagination; *enthúmēsis* (1761), deliberation, device; *epínoia* (1963), a design of the mind; *nóēma* (3540), a perception, thought; *dianóēma* (1270), a thought, plot, machination, sentiment.

1262. διαλύω, dialuō, *dee-al-oo´-o*; from 1223 and 3089; to *dissolve utterly*:—scatter.

1263. διαμαρτύρομαι, diamarturomai, *dee-am-ar-too´-rom-ahee*; from 1223 and 3140; to *attest* or *protest earnestly*, or (by implication) *hortatively*:—charge, testify (unto), witness.

From *diá* (1223), an intensive, and *martúromai* (3143), to witness, bear witness. To testify through and through, to bear full and complete witness. To admonish solemnly, to charge earnestly, to urge upon (Lk 16:28; Ac 2:40; 1Th 4:6; 1Ti 5:21; 2Ti 2:14; 4:1). Also, to testify fully, i.e. to declare fully, to teach earnestly, to enforce (Ac 8:25; 18:5; 20:21, 24; Heb 2:6).

Syn.: *diastéllomai* (1291), to admonish, literally to draw asunder; *embrimáomai* (1690), to charge strictly; *egkaléō* (1458), to accuse; *entéllomai* (1781), to command, give charge; *epitimáō* (2008), to rebuke; *paraggéllō* (3853), to command, give charge; *dierōtáō* (1331), to question so as to make sure.

1264. διαμάχομαι, diamachomai, *dee-am-akh´-om-ahee*; from 1223 and 3164; to *fight fiercely* (in altercation):—strive.

1265. διαμένω, diamenō, *dee-am-en´-o*; from 1223 and 3306; to *stay constantly* (in being or relation):—continue, remain.

1266. διαμερίζω, diamerizō, *dee-am-er-id´-zo*; from 1223 and 3307; to *partition thoroughly* (literal in distribution, figurative in dissension):—cloven, divide, part.

1267. διαμερισμός, diamerismos, *dee-am-er-is-mos´*; from 1266; *disunion* (of opinion and conduct):—division.

1268. διανέμω, dianemō, *dee-an-em´-o*; from 1223 and the base of 3551; to *distribute*, i.e. (of information) to *disseminate*:—spread.

1269. διανεύω, dianeuō, *dee-an-yoo´-o*; from 1223 and 3506; to *nod* (or *express* by signs) *across* an intervening space:—beckon.

1270. διανόημα, dianoēma, *dee-an-o´-ay-mah*; from a compound of 1223 and 3539; something *thought through*, i.e. a *sentiment*:—thought.

Noun from *dianoéomai* (n.f.), to agitate in mind, which is from *diá* (1223), denoting separation, and *noéō* (3539), to think over. Thought (Lk 11:17; Sept.: Isa 55:9).

Syn.: *enthúmēsis* (1761), an inward reasoning, generally evil surmising or supposition, device, usually imaginary; *énnoia* (1771), thoughtfulness, denoting inward intentions that involve moral understanding without any evil connotations; *logismós* (3053), the art of reckoning, reasoning; *dialogismós* (1261) refers to a more thorough reflection, thought, thinking something through; *phrónēsis* (5428), mental action or activity, intellectual insight, prudence; *phrónēma* (5427), that which one has in the mind, thought, an object of thought with a bad or good connotation.

1271. διάνοια, dianoia, *dee-an´-oy-ah*; from 1223 and 3563; *deep thought*, (properly) the faculty (*mind* or its *disposition*); (by implication) its exercise:—imagination, mind, understanding.

Noun from *dianoéomai* (n.f.), to agitate in mind, which is from *diá* (1223), denoting separation, and *noéō* (3539), to think over. Thought, mind, i.e. the power of thought:

(I) By metonymy: the mind, thoughts, intellect, i.e. the thinking faculty (Mt 22:37; Mk 12:30; Lk 10:27; Eph 1:18, only in some MSS; 4:18; Heb 8:10; 10:16 quoted from Jer 31:33; 1Pe 1:13; 2Pe 3:1; Sept.: Ge 17:17; 24:45).

(II) Intelligence, insight (1Jn 5:20; Sept.: Ex 35:25; 36:1).

(III) Mind, i.e. mode of thinking and feeling; the feelings, affections, disposition of mind (Eph 2:3; Col 1:21).

Syn.: *lógos* (3056), reason, intelligence; *phrónēma* (5427), the thought of the mind and the process of thinking and understanding; *phrónēsis* (5428), prudence; *epínoia* (1963), a thought or design for evil purposes; *nóēma* (3540), the product of the mind or thought; *dianóēma* (1270) an evil device; *enthúmēsis* (1761) a thought that involves the agitation of passion; *thumós* (2372), wrath; *logismós* (3053), the working out of the mind, imagination; *dialogismós* (1261), the results of the thorough exercise of the mind; *súnesis* (4907), discernment, understanding.

1272. διανοίγω, dianoigō, *dee-an-oy´-go*; from 1223 and 455; to *open thoroughly*, literal (as a firstborn) or figurative (to *expound*):—open.

1273. διανυκτερεύω, dianuktereuō, *dee-an-ook-ter-yoo´-o*; from 1223 and a derivative of 3571; to *sit up the whole night*:—continue all night.

1274. διανύω, dianuō, *dee-an-oo´-o*; from 1223 and **ἀνύω, *anuō*** (to *effect*); to *accomplish thoroughly*:—finish.

1275. διαπαντός, diapantos, *dee-ap-an-tos´*; from 1223 and the genitive of 3956; *through all* time, i.e. (adverb) *constantly*:—alway (-s), continually.

1276. διαπεράω, diaperaō, *dee-ap-er-ah´-o*; from 1223 and a derivative of the base of 4008; to *cross entirely*:—go over, pass (over), sail over.

1277. διαπλέω, diapleō, *dee-ap-leh´-o*; from 1223 and 4126; to *sail through*:—sail over.

1278. διαπονέω, diaponeō, *dee-ap-on-eh´-o*; from 1223 and a derivative of 4192; to *toil through*, i.e. (passive) *be worried*:—be grieved.

1279. διαπορεύομαι, diaporeuomai, *dee-ap-or-yoo´-om-ahee*; from 1223 and 4198; to *travel through*:—go through, journey in, pass by.

1280. διαπορέω, diaporeō, *dee-ap-or-eh´-o*; from 1223 and 639; to *be thoroughly nonplussed*:—(be in) doubt, be (much) perplexed.

1281. διαπραγματεύομαι, diapragmateuomai, *dee-ap-rag-mat-yoo´-om-ahee*; from 1223 and 4231; to *thoroughly occupy oneself*, i.e. (transitive and by implication) to *earn* in business:—gain by trading.

1282. διαπρίω, diapriō, *dee-ap-ree´-o*; from 1223 and the base of 4249; to *saw asunder*, i.e. (figurative) to *exasperate*:—cut (to the heart).

1283. διαρπάζω, diarpazō, *dee-ar-pad´-zo*; from 1223 and 726; to *seize asunder*, i.e. *plunder*:—spoil.

1284. διαῤῥήσσω, diarrhēssō, *dee-ar-hrayce´-so*; from 1223 and 4486; to *tear asunder*:—break, rend.

1285. διασαφέω, diasapheō, *dee-as-af-eh´-o*; from 1223 and **σαφής, *saphēs*** (*clear*); to *clear thoroughly*, i.e. (figurative) *declare*:—tell unto.

1286. διασείω, diaseiō, *dee-as-i´-o*; from 1223 and 4579; to *shake thoroughly*, i.e. (figurative) to *intimidate*:—do violence to.

1287. διασκορπίζω, diaskorpizō, *dee-as-kor-pid´-zo*; from 1223 and 4650; to *dissipate*, i.e. (genitive) to *rout* or *separate*; special to *winnow*; (figurative) to *squander*:—disperse, scatter (abroad), strew, waste.

1288. δεασπάω, deaspaō, *dee-as-pah´-o*; from 1223 and 4685; to *draw apart*, i.e. *sever* or *dismember*:—pluck asunder, pull in pieces.

1289. διασπείρω, diaspeirō, *dee-as-pi´-ro*; from 1223 and 4687; to *sow throughout*, i.e. (figurative) *distribute* in foreign lands:—scatter abroad.

1290. διασπορά, diaspora, *dee-as-por-ah´*; from 1289; *dispersion*, i.e. (special and concrete) the (converted) Israelite *resident* in Gentile countries:—(which are) scattered (abroad).

1291. διαστέλλομαι, diastellomai, *dee-as-tel´-lom-ahee*; middle from 1223 and 4724; to *set* (oneself) *apart* (figurative, *distinguish*), i.e. (by implication) to *enjoin*:—charge, that which was (give) commanded (-ment).

1292. διάστημα, diastēma, *dee-as´-tay-mah*; from 1339; an *interval*:—space.

1293. διαστολή, diastolē, *dee-as-tol-ay´*; from 1291; a *variation*:—difference, distinction.

1294. διαστρέφω, diastrephō, *dee-as-tref´-o*; from 1223 and 4762; to *distort*, i.e. (figurative) *misinterpret*, or (moral) *corrupt*:—perverse (-rt), turn away.

1295. διασώζω, diasōzō, *dee-as-odze´-o*; from 1223 and 4982; to *save thoroughly*, i.e. (by implication or analogy) to *cure, preserve, rescue*, etc.:—bring safe, escape (safe), heal, make perfectly whole, save.

From *diá* (1223), through, and *sṓzō* (4982), to save. To save through, to bring safely through danger or sickness; to preserve (Ac 27:43; 28:1, 4; 1Pe 3:20; Sept.: Nu 10:9; Dt 20:4; Job 29:12; Da 11:41). With the idea of motion, to bring safely through to any place or person; in the pass., to come to or reach safely (Ac 23:24; 27:44; Sept.: Ge 19:19; Isa 37:38). Of the sick, to bring safely through, to heal (Mt 14:36; Lk 7:3; Sept.: Jer 8:20).

Syn.: *exairéomai* (1807), to rescue; *diaphulássō* (1314), to protect; *rhúomai* (4506) to rescue; *peripoiéomai* (4046), to preserve; *therapeúō* (2323), to care for the sick, heal; *iáomai* (2390), to heal.

1296. διαταγή, diatagē, *dee-at-ag-ay´*; from 1299; *arrangement*, i.e. *institution*:—instrumentality.

Noun from *diatássō* (1299), to appoint. An ordering of things, a disposition, ordinance, arrangement:

(I) Particularly, referring to the dispositions or arrangements of angels (Ac 7:53, cf. Gal 3:19; Heb 2:2). The OT makes no mention of angels at the giving of the Law (Ex 20:1, 19, 22), but the above passages of the NT assume their instrumentality, in accordance also with Jewish tradition (Sept.: Dt 33:2).

(II) In the sense of ordinance, institute (Ro 13:2; Sept.: Ezr 4:11).

Syn.: *diátagma* (1297), an arrangement, edict, mandate, the result of *diatagḗ*.

1297. διάταγμα, diatagma, *dee-at´-ag-mah*; from 1299; an *arrangement*, i.e. (authoritative) *edict*:—commandment.

Noun from *diatássō* (1299), to command, arrange in its proper order. Ordinance, mandate, edict. Only in Heb 11:23; Sept.: Ezr 7:11.

1298. διαταράσσω, diatarassō, *dee-at-ar-as´-so*; from 1223 and 5015; to *disturb wholly*, i.e. *agitate* (with alarm):—trouble.

1299. διατάσσω, diatassō, *dee-at-as´-so*; from 1223 and 5021; to *arrange thoroughly*, i.e. (special) *institute, prescribe*, etc.:—appoint, command, give, (set in) order, ordain.

From *diá* (1223), through, and *tássō* (5021), to appoint, order. To arrange throughout, to place in order, as troops. In the NT, used figuratively: to set fully in order, to arrange, to appoint, to ordain (Gal 3:19). Also in the sense of to direct, to prescribe, to order (Mt 11:1; Lk 8:55; Ac 18:2; 1Co 9:14; 16:1).

Deriv.: *diatagḗ* (1296), an ordinance; *diátagma* (1297), that which is imposed by decree or law; *epidiatássomai* (1928), to arrange, appoint.

1300. διατελέω, diateleō, *dee-at-el-eh´-o*; from 1223 and 5055; to *accomplish thoroughly*, i.e. (subject) to *persist*:—continue.

1301. διατηρέω, diatēreō, *dee-at-ay-reh´-o*; from 1223 and 5083; to *watch thoroughly*, i.e. (positive and transitive) to *observe* strictly, or (negative and reflexive) to *avoid* wholly:—keep.

From *diá* (1223), an intensive, and *tēréō* (5083), to guard, watch. To watch carefully, keep with care. In the NT, used figuratively: to guard with care, to lay up, to retain (Lk 2:51; Sept.: Ge 37:11); to guard or keep oneself from something, to abstain from something (Ac 15:29).

Syn.: *phulássō* (5442), to guard; *diaphulássō* (1314), guard thoroughly or carefully; *phrouréō* (5432), to keep as if with a military guard; *kratéō* (2902), to hold fast.

1302. διατί, diati, *dee-at-ee´*; from 1223 and 5101; *through what* cause?, i.e. *why?*:—wherefore, why.

1303. διατίθεμαι, diatithemai, *dee-at-ith´-em-ahee*; middle from 1223 and 5087; to *put apart*, i.e. (figurative) *dispose* (by assignment, compact or bequest):—appoint, make, testator.

From *diá* (1223), an intensive, and *títhēmi* (5087), to place. To set out in order, to arrange. In the NT, used only in the middle: to arrange in one's own behalf.

(I) Generally: to appoint, to make over (Lk 22:29); so of a testamentary disposition: to devise, to bequeath by will, hence used of a testator, i.e. the one making the will (Heb 9:16, 17).

(II) Spoken of a covenant: to make an arrangement with, to institute or make a covenant with (Ac 3:25; Heb 8:10; 10:16; Sept.: Dt 5:3; Jos 9:6, 7; 2Sa 3:13).

Deriv.: *antidiatithēmi* (475), to set oneself opposite; *diathḗkē* (1242), a contract, covenant.

Syn.: *protíthemai* (4388), to propose, purpose; *skopéō* (4648), to aim, look at, mark; *apoblépō* (578), to intensely regard; *atenízō* (816), to set eyes on; *bouleúomai* (1011), to purpose; *thélō* (2309), to will; *logízomai* (3049), to reckon; *proorízō* (4309), to determine before.

1304. διατρίβω, diatribō, *dee-at-ree´-bo*; from 1223 and the base of 5147; to *wear through* (time), i.e. *remain*:—abide, be, continue, tarry.

1305. διατροφή, diatrophē, *dee-at-rof-ay´*; from a compound of 1223 and 5142; *nourishment*:—food.

1306. διαυγάζω, diaugazō, *dee-ow-gad´-zo*; from 1223 and 826; to *glimmer through*, i.e. *break* (as day):—dawn.

1307. διαφανής, diaphanēs, *dee-af-an-ace´*; from 1223 and 5316; *appearing through*, i.e. "*diapha-nous*":—transparent.

1308. διαφέρω, diapherō, *dee-af-er´-o*; from 1223 and 5342; to *bear through*, i.e. (literal) *transport*; usually to *bear apart*, i.e. (objective) to *toss about* (figurative) *report*; subject to "*differ*," or (by implication) *surpass*:—be better, carry, differ from, drive up and down, be (more) excellent, make matter, publish, be of more value.

1309. διαφεύγω, diapheugō, *dee-af-yoo´-go*; from 1223 and 5343; to *flee through*, i.e. *escape*:—escape.

1310. διαφημίζω, diaphēmizō, *dee-af-ay-mid´-zo*; from 1223 and a derivative of 5345; to *report thoroughly*, i.e. *divulgate*:—blaze abroad, commonly report, spread abroad, fame.

1311. διαφθείρω, diaphtheirō, *dee-af-thi´-ro*; from 1225 and 5351; to *rot thoroughly*, i.e. (by implication) to *ruin* (passive, *decay* utterly, figurative, *pervert*):—corrupt, destroy, perish.

1312. διαφθορά, diaphthora, *dee-af-thor-ah´*; from 1311; *decay*:—corruption.

1313. διάφορος, diaphoros, *dee-af´-or-os*; from 1308; *varying*; also *surpassing*:—differing, divers, more excellent.

1314. διαφυλάσσω, diaphulassō, *dee-af-oo-las´-so*; from 1223 and 5442; to *guard thoroughly*, i.e. *protect*:—keep.

1315. διαχειρίζομαι, diacheirizomai, *dee-akh-i-rid´-zom-ahee*; from 1223 and a derivative of 5495; to *handle thoroughly*, i.e. *lay* violent *hands* upon:—kill, slay.

1316. διαχωρίζομαι, diachōrizomai, *dee-akh-o-rid´-zom-ahee*; from 1223 and the middle of 5563; to *remove* (oneself) *wholly*, i.e. *retire*:—depart.

1317. διδακτικός, didaktikos, *did-ak-tik-os´*; from 1318; *instructive* ("didactic"):—apt to teach.

Adjective from *didáskō* (1321), to teach. Didactic, able to communicate Christian teaching, apt or skilled in teaching (1Ti 3:2; 2Ti 2:24).

1318. διδακτός, didaktos, *did-ak-tos´*; from 1321; (subject) *instructed* or (object) *communicated* by teaching:—taught, which … teacheth.

1319. διδασκαλία, didaskalia, *did-as-kal-ee´-ah*; from 1320; *instruction* (the function or the information):—doctrine, learning, teaching.

Noun from *didáskō* (1321), to teach. Teaching or instruction:

(I) The art or manner of teaching (Ro 12:7; 1Ti 4:13, 16; 5:17; Tit 2:7). With the sense of warning or admonition (Ro 15:4; 2Ti 3:16 [cf. 1Co 10:11]).

(II) The thing taught, instruction, precept, doctrine: as coming from men, perverse (Mt 15:9; Mk 7:7; Eph 4:14; Col 2:22; 1Ti 4:1; Sept.: Isa 29:13); from God: divine teaching (1Ti 1:10; 4:6; 6:1, 3; 2Ti 3:10; 4:3; Tit 1:9; 2:1, 10).

Syn.: *paideía* (3809), education or training; *kḗrugma* (2782), preaching; *lógos* (3056), word, speech, utterance, doctrine, precept, teaching; *parádosis* (3862), delivery, the act of delivering over from one to another, that delivery being in some instances instruction, teaching, precept, ordinance.

1320. διδάσκαλος, didaskalos, *did-as´-kal-os*; from 1321; an *instructor* (genitive or special):—doctor, master, teacher.

Noun from *didáskō* (1321), to teach. Instructor, master, teacher (Ro 2:20; Heb 5:12). So of Jewish doctors or lawyers (Mt 9:11; 10:24, 25; Lk 2:46; 6:40; Jn 3:10); hence equivalent to the title Rabbi (Jn 1:38; 20:16). Spoken of John the Baptist (Lk 3:12); of Jesus (Mt 8:19; 12:38; 17:24; Mk 5:35; 14:14; Jn 11:28); of the apostle Paul (1Ti 2:7); and of other Christian teachers (1Co 12:28, 29).

Deriv.: *heterodidaskaléō* (2085), to teach another doctrine; *kalodidáskalos* (2567), good teacher or teacher of good things; *nomo-*

didáskalos (3547), an expounder or teacher of the Jewish law; *pseudodidáskalos* (5572), a false teacher.

1321. διδάσκω, didaskō, *did-as´-ko*; a prolonged (causative) form of a primary verb **δάω, *daō*** (to *learn*); to *teach* (in the same broad application):—teach.

From *dáō* (n.f.), to know or teach. To teach, instruct:

(I) Generally and in an absolute sense (Mt 4:23; 5:2; 9:35; Mk 1:21; 9:31; Lk 4:15; Jn 7:35; 1Co 4:17; 11:14; Eph 4:21; 1Ti 4:11; Tit 1:11; Heb 5:12; 1Jn 2:27).

(II) In the sense of to tutor, to direct, to advise, to put in mind (Mt 28:15; Jn 9:34; Ac 21:21; Heb 8:11; Rev 2:20).

Deriv.: *didaktikós* (1317), instructive, didactic, skilled in teaching, communicative; *didaktós* (1318), capable of being taught, instructed; *didaskalía* (1319), instruction, teaching, either the manner of teaching or the content of teaching; *didáskalos* (1320), a teacher; *didachḗ* (1322), doctrine, instruction, the act or content of teaching which depends on the context in which it is found; *theodídaktos* (2312), taught by God.

Syn.: *paideúō* (3811), to instruct with discipline; *katēchéō* (2727), to teach orally, the word from which we derive our Eng. "catechize" and "catechism" which is religious instruction; *mathēteúō* (3100), to disciple, teach with the expectation of one's learning and appropriating; *muéō* (3453), to initiate into certain mysteries, learn a secret.

1322. διδαχή, didachē, *did-akh-ay´*; from 1321; *instruction* (the act or the matter):—doctrine, hath been taught.

Noun from *didáskō* (1321), to teach. The act of teaching, instructing, tutoring (Mk 4:2; 12:38; 1Co 14:6, 26; 2Ti 4:2); the manner or character of one's teaching (Mt 7:28; 22:33; Mk 1:22, 27; 11:18; Lk 4:32); the things taught, precept, doctrine (Mt 16:12; Jn 7:16, 17; Ac 17:19; Ro 6:17; Heb 6:2; 13:9).

Syn.: *lógos* (3056), word, doctrine or a discourse.

1323. δίδραχμον, didrachmon, *did´-rakh-mon*; from 1364 and 1406; a *double drachma* (*didrachm*):—tribute.

1324. Δίδυμος, Didumos, *did´-oo-mos*; prolonged from 1364; *double*, i.e. *twin; Didymus*, a Christian:—Didymus.

1325. δίδωμι, didōmi, *did´-o-mee*; a prolonged form of a primary verb (which is used as an alternative in most of the tenses); to *give* (used in a very wide application, properly or by implication, literal or figurative; greatly modified by the connection):—adventure, bestow, bring forth, commit, deliver (up), give, grant, hinder, make, minister, number, offer, have power, put, receive, set, shew, smite (+ with the hand), strike (+ with the palm of the hand), suffer, take, utter, yield.

1326. διεγείρω, diegeirō, *dee-eg-i´-ro*; from 1223 and 1453; to *wake fully*, i.e. *arouse* (literal or figurative):—arise, awake, raise, stir up.

1327. διέξοδος, diexodos, *dee-ex´-od-os*; from 1223 and 1841; an *outlet through*, i.e. probably an open *square* (from which roads diverge):—highway.

1328. διερμηνευτής, diermēneutēs, *dee-er-main-yoo-tace´*; from 1329; an *explainer*:—interpreter.

1329. διερμηνεύω, diermēneuō, *dee-er-main-yoo´-o*; from 1223 and 2059; to *explain thoroughly*; (by implication) to *translate*:—expound, interpret (-ation).

1330. διέρχομαι, dierchomai, *dee-er´-khom-ahee*; from 1223 and 2064; to *traverse* (literal):—come, depart, go (about, abroad, everywhere, over, through, throughout), pass (by, over, through, throughout), pierce through, travel, walk through.

1331. διερωτάω, dierōtaō, *dee-er-o-tah´-o*; from 1223 and 2065; to *question throughout*, i.e. *ascertain* by interrogation:—make enquiry for.

1332. διετής, dietēs, *dee-et-ace´*; from 1364 and 2094; *of two years* (in age):—two years old.

1333. διετία, dietia, *dee-et-ee´-a*; from 1332; a space of *two years* (*biennium*):—two years.

1334. διηγέομαι, diēgeomai, *dee-ayg-eh´-om-ahee*; from 1223 and 2233; to *relate fully*:—declare, shew, tell.

From *diá* (1223), through or an intensive, and *hēgéomai* (2233), to lead. To lead or conduct through to the end. To recount, tell, relate in full (Mk 5:16; 9:9; Lk 8:39; 9:10; Ac 8:33 [quoted from Isa 53:8]; 9:27; 12:17; Heb 11:32).

Deriv.: *diḗgēsis* (1335), a narrative and not a declaration; *ekdiēgéomai* (1555), to recount, rehearse or relate particularly.

Syn.: *anaggéllō* (312), to announce, report; *apaggéllō* (518), to announce or report from a person or place, declare; *diaggéllō* (1229), to announce thoroughly, declare fully; *kataggéllō* (2605), to proclaim; *dēlóō* (1213), to make plain, declare; *phrázō* (5419), to declare; *gnōrízō* (1107), to make known; *emphanízō* (1718), to declare plainly; *phaneróō* (5319), to manifest; *anatíthemai* (394), to declare, communicate; *mēnúō* (3377), to disclose something before unknown; *exaggéllō* (1804), to tell out, proclaim abroad; *légō* (3004), to tell; *megalúnō* (3170), to magnify; *exēgéomai* (1834), to declare by making plain; *diasaphéō*, (1285) to make clear.

1335. διήγεσις, diēgesis, *dee-ayg´-es-is*; from 1334; a *recital*:—declaration.

1336. διηνεκές, diēnekes, *dee-ah-nek-es´*; neuter of a compound of 1223 and a derivative of an alternate of 5342; *carried through*, i.e. (adverb with 1519 and 3588 prefix) *perpetually*:—+ continually, for ever.

1337. διθάλασσος, dithalassos, *dee-thal´-as-sos*; from 1364 and 2281; *having two seas*, i.e. a *sound* with a double outlet:—where two seas meet.

1338. διϊκνέομαι, diïkneomai, *dee-ik-neh´-om-ahee*; from 1223 and the base of 2425; to *reach through*, i.e. *penetrate*:—pierce.

1339. διΐστημε, diïstēme, *dee-is´-tay-mee*; from 1223 and 2476; to *stand apart*, i.e. (reflex.) to *remove, intervene*:—go further, be parted, after the space of.

1340. διϊσχυρίζομαι, diïschurizomai, *dee-is-khoo-rid´-zom-ahee*; from 1223 and a derivative of 2478; to *stout* it *through*, i.e. *asseverate*:—confidently (constantly) affirm.

1341. δικαιοκρισία, dikaiokrisia, *dik-ah-yok-ris-ee´-ah*; from 1342 and 2920; a *just sentence*:—righteous judgement.

Noun from *díkaios* (1342), just, righteous, and *krísis* (2920), judgement. Righteous judgement (Ro 2:5 [cf. Hos 6:5; 2Th 1:5]).

1342. δίκαιος, dikaios, *dik´-ah-yos*; from 1349; *equitable* (in character or act); (by implication) *innocent, holy* (absolute or relative):—just, meet, right (-eous).

Adjective from *díkē* (1349), right, just. Right, just, i.e. physically: like, even, equal, e.g., numbers. Also just as it should be, i.e. fit, proper, good. Hence usually and in the NT, in a moral sense: righteous, just; spoken:

(I) Of one who acts alike to all, who practices even-handed justice: just, equitable, impartial. Spoken of God (2Ti 4:8; Rev 16:5); of a judgement or decision (Jn 5:30; 7:24; Lk 12:57; 2Th 1:5, 6; Rev 16:7; 19:2; Sept.: Jer 42:5; Ps 12:2).

(II) Of character, conduct: just as it should be, i.e. upright, righteous, virtuous. Also, good in a general sense; however, *ho díkaios* is strictly one who does right, while *ho agathós* (18) is one who does good, a benefactor.

(A) Spoken of things righteous, just (Ro 7:12; 1Jn 3:12); what is right, proper (Mt 20:4, 7; Col 4:1).

(B) Spoken of persons: **(1)** In the usage of common life (Mt 5:45; Mk 2:17; Lk 5:32; 18:9; 20:20; Ac 10:22; Ro 5:7; 2Pe 2:7, 8); including the idea of innocent (Mt 27:19, 24); including the idea of mild, clement, kind (Mt 1:19; 1Jn 1:9). **(2)** Especially of those whose hearts are right with God: righteous, pious, godly (Mt 13:43; 23:29; 25:46; Mk 6:20; Lk 14:14; Ro 2:13; 3:10). **(3)** Spoken in the highest and most perfect sense of God (Jn 17:25; Ro 3:26; 1Jn 2:29); of Christ (Ac 3:14; 7:52; 1Jn 2:1; 3:7; Sept.: Ex 9:27; Dt 32:4; Ezr 9:15).

Deriv.: *dikaiokrisía* (1341), righteous judgement; *dikaiosúnē* (1343), righteousness; *dikaióō* (1344), to justify; *dikaíōs* (1346), justly.

Syn.: *agathós* (18), good; *hágios* (40), holy in the sense of blameless in character; *hósios* (3741), sacred, the performer of the ordinances. See *dikaiosúnē* (1343), righteousness, and *euthús* (2117), straight, true.

1343. δικαιοσύνη, dikaiosunē, *dik-ah-yos-oo´-nay*; from 1342; *equity* (of character or act); specially (Christian) *justification*:—righteousness.

Noun from *díkaios* (1342), just, righteous. Justice, righteousness:

(I) Doing alike to all, justice, equity, impartiality; spoken of a judge (Ac 17:31; Heb 11:33; Rev 19:11).

(II) Of character, conduct, etc.: being just as one should be, i.e. rectitude, uprightness, righteousness, virtue; equivalent to the adj. *díkaios* (1342), just, righteous.

(A) Of actions, duties, equivalent to *tó díkaion*, what is right, proper, fit (Mt 3:15).

(B) Of disposition or conduct in common life (Eph 5:9; 2Ti 6:11; 2Ti 2:22; Heb 1:9; 7:2; Rev 19:11; Sept.: 1Sa 26:23; Job 29:14; Ps 15:2; 50:6; Pr 8:18, 20). Including the idea of kindness, graciousness, liberality (2Co 9:9, 10; 2Pe 1:1 [cf. *díkaios*, just, righteous]).

(C) Spoken of that righteousness which has regard to God and the divine law: **(1)** Merely external, consisting of the observance of external precepts (Php 3:6). **(2)** Internal, where the heart is right with God, piety toward God, and hence righteousness, godliness (Mt 5:6, 10, 20; 6:33; 21:32; Lk 1:75; Ac 10:35; 24:25; Ro 6:16, 18f.; Heb 1:9; 5:13; Jas 3:18; Sept.: Ge 18:19; 1Ki 3:6; Ps 17:15; Eze 14:14). So used in the expression "to count or impute as righteousness," i.e. to regard as evidence of piety (Ro 4:3, 5, 6, 9, 22; Gal 3:6; Jas 2:23, all quoted from Ge 15:6). Spoken of the righteousness which is of (*ek* [1537], out of) or through (*diá* [1223]) faith in Christ, i.e. where faith is counted or imputed as righteousness or as evidence of piety (Ro 9:30; 10:6; Php 3:9; Heb 11:7); of Christ as the source or author of righteousness (1Co 1:30); of the righteousness of God, i.e. the righteousness which God approves, requires, bestows (Ro 1:17; 3:21, 22, 25, 26). Those on whom God bestows His righteousness become righteous before God (2Co 5:21; Sept.: Ps 5:8). **(3)** In the highest and most perfect sense, of God subjectively, i.e. as an attribute of His character (Ro 3:5); of Christ (Jn 16:8, 10).

(III) By metonymy, in the sense of being regarded as just, i.e. imputation of righteousness, justification, *dikaíōsis* (1347) being the act of justification (Ro 5:17, 21; 10:4, 5; 2Co 3:9).

Syn.: *euthútēs* (2118), rectitude, righteousness.

1344. δικαιόω, dikaioō, *dik-ah-yo´-o*; from 1342; to *render* (i.e. *show* or *regard* as) *just* or *innocent*:—free, justify (-ier), be righteous.

From *díkaios* (1342), just, righteous. To justify, i.e. to regard as just, to declare one to be just:

(I) As a matter of right or justice: to absolve, acquit, clear from any charge or imputation. (Mt 12:37; 1Co 4:4; Ac 13:39; Ro 6:7; Sept.: Ex 23:7; Dt 25:1; 1Ki 8:32). With *eautón* (*eautoú* [1438], oneself), to justify oneself, to excuse oneself (Lk 10:29).

(II) Spoken of character: to declare to be just as one should be, to pronounce right; of things, to regard as right and proper. In the NT, used only of persons: to acknowledge and declare anyone to be righteous, virtuous, good:

(A) By implication, to vindicate, approve, honour, glorify, and in the pass. to receive honour (Mt 11:19; Lk 7:29, 35; 1Ti 3:16).

(B) In relation to God and the divine Law: to declare righteous, to regard as pious. Spoken of the Pharisees, those who "justify themselves before men," i.e. those who profess themselves righteous and pious before men (Lk 16:15). Spoken especially of the justification bestowed by God on men through Christ, in which he is said to regard and treat them as righteous, i.e. to absolve from the consequences of sin and admit to the enjoyment of the divine favour (Ro 3:26, 30; 4:5; 8:30, 33; Gal 3:8). So in the pass.: to be justified (Ro 3:20, 24, 28; Gal 2:16; 3:11; Jas 2:21, 24, 25).

(III) In the sense of to make or cause to be upright. In the middle, to make oneself upright, i.e. to be upright, virtuous (Rev 22:11).

Deriv.: *dikaíōma* (1345), judgement, ordinance; *dikaíōsis* (1347), justification.

Syn.: *aphíēmi* (863), to forgive; *charízomai* (5483), to pardon; *charitóō* (5487), to supply with grace, make acceptable; *apallássō* (525), to deliver in a legal sense from the claims of an opponent; *lutróō* (3084), to redeem by paying ransom; *lúō* (3089), to loose, let go, and the compound *apolúō* (630), to dismiss, forgive, set at liberty; *rhúomai* (4506), to rescue. For further syn., see *dikaiosúnē* (1343), righteousness.

1345. δικαίωμα, dikaiōma, *dik-ah´-yo-mah*; from 1344; an *equitable deed*; (by implication) a *statute* or *decision*:—judgement, justification, ordinance, righteousness.

Noun from *dikaióō* (1344), to justify. Anything justly or rightly done, hence right, justice, equity:

(I) Spoken of a doing right or justice to someone, in a favourable sense: justification, acquittal (Ro 5:16); in an unfavourable sense: condemnation, judgement (Rev 15:4).

(II) Generally: a decree, as defining and establishing what is right and just, i.e. precept, law, ordinance (Lk 1:6; Ro 1:32; 2:26; 8:4; Heb 9:1, 10).

(III) Spoken of character: righteousness, virtue, piety toward God, e.g., of saints (Rev 19:8); of Christ, as manifested in his obedience (Ro 5:18).

Syn.: *diatagḗ* (1296), ordinance; *dógma* (1378), decree.

1346. δικαίως, dikaiōs, *dik-ah´-yoce*; adverb from 1342; *equitably*:—justly, (to) righteously (-ness).

Adverb from *díkaios* (1342), just. Justly, rightly (1Pe 2:23; Sept.: Dt 1:16; Pr 31:9); righteously, piously (1Th 2:10; Tit 2:12); with strict justice (Lk 23:41); as it is fit, proper, right (1Co 15:34).

Syn.: *euthéōs* (2112), straightly; *orthṓs* (3723), rightly.

1347. δικαίωσις, dikaiōsis, *dik-ah´-yo-sis*; from 1344; *acquittal* (for Christ's sake):—justification.

From *dikaióō* (1344), to justify. Justification, which God bestows on men through Christ (Ro 4:25; 5:18).

Syn.: *áphesis* (859), remission; *lútrōsis* (3085), redemption, deliverance from the guilt and power of sin; *apolútrōsis* (629), a releasing on payment of ransom; *hilastḗrion* (2435), propitiation; *hilasmós* (2434), expiation; *sōtēría* (4991), salvation.

1348. δικαστής, dikastēs, *dik-as-tace´*; from a derivative of 1349; a *judger*:—judge.

Noun from *dikázō* (n.f.), to give judgement, which is from *díkē* (1349), justice. A judge (Lk 12:14; Ac 7:27, 35; Sept.: Ex 2:14; 1Sa 8:1).

1349. δίκη, dikē, *dee´-kay*; probably from 1166; *right* (as self-*evident*), i.e. *justice* (the principle, a decision, or its execution):—judgement, punish, vengeance.

A noun meaning judgement, sentence, implying punishment (Ac 25:15 [TR]; 2Th 1:9; Jude 7). Justice, personified as *Díkē*, the daughter of the mythological Greek god Zeus and goddess Themis (Ac 28:4).

Deriv.: *ádikos* (94), unjust or unrighteous; *antídikos* (476), an opponent, adversary; *díkaios* (1342), just; *ékdikos* (1558), a punisher or one who carries out the verdict of an issue, an avenger; *éndikos* (1738), one who acts within his rights, fair, just; *hupódikos* (5267), under sentence, one who comes under judgement.

1350. δίκτυον, diktuon, *dik´-too-on*; probably from a primary verb **δίκω,** *dikō* (to *cast*); a *seine* (for fishing):—net.

A noun meaning net, a fish-net (Mt 4:20, 21; Mk 1:18, 19; Lk 5:2, 4–6; Jn 21:6, 8, 11).

1351. δίλογος, dilogos, *dil´-og-os*; from 1364 and 3056; *equivocal*, i.e. telling a different story:—double-tongued.

1352. διό, dio, *dee-o´*; from 1223 and 3739; *through which* thing, i.e. *consequently*:—for which cause, therefore, wherefore.

1353. διοδεύω, diodeuō, *dee-od-yoo´-o*; from 1223 and 3593; to *travel through*:—go throughout, pass through.

1354. Διονύσιος, Dionusios, *dee-on-oo´-see-os*; from **Διόνυσος,** ***Dionusos*** (*Bacchus*); *reveller*; *Dionysius*, an Athenian:—Dionysius.

1355. διόπερ, dioper, *dee-op´-er*; from 1352 and 4007; *on which very account*:—wherefore.

1356. διοπετής, diopetēs, *dee-op-et-ace´*; from the alternate of 2203 and the alternate of 4098; *sky-fallen* (i.e. an *aerolite*):—which fell down from Jupiter.

1357. διόρθωσις, diorthōsis, *dee-or´-tho-sis*; from a compound of 1223 and a derivative of 3717, meaning to *straighten thoroughly; rectification*, i.e. (special) the Messianic *restauration*:—reformation.

Noun from *diorthóō* (n.f.), to correct, amend. Amendment, correction, reformation, only in Heb 9:10, the time of a new and better dispensation under the Messiah.

Syn.: *táxis* (5010), order; *euprépeia* (2143), good suitableness.

1358. διορύσσω, diorussō, *dee-or-oos´-so*; from 1223 and 3736; to *penetrate* burglariously:—break through (up).

1359. Διόσκουροι, Dioskouroi, *dee-os´-koo-roy*; from the alternate of 2203 and a form of the base of 2877; *sons of Jupiter*, i.e. the twins *Dioscuri*:—Castor and Pollux.

1360. διότι, dioti, *dee-ot´-ee*; from 1223 and 3754; *on the very account that*, or *inasmuch as*:—because (that), for, therefore.

1361. Διοτρεφής, Diotrephēs, *dee-ot-ref-ace´*; from the alternate of 2203 and 5142; *Jove-nourished; Diotrephes*, an opponent of Christianity:—Diotrephes.

1362. διπλοῦς, diplous, *dip-looce´*; from 1364 and (probably) the base of 4119; *two-fold*:—double, two-fold more.

1363. διπλόω, diploō, *dip-lo´-o*; from 1362; to *render two-fold*:—double.

1364. δίς, dis, *dece*; adverb from 1417; *twice*:—again, twice.

1365. διστάζω, distazō, *dis-tad´-zo*; from 1364; properly to *duplicate*, i.e. (mental) to *waver* (in opinion):—doubt.

1366. δίστομος, distomos, *dis´-tom-os*; from 1364 and 4750; *double-edged*:—with two edges, two-edged.

1367. δισχίλιοι, dischilïoi, *dis-khil´-ee-oy*; from 1364 and 5507; *two thousand*:—two thousand.

1368. διϋλίζω, diulizō, *dee-oo-lid´-zo*; from 1223 and **ὑλίζω, hulizō,** *hoo-lid´-zo* (to *filter*); to *strain out*:—strain at [*probably by misprint*].

1369. διχάζω, dichazō, *dee-khad´-zo*; from a derivative of 1364; to *make apart*, i.e. *sunder* (figurative) *alienate*:—set at variance.

1370. διχοστασία, dichostasia, *dee-khos-tas-ee´-ah*; from a derivative of 1364 and 4714; *disunion*, i.e. (figurative) *dissension*:—division, sedition.

Noun from *dícha* (n.f.), separately, and *stásis* (4714), dissension. Dissention, discord (Ro 16:17; 1Co 3:3; Gal 5:20).

Syn.: *diamerismós* (1267), dissension, division, discord; *schísma* (4978), schism, division, tearing apart; *haíresis* (139), heresy, disunion; *merismós* (3311), a division, partition, separation.

1371. διχοτομέω, dichotomeō, *dee-khot-om-eh´-o*; from a compound of a derivative of 1364 and a derivative of **τέμνω, temnō** (to *cut*); to *bisect*, i.e. (by extension) to *flog* severely:—cut asunder (in sunder).

1372. διψάω, dipsaō, *dip-sah´-o*; from a variation of 1373; to *thirst* for (literal or figurative):—(be, be a-) thirst (-y).

1373. δίψος, dipsos, *dip´-sos*; of uncertain affinity; *thirst*:—thirst.

1374. δίψυχος, dipsuchos, *dip´-soo-khos*; from 1364 and 5590; *two-spirited*, i.e. *vacillating* (in opinion or purpose):—double minded.

Adjective from *dís* (1364), twice, and *psuchḗ* (5590), soul, mind. Double-minded, inconstant, wavering (Jas 1:8; 4:8).

Syn.: *akatástatos* (182), unstable.

1375. διωγμός, diōgmos, *dee-ogue-mos´*; from 1377; *persecution*:—persecution.

1376. διώκτης, diōktēs, *dee-oke´-tace*; from 1377; a *persecutor*:—persecutor.

1377. διώκω, diōkō, *dee-o´-ko*; a prolonged (and causative) form of a primary verb **δίω, diō** (to *flee*; compare the base of 1169 and 1249); to *pursue* (literal or figurative); (by implication) to *persecute*:—ensue, follow (after), given to, (suffer) persecute (-ion), press forward.

1378. δόγμα, dogma, *dog´-mah*; from the base of 1380; a *law* (civil, ceremonial or ecclesiastical):—decree, ordinance.

Noun from *dokéō* (1380), to think. A decree, edict, ordinance, e.g., of a prince (Lk 2:1; Ac 17:7); of the apostles (Ac 16:4); of the Mosaic Law, i.e. external precepts (Eph 2:15; Col 2:14; Sept.: Da 2:13; 3:10; 6:8, 13, 15).

Deriv.: *dogmatízō* (1379), to decree.

Syn.: *diatagḗ* (1296), ordinance; *parádosis* (3862), tradition, that which has been handed down; *archḗ* (746), principle; *kanṓn* (2583), rule, canon; *nómos* (3551), law; *alḗtheia* (225), truth; *pístis* (4102), faith.

1379. δογματίζω, dogmatizō, *dog-mat-id´-zo*; from 1378; to *prescribe* by statute, i.e. (reflexive) to *submit to* ceremonial *rule*:—be subject to ordinances.

From *dógma* (1378), decree, ordinance. To make a decree, to prescribe an ordinance. In the middle voice, *dogmatízomai*, to let oneself fall into a certain order, subject oneself to ordinances (Col 2:20).

Syn.: *kuróō* (2964), to ratify, confirm.

1380. δοκέω, dokeō, *dok-eh´-o*; a prolonged form of a primary verb **δόκω, dokō,** *dok´-o* (used only as an alternate in certain tenses; compare the base of 1166) of the same meaning; to *think*; (by implication) to *seem* (truthfully or uncertainly):—be accounted, (of own) please (-ure), be of reputation, seem (good), suppose, think, trow.

To seem, appear:

(I) With a reflexive pron. expressed or implied: to seem to oneself, i.e. to be of opinion, to think, suppose, believe (Mt 6:7; Lk 8:18; Ac 26:9; Heb 10:29).

(II) In reference to others: to seem, to appear (Lk 10:36; Ac 17:18; 1Co 12:22; 2Co 10:9; Heb 12:11). Spoken also, in the moderation and urbanity of the Greek manner, of what is real and certain (Mk 10:42; Lk 22:24; 1Co 11:16; Gal 2:9; Heb 4:1).

(III) Impersonally, *dokeí moi* ([3427], to me), it seems to me, that is:

(A) Personally to think, suppose. Used interrogatively in the expression "what do you think?" (Mt 17:25; 18:12; 21:28; 22:17, 42; 26:66; Jn 11:56). Without the interrogative (Ac 25:27).

(B) It seems good to me, it is my pleasure, equivalent to "determine" or "resolve" (Lk 1:3; Ac 15:22, 25, 28, 34). As a part.: what seems good to them, i.e. what seems their pleasure or will (Heb 12:10).

Deriv.: *dógma* (1378), a decree, ordinance; *dóxa* (1391), glory, esteem; *eudokéō* (2106), to think well of.

Syn.: *nomízō* (3543), to consider, suppose, think; *hupolambánō* (5274), to suppose; *huponoéō* (5282), to suspect, conjecture; *oíomai* (3633), to expect, imagine, suppose; *logízomai* (3049), to reckon, suppose; *hēgéomai* (2233), to account, to think; *noéō* (3539), to perceive, understand; *phronéō* (5426), to think; *ginṓskō* (1097), to come to know, recognize; *oída* (1492), to perceive; *epístamai* (1987), to know, understand; *gnōrízō* (1107), to discover, know.

1381. δοκιμάζω, dokimazō, *dok-im-ad´-zo*; from 1384; to *test* (literal or figurative); (by implication) to *approve*:—allow, discern, examine, × like, (ap-) prove, try.

From *dókimos* (1384), tested, approved. To try, prove:

(I) To make trial of, put to the proof, examine, e.g., metals, by fire (1Co 3:13; 1Pe 1:7; Sept.: Pr 17:3; Zec 13:9); other things, by use (Lk 14:19); generally, by any method (Ro 12:2; 1Co 11:28; 2Co 8:8, 22; 13:5; Gal 6:4; Eph 5:10; 1Th 2:4; 5:21; 2Ti 3:10; 1Jn 4:1; Sept.: Ps 17:3; 139:1, 23; Jer 11:20). By implication, to examine and judge, i.e. to estimate, distinguish (Lk 12:56; see Mt 16:3; Ro 2:18; Php 1:10; Sept.: Zec 11:13). Spoken with reference to God meaning to put to the proof, i.e. to tempt (Heb 3:9 [cf. Mal 3:15]).

(II) In the sense of to have proved, i.e. to hold as tried, to regard as proved, and generally to approve, judge fit and proper, e.g., persons (1Co 16:3; 1Th 2:4); things (Ro 14:22).

Deriv.: *apodokimázō* (593), to disapprove, reject.

Syn.: *apodeíknumi* (584), to show forth, approve; *anakrínō* (350), to investigate, usually judicially; *diakrínō* (1252), to discriminate, determine, decide.

1382. δοκιμή, dokimē, *dok-ee-may´*; from the same as 1384; *test* (abstract or concrete); (by implication) *trustiness*:—experience (-riment), proof, trial.

Noun from *dókimos* (1384), approved, tried. Proof, trial. The state of being tried (2Co 8:2); the state of having been tried, tried uprightness, approved integrity (Ro 5:4; 2Co 2:9; 9:13). Also, proof, in the sense of evidence, sign, token (2Co 13:3; 12:12).

Syn.: *éndeigma* (1730), the result of proving, the token; *tekmḗrion* (5039), the mark or sign which provides positive proof of the trial.

1383. δοκίμιον, dokimion, *dok-im´-ee-on*; neuter of a presumed derivative of 1382; a *testing*; (by implication) *trustworthiness*:—trial, trying.

Noun from *dókimos* (1384), approved, tried. Proof, trial; a trying or testing (Jas 1:3; 1Pe 1:7).

1384. δόκιμος, dokimos, *dok´-ee-mos*; from 1380; properly *acceptable* (*current* after assayal), i.e. *approved*:—approved, tried.

Adjective from *déchomai* (1209), to accept, receive. Receivable, current; spoken of money, etc. as having been tried and refined (Sept.: Ge 23:16; 1Ch 29:4; 2Ch 9:17). Hence in the NT: tried, proved; approved, and therefore genuine (Ro 14:18; 16:10; 1Co 11:19; 2Co 10:18; 13:7; 2Ti 2:15; Jas 1:12);

Deriv.: *adókimos* (96), unapproved, reprobate; *dokimázō* (1381), to prove, try; *dokimḗ* (1382), trial, proof; *dokímion* (1383), test.

Syn.: *áxios* (514), worthy; *hikanós* (2425), able; *eklektós* (1588), chosen; *akatákritos* (178), uncondemned; *ámemptos* (273), unblameable; *anepílēptos* (423), blameless; *amṓmētos* (298), unblameable; *ámōmos* (299), faultless; *áspilos* (784), spotless.

1385. δοκός, dokos, *dok-os´*; from 1209 (through the idea of *holding* up); a *stick* of timber:—beam.

1386. δόλιος, dolios, *dol´-ee-os*; from 1388; *guileful*:—deceitful.

1387. δολιόω, dolioō, *dol-ee-o´-o*; from 1386; to *be guileful*:—use deceit.

1388. δόλος, dolos, *dol´-os*; from an obsolete primary **δέλλω, dellō** (probably meaning to *decoy*; compare 1185); a *trick* (*bait*), i.e. (figurative) *wile*:—craft, deceit, guile, subtilty.

1389. δολόω, doloō, *dol-o´-o*; from 1388; to *ensnare*, i.e. (figurative) *adulterate*:—handle deceitfully.

From *dólos* (1388), deceit. To adulterate, to corrupt. Only in 2Co 4:2.

Syn.: *apatáō* (538), to beguile, deceive; *exapatáō* (1818), to beguile thoroughly, deceive wholly; *phrenapatáō* (5422), to cause deceit in the mind; *planáō* (4105), to cause to go astray, wander; *paralogízomai* (3884), to deceive by false reasoning; *deleázō* (1185), to catch by a bait (*délear*); *apoplanáō* (635), to cause to wander away from, lead astray.

1390. δόμα, doma, *dom´-ah*; from the base of 1325; a *present*:—gift.

Noun from *dídōmi* (1325), to give. A gift (Mt 7:11; Lk 11:13; Eph 4:8; Php 4:17; see Sept.: Ge 25:6; Ps 68:18; Pr 18:16; Da 2:48).

1391. δόξα, doxa, *dox´-ah*; from the base of 1380; *glory* (as very *apparent*), in a wide application (literal or figurative, object or subject):—dignity, glory (-ious), honour, praise, worship.

Noun from *dokéō* (1380), to think, recognize. A seeming, an appearance. In the NT, honour, glory:

(I) Spoken of honour due or rendered, i.e. praise, applause (Lk 14:10; Jn 5:41, 44; 7:18; 8:50, 54; 2Co 6:8; 1Th 2:6); of God, e.g., to the honour and glory of God, i.e. that God may be honored, glorified (Jn 11:4; Ro 3:7; 15:7; Php 1:11; Rev 4:11). In ascriptions of glory or praise to God (Lk 2:14; Ro 11:36; Gal 1:5; 1Pe 4:11; Sept.: 1Ch 16:28, 29 [cf. Ps 29:9; 104:35; 106:48]). By metonymy, spoken of the occasion or source of honour or glory (1Co 11:15; 2Co 8:23; Eph 3:13; 1Th 2:20).

(II) In the NT, spoken also of that which excites admiration or to which honour is ascribed:

(A) Of external conditions: dignity, splendour, glory (Heb 2:7, quoted from Ps 8:5; 1Pe 1:24). By metonymy: that which reflects, expresses or exhibits dignity (1Co 11:7). Spoken of kings: regal majesty, splendour, pomp, magnificence, e.g., of the expected temporal reign of the Messiah (Mk 10:37); of the glory of His Second Coming (Mt 19:28; 24:30; Mk 13:26; Lk 9:26; 21:27; Tit 2:13; Sept.: 1Sa 2:8; 1Ch 29:25; Isa 8:7; Da 11:21); of the accompaniments of royalty, e.g., splendid apparel (Mt 6:29; Lk 12:27; Sept.: Ex 28:2, 36; Est 5:1; Isa 61:3); of wealth, treasures (Mt 4:8; Lk 4:6; Rev 21:24, 26; Sept.: Ge 31:1; Isa 10:3). By metonymy spoken in the plural of persons in high honour, e.g., *dóxai*, dignitaries, i.e. kings, princes, magistrates (2Pe 2:10; Jude 8 [cf. Isa 5:13]).

(B) Of an external appearance: luster, brightness, dazzling light (Ac 22:11; 1Pe 5:4); the sun, stars (1Co 15:40, 41); Moses' face (2Co 3:7; Sept.: Ex 34:29, 30, 35); the celestial light which surrounds angels (Rev 18:1), or glorified saints (Lk 9:31, 32; 1Co 15:43; Php 3:21; Col 3:4). Spoken especially of the celestial splendour in which God sits enthroned and His divine effulgence, dazzling majesty, radiant glory (2Th 1:9; 2Pe 1:17; Rev 15:8; 21:11, 23 [cf. 22:5]); as visible to mortals (Lk 2:9; Jn 12:41, see Isa 6:1; Ac 7:55); as manifested in the Messiah's Second Coming (Mt 16:27; Mk 8:38; Sept.: Ex 16:10; 24:17; 1Ki 8:11 [cf. Ps 104:1ff.; Eze 1:26–28]).

(C) Of internal character: glorious moral attributes, excellence, perfection. As spoken of God: infinite perfection, divine majesty and holiness (Ac 7:2; Ro 1:23; Eph 1:17; Heb 1:3); of the divine perfections as manifested in the power of God (Jn 11:40; Ro 6:4; 9:23; Eph 1:12, 14, 18; 3:16; Col 1:11; 2Pe 1:3); of Jesus, as the brightness (*apaúgasma* [541]) of the divine character (Jn 1:14; 2:11; Heb 1:3); of things, in place of an adj.: excellent, splendid, glorious (2Co 3:7–9; Eph 1:6).

(D) Of that exalted state of blissful perfection which is the portion of those who dwell with God in heaven. As spoken of Christ and including the idea of His royal majesty as Messiah (Lk 24:26; Jn 17:5, 22, 24; 2Th 2:14; 1Ti 3:16; 1Pe 1:11); of glorified saints, i.e. salvation, eternal life (Ro 2:7, 10; 8:18; 1Co 2:7; 2Co 4:17; 1Th 2:12; 2Ti 2:10; Heb 2:10; 1Pe 5:1). By metonymy: the author or procurer of this glory for anyone, i.e. the author of salvation (Lk 2:32), the same as the Lord of glory (1Co 2:8 [see v. 7]).

Deriv.: *doxázō* (1392), to glorify; *éndoxos* (1741), glorious; *kenódoxos* (2755), self-conceited; *parádoxos* (3861), strange, contrary to expected appearance, equivalent to a miraculous manifestation.

Syn.: *agallíasis* (20), exultation; *chará* (5479), joy; *euphrosúnē* (2167), having a joyful attitude; *kléos* (2811), renown; *kaucháomai* (2744), to boast; *kaúchēsis* (2746), the act of boasting; *kaúchēma* (2745), the boast or the reason for boasting.

1392. δοξάζω, doxazō, *dox-ad´-zo*; from 1391; to *render* (or *esteem*) *glorious* (in a wide application):—(make) glorify (-ious), full of (have) glory, honour, magnify.

From *dóxa* (1391), glory. To glorify:

(I) To ascribe glory or honour to anyone, praise, celebrate (Mt 6:2; Lk 4:15; Jn 8:54; Ac 13:48; Heb 5:5; Rev 18:7; Sept.: 2Sa 6:22; La 1:8). To glorify God, meaning to render glory to Him; to celebrate with praises, worship, adoration (Mt 5:16; 9:8; 15:31; Mk 2:12; Lk 2:20; 5:25, 26; 7:16; 13:13; 17:15; 18:43; 23:47; Jn 13:31, 32; 14:13; 15:8; 17:4; 21:19; Ac 4:21; 11:18; 21:20; Ro 1:21; 15:6, 9; 1Co 6:20; 2Co 9:13; Gal 1:24; 1Pe 2:12; 4:11, 16); the name of God (Jn 12:28; Rev 15:4).

(II) To honour, bestow honour upon, exalt in dignity, render glorious:

(A) Used generally: to render excellent, splendid (1Co 12:26; 2Th 3:1; Sept.: 1Ch 19:3; Est 6:6, 7, 9, 11; Pr 13:18); in the pass. voice: to be excellent, splendid, glorious (Ro 11:13; 2Co 3:10; 1Pe 1:8; Sept.: Ex 34:29, 30, 35).

(B) Spoken of God and Christ, meaning to glorify, i.e. to render conspicuous and glorious the divine character and attributes; e.g., of God as glorified by the Son (Jn 12:28; 13:31, 32; 14:13; 17:1, 4); by Christians (Jn 15:8; 21:19); of Christ as glorified by the Father (Jn 8:54; 13:32; 17:1, 5; Ac 3:13); by the Spirit (Jn 16:14); by Christians (Jn 17:10); generally (Jn 11:4; 13:31; Sept.: Ex 15:6, 11; Le 10:3; Isa 5:16).

(C) Spoken of Christ and His followers: to glorify, i.e. to advance to that state of bliss and glory which is the portion of those who dwell with God in heaven, e.g., of Christ as the Messiah (Jn 7:39; 12:16, 23 [cf. Isa 52:13]).

Deriv.: *sundoxázō* (4888), to glorify together.

Syn.: *timáō* (5091), to honour; *megalúnō* (3170), to make great, magnify.

1393. Δορκάς, Dorkas, *dor-kas´*; *gazelle*; *Dorcas*, a Christian woman:—Dorcas.

1394. δόσις, dosis, *dos´-is*; from the base of 1325; a *giving*; by implication (concrete) a *gift*:—gift, giving.

Noun from *dídōmi* (1325), to give. A gift; the act of giving (Php 4:15; Jas 1:17). For a full discussion of all the cognate words see *dṓron* (1435), a gift.

1395. δότης, dotēs, *dot´-ace*; from the base of 1325; a *giver*:—giver.

1396. δουλαγωγέω, doulagōgeō, *doo-lag-ogue-eh´-o*; from a presumed compound of 1401 and 71; to *be a slave-driver*, i.e. to *enslave* (figurative, *subdue*):—bring into subjection.

From *doúlos* (1401), servant, and *ágō* (71), to lead, bring. To bring into subjection, to subdue. Only in 1Co 9:27.

Syn.: *doulóō* (1402), to make a slave, enslave; *katadoulóō* (2615), to bring into bondage; *hupotássō* (5293), to subject.

1397. δουλεία, douleia, *doo-li´-ah*; from 1398; *slavery* (ceremonial or figurative):—bondage.

Noun from *douleúō* (1398), to be a slave, to serve. Slavery, bondage. Spoken of the condition of those under the Mosaic Law (Gal 4:24). Used figuratively: a slavish spirit, in contrast to the spirit of sonship (Ro 8:15); of the condition of those who are subject to death (Ro 8:21); of those subject to the fear of death (Heb 2:15).

Deriv.: *ophthalmodouleía* (3787), eyeservice, implying an outward service only.

1398. δουλεύω, douleuō, *dool-yoo´-o*; from 1401; to *be a slave* to (literal or figurative, involuntary or voluntary):—be in bondage, (do) serve (-ice).

From *doúlos* (1401), servant. To be a slave or servant:

(I) Spoken of involuntary service (Mt 6:24; Lk 16:13; Eph 6:7; 1Ti 6:2; Sept.: Le 25:39; Dt 15:12); of a people meaning to be subject to (Jn 8:33; Ac 7:7; Ro 9:12 [cf. Ge 25:23; 27:40]; Sept.: Ge 14:4; Jgs 3:8, 14). Metaphorically, of those subject to the Mosaic Law (Gal 4:25).

(II) Metaphorically spoken of voluntary service: to obey, be devoted to (Lk 15:29; Ro 12:11; Gal 5:13; Php 2:22; Sept.: Ge 29:15, 18, 20, 25, 30). In a moral sense: to obey or be devoted to God (Mt 6:24; Lk 16:13; Ac 20:19; Ro 7:6; 1Th 1:9); to Christ (Ro 14:18; 16:18; Col 3:24); to the law of God (Ro 7:25; Sept.: Dt 13:4; Jgs 2:7; Mal 3:18). Spoken of false gods (Gal 4:8; Sept.: Ex 23:33); of things: to obey, follow, indulge in, e.g., mammon (Mt 6:24; Lk 16:13); sin (Ro 6:6); the belly, i.e. one's appetite (Ro 16:18); the elements (Gal 4:9). To indulge in one's lusts (Tit 3:3).

Deriv.: *douleía* (1397), slavery, bondage.

Syn.: *diakonéō* (1247), to minister; *leitourgéō* (3008), to render public service, do service to the gods; *latreúō* (3000), to serve for hire; *hupēretéō* (5256), to serve as an underling; *hierourgéō* (2418), to minister in priestly service; *ergázomai* (2038), to work.

1399. δούλη, doulē, *doo´-lay*; feminine of 1401; a *female slave* (involuntary or voluntary):—handmaid (-en).

1400. δοῦλον, doulon, *doo´-lon*; neuter of 1401; *subservient*:—servant.

1401. δοῦλος, doulos, *doo´-los*; from 1210; a *slave* (literal or figurative, involuntary or voluntary; frequently therefore in a qualified sense of *subjection* or *subserviency*):—bond (-man), servant.

A noun meaning slave, servant:

(I) Spoken of involuntary service: a slave as opposed to a free man (1Co 7:21; Gal 3:28; Col 3:11; Rev 6:15). Also generally: a servant (Mt 13:27, 28; Jn 4:51; Ac 2:18; Eph 6:5; 1Ti 6:1; Sept.: Le 25:44; Jos 9:23; Jgs 6:27). In Php 2:7, having taken "the form of a servant," means appearing in a humble and despised condition.

(II) Metaphorically, spoken of voluntary service: a servant, implying obedience, devotion (Jn 15:15; Ro 6:16). Implying modesty (2Co 4:5); in praise of modesty (Mt 20:27; Mk 10:44). Spoken of the true followers and worshippers of God, e.g., a servant of God: either of agents sent from God, as Moses (Rev 15:3; see Jos 1:1), prophets (Rev 10:7; 11:18; Sept.: Jos 24:29; Jer 7:25), or simply of the worshippers of God (Rev 2:20; 7:3; 19:5; Sept.: Ps 34:22; 134:1); the followers and ministers of Christ (Eph 6:6; 2Ti 2:24), especially applied to the apostles (Ro 1:1; Gal 1:10; 2Pe 1:1; Jude 1). Used instead of the personal pron. in the oriental style of addressing a superior (Lk 2:29; Ac 4:29; Sept.: 1Sa 3:9, 10; Ps 19:12). In respect of things, of one who indulges in or is addicted to something (Jn 8:34; Ro 6:16, 17; 2Pe 2:19).

(III) In the sense of minister, attendant; spoken of the officers of an oriental court (Mt 18:23, 26–28, 32; 22:3, 4, 6, 8, 10).

Deriv.: *doulagōgéō* (1396), to be a slave driver; *douleúō* (1398), to be a slave to, to serve; *doulóō* (1402), to make a slave or bring someone into slavery; *súndoulos* (4889), fellow slave.

Syn.: *diákonos* (1249), a deacon, servant, minister; *paîs* (3816), literally "a child," but also an attendant, servant; *oikétēs* (3610), a house servant; *hupērétēs* (5257), a servant; *therápōn* (2324), a healer, an attendant servant; *místhios* (3407) and *misthōtós* (3411), a hired servant.

1402. δουλόω, douloō, *doo-lo´-o*; from 1401; to *enslave* (literal or figurative):—bring into (be under) bondage, × given, become (make) servant.

From *doúlos* (1401), slave. To make a slave or servant, to bring into bondage (Ac 7:6; 1Co 9:19; Sept.: Ge 15:13); in the pass., to be subjugated, subdued (Ro 6:18, 22); in the perf. tense, to be dependent (Gal 4:3).

Deriv.: *katadoulóō* (2615), to enslave.

Syn.: *kurieúō* (2961), to exercise lordship over.

1403. δοχή, dochē, *dokh-ay´*; from 1209; a *reception*, i.e. convivial *entertainment*:—feast.

Noun from *déchomai* (1209), to receive. A reception, entertainment, banquet (Lk 5:29; 14:13; Sept.: Ge 26:30; Est 1:3; 5:4).

Syn.: *heortḗ* (1859), a feast or festival; *deípnon* (1173), the chief meal of the day, dinner or supper; *gámos* (1062), a wedding or a wedding feast; *agápē* (26), a love feast.

1404. δράκων, drakōn, *drak´-own*; probably from an alternate form of **δέρκομαι, *derkomai*** (*to look*); a fabulous kind of *serpent* (perhaps as supposed to *fascinate*):—dragon.

1405. δράσσομαι, drassomai, *dras´-som-ahee*; perhaps akin to the base of 1404 (through the idea of *capturing*); to *grasp*, i.e. (figurative) *entrap*:—take.

1406. δραχμή, drachmē, *drakh-may´*; from 1405; a *drachma* or (silver) coin (as *handled*):—piece (of silver).

1407. δρέπανον, drepanon, *drep´-an-on*; from **δρέπω, *drepō*** (*to pluck*); a gathering *hook* (especially for harvesting):—sickle.

1408. δρόμος, dromos, *drom´-os*; from the alternate of 5143; a *race*, i.e. (figurative) *career*:—course.

1409. Δρούσιλλα, Drousilla, *droo´-sil-lah*; a feminine diminutive of *Drusus* (a Roman name); *Drusilla*, a member of the Herodian family:—Drusilla.

1410. δύναμαι, dunamai, *doo´-nam-ahee*; of uncertain affinity; to *be able* or *possible*:—be able, can (do, + -not), could, may, might, be possible, be of power.

To be able, have power, both in a physical and moral sense (Mt 3:9; 2Ti 3:15), as depending either on the disposition or faculties of mind (1Th 2:6), the degree of strength or skill (Ro 15:14), or the nature and external circumstances of the case (Ac 24:8, 11).

Deriv.: *dúnamis* (1411), power, ability, strength; *dunástēs* (1413), ruler; *dunatós* (1415), powerful, strong.

Syn.: *ischúō* (2480), to be strong, prevail, but indicating a more forceful strength or ability than is involved in *dúnamai*; *exischúō* (1840), to be thoroughly strong; *katischúō* (2729), to overpower, prevail; *krataióō* (2901), to strengthen, sustain; *sthenóō* (4599), to strengthen.

1411. δύναμις, dunamis, *doo´-nam-is*; from 1410; *force* (literal or figurative); specially miraculous *power* (usually by implication, a *miracle* itself):—ability, abundance, meaning, might (-ily,

-y, -y deed), (worker of) miracle (-s), power, strength, violence, might (wonderful) work.

Noun from *dúnamai* (1410), to be able. Power, ability, strength, force:

(I) Spoken of intrinsic power, either physical or moral, as in the verb *dúnamai* (1410):

(A) Of the body (1Co 15:43; Heb 11:11; Sept.: Job 39:19, *dúnamis*; Job 40:11, *ischús*; Ps 29:4, *ischús* [2479], strength).

(B) Generally (Mt 25:15; Ac 6:8; 1Co 15:56; 2Ti 1:7); a spirit of strength, meaning manly vigour in opposition to a spirit of cowardice (Heb 1:3; 7:16; 11:34; Rev 1:16; Sept.: 2Ki 18:20; 1Ch 13:8; 29:2; Ezr 2:69; 10:13; Job 12:13). Also in various constructions with *katá* (2596): according to one's strength, meaning as far as one can (2Co 8:3). With *hupér* (5228), beyond: above one's strength (2Co 1:8; 8:3). With *en* (1722), in: with power, powerfully, mightily (Col 1:29; 2Th 1:11).

(C) Spoken of God: the great power of God, meaning His almighty energy (Mt 22:29; Mk 12:24; Lk 1:35; 5:17; Ro 1:20; 9:17; 1Co 6:14; 2Co 4:7; 13:4; Eph 1:19; 3:7, 20; 2Ti 1:8; 1Pe 1:5; 2Pe 1:3). Joined with *dóxa* [(1391), glory] it implies the greatness, omnipotence, and majesty of God (Rev 15:8. See Mt 26:64; Mk 14:62; Lk 22:69; Heb 1:3, "on the right hand of the Majesty"). By metonymy, spoken of a person or thing in whom the power of God is manifested, i.e. the manifestation of the power of God (Ac 8:10; see Ro 1:16; 1Co 1:18, 24). With phrase "of God" it expresses the source, i.e. power imparted from God (1Co 2:5; 2Co 6:7). Spoken of Jesus as exercising the power to heal (Mk 5:30; Lk 6:19; 8:46; 2Co 12:9). In the sense of power, omnipotent majesty (Mt 24:30; Mk 9:1; 13:26; Lk 21:27; 2Th 1:7; 2Pe 1:16); as spoken of the power of the Spirit, meaning the power imparted by the Spirit (Lk 4:14; Ro 15:13, 19); of prophets and apostles as empowered by the Holy Spirit (Lk 1:17; 24:49; Ac 1:8 [cf. Ac 2:4]).

(D) By metonymy of effect for cause, the plural *dunámeis*, powers, is often used for mighty deeds, miracles (Mt 7:22; 11:20, 21, 23; 13:54, 58; 14:2; Mk 6:2, 5, 14; Lk 10:13; 19:37; Ac 2:22; 8:13; 19:11; 1Co 12:10; 2Co 12:12; Gal 3:5; Heb 2:4; Sept.: Job 37:14; Ps 106:2). Hence, as abstract for concrete: a worker of miracles (1Co 12:28, 29).

(E) Spoken of the essential power, true nature or reality of something (Php 3:10; 2Ti 3:5). As opposed to *lógos* (3056), speech merely (1Co 4:19, 20; 1Th 1:5). Metaphorically of language: the power of a word, i.e. meaning, significance (1Co 14:11).

(II) Spoken of power as resulting from external sources and circumstances:

(A) Power, authority, might (Lk 4:36; 9:1; Ac 3:12; 2Pe 2:11; Rev 13:2; 17:13). Spoken of omnipotent sovereignty as due to God, e.g., in ascriptions (Mt 6:13; Rev 4:11; 5:12; 7:12; 11:17; 12:10; 19:1; Sept.: 1Ch 29:11). Joined with *ónoma* (3686), name (Ac 4:7; 1Co 5:4). By metonymy of abstract for concrete, put for "the one in authority," similar to the Eng. authorities, i.e. persons in authority, the mighty, the powerful (Ro 8:38; 1Co 15:24; Eph 1:21; 1Pe 3:22; Sept.: Est 2:18).

(B) With the meaning of number, quantity, abundance, wealth (in Rev 3:8, a small number of members or perhaps true believers [cf. Rev 18:3]). Metaphorically for enjoyment, happiness (Heb 6:5).

(C) Of warlike power, like the Eng. force, forces, i.e. host, army (Lk 10:19; Sept.: Ex 14:28; 15:4; 2Sa 10:7; 17:25; 20:23). By Hebraism, *dunámeis tṓn ouranṓn*, "the hosts of heaven" (see *ouranós* [3772], heaven), i.e. the sun, moon, and stars (Mt 24:29; Mk 13:25; Lk 21:26 [cf. Rev 6:13; Sept.: Isa 34:4; Da 8:10]).

Deriv.: *dunamóō* (1412), to strengthen.

Syn.: *ischús* (2479), strength, ability, force, somewhat stronger than *dúnamis*; *krátos* (2904), dominion, enduring strength; *exousía* (1849), authority; *archḗ* (746), rule, power; *megaleiótēs* (3168), majesty; with the meaning of miracle: *sēmeíon* (4592), sign, token; *téras* (5059), something strange, a marvel, wonder; *megaleíon* (3167), a great work; *éndoxon* (1741), a glorious work; *parádoxon* (3861), a strange work; *thaumásion* (2297), a marvelous work; *thaúma* (2295), a wonder, marvel; *érgon* (2041), work when referring to Christ's work.

1412. δυναμόω, dunamoō, *doo-nam-o´-o*; from 1411; to *enable*:—strengthen.

From *dúnamis* (1411), strength. To strengthen. In the NT, used in the pass., to be strengthened, grow strong morally (Col 1:11 [cf. Eph 3:16]).

Deriv.: *endunamóō* (1743), to make strong.

Syn.: *ischúō* (2480), to have strength; *enischúō* (1765), to strengthen; *krataióō* (2901), to strengthen; *sthenóō* (4599), to strengthen; *stereóō* (4732), to establish; *epistērízō* (1991), to establish, confirm; *stērízō* (4741), to establish, strengthen.

1413. δυνάστης, dunastēs, *doo-nas´-tace*; from 1410; a *ruler* or *officer*:—of great authority, mighty, potentate.

Noun from *dúnamai* (1410), to be able. One in power; a potentate, prince (Lk 1:52; 1Ti 6:15; Sept.: Pr 8:16; 14:28; 23:1); one in authority under a prince, a minister of a court (Ac 8:27; Sept.: Ge 50:4; Jer 34:19; Le 19:15).

Syn.: *dunatós* (1415), powerful, mighty, and *ischurós* (2478), strong; *krataiós* (2900), one who has dominion; *kúrios* (2962), lord, master; *despótēs* (1203), despot, master, lord; *megistán* (3175), great man, prince, lord.

1414. δυνατέω, dunateō, *doo-nat-eh´-o*; from 1415; to *be efficient* (figurative):—be mighty.

1415. δυνατός, dunatos, *doo-nat-os´*; from 1410; *powerful* or *capable* (literal or figurative); neuter *possible*:—able, could, (that is) mighty (man), possible, power, strong.

1416. δύνω, dunō, *doo´-no*; or **δῦμι**, ***dumi***, *doo´-mee*; prolonged forms of an obsolete primary **δύω**, ***duō***; *doo´-o* (to *sink*); to *go* "*down*":—set.

1417. δύο, duo, *doo´-o*; a primary numeral; "*two*":—both, twain, two.

1418. δυς, dus, *doos*; a primary inseparable particle of uncertain derivative; used only in composition as a prefix; *hard*, i.e. *with difficulty*:— + hard, + grievous, *etc.*

1419. δυσβάστακτος, dusbastaktos, *doos-bas´-tak-tos*; from 1418 and a derivative of 941; *oppressive*:—grievous to be borne.

1420. δυσεντερία, dusenteria, *doos-en-ter-ee´-ah*; from 1418 and a compound of 1787 (meaning a *bowel*); a "*dysentery*":—bloody flux.

1421. δυσερμήνευτος, dusermēneutos, *doos-er-mane´-yoo-tos*; from 1418 and a presumed derivative of 2059; *difficult of explanation*:—hard to be uttered.

1422. δύσκολος, duskolos, *doos´-kol-os*; from 1418 and **κόλον**, ***kolon*** (*food*); properly *fastidious about eating* (*peevish*), i.e. (genitive) *impracticable*:—hard.

1423. δυσκόλως, duskolōs, *doos-kol´-oce*; adverb from 1422; *impracticably*:—hardly.

1424. δυσμή, dusmē, *doos-may´*; from 1416; the sun-*set*, i.e. (by implication) the *western* region:—west.

1425. δυσνόητος, dusnoētos, *doos-no´-ay-tos*; from 1418 and a derivative of 3539; *difficult of perception*:—hard to be understood.

Adjective from *dus* (1418), hard, and *noētós* (n.f.), understood, which is from *noéō* (3539), to understand. Hard to be understood. Only in 2Pe 3:16.

Syn.: *dusermḗneutos* (1421), difficult to explain, hard to understand; *dúskolos* (1422), difficult; *sklērós* (4642), hard, difficult.

1426. δυσφημία, dusphēmia, *doos-fay-mee´-ah*; from a compound of 1418 and 5345; *defamation*:—evil report.

1427. δώδεκα, dōdeka, *do´-dek-ah*; from 1417 and 1176; *two* and *ten*, i.e. a *dozen*:—twelve.

1428. δωδέκατος, dōdekatos, *do-dek´-at-os*; from 1427; *twelfth*:—twelfth.

1429. δωδεκάφυλον, dōdekaphulon, *do-dek-af´-oo-lon*; from 1427 and 5443; the *commonwealth* of Israel:—twelve tribes.

1430. δῶμα, dōma, *do´-mah*; from **δέμο**, ***demō*** (to *build*); properly an *edifice*, i.e. (special) a *roof*:—housetop.

1431. δωρεά, dōrea, *do-reh-ah´*; from 1435; a *gratuity*:—gift.

Noun from *dídōmi* (1325), to give. A gift (Jn 4:10; Ac 2:38; 8:20; 10:45; 11:17; Ro 5:15, 17; 2Co 9:15; Eph 3:7; 4:7; Heb 6:4; Sept.: Da 2:6).

Deriv.: *dōreán* (1432), freely; *dōréomai* (1433), to make a gift of.

1432. δωρεάν, dōrean, *do-reh-an´*; accusative of 1431 as adverb; *gratuitously* (literal or figurative):—without a cause, freely, for naught, in vain.

1433. δωρέομαι, dōreomai, *do-reh´-om-ahee*; middle from 1435; to *bestow* gratuitously:—give.

1434. δώρημα, dōrēma, *do´-ray-mah*; from 1433; a *bestowment*:—gift.

Noun from *dōréō* (1433), to make a gift. A gift (Ro 5:16; Jas 1:17).

1435. δῶρον, dōron, *do´-ron*; a *present*; specially a *sacrifice*:—gift, offering.

Noun from *dídōmi* (1325), to give. Gift. Used of gifts given as an expression of honour (Mt 2:11); for support of the temple (Mt 15:5; Mk 7:11; Lk 21:1, 4); to God (Mt 5:23, 24; 8:4; 23:18, 19; Heb 5:1; 8:3, 4; 9:9; 11:4); as the gift of salvation (Eph 2:8); for celebrating (Rev 11:10).

1436. ἔα, ea, *eh´-ah*; apparently imperative of 1439; properly *let it be*, i.e. (as interject) *aha!*:—let alone.

1437. ἐάν, ean, *eh-an´*; from 1487 and 302; a *conditional* particle; *in case* that, *provided*, etc.; often used in connection with other particles to denote *indefiniteness* or *uncertainty*:—before, but, except, (and) if, (if) so, (what-, whither-) soever, though, when (-soever), whether (or), to whom, [who-] so (-ever). See 3361.

1438. ἑαυτοῦ, heautou, *heh-ow-too´* (including all the other cases); from a reflexive pronoun otherwise obsolete and the generic (dative or accusative) of 846; *him-* (*her-, it-, them-*, also [in conjunction with the personal pronoun of the other persons] *my-, thy-, our-, your-*) *self* (*selves*), etc.:—alone, her (own, -self), (he) himself, his (own), itself, one (to) another, our (thine) own (-selves), + that she had, their (own, own selves), (of) them (-selves), they, thyself, you, your (own, own conceits, own selves, -selves).

1439. ἐάω, eaō, *eh-ah´-o*; of uncertain affinity; to *let be*, i.e. *permit* or *leave* alone:—commit, leave, let (alone), suffer. See also 1436.

1440. ἑβδομήκοντα, hebdomēkonta, *heb-dom-ay´-kon-tah*; from 1442 and a modified form of 1176, *seventy*:—seventy, three score and ten.

1441. ἑβδομηκοντακίς, hebdomēkontakis, *heb-dom-ay-kon-tak-is´*; multiple adverb from 1440; *seventy times*:—seventy times.

1442. ἕβδομος, hebdomos, *heb´-dom-os*; ordinal from 2033; *seventh*:—seventh.

1443. Ἐβέρ, Eber, *eb-er´*; of Hebrew origin [5677]; *Eber*, a patriarch:—Eber.

1444. Ἑβραϊκός, Hebraïkos, *heb-rah-ee-kos´*; from 1443; *Hebraïc* or the *Jewish* language:—Hebrew.

1445. Ἑβραῖος, Hebraios, *heb-rah´-yos*; from 1443; a *Hebræan* (i.e. Hebrew) or *Jew*:—Hebrew.

1446. Ἑβραΐς, Hebraïs, *heb-rah-is´*; from 1443; the *Hebraistic* (i.e. *Hebrew*) or *Jewish* (*Chaldee*) language:—Hebrew.

1447. Ἑβραϊστί, Hebraïsti, *heb-rah-is-tee´*; adverb from 1446; *Hebraistically* or in the Jewish (Chaldee) language:—in (the) Hebrew (tongue).

1448. ἐγγίζω, eggizō, *eng-id´-zo*; from 1451; to make *near*, i.e. (reflexive) *approach*:—approach, be at hand, come (draw) near, be (come, draw) nigh.

From *eggús* (1451), near. To bring near, cause to approach. In the NT, used intransitively: to come near, approach (Lk 7:12; 15:1, 25; 22:47; Ac 10:9); in the perf., *ḗggika*, to be near, to be at hand (Mt 3:2; 4:17; 10:7; Mk 1:15; Lk 10:11).

(I) Spoken of persons (Mt 21:1; 26:46; Mk 11:1; 14:42; Lk 7:12; 12:33; 18:40; 19:37, 41; 24:15; Ac 10:9; 21:33; 23:15).

(II) Spoken of things, time (Mt 3:2; 4:17; 10:7; 21:34; 26:45; Mk 1:15; Lk 21:8, 20, 28; 22:1; Ac 7:17; Ro 13:12; Heb 10:25; Jas 5:8; 1Pe 4:7).

(III) Metaphorically (Php 2:30; Sept.: Job 33:22; Ps 88:3; 107:18).

(IV) The expression *eggízō tṓ Theṓ*, "to draw near to God" was often connected with offering sacrifices in the temple (Sept.: Ex 19:22; Eze 44:13). In the NT, it means to worship God with a pious heart (Mt 15:8; Heb 7:19; Jas 4:8, quoted from Isa 29:13). God is said to "approach men," which means to draw near to Christians, by the aid of His Spirit, grace (Jas 4:8; Sept.: Dt 4:7 [cf. Ps 145:18]).

Deriv.: *proseggízō* (4331), approaching, coming close to.

Syn.: *paraplēsíon* (3897), near; *plēsíon* (4139), near, neighbour; *pará* (3844), beside, along side, near; *prós* (4314), toward, on the side, near; *ephístēmi* (2186), to come near, be at hand; *prosérchomai* (4334), to draw near; *proságō* (4317), to draw near; *érchomai* (2064), to come, as contrasted to *hḗkō* (2240), to arrive and be present; *paragínomai* (3854), to arrive and be present; *aphiknéomai* (864), to arrive at a place; *katantáō* (2658), to come to; *parístēmi* (3936), to stand by or near; *phthánō* (5348), to come upon, arrive.

1449. ἐγγράφω, eggraphō, *eng-graf´-o*; from 1722 and 1125; to "*engrave*," i.e. *inscribe*:—write (in).

1450. ἔγγυος, egguos, *eng´-goo-os*; from 1722 and **γυῖον, guion** (a *limb*); *pledged* (as if *articulated* by a member), i.e. a *bondsman*:—surety.

Adjective from *eggúē* (n.f.), pledge, bail, security. Yielding a pledge. Only in Heb 7:22 (cf. Heb 7:21, 24, 25).

Syn.: *bebaíōsis* (951), confirmation; *plērophoría* (4136), assurance; *marturía* (3141), evidence; *apódeixis* (585), proof.

1451. ἐγγύς, eggus, *eng-goos´*; from a primary verb **ἄγχω, agchō** (to *squeeze* or *throttle*; akin to the base of 43); *near* (literal or figurative, of place or time):—from, at hand, near, nigh (at hand, unto), ready.

Adverb meaning close, near:

(I) Of place (Jn 3:23; 6:19, 23; 11:18, 54; 19:42; Lk 19:11; Ac 1:12; Sept.: Ge 45:10; Eze 23:12). Metaphorically: near, nigh (Php 4:5 [cf. Php 4:6 {see also Ps 34:18; 145:18}]; Heb 6:8; 8:13). Spoken of the Jews, "those who are near," i.e. having the knowledge and worship of the true God, as opposed to those who are far, the Gentiles (Eph 2:17; Sept.: Isa 57:19). Thus, to become near to God, by embracing the gospel (Eph 2:13).

(II) Of time: to be near, at hand (Mt 24:32, 33; Mk 13:28, 29; Rev 1:3; 22:10). Used of the Passover (Jn 2:13; 6:4; 11:55); the feast (Jn 7:2); the kingdom of God (Lk 21:31); the Lord (Php 4:5 [cf. Heb 10:37]). Used in the Sept. for *qārôb* (7138, OT): Eze 30:3; Joel 1:15; 2:1.

Deriv.: *eggízō* (1448), to bring near; *eggúteron* (1452), nearer.

1452. ἐγγύτερον, egguteron, *eng-goo´-ter-on*; neuter of the comparative of 1451; *nearer*:—nearer.

1453. ἐγείρω, egeirō, *eg-i´-ro*; probably akin to the base of 58 (through the idea of *collecting* one's faculties); to *waken* (transitive or intransitive), i.e. *rouse* (literal from sleep, from sitting or lying, from disease, from death; or figurative from obscurity, inactivity, ruins, nonexistence):—awake, lift (up), raise (again, up), rear up, (a-) rise (again, up), stand, take up.

To rise, to have risen:

(I) To rise from sleep, implying also the idea of rising up from the posture of sleep, i.e. from lying down (Mt 8:25; 25:7; Mk 4:27; Ac 12:7; Sept.: Ge 41:4, 7; Pr 6:9). Metaphorically, to wake up from sluggishness, lethargy (Ro 13:11 [cf. Eph 5:14]); from death, of which sleep is the emblem (Mt 27:52 [cf. Job 14:12; Da 12:2]). To raise the dead (Mt 10:8; Jn 5:21; Ac 26:8; 1Co 15:15, 16; 2Co 1:9). To rise from the dead (Mk 6:14, 16; Lk 9:7; Jn 2:22; see also Mt 16:21; 17:23; 27:63; Mk 16:14; Ac 5:30; Ro 4:25; 2Co 4:14; Sept.: 2Ki 4:31; Isa 26:19).

(II) The idea of sleep not being involved, it also means to cause to rise up, raise up, set upright, and in the middle to rise up, arise:

(A) Spoken of persons who are sitting (Ac 3:7) or reclining at a table (Jn 13:4), or prostrate or lying down (Mt 17:7; Lk 11:8; Ac 9:8; 10:26; Sept.: 2Sa 12:17); also of sick persons (Mt 8:15; Mk 1:31; 2:12), including the idea of convalescence, to set up again, i.e. to heal (Jas 5:15).

(**B**) By an oriental pleonasm, prefixed to verbs of going, of undertaking, or doing something (Mt 2:13, 14, "having risen take the child" [a.t.]; also Mt 2:20, 21; 9:19; Jn 11:29; Sept.: 1Ch 22:19).

(**C**) Metaphorically of persons, in the middle, to rise up against as does an adversary (Mt 24:7; Mk 13:8; Lk 21:10; Sept.: Isa 10:26; Jer 50:9). Also "to rise in the judgement with this generation" (a.t. [Mt 12:42; Lk 11:31]).

(**D**) Spoken of things, to raise up, e.g., out of a pit (Mt 12:11 [cf. Lk 14:5]). In Jn 2:19, 20, to erect, build.

(**III**) Metaphorically: to raise up, to cause to arise or exist; in the middle to arise, to appear (Lk 1:69; Ac 13:22, 23). In the middle, spoken of prophets (Mt 11:11; 24:11, 24; Mk 13:22; Lk 7:16; Jn 7:52; Sept.: Jgs 3:9, 15; Isa 41:25; 45:13). In the sense of to cause to be born, to create (Mt 3:9; Lk 3:8).

(**IV**) Intransitively: to awake, to arise; thus to awake from sleep or, figuratively, from sluggishness (Eph 5:14); also to rise up, arise from a sitting or reclining posture (Mk 2:9, 11; 3:3; 5:41; 10:49; Lk 5:23, 24; 6:8; Jn 5:8).

Deriv.: *grēgoréō* (1127), to watch, be vigilant; *diegeírō* (1326), awake from natural sleep; *égersis* (1454), stimulation, erection, awakening; *exegeírō* (1825), to raise from out of; *epegeírō* (1892), to rouse up, excite; *sunegeírō* (4891), to raise together.

Syn.: *diagrēgoréō* (1235), to be fully watchful by being wide awake; *agrupnéō* (69), to be awake, watchful; *agrupnía* (70), sleeplessness; *anístēmi* (450), to stand up or arise; *eknḗphō* (1594), to return to one's senses from drunkenness, become sober; *exupnízō* (1852), to arouse a person from sleep (Jn 11:11); *aírō* (142), to raise, take up, lift; *epaírō* (1869), to lift up, raise; *hupsóō* (5312), to lift or raise up; *anorthóō* (461), to set upright; *anakúptō* (352), to lift oneself up; *anabibázō* (307), to cause to go up or ascend; *exanístēmi* (1817), to raise up from among or to rise up; *anabaínō* (305), to go up; *anatéllō* (393), to rise, speaking of the sun; *katephístēmi* (2721), to rise up as in insurrection; *epanístamai* (1881), to rise up against; *hístēmi* (2476), to cause to stand; *stḗkō* (4739), to stand upright; *anakathízō* (339), to set up, intransitively to sit up.

1454. ἔγερσις, egersis, *eg´-er-sis*; from 1453; a *resurgence* (from death):—resurrection.

Noun from *egeírō* (1453), to wake up. Resurrection, reanimation of the dead (Mt 27:53).

Syn.: *anástasis* (386), resurrection; *exanástasis* (1815), resurrection out of.

1455. ἐγκάθετος, egkathetos, *eng-kath´-et-os*; from 1722 and a derivative of 2524; *subinduced*, i.e. surreptitiously *suborned* as a lier-in-wait:—spy.

1456. ἐγκαίνια, egkainia, *eng-kah´ee-nee-ah*; neuter plural of a presumed compound from 1722 and 2537; *innovatives*, i.e. (special) *renewal* (of religious services after the Antiochian interruption):—dedication.

Noun from *en* (1722), in or at, and *kainós* (2537), qualitatively new. Festival of dedication, only in Jn 10:22. This festival was instituted by Judas Maccabaeus to commemorate the purification of the temple and the renewal of the temple worship after the three years of profanation by Antiochus Epiphanes. It was held for eight days, beginning on the twenty-fifth day of the month of Kislev, which began the new moon of December. Josephus calls it *phṓta* (5457), i.e. the festival of lights or lanterns.

1457. ἐγκαινίζω, egkainizō, *eng-kahee-nid´-zo*; from 1456; to *renew*, i.e. *inaugurate*:—consecrate, dedicate.

From *en* (1722), in or at, and *kainízō* (n.f.), to make new. To dedicate, consecrate (Heb 9:18; 10:20; Sept.: Dt 20:5; 1Ki 8:64 [cf. 1Sa 11:14]). Also from *kainízō* (n.f.): *anakainízō* (340), to renew.

Syn.: *ananeóō* (365), to renew.

1458. ἐγκαλέω, egkaleō, *eng-kal-eh´-o*; from 1722 and 2564; to *call in* (as a debt or demand), i.e. *bring to account* (*charge, criminate*, etc.):—accuse, call in question, implead, lay to the charge.

From *en* (1722), in, and *kaléō* (2564), to call. To bring a charge against, call to account, accuse, arraign (Ac 19:38, 40; 23:28, 29; 26:2, 7; Ro 8:33).

Deriv.: *anégkalētos* (410), unaccused, blameless; *égklēma* (1462), a public accusation.

Syn.: *katēgoréō* (2723), to accuse; *diabállō* (1225), to accuse, defame; *katakrínō* (2632), to condemn; *elégchō* (1651), to reprove; *mémphomai* (3201), to find fault.

1459. ἐγκαταλείπω, egkataleipō, *eng-kat-al-i´-po*; from 1722 and 2641; to *leave behind in* some place, i.e. (in a good sense) *let remain over*, or (in a bad one) to *desert*:—forsake, leave.

1460. ἐγκατοικέω, egkatoikeō, *eng-kat-oy-keh´-o*; from 1722 and 2730; to *settle down in* a place, i.e. *reside*:—dwell among.

1461. ἐγκεντρίζω, egkentrizō, *eng-ken-trid´-zo*; from 1722 and a derivative of 2759; to *prick in*, i.e. *ingraft*:—graff in (-to).

1462. ἔγκλημα, egklēma, *eng´-klay-mah*; from 1458; an *accusation*, i.e. *offence* alleged:—crime laid against, laid to charge.

Noun from *egkaléō* (1458), to arraign. Charge, accusation (Ac 23:29), complaint, charge (Ac 25:16).

Syn.: *katēgoría* (2724), a criminal charge, an accusation.

1463. ἐγκομβόομαι, egkomboomai, *eng-kom-bo´-om-ahee*; middle from 1722 and **κομβόω, *komboō*** (to *gird*); to *engirdle* oneself (for labour), i.e. figurative (the apron being a badge of servitude) to *wear* (in token of mutual deference):—be clothed with.

1464. ἐγκοπή, egkopē, *eng-kop-ay´*; from 1465; a *hindrance*:—× hinder.

1465. ἐγκόπτω, egkoptō, *eng-kop´-to*; from 1722 and 2875; to *cut into*, i.e. (figurative) *impede, detain*:—hinder, be tedious unto.

1466. ἐγκράτεια, egkrateia, *eng-krat´-i-ah*; from 1468; *self-control* (especially *continence*):—temperance.

1467. ἐγκρατεύομαι, egkrateuomai, *eng-krat-yoo´-om-ahee*; middle from 1468; to *exercise self-restraint* (in diet and chastity):—can ([-not]) contain, be temperate.

1468. ἐγκρατής, egkratēs, *eng-krat-ace´*; from 1722 and 2904; *strong in* a thing (*masterful*), i.e. (figurative and reflex.) *self-controlled* (in appetite, etc.):—temperate.

1469. ἐγκρίνω, egkrinō, *eng-kree´-no*; from 1722 and 2919; to *judge in*, i.e. *count* among:—make of the number.

From *en* (1722), in or among, and *krínō* (2919), to judge, reckon, classify. To judge or classify among. Only in 2Co 10:12.

Syn.: *psēphízō* (5585), to compute, count; *logízomai* (3049), to reckon; *katalégō* (2639), to enroll, take into the number; *anagnōrízō* (319), to recognize; *paradéchomai* (3858), to accept, receive.

1470. ἐγκρύπτω, egkruptō, *eng-kroop´-to*; from 1722 and 2928; to *conceal in*, i.e. *incorporate with*:—hid in.

1471. ἔγκυος, egkuos, *eng´-koo-os*; from 1722 and the base of 2949; *swelling inside*, i.e. *pregnant*:—great with child.

1472. ἐγχρίω, egchriō, *eng-khree´-o*; from 1722 and 5548; to *rub in* (oil), i.e. *besmear*:—anoint.

1473. ἐγώ, egō, *eg-o´*; a primary pronoun of the first person *I* (only expressed when emphatic):—I, me. For the other cases and the plural see 1691, 1698, 1700, 2248, 2249, 2254, 2257, etc.

1474. ἐδαφίζω, edaphizō, *ed-af-id´-zo*; from 1475; to *raze*:—lay even with the ground.

1475. ἔδαφος, edaphos, *ed´-af-os*; from the base of 1476; a *basis* (*bottom*), i.e. the *soil*:—ground.

1476. ἑδραῖος, hedraios, *hed-rah´-yos*; from a derivative of **ἕζομαι, *hezomai*** (to *sit*); *sedentary*, i.e. (by implication) *immovable*:—settled, steadfast.

1477. ἑδραίωμα, hedraiōma, *hed-rah´-yo-mah*; from a derivative of 1476; a *support*, i.e. (figurative) *basis*:—ground.

1478. Ἐζεκίας, Ezekias, *ed-zek-ee´-as*; of Hebrew origin [2396]; *Ezekias* (i.e. *Hezekiah*), an Israelite:—Ezekias.

1479. ἐθελοθρησκεία, ethelothrēskeia, *eth-el-oth-race-ki´-ah*; from 2309 and 2356; *voluntary* (*arbitrary* and *unwarranted*) *piety*, i.e. *sanctimony*:—will worship.

1480. ἐθίζω, ethizō, *eth-id´-zo*; from 1485; to *accustom*, i.e. (neuter passive participle) *customary*:—custom.

1481. ἐθνάρχης, ethnarchēs, *eth-nar´-khace*; from 1484 and 746; the *governor* [not king] *of a district*:—ethnarch.

1482. ἐθνικός, ethnikos, *eth-nee-kos´*; from 1484; *national* ("*ethnic*"), i.e. (special) a *Gentile*:—heathen (man).

Adjective from *éthnos* (1484), nation. National, popular. In the NT, used in the Jewish sense of Gentile, heathen, spoken of all who are not Israelites (Mt 6:7; 18:17).

Deriv.: *ethnikṓs* (1483), in a manner of the Gentiles.

1483. ἐθνικῶς, ethnikōs, *eth-nee-koce´*; adverb from 1482; *as a Gentile*:—after the manner of Gentiles.

Adverb from *ethnikós* (1482), a heathen, Gentile. After the manner of the heathen or the Gentiles. Only in Gal 2:14.

1484. ἔθνος, ethnos, *eth´-nos*; probably from 1486; a *race* (as of the same *habit*), i.e. a *tribe*; specially a *foreign* (*non-Jewish*) one (usually by implication, *pagan*):—Gentile, heathen, nation, people.

A noun meaning multitude, people, race, belonging and living together.

(**I**) Generally, the people or inhabitants of Samaria (Ac 8:9, cf. v. 5); the whole race of mankind (Ac 17:26). See also 1Pe 2:9; Sept.: 2Ch 32:7; Isa 13:4.

(**II**) In the sense of nation, people, as distinct from all others (Mt 20:25; Mk 10:42; Lk 7:5; Jn 11:48, 50; Ac 7:7; 10:22; Sept.: Ge 12:2; Ex 1:9; 33:13; Dt 1:28).

(**III**) In the Jewish sense, *tá éthnē*, the nations, means the Gentile nations or the Gentiles in general as spoken of all who are not Israelites and implying idolatry and ignorance of the true God, i.e. the heathen, pagan nations (Mt 4:15; 10:5; Mk 10:33; Lk 2:32; Ac 4:27; 26:17; Ro 2:14; 3:29; Sept.: Ne 5:8, 9; Isa 9:1; Eze 4:13; 27:33, 36; 34:13; Jer 10:3).

Deriv.: *ethnárchēs* (1481), the governor of a district; *ethnikós* (1482), a heathen.

1485. ἔθος, ethos, *eth´-os*; from 1486; a *usage* (prescribed by habit or law):—custom, manner, be wont.

1486. ἔθω, ethō, *eth´-o*; a primary verb; to *be used* (by habit or conventionality); neuter perfect participle *usage*:—be custom (manner, wont).

1487. εἰ, ei, *i*; a primary particle of conditionality; *if, whether, that*, etc.:—forasmuch as, if, that, ([al-]) though, whether. Often used in connection or composition with other particles, especially as in 1489, 1490, 1499, 1508, 1509, 1512, 1513, 1536, 1537. See also 1437.

1488. εἶ, ei, *i*; second personal singular present of 1510; thou *art*:—art, be.

1489. εἴγε, eige, *i´-gheh*; from 1487 and 1065; *if indeed, seeing that, unless*, (with negative) *otherwise*:—if (so be that, yet).

1490. εἰ δὲ μή(γε), ei de mē(ge), *i deh may´-(gheh)*; from 1487, 1161 and 3361 (sometimes with 1065 added); *but if not*:—(or) else, if (not, otherwise), otherwise.

1491. εἶδος, eidos, *i´-dos*; from 1492; a *view*, i.e. *form* (literal or figurative):—appearance, fashion, shape, sight.

Noun from *eídō* (1492), to see. The act of seeing, the thing seen, external appearance. The object of sight, form, appearance (Lk 3:22; 9:29; Jn 5:37; Sept.: Ge 41:2f.; Ex 24:17; Nu 9:16; 1Sa 25:3; Est 2:7); manner, kind, species (1Th 5:22, Sept.: Jer 15:3).

Deriv.: *eídōlon* (1497), idol; *petrṓdēs* (4075), rock-like, stone-like.

Syn.: *schḗma* (4976), figure, fashion; *morphḗ* (3444), form, makeup; *homoíōma* (3667), likeness; *theōría* (2335), gaze, spectacle; *hórama* (3705), that which is seen, appearance.

1492. εἴδω, eidō, *i´-do*; a primary verb; used only in certain past tenses, the others being borrowed from the equivalent 3700 and 3708; properly to *see* (literal or figurative); by implication (in the perf. only) to *know*:—be aware, behold, × can (+ not tell), consider, (have) know (-ledge), look (on), perceive, see, be sure, tell, understand, wish, wot. Compare 3700.

To see. This verb is obsolete in the present act. for which *horáō* (3708), to see with perception, is used. The tenses derived from the meaning of *eídō* form two families, one of which has exclusively the meaning of to see, the other that of to know:

(**I**) To see, implying not the mere act of seeing but the actual perception of some object, and thus differing from *blépō* (991), to see:

(**A**) Particularly, spoken of persons or things (Mt 2:2; 5:1; Mk 9:9; 11:13, 20; Jn 1:48; Ac 8:39; Heb 3:9; Rev 1:2), and also in various modified senses: (**1**) To behold, look upon, contemplate (Mt 9:36; 28:6; Mk 8:33; Lk 24:39; Jn 20:27; Sept.: Nu 12:8). (**2**) To see in order to know, to look at or into, examine (Mk 5:14; 6:38; 12:15; Lk 8:35; 14:18; Jn 1:39, 46). (**3**) To see face to face, to see and talk with, to visit, i.e. to have personal acquaintance and relationship with (Lk 8:20; 9:9; Jn 12:21; Ac 16:40; Ro 1:11; 1Co 16:7; Gal 1:19; Php 1:27; 2:28). Also of a city, such as Rome (Ac 19:21). (**4**) To wait to see, watch, observe (Mt 26:58; 27:49; Mk 15:36). (**5**) To see take place, witness, to live to see (Mt 13:17; 24:33; Mk 2:12). Also "to see one's day," meaning to witness the events of his life and times (Lk 17:22; Jn 8:56).

(**B**) Metaphorically, spoken of the mind: to perceive by the senses, to be aware of, to remark (Mt 9:2, 4; Lk 17:15; Jn 7:52; Ro 11:22).

(**C**) To see, i.e. to experience either good (meaning to enjoy) or evil (meaning to suffer), referring to death in (Lk 2:26; Jn 3:3; Ac 2:27, 31; 13:35; Heb 11:5; Rev 18:7; 1Pe 3:10; Sept.: Ps 89:48).

(**II**) To know, i.e. to have seen, perceived, apprehended:

(**A**) To be acquainted with, spoken of things (Mt 25:13; Mk 10:19; Lk 18:20; Jn 4:22; Ro 7:7; 13:11; Jude 5, 10; Sept.: Ex 3:7; Job 8:9. See also 1Co 16:15; 1Th 2:1); of persons (Mt 25:12; Mk 1:34; Jn 6:42; Ac 7:18; Heb 10:30; 1Pe 1:8). Used in an absolute sense (Lk 11:44; 2Co 11:11). Before an indirect question (Mt 24:43; Mk 13:35; Lk 12:39; Col 4:6; 1Th 4:2; 2Th 3:7).

(**B**) In the sense of to perceive, be aware of, understand (Mt 12:25; Mk 4:13; 12:15; Lk 11:17).

(**C**) By implication: to know how, i.e. to be able (Mt 7:11; Lk 12:56; Php 4:12; 1Th 4:4; 1Ti 3:5; Jas 4:17; 2Pe 2:9).

(**D**) From the Hebrew, with the idea of volition: to know and approve or love; hence spoken of men: to care for, take an interest in (1Th 5:12; Sept.: Ge 39:6). Of God: to know God, i.e. to acknowledge and adore God (Gal 4:8; 1Th 4:5; 2Th 1:8; Tit 1:16; Heb 8:11; Sept.: 1Sa 2:12; Job 18:21; Jer 31:34).

Deriv.: *Hádēs* (86), Hades; *apeídō* (542), to see fully; *eídos* (1491), appearance, shape, sight; *íde* (2396) and *epeidon* (1896), behold, look upon; *idéa* or *eidéa* (2397), aspect, countenance, idea; *ísēmi* (2467), to confirm; *proeídō* (4275), foresee; *suneidō* (4894), to understand together, metaphorically meaning to become aware; *hupereidon* (5237), to overlook.

Syn.: *blépō* (991), to see, to perceive, take heed; *horáō* (3708), to see; *emblépō* (1689), to look earnestly; *theōréō* (2334), to scrutinize; *theáomai* (2300), to behold with wonder; *epopteúō* (2029), to witness as a spectator or overseer; *atenízō* (816), to gaze upon; *katanoéō* (2657), to comprehend, apprehend, perceive fully; *óptomai* (3700), to see, both objectively and subjectively, sometimes *optánō*, to allow oneself to be seen; *noéō* (3539), to perceive with the mind; *katanoéō* (2657), to perceive clearly; *logízomai* (3049), to consider, use one's mind, take into account; *analogízomai* (357), to consider well; *suníēmi* (4920), to understand, consider; *ginṓskō* (1097), to know; *proséchō* (4337), to pay attention to, take heed.

1493. εἰδωλεῖον, eidōleion, *i-do-li´-on*; neuter of a presumed derivative of 1497; an *image-fane*:—idol's temple.

1494. εἰδωλόθυτον, eidōlothuton, *i-do-loth´-oo-ton*; neuter of a compound of 1497 and a presumed derivative of 2380; an *image-sacrifice*, i.e. part of an *idolatrous offering*:—(meat, thing that is) offered (in sacrifice, sacrificed) to (unto) idols.

Noun from *eídōlon* (1497), idol, and *thúō* (2380), to sacrifice. Whatever is sacrificed or offered to an idol, such as flesh or heathen sacrifices (Ac 15:29; 21:25; 1Co 8:1, 4, 7, 10; 10:19, 28; Rev 2:14, 20).

1495. εἰδωλολατρεία, eidōlolatreia, *i-do-lol-at-ri´-ah*; from 1497 and 2999; *image-worship* (literal or figurative):—idolatry.

Noun from *eídōlon* (1497), idol, and *latreía* (2999), service, worship. Idolatry, idol worship. Used only in the NT and Patristic Gr. (1Co 10:14; Gal 5:20; Col 3:5; 1Pe 4:3).

1496. εἰδωλολάτρης, eidōlolatrēs, *i-do-lol-at´-race*; from 1497 and the base of 3000; an *image-* (*servant* or) *worshipper* (literal or figurative):—idolater.

Noun from *eídōlon* (1497), idol, and *látris* (n.f.), a servant, worshipper. Idolater, a worshipper of idols (1Co 5:10, 11; 6:9; 10:7; Eph 5:5; Rev 21:8; 22:15).

Syn.: *ethnikós* (1482), heathen, Gentile; *proskunētḗs* (4353), worshipper.

1497. εἴδωλον, eidōlon, *i´-do-lon*; from 1491; an *image* (i.e. for worship); (by implication) a heathen *god*, or (plural) the *worship* of such:—idol.

Noun from *eídos* (1491), a form, appearance. In Class. Gr., any image or figure. In the NT, an idol, either an idol-image (Ac 7:41; 1Co 12:2; Rev 9:20; Sept.: 2Ch 33:22; Isa 30:22), or an idol-god, a heathen deity (1Co 8:4, 7; 10:19; Sept.: Nu 25:2; 2Ki 17:12, 33; 21:11, 20). By implication: idol-worship, idolatry (Ro 2:22; 2Co 6:16; 1Th 1:9; 1Jn 5:21).

Deriv.: *eidōleíon* (1493), idol temple; *eidōlóthuton* (1494), that which is sacrificed to idols; *eidōlolatreía* (1495), idolatry; *eidōlolátrēs* (1496), an idolater; *kateídōlos* (2712), utterly idolatrous, given to idolatry.

Syn.: *eikṓn* (1504), statue, icon, resemblance, image, representation.

1498. εἴην, eiēn, *i´-ane*; optative (i.e. English subjunctive) present of 1510 (including the other person); *might* (*could, would* or *should*) *be*:—mean, + perish, should be, was, were.

1499. εἰ καί, ei kai, *i kahee*; from 1487 and 2532; *if also* (or *even*):—if (that), though.

1500. εἰκῆ, eikē, *i-kay´*; probably from 1502 (through the idea of *failure*); *idly*, i.e. *without reason* (or *effect*):—without a cause, (in) vain (-ly).

1501. εἴκοσι, eikosi, *i´-kos-ee*; of uncertain affinity; a *score*:—twenty.

1502. εἴκω, eikō, *i´-ko*; apparently a primary verb; properly to *be weak*, i.e. *yield*:—give place.

1503. εἴκω, eikō, *i´-ko*; apparently a primary verb [perhaps akin to 1502 through the idea of *faintness* as a copy]; to *resemble*:—be like.

1504. εἰκών, eikōn, *i-kone´*; from 1503; a *likeness*, i.e. (literal) *statue, profile*, or (figurative) *representation, resemblance*:—image.

Noun from *eíkō* (1503), to be like, resemble. Likeness, image, effigy, figure (Mt 22:20; Mk 12:16; Lk 20:24; Ro 1:23), an idol-image, statue (Rev 13:14, 15; 14:9, 11; 15:2; 16:2; 19:20; Sept.: Dt 4:16; Isa 40:18, 20; Eze 23:14). In the sense of copy, representation (1Co 11:7; 2Co 4:4; Col 1:15; Heb 10:1). A likeness to anyone, resemblance, similitude (Ro 8:29; 1Co 15:49; Col 3:10).

1505. εἰλικρίνεια, eilikrineia, *i-lik-ree´-ni-ah*; from 1506; *clearness*, i.e. (by implication) *purity* (figurative):—sincerity.

Noun from *eilikrinḗs* (1506), pure, sincere. Clearness. Used metaphorically: pureness, sincerity (1Co 5:8; 2Co 1:12; 2:17).

Syn.: *euthútēs* (2118), rectitude; *haplótēs* (572), sincerity.

1506. εἰλικρινής, eilikrinēs, *i-lik-ree-nace´*; from **εἵλη, heilē** (the sun's *ray*) and 2919; *judged by sunlight*, i.e. tested as *genuine* (figurative):—pure, sincere.

Adjective from *heílē* (n.f.), the shining or splendour of the sun, and *krínō* (2919), to judge, discern. Judged of in sunshine; by implication: clear as light, manifest. In the NT, pure, sincere (Php 1:10; 2Pe 3:1).

Deriv.: *eilikríneia* (1505), sincerity.

Syn.: *ádolos* (97), guileless, pure; *ákakos* (172), without evil; *gnḗsios* (1103), true, genuine, sincere; *alēthḗs* (227), manifest, unconcealed; *alēthinós* (228), genuine, real; *hagnós* (53), pure; *katharós* (2513), pure, cleansed; *haploús* (573), sincere; *anupókritos* (505), unhypocritical.

1507. εἱλίσσω, heilissō, *hi-lis´-so*; a prolonged form of a primary but defective verb **εἵλω, heilō** (of the same meaning); to *coil* or *wrap*:—roll together. See also 1667.

1508. εἰ μή, ei mē, *i may*; from 1487 and 3361; *if not*:—but, except (that), if not, more than, save (only) that, saving, till.

1509. εἰ μή τι, ei mē ti, *i may tee*; from 1508 and the neuter of 5100; *if not somewhat*:—except.

1510. εἰμί, eimi, *i-mee´*; first person singular presumed indicative; a prolonged form of a primary and defective verb; *I exist* (used only when emphatic):—am, have been, × it is I, was. See also 1488, 1498, 1511, 1527, 2070, 2071, 2075, 2076, 2258, 2468, 2771, 5600.

To be is the usual verb of existence, and also the usual logical copula or link, connecting subj. and predicate:

(I) As a verb of existence, to be, to have existence:

(A) Particularly and generally: **(1)** In the metaphysical sense (Mk 12:32; Jn 1:1; 8:50, 58; Ac 19:2; Heb 11:6). Spoken of life: to exist, to live (Mt 2:18; 23:30); not to die (Ac 17:28). **(2)** Generally: to be, to exist, to be found, as of persons (Mt 12:11; Lk 4:25, 27; Jn 3:1; Ro 3:10, 11). Of things: to be, to exist, to have place (Mt 6:30; 22:23; Mk 7:15; Lk 6:43; Ac 2:29; Ro 13:1). **(3)** Spoken of time, generally (Mk 11:13; Lk 23:44; Jn 1:40; Ac 2:15; 2Ti 4:3); of festivals (Mk 15:42; Ac 12:3).

(B) By implication and by force of the adjuncts, *eimí* means to come to be, come into existence, similar to *gínomai* (1096), to come about: **(1)** To come to pass, take place, occur, be done. The fut. *éstai* and other tenses also have similar meaning (Lk 12:55 [cf. 21:11, 25; Ac 11:28; 27:25]). **(2)** To become something (Mt 19:5; 2Co 6:18; Eph 5:31; Heb 8:10; Jas 5:3).

(C) It is proper, in one's power or convenient (1Co 11:20; Heb 9:5).

(II) As a logical copula or link connecting the subj. and predicate: to be, where the predicate specifies who or what a person or thing is in respect to nature, origin, office, condition, circumstances, state, place, habits, disposition of mind. But this all lies in the predicate and not in the copula, which merely connects the predicate with the subj., e.g., Mt 2:6; Ac 2:32. *Eimí* is also used in this sense to construct metaphorical expressions (Mt 5:13, 14; 12:50; Lk 8:11; 12:1; Jn 1:4). When used as a copula, the forms of *eimí* are often omitted (Mt 9:37; 13:54; Mk 9:23; 1Co 10:26; 11:12).

Deriv.: *ápeimi* (548), to be absent; *éneimi* (1751), to be within; *páreimi* (3918), to be present; *súneimi* (4895), to be with.

Syn.: *gínomai* (1096), to begin to be, to come to pass; *hupárchō* (5225), to be in existence.

1511. εἶναι, einai, *i´-nahee*; presumed infinitive from 1510; *to exist*:—am, are, come, is, × lust after, × please well, there is, to be, was.

1512. εἴ περ, ei per, *i per*; from 1487 and 4007; *if perhaps*:—if so be (that), seeing, though.

1513. εἴ πως, ei pōs, *i poce*; from 1487 and 4458; *if somehow*:—if by any means.

1514. εἰρηνεύω, eirēneuō, *i-rane-yoo´-o*; from 1515; to *be* (*act*) *peaceful*:—be at (have, live in) peace, live peaceably.

From *eirḗnē* (1515), peace. To make peace, be at peace (Sept.: 1Ki 22:44). In the NT, used metaphorically: to live in peace, harmony, accord. Used in an absolute sense in 2Co 13:11. In 1Th 5:13, "be at peace among yourselves"; Mk 9:50, "with each other" (a.t.); Ro 12:18, "with all."

Syn.: *sigáō* (4601), to be silent, to hold one's peace; *hēsucházō* (2270), hold one's peace; *phimóō* (5392), to muzzle, hold one's peace.

1515. εἰρήνη, eirēnē, *i-rah´-nay*; probably from a primary verb **εἴρω, eirō** (to *join*); *peace* (literal or figurative); (by implication) *prosperity*:—one, peace, quietness, rest, + set at one again.

(I) Peace, particularly in a civil sense, the opposite of war and dissension (Lk 14:32; Ac 12:20; Rev 6:4). Among individuals, peace, harmony (Mt 10:34; Lk 12:51; Ac 7:26; Ro 14:19; Heb 7:2). Metaphorically: peace of mind, tranquillity, arising from reconciliation with God and a sense of a divine favour (Ro 5:1; 15:13; Php 4:7 [cf. Isa 53:5]).

(II) By implication, a state of peace, tranquillity (Lk 2:29; 11:21; Jn 16:33; Ac 9:31; 1Co 14:33; 1Th 5:3; Sept.: Jgs 6:23; Isa 14:30; Eze 38:8, 11).

(III) Peace, meaning health, welfare, prosperity, every kind of good. In Lk 1:79, "the way of peace" means the way of happiness; 2:14; 10:6, "son of peace" means son of happiness, i.e. one worthy of it; 19:42; Ro 8:6; Eph 6:15, "gospel of peace" means gospel of bliss, i.e. which leads to bliss; 2Th 3:16. "The God of peace" means the author and giver of blessedness (Ro 15:33; 16:20; Php 4:9; 1Th 5:23; Heb 13:20 [cf. Sept.: Isa 9:6, "the Prince of Peace"]). "Your peace" means the good or blessing which you have in Christ and share through salutation and benediction (Mt 10:13; Lk 10:6; Jn 14:27). The expression "with peace" means with good wishes, benediction, kindness (Ac 15:33; Heb 11:31). Simply "in peace" (1Co 16:11; Sept.: Ge 26:29; Ex 18:23). As used in formulas of salutation, either at meeting or parting, see *aspázomai* (782), to embrace, to greet. Thus on meeting, the salutation is "Peace be unto you [*eirḗnē humín*]," meaning every good wish (Lk 24:36; Jn 20:19, 21, 26; Da 10:19). Also in letters (Ro 1:7; 2:10; 1Co 1:3; 2Co 1:2; Gal 1:3). In Lk 10:5, "Peace unto this house" (a.t.) means every good wish for this house; Sept.: Jgs 19:20; 1Ch 12:18. At parting, *húpage* (5217), go, meaning to go away in peace (Mk 5:34; Jas 2:16). The same with the verb *poreúou* from *poreúomai* (4198), to go in peace (Lk 7:50; 8:48; Ac 16:36; Sept.: Jgs 18:6; 1Sa 1:17; 20:42).

Deriv.: *eirēneúō* (1514), to bring peace, reconcile; *eirēnikós* (1516), peaceful; *eirēnopoiéō* (1517), to make peace without necessarily effecting a change in the person or persons involved.

Syn.: *hēsuchía* (2271), quietness; *galḗnē* (1055), tranquillity, calm.

1516. εἰρηνικός, eirēnikos, *i-ray-nee-kos´*; from 1515; *pacific*; (by implication) *salutary*:—peaceable.

Adjective from *eirḗnē* (1515), peace. Pertaining to peace, peaceable or peaceful (Heb 12:11, healthful, wholesome; Jas 3:17, peaceful, disposed to peace; Sept.: Dt 2:26; Ps 37:37; 120:7). The reference is to *eirḗnē* (1515), peace, as the blessing of salvation.

Syn.: *hēsúchios* (2272), quiet, peaceful; *homóphrōn* (3675), harmonious, of one mind; *isópsuchos* (2473), of one soul, agreeable, likeminded; *ḗremos* (2263), tranquil.

1517. εἰρηνοποιέω, eirēnopoieō, *i-ray-nop-oy-eh´-o*; from 1518; to *be a peace-maker*, i.e. (figurative) to *harmonize*:—make peace.

From *eirḗnē* (1515), peace, and *poiéō* (4160), to make. To make peace, reconciliation (Col 1:20; Sept.: Pr 10:10).

Deriv.: *eirēnopoiós* (1518), peacemaking or a peacemaker.

Syn.: *diallássō* (1259), to conciliate, reconcile; *katallássō* (2644), to reconcile man to God when the change occurs in man; *apokatallássō* (604), to reconcile fully.

1518. εἰρηνοποιός, eirēnopoios, *i-ray-nop-oy-os´*; from 1518 and 4160; *pacificatory*, i.e. (subjective) *peaceable*:—peacemaker.

Noun from *eirēnopoiéō* (1517), to make peace. Peacemaker, an ambassador who comes to bring peace. In the NT, used metaphorically. Only in Mt 5:9.

1519. εἰς, eis, *ice*; a primary preposition; *to* or *into* (indicating the point reached or entered), of place, time, or (figurative) purpose (result, etc.); also in adverbial phrases:—[abundant-] ly, against, among, as, at, [back-] ward, before, by, concerning, + continual, + far more exceeding, for [intent, purpose], fore, + forth, in (among, at, unto, -so much that, -to), to the intent that, + of one mind, + never, of, (up-) on, + perish, + set at one again, (so) that, therefore (-unto), throughout, till, to (be, the end, -ward), (here-) until (-to), ... ward, [where-] fore, with. Often used in composition with the same general import, but only with verbs (etc.) expressing motion (literal or figurative).

Preposition with the primary idea of motion into any place or thing; also of motion or direction to, toward or upon any place, thing. The antithesis is expressed by *ek* (1537), out of.

(I) Of place, which is the primary and most frequent use, meaning into, to:

(A) After verbs implying motion of any kind: into or to, toward, upon any place or object, e.g., verbs of going, coming, leading, following, sending, growing, placing, delivering over to and the like (Mt 2:12; 4:8; 5:1; 6:6; 8:18; 12:44; 15:11, 17; 20:17; 21:18; Mk 1:38; 5:21; 6:45; 9:31; 13:14; Lk 8:23, 26; Jn 1:9; 7:14; 16:21, "is born into the world"; Ac 16:16; 26:14; Ro 5:12; 10:18; Rev 2:22).

(B) After verbs implying duration: upon, or toward any place or object, e.g., verbs of hearing, calling, announcing, showing (Mt 10:27; 22:3, 4; Mk 5:14; 13:10; Lk 7:1; 24:47; Jn 8:26; Ac 11:22, "hearing in the ears" [a.t.]; 1Co 14:9; 2Co 8:24; 11:6). Especially after verbs of looking (Mt 5:35, "toward Jerusalem" [a.t.], i.e. turning or looking toward it; Mt 22:16; Jn 13:22; Ac 1:10, 11; 3:4; Heb 11:26). After nouns (Ac 9:2, "letters [directed] to Damascus"; Ro 15:31, "my service which I have for Jerusalem").

(C) Metaphorically of a state or condition into which one comes, after verbs of motion, duration (Mt 25:46; Mk 5:26; 9:43; Lk 22:33; 24:20; Jn 4:38; 5:24; 16:13; Ac 26:18; 2Co 10:5; Gal 1:6; Php 1:12; 3:11; 2Ti 2:4; 3:6; Heb 2:10).

(II) Of time:

(A) Time meaning when, implying a term, limit, i.e. to, up to, until (Mt 10:22; Ac 4:3; 13:42; Php 1:10; 2:16; 1Th 4:15; 2Th 2:6; 2Pe 2:4; 3:7).

(B) Time, indicating how long, or marking duration, commonly translated for or from (Lk 1:50; 12:19). A frequent occurrence of this use in the NT is in the phrase *eis tṓn aiṓna*, lit. "until the age" (see *aiṓn* [165]), which is often translated forever or everlasting (Mt 12:19; Mk 11:14; Jn 6:58; Ro 9:5; Heb 5:6; Rev 1:6), and in some cases, never (Mk 3:29; Jn 10:28).

(III) Figuratively, as marking the object or point to or toward which anything ends:

(A) Spoken of a result, effect, consequence, marking that which any person or thing inclines toward or becomes (Mt 13:30, "bind them in bundles"; Jn 17:23 "perfect in one"; Ac 2:20; 10:4, "Thy prayers and thine alms are come up for [*eis*] a memorial before God"; Ro 10:10; 1Co 11:17; 15:54; Eph 2:21, 22; Heb 6:6, 8; 1Pe 1:22; Rev 11:6).

(B) Spoken of measure, degree, extent, chiefly by way of periphrasis for an adverb as in Lk 13:11, *eis tó pantelés* (3838), i.e. entirely, at all. In Heb 7:25, with the idea of perpetuity. In 2Co 4:17, *eis huperbolḗn* (5236), hyperbole, exceeding or exceedingly. In 2Co 10:13, *eis tá ámetra* (280), beyond the measure, i.e. immoderately, extravagantly. In 2Co 13:2, *eis tó pálin* (3825), means simply again. Also *eis kenón* (2756), empty, vain, means in vain (2Co 6:1; Gal 2:2; Php 2:16).

(C) Spoken of a direction of mind, i.e. as marking an object of desire, goodwill, also aversion **(1)** In a good sense, toward, for, on behalf of (Mt 26:10, "she did a good work for my benefit" [a.t.]; Ro 10:1, "unto salvation" [a.t.] or for or toward salvation; Ro 12:16; 14:19; 2Co 10:1; Php 1:23, "desire to depart" or to die; 1Th 4:10; 5:15; 2Pe 3:9). Also after nouns, e.g., love on behalf of someone (Ro 5:8; 2Co 2:4, 8; Eph 1:15); the gift bestowed upon someone or for the good of someone (2Co 1:11). After an adj. (Eph 4:32 "kind one to another"; 1Pe 4:9 "hospitable one to another"). With the verbs *elpízō* (1679), to hope, and *pisteúō* (4100), to believe, with *eis*, usually with a dat., in which case these verbs imply an affection or direction of mind toward a person or thing, i.e. to place hope or confidence in or upon (Mt 18:6, those "which believe [or place confidence] in me"; Jn 2:11; 5:45; 2Co 1:10 [cf. Ac 24:15]). The substantive *elpís* (1680), hope, or *pístis* (4102), faith, *eis* followed by the accusative, hope or faith in someone (Ac 20:21; 24:24; 1Pe 1:21). With *pepoíthēsis* (4006), confidence (2Co 8:22). **(2)** In an unfriendly sense, "against" (Mt 18:15; Mk 3:29; Lk 12:10, "whosoever shall speak a word against the Son of man," against the Holy Spirit, indicated by *eis*; Ac 9:1; 1Co 6:18, to sin against; Col 3:9). Also after nouns as in Ac 23:30 with *epiboulḗ* (1917), a plan against; Ro 8:7 with *échthra* (2189), enmity against God; Heb 12:3 with *antilogía* (485), contradiction against him.

(D) Spoken of an intention, purpose, aim, end: **(1)** In the sense of unto, in order to or for, i.e. for the purpose of, for the sake of, on account of (Mt 8:4, 34; 27:7, 10; Mk 1:4; Lk 5:4; 22:19; 24:20; Jn 1:7; 9:39; Ac 4:30; 11:29; 14:26; Ro 1:16, 17; 5:21; 6:19; 9:21; 10:4; 15:18; 1Co 2:7; 2Co 2:12; Eph 4:12; 2Ti 1:16). In Mt 18:20, "gathered together in my name," means on My account, because of Me, for My sake, in order to promote My cause. Also before an inf. with the article, in order to, in order that (Mt 20:19; Mk 14:55; Lk 20:20; Ro 1:11; 11:11; Jas 1:18). With the accusative meaning to what end? wherefore? why? (Mt 14:31; Mk 15:34). With *toúto* (5124), this, *eis toúto*, meaning to this end, for this purpose, therefore (Mk 1:38; Ac 9:21; Ro 9:17). Followed by the relative pron. *hó*, *eis hó*, meaning to which end, whereunto (2Th 1:11;

1Pe 2:8). (2) In the sense of to or for, implying use, advantage (Mt 5:13; 10:10; 20:1, "to hire labourers into his vineyard"; Mk 8:19, 20; Lk 7:30, "against themselves," i.e. to their own detriment; 9:13; 14:35, "neither for serving the land nor for the dunghill" [a.t.]; Jn 6:9; Ac 2:22; Ro 11:36; 15:26; 16:6; 1Co 8:6, unto him, for him, i.e. for his honour and glory; 2Co 8:6; Gal 4:11; Eph 1:5; 3:2; 1Pe 1:4).

(E) Generally as marking the obj. of any reference, relation, allusion unto or toward, i.e. with reference to: **(1)** In accordance with, conformable to (Mt 10:41, 42, "He that receiveth a prophet in the name of a prophet" means in accordance with the character of a prophet, or as a prophet, or with the honour due of a prophet). In Mt 12:41; Lk 11:32, "they repented at [*eis*] the preaching of Jonah," where *eis*, into, means conformable to or at the preaching of Jonah. In Ac 7:53, "received the law by the disposition of angels," *eis* means conformable to or in consequence of the arrangements of angels. (See *diatagḗ* (1296), arrangement.) **(2)** In the sense meaning as, as to, in respect to, concerning (Lk 12:21, "not rich toward [*eis*] God" means in respect to God; Ac 2:25, "For David speaketh concerning [*eis*] him"; 25:20, "because I doubted of such manner of questions," *eis tḗn … zḗtēsin* [2214], searching, question, where *eis* [TR] means concerning; Ro 4:20; 13:14; 16:5, 19; 2Co 2:9; 9:8; Gal 6:4; Eph 3:16; 5:32; 1Th 5:18; 2Ti 2:14; Heb 7:14; 1Pe 3:21).

In composition, *eis* implies: **(a)** motion into, as *eisdéchomai* (1523), to take into one's favour, receive; *eíseimi* (1524), to enter into; *eisérchomai* (1525), to enter in; *eisphérō* (1533), to bring in; **(b)** motion or direction, direction to, toward, as *eisakoúō* (1522), to listen to, hear.

1520. εἷς, heis, *hice*; (including the neuter [etc.] **ἕν**, ***hen***); a primary numeral; *one*:—a (-n, -ny, certain), + abundantly, man, one (another), only, other, some. See also 1527, 3367, 3391, 3762.

Masculine form *heís;* feminine *mía*; neuter *hén*. One, the first cardinal numeral:

(I) Without the substantive (Lk 18:19, "No one is good except one, God" [a.t.]; 1Co 9:24; Gal 3:20). In Mt 25:15, "to one he gave five talents, to the one two, to the other one [omitting the substantive talent repeated]" (a.t.). With a substantive (Mt 5:41, "one mile" [a.t.]; 6:27, "one cubit"; Mk 10:8, the two into one flesh; Jn 11:50; Ac 17:26; 1Co 10:8. With a neg., equivalent to not one, none (Mt 5:18, "one jot or one tittle shall in no wise pass"; Ro 3:12, "not so much as one" [a.t.], not even one, quoted from Ps 14:3; 53:4; Sept.: Jgs 4:16 [cf. Ex 9:7]). The expression *oudé* (3761), nor, followed by *heís* in the masc. or in the neuter *oudé hén*, not one, not even one, more emphatic than *oudeís* (3762), not even one. See Mt 27:14; Jn 1:3; Ac 4:32; Ro 3:10; 1Co 6:5. With the article *ho heís*, masc., and *tó hén*, neuter, the one (Mt 25:18, 24; 1Co 10:17). In Mt 5:19, "one of these least commandments"; Mk 6:15, "one of the prophets"; Lk 5:3; Jn 12:2. Also with *ek* (1537), of, followed by the gen. (Mt 18:12, "one of them"; Mk 9:17; Ac 11:28; Rev 5:5).

(II) Used distributively:

(A) *Heís / heís*, one / one, i.e. one / the other (Mt 20:21; 24:41; 27:38; Jn 20:12), fem. *mía / mía*. Also with the article *ho heís / ho heís*, the one / the other (Mt 24:40). In 1Th 5:11, *heís tón héna*, one another. In 1Co 4:6, *heís hupér* (5228), above, *toú henós*, the one above the other. In Mt 17:4, *mían / mían / mían*, one tent for each of the three, Jesus, Moses, and Elijah. See Mk 4:8; Lk 9:33; Sept.: Le 12:8; 1Sa 10:3; 13:17, 18; 2Ch 3:17. With the article *ho heís / ho héteros*, the one / the other (Mt 6:24; Lk 7:41; Ac 23:6). In Rev 17:10, *ho heís / ho állos* (243), other, the one / the other.

(B) *Heís hékastos* (1538), each one, every one (Ac 2:6; 20:31; Col 4:6). Followed by the gen. partitively (Lk 4:40; Ac 2:3; Eph 4:7). In Rev 21:21, *aná* (303), on, upon, *heís hékastos* means each one of the gates. See *aná* (303, II).

(C) The expression *kath' héna* or *kath' hén*, one by one, singly (Jn 21:25; 1Co 14:31). In Eph 5:33, *hoi kath' héna*, every one of you. In Ac 21:19, *kath' hén hékaston*, each one singly, where *kath' hén* here qualifies *hékaston*, each one. The expression *hén kath' hén*, one by one, one after another, singly (Rev 4:8 [UBS]). The expression *heís kath' heís*, one by one, is irregularly used in the NT for *heís kath' héna* (Mk 14:19; Jn 8:9). In Ro 12:5, *ho dé kath' heís*, and every one.

(III) Emphatic, one, i.e.:

(A) Even one, one single, only one (Mt 5:36; 21:24; Mk 8:14; 10:21; 12:6; Jn 7:21; 1Co 10:17; 2Pe 3:8). The expression *apó* (575), from, *miás* in Lk 14:18 means with one accord or voice. In the sense of only, alone (Mk 2:7; Jas 4:12). In Jn 20:7, "in only one place" (a.t.).

(B) One and the same (Ro 3:30; 1Co 3:8; Gal 3:28; Php 2:2; Heb 2:11; Rev 17:13; Sept.: Ge 41:25, 26). Fully written, *hén kaí tó autó* (1Co 11:5; 12:11).

(IV) Indefinitely meaning one, someone, anyone, the same as *tis* (5100), someone (Mt 19:16). With the substantive (Mt 8:19, "a … scribe"; Mk 12:42, "a … widow"; Jn 6:9; Ro 9:10). Followed by the gen. partitive, one of many (Lk 5:3; 20:1; Sept.: Ge 22:2; 27:45; 42:16). *Heís tis*, a certain one (Mk 14:51, "a certain young man," followed by the gen. [see Mk 14:47]). Followed by *ek* (1537), of, from (Lk 22:50; Jn 11:49). In this use, *heís* sometimes has the force of our indefinite article "a" or "an" as in Mt 21:19, "a fig tree"; Jas 4:13, "a year"; Rev 8:13; 9:13; Sept.: Ezr 4:8; Da 2:31; 8:3.

(V) As an ordinal, the first, mostly spoken of the first day of the week as in Mt 28:1 where the noun *hēméra* (2250), day, is understood. See Mk 16:2; Lk 24:1; Ac 20:7; 1Co 16:2. In the Sept. used for the first of the month (Ge 1:5; 8:13; Ex 40:2, 17). In Rev 9:12, the "one" means the first.

Deriv.: *héndeka* (1733), eleven; *henótēs* (1775), oneness, unity.

1521. εἰσάγω, eisagō, *ice-ag´-o*; from 1519 and 71; to *introduce* (literal or figurative):—bring in (-to), (+ was to) lead into.

1522. εἰσακούω, eisakouō, *ice-ak-oo´-o*; from 1519 and 191; to *listen* to:—hear.

1523. εἰσδέχομαι, eisdechomai, *ice-dekh´-om-ahee*; from 1519 and 1209; to *take into* one's favour:—receive.

From *eis* (1519), into, and *déchomai* (1209), to receive. To receive into favour or communion (only in 2Co 6:17, "and I will gather you" [a.t.], quoted apparently from Jer 32:37, 38. See Jer 23:3; Eze 11:17; 20:34, 41, of God gathering the exiles of Israel into their own land).

Syn.: *lambánō* (2983), to receive; *paralambánō* (3880), to receive from another; *prosdéchomai* (4327), to accept fabourably; *proslambánō* (4355), to receive, take to oneself; *apodéchomai* (588), to receive gladly.

1524. εἴσειμι, eiseimi, *ice´-i-mee*; from 1519 and **εἶμι**, ***eimi*** (to *go*); to *enter*:—enter (go) into.

1525. εἰσέρχομαι, eiserchomai, *ice-er´-khom-ahee*; from 1519 and 2064; to *enter* (literal or figurative):— × arise, come (in, into), enter in (-to), go in (through).

1526. εἰσί, eisi, *i-see´*; third person plural presumed indicative of 1510; they *are*:—agree, are, be, dure, × is, were.

1527. εἷς καθ εἷς, heis kath heis, *hice kath hice*; from 1520 repeated with 2596 inserted; *severally*:—one by one.

1528. εἰσκαλέω, eiskaleō, *ice-kal-eh´-o*; from 1519 and 2564; to *invite* in:—call in.

1529. εἴσοδος, eisodos, *ice´-od-os*; from 1519 and 3598; an *entrance* (literal or figurative):—coming, enter (-ing) in (to).

1530. εἰσπηδάω, eispēdaō, *ice-pay-dah´-o*; from 1519 and **πηδάω**, ***pēdaō*** (to *leap*); to *rush in*:—run (spring) in.

1531. εἰσπορεύομαι, eisporeuomai, *ice-por-yoo´-om-ahee*; from 1519 and 4198; to *enter* (literal or figurative):—come (enter) in, go into.

1532. εἰστρέχω, eistrechō, *ice-trekh´-o*; from 1519 and 5143; to *hasten inward*:—run in.

1533. εἰσφέρω, eispherō, *ice-fer´-o*; from 1519 and 5342; to *carry inward* (literal or figurative):—bring (in), lead into.

1534. εἶτα, eita, *i´-tah*; of uncertain affinity; a particle of *succession* (in time or logical enumeration), *then, moreover*:—after that (-ward), furthermore, then. See also 1899.

1535. εἴτε, eite, *i´-teh*; from 1487 and 5037; *if too*:—if, or, whether.

1536. εἴ τις, ei tis, *i tis*; from 1487 and 5100; *if any*:—he that, if a (-ny) man ('s, thing, from any, ought), whether any, whosoever.

1537. ἐκ, ek, *ek*; or **ἐξ**, ***ex***, *ex*; a primary preposition denoting *origin* (the point *whence* motion or action proceeds), *from, out* (of place, time or cause; literal or figurative; direct or remote):—after, among, × are, at, betwixt (-yond), by (the means of), exceedingly, (+ abundantly above), for (-th), from (among, forth, up), + grudgingly, + heartily, × heavenly, × hereby, + very highly, in, … ly, (because, by reason) of, off (from), on, out among (from, of), over, since, × thenceforth, through, × unto, × vehemently, with (-out). Often used in composition, with the same general import; often of *completion*.

Before a vowel, it is spelled *ex*. Prep., primarily meaning out of, from, of, as spoken of such objects which before were in another, but are now seperated from it, either in respect of place, time, source, or origin. It is the direct opposite of *eis* (1519), into or in.

(I) Of place, which is the primary and most frequent use, meaning out of, from:

(A) After verbs implying motion of any kind, out of or from any place or object, e.g., verbs of going, coming, sending, throwing, following, gathering, separating, removing, and the like (Mt 2:6, 15, "out of Egypt"; 7:5; 13:49, "the wicked from among the just" [also Mt 13:52; 17:5; 24:17]; Mk 1:11; 9:7; 11:8; 13:15 [also Mk 13:27; 16:3]; Lk 2:4; 10:18; 17:24; 23:55; Jn 1:19; 2:15; 13:1; Ac 23:10; 27:29, 30; Ro 11:24; 2Th 2:7; Heb 3:16; Rev 2:5).

(B) After verbs implying direction, out of or from any place, thus marking the point from which the direction sets off or tends (Lk 5:3, "taught the people out of the ship," i.e. from the boat or while in the boat; Mk 11:20 [cf. Job 28:9; Jn 19:23; Ac 28:4]). As implying the direction in which one is placed in respect to a person or thing, as to sit, stand, or be *ek dexiás* (1188), right hand side, or *ex euōnúmōn* (2176), the left hand side, where in Eng. we use at or on (Mt 20:21, 23; 22:44; 25:33; 26:64; Mk 10:37; Lk 1:11; Ac 2:25, 34; Heb 1:13; Sept.: Ex 14:22, 29; 1Sa 23:19, 24; Ps 16:8).

(C) Metaphorically, of a state or condition out of which one comes or is brought. After verbs of motion or direction as in Jn 10:28, 39, "out of his hand"; Ac 4:2; 17:3, "resurrection from the dead"; Ro 6:4, 9, 13; 7:4, 24; 11:15; 13:11; Col 1:18.

(II) Of time, of the beginning of a period of time, a point from which onward anything takes place (Mt 19:12, "from their mother's womb"; 19:20, "from my youth"; Lk 8:27, for a "long time" is lit. "from years"; Jn 6:64; 9:1, 32; Ac 9:33; 15:21; 24:10; Sept.: Ps 22:10; 71:6).

(III) Of the origin or source of anything, i.e. the primary, direct, immediate source, in distinction from *apó* (575), which marks the secondary, indirect origin, and *hupó* (5259), by, which denotes the immediate efficient agent.

(A) Of persons: of the place, stock, family, condition, meaning out of which one is derived or to which he belongs, e.g.: **(1)** Of the place from which one is, where one resides (Lk 8:27, "out of the city"; 23:7, "that he belonged unto Herod's jurisdiction"; Jn 1:46; Ac 23:34). In Col 4:9, 12, *ho ex humṓn*, "of you" means of your city; Lk 11:13, *ho patḗr ho ex ouranoú*, "heavenly Father"; elsewhere usually *en* (1722), in, *ouranṓ*, in heaven (Mt 5:45; 6:9; 7:21). **(2)** Of family, race, ancestors (Lk 1:5, "a … priest of the course of Abijah," 27; 2:4, "of the house of David"; Ac 4:6; 13:21; Ro 9:5, 6, 24; Heb 7:14). *Ek spérmatos* (4690), seed, followed by the gen., means of or from the seed, i.e. family or race of someone (Jn 7:42; Ro 1:3; 2Ti 2:8; Sept.: Ru 4:12; 1Ki 11:14). Followed by the gen., of the mother, to be born of a woman (Mt 1:3, 5, 6, 16; Gal 4:4, 22, 23). **(3)** Of condition or state (Jn 8:41, "We be not born of [*ek*] fornication"). *Hoi ek peritomḗs pistoí*, "they of the circumcision which believed" (see *peritomḗs* (4061), circumcision; *pistoí* (4103), believing), i.e. the Jewish Christians (Ac 10:45; cf. Ro 4:12; Gal 2:12).

(B) Of the source, i.e. the person or thing, out of or from which anything proceeds, is derived, or to which it pertains. **(1)** Used generally (Mt 21:19; Mk 11:30, "The baptism of John, was it from [*ek*] heaven, or of [*ek*] men?"; Lk 1:78; 10:11; Jn 1:13; 3:25, 27, 31; 4:22; 7:22; 10:16, 32; Ac 5:38; 19:25; Ro 2:29; 10:17; 1Co 2:12; 15:47; 2Co 5:2; 8:7; 9:2; Heb 2:11; 7:6; 1Jn 4:7; Rev 15:8). Spoken of an affection or state of mind out of which an emotion flows (2Co 2:4, "out of much affliction"; 2Ti 1:5; 1Pe 1:22); of any source of knowledge (Mt 12:33; Lk 6:44; Jn 12:34; Ro 2:18); of proof (Jas 2:18, "I shall show you my faith by [*ek*] my works," thus proving it; 3:13); of the source from which any judgement is drawn: from, out of, whereas in Eng. we would translate it "by" or "according to" (Mt 12:37, "by thy words thou shalt be justified"; Lk 19:22; Rev 20:12; Sept.: Nu 26:56). **(2)** As marking not only the source and origin, but also the character of any person or thing as derived from that source, implying connection, dependence, adherence, devotion, likeness (Jn 3:6, 8, "of the flesh"; 3:31, "of the earth"; 7:17, "he shall know of the doctrine, whether it be of God"; 8:23; 8:44; 8:47, "He that is of God, heareth God's words," i.e. character shows origin; 17:14, 16, "not of the world"; 1Jn 2:16, 29; 3:8–10; 4:1–7). Metaphorically, used of the source of character or quality, implying adherence to, connection with (Jn 18:37, "everyone that is of the truth," i.e. whose source is truth; Gal 3:10, 12; 1Jn 2:21; 3:19). Hence, *ek* forms a periphrasis for an adj. or part., e.g., *ho ek písteōs*, literally "a person of faith," a believer, (Ro 3:26; 4:16, a person "of the faith of Abraham," who believes as he did; Gal 3:7, 9); *ho ek nómou* (3551), law, one of the law, i.e. one under the law, an adherent of it (Ro 4:14, 16).

(C) Of the motive, ground, occasion from whence anything proceeds, the incidental cause, "from," "out of," i.e. by reason of, because of, in consequence of (Jn 4:6, being tired as a result of walking; 2Co 13:4, "He was crucified because of weakness [physical], but He lives by reason of the power of God" [a.t.]; Php 1:16, 17; 2Ti 6:4; Heb 7:12; Jas 4:1; Rev 8:11, 13; 16:10, 11, 21). With the verb *dikaióō* (1344), to justify, or *dikaioúmai ek písteōs*, to justify or to be justified by, from, on account of, or through faith (Ro 3:30; 5:1; Gal 2:16; 3:24). Elsewhere with the gen. (Ro 3:20; 4:2; Gal 2:16), with the adj. *díkaios* (1342), just or righteous, *ek písteōs*, just or righteous by or on account of faith (Ro 1:17). With the noun *dikaiosúnē* (1343), righteousness, *ek písteōs* (Ro 3:26; 9:30; 10:6, righteousness out of or resulting from faith).

(D) Of the efficient cause or agent, that from which any action or thing proceeds, is produced or effected, i.e. from, by (Mt 1:18, 20; Jn 6:65, "except it were given to him of my Father," i.e. if the efficient cause is not the Father; 12:49, *ex emautoú* (1683), "of myself"; Ro 9:10; 1Co 8:6; 2Co 1:11; 2:2; 7:9; Gal 5:8; Eph 4:16; Php 1:23; Rev 2:11; 9:2, 18).

(E) Of the manner or mode in which anything is done, out of, from, or, as we would express in Eng., in, with (Mt 12:34; Mk 12:30, 33, "to love him with [*ek*] all the heart … and with all the soul"; Lk 10:27; Jn 3:31; 8:44; Ac 8:37; Ro 6:17, heartily; 14:23, "not out of faith" [a.t.], i.e. not in or with faith; 2Co 8:11, "out of that which ye have"; 8:14; Eph 6:6; 1Th 2:3; 1Pe 4:11; 1Jn 4:5). In an adverb sense, e.g., *ek perissoú* (4053), abundance, meaning abundantly, exceedingly (Mk 6:51; 14:31); *ek mérous* (3313), part, meaning in part, partly (1Co 12:27; 13:9, 10, 12); *ek métrou* (3358), measure, meaning measurably, moderately (Jn 3:34); *ek sumphṓnou* (4859), agreement, meaning by mutual consent (1Co 7:5).

(F) Of the means, instrument, instrumental cause: from, i.e. by means of, by, through, with (Lk 16:9, "by means of" [a.t.]; Jn 3:5, "out of water" [a.t.]; 9:6; 1Co 9:13, 14, "live of the gospel," i.e. to live by means of the gospel; Heb 11:35; Rev 3:18, "gold tried by means of fire [*ek purós* (4442)]" [a.t.]; 17:2, 6; 18:3, 19). Also with verbs of filling, being full (Mt 23:25; Jn 12:3; Rev 8:5); also of a price as a means of acquiring anything (Mt 20:2, 13, for one dinar; 27:7, "and by means of them [silver coins] they bought the field" [a.t.]; Ac 1:18, where *ek* with the gen. is equivalent to the simple gen. which is the usual construction).

(G) Of the material, of, out of, from (Mt 27:29, "crown made of thorns" [a.t.]; Jn 2:15; Ro 9:21; 1Co 11:8; Eph 5:30; Heb 11:3; Rev 18:12; 21:21).

(H) Of the whole in relation to a part, a whole from which a part is spoken of, i.e. partitively (1Co 12:15, 16, "I am not [part] of the body"; Ac 10:1). After *esthíō* (2068) or *phágomai* (5315), to eat, *pínō* (4095), to drink, meaning to eat or drink of anything, i.e. part of it (Mt 26:27, 29; Lk 22:16; Jn 4:12–14; 6:26; 1Co 9:7; 11:28; Rev 2:7; 14:10; 18:3). Spoken of a class or number out of which one is separated, of which he forms part (Mk 14:69, "He is out of them" [a.t.], he belongs to them but he is separated from them; Lk 22:3; Jn 1:24; Ac 6:9; 21:8; Ro 16:10; Php 4:22; 2Ti 3:6). See *eimí* (1510, IX, C). After a numeral or pron., e.g., *heís* (1520), one (Mt 10:29, "one of them" [a.t.]; Mk 9:17; Lk 15:4); two (Mt 25:2, "five of them" [a.t.]; Mk 16:12; Jn 1:35, "two of his disciples" [a.t.]; Ac 26:23, "first of those from the resurrection of the dead" [a.t.]; Heb 7:4, "the tenth of the spoils"). After *tis* (5100), one, indefinite (Heb 4:1, "if any of you" [a.t.]); *tinés*, plural (Lk 11:15; Ac 11:20; Ro 11:14; Jas 2:16). After *tis* (5101) as an interrogative, who, which (Mt 21:31, "who of the two" [a.t.]; Lk 11:5; Jn 8:46). After *oudeís* (3762), none (Jn 7:19). Also with *tis* (sing.) and *tinés* (pl. implied) (Mt 23:34; Lk 21:16; Jn 9:40; 16:17; Rev 3:9).

In composition *ek* implies: **(a)** removal out, from, off, or away, as *ekbállō* (1544), to eject or to put away or out of; *ekphérō* (1627), to bring forth or out; (**b**) continuance, as *ekteínō* (1614), to extend, put or stretch forth; *ektréphō* (1625), to nourish, bring up; (**c**) completion, meaning "in full," as *ekdapanáō* (1550), to spend everything, all that one has; (**d**) intensiveness, as *ékdēlos* (1552), wholly evident or manifest; *exapatáō* (1818), to completely deceive; *ektarássō* (1613), to disturb completely.

1538. ἕκαστος, hekastos, *hek´-as-tos*; as if a superlative of **ἕκας**, ***hekas*** (*afar*); *each* or *every*:—any, both, each (one), every (man, one, woman), particularly.

Adjective from *hékas* (n.f.), separate. Each, every one, of any number separately, as in Mt 16:27, "every man," i.e. each one separately (Mt 26:22; Lk 6:44; Jn 7:53; Ro 2:6). This idea of separation or singling out is expressed still more strongly by *heís hékastos*, each one (Lk 4:40; Ac 2:3; 20:31; Eph 4:16; Rev 21:21).

Deriv.: *hekástote* (1539), each time, always.

Syn.: *pás* (3956), every one, any and every; *idía*, the dat. of *ídios* (2398), self, individual, individually.

1539. ἑκάστοτε, hekastote, *hek-as´-tot-eh*; as if from 1538 and 5119; at *every time*:—always.

1540. ἑκατόν, hekaton, *hek-at-on´*; of uncertain affinity; a *hundred*:—hundred.

1541. ἑκατονταέτης, hekatontaetēs, *hek-at-on-tah-et´-ace*; from 1540 and 2094; *centenarian*:—hundred years old.

1542. ἑκατονταπλασίων, hekatontaplasiōn, *hek-at-on-ta-plah-see´-own*; from 1540 and a presumed derivative of 4111; a *hundred times*:—hundredfold.

1543. ἑκατοντάρχης, hekatontarchēs, *hek-at-on-tar´-khace*; or **ἑκατόνταρχος**, ***hekatontarchos***; *hek-at-on´-tar-khos*; from 1540 and 757; the *captain of one hundred men*:—centurion.

1544. ἐκβάλλω, ekballō, *ek-bal´-lo*; from 1537 and 906; to *eject* (literal or figurative):—bring forth, cast (forth, out), drive (out), expel, leave, pluck (pull, take, thrust) out, put forth (out), send away (forth, out).

1545. ἔκβασις, ekbasis, *ek´-bas-is*; from a compound of 1537 and the base of 939 (meaning to *go out*); an *exit* (literal or figurative):—end, way to escape.

1546. ἐκβολή, ekbolē, *ek-bol-ay´*; from 1544; *ejection*, i.e. (special) a *throwing overboard* of the cargo:— + lighten the ship.

1547. ἐκγαμίζω, ekgamizō, *ek-gam-id´-zo*; from 1537 and a form of 1061 [compare 1548]; to *marry off* a daughter:—give in marriage.

1548. ἐκγαμίσκω, ekgamiskō, *ek-gam-is´-ko*; from 1537 and 1061; the same as 1547:—give in marriage.

1549. ἔκγονον, ekgonon, *ek´-gon-on*; neuter of a derivative of a compound of 1537 and 1096; a *descendant*, i.e. (special) *grandchild*:—nephew.

1550. ἐκδαπανάω, ekdapanaō, *ek-dap-an-ah´-o*; from 1537 and 1159; to *expend* (wholly), i.e. (figurative) *exhaust*:—spend.

1551. ἐκδέχομαι, ekdechomai, *ek-dekh´-om-ahee*; from 1537 and 1209; to *accept from* some source, i.e. (by implication) to *await*:—expect, look (tarry) for, wait (for).

From *ek* (1537), out, and *déchomai* (1209), to receive. To watch for, expect, to be about to receive from any quarter (Jn 5:3; 1Co 16:11; Heb 11:10; Jas 5:7); expect, wait for (Ac 17:16; 1Co 11:33; Heb 10:13; 1Pe 3:20).

Deriv.: *apekdéchomai* (553), to look for, expect fully; *ekdochḗ* (1561), expectation.

Syn.: *anaménō* (362), to wait for in confident expectancy; *apekdéchomai* (553), to await or expect eagerly; *elpízō* (1679), to hope for; *periménō* (4037), to wait for; *prosdokáō* (4328), to watch toward, look for; *paredreúō* (4332), to wait upon with steadfastness; *proskarteréō* (4342), to wait on; *prosdéchomai* (4367), to expect, look for.

1552. ἔκδηλος, ekdēlos, *ek´-day-los*; from 1537 and 1212; *wholly evident*:—manifest.

1553. ἐκδημέω, ekdēmeō, *ek-day-meh´-o*; from a compound of 1537 and 1218; to *emigrate*, i.e. (figurative) *vacate* or *quit*:—be absent.

From *ékdēmos* (n.f.), away from home, which is from *ek* (1537), from or out of, and *dḗmos* (1218), people. To go out from one's people, to be absent from one's country. In the NT, generally to be absent from any place or person (2Co 5:6, 8, 9).

Deriv.: *sunékdēmos* (4898), absent or traveling.

Syn.: *apogínomai* (581), to be away from; *apodēméō* (589), to go abroad, go away from where one is; *apothnḗskō* (599), to die off or out; *thnḗskō* (2348), to die; *teleutáō* (5053), to reach the end of the present state of being.

1554. ἐκδίδωμι, ekdidōmi, *ek-did´-o-mee*; from 1537 and 1325; to *give forth*, i.e. (special) to *lease*:—let forth (out).

1555. ἐκδιηγέομαι, ekdiēgeomai, *ek-dee-ayg-eh´-om-ahee*; from 1537 and a compound of 1223 and 2233; to *narrate through* wholly:—declare.

1556. ἐκδικέω, ekdikeō, *ek-dik-eh´-o*; from 1558; to *vindicate, retaliate, punish*:—a (re-) venge.

From *ékdikos* (1558), avenger. To execute justice, defend one's cause, maintain one's right (Lk 18:3, 5; Sept.: Ps 37:28). To avenge, i.e. to make penal satisfaction (Ro 12:19; cf. Ro 12:17, 20). To take vengeance on, to punish, e.g., in the constructions "avenge the blood on" or "at the hand of" (a.t.) someone (Rev 6:10; 19:2. See Sept.: 2Ki 9:7 [cf. Dt 18:19; Hos 1:4]). In the sense of simply to punish (2Co 10:6; Sept.: Ex 21:20).

Deriv.: *ekdíkēsis* (1557), vengeance, the bringing forth of justice.

Syn.: *antapodídōmi* (467), to repay; *apodídōmi* (591), to requite.

1557. ἐκδίκησις, ekdikēsis, *ek-dik´-ay-sis*; from 1556; *vindication, retribution*:—(a-, re-) venge (-ance), punishment.

Noun from *ekdikéō* (1556), to execute justice. Execution of right, justice:

(**I**) Maintenance of right, support, protection, hence, *poiéō ekdíkēsin* (*poiéō* [4160], to do) is the same as *ekdikéō*, to maintain one's right, defend one's cause, followed by the gen. of person, meaning for whom (Lk 18:7, 8). Followed by the dat. of person, meaning against whom (Ac 7:24 [cf. Sept.: Jgs 11:36; 2Sa 22:48]).

(**II**) Vengeance, i.e. penal retribution (Ro 12:19; Heb 10:30; Sept.: 2Sa 4:8; Ps 79:10; Jer 11:20; Hos 9:7). In the sense of vindictive justice: punishment (Lk 21:22; 2Th 1:8; 1Pe 2:14). Referring to the evildoer (2Co 7:11 [cf. 2Co 7:12; Sept.: Mic 5:15]).

Syn.: *epitimía* (2009), penalty, punishment; *kólasis* (2851), punishment; *kríma* (2917), condemnation; *krísis* (2920), judgement; *timōría* (5098), vengeance, punishment which vindicates one's honour.

1558. ἔκδικος, ekdikos, *ek´-dik-os*; from 1537 and 1349; carrying *justice out*, i.e. a *punisher*:—a (re-) venger.

Noun from *ek* (1537), from, out, and *díkē* (1349), justice. Executing right and justice, hence an avenger, punisher (Ro 13:4; 1Th 4:6).

Deriv.: *ekdikéō* (1556), to execute justice.

Syn.: *dikastḗs* (1348), one who brings justice among people; *kritḗs* (2923), judge; *misthapodótēs* (3406), rewarder.

1559. ἐκδιώκω, ekdiōkō, *ek-dee-o´-ko*; from 1537 and 1377; to *pursue out*, i.e. *expel* or *persecute* implacably:—persecute.

1560. ἔκδοτος, ekdotos, *ek´-dot-os*; from 1537 and a derivative of 1325; *given out* or *over*, i.e. *surrendered*:—delivered.

1561. ἐκδοχή, ekdochē, *ek-dokh-ay´*; from 1551; *expectation*:—looking for.

Noun from *ekdéchomai* (1551), to expect. A looking for, expectation (Heb 10:27).

Syn.: *apokaradokía* (603), intense anticipation; *prosdokía* (4329), watching for, expectation; *elpís* (1680), hope.

1562. ἐκδύω, ekduō, *ek-doo´-o*; from 1537 and the base of 1416; to cause to *sink out* of, i.e. (specially as of clothing) to *divest*:—strip, take off from, unclothe.

1563. ἐκεῖ, ekei, *ek-i´*; of uncertain affinity; *there*; by extension *thither*:—there, thither (-ward), (to) yonder (place).

1564. ἐκεῖθεν, ekeithen, *ek-i´-then*; from 1563; *thence*:—from that place, (from) thence, there.

1565. ἐκεῖνος, ekeinos, *ek-i´-nos*; from 1563; *that* one (or [neuter] thing); often intensified by the article prefixed:—he, it, the other (same), selfsame, that (same, very), × their, × them, they, this, those. See also 3778.

1566. ἐκεῖσε, ekeise, *ek-i´-seh*; from 1563; *thither*:—there.

1567. ἐκζητέω, ekzēteō, *ek-zay-teh´-o*; from 1537 and 2212; to *search out*, i.e. (figurative) *investigate, crave, demand*, (by Hebrew) *worship*:—en- (re-) quire, seek after (carefully, diligently).

1568. ἐκθαμβέω, ekthambeō, *ek-tham-beh´-o*; from 1569; to *astonish* utterly:—affright, greatly (sore) amaze.

1569. ἔκθαμβος, ekthambos, *ek´-tham-bos*; from 1537 and 2285; *utterly astounded*:—greatly wondering.

1570. ἔκθετος, ekthetos, *ek´-thet-os*; from 1537 and a derivative of 5087; *put out*, i.e. *exposed* to perish:—cast out.

1571. ἐκκαθαίρω, ekkathairō, *ek-kath-ah´ee-ro*; from 1537 and 2508; to *cleanse thoroughly*:—purge (out).

1572. ἐκκαίω, ekkaiō, *ek-kah´-yo*; from 1537 and 2545; to *inflame* deeply:—burn.

1573. ἐκκακέω, ekkakeō, *ek-kak-eh´-o*; from 1537 and 2556; to *be* (*bad* or) *weak*, i.e. (by implication) to *fail* (in heart):—faint, be weary.

From *ek* (1537), out of, or an intensive, and *kakós* (2556), bad. To turn out to be a coward, to lose one's courage. In the NT, generally: to be fainthearted, to faint or despond in view of trial, difficulty. Intransitively (2Co 4:1, 16; Eph 3:13). In the sense of to be remiss or slothful in duty (Lk 18:1; Gal 6:9; 2Th 3:13).

Syn.: *apopsúchō* (674), to lose soul or heart, faint; *eklúō* (1590), to be faint, grow weary; *kámnō* (2577), to be weary.

1574. ἐκκεντέω, ekkenteō, *ek-ken-teh´-o*; from 1537 and the base of 2759; to *transfix*:—pierce.

1575. ἐκκλάω, ekklaō, *ek-klah´-o*; from 1537 and 2806; to *exscind*:—break off.

1576. ἐκκλείω, ekkleiō, *ek-kli´-o*; from 1537 and 2808; to *shut out* (literal or figurative):—exclude.

1577. ἐκκλησία, ekklēsia, *ek-klay-see´-ah*; from a compound of 1537 and a derivative of 2564; a *calling out*, i.e. (concretely) a popular *meeting*, especially a religious *congregation* (Jewish *synagogue*, or Christian community of members on earth or saints in heaven or both):—assembly, church.

Noun from *ékklētos* (n.f.), called out, which is from *ekkaléō* (n.f.), to call out. A convocation, assembly, congregation:

(I) Of persons legally called out or summoned (Ac 19:39, of the people); and hence also of a tumultuous assembly not necessarily legal (Ac 19:32, 41). In the Jewish sense: a congregation, assembly of the people for worship, e.g., in a synagogue (Mt 18:17), or generally (Ac 7:38; Heb 2:12 quoted from Ps 22:22; Sept.: Dt 18:16; 2Ch 1:3, 5).

(II) In the Christian sense: an assembly of Christians, generally (1Co 11:18, a church, the Christian church).

(A) A particular church, e.g., in Jerusalem (Ac 8:1; 11:22); Antioch (Ac 11:26; 13:1); Corinth (1Co 1:2; 2Co 1:1); Asia Minor (1Co 16:19); Galatia (Gal 1:2); Thessalonica (1Th 1:1; 2Th 1:1); Cenchrea (Ro 16:1). Also, "the churches of the nations" (a.t.) means churches of Gentile Christians (Ro 16:4); the church which meets at the house of someone (Ro 16:5; 1Co 16:19; Phm 2); the churches of Christ (Ro 16:16); the church of God at Corinth (1Co 1:2).

(B) The universal church (Mt 16:18; 1Co 12:28; Gal 1:13; Eph 1:22; 3:10; Heb 12:23); church of God (1Co 10:32; 11:22; 15:9; 2Ti 3:15 [cf. in the Sept. the church of the Lord {Dt 23:2, 3}]).

1578. ἐκκλίνω, ekklinō, *ek-klee´-no*; from 1537 and 2827; to *deviate*, i.e. (absolute) to *shun* (literal or figurative), or (relative) to *decline* (from piety):—avoid, eschew, go out of the way.

1579. ἐκκολυμβάω, ekkolumbaō, *ek-kol-oom-bah´-o*; from 1537 and 2860; to *escape* by *swimming*:—swim out.

1580. ἐκκομίζω, ekkomizō, *ek-kom-id´-zo*; from 1537 and 2865; to *bear forth* (to burial):—carry out.

1581. ἐκκόπτω, ekkoptō, *ek-kop´-to*; from 1537 and 2875; to *exscind*; (figurative) to *frustrate*:—cut down (off, out), hew down, hinder.

1582. ἐκκρέμαμαι, ekkremamai, *ek-krem´-am-ahee*; middle from 1537 and 2910; to *hang upon* the lips of a speaker, i.e. *listen closely*:—be very attentive.

1583. ἐκλαλέω, eklaleō, *ek-lal-eh´-o*; from 1537 and 2980; to *divulge*:—tell.

1584. ἐκλάμπω, eklampō, *ek-lam´-po*; from 1537 and 2989; to *be resplendent*:—shine forth.

1585. ἐκλανθάνομαι, eklanthanomai, *ek-lan-than´-om-ahee*; middle from 1537 and 2990; to *be* utterly *oblivious* of:—forget.

1586. ἐκλέγομαι, eklegomai, *ek-leg´-om-ahee*; middle from 1537 and 3004 (in its primary sense); to *select*:—make choice, choose (out), chosen.

From *ek* (1537), out, and *légō* (3004), to select, choose. To choose, select, choose for oneself. In the NT found only in the middle *eklégomai*:

(I) Generally, of things (Lk 10:42; 14:7). Followed by *hína* (2443), so that, of purpose (1Co 1:27, 28; Sept.: Ge 13:11); of persons (Jn 6:70; 15:16; Ac 1:2, 24; 6:5; 15:22, 25; Sept.: 1Sa 8:18; 10:24); followed by *ek* (1537), from (Jn 15:19); followed by *apó* (575), of (Lk 6:13). With an inf. implied (Jas 2:5 where the implied inf. is *eínai* [1511], to be). Followed by *en* (1722), among (Ac 15:7, "God made choice among us").

(II) By implication: to choose out, with the accessory idea of kindness, favour, love (Mk 13:20; Jn 13:18; Ac 13:17; Eph 1:4; Sept.: Dt 4:37; Ps 65:4; Zec 3:2). In some MSS, Lk 9:35 (TR) has *eklelegménos*, chosen, instead of *agapētós* (27), beloved.

Deriv.: *eklektós* (1588), chosen, elect.

Syn.: *hairéomai* (138), to prefer; *hairetízō* (140), to prefer, choose; *epilégomai* (1951), to select, choose for oneself.

1587. ἐκλείπω, ekleipō, *ek-li´-po*; from 1537 and 3007; to *omit*, i.e. (by implication) *cease* (*die*):—fail.

1588. ἐκλεκτός, eklektos, *ek-lek-tos´*; from 1586; *select*; (by implication) *favorite*:—chosen, elect.

Adjective from *eklégō* (1586), to choose, select. Chosen, select:

(I) Select, choice, excellent. Used as an adj. in regard to stone as in 1Pe 2:4, 6 quoted from Isa 28:16; see Ezr 5:8. Of persons, chosen or distinguished as in 1Pe 2:9, *génos eklektón* (*génos* [1085], generation), "a chosen generation," referring to the believers in Christ. See Sept.: Isa 43:20. Of angels in 2Ti 5:21, referring to them as chosen by God to minister to the special needs of believers.

(II) By implication meaning chosen, with the accessory idea of kindness, favour, love, equivalent to cherished, beloved (Lk 23:35, "the chosen of God"; Ro 16:13; Sept.: Ps 105:6; 1Ch 16:13). Hence *hoi eklektoí*, the elect, i.e. those chosen of God for salvation or as members of the kingdom of heaven, and who therefore enjoy his favour, and lead a holy life in communion with him. They are also called saints (Ro 1:7; 15:31); Christians (Ac 11:26; 26:28; 1Pe 4:16).

Deriv.: *suneklektós* (4899), elected together with.

1589. ἐκλογή, eklogē, *ek-log-ay´*; from 1586; (divine) *selection* (abstract or concrete):—chosen, election.

Noun from *eklégō* (1586), to choose, select. Election, choice, selection:

(I) Generally as in Ac 9:15, a chosen vessel, an instrument of usefulness.

(II) Election, the benevolent purpose of God by which any are chosen unto salvation so that they are led to embrace and persevere in

Christ's bestowed grace and the enjoyment of its privileges and blessings here and hereafter (Ro 11:15, 28; 1Th 1:4; 2Pe 2:10).

(III) By implication meaning free choice, free will, election. In Ro 9:11 we have the expression, "that the purpose of God according to election might stand." This means that God's intention (*próthesis* [4286]) was according to the principle of election which is God's free choice without being affected by any outside circumstances or the worth of the individuals concerned.

Syn.: *haíresis* (139), choice.

1590. ἐκλύω, ekluō, *ek-loo´-o*; from 1537 and 3089; to *relax* (literal or figurative):—faint.

1591. ἐκμάσσω, ekmassō, *ek-mas´-so*; from 1537 and the base of 3145; to *knead out*, i.e. (by analogy) to *wipe dry*:—wipe.

1592. ἐκμυκτερίζω, ekmukterizō, *ek-mook-ter-id´-zo*; from 1537 and 3456; to *sneer* outright at:—deride.

1593. ἐκνεύω, ekneuō, *ek-nyoo´-o*; from 1537 and 3506; (by analogy) to *slip off*, i.e. quietly *withdraw*:—convey self away.

1594. ἐκνήφω, eknēphō, *ek-nay´-fo*; from 1537 and 3525; (figurative) to *rouse* (oneself) *out* of stupor:—awake.

1595. ἑκούσιον, hekousion, *hek-oo´-see-on*; neuter of a derivative from 1635; *voluntariness*:—willingly.

Adjective from *hekṓn* (1635), willingly. Voluntary, willing. Only in Phm 14 where it means willingly, uncompelled, gladly (Sept.: Nu 15:3).

Deriv.: *hekousíōs* (1596), voluntarily.

Syn.: *authaíretos* (830), voluntary, willing; *hétoimos* (2092), ready; *próthumos* (4289), willing.

1596. ἑκουσίως, hekousiōs, *hek-oo-see´-oce*; adverb from the same as 1595; *voluntarily*:—wilfully, willingly.

Adverb from *hekoúsios* (1595), voluntary. Voluntarily, intentionally (Heb 10:26; 1Pe 5:2; Sept.: Ps 54:6).

Syn.: *hekṓn* (1635), voluntarily, willingly.

1597. ἔκπαλαι, ekpalai, *ek´-pal-ahee*; from 1537 and 3819; *long ago, for a long while*:—of a long time, of old.

1598. ἐκπειράζω, ekpeirazō, *ek-pi-rad´-zo*; from 1537 and 3985; to *test thoroughly*:—tempt.

From *ek* (1537), an intensive, and *peirázō* (3985), tempt. Try, prove, tempt, put to the test (Mt 4:7; Lk 4:12; 10:25; 1Co 10:9; Sept.: Dt 6:16; 8:16; Ps 78:18).

Syn.: *peirázō* (3985), to test; *dokimázō* (1381), to test, prove.

1599. ἐκπέμπω, ekpempō, *ek-pem´-po*; from 1537 and 3992; to *despatch*:—send away (forth).

1600. ἐκπετάννυμι, ekpetannumi, *ek-pet-an´-noo-mee*; from 1537 and a form of 4072; to *fly out*, i.e. (by analogy) *extend*:—stretch forth.

1601. ἐκπίπτω, ekpiptō, *ek-pip´-to*; from 1537 and 4098; to *drop away*; specially *be driven out* of one's course; (figurative) to *lose, become inefficient*:—be cast, fail, fall (away, off), take no effect.

1602. ἐκπλέω, ekpleō, *ek-pleh´-o*; from 1537 and 4126; to *depart* by ship:—sail (away, thence).

1603. ἐκπληρόω, ekplēroō, *ek-play-ro´-o*; from 1537 and 4137; to *accomplish* entirely:—fulfill.

From *ek* (1537), an intensive, and *pleróō* (4137), to fill, fulfill. To fulfill entirely, completely (Ac 13:33, "the promise").

Deriv.: *eklḗrōsis* (1604), accomplishment.

Syn.: *anaplēróō* (378), to fill up, fill completely; *empíplēmi* (1705), to fill full; *epiteléō* (2005), to fill further, finish; *plḗthō* (4130), to fill; *sunteléō* (4931), to complete, bring to completion; *teleióō* (5048), to bring to an end, fulfill; *teléō* (5055), to fulfill.

1604. ἐκπλήρωσις, ekplērōsis, *ek-play´-ro-sis*; from 1603; *completion*:—accomplishment.

Noun from *ekplēróō* (1603), to fulfill. A fulfilling, accomplishment (only in Ac 21:26 announcing the fulfillment [full observance] of the days, i.e. that he was about to keep in full the proper number of days; see Nu 6:9).

Syn.: *plḗrōma* (4138), a filling up, fulfillment; *teleíōsis* (5050), performance, fulfillment.

1605. ἐκπλήσσω, ekplēssō, *ek-place´-so*; from 1537 and 4141; to *strike* with astonishment:—amaze, astonish.

1606. ἐκπνέω, ekpneō, *ek-pneh´-o*; from 1537 and 4154; to *expire*:—give up the ghost.

1607. ἐκπορεύομαι, ekporeuomai, *ek-por-yoo´-om-ahee*; from 1537 and 4198; to *depart, be discharged, proceed, project*:—come (forth, out of), depart, go (forth, out), issue, proceed (out of).

1608. ἐκπορνεύω, ekporneuō, *ek-porn-yoo´-o*; from 1537 and 4203; to *be utterly unchaste*:—give self over to fornication.

1609. ἐκπτύω, ekptuō, *ek-ptoo´-o*; from 1537 and 4429; to *spit out*, i.e. (figurative) *spurn*:—reject.

1610. ἐκριζόω, ekrizoō, *ek-rid-zo´-o*; from 1537 and 4492; to *uproot*:—pluck up by the root, root up.

1611. ἔκστασις, ekstasis, *ek´-stas-is*; from 1839; a *displacement* of the mind, i.e. *bewilderment*, "*ecstasy*":— + be amazed, amazement, astonishment, trance.

From *exístēmi* (1839), to remove out of its place or state. A putting away, removal of anything out of a place. In the NT, used metaphorically: ecstasy, i.e. the state of being out of one's usual mind:

(I) Arising from any strong emotion, e.g., astonishment, amazement (Mk 5:42; 16:8; Lk 5:26; Ac 3:10; Sept.: Ge 27:33; Dt 28:28; 2Ch 14:14; Eze 27:35).

(II) A trance, i.e. a state in which the soul is unconscious of present objects, being rapt into visions of distant or future things (Ac 10:10; 11:5; 22:17 [cf. 2Co 12:2; Eze 1:1 {cf. Sept.: Ge 2:21}]).

Syn.: *aporía* (640), bewilderment; *thámbos* (2285), astonishment; *hórasis* (3706), gazing, vision; *phóbos* (5401), fear.

1612. ἐκστρέφω, ekstrephō, *ek-stref´-o*; from 1537 and 4762; to *pervert* (figurative):—subvert.

1613. ἐκταράσσω, ektarassō, *ek-tar-as´-so*; from 1537 and 5015; to *disturb wholly*:—exceedingly trouble.

1614. ἐκτείνω, ekteinō, *ek-ti´-no*; from 1537 and **τείνω, teinō** (to *stretch*); to *extend*:—cast, put forth, stretch forth (out).

1615. ἐκτελέω, ekteleō, *ek-tel-eh´-o*; from 1537 and 5055; to *complete* fully:—finish.

1616. ἐκτένεια, ekteneia, *ek-ten´-i-ah*; from 1618; *intentness*:—× instantly.

1617. ἐκτενέστερον, ektenesteron, *ek-ten-es´-ter-on*; neuter of the comparative of 1618; *more intently*:—more earnestly.

1618. ἐκτενής, ektenēs, *ek-ten-ace´*; from 1614; *intent*:—without ceasing, fervent.

Adjective from *ekteínō* (1614), to stretch out, extend. Stretched out, continual, intense (Ac 12:5 [TR]; 1Pe 4:8). The comparative: *ektenésteron* (1617), more intensely, earnestly.

Deriv.: *ektenṓs* (1619), intensely, earnestly.

Syn.: *adiáleiptos* (88), unceasing; *makrós* (3117), long; *spoudaíos* (4705), diligent, earnest.

1619. ἐκτενῶς, ektenōs, *ek-ten-oce´*; adverb from 1618; *intently*:—fervently.

1620. ἐκτίθημι, ektithēmi, *ek-tith´-ay-mee*; from 1537 and 5087; to *expose*; (figurative) to *declare*:—cast out, expound.

1621. ἐκτινάσσω, ektinassō, *ek-tin-as´-so*; from 1537 and **τινάσσω, tinassō** (to *swing*); to *shake* violently:—shake (off).

1622. ἐκτός, ektos, *ek-tos´*; from 1537; the *exterior*; figurative (as a preposition) *aside from, besides*:—but, except (-ed), other than, out of, outside, unless, without.

1623. ἕκτος, hektos, *hek´-tos*; ordinal from 1803; *sixth*:—sixth.

1624. ἐκτρέπω, ektrepō, *ek-trep´-o*; from 1537 and the base of 5157; to *deflect*, i.e. *turn away* (literal or figurative):—avoid, turn (aside, out of the way).

1625. ἐκτρέφω, ektrephō, *ek-tref´-o*; from 1537 and 5142; to *rear up* to maturity, i.e. (genitive) to *cherish* or *train*:—bring up, nourish.

1626. ἔκτρωμα, ektrōma, *ek´-tro-mah*; from a compound of 1537 and **τιτρώσκω,** ***titrōskō*** (to *wound*); a *miscarriage* (*abortion*), i.e. (by analogy) *untimely birth*:—born out of due time.

1627. ἐκφέρω, ekpherō, *ek-fer´o*; from 1537 and 5342; to *bear out* (literal or figurative):—bear, bring forth, carry forth (out).

1628. ἐκφεύγω, ekpheugō, *ek-fyoo´-go*; from 1537 and 5343; to *flee out*:—escape, flee.

1629. ἐκφοβέω, ekphobeō, *ek-fob-eh´-o*; from 1537 and 5399; to *frighten utterly*:—terrify.

1630. ἔκφοβος, ekphobos, *ek´-fob-os*; from 1537 and 5401; *frightened out* of one's wits:—sore afraid, exceedingly fearful.

1631. ἐκφύω, ekphuō, *ek-foo´-o*; from 1537 and 5453; to *sprout up*:—put forth.

1632. ἐκχέω, ekcheō, *ek-kheh´-o*; or (by varitation) **ἐκχύνω,** ***ekchunō***, *ek-khoo´-no*; from 1537 and **χέω,** ***cheō*** (to *pour*); to *pour forth*; (figurative) to *bestow*:—gush (pour) out, run greedily (out), shed (abroad, forth), spill.

1633. ἐκχωρέω, ekchōreō, *ek-kho-reh´-o*; from 1537 and 5562; to *depart*:—depart out.

1634. ἐκψύχω, ekpsuchō, *ek-psoo´-kho*; from 1537 and 5594; to *expire*:—give (yield) up the ghost.

From *ek* (1537), out, and *psúchō* (5594), to breathe. To expire, die, used intransitively (Ac 5:5, 10; 12:23; Sept.: Jgs 4:21; Eze 21:7).

Syn.: *apogínomai* (581), to be away from; *thnḗskō* (2348), to die; *apothnḗskō* (599), to die off or out; *koimáomai* (2837), to fall asleep; *teleutáō* (5053) and *apóllumi* (622) to die, expire.

1635. ἑκών, hekōn, *hek-own´*; of uncertain affinity; *voluntary*:—willingly.

Adjective meaning willing, voluntary (Ro 8:20; 1Co 9:17).

Deriv.: *ákōn* (210), unwillingly; *ekoúsios* (1595), willing, voluntary.

Syn.: *hekousíōs* (1596), willingly.

1636. ἐλαία, elaia, *el-ah´-yah*; feminine of a presumed derivative from an obsolete primary; an *olive* (the tree or the fruit):—olive (berry, tree).

1637. ἔλαιον, elaion, *el´-ah-yon*; neuter of the same as 1636; olive *oil*:—oil.

Noun from *elaía* (1636), olive tree. Olive oil. Used for lamps (Mt 25:3, 4, 8); for wounds and anointing the sick (Mk 6:13; Lk 10:34; Jas 5:14); as mixed with spices for anointing the head and body in token of honour (Lk 7:46; Heb 1:9); also an article of trade (Lk 16:6; Rev 8:13).

1638. ἐλαιών, elaiōn, *el-ah-yone´*; from 1636; an *olive-orchard*, i.e. (special) the *Mt. of Olives*:—Olivet.

1639. Ἐλαμίτης, Elamitēs, *el-am-ee´-tace*; of Hebrew origin [5867]; an *Elamite* or Persian:—Elamite.

1640. ἐλάσσων, elassōn, *el-as´-sone*; or **ἐλάττων,** ***elattōn***; *el-at-tone´*; comparative of the same as 1646; *smaller* (in size, quantity, age or quality):—less, under, worse, younger.

1641. ἐλαττονέω, elattoneō, *el-at-ton-eh´-o*; from 1640; to *diminish*, i.e. *fall short*:—have lack.

1642. ἐλαττόω, elattoō, *el-at-to´-o*; from 1640; to *lessen* (in rank or influence):—decrease, make lower.

1643. ἐλαύνω, elaunō, *el-ow´-no*; a prolonged form of a primary verb (obsolete except in certain tenses as an alternative of this) of uncertain affinity; to *push* (as wind, oars or dæmoniacal power):—carry, drive, row.

1644. ἐλαφρία, elaphria, *el-af-ree´-ah*; from 1645; *levity* (figurative), i.e. *fickleness*:—lightness.

1645. ἐλαφρός, elaphros, *el-af-ros´*; probably akin to 1643 and the base of 1640; *light*, i.e. *easy*:—light.

1646. ἐλάχιστος, elachistos, *el-akh´-is-tos*; superlative of **ἔλαχυς,** ***elachus*** (*short*); used as equivalent to 3398; *least* (in size, amount, dignity, etc.):—least, very little (small), smallest.

1647. ἐλαχιστότερος, elachistoteros, *el-akh-is-tot´-er-os*; comparative of 1646; *far less*:—less than the least.

1648. Ἐλεάζαρ, Eleazar, *el-eh-ad´-zar*; of Hebrew origin [499]; *Eleazar*, an Israelite:—Eleazar.

1649. ἔλεγξις, elegxis, *el´-eng-xis*; from 1651; *refutation*, i.e. *reproof*:—rebuke.

1650. ἔλεγχος, elegchos, *el´-eng-khos*; from 1651; *proof, conviction*:—evidence, reproof.

Noun from *elégchō* (1651), to convict. Conviction. Metonymically, meaning certain persuasion (Heb 11:1). In the sense of refutation of adversaries (2Ti 3:16; see Sept.: Job 13:6; 23:4; Hos 5:9).

Syn.: *dokimḗ* (1382), proof; *krísis* (2920), judgement; *momphḗ* (3437), fault.

1651. ἐλέγχω, elegchō, *el-eng´-kho*; of uncertain affinity; to *confute, admonish*:—convict, convince, tell a fault, rebuke, reprove.

To shame, disgrace, but only in Class. Gr. In the NT, to convict, to prove one in the wrong and thus to shame him. Transitively:

(I) To convict, to show to be wrong (Jn 8:9, 46; 16:8; 1Co 14:24; Jas 2:9). To convince of error, refute, confute (Tit 1:9, 13; 2:15; Sept.: Job 32:12; Pr 18:17).

(II) By implication: to reprove, rebuke, admonish (Mt 18:15; Lk 3:19; 1Ti 5:20; 2Ti 4:2; Sept.: Ge 21:25; Pr 9:8). To reprove by chastisement, correct, chastise in a moral sense (Rev 3:19); with *paideúō* (3811), train (Heb 12:5 from Pr 3:11, 12. See Sept.: Job 5:17; Ps 6:1; 38:1).

(III) By implication spoken of hidden things: to detect, demonstrate, make manifest (Jn 3:20 where *elegchthḗ* is parallel with *phanerōthḗ* [5319], to manifest in Jn 3:21 [Eph 5:11, 13]).

Deriv.: *élegxis* (1649), the act of rebuking; *élegchos* (1650), reproof; *exelégchō* (1827), to convict thoroughly.

Syn.: *apodokimázō* (593), to repudiate; *epikrínō* (1948), to adjudge; *kakologéō* (2551), to speak evil of; *katakrínō* (2632) or *katadikázō* (2613), to condemn; *katalaléō* (2635), to slander; *katēgoréō* (2723), to accuse; *krínō* (2919), to judge; *mémphomai* (3201), to find fault.

1652. ἐλεεινός, eleeinos, *el-eh-i-nos´*; from 1656; *pitiable*:—miserable.

Adjective from *éleos* (1656), mercy. Worthy of pity, pitiable, full of misery, wretched, miserable. In the NT used only in 1Co 15:19; Rev 3:17.

Syn.: *kakós* (2556), bad in character; *ponērós* (4190), evil, harmful; *saprós* (4550), corrupt, rotten; *phaúlos* (5337), slight, trivial.

1653. ἐλεέω, eleeō, *el-eh-eh´-o*; from 1656; to *compassionate* (by word or deed, specially by divine grace):—have compassion (pity on), have (obtain, receive, shew) mercy (on).

From *éleos* (1656), mercy. To show mercy, to show compassion. The general meaning is to have compassion or mercy on a person in unhappy circumstances. Used transitively in the pass., to be pitied, obtain mercy, implying not merely a feeling for the misfortunes of others involving sympathy (*oiktirmós* [3628], pity), but also an active desire to remove those miseries.

(I) Generally (Mt 5:7; 9:27; 15:22; 17:15; 18:33; 20:30, 31; Mk 5:19; 10:47, 48; Lk 16:24; 17:13; 18:38, 39; Php 2:27; Jude 22; Sept.: Dt 13:17; 2Sa 12:22; 2Ki 13:23; Ps 6:2; Isa 13:18). Spoken of those who had charge of the poor (Ro 12:8 [cf. Pr 14:21, 31; 28:8]); of those who are freed from deserved punishment, in the pass.: to obtain mercy, be spared (1Ti 1:13, 16; Sept.: Dt 7:2; Isa 9:19; Eze 7:4, 9). By implication: to be gracious toward, bestow kindness on (Ro 9:15, 16, 18 quoted from Ex 33:19; Sept.: Ge 43:29).

(**II**) Spoken of the mercy of God through Christ or salvation in Christ: to bestow salvation on; in the pass.: to obtain salvation (Ro 11:30–32; 1Co 7:25; 2Co 4:1; 1Pe 2:10).

Syn.: *hiláskomai* (2433), to be propitious, merciful, make reconciliation for; *lupéō* (3076), to be sad, sorry; *splagchnízomai* (4697), to have bowels of mercy or a yearning heart, feel sympathy, pity; *sumpathéō* (4834), to have sympathy, compassion; *sumpáschō* (4841), to suffer with.

1654. ἐλεημοσύνη, eleēmosunē, *el-eh-ay-mos-oo´-nay*; from 1656; *compassionateness*, i.e. (as exercised toward the poor) *beneficence*, or (concretely) a *benefaction*:—alms (-deeds).

From *eleḗmōn* (1655), merciful. Mercy, compassion (Sept.: Pr 21:21; Isa 38:18). In the NT by metonymy of effect for cause: alms, charity, money given to the poor (Mt 6:1 [TR]; 6:2–4; Lk 11:41; 12:33; Ac 3:2, 3, 10; 9:36; 10:2, 4, 31; 24:17; Sept.: Da 4:24).

1655. ἐλεήμων, eleēmōn, *el-eh-ay´-mone*; from 1653; *compassionate* (actively):—merciful.

Adjective from *éleos* (1656), mercy. Compassionate, merciful; benevolently merciful, involving thought and action (Mt 5:7; Sept.: Ex 22:27; Ps 103:8; 145:8; Jer 3:12).

Deriv.: *aneleḗmōn* (415), unmerciful; *eleēmosúnē* (1654), merciful.

Syn.: *oiktírmōn* (3629) feelings of compassion.

1656. ἔλεος, eleos, *el´-eh-os*; of uncertain affinity; *compassion* (human or divine, especially active):—(+ tender) mercy.

A noun meaning mercy, compassion:

(**I**) *Ho éleos*, gen. *éleou*, masc. noun:

(**A**) Mercy, compassion, active pity (Mt 23:23; Tit 3:5; Heb 4:16; Sept.: Isa 60:10).

(**B**) With the sense of goodness in general, especially piety (Mt 9:13; 12:7 quoted from Hos 6:6).

(**II**) *To éleos*, gen. *eléous*, neuter noun, found only in the Sept., the NT, and church writers in contrast to the noun in the masc. *ho éleos* which alone is used by Class. Gr. writers. Mercy, compassion, active pity:

(**A**) Generally (Lk 1:50, 78; Ro 9:23; 15:9; Eph 2:4; 1Pe 1:3; Jas 3:17; Sept.: Dt 13:17; Ne 13:22; Ps 51:1; Isa 63:7). With the verb *poiéō* (4160), to do mercy for someone, meaning to show mercy to, equivalent to the verb *eleéō* (1653), to have compassion on, show mercy (Lk 1:72; 10:37; Jas 2:13; Sept.: Ge 24:12; 1Sa 15:6). With the verb *megalúnō* (3170), to make great, magnify, show great mercy on someone (Lk 1:58). In the phrase, *mnēsthḗnai eléous*, lit. "to remember mercy" (from *mimnḗskō* [3403], to remember), meaning to give a new proof of mercy and favour to Israel, in reference to God's ancient mercies to that people (Lk 1:54 [cf. Ps 25:6; 89:28, 50; Sept.: 2Ch 6:42; Jer 2:2]). Spoken of mercy as a passing over of deserved punishment (Jas 2:13 [cf. Sept.: Nu 14:19]).

(**B**) Spoken of the mercy of God through Christ, i.e. salvation in the Christian sense from sin and misery (Jude 21, "the mercy of our Lord Jesus Christ" means salvation through Christ; see Ro 11:31). In benedictions, including the idea of mercies and blessings of every kind, e.g., "the Lord give mercy" (2Ti 1:16, 18). Also joined with *eirḗnē* (1515), peace (Gal 6:16; 1Ti 1:2; 2Ti 1:2; Tit 1:4; 2Jn 3; Jude 2).

Deriv.: *eleeinós* (1652), worthy of pity; *eleéō* (1653), to be merciful; *eleḗmōn* (1655), merciful.

Syn.: *oiktirmós* (3628), pity; *lúpē* (3077), sorrow; *splágchnon* (4698), affection, sympathy; *hilasmós* (2434), propitiation.

1657. ἐλευθερία, eleutheria, *el-yoo-ther-ee´-ah*; from 1658; *freedom* (legitimate or licentious, chiefly moral or ceremonial):—liberty.

Noun from *eleútheros* (1658), a free person. Freedom, as liberty to do as one pleases (1Co 10:29; 2Pe 2:19); freedom from the yoke of the Mosaic Law (2Co 3:17; Gal 2:4; 5:1, 13), so from the yoke of external observances in general (1Pe 2:16); from the dominion of sinful appetites and passions (Jas 1:25; 2:12); from a state of calamity and death (Ro 8:21).

Syn.: *politeía* (4174), citizenship, referring to the fact that a citizen was a free man; *cháris* (5485), grace.

1658. ἐλεύθερος, eleutheros, *el-yoo´-ther-os*; probably from the alternative of 2064; *unrestrained* (to *go* at pleasure), i.e. (as a citizen) *not a slave* (whether *freeborn* or *manumitted*), or (genitive) *exempt* (from obligation or liability):—free (man, woman), at liberty.

Adjective meaning "one who can go where he will," free, at liberty:

(**I**) In a civil sense:

(**A**) Freeborn (1Co 12:13; Gal 3:28; 4:22, 23, 30, 31; Eph 6:8; Col 3:11; Rev 6:15; 13:16; 19:18). Figuratively of the heavenly Jerusalem, meaning nobler (Gal 4:26; Sept.: Ne 13:17; Ecc 10:17).

(**B**) Freed, made free (Jn 8:33; 1Co 7:21, 22; Sept.: Ex 21:2, 26, 27).

(**C**) Free, exempt from an obligation or law (Mt 17:26; Ro 7:3; 1Co 7:39 [cf. Sept.: Dt 21:14]); free from external obligations in general, so as to act as one pleases (1Co 9:1, 19); in respect to the exercise of piety (1Pe 2:16).

(**II**) Metaphorically: free from the slavery of sin (Jn 8:36; Ro 6:18 [cf. Ro 6:20, "free from righteousness"]).

Deriv.: *apeleútheros* (558) free man; *eleuthería* (1657), freedom; *eleutheróō* (1659), to make free.

1659. ἐλευθερόω, eleutheroō, *el-yoo-ther-o´-o*; from 1658; to *liberate*, i.e. (figurative) to *exempt* (from moral, ceremonial or mortal liability):—deliver, make free.

From *eleútheros* (1658), free. To make free, liberate from the power and punishment of sin, the result of redemption (Jn 8:32, 36; Ro 6:18, 22); from a state of calamity and death (Ro 8:2, 21); from the power of condemnation by the Mosaic Law (Gal 5:1). For a full discussion, see *eleuthería* (1657), freedom, liberty.

Syn.: *charízō* (5483), to deliver; *apolúō* (630), to set free; *apallássō* (525), to release.

1660. ἔλευσις, eleusis, *el´-yoo-sis*; from the alternative of 2064; an *advent*:—coming.

1661. ἐλεφάντινος, elephantinos, *el-ef-an´-tee-nos*; from **ἔλεφας**, *elephas* (an "*elephant*"); *elephantine*, i.e. (by implication) composed of *ivory*:—of ivory.

1662. Ἐλιακείμ, Eliakeim, *el-ee-ak-ime´*; of Hebrew origin [471]; *Eliakim*, an Israelite:—Eliakim.

1663. Ἐλιέζερ, Eliezer, *el-ee-ed´-zer*; of Hebrew origin [461]; *Eliezer*, an Israelite:—Eliezer.

1664. Ἐλιούδ, Elioud, *el-ee-ood´*; of Hebrew origin [410 and 1935]; *God of majesty; Eliud*, an Israelite:—Eliud.

1665. Ἐλισάβετ, Elisabet, *el-ee-sab´-et*; of Hebrew origin [472]; *Elisabet*, an Israelitess:—Elisabeth.

1666. Ἐλισσαῖος, Elissaios, *el-is-sah´-yos*; of Hebrew origin [477]; *Elissæus*, an Israelite:—Elissæus.

1667. ἑλίσσω, helissō, *hel-is´-so*; a form of 1507; to *coil* or *wrap*:—fold up.

1668. ἕλκος, helkos, *hel´-kos*; probably from 1670; an *ulcer* (as if drawn together):—sore.

1669. ἑλκόω, helkoō, *hel-ko´-o*; from 1668; to *cause to ulcerate*, i.e. (passive) *be ulcerous*:—full of sores.

1670. ἑλκύω, helkuō, *hel-koo´-o*; or **ἕλκω**, ***helkō***, *hel´-ko*; probably akin to 138; to *drag* (literal or figurative):—draw. Compare 1667.

To draw, to drag (Jn 21:6, 11; 18:10). Of persons: to drag, to force before magistrates (Ac 16:19; Jas 2:6), or out of a place (Ac 21:30). Metaphorically: to draw, induce to come (Jn 6:44; 12:32).

Deriv.: *exélkō* (1828), to draw away.

1671. Ἑλλάς, Hellas, *hel-las´*; of uncertain affinity; *Hellas* (or *Greece*), a country of Europe:—Greece.

1672. Ἕλλην, Hellēn, *hel´-lane*; from 1671; a *Hellen* (*Grecian*) or inhabitant of Hellas; by extension a *Greek-speaking* person, especially a *non-Jew*:—Gentile, Greek.

1673. Ἑλληνικός, Hellēnikos, *hel-lay-nee-kos´*; from 1672; *Hellenic*, i.e. *Grecian* (in language):—Greek.

1674. Ἑλληνίς, Hellēnis, *hel-lay-nis´*; feminine of 1672; a *Grecian* (i.e. *non-Jewish*) woman:—Greek.

1675. Ἑλληνιστής, Hellēnistēs, *hel-lay-nis-tace´*; from a derivative of 1672; a *Hellenist* or Greek-speaking Jew:—Grecian.

1676. Ἑλληνιστί, Hellēnisti, *hel-lay-nis-tee´*; adverb from the same as 1675; *Hellenistically*, i.e. in the Grecian language:—Greek.

1677. ἐλλογέω, ellogeō, *el-log-eh´-o*; from 1722 and 3056 (in the sense of *account*); to *reckon in*, i.e. *attribute*:—impute, put on account.

From *en* (1722), in, and *lógos* (3056), word. To reckon in, to put to one's account (Phm 18). Metaphorically of sin: to impute (Ro 5:13).

Syn.: *logízomai* (3049), to reckon by calculation or imputation.

1678. Ἐλμωδάμ, Elmōdam, *el-mo-dam´*; of Hebrew origin [perhaps for 486]; *Elmodam*, an Israelite:—Elmodam.

1679. ἐλπίζω, elpizō, *el-pid´-zo*; from 1680; to *expect* or *confide*:—(have, thing) hope (-d) (for), trust.

From *elpís* (1680), hope. To hope, expect with desire (Lk 6:34; 23:8; Ac 26:7; Ro 15:24; 1Co 16:7; Php 2:19, 23; 1Ti 3:14; 2Jn 12; 3Jn 14); followed by the accusative of thing, to hope for (Ro 8:24, 25; 1Co 13:7). In the construction meaning to hope in someone, i.e. to trust in, confide in (Mt 12:21; Jn 5:45; Ro 15:12; 1Ti 6:17); spoken of those who put their trust in God (2Co 1:10; 1Ti 4:10; 5:5; 1Pe 3:5; Sept.: Ps 26:1; Isa 11:10); spoken of trusting in Christ (1Co 15:19; Sept.: 2Ki 18:5; Ps 33:21).

Deriv.: *apelpízō* (560), to bring to despair; *proelpízō* (4276), to hope before.

Syn.: *prosdokáō* (4328), to expect; *prosménō* (4357), to abide still, with an element of hope; *apekdéchomai* (553), to expect fully; *anaménō* (362), to wait for; *ekdéchomai* (1551), to await, expect, anticipate.

1680. ἐλπίς, elpis, *el-pece´*; from a primary **ἔλπω,** ***elpō*** (to *anticipate*, usually with pleasure); *expectation* (abstract or concrete) or *confidence*:—faith, hope.

A noun meaning hope, confident expectation of good:

(I) Generally (Ro 8:24; 2Co 10:15; Php 1:20). With a gen. of the thing hoped for (Ac 27:20). See Ac 16:19; 23:6, "of the hope and resurrection"; 26:6, 7. Of the person hoping (Ac 28:20; 2Co 1:7; Sept.: Job 14:7; 17:15; Isa 31:2; Eze 37:11). With *pará* (3844), against or in spite of, with the accusative *par' elpída*, against hope, i.e. without ground of hope (Ro 4:18). With *epí* (1909), upon, and the dat., *ep' elpídi*, literally on hope or in hope, i.e. with hope, full of hope and confidence (Ac 2:26; see Ro 4:18; 8:20; 1Co 9:10; Sept.: Ps 4:8; 16:9). By metonymy, spoken of the object of hope (Ro 8:24, "hope that is seen is not hope" [see *blépō* {991, I, B}, to see]). In 1Co 9:10 (TR), "should be partaker of his hope." See Sept.: Job 6:8.

(II) Spoken especially of those who experience the hope of salvation through Christ, eternal life, and blessedness (Ro 5:2, 4, 5; 12:12; 15:4, 13, "the God of hope," i.e. the author and source of hope, not the one who needs hope; see 1Co 13:13; 2Co 3:12; Eph 2:12; 4:4; 1Th 4:13; 5:8; 2Th 2:16; Tit 1:2; 3:7; Heb 3:6; 6:11; 10:23; 1Pe 1:3; 3:15). Followed by the gen. of the thing or person on which this hope rests (Eph 1:18; Col 1:23; 1Th 1:3). By metonymy, spoken of the object of this hope, i.e. salvation (Col 1:5). The hope or salvation resulting from justification by faith (Gal 5:5; see Tit 2:13; Heb 6:18; 7:19). By metonymy, also of the source, ground, author of hope, i.e. Christ (Col 1:27; 1Ti 1:1).

(III) Of a hope in or on someone, i.e. trust, confidence (Ac 24:15; 1Pe 1:21; 1Jn 3:3).

Deriv.: *elpízō* (1679), to trust, hope.

Syn.: *apokaradokía* (603), intense anticipation, earnest expectation; *ekdochḗ* (1561), expectation.

1681. Ἐλύμας, Elumas, *el-oo´-mas*; of foreign origin; *Elymas*, a wizard:—Elymas.

1682. ἐλοΐ, elōi, *el-o-ee´*; of Chaldee origin [426 with pronoun suffix]; *my God*:—Eloi.

1683. ἐμαυτοῦ, emautou, *em-ow-too´*; general compound of 1700 and 846; *of myself* (so likewise the dative **ἐμαυτῷ,** ***emautōi***, *em-ow-to´*; and accusative **ἐμαυτόν,** ***emauton***, *em-ow-ton´*):—me, mine own (self), myself.

1684. ἐμβαίνω, embainō, *em-ba´hee-no*; from 1722 and the base of 939; to *walk on*, i.e. *embark* (aboard a vessel), *reach* (a pool):—come (get) into, enter (into), go (up) into, step in, take ship.

1685. ἐμβάλλω, emballō, *em-bal´-lo*; from 1722 and 906; to *throw on*, i.e. (figurative) *subject to* (eternal punishment):—cast into.

1686. ἐμβάπτω, embaptō, *em-bap´-to*; from 1722 and 911; to *whelm on*, i.e. *wet* (a part of the person, etc.) by contact with a fluid:—dip.

1687. ἐμβατεύω, embateuō, *em-bat-yoo´-o*; from 1722 and a presumed derivative of the base of 939; equivalent to 1684; to *intrude on* (figurative):—intrude into.

1688. ἐμβιβάζω, embibazō, *em-bib-ad´-zo*; from 1722 and **βιβάζω,** ***bibazō*** (to *mount*; causative of 1684); to *place on*, i.e. *transfer* (aboard a vessel):—put in.

1689. ἐμβλέπω, emblepō, *em-blep´-o*; from 1722 and 991; to *look on*, i.e. (relative) to *observe* fixedly, or (absolute) to *discern* clearly:—behold, gaze up, look upon, (could) see.

1690. ἐμβριμάομαι, embrimaomai, *em-brim-ah´-om-ahee*; from 1722 and **βριμάομαι,** ***brimaomai*** (to *snort* with anger); to have *indignation on*, i.e. (transitive) to *blame*, (intransitive) to *sigh* with chagrin, (special) to sternly *enjoin*:—straitly charge, groan, murmur against.

1691. ἐμέ, eme, *em-eh´*; a prolonged form of 3165; *me*:—I, me, my (-self).

1692. ἐμέω, emeō, *em-eh´-o*; of uncertain affinity; to *vomit*:—(will) spue.

1693. ἐμμαίνομαι, emmainomai, *em-mah´ee-nom-ahee*; from 1722 and 3105; to *rave on*, i.e. *rage at*:—be mad against.

1694. Ἐμμανουήλ, Emmanouēl, *em-man-oo-ale´*; of Hebrew origin [6005]; *God with us; Emmanuel*, a name of Christ:—Emmanuel.

1695. Ἐμμαούς, Emmaous, *em-mah-ooce´*; probably of Hebrew origin [compare 3222]; *Emmaüs*, a place in Palestine:—Emmaus.

1696. ἐμμένω, emmenō, *em-men´-o*; from 1722 and 3306; to *stay in* the same place, i.e. (figurative) to *persevere*:—continue.

From *en* (1722), in, and *ménō* (3306), to remain. To remain, persevere in (Ac 14:22; Gal 3:10; Heb 8:9; Sept.: Dt 27:26).

Syn.: *epiménō* (1961), to continue in, metaphorically to persevere; *kartetéō* (2594), to endure; *diaménō* (1265), to stay through, remain; *paraménō* (3887), to persevere; *diateléō* (1300), to persist, continue.

1697. Ἐμμόρ, Emmor, *em-mor´*; of Hebrew origin [2544]; *Emmor* (i.e. *Chamor*), a Canaanite:—Emmoral.

1698. ἐμοί, emoi, *em-oy´*; a prolonged form of 3427; *to me*:—I, me, mine, my.

1699. ἐμός, emos, *em-os´*; from the oblique cases of 1473 (1698, 1700, 1691); *my*:—of me, mine (own), my.

1700. ἐμοῦ, emou, *em-oo´*; a prolonged form of 3449; *of me*:—me, mine, my.

1701. ἐμπαιγμός, empaigmos, *emp-aheeg-mos´*; from 1702; *derision*:—mocking.

1702. ἐμπαίζω, empaizō, *emp-aheed´-zo*; from 1722 and 3815; to *jeer at*, i.e. *deride*:—mock.

1703. ἐμπαίκτης, empaiktēs, *emp-aheek-tace´*; from 1702; a *derider*, i.e. (by implication) a *false teacher*:—mocker, scoffer.

1704. ἐμπεριπατέω, emperipateō, *em-per-ee-pat-eh´-o*; from 1722 and 4043; to *perambulate on* a place, i.e. (figurative) to *be occupied among* persons:—walk in.

1705. ἐμπίπλημι, empiplēmi, *em-pip´-lay-mee*; or **ἐμπλήθω, *emplēthō***, *em-play´-tho*; from 1722 and the base of 4118; to *fill in* (*up*), i.e. (by implication) to *satisfy* (literal or figurative):—fill.

1706. ἐμπίπτω, empiptō, *em-pip´-to*; from 1722 and 4098; to *fall on*, i.e. (literal) *be entrapped by*, or (figurative) *be overwhelmed with*:—fall among (into).

1707. ἐμπλέκω, emplekō, *em-plek´-o*; from 1722 and 4120; to *entwine*, i.e. (figurative) *involve* with:—entangle (in, self with).

1708. ἐμπλοκή, emplokē, *em-plok-ay´*; from 1707; elaborate *braiding* of the hair:—plaiting.

1709. ἐμπνέω, empneō, *emp-neh´-o*; from 1722 and 4154; to *inhale*, i.e. (figurative) to *be animated by* (*bent upon*):—breathe.

1710. ἐμπορεύομαι, emporeuomai, *em-por-yoo´-om-ahee*; from 1722 and 4198; to *travel in* (a country as a pedlar), i.e. (by implication) to *trade*:—buy and sell, make merchandise.

1711. ἐμπορία, emporia, *em-por-ee´-ah*; feminine from 1713; *traffic*:—merchandise.

1712. ἐμπόριον, emporion, *em-por´-ee-on*; neuter from 1713; a *mart* ("*emporium*"):—merchandise.

1713. ἔμπορος, emporos, *em´-por-os*; from 1722 and the base of 4198; a (wholesale) *tradesman*:—merchant.

1714. ἐμπρήθω, emprēthō, *em-pray´-tho*; from 1722 and **πρήθω, *prēthō*** (to *blow* a flame); to *enkindle*, i.e. *set on fire*:—burn up.

1715. ἔμπροσθεν, emprosthen, *em´-pros-then*; from 1722 and 4314; *in front of* (in place [literal or figurative] or time):—against, at, before, (in presence, sight) of.

1716. ἐμπτύω, emptuō, *emp-too´-o*; from 1722 and 4429; to *spit at* or *on*:—spit (upon).

1717. ἐμφανής, emphanēs, *em-fan-ace´*; from a compound of 1722 and 5316; *apparent in* self:—manifest, openly.

1718. ἐμφανίζω, emphanizō, *em-fan-id´-zo*; from 1717; to *exhibit* (in person) or *disclose* (by words):—appear, declare (plainly), inform, (will) manifest, shew, signify.

1719. ἔμφοβος, emphobos, *em´-fob-os*; from 1722 and 5401; *in fear*, i.e. *alarmed*:—affrighted, afraid, tremble.

1720. ἐμφυσάω, emphusaō, *em-foo-sah´-o*; from 1722 and **φυσάω, *phusaō*** (to *puff*) [compare 5453]; to *blow at* or *on*:—breathe on.

1721. ἔμφυτος, emphutos, *em´-foo-tos*; from 1722 and a derivative of 5453; *implanted* (figurative):—engrafted.

1722. ἐν, en, *en*; a primary preposition denoting (fixed) *position* (in place, time or state), and (by implication) *instrumentality* (medially or constructively), i.e. a relation of *rest* (intermediate between 1519 and 1537); "*in*," *at*, (up-) *on*, *by*, etc.:—about, after, against, + almost, × altogether, among, × as, at, before, between, (here-) by (+ all means), for (… sake of), + give self wholly to, (here-) in (-to, -wardly), × mightily, (because) of, (up-) on, [open-] ly, × outwardly, one, × quickly, × shortly, [speedi-] ly, × that, × there (-in, -on), through (-out), (un-) to (-ward), under, when, where (-with), while, with (-in). Often used in compounds, with substantially the same import; rarely with verbs of motion, and then not to indicate direction, except (elliptically) by a separate (and different) preposition.

Preposition meaning in, on, at, by any place or thing, with the primary idea of rest. As compared with *eis* (1519), into or unto, and *ek* (1537), out of or from, it stands between the two; *eis* implies motion into, and *ek* motion out of, while *en* means remaining in place.

(I) Of place, which is the primary and most frequent use and spoken of everything which is conceived as being, remaining, taking place, meaning within some definite space or limits: in, on, at, by:

(A) Particularly with the meaning of in or within (Mt 4:21) as in a ship; in the synagogues (Mt 4:23); in the corners of the streets (Mt 6:5); at home (Mt 8:67); in the prison (Mt 11:2); in the market (Mt 11:16; Lk 7:32); in his field (Mt 13:24, 27); in the tomb (Mk 5:3; Jn 5:28; 11:17; 19:41); in a certain place (Lk 11:1); in their midst (Lk 22:5); in the temple (Ac 2:46); in the praetorium (Php 1:13). With the names of cities, countries, places (Mt 2:1, 5, 19; 3:1, 3; 4:13; 9:31; Ac 7:36; 9:36; 10:1; Ro 1:7; 1Th 1:7, 8). In hell (*Hádēs* [86]) (Lk 16:23 [cf. Mt 10:28; Rev 21:8]); in earth, in heaven (Mt 5:12; 6:10, 20; 16:19; Lk 15:7); your Father which is in heaven (Mt 5:45; 7:11 [cf. 18:35]); in the kingdom of heaven (Mt 5:19; 8:11); in the earth (Mt 25:18, 25; Jn 13:1; Ro 9:17; Col 1:6); in the sea (Mk 5:13; Mk 6:47; 2Co 11:25). Of a book, writing (Mk 12:26; Lk 2:23; 20:42; Jn 6:45; Ac 13:33; Ro 11:2, in the section respecting Elijah; Heb 4:5, 7; 5:6). Of the body and its parts (Mt 1:18, 23; 3:12; 7:3, 4; Lk 1:44; Ro 6:12; 2Co 12:2; 1Pe 2:22; Rev 6:5). Spoken of persons, particularly in one's body (Mt 1:20; Ac 19:16; 20:10; figuratively, Mt 6:23; Ro 7:17, 18, 20; 1Pe 2:22).

(B) Spoken of elevated objects, a surface, meaning in, i.e. on, upon, as a fig tree (Mk 11:13); a mountain (Lk 8:32; Jn 4:20; Heb 8:5; Sept.: Ex 31:18); "engraven in stones" (2Co 3:7); "in my throne" (Rev 3:21); See Lk 12:51; Jn 20:25; Ac 7:33; Rev 13:12; 18:19. Figuratively, Jude 12.

(C) In a somewhat wider sense, simply implying contact, close proximity, meaning in, at, on, by, near, with, equivalent to *pará* (3844), near (Mt 6:5; 7:6, at or under the feet; Lk 13:4; 16:23; Jn 11:10; 15:4, remains on, attached to the vine; 19:41; Ac 2:19; Ro 8:34; Heb 1:3; 8:1; 10:12; Rev 9:10). **(1)** Of those with whom someone is in near connection, intimate union, oneness of heart, mind, purpose, especially of Christians, in union with Christ by faith and who are become as branches in the true vine (Jn 15:2, 4, 5; see Jn 6:56; 14:20; Ro 16:7, 11; 1Co 1:30; 9:1, 2; 2Co 5:17; Eph 2:13; 1Th 4:16, those who died in union with Christ by faith, as Christians [cf. 1Co 15:18; Rev 14:13]). Hence, those "in Christ" means Christians (2Co 12:2; Gal 1:22; 1Pe 5:14). Generally those in connection with Christ, in the Christian faith (Ro 12:5; Gal 3:28; 5:6; 6:15; Php 4:1; 1Th 3:8; 1Jn 2:24). Christ is in the believer and vice versa, in consequence of faith in Him (Jn 6:56; 14:20; 15:4, 5; 17:23, 26; Ro 8:9; Gal 2:20); of the believer's union with God (1Th 1:1; 1Jn 2:24; 3:6, 24; 4:13, 15, 16); of the mutual union of God and Christ (Jn 10:38; 14:10, 11, 20); of the Holy Spirit in Christians (Jn 14:17; Ro 8:9, 11; 1Co 3:16; 6:19). **(2)** Of those in, with, on whom, i.e. in whose person or character anything exists, is done (cf. *pará* [3844], near), e.g., in one's external life and conduct (Jn 18:38; 19:4, 6; Ac 24:20; 25:5; 1Co 4:2; 1Jn 2:10). Generally of any power, influence, efficiency, e.g., from God, the Spirit (Mt 14:2; Jn 1:4; 14:13, 30; 17:26; 1Co 12:6; 2Co 4:4, 12; 6:12; Gal 4:19; Php 2:5, 13; Col 1:19; Heb 13:21; 1Jn 3:9, 15); also *en heautṓ* ([1438], himself, in the dat.), meaning in, with, or of oneself (Mt 13:21; Jn 5:26; 6:53; 2Co 1:9). **(3)** Of those in or with whom, i.e. in whose mind, heart, soul, anything exists or takes place (cf. *pará* [3844], near) as virtues, vices, faculties (Jn 1:47; 4:14, meaning in his soul; 17:13; Ro 7:8; 1Co 2:11; 8:7; 2Co 11:10; Eph 4:18). "Your life is hid with Christ in God" (Col 3:3) means in the mind and counsels of God. See Eph 3:9. The expression *en heautṓ*, *en heautoís*, in or with oneself or themselves, means in one's heart (Mt 3:9; Lk 7:39, 49; Ro 8:23; Jas 2:4).

(D) Of a number or multitude, as indicating place, meaning in, among, with, equivalent to *en mésō* (3319), in the midst (Mt 2:6). With the same meaning of among (Mt 11:11, 21; 20:27; Mk 10:43; Lk 1:1; Jn 1:14; 11:54; Ac 2:29; 20:32; Ro 1:5, 6; 1Co 11:18; Eph 5:3; 1Pe 5:1, 2; 2Pe 2:8). Also in the dat. plural *en heautoís* (1438), in themselves, meaning among themselves (Mt 9:3; 21:38; Ac 28:29); *en allḗlois* (240), one another, meaning with one another (Mk 9:50; Jn 13:35; Ro 15:5). With the dat. sing. of a coll. noun (Lk 1:61; 2:44; 4:25, 27, "in Israel"; Jn 7:43; Ac 10:35; Eph 3:21; 2Pe 2:1; Sept.: Ge 23:6; Le 16:29; 2Ki 18:5). Hence with dat. plural of person by whom one is accompanied, escorted (Lk 14:31; Jude 14; Sept.: Nu 20:19). With the dat. plural of thing (1Co 15:3, adverb, "first of all," among the first).

(E) Of persons, by implication meaning before, in the presence of (Mk 8:38; Lk 1:25; Ac 6:8; 24:21, as before judges; 1Co 2:6; 2Co 10:1). Figuratively (Lk 4:21 [cf. Sept.: Dt 5:1]), hence metaphorically, meaning in the sight of someone, he being judge (Lk 16:15, "in the sight of," or judgement of men; 1Co 14:11; Col 3:20). Also, by Hebraism, *en ophthalmoís humṓn* (see *ophthalmós* [3788], eye; *humṓn* [5216], of you), meaning before your eyes, i.e. in your judgement (Mt 21:42; Mk 12:11; Sept.: Ps 118:23).

(**F**) Spoken of that by which one is surrounded or enveloped, meaning in, with (Mt 16:27; 25:31; Mk 13:26; Lk 21:27; Ac 7:30); of clothing (Mt 7:15; 11:8; Mk 12:38; Heb 11:37; Jas 2:2); ornaments (1Ti 2:9); bonds (Eph 6:20). Also *en sarkí* (4561), flesh, meaning in the flesh, clothed in flesh, in the body (1Jn 4:2; 2Jn 7); to live in the flesh (Gal 2:20; Php 1:22; Sept.: Dt 22:12; Ps 147:8). Hence of that with which one is furnished, which he carries with him (1Co 4:21; Heb 9:25). Metaphorically (Lk 1:17; Ro 15:29; Eph 6:2; Sept.: Jos 22:8; 1Sa 1:24; Ps 66:13).

(**II**) Of time:

(**A**) When, i.e. a definite point or period in, during, on, at which anything takes place (Mt 2:1; 3:1; 8:13; 12:1, 2; Ac 20:7; 1Co 11:23; Jn 11:9, 10, by day, by night). With a neuter adj. (Ac 7:13; 2Co 11:6; Php 4:6). With a pron. used in an absolute sense, *en hṓ* (3739), in which, in the dat. sing. implying *chrónō*, the dat. sing. of *chrónos* (5550), time (Mk 2:19; Jn 5:7). With the article and adverb (Lk 7:11; 8:1; Jn 4:31). Spoken of an action or event which serves to mark a definite time (Mt 22:28; Lk 11:31, 32; Jn 21:20; 1Co 15:52; 2Th 1:7; 1Jn 2:28). With *en hoís* (see *hós* [3739], which) implying *prágmasi* (*prágma* [4229], affair, matter, thing), meaning during which things, meanwhile (Lk 12:1). Especially with the dat. article and inf., *en* is used to mean on or at an action or event, while it is taking place (Lk 1:8; 2:6; 5:1; 9:36; 24:51; Ac 8:6; Sept.: 1Sa 1:7).

(**B**) Meaning how long a space or period which anything takes place in or within, such as within or in three days (Mt 27:40; Mk 15:29; Sept.: Isa 16:14).

(**III**) Figuratively of the state, condition or manner in which one is, moves, acts; of the ground, occasion, means, on, in, by, or through which one is affected, moved, acted upon:

(**A**) Of the state, condition, or circumstances in which a person or thing is: (**1**) Generally, of an external state (Lk 2:29; 8:43; 11:21 [cf. Lk 16:23; 23:12, 40; Ro 1:4; 8:37; 1Co 7:18, 20, 24; 15:42, 43; 2Co 6:4, 5; Gal 1:14; Php 2:7]; 2Th 3:16, in every state, at every turn; 1Ti 2:2); of an internal state of the mind or feelings (Ac 11:5; Ro 15:32; 1Co 1:10; 2:3; 14:6, in the state or condition of one who receives and utters a revelation; 2Co 11:17, 21; Eph 3:12; 5:21; 1Th 2:17; 1Ti 1:13; 2:11; Heb 3:11; Jas 1:21; 2:1; Jude 24). In this usage *en* with its dat. is often equivalent to an adj. (Ro 4:10; 2Co 3:7, 8; Php 4:19; 1Ti 2:7, 12, 14; Tit 1:6; 3:5); an adverb (Ac 5:23; Ro 2:28, 29; Eph 6:24). (**2**) Of the business, employment or actions in which one is engaged (Mt 20:15, *en toís emoís*, lit. "in my own things, affairs"; 21:22; 22:15; 23:30; Mk 4:2; 8:27; Lk 16:10; 24:35; Jn 8:3; Ac 6:1; 24:16; Ro 1:9, "labouring in the gospel" [a.t.]; 14:18; 1Co 15:58; 2Co 7:11; Col 1:10; 4:2; 1Ti 4:15; 5:17; Heb 6:18; 11:34; Jas 1:8; 4:3). Also with the dat. of person, meaning in the work, business, cause of someone (Ro 16:12; 1Co 4:17; Eph 6:21). (**3**) Implying in the power of someone (Ac 4:12; 5:4 [cf. 1:7; Jn 3:35]); in the power or under the influence of the Spirit (*en pneúmati*, the dat. sing. of *pneúma* [4151], spirit) in Mt 12:28; 22:43; Mk 12:36; Lk 2:27; 4:1; 1Co 12:3; Rev 1:10; 4:2; 17:3; of demoniacs, *en pneúmati akathártō* (dat. sing. of *akáthartos* [169], unclean), in the power of or possessed by an unclean spirit (Mk 1:23; 5:2); of one's sound mind, *genómenos en heautṓ* (*gínomai* [1096], to become; *heautṓ* [1438] in the dat. sing., himself), having come to himself (Ac 12:11).

(**B**) Of manner or mode, i.e. the external or internal state or circumstances by which any action is accompanied, in, with or in reference to which it is performed: (**1**) Generally of manner (cf. *ek* [1537, III, E]; Mt 22:37, quoted from Dt 6:5; Mk 4:2; Lk 2:36; 21:25; Jn 16:25; Ac 2:46; 10:48 [cf. *baptízō* {907, III}; Ro 1:9; 9:22; 15:6; 1Co 2:4, 7; 14:21; 2Co 3:7; Col 3:22; 1Pe 2:24; 2Pe 2:3; 1Jn 5:6]). In an adverb sense (Mt 22:16, *en alētheía didáskeis*, lit. "in truth you teach," i.e. you teach truly; Mk 9:1; Ac 12:7; 22:18; Eph 6:19, *en parrēsía*, lit. "with/in boldness," i.e. boldly; Col 4:5; Rev 18:2; 19:11). (**2**) Of a rule, law, standard, in, by, according to, conformable to (Mt 7:2; Lk 1:8; 1Co 15:23; Php 1:8; 1Th 4:15; 1Ti 1:18; Heb 4:11). Of a rule of life (Lk 1:6). With the dat. of person (2Co 10:12). In conformity with the will, law or precept of someone (Jn 3:21; 1Co 7:39; Eph 6:1). (**3**) In the sense meaning in respect to, as to (Lk 1:7, 18; Eph 2:11; Tit 1:13; Jas 2:10; 3:2). Also *en pantí* (dat. sing. of *pás* [3956], all), in every respect (2Co 8:7; 9:8, 11); *en mēdení* (dat. sing. of *mēdén*, the neuter of *mēdeís* [3367], no one) meaning in no respect (2Co 7:9; Jas 1:4); and *en oudení* (dat. sing. of *oudén*, the neuter of *oudeís* [3762], no one), in a more absolute way, meaning in no way or respect (Php 1:20). After words meaning plenty or want (Ro 15:13; 1Co 1:5, 7; 2Co 3:9; 8:7; Eph 2:4; Col 2:7; 1Ti 6:18).

(**C**) Of the ground, basis, occasion, in, on or upon which anything rests, exists, takes place. (**1**) Of a person or thing (1Co 2:5, *en sophía anthrṓpōn*, "in the wisdom of men"; 2Co 4:10; Gal 4:14; Eph 2:11); in the person or case of someone: in or by his example (Lk 22:37; Jn 9:3; Ac 4:2; Ro 9:17; 1Co 4:6; 2Co 4:3; Eph 1:20; Php 1:30). After verbs implying to do anything in one's case, i.e. to or for one where the accusative or dat. might stand (Mt 17:12; Lk 23:31; 1Co 9:15; 1Th 5:12, for your benefit). With the verb *homologéō* (3670), to confess, followed by *en* and the dat. means to confess in one's case or cause, to acknowledge (Mt 10:32; Lk 12:8). With the verb *skandalízomai* (4624), to be offended, followed by *en* and the dat. sing. meaning to take offence in someone, in his case or cause (Mt 11:6; 13:57; 26:31, 33). Spoken of that in which anything consists, is comprised, fulfilled, manifested (Jn 9:30; Ro 13:9; Gal 5:14; Eph 2:7; 5:9; Heb 3:12; 1Pe 3:4; 1Jn 3:10; 4:9, 10, 17). After verbs of swearing, to mark the ground, basis, or object on which the oath rests, expressed in Eng. as "by," or "upon" (Mt 5:34–36; 23:16, 18, 20; Rev 10:6; Sept.: 1Sa 24:22; 2Sa 19:7; 1Ki 2:8). (**2**) Of the ground, motive or exciting cause in consequence of which any action is performed, in, on, at, by, i.e. because of, on account of (Mt 6:7; Ac 7:29; 1Co 11:22; 2Co 6:12; 1Pe 4:14, 16 [cf. Mk 9:41; Sept.: 2Ch 16:7]). *En toútō*, sing. dat. of *toúto* (5124), this, meaning herein, hereby, on this account, therefore (Jn 15:8; 16:30; Ac 24:16; 1Co 4:4, to know herein, hereby, by this. See Jn 13:35; 1Jn 2:3, 5). When the relative pron. *en hṓ* is used, it is equivalent to *en toútō* followed by *hóti* (3754), that, meaning herein that, in that, because (Ro 8:3; Heb 2:18; 6:17, wherefore; 1Pe 2:12). In this sense, *en* does not occur with the dat. of person. Spoken also of the authority in consequence of which anything is done, in, by, under, i.e. by virtue of (Mt 21:9; Lk 20:2; Jn 5:43; 10:25; 12:13; 14:26; Ac 4:7; 1Co 5:4; 2Th 3:6). (**3**) Of the ground or occasion of an emotion of mind, after words expressing joy, wonder, hope, confidence, and the reverse. With the dat. of thing (Mt 12:21; Mk 1:15; Lk 10:20; Ac 7:41; Ro 2:23; Eph 3:13; Php 3:3, 4; Sept.: Ps 33:21; Jer 48:7); of person (Ro 5:11; 1Co 15:19; 2Co 7:16; Eph 1:12; 1Ti 6:17; Sept.: 2Ki 18:5; Hos 10:13).

(**D**) Of the means, by the aid or intervention of which anything takes place, is done, meaning in, by means of. (**1**) With the dat. of person, by whose aid or intervention, in, by, with, through whom, anything is done (Mt 9:34; Ac 4:9; 17:28, 31; 1Co 15:22; Gal 3:8, lit. "shall be blessed in you all nations," i.e. in and through you [cf. Ac 3:25; Heb 1:1; 1Jn 5:11]). (**2**) With the dat. of thing, but used strictly only of such means as imply that the obj. affected is actually in, among, surrounded by them, particularly in and through (Mt 8:32, "in [and by] the waters"; 1Co 3:13; Rev 14:10; 16:8; Sept.: Le 8:32). Hence generally where the obj. is conceived as being in or in contact or connection with the means (Mt 3:11, "baptize you in water" [a.t.]; 5:13; 17:21; 25:16; Lk 21:34; Ac 7:35, in or "by the hand" of someone; 11:14; 20:19; Ro 10:5, 9; 12:21; 1Co 6:20; Gal 3:19; Heb 10:29; 13:20; Rev 1:5; Sept.: Nu 36:2; Jgs 16:7; Job 18:8). Hence in the NT and later writers, simply of the instrument, where Class. Gr. writers usually use the dat. alone (Lk 22:49; Ro 16:16; Jas 3:9; Rev 6:8; 12:5; 13:10; Sept.: Ge 48:22; Dt 15:19; Jer 14:12; Hos 1:7). (**3**) Spoken of price or exchange, of that by means by which or with which anything is purchased or exchanged (Ro 1:23, "exchanged the glory of God for [*en*] an image," 25; Rev 5:9; Sept.: 1Sa 24:20; Ecc 4:9; La 5:4).

(**IV**) Sometimes *en* with the dat. is where the natural construction would seem to require *eis* (1519), unto, into, with the accusative as after verbs which imply, not rest in a place or state, but motion or direction into or toward an object. In such cases, the idea of arrival and subsequent rest in that place or state is either actually expressed or is implied in the context. See the converse of this in *eis* (1519, V). After verbs of motion (Mt 10:16, "in the midst of wolves," by whom you are already surrounded; 14:3, to put in prison or into prison; Mk 1:16; 15:46 [cf. Lk 23:53, they placed him in the tomb]; Lk 5:16, He withdrew and abode in deserts; 7:17, went out, spread abroad, in the whole land; Jn 3:35; 5:4; Rev 11:12; Sept.: Jgs 6:35; Ezr 7:10). Metaphorically, after words expressing an affection of mind toward someone (2Co 8:7; 1Jn 4:9, 16); wrath upon the people (Lk 21:23 [{TR} cf. Sept.: 2Sa 24:17]).

In composition *en* implies: (**a**) A being or resting in, as *éneimi* (1751), to be within; *emménō* (1696), to stay in the same place, persevere; (**b**) Into, when compounded with verbs of motion, as *embaínō* (1684), to walk on, embark, come into, step in; (**c**) Conformity, as *éndikos* (1738), equitable, just; *énnomos* (1772), lawful; (**d**) Participation, as *énochos* (1777), guilty of.

1723. ἐναγκαλίζομαι, enagkalizomai, *en-ang-kal-id´-zom-ahee*; from 1722 and a derivative of 43; to *take in* one's *arms*, i.e. *embrace*:—take up in arms.

1724. ἐνάλιος, enalios, *en-al´-ee-os*; from 1722 and 251; *in the sea*, i.e. *marine*:—thing in the sea.

1725. ἔναντι, enanti, *en´-an-tee*; from 1722 and 473; *in front* (i.e. figurative, *presence*) *of*:—before.

1726. ἐναντίον, enantion, *en-an-tee´-on*; neuter of 1727; (adverb) *in the presence* (*view*) *of*:—before, in the presence of.

1727. ἐναντίος, enantios, *en-an-tee´-os*; from 1725; *opposite*; (figurative) *antagonistic*:—(over) against, contrary.

1728. ἐνάρχομαι, enarchomai, *en-ar´-khom-ahee*; from 1722 and 756; to *commence on*:—rule [*by mistake* for 757].

1729. ἐνδεής, endeēs, *en-deh-ace´*; from a compound of 1722 and 1210 (in the sense of *lacking*); *deficient in*:—lacking.

1730. ἔνδειγμα, endeigma, *en´-dighe-mah*; from 1731; an *indication* (concrete):—manifest token.

1731. ἐνδείκνυμι, endeiknumi, *en-dike´-noo-mee*; from 1722 and 1166; to *indicate* (by word or act):—do, show (forth).

1732. ἔνδειξις, endeixis, *en´-dike-sis*; from 1731; *indication* (abstract):—declare, evident token, proof.

1733. ἕνδεκα, hendeka, *hen´-dek-ah*; from (the neuter of) 1520 and 1176; *one* and *ten*, i.e. *eleven*:—eleven.

1734. ἑνδέκατος, hendekatos, *hen-dek´-at-os*; order from 1733; *eleventh*:—eleventh.

1735. ἐνδέχεται, endechetai, *en-dekh´-et-ahee*; third person singular presumed of a compound of 1722 and 1209; (impersonally) *it is accepted in*, i.e. *admitted* (*possible*):—can (+ not) be.

From the prep. *en* (1722), in, upon, and *déchomai* (1209), to receive. As an impersonal verb *endéchetai*, used with the neg., it is not possible, it may not be (Lk 13:33).

Deriv.: *anéndektos* (418), impossible.

Syn.: *dúnamai* (1410), to be able; *ischúō* (2480), to be strong.

1736. ἐνδημέω, endēmeō, *en-day-meh´-o*; from a compound of 1722 and 1218; to *be in* one's own *country*, i.e. *home* (figurative):—be at home (present).

1737. ἐνδιδύσκω, endiduskō, *en-did-oos´-ko*; a prolonged form of 1746; to *invest* (with a garment):—clothe in, wear.

1738. ἔνδικος, endikos, *en´-dee-kos*; from 1722 and 1349; *in* the *right*, i.e. *equitable*:—just.

Adjective from *en* (1722), in, and *díkē* (1349), justice. Conformable to right, i.e. right, just (Heb 2:2). In Ro 3:8, *éndikon* presupposes that which has been decided justly.

Syn.: *díkaios* (1342), just; *dikaíōs* (1346), justly, is that which leads to the just sentence.

1739. ἐνδόμησις, endomēsis, *en-dom´-ay-sis*; from a compound of 1722 and a derivative of the base of 1218; a *housing in* (*residence*), i.e. *structure*:—building.

1740. ἐνδοξάζω, endoxazō, *en-dox-ad´-zo*; from 1741; to *glorify*:—glorify.

From *éndoxos* (1741), glorious. To glorify. Used only in 2Th 1:10, 12.

Syn.: *megalúnō* (3170), to make great; *peripoiéomai* (4046), to make something of oneself.

1741. ἔνδοξος, endoxos, *en´-dox-os*; from 1722 and 1391; *in glory*, i.e. *splendid*, (figurative) *noble*:—glorious, gorgeous [-ly], honourable.

Adjective from *en* (1722), in, and *dóxa* (1391), glory. Glorious, splendid:

(**I**) Of persons: honored, respected, noble (1Co 4:10; Sept.: 1Sa 9:6; Isa 23:8). Of deeds, in the neuter plural *tá éndoxa*, glorious, memorable (Lk 13:17; Sept.: Ex 34:10; Job 5:9; Isa 12:4).

(**II**) Of external appearance: splendid, glorious, as of raiment (Lk 7:25; Sept.: 2Ch 2:9; Isa 22:17; 23:9). Metaphorically: a glorious Church, signifying the Church adorned in pure and splendid raiment as a bride (Eph 5:27 [cf. Eph 5:25, as well as Rev 19:7, 8; 21:9]).

Deriv.: *endoxázō* (1740), to glorify.

Syn.: *tá éndoxa* implying glorious things, miracles, unusual acts; *sēmeía* (4592), signs; *dunámeis* (1411), mighty works; *megaleía* (3167), great works; *parádoxa* (3861), strange works; *thaumásia* (2297), admirable works; *tímios* (5093), precious, valuable, honourable; *éntimos* (1784), honourable; *euschḗmōn* (2158), comely, honourable; *kalós* (2570), good; *semnós* (4586), honourable, grave, modest.

1742. ἔνδυμα, enduma, *en´-doo-mah*; from 1746; *apparel* (especially the outer *robe*):—clothing, garment, raiment.

1743. ἐνδυναμόω, endunamoō, *en-doo-nam-o´-o*; from 1722 and 1412; to *empower*:—enable, (increase in) strength (-en), be (make) strong.

From *en* (1722), in, and *dunamóō* (1412), to strengthen. Found only in biblical and ecclesiastical Gr. meaning to make strong, vigorous, to strengthen. Used in the pass., to be strengthened, become strong. Of the body, as made strong out of weakness (Heb 11:34 [TR]). Metaphorically, of the mind (Ac 9:22; Ro 4:20; Eph 6:10; Php 4:13; 1Ti 1:12; 2Ti 2:1; 4:17; Sept.: Ps 52:9).

Syn.: *ischúō* (2480), to strengthen, enable; *enischúō* (1765), to strengthen fully; *epischúō* (2001), to make strong; *krataióō* (2901), to strengthen with the implied meaning of to establish; *sthenóō* (4599), to strengthen; *stērízō* (4741), to establish; *epistērízō* (1991), to confirm, establish; *stereóō* (4732), to make stable.

1744. ἐνδύνω, endunō, *en-doo´-no*; from 1772 and 1416; to *sink* (by implication, *wrap* [compare 1746] *on*, i.e. (figurative) *sneak*:—creep.

1745. ἔνδυσις, endusis, *en´-doo-sis*; from 1746; *investment* with clothing:—putting on.

1746. ἐνδύω, enduō, *en-doo´-o*; from 1722 and 1416 (in the sense of *sinking* into a garment); to *invest* with clothing (literal or figurative):—array, clothe (with), endue, have (put) on.

1747. ἐνέδρα, enedra, *en-ed´-rah*; feminine from 1722 and the base of 1476; an *ambuscade*, i.e. (figurative) murderous *purpose*:—lay wait. See also 1749.

1748. ἐνεδρεύω, enedreuō, *en-ed-ryoo´-o*; from 1747; to *lurk*, i.e. (figurative) *plot* assassination:—lay wait for.

1749. ἔνεδρον, enedron, *en´-ed-ron*; neuter of the same as 1747; an *ambush*, i.e. (figurative) murderous *design*:—lying in wait.

1750. ἐνειλέω, eneileō, *en-i-leh´-o*; from 1772 and the base of 1507; to *enwrap*:—wrap in.

1751. ἔνειμι, eneimi, *en´-i-mee*; from 1772 and 1510; to *be within* (neuter participle plural):—such things as … have. See also 1762.

1752. ἕνεκα, heneka, *hen´-ek-ah*; or **ἕνεκεν,** ***heneken***, *hen´-ek-en*; or **εἵνεκεν,** ***heineken***, *hi´-nek-en*; of uncertain affinity; *on account of*:—because, for (cause, sake), (where-) fore, by reason of, that.

1753. ἐνέργεια, energeia, *en-erg´-i-ah*; from 1756; *efficiency* ("energy"):—operation, strong, (effectual) working.

1754. ἐνεργέω, energeō, *en-erg-eh´-o*; from 1756; to *be active, efficient*:—do, (be) effectual (fervent), be mighty in, shew forth self, work (effectually in).

From *energḗs* (1756), in work, operative, active. To be at work, to be effective, operative:

(**I**) To work, be active, produce an effect, spoken of things (Mt 14:2; Mk 6:14, "mighty works do show forth themselves in him"; see Eph 1:20; 2:2; Php 2:13); of persons (Gal 2:8, "he that wrought effectually in Peter."

(II) Transitively: to work, to effect, produce, spoken of persons (1Co 12:6, "which worketh all"; see 1Co 12:11; Gal 3:5; Eph 1:11; Php 2:13; Sept.: Pr 21:6; Isa 41:4).

(III) Middle: to show activity, i.e. to work, be active, operate, spoken only of things (Ro 7:5; 2Co 1:6; 4:12; Gal 5:6; Eph 3:20; Col 1:29; 1Th 2:13; 2Th 2:7). In the part. *energouménē* as adj., working, effective (Jas 5:16, "an effective supplication" [a.t.]).

Deriv.: *enérgēma* (1755), operation, working, an effect.

Syn.: *ergázomai* (2038), work; *katergázomai* (2716), to achieve, effect by toil; *douleúō* (1398), work; *poiéō* (4160), to do; *dunatéō* (1414), to be powerful, be able; *ischúō* (2480), to prevail, able to do; *epiteléō* (2005), accomplish, perform; *prássō* (4238), to execute, accomplish; *kámnō* (2577), to toil.

1755. ἐνέργημα, energēma, *en-erg´-ay-mah*; from 1754; an *effect*:—operation, working.

Noun from *energéō* (1754), to effect. Effect produced, operation. In the NT, used only in 1Co 12:6, 10 of the results of the energy of God in the believer. Though *enérgēma* is translated "operation," it is actually the results energized by God's grace.

1756. ἐνεργής, energēs, *en-er-gace´*; from 1722 and 2041; *active, operative*:—effectual, powerful.

Adjective from *en* (1722), in, and *érgon* (2041), work. Working, operative, active, effective (1Co 16:9; Phm 6; Heb 4:12).

Deriv.: *enérgeia* (1753), operation, working; *energéō* (1754), to be active, efficient.

1757. ἐνευλογέω, eneulogeō, *en-yoo-log-eh´-o*; from 1722 and 2127; to *confer a benefit on*:—bless.

1758. ἐνέχω, enechō, *en-ekh´-o*; from 1722 and 2192; to *hold in* or *upon*, i.e. *ensnare*; (by implication) to *keep a grudge*:—entangle with, have a quarrel against, urge.

From *en* (1722), in or upon, and *échō* (2192), to have. To have in oneself, implying a disposition of mind toward a person or thing, either favourable or unfavourable (Mk 6:19; Lk 11:53). In the pass.: to be held in or by something; figuratively, to be entangled in, subject to (Gal 5:1).

Deriv.: *énochos* (1777), to be held fast, bound, obliged.

Syn.: *pagideúō* (3802), to ensnare; *emplékō* (1707), to entangle.

1759. ἐνθάδε, enthade, *en-thad´-eh*; from a prolonged form of 1722; properly *within*, i.e. (of place) *here, hither*:—(t-) here, hither.

1760. ἐνθυμέομαι, enthumeomai, *en-thoo-meh´-om-ahee*; from a compound of 1722 and 2372; to *be inspirited*, i.e. *ponder*:—think.

1761. ἐνθύμησις, enthumēsis, *en-thoo´-may-sis*; from 1760; *deliberation*:—device, thought.

1762. ἔνι, eni, *en´-ee*; contracted from third person singular presumed indicative of 1751; impersonal *there is* in or among:—be, (there) is.

1763. ἐνιαυτός, eniautos, *en-ee-ow-tos´*; prolonged from a primary **ἔνος**, *enos* (a *year*); a *year*:—year.

1764. ἐνίστημι, enistēmi, *en-is´-tay-mee*; from 1722 and 2476; to *place on* hand, i.e. (reflexive) *impend*, (participle) be *instant*:—come, be at hand, present.

From *en* (1722), in, with, and *hístēmi* (2476), to stand. In the NT, used metaphorically: to stand near, i.e. to be at hand, to impend (2Th 2:2; 2Ti 3:1). Instant, present (Ro 8:38; 1Co 3:22; 7:26; Gal 1:4; Heb 9:9).

Syn.: *hḗkō* (2240), to come, be present; *ephístēmi* (2186), to arrive; *parístēmi* (3936), to be near at hand; *proseggízō* (4331), to come near; *páreimi* (3918), to be near.

1765. ἐνισχύω, enischuō, *en-is-khoo´-o*; from 1722 and 2480; to *invigorate* (transitive or reflexive):—strengthen.

1766. ἔννατος, ennatos, *en´-nat-os*; order from 1767; *ninth*:—ninth.

1767. ἐννέα, ennea, *en-neh´-ah*; a primary number; *nine*:—nine.

1768. ἐννενηκονταεννέα, ennenēkontaennea, *en-nen-ay-kon-tah-en-neh´-ah*; from a (tenth) multiple of 1767 and 1767 itself; *ninety-nine*:—ninety and nine.

1769. ἐννεός, enneos, *en-neh-os´*; from 1770; *dumb* (as *making signs*), i.e. *silent* from astonishment:—speechless.

1770. ἐννεύω, enneuō, *en-nyoo´-o*; from 1722 and 3506; to *nod at*, i.e. *beckon* or *communicate by gesture*:—make signs.

1771. ἔννοια, ennoia, *en´-noy-ah*; from a compound of 1722 and 3563; *thoughtfulness*, i.e. moral *understanding*:—intent, mind.

Noun from *en* (1722), in, and *noús* (3563), mind. What is in the mind, e.g., idea, notion, intention, purpose (Heb 4:12; 1Pe 4:1; Sept.: Pr 3:21 [cf. Pr 23:19]).

Syn.: *lógos* (3056), reason, cause, intent; *aitía* (156), cause; *aítion* (158), fault; *enthúmēsis* (1761), device, thought; *epínoia* (1963), a thought by way of design; *nóēma* (3540), a purpose, a device of the mind; *dianóēma* (1270), a thought, machination; *logismós* (3053), imagination; *dialogismós* (1261), reasoning.

1772. ἔννομος, ennomos, *en´-nom-os*; from 1722 and 3551; (subject) *legal*, or (object) *subject* to:—lawful, under law.

Adjective from *en* (1722), in, and *nómos* (3551), law. What is within range of law or conformable to law. Legal, legitimate (Ac 19:39); subject to law (1Co 9:21).

Syn.: *éndikos* (1738), equitable, just.

1773. ἔννυχον, ennuchon, *en´-noo-khon*; neuter of a compound of 1722 and 3571; (adverb) *by night*:—before day.

1774. ἐνοικέω, enoikeō, *en-oy-keh´-o*; from 1722 and 3611; to *inhabit* (figurative):—dwell in.

1775. ἑνότης, henotēs, *hen-ot´-ace*; from 1520; *oneness*, i.e. (figurative) *unanimity*:—unity.

1776. ἐνοχλέω, enochleō, *en-okh-leh´-o*; from 1722 and 3791; to *crowd in*, i.e. (figurative) to *annoy*:—trouble.

1777. ἔνοχος, enochos, *en´-okh-os*; from 1758; *liable* to (a condition, penalty or imputation):—in danger of, guilty of, subject to.

1778. ἔνταλμα, entalma, *en´-tal-mah*; from 1781; an *injunction*, i.e. religious *precept*:—commandment.

Noun from *entéllomai* (1781), to charge, command. A mandate, precept, ordinance (Mt 15:9; Mk 7:7; Col 2:22; Sept.: Job 23:11, 12; Isa 29:13).

Syn.: *diátagma* (1297), that which is imposed by decree or law; *diatagḗ* (1296), a decree; *epitagḗ* (2003), command; *paraggelía* (3852), a proclamation, charge; *nómos* (3851), law.

1779. ἐνταφιάζω, entaphiazō, *en-taf-ee-ad´-zo*; from a compound of 1722 and 5028; to *inswathe* with cerements for interment:—bury.

1780. ἐνταφιασμός, entaphiasmos, *en-taf-ee-as-mos´*; from 1779; *preparation* for interment:—burying.

1781. ἐντέλλομαι, entellomai, *en-tel´-lom-ahee*; from 1722 and the base of 5056; to *enjoin*:—(give) charge, (give) command (-ments), injoin.

1782. ἐντεύθεν, enteuthen, *ent-yoo´-then*; from the same as 1759; *hence* (literal or figurative); (repeated) *on both sides*:—(from) hence, on either side.

1783. ἔντευξις, enteuxis, *ent´-yook-sis*; from 1793; an *interview*, i.e. (special) *supplication*:—intercession, prayer.

Noun from *entugchánō* (1793), to chance upon, to entreat. A falling in with, meeting with, coming together. In the NT, intercession, prayer (1Ti 2:1; 4:5, prayer according to God's will).

1784. ἔντιμος, entimos, *en´-tee-mos*; from 1722 and 5092; *valued* (figurative):—dear, more honourable, precious, in reputation.

1785. ἐντολή, entolē, *en-tol-ay´*; from 1781; *injunction*, i.e. an authoritative *prescription*:—commandment, precept.

Noun from *entéllomai* (1781), to charge, command. Commandment, whether of God or man:

(I) Charge, commission, direction (Jn 10:18; 12:49, 50; Ac 17:15; Col 4:10; Heb 7:5; Sept.: 2Ki 18:36; 2Ch 8:15). With the meaning of a public charge or edict from magistrates (Jn 11:57; Sept.: 2Ch 35:16).

(II) In the sense of precept, commandment, law as spoken of:

(A) The traditions of the rabbis (Tit 1:14).

(B) The precepts and teachings of Jesus (Jn 13:34; 15:12; 1Co 14:37; 1Jn 2:8).

(C) The precepts and commandments of God in general (1Co 7:19; 1Jn 3:22, 23; Sept.: Dt 4:2, 40).

(D) The precepts of the Mosaic Law, in whole or in part (Mt 5:19; 19:17; 22:36, 38, 40; Mk 10:5, 19; Ro 7:8–13).

(E) Generally and collectively, *hē entolḗ* or *hē entolḗ Theoú*, the commandment of God, used either for the Mosaic Law (Mt 15:3, 6; Mk 7:8, 9; Lk 23:56; Sept.: 2Ki 21:8; 2Ch 12:1) or for the precepts given to Christians, Christian doctrines and duties (1Ti 6:14; 2Pe 2:21; 3:2).

Syn.: *prostássō* (4367), to charge; *éntalma* (1778), a religious commandment; *diátagma*, (1297), edict, decree; *diatagḗ* (1296), ordinance, disposition; *epitagḗ* (2003), commanding authority, order, command; *paraggelía* (3852), charge.

1786. ἐντόπιος, entopios, *en-top´-ee-os*; from 1722 and 5117; a *resident*:—of that place.

1787. ἐντός, entos, *en-tos´*; from 1722; *inside* (adverb or noun):—within.

1788. ἐντρέπω, entrepō, *en-trep´-o*; from 1722 and the base of 5157; to *invert*, i.e. (figurative and reflexive) in a good sense, to *respect*; or in a bad one, to *confound*:—regard, (give) reverence, shame.

1789. ἐντρέφω, entrephō, *en-tref´-o*; from 1722 and 5142; (figurative) to *educate*:—nourish up in.

1790. ἔντρομος, entromos, *en´-trom-os*; from 1722 and 5156; *terrified*:— × quake, × trembled.

1791. ἐντροπή, entropē, *en-trop-ay´*; from 1788; *confusion*:—shame.

Noun from *entrépō* (1788), to withdraw. Shame, a putting to shame (1Co 6:5; 15:34; Sept.: Ps 35:26; 69:8, 20).

Syn.: *óneidos* (3681), reproach; *atimía* (819), dishonour, shame; *spílos* (4696), disgrace, spot; *stígma* (4742), scar; *skándalon* (4625), scandal, offence; *aischúnē* (152), shame.

1792. ἐντρυφάω, entruphaō, *en-troo-fah´-o*; from 1722 and 5171; to *revel in*:—sporting selves.

1793. ἐντυγχάνω, entugchanō, *en-toong-khan´-o*; from 1722 and 5177; to *chance upon*, i.e. (by implication) *confer with*; by extension to *entreat* (in favour or against):—deal with, make intercession.

1794. ἐντυλίσσω, entulissō, *en-too-lis´-so*; from 1722 and **τυλίσσω**, *tulissō* (to *twist*; probably akin to 1507); to *entwine*, i.e. *wind* up in:—wrap in (together).

1795. ἐντυπόω, entupoō, *en-too-po´-o*; from 1722 and a derivative of 5179; to *enstamp*, i.e. *engrave*:—engrave.

1796. ἐνυβρίζω, enubrizō, *en-oo-brid´-zo*; from 1722 and 5195; to *insult*:—do despite unto.

1797. ἐνυπνιάζομαι, enupniazomai, *en-oop-nee-ad´-zom-ahee*; middle from 1798; to *dream*:—dream (-er).

1798. ἐνύπνιον, enupnion, *en-oop´-nee-on*; from 1722 and 5258; something seen *in sleep*, i.e. a *dream* (*vision* in a dream):—dream.

1799. ἐνώπιον, enōpion, *en-o´-pee-on*; neuter of a compound of 1722 and a derivative of 3700; *in* the *face* of (literal or figurative):—before, in the presence (sight) of, to.

1800. 'Ενώς, Enōs, *en-oce´*; of Hebrew origin [583]; *Enos* (i.e. *Enosh*), a patriarch:—Enos.

1801. ἐνωτίζομαι, enōtizomai, *en-o-tid´-zom-ahee*; middle from a compound of 1722 and 3775; to take *in one's ear*, i.e. to *listen*:—hearken.

1802. 'Ενώχ, Enōch, *en-oke´*; of Hebrew origin [2585]; *Enoch* (i.e. *Chanok*), an antediluvian:—Enoch.

1803. ἕξ, hex, *hex*; a primary numeral; *six*:—six.

1804. ἐξαγγέλλω, exaggellō, *ex-ang-el´-lo*; from 1537 and the base of 32; to *publish* i.e. *celebrate*:—shew forth.

From *ek* (1537), out, and *aggéllō* (n.f., see *anaggéllō* [312]), to tell, declare. To declare abroad, make widely known (1Pe 2:9; Sept.: Ps 9:14; 79:13).

Syn.: *phaneróō* (5319), to manifest; *dēlóō* (1213), to make plain; *diēgéomai* (1334), to declare; *légō* (3004), to tell; *apaggéllō* (518), to declare, tell; *kērússō* (2784), to proclaim, preach; *kataggéllō* (2605), to proclaim; *marturéō* (3140), to witness.

1805. ἐξαγοράζω, exagorazō, *ex-ag-or-ad´-zo*; from 1537 and 59; to *buy up*, i.e. *ransom*; (figurative) to *rescue* from loss (*improve* opportunity):—redeem.

From *ek* (1537), out or from, and *agorázō* (59), to buy. To purchase out, to buy up from the possession or power of someone. In the NT, to redeem, to set free from service or bondage (Gal 3:13; 4:5); in the middle voice, to redeem for one's use, used metaphorically in Eph 5:16; Col 4:5.

Syn.: *lutróō* (3084), to release on receipt of ransom, redeem.

1806. ἐξάγω, exagō, *ex-ag´-o*; from 1537 and 71; to *lead forth*:—bring forth (out), fetch (lead) out.

1807. ἐξαιρέω, exaireō, *ex-ahee-reh´-o*; from 1537 and 138; active to *tear out*; middle to *select*; (figurative) to *release*:—deliver, pluck out, rescue.

1808. ἐξαίρω, exairō, *ex-ah´ee-ro*; from 1537 and 142; to *remove*:—put (take) away.

1809. ἐξαιτέομαι, exaiteomai, *ex-ahee-teh´-om-ahee*; middle from 1537 and 154; to *demand* (for trial):—desire.

From *ek* (1537), out, and *aitéō* (154), to ask, require or demand. To claim back, require something to be delivered up. In the middle voice as a deponent verb, *exaitéomai*, to claim back for oneself (Lk 22:31).

Syn.: *epithuméō* (1937), to covet, desire; *zētéō* (2212), to require; *epizētéō* (1934), to crave; *diṓkō* (1377), to seek; *axióō* (515), to deem entitled; *apaitéō* (523), to demand back.

1810. ἐξαίφνης, exaiphnēs, *ex-ah´eef-nace*; from 1537 and the base of 160; *of a sudden* (*unexpectedly*):—suddenly. Compare 1819.

1811. ἐξακολουθέω, exakoloutheō, *ex-ak-ol-oo-theh´-o*; from 1537 and 190; to *follow out*, i.e. (figurative) to *imitate*, *obey*, yield to:—follow.

1812. ἑξακόσιοι, hexakosioi, *hex-ak-os´-ee-oy*; plural ordinal from 1803 and 1540; *six hundred*:—six hundred.

1813. ἐξαλείφω, exaleiphō, *ex-al-i´-fo*; from 1537 and 218; to *smear out*, i.e. *obliterate* (*erase* tears; figurative, *pardon* sin):—blot out, wipe away.

1814. ἐξάλλομαι, exallomai, *ex-al´-lom-ahee*; from 1537 and 242; to *spring forth*:—leap up.

1815. ἐξανάστασις, exanastasis, *ex-an-as´-tas-is*; from 1817; a *rising from* death:—resurrection.

Noun from *exanístēmi* (1817), to rise up. The resurrection from among the dead (Php 3:11).

1816. ἐξανατέλλω, exanatellō, *ex-an-at-el´-lo*; from 1537 and 393; to *start up out* of the ground, i.e. *germinate*:—spring up.

1817. ἐξανίστημι, exanistēmi, *ex-an-is´-tay-mee*; from 1537 and 450; objective to *produce*, i.e. (figurative) *beget*; subject to *arise*, i.e. (figurative) *object*:—raise (rise) up.

From *ek* (1537), out of or from, and *anístēmi* (450), to rise up. To rise up from among others (Ac 15:5; Sept.: Ge 18:16; 19:1; Jgs 3:20); transitively, to raise up seed from a woman (Mk 12:19; Lk 20:28; Sept.: Ge 4:25; 19:32, 34).

Deriv.: *exanástasis* (1815), resurrection.

Syn.: *exegeírō* (1825), to arouse fully, awaken; *anorthóō* (461), to straighten up; *stḗkō* (4739), to stand; *exanatéllō* (1816), to spring from.

1818. ἐξαπατάω, exapataō, *ex-ap-at-ah´-o*; from 1537 and 538; to *seduce wholly*:—beguile, deceive.

1819. ἐξάπινα, exapina, *ex-ap´-ee-nah*; from 1537 and a derivative of the same as 160; *of a sudden*, i.e. *unexpectedly*:—suddenly. Compare 1810.

1820. ἐξαπορέομαι, exaporeomai, *ex-ap-or-eh´-om-ahee*; middle from 1537 and 639; to *be utterly at a loss*, i.e. *despond*:—(in) despair.

1821. ἐξαποστέλλω, exapostellō, *ex-ap-os-tel´-lo*; from 1537 and 649; to *send away forth*, i.e. (on a mission) to *despatch*, or (peremptorily) to *dismiss*:—send (away, forth, out).

1822. ἐξαρτίζω, exartizō, *ex-ar-tid´-zo*; from 1537 and a derivative of 739; to *finish out* (time); (figurative) to *equip fully* (a teacher):—accomplish, thoroughly furnish.

From *ek* (1537), an intensive, and *artízō* (n.f.), to put in appropriate condition. To complete entirely. Spoken of time: to finish, to bring to an end (Ac 21:5); of a religious teacher: to make thoroughly perfect, to furnish out (2Ti 3:17).

Syn.: *kataskeuázō* (2680), to make, fit, prepare; *katartízō* (2675), to fit, frame, prepare; *sunistéō* (4921), to set together; *sunarmologéō* (4883), to fit together; *plēróō* (4137), to bring to completion; *teléō* (5055), to accomplish, complete.

1823. ἐξαστράπτω, exastraptō, *ex-as-trap´-to*; from 1537 and 797; to *lighten forth*, i.e. (figurative) to *be radiant* (of very white garments):—glistening.

1824. ἐξαύτης, exautēs, *ex-ow´-tace*; from 1537 and the generic singular feminine of 846 (5610 being understood); *from that* hour, i.e. *instantly*:—by and by, immediately, presently, straightway.

1825. ἐξεγείρω, exegeirō, *ex-eg-i´-ro*; from 1537 and 1453; to *rouse fully*, i.e. (figurative) to *resuscitate* (from death), *release* (from infliction):—raise up.

From *ek* (1537), out, and *egeírō* (1453), to raise. To raise up, wake out of sleep. In the NT, used metaphorically: to raise up out of death (1Co 6:14); to raise up, i.e. to cause to arise or exist (Ro 9:17, quoted from Ex 9:16).

Syn.: *anorthóō* (461), to raise up; *exanístēmi* (1817), to rise up.

1826. ἔξειμι, exeimi, *ex´-i-mee*; from 1537 and **εἶμι, eimi** (to *go*); to *issue*, i.e. *leave* (a place), *escape* (to the shore):—depart, get [*to land*], go out.

1827. ἐξελέγχω, exelegchō, *ex-el-eng´-kho*; from 1537 and 1651; to *convict fully*, i.e. (by implication) to *punish*:—convince.

1828. ἐξέλκω, exelkō, *ex-el´-ko*; from 1537 and 1670; to *drag forth*, i.e. (figurative) to *entice* (to sin):—draw away.

1829. ἐξέραμα, exerama, *ex-er´-am-ah*; from a compound of 1537 and a presumed **ἐραω, eraō** (to *spew*); *vomit*, i.e. *food disgorged*:—vomit.

1830. ἐξερευνάω, exereunaō, *ex-er-yoo-nah´-o*; from 1537 and 2045; to *explore* (figurative):—search diligently.

1831. ἐξέρχομαι, exerchomai, *ex-er´-khom-ahee*; from 1537 and 2064; to *issue* (literal or figurative):—come (forth, out), depart (out of), escape, get out, go (abroad, away, forth, out, thence), proceed (forth), spread abroad.

1832. ἔξεστι, exesti, *ex´-es-tee*; third person singular presumed indicative of a compound of 1537 and 1510; so also **ἐξόν, exon,** *ex-on´*; neuter presumed participle of the same (with or without some form of 1510 expressed); impersonal *it is right* (through the figurative idea of *being out* in public):—be lawful, let, × may (-est).

1833. ἐξετάζω, exetazō, *ex-et-ad´-zo*; from 1537 and **ἐτάζω, etazō** (to *examine*); to *test thoroughly* (by questions), i.e. *ascertain* or *interrogate*:—ask, enquire, search.

1834. ἐξηγέομαι, exēgeomai, *ex-ayg-eh´-om-ahee*; from 1537 and 2233; to *consider out* (aloud), i.e. *rehearse, unfold*:—declare, tell.

Middle deponent from *ek* (1537), out, or an intensive, and *hēgéomai* (2233), to tell, lead forward. To bring or lead out, to take the lead, be the leader. In the NT, to bring out, i.e. to make known, to declare:

(I) To unfold, reveal, make known, as a teacher (Jn 1:18 [cf. Mt 11:27; Sept.: Le 14:57]).

(II) To tell, narrate, recount (Lk 24:35; Ac 10:8; 15:12, 14; 21:19; Sept.: Jgs 7:13).

Syn.: *diasaphéō* (1285), to make clear; *phaneróō* (5319), to manifest.

1835. ἑξήκοντα, hexēkonta, *hex-ay´-kon-tah*; the tenth multiple of 1803; *sixty*:—sixty [-fold], threescore.

1836. ἑξῆς, hexēs, *hex-ace´*; from 2192 (in the sense of *taking hold* of, i.e. *adjoining*); *successive*:—after, following, × morrow, next.

1837. ἐξηχέομαι, exēcheomai, *ex-ah-kheh´-om-ahee*; middle from 1537 and 2278; to "*echo*" *forth*, i.e. *resound* (*be* generally *reported*):—sound forth.

1838. ἕξις, hexis, *hex´-is*; from 2192; *habit*, i.e. (by implication) *practice*:—use.

1839. ἐξίστημι, existēmi, *ex-is´-tay-mee*; from 1537 and 2476; to *put* (*stand*) *out* of wits, i.e. *astound*, or (reflexive) *become astounded, insane*:—amaze, be (make) astonished, be beside self (selves), bewitch, wonder.

From *ek* (1537), out, and *hístēmi* (2476), to stand. To put out of place. In the NT, used only metaphorically: to put out of oneself, i.e. to astonish, fill with wonder (Lk 24:22; Ac 8:9, 11); to be beside oneself, to be put out of one's mind (Mk 3:21; 2Co 5:13; Sept.: Job 12:17); to be astonished, amazed, filled with wonder (Mt 12:23; Mk 2:12; 5:42; 6:51; Lk 8:56; Sept.: Ge 27:33).

Deriv.: *ékstasis* (1611), bewilderment, wonder.

Syn.: *ekplḗssomai* (1605), to be astonished; *thambéomai* (2284), to be amazed; *ekthambéomai* (1568), to be utterly amazed; *maínomai* (3105), to rave; *paraphronéō* (3912), to act as a fool; *thaumázō* (2296), to marvel.

1840. ἐξισχύω, exischuō, *ex-is-khoo´-o*; from 1537 and 2480; to *have full strength*, i.e. *be entirely competent*:—be able.

1841. ἔξοδος, exodos, *ex´-od-os*; from 1537 and 3598; an *exit*, i.e. (figurative) *death*:—decease, departing.

1842. ἐξολοθρεύω, exolothreuō, *ex-ol-oth-ryoo´-o*; from 1537 and 3645; to *extirpate*:—destroy.

1843. ἐξομολογέω, exomologeō, *ex-om-ol-og-eh´-o*; from 1537 and 3670; to *acknowledge* or (by implication of *assent*) *agree fully*:—confess, profess, promise.

From *ek* (1537), out, and *homologéō* (3670), to assent. Similar to *homologéō*, but stronger: to speak out the same things as another; hence in the NT:

(I) To concede, to acknowledge, to confess fully (Mt 3:6; Mk 1:5; Ac 19:18; Jas 5:16; Sept.: Da 9:4); to acknowledge openly, to profess (Php 2:11; Rev 3:5). In the middle, to make acknowledgement for benefits, i.e. to give thanks, to praise (Mt 11:25; Lk 10:21; Ro 14:11; 15:9 quoted from Ps 18:49, 50; Sept.: 1Ch 16:4; 2Ch 30:22; Ps 57:9, 10).

(II) To assent fully, to agree, to promise (Lk 22:6).

Syn.: *homologéō* (3670), to speak the same thing, confess, declare, admit; *epineúō* (1962), to nod to, express approval; *sumphōnéō* (4856), to agree; *egkrínō* (1469), judge in; *apodéchomai* (588), to accept; *anagnōrízō* (319), to recognize.

1844. ἐξορκίζω, exorkizō, *ex-or-kid´-zo*; from 1537 and 3726; to *exact an oath*, i.e. *conjure*:—adjure.

1845. ἐξορκιστής, exorkistēs, *ex-or-kis-tace´*; from 1844; *one that binds by an oath* (or *spell*), i.e. (by implication) an "*exorcist*" (*conjurer*):—exorcist.

1846. ἐξορύσσω, exorussō, *ex-or-oos´-so*; from 1537 and 3736; to *dig out*, i.e. (by extension) to *extract* (an eye), *remove* (a roofing):—break up, pluck out.

1847. ἐξουδενόω, exoudenoō, *ex-oo-den-o´-o*; from 1537 and a derivative of the neuter of 3762; to *make utterly nothing of*, i.e. *despise*:—set at nought. See also 1848.

1848. ἐξουθενέω, exoutheneō, *ex-oo-then-eh´-o*; a variation of 1847 and meaning the same:—contemptible, despise, least esteemed, set at nought.

1849. ἐξουσία, exousia, *ex-oo-see´-ah*; from 1832 (in the sense of *ability*); *privilege*, i.e. (subject) *force, capacity, competency, freedom*, or (object) *mastery* (concrete *magistrate, superhuman, potentate, token of control*), delegated *influence*:—authority, jurisdiction, liberty, power, right, strength.

Noun from *éxesti* (1832), it is permissible, allowed. Power:

(I) The power of doing something, ability, faculty (Mt 9:6, 8; Mk 2:10; Lk 5:24; 10:19; 12:5; Jn 10:18; 19:11; Ac 8:19; Rev 13:12). With the meaning of strength, force, efficiency (Mt 7:29; Mk 1:22; Rev 9:3, 19), with the prep. *en* (1722), in, and the dat., *en exousía* as adjunct, powerful (Lk 4:32); with the prep. *katá* (2596), according to, *kat' exousían* being equivalent to *en exousía*, as adverb, i.e. with intensive strength, with point and effect (Mk 1:27 [cf. Lk 4:36]).

(II) Power of doing or not doing, i.e. license, liberty, free choice (Ac 1:7; 5:4; Ro 9:21; 1Co 7:37; 8:9; 9:4–6, 12, 18; 2Th 3:9; Rev 22:14).

(III) Power as entrusted, i.e. commission, authority, right, full power (Mt 8:9; 21:23, 24, 27; Mk 3:15; 11:28, 29, 33; Lk 20:2, 8; Jn 1:12; Ac 9:14; 26:10, 12; 2Co 10:8; 13:10; Heb 13:10; Rev 13:5).

(IV) Power over persons and things, dominion, authority, rule.

(A) Particularly and generally (Mt 28:18; Mk 13:34; Lk 7:8; Jude 25; Rev 13:2, 4; 17:12, 13; 18:1; Sept.: Ps 136:8, 9; Da 3:33; 4:31). Before the gen. of person to whom the power belongs (Lk 20:20; 22:53; Ac 26:18; Col 1:13; Rev 12:10). Followed by the gen. of the object subjected to the power (Mt 10:1; Mk 6:7, "power over unclean spirits"; Jn 17:2).

(B) As a metonym used for: **(1)** What is subject to one's rule, dominion, domain, jurisdiction (Lk 4:6; 23:7; Sept.: 2Ki 20:13; Ps 114:2). **(2)** In plural or coll., those invested with power, as rulers, magistrates (Lk 12:11; Ro 13:1–3; Tit 3:1). For the celestial and infernal powers, princes, potentates, e.g., angels, archangels (Eph 1:21; 3:10; Col 1:16; 2:10; 1Pe 3:22); demons (Eph 6:12; Col 2:15). Generally, of the powerful adversaries of the gospel (1Co 15:24 [cf. *arché* {746}, principality]). **(3)** In 1Co 11:10, where *exousía* is used as an emblem of power, i.e. a veil or covering (cf. 1Co 11:13, 16) as an emblem of subjection to the power of a husband, a token of modest adherence to duties and usages established by law or custom lest spies or evil-minded persons should take advantage of any impropriety in the meetings of the Christians (cf. *timḗ* [5092], honour).

Syn.: *krátos* (2904), dominion; *dúnamis* (1411), power. *Exousía* denotes the executive power while *archḗ* (746), rule, represents the authority granting the power.

Deriv.: *exousiázō* (1850), to exercise authority.

1850. ἐξουσιάζω, exousiazō, *ex-oo-see-ad´-zo*; from 1849; to *control*:—exercise authority upon, bring under the (have) power of.

1851. ἐξοχή, exochē, *ex-okh-ay´*; from a compound of 1537 and 2192 (meaning to *stand out*); *prominence* (figurative):—principal.

1852. ἐξυπνίζω, exupnizō, *ex-oop-nid´-zo*; from 1853; to *waken*:—awake out of sleep.

1853. ἔξυπνος, exupnos, *ex´-oop-nos*; from 1537 and 5258; *awake*:— × out of sleep.

1854. ἔξω, exō, *ex´-o*; adverb from 1537; *out* (*-side, of doors*), literal or figurative:—away, forth, (with-) out (of, -ward), strange.

1855. ἔξωθεν, exōthen, *ex´-o-then*; from 1854; *external* (*-ly*):—out (-side, -ward, -wardly), (from) without.

1856. ἐξωθέω, exōtheō, *ex-o-theh´-o*; or **ἐξώθω, *exōthō*,** *ex-o´-tho*; from 1537 and **ὠθέω,** *ōtheō* (to *push*); to *expel*; (by implication) to *propel*:—drive out, thrust in.

1857. ἐξώτερος, exōteros, *ex-o´-ter-os*; comparative of 1854; *exterior*:—outer.

1858. ἑορτάζω, heortazō, *heh-or-tad´-zo*; from 1859; to *observe a festival*:—keep the feast.

1859. ἑορτή, heortē, *heh-or-tay´*; of uncertain affinity; a *festival*:—feast, holy day.

1860. ἐπαγγελία, epaggelia, *ep-ang-el-ee´-ah*; from 1861; an *announcement* (for information, assent or pledge; especially a divine *assurance* of good):—message, promise.

Noun from *epaggéllō* (1861), to announce. Annunciation, announcement:

(I) Particularly in 1Jn 1:5 (TR), where later editions have *aggelia* (31), message (Sept.: Eze 7:26).

(II) By implication, a promise:

(A) Particularly a promise given (2Co 1:20; Eph 1:13; 6:2; 1Ti 4:8; 2Pe 3:4, 9; Sept.: Est 4:7). Of special promises, e.g., made to Abraham (Ac 7:6, 17; Ro 4:16, 20; Heb 6:12, 15; 7:6; 11:9, Promised Land); in respect to Isaac (Ro 9:9; Gal 4:23); of a spiritual seed (Ro 9:8; Gal 4:28); as made to Abraham and the Jewish patriarchs and prophets in general, e.g., of a future Saviour (Ac 13:23, 32; 26:6); of future blessings and the enjoyment of God's favour (Ac 2:39; Ro 4:13, 14, 16; 9:4; 15:8; 2Co 7:1; Gal 3:16–18, 21, 22, 29; Eph 2:12; 3:6; Heb 6:12, 17; 11:17); of salvation in Christ (2Ti 1:1); an apostle in respect to the promise of eternal life in Christ, that is, appointed to announce it (Heb 4:1; 8:6; 9:15; 1Jn 2:25).

(B) Metonymically, used for the thing promised (Heb 11:13, 33, 39); of salvation in Christ (Heb 10:36); of the Holy Spirit (Lk 24:49; Ac 1:4). In Ac 2:33; Gal 3:14, "having received the promise of the Spirit" (a.t.) means having received the promised effusions of the Spirit.

1861. ἐπαγγέλλω, epaggellō, *ep-ang-el´-lo*; from 1909 and the base of 32; to *announce upon* (reflexive), i.e. (by implication) to *engage* to do something, to *assert* something respecting oneself:—profess, (make) promise.

From *epí* (1909), an intensive, and *aggéllō* (n.f., see *anaggéllō* [312]), to tell, declare. To proclaim, to announce a message. In the NT, used only in the middle voice, *epaggéllomai*, meaning to announce oneself, offer oneself for a responsibility or service. Used primarily as "to promise" in Mk 14:11; Ac 7:5; Ro 4:21, *apéggelmai*, with middle meaning; 2Pe 2:19, and "to profess" in 1Ti 2:10; 6:21 with the meaning of pretending. When used with this special meaning, the word and its deriv. refer to God's divine promise of spontaneous salvation. To render a service. (See Ac 1:4, *epaggelían* [1860] "the promise"; 7:5; Ro 4:21; Tit 1:2; Heb 12:26; Jas 1:12; 2:5; 1Jn 2:25.) Used in an absolute sense, meaning to give a promise (Gal 3:19 with pass. meaning; Heb 6:13; 10:23; 11:11; Sept.: Est 4:7).

Deriv.: *epaggelía* (1860), an announcement, message; *epággelma* (1862), promise; *proepaggéllō* (4279), to promise before.

1862. ἐπάγγελμα, epaggelma, *ep-ang´-el-mah*; from 1861; a *self-committal* (by *assurance* of conferring some good):—promise.

Noun from *epaggéllō* (1861), to proclaim. A promise. Found only in 2Pe 1:4; 3:13.

1863. ἐπάγω, epagō, *ep-ag´-o*; from 1909 and 71; to *superinduce*, i.e. *inflict* (an evil), *charge* (a crime):—bring upon.

1864. ἐπαγωνίζομαι, epagōnizomai, *ep-ag-o-nid´-zom-ahee*; from 1909 and 75; to *struggle for*:—earnestly contend for.

From *epí* (1909), for, and *agōnízomai* (75), to strive, contend earnestly. To fight for or in reference to something, with the dat. of that which gives the occasion (Jude 3).

Syn.: *máchomai* (3164), to fight; *diamáchomai* (1264), to struggle against; *erízō* (2051), to strive; *athléō* (118), to contend in games; *poleméō* (4170), to fight in war.

1865. ἐπαθροίζω, epathroizō, *ep-ath-roid´-zo*; from 1909 and **ἀθροίζω,** ***athroizō*** (to *assemble*); to *accumulate*:—gather thick together.

1866. Ἐπαίνετος, Epainetos, *ep-a´hee-net-os*; from 1867; *praised; Epænetus*, a Christian:—Epenetus.

1867. ἐπαινέω, epaineō, *ep-ahee-neh´-o*; from 1909 and 134; to *applaud*:—commend, laud, praise.

1868. ἔπαινος, epainos, *ep´-ahee-nos*; from 1909 and the base of 134; *laudation*; concretely a *commendable* thing:—praise.

1869. ἐπαίρω, epairō, *ep-ahee´-ro*; from 1909 and 142; to *raise up* (literal or figurative):—exalt self, poise (lift, take) up.

1870. ἐπαισχύνομαι, epaischunomai, *ep-ahee-skhoo´-nom-ahee*; from 1909 and 153; to *feel shame for* something:—be ashamed.

1871. ἐπαιτέω, epaiteō, *ep-ahee-teh´-o*; from 1909 and 154; to *ask for*:—beg.

From *epí* (1909), an intensive, and *aitéō* (154), to ask, implore, claim. To beg, ask for alms (Lk 16:3; Sept.: Ps 109:10).

Syn.: *zētéō* (2212), to ask; *epithuméō* (1937), to desire; *exaitéomai* (1809), to desire, demand; *axióō* (515), to consider oneself entitled to; *apaitéō* (523), to demand back, ask again, require; *epizētéō* (1934), to inquire for.

1872. ἐπακολουθέω, epakoloutheō, *ep-ak-ol-oo-theh´-o*; from 1909 and 190; to *accompany*:—follow (after).

1873. ἐπακούω, epakouō, *ep-ak-oo´-o*; from 1909 and 191; to *hearken* (fabourably) *to*:—hear.

1874. ἐπακροάομαι, epakroaomai, *ep-ak-ro-ah´-om-ahee*; from 1909 and the base of 202; to *listen* (intently) *to*:—hear.

1875. ἐπάν, epan, *ep-an´*; from 1909 and 302; a particle of indefinite contemporaneousness; *whenever, as soon as*:—when.

1876. ἐπάναγκες, epanagkes, *ep-an´-ang-kes*; neuter of a presumed compound of 1909 and 318; (adverb) *on necessity*, i.e. *necessarily*:—necessary.

Adverb from *epí* (1909), upon, on account of, and *anágkē* (318), necessity. Necessarily. With the article it assumes the meaning of a noun, *tó epánagkes*, necessities or things of necessity (Ac 15:28).

Syn.: *anagkaíos* (316), necessary; *deí* (1163), that which must be; *prépon* (4241), that which is proper; *chreía* (5532), need, necessity.

1877. ἐπανάγω, epanagō, *ep-an-ag´-o*; from 1909 and 321; to *lead up on*, i.e. (technical) to *put out* (to sea); (intransitive) to *return*:—launch (thrust) out, return.

1878. ἐπαναμιμνήσκω, epanamimnēskō, *ep-an-ah-mim-nace´-ko*; from 1909 and 363; to *remind of*:—put in mind.

1879. ἐπαναπαύομαι, epanapauomai, *ep-an-ah-pow´-om-ahee*; middle from 1909 and 373; to *settle on*; literal (*remain*) or figurative (*rely*):—rest in (upon).

From *epí* (1909), upon, and *anapaúomai* (373), to rest. In the NT, only in the middle *epanapaúomai*. To rely, rest, repose oneself upon (Ro 2:17; Sept.: Mic 3:11); to rest with the sense of remaining upon (Lk 10:6; Sept.: Nu 11:25, 26; 2Ki 2:15).

1880. ἐπανέρχομαι, epanerchomai, *ep-an-er´-khom-ahee*; from 1909 and 424; to *come up on*, i.e. *return*:—come again, return.

1881. ἐπανίσταμαι, epanistamai, *ep-an-is´-tam-ahee*; middle from 1909 and 450; to *stand up on*, i.e. (figurative) to *attack*:—rise up against.

1882. ἐπανόρθωσις, epanorthōsis, *ep-an-or´-tho-sis*; from a compound of 1909 and 461; a *straightening up again*, i.e. (figurative) *rectification* (*reformation*):—correction.

Noun from *epanorthóō* (n.f.), to set right again, correct, which is from *epí* (1909), upon, and *anorthóō* (461), to make straight. A setting to rights, reparation, restitution. Only in 2Ti 3:16.

Syn.: *nouthesía* (3559), admonition; *paideía* (3809), instruction; *apokatástasis* (605), restitution.

1883. ἐπάνω, epanō, *ep-an´-o*; from 1909 and 507; *up above*, i.e. *over* or *on* (of place, amount, rank, etc.):—above, more than, (up-) on, over.

1884. ἐπαρκέω, eparkeō, *ep-ar-keh´-o*; from 1909 and 714; to *avail for*, i.e. *help*:—relieve.

1885. ἐπαρχία, eparchia, *ep-ar-khee´-ah*; from a compound of 1909 and 757 (meaning a *governor* of a district, "eparch"); a special *region* of government, i.e. a Roman *præfecture*:—province.

1886. ἔπαυλις, epaulis, *ep´-ow-lis*; from 1909 and an equivalent of 833; a *hut over* the head, i.e. a *dwelling*.

1887. ἐπαύριον, epaurion, *ep-ow´-ree-on*; from 1909 and 839; occurring *on* the *succeeding* day, i.e. (2250 being implied) *to-morrow*:—day following, morrow, next day (after).

1888. ἐπαυτοφώρῳ, epautophōrōi, *ep-ow-tof-o´-ro*; from 1909 and 846 and (the dative singular of) a derivative of **φώρ,** ***phōr*** (a *thief*); *in theft itself*, i.e. (by analogy) *in actual crime*:—in the very act.

1889. Ἐπαφρᾶς, Epaphras, *ep-af-ras´*; contrete from 1891; *Epaphras*, a Christian:—Epaphras.

1890. ἐπαφρίζω, epaphrizō, *ep-af-rid´-zo*; from 1909 and 875; to *foam upon*, i.e. (figurative) to *exhibit* (a vile passion):—foam out.

1891. Ἐπαφρόδιτος, Epaphroditos, *ep-af-rod´-ee-tos*; from 1909 (in the sense of *devoted* to) and **Ἀφροδίτη,** ***Aphroditē*** (*Venus*); *Epaphroditus*, a Christian:—Epaphroditus. Compare 1889.

1892. ἐπεγείρω, epegeirō, *ep-eg-i´-ro*; from 1909 and 1453; to *rouse upon*, i.e. (figurative) to *excite* against:—raise, stir up.

1893. ἐπεί, epei, *ep-i´*; from 1909 and 1487; *thereupon*, i.e. *since* (of time or cause):—because, else, for that (then, -asmuch as), otherwise, seeing that, since, when.

1894. ἐπειδή, epeidē, *ep-i-day´*; from 1893 and 1211; *since now*, i.e. (of time) *when* or (of cause) *whereas*:—after that, because, for (that, -asmuch as), seeing, since.

1895. ἐπειδήπερ, epeidēper, *ep-i-day´-per*; from 1894 and 4007; *since indeed* (of cause):—forasmuch.

1896. ἐπεῖδον, epeidon, *ep-i´-don*; and other moods and persons of the same tense; from 1909 and 1492; to *regard* (fabourably or otherwise):—behold, look upon.

Second aor. 1st person of *ephoráō* ([n.f.], to look upon fabourably), from *epí* (1909), upon, and or *eídō* (1492), to look. In the NT, from the Hebrew: to look upon, to regard, to attend to, especially with kindness (Lk 1:25; Sept.: Ex 2:25; Ps 31:7); or unfabourably, for evil (Ac 4:29).

1897. ἐπείπερ, epeiper, *ep-i´-per*; from 1893 and 4007; *since* indeed (of cause):—seeing.

1898. ἐπεισαγωγή, epeisagōgē, *ep-ice-ag-o-gay´*; from a compound of 1909 and 1521; a *superintroduction*:—bringing in.

1899. ἔπειτα, epeita, *ep´-i-tah*; from 1909 and 1534; *thereafter*:—after that (-ward), then.

1900. ἐπέκεινα, epekeina, *ep-ek´-i-nah*; from 1909 and (the accusative plural neuter of) 1565; *upon those* parts of, i.e. *on the further side of*:—beyond.

1901. ἐπεκτείνομαι, epekteinomai, *ep-ek-ti´-nom-ahee*; middle from 1909 and 1614; to *stretch* (oneself) forward *upon*:—reach forth.

1902. ἐπενδύομαι, ependuomai, *ep-en-doo´-om-ahee*; middle from 1909 and 1746; to *invest upon* oneself:—be clothed upon.

1903. ἐπενδύτης, ependutēs, *ep-en-doo´-tace*; from 1902; a *wrapper*, i.e. outer garment:—fisher's coat.

1904. ἐπέρχομαι, eperchomai, *ep-er´-khom-ahee*; from 1909 and 2064; to *supervene*, i.e. *arrive, occur, impend, attack*, (figurative) *influence*:—come (in, upon).

1905. ἐπερωτάω, eperōtaō, *ep-er-o-tah´-o*; from 1909 and 2065; to *ask for*, i.e. *inquire, seek*:—ask (after, questions), demand, desire, question.

From *epí* (1909), an intensive, and *erōtáō* (2065), to ask, inquire of, beg of:

(I) Generally (Mk 7:17; 11:29; Lk 20:40; Sept.: 2Sa 14:18); to speak, say, saying, or the question itself (Mt 12:10; Mk 5:9; Lk 3:10, 14; Ac 1:6; 1Co 14:35). Used in an absolute sense (Mt 22:35; Ac 23:34; Sept.: Ge 38:21; 43:7). In the sense of to require, demand (Mt 16:1; Sept.: Ps 137:3).

(II) In a judicial sense: to question, interrogate (Mt 27:11; Jn 18:21; Ac 5:27). Used in an absolute sense (Lk 23:6).

(III) To ask or inquire after God, i.e. to seek God, the same as *ekzētéō* (1567), to seek after (Ro 10:20 quoted from Isa 65:1).

Deriv.: *eperṓtēma* (1906), inquiry.

Syn.: *ereunáō* (2045), to investigate.

1906. ἐπερώτημα, eperōtēma, *ep-er-o´-tay-mah*; from 1905; an *inquiry*:—answer.

1907. ἐπέχω, epechō, *ep-ekh´-o*; from 1909 and 2192; to *hold upon*, i.e. (by implication) to *retain*; (by extension) to *detain*; (with implication of 3563) to *pay attention to*:—give (take) heed unto, hold forth, mark, stay.

1908. ἐπηρεάζω, epēreazō, *ep-ay-reh-ad´-zo*; from a compound of 1909 and (probably) **ἀρειά**, ***areia*** (*threats*); to *insult, slander*:—use despitefully, falsely accuse.

1909. ἐπί, epi, *ep-ee´*; a primary preposition properly meaning *superimposition* (of time, place, order, etc.), as a relation of *distribution* [with the genitive], i.e. *over, upon*, etc.; of *rest* (with the dative) *at, on*, etc.; of *direction* (with the accusative) *toward, upon*, etc.:—about (the times), above, after, against, among, as long as (touching), at, beside, × have charge of, (be-, [where-]) fore, in (a place, as much as, the time of, -to), (because) of, (up-) on (behalf of), over, (by, for) the space of, through (-out), (un-) to (-ward), with. In compounds it retains essentially the same import, *at, upon*, etc. (literal or figurative).

1910. ἐπιβαίνω, epibainō, *ep-ee-bah´ee-no*; from 1909 and the base of 939; to *walk upon*, i.e. *mount, ascend, embark, arrive*:—come (into), enter into, go abroad, sit upon, take ship.

From *epí* (1909), upon, to, and *bainō* (n.f.), to go. To go upon, mount, as upon a donkey (Mt 21:5); aboard ship (Ac 21:2, 6 [TR]; 27:2); to set foot upon, to come upon or, enter into (Ac 20:18; 25:1).

Syn.: *epérchomai* (1904), to come or go upon; *ephístēmi* (2186), to come up; *eíseimi* (1524) and *eisporeúomai* (1531), to go into; *eisérchomai* (1525), to come into; *embaínō* (1684), to go into, step in; *embibázō* (1688), to place on, transfer, put on board ship.

1911. ἐπιβάλλω, epiballō, *ep-ee-bal´-lo*; from 1909 and 906; to *throw upon* (literal or figurative, transitive or reflexive; usually with more or less force); specially (with 1438 implied) to *reflect*; impersonally to *belong to*:—beat into, cast (up-) on, fall, lay (on), put (unto), stretch forth, think on.

1912. ἐπιβαρέω, epibareō, *ep-ee-bar-eh´-o*; from 1909 and 916; to *be heavy upon*, i.e. (pecuniarily) to *be expensive to*; (figurative) to *be severe toward*:—be chargeable to, overcharge.

1913. ἐπιβιβάζω, epibibazō, *ep-ee-bee-bad´-zo*; from 1909 and a reduplicated derivative of the base of 939 [compare 307]; to *cause to mount* (an animal):—set on.

1914. ἐπιβλέπω, epiblepō, *ep-ee-blep´-o*; from 1909 and 991; to *gaze at* (with favour, pity or partiality):—look upon, regard, have respect to.

1915. ἐπίβλημα, epiblēma, *ep-ib´-lay-mah*; from 1911; a *patch*:—piece.

1916. ἐπιβοάω, epiboaō, *ep-ee-bo-ah´-o*; from 1909 and 994; to *exclaim against*:—cry.

1917. ἐπιβουλή, epiboulē, *ep-ee-boo-lay´*; from a presumed compound of 1909 and 1014; a *plan against* someone, i.e. a *plot*:—laying (lying) in wait.

1918. ἐπιγαμβρεύω, epigambreuō, *ep-ee-gam-bryoo´-o*; from 1909 and a derivative of 1062; to *form affinity with*, i.e. (special) in a levirate way:—marry.

1919. ἐπίγειος, epigeios, *ep-ig´-i-os*; from 1909 and 1093; *worldly* (physical or moral):—earthly, in earth, terrestrial.

Adjective from *epí* (1909), upon, and *gḗ* (1093), the earth. Earthly, terrestrial; belonging on earth or to earth (1Co 15:40; 2Co 5:1 [cf. Job 4:19]); spoken of persons (Php 2:10); *tá epígeia*, earthly things, things relating to this life (Jn 3:12; Php 3:19); *sophía epígeios* (*sophía* [4678], wisdom), earthly wisdom, i.e. imperfect and perverse (Jas 3:15).

1920. ἐπιγίνομαι, epiginomai, *ep-ig-in´-om-ahee*; from 1909 and 1096; to *arrive upon*, i.e. *spring up* (as a wind):—blow.

1921. ἐπιγινώσκω, epiginōskō, *ep-ig-in-oce´-ko*; from 1909 and 1097; to *know upon* some mark, i.e. *recognise*; (by implication) to *become fully acquainted with*, to *acknowledge*:—(ac-, have, take) know (-ledge, well), perceive.

1922. ἐπίγνωσις, epignōsis, *ip-ig´-no-sis*; from 1921; *recognition*, i.e. (by implication) full *discernment, acknowledgment*:—(ac-) knowledge (-ing, -ment).

Noun from *epiginṓskō* (1921), to recognize. Full knowledge; the act of coming to a full knowledge of something; cognition, acknowledgement (1Ti 2:4; 2Ti 2:25; 3:7; Tit 1:1; Phm 6 [UBS]; 2Pe 1:3; 2:20); full knowledge, as spoken of what is known in the NT of God, Christ, divine things (Ro 1:28; 10:2; Eph 1:17; 4:13; Col 1:9, 10; 2:2; 1Ti 2:4; 2Ti 2:25; 3:7; Tit 1:1; Heb 10:26; 2Pe 1:2, 3).

Syn.: *pístis* (4102), faith, since it is the means of the acceptance of divine revelation as *epígnōsis* can be said to be the comprehension of divine revelation to man; *gnṓsis* (1108), knowledge. See the contrasting use of *ginṓskō* in Ro 1:21 and *epígnōsis* in Ro 1:28.

1923. ἐπιγραφή, epigraphē, *ep-ig-raf-ay´*; from 1924; an *inscription*:—superscription.

1924. ἐπιγράφω, epigraphō, *ep-ee-graf´-o*; from 1909 and 1125; to *inscribe* (physical or mental):—inscription, write in (over, thereon).

1925. ἐπιδείκνυμι, epideiknumi, *ep-ee-dike´-noo-mee*; from 1909 and 1166; to *exhibit* (physical or mental):—shew.

1926. ἐπιδέχομαι, epidechomai, *ep-ee-dekh´-om-ahee*; from 1909 and 1209; to *admit* (as a guest or [figurative] teacher):—receive.

1927. ἐπιδημέω, epidēmeō, *ep-ee-day-meh´-o*; from a compound of 1909 and 1218; to *make oneself at home*, i.e. (by extension) to *reside* (in a foreign country):—[be] dwelling (which were) there, stranger.

1928. ἐπιδιατάσσομαι, epidiatassomai, *ep-ee-dee-ah-tas´-som-ahee*; middle from 1909 and 1299; to *appoint besides*, i.e. *supplement* (as a codicil):—add to.

1929. ἐπιδίδωμι, epididōmi, *ep-ee-did´-o-mee*; from 1909 and 1325; to *give over* (by hand or surrender):—deliver unto, give, let (+ [her drive]), offer.

1930. ἐπιδιορθόω, epidiorthoō, *ep-ee-dee-or-tho´-o*; from 1909 and a derivative of 3717; to *straighten further*, i.e. (figurative) *arrange additionally*:—set in order.

From *epí* (1909), besides, above, and *diorthóō* (n.f.), to correct. Only in Tit 1:5, meaning to proceed in correcting or setting in order. See *diórthōsis* (1357), an amendment, restoration.

Syn.: *paideúō* (3811), to train up, correct; *morphóō* (3445), to fashion.

1931. ἐπιδύω, epiduō, *ep-ee-doo´-o*; from 1909 and 1416; to *set* fully (as the sun):—go down.

1932. ἐπιείκεια, epieikeia, *ep-ee-i´-ki-ah*; from 1933; *suitableness*, i.e. (by implication) *equity, mildness*:—clemency, gentleness.

Noun from *epieikḗs* (1933), fitting, appropriate. Clemency or gentleness (Ac 24:4; 2Co 10:1).

Syn.: contrast *ḗpios* (2261), mild; *anochḗ* (463), forbearance; *makrothumía* (3115), long-suffering; *hupomonḗ* (5281), patience; *praótēs* (4236), meekness.

1933. ἐπιεικής, epieikēs, *ep-ee-i-kace´*; from 1909 and 1503; *appropriate*, i.e. (by implication) *mild*:—gentle, moderation, patient.

1934. ἐπιζητέω, epizēteō, *ep-eed´-zay-teh´-o*; from 1909 and 2212; to *search* (*inquire*) *for*; intensive to *demand*, to *crave*:—desire, enquire, seek (after, for).

1935. ἐπιθανάτιος, epithanatios, *ep-ee-than-at´-ee-os*; from 1909 and 2288; doomed *to death*:—appointed to death.

1936. ἐπίθεσις, epithesis, *ep-ith´-es-is*; from 2007; an *imposition* (of hands officially):—laying (putting) on.

1937. ἐπιθυμέω, epithumeō, *ep-ee-thoo-meh´-o*; from 1909 and 2372; to set the *heart upon*, i.e. *long* for (rightfully or otherwise):—covet, desire, would fain, lust (after).

From *epí* (1909), in, and *thumós* (2372), the mind. To fix the desire on, to desire earnestly, to long for. Generally (Lk 17:22; Gal 5:17; Rev 9:6). To desire in a good sense (Mt 13:17; Lk 22:15; 1Ti 3:1; Heb 6:11; 1Pe 1:12); as a result of physical needs (Lk 15:16; 16:21); in a bad sense of coveting and lusting after (Mt 5:28; Ro 7:7; 13:9; 1Co 10:6 [cf. Jas 4:2; Sept.: Ex 20:17; Dt 5:21; 14:26; 2Sa 3:21; Pr 21:26]).

Deriv.: *epithumētḗs* (1938), one who desires; *epithumía* (1939), desire.

Syn.: *sumpathéō* (4834), to like, sympathize; *agapáō* (25), to love; *homeíromai* or *himeíromai* (2442), to have a strong affection for, yearn after; *orégomai* (3713) or *epipothéō* (1971), to long after; *thélō* (2309), to wish, implying volition and purpose; *boúlomai* (1014), to will deliberately, design; *thélō*; *zēlóō* (2206), to have a zeal for; *aitéō* (154), to ask, desire; *epizētéō* (1934), to seek earnestly; *exaitéomai* (1809), to desire earnestly.

1938. ἐπιθυμητής, epithumētēs, *ep-ee-thoo-may-tace´*; from 1937; a *craver*:— + lust after.

1939. ἐπιθυμία, epithumia, *ep-ee-thoo-mee´-ah*; from 1937; a *longing* (especially for what is forbidden):—concupiscence, desire, lust (after).

Noun from *epithuméō* (1937), to desire greatly. Strong desire, longing, lust:

(I) Generally: longing (Lk 22:15; Php 1:23; 1Th 2:17; Rev 18:14; Sept.: Pr 10:24; 11:23; Da 9:23; 10:3, 11).

(II) More frequently in a bad sense: irregular and inordinate desire, appetite, lust.

(A) Generally (Mk 4:19; Ro 6:12; 7:7, 8; 13:14; Col 3:5; 1Ti 6:9; 2Ti 3:6; 4:3; Tit 3:3; Jas 1:14, 15; 1Pe 1:14; 4:2, 3; 2Pe 1:4; 3:3; Jude 16, 18). The lust of the flesh means carnal desires, appetites (Gal 5:16, 24; Eph 2:3; 2Pe 2:18; 1Jn 2:16). Also *epithumíai sarkikaí* (4559), carnal, fleshly (1Pe 2:11) referring to worldly desires; desires of the eyes (1Jn 2:16); polluted desires (2Pe 2:10); "lusts of deceit" (a.t.) means "deceitful lusts" (Eph 4:22); "youthful lusts" (2Ti 2:22); see Sept.: Pr 21:25, 26. All these refer to the desires which are fixed on sensual objects as pleasures, profits, honours.

(B) Spoken of impure desire: lewdness (Ro 1:24; 1Th 4:5).

(C) By metonymy: lust, i.e. an object of impure desire, that which is lusted after (Jn 8:44; 1Jn 2:17; Sept.: Da 11:37).

Syn.: *eudokía* (2107), good pleasure or will; *epipóthēsis* (1972), an earnest desire; *epipothía* (1974), a great desire; *thélēma* (2307), a will; *boúlēma* (1013), desire, purpose; *órexis* (3715), desire of any kind with an evil connotation; *hēdonḗ* (2237), lust, pleasure; *páthēma* (3804), passion.

1940. ἐπικαθίζω, epikathizō, *ep-ee-kath-id´-zo*; from 1909 and 2523; to *seat upon*:—set upon.

1941. ἐπικαλέομαι, epikaleomai, *ep-ee-kal-eh´-om-ahee*; middle from 1909 and 2564; to *entitle*; (by implication) to *invoke* (for aid, worship, testimony, decision, etc.):—appeal (unto), call (on, upon), surname.

From *epí* (1909), upon, and *kaléō* (2564), to call, to surname. To call upon:

(I) To call upon for aid. In the NT, only in the middle: to call upon for aid in one's own behalf, to invoke:

(A) Particularly of invocation addressed to Christ for aid (Ac 7:59; see Sept.: 1Sa 12:17, 18; 2Sa 22:7). Generally: to invoke, pray to, worship, spoken of God (Ro 10:12, 14; 2Ti 2:22); followed by "the name" (Ac 2:21; 9:14; Ro 10:13; Sept.: Ge 4:26; 26:25; Dt 33:19; Joel 2:32); of Christ, followed by "the name," implying the Lord Jesus Christ (Ac 9:21; 22:16; 1Co 1:2).

(B) In adjurations, imprecations: to call upon, invoke, as a witness (2Co 1:23).

(C) In a judicial sense: to call upon, invoke a higher tribunal or judge, i.e. to appeal to, e.g., Caesar (Ac 25:11, 12, 25; 26:32; 28:19). Followed by an inf. (Ac 25:21, "demanding by appeal that" [a.t.]).

(II) To call a name upon, i.e. to name in addition, to surname (Mt 10:25 [UBS]; Sept.: Nu 21:3; Jgs 6:32, the simple verb *ekálesen*). In the middle, in 1Pe 1:17, "if ye call him your Father" (a.t. [cf. Jer 3:19]).

(A) Particularly in Mt 10:3; Lk 22:3; Ac 1:23; 4:36; 10:5, 18, 32; 11:13; 12:12, 25; 15:22; Heb 11:16; Sept.: Da 10:1; Mal 1:4.

(B) "Upon whom my name is called" (Ac 15:17, i.e. who are called or surnamed by my name, implying property, relation, quoted from Am 9:12; Jas 2:7; see 2Sa 12:28, the simple verb *klēthḗ*, Jer 14:9).

Syn.: *aitéō* (154), to ask, call for; *phōnéō* (5455), to cry out; *krázō* (2896), to call aloud, cry; *kraugázō* (2905), to shout; *onomázō* (3687), to name; *eponomázō* (2028), to surname; *prosagoreúō* (4316), to salute or call upon by name; *prosphōnéō* (4377), to call unto.

1942. ἐπικάλυμα, epikaluma, *ep-ee-kal´-oo-mah*; from 1943; a *covering*, i.e. (figurative) *pretext*:—cloke.

1943. ἐπικαλύπτω, epikaluptō, *ep-ee-kal-oop´-to*; from 1909 and 2572; to *conceal*, i.e. (figurative) *forgive*:—cover.

1944. ἐπικατάρατος, epikataratos, *ep-ee-kat-ar´-at-os*; from 1909 and a derivative of 2672; *imprecated*, i.e. *execrable*:—accursed.

Adjective from *epí* (1909), upon, and *katáratos* (n.f.), cursed. Accursed, under a curse, doomed to punishment (Jn 7:49; Gal 3:10 quoted from Dt 27:26; Sept.: Ge 9:25; Dt 27:15).

Syn.: *epáratos*, accursed.

1945. ἐπίκειμαι, epikeimai, *ep-ik´-i-mahee*; from 1909 and 2749; to *rest upon* (literal or figurative):—impose, be instant, (be) laid (there-, up-) on, (when) lay (on), lie (on), press upon.

1946. Ἐπικούρειος, Epikoureios, *ep-ee-koo´-ri-os*; from **Ἐπίκουρος,** *Epikouros*; [compare 1947] (a noted philosopher); an *Epicurean* or follower of Epicurus:—Epicurean.

1947. ἐπικουρία, epikouria, *ep-ee-koo-ree´-ah*; from a compound of 1909 and a (prolonged) form of the base of 2877 (in the sense of *servant*); *assistance*:—help.

1948. ἐπικρίνω, epikrinō, *ep-ee-kree´-no*; from 1909 and 2919; to *adjudge*:—give sentence.

1949. ἐπιλαμβάνομαι, epilambanomai, *ep-ee-lam-ban´-om-ahee*; middle from 1909 and 2983; to *seize* (for help, injury, attainment or any other purpose; literal or figurative):—catch, lay hold (up-) on, take (by, hold of, on).

From *epí* (1909), upon, and *lambánō* (2983), to take. To take hold upon, lay hold of in order to hold or detain oneself:

(I) Generally: to take hold of, e.g., to take the hand or take by the hand (Mk 8:23; Ac 23:19). Metaphorically (Heb 8:9; Sept.: Jer 31:32; Zec 14:13). To lay hold on, e.g., in order to lead, conduct (Lk 9:47; Ac 9:27; 17:19); in order to succor, heal (Mt 14:31; Lk 14:4). With the idea of violence: to lay hold on, to seize by force as a prisoner (Lk 23:26; Ac 16:19; 18:17; 21:30, 33) Figuratively spoken of language: to lay hold on another's words, i.e. to censure (Lk 20:20, 26).

(II) Metaphorically: to lay hold of in order to obtain and possess (1Ti 6:12, 19).

Deriv.: *anepílēptos* (423), blameless.

Syn.: *sullambánō* (4815), to seize; *harpázō* (726), to snatch or catch away; *sunarpázō* (4884), to snatch, seize, keep a firm grip on; *katéchō* (2722), to hold firmly, fast; *kratéō* (2902), to prevail; *tēréō* (5083), to keep; *bastázō* (941), to bear; *epiphérō* (2018), to bring against.

1950. ἐπιλανθάνομαι, epilanthanomai, *ep-ee-lan-than´-om-ahee*; middle from 1909 and 2990; to *lose out* of mind; (by implication) to *neglect*:—(be) forget (-ful of).

1951. ἐπιλέγομαι, epilegomai, *ep-ee-leg´-om-ahee*; middle from 1909 and 3004; to *surname, select*:—call, choose.

From *epí* (1909), upon, moreover, and *légō* (3004), to say. To speak or say upon, i.e. moreover, besides, in addition to. To say or speak upon, i.e. by implication, to name, call (Jn 5:2). To choose, either in addition to or in succession to another (Ac 15:40, to choose for oneself, with the accusative; Sept.: 2Sa 10:9).

Syn.: *eklégomai* (1586), to select out of; *hairéomai* (138), to choose in preference; *hairetízō* (140), to elect in preference; *kaléō* (2564), to call.

1952. ἐπιλείπω, epileipō, *ep-ee-li´-po*; from 1909 and 3007; to *leave upon*, i.e. (figurative) to *be insufficient for*:—fail.

1953. ἐπιλησμονή, epilēsmonē, *ep-ee-lace-mon-ay´*; from a derivative of 1950; *negligence*:— × forgetful.

1954. ἐπίλοιπος, epiloipos, *ep-il´-oy-pos*; from 1909 and 3062; *left over*, i.e. *remaining*:—rest.

1955. ἐπίλυσις, epilusis, *ep-il´-oo-sis*; from 1956; *explanation*, i.e. *application*:—interpretation.

1956. ἐπιλύω, epiluō, *ep-ee-loo´-o*; from 1909 and 3089; to *solve further*, i.e. (figurative) to *explain, decide*:—determine, expound.

1957. ἐπιμαρτυρέω, epimartureō, *ep-ee-mar-too-reh´-o*; from 1909 and 3140; to *attest further*, i.e. *corroborate*:—testify.

From *epí* (1909), an intensive, and *marturéō* (3140), to witness. To testify, to attest (1Pe 5:12).

Deriv.: *sunepimarturéō* (4901), to bear further witness with someone.

Syn.: *bebaióō* (950), to assure; *kuróō* (2964), to ratify, confirm.

1958. ἐπιμέλεια, epimeleia, *ep-ee-mel´-i-ah*; from 1959; *carefulness*, i.e. kind *attention* (*hospitality*):— + refresh self.

1959. ἐπιμελέομαι, epimeleomai, *ep-ee-mel-eh´-om-ahee*; middle from 1909 and the same as 3199; to *care for* (physical or otherwise):—take care of.

1960. ἐπιμελῶς, epimelōs, *ep-ee-mel-oce´*; adverb from a derivative of 1959; *carefully*:—diligently.

1961. ἐπιμένω, epimenō, *ep-ee-men´-o*; from 1909 and 3306; to *stay over*, i.e. *remain* (figurative, *persevere*):—abide (in), continue (in), tarry.

1962. ἐπινεύω, epineuō, *ep-een-yoo´-o*; from 1909 and 3506; to *nod at*, i.e. (by implication) to *assent*:—consent.

1963. ἐπίνοια, epinoia, *ep-in´-oy-ah*; from 1909 and 3563; *attention* of the mind, i.e. (by implication) *purpose*:—thought.

Noun from *epinoéō* (n.f.), to think upon, from *epí* (1909), upon, and *noús* (3563), mind. A thought, purpose, cogitation (Ac 8:22).

Syn.: *nóēma* (3540), a purpose, device of the mind; *dianóēma* (1270), a plan, machination; *enthúmēsis* (1761), thought, device; *logismós* (3053), thought, imagination; *dialogismós* (1261), reasoning.

1964. ἐπιορκέω, epiorkeō, *ep-ee-or-keh´-o*; from 1965; to *commit perjury*:—forswear self.

1965. ἐπίορκος, epiorkos, *ep-ee´-or-kos*; from 1909 and 3727; *on oath*, i.e. (falsely) a *forswearer*:—perjured person.

1966. ἐπιοῦσα, epiousa, *ep-ee-oo´-sah*; feminine singular participle of a compound of 1909 and **εἶμι, *heimi*** (to *go*); *supervening*, i.e. (2250 or 3571 being expressed or implied) the *ensuing* day or night:—following, next.

1967. ἐπιούσιος, epiousios, *ep-ee-oo´-see-os*; perhaps from the same as 1966; *to-morrow's*; but more probably from 1909 and a derivative of the presumed participle feminine of 1510; *for subsistence*, i.e. *needful*:—daily.

Adjective from *epí* (1909), for or into, and *ousía* (3776), being, substance. Daily, used as an adj. Occurs only in the Lord's Prayer (Mt 6:11; Lk 11:3). The Greek Church Father, Chrysostom, explains the *epioúsion árton* (740) as that bread which is needed for our daily support of life. It is that bread which is needful to the *ousia*, substance, of our being, that will sustain us. Other interpreters derive it from *epioúsa* (1966), the next, fem. referring to *hēméra* (2250), day, but in the masc. for *ártos* (740), bread, bread for the coming day.

Syn.: *ephḗmeros* (2184), for the day; *kathēmerinós* (2522), daily; *sḗmeron* (4594), today, this day; *tḗs sḗmeron hēméras*, unto this very day; *tás hēméras*, every day, in the daytime; *pásan hēméran*, every day; *kath' hekástēn hēméran*, literally according to each day, day by day.

1968. ἐπιπίπτω, epipiptō, *ep-ee-pip´-to*; from 1909 and 4098; to *embrace* (with affection) or *seize* (with more or less violence; literal or figurative):—fall into (on, upon), lie on, press upon.

1969. ἐπιπλήσσω, epiplēssō, *ep-ee-place´-so*; from 1909 and 4141; to *chastise*, i.e. (with words) to *upbraid*:—rebuke.

1970. ἐπιπνίγω, epipnigō, *ep-ee-pnee´-go*; from 1909 and 4155; to *throttle upon*, i.e. (figurative) *overgrow*:—choke.

1971. ἐπιποθέω, epipotheō, *ep-ee-poth-eh´-o*; from 1909 and **ποθέω, *potheō*** (to *yearn*); to *dote upon*, i.e. *intensely crave* possession (lawfully or wrongfully):—(earnestly) desire (greatly), (greatly) long (after), lust.

1972. ἐπιπόθησις, epipothēsis, *ep-ee-poth´-ay-sis*; from 1971; a *longing for*:—earnest (vehement) desire.

1973. ἐπιπόθητος, epipothētos, *ep-ee-poth´-ay-tos*; from 1909 and a derivative of the latter part of 1971; *yearned upon*, i.e. *greatly loved*:—longed for.

1974. ἐπιποθία, epipothia, *ep-ee-poth-ee´-ah*; from 1971; *intense longing*:—great desire.

1975. ἐπιπορεύομαι, epiporeuomai, *ep-ee-por-yoo´-om-ahee*; from 1909 and 4198; to *journey further*, i.e. *travel on* (*reach*):—come.

1976. ἐπιῤῥάπτω, epirrhaptō, *ep-ir-hrap´-to*; from 1909 and the base of 4476; to *stitch upon*, i.e. *fasten* with the needle:—sew on.

1977. ἐπιῤῥίπτω, epirrhiptō, *ep-ir-hrip´-to*; from 1909 and 4496; to *throw upon* (literal or figurative):—cast upon.

1978. ἐπίσημος, episēmos, *ep-is´-ay-mos*; from 1909 and some form of the base of 4591; *remarkable*, i.e. (figurative) *eminent*:—notable, of note.

1979. ἐπισιτισμός, episitismos, *ep-ee-sit-is-mos´*; from a compound of 1909 and a derivative of 4621; a *provisioning*, i.e. (concretely) *food*:—victuals.

1980. ἐπισκέπτομαι, episkeptomai, *ep-ee-skep´-tom-ahee*; middle from 1909 and the base of 4649; to *inspect*, i.e. (by implication) to *select*; by extension to *go to see, relieve*:—look out, visit.

From *epí* (1909), upon, and *sképtomai* (n.f.), to look. To look at something, examine closely, inspect, observe:

(I) To look upon with mercy, favour, regard (Lk 1:68, 78; 7:16; Ac 15:14; Heb 2:6 quoted from Ps 8:5; see Ge 50:24, 25; Ps 106:4).

(II) To visit in order to punish (Sept.: Ps 89:32).

(III) To look after, take care of, tend (Ac 7:23; 15:36; Sept.: Jgs 15:1). Frequently used in the Class. Gr. for taking care of or nursing the sick (Mt 25:36, 43; Jas 1:27).

(IV) To look at accurately or diligently, with the meaning to look for, seek out, as persons for office, transitively (Ac 6:3; Sept.: Le 13:36; Ezr 6:1; Eze 20:40).

Syn.: *historéō* (2477), to visit, in order to be acquainted with; *epiphérō* (2018), to bear upon, add, bring against.

1981. ἐπισκηνόω, episkēnoō, *ep-ee-skay-no´-o*; from 1909 and 4637; to *tent upon*, i.e. (figurative) *abide with*:—rest upon.

1982. ἐπισκιάζω, episkiazō, *ep-ee-skee-ad´-zo*; from 1909 and a derivative of 4639; to *cast a shade upon*, i.e. (by analogy) to *envelop* in a haze of brilliancy; (figurative) to *invest* with preternatural influence:—overshadow.

1983. ἐπισκοπέω, episkopeō, *ep-ee-skop-eh´-o*; from 1909 and 4648; to *oversee*; (by implication) to *beware*:—look diligently, take the oversight.

From *epí* (1909), upon, and *skopéō* (4648), to regard, give attention to. To look upon, observe, examine the state of affairs of something, look after, oversee. In the NT, to look after, to see to, to take care of (Heb 12:15; 1Pe 5:2; Sept.: Dt 11:12).

Deriv.: *episkopḗ* (1984), the office of a bishop.

Syn.: *poimaínō* (4165), to shepherd, tend a flock; *bóskō* (1006), to lead to pasture, fodder; *epimeléomai* (1959), to show concern over; *merimnáō* (3309) to be concerned.

1984. ἐπισκοπή, episkopē, *ep-is-kop-ay´*; from 1980; *inspection* (for relief); (by implication) *superintendence*; specially the Christian "*episcopate*":—the office of a "bishop," bishoprick, visitation.

Noun from *episkopéō* (1983), to look after. Visitation, or the act of visiting or being visited or inspected. In the NT, used metaphorically of God, who is said to visit men for good (Lk 19:44; 1Pe 2:12; Sept.: Job 10:12; 34:9). Of the duty of visiting or inspecting, i.e. charge, office (Ac 1:20, quoted from Ps 109:8). Spoken of the office of an *epískopos*, overseer, i.e. the care and oversight of a Christian church (1Ti 3:1).

1985. ἐπίσκοπος, episkopos, *ep-is´-kop-os*; from 1909 and 4649 (in the sense of 1983); a *superintendent*, i.e. Christian officer in general charge of a (or the) church (literal or figurative):—bishop, overseer.

Noun from *epí* (1909), upon, and *skopós* (4649), a watchman. Superintendent, overseer. The overseer of public works (Sept.: 2Ch 34:12, 17); of cities, e.g., a prefect (Isa 60:17). In Athens *epískopoi* (pl.) were magistrates sent to outlying cities to organize and govern them. In the NT, used of officers in the local churches, overseers, superintendents (Ac 20:28; Php 1:1; 1Ti 3:2; Tit 1:7). Used figuratively of Jesus (1Pe 2:25). This name was originally simply the Greek term equal to *presbúteros* (4245), which was derived from the Jewish polity.

Deriv.: *allotrioepískopos* (244), a busybody.

Syn.: *presbúteros* (4245), elder; *poimḗn* (4166), shepherd; *diákonos* (1249), minister.

1986. ἐπισπάομαι, epispaomai, *ep-ee-spah´-om-ahee*; from 1909 and 4685; to *draw over*, i.e. (with 203 implied) *efface* the mark of *circumcision* (by recovering with the foreskin):—become uncircumcised.

1987. ἐπίσταμαι, epistamai, *ep-is´-tam-ahee*; apparently a middle of 2186 (with 3563 implied); to *put* the mind *upon*, i.e. *comprehend*, or *be acquainted with*:—know, understand.

1988. ἐπιστάτης, epistatēs, *ep-is-tat´-ace*; from 1909 and a presumed derivative of 2476; an *appointee over*, i.e. *commander* (*teacher*):—master.

1989. ἐπιστέλλω, epistellō, *ep-ee-stel´-lo*; from 1909 and 4724; to *enjoin* (by writing), i.e. (genitive) to *communicate by letter* (for any purpose):—write (a letter, unto).

1990. ἐπιστήμων, epistēmōn, *ep-ee-stay´-mone*; from 1987; *intelligent*:—endued with knowledge.

1991. ἐπιστηρίζω, epistērizō, *ep-ee-stay-rid´-zo*; from 1909 and 4741; to *support further*, i.e. *reëstablish*:—confirm, strengthen.

1992. ἐπιστολή, epistolē, *ep-is-tol-ay´*; from 1989; a *written message*:—"epistle," letter.

1993. ἐπιστομίζω, epistomizō, *ep-ee-stom-id´-zo*; from 1909 and 4750; to put something *over* the *mouth*, i.e. (figurative) to *silence*:—stop mouths.

1994. ἐπιστρέφω, epistrephō, *ep-ee-stref´-o*; from 1909 and 4762; to *revert* (literal, figurative or moral):—come (go) again, convert, (re-) turn (about, again).

From *epí* (1909), to, and *stréphō* (4762), to turn. To turn upon, toward:

(I) In a moral sense: to turn upon or convert unto (Lk 1:16, 17; Sept.: Ezr 6:22). In the sense of to turn back again upon, to cause to return from error (Jas 5:19, 20; Sept.: 1Ki 13:18–20).

(II) To turn oneself upon or toward, i.e. to turn toward or unto:

(A) Act. intransitively (Ac 9:40): **(1)** Figuratively: to turn to the service and worship of the true God (Ac 9:35; 11:21; 14:15; 15:19; 26:18, 20); to the Lord (2Co 3:16; 1Th 1:9); to the shepherd (1Pe 2:25; Sept.: Ge 24:49; Dt 31:18, where is found the verb *apostréphō* [654], to turn away; Jos 19:34; 1Ch 12:19; Hos 5:4; Am 4:6, 8). **(2)** By implication, to turn about, upon or toward (Rev 1:12). Used in an absolute sense (Ac 16:18; Sept.: Jgs 18:21). **(3)** To turn back upon, return unto, and followed by *opísō* (3694), back (Mt 24:18); *eis tá opísō*, backward (Mk 13:16; Lk 17:31); by *eis* (1519), unto, with the accusative (Mt 12:44); by *epí* (1909), upon, with the accusative (Lk 17:4; 2Pe 2:22). Used in an absolute sense (Lk 2:20 [TR]; Ac 15:36). Of the breath or spirit returning to a dead body (Lk 8:55; Sept.: Ru 1:7, 10; 2Sa 6:20; 1Ki 2:30). Metaphorically, spoken of a return to good: to return, be converted, used in an absolute sense (Lk 22:32; Ac 3:19; also Mt 13:15; Mk 4:12; Ac 28:27, all quoted from Isa 6:10); also to turn back unto evil (Gal 4:9; 2Pe 2:21).

(B) Middle, intransitively: **(1)** By implication: to turn about, upon or toward (Mt 9:22; Mk 8:33; Jn 21:20); by *en* (1722), in (Mk 5:30; Sept.: Nu 23:5). **(2)** To turn back upon, return unto (Mt 10:13; Sept.: Ru 1:11, 12, 15). Metaphorically, to return to good, be converted (Jn 12:40 [cf. Isa 6:10]).

Deriv.: *epistrophḗ* (1995), conversion.

Syn.: *epanérchomai* (1880), to come back again; *anakámptō* (344), to return; *metastréphō* (3344), to change into something different.

1995. ἐπιστροφή, epistrophē, *ep-is-trof-ay´*; from 1994; *reversion*, i.e. moral *revolution*:—conversion.

Noun from *epistréphō* (1994), to turn about. A turning around, conversion. Occurs only in Ac 15:3.

1996. ἐπισυνάγω, episunagō, *ep-ee-soon-ag´-o*; from 1909 and 4863; to *collect upon* the same place:—gather (together).

1997. ἐπισυναγωγή, episunagōgē, *ep-ee-soon-ag-o-gay´*; from 1996; a complete *collection*; specially a Christian *meeting* (for worship):—assembling (gathering) together.

Noun from *episunágō* (1996), to gather together. The act of gathering or assembling together (2Th 2:1 [cf. 1Th 4:17]; Heb 10:25).

Syn.: *sunagōgḗ* (4864), a gathering of Jews for worship, a synagogue; *ekklēsía* (1577), an assembly, church; *sunédrion* (4892), a council; *panḗguris* (3831), a festive assembly; *sunodía* (4923), synod, companionship on a journey.

1998. ἐπισυντρέχω, episuntrechō, *ep-ee-soon-trekh΄-o*; from 1909 and 4936; to *hasten together upon* one place (or a participle occasion):—come running together.

1999. ἐπισύστασις, episustasis, *ep-ee-soo΄-stas-is*; from the middle of a compound of 1909 and 4921; a *conspiracy*, i.e. *concourse* (riotous or friendly):—that which cometh upon, + raising up.

Noun from *episunístēmi* (n.f.), to come together upon, which is from *epí* (1909), an intensive, and *sunístēmi* (4921), to approve. A concourse, crowd. In Ac 24:12, *poieín episústasin*, to excite a crowd, raise a tumult (see *poiéō* [4160], to make, do). Spoken of a crowd: constant ingress of persons coming to someone (2Co 11:28).

Syn.: *próskomma* (4348), stumbling; *proskopḗ* (4349), offence; *phragmós* (5418), a barrier.

2000. ἐπισφαλής, episphalēs, *ep-ee-sfal-ace΄*; from a compound of 1909 and **σφάλλω**, *sphallō* (to *trip*); (figurative) *insecure*:—dangerous.

2001. ἐπισχύω, epischuō, *ep-is-khoo΄-o*; from 1909 and 2480; to *avail further*, i.e. (figurative) *insist stoutly*:—be the more fierce.

2002. ἐπισωρεύω, episōreuō, *ep-ee-so-ryoo΄-o*; from 1909 and 4987; to *accumulate further*, i.e. (figurative) *seek* additionally:—heap.

2003. ἐπιταγή, epitagē, *ep-ee-tag-ay΄*; from 2004; an *injunction* or *decree*; (by implication) *authoritativeness*:—authority, commandment.

Noun from *epitássō* (2004), to command, arrange upon. Authority, command imposed upon someone. Command of Christ (1Co 7:6, 25; 2Co 8:8); of God, will, decree (Ro 16:26 [TR]; 1Ti 1:1; Tit 1:3); generally (Tit 2:15, "with all injunction" [a.t.], i.e. strongly, severely).

Syn.: *diatagḗ* (1296), an order, ordinance, disposition; *diátagma* (1297), commandment, that which is imposed by decree or law; *entolḗ* (1785), a general injunction, charge, precept of moral and religious nature; *éntalma* (1778), the thing commanded, a commission, precept.

2004. ἐπιτάσσω, epitassō, *ep-ee-tas΄-so*; from 1909 and 5021; to *arrange upon*, i.e. *order*:—charge, command, injoin.

From *epí* (1909), upon, over, and *tássō* (5021), to arrange, appoint or place appropriately. To give an order; put upon one as a duty, enjoin (Mk 1:27; 6:27, 39; 9:25; Lk 4:36; 8:25, 31; 14:22; Ac 23:2; Phm 8).

Deriv.: *epitagḗ* (2003), injunction, command.

Syn.: *diastéllomai* (1291), to charge, enjoin; *diatássō* (1299), to set in order, command; *entéllomai* (1781), to order, command, enjoin; *keleúō* (2753), to order, bid; *paraggéllō* (3853), to order, give a charge; *prostássō* (4367), to prescribe, give command.

2005. ἐπιτελέω, epiteleō, *ep-ee-tel-eh΄-o*; from 1909 and 5055; to *fulfill further* (or *completely*), i.e. *execute*; (by implication) to *terminate, undergo*:—accomplish, do, finish, (make) (perfect), perform (× -ance).

From *epí* (1909), an intensive, and *teléō* (5055), to complete. To bring through to an end, to finish, to perform. Spoken of a work, business, course, etc. (Lk 13:32; Ro 15:28; 2Co 7:1; 8:6, 11; Php 1:6; Heb 8:5; 9:6). In the middle: to come to an end, to finish (Gal 3:3). Figuratively, spoken of sufferings: to accomplish, i.e. to undergo, to endure (1Pe 5:9).

Syn.: *apoteléō* (658), to perfect, finish; *eklēróō* (1603), to fulfill, accomplish entirely; *ekteléō* (1615), to finish out or complete; *plēróō* (4137), to complete, fulfill, carry out; *sunteléō* (4931), to bring to fulfillment, effect in concord with; *teleióō* (5048), to make perfect, complete, accomplish.

2006. ἐπιτήδειος, epitēdeios, *ep-ee-tay΄-di-os*; from **ἐπιτηδές**, *epitēdes* (*enough*); *serviceable*, i.e. (by implication) *requisite*:—things which are needful.

2007. ἐπιτίθημι, epitithēmi, *ep-ee-tith΄-ay-mee*; from 1909 and 5087; to *impose* (in a friendly or hostile sense):—add unto, lade, lay upon, put (up) on, set on (up), + surname, × wound.

2008. ἐπιτιμάω, epitimaō, *ep-ee-tee-mah΄-o*; from 1909 and 5091; to *tax upon*, i.e. *censure* or *admonish*; (by implication) *forbid*:—(straitly) charge, rebuke.

From *epí* (1909), upon, and *timáō* (5091), to evaluate. In the NT, to punish, rebuke, charge:

(I) Generally (Mt 16:22; 19:13; 20:31; Mk 8:32; 10:13, 48; Lk 18:15, 39; 19:39). With the idea of punishment (Jude 9). With the idea of restraining: spoken of winds and waves (Mt 8:26; Mk 4:39; Lk 8:24); of a fever (Lk 4:39).

(II) By implication, to admonish strongly, with urgency, authority, i.e. to enjoin upon, charge strictly: e.g., not to tell something (Mt 12:16; Mk 3:12; 8:30; Lk 9:21); with the idea of censure implied, e.g., demons (Mt 17:18; Mk 1:25; 9:25; Lk 4:35, 41; 9:42).

Deriv.: *epitimía* (2009), punishment.

Syn.: *elégchō* (1651), to reprove with conviction; *embrimáomai* (1690), to charge strictly, rebuke sternly; *epiplḗssō* (1969), to strike at, rebuke.

2009. ἐπιτιμία, epitimia, *ep-ee-tee-mee΄-ah*; from a compound of 1909 and 5092; properly *esteem*, i.e. *citizenship*; used (in the sense of 2008) of a *penalty*:—punishment.

2010. ἐπιτρέπω, epitrepō, *ep-ee-trep΄-o*; from 1909 and the base of 5157; to *turn over* (*transfer*), i.e. *allow*:—give leave (liberty, license), let, permit, suffer.

2011. ἐπιτροπή, epitropē, *ep-ee-trop-ay΄*; from 2010; *permission*, i.e. (by implication) full *power*:—commission.

2012. ἐπίτροπος, epitropos, *ep-it΄-rop-os*; from 1909 and 5158 (in the sense of 2011); a *commissioner*, i.e. domestic *manager*, *guardian*:—steward, tutor.

2013. ἐπιτυγχάνω, epitugchanō, *ep-ee-toong-khan΄-o*; from 1909 and 5177; to *chance upon*, i.e. (by implication) *attain*:—obtain.

2014. ἐπιφαίνω, epiphainō, *ep-ee-fah΄ee-no*; from 1909 and 5316; to *shine upon*, i.e. *become* (literal) *visible* or (figurative) *known*:—appear, give light.

From *epí* (1909), over, upon or to, and *phaínō* (5316), to shine. To cause to appear upon or to; to show before, to exhibit. In the NT, to show oneself upon or to, i.e. to appear upon or to. Spoken of light: to shine upon (Lk 1:79; Ac 27:20). Metaphorically: to be conscious, to be known and manifest; spoken of God's grace (Tit 2:11); spoken of God's love (Tit 3:4).

Deriv.: *epipháneia* (2015), appearing; *epiphanḗs* (2016), memorable, notable.

Syn.: *emphanízō* (1718), to cause to appear; *óptomai, optánomai* (3700), to appear; *phaneróō* (5319), to manifest.

2015. ἐπιφάνεια, epiphaneia, *ep-if-an΄-i-ah*; from 2016; a *manifestation*, i.e. (special) the *advent* of Christ (past or future):—appearing, brightness.

Noun from *epiphaínō* (2014), to appear. An appearing, appearance. Spoken of the advent of Jesus (2Ti 1:10); of his future advent (2Th 2:8; 1Ti 6:14; 2Ti 4:1, 8; Tit 2:13).

Syn.: *apokálupsis* (602), revelation, unveiling; *parousía* (3952), appearance, appearing, presence.

2016. ἐπιφανής, epiphanēs, *ep-if-an-ace΄*; from 2014; *conspicuous*, i.e. (figurative) *memorable*:—notable.

2017. ἐπιφαύω, epiphauō, *ep-ee-fow΄-o*; a form of 2014; to *illuminate* (figurative):—give light.

2018. ἐπιφέρω, epipherō, *ep-ee-fer΄-o*; from 1909 and 5342; to *bear upon* (or *further*), i.e. *adduce* (personally or judicially [*accuse, inflict*]), *superinduce*:—add, bring (against), take.

2019. ἐπιφωνέω, epiphōneō, *ep-ee-fo-neh΄-o*; from 1909 and 5455; to *call at* something, i.e. *exclaim*:—cry (against), give a shout.

2020. ἐπιφώσκω, epiphōskō, *ep-ee-foce΄-ko*; a form of 2017; to begin to *grow light*:—begin to dawn, × draw on.

2021. ἐπιχειρέω, epicheireō, *ep-ee-khi-reh´-o*; from 1909 and 5495; to put the *hand upon,* i.e. *undertake:*—go about, take in hand (upon).

2022. ἐπιχέω, epicheō, *ep-ee-kheh´-o*; from 1909 and **χέω,** *cheō* (to *pour*); to *pour upon:*—pour in.

2023. ἐπιχορηγέω, epichorēgeō, *ep-ee-khor-ayg-eh´-o*; from 1909 and 5524; to *furnish besides,* i.e. fully *supply,* (figurative) *aid* or *contribute:*—add, minister (nourishment, unto).

2024. ἐπιχορηγία, epichorēgia, *ep-ee-khor-ayg-ee´-ah*; from 2023; *contribution:*—supply.

2025. ἐπιχρίω, epichriō, *ep-ee-khree´-o*; from 1909 and 5548; to *smear over:*—anoint.

2026. ἐποικοδομέω, epoikodomeō, *ep-oy-kod-om-eh´-o*; from 1909 and 3618; to *build upon,* i.e. (figurative) to *rear up:*—build thereon (thereupon, on, upon).

From *epí* (1909), upon, and *oikodoméō* (3618), to build. To build upon, to erect a foundation. In the NT, only figuratively: to build upon, spoken of the Christian faith and Christian life, both the whole church and its individual members as built upon the only foundation, Christ, and implying the constant internal development of the kingdom of God and the visible church, like a holy temple progressively and unceasingly built up from the foundation (1Co 3:10, 12, 14; Eph 2:20; Col 2:7). By implication: to build up further in the faith and upon Christ (Ac 20:32; Jude 20).

Syn.: *anoikodoméō* (456), to rebuild; *epoikodoméō* (2026), to build upon, edify; *kataskeuázō* (2680), to construct, build.

2027. ἐποκέλλω, epokellō, *ep-ok-el´-lo*; from 1909 and **ὀκέλλω,** *okellō* (to *urge*); to *drive upon* the shore, i.e. to *beach* a vessel:—run aground.

2028. ἐπονομάζω, eponomazō, *ep-on-om-ad´-zo*; from 1909 and 3687; to *name further,* i.e. *denominate:*—call.

2029. ἐποπτεύω, epopteuō, *ep-opt-yoo´-o*; from 1909 and a derivative of 3700; to *inspect,* i.e. *watch:*—behold.

2030. ἐπόπτης, epoptēs, *ep-op´-tace*; from 1909 and a presumed derivative of 3700; a *looker- on:*—eyewitness.

2031. ἔπος, epos, *ep´-os*; from 2036; a *word:*— × say.

2032. ἐπουράνιος, epouranios, *ep-oo-ran´-ee-os*; from 1909 and 3772; *above* the *sky:*—celestial, (in) heaven (-ly), high.

Adjective from *epí* (1909), upon, in, and *ouranós* (3772), heaven. Heavenly, celestial. Spoken of those who dwell in heaven (Mt 18:35; Php 2:10); of those who come from heaven (1Co 15:48, 49); of heavenly or celestial bodies, the sun, moon (1Co 15:40 [see 1Co 15:44]). The neuter plural with the definite article: the heavens, heaven (Eph 1:20; 2:6; 3:10). Of the lower heavens, the sky or air as the seat of evil spirits (Eph 6:12). Spoken of the kingdom of heaven and whatever pertains to it (2Ti 4:18). Also Jn 3:12; Eph 1:3; Heb 3:1; 6:4; 8:5; 9:23; 11:16; 12:22.

2033. ἑπτά, hepta, *hep-tah´*; a primary number; *seven:*—seven.

2034. ἑπτακίς, heptakis, *hep-tak-is´*; adverb from 2033; *seven times:*—seven times.

2035. ἑπτακισχίλιοι, heptakischilioi, *hep-tak-is-khil´-ee-oy*; from 2034 and 5507; *seven times a thousand:*—seven thousand.

2036. ἔπω, epō, *ep´-o*; a primary verb (used only in the definite past tense, the others being borrowed from 2046, 4483 and 5346); to *speak* or *say* (by word or writing):—answer, bid, bring word, call, command, grant, say (on), speak, tell. Compare 3004.

2037. Ἔραστος, Erastos, *er´-as-tos*; from **ἐράω,** *Eraō* (to *love*); *beloved; Erastus,* a Christian:—Erastus.

2038. ἐργάζομαι, ergazomai, *er-gad´-zom-ahee*; middle from 2041; to *toil* (as a task, occupation, etc.), (by implication) *effect, be engaged in* or *with,* etc.:—commit, do, labour for, minister about, trade (by), work.

Middle deponent from *érgon* (2041), work. To work, labour:

(I) Intransitively, to work, labour, that is:

(A) Particularly in a field (Mt 21:28); at a trade (Ac 18:3; 1Co 4:12; 1Th 2:9; 2Th 3:8); generally (Lk 13:14; Jn 9:4; 1Co 9:6; 1Th 4:11; 2Th 3:10–12).

(B) In the sense of being active, i.e. to exert one's powers and faculties (Jn 5:17; Ro 4:5).

(C) Also to do business, i.e. to trade, to deal (Mt 25:16).

(II) Transitively, to work, perform by labour, to do, produce:

(A) Of things wrought, done, performed, e.g., miracles (Jn 6:30; Ac 13:41); of sacred rites (1Co 9:13); generally (Eph 4:28; Col 3:23). To work the works of God, or a good work (Mt 26:10; Mk 14:6; Jn 3:21; 6:28; 9:4; 1Co 16:10; 3Jn 5). Also Mt 7:23; Ac 10:35; Ro 2:10; 13:10; Gal 6:10; Heb 11:33; Jas 2:9).

(B) In the sense of to till, cultivate, e.g., the earth (Sept.: Ge 2:5, 15). In the NT, metaphorically spoken only of the sea: to cultivate the sea, i.e. to ply or follow the sea as an occupation as sailors, mariners (Rev 18:17).

(C) In the sense of to work for, labour for, earn, e.g., one's food (Jn 6:27; 2Jn 8).

Deriv.: *ergasía* (2039), craft, diligence, gain; *ergátēs* (2040), labourer; *katergázomai* (2716), to work fully, accomplish; *periergázomai* (4020), to be a busybody; *prosergázomai* (4333), to gain, acquire besides.

Syn.: *energéō* (1754), to work in; *epiteléō* (2005), to perform; *katergázomai* (2716), to work; *kopiáō* (2872), to toil; *poiéō* (4160), to do; *pragmateúomai* (4231), to trade; *prássō* (4238), to do work; *prosergázomai* (4333), to work out in addition.

2039. ἐργασία, ergasia, *er-gas-ee´-ah*; from 2040; *occupation;* (by implication) *profit, pains:*—craft, diligence, gain, work.

2040. ἐργάτης, ergatēs, *er-gat´-ace*; from 2041; a *toiler;* (figurative) a *teacher:*—labourer, worker (-men).

2041. ἔργον, ergon, *er´-gon*; from a primary (but obsolete) **ἔργω,** *ergō* (to *work*); *toil* (as an effort or occupation); (by implication) an *act:*—deed, doing, labour, work.

Noun from *érgō* (n.f.), to work. Work, performance, the result or object of employment, making or working:

(I) A labour, business, employment, something to be done.

(A) Generally (Mk 13:34; Eph 4:12; 1Ti 3:1); of the work which Jesus was sent to fulfill on earth (Jn 5:20, 36; 10:38; 17:4); that which one has been called or ordained to accomplish (Jn 4:34; 6:28, 29; 9:4; 17:4; Ac 13:2; 14:26; 15:38; 1Co 15:58; 16:10; Php 1:22; 2:30; Rev 2:26).

(B) In the sense of undertaking, attempt (Ac 5:38).

(II) Work, i.e. deed, act, action, something done:

(A) Generally: to work a work, do a deed (Ac 13:41 quoted from Hab 1:5); of the works of Jesus: miracles, mighty deeds (Mt 11:2; Jn 7:3, 21; 14:10–12; 15:24); of God (Heb 3:9 from Ps 95:9).

(B) An action or deed as contrasted to *lógos* (3056), word (Lk 24:19; Ac 7:22; Ro 15:18; 2Co 10:11; Col 3:17; Tit 1:16). By implication in Jas 1:25, not a hearer, "but a doer of the work" or the deed.

(C) Of the works of men in reference to right and wrong as judged by the moral law, the precepts of the gospel: **(1)** Generally (Mt 23:3, 5; Jn 3:20, 21; Ac 26:20; Ro 2:6; 3:27; 2Co 11:15; Gal 6:4; 1Pe 1:17; Rev 20:12). **(2)** Of good works, with various adjectives (Mt 5:16; Mk 14:6; Ac 9:36; Ro 2:7; Eph 2:10; 2Th 2:17; 1Ti 6:18; Tit 2:7; 3:5; Heb 13:21; Jas 1:4). **(3)** Of evil works with various adjectives (Jn 3:19; Ro 13:12; Gal 5:19; Col 1:21; 2Ti 4:18; Heb 6:1; 2Pe 2:8; 1Jn 3:12; Jude 15). **(4)** Of works of the law, meaning works required or conformable to the Mosaic moral law and required by this law (Ro 2:15; 3:20; 4:2, 6; 9:11; 11:6; Gal 2:16; Eph 2:9; 2Ti 1:9). **(5)** Of works of faith, meaning springing from faith, combined with faith (1Th 1:3; 2Th 1:11; Heb 6:10; Jas 2:14, 17–26).

(III) Work, i.e. the thing wrought, something made or created generally by men, such as an idol (Ac 7:41). Of the works of God, generally (Ac 15:18; Ro 14:20; Php 1:6; Heb 1:10; Rev 15:3). Also of works implying power, and used for power or might, e.g., of God (Jn 9:3); of Satan (1Jn 3:8).

Deriv.: *ampelourgós* (289), vine-dresser; *argós* (692), idle, barren; *geōrgós* (1092), husbandman; *dēmiourgós* (1217), one who works for the public; *energḗs* (1756), active; *ergázomai* (2038), to work; *euergétēs* (2110), benefactor; *leitourgós* (3011), public servant, minister; *panoúr-*

gos (3835), crafty; *períergos* (4021), busybody; *sunergós* (4904), work-fellow.

Syn.: *dúnamis* (1411), miracle, a powerful deed or act; *ergasía* (2039), a working, business; *ktísma* (2938), product, creature; *poíēsis* (4162), a doing, deed; *prágma* (4229), an accomplished act, deed; *práxis* (4234), transaction, a deed; *téchnē* (5078) craft, occupation.

2042. ἐρεθίζω, erethizō, *er-eth-id´-zo*; from a presumed prolonged form of 2054; to *stimulate* (especially to anger):—provoke.

2043. ἐρείδω, ereidō, *er-i´-do*; of obscure affinity; to *prop*, i.e. (reflexive) *get fast*:—stick fast.

2044. ἐρεύγομαι, ereugomai, *er-yoog´-om-ahee*; of uncertain affinity; to *belch*, i.e. (figurative) to *speak out*:—utter.

2045. ἐρευνάω, ereunaō, *er-yoo-nah´-o*; apparently from 2046 (through the idea of *inquiry*); to *seek*, i.e. (figurative) to *investigate*:—search.

2046. ἐρέω, ereō, *er-eh´-o*; probably a fuller form of 4483; an alternate for 2036 in certain tenses; to *utter*, i.e. *speak* or *say*:—call, say, speak (of), tell.

Some tenses use *rhéō* (4483) or *épō* (2036). To say, declare (Mt 26:75; Lk 2:24; 22:13; Jn 4:18; Ro 4:1). To promise (Heb 13:5); to call (Jn 15:15).

Deriv.: *proeréō* (4280), to say before, foretell.

Syn.: *laléō* (2980), to talk; *phēmí* (5346), to speak, affirm.

2047. ἐρημία, erēmia, *er-ay-mee´-ah*; from 2048; *solitude* (concrete):—desert, wilderness.

2048. ἔρημος, erēmos, *er´-ay-mos*; of uncertain affinity; *lonesome*, i.e. (by implication) *waste* (usually as a noun, 5561 being implied):—desert, desolate, solitary, wilderness.

2049. ἐρημόω, erēmoō, *er-ay-mo´-o*; from 2048; to *lay waste* (literal or figurative):—(bring to, make) desolate (-ion), come to nought.

2050. ἐρήμωσις, erēmōsis, *er-ay´-mo-sis*; from 2049; *despoliation*:—desolation.

2051. ἐρίζω, erizō, *er-id´-zo*; from 2054; to *wrangle*:—strive.

2052. ἐριθεία, eritheia, *er-ith-i´-ah*; perhaps from the same as 2042; properly *intrigue*, i.e. (by implication) *faction*:—contention (-ious), strife.

Noun from *eritheúō* (n.f.), to work for hire. Contention, party-strife, rivalry (Php 1:16; 2:3). It also means canvassing for public office, scheming, promoting political factions (Ro 2:8; 2Co 12:20; Gal 5:20; Jas 3:14, 16).

Syn.: *éris* (2054), strife, quarrel, rivalry; *logomachía* (3055), strife of words; *paroxusmós* (3948), paroxysm, contention, irritation; *philoneikía* (5379), dispute, quarrelsomeness.

2053. ἔριον, erion, *er´-ee-on*; of obscure affinity; *wool*:—wool.

2054. ἔρις, eris, *er´-is*; of uncertain affinity; a *quarrel*, i.e. (by implication) *wrangling*:—contention, debate, strife, variance.

2055. ἐρίφιον, eriphion, *er-if´-ee-on*; from 2056; a *kidling*, i.e. (genitive) *goat* (symbolical *wicked* person):—goat.

2056. ἔριφος, eriphos, *er´-if-os*; perhaps from the same as 2053 (through the idea of *hairiness*); a *kid* or (generic) *goat*:—goat, kid.

2057. Ἑρμᾶς, Hermas, *her-mas´*; probably from 2060; *Hermas*, a Christian:—Hermas.

2058. ἑρμηνεία, hermēneia, *her-may-ni´-ah*; from the same as 2059; *translation*:—interpretation.

2059. ἑρμηνεύω, hermēneuō, *her-mayn-yoo´-o*; from a presumed derivative of 2060 (as the god of language); to *translate*:—interpret.

2060. Ἑρμῆς, Hermēs, *her-mace´*; perhaps from 2046; *Hermes*, the name of the messenger of the Greek deities; also of a Christian:—Hermes, Mercury.

2061. Ἑρμογενης, Hermōgenēs, *her-mog-en´-ace*; from 2060 and 1096; *born of Hermes; Hermogenes*, an apostate Christian:—Hermogenes.

2062. ἑρπετόν, herpeton, *her-pet-on´*; neuter of a derivative of **ἕρπω, herpō** (to *creep*); a *reptile*, i.e. (by Hebrew [compare 7431]) a small *animal*:—creeping thing, serpent.

2063. ἐρυθρός, eruthros, *er-oo-thros´*; of uncertain affinity; *red*, i.e. (with 2281) the *Red* Sea:—red.

2064. ἔρχομαι, erchomai, *er´-khom-ahee*; middle of a primary verb (used only in the present and imperfect tenses, the others being supplied by a kindred [middle] **ἐλεύθομαι, *eleuthomai***, *el-yoo´- thom-ahee*; or [active] **ἔλθω, *elthō***, *el´-tho*; which do not otherwise occur); to *come* or *go* (in a great variety of applications, literal and figurative):—accompany, appear, bring, come, enter, fall out, go, grow, × light, × next, pass, resort, be set.

To come, to go, move or pass along in any direction, as marked by the adjuncts or often simply by the context. The forms of the 2d aor., however, more frequently signify to come, and are rarely used of one who goes from or away.

(I) To go, with adjuncts implying motion from a place or person to another: to go, to go to (Mk 11:13; Lk 2:44; Jn 6:17; Ac 9:17; Heb 11:8).

(II) To come, with adjuncts implying motion to or toward any person or place:

(A) As spoken of persons: in an absolute sense (Mt 8:9; Mk 4:4; Jn 1:39). In the present in a historical sense, that is, instead of the aor. (Mt 25:11, 19; Mk 2:18; Jn 20:18; 3Jn 3); in a fut. sense, apparently, but only of what is certain to take place (Jn 4:25; 14:3, 30; Rev 1:7). Especially in the phrase *ho erchómenos*, the coming One, i.e. the future One, He who shall come, the Messiah (Mt 11:3; 21:9; Lk 7:19, 20; Jn 6:14; 11:27; 12:13).

(B) In the sense of to come forth before the public: to appear, make one's appearance (Mt 11:14, 19; 17:11; 24:5; Mk 9:11, 12; Jn 1:31; Gal 3:19; 2Pe 3:3; 1Jn 4:2).

(C) In the sense of to come again, come back, to return: (Mt 2:21; 5:24; Lk 15:30; 19:13; Jn 7:45; 9:7; 14:18, 28; 21:22; Ro 9:9; 2Th 1:10; Heb 13:25).

(D) Metaphorically spoken of things, for example: **(1)** Of time (Mt 9:15; Lk 23:29; Jn 4:35; 9:4; 16:4, 32; Ac 2:20; 3:19; Heb 8:8). **(2)** Of the kingdom of God, to come, i.e. to be established (Mt 6:10; Mk 11:10).

Deriv.: *anérchomai* (424), to go up; *apérchomai* (565), to go away or from; *diérchomai* (1330), to come or go through; *eisérchomai* (1525), to go or come into; *éleusis* (1660), advent, coming; *exérchomai* (1831), to come out; *epérchomai* (1904), to come or go upon; *katérchomai* (2718), to come down; *parérchomai* (3928), to pass by; *periérchomai* (4022), to come or go all around; *proérchomai* (4281), to go before, precede; *prosérchomai* (4334), to come or go near; *sunérchomai* (4905), to come together.

Syn.: *paragínomai* (3854), to arrive, be present. Also *aphiknéomai* (864), to arrive at a place; *hḗkō* (2240), to come, with the emphasis of being present.

2065. ἐρωτάω, erōtaō, *er-o-tah´-o*; apparently from 2046 [compare 2045]; to *interrogate*; (by implication) to *request*:—ask, beseech, desire, intreat, pray. Compare 4441.

From *éromai* (n.f.), to ask, inquire. To ask:

(I) To interrogate, inquire of (Mt 16:13; 21:24; Mk 4:10; Lk 9:45; 20:3; 22:68; Jn 1:19; 16:5).

(II) To request, entreat, beseech (Mt 15:23; Lk 5:3; 7:3, 36; 14:18, 19; Jn 4:40, 47; 12:21; Ac 3:3; 23:20; Php 4:3; 1Th 4:1; 5:12; 2Th 2:1).

Deriv.: *dierōtáō* (1331), to inquire; *eperōtáō* (1905), to interrogate, inquire of.

Syn.: *akribóō* (198), to learn by diligent or exact inquiry; *déomai* (1189), to beseech; *parakaléō* (3870), to beseech; *diaginṓskō* (1231), to inquire; *exaitéomai* (1809), to demand, desire; *exetázō* (1833), to search out; *epaitéō* (1871), to ask for, beg; *punthánomai* (4441), to ask by way of inquiry.

2066. ἐσθής, esthēs, *es-thace´*; from **ἕννυμι, *hennumi*** (to *clothe*); *dress*:—apparel, clothing, raiment, robe.

2067. ἔσθησις, esthēsis, *es´-thay-sis*; from a derivative of 2066; *clothing* (concrete):—government.

2068. ἐσθίω, esthiō, *es-thee´-o*; strengthened for a primary **ἔδω, *edō*** (to *eat*); used only in certain tenses, the rest being supplied by 5315; to *eat* (usually literal):—devour, eat, live.

2069. 'Εσλί, Esli, *es-lee´*; of Hebrew origin [probably for 454]; *Esli*, an Israelite:—Esli.

2070. ἐσμέν, esmen, *es-men´*; first person plural indicative of 1510; we *are*:—are, be, have our being, × have hope, + [the gospel] was [preached unto] us.

2071. ἔσομαι, esomai, *es´-om-ahee*; future of 1510; *will be*:—shall (should) be (have), (shall) come (to pass), × may have, × fall, what would follow, × live long, × sojourn.

2072. ἔσοπτρον, esoptron, *es´-op-tron*; from 1519 and a presumed derivative of 3700; a *mirror* (for *looking into*):—glass. Compare 2734.

2073. ἑσπέρα, hespera, *hes-per´-ah*; feminine of an adjective **ἑσπερός, *hesperos*** (*evening*); the *eve* (5610 being implication):—evening (-tide).

2074. 'Εσρώμ, Esrōm, *es-rome´*; of Hebrew origin [2696]; *Esrom* (i.e. *Chetsron*), an Israelite:—Esrom.

2075. ἐστέ, este, *es-teh´*; second person plural presumed indicative of 1510; ye *are*:—be, have been, belong.

2076. ἐστί, esti, *es-tee´*; third person singular presumed indicative of 1510; he (she or it) *is*; also (with neuter plural) they *are*:—are, be (-long), call, × can [-not], come, consisteth, × dure for awhile, + follow, × have, (that) is (to say), make, meaneth, × must needs, + profit, + remaineth, + wrestle.

2077. ἔστω, estō, *es´-to*; second person singular presumed imperative of 1510; *be* thou; also **ἔστωσαν, *estōsan***, *es´-to-san*; third person of the same; *let* them *be*:—be.

2078. ἔσχατος, eschatos, *es´-khat-os*; a superlative probably from 2192 (in the sense of *contiguity*); *farthest, final* (of place or time):—ends of, last, latter end, lowest, uttermost.

Noun probably from *ek* (1537), from, in the sense of farthest. The extreme, most remote, spoken of place and time:

(I) Of place:

(A) Particularly extreme, most remote, the neuter as substantive, the extremity (Ac 1:8; 13:47; Sept.: Dt 28:49; Isa 48:20; Jer 16:19).

(B) Metaphorically implying rank or dignity, the last, lowest, least (Lk 14:9, 10). Generally (Mt 19:30; Mk 9:35; 10:31; Lk 13:30; Jn 8:9; 1Co 4:9).

(C) Of order or number, the last, utmost (Mt 5:26; Lk 12:59).

(II) Of time, the last or latest:

(A) Generally of persons (Mt 20:8, 12, 14, 16; Mk 12:6, 22; 1Co 15:26, 45). In an adverb sense (Mk 12:6, 22, "the last to die being the woman" [a.t.]). Of things, the last or the latter one or thing (1Co 15:52; Rev 2:19; 15:1; 21:9); the latter state or condition of anyone or anything (Mt 12:45; 27:64; Lk 11:26; 2Pe 2:20). In the neuter as an adverb, "last of all" (1Co 15:8).

(B) With a noun of time, as the last day, e.g., of a festival (Jn 7:37); of the world, the day of judgement (Jn 6:39, 40, 44, 54; 11:24; 12:48). The last days, the last time, the last hour (Ac 2:17; 2Ti 3:1; Heb 1:2; Jas 5:3; 1Pe 1:5, 20; 2Pe 3:3; 1Jn 2:18; Jude 18). All the above refer to the last times of this age. These are the times since the coming of Christ in which the power of this world is in part broken, and will be wholly destroyed only at Christ's Second Advent, designated in 1Co 10:11 as the ends of the ages or the end of the age. These expressions cover the whole interval between the first and the final advent of Christ; but they sometimes refer more particularly to the period in which the sacred writers lived, adjacent to the first coming (Ac 2:17; Heb 1:2; 1Pe 1:20; Jude 18), and elsewhere more to later times, before the Second Coming (2Ti 3:1; Jas 5:3; 1Pe 1:5; 2Pe 3:3).

(C) The phrase *ho prṓtos kaí ho éschatos* (*ho* [3588], the; *prṓtos* [4413], first; *kaí* [2532], and), the first and the last, is spoken of the Messiah in glory (Rev 1:17; 2:8; 22:13) in the sense of eternal, the beginning and the end.

Deriv.: *eschátōs* (2079), extremely, used idiomatically of being at the point of death.

Syn.: *péras* (4009), extremity, end; *télos* (5056), end.

2079. ἐσχάτως, eschatōs, *es-khat´-oce*; adverb from 2078; *finally*, i.e. (with 2192) *at the extremity* of life:—point of death.

2080. ἔσω, esō, *es´-o*; from 1519; *inside* (as preposition or adjective):—(with-) in (-ner, -to, -ward).

2081. ἔσωθεν, esōthen, *es´-o-then*; from 2080; *from inside*; also used as equivalent to 2080 (*inside*):—inward (-ly), (from) within, without.

2082. ἐσώτερος, esōteros, *es-o´-ter-os*; comparative of 2080; *interior*:—inner, within.

2083. ἑταῖρος, hetairos, *het-ah´ee-ros*; from **ἔτης, *etēs*** (a *clansman*); a *comrade*:—fellow, friend.

2084. ἑτερόγλωσσος, heteroglōssos, *het-er-og´-loce-sos*; from 2087 and 1100; *other-tongued*, i.e. a *foreigner*:—man of other tongue.

Adjective from *héteros* (2087), another of a different kind, and *glṓssa* (1100), a tongue, language. One of another tongue or language (1Co 14:21, equal to *glṓssais hetérais* [pl. of *héteros* {2087}], with other languages, an allusion to Isa 28:11).

2085. ἑτεροδιδασκαλέω, heterodidaskaleō, *het-er-od-id-as-kal-eh´-o*; from 2087 and 1320; to *instruct differently*:—teach other doctrine (-wise).

From *héteros* (2087), another of a different kind, and *didáskalos* (1320), teacher. To teach a doctrine different from one's own (1Ti 1:3; 6:3). Equal to the phrase *hétera didáskō* ([1321], to teach), to teach differently. The context implies that the doctrine taught is false.

2086. ἑτεροζυγέω, heterozugeō, *het-er-od-zoog-eh´-o*; from a compound of 2087 and 2218; to *yoke* up *differently*, i.e. (figurative) to *associate discordantly*:—unequally yoke together with.

From *héteros* (2087), another of a different kind, and *zugóō* (2218), to yoke. To yoke unequally, that is, to yoke two different kinds of animals together to pull a load (see Dt 22:10). In the NT, only figuratively of Christians living in improper alliances with pagan idolators. Used only in 2Co 6:14.

2087. ἕτερος, heteros, *het´-er-os*; of uncertain affinity; (an-, the) *other* or *different*:—altered, else, next (day), one, (an-) other, some, strange.

Correlative pronoun. The other:

(I) Particularly and definitely with the article, *ho héteros*: the other of two where one has been already mentioned (Mt 6:24; Lk 5:7; 7:41; 23:40; 1Co 14:17; Gal 6:4). In Lk 4:43, in those "other [*hetérais*] cities" where the gospel has not yet been preached. In distinction from oneself, another person (Ro 2:1; 1Co 4:6; 14:17).

(II) Indefinite and without the article: other, another, some other, equivalent to *állos* (243), another, but with a stronger expression of difference.

(A) Another, with limited emphasis on dissimilarities (Mt 8:21; 16:14; Lk 8:3; 11:16; 14:19, 20; Jn 19:37; Ac 1:20; 7:18; 8:34; 27:1; Ro 8:39; 1Co 12:9; 15:40; Eph 3:5; 1Ti 1:10).

(B) With more emphasis on dissimilarities, of another kind, another, different, in another form (Mk 16:12; Ro 7:23; Gal 1:6; Jas 2:25); of a priest from a different line or family (Heb 7:11, 15). In the sense of foreign, strange (Jude 7; of other languages (Ac 2:4; 1Co 14:21). Different, altered (Lk 9:29).

Deriv.: *heteróglōssos* (2084), one of a different tongue; *heterozugéō* (2086), to yoke unequally; *heterodidaskaléō* (2085), to teach a doctrine different than one's own; *heterozugéō hetérōs* (2088), otherwise, differently.

2088. ἑτέρως, heterōs, *het-er´-oce*; adverb from 2087; *differently*:—otherwise.

Adverb from *héteros* (2087), a different one, another of a different quality. Otherwise. Only in Php 3:15.

2089. ἔτι, eti, *et´-ee*; perhaps akin to 2094; "*yet*," *still* (of time or degree):—after that, also, ever, (any) further, (t-) henceforth (more), hereafter, (any) longer, (any) more (-one), now, still, yet.

2090. ἑτοιμάζω, hetoimazō, *het-oy-mad´-zo*; from 2092; to *prepare*:—prepare, provide, make ready. Compare 2680.

2091. ἑτοιμασία, hetoimasia, *het-oy-mas-ee´-ah*; from 2090; *preparation*:—preparation.

2092. ἑτοιμος, hetoimos, *het-oy´-mos*; from an old noun **ἔτεος**, *heteos* (*fitness*); *adjusted*, i.e. *ready*:—prepared, (made) ready (-iness, to our hand).

2093. ἑτοίμως, hetoimōs, *het-toy´-moce*; adverb from 2092; *in readiness*:—ready.

2094. ἔτος, etos, *et´-os*; apparently a primary word; a *year*:—year.

2095. εὖ, eu, *yoo*; neuter of a primary **εὖς**, *eus* (*good*); (adverb) *well*:—good, well (done).

Adverb, neuter of *eús* (n.f.), good, brave, noble. Well, good.

(I) Particularly with verbs, with the verb *gínomai* (1096), to become, to be prosperous (Eph 6:3); with verbs of doing: to do good, to do right (Mk 14:7; Ac 15:29).

(II) In commendations, the equivalent of "Well done!" (Mt 25:21, 23; Lk 19:17).

(III) Used extensively as a prefix to compound verbs with the meaning of well, good, and hence often used as an intensive, e.g., *eulogéō* (2127), to eulogise, bless; *eukairía* (2120), good or appropriate opportunity.

Syn.: *kalṓs* (2573), well.

2096. Εὔα, Eua, *yoo´-ah*; of Hebrew origin [2332]; *Eua* (or *Eva*, i.e. *Chavvah*), the first woman:—Eve.

2097. εὐαγγελίζω, euaggelizō, *yoo-ang-ghel-id´-zo*; from 2095 and 32; to *announce good* news ("evangelize") especially the gospel:—declare, bring (declare, show) glad (good) tidings, preach (the gospel).

From *euággelos* (n.f.), bringing good news, which is from *eu* (2095), good, well, and *aggéllō* (n.f.), to proclaim, tell. To bring glad tidings, declare as a matter of joy:

(I) To announce, publish, as glad tidings (Lk 1:19; 4:18; Ac 10:36; 13:32; Ro 10:15; Eph 2:17; 1Th 3:6).

(II) Spoken of the annunciation of the gospel of Christ and all that pertains to it: to preach, proclaim, the idea of glad tidings being implied:

(A) To preach the kingdom of God, meaning the things concerning the kingdom of God (Lk 4:43; 8:1; Ac 8:12). With the kingdom implied (Lk 3:18; 9:6; 20:1).

(B) To preach Jesus Christ or the Lord Jesus (Ac 5:42; 8:35; 11:20; 17:18; Gal 1:16; Eph 3:8).

(C) Generally, to preach the gospel, the Word, the faith (Ac 8:4, 25, 40; 14:7, 15, 21; 15:35; 16:10; Ro 1:15; 15:20; 1Co 1:17; 9:16, 18; 15:1, 2; 2Co 10:16; 11:7; Gal 1:8, 9, 23; 4:13; 1Pe 1:12).

Deriv.: *euaggelistḗs* (2099), evangelist; *proeuaggelízomai* (4283), announce good news beforehand.

2098. εὐαγγέλιον, euaggelion, *yoo-ang-ghel´-ee-on*; from the same as 2097; a *good message*, i.e. the *gospel*:—gospel.

Noun from *euággelos* (n.f.), bringing good news, which is from *eú* (2095), good, well, and *aggéllō* (n.f.), to proclaim, tell. Originally a reward for good news, later becoming good news. In the NT, spoken only of the glad tidings of Christ and His salvation, the gospel.

(I) In the books of the NT, outside the writings of Paul, in the sense of glad tidings:

(A) The gospel of the kingdom of God (Mt 4:23; 9:35; 24:14; Mk 1:14). By implication (Mt 26:13; Mk 1:15; 13:10; 14:9; Rev 14:6).

(B) The glad tidings of the coming and life of Jesus as the Messiah (Mk 8:35; 10:29; 16:15; Ac 15:7). Later, *euaggélion* came to mean "gospel" in the sense of "a history of Jesus' life" such as we have in the Gospels of Matthew, Mark, Luke and John.

(II) In the writings of Paul, and once in the writings of Peter, the gospel, that is:

(A) Generally, the gospel plan of salvation, its doctrines, declarations, precepts, promises (Ro 2:16; 11:28; 16:25; 1Co 9:14, 18; 15:1; 2Co 4:3, 4; 9:13; 10:14; Gal 1:11; 2:2, 5, 14; Eph 1:13; 3:6; 6:19; Php 1:5, 7, 17, 27; 2:22; Col 1:5, 23; 1Th 1:5; 2:4; 2Ti 1:10; 2:8). The gospel of Christ made known by Him as its founder and chief cornerstone (Ro 15:19, 29; 1Co 9:12, 18; Gal 1:7; 1Th 3:2; 2Th 1:8). The gospel of God, of which God is the Author through Christ (Ro 15:16; 2Co 11:7; 1Th 2:2, 8, 9; 1Ti 1:11; 1Pe 4:17). By antithesis, *héteron* (2087), another but different gospel, including other precepts (2Co 11:4; Gal 1:6).

(B) By metonymy: the gospel work, i.e. the preaching of the gospel, labour in the gospel (Ro 1:1, 9, 16; 1Co 4:15; 9:14, 23; 2Co 2:12; 8:18; Gal 2:2; Eph 6:15; Php 1:12; 4:3, 15; 2Th 2:14; 2Ti 1:8; Phm 13).

2099. εὐαγγελιστής, euaggelistēs, *yoo-ang-ghel-is-tace´*; from 2097; a *preacher* of the gospel:—evangelist.

Noun from *eauggelízō* (2097), to evangelize. An evangelist, a preacher of the gospel. He was often not located in any particular place but traveled as a missionary to preach the gospel and establish churches (Ac 21:8; Eph 4:11; 2Ti 4:5).

Syn.: *kḗrux* (2783), preacher. Also *ággelos* (32), messenger.

2100. εὐαρεστέω, euaresteō, *yoo-ar-es-teh´-o*; from 2101; to *gratify entirely*:—please (well).

From *euárestos* (2101), well pleasing. To please well as Enoch pleased God through his faith (Heb 11:5, 6; see Ge 5:22, 24). In the middle, to take pleasure in, to be pleased with (Heb 13:16).

2101. εὐάρεστος, euarestos, *yoo-ar´-es-tos*; from 2095 and 701; *fully agreeable*:—acceptable (-ted), well-pleasing.

Adjective from *eu* (2095), well, and *aréskō* (700), to please. Well-pleasing, acceptable. We are to strive to make our lives acceptable and well-pleasing to God (Ro 12:1, 2; 14:18; 2Co 5:9; Eph 5:10; Php 4:18; Col 3:20; Heb 13:21); slaves are to strive to please their masters (Tit 2:9).

Deriv.: *euarestéō* (2100), to please well; *euaréstōs* (2102), acceptably.

Syn.: *euprósdektos* (2144), acceptable.

2102. εὐαρέστως, euarestōs, *yoo-ar-es´-toce*; adverb from 2101; *quite agreeably*:—acceptably, + please well.

Adverb from *euárestos* (2101), pleasing, well-pleasing. Pleasingly, acceptably (Heb 12:28).

2103. Εὔβουλος, Euboulos, *yoo´-boo-los*; from 2095 and 1014; *good-willer; Eubulus*, a Christian:—Eubulus.

2104. εὐγένης, eugenēs, *yoog-en´-ace*; from 2095 and 1096; *well born*, i.e. (literal) *high* in rank, or (figurative) *generous*:—more noble, nobleman.

2105. εὐδία, eudia, *yoo-dee´-ah*; feminine from 2095 and the alternate of 2203 (as the god of the weather); a *clear sky*, i.e. *fine weather*:—fair weather.

2106. εὐδοκέω, eudokeō, *yoo-dok-eh´-o*; from 2095 and 1380; to *think well* of, i.e. *approve* (an act); specially to *approbate* (a person or thing):—think good, (be well) please (-d), be the good (have, take) pleasure, be willing.

From *eú* (2095), well, good, and *dokéō* (1380), to think. In the NT, to think good, i.e. to please, like, take pleasure in:

(I) Generally: to view with favour (Mt 3:17; 12:18; 17:5; Mk 1:11; Lk 3:22; 1Co 10:5; 2Co 12:10; 2Th 2:12; Heb 10:6, 8, 38; 2Pe 1:17).

(II) In the sense of to will, desire, followed by the inf. expressed or implied:

(A) Generally, to be willing, ready (2Co 5:8; 1Th 2:8).

(B) By implication to determine, resolve, choose with pleasure to do something, with the idea of benevolence being implied (Ro 15:26, 27; 1Th 3:1). Spoken of God (Lk 12:32; 1Co 1:21; Gal 1:15; Col 1:19).

Deriv.: *eudokía* (2107), goodwill, pleasure; *suneudokéō* (4909), to think well of with others.

Syn.: *euarestéō* (2100), gratify, please.

2107. εὐδοκία, eudokia, *yoo-dok-ee´-ah*; from a presumed compound of 2095 and the base of 1380; *satisfaction*, i.e. (subject) *delight*, or (object) *kindness, wish, purpose*:—desire, good pleasure (will), × seem good.

Noun from *eudokéō* (2106), to please, favour. goodwill, good pleasure:

(I) Particular delight in any person or thing and hence goodwill, favour (Lk 2:14, "goodwill toward men" on the part of God). See *eudokéō* (2106, I). Of men, goodwill, kind intention (Php 1:15). By implication, desire, longing (Ro 10:1).

(II) In the sense of good pleasure, will, purpose, the idea of benevolence being included. Spoken of God (Mt 11:26; Lk 10:21; Eph 1:5, 9; Php 2:13; 2Th 1:11).

Syn.: *apólausis* (619), enjoyment in regard to pleasures; *boúlēma* (1013), deliberate design, purpose; *epipóthēsis* (1972), an earnest desire, and with the same meaning *epipothía* (1974); *eúnoia* (2133), goodwill; *hēdonḗ* (2237), pleasure, but only in respect to lust; *thélēma* (2307), will, pleasure, favour.

2108. εὐεργεσία, euergesia, *yoo-erg-es-ee´-ah*; from 2110; *beneficence* (genitive or special):—benefit, good deed done.

2109. εὐεργετέω, euergeteō, *yoo-erg-et-eh´-o*; from 2110; to *be philanthropic*:—do good.

2110. εὐεργέτης, euergetēs, *yoo-erg-et´-ace*; from 2095 and the base of 2041; a *worker of good*, i.e. (special) a *philanthropist*:—benefactor.

2111. εὔθετος, euthetos, *yoo´-thet-os*; from 2095 and a derivative of 5087; *well placed*, i.e. (figurative) *appropriate*:—fit, meet.

2112. εὐθέως, eutheōs, *yoo-theh´-oce*; adverb from 2117; *directly*, i.e. *at once* or *soon*:—anon, as soon as, forthwith, immediately, shortly, straightway.

2113. εὐθυδρομέω, euthudromeō, *yoo-thoo-drom-eh´-o*; from 2117 and 1408; to *lay a straight course*, i.e. *sail direct*:—(come) with a straight course.

2114. εὐθυμέω, euthumeō, *yoo-thoo-meh´-o*; from 2115; to *cheer up*, i.e. (intransitive) *be cheerful*; neuter comparative (adverb) *more cheerfully*:—be of good cheer (merry).

2115. εὔθυμος, euthumos, *yoo´-thoo-mos*; from 2095 and 2372; in *fine spirits*, i.e. *cheerful*:—of good cheer, the more cheerfully.

2116. εὐθύνω, euthunō, *yoo-thoo´-no*; from 2117; to *straighten* (*level*); technically to *steer*:—governor, make straight.

2117. εὐθύς, euthus, *yoo-thoos´*; perhaps from 2095 and 5087; *straight*, i.e. (literal) *level*, or (figurative) *true*; adverb (of time) *at once*:—anon, by and by, forthwith, immediately, straightway.

2118. εὐθύτης, euthutēs, *yoo-thoo´-tace*; from 2117; *rectitude*:—righteousness.

2119. εὐκαιρέω, eukaireō, *yoo-kahee-reh´-o*; from 2121; to *have good time*, i.e. *opportunity* or *leisure*:—have leisure (convenient time), spend time.

2120. εὐκαιρία, eukairia, *yoo-kahee-ree´-ah*; from 2121; a favourable *occasion*:—opportunity.

Noun from *eúkairos* (2121), convenient, which is from *eú* (2095), good, well, and *kairós* (2540), time, season. The right and suitable time or convenient opportunity; used in the NT only of Judas seeking a good opportunity to betray Jesus (Mt 26:16; Lk 22:6).

2121. εὔκαιρος, eukairos, *yoo´-kahee-ros*; from 2095 and 2540; *well-timed*, i.e. *opportune*:—convenient, in time of need.

2122. εὐκαίρως, eukairōs, *yoo-kah´ee-roce*; adverb from 2121; *opportunely*:—conveniently, in season.

2123. εὐκοπώτερος, eukopōteros, *yoo-kop-o´-ter-os*; comparative of a compound of 2095 and 2873; *better for toil*, i.e. *more facile*:—easier.

2124. εὐλάβεια, eulabeia, *yoo-lab´-i-ah*; from 2126; properly *caution*, i.e. (religiously) *reverence* (*piety*); (by implication) *dread* (concrete):—fear (-ed).

Noun from *eulabḗs* (2126), devout, pious. In the NT, fear of God, reverence, piety. Spoken of Jesus (Heb 5:7); spoken as a challenge to us (Heb 12:28).

2125. εὐλαβέομαι, eulabeomai, *yoo-lab-eh´-om-ahee*; middle from 2126; to *be circumspect*, i.e. (by implication) to *be apprehensive*; religiously, to *reverence*:—(moved with) fear.

From *eulabḗs* (2126), devout, pious. To act with caution, to be circumspect. In the NT, to fear (Ac 23:10). In respect of God: to fear, to reverence spoken of Noah (Heb 11:7).

2126. εὐλαβής, eulabēs, *yoo-lab-ace´*; from 2095 and 2983; *taking well* (*carefully*), i.e. *circumspect* (religiously, *pious*):—devout.

Adjective from *eú* (2095), good, well, right, rightly, and *lambánō* (2983), to take. Cautious, circumspect. In the NT, spoken only in reference to God: God fearing, pious, devout (Lk 2:25; Ac 2:5; 8:2).

Deriv.: *eulábeia* (2124), right attitude, reverence; *eulabéomai* (2125), to act with caution, to fear.

2127. εὐλογέω, eulogeō, *yoo-log-eh´-o*; from a compound of 2095 and 3056; to *speak well of*, i.e. (religiously) to *bless* (*thank* or *invoke a benediction upon, prosper*):—bless, praise.

From *eú* (2095), good, well, and *lógos* (3056), word. To bless, speak well of:

(I) Of men toward God: to bless, i.e. to praise, speak well of with praise and thanksgiving (Lk 1:64; 2:28; 24:53; 1Co 14:16; Jas 3:9).

(II) Of men toward men and things: to bless, speak well of with praise and thanksgiving, to invoke God's blessing upon:

(A) To pray for one's welfare as God perceives it for His actions in their lives (Mt 5:44; Mk 10:16; Lk 6:28; Ro 12:14; 1Co 4:12; 1Pe 3:9).

(B) Spoken of food: to bless, i.e. to ask God's blessing upon (Mt 14:19; Mk 6:41; 8:7; Lk 9:16). Of the Lord's Supper where we may render by implication the meaning of to consecrate (Mt 26:26; Mk 14:22; Lk 24:30; 1Co 10:16).

(III) Of God toward men: to bless, i.e. to distinguish with favour, to prosper, to make happy (Ac 3:26; Eph 1:3; Heb 6:14). Blessed, favored of God, happy; used in joyful salutations, of the Messiah and his reign (Mt 21:9; 23:39; Mk 11:9, 10; Lk 13:35; 19:38; Jn 12:13).

Deriv.: *eneulogéō* (1757), to bless, blessed; *eulogētós* (2128), blessed; *eulogía* (2129), blessing.

Syn.: *makarízō* (3106), to pronounce as blessed; *humnéō* (5214), to sing, laud, praise.

2128. εὐλογητός, eulogētos, *yoo-log-ay-tos´*; from 2127; *adorable*:—blessed.

Adjective from *eulogéō* (2127), to bless. Blessed. In the NT, only of God, i.e. worthy of praise. Used as a doxology: blessed be God (Lk 1:68; 2Co 1:3; Eph 1:3; 1Pe 1:3); spoken of Christ as God (Ro 9:5). Also Mk 14:61; Ro 1:25; 2Co 11:31.

2129. εὐλογία, eulogia, *yoo-log-ee´-ah*; from the same as 2127; *fine speaking*, i.e. *elegance of language; commendation* ("*eulogy*"), i.e. (reverentially) *adoration*; religiously, *benediction*; (by implication) *consecration*; by extension *benefit* or *largess*:—blessing (a matter of) bounty (× -tifully), fair speech.

Noun from *eulogéō* (2127), to bless. Commendation, blessing:

(I) In the NT, only once in a bad sense, spoken of as used by false teachers, flattering words (Ro 16:18). Elsewhere in the NT, blessing.

(II) Blessing God or ascribing praise, implying also thanksgiving (Rev 5:12, 13; 7:12), speaking well of and glorifying our God.

(III) From men toward men, i.e. blessing, benediction, petition for good from God upon persons (Heb 12:17); upon things: the cup of the Lord's Supper (1Co 10:16, see Mt 26:27).

(IV) By metonymy, blessing, favour conferred, gift, benefit, bounty:

(A) From God to men (Ro 15:29; Gal 3:14; Eph 1:3; Heb 6:7; 1Pe 3:9; Sept.: Ge 49:25; Isa 65:8).

(B) From men to men: a gift, bounty, present (2Co 9:5). Hence, by implication, for liberality, generosity (2Co 9:5, 6).

Syn.: *makarismós* (3108), blessedness or the action of becoming blessed.

2130. εὐμετάδοτος, eumetadotos, *yoo-met-ad´-ot-os*; from 2095 and a presumed derivative of 3330; *good at imparting*, i.e. *liberal*:—ready to distribute.

2131. Εὐνίκη, Eunikē, *yoo-nee´-kay*; from 2095 and 3529; *victorious; Eunice*, a Jewess:—Eunice.

2132. εὐνόεω, eunoeō, *yoo-no-eh´-o*; from a compound of 2095 and 3563; to *be well-minded*, i.e. *reconcile*:—agree.

From *eúnoos* (n.f.), benevolent, kindly, which is from *eú* (2095), well, and *noús* (3563), mind. To be well-disposed or well-intentioned toward another (Mt 5:25).

Deriv.: *eúnoia* (2133), benevolence.

Syn.: *eudokéō* (2106), to think well of.

2133. εὔνοια, eunoia, *yoo´-noy-ah*; from the same as 2132; *kindness*; euphemism *conjugal duty*:—benevolence, goodwill.

Noun from *eunoéō* (2132), to favour. Benevolence, goodwill (1Co 7:3; Eph 6:7).

Syn.: *eudokía* (2107), pleasure, good thought.

2134. εὐνουχίζω, eunouchizō, *yoo-noo-khid´-zo*; from 2135; to *castrate* (figurative, *live unmarried*):—make … eunuch.

2135. εὐνοῦχος, eunouchos, *yoo-noo´-khos*; from **εὐνή, eunē** (a *bed*) and 2192; a *castrated* person (such being employed in Oriental bed-chambers); by extension an *impotent* or *unmarried* man; (by implication) a *chamberlain* (*state-officer*):—eunuch.

2136. Εὐοδία, Euodia, *yoo-od-ee´-ah*; from the same as 2137; *fine travelling; Euodia*, a Christian woman:—Euodias.

2137. εὐοδόω, euodoō, *yoo-od-o´-o*; from a compound of 2095 and 3598; to *help* on the *road*, i.e. (passive) *succeed in reaching*; (figurative) to *succeed* in business affairs:—(have a) prosper (-ous journey).

2138. εὐπειθής, eupeithēs, *yoo-pi-thace´*; from 2095 and 3982; *good* for *persuasion*, i.e. (intransitive) *compliant*:—easy to be intreated.

2139. εὐπερίστατος, euperistatos, *yoo-per-is´-tat-os*; from 2095 and a derivative of a presumed compound of 4012 and 2476; *well standing around*, i.e. (a *competitor*) *thwarting* (a racer) in every direction (figurative, of sin in general):—which doth so easily beset.

2140. εὐποιΐα, eupoiïa, *yoo-poy-ee´-ah*; from a compound of 2095 and 4160; *well doing*, i.e. *beneficence*:—to do good.

2141. εὐπορέω, euporeō, *yoo-por-eh´-o*; from a compound of 2090 and the base of 4197; (intransitive) to *be good* for *passing* through, i.e. (figurative) *have* pecuniary *means*:—ability.

From *eúporos* (n.f.), prosperous, which is from *eú* (2095), good, well, and *poreía* (4197), journey. To prosper. Used only in Ac 11:29.

Deriv.: *euporía* (2142), pecuniary resources, abundance, wealth.

Syn.: *perisseúō* (4052), to abound; *pleonázō* (4121), to have more, increase.

2142. εὐπορία, euporia, *yoo-por-ee´-ah*; from the same as 2141; pecuniary *resources*:—wealth.

2143. εὐπρέπεια, euprepeia, *yoo-prep´-i-ah*; from a compound of 2095 and 4241; *good suitableness*, i.e. *gracefulness*:—grace.

2144. εὐπρόσδεκτος, euprosdektos, *yoo-pros´-dek-tos*; from 2095 and a derivative of 4327; *well-received*, i.e. *approved*, *favourable*:—acceptable (-ted).

Adjective from *eú* (2095), well, and *prosdéchomai* (4327), to receive, accept. Well-received, acceptable, approved: spoken concerning gifts (Ro 15:16, 31; 2Co 8:12); spoken concerning the present time (2Co 6:2); spoken concerning our spiritual sacrifices (1Pe 2:5).

Syn.: *apodektós* (587), acceptable; *arestós* (701), pleasing, agreeable; *dektós* (1184), acceptable, favourable; *euárestos* (2101), well-pleasing, acceptable.

2145. εὐπρόσεδρος, euprosedros, *yoo-pros´-ed-ros*; from 2095 and the same as 4332; *sitting well toward*, i.e. (figurative) *assiduous* (neuter *diligent service*):—× attend upon.

2146. εὐπροσωπέω, euprosōpeō, *yoo-pros-o-peh´-o*; from a compound of 2095 and 4383; to *be of good countenance*, i.e. (figurative) to *make a display*:—make a fair show.

From *euprósōpos* (n.f.), good-looking, pleasant in appearance, which is from *eú* (2095), well, and *prósōpon* (4383), a face, appearance. Only in Gal 6:12, meaning to make a fair show, to strive to please. In this case, desiring to please other men, not God.

2147. εὑρίσκω, heuriskō, *hyoo-ris´-ko*; a prolonged form of a primary **εὕρω, heurō**, *hyoo´-ro*; which (together with another cognate form **εὑρέω, heureō**, *hyoo-reh´-o*) is used for it in all the tenses except the present and imperfect; to *find* (literal or figurative):—find, get, obtain, perceive, see.

To find:

(I) Generally: to find without seeking, meet with, light upon:

(A) Particularly (Mt 13:44; Lk 4:17; 18:8; Jn 12:14; Ac 9:33; 21:2; 28:14).

(B) Metaphorically: to find, i.e. to perceive or learn by experience that a person or thing is or does a particular thing (Mt 12:44; Mk 7:30; Lk 8:35; 24:2; Jn 11:17; Ac 5:10; 9:2; 2Co 9:4; 1Pe 1:7; Rev 5:4).

(II) To find by search, inquiry, to find out, discover:

(A) Particularly and in an absolute sense (Mt 7:7, 8, 14; 12:43; 13:46; Mk 1:37; 11:13; Lk 2:45; 15:4; Jn 7:34, 35; 10:9; Ac 5:22; 7:11). Of a judge: to find innocent after examination (Jn 18:38; 19:4, 6; Ac 13:28; 23:9).

(B) In various figurative senses: **(1)** To find God, be accepted by Him when humbly and sincerely turning to Him (Ac 17:27; Ro 10:20). **(2)** Spoken of computation, measurement, to find, figure out a value, a distance, etc. (Ac 19:19; 27:28). **(3)** To find out mentally, i.e. to invent, contrive, to find a way to do something (Lk 5:19; 19:48; Ac 4:21).

(III) Middle, to find for oneself, i.e. to acquire, obtain, get for oneself or another (Mt 10:39; 11:29; Lk 9:12; Jn 21:6; Ac 7:46; Ro 4:1; Heb 9:12; 12:17; Rev 9:6; 18:14). To find grace or mercy, meaning to obtain favour with God (Lk 1:30; 2Ti 1:18; Heb 4:16).

Deriv.: *aneurískō* (429), to find out by search, discover.

Syn.: *ktáomai* (2932), to acquire.

2148. Εὐροκλύδων, Eurokludōn, *yoo-rok-loo´-dohn*; from **Εὖρος**, *Euros* (the *east* wind) and 2830; a *storm from the East* (or Southeast), i.e. (in modern phrase) a *Levanter*:—Euroklydon.

2149. εὐρύχωρος, euruchōros, *yoo-roo´-kho-ros*; from **εὐρύς, eurus** (*wide*) and 5561; *spacious*:—broad.

2150. εὐσέβεια, eusebeia, *yoo-seb´-i-ah*; from 2152; *piety*; specially the *gospel* scheme:—godliness, holiness.

Noun from *eusebḗs* (2152), devout, godly. Piety, reverence, in the NT, only as directed toward God and denoting the spontaneous feeling of the heart (Ac 3:12; 1Ti 2:2; 4:7, 8; 6:3, 5, 6, 11; Tit 1:1; 2Pe 1:3, 6, 7; 3:11). By metonymy: religion, the gospel plan (1Ti 3:16).

Syn.: *eulábeia* (2124), piety, reverence motivated by the fear of God or caution, more than by love for God, as *eusébeia*.

2151. εὐσεβέω, eusebeō, *yoo-seb-eh´-o*; from 2152; to *be pious*, i.e. (toward God) to *worship*, or (toward parents) to *respect* (*support*):—show piety, worship.

From *eusebḗs* (2152), devout, godly.

(I) To be reverent, pious: spoken of the attitude of the Athenians toward the Unknown God (Ac 17:23).

(II) To respect, honour: spoken of the proper attitude toward parents (1Ti 5:4).

Syn.: *latreúō* (3000), to serve religiously, worship; *proskunéō* (4352), to make obeisance, do reverence to; *sebázomai* (4573), to honour, worship.

2152. εὐσεβής, eusebēs, *yoo-seb-ace´*; from 2095 and 4576; *well-reverent*, i.e. *pious*:—devout, godly.

Adjective from *eú* (2095), well, and *sébomai* (4576), to revere. Pious. In the NT, toward God: religious, devout (2Pe 2:9). Spoken as an attribute of Cornelius (Ac 10:2, 7). Spoken as an attribute of Ananias (Ac 22:12).

Deriv.: *eusébeia* (2150), piety, reverence; *eusebéō* (2151), to be pious; *eusebō̃s* (2153), in a godly manner.

2153. εὐσεβῶς, eusebōs, *yoo-seb-oce´*; adverb from 2152; *piously*:—godly.

2154. εὔσημος, eusēmos, *yoo´-say-mos*; from 2095 and the base of 4591; *well indicated*, i.e. (figurative) *significant*:—easy to be understood.

2155. εὔσπλαγχνος, eusplagchnos, *yoo´-splangkh-nos*; from 2095 and 4698; *well compassioned*, i.e. *sympathetic*:—pitiful, tender-hearted.

2156. εὐσχημόνως, euschēmonōs, *yoo-skhay-mon´-oce*; adverb from 2158; *decorously*:—decently, honestly.

2157. εὐσχημοσύνη, euschēmosunē, *yoo-skhay-mos-oo´-nay*; from 2158; *decorousness*:—comeliness.

2158. εὐσχήμων, euschēmōn, *yoo-skhay´-mone*; from 2095 and 4976; *well-formed*, i.e. (figurative) *decorous, noble* (in rank):—comely, honourable.

2159. εὐτόνως, eutonōs, *yoo-ton´-oce*; adverb from a compound of 2095 and a derivative of **τείνω**, ***teinō*** (to *stretch*); *in a well-strung manner*, i.e. (figurative) *intensely* (in a good sense, *cogently*; in a bad one, *fiercely*):—mightily, vehemently.

2160. εὐτραπελία, eutrapelia, *yoo-trap-el-ee´-ah*; from a compound of 2095 and a derivative of the base of 5157 (meaning *well-turned*, i.e. *ready at repartee, jocose*); *witticism*, i.e. (in a vulgar sense) *ribaldry*:—jesting.

Noun from *eutrápelos* (n.f.), courteous, sportive, which is from *eú* (2095), easily, and *trépō* (n.f.), to turn. Humor, wit. In the NT used in a bad sense: levity, jesting; frivolous and indecent discourse. Only in Eph 5:4.

2161. Εὔτυχος, Eutuchos, *yoo´-too-khos*; from 2095 and a derivative of 5177; *well-fated*, i.e. *fortunate; Eutychus*, a young man:—Eutychus.

2162. εὐφημία, euphēmia, *yoo-fay-mee´-ah*; from 2163; *good language* ("*euphemy*"), i.e. *praise* (*repute*):—good report.

2163. εὔφημος, euphēmos, *yoo´-fay-mos*; from 2095 and 5345; *well spoken of*, i.e. *reputable*:—of good report.

2164. εὐφορέω, euphoreō, *yoo-for-eh´-o*; from 2095 and 5409; to *bear well*, i.e. *be fertile*:—bring forth abundantly.

2165. εὐφραίνω, euphrainō, *yoo-frah´ee-no*; from 2095 and 5424; to *put* (middle or passive *be*) *in a good* frame of *mind*, i.e. *rejoice*:—fare, make glad, be (make) merry, rejoice.

From *eú* (2095), good, well, and *phrḗn* (5424), mind. To make glad-minded, to make glad, to cause to rejoice (2Co 2:2); in the middle, to be glad, joyful (Ac 2:26; Ro 15:10; Gal 4:27). As connected with feasting: to be joyful or merry, in a natural sense (Lk 15:23, 24, 29, 32) or in a bad sense (Lk 12:19; Ac 7:41).

Deriv.: *euphrosúnē* (2167), gladness.

Syn.: *agalliáō* (21), to exult, rejoice greatly; *euthuméō* (2114), to make cheerful; *chaírō* (5463), to rejoice.

2166. Εὐφράτης, Euphratēs, *yoo-frat´-ace*; of foreign origin [compare 6578]; *Euphrates*, a river of Asia:—Euphrates.

2167. εὐφροσύνη, euphrosunē, *yoo-fros-oo´-nay*; from the same as 2165; *joyfulness*:—gladness, joy.

Noun from *eúphron* (n.f.), gladsome, cheerful, which is from *eu* (2095), well, and *phrḗn* (5424), mind. Joy, joyfulness, gladness (Ac 2:28; 14:17). Also from *eúphrōn* (n.f.): *euphrainō* (2165), to rejoice.

Syn.: *agallíasis* (20), exultation, exuberant joy; *chará* (5479), joy, delight.

2168. εὐχαριστέω, eucharisteō, *yoo-khar-is-teh´-o*; from 2170; to *be grateful*, i.e. (active) to *express gratitude* (toward); specially to *say grace* at a meal:—(give) thank (-ful, -s).

From *eucháristos* (2170), thankful, grateful, well-pleasing. To show oneself grateful, to be thankful, to give thanks (Lk 17:16; Ro 16:4). Elsewhere in the NT, used only in reference to God: to give thanks to God (Lk 18:11; Jn 11:41; Ac 28:15; Ro 7:25; 1Co 1:14; 14:18; 2Co 1:11; Eph 1:16; 5:20; Col 1:3, 12; 3:17; 1Th 2:13; 5:18; Phm 4; Rev 11:17). Spoken of giving thanks before meals (Mt 15:36; 26:27; Mk 8:6; 14:23; Lk 22:17, 19; Jn 6:11, 23; Ac 27:35; Ro 14:6; 1Co 10:30; 11:24).

Syn.: *eulogéō* (2127), to bless, praise.

2169. εὐχαριστία, eucharistia, *yoo-khar-is-tee´-ah*; from 2170; *gratitude*; active *grateful language* (to God, as an act of worship):—thankfulness, (giving of) thanks (-giving).

Noun from *euchāristos* (2170), thankful, grateful, well-pleasing. Gratitude, thankfulness (Ac 24:3). In Paul's writings and in the Book of the Revelation, it means the giving of thanks, the expression of gratitude to God (1Co 14:16; 2Co 4:15; 9:11, 12; Eph 5:4; Php 4:6; Col 2:7; 4:2; 1Th 3:9; 1Ti 2:1; 4:3, 4; Rev 7:12).

2170. εὐχάριστος, eucharistos, *yoo-khar´-is-tos*; from 2095 and a derivative of 5483; *well favored*, i.e. (by implication) *grateful*:—thankful.

Adjective from *eú* (2095), well, and *charízomai* (5483), to grant, give. Thankful, grateful, well-pleasing (Col 3:15; Sept.: Pr 11:16). Some attribute to it, by implication, the meaning of well-pleasing, acceptable to God, and others the meaning of generous.

Deriv.: *eucharistéō* (2168), to be thankful; *eucharistía* (2169), thankfulness, giving of thanks.

2171. εὐχή, euchē, *yoo-khay´*; from 2172; properly a *wish*, expressed as a *petition* to God, or in *votive* obligation:—prayer, vow.

2172. εὔχομαι, euchomai, *yoo´-khom-ahee*; middle of a primary verb; to *wish*; (by implication) to *pray* to God:—pray, will, wish.

2173. εὔχρηστος, euchrēstos, *yoo´-khrays-tos*; from 2095 and 5543; *easily used*, i.e. *useful*:—profitable, meet for use.

Adjective from *eú* (2095), well, and *chráomai* (5530), to furnish what is needful. Useful or very useful. Spoken in the NT of Christian service (2Ti 2:21; 4:11; Phm 11).

Syn.: *chrḗsimos* (5539), serviceable, profitable, useful.

2174. εὐψυχέω, eupsucheō, *yoo-psoo-kheh´-o*; from a compound of 2095 and 5590; to *be in good spirits*, i.e. *feel encouraged*:—be of good comfort.

2175. εὐωδία, euōdia, *yoo-o-dee´-ah*; from a compound of 2095 and a derivative of 3605; *good-scentedness*, i.e. *fragrance*:—sweet savour (smell, -smelling).

2176. εὐώνυμος, euōnumos, *yoo-o´-noo-mos*; from 2095 and 3686; properly *well-named* (*good-omened*), i.e. the *left* (which was the *lucky* side among the pagan Greeks); neuter as adverb *at the left* hand:—(on the) left.

2177. ἐφάλλομαι, ephallomai, *ef-al´-lom-ahee*; from 1909 and 242; to *spring upon*:—leap on.

2178. ἐφάπαξ, ephapax, *ef-ap´-ax*; from 1909 and 530; *upon one occasion* (only):—(at) once (for all).

2179. Ἐφεσῖνος, Ephesinos, *ef-es-ee´-nos*; from 2181; *Ephesine*, or situated at Ephesus:—of Ephesus.

2180. Ἐφέσιος, Ephesios, *ef-es´-ee-os*; from 2181; an *Ephesian* or inhabitant of Ephesus:—Ephesian, of Ephesus.

2181. Ἔφεσος, Ephesos, *ef´-es-os*; probably of foreign origin; *Ephesus*, a city of Asia Minor:—Ephesus.

2182. ἐφευρέτης, epheuretēs, *ef-yoo-ret´-ace*; from a compound of 1909 and 2147; a *discoverer*, i.e. *contriver*:—inventor.

2183. ἐφημερία, ephēmeria, *ef-ay-mer-ee´-ah*; from 2184; *diurnality*, i.e. (special) the quotidian *rotation* or *class* of the Jewish priests' service at the temple, as distributed by families:—course.

2184. ἐφήμερος, ephēmeros, *ef-ay´-mer-os*; from 1909 and 2250; *for a day* ("ephemeral"), i.e. *diurnal*:—daily.

2185. ἐφικνέομαι, ephikneomai, *ef-ik-neh´-om-ahee*; from 1909 and a cognate of 2240; to *arrive upon*, i.e. *extend to*:—reach.

2186. ἐφίστημι, ephistēmi, *ef-is´-tay-mee*; from 1909 and 2476; to *stand upon*, i.e. *be present* (in various applications, friendly or otherwise, usually literal):—assault, come (in, to, unto, upon), be at hand (instant), present, stand (before, by, over).

2187. Ἐφραΐμ, Ephraïm, *ef-rah-im´*; of Hebrew origin [669 or better 6085]; *Ephraïm*, a place in Palestine:—Ephraim.

2188. ἐφφαθά, ephphatha, *ef-fath-ah´*; of Chaldee origin [6606]; *be opened!*:—Ephphatha.

2189. ἔχθρα, echthra, *ekh´-thrah*; feminine of 2190; *hostility*; (by implication) a reason for *opposition*:—enmity, hatred.

2190. ἐχθρός, echthros, *ekh-thros´*; from a primary **ἔχθω,** ***echthō*** (to *hate*); *hateful* (passive *odious*, or active *hostile*); usually as a noun, an *adversary* (especially *Satan*):—enemy, foe.

2191. ἔχιδνα, echidna, *ekh´-id-nah*; of uncertain origin; an *adder* or other poisonous snake (literal or figurative):—viper.

2192. ἔχω, echō, *ekh´-o*; (including an alternate form **σχέω,** ***scheō***, *skheh´-o*; used in certain tenses only); a primary verb; to *hold* (used in very various applications, literal or figurative, direct or remote; such as *possession, ability, contiguity, relation* or *condition*):—be (able, × hold, possessed with), accompany, + begin to amend, can (+ -not), × conceive, count, diseased, do, + eat, + enjoy, + fear, following, have, hold, keep, + lack, + go to law, lie, + must needs, + of necessity, + need, next, + recover, + reign, + rest, return, × sick, take for, + tremble, + uncircumcised, use.

To have, to hold, i.e. to have and hold, implying continued possession:

(I) Particularly and primarily to have in one's hands, to hold in the hand (Mt 26:7; Heb 8:3; Rev 1:16; 5:8; 6:2, 5; 8:3, 6; 9:14; 10:2; 17:4).

(II) Generally and most frequently, to have, to possess externally, to have in one's possession, power, charge, control: for example, property (Mt 13:12; 19:21, 22; Mk 10:22, 23; Lk 18:24; 21:4). In figurative phrases: to have years means to be so many years old (Jn 8:57); to have a certain distance means to be a certain distance away (Ac 1:12).

(III) Spoken of what one is said to have in, on, by, or with himself, i.e. of any condition, circumstance, or state either external or internal in which one is:

(A) Generally of any obligation, duty, course (Lk 12:50; Ac 18:18; 21:23; Ro 12:4; 2Co 4:1); of sin, guilt (Jn 9:41; 15:22; Ac 23:29; 1Ti 5:12); lawsuits (1Co 6:4, 7; see Ac 28:29).

(B) Of any condition or affection of body or mind: **(1)** Of the body, to have disease, infirmity (Mk 3:10; Ac 28:9; Heb 7:28; Rev 13:14, wounds); to have a demon or devil, meaning to be possessed (Mt 11:18; Mk 3:22, 30; 9:17; Lk 13:11; Ac 16:16; 19:13). **(2)** Of the mind, e.g., to have love (Jn 5:42; 13:35). Also Lk 17:9; Php 1:23; Col 4:13; 1Ti 5:20; 2Ti 1:12; 3Jn 4). An affection or emotion in Gr. writings is often said to have or to possess a person. In the NT, only in Mk 16:8, literally: "fear and trembling had them."

(C) Particularly of things which one has in, on, or about himself, including the idea of to bear, carry, e.g., in oneself, as in the womb, to be pregnant (Mt 1:18; Rev 12:2).

(IV) Metaphorically and intensively: to have firmly in mind, to hold to, hold fast:

(A) Generally, of things, e.g., Christ's commandments (Jn 14:21). Also 1Co 11:16; Php 3:9; 1Ti 3:9; 2Ti 1:13; Heb 6:19; 1Pe 2:12; Rev 2:24, 25. To have God and Christ, to hold fast to Them, i.e. to acknowledge with love and devotion (1Jn 2:23; 5:12; 2Jn 9).

(B) By implication: to hold for or as, to regard someone as something, e.g., to regard John the Baptist as a prophet (Mt 14:5; 21:26; Mk 11:32).

(V) In the middle, to be near to, adjacent, contiguous. In the NT, only in the participle, meaning near, next, e.g., of place (Mk 1:38, adjacent to, next); of time, with *hēméra* (2250), day, stated or implied, the next day (Lk 13:33; Ac 20:15; 21:26).

Deriv.: *anéchomai* (430), to tolerate, put up with, bear with, endure; *antéchō* (472), to hold firmly, cleave to, support; *apéchō* (568), to have in full; *enéchō* (1758), to hold fast, entangle; *hexḗs* (1836), next; *héxis* (1838), habit, practice; *epéchō* (1907), to hold fast, heed; *eunoúchos* (2135), a eunuch; *kakouchéō* (2558), to mistreat; *katéchō* (2722), to hold firmly, hold down, hold fast; *metéchō* (3348), to be partaker of, share, participate; *paréchō* (3930), to give from one to another; *periéchō* (4023), to include, contain; *pleonektéō* (4122), to take advantage, defraud; *pleonexía* (4124), covetousness, greediness; *proéchō* (4284), to excel, be better; *proséchō* (4337), to take heed; *rhabdoúchos* (4465), a rod-holder, officer; *sunéchō* (4912), to hold together, compress, arrest, afflict, be in a strait; *schedón* (4975), nigh, almost; *schḗma* (4976), shape, fashion, figure; *huperéchō* (5242), to be superior; *hupéchō* (5254), to suffer, endure.

2193. ἕως, heōs, *heh´-oce*; of uncertain affinity; a conjunction, preposition and adverb of continuance, *until* (of time and place):—even (until, unto), (as) far (as), how long, (un-) til (-l), (hither-, un-, up) to, while (-s).

2194. Ζαβουλών, Zaboulōn, *dzab-oo-lone´*; of Hebrew origin [2074]; *Zabulon* (i.e. *Zebulon*), a region of Palestine:—Zabulon.

2195. Ζακχαῖος, Zakchaios, *dzak-chah´ee-os*; of Hebrew origin [compare 2140]; *Zacchæus*, an Israelite:—Zacchæus.

2196. Ζαρά, Zara, *dzar-ah´*; of Hebrew origin [2226]; *Zara* (i.e. *Zerach*), an Israelite:—Zara.

2197. Ζαχαρίας, Zacharias, *dzakh-ar-ee´-as*; of Hebrew origin [2148]; *Zacharias* (i.e. *Zechariah*), the name of two Israelites:—Zacharias.

2198. ζάω, zaō, *dzah´-o*; a primary verb; to *live* (literal or figurative):—life (-time), (a-) live (-ly), quick.

(I) To live, have life, spoken of physical life and existence as opposed to death or nonexistence, and implying always some duration:

(A) Generally, of human life (Ac 10:42; 17:28; 22:22; Ro 7:1–3; 14:9; 1Co 15:45; Heb 9:17; 1Pe 4:5). Of persons raised from the dead (Mt 9:18; Mk 16:11; Jn 5:25; Ac 1:3; 9:41; Rev 20:4); of those restored from sickness, not to die; by implication to be well (Jn 4:50, 51, 53).

(B) In the sense of to exist, in an absolute sense and without end, now and hereafter: to live forever; of human beings (Mt 22:32; Mk 12:27; Lk 20:38; Jn 11:25; 1Th 5:10; 1Pe 4:6); of Jesus (Jn 6:57; 14:19; Ro 6:10; 2Co 13:4; Heb 7:8, 25; Rev 1:18; 2:8); of God (Mt 16:16; Jn 6:57; Ac 14:15; Ro 9:26; 14:11; 1Th 1:9; 1Ti 6:17; Heb 3:12; 12:22; Rev 4:9, 10; 10:6).

(C) Metaphorically, of things, only in the part. *zṓn*: living, lively, active, also enduring, opposed to what is dead, inactive, or transient (Ro 12:1; Heb 4:12; 1Pe 1:3, 23; 2:4, 5). "Living water" means the water of running streams and fountains, as opposed to that of stagnant cisterns, pools or marshes (Jn 4:10, 11; 7:38; Rev 7:17).

(II) To live, to sustain life, to live on or by anything (Mt 4:4; 1Co 9:14).

(III) To live in a certain way, to pass one's life in a certain manner (Lk 15:13; Ac 26:5; Ro 7:9; Gal 2:14; 2Ti 3:12; Tit 2:12).

Deriv.: *anazáō* (326), to revive; *zōḗ* (2222), life; *suzáō* (4800), to live with.

Syn.: *bióō* (980), to live; *diágō* (1236), to spend one's life; *hupárchō* (5225), to be in existence.

2199. Ζεβεδαῖος, Zebedaios, *dzeb-ed-ah´-yos*; of Hebrew origin [compare 2067]; *Zebedæus*, an Israelite:—Zebedee.

2200. ζεστός, zestos, *dzes-tos´*; from 2204; *boiled*, i.e. (by implication) *calid* (figurative, *fervent*):—hot.

Adjective from *zéō* (2204), to be hot. Hot, used figuratively, meaning fervent in Rev 3:15, 16.

Syn.: *ektenḗs* (1618), strained, stretched, fervent; *thérmē* (2329), heat.

2201. ζεῦγος, zeugos, *dzyoo´-gos*; from the same as 2218; a *couple*, i.e. a *team* (of oxen yoked together) or *brace* (of birds tied together):—yoke, pair.

2202. ζευκτηρία, zeuktēria, *dzyook-tay-ree´-ah*; feminine of a derivative (at the second stage) from the same as 2218; a *fastening* (*tiller-rope*):—band.

2203. Ζεύς, Zeus, *dzyooce*; of uncertain affinity; in the oblique cases there is used instead of it a (probably cognate) name **Δίς, Dis**, *deece*; which is otherwise obsolete; *Zeus* or *Dis* (among the Latins *Jupiter* or *Jove*), the supreme deity of the Greeks:—Jupiter.

2204. ζέω, zeō, *dzeh´-o*; a primary verb; to *be hot* (*boil*, of liquids; or *glow*, of solids), i.e. (figurative) *be fervid* (*earnest*):—be fervent.

To seethe, bubble, boil, from the sound of boiling water. In the NT, only applied spiritually, meaning to be fervent (Ac 18:25; Ro 12:11).

Deriv.: *zestós* (2200), fervent, hot; *zē̃los* (2205), zeal.

2205. ζῆλος, zēlos, *dzay´-los*; from 2204; properly *heat*, i.e. (figurative) "*zeal*" (in a favourable sense, *ardor*; in an unfavourable one, *jealousy*, as of a husband [figurative of God], or an enemy, *malice*):—emulation, envy (-ing), fervent mind, indignation, jealousy, zeal.

Noun from *zéō* (2204), to be hot, fervent. Zeal, used in a good sense (Jn 2:17; Ro 10:2; 2Co 7:7, 11; 11:2; Col 4:13), but often in an evil sense, meaning envy, jealousy, anger (Ac 5:17; 13:45; Ro 13:13; 1Co 3:3; Gal 5:20; Php 3:6; Heb 10:27; Jas 3:14, 16).

Deriv.: *zēlóō* (2206), to be zealous or jealous.

Syn.: *órexis* (3715), excitement of the mind, a longing after; *prothumía* (4288), willingness, readiness of mind; *spoudḗ* (4710), diligence, forwardness.

2206. ζηλόω, zēloō, *dzay-lo´-o*; from 2205; to *have warmth* of feeling for or against:—affect, covet (earnestly), (have) desire, (move with) envy, be jealous over, (be) zealous (-ly affect).

2207. ζηλωτής, zēlōtēs, *dzay-lo-tace´*; from 2206; a "*zealot*":—zealous.

2208. Ζηλωτής, Zēlōtēs, *dzay-lo-tace´*; the same as 2208; a *Zealot*, i.e. (special) *partisan* for Jewish political independence:—Zelotes.

2209. ζημία, zēmia, *dzay-mee´-ah*; probably akin to the base of 1150 (through the idea of *violence*); *detriment*:—damage, loss.

2210. ζημιόω, zēmioō, *dzay-mee-o´-o*; from 2209; to *injure*, i.e. (reflexive or passive) to *experience detriment*:—be cast away, receive damage, lose, suffer loss.

2211. Ζηνᾶς, Zēnas, *dzay-nas´*; probably contrete from a poetic form of 2203 and 1435; *Jove-given; Zenas*, a Christian:—Zenas.

2212. ζητέω, zēteō, *dzay-teh´-o*; of uncertain affinity; to *seek* (literal or figurative); specially (by Hebrew) to *worship* (God), or (in a bad sense) to *plot* (against life):—be (go) about, desire, endeavour, enquire (for), require, (× will) seek (after, for, means). Compare 4441.

2213. ζήτημα, zētēma, *dzay´-tay-mah*; from 2212; a *search* (properly concrete), i.e. (in words) a *debate*:—question.

2214. ζήτησις, zētēsis, *dzay´-tay-sis*; from 2212; a *searching* (properly the act), i.e. a *dispute* or its *theme*:—question.

2215. ζιζάνιον, zizanion, *dziz-an´-ee-on*; of uncertain origin; *darnel* or false grain:—tares.

2216. Ζοροβάβελ, Zorobabel, *dzor-ob-ab´-el*; of Hebrew origin [2216]; *Zorobabel* (i.e. *Zerubbabel*), an Israelite:—Zorobabel.

2217. ζόφος, zophos, *dzof´-os*; akin to the base of 3509; *gloom* (as shrouding like a *cloud*):—blackness, darkness, mist.

2218. ζυγός, zugos, *dzoo-gos´*; from the root of **ζεύγνυμι, zeugnumi** (to *join*, especially by a "yoke"); a *coupling*, i.e. (figurative) *servitude* (a *law* or *obligation*); also (literal) the *beam* of the balance (as *connecting* the scales):—pair of balances, yoke.

2219. ζύμη, zumē, *dzoo´-may*; probably from 2204; *ferment* (as if *boiling* up):—leaven.

A noun meaning leaven, sourdough (Mt 13:33; Lk 13:21). As leaven causes to ferment and turn sour, spoken proverbially: "a little leaven leaveneth the whole lump" (1Co 5:7; Gal 5:9), i.e. a few bad men corrupt a multitude. Used figuratively of corruptness, perverseness of life, doctrine, heart, etc. (Mt 16:6, 11; Mk 8:15; Lk 12:1; 1Co 5:7, 8).

Deriv.: *ázumos* (106), unleavened; *zumóō* (2220), to leaven, mix with leaven.

2220. ζυμόω, zumoō, *dzoo-mo´-o*; from 2219; to *cause to ferment*:—leaven.

From *zúmē* (2219), leaven. To leaven, mix with leaven (Mt 13:33; Lk 13:21; 1Co 5:6; Gal 5:9). See *zúme* (2219), leaven.

2221. ζωγρέω, zōgreō, *dzogue-reh´-o*; from the same as 2226 and 64; to *take alive* (*make a prisoner of war*), i.e. (figurative) to *capture* or *ensnare*:—take captive, catch.

2222. ζωή, zōē, *dzo-ay´*; from 2198; *life* (literal or figurative):—life (-time). Compare 5590.

Noun from *záō* (2198), to live. Life:

(I) Generally, physical life and existence as opposed to death and nonexistence:

(A) Particularly and generally of human life (Lk 16:25; Ac 17:25; 1Co 3:22; 15:19; Heb 7:3; Jas 4:14; Rev 11:11). Of life or existence after rising from the dead, only of Christ (Ro 5:10; 2Co 4:10–12). Metaphorically of the Jewish people (Ro 11:15).

(B) In the sense of existence, life, in an absolute sense and without end (Jn 1:4; 5:26; Ro 6:4; Eph 4:18; Heb 7:16; 2Pe 1:3; 1Jn 1:1, 2; Rev 2:7; 21:6; 22:1, 2, 14, 17).

(II) Life, i.e. blessed life, life that satisfies:

(A) Generally (Lk 12:15; Jn 6:51; Ac 2:28; 2Co 2:16; 1Pe 3:10).

(B) In the Christian sense of eternal life, i.e. that life of bliss and glory in the kingdom of God which awaits the true disciples of Christ after the resurrection (Mt 7:14; 18:8, 9; 19:16, 17; Jn 3:15, 16; 5:24; Ro 5:17, 18; 8:2, 6, 10; Php 2:16; 1Ti 4:8; 6:19; 2Ti 1:1; 1Jn 3:14; 5:12, 13, 16).

Syn.: *bíos* (979), the period or duration of life; *psuchḗ* (5590), literally soul, the breath of life, natural life, the seat of personality. Also *bíōsis* (981), manner of life.

2223. ζώνη, zōnē, *dzo´-nay*; probably akin to the base of 2218; a *belt*; (by implication) a *pocket*:—girdle, purse.

2224. ζώννυμι, zōnnumi, *dzone´-noo-mi*; from 2223; to *bind about* (especially with a belt):—gird.

2225. ζωογονέω, zōogoneō, *dzo-og-on-eh´-o*; from the same as 2226 and a derivative of 1096; to *engender alive*, i.e. (by analogy) to *rescue* (passive *be saved*) from death:—live, preserve.

From *zōogónos* (n.f.), life-giving. To give birth to living creatures, give life, make alive. In the NT, to retain, preserve life (Lk 17:33; Ac 7:19).

Syn.: *zōopoiéō* (2227), to cause to live; *suzōopoiéō* (4806), to quicken together or make alive with; *anazōpuréō* (329), to revive.

2226. ζῶον, zōon, *dzo´-on*; neuter of a derivative of 2198; a *live* thing, i.e. an *animal*:—beast.

Noun from *zōós* (n.f.), alive. A living creature, an animal (Heb 13:11; 2Pe 2:12; Jude 10). One of four angelic beings which John saw serving and praising God in heaven with the twenty-four elders (Rev 4:6–9; 5:6, 8, 11, 14; 6:1, 3, 5–7; 7:11; 14:3; 15:7; 19:4).

Syn.: *thḗrion* (2342), a wild beast; *ktḗnos* (2934), a pack animal or beast of any kind; *tetrápous* (5074), a four-footed beast.

2227. ζωοποιέω, zōopoieō, *dzo-op-oy-eh´-o*; from the same as 2226 and 4160; to (*re-*) *vitalize* (literal or figurative):—make alive, give life, quicken.

From *zōós* (n.f.), alive, and *poiéō* (4160), to make. To make alive, endue with life, to quicken:

(I) Particularly (1Ti 6:13); of the dead: to recall to life, to quicken, to reanimate (Jn 5:21; Ro 4:17; 8:11; 1Co 15:22; 1Pe 3:18); of seeds: to quicken, to germinate (1Co 15:36).

(II) By implication: to give eternal life, to make alive forever in the bliss and privileges of the Redeemer's kingdom (Jn 6:63; 1Co 15:45; 2Co 3:6; Gal 3:21).

Deriv.: *suzōopoiéō* (4806), to quicken together or make alive with.
Syn.: *zōogonéō* (2225), to give life, produce or preserve alive.

2228. ἤ, ē, *ay*; a primary particle of distinction between two connected terms; disjunctive, *or*; comparative, *than*:—and, but (either), (n-) either, except it be, (n-) or (else), rather, save, than, that, what, yea. Often used in connection with other particles. Compare especially 2235, 2260, 2273.

2229. ἦ, ē, *ay*; an adverb of *confirmation*; perhaps intensive of 2228; used only (in the NT) before 3303; *assuredly*:—surely.

2230. ἡγεμονεύω, hēgemoneuō, *hayg-em-on-yoo´-o*; from 2232; to *act as ruler*:—be governor.

2231. ἡγεμονία, hēgemonia, *hayg-em-on-ee´-ah*; from 2232; *government*, i.e. (in time) official *term*:—reign.

2232. ἡγεμών, hēgemōn, *hayg-em-ohn´*; from 2233; a *leader*, i.e. *chief* person (or figurative, place) of a province:—governor, prince, ruler.

2233. ἡγέομαι, hēgeomai, *hayg-eh´-om-ahee*; middle of a (presumed) strengthened form of 71; to *lead*, i.e. *command* (with official authority); (figurative) to *deem*, i.e. *consider*:—account, (be) chief, count, esteem, governor, judge, have the rule over, suppose, think.

Middle deponent of *ágō* (71), to lead. To lead or go before, go first, lead the way. In the NT:

(I) To be a leader, chief, generally only in the participle with the article, a leader, chief, equivalent to *hēgemṓn* (2232), leader, chief (Ac 14:12). Spoken generally of those who have influence and authority (Lk 22:26; Ac 15:22); of officers and teachers in the churches (Heb 13:7, 17, 24); of a chief magistrate such as Joseph in Egypt (Ac 7:10); the Messiah, a ruler, prince (Mt 2:6).

(II) Figuratively, to lead out before the mind, i.e. to view, regard, esteem, consider (2Co 9:5; Php 2:3, 6; 3:7, 8; 1Th 5:13; 2Th 3:15; 1Ti 1:12; 6:1; Heb 10:29; 11:11, 26; Jas 1:2; 2Pe 1:13; 2:13; 3:9, 15).

Deriv.: *diēgéomai* (1334), to declare, show; *exēgéomai* (1834), to bring forth, thoroughly explain; *hēgemṓn* (2232), governor; *proēgéomai* (4285), to prefer or go before another; *hodēgós* (3595), a guide.

Syn.: For **(I)**: *árchō* (757), to rule; *hēgemoneúō* (2230), to be a ruler; *oikodespotéō* (3616), to be ruler of the house; *proḯstēmi* (4291), to stand over or before, to rule; *poimaínō* (4165), to shepherd. For **(II)**: *dokéō* (1380), to be of an opinion, think; *krínō* (2919), to judge, esteem; *logízomai* (3049), to reckon; *nomízō* (3543), to suppose, think; *phronéō* (5426), to think.

2234. ἡδέως, hēdeōs, *hay-deh´-oce*; adverb from a derivative of the base of 2237; *sweetly*, i.e. (figurative) *with pleasure*:—gladly.

2235. ἤδη, ēdē, *ay´-day*; apparently from 2228 (or possibly 2229) and 1211; *even now*:—already, (even) now (already), by this time.

2236. ἥδιστα, hēdista, *hay´-dis-tah*; neuter plural of the superlative of the same as 2234; *with great pleasure*:—most (very) gladly.

2237. ἡδονή, hēdonē, *hay-don-ay´*; from **ἁνδάνω, handanō** (to *please*); sensual *delight*; (by implication) *desire*:—lust, pleasure.

2238. ἡδύοσμον, hēduosmon, *hay-doo´-os-mon*; neuter of a compound of the same as 2234 and 3744; a *sweet-scented* plant, i.e. *mint*:—mint.

2239. ἦθος, ēthos, *ay´-thos*; a strengthened form of 1485; *usage*, i.e. (plural) moral *habits*:—manners.

2240. ἥκω, hēkō, *hay´-ko*; a primary verb; to *arrive*, i.e. *be present* (literal or figurative):—come.

2241. ἠλί, ēli, *ay-lee´*; of Hebrew origin [410 with pronoun suffix]; *my God*:—Eli.

2242. Ἡλί, Hēli, *hay-lee´*; of Hebrew origin [5941]; *Heli* (i.e. *Eli*), an Israelite:—Heli.

2243. Ἡλίας, Hēlias, *hay-lee´-as*; of Hebrew origin [452]; *Helias* (i.e. *Elijah*), an Israelite:—Elias.

2244. ἡλικία, hēlikia, *hay-lik-ee´-ah*; from the same as 2245; *maturity* (in years or size):—age, stature.

2245. ἡλίκος, hēlikos, *hay-lee´-kos*; from **ἧλιξ, hēlix** (a *comrade*, i.e. one of the same age); *as big as*, i.e. (interjectively) *how much*:—how (what) great.

2246. ἥλιος, hēlios, *hay´-lee-os*; from **ἕλη, helē** (a *ray*; perhaps akin to the alternate of 138); the *sun*; (by implication) *light*:— + east, sun.

2247. ἧλος, hēlos, *hay´-los*; of uncertain affinity; a *stud*, i.e. *spike*:—nail.

2248. ἡμᾶς, hēmas, *hay-mas´*; accusative plural of 1473; *us*:—our, us, we.

2249. ἡμεῖς, hēmeis, *hay-mice´*; nominal plural of 1473; *we* (only used when emphatic):—us, we (ourselves).

2250. ἡμέρα, hēmera, *hay-mer´-ah*; feminine (with 5610 implied) of a derivative of **ἧμαι, hēmai** (to *sit*; akin to the base of 1476) meaning *tame*, i.e. *gentle*; *day*, i.e. (literal) the time space between dawn and dark, or the whole twenty-four hours (but several days were usually reckoned by the Jews as inclusive of the parts of both extremes); (figurative) a *period* (always defined more or less clearly by the context):—age, + alway, (mid-) day (by day, [-ly]), + for ever, judgement, (day) time, while, years.

A noun meaning day, daytime, occasion, time:

(I) Day, particularly the time from one sunrise or sunset to another, equal to *nuchthḗmeron* (3574), a day and a night, a full twenty-four-hour day or only a part of it.

(A) Generally (Mk 6:21; Lk 4:16; 9:28; 22:7; 24:21; Ac 21:26; Ro 14:5, 6; 1Co 15:31; Jas 5:5; Rev 2:10).

(B) Emphatically, a certain or set day (Ac 17:31; 1Co 4:3, "man's judgement," lit. "man's day," i.e. human day of trial, meaning a court day; Heb 4:7).

(C) Specifically, *hēméra toú kuríou* (*toú* [3588], the; *kuríou* [2962], Lord), Day of the Lord when Christ will return to judge the world and fully establish His kingdom (1Co 1:8; 5:5; 2Co 1:14; 1Th 5:2, 4; 2Pe 3:10); the great day of judgement (Mt 7:22; 10:15; 11:22, 24; 12:36; Mk 13:32; Ac 2:20; Ro 2:16; 2Th 1:10; Jude 6); the day of wrath (Ro 2:5; Rev 6:17); "the day of redemption" (Eph 4:30); "the last day" (Jn 6:39, 40); "the day of God," by whose authority Christ sits as judge (2Pe 3:12).

(D) Day, daylight, from sunrise to sunset: in antithesis with *núx* (3571), night (Lk 4:42; 21:37; Jn 9:4; Ac 12:18; 16:35; 26:13; Rev 8:12); night and day, meaning continually (Mk 4:27; 5:5; Lk 2:37; 18:7; Ac 9:24; 20:31; 26:7; 1Th 2:9); metaphorically for the light of true and higher knowledge, moral light (Ro 13:12; 1Th 5:5, 8; 2Pe 1:19).

(II) Time in general, nearly equivalent to *chrónos* (5550), time:

(A) In the singular, of a point or period of time (Eph 6:13). Followed by the gen. of person (Lk 19:42, "in this thy time" [a.t.], meaning while you yet are living); followed by the possessive pronoun and the article (Jn 8:56, "so that he may see my day" [a.t.], meaning my time, the time of my manifestation).

(B) In the plural, *hēmérai*, days, i.e. time: **(1)** Generally (Mt 9:15; Lk 17:22); "the last days" (Ac 2:17; Jas 5:3); "these days" (Ac 3:24); "those days" (Mt 3:1; Mk 13:24; Rev 9:6); "the former days" (Heb 10:32). Followed by the gen. of person, e.g., "the days of John the Baptist" (Mt 11:12). Also see Lk 4:25; Ac 7:45. **(2)** Specifically the time of one's life, i.e. one's days, years, age, life, e.g., fully (Lk 1:75 [cf. Ge 47:8, 9]). Elizabeth is spoken of three times as being advanced in her days, meaning old (Lk 1:7, 18; 2:36).

Deriv.: *ephḗmeros* (2184), for a day, daily; *kathēmerinós* (2522), daily; *mesēmbría* (3314), midday, noon; *nuchthḗmeron* (3574), a day and night; *oktaḗmeros* (3637), eighth day.

Syn.: *kairós* (2540), season; *chrónos* (5550), time; *hṓra* (5610), hour.

2251. ἡμέτερος, hēmeteros, *hay-met´-er-os*; from 2349; *our*:—our, your [*by a different reading*].

2252. ἤμην, ēmēn, *ay´-mane*; a prolonged form of 2358; I *was*:—be, was. [*Sometimes unexpressed*].

2253. ἡμιθανής, hēmithanēs, *hay-mee-than-ace´*; from a presumed compound of the base of 2255 and 2348; *half dead*, i.e. *entirely exhausted*:—half dead.

2254. ἡμῖν, hēmin, *hay-meen´*; dative plural of 1473; *to* (or *for, with, by*) *us*:—our, (for) us, we.

2255. ἥμισυ, hēmisu, *hay´-mee-soo*; neuter of a derivative from an inseparable prefix akin to 260 (through the idea of *partition* involved in *connection*) and meaning *semi-*; (as noun) *half*:—half.

2256. ἡμιώριον, hēmiōrion, *hay-mee-o´-ree-on*; from the base of 2255 and 5610; a *half hour*:—half an hour.

2257. ἡμῶν, hēmōn, *hay-mone´*; generic plural of 1473; *of* (or *from*) *us*:—our (company), us, we.

2258. ἦν, ēn, *ane*; imperfect of 1510, *I* (*thou*, etc.) *was* (*wast* or *were*):— + agree, be, × have (+ charge of), hold, use, was (-t), were.

2259. ἡνίκα, hēnika, *hay-nee´-kah*; of uncertain affinity; *at which time*:—when.

2260. ἤπερ, ēper, *ay´-per*; from 2228 and 4007; *than at all* (or *than perhaps, than indeed*):—than.

2261. ἤπιος, ēpios, *ay´-pee-os*; probably from 2031; properly *affable*, i.e. *mild* or *kind*:—gentle.

Adjective meaning placid, gentle, mild, easy, compliant (1Th 2:7); given as an attribute of any good servant of God (2Ti 2:24).

Syn.: *práos* (4235), meek; *praús* (4239), meek; *epieikḗs* (1933), gentle, tolerant; *hēsúchios* (2272), peaceable, quiet; *ḗremos* (2263), composed, peaceful.

2262. Ἤρ, Ēr, *ayr*; of Hebrew origin [6147]; *Er*, an Israelite:—Er.

2263. ἤρεμος, ēremos, *ay´-rem-os*; perhaps by transposition from 2048 (through the idea of *stillness*); *tranquil*:—quiet.

2264. Ἡρώδης, Hērōdēs, *hay-ro´-dace*; compound of **ἥρως, *Hērōs*** (a "*hero*") and 1491; *heroic; Herodes*, the name of four Jewish kings:—Herod.

2265. Ἡρωδιανοί, Hērōdianoi, *hay-ro-dee-an-oy´*; plural of a derivative of 2264; *Herodians*, i.e. partisans of Herodes:—Herodians.

2266. Ἡρωδιάς, Hērōdias, *hay-ro-dee-as´*; from 2264; *Herodias*, a woman of the Herodian family:—Herodias.

2267. Ἡροδίων, Hērōdiōn, *hay-ro-dee´-ohn*; from 2264; *Herodion*, a Christian:—Herodion.

2268. Ἡσαΐας, Hēsaïas, *hay-sah-ee´-as*; of Hebrew origin [3470]; *Hesaias* (i.e. *Jeshajah*), an Israelite:—Esaias.

2269. Ἠσαῦ, Ēsau, *ay-sow´*; of Hebrew origin [6215]; *Esau*, an Edomite:—Esau.

2270. ἡσυχάζω, hēsuchazō, *hay-soo-khad´-zo*; from the same as 2272; to *keep still* (intransitive), i.e. *refrain* from labour, meddlesomeness or speech:—cease, hold peace, be quiet, rest.

From *hḗsuchos* (n.f.), quiet, still. To be quiet, live quietly (1Th 4:11). By implication: to rest from labour (Lk 23:56); to be silent, not speaking, keep one's self from speaking out (Lk 14:4); to acquiesce (Ac 11:18; 21:14).

Syn.: *katapaúō* (2664), to rest, restrain; *paúō* (3973), to stop; *sigáō* (4601), to be silent; *siōpáō* (4623), to keep silence.

2271. ἡσυχία, hēsuchia, *hay-soo-khee´-ah*; feminine of 2272; (as noun) *stillness*, i.e. desistance from bustle or language:—quietness, silence.

2272. ἡσύχιος, hēsuchios, *hay-soo´-khee-os*; a prolonged form of a compound probably of a derivative of the base of 1476 and perhaps 2192; properly *keeping* one's *seat* (*sedentary*), i.e. (by implication) *still* (*undisturbed, undisturbing*):—peaceable, quiet.

2273. ἤτοι, ētoi, *ay´-toy*; from 2228 and 5104; *either indeed*:—whether.

2274. ἡττάω, hēttaō, *hayt-tah´-o*; from the same as 2276; to *make worse*, i.e. *vanquish* (literal or figurative); (by implication) to *rate lower*:—be inferior, overcome.

2275. ἥττημα, hēttēma, *hayt´-tay-mah*; from 2274; a *deterioration*, i.e. (object) *failure* or (subject) *loss*:—diminishing, fault.

2276. ἧττον, hētton, *hate´-ton*; neuter of comparative of **ἧκα, *hēka*** (*slightly*) used for that of 2556; *worse* (as noun); (by implication) *less* (as adverb):—less, worse.

2277. ἤτω, ētō, *ay´-to*; third person singular imperative of 1510; *let him* (or *it*) *be*:—let … be.

2278. ἠχέω, ēcheō, *ay-kheh´-o*; from 2279; to *make a* loud *noise*, i.e. *reverberate*:—roar, sound.

2279. ἦχος, ēchos, *ay´-khos*; of uncertain affinity; a loud or confused *noise* ("*echo*"), i.e. *roar*; (figurative) a *rumour*:—fame, sound.

2280. Θαδδαῖος, Thaddaios, *thad-dah´-yos*; of uncertain origin; *Thaddæus*, one of the apostles:—Thaddæus.

2281. θάλασσα, thalassa, *thal´-as-sah*; probably prolonged from 251; the *sea* (general or special):—sea.

Noun probably from *háls* (251), salt. The sea, a sea:

(I) Generally, and as implying the vicinity of land (Mt 13:47; 18:6, "expanse of the sea" [a.t.]; Mk 9:42; Lk 21:25; Ro 9:27; 2Co 11:26; Rev 18:17; 20:13; 21:1); the land and sea standing for the whole earth (Rev 7:1–3; 12:12). The heaven, the earth, and the sea standing for the universe (Ac 4:24; 14:15; Rev 5:13). Poetically, because of the appearance of that upon which the throne of God is said to be founded, a crystal sea (Rev 4:6; 15:2).

(II) Of particular seas and lakes:

(A) By implication the Mediterranean (Ac 10:6, 32; 17:14).

(B) The Red Sea (Ac 7:36; 1Co 10:1, 2).

(C) The Sea of Galilee or Tiberias (Mt 4:15, 18; Mk 1:16; Jn 6:6–19; 21:1).

Deriv.: *dithálassos* (1337), between two seas; *parathalássios* (3864), along the sea.

Syn.: *límnē* (3041), lake.

2282. θάλπω, thalpō, *thal´-po*; probably akin to **θάλλω, *thallō*** (to *warm*); to *brood*, i.e. (figurative) to *foster*:—cherish.

2283. Θάμαρ, Thamar, *tham´-ar*; of Hebrew origin [8559]; *Thamar* (i.e. *Tamar*), an Israelitess:—Thamar.

2284. θαμβέω, thambeō, *tham-beh´-o*; from 2285; to *stupefy* (with surprise), i.e. *astound*:—amaze, astonish.

2285. θάμβος, thambos, *tham´-bos*; akin to an obsolete **τάφω, *taphō*** (to *dumbfound*); *stupefaction* (by surprise), i.e. *astonishment*:— × amazed, + astonished, wonder.

2286. θανάσιμος, thanasimos, *than-as´-ee-mos*; from 2288; *fatal*, i.e. *poisonous*:—deadly.

2287. θανατήφορος, thanatēphoros, *than-at-ay´-for-os*; from (the feminine form of) 2288 and 5342; *death-bearing*, i.e. *fatal*:—deadly.

2288. θάνατος, thanatos, *than´-at-os*; from 2348; (properly an adjective used as a noun) *death* (literal or figurative):— × deadly, (be …) death.

Noun from *thnḗskō* (2348), to die. Death, the extinction of life, naturally or by violence:

(I) Generally, and of natural death (Jn 11:4, 13; Ro 8:38; Php 1:20; Heb 7:23). To taste or to experience death (Mt 26:38; Mk 14:34; Jn 12:33; 18:32; 21:19; Rev 13:3). Figuratively, exposure to death (2Co 11:23). Used by metonymy for plague, pestilence (Rev 6:8; 18:8).

(II) Spoken of a violent death.

(A) Of punishment: guilty of death (Mt 26:66; Mk 14:64); worthy of death (Lk 23:15; Ac 23:29); to sentence someone to death (Mt

20:18; Mk 10:33); death on the cross (Php 2:8). Also Mt 10:21; 15:4; Mk 7:10; 13:12; Lk 23:22; 24:20; Ac 22:4; 2Co 1:9, 10; Rev 2:10, 23.

(B) Of the death of Jesus (Ro 5:10; 1Co 11:26; Php 2:8; Col 1:22; Heb 2:9, 14; 9:15).

(III) Often in the Sept., *thánatos* has the sense of destruction, perdition, misery, implying both physical death and exclusion from the presence and favour of God in consequence of sin and disobedience. Opposed to *zōḗ* (2222), life and blessedness (Sept.: Dt 30:19; Pr 11:19; 12:28). In the NT, this sense is applied with more definitiveness to the gospel plan of salvation, and as *zōḗ* is used to denote the bliss and glory of the kingdom of God including the idea of a joyful resurrection, so *thánatos* is used for the opposite, i.e. rejection from the kingdom of God. This includes the idea of physical death as aggravated by eternal condemnation; sometimes with the idea of physical death being more prominent, and other times subsequent perdition being more prominent (Jn 8:51; Ro 6:16, 21, 23; 7:5, 10; 8:2, 6; 2Co 2:16; 3:7; 2Ti 1:10; Heb 2:15; Jas 5:20; 1Jn 3:14; 5:16, 17). Called also the second death (Rev 2:11; 20:6, 14; 21:8), referring to eternal spiritual separation from God. In this sense *ho thánatos* is used as a kind of personification, the idea of physical death being prominent (Ro 5:12, 14, 17, 21; 1Co 15:26, 54–56).

(IV) Poetically, death as the king of Hades (86), *ho thánatos* being personified (Rev 6:8; 20:13). See Rev 1:18.

Deriv.: *epithanátios* (1935), appointed to die; *thanásimos* (2286), deadly; *thanatēphóros* (2287), death-bearing, deadly; *thanatóō* (2289), to put to death.

Syn.: *nékrōsis* (3500), a deadness; *teleutḗ* (5054), an end, death.

2289. θανατόω, thanatoō, *than-at-o´-o*; from 2288; to *kill* (literal or figurative):—become dead, (cause to be) put to death, kill, mortify.

2290. θάπτω, thaptō, *thap´-to*; a primary verb; to *celebrate funeral rites*, i.e. *inter*:—bury.

2291. Θάρα, Thara, *thar´-ah*; of Hebrew origin [8646]; *Thara* (i.e. *Terach*), the father of Abraham:—Thara.

2292. θαῤῥέω, tharrheō, *thar-hreh´-o*; another form for 2293; to *exercise courage*:—be bold, × boldly, have confidence, be confident. Compare 5111.

2293. θαρσέω, tharseō, *thar-seh´-o*; from 2294; to *have courage*:—be of good cheer (comfort). Compare 2292.

2294. θάρσος, tharsos, *thar´-sos*; akin (by transposition) to **θράσος**, *thrasos* (*daring*); boldness (subjective):—courage.

2295. θαῦμα, thauma, *thou´-mah*; apparently from a form of 2300; *wonder* (properly, concrete; but by implication, abstract):—admiration.

2296. θαυμάζω, thaumazō, *thou-mad´-zo*; from 2295; to *wonder*; (by implication) to *admire*:—admire, have in admiration, marvel, wonder.

2297. θαυμάσιος, thaumasios, *thow-mas´-ee-os*; from 2295; *wondrous*, i.e. (neuter as noun) a *miracle*:—wonderful thing.

Adjective from *thaumázō* (2296), to admire. Wonderful, admirable. In the NT, a wonder, miracle. Only in Mt 21:15.

Syn.: *éndoxos* (1741), glorious; *thaumastós* (2298), wonderful, marvelous, worthy of admiration; *parádoxos* (3861), strange, astonishing work.

2298. θαυμαστός, thaumastos, *thow-mas-tos´*; from 2296; *wondered* at, i.e. (by implication) *wonderful*:—marvel (-lous).

2299. θεά, thea, *theh-ah´*; feminine of 2316; a female *deity*:—goddess.

2300. θεάομαι, theaomai, *theh-ah´-om-ahee*; a prolonged form of a primary verb; to *look* closely at, i.e. (by implication) to *perceive* (literal or figurative); by extension to *visit*:—behold, look (upon), see. Compare 3700.

Middle deponent from *tháomai* (n.f.) to wonder. To behold, to see, to look at:

(I) Simply to see, perceive with the eyes (Mk 16:11, 14; Lk 5:27; Jn 8:10; Ac 1:11; 21:27; 22:9; 1Jn 4:12, 14).

(II) Involving more than merely seeing and including the idea of desire, interest, pleasure (Mt 6:1; 11:7; 22:11; 23:5; Lk 7:24; 23:55; Jn 1:14; 4:35).

Deriv.: *théatron* (2302), theater.

Syn.: *atenízō* (816), to gaze intently; *blépō* (991) to see; *emblépō* (1689), to look earnestly upon and learn from; *epopteúō* (2029), to oversee; *theōréō* (2334), to look at a thing with interest and attention to details, to consider; *katanoéō* (2657), to comprehend with the mind.

2301. θεατρίζω, theatrizō, *theh-at-rid´-zo*; from 2302; to *expose as a spectacle*:—make a gazing stock.

2302. θέατρον, theatron, *theh´-at-ron*; from 2300; *a place for public show* ("*theatre*"), i.e. general *audience-room*; (by implication) a *show* itself (figurative):—spectacle, theatre.

2303. θεῖον, theion, *thi´-on*; probably neuter of 2304 (in its origin sense of *flashing*); *sulphur*:—brimstone.

2304. θεῖος, theios, *thi´-os*; from 2316; *godlike* (neuter as noun, *divinity*):—divine, godhead.

Adjective from *Theós* (2316), God. Divine, what is uniquely God's and proceeds from Him (2Pe 1:3, 4); the divine nature, divinity (Ac 17:29).

2305. θειότης, theiotēs, *thi-ot´-ace*; from 2304; *divinity* (abstract):—godhead.

Noun from *Theíos* (2304), divine. Divinity, divine nature. Used only in Ro 1:20.

2306. θειώδης, theiōdēs, *thi-o´-dace*; from 2303 and 1491; *sulphur-like*, i.e. *sulphurous*:—brimstone.

2307. θέλημα, thelēma, *thel´-ay-mah*; from the prolonged form of 2309; a *determination* (properly the thing), i.e. (active) *choice* (special *purpose, decree*; abstract *volition*) or (passive) *inclination*:—desire, pleasure, will.

Noun from *thélō* (2309), to will. Will, active volition:

(I) Will, the act of willing, what one wills or prefers, wish, good pleasure (Mt 26:42; Jn 1:13; Ac 21:14; 1Co 16:12; Eph 5:17; 1Pe 2:15; 4:2, 3, 19; 1Jn 5:14).

(II) By metonymy: will, what one wills or determines to do or have done (Mt 7:21; 12:50; 21:31; Mk 3:35; Jn 5:30; 6:38; Ac 13:22; Ro 12:2; Eph 6:6; Heb 13:21); the desires of the flesh (Eph 2:3; Sept.: 1Ki 5:8, 9; Ps 103:21; 143:10). By implication: will, i.e. purpose, counsel, decree, law (Mt 18:14; Jn 6:39, 40; Ac 22:14; Heb 10:7, 9, 10, 36). Hence, the will of God, i.e. the counsels or eternal purposes of God (Mt 6:10; Lk 11:2).

(III) By metonymy: will, the faculty of willing, free will (Lk 23:25; 1Co 7:37; 2Pe 1:21); of God (Eph 1:5, 11; 1Pe 3:17).

Syn.: *boulḗ* (1012), counsel, purpose, will. Also *boúlēma* (1013), resolve, purpose, will; *epithumía* (1939), longing, desire, passion; *epipóthēsis* (1972), earnest desire; *thélēsis* (2308), determination, act of will.

2308. θέλησις, thelēsis, *thel´-ay-sis*; from 2309; *determination* (properly the act), i.e. *option*:—will.

2309. θέλω, thelō, *thel´-o*; or **ἐθέλω**, *ethelō*, *eth-el´-o*; in certain tenses **θελέω**, *theleō*, *thel-eh´-o*; and **ἐθελέω**, *etheleō*, *eth-el-eh´-o*; which are otherwise obsolete; apparently strengthened from the alternate form of 138; to *determine* (as an active *option* from subjective impulse; whereas 1014 properly denotes rather a passive *acquiescence* in objective considerations), i.e. *choose* or *prefer* (literal or figurative); (by implication) to *wish*, i.e. *be inclined* to (sometimes adverbially *gladly*); impersonally for the future tense, to *be about to*; by Hebrew to *delight in*:—desire, be disposed (forward), intend, list, love, mean, please, have rather, (be) will (have, -ling, -ling [ly]).

To will, wish, desire, implying active volition and purpose; differing from *boúlomai* (1014), to wish, desire, in that *boúlomai* expresses a more passive desire or willingness.

(I) To will, i.e. to have in mind, to purpose, intend, be pleased:

(A) Of God and Christ (Jn 5:21; Ac 18:21; Ro 9:22; 1Co 4:19; Col 1:27; 1Ti 2:4; Jas 4:15).

(B) Of men (Mt 2:18; 5:40; 19:21; Mk 3:13; 6:19, 26; 7:24; Lk 8:20; 15:28; Ac 10:10; Gal 4:20; Rev 11:6).

(C) Used metaphorically of the wind (Jn 3:8).

(II) Generally: to wish, desire, choose (Mt 5:42; 7:12; 19:17; 20:32; Mk 6:25; Jn 16:19; 17:24; 1Co 7:7; 11:3; Gal 4:20). Sometimes *thélō* is rendered as an adverb, i.e. "willingly," "gladly," (Jn 6:21).

(III) By implication: to be disposed or inclined toward anything, delight in, love, in which case it is a syn. of *philéō* (5368), to love (Mt 9:13; 12:7; 27:43; Lk 20:46; Jn 3:8). Followed by *en* ([1722], in), to delight in anything (Col 2:18).

(IV) By implication: to be of a particular mind or opinion, to affirm (2Pe 3:5, "for they want to be ignorant" [a.t. {cf. 2Pe 3:4}]).

Deriv.: *ethelothrēskeía* (1479), voluntary; *thélēma* (2307), will; *thélēsis* (2308), the act of the will, pleasure, desire.

Syn.: *aitéō* (154), to ask, desire; *exaitéomai* (1809), to demand, desire; *epithuméō* (1937), to desire earnestly; *epipothéō* (1971), to long after; *erōtáō* (2065), to request, ask; *zēlóō* (2206), to have a zeal for, be jealous, desire earnestly; *himeíromai* (2442), to have a strong desire for; *orégomai* (3713), to desire.

2310. θεμέλιος, themelios, *them-el´-ee-os*; from a derivative of 5087; something *put* down, i.e. a *substruction* (of a building, etc.), (literal or figurative):—foundation.

2311. θεμελιόω, themelioō, *them-el-ee-o´-o*; from 2310; to *lay a basis* for, i.e. (literal) *erect*, or (figurative) *consolidate*:—(lay the) found (-ation), ground, settle.

2312. θεοδίδακτος, theodidaktos, *theh-od-id´-ak-tos*; from 2316 and 1321; *divinely instructed*:—taught of God. **θεολόγος *theologos***, *theh-ol-og´-os*, from 2316 and 3004; a "*theologian*":—divine.

2313. θεομαχέω, theomacheō, *theh-o-makh-eh´-o*; from 2314; to *resist deity*:—fight against God.

2314. θεόμαχος, theomachos, *theh-om´-akh-os*; from 2316 and 3164; an *opponent of deity*:—to fight against God.

2315. θεόπνευστος, theopneustos, *theh-op´-nyoo-stos*; from 2316 and a presumed derivative of 4154; *divinely breathed* in:—given by inspiration of God.

Adjective from *theós* (2316), God, and *pnéō* (4154), to breathe or blow. Literally, "breathed by God." Given by God, divinely inspired. Occurs only in 2Ti 3:16.

2316. θεός, theos, *theh´-os*; of uncertain affinity; a *deity*, especially (with 3588) *the* supreme *Divinity*; (figurative) a *magistrate*; by Hebrew *very*:— × exceeding, God, god [-ly, -ward].

(I) God of all, Jehovah (Mt 1:23; 6:24; Lk 2:14, 52; Jn 3:2; 4:24; Ro 16:26; 1Co 4:1). Also "the Lord God" (Mt 4:10; 22:37; Mk 12:29, 30; Lk 1:16, 32; 1Pe 3:15; Rev 4:8). In construction:

(A) Of persons: the God of someone, i.e. his protector, benefactor, the object of his worship (Mt 22:32; Mk 12:26; Lk 1:68; Ac 5:30); of things, i.e. God as the author and giver, the source (Ro 15:5; Php 4:9; Heb 13:20; 1Pe 5:10).

(B) Spoken of what comes forth, is sent, given, appointed from God (Mt 3:16; Lk 11:49; Ac 23:4; 2Ti 3:17).

(II) Spoken of Christ, the logos, who is declared to be God (Jn 1:1; 20:28; Ro 9:5; Php 2:6; 1Ti 3:16; Heb 1:8; 1Jn 5:20).

(III) From the Hebrew, spoken of the leaders of Israel as representatives of God in the Jewish theocracy (Jn 10:34, 35, quoted from Ps 82:1, 6).

(IV) In the Greek sense: a god, a deity (Ac 7:43; 12:22; 14:11; 19:26; 1Co 8:4, 5; Gal 4:8). So Satan is called "the god of this world," its leader, etc. (2Co 4:4).

Deriv.: *átheos* (112), without God; *theá* (2299), goddess; *theíos* (2304), divine; *theiótēs* (2305), divinity, referring to the power of God but not to His essential character and nature; *theodídaktos* (2312), taught of God; *theomáchos* (2314), one fighting against God; *theópneustos* (2315), inspired of God; *theosebḗs* (2318), reverent of God; *theostugḗs* (2319), one hating God; *theótēs* (2320), divinity, referring to the essence and nature of God; *philótheos* (5377), fond of God, lover or friend of God.

Syn.: *kúrios* (2962), God, Lord, master, supreme in authority; *pantokrátōr* (3841), Omnipotent, Almighty.

2317. θεοσέβεια, theosebeia, *theh-os-eb´-i-ah*; from 2318; *devoutness*, i.e. *piety*:—godliness.

2318. θεοσεβής, theosebēs, *theh-os-eb-ace´*; from 2316 and 4576; *reverent of God*, i.e. *pious*:—worshipper of God.

Adjective from *theós* (2316), God, and *sébomai* (4576), to reverence. Godly, devout, translated "worshipper of God" (Jn 9:31).

Deriv.: *theosébeia* (2317), godliness.

Syn.: *eulabḗs* (2126), one who receives something well, devout but in a more passive way than *eusebḗs*; *eusebḗs* (2152), pious, reverent, devout, showing one's reverence in a worshipful attitude; *philótheos* (5377), fond or a friend of God. Also *theóphilos* (2321), a friend of God, used only as the proper name Theophilus.

2319. θεοστυγής, theostugēs, *theh-os-too-gace´*; from 2316 and the base of 4767; *hateful to God*, i.e. *impious*:—hater of God.

Adjective from *theós* (2316), God, and *stugéō* (n.f., see *apostugéō* [655]), to hate, abhor. In the NT: hating God, impious. Occurs only in Ro 1:30.

2320. θεότης, theotēs, *theh-ot´-ace*; from 2316; *divinity* (abstract):—godhead.

Noun from *Theós* (2316), God. Deity, the divine nature and perfections. Only in Col 2:9.

2321. Θεόφιλος, Theophilos, *theh-of´-il-os*; from 2316 and 5384; *friend of God; Theophilus*, a Christian:—Theophilus.

2322. θεραπεία, therapeia, *ther-ap-i´-ah*; from 2323; *attendance* (specially medical, i.e. *cure*); (figurative and collective) *domestics*:—healing, household.

2323. θεραπεύω, therapeuō, *ther-ap-yoo´-o*; from the same as 2324; to *wait upon* menially, i.e. (figurative) to *adore* (God), or (special) to *relieve* (of disease):—cure, heal, worship.

From *therápōn* (2324), attendant, servant. To wait upon, minister to, render voluntary service:

(I) With the root idea: only once, in the passive: to be served, ministered to (Ac 17:25).

(II) With the derived idea of to take care of the sick, to tend, with the more general meaning of to heal, cure (Mt 4:23, 24; 10:1, 8; 12:10; Mk 1:34; Lk 6:7; 7:21; 8:2; Ac 4:14; Rev 13:3, 12).

Deriv.: *therapeía* (2322), service, healing.

Syn.: *iáomai* (2390), to heal; *sṓzō* (4982), to save, heal.

2324. θεράπων, therapōn, *ther-ap´-ohn*; apparently a participle from an otherwise obsolete derivative of the base of 2330; a menial *attendant* (as if *cherishing*):—servant.

A noun meaning servant, attendant, minister, implying always voluntary service and attendance, and therefore different from *doúlos* (1401), a slave, which is often used to refer to involuntary service. Used once, of Moses (Heb 3:5).

Deriv.: *therapeúō* (2323), to voluntarily serve.

2325. θερίζω, therizō, *ther-id´-zo*; from 2330 (in the sense of the *crop*); to *harvest*:—reap.

2326. θερισμός, therismos, *ther-is-mos´*; from 2325; *reaping*, i.e. the *crop*:—harvest.

2327. θεριστής, theristēs, *ther-is-tace´*; from 2325; a *harvester*:—reaper.

2328. θερμαίνω, thermainō, *ther-mah´ee-no*; from 2329; to *heat* (oneself):—(be) warm (-ed, self).

2329. θέρμη, thermē, *ther´-may*; from the base of 2330; *warmth*:—heat.

2330. θέρος, theros, *ther´-os*; from a primary **θέρω, *therō*** (to *heat*); properly *heat*, i.e. *summer*:—summer.

2331. Θεσσαλονικεύς, Thessalonikeus, *thes-sal-on-ik-yoos´*; from 2332; a *Thessalonican*, i.e. inhabitant of Thessalonice:—Thessalonian.

2332. Θεσσαλονίκη, Thessalonikē, *thes-sal-on-ee´-kay*; from **Θεσσαλός**, *Thessalos* (a *Thessalian*) and 3529; *Thessalonice*, a place in Asia Minor:—Thessalonica.

2333. Θευδᾶς, Theudas, *thyoo-das´*; of uncertain origin; *Theudas*, an Israelite:—Theudas.

2334. θεωρέω, theōreō, *theh-o-reh´-o*; from a derivative of 2300 (perhaps by addition of 3708); to *be a spectator* of, i.e. *discern* (literal, figurative [*experience*] or intensive [*acknowledge*]):—behold, consider, look on, perceive, see. Compare 3700.

From *theōrós* (n.f.), a spectator, from *theáomai* (2300), to look closely at. To be a spectator of, i.e. to look on or at, to behold:

(I) Simply to see, perceive with the eyes, behold, nearly equivalent to *blépō* (991), to look.

(A) Generally: to see a person or thing (Mk 3:11; 5:15; Lk 10:18; 21:6; 24:37; Jn 7:3; 9:8; 14:19; 16:10, 16, 17, 19; Ac 3:16; 9:7; 20:38; 25:24).

(B) To see something happening (Mk 5:38; 16:4; Jn 10:12; 20:6; Ac 7:56; 10:11; 1Jn 3:17).

(II) Figuratively, to perceive with the mind:

(A) To recognize a present situation (Jn 4:19; Ac 17:16; 21:20).

(B) To perceive a danger, future reality (Ac 27:10).

(III) Metaphorically, to comprehend, consider, experience:

(A) To see in the sense of comprehending, recognizing, acknowledging (Jn 6:40; 12:45; 14:17).

(B) To consider (Heb 7:4).

(C) To experience, e.g., death (Jn 8:51); to experience in the sense of partaking of something, e.g., Christ's glory (Jn 17:24).

Deriv.: *anatheōréō* (333), to look again; *theōría* (2335), spectacle, sight; *paratheōréo* (3865), to overlook, neglect.

Syn.: *atenízō* (816), to gaze intently; *blépō* (991), to look; *diablépō* (1227), to see through clearly; *eídō* (1492), to know, consider, perceive; *emblépō* (1689), to look earnestly; *epopteúō* (2029), to oversee; *kathoráō* (2529), to discern clearly; *katalambánō* (2638), to comprehend, perceive; *katanoéō* (2657), to perceive.

2335. θεωρία, theōria, *theh-o-ree´-ah*; from the same as 2334; *spectatorship*, i.e. (concrete) a *spectacle*:—sight.

2336. θήκη, thēkē, *thay´-kay*; from 5087; a *receptacle*, i.e. *scabbard*:—sheath.

2337. θηλάζω, thēlazō, *thay-lad´-zo*; from **θηλή**, *thēlē* (the *nipple*); to *suckle*; (by implication) to *suck*:—(give) suck (-ling).

2338. θῆλυς, thēlus, *thay´-loos*; from the same as 2337; *female*:—female, woman.

Adjective meaning female, as contrasted with *arsēn* (730), male. God created the human race, male and female (Mt 19:4; Mk 10:6); in one sense, male and female are equal in Christ (Gal 3:28). Also used two times in referring to homosexual abuses of God's plan for marriage (Ro 1:26, 27).

Syn.: *gunḗ* (1135), woman or wife.

2339. θήρα, thēra, *thay´-rah*; from **θήρ**, *thēr* (a wild *animal*, as *game*); *hunting*, i.e. (figurative) *destruction*:—trap.

2340. θηρεύω, thēreuō, *thay-ryoo´-o*; from 2339; to *hunt* (an animal), i.e. (figurative) to *carp at*:—catch.

2341. θηριομαχέω, thēriomacheō, *thay-ree-om-akh-eh´-o*; from a compound of 2342 and 3164; to *be a beast-fighter* (in the gladiatorial show), i.e. (figurative) to *encounter* (furious men):—fight with wild beasts.

2342. θηρίον, thērion, *thay-ree´-on*; diminutive from the same as 2339; a *dangerous animal*:—(venomous, wild) beast.

Noun meaning wild beast (Mk 1:13; Ac 10:12; 11:6; Rev 6:8). Used metaphorically of brutal, savage men (Tit 1:12); used symbolically in the Apocalypse (Rev 11:7; 13:1ff.; 14:9; 17:3ff.; 19:19, 20; 20:4, 10).

Deriv.: *thēriomachéō* (2341), to fight with wild beasts.

2343. θησαυρίζω, thēsaurizō, *thay-sow-rid´-zo*; from 2344; to *amass* or *reserve* (literal or figurative):—lay up (treasure), (keep) in store, (heap) treasure (together, up).

2344. θησαυρός, thēsauros, *thay-sow-ros´*; from 5087; a *deposit*, i.e. *wealth* (literal or figurative):—treasure.

2345. θιγγάνω, thigganō, *thing-gan´-o*; a prolonged form of an obsolete primary **θίγω**, *thigō* (to *finger*); to *manipulate*, i.e. *have to do with*; (by implication) to *injure*:—handle, touch.

Verb meaning to touch. Spoken of ascetic prohibitions not to handle (Col 2:21); spoken of animals forbidden to touch Mt. Sinai while God gave the Law (Heb 12:20). Intensive: to touch forcibly, i.e. to smite, to harm (Heb 11:28).

Syn.: *háptomai* (680), to touch; *prospsaúō* (4379), to touch upon, touch slightly; *psēlapháō* (5584), to touch lightly, to search for.

2346. θλίβω, thlibō, *thlee´-bo*; akin to the base of 5147; to *crowd* (literal or figurative):—afflict, narrow, throng, suffer tribulation, trouble.

2347. θλίψις, thlipsis, *thlip´-sis*; from 2346; *pressure* (literal or figurative):—afflicted (-tion), anguish, burdened, persecution, tribulation, trouble.

Noun from *thlíbō* (2346), to crush, press, compress, squeeze, which is from *thláō* (n.f.), to break. Pressure, compression. In the NT, only figuratively: pressure from evils, i.e. affliction, distress (Jn 16:21; 2Co 2:4; Php 1:16). More often, by metonymy: evils by which one is pressed, affliction, distress, calamity, persecution; tribulation (Mt 13:21; Ac 7:10, 11; Ro 5:3; 2Co 1:4; Heb 10:33).

Syn.: *báros* (922), heavy, burdensome weight; *diōgmós* (1375), persecution; *kakopátheia* (2552), the suffering of affliction; *kákōsis* (2561), ill treatment; *páthēma* (3804), affliction, that which one suffers; *sunochḗ* (4928), anguish, distress; *tarachḗ* (5016), agitation, disturbance, trouble; *phortíon* (5413), a weight which one may bear without it becoming a burden or causing distress.

2348. θνήσκω, thnēskō, *thnay´-sko*; a strengthened form of a simpler primary **θάνω**, *thanō*, *than´-o* (which is used for it only in certain tenses); to *die* (literal or figurative):—be dead, die.

To die; naturally (Mt 2:20; Mk 15:44; Lk 7:12; 8:49; Jn 11:21, 39, 41, 44; 12:1; 19:33; Ac 14:19; 25:19; Sept.: 2Sa 12:18). Figuratively, to be dead spiritually, though physically alive (1Ti 5:6).

Deriv.: *apothnḗskō* (599), to die off; *hēmithanḗs* (2253), half dead; *thánatos* (2288), death; *thnētós* (2349), mortal.

Syn.: *apogenómenos* (581), to no longer be in one's present existence; *koimáō* (2837), to sleep, metaphorically used with the meaning of to die; *teleutáō* (5053), to end one's life.

2349. θνητός, thnētos, *thnay-tos´*; from 2348; *liable to die*:—mortal (-ity).

Adjective from *thnḗskō* (2348), to die. Mortal, subject to death (Ro 6:12; 8:11; 2Co 4:11); as a substantive with the article: mortal nature, mortality (1Co 15:53, 54; 2Co 5:4).

Syn.: *phthartós* (5349), corruptible.

2350. θορυβέω, thorubeō, *thor-oo-beh´-o*; from 2351; to *be in tumult*, i.e. *disturb, clamor*:—make ado (a noise), trouble self, set on an uproar.

2351. θόρυβος, thorubos, *thor´-oo-bos*; from the base of 2360; a *disturbance*:—tumult, uproar.

2352. θραύω, thrauō, *throw´-o*; a primary verb; to *crush*:—bruise. Compare 4486.

2353. θρέμμα, thremma, *threm´-mah*; from 5142; *stock* (as *raised* on a farm):—cattle.

2354. θρηνέω, thrēneō, *thray-neh´-o*; from 2355; to *bewail*:—lament, mourn.

From *thrḗnos* (2355), lamentation. To weep aloud, wail, mourn, as at a funeral:

(I) Intransitively (Mt 11:17; Lk 7:32; Jn 16:20).

(II) Transitively, to mourn for someone (Lk 23:27).

Syn.: *dakrúō* (1145), to shed tears; *klaíō* (2799), to weep; *stenázō* (4727), to groan.

2355. θρῆνος, thrēnos, *thray´-nos*; from the base of 2360; *wailing*:—lamentation.

2356. θρησκεία, thrēskeia, *thrace-ki´-ah*; from a derivative of 2357; ceremonial *observance*:—religion, worshipping.

2357. θρῆσκος, thrēskos, *thrace´-kos*; probably from the base of 2360; *ceremonious* in worship (as *demonstrative*), i.e. *pious*:—religious.

Adjective meaning fearing God, pious, religious. Only in Jas 1:26.

Syn.: *eulabḗs* (2126), reverent [toward God], one who accepts God's will; *eusebḗs* (2152), pious, devout; *theosebḗs* (2318), reverent toward God, pious, worshipful; *philótheos* (5377) and *theóphilos* (2321), a friend of God.

2358. θριαμβεύω, thriambeuō, *three-am-byoo´-o*; from a prolonged compound of the base of 2360 and a derivative of 680 (meaning a *noisy iambus,* sung in honour of Bacchus); to *make an acclamatory procession*, i.e. (figurative) to *conquer* or (by Hebrew) to *give victory*:—(cause) to triumph (over).

2359. θρίξ, thrix, *threeks*; generic **τριχός**, ***trichos***, etc.; of uncertain derivative; *hair*:—hair. Compare 2864.

2360. θροέω, throeō, *thro-eh´-o*; from **θρέομαι**, ***threomai*** (to *wail*); to *clamor*, i.e. (by implication) to *frighten*:—trouble.

2361. θρόμβος, thrombos, *throm´-bos*; perhaps from 5142 (in the sense of *thickening*); a *clot*:—great drop.

2362. θρόνος, thronos, *thron´-os*; from **θράω**, ***thraō*** (to *sit*); a stately *seat* ("*throne*"); (by implication) *power* or (concrete) a *potentate*:—seat, throne.

2363. Θυάτειρα, Thuateira, *thoo-at´-i-rah*; of uncertain derivative; *Thyatira*, a place in Asia Minor:—Thyatira.

2364. θυγάτηρ, thugatēr, *thoo-gat´-air*; apparently a primary word [compare "daughter"]; a *female child*, or (by Hebrew) *descendant* (or *inhabitant*):—daughter.

2365. θυγάτριον, thugatrion, *thoo-gat´-ree-on*; from 2364; a *daughterling*:—little (young) daughter.

2366. θύελλα, thuella, *thoo´-el-lah*; from 2380 (in the sense of *blowing*) a storm:—tempest.

Noun from *thúō* (n.f.), to rush on or along, spoken of wind or a storm. Tempest. Only in Heb 12:18. Also from *thúō* (n.f.): *thumós* (2372), anger, wrath.

Syn.: *pnoḗ* (4157), wind; *laílaps* (2978), storm, tempest.

2367. θύϊνος, thuïnos, *thoo´-ee-nos*; from a derivative of 2380 (in the sense of *blowing*; denoting a certain *fragrant* tree); made of *citron*-wood:—thyine.

2368. θυμίαμα, thumiama, *thoo-mee´-am-ah*; from 2370; an *aroma*, i.e. fragrant *powder* burnt in religious service; (by implication) the *burning* itself:—incense, odour.

2369. θυμιαστήριον, thumiastērion, *thoo-mee-as-tay´-ree-on*; from a derivative of 2370; a *place of fumigation*, i.e. the *altar of incense* (in the temple):—censer.

2370. θυμιάω, thumiaō, *thoo-mee-ah´-o*; from a derivative of 2380 (in the sense of *smoking*); to *fumigate*, i.e. *offer* aromatic *fumes*:—burn incense.

2371. θυμομαχέω, thumomacheō, *thoo-mom-akh-eh´-o*; from a presumed compound of 2372 and 3164; to *be in a furious fight*, i.e. (figurative) to *be exasperated*:—be highly displeased.

2372. θυμός, thumos, *thoo-mos´*; from 2380; *passion* (as if *breathing* hard):—fierceness, indignation, wrath. Compare 5590.

Noun from *thúō* (n.f.), to move impetuously. In Classical Greek: mind, soul, e.g., as the principle of life, as the seat of the will, desire, emotions, passions, etc. Hence generally, and in the NT: passion, i.e. violent commotion of mind, indignation, anger, wrath; differing from *orgḗ* (3709) in the mode of conception rather than in the thing signified, with *thumós* picturing the inward feeling, and *orgḗ* representing the outward emotion (Lk 4:28; Ac 19:28; Eph 4:31; Col 3:8; Heb 11:27; Rev 12:12). In the plural, "bursts of anger" (2Co 12:20; Gal 5:20). Spoken of God, and including the idea of punishment, punitive judgements (Ro 2:8; Rev 15:1). Further, by the Hebrew prophets Jehovah is represented as giving to the nations in His wrath an intoxicating cup, so that they reel and stagger to destruction; hence also in the NT, the expression "the wine of the wrath (*thumós*) of God" (Rev 14:10; 16:19; with "wine" implied, 15:7; 16:1). By a similar figure, "the wine press of the wrath of God" (Rev 14:19; 19:15, in allusion to Isa 63:3).

Deriv.: *enthuméomai* (1760), to think upon; *epithuméō* (1937), to desire; *eúthumos* (2115), cheerful; *thumomachéō* (2371), to fight fiercely; *thumóō* (2373), to provoke to anger; *próthumos* (4289), predisposed, ready, willing; *prothúmōs* (4290), readily, willingly.

Syn.: *aganáktēsis* (24), irritation, indignation; *parorgismós* (3950), wrath.

2373. θυμόω, thumoō, *thoo-mo´-o*; from 2372; to *put in a passion*, i.e. *enrage*:—be wroth.

2374. θύρα, thura, *thoo´-rah*; apparently a primary word [compare "door"]; a *portal* or entrance (the opening or the closure, literal or figurative):—door, gate.

2375. θυρεός, thureos, *thoo-reh-os´*; from 2374; a large *shield* (as *door*-shaped):—shield.

2376. θυρίς, thuris, *thoo-rece´*; from 2374; an *aperture*, i.e. *window*:—window.

2377. θυρωρός, thurōros, *Thoo-ro-ros´*; from 2374 and **οὖρος**, ***ouros*** (a *watcher*); a *gate-warden*:—that kept the door, porter.

2378. θυσία, thusia, *thoo-see´-ah*; from 2380; *sacrifice* (the act or the victim, literal or figurative):—sacrifice.

Noun from *thúō* (2380), to sacrifice. Sacrifice:

(I) The act and rite of sacrificing (Mt 9:13; 12:7; Heb 9:26; 10:5, 8, quoted from Ps 40:6, 7).

(II) By metonymy: the thing sacrificed, victim, the flesh of victims, part of which was burned on the altar and part given to the priests (Mk 9:49 [cf. Le 2:13]; Mk 12:33; Lk 13:1; Ac 7:41, 42; 1Co 10:18); of an expiatory sacrifice for sin (Eph 5:2; Heb 5:1; 7:27; 8:3; 9:9, 23; 10:1, 11, 12, 26).

(III) Metaphorically, of service, obedience, praise offered to God, an offering, oblation (Ro 12:1; Php 2:17; 4:18; Heb 13:15, 16; 1Pe 2:5).

2379. θυσιαστήριον, thusiastērion, *thoo-see-as-tay´-ree-on*; from a derivative of 2378; a *place of sacrifice*, i.e. an *altar* (special or genitive, literal or figurative):—altar.

Noun from *thusiázō* (n.f.), to sacrifice. An altar (Mt 5:23, 24; 23:18–20; Ro 11:3; Heb 7:13; Jas 2:21). Used specifically of the altar for burnt offerings in the temple (Mt 23:35; Lk 11:51; 1Co 9:13; 10:18; Heb 13:10). Symbolically, in heaven (Rev 6:9; 8:3, 5; 9:13; 11:1; 14:18; 16:7); of the altar of incense in the temple, made of gold (Lk 1:11).

Syn.: *bōmós* (1041), an altar.

2380. θύω, thuō, *thoo´-o*; a primary verb; properly to *rush* (*breathe* hard, *blow, smoke*), i.e. (by implication) to *sacrifice* (properly by fire, but genitive); by extension to *immolate* (*slaughter* for any purpose):—kill, (do) sacrifice, slay.

To sacrifice, to kill and offer in sacrifice (Ac 14:13, 18; 1Co 10:20). "To sacrifice the passover" means to kill the Paschal Lamb as a species of sacrifice (Mk 14:12; Lk 22:7; 1Co 5:7). In a derived sense: to slay (Mt 22:4; Lk 15:23, 27, 30; Jn 10:10; Ac 10:13; 11:7).

Deriv.: *eidōlóthuton* (1494), sacrifice; *thusia* (2378), sacrifice.

Syn.: *anairéō* (337), to kill, used physically only; *apokteínō* (615), to kill; *diacheirízō* (1315), to lay violent hands upon, to kill; *thanatóō* (2289), to put to death; *spházō* (4969), to slay, slaughter.

2381. Θωμᾶς, Thōmas, *tho-mas´*; of Chaldee origin [compare 8380]; *the twin; Thomas*, a Christian:—Thomas.

2382. θώραξ, thōrax, *tho´-rax*; of uncertain affinity; the *chest* ("*thorax*"), i.e. (by implication) a *corslet*:—breastplate.

2383. Ἰάειρος, Iaeiros, *ee-ah´-i-ros*; of Hebrew origin (2971, i.e. *Jair*), an Israelite:—Jairus.

2384. Ἰακώβ, Iakōb, *ee-ak-obe´*; of Hebrew origin [3290]; *Jacob* (i.e. *Ja'akob*), the progenitor of the Israelite; also an Israelite:—Jacob.

2385. Ἰάκωβος, Iakōbos, *ee-ak´-o-bos*; the same as 2384 Græcized; *Jacobus*, the name of three Israelites:—James.

2386. ἴαμα, iama, *ee´-am-ah*; from 2390; a *cure* (the effect):—healing.

2387. Ἰαμβρῆς, Iambrēs, *ee-am-brace´*; of Egyptian origin; *Jambres*, an Egyptian:—Jambres.

2388. Ἰαννά, Ianna, *ee-an-nah´*; probably of Hebrew origin [compare 3238]; *Janna*, an Israelite:—Janna.

2389. Ἰαννῆς, Iannēs, *ee-an-nace´*; of Egyptian origin; *Jannes*, an Egyptian:—Jannes.

2390. ἰάομαι, iaomai, *ee-ah´-om-ahee*; middle of apparently a primary verb; to *cure* (literal or figurative):—heal, make whole.

Verb meaning to heal, cure, restore to bodily health (Mt 8:8, 13; Lk 5:17; 6:19; 9:2, 11, 42; 14:4; 22:51; Jn 4:47; 5:13; Ac 10:38; 28:8; Jas 5:16). Metaphorically, of moral diseases: to heal or save from the consequences of sin (Mt 13:15; Jn 12:40; Ac 28:27; Lk 4:18 [cf. Isa 61:1]; Heb 12:13; 1Pe 2:24).

Deriv.: *íama* (2386), the means of healing; *íasis* (2392), the act or process of healing; *iatrós* (2395), physician.

Syn.: *therapeúō* (2323), to heal with the additional meaning of caring for; *sṓzō* (4982), to save, with the additional meaning of rescuing from the effects of disease.

2391. Ἰάρεδ, Iared, *ee-ar´-ed*; of Hebrew origin [3382]; *Jared* (i.e. *Jered*), an antediluvian:—Jared.

2392. ἴασις, iasis, *ee´-as-is*; from 2390; *curing* (the act):—cure, heal (-ing).

2393. ἴασπις, iaspis, *ee´-as-pis*; probably of foreign origin [see 3471]; "*jasper*," a gem:—jasper.

2394. Ἰάσων, Iasōn, *ee-as´-oan*; future active participle masculine of 2390; *about to cure; Jason*, a Christian:—Jason.

2395. ἰατρός, iatros, *ee-at-ros´*; from 2390; a *physician*:—physician.

2396. ἴδε, ide, *id´-eh*; second person singular imperfect active of 1492; used as interjection to denote *surprise; lo!*:—behold, lo, see.

The later form for *idé*, 2d aor. of imper. of *eídō* (1492), to see, calling attention to what may be seen or heard or mentally apprehended in any way. In the NT, often as a particle of exclamation: see, lo, behold!, calling attention to something present (Mt 25:20, 22, 25; Mk 3:34; 11:21; Jn 1:29; 7:26; 11:36; 19:4, 5, 14). In the sense of behold, observe, consider (Mk 15:4; Jn 5:14; Ro 2:17; Gal 5:2).

Syn.: *atenízō* (816), to gaze intently; *blépō* (991), to see; *emblépō* (1689), to earnestly look; *epopteúō* (2029), to be an eyewitness; *theáomai* (2300), to view attentively, contemplate; *theōréō* (2334), to look with careful observation to details; *katanoéō* (2657), to perceive; *paratēréō* (3906), to note, observe.

2397. ἰδέα, idea, *id-eh´-ah*; from 1492; a *sight* [compare figurative "idea"], i.e. *aspect*:—countenance.

Noun from *eídō* (1492), to see. Aspect, appearance, countenance. Only in Mt 28:3.

2398. ἴδιος, idios, *id´-ee-os*; of uncertain affinity; *pertaining to self*, i.e. one's *own*; (by implication) *private* or *separate*:— × his acquaintance, when they were alone, apart, aside, due, his (own, proper, several), home, (her, our, thine, your) own (business), private (-ly), proper, severally, their (own).

Adjective meaning properly one's own:

(I) As belonging to oneself and not to another, one's own, peculiar:

(A) Denoting ownership, that of which one is himself the owner, possessor, producer, as: my own, your own, his own. Of things (Mt 22:5; 25:15; Mk 15:20; Lk 6:41, 44; Jn 5:43; 7:18; 10:3, 4; Ac 20:28; 28:30; Ro 10:3; 14:5; 1Ti 3:4, 5; 2Pe 1:20; 3:17). Hence, with the plural neuter article *tá ídia*, generally possessions, property, specifically one's own house or home (Jn 16:32; 19:27; Ac 21:6); own nation, people (Jn 1:11 which also includes the world, the total humanity that Christ made). Spoken of persons, e.g., denoting one's brother, father, etc. (Jn 1:41; 5:18). Also Mt 25:14; Jn 1:11; 13:1; Ro 8:32; 14:4; 1Co 7:2; 1Ti 6:1; 5:8).

(B) In the sense of peculiar, particular, as distinguishing one person from others, e.g., one's own dialect (Ac 1:19; 2:6, 8) or superstition (Ac 25:19).

(C) As denoting that which in its nature or by appointment pertains in any way to a person or thing, e.g., in Ac 1:25, "to his own place," i.e. proper and appointed for him; "his own generation" in which he lived (Ac 13:36); "his own reward" (1Co 3:8); see 1Co 15:23; Jude 6. Also *kairós* ([2540], occasion, opportunity, appropriate time) *ídios*, or in the plural *kairoí ídioi*, own times or opportunities, i.e. due or proper time as determined by God (Gal 6:9; 1Ti 2:6; 6:15; Tit 1:3).

(II) As pertaining to a private person and not to the public: private, particular, individual, as opposed to *dēmósios* (1219), public, open, and *koinós* (2839), common. Hence, in the NT, used adverbially:

(A) *Idía*, individually, severally, to each one (1Co 12:11).

(B) *Kat' idían* with the prep. *katá* (2596), according to, meaning privately, by oneself, apart from others (Mt 14:13, 23; 17:1, 19; Mk 4:34; 6:31; 9:2, 28; Ac 23:19; Gal 2:2).

Deriv.: *idiṓtēs* (2399), a common or private man.

2399. ἰδιώτης, idiōtēs, *id-ee-o´-tace*; from 2398; a *private* person, i.e. (by implication) an *ignoramus* (compare "idiot"):—ignorant, rude, unlearned.

Noun from *ídios* (2398), one's own. A private citizen, as opposed to someone in a public office. In the NT: plebeian, i.e. unlettered, unlearned, an amateur rather than a professional (Ac 4:13; 2Co 11:6). One who has not been initiated into Christian truth (1Co 14:16, 23, 24).

2400. ἰδού, idou, *id-oo´*; second person singular imperfect middle of 1492; used as imperonal *lo!*:—behold, lo, see.

2401. Ἰδουμαία, Idoumaia, *id-oo-mah´-yah*; of Hebrew origin [123]; *Idumæa* (i.e. *Edom*), a region East (and South) of Palestine:—Idumæa.

2402. ἱδρός, hidros, *hid-roce´*; a strengthened form of a primary ἴδος, *idos* (*sweat*); *perspiration*:—sweat.

2403. Ἰεζαβήλ, Iezabēl, *ee-ed-zab-ale´*; of Hebrew origin [348]; *Jezabel* (i.e. *Jezebel*), a Tyrian woman (used as a synonym of a termagant or false teacher):—Jezabel.

2404. Ἱεράπολις, Hierapolis, *hee-er-ap´-ol-is*; from 2413 and 4172; *holy city; Hierapolis*, a place in Asia Minor:—Hierapolis.

2405. ἱερατεία, hierateia, *hee-er-at-i´-ah*; from 2407; *priestliness*, i.e. the *sacerdotal function*:—office of the priesthood, priest's office.

2406. ἱεράτευμα, hierateuma, *hee-er-at´-yoo-mah*; from 2407; the *priestly fraternity*, i.e. a *sacerdotal order* (figurative):—priesthood.

2407. ἱερατεύω, hierateuō, *hee-er-at-yoo´-o*; prolonged from 2409; to *be a priest*, i.e. *perform his functions*:—execute the priest's office.

2408. Ἱερεμίας, Hieremias, *hee-er-em-ee´-as*; of Hebrew origin [3414]; *Hieremias* (i.e. *Jermijah*), an Israelite:—Jeremiah.

2409. ἱερεύς, hiereus, *hee-er-yooce´*; from 2413; a *priest* (literal or figurative):—(high) priest.

Noun from *hierós* (2413), sacred. A priest, one who performs the sacred rites:

(I) Used of heathen priests (Ac 14:13).

(II) Used also to denote the Jewish priests, the descendants of Aaron generally (Mt 8:4; 12:4, 5; Mk 1:44; 2:26; Lk 1:5; 5:14; 6:4; 10:31; 17:14; Jn 1:19; Ac 6:7; Heb 9:6). They were divided into twenty-four classes for the service of the temple (1Ch 24), and the heads of these classes were sometimes called *archiereís* (749), chief priests. These seem to be referred to in Ac 4:1. See Le 1:5. Spoken of the high priest (Heb 7:21, 23; 8:4; 10:11, 21).

(III) Of Melchizedek as a high priest of God (Heb 7:1, 3; see Ge 14:18; Ps 110:4); of Jesus as the spiritual High Priest (Heb 5:6; 7:11, 15, 17, 21; 10:21).

(IV) Figuratively, Christians are also called priests unto God as offering Him spiritual sacrifices (Rev 1:6; 5:10; 20:6 [cf. 1Pe 2:5]).

Deriv.: *archiereús* (749), high priest; *hierateúō* (2407), to officiate as a priest.

Syn.: *Levítēs* (3019), Levite, a servant of the priests.

2410. Ἱεριχώ, Hierichō, *hee-er-ee-kho´*; of Hebrew origin [3405]; *Jericho*, a place in Palestine:—Jericho.

2411. ἱερόν, hieron, *hee-er-on´*; neuter of 2413; a *sacred* place, i.e. the entire precincts (whereas 3485 denotes the central *sanctuary* itself) of the *temple* (at Jerusalem or elsewhere):—temple.

Noun from *hierós* (2413), sacred. temple.

(I) A temple, whether of the true God (Mt 12:5, 6) or an idol (Ac 19:27). It often includes not only the building but the courts and all the sacred ground or enclosure.

(II) In the NT, it always refers to the temple as rebuilt by Herod the Great, and minutely described by Josephus (Ant. 15.11.3). According to him, the temple consisted of three parts or enclosures with the temple proper or *naós* (3485) in the center and two circular courts or areas around it, one exterior to the other. Only the priests could enter the *naós,* which was divided into two parts (*tó hágion* [39], the sanctuary, and *tó Hágion Hagíōn*, the Holy of Holies). The whole temple, therefore, consisted strictly of two parts: the physical structure (*ho naós*) and the courts leading into it. Hence, *tó hierón* is used for the whole and also for the courts, but not for the *naós* exclusively.

(A) Generally, and for the whole (Mt 24:1; Mk 13:1, 3; Lk 21:5; 22:52).

(B) Of the courts (Mt 12:5; Mk 11:11; Lk 2:27, 37; 18:10; Ac 2:46; 3:1; 21:26).

(C) Of the outer court where things were bought and sold (Mt 21:12, 14, 15; Mk 11:15, 16). It was here that Jesus disputed and taught (Mt 21:23; 26:55; Mk 11:27; Lk 2:46; Jn 5:14; 7:14, 28); also the apostles (Ac 5:20, 21, 25, 42). The pinnacle of the temple (Mt 4:5; Lk 4:9) is probably a reference to the apex or summit of Solomon's porch which Josephus describes as being exterior to the temple itself on the east side and built up to the height of 400 cubits (600 feet) from the foundation in the Valley of Kidron below.

Deriv.: *hierósulos* (2417), one who robs churches or temples.

Syn.: *naós* (3485), temple.

2412. ἱεροπρεπής, hieroprepēs, *hee-er-op-rep-ace´*; from 2413 and the same as 4241; *reverent*:—as becometh holiness.

Adjective from *hierós* (2413), sacred, and *prépō* (4241), to suit, become. Fitting or appropriate for a sacred place or person, venerable. Only in Tit 2:3, older women ought to adorn their profession of Christ with their behaviour.

Syn.: *sebastós* (4575), venerable, august; *eulabḗs* (2126), pious, devout; *semnós* (4586), honourable, venerable.

2413. ἱερός, hieros, *hee-er-os´*; of uncertain affinity; *sacred*:—holy.

Adjective meaning sacred, dedicated to God:

(I) Used of the sacred Scriptures (2Ti 3:15).

(II) Used of the sacred services, sacred rites (1Co 9:13).

Deriv.: *hiereús* (2409), priest.

Syn.: *hósios* (3741), sacred.

2414. Ἱεροσόλυμα, Hierosoluma, *hee-er-os-ol´-oo-mah*; of Hebrew origin [3389]; *Hierosolyma* (i.e. *Jerushalaïm*), the capital of Palestine:—Jerusalem. Compare 2419.

2415. Ἱεροσολυμίτης, Hierosolumitēs, *hee-er-os-ol-oo-mee´-tace*; from 2414; a *Hierosolymite*, i.e. inhabitant of Hierosolyma:—of Jerusalem.

2416. ἱεροσυλέω, hierosuleō, *hee-er-os-ool-eh´-o*; from 2417; to *be a temple-robber* (figurative):—commit sacrilege.

From *hierósulos* (2417), a sacrilegious person, which is from *hierón* (2411), the temple, and *suláō* (4813), to rob. To rob temples, commit sacrilege. Only in Ro 2:22, where some believe it refers to robbing idol temples with no concern for the defilement caused by coming into contact with idolatry, while others believe it refers to a profaning of the temple of God (see Ne 13:10; Mal 3:8; Mt 21:12).

2417. ἱερόσυλος, hierosulos, *hee-er-os´-oo-los*; from 2411 and 4813; a *temple-despoiler*:—robber of churches.

Adjective from *hierón* (2411), temple, and *suláō* (4813), to rob, spoil. A robber of a temple, a sacrilegious person. Only in Ac 19:37.

Deriv.: *hierosuléō* (2416), to commit sacrilege.

2418. ἱερουργέω, hierourgeō, *hee-er-oorg-eh´-o*; from a compound of 2411 and the base of 2041; to *be a temple-worker*, i.e. *officiate as a priest* (figurative):—minister.

From *hierourgós* (n.f.), sacrificing, which is from *hierón* (2411), temple, and *érgon* (2041), work. To perform sacred rites, especially sacrifice; to officiate as a priest. Occurs only in Ro 15:16.

2419. Ἱερουσαλήμ, Hierousalēm, *hee-er-oo-sal-ame´*; of Hebrew origin [3389]; *Hierusalem* (i.e. *Jerushalem*), the capital of Palestine:—Jerusalem. Compare 2414.

2420. ἱερωσύνη, hierōsunē, *hee-er-o-soo´-nay*; from 2413; *sacredness*, i.e. (by implication) the *priestly office*:—priesthood.

2421. Ἰεσσαί, Iessai, *es-es-sah´ee*; of Hebrew origin [3448]; *Jessæ* (i.e. *Jishai*), an Israelite:—Jesse.

2422. Ἰεφθάε, Iephthae, *ee-ef-thah´-eh*; of Hebrew origin [3316]; *Jephthaë* (i.e. *Jiphtach*), an Israelite:—Jephthah.

2423. Ἰεχονίας, Iechonias, *ee-ekh-on-ee´-as*; of Hebrew origin [3204]; *Jechonias* (i.e. *Jekonjah*), an Israelite:—Jechonias.

2424. Ἰησοῦς, Iēsous, *ee-ay-sooce´*; of Hebrew origin [3091]; *Jesus* (i.e. *Jehoshua*), the name of our Lord and two (three) other Israelites:—Jesus.

2425. ἱκανός, hikanos, *hik-an-os´*; from ἵκω *hikō* [ἱκάνω or ἱκνέομαι; akin to 2240] (to *arrive*); *competent* (as if *coming* in season), i.e. *ample* (in amount) or *fit* (in character):—able, + content, enough, good, great, large, long (while), many, meet, much, security, sore, sufficient, worthy.

Adjective from *hiknéomai* (n.f.), to come. Sufficient:

(I) Of things: enough (Lk 22:38). Hence *tó hikanón*, satisfaction, as in to do or make satisfaction, to satisfy (Mk 15:15); to take satisfaction or security (Ac 17:9).

(II) Of persons: sufficient, adequate, capable (2Co 2:16; 3:5; 2Ti 2:2). With the meaning of worthy (Mt 3:11; 8:8; Mk 1:7; Lk 3:16; 7:6; 1Co 15:9).

(III) Referring to number: many (Mt 28:12, literally many pieces of silver; Lk 8:32; 23:9; Ac 12:12; 14:21; 19:19; 20:8; 1Co 11:30); with the plural of *hēméra* (2250), day, many days (Ac 9:23, 43; 18:18).

(IV) Referring to magnitude: abundant, great, much (Ac 22:6); with *óchlos* (3793), crowd, a great crowd, many people (Mk 10:46; Lk 7:12; Ac 11:24, 26; 19:26); with *chrónos* (5550), time, a long time (Lk 8:27; 23:8; Ac 8:11; 27:9).

Deriv.: *hikanótēs* (2426), sufficiency, ability, fitness; *hikanóō* (2427), to make sufficient or fit, equip.

Syn.: *arketós* (713), enough.

2426. ἱκανότης, hikanotēs, *hik-an-ot´-ace*; from 2425; *ability*:—sufficiency.

2427. ἱκανόω, hikanoō, *hik-an-o´-o*; from 2425; to *enable*, i.e. *qualify*:—make able (meet).

2428. ἱκετηρία, hiketēria, *hik-et-ay-ree´-ah*; from a derivative of the base of 2425 (through the idea of *approaching* for a favour); *intreaty*:—supplication.

Noun from *hikétēs* (n.f.), a suppliant. Supplication. Only in Heb 5:7.

Syn.: *déēsis* (1162), supplication for a particular need; *énteuxis* (1783), intercession; *paráklēsis* (3874), entreaty; *proseuchḗ* (4335), prayer to God.

2429. ἰκμάς, hikmas, *hik-mas´*; of uncertain affinity; *dampness*:—moisture.

2430. Ἰκόνιον, Ikonion, *ee-kon´-ee-on*; perhaps from 1504; *image-like*; *Iconium*, a place in Asia Minor:—Iconium.

2431. ἱλαρός, hilaros, *hil-ar-os´*; from the same as 2436; *propitious* or *merry* ("*hilarious*"), i.e. *prompt* or *willing*:—cheerful.

2432. ἱλαρότης, hilarotēs, *hil-ar-ot´-ace*; from 2431; *alacrity*:—cheerfulness.

2433. ἱλάσκομαι, hilaskomai, *hil-as´-kom-ahee*; middle from the same as 2436; to *conciliate*, i.e. (transitive) to *atone* for (sin), or (intransitive) *be propitious*:—be merciful, make reconciliation for.

From *hílaos* (n.f., see *híleōs* [2436]), propitious. To reconcile to oneself, to be propitious, gracious, as of gods; of men: to be kind, gentle, gracious. In the NT: to propitiate, make propitiation for sins (Heb 2:17). In the passive sense, to be propitious, merciful (Lk 18:13).

Deriv.: *hilasmós* (2434), propitiation; *hilastḗrion* (2435), propitiation, mercy seat.

Syn.: *eleéō* (1653), to show mercy; *oikteírō* (3627), to have compassion on.

2434. ἱλασμός, hilasmos, *hil-as-mos´*; *atonement*, i.e. (concretely) an *expiator*:—propitiation.

Noun from *hiláskomai* (2433), to propitiate, expiate. Propitiation, that which appeases anger and brings reconciliation with someone who has reason to be angry with one (1Jn 2:2; 4:10).

2435. ἱλαστήριον, hilastērion, *hil-as-tay´-ree-on*; neuter of a derivative of 2433; an *expiatory* (place or thing), i.e. (concretely) an atoning *victim*, or (special) the *lid* of the Ark (in the temple):—mercyseat, propitiation.

From *hiláskomai* (2433), to propitiate, expiate. Propitiatory, expiatory. In the NT in the neuter: a propitiator, one who makes propitiation (Ro 3:25); with the article, mercy seat (Heb 9:5), the lid or cover of the Ark of the Covenant, where the high priest would make propitiation once a year by sprinkling blood upon the mercy seat (Ex 25:17–22; Le 16:11–15).

2436. ἵλεως, hileōs, *hil´-eh-oce*; perhaps from the alternate form of 138; *cheerful* (as *attractive*), i.e. *propitious*; adverb (by Hebrew) God be *gracious!*, i.e. (in averting some calamity) *far* be it:—be it far, merciful.

Adjective, the Attic for *hílaos* (n.f.). Appeased, merciful, as of gods; cheerful, propitious, favourable, merciful. In the NT, of God: propitious, merciful (Heb 8:12). Used by Peter in Mt 16:22 as an exclamation, *híleōs soi,* literally "mercy to you" (see *soi* [4671], to you), meaning "May God have mercy on you and never allow this to happen."

Deriv.: *aníleōs* (448), unmerciful.

2437. Ἰλλυρικόν, Illurikon, *il-loo-ree-kon´*; neuter of an adjective from a name of uncertain derivative; (the) *Illyrican* (shore), i.e. (as a name itself) *Illyricum*, a region of Europe:—Illyricum.

2438. ἱμάς, himas, *hee-mas´*; perhaps from the same as 260; a *strap*, i.e. (special) the *tie* (of a sandal) or the *lash* (of a scourge):—latchet, thong.

2439. ἱματίζω, himatizō, *him-at-id´-zo*; from 2440; to *dress*:—clothe.

2440. ἱμάτιον, himation, *him-at´-ee-on*; neuter of a presumed derivative of **ἕννυμι**, *ennumi* (to *put on*); a *dress* (inner or outer):—apparel, cloke, clothes, garment, raiment, robe, vesture.

(I) Generally any garment (Mt 9:16; 11:8; Mk 2:21; Lk 5:36; 7:25; Heb 1:11). Plural with article: one's garments, clothing, raiment including the outer and inner garment, cape and shirt or coat (Mt 17:2; 24:18; 26:65; 27:31, 35; Mk 15:24; Jn 13:4, 12; Ac 14:14; 16:22; 22:23; Jas 5:2; Rev 4:4).

(II) The outer garment, mantle, cape (different from the tunic or *chitṓn* [5509]), a shirt over which the *himátion* is worn (cf. Ac 9:39). The *himátion* seems to have been a large piece of woolen cloth nearly square, which was wrapped around the body or fastened about the shoulders, and served also to wrap oneself in at night (Ex 22:26, 27); hence it might not be taken by a creditor, though the tunic could be (cf. Mt 5:40; Lk 6:29). See also Mt 9:20, 21; 21:7, 8; 14:36; Jn 19:2; Ac 7:58; 12:8; 22:20.

Deriv.: *himatízō* (2439), to clothe.

Syn.: *énduma* (1742), a garment of any kind; *ependútēs* (1903), an upper or outer garment which sometimes fishermen wore when at work; *esthḗs* (2066) and *ésthēsis* (2067), clothing; *himatismós* (2441), clothing, apparel; *katastolḗ* (2689), long robe of dignity; *peribólaion* (4018), a wrap or cape, a garment thrown around one; *podḗrēs* (4158), an outer garment reaching to the feet; *sképasma* (4629), a covering, raiment; *stolḗ* (4749), a stately robe or uniform, a long gown worn as a mark of dignity; *phelónēs* (5341), a mantle, traveling robe for protection against stormy weather, overcoat; *chlamús* (5511), a military cloak worn over the *chitṓn* by emperors, kings, magistrates, military officers; *chitṓn* (5509), tunic.

2441. ἱματισμός, himatismos, *him-at-is-mos´*; from 2439; *clothing*:—apparel (× -led), array, raiment, vesture.

Noun from *himatízō* (2439), to clothe. Clothing, raiment. Garments stately and costly (Mt 27:35; Lk 7:25; 9:29; Jn 19:24; Ac 20:33; 1Ti 2:9).

Syn.: For a list of various types of clothing, see the synonyms under *himátion* (2440), garment.

2442. ἱμείρομαι, himeiromai, *him-i´-rom-ahee*; middle from **ἵμερος**, *himeros* (a *yearning*; of uncertain affinity); to *long for*:—be affectionately desirous.

2443. ἵνα, hina, *hin´-ah*; probably from the same as the former part of 1438 (through the *demonstrative* idea; compare 3588); in order *that* (denoting the *purpose* or the *result*):—albeit, because, to the intent (that), lest, so as, (so) that, (for) to. Compare 3363.

2444. ἱνατί, hinati, *hin-at-ee´*; from 2443 and 5101; *for what* reason?, i.e. *why?*:—wherefore, why.

2445. Ἰόππη, Ioppē, *ee-op´-pay*; of Hebrew origin [3305]; *Joppe* (i.e. *Japho*), a place in Palestine:—Joppa.

2446. Ἰορδάνης, Iordanēs, *ee-or-dan´-ace*; of Hebrew origin [3383]; the *Jordanes* (i.e. *Jarden*), a river of Palestine:—Jordan.

2447. ἰός, ios, *ee-os´*; perhaps from **εἶμι**, *eimi* (to *go*) or **ἵημι**, *hiēmi* (to *send*); *rust* (as if *emitted* by metals); also *venom* (as *emitted* by serpents):—poison, rust.

2448. Ἰουδά, Iouda, *ee-oo-dah´*; of Hebrew origin [3063 or perhaps 3194]; *Judah* (i.e. *Jehudah* or *Juttah*), a part of (or place in) Palestine:—Judah.

2449. Ἰουδαία, Ioudaia, *ee-oo-dah´-yah*; feminine of 2453 (with 1093 implication); the *Judæan* land (i.e. *Judæa*), a region of Palestine:—Judæa.

2450. Ἰουδαΐζω, Ioudaïzō, *ee-oo-dah-id´-zo*; from 2453; to *become a Judæan*, i.e. "*Judaize*":—live as the Jews.

2451. Ἰουδαϊκός, Ioudaïkos, *ee-oo-dah-ee-kos´*; from 2453; *Judaïc*, i.e. *resembling a Judæan*:—Jewish.

2452. Ἰουδαϊκῶς, Ioudaïkōs, *ee-oo-dah-ee-koce´*; adverb from 2451; *Judaïcally* or *in a manner resembling a Judæan*:—as do the Jews.

2453. Ἰουδαῖος, Ioudaios, *ee-oo-dah´-yos*; from 2448 (in the sense of 2455 as a country); *Judæan*, i.e. belonging to *Jehudah*:—Jew (-ess), of Judæa.

2454. Ἰουδαϊσμός, Ioudaismos, *ee-oo-dah-is-mos´*; from 2450; "*Judaïsm,*" i.e. the *Jewish faith* and usages:—Jews' religion.

2455. Ἰουδάς, Ioudas, *ee-oo-das´*; of Hebrew origin [3063]; *Judas* (i.e. *Jehudah*), the name of ten Israelites; also of the posterity of one of them and its region:—Juda (-h, -s); Jude.

2456. Ἰουλία, Ioulia, *ee-oo-lee´-ah*; feminine of the same as 2457; *Julia*, a Christian woman:—Julia.

2457. Ἰούλιος, Ioulios, *ee-oo´-lee-os*; of Latin origin; *Julius*, a centurion:—Julius.

2458. Ἰουνίας, Iounias, *ee-oo-nee´-as*; of Latin origin; *Junias*, a Christian:—Junias.

2459. Ἰοῦστος, Ioustos, *ee-ooce´-tos*; of Latin origin ("*just*"); *Justus*, the name of three Christians:—Justus.

2460. ἱππεύς, hippeus, *hip-yooce´*; from 2462; an *equestrian*, i.e. member of a *cavalry* corps:—horseman.

2461. ἱππικόν, hippikon, *hip-pee-kon´*; neuter of a derivative of 2462; the *cavalry* force:—horse [-men].

2462. ἵππος, hippos, *hip´-pos*; of uncertain affinity; a *horse*:—horse.

2463. ἶρις, iris, *ee´-ris*; perhaps from 2046 (as a symbol of the female *messenger* of the pagan deities); a *rainbow* ("*iris*"):—rainbow.

2464. Ἰσαάκ, Isaak, *ee-sah-ak´*; of Hebrew origin [3327]; *Isaac* (i.e. *Jitschak*), the son of Abraham:—Isaac.

2465. ἰσάγγελος, isaggelos, *ee-sang´-el-los*; from 2470 and 32; *like an angel*, i.e. *angelic*:—equal unto the angels.

Adjective from *ísos* (2470), similar or equal, and *ággelos* (32) angel. Angel-like. Only in Lk 20:36.

2466. Ἰσαχάρ, Isachar, *ee-sakh-ar´*; of Hebrew origin [3485]; *Isachar* (i.e. *Jissaskar*), a son of Jacob (figurative, his descendant):—Issachar.

2467. ἴσημι, isēmi, *is´-ay-mee*; assumed by some as the base of certain irregular forms of 1942; to *know*:—know.

2468. ἴσθι, isthi, *is´-thee*; second person imperfect preson of 1510; *be* thou:— + agree, be, × give thyself wholly to.

2469. Ἰσκαριώτης, Iskariōtēs, *is-kar-ee-o´-tace*; of Hebrew origin [probably 377 and 7149]; *inhabitant of Kerioth*; *Iscariotes* (i.e. *Keriothite*), an epithet of Judas the traitor:—Iscariot.

2470. ἴσος, isos, *ee´-sos*; probably from 1492 (through the idea of *seeming*); *similar* (in amount or kind):— + agree, as much, equal, like.

2471. ἰσότης, isotēs, *ee-sot´-ace*; *likeness* (in condition or proportion); (by implication) *equity*:—equal (-ity).

2472. ἰσότιμος, isotimos, *ee-sot´-ee-mos*; from 2470 and 5092; *of equal value* or *honour*:—like precious.

2473. ἰσόψυχος, isopsuchos, *ee-sop´-soo-khos*; from 2470 and 5590; *of similar spirit*:—like-minded.

Adjective from *ísos* (2470), equal, and *psuchḗ* (5590), soul, mind. Like-minded. Only in Php 2:20.

Syn.: *homóphrōn* (3675), like-minded.

2474. Ἰσραήλ, Israēl, *is-rah-ale´*; of Hebrew origin [3478]; *Israel* (i.e. *Jisrael*), the adopted name of Jacob, including his descendant (literal or figurative):—Israel.

2475. Ἰσραηλίτης, Israēlitēs, *is-rah-ale-ee´-tace*; from 2474; an "*Israelite*," i.e. descendant of Israel (literal or figurative):—Israelite.

2476. ἵστημι, histēmi, *his´-tay-mee*; a prolonged form of a primary **στάω**, ***staō***, *stah´-o* (of the same meaning, and used for it in certain tenses); to *stand* (transitive or intransitive), used in various applications (literal or figurative):—abide, appoint, bring, continue, covenant, establish, hold up, lay, present, set (up), stanch, stand (by, forth, still, up). Compare 5087.

To stand, to place:

(I) Transitively: to cause to stand, to set or place:

(A) With adjuncts implying the place where (Mt 4:5; 25:33; Lk 9:47; Ac 5:27; 22:30). Generally: to cause to stand forth (Ac 1:23; 6:13; Ro 14:4).

(B) To establish, confirm (Ro 3:31; 10:3; Heb 10:9). Of time: to fix, appoint (Ac 17:31).

(C) To place in a balance, i.e. to weigh out (Mt 26:15). Metaphorically: to impute, e.g., sin unto someone (Ac 7:60).

(D) In the passive: to be established, stand firm, stand (Mt 12:25, 26; Mk 3:25); to be confirmed (Mt 18:16; 2Co 13:1).

(II) Intransitively: to stand:

(A) As opposed to falling (1Co 10:12); also standing in prayer or sacrifice (Mt 6:5; Heb 10:11). With adjuncts implying the place where (Mt 12:46; 13:2; Mk 11:5; Lk 1:11; 6:17; 9:27; Jn 20:11, 19; Ac 5:20, 23; 24:21; Rev 7:9, 11; 10:5). Without an adjunct of place expressed, but in the sense of to stand by, near, there, according to the context, i.e. to be present (Mt 26:73; Lk 19:8; 23:35; Jn 1:35; 3:29; 7:37; 18:18; Ac 2:14). Of persons standing before a judge, either as accusers (Lk 23:10) or as accused (Ac 26:6). Also before Christ as Judge, where it is (by implication) to stand firm in the consciousness of acquittal and final approval (Lk 21:36). Spoken of fishing boats: to stand or be stationed, lie (Lk 5:2).

(B) Figuratively: to stand fast, i.e. to continue, endure, persist, e.g., of things (Mt 12:25; Lk 11:18; 2Ti 2:19); of persons (Ac 26:22; 1Co 7:37; Col 4:12; Rev 6:17). To stand fast against an enemy, as opposed to *pheúgō* (5343), to run away (Eph 6:11, 13). In the sense of to be established, confirmed (Mt 18:16; 2Co 13:1).

(C) In the aorist tense, to stand still, stop, e.g., of persons (Mt 20:32; Mk 10:49; Lk 7:14; 18:40); of things (Mt 2:9; Ac 8:38); to cease (Lk 8:44); to remain, abide, continue (Jn 8:44).

Deriv.: *anthístēmi* (436), to oppose; *anístēmi* (450), to raise (transitively), and to rise (intransitively); *aphístēmi* (868), to withdraw from or stand away from; *diḯstēmi* (1339), to remove; *enístēmi* (1764), to be present; *exístēmi* (1839), to be amazed; *epístamai* (1987), to understand; *ephístēmi* (2186), to approach, be present; *kathístēmi* (2525), to appoint a person to a position; *methístēmi* or *methistánō* (3179), to remove; *parístēmi* or *paristánō* (3936), to stand by or beside; *periḯstēmi* (4026), to stand around; *proḯstēmi* (4291), to preside, rule; *prōtostátēs* (4414), a leader or captain; *stádios* (4712), furlong, race; *stámnos* (4713), a jar, earthen pot; *stásis* (4714), an uprising; *statḗr* (4715), piece of money; *staurós* (4716), stake, cross; *stḗthos* (4738), the breast; *stḗkō* (4739), to stand firm; *stērízō* (4741), to set fast, to fix firmly; *stoá* (4745), a pillar, column; *sunistánō* (4921), to commend, consist.

Syn.: *anorthóō* (461), to set straight or up; *bebaióō* (950), to confirm, establish; *egeírō* (1453), to raise; *keímai* (2749), to lie, set; *ménō* (3306), abide, continue, stand; *paragínomai* (3854), to be beside, present; *stereóō* (4732), to make firm; *stērízō* (4741), to fix, make fast, set; *tássō* (5021), to place in order.

2477. ἱστορέω, historeō, *his-tor-eh´-o*; from a derivative of 1492; to *be knowing* (*learned*), i.e. (by implication) to *visit* for information (*interview*):—see.

2478. ἰσχυρός, ischuros, *is-khoo-ros´*; from 2479; *forcible* (literal or figurative):—boisterous, mighty (-ier), powerful, strong (-er, man), valiant.

2479. ἰσχύς, ischus, *is-khoos´*; from a derivative of **ἴς**, ***his*** (*force*; compare **ἔσχον**, ***eschon***, a form of 2192); *forcefulness* (literal or figurative):—ability, might ([-ily]), power, strength.

Noun from *is* (n.f.), strength, and *échō* (2192), to have. Strength, might, power, both of body and mind. Physical (Rev 18:2, literally, "with a mighty voice"); mental and moral (Mk 12:30, 33; Lk 10:27; 1Pe 4:11). Also generally: power, potency, preeminence (Eph 1:19; 2Th 1:9; 2Pe 2:11). So in ascriptions to God (Rev 5:12; 7:12).

Deriv.: *ischúō* (2480), to be strong.

Syn.: *dúnamis* (1411), power; *enérgeia* (1753), energy, efficiency, effectual working; *exousía* (1849), authority or the right to exercise power; *krátos* (2904), dominion, the outward manifestation of power; *megaleiótēs* (3168), greatness, mighty power.

2480. ἰσχύω, ischuō, *is-khoo´-o*; from 2479; to *have* (or *exercise*) *force* (literal or figurative):—be able, avail, can do ([-not]), could, be good, might, prevail, be of strength, be whole, + much work.

From *ischús* (2479), strength. To be strong, i.e. to have strength, ability, power, both physical and moral:

(I) Physically: to be strong, robust (Mt 9:12; Mk 2:17).

(II) Generally: to be able, followed by the inf. (Mt 8:28; 26:40; Mk 5:4; 14:37; Lk 6:48; 8:43; 14:6, 29, 30; 16:3; 20:26; Jn 21:6; Ac 6:10; 15:10; 25:7; 27:16). With the inf. implied (Mk 9:18; Lk 13:24; Php 4:13, either "I can do all things" or "I can endure all things").

(III) To have efficacy, to avail, have force and value (Gal 5:6; 6:15; Heb 9:17; Jas 5:16).

(IV) To prevail against or over anyone (Ac 19:16; Rev 12:8). Figuratively: to spread abroad, to acquire strength and be effective (Ac 19:20).

Deriv.: *enischúō* (1765), to be strong; *exischúō* (1840), to be able; *epischúō* (2001), to be stronger; *ischurós* (2478), strong, powerful; *katischúō* (2729), to overpower, prevail against.

Syn.: *dúnamai* (1410), to be able, have power; *dunatéō* (1414), to show oneself powerful; *krataióō* (2901), to become strong; *nikáō* (3528), to conquer, prevail; *stereóō* (4732), to confirm, make firm; *hugiaínō* (5198), to be in good health.

2481. ἴσως, isōs, *ee´-soce*; adverb from 2470; *likely*, i.e. *perhaps*:—it may be.

2482. Ἰταλία, Italia, *ee-tal-ee´-ah*; probably of foreign origin; *Italia*, a region of Europe:—Italy.

2483. Ἰταλικός, Italikos, *ee-tal-ee-kos´*; from 2482; *Italic*, i.e. belonging to Italia:—Italian.

2484. Ἰτουραῖα, Itouraia, *ee-too-rah´-yah*; of Hebrew origin [3195]; *Ituræa* (i.e. *Jetur*), a region of Palestine:—Ituræa.

2485. ἰχθύδιον, ichthudion, *ikh-thoo´-dee-on*; diminutive from 2486; a *petty fish*:—little (small) fish.

2486. ἰχθύς, ichthus, *ikh-thoos´*; of uncertain affinity; a *fish*:—fish.

2487. ἴχνος, ichnos, *ikh´-nos*; from **ἰκνέομαι, *ikneomai*** (to *arrive*; compare 2240); a *track* (figurative):—step.

2488. Ἰωαθαμ, Iōatham, *ee-o-ath´-am*; of Hebrew origin [3147]; *Joatham* (i.e. *Jotham*), an Israelite:—Joatham.

2489. Ἰωάννα, Iōanna, *ee-o-an´-nah*; feminine of the same as 2491; *Joanna*, a Christian:—Joanna.

2490. Ἰωαννᾶς, Iōannas, *ee-o-an-nas´*; a form of 2491; *Joannas*, an Israelite:—Joannas.

2491. Ἰωάννης, Iōannēs, *ee-o-an´-nace*; of Hebrew origin [3110]; *Joannes* (i.e. *Jochanan*), the name of four Israelites:—John.

2492. Ἰώβ, Iōb, *ee-obe´*; of Hebrew origin [347]; *Job* (i.e. *Ijob*), a patriarch:—Job.

2493. Ἰωήλ, Iōēl, *ee-o-ale´*; of Hebrew origin [3100]; *Joel*, an Israelite:—Joel.

2494. Ἰωνάν, Iōnan, *ee-o-nan´*; probably for 2491 or 2495; *Jonan*, an Israelite:—Jonan.

2495. Ἰωνᾶς, Iōnas, *ee-o-nas´*; of Hebrew origin [3124]; *Jonas* (i.e. *Jonah*), the name of two Israelites:—Jonas.

2496. Ἰωράμ, Iōram, *ee-o-ram´*; of Hebrew origin [3141]; *Joram*, an Israelite:—Joram.

2497. Ἰωρείμ, Iōreim, *ee-o-rime´*; perhaps for 2496; *Jorim*, an Israelite:—Jorim.

2498. Ἰωσαφάτ, Iōsaphat, *ee-o-saf-at´*; of Hebrew origin [3092]; *Josaphat* (i.e. *Jehoshaphat*), an Israelite:—Josaphat.

2499. Ἰωσή, Iōsē, *ee-o-say´*; genitive of 2500; *Jose*, an Israelite:—Jose.

2500. Ἰωσῆς, Iōsēs, *ee-o-sace´*; perhaps for 2501; *Joses*, the name of two Israelites:—Joses. Compare 2499.

2501. Ἰωσήφ, Iōsēph, *ee-o-safe´*; of Hebrew origin [3130]; *Joseph*, the name of seven Israelites:—Joseph.

2502. Ἰωσίας, Iōsias, *ee-o-see´-as*; of Hebrew origin [2977]; *Josias* (i.e. *Joshiah*), an Israelite:—Josias.

2503. ἰῶτα, iōta, *ee-o´-tah*; of Hebrew origin [the tenth letter of the Hebrew alphabet]; "*iota*," the name of the eighth letter of the Greek alphabet, put (figurative) for a very small part of anything:—jot.

2504. κἀγώ, kagō, *kag-o´*; from 2532 and 1473 (so also the dative **κἀμοί, *kamoi***, *kam-oy´*; and accusative **κἀμέ, *kame***, *kam-eh´*); *and* (or *also, even*, etc.) *I*, (*to*) *me*:—(and, even, even so, so) I (also, in like wise), both me, me also.

2505. καθά, katha, *kath-ah´*; from 2596 and the neuter plural of 3739; *according to which* things, i.e. *just as*:—as.

2506. καθαίρεσις, kathairesis, *kath-ah´ee-res-is*; from 2507; *demolition*; (figurative) *extinction*:—destruction, pulling down.

2507. καθαιρέω, kathaireō, *kath-ahee-reh´-o*; from 2596 and 138 (including its alternate); to *lower* (or with violence) *demolish* (literal or figurative):—cast (pull, put, take) down, destroy.

2508. καθαίρω, kathairō, *kath-ah´ee-ro*; from 2513; to *cleanse*, i.e. (special) to *prune*; (figurative) to *expiate*:—purge.

From *katharós* (2513), pure, clean, without stain or spot. To cleanse from filth, purify. In the NT: to cleanse a tree or vine from useless branches, to prune (Jn 15:2). Figuratively, to cleanse from sin, to purify by making atonement (Heb 10:2).

Deriv.: *akáthartos* (169), unclean; *ekkathaírō* (1571), to purge out, cleanse thoroughly.

Syn.: *katharízō* (2511), to cleanse, make free from admixture. Also *hagnízō* (48), to cleanse from defilement, to purify ceremonially or morally.

2509. καθάπερ, kathaper, *kath-ap´-er*; from 2505 and 4007; *exactly as*:—(even, as well) as.

2510. καθάπτω, kathaptō, *kath-ap´-to*; from 2596 and 680; to *seize upon*:—fasten on.

2511. καθαρίζω, katharizō, *kath-ar-id´-zo*; from 2513; to *cleanse* (literal or figurative):—(make) clean (-se), purge, purify.

From *katharós* (2513), pure. To cleanse, free from filth:

(I) Particularly (Mt 23:25, 26; Lk 11:39). Spoken of lepers afflicted with a filthy disease and accounted as unclean: to cleanse, i.e. to heal (Mt 8:2, 3; 10:8; 11:5; Mk 1:40–42; Lk 4:27; 17:14, 17).

(II) Figuratively: to cleanse in a moral sense, i.e. from sin or pollution, by blood atonement (Heb 9:14, 22, 23; 1Jn 1:7); with no reference to blood atonement: to purify (Ac 15:9; 2Co 7:1; Jas 4:8); in the sense of to declare clean, i.e. Levitically: to make lawful (Mk 7:19; Ac 10:15; 11:9).

Deriv.: *diakatharízō* (1245), to cleanse thoroughly; *katharismós* (2512), the action or the result of cleansing, purification.

2512. καθαρισμός, katharismos, *kath-ar-is-mos´*; from 2511; a *washing* off, i.e. (ceremonial) *ablution*, (moral) *expiation*:—cleansing, + purge, purification, (-fying).

Noun from *katharízō* (2511), to make clean. Purification:

(I) Particularly, e.g., of the Jewish washings before meals (Jn 2:6); figuratively, of the ceremonial purification of lepers (Mk 1:44; Lk 5:14). Also of a woman after childbirth (Lk 2:22) and of baptism as a rite of purification (Jn 3:25).

(II) Metaphorically: purification from sin, expiation (Heb 1:3; 2Pe 1:9).

Syn.: *hagnismós* (49), ceremonial cleansing, purification; *baptismós* (909), ablution.

2513. καθαρός, katharos, *kath-ar-os´*; of uncertain affininity; *clean* (literal or figurative):—clean, clear, pure.

Adjective meaning clean, pure, in a natural sense: unsoiled, unalloyed:

(I) Particularly (Mt 27:59; Jn 13:10; Heb 10:22; Rev 15:6; 19:8, 14; 21:18, 21; 22:1). Used figuratively, in the Levitical sense (Jn 13:10); by implication: lawful, not forbidden (Ro 14:20; Tit 1:15).

(II) Metaphorically: clean, pure, in a moral sense, i.e. guiltless, innocent (Ac 18:6; 20:26); sincere, upright, void of evil (Mt 5:8; Jn 13:11; 1Ti 1:5; 3:9; 2Ti 1:3; 2:22; 1Pe 1:22).

Deriv.: *kathaírō* (2508), to cleanse; *katharízō* (2511) to make clean; *katharótēs* (2514), purity.

2514. καθαρότης, katharotēs, *kath-ar-ot´-ace*; from 2513; *cleanness* (ceremonial):—purification.

Noun from *katharós* (2513), pure. Purity. Only in Heb 9:13.

Deriv.: *akathártēs* (168), uncleanness.

2515. καθέδρα, kathedra, *kath-ed´-rah*; from 2596 and the same as 1476; a *bench* (literal or figurative):—seat.

2516. καθέζομαι, kathezomai, *kath-ed´-zom-ahee*; from 2596 and the base of 1476; to *sit down*:—sit.

2517. καθεξῆς, kathexēs, *kath-ex-ace´*; from 2596 and 1836; *thereafter*, i.e. *consecutively*; as a noun (by ellipsis of noun) a *subsequent* person or time:—after (-ward), by (in) order.

2518. καθεύδω, katheudō, *kath-yoo´-do*; from 2596 and **εὕδω, *heudō*** (to *sleep*); to lie *down to rest*, i.e. (by implication) to *fall asleep* (literal or figurative):—(be a-) sleep.

2519. καθηγητής, kathēgētēs, *kath-ayg-ay-tace´*; from a compound of 2596 and 2233; a *guide*, i.e. (figurative) a *teacher*:—master.

2520. καθήκω, kathēkō, *kath-ay´-ko*; from 2596 and 2240; to *reach to*, i.e. (neuter of presumed active participle, figurative as adjective) *becoming*:—convenient, fit.

2521. κάθημαι, kathēmai, *kath´-ay-mahee*; from 2596 and **ἧμαι, *hēmai*** (to *sit*; akin to the base of 1476); to *sit down*; (figurative) to *remain, reside*:—dwell, sit (by, down).

2522. καθημερινός, kathēmerinos, *kath-ay-mer-ee-nos´*; from 2596 and 2250; *quotidian*:—daily.

2523. καθίζω, kathizō, *kath-id´-zo*; another (active) form for 2516; to *seat down*, i.e. *set* (figurative, *appoint*); intransitive to *sit* (down); (figurative) to *settle* (*hover, dwell*):—continue, set, sit (down), tarry.

2524. καθίημι, kathiēmi, *kath-ee´-ay-mee*; from 2596 and **ἵημι, *hiēmi*** (to *send*); to *lower*:—let down.

2525. καθίστημι, kathistēmi, *kath-is´-tay-mee*; from 2596 and 2476; to *place down* (permanently), i.e. (figurative) to *designate, constitute, convoy*:—appoint, be, conduct, make, ordain, set.

From *katá* (2596), down, and *hístēmi* (2476), to stand. To set, set down, place:

(I) To set, place. Transitively: to set down, bring to pass, cause to stand (Ac 17:15). Metaphorically: to stand, to be set, i.e. to be (Jas 3:6; 4:4). To cause to be, to make (2Pe 1:8); pass.: to be made, to become, Ro 5:19).

(II) Of persons: to set, to appoint, to place in charge of something (Mt 24:45, 47; 25:21, 23; Lk 12:42, 44; Ac 6:3); with double accusative: to appoint someone to a position, to put in a situation or position (Lk 12:14; Ac 7:10, 27, 35; Heb 7:28).

Deriv.: *akatástatos* (182), unstable; *antikathístēmi* (478), to resist; *apokathístēmi* (600), to restore; *katástēma* (2688), behaviour.

Syn.: *anadeíknumi* (322), to appoint to a position or a service; *diatássō* (1299), to appoint, prescribe; *tássō* (5021), to place in order; *títhēmi* (5087), to put; *cheirotonéō* (5500), to appoint by placing hands on as in the appointment of elders.

2526. καθό, katho, *kath-o´*; from 2596 and 3739; *according to which* thing, i.e. *precisely as, in proportion as*:—according to that, (inasmuch) as. And **καθολικός *katholikos***, *kath-ol-ee-kos´*, from 2527; *universal*:—general.

2527. καθόλου, katholou, *kath-ol´-oo*; from 2596 and 3650; *on the whole*, i.e. *entirely*:—at all.

2528. καθοπλίζω, kathoplizō, *kath-op-lid´-zo*; from 2596 and 3695; to *equip fully* with armour:—arm.

2529. καθοράω, kathoraō, *kath-or-ah´-o*; from 2596 and 3708; to *behold fully*, i.e. (figurative) *distinctly apprehend*:—clearly see.

2530. καθότι, kathoti, *kath-ot´-ee*; from 2596 and 3739 and 5100; *according to which certain* thing, i.e. *as far* (or *inasmuch*) *as*:—(according, forasmuch) as, because (that).

2531. καθώς, kathōs, *kath-oce´*; from 2596 and 5613; *just* (or *inasmuch*) *as, that*:—according to, (according, even) as, how, when.

2532. καί, kai, *kahee*; apparently a primary particle, having a *copulative* and sometimes also a *cumulative* force; *and, also, even, so, then, too*, etc.; often used in connection (or composition) with other particles or small words:—and, also, both, but, even, for, if, or, so, that, then, therefore, when, yet.

2533. Καϊάφας, Kaïaphas, *kah-ee-af´-as*; of Chaldee origin; *the dell*; *Caïaphas* (i.e. *Cajepha*), an Israelite:—Caiaphas.

2534. καίγε, kaige, *ka´hee-gheh*; from 2532 and 1065; *and at least* (or *even, indeed*):—and, at least.

2535. Κάϊν, Kaïn, *kah´-in*; of Hebrew origin [7014]; *Caïn* (i.e. *Cajin*), the son of Adam:—Cain.

2536. Καϊνάν, Kaïnan, *Kah-ee-nan´*; of Hebrew origin [7018]; *Caïnan* (i.e. *Kenan*), the name of two patriarchs:—Cainan.

2537. καινός, kainos, *kahee-nos´*; of uncertain affinity; *new* (especially in *freshness*; while 3501 is properly so with respect to *age*):—new.

(I) Newly made, not impaired by time or use, spoken of: new skins used as containers (Mt 9:17; Mk 2:22; Lk 5:38); a grave or sepulchre (Mt 27:60; Jn 19:41); a garment (Lk 5:36). Also Mt 13:52, "treasures new and old."

(II) New, i.e. current or not before known, newly introduced. Spoken of a new: doctrine (Mk 1:27; Ac 17:19); commandment or precept (Jn 13:34; 1Jn 2:7, 8; 2Jn 5); name (Rev 2:17; 3:12). In the comparative degree, i.e. newer (Ac 17:21). In the sense of other, i.e. foreign or different, spoken of tongues or languages (Mk 16:17).

(III) New, as opposed to old or former and hence also implying better, as *kainḗ diathḗkē* ([1242] testament), a new and better covenant (Mt 26:28; Mk 14:24; Lk 22:20; 1Co 11:25; Heb 8:8, 13); "a new song," i.e. a nobler, loftier strain (Rev 5:9; 14:3). Also for renewed, made new, and therefore superior, more splendid, e.g. "new heavens and a new earth" (2Pe 3:13; Rev 21:1); the "new Jerusalem" (Rev 3:12; 21:2). Metaphorically, speaking of Christians who are renewed and changed from evil to good by the Spirit of God: a new creation (2Co 5:17; Gal 6:15), a new man (Eph 2:15; 4:24).

Deriv.: *egkaínia* (1456), dedication; *kainótēs* (2538), newness.

Syn.: *néos* (3501), new.

2538. καινότης, kainotēs, *kahee-not´-ace*; from 2537; *renewal* (figurative):—newness.

Noun from *kainós* (2537), new. Newness. In the NT used in a moral sense (Ro 6:4; 7:6). See *kainós* (2537, III).

Syn.: *neótēs* (3503), newness, youthfulness; *anakaínōsis* (342), renewing.

2539. καίπερ, kaiper, *kah´ee-per*; from 2532 and 4007; *and indeed*, i.e. *nevertheless* or *notwithstanding*:—and yet, although.

2540. καιρός, kairos, *kahee-ros´*; of uncertain affinity; an *occasion*, i.e. *set* or *proper* time:— × always, opportunity, (convenient, due) season, (due, short, while) time, a while. Compare 5550.

Right proportion, just measure. In the NT, used only of time, season:

(I) Fit time, proper season:

(A) Generally equivalent to opportunity, occasion (Ac 24:25; 2Co 6:2; Gal 6:10; Eph 5:16; Col 4:5; Heb 11:15).

(B) Appointed time, set time, certain season, equivalent to a fixed and definite time or season (Mt 13:30; 21:34, 41; 26:18; Mk 11:13; Lk 8:13; 19:44; Jn 7:6; Ac 3:19; Gal 6:9; 2Ti 4:6; Heb 9:10; 11:11; Rev 11:18). With a demonstrative article or pron., e.g., this present time, that time, definitely marked out and expressed (Mt 11:25; 12:1; 14:1; Mk 10:30; Lk 13:1; 18:30; Ro 11:5; 2Co 8:14). Generally (Mk 12:2; Ac 17:26; Gal 4:10; 2Ti 4:3; Rev 12:12). So in allusion to the set time for the coming of the Messiah in His kingdom or for judgement (Mt 8:29; 16:3; Mk 1:15; 13:33; Lk 12:56; 21:8; Ac 1:7; Ro 13:11; 1Co 7:29; Eph 1:10; 1Th 5:1; 1Pe 1:11; 4:17; Rev 1:3; 22:10).

(II) Generally meaning time, season, equivalent to *chrónos* (5550):

(A) Particularly (Lk 21:36; Eph 6:18); a season of the year (Ac 14:17); in a prophetic style as used for a year (Rev 12:14).

Deriv.: *akairéomai* (170), to lack opportunity; *akaírōs* (171), inopportunely, out of season; *eúkairos* (2121), well-timed; *próskairos* (4340), recent, temporary, temporal, for a season.

Syn.: *chrónos* (5550), time, duration of a period; *hēméra* (2250), day as a point in time, era; *hṓra* (5610), hour, used sometimes with the meaning of season, opportunity.

2541. Καῖσαρ, Kaisar, *Kah´ee-sar*; of Latin origin; *Cæsar*, a title of the Roman emperor:—Cæsar.

2542. Καισάρεια, Kaisareia, *kahee-sar´-i-a*; from 2541; *Cæsaria*, the name of two places in Palestine:—Cæsarea.

2543. καίτοι, kaitoi, *kah´ee-toy*; from 2532 and 5104; *and yet*, i.e. *nevertheless*:—although.

2544. καίτοιγε, kaitoige, *kah´ee-toyg-eh*; from 2543 and 1065; *and yet indeed*, i.e. *although really*:—nevertheless, though.

2545. καίω, kaiō, *kah´-yo*; apparently a primary verb; to *set on fire*, i.e. *kindle* or (by implication) *consume*:—burn, light.

2546. κἀκεῖ, kakei, *kak-i´*; from 2532 and 1563; *likewise in that place*:—and there, there (thither) also.

2547. κἀκεῖθεν, kakeithen, *kak-i´-then*; from 2532 and 1564; *likewise from that place* (or *time*):—and afterward (from) (thence), thence also.

2548. κακεῖνος, kakeinos, *kak-i´-nos*; from 2532 and 1565; *likewise that* (or *those*):—and him (other, them), even he, him also, them (also), (and) they.

2549. κακία, kakia, *kak-ee´-ah*; from 2556; *badness*, i.e. (subject) *depravity*, or (active) *malignity*, or (passive) *trouble*:—evil, malice (-iousness), naughtiness, wickedness.

Noun from *kakós* (2556), bad. Badness. In the NT: evil in a moral sense:

(I) Wickedness of heart, life, and character (Ac 8:22; 1Co 14:20; Jas 1:21; 1Pe 2:16).

(II) In an act. sense: malice, the desire to do evil to others (1Co 5:8; Eph 4:31; Col 3:8; Tit 3:3; 1Pe 2:1).

(III) Evil, i.e. trouble, affliction (Mt 6:34).

Syn.: *adíkēma* (92), injustice, iniquity; *adikía* (93), unrighteousness; *hamartía* (266), sin; *anomía* (458), lawlessness; *paranomía* (3892), transgression.

2550. κακοήθεια, kakoētheia, *kak-o-ay´-thi-ah*; from a compound of 2556 and 2239; *bad character*, i.e. (special) *mischievousness*:—malignity.

Noun from *kakoḗthēs* (n.f.), mischievous, which is from *kakós* (2556), bad, evil, and *ḗthos* (2239), disposition, custom. Mischief, malignity, evil habit, the desire to do evil to others. Occurs only in Ro 1:29.

2551. κακολογέω, kakologeō, *kak-ol-og-eh´-o*; from a compound of 2556 and 3056; to *revile*:—curse, speak evil of.

2552. κακοπάθεια, kakopatheia, *kak-op-ath´-i-ah*; from a compound of 2556 and 3806; *hardship*:—suffering affliction.

Noun from *kakopathéō* (2553), to suffer misfortune, hardship. A suffering of evil, i.e. suffering, affliction (Jas 5:10).

Syn.: *diōgmós* (1375), persecution; *thlípsis* (2347), pressure and hence affliction, being squeezed from the outside, constriction; *kákōsis* (2561), affliction, ill-treatment; *páthēma* (3804), suffering, affliction; *stenochōría* (4730), anguish; *sunochḗ* (4928), being in straits, distress; *tarachḗ* (5016), agitation, disturbance, trouble.

2553. κακοπαθέω, kakopatheō, *kak-op-ath-eh´-o*; from the same as 2552; to *undergo hardship*:—be afflicted, endure afflictions (hardness), suffer trouble.

From *kakopathḗs* (n.f.), suffering ill, which is from *kakós* (2556), evil, and *páthos* (3806), passion. To suffer evil or afflictions, to be afflicted (2Ti 2:9; Jas 5:13). Especially of soldiers and others: to endure hardships (2Ti 2:3; 4:5).

Deriv.: *kakopátheia* (2552), suffering, affliction; *sugkakopathéō* (4777), to suffer hardship with someone.

Syn.: *basanízō* (928), to toil, be tormented; *odunáō* (3600) to be tormented; *talaipōréō* (5003), to be afflicted, suffer hardship, be miserable.

2554. κακοποιέω, kakopoieō, *kak-op-oy-eh´-o*; from 2555; to *be a bad-doer*, i.e. (object) to *injure*, or (genitive) to *sin*:—do (-ing) evil.

From *kakopoiós* (2555), evildoer. To do evil to others, i.e. to injure, to harm (Mk 3:4; Lk 6:9); generally: to commit sin (1Pe 3:17; 3Jn 11).

Syn.: *kakóō* (2559), to ill-treat, exasperate, vex, afflict; *basanízo* (928), to torment; *bláptō* (984), to injure, hurt.

2555. κακοποιός, kakopoios, *kak-op-oy-os´*; from 2556 and 4160; a *bad-doer*; (special) a *criminal*:—evildoer, malefactor.

Adjective from *kakós* (2556), evil, and *poiéō* (4160), to do or make. An evildoer (1Pe 2:12, 14; 3:16; 4:15). Spoken falsely of Christ (Jn 18:30).

Deriv.: *kakopoiéō* (2554), to do evil.

Syn.: *kakoúrgos* (2557), evil worker, malefactor; *ponērós* (4190), one of the names attributed to Satan, malevolent.

2556. κακός, kakos, *kak-os´*; apparently a primary word; *worthless* (*intrinsically* such; whereas 4190 properly refers to *effects*), i.e. (subject) *depraved*, or (object) *injurious*:—bad, evil, harm, ill, noisome, wicked.

Adjective meaning bad, worthless externally. Of a soldier, cowardly. In the NT evil, wicked:

(I) In a moral sense: wicked, vicious, bad in heart, conduct, and character (Mt 21:41; 24:48; Php 3:2; Rev 2:2). Of things such as thoughts and works (Mk 7:21; Ro 13:3; 1Co 15:33; Col 3:5). In the neuter, evil, evil things, wickedness, fault, crime (Mt 27:23; Mk 15:14; Lk 23:22; Jn 18:23; Ac 23:9; Ro 1:30; 2:9; 3:8; 7:19, 21; 13:4; 16:19; 1Co 10:6; 2Co 13:7; 1Ti 6:10; Heb 5:14; Jas 1:13; 1Pe 3:12; 3Jn 11).

(II) Actively causing evil, i.e. hurtful, harmful (Ro 14:20; Tit 1:12; Rev 16:2). In the neuter, evil, i.e. cause or source of evil (Jas 3:8); evil done to anyone, harm, injury (Ac 16:28; 28:5; Ro 12:17, 21; 13:10; 1Co 13:5; 1Th 5:15; 1Pe 3:9). In words, evil speaking (1Pe 3:10). In the plural, evils, i.e. troubles, afflictions (Lk 16:25; Ac 9:13; 2Ti 4:14).

Deriv.: *ákakos* (172), one without evil, upright; *anexíkakos* (420), without evil, long-suffering; *ekkakéō* or *egkakéō* (1573), to become discouraged; *kakía* (2549), wickedness, trouble; *kakopoiós* (2555), evildoer; *kakoúrgos* (2557), one who works evil; *kakouchéō* (2558), to suffer adversity; *kakóō* (2559), to ill-treat; *kakō̂s* (2560), badly.

Syn.: *ánomos* (459), lawless as a characterization of the person himself in regard to obedience to the law; *kakía* (2549), wickedness, iniquity, evil, affliction; *ponērós* (4190), malicious with willful harm to others, an element not necessarily found in *kakós*.; *saprós* (4550), corrupt, rotten, unfit for use, putrid; *phaúlos* (5337), trivial, bad in the sense of being worthless.

2557. κακοῦργος, kakourgos, *kak-oor´-gos*; from 2556 and the base of 2041; a *wrong-doer*, i.e. *criminal*:—evildoer, malefactor.

Noun from *kakós* (2556), bad, and *érgō* (n.f.), to work, which is the obsolete root of *érgon* (2041), work. An evildoer, malefactor; spoken of the two thieves who were crucified beside Jesus (Lk 23:32, 33, 39); spoken of Paul suffering wrongly as an evildoer (2Ti 2:9).

Syn.: *kakopoiós* (2555), an evildoer; *lēstḗs* (3027), a robber, plunderer.

2558. κακουχέω, kakoucheō, *kak-oo-kheh´-o*; from a presumed compound of 2556 and 2192; to *maltreat*:—which suffer adversity, torment.

2559. κακόω, kakoō, *kak-o´-o*; from 2556; to *injure*; (figurative) to *exasperate*:—make evil affected, entreat evil, harm, hurt, vex.

From *kakós* (2556), bad, evil. Physically, to do evil to someone, to maltreat, to harm, afflict (Ac 7:6, 19; 12:1; 18:10; 1Pe 3:13); also, in the NT, in a moral sense: to make evil-affected, i.e. to embitter (Ac 14:2).

Deriv.: *kákōsis* (2561), distress, affliction.

Syn.: *kakopoiéō* (2554), to do evil.

2560. κακῶς, kakōs, *kak-oce´*; adverb from 2556; *badly* (physical or moral):—amiss, diseased, evil, grievously, miserably, sick, sore.

Adverb from *kakós* (2556), bad, evil. Badly:

(I) Physically: with *échō* (2192), to have, meaning to be ill (Mt 4:24; 8:16; 9:12; 14:35; Mk 1:32, 34; 2:17; 6:55; Lk 5:31; 7:2).

(II) Used with various action verbs: badly, grievously, miserably (Mt 15:22; 17:15; 21:41).

(III) Used with verbs denoting speech: to speak evil of anyone, revile (Ac 23:5); to speak evil words (Jn 18:23); to ask amiss, badly, improperly (Jas 4:3).

Syn.: *árrōstos* (732), infirm, sick; *asthenḗs* (772), without strength, weak; *deinṓs* (1171), grievously, severely.

2561. κάκωσις, kakōsis, *kak´-o-sis*; from 2559; *maltreatment*:—affliction.

2562. καλάμη, kalamē, *kal-am´-ay*; feminine of 2563; a *stalk* of grain, i.e. (collective) *stubble*:—stubble.

2563. κάλαμος, kalamos, *kal´-am-os*; of uncertain affinity; a *reed* (the plant or its stem, or that of a similar plant); (by implication) a *pen*:—pen, reed.

2564. καλέω, kaleō, *kal-eh´-o*; akin to the base of 2753; to "*call*" (properly aloud, but used in a variety of applications, dirivative or otherwise):—bid, call (forth), (whose, whose sur-) name (was [called]).

To call:

(I) To call to someone in order that he may come or go somewhere:

(A) Particularly with the actual voice (Mt 4:21; 20:8; Mk 1:20; Lk 19:13); as a shepherd calls his flock (Jn 10:3).

(B) Generally: to call in some way, send for, direct to come (Mt 2:7, 15; Heb 11:8).

(C) To call authoritatively, to call forth, summon, e.g., before a judge (Ac 4:18; 24:2). Figuratively, of God calling forth and disposing of things that are not, even as though they were, i.e. calling them into existence (Ro 4:17).

(D) In the sense of to invite, particularly to a banquet (Mt 22:3, 8, 9; Lk 7:39; 14:8, 17; Jn 2:2; 1Co 10:27). Metaphorically: to call or invite to anything, e.g., of Jesus, to call to repentance, etc. (Mt 9:13; Mk 2:17); of God (Ro 9:24; 1Co 1:9; 7:15, 17ff.; Gal 5:8, 13; 1Th 2:12; 2Th 2:14; 1Ti 6:12; 2Ti 1:9; Heb 9:15; 1Pe 2:9, 21; 5:10; Rev 19:9).

(E) In the sense of to call to any position, i.e. to appoint, choose (Gal 1:15; Heb 5:4).

(II) To call, i.e. to name, to give a name to any person or thing:

(A) Particularly as spoken of: **(1)** A proper name or surname, e.g., of persons (Mt 1:21, 23, 25; Lk 1:13; 2:21; Ac 1:23; Ro 9:7; Heb 11:18; Rev 19:13. Of places (Mt 27:8; Lk 2:4; Ac 3:11; 28:1; Rev 1:9). **(2)** An epithet, descriptive adj., or appellation, e.g., a Nazarene (Mt 2:23). Also Mt 22:43; 23:7, 8, 10; Lk 6:15; 15:19, 21; Ac 10:1; Ro 9:26; Jas 2:23; 1Jn 3:1).

(B) Passive, in the sense of to be regarded, accounted, meaning to be (Mt 5:9, 19; 21:13; Mk 11:17; Lk 1:32, 35; 2:23; Heb 3:13).

Deriv.: *antikaléō* (479), to invite in return; *egkaléō* (1458), to accuse; *eiskaléō* (1528), to invite; *epikaléomai* (1941), to call upon, to be surnamed; *klḗsis* (2821), calling; *klētós* (2822), called; *metakaléō* (3333), to call; *parakaléō* (3870), to call near, to comfort; *prokaléō* (4292), to provoke; *proskaléō* (4341), to invite; *sugkaléō* (4779), to call together.

Syn.: *eponomázō* (2028), to surname; *onomázō* (3687), to name, call, command; *prosphōnéō* (4377), to call unto; *phōnéō* (5455), to call with a loud voice.

2565. καλλιέλαιος, kallielaios, *kal-le-el´-ah-yos*; from the base of 2566 and 1636; a *cultivated olive* tree, i.e. a *domesticated* or *improved* one:—good olive tree.

2566. καλλίον, kallion, *kal-lee´-on*; neuter of the (irregular) comparative of 2570; (adverb) *better* than many:—very well.

2567. καλοδιδάσκαλος, kalodidaskalos, *kal-od-id-as´-kal-os*; from 2570 and 1320; a *teacher of* the *right*:—teacher of good things.

2568. Καλοὶ Λιμένες, Kaloi Limenes, *kal-oy´ lee-man´-es*; plural of 2570 and 3040; *Good Harbors*, i.e. *Fairhaven*, a bay of Crete:—fair havens.

2569. καλοποιέω, kalopoieō, *kal-op-oy-eh´-o*; from 2570 and 4160; to *do well*, i.e. live virtuously:—well doing.

2570. καλός, kalos, *kal-os´*; of uncertain affinity; properly *beautiful*, but chiefly (figurative) *good* (literal or moral), i.e. *valuable* or *virtuous* (for *appearance* or *use*, and thus distinguished from 18, which is properly *intrinsic*):— × better, fair, good (-ly), honest, meet, well, worthy.

Adjective meaning handsome, beautiful, primarily as to external form and appearance. In the NT, of quality: good, handsome, excellent:

(I) Good as to quality and character:

(A) Generally, the soil of the earth (Mt 13:8, 23; Mk 4:8, 20; Lk 8:15); a tree (Mt 12:33; Lk 6:43); seed (Mt 13:24, 27, 37, 38); a measure, i.e. bountiful, proper measure (Lk 6:38).

(B) By implication: choice, excellent, e.g., fruit (Mt 3:10; 7:17–19; Lk 3:9; 6:43); wine (Jn 2:10); pearls (Mt 13:45); stones (Lk 21:5). See Mt 13:48; Ro 7:16; 1Th 5:21; 1Ti 3:1, 13; 4:6, "good doctrine"; 6:12, 13, 19; 2Ti 1:14; Heb 6:5).

(C) With a meaning of honourable, distinguished (1Ti 1:18; 3:7; Jas 2:7).

(II) Good as to effect or influence, useful, profitable (Mk 9:50; Lk 14:34). Hence the expression *kalón ésti* (1510), meaning it is good, profitable, and in some contexts, it is better (Mt 17:4; 18:8, 9; 26:24; Mk 9:5, 42; 14:21; Lk 9:33; 1Co 7:1, 8; 9:15).

(III) Good in a moral sense, virtuous:

(A) Spoken of thoughts, feelings, actions, e.g., a good conscience (Heb 13:18); good conduct (Jas 3:13; 1Pe 2:12); "the good fight" (1Ti 6:12; 2Ti 4:7). In 1Ti 2:3; 5:4, "it is good in the sight of [*enṓpion* {1799}, before] God" (a.t.); in Lk 8:15 of the heart being both *kalḗ* (2570), inherently good, and *agathḗ* (18), benevolent, able to externalize its qualities. Also used of work or works: **(1)** Generally meaning well-doing, virtue, as in Eng., a good or noble deed or deeds (Mt 5:16; 1Ti 5:25; Tit 2:7, 14; 3:8; Heb 10:24; 1Pe 2:12); **(2)** In the sense of useful work, i.e. benefit (Mt 26:10; Mk 14:6; Jn 10:32, 33; 1Ti 5:10; 6:18; Tit 3:8, 14). Hence, *kalón esti* (1510), it is good, meaning it is right (Mt 15:26; Mk 7:27; Ro 14:21; Gal 4:18; Heb 13:9).

(B) Spoken of persons in reference to the performance of duty, e.g., "the good shepherd" (Jn 10:11, 14). See also 1Ti 4:6; 2Ti 2:3; 1Pe 4:10.

Deriv.: *kállion* (2566), very well; *kalopoiéō* (2569), to do well, excellently; *kalṓs* (2573), well.

Syn.: *agathós* (18), good, benevolent; *áxios* (514), worthy; *arestós* (701), agreeable, pleasing; *chrēstós* (5543), good, kind.

2571. κάλυμα, kaluma, *kal´-oo-mah*; from 2572; a *cover*, i.e. *veil*:—vail.

2572. καλύπτω, kaluptō, *kal-oop´-to*; akin to 2813 and 2928; to *cover* up (literal or figurative):—cover, hide.

To envelop, to cover over:

(I) To cover (Mt 8:24; Lk 8:16; 23:30).

(II) By implication: to hide, the same as *krúptō* (2928), to hide (Mt 10:26; 2Co 4:3; Jas 5:20; 1Pe 4:8; in the two latter cases, it means to cause a multitude of sins to be overlooked and not punished.

Deriv.: *anakalúptō* (343), to uncover; *apokalúptō* (601), to disclose, reveal; *epikalúptō* (1943), to cover up or over; *kálumma* (2571), covering, veil; *katakalúptō* (2619), to cover completely; *parakalúptō* (3871), to hide; *perikalúptō* (4028), to cover around; *sugkalúptō* (4780), to cover up, conceal.

Syn.: *apokrúptō* (613), to conceal from; *egkrúptō* (1470), to hide in something; *krúptō* (2928), to keep secret, hide; *parakalúptō* (3871), to cover with a veil, hide.

2573. καλῶς, kalōs, *kal-oce´*; adverb from 2570; *well* (usually moral):—(in a) good (place), honestly, + recover, (full) well.

2574. κάμηλος, kamēlos, *kam´-ay-los*; of Hebrew origin [1581]; a "*camel*":—camel.

2575. κάμινος, kaminos, *kam´-ee-nos*; probably from 2545; a *furnace*:—furnace.

2576. καμμύω, kammuō, *kam-moo´-o*; for a compound of 2596 and the base of 3466; to *shut down*, i.e. *close* the eyes:—close.

2577. κάμνω, kamnō, *kam´-no*; apparently a primary verb; properly to *toil*, i.e. (by implication) to *tire* (figurative, *faint, sicken*):—faint, sick, be wearied.

Primarily to be weary from constant work (Heb 12:3). Also, to be sick (Jas 5:15; Rev 2:3).

Syn.: *apopsúchō* (674), to be faint at heart; *asthenéō* (770), to be weak, sick; *ekkakéō* or *egkakéō* (1573), to be faint-hearted, weary; *eklúō* (1590), to become feeble, grow weary; the expression *échō kakṓs* (*échō* [2192], to have; *kakṓs* [2560], bad) to have it badly or to be sick; *kopiáō* (2872), to grow weary, to toil; *noséō* (3552), to be sick.

2578. κάμπτω, kamptō, *kamp´-to*; apparently a primary verb; to *bend*:—bow.

2579. κἄν, kan, *kan*; from 2532 and 1437; *and* (or *even*) *if*:—and (also) if (so much as), if but, at the least, though, yet.

2580. Κανᾶ, Kana, *kan-ah´*; of Hebrew origin [compare 7071]; *Cana*, a place in Palestine:—Cana.

2581. Κανανίτης, Kananitēs, *kan-an-ee´-tace*; of Chaldee origin [compare 7067]; *zealous; Cananitès*, an epithet:—Canaanite [*by mistake for a derivative from* 5477].

2582. Κανδάκη, Kandakē, *kan-dak´-ay*; of foreign origin; *Candacè*, an Egyptian queen:—Candace.

2583. κανών, kanōn, *kan-ohn´*; from **κάνη**, ***kanē*** (a straight *reed*, i.e. *rod*); a *rule* ("*canon*"), i.e. (figurative) a *standard* (of faith and practice); (by implication) a *boundary*, i.e. (figurative) a *sphere* (of activity):—line, rule.

2584. Καπερναούμ, Kapernaoum, *cap-er-nah-oom´*; of Hebrew origin [probably 3723 and 5151]; *Capernaüm*, i.e. *Caphanachum*), a place in Palestine:—Capernaum.

2585. καπηλεύω, kapēleuō, *kap-ale-yoo´-o*; from **κάπηλος**, ***kapēlos*** (a *huckster*); to *retail*, i.e. (by implication) to *adulterate* (figurative):—corrupt.

From *kápēlos* (n.f.), a retailer, huckster, vintner, inn-keeper. To peddle; for profit. Only in 2Co 2:17. The *kápēloi* were notorious for adulterating their commodities, and *kapēleúō*, may have a figurative implication here, meaning, to adulterate, to corrupt.

Syn.: *phtheírō* (5351), to corrupt; *kataphtheírō* (2704), to corrupt; *diaphtheírō* (1311), to corrupt.

2586. καπνός, kapnos, *kap-nos´*; of uncertain affinity; *smoke*:—smoke.

2587. Καππαδοκία, Kappadokia, *kap-pad-ok-ee´-ah*; of foreign origin; *Cappadocia*, a region of Asia Minor:—Cappadocia.

2588. καρδία, kardia, *kar-dee´-ah*; prolonged from a primary **κάρ**, *kar* (Latin *cor*, "*heart*"); the *heart*, i.e. (figurative) the *thoughts* or *feelings* (*mind*); also (by analogy) the *middle*:—(+ broken-) heart (-ed).

Noun meaning heart. The seat and center of circulation, and therefore of human life. In the NT, used only figuratively:

(I) As the seat of the desires, feelings, affections, passions, impulses, i.e. the heart or mind:

(A) Generally (Mt 5:8, 28; 6:21; Mk 4:15; Lk 1:17; Jn 14:1; Ac 11:23; 2Ti 2:22; Heb 3:8; 10:22).

(B) In phrases: as out of or from the heart, meaning willingly (Mt 18:35; Ro 6:17); with the whole heart (Mt 22:37; Mk 12:30; Sept.: Dt 6:5; Ps 119:34); of one heart and soul, i.e. entire unanimity (Ac 4:32).

(C) Used for the person himself in cases where values, affections or passions are attributed to the heart or mind (Mt 24:48; Jn 16:22; Ac 2:26; 14:17; Ro 10:6; Col 2:2; 2Th 2:17; Jas 1:26; 5:5; Rev 18:7).

(II) As the seat of the intellect meaning the mind, understanding (Mt 13:15; Mk 6:52; Lk 1:66; 2:51; 24:25; Jn 12:40; Ro 1:21; Eph 4:18; 2Pe 1:19). In the sense of conscience (Ro 2:15; 1Jn 3:20, 21).

(III) Figuratively: the heart of something, the middle or central part, i.e. the heart of the earth (Mt 12:40).

Deriv.: *kardiognṓstēs* (2589), heart-knower, heart-searcher; *sklērokardía* (4641), hardening of the heart, stubbornness.

Syn.: *noús* (3563), mind; *súnesis* (4907), understanding, prudence; *psuchḗ* (5590), soul.

2589. καρδιογνώστης, kardiognōstēs, *kar-dee-og-noce´-tace*; from 2588 and 1097; a *heart-knower*:—which knowest the hearts.

Noun from *kardía* (2588), heart, and *ginṓskō* (1097), to know. One who knows the heart, searcher of hearts (Ac 1:24; 15:8).

2590. καρπός, karpos, *kar-pos´*; probably from the base of 726; *fruit* (as *plucked*), literal or figurative:—fruit.

2591. Κάρπος, Karpos, *kar´-pos*; perhaps for 2590; *Carpus*, probably a Christian:—Carpus.

2592. καρποφορέω, karpophoreō, *kar-pof-or-eh´-o*; from 2593; to *be fertile* (literal or figurative):—be (bear, bring forth) fruit (-ful).

2593. καρποφόρος, karpophoros, *kar-pof-or´-os*; from 2590 and 5342; *fruitbearing* (figurative):—fruitful.

2594. καρτερέω, kartereō, *kar-ter-eh´-o*; from a derivative of 2904 (transposed); to *be strong*, i.e. (figurative) *steadfast* (*patient*):—endure.

From *karterós* (n.f.), strength. To be strong, steadfast, firm, to endure, hold out, bear the burden. Only in Heb 11:27.

Deriv.: *proskarteréō* (4342), to persist, hold fast.

Syn.: *anéchō* (430), to hold up; *makrothuméō* (3114) to be long-suffering toward people; *ménō* (3306), to abide, endure; *hupoménō* (5278), to abide under, endure circumstances; *hupophérō* (5297), to bear up under, to endure trial or suffering.

2595. κάρφος, karphos, *kar´-fos*; from **κάρφω**, ***karpho*** (to *wither*); a dry *twig* or *straw*:—mote.

2596. κατά, kata, *kat-ah´*; a primary particle; (preposition) *down* (in place or time), in varied relations (according to the case [general, dative or accusative] with which it is joined):—about, according as (to), after, against, (when they were) × alone, among, and, × apart, (even, like) as (concerning, pertaining to, touching), × aside, at, before, beyond, by, to the charge of, [charita-] bly, concerning, + covered, [dai-] ly, down, every, (+ far more) exceeding, × more excellent, for, from … to, godly, in (-asmuch, divers, every, -to, respect of), … by, after the manner of, + by any means, beyond (out of) measure, × mightily, more, × natural, of (up-) on (× part), out (of every), over against, (+ your) × own, + particularly, so, through (-out, -out every), thus, (un-) to (-gether, -ward), × uttermost, where (-by), with. In composition it retains many of these applications, and frequently denotes *opposition, distribution* or *intensity*.

Preposition with the primary meaning of down. Down from, down upon, down in:

(I) With the gen.:

(A) Of place: **(1)** Indicating motion meaning down from a higher to a lower place, e.g., down a precipice into the sea (Mt 8:32; Mk 5:13; Lk 8:33). **(2)** Generally of motion or direction upon, toward or through any place or object: **(a)** Particularly in the sense of upon, against (Ac 27:14). **(b)** In the sense of through, throughout (Lk 4:14; 23:5; Ac 9:31, 42; 10:37). **(c)** After verbs of swearing, i.e. to swear upon or by anything, at the same time stretching out the hand over, upon, or toward it (Mt 26:63; Heb 6:13, 16).

(B) Figuratively, of the object toward or upon which something tends or aims: upon, in respect to (1Co 15:15; Jude 15). More usually in a hostile sense: against; or after words of speaking, accusing, warring, and the like (Mt 5:11, 23; 10:35; 12:14; 26:59; Mk 11:25; 14:55ff.; Ac 4:26; 16:22; 2Co 13:8; Gal 5:17).

(II) With the accusative, where the primary and general idea is down upon, out over:

(A) Of place, that is: **(1)** Of motion expressed or implied or of extension out over, through, or throughout a place (Lk 8:39; 15:14; Ac 5:15; 8:1; 11:1; 15:23; 24:12). With *hodós* (3598), way, meaning along or by the way, while traveling upon it (Lk 10:4; Ac 25:3; 26:13). Hence, from the idea of motion throughout every part of the whole arises the distributive sense of *katá*, e.g., *katá pólin kaí kṓmēn*, "throughout every city and village" (Lk 8:1; see *pólis* (4172), city; *kai* (2532), and *kṓmē*

(2968), village. *Kat' oíkon*, "from house to house" (*katá*; *oikos* [3624], house). See also Lk 8:4; 9:6; 13:22; Ac 8:3; 14:23; 15:21; 22:19). **(2)** Of motion referring to situation upon, at, near to, or adjacent to (Lk 10:32, 33; Ac 2:10; 16:7; 27:2; 27:7). **(3)** Of motion or direction, upon, i.e. toward any place (Ac 8:26; 27:12; Php 3:14).

(B) Of time, i.e. of a period or point of time: down upon which, e.g., in, at, or during which anything takes place; *katá kairón* ([2540], occasion, season, opportune time), in due time (Jn 5:4; Ro 5:6); about midnight (Ac 16:25; 27:27); *kat' archás* ([746], beginning) in the beginning (Heb 1:10). Also used in a distributive sense with various designations of time. Thus: every day (Mt 26:55; Mk 14:49; Lk 11:3; 19:47; Ac 2:46; 17:17); every year (Lk 2:41; Heb 9:25; 10:1, 3); every feast (Mt 27:15; Lk 23:17); every Sabbath (Ac 18:4); every first day of the week (1Co 16:2).

(C) In a distributive sense, derived strictly from the idea of pervading all the parts of the whole; as of place, see I, A above, and of time, see I, B. Also generally of any parts, number, e.g., *katá méros* ([3313], part), i.e. part for part, particularly (Heb 9:5). Of number, *kath' héna* ([1520], one), meaning one by one (1Co 14:31). Also *katá dúo* ([1417], two), meaning two at a time, in a session (1Co 14:27).

(D) Metaphorically, as expressing the relation in which one thing stands toward another, thus also everywhere implying manner. Spoken of: **(1)** Accordance, conformity, e.g., **(a)** Of a norm, rule, standard of comparison: according to, conformable to, after: "According to your faith be it unto you" (Mt 9:29; 23:3; Mk 7:5; Lk 2:22, 39; 23:56; Jn 8:15; 19:7; Ac 22:12; 23:31; 26:5; Ro 2:2; 8:4, 5, 27; 10:2; Eph 4:22; Col 2:8; 3:22; Heb 5:6, 10). In composition, *katá* denotes: **(a)** motion downwards, as *katabaínō* (2597), to descend; *kathairéō* (2507), to demolish, put down, destroy; *katapíptō* (2667), to fall down **(b)** opposition against in a hostile sense as *kataginṓskō* (2607), to blame; *katēgoréō* (2723), to accuse; *katalaléō* (2635), to slander **(c)** distribution as *kataklērodotéō* (2624), to apportion an estate by casting lots.

2597. καταβαίνω, katabainō, *kat-ab-ah´ee-no*; from 2596 and the base of 939; to *descend* (literal or figurative):—come (get, go, step) down, fall (down).

From *katá* (2596), down, and *baínō* (n.f.), to go or come. To come or go down, descend from a higher to a lower place:

(I) Spoken of persons, followed by *apó* ([575], from): to descend from somewhere (Mt 8:1; 14:29; 17:9; Mk 9:9; 15:30). Spoken of those who descend or come down from heaven, e.g.: of God as affording aid to the oppressed (Ac 7:34); of the Son of Man (Jn 6:38, 42; 1Th 4:16); of the Holy Spirit (Lk 3:22; Jn 1:32, 33); of angels (Mt 28:2; Jn 1:51; 5:4); of Satan as cast down from heaven (Rev 12:12).

(II) Spoken of things: a way leading down from a higher to a lower tract of country as the way coming down from Jerusalem unto Gaza (Ac 8:26). Of things descending from heaven, i.e. let down or sent down from God as a vessel (Ac 10:11; 11:5); spiritual gifts (Jas 1:17); the New Jerusalem, the one descending out of heaven from God (Rev 3:12).

Deriv.: *katábasis* (2600), descent; *sugkatabaínō* (4782), to go down with.

Syn.: *katérchomai* (2718), to come down.

2598. καταβάλλω, kataballō, *kat-ab-al´-lo*; from 2596 and 906; to *throw down*:—cast down, lay.

2599. καταβαρέω, katabareō, *kat-ab-ar-eh´-o*; from 2596 and 916; to *impose upon*:—burden.

2600. κατάβασις, katabasis, *kat-ab´-as-is*; from 2597; a *declivity*:—descent.

2601. καταβιβάζω, katabibazō, *kat-ab-ib-ad´-zo*; from 2596 and a derivative of the base of 939; to *cause to go down*, i.e. *precipitate*:—bring (thrust) down.

2602. καταβολή, katabolē, *kat-ab-ol-ay´*; from 2598; a *deposition*, i.e. *founding*; (figurative) *conception*:—conceive, foundation.

Noun from *katabállō* (2598), to cast down. A casting or laying down:

(I) A laying down, founding, foundation. In the phrase, *katabolḗ toú kósmou*, the foundation of the world (*kósmos* [2889], world), i.e. the beginning of creation (Mt 13:35; 25:34; Lk 11:50; Jn 17:24; Eph 1:4; Heb 4:3; 9:26; 1Pe 1:20; Rev 13:8; 17:8).

(II) Of seed, a casting in; used metaphorically in Heb 11:11, conception.

Syn.: For **(I)**: *archḗ* (746), beginning (a syn. for foundation); *ktísis* (2937), creation. For **(II)**: *sullambánō* (4815), to take together.

2603. καταβραβεύω, katabrabeuō, *kat-ab-rab-yoo´-o*; from 2596 and 1018 (in its original sense); to *award* the price *against*, i.e. (figurative) to *defraud* (of salvation):—beguile of reward.

2604. καταγγελεύς, kataggeleus, *kat-ang-gel-yooce´*; from 2605; a *proclaimer*:—setter forth.

Noun from *kataggéllō* (2605) to proclaim. A proclaimer, publisher. Only in Ac 17:18.

Syn.: *kḗrux* (2783), a herald, preacher.

2605. καταγγέλλω, kataggellō, *kat-ang-gel´-lo*; from 2596 and the base of 32; to *proclaim, promulgate*:—declare, preach, shew, speak of, teach.

From *katá* (2596), an intensive, and *aggéllō* (n.f., see *anaggéllō* [312]), to tell, declare. To declare plainly, openly, or aloud:

(I) To announce, proclaim (Ac 13:38). To celebrate (Ro 1:8; 1Co 11:26).

(II) By implication: to preach, set forth, to implant in the mind by repetition (Ac 4:2; 13:5, 38; 15:36; 16:17, 21; 17:3, 13, 23; 26:23; 1Co 2:1; 9:14; Php 1:16, 18; Col 1:28).

Deriv.: *kataggeleús* (2604), a proclaimer, publisher; *prokataggéllō* (4293), to foretell.

Syn.: *kērússō* (2784), to preach, proclaim.

2606. καταγελάω, katagelaō, *kat-ag-el-ah´-o*; to *laugh down*, i.e. *deride*:—laugh to scorn.

2607. καταγινώσκω, kataginōskō, *kat-ag-in-o´-sko*; from 2596 and 1097; to *note against*, i.e. *find fault with*:—blame, condemn.

From *katá* (2596), against, and *ginṓskō* (1097), to know. To think ill of, to condemn, to blame (1Jn 3:20, 21). In the passive, to incur blame, be worthy of blame, spoken of Peter's withdrawing from the fellowship of Gentile Christians in Antioch (Gal 2:11).

Deriv.: *akatágnōstos* (176), unblameable.

Syn.: *katadikázō* (2613), to pronounce judgement, condemn; *katakrínō* (2632), to condemn; *mémphomai* (3201), to find fault; *mōmáomai* (3469), to find fault with, blame.

2608. κατάγνυμι, katagnumi, *kat-ag´-noo-mee*; from 2596 and the base of 4486; to *rend in pieces*, i.e. *crack apart*:—break.

2609. κατάγω, katagō, *kat-ag´-o*; from 2596 and 71; to *lead down*; specially to *moor* a vessel:—bring (down, forth), (bring to) land, touch.

2610. καταγωνίζομαι, katagōnizomai, *kat-ag-o-nid´-zom-ahee*; from 2596 and 75; to *struggle against*, i.e. (by implication) to *overcome*:—subdue.

From *katá* (2596), against, and *agōnízomai* (75), to contend for victory in the public games. To contend against; and by implication, to conquer, subdue. Only in Heb 11:33.

Syn.: *nikáō* (3528), to be victorious; *hupotássō* (5293), to subdue or bring into subjection. Also, *katakurieúō* (2634), to conquer, master; *hupernikáō* (5245), to be more than a conqueror.

2611. καταδέω, katadeō, *kat-ad-eh´-o*; from 2596 and 1210; to *tie down*, i.e. *bandage* (a wound):—bind up.

2612. κατάδηλος, katadēlos, *kat-ad´-ay-los*; from 2596 intensive and 1212; *manifest*:—far more evident.

2613. καταδικάζω, katadikazō, *kat-ad-ik-ad´-zo*; from 2596 and a derivative of 1349; to *adjudge against*, i.e. *pronounce guilty*:—condemn.

From *katá* (2596), against, and *dikázō* (n.f.), to judge, pronounce sentence, which is from *díkē* (1349), judgement. To give judgement against a person, pass sentence, condemn (Mt 12:7, 37; Lk 6:37; Jas 5:6).

Syn.: *kataginṓskō* (2607), to know something against, to condemn; *katakrínō* (2632), to give judgement against, pass sentence on, condemn; *krínō* (2919), to judge, distinguish, to condemn.

2614. καταδιώκω, katadiōkō, *kat-ad-ee-o´-ko*; from 2596 and 1377; to *hunt down*, i.e. *search for*:—follow after.

2615. καταδουλόω, katadouloō, *kat-ad-oo-lo´-o*; from 2596 and 1402; to *enslave utterly*:—bring into bondage.

From *katá* (2596), an intensive, and *doulóō* (1402), to enslave. To enslave utterly, reduce to absolute slavery (2Co 11:20); in the middle to make a slave for oneself (Gal 2:4).

Syn.: *doulagōgéō* (1396), to lead into slavery, bondage, to subject.

2616. καταδυναστεύω, katadunasteuō, *kat-ad-oo-nas-tyoo´-o*; from 2596 and a derivative of 1413; to *exercise dominion against*, i.e. *oppress*:—oppress.

2617. καταισχύνω, kataischunō, *kat-ahee-skhoo´-no*; from 2596 and 153; to *shame down*, i.e. *disgrace* or (by implication) *put to the blush*:—confound, dishonour, (be a-, make a-) shame (-d).

2618. κατακαίω, katakaiō, *kat-ak-ah´ee-o*; from 2596 and 2545; to *burn down* (to the ground), i.e. *consume wholly*:—burn (up, utterly).

2619. κατακαλύπτω, katakaluptō, *kat-ak-al-oop´-to*; from 2596 and 2572; to *cover wholly*, i.e. *veil*:—cover, hide.

2620. κατακαυχάομαι, katakauchaomai, *kat-ak-ow-khah´-om-ahee*; from 2596 and 2744; to *exult against* (i.e. *over*):—boast (against), glory, rejoice against.

2621. κατάκειμαι, katakeimai, *kat-ak´-i-mahee*; from 2596 and 2749; to *lie down*, i.e. (by implication) *be sick*; specially to *recline* at a meal:—keep, lie, sit at meat (down).

2622. κατακλάω, kataklaō, *kat-ak-lah´-o*; from 2596 and 2806; to *break down*, i.e. *divide*:—break.

2623. κατακλείω, katakleiō, *kat-ak-li´-o*; from 2596 and 2808; to *shut down* (in a dungeon), i.e. *incarcerate*:—shut up.

2624. κατακληροδοτέω, kataklērodoteō, *kat-ak-lay-rod-ot-eh´-o*; from 2596 and a derivative of a compound of 2819 and 1325; to *be a giver of lots to each*, i.e. (by implication) to *apportion an estate*:—divide by lot.

From *katá* (2596), according to, a distributive, and *klērodotéō* (n.f.), to distribute by lot, which is from *klḗros* (2819), part, lot, and *dídōmi* (1325), to give. To distribute by lot (Ac 13:19).

Syn.: *diadídōmi* (1239), to distribute; *diairéō* (1244), to divide into parts, distribute; *merízō* (3307), to divide into parts.

2625. κατακλίνω, kataklinō, *kat-ak-lee´-no*; from 2596 and 2827; to *recline down*, i.e. (special) to *take a place* at table:—(make) sit down (at meat).

2626. κατακλύζω, katakluzō, *kat-ak-lood´-zo*; from 2596 and the base of 2830; to *dash* (*wash*) *down*, i.e. (by implication) to *deluge*:—overflow.

2627. κατακλυσμός, kataklusmos, *kat-ak-looce-mos´*; from 2626; an *inundation*:—flood.

2628. κατακολουθέω, katakoloutheō, *kat-ak-ol-oo-theh´-o*; from 2596 and 190; to *accompany closely*:—follow (after).

2629. κατακόπτω, katakoptō, *kat-ak-op´-to*; from 2596 and 2875; to *chop down*, i.e. *mangle*:—cut.

2630. κατακρημνίζω, katakrēmnizō, *kat-ak-rame-nid´-zo*; from 2596 and a derivative of 2911; to *precipitate down*:—cast down headlong.

2631. κατάκριμα, katakrima, *kat-ak´-ree-mah*; from 2632; an *adverse sentence* (the verdict):—condemnation.

From *katakrínō* (2632), to condemn. Judgement against, condemnation. Spoken of as the result of Adam's fall (Ro 5:16, 18). Spoken of as being completely absent for the Christian walking after the spirit (Ro 8:1).

Syn.: *katákrisis* (2633), the process of judging which leads to condemnation; *kríma* (2917), the verdict or sentence pronounced, condemnation; *krísis* (2920), the process of investigation in the execution of justice.

2632. κατακρίνω, katakrinō, *kat-ak-ree´-no*; from 2596 and 2919; to *judge against*, i.e. *sentence*:—condemn, damn.

From *katá* (2596), against, and *krínō* (2919), to judge. To pronounce sentence against, condemn:

(I) Of persons, with an explicit punishment (Mt 20:18; Mk 10:33; 14:64; 2Pe 2:6); with the crime or punishment implied (Jn 8:10, 11; Ro 2:1). Used in an absolute sense (Mt 27:3; Ro 8:34). Of the last judgement (Mk 16:16; 1Co 11:32). Figuratively (Ro 8:3).

(II) By implication: to condemn by contrast, i.e. to show by one's good conduct that others are guilty of misconduct and deserve condemnation (Mt 12:41, 42; Lk 11:31, 32; Heb 11:7).

Deriv.: *akatákritos* (178), without trial, uncondemned; *autokatákritos* (843), self-condemned; *katákrima* (2631), condemnation; *katákrisis* (2633), the act of condemning.

Syn.: *kataginṓskō* (2607), to know something against, to condemn; *katadikázō* (2613), to pronounce judgement, condemn.

2633. κατάκρισις, katakrisis, *kat-ak´-ree-sis*; from 2632; *sentencing adversely* (the act):—condemn (-ation).

Noun from *katakrínō* (2632), to condemn. Condemnation, as brought by the Mosaic Law (2Co 3:9); in the sense of censure, blame (2Co 7:3).

2634. κατακυριεύω, katakurieuō, *kat-ak-oo-ree-yoo´-o*; from 2596 and 2961; to *lord against*, i.e. *control, subjugate*:—exercise dominion over (lordship), be lord over, overcome.

2635. καταλαλέω, katalaleō, *kat-al-al-eh´-o*; from 2637; to *be a traducer*, i.e. to *slander*:—speak against (evil of).

From *katá* (2596), against, and *laléō* (2980), to speak. To speak against, to speak evil of, to slander (1Pe 2:12; 3:16). Forbidden for Christians (Jas 4:11).

Deriv.: *katalalía* (2636), backbiting, defamation; *katálalos* (2637), a backbiter.

Syn.: *blasphēméō* (987), to blaspheme, revile; *diabállō* (1225), to falsely accuse; *egkaléō* (1458), to accuse in court; *kakologéō* (2551), to speak evil; *kataginṓskō* (2607), to blame, condemn; *katēgoréō* (2723), to accuse; *sukophantéō* (4811), to accuse falsely.

2636. καταλαλία, katalalia, *kat-al-al-ee´-ah*; from 2637; *defamation*:—backbiting, evil speaking.

2637. κατάλαλος, katalalos, *kat-al´-al-os*; from 2596 and the base of 2980; *talkative against*, i.e. a *slanderer*:—backbiter.

Adjective, from *katalaléō* (2635), to speak against. Slanderous. Used as a substantive, a slanderer, backbiter (Ro 1:30).

Syn.: *blásphēmos* (989), blasphemer; *diábolos* (1228), devil, slanderer; *katḗgoros* (2725), accuser; *kritikós* (2924), critical; *hubristḗs* (5197), insulter.

2638. καταλαμβάνω, katalambanō, *kat-al-am-ban´-o*; from 2596 and 2983; to *take eagerly*, i.e. *seize, possess*, etc. (literal or figurative):—apprehend, attain, come upon, comprehend, find, obtain, perceive, (over-) take.

From *katá* (2596), an intensive, and *lambánō* (2983), to take. To take; to receive, with the idea of eagerness:

(I) To lay hold of, seize, with eagerness, suddenness: spoken of the taking of the woman caught in adultery (Jn 8:3, 4); spoken of an evil spirit taking possession of a person (Mk 9:18). Spoken figuratively of darkness or evil suddenly coming upon someone (Jn 12:35; 1Th 5:4).

(II) In allusion to the public games: to obtain the prize with the idea of eager and strenuous exertion, to grasp, seize upon (Ro 9:30; 1Co 9:24; Php 3:12, 13).

(III) Figuratively: to seize with the mind, to comprehend, to perceive (Jn 1:5; Ac 4:13; 10:34; 25:25; Eph 3:18).

Syn.: *aisthánomai* (143) to understand, perceive through the senses; *harpázō* (726), to pluck, seize, take by force; *ginṓskō* (1097), to know by experience and observation; *epiginṓskō* (1921), to gain full knowledge; *katanoéō* (2657), to perceive fully; *kratéō* (2902), to get possession of, to hold; *noéō* (3539), to perceive with the mind; *piázō* (4084), to seize; *phthánō* (5348), to attain.

2639. καταλέγω, katalegō, *kat-al-eg´-o*; from 2596 and 3004 (in its original meaning); to *lay down*, i.e. (figurative) to *enroll*:—take into the number.

2640. κατάλειμμα, kataleimma, *kat-al´-ime-mah*; from 2641; a *remainder*, i.e. (by implication) a *few*:—remnant.

2641. καταλείπω, kataleipō, *kat-al-i´-po*; from 2596 and 3007; to *leave down*, i.e. *behind*; (by implication) to *abandon, have remaining*:—forsake, leave, reserve.

2642. καταλιθάζω, katalithazō, *kat-al-ith-ad´-zo*; from 2596 and 3034; to *stone down*, i.e. *to death*:—stone.

2643. καταλλαγή, katallagē, *kat-al-lag-ay´*; from 2644; *exchange* (figurative, *adjustment*), i.e. *restoration* to (the divine) favour:—atonement, reconciliation (-ing).

Noun from *katallássō* (2644), to reconcile. Reconciliation, restoration to the divine favour (Ro 5:11; 2Co 5:18, 19); the means, occasion of reconciling the world to God (Ro 11:15).

2644. καταλλάσσω, katallassō, *kat-al-las´-so*; from 2596 and 236; to *change mutually*, i.e. (figurative) to *compound* a difference:—reconcile.

From *katá* (2596), an intensive, and *allássō* (236), to change. In the NT, to change toward, i.e. one person toward another; to reconcile to someone, differing from *diallássō* (1259), reconcile, which implies mutual change (Ro 5:10; 1Co 7:11; 2Co 5:20). Spoken also of God reconciling the world to Himself (2Co 5:18, 19).

Deriv.: *apokatallássō* (604), to reconcile fully; *katallagḗ* (2643), reconciliation.

Syn.: *diallássō* (1259), to reconcile when the fault may lie on the part of both parties concerned; *apokatallássō* (604), to reconcile completely and change from one condition to another; *apokathístēmi* (600), to restore, reclaim.

2645. κατάλοιπος, kataloipos, *kat-al´-oy-pos*; from 2596 and 3062; *left down* (*behind*) i.e. *remaining* (plural the *rest*):—residue.

2646. κατάλυμα, kataluma, *kat-al´-oo-mah*; from 2647; properly a *dissolution* (breaking up of a journey), i.e. (by implication) a *lodging-place*:—guestchamber, inn.

2647. καταλύω, kataluō, *kat-al-oo´-o*; from 2596 and 3089; to *loosen down* (*disintegrate*), i.e. (by implication) to *demolish* (literal or figurative); specially [compare 2646] to *halt* for the night:—destroy, dissolve, be guest, lodge, come to nought, overthrow, throw down.

From *katá* (2596), an intensive, and *lúō* (3089), to loose. To loosen:

(I) Particularly: to dissolve, to disunite the parts of something; hence spoken of buildings: to pull down, to destroy (Mt 26:61; 27:40; Mk 13:2; 14:58; 15:29; Lk 21:6; Ac 5:38, 39; 6:14). Used figuratively in Gal 2:18.

(II) In the Septuagint OT, to unbind; hence of caravans, travelers, etc.: to halt for rest or for the night, to put up for the night, i.e. when the beasts of burden are unharnessed and unloaded (Sept.: Ge 42:27; 43:21). In the NT, generally: to lodge, to take lodging (Lk 9:12; 19:7).

Deriv.: *akatálutos* (179), indissoluble; *katáluma* (2646), lodging place.

Syn.: *analískō* (355), to destroy, consume; *anatrépō* (396), to overthrow, upset; *apóllumi* (622), to destroy; *dialúō* (1262), to dissolve utterly, scatter; *diaphtheírō* (1311), to utterly destroy; *erēmóō* (2049), to make desolate; *kathairéō* (2507), to put down; *katastréphō* (2690), to overthrow, ruin; *katastrṓnnumi* (2693), to overthrow.

2648. καταμανθάνω, katamanthanō, *kat-am-an-than´-o*; from 2596 and 3129; to *learn thoroughly*, i.e. (by implication) to *note carefully*:—consider.

2649. καταμαρτυρέω, katamartureō, *kat-am-ar-too-reh´-o*; from 2596 and 3140; to *testify against*:—witness against.

2650. καταμένω, katamenō, *kat-am-en´-o*; from 2596 and 3306; to *stay fully*, i.e. *reside*:—abide.

2651. καταμόνας, katamonas, *kat-am-on´-as*; from 2596 and accusative plural feminine of 3441 (with 5561 implied); *according to sole* places, i.e. (adverb) *separately*:—alone.

2652. κατανάθεμα, katanathema, *kat-an-ath´-em-ah*; from 2596 (intensive) and 331; an *imprecation*:—curse.

2653. καταναθεματίζω, katanathematizō, *kat-an-ath-em-at-id´-zo*; from 2596 (intensive) and 332; to *imprecate*:—curse.

2654. καταναλίσκω, katanaliskō, *kat-an-al-is´-ko*; from 2596 and 355; to *consume utterly*:—consume.

2655. καταναρκάω, katanarkaō, *kat-an-ar-kah´-o*; from 2596 and **ναρκάω**, ***narkaō*** (to *be numb*); to *grow utterly torpid*, i.e. (by implication) *slothful* (figurative, *expensive*):—be burdensome (chargeable).

2656. κατανεύω, kataneuō, *kat-an-yoo´-o*; from 2596 and 3506; to *nod down* (*toward*), i.e. (by analogy) to *make signs* to:—beckon.

2657. κατανοέω, katanoeō, *kat-an-o-eh´-o*; from 2596 and 3539; to *observe fully*:—behold, consider, discover, perceive.

From *katá* (2596), an intensive, and *noéō* (3539), to think. To see or discern distinctly, to perceive clearly (Mt 7:3; Lk 6:41; Ac 27:39); to take notice accurately, to observe, to consider (Lk 12:24, 27; 20:23; Ac 7:31, 32; 11:6; Heb 3:1; Jas 1:23, 24). In the sense of having respect for, to regard (Ro 4:19; Heb 10:24).

Syn.: *theōréō* (2334), discern; *katalambánō* (2638), to apprehend, comprehend, perceive; *katamanthánō* (2648), to learn thoroughly or consider accurately.

2658. καταντάω, katantaō, *kat-an-tah´-o*; from 2596 and a derivative of 473; to *meet against*, i.e. *arrive* at (literal or figurative):—attain, come.

2659. κατάνυξις, katanuxis, *kat-an´-oox-is*; from 2660; a *prickling* (sensation, as of the limbs *asleep*), i.e. (by implication [perhaps by some confusion with 3506 or even with 3571]) *stupor* (*lethargy*):—slumber.

2660. κατανύσσω, katanussō, *kat-an-oos´-so*; from 2596 and 3572; to *pierce thoroughly*, i.e. (figurative) to *agitate* violently ("sting to the quick"):—prick.

2661. καταξιόω, kataxioō, *kat-ax-ee-o´-o*; from 2596 and 515; to *deem entirely deserving*:—(ac-) count worthy.

2662. καταπατέω, katapateō, *kat-ap-at-eh´-o*; from 2596 and 3961; to *trample down*; (figurative) to *reject* with disdain:—trample, tread (down, underfoot).

2663. κατάπαυσις, katapausis, *kat-ap´-ow-sis*; from 2664; *reposing down*, i.e. (by Hebrew) *abode*:—rest.

Noun from *katapaúō* (2664), to make to cease. The act of resting, rest. From the Hebrew rest, i.e. place of rest, fixed abode, dwelling (Ac 7:49, alluding to a temple). Also of the rest or fixed abode of the Israelites in the Promised Land after their wanderings (Heb 3:11, 18; 4:3, 5). Hence, figuratively, the quiet abode of those who will dwell with God in heaven, in allusion to the Sabbath rest (Heb 4:1, 3, 10, 11).

Syn.: *hēsuchía* (2271), quietness.

2664. καταπαύω, katapauō, *kat-ap-ow´-o*; from 2596 and 3973; to *settle down*, i.e. (literal) to *colonize*, or (figurative) to (*cause to*) *desist*:—cease, (give) rest (-rain).

From *katá* (2596), an intensive, and *paúō* (3973), to make to cease. To quiet down:

(I) Transitively, to cause to rest, give rest (Heb 4:8 [cf. Heb 4:1, 9]).

(II) To restrain (Ac 14:18).

(III) Intransitively, to rest entirely (Heb 4:4, 10).

Deriv.: *akatápaustos* (180), incessant; *katápausis* (2663), cessation from work, rest.

Syn.: *anapaúō* (373), to rest inwardly, but not necessarily from a cessation of work as is expressed by *katapaúō*; *aníēmi* (447), to rest from endurance and suffering or persecution; *dialeípō* (1257), to pause awhile, intermit, desist, cease; *hēsucházō* (2270), to be quiet, still, at rest; *kopázō* (2869), to relax from toil, to cease raging.

2665. καταπέτασμα, katapetasma, *kat-ap-et´-as-mah*; from a compound of 2596 and a congener of 4072; something *spread thoroughly*, i.e. (special) the door *screen* (to the Most Holy Place) in the Jewish Temple:—vail.

2666. καταπίνω, katapinō, *kat-ap-ee´-no*; from 2596 and 4095; to *drink down*, i.e. *gulp entire* (literal or figurative):—devour, drown, swallow (up).

2667. καταπίπτω, katapiptō, *kat-ap-ip´-to*; from 2596 and 4098; to *fall down*:—fall (down).

2668. καταπλέω, katapleō, *kat-ap-leh´-o*; from 2596 and 4126; to *sail down* upon a place, i.e. to *land* at:—arrive.

2669. καταπονέω, kataponeō, *kat-ap-on-eh´-o*; from 2596 and a derivative of 4192; to *labour down* i.e. *wear with toil* (figurative, *harass*):—oppress, vex.

2670. καταποντίζω, katapontizō, *kat-ap-on-tid´-zo*; from 2596 and a derivative of the same as 4195; to *plunge down*, i.e. *submerge*:—drown, sink.

2671. κατάρα, katara, *kat-ar´-ah*; from 2596 (intensive) and 685; *imprecation, execration*:—curse (-d, -ing).

Noun from *katá* (2596), against, and *ará* (685), a curse. To invoke evil upon, to curse:

(I) Particularly and generally: cursing (Jas 3:10).

(II) From the Hebrew curse, i.e. a devoting or dooming to utter destruction (see *anáthema* [331], curse); hence condemnation, doom, punishment (Gal 3:10, 13); by metonymy: accursed (2Pe 2:14). Also of the earth: accursed, i.e. doomed to sterility (Heb 6:8).

Syn.: *anáthema* (331) which translates the Hebrew *chērem* (2764, OT), a thing devoted to God such as sacrifices; a votive offering, gift, or for its destruction as an idol, a city. In the NT, it is used with this latter meaning as also *anathematízō* (332), to curse; *katáthema* (2652), sometimes *katanáthema*, an accursed thing from which is derived *katanathematízō* (2653), to utter a curse against.

2672. καταράομαι, kataraomai, *kat-ar-ah´-om-ahee*; middle from 2671; to *execrate*; (by analogy) to *doom*:—curse.

From *katára* (2671), a curse. To wish anyone evil or ruin, the opposite of *eulogéō* (Mt 5:44; Lk 6:28; Ro 12:14; Jas 3:9). To devote to destruction, as with *anáthema* (331), accursed thing (Mk 11:21). In the perf. pass., to be cursed (Mt 25:41).

Syn.: *anathematízō* (332), to declare something to be devoted to destruction, to curse; *kakologéō* (2551), to speak evil; *katanathematízō* (2653), to utter curses against.

2673. καταργέω, katargeō, *kat-arg-eh´-o*; from 2596 and 691; to *be* (*render*) *entirely idle* (*useless*), literal or figurative:—abolish, cease, cumber, deliver, destroy, do away, become (make) of no (none, without) effect, fail, loose, bring (come) to nought, put away (down), vanish away, make void.

From *katá* (2596), an intensive, and *argéō* (691), to be idle. To render inactive, idle, useless, ineffective:

(I) Particularly of land: to use up ineffectively (Lk 13:7); metaphorically: to make without effect, to make vain, void, fruitless (Ro 3:3, 31; 4:14; 1Co 1:28; Gal 3:17; Eph 2:15).

(II) By implication: to cause to cease, to do away, to put an end to (1Co 6:13). Hence to abolish, to destroy (Ro 6:6; 1Co 15:24, 26; 2Th 2:8; 2Ti 1:10; Heb 2:14). In the pass.: to cease, to be done away (1Co 2:6; 13:8, 10; 2Co 3:7, 11, 13, 14; Gal 5:11); to cease being under or connected with some person or thing (Ro 7:2, 6).

Syn.: *athetéō* (114), to set aside, reject; *akuróō* (208), to render void, deprive of force or authority; *kenóō* (2758), to make empty, of no effect; *lúō* (3089), to loose, dissolve, sever.

2674. καταριθμέω, katarithmeō, *kat-ar-ith-meh´-o*; from 2596 and 705; to *reckon among*:—number with.

2675. καταρτίζω, katartizō, *kat-ar-tid´-zo*; from 2596 and a derivative of 739; to *complete thoroughly*, i.e. *repair* (literal or figurative) or *adjust*:—fit, frame, mend, (make) perfect (-ly join together), prepare, restore.

From *katá* (2596), with, and *artízō* (n.f.), to adjust, fit, finish, which is from *ártios* (739), fit, complete. To put in full order, to make fully ready, to make complete:

(I) To refit, repair, mend that which is broken, e.g., nets (Mt 4:21; Mk 1:19). Spoken figuratively of a person in error, to restore, set right (Gal 6:1). To be suitable, such as one should be, deficient in no part: spoken of persons (Lk 6:40; 1Co 1:10; 2Co 13:11; Heb 13:21; 1Pe 5:10); spoken of things, to fill out, supply (1Th 3:10).

(II) Generally to prepare, set in order, constitute, only in the pass. and middle (Mt 21:16; Ro 9:22; Heb 10:5; 11:3).

Deriv.: *katártisis* (2676), the act of completion, making fit; *katartismós* (2677), complete furnishing, fitting; *prokatartízō* (4294), to perfect or make fit beforehand, make right, equip beforehand.

Syn.: *exartízō* (1822), to accomplish, equip fully; *sunarmologéō* (4883), to fit or frame together.

2676. κατάρτισις, katartisis, *kat-ar´-tis-is*; from 2675; *thorough equipment* (subject):—perfection.

Noun from *katartízō* (2675), to make fully ready, put in order. The act of completing, perfecting (2Co 13:9).

Syn.: *teleíōsis* (5050), a fulfillment, completion, perfection, an end accomplished as the effect of a process.

2677. καταρτισμός, katartismos, *kat-ar-tis-mos´*; from 2675; *complete furnishing* (object):—perfecting.

Noun from *katartízō* (2675), to make fully ready. A perfecting, i.e. the act of making perfect. Used only in Eph 4:12.

Syn.: *teleíōsis* (5050), a fulfillment, completion, perfection, an end accomplished as the effect of a process.

2678. κατασείω, kataseiō, *kat-as-i´-o*; from 2596 and 4579; to *sway downward*, i.e. *make a signal*:—beckon.

2679. κατασκάπτω, kataskaptō, *kat-as-kap´-to*; from 2596 and 4626; to *undermine*, i.e. (by implication) *destroy*:—dig down, ruin.

2680. κατασκευάζω, kataskeuazō, *kat-ask-yoo-ad´-zo*; from 2596 and a derivative of 4632; to *prepare thoroughly* (properly by external *equipment*; whereas 2090 refers rather to internal *fitness*); (by implication) to *construct, create*:—build, make, ordain, prepare.

2681. κατασκηνόω, kataskēnoō, *kat-as-kay-no´-o*; from 2596 and 4637; to *camp down*, i.e. *haunt*; (figurative) to *remain*:—lodge, rest.

2682. κατασκήνωσις, kataskēnōsis, *kat-as-kay´-no-sis*; from 2681; an *encamping*, i.e. (figurative) a *perch*:—nest.

2683. κατασκιάζω, kataskiazō, *kat-as-kee-ad´-zo*; from 2596 and a derivative of 4639; to *overshade*, i.e. *cover*:—shadow.

2684. κατασκοπέω, kataskopeō, *kat-as-kop-eh´-o*; from 2685; to *be a sentinel*, i.e. to *inspect* insidiously:—spy out.

2685. κατάσκοπος, kataskopos, *kat-as´-kop-os*; from 2596 (intensive) and 4649 (in the sense of a *watcher*); a *reconnoiterer*:—spy.

2686. κατασοφίζομαι, katasophizomai, *kat-as-of-id´-zom-ahee*; middle from 2596 and 4679; to *be crafty against*, i.e. *circumvent*:—deal subtilly with.

2687. καταστέλλω, katastellō, *kat-as-tel´-lo*; from 2596 and 4724; to *put down*, i.e. *quell*:—appease, quiet.

2688. κατάστημα, katastēma, *kat-as´-tay-mah*; from 2525; properly a *position* or *condition*, i.e. (subject) *demeanour*:—behaviour.

2689. καταστολή, katastolē, *kat-as-tol-ay´*; from 2687; a *deposit*, i.e. (special) *costume*:—apparel.

2690. καταστρέφω, katastrephō, *kat-as-tref´-o*; from 2596 and 4762; to *turn* upside *down*, i.e. *upset*:—overthrow.

2691. καταστρηνιάω, katastrēniaō, *kat-as-tray-nee-ah´-o*; from 2596 and 4763; to *become voluptuous against*:—begin to wax wanton against.

2692. καταστροφή, katastrophē, *kat-as-trof-ay´*; from 2690; an *overturn* ("*catastrophe*"), i.e. *demolition*; (figurative) *apostasy*:—overthrow, subverting.

2693. καταστρώννυμι, katastrōnnumi, *kat-as-trone´-noo-mee*; from 2596 and 4766; to *strew down*, i.e. (by implication) to *prostrate* (*slay*):—overthrow.

2694. κατασύρω, katasurō, *kat-as-oo´-ro*; from 2596 and 4951; to *drag down*, i.e. *arrest* judicially:—hale.

2695. κατασφάττω, katasphattō, *kat-as-fat´-to*; from 2596 and 4969; to *kill down*, i.e. *slaughter*:—slay.

2696. κατασφραγίζω, katasphragizō, *kat-as-frag-id´-zo*; from 2596 and 4972; to *seal closely*:—seal.

2697. κατάσχεσις, kataschesis, *kat-as´-khes-is*; from 2722; a *holding down*, i.e. *occupancy*:—possession.

2698. κατατίθημι, katatithēmi, *kat-at-ith´-ay-mee*; from 2596 and 5087; to *place down*, i.e. *deposit* (literal or figurative):—do, lay, shew.

2699. κατατομή, katatomē, *kat-at-om-ay´*; from a compound of 2596 and **τέμνω,** *temnō* (to *cut*); a *cutting down* (*off*), i.e. *mutilation* (ironically):—concision. Compare 609.

Noun from *katatémnō* (n.f.), to cut through or off. A cutting off, mutilation. Used contemptuously in Php 3:2, of the Jewish circumcision in contrast with the true spiritual circumcision in v. 3.

2700. κατατοξεύω, katatoxeuō, *kat-at-ox-yoo´-o*; from 2596 and a derivative of 5115; to *shoot down* with an arrow or other missile:—thrust through.

2701. κατατρέχω, katatrechō, *kat-at-rekh´-o*; from 2596 and 5143; to *run down*, i.e. *hasten* from a tower:—run down.

2702. καταφέρω, katapherō, *kat-af-er´-o*; from 2596 and 5342 (including its alternate); to *bear down*, i.e. (figurative) *overcome* (with drowsiness); specially to *cast* a vote:—fall, give, sink down.

2703. καταφευγω, katapheugō, *kat-af-yoo´-go*; from 2596 and 5343; to *flee down* (*away*):—flee.

2704. καταφθείρω, kataphtheirō, *kat-af-thi´-ro*; from 2596 and 5351; to *spoil entirely*, i.e. (literal) to *destroy*; or (figurative) to *deprave*:—corrupt, utterly perish.

2705. καταφιλέω, kataphileō, *kat-af-ee-leh´-o*; from 2596 and 5368; to *kiss earnestly*:—kiss.

2706. καταφρονέω, kataphroneō, *kat-af-ron-eh´-o*; from 2596 and 5426; to *think against*, i.e. *disesteem*:—despise.

2707. καταφροντής, kataphrontēs, *kat-af-ron-tace´*; from 2706; a *contemner*:—despiser.

2708. καταχέω, katacheō, *kat-akh-eh´-o*; from 2596 and **χέω,** *cheō* (to *pour*); to *pour down* (*out*):—pour.

2709. καταχθόνιος, katachthonios, *kat-akh-thon´-ee-os*; from 2596 and **χθών,** *chthōn* (the *ground*); *subterranean*, i.e. *infernal* (belonging to the world of departed spirits):—under the earth.

2710. καταχράομαι, katachraomai, *kat-akh-rah´-om-ahee*; from 2596 and 5530; to *overuse* i.e. *misuse*:—abuse.

From *katá* (2596), against, denoting wrong, or an intensive, denoting excess, and *chráomai* (5530), to use. To fail to use thoroughly, or to overuse, thus to misuse, abuse (1Co 7:31; 9:18).

2711. καταψύχω, katapsuchō, *kat-ap-soo´-kho*; from 2596 and 5594; to *cool down* (*off*), i.e. *refresh*:—cool.

From *katá* (2596), an intensive, and *psúchō* (5594), to cool. To cool, refresh. Used only in Lk 16:24.

Syn.: *anapsúchō* (404), to refresh.

2712. κατείδωλος, kateidōlos, *kat-i´-do-los*; from 2596 (intensive) and 1497; *utter idolatrous*:—wholly given to idolatry.

Adjective from *katá* (2596), an intensive, and *eídōlon* (1497), idol. Full of idols. Used only in Ac 17:16.

2713. κατέναντι, katenanti, *kat-en´-an-tee*; from 2596 and 1725; *directly opposite*:—before, over against.

2714. κατενώπιον, katenōpion, *kat-en-o´-pee-on*; from 2596 and 1799; *directly in front of*:—before (the presence of), in the sight of.

2715. κατεξουσιάζω, katexousiazō, *kat-ex-oo-see-ad´-zo*; from 2596 and 1850; to *have* (*wield*) *full privilege over*:—exercise authority.

2716. κατεργάζομαι, katergazomai, *kat-er-gad´-zom-ahee*; from 2596 and 2038; to *work fully*, i.e. *accomplish*; (by implication) to *finish, fashion*:—cause, do (deed), perform, work (out).

2717. *This number was omitted in Strong's Dictionary of the Greek Testament.*

2718. κατέρχομαι, katerchomai, *kat-er´-khom-ahee*; from 2596 and 2064 (including its alternate); to *come* (or *go*) *down* (literal or figurative):—come (down), depart, descend, go down, land.

2719. κατεσθίω, katesthiō, *kat-es-thee´-o*; from 2596 and 2068 (including its alternate); to *eat down*, i.e. *devour* (literal or figurative):—devour.

2720. κατευθύνω, kateuthunō, *kat-yoo-thoo´-no*; from 2596 and 2116; to *straighten fully*, i.e. (figurative) *direct*:—guide, direct.

2721. κατεφίστημι, katephistēmi, *kat-ef-is´-tay-mee*; from 2596 and 2186; to *stand over against*, i.e. *rush upon* (*assault*):—make insurrection against.

2722. κατέχω, katechō, *kat-ekh´-o*; from 2596 and 2192; to *hold down* (*fast*), in various applications (literal or figurative):—have, hold (fast), keep (in memory), let, × make toward, possess, retain, seize on, stay, take, withhold.

From *katá* (2596), an intensive, and *échō* (2192), to have, hold. Hold fast, retain, or hold down:

(I) To retain, detain a person (Lk 4:42; Phm 13). Used in the sense of to hinder, to repress (2Th 2:6, 7).

(II) To possess, i.e. to hold in secure possession (1Co 7:30; 2Co 6:10). Romans 1:18 is probably to be understood as possessing a knowledge of the truth, but living in unrighteousness.

(III) Figuratively: to hold fast in one's mind and heart (Lk 8:15; 1Co 11:2; 15:2; 1Th 5:21; Heb 3:6, 14; 10:23 [cf. Ro 7:6]). In the passive: to be held fast, bound, e.g., by a law (Ro 7:6), by a disease (Jn 5:4).

(IV) As a nautical term, to hold a ship firm toward the land, i.e. to steer toward land (Ac 27:40).

(V) By implication: to lay fast hold of, to seize (Mt 21:38; Lk 14:9).

Deriv.: *akatáschetos* (183), unrestrainable, unruly; *katáschesis* (2697), possession.

Syn.: *katalambánō* (2638), to comprehend, to apprehend; *kratéō* (2902), to hold fast; *lambánō* (2983), to lay hold of; *piázō* (4084), to lay hold of forcefully.

2723. κατηγορέω, katēgoreō, *kat-ay-gor-eh´-o*; from 2725; to *be a plaintiff*, i.e. to *charge* with some offence:—accuse, object.

From *katá* (2596), against, and *agoreúō* (n.f.), to speak. To speak openly against, to condemn or accuse mainly in a legal sense (Mt 12:10; Mk 3:2; 15:3; Lk 23:2, 10, 14; Jn 5:45; 8:6; Ac 22:30; 24:2, 8, 19; 25:5, 11; 28:19; Ro 2:15; Rev 12:10).

Deriv.: *katēgoría* (2724), accusation, incrimination; *katḗgoros* (2725), accuser.

2724. κατηγορία, katēgoria, *kat-ay-gor-ee´-ah*; from 2725; a *complaint* ("category"), i.e. criminal *charge*:—accusation (× -ed).

Noun from *katēgoréō* (2723), to accuse. Accusation, incrimination of a person (Lk 6:7; Jn 18:29; 1Ti 5:19; Tit 1:6).

Syn.: *aitía* (156), cause, accusation; *aitíama* (157), a complaint or accusation; *égklēma* (1462), accusation.

2725. κατήγορος, katēgoros, *kat-ay´-gor-os*; from 2596 and 58; *against* one in the *assembly*, i.e. a *complainant* at law; specially *Satan*:—accuser.

Noun from *katēgoréō* (2723), to accuse. Accuser (Jn 8:10; Ac 23:30, 35; 24:8; 25:16, 18; Rev 12:10).

Syn.: *diábolos* (1228), slanderer, the devil.

2726. κατήφεια, katēpheia, *kat-ay´-fi-ah*; from a compound of 2596 and perhaps a derivative of the base of 5316 (meaning *downcast* in look); *demureness*, i.e. (by implication) *sadness*:—heaviness.

2727. κατηχέω, katēcheō, *kat-ay-kheh´-o*; from 2596 and 2279; to *sound down* into the ears, i.e. (by implication) to *indoctrinate* ("catechize") or (genitive) to *apprise* of:—inform, instruct, teach.

2728. κατιόω, katioō, *kat-ee-o´-o*; from 2596 and a derivative of 2447; to *rust down*, i.e. *corrode*:—canker.

2729. κατισχύω, katischuō, *kat-is-khoo´-o*; from 2596 and 2480; to *overpower*:—prevail (against).

2730. κατοικέω, katoikeō, *kat-oy-keh´-o*; from 2596 and 3611; to *house permanently*, i.e. *reside* (literal or figurative):—dwell (-er), inhabitant (-ter).

From *katá* (2596), an intensive, and *oikéō* (3611), to dwell. To settle down in a fixed dwelling, to dwell permanently:

(I) To dwell permanently in, inhabit a house or place (Mt 2:23; 4:13; 12:45; Lk 13:4; Ac 1:20; 7:4; Heb 11:9; Rev 3:10; 6:10; 17:8).

(II) Metaphorically of God (Ac 7:48; 17:24); of Christ as being ever present by His Spirit in the hearts of Christians (Eph 3:17); of the fullness of the Godhead which was in Jesus (Col 1:19; 2:9); of the Spirit dwelling in man (Jas 4:5); of the righteousness dwelling in the new heavens and the new earth (2Pe 3:13).

Deriv.: *egkatoikéō* (1460), to dwell among; *katoíkēsis* (2731), the act of coming to dwell, a dwelling, habitation; *katoikētḗrion* (2732), a habitation; *katoikía* (2733), habitation, house.

Syn.: *enoikéō* (1774), to dwell in; *kataskēnóō* (2681), to pitch one's tent and lodge in it; *ménō* (3306), to abide, remain; *perioikéō* (4039), to dwell around; *skēnóō* (4637), to live in a tent; *sunoikéō* (4924), to dwell with.

2731. κατοίκησις, katoikēsis, *kat-oy´-kay-sis*; from 2730; *residence* (properly, the act; but by implication concretely, the mansion):—dwelling.

2732. κατοικητήριον, katoikētērion, *kat-oy-kay-tay´-ree-on*; from a derivative of 2730; a *dwelling-place*:—habitation.

2733. κατοικία, katoikia, *kat-oy-kee´-ah*; *residence* (properly, the condition; but by implication, the abode itself):—habitation.

2734. κατοπτρίζομαι, katoptrizomai, *kat-op-trid´-zom-ahee*; middle from a compound of 2596 and a derivative of 3700 [compare 2072]; to *mirror oneself*, i.e. to *see reflected* (figurative):—behold as in a glass.

2735. κατόρθωμα, katorthōma, *kat-or´-tho-mah*; from a compound of 2596 and a derivative of 3717 [compare 1357]; something *made fully upright*, i.e. (figurative) *rectification* (specially *good* public *administration*):—very worthy deed.

2736. κάτω, katō, *kat´-o*; also (comparative) **κατωτέρω, *katōterō***, *kat-o-ter´-o* [compare 2737]; adverb from 2596; *downwards*:—beneath, bottom, down, under.

Adverb of place, from *katá* (2596), down. Downwards, below. The comparative is *katṓteros* (2737), lower:

(I) Of place, implying motion: down (Mt 4:6; Lk 4:9; Jn 8:6; Ac 20:9; Sept.: Ecc 3:21; Isa 37:31); below, underneath (Mt 27:51; Mk 14:66; 15:38; Ac 2:19). Used as an adj.: that which is below, i.e. earthly (Jn 8:23).

(II) Of time: comparatively, *katōtérō*, below a certain age (Mt 2:16).

Deriv.: *hupokátō* (5270), under.

2737. κατώτερος, katōteros, *kat-o´-ter-os*; comparative from 2736; *inferior* (locally, of Hades):—lower.

2738. καῦμα, kauma, *kow´-mah*; from 2545; properly a *burn* (concrete), but used (abstract) of a *glow*:—heat.

2739. καυματίζω, kaumatizō, *kow-mat-id´-zo*; from 2738; to *burn*:—scorch.

2740. καῦσις, kausis, *kow´-sis*; from 2545; *burning* (the act):—be burned.

2741. καυσόω, kausoō, *kow-so´-o*; from 2740; to *set on fire*:—with fervent heat.

2742. καύσων, kausōn, *kow´-sone*; from 2741; a *glare*:—(burning) heat.

2743. καυτηριάζω, kautēriazō, *kow-tay-ree-ad´-zo*; from a derivative of 2545; to *brand* ("*cauterize*"), i.e. (by implication) to *render unsensitive* (figurative):—sear with a hot iron.

2744. καυχάομαι, kauchaomai, *kow-khah´-om-ahee*; from some (obsolete) base akin to that of **αὐχέω, *aucheō*** (to *boast*) and 2172; to *vaunt* (in a good or a bad sense):—(make) boast, glory, joy, rejoice.

2745. καύχημα, kauchēma, *kow´-khay-mah*; from 2744; a *boast* (properly, the object; by implication, the act) in a good or a bad sense:—boasting, (whereof) to glory (of), glorying, rejoice (-ing).

2746. καύχησις, kauchēsis, *kow´-khay-sis*; from 2744; *boasting* (properly, the act; by implication, the object), in a good or a bad sense:—boasting, whereof I may glory, glorying, rejoicing.

2747. Κεγχρεαί, Kegchreai, *keng-khreh-a´hee*; probably from **κέγχρος**, *Kegchros* (*millet*); *Cenchre'*, a port of Corinth:—Cenchrea.

2748. Κεδρών, Kedrōn, *ked-rone´*; of Hebrew origin [6939]; *Cedron* (i.e. *Kidron*), a brook near Jerusalem:—Cedron.

2749. κεῖμαι, keimai, *ki´-mahee*; middle of a primary verb; to *lie* outstretched (literal or figurative):—be (appointed, laid up, made, set), lay, lie. Compare 5087.

To lie, be laid down:

(I) To lie down, be laid down (Mt 28:6; Lk 2:12, 16; 23:53; 24:12; Jn 11:41; 20:5–7, 12; 21:9).

(II) To be placed or set (Mt 5:14; Jn 2:6; 19:29; 2Co 3:15; Rev 4:2); to be laid, applied, e.g., an ax laid to a tree (Mt 3:10; Lk 3:9); to be laid, as a foundation (1Co 3:11); to be stored up (Lk 12:19); to be set, appointed (Lk 2:34; Php 1:17; 1Th 3:3); to be made or promulgated as a law (1Ti 1:9).

(III) To be in the power of someone (1Jn 5:19).

Deriv.: *anákeimai* (345), to rest on; *antíkeimai* (480), to lie over against or to oppose; *apókeimai* (606), to be laid, reserved, appointed; *epíkeimai* (1945), to rest upon, impose, be instant, press upon; *katákeimai* (2621), to lie down; *kṓmē* (2968), a village; *parákeimai* (3873), to lie ready; *períkeimai* (4029), to lie around; *prókeimai* (4295), to lie before, set forth, to lie in front of.

Syn.: *kataklínō* (2625), to recline, sit down to eat.

2750. κειρία, keiria, *ki-ree´-ah*; of uncertain affinity; a *swathe*, i.e. *winding-sheet*:—graveclothes.

2751. κείρω, keirō, *ki´-ro*; a primary verb; to *shear*:—shear (-er).

2752. κέλευμα, keleuma, *kel´-yoo-mah*; from 2753; a *cry* of incitement:—shout.

2753. κελεύω, keleuō, *kel-yoo´-o*; from a primary **κέλλω, *kellō*** (to *urge* on); "hail"; to *incite* by word, i.e. *order*:—bid, (at, give) command (-ment).

2754. κενοδοξία, kenodoxia, *ken-od-ox-ee´-ah*; from 2755; *empty glorying*, i.e. *self-conceit*:—vain-glory.

2755. κενόδοξος, kenodoxos, *ken-od´-ox-os*; from 2756 and 1391; *vainly glorifying*, i.e. *self-conceited*:—desirous of vain-glory.

2756. κενός, kenos, *ken-os´*; apparently a primary word; *empty* (literal or figurative):—empty, (in) vain.

(I) Empty, the opposite of *pleres* (4134), full (Mk 12:3; Lk 1:53; 20:10, 11).

(II) Figuratively, meaning empty, vain: fruitless, without usefulness or success (Ac 4:25; 1Co 15:10, 14, 58; 2Co 6:1; Gal 2:2; Php 2:16; 1Th 2:1; 3:5).

(III) Of that in which there is nothing of truth or reality, false, fallacious, e.g., empty words meaning false words, deceitful (Eph 5:6; Col 2:8); of persons, meaning empty, foolish (Jas 2:20).

Deriv.: *kenódoxos* (2755), self-conceited; *kenophōnía* (2757), empty speaking; *kenóō* (2758), to be in vain; *kenō̂s* (2761), in vain.

2757. κενοφωνία, kenophōnia, *ken-of-o-nee´-ah*; from a presumed compound of 2756 and 5456; *empty sounding*, i.e. *fruitless discussion*:—vain.

Noun from *kenós* (2756), vain, and *phōnḗ* (5456), a voice. Empty or fruitless speaking (1Ti 6:20; 2Ti 2:16).

2758. κενόω, kenoō, *ken-o´-o*; from 2756; to *make empty*, i.e. (figurative) to *abase, neutralize, falsify*:—make (of no effect, of no reputation, void), be in vain.

From *kenós* (2756), empty, void. To make empty, to empty. In the NT, used figuratively:

(I) To empty oneself, i.e. divest oneself of rightful dignity by descending to an inferior condition, to abase oneself (Php 2:7).

(II) To make empty, vain, fruitless (Ro 4:14; 1Co 1:17). Hence to show that something is without ground, fallacious (1Co 9:15; 2Co 9:3).

Syn.: *mataióō* (3154), to render vain, without meaning or fulfillment.

2759. κέντρον, kentron, *ken´-tron*; from **κεντέω**, *kenteō* (to *prick*); a *point* ("centre"), i.e. a *sting* (figurative, *poison*) or *goad* (figurative, divine *impulse*):—prick, sting.

2760. κεντυρίων, kenturiōn, *ken-too-ree´-ohn*; of Latin origin; a *centurion*, i.e. *captain* of one hundred soldiers:—centurion.

2761. κενῶς, kenōs, *ken-oce´*; adverb from 2756; *vainly*, i.e. *to no purpose*:—in vain.

2762. κεραία, keraia, *ker-ah´-yah*; feminine of a presumed derivative of the base of 2768; something *horn-like*, i.e. (special) the *apex* of a Hebrew letter (figurative, the least *particle*):—tittle.

2763. κεραμεύς, kerameus, *ker-am-yooce´*; from 2766; a *potter*:—potter.

2764. κεραμικός, keramikos, *ker-am-ik-os´*; from 2766; *made of clay*, i.e. *earthen*:—of a potter.

2765. κεράμιον, keramion, *ker-am´-ee-on*; neuter of a presumed derivative of 2766; an *earthenware* vessel, i.e. *jar*:—pitcher.

2766. κέραμος, keramos, *ker´-am-os*; probably from the base of 2767 (through the idea of *mixing* clay and water); *earthenware*, i.e. a *tile* (by analogy, a thin *roof* or *awning*):—tiling.

2767. κεράννυμι, kerannumi, *ker-an´-noo-mee*; a prolonged form of a more primary **κεράω**, *keraō*, *ker-ah´-o* (which is used in certain tenses); to *mingle*, i.e. (by implication) to *pour* out (for drinking):—fill, pour out. Compare 3396.

2768. κέρας, keras, *ker´-as*; from a primary **κάρ**, *kar* (the *hair* of the head); a *horn* (literal or figurative):—horn.

2769. κεράτιον, keration, *ker-at´-ee-on*; neuter of a presumed derivative of 2768; something *horned*, i.e. (special) the *pod* of the carob-tree:—husk.

2770. κερδαίνω, kerdainō, *ker-dah´ee-no*; from 2771; to *gain* (literal or figurative):—(get) gain, win.

2771. κέρδος, kerdos, *ker´-dos*; of uncertain affinity; *gain* (pecuniary or genitive):—gain, lucre.

2772. κέρμα, kerma, *ker´-mah*; from 2751; a *clipping* (*bit*), i.e. (special) a *coin*:—money.

2773. κερματιστής, kermatistēs, *ker-mat-is-tace´*; from a derivative of 2772; a *handler of coins*, i.e. *money-broker*:—changer of money.

2774. κεφάλαιον, kephalaion, *kef-al´-ah-yon*; neuter of a derivative of 2776; a *principal* thing, i.e. *main point*; specially an *amount* (of money):—sum.

2775. κεφαλαιόω, kephalaioō, *kef-al-ahee-o´-o*; from the same as 2774; (special) to *strike on the head*:—wound in the head.

2776. κεφαλή, kephalē, *kef-al-ay´*; probably from the primary **κάπτω**, *kaptō* (in the sense of *seizing*); the *head* (as the part most readily *taken* hold of), literal or figurative:—head.

Noun meaning the head:

(I) Particularly of a man or woman (Mt 6:17; 8:20; 27:30; Lk 7:38); as cut off (Mt 14:11; Mk 6:27); of animals (Rev 9:17, 19; 12:3); as the principal part, but emphatically for the whole person (Ac 18:6, "Your blood be upon your own heads," meaning the guilt for your destruction rests upon yourselves; Ro 12:20). Figuratively of things: the head, top, summit, e.g., the head of the corner, meaning the chief stone of the corner, the cornerstone, the same as *akrogōniaíos* (204), belonging to the extreme corner, chief corner (Mt 21:42; Mk 12:10; Lk 20:17; Ac 4:11; 1Pe 2:7).

(II) Figuratively of persons, i.e. the head, chief, one to whom others are subordinate, e.g., the husband in relation to his wife (1Co 11:3; Eph 5:23); of Christ in relation to His Church which is His body, and its members are His members (Eph 1:22; 4:15; 5:23; Col 1:18; 2:10, 19); of God in relation to Christ (1Co 11:3).

Deriv.: *apokephalízō* (607), to decapitate, behead; *kephalís* (2777), a knob, roll, volume; *perikephalaía* (4030), helmet.

Syn.: *hēgemṓn* (2232), a leader, ruler.

2777. κεφαλίς, kephalis, *kef-al-is´*; from 2776; properly a *knob*, i.e. (by implication) a *roll* (by extension from the *end* of a stick on which the manuscript was rolled):—volume.

2778. κῆνσος, kēnsos, *kane´-sos*; of Latin origin; properly an *enrollment* ("*census*"), i.e. (by implication) a *tax*:—tribute.

2779. κῆπος, kēpos, *kay´-pos*; of uncertain affinity; a *garden*:—garden.

2780. κηπουρός, kēpouros, *kay-poo-ros´*; from 2779 and **οὖρος**, *ouros* (a *warden*); a *garden-keeper*, i.e. *gardener*:—gardener.

2781. κηρίον, kērion, *kay-ree´-on*; diminutive from **κηός**, *kēos* (*wax*); a *cell* for honey, i.e. (collective) the *comb*:—[honey-] comb.

2782. κήρυγμα, kērugma, *kay´-roog-mah*; from 2784; a *proclamation* (especially of the gospel; (by implication) the *gospel* itself):—preaching.

Noun from *kērússō* (2784), to preach, discharge a herald's office, cry out, proclaim. Proclamation by a herald. In the NT, annunciation, preaching, spoken of prophets (Mt 12:41; Lk 11:32); of Christ and his apostles: preaching the gospel, public instruction (1Co 1:21; 2:4; 15:14; Tit 1:3); used by metonymy for the gospel preached (Ro 16:25; 2Ti 4:17).

Syn.: *aggelía* (31), a message, proclamation, news; *epaggelía* (1860), a promise, message.

2783. κήρυξ, kērux, *kay´-roox*; from 2784; a *herald*, i.e. of divine truth (especially of the gospel):—preacher.

Noun from *kērússō* (2784), to preach. A herald, public crier. In the NT: a preacher, public instructor of the divine will and precepts, as Noah (2Pe 2:5), of the gospel, as Paul (1Ti 2:7; 2Ti 1:11).

2784. κηρύσσω, kērussō, *kay-roos´-so*; of uncertain affinity; to *herald* (as a public *crier*), especially divine truth (the gospel):—preach (-er), proclaim, publish.

To preach, to herald, proclaim:

(I) Generally, to proclaim, announce publicly (Mt 10:27; Lk 12:3; Ac 10:42; Rev 5:2). In the sense of to publish abroad, announce publicly (Mk 1:45; 5:20; 7:36; Lk 8:39).

(II) Especially to preach, publish, or announce religious truth, the gospel with its attendant privileges and obligations, the gospel dispensation:

(A) Generally of John the Baptist (Mt 3:1; Mk 1:4, 7; Lk 3:3; Ac 10:37); of Jesus (Mt 4:17, 23; 9:35; 11:1; Mk 1:14, 38, 39; Lk 4:44; 8:1; 1Pe 3:19); of apostles and teachers (Mt 10:7; 24:14; 26:13; Mk 3:14; 6:12; 13:10; 14:9; 16:15, 20; Lk 9:2; 24:47; Ac 20:25; 28:31; Ro 10:8, 14, 15; 1Co 9:27; 15:11; Gal 2:2; Col 1:23; 1Th 2:9; 2Ti 4:2). "To preach Christ" means to announce Him as the Messiah and urge the reception of His gospel (Ac 8:5; 9:20; 19:13; 1Co 1:23; 15:12; 2Co 1:19; 4:5; 11:4; Php 1:15; 1Ti 3:16).

(B) In allusion to the Mosaic and prophetic institutions, to preach, teach (Lk 4:18, 19; Ac 15:21; Ro 2:21; Gal 5:11).

Deriv.: *kḗrugma* (2782), the message of a herald, denotes preaching, the substance of which is distinct from the act; *kḗrux* (2783), a herald, a preacher; *prokērússō* (4296), to proclaim before or ahead.

Syn.: *diaggéllō* (1229), to herald thoroughly, declare, preach, signify; *diamartúromai* (1263), to testify thoroughly; *euaggelízō* (2097), to proclaim the good news, evangelize; *kataggéllō* (2605), to proclaim, promulgate, declare; *parrēsiázomai* (3955), to speak or preach boldly.

2785. κῆτος, kētos, *kay´-tos*; probably from the base of 5490; a huge *fish* (as *gaping* for prey):—whale.

2786. Κηφᾶς, Kēphas, *kay-fas´*; of Chaldee origin [compare 3710]; *the Rock; Cephas* (i.e. *Kepha*), a surname of Peter:—Cephas.

2787. κιβωτός, kibōtos, *kib-o-tos´*; of uncertain derivative; a *box*, i.e. the sacred *ark* and that of Noah:—ark.

2788. κιθάρα, kithara, *kith-ar´-ah*; of uncertain affinity; a *lyre*:—harp.

2789. κιθαρίζω, kitharizō, *kith-ar-id´-zo*; from 2788; to *play on a lyre*:—harp.

2790. κιθαρῳδός, kitharōidos, *kith-ar-o-dos´*; from 2788 and a derivative of the same as 5603; a *lyre-singer* (*-player*), i.e. *harpist*:—harper.

2791. Κιλικία, Kilikia, *kil-ik-ee´-ah*; probably of foreign origin; *Cilicia*, a region of Asia Minor:—Cilicia.

2792. κινάμωμον, kinamōmon, *kin-am´-o-mon*; of foreign origin [compare 7076]; *cinnamon*:—cinnamon.

2793. κινδυνεύω, kinduneuō, *kin-doon-yoo´-o*; from 2794; to *undergo peril*:—be in danger, be (stand) in jeopardy.

2794. κίνδυνος, kindunos, *kin´-doo-nos*; of uncertain derivative; *danger*:—peril.

2795. κινέω, kineō, *kin-eh´-o*; from **κίω, kiō** (poetic for **εἶμι, *eimi***, to go); to *stir* (transitive), literal or figurative:—(re-) move (-r), way.

2796. κίνησις, kinēsis, *kin´-ay-sis*; from 2795; a *stirring*:—moving.

2797. Κίς, Kis, *kis*; of Hebrew origin [7027]; *Cis* (i.e. *Kish*), an Israelite:—Cis.

2798. κλάδος, klados, *klad´-os*; from 2806; a *twig* or *bough* (as if broken off):—branch.

2799. κλαίω, klaiō, *klah´-yo*; of uncertain affinity; to *sob*, i.e. *wail* aloud (whereas 1145 is rather to *cry* silently):—bewail, weep.

2800. κλάσις, klasis, *klas´-is*; from 2806; *fracture* (the act):—breaking.

Noun from *kláō* (2806), to break. The act of breaking, particularly with reference to the bread in the Lord's Supper (Lk 24:35; Ac 2:42).

2801. κλάσμα, klasma, *klas´-mah*; from 2806; a *piece* (*bit*):—broken, fragment.

Noun from *kláō* (2806), to break. That which is broken off, a fragment, crumb; used of the fragments collected after the miraculous feedings (Mt 14:20; 15:37; Mk 6:43; 8:8, 19, 20; Lk 9:17; Jn 6:12, 13).

2802. Κλαύδη, Klaudē, *klow´-day*; of uncertain derivative; *Claude*, an island near Crete:—Clauda.

2803. Κλαυδία, Klaudia, *klow-dee´-ah*; feminine of 2804; *Claudia*, a Christian woman:—Claudia.

2804. Κλαύδιος, Klaudios, *klow´-dee-os*; of Latin origin; *Claudius*, the name of two Romans:—Claudius.

2805. κλαυθμός, klauthmos, *klowth-mos´*; from 2799; *lamentation*:—wailing, weeping, × wept.

2806. κλάω, klaō, *klah´-o*; a primary verb; to *break* (specially of bread):—break.

Verb meaning to break. In the NT, used only of the breaking of bread for distribution before a meal, the Jewish bread being in the form of thin cakes (Mt 14:19; 15:36; Mk 8:6, 19; Lk 24:30; Ac 27:35; Sept.: Jer 16:7); used in the Lord's Supper and *agápē* (26), love feast (Mt 26:26; Mk 14:22; Lk 22:19; Ac 2:46; 20:7, 11; 1Co 10:16; 11:24).

Deriv.: *ekkláō* (1575), to break off; *katakláō* (2622), to break bread; *kládos* (2798), branch; *klásis* (2800), the breaking; *klásma* (2801), that which is broken off, fragment, crumb; *klḗma* (2814), branch.

Syn.: *katágnumi* (2608), to break, crack apart; *suntríbō* (4937), to shatter, break in pieces by crushing.

2807. κλείς, kleis, *klice*; from 2808; a *key* (as *shutting* a lock), literal or figurative:—key.

2808. κλείω, kleiō, *kli´-o*; a primary verb; to *close* (literal or figurative):—shut (up).

2809. κλέμμα, klemma, *klem´-mah*; from 2813; *stealing* (properly the thing stolen, but used of the act):—theft.

2810. Κλεόπας, Kleopas, *kleh-op´-as*; probably contrete from **Κλεόπατρος**, ***Kleopatros*** (compound of 2811 and 3962); *Cleopas*, a Christian:—Cleopas.

2811. κλέος, kleos, *kleh´-os*; from a shorter form of 2564; *renown* (as if *being called*):—glory.

2812. κλέπτης, kleptēs, *klep´-tace*; from 2813; a *stealer* (literal or figurative):—thief. Compare 3027.

From *kléptō* (2813), to steal. Thief (Mt 6:19, 20; Lk 12:33, 39; 1Co 6:10; 1Th 5:2, 4; 1Pe 4:15; 2Pe 3:10; Rev 3:3; 16:15). Occurring along with *lēstḗs* (3027), robber (Jn 10:1, 8). The *kléptēs* steals secretly, as would a burglar (Mt 24:43) or an embezzler (Jn 12:6), while the *lēstḗs* robs forcefully with violence. Figuratively, of false teachers or deceivers who steal men away from the truth (Jn 10:8, 10).

Syn.: *hárpax* (727), extortioner.

2813. κλέπτω, kleptō, *klep´-to*; a primary verb; to *filch*:—steal.

2814. κλῆμα, klēma, *klay´-mah*; from 2806; a *limb* or *shoot* (as if *broken* off):—branch.

Noun from *kláō* (2806), to break. A shoot, sprout, branch, such as are easily broken off. In the NT, of the vine: a shoot, tendril (Jn 15:2, 4–6; Sept.: Eze 15:2; 17:6, 7).

Syn.: *kládos* (2798), young tender shoot, branch; *stoibás* (4746), a branch full of leaves or a layer of leaves.

2815. Κλήμης, Klēmēs, *klay´-mace*; of Latin origin; *merciful; Clemes* (i.e. *Clemens*), a Christian:—Clement.

2816. κληρονομέω, klēronomeō, *klay-ron-om-eh´-o*; from 2818; to *be* an *heir* to (literal or figurative):—be heir, (obtain by) inherit (-ance).

From *klēronómos* (2818), an heir. To be an heir, to inherit. In the Septuagint OT, used originally of receiving an inheritance by lot, of the division of the land of Canaan among the twelve tribes (Nu 26:55; Jos 16:4). Hence, in the NT generally:

(I) To inherit, to be heir, in an absolute sense (Gal 4:30).

(II) To obtain, acquire, possess. In the NT, spoken of the friends of God as receiving admission to the kingdom of heaven and its attendant privileges (Mt 5:5; 25:34). To inherit eternal life (Mt 19:29; Mk 10:17; Lk 10:25; 18:18). Used with the negative to describe those who will not inherit (1Co 6:9, 10; 15:50; Gal 5:21). See also Heb 1:4, 14; 6:12; 12:17; 1Pe 3:9; Rev 21:7.

Syn.: *klēróō* (2820), to determine by lot.

2817. κληρονομία, klēronomia, *klay-ron-om-ee´-ah*; from 2818; *heirship*, i.e. (concrete) a *patrimony* or (genitive) a *possession*:—inheritance.

Noun from *klēronómos* (2818), an heir. Inheritance (Mt 21:38; Mk 12:7; Lk 12:13; 20:14). Generally: portion, possession, especially of the land of Canaan as the possession of Abraham and his descendants (Ac 7:5; Heb 11:8); hence figuratively of admission to the kingdom of God and its attendant privileges (Ac 20:32; Gal 3:18; Eph 1:14, 18; 5:5; Col 3:24; Heb 9:15; 1Pe 1:4). See *klēronoméō* (2816), to be an heir.

2818. κληρονόμος, klēronomos, *klay-ron-om´-os*; from 2819 and the base of 3551 (in its original sense of *partitioning*, i.e. [reflexive] *getting* by apportionment); a *sharer by lot*, i.e. an *inheritor* (literal or figurative); (by implication) a *possessor*:—heir.

Noun from *klḗros* (2819), lot, and *nómos* (3551), law, anything established. An heir, originally of an inheritance divided by lot, but later spoken of any heir (Mt 21:38; Mk 12:7; Lk 20:14; Gal 4:1). Figuratively, a partaker of the blessings which God bestows upon His children, implying admission to the kingdom of heaven and its privileges (Ro 4:13, 14; 8:17; Gal 3:29; 4:7; Tit 3:7; Heb 1:2; 6:17; 11:7; Jas 2:5). See *klēronoméō* (2816), to be an heir.

Deriv.: *klēronoméō* (2816), to be an heir; *klēronomía* (2817), that which constitutes one as heir, inheritance; *sugklēronómos* (4789), he who participates in the same inheritance or lot, joint-heir.

2819. κλῆρος, klēros, *klay´-ros*; probably from 2806 (through the idea of using *bits* of wood, etc., for the purpose); a *die* (for drawing chances); (by implication) a *portion* (as if so secured); by extension an *acquisition* (especially a *patrimony*, figurative):—heritage, inheritance, lot, part.

Noun probably from *kláō* (2806), to break. A lot:

(I) A lot, die, anything used in determining chances. Spoken of the lot cast by the soldiers gambling for Christ's clothing at the cross (Mt 27:35; Mk 15:24; Lk 23:34; Jn 19:24); spoken of the lot used to choose Judas's successor (Ac 1:26).

(II) A lot, allotment, portion, or share to which one is appointed by lot or otherwise (Ac 1:17, 25; 8:21). Hence, generally, a portion, possession, heritage (Ac 26:18; Col 1:12; 1Pe 5:3).

Deriv.: *klēronómos* (2818), one who has an inheritance, a lot; *klēróō* (2820), to cast lots, determine by lot; *naúklēros* (3490), an owner of a ship; *holóklēros* (3648), an entire portion, intact.

Syn.: *merís* (3310), part, share; *méros* (3313), a part, portion of the whole.

2820. κληρόω, klēroō, *klay-ro´-o*; from 2819; to *allot*, i.e. (figurative) to *assign* (a privilege):—obtain an inheritance.

From *klḗros* (2819), a lot. In the passive, to obtain an inheritance, as through the casting of lots. Only in Eph 1:11. See *klēronoméō* (2816), to be an heir.

Deriv.: *prosklēróō* (4345), to give or assign by lot.

2821. κλῆσις, klēsis, *klay´-sis*; from a shorter form of 2564; an *invitation* (figurative):—calling.

Noun from *kaléō* (2564), to call. A call, an invitation to a banquet. In the NT, used metaphorically: a call, invitation to the kingdom of God and its privileges, i.e. the divine call by which Christians are introduced into the privileges of the gospel (Ro 11:29; 1Co 1:26; 7:20; Eph 1:18; 4:1, 4; Php 3:14; 2Th 1:11; 2Ti 1:9; Heb 3:1; 2Pe 1:10).

2822. κλητός, klētos, *klay-tos´*; from the same as 2821; *invited*, i.e. *appointed*, or (special) a *saint*:—called.

Verbal adj. from *kaléō* (2564), to call. Called, invited, e.g., to a banquet as guests. Hence In the NT, used figuratively: called, invited to the kingdom of heaven and its privileges: generally (Mt 20:16; 22:14); also emphatically of those who have obeyed this call, i.e. saints, Christians (Ro 1:6, 7; 1Co 1:2, 24; Jude 1; Rev 17:14). In the sense of appointed, chosen to an office (Ro 1:1; 1Co 1:1).

2823. κλίβανος, klibanos, *klib´-an-os*; of uncertain derivative; an earthen *pot* used for baking in:—oven.

2824. κλίμα, klima, *klee´-mah*; from 2827; a *slope*, i.e. (special) a "*clime*" or *tract* of country:—part, region.

2825. κλίνη, klinē, *klee´-nay*; from 2827; a *couch* (for sleep, sickness, sitting or eating):—bed, table.

2826. κλινίδιον, klinidion, *klin-id´-ee-on*; neuter of a presumed derivative of 2825; a *pallet* or *little couch*:—bed.

2827. κλίνω, klinō, *klee´-no*; a primary verb; to *slant* or *slope*, i.e. *incline* or *recline* (literal or figurative):—bow (down), be far spent, lay, turn to flight, wear away.

2828. κλισία, klisia, *klee-see´-ah*; from a derivative of 2827; properly *reclination*, i.e. (concrete and specific) a *party* at a meal:—company.

2829. κλοπή, klopē, *klop-ay´*; from 2813; *stealing*:—theft.

2830. κλύδων, kludōn, *kloo´-dohn*; from **κλύζω, kluzō** (to *billow* or *dash* over); a *surge* of the sea (literal or figurative):—raging, wave.

2831. κλυδωνίζομαι, kludōnizomai, *kloo-do-nid´-zom-ahee*; middle from 2830; to *surge*, i.e. (figurative) to *fluctuate*:—toss to and fro.

2832. Κλωπᾶς, Klōpas, *klo-pas´*; of Chaldee origin (corresponding to 256); *Clopas*, an Israelite:—Clopas.

2833. κνήθω, knēthō, *knay´-tho*; from a primary **κνάω, knaō** (to *scrape*); to *scratch*, i.e. (by implication) to *tickle*:—× itching.

2834. Κνίδος, Knidos, *knee´-dos*; probably of foreign origin; *Cnidus*, a place in Asia Minor:—Cnidus.

2835. κοδράντης, kodrantēs, *kod-ran´-tace*; of Latin origin; a *quadrans*, i.e. the fourth part of an *assarius* (787):—farthing.

2836. κοιλία, koilia, *koy-lee´-ah*; from **κοῖλος, koilos** ("*hollow*"); a *cavity*, i.e. (special) the *abdomen*; (by implication) the *matrix*; (figurative) the *heart*:—belly, womb.

2837. κοιμάω, koimaō, *koy-mah´-o*; from 2749; to *put to sleep*, i.e. (passive or reflexive) to *slumber*; (figurative) to *decease*:—(be a-, fall a-, fall on) sleep, be dead.

2838. κοίμησις, koimēsis, *koy´-may-sis*; from 2837; *sleeping*, i.e. (by implication) *repose*:—taking of rest.

2839. κοινός, koinos, *koy-nos´*; probably from 4862; *common*, i.e. (literally) shared by all or several, or (ceremonial) *profane*:—common, defiled, unclean, unholy.

Adjective meaning common.

(I) Particularly, pertaining equally to all (Ac 2:44; 4:32); spoken of the common faith (Tit 1:4) and of the common salvation (Jude 3).

(II) In the Levitical sense: not permitted by the Mosaic precepts, and therefore common, i.e. not sacred; hence the same as ceremonially unclean, unholy, profane (Mk 7:2; Ac 10:14, 28; 11:8; Ro 14:14). Figuratively, unholy, unconsecrated (Heb 10:29).

Deriv.: *koinóō* (2840), to make common, unclean; *koinōnós* (2844), an associate, companion, partner, participant.

Syn.: *akáthartos* (169), unclean; *anósios* (462), unholy, profane.

2840. κοινόω, koinoō, *koy-no´-o*; from 2839; to *make* (or *consider*) *profane* (ceremonial):—call common, defile, pollute, unclean.

From *koinós* (2839), common. To make common, unclean, pollute or defile (Mt 15:11, 18, 20; Mk 7:15, 18, 20, 23; Ac 21:28; Heb 9:13; Rev 21:27); to pronounce or call common or unclean (Ac 10:15; 11:9). See *koinós* (2839, II), common.

Syn.: *miaínō* (3392), to stain, defile; *molúnō* (3435), to besmear; *spilóō* (4695), to defile, spot.

2841. κοινωνέω, koinōneō, *koy-no-neh´-o*; from 2844; to *share* with others (object or subject):—communicate, distribute, be partaker.

From *koinōnós* (2844), an associate, partaker. To be a partaker of or in anything with someone else, i.e. to share in common (Ro 15:27;

Heb 2:14); to share resources with others (Ro 12:13; Gal 6:6; Php 4:15); in an adverse sense, to share guilt (1Ti 5:22; 2Jn 11).

Deriv.: *koinōnía* (2842), fellowship; *sugkoinōnéō* (4790), to share with.

Syn.: *metéchō* (3348), to partake of, share; *summerízomai* (4829), to have a share in, be a partaker with.

2842. κοινωνία, koinōnia, *koy-nohn-ee´-ah*; from 2844; *partnership*, i.e. (literal) *participation*, or (social) *intercourse*, or (pecuniary) *benefaction*:—(to) communicate (-ation), communion, (contri-) distribution, fellowship.

Noun from *koinōnéō* (2841), to share in. Act of partaking, sharing, because of a common interest:

(I) Participation, communion, fellowship (Ac 2:42; 1Co 1:9; 10:16; 2Co 6:14; 13:14; Gal 2:9; Eph 3:9; Php 1:5; 2:1; 3:10; Phm 6; 1Jn 1:3, 6, 7).

(II) Sharing, distribution. In the NT, a metonym for contribution, collection of money in behalf of poorer churches (Ro 15:26; 2Co 8:4; 9:13; Heb 13:16).

Syn.: *eleēmosúnē* (1654), compassion, beneficence, alms; *metochḗ* (3352), partnership.

2843. κοινωνικός, koinōnikos, *koy-no-nee-kos´*; from 2844; *communicative*, i.e. (pecuniarily) *liberal*:—willing to communicate.

2844. κοινωνός, koinōnos, *koy-no-nos´*; from 2839; a *sharer*, i.e. *associate*:—companion, × fellowship, partaker, partner.

Adjective from *koinós* (2839), common. A partaker, partner, companion:

(I) Generally, of partners (Mt 23:20; Lk 5:10; 2Co 8:23; Phm 17).

(II) Figuratively, of those who eat meats offered to idols, partakers or companions either with God or with demons (1Co 10:18, 20).

(III) Figuratively, of those who serve Christ, partakers of divine blessings (2Co 1:7; 1Pe 5:1; 2Pe 1:4).

Deriv.: *koinōnéō* (2841), to share in; *koinōnikós* (2843), communicative, generous; *sugkoinōnós* (4791), joint participator, companion.

Syn.: *métochos* (3353), partner.

2845. κοίτη, koitē, *koy´-tay*; from 2749; a *couch*; by extension *cohabitation*; (by implication) the male *sperm*:—bed, chambering, × conceive.

2846. κοιτών, koitōn, *koy-tone´*; from 2845; a *bedroom*:—+ chamberlain.

2847. κόκκινος, kokkinos, *kok´-kee-nos*; from 2848 (from the *kernel*-shape of the insect); *crimson*-coloured:—scarlet (colour, coloured).

2848. κόκκος, kokkos, *kok´-kos*; apparently a primary word; a *kernel* of seed:—corn, grain.

2849. κολάζω, kolazō, *kol-ad´-zo*; from **κόλος**, ***kolos*** (*dwarf*); properly to *curtail*, i.e. (figurative) to *chastise* (or *reserve* for infliction):—punish.

2850. κολακεία, kolakeia, *kol-ak-i´-ah*; from a derivative of **κόλαξ**, ***kolax*** (a *fawner*); *flattery*:— × flattering.

2851. κόλασις, kolasis, *kol´-as-is*; from 2849; penal *infliction*:—punishment, torment.

Noun from *kolázō* (2849), to punish. Mutilation, pruning. In the NT, punishment. Spoken of eternal punishment for those condemned by Christ (Mt 25:46); spoken of the temporary torment produced by fear in the soul of one conscious of sin before the love of God brings peace at salvation (1Jn 4:18).

Syn.: *díkē* (1349), judgement, the execution of a sentence; *ekdíkēsis* (1557), vengeance, punishment; *epitimía* (2009), penalty.

2852. κολαφίζω, kolaphizō, *kol-af-id´-zo*; from a derivative of the base of 2849; to *rap* with the fist:—buffet.

2853. κολλάω, kollaō, *kol-lah´-o*; from **κόλλα**, ***kolla*** ("*glue*"); to *glue*, i.e. (passive or reflexive) to *stick* (figurative):—cleave, join (self), keep company.

2854. κολλούριον, kollourion, *kol-loo´-ree-on*; neuter of a presumed derivative of **κολλύρα**, ***kollura*** (a *cake*; probably akin to the base of 2853); properly a *poultice* (as made of or in the form of *crackers*), i.e. (by analogy) a *plaster*:—eyesalve.

2855. κολλυβιστής, kollubistēs, *kol-loo-bis-tace´*; from a presumed derivative of **κόλλυβος**, ***kollubos*** (a small *coin*; probably akin to 2854); a *coin-dealer*:—(money-) changer.

2856. κολοβόω, koloboō, *kol-ob-o´-o*; from a derivative of the base of 2849; to *dock*, i.e. (figurative) *abridge*:—shorten.

2857. Κολοσσαί, Kolossai, *kol-os-sah´ee*; apparently feminine plural of **κολοσσός**, *Kolossos* ("*colossal*"); *Colossæ*, a place in Asia Minor:—Colosse.

2858. Κολοσσαεύς, Kolossaeus, *kol-os-sayoos´*; from 2857; a *Colossæan*, i.e. inhabitant of Colossæ:—Colossian.

2859. κόλπος, kolpos, *kol´-pos*; apparently a primary word; the *bosom*; (by analogy) a *bay*:—bosom, creek.

2860. κολυμβάω, kolumbaō, *kol-oom-bah´-o*; from **κολυμβος**, ***kolumbos*** (a *diver*); to *plunge* into water:—swim.

2861. κολυμβήθρα, kolumbēthra, *kol-oom-bay´-thrah*; from 2860; a *diving-place*, i.e. *pond* for bathing (or swimming):—pool.

2862. κολωνία, kolōnia, *kol-o-nee´-ah*; of Latin origin; a Roman "*colony*" for veterans:—colony.

2863. κομάω, komaō, *kom-ah´-o*; from 2864; to *wear tresses* of hair:—have long hair.

2864. κόμη, komē, *kom´-ay*; apparently from the same as 2865; the *hair* of the head (*locks*, as *ornamental*, and thus differing from 2359, which properly denotes merely the *scalp*):—hair.

2865. κομίζω, komizō, *kom-id´-zo*; from a primary **κομέω**, ***komeō*** (to *tend*, i.e. take care of); properly to *provide* for, i.e. (by implication) to *carry* off (as if from harm; genitive *obtain*):—bring, receive.

2866. κομψότερον, kompsoteron, *komp-sot´-er-on*; neuter comparative of a derivative of the base of 2865 (meaning properly *well dressed*, i.e. *nice*); (figurative) *convalescent*:— + began to amend.

2867. κονιάω, koniaō, *kon-ee-ah´-o*; from **κονία**, ***konia*** (*dust*; by analogy, *lime*); to *whitewash*:—whiten.

2868. κονιορτός, koniortos, *kon-ee-or-tos´*; from the base of 2867 and **ὄρνυμι**, ***ornumi*** (to "*rouse*"); *pulverulence* (as *blown* about):—dust.

2869. κοπάζω, kopazō, *kop-ad´-zo*; from 2873; to *tire*, i.e. (figurative) to *relax*:—cease.

From *kópos* (2873), labour, fatigue. To be weary; hence to relax, to remit, to cease. In the NT, of the wind: to become calm (Mt 14:32; Mk 4:39; 6:51).

Syn.: *katapaúō* (2664), to cease or rest completely; *paúō* (3973), to stop.

2870. κοπετός, kopetos, *kop-et-os´*; from 2875; *mourning* (properly by *beating* the breast):—lamentation.

2871. κοπή, kopē, *kop-ay´*; from 2875; *cutting*, i.e. *carnage*:—slaughter.

2872. κοπιάω, kopiaō, *kop-ee-ah´-o*; from a derivative of 2873; to *feel fatigue*; (by implication) to *work hard*:—(bestow) labour, toil, be wearied.

2873. κόπος, kopos, *kop´-os*; from 2875; a *cut*, i.e. (by analogy) *toil* (as *reducing* the strength), literal or figurative; (by implication) *pains*:—labour, + trouble, weariness.

From *kóptō* (2875), to strike. Toil, labour, from an original meaning of beating, wailing, grief with beating the breast. In the NT, toil, labour, i.e. wearisome effort (Jn 4:38; 1Co 3:8; 15:58; 2Co 6:5; 10:15; 11:23, 27; 1Th 1:3; 2:9; 3:5; 2Th 3:8; Heb 6:10; Rev 2:2; 14:13). In the sense of trouble, vexation (Mt 26:10; Mk 14:6; Lk 11:7; 18:5; Gal 6:17).

Deriv.: *eukopṓteros* (2123), easier, lighter; *kopázō* (2869), to tire, cease; *kopiáō* (2872), to feel fatigue from labour.

Syn.: *móchthos* (3449), the everyday word for human labour; *pónos* (4192), pain, work.

2874. κοπρία, kopria, *kop-ree´-ah*; from **κόπρος, *kopros*** (*ordure*; perhaps akin to 2875); *manure*:—dung (-hill).

2875. κόπτω, koptō, *kop´-to*; a primary verb; to "*chop*"; specially to *beat* the breast in grief:—cut down, lament, mourn, (be-) wail. Compare the base of 5114.

To cut, to strike, to smite.

(I) To cut off or down, as branches of a tree (Mt 21:8; Mk 11:8).

(II) In the middle: to strike or beat one's body, particularly the breast, with the hands in lamentation, to lament, wail (Mt 11:17; 24:30; Lk 23:27; Rev 1:7; 18:9).

Deriv.: *anakóptō* (348), to hinder, beat back; *apokóptō* (609), to cut off; *argurokópos* (695), silversmith; *egkóptō* (1465), to cut into, hinder; *ekkóptō* (1581), to cut or strike out; *katakóptō* (2629), to cut down; *kopetós* (2870), beating, mourning; *kopḗ* (2871), slaughter; *kópos* (2873), labour, weariness; *kōphós* (2974), deaf, dumb, speechless; *prokóptō* (4298), to advance, increase; *próskomma* (4348), offence, stumbling block; *proskóptō* (4350), to strike at, trip.

Syn.: *thrēnéō* (2354), to mourn, wail; *klaíō* (2799), to weep; *penthéō* (3996), to mourn; *stenázō* (4727), to groan.

2876. κόραξ, korax, *kor´-ax*; perhaps from 2880; a *crow* (from its *voracity*):—raven.

2877. κοράσιον, korasion, *kor-as´-ee-on*; neuter of a presumed derivative of **κόρη, *korē*** (a *maiden*); a (little) *girl*:—damsel, maid.

2878. κορβᾶν, korban, *kor-ban´*; and **κορβανᾶς, *korbanas***, *kor-ban-as´*; of Hebrew and Chaldee origin respectively [7133]; a votive *offering* and *the offering*; a *consecrated present* (to the temple fund); by extension (the latter term) the *Treasury* itself, i.e. the room where the contribution boxes stood:—Corban, treasury.

2879. Κορέ, Kore, *kor-eh´*; of Hebrew origin [7141]; *Corè* (i.e. *Korach*), an Israelite:—Core.

2880. κορέννυμι, korennumi, *kor-en´-noo-mee*; a primary verb; to *cram*, i.e. *glut* or *sate*:—eat enough, full.

To sate, satisfy with food and drink. Passive: to be sated, to be full (Ac 27:38; 1Co 4:8).

Syn.: *gemízō* (1072), to fill; *empíplēmi* (1705), to fill full, satisfy, fill the hungry; *mestóō* (3325), to fill to the brim; *plḗthō* (4130), to fill; *plēróō* (4137), to make full, to fill; *chortázō* (5526), to fill or satisfy with food.

2881. Κορίνθιος, Korinthios, *kor-in´-thee-os*; from 2882; a *Corinthian*, i.e. inhabitant of Corinth:—Corinthian.

2882. Κόρινθος, Korinthos, *kor´-in-thos*; of uncertain derivative; *Corinthus*, a city of Greece:—Corinth.

2883. Κορνήλιος, Kornēlios, *kor-nay´-lee-os*; of Latin origin; *Cornelius*, a Roman:—Cornelius.

2884. κόρος, koros, *kor´-os*; of Hebrew origin [3734]; a *cor*, i.e. a specific measure:—measure.

2885. κοσμέω, kosmeō, *kos-meh´-o*; from 2889; to *put in* proper *order*, i.e. *decorate* (literal or figurative); specially to *snuff* (a wick):—adorn, garnish, trim.

2886. κοσμικός, kosmikos, *kos-mee-kos´*; from 2889 (in its secondary sense); *terrene* ("*cosmic*"), literal (*mundane*) or figurative (*corrupt*):—worldly.

From *kósmos* (2889), world. Worldly, terrestrial, that which belongs to the world. In the NT, it corresponds to the idea of *kósmos* (2889), world, as the opposite of heavenly and spiritual (Heb 9:1). Used figuratively in the sense of worldly, conforming to this world, belonging to the men of this world (Tit 2:12).

Syn.: *sarkikós* (4559), fleshly, carnal; *sōmatikós* (4984), bodily; *phusikós* (5446), physical.

2887. κόσμιος, kosmios, *kos´-mee-os*; from 2889 (in its primary sense); *orderly*, i.e. *decorous*:—of good behaviour, modest.

Adjective from *kósmos* (2889), order, arrangement. Well-ordered, decorous, modest, in a moral sense. Spoken of modest clothing (1Ti 2:9); spoken of modest behaviour (1Ti 3:2).

Syn.: *eulabḗs* (2126), reverent, circumspect; *hieroprepḗs* (2412), acting in a way befitting holiness; *euschḗmōn* (2158), decorous, honourable.

2888. κοσμοκράτωρ, kosmokratōr, *kos-mok-rat´-ore*; from 2889 and 2902; a *world-ruler*, an epithet of Satan:—ruler.

Noun from *kósmos* (2889), world, and *kratéō* (2902), to hold. Lord of the world. Used in the NT of Satan as the prince of this world. Only in Eph 6:12, in the plural, referring to Satan and his angels.

Syn.: *pantokrátōr* (3841), the Almighty, the ruler of everything, a title used only of God. Also *árchōn* (758), ruler; *basileús* (935), king; *despótēs* (1203), master, absolute ruler; *kúrios* (2962), God, Lord, master.

2889. κόσμος, kosmos, *kos´-mos*; probably from the base of 2865; orderly *arrangement*, i.e. *decoration*; (by implication) the *world* (in a wide or narrow sense, including its inhabitant, literal or figurative [moral]):—adorning, world.

Noun probably from *koméō* (n.f.), to tend, to take care of. Order, regular disposition and arrangement:

(I) Order of the universe, the world:

(A) The universe, heavens and earth (Mt 13:35; 24:21; Lk 11:50; Jn 17:5, 24; Ac 17:24; Ro 1:20; Heb 4:3). Used as a metonym for the inhabitants of the universe (1Co 4:9). Figuratively and symbolically: a world of something, as an aggregate such as in Jas 3:6, "a world of iniquity."

(B) The earth, this lower world as the abode of man: **(1)** The then-known world and particularly the people who lived in it (Mt 4:8; Mk 16:15; Jn 3:17, 19; 16:21, 28; 21:25; 1Ti 3:16; 1Pe 5:9; 2Pe 3:6). **(2)** Metonymically, inhabitants of the earth, men, mankind (Mt 5:14; 13:38; Jn 1:29; 3:16; Ro 3:6, 19; 1Co 4:13; 2Co 5:19; Heb 11:7; 2Pe 2:5; 1Jn 2:2). As a hyperbole, the world, everybody, when in fact, a smaller group is visualized (Jn 7:4; 12:19). It also stands for the heathen world, the same as *tá éthnē* (1484), "the nations" (Ro 11:12, 15).

(C) In the Jewish mode of speaking: the present world, the present order of things, as opposed to the kingdom of Christ; and hence, always with the idea of transience, worthlessness, and evil both physical and moral, the seat of cares, temptations, irregular desires. **(1)** Generally (Jn 12:25; 18:36; 1Co 5:10; Eph 2:2; 1Jn 4:17). Specifically: the wealth and enjoyments of this world, this life's goods (Mt 16:26; Mk 8:36; Lk 9:25; 1Co 3:22; 7:31, 33, 34; Gal 6:14; Jas 4:4; 1Jn 2:17). **(2)** Used metonymically for the men of this world as opposed to those who seek the kingdom of God (Jn 7:7; 14:17; 16:8; 17:6, 9; 1Co 1:20, 21; 3:19; 2Co 7:10; Php 2:15; Jas 1:27); as subject to Satan, the ruler of this world (Jn 12:31; 14:30; 16:11).

(II) Adornment, adorning (1Pe 3:3).

Deriv.: *kosméō* (2885), to order, put in order, decorate, adorn; *kosmikós* (2886), worldly, earthly; *kósmios* (2887), well-ordered, well-mannered, decorous; *kosmokrátor* (2888), a world ruler.

Syn.: *aiṓn* (165), age; *oikouménē* (3625), the inhabited earth, civilization; *gḗ* (1093), earth as arable land, but also the earth as a whole, the world in contrast to the heavens.

2890. Κούαρτος, Kouartos, *koo´-ar-tos*; of Latin origin (*fourth*); *Quartus*, a Christian:—Quartus.

2891. κοῦμι, koumi, *koo´-mee*; of Chaldee origin [6966]; *cumi* (i.e. *rise!*):—cumi.

2892. κουστωδία, koustōdia, *koos-to-dee´-ah*; of Latin origin; "*custody*," i.e. a Roman *sentry*:—watch.

2893. κουφίζω, kouphizō, *koo-fid´-zo*; from **κοῦφος, *kouphos*** (*light* in weight); to *unload*:—lighten.

2894. κόφινος, kophinos, *kof´-ee-nos*; of uncertain derivative; a (small) *basket*:—basket.

2895. κράββατος, krabbatos, *krab´-bat-os*; probably of foreign origin; a *mattress*:—bed.

2896. κράζω, krazō, *krad´-zo*; a primary verb; properly to "*croak*" (as a raven) or *scream*, i.e. (genitive) to *call* aloud (*shriek, exclaim, intreat*):—cry (out).

2897. κραιπάλη, kraipalē, *krahee-pal´-ay*; probably from the same as 726; properly a *headache* (as a *seizure* of pain) from drunkenness, i.e. (by implication) a *debauch* (by analogy, a *glut*):—surfeiting.

Noun meaning headache, a hangover, a shooting pain or a confusion in the head arising from intoxication and its consequences. Constant reveling, carousing. Only in Lk 21:34.

Syn.: *kṓmos* (2970), revelings and riotings; *méthē* (3178), drunkenness; *oinophlugía* (3632), excess of wine; *pótos* (4224), a drinking bout leading possibly to excess.

2898. κρανίον, kranion, *kran-ee´-on*; diminutive of a derivative of the base of 2768; a *skull* ("*cranium*"):—Calvary, skull.

2899. κράσπεδον, kraspedon, *kras´-ped-on*; of uncertain derivative; a *margin*, i.e. (special) a *fringe* or *tassel*:—border, hem.

2900. κραταιός, krataios, *krat-ah-yos´*; from 2904; *powerful*:—mighty.

2901. κραταιόω, krataioō, *krat-ah-yo´-o*; from 2900; to *empower*, i.e. (passive) *increase in vigour*:—be strengthened, be (wax) strong.

2902. κρατέω, krateō, *krat-eh´-o*; from 2904; to *use strength*, i.e. *seize* or *retain* (literal or figurative):—hold (by, fast), keep, lay hand (hold) on, obtain, retain, take (by).

From *krátos* (2904), strength. To be strong, mighty, powerful; to have power over, to rule over:

(I) To have power over, to gain, attain to (Ac 27:13); to hold fast (Heb 4:14). To take the hand of someone (Mt 9:25; Mk 1:31; 5:41; 9:27; Lk 8:54) to hold by the feet (Mt 28:9).

(II) To have power over, to be or become the master of, always implying a certain degree of force with which one brings a person or thing wholly under his power, even when resistance is encountered. Generally: to bring under one's power, lay hold of, seize, or take a person (Mt 14:3; 18:28; 21:46; 22:6; 26:4, 48, 50, 55, 57; Mk 3:21; 6:17; 12:12; 14:1, 44, 46, 49, 51; Ac 24:6; Rev 20:2); an animal (Mt 12:11).

(III) To have in one's power, be master of, i.e. to hold, hold fast, not to let go, e.g., of things (Rev 2:1; 7:1); of persons: to hold in subjection (pass., Ac 2:24). To hold one fast, i.e. to hold fast to someone, cleave to him, for example, in person (Ac 3:11), or in faith hold on to Christ (Col 2:19). Metaphorically spoken of sins: to retain, not to forgive (Jn 20:23). To keep to oneself, e.g., the word (Mk 9:10). Generally: to hold fast in mind, observe (Mk 7:3, 4, 8; 2Th 2:15; Rev 2:13–15, 25; 3:11). In the passive, concerning the eyes: "to be held," i.e. prevented from recognizing (Lk 24:16).

Deriv.: *kosmokrátōr* (2888), a world ruler.

Syn.: *antéchomai* (472), to hold firmly to; *harpázō* (726), to take by force suddenly; *epilambánō* (1949), to lay hold of; *katéchō* (2722), to hold firmly; *piázō* (4084), to take hold, apprehend; *sunéchō* (4912), to hold a prisoner.

2903. κράτιστος, kratistos, *krat´-is-tos*; superl. of a derivative of 2904; *strongest*, i.e. (in dignity) *very honourable*:—most excellent (noble).

2904. κράτος, kratos, *krat´-os*; perhaps a primary word; *vigour* ["great"] (literal or figurative):—dominion, might [-ily], power, strength.

Noun meaning strength, might:

(I) Generally: might or power, strength (Ac 19:20; Eph 1:19; 6:10; Col 1:11). Used metonymically for might, for mighty deeds (Lk 1:51).

(II) Power, dominion, ruling control. Spoken of God (1Ti 6:16; 1Pe 4:11; 5:11; Jude 25; Rev 1:6; 5:13); spoken of the devil having temporary dominion over death (Heb 2:14).

Deriv.: *akratḗs* (193), without self-control; *egkratḗs* (1468), temperate; *kratéō* (2902), to be strong, to seize; *krátistos* (2903), most excellent; *pantokrátōr* (3841), ruler over all, Almighty.

Syn.: *dúnamis* (1411), strength, power and its execution; *exousía* (1849), authority; *ischús* (2479), strength possessed.

2905. κραυγάζω, kraugazō, *krow-gad´-zo*; from 2906; to *clamor*:—cry out.

2906. κραυγή, kraugē, *krow-gay´*; from 2896; an *outcry* (in notification, tumult or grief):—clamour, cry (-ing).

2907. κρέας, kreas, *kreh´-as*; perhaps a primary word; (butcher's) *meat*:—flesh.

2908. κρεῖσσον, kreisson, *krice´-son*; neuter of an alternate form of 2909; (as noun) *better*, i.e. *greater advantage*:—better.

The neuter of *kreíssōn* (2909) used as an adverb. Better, in the sense of more useful, more profitable. Used only in 1Co 7:38.

2909. κρείττων, kreittōn, *krite´-tohn*; comparative of a derivative of 2904; *stronger*, i.e. (figurative) *better*, i.e. *nobler*:—best, better.

Adjective, the comparative of *kratús* (n.f.), strong, which is from *krátos* (2904), power, and used as a comparative of *agathós* (18), benevolently good. Better in value or dignity, nobler, more excellent (1Co 7:9; 11:17; 12:31; Php 1:23; Heb 1:4; 6:9; 7:7, 19, 22; 8:6; 9:23; 10:34; 11:16, 35, 40; 12:24; 1Pe 3:17; 2Pe 2:21).

Syn.: *meízōn* (3187), greater.

2910. κρεμάννυμι, kremannumi, *krem-an´-noo-mee*; a prolonged form of a primary verb; to *hang*:—hang.

2911. κρημνός, krēmnos, *krame-nos´*; from 2910; *overhanging*, i.e. a *precipice*:—steep place.

2912. Κρής, Krēs, *krace*; from 2914; a *Cretan*, i.e. inhabitant of Crete:—Crete, Cretian.

2913. Κρήσκης, Krēskēs, *krace´-kace*; of Latin origin; *growing*; *Cresces* (i.e. *Crescens*), a Christian:—Crescens.

2914. Κρήτη, Krētē, *kray´-tay*; of uncertain derivative; *Cretè*, an island in the Mediterranean:—Crete.

2915. κριθή, krithē, *kree-thay´*; of uncertain derivative; *barley*:—barley.

2916. κρίθινος, krithinos, *kree´-thee-nos*; from 2915; consisting *of barley*:—barley.

2917. κρίμα, krima, *kree´-mah*; from 2919; a *decision* (the function or the effect, for or against ["crime"]):—avenge, condemned, condemnation, damnation, + go to law, judgement.

Noun from *krínō* (2919), to judge. Judgement, sentence, the reason for judgement:

(I) The act of judging, giving judgement, equivalent to *krísis* (2920), judgement (1Pe 4:17). Spoken in reference to future reward and punishment (Jn 9:39); of the judgement of the last day (Ac 24:25; Heb 6:2). Used metonymically for the power of judgement (Rev 20:4).

(II) Judgement given, decision, award, sentence:

(A) Generally (Mt 7:2; Ro 5:16; 11:33).

(B) More often, a sentence of punishment or condemnation, implying also the punishment itself as a certain consequence (Mt 23:14; Mk 12:40; Lk 20:47; 23:40; 24:20; Ro 2:2, 3; 3:8; 13:2; 1Co 11:29, 34; Gal 5:10; 1Ti 3:6; 5:12; Jas 3:1; 2Pe 2:3; Jude 4; Rev 17:1; 18:20).

(C) Lawsuit, cause, something to be judged (1Co 6:7).

Syn.: *apókrima* (610), sentence; *díkē* (1349), judgement, a decision or its execution.

2918. κρίνον, krinon, *kree´-non*; perhaps a primary word; a *lily*:—lily.

2919. κρίνω, krinō, *kree´-no*; properly to *distinguish*, i.e. *decide* (mentally or judicially); (by implication) to *try, condemn, punish*:—avenge, conclude, condemn, damn, decree, determine, esteem, judge, go to (sue at the) law, ordain, call in question, sentence to, think.

To separate, distinguish, discriminate between good and evil, select, choose out the good. In the NT, it means to judge, to form or give an opinion after separating and considering the particulars of a case:

(I) To judge in one's own mind as to what is right, proper, expedient; to deem, decide, determine (Lk 7:43; 12:57; Ac 3:13; 4:19; 15:19; 20:16; 25:25; 27:1; Ro 14:5; 1Co 2:2; 10:15; Tit 3:12; Rev 16:5).

(II) To form and express a judgement or opinion as to any person or thing, more commonly unfavourable (Jn 7:24; 8:15; Ro 2:1, 3, 27; 14:3, 4, 10, 13, 22; 1Co 4:5; 10:29; Col 2:16; Jas 4:11, 12); in an absolute sense (Mt 7:1, 2; Lk 6:37; Jn 8:16).

(III) To judge in a judicial sense:

(A) To sit in judgement on any person, to try (Jn 18:31; Ac 23:3; 24:6; 1Co 5:12). In the pass. *krínomai*: to be judged, tried, be on trial (Ac 23:6; 24:21; 25:9, 10; 26:6; Ro 3:4). Spoken in reference to the gospel dispensation, to the judgement of the great day of God's judging the world through Christ (Jn 5:22; 8:50; Ac 17:31; Ro 2:16; 3:6; 1Co 5:13; 2Ti 4:1; 1Pe 1:17; 2:23; 4:5; Rev 11:18; 19:11; 20:12, 13).

(B) In the sense of to pass judgement upon, condemn (Lk 19:22; Jn 7:51; Ac 13:27). As also implying punishment (1Co 11:31, 32; 1Pe 4:6). Of the condemnation of the wicked and including the idea of punishment as a certain consequence, meaning to punish, take vengeance on. Spoken of God as judge (Ac 7:7 quoted from Ge 15:14; Ro 2:12; 2Th 2:12; Heb 13:4; Rev 6:10; 18:8, 20; 19:2).

(C) To vindicate, avenge (Heb 10:30).

(IV) In the passive, particularly: to let oneself be judged, i.e. to have a lawsuit, go to law (Mt 5:40); to be judged before someone (1Co 6:1, 6).

Deriv.: *anakrínō* (350), to judicially investigate, examine; *apokrínomai* (611), to answer, respond; *diakrínō* (1252), to discriminate, make to differ, judge thoroughly; *egkrínō* (1469), to class with, count among, approve; *eilikrinḗs* (1506), pure, sincere; *epikrínō* (1948), to give sentence; *katakrínō* (2632), to judge against, condemn; *kríma* (2917), judicial decision; *krísis* (2920), judgement; *kritḗs* (2923), judge; *sugkrínō* (4793), to judge one thing comparing it with another, to interpret; *hupokrínomai* (5271), to speak or act under false identity.

Syn.: *diaginṓskō* (1231), to ascertain exactly; *diakrínō* (1252), to discern; *kataginṓskō* (2607), to think ill of, condemn, find fault with; *katadikázō* (2613), to pronounce judgement, condemn.

2920. κρίσις, krisis, *kree´-sis*; *decision* (subject or object, for or against); by extension a *tribunal*; (by implication) *justice* (specially divine *law*):—accusation, condemnation, damnation, judgement.

Noun from *krínō* (2919), to judge. Judgement:

(I) Generally: an opinion formed and expressed (Jn 7:24; 8:16).

(II) Judgement, in a judicial sense:

(A) The act of judging in reference to the final judgement, as the day of judgement (Mt 10:15; 11:22, 24; 12:36; Mk 6:11; 2Pe 2:9; 3:7; 1Jn 4:17); as the hour of judgement (Rev 14:7); as the judgement of the great day (Jude 6). Simply *krísis* standing for the judgement of the great day (Mt 12:41, 42; Lk 10:14; 11:31, 32; Heb 9:27). Used metonymically for the power of judgement (Jn 5:22).

(B) Judgement given, sentence pronounced (Jn 5:30; 2Pe 2:11; Jude 9). Specifically: sentence of punishment or condemnation, e.g., to death (Ac 8:33). Usually implying also punishment as a certain consequence (Mt 23:33; Mk 3:29; Jn 3:19; 5:24, 29; 1Ti 5:24; Heb 10:27; Jas 2:13; 2Pe 2:4; Rev 16:7; 18:10; 19:2).

(C) Used metonymically for a court of justice, a tribunal, judges, i.e. the smaller tribunals established in the cities of Palestine and subordinate to the Sanhedrin (Mt 5:21, 22).

(III) Right, justice, equity (Mt 23:23; Lk 11:42). Also for law, statutes, i.e. the divine law, the religion of Jehovah as developed in the gospels (Mt 12:18, 20).

Syn.: *aísthēsis* (144), discernment, judgement as through the senses.

2921. Κρίσπος, Krispos, *kris´-pos*; of Latin origin; "*crisp*"; *Crispus*, a Corinthian:—Crispus.

2922. κριτήριον, kritērion, *kree-tay´-ree-on*; neuter of a presumed derivative of 2923; a *rule* of judging ("*criterion*"), i.e. (by implication) a *tribunal*:—to judge, judgement (seat)

Noun from *kritḗs* (2923), a judge. Criterion, rule of judging. In the NT, used metaphorically: court of justice, tribunal (1Co 6:2; Jas 2:6); by implication: cause, lawsuit (1Co 6:4).

Syn.: *bḗma* (968), judgement seat, tribunal.

2923. κριτής, kritēs, *kree-tace´*; from 2919; a *judge* (general or special):—judge.

Noun from *krínō* (2919), to judge. He who decides, a judge:

(I) Generally (Mt 12:27; Lk 11:19; Jas 2:4); in an unfavourable sense (Jas 4:11).

(II) In a judicial sense: one who sits to render justice (Mt 5:25; Lk 12:58; 18:2, 6; Ac 18:15; 24:10). Of Christ the final judge (Ac 10:42; 2Ti 4:8; Jas 5:9); of God (Heb 12:23).

(III) A leader, ruler, chief, spoken of the Hebrew judges from Joshua to Samuel (Ac 13:20).

Deriv.: *kritḗrion* (2922), judgement, tribunal; *kritikós* (2924), discerner.

Syn.: *dikastḗs* (1348), a judicial judge.

2924. κριτικός, kritikos, *krit-ee-kos´*; from 2923; *decisive* ("*critical*"), i.e. *discriminative*:—discerner.

Adjective from *kritḗs* (2923), a judge. Able to discern or decide correctly, skilled in judging. Used only in Heb 4:12.

2925. κρούω, krouō, *kroo´-o*; apparently a primary verb; to *rap*:—knock.

2926. κρυπτή, kruptē, *kroop-tay´*; feminine of 2927; a *hidden* place, i.e. *cellar* ("*crypt*"):—secret.

2927. κρυπτός, kruptos, *kroop-tos´*; from 2928; *concealed*, i.e. *private*:—hid (-den), inward [-ly], secret.

2928. κρύπτω, kruptō, *kroop´-to*; a primary verb; to *conceal* (properly by *covering*):—hide (self), keep secret, secret [-ly].

2929. κρυσταλλίζω, krustallizō, *kroos-tal-lid´-zo*; from 2930; to *make* (i.e. intransitive *resemble*) *ice* ("crystallize"):—be clear as crystal.

2930. κρύσταλλος, krustallos, *kroos´-tal-los*; from a derivative of **κρύος**, ***kruos*** (*frost*); *ice*, i.e. (by analogy) rock "*crystal*":—crystal.

2931. κρυφῆ, kruphē, *kroo-fay´*; adverb from 2928; *privately*:—in secret.

2932. κτάομαι, ktaomai, *ktah´-om-ahee*; a primary verb; to *get*, i.e. *acquire* (by any means; *own*):—obtain, possess, provide, purchase.

2933. κτῆμα, ktēma, *ktay´-mah*; from 2932; an *acquirement*, i.e. *estate*:—possession.

2934. κτῆνος, ktēnos, *ktay´-nos*; from 2932; *property*, i.e. (special) a domestic *animal*:—beast.

2935. κτήτωρ, ktētōr, *ktay´-tore*; from 2932; an *owner*:—possessor.

2936. κτίζω, ktizō, *ktid´-zo*; probably akin to 2932 (through the idea of the *proprietorship* of the *manufacturer*); to *fabricate*, i.e. *found* (*form* originally):—create, Creator, make.

To bring under tillage and settlement. In the NT: to establish, to create, produce from nothing (Mk 13:19; Ro 1:25; Eph 3:9; Col 1:16; 3:10; 1Ti 4:3; Rev 4:11; 10:6); to form out of preexistent matter (1Co 11:9); to make, compose (Eph 2:15); to create and form in a spiritual sense, regeneration or renewal (Eph 2:10; 4:24).

Deriv.: *ktísis* (2937), creation; *ktísma* (2938), creature; *ktístēs* (2939), creator, founder, inventor.

Syn.: *kataskeuázō* (2680), to prepare, make ready, build; *poiéō* (4160), to make.

2937. κτίσις, ktisis, *ktis´-is*; from 2936; original *formation* (properly, the act; by implication, the thing, literal or figurative):—building, creation, creature, ordinance.

Noun from *ktízō* (2936), to create, form or found. A founding of cities. In the NT: creation, i.e. the act of creation (Ro 1:20). Generally: a created thing, and collectively: created things (Ro 1:25; 8:39; Heb 4:13). Also in the sense of creation in general, the universe (Mk 10:6; 13:19; Col 1:15; 2Pe 3:4; Rev 3:14); specifically: the visible creation (Heb 9:11). Used metonymically for man, mankind (Mk 16:15; Ro 8:19–22; 2Co 5:17; Gal 6:15; Col 1:23). By implication: ordinance, institution (1Pe 2:13).

2938. κτίσμα, ktisma, *ktis´-mah*; from 2936; an original *formation* (concrete), i.e. *product* (created thing):—creature.

Noun from *ktízō* (2936), to create, form or found. In the NT: creature, created thing. Spoken of animals as a source of food (1Ti 4:4); spoken of mankind (Jas 1:18); spoken of every living being in the sea (Rev 8:9); spoken of every living being in the universe (Rev 5:13).

Syn.: *plásma* (4110), something molded or formed; *poíēma* (4161), a product.

2939. κτιστής, ktistēs, *ktis-tace´*; from 2936; a *founder*, i.e. *God* (as author of all things):—Creator.

Noun from *ktízō* (2936), to create, form or found. Creator, founder, inventor. Only in 1Pe 4:19, a creator.

Syn.: *dēmiourgós* (1217), builder, maker; *technítēs* (5079), architect, designer.

2940. κυβεία, kubeia, *koo-bi´-ah*; from **κύβος, *kubos*** (a "*cube*," i.e. *die* for playing); *gambling*, i.e. (figurative) *artifice* or *fraud*:—sleight.

2941. κυβέρνησις, kubernēsis, *koo-ber´-nay-sis*; from **κυβερνάω, *kubernaō*** (of Latin origin, to *steer*); *pilotage*, i.e. (figurative) *directorship* (in the church):—government.

2942. κυβερνήτης, kubernētēs, *koo-ber-nay´-tace*; from the same as 2941; *helmsman*, i.e. (by implication) *captain*:—(ship) master.

2943. κυκλόθεν, kuklothen, *koo-kloth´-en*; adverb from the same as 2945; *from* the *circle*, i.e. *all around*:—(round) about.

2944. κυκλόω, kukloō, *koo-klo´-o*; from the same as 2945; to *encircle*, i.e. *surround*:—compass (about), come (stand) round about.

2945. κύκλῳ, kuklōi, *koo´-klo*; as if dative of **κύκλος, *kuklos*** (a *ring*, "*cycle*"; akin to 2947); i.e. *in a circle* (by implication of 1722), i.e. (adverb) *all around*:—round about.

2946. κύλισμα, kulisma, *koo´-lis-mah*; from 2947; a *wallow* (the effect of *rolling*), i.e. *filth*:—wallowing.

2947. κυλιόω, kulioō, *koo-lee-o´-o*; from the base of 2949 (through the idea of *circularity*; compare 2945, 1507); to *roll* about:—wallow.

2948. κυλλός, kullos, *kool-los´*; from the same as 2947; *rocking* about, i.e. *crippled* (*maimed*, in feet or hands):—maimed.

2949. κῦμα, kuma, *koo´-mah*; from **κύω, *kuō*** (to *swell* [with young], i.e. *bend, curve*); a *billow* (as *bursting* or *toppling*):—wave.

2950. κύμβαλον, kumbalon, *koom´-bal-on*; from a derivative of the base of 2949; a "*cymbal*" (as *hollow*):—cymbal.

2951. κύμινον, kuminon, *koo´-min-on*; of foreign origin [compare 3646]; *dill* or *fennel* ("cummin"):—cummin.

2952. κυνάριον, kunarion, *koo-nar´-ee-on*; neuter of a presumed derivative of 2965; a *puppy*:—dog.

2953. Κύπριος, Kuprios, *koo´-pree-os*; from 2954; a *Cyprian* (*Cypriot*), i.e. inhabitant of Cyprus:—of Cyprus.

2954. Κύπρος, Kupros, *koo´-pros*; of uncertain origin; *Cyprus*, an island in the Mediterranean:—Cyprus.

2955. κύπτω, kuptō, *koop´-to*; probably from the base of 2949; to *bend* forward:—stoop (down).

To stoop, to bow down oneself. To stoop in subservience to tie another's sandal strings (Mk 1:7); to stoop to write on the ground (Mk 1:7; Jn 8:6, 8).

Deriv.: *anakúptō* (352), to lift up; *parakúptō* (3879), to stoop to look into; *sugkúptō* (4794), to bend or bow down over.

Syn.: *klínō* (2827), to bow down.

2956. Κυρηναῖος, Kurēnaios, *koo-ray-nah´-yos*; from 2957; a *Cyrenæan*, i.e. inhabitant of Cyrene:—of Cyrene, Cyrenian.

2957. Κυρήνη, Kurēnē, *koo-ray´-nay*; of uncertain derivative; *Cyrenè*, a region of Africa:—Cyrene.

2958. Κυρήνιος, Kurēnios, *koo-ray´-nee-os*; of Latin origin; *Cyrenius* (i.e. *Quirinus*), a Roman:—Cyrenius.

2959. Κυρία, Kuria, *koo-ree´-ah*; feminine of 2962; *Cyria*, a Christian woman:—lady.

2960. κυριακός, kuriakos, *koo-ree-ak-os´*; from 2962; *belonging to* the *Lord* (Jehovah or Jesus):—Lord's.

From *kúrios* (2962), God, Lord, master. Belonging to a lord or ruler. Spoken of the Lord's Supper (1Co 11:20), and of the Lord's day (Rev 1:10), as belonging to Christ, to the Lord, having special reference to Him.

2961. κυριεύω, kurieuō, *koo-ree-yoo´-o*; from 2962; to *rule*:—have dominion over, lord, be lord of, exercise lordship over.

2962. κύριος, kurios, *koo´-ree-os*; from **κῦρος, *kuros*** (*supremacy*); *supreme* in authority, i.e. (as noun) *controller*; (by implication) *Mr.* (as a respectful title):—God, Lord, master, Sir.

Noun from *kúros* (n.f.), might, power. Lord, master, owner:

(I) Generally:

(A) As the possessor, owner, master, e.g., of property (Mt 20:8; 21:40; Gal 4:1); master or head of a house (Mt 15:27; Mk 13:35); of persons, servants, slaves (Mt 10:24; 24:45, 46, 48, 50; Ac 16:16, 19; Ro 14:4; Eph 6:5, 9; Col 3:22; 4:1). Spoken of a husband (1Pe 3:6). Lord, master of something and having absolute authority over it, e.g., master of the harvest (Mt 9:38; Lk 10:2); master of the Sabbath (Mt 12:8; Mk 2:28).

(B) Of a supreme lord, sovereign, e.g., the Roman emperor (Ac 25:26); the heathen gods (1Co 8:5).

(C) As an honorary title of address, especially to superiors, equivalent to mister, sir, as a servant to his master (Mt 13:27; Lk 13:8); a son to his father (Mt 21:30); a student or follower to a teacher, master (Mt 8:25; Lk 9:54). See also Mt 7:21, 22; Lk 6:46. Spoken to a person of dignity and authority (Mk 7:28; Jn 4:11, 15, 19, 49); to a Roman procurator (Mt 27:63). Spoken when addressing someone respectfully (Jn 12:21; 20:15; Ac 16:30).

(II) Spoken of God and Christ:

(A) Of God as the supreme Lord and Sovereign of the universe, usually in the Sept. for the Hebrew *Yehōwāh* (3068, OT), Jehovah, Lord. With the article *ho Kúrios* (Mt 1:22; 5:33; Mk 5:19; Lk 1:6, 28; Ac 7:33; Heb 8:2; Jas 4:15). Without the article *Kúrios* (Mt 27:10; Mk 13:20; Lk 1:58; Ac 7:49; Ro 4:8; Heb 7:21; 1Pe 1:25). With adjuncts, e.g., *Kúrios ho Theós* ([2316], God), the Lord God (Mt 4:7, 10; 22:37; Lk 1:16); *Kúrios Sabaṓth* ([4519], armies), Lord of hosts, armies; a military appellation of God (Ro 9:29; Jas 5:4); *Kúrios Pantokrátōr* (3841), Lord Almighty or ruler of all (2Co 6:18); *Kúrios ho Theós ho Pantokrátōr*, Lord, the God, the Almighty (Rev 4:8; 11:17); *Kúrios tṓn kurieuóntōn* (2961), Lord of lords, referring to those who are ruling (1Ti 6:15); Lord of heaven and earth (Mt 11:25; Lk 10:21; Ac 17:24).

(B) Of the Lord Jesus Christ: **(1)** In reference to His abode on earth as a master and teacher, equivalent to *rhabbí* (4461), rabbi, and *epistátēs* (1988), master, superintendent (Mt 17:4 [cf. Mk 9:5; Lk 9:33]. See also Jn 13:13, 14). Chiefly in the gospels before the resurrection of Christ (Mt 21:3; 28:6; Lk 7:13; 10:1; Jn 4:1; 20:2, 13; Ac 9:5; 1Co 9:5). With adjuncts, e.g., *ho Kúrios kaí ho didáskalos* ([1320], teacher), the Lord and teacher (Jn 13:13, 14); *ho Kúrios Iēsoús* (2424), the Lord Jesus (Lk 24:3; Ac 1:21; 4:33; 1Co 11:23). **(2)** As the supreme Lord of the gospel dispensation, "head over all things to the church" (Ro 10:12; Rev 17:14); as simply "Lord" or "the Lord" (Mt 22:44; Mk 16:20; Ac 8:25; 19:10; 2Co 3:16, 17; Eph 5:10; Col 3:23; 4:1; 2Th 3:1, 5; 2Ti 4:8; Heb 7:14; Jas 5:7; 2Pe 3:10; Rev 11:8). With adjuncts, e.g. "the Lord Jesus" (Ro 4:24; 10:9; 1Co 5:5; Php 2:19; Heb 13:20); "the Lord Jesus Christ" or "Jesus Christ the Lord" (Ac 16:31; Ro 1:3, 7; 13:14; 16:18; 1Co 1:2, 9, 10; Gal 6:18; Eph 3:11; Php 1:2; 1Ti 1:2); *Christós Kúrios*, meaning the Messiah (Lk 2:11).

Deriv.: *kuría* (2959), lady; *kuriakós* (2960), the Lord's; *kurieúō* (2961), to be lord; *kuriótēs* (2963), lordship, dominion.

Syn.: *archēgós* (747), leader; *árchōn* (758), ruler; *despótēs* (1203), master; *ethnárchēs* (1481), leader of a nation; *hēgemṓn* (2232), governor, ruler; *kosmokrátōr* (2888), world ruler; *pantokrátōr* (3841), Almighty.

2963. κυριότης, kuriotēs, *koo-ree-ot´-ace*; from 2962; *mastery*, i.e. (concrete and collective) *rulers*:—dominion, government.

Noun from *kúrios* (2962), God, Lord, master. Dominion, civil power, authority. Spoken of as despised by wicked men (2Pe 2:10; Jude 8); spoken of as created by Christ (Col 1:16), who has been placed above them (Eph 1:21).

Syn.: *archḗ* (746), rule; *exousía* (1849), authority; *hēgemonía* (2231), government; *krátos* (2904), dominion; *kubérnēsis* (2941), government.

2964. κυρόω, kuroō, *koo-ro´-o*; from the same as 2962; to *make authoritative*, i.e. *ratify*:—confirm.

2965. κύων, kuōn, *koo´-ohn*; a primary word; a *dog* ["*hound*"] (literal or figurative):—dog.

2966. κῶλον, kōlon, *ko´-lon*; from the base of 2849; a *limb* of the body (as if *lopped*):—carcase.

2967. κωλύω, kōluō, *ko-loo´-o*; from the base of 2849; to *estop*, i.e. *prevent* (by word or act):—forbid, hinder, keep from, let, not suffer, withstand.

2968. κώμη, kōmē, *ko´-may*; from 2749; a *hamlet* (as if *laid* down):—town, village.

2969. κωμόπολις, kōmopolis, *ko-mop´-ol-is*; from 2968 and 4172; an unwalled *city*:—town.

2970. κῶμος, kōmos, *ko´-mos*; from 2749; a *carousal* (as if a *letting loose*):—reveling, rioting.

Noun meaning feasting. In the NT: reveling and carousing (Ro 13:13; Gal 5:21; 1Pe 4:3); a carousing or merrymaking after supper, the guests often moving out into the streets and going through the city with torches, music, and songs in honour of Bacchus, etc.

Syn.: *kraipálē* (2897), giddiness caused by overindulgence in wine; *méthē* (3178), drunkenness; *oinophlugía* (3632), excess of wine; *pótos* (4224), a drinking bout or banquet.

2971. κώνωψ, kōnōps, *ko´-nopes*; apparently from a derivative of the base of 2759 and a derivative of 3700; a *mosquito* (from its *stinging proboscis*):—gnat.

2972. Κῶς, Kōs, *koce*; of uncertain origin; *Cos*, an island in the Mediterranean:—Cos.

2973. Κωσάμ, Kōsam, *ko-sam´*; of Hebrew origin [compare 7081]; *Cosam* (i.e. *Kosam*), an Israelite:—Cosam.

2974. κωφός, kōphos, *ko-fos´*; from 2875; *blunted*, i.e. (figurative) of hearing (*deaf*) or speech (*dumb*):—deaf, dumb, speechless.

2975. λαγχάνω, lagchanō, *lang-khan´-o*; a prolonged form of a primary verb, which is only used as an alternate in certain tenses; to *lot*, i.e. *determine* (by implication, *receive*) especially by lot:—his lot be, cast lots, obtain.

2976. Λάζαρος, Lazaros, *lad´-zar-os*; probably of Hebrew origin [499]; *Lazarus* (i.e. *Elazar*), the name of two Israelites (one imaginary):—Lazarus.

2977. λάθρα, lathra, *lath´-rah*; adverb from 2990; *privately*:—privily, secretly.

2978. λαῖλαψ, lailaps, *lah´ee-laps*; of uncertain derivative; a *whirlwind* (*squall*):—storm, tempest.

Noun meaning fierce tempest with driving wind and rain, a whirlwind, hurricane. Spoken of storms on the sea of Galilee (Mk 4:37; Lk 8:23); used metaphorically to describe wicked false teachers (2Pe 2:17).

Syn.: *thúella* (2366), hurricane, cyclone; *cheimṓn* (5494), winter storm.

2979. λακτίζω, laktizō, *lak-tid´-zo*; from adverb **λάξ**, *lax* (*heelwise*); to *recalcitrate*:—kick.

2980. λαλέω, laleō, *lal-eh´-o*; a prolonged form of an otherwise obsolete verb; to *talk*, i.e. *utter* words:—preach, say, speak (after), talk, tell, utter. Compare 3004.

To speak, to talk; to use the voice without any necessary reference to the words spoken, thus differing from *légō* (3004). In Class. Gr., especially of children: to talk too much, to prattle. In the NT, generally: to speak, to talk:

(I) Particularly, simply to speak, e.g., spoken of those formerly deaf and dumb (Mt 9:33; 12:22; 15:31). See also Mk 7:35; Lk 7:15; Jn 7:26; Ac 2:6; 7:6; 18:9; 1Co 12:3; 14:9; Jas 1:19). To speak to or with someone (Mt 12:47; Mk 6:50; Lk 1:22; Jn 4:27; 9:29, 37; 19:10; Ac 7:38; Ro 7:1; 2Jn 12; Rev 21:9).

(II) As modified by the context where the meaning lies not so much in the verb itself, *laléō*, as in the adjuncts:

(A) To teach, preach (Mt 13:10; Lk 5:4; Jn 7:17; 12:50; Ac 14:1; 1Co 3:1; 14:34, 35; 1Pe 4:11).

(B) To tell, relate, declare, announce something (Mt 26:13; Lk 2:20; Jn 1:37; Ac 4:20; 27:25).

(C) To foretell, declare (Lk 1:55, 70; 24:25; Jn 16:1, 4; Ac 3:24; 26:22; 28:25; Jas 5:10; 2Pe 1:21).

(D) Figuratively: to speak by writing or letter (2Co 11:17; Heb 2:5; 2Pe 3:16); also spoken of one dead who speaks or exhorts by his example (Heb 11:4).

(III) By metonymy of things, e.g.:

(A) Spoken of the law in the sense of to prescribe (Ro 3:19).

(B) Spoken of the expiatory blood of Jesus in the sense of to accomplish (Heb 12:24).

Deriv.: *alálētos* (215), unspeakable; *álalos* (216), unable to speak; *dialaléō* (1255), to converse; *eklaléō* (1583), to speak out; *katalaléō* (2635), to speak against; *laliá* (2981), saying, speech; *mogilálos* (3424), speaking with difficulty, a stutterer; *proslaléō* (4354), to speak to or with; *sullaléō* (4814), to speak with.

Syn.: *anaggéllō* (312), to announce, declare; *apaggéllō* (518), to announce, declare, report; *apophthéggomai* (669), to speak forth; *diēgéomai* (1334), to declare, report, narrate; *eréō* (2046), to speak; *légō* (3004), to speak thoughtfully; *homiléō* (3656), to talk, converse; *phēmí* (5346), to declare; *phthéggomai* (5350), to utter a sound or voice, to proclaim.

2981. λαλιά, lalia, *lal-ee-ah´*; from 2980; *talk*:—saying, speech.

2982. λαμά, lama, *lam-ah´*; or **λαμμᾶ**, *lamma*, *lam-mah´*; of Hebrew origin [4100 with prepositional prefix]; *lama* (i.e. *why*):—*lama*.

2983. λαμβάνω, lambanō, *lam-ban´-o*; a prolonged form of a primary verb, which is used only as an alternate in certain tenses; to *take* (in very many applications, literal and figurative [properly object or active, to *get hold* of; whereas 1209 is rather subject or passive, to *have offered* to one; while 138 is more violent, to *seize* or *remove*]):—accept, + be amazed, assay, attain, bring, × when I call, catch, come on (× unto), + forget, have, hold, obtain, receive (× after), take (away, up).

To take in whatever manner:

(I) To take:

(A) Particularly with the hand: **(1)** Generally (Mt 14:19; 25:1; 26:26, 52; 27:6, 30, 48; Mk 9:36; Lk 22:17; Jn 12:3, 13; 13:4, 12, 30; 1Co 11:23; Rev 5:8; 22:17). Figuratively: to receive honour unto oneself (Heb 5:4); power (Rev 11:17). **(2)** Of taking food or drink (Mk 15:23; Jn 19:30; Ac 9:19; 1Ti 4:4). **(3)** With the meaning of to make provision for or take with (Mt 16:5, 7; 25:4; Jn 18:3). To take a wife (Mk 12:19, 21; Lk 20:28). **(4)** Figuratively, to take upon oneself, to bear, e.g., the cross (Mt 10:38); our sicknesses (Mt 8:17). **(5)** To take up, gather up (Mt 16:9, 10). Figuratively, to take the soul, as opposed to *títhēmi* (5087), to place, lay down (Jn 10:17, 18).

(B) To take out from a number, i.e. to choose (Ac 15:14).

(C) To take, i.e. to seize, lay hold of, with the idea of force or violence. **(1)** Particularly (Mt 21:35, 39; Mk 12:3, 8; 2Co 11:20). In hunting or fishing: to take, catch (Lk 5:5); metaphorically (2Co 12:16). **(2)** Figuratively: to seize, to come or to fall upon someone, spoken of temptation (1Co 10:13); spoken of an evil spirit, demon (Lk 9:39). Also, of a strong affection or emotion, e.g., ecstasy fell upon all (Lk 5:26); fear (Lk 7:16).

(D) To take away, e.g., from someone by force (Mt 5:40; Rev 3:11; 6:4).

(E) To take up with a person, i.e. to receive him as a friend or guest into one's house or society, equivalent to *déchomai* (1209), to accept:

(1) Generally (Jn 19:27; 2Jn 10). Metaphorically of a teacher: to receive, acknowledge, embrace and follow his instructions (Jn 1:12; 5:43; 13:20; 14:17); of doctrine: to embrace, admit, e.g., the word (Mt 13:20; Mk 4:16); the witness (Jn 3:11, 32, 33); the words (Jn 12:48; 17:8; 1Jn 5:9). (2) To receive the person of someone, used only in a bad sense in the NT: to accept one's person, meaning to be partial toward him (Lk 20:21; Gal 2:6).

(F) Figuratively, with *lḗthēn* [3024], forgetfulness, "to take forgetfulness," i.e. to forget (2Pe 1:9); with *peíran* ([3984], trial, attempt, "to take an attempt," i.e. to make an attempt (Heb 11:29).

(II) To receive what is given or imparted or imposed, to obtain, partake of:

(A) Generally (Mt 7:8; 10:8; Mk 10:30; Jn 16:24; Ac 2:33; Ro 4:11; 1Co 4:7; Gal 3:14; Jas 1:7; 1Jn 2:27; Rev 18:4).

(B) Of those who receive an office, station, position (Lk 19:12, 15; Ac 1:20, 25; Heb 7:5).

(C) Of persons appointed to receive tribute, rent, etc.: to collect, exact (Mt 17:24, 25; 21:34; Heb 7:8).

(D) Figuratively: to receive instruction, i.e. to be instructed, to learn (Rev 3:3).

Deriv.: *analambánō* (353), to take up; *antilambánō* (482), to take hold of, support; *apolambánō* (618), to receive, take back; *dexiolábos* (1187), a spearman; *epilambánomai* (1949), to grasp; *eulabḗs* (2126), devout; *katalambánō* (2638), to seize, comprehend, attain; *lḗpsis* (3028), a receiving; *metalambánō* (3335), to take part, share; *paralambánō* (3880), to take or receive from another; *prolambánō* (4301), to anticipate; *proslambánō* (4355), to receive or take to oneself; *prosōpolḗptēs* (4381), a respector of persons; *sullambánō* (4815), to seize, catch; *hupolambánō* (5274), to assume.

Syn.: *déchomai* (1209), to receive. Also *anadéchomai* (324), to receive; *apéchō* (568), to receive, to have in full; *apodéchomai* (588), to receive, to accept gladly; *eisdéchomai* (1523), to receive into favour; *epidéchomai* (1926), to accept; *komízō* (2865), to receive; *paradéchomai* (3858), to receive or admit with approval; *prosdéchomai* (4327), to receive to oneself; *hupodéchomai* (5264), to receive as a guest.

2984. Λάμεχ, Lamech, *lam´-ekh*; of Hebrew origin [3929]; *Lamech* (i.e. *Lemek*), a patriarch:—Lamech.

2985. λαμπάς, lampas, *lam-pas´*; from 2989; a "*lamp*" or *flambeau*:—lamp, light, torch.

Noun from *lámpō* (2989), to light, shine. A torch, lamp. Spoken of torches (Jn 18:3); spoken of lights, where the context implies lamps on lampstands (Ac 20:8; Rev 4:5); spoken of lamps or special torches fed with oil (Mt 25:1, 3, 4, 7, 8); used figuratively of a burning star (Rev 8:10).

2986. λαμπρός, lampros, *lam-pros´*; from the same as 2985; *radiant*; (by analogy) *limpid*; (figurative) *magnificent* or *sumptuous* (in appearance):—bright, clear, gay, goodly, gorgeous, white.

2987. λαμπρότης, lamprotēs, *lam-prot´-ace*; from 2896; *brilliancy*:—brightness.

2988. λαμπρῶς, lamprōs, *lam-proce´*; adverb from 2986; *brilliantly*, i.e. (figurative) *luxuriously*:—sumptuously.

2989. λάμπω, lampō, *lam´-po*; a primary verb; to *beam*, i.e. *radiate* brilliancy (literal or figurative):—give light, shine.

2990. λανθάνω, lanthanō, *lan-than´-o*; a prolonged form of a primary verb, which is used only as an alternate in certain tenses; to *lie hid* (literal or figurative); often used adverb *unwittingly*:—be hid, be ignorant of, unawares.

2991. λαξευτός, laxeutos, *lax-yoo-tos´*; from a compound of **λᾶς**, *las* (a *stone*) and the base of 3584 (in its origin sense of *scraping*); *rock-quarried*:—hewn in stone.

2992. λαός, laos, *lah-os´*; apparently a primary word; a *people* (in genitive; thus differing from 1218, which denotes one's *own* populace):—people.

Noun meaning people:

(I) A people, nation, tribe, i.e. the mass of any people, and not like *dḗmos* (1218), which would be limited to a community of free citizens (Lk 2:10; Ac 4:25; Rev 5:9). Specifically of the Jews as the people of God's choice (Mt 1:21; 2:4, 6; Mk 7:6; Lk 2:32; Jn 11:50; Heb 7:5). Figuratively, of Christians as God's spiritual Israel (Tit 2:14; Heb 2:17; 4:9; 13:12).

(II) Generally: the people, i.e. the multitude, the public, either indefinitely or of a multitude collected in one place (Lk 7:29; 8:47; 9:13; Ac 3:9, 11, 12); especially the common people, the populace, the inhabitants of any city or territory, e.g., Jerusalem (Ac 2:47; 21:30, 36); of Galilee (Mt 4:23; 9:35); as distinguished from magistrates, etc. (Mt 26:5; 27:25, 64; Mk 11:32; Lk 19:48; 23:13; Ac 6:12).

Syn.: *éthnos* (1484), nation, used in the plural to signify the heathen or Gentiles as distinguished from the Jews or believers. Also, *dḗmos* (1218) a community of free citizens, a people commonly bound together; *óchlos* (3793), a disorganized crowd or multitude.

2993. Λαοδίκεια, Laodikeia, *Lah-od-ik´-i-ah*; from a compound of 2992 and 1349; *Laodicia*, a place in Asia Minor:—Laodicea.

2994. Λαοδικεύς, Laodikeus, *lah-od-ik-yooce´*; from 2993; a *Laodicean*, i.e. inhabitant of Laodicia:—Laodicean.

2995. λάρυγξ, larugx, *lar´-oongks*; of uncertain derivative; the *throat* ("*larynx*"):—throat.

2996. Λασαία, Lasaia, *las-ah´-yah*; of uncertain origin; *Lasæa*, a place in Crete:—Lasea.

2997. λάσχω, laschō, *las´-kho*; a strengthened form of a primary verb, which only occurs in this and another prolonged form as alternate in certain tenses; to *crack* open (from a fall):—burst asunder.

2998. λατομέω, latomeō, *lat-om-eh´-o*; from the same as the first part of 2991 and the base of 5114; to *quarry*:—hew.

2999. λατρεία, latreia, *lat-ri´-ah*; from 3000; *ministration* of God, i.e. *worship*:—(divine) service.

Noun from *latreúō* (3000), to serve for hire, to worship. Service for hire or as a slave. In the NT, only in respect to God, divine service (Jn 16:2); spoken of the priest's service in the sacrifices (Ro 9:4; Heb 9:1, 6); used figuratively of the Christian's offering himself as a living sacrifice (Ro 12:1).

Deriv.: *eidōlolatreía* (1495), idolatry.

Syn.: *diakonía* (1248), service, ministry; *thrēskeia* (2356), religion, worship; *leitourgía* (3009), public ministry.

3000. λατρεύω, latreuō, *lat-ryoo´-o*; from **λάτρις**, *latris* (a hired *menial*); to *minister* (to God), i.e. *render* religious *homage*:—serve, do the service, worship (-per).

From *latrís* (n.f.), one hired. To serve, in a religious sense to serve and to worship God (Mt 4:10; Lk 1:74; 2:37; 4:8; Ac 7:7; 24:14; 26:7; 27:23; Ro 1:9; Php 3:3; 2Ti 1:3; Heb 9:14; 12:28; Rev 22:3); used in a negative sense: to worship the host of heaven, i.e. the sun, moon, and stars (Ac 7:42); to worship the creature rather than the Creator (Ro 1:25). Used of those who served in offering the OT sacrifices (Heb 8:5; 9:9; 10:2; 13:10) and of those serving the celestial temple (Rev 7:15).

Deriv.: *latreía* (2999), service, worship.

Syn.: *eusebéō* (2151), to act piously toward, worship; *proskunéō* (4352), to make obeisance, do reverence to, worship, do homage; *sebázomai* (4573), to honour religiously, render reverence; *sébomai* (4576), to revere, render devotion. With the meaning of rendering service: *diakonéō* (1247), to minister; *leitourgéō* (3008), to minister publicly in sacred service.

3001. λάχανον, lachanon, *lakh´-an-on*; from **λαχαίνω**, *lachainō* (to *dig*); a *vegetable*:—herb.

3002. Λεββαῖος, Lebbaios, *leb-bah´-yos*; of uncertain origin; *Lebbæus*, a Christian:—Lebbæus.

3003. λεγεών, legeōn, *leg-eh-ohn´*; of Latin origin; a "*legion*," i.e. Roman *regiment* (figurative):—legion.

3004. λέγω, legō, *leg´-o*; a primary verb; properly to "*lay*" forth, i.e. (figurative) *relate* (in words [usually of systematic or set *discourse*; whereas 2036 and 5346 generally refer to an *individual* expression or speech respectively; while 4483 is properly to *break silence* merely, and 2980 means an *extended* or random harangue]); (by implication) to *mean*:—ask, bid, boast, call, describe, give out, name, put forth, say (-ing, on), shew, speak, tell, utter.

Originally: to lay or let lie down for sleep, to lay together, i.e. to collect; later: to relate, recount; and hence the meaning of to say, speak, i.e. to utter definite words, connected and significant discourse. It thus differs from *laléō* (2980), which refers primarily to words spoken and not to their connected sense. In the NT:

(I) To lay before, i.e. to relate, e.g., a parable, to put forth, propound (Lk 12:41; 13:6; 14:7; 18:1). Of events: to narrate, tell (Lk 24:10).

(II) To say, speak, discourse:

(A) Generally (Mt 16:13; 27:11; 21:16; Mk 9:11; 11:23; Lk 8:8; 9:7; Jn 4:20; 5:34; 18:37; Ac 4:32; 8:6; Ro 10:8; Eph 5:12).

(B) As modified by the context, where the meaning lies not so much in *légō*, as in the adjuncts, e.g.: **(1)** Before questions: to ask, inquire (Mt 9:14; Mk 5:30; 6:37; 14:14; Lk 7:20; 16:5; 22:11; Jn 7:11; Ac 25:20; Ro 10:19). **(2)** Before replies: to answer, reply (Mt 17:25; 18:22; 20:7, 21; Jn 18:17). **(3)** In affirmations: to affirm, maintain (Mt 22:23; Mk 14:31; Lk 24:23; Gal 4:1; Jas 2:14; 1Jn 2:4, 6, 9). In the formulas "I say unto thee" (or unto you), in solemn affirmations, generally (Mt 11:9, 22; Mk 11:24; Lk 4:25; 7:14; 15:10; Jn 3:11). **(4)** Figuratively: to say or speak by writing, by letter, e.g., with the words written (Lk 1:63; 20:42; 1Co 7:6; 15:51; 2Co 6:13; Php 4:11; 1Th 4:15; Phm 21).

(III) To call, to name, similar to *kaléō* [(2564), to call]; particularly: to speak of as being something or being called something (Mt 19:17; Mk 15:12; Lk 20:37; Jn 5:18; 15:15; Ac 10:28; Heb 11:24). Passive participle: called, named (Mt 2:23; 9:9; 26:3, 14; Mk 15:7; Jn 4:5; 9:11; 21:2; Ac 3:2; Eph 2:11). Also surnamed (Mt 4:18; 10:2; Col 4:11). With the idea of translation into another language (Jn 1:38; 4:25; 11:16; 19:17; 20:16; Ac 9:36).

Deriv.: *antilégō* (483), to contradict, speak against; *genealogéō* (1075), to reckon by generation; *dialégomai* (1256), to discuss, reason; *dílogos* (1351), double-tongued; *eklégomai* (1586), to choose, elect; *epilégō* (1951), to call, select; *katalégō* (2639), to reckon among, to count in; *logía* (3048), collection, gathering; *lógos* (3056), word, reason, expression; *mataiológos* (3151), one talking lightly; *paralégō* (3881), to pass, sail by; *prolégō* (4302), to tell before, foretell; *spermológos* (4691), babbler; *stratologéō* (4758), to enlist; *sullégō* (4816), to collect; *Philólogos* (5378), a proper name: lover of the word; *pseudológos* (5573), one speaking lies.

Syn.: *laléō* (2980), to say something (sometimes in contrast with *légō*, the former indicating a mere utterance of sounds, breaking silence, or speaking). Also, *anaggéllō* (312), to announce, report; *antapokrínomai* (470), to reply against; *apaggéllō* (518), to announce, report; *apokrínomai* (611), to give an answer to a question; *dēlóō* (1213), to make plain; *diēgéomai* (1334), to narrate; *diaggéllō* (1229), to announce, declare; *diasaphéō* (1285), to make clear; *ekdiēgéomai* (1555), to narrate in full; *exaggéllō* (1804), to publish, proclaim; *exēgéomai* (1834), to declare, bring out the meaning; *epaggéllō* (1861), to announce, proclaim; *eréō* (2046), to tell, say; *euaggelízō* (2097), to evangelize; *kataggéllō* (2605), to declare, proclaim; *kērússō* (2784), to preach, herald; *homiléō* (3656), to converse with; *paraggéllō* (3853), to charge, command; *parrēsiázomai* (3955), to be bold in speech; *plērophoréō* (4135), to inform fully; *prophēteúō* (4395), to prophesy; *suzētéō* (4802), to discuss; *pháskō* (5335), to affirm; *phēmí* (5346), to say by way of enlightening, explaining, affirming; *phrázō* (5419), to declare.

3005. λεῖμμα, leimma, *lime´-mah*; from 3007; a *remainder*:—remnant.

3006. λεῖος, leios, *li´-os*; apparently a primary word; *smooth*, i.e. "*level*":—smooth.

3007. λείπω, leipō, *li´-po*; a primary verb; to *leave*, i.e. (intransitive or passive) to *fail* or *be absent*:—be destitute (wanting), lack.

3008. λειτουργέω, leitourgeō, *li-toorg-eh´-o*; from 3011; to be a *public servant*, i.e. (by analogy) to *perform* religious or charitable *functions* (*worship, obey, relieve*):—minister.

From *leitourgós* (3011), public servant. To perform a public service. In the NT: to minister, to serve publicly in religious worship, e.g., the priests of the OT (Heb 10:11), Christian teachers (Ac 13:2). By implication, in a more private sense: to minister to anyone, to supply monetary aid (Ro 15:27).

Syn.: *diakonéō* (1247), to minister voluntarily; *douleúō* (1398), to serve as a slave, and therefore to serve by compulsion; *latreúō* (3000), primarily to work for hire, but when it involves service to God, it is also part of worship; *hupēretéō* (5256), to serve.

3009. λειτουργία, leitourgia, *li-toorg-ee´-ah*; from 3008; *public function* (as priest ["liturgy"] or almsgiver):—ministration (-try), service.

3010. λειτουργικός, leitourgikos, *li-toorg-ik-os´*; from the same as 3008; *functional publicly* ("liturgic"), i.e. *beneficent*:—ministering.

3011. λειτουργός, leitourgos, *li-toorg-os´*; from a derivative of 2992 and 2041; a *public servant*, i.e. a *functionary* in the temple or gospel, or (genitive) a *worshipper* (of God) or *benefactor* (of man):—minister (-ed).

3012. λέντιον, lention, *len´-tee-on*; of Latin origin; a "*linen*" cloth, i.e. *apron*:—towel.

3013. λεπίς, lepis, *lep-is´*; from **λέπω, *lepō*** (to *peel*); a *flake*:—scale.

3014. λέπρα, lepra, *lep´-rah*; from the same as 3013; *scaliness*, i.e. "*leprosy*":—leprosy.

3015. λεπρός, lepros, *lep-ros´*; from the same as 3014; *scaly*, i.e. *leprous* (a *leper*):—leper.

3016. λεπτόν, lepton, *lep-ton´*; neuter of a derivative of the same as 3013; something *scaled* (*light*), i.e. a small *coin*:—mite.

3017. Λευΐ, Leuï, *lyoo-ee´*; of Hebrew origin [3878]; *Levi*, the name of three Israelites:—Levi. Compare 3018.

3018. Λευΐς, Leuïs, *lyoo-is´*; a form of 3017; *Lewis* (i.e. *Levi*), a Christian:—Levi.

3019. Λευΐτης, Leuïtēs, *lyoo-ee´-tace*; from 3017; a *Levite*, i.e. descendant of Levi:—Levite.

3020. Λευϊτικός, Leuïtikos, *lyoo-it´-ee-kos´*; from 3019; *Levitic*, i.e. relating to the Levites:—Levitical.

3021. λευκαίνω, leukainō, *lyoo-kah´ee-no*; from 3022; to *whiten*:—make white, whiten.

3022. λευκός, leukos, *lyoo-kos´*; from **λύκη, *lukē*** ("*light*"); *white*:—white.

3023. λεών, leōn, *leh-ohn´*; a primary word; a "*lion*":—lion.

3024. λήθη, lēthē, *lay´-thay*; from 2990; *forgetfulness*:— + forget.

3025. ληνός, lēnos, *lay-nos´*; apparently a primary word; a *trough*, i.e. wine-*vat*:—winepress.

3026. λῆρος, lēros, *lay´-ros*; apparently a primary word; *twaddle*, i.e. an *incredible* story:—idle tale.

3027. ληστης, lēistēs, *lace-tace´*; from **ληΐζομαι, *lēizomai*** (to *plunder*); a *brigand*:—robber, thief.

Noun from *leízomai* (n.f.), to plunder. A plunderer, robber (Mt 21:13; 26:55; 27:38, 44; Mk 11:17; 14:48; 15:27; Lk 10:30, 36; 19:46; 22:52; Jn 10:1; 18:40; 2Co 11:26; Sept.: Jer 7:11); metaphorically of false teachers (Jn 10:8). See *kléptēs* (2812), thief.

Syn.: *kléptēs* (2812), thief. Also, *hierósulos* (2417), a robber of temples; *kakopoiós* (2555), an evildoer; *kakoúrgos* (2557), an evil worker, malefactor.

3028. λῆψις, lēpsis, *lape´-sis*; from 2983; *receipt* (the act):—receiving.

3029. λίαν, lian, *lee´-an*; of uncertain affinity; *much* (adverb):—exceeding, great (-ly), sore, very (+ chiefest).

3030. λίβανος, libanos, *lib´-an-os*; of foreign origin [3828]; the *incense*-tree, i.e. (by implication) *incense* itself:—frankincense.

3031. λιβανωτός, libanōtos, *lib-an-o-tos´*; from 3030; *frankincense*, i.e. (by extension) a *censer* for burning it:—censer.

3032. Λιβερτῖνος, Libertinos, *lib-er-tee´-nos*; of Latin origin; a Roman *freedman*:—Libertine.

3033. Λιβύη, Libuē, *lib-oo´-ay*; probably from 3047; *Libye*, a region of Africa:—Libya.

3034. λιθάζω, lithazō, *lith-ad´-zo*; from 3037; to *lapidate*:—stone.

3035. λίθινος, lithinos, *lith´-ee-nos*; from 3037; *stony*, i.e. made of *stone*:—of stone.

3036. λιθοβολέω, lithoboleō, *lith-ob-ol-eh´-o*; from a compound of 3037 and 906; to *throw stones*, i.e. *lapidate*:—stone, cast stones.

3037. λίθος, lithos, *lee´-thos*; apparently a primary word; a *stone* (literal or figurative):—(mill-, stumbling-) stone.

3038. λιθόστρωτος, lithostrōtos, *lith-os´-tro-tos*; from 3037 and a derivative of 4766; *stone-strewed*, i.e. a tessellated *mosaic* on which the Roman tribunal was placed:—Pavement.

3039. λικμάω, likmaō, *lik-mah´-o*; from **λικμός, *likmos***, the equivalent of **λίκνον, *liknon*** (a winnowing *fan* or basket); to *winnow*, i.e. (by analogy) to *triturate*:—grind to powder.

3040. λιμήν, limēn, *lee-mane´*; apparently a primary word; a *harbor*:—haven. Compare 2568.

3041. λίμνη, limnē, *lim´-nay*; probably from 3040 (through the idea of the nearness of shore); a *pond* (large or small):—lake.

3042. λιμός, limos, *lee-mos´*; probably from 3007 (through the idea of *destitution*); a *scarcity* of food:—dearth, famine, hunger.

3043. λίνον, linon, *lee´-non*; probably a primary word; *flax*, i.e. (by implication) "*linen*":—linen.

3044. Λῖνος, Linos, *lee´-nos*; perhaps from 3043; *Linus*, a Christian:—Linus.

3045. λιπαρός, liparos, *lip-ar-os´*; from **λιπος, *lipos*** (*grease*); *fat*, i.e. (figurative) *sumptuous*:—dainty.

3046. λίτρα, litra, *lee´-trah*; of Latin origin [*libra*]; a *pound* in weight:—pound.

3047. λίψ, lips, *leeps*; probably from **λείβω, *leibō*** (to *pour* a "libation"); the *south* (-west) wind (as bringing rain, i.e. (by extension) the *south* quarter:—southwest.

3048. λογία, logia, *log-ee´-ah*; from 3056 (in the commercial sense); a *contribution*:—collection, gathering.

3049. λογίζομαι, logizomai, *log-id´-zom-ahee*; middle from 3056; to *take an inventory*, i.e. *estimate* (literal or figurative):—conclude, (ac-) count (of), + despise, esteem, impute, lay, number, reason, reckon, suppose, think (on).

From *lógos* (3056), reason, word, account. To reason, to think, consider, reckon:

(I) Generally to think upon, to consider (Mk 11:31; 2Co 10:7; Php 4:8; Heb 11:19). In the sense of to reason out, to think out, to find out by thinking (2Co 3:5).

(II) Of the result of reasoning: to conclude, to judge, to suppose, to hold (Ro 3:28; 2Co 11:5; 12:6; Php 3:13; 1Pe 5:12). So generally: to reason, to judge (1Co 13:11); also in the sense of to purpose (2Co 10:2).

(III) To reckon someone to be in a particular group: e.g., to consider Christ as a transgressor (Mk 15:28; Lk 22:37). To count, regard, to hold (Ac 19:27; Ro 8:36; 1Co 4:1; 2Co 10:2).

(IV) To reckon or count to someone, particularly: to put to one's account (Ro 4:4); hence figuratively: to impute, to attribute:

(A) Generally, of God's imputing righteousness (Ro 4:6, 11). So of evil: to impute, to lay to one's charge; and with a neg., not to impute, i.e. to overlook, to forgive (Ro 4:8; 2Co 5:19; 2Ti 4:16).

(B) Also followed by that which is imputed, laid to one's charge, e.g., imputing Abraham's faith to him as righteousness; i.e. treating him as righteous on account of his faith (Ro 4:3, 9, 22; Gal 3:6; Jas 2:23).

Deriv.: *analogízomai* (357), to consider; *dialogízomai* (1260), to reckon distributively, to settle with one, to consider, deliberate; *logismós* (3053), a thought; *paralogízomai* (3884), to beguile, deceive; *sullogízomai* (4817), to reason with.

Syn.: *dialégomai* (1256), to dispute or reason with; *dokéō* (1380), to think, suppose; *egkrínō* (1469), to judge, to classify; *ellogéō* (1677), to put to a person's account, to reckon, impute; *katalégō* (2639), to count in; *kataxióō* (2661), to count worthy; *katarithméō* (2674), to number with, count among; *krínō* (2919), to judge, reckon; *nomízō* (3543), to suppose; *oíomai* (3633) I suppose, think; *sugkatapsēphízō* (4785), to reckon together with; *sullogízomai* (4817), to reckon, reason; *huponoéō* (5282), to suppose, surmise, think; *phronéō* (5426), to think.

3050. λογικός, logikos, *log-ik-os´*; from 3056; *rational* ("*logical*"):—reasonable, of the word.

Adjective from *lógos* (3056), reason, word. Literally, "of the Word": rational, pertaining to the reason, mind, understanding. Used in Ro 12:1 concerning the presentation of our bodies to be a living sacrifice to God as our *logikēn latreian,* "rational service," i.e. the service or worship which is made by our mind (see *latreía* [2999], service or worship), stressing the inner motive and desires of our sacrifice more than outward deeds. Also used in 1Pe 2:2 in the phrase, *logikón ádolon gála,* which can be rendered either "the pure milk of the word" or "the pure milk for [or fitted for] the mind" (see *ádolos* [97], pure; *gála* [1051], milk).

3051. λόγιον, logion, *log´-ee-on*; neuter of 3052; an *utterance* (of God):—oracle.

Noun from *lógios* (3052) eloquent. Something uttered or spoken. Of God: an oracle, divine communication, e.g., of the oracles in the OT (Ac 7:38; Ro 3:2). So through Christ, the doctrines of the gospel (Heb 5:12; 1Pe 4:11).

3052. λόγιος, logios, *log´-ee-os*; from 3056; *fluent*, i.e. an *orator*:—eloquent.

3053. λογισμός, logismos, *log-is-mos´*; from 3049; *computation*, i.e. (figurative) *reasoning* (*conscience, conceit*):—imagination, thought.

Noun from *logízomai* (3049), to count, reckon, take an inventory. A reckoning, calculation. In the NT: reasoning, thought, meditation (Ro 2:15). Also in the sense of devices, counsels against God (2Co 10:5).

Syn.: *boulḗ* (1012), purpose, plan; *nóema* (3540), thought.

3054. λογομαχέω, logomacheō, *log-om-akh-eh´-o*; from a compound of 3056 and 3164; to *be disputatious* (on trifles):—strive about words.

3055. λογομαχία, logomachia, *log-om-akh-ee´-ah*; from the same as 3054; *disputation* about trifles ("*logomachy*"):—strife of words.

3056. λόγος, logos, *log´-os*; from 3004; something *said* (including the *thought*); (by implication) a *topic* (subject of discourse), also *reasoning* (the mental faculty or *motive*; by extension a *computation*; specially (with the art. in John) the Divine *Expression* (i.e. *Christ*):—account, cause, communication, × concerning, doctrine, fame, × have to do, intent, matter, mouth, preaching, question, reason, + reckon, remove, say (-ing), shew, × speaker, speech, talk, thing, + none of these things move me, tidings, treatise, utterance, word, work.

Noun from *légō* (3004), to speak intelligently. A word, as spoken; anything spoken; also reason as manifesting itself in the power of speech:

(I) A word, both the act of speaking and the thing spoken:

(A) A word, as uttered by the living voice, a speaking, speech, utterance (Mt 8:8; Lk 7:7; 23:9; 1Co 14:9; Heb 12:19); a saying, discourse, conversation (Mt 12:37; 15:12; 19:22; 22:15; 26:1; Ac 5:24).

Metonymically, the power of speech, delivery, oratory, eloquence (1Co 12:8; 2Co 11:6; Eph 6:19). The Word of God, meaning His omnipotent voice, decree (2Pe 3:5, 7; Sept.: Ps 32:6 [cf. Ge 1:3; Ps 148:5]).

(**B**) A saying, declaration, sentiment uttered: (**1**) Generally (Mt 10:14; Lk 4:22; 20:20; Jn 6:60). In reference to words or declarations, e.g., which precede (Mt 7:24, 26; Mk 7:29; Jn 2:22; 6:60; 7:40; 10:19; 12:38; Ac 5:24; 20:35; Ro 9:9; 13:9; 1Co 15:54; 1Ti 3:1; Tit 3:8; Rev 19:9). The word, declaration of a prophet, meaning prediction, prophecy (Lk 3:4; Jn 12:38; Ac 15:15; 2Pe 1:19; Rev 1:3); a proverb, maxim (Jn 4:37). (**2**) In reference to religion, religious duties, i.e. doctrine, precept (Ac 15:24; 18:15; 1Ti 4:6; Tit 1:9; Heb 2:2); especially of God, the Word of God, meaning divine revelation and declaration, oracle (Mk 7:13; Lk 5:1; Jn 5:38; 10:35; 17:6; Ac 4:29; Ro 9:6, 28; 1Co 14:36; 2Co 4:2; Col 1:25; 1Th 2:13; Tit 1:3; Heb 4:2, 12; 13:7).

(**II**) Reason, the reasoning faculty as that power of the soul which is the basis of speech. In the NT:

(**A**) A reason, ground, cause (Mt 5:32; Ac 10:29; 18:14).

(**B**) Reason as demanded or assigned, i.e. a reckoning, an account (Mt 18:23; 25:19; Lk 16:2; Ac 19:40; 20:24; Heb 13:17; 1Pe 3:15; 4:5).

(**III**) The Word, the *Lógos* in the writings of John (Jn 1:1, 14; 1Jn 1:1; Rev 19:13); it here stands for the preexistent nature of Christ, i.e. that spiritual and divine nature spoken of in the Jewish writings before and about the time of Christ, under various names, e.g., Son of Man (Da 7:13); Word of Jehovah (used in the Aramaic Targums, the translations which were used in the Jewish synagogues along with the Hebrew Scriptures). On this divine word, the Jews of that age would appear to have had much subtle discussion; and therefore probably the apostle sets out with affirming, "In the beginning was the Word, and the Word was with God, and the Word was God" (Jn 1:1); and then also declares that this Word became flesh and was thus the Messiah (Jn 1:14).

Deriv.: *álogos* (249), irrational, without intelligence; *analogía* (356), analogy; *analogízomai* (357), to contemplate, consider; *apologéomai* (626), to answer back, defend oneself; *battologéō* (945), to use vain repetitions; *ellogéō* (1677), to account, reckon in; *eulogéō* (2127), to speak well of, bless; *logízomai* (3049), to reckon, impute; *logikós* (3050), reasonable; *lógios* (3052), fluent, orator, intelligent person; *polulogía* (4180), much speaking.

Syn.: *rhḗma* (4487), word, utterance. Also, *aggelía* (31), message, announcement; *eperṓtēma* (1906), an inquiry, answer; *laliá* (2981), speech; *homilía* (3657), homily, communication, speech; *prophēteía* (4394), prophecy, something spoken ahead of its occurrence or spoken forth; *suzḗtēsis* (4803), mutual questioning; *phḗmē* (5345), fame, report, that which is being said about someone.

3057. λόγχη, logchē, *long´-khay*; perhaps a primary word; a "*lance*":—spear.

3058. λοιδορέω, loidoreō, *loy-dor-eh´-o*; from 3060; to *reproach*, i.e. *vilify*:—revile.

From *loídoros* (3060), a reviler. To revile, reproach (Jn 9:28; Ac 23:4; 1Co 4:12; 1Pe 2:23).

Deriv.: *antiloidoréō* (486), to revile again.

Syn.: *atimázō* (818), to dishonour; *blasphēméō* (987), to revile, blaspheme; *empaízō* (1702), to mock, jeer; *theatrízō* (2301), to expose as a spectacle; *katageláō* (2606), to deride, laugh to scorn; *muktērízō* (3456), to ridicule; *oneidízō* (3679), to reproach; *hubrízō* (5195), to insult, to use despitefully or shamefully; *chleuázō* (5512), to mock.

3059. λοιδορία, loidoria, *loy-dor-ee´-ah*; from 3060; *slander* or *vituperation*:—railing, reproach [-fully].

3060. λοίδορος, loidoros, *loy´-dor-os*; from **λοιδός, loidos** (*mischief*); *abusive*, i.e. a *blackguard*:—railer, reviler.

3061. λοιμός, loimos, *loy-mos´*; of uncertain affinity; a *plague* (literal, the *disease*; or figurative, a *pest*):—pestilence (-t).

3062. λοιποί, loipoi, *loy-poy´*; masculine plural of a derivative of 3007; *remaining* ones:—other, which remain, remnant, residue, rest.

3063. λοιπόν, loipon, *loy-pon´*; neuter singular of the same as 3062; something *remaining* (adverb):—besides, finally, furthermore, (from) henceforth, moreover, now, + it remaineth, then.

3064. λοιποῦ, loipou, *loy-poo´*; generic singular of the same as 3062; *remaining* time:—from henceforth.

3065. Λουκᾶς, Loukas, *loo-kas´*; contracted from Latin *Lucanus; Lucas*, a Christian:—Lucas, Luke.

3066. Λούκιος, Loukios, *loo´-kee-os*; of Latin origin; *illuminative; Lucius*, a Christian:—Lucius.

3067. λουτρόν, loutron, *loo-tron´*; from 3068; a *bath*, i.e. (figurative) *baptism*:—washing.

Noun from *loúō* (3068), to bathe. The act of bathing, washing, ablution. Spoken of the washing of the word of God as a cleansing instrument (Eph 5:26); spoken of the cleansing which takes place at salvation (Tit 3:5).

Syn.: *katharismós* (2512), cleansing.

3068. λούω, louō, *loo´-o*; a primary verb; to *bathe* (the *whole* person; whereas 3538 means to wet a *part* only, and 4150 to wash, cleanse *garments* exclusively):—wash.

To bathe, to wash (Jn 13:10; Ac 9:37; 16:33; Heb 10:22; 2Pe 2:22). Metaphorically: to cleanse and purify from sin, as in being washed by Christ's blood (Rev 1:5).

Deriv.: *apoloúō* (628), to wash away; *loutrón* (3067), bath.

Syn.: *katharízō* (2511), to cleanse.

3069. Λύδδα, Ludda, *lud´-dah*; of Hebrew origin [3850]; *Lydda* (i.e. *Lod*), a place in Palestine:—Lydda.

3070. Λυδία, Ludia, *loo-dee´-ah*; properly feminine of **Λύδιος, *Ludios***; [of foreign origin] (a *Lydian*, in Asia Minor); *Lydia*, a Christian woman:—Lydia.

3071. Λυκαονία, Lukaonia, *loo-kah-on-ee´-ah*; perhaps remotely from 3074; *Lycaonia*, a region of Asia Minor:—Lycaonia.

3072. Λυκαονιστί, Lukaonisti, *loo-kah-on-is-tee´*; adverb from a derivative of 3071; *Lycaonistically*, i.e. in the language of the Lycaonians:—in the speech of Lycaonia.

3073. Λυκία, Lukia, *loo-kee´-ah*; probably remotely from 3074; *Lycia*, a province of Asia Minor:—Lycia.

3074. λύκος, lukos, *loo´-kos*; perhaps akin to the base of 3022 (from the *whitish* hair); a *wolf*:—wolf.

3075. λυμαίνομαι, lumainomai, *loo-mah´ee-nom-ahee*; middle from a probable derivative of 3089 (meaning *filth*); properly to *soil*, i.e. (figurative) *insult* (*maltreat*):—make havock of.

3076. λυπέω, lupeō, *loo-peh´-o*; from 3077; to *distress*; reflexive or passive to *be sad*:—cause grief, grieve, be in heaviness, (be) sorrow (-ful), be (make) sorry.

From *lúpē* (3077), sorrow. To grieve, afflict with sorrow; middle or passive, to be grieved, sad, sorrowful (Mt 14:9; 17:23; 18:31; 19:22; 26:22, 37; Mk 10:22; 14:19; Jn 16:20; 21:17; Ro 14:15; 2Co 2:2, 4; 6:10; 7:9, 11; 1Th 4:13; 1Pe 1:6). With the meaning of to cause grief, offend (2Co 2:5; 7:8; Eph 4:30).

Deriv.: *sullupéō* (4818), to sorrow together.

Syn.: *adēmonéō* (85), to be in distress; *diaponéō* (1278), in the pass., to be troubled as the result of pain and toil; *enochléō* (1776), to vex; *thlíbō* (2346), to squeeze, to afflict; *thrēnéō* (2354), bewail; *kóptō* (2875), to beat the breast, an outward sign of an inward grief; *odunáō* (3600), to cause pain, be in anguish; *penthéō* (3996), mourn; *tarássō* (5015), to trouble; *turbázō* (5182), to disturb, trouble.

3077. λύπη, lupē, *loo´-pay*; apparently a primative word; *sadness*:—grief, grievous, + grudgingly, heaviness, sorrow.

3078. Λυσανίας, Lusanias, *loo-san-ee´-as*; from 3080 and **ἀνία, *Ania*** (*trouble*); *grief-dispelling; Lysanias*, a governor of Abilene:—Lysanias.

3079. Λυσίας, Lusias, *loo-see´-as*; of uncertain affinity; *Lysias*, a Roman:—Lysias.

3080. λύσις, lusis, *loo´-sis*; from 3089; a *loosening*, i.e. (special) *divorce*:—to be loosed.

3081. λυσιτελεῖ, lusitelei, *loo-sit-el-i´*; third person singular present indicative active of a derivative of a composition of 3080 and 5056; impersonal it *answers* the *purpose*, i.e. *is advantageous:*—it is better.

3082. Λύστρα, Lustra, *loos´-trah*; of uncertain origin; *Lystra*, a place in Asia Minor:—Lystra.

3083. λύτρον, lutron, *loo´-tron*; from 3089; something to *loosen* with, i.e. a redemption *price* (figurative, *atonement*):—ransom.

Noun from *lúō* (3089), to loose. Ransom, lit. "loosing-money," i.e. price paid for redeeming captives. Used metaphorically for the ransom paid by Christ for the delivering of men from the bondage of sin and death (Mt 20:28; Mk 10:45).

Deriv.: *antílutron* (487), ransom; *lutróō* (3084), to ransom.

Syn.: *timḗ* (5092), price.

3084. λυτρόω, lutroō, *loo-tro´-o*; from 3083; to *ransom* (literal or figurative):—redeem.

From *lútron* (3083), a ransom. To ransom, i.e. to let go free for a ransom. In the NT, used in the middle voice: to ransom, to redeem, to deliver; used metaphorically of Christ's purchasing our salvation (Lk 24:21; Tit 2:14; 1Pe 1:18).

Deriv.: *lútrōsis* (3085), the act of redemption or deliverance; *lutrōtḗs* (3086), redeemer.

Syn.: *apallássō* (525), to release, deliver; *diasṓzō* (1295), to rescue, bring through safely; *eleutheróō* (1659), to free; *sṓzō* (4982), to save, deliver.

3085. λύτρωσις, lutrōsis, *loo´-tro-sis*; from 3084; a *ransoming* (figurative):— + redeemed, redemption.

Noun from *lutróō* (3084), to release on receipt of a ransom. Redemption, deliverance; spoken of the redemption of Israel (Lk 1:68; 2:38). Used metaphorically: redemption from sin and its consequences (Heb 9:12).

Syn.: *áphesis* (859), release, forgiveness; *dikaíōsis* (1347), justification; *sōtēría* (4991), salvation, rescuing; *sōtḗrion* (4992), the means of salvation.

3086. λυτρωτής, lutrōtēs, *loo-tro-tace´*; from 3084; a *redeemer* (figurative):—deliverer.

Noun from *lutróō* (3084), to release on receipt of a ransom. Redeemer, liberator. In the NT, used only in Ac 7:35 of Moses.

Syn.: *sōtḗr* (4990), savior.

3087. λυχνία, luchnia, *lookh-nee´-ah*; from 3088; a *lamp-stand* (literal or figurative):—candlestick.

3088. λύχνος, luchnos, *lookh´-nos*; from the base of 3022; a portable *lamp* or other *illuminator* (literal or figurative):—candle, light.

Noun meaning portable light, as a candle, lamp, lantern, etc. (Mt 5:15; Mk 4:21; Lk 8:16; 11:33, 36; 12:35; 15:8; 2Pe 1:19; Rev 18:23; 22:5). "The lamp of the body" (a.t.) represents the eye (Mt 6:22; Lk 11:34). Metaphorically, of John the Baptist as a distinguished teacher (Jn 5:35); of the Messiah, the Lamb in the new Jerusalem (Rev 21:23).

Deriv.: *luchnía* (3087), lampstand.

Syn.: *lampás* (2985), a torch, but frequently fed like a lamp with oil from a little vessel used for the purpose; *phanós* (5322), a lantern or torch.

3089. λύω, luō, *loo´-o*; a primary verb; to "*loosen*" (literal or figurative):—break (up), destroy, dissolve, (un-) loose, melt, put off. Compare 4486.

To loose, loosen what is bound, meaning to unbind, untie:

(I) Particularly, of loosing something fastened; e.g., sandal straps (Mk 1:7; Lk 3:16; Jn 1:27; Ac 7:33; 13:25); figuratively, the impediment of the tongue (Mk 7:35); the pains of death (Ac 2:24); also, of animals tied, e.g., a colt (Mt 21:2; Mk 11:2, 4; Lk 19:30, 31, 33); of a person swathed in bandages or graveclothes (Jn 11:44); of persons bound in sin and wickedness, who are loosed through the preaching of and a saving relationship with Jesus Christ and are judged or disciplined by the church based on their works (Mt 16:19; 18:18).

(II) Spoken of persons bound: to let go, loose, set free, e.g., prisoners (Ac 22:30; 24:26; Rev 20:3, 7); figuratively (Lk 13:16; 1Co 7:27).

(III) To loosen, dissolve, i.e. to sever, break (Ac 27:41; Rev 5:2, 5); figuratively of an assembly: to dissolve or break up (Ac 13:43).

(IV) By implication: to destroy, e.g., buildings, to demolish (Jn 2:19; Eph 2:14); figuratively (1Jn 3:8); of the world: to be destroyed by fire, to dissolve, melt (2Pe 3:10–12); figuratively of a law or institution: to loosen its obligation, i.e. either to make void, to do away (Mt 5:19; Jn 10:35), or to break, to violate (Jn 7:23).

Deriv.: *analúō* (360), to return; *apolúō* (630), to dismiss, release; *dialúō* (1262), to dissolve, scatter; *eklúō* (1590), to set free from; *epilúō* (1956), to unloose, explain, dissolve; *katalúō* (2647), to destroy, throw down; *lúsis* (3080), a loosening, divorce; *lútron* (3083), ransom; *paralúō* (3886), to loosen, become feeble, paralyzed.

Syn.: *apallássō* (525), to release, deliver; *apekdúō* (554), to strip off clothes, put off; *apochōrízō* (673), to separate off; *diachōrízō* (1316), to depart, remove oneself; *methístēmi* (3179), to remove; *chōrízō* (5563), to separate.

3090. Λωΐς, Lōis, *lo-ece´*; of uncertain origin; *Loïs*, a Christian woman:—Lois.

3091. Λώτ, Lōt, *lote*; of Hebrew origin [3876]; *Lot*, a patriarch:—Lot.

3092. Μαάθ, Maath, *mah-ath´*; probably of Hebrew origin; *Maath*, an Israelite:—Maath.

3093. Μαγδαλά, Magdala, *mag-dal-ah´*; of Chaldee origin [compare 4026]; *the tower; Magdala* (i.e. *Migdala*), a place in Palestine:—Magdala.

3094. Μαγδαληνή, Magdalēnē, *mag-dal-ay-nay´*; feminine of a derivative of 3093; a female *Magda-lene*, i.e. inhabitant of Magdala:—Magdalene.

3095. μαγεία, mageia, *mag-i´-ah*; from 3096; "*magic*":—sorcery.

3096. μαγεύω, mageuō, *mag-yoo´-o*; from 3097; to *practice magic:*—use sorcery.

3097. μάγος, magos, *mag´-os*; of foreign origin [7248]; a *Magian*, i.e. Oriental *scientist*; (by implication) a *magician:*—sorcerer, wise man.

3098. Μαγώγ, Magōg, *mag-ogue´*; of Hebrew origin [4031]; *Magog*, a foreign nation, i.e. (figurative) an Antichristian party:—Magog.

3099. Μαδιάν, Madian, *mad-ee-an´*; of Hebrew origin [4080]; *Madian* (i.e. *Midian*), a region of Arabia:—Madian.

3100. μαθητεύω, mathēteuō, *math-ayt-yoo´-o*; from 3101; intransitive to *become a pupil*; transitive to *disciple*, i.e. enroll as scholar:—be disciple, instruct, teach.

From *mathētḗs* (3101), disciple. To be the disciple of someone (Mt 27:57); to train as a disciple; to teach, to instruct; e.g., the Great Commission (Mt 28:19). Also Mt 13:52; Ac 14:21.

Syn.: *didáskō* (1321), to give instruction, teach; *heterodidaskaléō* (2085), to teach a different doctrine; *katēchéō* (2727), to teach orally, instruct, catechize; *paideúō* (3811), to instruct and train, to discipline.

3101. μαθητής, mathētēs, *math-ay-tes´*; from 3129; a *learner*, i.e. *pupil:*—disciple.

Noun from *manthánō* (3129), to learn, to understand. A disciple, scholar, follower of a teacher; generally (Mt 10:24); of the Pharisees (Mt 22:16); of John the Baptist (Mt 9:14; Mk 2:18; Lk 5:33; Jn 3:25); of Jesus (Mt 5:1; Mk 8:27; Lk 8:9; Jn 3:22); specifically of the twelve apostles (Mt 10:1; 11:1; 20:17; Lk 9:1); emphatically for true disciples (Jn 13:35; 15:8). After Christ's death, the term disciple takes the broader sense of follower, believer, i.e. Christian (Ac 6:1, 2; 11:26). **Deriv.**: *mathēteúō* (3100), to disciple; *summathētḗs* (4827), a fellow disciple.

3102. μαθήτρια, mathētria, *math-ay´-tree-ah*; feminine from 3101; a female *pupil:*—disciple.

3103. Μαθουσάλα, Mathousala, *math-oo-sal´-ah*; of Hebrew origin [4968]; *Mathusala* (i.e. *Methu-shelach*), an antediluvian:—Mathusala.

3104. Μαϊνάν, Maïnan, *mahee-nan´*; probably of Hebrew origin; *Maïnan*, an Israelite:—Mainan.

3105. μαίνομαι, mainomai, *mah´ee-nom-ahee*; middle from a primary **μάω,** ***maō*** (to *long* for; through the idea of insensate *craving*); to *rave* as a "maniac":—be beside self (mad).

3106. μακαρίζω, makarizō, *mak-ar-id´-zo*; from 3107; to *beatify*, i.e. *pronounce* (or *esteem*) *fortunate*:—call blessed, count happy.

From *mákar* (n.f.), the poetic form of *makários* (3107), blessed. To call happy, blessed, to congratulate (Lk 1:48; Jas 5:11).

Deriv.: *makarismós* (3108), a state of blessedness.

Syn.: *eulogéō* (2127), to speak well of, bless.

3107. μακάριος, makarios, *mak-ar´-ee-os*; a prolonged form of the poetical **μάκαρ,** ***makar*** (meaning the same); supremely *blest*; by extension *fortunate, well off*:—blessed, happy (× -ier).

A prose form of the poetic *mákar* (n.f.), blessed one. Happy, fortunate, blessed. Spoken in the Beatitudes of those receiving God's favour, regardless of what their circumstances may be (Mt 5:3–11). See also Lk 1:45; 6:20–22; Ac 20:35; Ro 4:7; 1Co 7:40. Used to refer to God as being well-spoken of, praised (1Ti 1:11).

Deriv.: *makarízō* (3106), to declare blessed.

Syn.: *eulogētós* (2128), blessed, well-spoken of; *eulogēménos*, blessed, passive participle of *eulogéō* (2127), to eulogise, bless, thank.

3108. μακαρισμός, makarismos, *mak-ar-is-mos´*; from 3106; *beatification*, i.e. *attribution of good fortune*:—blessedness.

3109. Μακεδονία, Makedonia, *mak-ed-on-ee´-ah*; from 3110; *Macedonia*, a region of Greece:—Macedonia.

3110. Μακεδών, Makedōn, *mak-ed-ohn´*; of uncertain derivative; a *Macedon* (*Macedonian*), i.e. inhabitant of Macedonia:—of Macedonia, Macedonian.

3111. μάκελλον, makellon, *mak´-el-lon*; of Latin origin [*macellum*]; a *butcher's stall, meat market* or *provision-shop*:—shambles.

3112. μακράν, makran, *mak-ran´*; feminine accusative singular of 3117 (3598 being implied); *at a distance* (literal or figurative):—(a-) far (off), good (great) way off.

3113. μακρόθεν, makrothen, *mak-roth´-en*; adverb from 3117; *from a distance* or *afar*:—afar off, from far.

3114. μακροθυμέω, makrothumeō, *mak-roth-oo-meh´-o*; from the same as 3116; to *be long-spirited*, i.e. (objective) *forbearing* or (subjective) *patient*:—bear (suffer) long, be long-suffering, have (long) patience, be patient, patiently endure.

From *makróthumos* (n.f.), long-suffering, which is from *makrós* (3117), long, and *thumós* (2372), wrath, anger. To be long-minded, i.e. slow to anger; to be long-suffering, to be patient (Mt 18:26, 29; 1Co 13:4; 1Th 5:14; 2Pe 3:9), to wait patiently (Heb 6:15; Jas 5:7, 8).

Deriv.: *makrothumía* (3115), long-suffering.

Syn.: *hupoménō* (5278), to endure. Also, *anéchomai* (430), to tolerate; endure; *karteréō* (2594), to endure; *pheídomai* (5339), to spare.

3115. μακροθυμία, makrothumia, *mak-roth-oo-mee´-ah*; from the same as 3116; *longanimity*, i.e. (objective) *forbearance* or (subjective) *fortitude*:—long-suffering, patience.

Noun from *makrothuméō* (3114), to be long-suffering. Forbearance, long-suffering, patient endurance when others attack or make our lives difficult. *Makrothumía* describes patience with people, while *hupomonē* (5281), patience, describes more patience with circumstances. Used of God (Ro 2:4; 9:22; 1Pe 3:20; 2Pe 3:15). Spoken of as one of the fruits of the Spirit (Gal 5:22). Also 2Co 6:6; Eph 4:2; Col 1:11; 3:12; 1Ti 1:16; 2Ti 3:10; 4:2; Heb 6:12; Jas 5:10).

Syn.: *anochḗ* (463), tolerance; *epieíkeia* (1932), gentleness.

3116. μακροθυμώς, makrothumōs, *mak-roth-oo-moce´*; adverb of a compound of 3117 and 2372; *with long (enduring) temper*, i.e. *leniently*:—patiently.

Adverb from *makróthumos* (n.f.), long-suffering, which is from *makrós* (3117), long, and *thumós* (2372), wrath, anger. Patiently, i.e. with forbearance, with clemency. Used only in Ac 26:3. See *makrothumía* (3115), long-suffering.

3117. μακρός, makros, *mak-ros´*; from 3372; *long* (in place [*distant*] or time [neuter plural]):—far, long.

3118. μακροχρόνιος, makrochronios, *mak-rokh-ron´-ee-os*; from 3117 and 5550; *long-timed*, i.e. *long-lived*:—live long.

3119. μαλακία, malakia, *mal-ak-ee´-ah*; from 3120; *softness*, i.e. *enervation (debility)*:—disease.

Noun from *malakós* (3120), soft. Softness, used figuratively for timidity, effeminacy, luxury. In the NT: weakness, disease (Mt 4:23; 9:35; 10:1).

Syn.: *asthéneia* (769), disease, weakness; *nósēma* (3553), ailment, disease; *nósos* (3554), malady, infirmity.

3120. μαλακός, malakos, *mal-ak-os´*; of uncertain affinity.; *soft*, i.e. *fine* (clothing); (figurative) a *catamite*:—effeminate, soft.

3121. Μαλελεήλ, Maleleēl, *mal-el-eh-ale´*; of Hebrew origin [4111]; *Maleleël* (i.e. *Mahalalel*), an antediluvian:—Maleleel.

3122. μάλιστα, malista, *mal´-is-tah*; neuter plural of the superlative of an apparently primary adverb **μάλα,** ***mala*** (*very*); (adverb) *most (in the greatest degree)* or *particularly*:—chiefly, most of all, (e-) specially.

3123. μᾶλλον, mallon, *mal´-lon*; neuter of the comparative of the same as 3122; (adverb) *more* (*in a greater degree*) or *rather*:— + better, × far, (the) more (and more), (so) much (the more), rather.

3124. Μάλχος, Malchos, *mal´-khos*; of Hebrew origin [4429]; *Malchus*, an Israelite:—Malchus.

3125. μάμμη, mammē, *mam´-may*; of native origin ["mammy"]; a *grandmother*:—grandmother.

3126. μαμμωνᾶς, mammōnas, *mam-mo-nas´*; of Chaldee origin (*confidence*; i.e. figurative, *wealth*, personified); *mammonas*, i.e. *avarice* (deified):—mammon.

From the Aramaic *māmôn* (n.f.), mammon, the comprehensive word for all kinds of possessions, earnings, and gains; wealth, riches (Lk 16:9, 11). Also personified, like the Gr. *ploútos* (4149), wealth, as that which one serves if he doesn't serve God (Mt 6:24; Lk 16:13).

3127. Μαναήν, Manaēn, *man-ah-ane´*; of uncertain origin; *Manaën*, a Christian:—Manaen.

3128. Μανασσῆς, Manassēs, *man-as-sace´*; of Hebrew origin [4519]; *Manasses* (i.e. *Menashsheh*), an Israelite:—Manasses.

3129. μανθάνω, manthanō, *man-than´-o*; prolonged from a primary verb, another form of which, **μαθέω,** ***matheō***, is used as an alternate in certain tenses; to *learn* (in any way):—learn, understand.

(I) Particularly: intellectually, from others or from study and observation (Mt 9:13; 11:29; 24:32; Mk 13:28; 1Ti 5:4, 13; 2Ti 3:14). To learn someone, i.e. his doctrines, precepts (Eph 4:20). In the sense of to learn by information, to be informed (Ac 23:27; Gal 3:2); also to understand, to comprehend (Rev 14:3).

(II) Morally: to learn from experience, with the idea of to do habitually, to be wont (Php 4:11; Tit 3:14; Heb 5:8).

Deriv.: *amathḗs* (261), unlearned; *katamanthánō* (2648), to learn, to understand thoroughly; *mathētḗs* (3101), disciple.

3130. μανία, mania, *man-ee´-ah*; from 3105; *craziness*:—[+ make] × mad.

3131. μάννα, manna, *man´-nah*; of Hebrew origin [4478]; *manna* (i.e. *man*), an edible gum:—manna.

3132. μαντεύομαι, manteuomai, *mant-yoo´-om-ahee*; from a derivative of 3105 (meaning a *prophet*, as supposed to *rave* through *inspiration*); to *divine*, i.e. *utter spells* (under pretence of foretelling):—by soothsaying.

From *mántis* (n.f.), a soothsayer, diviner, which is from *maínomai* (3105), to be mad, beside oneself. To utter responses from an oracle, to divine, foretell. Only in Ac 16:16.

Syn.: *proginṓskō* (4267), to foreknow; *prolégō* (4302), to foretell; *proorā́ō* (4308), to behold in advance; *prophēteúō* (4395), to prophesy.

3133. μαραίνω, marainō, *mar-ah´ee-no*; of uncertain affinity; to *extinguish* (as fire), i.e. (figurative and passive) to *pass away*:—fade away.

3134. μαρὰν ἀθά, maran atha, *mar´-an ath´-ah*; of Chaldee origin (meaning *our Lord has come*); *maranatha,* i.e. an exclamation of the approaching *divine judgement*:—Maranatha.

3135. μαργαρίτης, margaritēs, *mar-gar-ee´-tace*; from **μάργαρος,** *margaros* (a pearl-*oyster*); a *pearl*:—pearl.

3136. Μάρθα, Martha, *mar´-thah*; probably of Chaldee origin (meaning *mistress*); *Martha,* a Christian woman:—Martha.

3137. Μαρία, Maria, *mar-ee´-ah*; or **Μαριάμ,** *Mariam, mar-ee-am´*; of Hebrew origin [4813]; *Maria* or *Mariam* (i.e. *Mirjam*), the name of six Christian females:—Mary.

3138. Μάρκος, Markos, *mar´-kos*; of Latin origin; *Marcus,* a Christian:—Marcus, Mark.

3139. μάρμαρος, marmaros, *mar´-mar-os*; from **μαρμαίρω,** ***marmairō*** (to *glisten*); *marble* (as sparkling *white*):—marble.

μάρτυρ, *martur*. See 3144.

3140. μαρτυρέω, martureō, *mar-too-reh´-o*; from 3144; to *be a witness,* i.e. *testify* (literal or figurative):—charge, give [*evidence*], bear record, have (obtain, of) good (honest) report, be well reported of, testify, give (have) testimony, (be, bear, give, obtain) witness.

From *mártus* (3144), witness. To be a witness, bear witness:

(I) To bear witness, to testify to the truth of what one has seen, heard, or knows:

(A) Particularly and generally: to bear witness concerning a person or thing (Jn 1:7, 8, 15; 2:25; 8:13, 14, 18; 21:24; 1Co 15:15; 1Jn 4:14); to testify something (Jn 3:11; 3:32; Ac 26:5; Heb 10:15; 1Jn 1:2; 5:6–8; Rev 1:2; 22:16, 20); to prove by testimony (Jn 18:23).

(B) Figuratively: of God as testifying by His Spirit through signs and miracles. (Jn 5:37; 8:18; 1Jn 5:9, 10). Of the Scriptures or prophets (Jn 5:39; Ac 10:43). Of one's deeds, works (Jn 5:36; 10:25).

(II) Emphatically: to testify strongly, bear honourable testimony; and pass., to be well-testified about, to have good witness (Heb 7:8; 11:4, 5). Generally: to speak well of, applaud (Lk 4:22; Ac 15:8; Heb 11:4; 3Jn 12). In the pass., meaning to be lauded, to be of good report (Ac 6:3; 10:22; 16:2; 22:12; 1Ti 5:10; Heb 11:2; 3Jn 12).

Deriv.: *epimarturéō* (1957), to bear witness to; *katamarturéō* (2649), to bear witness against; *marturía* (3141), a testimony; *martúrion* (3142), a declaration of facts, proof, a testimony; *summarturéō* (4828), to bear witness with; *pseudomarturéō* (5576), to bear false witness.

Syn.: *bebaióō* (950), to assure; *plērophoréō* (4135), to inform fully; *phaneróō* (5319), to manifestly declare.

3141. μαρτυρία, marturia, *mar-too-ree´-ah*; from 3144; *evidence* given (judicially or generic):—record, report, testimony, witness.

Noun from *marturéō* (3140), to witness. Witness, testimony, as borne, given:

(I) Particularly: judicial testimony in court (Mk 14:55, 56, 59; Lk 22:71; Jn 8:17).

(II) Generally, testimony to the truth of anything (Jn 19:35; 21:24; 3Jn 12). So of a poet (Tit 1:13). Elsewhere only in reference to Jesus and his doctrines, i.e. to the truth of his mission and gospel (Jn 5:34); so from John the Baptist (Jn 1:7, 19; 5:36), from other teachers (Ac 22:18; Rev 11:7; 12:11), also from God (Jn 5:32; 1Jn 5:9–11). Of Christ's testimony respecting himself (Jn 3:11, 32, 33; 5:31; 8:13, 14).

(III) Emphatically: honourable testimony, good report (1Ti 3:7).

Deriv.: *pseudomarturía* (5577), a false witness.

Syn.: *martúrion* (3142), testimony.

3142. μαρτύριον, marturion, *mar-too´-ree-on*; neuter of a presumed derivative of 3144; something *evidential,* i.e. (genitive) *evidence* given or (special) the *Decalogue* (in the sacred tabernacle):—to be testified, testimony, witness.

Noun from *marturéō* (3140), to witness. Witness, testimony, as borne, given, equivalent to *marturía* (3141):

(I) Generally (2Co 1:12). So historically (Ac 4:33). In reference to Jesus and his doctrines (1Co 1:6; 2:1; 2Th 1:10; 2Ti 1:8). Generally in the sense of testimony, evidence, proof (Mt 8:4; 10:18; 24:14; Mk 1:44; 6:11; Lk 5:14; 21:13; Jas 5:3).

(II) Used as a designation of the Mosaic tabernacle (Ac 7:44; Rev 15:5).

Syn.: *bebaíōsis* (951), confirmation; *marturía* (3141), testimony.

3143. μαρτύρομαι, marturomai, *mar-too´-rom-ahee*; middle from 3144; to *be adduced* as *a witness,* i.e. (figurative) to *obtest* (in affirmation or exhortation):—take to record, testify.

From *mártus* (3144), witness. To call to witness, to invoke as witness. In the NT: to testify, to solemnly affirm, to make an earnest and solemn appeal (Ac 20:26; Gal 5:3); also to exhort solemnly (Eph 4:17).

Deriv.: *diamartúromai* (1263), to bear witness, to charge; *promartúromai* (4303), to witness beforehand.

Syn.: *bebaióō* (950), to confirm; *dēlóō* (1213), to declare.

3144. μάρτυς, martus, *mar´-toos*; of uncertain affinity; a *witness* (literal [judicially] or figurative [genitive]); (by analogy) a "*martyr*":—martyr, record, witness.

(I) Particularly, in a judicial sense (Mt 18:16; 26:65; Mk 14:63; Ac 6:13; 7:58; 2Co 13:1; Heb 10:28).

(II) Generally, one who testifies or can testify to the truth of what he has seen, heard, knows (Ro 1:9; 2Co 1:23; Php 1:8; 1Th 2:10; 1Ti 6:12); so in allusion to those who witness a public game (Heb 12:1). Especially of those who witnessed the life, death, and resurrection of Jesus, who bear witness to the truth as it is in Jesus (Lk 24:48; Ac 1:8, 22; 2:32; 5:32; 26:16; 2Ti 2:2); so of one who bears witness for God, and testifies to the world what God reveals through him, i.e. a teacher, prophet (Rev 1:5; 3:14; 11:3).

(III) A martyr, one who by his death bears witness to the truth (Ac 22:20; Rev 2:13; 17:6).

Deriv.: *amárturos* (267), without a witness; *marturéō* (3140), to witness; *martúromai* (3143), to summon as a witness, adjure; *pseudomártur* (5575), a person who bears false witness.

Syn.: *autóptēs* (845), eyewitness.

3145. μασσάομαι, massaomai, *mas-sah´-om-ahee*; from a primary **μάσσω,** *massō* (to *handle* or *squeeze*); to *chew*:—gnaw.

3146. μαστιγόω, mastigoō, *mas-tig-o´-o*; from 3148; to *flog* (literal or figurative):—scourge.

3147. μαστίζω, mastizō, *mas-tid´-zo*; from 3149; to *whip* (literal):—scourge.

3148. μάστιξ, mastix, *mas´-tix*; probably from the base of 3145 (through the idea of *contact*); a *whip* (literal, the Roman *flagellum* for criminals; figurative, a *disease*):—plague, scourging.

3149. μαστός, mastos, *mas-tos´*; from the base of 3145; a (properly female) *breast* (as if *kneaded* up):—pap.

3150. ματαιολογία, mataiologia, *mat-ah-yol-og-ee´-ah*; from 3151; *random talk,* i.e. *babble*:—vain jangling.

3151. ματαιολόγος, mataiologos, *mat-ah-yol-og´-os*; from 3152 and 3004; an *idle* (i.e. *senseless* or *mischievous*) *talker,* i.e. a *wrangler*:—vain talker.

Adjective from *mátaios* (3152), vain, and *légō* (3004), to speak. Given to vain talking; vain talker, empty wrangler. Used only in Tit 1:10.

Deriv.: *mataiología* (3150), vain talk.

3152. μάταιος, mataios, *mat´-ah-yos*; from the base of 3155; *empty,* i.e. (literal) *profitless,* or (special) an *idol*:—vain, vanity.

Adjective from *mátēn* (3155), to no purpose, in vain. Useless, worthless, vain, empty (1Co 3:20; 15:17; Tit 3:9; Jas 1:26; 1Pe 1:18). *Mátios* carries the idea of aimless, fruitless, and misleading, whereas *kenós* (2756), vain, emphasizes something's emptiness and hollowness. As a substantive in the plural: "vanities, nothings," for idols, idolatry (Ac 14:15).

Deriv.: *mataiológos* (3151), one who talks vainly; *mataiótēs* (3153), vanity; *mataióō* (3154), to become vain.

Syn.: *kenós* (2756), empty, vacant, inane. Also, *ákarpos* (175), unfruitful; *alazṓn* (213), braggart, boastful; *alusitelḗs* (255) and *anōphelḗs* (512), unprofitable; *kenódoxos* (2755), self-centered, conceited, vain.

3153. ματαιότης, mataiotēs, *mat-ah-yot´-ace*; from 3152; *inutility*; (figurative) *transientness*; (moral) *depravity*:—vanity.

Noun from *mátaios* (3152), vain. Vanity, emptiness (2Pe 2:18). In the sense of frailty, transientness (Ro 8:20). From the Hebrew for folly, perverseness, wickedness (Eph 4:17).

3154. ματαιόω, mataioō, *mat-ah-yo´-o*; from 3152; to *render* (passive *become*) *foolish*, i.e. (moral) *wicked* or (special) *idolatrous*:—become vain.

From *mátaios* (3152), vain. To make vain or worthless. In the NT, only passive: to become vain, i.e. foolish, perverse, wicked. Used only in Ro 1:21. See *mátaios* (3152), vain.

Syn.: *paraphronéō* (3912), to act foolishly, thoughtlessly.

3155. μάτην, matēn, *mat´-ane*; accusative of a derivative of the base of 3145 (through the idea of tentative *manipulation*, i.e. unsuccessful *search*, or else of *punishment*); *folly*, i.e. (adverb) *to no purpose*:—in vain.

Adverb meaning in vain, to no purpose, fruitlessly (Mt 15:9; Mk 7:7). See *mátaios* (3152), vain.

Deriv.: *mátaios* (3152), vain.

Syn.: *kenṓs* (2761), in vain.

3156. Ματθαῖος, Matthaios, *mat-thah´-yos*; a shorter form of 3161; *Matthæus* (i.e. *Matthitjah*), an Israelite and Christian:—Matthew.

3157. Ματθάν, Matthan, *mat-than´*; of Hebrew origin [4977]; *Matthan* (i.e. *Mattan*), an Israelite:—Matthan.

3158. Ματθάτ, Matthat, *mat-that´*; probably a shortened form of 3161; *Matthat* (i.e. *Mattithjah*), the name of two Israelites:—Mathat.

3159. Ματθίας, Matthias, *mat-thee´-as*; apparently a shortened form of 3161; *Matthias* (i.e. *Mattithjah*), an Israelite:—Matthias.

3160. Ματταθά, Mattatha, *mat-tath-ah´*; probably a shortened form of 3161 [compare 4992]; *Mattatha* (i.e. *Mattithjah*), an Israelite:—Mattatha.

3161. Ματταθίας, Mattathias, *mat-tath-ee´-as*; of Hebrew origin [4993]; *Mattathias* (i.e. *Mattithjah*), an Israelite and Christian:—Mattathias.

3162. μάχαιρα, machaira, *makh´-ahee-rah*; probably feminine of a presumed derivative of 3163; a *knife*, i.e. *dirk*; (figurative) *war*, judicial *punishment*:—sword.

3163. μάχη, machē, *makh´-ay*; from 3164; a *battle*, i.e. (figurative) *controversy*:—fighting, strive, striving.

Noun from *máchomai* (3164), to fight. A fight, battle. In the NT, generally: strife, contest, controversy (2Co 7:5; 2Ti 2:23; Jas 4:1); controversies respecting the Mosaic Law (Tit 3:9).

Deriv.: *ámachos* (269), not contentious.

Syn.: *agṓn* (73), strife, fight; *logomachía* (3055), strife of words; *pálē* (3823), wrestling; *pólemos* (4171), war; *stásis* (4714), insurrection or sedition as a civil war.

3164. μάχομαι, machomai, *makh´-om-ahee*; middle of an apparently primary verb; to *war*, i.e. (figurative) to *quarrel, dispute*:—fight, strive.

3165. μέ, me, *meh*; a shorter (and probably original) form of 1691; *me*:—I, me, my.

3166. μεγαλαυχέω, megalaucheō, *meg-al-ow-kheh´-o*; from a compound of 3173 and **αὐχέω**, ***aucheō*** (to *boast*; akin to 837 and 2744); to *talk big*, i.e. *be grandiloquent* (*arrogant, egotistic*):—boast great things.

3167. μεγαλεῖος, megaleios, *meg-al-i´-os*; from 3173; *magnificent*, i.e. (neuter plural as noun) a conspicuous *favour*, or (subject) *perfection*:—great things, wonderful works.

Adjective from *mégas* (3173), great, indicating great works or miracles. Great, glorious, wonderful. As a substantive: great things, wonderful works (Lk 1:49; Ac 2:11).

Deriv.: *megaleiótēs* (3168), majesty.

Syn.: In the plural as great things, miracles: *sēmeía* (4592), signs. Also, *dunámeis* (1411), mighty works; *éndoxa* (1741), glorious things; *thaumásia* (2297), astonishing things; *parádoxa* (3861), strange or extraordinary things; *térata* (5059), wonders.

3168. μεγαλειότης, megaleiotēs, *meg-al-i-ot´-ace*; from 3167; *superbness*, i.e. *glory* or *splendour*:—magnificence, majesty, mighty power.

3169. μεγαλοπρεπής, megaloprepēs, *meg-al-op-rep-ace´*; from 3173 and 4241; *befitting greatness* or *magnificence* (*majestic*):—excellent.

3170. μεγαλύνω, megalunō, *meg-al-oo´-no*; from 3173; to *make* (or *declare*) *great*, i.e. *increase* or (figurative) *extol*:—enlarge, magnify, shew great.

3171. μεγάλως, megalōs, *meg-al´-oce*; adverb from 3173; *much*:—greatly.

3172. μεγαλωσύνη, megalōsunē, *meg-al-o-soo´-nay*; from 3173; *greatness*, i.e. (figurative) *divinity* (often *God* himself):—majesty.

3173. μέγας, megas, *meg´-as*; [including the prolonged forms, feminine **μεγάλη**, ***megalē***, plural **μέγάλοι**, ***megaloi***, etc.; compare also 3176, 3187]; *big* (literal or figurative, in a very wide application):—(+ fear) exceedingly, great (-est), high, large, loud, mighty, + (be) sore (afraid), strong, × to years.

3174. μέγεθος, megethos, *meg´-eth-os*; from 3173; *magnitude* (figurative):—greatness.

3175. μεγιστᾶνες, megistanes, *meg-is-tan´-es*; plural from 3176; *grandees*:—great men, lords.

3176. μέγιστος, megistos, *meg´-is-tos*; superlative of 3173; *greatest* or *very great*:—exceeding great.

3177. μεθερμηνεύω, methermēneuō, *meth-er-mane-yoo´-o*; from 3326 and 2059; to *explain over*, i.e. *translate*:—(by) interpret (-ation).

3178. μέθη, methē, *meth´-ay*; apparently a primary word; an *intoxicant*, i.e. (by implication) *intoxication*:—drunkenness.

Noun from *méthu* (n.f., see below). Drunkenness (Lk 21:34; Ro 13:13; Gal 5:21).

Deriv. of *méthu* (n.f.): *methúskō* (3182), to make or become drunk; *méthusos* (3183), a drunkard; *methúō* (3184), to be drunk.

Syn.: *oinophlugía* (3632), excess of wine. Also, *kraipálē* (2897), dissipation, excess, a headache from drunkenness; *pósis* (4213), the act of drinking; *pótos* (4224), banqueting or a drinking party.

3179. μεθίστημι, methistēmi, *meth-is´-tay-mee*; or (1Co 13:2) **μεθιστάνω**, ***methistanō***, *meth-is-tan´-o*; from 3326 and 2476; to *transfer*, i.e. *carry away, depose* or (figurative) *exchange, seduce*:—put out, remove, translate, turn away.

From *metá* (3326), denoting change of place or condition, and *hístēmi* (2476), to place, stand. To set or move over from one place to another, to transfer, to remove. In the NT, to move physically (1Co 13:2); in a spiritual sense: to move into the kingdom of God (Col 1:13). Metaphorically: to draw over to another side or party, to seduce (Ac 19:26). Of persons: to remove from office, to depose (Ac 13:22); of a steward: to dismiss (Lk 16:4).

Syn.: *ekchōréō* (1633), to depart; *metakinéō* (3334), to move away; *metatíthēmi* (3346), to transport, change, remove.

3180. μεθοδεία, methodeia, *meth-od-i´-ah*; from a compound of 3326 and 3593 [compare "method"]; *travelling over*, i.e. *travesty* (*trickery*):—wile, lie in wait.

Noun from *methodeúō* (n.f.), to work by method. To trace out with method and skill, to treat methodically; to use art, to deal artfully; hence method, in the sense of art, wile (Eph 4:14; 6:11).

Syn.: *apátē* (539), deceit; *dólos* (1388), wile, craft; *panourgía* (3834), trickery, craftiness.

3181. μεθόριος, methorios, *meth-or´-ee-os*; from 3326 and 3725; *bounded alongside*, i.e. *contiguous* (neuter plural as noun, *frontier*):—border.

3182. μεθύσκω, methuskō, *meth-oos´-ko*; a prolonged (transitive) form of 3184; to *intoxicate*:—be drunk (-en).

3183. μέθυσος, methusos, *meth´-oo-sos*; from 3184; *tipsy*, i.e. (as noun) a *sot*:—drunkard.

3184. μεθύω, methuō, *meth-oo´-o*; from another form of 3178; to *drink* to *intoxication*, i.e. *get drunk*:—drink well, make (be) drunk (-en).

3185. μεῖζον, meizon, *mide´-zon*; neuter of 3187; (adverb) in a *greater* degree:—the more.

3186. μειζότερος, meizoteros, *mide-zot´-er-os*; continued comparative of 3187; *still larger* (figurative):—greater.

3187. μείζων, meizōn, *mide´-zone*; irregular comparative of 3173; *larger* (literal or figurative, specially in age):—elder, greater (-est), more.

3188. μέλαν, melan, *mel´-an*; neuter of 3189 as noun; *ink*:—ink.

3189. μέλας, melas, *mel´-as*; apparently a primary word; *black*:—black.

3190. Μελεᾶς, Meleas, *mel-eh-as´*; of uncertain origin; *Meleas*, an Israelite:—Meleas.

3191. μελετάω, meletaō, *mel-et-ah´-o*; from a presumed derivative of 3199; to *take care of*, i.e. (by implication) *revolve* in the mind:—imagine, (pre-) meditate.

3192. μέλι, meli, *mel´-ee*; apparently a primary word; *honey*:—honey.

3193. μελίσσιος, melissios, *mel-is´-see-os*; from 3192; *relating to honey*, i.e. *bee* (comb):—honeycomb.

3194. Μελίτη, Melitē, *mel-ee´-tay*; of uncertain origin; *Melita*, an island in the Mediterranean:—Melita.

3195. μέλλω, mellō, *mel´-lo*; a strengthened form of 3199 (through the idea of *expectation*); to *intend*, i.e. *be about* to be, do, or suffer something (of persons or things, especially events; in the sense of *purpose, duty, necessity, probability, possibility*, or *hesitation*):—about, after that, be (almost), (that which is, things, + which was for) to come, intend, was to (be), mean, mind, be at the point, (be) ready, + return, shall (begin), (which, that) should (after, afterwards, hereafter) tarry, which was for, will, would, be yet.

To be about to do or suffer anything; to be on the point of doing, usually followed by an infinitive expressing what one is going to do:

(I) Generally (Lk 7:2; Jn 4:47; Ac 21:27; 27:33; Rev 3:2). Also implying purpose, i.e. to have in mind, to intend, to will (Ac 12:6). Also Mt 2:13; Lk 10:1; Jn 6:6; Ac 3:3; Rev 10:4.

(II) With the idea of ought, should, must; implying necessity, accordance with the nature of things or with divine appointment, and therefore certain, destined to take place (Mt 11:14; Mk 10:32; Lk 9:31, 44; Jn 11:51; Ac 28:6; Heb 1:14; Rev 2:10); hence the participle without an infinitive: impending, future (Mt 3:7; 12:32; Lk 13:9; Ro 5:14; 8:38; 1Co 3:22; 1Ti 4:8; Heb 9:11).

(III) To be ever about to do a thing, i.e. to linger, to delay (Ac 22:16).

3196. μέλος, melos, *mel´-os*; of uncertain affinity; a *limb* or *part* of the body:—member.

3197. Μελχί, Melchi, *mel-khee´*; of Hebrew origin [4428 with pronoun suffix, *my king*]; *Melchi* (i.e. *Malki*), the name of two Israelites:—Melchi.

3198. Μελχισεδέκ, Melchisedek, *mel-khis-ed-ek´*; of Hebrew origin [4442]; *Melchisedek* (i.e. *Malkitsedek*), a patriarch:—Melchisedec.

3199. μέλω, melō, *mel´-o*; a primary verb; to *be of interest* to, i.e. to *concern* (only third person singular presumed indicative used impersonal *it matters*):—(take) care.

3200. μεμβράνα, membrana, *mem-bran´-ah*; of Latin origin ("*membrane*"); a (written) sheep-*skin*:—parchment.

3201. μέμφομαι, memphomai, *mem´-fom-ahee*; middle of an apparently primary verb; to *blame*:—find fault.

3202. μεμψίμοιρος, mempsimoiros, *mem-psim´-oy-ros*; from a presumed derivative of 3201 and **μοῖρα, *moira*** (*fate*; akin to the base of 3313); *blaming fate*, i.e. *querulous* (*discontented*):—complainer.

3203–3302. *These numbers were omitted in Strong's Dictionary of the Greek Testament.*

3303. μέν, men, *men*; a primary particle; properly indicative of *affirmation* or *concession* (*in fact*); usually followed by a *contrasted* clause with 1161 (*this* one, the *former*, etc.):—even, indeed, so, some, truly, verily. Often compounded with other particles in an *intensive* or *asseverative* sense.

3304. μενοῦνγε, menounge, *men-oon´-geh*; from 3303 and 3767 and 1065; *so then at least*:—nay but, yea doubtless (rather, verily).

3305. μέντοι, mentoi, *men´-toy*; from 3303 and 5104; *indeed though*, i.e. *however*:—also, but, howbeit, nevertheless, yet.

3306. μένω, menō, *men´-o*; a primary verb; to *stay* (in a given place, state, relation or expectancy):—abide, continue, dwell, endure, be present, remain, stand, tarry (for), × thine own.

To remain, abide, dwell, live.

(I) Intransitively, to remain, dwell:

(A) Of place, i.e. of a person dwelling or lodging in a place (Mt 10:11; 26:38; Lk 8:27; 19:5; 24:29; Jn 1:38, 39; 2:12; 7:9; 8:35; Ac 16:15; 20:15; 28:16; 2Ti 4:20). With the meaning of staying in one place (Mt 26:38; Ac 27:31). Of bodies remaining (Jn 19:31). Figuratively of a veil remaining over the eyes (2Co 3:14).

(B) Of a state or condition, i.e. of a person remaining in a state or condition (Jn 12:46; Ac 5:4; 1Co 7:8, 40; Php 1:25; 2Ti 2:13; Heb 7:3; 1Jn 3:14). To continue to exist, to remain in force, to endure, with the adjunct of time during or to which a person or thing remains, continues, endures (Jn 21:22, 23; 1Co 15:6; 2Co 9:9; 1Pe 1:25; Rev 17:10). Used in an absolute sense, with the idea of perpetuity, i.e. to remain or endure forever, to be perpetual, e.g., Christian graces, "faith, hope, love" (1Co 13:13). See Jn 15:16; 2Co 3:11; Heb 10:34; 12:27; 13:1.

(C) Of the relation in which one person or thing stands with another, chiefly in John's writings; thus to remain in or with someone, i.e. to be and remain united with him, one with him in heart, mind, and will (Jn 6:56; 14:10; 15:4–7; 1Jn 2:6; 3:24; 4:15, 16). Also: to remain in something, equivalent to remaining steadfast, persevering in it (Jn 8:31; 15:9; 1Ti 2:15; 1Jn 2:10; 4:16; 2Jn 9). Conversely and in a like general sense, something may be said to remain in a person (Jn 5:38; 15:11; 1Jn 2:14; 3:15, 17; 2Jn 2).

(II) Transitively: to remain for someone, wait for, await (Ac 20:5, 23).

Deriv.: *anaménō* (362), to await; *diaménō* (1265), to continue abiding; *emménō* (1696), to persevere; *epiménō* (1961), to continue in, tarry; *kataménō* (2650), to remain or abide; *monḗ* (3438), an abode, place to stay; *paraménō* (3887), to remain beside, endure; *periménō* (4037), to stay around, wait for; *prosménō* (4357), to abide with, continue with; *hupoménō* (5278), to be patient, endure trials and afflictions.

Syn.: *agrauléō* (63), to lodge in a fold or in a field; *anastréphō* (390), to abide; *apoleípō* (620), to remain; *aulízomai* (835), to pass the night in the open air; *dianuktereúō* (1273), to pass the night; *diatríbō* (1304), to spend or pass time, stay.

3307. μερίζω, merizō, *mer-id´-zo*; from 3313; to *part*, i.e. (literal) to *apportion, bestow, share*, or (figurative) to *disunite, differ*:—deal, be difference between, distribute, divide, give part.

3308. μέριμνα, merimna, *mer´-im-nah*; from 3307 (through the idea of *distraction*); *solicitude*:—care.

3309. μεριμνάω, merimnaō, *mer-im-nah´-o*; from 3308; to *be anxious* about:—(be, have) care (-ful), take thought.

3310. μερίς, meris, *mer-ece´*; feminine of 3313; a *portion*, i.e. *province, share* or (abstract) *participation*:—part (× -akers).

3311. μερισμός, merismos, *mer-is-mos´*; from 3307; a *separation* or *distribution*:—dividing asunder, gift.

Noun from *merízō* (3307), to divide into parts. Partition, division, i.e. separation (Heb 4:12); also distribution, and so put for a gift which is distributed (Heb 2:4).

Syn.: *analogía* (356), analogy, proportion; *diaíresis* (1243), division, distribution; *klēronomía* (2817), inheritance, heirship.

3312. μεριστής, meristēs, *mer-is-tace´*; from 3307; an *apportioner* (*administrator*):—divider.

3313. μέρος, meros, *mer´-os*; from an obsolete but more primary form of **μείρομαι**, ***meiromai*** (to *get* as a *section* or *allotment*); a *division* or *share* (literal or figurative, in a wide application):—behalf, coast, course, craft, particular (+ -ly), part (+ -ly), piece, portion, respect, side, some sort (-what).

3314. μεσημβρία, mesēmbria, *mes-ame-bree´-ah*; from 3319 and 2250; *midday*; (by implication) the *south*:—noon, south.

3315. μεσιτεύω, mesiteuō, *mes-it-yoo´-o*; from 3316; to *interpose* (as arbiter), i.e. (by implication) to *ratify* (as surety):—confirm.

From *mesítēs* (3316), mediator. To be a mediator between two contending parties. Only in Heb 6:17, where it has the idea of pledging oneself as surety.

3316. μεσίτης, mesitēs, *mes-ee´-tace*; from 3319; a *go-between*, i.e. (simply) an *internunciator*, or (by implication) a *reconciler* (*intercessor*):—mediator.

Noun from *mésos* (3319), middle, in the midst. A go-between, a mediator; one who intervenes between two parties, i.e. an interpreter, a medium of communication (Gal 3:19, 20), an intercessor, reconciler, especially used of Christ (1Ti 2:5; Heb 8:6; 9:15; 12:24).

Deriv.: *mesiteúō* (3315), to mediate, intercede.

3317. μεσονύκτιον, mesonuktion, *mes-on-ook´-tee-on*; neuter of a compound of 3319 and 3571; *midnight* (especially as a watch):—midnight.

3318. Μεσοποταμία, Mesopotamia, *mes-op-ot-am-ee´-ah*; from 3319 and 4215; *Mesopotamia* (as lying between the Euphrates and the Tigris; compare 763), a region of Asia:—Mesopotamia.

3319. μέσος, mesos, *mes´-os*; from 3326; *middle* (as adjective or [neuter] noun):—among, × before them, between, + forth, mid [-day, -night], midst, way.

Adjective meaning middle, in the midst. Used to indicate the middle part of something: e.g., the middle of the night (Mt 25:6); the middle of the day (Ac 26:13); the middle of the veil (Lk 23:45). Used in the sense of in the midst, among: e.g., "in the midst of wolves" (Mt 10:16; Lk 10:3). Also Mt 14:24; 18:2; Mk 6:47; Jn 1:26; 19:18; Rev 1:13).

Deriv.: *mesēmbría* (3314), midday; *mesítēs* (3316), mediator, one standing in the middle, a go-between; *mesonúktion* (3317), midnight; *mesótoichon* (3320), a partition, middle wall; *mesouránēma* (3321), mid-sky, midst of heaven; *mesóō* (3322), to be in the middle; *metaxú* (3342), in the midst of.

3320. μεσότοιχον, mesotoichon, *mes-ot´-oy-khon*; from 3319 and 5109; a *partition* (figurative):—middle wall.

3321. μεσουράνημα, mesouranēma, *mes-oo-ran´-ay-mah*; from a presumed compound of 3319 and 3772; *mid-sky*:—midst of heaven.

3322. μεσόω, mesoō, *mes-o´-o*; from 3319; to *form* the *middle*, i.e. (in point of time), to *be halfway* over:—be about the midst.

3323. Μεσσίας, Messias, *mes-see´-as*; of Hebrew origin [4899]; the *Messias* (i.e. *Mashiach*), or Christ:—Messias.

3324. μεστός, mestos, *mes-tos´*; of uncertain derivative; *replete* (literal or figurative):—full.

3325. μεστόω, mestoō, *mes-to´-o*; from 3324; to *replenish*, i.e. (by implication) to *intoxicate*:—fill.

3326. μετά, meta, *met-ah´*; a primary preposition (often used adverb); properly denoting *accompaniment*; "*amid*" (local or causal); modified variously according to the case (general *association*, or accusative *succession*) with which it is joined; occupying an intermediate position between 575 or 1537 and 1519 or 4314; less intimate than 1722, and less close than 4862):—after (-ward), × that be again, against, among, × and, + follow, hence, hereafter, in, of, (up-) on, + our, × and setting, since, (un-) to, + together, when, with (+ -out). Often used in composition, in substantially the same relations of *participation* or *proximity*, and *transfer* or *sequence*.

Preposition governing the gen. and accusative. Its primary meaning is mid, amid, in the midst, with, among, implying accompaniment and thus differing from *sún* (4862), which expresses conjunction, union:

(I) With the genitive, implying companionship, fellowship:

(A) With, in the sense of amid, among, in the midst of, as where one is said to be, sit, or stand (Mt 26:58; Mk 1:13; 14:54, 62; Lk 24:5; Jn 18:5; Ac 20:18; Rev 21:3).

(B) With, in the sense of together with: **(1)** Particularly, of persons: **(a)** Where one is said to be, go, remain, sit, or stand with someone, in his company; so also with the notation of place added (Mt 5:25; 9:15; Mk 5:18; Lk 11:7; 15:31; 22:21; Jn 3:26; 7:33; 11:31; 2Ti 4:11; Rev 3:21). **(b)** Where one is said to do or suffer something with another, implying joint or mutual action, influence, suffering (Mt 2:3; 12:30, 41; 18:23; Mk 3:6, 7; Lk 5:30; Jn 11:16; 19:18; Ac 24:1; Ro 12:15; 1Th 3:13; Heb 13:23; Rev 3:20). **(2)** Figuratively, of things: **(a)** As designating the state or emotion of the mind which accompanies the doing of something or with which one acts, e.g., fear (Mt 28:8). Also Mk 3:5; Lk 14:9; Ac 20:19; 24:3; Eph 4:2; 2Th 3:12; 1Ti 2:9; Heb 10:22. **(b)** As designating an external action, circumstance, or condition with which another action or event is accompanied, e.g., with an oath (Mt 14:7). Also 24:31; 27:66; Mk 6:25; 10:30; Lk 9:39; 17:20; Ac 5:26; 13:17; 14:23; 24:18; 2Co 8:4; 1Ti 4:14; Heb 5:7; 7:21. Also often where it is equivalent to *kai* (2532), and (Eph 6:23; Col 1:11; 1Ti 1:14; 2:15; 3:4; 2Ti 2:10; Heb 9:19).

(II) With the accusative, *metá* strictly implies motion toward the middle or into the midst of something, and also motion after a person or thing, i.e. either so as to follow and be with a person or to fetch a person or thing. Hence also spoken of succession either in place or time, meaning after:

(A) Of succession in place meaning after, behind (Heb 9:3).

(B) Of succession in time: With a noun of time, e.g., "after six days" (Mt 17:1); also Mt 25:19; Mk 8:31; Lk 15:13; Ac 12:4; 28:11; Gal 1:18). With a noun of person (Ac 5:37; 19:4); with a noun marking an event or point of time (Mt 1:12; Mk 13:24; Lk 9:28; Jn 13:27; 2Pe 1:15).

In composition *metá* denotes: **(a)** fellowship, partnership, as *metadídōmi* (3330), to impart; *metalambánō* (3335), to participate; *metéchō* (3348), to partake; **(b)** proximity, contiguity, as *methórios* (3181), border; **(c)** motion or direction after, as *metapémpō* (3343), to summon or invite; **(d)** transition, transposition, change, meaning over as in *methistēmi* (3179), to carry away, transfer, remove; *metabaínō* (3327), to go over, depart; *metatíthēmi* (3346), to remove.

3327. μεταβαίνω, metabainō, *met-ab-ah´ee-no*; from 3326 and the base of 939; to *change place*:—depart, go, pass, remove.

From *metá* (3326), denoting change of place or condition, and *baínō* (n.f.), to go or come. To pass or go from one place to another (Mt 17:20; Lk 10:7); to go away, depart (Mt 8:34; 11:1; 12:9; 15:29; Jn 7:3; 13:1; Ac 18:7). Figuratively, spoken of passing from death to life (Jn 5:24; 1Jn 3:14).

Syn.: *analúō* (360), to depart; *anachōréō* (402), to depart, retire; *apérchomai* (565), to go away; *aphístēmi* (868), to stand off, depart from someone; *metaírō* (3332), to remove; *poreúomai* (4198), to go one's way; *hupágō* (5217), to depart, go; *chōrízō* (5563), to separate, depart.

3328. μεταβάλλω, metaballō, *met-ab-al´-lo*; from 3326 and 906; to *throw over*, i.e. (middle figurative) to *turn about* in opinion:—change mind.

3329. μετάγω, metagō, *met-ag´-o*; from 3326 and 71; to *lead over*, i.e. *transfer* (*direct*):—turn about.

3330. μεταδίδωμι, metadidōmi, *met-ad-id´-o-mee*; from 3326 and 1325; to *give over*, i.e. *share*:—give, impart.

3331. μετάθεσις, metathesis, *met-ath´-es-is*; from 3346; *transposition*, i.e. *transferral* (to heaven), *disestablishment* (of a law):—change, removing, translation.

3332. μεταίρω, metairō, *met-ah´ee-ro*; from 3326 and 142; to *betake* oneself, i.e. *remove* (locally):—depart.

3333. μετακαλέω, metakaleō, *met-ak-al-eh´-o*; from 3326 and 2564; to *call elsewhere*, i.e. *summon*:—call (for, hither).

From *metá* (3326), denoting change of place or condition, and *kaléō* (2564), to call from one place to another, summon. As used in the middle voice, to call to oneself, to call for, to invite (Ac 7:14; 10:32; 20:17; 24:25).

Syn.: *metapémpō* (3343), to send after or for.

3334. μετακινέω, metakineō, *met-ak-ee-nah´-o*; from 3326 and 2795; to *stir* to a place *elsewhere*, i.e. *remove* (figurative):—move away.

3335. μεταλαμβάνω, metalambanō, *met-al-am-ban´-o*; from 3326 and 2983; to *participate*; genitive to *accept* (and use):—eat, have, be partaker, receive, take.

3336. μετάληψις, metalēpsis, *met-al´-ape-sis*; from 3335; *participation*:—taking.

3337. μεταλλάσσω, metallassō, *met-al-las´-so*; from 3326 and 236; to *exchange*:—change.

From *metá* (3326), denoting change of place or condition, and *allássō* (236), to change. To exchange one thing for another. Used only in a negative sense, exchanging God's revelation for a lie, and exchanging God's plan for man's sexual nature into homosexuality (Ro 1:25, 26).

3338. μεταμέλλομαι, metamellomai, *met-am-el´-lom-ahee*; from 3326 and the middle of 3199; to *care afterwards*, i.e. *regret*:—repent (self).

From *metá* (3326), denoting change of place or condition, and *mélomai*, middle of *mélō* (3199), to concern, to be concerned. To change one's care, etc. Hence to change one's mind or purpose after having done anything (Mt 21:29, 32; Heb 7:21). With the idea of regret, sorrow: to feel sorrow, remorse (Mt 27:3, of Judas; 2Co 7:8).

Deriv.: *ametamélētos* (278), not regretted.

3339. μεταμορφόω, metamorphoō, *met-am-or-fo´-o*; from 3326 and 3445; to *transform* (literal or figurative "metamorphose"):—change, transfigure, transform.

From *metá* (3326), denoting change of place or condition, and *morphóō* (3445), to form. To transform, transfigure, change one's form. In the NT, only in the passive: to be transfigured, transformed. Spoken literally of Christ's transfiguration on the mount (Mt 17:2; Mk 9:2). Spoken figuratively of our being transformed in mind and heart (Ro 12:2; 2Co 3:18).

Syn.: *metastréphō* (3344), to turn from, change; *metaschēmatízō* (3345), to change one's outward form.

3340. μετανοέω, metanoeō, *met-an-o-eh´-o*; from 3326 and 3539; to *think differently* or *afterwards*, i.e. *reconsider* (moral *feel compunction*):—repent.

From *metá* (3326), denoting change of place or condition, and *noéō* (3539), to perceive with the mind, think, comprehend. To repent, change the mind, relent; implying the feeling of regret, sorrow. Distinguished from *metamélomai* (3338), which may mean only to regret, to have remorse:

(I) Generally (Lk 17:3, 4; 2Co 12:21).

(II) In a religious sense, implying pious sorrow for unbelief and sin and a turning from them unto God and the gospel of Christ (Mt 3:2; 4:17; 11:20, 21; 12:41; Mk 1:15; 6:12; Lk 13:3, 5; 15:7, 10; 16:30; Ac 2:38; 3:19; 17:30; 26:20; Rev 2:5, 16, 21; 3:3, 19; 16:9).

Deriv.: *ametanóētos* (279), impenitent *metánoia* (3341), a change of mind, repentance.

3341. μετάνοια, metanoia, *met-an´-oy-ah*; from 3340; (subject) *compunction* (for guilt, including *reformation*); (by implication) *reversal* (of [another's] decision):—repentance.

Noun from *metanoéō* (3340), to repent. A change of mind, repentance: generally (Heb 12:17); in a religious sense, implying pious sorrow for unbelief and sin and a turning from them unto God and the gospel of Christ (Mt 3:8, 11; 9:13; Mk 2:17; Lk 3:8; 5:32; 15:7; Ac 5:31; 20:21; 26:20; Ro 2:4; Heb 6:6; 2Pe 3:9).

3342. μεταξύ, metaxu, *met-ax-oo´*; from 3326 and a form of 4862; *betwixt* (of place or person); (of time) as adjective *intervening*, or (by implication) *adjoining*:—between, meanwhile, next.

3343. μεταπέμπω, metapempō, *met-ap-emp´-o*; from 3326 and 3992; to *send* from *elsewhere*, i.e. (middle) to *summon* or *invite*:—call (send) for.

3344. μεταστρέφω, metastrephō, *met-as-tref´-o*; from 3326 and 4762; to *turn across*, i.e. *transmute* or (figurative) *corrupt*:—pervert, turn.

3345. μετασχηματίζω, metaschēmatizō, *met-askh-ay-mat-id´-zo*; from 3326 and a derivative of 4976; to *transfigure* or *disguise*; (figurative) to *apply* (by accommodation):—transfer, transform (self).

From *metá* (3326), denoting change of place or condition, and *schēmatízō* (n.f.), to form, which is from *schḗma* (4976), shape, outward form. To transform, change the outward form or appearance of something (1Co 4:6). Used in a negative sense of false apostles changing their appearance into apostles of Christ and ministers of righteousness (2Co 11:13, 14); and of Satan appearing as an angel of light (2Co 11:15). Used once of the awaited transformation of the bodies of believers into immortal bodies, fitted to the glory of Christ (Php 3:21).

3346. μετατίθημι, metatithēmi, *met-at-ith´-ay-mee*; from 3326 and 5087; to *transfer*, i.e. (literal) *transport*, (by implication) *exchange*, (reflexive) *change sides*, or (figurative) *pervert*:—carry over, change, remove, translate, turn.

3347. μετέπειτα, metepeita, *met-ep´-i-tah*; from 3326 and 1899; *thereafter*:—afterward.

3348. μετέχω, metechō, *met-ekh´-o*; from 3326 and 2192; to *share* or *participate*; (by implication) *belong* to, *eat* (or *drink*):—be partaker, pertain, take part, use.

From *metá* (3326), with, denoting association, and *échō* (2192), have. To have together with others, to partake of, share in. Generally (1Co 9:10, 12; 10:30; Heb 5:13). Spoken of Christ's partaking of flesh and blood, i.e. becoming flesh and blood like us (Heb 2:14); spoken of partaking of the Lord's Supper (1Co 10:17, 21); spoken of Christ belonging to a tribe other than the one appointed for the priesthood (Heb 7:13).

Deriv.: *metochḗ* (3352), a partaking, participation, fellowship; *métochos* (3353), a partaker, an associate.

Syn.: *koinōnéō* (2841), to participate, share.

3349. μετεωρίζω, meteōrizō, *met-eh-o-rid´-zo*; from a compound of 3326 and a collative form of 142 or perhaps rather of

109 (compare "meteor"); to *raise in mid-air,* i.e. (figurative) *suspend* (passive *fluctuate* or *be anxious*):—be of doubtful mind.

3350. μετοικεσία, metoikesia, *met-oy-kes-ee´-ah*; from a derivative of a compound of 3326 and 3624; a *change of abode,* i.e. (special) *expatriation*:—× brought, carried (-ying) away (in-) to.

3351. μετοικίζω, metoikizō, *met-oy-kid´-zo*; from the same as 3350; to *transfer* as a *settler* or *captive,* i.e. *colonize* or *exile*:—carry away, remove into.

3352. μετοχή, metochē, *met-okh-ay´*; from 3348; *participation,* i.e. *intercourse*:—fellowship.

3353. μέτοχος, metochos, *met´-okh-os*; from 3348; *participant,* i.e. (as noun) a *sharer*; (by implication) an *associate*:—fellow, partaker, partner.

3354. μετρέω, metreō, *met-reh´-o*; from 3358; to *measure* (i.e. ascertain in size by a fixed standard); (by implication) to *admeasure* (i.e. allot by rule); (figurative) to *estimate*:—measure, mete.

3355. μετρητής, metrētēs, *met-ray-tace´*; from 3354; a *measurer,* i.e. (special) a certain standard *measure* of capacity for liquids:—firkin.

3356. μετριοπαθέω, metriopatheō, *met-ree-op-ath-eh´-o*; from a compound of the base of 3357 and 3806; to *be moderate in passion,* i.e. *gentle* (to *treat indulgently*):—have compassion.

From *metriopathḗs* (n.f.), moderate in passions, which is from *métrios* (n.f.), moderate, and *páthos* (3806), passion. To be moderate in one's passions, to have one's passions moderated; hence to be gentle, indulgent, compassionate. Only in Heb 5:2.

Syn.: *anéchomai* (430), to bear with tolerance; *eleéō* (1653), to have mercy; *makrothuméō* (3114), to be long-suffering; *oikteírō* (3627), to have pity; *splagchnízomai* (4697), to be moved with compassion; *sumpathéō* (4834), to suffer with another, commiserate.

3357. μετρίως, metriōs, *met-ree´-oce*; adverb from a derivative of 3358; *moderately,* i.e. *slightly*:—a little.

3358. μέτρον, metron, *met´-ron*; an apparently primary word; a *measure* ("metre"), literal or figurative; (by implication) a limited *portion* (*degree*):—measure.

3359. μέτοπον, metopon, *met´-o-pon*; from 3326 and **ὤψ, *ōps*** (the *face*); the *forehead* (as *opposite* the *countenance*):—forehead.

3360. μέχρι, mechri, *mekh´-ree*; or **μεχρίς, *mechris,*** *mekh-ris´*; from 3372; *as far as,* i.e. *up to* a certain point (as preposition of extent [denoting the *terminus,* whereas 891 refers especially to the *space* of time or place intervening] or conjecture):—till, (un-) to, until.

3361. μή, mē, *may*; a primary particle of qualified *negation* (whereas 3756 expresses an absolute denial); (adverb) *not,* (conjunction) *lest*; also (as interrogative implying a *negative* answer [whereas 3756 expects an *affirmative* one]) *whether*:—any, but (that), × forbear, + God forbid, + lack, lest, neither, never, no (× wise in), none, nor, [can-] not, nothing, that not, un [-taken], without. Often used in compounds in substantially the same relations. See also 3362, 3363, 3364, 3372, 3373, 3375, 3378.

3362. ἐὰν μή, ean mē, *eh-an´ may*; i.e. 1437 and 3361; *if not,* i.e. *unless*:—× before, but, except, if no, (if, + whosoever) not.

3363. ἵνα μή, hina mē, *hin´-ah may*; i.e. 2443 and 3361; *in order* (or *so*) *that not*:—albeit not, lest, that no (-t, [-thing]).

3364. οὐ μή, ou mē, *oo may*; i.e. 3756 and 3361; a double negative strengthening the denial; *not at all*:—any more, at all, by any (no) means, neither, never, no (at all), in no case (wise), nor ever, not (at all, in any wise). Compare 3378.

3365. μηδαμῶς, mēdamōs, *may-dam-oce´*; adverb from a compound of 3361 and **ἀμός, *amos*** (*somebody*); *by no means*:—not so.

3366. μηδέ, mēde, *may-deh´*; from 3361 and 1161; *but not, not even*; in a continued negation, *nor*:—neither, nor (yet), (no) not (once, so much as).

3367. μηδείς, mēdeis, *may-dice´*; including the irregular feminine **μηδεμία, *mēdemia,*** *may-dem-ee´-ah,* and the neuter **μηδέν, *mēden,*** *may-den´*; from 3361 and 1520; *not even one* (man, woman, thing):—any (man, thing), no (man), none, not (at all, any man, a whit), nothing, + without delay.

Adjective from *mēdé* (3366), and not, also not, and *heís* (1520), one. Not even one, no one, i.e. no one whoever he may be. Used with other moods which express potentiality where *oudeís* (3762), no one, would be used with the indicative mood to express actuality.

(I) Generally (Mt 16:20; Mk 6:8; 11:14; Jn 8:10; Ac 4:17, 21; Ro 13:8; 1Co 1:7; 3:18, 21; 2Co 6:3; Php 2:3; Tit 2:15; Heb 10:2; Jas 1:13; 1Pe 3:6).

(II) Neuter *mēdén,* nothing: After verbs of profit or loss, deficiency (Mk 5:26; Lk 4:35; 2Co 11:5; Php 4:6); As an adverb, not at all, in no respect, e.g., without doubting at all (Ac 10:20; 11:12; Jas 1:6).

Syn.: *oudeís* (3762), no one. Also, *mḗtis* (3387), no man, not anyone.

3368. μηδέποτε, mēdepote, *may-dep´-ot-eh*; from 3366 and 4218; *not even ever*:—never.

3369. μηδέπω, mēdepō, *may-dep´-o*; from 3366 and 4452; *not even yet*:—not yet.

3370. Μῆδος, Mēdos, *may´-dos*; of foreign origin [compare 4074]; a *Median,* or inhabitant of Media:—Mede.

3371. μηκέτι, mēketi, *may-ket´-ee*; from 3361 and 2089; *no further*:—any longer, (not) henceforth, hereafter, no henceforward (longer, more, soon), not any more.

3372. μῆκος, mēkos, *may´-kos*; probably akin to 3173; *length* (literal or figurative):—length.

3373. μηκύνω, mēkunō, *may-koo´-no*; from 3372; to *lengthen,* i.e. (middle) to *enlarge*:—grow up.

3374. μηλωτή, mēlōtē, *may-lo-tay´*; from **μῆλον, *mēlon*** (a *sheep*); a *sheep-skin*:—sheepskin.

3375. μήν, mēn, *mane*; a stronger form of 3303; a particle of affirmation (only with 2229); *assuredly*:—+ surely.

3376. μήν, mēn, *mane*; a primary word; a *month*:—month.

3377. μηνύω, mēnuō, *may-noo´-o*; probably from the same base as 3145 and 3415 (i.e. **μάω, *maō,*** to *strive*); to *disclose* (through the idea of mental *effort* and thus calling to *mind*), i.e. *report, declare, intimate*:—shew, tell.

3378. μὴ οὐκ, mē ouk, *mē ook*; i.e. 3361 and 3756; as interrogative and negative *is it not that?*:—neither (followed by *no*), + never, not. Compare 3364.

3379. μήποτε, mēpote, *may´-pot-eh*; or **μή ποτε, *mē pote,*** *may pot´-eh*; from 3361 and 4218; *not ever*; also *if* (or *lest*) *ever* (or *perhaps*):—if peradventure, lest (at any time, haply), not at all, whether or not.

3380. μήπω, mēpō, *may´-po*; from 3361 and 4452; *not yet*:—not yet.

3381. μήπως, mēpōs, *may´-poce*; or **μή πως, *mē pōs,*** *may poce*; from 3361 and 4458; *lest somehow*:—lest (by any means, by some means, haply, perhaps).

3382. μηρός, mēros, *may-ros´*; perhaps a primary word; a *thigh*:—thigh.

3383. μήτε, mēte, *may´-teh*; from 3361 and 5037; *not too,* i.e. (in continued negation) *neither* or *nor*; also, *not even*:—neither, (n-) or, so much as.

3384. μήτηρ, mētēr, *may´-tare*; apparently a primary word; a "*mother*" (literal or figurative, immediate or remote):—mother.

3385. μήτι, mēti, *may´-tee*; from 3361 and the neuter of 5100; *whether at all*:—not [*the particle usually not expressed, except by the form of the question*].

3386. μήτιγε, mētige, *may´-tig-eh*; from 3385 and 1065; *not at all then*, i.e. *not to say* (*the rather still*):—how much more.

3387. μήτις, mētis, *may´-tis*; or **μή τις,** *mē tis*, *may tis*; from 3361 and 5100; *whether any*:—any [*sometimes unexpressed except by the simple interrogative form of the sentence*].

3388. μήτρα, mētra, *may´-trah*; from 3384; the *matrix*:—womb.

3389. μητραλῴας, mētralōias, *may-tral-o´-as*; from 3384 and the base of 257; a *mother-thresher*, i.e. *matricide*:—murderer of mothers.

3390. μητρόπολις, mētropolis, *may-trop´-ol-is*; from 3384 and 4172; a *mother city*, i.e. "*metropolis*":—chiefest city.

3391. μία, mia, *mee´-ah*; irregular feminine of 1520; *one* or *first*:—a (certain), + agree, first, one, × other.

3392. μιαίνω, miainō, *me-ah´ee-no*; perhaps a primary verb; to *sully* or *taint*, i.e. *contaminate* (ceremonial or morally):—defile.

To stain with colour, to tinge. In the NT: pollute, defile:

(I) In the Levitical sense (Jn 18:28).

(II) In a moral sense (Jude 8). Pass.: to be polluted, corrupt (Tit 1:15; Heb 12:15).

Deriv.: *amiantos* (283), undefiled; *miasma* (3393), defilement; *miasmós* (3394), the act of defiling.

Syn.: *molúnō* (3435), to besmear or soil. Also, *diaphtheírō* (1311), to corrupt completely; *kataphtheírō* (2704), to corrupt utterly; *koinóō* (2840), to make common, render unholy or unclean in a ceremonial sense; *sḗpō* (4595), to make corrupt, to render rotten; *spilóō* (4695), to defile; *phtheírō* (5351), to corrupt.

3393. μίασμα, miasma, *mee´-as-mah*; from 3392 ("*miasma*"); (moral) *foulness* (properly the effect):—pollution.

Noun from *miaínō* (3392), to defile. A colouring, staining; hence pollution, defilement, in a moral sense (2Pe 2:20).

Syn.: *alísgēma* (234), pollution, contamination; *molusmós* (3436), defilement; *spílos* (4696), a spot, moral blemish; *phthorá* (5356), corruption.

3394. μιασμός, miasmos, *mee-as-mos´*; from 3392; (morally) *contamination* (properly the act):—uncleanness.

Noun from *miaínō* (3392), to pollute, defile. Pollution, defilement in a moral sense. Primarily indicates the act of polluting which results in the *miasma* (3393), defilement. Used only in 2Pe 2:10, where it refers to lusts which are polluted.

Syn.: *alísgēma* (234), pollution, contamination; *diaphthorá* (1312), thorough corruption; *molusmós* (3436), defilement; *spílos* (4696), a moral blemish; *phthorá* (5356), corruption.

3395. μίγμα, migma, *mig´-mah*; from 3396; a *compound*:—mixture.

3396. μίγνυμι, mignumi, *mig´-noo-mee*; a primary verb; to *mix*:—mingle.

3397. μικρόν, mikron, *mik-ron´*; masculine or neuter singular of 3398 (as noun); a *small* space of *time* or *degree*:—a (little) (while).

3398. μικρός, mikros, *mik-ros´*; including the comparative **μικρότερος,** *mikroteros*, *mik-rot´-er-os*; apparently a primary word; *small* (in size, quantity, number or [figurative] dignity):—least, less, little, small.

3399. Μίλητος, Milētos, *mil´-ay-tos*; of uncertain origin; *Miletus*, a city of Asia Minor:—Miletus.

3400. μίλιον, milion, *mil´-ee-on*; of Latin origin; a *thousand* paces, i.e. a "*mile*":—mile.

3401. μιμέομαι, mimeomai, *mim-eh´-om-ahee*; middle from **μῖμος,** *mimos* (a "*mimic*"); to *imitate*:—follow.

3402. μιμητής, mimētēs, *mim-ay-tace´*; from 3401; an *imitator*:—follower.

3403. μιμνήσκω, mimnēskō, *mim-nace´-ko*; a prolonged form of 3415 (from which some of the tenses are borrowed); to *remind*, i.e. (middle) to *recall to mind*:—be mindful, remember.

3404. μισέω, miseō, *mis-eh´-o*; from a primary **μῖσος,** *misos* (*hatred*); to *detest* (especially to *persecute*); by extension to *love less*:—hate (-ful).

3405. μισθαποδοσία, misthapodosia, *mis-thap-od-os-ee´-ah*; from 3406; *requital* (good or bad):—recompence of reward.

Noun from *misthapodótēs* (3406), rewarder. A recompense, whether a reward (Heb 10:35; 11:26) or a punishment (Heb 2:2).

Syn.: With the meaning of reward: *amoibḗ* (287), recompense; *antapódoma* (468), reward or punishment; *antapódosis* (469), rewards, recompense or punishment; *antimisthía* (489), a reward, requital; *opsṓnion* (3800), a soldier's pay. With the meaning of punishment: *díkē* (1349), justice, a sentence; *epitimía* (2009), penalty, punishment; *kólasis* (2851), punishment, the negation of the enjoyment of life; *timōría* (5098), vengeance, punishment, the vindication of honour.

3406. μισθαποδότης, misthapodotēs, *mis-thap-od-ot´-ace*; from 3409 and 591; a *remunerator*:—rewarder.

Noun from *misthós* (3408), a reward, and *apodídōmi* (591), to render. A recompenser, rewarder. Used only in Heb 11:6.

Deriv.: *misthapodosía* (3405), a punishment, recompense.

3407. μίσθιος, misthios, *mis´-thee-os*; from 3408; a *wage-earner*:—hired servant.

Adjective from *misthós* (3408), hire, pay, reward. Hired servant. Used only in Lk 15:17, 19.

Syn.: *ergátēs* (2040), a worker.

3408. μισθός, misthos, *mis-thos´*; apparently a primary word; *pay* for service (literal or figurative), good or bad:—hire, reward, wages.

Noun meaning wages, hire, reward:

(I) Particularly and generally (Mt 20:8; Lk 10:7; Ac 1:18; Ro 4:4; 1Co 3:8; 1Ti 5:18; Jas 5:4; 2Pe 2:15; Jude 11).

(II) In the sense of reward to be received hereafter (Mt 5:12, 46; 6:1, 2, 5, 16; 10:41, 42; Mk 9:41; Lk 6:23, 35; Jn 4:36; 1Co 3:14; 9:17, 18; 2Jn 8; Rev 11:18; 22:12).

(III) In the sense of retribution, punishment (2Pe 2:13).

Deriv.: *antimisthía* (489), reward, penalty; *misthapodótēs* (3406), rewarder; *místhios* (3407), a day labourer, one paid by the day; *misthóō* (3409), to hire; *misthōtós* (3411), a hired worker.

Syn.: *amoibḗ* (287), recompense; *antapódoma* (468), recompense, what one receives in reward or punishment; *antapódosis* (469), the act of recompensing; *opsṓnion* (3800), rations for soldiers, wages.

3409. μισθόω, misthoō, *mis-tho´-o*; from 3408; to *let* out for wages, i.e. (middle) to *hire*:—hire.

3410. μίσθωμα, misthōma, *mis´-tho-mah*; from 3409; a *rented* building:—hired house.

3411. μισθωτός, misthōtos, *mis-tho-tos´*; from 3409; a *wage-worker* (good or bad):—hired servant, hireling.

Noun from *misthóō* (3409), to hire. One hired, a hired servant (Mk 1:20). Spoken of the hired servant who will leave the sheep in the face of danger (Jn 10:12, 13).

Syn.: *misthios* (3407), hired servant; *ergátēs* (2040), worker.

3412. Μιτυλήνη, Mitulēnē, *mit-oo-lay´-nay*; for **μυτιλήνη,** *Mutilēnē* (*abounding in shell-fish*); *Mitylene* (or *Mytilene*), a town in the island Lesbos:—Mitylene.

3413. Μιχαήλ, Michaēl, *mikh-ah-ale´*; of Hebrew origin [4317]; *Michaël*, an archangel:—Michael.

3414. μνᾶ, mna, *mnah*; of Latin origin; a *mna* (i.e. *mina*), a certain *weight*:—pound.

3415. μνάομαι, mnaomai, *mnah´-om-ahee*; middle of a derivative of 3306 or perhaps of the base of 3145 (through the idea of *fixture* in the mind or of mental *grasp*); to *bear in mind*, i.e. *recollect*; (by implication) to *reward* or *punish*:—be mindful, remember, come (have) in remembrance. Compare 3403.

3416. Μνάσων, Mnasōn, *mnah´-sohn*; of uncertain origin; *Mnason*, a Christian:—Mnason.

3417. μνεία, mneia, *mni´-ah*; from 3415 or 3403; *recollection*; (by implication) *recital*:—mention, remembrance.

3418. μνῆμα, mnēma, *mnay´-mah*; from 3415; a *memorial*, i.e. sepulchral *monument* (*burial-place*):—grave, sepulchre, tomb.

3419. μνημεῖον, mnēmeion, *mnay-mi´-on*; from 3420; a *remembrance*, i.e. *cenotaph* (*place of interment*):—grave, sepulchre, tomb.

3420. μνήμη, mnēmē, *mnay´-may*; from 3403; *memory*:—remembrance.

3421. μνημονεύω, mnēmoneuō, *mnay-mon-yoo´-o*; from a derivative of 3420; to *exercise memory*, i.e. *recollect*; (by implication) to *punish*; also to *rehearse*:—make mention, be mindful, remember.

3422. μνημόσυνον, mnēmosunon, *mnay-mos´-oo-non*; from 3421; a *reminder* (*memorandum*), i.e. *record*:—memorial.

3423. μνηστεύω, mnēsteuō, *mnace-tyoo´-o*; from a derivative of 3415; to *give a souvenir* (engagement present), i.e. *betroth*:—espouse.

3424. μογιλάλος, mogilalos, *mog-il-al´-os*; from 3425 and 2980; *hardly talking*, i.e. *dumb* (*tongue-tied*):—having an impediment in his speech.

3425. μόγις, mogis, *mog´-is*; adverb from a primary **μόγος, *mogos*** (*toil*); *with difficulty*:—hardly.

3426. μόδιος, modios, *mod´-ee-os*; of Latin origin; a *modius*, i.e. certain measure for things dry (the quantity or the utensil):—bushel.

3427. μοί, moi, *moy*; the simpler form of 1698; *to me*:—I, me, mine, my.

3428. μοιχαλίς, moichalis, *moy-khal-is´*; a prolonged form of the feminine of 3432; an *adulteress* (literal or figurative):—adulteress (-ous, -y).

3429. μοιχάω, moichaō, *moy-khah´-o*; from 3432; (middle) to *commit adultery*:—commit adultery.

3430. μοιχεία, moicheia, *moy-khi´-ah*; from 3431; *adultery*:—adultery.

3431. μοιχεύω, moicheuō, *moy-khyoo´-o*; from 3432; to *commit adultery*:—commit adultery.

3432. μοιχός, moichos, *moy-khos´*; perhaps a primary word; a (male) *paramour*; (figurative) *apostate*:—adulterer.

3433. μόλις, molis, *mol´-is*; probably by variation for 3425; *with difficulty*:—hardly, scarce (-ly), + with much work.

3434. Μολόχ, Moloch, *mol-okh´*; of Hebrew origin [4432]; *Moloch* (i.e. *Molek*), an idol:—Moloch.

3435. μολύνω, molunō, *mol-oo´-no*; probably from 3189; to *soil* (figurative):—defile.

To defile, besmear or soil as with mud or filth (1Co 8:7; Rev 3:4; 14:4).

Deriv.: *molusmós* (3436), defilement, the act of defiling.

Syn.: *miaínō* (3392), to contaminate, defile; *spilóō* (4695), to spot, pollute.

3436. μολυσμός, molusmos, *mol-oos-mos´*; from 3435; a *stain*, i.e. (figurative) *immorality*:—filthiness.

Noun from *molúnō* (3435), to defile. A soiling: defilement, pollution in a moral sense, filthiness. Used only in 2Co 7:1.

Syn.: *diaphthorá* (1312), complete corruption; *míasma* (3393), defilement, the result of defilement; *miasmós* (3394), uncleanness; *phthorá* (5356), corruption.

3437. μομφή, momphē, *mom-fay´*; from 3201; *blame*, i.e. (by implication) a *fault*:—quarrel.

3438. μονή, monē, *mon-ay´*; from 3306; a *staying*, i.e. *residence* (the act or the place):—abode, mansion.

Noun from *ménō* (3306), to remain, dwell. A dwelling place, habitation, abode. Used in Jn 14:2 in the sense of rooms, apartments. Spoken of figuratively in Jn 14:23 in the sense of Jesus and the Father making the believer their resting place.

Syn.: *épaulis* (1886), a country house, cottage, cabin; *katoikētḗrion* (2732), a habitation; *katoikía* (2733), dwelling place; *oikētḗrion* (3613), a habitation; *skēnḗ* (4633), a tent or tabernacle; *skḗnōma* (4638), a pitched tent, metaphorically referring to the body.

3439. μονογενής, monogenēs, *mon-og-en-ace*; from 3441 and 1096; *only-born*, i.e. *sole*:—only (begotten, child).

Adjective from *mónos* (3441), only, and *génos* (1085), kind, which is from the root of *gínomai* (1096), to become. Only-born, only begotten, i.e. only child (Lk 7:12; 8:42; 9:38; Heb 11:17). In John's writings, spoken only of *ho Lógos* (3056), The Word, the only begotten Son of God in the highest sense, as alone knowing and revealing the essence of the Father (Jn 1:14, 18; 3:16, 18; 1Jn 4:9).

3440. μόνον, monon, *mon´-on*; neuter of 3441 as adverb; *merely*:—alone, but, only.

3441. μόνος, monos, *mon´-os*; probably from 3306; *remaining*, i.e. *sole* or *single*; (by implication) *mere*:—alone, only, by themselves.

3442. μονόφθαλμος, monophthalmos, *mon-of´-thal-mos*; from 3441 and 3788; *one-eyed*:—with one eye.

3443. μονόω, monoō, *mon-o´-o*; from 3441; to *isolate*, i.e. *bereave*:—be desolate.

3444. μορφή, morphē, *mor-fay´*; perhaps from the base of 3313 (through the idea of *adjustment* of parts); *shape*; (figurative) *nature*:—form.

Noun meaning form, shape. Spoken of Jesus appearing in another form, one that was not recognized, to the two disciples on the road to Emmaus (Mk 16:12, see *héteros* [2087], another). Used in the sense of *phúsis* (5449), nature, rather than simply form or shape: spoken of Jesus having been in the "form of God" (Php 2:6, see *Theós* [2316], God), a clear affirmation of His divine nature; contrastly, spoken of Jesus having taken on Himself the "form of a slave" (Php 2:7, see *doulos* [1401], slave) at the incarnation, a clear affirmation of His human nature.

Deriv.: *morphóō* (3445), to form, fashion; *súmmorphos* (4832), conformed to.

3445. μορφόω, morphoō, *mor-fo´-o*; from the same as 3444; to *fashion* (figurative):—form.

From *morphḗ* (3444), form, shape. To form, fashion. Found only in Gal 4:19 where the Christian is described as a little child who needs to mature until his character and conduct project the very image of Christ.

Deriv.: *metamorphóō* (3339), to transform, transfigure; *mórphōsis* (3446), formulation, impression.

Syn.: *plássō* (4111), to shape, form.

3446. μόρφωσις, morphōsis, *mor´-fo-sis*; from 3445; *formation*, i.e. (by implication) *appearance* (*semblance* or [concrete] *formula*):—form.

Noun from *morphóō* (3445), to form. A forming; hence form, appearance, e.g., mere external form (2Ti 3:5); by implication: a prescribed form, a norm (Ro 2:20).

Syn.: *schēma* (4976), fashion; *charaktēr* (5481), exact image.

3447. μοσχοποιέω, moschopoieō, *mos-khop-oy-eh´-o*; from 3448 and 4160; to *fabricate* the image of a *bullock*:—make a calf.

3448. μόσχος, moschos, *mos´-khos*; probably strengthened for **ὄσχος**, *oschos* (a *shoot*); a young *bullock*:—calf.

3449. μόχθος, mochthos, *mokh´-thos*; from the base of 3425; *toil*, i.e. (by implication) *sadness*:—painfulness, travail.

Noun from *mógos* (n.f.), labour, toil. Wearisome labour, travail; including the idea of painful effect, sorrow. In the NT, always coupled with *kópos* (2873), weariness, labour (2Co 11:27; 1Th 2:9; 2Th 3:8).

3450. μοῦ, mou, *moo*; the simpler form of 1700; *of me*:—I, me, mine (own), my.

3451. μουσικός, mousikos, *moo-sik-os´*; from **μουσς**, *Mousa* (a *Muse*); "*musical,*" i.e. (as noun) a *minstrel*:—musician.

3452. μυελός, muelos, *moo-el-os´*; perhaps a primary word; the *marrow*:—marrow.

3453. μυέω, mueō, *moo-eh´-o*; from the base of 3466; *to initiate*, i.e. (by implication) to *teach*:—instruct.

3454. μῦθος, muthos, *moo´-thos*; perhaps from the same as 3453 (through the idea of *tuition*); a *tale*, i.e. *fiction* ("*myth*"):—fable.

Noun meaning speech, discourse. In the NT: fable, fiction, a mythic tale which will lead men astray from the truth (1Ti 1:4; 4:7; 2Ti 4:4; Tit 1:14; 2Pe 1:16).

3455. μυκάομαι, mukaomai, *moo-kah´-om-ahee*; from a presumed derivative of **μύζω**, *muzō* (to "*moo*"); to *bellow* (*roar*):—roar.

3456. μυκτηρίζω, mukterizō, *mook´-tay-rid´-zo*; from a derivative of the base of 3455 (meaning *snout*, as that whence *lowing* proceeds); to *make mouths* at, i.e. *ridicule*:—mock.

3457. μυλικός, mulikos, *moo-lee-kos´*; from 3458; *belonging to a mill*:—mill [-stone].

3458. μύλος, mulos, *moo´-los*; probably ultimately from the base of 3433 (through the idea of *hardship*); a "*mill,*" i.e. (by implication) a *grinder* (*millstone*):—millstone.

3459. μύλων, mulōn, *moo´-lone*; from 3458; a *mill-house*:—mill.

3460. Μύρα, Mura, *moo´-rah*; of uncertain derivative; *Myra*, a place in Asia Minor:—Myra.

3461. μυρίας, murias, *moo-ree´-as*; from 3463; a *ten-thousand*; by extension a "*myriad*" or indefinite number:—ten thousand.

3462. μυρίζω, murizō, *moo-rid´-zo*; from 3464; to *apply* (perfumed) *unguent* to:—anoint.

3463. μύριοι, murioi, *moo´-ree-oi*; plural of an apparently primary word (properly meaning *very many*); *ten thousand*; by extension *innumerably* many:—ten thousand.

3464. μύρον, muron, *moo´-ron*; probably of foreign origin [compare 4753, 4666]; "*myrrh,*" i.e. (by implication) *perfumed oil*:—ointment.

Any aromatic resin distilling of itself from a tree or plant, especially myrrh. In the NT, generally: ointment, i.e. perfumed oil typically used to anoint oneself for special occasions, or to prepare a body for burial (Mt 26:7, 9, 12; Mk 14:3, 4; Lk 7:37, 38; 23:56; Jn 11:2; 12:3, 5; Rev 18:13).

Deriv.: *murízō* (3462), to anoint for burial, embalm.

3465. Μυσία, Musia, *moo-see´-ah*; of uncertain origin; *Mysia*, a region of Asia Minor:—Mysia.

3466. μυστήριον, mustērion, *moos-tay´-ree-on*; from a derivative of **μύω**, *muō* (to *shut* the mouth); a *secret* or "*mystery*" (through the idea of *silence* imposed by *initiation* into religious rites):—mystery.

Noun from *mústēs* (n.f.), a person initiated into sacred mysteries, which is from *muéō* (3453), to initiate, learn a secret. A mystery, i.e. something into which one must be initiated or instructed before it can be known; something of itself not obvious and above human insight. In the NT, spoken of facts, doctrines, principles, etc. not previously revealed:

(I) Generally (Mt 13:11; Mk 4:11; Lk 8:10; 1Co 14:2; Eph 5:32; 2Th 2:7; Rev 1:20; 17:5, 7).

(II) Specifically, of the gospel, the Christian dispensation, as having been long hidden and first revealed in later times (Ro 16:25; 1Co 2:7; Eph 3:3, 4, 9; Col 2:2; 4:3; 1Ti 3:9); so of particular doctrines or parts of the gospel (Ro 11:25; 1Co 15:51; Eph 1:9; 1Ti 3:16).

3467. μυωπάζω, muōpazō, *moo-ope-ad´-zo*; from a compound of the base of 3466 and **ὤψ**, *ōps* (the *face*; from 3700); to *shut* the *eyes*, i.e. *blink* (*see indistinctly*):—cannot see afar off.

3468. μώλωψ, mōlōps, *mo´-lopes*; from **μῶλος**, *mōlos* ("*moil*"; probably akin to the base of 3433) and probably **ὤψ**, *ōps* (the *face*; from 3700); a *mole* ("black eye") or *blow-mark*:—stripe.

3469. μωμάομαι, mōmaomai, *mo-mah´-om-ahee*; from 3470; to *carp* at, i.e. *censure* (*discredit*):—blame.

3470. μῶμος, mōmos, *mo´-mos*; perhaps from 3201; a *flaw* or *blot*, i.e. (figurative) *disgraceful* person:—blemish.

Blame, fault, blemish, disgrace. Used only in 2Pe 2:13. See *ámōmos* (299), without spot.

Deriv.: *ámōmos* (299), blameless, without spot; *momáomai* (3469), to find fault with, blame.

3471. μωραίνω, mōrainō, *mo-rah´ee-no*; from 3474; to *become insipid*; (figurative) to *make* (passive *act*) as a *simpleton*:—become fool, make foolish, lose savour.

3472. μωρία, mōria, *mo-ree´-ah*; from 3474; *silliness*, i.e. *absurdity*:—foolishness.

3473. μωρολογία, mōrologia, *mo-rol-og-ee´-ah*; from a compound of 3474 and 3004; *silly talk*, i.e. *buffoonery*:—foolish talking.

Noun from *mōrológos* (n.f.), speaking foolishly, which is from *mōrós* (3474), foolish, and *légō* (3004), to speak. Foolish talking, empty discourse (Eph 5:4).

3474. μωρός, mōros, *mo-ros´*; probably from the base of 3466; *dull* or *stupid* (as if *shut* up), i.e. *heedless*, (moral) *blockhead*, (apparently) *absurd*:—fool (-ish, × -ishness).

Adjective meaning dull, not acute, e.g., of impressions of the taste: insipid, tasteless. In the NT, of the mind: stupid, foolish; and as a substantive: a fool (Mt 5:22; 7:26; 23:17, 19; 25:2, 3, 8; 1Co 3:18; 4:10). Of things: foolishness (1Co 1:25); foolish things (1Co 1:27; 2Ti 2:23; Tit 3:9).

Deriv.: *mōraínō* (3471), to become dull; *mōría* (3472), foolishness as a personal quality.

Syn.: *anóētos* (453), senseless, one lacking understanding; *ásophos* (781), unwise; *asúnetos* (801), without discernment; *áphrōn* (878), foolish, a fool.

3475. Μωσεύς, Mōseus, *moce-yoos´*; or **Μωσῆς**, *Mōsēs*, *mo-sace´*; or **Μωϋσῆς**, *Mōüsēs*, *mo-oo-sace´*; of Hebrew origin; [4872]; *Moseus, Moses* or *Moüses* (i.e. *Mosheh*), the Hebrew lawgiver:—Moses.

3476. Ναασσών, Naassōn, *nah-as-sone´*; of Hebrew origin [5177]; *Naasson* (i.e. *Nachshon*), an Israelite:—Naasson.

3477. Ναγγαί, Naggai, *nang-gah´ee*; probably of Hebrew origin [compare 5052]; *Nangæ* (i.e. perhaps *Nogach*), an Israelite:—Nagge.

3478. Ναζαρέθ, Nazareth, *nad-zar-eth´*; or **Ναζαρέτ**, *Nazaret*, *nad-zar-et´*; of uncertain derivative; *Nazareth* or *Nazaret*, a place in Palestine:—Nazareth.

3479. Ναζαρηνός, Nazarēnos, *nad-zar-ay-nos´*; from 3478; a *Nazarene*, i.e. inhabitant of Nazareth:—of Nazareth.

3480. Ναζωραῖος, Nazōraios, *nad-zo-rah´-yos*; from 3478; a *Nazoræan*, i.e. inhabitant of Nazareth; by extension a *Christian*:—Nazarene, of Nazareth.

3481. Ναθάν, Nathan, *nath-an´*; of Hebrew origin [5416]; *Nathan*, an Israelite:—Nathan.

3482. Ναθαναήλ, Nathanaēl, *nath-an-ah-ale´*; of Hebrew origin [5417]; *Nathanaël* (i.e. *Nathanel*), an Israelite and Christian:—Nathanael.

3483. ναί, nai, *nahee*; a primary particle of strong affirmation; *yes*:—even so, surely, truth, verily, yea, yes.

3484. Ναΐν, Naïn, *nah-in´*; probably of Hebrew origin [compare 4999]; *Naïn*, a place in Palestine:—Nain.

3485. ναός, naos, *nah-os´*; from a primary **ναίω**, ***naiō*** (to *dwell*); a *fane, shrine, temple*:—shrine, temple. Compare 2411.

Noun from *naiō* (n.f.), to dwell. A dwelling, temple, as the dwelling of a god:

(I) Generally, of any temple (Ac 7:48; 17:24; 19:24, referring to the miniature copies of the temple of Diana at Ephesus containing a small image of the goddess. Such shrines of other gods were also common, made of gold, silver or wood, and were purchased by pilgrims and travelers, probably as souvenirs or to be used in their devotions).

(II) Of the temple in Jerusalem or in allusion to it, but only of the actual edifice; in distinction from *hierón* (2411), temple, which included the courts and other appurtenances, *naós* refers to the building itself (Mt 23:16, 17, 21, 35; 26:61; 27:5; 27:40, 51; Mk 14:58; 15:29; Lk 1:9, 21, 22; 23:45; Jn 2:19, 20; 2Th 2:4). See also Rev 11:1, 2.

(III) Of the temple of God in heaven (cf. Rev 3:12; 7:15; 11:19; 14:15, 17; 15:5, 6, 8; 16:1, 17; 21:22).

(IV) Metaphorically, of persons in whom God or His Spirit is said to dwell or act, e.g., the body of Jesus (Jn 2:19, 21); of Christians (1Co 3:16, 17; 6:19; 2Co 6:16; Eph 2:21).

Deriv.: *neōkóros* (3511), a temple servant, worshipper.

Syn.: *tó hágion* (39) the holy place, sanctuary, spoken of the temple.

3486. Ναούμ, Naoum, *nah-oom´*; of Hebrew origin [5151]; *Naüm* (i.e. *Nachum*), an Israelite:—Naum.

3487. νάρδος, nardos, *nar´-dos*; of foreign origin [compare 5373]; "*nard*":—[spike-] nard.

3488. Νάρκισσος, Narkissos, *nar´-kis-sos*; a flower of the same name, from **νάρκη**, ***Narkē*** (*stupefaction*, as a "narcotic"); *Narcissus*, a Roman:—Narcissus.

3489. ναυαγέω, nauageō, *now-ag-eh´-o*; from a compound of 3491 and 71; to *be shipwrecked* (*stranded*, "navigate"), literal or figurative:—make (suffer) shipwreck.

3490. ναύκληρος, nauklēros, *now´-klay-ros*; from 3491 and 2819 ("clerk"); a *captain*:—owner of a ship.

3491. ναῦς, naus, *nowce*; from **νάω**, ***naō***; or **νέω**, ***neō*** (to *float*); a *boat* (of any size):—ship.

3492. ναύτης, nautēs, *now´-tace*; from 3491; a *boatman*, i.e. *seaman*:—sailor, shipman.

3493. Ναχώρ, Nachōr, *nakh-ore´*; of Hebrew origin [5152]; *Nachor*, the grandfather of Abraham:—Nachor.

3494. νεανίας, neanias, *neh-an-ee´-as*; from a derivative of 3501; a *youth* (up to about forty years):—young man.

3495. νεανίσκος, neaniskos, *neh-an-is´-kos*; from the same as 3494; a *youth* (under forty):—young man.

3496. Νεάπολις, Neapolis, *neh-ap´-ol-is*; from 3501 and 4172; *new town*; *Neäpolis*, a place in Macedonia:—Neapolis.

3497. Νεεμάν, Neeman, *neh-eh-man´*; of Hebrew origin [5283]; *Neëman* (i.e. *Naaman*), a Syrian:—Naaman.

3498. νεκρός, nekros, *nek-ros´*; from an apparently primary **νέκυς**, ***nekus*** (a *corpse*); *dead* (literal or figurative; also as noun):—dead.

Adjective from *nékus* (n.f.), a corpse. Dead:

(I) As a substantive: a dead person, dead body, corpse (Mt 23:27; Rev 20:13).

(A) As yet unburied (Mt 8:22; Lk 7:15); one slain (Rev 16:3).

(B) As buried, laid in a sepulchre, and therefore the spirit being in Hades (Lk 16:30; Jn 5:25; Ac 10:42; Ro 14:9; 1Th 4:16; Heb 11:35).

(C) Figuratively in the plural, those dead to Christ and His gospel, meaning spiritually dead (Mt 8:22, "Let the spiritually dead bury their dead" [a.t.], meaning let no lesser duty keep you from the one great duty of following Me; Lk 9:60; Ro 6:13; 11:15; Eph 5:14).

(II) As an adjective:

(A) Particularly (Mt 28:4; Ac 20:9; 28:6; Rev 1:17). Figuratively for lost, perished, given up as dead, e.g., the prodigal son (Lk 15:24, 32).

(B) Figuratively, in opposition to the life of the gospel, e.g.: **(1)** Of persons: dead to Christ and His gospel and thus exposed to punishment, spiritually dead (Eph 2:1, 5; Col 2:13; Rev 3:1). Used in the opposite sense, dead to sin, i.e. no longer willingly subject to it (Ro 6:11). **(2)** Of things, dead, i.e. inactive, inoperative (Ro 7:8; Heb 6:1; 9:14; Jas 2:17, 20, 26).

Deriv.: *nekróō* (3499), to put to death.

3499. νεκρόω, nekroō, *nek-ro´-o*; from 3498; to *deaden*, i.e. (figurative) to *subdue*:—be dead, mortify.

3500. νέκρωσις, nekrōsis, *nek´-ro-sis*; from 3499; *decease*; (figurative) *impotency*:—deadness, dying.

Noun from *nekróō* (3499), to mortify. The act of killing, putting to death (2Co 4:10, "always carrying about in the body the putting to death of the Lord Jesus" [a.t.], i.e. being exposed to cruelties resembling those which He sustained in His last sufferings). Figuratively: the state of deadness, barrenness as spoken of the womb (Ro 4:19).

3501. νέος, neos, *neh´-os*; including the comparative **νεώτερος**, ***neōteros***, *neh-o´-ter-os*; a primary word; "*new*," i.e. (of persons) *youthful*, or (of things) *fresh*; (figurative) *regenerate*:—new, young.

Adjective meaning young, new:

(I) Particularly of persons: young, youthful (Tit 2:4). In the comparative form: younger (Jn 21:18); in the comparative plural, the younger, the young, as opposed to those older (Ac 5:6; 1Ti 5:1, 2, 11, 14; Tit 2:6; 1Pe 5:5). As implying inferior dignity (Lk 22:26).

(II) Of things: new, recent, e.g., wine (Mt 9:17; Mk 2:22; Lk 5:37, 38, 39). Figuratively of the heart, disposition, nature, as renewed and therefore better: e.g., the new man (Col 3:10); the new covenant (Heb 12:24); Also 1Co 5:7.

Deriv.: *neanías* (3494), a youth; *neanískos* (3495), a youth under forty; *neossós* (3502), a young bird; *neótēs* (3503), youthful age; *neóphutos* (3504), newly planted; *neōterikós* (3512), youthful; *noumēnía* (3561), new moon.

Syn.: *kainós* (2537), new. Also, *prósphatos* (4372), recent, new in the sense of time.

3502. νεοσσός, neossos, *neh-os-sos´*; from 3501; a *youngling* (*nestling*):—young.

Masculine noun from *néos* (3501), young. A young animal, or often specifically a young bird. Used only in Lk 2:24.

Deriv.: *nossiá* (3555), a nest of young birds; *nossíon* (3556), a young bird.

3503. νεότης, neotēs, *neh-ot´-ace*; from 3501; *newness*, i.e. *youthfulness*:—youth.

Noun from *néos* (3501), young. Youth, age or time of youth (Mt 19:20; Mk 10:20; Lk 18:21; Ac 26:4); youthfulness, thus Timothy is told to conduct his leadership in such a way that no man despises his *neótēs* (1Ti 4:12). He is at least thirty years old, but leading men much older.

3504. νεόφυτος, neophutos, *neh-of´-oo-tos*; from 3501 and a derivative of 5453; *newly planted*, i.e. (figurative) a *young convert* ("*neophyte*"):—novice.

Adjective from *néos* (3501), new, and *phúō* (5453), to germinate. Newly sprung up or, figuratively, a neophyte, new convert (1Ti 3:6).

Syn.: *ápeiros* (552), inexperienced.

3505. Νέρων, Nerōn, *ner´-ohn*; of Latin origin; *Neron* (i.e. *Nero*), a Roman emperor:—Nero.

3506. νεύω, neuō, *nyoo´-o*; apparently a primary verb; to "*nod*," i.e. (by analogy) to *signal*:—beckon.

3507. νεφέλη, nephelē, *nef-el´-ay*; from 3509; properly *cloudiness*, i.e. (concrete) a *cloud*:—cloud.

3508. Νεφθαλείμ, Nephthaleim, *nef-thal-ime´*; of Hebrew origin [5321]; *Nephthaleim* (i.e. *Naph-thali*), a tribe in Palestine:—Nephthalim.

3509. νέφος, nephos, *nef´-os*; apparently a primary word; a *cloud*:—cloud.

3510. νεφρός, nephros, *nef-ros´*; of uncertain affinity; a *kidney* (plural), i.e. (figurative) the inmost *mind*:—reins.

3511. νεωκόρος, neōkoros, *neh-o-kor´-os*; from a form of 3485 and **κορέω**, ***koreō*** (to *sweep*); a *temple-servant*, i.e. (by implication) a *votary*:—worshipper.

3512. νεωτερικός, neōterikos, *neh-o-ter´-ik-os*; from the comparative of 3501; *appertaining to younger* persons, i.e. *juvenile*:—youthful.

3513. νή, nē, *nay*; probably an intensive form of 3483; a particle of attestation (accompanied by the object invoked or appealed to in confirmation); *as sure as*:—I protest by.

3514. νήθω, nēthō, *nay´-tho*; from **νέω**, ***neō*** (of like meaning); to *spin*:—spin.

3515. νηπιάζω, nēpiazō, *nay-pee-ad´-zo*; from 3516; to *act* as a *babe*, i.e. (figurative) *innocently*:—be a child.

3516. νήπιος, nēpios, *nay´-pee-os*; from an obsolete particle **νη**, ***ne*** (implying *negation*) and 2031; *not speaking*, i.e. an *infant* (*minor*); (figurative) a *simple-minded* person, an *immature* Christian:—babe, child (+ -ish).

Adjective from *nḗ-*, not, and *épos* (2031), word. One who cannot speak, hence, an infant, child, baby without any definite limitation of age.

(I) Particularly (Mt 21:16; 1Co 13:11). By implication: a minor, one not yet of age (Gal 4:1).

(II) Metaphorically: a babe, one unlearned, unenlightened, simple, innocent (Mt 11:25; Lk 10:21; Ro 2:20; Gal 4:3). Implying censure (1Co 3:1; Eph 4:14; Heb 5:13).

Deriv.: *nēpiázō* (3515), to be as a child.

Syn.: *bréphos* (1025), an unborn or a newborn child, infant; *teknı́on* (5040), little child; *téknon* (5043), child.

3517. Νηρεύς, Nēreus, *nare-yoos´*; apparently from a derivative of the base of 3491 (meaning *wet*); *Nereus*, a Christian:—Nereus.

3518. Νηρί, Nēri, *nay-ree´*; of Hebrew origin [5374]; *Neri* (i.e. *Nerijah*), an Israelite:—Neri.

3519. νησίον, nēsion, *nay-see´-on*; diminutive of 3520; an *islet*:—island.

3520. νῆσος, nēsos, *nay´-sos*; probably from the base of 3491; an *island*:—island, isle.

3521. νηστεία, nēsteia, *nace-ti´-ah*; from 3522; *abstinence* (from lack of food, or voluntary and religious); specially the *fast* of the Day of Atonement:—fast (-ing).

3522. νηστεύω, nēsteuō, *nace-tyoo´-o*; from 3523; to *abstain* from food (religiously):—fast.

3523. νῆστις, nēstis, *nace´-tis*; from the inseparable negative particle **νη**, ***nē*** (*not*) and 2068; *not eating*, i.e. *abstinent* from food (religiously):—fasting.

3524. νηφάλεος, nēphaleos, *nah-fal´-eh-os*; or **νηφάλιος**, ***nēphalios***, *nay-fal´-ee-os*; from 3525; *sober*, i.e. (figurative) *circumspect*:—sober.

3525. νήφω, nēphō, *nay´-fo*; of uncertain affinity; to *abstain* from wine (*keep sober*), i.e. (figurative) *be discreet*:—be sober, watch.

3526. Νίγερ, Niger, *neeg´-er*; of Latin origin; *black; Niger*, a Christian:—Niger.

3527. Νικάνωρ, Nikanōr, *nik-an´-ore*; probably from 3528; *victorious; Nicanor*, a Christian:—Nicanor.

3528. νικάω, nikaō, *nik-ah´-o*; from 3529; to *subdue* (literal or figurative):—conquer, overcome, prevail, get the victory.

3529. νίκη, nikē, *nee´-kay*; apparently a primary word; *conquest* (abstract), i.e. (figurative) the *means of success*:—victory.

3530. Νικόδημος, Nikodēmos, *nik-od´-ay-mos*; from 3534 and 1218; *victorious* among his *people; Nicodemus*, an Israelite:—Nicodemus.

3531. Νικολαΐτης, Nikolaïtēs, *nik-ol-ah-ee´-tace*; from 3532; a *Nicolaïte*, i.e. adherent of *Nicolaüs*:—*Nicolaitane*.

3532. Νικόλαος, Nikolaos, *nik-ol´-ah-os*; from 3534 and 2994; *victorious* over the *people; Nicolaüs*, a heretic:—Nicolaus.

3533. Νικόπολις, Nikopolis, *nik-op´-ol-is*; from 3534 and 4172; *victorious city; Nicopolis*, a place in Macedonia:—Nicopolis.

3534. νῖκος, nikos, *nee´-kos*; from 3529; a *conquest* (concrete), i.e. (by implication) *triumph*:—victory.

3535. Νινευΐ, Nineuï, *nin-yoo-ee´*; of Hebrew origin [5210]; *Ninevi* (i.e. *Nineveh*), the capital of Assyria:—Nineve.

3536. Νινευΐτης, Nineuïtēs, *nin-yoo-ee´-tace*; from 3535; a *Ninevite*, i.e. inhabitant of Nineveh:—of Nineve, Ninevite.

3537. νιπτήρ, niptēr, *nip-tare´*; from 3538; a *ewer*:—bason.

3538. νίπτω, niptō, *nip´-to*; to *cleanse* (especially the hands or the feet or the face); ceremony to *perform ablution*:—wash. Compare 3068.

To wash some part of the body, as the face, hands or feet. Washing of the hands and feet was very common with the Jews, e.g., of the hands before eating; of the feet, as a mark of hospitality offered to a guest on his arrival, and performed by menial servants or slaves. *Níptō* usually expresses the washing of a part of the body as the hands (Mt 15:2; Mk 7:3), the feet (Jn 13:5, 6, 8, 10, 12, 14; 1Ti 5:10), the face (Mt 6:17), the eyes (Jn 9:7, 11, 15).

Deriv.: *ániptos* (449), unwashed; *aponíptō* (633), to wash off; *niptḗr* (3537), a washbasin.

Syn.: *loúō* (3068), to wash, bathe. Also, *baptízō* (907), baptize, wash ceremonially; *bréchō* (1026), to wet; *plúnō* (4150), to wash things; *rhantízō* (4472), to sprinkle.

3539. νοιέω, noieō, *noy-eh´-o*; from 3563; to *exercise* the *mind* (*observe*), i.e. (figurative) to *comprehend, heed*:—consider, perceive, think, understand.

From *noús* (3563), the mind. To see with the eyes; to perceive, observe. In the NT, used figuratively: to see with the mind, i.e.:

(I) To perceive, understand, comprehend (Mt 15:17; 16:9, 11; Mk 7:18; 8:17; Jn 12:40; Ro 1:20; Eph 3:4, 20; 1Ti 1:7; Heb 11:3).

(II) To have in mind, think about, consider (Mt 24:15; Mk 13:14; 2Ti 2:7).

Deriv.: *agnoéō* (50), not to understand, not know; *anóētos* (453), foolish, unintelligent; *katanoéō* (2657), to ponder, study; *metanoéō* (3340), to repent, change one's mind; *nóēma* (3540), perception, meaning, thought; *pronoéō* (4306), to provide for; *huponoéō* (5282), to conjecture, think, suppose.

Syn.: *ginṓskō* (1097) to know experientially; *diaginṓskō* (1231), to determine, ascertain exactly, inquire; *dokéō* (1380), to suppose, think; *oída* (1492), to know intuitively or instinctively; *epístamai* (1987), to know; *logízomai* (3049), to reckon, take into account; *punthánomai* (4441), to inquire, understand; *suníēmi* (4920), to understand; *phronéō* (5426), to think.

3540. νόημα, noēma, *no´-ay-mah*; from 3539; a *perception*, i.e. *purpose*, or (by implication) the *intellect, disposition*, itself:—device, mind, thought.

Noun from *noéō* (3539), to perceive. A thought. That which is thought out, planned, devised, in a negative sense (2Co 2:11; 10:5). By metonymy: the mind itself, the understanding (2Co 3:14; 4:4; 11:3; Php 4:7).

Syn.: *dialogismós* (1261), reasoning, thought; *dianóēma* (1270), a thought, machination; *diánoia* (1271), understanding; *enthúmēsis* (1761), an inward reasoning, device, thought; *énnoia* (1771), an inward thought; *epínoia* (1963), a thought; *logismós* (3053), thought, imagination.

3541. νόθος, nothos, *noth´-os*; of uncertain affinity; a *spurious* or *illegitimate* son:—bastard.

3542. νομή, nomē, *nom-ah´*; feminine from the same as 3551; *pasture*, i.e. (the act) *feeding* (figurative, *spreading* of a gangrene), or (the food) *pasturage*:— × eat, pasture.

3543. νομίζω, nomizō, *nom-id´-zo*; from 3551; properly to *do* by *law* (*usage*), i.e. to *accustom* (passive, *be usual*); by extension to *deem* or *regard*:—suppose, think, be wont.

3544. νομικός, nomikos, *nom-ik-os´*; from 3551; *according* (or *pertaining*) *to law*, i.e. *legal* (ceremony); as noun, an *expert in* the (Mosaic) *law*:—about the law, lawyer.

Adjective from *nómos* (3551), law. Pertaining to the law. Generally (Tit 3:9); of persons: one skilled in the law, a lawyer (Tit 3:13). In the Jewish sense: an interpreter and teacher of the Mosaic Law (Mt 22:35; Lk 7:30; 10:25; 11:45, 46, 52; 14:3).

Syn.: *grammateús* (1122), scribe; *nomodidáskalos* (3547), teacher of the law; *nomothétēs* (3550), a lawyer, legislator.

3545. νομίμως, nomimōs, *nom-im´-oce*; adverb from a derivative of 3551; *legitimately* (specially agreeably to the rules of the lists):—lawfully.

3546. νόμισμα, nomisma, *nom´-is-mah*; from 3543; *what is reckoned* as of value (after the Latin *numisma*), i.e. current *coin*:—money.

3547. νομοδιδάσκαλος, nomodidaskalos, *nom-od-id-as´-kal-os*; from 3551 and 1320; an *expounder of* the (Jewish) *law*, i.e. a *Rabbi*:—doctor (teacher) of the law.

3548. νομοθεσία, nomothesia, *nom-oth-es-ee´-ah*; from 3550; *legislation* (specially the *institution of* the Mosaic *code*):—giving of the law.

3549. νομοθετέω, nomotheteō, *nom-oth-et-eh´-o*; from 3550; to *legislate*, i.e. (passive) to *have* (the Mosaic) *enactments* injoined, *be sanctioned* (by them):—establish, receive the law.

3550. νομοθέτης, nomothetēs, *nom-oth-et´-ace*; from 3551 and a derivative of 5087; a *legislator*:—lawgiver.

3551. νόμος, nomos, *nom´-os*; from a primary **νέμω, nemō** (to *parcel* out, especially *food* or *grazing* to animals); *law* (through the idea of prescriptive *usage*), general (*regulation*), special (of Moses [including the volume]; also of the gospel), or figurative (a *principle*):—law.

Noun from *némō* (n.f., see *aponémō* [632]), to divide among, parcel out, allot. Something divided out, allotted; what one has in use and possession; hence, usage, custom. In the NT, law:

(I) Generally, without reference to a particular people or state (Ro 4:15; 5:13; 7:8; 1Ti 1:9).

(II) Specifically, of particular laws, statutes, ordinances, spoken in the NT mostly of the Mosaic statutes:

(A) Spoken of laws relating to civil rights and duties (Jn 7:51; 8:5; Jn 19:7; Ac 23:3; 24:6); spoken of the law of marriage (Ro 7:2, 3; 1Co 7:39); the Levitical priesthood (Heb 7:16); spoken of the ordinance or command respecting the promulgation of the Law (Heb 9:19).

(B) Of laws relating to external religious rites, e.g., purification (Lk 2:22; Heb 9:22); circumcision (Jn 7:23; Ac 15:5; 21:20, 24); sacrifices (Heb 10:8).

(C) Of laws relating to the hearts and conduct of men (Ro 7:7; Heb 8:10; 10:16; Jas 2:8).

(D) By implication for a written law, a law expressly given, i.e. in writing (Ro 2:14).

(III) The Law, i.e. a code or body of laws. In the NT used only of the Mosaic code:

(A) Specifically (Mt 5:18; 22:36; Lk 16:17; Jn 1:17; 7:19; Ac 7:53; Ro 2:13ff.; 5:13; 1Co 15:56; Gal 3:10ff.; 1Ti 1:8; Jas 2:9, 11).

(B) Metaphorically for the Mosaic dispensation (Ro 10:4; Heb 7:12; 10:1).

(C) By metonymy: the Book of the Law, i.e. particularly the books of Moses, the Pentateuch (Mt 12:5; Lk 2:23; 10:26; 1Co 9:8, 9; 14:34). As forming part of the OT, the Law and the prophets (Mt 5:17; Lk 16:16; Jn 1:45; Ac 13:15; 28:23; Ro 3:21); the Law, the prophets, and the Psalms (Lk 24:44); also simply the Law for the OT (Jn 10:34; 12:34; 15:25; 1Co 14:21).

(IV) Metaphorically: the perfect law, meaning the more perfect law for the Christian dispensation, in contrast with that of Moses (Jas 1:25; 2:12; 4:11); of the laws and precepts established by the gospel, e.g., the law of Christ (Ro 13:8, 10; Gal 5:23; 6:2).

(V) Metaphorically, the law, i.e. rule, norm or standard of judging or acting (Ro 3:27; 7:23, 25; 8:2, 7; 9:31). In the sense of a rule of life, discipline (Php 3:5).

Deriv.: *ánomos* (459), without law; *énnomos* (1772), lawful; *nomízō* (3543), to suppose, to think; *nomikós* (3544), lawyer, one learned in the law; *nomodidáskalos* (3547), teacher of the law; *nomothétēs* (3550), a lawgiver.

Syn.: *dógma* (1378), decree, a law; *kanṓn* (2583), rule.

3552. νοσέω, noseō, *nos-eh´-o*; from 3554; to *be sick*, i.e. (by implication of a diseased appetite) to *hanker* after (figurative, to *harp* upon):—dote.

3553. νόσημα, nosēma, *nos´-ah-ma*; from 3552; an *ailment*:—disease.

3554. νόσος, nosos, *nos´-os*; of uncertain affinity; a *malady* (rarely figurative of moral *disability*):—disease, infirmity, sickness.

Noun meaning disease, sickness (Mt 4:23, 24; 9:35; 10:1; Mk 1:34; 3:15; Lk 4:40; 6:17; 7:21; 9:1; Ac 19:12). Figuratively: pain, sorrow, evil (Mt 8:17).

Deriv.: *noséō* (3552), to be sick.

Syn.: *árrōstos* (732), sick or ill, a disease of a more grievous kind; *asthéneia* (769), sickness, weakness; *malakía* (3119), a slighter infirmity.

3555. νοσσιά, nossia, *nos-see-ah´*; from 3502; a *brood* (of chickens):—brood.

3556. νοσσίον, nossion, *nos-see´-on*; diminutive of 3502; a *birdling*:—chicken.

3557. νοσφίζομαι, nosphizomai, *nos-fid´-som-ahee*; middle from **νοσφί, nosphi** (*apart* or *clandestinely*); to *sequestrate* for oneself, i.e. *embezzle*:—keep back, purloin.

From *nósphi* (n.f.), apart, separated. In the NT, only in the middle, to embezzle, keep back something which belongs to another. Spoken of Ananias and Sapphira keeping back part of the sale price of their property while claiming to give all (Ac 5:2, 3); spoken as a prohibition for Christian slaves (Tit 2:10).

Syn.: *aposteréō* (650), to deprive by fraud; *kléptō* (2813), to steal.

3558. νότος, notos, *not´-os*; of uncertain affinity; the *south* (*-west*) *wind*; by extension the *southern quarter* itself:—south (wind).

3559. νουθεσία, nouthesia, *noo-thes-ee´-ah*; from 3563 and a derivative of 5087; calling *attention* to, i.e. (by implication) mild *rebuke* or *warning*:—admonition.

Feminine noun from *noutheteō* (3560), to admonish. A putting in mind, i.e. admonition, warning, exhortation (1Co 10:11; Tit 3:10). Linked with *paideía* (3809), discipline, and training (Eph 6:4). *Nouthesía* refers to instruction by word, while *paideía* refers to the wider area of training a child.

Syn.: *epanórthōsis* (1882), correction.

3560. νουθετέω, noutheteō, *noo-thet-eh´-o*; from the same as 3559; to *put in mind*, i.e. (by implication) to *caution* or *reprove* gently:—admonish, warn.

From *noús* (3563), mind, and *títhēmi* (5087), to place. To put in mind, to put in one's heart; hence to warn, admonish, exhort (Ac 20:31; Ro 15:14; 1Co 4:14; Col 1:28; 3:16; 1Th 5:12, 14; 2Th 3:15). See *nouthesía* (3559), admonition.

Syn.: *epitimáō* (2008), to rebuke; *paideúō* (3811), to correct by discipline; *parainéō* (3867), to admonish, exhort; *sumbouleúō* (4823), to consult jointly, to counsel; *hupodeíknumi* (5263), forewarn; *chrēmatízō* (5537), to be warned, be admonished.

3561. νουμηνία, noumēnia, *noo-may-nee´-ah*; feminine of a compound of 3501 and 3376 (as noun, by implication of 2250); the festival of *new moon*:—new moon.

3562. νουνεχῶς, nounechōs, *noon-ekh-oce´*; adverb from a compound of the accusative of 3563 and 2192; in a *mind-having* way, i.e. *prudently*:—discreetly.

Adverb from *nounechḗs* (n.f.), wise, discreet, which is from *noús* (3563), mind, and *échō* (2192), have. Wisely, discreetly, sensibly, as possessing discernment (Mk 12:34).

Syn.: *sōphrónōs* (4996), with sound mind; *phronímōs* (5430), prudently.

3563. νοῦς, nous, *nooce*; probably from the base of 1097; the *intellect*, i.e. *mind* (divine or human; in thought, feeling, or will); (by implication) *meaning*:—mind, understanding. Compare 5590.

Noun meaning the mind:

(I) As the seat of emotions and affections, mode of thinking and feeling, disposition, moral inclination, equivalent to the heart (Ro 1:28; 12:2; 1Co 1:10; Eph 4:17, 23; Col 2:18; 1Ti 6:5; 2Ti 3:8; Tit 1:15); firmness or presence of mind (2Th 2:2); implying heart, reason, conscience, in opposition to fleshly appetites (Ro 7:23, 25).

(II) Understanding, intellect (Lk 24:45; 1Co 14:14, 15, 19; Php 4:7; Rev 13:18).

(III) Metonymically for what is in the mind, thought, counsel, purpose, opinion, of God or Christ (Ro 11:34; 1Co 2:16); of men (Ro 14:5).

(IV) Metaphorically of things: sense, meaning (Rev 17:9).

Deriv.: *ánoia* (454), madness, folly; *énnoia* (1771), notion, intention; *epínoia* (1963), a thought; *noéō* (3539), to perceive, think; *nouthetéō* (3560), to admonish.

Syn.: *diánoia* (1271), the faculty of the mind, intelligence; *nóēma* (3540), thought, intellect; *súnesis* (4907), understanding; *phrónēma* (5427), state of mind, manner of thinking; *phrónēsis* (5428), insight, prudence.

3564. Νυμφᾶς, Numphas, *noom-fas´*; probably contracted from a compound of 3565 and 1435; *nymph-given* (i.e. *-born*); *Nymphas*, a Christian:—Nymphas.

3565. νύμφη, numphē, *noom-fay´*; from a primary but obsolete verb ***νύπτω, nuptō*** (to *veil* as a bride; compare Latin "*nupto*," to *marry*); a young *married* woman (as *veiled*), including a *betrothed* girl; (by implication) a *son's wife*:—bride, daughter-in-law.

3566. νυμφίος, numphios, *noom-fee´-os*; from 3565; a *bridegroom* (literal or figurative):—bridegroom.

3567. νυμφών, numphōn, *noom-fohn´*; from 3565; the *bridal* room:—bridechamber.

3568. νῦν, nun, *noon*; a primary particle of present time; "*now*" (as adverb of date, a transition or emphasis); also as noun or adjective *present* or *immediate*:—henceforth, + hereafter, of late, soon, present, this (time). See also 3569, 3570.

3569. τανῦν, tanun, *tan-oon´*; or ***τὰ νῦν, ta nun***, *tah noon*; from neuter plural of 3588 and 3568; *the* things *now*, i.e. (adverb) *at present*:—(but) now.

3570. νυνί, nuni, *noo-nee´*; a prolonged form of 3568 for emphasis; *just now*:—now.

3571. νύξ, nux, *noox*; a primary word; "*night*" (literal or figurative):—(mid-) night.

3572. νύσσω, nussō, *noos´-so*; apparently a primary word; to *prick* ("nudge"):—pierce.

3573. νυστάζω, nustazō, *noos-tad´-zo*; from a presumed derivative of 3506; to *nod*, i.e. (by implication) to *fall asleep*; (figurative) to *delay*:—slumber.

3574. νυχθήμερον, nuchthēmeron, *nookh-thay´-mer-on*; from 3571 and 2250; a *day*-and-*night*, i.e. full *day* of twenty-four hours:—night and day.

3575. Νῶε, Nōe, *no´-eh*; of Hebrew origin [5146]; *Noë* (i.e. *Noäch*), a patriarch:—Noe.

3576. νωθρός, nōthros, *no-thros´*; from a derivative of 3541; *sluggish*, i.e. (literal) *lazy*, or (figurative) *stupid*:—dull, slothful.

Adjective meaning slow, sluggish. Used figuratively in the NT, of the mind: dull, stupid (Heb 5:11; 6:12).

Syn.: *argós* (692), idle, lazy; *bradús* (1021), slow, sluggish; *oknērós* (3636), lazy.

3577. νῶτος, nōtos, *no´-tos*; of uncertain affinity; the *back*:—back.

3578. ξενία, xenia, *xen-ee´-ah*; from 3581; *hospitality*, i.e. (by implication) a *place of entertainment*:—lodging.

3579. ξενίζω, xenizō, *xen-id´-xo*; from 3581; to *be a host* (passive a *guest*); (by implication) *be* (*make, appear*) *strange*:—entertain, lodge, (think it) strange.

3580. ξενοδοχέω, xenodocheō, *xen-od-okh-eh´-o*; from a compound of 3581 and 1209; to *be hospitable*:—lodge strangers.

3581. ξένος, xenos, *xen´-os*; apparently a primary word; *foreign* (literal, *alien*, or figurative, *novel*); (by implication) a *guest* or (vice-versa) *entertainer*:—host, strange (-r).

3582. ξέστης, xestēs, *xes´-tace*; as if from ***ξέω, xeō*** (properly to *smooth*; by implication [of *friction*] to *boil* or *heat*); a *vessel* (as *fashioned* or for *cooking*) [or perhaps by corruption from the Latin *sextarius*, the *sixth* of a modius, i.e. about a *pint*], i.e. (special) a *measure* for liquids or solids (by analogy, a *pitcher*):—pot.

3583. ξηραίνω, xērainō, *xay-rah´ee-no*; from 3584; to *desiccate*; (by implication) to *shrivel*, to *mature*:—dry up, pine away, be ripe, wither (away).

3584. ξηρός, xēros, *xay-ros´*; from the base of 3582 (through the idea of *scorching*); *arid*; (by implication) *shrunken*, *earth* (as opposed to water):—dry, land, withered.

3585. ξύλινος, xulinos, *xoo´-lin-os*; from 3586; *wooden*:—of wood.

3586. ξύλον, xulon, *xoo´-lon*; from another form of the base of 3582; *timber* (as fuel or material); (by implication) a *stick, club* or *tree* or other wooden article or substance:—staff, stocks, tree, wood.

3587. ξυράω, xuraō, *xoo-rah´-o*; from a derivative of the same as 3586 (meaning a *razor*); to *shave* or "*shear*" the hair:—shave.

3588. ὁ, ho, *ho*; including the feminine **ἡ**, ***hē***, *hay*; and the neuter **τό**, *to*, *to*; in all their inflections; the definite article; *the* (sometimes to be supplied, at others omitted, in English idiom):—the, this, that, one, he, she, it, etc.

3589. ὀγδοήκοντα, ogdoēkonta, *og-do-ay´-kon-tah*; from 3590; *ten times eight*:—fourscore.

3590. ὄγδοος, ogdoos, *og´-do-os*; from 3638; the *eighth*:—eighth.

3591. ὄγκος, ogkos, *ong´-kos*; probably from the same as 43; a *mass* (as *bending* or *bulging* by its load), i.e. *burden* (*hindrance*):—weight.

3592. ὅδε, hode, *hod´-eh*; including the feminine **ἥδε**, ***hēde***, *hay´-deh*; and the neuter **τόδε**, ***tode***, *tod´-e*; from 3588 and 1161; the *same*, i.e. *this* or *that* one (plural *these* or *those*); often used as personal pronoun:—he, she, such, these, thus.

3593. ὁδεύω, hodeuō, *hod-yoo´-o*; from 3598; to *travel*:—journey.

3594. ὁδηγέω, hodēgeō, *hod-ayg-eh´-o*; from 3595; to *show* the *way* (literal or figurative [*teach*]):—guide, lead.

3595. ὁδηγός, hodēgos, *hod-ayg-os´*; from 3598 and 2233; a *conductor* (literal or figurative [*teacher*]):—guide, leader.

3596. ὁδοιπορέω, hodoiporeō, *hod-oy-por-eh´-o*; from a compound of 3598 and 4198; to *be a wayfarer*, i.e. *travel*:—go on a journey.

3597. ὁδοιπορία, hodoiporia, *hod-oy-por-ee´-ah*; from the same as 3596; *travel*:—journey (-ing).

3598. ὁδός, hodos, *hod-os´*; apparently a primary word; a *road*; (by implication) a *progress* (the route, act or distance); (figurative) a *mode* or *means*:—journey, (high-) way.

(I) In respect to place: a way, highway, road, street:

(A) Used generally (Mt 2:12; 8:28; Mk 2:23; Lk 10:4; Ac 8:26, 36; 25:3; Jas 2:25). Spoken of a pathway between fields (Mt 13:4, 19; Mk 4:4, 15; spoken of a street in a city (Mt 22:9, 10; Lk 14:23). Metonymically for the whole region through which the way leads (Mt 4:15; 10:5).

(B) Figuratively: the way of access, e.g., into the direct presence of God (Heb 9:8).

(C) Figuratively: the way in front of one. Spoken of as the way for a monarch, which is prepared and straightened by envoys beforehand to fill in holes and smooth over rough places, as described in Isa 40:3 (Mt 3:3; 11:10; Mk 1:2, 3; Jn 1:23). Also Rev 16:12.

(D) Spoken by metonymy of Jesus as the way, i.e. the author and medium of access to God and eternal life (Jn 14:6).

(II) In action: a going, journey, progress, course.

(A) Generally: (Mt 15:32; Mk 2:23; 8:3, 27; Lk 9:3; 11:6; Ac 8:39; 9:17, 27; 25:3; 26:13; 1Th 3:11).

(B) Following expressions of time, e.g., a day's journey, the distance covered in one day (Lk 2:44); a Sabbath day's journey, the distance permitted by Rabbinical interpreters, a little less than a mile (Ac 1:12).

(III) Figuratively, a way of life and conduct, a lifestyle:

(A) Spoken of in terms of the people following them; e.g., the way of Baalam (2Pe 2:15). Also Ac 14:16; Ro 3:16, 17; 1Co 4:17; Jas 1:8; 5:20; Jude 1:11).

(B) Spoken of in terms of their characteristics or goals (Mt 21:32; Lk 1:79; Ac 2:28; 16:17; 2Pe 2:2, 21).

(C) The way of God, the way of the Lord, i.e. the way which he approves (Mt 22:16; Lk 20:21; Ac 18:25, 26). Also Mt 21:32; Ac 13:10; Ro 11:33; Heb 3:10; Rev 15:3.

(D) Hence used in an absolute sense for the Christian way, the Christian religion (Ac 9:2; 19:9, 23; 22:4; 24:14, 22).

Deriv.: *ámphodon* (296), place where two roads meet; *eísodos* (1529), entrance, access; *éxodos* (1841), way out, exodus, an exit; *hodeúō* (3593), to travel, journey; *hodēgós* (3595), guide, leader; *párodos* (3938), a passing or passage; *sunodía* (4923), a caravan.

Syn.: *drómos* (1408), a race, running, career, course; *tríbos* (5147), a worn path; *trochiá* (5163), a track of a wheel, used idiomatically of keeping on the straight path.

3599. ὀδούς, odous, *od-ooce*; perhaps from the base of 2068; a "*tooth*":—tooth.

3600. ὀδυνάω, odunaō, *od-oo-nah´-o*; from 3601; to *grieve*:—sorrow, torment.

3601. ὀδύνη, odunē, *od-oo´-nay*; from 1416; *grief* (as *dejecting*):—sorrow.

3602. ὀδυρμός, odurmos, *od-oor-mos´*; from a derivative of the base of 1416; *moaning*, i.e. *lamentation*:—mourning.

3603. ὅ ἐστι, ho esti, *ho es-tee´*; from the neuter of 3739 and the third person singular presumed indicative of 1510; *which is*:—called, which is (make), that is (to say).

3604. Ὀζίας, Ozias, *od-zee´-as*; of Hebrew origin [5818]; *Ozias* (i.e. *Uzzijah*), an Israelite:—Ozias.

3605. ὄζω, ozō, *od´-zo*; a primary verb (in a strengthened form); to *scent* (usually an ill "odour"):—stink.

3606. ὅθεν, hothen, *hoth´-en*; from 3739 with the directive enclitic of source; *from which* place or source or cause (adverb or conjecture):—from thence, (from) whence, where (-by, -fore, -upon).

3607. ὀθόνη, othonē, *oth-on´-ay*; of uncertain affinity; a *linen* cloth, i.e. (especially) a *sail*:—sheet.

3608. ὀθόνιον, othonion, *oth-on´-ee-on*; neuter of a presumed derivative of 3607; a linen *bandage*:—linen clothes.

3609. οἰκεῖος, oikeios, *oy-ki´-os*; from 3624; *domestic*, i.e. (as noun), a *relative, adherent*:—(those) of the (his own) house (-hold).

Adjective from *oíkos* (3624), a house or household. Belonging to the household. In the NT, only in the plural: belonging to a certain household (1Ti 5:8). Used figuratively in the NT for associates, kindred of God, children of God (Gal 6:10; Eph 2:19). See *oikétēs* (3610), a household servant.

Syn.: *oikiakós* (3615), belonging to one's household; *suggenḗs* (4773), a relative.

3610. οἰκέτης, oiketēs, *oy-ket´-ace*; from 3611; a fellow *resident*, i.e. menial *domestic*:—(household) servant.

Noun from *oíkos* (3624), house. A domestic servant (Lk 16:13; Ac 10:7; Ro 14:4; 1Pe 2:18).

Syn.: *diákonos* (1249), a servant, minister, deacon; *doúlos* (1401), slave; *therápōn* (2324), attendant; *místhios* (3407), hired servant; *misthōtós* (3411), hired servant; *país* (3816), an attendant, boy, one acting as a servant; *hupērétēs* (5257), an officer, a servant.

3611. οἰκέω, oikeō, *oy-key´-o*; from 3624; to *occupy a house*, i.e. *reside* (figurative, *inhabit, remain, inhere*); (by implication) to *cohabit*:—dwell. See also 3625.

From *oíkos* (3624), a dwelling. To reside, dwell, abide:

(I) To dwell in: spoken figuratively of the Holy Spirit abiding in Christians (Ro 8:9, 11; 1Co 3:16); spoken figuratively also of sin or a sinful propensity abiding in men (Ro 7:17, 18, 20); spoken of God dwelling in unapproachable light (1Ti 6:16).

(II) To dwell with someone, and as spoken of man and wife, to live together, cohabit (1Co 7:12, 13; Sept.: Pr 21:19 [cf. 1Ki 3:17]).

Deriv.: *enoikéō* (1774), to dwell in; *katoikéō* (2730), to settle down in a dwelling; *oíkēma* (3612), a room, a prison cell; *oikḗterion* (3613), habitation; *oikouménē* (3625), the inhabited world; *paroikéō* (3939), to sojourn, dwell temporarily; *perioikéō* (4039), to dwell around, as a neighbour; *sunoikéō* (4924), to dwell with.

Syn.: *kataskēnóō* (2681), to lodge; *ménō* (3306), to abide, remain; *skēnóō* (4637), to dwell as if in a tent.

3612. οἴκημα, oikēma, *oy´-kay-mah*; from 3611; a *tenement*, i.e. (special) a *jail*:—prison.

Noun from *oikéō* (3611), to dwell. A house, dwelling. In the NT, and polite Attic Greek usage: a prison (Ac 12:7).

3613. οἰκητήριον, oikētērion, *oy-kay-tay´-ree-on*; neuter of a presumed derivative of 3611 (equivalent to 3612); a *residence* (literal or figurative):—habitation, house.

3614. οἰκία, oikia, *oy-kee´-ah*; from 3624; properly *residence* (abstract), but usually (concrete) an *abode* (literal or figurative); (by implication) a *family* (especially *domestics*):—home, house (-hold).

Noun from *oíkos* (3624), a house. A building, house, dwelling:

(I) In the NT *oikía* is used for an actual house (Mt 2:11; 26:6; Mk 1:29; 14:3; Lk 4:38; 10:5, 7; 22:10, 11; Jn 11:31; 12:3; Ac 4:34; 18:7; 1Co 11:22; 1Ti 5:13; 2Ti 2:20; 3:6; 2Jn 10). Figuratively: spoken of heaven as the dwelling of God (Jn 14:2); spoken of the body as the habitation of the soul (2Co 5:1).

(II) Figuratively: a family, household (Mt 10:13; 12:25; Mk 6:4; 13:35; Jn 4:53; 1Co 16:15). In Mk 10:29 *oikía* may refer to the whole family.

(III) By metonymy: possessions, one's belongings (Mt 23:14; Mk 12:40; Lk 20:47).

Deriv.: *oikiakós* (3615), a relative, pertaining to one's family or household.

3615. οἰκιακός, oikiakos, *oy-kee-ak-os´*; from 3614; *familiar,* i.e. (as noun) *relatives*:—they (them) of (his own) household.

3616. οἰκοδεσποτέω, oikodespoteō, *oy-kod-es-pot-eh´-o*; from 3617; to *be* the *head of* (i.e. *rule*) *a family*:—guide the house.

3617. οἰκοδεσπότης, oikodespotēs, *oy-kod-es-pot´-ace*; from 3624 and 1203; *the head of a family*:—goodman (of the house), householder, master of the house.

Noun from *oíkos* (3624), a house and *despótēs* (1203), a lord, master. The master of the house, head of a family (Mt 10:25; 24:43; Mk 14:14; Lk 12:39; 13:25; 14:21; 22:11); also a landowner (Mt 13:27; 20:1, 11; 21:33).

Deriv.: *oikodespotéō* (3616), to be head of the house or family.

Syn.: *despótēs* (1203), absolute owner, master; *kúrios* (2962), God, Lord, master.

3618. οἰκοδομέω, oikodomeō, *oy-kod-om-eh´-o*; from the same as 3619; to *be* a *house-builder,* i.e. *construct* or (figurative) *confirm*:—(be in) build (-er, -ing, up), edify, embolden.

From *oikodómos* (n.f.), builder. To build, construct, erect:

(I) Particularly, to build: e.g., a house (Mt 7:24, 26; Lk 6:48, 49); a tower (Mt 21:33; Mk 12:1; Lk 14:28); a temple (Mk 14:58; Jn 2:20); a barn (Lk 12:18); a synagogue (Lk 7:5). See also Lk 14:30; 17:28; Ac 7:47, 49. The plural participle: builders (Mt 21:42; Mk 12:10; Lk 20:17; Ac 4:11; 1Pe 2:7). Spoken figuratively, to build: of a system of instruction or doctrine (Ro 15:20; Gal 2:18).

(II) By implication: to rebuild or renew a building decayed or destroyed such as the sepulchres of the prophets (Mt 23:29; Lk 11:47, 48). See also Mt 26:61; 27:40; Mk 15:29.

(III) Figuratively: to build up, establish, confirm. Spoken of the Christian Church and its members who are thus compared to a building, a temple of God, erected upon the one and only foundation, Jesus Christ (cf. 1Co 3:9, 10) and ever built up progressively and unceasingly more and more from the foundation:

(A) Externally (Mt 16:18; Ac 9:31; 1Pe 2:5).

(B) Internally, in a good sense: to build up in the faith, to edify, to cause to advance in the divine light (1Co 8:1; 10:23; 14:4, 17; 1Th 5:11). In a bad sense: to embolden (1Co 8:10).

Deriv.: *anoikodoméō* (456), to build again; *epoikodoméō* (2026), to build upon; *sunoikodoméō* (4925), to build together.

Syn.: *kataskeuázō* (2680), to prepare, establish, build; *ktízō* (2936), to create, make.

3619. οἰκοδομή, oikodomē, *oy-kod-om-ay´*; feminine (abstract) of a compound of 3624 and the base of 1430; *architecture,* i.e. (concrete) a *structure*; (figurative) *confirmation*:—building, edify (-ication, -ing).

Noun from *oikódomos,* (n.f.), builder, which is from *oíkos* (3624), house, and *duméō,* to build.

(I) A building up; the act of building. In the NT, only metaphorically: a building up in the faith, edification, advancement in the divine life, spoken of the Christian church and its members (Ro 14:19; 15:2; 1Co 14:5, 12, 26; 2Co 10:8; 12:19; Eph 4:12, 16, 29).

(II) A building, an edifice (Mt 24:1; Mk 13:1, 2). Figuratively, of the Christian church as the temple of God (1Co 3:9; Eph 2:21). Spoken of the future spiritual body as the abode of the soul (2Co 5:1).

Syn.: *endṓmēsis* (1739), a thing built, structure; *ktísis* (2937), a creation.

3620. οἰκοδομία, oikodomia, *oy-kod-om-ee´-ah*; from the same as 3619; *confirmation*:—edifying.

3621. οἰκονομέω, oikonomeō, *oy-kon-om-eh´-o*; from 3623; to *manage* (a house, i.e. an estate):—be steward.

3622. οἰκονομία, oikonomia, *oy-kon-om-ee´-ah*; from 3623; *administration* (of a household or estate); specially a (religious) "*economy*":—dispensation, stewardship.

Noun from *oikonoméō* (3621), to be a manager of a household. Management of a household or of household affairs. Particularly: stewardship, administration (Lk 16:2); figuratively: of the apostolic office (1Co 9:17; Eph 1:10; 3:2; Col 1:25). Also, an economy, i.e. a disposition or arrangement of things, a dispensation, scheme (Eph 1: 10).

3623. οἰκονόμος, oikonomos, *oy-kon-om´-os*; from 3624 and the base of 3551; a *house-distributor* (i.e. *manager*), or *overseer,* i.e. an employee in that capacity; by extension a fiscal *agent* (*treasurer*); (figurative) a *preacher* (of the gospel):—chamberlain, governor, steward.

Noun from *oíkos* (3624), house, and *némō* (n.f., see *aponémō* [632]), to deal out, distribute, apportion. An administrator, a house manager, overseer, steward:

(I) Particularly: one who has authority over the servants or slaves of a family to assign their tasks and portions. Along with this was the general management of affairs and accounts (Lk 12:42; 1Co 4:2). Such persons were themselves usually slaves (cf. Eliezer [Ge 15:2] and Joseph [Ge 39:4]). However, free persons appear also to have been thus employed (Lk 16:1, 3, 8; cf. also below in II). The *oikonómoi* also had some charge over the sons of a family, probably in respect to monetary matters, thus differing from the *epítropoi* (2012), guardians or tutors (Gal 4:2 [cf. Ge 24:3]).

(II) In a wider sense: one who administers a public charge or office, a steward, minister, agent; of the fiscal officer of a city or state, treasurer (Ro 16:23). Metaphorically of the apostles and other teachers as stewards or ministers of the gospel (1Co 4:1; Tit 1:7; 1Pe 4:10).

Deriv.: *oikonoméō* (3621), to be a manager of a household.

Syn.: *epítropos* (2012), guardian.

3624. οἶκος, oikos, *oy´-kos*; of uncertain affinity; a *dwelling* (more or less extensive, literal or figurative); (by implication), a *family* (more or less related, literal or figurative):—home, house (-hold), temple.

Noun meaning house, dwelling, home:

(I) Generally (Mt 9:6, 7; Mk 5:19; Lk 1:40; Jn 7:53; Ac 2:46; 5:42; 8:3; 10:22; 20:20; Ro 16:5). With the preposition *en* ([1722] in), *en oíkō,* at home (1Co 11:34; 14:35). Spoken of various kinds of houses or edifices, such as the house of the king, a palace (Mt 11:8). A house of commerce, meaning a bazaar (Jn 2:16). Specifically, house of God, meaning the tabernacle or temple where the presence of God was manifested and where God was said to dwell, e.g., the tabernacle (Mt 12:4; Mk 2:26; Lk 6:4); the temple at Jerusalem (Mt 21:13; Jn 2:16, 17; Ac 7:47, 49); the *ho naós,* sanctuary (Lk 11:51). Figuratively: of Christians as the spiritual house or temple of God (1Pe 2:5); conversely, of one in whom evil spirits dwell (Mt 12:44; Lk 11:24).

(II) By metonymy: a household, family, those who live together in a house (Lk 10:5; Ac 10:2; 11:14; 16:15; 1Co 1:16; 2Ti 1:16; Tit 1:11). Including the idea of household affairs (Ac 7:10; 1Ti 3:4, 5, 12). Metaphorically: *oíkos tou Theoú,* the household of God, i.e. the Christian Church, Christians (1Ti 3:15; Heb 3:6; 10:21; 1Pe 4:17); the Jewish assembly (Heb 3:2, 5).

(III) In a collective sense: the houses and inhabitants of a city or country (Mt 23:38; Lk 13:35).

(IV) By metonymy: family, lineage, posterity, descended from one head or ancestor; e.g., the house of David (Lk 1:27, 69; 2:4). A whole people or nation as descended from one ancestor such as the house or people of Israel (Mt 10:6; 15:24); the house of Jacob (Lk 1:33); the house of Judah (Heb 8:8).

Deriv.: *oikeíos* (3609), of one's own household; *oikétēs* (3610), a fellow resident, a domestic servant; *oikéō* (3611), to reside; *oikía* (3614), a house; *oikodespótēs* (3617), the master of the house; *oikonómos* (3623), steward, manager; *oikourós* (3626), one who stays at home and takes care of it; *panoikí* (3832), with all the house; *pároikos* (3941), a sojourning; *períoikos* (4040), someone living near, a neighbour.

Syn.: *skēnḗ* (4633), a tabernacle, tent, temporary dwelling place; *skḗnos* (4636), used of the body as a tabernacle of the soul; *skḗnōma* (4638), a temporary habitation.

3625. οἰκουμένη, oikoumenē, *oy-kou-men´-ay*; feminine participle presumed passive of 3611 (as noun, by implication of 1093); *land,* i.e. the (terrene part of the) *globe*; specially the Roman *empire*:—earth, world.

Noun from *oikéō* (3611), to dwell, abide. The inhabited earth, the world:

(I) Particularly as inhabited by the Greeks, and later by the Greeks and Romans; hence spoken of the Roman empire (Ac 17:6; 24:5), of Palestine and the adjacent countries (Lk 2:1; 21:26; Ac 11:28).

(II) Generally, in later usage: the habitable globe, the earth, the world (Mt 24:14; Ro 10:18; Heb 1:6; Rev 16:14). Metaphorically: the world, for the inhabitants of the earth, mankind (Ac 17:31; 19:27; Rev 3:10; 12:9). Figuratively with *mello* (3195), about to be: the world to come (Heb 2:5).

3626. οἰκουρός, oikouros, *oy-koo-ros´*; from 3624 and **οὖρος, *ouros*** (a *guard*; be "ware"); a *stayer at home*, i.e. *domestically inclined* (a "good housekeeper"):—keeper at home.

Adjective from *oíkos* (3624), house, and *ourós* (n.f.), a keeper. In the NT, keeping the house, i.e. one who keeps at home, domestic. Used only in Tit 2:5.

3627. οἰκτείρω, oikteirō, *oyk-ti´-ro*; also (in certain tenses) prolonged **οἰκτερέω, *oiktereō***, *oyk-ter-eh´-o*; from **οἶκτος, *oiktos*** (*pity*); to *exercise pity*:—have compassion on.

3628. οἰκτιρμός, oiktirmos, *oyk-tir-mos´*; from 3627; *pity*:—mercy.

3629. οἰκτίρμων, oiktirmōn, *oyk-tir´-mone*; from 3627; *compassionate*:—merciful, of tender mercy.

3630. οἰνοπότης, oinopotēs, *oy-nop-ot´-ace*; from 3631 and a derivative of the alternate of 4095; a *tippler*:—winebibber.

3631. οἶνος, oinos, *oy´-nos*; a primary word (or perhaps of Hebrew origin [3196]); "*wine*" (literal or figurative):—wine.

Noun meaning wine:

(I) Particularly as *oínos néos*, new wine (Mt 9:17; Mk 2:22; Lk 5:37, 38). Also Mk 15:23; Lk 1:15; 10:34; Jn 2:3; 4:46; Ro 14:21; Eph 5:18; 1Ti 3:8; Tit 2:3; Rev 6:6; 18:13.

(II) Figuratively: "the wine of the wrath of God"—the intoxicating cup which God in wrath presents to the nations, and which causes them to reel and stagger to their destruction (Rev 14:10; 16:19; 19:15). Also figuratively: "the wine of wrath of fornication," i.e. a love potion, with which a harlot seduces to fornication (idolatry), and thus brings upon men the wrath of God (Rev 14:8; 18:3; also elliptically in Rev 17:2).

Deriv.: *oinopótēs* (3630), a drinker of wine; *pároinos* (3943), a heavy drinker.

Syn.: *gleúkos* (1098), sweet new wine; *síkera* (4608), strong drink.

3632. οἰνοφλυγία, oinophlugia, *oy-nof-loog-ee´-ah*; from 3631 and a form of the base of 5397; an *overflow* (or surplus) of *wine*, i.e. *vinolency* (*drunkenness*):—excess of wine.

3633. οἴομαι, oiomai, *oy´-om-ahee*; or (shorter) **οἶμαι, *oimai***, *oy´-mahee*; middle apparently from 3634; to *make like* (oneself), i.e. *imagine* (*be of* the *opinion*):—suppose, think.

3634. οἷος, oios, *hoy´-os*; probably akin to 3588, 3739 and 3745; *such* or *what sort* of (as a correlation or exclamation); especially the neuter (adverb) with negative not *so*:—so (as), such as, what (manner of), which.

3635. ὀκνέω, okneō, *ok-neh´-o*; from **ὄκνος, *oknos*** (*hesitation*); to *be slow* (figurative, *loath*):—delay.

3636. ὀκνηρός, oknēros, *ok-nay-ros´*; from 3635; *tardy*, i.e. *indolent*; (figurative) *irksome*:—grievous, slothful.

3637. ὀκταήμερος, oktaēmeros, *ok-tah-ay´-mer-os*; from 3638 and 2250; an *eight-day* old person or act:—the eighth day.

3638. ὀκτώ, oktō, *ok-to´*; a primary numeral; "*eight*":—eight.

3639. ὄλεθρος, olethros, *ol´-eth-ros*; from a primary **ὄλλυμι, *ollumi*** (to *destroy*; a prolonged form); *ruin*, i.e. *death, punishment*:—destruction.

Noun from *óllumi* (n.f.), to destroy, kill. Destruction, ruin, death. Spoken of permanent divine punishment (1Th 5:3; 2Th 1:9; 1Ti 6:9); spoken of a temporal destruction of the flesh, leading to restoration and salvation of the soul (1Co 5:5). Some believe *ólethros* here refers to the conquest of fleshly appetites and rebellion against God (cf. 2Co 2:5–11), while others believe that it refers to bodily harm or sickness (cf. Ac 13:9–11).

Deriv.: *olothreúō* (3645), to destroy.

Syn.: *apṓleia* (684), damnation, destruction; *diaphthorá* (1312), corruption, destruction; *phthorá* (5356), corruption.

3640. ὀλιγόπιστος, oligopistos, *ol-ig-op´-is-tos*; from 3641 and 4102; *incredulous*, i.e. *lacking confidence* (in Christ):—of little faith.

Adjective from *olígos* (3641), little, and *pistis* (4102), faith. Of little faith; spoken only by the Lord to believers as a gentle rebuke for anxiety (Mt 6:30; 8:26; 14:31; 16:8; Lk 12:28).

3641. ὀλίγος, oligos, *ol-ee´-gos*; of uncertain affinity; *puny* (in extent, degree, number, duration or value); especially neuter (adverb) *somewhat*:— + almost, brief [-ly], few, (a) little, + long, a season, short, small, a while.

3642. ὀλιγόψυχος, oligopsuchos, *ol-ig-op´-soo-khos*; from 3641 and 5590; *little-spirited*, i.e. *faint-hearted*:—feebleminded.

Adjective from *olígos* (3641), small or little, and *psuchḗ* (5590), soul, mind. Low-spirited, fainthearted, discouraged. Used only in 1Th 5:14.

Syn.: *deilós* (1169), timid, fearful; *ékphobos* (1630), terrified; *éntromos* (1790), terror-stricken.

3643. ὀλιγωρέω, oligōreō, *ol-ig-o-reh´-o*; from a compound of 3641 and **ὥρα, *ōra*** ("*care*"); to *have little regard* for, i.e. to *disesteem*:—despise.

3644. ὀλοθρευτής, olothreutēs, *ol-oth-ryoo-tace´*; from 3645; a *ruiner*, i.e. (special) a venomous *serpent*:—destroyer.

3645. ὀλοθρεύω, olothreuō, *ol-oth-ryoo´-o*; from 3639; to *spoil*, i.e. *slay*:—destroy.

3646. ὁλοκαύτωμα, holokautōma, *hol-ok-ow´-to-mah*; from a derivative of a compound of 3650 and a derivative of 2545; a *wholly-consumed* sacrifice ("holocaust"):—(whole) burnt offering.

3647. ὁλοκληρία, holoklēria, *hol-ok-lay-ree´-ah*; from 3648; *integrity*, i.e. physical *wholeness*:—perfect soundness.

3648. ὁλόκληρος, holoklēros, *hol-ok´-lay-ros*; from 3650 and 2819; *complete* in every *part*, i.e. perfectly *sound* (in body):—entire, whole.

Adjective from *hólos* (3650), all, the whole, and *klḗros* (2819), a part, share. Whole in every part, i.e. generally: whole, entire, perfect (1Th 5:23). Figuratively, whole, complete, in a moral sense (Jas 1:4).

Deriv.: *holoklēría* (3647), soundness.

Syn.: *hólos* (3650), whole, complete; *holotelḗs* (3651), complete in every respect; *pantelḗs* (3838), entire, complete.

3649. ὀλολύζω, ololuzō, *ol-ol-ood´-zo*; a reduplicated primary verb; to "*howl*" or "*halloo*," i.e. *shriek*:—howl.

3650. ὅλος, holos, *hol´-os*; a primary word; "*whole*" or "*all*," i.e. *complete* (in extent, amount, time or degree), especially (neuter) as noun or adverb:—all, altogether, every whit, + throughout, whole.

Adjective meaning whole, the whole, all, including every part, e.g., of space, extent, amount (Mt 4:23; 5:29; 16:26; 22:40; Mk 1:33; Lk 1:65; 13:21; Jn 4:53; 19:23; 1Co 5:6). Used of time (Mt 20:6; Lk 5:5; Ac 11:26; 28:30); used of an affection, emotion, condition, e.g., with your whole heart (Mt 22:37; Lk 10:27). Also Jn 9:34; 13:10.

Deriv.: *kathólou* (2527), wholly, entirely; *holóklēros* (3648), entire; *holotelḗs* (3651), wholly, through and through; *hólōs* (3654), at all.

Syn.: *hápas* (537), the whole; *pás* (3956), all; *plḗrōma* (4138), fullness.

3651. ὁλοτελής, holotelēs, *hol-ot-el-ace´*; from 3650 and 5056; *complete* to the *end*, i.e. *absolutely perfect*:—wholly.

Adjective from *hólos* (3650), all, the whole, and *télos* (5056), completion. All or the whole, completely or entirely. Used only in 1Th 5:23.

Syn.: *ártios* (739), complete, perfect; *holóklēros* (3648), whole; *pantelḗs* (3838), entire; *plḗrēs* (4134), full; *téleios* (5046), perfect.

3652. Ὀλυμπᾶς, Olumpas, *ol-oom-pas´*; probably a contracted from **Ὀλυμπιόδωρος, *Olumpiodōros*** (*Olympian-bestowed*, i.e. *heaven-descended*); *Olympas*, a Christian:—Olympas.

3653. ὄλυνθος, olunthos, *ol´-oon-thos*; of uncertain derivative; an *unripe* (because out of season) *fig*:—untimely (figurative).

3654. ὅλως, holōs, *hol´-oce*; adverb from 3650; *completely*, i.e. *altogether*; (by analogy) *everywhere*; (negative) not *by any means*:—at all, commonly, utterly.

3655. ὄμβρος, ombros, *om´-bros*; of uncertain affinity; a thunder *storm*:—shower.

3656. ὁμιλέω, homileō, *hom-il-eh´-o*; from 3658; to *be in company* with, i.e. (by implication) to *converse*:—commune, talk.

3657. ὁμιλία, homilia, *hom-il-ee´-ah*; from 3658; *companionship* ("homily"), i.e. (by implication) *intercourse*:—communication.

3658. ὅμιλος, homilos, *hom´-il-os*; from the base of 3674 and a derivative of the alternate of 138 (meaning a *crowd*); *association together*, i.e. a *multitude*:—company.

3659. ὄμμα, omma, *om´-mah*; from 3700; a *sight*, i.e. (by implication) the *eye*:—eye.

3660. ὀμνύω, omnuō, *om-noo´-o*; a prolonged form of a primary but obsolete **ὄμω, *omō***, for which another prolonged form (**ὀμόω, *omoō***, *om-o´-o*) is used in certain tenses; to *swear*, i.e. *take* (or *declare on*) *oath*:—swear.

3661. ὁμοθυμαδόν, homothumadon, *hom-oth-oo-mad-on´*; adverb from a compound of the base of 3674 and 2372; *unanimously*:—with one accord (mind).

3662. ὁμοιάζω, homoiazō, *hom-oy-ad´-zo*; from 3664; to *resemble*:—agree.

3663. ὁμοιοπαθής, homoiopathēs, *hom-oy-op-ath-ace´*; from 3664 and the alternate of 3958; *similarly affected*:—of (subject to) like passions.

3664. ὅμοιος, homoios, *hom´-oy-os*; from the base of 3674; *similar* (in appearance or character):—like, + manner.

Adjective from *homós* (n.f., see *homologeō* [3670]), one and the same. Like, similar:

(I) Generally, similar in external form and appearance (Jn 9:9; Rev 1:13, 15; 9:7, 10, 19; 13:2, 11; 14:14; 21:11, 18); in kind or nature (Ac 17:29; Gal 5:21); in conduct, character (Mt 11:16; 13:52; Lk 7:31, 32; 12:36; 1Jn 3:2); in conditions, circumstances (Mt 13:31, 33, 44, 45, 47; 20:1; Lk 6:47–49; 13:18, 19, 21; Rev 18:18).

(II) Just like, equal, the same with: in kind or nature (Jude 7); in conduct, character (Jn 8:55); in authority, dignity, power (Mt 22:39; Mk 12:31; Rev 13:4).

Deriv.: *homoiázō* (3662), to resemble; *homoiopathḗs* (3663), similarly affected, affected in a like fashion; *homoiótēs* (3665), similarity; *homoióō* (3666), to make like; *homoíōs* (3668), in a similar way, likewise; *parómoios* (3946), similar, much like.

Syn.: *ísos* (2470), equal; *hoíos* (3634), such as; *hopoíos* (3697), what manner; *toiósde* (5107), such, like; *toioútos* (5108), such, of this kind.

3665. ὁμοιότης, homoiotēs, *hom-oy-ot´ace*; from 3664; *resemblance*:—like as, similitude.

3666. ὁμοιόω, homoioō, *hom-oy-o´-o*; from 3664; to *assimilate*, i.e. *compare*; passive to *become similar*:—be (make) like, (in the) liken (-ess), resemble.

3667. ὁμοίωμα, homoiōma, *hom-oy´-o-mah*; from 3666; a *form*; abstract *resemblance*:—made like to, likeness, shape, similitude.

Noun from *homoióō* (3666), to make like. Something made like, a likeness:

(I) Generally: likeness, resemblance, similarity, made in the same way (Ro 1:23; 5:14; 6:5; 8:3; Rev 9:7).

(II) Particularly: in Php 2:7 *homoiōma* describes more than a mere similarity or resemblance. Jesus became a man. Perhaps *homoiōma* is used here to stress the fact that His humanity did differ from ours in the sense that Jesus' humanity was a sinless one, as was the human nature of Adam and Eve before the Fall (cf. Ro 8:3; Heb 4:15).

Syn.: *morphḗ* (3444), form, nature. Also *schḗma* (4976), form, fashion; *homoiótēs* (3665), similarity but not identical substance, hence, in Jesus, a similar human nature but without participation in man's sinfulness; *homoíōsis* (3669), the action of making alike, similitude, likeness.

3668. ὁμοίως, homoiōs, *hom-oy´-oce*; adverb from 3664; *similarly*:—likewise, so.

Adverb from *hómoios* (3664), like, resembling. In like manner, likewise, in the same way (Mt 22:26; 26:35; 27:41; Mk 4:16; 15:31; Lk 3:11; 5:10, 33; 6:31; 10:32, 37; 13:5; 16:25; 17:28, 31; 22:36; Jn 5:19; 6:11; 21:13; Ro 1:27; 1Co 7:3, 4, 22; Heb 9:21; Jas 2:25; 1Pe 3:1, 7; 5:5; Jude 8; Rev 8:12).

Syn.: *paraplēsíōs* (3898), similarly; *hōsaútōs* (5615), thus, in the same way.

3669. ὁμοίωσις, homoiōsis, *hom-oy´-o-sis*; from 3666; *assimilation*, i.e. *resemblance*:—similitude.

Noun from *homoióō* (3666), to make like. A likening, comparison. In the NT: likeness, resemblance. Only in Jas 3:9, in allusion to Ge 1:26.

Syn.: *antítupon* (499), an antitype, something that is stamped out as a true likeness; *eikṓn* (1504), a physical representation, image; *homoiótēs* (3665), likeness, similitude; *homoíōma* (3667), the likeness of something, a resemblance.

3670. ὁμολογέω, homologeō, *hom-ol-og-eh´-o*; from a compound of the base of 3674 and 3056; to *assent*, i.e. *covenant*, *acknowledge*:—con- (pro-) fess, confession is made, give thanks, promise.

From *homólogos* (n.f.), assenting, which is from *homoú* (3674), together with, and *lógos* (3056), word. To speak or say the same with another, e.g., to say the same things, i.e. to assent, accord, to agree with:

(I) To concede, admit, confess (Ac 24:14); of sins (1Jn 1:9). Hence, to confess publicly, acknowledge openly, profess (Mt 7:23; Jn 9:22; 12:42; Ac 23:8; Ro 10:9, 10; Heb 11:13). Followed by *en* ([1722], in), to confess Christ personally, meaning to profess or acknowledge Him (Mt 10:32; Lk 12:8). Followed by reference to a person: to acknowledge in honour of someone, i.e. to give thanks, to praise (Heb 13:15).

(II) To be in accord with someone, to promise (Mt 14:7).

Deriv.: *anthomologéomai* (437), to confess in return, respond in praise; *exomologéō* (1843), to confess verbally, to profess or acknowledge, promise, praise; *homologia* (3671), confession; *homologouménōs* (3672), confessedly, surely, without controversy.

Syn.: *epaggéllō* (1861), to announce, promise, profess; *eulogéō* (2127), to speak well of; *pháskō* (5335), to assert, affirm, profess.

3671. ὁμολογία, homologia, *hom-ol-og-ee´-ah*; from the same as 3670; *acknowledgment*:—con- (pro-) fession, professed.

Noun from *homologéō* (3670), to agree, confess, say the same. Assent, accord, agreement. In the NT: confession, profession (2Co 9:13; 1Ti 6:12, 13; Heb 10:23). Spoken by metonymy the thing professed, i.e. the Christian religion (Heb 3:1; 4:14).

3672. ὁμολογουμένως, homologoumenōs, *hom-ol-og-ow-men´-oce*; adverb of presumed passive participle of 3670; *confessedly*:—without controversy.

Adverb from *homologéō* (3670), to confess. By consent of all, confessedly, without controversy. Used only in 1Ti 3:16).

Syn.: *alēthṓs* (230), truly; *anantirrḗtōs* (369), without objection; *asphalṓs* (806), assuredly; *óntōs* (3689), verily, certainly; *pántōs* (3843), surely, altogether.

3673. ὁμότεχνος, homotechnos, *hom-ot´-ekh-nos*; from the base of 3674 and 5078; a *fellow artificer*:—of the same craft.

3674. ὁμοῦ, homou, *hom-oo´*; generic of **ὁμός, *homos*** (the *same*; akin to 260) as adverb; *at* the *same* place or time:—together.

3675. ὁμόφρων, homophrōn, *hom-of´-rone*; from the base of 3674 and 5424; *like-minded*, i.e. *harmonious*:—of one mind.

3676. ὅμως, homōs, *hom´-oce*; adverb from the base of 3674; *at* the *same* time, i.e. (conjecture) *notwithstanding, yet still*:—and even, nevertheless, though, but.

3677. ὄναρ, onar, *on´-ar*; of uncertain derivative; a *dream*:—dream.

3678. ὀνάριον, onarion, *on-ar´-ee-on*; neuter of a presumed derivative of 3688; a *little ass*:—young ass.

3679. ὀνειδέζω, oneidezō, *on-i-did´-zo*; from 3681; to *defame*, i.e. *rail at, chide, taunt*:—cast in teeth, (suffer) reproach, revile, upbraid.

3680. ὀνειδισμός, oneidismos, *on-i-dis-mos´*; from 3679; *contumely*:—reproach.

3681. ὄνειδος, oneidos, *on´-i-dos*; probably akin to the base of 3686; *notoriety*, i.e. a *taunt* (*disgrace*):—reproach.

3682. Ὀνήσιμος, Onēsimos, *on-ay´-sim-os*; from 3685; *profitable; Onesimus*, a Christian:—Onesimus.

3683. Ὀνησίφορος, Onēsiphoros, *on-ay-sif´-or-os*; from a derivative of 3685 and 5411; *profit-bearer; Onesiphorus*, a Christian:—Onesiphorus.

3684. ὀνικός, onikos, *on-ik-os´*; from 3688; *belonging to* an *ass*, i.e. *large* (so as to be turned by an ass):—millstone.

3685. ὀνίνημι, oninēmi, *on-in´-ay-mee*; a prolonged form of an apparent primary verb (**ὄνομαι**, ***onomai***, to slur); for which another prolonged form (**ὀνάω**, ***onaō***); is used as an alternate in some tenses [unless indeed it be identical with the base of 3686 through the idea of *notoriety*]; to *gratify*, i.e. (middle) to *derive pleasure* or *advantage* from:—have joy.

3686. ὄνομα, onoma, *on´-om-ah*; from a presumed derivative of the base of 1097 (compare 3685); a "*name*" (literal or figurative) [*authority, character*]:—called, (+ sur-) name (-d).

Noun meaning name; the proper name or appellation of a person:

(I) Particularly and generally (Mt 1:21, 23, 25; 10:2; Mk 3:16, 17; 6:14; Lk 1:61, 63; 10:20; Ac 13:8; 1Co 1:13, 15; Php 4:3; Rev 13:1; 17:3; 21:14). By metonymy, "name" is sometimes put for the person or persons bearing that name (Lk 6:22; Ac 1:15; Rev 3:4; 11:13).

(II) Used to imply authority, e.g., to come or to do something in or by the name of someone, meaning using his name; as his messenger, envoy, representative; by his authority, with his sanction (Mt 10:41, 42; 18:5; 21:9; 23:39; Mk 9:39; 16:17; Lk 9:49; 10:17; 24:47; Jn 5:43; 10:25; 14:13, 14, 26; Ac 3:6; 4:7, 17, 18; 5:28, 40; 9:27; 1Co 5:4; 2Th 3:6; Jas 5:14). Of impostors (Mt 7:22; Mk 9:38 [presumed]; 13:6; Lk 21:8).

(III) Used to imply character, dignity, referring to an honourable appellation, title (Eph 1:21; Php 2:9). See Ac 4:12; Heb 1:4; Rev 19:16. A mere name, as opposed to reality (Rev 3:1).

(IV) Used emphatically: the name of God, of the Lord, of Christ, by metonymy as the total expression of God Himself, Christ Himself, in all their being, attributes, relations, manifestations (Mt 6:9; 18:20; 28:19):

(A) Spoken of God, where His name is said to be hallowed, revealed, invoked, honored (Mt 6:9; Lk 1:49; 11:2; Jn 12:28; 17:6, 11, 12; Ac 2:21; 9:14, 21; 15:14, 17; Ro 9:17; 10:13; 15:9; 1Co 1:2; Heb 2:12; 6:10; 13:15; Rev 11:18); to baptize in the name of the Lord (Mt 28:19; Ac 2:38; 8:16; 10:48; 19:5); by antithesis, to baptize in the name of Paul (1Co 1:13, 15); the blaspheming of His name (Ro 2:24; 1Ti 6:1).

(B) Spoken of Christ as the Messiah where His name is said to be honored, revered, believed on, invoked (Mt 12:21; 18:20; Jn 1:12; 2:23; Ac 8:12; 19:17; Ro 1:5; Php 2:10; 2Th 1:12; Rev 2:13; 3:8); where benefits are said to be received in or through the name of Christ (Jn 20:31; Ac 4:10, 30; 10:43; 1Co 6:11; 1Jn 2:12); where something is done in His name, meaning for His sake, or in and through Him, through faith in Him (Eph 5:20; Col 3:17; 3Jn 7). Where evils and sufferings are endured for the name of Christ (Mt 10:22; 19:29; Mk 13:13; Lk 21:12; Jn 15:21; Ac 5:41; 9:16; 21:13; 1Pe 4:14; Rev 2:3). Where one opposes and blasphemes the name of Christ (Ac 26:9; Jas 2:7).

(C) Spoken of the Holy Spirit, to baptize in His name (Mt 28:19).

Deriv.: *euṓnumos* (2176), of good name; *onomázō* (3687), to name; *pseudṓnumos* (5581), bearing a false name.

3687. ὀνομάζω, onomazō, *on-om-ad´-zo*; from 3686; to *name*, i.e. *assign an appellation*; by extension to *utter, mention, profess*:—call, name.

3688. ὄνος, onos, *on´-os*; apparently a primary word; a *donkey*:—ass.

3689. ὄντως, ontōs, *on´-toce*; adverb of the oblique cases of 5607; *really*:—certainly, clean, indeed, of a truth, verily.

3690. ὄξος, oxos, *ox´-os*; from 3691; *vinegar*, i.e. *sour* wine:—vinegar.

3691. ὀξύς, oxus, *ox-oos´*; probably akin to the base of 188 ["*acid*"]; *keen*; (by analogy) *rapid*:—sharp, swift.

3692. ὀπή, opē, *op-ay´*; probably from 3700; a *hole* (as if for light), i.e. *cavern*; (by analogy) a *spring* (of water):—cave, place.

3693. ὄπισθεν, opisthen, *op´-is-then*; from **ὄπις**, ***opis*** (*regard*; from 3700) with enclitic of source; *from the rear* (as a secure *aspect*), i.e. *at* the *back* (adverb and preposition of place or time):—after, backside, behind.

3694. ὀπίσω, opisō, *op-is´-o*; from the same as 3693 with enclitic of direction; *to* the *back*, i.e. *aback* (as adverb or preposition of time or place; or as noun):—after, back (-ward), (+ get) behind, + follow.

3695. ὁπλίζω, hoplizō, *hop-lid´-zo*; from 3696; to *equip* (with weapons [middle and figurative]):—arm self.

3696. ὅπλον, hoplon, *hop´-lon*; probably from a primary **ἕπω**, ***hepō*** (to be *busy* about); an *implement* or *utensil* or *tool* (literal or figurative, especially offensive for war):—armour, instrument, weapon.

3697. ὁποῖος, hopoios, *hop-oy´-os*; from 3739 and 4169; of *what* kind *that*, i.e. *how* (*as*) *great* (*excellent*) (specially as indefinite correlation to antecedent definite 5108 of quality):—what manner (sort) of, such as, whatsoever.

3698. ὁπότε, hopote, *hop-ot´-eh*; from 3739 and 4218; *what* (-ever) *then*, i.e. (of time) *as soon as*:—when.

3699. ὅπου, hopou, *hop´-oo*; from 3739 and 4225; *what* (-ever) *where*, i.e. *at whichever* spot:—in what place, where (-as, -soever), whither (+ soever).

3700. ὀπτάνομαι, optanomai, *op-tan´-om-ahee*; a (middle) prolonged form of the primary (middle) **ὄπτομαι**, ***optomai***, *op´-tom-ahee*; which is used for it in certain tenses; and both as alternate of 3708; to *gaze* (i.e. with wide-open eyes, as at something remarkable; and thus differing from 991, which denotes simply *voluntary* observation; and from 1492, which expresses merely mechanical, passive or casual vision; while 2300, and still more emphatically its intensive 2334, signifies an earnest but more continued *inspection*; and 4648 a watching *from a distance*):—appear, look, see, shew self.

3701. ὀπτασία, optasia, *op-tas-ee´-ah*; from a presumed derivative of 3700; *visuality*, i.e. (concretely) an *apparition*:—vision.

3702. ὀπτός, optos, *op-tos´*; from an obsolete verb akin to **ἕψω**, ***hepsō*** (to "*steep*"); *cooked*, i.e. *roasted*:—broiled.

3703. ὀπώρα, opōra, *op-o´-rah*; apparently from the base of 3796 and 5610; properly *even-tide* of the (summer) season (*dog-days*), i.e. (by implication) *ripe* fruit:—fruit.

3704. ὅπως, hopōs, *hop´-oce*; from 3739 and 4459; *what* (-ever) *how*, i.e. *in* the *manner that* (as adverb or conjecture of coincidence, intentional or actual):—because, how, (so) that, to, when.

3705. ὅραμα, horama, *hor´-am-ah*; from 3708; *something gazed at*, i.e. a *spectacle* (especially supernatural):—sight, vision.

3706. ὅρασις, horasis, *hor´-as-is*; from 3708; the act of *gazing*, i.e. (external) an *aspect* or (internal) an inspired *appearance*:—sight, vision.

3707. ὁρατός, horatos, *hor-at-os´*; from 3708; *gazed at*, i.e. (by implication) *capable of being seen*:—visible.

3708. ὁράω, horaō, *hor-ah´-o*; properly to *stare* at [compare 3700], i.e. (by implication) to *discern* clearly (physical or mental); by extension to *attend* to; by Hebrew to *experience*; passive to *appear*:—behold, perceive, see, take heed.

To see, perceive with the eyes, look at, not emphasizing the mere act of seeing, but the actual perception of some object, thus differing from *blépō* (991), to see:

(I) To see with the eyes:

(A) Particularly, persons or things (Lk 1:22; 9:36; 16:23; 24:23; Jn 4:45; 5:37; 20:18, 25, 29; Ac 7:44; 22:15; Heb 2:8; 1Pe 1:8; 1Jn 1:1).

(B) In various modified senses: **(1)** To see face-to-face, to see and converse with, i.e. have personal acquaintance and fellowship with (Jn 6:36; 8:57; 14:9; 15:24; Ac 20:25; Col 2:1). **(2)** To look upon, to behold, to contemplate (Jn 19:37). **(3)** To see take place, to witness (Lk 17:22).

(C) Passive: to be seen by someone, to appear to someone: **(1)** Particularly, spoken of things (Rev 11:19; 12:1, 3); spoken of persons, e.g., angels (Lk 1:11; 22:43; Ac 7:30, 35); of God (Ac 7:2); of persons dead (Mt 17:3; Mk 9:4; Lk 9:31); of Jesus after his resurrection (Lk 24:34; Ac 1:3; 26:16; 1Co 15:5–8; 1Ti 3:16), or of Jesus in the Second Coming (Heb 9:28). **(2)** Middle: to show oneself, present oneself to or before someone (Ac 7:26).

(II) Figuratively, to perceive with the mind or senses.

(A) Particularly, to see God, meaning to know Him, be acquainted with Him, know His character; only in John's writings (Jn 1:18; 6:46; 14:7, 9; 15:24; 1Jn 3:6; 4:20; 3Jn 11). In a wider sense: to see God, i.e. to be admitted to his presence, to enjoy his fellowship and special favour, the figure being drawn from the customs of oriental courts (Mt 5:8; Heb 12:14; Rev 22:4).

(B) Generally: to be aware of, observe (Ac 8:23; Jas 2:24).

(C) Spoken of things: to see and know, to come to know, learn (Jn 3:11, 32; 8:38; Col 2:18).

(D) By Hebraism: to experience, e.g., good, to attain to, to enjoy (Jn 3:36).

(E) In an absolute sense: to see to it, take care, take heed (Heb 8:5); usually followed by *mḗ* ([3361], not), meaning take heed lest, beware (Mt 18:10; 24:6; 1Th 5:15; Rev 19:10; 22:9). Also Mt 8:4; 9:30; Mk 1:44.

Deriv.: *aóratos* (517), invisible; *aphoráō* (872), to look away from one thing so as to see another; *kathoráō* (2529), to see clearly; *hórama* (3705), a spectacle, appearance, vision; *hórasis* (3706), vision, sight; *horatós* (3707), visible; *prooráō* (4308), to foresee.

Syn.: *blépō* (991), to see; *eídō* (1492), to see, perceive; *paratēréō* (3906), to observe; *theáomai* (2300), to look closely; *theōréō* (2334), to see, discern, perceive.

3709. ὀργή, orgē, *or-gay´*; from 3713; properly *desire* (as a *reaching* forth or *excitement* of the mind), i.e. (by analogy) violent *passion* (*ire*, or [justifiable] *abhorrence*); (by implication) *punishment*:—anger, indignation, vengeance, wrath.

Noun from *orégō* (3713), to covet after, desire. The native character, disposition, temper of the mind; impulse, impetus. Hence in the NT: passion, i.e. any violent commotion of mind; indignation, anger, wrath, especially as including desire for vengeance, punishment, and therein differing from *thumós* (2372), wrath:

(I) Generally (Mk 3:5; Ro 12:19; Eph 4:31; Col 3:8; 1Ti 2:8; Jas 1:19, 20). Spoken of God, as implying utter abhorrence of sin and aversion to those who live in it (Ro 9:22; Heb 3:11; 4:3).

(II) By metonymy: wrath, as including the idea of punishment, e.g., as the penalty of law (Ro 4:15; 13:4, 5). Also of the punitive wrath of God, the divine judgements to be inflicted upon the wicked (Mt 3:7; Lk 3:7; 21:23; Jn 3:36; Ro 2:8; 3:5; 5:9; 9:22; Eph 5:6; Col 3:6; 1Th 1:10).

Deriv.: *orgízō* (3710), to make angry, provoke; *orgílos* (3711), angry, quick-tempered.

Syn.: *thumós* (2372), wrath. Also *aganáktēsis* (24), indignation; *eritheia* (2052), partisan strife.

3710. ὀργίζω, orgizō, *or-gid´-zo*; from 3709; to *provoke* or *enrage*, i.e. (passive) *become exasperated*:—be angry (wroth).

3711. ὀργίλος, orgilos, *org-ee´-los*; from 3709; *irascible*:—soon angry.

3712. ὀργυιά, orguia, *org-wee-ah´*; from 3713; a *stretch* of the arms, i.e. a *fathom*:—fathom.

3713. ὀρέγομαι, oregomai, *or-eg´-om-ahee*; middle of apparently a prolonged form of an obsolete primary [compare 3735]; to *stretch* oneself, i.e. *reach* out after (*long* for):—covet after, desire.

3714. ὀρεινός, oreinos, *or-i-nos´*; from 3735; *mountainous*, i.e. (feminine, by implication of 5561) the *Highlands* (of Judæa):—hill country.

3715. ὄρεξις, orexis, *or´-ex-is*; from 3713; *excitement* of the mind, i.e. *longing* after:—lust.

Noun from *orégō* (3713), to desire. A reaching after. Figuratively: longing, lust. Used only in Ro 1:27, spoken of homosexual lust.

Syn.: *epithumía* (1939), desire, longing, lust.

3716. ὀρθοποδέω, orthopodeō, *or-thop-od-eh´-o*; from a compound of 3717 and 4228; to *be straight-footed*, i.e. (figurative) to *go directly* forward:—walk uprightly.

3717. ὀρθός, orthos, *or-thos´*; probably from the base of 3735; *right* (as *rising*), i.e. (perpendicularly) *erect* (figurative, *honest*), or (horizontally) *level* or *direct*:—straight, upright.

Adjective meaning straight. Spoken of standing straight, erect (Ac 14:10). Straight and level; not crooked or uneven. Used figuratively of paths (Heb 12:13).

Deriv.: *anorthóō* (461), to make straight or upright again; *orthotoméō* (3718), to rightly divide; *orthṓs* (3723), rightly.

Syn.: *euthús* (2117), straight.

3718. ὀρθοτομέω, orthotomeō, *or-thot-om-eh´-o*; from a compound of 3717 and the base of 5114; to *make* a *straight cut*, i.e. (figurative) to *dissect* (*expound*) *correctly* (the divine message):—rightly divide.

From *orthós* (3717), right and *témnō* (n.f., see below), to cut or divide. To cut straight, to divide right. In the NT, used figuratively: to handle correctly, skillfully; to correctly teach the word of truth. Used only in 2Ti 2:15.

Deriv. of *témnō* (n.f.): *peritémnō* (4059), to circumcise; *suntémnō* (4932), to cut short; *tomṓteros* (5114), finer edged, sharper.

3719. ὀρθρίζω, orthrizō, *or-thrid´-zo*; from 3722; to *use* the *dawn*, i.e. (by implication) to *repair betimes*:—come early in the morning.

3720. ὀρθρινός, orthrinos, *or-thrin-os´*; from 3722; *relating to* the *dawn*, i.e. *matutinal* (as an epithet of Venus, especially brilliant in the early day):—morning.

3721. ὄρθριος, orthrios, *or´-three-os*; from 3722; *in the dawn*, i.e. up *at day-break*:—early.

3722. ὄρθρος, orthros, *or´-thros*; from the same as 3735; *dawn* (as *sunrise*, *rising* of light); by extension *morn*:—early in the morning.

3723. ὀρθῶς, orthōs, *or-thoce´*; adverb from 3717; *in a straight* manner, i.e. (figurative) *correctly* (also morally):—plain, right (-ly).

3724. ὁρίζω, horizō, *hor-id´-zo*; from 3725; to *mark* out or *bound* ("horizon"), i.e. (figurative) to *appoint, decree, specify*:—declare, determine, limit, ordain.

From *hóros* (n.f., see *methórios* [3181]), boundary, limit. To mark out definitely, determine, appoint, set up. Of persons: to set up, appoint (Ro 1:4; Ac 10:42; 17:31); in respect to time, to determine the time (Ac 17:26; Heb 4:7). To determine, resolve, decree (Lk 22:22; Ac 2:23; 11:29).

Deriv.: *aphorízō* (873), to set off by boundary, exclude, separate; *proorízō* (4309), foreordain.

Syn.: *tássō* (5021), ordain, appoint. Also *aphorízō* (873), to set off by boundary, exclude; *diatássō* (1299), to arrange thoroughly; *diachōrízō* (1316), to apportion, separate.

3725. ὅριον, horion, *hor´-ee-on*; neuter of a derivative of an apparently primary **ὅρος,** ***horos*** (a *bound* or *limit*); a *boundary-line*, i.e. (by implication) a *frontier* (*region*):—border, coast.

3726. ὁρκίζω, horkizō, *hor-kid´-zo*; from 3727; to *put on oath*, i.e. *make swear*; (by analogy) to solemnly *enjoin*:—adjure, charge.

3727. ὅρκος, horkos, *hor´-kos*; from **ἕρκος,** ***herkos*** (a *fence*; perhaps akin to 3725); a *limit*, i.e. (sacred) *restraint* (special *oath*):—oath.

3728. ὁρκωμοσία, horkōmosia, *hor-ko-mos-ee´-ah*; from a compound of 3727 and a derivative of 3660; *asseveration on oath*:—oath.

3729. ὁρμάω, hormaō, *hor-mah´-o*; from 3730; to *start*, *spur* or *urge* on, i.e. (reflexive) to *dash* or *plunge*:—run (violently), rush.

3730. ὁρμή, hormē, *hor-may´*; of uncertain affinity; a violent *impulse*, i.e. *onset*:—assault.

Noun from *órnumi* (n.f.), to excite, arouse. A rushing on, onset, impetus, attempt (Ac 14:5). Figuratively, of the mind: impulse, will, desire (Ac 14:5; Jas 3:4).

Deriv.: *aphormḗ* (874), an occasion; *hormáō* (3729), to rush violently, incite.

Syn.: *bía* (970), force, violence.

3731. ὅρμημα, hormēma, *hor´-may-mah*; from 3730; an *attack*, i.e. (abstract) *precipitancy*:—violence.

3732. ὄρνεον, orneon, *or´-neh-on*; neuter of a presumed derivative of 3733; a *birdling*:—bird, fowl.

3733. ὄρνις, ornis, *or´-nis*; probably from a prolonged form of the base of 3735; a *bird* (as *rising* in the air), i.e. (special) a *hen* (or female domestic fowl):—hen.

3734. ὁροθεσία, horothesia, *hor-oth-es-ee´-ah*; from a compound of the base of 3725 and a derivative of 5087; a *limit-placing*, i.e. (concrete) *boundary-line*:—bound.

3735. ὄρος, oros, *or´-os*; probably from an obsolete **ὄρω,** ***orō*** (to *rise* or "*rear*"; perhaps akin to 142; compare 3733); a *mountain* (as *lifting* itself above the plain):—hill, mount (-ain).

3736. ὀρύσσω, orussō, *or-oos´-so*; apparently a primary verb; to "*burrow*" in the ground, i.e. *dig*:—dig.

3737. ὀρφανός, orphanos, *or-fan-os´*; of uncertain affinity; *bereaved* ("*orphan*"), i.e. *parentless*:—comfortless, fatherless.

3738. ὀρχέομαι, orcheomai, *or-kheh´-om-ahee*; middle from **ὄρχος,** ***orchos*** (a *row* or *ring*); to *dance* (from the *ranklike* or *regular* motion):—dance.

3739. ὅς, hos, *hos*; including feminine **ἥ,** ***hē***, *hay*; and neuter **ὅ,** ***ho***, *ho*; probably a primary word (or perhaps a form of the article 3588); the relative (sometimes demonstrative) pronoun, *who, which, what, that*:—one, (an-, the) other, some, that, what, which, who (-m, -se), etc. See also 3757.

3740. ὁσάκις, hosakis, *hos-ak´-is*; multiple adverb from 3739; *how* (i.e. with 302, *so*) *many times* as:—as oft (-en) as.

3741. ὅσιος, hosios, *hos´-ee-os*; of uncertain affinity; properly *right* (by intrinsic or divine character; thus distinguished from 1342, which refers rather to *human* statutes and relations; from 2413, which denotes formal *consecration*; and from 40, which relates to *purity* from defilement), i.e. *hallowed* (*pious, sacred, sure*):—holy, mercy, shalt be.

Adjective meaning holy, righteous, unpolluted with wickedness, right as conformed to God and His laws, thus distinguished from *díkaios* (1342), which refers more to human laws and duties. Used in the NT:

(I) Of God (Rev 15:4; 16:5; Sept.: Dt 32:4; Ps 145:17); of Christ (Ac 2:27; 13:35; Heb 7:26); of men, meaning pious, godly, careful of all duties toward God (Tit 1:8).

(II) Of things, meaning holy, sacred (1Ti 2:8; Sept.: Pr 22:11). In Ac 13:34, "the sure mercies of David," *hósios* refers to the holy promises (see v. 35; Isa 55:3).

Deriv.: *anósios* (462), unholy, ungodly; *hosiótēs* (3742), sacredness, holiness; *hosíōs* (3743), piously.

Syn.: *hágios* (40), holy with the implication of purity; *áspilos* (784), unblemished; *hieroprepḗs* (2412), reverent, as is becoming to sacredness.

3742. ὁσιότης, hosiotēs, *hos-ee-ot´-ace*; from 3741; *piety*:—holiness.

Noun from *hósios* (3741), holy, righteous. Holiness manifesting itself in the discharge of pious duties in religious and social life. Twice in the NT joined with *dikaiosúnē* (1343), righteousness (Lk 1:75; Eph 4:24).

Syn.: *hagiótēs* (41), inherent holiness implying pure moral character; *hagiōsúne* (42), holiness; *theiótēs* (2305), divinity, divine nature.

3743. ὁσίως, hosiōs, *hos-ee´-oce*; adverb from 3741; *piously*:—holily.

3744. ὀσμή, osmē, *os-may´*; from 3605; *fragrance* (literal or figurative):—odour, savour.

3745. ὅσος, hosos, *hos´-os*; by reduplicated from 3739; *as* (*much, great, long*, etc.) *as*:—all (that), as (long, many, much) (as), how great (many, much), [in-] asmuch as, so many as, that (ever), the more, those things, what (great, -soever), wheresoever, wherewithsoever, which, × while, who (-soever).

3746. ὅσπερ, hosper, *hos´-per*; from 3739 and 4007; *who especially*:—whomsoever.

3747. ὀστέον, osteon, *os-teh´-on*; or contrete **ὀστοῦν,** ***ostoun***, *os-toon´*; of uncertain affinity; a *bone*:—bone.

3748. ὅστις, hostis, *hos´-tis*; including the feminine **ἥτις,** ***hētis***, *hay´-tis*; and the neuter **ὅ τι,** ***ho ti***, *hot´-ee*; from 3739 and 5100; *which some*, i.e. *any that*; also (definite) *which same*:—× and (they), (such) as, (they) that, in that they, what (-soever), whereas ye, (they) which, who (-soever). Compare 3754.

Indefinite relative pronoun from *hós* (3739), he who, and *tis* (5100), anyone, someone. Anyone who, someone who, whoever, whatever, differing from *hós* (3739) in referring to a subject only generally as one of a class and not definitely, thus serving to render a proposition as general; usually translated whoever, etc.

(I) When modifying a noun which is already indefinite, *hóstis* will generally be translated in its own clause as if it were a definite relative pronoun, "who, which" (Ac 16:16). Also Mt 7:26; 13:52; 16:28; 25:1; Lk 7:37; Ac 16:16; 24:1; Ro 16:6, 12; 1Co 6:20; 7:13; Php 2:20).

(II) When *hóstis* is used as a substantive in an introductory clause, it will have the idea of everyone who, all who, whosoever, whatsoever: e.g., "whosoever shall exalt himself shall be abased" (Mt 23:12). Also Mt 5:39, 41; 7:24; 10:32, 33; 13:12; 18:4; 23:12; Mk 4:20; 8:34; Lk 14:27; Ac 3:23; Gal 5:10; Rev 1:7.

(III) However, sometimes *hóstis* refers to a definite subject and is then apparently equal to *hós*, who, which: e.g., "the city of David, which is called Bethlehem" (Lk 2:4). Also Jn 8:53; Ac 11:28; 16:12; Ro 16:6, 12; Rev 1:12; 11:8.

3749. ὀστράκινος, ostrakinos, *os-tra´-kin-os*; from **ὄστρακον,** ***ostrakon***; ["oyster"] (a *tile*, i.e. *terra cotta*); *earthen*-ware, i.e. *clayey*; (by implication) *frail*:—of earth, earthen.

3750. ὄσφρησις, osphrēsis, *os´-fray-sis*; from a derivative of 3605; *smell* (the sense):—smelling.

3751. ὀσφύς, osphus, *os-foos´*; of uncertain affinity; the *loin* (external), i.e. the *hip*; internal (by extension) *procreative power*:—loin.

3752. ὅταν, hotan, *hot´-an*; from 3753 and 302; *whenever* (implying *hypothesis* or more or less *uncertainty*); also causative (conjecture) *inasmuch as*:—as long (soon) as, that, + till, when (-soever), while.

3753. ὅτε, hote, *hot´-eh*; from 3739 and 5037; at *which* (thing) *too*, i.e. *when*:—after (that), as soon as, that, when, while. **ὅτε, *ho te***, *ho´-teh*; also feminine **ἥτε, *hē te***, *hay´-teh*; and neuter **τό τε, *tō te***, *tot´-eh*; simply the article 3588 followed by 5037; so written (in some editions) to distinguish them from 3752 and 5119.

3754. ὅτι, hoti, *hot´-ee*; neuter of 3748 as conjecture; demonstrative *that* (sometimes redundant); causative *because*:—as concerning that, as though, because (that), for (that), how (that), (in) that, though, why.

Conjunction meaning that (demonstrative), because (causal). As a demonstrative it introduces the object, contents, or argument to which the preceding words refer. As a causal, it assigns the cause, motive, ground of something:

(I) As a demonstrative conjunction:

(A) Particularly after demonstrative pronouns (Jn 3:19, "And this is the condemnation, that (*hóti*) light is come into the world . . ."; Ro 2:3; 2Co 5:14; Rev 2:6); after interrogative pronouns (Lk 2:49, "How is it that ye sought me?" Also Mk 2:16; Lk 8:25; Jn 14:22; Ac 5:4, 9; Heb 2:6).

(B) Most frequently *hóti* is put after certain classes of verbs to express the obj. or reference of the verb, e.g., "Moreover I call God for a record upon my soul, that (*hóti*) to spare you I came not as yet unto Corinth" (2Co 1:23); "His disciples remembered that (*hóti*) he had said this unto them" (Jn 2:22). Also Mt 16:21; Mk 2:8, 10; Jn 16:4; Ac 24:26; Ro 8:28, 38; Php 2:24; Heb 11:19; Jas 1:7).

(II) As a causal conjunction: *hóti* is put after certain classes of verbs and also generally to express the cause, reason, motive, occasion of the action or event mentioned, often translated "that," "because," or "for," e.g., "My name is Legion, for [*hóti*] we are many" (Mk 5:9). Also Mt 2:18; Mk 1:27; Lk 4:36; 11:42, 43; 16:3; 23:40; Ro 6:17; 1Co 11:2, 17; 2Co 7:9; Gal 1:6; Rev 5:4; 18:11.

Deriv.: *dióti* (1360), because, for.

3755. ὅτου, hotou, *hot´-oo*; for the generic of 3748 (as adverb); during *which same* time, i.e. *whilst*:—whiles.

3756. οὐ, ou, *oo*; also (before a vowel) **οὐκ**, ***ouk***, *ook*; and (before an aspirate) **οὐχ**, ***ouch***, *ookh*; a primary word; the absolute negative [compare 3361] adverb; *no* or *not*:— + long, nay, neither, never, no (× man), none, [can-] not, + nothing, + special, un ([-worthy]), when, + without, + yet but. See also 3364, 3372.

3757. οὗ, hou, *hoo*; generic of 3739 as adverb; at *which* place, i.e. *where*:—where (-in), whither ([-soever]).

3758. οὐά, oua, *oo-ah´*; a primary exclamation of surprise; "*ah*":—ah.

3759. οὐαί, ouai, *oo-ah´ee*; a primary exclamation of grief; "*woe*":—alas, woe.

3760. οὐδαμῶς, oudamōs, *oo-dam-oce´*; adverb from (the feminine) of 3762; *by no means*:—not.

3761. οὐδέ, oude, *oo-deh´*; from 3756 and 1161; *not however*, i.e. *neither, nor, not even*:—neither (indeed), never, no (more, nor, not), nor (yet), (also, even, then) not (even, so much as), + nothing, so much as.

3762. οὐδείς, oudeis, *oo-dice´*; including feminine **οὐδεμία**, ***oudemia***, *oo-dem-ee´-ah*; and neuter **οὐδέν**, ***ouden***, *oo-den´*; from 3761 and 1520; *not even one* (man, woman or thing), i.e. *none, nobody, nothing*:—any (man), aught, man, neither any (thing), never (man), no (man), none (+ of these things), not (any, at all, -thing), nought.

Adjective from *ou* (3756), not, and *heís* (1520), one. Not even one, not the least. When it is used in the neuter, *oudén*, it means nothing or not a thing. *Oudeís* is used with the indicative mood to state objectively, where *mēdeís* (3367), not even one, is used with all other moods to state potentially. This distinction parallels the use of the two simple negatives *ou* (3756), not, and *mḗ* (3361), not. Generally it means no one, nothing, none at all; particularly and emphatically: not even one, not the least.

(I) As a negative adj.: not one, no (Lk 4:24; 23:4; Jn 10:41; 16:29; 18:38; 1Co 8:4).

(II) Used in an absolute sense, as a substantive, *oudeís* means no one, no man, no person (Mt 6:24; 22:16; Mk 5:4; Lk 4:26, 27; 5:36, 37, 39; Jn 5:22; 8:15; 17:12; 18:9; Ac 4:12; 5:13; 9:8; 18:17; 1Co 1:14; 9:15; 2Co 11:9; Eph 5:29; Rev 2:17).

(III) Neuter *oudén*, used in an absolute sense, generally means "nothing" (Mt 10:26; 27:24; Mk 14:60; Lk 4:2; 22:35; Jn 3:27; 8:28; Ac 15:9; 26:26; Gal 2:6; Heb 2:8). The accusative *oudén* as an adverb means in no way, in no respect (2Co 12:11).

Syn.: *mēdeís* (3367), none.

3763. οὐδέποτε, oudepote, *oo-dep´-ot-eh*; from 3761 and 4218; *not even at any time*, i.e. *never at all*:—neither at any time, never, nothing at any time.

3764. οὐδέπω, oudepō, *oo-dep´-o*; from 3761 and 4452; *not even yet*:—as yet not, never before (yet), (not) yet.

3765. οὐκέτι, ouketi, *ook-et´-ee*; also (separately) **οὐκ ἔτι, *ouk eti***, *ook et´-ee*; from 3756 and 2089; *not yet, no longer*:—after that (not), (not) any more, henceforth (hereafter) not, no longer (more), not as yet (now), now no more (not), yet (not).

3766. οὐκοῦν, oukoun, *ook-oon´*; from 3756 and 3767; is it *not therefore* that, i.e. (affirmative) *hence* or *so*:—then.

3767. οὖν, oun, *oon*; apparently a primary word; (adverb) *certainly*, or (conjecture) *accordingly*:—and (so, truly), but, now (then), so (likewise then), then, therefore, verily, wherefore.

3768. οὔπω, oupō, *oo´-po*; from 3756 and 4452; *not yet*:—hitherto not, (no . . .) as yet, not yet.

3769. οὐρά, oura, *oo-rah´*; apparently a primary word; a *tail*:—tail.

3770. οὐράνιος, ouranios, *oo-ran´-ee-os*; from 3772; *celestial*, i.e. *belonging to* or *coming from* the *sky*:—heavenly.

Adjective from *ouranós* (3772), heaven. Celestial, heavenly, i.e. dwelling in heaven, as the "Heavenly Father" (Mt 6:14, 26, 32; 15:13), the "heavenly host" (Lk 2:13); a heavenly vision (Ac 26:19).

Syn.: *epouránios* (2032), heavenly.

3771. οὐρανόθεν, ouranothen, *oo-ran-oth´-en*; from 3772 and the enclitic of source; *from* the *sky*:—from heaven.

3772. οὐρανός, ouranos, *oo-ran-os´*; perhaps from the same as 3735 (through the idea of *elevation*); the *sky*; by extension *heaven* (as the abode of God); (by implication) *happiness, power, eternity*; specially the *gospel* (*Christianity*):—air, heaven ([-ly]), sky.

Noun meaning heaven, sky, air. Often used in the plural, *hoi ouranoí*, "the heavens," in imitation of the Heb use of the plural *šāmayim* (8064, OT; heavens). The plural is found most often in Matthew, less often in Mark and the epistles of Paul and Peter, only six times in Luke's writings, and not at all in the writings of John and James. However, the singular and plural are used similarly and interchangeably, with no significant difference in meaning between them. In the Hebrew usage, the term was used to speak of the expanse of the sky above, which was regarded as solid and fixed, i.e. the firmament; but was also commonly used to include the regions above the sky where God was said to dwell, and likewise the region underneath and next to the firmament, where the clouds are gathered, the birds fly, etc. Thus, in the NT, *ouranós* is used:

(I) Of the visible heavens and all their phenomena; so where heaven and earth are spoken of together, e.g., as opposites (1Co 8:5; Heb 12:26; 2Pe 3:5); as "heaven and earth," i.e. the universe (Mt 5:18; Mk 13:31; Lk 10:21; Ac 4:24; Col 1:16; Rev 10:6; 14:7). Further, in expressions such as the "present heavens," which are to be destroyed at the final consummation of all things, after which the "new heavens" are to appear (2Pe 3:7, 13; Rev 21:1). Sometimes more than one heaven is spoken of (Eph 4:10; Heb 4:14; 7:26; see more fully in IV, below). Used figuratively in expressions such as "to be exalted to heaven," i.e. to be highly distinguished, renowned (Mt 11:23; Lk 10:15).

(II) Of the firmament itself, the starry heaven, in which the sun, moon, and stars are fixed (Mk 13:25; Heb 11:12). Hence "the powers of heaven," i.e. the host or hosts of heaven; the sun, moon, and stars (Mt 24:29; Mk 13:25; Lk 21:26). Further, the stars are said to "fall from heaven," as emblematic of great commotions and revolutions (Mt 24:29; Rev 6:13; 8:10; 9:1). The firmament itself, which is spread out over the earth as a tent or curtain (Ps 104:2; Isa 40:22), is likewise said to be rolled together as a scroll (Rev 6:14). Used figuratively in Lk 10:18, where the form of expression is in allusion to Isa 14:12, the lightning being emblematic of swiftness.

(III) Of the lower heaven, or region below the firmament, i.e. the air, atmosphere, where clouds and storms are gathered and lightning breaks forth, where the birds fly, etc. Of clouds, i.e. "sky" (Mt 16:2, 3; Mk 14:62; Lk 12:56); of rain and hail (Rev 16:21); of lightning or fire from heaven (Lk 9:54; 17:29; Rev 20:9); of signs, wonders (Mt 16:1; Mk 8:11; Lk 11:16; Ac 2:19; Rev 12:1, 3); of birds (Mt 6:26; 8:20; Lk 8:5; 9:58). Figuratively, in the expression "to shut up the heavens," i.e. to withhold rain (Lk 4:25; Rev 11:6).

(IV) Of the upper or superior heaven, beyond the visible firmament, the abode of God and his glory, of the Messiah, of the angels, the spirits of the righteous after death, and generally everything which is said to be with God:

(A) Generally, e.g., of God (Mt 5:16, 34, 45; 23:22; Mk 11:25, 26; Lk 10:21; Ac 7:49; Eph 6:9; Col 4:1; Heb 8:1; Rev 11:13; 16:11); of the Messiah, the son of God, as coming from heaven (Jn 3:13, 31; 6:33, 38, 41), or as returning there after his resurrection (Mk 16:19; Lk 24:51; Ac 1:10, 11), whence he will again come to judge the world (1Th 1:10; 4:16; 2Th 1:7); of the Holy Spirit (Mt 3:16; Jn 1:32; 1Pe 1:12); of angels (Mt 18:10; 24:36; Mk 12:25; Lk 22:43; Gal 1:8); of the righteous after death, as the seat of their final glorious reward (Mt 5:12; 6:20; Lk 10:20; 2Co 5:1; Col 1:5; 1Pe 1:4). In heaven also is the spiritual temple with its sacred utensils (Heb 9:23, 24; Rev 11:19; 14:17; 15:5; 16:17); and there also the new Jerusalem is prepared and adorned (Rev 3:12; 21:2, 10). Poetically, the heavens are said to rejoice (Rev 12:12; 18:20).

(B) The expression "caught up to the third heaven" (2Co 12:2), probably in allusion to the three heavens as above specified: the lower, the middle or firmament, and the superior; hence the "third heaven," i.e. the highest heaven, the abode of God and angels and glorified spirits; the spiritual paradise (see 2Co 12:4).

(C) By metonymy, as in Eng., heaven, as the abode of God, is often put for God himself (Mt 21:25; Mk 11:30; Lk 20:4, 5). Also in the formula found so frequently in Matthew, "the kingdom of heaven" (Mt 3:2; 4:17; 5:3, 10; et al.).

Deriv.: *epouránios* (2032), heavenly, what pertains to or is in heaven; *ouránios* (3770), heavenly; *ouranóthen* (3771), from heaven; *messouránēma* (3321), mid-heaven, the midst of the heavens.

Syn.: *parádeisos* (3857), paradise.

3773. Οὐρβανός, Ourbanos, *oor-ban-os´*; of Latin origin; *Urbanus* (*of* the *city*, "*urbane*"), a Christian:—Urbanus.

3774. Οὐρίας, Ourias, *oo-ree´-as*; of Hebrew origin [223]; *Urias* (i.e. *Urijah*), a Hittite:—Urias.

3775. οὖς, ous, *ooce*; apparently a primary word; the *ear* (physical or mental):—ear.

3776. οὐσία, ousia, *oo-see´-ah*; from the feminine of 5607; *substance*, i.e. *property* (*possessions*):—goods, substance.

3777. οὔτε, oute, *oo´-teh*; from 3756 and 5037; *not too*, i.e. *neither* or *nor*; (by analogy) *not even*:—neither, none, nor (yet), (no, yet) not, nothing.

3778. οὗτος, houtos, *hoo´-tos*; including nominal masculine plural **οὗτοι**, ***houtoi***, *hoo´-toy*; nominal feminine singular **αὕτη**, ***hautē***, *how´-tay*; and nominal feminine plural **αὗται**, ***hautai***, *how´-tahee*; from the article 3588 and 846; *the he* (*she* or *it*), i.e. *this* or *that* (often with article repeated):—he (it was that), hereof, it, she, such as, the same, these, they, this (man, same, woman), which, who.

3779. οὕτω, houtō, *hoo´-to*; or (before a vowel) **οὕτως**, ***houtōs***, *hoo´-toce*; adverb from 3778; *in this way* (referring to what precedes or follows):—after that, after (in) this manner, as, even (so), for all that, like (-wise), no more, on this fashion (-wise), so (in like manner), thus, what.

3780. οὐχί, ouchi, *oo-khee´*; intensive of 3756; *not indeed*:—nay, not.

3781. ὀφειλέτης, opheiletēs, *of-i-let´-ace*; from 3784; an *ower*, i.e. person *indebted*; (figurative) a *delinquent*; morally a *transgressor* (against God):—debtor, which owed, sinner.

Noun from *opheílō* (3784), to owe. A debtor:

(I) One owing money (Mt 18:24). One indebted for favors (Ro 15:27).

(II) One morally bound to the performance of any duty (Ro 1:14; 8:12; Gal 5:3).

(III) Delinquent, one who fails in the performance of duty (Mt 6:12, meaning those who fail in their duty toward us). Generally: a transgressor, sinner (Lk 13:4 [cf. 13:2]).

Deriv.: *chreōpheilétēs* (5533), one who owes a debt.

Syn.: *chreopheilétes* (5533), debtor.

3782. ὀφειλή, opheilē, *of-i-lay´*; from 3784; *indebtedness*, i.e. (concrete) a *sum* owed; (figurative) *obligation*, i.e. (conjugal) *duty*:—debt, due.

Noun from *opheílō* (3784), to owe. A debt which must be paid (Mt 18:32), obligation, a service which one owes someone (Ro 13:7; 1Co 7:3).

Syn.: *opheílēma* (3783), an amount due.

3783. ὀφείλημα, opheilēma, *of-i´-lay-mah*; from (the alternate of) 3784; *something owed*, i.e. (figurative) a *due*; morally a *fault*:—debt.

Noun from *opheílō* (3784), to owe. A debt, that which is owed, which is strictly due (Ro 4:4). Also an offence; a trespass which requires reparation (Mt 6:12, cf. 6:14).

3784. ὀφείλω, opheilō, *of-i´-lo*; or (in certain tenses) its prolonged form **ὀφειλέω**, ***opheileō***, *of-i-leh´-o*; probably from the base of 3786 (through the idea of *accruing*); to *owe* (pecuniarily); (figurative) to *be under obligation* (*ought, must, should*); (morally) to *fail* in duty:—behove, be bound, (be) debt (-or), (be) due (-ty), be guilty (indebted), (must) need (-s), ought, owe, should. See also 3785.

To owe, to be indebted:

(I) Primarily of money (Mt 18:28; Lk 7:41; 16:5, 7; Phm 18). Passive participle: what is owed, debt, due (Mt 18:30, 34; 1Co 7:3).

(II) Figuratively, to be bound or obligated to perform a duty, meaning I ought, must. Of what is required by law or duty in general (Mt 23:16, 18; Lk 17:10; Jn 13:14; 19:7; Ro 15:1, 27; 2Co 12:14; Eph 5:28; 2Th 1:3; 2:13; 1Jn 2:6; 3:16; 4:11; 3Jn 8). Also of what the circumstances of time, place, or person render proper: to be fit and proper (Ac 17:29; 1Co 7:36; 11:7, 10; 2Co 12:11; Heb 2:17; 5:3, 12); what is from the nature of the case necessary (1Co 5:10; 9:10).

(III) By implication: to fail in duty, be delinquent, be indebted to someone (Lk 11:4).

Deriv.: *opheilétēs* (3781), debtor; *opheilḗ* (3782), debt, obligation; *opheílēma* (3783), that which is owed, obligation; *óphelon* (3785), what one wishes to happen; *prosopheílō* (4359), to owe in addition to.

Syn.: *anagkázomai* (315), to be compelled, to have to; *dei* (1163), it is necessary, an obligation out of necessity or inevitability; *prépō* (4241), it is proper or right; *chrḗ* (5534), it needs be, ought; *chrḗzō* (5535), to need.

3785. ὄφελον, ophelon, *of´-el-on*; first person singular of a past tense of 3784; *I ought* (*wish*), i.e. (interjection) *oh that!*:—would (to God).

3786. ὄφελος, ophelos, *of´-el-os*; from **ὀφέλλω**, ***ophellō*** (to *heap* up, i.e. *accumulate* or *benefit*); *gain*:—advantageth, profit.

3787. ὀφθαλμοδουλεία, ophthalmodouleia, *of-thal-mod-oo-li´-ah*; from 3788 and 1397; *sight-labour*, i.e. that needs watching (*remissness*):—eye-service.

Noun from *ophthalmós* (3788), eye, and *douleía* (1397), service. Eyeservice, i.e. that is work or service rendered only under the master's eye (Eph 6:6; Col 3:22).

3788. ὀφθαλμός, ophthalmos, *of-thal-mos´*; from 3700; the *eye* (literal or figurative); (by implication) *vision*; (figurative) *envy* (from the jealous side-glance):—eye, sight.

3789. ὄφις, ophis, *of´-is*; probably from 3700 (through the idea of *sharpness* of vision); a *snake*, figurative (as a type of sly cunning) an artful *malicious* person, especially *Satan*:—serpent.

3790. ὀφρύς, ophrus, *of-roos´*; perhaps from 3700 (through the idea of the shading or proximity to the organ of *vision*); the eye-"*brow*" or *forehead*, i.e. (figurative) the *brink* of a precipice:—brow.

3791. ὀχλέω, ochleō, *okh-leh´-o*; from 3793; to *mob*, i.e. (by implication) to *harass*:—vex.

3792. ὀχλοποιέω, ochlopoieō, *okh-lop-oy-eh´-o*; from 3793 and 4160; to *make a crowd*, i.e. *raise a* public *disturbance*:—gather a company.

3793. ὄχλος, ochlos, *okh´-los*; from a derivative of 2192 (meaning a *vehicle*); a *throng* (as *borne* along); (by implication) the *rabble*; by extension a *class* of people; (figurative) a *riot*:—company, multitude, number (of people), people, press.

Noun meaning crowd, a group of people. The size of an *óchlos* is relative. E.g., the *óchlos* of the disciples gathered in the upper room after Christ's ascension is about 120 people, while the crowd described in Lk 12:1 is several thousand.

(I) A crowd, throng, confused multitude. Used in the singular (Mt 9:23, 25; 14:14; 15:33; Mk 2:4; 8:1; Lk 5:1, 29; 6:17; 12:1; Jn 5:13; 12:9; Ac 6:7; 11:24, 26; 14:14; 19:26). Used intensively in the plural with the same sense as the singular: crowds, multitude (Mt 4:25; 5:1; 7:28; Lk 4:42; 5:3, 15; Jn 7:12; Ac 8:6; 17:13).

(II) Sometimes used for the common people, the rabble (Mt 14:5; 21:26; Mk 12:12; Jn 7:12, 49; Ac 16:22; 24:12).

Deriv.: *ochléō* (3791), to excite a crowd, to vex, to harass with crowds; *ochlopoiéō* (3792), to raise a public disturbance.

Syn.: *dēmos* (1218), a mass of people assembled in a public place; *laós* (2992), people; *plēthos* (4128), a multitude of people, populace.

3794. ὀχύρωμα, ochurōma, *okh-oo´-ro-mah*; from a remote derivative of 2192 (meaning to *fortify*, through the idea of *holding* safely); a *castle* (figurative, *argument*):—stronghold.

3795. ὀψάριον, opsarion, *op-sar´-ee-on*; neuter of a presumed derivative of the base of 3702; a *relish* to other food (as if cooked *sauce*), i.e. (special) *fish* (presumably salted and dried as a condiment):—fish.

3796. ὀψέ, opse, *op-seh´*; from the same as 3694 (through the idea of *backwardness*); (adverb) *late* in the day; by extension *after the close* of the day:—(at) even, in the end.

3797. ὄψιμος, opsimos, *op´-sim-os*; from 3796; *later*, i.e. *vernal* (showering):—latter.

3798. ὄψιος, opsios, *op´-see-os*; from 3796; *late*; feminine (as noun) *afternoon* (early eve) or *nightfall* (later eve):—even (-ing, [-tide]).

3799. ὄψις, opsis, *op´-sis*; from 3700; properly *sight* (the act), i.e. (by implication) the *visage*, an external *show*:—appearance, countenance, face.

3800. ὀψώνιον, opsōnion, *op-so´-nee-on*; neuter of a presumed derivative of the same as 3795; *rations* for a soldier, i.e. (by extension) his *stipend* or *pay*:—wages.

Noun from *ópson* (n.f.), meat, and *ōnéomai* (n.f.), to buy. It primarily signifies whatever is bought to be eaten with bread, provisions, supplies for a soldier's pay (Lk 3:14; 1Co 9:7). Metaphorically, it means general wages, recompense (Ro 6:23; 2Co 11:8).

Deriv.: *paropsís* (3953), a dish.

Syn.: *misthós* (3408), pay, wages.

3801. ὁ ὢν ὁ ἦν ὁ ἐρχόμενος, ho ōn ho ēn ho erchomenos, *ho own ho ane ho er-khom´-enos*; a phrase combining 3588 with the presumed participle and imperfect of 1510 and the presumed participle of 2064 by means of 2532; *the* one *being and the* one that *was and the* one *coming*, i.e. *the Eternal*, as a divine epithet of Christ:—which art (is, was), and (which) wast (is, was), and art (is) to come (shalt be).

3802. παγιδεύω, pagideuō, *pag-id-yoo´-o*; from 3803; to *ensnare* (figurative):—entangle.

3803. παγίς, pagis, *pag-ece´*; from 4078; a *trap* (as *fastened* by a noose or notch); (figurative) a *trick* or *strategem* (*temptation*):—snare.

3804. πάθημα, pathēma, *path´-ay-mah*; from a presumed derivative of 3806; something *undergone*, i.e. *hardship* or *pain*; subject an *emotion* or *influence*:—affection, affliction, motion, suffering.

Noun from *páschō* (3958), to suffer. Suffering, affliction:

(I) Particularly: evil suffered, affliction, distress. Singular (Heb 2:9); plural (Ro 8:18; 2Co 1:5–7; Php 3:10; Col 1:24; 2Ti 3:11; Heb 2:10; 10:32; 1Pe 1:11; 4:13; 5:1, 9).

(II) By metonymy: a passion, i.e. an affection of mind, emotion (Ro 7:5; Gal 5:24).

Syn.: *kakopátheia* (2552), affliction; *páthos* (3806), suffering, passion, lust.

3805. παθητός, pathētos, *path-ay-tos´*; from the same as 3804; *liable* (i.e. *doomed*) *to* experience *pain*:—suffer.

Adjective from *páschō* (3958), to suffer, to undergo pain, inconvenience, or punishment. Liable to suffering. In the NT: destined to suffer (Ac 26:23). See *páthēma* (3804), suffering.

3806. πάθος, pathos, *path´-os*; from the alternate of 3958; properly *suffering* ("*pathos*"), i.e. (subject) a *passion* (especially *concupiscence*):—(inordinate) affection, lust.

Noun from *páschō* (3958), to suffer. Suffering, affliction. In the NT: passion, i.e. affliction of the mind, emotion, especially lustful compassion (Ro 1:26; Col 3:5; 1Th 4:5).

Deriv.: *sumpathḗs* (4835), compassionate, sympathizing; *homoiopathḗs* (3663), of like passions.

Syn.: *asélgeia* (766), licentiousness; *epithumía* (1939), desire; *órexis* (3715), a longing after; *hormḗ* (3730), violent impulse.

3807. παιδαγωγός, paidagōgos, *pahee-dag-o-gos´*; from 3816 and a reduplicated form of 71; a *boy-leader*, i.e. a servant whose office it was to take the children to school; (by implication [figurative] a *tutor* ["*pædagogue*"]):—instructor, schoolmaster.

Noun from *país* (3816), a child, and *agōgós* (n.f.), a leader, which is from *ágō* (71), to lead. An instructor or teacher of children, a schoolmaster, a pedagogue (1Co 4:15). Usually a slave or freedman to whose care the boys of a family were committed, who trained them up, instructed them at home, and accompanied them to the public schools. In the NT, used figuratively of the Mosaic Law (Gal 3:24, 25).

Syn.: *paideutḗs* (3810), a trainer, instructor. Also *didáskalos* (1320), teacher; *epítropos* (2012), guardian; *kathēgētḗs* (2519), a guide, teacher, master.

3808. παιδάριον, paidarion, *pahee-dar´-ee-on*; neuter of a presumed derivative of 3816; a *little boy*:—child, lad.

3809. παιδεία, paideia, *pahee-di´-ah*; from 3811; *tutorage*, i.e. *education* or *training*; (by implication) disciplinary *correction*:—chastening, chastisement, instruction, nurture.

Noun from *paideúō* (3811), to instruct. Training of a child, and hence generally: education, discipline; instruction as consisting of teaching, admonition, rewards, punishments, etc. Generally (Eph 6:4; 2Ti 3:16); by synecdoche of the part for whole: correction, chastisement (Heb 12:5, 7, 8, 11).

Syn.: *epanórthōsis* (1882), correction; *nouthesía* (3559), instruction, admonition.

3810. παιδευτής, paideutēs, *pahee-dyoo-tace´*; from 3811; a *trainer*, i.e. *teacher* or (by implication) *discipliner*:—which corrected, instructor.

Noun from *paideúō* (3811), to instruct, correct, chastise. An instructor (Ro 2:20); a corrector, a chastiser (Heb 12:9).

Syn.: *paidagōgós* (3807), instructor. Also *didáskalos* (1320), an instructor, teacher; *kathēgētḗs* (2519), a guide, master, teacher.

3811. παιδεύω, paideuō, *pahee-dyoo´-o*; from 3816; to *train* up a child, i.e. *educate*, or (by implication) *discipline* (by punishment):—chasten (-ise), instruct, learn, teach.

From *país* (3816), child. To train up a child, and hence generally: to educate, to discipline, to instruct:

(I) Generally (Ac 7:22; 22:3). In the sense of to teach; to admonish, by word or deed (1Ti 1:20; 2Ti 2:25; Tit 2:12).

(II) By synecdoche of part for the whole: to correct, to chastise, to chasten, e.g., as children (Heb 12:7, 10). Spoken of chastening from God by afflictions, calamities (1Co 11:32; 2Co 6:9; Heb 12:6; Rev 3:19). Of prisoners: to scourge (Lk 23:16, 22).

Deriv.: *apaídeutos* (521), unlearned; *paideía* (3809), training, chastening; *paideutḗs* (3810), instructor, trainer.

Syn.: *gumnázō* (1128), to train; *didáskō* (1321), to teach; *ektréphō* (1625), to bring up a child; *mastigóō* (3146), to scourge, whip; *hodēgéō* (3594), to show the way, lead, guide; *tréphō* (5142), to bring up a child.

3812. παιδιόθεν, paidiothen, *pahee-dee-oth´-en*; adverb (of *source*) from 3813; *from infancy*:—of a child.

3813. παιδίον, paidion, *pahee-dee´-on*; neuter diminutive of 3816; a *childling* (of either sex), i.e. (properly) an infant, or (by extension) a half-grown *boy* or *girl*; (figurative) an *immature* Christian:—(little, young) child, damsel.

3814. παιδίσκη, paidiskē, *pahee-dis´-kay*; feminine diminutive of 3816; a *girl*, i.e. (special) a *female slave* or *servant*:—bondmaid (-woman), damsel, maid (-en).

3815. παίζω, paizō, *paheed´-zo*; from 3816; to *sport* (as a boy):—play.

3816. παῖς, pais, *paheece*; perhaps from 3817; a *boy* (as often *beaten* with impunity), or (by analogy) a *girl*, and (genitive) a *child*; specially a *slave* or *servant* (especially a *minister* to a king; and by eminence to God):—child, maid (-en), (man) servant, son, young man.

Noun meaning child, male or female; a boy, youth; a girl, maiden. Spoken of all ages from infancy to full grown youth (cf. Mt 2:16, children under two years of age; Ac 20:12, young man):

(I) Particularly and generally (Mt 2:16; 17:18; 21:15; Lk 2:43; 8:51, 54; 9:42; Jn 4:51; Ac 20:12).

(II) Boy, servant:

(A) Particularly and generally, equivalent to *doúlos* (1401), a servant, slave (Mt 8:6, 8, 13 [cf. Lk 7:3]; Lk 7:7 [cf. v. 3]; Lk 12:45; 15:26).

(B) An attendant, minister, as of a king (Mt 14:2; Sept.: Ge 41:38).

(C) The servant of God, spoken of a minister or ambassador of God, called and beloved of God, and sent by Him to perform any service, e.g., of David (Lk 1:69; Ac 4:25); of Israel (Lk 1:54); of Jesus the Messiah (Mt 12:18; Ac 3:13, 26; 4:27, 30).

Deriv.: *paidagōgós* (3807), schoolmaster; *paideúō* (3811), to train, chasten; *paízō* (3815), to play.

Syn.: As a child: *bréphos* (1025), infant; *téknon* (5043), child; *teknίon* (5040), small child. As a servant: *therápōn* (2324), a servant; *oikétēs* (3610), a domestic servant; *paidiskē* (3814), a maidservant; *hupērétēs* (5257), a subordinate servant.

3817. παίω, paiō, *pah´-yo*; a primary verb; to *hit* (as if by a single blow and less violently than 5180); specially to *sting* (as a scorpion):—smite, strike.

3818. Πακατιανή, Pakatianē, *pak-at-ee-an-ay´*; feminine of an adjective of uncertain derivative; *Pacatianian*, a section of Phrygia:—Pacatiana.

3819. πάλαι, palai, *pal´-ahee*; probably another form for 3825 (through the idea of *retrocession*); (adverb) *formerly*, or (by relative) *sometime since*; (elliptically as adjective) *ancient*:—any while, a great while ago, (of) old, in time past.

Adverb of time. In the past, long ago, of olden times, formerly, long before now. Particularly (Mt 11:21; Lk 10:13; Heb 1:1; Jude 4). Spoken relative to the present moment: already, at the present time (Mk 15:44).

Deriv.: *ékpalai* (1597), of old; *palaiós* (3820), old.

Syn.: *ékpalai* (1597), of old; *poté* (4218), in time past.

3820. παλαιός, palaios, *pal-ah-yos´*; from 3819; *antique*, i.e. *not recent, worn out*:—old.

Adjective from *pálai* (3819), in the past, long ago. Old, not new, what is of long standing:

(I) In age or time, old, former, not recent. Spoken of wine (Lk 5:39); leaven (1Co 5:7, 8); testament (2Co 3:14); a commandment (1Jn 2:7); man (Ro 6:6; Eph 4:22; Col 3:9).

(II) From use, meaning old, worn-out, spoken of a garment (Mt 9:16; Mk 2:21; Lk 5:36); wineskins (Mt 9:17; Mk 2:22; Lk 5:37). See also Mt 13:52.

Deriv.: *palaiótēs* (3821), aged, obsolete; *palaióō* (3822), to make old.

Syn.: *archaíos* (744), old, ancient, original, what has exited from the beginning. *Palaiós* is not necessarily from the beginning but just old.

3821. παλαιότης, palaiotēs, *pal-ah-yot´-ace*; from 3820; *antiquatedness*:—oldness.

Noun from *palaiós* (3820), old. Age, antiquity, lengthy existence. Used only in Ro 7:6.

3822. παλαιόω, palaioō, *pal-ah-yo´-o*; from 3820; to *make* (passive *become*) *worn out*, or *declare obsolete*:—decay, make (wax) old.

From *palaiós* (3820), old. In the active, to make old, render obsolete, abrogate (Heb 8:13). In the passive, to grow old, become worn out (Lk 12:33; Heb 1:11).

3823. πάλη, palē, *pal´-ay*; from **πάλλω, *pallō*** (to *vibrate*; another form for 906); *wrestling*:— + wrestle.

3824. παλιγγενεσία, paliggenesia, *pal-ing-ghen-es-ee´-ah*; from 3825 and 1078; (spiritual) *rebirth* (the state or the act), i.e. (figurative) spiritual *renovation*; specially Messianic *restoration*:—regeneration.

Noun from *pálin* (3825), again, and *génesis* (1078), generation, source. Regeneration, restoration, renewal. In a moral sense: regeneration, new birth, i.e. change by grace from a carnal nature to a Christian life (Tit 3:5). In the sense of renovation, restoration, restitution to a former state; spoken of the complete eternal manifestation of the Messiah's kingdom when all things are to be delivered from their present corruption and restored to spiritual purity and splendour (Mt 19:28).

Syn.: *anakaínōsis* (342), renewing.

3825. πάλιν, palin, *pal´-in*; probably from the same as 3823 (through the idea of *oscillatory* repetition); (adverb) *anew*, i.e. (of place) *back*, (of time) *once more*, or (conjecture) *furthermore* or *on the other hand*:—again.

3826. παμπληθεί, pamplēthei, *pam-play-thi´*; dative (adverb) of a compound of 3956 and 4128; *in full multitude*, i.e. *concertedly* or *simultaneously*:—all at once.

3827. πάμπολυς, pampolus, *pam´-pol-ooce*; from 3956 and 4183; *full many*, i.e. *immense*:—very great.

3828. Παμφυλία, Pamphulia, *pam-fool-ee´-ah*; from a compound of 3956 and 5443; *every-tribal*, i.e. *heterogeneous* (5561 being implication); *Pam-phylia*, a region of Asia Minor:—Pamphylia.

3829. πανδοχεῖον, pandocheion, *pan-dokh-i´-on*; neuter of a presumed compound of 3956 and a derivative of 1209; *all-receptive*, i.e. a public *lodging*-place (*caravanserai* or *khan*):—inn.

3830. πανδοχεύς, pandocheus, *pan-dokh-yoos´*; from the same as 3829; an *innkeeper* (*warden of a caravanserai*):—host.

3831. πανήγυρις, panēguris, *pan-ay´-goo-ris*; from 3956 and a derivative of 58; a *mass-meeting*, i.e. (figurative) *universal companionship*:—general assembly.

Noun from *pás* (3956), all, and *águris* (n.f.), an assembly, which is from *agorá* (58), public square, marketplace. An assembly or convocation of the whole people in order to celebrate any public festival or solemnity, as the public games, sacrifices, etc. Hence generally: a festive convocation, joyful assembly. In the NT, used only in Heb 12:23.

Syn.: *ekklēsía* (1577), church, assembly; *sunagōgḗ* (4864), synagogue. These words, however, do not inherently imply gatherings for festivities as *panḗguris* does.

3832. πανοικί, panoiki, *pan-oy-kee´*; adverb from 3956 and 3624; *with* the *whole family*:—with all his house.

3833. πανοπλία, panoplia, *pan-op-lee´-ah*; from a compound of 3956 and 3696; *full armour* ("*panoply*"):—all (whole) armour.

3834. πανουργία, panourgia, *pan-oorg-ee´-ah*; from 3835; *adroitness*, i.e. (in a bad sense) *trickery* or *sophistry*:—(cunning) craftiness, subtlety.

3835. πανοῦργος, panourgos, *pan-oor´-gos*; from 3956 and 2041; *all-working*, i.e. *adroit* (*shrewd*):—crafty.

3836. πανταχόθεν, pantachothen, *pan-takh-oth´-en*; adverb (of *source*) from 3837; *from all* directions:—from every quarter.

3837. πανταχοῦ, pantachou, *pan-takh-oo´*; generic (as adverb of *place*) of a presumed derivative of 3956; *universally*:—in all places, everywhere.

3838. παντελής, pantelēs, *pan-tel-ace´*; from 3956 and 5056; *full-ended*, i.e. *entire* (neuter as noun, *completion*):— + in [no] wise, uttermost.

Adjective from *pás* (3956), any, all, and *télos* (5056), end. Complete, whole, entire. In the NT, used adverbially: wholly, entirely, as referring to time: always (Heb 7:25); with a negative, not at all (Lk 13:11).

Syn.: *téleios* (5046), complete. Also *aiṓnios* (166), forever, eternal.

3839. πάντη, pantē, *pan´-tay*; adverb (of *manner*) from 3956; *wholly*:—always.

3840. παντόθεν, pantothen, *pan-toth´-en*; adverb (of *source*) from 3956; *from* (i.e. *on*) *all* sides:—on every side, round about.

3841. παντοκράτωρ, pantokratōr, *pan-tok-rat´-ore*; from 3956 and 2904; the *all-ruling*, i.e. *God* (as absolute and universal *sovereign*):—Almighty, Omnipotent.

3842. πάντοτε, pantote, *pan´-tot-eh*; from 3956 and 3753; *every when*, i.e. *at all* times:—alway (-s), ever (-more).

3843. πάντως, pantōs, *pan´-toce*; adverb from 3956; *entirely*; specially *at all events*, (with negative following) *in* no *event*:—by all means, altogether, at all, needs, no doubt, in [no] wise, surely.

3844. παρά, para, *par-ah´*; a primary preposition; properly *near*, i.e. (with general) *from beside* (literal or figurative), (with dative) *at* (or *in*) the *vicinity* of (object or subject), (with accusative) to the *proximity* with (local [especially *beyond* or *opposed* to] or causal [*on account* of]):—above, against, among, at, before, by, contrary to, × friend, from, + give [such things as they], + that [she] had, × his, in, more than, nigh unto, (out) of, past, save, side … by, in the sight of, than, [there-] fore, with. In compounds it retains the same variety of application.

Preposition with the primary meaning of near, nearby, expressing the notion of immediate vicinity or proximity which is differently modified according to the force of each case:

(I) With the gen., expressing the meaning from near, from with. In the NT, only with a gen. of person, implying a going forth or proceeding from the near vicinity of someone, from the presence or side of someone. From:

(A) Particularly after verbs of motion, as of coming, sending (Mk 14:43; Lk 6:19; 8:49; Jn 15:26; 17:8). Also Jn 1:14; 6:46; 7:29.

(B) Figuratively, after verbs of asking, receiving, or those which imply these ideas. After verbs of asking, seeking (Mt 2:4, 7; 20:20; Mk 8:11; Lk 12:48; Jn 1:40; 17:7; Ac 26:22; 28:22; Gal 1:12; Eph 6:8; Php 4:18; 2Pe 1:17).

(C) Figuratively, with the gen. of person as the source, author, director, meaning from whom something proceeds or is derived (Mt 21:42; Lk 1:45; 2:1; Jn 1:6; Ac 22:30).

(II) With the dat. both of person and thing, expressing rest or position, near, hard by, with; and with the dat. plural, meaning among.

(A) Particularly of place, after verbs implying rest or remaining in a place (Mt 6:1; 22:25; 28:15; Lk 9:47; 19:7; Jn 1:39; 8:38; 19:25; Ac 10:6; Col 4:16; 2Ti 4:13; Rev 2:13).

(B) With the dat. of person, the reference being to the person himself without regard to place. **(1)** Particularly and generally meaning with, among (Mt 19:26; 21:25; Lk 1:30; 2:52; Ro 2:11, 13; 1Co 3:19; 2Co 1:17; Gal 3:11; Jas 1:27; 1Pe 2:4, 20; 2Pe 2:11; 3:8).

(III) With the accusative, particularly expressing motion near a place.

(A) Particularly implying motion along the side of something, meaning nearby, by, along (Mt 4:18; 13:4; Mk 2:13; 4:15).

(B) As expressing motion to a place, near to, to, at (Mt 15:29; Lk 8:41; Ac 4:35; 7:58).

(C) Sometimes also expressing the idea of rest or remaining near a place, near, by, at (Mt 13:1; Mk 4:1; 5:21; Lk 5:1; 7:38; Ac 22:3; Heb 11:12). **(2)** Metaphorically, of the ground or reason by or along with which a conclusion follows by reason of, because of, meaning thereby, therefore, on this account (1Co 12:15, 16).

(D) As denoting motion by or past a place. In the NT, only figuratively, as implying a failure to reach the exact point of aim, either falling short or with the general meaning of "other than." **(1)** Aside from, away from, i.e. contrary to, against (Ac 18:13; Ro 1:26; 4:18; 11:24; 16:17; Gal 1:8, 9). **(2)** Beside, with the meaning of falling short (2Co 11:24). **(3)** Past, in the sense of beyond, past (Heb 11:11). More commonly, in the sense of more than, above, beyond (Lk 13:2; Ro 1:25; 12:3; 14:5; Heb 1:4; 2:7; 11:4; 12:24).

(IV) In composition, *pará* implies:

(A) Nearness, proximity, near, by, as in *parakathízō* (3869), to sit down near; *parístēmi* (3936), to stand beside, to aid; *parathalássios* (3864), along the sea.

(B) Motion or direction, near to, by, as in *paraballō* (3846), to throw alongside, compare; *paradídōmi* (3860), to surrender, betray; *paréchō* (3930), to hold near, bring, offer; *parateínō* (3905), to extend along.

(C) Motion, by or past any place, going beyond, as *parágō* (3855), to go beyond; *parérchomai* (3928), to go by, pass by; *parapléō* (3896), to sail by. Used metaphorically, of coming short of or going beyond the true point: *parakoúō* (3878), to mishear, disobey; *paratheōréō* (3865), to overlook, disregard; implying violation, as *parabaínō* (3845), to disobey a command.

Syn.: *eggús* (1451), near; *paraplḗsion* (3897), close by; *plēsíon* (4139), nearby; *prós* (4314), toward, near; *schedón* (4975), nigh, almost.

3845. παραβαίνω, parabainō, *par-ab-ah´ee-no*; from 3844 and the base of 939; to *go contrary to*, i.e. *violate* a command:—(by) transgress (-ion).

From *pará* (3844), beyond or contrary to, and *bainō* (n.f., see *metabaínō* [3327]), to go away from, to move. To go aside from, transgress, violate (Mt 15:2, 3; 2Jn 1:9). To lose one's office or position by transgression (Ac 1:25).

Deriv.: *aparábatos* (531), unchangeable; *parábasis* (3847), transgression; *parabátēs* (3848), transgressor.

Syn.: *hamartánō* (264), to sin; *apistéō* (569), to disbelieve; *paranoméō* (3891), to transgress the law.

3846. παραβάλλω, paraballō, *par-ab-al´-lo*; from 3844 and 906; to *throw alongside*, i.e. (reflexive) to *reach* a place, or (figurative) to *liken*:—arrive, compare.

From *pará* (3844), near, and *bállō* (906), to cast, put. To throw or place side by side; figuratively, to compare (Mk 4:30). Hence, as a nautical term, to come to a place, arrive at (Ac 20:15).

Deriv.: *parabolḗ* (3850), comparison, parable.

Syn.: *homoióō* (3666), to resemble, make similar; *sugkrínō* (4793), to compare.

3847. παράβασις, parabasis, *par-ab´-as-is*; from 3845; *violation*:—breaking, transgression.

Noun from *parabaínō* (3845), to transgress. Transgression, wrongdoing, lawbreaking, a deliberate stepping over a boundary (Ro 2:23; 4:15; 5:14; Gal 3:19; 1Ti 2:14; Heb 2:2; 9:15).

Syn.: *paranomía* (3892), lawbreaking; *paráptōma* (3900), a fault, mistake, error, sin. Also *hamártēma* (265), act of sin; *hamartía* (266), sin.

3848. παραβάτης, parabatēs, *par-ab-at´-ace*; from 3845; a *violator*:—breaker, transgress (-or).

Noun from *parabaínō* (3845), to transgress. Transgressor, violator of the law; used with reference to the imputation of sin to those who having known the law transgress it and deviate from the truth (Ro 2:25, 27; Gal 2:18; Jas 2:9, 11).

Syn.: *hamartōlós* (268), a sinner; *ánomos* (459), lawless person, transgressor.

3849. παραβιάζομαι, parabiazomai, *par-ab-ee-ad´-zom-ahee*; from 3844 and the middle of 971; to *force contrary* to (nature), i.e. *compel* (by entreaty):—constrain.

3850. παραβολή, parabolē, *par-ab-ol-ay´*; from 3846; a *similitude* ("*parable*"), i.e. (symbolic) *fictitious narrative* (of common life conveying a moral), *apothegm* or *adage*:—comparison, figure, parable, proverb.

Noun from *parabállō* (3846), to compare. A parable, a placing side by side. In the NT, a comparison, similitude, parable.

(I) Generally, a comparison (Mk 4:30). In the sense of image, figure, symbol, equivalent to *túpos* (5179), a type (Heb 9:9; 11:19).

(II) Specifically, a parable, i.e. a short story under which something else is figured or in which the fictitious is used to represent and illustrate the real. This common oriental method of teaching was much used by Christ (Mt 13:24, 31, 33; 15:15; 21:33; 22:1; Mk 4:10, 11, 13; 7:17; 12:12; Lk 5:36; 6:39; 8:9–11; 12:16, 41; 13:6; 15:3; 18:1, 9; 19:11; 20:9, 19; 21:29). Parables may be short, one-sentence statements (Mt 13:31, 33), or longer, more involved stories (Mt 13:24–30; 22:1–14; Lk 20:9–19). Although a *parabállō* is usually a positive comparison statement, it may also occur in the form of a question (Lk 6:39), or a proverbial saying (Lk 4:23).

Syn.: *paroimía* (3942), a proverb.

3851. παραβουλεύομαι, parabouleuomai, *par-ab-ool-yoo´-om-ahee*; from 3844 and the middle of 1011; to *misconsult*, i.e. *disregard*:—not (to) regard (-ing).

3852. παραγγελία, paraggelia, *par-ang-gel-ee´-ah*; from 3853; a *mandate*:—charge, command.

Noun from *paraggéllō* (3853), to command. A proclamation, command from a superior. Spoken of those from secular magistrates (Ac 5:28; 16:24), and of those from Paul (1Th 4:2; 1Ti 1:5, 18).

Syn.: *diatagḗ* (1296), arrangement, order; *diátagma* (1297), edict; *éntalma* (1778), an injunction; *entolḗ* (1785), command, precept.

3853. παραγγέλλω, paraggellō, *par-ang-gel´-lo*; from 3844 and the base of 32; to *transmit a message*, i.e. (by implication) to *enjoin*:—(give in) charge, (give) command (-ment), declare.

From *pará* (3844), to the side of, and *aggéllō* (n.f., see *anaggéllō* [312]), to tell, declare. To bring word to anyone. In the NT, to direct, to charge or command (Mk 8:6; Lk 8:29; Ac 10:42; 15:5; 16:18, 23; 17:30; 23:30; 1Co 11:17; 1Th 4:11; 2Th 3:4, 6, 10, 12; 1Ti 5:7; 6:13). Followed by *mḗ* (3361), not, meaning to prohibit (Mt 10:5; Mk 6:8; Lk 8:56; 9:21; Ac 1:4; 4:18; 5:28, 40; 23:22; 1Co 7:10; 1Ti 1:3; 6:17).

Deriv.: *paraggelía* (3852), a commandment.

Syn.: *entéllomai* (1781), to command; *keleúō* (2753), to command, to order.

3854. παραγίνομαι, paraginomai, *par-ag-in´-om-ahee*; from 3844 and 1096; to *become near*, i.e. *approach* (*have arrived*); (by implication) to *appear* publicly:—come, go, be present.

3855. παράγω, paragō, *par-ag´-o*; from 3844 and 71; to *lead near*, i.e. (reflexive or intransitive) to *go along* or *away*:—depart, pass (away, by, forth).

3856. παραδειγματίζω, paradeigmatizō, *par-ad-igue-mat-id´-zo*; from 3844 and 1165; to *show alongside* (the public), i.e. *expose to infamy*:—make a public example, put to an open shame.

3857. παράδεισος, paradeisos, *par-ad´-i-sos*; of Oriental origin [compare 6508]; a *park*, i.e. (special) an *Eden* (place of future happiness, "*paradise*"):—paradise.

3858. παραδέχομαι, paradechomai, *par-ad-ekh´-om-ahee*; from 3844 and 1209; to *accept near*, i.e. *admit* or (by implication) *delight* in:—receive.

From *pará* (3844), from, and *déchomai* (1209), to receive. In the NT, to receive, to accept, to approve something (Mk 4:20; Ac 16:21; 22:18; 1Ti 5:19). Of persons, to receive, to accept as one's child (Heb 12:6).

Syn.: *apodéchomai* (588), to approve, welcome; *anagnōrízō* (319), to recognize.

3859. παραδιατριβή, paradiatribē, *par-ad-ee-at-ree-bay´*; from a compound of 3844 and 1304; *misemployment*, i.e. *meddlesomeness*:—perverse disputing.

3860. παραδίδωμι, paradidōmi, *par-ad-id´-o-mee*; from 3844 and 1325; to *surrender*, i.e. *yield up, intrust, transmit*:—betray, bring forth, cast, commit, deliver (up), give (over, up), hazard, put in prison, recommend.

3861. παράδοξος, paradoxos, *par-ad´-ox-os*; from 3844 and 1391 (in the sense of *seeming*); *contrary to expectation*, i.e. *extraordinary* ("*paradox*"):—strange.

Adjective from *pará* (3844), beyond, and *dóxa* (1391), opinion, expectation, glory. Paradoxical, strange. When used as a noun, something beyond one's expectation, a miracle. Used only in Lk 5:26.

Syn.: *dúnamis* (1411), power, miracle; *éndoxos* (1741), something glorious; *thaumásios* (2297), wonderful thing; *megaleíos* (3167), magnificent thing; *sēmeíon* (4592), sign; *téras* (5059), wonderful thing.

3862. παράδοσις, paradosis, *par-ad´-os-is*; from 3860; *transmission*, i.e. (concrete) a *precept*; specially the Jewish *traditionary law*:—ordinance, tradition.

3863. παραζηλόω, parazēloō, *par-ad-zay-lo´-o*; from 3844 and 2206; to *stimulate alongside*, i.e. *excite to rivalry*:—provoke to emulation (jealousy).

3864. παραθαλάσσιος, parathalassios, *par-ath-al-as´-see-os*; from 3844 and 2281; *along* the *sea*, i.e. *maritime* (*lacustrine*):—upon the sea coast.

3865. παραθεωρέω, paratheōreō, *par-ath-eh-o-reh´-o*; from 3844 and 2334; to *overlook* or *disregard*:—neglect.

3866. παραθήκη, parathēkē, *par-ath-ah´-kay*; from 3908; a *deposit*, i.e. (figurative) *trust*:—committed unto.

3867. παραινέω, paraineō, *par-ahee-neh´-o*; from 3844 and 134; to *mispraise*, i.e. *recommend* or *advise* (a different course):—admonish, exhort.

3868. παραιτέομαι, paraiteomai, *par-ahee-teh´-om-ahee*; from 3844 and the middle of 154; to *beg off*, i.e. *deprecate, decline, shun*:—avoid, (make) excuse, entreat, refuse, reject.

From *pará* (3844) aside, implying something more than is proper, hence, wrongly, and *aitéō* (154), to ask, beg. To ask near anyone, i.e. at his hands, to obtain by asking. In the NT, to ask aside or away, to get rid of by asking, similar to the English expression, to beg off of one.

(I) Primarily and generally, to entreat that something may not take place (Ac 25:11; Heb 12:19).

(II) To excuse oneself from an invitation (Lk 14:18, 19).

(III) By implication, not to receive, i.e. to refuse, to reject (1Ti 4:7; 5:11; Heb 12:25). In the sense of to avoid, to shun (2Ti 2:23; Tit 3:10).

Syn.: *egkataleípō* (1459), to forsake, give up.

3869. παρακαθίζω, parakathizō, *par-ak-ath-id´-zo*; from 3844 and 2523; to *sit down near*:—sit.

3870. παρακαλέω, parakaleō, *par-ak-al-eh´-o*; from 3844 and 2564; to *call near*, i.e. *invite, invoke* (by *imploration, hortation* or *consolation*):—beseech, call for, (be of good) comfort, desire, (give) exhort (-ation), entreat, pray.

From *pará* (3844), to the side of, and *kaléō* (2564), to call. To aid, help, comfort, encourage. Translated: to comfort, exhort, desire, call for, beseech with a stronger force than *aitéō* (154).

(I) To invite to come (Ac 28:20).

(II) To call for or upon someone as for aid, to invoke God, to beseech, entreat (Mt 8:5, 31, 34; 18:32; Mk 1:40; 5:17, 18, 23; Lk 8:31; Ac 8:31; 9:38; 16:15, 39; 19:31; 21:12; 24:4; 25:2; 1Co 16:12; 2Co 12:8, 18; Phm 10).

(III) To call upon someone to do something, to exhort, admonish, with the accusative of person (Lk 3:18; Ac 2:40; 11:23; 15:32; 27:33, 34; Ro 12:1, 8; 1Co 1:10; 4:16; 14:31; 2Co 2:8; 5:20; 6:1; 8:6; 10:1; 13:11; Eph 4:1; Php 4:2; 1Th 2:11; 4:1; 1Ti 2:1; 5:1; 6:2; Tit 1:9; 2:15; Heb 3:13; 10:25; 13:19; 1Pe 2:11; 5:1).

(IV) To exhort in the way of consolation, encouragement, to console, comfort (Mt 2:18; 5:4; 2Co 1:4; 2:7; 7:6; Eph 6:22; Col 4:8; 1Th 3:7; 4:18; 2Th 2:17). In the sense of to make glad, in the pass., to be glad, rejoice (Lk 16:25; Ac 20:12).

Deriv.: *paráklēsis* (3874), exhortation, consolation, comfort; *paráklētos* (3875), a counselor, an advocate, a comforter; *sumparakaléō* (4837), to comfort together.

Syn.: *noutheteō* (3560), to warn, admonish; *paramuthéomai* (3888), to console, comfort.

3871. παρακαλύπτω, parakaluptō, *par-ak-al-oop´-to*; from 3844 and 2572; to *cover alongside*, i.e. *veil* (figurative):—hide.

3872. παρακαταθήκη, parakatathēkē, *par-ak-at-ath-ay´-kay*; from a compound of 3844 and 2698; something *put down alongside*, i.e. a *deposit* (sacred *trust*):—that (thing) which is committed (un-) to (trust).

3873. παράκειμαι, parakeimai, *par-ak´-i-mahee*; from 3844 and 2749; to *lie near*, i.e. *be at hand* (figurative, *be prompt* or *easy*):—be present.

3874. παράκλησις, paraklēsis, *par-ak´-lay-sis*; from 3870; *imploration, hortation, solace*:—comfort, consolation, exhortation, entreaty.

Noun from *parakaléō* (3870), to beseech. The act of exhortation, encouragement, comfort.

(I) An entreaty, petition, appeal (2Co 8:4, 17 [cf. v. 6]).

(II) Exhortation, admonition (Ro 12:8; 1Co 14:3; 1Ti 4:13; Heb 12:5; 13:22). In the sense of instruction, teaching, especially teaching that encourages (Ac 13:15; 15:31; 1Th 2:3). This is probably the significance of Ac 4:36 where Barnabas is described as the son of *parakléseos*, i.e. son of exhortation, the Aramaic name, Barnabas, probably signifying "son of prophecy."

(III) Consolation, comfort, solace (Ac 9:31; Ro 15:4, 5; 2Co 1:3–7; 7:4, 7, 13; Php 2:1; 2Th 2:16; Phm 7; Heb 6:18). By metonymy, the Messiah as the author of spiritual aid and consolation (Lk 2:25). By implication, joy, gladness (Lk 6:24).

Syn.: *nouthesía* (3559), warning, admonition; *paramuthía* (3889), consolation, comfort.

3875. παράκλητος, paraklētos, *par-ak´-lay-tos*; an *intercessor, consoler*:—advocate, comforter.

Noun from *parakaléō* (3870), to comfort, encourage or exhort. One called upon to help.

(I) An advocate, intercessor; one who pleads the cause of anyone before a judge (1Jn 2:1).

(II) A comforter, bestowing spiritual aid and consolation, spoken of the Holy Spirit (Jn 14:16, 26; 15:26; 16:7).

3876. παρακοή, parakoē, *par-ak-o-ay´*; from 3878; *inattention*, i.e. (by implication) *disobedience*:—disobedience.

Noun from *parakoúō* (3878), to disobey. In its strictest sense, it means a failing to hear or mishearing. In the NT, neglect to hear, emphasizing the active disobedience which follows this inattentive or careless hearing (cf. Ro 5:19; 2Co 10:6; Heb 2:2).

Syn.: *apeítheia* (543), disobedience; *parábasis* (3847), transgression.

3877. παρακολουθέω, parakoloutheō, *par-ak-ol-oo-theh´-o*; from 3844 and 190; to *follow near*, i.e. (figurative) *attend* (as a result), *trace out, conform* to:—attain, follow, fully know, have understanding.

3878. παρακούω, parakouō, *par-ak-oo´-o*; from 3844 and 191; to *mishear*, i.e. (by implication) to *disobey*:—neglect to hear.

3879. παρακύπτω, parakuptō, *par-ak-oop´-to*; from 3844 and 2955; to *bend beside*, i.e. *lean over* (so as to *peer within*):—look (into), stoop down.

3880. παραλαμβάνω, paralambanō, *par-al-am-ban´-o*; from 3844 and 2983; to *receive near*, i.e. *associate with* oneself (in any familiar or intimate act or relation); (by analogy) to *assume* an office; (figurative) to *learn*:—receive, take (unto, with).

3881. παραλέγομαι, paralegomai, *par-al-eg´-om-ahee*; from 3844 and the middle of 3004 (in its original sense); (special) to *lay* one's course *near*, i.e. *sail past*:—pass, sail by.

3882. παράλιος, paralios, *par-al´-ee-os*; from 3844 and 251; *beside* the *salt* (*sea*), i.e. *maritime*:—sea coast.

3883. παραλλαγή, parallagē, *par-al-lag-ay´*; from a compound of 3844 and 236; *transmutation* (of phase or orbit), i.e. (figurative) *fickleness*:—variableness.

3884. παραλογίζομαι, paralogizomai, *par-al-og-id´-zom-ahee*; from 3844 and 3049; to *misreckon*, i.e. *delude*:—beguile, deceive.

3885. παραλυτικός, paralutikos, *par-al-oo-tee-kos´*; from a derivative of 3886; as if *dissolved*, i.e. "*paralytic*":—that had (sick of) the palsy.

3886. παραλύω, paraluō, *par-al-oo´-o*; from 3844 and 3089; to *loosen beside*, i.e. *relax* (perfect passive participle *paralyzed* or *enfeebled*):—feeble, sick of the (taken with) palsy.

3887. παραμένω, paramenō, *par-am-en´-o*; from 3844 and 3306; to *stay near*, i.e. *remain* (literal, *tarry*; or figurative, *be permanent, persevere*):—abide, continue.

From *pará* (3844), with, and *ménō* (3306), to remain. To stay, remain nearby with someone, abide (1Co 16:6); to remain, to continue in an office or position; e.g., the priest's office (Heb 7:23). Figuratively, to continue, persevere, e.g., in the law of liberty (Jas 1:25).

Deriv.: *sumparaménō* (4839), to remain together.

Syn.: *diaménō* (1265), to remain throughout or constant; *diateléō* (1300), to continue.

3888. παραμυθέομαι, paramutheomai, *par-am-oo-theh´-om-ahee*; from 3844 and the middle of a derivative of 3454; to *relate near*, i.e. (by implication) *encourage, console*:—comfort.

3889. παραμυθία, paramuthia, *par-am-oo-thee´-ah*; from 3888; *consolation* (properly abstract):—comfort.

3890. παραμύθιον, paramuthion, *par-am-oo´-thee-on*; neuter of 3889; *consolation* (properly concrete):—comfort.

3891. παρανομέω, paranomeō, *par-an-om-eh´-o*; from a compound of 3844 and 3551; to *be opposed to law*, i.e. to *transgress*:—contrary to law.

3892. παρανομία, paranomia, *par-an-om-ee´-ah*; from the same as 3891; *transgression*:—iniquity.

Noun from *paranoméō* (3891), to transgress the law, which is from *pará* (3844), beyond, and *nómos* (3551), law. A transgression or an offence of the law. Used only in 2Pe 2:16. The verb *paranoméō* (3891) occurs in Ac 23:3.

Syn.: *adikía* (93), unrighteousness, injustice, wrong; *hamartía* (266), sin; *anomía* (458), lawlessness; *parábasis* (3847), the act of transgression; *parakoḗ* (3876), disobedience; *paráptōma* (3900), transgression.

3893. παραπικραίνω, parapikrainō, *par-ap-ik-rah´ee-no*; from 3844 and 4087; to *embitter alongside*, i.e. (figurative) to *exasperate*:—provoke.

3894. παραπικρασμός, parapikrasmos, *par-ap-ik-ras-mos´*; from 3893; *irritation*:—provocation.

3895. παραπίπτω, parapiptō, *par-ap-ip´-to*; from 3844 and 4098; to *fall aside*, i.e. (figurative) to *apostatize*:—fall away.

From *pará* (3844), to the side of or from, implying error, and *píptō* (4098), to fall. In the NT, figuratively, to fall away from the path of duty, to abandon the faith, to apostatize. Used only in Heb 6:6.

Deriv.: *paráptōma* (3900), transgression.

Syn.: *katapíptō* (2667), to fall down.

3896. παραπλέω, parapleō, *par-ap-leh´-o*; from 3844 and 4126; to *sail near*:—sail by.

3897. παραπλήσιον, paraplēsion, *par-ap-lay´-see-on*; neuter of a compound of 3844 and the base of 4139 (as adverb); *close by*, i.e. (figurative) *almost*:—nigh unto.

3898. παραπλησίως, paraplēsiōs, *par-ap-lay-see´-oce*; adverb from the same as 3897; *in a manner near by*, i.e. (figurative) *similarly*:—likewise.

3899. παραπορεύομαι, paraporeuomai, *par-ap-or-yoo´-om-ahee*; from 3844 and 4198; to *travel near*:—go, pass (by).

3900. παράπτωμα, paraptōma, *par-ap´-to-mah*; from 3895; a *side-slip* (*lapse* or *deviation*), i.e. (unintentional) *error* or (willful) *transgression*:—fall, fault, offence, sin, trespass.

Noun from *parapíptō* (3895), to fall by the wayside. A falling aside or away as from right, truth, duty; a lapse, error, fault.

(I) Transgressions committed out of ignorance or carelessness (Mt 6:14, 15; 18:35; Mk 11:25, 26; Gal 6:1; Jas 5:16).

(II) Transgressions which are deliberate, intentional; sins (Ro 4:25; 5:15–18, 20; 11:11, 12; 2Co 5:19; Eph 1:7; 2:1, 5; Col 2:13).

Syn.: *hamartía* (266), offence, sin; *parábasis* (3847), violation, transgression.

3901. παραῤῥυέω, pararrhueō, *par-ar-hroo-eh´-o*; from 3844 and the alternate of 4482; to *flow by*, i.e. (figurative) carelessly *pass* (*miss*):—let slip.

3902. παράσημος, parasēmos, *par-as´-ay-mos*; from 3844 and the base of 4591; *side-marked*, i.e. *labelled* (with a *badge* [*figure-head*] of a ship):—sign.

3903. παρασκευάζω, paraskeuazō, *par-ask-yoo-ad´-zo*; from 3844 and a derivative of 4632; to *furnish aside*, i.e. *get ready*:—prepare self, be (make) ready.

3904. παρασκευή, paraskeuē, *par-ask-yoo-ay´*; as if from 3903; *readiness*:—preparation.

3905. παρατείνω, parateinō, *par-at-i´-no*; from 3844 and **τείνω,** ***teinō*** (to *stretch*); to *extend along*, i.e. *prolong* (in point of time):—continue.

3906. παρατηρέω, paratēreō, *par-at-ay-reh´-o*; from 3844 and 5083; to *inspect alongside*, i.e. *note insidiously* or *scrupulously*:—observe, watch.

From *pará* (3844), near or close to, and *tēréō* (5083), to keep, observe. To watch closely.

(I) To watch closely with a sinister intent. Spoken of the Pharisees watching Jesus to catch him doing anything which they could accuse him of (Mk 3:2; Lk 6:7; 14:1; 20:20). Spoken of the Jews watching the city gates to seize Paul as he left the city (Ac 9:24).

(II) To observe religious days scrupulously, to keep them superstitiously (Gal 4:10).

Deriv.: *paratḗrēsis* (3907), attentive watching.

Syn.: *blépō* (991), look at; *theáomai* (2300), to look closely at, perceive; *theōréō* (2334), to behold intensely, consider, perceive, see; *horáō* (3708), to see.

3907. παρατήρησις, paratērēsis, *par-at-ay´-ray-sis*; from 3906; *inspection*, i.e. *ocular evidence*:—observation.

Noun from *paratēréō* (3906), to watch closely. Close watching, accurate observation. Used only in Lk 17:20.

3908. παρατίθημι, paratithēmi, *par-at-ith´-ay-mee*; from 3844 and 5087; to *place alongside*, i.e. *present* (food, truth); (by implication) to *deposit* (as a trust or for protection):—allege, commend, commit (the keeping of), put forth, set before.

3909. παρατυγχάνω, paratugchanō, *par-at-oong-khan´-o*; from 3844 and 5177; to *chance near*, i.e. *fall in with*:—meet with.

3910. παραυτίκα, parautika, *par-ow-tee´-kah*; from 3844 and a derivative of 846; *at* the *very* instant, i.e. *momentary*:—but for a moment.

3911. παραφέρω, parapherō, *par-af-er´-o*; from 3844 and 5342 (including its alternate forms); to *bear along* or *aside*, i.e. *carry off* (literal or figurative); (by implication) to *avert*:—remove, take away.

3912. παραφρονέω, paraphroneō, *par-af-ron-eh´-o*; from 3844 and 5426; to *misthink*, i.e. *be insane* (*silly*):—as a fool.

3913. παραφρονία, paraphronia, *par-af-ron-ee´-ah*; from 3912; *insanity*, i.e. *foolhardiness*:—madness.

3914. παραχειμάζω, paracheimazō, *par-akh-i-mad´-zo*; from 3844 and 5492; to *winter near*, i.e. *stay* with over the *rainy* season:—winter.

3915. παραχειμασία, paracheimasia, *par-akh-i-mas-ee´-ah*; from 3914; a *wintering* over:—winter in.

3916. παραχρῆμα, parachrēma, *par-akh-ray´-mah*; from 3844 and 5536 (in its original sense); *at the thing* itself, i.e. *instantly*:—forthwith, immediately, presently, straightway, soon.

3917. πάρδαλις, pardalis, *par´-dal-is*; feminine of **πάρδος,** ***pardos*** (a *panther*); a *leopard*:—leopard.

3918. πάρειμι, pareimi, *par´-i-mee*; from 3844 and 1510 (including its various forms); to *be near*, i.e. *at hand*; neuter presumed participle (singular) *time being*, or (plural) *property*:—come, × have, be here, + lack, (be here) present.

3919. παρεισάγω, pareisagō, *par-ice-ag´-o*; from 3844 and 1521; to *lead in aside*, i.e. *introduce surreptitiously*:—privily bring in.

3920. παρείσακτος, pareisaktos, *par-ice´-ak-tos*; from 3919; *smuggled in*:—unawares brought in.

3921. παρεισδύνω, pareisdunō, *par-ice-doo´-no*; from 3844 and a compound of 1519 and 1416; to *settle in alongside*, i.e. *lodge stealthily*:—creep in unawares.

3922. παρεισέρχομαι, pareiserchomai, *par-ice-er´-khom-ahee*; from 3844 and 1525; to *come in alongside*, i.e. *supervene additionally* or *stealthily*:—come in privily, enter.

3923. παρεισφέρω, pareispherō, *par-ice-fer´-o*; from 3844 and 1533; to *bear in alongside*, i.e. *introduce simultaneously*:—give.

3924. παρεκτός, parektos, *par-ek-tos´*; from 3844 and 1622; *near outside*, i.e. *besides*:—except, saving, without.

3925. παρεμβολή, parembolē, *par-em-bol-ay´*; from a compound of 3844 and 1685; a *throwing in beside (juxtaposition)*; i.e. (special) *battle-array, encampment* or *barracks* (tower Antonia):—army, camp, castle.

3926. παρενοχλέω, parenochleō, *par-en-okh-leh´-o*; from 3844 and 1776; to *harass further*, i.e. *annoy*:—trouble.

3927. παρεπίδημος, parepidēmos, *par-ep-id´-ay-mos*; from 3844 and the base of 1927; an *alien alongside*, i.e. a *resident foreigner*:—pilgrim, stranger.

Adjective from *pará* (3844), near or close to, and *epídēmos* (n.f.), stranger, which is from *epí* (1909), in or among, and *dḗmos* (1218), a people. A stranger, sojourner; one living among a people not one's own (Heb 11:13; 1Pe 1:1; 2:11). Also from *epídēmos* (n.f.): *epidēméō* (1927), to reside as a stranger, used in Ac 2:10; 17:21.

Syn.: *allogenḗs* (241), one of a different race; *allótrios* (245), stranger; *apódēmos* (590), sojourner, living in another country; *xénos* (3581), a stranger, foreigner; *pároikos* (3941), alien, sojourner.

3928. παρέρχομαι, parerchomai, *par-er´-khom-ahee*; from 3844 and 2064; to *come near* or *aside*, i.e. to *approach* (*arrive*), go *by* (or *away*), (figurative) *perish* or *neglect*, (causative) *avert*:—come (forth), go, pass (away, by, over), past, transgress.

3929. πάρεσις, paresis, *par´-es-is*; from 2935; *prætermission*, i.e. *toleration*:—remission.

Noun from *paríēmi* (3935), to let pass by. A letting pass, remission in the sense of overlooking, not punishing. Used only in Ro 3:25. *Páresis* differs from *áphesis* (859), which implies pardon or forgiveness, i.e. not just an absence of punishment, but the removal of guilt.

3930. παρέχω, parechō, *par-ekh´-o*; from 3844 and 2192; to *hold near*, i.e. *present, afford, exhibit, furnish occasion*:—bring, do, give, keep, minister, offer, shew, + trouble.

From *pará* (3844), unto, at, near, and *échō* (2192), to have, hold. To hold out toward someone, to present, offer.

(I) Particularly to offer, e.g., one's cheek (Lk 6:29). Also 1Ti 6:17.

(II) Figuratively, meaning to be the cause, source, occasion of something to a person, to make or do, to give or bestow, to occasion something in one's behalf. E.g., with *kópos* (2873), trouble, to give one trouble, to vex (Mt 26:10; Mk 14:6; Lk 11:7; 18:5; Gal 6:17). Also Lk 7:4; Ac 16:16; 17:31; 19:24; 22:2; 28:2; Col 4:1; 1Ti 1:4; Tit 2:7.

Syn.: *prosphérō* (4374), to bring, present, offer.

3931. παρηγορία, parēgoria, *par-ay-gor-ee´-ah*; from a compound of 3844 and a derivative of 58 (meaning to *harangue* an assembly); an *address alongside*, i.e. (special) *consolation*:—comfort.

3932. παρθενία, parthenia, *par-then-ee´-ah*; from 3933; *maidenhood*:—virginity.

3933. παρθένος, parthenos, *par-then´-os*; of unknown origin; a *maiden*; (by implication) an unmarried *daughter*:—virgin.

3934. Πάρθος, Parthos, *par´-thos*; probably of foreign origin; a *Parthian*, i.e. inhabitant of Parthia:—Parthian.

3935. παρίημι, pariēmi, *par-ee´-ay-mi*; from 3844 and **ἵημι,** ***hiēmi*** (to *send*); to *let by*, i.e. *relax*:—hang down.

3936. παρίστημι, paristēmi, *par-is´-tay-mee*; or prolonged **παριστάνω,** ***paristanō***, *par-is-tan´-o*; from 3844 and 2476; to *stand beside*, i.e. (transitive) to *exhibit, proffer*, (special) *recommend*, (figurative) *substantiate*; or (intransitive) to *be at hand* (or *ready*), *aid*:—assist, bring before, command, commend, give presently, present, prove, provide, shew, stand (before, by, here, up, with), yield.

3937. Παρμενᾶς, Parmenas, *par-men-as´*; probably by contraction for **Παρμενίδης,** ***Parmenidēs*** (a derivative of a compound of 3844 and 3306); *constant; Parmenas*, a Christian:—Parmenas.

3938. πάροδος, parodos, *par´-od-os*; from 3844 and 3598; a *byroad*, i.e. (active) a *route*:—way.

3939. παροικέω, paroikeō, *par-oy-keh´-o*; from 3844 and 3611; to *dwell near*, i.e. *reside* as a *foreigner*:—sojourn in, be a stranger.

From *pará* (3844), near or at, and *oikéō* (3611), to dwell. To dwell near, to be a neighbour. To dwell or sojourn as a stranger (Lk 24:18; Heb 11:9).

Syn.: *epidēméō* (1927), to reside in a foreign country.

3940. παροικία, paroikia, *par-oy-kee´-ah*; from 3941; *foreign residence*:—sojourning, × as strangers.

3941. πάροικος, paroikos, *par´-oy-kos*; from 3844 and 3624; having a *home near*, i.e. (as noun) a *by-dweller* (*alien resident*):—foreigner, sojourn, stranger.

Adjective from *pará* (3844), near or at, and *oíkos* (3624), house. Dwelling near, neighboring; as a substantive: a sojourner, one without the right of citizenship, a foreigner (Ac 7:6, 29). Figuratively, spoken of the saints: as sojourners in this world (1Pe 2:11); as strangers outside the church (Eph 2:19).

Deriv.: *paroikía* (3940), a sojourning.

Syn.: *allótrios* (245), stranger; *parepídēmos* (3927), one sojourning in a strange place. Also *allogenḗs* (241), one of a different race; *xénos* (3581), a stranger, foreigner.

3942. παροιμία, paroimia, *par-oy-mee´-ah*; from a compound of 3844 and perhaps a derivative of 3633; apparently a state *alongside of supposition*, i.e. (concrete) an *adage*; specially an enigmatical or fictitious *illustration*:—parable, proverb.

3943. πάροινος, paroinos, *par´-oy-nos*; from 3844 and 3631; staying *near wine*, i.e. *tippling* (a *toper*):—given to wine.

3944. παροίχομαι, paroichomai, *par-oy´-khom-ahee*; from 3844 and **οἴχομαι,** ***oichomai*** (to *depart*); to *escape along*, i.e. *be gone*:—past.

3945. παρομοιάζω, paromoiazō, *par-om-oy-ad´-zo*; from 3946; to *resemble*:—be like unto.

3946. παρόμοιος, paromoios, *par-om´-oy-os*; from 3844 and 3664; *alike nearly*, i.e. *similar*:—like.

3947. παροξύνω, paroxunō, *par-ox-oo´-no*; from 3844 and a derivative of 3691; to *sharpen alongside*, i.e. (figurative) to *exasperate*:—easily provoke, stir.

3948. παροξυσμός, paroxusmos, *par-ox-oos-mos´*; from 3947 ("*paroxysm*"); *incitement* (to good), or *dispute* (in anger):—contention, provoke unto.

3949. παροργίζω, parorgizō, *par-org-id´-zo*; from 3844 and 3710; to *anger alongside*, i.e. *enrage*:—anger, provoke to wrath.

3950. παροργισμός, parorgismos, *par-org-is-mos´*; from 3949; *rage*:—wrath.

Noun from *parorgízō* (3949), to make angry, provoke to violent or bitter anger. Anger provoked, indignation, wrath. Used only in Eph 4:26.

Syn.: *aganáktēsis* (24), indignation.

3951. παροτρύνω, parotrunō, *par-ot-roo´-no*; from 3844 and **ὀτρύνω,** ***otrunō*** (to *spur*); to *urge along*, i.e. *stimulate* (to hostility):—stir up.

3952. παρουσία, parousia, *par-oo-see´-ah*; from the presumed participle of 3918; a *being near*, i.e. *advent* (often, *return*; specially of Christ to punish Jerusalem, or finally the wicked); (by implication) physical *aspect*:—coming, presence.

Noun from *parṓn* (participle of *páreimi* [3918], to be present), present, presence, a being present, a coming to a place. Presence, coming or arrival.

(I) Presence, the state of being present rather than absent (2Co 10:10; Php 2:12).

(II) A coming or visit (1Co 16:17; 2Co 7:6, 7; Php 1:26).

(III) Used of the Second Coming of Christ (Mt 24:3; 1Co 15:23; 1Th 2:19; 2Th 2:8; 2Pe 3:4; 1Jn 2:28); the Son of Man (Mt 24:27, 37, 39); the Lord (1Th 3:13; 4:15; 5:23; 2Th 2:1; Jas 5:7, 8; 2Pe 1:16); the day of God (2Pe 3:12). The term *parousia* is used of Christ's Second Coming as a whole, and of individual events (e.g., the Rapture); only context can determine which is being discussed.

(IV) Of the coming or manifestation of the man of sin (2Th 2:9 [cf. 2Th 2:3]).

Syn.: *éleusis* (1660), coming.

3953. παροψίς, paropsis, *par-op-sis´*; from 3844 and the base of 3795; a *side-dish* (the receptacle):—platter.

3954. παῤῥησία, parrhēsia, *par-rhay-see´-ah*; from 3956 and a derivative of 4483; *all* out-*spokenness*, i.e. *frankness, bluntness, publicity*; (by implication) *assurance*:—bold (× -ly, -ness, -ness of speech), confidence, × freely, × openly, × plainly (-ness).

Noun from *pás* (3956), all, and *rhḗsis* (n.f.), the act of speaking. Literally, "the speaking all one is thinking," i.e. freespokenness as a characteristic of a frank and fearless mind; hence freeness, frankness, boldness in speech and action.

(I) Particularly, boldness (Ac 4:13; 2Co 3:12). In adverbial phrases, with openness, openly, plainly (Mk 8:32; Jn 7:4, 13, 26; 10:24; 11:14, 54; 16:25, 29; 18:20; Col 2:15); with boldness, boldly (Ac 2:29; 4:29, 31; 28:31; Eph 6:19; Php 1:20).

(II) By implication, the right or authority to speak boldly (1Ti 3:13; Phm 8).

(III) By implication, frank reliance, confidence, assurance (2Co 7:4; Eph 3:12; Heb 3:6; 4:16; 10:19, 35; 1Jn 2:28; 3:21; 4:17; 5:14).

Deriv.: *parrēsiázomai* (3955), to speak boldly or freely.

Syn.: *thársos* (2294), courage; *pepoíthēsis* (4006), persuasion, assurance, confidence.

3955. παῤῥησιάζομαι, parrhēsiazomai, *par-hray-see-ad´-zom-ahee*; middle from 3954; to *be frank* in utterance, or *confident* in spirit and demeanour:—be (wax) bold, (preach, speak) boldly.

From *parrēsía* (3954), freedom or frankness in speaking. To be freespoken, to speak freely, openly, boldly, in speech and action (Ac 9:27, 29; 13:46; 14:3; 18:26; 19:8; 26:26; Eph 6:20; 1Th 2:2).

Syn.: *apotolmáō* (662), to be very bold, to speak boldly; *tharréō* (2292), to be bold, courageous; *tolmáō* (5111), to dare.

3956. πᾶς, pas, *pas*; including all the forms of declension; apparently a primary word; *all, any, every,* the *whole*:—all (manner of, means), alway (-s), any (one), × daily, + ever, every (one, way), as many as, + no (-thing), × thoroughly, whatsoever, whole, whosoever.

Adjective meaning all.

(I) Includes the idea of oneness, a totality or the whole, the same as *hólos* (3650), the whole.

(A) The singular may have the idea of "whole" (Mt 8:32); "every" (Ro 3:19); "all" reference to qualitative nouns, e.g., "all" judgement (Jn 5:22). Also Mt 6:29; Mk 5:33; Lk 1:10; 4:25; Ac 1:8. Used by metonymy with the names of cities or countries to speak of the inhabitants (Mt 3:5; Mk 1:5; Lk 2:1).

(B) In the plural, to signify all of those in a group (Mt 1:17; 4:8; Mk 3:28; Lk 1:6; Ac 5:20; 22:15; Ro 1:5; 5:12, 18).

(II) Also includes the idea of plurality meaning all or every, equivalent to *hékastos* (1538), each one. Everyone who falls into a certain classification.

(A) With the relative pronoun, *hós* (3739), who, everyone who, whoever (Mt 7:24; Jn 6:37, 39; 17:2; Ac 2:21; Ro 10:13; 14:23; Gal 3:10; Col 3:17).

(B) With a participle with the article, it becomes a substantive expressing a class, e.g., everyone who is angry (Mt 5:22). Also Lk 6:47; Jn 6:45; Ac 10:43; Ro 2:10.

(III) All, meaning of all kinds, of every kind and sort including every possible variety.

(A) Generally (Mt 4:23; Ro 1:18, 29; 1Ti 6:10; 1Pe 2:1).

(B) In the sense of all possible, the greatest, utmost, supreme (Mt 28:18; Ac 5:23; 17:11; 23:1; 2Co 12:12; Php 1:20; 2:29; 1Ti 2:2; 2Ti 4:2; Jas 1:2; 1Pe 2:18; Jude 3).

Deriv.: *hápas* (537), whole, all; *diapantós* (1275), continually, always.

Syn.: *hólos* (3650), all, whole. Also *hápas* (537), absolutely all; *hékastos* (1538), each one; *holóklēros* (3648), complete in every part, entire.

3957. πάσχα, pascha, *pas´-khah*; of Chaldee origin [compare 6453]; the *Passover* (the meal, the day, the festival or the special sacrifices connected with it):—Easter, Passover.

3958. πάσχω, paschō, *pas´-kho*; including the forms (**πάθω,** ***pathō***, *path´-o*) and (**πένθω,** ***penthō***, *pen´-tho*), used only in certain tenses for it; apparently a primary verb; to *experience* a sensation or impression (usually painful):—feel, passion, suffer, vex.

In the most general sense, to be affected by something from without, to be acted upon, to undergo an experience. In the NT, used of evil, meaning to suffer, be subjected to evil (Mt 17:12; 27:19; Mk 5:26; Lk 13:2; Ac 9:16; 28:5; 1Co 12:26; Gal 3:4; Php 1:29; 1Th 2:14; 2Th 1:5; 2Ti 1:12; Heb 2:18; 5:8; 1Pe 2:19, 20, 23; 3:14, 17; 4:19; 5:10; Rev 2:10). Spoken of the suffering and death of Christ (Mt 16:21; 17:12; Mk 9:12; Lk 17:25; 22:15; 24:26, 46; Ac 1:3; 3:18; 17:3; Heb 9:26; 13:12; 1Pe 2:21; 3:18; 4:1).

Deriv.: a fellow sufferer; *páthēma* (3804), suffering; *pathētós* (3805), subject to suffering; *páthos* (3806), suffering; *propáschō* (4310), to have suffered before; *sumpáschō* (4841), to suffer with.

Syn.: *basanízomai* (the passive of *basanízō* [928]), to be tormented; *kakouchéomai* (the passive of *kakouchéō* [2558]), to be inflicted with harm; *kataponéomai* (the passive of *kataponéō* [2669]), to be oppressed, be vexed; *talaipōréō* (5003), to be afflicted.

3959. Πάταρα, Patara, *pat´-ar-ah*; probably of foreign origin; *Patara*, a place in Asia Minor:—Patara.

3960. πατάσσω, patassō, *pat-as´-so*; probably prolonged from 3817; to *knock* (gently or with a weapon or fatally):—smite, strike. Compare 5180.

3961. πατέω, pateō, *pat-eh´-o*; from a derivative probably of 3817 (meaning a "*path*"); to *trample* (literal or figurative):—tread (down, under foot).

From *pátos* (n.f.), a path, a beaten way. To tread with the feet.

(I) To tread down, to trample under foot, i.e. to lay waste (Lk 21:24; Rev 11:2). In the sense of to tread out, as grapes in a wine vat (Rev 14:20; 19:15).

(II) To tread on, as to tread upon serpents (Lk 10:19).

Deriv.: *katapatéō* (2662), to trample; *peripatéō* (4043), to walk around.

3962. πατήρ, patēr, *pat-ayr´*; apparently a primary word; a "*father*" (literal or figurative, near or more remote):—father, parent.

A noun, the etymology of which is uncertain. A father, spoken generally of men and in a special sense of God. Progenitor, ancestor, father, mentor, or model.

(I) Generally.

(A) Particularly one's father, by whom one is begotten (Mt 2:22; 19:5; Mk 5:40; Jn 4:53; Heb 7:10). Plural, parents, both father and mother (Heb 11:23; perhaps Eph 6:4). Of one reputed to be a father or stepfather (Lk 2:48).

(B) Of a remote ancestor, forefather, progenitor, or founder of a tribe or people, patriarch. Singular (Mt 3:9; Mk 11:10; Lk 1:32, 73; Jn 4:12; 7:22; Ac 3:13; Ro 9:5; Heb 1:1). Figuratively in a spiritual and moral sense, spoken of Abraham as the father of all who believe (Ro 4:11, 12, 16); spoken of one who leads another to Christ (1Co 4:15). Spoken of Satan as the father of wicked and depraved men (Jn 8:38, 41, 44). He is the model whom sinners resemble, i.e. they have like evil character.

(C) As a title of respect and reverence, in direct address (Lk 16:24, 27, 30); of a teacher as exercising paternal care, authority and affection (Mt 23:9; 1Co 4:15 [cf. Php 2:22; 1Th 2:11]. In the plural, fathers, as an honorary title of address used toward older persons (1Jn 2:13, 14); also toward magistrates, members of the Sanhedrin (Ac 7:2; 22:1).

(D) Metaphorically with the gen. of a thing; the author, source, beginner of something (Jn 8:44; Ro 4:12).

(II) Of God generally as the creator, preserver, governor of all men and things, watching over them with paternal love and care. Thus in the NT God is called Father.

(A) Claimed improperly by unsaved Jews (Jn 9:41 [cf. v. 42]).

(B) Properly ascribed for all those who are saved (Mt 6:4, 6, 8, 14, 15, 18; Ro 1:7; 8:15; 1Co 1:3; 2Co 6:18).

(C) Specifically, God is called the Father of our Lord Jesus Christ in respect to that particular relation in which Christ is the Son of God. See *huiós* (5207), son, where the Father and Son are expressly distinguished (Mt 11:27; 28:19; Mk 13:32; Lk 9:26; 10:22; Jn 1:14, 18; 3:35; 5:26; Ro 15:6; 2Co 1:3; 11:31; Eph 1:3; Col 1:3; Heb 1:5; 1Pe 1:3; 1Jn 2:22; 4:14; 2Jn 3, 9).

(D) Metaphorically in Jas 1:17, "the Father of lights" meaning the author or creator of the heavenly luminaries.

Deriv.: *apátōr* (540), literally without father; *patralǿas* (3964), a murderer of fathers; *patriá* (3965), paternal descent; *patriárchēs* (3966), patriarch, progenitor; *patrikós* (3967), paternal, ancestral; *patrís* (3968), a fatherland, native country, town, home; *patroparádotos* (3970), handed down from one's fathers.

Syn.: Related words on family: *mḗtēr* (3384), mother; *huiós* (5207), son; *thugátēr* (2364), daughter; *adelphós* (80), brother; *adelphḗ* (79), sister; *pentherá* (3994), mother-in-law; *631pentherós* (3995), father-in-law; *ékgonos* (1549), grandchild, literally a descendant; *mámmē* (3125), a grandmother; *anepsiós* (431), a cousin; *suggenḗs* (4773), a relative; *génos* (1085), family, stock; *oíkos* (3624), family; *goneús* (1118), a parent; *prógonos* (4269), an ancestor, forefather.

3963. Πάτμος, Patmos, *pat´-mos*; of uncertain derivative; *Patmus*, an islet in the Mediterranean:—Patmos.

3964. πατραλῴας, patralōias, *pat-ral-o´-as*; from 3962 and the same as the latter part of 3389; a *parricide*:—murderer of fathers.

3965. πατριά, patria, *pat-ree-ah´*; as if feminine of a derivative of 3962; paternal *descent*, i.e. (concretely) a *group* of families or a whole *race* (*nation*):—family, kindred, lineage.

Noun from *patḗr* (3962), father. Paternal, descent, lineage. In the NT, a family.

(I) Particularly, a family which may include several households (Lk 2:4; Eph 3:15).

(II) In a wider sense, a tribe, people, nation (Ac 3:25).

Deriv.: *patriárchēs* (3966), patriarch.

Syn.: *phulḗ* (5443), tribe, race, clan. Also *geneá* (1074), age, generation; *génos* (1085), stock, race, kind; *oíkos* (3624), family.

3966. πατριάρχης, patriarchēs, *pat-ree-arkh´-ace*; from 3965 and 757; a *progenitor* ("patriarch"):—patriarch.

3967. πατρικός, patrikos, *pat-ree-kos´*; from 3962; *paternal*, i.e. *ancestral*:—of fathers.

3968. πατρίς, patris, *pat-rece´*; from 3962; a *father-land*, i.e. *native town*; (figurative) heavenly *home*:—(own) country.

3969. Πατρόβας, Patrobas, *pat-rob´-as*; perhaps contraction for **Πατρόβιος *Patrobios*** (a compound of 3962 and 979); *father's life; Patrobas*, a Christian:—Patrobas.

3970. πατροπαράδοτος, patroparadotos, *pat-rop-ar-ad´-ot-os*; from 3962 and a derivative of 3860 (in the sense of *handing over* or *down*); *traditionary*:—received by tradition from fathers.

3971. πατρῷος, patrōios, *pat-ro´-os*; from 3962; *paternal*, i.e. *hereditary*:—of fathers.

3972. Παῦλος, Paulos, *pow´-los*; of Latin origin; (*little*; but remotely from a derivative of 3973, meaning the same); *Paulus*, the name of a Roman and of an apostle:—Paul, Paulus.

3973. παύω, pauō, *pow´-o*; a primary verb ("*pause*"); to *stop* (transitive or intransitive), i.e. *restrain, quit, desist, come to an end*:—cease, leave, refrain.

To stop, pause, make an end.

(I) Active, to make one pause, to make one leave off, to restrain. Only in 1Pe 3:10.

(II) More commonly in the middle, to pause, to leave off, to refrain (Lk 5:4; 11:1; Ac 5:42; 6:13; 13:10; 21:32; Eph 1:16; Col 1:9; Heb 10:2; 1Pe 4:1); to cease, to come to an end (Lk 8:24; Ac 20:1; 1Co 13:8).

Deriv.: *anapaúō* (373), to rest; *katapaúō* (2664), to rest.

Syn.: *dialeípō* (1257), to leave off for a time; *hēsucházō* (2270), to become quiet, still, at rest; *katargéō* (2673), to render inactive, abolish; *kopázō* (2869), to cease as a result of being tired, relax, subside.

3974. Πάφος, Paphos, *paf´-os*; of uncertain derivative; *Paphus*, a place in Cyprus:—Paphos.

3975. παχύνω, pachunō, *pakh-oo´-no*; from a derivative of 4078 (meaning *thick*); to *thicken*, i.e. (by implication) to *fatten* (figurative, *stupefy* or *render callous*):—wax gross.

3976. πέδη, pedē, *ped´-ay*; ultimately from 4228; a *shackle* for the feet:—fetter.

3977. πεδινός, pedinos, *ped-ee-nos´*; from a derivative of 4228 (meaning the *ground*); *level* (as easy for the *feet*):—plain.

3978. πεζεύω, pezeuō, *ped-zyoo´-o*; from the same as 3979; to *foot* a journey, i.e. *travel* by land:—go afoot.

3979. πεζῇ, pezēi, *ped-zay´*; dative feminine of a derivative of 4228 (as adverb); *foot-wise*, i.e. by *walking*:—a- (on) foot.

3980. πειθαρχέω, peitharcheō, *pi-tharkh-eh´-o*; from a compound of 3982 and 757; to *be persuaded* by a *ruler*, i.e. (general) to *submit* to authority; (by analogy) to *conform* to advice:—hearken, obey (magistrates).

3981. πειθός, peithos, *pi-thos´*; from 3982; *persuasive*:—enticing.

3982. πείθω, peithō, *pi´-tho*; a primary verb; to *convince* (by argument, true or false); (by analogy) to *pacify* or *conciliate* (by other fair means); reflexive or passive to *assent* (to evidence or authority), to *rely* (by inward certainty):—agree, assure, believe, have confidence, be (wax) confident, make a friend, obey, persuade, trust, yield.

To persuade, particularly to move or affect by kind words or motives.

(I) Active voice, to persuade.

(A) Generally, to persuade another to receive a belief, meaning to convince (Mt 27:20; Ac 13:43; 14:19; 18:4; 19:8, 26; 26:28; 28:23; 2Co 5:11).

(B) To bring over to kind feelings, to conciliate. **(1)** Generally, to pacify or quiet an accusing conscience, "our heart" (1Jn 3:19). **(2)** To win over, gain the favour of, make a friend of, with the accusative of person (Gal 1:10); by presents, bribes (Mt 28:14; Ac 12:20).

(II) Middle/passive, meaning to let oneself be persuaded, to be persuaded.

(A) Generally of any truth. Used in an absolute sense, to be convinced, believe (Lk 16:31; 20:6; Ac 17:4; 21:14; Ro 8:38; 14:14; 15:14; 2Ti 1:5, 12; Heb 6:9; 11:13).

(B) To assent to, obey, follow (Ac 5:36, 37; 23:21; 27:11; Ro 2:8; Gal 3:1; 5:7; Heb 13:17; Jas 3:3).

(III) In the perfect tense, to be persuaded, to trust.

(A) To be confident, assured (Ro 2:19; 2Co 2:3; Gal 5:10; Php 1:6, 25; 2Th 3:4; Heb 13:18).

(B) To confide in, rely upon (Mt 27:43; Mk 10:24; Lk 11:22; 18:9; 2Co 1:9; 10:7; Php 1:14; 3:3, 4; Php 1:14; Phm 21; Heb 2:13).

Deriv.: *anapeíthō* (374), to persuade or induce in an evil sense; *apeithḗs* (545), disobedient; *eupeithḗs* (2138), easy to be entreated; *peithós* (3981), persuasive, enticing; *peismonḗ* (3988), persuasion; *pepoíthēsis* (4006), trust, confidence; *pístis* (4102), faith, belief; *pistós* (4103), faithful.

Syn.: *parotrúnō* (3951), to urge along, stimulate; *pisteúō* (4100), to believe, be persuaded of; *pistóō* (4104), to trust or give assurance to; *plērophoréō* (4135), to be fully assured; *sugkatatíthēmi* (4784), to consent; *sumbouleúō* (4823), to give counsel; *sumphōnéō* (4856), to agree; *suntíthēmi* (4934), to assent.

3983. πεινάω, peinaō, *pi-nah´-o*; from the same as 3993 (through the idea of pinching *toil*; "*pine*"); to *famish* (absolute or comparatively); (figurative) to *crave*:—be an hungered.

3984. πεῖρα, peira, *pi´-rah*; from the base of 4008 (through the idea of *piercing*); a *test*, i.e. *attempt, experience*:—assaying, trial.

Noun from *peírō* (n.f.), to perforate, pierce. An attempt, an experience. In the NT, used only with *lambánō* (2983), to take or make an attempt (Heb 11:29); to take or receive an experience (Heb 11:36).

Deriv.: *ápeiros* (552), inexperienced, unskilled; *peirázō* (3985), to tempt or test; *peiráō* (3987), to try, test, tempt.

Syn.: *dokimḗ* (1382), experience, trial; *dokímion* (1383), trial, proof.

3985. πειράζω, peirazō, *pi-rad´-zo*; from 3984; to *test* (object), i.e. *endeavour, scrutinize, entice, discipline*:—assay, examine, go about, prove, tempt (-er), try.

From *peíra* (3984), experience, trial. To make trial of, to try. Similar to *peiráō* (3987), to assay.

(I) Of actions, to attempt, to make an effort (Ac 16:7; 24:6).

(II) Of persons, to tempt, prove, put to the test.

(A) Generally and in a good sense in order to ascertain the character, views, or feelings of someone (Mt 22:35; Jn 6:6; Rev 2:2).

(B) In a bad sense, with ill intent (Mk 8:11; 10:2; 12:15; Lk 11:16; 20:23; Jn 8:6). Hence by implication, to try one's virtue, tempt, solicit to sin (Gal 6:1; Jas 1:13, 14; Rev 2:10); especially by Satan (Mt 4:1, 3; Mk 1:13; Lk 4:2; 1Co 7:5; 1Th 3:5).

(C) In summary, God is said to try men by adversity, to test their faith and confidence in Him (1Co 10:13; Heb 2:18; 11:17, 37; Rev 3:10). Men are said to prove or tempt God by doubting, distrusting His power and aid (1Co 10:9; Heb 3:9); lying to Him (Ac 5:9); and refusing to follow His guidance (Ac 15:10).

Deriv.: *apeírastos* (551), incapable of being tempted; *ekpeírázō* (1598), to try, put to the test; *peirasmós* (3986), testing, temptation.

Syn.: *anakrínō* (350), to examine; *dokimázō* (1381), to prove, test, approve; *exetázō* (1833), to search, question.

3986. πειρασμός, peirasmos, *pi-ras-mos´*; from 3985; a putting to *proof* (by experiment [of good], *experience* [of evil], solicitation, discipline or provocation); (by implication) *adversity*:—temptation, × try.

Noun from *peirázō* (3985), to make trial of, try, tempt. Trial, a trial, proof, a putting to the test, spoken of persons only.

(I) Generally, trial of one's character (1Pe 4:12). By implication, trial of one's virtue, temptation, solicitation to sin, especially from Satan (Lk 4:13; 1Ti 6:9).

(II) Trial, temptation.

(A) A state of trial in which God brings His people through adversity and affliction in order to encourage and prove their faith and confidence in Him (1Co 10:13; Jas 1:2, 12; 1Pe 1:6; 2Pe 2:9). Hence used by metonymy for adversity, affliction, sorrow (Lk 22:28; Ac 20:19; Gal 4:14; Rev 3:10). When Christ urges us to pray that God would not lead us or allow us to go into *peirasmós* (Mt 6:13; 26:41; Mk 14:38; Lk 8:13; 11:4; 22:40, 46), he is evidently referring to those enticements to sin that we might not be able to resist in our present stage of spiritual growth.

(B) In the opposite way, man "tempts" God by distrusting Him and complaining to Him (Heb 3:8).

Syn.: *dokimḗ* (1382), trial; *dokímion* (1383), proof.

3987. πειράω, peiraō, *pi-rah´-o*; from 3984; to *test* (subject), i.e. (reflexive) to *attempt*:—assay.

From *peíra* (3984), trial. To try to do something (Ac 9:26; 26:21).

3988. πεισμονή, peismonē, *pice-mon-ay´*; from a presumed derivative of 3982; *persuadableness*, i.e. *credulity*:—persuasion.

3989. πέλαγος, pelagos, *pel´-ag-os*; of uncertain affinity; deep or open *sea*, i.e. the *main*:—depth, sea.

A noun meaning wide expanse of water, the open sea (Ac 27:5). Used with *thálassa* (2281), sea, meaning far out into the sea (Mt 18:6).

3990. πελεκίζω, pelekizō, *pel-ek-id´-zo*; from a derivative of 4141 (meaning an *axe*); to *chop* off (the head), i.e. *truncate*:—behead.

3991. πέμπτος, pemptos, *pemp´-tos*; from 4002; *fifth*:—fifth.

3992. πέμπω, pempō, *pem´-po*; apparently a primary verb; to *dispatch* (from the subject view or point of *departure*, whereas **ἵημι**, ***hiēmi***; [as a stronger form of **εἶμι**, ***eimi***] refers rather to the object point or *terminus ad quem*, and 4724 denotes properly the *orderly* motion involved), especially on a temporary errand; also to *transmit, bestow*, or *wield*:—send, thrust in.

3993. πένης, penēs, *pen´-ace*; from a primary **πένηο**, ***peno*** (to *toil* for daily subsistence); *starving*, i.e. *indigent*:—poor. Compare 4434.

Adjective from *pénomai* (n.f), to work for a living. Poor, needy. Only in 2Co 9:9.

Syn.: *endeḗs* (1729), needy, destitute; *ptōchós* (4434), destitute.

3994. πενθερά, penthera, *pen-ther-ah´*; feminine of 3995; a *wife's mother*:—mother-in-law, wife's mother.

3995. πενθερός, pentheros, *pen-ther-os´*; of uncertain affinity; a *wife's father*:—father-in-law.

3996. πενθέω, pentheō, *pen-theh´-o*; from 3997; to *grieve* (the feeling or the act):—mourn, (be-) wail.

From *pénthos* (3997), mourning. To mourn, lament.

(I) To bewail someone, to grieve for him (2Co 12:21).

(II) To mourn at the death of a friend (Mk 16:10); generally, to be sad, sorrowful (Mt 5:4; 9:15; 1Co 5:2), with *klaíō* (2799), to weep (Lk 6:25; Jas 4:9; Rev 18:11, 15, 19).

Syn.: *thrēnéō* (2354), to bewail; *kóptō* (2875), to beat the breast as an outward sign of inward grief; *lupéō* (3076), to grieve.

3997. πένθος, penthos, *pen´-thos*; strengthened from the alternate of 3958; *grief*:—mourning, sorrow.

3998. πεντιχρός, pentichros, *pen-tikh-ros´*; prolonged from the base of 3993; *necessitous*:—poor.

3999. πεντακίς, pentakis, *pen-tak-ece´*; multiple adverb from 4002; *five times*:—five times.

4000. πεντακισχίλιοι, pentakischilioi, *pen-tak-is-khil´-ee-oy*; from 3999 and 5507; *five times a thousand*:—five thousand.

4001. πεντακόσιοι, pentakosioi, *pen-tak-os´-ee-oy*; from 4002 and 1540; *five hundred*:—five hundred.

4002. πέντε, pente, *pen´-teh*; a primary number; "*five*":—five.

4003. πεντεκαιδέκατος, pentekaidekatos, *pen-tek-ahee-dek´-at-os*; from 4002 and 2532 and 1182; *five and tenth*:—fifteenth.

4004. πεντήκοντα, pentēkonta, *pen-tay´-kon-tah*; multiple of 4002; *fifty*:—fifty.

4005. πεντηκοστή, pentēkostē, *pen-tay-kos-tay´*; feminine of the order of 4004; *fiftieth* (2250 being implied) from Passover, i.e. the festival of "*Pentecost*":—Pentecost.

4006. πεποίθησις, pepoithēsis, *pep-oy´-thay-sis*; from the perfect of the alternate of 3958; *reliance*:—confidence, trust.

Noun meaning trust, confidence (2Co 1:15; 3:4; 8:22; 10:2; Eph 3:12; Php 3:4). See *peíthō* (3982, III), to persuade.

Syn.: *elégchos* (1650), conviction; *plērophoría* (4136), full assurance; *pístis* (4102), faith; *peismonḗ* (3988), persuasion.

4007. περ, per, *per*; from the base of 4008; an enclitic particle significant of *abundance* (*thoroughness*), i.e. *emphasis; much, very* or *ever*:—[whom-] soever.

4008. πέραν, peran, *per´-an*; apparently accusative of an obsolete derivative of **πείρω**, ***peirō*** (to "*pierce*"); *through* (as adverb or prep.), i.e. *across*:—beyond, farther (other) side, over.

4009. πέρας, peras, *per´-as*; from the same as 4008; an *extremity*:—end, ut- (ter-) most part.

4010. Πέργαμος, Pergamos, *per´-gam-os*; from 4444; *fortified; Pergamus*, a place in Asia Minor:—Pergamos.

4011. Πέργη, Pergē, *perg´-ay*; probably from the same as 4010; a *tower; Perga*, a place in Asia Minor:—Perga.

4012. περί, peri, *per-ee´*; from the base of 4008; properly *through* (all *over*), i.e. *around*; (figurative) *with respect* to; used in various applications, of place, cause or time (with the generic denoting the *subject* or *occasion* or *superlative* point; with the accusative the *locality, circuit, matter, circumstance* or general *period*):—(there-) about, above, against, at, on behalf of, × and his company, which concern, (as) concerning, for, × how it will go with, ([there-, where-]) of, on, over, pertaining (to), for sake, × (e-) state, (as) touching, [where-] by (in), with. In comparison it retains substantially the same meaning of circuit (*around*), excess (*beyond*), or completeness (*through*).

4013. περιάγω, periagō, *per-ee-ag´-o*; from 4012 and 71; to *take around* (as a companion); reflex. to *walk around*:—compass, go (round) about, lead about.

4014. περιαιρέω, periaireō, *per-ee-ahee-reh´-o*; from 4012 and 138 (including its alternate); to *remove* all *around*, i.e. *unveil, cast off* (anchor); (figurative) to *expiate*:—take away (up).

From *perí* (4012), around, suggesting completeness, and *hairéomai* (138), to lift up and take away. To take away, abandon.

(I) Used transitively (Ac 27:40, "taking up the anchors round about" [a.t. {cf. 27:29}]); of a veil, to remove (2Co 3:16, an allusion to Ex 34:34. Sept.: Ge 41:42; Est 3:10; Jnh 3:6).

(II) Metaphorically, to take away completely (Heb 10:11, "completely take away sins" [a.t.], to make complete expiation for sins [cf. Heb 10:4]).

Syn.: *periphérō* (4064), to bear about; *sunépomai* (4902), to accompany; *leípō* (3007), to leave; *kataleípō* (2641), to forsake; *apoleípō* (620), to leave behind; *egkataleípō* (1459), to abandon; *aphíēmi* (863), to leave; *eáō* (1439), to leave alone.

4015. περιαστράπτω, periastraptō, *per-ee-as-trap´-to*; from 4012 and 797; to *flash* all *around,* i.e. *envelop in light:*—shine round (about).

4016. περιβάλλω, periballō, *per-ee-bal´-lo*; from 4012 and 906; to *throw* all *around,* i.e. *invest* (with a palisade or with clothing):—array, cast about, clothe (-d me), put on.

4017. περιβλέπω, periblepō, *per-ee-blep´-o*; from 4012 and 991; to *look* all *around:*—look (round) about (on).

4018. περιβόλαιον, peribolaion, *per-ib-ol´-ah-yon*; neuter of a presumed derivative of 4016; something *thrown around* one, i.e. a *mantle, veil:*—covering, vesture.

4019. περιδέω, perideō, *per-ee-deh´-o*; from 4012 and 1210; to *bind around* one, i.e. *enwrap:*—bind about.

4020. περιεργάζομαι, periergazomai, *per-ee-er-gad´-zom-ahee*; from 4012 and 2038; to *work* all *around,* i.e. *bustle about (meddle):*—be a busybody.

4021. περίεργος, periergos, *per-ee´-er-gos*; from 4012 and 2041; *working* all *around,* i.e. *officious* (*meddlesome,* neuter plural *magic*):—busybody, curious arts.

4022. περιέρχομαι, perierchomai, *per-ee-er´-khom-ahee*; from 4012 and 2064 (including its alternate); to *come* all *around,* i.e. *stroll, vacillate, veer:*—fetch a compass, vagabond, wandering about.

4023. περιέχω, periechō, *per-ee-ekh´-o*; from 4012 and 2192; to *hold* all *around,* i.e. *include, clasp* (figurative):— + astonished, contain, after [this manner].

4024. περιζώννυμι, perizōnnumi, *per-id-zone´-noo-mee*; from 4012 and 2224; to *gird* all *around,* i.e. (middle or passive) to *fasten on one's belt* (literal or figurative):—gird (about, self).

4025. περίθεσις, perithesis, *per-ith´-es-is*; from 4060; a *putting* all *around,* i.e. *decorating* oneself with:—wearing.

4026. περιΐστημι, periistēmi, *per-ee-is´-tay-mee*; from 4012 and 2476; to *stand* all *around,* i.e. (near) to *be a bystander,* or (aloof) to *keep away* from:—avoid, shun, stand by (round about).

4027. περικάθαρμα, perikatharma, *per-ee-kath´-ar-mah*; from a compound of 4012 and 2508; something *cleaned* off all *around,* i.e. *refuse* (figurative):—filth.

Noun from *perikathaírō* (n.f.), to purge or cleanse all around, which is from *perí* (4012), around, and *kathaírō* (2508), to cleanse. The filth or defilement washed away by cleansing; see *katharismós* (2512), the process of purification. It may be used to denote an expiatory victim or ransom, as cleansing from guilt and punishment (Sept.: Pr 21:18). It is used metonymically in the NT of wretches or outcasts. Paul, in 1Co 4:13, mentions that the disciples of Christ are considered to be the refuse or outcasts of the world.

Syn.: *rhúpos* (4509), dirt, filth; *rhuparía* (4507), filthiness.

4028. περικαλύπτω, perikaluptō, *per-ee-kal-oop´-to*; from 4012 and 2572; to *cover* all *around,* i.e. *entirely* (the face, a surface):—blindfold, cover, overlay.

4029. περίκειμαι, perikeimai, *per-ik´-i-mahee*; from 4012 and 2749; to *lie* all *around,* i.e. *inclose, encircle, hamper* (literal or figurative):—be bound (compassed) with, hang about.

4030. περικεφαλαία, perikephalaia, *per-ee-kef-al-ah´-yah*; feminine of a compound of 4012 and 2776; *encirclement of* the *head,* i.e. a *helmet:*—helmet.

4031. περικρατής, perikratēs, *per-ee-krat-ace´*; from 4012 and 2904; *strong* all *around,* i.e. a *master* (*manager*):— + come by.

4032. περικρύπτω, perikruptō, *per-ee-kroop´-to*; from 4012 and 2928; to *conceal* all *around,* i.e. *entirely:*—hide.

4033. περικυκλόω, perikukloō, *per-ee-koo-klo´-o*; from 4012 and 2944; to *encircle* all *around,* i.e. *blockade completely:*—compass round.

4034. περιλάμπω, perilampō, *per-ee-lam´-po*; from 4012 and 2989; to *illuminate* all *around,* i.e. *invest with a halo:*—shine round about.

4035. περιλείπω, perileipō, *per-ee-li´-po*; from 4012 and 3007; to *leave* all *around,* i.e. (passive) *survive:*—remain.

4036. περίλυπος, perilupos, *per-il´-oo-pos*; from 4012 and 3077; *grieved* all *around,* i.e. *intensely sad:*—exceeding (very) sorry (-owful).

4037. περιμένω, perimenō, *per-ee-men´-o*; from 4012 and 3306; to *stay around,* i.e. *await:*—wait for.

From *perí* (4012), concerning, for, about, and *ménō* (3306), to remain, wait. To wait around. Transitively with an accusative, to wait for (Ac 1:4, waiting for the fulfillment of the promise of the Holy Spirit). See Sept.: Ge 49:18.

Syn.: *ekdéchomai* (1551), expect; *apekdéchomai* (553), to await or expect eagerly; *prosdéchomai* (4327), to look for with patience; *prosdokáō* (4328), to anticipate, await; *anaménō* (362), to wait with expectancy; *epiménō* (1961), to persevere; *prosménō* (4357), to persevere in, stay further in, continue in; *epéchō* (1907), to give heed to; *diatríbō* (1304), to tarry; *proskarteréō* (4342), to continue steadfastly in, wait; *prosedreúō* ([4332] TR) or *paredreúō* (UBS), to sit constantly beside, wait upon, expect.

4038. πέριξ, perix, *per´-ix*; adverb from 4012; all *around,* i.e. (as adjective) *circumjacent:*—round about.

4039. περιοικέω, perioikeō, *per-ee-oy-keh´-o*; from 4012 and 3611; to *reside around,* i.e. *be a neighbour:*—dwell round about.

4040. περίοικος, perioikos, *per-ee´-oy-kos*; from 4012 and 3611; *housed around,* i.e. *neighboring* (elliptically as noun):—neighbour.

4041. περιούσιος, periousios, *per-ee-oo´-see-os*; from the presumed participle feminine of a compound of 4012 and 1510; *being beyond* usual, i.e. *special* (one's *own*):—peculiar.

Adjective from *periousía* (n.f.), what is over and above, abundance, which is from *perí* (4012), beyond, and *ousía* (3776), substance. Having abundance, superabundant. Used only in Tit 2:14 where by implication, one's own, special, abundant, chosen.

Syn.: *eklektós* (1588), chosen, elect; *polútimos* (4186), extremely valuable.

4042. περιοχή, periochē, *per-ee-okh-ay´*; from 4023; a *being held around,* i.e. (concretely) a *passage* (of Scripture, as *circumscribed*):—place.

4043. περιπατέω, peripateō, *per-ee-pat-eh´-o*; from 4012 and 3961; to *tread* all *around,* i.e. *walk* at large (especially as proof of ability); (figurative) to *live, deport oneself, follow* (as a companion or votary):—go, be occupied with, walk (about).

4044. περιπείρω, peripeirō, *per-ee-pi´-ro*; from 4012 and the base of 4008; to *penetrate entirely,* i.e. *transfix* (figurative):—pierce through.

4045. περιπίπτω, peripiptō, *per-ee-pip´-to*; from 4012 and 4098; to *fall* into something that is all *around,* i.e. *light among* or *upon, be surrounded with:*—fall among (into).

4046. περιποιέομαι, peripoieomai, *per-ee-poy-eh´-om-ahee*; middle from 4012 and 4160; to *make around oneself,* i.e. *acquire* (*buy*):—purchase.

4047. περιποίησις, peripoiēsis, *per-ee-poy´-ay-sis*; from 4046; *acquisition* (the act or the thing); by extension *preservation*:—obtain (-ing), peculiar, purchased, possession, saving.

4048. περιῤῥήγνυμι, perirrhēgnumi, *per-ir-hrayg´-noo-mee*; from 4012 and 4486; to *tear* all *around*, i.e. *completely away*:—rend off.

4049. περισπάω, perispaō, *per-ee-spah´-o*; from 4012 and 4685; to *drag* all *around*, i.e. (figurative) to *distract* (with care):—cumber.

4050. περισσεία, perisseia, *per-is-si´-ah*; from 4052; *surplusage*, i.e. *superabundance*:—abundance (-ant, [-ly]), superfluity.

Noun from *perissós* (4053), over and above. A superabundance, more than enough (2Co 10:15); spoken of grace (Ro 5:17), joy (2Co 8:2), wickedness (Jas 1:21).

Syn.: *hadrótēs* (100), bounty, abundance; *perísseuma* (4051), abundance, that which remains over; *huperbolḗ* (5236), excess, a great measure, more than necessary.

4051. περίσσευμα, perisseuma, *per-is´-syoo-mah*; from 4052; a *surplus*, or *superabundance*:—abundance, that was left, over and above.

Noun from *perisseúō* (4052), to abound. More than enough, abundance.

(I) What is left over, remainder (Mk 8:8).

(II) What is laid up, superabundance. Spoken of material possessions (2Co 8:12). Figuratively, spoken of the thoughts that fill the heart (Mt 12:34; Lk 6:45).

4052. περισσεύω, perisseuō, *per-is-syoo´-o*; from 4053; to *superabound* (in quantity or quality), *be in excess, be superfluous*; also (transposed) to *cause to superabound* or *excel*:—(make, more) abound, (have, have more) abundance, (be more) abundant, be the better, enough and to spare, exceed, excel, increase, be left, redound, remain (over and above).

4053. περισσός, perissos, *per-is-sos´*; from 4012 (in the sense of *beyond*); *superabundant* (in quantity) or *superior* (in quality); (by implication) *excessive*; adverb (with 1537) *violently*; neuter (as noun) *preeminence*:—exceeding abundantly above, more abundantly, advantage, exceedingly, very highly, beyond measure, more, superfluous, vehement [-ly].

Adjective from *perí* (4012), around, above. Over and above, more than enough.

(I) Particularly as exceeding a certain measure, more than (Mt 5:37, 47). In the sense of superfluous (2Co 9:1).

(II) Generally, superabundant, abundant, much, great.

(A) Positively, as an adverb, abundantly, in superabundance (Jn 10:10). With the prep. *ek* (1537), by means of, or expressing measure, beyond measure, exceedingly (Mk 6:51; 14:31; Eph 3:20; 1Th 3:10; 5:13).

(B) By implication, in a comparative sense, advantage (Ro 3:1).

Deriv.: *perisseía* (4050), a superfluity, an overflowing; *perisseúō* (4052), to abound, be exceeding.

Syn.: *mállon* (3123), very much; *meízōn* (3187), greater; *pleíōn* (4119), more than.

4054. περισσότερον, perissoteron, *per-is-sot´-er-on*; neuter of 4055 (as adverb); in a *more superabundant* way:—more abundantly, a great deal, far more.

4055. περισσότερος, perissoteros, *per-is-sot´-er-os*; comparative of 4053; *more superabundant* (in number, degree or character):—more abundant, greater (much) more, overmuch.

4056. περισσοτέρως, perissoterōs, *per-is-sot-er´-oce*; adverb from 4055; *more superabundantly*:—more abundant (-ly), × the more earnest, (more) exceedingly, more frequent, much more, the rather.

4057. περισσῶς, perissōs, *per-is-soce´*; adverb from 4053; *superabundantly*:—exceedingly, out of measure, the more.

4058. περιστερά, peristera, *per-is-ter-ah´*; of uncertain derivative; a *pigeon*:—dove, pigeon.

4059. περιτέμνω, peritemnō, *per-ee-tem´-no*; from 4012 and the base of 5114; to *cut around*, i.e. (special) to *circumcise*:—circumcise.

From *perí* (4012), around, about, and *témnō* (n.f.), to cut off. To cut off or around, to circumcise, to remove the foreskin of the male (Lk 1:59; 2:21; Jn 7:22; Ac 7:8; 15:5; 16:3; 21:21). In the passive (Ac 15:1, 24; 1Co 7:18; Gal 2:3; 5:2, 3; 6:12, 13). Metaphorically in a spiritual sense, meaning to put away impurity (Col 2:11).

Deriv.: *aperítmētos* (564), uncircumcised; *peritomḗ* (4061), circumcision.

4060. περιτίθημι, peritithēmi, *per-ee-tith´-ay-mee*; from 4012 and 5087; to *place around*; (by implication) to *present*:—bestow upon, hedge round about, put about (on, upon), set about.

4061. περιτομή, peritomē, *per-it-om-ay´*; from 4059; *circumcision* (the rite, the condition or the people, literal or figurative):— × circumcised, circumcision.

Noun from *peritémnō* (4059), to cut around, circumcise. Circumcision. It was practiced by the Jews as a distinguishing sign of the Jewish nation from Abraham on (Ge 17:10f.; Le 12:3; Lk 1:59), and also by several ancient oriental nations and by all of the Muslims.

(I) Spoken of the act of circumcision or cutting off the foreskin (Jn 7:22, 23; Ac 7:8; Ro 4:11; Gal 5:11; Php 3:5).

(II) Spoken of the state of being circumcised (Ro 2:25–27; 3:1; 4:10, 12; 1Co 7:19; Gal 2:12; 5:6; 6:15; Col 4:11; Tit 1:10).

(III) Used figuratively of persons practicing circumcision, the Jews, as opposed to the uncircumcised Gentiles (Ro 3:30; 4:9, 12; 15:8; Gal 2:7–9; Eph 2:11; Col 3:11).

(IV) Spoken figuratively of the spiritual circumcision of the heart and affections, by putting the sins of the flesh off from the body (Ro 2:28, 29; Php 3:3; Col 2:11).

4062. περιτρέπω, peritrepō, *per-ee-trep´-o*; from 4012 and the base of 5157; to *turn around*, i.e. (mental) to *craze*:— + make mad.

4063. περιτρέχω, peritrechō, *per-ee-trekh´-o*; from 4012 and 5143 (including its alternate); to *run around*, i.e. *traverse*:—run through.

4064. περιφέρω, peripherō, *per-ee-fer´-o*; from 4012 and 5342; to *convey around*, i.e. *transport hither and thither*:—bear (carry) about.

4065. περιφρονέω, periphroneō, *per-ee-fron-eh´-o*; from 4012 and 5426; to *think beyond*, i.e. *depreciate* (*condemn*):—despise.

4066. περίχωρος, perichōros, *per-ikh´-o-ros*; from 4012 and 5561; *around* the *region*, i.e. *circumjacent* (as noun, with 1093 implication *vicinity*):—country (round) about, region (that lieth) round about.

4067. περίψωμα, peripsōma, *per-ip´-so-mah*; from a compound of 4012 and **ψάω** ***psaō*** (to *rub*); something *brushed* all *around*, i.e. *off-scrapings* (figurative, *scum*):—offscouring.

4068. περπερεύομαι, perpereuomai, *per-per-yoo´-om-ahee*; middle from **πέρπερος, *perperos*** (*braggart*; perhaps by reduplication of the base of 4008); to *boast*:—vaunt itself.

From *pérperos* (n.f.), braggart. To brag or boast (1Co 13:4).

Syn.: *tuphóō* (5187), to be lifted up with pride; *huperaíromai* (5229), to become haughty; *huperphronéō* (5252), to think too highly.

4069. Περσίς, Persis, *per-sece´*; a *Persian* woman; *Persis*, a Christian female:—Persis.

4070. πέρυσι, perusi, *per´-oo-si*; adverb from 4009; the *bygone*, i.e. (as noun) *last year*:— + a year ago.

4071. πετεινόν, peteinon, *pet-i-non´*; neuter of a derivative of 4072; a *flying* animal, i.e. *bird*:—bird, fowl.

4072. πέτομαι, petomai, *pet´-om-ahee*; or prolonged **πετάομαι, *petaomai***, *pet-ah´-om-ahee*; or contracted **πτάομαι,**

ptaomai, ptah´-om-ahee; middle of a primary verb; to *fly*:—fly (-ing).

4073. πέτρα, petra, *pet´-ra*; feminine of the same as 4074; a (mass of) *rock* (literal or figurative):—rock.

4074. Πέτρος, Petros, *pet´-ros*; apparently a primary word; a (piece of) *rock* (larger than 3037); as a name, *Petrus*, an apostle:—Peter, rock. Compare 2786.

4075. πετρώδης, petrōdēs, *pet-ro´-dace*; from 4073 and 1491; *rock-like*, i.e. *rocky*:—stony.

4076. πήγανον, pēganon, *pay´-gan-on*; from 4078; *rue* (from its *thick* or *fleshy* leaves):—rue.

4077. πηγή, pēgē, *pay-gay´*; probably from 4078 (through the idea of *gushing* plumply); a *fount* (literal or figurative), i.e. *source* or *supply* (of water, blood, enjoyment) (not necessarily the original spring):—fountain, well.

Noun meaning fountain, source of water.

(I) Generally, a fountain of water (Jas 3:11, 12; Rev 8:10; 14:7; 16:4). Figuratively of life-giving water (Jn 4:14); also, an emblem of the highest enjoyment (Rev 7:17; 21:6).

(II) A well (Jn 4:6; 2Pe 2:17).

(III) A discharge or flow of blood from the body (Mk 5:29; Lk 8:44).

4078. πήγνυμι, pēgnumi, *payg´-noo-mee*; a prolonged form of a primary verb (which in its simpler form occurs only as an alternate in certain tenses); to *fix* ("*peg*"), i.e. (special) to *set up* (a tent):—pitch.

4079. πηδάλιον, pēdalion, *pay-dal´-ee-on*; neuter of a (presumed) derivative of **πηδόν**, ***pēdon*** (the *blade* of an oar; from the same as 3976); a "*pedal*," i.e. *helm*:—rudder.

4080. πηλίκος, pēlikos, *pay-lee´-kos*; a quantitative form (the feminine) of the base of 4225; *how much* (as indefinite), i.e. in size or (figurative) dignity:—how great (large).

4081. πηλός, pēlos, *pay-los´*; perhaps a primary word; *clay*:—clay.

4082. πήρα, pēra, *pay´-rah*; of uncertain affinity; a *wallet* or leather *pouch* for food:—scrip.

4083. πῆχυς, pēchus, *pay´-khoos*; of uncertain affinity; the *forearm*, i.e. (as a measure) a *cubit*:—cubit.

4084. πιάζω, piazō, *pee-ad´-zo*; probably another form of 971; to *squeeze*, i.e. *seize* (gently by the hand [*press*], or officially [*arrest*], or in hunting [*capture*]):—apprehend, catch, lay hand on, take. Compare 4085.

4085. πιέζω, piezō, *pee-ed´-zo*; another form for 4084; to *pack*:—press down.

4086. πιθανολογία, pithanologia, *pith-an-ol-og-ee´-ah*; from a compound of a derivative of 3982 and 3056; *persuasive language*:—enticing words.

4087. πικραίνω, pikrainō, *pik-rah´ee-no*; from 4089; to *embitter* (literal or figurative):—be (make) bitter.

4088. πικρία, pikria, *pik-ree´-ah*; from 4089; *acridity* (especially *poison*), literal or figurative:—bitterness.

4089. πικρός, pikros, *pik-ros´*; perhaps from 4078 (through the idea of *piercing*); *sharp* (*pungent*), i.e. *acrid* (literal or figurative):—bitter.

4090. πικρῶς, pikrōs, *pik-roce´*; adverb from 4089; *bitterly*, i.e. (figurative) *violently*:—bitterly.

4091. Πιλάτος, Pilatos, *pil-at´-os*; of Latin origin; *close-pressed*, i.e. *firm; Pilatus*, a Roman:—Pilate.

4092. πίμπρημι, pimprēmi, *pim´-pray-mee*; a reduplicated and prolonged form of a primary **πρέω**, ***preō***, *preh´-o* (which occurs only as an alternate in certain tenses); to *fire*, i.e. *burn* (figurative and passive *become inflamed* with fever):—be (× should have) swollen.

4093. πινακίδιον, pinakidion, *pin-ak-id´-ee-on*; diminitive of 4094; a *tablet* (for writing on):—writing table.

4094. πίναξ, pinax, *pin´-ax*; apparently a form of 4109; a *plate*:—charger, platter.

4095. πίνω, pinō, *pee´-no*; a prolonged form of **πίω**, ***piō***, *pee´-o*; which (together with another form **πόω**, ***poō***, *po´-o*) occurs only as an alternate in certain tenses; to *imbibe* (literal or figurative):—drink.

4096. πιότης, piotēs, *pee-ot´-ace*; from **πίων**, ***piōn*** (*fat*; perhaps akin to the alternate of 4095 through the idea of *repletion*); *plumpness*, i.e. (by implication) *richness* (*oiliness*):—fatness.

4097. πιπράσκω, pipraskō, *pip-ras´-ko*; a reduplicated and prolonged form of **πράω**, ***praō***, *prah´-o* (which occurs only as an alternate in certain tenses); contracted from **περάω**, ***peraō*** (to *traverse*; from the base of 4008); to *traffic* (by *travelling*), i.e. *dispose* of as merchandise or into slavery (literal or figurative):—sell.

4098. πίπτω, piptō, *pip´-to*; a reduplicated and contracted form of **πέτω**, ***petō***, *pet´-o* (which occurs only as an alternate in certain tenses); probably akin to 4072 through the idea of *alighting*; to *fall* (literal or figurative):—fail, fall (down), light on.

To fall.

(I) Particularly, to fall from a higher to a lower place, spoken of persons and things (Mt 10:29; 13:5, 7, 8; 21:44; 24:29; Mk 4:4, 5; Lk 8:5–8; 20:18; 23:30; Jn 12:24). Figuratively, to fall upon, to seize (Rev 6:13; 11:11).

(II) Of persons, meaning to fall down or prostrate (Mt 2:11; 4:9; 17:6; 18:26, 29; Mk 5:22; 9:20; 14:35; Lk 5:12; 8:41; 17:16; Jn 11:32; 18:6; Ac 5:5; 9:4; 10:25; 22:7; 1Co 14:25; Rev 1:17; 4:10; 5:8; 19:10; 22:8). Spoken of those who fall dead (Lk 21:24; 1Co 10:8; Heb 3:17; Rev 17:10).

(III) Of edifices, meaning to fall, to fall in ruins (Mt 7:25, 27; Lk 6:49; 13:4; Heb 11:30). Figuratively (Lk 11:17; Ac 15:16); in prophetic imagery (Rev 11:13; 14:8; 16:19; 18:2).

(IV) Of a lot, meaning to fall to or upon someone (Ac 1:26).

(V) Metaphorically of persons, meaning to fall from grace or favour (Ro 11:11, 22; 14:4; 1Co 10:12; Heb 4:11; Jas 5:12). Of things, meaning to fall to the ground, to fail, become void (Lk 16:17).

Deriv.: *anapíptō* (377), to fall back, sit down; *antipíptō* (496), to resist; *apopíptō* (634), to fall from; *gonupetéō* (1120), to bow down; *ekpíptō* (1601), to fall out of; *empíptō* (1706), to fall into or among; *epipíptō* (1968), to fall upon; *katapíptō* (2667), to fall down; *parapípto* (3895), to fall beside, to fall down; *peripíptō* (4045), to fall among; *prospíptō* (4363), to fall toward; *ptṓma* (4430), a ruin, corpse, dead body; *ptṓsis* (4431), the act of falling.

Syn.: *katapontízō* (2670), to sink; *rhíptomai* (4496), to fling oneself, to deliberately fall or throw oneself.

4099. Πισιδία, Pisidia, *pis-id-ee´-ah*; probably of foreign origin; *Pisidia*, a region of Asia Minor:—Pisidia.

4100. πιστεύω, pisteuō, *pist-yoo´-o*; from 4102; to *have faith* (in, upon, or with respect to, a person or thing), i.e. *credit*; (by implication) to *entrust* (especially one's spiritual well-being to Christ):—believe (-r), commit (to trust), put in trust with.

From *pístis* (4102), faith. To believe, have faith in, trust. NT meanings:

(I) Particularly, to be firmly persuaded as to something, to believe (Mk 11:23; Ro 6:8; 10:9; 14:2). With the idea of hope and certain expectation (Ac 18:8).

(A) More commonly used of words spoken and things, followed by the dat. of the person whose words one believes and trusts in (Mk 16:13; Jn 4:21; 5:46; Ac 8:12; 1Jn 4:1).

(B) With an adjunct of the words or thing spoken (Mk 1:15; Lk 1:20; 24:25; Jn 4:50; Ac 13:41; 24:14; 2Th 2:11).

(C) With an adjunct of the thing believed (Jn 9:18; 11:26; 14:10; Ro 10:9; 1Co 13:7; 2Th 1:10; 1Jn 4:16).

(D) Used in an absolute sense where the case of person or thing is implied from the context (Mt 24:23; Mk 13:21; Jn 12:47).

(II) Of God, to believe in God, to trust in Him as able and willing to help and answer prayer (Jn 5:24; 14:1; Ac 16:34; 27:25; Ro 4:17, 18, 24; 1 Jn 5:10; 1Pe 1:21).

(III) Of a messenger from God, to believe on and trust in him (when applied to a merely human messenger of God, to credit and trust him, as coming from God and acting under divine authority).

(A) Of John the Baptist, with the dat. (Mt 21:25, 32; Lk 20:5).

(B) Of Jesus as the Messiah, able and ready to help His followers (Mt 8:13; 9:28; Mk 5:36; Jn 4:48; 14:1). **(1)** Generally, of Jesus as a teacher and the Messiah sent from God (Mt 18:6; Mk 9:42; Jn 1:12; 2:23; 5:38; 8:31; 10:37, 38; 16:27, 30; 17:8, 21; 20:31; Ac 10:43; Ro 10:14; Gal 2:16; 1Pe 1:8). **(2)** Used in an absolute sense, to believe, meaning to become a Christian (Mk 15:32; Lk 22:67; Jn 1:7; 12:39; Ac 2:44; 4:4, 32; 14:1; 17:12, 34; 19:18; Ro 4:11; 1Co 1:21; Gal 3:22; 1Th 1:7; 1Pe 2:7).

(IV) Transitively, to entrust, commit in trust to someone (Lk 16:11; Jn 2:24). In the passive, to be entrusted with something, to have something committed to one's trust or charge (Ro 3:2; 1Co 9:17; Gal 2:7; 1Th 2:4; 1Ti 1:11; Tit 1:3).

Syn.: *peíthomai* (3982), to be convinced.

4101. πιστικός, pistikos, *pis-tik-os´*; from 4102; *trustworthy*, i.e. *genuine* (*unadulterated*):—spike- [nard].

4102. πίστις, pistis, *pis´-tis*; from 3982; *persuasion*, i.e. *credence*; moral *conviction* (of *religious* truth, or the truthfulness of God or a religious teacher), especially *reliance* upon Christ for salvation; abstract *constancy* in such profession; by extension the system of religious (gospel) *truth* itself:—assurance, belief, believe, faith, fidelity.

Noun from *peíthō* (3982), to win over, persuade. Faith, trust, firm persuasion, confiding belief in the truth, veracity, reality of any person or thing.

(I) In the common Greek usage:

(A) Particularly and generally, a firm persuasion, a belief in the truth of someone or something (Heb 11:1). See also Ro 14:22, 23; 2Co 5:7; 2Th 2:13; 1Pe 1:5. A ground of confidence, reason for belief, proof (Ac 17:31).

(B) Good faith, faithfulness, sincerity (Mt 23:23; Ro 3:3; Gal 5:22; 1Ti 1:19; 2:7; 2Ti 2:22; 3:10; Tit 2:10; Rev 2:19; 13:10).

(II) As a technical term indicative of the means of appropriating what God in Christ has for man, resulting in the transformation of man's character and way of life. Such can be termed gospel faith or Christian faith (Ro 3:22ff.).

(A) Of God, meaning faith in, on, or toward God (Mt 17:20; 21:21; Mk 11:22; Lk 17:5, 6; Ro 1:17; Col 2:12; 1Th 1:8; Heb 4:2; 6:1; 10:22, 38; Jas 1:6; 5:15; 1Pe 1:21). Spoken by analogy of the faith of the patriarchs and pious men from the Old Testament who looked forward in faith and hope to the blessings of the gospel: spoken of Abraham (Ro 4:5, 9, 11–14, 16, 19, 20; Heb 6:12; 11:8, 9), spoken of others (11:4, 5, 7, 11, 13, 17, 20–24, 27–31, 33, 39).

(B) Of Christ, faith in Christ: **(1)** As able to work miracles, to heal the sick (Mt 8:10; 9:2, 22, 29; 15:28; Mk 2:5; 5:34; 10:52; Lk 5:20; 7:9, 50; 8:48; 17:19; 18:42; Ac 3:16). **(2)** Of faith in Christ's death, as the ground of justification before God, saving faith, found only in Paul's writings (Ro 3:22, 25–28, 30, 31; 1Co 15:14, 17). Generally (Ro 1:17; 5:1, 2; 9:30, 32; 10:6, 17; Gal 2:16, 20; 3:2, 5, 7–9, 11, 12, 14, 22, 24; 5:5, 6; Eph 2:8; 3:12; Php 3:9. (Of the faith of Old Testament saints, see A above.)

(C) By metonymy of the object of Christian faith, meaning the doctrines received and believed, Christian doctrine, the gospel, all that Christianity stands for (Ac 6:7; 14:27; 24:24; Ro 1:5; 10:8; 2Co 1:24; Gal 1:23; 3:23, 25; Eph 4:5; 1Ti 1:2, 4, 19; 3:9; 6:21; Tit 1:4; 2Pe 1:1; 1Jn 5:4; Jude 3, 20).

Deriv.: *oligópistos* (3640), having but little faith; *pisteúō* (4100), to believe, have faith in; *pistikós* (4101), persuasive, faithful.

Syn.: *bebaíōsis* (951), the act of assurance, confirmation; *pepoíthēsis* (4006), reliance, confidence.

4103. πιστός, pistos, *pis-tos´*; from 3982; object *trustworthy*; subject *trustful*:—believe (-ing, -r), faithful (-ly), sure, true.

Adjective from *peíthō* (3982), to win over, persuade. Worthy of belief, trust, or confidence, faithful.

(I) Trustworthy, true, believable, worthy of credit (1Co 7:25; 1Ti 1:12; 2Ti 2:2; 1Pe 4:19; Rev 1:5; 2:13; 3:14; 19:11). Of things, true, sure (Ac 13:34). Used with *lógos* [3056], word or saying (1Ti 1:15; 3:1; 4:3; 2Ti 2:11; Tit 1:9; 3:8; Rev 21:5; 22:6).

(II) Faithful in duty to oneself and to others, of true fidelity (Col 4:9; 1Pe 5:12; Rev 2:10). Of God as faithful to His promises (1Co 1:9; 10:13; 2Co 1:18; 1Th 5:24; 2Th 3:3; Heb 10:23; 11:11; 1Jn 1:9); of Christ (2Ti 2:13). Especially of servants, ministers, who are faithful in the performance of duty (Mt 24:45; 25:21, 23; Lk 12:42; 16:10–12; 19:17; 1Co 4:2; Eph 1:1; 6:21; Col 1:2, 7; 4:7, 9; 1Ti 3:11; Heb 2:17; 3:2, 5).

(III) With an act. sense, firm in faith, confiding, trusting, believing, equivalent to the present participle of *pisteúō* (4100), to believe (Jn 20:27; Gal 3:9). Followed by the dative (1Co 4:17). Used in an absolute sense (Jn 20:20; Ac 10:45; 16:1, 15; 1Co 4:17; 2Co 6:15; Gal 3:9; 1Ti 4:3, 10, 12; 5:16; 6:2; Tit 1:6; Rev 17:14). Used adverbially, faithfully (3Jn 5).

Deriv.: *ápistos* (571), untrustworthy; *pistóō* (4104), to confirm, establish.

Syn.: *áxios* (514), worthy; *aklinḗs* (186), firm, without wavering; *alēthḗs* (227), true; *alēthinós* (228), truthful; *ámemptos* (273), blameless; *anepílēmptos* (423), irreproachable; *apseudḗs* (893), truthful; *bébaios* (949), steadfast, sure; *eilikrinḗs* (1506), sincere.

4104. πιστόω, pistoō, *pis-to´-o*; from 4103; to *assure*:—assure of.

From *pistós* (4103), faithful. To make one faithful, trustworthy. Passive: to be made confident, believing; to be assured. Only in 2Ti 3:14.

Syn.: *bebaióō* (950), to confirm, establish; *diabebaióō* (1236), to strongly affirm; *kuróō* (2964), to ratify.

4105. πλανάω, planaō, *plan-ah´-o*; from 4106; to (properly *cause* to) *roam* (from safety, truth, or virtue):—go astray, deceive, err, seduce, wander, be out of the way.

4106. πλάνη, planē, *plan´-ay*; feminine of 4108 (as abstract); object *fraudulence*; subject a *straying* from orthodoxy or piety:—deceit, to deceive, delusion, error.

4107. πλανήτης, planētēs, *plan-ay´-tace*; from 4108; a *rover* ("planet"), i.e. (figurative) an *erratic* teacher:—wandering.

4108. πλάνος, planos, *plan´-os*; of uncertain affinity; *roving* (as a *tramp*), i.e. (by implication) an *impostor* or *misleader*:—deceiver, seducing.

4109. πλάξ, plax, *plax*; from 4111; a *moulding-board*, i.e. *flat* surface ("*plate*," or *tablet*, literal or figurative):—table.

4110. πλάσμα, plasma, *plas´-mah*; from 4111; something *moulded*:—thing formed.

4111. πλάσσω, plassō, *plas´-so*; a primary verb; to *mould*, i.e. *shape* or *fabricate*:—form.

4112. πλαστός, plastos, *plas-tos´*; from 4111; *moulded*, i.e. (by implication) *artificial* or (figurative) *fictitious* (*false*):—feigned.

4113. πλατεῖα, plateia, *plat-i´-ah*; feminine of 4116; a *wide* "*plat*" or "*place*," i.e. open *square*:—street.

4114. πλάτος, platos, *plat´-os*; from 4116; *width*:—breadth.

4115. πλατύνω, platunō, *plat-oo´-no*; from 4116; to *widen* (literal or figurative):—make broad, enlarge.

4116. πλατύς, platus, *plat-oos´*; from 4111; spread out "*flat*" ("plot"), i.e. *broad*:—wide.

4117. πλέγμα, plegma, *pleg´-mah*; from 4120; a *plait* (of hair):—broidered hair.

4118. πλεῖστος, pleistos, *plice´-tos*; irregular superlative of 4183; the *largest number* or *very large*:—very great, most.

4119. πλείων, pleiōn, *pli´-own*; neuter **πλεῖον**, ***pleion***, *pli´-on*; or **πλέον**, ***pleon***, *pleh´-on*; comparative of 4183; *more* in quantity, number, or quality; also (in plural) the *major portion*:—× above, + exceed, more excellent, further, (very) great (-er), long (-er), (very) many, greater (more) part, + yet but.

4120. πλέκω, plekō, *plek´-o*; a primary word; to *twine* or *braid*:—plait.

4121. πλεονάζω, pleonazō, *pleh-on-ad´-zo*; from 4119; to *do, make* or *be more*, i.e. *increase* (transitive or intransitive); by extension to *superabound*:—abound, abundant, make to increase, have over.

4122. πλεονεκτέω, pleonekteō, *pleh-on-ek-teh´-o*; from 4123; to *be covetous*, i.e. (by implication) to *overreach*:—get an advantage, defraud, make a gain.

4123. πλεονέκτης, pleonektēs, *pleh-on-ek´-tace*; from 4119 and 2192; *holding (desiring) more*, i.e. *eager for gain (avaricious*, hence a *defrauder)*:—covetous.

4124. πλεονεξία, pleonexia, *pleh-on-ex-ee´-ah*; from 4123; *avarice*, i.e. (by implication) *fraudulency, extortion*:—covetous (-ness) practices, greediness.

Noun from *pleonéktēs* (4123), covetous, which is from *pleíōn* (4119), more, and *échō* (2192), to have. The state of having more, a larger portion, advantage. In the NT, the will to have more, i.e. covetousness, greediness for gain, which leads a person to defraud others (Mk 7:22; Lk 12:15; Ro 1:29; 2Co 9:5; Eph 4:19; 5:3; Col 3:5; 1Th 2:5; 2Pe 2:3, 14).

Syn.: *epithumía* (1939), desire, lust; *órexis* (3715), appetite.

4125. πλευρά, pleura, *plyoo-rah´*; of uncertain affinity; a *rib*, i.e. (by extension) *side*:—side.

4126. πλέω, pleō, *pleh´-o*; another form for **πλεύω, *pleuō***, *plyoo´-o*, which is used as an alternate in certain tenses; probably a form of 4150 (through the idea of *plunging* through the water); to *pass* in a vessel:—sail. See also 4130.

4127. πληγή, plēgē, *play-gay´*; from 4141; a *stroke*; (by implication) a *wound*; (figurative) a *calamity*:—plague, stripe, wound (-ed).

4128. πλῆθος, plēthos, *play´-thos*; from 4130; a *fulness*, i.e. a *large number, throng, populace*:—bundle, company, multitude.

4129. πληθύνω, plēthunō, *play-thoo´-no*; from another form of 4128; to *increase* (transitive or intransitive):—abound, multiply.

4130. πλήθω, plēthō, *play´-tho*; a prolonged form of a primary **πλέω, *pleō***, *pleh´-o* (which appears only as an alternate in certain tenses and in the reduplication form **πίμπλημι, *pimplēmi***; to "*fill*" (literal or figurative [*imbue, influence, supply*]); specially to *fulfil* (time):—accomplish, full (… come), furnish.

4131. πλήκτης, plēktēs, *plake´-tace*; from 4141; a *smiter*, i.e. *pugnacious (quarrelsome)*:—striker.

4132. πλημμύρα, plēmmura, *plame-moo´-rah*; prolonged from 4130; *flood-tide*, i.e. (by analogy) a *freshet*:—flood.

4133. πλήν, plēn, *plane*; from 4119; *moreover (besides)*, i.e. *albeit, save that, rather, yet*:—but (rather), except, nevertheless, notwithstanding, save, than.

4134. πλήρης, plērēs, *play´-race*; from 4130; *replete*, or *covered* over; (by analogy) *complete*:—full.

Adjective from *pléos* (n.f.), full. Full, filled.

(I) Particularly of hollow vessels, e.g., baskets filled with fragments (Mt 14:20; 15:37; Mk 6:43; 8:19). Of a surface, full, fully covered (Lk 5:12).

(II) Figuratively, full, abounding. Spoken of men being filled with something, e.g., of the Holy Spirit (Lk 4:1; Ac 6:3, 5; 7:55; 11:24). See also Jn 1:14; Ac 6:8; 9:36; 13:10; 19:28.

(III) Figuratively, full in the sense of being complete, perfect. Spoken of a full kernel of grain (Mk 4:28); spoken of a full reward (2Jn 8).

Syn.: *mestós* (3324), full.

4135. πληροφορέω, plērophoreō, *play-rof-or-eh´-o*; from 4134 and 5409; to *carry out fully* (in evidence), i.e. *completely assure* (or *convince*), *entirely accomplish*:—most surely believe, fully know (persuade), make full proof of.

From *plḗrēs* (4134), full, and *phoréō* (5409), to fill. To persuade fully, give full assurance.

(I) Of persons, in the passive, to be fully assured, persuaded (Ro 4:21; 14:5).

(II) Of things, to make fully assured, give full proof of, confirm fully (2Ti 4:5); passive, to be fully established as true (Lk 1:1; 2Ti 4:17).

Deriv.: *plērophoría* (4136), perfect certitude, full conviction.

Syn.: *apodeíknumi* (584), to demonstrate, accredit; *bebaióō* (950), to assure, establish; *kuróō* (2964), to ratify, confirm; *pistóō* (4104), to assure.

4136. πληροφορία, plērophoria, *play-rof-or-ee´-ah*; from 4135; *entire confidence*:—(full) assurance.

Noun from *plērophoréō* (4135), to fulfill. Full assurance, firm persuasion (Col 2:2; 1Th 1:5; Heb 6:11; 10:22).

Syn.: *pepoíthēsis* (4006), reliance, confidence; *pístis* (4102), faith, confidence, dependability.

4137. πληρόω, plēroō, *play-ro´-o*; from 4134; to *make replete*, i.e. (literal) to *cram* (a net), *level* up (a hollow), or (figurative) to *furnish* (or *imbue, diffuse, influence*), *satisfy, execute* (an office), *finish* (a period or task), *verify* (or *coincide* with a prediction), etc.:—accomplish, × after, (be) complete, end, expire, fill (up), fulfil, (be, make) full (come), fully preach, perfect, supply.

From *plḗrēs* (4134), full. To make full, fill, to fill up.

(I) Particularly, to fill a vessel or hollow place; passive (Mt 13:48; Lk 3:5). Figuratively (Mt 23:32, sins). Generally of a place, to fill by diffusing something throughout (Jn 12:3; Ac 2:2; 5:28). Figuratively, to fill one's heart, to take possession of it (Jn 14:6; Ac 5:3).

(II) Figuratively, to fill, supply abundantly with something, impart richly, imbue with; e.g., to fill with joy (Ac 2:28; 13:52; 2Ti 1:4). See also Lk 2:40; Ro 1:29; 15:13, 14; 2Co 7:4; Eph 1:23; 3:19; 4:10; 5:18; Php 1:11; 4:18, 19; Col 1:9; 2:10).

(III) To fulfill, perform fully.

(A) Spoken of duty or obligation (Mt 3:15; Ac 12:25; Col 4:17).

(B) Of a declaration or prophecy, to fulfill or accomplish (Ac 3:18; 13:27). More often in the passive, to be fulfilled, accomplished, to have been accomplished (Mt 2:17; 26:54; 27:9; Mk 15:28; Lk 1:20; 4:21; 21:22; 24:44; Ac 1:16; Jas 2:23).

(IV) To fulfill, bring to a full end, accomplish, complete.

(A) In the passive, of time, to be fulfilled, completed, ended (Mk 1:15; Lk 21:24; Jn 7:8; Ac 7:23, 30; 9:23; 24:27).

(B) Of a business or work, to accomplish, finish, complete (Lk 7:1; 9:31; Ac 13:25; 14:26; 19:21, Ro 15:19; Col 1:25; Rev 6:11).

(C) By implication, to fill out, complete, make perfect, accomplish an end (Mt 5:17; Php 2:2; 2Th 1:11). In the passive, to be made full, complete (Lk 22:16; Jn 3:29; 15:11; 16:24; 17:13; 2Co 10:6; Col 4:12; 1Jn 1:4; 2Jn 12; Rev 3:2).

Deriv.: *anaplēróō* (378), to fill up; *ekplēróō* (1603), to fill, fulfill; *plḗrōma* (4138), fullness; *sumplēróō* (4845), to fill completely.

Syn.: *anaplēróō* (378), to complete, supply, fill up; *gémō* (1073), to be full; *ekplēróō* (1603), to accomplish entirely, fulfill; *epiteléō* (2005), to fulfill, complete, perform; *kuróō* (2964), to make authoritative, ratify; *mestóō* (3325), to fill; *pímplēmi* or *plḗthō* (4130), to fill, accomplish; *teleióō* (5048), to complete, fulfill, finish; *teléō* (5055), to complete, execute, conclude, finish.

4138. πλήρωμα, plērōma, *play´-ro-mah*; from 4137; *repletion* or *completion*, i.e. (subject) what *fills* (as contents, supplement, copiousness, multitude), or (object) what is *filled* (as container, performance, period):—which is put in to fill up, piece that filled up, fulfilling, full, fulness.

Noun from *plēróō* (4137), to make full, fill, fill up. Fullness, filling; basically, that with which anything is filled or of which it is full, the contents.

(I) Particularly meaning the contents of the earth (1Co 10:26, 28); of baskets (Mk 8:20); supplement, that which fills up, such as a patch (*epíblēma* [1915]) (Mt 9:16; Mk 2:21).

(II) Figuratively meaning fullness, full measure, abundance.

(A) Generally, of grace and God's provisions (Jn 1:16; Ro 11:12; 15:29; Eph 3:19); of divine perfections (Col 2:9).

(B) Of persons, full number, complement, multitude (Ro 11:25; Eph 1:23).

(III) Fulfillment, full end, completion.

(A) Of time, full period (Gal 4:4; Eph 1:10).

(B) By implication, meaning completeness, reaching the intended goal (Ro 13:10; Eph 1:23; 4:13).

Syn.: *eklḗrōsis* (1604), completion, accomplishment; *teleiótēs* (5047), completeness; *télos* (5056), end, goal.

4139. πλησίον, plēsion, *play-see´-on*; neuter of a derivative of **πέλας**, ***pelas*** (*near*); (adverb) *close* by; as noun, a *neighbour*, i.e. *fellow* (as man, countryman, Christian or friend):—near, neighbour.

Adverb from *pélas* (n.f.), near, near to. Near, nearby.

(I) Particularly, of places, near, neighboring (Jn 4:5).

(II) Figuratively, used as a substantive, of people: one near, a neighbour, fellow, another person of the same nature, country, class.

(A) Generally, a fellow man, any other member of the human family, as in the precept "Thou shalt love thy neighbour as thyself" (Mt 19:19; 22:39; Mk 12:31; Ro 13:9; Gal 5:14; Jas 2:8). See also Mk 12:33; Lk 10:27, 29, 36; Ro 13:10; Eph 4:25; Heb 8:11.

(B) One of the same people or country, a fellow countryman (Ac 7:27 [cf. 7:24, 26]).

(C) One of the same faith, a fellow Christian (Ro 15:2).

(D) A friend, associate, the opposite of *echthrós* (2190), enemy (Mt 5:43), and the same as *phílos* (5384), friend.

Deriv.: *paraplḗsion* (3897), nearby, close to.

Syn.: *geítōn* (1069), neighbour; *eggús* (1451), near.

4140. πλησμονή, plēsmonē, *place-mon-ay´*; from a presumed derivative of 4130; a *filling* up, i.e. (figurative) *gratification*:—satisfying.

4141. πλήσσω, plēssō, *place´-so*; apparently another form of 4111 (through the idea of *flattening* out); to *pound*, i.e. (figurative) to *inflict* with (calamity):—smite. Compare 5180.

4142. πλοιάριον, ploiarion, *ploy-ar´-ee-on*; neuter of a presumed derivative of 4143; a *boat*:—boat, little (small) ship.

4143. πλοῖον, ploion, *ploy´-on*; from 4126; a *sailer*, i.e. *vessel*:—ship (-ping).

4144. πλόος, ploos, *plo´-os*; from 4126; a *sail*, i.e. *navigation*:—course, sailing, voyage.

4145. πλούσιος, plousios, *ploo´-see-os*; from 4149; *wealthy*; (figurative) *abounding* with:—rich.

4146. πλουσίως, plousiōs, *ploo-see´-oce*; adverb from 4145; *copiously*:—abundantly, richly.

4147. πλουτέω, plouteō, *ploo-teh´-o*; from 4148; to *be* (or *become*) *wealthy* (literal or figurative):—be increased with goods, (be made, wax) rich.

From *ploútos* (4149), wealth. To be rich, restore.

(I) Particularly, to be rich in material possessions (Lk 1:53; 1Co 4:8; 1Ti 6:9; Rev 3:17; 18:5, 15, 19).

(II) Figuratively, to be rich in something spiritual, to be rich in God's blessings (Ro 10:12; 2Co 8:9; Rev 3:18). To be rich in good works (1Ti 6:18); to be rich toward God, in the sense of laying up treasures in heaven by doing good works (Lk 12:21).

4148. πλουτίζω, ploutizō, *ploo-tid´-zo*; from 4149; to *make wealthy* (figurative):—en- (make) rich.

4149. πλοῦτος, ploutos, *ploo´-tos*; from the base of 4130; *wealth* (as *fulness*), i.e. (literal) *money, possessions*, or (figurative) *abundance, richness*, (special) valuable *bestowment*:—riches.

4150. πλύνω, plunō, *ploo´-no*; a prolonged form of an obsolete **πλύω**, ***pluō*** (to "*flow*"); to "*plunge*," i.e. *launder* clothing:—wash. Compare 3068, 3538.

To wash, as garments (Rev 7:14).

Deriv.: *apoplúnō* (637), to wash out.

Syn.: *loúō* (3068), bathe; *níptō* (3538), to wash (part of the body). Also *apoloúō* (628), to bathe off; *aponíptō* (634), to wash off; *bréchō* (1026), to wet, wash; *katharízō* (2511), to cleanse; *kathaírō* (2508), to cleanse, purge.

4151. πνεῦμα, pneuma, *pnyoo´-mah*; from 4154; a *current* of air, i.e. *breath* (*blast*) or a *breeze*; (by analogy or figurative) a *spirit*, i.e. (human) the rational *soul*, (by implication) *vital principle*, mental *disposition*, etc., or (superhuman) an *angel, dæmon*, or (divine) *God*, Christ's *spirit*, the Holy *Spirit*:—ghost, life, spirit (-ual, -ually), mind. Compare 5590.

Noun from *pnéō* (4154), to breathe, to blow.

(I) Breath.

(A) Of the mouth or nostrils, a breathing, blast. Spoken of the destroying power of God (2Th 2:8). Spoken of the vital breath of life (Rev 11:11).

(B) Breath of air, air in motion, a breeze, blast, the wind (Jn 3:8).

(II) Spirit.

(A) The vital spirit or life, the principle of life residing in man. The breath breathed by God into man and again returning to God, the spiritual entity in man (Mt 27:50; Lk 8:55; 23:46; Jn 19:30; Ac 7:59; 1Co 15:45; Rev 13:15).

(B) The rational spirit, mind, element of life. **(1)** Generally, spirit distinct from the body and soul. In 1Th 5:23, *pneúma, psuchḗ* (soul [5590]), and *sṓma* (body [4983]) are listed together in describing the whole man. Hebrews 4:12 also describes them as being distinct from one another. **(2)** As referring to the disposition, feeling, temper of mind; e.g., the spirit of gentleness (1Co 4:21; Gal 6:1). Also Lk 9:55; Ro 8:15; 11:8; 1Co 4:21; 2Co 4:13; 12:18; Eph 2:2; 4:23; Php 1:27; 2:1; 2Ti 1:7; Jas 4:5; 1Pe 3:4). **(3)** As including the understanding, intellect (Mk 2:8; Lk 1:80; 2:40; 1Co 2:11, 12).

(III) A spirit; a simple, incorporeal, immaterial being (thought of as possessing higher capacities than man does in his present state).

(A) Spoken of created spirits: **(1)** Of the human soul or spirit, after its departure from the body and as existing in a separate state (Heb 12:23; 1Pe 3:19). Of the soul of a person reappearing after death, a spirit, ghost (Lk 24:37, 39; Ac 23:8, 9). **(2)** Of an evil spirit, demon (Mt 8:16; Mk 9:20; Lk 9:39; 10:20). Used mostly with the adjective *akátharton* (169), unclean, as an unclean spirit (Mt 10:1; 12:43, 45; Mk 1:23, 26, 27; 3:11, 30; 5:2, 8, 13; 6:7; 7:25; Lk 4:36; 6:18; 8:29; 9:42; 11:24, 26; Ac 5:16; 8:7; Rev 16:13; 18:2). Described as evil spirits (Lk 7:21; 8:2; 19:12, 13, 15, 16); as spirits of demons (Lk 4:35; Rev 16:14). Identified on the basis of what they produce: an unspeaking spirit (Mk 9:17); an unspeaking and deaf spirit (Lk 9:25); a spirit causing weakness or sickness (Lk 13:11); a spirit of divination or fortune-telling (Ac 16:16). **(3)** Less often in the plural, of angels as God's ministering spirits (Heb 1:14; Rev 1:4; 3:1; 4:5; 5:6).

(B) Of God in reference to His incorporeality (Jn 4:24).

(C) Of the Spirit of God. In the NT, referred to as "the Spirit of God," "the Holy Spirit," in an absolute sense as "the Spirit"; the Spirit of Christ as being communicated by Him after His resurrection and ascension. The same as the Spirit of Christ (Ro 8:9; 1Pe 1:11); the Spirit of Jesus Christ (Php 1:19); the Spirit of the Lord (2Co 3:17); the Spirit of God's Son (Gal 4:6). The Holy Spirit is everywhere represented as being in intimate union with God the Father and God the Son. The passages with this meaning in the NT may be divided into two classes: those in which being, intelligence, and agency are predicated of the Spirit; and, metonymically, those in which the effects and consequences of this agency are spoken about. **(1)** The Holy Spirit as possessing being, intelligence, agency. **(a)** Joined with the Father and the Son, with the same or with different predicates (Mt 28:19; 1Co 12:4–6; 2Co 13:14; 1Pe 1:2; Jude 20, 21; 1Jn 5:7). **(b)** Spoken of in connection with God the Father, as having intimate union or oneness with Him (Jn 15:26; 1Co 2:10, 11). Described as speaking through the prophets of the OT and the apostles (Ac 1:16; 28:25; Heb 3:7; 9:8; 10:15). Spoken of as imparting new spiritual life to those who believe in the gospel (Jn 3:5, 6, 8), and then dwelling in Christians (Ro 8:9, 11; 1Co 3:16; 6:19; 2Ti 1:14). The Spirit and God the Father are interchanged (Ac 5:3, 9 [cf. 5:4]; Eph 6:17). **(c)** Spoken in connection with or in reference to Christ as an equal, in the form of an oath (Ro 15:30; 1Co 6:11; 2Co 3:17; Heb 10:29). The Holy Spirit is described as descending in a bodily form upon Jesus after His baptism (Mt 3:16; Mk 1:10; Lk 3:22; Jn 1:32, 33). **(d)** As coming to and acting upon Christians, illuminating and empowering them, and remaining with them, imparting to them spiritual knowledge, aid, consolation, sanctification, and making intercession with and for them (Jn 14:17, 26; 15:26; 16:13; Ro 8:14, 16, 26, 27; 14:17; 15:13, 16; 2Co 1:22; 5:5; Eph 3:16; 6:18; 1Th 1:6; 2Th 2:13). Described as the author of revelations to men through the prophets of the OT, being the authority through which prophets and holy men were motivated when they spoke or acted in the Spirit or through the Spirit (Mt 22:43; Mk 12:36; Ac 10:19; 20:23; 21:11; 1Ti 4:1; Rev 19:10). **(2)** The Holy Spirit's influence and effect upon others, such as the power of the Holy Spirit (Ac 1:8). Spoken: **(a)** Of the role of the Holy Spirit in the miraculous conception of the Lord Jesus (Lk 1:35). See also Mt 1:18, 20. **(b)** Of that special authority which rested upon and empowered the Lord Jesus after the descent of the Holy Spirit upon Him at His baptism (Lk 4:1). See also Mt 12:18; Lk 4:18; Jn 3:34; Ac 10:38. As prompting Him to various actions, such as going into the desert and being tempted (Mt 4:1; Mk 1:12; Lk 4:1). See also Mt 12:28; Lk 4:14. **(c)** Of His filling and empowering others (Lk 1:15; 1:41; 1:67; 2:25–27). The technical expression "to be baptized in [or with] the Holy Spirit" refers to the spiritual baptism into the body of Christ for all those who were truly saved (Mt 3:11; Mk 1:8; Lk 3:16; Jn 1:33; Ac 1:5; 11:16; 1Co 12:13). **(d)** Of that authority of the Holy Spirit by which the apostles were qualified to act as directors of the church of Christ (Jn 20:22). Specifically, of the empowerment imparted by the Holy Spirit on and after the Day of Pentecost, by which the apostles and early Christians were endowed with high supernatural qualifications for their work; knowledge equivalent to a full knowledge of gospel truth and the power of prophesying, working miracles, and speaking with languages previously unknown to them; all done in evidence of the baptism of the Holy Spirit (Ac 2:4, 17, 18, 33, 38; 5:32; 8:15, 17–19; 10:44, 45, 47; 11:15, 24; 13:9; 15:8; 19:6; Ro 15:19; 1Co 2:4; 7:40; 12:7–9; 14:2, 32; Gal 3:2, 3, 5, 14; Eph 1:13; 1Th 1:5; 4:8; 5:19; Heb 2:4; 1Pe 1:12). The Holy Spirit prompts one to do or restrain from doing particular actions (Ac 8:29, 39; 13:2, 4; 15:28; 16:6, 7); encourages holy boldness, energy, and zeal in speaking and acting (Ac 4:8, 31); serves the medium of divine communications and revelations (Ac 7:55; 11:28; 21:4; Eph 3:5); and is the source of support, comfort, Christian joy and triumph (Eph 5:18; Php 1:19). **(3)** Metonymically spoken of a person or teacher who acts or professes to act under the inspiration of the Holy Spirit by divine inspiration (1Co 12:10, "discerning of spirits" of teachers, a critical faculty of the mind quickened by the Holy Spirit, consisting not only of the power of discerning who was a prophet and who was not, but also of a distinguishing in the discourses of a teacher what proceeded from the Holy Spirit and what did not. Also 1Jn 4:1–3, 6).

Deriv.: *pneumatikós* (4152), spiritual.

Syn.: *pnoḗ* (4157), breath, wind.

4152. πνευματικός, pneumatikos, *phyoo-mat-ik-os´*; from 4151; *non-carnal*, i.e. (humanly) *ethereal* (as opposed to gross), or (demonically) a *spirit* (concretely), or (divinely) *supernatural, regenerate, religious*:—spiritual. Compare 5591.

Adjective from *pneúma* (4151), spirit. Spiritual.

(I) Pertaining to the nature of spirits. Spoken of "a spiritual body" (1Co 15:44), i.e. a body dominated by the Spirit or fit for the Spirit, in contrast to a natural or animal body, which obeys one's natural instincts. Spoken of the spiritual forces of wickednesses (Eph 6:12).

(II) Pertaining to or proceeding from the Holy Spirit.

(A) Of persons who are spiritual, i.e. enlightened by the Holy Spirit, enjoying the influences, graces, and gifts of the Holy Spirit (1Co 2:15; 3:1; 14:37; Gal 6:1).

(B) Of things spiritual, i.e. communicated or imparted by the Holy Spirit (Ro 1:11; 7:14; 15:27; 1Co 2:13; 9:11; 12:1; 14:1; Eph 1:3; 5:19; Col 1:9; 3:16). Also spoken of things in a higher and spiritual sense, not literal or corporeal, including also a reference to the Holy Spirit (1Co 10:3, 4; 1Pe 2:5).

Deriv.: *pneumatikṓs* (4153), spiritually.

4153. πνευματικῶς, pneumatikōs, *pnyoo-mat-ik-oce´*; adverb from 4152; *non-physically*, i.e. *divinely*, figuratively:—spiritually.

Adverb from *pneumatikós* (4152), spiritual. Spiritually, by the assistance of the Holy Spirit (1Co 2:14), prophetically, allegorically, mystically (Rev 11:8 [cf. Rev 17:5, 7]).

4154. πνέω, pneō, *pneh´-o*; a primary word; to *breathe* hard, i.e. *breeze*:—blow. Compare 5594.

To blow upon, as the wind or air (Mt 7:25, 27; Lk 12:55; Jn 3:8; 6:18; Ac 27:40; Rev 7:1).

Deriv.: *ekpnéō* (1606), to die, expire; *empnéō* (1709), to inhale, breathe, to inspire; *theópneustos* (2315), God-breathed, inspired; *pneúma* (4151), wind, breath, life, spirit; *pnoḗ* (4157), wind, breath; *hupopnéō* (5285), to blow gently or softly.

Syn.: *rhipízō* (4494), to fan up, to agitate, toss.

4155. πνίγω, pnigō, *pnee´-go*; strengthened from 4154; to *wheeze*, i.e. (causative by implication) to *throttle* or *strangle* (*drown*):—choke, take by the throat.

4156. πνικτός, pniktos, *pnik-tos´*; from 4155; *throttled*, i.e. (neuter concrete) an animal *choked* to death (*not bled*):—strangled.

4157. πνοή, pnoē, *pno-ay´*; from 4154; *respiration*, a *breeze*:—breath, wind.

Noun from *pnéō* (4154), to breathe, blow. Wind, vital breath, respiration, the ability to breathe (Ac 17:25; a breath of air, a blast of wind (Ac 2:2).

Syn.: *aḗr* (109), air; *ánemos* (417), violent wind; *pneúma* (4151), wind.

4158. ποδήρης, podērēs, *pod-ay´-race*; from 4228 and another element of uncertain affinity; a *dress* (2066 implied) *reaching* the *ankles*:—garment down to the foot.

Adjective from *poús* (4228), foot, and *arṓ* (n.f.), to join, fasten, fit. Reaching down to the feet, spoken of long flowing robes. Used only in Rev 1:13.

Syn.: *stolḗ* (4749), a long robe worn by people of rank as a mark of distinction. For a list of various types of clothing, see the synonyms under *himátion* (2440), garment.

4159. πόθεν, pothen, *poth´-en*; from the base of 4213 with enclitic adverb of origin; *from which* (as interrogative) or *what* (as relative) place, state, source or cause:—whence.

4160. ποιέω, poieō, *poy-eh´-o*; apparently a prolonged form of an obsolete primary; to *make* or *do* (in a very wide application, more or less direct):—abide, + agree, appoint, × avenge, + band together, be, bear, + bewray, bring (forth), cast out, cause, commit, + content, continue, deal, + without any delay, (would) do (-ing), execute, exercise, fulfil, gain, give, have, hold, × journeying, keep, + lay wait, + lighten the ship, make, × mean, + none of these things move me, observe, ordain, perform, provide, + have purged, purpose, put, + raising up, × secure, shew, × shoot out, spend, take, tarry, + transgress the law, work, yield. Compare 4238.

To make, do, expressing action either as completed or continued.

(I) To make, i.e. to form, produce, bring about, cause; spoken of any external act as manifested in the production of something tangible, corporeal, obvious to the senses, i.e. completed action.

(A) Generally: **(1)** Particularly and with the accusative (Mt 17:4; Jn 9:11; 18:18; 19:23; Ac 7:40; 9:39; 19:24; Ro 9:20; Heb 12:13; Rev 13:14). **(2)** Spoken of God, to make, create, with the accusative (Mt 19:4; Lk 11:40; Ac 4:24; 7:50; 14:15; 17:24; Heb 1:2; Rev 14:7).

(B) Figuratively spoken of a state or condition, or of things intangible and incorporeal, and generally of such things as are produced by an inward act of the mind or will; to make, to cause, to bring about, to occasion. **(1)** Generally to cause, to bring about, e.g., to make peace (Eph 2:15). See also Lk 1:68; Ac 15:3; 24:12; Ro 16:17; 1Co 10:13; Heb 8:9; Ro 15:26; Heb 1:3. Used of mighty deeds, wonders, miracles (Mt 7:22; 13:58; Lk 1:51; Jn 2:11, 23; 4:54; 5:36; 6:30; 11:47; Ac 6:8; 7:36; 15:12). **(2)** Spoken of a course of action or conduct, to do, execute, exercise, practice; e.g., with *krísin* (2920), judgement, to execute judgement (Jn 5:27; Jude 15). Specifically of right, duty, virtue (Jn 3:21; 5:29; Ro 2:14; 7:19; 10:5; Eph 6:8; Jas 4:17; 1Jn 1:6; 2:29; 3:7; 3Jn 5). **(3)** Of evil deeds or conduct, to do, commit or practice sin (Mt 13:41; Lk 12:48; Jn 8:34; Ro 1:32; 2:3; 1Co 6:18; 2Co 11:7; 1Jn 3:4; Rev 21:27).

(C) To cause to exist, as spoken of generative power, to beget, to bring forth, to bear. **(1)** Of trees and plants, to germinate, bring forth fruit, yield (Mt 3:10; 7:17; 13:23, 26; Lk 3:9; Rev 22:2). Metaphorically (Mt 3:8; 21:43; Lk 3:8). Of branches, to shoot forth (Mk 4:32); of a fountain pouring out water (Jas 3:12). **(2)** Figuratively of persons, to make for oneself, to get, acquire, gain (Lk 12:33; 16:9; Jn 4:1). To profit, advantage, gain (Mt 25:16; Lk 19:18; 1Co 15:29).

(D) Causative, to cause to do or be. E.g., to make someone sit down (Jn 6:10). See also Mt 5:32; 21:13; Mk 1:17; 7:37; 8:25; Lk 5:34; Jn 4:46; 6:15; 11:37; Ac 3:12; 17:26; 1Co 6:15; Col 4:16; Heb 1:7; Rev 13:13).

(II) To do, expressing an action as continued or not yet completed, sometimes, what one does repeatedly, habitually, like *prássō* (4238), to practice.

(A) Followed by the accusative of thing, and without reference to a person as the remote object. **(1)** Followed by the accusative pron., to do, generally (Mt 5:47; 8:9; 9:28; Mk 11:3; Lk 6:2; 7:8; 20:2; Ac 1:1; 14:11, 15; 1Co 7:36; Gal 2:10; Eph 6:9; Php 2:14; Col 3:17; 1Ti 5:21; Jas 4:15).

(B) Intransitively to do, act, always with an adverbial modifier telling how one acts; e.g., to act prudently (Lk 16:8). See also Mt 1:24; 12:12; 23:3; 28:15; Lk 2:27; 12:47; Jn 14:31; 1Co 7:37, 38; 16:1).

(C) Followed by the accusative of time, meaning to do or act for a certain time, up to a certain time, to spend, pass (Mt 20:12; Ac 15:33; 18:23; 20:3; 2Co 11:25; Jas 4:13; Rev 13:5).

Deriv.: *eirēnopoiéō* (1517), to make peace; *zōopoiéō* (2227), to make alive; *kakopoiós* (2555), evildoer; *kalopoiéō* (2569), to live virtuously; *moschopoiéō* (3447), to make a calf; *ochlopoiéō* (3792), to make a crowd; *peripoiéō* (4046), to purchase, acquire, preserve, keep; *poíēma* (4161), creation, work, action; *poíēsis* (4162), performance, action; *poiētḗs* (4163), creator, maker, doer; *prospoiéomai* (4364), to pretend; *skēnopoiós* (4635), tentmaker; *cheiropoíētos* (5499), make by hands.

Syn.: *prássō* (4238), to do, to practice, perform. Also *apoteléō* (658), to finish; *douleúō* (1398), to labour as a slave; *ekteléō* (1615), to finish; *energéō* (1754), to be active, efficient; *epiteléō* (2005), to fulfill, perform completely; *ergázomai* (2038), to work; *katergázomai* (2716), to work fully, accomplish; *teléō* (5055), to complete, conclude.

4161. ποίημα, poiēma, *poy´-ay-mah*; from 4160; a *product*, i.e. *fabric* (literal or figurative):—thing that is made, workmanship.

4162. ποίησις, poiēsis, *poy´-ay-sis*; from 4160; *action*, i.e. *performance* (of the law):—deed.

4163. ποιητής, poiētēs, *poy-ay-tace´*; from 4160; a *performer*; specially a "*poet*":—doer, poet.

4164. ποικίλος, poikilos, *poy-kee´-los*; of uncertain derivative; *motley*, i.e. *various* in character:—divers, manifold.

4165. ποιμαίνω, poimainō, *poy-mah´ee-no*; from 4166; to *tend* as a shepherd (or figurative, *supervisor*):—feed (cattle), rule.

From *poimḗn* (4166), shepherd. To feed a flock or herd, to tend. Used particularly (Lk 17:7, shepherding). Used figuratively, to care for, provide: referring to kings and princes in regard to their people (Mt 2:6; Rev 7:17); in regard to pastors and teachers in the church (Jn 21:16; Ac 20:28; 1Pe 5:2). From the context, to rule, to govern with severity, spoken of Christ ruling with a rod of iron (Rev 2:27; 12:5; 19:15). In a bad sense, with *heautón* (1438), himself, to feed or cherish oneself, to take care of oneself at the expense of others (Jude 12).

Syn.: *bóskō* (1006), to feed, distinguished from *poimaínō* in that the latter implies the whole office of the shepherd as guiding, guarding, and placing the flock in the fold, as well as leading it to nourishment; *hēgemoneúō* (2230), to act as ruler; *hēgéomai* (2233), to lead; *kateuthúnō* (2720), to guide, direct.

4166. ποιμήν, poimēn, *poy-mane´*; of uncertain affinity; a *shepherd* (literal or figurative):—shepherd, pastor.

Noun meaning shepherd, one who generally cares for flocks.

(I) Particularly (Mt 9:36; 25:32; Mk 6:34; Lk 2:8, 15, 18, 20).

(II) Figuratively of Jesus as the Great Shepherd who watches over and provides for the welfare of the Church, His flock (Mt 26:31; Mk 14:27; Jn 10:2, 11, 12, 14, 16; Heb 13:20; 1Pe 2:25); spoken also of the spiritual guide of a particular church (Eph 4:11).

Deriv.: *archipoímēn* (750), chief shepherd; *poimaínō* (4165), to tend, take general care of the flock; *poímnē* (4167) and *poímnion* (4168), flock.

Syn.: *archēgós* (747), leader; *didáskalos* (1320), teacher; *epískopos* (1985), overseer, superintendent; *hēgemṓn* (2232), a leader; *presbúteros* (4245), elder, spiritual leader.

4167. ποίμνη, poimnē, *poym´-nay*; contracted from 4165; a *flock* (literal or figurative):—flock, fold.

Noun from *poimḗn* (4166), shepherd. A flock of sheep (Lk 2:8; 1Co 9:7). Figuratively, the flock of Christ, His disciples, the Church (Mt 26:31; Jn 10:16).

Syn.: *poímnion* (4168), a flock. Also *ekklēsía* (1577), church, assembly.

4168. ποίμνιον, poimnion, *poym´-nee-on*; neuter of a presumed derivative of 4167; a *flock*, i.e. (figurative) *group* (of believers):—flock.

Noun from *poimḗn* (4166), shepherd. A flock. In the NT, it is applied only figuratively for the flock of Christ, his disciples, the Church (Lk 12:32; Ac 20:28, 29; 1Pe 5:2, 3). A diminutive of *poímnē* (4167).

Syn.: *poímnē* (4167), flock. Also *ekklēsía* (1577), church.

4169. ποῖος, poios, *poy´-os*; from the base of 4226 and 3634; individualizing interrogative (of character) *what* sort of, or (of number) *which* one:—what (manner of), which.

4170. πολεμέω, polemeō, *pol-em-eh´-o*; from 4171; to *be* (engaged) in *warfare*, i.e. to *battle* (literal or figurative):—fight, (make) war.

4171. πόλεμος, polemos, *pol´-em-os*; from **πέλομαι, pelomai** (to *bustle*); *warfare* (literal or figurative; a single encounter or a series):—battle, fight, war.

(I) Generally, war (Mt 24:6; Mk 13:7; Lk 14:31; 21:9; Rev 11:7; 12:7, 17; 13:7; 19:19).

(II) Particularly, a fight, a battle (1Co 14:8; Heb 11:34; Rev 9:7, 9; 16:14; 20:8). As a hyperbole: referring to strife (Jas 4:1).

Deriv.: *poleméō* (4170), to make war, fight.

Syn.: While *pólemos* embraces the whole course of hostilities, *máchē* (3163), battle, includes the use of arms of hostile armies.

4172. πόλις, polis, *pol´-is*; probably from the same as 4171, or perhaps from 4183; a *town* (properly with walls, of greater or less size):—city.

4173. πολιτάρχης, politarchēs, *pol-it-ar´-khace*; from 4172 and 757; a *town-officer*, i.e. *magistrate*:—ruler of the city.

4174. πολιτεία, politeia, *pol-ee-ti´-ah*; from 4177 ("*polity*"); *citizenship*; concretely a *community*:—commonwealth, freedom.

4175. πολίτευμα, politeuma, *pol-it´-yoo-mah*; from 4176; a *community*, i.e. (abstract) *citizenship* (figurative):—conversation.

4176. πολιτεύομαι, politeuomai, *pol-it-yoo´-om-ahee*; middle of a derivative of 4177; to *behave* as a citizen (figurative):—let conversation be, live.

4177. πολίτης, politēs, *pol-ee´-tace*; from 4172; a *townsman*:—citizen.

4178. πολλάκις, pollakis, *pol-lak´-is*; multiple adverb from 4183; *many times*, i.e. *frequently*:—oft (-en, -entimes, -times).

4179. πολλαπλασίων, pollaplasiōn, *pol-lap-las-ee´-ohn*; from 4183 and probably a derivative of 4120; *manifold*, i.e. (neuter as noun) *very much more*:—manifold more.

4180. πολυλογία, polulogia, *pol-oo-log-ee´-ah*; from a compound of 4183 and 3056; *loquacity*, i.e. *prolixity*:—much speaking.

4181. πολυμέρως, polumerōs, *pol-oo-mer´-oce*; adverb from a compound of 4183 and 3313; *in many portions*, i.e. *variously* as to time and agency (*piecemeal*):—at sundry times.

4182. πολυποίκιλος, polupoikilos, *pol-oo-poy´-kil-os*; from 4183 and 4164; *much variegated*, i.e. *multifarious*:—manifold.

4183. πολύς, polus, *pol-oos´*; including the forms from the alternate **πολλός, polos** (singular) *much* (in any respect) or (plural) *many*; neuter (singular) as adverb *largely*; neuter (plural) as adverb or noun *often, mostly, largely*:—abundant, + altogether, common, + far (passed, spent), (+ be of a) great (age, deal, -ly, while), long, many, much, oft (-en [-times]), plenteous, sore, straitly. Compare 4118, 4119.

4184. πολύσπλαγχνος, polusplagchnos, *pol-oo´-splankh-nos*; from 4183 and 4698 (figurative); *extremely compassionate*:—very pitiful.

4185. πολυτελής, polutelēs, *pol-oo-tel-ace´*; from 4183 and 5056; *extremely expensive*:—costly, very precious, of great price.

4186. πολύτιμος, polutimos, *pol-oot´-ee-mos*; from 4183 and 5092; *extremely valuable*:—very costly, of great price.

4187. πολυτρόπως, polutropōs, *pol-oot-rop´-oce*; adverb from a compound of 4183 and 5158; *in many ways*, i.e. *variously* as to method or form:—in divers manners.

4188. πόμα, poma, *pom´-ah*; from the alternate of 4095; a *beverage*:—drink.

4189. πονηρία, ponēria, *pon-ay-ree´-ah*; from 4190; *depravity*, i.e. (special) *malice*; plural (concrete) *plots, sins*:—iniquity, wickedness.

Noun from *ponērós* (4190) evil, malicious. Evil nature, badness. In the NT, only in a moral sense, evil disposition, wickedness, malice (Mt 22:18; Lk 11:39; Ro 1:29; 1Co 5:8; Eph 6:12). In the plural: wicked counsels, wicked deeds (Mk 7:22; Ac 3:26).

Syn.: *kakía* (2549), evil, badness. Also *adíkēma* (92), injustice, misdeed; *adikía* (93), unrighteousness; *hamartía* (266), sin, missing the mark; *anomía* (458), lawlessness; *paranomía* (3892), law-breaking; *parábasis* (3847), an overstepping, transgression.

4190. πονηρός, ponēros, *pon-ay-ros´*; from a derivative of 4192; *hurtful*, i.e. *evil* (properly in effect or influence, and thus differing from 2556, which refers rather to *essential* character, as well as from 4550, which indicates *degeneracy* from original virtue); (figurative) *calamitous*; also (passive) *ill*, i.e. *diseased*; but especially (morally) *culpable*, i.e. *derelict, vicious, facinorous*; neuter (singular) *mischief, malice*, or (plural) *guilt*; masculine (singular) the *devil*, or (plural) *sinners*:—bad, evil, grievous, harm, lewd, malicious, wicked (-ness). See also 4191.

Adjective from *pónos* (4192), labour, sorrow, pain. Evil in a moral or spiritual sense, wicked, malicious, mischievous.

(I) In an active sense, evil which causes evil to others, evil-disposed, malevolent, malignant, wicked.

(A) Of persons (Mt 5:45; 7:11; 12:34, 35; 13:49; 18:32; Lk 6:35, 45; 11:13; Ac 17:5; 2Th 3:2). With *pneúma* [4151], spirit: evil spirits, malignant demons (Lk 7:21; 8:2; Ac 19:12, 13, 15, 16). With the definite article, the evil one, Satan (Mt 13:19, 38; Eph 6:16; 1Jn 2:13, 14; 3:12; 5:18). Other verses that could be interpreted this way: Mt 5:37; 6:13; Lk 11:4; Jn 17:15; 1Jn 5:19.

(B) Of things, such as the eye, an evil eye referring to envy (Mt 20:15; Mk 7:22); evil thoughts (1Ti 6:4; Jas 2:4). Particularly as causing pain or hurt, hurtful, with injurious words (Mt 5:11; Ac 28:21; 3Jn 10). Also painful, grievous (Rev 16:2). The neuter with the definite article: evil, evil intent, malice, wickedness (Mt 5:37, 39). Also evil as inflicted, calamity, affliction.

(II) In the passive sense, evil, made evil, evil in nature or quality, bad, ill, vicious.

(A) Morally, wicked, corrupt (Mt 12:39, 45; 16:4; Lk 11:29; 1Co 5:13; Gal 1:4; 2Ti 3:13); of a servant, remiss, slothful (Mt 25:26; Lk 19:22); of things, wicked, corrupt, as of works (Jn 3:19; 7:7; Col 1:21; 2Ti 4:18; 1Jn 3:12; 2Jn 11), also Ac 18:14; 1Th 5:22; Heb 3:12; 10:22; Jas 4:16. Used of times, particularly as full of sorrow and affliction, evil, calamitous (Eph 5:16; 6:13). In the neuter with the definite article: in the singular, evil, wickedness, guilt (Lk 6:45; Ro 12:9; 1Jn 5:19); in the plural, evil things, wicked deeds (Mk 7:23).

(B) In a physical sense, as of external quality and condition, evil, bad, bad fruit (Mt 7:17, 18). Of persons in reference to external state, dress (Mt 22:10).

Deriv.: *ponēría* (4189), evil, wickedness, maliciousness.

Syn.: *kakós* (2556), bad character but not necessarily hurtful or malicious. Also *ádikos* (94), unrighteous; *áthesmos* (113), lawless, contrary to custom; *hamartōlós* (268), a sinner; *anáxios* (370), unworthy; *ánomos* (459), lawless; *kakopoiós* (2555), an evildoer; *kakoúrgos* (2557), an evil worker, malefactor; *parabátēs* (3848), a transgressor; *phaúlos* (5337), slight, trivial, mean, bad, in the sense of being worthless, contemptible.

4191. πονηρότερος, ponēroteros, *pon-ay-rot´-er-os*; comparative of 4190; *more evil*:—more wicked.

4192. πόνος, ponos, *pon´-os*; from the base of 3993; *toil*, i.e. (by implication) *anguish*:—pain.

Noun from *pénomai* (n.f., see *pénēs* [3993]), to labour. Labor, toil, travail. Hence sorrow, pain, anguish (Rev 16:10, 11; 21:4).

Deriv.: *ponērós* (4190), evil, wicked.

Syn.: *kópos* (2873), the weariness resulting from labour; *lúpē* (3077), grief, sorrow; *odúnē* (3601), pain, distress; *pénthos* (3997), mourning, sorrow; *ōdín* (5604), pain, especially of childbirth.

4193. Ποντικός, Pontikos, *pon-tik-os´*; from 4195; a *Pontican*, i.e. native of Pontus:—born in Pontus.

4194. Πόντιος, Pontios, *pon´-tee-os*; of Latin origin; apparently *bridged; Pontius*, a Roman:—Pontius.

4195. Πόντος, Pontos, *pon´-tos*; a *sea; Pontus*, a region of Asia Minor:—Pontus.

4196. Πόπλιος, Poplios, *pop´-lee-os*; of Latin origin; apparently "*popular*"; *Poplius* (i.e. *Publius*), a Roman:—Publius.

4197. πορεία, poreia, *por-i´-ah*; from 4198; *travel* (by land); figurative (plural) *proceedings*, i.e. *career*:—journey [-ing], ways.

4198. πορεύομαι, poreuomai, *por-yoo´-om-ahee*; middle from a derivative of the same as 3984; to *traverse*, i.e. *travel* (literal or figurative; especially to *remove* [figurative, *die*], *live*, etc.)—depart, go (away, forth, one's way, up), (make a, take a) journey, walk.

4199. πορθέω, portheō, *por-theh´-o*; prolonged from **πέρθω**, ***porthō*** (to *sack*); to *ravage* (figurative):—destroy, waste.

4200. πορισμός, porismos, *por-is-mos´*; from a derivative of **πόρος**, *poros* (a *way*, i.e. *means*); *furnishing* (*procuring*), i.e. (by implication) *money-getting* (*acquisition*):—gain.

4201. Πόρκιος, Porkios, *por´-kee-os*; of Latin origin; apparently *swinish; Porcius*, a Roman:—Porcius.

4202. πορνεία, porneia, *por-ni´-ah*; from 4203; *harlotry* (including *adultery* and *incest*); (figurative) *idolatry*:—fornication.

4203. πορνεύω, porneuō, *porn-yoo´-o*; from 4204; to *act* the *harlot*, i.e. (literal) *indulge* unlawful *lust* (of either sex), or (figurative) *practise idolatry*:—commit (fornication).

4204. πόρνη, pornē, *por´-nay*; feminine of 4205; a *strumpet*; (figurative) an *idolater*:—harlot, whore.

4205. πόρνος, pornos, *por´-nos*; from **πέρνημι**, ***pernēmi*** (to *sell*; akin to the base of 4097); a (male) *prostitute* (as *venal*), i.e. (by analogy) a *debauchee* (*libertine*):—fornicator, whoremonger.

4206. πόῤῥω, porrhō, *por´-rho*; adverb from 4253; *forwards*, i.e. *at a distance*:—far, a great way off. See also 4207.

4207. πόῤῥωθεν, porrhōthen, *por´-rho-then*; from 4206 with adverb enclitic of source; *from far*, or (by implication) *at a distance*, i.e. *distantly*:—afar off.

4208. πоῤῥωτέρω, porrhōterō, *por-rho-ter´-o*; adverb comparative of 4206; *farther*, i.e. *a greater distance*:—further.

4209. πορφύρα, porphura, *por-foo´-rah*; of Latin origin; the "*purple*" mussel, i.e. (by implication) the *red-blue* colour itself, and finally a garment dyed with it:—purple.

4210. πορφυροῦς, porphurous, *por-foo-rooce´*; from 4209; *purpureal*, i.e. *bluish red*:—purple.

4211. πορφυρόπωλις, porphuropōlis, *por-foo-rop´-o-lis*; feminine of a compound of 4209 and 4453; a *female trader in purple* cloth:—seller of purple.

4212. ποσάκις, posakis, *pos-ak´-is*; multiple from 4214; *how many times*:—how oft (-en).

4213. πόσις, posis, *pos´-is*; from the alternate of 4095; a *drinking* (the act), i.e. (concretely) a *draught*:—drink.

4214. πόσος, posos, *pos´-os*; from an obsolete **πός** ***pos*** (*who, what*) and 3739; interrogative pronoun (of amount) *how much* (*large, long* or [plural] *many*):—how great (long, many), what.

4215. ποταμός, potamos, *pot-am-os´*; probably from a derivative of the alternate of 4095 (compare 4224); a *current, brook* or *freshet* (as *drinkable*), i.e. *running water*:—flood, river, stream, water.

4216. ποταμοφόρητος, potamophorētos, *pot-am-of-or´-ay-tos*; from 4215 and a derivative of 5409; *riverborne*, i.e. *overwhelmed by a stream*:—carried away of the flood.

4217. ποταπός, potapos, *pot-ap-os´*; apparently from 4219 and the base of 4226; interrogative *whatever*, i.e. of *what possible* sort:—what (manner of).

4218. ποτέ, pote, *pot-eh´*; from the base of 4225 and 5037; indefinite adverb, at *sometime, ever*:—afore- (any, some-) time (-s), at length (the last), (+ n-) ever, in the old time, in time past, once, when.

4219. πότε, pote, *pot´-eh*; from the base of 4225 and 5037; interrogative adverb, at *what time*:— + how long, when.

4220. πότερον, poteron, *pot´-er-on*; neuter of a comparative of the base of 4226; interrogative as adverb, *which* (of two), i.e. *is it* this or that:—whether.

4221. ποτήριον, potērion, *pot-ay´-ree-on*; neuter of a derivative of the alternate of 4095; a *drinking-vessel*; by extension the contents thereof, i.e. a *cupful* (*draught*); (figurative) a *lot* or *fate*:—cup.

4222. ποτίζω, potizō, *pot-id´-zo*; from a derivative of the alternate of 4095; to *furnish drink, irrigate*:—give (make) to drink, feed, water.

4223. Ποτίολοι, Potioloi, *pot-ee´-ol-oy*; of Latin origin; *little wells*, i.e. *mineral springs; Potioli* (i.e. *Puteoli*), a place in Italy:—Puteoli.

4224. πότος, potos, *pot´-os*; from the alternate of 4095; a *drinking-bout* or *carousal*:—banqueting.

Noun from *pínō* (4095), to drink. A drinking match, a drunken bout (1Pe 4:3).

Syn.: *kraipálē* (2897), debauchery, dissipation; *kṓmos* (2970), rioting or reveling; *méthē* (3178), drunkeness; *oinophlugía* (3632), excess of wine.

4225. πού, pou, *poo*; generic of an indefinite pronoun **πός**, ***pos*** (*some*) otherwise obsolete (compare 4214); as adverb of place, *somewhere*, i.e. *nearly*:—about, a certain place.

4226. ποῦ, pou, *poo*; generic of an interrogative pronoun **πός**, ***pos*** (*what*) otherwise obsolete (perhaps the same as 4225 used with the rising slide of inquiry); as adverb of place; *at* (by implication, *to*) *what* locality:—where, whither.

4227. Πούδης, Poudēs, *poo´-dace*; of Latin origin; *modest; Pudes* (i.e. *Pudens*), a Christian:—Pudens.

4228. πούς, pous, *pooce*; a primary word; a "*foot*" (figurative or literal):—foot (-stool).

4229. πρᾶγμα, pragma, *prag´-mah*; from 4238; a *deed*; (by implication) an *affair*; by extension an *object* (material):—business, matter, thing, work.

4230. πραγματεία, pragmateia, *prag-mat-i´-ah*; from 4231; a *transaction*, i.e. *negotiation*:—affair.

4231. πραγματεύομαι, pragmateuomai, *prag-mat-yoo´-om-ahee*; from 4229; to *busy oneself* with, i.e. to *trade*:—occupy.

4232. πραιτώριον, praitōrion, *prahee-to´-ree-on*; of Latin origin; the *prætorium* or governor's *courtroom* (sometimes including the whole *edifice* and *camp*):—(common, judgement) hall (of judgement), palace, prætorium.

4233. πράκτωρ, praktōr, *prak´-tore*; from a derivative of 4238; a *practiser*, i.e. (special) an official *collector*:—officer.

4234. πρᾶξις, praxis, *prax´-is*; from 4238; *practice*, i.e. (concretely) an *act*; by extension a *function*:—deed, office, work.

4235. πρᾶος, praios, *prah´-os*; a form of 4239, used in certain parts; *gentle*, i.e. *humble*:—meek.

4236. πρᾳότης, praiotēs, *prah-ot´-ace*; from 4235; *gentleness*; (by implication) *humility*:—meekness.

4237. πρασιά, prasia, *pras-ee-ah´*; perhaps from **πράσον, *prason*** (a *leek*, and so an *onion-patch*); a garden-*plot*, i.e. (by implication, of regular *beds*) a *row* (repeated in plural by Hebrew to indicate an arrangement):—in ranks.

4238. πράσσω, prassō, *pras´-so*; a primary verb; to "*practise*," i.e. *perform repeatedly* or *habitually* (thus differing from 4160, which properly refers to a *single* act); (by implication) to *execute, accomplish*, etc.; specially to *collect* (dues), *fare* (personally):—commit, deeds, do, exact, keep, require, use arts.

To do, make, perform in general, expressing an action as continued or not yet completed, what one does repeatedly, continually, habitually, like *poiéō* (4160, II). Found in Jn 3:20; 5:29; elsewhere only in the writings of Luke and Paul.

(I) With the accusative of thing, without reference to a person as the remote object:

(A) Spoken of particular deeds, acts, or works done repeatedly or continually, to do, perform, to practice; e.g., to practice magic (Ac 19:19). See also Ac 26:26; 1Th 4:11; 1Co 9:17. Sometimes spoken of doing a single action (Ac 19:36).

(B) Spoken of a course of action or conduct, especially of right, duty, virtue, to do, meaning to exercise, to practice (Ac 26:20; Ro 2:25; 7:15; 9:11; 2Co 5:10; Php 4:9).

(C) More often spoken of evil deeds or conduct, to do, meaning to commit, practice (Lk 22:23; 23:15, 41; Jn 3:20; 5:29; Ac 25:11, 25; 26:31; Ro 1:32; 2:1–3; 7:19; 13:4; 2Co 12:21; Gal 5:21).

(II) Intransitively, to do.

(A) To do or act in a certain way, e.g., ignorantly (Ac 3:17); contrary to the decrees of Caesar (Ac 17:7).

(B) To do, fare, get along in a certain way (Ac 15:29; Eph 6:21).

(III) Spoken in reference to a person, to do something harmful or evil to someone (Ac 5:35; 16:28; 26:9). To change or exact money from someone (Lk 3:13; 19:23).

Deriv.: *prágma* (4229), deed, event, task; *práktōr* (4233), agent; *práxis* (4234), action, deed.

Syn.: *poiéō* (4160), to do. Also *apoteléō* (658), to perform completely; *energéō* (1754), to work energetically; *epiteléō* (2005), to perform fully; *ergázomai* (2038), to work; *katergázomai* (2716), to accomplish.

4239. πραΰς, praüs, *prah-ooce´*; apparently a primary word; *mild*, i.e. (by implication) *humble*:—meek. See also 4235.

Adjective meaning meek, mild, gentle (Mt 5:5; 21:5; 1Pe 3:4). See *praṹtēs* (4240), meekness for a full discussion of the meaning.

Deriv.: *praṹtēs* (4240), meekness.

Syn.: *ḗpios* (2261), gentle, of a soothing disposition; *epieikḗs* (1933), gentle, mild, forbearing; *tapeinós* (5011), humble.

4240. πραΰτης, praütēs, *prah-oo´-tace*; from 4239; *mildness*, i.e. (by implication) *humility*:—meekness.

Noun from *praṹs* (4239), meek. Meekness, mildness, forbearance. In the NT it expresses a meekness which differs from the usual connotation of the word in English. *Praṹtēs*, according to Aristotle, is the middle standing between two extremes, getting angry without reason (*orgilótēs* [n.f.]), and not getting angry at all (*aorgēsía* [n.f.]). It is the result of a strong man's choice to control his reactions in submission to

God. It is a balance born in strength of character, stemming from confident trust in God, not from weakness or fear (Jas 1:21; 3:13; 1Pe 3:15).

Syn.: *epieíkeia* (1932), fairness, moderation, gentleness; *tapeinophrosúnē* (5012), humility.

4241. πρέπω, prepō, *prep´-o*; apparently a primary verb; to *tower* up (*be conspicuous*), i.e. (by implication) to *be suitable* or *proper* (third person singular presumed indicative, often used impersonally, it is *fit* or *right*):—become, comely.

4242. πρεσβεία, presbeia, *pres-bi´-ah*; from 4243; *seniority* (*eldership*), i.e. (by implication) an *embassy* (concrete *ambassadors*):—ambassage, message.

4243. πρεσβεύω, presbeuō, *pres-byoo´-o*; from the base of 4245; to be a *senior*, i.e. (by implication) *act as a representative* (figurative, *preacher*):—be an ambassador.

4244. πρεσβυτέριον, presbuterion, *pres-boo-ter´-ee-on*; neuter of a presumed derivative of 4245; the *order of elders*, i.e. (special) Israelite *Sanhedrin* or Christian "*presbytery*":—(estate of) elder (-s), presbytery.

Noun from *presbúteros* (4245), elder. Presbytery, an assembly of aged men, a council of elders, a senate. Spoken of the Jewish Sanhedrin (Lk 22:66; Ac 22:5), which is otherwise called *sunédrion* (4892), a joint session, a council. Spoken of the elders of the Christian church, a governing ecclesiastical body comprised of *presbúteroi* (4245), apparently with reference to the council of elders in a given area (1Ti 4:14). Along with elders there were also *diákonoi* (pl.) (1249), deacons in the local church (Php 1:1). Deacons are never presented as a governing council as are the elders; they exist to assist the elders.

4245. πρεσβύτερος, presbuteros, *pres-boo´-ter-os*; comparative of **πρέσβυς**, *presbus* (*elderly*); *older*; as noun, a *senior*; specially an Israelite *Sanhedrist* (also figurative, member of the celestial council) or Christian "*presbyter*":—elder (-est), old.

Adjective, the comparative of *présbus* (n.f.), an old man, an ambassador. Older, aged.

(I) Particularly as a comparative adjective (Lk 15:25). As a substantive an older person, senior; in the plural, old men, seniors, the aged (Ac 2:17; 1Ti 5:1, 2; 1Pe 5:5). In the plural, the ancients, the fathers, ancestors (Mt 15:2; Mk 7:3, 5; Heb 11:2).

(II) As a substantive in the Jewish and Christian usage, a title of dignity, an elder, plural elders, meaning persons of ripe age and experience who were called to take part in the management of public affairs. In the NT spoken of:

(A) The members of the Jewish Sanhedrin at Jerusalem (Mt 16:21; 21:23; 26:3, 47, 57, 59; 27:1, 3, 12, 20, 41; 28:11, 12; Mk 8:31; 11:27; 14:43, 53; 15:1; Lk 9:22; 20:1; 22:52; Ac 4:5, 8, 23; 23:14; 24:1; 25:15).

(B) The elders in other cities, such as Capernaum (Lk 7:3).

(C) The elders of Christian churches, presbyters, to whom was committed the direction and government of individual churches (Ac 11:30; 14:23; 15:2, 4, 6, 22, 23; 16:4; 20:17 [cf. 20:28]; 21:18; 1Ti 5:17; Tit 1:5; Jas 5:14; 1Pe 5:1). In the sing., *presbúteros* (1Ti 5:19; 2Jn 1; 3Jn 1).

(D) The twenty-four elders around the throne of God in heaven (Rev 4:4, 10; 5:5, 6, 8, 11, 14; 7:11, 13; 11:16; 14:3; 19:4).

Deriv.: *presbutérion* (4244), a council of elders, an assembly of aged men which acted as the governing body of the church; *sumpresbúteros* (4850), a fellow elder.

Syn.: *epískopos* (1985), overseer, bishop. Also *didáskolos* (1320), teacher; *poimḗn* (4166), shepherd, pastor.

4246. πρεσβύτης, presbutēs, *pres-boo´-tace*; from the same as 4245; an *old man*:—aged (man), old man.

4247. πρεσβῦτις, presbutis, *pres-boo´-tis*; feminine of 4246; an *old woman*:—aged woman.

4248. πρηνής, prēnēs, *pray-nace´*; from 4253; *leaning* (*falling*) *forward* ("*prone*"), i.e. *head foremost*:—headlong.

4249. πρίζω, prizō, *prid´-zo*; a strengthened form of a primary **πρίω**, *priō* (to *saw*); to *saw* in two:—saw asunder.

4250. πρίν, prin, *prin*; adverb from 4253; *prior, sooner*:—before (that), ere.

4251. Πρίσκα, Priska, *pris´-kah*; of Latin origin; feminine of *Priscus, ancient; Priska*, a Christian woman:—Prisca. See also 4252.

4252. Πρίσκιλλα, Priscilla, *pris´-cil-lah*; diminutive of 4251; *Priscilla* (i.e. *little Prisca*), a Christian woman:—Priscilla.

4253. πρό, pro, *pro*; a primary preposition; "*fore*," i.e. *in front of, prior* (figurative, *superior*) *to*:—above, ago, before, or ever. In comparative it retains the same significations.

4254. προάγω, proagō, *pro-ag´-o*; from 4253 and 71; to *lead forward* (magisterially); intransitive to *precede* (in place or time [participle *previous*]):—bring (forth, out), go before.

From *pró* (4253), before or forth, and *ágō* (71), to go. To go before, bring out.

(I) Transitively, to lead or bring forth, as a prisoner out of prison (Ac 16:30); in a judicial sense, to bring forth to execute (Ac 12:6) or to judge (25:26).

(II) Intransitively, to go before, referring either to place or time.

(A) Of place, to go before, in front or in advance (Mt 2:9; 21:9; Mk 10:32; 11:9; Lk 18:39).

(B) In time, to go first, precede (Mt 14:22; 21:31; 26:32; 28:7; Mk 6:45; 14:28; 16:7; 1Ti 1:18; 5:24; Heb 7:18).

Syn.: *progínomai* (4266), to have transpired already, be past; *proérchomai* (4281), to go before, precede; *proporeúomai* (4313), to go before; *protréchō* (4390), to run forward, precede.

4255. προαιρέομαι, proaireomai, *pro-ahee-reh´-om-ahee*; from 4253 and 138; to *choose* for oneself *before* another thing (*prefer*), i.e. (by implication) to *propose* (*intend*):—purpose.

4256. προαιτιάομαι, proaitiaomai, *pro-ahee-tee-ah´-om-ahee*; from 4253 and a derivative of 156; to *accuse already*, i.e. *previously charge*:—prove before.

4257. προακούω, proakouō, *pro-ak-oo´-o*; from 4253 and 191; to *hear already*, i.e. *anticipate*:—hear before.

4258. προαμαρτάνω, proamartanō, *pro-am-ar-tan´-o*; from 4253 and 264; to *sin previously* (to conversion):—sin already, heretofore sin.

4259. προαύλιον, proaulion, *pro-ow´-lee-on*; neuter of a presumed compound of 4253 and 833; a *forecourt*, i.e. *vestibule* (*alley-way*):—porch.

4260. προβαίνω, probainō, *prob-ah´ee-no*; from 4253 and the base of 939; to *walk forward*, i.e. *advance* (literally or in years):—+ be of a great age, go farther (on), be well stricken.

4261. προβάλλω, proballō, *prob-al´-lo*; from 4253 and 906; to *throw forward*, i.e. *push to the front, germinate*:—put forward, shoot forth.

4262. προβατικος, probatikos, *prob-at-ik-os´*; from 4263; *relating to sheep*, i.e. (a *gate*) through which they were led into Jerusalem:—sheep (market).

4263. πρόβατον, probaton, *prob´-at-on*; properly neuter of a presumed derivative of 4260; *something that walks forward* (a *quadruped*), i.e. (special) a *sheep* (literal or figurative):—sheep ([-fold]).

4264. προβιβάζω, probibazō, *prob-ib-ad´-zo*; from 4253 and a reduplicated form of 971; to *force forward*, i.e. *bring to the front, instigate*:—draw, before instruct.

4265. προβλέπω, problepō, *prob-lep´-o*; from 4253 and 991; to *look out beforehand*, i.e. *furnish in advance*:—provide.

4266. προγίνομαι, proginomai, *prog-in´-om-ahee*; from 4253 and 1096; to *be already*, i.e. *have previously transpired*:—be past.

4267. προγινώσκω, proginōskō, *prog-in-oce´-ko*; from 4253 and 1097; to *know beforehand*, i.e. *foresee*:—foreknow (ordain), know (before).

From *pró* (4253), before, and *ginṓskō* (1097), to know. To perceive or recognize beforehand, know previously, take into account or specially consider beforehand, to grant prior acknowledgement or recognition to someone, to foreknow.

(I) Generally, to know already, to be acquainted with a person or fact beforehand (Ac 26:5; 2Pe 3:17).

(II) Used of God's eternal counsel it includes all that He has considered and purposed to do prior to human history. In the language of Scripture, something foreknown is not simply that which God was aware of prior to a certain point. Rather, it is presented as that which God gave prior consent to, that which received His favourable or special recognition. Hence, this term is reserved for those matters which God fabourably, deliberately and freely chose and ordained.

(A) Used of persons, to approve of beforehand, to make a previous choice of, as of a special people (Ro 8:29; 11:2). The salvation of every believer is known and determined in the mind of God before its realization in time. *Proginṓskō* essentially entails a gracious self-determining on God's part from eternity to extend fellowship with Himself to undeserving sinners. It emphasizes the exercise of God's wisdom and intelligence in regard to His eternal purpose. Compare *proorízō* (4309) which emphasizes the exercise of God's will in regard to these things (Ro 8:29). What He has decreed is what He has decided. He foreordains unto salvation those whom He specially considered and chose in eternity past (see Mt 7:23; Jn 10:14; Ro 11:2; 1Co 8:3; Gal 4:9; 2Ti 2:19).

(B) Used of events, to previously decide or plan, to foreknow for God is to foreordain. First Peter 1:19, 20 presents Christ as the "Lamb of God foreknown from the foundation of the world" (a.t.). He is said to be foreknown because God had planned and determined in His eternal counsel to provide His Son as a sacrifice for His people. It is not merely that God knew ahead of time that Christ would so come and die; God's foreknowledge is given here as the cause for His Son's sacrifice—because He planned and decreed it.

Deriv.: *prógnōsis* (4268), foreknowledge.

Syn.: *problépō* (4265), to look out beforehand, to supply in advance, foresee; *proeidō* (4275) to foresee; *proetoimázō* (4282), to ordain or prepare before; *prolégō* (4302), to tell or say beforehand; *promerimnáō* (4305), to take thought or care beforehand; *pronoéō* (4306), to know or consider in advance; *prooráō* (4308), to foresee; *proorízō* (4309), to set limits in advance, ordain beforehand, predestinate.

4268. πρόγνωσις, prognōsis, *prog´-no-sis*; from 4267; *forethought*:—foreknowledge.

Noun from *proginṓskō* (4267), to know beforehand. Foreknowledge, recognition or consideration beforehand. In the NT, it is used to denote the foreordained purpose and counsel of God in salvation (Ac 2:23; 1Pe 1:2).

Syn.: *prónoia* (4307), forethought, providence. Also *próthesis* (4286), a setting forth beforehand.

4269. πρόγονος, progonos, *prog´-on-os*; from 4266; an *ancestor*, (*grand-*) *parent*:—forefather, parent.

4270. προγράφω, prographō, *prog-raf´-o*; from 4253 and 1125; to *write previously*; (figurative) to *announce, prescribe*:—before ordain, evidently set forth, write (afore, aforetime).

4271. πρόδηλος, prodēlos, *prod´-ay-los*; from 4253 and 1212; *plain before* all men, i.e. *obvious*:—evident, manifest (open) beforehand.

4272. προδίδωμι, prodidōmi, *prod-id´-o-mee*; from 4253 and 1325; to *give before* the other party has given:—first give.

4273. προδότης, prodotēs, *prod-ot´-ace*; from 4272 (in the sense of *giving forward* into another's [the enemy's] hands); a *surrender*:—betrayer, traitor.

4274. πρόδρομος, prodromos, *prod´-rom-os*; from the alternate of 4390; a *runner ahead*, i.e. *scout* (figurative, *precursor*):—forerunner.

4275. προείδω, proeidō, *pro-i´-do*; from 4253 and 1492; *foresee*:—foresee, saw before.

4276. προελπίζω, proelpizō, *pro-il-pid´-zo*; from 4253 and 1679; to *hope in advance* of other confirmation:—first trust.

4277. προέπω, proepō, *pro-ep´-o*; from 4253 and 2036; to *say already*, to *predict*:—forewarn, say (speak, tell) before. Compare 4280.

4278. προενάρχομαι, proenarchomai, *pro´-en-ar´-khom-ahee*; from 4253 and 1728; to *commence already*:—begin (before).

4279. προεπαγγέλλομαι, proepaggellomai, *pro-ep-ang-ghel´-lom-ahee*; middle from 4253 and 1861; to *promise of old*:—promise before.

From *pró* (4253), before, and *epaggéllō* (1861), to bring word to, to announce, promise. In the NT, only in the middle *proepaggéllomai*, to proclaim or promise beforehand. Used only in Ro 1:2.

4280. προερέω, proereō, *pro-er-eh´-o*; from 4253 and 2046; used as alternate of 4277; to *say already, predict*:—foretell, say (speak, tell) before.

4281. προέρχομαι, proerchomai, *pro-er´-khom-ahee*; from 4253 and 2064 (including its alternate); to *go onward, precede* (in place or time):—go before (farther, forward), outgo, pass on.

4282. προετοιμάζω, proetoimazō, *pro-et-oy-mad´-zo*; from 4253 and 2090; to *fit up in advance* (literal or figurative):—ordain before, prepare afore.

4283. προευαγγελίζομαι, proeuaggelizomai, *pro-yoo-ang-ghel-id´-zom-ahee*; middle from 4253 and 2097; to *announce* glad news *in advance*:—preach before the gospel.

From *pró* (4253), before, and *euaggelízō* (2097), to preach the gospel or the good news. To proclaim the gospel beforehand. Only in Gal 3:8.

Syn.: *prokērússō* (4296), to preach, announce beforehand.

4284. προέχομαι, proechomai, *pro-ekh-om-ahee*; middle from 4253 and 2192; to *hold* oneself *before* others, i.e. (figurative) to *excel*:—be better.

4285. προηγέομαι, proēgeomai, *pro-ay-geh´-om-ahee*; from 4253 and 2233; to *lead the way* for others, i.e. *show deference*:—prefer.

4286. πρόθεσις, prothesis, *proth´-es-is*; from 4388; a *setting forth*, i.e. (figurative) *proposal* (*intention*); specially the *show-bread* (in the temple) as *exposed* before God:—purpose, shew [-bread].

Noun from *protíthēmi* (4388), to purpose or plan. A setting forth, an exposition, a placing in view or openly displaying something.

(I) Particularly, as of food, in an adjectival sense. Spoken of the shewbread, the twelve loaves of bread which were set out fresh every morning on a table in the sanctuary (Mt 12:4; Mk 2:26; Lk 6:4; Heb 9:2). See Le 24:5–9.

(II) Figuratively, what one proposes in one's mind or purposes to himself. Spoken of a purpose, an intent (Ac 27:13); spoken of a firm resolve, a design (Ac 11:23; 2Ti 3:10); spoken of the eternal purpose and counsel of God (Ro 8:28; 9:11; Eph 1:11; 3:11; 2Ti 1:9).

Syn.: *boúlēma* (1013), purpose, will; *thélēma* (2307), desire or will with the power to execute that will; *prógnōsis* (4268), forethought, foreknowledge; *prónoia* (4307), provision, providence, forethought.

4287. προθέσμιος, prothesmios, *proth-es´-mee-os*; from 4253 and a derivative of 5087; *fixed beforehand*, i.e. (feminine with 2250 implication) a *designated* day:—time appointed.

Noun from *pró* (4253), before, and *thesmós* (n.f.), custom, ordinance, which is from *títhēmi* (5087), to set, place, lay. A pre-appointed day or time, the day or time being understood. Used only in Gal 4:2.

4288. προθυμία, prothumia, *proth-oo-mee´-ah*; from 4289; *predisposition*, i.e. *alacrity*:—forwardness of mind, readiness (of mind), ready (willing) mind.

4289. πρόθυμος, prothumos, *proth´-oo-mos*; from 4253 and 2372; *forward* in *spirit*, i.e. *predisposed*; neuter (as noun) *alacrity*:—ready, willing.

4290. προθύμως, prothumōs, *proth-oo´-moce*; adverb from 4289; *with alacrity*:—willingly.

4291. προΐστημι, proïstēmi, *pro-is´-tay-mee*; from 4253 and 2476; to *stand before*, i.e. (in rank) to *preside*, or (by implication) to *practise*:—maintain, be over, rule.

4292. προκαλέομαι, prokaleomai, *prok-al-eh´-om-ahee*; middle from 4253 and 2564; to *call forth to oneself* (*challenge*), i.e. (by implication) to *irritate*:—provoke.

4293. προκαταγγέλλω, prokataggellō, *prok-at-ang-ghel´-lo*; from 4253 and 2605; to *announce beforehand*, i.e. *predict, promise*:—foretell, have notice, (shew) before.

From *pró* (4253), before, and *kataggéllō* (2605), declare, publish. To announce beforehand, foretell (Ac 3:18, 24; 7:52). To announce beforehand in the sense of promising (2Co 9:5).

Syn.: *proépō* (4277), to tell before; *prolégō* (4302), foretell; *prophēteúō* (4395), to prophesy.

4294. προκαταρτίζω, prokatartizō, *prok-at-ar-tid´-zo*; from 4253 and 2675; to *prepare in advance*:—make up beforehand.

From *pró* (4253), before, and *katartízō* (2675), to establish, set up. To make ready beforehand, make right. Used only in 2Co 9:5 of the offerings for the Jerusalem church which Paul wished to find already prepared.

Syn.: *hetoimázō* (2090), to prepare; *kataskeuázō* (2680), to prepare, make ready or fitting; *paraskeuázō* (3903), to prepare, make ready; *proetoimázō* (4282), to prepare beforehand.

4295. πρόκειμαι, prokeimai, *prok´-i-mahee*; from 4253 and 2749; to *lie before* the view, i.e. (figurative) to *be present* (to the mind), to *stand forth* (as an example or reward):—be first, set before (forth).

4296. προκηρύσσω, prokērussō, *prok-ay-rooce´-so*; from 4253 and 2784; to *herald* (i.e. *proclaim*) *in advance*:—before (first) preach.

4297. προκοπή, prokopē, *prok-op-ay´*; from 4298; *progress*, i.e. *advancement* (subject or object):—furtherance, profit.

4298. προκόπτω, prokoptō, *prok-op´-to*; from 4253 and 2875; to *drive forward* (as if by beating), i.e. (figurative and intransitive) to *advance* (in amount, to *grow*; in time, to *be well along*):—increase, proceed, profit, be far spent, wax.

4299. πρόκριμα, prokrima, *prok´-ree-mah*; from a compound of 4253 and 2919; a *prejudgment* (*prejudice*), i.e. *prepossession*:—prefer one before another.

Noun from *prokrínō* (n.f.), to prefer, which is from *pró* (4253), before, and *krínō* (2919), to judge. A preferring before, a judging beforehand, prejudice. It is an unfavourable prejudgment against one, partiality being the chief attitude of this prejudgment (1Ti 5:21).

4300. προκυρόω, prokuroō, *prok-oo-ro´-o*; from 4253 and 2964; to *ratify previously*:—confirm before.

4301. προλαμβάνω, prolambanō, *prol-am-ban´-o*; from 4253 and 2983; to *take in advance*, i.e. (literal) *eat before* others have an opportunity; (figurative) to *anticipate, surprise*:—come aforehand, overtake, take before.

4302. προλέγω, prolegō, *prol-eg´-o*; from 4253 and 3004; to *say beforehand*, i.e. *predict, forewarn*:—foretell, tell before.

4303. προμαρτύρομαι, promarturomai, *prom-ar-too´-rom-ahee*; from 4253 and 3143; to *be a witness in advance*, i.e. *predict*:—testify beforehand.

4304. προμελετάω, promeletaō, *prom-el-et-ah´-o*; from 4253 and 3191; to *premeditate*:—meditate before.

4305. προμεριμνάω, promerimnaō, *prom-er-im-nah´-o*; from 4253 and 3309; to *care* (anxiously) *in advance*:—take thought beforehand.

4306. προνοέω, pronoeō, *pron-o-eh´-o*; from 4253 and 3539; to *consider in advance*, i.e. *look* out for *beforehand* (active by way of *maintenance* for others; middle by way of *circumspection* for oneself):—provide (for).

From *pró* (4253), before, and *noéō* (3539), to think, comprehend. To foresee, to perceive beforehand. In the NT, figuratively, to see to beforehand, to care for, to provide for (1Ti 5:8). In the middle voice, to provide for in one's behalf, to apply one's self, to practice diligently (Ro 12:17; 2Co 8:21).

Deriv.: *prónoia* (4307), forethought, providential care.

Syn.: *problépō* (4265) or *proorá̄ō* (4308), to foresee.

4307. πρόνοια, pronoia, *pron´-oy-ah*; from 4306; *forethought*, i.e. provident *care* or *supply*:—providence, provision.

Noun from *pronoéō* (4306), to know ahead. Foresight, providence, care (Ac 24:2); provision, forethought, spoken of in reference to gratifying the lusts of the flesh (Ro 13:14).

Syn.: *epiméleia* (1958), carefulness, attention.

4308. προοράω, prooraō, *pro-or-ah´-o*; from 4253 and 3708; to *behold in advance*, i.e. (active) to *notice* (another) *previously*, or (middle) to *keep in* (one's own) *view*:—foresee, see before.

4309. προορίζω, proorizō, *pro-or-id´-zo*; from 4253 and 3724; to *limit in advance*, i.e. (figurative) *predetermine*:—determine before, ordain, predestinate.

From *pró* (4253), before, and *horízō* (3724), to determine. To decide or determine beforehand, to foreordain, to predetermine. Used in proclaiming that the actions of Herod and Pontius Pilate in crucifying Jesus Christ were predetermined by the hand and will of God (Ac 4:28). *Proorízō* is used to declare God's eternal decrees of both the objects and goal of His plan of salvation (Ro 8:29, 30), of the glorious benefits that will come from that salvation (1Co 2:7), and of our adoption and inheritance as sons of God (Eph 1:5, 11).

Syn.: *proetoimázō* (4282), to prepare before; *protássō* (4384), to appoint before; *procheirízō* (4400), to appoint beforehand.

4310. προπάσχω, propaschō, *prop-as´-kho*; from 4253 and 3958; to *undergo* hardship *previously*:—suffer before.

4311. προπέμπω, propempō, *prop-em´-po*; from 4253 and 3992; to *send forward*, i.e. *escort* or *aid* in travel:—accompany, bring (forward) on journey (way), conduct forth.

4312. προπετής, propetēs, *prop-et-ace´*; from a compound of 4253 and 4098; *falling forward*, i.e. *headlong* (figurative, *precipitate*):—heady, rash [-ly].

4313. προπορεύομαι, proporeuomai, *prop-or-yoo´-om-ahee*; from 4253 and 4198; to *precede* (as guide or herald):—go before.

4314. πρός, pros, *pros*; a strengthened form of 4253; a preposition of direction; *forward to*, i.e. *toward* (with the genitive *the side of*, i.e. *pertaining to*; with the dative *by the side of*, i.e. *near to*; usually with the accusative the place, time, occasion, or respect, which is the *destination* of the relation, i.e. *whither* or *for* which it is predicated):—about, according to, against, among, at, because of, before, between, ([where-]) by, for, × at thy house, in, for intent, nigh unto, of, which pertain to, that, to (the end that), + together, to ([you]) -ward, unto, with (-in). In comparative it denotes essentially the same applications, namely, motion *toward*, accession *to*, or nearness *at*.

Preposition meaning toward, to, unto.

(I) Marking the object toward or to which something moves or is directed.

(A) Of place, thing, or person meaning toward, to, unto. **(1)** Particularly of motion or direction after verbs of going, coming, departing (Mt 11:28; 21:34; 26:57; Mk 10:1; Lk 23:7; Jn 3:20; 10:35; 16:7; Ac 9:2; 13:32; 15:25; 22:5; Ro 1:10; 2Co 3:1; Gal 1:17). **(2)** With verbs of falling (Mk 5:22; Lk 16:20; Ac 3:2). **(3)** After verbs implying motion or direction in a close proximity as turning, reaching, looking (Lk 7:44; Ac 9:40; Ro 10:21). **(4)** With verbs of speaking, answering, and praying (Mt 3:15; Lk 1:19; 22:70; Ac 2:38; 3:12; 8:24; Ro 10:1).

(**B**) Of time: (**1**) Spoken of a time when, meaning toward, near (Lk 24:29). (**2**) Spoken of a time during which, meaning for, at (Lk 8:13; Jn 5:35; 1Co 7:5; Gal 2:5; Heb 12:10, 11; Jas 4:14).

(**II**) Used figuratively:

(**A**) After verbs and words implying direction of the mind or will, an affection or disposition toward someone. (**1**) Favorable, meaning toward, to, implying goodwill, confidence (2Co 3:4; 7:4; Col 4:5; 1Th 1:8; 4:12; 5:14; 2Ti 2:24; Tit 3:2; Phm 5). (**2**) Unfavorable, meaning against (Ac 24:19; 25:19; 1Co 6:1; Eph 6:11; Col 3:13, 19; Heb 12:4; Rev 13:6).

(**B**) Denoting the direction, reference, or relation which one object has toward or to another. (**1**) Toward, in reference or respect to, as to, implying the direction or remote object of an action. (**a**) With reference to persons; e.g., "What is that to us?" (Mt 27:4). See also Jn 21:22, 23. (**b**) With reference to things relating or pertaining to any person or thing or condition, e.g., "things which make for peace" (Lk 19:42). See also Lk 14:32; Ac 28:10; 2Pe 1:3. The things pertaining to God, i.e. divine things (Ro 15:17; Heb 2:17; 5:1). (**2**) Spoken of a rule, norm, or standard, meaning according to, in conformity with (Lk 12:47; 2Co 5:10; Gal 2:14). (**3**) Of the motive, ground, or occasion of an action, meaning on account of, because of, for (Mt 19:8; Mk 10:5). (**4**) As marking the end result, the aim or purpose of an action, meaning for what, why, to what end, for what purpose (Jn 13:28). After verbs expressing the end, aim, tendency of an action or quality (Ac 3:10; Ro 3:26; 15:2; 1Co 6:5; 7:35; 10:11; 2Co 1:20; Eph 4:12; 1Ti 1:16; 4:7; Heb 5:14; 6:11; 1Pe 4:12). Also after nouns and adjectives that express such ends, aims, or tendencies (Jn 4:35; 11:4; Ac 27:12, 34; 2Co 10:4; Eph 4:14, 29; Col 2:23; 2Ti 3:17; Tit 1:16; 1Pe 3:15; 2Pe 3:16; 1Jn 5:16, 17). Followed by the inf. with the neuter definite article *tó*, meaning in order that (Mt 5:28; 6:1; 13:30; 23:5; Mk 13:22; Eph 6:11; Jas 3:3).

(**III**) Sometimes used after verbs which express simply rest:

(**A**) Used of places, meaning at, by, in a place (Mk 2:2; 4:1; 5:11; 11:4; 14:54; Lk 19:37; Jn 18:16; 20:12; Rev 1:13).

(**B**) With persons, meaning with, by, among (Mt 13:56; 26:55; Mk 6:3; 14:49; Jn 1:1; 1Co 16:7; 2Co 1:12; Gal 1:18; 2:5; 4:18; 2Th 2:5; Phm 13).

(**IV**) In composition *prós* implies:

(**A**) Motion, direction, reference, meaning toward, to, at, as *prosérchomai* (4334), to come near; *prosdokáō* (4328), to expect, wait for; *proságō* (4317), to lead toward, to approach, bring near; *proseggízō* (4331), to approach near; *prosphilḗs* (4375), friendly toward, acceptable, lovely.

(**B**) Accession, addition, meaning thereto, over and above, moreover, further, as *prosaitéō* (4319), to ask besides, to beg; *prosapeiléō* (4324), to threaten further. Used intensively as *próspeinos* (4361), intensely hungry.

(**C**) Nearness, a being or remaining near, at, by, as *prosedreúō* (4332), to attend as a servant, wait on; *prosménō* (4357), remain in a place with someone, abide still.

Syn.: *epí* (1909), upon, at; *eis* (1519), to.

4315. προσάββατον, prosabbaton, *pros-ab´-bat-on*; from 4253 and 4521; a *fore-sabbath*, i.e. the *Sabbath-eve*:—day before the sabbath. Compare 3904.

4316. προσαγορεύω, prosagoreuō, *pros-ag-or-yoo´-o*; from 4314 and a derivative of 58 (meaning to *harangue*); to *address*, i.e. salute by *name*:—call.

From *prós* (4314), to, and *agoreúō* (n.f.), to address, which is from *agorá* (58), the marketplace, also the town square which provided a public platform for speakers. To address, greet. In the NT, to call by name, give a name to. Used only in Heb 5:10.

Syn.: *kaléō* (2564), to call, call a name; *onamázō* (3687), to name.

4317. προσάγω, prosagō, *pros-ag´-o*; from 4314 and 71; to *lead toward*, i.e. (transitive) to *conduct near* (*summon, present*), or (intransitive) to *approach*:—bring, draw near.

From *prós* (4314), to or toward, and *ágō* (71), to bring, come. To lead or conduct to someone, to bring near.

(**I**) To bring to (Lk 9:41; Ac 16:20); figuratively, to bring near to God, present before God (1Pe 3:18).

(**II**) To draw near, to approach (Ac 27:27).

Deriv.: *prosagōgḗ* (4318), access, approach.

Syn.: *anágō* (321), to lead or bring up to; *eiságō* (1521), to lead in, bring in; *epiphérō* (2018), to bring upon, bring forward; *prosérchomai* (4334), to come near, approach; *prosphérō* (4374), to bring to, approach.

4318. προσαγωγή, prosagōgē, *pros-ag-ogue-ay´*; from 4317 (compare 72); *admission*:—access.

Noun from *proságō* (4317), to bring near. A leading or bringing to. In the NT, approach, access, admission, used always of access to God (Ro 5:2; Eph 2:18; 3:12).

Syn.: *eísodos* (1529), entrance.

4319. προσαιτέω, prosaiteō, *pros-ahee-teh´-o*; from 4314 and 154; to *ask repeatedly* (*importune*), i.e. *solicit*:—beg.

From *prós* (4314), for, adding intensity, and *aitéō* (154), to ask, beg. To ask in addition, to demand besides. In the NT, to beg (Mk 10:46; Lk 18:35; Jn 9:8).

4320. προσαναβαίνω, prosanabainō, *pros-an-ab-ah´ee-no*; from 4314 and 305; to *ascend farther*, i.e. *be promoted* (*take an upper* [*more honourable*] *seat*):—go up.

4321. προσαναλίσκω, prosanaliskō, *pros-an-al-is´-ko*; from 4314 and 355; to *expend further*:—spend.

4322. προσαναπληρόω, prosanaplēroō, *pros-an-ap-lay-ro´-o*; from 4314 and 378; to *fill up further*, i.e. *furnish fully*:—supply.

From *prós* (4314), beside, meaning in addition to, and *anaplēróō* (378), to supply. To fill up by adding, to supply fully that which one lacks or needs (2Co 9:12; 11:9).

Syn.: *empíplēmi* (1705), to fill up; *epichorēgéō* (2023), to supply fully, abundantly.

4323. προσανατίθημι, prosanatithēmi, *pros-an-at-ith´-ay-mee*; from 4314 and 394; to *lay up in addition*, i.e. (middle and figurative) to *impart* or (by implication) to *consult*:—in conference add, confer.

4324. προσαπειλέω, prosapeileō, *pros-ap-i-leh´-o*; from 4314 and 546; to *menace additionally*:—threaten further.

4325. προσδαπανάω, prosdapanaō, *pros-dap-an-ah´-o*; from 4314 and 1159; to *expend additionally*:—spend more.

4326. προσδέομαι, prosdeomai, *pros-deh´-om-ahee*; from 4314 and 1189; to *require additionally*, i.e. *want further*:—need.

4327. προσδέχομαι, prosdechomai, *pros-dekh´-om-ahee*; from 4314 and 1209; to *admit* (to intercourse, hospitality, credence or [figurative] endurance); (by implication) to *await* (with confidence or patience):—accept, allow, look (wait) for, take.

From *prós* (4314), unto or for, and *déchomai* (1209), to receive or accept. To receive to oneself, to accept.

(**I**) Of things, figuratively, to admit, to allow (Ac 24:15; Heb 11:35); of evils, to put up with, endure (Heb 10:34).

(**II**) Of persons, to receive, to accept into one's presence and kindness (Lk 15:2; Ro 16:2; Php 2:29).

(**III**) Of things future, to wait for, to expect (Mk 15:43; Lk 2:25, 38; 12:36; 23:51; Ac 23:21; Tit 2:13; Jude 21).

Deriv.: *euprósdektos* (2144), acceptable.

Syn.: *apodéchomai* (588), to accept; *déchomai* (1209), to receive; *lambánō* (2983), to receive; *paralambánō* (3880), to receive from; *proslambánō* (4355), to welcome.

4328. προσδοκάω, prosdokaō, *pros-dok-ah´-o*; from 4314 and **δοκεύω,** *dokeuō* (to *watch*); to *anticipate* (in thought, hope or fear); (by implication) to *await*:—(be in) expect (-ation), look (for), when looked, tarry, wait for.

From *prós* (4314), unto or for, and *dokeúō* (n.f.), to look for. To look for, to wait for.

(**I**) To expect one's coming (Mt 24:50; Lk 3:15; 12:46; Ac 28:6).

(**II**) To wait for with hope (Mt 11:3; Lk 1:21; 7:19, 20; 8:40; Ac 3:5; 10:24; 27:33; 28:6; 2Pe 3:12–14).

Deriv.: *prosdokía* (4329) looking for, expectation.

Syn.: *anaménō* (362), to wait for; *elpízō* (1679), to hope; *apekdéchomai* (553), to expect fully, look for.

4329. προσδοκία, prosdokia, *pros-dok-ee´-ah*; from 4328; *apprehension* (of evil); (by implication) *infliction* anticipated:—expectation, looking after.

Noun from *prosdokáō* (4328), to wait, expect. A looking for, an expectation, in the NT only of evils (Lk 21:26; Ac 12:11).

Syn.: *apokaradokía* (603), expectancy, eager longing; *ekdoché̄* (1561), expectation.

4330. προσεάω, proseaō, *pros-eh-ah´-o*; from 4314 and 1439; to *permit further* progress:—suffer.

4331. προσεγγίζω, proseggizō, *pros-eng-ghid´-zo*; from 4314 and 1448; to *approach near*:—come nigh.

From *prós* (4314), to, and *eggízō* (1448), to approach. To approach or come near to (Mk 2:4).

Syn.: *proságō* (4317), to draw near; *prosérchomai* (4334), to draw near.

4332. προσεδρεύω, prosedreuō, *pros-ed-ryoo´-o*; from a compound of 4314 and the base of 1476; to *sit near*, i.e. *attend* as a servant:—wait at.

4333. προσεργάζομαι, prosergazomai, *pros-er-gad´-zom-ahee*; from 4314 and 2038; to *work additionally*, i.e. (by implication) *acquire besides*:—gain.

4334. προσέρχομαι, proserchomai, *pros-er´-khom-ahee*; from 4314 and 2064 (including its alternate); to *approach*, i.e. (literal) *come near, visit*, or (figurative) *worship, assent to*:—(as soon as he) come (unto), come thereunto, consent, draw near, go (near, to, unto).

From *prós* (4314), to, and *érchomai* (2064), to come. To come to or near any place or person.

(I) Particularly, to come to, approach (Mt 4:3, 11; 8:5; Mk 1:31; 14:45; Lk 8:24; 10:34; 23:52; Jn 12:21; Ac 7:31; 9:1; 28:9; Heb 12:18, 22). With the expanded meaning of to visit, to have conversation with (Ac 10:28; 24:23).

(II) Figuratively:

(A) To come to God, draw near unto Him in prayer, sacrifice, worship, devotion of heart and life (Heb 4:16; 7:25; 11:6); to come to Christ (1Pe 2:4).

(B) To assent to, embrace, accept (1Ti 6:3).

Deriv.: *prosḗlutos* (4339), a stranger, foreigner.

Syn.: *paragínomai* (3854), to arrive, to be present; *proságō* (4317), to draw or lead near; *proseggízō* (4331), to approach, come near; *prosporeúomai* (4365), to come near to.

4335. προσευχή, proseuchē, *pros-yoo-khay´*; from 4336; *prayer* (*worship*); by implication an *oratory* (*chapel*):—× pray earnestly, prayer.

Noun from *proseúchomai* (4336), to offer prayer. Prayer, prayer to God.

(I) Particularly: in the singular (Mt 17:21; 21:13; 21:22; Mk 9:29; 11:17; Lk 6:12; 19:46; 22:45; Ac 1:14; 3:1; 6:4; 10:31; 12:5; Ro 12:12; 1Co 7:5; Eph 6:18; Php 4:6; Col 4:2; Jas 5:17); in the plural (Ac 2:42; 10:4; Ro 1:10; 15:30; Eph 1:16; Col 4:12; 1Th 1:2; 1Ti 2:1; 5:5; Phm 4, 22; 1Pe 3:7; 4:7; Rev 5:8; 8:3, 4).

(II) Spoken by metonymy for a house or a place of prayer (Ac 16:13, 16). Such places for social prayer and devotion were in the outskirts of those towns where the Jews were unable or not permitted to have a synagogue, and were usually near a river or the seashore for the convenience of ablution (to which the Jews were dedicated).

Syn.: *déēsis* (1162), supplication; *paráklēsis* (3874), entreaty.

4336. προσεύχομαι, proseuchomai, *pros-yoo´-khom-ahee*; from 4314 and 2172; to *pray to* God, i.e. *supplicate, worship*:—pray (× earnestly, for), make prayer.

From the preposition *prós* (4314), to, and *eúchomai* (2172), to wish, pray. To pray to God, offer prayer.

(I) In the NT, *proseúchomai* is always directed toward God, whether stated or implied (Mt 6:5–7; 14:23; Mk 1:35; Lk 3:21; Ac 6:6; 1Co 11:4; 1Th 5:17; 1Ti 2:8; Jas 5:13, 18).

(II) The manner in which one prays is expressed either by the dative (1Co 11:5; 14:14, 15; Jas 5:17); or with *en* (1722), in (Eph 6:18; Jude 20).

(III) The object or thing prayed for is put after *hína* (2443), so that (Mt 24:20, neg.; Mk 13:18; 14:35, 38; 1Co 14:13; Php 1:9; Col 1:9), or expressed by the infinitive (Lk 22:40; Jas 5:17).

Deriv.: *proseuché̄* (4335), prayer.

Syn.: *aitéomai* (154), to ask, as from an inferior to a superior; *déomai* (1189), to make request for particular needs; *erōtáō* (2065), to ask.

4337. προσέχω, prosechō, *pros-ekh´-o*; from 4314 and 2192; (figurative) to *hold* the mind (3563 implication) *toward*, i.e. *pay attention to, be cautious about, apply oneself* to, *adhere to*:—(give) attend (-ance, -ance at, -ance to, unto), beware, be given to, give (take) heed (to, unto) have regard.

4338. προσηλόω, prosēloō, *pros-ay-lo´-o*; from 4314 and a derivative of 2247; to *peg to*, i.e. *spike* fast:—nail to.

4339. προσήλυτος, prosēlutos, *pros-ah´-loo-tos*; from the alternate of 4334; an *arriver* from a foreign region, i.e. (special) an *acceder* (*convert*) to Judaism ("*proselyte*"):—proselyte.

Noun from *prosérchomai* (4334), to come near, come to. One who comes to another country or people, a stranger, sojourner. In the NT, it is used in the later Jewish sense of the term, for a proselyte, a convert from Paganism to Judaism (Mt 23:15; Ac 2:10; 6:5; 13:43).

4340. πρόσκαιρος, proskairos, *pros´-kahee-ros*; from 4314 and 2540; *for* the *occasion* only, i.e. *temporary*:—dur- [eth] for awhile, endure for a time, for a season, temporal.

4341. προσκαλέομαι, proskaleomai, *pros-kal-eh´-om-ahee*; middle from 4314 and 2564; to *call toward oneself*, i.e. *summon, invite*:—call (for, to, unto).

From *prós* (4314), to, and *kaléō* (2564), to call. To call someone to oneself, bid to come, to summon (Mt 10:1; 15:10, 32; 18:2, 32; 20:25; Mk 3:13, 23; 6:7; 7:14; 8:1, 34; 10:42; 12:43; 15:44; Lk 7:19; 15:26; 16:5; 18:16; Ac 5:40; 6:2; 13:7; 20:1; 23:17, 18, 23; Jas 5:14). Figuratively, to invite men to embrace the gospel (Ac 2:39). Also, to call one to an office or duty, to appoint, to choose (Ac 13:2; 16:10).

Syn.: *metakaléō* (3333), to summon hither, recall; *prosphōnéō* (4377), to call unto.

4342. προσκαρτερέω, proskartereō, *pros-kar-ter-eh´-o*; from 4314 and 2594; to *be earnest toward*, i.e. (to a thing) to *persevere, be constantly* diligent, or (in a place) to *attend* assiduously all the exercises, or (to a person) to *adhere* closely *to* (as a servitor):—attend (give self) continually (upon), continue (in, instant in, with), wait on (continually).

From *prós* (4314), to, and *karteréō* (2594), to endure. To be strong or firm toward anything, to endure or persevere, to be continually with a person or work.

(I) Spoken of a work or business; to continue or persevere. (Ac 1:14; 2:42, 46; 6:4; Ro 12:12; 13:6; Col 4:2).

(II) Spoken of persons, to remain near, to wait upon, to be in readiness (Mk 3:9; Ac 8:13; 10:7).

Deriv.: *proskartérēsis* (4343), perseverance.

Syn.: *diateléō* (1300), to bring through to an end, to accomplish; *ménō* (3306), to remain; *diaménō* (1265), to continue throughout; *emménō* (1696), to remain in; *epiménō* (1961), to continue in; *paraménō* (3887), to remain by or near; *prosménō* (4357), to remain with.

4343. προσκαρτέρησις, proskarterēsis, *pros-kar-ter´-ay-sis*; from 4342; *persistency*:—perseverance.

4344. προσκεφάλαιον, proskephalaion, *pros-kef-al´-ahee-on*; neuter of a presumed compound of 4314 and 2776; something *for* the *head*, i.e. a *cushion*:—pillow.

4345. προσκληρόω, prosklēroō, *pros-klay-ro´-o*; from 4314 and 2820; to *give* a common *lot to*, i.e. (figurative) to *associate with*:—consort with.

4346. πρόσκλισις, prosklisis, *pros´-klis-is*; from a compound of 4314 and 2827; a *leaning toward*, i.e. (figurative) *proclivity* (*favoritism*):—partiality.

4347. προσκολλάω, proskollaō, *pros-kol-lay´-o*; from 4314 and 2853; to *glue to*, i.e. (figurative) to *adhere*:—cleave, join (self).

4348. πρόσκομμα, proskomma, *pros´-kom-mah*; from 4350; a *stub*, i.e. (figurative) *occasion of apostasy*:—offence, stumbling (block, [-stone]).

4349. προσκοπή, proskopē, *pros-kop-ay´*; from 4350; a *stumbling*, i.e. (figurative and concrete) *occasion of sin*:—offence.

4350. προσκόπτω, proskoptō, *pros-kop´-to*; from 4314 and 2875; to *strike at*, i.e. *surge against* (as water); specially to *stub on*, i.e. *trip up* (literal or figurative):—beat upon, dash, stumble (at).

From *prós* (4314), to, against, and *kóptō* (2875), to cut, strike. To beat upon anything, to strike against.

(I) Generally, to beat against, as floods and winds against a house (Mt 7:27).

(II) Particularly, to strike the foot against anything (Mt 4:6; Lk 4:11); to stumble after striking the foot against anything (Jn 11:9, 10). Figuratively, to take offence at something, so as to fall into error and sin (Ro 9:32; 14:21; 1Pe 2:8).

Deriv.: *apróskopos* (677), void of offence, faultless; *próskomma* (4348), a stumbling block, offence, hindrance; *proskopḗ* (4349), stumbling block, offence.

Syn.: *ptaíō* (4417), to stumble; *skandalízō* (4624), to put a snare or stumbling block in the way.

4351. προσκυλίω, proskuliō, *pros-koo-lee´-o*; from 4314 and 2947; to *roll toward*, i.e. *block against*:—roll (to).

4352. προσκυνέω, proskuneō, *pros-koo-neh´-o*; from 4314 and a probable derivative of 2965 (meaning to *kiss*, like a dog *licking* his master's hand); to *fawn* or *crouch to*, i.e. (literal or figurative) *prostrate* oneself in homage (*do reverence* to, *adore*):—worship.

4353. προσκυνητής, proskunētēs, *pros-koo-nay-tace´*; from 4352; an *adorer*:—worshipper.

4354. προσλαλέω, proslaleō, *pros-lal-eh´-o*; from 4314 and 2980; to *talk to*, i.e. *converse with*:—speak to (with).

4355. προσλαμβάνω, proslambanō, *pros-lam-ban´-o*; from 4314 and 2983; to *take to* oneself, i.e. *use* (food), *lead* (aside), *admit* (to friendship or hospitality):—receive, take (unto).

4356. πρόσληψις, proslēpsis, *pros´-lape-sis*; from 4355; *admission*:—receiving.

4357. προσμένω, prosmenō, *pros-men´-o*; from 4314 and 3306; to *stay further*, i.e. *remain* in a place, with a person: (figurative) to *adhere* to, *persevere* in:—abide still, be with, cleave unto, continue in (with).

From *prós* (4314), to, with, and *ménō* (3306), to remain. To remain at a place (Ac 18:18; 1Ti 1:3); to remain or continue with a person (Mt 15:32; Mk 8:2). In a figurative sense, to remain faithful to someone (Ac 11:23); to continue in, i.e. to be constant in, to persevere (1Ti 5:5).

Syn.: *proskarteréō* (4342), to continue in, remain constant.

4358. προσορμίζω, prosormizō, *pros-or-mid´-zo*; from 4314 and a derivative of the same as 3730 (meaning to *tie* [*anchor*] or *lull*); to *moor to*, i.e. (by implication) *land at*:—draw to the shore.

4359. προσοφείλω, prosopheilō, *pros-of-i´-lo*; from 4314 and 3784; to *be indebted additionally*:—over besides.

4360. προσοχθίζω, prosochthizō, *pros-okh-thid´-zo*; from 4314 and a form of **ὀχθέω**, *ochtheō* (to *be vexed* with something irksome); to *feel indignant at*:—be grieved with.

4361. πρόσπεινος, prospeinos, *pros´-pi-nos*; from 4314 and the same as 3983; *hungering further*, i.e. *intensely hungry*:—very hungry.

4362. προσπήγνυμι, prospēgnumi, *pros-payg´-noo-mee*; from 4314 and 4078; to *fasten to*, i.e. (special) to *impale* (on a cross):—crucify.

4363. προσπίπτω, prospiptō, *pros-pip´-to*; from 4314 and 4098; to *fall toward*, i.e. (gently) *prostrate* oneself (in supplication or homage), or (violently) to *rush* upon (in storm):—beat upon, fall (down) at (before).

4364. προσποιέομαι, prospoieomai, *pros-poy-eh´-om-ahee*; middle from 4314 and 4160; to *do forward for oneself*, i.e. *pretend* (as if about to do a thing):—make as though.

4365. προσπορεύομαι, prosporeuomai, *pros-por-yoo´-om-ahee*; from 4314 and 4198; to *journey toward*, i.e. *approach* [not the same as 4313]:—go before.

4366. προσρήγνυμι, prosrēgnumi, *pros-rayg´-noo-mee*; from 4314 and 4486; to *tear toward*, i.e. *burst upon* (as a tempest or flood):—beat vehemently against (upon).

4367. προστάσσω, prostassō, *pros-tas´-so*; from 4314 and 5021; to *arrange toward*, i.e. (figurative) *enjoin*:—bid, command.

4368. προστάτις, prostatis, *pros-tat´-is*; feminine of a derivative of 4291; a *patroness*, i.e. *assistant*:—succourer.

4369. προστίθημι, prostithēmi, *pros-tith´-ay-mee*; from 4314 and 5087; to *place additionally*, i.e. *lay beside, annex, repeat*:—add, again, give more, increase, lay unto, proceed further, speak to any more.

4370. προστρέχω, prostrechō, *pros-trekh´-o*; from 4314 and 5143 (including its alternate); to *run toward*, i.e. *hasten* to meet or join:—run (thither to, to).

4371. προσφάγιον, prosphagion, *pros-fag´-ee-on*; neuter of a presumed derivative of a compound of 4314 and 5315; something *eaten in addition* to bread, i.e. a *relish* (specially *fish*; compare 3795):—meat.

4372. πρόσφατος, prosphatos, *pros´-fat-os*; from 4253 and a derivative of 4969; *previously* (*recently*) *slain* (*fresh*), i.e. (figurative) *lately made*:—new.

4373. προσφάτως, prosphatōs, *pros-fat´-oce*; adverb from 4372; *recently*:—lately.

4374. προσφέρω, prospherō, *pros-fer´-o*; from 4314 and 5342 (including its alternate); to *bear toward*, i.e. *lead to, tender* (especially to God), *treat*:—bring (to, unto) deal with, do, offer (unto, up), present unto, put to.

4375. προσφιλής, prosphilēs, *pros-fee-lace´*; from a presumed compound of 4314 and 5368; *friendly toward*, i.e. *acceptable*:—lovely.

4376. προσφορά, prosphora, *pros-for-ah´*; from 4374; *presentation*; concretely an *oblation* (bloodless) or *sacrifice*:—offering (up).

4377. προσφωνέω, prosphōneō, *pros-fo-neh´-o*; from 4314 and 5455; to *sound toward*, i.e. *address, exclaim, summon*:—call unto, speak (un-) to.

4378. πρόσχυσις, proschusis, *pros´-khoo-sis*; from a compound of 4314 and **χέω**, *cheō* (to *pour*); a *shedding forth*, i.e. *affusion*:—sprinkling.

4379. προσψαύω, prospsauo, *pros-psow´-o*; from 4314 and **ψαύω**, *psauō* (to *touch*); to *impinge*, i.e. *lay a finger on* (in order to relieve):—touch.

4380. προσωποληπτέω, prosōpolēpteō, *pros-o-pol-ape-teh´-o*; from 4381; to *favour an individual*, i.e. *show partiality*:—have respect to persons.

4381. προσωπολήπτης, prosōpolēptēs, *pros-o-pol-ape´-tace*; from 4383 and 2983; an *accepter of a face* (*individual*), i.e. (special) one *exhibiting partiality*:—respecter of persons.

4382. προσωποληψία, prosōpolēpsia, *pros-o-pol-ape-see´-ah*; from 4381; *partiality*, i.e. *favoritism*:—respect of persons.

Noun which comes from *prosōpolēptéō* (4380), to show partiality which is from *prósōpon* (4383), face, and *lambánō* (2983), to receive. A respecting of persons, partiality, favoritism (Ro 2:11; Eph 6:9; Col 3:25; Jas 2:1). This Greek word is found only in the NT.

4383. πρόσωπον, prosōpon, *pros´-o-pon*; from 4314 and **ὤψ**, ***ōps*** (the *visage*; from 3700); the *front* (as being *toward view*), i.e. the *countenance, aspect, appearance, surface*; by implication *presence, person*:—(outward) appearance, × before, countenance, face, fashion, (men's) person, presence.

Noun from *prós* (4314), toward, and *ṓps* (n.f.), the eye or face, which is from *óptomai* (3700), to see. Literally the part toward, at, or around the eye. Hence, the face, countenance.

(I) Particularly (Mt 6:16, 17; 17:2; 26:67; Mk 14:65; Lk 9:29; 22:64; 24:5; Ac 6:15; 2Co 3:7, 13, 18; 4:6; 11:20; Gal 1:22; Jas 1:23; Rev 4:7; 9:7; 10:1). Figuratively, to set the face toward, meaning to set forth with fixed purpose toward something (Lk 9:51, 53), to set the face against, meaning to oppose someone or something (1Pe 3:12). *Prósōpon* is used in antithesis to *kardía* (2588), heart, in 1Th 2:17, being separated "in face, not heart," meaning separated physically, but not in spirit or thought. In 2Co 5:12, boasting "in face and not in heart," meaning in external appearances and not in internal realities.

(II) Used by metonymy for presence, person:

(A) Adverbially: **(1)** from the face, meaning from the presence of someone (Ac 3:19; 5:41; 7:45; 2Th 1:9; Rev 6:16; 12:14; 20:11); **(2)** in the face, meaning in the presence of someone (Lk 2:31; Ac 2:28; 3:13; 2Co 2:10; 8:24); **(3)** before the face, meaning before the presence, spoken of messengers who go before someone to announce his coming (Mt 11:10; Mk 1:2; Lk 1:76; 7:27; 9:52; 10:1; Ac 13:24).

(B) As a verbal object: **(1)** to see the face of someone, meaning to see him, to converse with him (Col 2:1); **(2)** to behold the face of God, meaning to have access to Him, to be in His presence (Mt 18:10; Rev 22:4); **(3)** to see the face or receive the face of someone, meaning to regard the external appearance and become partial toward someone, to show favoritism (Mt 22:16; Mk 12:14; Lk 20:21; Gal 2:6).

(C) Once used in an absolute sense as in the later Gr., meaning a person (2Co 1:11, from many faces, meaning from many persons).

(III) Of things meaning face, surface: e.g., the face of the earth, meaning the whole earth (Lk 21:35; Ac 17:26). Hence, equal to the exterior or external appearance: e.g., the face of the sky (Mt 16:3; Lk 12:56); the face of a flower (Jas 1:11).

Deriv.: *prosōpolḗptēs* (4381), one who shows partiality.

Syn.: *eídos* (1491), that which strikes the eye, is exposed to view, external appearance, form, shape.

4384. προτάσσω, protassō, *prot-as´-so*; from 4253 and 5021; to *pre-arrange*, i.e. *prescribe*:—before appoint.

From *pró* (4253), forth, and *tássō* (5021), to arrange, order. To arrange or set in order before or in front, to appoint before, spoken of times or seasons being marked out beforehand. Used only in Ac 17:26.

Syn.: *proginṓskō* (4267), to foreknow, to consider beforehand; *proetoimázō* (4282), to prepare before; *procheirízō* (4400), to appoint beforehand; *proorízō* (4309), to appoint or decree beforehand.

4385. προτείνω, proteinō, *prot-i´-no*; from 4253 and **τείνω**, ***teinō*** (to *stretch*); to *protend*, i.e. *tie prostrate* (for scourging):—bind.

4386. πρότερον, proteron, *prot´-er-on*; neuter of 4387 as adverb (with or without the article); *previously*:—before, (at the) first, former.

4387. πρότερος, proteros, *prot´-er-os*; comparative of 4253; *prior* or *previous*:—former.

4388. προτίθεμαι, protithemai, *prot-ith´-em-ahee*; middle from 4253 and 5087; to *place before*, i.e. (for oneself) to *exhibit*; (to oneself) to *propose* (*determine*):—purpose, set forth.

From *pró* (4253), before, forth, and *títhēmi* (5087), to place. To set before someone. In the NT, only in the middle *protíthemai*. To propose, set forth or before the eyes, publicly, for all to see (Ro 3:25); to propose to oneself, to purpose, to plan beforehand (Ro 1:13; Eph 1:9).

Deriv.: *próthesis* (4286), a setting forth, a purpose.

Syn.: *bouleúō* (1011), to resolve, determine, purpose; *boúlomai* (1014), to will, be disposed, intend; *thélō* (2309), to desire, to will.

4389. προτρέπομαι, protrepomai, *prot-rep´-om-ahee*; middle from 4253 and the base of 5157; to *turn forward* for oneself, i.e. *encourage*:—exhort.

4390. προτρέχω, protrechō, *prot-rekh´-o*; from 4253 and 5143 (including its alternate); to *run forward*, i.e. *outstrip, precede*:—outrun, run before.

4391. προϋπάρχω, proüparchō, *pro-oop-ar´-kho*; from 4253 and 5225; to *exist before*, i.e. (adverb) to *be* or *do* something *previously*:— + be before (-time).

4392. πρόφασις, prophasis, *prof´-as-is*; from a compound of 4253 and 5316; an *outward showing*, i.e. *pretext*:—cloke, colour, pretence, show.

4393. προφέρω, propherō, *prof-er´-o*; from 4253 and 5342; to *bear forward*, i.e. *produce*:—bring forth.

4394. προφητεία, prophēteia, *prof-ay-ti´-ah*; from 4396 ("*prophecy*"); *prediction* (scriptural or other):—prophecy, prophesying.

Noun from *prophēteúō* (4395), to prophesy. A prophesying or prophecy.

(I) Particularly prediction, the foretelling of future events, including the declarations, exhortations, and warnings uttered by the prophets while acting under divine influence; of the prophecies of the OT (Mt 13:14; 2Pe 1:20, 21); the revelations and warnings of the Book of Revelation (Rev 1:3; 22:7, 10, 18, 19). In 1Ti 1:18; 4:14, *prophēteía* seems to refer to the prophetic revelations or directions of the Holy Spirit by which persons were designated as officers and teachers in the primitive church.

(II) Prophecy, meaning the prophetic office, the prophetic gift, spoken in the NT of the special spiritual gift imparted to the teachers of the early church (Ro 12:6; 1Co 12:10; 13:2, 8; 14:22).

(III) By metonymy, the act of prophesying, the exercise of the prophetic office, the acting as an ambassador of God and the interpreter of His mind and will (Rev 11:6). Specifically the exercise of the prophetic gift or charisma in the early church (1Co 14:6; 1Th 5:20).

Syn.: *apokálupsis* (602), revelation.

4395. προφητεύω, prophēteuō, *prof-ate-yoo´-o*; from 4396; to *foretell* events, *divine, speak* under *inspiration, exercise* the prophetic *office*:—prophesy.

From *prophḗtēs* (4396), prophet. To prophesy.

(I) Particularly, to foretell future events, to predict, often representing the idea from the OT of exhorting, reproving, threatening, and everything spoken by the prophets while they were acting under the divine influence as ambassadors of God and as interpreters of His mind and will. Spoken of the OT prophets (Mt 11:13; 15:7; Mk 7:6; 1Pe 1:10; Jude 14), and of the NT prophets (Lk 1:67; Rev 10:11; 11:3). See also Ac 2:17, 18. Spoken once of the high priest, with whose office the gift of prophecy was supposed to be connected (Jn 11:51). Spoken also of false prophets (Mt 7:22). Spoken in mockery by the soldiers commanding Jesus to prophesy and identify who had hit Him while He was blindfolded (Mt 26:68; Mk 14:65; Lk 22:64).

(II) Specifically of the prophetic gift imparted by the Holy Spirit to the early Christians (Ac 19:6; 21:9; 1Co 11:4, 5; 13:9; 14:1, 3–5, 24, 31, 39).

Deriv.: *prophēteía* (4394), a prophecy.

Syn.: *apokalúptō* (601), to reveal; *prolégō* (4302), to foretell.

4396. προφήτης, prophētēs, *prof-ay´-tace*; from a compound of 4253 and 5346; a *foreteller* ("*prophet*"); (by analogy) an *inspired speaker*; by extension a *poet*:—prophet.

Noun from *próphēmi* (n.f.), to tell beforehand, which is from *pró* (4253), before or forth, and *phēmí* (5346), to tell. A prophet, a foreteller of future events, also an interpreter. In the NT *prophḗtēs* corresponds to the person who in the OT spoke under divine influence and inspiration. This included the foretelling of future events and the exhorting, reproving, and threatening of individuals or nations as the ambassador of God and as the interpreter of His will to men (Eze 2). Hence the prophet spoke not his own thoughts but what he received from God, retaining, however, his own consciousness and self-possession (Ex 7:1; 2Pe 1:20, 21; especially 1Co 14:32).

(I) In the NT as spoken of the prophets of the OT:

(A) Used particularly of Isaiah (Mt 1:22; 3:3; Lk 3:4; Jn 1:23); Jeremiah (Mt 2:17); Joel (Ac 2:16); Micah (Mt 2:5); Jonah (Mt 12:39; Lk 11:29); Zechariah (Mt 21:4); Daniel (Mt 24:15; Mk 13:14); Samuel (Ac 13:20); David (Ac 2:30); Elisha (Lk 4:27); Asaph (Mt 13:35); Balaam (2Pe 2:16). In the plural and generally (Mt 2:23; 5:12; 23:29–31, 34, 37; Mk 8:28; Lk 1:70; Ro 1:2; Heb 1:1; Jas 5:10; 1Pe 1:10).

(B) Spoken by metonymy of the prophetic books of the OT (Mt 26:56); generally (Mt 5:17; Mk 1:2; Lk 16:29, 31; 24:27, 44; Ac 8:28; 28:23; Ro 3:21); of the doctrines contained in the prophetic books (Mt 7:12; 22:40; Ac 26:27).

(II) Spoken generally of persons acting by divine influence as prophets and ambassadors of God under the new dispensation, equivalent to a teacher sent from God (Mt 10:41; 13:57; Mk 6:4; Lk 4:24; 13:33; Jn 7:52; Rev 11:10; 16:6; 18:20, 24); specifically of John the Baptist (Mt 11:9; 14:5; Mk 11:32; Lk 1:76; 20:6); of Jesus (Mt 21:11, 46; Lk 7:16; 24:19; Jn 9:17); the Messiah as a prophet coming into the world (Jn 1:21, 25; 6:14).

(III) Spoken specifically of those who possessed the prophetic gift or charisma imparted by the Holy Spirit to the early churches. Prophets were a class of instructors or preachers who were next in rank to the apostles and before the teachers (1Co 12:28). Like the apostles, however, they did not remain in one place as the teachers did. They seem to have differed from the teachers in that while the latter spoke in a calm, connected, didactic discourse, adapted to instruct and enlighten the hearers, the prophets spoke more from the impulse of sudden inspiration, from the light of a sudden revelation at the moment, as indicated in 1Co 14:30. It seems that this discourse was probably more adapted by means of powerful exhortations to awaken the feeling and consciousness of the hearers. The idea of speaking from an immediate revelation seems here to be fundamental, as relating either to future events or to the mind of the Spirit in general. See also Ac 11:27; see 13:1; 1Co 12:28, 29; 14:29, 32, 37; Eph 2:20; 3:5; 4:11).

(IV) Spoken once in the Greek secular sense of a spokesman of the gods (Tit 1:12).

Deriv.: *prophēteúō* (4395), to prophesy; *prophētikós* (4397), prophetic; *pseudoprophḗtēs* (5578), a false prophet.

4397. προφητικός, prophētikos, *prof-ay-tik-os´*; from 4396; *pertaining to a foreteller* ("*prophetic*"):—of prophecy, of the prophets.

4398. προφῆτις, prophētis, *prof-ay´-tis*; feminine of 4396; a *female foreteller* or an *inspired woman*:—prophetess.

4399. προφθάνω, prophthanō, *prof-than´-o*; from 4253 and 5348; to *get* an *earlier start of*, i.e. *anticipate*:—prevent.

4400. προχειρίζομαι, procheirizomai, *prokh-i-rid´-zom-ahee*; middle from 4253 and a derivative of 5495; to *handle* for oneself *in advance*, i.e. (figurative) to *purpose*:—choose, make.

4401. προχειροτονέω, procheirotoneō, *prokh-i-rot-on-eh´-o*; from 4253 and 5500; to *elect in advance*:—choose before.

4402. Πρόχορος, Prochoros, *prokh´-or-os*; from 4253 and 5525; *before* the *dance*; *Prochorus*, a Christian:—Prochorus.

4403. πρύμνα, prumna, *proom´-nah*; feminine of **πρυμνύς, *prumnus*** (*hindmost*); the *stern* of a ship:—hinder part, stern.

4404. πρωΐ, prōï, *pro-ee´*; adverb from 4253; at *dawn*; by implication the *day-break* watch:—early (in the morning), (in the) morning.

4405. πρωΐα, prōïa, *pro-ee´-ah*; feminine of a derivative of 4404 as noun; *day-dawn*:—early, morning.

4406. πρώϊμος, prōïmos, *pro´-ee-mos*; from 4404; *dawning*, i.e. (by analogy) *autumnal* (showering, the first of the rainy season):—early.

4407. πρωϊνός, prōïnos, *pro-ee-nos´*; from 4404; pertaining to the *dawn*, i.e. *matutinal*:—morning.

4408. πρώρα, prōra, *pro´-ra*; feminine of a presumed derivative of 4253 as noun; the *prow*, i.e. forward part of a vessel:—forepart (-ship).

4409. πρωτεύω, prōteuō, *prote-yoo´-o*; from 4413; to *be first* (in rank or influence):—have the preeminence.

4410. πρωτοκαθεδρία, prōtokathedria, *pro-tok-ath-ed-ree´-ah*; from 4413 and 2515; a *sitting first* (in the front row), i.e. *preeminence* in council:—chief (highest, uppermost) seat.

4411. πρωτοκλισία, prōtoklisia, *pro-tok-lis-ee´-ah*; from 4413 and 2828; a *reclining first* (in the place of honour) at the dinner-bed, i.e. *preeminence* at meals:—chief (highest, uppermost) room.

4412. πρῶτον, prōton, *pro´-ton*; neuter of 4413 as adverb (with or without 3588); *firstly* (in time, place, order, or importance):—before, at the beginning, chiefly, (at, at the) first (of all).

The neuter of *prṓtos* (4413), first, used as an adverb. First.

(I) Particularly of place, order, time, usually without the article.

(A) Generally (Mt 17:10, 11; Mk 7:27; Lk 9:59, 61; Jn 18:13; Ac 7:12; 15:14; 1Co 11:18; 1Pe 4:17).

(B) Emphatically meaning first of all, before all (Mt 23:26; Ac 13:46; Ro 1:8).

(C) In division or distribution, as referring to a series or succession of circumstances and followed by other adverb of order or time expressed or implied: "First apostles, secondarily …" (1Co 12:28). See also Mt 5:24; 7:5; Mk 3:27; 4:28; Lk 6:42; 1Th 4:16; Jas 3:17.

(D) Rarely with the article *tó prṓton*, the first, at first, formerly (Jn 10:40; 12:16; 19:39).

(II) Figuratively of dignity or importance, first, first of all, chiefly, especially (Mt 6:33; Ro 3:2; 1Ti 2:1; 2Pe 1:20; 3:3).

4413. πρῶτος, prōtos, *pro´-tos*; contracted superlative of 4253; *foremost* (in time, place, order or importance):—before, beginning, best, chief (-est), first (of all), former.

Adjective, the superlative of *pró* (4253), forward. Foremost, hence first, the first.

(I) Generally as an adj. spoken of place, order, time. First (Mt 20:8, 10; 21:36; 26:17; Mk 14:12; 16:9; Lk 2:2; Ac 1:1; 12:10; 1Co 15:3, 45; Eph 6:2; Php 1:5; Heb 9:2, 6, 8; Rev 1:17; 4:1, 7; 8:7). *Prṓtos* sometimes takes on the idea of former, that which used to be (Mt 12:45; 1Ti 5:12; 2Pe 2:20; Rev 2:4; 21:4). In this respect *prṓtos* stands in direct opposition to *kainós* (2537), qualitatively new (Heb 8:13; Rev 21:1).

(II) In an adverbial sense, first, i.e. in the first place (Mt 10:2; Jn 1:41; 8:7; Ac 26:23; Ro 10:19; 1Jn 4:19). Used for the comparative *próteros*, before (Jn 1:15, 30).

(III) Figuratively of rank or dignity, meaning first in importance (Mt 20:27; 22:38; Mk 6:21; 10:44; 12:28–30; Lk 15:22; 19:47; Ac 13:50; 16:12; 17:4; 28:7, 17; Eph 6:2; 1Ti 1:15). Contrasted with *éschatos* [2078], last, in expressions that state that the first shall be last and the last shall be first, meaning those who seem or claim to be first shall be last (Mt 19:30; 20:16; Mk 10:31; Lk 13:30).

Deriv.: *deuteróprōtos* (1207), the second after the first; *prōteúō* (4409), to be first; *prōtokathedría* (4410), the first seat or the best seat; *prōtoklisia* (4411), the first place; *prṓton* (4412), first, at first; *prōtostátēs* (4414), a leader or captain; *prōtótokos* (4416), firstborn, chief in rank, heir.

Syn.: *archḗ* (746), beginning.

4414. πρωτοστάτης, prōtostatēs, *pro-tos-tat´-ace*; from 4413 and 2476; one *standing first* in the ranks, i.e. a *captain* (*champion*):—ringleader.

4415. πρωτοτόκια, prōtotokia, *pro-tot-ok´-ee-ah*; from 4416; *primogeniture* (as a privilege):—birthright.

4416. πρωτοτόκος, prōtotokos, *pro-tot-ok´-os*; from 4413 and the alternate of 5088; *firstborn* (usually as noun, literal or figurative):—firstbegotten (-born).

Noun from *prṓtos* (4413), first, and *tíktō* (5088), to bear, bring forth. Firstborn, preeminent.

(I) Particularly the firstborn of a father or mother (Mt 1:25; Lk 2:7).

(II) Figuratively, the firstborn in the sense of the chief one, the one highly distinguished, so of Christ, as the beloved Son of God before the creation of the world (Col 1:15 [cf. v. 16]; Heb 1:6 [cf. v. 5]), or in relation to His followers (Ro 8:29). Or, as the first to rise from the dead, the leader and prince of those who shall arise (Col 1:18; Rev 1:5).

(III) Firstborn of the saints in heaven, probably those formerly highly distinguished on earth by the favour and love of God, such as patriarchs, prophets, apostles (Heb 12:23).

Deriv.: *prōtotókia* (4415), the rights of the firstborn.

4417. πταίω, ptaiō, *ptah´-yo*; a form of 4098; to *trip*, i.e. (figurative) to *err, sin, fail* (of salvation):—fall, offend, stumble.

4418. πτέρνα, pterna, *pter´-nah*; of uncertain derivative; the *heel* (figurative):—heel.

4419. πτερύγιον, pterugion, *pter-oog´-ee-on*; neuter of a presumed derivative of 4420; a *winglet*, i.e. (figurative) *extremity* (top corner):—pinnacle.

4420. πτέρυξ, pterux, *pter´-oox*; from a derivative of 4072 (meaning a *feather*); a *wing*:—wing.

4421. πτηνόν, ptēnon, *ptay-non´*; contracted from 4071; a *bird*:—bird.

4422. πτοέω, ptoeō, *pto-eh´-o*; probably akin to the alternate of 4098 (through the idea of causing to *fall*) or to 4072 (through that of causing to *fly* away); to *scare*:—frighten.

4423. πτόησις, ptoēsis, *pto´-ay-sis*; from 4422; *alarm*:—amazement.

4424. Πτολεμαΐς, Ptolemaïs, *ptol-em-ah-is´*; from **Πτολεμαῖος** ***Ptolemaios*** (*Ptolemy*, after whom it was named); *Ptolemaïs*, a place in Palestine:—Ptolemais.

4425. πτύον, ptuon, *ptoo´-on*; from 4429; a *winnowing-fork* (as *scattering* like spittle):—fan.

4426. πτύρω, pturō, *ptoo´-ro*; from a presumed derivative of 4429 (and thus akin to 4422); to *frighten*:—terrify.

4427. πτύσμα, ptusma, *ptoos´-mah*; from 4429; *saliva*:—spittle.

4428. πτύσσω, ptussō, *ptoos´-so*; probably akin to **πετάννυμι**, ***petannumi*** (to *spread*; and thus apparently allied to 4072 through the idea of *expansion*, and to 4429 through that of *flattening*; compare 3961); to *fold*, i.e. *furl* a scroll:—close.

4429. πτύω, ptuō, *ptoo´-o*; a primary verb (compare 4428); to *spit*:—spit.

4430. πτῶμα, ptōma, *pto´-mah*; from the alternate of 4098; a *ruin*, i.e. (special) lifeless *body* (*corpse, carrion*):—dead body, carcase, corpse.

4431. πτῶσις, ptōsis, *pto´-sis*; from the alternate of 4098; a *crash*, i.e. *downfall* (literal or figurative):—fall.

4432. πτωχεία, ptōcheia, *pto-khi´-ah*; from 4433; *beggary*, i.e. *indigence* (literal or figurative):—poverty.

4433. πτωχεύω, ptōcheuō, *pto-khyoo´-o*; from 4434; to *be a beggar*, i.e. (by implication) to *become indigent* (figurative):—become poor.

4434. πτωχός, ptōchos, *pto-khos´*; from **πτώσσω, *ptōssō*** (to *crouch*; akin to 4422 and the alternate of 4098); a *beggar* (as *cringing*), i.e. *pauper* (strictly denoting absolute or public *mendicancy*, although also used in a qualified or relative sense; whereas 3993 properly means only *straitened* circumstances in private), literal (often as noun) or figurative (*distressed*):—beggar (-ly), poor.

Adjective from *ptṓssō* (n.f.), to crouch, cower like a beggar. Poor and helpless.

(I) Particularly and often as substantive:

(A) A poor, helpless man and therefore a beggar (Lk 14:13, 21; 16:20, 22; Jn 9:8). Figuratively (Rev 3:17).

(B) In the plural, the poor, meaning the needy, those destitute of the necessities of life and subsisting on the alms from others (Mt 19:21; 26:9, 11; Mk 10:21; 14:5, 7; Lk 6:20; 18:22; 19:8; Jn 12:5, 6, 8; 13:29; Sept.: Est 9:22; Pr 28:27; 31:20).

(C) Generally, poor, needy, contrasted with *pénēs* (3993), one who may be poor but earns his bread by daily labour; also spoken of true poverty, as opposed to the rich, without the idea of begging (Mk 12:42, 43; Lk 21:3; Ro 15:26; 2Co 6:10; Gal 2:10; Jas 2:2, 3, 5, 6; Rev 13:16).

(II) By implication, poor, low, humble, of low estate, including also the idea of being afflicted, distressed (Mt 11:5; Lk 4:18). Figuratively in Mt 5:3, "poor in spirit" means those who recognize their spiritual helplessness.

(III) Figuratively, of things worthless, poor, imperfect (Gal 4:9).

Deriv.: *ptōcheia* (4432), poverty, want, helplessness; *ptocheúō* (4433), to be or become poor.

Syn.: *endeḗs* (1729), lacking, needy.

4435. πυγμή, pugmē, *poog-may´*; from a primary **πύξ, *pux*** (the *fist* as a weapon); the clenched *hand*, i.e. (only in dative as adverb) *with* the *fist* (hard *scrubbing*):—oft.

4436. Πύθων, Puthōn, *poo´-thone*; from **Πυθώ, *Puthō*** (the name of the region where Delphi, the seat of the famous *oracle*, was located); a *Python*, i.e. (by analogy with the supposed *diviner* there) *inspiration* (*soothsaying*):—divination.

4437. πυκνός, puknos, *pook-nos´*; from the same as 4635; *clasped* (*thick*), i.e. (figurative) *frequent*; neuter plural (as adverb) *frequently*:—often (-er).

4438. πυκτέω, pukteō, *pook-teh´-o*; from a derivative of the same as 4435; to *box* (with the fist), i.e. *contend* (as a boxer) at the games (figurative):—fight.

4439. πύλη, pulē, *poo´-lay*; apparently a primary word; a *gate*, i.e. the leaf or wing of a folding *entrance* (literal or figurative):—gate.

4440. πυλών, pulōn, *poo-lone´*; from 4439; a *gateway, door-way* of a building or city; by implication a *portal* or *vestibule*:—gate, porch.

4441. πυνθάνομαι, punthanomai, *poon-than´-om-ahee*; middle prolonged from a primary **πύθω, *puthō*** (which occurs only as an alternate in certain tenses); to *question*, i.e. *ascertain* by inquiry (as a matter of *information* merely; and thus differing from 2065, which properly means a *request* as a favour; and from 154, which is strictly a *demand* of something due; as well as from 2212, which implies a *search* for something hidden; and from 1189, which involves the idea of urgent *need*); by implication to *learn* (by casual intelligence):—ask, demand, enquire, understand.

4442. πῦρ, pur, *poor*; a primary word; "*fire*" (literal or figurative, specially *lightning*):—fiery, fire.

4443. πυρά, pura, *poo-rah´*; from 4442; a *fire* (concrete):—fire.

4444. πύργος, purgos, *poor´-gos*; apparently a primary word ("*burgh*"); a *tower* or *castle*:—tower.

4445. πυρέσσω, puressō, *poo-res´-so*; from 4443; to *be on fire*, i.e. (special) to *have a fever*:—be sick of a fever.

4446. πυρετός, puretos, *poo-ret-os´*; from 4445; *inflamed*, i.e. (by implication) *feverish* (as noun, *fever*):—fever.

4447. πύρινος, purinos, *poo´-ree-nos*; from 4443; *fiery*, i.e. (by implication) *flaming*:—of fire.

4448. πυρόω, puroō, *poo-ro´-o*; from 4442; to *kindle*, i.e. (passive) to *be ignited, glow* (literal), *be refined* (by implication), or (figurative) to *be inflamed* (with anger, grief, lust):—burn, fiery, be on fire, try.

4449. πυῤῥάζω, purrhazō, *poor-hrad´-zo*; from 4450; to *redden* (intransitive):—be red.

4450. πυῤῥός, purrhos, *poor-hros´*; from 4442; *fire-like*, i.e. (special) *flame-coloured*:—red.

4451. πύρωσις, purōsis, *poo´-ro-sis*; from 4448; *ignition*, i.e. (special) *smelting* (figurative, *conflagration, calamity* as a *test*):—burning, trial.

4452. -πω, -pō, *po*; another form of the base of 4458; an enclitic particle of indefiniteness; *yet, even*; used only in comparative. See 3369, 3380, 3764, 3768, 4455.

4453. πωλέω, pōleō, *po-leh´-o*; probably ultimately from **πέλομαι, *pelomai*** (to *be busy*, to *trade*); to *barter* (as a *pedlar*), i.e. to *sell*:—sell, whatever is sold.

4454. πῶλος, pōlos, *po´-los*; apparently a primary word; a "*foal*" or "*filly*," i.e. (special) a *young ass*:—colt.

4455. πώποτε, pōpote, *po´-pot-e*; from 4452 and 4218; *at any time*, i.e. (with negative particle) *at no time*:—at any time, + never (… to any man), + yet never man.

4456. πωρόω, pōroō, *po-ro´-o*; apparently from **πῶρος, *pōros*** (a kind of *stone*); to *petrify*, i.e. (figurative) to *indurate* (*render stupid* or *callous*):—blind, harden.

From *pṓros* (n.f.), a kind of stone. The verb means to harden, make hard like a stone, or callous and insensible to the touch. In the NT only figuratively, to harden, to make dull or stupid. Spoken of the heart being hardened (Mk 6:52; 8:17; Jn 12:40). Spoken of the mind being hardened (2Co 3:14). Its use in Ro 11:7 seems to be an instance where both the heart and the understanding were hardened.

Deriv.: *pṓrōsis* (4457), hardening.

Syn.: *sklērúnō* (4645), to harden.

4457. πώρωσις, pōrōsis, *po´-ro-sis*; from 4456; *stupidity* or *callousness*:—blindness, hardness.

Noun from *pōróō* (4456), to harden, petrify, render insensitive. A hardening. In the NT, used only figuratively, hardness of heart or mind, insensitivity (Mk 3:5; Ro 11:25; Eph 4:18).

Syn.: *sklērótēs* (4643), hardness. Also *sklērokardía* (4641), hardness of heart.

4458. πώς, pōs, *poce*; adverb from the base of 4225; an enclitic particle of indefiniteness of manner; *somehow* or *anyhow*; used only in comparative:—haply, by any (some) means, perhaps. See 1513, 3381. Compare 4459.

4459. πῶς, pōs, *poce*; adverb from the base of 4226; an interrogative particle of manner; *in what way?* (sometimes the question is indirect, *how?*); also as exclamation, *how much!*:—how, after (by) what manner (means), that. [*Occasionally unexpressed in English.*]

4460. Ῥαάβ, Rhaab, *hrah-ab´*; of Hebrew origin [7343]; *Raab* (i.e. *Rachab*), a Canaanitess:—Rahab. See also 4477.

4461. ῥαββί, rhabbi, *hrab-bee´*; of Hebrew origin [7227 with pronoun suffix]; *my master*, i.e. *Rabbi*, as an official title of honour:—Master, Rabbi.

4462. ῥαββονί, rhabboni, *hrab-bon-ee´*; or **ῥαββουνί, *rhabbouni***, *hrab-boo-nee´*; of Chaldee origin; corresponding to 4461:—Lord, Rabboni.

4463. ῥαβδίζω, rhabdizō, *hrab-did´-zo*; from 4464; to *strike with a stick*, i.e. *bastinado*:—beat (with rods).

4464. ῥάβδος, rhabdos, *hrab´-dos*; from the base of 4474; a *stick* or *wand* (as a *cudgel*, a *cane* or a *baton* of royalty):—rod, sceptre, staff.

4465. ῥαβδοῦχος, rhabdouchos, *hrab-doo´-khos*; from 4464 and 2192; a *rod-* (the Latin *fasces*) *holder*, i.e. a Roman *lictor* (*constable* or *executioner*):—sergeant.

4466. Ῥαγαῦ, Rhagau, *hrag-ow´*; of Hebrew origin [7466]; *Ragau* (i.e. *Reü*), a patriarch:—Ragau.

4467. ῥᾳδιούργημα, rhaidiourgēma, *hrad-ee-oorg´-ay-mah*; from a compound of **ῥᾴδιος, *rhaidios*** (*easy*, i.e. *reckless*) and 2041; *easy-going behaviour*, i.e. (by extension) a *crime*:—lewdness.

4468. ῥᾳδιουργία, rhaidiourgia, *hrad-ee-oorg-ee´-a*; from the same as 4467; *recklessness*, i.e. (by extension) *malignity*:—mischief.

4469. ῥακά, rhaka, *rhak-ah´*; of Chaldee or [compare 7386]; O *empty* one, i.e. thou *worthless* (as a term of utter vilification):—Raca.

4470. ῥάκος, rhakos, *hrak´-os*; from 4486; a "*rag*," i.e. *piece* of cloth:—cloth.

4471. Ῥαμᾶ, Rhama, *hram-ah´*; of Hebrew origin [7414]; *Rama* (i.e. *Ramah*), a place in Palestine:—Rama.

4472. ῥαντίζω, rhantizō, *hran-tid´-zo*; from a derivative of **ῥαίνω, *rhainō*** (to *sprinkle*); to *render besprinkled*, i.e. *asperse* (ceremonial or figurative):— sprinkle.

From *rhainō* (n.f.), to sprinkle. To sprinkle. Spoken of the water of purification made from the ashes of a heifer, and compared to the cleansing power of Christ's blood (Heb 9:13; cf. Nu 19). It is also spoken of the blood of sacrificial animals sprinkled for purification, and compared with the atoning power of Christ's blood, the blood of the new covenant (Heb 9:19, 21; cf. Ex 24:6, 8). Figuratively, spoken of our hearts being sprinkled with the blood of Christ in cleansing from an impure conscience (Heb 10:22). The purpose of describing Christ's redemptive work in terms of Levitical ritualism is to explain how Christ in His atoning death (and triumphant resurrection) accomplished what these things represented, their essential significance, and to say that those rituals are therefore irrelevant and unnecessary. Calvary was both the altar and the mercy seat; Christ was both the priest and the sacrifice.

Deriv.: *rhantismós* (4473), sprinkling.

4473. ῥαντισμός, rhantismos, *hran-tis-mos´*; from 4472; *aspersion* (ceremonial or figurative):—sprinkling.

Noun from *rhantízō* (4472), to sprinkle. Sprinkling. In the NT, it is used to identify the blood of Christ as the "blood of sprinkling," corresponding to the OT blood of sprinkling (Heb 12:24; 1Pe 1:2 [cf. Nu 19:9, 13, 20, 21]), even to the blood of Abel's righteous sacrifice, which pointed forward to the sacrifice made by Christ.

4474. ῥαπίζω, rhapizō, *hrap-id´-zo*; from a derivative of a primary **ῥέπω, *rhepō*** (to *let fall*, "*rap*"); to *slap*:—smite (with the palm of the hand). Compare 5180.

4475. ῥάπισμα, rhapisma, *hrap´-is-mah*; from 4474; a *slap*:—(+ strike with the) palm of the hand, smite with the hand.

4476. ῥαφίς, rhaphis, *hraf-ece´*; from a primary **ῥάπτω, *rhaptō*** (to *sew*; perhaps rather akin to the base of 4474 through the idea of *puncturing*); a *needle*:—needle.

4477. Ῥαχάβ, Rhachab, *hrakh-ab´*; from the same as 4460; *Rachab*, a Canaanitess:—Rachab.

4478. Ῥαχήλ, Rhachēl, *hrakh-ale´*; of Hebrew origin [7354]; *Rachel*, the wife of Jacob:—Rachel.

4479. Ῥεβέκκα, Rhebekka, *hreb-bek´-kah*; of Hebrew origin [7259]; *Rebecca* (i.e. *Ribkah*), the wife of Isaac:—Rebecca.

4480. ῥέδα, rheda, *hred´-ah*; of Latin origin; a *rheda*, i.e. four-wheeled *carriage* (*wagon* for riding):—chariot.

4481. Ῥεμφάν, Rhemphan, *hrem-fan´*; by incorrect transliteration for a word of Hebrew origin [3594]; *Remphan* (i.e. *Kijun*), an Egyptian idol:—Remphan.

4482. ῥέω, rheō, *hreh´-o*; a primary verb; for some tenses of which a prolonged form **ῥεύω, *rheuō***, *hryoo´-o*, is used; to *flow* ("*run*," as water):—flow.

4483. ῥέω, rheō, *hreh´-o*; for certain tenses of which a prolonged form **ἐρέω, *ereō***, *er-eh´-o*, is used; and both as alternate for 2036; perhaps akin (or identical) with 4482 (through the idea of *pouring* forth); to *utter*, i.e. *speak* or *say*:—command, make, say, speak (of). Compare 3004.

4484. Ῥήγιον, Rhēgion, *hrayg´-ee-on*; of Latin origin; *Rhegium*, a place in Italy:—Rhegium.

4485. ῥῆγμα, rhēgma, *hrayg´-mah*; from 4486; something *torn*, i.e. a *fragment* (by implication and abstract a *fall*):—ruin.

4486. ῥήγνυμι, rhēgnumi, *hrayg´-noo-mee*; or **ῥήσσω,** *rhēssō, hrace´-so*; both prolonged forms of **ῥήκω,** *rhēko* (which appears only in certain forms, and is itself probably a strengthened form of **ἄγνυμι,** *agnumi*; [see in 2608]); to "*break*," "*wreck*" or "*crack*," i.e. (especially) to *sunder* (by *separation* of the parts; 2608 being its intensive [with the preposition in comparative], and 2352 a *shattering* to minute fragments; but not a *reduction* to the constituent particles, like 3089) or *disrupt, lacerate*; by implication to *convulse* (with *spasms*); (figurative) to *give vent* to joyful emotions:—break (forth), burst, rend, tear.

4487. ῥῆμα, rhēma, *hray´-mah*; from 4483; an *utterance* (individual, collective or special); by implication a *matter* or *topic* (especially of narration, command or dispute); with a negative *naught* whatever:— + evil, + nothing, saying, word.

Noun from *rhéō* (4483), to speak. That which is spoken, a statement, word.

(I) Particularly a word as uttered by a living voice: a saying, speech, or discourse (Mt 12:36; 26:75; Mk 9:32; 14:72; Lk 1:38; 2:17, 50; 9:45; 18:34; 20:26; Ac 11:16; 28:25). In the plural, words (Lk 2:19, 51; 7:1; 24:8, 11; Ac 2:14; 6:11, 13; 10:44; 16:38; 26:25; Ro 10:18; 2Co 12:4; Heb 12:19).

(II) In the NT, *rhḗma* often takes on a particular meaning from its adjuncts or context:

(A) Charge, accusation (Mt 5:11; 18:16; 27:14; 2Co 13:1).

(B) Prediction, prophecy (2Pe 3:2; Jude 17). Also, the sayings of God (Rev 17:17).

(C) Promise from God (Lk 2:29; Heb 6:5).

(D) Command (Lk 5:5; Heb 1:3; 11:3). Alsos Mt 4:4; Lk 4:4, where *rhḗma* is used in metonymy for everything which God decrees.

(E) Teaching, precept, doctrine (Lk 3:2; Jn 3:37; 5:47; 6:63, 68; 8:47; 10:21; 12:47, 48; 14:10; 15:7; 17:8; Ac 5:20; 10:22, 37; Ro 10:17; Eph 5:26; 6:17; 1Pe 1:25).

(II) Spoken by metonymy for things spoken of: a matter, a happening (Lk 1:37; 65; 2:15; Ac 5:32).

Syn.: *lógos* (3056), word. Also *épos* (2031), a word.

4488. Ῥησά, Rhēsa, *hray-sah´*; probably of Hebrew origin [apparently for 7509]; *Resa* (i.e. *Rephajah*), an Israelite:—Rhesa.

4489. ῥήτωρ, rhētōr, *hray´-tore*; from 4483; a *speaker*, i.e. (by implication) a forensic *advocate*:—orator.

4490. ῥητῶς, rhētōs, *hray-toce´*; adverb from a derivative of 4483; out-*spokenly*, i.e. *distinctly*:—expressly.

4491. ῥίζα, rhiza, *hrid´-zah*; apparently a primary word; a "*root*" (literal or figurative):—root.

4492. ῥιζόω, rhizoō, *hrid-zo´-o*; from 4491; to *root* (figurative, *become stable*):—root.

4493. ῥιπή, rhipē, *hree-pay´*; from 4496; a *jerk* (of the eye, i.e. [by analogy] an *instant*):—twinkling.

4494. ῥιπίζω, rhipizō, *hrip-id´-zo*; from a derivative of 4496 (meaning a *fan* or *bellows*); to *breeze up*, i.e. (by analogy) to *agitate* (into waves):—toss.

4495. ῥιπτέω, rhipteō, *hrip-teh´-o*; from a derivative of 4496; to *toss* up:—cast off.

4496. ῥίπτω, rhiptō, *hrip´-to*; a primary verb (perhaps rather akin to the base of 4474, through the idea of sudden *motion*); to *fling* (properly with a quick *toss*, thus differing from 906, which denotes a *deliberate* hurl; and from **τείνω,** *teinō*; [see in 1614], which indicates an *extended* projection); by qualification, to *deposit* (as if a load); by extension to *disperse*:—cast (down, out), scatter abroad, throw.

4497. Ῥοβοάμ, Rhoboam, *hrob-o-am´*; of Hebrew origin [7346]; *Roboäm* (i.e. *Rechabam*), an Israelite:—Roboam.

4498. Ῥόδη, Rhodē, *hrod´-ay*; probably for **ῥόδη,** *Rhodē* (a *rose*); *Rode*, a servant girl:—Rhoda.

4499. Ῥόδος, Rhodos, *hrod´-os*; probably from **ῥόδον,** *Rhodon* (a *rose*); *Rhodus*, an island of the Mediterranean:—Rhodes.

4500. ῥοιζηδόν, rhoizēdon, *hroyd-zay-don´*; adverb from a derivative of **ῥοῖζος,** *rhoizos* (a *whir*); *whizzingly*, i.e. *with a crash*:—with a great noise.

4501. ῥομφαία, rhomphaia, *hrom-fah´-yah*; probably of foreign origin; a *sabre*, i.e. a long and broad *cutlass* (any *weapon* of the kind, literal or figurative):—sword.

4502. Ῥουβήν, Rhoubēn, *hroo-bane´*; of Hebrew origin [7205]; *Ruben* (i.e. *Reuben*), an Israelite:—Reuben.

4503. Ῥούθ, Rhouth, *hrooth*; of Hebrew origin [7827]; *Ruth*, a Moabitess:—Ruth.

4504. Ῥοῦφος, Rhouphos, *hroo´-fos*; of Latin origin; *red; Rufus*, a Christian:—Rufus.

4505. ῥύμη, rhumē, *hroo´-may*; prolonged from 4506 in its original sense; an *alley* or *avenue* (as crowded):—lane, street.

4506. ῥύομαι, rhuomai, *rhoo´-om-ahee*; middle of an obsolete verb, akin to 4482 (through the idea of a *current*; compare 4511); to *rush* or *draw* (for oneself), i.e. *rescue*:—deliver (-er).

From *rhúō* (n.f., see *rhúmē* [4505]), to draw, drag along the ground. To draw or snatch from danger, rescue, deliver. In the NT, it is used of God's delivering His saints (Mt 6:13; 27:43; Lk 1:74; 11:4; Ro 7:24; 11:26; 15:31; 2Co 1:10; Col 1:13; 1Th 1:10; 2Th 3:2; 2Ti 3:11; 4:17, 18; 2Pe 2:7, 9).

Syn.: *apallássō* (525), to free from, release, deliver; *apolúō* (630), to dismiss, set free; *eleutheróō* (1659), to deliver, free; *exairéō* (1807), to take out, deliver; *lutróō* (3084), to ransom, redeem; *lúō* (3089), to loose; *sṓzō* (4982), to save, deliver, rescue.

4507. ῥυπαρία, rhuparia, *hroo-par-ee´-ah*; from 4508; *dirtiness* (moral):—turpitude.

4508. ῥυπαρός, rhuparos, *rhoo-par-os´*; from 4509; *dirty*, i.e. (relative) *cheap* or *shabby*; moral *wicked*:—vile.

4509. ῥύπος, rhupos, *hroo´-pos*; of uncertain affinity; *dirt*, i.e. (moral) *depravity*:—filth.

4510. ῥυπόω, rhupoō, *rhoo-po´-o*; from 4509; to *soil*, i.e. (intransitive) to *become dirty* (moral):—be filthy.

4511. ῥύσις, rhusis, *hroo´-sis*; from 4506 in the sense of its congener 4482; a *flux* (of blood):—issue.

4512. ῥυτίς, rhutis, *hroo-tece´*; from 4506; a *fold* (as *drawing* together), i.e. a *wrinkle* (especially on the face):—wrinkle.

4513. Ῥωμαϊκός, Rhōmaïkos, *rho-mah-ee-kos´*; from 4514; *Romaïc*, i.e. *Latin*:—Latin.

4514. Ῥωμαῖος, Rhōmaios, *hro-mah´-yos*; from 4516; *Romæan*, i.e. *Roman* (as noun):—Roman, of Rome.

4515. Ῥωμαϊστί, Rhōmaïsti, *hro-mah-is-tee´*; adverb from a presumed derivative of 4516; *Romaïsti-cally*, i.e. *in* the *Latin* language:—Latin.

4516. Ῥώμη, Rhōmē, *hro´-may*; from the base of 4517; *strength; Roma*, the capital of Italy:—Rome.

4517. ῥώννυμι, rhōnnumi, *hrone´-noo-mee*; prolonged from **ῥώομαι,** *rhōomai* (to *dart*; probably akin to 4506); to *strengthen*, i.e. (impersonal passive) *have health* (as a parting exclamation, *good-bye*):—farewell.

4518. σαβαχθανί, sabachthani, *sab-akh-than-ee´*; of Chaldee origin [7662 with pronoun suffix]; *thou hast left me; sabachthani* (i.e. *shebakthani*), a cry of distress:—sabachthani.

4519. σαβαώθ, sabaōth, *sab-ah-owth´*; of Hebrew origin [6635 in feminine plural]; *armies; sabaoth* (i.e. *tsebaoth*), a military epithet of God:—sabaoth.

4520. σαββατισμός, sabbatismos, *sab-bat-is-mos´*; from a derivative of 4521; a "*sabbatism*," i.e. (figurative) the *repose* of Christianity (as a type of heaven):—rest.

4521. σάββατον, sabbaton, *sab´-bat-on*; of Hebrew origin [7676]; the *Sabbath* (i.e. *Shabbath*), or day of weekly *repose* from secular avocations (also the observance or institution itself); by extension a *se'nnight*, i.e. the interval between two Sabbaths; likewise the plural in all the above applications:—sabbath (day), week.

4522. σαγήνη, sagēnē, *sag-ay´-nay*; from a derivative of **σάττω**, *sattō* (to *equip*) meaning *furniture*, especially a *pack-saddle* (which in the East is merely a bag of *netted* rope); a "*seine*" for fishing:—net.

Noun meaning large net, dragnet, seine, used in fishing. It had floats on top and weights on the bottom and was capable of catching many different kinds of fish at once. It could be drawn in either from boats or from the shore. Only used in Mt 13:47.

Syn.: *díktuon* (1350), a net in a general sense; *amphíblēstron* (293), casting net.

4523. Σαδδουκαῖος, Saddoukaios, *sad-doo-kah´-yos*; probably a derivative from 4524; a *Sadducæan* (i.e. *Tsadokian*), or follower of a certain heretical Israelite:—Sadducee.

4524. Σαδώκ, Sadōk, *sad-oke´*; of Hebrew origin [6659]; *Sadoc* (i.e. *Tsadok*), an Israelite:—Sadoc.

4525. σαίνω, sainō, *sah´ee-no*; akin to 4579; to *wag* (as a dog its tail fawningly), i.e. (genitive) to *shake* (figurative, *disturb*):—move.

4526. σάκκος, sakkos, *sak´-kos*; of Hebrew origin [8242]; "*sack*"-*cloth*, i.e. *mohair* (the material or garments made of it, worn as a sign of grief):—sackcloth.

4527. Σαλά, Sala, *sal-ah´*; of Hebrew origin [7974]; *Sala* (i.e. *Shelach*), a patriarch:—Sala.

4528. Σαλαθιήλ, Salathiēl, *sal-ath-ee-ale´*; of Hebrew origin [7597]; *Salathiël* (i.e. *Sheältiël*), an Israelite:—Salathiel.

4529. Σαλαμίς, Salamis, *sal-am-ece´*; probably from 4535 (from the *surge* on the shore); *Salamis*, a place in Cyprus:—Salamis.

4530. Σαλείμ, Saleim, *sal-ime´*; probably from the same as 4531; *Salim*, a place in Palestine:—Salim.

4531. σαλεύω, saleuō, *sal-yoo´-o*; from 4535; to *waver*, i.e. *agitate, rock, topple* or (by implication) *destroy*; (figurative) to *disturb, incite*:—move, shake (together), which can [-not] be shaken, stir up.

4532. Σαλήμ, Salēm, *sal-ame´*; of Hebrew origin [8004]; *Salem* (i.e. *Shalem*), a place in Palestine:—Salem.

4533. Σαλμών, Salmōn, *sal-mone´*; of Hebrew origin [8012]; *Salmon*, an Israelite:—Salmon.

4534. Σαλμώνη, Salmōnē, *sal-mo´-nay*; perhaps of similar origin to 4529; *Salmone*, a place in Crete:—Salmone.

4535. σάλος, salos, *sal´-os*; probably from the base of 4525; a *vibration*, i.e. (special) *billow*:—wave.

4536. σάλπιγξ, salpigx, *sal´-pinx*; perhaps from 4535 (through the idea of *quavering* or *reverberation*); a *trumpet*:—trump (-et).

4537. σαλπίζω, salpizō, *sal-pid´-zo*; from 4536; to *trumpet*, i.e. *sound a blast* (literal or figurative):—(which are yet to) sound (a trumpet).

4538. σαλπιστής, salpistēs, *sal-pis-tace´*; from 4537; a *trumpeter*:—trumpeter.

4539. Σαλώμη, Salōmē, *sal-o´-may*; probably of Hebrew origin [feminine from 7965]; *Salomè* (i.e. *Shelomah*), an Israelitess:—Salome.

4540. Σαμάρεια, Samareia, *sam-ar´-i-ah*; of Hebrew origin [8111]; *Samaria* (i.e. *Shomeron*), a city and region of Palestine:—Samaria.

4541. Σαμαρείτης, Samareitēs, *sam-ar-i´-tace*; from 4540; a *Samarite*, i.e. inhabitant of Samaria:—Samaritan.

4542. Σαμαρεῖτις, Samareitis, *sam-ar-i´-tis*; feminine of 4541; a *Samaritess*, i.e. woman of Samaria:—of Samaria.

4543. Σαμοθράκη, Samothraikē, *sam-oth-rak´-ay*; from 4544 and **Θρᾴκη**, *Thraikē* (*Thrace*); *Samo-thracè* (*Samos of Thrace*), an island in the Mediterranean:—Samothracia.

4544. Σάμος, Samos, *sam´-os*; of uncertain affinity; *Samus*, an island of the Mediterranean:—Samos.

4545. Σαμουήλ, Samouēl, *sam-oo-ale´*; of Hebrew origin [8050]; *Samuel* (i.e. *Shemuel*), an Israelite:—Samuel.

4546. Σαμψών, Sampsōn, *samp-sone´*; of Hebrew origin [8123]; *Sampson* (i.e. *Shimshon*), an Israelite:—Samson.

4547. σανδάλιον, sandalion, *san-dal´-ee-on*; neuter of a derivative of **σάνδαλον**, *sandalon* (a "*sandal*"; of uncertain origin); a *slipper* or *sole-pad*:—sandal.

4548. σανίς, sanis, *san-ece´*; of uncertain affinity; a *plank*:—board.

4549. Σαούλ, Saoul, *sah-ool´*; of Hebrew origin [7586]; *Saül* (i.e. *Shaül*), the Jewish name of *Paul*:—Saul. Compare 4569.

4550. σαπρός, sapros, *sap-ros´*; from 4595; *rotten*, i.e. *worthless* (literal or moral):—bad, corrupt. Compare 4190.

4551. Σαπφείρη, Sappheirē, *sap-fi´-ray*; feminine of 4552; *Sapphirè*, an Israelitess:—Sapphira.

4552. σάπφειρος, sappheiros, *sap´-fi-ros*; of Hebrew origin [5601]; a "*sapphire*" or *lapis-lazuli* gem:—sapphire.

4553. σαργάνη, sarganē, *sar-gan´-ay*; apparently of Hebrew origin [8276]; a *basket* (as *interwoven* or *wicker*-work):—basket.

4554. Σάρδεις, Sardeis, *sar´-dice*; plural of uncertain derivative; *Sardis*, a place in Asia Minor:—Sardis.

4555. σάρδινος, sardinos, *sar´-dee-nos*; from the same as 4556; *sardine* (3037 being implication), i.e. a gem, so called:—sardine.

4556. σάρδιος, sardios, *sar´-dee-os*; properly adjective from an uncertain base; *sardian* (3037 being implication), i.e. (as noun) the gem so called:—sardius.

4557. σαρδόνυξ, sardonux, *sar-don´-oox*; from the base of 4556 and **ὄνυξ**, *onux* (the *nail* of a finger; hence the "*onyx*" stone); a "*sardonyx*," i.e. the gem so called:—sardonyx.

4558. Σάρεπτα, Sarepta, *sar´-ep-tah*; of Hebrew origin [6886]; *Sarepta* (i.e. *Tsarephath*), a place in Palestine:—Sarepta.

4559. σαρκικός, sarkikos, *sar-kee-kos´*; from 4561; *pertaining to flesh*, i.e. (by extension) *bodily, temporal*, or (by implication) *animal, unregenerate*:—carnal, fleshly.

Adjective from *sárx* (4561), flesh. Fleshly, carnal, pertaining to the flesh or body, the opposite of *pneumatikós* (4152), spiritual. Used only in the epistles.

(I) Generally, spoken of things, things of the body, external, temporal (Ro 15:27; 1Co 9:11).

(II) Implying weakness, frailty, imperfection: e.g., of persons as being carnal, worldly (1Co 3:1, 3, 4); of things as carnal, human, frail, transient, temporary (2Co 1:12; 10:4; Heb 7:16).

(III) Spoken of a tendency to satisfy the flesh, implying sinfulness, sinful inclination, carnal (Ro 7:14; 1Pe 2:11).

Syn.: *sōmatikós* (4984), bodily; *phusikós* (5446), physical; *psuchikós* (5591), natural, pertaining to our present body or existence.

4560. σάρκινος, sarkinos, *sar´-kee-nos*; from 4561; *similar to flesh*, i.e. (by analogy) *soft*:—fleshly.

Adjective from *sárx* (4561), flesh, body. Fleshly, material, and therefore soft, yielding to an impression. Only in 2Co 3:3.

4561. σάρξ, sarx, *sarx*; probably from the base of 4563; *flesh* (as *stripped* of the skin), i.e. (strictly) the *meat* of an animal (as food), or (by extension) the *body* (as opposed to the soul [or spirit], or as the symbol of what is external, or as the means of kindred), or (by implication) *human nature* (with its frailties [physical or moral] and passions), or (special) a *human being* (as such):—carnal (-ly, + -ly minded), flesh ([-ly]).

Noun meaning flesh of a living creature in distinction from that of a dead one, which is *kréas* (2907), meat.

(I) Specifically flesh, as one of the constituent parts of the body (Lk 24:39; 1Co 15:39). In the plural, fleshy parts, spoken of as being consumed (Jas 5:3; Rev 17:16; 19:18).

(II) By metonymy, flesh as used for the body, the corpus, the material nature as distinguished from the spiritual and intangible (*pneúma* [4151], the spirit). This usage of *sárx* is far more frequent in the NT than in classical writers.

(A) Generally and without any good or evil quality implied. **(1)** The opposite of *to pneúma*, the spirit expressed (Jn 6:52; Ac 2:26, 31; 1Co 5:5; 2Co 7:1; 12:7; Col 1:24; 2:1, 5, 23; Heb 2:14; 9:10, 13; 1Pe 3:21; Jude 8, 23). Metaphorically in Jn 6:51, "and the bread … is my flesh," meaning that Jesus Himself is the principle of life and nutrition to the regenerated soul (see vv. 53–56). Specifically used of the mortal body in distinction from a future and spiritual existence (2Co 4:11; Gal 2:20; Php 1:22, 24; 1Pe 4:2). **(2)** Used for that which is merely external or only apparent, in opposition to what is spiritual or real (Jn 6:63; 8:15; 1Co 1:26; 2Co 5:16; Eph 6:5; Col 3:22; Phm 16); of outward affliction, trials (1Co 7:28; 2Co 7:5; Gal 4:13, 14; 1Pe 4:1); specifically of the meticulous observance of Judaism as an attempt to earn salvation (Ro 2:28; 4:1; 2Co 11:18; Gal 3:3; Gal 6:12, 13; Eph 2:11; Php 3:3, 4; Col 2:13). **(3)** As the medium of natural generation and descent, and consequently kindred or natural descendants (Jn 1:13; Ac 2:30; Ro 9:3, 8; 1Co 10:18; Gal 4:23, 29; Heb 12:9). Of one's own countrymen (Ro 11:14).

(B) As implying weakness, frailty, imperfection, both physical and moral; the opposite being *pneúma* (4151), the spirit (Mt 16:7; 26:41; Mk 14:38; Jn 3:6; Ro 6:19; 1Co 15:15; 2Co 1:17; 10:2, 3; Gal 1:16; Eph 6:12).

(C) As implying sinfulness, proneness to sin, the carnal nature, the seat of carnal appetites and desires, of sinful passions and affections whether physical or moral (Ro 7:5, 18, 25; 8:3, 7, 8, 12; 13:14; Gal 5:13; Eph 2:3; Col 2:1, 18; 2Pe 2:10, 18; 1Jn 2:16). The Greeks ascribed a similar influence to the body (*sō̂ma* [4983]), as opposed to *Pneúma* (4151), the Spirit, referring to the Holy Spirit or His influences (Ro 8:1, 4–6, 9, 13; Gal 5:16, 17, 19, 24; 6:8).

(III) By metonymy, flesh, human nature, man (Mt 24:22; Mk 13:20; Lk 3:6; Jn 17:2; Ac 2:17; Ro 3:20; 1Co 1:29; Gal 2:16; 1Pe 1:24). Figuratively, of the union of husband and wife as one flesh (Mt 19:5, 6; Mk 10:8; 1Co 6:16; Eph 5:31). Compare Jude 7. Used specifically of the incarnation of Christ, His incarnate human nature (Jn 1:14; Ro 1:3; 9:5; Eph 2:15; Col 1:22; 1Ti 3:16; Heb 5:7; 10:20; 1Pe 3:18; 4:1; 1Jn 4:2, 3; 2Jn 7).

Deriv.: *sarkikós* (4559), fleshy, pertaining to the flesh, carnal, sensual; *sárkinos* (4560), of the flesh, made of flesh.

Syn.: *sō̂ma* (4983), body. Also *kréas* (2907), flesh in the sense of meat; *ptō̂ma* (4430), a corpse; *chrṓs* (5559), the body, but referring rather to the exterior of it, the surface.

4562. Σαρούχ, Sarouch, *sar-ooch´*; of Hebrew origin [8286]; *Saruch* (i.e. *Serug*), a patriarch:—Saruch.

4563. σαρόω, saroō, *sar-o´-o*; from a derivative of **σαιρω**, *sairō* (to *brush* off; akin to 4951) meaning a *broom*; to *sweep*:—sweep.

4564. Σάῤῥα, Sarrha, *sar´-hrah*; of Hebrew origin [8283]; *Sarra* (i.e. *Sarah*), the wife of Abraham:—Sara, Sarah.

4565. Σάρων, Sarōn, *sar´-one*; of Hebrew origin [8289]; *Saron* (i.e. *Sharon*), a district of Palestine:—Saron.

4566. Σατᾶν, Satan, *sat-an´*; of Hebrew origin [7854]; *Satan*, i.e. the *devil*:—Satan. Compare 4567.

4567. Σατανᾶς, Satanas, *sat-an-as´*; of Chaldee origin corresponding to 4566 (with the definite affix); *the accuser*, i.e. the *devil*:—Satan.

Noun transliterated from the Hebrew *Sātān* (7854, OT), adversary. Satan. In the NT, as a transliteration of the Hebrew proper name for the Devil (see *diábolos* [1228], devil). Satan (Mt 4:10; 12:26; Mk 4:15; Lk 10:18; 22:31; 26:18; et al.). As present in men, tempting them to evil (Mt 16:23; Mk 8:33; Lk 22:3; Jn 13:27; Ac 5:3; 2Co 11:14; Rev 12:9).

4568. σάτον, saton, *sat´-on*; of Hebrew origin [5429]; a certain *measure* for things dry:—measure.

4569. Σαῦλος, Saulos, *sow´-los*; of Hebrew origin, the same as 4549; *Saulus* (i.e. *Shaül*), the Jewish name of *Paul*:—Saul.

4570. σβέννυμι, sbennumi, *sben´-noo-mee*; a prolonged form of an apparently primary verb; to *extinguish* (literal or figurative):—go out, quench.

4571. σέ, se, *seh*; accusative singular of 4771; *thee*:—thee, thou, × thy house.

4572. σεαυτοῦ, seautou, *seh-ow-too´*; genitive from 4571 and 846; also dative of the same, **σεαυτῷ**, *seautōi*, *seh-ow-to´*; and accusative **σεαυτόν**, *seauton*, *seh-ow-ton´*; likewise contracted **σαυτοῦ**, *sautou*, *sow-too´*; **σαυτῷ**, *sautōi*, *sow-to´*; and **σαυτόν**, *sauton*, *sow-ton´*; respectively; *of* (*with, to*) *thyself*:—thee, thine own self, (thou) thy (-self).

4573. σεβάζομαι, sebazomai, *seb-ad´-zom-ahee*; middle from a derivative of 4576; to *venerate*, i.e. *adore*:—worship.

Middle deponent from *sébas* (n.f.), reverential awe, which is from *sébomai* (4576), to worship, to pay high respect. To be in worship of, to fear. In the NT, to stand in awe of someone, to reverence, venerate, worship. Used only in Ro 1:25.

Deriv.: *sébasma* (4574), object of worship; *sebastós* (4575), venerable, august.

Syn.: *eulabéomai* (2125), to reverence inwardly; *therapeúō* (2323), to serve; *proskunéō* (4352), to make obeisance, worship, reverence; *latreúō* (3000), to perform (religious) service.

4574. σέβασμα, sebasma, *seb´-as-mah*; from 4573; something *adored*, i.e. an *object of worship* (god, altar, etc.):—devotion, that is worshipped.

Noun from *sebázomai* (4573), to worship, venerate. An object of worship, anything venerated and worshiped, e.g., a god (Ac 17:23; 2Th 2:4).

4575. σεβαστός, sebastos, *seb-as-tos´*; from 4573; *venerable* (*august*), i.e. (as noun) a title of the Roman *Emperor*, or (as adjective) *imperial*:—Augustus (-').

4576. σέβομαι, sebomai, *seb´-om-ahee*; middle of an apparently primary verb; to *revere*, i.e. *adore*:—devout, religious, worship.

To worship, to reverence. In the NT, only in the middle voice (Mt 15:9; Mk 7:7; Ac 16:14; 18:13; 19:27). The participle, used as a substantive, a worshipper of the true God, spoken of Gentile proselytes and the Jews (Ac 13:43, 50; 16:14; 17:4, 17; 18:7).

Deriv.: *asebḗs* (765), godless; *eusebḗs* (2152), devout, godly; *theosebḗs* (2318), godly; *semnós* (4586), worthy of respect.

Syn.: *eulabéomai* (2125), to reverence inwardly; *latreúō* (3000), to perform (religious) service; *proskunéō* (4352), to make obeisance, worship, reverence.

4577. σειρά, seira, *si-rah´*; probably from 4951 through its congener **εἴρω**, *eirō* (to *fasten*; akin to 138); a *chain* (as *binding* or *drawing*):—chain.

4578. σεισμός, seismos, *sice-mos´*; from 4579; a *commotion,* i.e. (of the air) a *gale,* (of the ground) an *earthquake*:—earthquake, tempest.

Noun from *seíō* (4579), to shake. Earthquake, a shaking.

(I) Generally, in the sea meaning a tempest, tornado (Mt 8:24).

(II) Specifically, an earthquake (Mt 24:7; 27:54; 28:2; Mk 13:8; Lk 21:11; Ac 16:26; Rev 6:12; 8:5; 11:13, 19; 16:18).

Syn.: *thúella* (2366), storm, tempest; *laílaps* (2978), a tempest, hurricane; *cheimṓn* (5494), a winter storm.

4579. σείω, seiō, *si´-o*; apparently a primary verb; to *rock* (*vibrate,* properly sideways or to and fro), i.e. (genitive) to *agitate* (in any direction; cause to *tremble*); (figurative) to throw into a *tremor* (of fear or concern):—move, quake, shake.

4580. Σεκοῦνδος, Sekoundos, *sek-oon´-dos*; of Latin origin; "*second*"; *Secundus,* a Christian:—Secundus.

4581. Σελεύκεια, Seleukeia, *sel-yook´-i-ah*; from **Σέλευκος, *Seleukos*** (*Seleucus,* a Syrian king); *Seleuceia,* a place in Syria:—Seleucia.

4582. σελήνη, selēnē, *sel-ay´-nay*; from **σέλας, *selas*** (*brilliancy*; probably akin to the alternate of 138, through the idea of *attractiveness*); the *moon*:—moon.

4583. σεληνιάζομαι, selēniazomai, *sel-ay-nee-ad´-zom-ahee*; middle or passive from a presumed derivative of 4582; to *be moon-struck,* i.e. *crazy*:—be lunatic.

4584. Σεμΐ, Semi, *sem-eh-ee´*; of Hebrew origin [8096]; *Semeï* (i.e. *Shimi*), an Israelite:—Semei.

4585. σεμίδαλις, semidalis, *sem-id´-al-is*; probably of foreign origin; fine wheaten *flour*:—fine flour.

4586. σεμνός, semnos, *sem-nos´*; from 4576; *venerable,* i.e. *honourable*:—grave, honest.

Adjective from *sébomai* (4576), to worship, venerate. Venerable, respectable, honourable, dignified. In the NT, spoken of things: honourable, reputable (Php 4:8); spoken of persons: grave, dignified (1Ti 3:8, 11; Tit 2:2).

Deriv.: *semnótēs* (4587), gravity.

Syn.: *éntimos* (1784), honourable; *eugenḗs* (2104), noble; *euschḗmōn* (2158), honourable, decorous; *hieroprepḗs* (2412), reverent.

4587. σεμνότης, semnotēs, *sem-not´-ace*; from 4586; *venerableness,* i.e. *probity*:—gravity, honesty.

Noun from *semnós* (4586), venerable. Dignity, honesty, seriousness. Aristotle defined *semnótēs* as standing between not caring if you please anyone and endeavoring at all costs to please everybody (1Ti 2:2; 3:4; Tit 2:7).

Syn.: *aidṓs* (127), modesty, reverence toward God; *euprépeia* (2143), gracefulness; *eusébeia* (2150), godliness, piety.

4588. Σέργιος, Sergios, *serg´-ee-os*; of Latin origin; *Sergius,* a Roman:—Sergius.

4589. Σήθ, Sēth, *sayth*; of Hebrew origin [8352]; *Seth* (i.e. *Sheth*), a patriarch:—Seth.

4590. Σήμ, Sēm, *same*; of Hebrew origin [8035]; *Sem* (i.e. *Shem*), a patriarch:—Sem.

4591. σημαίνω, sēmainō, *say-mah´ee-no*; from **σῆμα, *sēma*** (a *mark*; of uncertain derivative); to *indicate*:—signify.

4592. σημεῖον, sēmeion, *say-mi´-on*; neuter of a presumed derivative of the base of 4591; an *indication,* especially ceremonial or supernatural:—miracle, sign, token, wonder.

Noun meaning sign of something past, a memorial, a monument. In the NT, a sign, a mark, a token.

(I) Particularly a sign by which something is designated, distinguished, known (Mt 26:48; Ro 4:11). Specifically a sign by which the character and truth of any person or thing is known, a token, proof (Lk 2:12; 2Co 12:12; 2Th 3:17).

(II) A sign by which the divine power in majesty is made known, a supernatural event or act, a token, wonder, or miracle by which the power and presence of God is manifested, either directly or through the agency of those whom He sends (Sept.: Ex 4:8, 17, 28, 30).

(A) As wrought of God (Mt 12:39; 16:4; Lk 11:29; 1Co 14:22). Spoken by metonymy of persons sent from God, whose character and acts are a manifestation of the divine power (Lk 2:34; 11:30). Of signs, wonders, miracles which God did through someone, joined with *térata* (5059), things out of the ordinary, wonders (Ac 2:22, 43; 4:30; 5:12; 14:3; 15:12). Specifically as revealing future events, a sign of future things, a portent, presage (Mt 16:3), the miraculous events and deeds which reveal the coming of the Messiah in His kingdom (Mt 24:3, 30; Mk 13:4; Lk 21:7, 11, 25; Ac 2:19; Rev 12:1, 3; 15:1).

(B) Of signs, wonders, miracles wrought by Jesus and His apostles and the prophets in proof and furtherance of their divine mission (Mt 12:38, 39; 16:1, 4; Mk 8:11, 12; 16:17, 20; Lk 11:16, 29; 23:8; Ac 4:16, 22; 8:6; 1Co 1:22). In John the word is used only in this sense (Jn 2:11, 18, 23; 3:2; 4:54; 6:2, 14, 26, 30; 7:31; 9:16; 10:41; 11:47; 12:18, 37; 20:30).

(C) Spoken by analogy of signs, wonders, wrought by false prophets claiming to act by divine authority (Rev 13:13, 14; 16:14; 19:20); with *térata* (Mt 24:24; Mk 13:22; 2Th 2:9).

Deriv.: *sēmeióō* (4593), to denote, signify.

Syn.: *dúnamis* (1411), mighty work, miracle; *thaúma* (2295), wonder; *thaumásios* (2297), a miracle; *megaleíon* (3167), great work; *téras* (5059), wonder.

4593. σημειόω, sēmeioō, *say-mi-o´-o*; from 4592; to *distinguish,* i.e. *mark* (for avoidance):—note.

4594. σήμερον, sēmeron, *say´-mer-on*; neuter (as adverb) of a presumed compound of the article 3588 (4595, **τ** changed to **σ**) and 2250; on *the* (i.e. *this*) *day* (or *night* current or just passed); general *now* (i.e. at *present, hitherto*):—this (to-) day.

4595. σήπω, sēpō, *say´-po*; apparently a primary verb; to *putrefy,* i.e. (figurative) *perish*:—be corrupted.

4596. σηρικός, sērikos, *say-ree-kos´*; from **Σήρ, *Sēr*** (an Indian tribe from whom *silk* was procured; hence the name of the *silkworm*); *Seric,* i.e. *silken* (neuter as noun, a *silky* fabric):—silk.

4597. σής, sēs, *sace*; apparently of Hebrew origin [5580]; a *moth*:—moth.

4598. σητόβρωτος, sētobrōtos, *say-tob´-ro-tos*; from 4597 and a derivative of 977; *moth-eaten*:—motheaten.

4599. σθενόω, sthenoō, *sthen-o´-o*; from **σθένος, *sthenos*** (bodily *vigour*; probably akin to the base of 2476); to *strengthen,* i.e. (figurative) *confirm* (in spiritual knowledge and power):—strengthen.

From *sthénos* (n.f.), strength. To strengthen, to make one more able to do something. Used only in 1Pe 5:10, where along with *stērízō* (4741), to make firm, it is used to speak of the strength Christ gives those who have endured suffering. The idea of these two Greek words is very similar. However, *stērízō* is used of making one firm, making them more resolved in their belief in the truth, while *sthenóō* is used of making one more capable, more able to endure trials.

Syn.: *endunamóō* (1743), to make strong; *epischúō* (2001), to reinforce, to strengthen more.

4600. σιαγών, siagōn, *see-ag-one´*; of uncertain derivative; the *jaw*-bone, i.e. (by implication) the *cheek* or side of the face:—cheek.

4601. σιγάω, sigaō, *see-gah´-o*; from 4602; to keep silent (transitive or intransitive):—keep close (secret, silence), hold peace.

4602. σιγή, sigē, *see-gay´*; apparently from **σίζω, *sizō*** (to *hiss,* i.e. *hist* or *hush*); *silence*:—silence. Compare 4623.

4603. σιδήρεος, sidēreos, *sid-ay´-reh-os*; from 4604; made *of iron*:—(of) iron.

4604. σίδηρος, sidēros, *sid´-ay-ros*; of uncertain derivative; *iron*:—iron.

4605. Σιδών, Sidōn, *sid-one´*; of Hebrew origin [6721]; *Sidon* (i.e. *Tsidon*), a place in Palestine:—Sidon.

4606. Σιδώνιος, Sidōnios, *sid-o´-nee-os*; from 4605; a *Sidonian*, i.e. inhabitant of Sidon:—of Sidon.

4607. σικάριος, sikarios, *sik-ar´-ee-os*; of Latin origin; a *dagger-man* or *assassin*; a *freebooter* (Jewish *fanatic* outlawed by the Romans):—murderer. Compare 5406.

Noun from the Latin *sicarius,* which is from *sica,* dagger. An assassin, murderer. Only in Ac 21:38. Bands of robbers of this character and referred to by this name were common in Judea under the Roman governors.

4608. σίκερα, sikera, *sik´-er-ah*; of Hebrew origin [7941]; an *intoxicant*, i.e. intensely fermented *liquor*:—strong drink.

Indeclinable noun transliterated from the Hebrew *shēkār* (7941, OT), strong drink. Strong drink, any intoxicating liquor, usually in reference to those prepared from grain, fruit, honey, or dates (Lk 1:15, where it occurs together with *oínos* [3631], wine).

4609. Σίλας, Silas, *see´-las*; contracted from 4610; *Silas*, a Christian:—Silas.

4610. Σιλουανός, Silouanos, *sil-oo-an-os´*; of Latin origin; "*silvan*"; *Silvanus*, a Christian:—Silvanus. Compare 4609.

4611. Σιλωάμ, Silōam, *sil-o-am´*; of Hebrew origin [7975]; *Siloäm* (i.e. *Shiloäch*), a pool of Jerusalem:—Siloam.

4612. σιμικίνθιον, simikinthion, *sim-ee-kin´-thee-on*; of Latin origin; a *semicinctium* or *half-girding*, i.e. narrow covering (*apron*):—apron.

4613. Σίμων, Simōn, *see´-mone*; of Hebrew origin [8095]; *Simon* (i.e. *Shimon*), the name of nine Israelites:—Simon. Compare 4826.

4614. Σινᾶ, Sina, *see-nah´*; of Hebrew origin [5514]; *Sina* (i.e. *Sinai*), a mountain in Arabia:—Sina.

4615. σίναπι, sinapi, *sin´-ap-ee*; perhaps from **σίνομαι**, ***sinomai*** (to *hurt*, i.e. *sting*); *mustard* (the plant):—mustard.

4616. σινδών, sindōn, *sin-done´*; of uncertain (perhaps foreign) origin; *byssos*, i.e. bleached *linen* (the cloth or a garment of it):—(fine) linen (cloth).

4617. σινιάζω, siniazō, *sin-ee-ad´-zo*; from **σινιον**, ***sinion*** (a *sieve*); to *riddle* (figurative):—sift.

4618. σιτευτός, siteutos, *sit-yoo-tos´*; from a derivative of 4621; *grain-fed*, i.e. *fattened*:—fatted.

4619. σιτιστός, sitistos, *sit-is-tos´*; from a derivative of 4621; *grained*, i.e. *fatted*:—fatling.

4620. σιτόμετρον, sitometron, *sit-om´-et-ron*; from 4621 and 3358; a *grain-measure*, i.e. (by implication) *ration* (*allowance* of food):—portion of meat.

4621. σῖτος, sitos, *see´-tos*; plural irregular neuter **σῖτα**, ***sita***, *see´-tah*; of uncertain derivative; *grain*, especially *wheat*:—corn, wheat.

4622. Σιών, Siōn, *see-own´*; of Hebrew origin [6726]; *Sion* (i.e. *Tsijon*), a hill of Jerusalem; (figurative) the *Church* (militant or triumphant):—Sion.

4623. σιωπάω, siōpaō, *see-o-pah´-o*; from **σιωπη**, ***siōpē*** (*silence*, i.e. a *hush*; properly *muteness*, i.e. *involuntary* stillness, or *inability* to speak; and thus differing from 4602, which is rather a voluntary *refusal* or *indisposition* to speak, although the terms are often used synonymously); to *be dumb* (but not *deaf* also, like 2974 properly); (figurative) to *be calm* (as *quiet water*):—dumb, (hold) peace.

4624. σκανδαλίζω, skandalizō, *skan-dal-id´-zo*; ("scandalize"); from 4625; to *entrap*, i.e. *trip* up (figurative, *stumble* [transitive] or *entice* to sin, apostasy or displeasure):—(make to) offend.

From *skándalon* (4625), a trap, stumbling block. To cause to stumble and fall, not found in Greek writers. In the NT, figuratively, in a moral sense, to be a stumbling block to someone, to cause to stumble at or in something, to give a cause of offence to someone.

Transitively:

(I) Generally, to offend, vex, particularly to scandalize (Mt 17:27; Jn 6:61; 1Co 8:13); in the passive voice, to be offended by someone, to take offence at his character, words, conduct, so as to reject him (Mt 11:6; 13:57; 15:12; 26:31, 33; Mk 6:3; 14:27; Lk 7:23).

(II) Causative, to cause to offend, lead astray, lead into sin, be a stumbling block or the occasion of one's sinning (Mt 5:29, 30; 18:6, 8, 9; Mk 9:42, 43, 45, 47; Lk 17:2). Hence in the passive, to be offended, be led astray or into sin, fall away from the truth (Mt 13:21; 24:10; Mk 4:17; Jn 16:1; Ro 14:1; 2Co 11:29).

Syn.: *píptō* (4098), to fail or fall; *proskóptō* (4350), to stumble; *ptaíō* (4417), to offend, stumble, sin.

4625. σκάνδαλον, skandalon, *skan´-dal-on*; ("scandal"); probably from a derivative of 2578; a *trap-stick* (*bent* sapling), i.e. *snare* (figurative, *cause* of displeasure or sin):—occasion to fall (of stumbling), offence, thing that offends, stumbling block.

Noun meaning the trigger of a trap on which the bait is placed, and which, when touched by the animal, springs and causes it to close causing entrapment. In the NT, stumbling block, offence, only figuratively in a moral sense.

(I) Generally as a cause of stumbling, falling, ruin, morally and spiritually. Spoken of Christ as the rock of stumbling (Ro 9:33; 11:9; 1Pe 2:7).

(II) As a cause of offence and indignation (Mt 16:23; 1Co 1:23; Gal 5:11).

(III) As a cause or occasion of sinning or of falling away from the truth (Mt 18:7; Lk 17:1; Ro 14:13; 16:17; 1Jn 2:10; Rev 2:14). By metonymy, spoken of persons (Mt 13:41).

Deriv.: *skandalízō* (4624), to cause to stumble.

Syn.: *próskomma* (4348), an obstacle; *proskopḗ* (4349), occasion of stumbling.

4626. σκάπτω, skaptō, *skap´-to*; apparently a primary verb; to *dig*:—dig.

4627. σκάφη, skaphē, *skaf´-ay*; a "*skiff*" (as if *dug* out), or *yawl* (carried aboard a large vessel for landing):—boat.

4628. σκέλος, skelos, *skel´-os*; apparently from **σκέλλω**, ***skellō*** (to *parch*; through the idea of *leanness*); the *leg* (as *lank*):—leg.

4629. σκέπασμα, skepasma, *skep´-as-mah*; from a derivative of **σκέπας** ***skepas*** (a *covering*; perhaps akin to the base of 4649 through the idea of *noticeableness*); *clothing*:—raiment.

4630. Σκευᾶς, Skeuas, *skyoo-as´*; apparently of Latin origin; *left-handed; Scevas* (i.e. *Scævus*), an Israelite:—Sceva.

4631. σκευή, skeuē, *skyoo-ay´*; from 4632; *furniture*, i.e. spare *tackle*:—tackling.

4632. σκεῦος, skeuos, *skyoo´-os*; of uncertain affinity; a *vessel*, *implement*, *equipment* or *apparatus* (literal or figurative [specially a *wife* as contributing to the usefulness of the husband]):—goods, sail, stuff, vessel.

4633. σκηνή, skēnē, *skay-nay´*; apparently akin to 4632 and 4639; a *tent* or cloth hut (literal or figurative):—habitation, tabernacle.

4634. σκηνοπηγία, skēnopēgia, *skay-nop-ayg-ee´-ah*; from 4636 and 4078; the *Festival of Tabernacles* (so called from the custom of erecting booths for temporary homes):—tabernacles.

4635. σκηνοποιός, skēnopoios, *skay-nop-oy-os´*; from 4633 and 4160; a *manufacturer of tents*:—tentmaker.

4636. σκῆνος, skēnos, *skay´-nos*; from 4633; a *hut* or *temporary* residence, i.e. (figurative) the human *body* (as the abode of the spirit):—tabernacle.

4637. σκηνόω, skēnoō, *skay-no´-o*; from 4636; to *tent* or *encamp*, i.e. (figurative) to *occupy* (as a mansion) or (special) to *reside* (as God did in the tabernacle of old, a symbol of protection and communion):—dwell.

4638. σκήνωμα, skēnōma, *skay´-no-mah*; from 4637; an *encampment*, i.e. (figurative) the *temple* (as God's residence), the *body* (as a tenement for the soul):—tabernacle.

4639. σκιά, skia, *skee´-ah*; apparently a primary word; "*shade*" or a shadow (literal or figurative [darkness of *error* or an *adumbration*]):—shadow.

4640. σκιρτάω, skirtaō, *skeer-tah´-o*; akin to **σκαίρω, *skairō*** (to *skip*); to *jump*, i.e. sympathetically *move* (as the *quickening* of a foetus):—leap (for joy).

4641. σκληροκαρδία, sklērokardia, *sklay-rok-ar-dee´-ah*; feminine of a compound of 4642 and 2588; *hardheartedness*, i.e. (special) *destitution of* (spiritual) *perception*:—hardness of heart.

Noun from *sklērós* (4642), hard, and *kardía* (2588), heart. Hardness of heart, stubbornness, obstinacy, perverseness. Spoken of the Jews (Mt 19:8; Mk 10:5). Spoken of the refusal of the disciples to believe those who had seen the resurrected Christ (Mk 16:14).

Syn.: *ástorgos* (794), without natural affection, hard-hearted; *pṓrōsis* (4457), dullness of heart; *sklērótēs* (4643), callousness.

4642. σκληρός, sklēros, *sklay-ros´*; from the base of 4628; *dry*, i.e. *hard* or *tough* (figurative, *harsh, severe*):—fierce, hard.

Adjective from *skéllō* (n.f.), to harden, dry up. Dried up, dry, hard, stiff; of the voice or sounds as hoarse or harsh; of things as hard, tough, not soft. Hence, in the NT, hard.

(I) Of winds as fierce, violent (Jas 3:4).

(II) Of things spoken as hard, harsh, offensive, such as words (Jn 6:60; Jude 15). Of things done as being hard, difficult, grievous (Ac 9:5; 26:14).

(III) Of persons as harsh, stern, severe (Mt 25:24).

Deriv.: *sklērokardía* (4641), hardness of heart; *sklērótēs* (4643), hardness; *sklērotráchēlos* (4644), stiff-necked; *sklērúnō* (4645), to make stubborn or hard.

Syn.: *austērós* (840), rough, severe, austere (*Sklērós* always indicates a harsh, brutal character which is not the case with *austērós*); *dúskolos* (1422), difficult, finicky; *chalepós* (5467), perilous.

4643. σκληρότης, sklērotēs, *sklay-rot´-ace*; from 4642; *callousness*, i.e. (figurative) *stubbornness*:—hardness.

Noun from *sklērós* (4642), dry, hard. Hardness, dryness. In the NT, only in Ro 2:5, figuratively of hardness of heart, obstinacy.

Syn.: *pṓrōsis* (4457), a hardening, dullness of the heart.

4644. σκληροτράχηλος, sklērotrachēlos, *sklay-rot-rakh´-ah-los*; from 4642 and 5137; *hardnaped*, i.e. (figurative) *obstinate*:—stiffnecked.

4645. σκληρύνω, sklērunō, *sklay-roo´-no*; from 4642; to *indurate*, i.e. (figurative) *render stubborn*:—harden.

From *sklērós* (4642), hard. To make hard or stiff, make obdurate. In the NT applied only figuratively in a moral sense, to harden, to make obstinate, perverse (Ac 19:9; Ro 9:18; Heb 3:8, 13, 15; 4:7).

Syn.: *pōróō* (4456), to make hard, callous.

4646. σκολιός, skolios, *skol-ee-os´*; from the base of 4628; *warped*, i.e. *winding*; (figurative) *perverse*:—crooked, froward, untoward.

4647. σκόλοψ, skolops, *skol´-ops*; perhaps from the base of 4628 and 3700; *withered* at the *front*, i.e. a *point* or *prickle* (figurative, a bodily *annoyance* or *disability*):—thorn.

4648. σκοπέω, skopeō, *skop-eh´-o*; from 4649; to take *aim* at (*spy*), i.e. (figurative) *regard*:—consider, take heed, look at (on), mark. Compare 3700.

From *skopós* (4649), mark, observer. To look, to watch. In the NT, to look at or upon, to behold, to regard (Lk 11:35; 2Co 4:18; Gal 6:1; Php 2:4), to mark to note (Ro 16:17; Php 3:17).

Deriv.: *episkopéō* (1983), to look after; *kataskopéō* (2684), to spy out.

Syn.: *blépō* (991), to watch; *epéchō* (1907), give attention to, mark; *horáō* (3708), to discern clearly; *proséchō* (4337), take heed, beware; *sēmeióō* (4593), to mark, note.

4649. σκοπός, skopos, *skop-os´*; ("scope"); from **σκέπτομαι, *skeptomai*** (to *peer* about ["skeptic"]; perhaps akin to 4626 through the idea of *concealment*; compare 4629); a *watch* (*sentry* or *scout*), i.e. (by implication) a *goal*:—mark.

Noun from *sképtomai* (n.f.), to look about. Goal, the mark at the end of a race. Particularly, an object set up in the distance, at which one looks and aims, e.g., a mark, a goal. Only in Php 3:14.

Deriv.: *epískopos* (1985), overseer, bishop; *skopéō* (4648), to look toward a goal, give heed.

Syn.: *télos* (5056), the point aimed at, end.

4650. σκορπίζω, skorpizō, *skor-pid´-zo*; apparently from the same as 4651 (through the idea of *penetrating*); to *dissipate*, i.e. (figurative) *put to flight, waste, be liberal*:—disperse abroad, scatter (abroad).

4651. σκορπίος, skorpios, *skor-pee´-os*; probably from an obsolete **σκέρπω, *skerpō*** (perhaps strengthened from the base of 4649 and meaning to *pierce*); a "*scorpion*" (from its *sting*):—scorpion.

4652. σκοτεινός, skoteinos, *skot-i-nos´*; from 4655; *opaque*, i.e. (figurative) *benighted*:—dark, full of darkness.

4653. σκοτία, skotia, *skot-ee´-ah*; from 4655; *dimness, obscurity* (literal or figurative):—dark (-ness).

Noun from *skótos* (4655), darkness. Darkness, the absence of light (Mt 10:27; Lk 12:3; Jn 6:17; 20:1; 1Jn 2:8, 9, 11). By metonymy, spoken of persons in moral darkness (Jn 1:5).

4654. σκοτίζω, skotizō, *skot-id´-zo*; from 4655; to *obscure* (literal or figurative):—darken.

4655. σκότος, skotos, *skot´-os*; from the base of 4639; *shadiness*, i.e. *obscurity* (literal or figurative):—darkness.

Noun meaning darkness.

(I) Particularly, spoken of physical darkness, such as the darkness that accompanied the crucifixion (Mt 27:45; Mk 15:33; Lk 23:44). Also Ac 2:20; 13:11; 1Co 4:5. Spoken of a dark place where darkness reigns, a place of eternal darkness and punishment called "outer darkness" in the parables of Jesus (Mt 13:12; 22:13; 25:31). See also 2Pe 2:17; Jude 13.

(II) Spoken figuratively of moral darkness, the absence of spiritual light and truth, including the idea of sinfulness and consequent calamity (Mt 4:16; 6:23; Lk 1:79; 11:35; Jn 3:19; Ac 26:18; Ro 2:19; 13:12; 2Co 4:6; 6:14; Eph 5:11). Spoken figuratively of persons in a state of moral darkness, wicked men under the influence of Satan (Lk 22:53; Eph 5:8; 6:12; Col 1:13).

Deriv.: *skoteinós* (4652), dark; *skotía* (4653), darkness; *skotízō* (4654), to darken, deprive of light; *skotóō* (4656), to darken.

Syn.: *achlús* (887), a thick mist, fog; *gnóphos* (1105), a thick dark cloud; *zóphos* (2217), gloom, darkness.

4656. σκοτόω, skotoō, *skot-o´-o*; from 4655; to *obscure* or *blind* (literal or figurative):—be full of darkness.

4657. σκύβαλον, skubalon, *skoo´-bal-on*; neuter of a presumed derivative of 1519 and 2965 and 906; what is *thrown to* the *dogs*, i.e. *refuse* (*ordure*):—dung.

4658. Σκύθης, Skuthēs, *skoo´-thace*; probably of foreign origin; a *Scythene* or *Scythian*, i.e. (by implication) a *savage*:—Scythian.

4659. σκυθρωπός, skuthrōpos, *skoo-thro-pos´*; from **σκυθρός, *skuthros*** (*sullen*) and a derivative of 3700; *angry-visaged*, i.e. *gloomy* or affecting a *mournful* appearance:—of a sad countenance.

4660. σκύλλω, skullō, *skool´-lo*; apparently a primary verb; to *flay*, i.e. (figurative) to *harass*:—trouble (self).

4661. σκῦλον, skulon, *skoo´-lon*; neuter from 4660; something *stripped* (as a *hide*), i.e. *booty*:—spoil.

4662. σκωληκόβρωτος, skōlēkobrōtos, *sko-lay-kob´-ro-tos*; from 4663 and a derivative of 977; *worm-eaten*, i.e. *diseased with maggots*:—eaten of worms.

4663. σκώληξ, skōlēx, *sko´-lakes*; of uncertain derivative; a *grub, maggot* or *earth-worm*:—worm.

4664. σμαράγδινος, smaragdinos, *smar-ag´-dee-nos*; from 4665; consisting *of emerald*:—emerald.

4665. σμάραγδος, smaragdos, *smar´-ag-dos*; of uncertain derivative; the *emerald* or green gem so called:—emerald.

4666. σμύρνα, smurna, *smoor´-nah*; apparently strengthened for 3464; *myrrh*:—myrrh.

4667. Σμύρνα, Smurna, *smoor´-nah*; the same as 4666; *Smyrna*, a place in Asia Minor:—Smyrna.

4668. Σμυρναῖος, Smurnaios, *smmor-nah´-yos*; from 4667; a *Smyrnæan*:—in Smyrna.

4669. σμυρνίζω, smurnizō, *smoor-nid´-zo*; from 4667; to *tincture with myrrh*, i.e. *embitter* (as a narcotic):—mingle with myrrh.

4670. Σόδομα, Sodoma, *sod´-om-ah*; plural of Hebrew origin [5467]; *Sodoma* (i.e. *Sedom*), a place in Palestine:—Sodom.

4671. σοί, soi, *soy*; dative of 4771; *to thee*:—thee, thine own, thou, thy.

4672. Σολομών, Solomōn, *sol-om-one´*; or **Σολομῶν,** ***Solomōn***; of Hebrew origin [8010]; *Solomon* (i.e. *Shelomoh*), the son of David:—Solomon.

4673. σορός, soros, *sor-os´*; probably akin to the base of 4987; a *funereal receptacle* (*urn, coffin*), i.e. (by analogy) a *bier*:—bier.

4674. σός, sos, *sos*; from 4771; *thine*:—thine (own), thy (friend).

4675. σοῦ, sou, *soo*; genitive of 4771; *of thee, thy*:— × home, thee, thine (own), thou, thy.

4676. σουδάριον, soudarion, *soo-dar´-ee-on*; of Latin origin; a *sudarium* (*sweat-cloth*), i.e. *towel* (for wiping the perspiration from the face, or binding the face of a corpse):—handkerchief, napkin.

4677. Σουσάννα, Sousanna, *soo-san´-nah*; of Hebrew origin [7799 feminine]; *lily; Susannah* (i.e. *Shoshannah*), an Israelitess:—Susanna.

4678. σοφία, sophia, *sof-ee´-ah*; from 4680; *wisdom* (higher or lower, worldly or spiritual):—wisdom.

Noun from *sophós* (4680), wise. Wisdom, skill, tact, expertise in any article.

In the NT, it refers to wisdom:

(I) Skill in the affairs of life, practical wisdom, wise management as shown in forming the best plans and selecting the best means, including the idea of sound judgement and good sense (Lk 21:15; Ac 6:3; 7:10: Col 1:28; 3:16; 4:5).

(II) In a higher sense, wisdom, deep knowledge, natural and moral insight, learning, science, implying cultivation of mind and enlightened understanding.

(A) Generally (Mt 12:42; Lk 11:31; Ac 7:22). Implying learned research and a knowledge of hidden things, of enigmatic and symbolic language (Col 2:23; Rev 13:18; 17:9).

(B) Specifically of the learning and philosophy current among the Greeks and Romans in the apostolic age intended to draw away the minds of men from divine truth, and which stood in contrast to the simplicity of the gospel (1Co 1:17, 19–22; 2:1, 4–6, 13; 3:19; 2Co 1:12).

(C) In respect to divine things, wisdom, knowledge, insight, deep understanding, represented everywhere as a divine gift, and including the idea of practical application (Mt 13:54; Mk 6:2; Ac 6:10). *Sophía* stands for divine wisdom, the ability to regulate one's relationship with God (Lk 2:40; 1Co 1:30; 2:6, 7; 12:8; Eph 1:17; Col 1:9; Jas 1:5; 3:13, 15, 17; 2Pe 3:15).

(III) The wisdom of God means the divine wisdom, including the ideas of infinite skill, insight, knowledge, purity (Ro 11:33; 1Co 1:21, 24; Eph 1:8; 3:10; Col 2:3; Rev 5:12; 7:12). Of the divine wisdom as revealed and manifested in Christ and His gospel (Mt 11:19; Lk 7:35; 11:49).

Deriv.: *philósophos* (5386), philosopher.

Syn.: *súnesis* (4907), the capacity for reasoning, intelligence, understanding; *sōphrosúnē* (4997), soundness of mind; *phrónēsis* (5428), prudence, moral insight.

4679. σοφίζω, sophizō, *sof-id´-zo*; from 4680; to *render wise*; in a sinister acceptation, to *form* "*sophisms*," i.e. *continue plausible error*:—cunningly devised, make wise.

4680. σοφός, sophos, *sof-os´*; akin to **σαφής,** ***saphēs*** (*clear*); *wise* (in a most general application):—wise. Compare 5429.

Adjective meaning wise, not necessarily implying brilliance or scholastic training, but rather the ability to apply with skill what one knows. In the NT, particularly used of applying spiritual truth in one's life. Hence, the following meanings:

(I) Skillful, expert (1Co 3:10).

(II) Skilled in the affairs of life, discreet, judicious, practically wise (1Co 6:5).

(III) Skilled in learning, learned, intelligent, enlightened, in respect to things human and divine.

(A) Generally, as to things human (Mt 11:25; Lk 10:21; Ro 1:14; 16:19; 1Co 1:25).

(B) Specifically as to the philosophy current among the Greeks and Romans (Ro 1:22; 1Co 1:19, 20, 26, 27; 3:18–20).

(C) In respect to divine things, wise, enlightened, as accompanying purity of heart and life (Eph 5:15; Jas 3:13).

(IV) Spoken of God as surpassing all others in wisdom, being infinite in skill, insight, knowledge, purity (Ro 16:27; 1Ti 1:17; Jude 1:25).

Deriv.: *ásophos* (781), unwise, foolish; *sophízō* (4679), to make wise, instruct.

Syn.: *logikós* (3050), reasonable; *sunetós* (4908), intelligent, prudent; *sṓphrōn* (4998), of sound mind; *phrónimos* (5429), prudent, ethical, well-behaved; *epistḗmōn* (1990), scientific, intelligent.

4681. Σπανία, Spania, *span-ee´-ah*; probably of foreign origin; *Spania*, a region of Europe:—Spain.

4682. σπαράσσω, sparassō, *spar-as´-so*; prolonged from **σπαίρω,** ***spairō*** (to *gasp*; apparently strengthened from 4685 through the idea of *spasmodic* contraction); to *mangle*, i.e. *convulse* with epilepsy:—rend, tear.

4683. σπαργανόω, sparganoō, *spar-gan-o´-o*; from **σπάργανον,** ***sparganon*** (a *strip*; from a derivative of the base of 4682 meaning to *strap* or *wrap* with strips); to *swathe* (an infant after the Oriental custom):—wrap in swaddling clothes.

4684. σπαταλάω, spatalaō, *spat-al-ah´-o*; from **σπατάλη,** ***spatalē*** (*luxury*); to *be voluptuous*:—live in pleasure, be wanton.

From *spatálē* (n.f.), luxury in eating and drinking. To live in luxury or pleasure, be self-indulgent. Paul counsels Timothy about the widows who live in pleasure or self-gratification (1Ti 5:6). Also used of wicked rich men (Jas 5:5).

Syn.: *strēniáō* (4763), to live luxuriously, sensuously; *trupháō* (5171), to live in pleasure, self-indulgence.

4685. σπάω, spaō, *spah´-o*; a primary verb; to *draw*:—draw (out).

4686. σπεῖρα, speira, *spi´-rah*; of immediate Latin origin, but ultimately a derivative of 138 in the sense of its cognative 1507; a *coil* (*spira*, "spire"), i.e. (figurative) a *mass* of men (a Roman military *cohort*; also [by analogy] a *squad* of Levitical janitors):—band.

4687. σπείρω, speirō, *spi´-ro*; probably strengthened from 4685 (through the idea of *extending*); to *scatter*, i.e. *sow* (literal or figurative):—sow (-er), receive seed.

4688. σπεκουλάτωρ, spekoulatōr, *spek-oo-lat´-ore*; of Latin origin; a *speculator*, i.e. military *scout* (*spy* or [by extension] *life-guardsman*):—executioner.

4689. σπένδω, spendō, *spen´-do*; apparently a primary verb; to *pour* out as a libation, i.e. (figurative) to *devote* (one's life or blood, as a sacrifice) ("*spend*"):—(be ready to) be offered.

4690. σπέρμα, sperma, *sper´-mah*; from 4687; something *sown*, i.e. *seed* (including the male "*sperm*"); by implication *offspring*; specially a *remnant* (figurative, as if kept over for planting):—issue, seed.

Noun from *speírō* (4687), to sow. Seed, as sown or scattered, whether of grains, plants or trees.

(I) Particularly, the seed sown (Mt 13:24, 27, 32, 37, 38; Mk 4:31; 1Co 15:38; 2Co 9:10). Used figuratively in 1Jn 3:9 of the work of the indwelling Holy Spirit in Christians that keeps them from practicing sin.

(II) Figuratively of the fertilized egg, the seed of conception (Heb 11:11). Hence, by metonymy, in the sense of children, offspring (Mt 22:24, 25; Mk 12:19–22; Lk 20:28). Generally, seed in the sense of posterity (Lk 1:55; Jn 7:42; 8:33, 37; Ac 3:25; 7:5, 6; 13:23; Ro 1:3; 4:13, 18; 11:1; 2Co 11:22; Gal 3:16, 19; 2Ti 2:8; Heb 2:16; 11:18; Rev 12:17). Hence, Christians are referred to as "the seed of Abraham," in that they are the spiritual children of Abraham, and by faith are heirs of the promises made to him (Ro 4:16; 9:8; Gal 3:29).

(III) By implication, seed in the sense of a remnant, a few survivors, like seed that is kept over from a former year (Ro 9:29).

Deriv.: *spermológos* (4691), seed-gathering, chatterer, babbler.

Syn.: *spóros* (4703), seed; *sporá* (4701), seed, a sowing.

4691. σπερμολόγος, spermologos, *sper-mol-og´-os*; from 4690 and 3004; a *seed-picker* (as the crow), i.e. (figurative) a *sponger, loafer* (specially a *gossip* or *trifler* in talk):—babbler.

4692. σπεύδω, speudō, *spyoo´-do*; probably strengthened from 4228; to "*speed*" ("study"), i.e. *urge* on (diligently or earnestly); by implication to *await* eagerly:—(make, with) haste unto.

4693. σπήλαιον, spēlaion, *spay´-lah-yon*; neuter of a presumed derivative of **σπέος,** ***speos*** (a *grotto*); a *cavern*; by implication a *hiding-place* or *resort*:—cave, den.

4694. σπιλάς, spilas, *spee-las´*; of uncertain derivative; a *ledge* or *reef* of rock in the sea:—spot [*by confusion with* 4696].

4695. σπιλόω, spiloō, *spee-lo´-o*; from 4696; to *stain* or *soil* (literal or figurative):—defile, spot.

From *spílos* (4696), a spot, stain. To defile, spot, stain (Jas 3:6; Jude 23).

Syn.: *miaínō* (3392), to defile; *molúnō* (3435), to soil, defile; *rhupóō* (4510), to soil, become dirty.

4696. σπίλος, spilos, *spee´-los*; of uncertain derivative; a *stain* or *blemish*, i.e. (figurative) *defect, disgrace*:—spot.

4697. σπλαγχνίζομαι, splagchnizomai, *splangkh-nid´-zom-ahee*; middle from 4698; to have the *bowels* yearn, i.e. (figurative) *feel sympathy*, to *pity*:—have (be moved with) compassion.

4698. σπλάγχνον, splagchnon, *splangkh´-non*; probably strengthened from **σπλήν,** ***splēn*** (the "*spleen*"); an *intestine* (plural); (figurative) *pity* or *sympathy*:—bowels, inward affection, + tender mercy.

4699. σπόγγος, spoggos, *spong´-gos*; perhaps of foreign origin; a "*sponge*":—spunge.

4700. σποδός, spodos, *spod-os´*; of uncertain derivative; *ashes*:—ashes.

4701. σπορά, spora, *spor-ah´*; from 4687; a *sowing*, i.e. (by implication) *parentage*:—seed.

4702. σπόριμος, sporimos, *spor´-ee-mos*; from 4703; *sown*, i.e. (neuter plural) a planted *field*:—corn (-field).

4703. σπόρος, sporos, *spor´-os*; from 4687; a *scattering* (of seed), i.e. (concrete) *seed* (as sown):—seed (× sown).

4704. σπουδάζω, spoudazō, *spoo-dad´-zo*; from 4710; to *use speed*, i.e. to *make effort, be prompt* or *earnest*:—do (give) diligence, be diligent (forward), endeavour, labour, study.

4705. σπουδαῖος, spoudaios, *spoo-dah´-yos*; from 4710; *prompt, energetic, earnest*:—diligent.

4706. σπουδαιότερον, spoudaioteron, *spoo-dah-yot´-er-on*; neuter of 4707 as adverb; *more earnestly* than others), i.e. very *promptly*:—very diligently.

4707. σπουδαιότερος, spoudaioteros, *spoo-dah-yot´-er-os*; comparative of 4705; *more prompt, more earnest*:—more diligent (forward).

4708. σπουδαιοτέρως, spoudaioterōs, *spoo-dah-yot-er´-oce*; adverb from 4707; *more speedily*, i.e. *sooner* than otherwise:—more carefully.

4709. σπουδαίως, spoudaiōs, *spoo-dah´-yoce*; adverb from 4705; *earnestly, promptly*:—diligently, instantly.

4710. σπουδή, spoudē, *spoo-day´*; from 4692; "*speed*," i.e. (by implication) *despatch, eagerness, earnestness*:—business, (earnest) care (-fulness), diligence, forwardness, haste.

4711. σπυρίς, spuris, *spoo-rece´*; from 4687 (as *woven*); a *hamper* or *lunch-receptacle*:—basket.

4712. στάδιον, stadion, *stad´-ee-on*; or masculine (in plural) **στάδιος,** ***stadios***, *stad´-ee-os*; from the base of 2476 (as *fixed*); a *stade* or certain measure of distance; by implication a *stadium* or *race-course*:—furlong, race.

4713. στάμνος, stamnos, *stam´-nos*; from the base of 2476 (as *stationary*); a *jar* or earthen *tank*:—pot.

4714. στάσις, stasis, *stas´-is*; from the base of 2476; a *standing* (properly the act), i.e. (by analogy) *position* (*existence*); by implication a popular *uprising*; (figurative) *controversy*:—dissension, insurrection, × standing, uproar.

Noun from *hístēmi* (2476), to stand. A setting up, an erecting, as of a statue. In the NT, a standing.

(I) The act of standing, with *échō* (2192), to have, to stand (Heb 9:8).

(II) In the sense of an uproar:

(A) Particularly, of a public commotion, sedition, insurrection (Mk 15:7; Lk 23:19, 25; Ac 19:40; 24:5).

(B) In a more private sense, dissension, contentions, controversy, with the idea of violence threatened (Ac 15:2; 23:7, 10).

Deriv.: *sustasiastḗs* (4955), a fellow insurgent; *dichostasía* (1370), division, separation.

4715. στατήρ, statēr, *stat-air´*; from the base of 2746; a *stander* (*standard* of value), i.e. (special) a *stater* or certain coin:—piece of money.

4716. σταυρός, stauros, *stow-ros´*; from the base of 2476; a *stake* or *post* (as *set* upright), i.e. (special) a *pole* or *cross* (as an instrument of capital punishment); (figurative) *exposure to death*, i.e. *self-denial*; by implication the *atonement* of Christ:—cross.

Noun from *hístēmi* (2476), to stand. A cross, a stake, often with a crosspiece, on which criminals were nailed for execution. This mode of punishment was known to the Persians (Ezr 6:11; Est 7:10); and the Carthaginians. However, it was most common among the Romans for slaves and criminals, and was introduced among the Jews by the Romans. It was not abolished until the time of Constantine who did so out of regard for Christianity.

Persons sentenced to be crucified were first scourged and then made to bear their own cross to the place of execution. A label or title was usually placed on the chest of or over the criminal.

(I) Particularly, the crosspiece which was fitted upon the upright stake, which Simon was compelled to carry for Jesus (Mt 27:32; Mk 15:21; Lk 23:26; Jn 19:17). Also, the total structure of the cross on which Jesus hung (Mt 27:40, 42; Mk 15:30, 32; Jn 19:19, 25, 31; Php 2:8; Col 1:20; 2:14). Figuratively, in phrases such as "to take up one's cross," or "to bear one's cross," meaning to undergo suffering, trial, punishment; to expose oneself to reproach and death (Mt 10:38; 16:24; Mk 8:34; 10:21; Lk 9:23; 14:27).

(II) By metonymy, spoken of the total experience of dying on the cross. Spoken only of Christ's death as the atonement for our sins (1Co 1:17, 18; Gal 5:11; 6:12, 14; Eph 2:16; Php 3:18; Heb 12:2).

Deriv.: *stauróō* (4717), to crucify.
Syn.: *xúlon* (3586), tree, cross.

4717. σταυρόω, stauroō, *stow-ro´-o*; from 4716; to *impale* on the cross; (figurative) to *extinguish* (*subdue*) passion or selfishness:—crucify.

From *staurós* (4716), cross. To crucify:

(I) Particularly, to crucify, to nail to a cross (Mt 20:19; 23:34; 26:2; 27:22ff.; 28:5; Mk 15:13ff.; 16:6; Lk 23:21ff.; 24:7, 20; Jn 19:6; Ac 2:36).

(II) Figuratively, to crucify the flesh with its affections and lusts, meaning to mortify them, to put them to death, to destroy the power of sinful desires (Gal 5:24; 6:14).

Deriv.: *anastauróō* (388), to recrucify; *sustauróō* (4957), to crucify with.

4718. σταφυλή, staphulē, *staf-oo-lay´*; probably from the base of 4735; a *cluster* of grapes (as if *intertwined*):—grapes.

4719. στάχυς, stachus, *stakh´-oos*; from the base of 2476; a *head* of grain (as *standing* out from the stalk):—ear (of corn).

4720. Στάχυς, Stachus, *stakh´-oos*; the same as 4719; *Stachys*, a Christian:—Stachys.

4721. στέγη, stegē, *steg´-ay*; strengthened from a primary **τέγος**, *tegos* (a "*thatch*" or "*deck*" of a building); a *roof*:—roof.

4722. στέγω, stegō, *steg´-o*; from 4721; to *roof* over, i.e. (figurative) to *cover* with silence (*endure* patiently):—(for-) bear, suffer.

4723. στεῖρος, steiros, *sti´-ros*; as contracted from 4731 (as *stiff* and *unnatural*); "*sterile*":—barren.

4724. στέλλω, stellō, *stel´-lo*; probably strengthened from the base of 2476; properly to *set* fast ("*stall*"), i.e. (figurative) to *repress* (reflexive *abstain* from associating with):—avoid, withdraw self.

To set, place, appoint to a position (such as soldiers in battle array). From this original idea of motion into a place comes the usual Greek significance of to send, to dispatch. In the NT, used only in the middle voice, of persons, to shrink from, to withdraw from, to avoid (2Co 8:20; 2Th 3:6).

Deriv.: *apostéllō* (649), to commission, send; *diastéllō* (1291), to differentiate, set oneself apart, order; *epistéllō* (1989), to send one a message; *katastéllō* (2687), repress, curb; *stolḗ* (4749), a robe, clothing of distinction; *sustéllō* (4958), to draw together, to contract, shorten; *hupostéllō* (5288), to hold back, to lower, draw back.

Syn.: *anachōréō* (402), to withdraw; *apochōréō* (672), to depart, withdraw; *apochōrízō* (673), to separate.

4725. στέμμα, stemma, *stem´-mah*; from the base of 4735; a *wreath* for show:—garland.

4726. στεναγμός, stenagmos, *sten-ag-mos´*; from 4727; a *sigh*:—groaning.

4727. στενάζω, stenazō, *sten-ad´-zo*; from 4728; to *make* (intransitive *be*) *in straits*, i.e. (by implication) to *sigh, murmur, pray* inaudibly:—with grief, groan, grudge, sigh.

4728. στενός, stenos, *sten-os´*; probably from the base of 2476; *narrow* (from obstacles *standing* close about):—strait.

4729. στενοχωρέω, stenochōreō, *sten-okh-o-reh´-o*; from the same as 4730; to *hem* in closely, i.e. (figurative) *cramp*:—distress, straiten.

4730. στενοχωρία, stenochōria, *sten-okh-o-ree´-ah*; from a compound of 4728 and 5561; *narrowness of room*, i.e. (figurative) *calamity*:—anguish, distress.

Noun from *stenós* (4728), narrow, and *chṓra* (5561), territory, a space. Distress, trouble, worry, anguish. In most of the verses where *stenochōría* is used in the NT, the word *thlípsis* (2347), tribulation, is also used (Ro 2:9; 8:35; 2Co 6:4). *Thlípsis* refers to troubles from without, such as persecution, affliction, or tribulation. *Stenochōría* has in view distress that arises from within (often caused by *thlípsis*), such as anguish or worry. In 2Co 12:10, Paul lists *stenochōría* as one of the forms of suffering for Christ through which we will be made strong in Him.

Syn.: *kakopátheia* (2552), hardship; *páthēma* (3804), misfortune, affliction; *sunochḗ* (4928), a restraint, distress, anguish; *talaipōría* (5004), hardship, misery.

4731. στερεός, stereos, *ster-eh-os´*; from 2476; *stiff*, i.e. *solid, stable* (literal or figurative):—steadfast, strong, sure.

4732. στερεόω, stereoō, *ster-eh-o´-o*; from 4731; to *solidify*, i.e. *confirm* (literal or figurative):—establish, receive strength, make strong.

4733. στερέωμα, stereōma, *ster-eh´-o-mah*; from 4732; something *established*, i.e. (abstract) *confirmation* (*stability*):—steadfastness.

4734. Στεφανᾶς, Stephanas, *stef-an-as´*; probably contraction for **στεφανωτός**, ***Stephanōtos*** (*crowned*; from 4737); *Stephanas*, a Christian:—Stephanas.

4735. στέφανος, stephanos, *stef´-an-os*; from an apparently primary **στέφω** ***stephō*** (to *twine* or *wreathe*); a *chaplet* (as a badge of royalty, a prize in the public games or a symbol of honour generally; but more conspicuous and elaborate than the simple *fillet*, 1238), literal or figurative:—crown.

A noun meaning crown, wreath.

(I) As the emblem of royal dignity (Rev 6:2; 12:1; 14:14). Ascribed to saints in heaven, elsewhere called kings (see Rev 4:4, 10). Of the crown of thorns set upon Christ in derision as King of the Jews (Mt 27:29; Mk 15:17; Jn 19:2, 5).

(II) As the prize conferred on victors in public games and elsewhere, a wreath (1Co 9:25). Figuratively, a symbol of the reward of eternal life (2Ti 4:8; Jas 1:12; 1Pe 5:4; Rev 2:10; 3:11).

(III) Figuratively, an ornament, honour, glory, that in which one may glory (Php 4:1; 1Th 2:19).

Deriv.: *stephanóō* (4737), to crown.
Syn.: *diádēma* (1238), diadem, a crown marking royal dignity.

4736. Στέφανος, Stephanos, *stef´-an-os*; the same as 4735; *Stephanus*, a Christian:—Stephen.

4737. στεφανόω, stephanoō, *stef-an-o´-o*; from 4735; to *adorn with* an honorary *wreath* (literal or figurative):—crown.

4738. στῆθος, stēthos, *stay´-thos*; from 2476 (as *standing* prominently); the (entire external) *bosom*, i.e. *chest*:—breast.

4739. στήκω, stēkō, *stay´-ko*; from the perfect tense of 2476; to *be stationary*, i.e. (figurative) to *persevere*:—stand (fast).

4740. στηριγμός, stērigmos, *stay-rig-mos´*; from 4741; *stability* (figurative):—steadfastness.

4741. στηρίζω, stērizō, *stay-rid´-zo*; from a presumed derivative of 2476 (like 4731); to *set fast*, i.e. (literal) to *turn resolutely* in a certain direction, or (figurative) to *confirm*:—fix, (e-) stablish, steadfastly set, strengthen.

4742. στίγμα, stigma, *stig´-mah*; from a primary **στίζω, *stizō*** (to "*stick*," i.e. *prick*); a *mark* incised or punched (for recognition of ownership), i.e. (figurative) *scar* of service:—mark.

4743. στιγμή, stigmē, *stig-may´*; feminine of 4742; a *point* of time, i.e. an *instant*:—moment.

4744. στίλβω, stilbō, *stil´-bo*; apparently a primary verb; to *gleam*, i.e. *flash* intensely:—shining.

4745. στοά, stoa, *sto-ah´*; probably from 2476; a *colonnade* or interior *piazza*:—porch.

4746. στοιβάς, stoibas, *stoy-bas´*; from a primary **στείβω, *steibō*** (to "*step*" or "*stamp*"); a *spread* (as if *tramped* flat) of loose materials for a couch, i.e. (by implication) a *bough* of a tree so employed:—branch.

4747. στοιχεῖον, stoicheion, *stoy-khi´-on*; neuter of a presumed derivative of the base of 4748; something *orderly* in arrangement, i.e. (by implication) a *serial* (*basal, fundamental,* *initial*) constituent (literal), proposition (figurative):—element, principle, rudiment.

Noun, a diminutive of *stoíchos* (n.f.), a row. Literally, one in a row, one in a series. In the NT, always used in the plural, the basic parts, elements, or components of something.

(I) Generally, the elements of nature, the component parts of the physical world (2Pe 3:10, 12).

(II) Spoken of elementary instruction, in particular of the first principles of Christian doctrine (Heb 5:12). Spoken of the principles of life, philosophy, and religion, particularly in contrasting ceremonial ordinances and the traditions and commandments of men with a true knowledge of Christ (Gal 4:3, 9; Col 2:8, 20).

4748. στοιχέω, stoicheō, *stoy-kheh´-o*; from a derivative of **στείχω**, *steichō* (to *range* in regular line); to *march* in (military) rank (*keep step*), i.e. (figurative) to *conform* to virtue and piety:—walk (orderly).

4749. στολή, stolē, *stol-ay´*; from 4724; *equipment*, i.e. (special) a "*stole*" or long-fitting *gown* (as a mark of dignity):—long clothing (garment), (long) robe.

Noun from *stéllō* (4724), to send. A long flowing robe reaching to the feet, generally worn by persons of high social rank or dignity (Mk 12:38; 16:5; Lk 15:22; 20:46; Rev 6:11; 7:9, 13, 14).

Deriv.: *katastolḗ* (2689), long robe of dignity.

Syn.: *podḗrēs* (4158), an outer garment reaching to the feet. For a list of various types of clothing, see the synonyms under *himátion* (2440), garment.

4750. στόμα, stoma, *stom´-a*; probably strengthened from a presumed derivative of the base of 5114; the *mouth* (as if a *gash* in the face); by implication *language* (and its relations); (figurative) an *opening* (in the earth); specially the *front* or *edge* (of a weapon):—edge, face, mouth.

4751. στόμαχος, stomachos, *stom´-akh-os*; from 4750; an *orifice* (the *gullet*), i.e. (special) the "*stomach*":—stomach.

4752. στρατεία, strateia, *strat-i´-ah*; from 4754; military *service*, i.e. (figurative) the apostolic *career* (as one of hardship and danger):—warfare.

4753. στράτευμα, strateuma, *strat´-yoo-mah*; from 4754; an *armament*, i.e. (by implication) a body of *troops* (more or less extensive or systematic):—army, soldier, man of war.

4754. στρατεύομαι, strateuomai, *strat-yoo´-om-ahee*; middle from the base of 4756; to *serve* in a military campaign; (figurative) to *execute the apostolate* (with its arduous duties and functions), to *contend* with carnal inclinations:—soldier, (go to) war (-fare).

4755. στρατηγός, stratēgos, *strat-ay-gos´*; from the base of 4756 and 71 or 2233; a *general*, i.e. (by implication or analogy) a (military) *governor* (*prætor*), the *chief* (*præfect*) of the (Levitical) temple-wardens:—captain, magistrate.

4756. στρατία, stratia, *strat-ee´-ah*; feminine of a derivative of **στρατός**, *stratos* (an *army*; from the base of 4766, as *encamped*); *camp-likeness*, i.e. an *army*, i.e. (figurative) the *angels*, the celestial *luminaries*:—host.

4757. στρατιώτης, stratiōtēs, *strat-ee-o´-tace*; from a presumed derivative of the same as 4756; a *camperout*, i.e. a (common) *warrior* (literal or figurative):—soldier.

4758. στρατολογέω, stratologeō, *strat-ol-og-eh´-o*; from a compound of the base of 4756 and 3004 (in its original sense); to *gather* (or *select*) as a *warrior*, i.e. *enlist* in the army:—choose to be a soldier.

4759. στρατοπεδάρχης, stratopedarchēs, *strat-op-ed-ar´-khace*; from 4760 and 757; a *ruler of an army*, i.e. (special) a Prætorian *præfect*:—captain of the guard.

4760. στρατόπεδον, stratopedon, *strat-op´-ed-on*; from the base of 4756 and the same as 3977; a *camping-ground*, i.e. (by implication) a body of *troops*:—army.

4761. στρεβλόω, strebloō, *streb-lo´-o*; from a derivative of 4762; to *wrench*, i.e. (special) to *torture* (by the rack), but only figurative, to *pervert*:—wrest.

4762. στρέφω, strephō, *stref´-o*; strengthened from the base of 5157; to *twist*, i.e. *turn* quite around or *reverse* (literal or figurative):—convert, turn (again, back again, self, self about).

To turn, turn about.

(I) To turn oneself, turn about (Mt 5:39; 7:6; 16:23; Lk 7:9, 44; 9:55; 10:23; 14:25; 22:61; 23:28; Jn 1:38; 20:14, 16; Ac 7:39, 42; 13:46).

(II) Figuratively, to turn into something, meaning to convert or change, such as waters into blood (Rev 11:6); of persons, to turn in mind, be converted or changed, become another kind of person, e.g., to become like children (Mt 18:3).

Deriv.: *anastréphō* (390), to overturn, to sojourn; *apostréphō* (654), to turn away or back; *diastréphō* (1294), to turn, twist throughout, pervert; *ekstréphō* (1612), to subvert, pervert; *epistréphō* (1994), to turn back again, turn about; *katastréphō* (2690), to ruin; *metastréphō* (3344), to turn around, change; *sustréphō* (4962), to roll together, to gather; *hupostréphō* (5290), to turn back, return.

Syn.: *metabállō* (3328), to turn about.

4763. στρηνιάω, strēniaō, *stray-nee-ah´-o*; from a presumed derivative of 4764; to *be luxurious*:—live deliciously.

From *strḗnos* (4764), excessive luxury (Rev 18:3). To revel, to live luxuriously, act with wantonness from abundance (Rev 18:7, 9).

Deriv.: *katastrēniáō* (2691), to become lascivious against.

Syn.: *spataláō* (4684), to live in pleasure, be wanton; *trupháō* (5171), to live in pleasure and luxury.

4764. στρῆνος, strēnos, *stray´-nos*; akin to 4731; a "*straining*," "*strenuousness*" or "strength," i.e. (figurative) *luxury* (*voluptuousness*):—delicacy.

4765. στρουθίον, strouthion, *stroo-thee´-on*; diminutive of **στρουθός**, *strouthos* (a *sparrow*); a *little sparrow*:—sparrow.

4766. στρώννυμι, strōnnumi, *strone´-noo-mee*; or simpler **στρωννύω**, *strōnnuō*, *strone-noo´-o*; prolonged from a still simpler **στρόω**, *stroō*, *stro´-o* (used only as an alternate in certain tenses; probably akin to 4731 through the idea of *positing*); to "*strew*," i.e. *spread* (as a carpet or couch):—make bed, furnish, spread, strew.

4767. στυγνητός, stugnētos, *stoog-nay-tos´*; from a derivative of an obsolete apparently primary **στύγω**, *stugō* (to *hate*); *hated*, i.e. *odious*:—hateful.

4768. στυγνάζω, stugnazō, *stoog-nad´-zo*; from the same as 4767; to *render gloomy*, i.e. (by implication) *glower* (*be overcast* with clouds, or *sombreness* of speech):—lower, be sad.

4769. στῦλος, stulos, *stoo´-los*; from **στύω**, *stuō* (to *stiffen*; properly akin to the base of 2476); a *post* ("*style*"), i.e. (figurative) *support*:—pillar.

4770. Στωϊκός, Stōïkos, *sto-ik-os´*; from 4745; a "*Stoïc*" (as occupying a particular porch in Athens), i.e. adherent of a certain philosophy:—Stoick.

4771. σύ, su, *soo*; the personal pronoun of the second person singular; *thou*:—thou. See also 4571, 4671, 4675; and for the plural 5209, 5210, 5213, 5216.

4772. συγγένεια, suggeneia, *soong-ghen´-i-ah*; from 4773; *relationship*, i.e. (concrete) *relatives*:—kindred.

4773. συγγενής, suggenēs, *soong-ghen-ace´*; from 4862 and 1085; a *relative* (by blood); by extension a fellow *countryman*:—cousin, kin (-sfolk, -sman).

4774. συγγνώμη, suggnōmē, *soong-gno´-may*; from a compound of 4862 and 1097; *fellow knowledge*, i.e. *concession*:—permission.

Noun from *sugginṓskō* (n.f.), to think alike, agree with, which is from *sún* (4862), with, and *ginṓskō* (1097), to know. Concession, permission. Used only in 1Co 7:6.

4775. συγκάθημαι, sugkathēmai, *soong-kath´-ay-mahee*; from 4862 and 2521; to *seat oneself* in company *with*:—sit with.

4776. συγκαθίζω, sugkathizō, *soong-kath-id´-zo*; from 4862 and 2523; to *give* (or *take*) *a seat* in company *with*:—(make) sit (down) together.

4777. συγκακοπαθέω, sugkakopatheō, *soong-kak-op-ath-eh´-o*; from 4862 and 2553; to *suffer hardship* in company *with*:—be partaker of afflictions.

From *sún* (4862), together, or with, and *kakopathéō* (2553), to suffer evil or affliction. To suffer hardship, evil or affliction along with someone. Only in 2Ti 1:8.

Syn.: *sugkakouchéō* (4778), to suffer affliction with; *sullupéō* (4818), to sorrow with; *sumpáschō* (4841), to suffer with; *sunōdínō* (4944), to travail in pain together; *sustenázō* (4959), to groan together.

4778. συγκακουχέω, sugkakoucheō, *soong-kak-oo-kheh´-o*; from 4862 and 2558; to *maltreat* in company *with*, i.e. (passive) *endure persecution together*:—suffer affliction with.

4779. συγκαλέω, sugkaleō, *soong-kal-eh´-o*; from 4862 and 2564; to *convoke*:—call together.

From *sún* (4862), together, and *kaléō* (2564), to call. To call together (Mk 15:16; Lk 9:1; 15:6, 9; 23:13; Ac 5:21; 10:24; 28:17).

4780. συγκαλύπτω, sugkaluptō, *soong-kal-oop´-to*; from 4862 and 2572; to *conceal altogether*:—cover.

4781. συγκάμπτω, sugkamptō, *soong-kamp´-to*; from 4862 and 2578; to *bend together*, i.e. (figurative) to *afflict*:—bow down.

4782. συγκαταβαίνω, sugkatabainō, *soong-kat-ab-ah´ee-no*; from 4862 and 2597; to *descend* in company *with*:—go down with.

4783. συγκατάθεσις, sugkatathesis, *soong-kat-ath´-es-is*; from 4784; a *deposition* (of sentiment) in company *with*, i.e. (figurative) *accord* with:—agreement.

4784. συγκατατίθεμαι, sugkatatithemai, *soong-kat-at-ith´-em-ahee*; middle from 4862 and 2698; to *deposit* (one's vote or opinion) in company *with*, i.e. (figurative) to *accord* with:—consent.

4785. συγκαταψηφίζω, sugkatapsēphizō, *soong-kat-aps-ay-fid´-zo*; from 4862 and a compound of 2596 and 5585; to *count down* in company *with*, i.e. *enroll among*:—number with.

4786. συγκεράννυμι, sugkerannumi, *soong-ker-an´-noo-mee*; from 4862 and 2767; to *commingle*, i.e. (figurative) to *combine* or *assimilate*:—mix with, temper together.

4787. συγκινέω, sugkineō, *soong-kin-eh´-o*; from 4682 and 2795; to *move together*, i.e. (special) to *excite* as a mass (to sedition):—stir up.

4788. συγκλείω, sugkleiō, *soong-kli´-o*; from 4862 and 2808; to *shut together*, i.e. *include* or (figurative) *embrace* in a common subjection to:—conclude, inclose, shut up.

4789. συγκληρονόμος, sugklēronomos, *soong-klay-ron-om´-os*; from 4862 and 2818; a *co-heir*, i.e. (by analogy) *participant in common*:—fellow (joint) -heir, heir together, heir with.

Noun from *sún* (4862), together, and *klēronómos* (2818), an heir, a sharer by lot. A co-heir, joint heir, a joint possessor (Ro 8:17; Heb 11:9; 1Pe 3:7). Spoken of the Gentiles as being joint heirs with Israel (Eph 3:6).

Syn.: *summétochos* (4830), a co-participant; *sugkoinōnós* (4791), a partaker with.

4790. συγκοινωνέω, sugkoinōneō, *soong-koy-no-neh´-o*; from 4862 and 2841; to *share* in company *with*, i.e. *co-participate* in:—communicate (have fellowship) with, be partaker of.

From *sún* (4862), with, and *koinōnéō* (2841), to partake. To participate in something with others, to share with others in anything. Spoken of in a good sense: sharing material things with someone in need (Php 4:14). Spoken of in a bad sense: sharing guilt with sinners (Eph 5:11; Rev 18:4).

Syn.: *summerízomai* (4829), to share jointly.

4791. συγκοινωνός, sugkoinōnos, *soong-koy-no-nos´*; from 4862 and 2844; a *co-participant*:—companion, partake (-r, -r with).

4792. συγκομίζω, sugkomizō, *soong-kom-id´-zo*; from 4862 and 2865; to *convey together*, i.e. *collect* or *bear* away in company *with* others:—carry.

4793. συγκρίνω, sugkrinō, *soong-kree´-no*; from 4862 and 2919; to *judge* of one thing in connection *with* another, i.e. *combine* (spiritual ideas with appropriate expressions) or *collate* (one person with another by way of contrast or resemblance):—compare among (with).

From *sún* (4862), together, and *krínō* (2919), to judge. Literally, to compare one thing with another by noting similarities and differences. In the NT, to place together and estimate the value of each (2Co 10:12). By extension, in the sense of to explain (by comparison), to interpret, to combine into one, e.g., interpreting spiritual things by spiritual things (1Co 2:13).

4794. συγκύπτω, sugkuptō, *soong-koop´-to*; from 4862 and 2955; to *stoop altogether*, i.e. *be completely overcome* by:—bow together.

4795. συγκυρία, sugkuria, *soong-koo-ree´-ah*; from a compound of 4862 and **κυρέω**, *ureō* (to *light* or *happen*; from the base of 2962); *concurrence*, i.e. *accident*:—chance.

4796. συγχαίρω, sugchairō, *soong-khah´ee-ro*; from 4862 and 5463; to *sympathize in gladness*, *congratulate*:—rejoice in (with).

4797. συγχέω, sugcheō, *soong-kheh´-o*; or **συγχύνω, sugchunō,** *soong-khoo´-no*; from 4862 and **χέω**, *cheō* (to *pour*) or its alternate; to *commingle* promiscuously, i.e. (figurative) to *throw* (an assembly) *into disorder*, to *perplex* (the mind):—confound, confuse, stir up, be in an uproar.

4798. συγχράομαι, sugchraomai, *soong-khrah´-om-ahee*; from 4862 and 5530; to *use jointly*, i.e. (by implication) to *hold intercourse in common*:—have dealings with.

4799. σύγχυσις, sugchusis, *soong´-khoo-sis*; from 4797; *commixture*, i.e. (figurative) riotous *disturbance*:—confusion.

4800. συζάω, suzaō, *sood-zah´-o*; from 4862 and 2198; to continue to *live* in common *with*, i.e. *co-survive* (literal or figurative):—live with.

4801. συζεύγνυμι, suzeugnumi, *sood-zyoog´-noo-mee*; from 4862 and the base of 2201; to *yoke together*, i.e. (figurative) *conjoin* (in marriage):—join together.

4802. συζητέω, suzēteō, *sood-zay-teh´-o*; from 4862 and 2212; to investigate *jointly*, i.e. *discuss*, *controvert*, *cavil*:—dispute (with), enquire, question (with), reason (together).

4803. συζήτησις, suzētēsis, *sood-zay´-tay-sis*; from 4802; *mutual questioning*, i.e. *discussion*:—disputation (-ting), reasoning.

4804. συζητητής, suzētētēs, *sood-zay-tay-tace´*; from 4802; a *disputant*, i.e. *sophist*:—disputer.

4805. σύζυγος, suzugos, *sood´-zoo-gos*; from 4801; *co-yoked*, i.e. (figurative) as noun, a *colleague*; probably rather as proper name; *Syzygus*, a Christian:—yokefellow.

4806. συζωοποιέω, suzōopoieō, *sood-zo-op-oy-eh´-o*; from 4862 and 2227; to *reanimate conjointly* with (figurative):—quicken together with.

4807. συκάμινος, sukaminos, *soo-kam´-ee-nos*; of Hebrew origin [8256] in imitation of 4809; a *sycamore*-fig tree:—sycamine tree.

4808. συκῆ, sukē, *soo-kay´*; from 4810; a *fig tree*:—fig tree.

4809. συκομωραία, sukomōraia, *soo-kom-o-rah´-yah*; from 4810 and **μόρον, *moron*** (the *mulberry*); the "*sycamore*"-fig tree:—sycamore tree. Compare 4807.

4810. σῦκον, sukon, *soo´-kon*; apparently a primary word; a *fig*:—fig.

4811. συκοφαντέω, sukophanteō, *soo-kof-an-teh´-o*; from a compound of 4810 and a derivative of 5316; to *be a fig-informer* (reporter of the law forbidding the exportation of figs from Greece), "*sycophant*," i.e. (general and by extension) to *defraud* (*exact* unlawfully, *extort*):—accuse falsely, take by false accusation.

4812. συλαγωγέω, sulagōgeō, *soo-lag-ogue-eh´-o*; from the base of 4813 and (the reduplicated form of) 71; to *lead* away as *booty*, i.e. (figurative) *seduce*:—spoil.

4813. συλάω, sulaō, *soo-lah´-o*; from a derivative of **σύλλω, *sullō*** (to *strip*; probably akin to 138; compare 4661); to *despoil*:—rob.

4814. συλλαλέω, sullaleō, *sool-lal-eh´-o*; from 4862 and 2980; to *talk together*, i.e. *converse*:—commune (confer, talk) with, speak among.

4815. συλλαμβάνω, sullambanō, *sool-lam-ban´-o*; from 4862 and 2983; to *clasp*, i.e. *seize* (*arrest, capture*); specially to *conceive* (literal or figurative); by implication to *aid*:—catch, conceive, help, take.

4816. συλλέγω, sullegō, *sool-leg´-o*; from 4862 and 3004 in its original sense; to *collect*:—gather (together, up).

4817. συλλογίζομαι, sullogizomai, *sool-log-id´-zom-ahee*; from 4862 and 3049; to *reckon together* (with oneself), i.e. *deliberate*:—reason with.

4818. συλλυπέω, sullupeō, *sool-loop-eh´-o*; from 4862 and 3076; to *afflict jointly*, i.e. (passive) *sorrow at* (on account of) someone:—be grieved.

4819. συμβαίνω, sumbainō, *soom-bah´ee-no*; from 4862 and the base of 939; to *walk* (figurative, *transpire*) *together*, i.e. *concur* (*take place*):—be (-fall), happen (unto).

4820. συμβάλλω, sumballō, *soom-bal´-lo*; from 4862 and 906; to *combine*, i.e. (in speaking) to *converse, consult, dispute*, (mentally) to *consider*, (by implication) to *aid*, (personally) to *join, attack*:—confer, encounter, help, make, meet with, ponder.

4821. συμβασιλεύω, sumbasileuō, *soom-bas-il-yoo´-o*; from 4862 and 936; to *be co-regent* (figurative):—reign with.

4822. συμβιβάζω, sumbibazō, *soom-bib-ad´-zo*; from 4862 and **βιβάζω, *bibazō*** (to *force*; causative [by reduplication] of the base of 939); to *drive together*, i.e. *unite* (in association or affection), (mentally) to *infer, show, teach*:—compact, assuredly gather, intrust, knit together, prove.

4823. συμβουλεύω, sumbouleuō, *soom-bool-yoo´-o*; from 4862 and 1011; to *give* (or *take*) *advice jointly*, i.e. *recommend, deliberate* or *determine*:—consult, (give, take) counsel (together).

4824. συμβούλιον, sumboulion, *soom-boo´-lee-on*; neuter of a presumed derivative of 4825; *advisement*; specially a *deliberative* body, i.e. the provincial *assessors* or lay-court:—consultation, counsel, council.

4825. σύμβουλος, sumboulos, *soom´-boo-los*; from 4862 and 1012; a *consultor*, i.e. *adviser*:—counsellor.

4826. Συμεών, Sumeōn, *soom-eh-one´*; from the same as 4613; *Symeon* (i.e. *Shimon*), the name of five Israelites:—Simeon, Simon.

4827. συμμαθητής, summathētēs, *soom-math-ay-tace´*; from a compound of 4862 and 3129; a *co-learner* (of Christianity):—fellow disciple.

4828. συμμαρτυρέω, summartureō, *soom-mar-too-reh´-o*; from 4862 and 3140; to *testify jointly*, i.e. *corroborate* by (concurrent) evidence:—testify unto, (also) bear witness (with).

4829. συμμερίζομαι, summerizomai, *soom-mer-id´-zom-ahee*; middle from 4862 and 3307; to *share jointly*, i.e. *participate* in:—be partaker with.

4830. συμμέτοχος, summetochos, *soom-met´-okh-os*; from 4862 and 3353; a *co-participant*:—partaker.

4831. συμμιμητής, summimētēs, *soom-mim-ay-tace´*; from a presumed compound of 4862 and 3401; a *co-imitator*, i.e. *fellow votary*:—follower together.

4832. σύμμορφος, summorphos, *soom-mor-fos´*; from 4862 and 3444; *jointly formed*, i.e. (figurative) *similar*:—conformed to, fashioned like unto.

Adjective from *sún* (4862), together with, and *morphḗ* (3444), form. Having like form with or being conformed to something. In the NT, spoken of twice in the sense of our becoming conformed to Christ: our being conformed to his likeness (Ro 8:29), and our bodies being conformed to his glorious body (Php 3:21).

Deriv.: *summorphóō* (4833), becoming conformed.

4833. συμμορφόω, summorphoō, *soom-mor-fo´-o*; from 4832; to *render like*, i.e. (figurative) to *assimilate*:—make conformable unto.

4834. συμπαθέω, sumpatheō, *soom-path-eh´-o*; from 4835; to *feel "sympathy"* with, i.e. (by implication) to *commiserate*:—have compassion, be touched with a feeling of.

From *sumpathḗs* (4835), sympathizing. To sympathize with, be compassionate, have compassion upon anyone, to offer sympathizing aid (Heb 4:15; 10:34).

Syn.: *splagchnízomai* (4697), to feel sympathy, to pity, have compassion; *sullupéomai* (the middle of *sullupéō* [4818]), to experience sorrow with, console.

4835. συμπαθής, sumpathēs, *soom-path-ace´*; from 4841; *having a fellow-feeling* ("*sympathetic*"), i.e. (by implication) *mutually commiserative*:—having compassion one of another.

Adjective from *sún* (4862), together or with, and *páthos* (3806), suffering, misfortune. Compassionate, sympathizing (1Pe 3:8).

Deriv.: *sumpathéō* (4834), to be compassionate.

4836. συμπαραγίνομαι, sumparaginomai, *soom-par-ag-in´-om-ahee*; from 4862 and 3854; to *be present together*, i.e. to *convene*; by implication to *appear in aid*:—come together, stand with.

4837. συμπαρακαλέω, sumparakaleō, *soom-par-ak-al-eh´-o*; from 4862 and 3870; to *console jointly*:—comfort together.

4838. συμπαραλαμβάνω, sumparalambanō, *soom-par-al-am-ban´-o*; from 4862 and 3880; to *take along in company*:—take with.

4839. συμπαραμένω, sumparamenō, *soom-par-am-en´-o*; from 4862 and 3887; to *remain in company*, i.e. *still live*:—continue with.

4840. συμπάρειμι, sumpareimi, *soom-par´-i-mee*; from 4862 and 3918; to *be at hand together*, i.e. *now present*:—be here present with.

4841. συμπάσχω, sumpaschō, *soom-pas´-kho*; from 4862 and 3958 (including its alternate); to *experience pain jointly* or of the *same kind* (specially *persecution*; to "*sympathize*"):—suffer with.

From *sún* (4862), together with, and *páschō* (3958), to suffer. To sympathize with, to suffer together with (1Co 12:26). To endure like sufferings (Ro 8:17).

4842. συμπέμπω, sumpempō, *soom-pem´-po*; from 4862 and 3992; to *despatch in company*:—send with.

4843. συμπεριλαμβάνω, sumperilambanō, *soom-per-ee-lam-ban´-o*; from 4862 and a compound of 4012 and 2983; to *take by inclosing altogether*, i.e. *earnestly throw the arms about one*:—embrace.

4844. συμπίνω, sumpinō, *soom-pee´-no*; from 4862 and 4095; to *partake a beverage in company*:—drink with.

4845. συμπληρόω, sumplēroō, *soom-play-ro´-o*; from 4862 and 4137; to *implenish completely*, i.e. (of space) to *swamp* (a boat), or (of time) to *accomplish* (passive be *complete*):—(fully) come, fill up.

From *sún* (4862), an intensive, and *plēróō* (4137), to fill. To fill to the brim. Used in the passive, to be filled completely, as with water (Lk 8:23). In the passive, used of time, to be fulfilled or fully come (Lk 9:51; Ac 2:1).

Syn.: *apoteléō* (658), to complete fully; *gemízō* (1072), to fill full; *empíplēmi* or *emplḗthō* (1705), to fill full; *pímplēmi* or *plḗthō* (4130), to fill up; *sunteléō* (4931), to complete fully; *teleióō* (5048), to complete.

4846. συμπνίγω, sumpnigō, *soom-pnee´-go*; from 4862 and 4155; to *strangle completely*, i.e. (literal) to *drown*, or (figurative) to *crowd*:—choke, throng.

4847. συμπολίτης, sumpolitēs, *soom-pol-ee´-tace*; from 4862 and 4177; a *native of the same town*, i.e. (figurative) *co-religionist* (*fellow Christian*):—fellow citizen.

4848. συμπορεύομαι, sumporeuomai, *soom-por-yoo´-om-ahee*; from 4862 and 4198; to *journey together*; by implication to *assemble*:—go with, resort.

4849. συμπόσιον, sumposion, *soom-pos´-ee-on*; neuter of a derivative of the alternate of 4844; a *drinking*-party ("*symposium*"), i.e. (by extension) a *room* of guests:—company.

4850. συμπρεσβύτερος, sumpresbuteros, *soom-pres-boo´-ter-os*; from 4862 and 4245; a *co-presbyter*:—presbyter, also an elder.

Noun from *sún* (4862), together with, and *presbúteros* (4245), an elder. A fellow elder (1Pe 5:1). Peter reminds the elders of the dignity of their office that they might not forget their duties (5:2, 3).

4851. συμφέρω, sumpherō, *soom-fer´-o*; from 4862 and 5342 (including its alternate); to *bear together* (*contribute*), i.e. (literal) to *collect*, or (figurative) to *conduce*; especially (neuter participle as noun) *advantage*:—be better for, bring together, be expedient (for), be good, (be) profit (-able for).

From *sún* (4862), together, and *phérō* (5342), to bring. To bring together.

(I) To bring together in one place (Ac 19:19).

(I) Figuratively, to bring together for anyone, in the sense of contributing, being advantageous, expedient, profitable (Mt 5:29, 30; 18:6; 19:10; Jn 11:50; 16:7; 1Co 6:12; 10:23; 2Co 8:10). The neuter participle may be used as a substantive: in the singular, meaning advantage, profit, benefit (1Co 7:35; 10:33; 12:7; Heb 12:10); or in the plural, meaning things profitable (Ac 20:20).

Syn.: *ōpheléō* (5623), to be useful, to benefit. Also *lusiteléō* (3081), to be advantageous, answer the purpose.

4852. σύμφημι, sumphēmi, *soom´-fay-mee*; from 4862 and 5346; to *say jointly*, i.e. *assent to*:—consent unto.

4853. συμφυλέτης, sumphuletēs, *soom-foo-let´-ace*; from 4862 and a derivative of 5443; a *co-tribesman*, i.e. *native of the same country*:— countryman.

4854. σύμφυτος, sumphutos, *soom´-foo-tos*; from 4862 and a derivative of 5453; *grown* along *with* (*connate*), i.e. (figurative) closely *united* to:—planted together.

Adjective from *sumphúō* (4855), to grow together, which is from *sún* (4862), together, and *phúō* (5453), to spring up, produce. Brought forth or grown together. In the NT, used only once in a figurative sense, united, at one with, e.g., oneness with Christ in the likeness of His death (Ro 6:5).

4855. συμφύω, sumphuō, *soom-foo´-o*; from 4862 and 5453; passive to *grow jointly*:—spring up with.

4856. συμφωνέω, sumphōneō, *soom-fo-neh´-o*; from 4859; to be *harmonious*, i.e. (figurative) to *accord* (*be suitable, concur*) or *stipulate* (by compact):—agree (together, with).

4857. συμφόνησις, sumphonēsis, *soom-fo´-nay-sis*; from 4856; *accordance*:—concord.

4858. συμφωνία, sumphōnia, *soom-fo-nee´-ah*; from 4859; *unison* of sound ("*symphony*"), i.e. a *concert* of instruments (harmonious *note*):—music.

4859. σύμφωνος, sumphōnos, *soom´-fo-nos*; from 4862 and 5456; *sounding together* (*alike*), i.e. (figurative) *accordant* (neuter as noun, *agreement*):—consent.

4860. συμψηφίζω, sumpsēphizō, *soom-psay-fid´-zo*; from 4862 and 5585; to *compute jointly*:—reckon.

4861. σύμψυχος, sumpsuchos, *soom´-psoo-khos*; from 4862 and 5590; *co-spirited*, i.e. *similar in sentiment*:—like-minded.

Adjective from *sún* (4862), together, and *psuchḗ* (5590), soul. Of one mind, joined together, at peace or harmony. Found only in Php 2:2, where it is used to encourage believers to unity and love. In the context of Philippians 2, *súmpsuchos* seems to imply a harmony of feeling as well as thought.

Syn.: *isópsuchos* (2473), like-minded; *súmphōnos* (4859), agreeing, of one accord; *homóphrōn* (3675), like-minded.

4862. σύν, sun, *soon*; a primary preposition denoting *union; with* or *together* (but much closer than 3326 or 3844), i.e. by association, companionship, process, resemblance, possession, instrumentality, addition, etc.:—beside, with. In comparative it has similar applications, including *completeness*.

A preposition. Together, with, together with, implying a nearer and closer connection than the preposition *metá* (3326), with.

(I) Particularly of society, companionship, consort, where one is said to be, do, suffer with someone, in connection and company with him. After verbs of sitting, standing, being or remaining with someone (Mk 4:10; Lk 1:56; 2:13; 7:12; 24:29; Ac 4:14; 14:4, 28; 21:16; 1Co 16:4; Col 2:5; 1Th 4:14).

(II) Figuratively of connection, association, as arising from similarity of experiences, from a common lot or event, with, in like manner with, like, e.g., to be dead with Christ (Ro 6:8; Col 2:20). Also 2Co 13:4; Gal 3:9; Col 2:13.

(III) Implying addition, accession, meaning besides, over and above (Lk 24:21).

(IV) In composition *sún* implies:

(A) Company, companionship, association with, together, same as the English prefix "con-" as in *sunágō* (4863), to bring together, gather. Also *sugkáthēmai* (4775), to sit with; *sunesthíō* (4906), to eat with.

(B) Completeness of an action, meaning altogether, round about, on every side, wholly, and thus intensive as in *sugkalúptō* (4780), to conceal completely; *sumplēróō* (4845), to fill up.

Syn.: *metá* (3326), with; *pará* (3844), near, beside. Also *homoú* (3674), together.

4863. συνάγω, sunagō, *soon-ag´-o*; from 4862 and 71; to *lead together*, i.e. *collect* or *convene*; specially to *entertain* (hospitably):— + accompany, assemble (selves, together), bestow, come together, gather (selves together, up, together), lead into, resort, take in.

From *sún* (4862), with, and *ágō* (71), to lead, assemble, gather together.

(I) Generally, to gather things or other people together. Spoken of one gathering things (Mt 3:12; 6:26; 12:30; 13:30, 47; 25:24, 26; Lk 3:17; 11:23; 12:17; 15:13; Jn 4:36; 6:12, 13). Spoken of one gathering people together (Mt 2:4; 22:10; 27:27; Ac 14:27; 15:30; Rev 13:10; 16:14, 16; 20:8). Passive: to be gathered by another (Mt 25:32).

(II) To take into one's house, meaning to give hospitality and protection (Mt 25:35, 38, 43).

Deriv.: *episunágō* (1996), to gather together in one place; *sunagōgḗ* (4864), a gathering, synagogue.

Syn.: *epathroízō* (1865), to accumulate; *sullégō* (4816), to collect or gather up; *sunathroízō* (4867), to gather together; *trugáō* (5166), to gather in as harvest or vintage.

4864. συναγωγή, sunagōgē, *soon-ag-o-gay´*; from (the reduplicated form of) 4863; an *assemblage* of persons; specially a Jewish "*synagogue*" (the meeting or the place); (by analogy) a Christian *church*:—assembly, congregation, synagogue.

Noun from *sunágō* (4863), to lead together, assemble. An assembly, a congregation, a synagogue. Spoken of the Jewish Christians. In other places in the NT, it is used as the assembly place of the Jews.

(I) Of a Jewish assembly or congregation, held in the synagogue buildings for prayer, reading the Scriptures, and exercising certain judicial powers (Mt 10:17; Mk 13:9; Lk 8:41; 12:11; 21:12; Ac 9:2; 13:42, 43; 22:19; 26:11).

(II) By metonymy of a Jewish place of worship, a synagogue, house of assembly. Synagogues appear to have been first introduced during the Babylonian exile when the people were deprived of their usual rites of worship and were accustomed to assemble on the Sabbath to hear portions of the Law read and expounded. After their return from exile, the same custom was continued in Palestine (cf. Ne 8:1ff.).

Assemblies were held in these at first only on the Sabbath and feast days; but subsequently also on the second and fifth days of the week, Mondays and Thursdays. The exercises consisted chiefly in prayers and the public reading of the OT which was expounded from the Hebrew into the vernacular tongue, with suitable exhortation (cf. Lk 4:16ff.; Ac 13:14ff.). The meeting was closed by a short prayer and benediction, to which the assembly responded with "Amen." See Mt 4:23; 6:2, 5; 9:35; 12:9; 13:54; 23:6, 34; Mk 1:21, 23, 29, 39; 3:1; 6:2; 12:39; Lk 4:15, 16, 20, 28, 33, 38, 44; 6:6; 7:5; 11:43; 13:10; 20:46; Jn 6:59; 18:20; Ac 6:9; 9:20; 13:5, 14; 14:1; 15:21; 17:1, 10, 17; 18:4, 7, 19, 26; 19:8; 24:12.

(III) Though synagogue denotes primarily the religious community of Jews (Lk 12:11; Ac 9:2; 26:11), it was also used of Judeo-Christian assemblies or churches (Jas 2:2). Through the Pauline writings, *ekklēsía* became the predominant name for the Christian church.

Deriv.: *aposunágōgos* (656), put out of the synagogue; *archisunágōgos* (752), ruler of the synagogue.

Syn.: *ekklēsía* (1577), church, assembly.

4865. συναγωνίζομαι, sunagōnizomai, *soon-ag-o-nid´-zom-ahee*; from 4862 and 75; to *struggle* in company *with*, i.e. (figurative) to *be a partner* (*assistant*):—strive together with.

From *sún* (4862), together, and *agōnízomai* (75), to strive, contend for victory, as in the public games. To exert oneself in company with another, to strive alongside, in the sense of aiding or helping. Used only in Ro 15:30, where Paul exhorts others to strive with him through prayer.

Syn.: *sunathléō* (4866), to wrestle in company with, strive together.

4866. συναθλέω, sunathleō, *soon-ath-leh´-o*; from 4862 and 118; to *wrestle* in company *with*, i.e. (figurative) to *seek jointly*:—labour with, strive together for.

4867. συναθροίζω, sunathroizō, *soon-ath-royd´-zo*; from 4862 and **ἀθροίζω**, *athroizō* (to *hoard*); to *convene*:—call (gather) together.

4868. συναίρω, sunairō, *soon-ah´ee-ro*; from 4862 and 142; to *make up together*, i.e. (figurative) to *compute* (an account):—reckon, take.

4869. συναιχμάλωτος, sunaichmalōtos, *soon-aheekh-mal´-o-tos*; from 4862 and 164; a *co-captive*:—fellow prisoner.

4870. συνακολουθέω, sunakoloutheō, *soon-ak-ol-oo-theh´-o*; from 4862 and 190; to *accompany*:—follow.

4871. συναλίζω, sunalizō, *soon-al-id´-zo*; from 4862 and **ἁλίζω**, *alizō* (to *throng*); to *accumulate*, i.e. *convene*:—assemble together.

4872. συναναβαίνω, sunanabainō, *soon-an-ab-ah´ee-no*; from 4862 and 305; to *ascend* in company *with*:—come up with.

4873. συνανάκειμαι, sunanakeimai, *soon-an-ak´-i-mahee*; from 4862 and 345; to *recline* in company *with* (at a meal):—sit (down, at the table, together) with (at meat).

4874. συναναμίγνυμι, sunanamignumi, *soon-an-am-ig´-noo-mee*; from 4862 and a compound of 303 and 3396; to *mix up together*, i.e. (figurative) *associate with*:—(have, keep) company (with).

4875. συναναπαύομαι, sunanapauomai, *soon-an-ap-ow´-om-ahee*; middle from 4862 and 373; to *recruit oneself* in company *with*:—refresh with.

4876. συναντάω, sunantaō, *soon-an-tah´-o*; from 4862 and a derivative of 473; to *meet with*; (figurative) to *occur*:—befall, meet.

4877. συνάντησις, sunantēsis, *soon-an´-tay-sis*; from 4876; a *meeting with*:—meet.

4878. συναντιλαμβάνομαι, sunantilambanomai, *soon-an-tee-lam-ban´-om-ahee*; from 4862 and 482; to *take* hold of *opposite together*, i.e. *co-operate* (*assist*):—help.

4879. συναπαγω, sunapagō, *soon-ap-ag´-o*; from 4862 and 520; to *take off together*, i.e. *transport with* (*seduce*, passive *yield*):—carry (lead) away with, condescend.

4880. συναποθνήσκω, sunapothnēskō, *soon-ap-oth-nace´-ko*; from 4862 and 599; to *decease* (literal) in company *with*, or (figurative) similarly *to*:—be dead (die) with.

4881. συναπόλλυμι, sunapollumi, *soon-ap-ol´-loo-mee;* from 4862 and 622; to *destroy* (middle or passive *be slain*) in company *with*:—perish with.

4882. συναποστέλλω, sunapostellō, *soon-ap-os-tel´-lo*; from 4862 and 649; to *despatch* (on an errand) in company *with*:—send with.

4883. συναρμολογέω, sunarmologeō, *soon-ar-mol-og-eh´-o*; from 4862 and a derivative of a compound of 719 and 3004 (in its original sense of *laying*); to *render close-jointed together*, i.e. *organize compactly*:—be fitly framed (joined) together.

4884. συναρπάζω, sunarpazō, *soon-ar-pad´-zo*; from 4862 and 726; to *snatch together*, i.e. *seize*:—catch.

4885. συναυξάνω, sunauxanō, *soon-owx-an´-o*; from 4862 and 837; to *increase* (*grow up*) *together*:—grow together.

4886. σύνδεσμος, sundesmos, *soon´-des-mos*; from 4862 and 1199; a *joint tie*, i.e. *ligament*, (figurative) *uniting principle, control*:—band, bond.

4887. συνδέω, sundeō, *soon-deh´-o*; from 4862 and 1210; to *bind with*, i.e. (passive) *be a fellow prisoner* (figurative):—be bound with.

4888. συνδοξάζω, sundoxazō, *soon-dox-ad´-zo*; from 4862 and 1392; to *exalt* to dignity in company (i.e. *similarly*) *with*:—glorify together.

From *sún* (4862), together, and *doxázō* (1392), to glorify. To glorify together. In the NT used only in Ro 8:17, in the passive, meaning to share in the glory of another. It is used there to express the privilege given to believers in Christ to share in His glory (cf. Jn 17:22).

4889. σύνδουλος, sundoulos, *soon´-doo-los*; from 4862 and 1401; a *co-slave*, i.e. *servitor* or *ministrant of the same master* (human or divine):—fellow servant.

Noun from *sún* (4862), together, and *doúlos* (1401), slave. A fellow slave, fellow servant. Also see the entry for *doúlos*.

(I) Particularly spoken of those in involuntary service (Mt 24:29).

(II) Spoken of those in voluntary service: of Christians serving Christ together (Col 1:7; 4:7; Rev 6:11); of angels serving the Lord God (Rev 19:10; 22:9); and of officials in an oriental court (Mt 18:28, 29, 31, 33).

4890. συνδρομή, sundromē, *soon-drom-ay´*; from (the alternate of) 4936; a *running together*, i.e. (riotous) *concourse*:—run together.

4891. συνεγείρω, sunegeirō, *soon-eg-i´-ro*; from 4862 and 1453; to *rouse* (from death) in company *with*, i.e. (figurative) to *revivify* (spiritually) in resemblance to:—raise up together, rise with.

From *sún* (4862), together, and *egeírō* (1453), to raise. To raise up together. Used in the NT of being raised up together with Christ. *Sunegeírō* does not refer to merely being raised in the likeness of Christ's resurrection, but rather, it points to a condition or work effected by union with Christ in His resurrection, taking place in and proceeding from it (Eph 2:6; Col 2:12; 3:1). The term, as it is used in the NT, is synonymous with justification (see Ro 4:25; 5:1; Col 2:12, 13).

4892. συνέδριον, sunedrion, *soon-ed´-ree-on*; neuter of a presumed derivative of a compound of 4862 and the base of 1476; a *joint session*, i.e. (special) the Jewish *Sanhedrin*; (by analogy) a subordinate *tribunal*:—council.

4893. συνείδησις, suneidēsis, *soon-i´-day-sis*; from a prolonged form of 4894; *co-perception*, i.e. moral *consciousness*:—conscience.

Noun from *suneidō* (4894), to be conscious of. Conscience.

(I) A knowing of oneself, consciousness; and hence conscience, that faculty of the soul which distinguishes between right and wrong and prompts one to choose the former and avoid the latter (Jn 8:9; Ro 2:15; 9:1; 13:5; 1Co 10:25, 27–29; 2Co 1:12; 8:7; 1Ti 4:2; Tit 1:15; Heb 9:9, 14; 10:2, 22). Spoken of a good conscience (Ac 23:1; 1Ti 1:5, 19; Heb 13:18; 1Pe 3:16, 21); a pure conscience (1Ti 3:9; 2Ti 1:3); a conscience void of offence (Ac 24:16); a weak conscience (1Co 8:7, 10, 12); an evil conscience (Heb 10:22).

(II) Used by metonymy of approval by the consciences of others (2Co 4:2; 5:11).

4894. συνείδω, suneidō, *soon-i´-do*; from 4862 and 1492; to *see completely*; used (like its primary) only in two past tenses, respectively meaning to *understand* or *become aware*, and to *be conscious* or (clandestinely) *informed of*:—consider, know, be privy, be ware of.

From *sún* (4862), together, and *eídō* (1492), to know. To know together, to become aware of.

(I) To know together with someone, to share information (Ac 5:2). To know within oneself, be conscious of (1Co 4:4).

(II) Figuratively, to see in one's own mind, to perceive within oneself, to be aware of (Ac 12:12; 14:6).

Deriv.: *suneidēsis* (4893), conscience.

4895. σύνειμι, suneimi, *soon´-i-mee*; from 4862 and 1510 (including its various inflections); to *be* in company *with*, i.e. *present* at the time:—be with.

4896. σύνειμι, suneimi, *soon´-i-mee*; from 4862 and **εἶμι, *eimi*** (to *go*); to *assemble*:—gather together.

4897. συνεισέρχομαι, suneiserchomai, *soon-ice-er´-khom-ahee*; from 4862 and 1525; to *enter* in company *with*:—go in with, go with into.

4898. συνέκδημος, sunekdēmos, *soon-ek´-day-mos*; from 4862 and the base of 1553; a *co-absentee* from home, i.e. *fellow traveller*:—companion in travel, travel with.

4899. συνεκλεκτός, suneklektos, *soon-ek-lek-tos´*; from a compound of 4862 and 1586; *chosen* in company *with*, i.e. *co-elect* (*fellow Christian*):—elected together with.

4900. συνελαύνω, sunelaunō, *soon-el-ow´-no*; from 4862 and 1643; to *drive together*, i.e. (figurative) *exhort* (to reconciliation):—+ set at one again.

4901. συνεπιμαρτυρέω, sunepimartureō, *soon-ep-ee-mar-too-reh´-o*; from 4862 and 1957; to *testify further jointly*, i.e. *unite in adding evidence*:—also bear witness.

4902. συνέπομαι, sunepomai, *soon-ep´-om-ahee*; middle from 4862 and a primary **ἕπω, *epō*** (to *follow*); to *attend* (*travel*) in company *with*:—accompany.

4903. συνεργέω, sunergeō, *soon-erg-eh´-o*; from 4904; to *be a fellow worker*, i.e. *co-operate*:—help (work) with, work (-er) together.

4904. συνεργός, sunergos, *soon-er-gos´*; from a presumed compound of 4862 and the base of 2041; a *co-labourer*, i.e. *coadjutor*:—companion in labour, (fellow-) helper (-labourer, -worker), labourer together with, workfellow.

4905. συνέρχομαι, sunerchomai, *soon-er´-khom-ahee*; from 4862 and 2064; to *convene, depart* in company *with, associate* with, or (special) *cohabit* (conjugally):—accompany, assemble (with), come (together), come (company, go) with, resort.

4906. συνεσθίω, sunesthiō, *soon-es-thee´-o*; from 4862 and 2068 (including its alternate); to *take food* in company *with*:—eat with.

4907. σύνεσις, sunesis, *soon´-es-is*; from 4920; a mental *putting together*, i.e. *intelligence* or (concretely) the *intellect*:—knowledge, understanding.

Noun from *suníēmi* (4920), to comprehend, reason out. Literally, a sending or putting together. In the NT, a putting together in the mind, i.e. intelligence, discernment, understanding (Lk 2:47; 1Co 1:19; Eph 3:4; Col 1:9; 2:2; 2Ti 2:7). By metonymy, the mind itself (Mk 12:33).

Syn.: *diánoia* (1271), understanding; *sophía* (4678), wisdom; *phrḗn* (5424), mind, mental perception; *phrónesis* (5428), prudence.

4908. συνετός, sunetos, *soon-et´-os*; from 4920; mentally *put* (or *putting*) *together*, i.e. *sagacious*:—prudent. Compare 5429.

Adjective from *suníēmi* (4920), to reason out, perceive, understand. Literally, capable of putting together in the mind. Hence, intelligent, perceptive, discerning. Having *súnesis* (4907), comprehension (Mt 11:25; Lk 10:21; Ac 13:7; 1Co 1:19).

Deriv.: *asúnetos* (801), unwise, without discernment or understanding.

Syn.: *sophós* (4680), wise; *phrónimos* (5429), discreet, prudent.

4909. συνευδοκέω, suneudokeō, *soon-yoo-dok-eh´-o*; from 4862 and 2106; to *think well of in common*, i.e. *assent* to, *feel gratified with*:—allow, assent, be pleased, have pleasure.

4910. συνευωχέω, suneuōcheō, *soon-yoo-o-kheh´-o*; from 4862 and a derivative of a presumed compound of 2095 and a derivative of 2192 (meaning to *be in good condition*, i.e. [by implication] to *fare well*, or *feast*); to *entertain* sumptuously in company *with*, i.e. (middle or passive) to *revel together*:—feast with.

4911. συνεφίστημι, sunephistēmi, *soon-ef-is´-tay-mee*; from 4862 and 2186; to *stand up together*, i.e. to *resist* (or *assault*) *jointly*:—rise up together.

4912. συνέχω, sunechō, *soon-ekh´-o*; from 4862 and 2192; to *hold together*, i.e. to *compress* (the ears, with a crowd or siege) or *arrest* (a prisoner); (figurative) to *compel, perplex, afflict, preoccupy*:—constrain, hold, keep in, press, lie sick of, stop, be in a strait, straiten, be taken with, throng.

From *sún* (4862), an intensive, and *échō* (2192), to have. To hold together, press together; to hold fast, to shut something up:

(I) Particularly, to cover one's ears (Ac 7:57), or of a city besieged, to shut it up (Lk 19:43); of a crowd, to press together (Lk 8:45); of persons having a prisoner in custody, to hold fast (Lk 22:63).

(II) Figuratively, to constrain, compel, press in on (2Co 5:14); in the passive, to be in constraint, distressed, perplexed (Lk 12:50; Ac 28:5; Php 1:23). With the meaning of to be seized, affected, afflicted: with fear (Lk 8:37), with diseases (Mt 4:24; Lk 4:38; Ac 28:8).

Deriv.: *sunochḗ* (4928), a holding together, a shutting up of the womb.

Syn.: *thlíbō* (2346), to distress, afflict; *piézō* (4885), to press down together; *anagkázō* (315), to compel; *parabiázō* (3849), to constrain.

4913. συνήδομαι, sunēdomai, *soon-ay´-dom-ahee*; middle from 4862 and the base of 2237; to *rejoice* in *with* oneself, i.e. *feel satisfaction* concerning:—delight.

4914. συνήθεια, sunētheia, *soon-ay´-thi-ah*; from a compound of 4862 and 2239; *mutual habituation*, i.e. *usage*:—custom.

4915. συνηλικιώτης, sunēlikiōtēs, *soon-ay-lik-ee-o´-tace*; from 4862 and a derivative of 2244; a *co-aged* person, i.e. *alike* in years:—equal.

4916. συνθάπτω, sunthaptō, *soon-thap´-to*; from 4862 and 2290; to *inter* in company *with*, i.e. (figurative) to *assimilate* spiritually (to Christ by a sepulture as to sin):—bury with.

4917. συνθλάω, sunthlaō, *soon-thlah´-o*; from 4862 and **θλάω,** ***hlaō*** (to *crush*); to *dash together*, i.e. *shatter*:—break.

4918. συνθλίβω, sunthlibō, *soon-thlee´-bo*; from 4862 and 2346; to *compress*, i.e. *crowd* on all sides:—throng.

4919. συνθρύπτω, sunthruptō, *soon-throop´-to*; from 4862 and **θρύπτω,** ***thruptō*** (to *crumble*); to *crush together*, i.e. (figurative) to *dispirit*:—break.

4920. συνίημι, suniēmi, *soon-ee´-ay-mee*; from 4862 and **ἵημι,** ***hiēmi*** (to *send*); to *put together*, i.e. (mentally) to *comprehend*; by implication to *act piously*:—consider, understand, be wise.

From *sún* (4862), together or together with, and *híēmi* (n.f.), to send or put. Literally, to send or bring together, as soldiers for a battle. Figuratively, to bring together in the mind, to grasp concepts and see the proper relation between them. Hence, to comprehend, understand, perceive.

In the NT, generally to understand, comprehend (Mt 13:13–15, 19, 23; 15:10; Mk 4:12; 6:52; Lk 8:10; Ac 28:26, 27; Ro 15:21; 2Co 10:12). Followed by those ideas or concepts which are understood (Mt 13:51; 16:12; 17:13; Lk 2:50; 18:34; 24:45; Ac 7:25; Eph 5:17). To understand, be wise, in respect to duty toward God to be upright, righteous, godly (Ro 3:11).

Deriv.: *súnesis* (4907), understanding; *sunetós* (4908), a person who understands.

Syn.: *ginṓskō* (1097), to know; *diaginṓskō* (1231), to know exactly; *eídō* (1492), to know intuitively; *epiginṓskō* (1921), to know fully, discern; *epístamai* (1987), to know well; *suneídō* (4894), to know intuitively, be conscious of; *phronéō* (5426), to think, understand.

4921. συνιστάω, sunistaō, *soon-is-tah´-o*; or (strengthened) **συνιστάνω,** ***sunistanō***, *soon-is-tan´-o*; or **συνίστημι,** ***sunistēmi***, *soon-is´-tay-mee*; from 4862 and 2476 (including its collective forms); to *set together*, i.e. (by implication) to *introduce* (fabourably), or (figurative) to *exhibit*; intransitive to *stand near*, or (figurative) to *constitute*:—approve, commend, consist, make, stand (with).

From *sún* (4862), together with, and *hístēmi* (2476), to set, place, stand. Transitively, to cause to stand with; intransitively, to stand with. *Sunistánō* and *sunistáō* are later forms of *sunístēmi*.

(I) Transitively, to cause to stand with, to place together. In the NT, to place with or before someone.

(A) Of persons, to introduce, present to one's acquaintance for favourable notice; hence, to commend, to present as worthy (Ro 16:1; 2Co 3:1; 4:2; 5:12; 10:12, 18; 12:11).

(B) Figuratively, to set forth with or before someone, to declare, show, make known and conspicuous (Ro 3:5; 5:8; 2Co 6:4; 7:11; Gal 2:18).

(II) Intransitively, to stand with, together.

(A) Particularly of persons (Lk 9:32; Sept.: 1Sa 17:26).

(B) Figuratively, from the transitive, to join parts together into a whole, to constitute, restore. In the NT, to be constituted, created, to exist (Col 1:17; 2Pe 3:5).

Deriv.: *sustatikós* (4956), commendatory.

Syn.: *apodeíknumi* (584), to prove by demonstration; *epainéō* (1867), to commend.

4922. συνοδεύω, sunodeuō, *soon-od-yoo´-o*; from 4862 and 3593; to *travel* in company *with*:—journey with.

4923. συνοδία, sunodia, *soon-od-ee´-ah*; from a compound of 4862 and 3598 ("*synod*"); *companionship* on a journey, i.e. (by implication) a *caravan*:—company.

4924. συνοικέω, sunoikeō, *soon-oy-key´-o*; from 4862 and 3611; to *reside together* (as a family):—dwell together.

4925. συνοικοδομέω, sunoikodomeō, *soon-oy-kod-om-eh´-o*; from 4862 and 3618; to *construct*, i.e. (passive) to *compose* (in company with other Christians, figurative):—build together.

4926. συνομιλέω, sunomileō, *soon-om-il-eh´-o*; from 4862 and 3656; to *converse* mutually:—talk with.

4927. συνομορέω, sunomoreō, *soon-om-or-eh´-o*; from 4862 and a derivative of a compound of the base of 3674 and the base of 3725; to *border together*, i.e. *adjoin*:—join hard.

4928. συνόχη, sunochē, *soon-okh´-ay*; from 4912; *restraint*, i.e. (figurative) *anxiety*:—anguish, distress.

4929. συντάσσω, suntassō, *soon-tas´-so*; from 4862 and 5021; to *arrange jointly*, i.e. (figurative) to *direct*:—appoint.

4930. συντέλεια, sunteleia, *soon-tel´-i-ah*; from 4931; *entire completion*, i.e. *consummation* (of a dispensation):—end.

Noun from *sunteléō* (4931), to accomplish. A full end, completion. In the NT, generally, the end, consummation, used only in the expressions *suntéleia toú aiṓnos*, "the completion of the age" (Mt 13:39, 40, 49; 24:3; 28:20) and *suntéleia tṓn aiṓnōn*, "the completion of the ages" (Heb 9:26). The word *aiṓn* (165), age, usually translated world, refers to a period of time.

Syn.: *télos* (5056), the end, goal.

4931. συντελέω, sunteleō, *soon-tel-eh´-o*; from 4862 and 5055; to *complete entirely*; genitive to *execute* (literal or figurative):—end, finish, fulfill, make.

From *sún* (4862), together or an intensive, and *teléō* (5055), to finish. In the NT, to end altogether, to finish wholly, to complete.

(I) Generally, spoken of finishing an activity (Mt 7:28; Lk 4:13). Spoken of time being ended (Lk 4:2; Ac 21:27). In the sense of to fulfill, to accomplish, e.g., a promise or prophecy (Mk 13:14; Ro 9:28).

(II) To finish, to complete in the sense of to make (Heb 8:8).

Deriv.: *suntéleia* (4930), a finishing, consummation, end.

Syn.: *apoteléō* (658), to finish, bring to a goal; *diateléō* (1300), to bring through to an end; *eklēróō* (1603), to fulfill; *ekteléō* (1615), to finish out, complete; *exartízō* (1822), to fit out, accomplish; *epiteléō* (2005), to complete, accomplish; *pímplēmi* or *plḗthō* (4130), to fill; *plēróō* (4137), to fulfill, complete; *poiéō* (4160), to do, fulfill; *sumplēróō* (4845), to fill completely; *teleióō* (5048), to accomplish.

4932. συντέμνω, suntemnō, *soon-tem´-no*; from 4862 and the base of 5114; to *contract* by cutting, i.e. (figurative) *do concisely* (*speedily*):—(cut) short.

4933. συντηρέω, suntēreō, *soon-tay-reh´-o*; from 4862 and 5083; to *keep* closely *together*, i.e. (by implication) to *conserve* (from ruin); mentally to *remember* (and *obey*):—keep, observe, preserve.

From *sún* (4862), an intensive, and *tēréō* (5083), to guard, keep. To watch or keep together with someone. In the NT:

(I) To watch or keep in the sense of to keep for oneself. Spoken of Herod keeping John the Baptist in close custody (Mk 6:20). Figuratively, to keep or lay up with oneself in mind (Lk 2:19).

(II) To keep or preserve together, from loss or destruction. Spoken of wine and the skin bottles in which it is kept (Mt 9:17; Lk 5:38).

Syn.: *diaphulássō* (1314), to guard carefully; *phulássō* (5442), to preserve.

4934. συντίθεμαι, suntithemai, *soon-tith´-em-ahee*; middle from 4862 and 5087; to *place jointly*, i.e. (figurative) to *consent* (*bargain, stipulate*), *concur*:—agree, assent, covenant.

4935. συντόμως, suntomōs, *soon-tom´-oce;* adverb from a derivative of 4932; *concisely* (*briefly*):—a few words.

4936. συντρέχω, suntrechō, *soon-trekh´-o;* from 4862 and 5143 (including its alternate); to *rush together* (hastily *assemble*) or *headlong* (figurative):—run (together, with).

4937. συντρίβω, suntribō, *soon-tree´-bo;* from 4862 and the base of 5147; to *crush completely,* i.e. to *shatter* (literal or figurative):—break (in pieces), broken to shivers (+ -hearted), bruise.

4938. σύντριμμα, suntrimma, *soon-trim´-mah;* from 4937; *concussion* or utter *fracture* (properly concrete), i.e. complete *ruin:*—destruction.

4939. σύντροφος, suntrophos, *soon´-trof-os;* from 4862 and 5162 (in a passive sense); a *fellow-nursling,* i.e. *comrade:*—brought up with.

4940. συντυγχάνω, suntugchanō, *soon-toong-khan´-o;* from 4862 and 5177; to *chance together,* i.e. *meet* with (*reach*):—come at.

4941. Συντύχη, Suntuchē, *soon-too´-khay;* from 4940; an *accident; Syntyche,* a Christian female:—Syntyche.

4942. συνυποκρίνομαι, sunupokrinomai, *soon-oo-pok-rin´-om-ahee;* from 4862 and 5271; to *act hypocritically* in concert *with:*—dissemble with.

4943. συνυπουργέω, sunupourgeō, *soon-oop-oorg-eh´-o;* from 4862 and a derivative of a compound of 5259 and the base of 2041; to *be a co-auxiliary,* i.e. *assist:*—help together.

4944. συνωδίνω, sunōdinō, *soon-o-dee´-no;* from 4862 and 5605; to *have* (parturition) *pangs* in company (concert, simultaneously) *with,* i.e. (figurative) to *sympathize* (in expectation of relief from suffering):—travail in pain together.

4945. συνωμοσία, sunōmosia, *soon-o-mos-ee´-ah;* from a compound of 4862 and 3660; a *swearing together,* i.e. (by implication) a *plot:*—conspiracy.

4946. Συράκουσαι, Surakousai, *soo-rak´-oo-sahee;* plural of uncertain derivative; *Syracusæ,* the capital of Sicily:—Syracuse.

4947. Συρία, Suria, *soo-ree´-ah;* probably of Hebrew origin [6865]; *Syria* (i.e. *Tsyria* or *Tyre*), a region of Asia:—Syria.

4948. Σύρος, Suros, *soo´-ros;* from the same as 4947; a *Syran* (i.e. probably *Tyrian*), a native of Syria:—Syrian.

4949. Συροφοίνισσα, Surophoinissa, *soo-rof-oy´-nis-sah;* feminine of a compound of 4948 and the same as 5403; a *Syro-phoenician* woman, i.e. a female native of Phoenicia in Syria:—Syrophenician.

4950. σύρτις, surtis, *soor´-tis;* from 4951; a *shoal* (from the sand *drawn* thither by the waves), i.e. the *Syrtis* Major or great bay on the north coast of Africa:—quicksands.

4951. σύρω, surō, *soo´-ro;* probably akin to 138; to *trail:*—drag, draw, hale.

To draw, drag, drag away, to haul. Spoken of things (Jn 21:8; Rev 12:4; Sept.: 2Sa 17:13) or of persons, to drag by force before magistrates or to punishment (Ac 8:3; 14:19; 17:6).

Deriv.: *katasúrō* (2694), to drag down, hale; *súrtis* (4950), a sandbank.

4952. συσπαράσσω, susparassō, *soos-par-as´-so;* from 4862 and 4682; to *rend completely,* i.e. (by analogy) to *convulse* violently:—throw down.

4953. σύσσημον, sussēmon, *soos´-say-mon;* neuter of a compound of 4862 and the base of 4591; a *sign in common,* i.e. preconcerted *signal:*—token.

4954. σύσσωμος, sussōmos, *soos´-so-mos;* from 4862 and 4983; *of* a *joint body,* i.e. (figurative) a *fellow member* of the Christian community:—of the same body.

Adjective from *sún* (4862), together with, and *sō̂ma* (4983), body. Of the same body with another. Figuratively, spoken in respect to the Christian church as the body of Christ and of the Gentiles as partakers in it. Used only in Eph 3:6.

Syn.: *adelphós* (80), brother.

4955. συστασιαστής, sustasiastēs, *soos-tas-ee-as-tace´;* from a compound of 4862 and a derivative of 4714; a *fellow insurgent:*—make insurrection with.

4956. συστατικός, sustatikos, *soos-tat-ee-kos´;* from a derivative of 4921; *introductory,* i.e. *recommendatory:*—of commendation.

4957. συσταυρόω, sustauroō, *soos-tow-ro´-o;* from 4862 and 4717; to *impale* in company *with* (literal or figurative):—crucify with.

From *sún* (4862), together with, and *stauróō* (4717), to crucify. To crucify with anyone (Mt 27:44; Mk 15:32; Jn 19:32). Figuratively, spoken of the old human nature, which lost its power when Christ was crucifed (Ro 6:6; Gal 2:20).

4958. συστέλλω, sustellō, *soos-tel´-lo;* from 4862 and 4724; to *send* (*draw*) *together,* i.e. *enwrap* (*enshroud* a corpse for burial), *contract* (an interval):—short, wind up.

4959. συστενάζω, sustenazō, *soos-ten-ad´-zo;* from 4862 and 4727; to *moan jointly,* i.e. (figurative) *experience a common calamity:*—groan together.

4960. συστοιχέω, sustoicheō, *soos-toy-kheh´-o;* from 4862 and 4748; to *file together* (as soldiers in ranks), i.e. (figurative) to *correspond* to:—answer to.

4961. συστρατιώτης, sustratiōtēs, *soos-trat-ee-o´-tace;* from 4862 and 4757; a *co-campaigner,* i.e. (figurative) an *associate* in Christian toil:—fellowsoldier.

4962. συστρέφω, sustrephō, *soos-tref´-o;* from 4862 and 4762; to *twist together,* i.e. *collect* (a bundle, a crowd):—gather.

4963. συστροφή, sustrophē, *soos-trof-ay´;* from 4962; a *twisting together,* i.e. (figurative) a secret *coalition,* riotous *crowd:*—+ band together, concourse.

4964. συσχηματίζω, suschēmatizō, *soos-khay-mat-id´-zo;* from 4862 and a derivative of 4976; to *fashion alike,* i.e. *conform* to the same pattern (figurative):—conform to, fashion self according to.

From *sún* (4862), together with, and *schēmatízō* (n.f.), to fashion. To give the same form with, to conform to anything. In the NT, used only in the middle or passive: to conform oneself (1Pe 1:14) or to be conformed to anything (Ro 12:2).

Syn.: *summorphóō* (4833), to be conformed to.

4965. Συχάρ, Suchar, *soo-khar´;* of Hebrew origin [7941]; *Sychar* (i.e. *Shekar*), a place in Palestine:—Sychar.

4966. Συχέμ, Suchem, *soo-khem´;* of Hebrew origin [7927]; *Sychem* (i.e. *Shekem*), the name of a Canaanite and of a place in Palestine:—Sychem.

4967. σφαγή, sphagē, *sfag-ay´;* from 4969; *butchery* (of animals for food or sacrifice, or [figurative] of men [*destruction*]):—slaughter.

4968. σφάγιον, sphagion, *sfag´-ee-on;* neuter of a derivative of 4967; a *victim* (in sacrifice):—slain beast.

4969. σφάζω, sphazō, *sfad´-zo;* a primary verb; to *butcher* (especially an animal for food or in sacrifice) or (genitive) to *slaughter,* or (special) to *maim* (violently):—kill, slay, wound.

4970. σφόδρα, sphodra, *sfod´-rah*; neuter plural of **σφοδρός,** ***sphodros*** (*violent*; of uncertain derivative) as adverb; *vehemently*, i.e. in *a high degree, much*:—exceeding (-ly), greatly, sore, very.

4971. σφοδρῶς, sphodrōs, *sfod-roce´*; adverb from the same as 4970; *very much*:—exceedingly.

4972. σφραγίζω, sphragizō, *sfrag-id´-zo*; from 4973; to *stamp* (with a signet or private mark) for security or preservation (literal or figurative); by implication to *keep secret*, to *attest*:—(set a, set to) seal up, stop.

4973. σφραγίς, sphragis, *sfrag-ece´*; probably strengthened from 5420; a *signet* (as *fencing* in or protecting from misappropriation); by implication the *stamp* impressed (as a mark of privacy, or genuineness), literal or figurative:—seal.

4974. σφυρόν, sphuron, *sfoo-ron´*; neuter of a presumed derivative probably of the same as **σφαῖρα**, ***sphaira*** (a *ball*, "*sphere*"; compare the feminine **σφῦρα**, ***sphura***, a *hammer*); the *ankle* (as *globular*):—ankle bone.

4975. σχεδόν, schedon, *skhed-on´*; neuter of a presumed derivative of the alternate of 2192 as adverb; *nigh*, i.e. *nearly*:—almost.

4976. σχῆμα, schēma, *skhay´-mah*; from the alternate of 2192; a *figure* (as a *mode* or *circumstance*), i.e. (by implication) external *condition*:—fashion.

Noun from *schein* (n.f.), the 2 aor. inf. of *échō* (2192), have. Fashion, external form, appearance.

In the NT, spoken of specific external circumstances, the state or condition of something (1Co 7:31). In Php 2:8, it refers to the Lord Jesus' whole outward appearance or condition, which bore no difference to that of other men.

Deriv.: *aschḗmōn* (809), shapeless, uncomely; *euschḗmōn* (2158), comely, well-formed.

4977. σχίζω, schizō, *skhid´-zo*; apparently a primary verb; to *split* or *sever* (literal or figurative):—break, divide, open, rend, make a rent.

4978. σχίσμα, schisma, *skhis´-mah*; from 4977; a *split* or *gap* ("*schism*"), literal or figurative:—division, rent, schism.

Noun from *schízō* (4977), to split, tear. A schism, a rip, a tear, as in a piece of cloth (Mt 9:16; Mk 2:21). Figuratively, a schism, dissension, division as to opinion (Jn 7:43; 9:16; 10:19; 1Co 1:10; 11:18; 12:25).

Syn.: *dichostasía* (1370), division, dissension.

4979. σχοινίον, schoinion, *skhoy-nee´-on*; diminitive of **σχοῖνος**, ***schoinos*** (a *rush* or *flag*-plant; of uncertain derivative); a *rushlet*, i.e. *grass-withe* or *tie* (general):—small cord, rope.

4980. σχολάζω, scholazō, *skhol-ad´-zo*; from 4981; to *take a holiday*, i.e. *be at leisure* for (by implication *devote oneself* wholly to); figurative, to *be vacant* (of a house):—empty, give self.

4981. σχολή, scholē, *schol-ay´*; probably feminine of a presumed derivative of the alternate of 2192; properly *loitering* (as a *withholding* of oneself from work) or *leisure*, i.e. (by implication) a "*school*" (as *vacation* from physical employment):—school.

4982. σώζω, sozō, *sode´-zo*; from a primary **σῶς**, ***sōs*** (contracted from obsolete **σάος**, ***saos***, "*safe*"); to *save*, i.e. *deliver* or *protect* (literal or figurative):—heal, preserve, save (self), do well, be (make) whole.

From *sṓs* (n.f.), safe, delivered. To save, deliver, make whole, preserve safe from danger, loss, destruction.

(I) Used particularly of persons, to keep safe, to preserve or deliver out of physical death (Mt 8:25; 14:30; 16:25; 24:22; 27:40, 42; Mk 3:4; 8:35; 13:20; Lk 6:9; 9:24; Jn 12:27; Ac 27:20, 31; Heb 5:7; Jude 5).

(II) Of sick persons, to save from death and (by implication) to heal, restore to health; passively, to be healed, recover (Mt 9:21, 22; Mk 5:23, 28, 34; Lk 7:50; 8:36, 48; Jn 11:12; Ac 4:9; Jas 5:15).

(III) Specifically of salvation from eternal death, sin, and the punishment and misery consequent to sin. To save, and (by implication), to give eternal life (Mt 1:21; 10:22; 18:11; 19:25; 24:13; Mk 10:26; 13:13; 16:16; Lk 8:12; Jn 5:34; 10:9; Ac 2:40; Ro 5:9, 10; 11:14; 1Co 1:21; 5:5; 1Ti 2:15; 4:16; 2Ti 4:18; Heb 7:25; Jas 1:21; 5:20). The participle is used substantively to refer to those being saved, those who have obtained salvation through Christ and are kept by Him (Lk 13:23; Ac 2:47; 1Co 1:18; 2Co 2:15; Rev 21:24).

Deriv.: *diasṓzō* (1295), to bring safely through; *sōtḗr* (4990), Saviour.

Syn.: *anagennáō* (313), to beget again from above; *diasṓzō* (1295), to bring safely through; *therapeúō* (2323), to care for the sick for the purpose of healing; *iáomai* (2390), to heal both physically and spiritually; *phulássō* (5442), to preserve.

4983. σῶμα, sōma, *so´-mah*; from 4982; the *body* (as a *sound* whole), used in a very wide application, literal or figurative:—bodily, body, slave.

A noun meaning body, an organized whole made up of parts and members.

(I) Generally of any material body: spoken of plants (1Co 15:37, 38) and also of celestial bodies: the sun, moon, stars (1Co 15:40 [cf. 41]).

(II) Specifically of creatures, living or dead.

(A) Spoken of a human body, different from *sárx* (4561), flesh, which word denotes the material of the body. **(1)** A living body (Mt 5:29, 30; 6:25; 26:12; Mk 5:29; 14:8; Lk 12:22, 23; Jn 2:21; Ro 1:24; 4:19; 1Co 6:13; 15:44; 2Co 4:10; 10:10; Col 1:22; 2:23; Heb 10:5; 1Pe 2:24). Spoken in antithesis to *psuchḗ* (5590), soul (Mt 10:28; Lk 12:4), and *pneúma* (4151), spirit (Ro 8:10; 1Co 5:3; 7:34); also used along with *sṓma, psuchḗ* and *pneúma* as a periphrasis for the whole man (1Th 5:23). Spoken of the seat of sinful affections and appetites (cf. *sárx* [4561], II, C). See Ro 6:6; 7:24 [cf. v. 23]; 8:13; Col 2:11. **(2)** A dead body, corpse, generally (Mt 14:12; 27:52, 58, 59; Lk 23:52, 55; 24:3, 23; Jn 19:31; Ac 9:40; Jude 9). Specifically spoken of the body of Christ as crucified for the salvation of man (Ro 7:4); spoken figuratively of the communion bread as representing the body of Christ as crucified for the salvation of man (Mt 26:26; Mk 14:22; Lk 22:19; 1Co 10:16; 11:24, 27, 29).

(B) Spoken of living beasts (Jas 3:3); also of the dead body of a beast, meaning a carcass (Lk 17:37; of victims slain as sacrifices (Heb 13:11).

(III) By metonymy, spoken of the body as the external man, to which is ascribed that which strictly belongs to the person, man, individual; forming a periphrasis for the person himself (Mt 6:22, 23; Lk 11:34, 36; Ro 12:1; Eph 5:28; Php 1:20). Spoken in a figurative sense of anyone having sexual union with a harlot as becoming part of one body with that harlot (1Co 6:16). Spoken of slaves (Rev 18:13).

(IV) Spoken figuratively for a body, meaning a whole, aggregate, collective mass, as spoken of the Christian church, the whole body of Christians collectively, of which Christ is the head (Ro 12:5; 1Co 10:17; 12:13, 27; Eph 1:23; 2:16; 4:4, 12, 16; 5:23, 30; Col 1:18, 24; 2:19; 3:15).

(V) Spoken figuratively in the sense of body, substance, reality as opposed *hē skiá* (4639), the shadow or type of future things (Col 2:17).

Deriv.: *sússōmos* (4954), belonging to the same body, of the same body; *sōmatikós* (4984), corporeal, physical.

4984. σωματικός, sōmatikos, *so-mat-ee-kos´*; from 4983; *corporeal* or *physical*:—bodily.

Adjective from *sṓma* (4983), body. Bodily, corporeal, having a shape of (Lk 3:22); pertaining to the body (1Ti 4:8).

Deriv.: *sōmatikṓs* (4985), corporeally, physically, bodily.

Syn.: *sarkikós* (4559), bodily, carnal, fleshly; *sárkinos* (4560), made of flesh; *phusikós* (5446), physical, material, natural.

4985. σωματικῶς, sōmatikōs, *so-mat-ee-koce´*; adverb from 4984; *corporeally* or *physically*:—bodily.

4986. Σώπατρος, Sōpatros, *so´-pat-ros*; from the base of 4982 and 3962; *of a safe father*; *Sopatrus*, a Christian:—Sopater. Compare 4989.

4987. σωρεύω, sōreuō, *sore-yoo´-o*; from another form of 4673; to *pile* up (literal or figurative):—heap, load.

4988. Σωσθένης, Sōsthenēs, *soce-then´-ace*; from the base of 4982 and that of 4599; *of safe strength; Sosthenes*, a Christian:—Sosthenes.

4989. Σωσίπατρος, Sōsipatros, *so-sip´-at-ros*; prolonged for 4986; *Sosipatrus*, a Christian:—Sosipater.

4990. σωτήρ, sōtēr, *so-tare´*; from 4982; a *deliverer*, i.e. God or Christ:—saviour.

Noun from *sṓzō* (4982), to save. A savior, deliverer, preserver, one who saves from danger or destruction and brings into a state of prosperity and happiness. In Gr. writers, the deliverer and benefactor of an estate. The ancient mythological gods (such as Zeus) were also called *sōtḗr*. In the NT, spoken:

(I) Of God as Saviour (Lk 1:47; 1Ti 1:1; 2:3; 4:10; Tit 1:3; 2:10; 3:4; Jude 25).

(II) Of Jesus as the Messiah, the Saviour of men, who saves His people from the guilt and power of sin and from eternal death, from punishment and misery as the consequence of sin, and gives them eternal life and blessedness in His kingdom (Lk 2:11; Jn 4:42; Ac 5:31; 13:23; Eph 5:23; Php 3:20; 2Ti 1:10; Tit 1:4; 2:13; 3:6; 2Pe 1:1, 11; 2:20; 3:2, 18; 1Jn 4:14).

Deriv.: *sōtēría* (4991), salvation; *sōtḗrion* (4992), the means of salvation.

Syn.: *lutrōtḗs* (3086), redeemer; *Messías* (3323), Messiah.

4991. σωτηρία, sōtēria, *so-tay-ree´-ah*; feminine of a derivative of 4990 as (properly abstract) noun; *rescue* or *safety* (physical or morally):—deliver, health, salvation, save, saving.

Noun from *sōtḗr* (4990), a savior, deliverer. Safety, deliverance, preservation from danger or destruction.

(I) Particularly and generally: deliverance from danger, slavery, or imprisonment (Lk 1:69, 71; Ac 7:25; Php 1:19; Heb 11:7). By implication victory (Rev 7:10; 12:10; 19:1).

(II) In the Christian sense, *sōtēría* is deliverance from sin and its spiritual consequences and admission to eternal life with blessedness in the kingdom of Christ (Lk 1:77; 19:9; Jn 4:22; Ac 4:12; 13:26; 16:17; Ro 1:16; 10:1, 10; 11:11; 13:11; 2Co 1:6; 7:10; Eph 1:13; Php 1:28; 2:12; 1Th 5:8, 9; 2Th 2:13; 2Ti 2:10; 3:15; Heb 1:14; 2:3, 10; 5:9; 6:9; 9:28; 1Pe 1:5, 9, 10; Jude 3). By metonymy, a source or bringer of salvation, Saviour (Ac 13:47).

Syn.: *lútrōsis* (3085), a ransoming, redemption; *apolútrōsis* (629), salvation, ransom in full; *sōtḗrion* (4992), the means of salvation.

4992. σωτήριον, sōtērion, *so-tay´-ree-on*; neuter of the same as 4991 as (properly concrete) noun; *defender* or (by implication) *defence*:—salvation.

Adjective from *sōtḗr* (4990), a savior, deliverer. Delivering, saving, bringing salvation. In the NT, only in the Christian sense of saving, bringing salvation (Tit 2:11). Hence, the neuter with the article is used as a substantive for salvation (Eph 6:17), for the doctrine of salvation (Ac 28:28), and, by metonymy, the Saviour (Lk 2:30; 3:6).

Syn.: *antílutron* (487), a redemption price, ransom; *apolútrōsis* (629), redemption, deliverance, salvation; *lútron* (3083), ransom.

4993. σωφρονέω, sōphroneō, *so-fron-eh´-o*; from 4998; to *be of sound mind*, i.e. *sane*, (figurative) *moderate*:—be in right mind, be sober (minded), soberly.

4994. σωφρονίζω, sōphronizō, *so-fron-id´-zo*; from 4998; to *make of sound mind*, i.e. (figurative) to *discipline* or *correct*:—teach to be sober.

4995. σωφρονισμός, sōphronismos, *so-fron-is-mos´*; from 4994; *discipline*, i.e. *self-control*:—sound mind.

4996. σωφρόνως, sōphronōs, *so-fron´-oce*; adverb from 4998; *with sound mind*, i.e. *moderately*:—soberly.

4997. σωφροσύνη, sōphrosunē, *so-fros-oo´-nay*; from 4998; *soundness of mind*, i.e. (literal) *sanity* or (figurative) *self-control*:—soberness, sobriety.

4998. σώφρων, sōphrōn, *so´-frone*; from the base of 4982 and that of 5424; *safe* (*sound*) *in mind*, i.e. *self-controlled* (*moderate* as to opinion or passion):—discreet, sober, temperate.

Adjective from *sṓs* (n.f.), sound, and *phrḗn* (5424), understanding. Discreet, sober, of a sound mind. Hence, spoken of one who follows sound reason and restrains his passions. In the NT, sober minded, having the mind's desires and passions under control (1Ti 3:2; Tit 1:8; 2:2, 5).

Deriv.: *sōphronéō* (4993), to be of sound mind; *sōphronízō* (4994), to teach to be discreet; *sōphrónōs* (4996), temperately; *sōphrosúnē* (4997), sobriety, sanity.

Syn.: *nēphálios* (3524), circumspect, sober; *sophós* (4680), wise; *phrónimos* (5429), prudent.

4999. Ταβέρναι, Tabernai, *tab-er´-nahee*; plural of Latin origin; *huts* or *wooden-walled* buildings; *Tabernæ*:—taverns.

5000. Ταβιθά, Tabitha, *tab-ee-thah´*; of Chaldee origin [compare 6646]; *the gazelle; Tabitha* (i.e. *Tabjetha*), a Christian female:—Tabitha.

5001. τάγμα, tagma, *tag´-mah*; from 5021; something orderly in *arrangement* (a *troop*), i.e. (figurative) a *series* or *succession*:—order.

Noun from *tássō* (5021), to arrange in an orderly manner. Anything arranged in order or in array such as a body of troops, a band, cohort. In the NT, order, sequence, or turn (1Co 15:23).

Syn.: *táxis* (5010), regular arrangement, succession.

5002. τακτός, taktos, *tak-tos´*; from 5021; *arranged*, i.e. *appointed* or *stated*:—set.

5003. ταλαιπωρέω, talaipōreō, *tal-ahee-po-reh´-o*; from 5005; to *be wretched*, i.e. *realize* one's own *misery*:—be afflicted.

5004. ταλαιπωρία, talaipōria, *tal-ahee-po-ree´-ah*; from 5005; *wretchedness*, i.e. *calamity*:—misery.

5005. ταλαίπωρος, talaipōros, *tal-ah´ee-po-ros*; from the base of 5007 and a derivative of the base of 3984; *enduring trial*, i.e. *miserable*:—wretched.

5006. ταλαντιαῖος, talantiaios, *tal-an-tee-ah´-yos*; from 5007; *talent-like* in weight:—weight of a talent.

5007. τάλαντον, talanton, *tal´-an-ton*; neuter of a presumed derivative of the original form of **τλάω**, ***tlao*** (to *bear*; equivalent to 5342); a *balance* (as *supporting* weights), i.e. (by implication) a certain *weight* (and thence a *coin* or rather *sum* of money) or "*talent*":—talent.

5008. ταλιθά, talitha, *tal-ee-thah´*; of Chaldee origin [compare 2924]; *the fresh*, i.e. young *girl; talitha* (*O maiden*):—talitha.

5009. ταμεῖον, tameion, *tam-i´-on*; neuter contraction of a presumed derivative of **ταμίας**, ***tamias*** (a *dispenser* or *distributor*; akin to **τέμνω**, *temnō*, to *cut*); a *dispensary* or *magazine*, i.e. a chamber on the ground-floor or interior of an Oriental house (generally used for *storage* or *privacy*, a spot for retirement):—secret chamber, closet, storehouse.

5010. τάξις, taxis, *tax´-is*; from 5021; regular *arrangement*, i.e. (in time) fixed *succession* (of rank or character), official *dignity*:—order.

Noun from *tássō* (5021), to arrange in order. A setting in order; hence, order, arrangement, disposition, especially of troops; an order or rank in a state or in society. In the NT:

(I) Arrangement, disposition, series (Lk 1:8; 1Co 14:40, in proper order, orderly). Figuratively, good order, well-regulated life (Col 2:5).

(II) Rank, quality, character, as in the phrase "a priest according to the order of Melchisedeck" (Heb 5:6, 10; 6:20; 7:11, 17, 21) which means a priest of the same order, rank, or quality as Melchizedek. Also Heb 7:11, not according to the order or rank of Aaron.

Syn.: *tágma* (5001), a group of people that has been arranged in an orderly fashion.

5011. ταπεινός, tapeinos, *tap-i-nos´*; of uncertain derivative; *depressed*, i.e. (figurative) *humiliated* (in circumstances or disposition):—base, cast down, humble, of low degree (estate), lowly.

Adjective. Low, not high, particularly of attitude and social positions.

(I) Of condition or lot, meaning humble, poor, of low degree (Lk 1:52; Jas 1:9).

(II) Of the mind, meaning lowly, humble, modest, including the idea of affliction, depression of mind (Ro 12:16; 2Co 10:1). Elsewhere with an accompanying idea of piety toward God (Mt 11:29; 2Co 7:6; Jas 4:6; 1Pe 5:5).

Deriv.: *tapeinóō* (5013), to humble.

5012. ταπεινοφροσύνη, tapeinophrosunē, *tap-i-nof-ros-oo´-nay*; from a compound of 5011 and the base of 5424; *humiliation of mind*, i.e. *modesty*:—humbleness of mind, humility (of mind), lowliness (of mind).

Noun from *tapeinóphrōn* (n.f.), low-minded, humble, which is from *tapeinós* (5011), lowly, humble. Humility, lowliness of mind, modesty of mind and deportment. Spoken of a genuine humility (Ac 20:19; Eph 4:2; Php 2:3; Col 2:18, 23; 3:12; 1Pe 5:5). Spoken of a mock humility or self-abasement for the wrong reasons (Col 2:18, 23).

Syn.: *praΰtēs* (4240), meekness.

5013. ταπεινόω, tapeinoō, *tap-i-no´-o*; from 5011; to *depress*; (figurative) to *humiliate* (in condition or heart):—abase, bring low, humble (self).

From *tapeinós* (5011), humble. To humble, bring low:

(I) Particularly, spoken of mountains and hills, to be made level (Lk 3:5).

(II) Figuratively as to condition, circumstances, to bring low, to humble, abase. With the reflexive pronoun *heautoú* (1438) oneself, to humble oneself, to make oneself of low condition, to become poor and needy (Mt 18:4; Lk 14:11; 18:14; 2Co 11:7; Php 2:8). In the passive, to be abased, brought low (Php 4:12). Spoken of the mind, to make humble through disappointment (2Co 12:21). In the passive, to be humiliated through disappointment or exposure to shame (Mt 23:12; Lk 14:11; 18:14). Also in the passive, with the idea of contrition and penitence toward God, to humble oneself (Jas 4:10; 1Pe 5:6).

Deriv.: *tapeínōsis* (5014), humility.

Syn.: *kataischúnō* (2617), to shame, disgrace, dishonour.

5014. ταπείνωσις, tapeinōsis, *tap-i´-no-sis*; from 5013; *depression* (in rank or feeling):—humiliation, be made low, low estate, vile.

Noun from *tapeinóō* (5013), to humble, abase. A making low, humiliation. In the NT, the act of being brought low, humiliation (Jas 1:10); spoken of Christ's humiliation (Ac 8:33); a being low, of humble condition (Php 3:21); spoken by Mary of her unworthiness (Lk 1:48).

Syn.: *aischúnē* (152), shame, disgrace; *atimía* (819), indignity, disgrace.

5015. ταράσσω, tarassō, *tar-as´-so*; of uncertain affinity; to *stir* or *agitate* (*roil* water):—trouble.

5016. ταραχή, tarachē, *tar-akh-ay´*; feminine from 5015; *disturbance*, i.e. (of water) *roiling*, or (of a mob) *sedition*:—trouble (-ing).

5017. τάραχος, tarachos, *tar´-akh-os*; masculine from 5015; a *disturbance*, i.e. (popular) *tumult*:—stir.

5018. Ταρσεύς, Tarseus, *tar-syoos´*; from 5019; a *Tarsean*, i.e. native of Tarsus:—of Tarsus.

5019. Ταρσός, Tarsos, *tar-sos´*; perhaps the same as **ταρσός**, ***Tarsos*** (a *flat* basket); *Tarsus*, a place in Asia Minor:—Tarsus.

5020. ταρταρόω, tartaroō, *tar-tar-o´-o*; from **Τάρταρος**, ***Tartarοs̄*** (the deepest *abyss* of Hades); to *incarcerate* in eternal torment:—cast down to hell.

From *tártaros* (n.f.), the lower part of Hades in Greek mythology where the spirits of the wicked were imprisoned and tormented. In the NT, to thrust down to Tarturus, to cast into Gehenna. Used only in 2Pe 2:4.

5021. τάσσω, tassō, *tas´-so*; a prolonged form of a primary verb (which later appears only in certain tenses); to *arrange* in an orderly manner, i.e. *assign* or *dispose* (to a certain position or lot):—addict, appoint, determine, ordain, set.

To place, arrange, set in order, e.g., to arrange soldiers in order or ranks. In the NT, used figuratively, meaning to set in a certain order, constitute, appoint, used transitively:

(I) Generally, to appoint, ordain to a position or duty (Lk 7:8; Ac 15:2; Ro 13:1; 1Co 16:15); spoken of those appointed to eternal life (Ac 13:48).

(II) To arrange, to appoint details of life; e.g., to arrange a meeting place (Mt 28:16); to arrange a meeting time (Ac 28:23); to ordain things to be done (Ac 22:10).

Deriv.: *anatássomai* (392), to compose in an orderly manner; *antitássō* (498), to resist; *apotássō* (657), to set apart; *átaktos* (813), disorderly, irregular; *diatássō* (1299), set in order, issue orderly and detailed instructions; *epitássō* (2004), to order; *prostássō* (4367), to command; *protássō* (4384), to foreordain; *suntássō* (4929), to arrange or set in order together; *tágma* (5001), an order, arrangement; *taktós* (5002), arranged, appointed; *táxis* (5010), an arrangement; *hupotássō* (5293), to place under, to make subject to.

Syn.: *apókeimai* (606), to be reserved, appointed, laid aside for a certain purpose; *diatíthemai* (1303), to set apart, to appoint; *kathístēmi* (2525), to designate, appoint, place; *títhēmi* (5087), to place, appoint, settle, ordain.

5022. ταῦρος, tauros, *tow´-ros*; apparently a primary word [compare 8450, "*steer*"]; a *bullock*:—bull, ox.

5023. ταῦτα, tauta, *tow´-tah*; nominal or accusative neuter plural of 3778; *these* things:— + afterward, follow, + hereafter, × him, the same, so, such, that, then, these, they, this, those, thus.

5024. ταὐτά, tauta, *tow-tah´*; neuter plural of 3588 and 846 as adverb; in *the same* way:—even thus, (manner) like, so.

5025. ταύταις, tautais, *tow´-taheece*; and **ταύτας**, ***tautas***, *tow´-tas*; dative and accusative feminine plural respectively of 3778; (*to* or *with* or *by*, etc.) *these*:—hence, that, then, these, those.

5026. ταύτῃ, tautēi, *tow-´tay*; and **ταύτην**, ***tautēn***, *tow´-tane*; and **ταύτης**, ***tautēs***, *tow´-tace*; dative, accusative and genitive respectively of the feminine singular of 3778; (*toward* or *of*) *this*:—her, + hereof, it, that, + thereby, the (same), this (same).

5027. ταφή, taphē, *taf-ay´*; feminine from 2290; *burial* (the act):— × bury.

5028. τάφος, taphos, *taf´-os*; masculine from 2290; a *grave* (the place of interment):—sepulchre, tomb.

5029. τάχα, tacha, *takh´-ah*; as if neuter plural of 5036 (adverb); *shortly*, i.e. (figurative) *possibly*:—peradventure (-haps).

5030. ταχέως, tacheōs, *takh-eh´-oce*; adverb from 5036; *briefly*, i.e. (in time) *speedily*, or (in manner) *rapidly*:—hastily, quickly, shortly, soon, suddenly.

5031. ταχινός, tachinos, *takh-ee-nos´*; from 5034; *curt*, i.e. *impending*:—shortly, swift.

5032. τάχιον, tachion, *takh´-ee-on*; neuter singular of the comparative of 5036 (as adverb); *more swiftly*, i.e. (in manner) *more rapidly*, or (in time) *more speedily*:—out [run], quickly, shortly, sooner.

5033. τάχιστα, tachista, *takh´-is-tah*; neuter plural of the superlative of 5036 (as adverb); *most quickly*, i.e. (with 5613 prefixed) *as soon* as possible:— + with all speed.

5034. τάχος, tachos, *takh´-os*; from the same as 5036; a *brief* space (of time), i.e. *with* 1722 (prefixed) in *haste*:— + quickly, + shortly, + speedily.

5035. ταχύ, tachu, *takh-oo´*; neuter singular of 5036 (as adverb); *shortly*, i.e. *without delay, soon*, or (by surprise) *suddenly*, or (by implication of ease) *readily*:—lightly, quickly.

5036. ταχύς, tachus, *takh-oos´*; of uncertain affinity; *fleet*, i.e. (figurative) *prompt* or *ready*:—swift.

5037. τε, te, *teh*; a primary particle (enclitic) of connection or addition; *both* or *also* (properly as correlation of 2532):—also, and, both, even, then, whether. Often used in comparative, usually as the latter part.

5038. τεῖχος, teichos, *ti´-khos*; akin to the base of 5088; a *wall* (as *formative* of a house):—wall.

5039. τεκμήριον, tekmērion, *tek-may´-ree-on*; neuter of a presumed derivative of **τεκμάρ,** ***tekmar*** (a *goal* or fixed *limit*); a *token* (as *defining* a fact), i.e. *criterion* of certainty:—infallible proof.

5040. τεκνίον, teknion, *tek-nee´-on*; diminutive of 5043; an *infant*, i.e. (plural figurative) *darlings* (Christian *converts*):—little children.

A noun, the diminutive of *téknon* (5043), child. A little child. Used only figuratively and always in the plural. A term of affection by a teacher to his disciples (Jn 13:33; Gal 4:19; 1Jn 2:1, 12, 28; 3:7, 18; 4:4; 5:21).

5041. τεκνογονέω, teknogoneō, *tek-nog-on-eh´-o*; from a compound of 5043 and the base of 1096; to *be a child-bearer*, i.e. *parent* (*mother*):—bear children.

5042. τεκνογονία, teknogonia, *tek-nog-on-ee´-ah*; from the same as 5041; *childbirth* (*parentage*), i.e. (by implication) *maternity* (the performance of *maternal duties*):—childbearing.

5043. τέκνον, teknon, *tek´-non*; from the base of 5098; a *child* (as *produced*):—child, daughter, son.

Noun from *tíktō* (5088), to bring forth, bear children. A child, male or female, son or daughter.

(I) Particularly:

(A) Generally, a child (Mt 10:21; Mk 12:19; Lk 1:7; 7:35; Ac 21:5; Tit 1:6; 2Jn 4, 13; Rev 12:4).

(B) Specifically of a son (Mt 21:28; Ac 21:21; Php 2:22; Rev 12:5).

(II) Spoken in the plural, children, in a wider sense meaning descendants, posterity (Mt 3:9; Lk 1:17; 3:8; Ac 2:39; Ro 9:7, 8; Gal 4:28, 31). Emphatically it means true children, genuine descendants (Jn 8:39; 1Pe 3:6).

(III) Spoken figuratively of one who is the object of parental love and care, or who yields filial love and reverence toward another.

(A) As a tender term of address, equivalent to "my child" or "my son" as from a friend or teacher (Mt 9:2; Mk 2:5; Lk 16:25).

(B) Generally for a pupil, disciple, the spiritual child of someone (1Co 4:14, 17; 1Ti 1:2, 18; 2Ti 1:2; Tit 1:4; 3Jn 4).

(C) Spoken in reference to children of God (see *Theos* [2316], God) in the sense of those whom God loves and cherishes as a Father. Generally of the devout worshippers of God, the righteous, saints, Christians (Jn 1:12; Ro 8:16, 17, 21; 9:8; Eph 5:1; 1Jn 3:1, 2, 10; 5:2). Also spoken of the Jews (Jn 11:52).

(D) Spoken in reference to the children of the devil (see *diábolos* [1228], devil), in the sense of his followers, subjects, in contrast to *tá tékna toú Theoú*, the children of God (1Jn 3:10).

(IV) Spoken in connection with the name of a city or village of a native, an inhabitant, one born or living in that city; e.g., children of Jerusalem (Mt 23:37; Lk 13:34; 19:44). Also see Gal 4:25; Rev 2:23.

(V) Spoken figuratively in connection with a genitive noun in the sense of a child of anything, meaning one connected with, partaking of, or exposed to that thing: e.g., children of light (Eph 5:8); of wisdom (Mt 11:19; Lk 7:35); of obedience (1Pe 1:14); of wrath (Eph 2:3), of a curse (2Pe 2:14).

Deriv.: *áteknos* (815), childless; *teknotrophéō* (5044), to bring up children; *philóteknos* (5388), loving one's children.

5044. τεκνοτροφέω, teknotropheō, *tek-not-rof-eh´-o*; from a compound of 5043 and 5142; to *be a child-rearer*, i.e. *fulfill* the duties of *a female parent*:—bring up children.

5045. τέκτων, tektōn, *tek´-tone*; from the base of 5098; an *artificer* (as *producer* of fabrics), i.e. (special) a *craftsman* in wood:—carpenter.

5046. τέλειος, teleios, *tel´-i-os*; from 5056; *complete* (in various applications of labour, growth, mental and moral character, etc.); neuter (as noun, with 3588) *completeness*:—of full age, man, perfect.

Adjective from *télos* (5056), goal, purpose. Finished, that which has reached its end, term, limit; hence, complete, full, lacking nothing.

(I) Generally (Jas 1:4, 17, 25; 1Jn 4:18). Figuratively, in a moral sense, of persons (Mt 5:48; Mt 19:21; Col 1:28; 4:12; Jas 1:4; 3:2); the will of God (Ro 12:2; Sept.: Ge 6:9; 1Ki 11:4).

(II) Specifically of persons meaning full age, adulthood, full-grown. In the NT, figuratively meaning full-grown in mind and understanding (1Co 14:20); in knowledge of the truth (1Co 2:6; 13:10; Php 3:15; Heb 5:14); in Christian faith and virtue (Eph 4:13).

Deriv.: *teleiótēs* (5047), completeness, perfection; *teleióō* (5048), to complete, perfect; *teleíōs* (5049), completely, without wavering, to the end.

Syn.: *ámemptos* (273), irreproachable, blameless; *ártios* (739), fitted, complete, perfect; *holóklēros* (3648), entire, whole; *plḗrēs* (4134), complete, full. *Téleios* is not to be confused with *anamártētos* (361), without sin or sinless.

5047. τελειότης, teleiotēs, *tel-i-ot´-ace*; from 5046; (the state) *completeness* (mental or moral):—perfection (-ness).

Noun from *téleios* (5046), perfect, one who reaches a goal. Perfection or perfectness, completeness (Col 3:14; Heb 6:1).

Syn.: *apartismós* (535), completion, finishing; *katartismós* (2677), the act of completing; *plḗrōma* (4138), a filling up, fulfillment, fullness.

5048. τελειόω, teleioō, *tel-i-o´-o*; from 5046; to *complete*, i.e. (literal) *accomplish*, or (figurative) *consummate* (in character):—consecrate, finish, fulfill, make) perfect.

From *téleios* (5046), complete, mature. To complete, make perfect by reaching the intended goal. Transitively:

(I) Particularly with the meaning to bring to a full end, completion, reaching the intended goal, to finish a work or duty (Lk 13:22; Jn 4:34; 5:36; 17:4); to finish a race or course (Ac 20:24; Php 3:12, probably reflects the same meaning). Of time (Lk 2:43); of prophecy, fulfilled (Jn 19:28).

(II) Figuratively meaning to make perfect in the sense of bringing to a state of completion or fulfillment.

(A) Generally (Jn 17:23; 2Co 12:9; Jas 2:22; 1Jn 2:5; 4:12, 17, 18).

(B) Used in the epistle to the Hebrews in a moral sense meaning to make perfect, to fully cleanse from sin, in contrast to ceremonial cleansing. Moral expiation is the completion or realization of the ceremonial one (Heb 7:19; 9:9; 10:1, 14). Also used of Christ as exalted to be head over all things (Heb 2:10; 5:9; 7:28); of saints advanced to glory (Heb 11:40; 12:23).

Deriv.: *teleíōsis* (5050), the act of completion; *teleiōtḗs* (5051), a completer, perfecter.

Syn.: *apoteléō* (658), to complete entirely, consummate, finish; *plēróō* (4137), to fill, satisfy, execute, finish, accomplish, complete, fulfill; *sumplēróō* (4845), to fill to the brim, accomplish, fill up, complete; *sunteléō* (4931), to complete entirely, finish, fulfill.

5049. τελείως, teleiōs, *tel-i´-oce*; adverb from 5046; *completely*, i.e. (of hope) *without wavering*:—to the end.

Adverb from *téleios* (5046), perfect, complete. Perfectly, entirely, steadfastly, unwaveringly. Used only in 1Pe 1:13.

Syn.: *hólōs* (3654), completely, altogether, utterly, by any means; *póntē* (3839), wholly, always.

5050. τελείωσις, teleiōsis, *tel-i´-o-sis*; from 5448; (the act) *completion*, i.e. (of prophecy) *verification*, or (of expiation) *absolution*:—perfection, performance.

Noun from *teleióō* (5048), to complete. Completion, perfection. Spoken of a prediction: fulfillment (Lk 1:45). Also spoken of perfect expiation (Heb 7:11).

Syn.: *holoklēría* (3647), integrity, wholeness, soundness; *suntéleia* (4930), completion, consummation.

5051. τελειωτής, teleiōtēs, *tel-i-o-tace´*; from 5048; a *completer*, i.e. *consummater*:—finisher.

Noun from *teleióō* (5048), to complete. A completer, perfecter, particularly one who reaches a goal so as to win the prize. Used only once in Scripture in Heb 12:2 where Jesus is called the "author and finisher of our faith." Compare Heb 2:10 where he is said to bring many sons to glory.

5052. τελεσφορέω, telesphoreō, *tel-es-for-eh´-o*; from a compound of 5056 and 5342; to *be a bearer to completion* (maturity), i.e. to *ripen* fruit (figurative):—bring fruit to perfection.

From *télos* (5056), end, goal, perfection, and *phérō* (5342), to bring, bear. To bring to perfection or maturity, e.g., fruit, grain, etc., to ripen. Used figuratively, only in Lk 8:14.

5053. τελευτάω, teleutaō, *tel-yoo-tah´-o*; from a presumed derivative of 5055; to *finish* life (by implication of 979), i.e. *expire* (*demise*):—be dead, decease, die.

From *teleutḗ* (5054), death, an end, accomplishment. To end, finish, complete. Intransitively, to end. In the NT, intransitively or with *bíon* (979), earthly life, implied, meaning to end one's life, die (Mt 2:19; 9:18; 22:25; Mk 9:44, 46, 48; Lk 7:2; Ac 2:29; 7:15; Heb 11:22). Of a violent death (Mt 15:4; Mk 7:10).

Syn.: *apothnḗskō* (599), to die off; *thnḗskō* (2348), to die; *sunapothnḗskō* (4880), to die with, together.

5054. τελευτή, teleutē, *tel-yoo-tay´*; from 5053; *decease*:—death.

Noun from *teléō* (5055), to accomplish or complete something. An end, figurative for death. In Mt 2:15, the end of life, death, decease (Sept.: Ge 27:2; Jos 1:1; Jgs 1:1).

Deriv.: *teleutáō* (5053), to end, finish, complete.

Syn.: *thánatos* (2288), death.

5055. τελέω, teleō, *tel-eh´-o*; from 5056; to *end*, i.e. *complete, execute, conclude, discharge* (a debt):—accomplish, make an end, expire, fill up, finish, go over, pay, perform.

From *télos* (5056), end, goal. To make an end or to accomplish, to complete something.

(I) Generally (Mt 10:23; 11:1; 13:53; 19:1; 26:1; Lk 2:39; 2Ti 4:7; Rev 11:7). In the passive (Lk 12:50; Jn 19:28, 30; Rev 10:7; 15:1, 8). Of time in the passive, meaning to be ended, fulfilled (Rev 20:3, 5, 7).

(II) To accomplish, fulfill, execute fully, e.g., a rule or law (Ro 2:27; Gal 5:16; Jas 2:8). Spoken of declarations, prophecy (Lk 18:31; 22:37; Ac 13:29; Rev 17:17).

(III) By implication, to pay off or in full, such as taxes, tribute (Mt 17:24; Ro 13:6).

Deriv.: *apoteléō* (658), to perfect; *diateléō* (1300), to finish completely; *ekteléō* (1615), to complete fully; *epiteléō* (2005), to complete, finish; *sunteléō* (4931), to finish entirely; *teleutḗ* (5054), an end, death.

Syn.: *sumplēróō* (4845), to fill up completely; *teleióō* (5048), to complete, accomplish, consecrate, perfect.

5056. τέλος, telos, *tel´-os*; from a primary **τέλλω,** ***tellō*** (to *set out* for a definite point or *goal*); properly the point aimed at as a *limit*, i.e. (by implication) the *conclusion* of an act or state (*termination* [literal, figurative or indefinite], *result* [immediate, ultimate or prophetic], *purpose*); specially an *impost* or *levy* (as *paid*):— + continual, custom, end (-ing), finally, uttermost. Compare 5411.

A noun meaning an end, a term, a termination, completion. Particularly only in respect to time.

(I) Generally (Mt 10:22; 24:6, 13; Mk 3:26; 13:7, 13; Lk 1:33; 21:9; 1Co 1:8; 10:11; 15:24; 2Co 1:13; 3:13; Heb 3:6, 14; 6:11; 7:3; 1Pe 4:7; Rev 2:26). Adverbially in the accusative, finally, at last (1Pe 3:8). With the prep. *eis* (1519), in, unto: to the end, continually, perpetually, forever (Lk 18:5; 1Th 2:16).

(II) Figuratively it means end, outcome, result (Mt 26:58; Lk 22:37; Ro 6:21, 22; 1Co 15:24; 2Co 11:15; Php 3:19; Heb 6:8; 7:3; Jas 5:11; 1Pe 1:9; 4:7, 17).

(III) Figuratively, the meaning can be extended to convey the end or final purpose, that to which all the parts tend and in which they terminate, the sum total (1Ti 1:5).

(IV) Figuratively, it can also be used for a tax, toll, custom, tribute, particularly what is paid for public purposes for the maintenance of the state (Mt 17:25; Ro 13:7).

Deriv.: *entéllomai* (1781), to charge, command; *pantelḗs* (3838), complete, whole, entire; *polutelḗs* (4185), very expensive, costly; *téleios* (5046), finished, complete; *telesphoréō* (5052), to bring to an intended perfection or goal; *teléō* (5055), to finish, complete; *telṓnēs* (5057), a gatherer of taxes or customs.

Syn.: *péras* (4009), a limit, boundary, uttermost part; *suntéleia* (4930), a completion, consummation, fulfillment; *ōméga* (5598), the last letter of the Greek alphabet.

5057. τελώνης, telōnēs, *tel-o´-nace*; from 5056 and 5608; a *tax-farmer*, i.e. *collector of* public *revenue*:—publican.

5058. τελώνιον, telōnion, *tel-o´-nee-on*; neuter of a presumed derivative of 5057; a *tax-gatherer's* place of business:—receipt of custom.

5059. τέρας, teras, *ter´-as*; of uncertain affinity; a *prodigy* or *omen*:—wonder.

A noun meaning wonder or omen. In the NT, it is always associated with *sēmeíon* (4592), sign, and always in the plural translated "wonders" (Ac 2:19, 22). Used of the miracles of Moses (Ac 7:36); of Christ (Jn 4:48); of the apostles and teachers (Ac 2:43; 4:30; 5:12; 6:8; 14:3; 15:12; Ro 15:19; 2Co 12:12; Heb 2:4); and of false prophets or teachers (Mt 24:24; Mk 13:22; 2Th 2:9).

Syn.: *dúnamis* (1411), mighty work, miracle; *thaúma* (2295), wonder; *thaumásios* (2297), a miracle; *megaleíos* (3167), something great; *sēmeíon* (4592), sign.

5060. Τέρτιος, Tertios, *ter´-tee-os*; of Latin origin; *third; Tertius*, a Christian:—Tertius.

5061. Τέρτυλλος, Tertullos, *ter´-tool-los*; of uncertain derivative; *Tertullus*, a Roman:—Tertullus.

5062. τεσσαράκοντα, tessarakonta, *tes-sar-ak´-on-tah*; the decade of 5064; *forty*:—forty.

5063. τεσσαρακονταετής, tessarakontaetēs, *tes-sar-ak-on-tah-et-ace´*; from 5062 and 2094; *of forty years* of age:—(+ full, of) forty years (old).

5064. τέσσαρες, tessares, *tes´-sar-es*; neuter **τέσσαρα,** ***tessara***, *tes´-sar-ah*; a plural number; *four*:—four.

5065. τεσσαρεσκαιδέκατος, tessareskaidekatos, *tes-sar-es-kahee-dek´-at-os*; from 5064 and 2532 and 1182; *fourteenth*:—fourteenth.

5066. τεταρταῖος, tetartaios, *tet-ar-tah´-yos*; from 5064; pertaining to the *fourth* day:—four days.

5067. τέταρτος, tetartos, *tet´-ar-tos*; order from 5064; *fourth*:—four (-th).

5068. τετράγωνος, tetragōnos, *tet-rag´-on-nos*; from 5064 and 1137; *four-cornered*, i.e. *square*:—foursquare.

5069. τετράδιον, tetradion, *tet-rad´-ee-on*; neuter of a presumed derivative of **τέτρας,** ***tetras*** (a *tetrad*; from 5064); a *quaternion* or squad (picket) of four Roman soldiers:—quaternion.

5070. τετρακισχίλιοι, tetrakischilioi, *tet-rak-is-khil´-ee-oy*; from the multiple adverb of 5064 and 5507; *four times a thousand*:—four thousand.

5071. τετρακόσιοι, tetrakosioi, *tet-rak-os´-ee-oy*; neuter **τετρακόσια,** *tetrakosia*, *tet-rak-os´-ee-ah*; plural from 5064 and 1540; *four hundred*:—four hundred.

5072. τετράμηνον, tetramēnon, *tet-ram´-ay-non*; neuter of a compound of 5064 and 3376; a *four months'* space:—four months.

5073. τετραπλόος, tetraploos, *tet-rap-lo´-os*; from 5064 and a derivative of the base of 4118; *quadruple*:—fourfold.

5074. τετράπους, tetrapous, *tet-rap´-ooce*; from 5064 and 4228; a *quadruped*:—four-footed beast.

5075. τετραρχέω, tetrarcheō, *tet-rar-kheh´-o*; from 5076; to *be a tetrarch*:—(be) tetrarch.

5076. τετράρχης, tetrarchēs, *tet-rar´-khace*; from 5064 and 757; the *ruler of a fourth* part of a country ("*tetrarch*"):—tetrarch.

5077. τεφρόω, tephroō, *tef-ro´-o*; from **τέφρα**, ***tephra*** (*ashes*); to *incinerate*, i.e. *consume*:—turn to ashes.

5078. τέχνη, technē, *tekh´-nay*; from the base of 5088; *art* (as *productive*), i.e. (special) a *trade*, or (genitive) *skill*:—art, craft, occupation.

5079. τεχνίτης, technitēs, *tekh-nee´-tace*; from 5078; an *artisan*; (figurative) a *founder* (*Creator*):—builder, craftsman.

5080. τήκω, tēkō, *tay´-ko*; apparently a primary verb; to *liquefy*:—melt.

5081. τηλαυγῶς, tēlaugōs, *tay-low-goce*; adverb from a compound of a derivative of 5056 and 827; in a *far-shining* manner, i.e. *plainly*:—clearly.

5082. τηλικοῦτος, tēlikoutos, *tay-lik-oo´-tos*; feminine **τηλικαύτη**, ***tēlikautē***, *tay-lik-ow´-tay*; from a compound of 3588 with 2245 and 3778; *such as this*, i.e. (in [figurative] magnitude) *so vast*:—so great, so mighty.

5083. τηρέω, tēreō, *tay-reh´-o*; from **τηρός**, ***teros*** (a *watch*; perhaps akin to 2334); to *guard* (from *loss* or *injury*, properly by keeping *the eye* upon; and thus differing from 5442, which is properly to *prevent* escaping; and from 2892, which implies a *fortress* or full military lines of apparatus), i.e. to *note* (a prophecy; figurative, to *fulfill* a command); by implication to *detain* (in custody; figurative, to *maintain*); by extension to *withhold* (for personal ends; figurative, to *keep unmarried*):—hold fast, keep (-er), (pre-, re-) serve, watch.

From *tērós* (n.f.), a warden, guard. To keep an eye on, to watch, and hence to guard, keep, obey, transitively:

(I) Particularly to watch, observe attentively, keep the eyes fixed upon, with the accusative (Rev 1:3, keeping for the fulfillment of the prophecy; 22:7, 9). Figuratively, to obey, observe, keep, fulfill a duty, precept, law, custom, or custom meaning to perform watchfully, vigilantly, spoken of keeping: commandments (Mt 19:17; Jn 14:15, 21; 15:10; 1Ti 6:14; 1Jn 2:3, 4; 3:22, 24; 5:2, 3; Rev 12:17; 14:12); a saying or words (Jn 8:51, 52, 55; 14:23, 24; 15:20; 17:6; 1Jn 2:5; Rev 3:8, 10); the law (Ac 15:5, 24; Jas 2:10); tradition (Mk 7:9); the Sabbath (Jn 9:16). See also Mt 23:3; 28:20; Ac 21:25; Rev 2:26; 3:3).

(II) To keep, guard, e.g., a prisoner (Mt 27:36, 54; 28:4; Ac 12:5, 6; 16:23; 24:23; 25:4, 21). Figuratively, to guard in the sense of keeping someone safe, preserving (Jn 17:11, 12, 15; 1Th 5:23; Jude 1; Rev 3:10). Figuratively, to guard in the sense of preserving something, e.g., the faith (2Ti 4:7); see also Eph 4:3; Jude 6. Figuratively, to guard oneself in the sense of keeping oneself from defilement (1Ti 5:22; Jas 1:27; 1Jn 5:18; Jude 21; Rev 16:15).

(III) To keep back or in store, reserve for later use (Jn 2:10; 12:7; 1Pe 1:4; to keep a daughter at home, unmarried, as opposed to giving her in marriage (1Co 7:37). In a negative sense, to reserve the blackness of eternal condemnation for the wicked (2Pe 2:17; Jude 13); to reserve the wicked for eternal judgement (2Pe 2:4, 9; 3:7).

Deriv.: *diatēréō* (1301) keep, store up; *paratēréō* (3906), to watch closely, guard; *suntēréō* (4933), conserve, keep, protect, preserve; *tḗrēsis* (5084), watch, custody.

Syn.: *phulássō* (5442), to guard, watch, keep by way of protection, observe, protect. Also *diaphulássō* (1314), to guard carefully; *kratéō* (2902), to get possession of, hold fast, keep; *phrouréō* (5432), to keep with a military guard.

5084. τήρησις, tērēsis, *tay´-ray-sis*; from 5083; a *watching*, i.e. (figurative) *observance*, or (concretely) a *prison*:—hold.

Noun from *tēréō* (5083), to keep watch. A custody, keeping, watching.

(I) Figuratively, observance, performance, of precepts (1Co 7:19).

(II) A keeping in the sense of a guarding. In the NT, by metonymy, a place of guarding, a prison (Ac 4:3; 5:18).

Syn.: *desmōtḗrion* (1201), a place of bonds, prison; *phulakḗ* (5438), a guarding or guard, prison, hold.

5085. Τιβεριάς, Tiberias, *tib-er-ee-as´*; from 5086; *Tiberias*, the name of a town and a lake in Palestine:—Tiberias.

5086. Τιβέριος, Tiberios, *tib-er´-ee-os*; of Latin origin; probably *pertaining to the* river *Tiberis* or *Tiber; Tiberius*, a Roman emperor:—Tiberius.

5087. τίθημι, tithēmi, *tith´-ay-mee*; a prolonged form of a primary **θέω**, ***theō***, *theh´-o* (which is used only as alternate in certain tenses); to place (in the widest application, literal and figurative; properly in a passive or horizontal posture, and thus different from 2476, which properly denotes an upright and active position, while 2749 is properly reflexive and utterly prostrate):— + advise, appoint, bow, commit, conceive, give, × kneel down, lay (aside, down, up), make, ordain, purpose, put, set (forth), settle, sink down.

To set, put, place, lay.

(I) Particularly, to set, put, or place a person or thing. To place under a basket (Mt 5:15; Mk 4:21) or under a bed (Lk 8:16). See also Lk 11:33; Jn 2:10; 19:19; Rev 10:2. In the middle, meaning to set or place on one's own behalf, or by one's own order; to put persons in prison (Mt 14:3; Ac 4:3; 5:25; 12:4).

(II) More often of things, to set, put, or lay down. To set in the proper place, assign a place (1Co 12:18).

(A) Particularly spoken of a foundation (Lk 6:48; 14:29; 1Co 3:10, 11); a stone, stumbling stone (Ro 9:33; 1Pe 2:6). Spoken of dead bodies: to lay in a tomb or sepulchre (Mt 27:60; Mk 6:29; 15:47; 16:6; Lk 23:53, 55; Jn 11:34; 19:41, 42; 20:2, 13, 15; Ac 7:16; 13:29; Rev 11:9). Spoken of the knees: to place the knees, to kneel (Mk 15:19; Lk 22:41; Ac 7:60; 9:40; 20:36; 21:5). To place in the sense of to lay off or aside, such as garments (Jn 13:4). See also Mk 10:16; Lk 5:18; Ac 3:2; 4:35, 37; 5:2, 15; 9:37; 1Co 15:25; 16:2; 2Co 3:13.

(B) Figuratively, to lay down one's life (Jn 10:11, 15, 17, 18; 13:37, 38; 15:13; 1Jn 3:16). To place something in the heart or spirit, in the sense of to resolve, to purpose (Lk 21:14; Ac 5:4; 19:21), or in the sense of to ponder (Lk 1:66). See also Mt 12:18; Lk 9:44; 2Co 5:19.

(C) Figuratively, to set, to place in the sense of to appoint, ordain, e.g., to ordain times and seasons (Ac 1:7). To place or ordain someone in a position, to make somebody something; e.g., to make Abraham the father of many nations (Ro 4:17), to make the Son heir of all things (Heb 1:2). To place one into a position of privilege or ministry (Jn 15:16; Ac 13:47; 20:28; 1Co 12:28; 1Ti 1:12; 2:7; 2Ti 1:11). To place or decree a place of subordination for someone (Mt 22:44; Mk 12:36; Lk 20:43; Ac 2:35; Heb 1:13; 10:13) or a punishment for someone (Mt 24:51; Lk 12:46; 1Pe 2:8). To place or give counsel, to advise (Ac 27:12); to place something for others in a certain way, as to give the gospel out freely (1Co 9:18).

Deriv.: *anatíthēmi* (394), to put up or before; *apotíthēmi* (659), to put off from oneself; *diatíthemai* (1303), dispose of, bequest, to appoint a testator; *ektíthēmi* (1620), to expose, set out; *epitíthēmi* (2007), to lay on; *eúthetos* (2111), well placed, proper; *thḗkē* (2336), receptacle; *thēsaurós* (2344), a receptacle for treasure; *katatíthēmi* (2698), to lay down; *metatíthēmi* (3346), to transfer, transport, change, remove; *nomothétēs* (3550), a lawgiver; *nouthetéō* (3560), to admonish; *horothesía* (3734), bound; *paratíthēmi* (3908), to place alongside, present, commit, set before; *peritíthēmi* (4060), to place or put around; *prostíthēmi* (4369), to place additionally, lay beside, annex, add to; *protíthemai* (4388), to place before for oneself, propose, purpose; *suntíthemai* (4934), agree, assent, covenant; *huiothesía* (5206) adoption; *hupotíthēmi* (5294), to place under, lay down.

Syn.: *apókeimai* (606), to be laid up, reserved, appointed; *hístēmi* (2476), to make to stand, appoint; *kathízō* (2523), to seat someone, set, appoint; *kathístēmi* (2525), to cause to stand, appoint a person to a position, ordain, set down; *horízō* (3724), to mark by a limit, determine, ordain, define; *procheirízō* (4400), to deliver up, appoint; *tássō* (5021), to place or arrange in order; *cheirotonéō* (5500), to place the hands on, choose by raising of hands, ordain.

5088. τίκτω, tiktō, *tik´-to*; a strengthened form of a primary **τέκω**, ***tekō***, *tek´-o* (which is used only as alternate in certain tenses); to *produce* (from seed, as a mother, a plant, the earth, etc.), literal or figurative:—bear, be born, bring forth, be delivered, be in travail.

To bring forth, bear, bring.

(I) Of women (Mt 1:21, 23, 25; 2:2; Lk 1:31, 57; 2:6, 7, 11; Jn 16:21; Gal 4:27; Heb 11:11; Rev 12:2, 4, 5, 13). Metaphorically of irregular desire as exciting to sin (Jas 1:15).

(II) Of the earth (Heb 6:7).

Deriv.: *prōtótokos* (4416), firstborn; *téknon* (5043), a child; *téchne* (5078), an art, trade, craft, skill; *tókos* (5110), a bringing forth, birth.

Syn.: *apokuéō* (616), to bring forth; *gennáō* (1080), to give birth; *phérō* (5342), to bring or bear.

5089. τίλλω, tillō, *til´-lo*; perhaps akin to the alternate of 138, and thus to 4951; to *pull* off:—pluck.

5090. Τίμαιος, Timaios, *tim´-ah-yos*; probably of Chaldee origin [compare 2931]; *Timæus* (i.e. *Timay*), an Israelite:—Timæus.

5091. τιμάω, timaō, *tim-ah´-o*; from 5093; to *prize*, i.e. *fix* a *valuation* upon; by implication to *revere*:—honour, value.

5092. τιμή, timē, *tee-may´*; from 5099; a *value*, i.e. *money* paid, or (concretely and collective) *valuables*; (by analogy) *esteem* (especially of the highest degree), or the *dignity* itself:—honour, precious, price, some.

5093. τίμιος, timios, *tim´-ee-os*; including the comparative **τιμιώτερος**, *timiōteros*, *tim-ee-o´-ter-os*; and the superlative **τιμιώτατος**, *timiōtatos*, *tim-ee-o´-tat-os*; from 5092; *valuable*, i.e. (object) *costly*, or (subject) *honored, esteemed*, or (figurative) *beloved*:—dear, honourable, (more, most) precious, had in reputation.

5094. τιμιότης, timiotēs, *tim-ee-ot´-ace*; from 5093; *expensiveness*, i.e. (by implication) *magnificence*:—costliness.

5095. Τιμόθεος, Timotheos, *tee-moth´-eh-os*; from 5092 and 2316; *dear to God; Timotheus*, a Christian:—Timotheus, Timothy.

5096. Τίμων, Timōn, *tee´-mone*; from 5092; *valuable; Timon*, a Christian:—Timon.

5097. τιμωρέω, timōreō, *tim-o-reh´-o*; from a compound of 5092 and **οὖρος**, *ouros* (a *guard*); properly to *protect* one's *honour*, i.e. to *avenge* (*inflict a penalty*):—punish.

5098. τιμωρία, timōria, *tee-mo-ree´-ah*; from 5097; *vindication*, i.e. (by implication) a *penalty*:—punishment.

Noun from *timōréō* (5097), to punish. Vindication, retaliation, from the idea of watching out for one's honour, protecting the honour of someone and avenging any violations of one's honour. In the NT, punishment. Used only in Heb 10:29.

Syn.: *díkē* (1349), justice, the execution of a sentence, punishment; *ekdíkēsis* (1557), punishment, retribution; *epitimía* (2009), penalty, punishment; *kólasis* (2851), torment.

5099. τίνω, tinō, *tee´-no*; strengthened for a primary **τίω**, *tiō*, *tee´-o* (which is only used as an alternate in certain tenses); to *pay* a price, i.e. as a *penalty*:—be punished with.

5100. τὶς, tis, *tis*; an encliteral indefinite pronoun; *some* or *any* person or object:—a (kind of), any (man, thing, thing at all), certain (thing), divers, he (every) man, one (× thing), ought, + partly, some (man, -body, -thing, -what), (+ that no-) thing, what (-soever), × wherewith, whom [-soever], whose ([-soever]).

Indefinite pronoun meaning one, someone, a certain one.

(I) Particularly and generally of some person or thing whom one cannot or does not wish to name or specify particularly. It is used in various constructions:

(A) Simply (Mt 12:29, 47; Lk 9:7–8; Jn 2:25; Ac 5:25; Ro 3:3; 1Co 4:18; 15:12; Php 1:15; Heb 4:6).

(B) Joined with a substantive or adjective taken substantively, a certain person or thing, someone or something (Lk 8:2, 27; 9:19; 17:12; Jn 4:46; Ac 9:19; Gal 6:1; Jude 4).

(C) Followed by the genitive of class or partition of which *tis* expresses a part, e.g., certain of the scribes (Mt 9:3). See also Mt 27:47; Mk 14:47; Lk 14:15; Jn 7:25; 9:16; Ro 11:14; 2Co 10:12.

(II) Emphatically meaning somebody, something, some person or thing of weight and importance, some great one (Ac 5:36; 8:9; 1Co 3:7; 8:2; 10:19; Gal 2:6; 6:15; Heb 10:27).

(III) *Tis* with a substantive or adjective sometimes serves to limit or modify the full meaning, with the idea of somewhat, in some measure, a kind of (Ro 1:11, 13; Jas 1:18).

5101. τίς, tis, *tis*; probably emphatical of 5100; an interrogative pronoun, *who, which* or *what* (in direct or indirect questions):—every man, how (much), + no (-ne, thing), what (manner, thing), where ([-by, -fore, -of, -unto, -with, -withal]), whether, which, who (-m, -se), why.

An interrogative pronoun meaning who?, which?, or what? As an interrogative pronoun it is always written with the acute accent, and is thus distinguished from *tis* or *ti*, as an indefinite pronoun. See *tis* (5100).

(I) Used in direct questions:

(A) Generally: **(1)** As a substantive: e.g., "who hath warned you" (Mt 3:7). See also Mt 21:23; 27:24; Mk 1:27; 2:7; 9:10; Lk 10:29; 16:2; Jn 1:22, 38; 2:4; 13:25; Ac 7:27; 19:3; Eph 4:9; Heb 3:17, 18; Rev 6:17. **(2)** With a substantive as an interrogative adjective modifier: e.g., "what man is there ... ?" (Mt 7:9). See also (Mt 5:46; 27:23; Lk 11:11; 14:31; Jn 2:18; Ro 6:21; Heb 7:11). **(3)** Followed by the gen. of class or of partition, of which *tís* expresses a part: e.g., "which of the prophets?" (Ac 7:52). See also Mt 6:27; 22:28; Lk 10:36; Jn 8:46; Heb 1:5, 13.

(B) The neuter *ti* is sometimes used as an adverb of interrogation. **(1)** Wherefore? why? for what cause? equivalent to *diá tí*, "because (*dia* [1223]) of what?" (Mt 7:3; 8:26; 17:10; Mk 11:3; Lk 6:2, 41; Jn 1:25; 7:19; Ac 26:14; 1Co 4:7; 10:30; 15:29, 30; Gal 3:19). **(2)** As to what? how? in what respect? equal to *katá ti*, "according to (*katá* [2596]) what?" (Mt 16:26; 19:20; 22:17; Mk 8:36; Lk 9:25; 1Co 7:16). Also as an intensive meaning how! how greatly! (Lk 12:49).

(C) Equivalent to *póteros* (4220), an interrogative pron. meaning which of two, where two are spoken about meaning who or which of the two? (Mt 9:5; 21:31; 27:21; 23:17, 19; Lk 7:42; 1Co 4:21).

(D) *Tís* with the indicative through the force of the context sometimes approaches to the sense of *poíos* (4169), meaning of what kind or sort? Of persons (Mt 16:13, 15; Mk 8:27, 29; Lk 1:66; 4:36; 24:17; Jn 7:36; Jas 4:12).

(II) Used in indirect questions where it is often equivalent to the indefinite relative pronoun *hóstis* (3748), who or which: e.g., "Let not thy left hand know what thy right hand doeth" where the original question was "What is the right hand doing?" (Mt 6:3). See also Mt 6:25; 9:13; 10:11, 19; Mk 15:24; Lk 6:47; 7:39; 8:9; Jn 19:24; Ac 21:33; Ro 8:26–27; Eph 3:18; Heb 5:12; 1Pe 5:8.

Deriv.: *diatí* (1302), why?, wherefore?

5102. τίτλος, titlos, *tit´-los*; of Latin origin; a *titulus* or "*title*" (*placard*):—title.

5103. Τίτος, Titos, *tee´-tos*; of Latin origin but uncertain significance; *Titus*, a Christian:—Titus.

5104. τοί, toi, *toy*; probably for the dative of 3588; an encliteral particle of *asseveration* by way of contrast; *in sooth*:—[*used only with other particles in comparative, as* 2544, 3305, 5105, 5106, etc.].

5105. τοιγαροῦν, toigaroun, *toy-gar-oon´*; from 5104 and 1063 and 3767; *truly for then*, i.e. *consequently*:—there- (where-) fore.

5106. τοίνυν, toinun, *toy´-noon*; from 5104 and 3568; *truly now*, i.e. *accordingly*:—then, therefore.

5107. τοιόσδε, toiosde, *toy-os´-deh*; (including the other inflections); from a derivative of 5104 and 1161; *such-like then*, i.e. *so great*:—such.

5108. τοιοῦτος, toioutos, *toy-oo´-tos*; (including the other inflections); from 5104 and 3778; *truly this*, i.e. *of this sort* (to denote character or individuality):—like, such (an one).

5109. τοῖχος, toichos, *toy´-khos*; another form of 5038; a *wall*:—wall.

5110. τόκος, tokos, *tok´-os*; from the base of 5088; *interest* on money loaned (as a *produce*):—usury.

5111. τολμάω, tolmaō, *tol-mah´-o*; from **τόλμα**, ***tolma*** (*boldness*; probably itself from the base of 5056 through the idea of *extreme* conduct); to *venture* (object or in *act*; while 2292 is rather subject or in *feeling*); by implication to be *courageous*:—be bold, boldly, dare, durst.

5112. τολμηρότερον, tolmēroteron, *tol-may-rot´-er-on*; neuter of the comparative of a derivative of the base of 5111 (as adverb); *more daringly*, i.e. *with greater confidence* than otherwise:—the more boldly.

5113. τολμητής, tolmētēs, *tol-may-tace´*; from 5111; a *daring* (*audacious*) man:—presumptuous.

5114. τομώτερος, tomōteros, *tom-o´-ter-os*; comparative of a derivative of the primary **τέμνω**, ***temnō*** (to *cut*, more comprehensive or decisive than 2875, as if by a *single* stroke; whereas that implies repeated blows, like *hacking*); *more keen*:—sharper.

5115. τόξον, toxon, *tox´-on*; from the base of 5088; a *bow* (apparently as the simplest fabric):—bow.

5116. τοπάζιον, topazion, *top-ad´-zee-on*; neuter of a presumed derivative (alternate) of **τόπάζος**, ***topazos*** (a "*topaz*"; of uncertain origin); a gem, probably the *chrysolite*:—topaz.

5117. τόπος, topos, *top´-os*; apparently a primary word; a *spot* (genitive in *space*, but limited by occupancy; whereas 5561 is a larger but particular *locality*), i.e. *location* (as a position, home, tract, etc.); (figurative) *condition, opportunity*; specially a *scabbard*:—coast, licence, place, × plain, quarter, + rock, room, where.

5118. τοσοῦτος, tosoutos, *tos-oo´-tos*; from **τόσος**, ***tosos*** (*so much*; apparently from 3588 and 3739) and 3778 (including its variations); so *vast as this*, i.e. *such* (in quantity, amount, number or space):—as large, so great (long, many, much), these many.

5119. τότε, tote, *tot´-eh*; from (the neuter of) 3588 and 3753; *the when*, i.e. *at the time* that (of the past or future, also in consecution):—that time, then.

5120. τοῦ, tou, *too*; properly the generic of 3588; sometimes used for 5127; *of this person*:—his.

5121. τοὐναντίον, tounantion, *too-nan-tee´-on*; contracted from the neuter of 3588 and 1726; *on the contrary*:—contrariwise.

5122. τοὔνομα, tounoma, *too´-no-mah*; contracted from the neuter of 3588 and 3686; *the name* (is):—named.

5123. τουτέστι, toutesti, *toot-es´-tee*; contracted from 5124 and 2076; *that is*:—that is (to say).

5124. τοῦτο, touto, *too´-to*; neuter singular nominal or accusative of 3778; *that* thing:—here [-unto], it, partly, self [-same], so, that (intent), the same, there [-fore, -unto], this, thus, where [-fore].

5125. τούτοις, toutois, *too´-toice*; dative plural masculine or neuter of 3778; *to* (*for, in, with* or *by*) *these* (persons or things):—such, them, there [-in, -with], these, this, those.

5126. τοῦτον, touton, *too´-ton*; accusative singular masculine of 3778; *this* (person, as object of verb or preposition):—him, the same, that, this.

5127. τούτου, toutou, *too´-too*; genitive singular masculine or neuter of 3778; *of* (*from* or *concerning*) *this* (person or thing):—here [-by], him, it, + such manner of, that, thence [-forth], thereabout, this, thus.

5128. τούτους, toutous, *too´-tooce*; accusative plural masculine of 3778; *these* (persons, as object of verb or preposition):—such, them, these, this.

5129. τούτῳ, toutōi, *too´-to*; dative singular masculine or neuter of 3778; *to* (*in, with or by*) *this* (person or thing):—here [-by, -in], him, one, the same, there [-in], this.

5130. τούτων, toutōn, *too´-tone*; genitive plural masculine or neuter of 3778; *of* (*from* or *concerning*) *these* (persons or things):—such, their, these (things), they, this sort, those.

5131. τράγος, tragos, *trag´-os*; from the base of 5176; a *he-goat* (as a *gnawer*):—goat.

5132. τράπεζα, trapeza, *trap´-ed-zah*; probably contracted from 5064 and 3979; a *table* or *stool* (as being *four-legged*), usually for food (figurative, a *meal*); also a *counter* for money (figurative, a broker's *office* for loans at interest):—bank, meat, table.

5133. τραπεζίτης, trapezitēs, *trap-ed-zee´-tace*; from 5132; a money-*broker* or *banker*:—exchanger.

5134. τραῦμα, trauma, *trow´-mah*; from the base of **τιτρώσκω**, ***titrōskō*** (to *wound*; akin to the base of 2352, 5147, 5149, etc.); a *wound*:—wound.

5135. τραυματίζω, traumatizō, *trow-mat-id´-zo*; from 5134; to *inflict a wound*:—wound.

5136. τραχηλίζω, trachēlizō, *trakh-ay-lid´-zo*; from 5137; to *seize* by *the throat* or *neck*, i.e. to *expose* the *gullet* of a victim for killing (genitive to *lay bare*):—opened.

5137. τράχηλος, trachēlos, *trakh´-ay-los*; probably from 5143 (through the idea of *mobility*); the *throat* (*neck*), i.e. (figurative) *life*:—neck.

5138. τραχύς, trachus, *trakh-oos´*; perhaps strengthened from the base of 4486 (as if *jagged* by rents); *uneven, rocky* (*reefy*):—rock, rough.

5139. Τραχωνῖτις, Trachōnitis, *trakh-o-nee´-tis*; from a derivative of 5138; *rough* district; *Trachonitis*, a region of Syria:—Trachonitis.

5140. τρεῖς, treis, *trice*; neuter **τρία**, ***tria***, *tree´-ah*; a primary (plural) number; "*three*":—three.

5141. τρέμω, tremō, *trem´-o*; strengthened from a primary **τρέω**, ***treō*** (to "*dread*," "*terrify*"); to "*tremble*" or *fear*:—be afraid, trembling.

5142. τρέφω, trephō, *tref´-o*; a primary verb (properly **θρέφω**, ***threphō***; but perhaps strength from the base of 5157 through the idea of *convolution*); properly to *stiffen*, i.e. *fatten* (by implication to *cherish* [with food, etc.], *pamper, rear*):—bring up, feed, nourish.

5143. τρέχω, trechō, *trekh´-o*; apparently a primary verb (properly **θρέχω**, ***threchō***; compare 2359); which uses **δρέμω**, ***dremō***, *drem´-o* (the base of 1408) as alternate in certain tenses; to *run* or *walk hastily* (literal or figurative):—have course, run.

5144. τριάκοντα, triakonta, *tree-ak´-on-tah*; the decade of 5140; *thirty*:—thirty.

5145. τριακόσιοι, triakosioi, *tree-ak-os´-ee-oy*; plural from 5140 and 1540; *three hundred*:—three hundred.

5146. τρίβολος, tribolos, *trib´-ol-os*; from 5140 and 956; properly a *crow-foot* (*three-pronged* obstruction in war), i.e. (by analogy) a *thorny* plant (*caltrop*):—brier, thistle.

5147. τρίβος, tribos, *tree´-bos*; from **τρίβω**, ***tribō*** (to "*rub*"; akin to **τείρω**, ***teirō***; **τρύω**, ***truō***; and the base of 5131, 5134); a *rut* or worn *track*:—path.

5148. τριετία, trietia, *tree-et-ee´-ah*; from a compound of 5140 and 2094; a *three years' period* (*triennium*):—space of three years.

5149. τρίζω, trizo, *trid´-zo*; apparently a primary verb; to *creak* (*squeak*), i.e. (by analogy) to *grate* the teeth (in frenzy):—gnash.

5150. τρίμηνον, trimēnon, *trim´-ay-non*; neuter of a compound of 5140 and 3376 as noun; a *three months'* space:—three months.

5151. τρίς, tris, *trece*; adverb from 5140; *three times*:—three times, thrice.

5152. τρίστεγον, tristegon, *tris´-teg-on*; neuter of a compound of 5140 and 4721 as noun; a *third roof* (*story*):—third loft.

5153. τρισχίλιοι, trischilioi, *tris-khil´-ee-oy*; from 5151 and 5507; *three times a thousand*:—three thousand.

5154. τρίτος, tritos, *tree´-tos*; order from 5140; *third*; neuter (as noun) a *third part*, or (as adverb) a (or the) *third* time, *thirdly*:—third (-ly).

5155. τρίχινος, trichinos, *trikh´-ee-nos*; from 2359; *hairy*, i.e. made *of hair* (*mohair*):—of hair.

5156. τρόμος, tromos, *trom´-os*; from 5141; a "*trembling*," i.e. quaking with *fear*:— + tremble (-ing).

5157. τροπή, tropē, *trop-ay´*; from an apparently primary **τρέπω,** ***trepō*** (to *turn*); a *turn* ("trope"), i.e. *revolution* (figurative, *variation*):—turning.

5158. τρόπος, tropos, *trop´-os*; from the same as 5157; a *turn*, i.e. (by implication) *mode* or *style* (especially with preposition or relative prefix as adverb *like*); (figurative) *deportment* or *character*:—(even) as, conversation, [+ like] manner (+ by any) means, way.

5159. τροποφορέω, tropophoreō, *trop-of-or-eh´-o*; from 5158 and 5409; to *endure* one's *habits*:—suffer the manners.

5160. τροφή, trophē, *trof-ay´*; from 5142; *nourishment* (literal or figurative); by implication *rations* (*wages*):—food, meat.

5161. Τρόφιμος, Trophimos, *trof´-ee-mos*; from 5160; *nutritive; Trophimus*, a Christian:—Trophimus.

5162. τροφός, trophos, *trof-os´*; from 5142; a *nourisher*, i.e. *nurse*:—nurse.

5163. τροχιά, trochia, *trokh-ee-ah´*; from 5164; a *track* (as a wheel-*rut*), i.e. (figurative) a *course* of conduct:—path.

5164. τροχός, trochos, *trokh-os´*; from 5143; a *wheel* (as a *runner*), i.e. (figurative) a *circuit* of physical effects:—course.

5165. τρύβλιον, trublion, *troob´-lee-on*; neuter of a presumed derivative of uncertain affinity; a *bowl*:—dish.

5166. τρυγάω, trugaō, *troo-gah´-o*; from a derivative of **τρύγω,** ***trugō*** (to *dry*) meaning ripe *fruit* (as if *dry*); to *collect* the vintage:—gather.

5167. τρυγών, trugōn, *troo-gone´*; from **τρύζω,** ***truzō*** (to *murmur*; akin to 5149, but denoting a *duller* sound); a *turtle-dove* (as *cooing*):—turtle-dove.

5168. τρυμαλιά, trumalia, *troo-mal-ee-ah´*; from a derivative of **τρύω,** ***truō*** (to *wear* away; akin to the base of 5134, 5147 and 5176); an *orifice*, i.e. a needle's *eye*:—eye. Compare 5169.

5169. τρύπημα, trupēma, *troo´-pay-mah*; from a derivative of the base of 5168; an *aperture*, i.e. a needle's *eye*:—eye.

5170. Τρύφαινα, Truphaina, *troo´-fahee-nah*; from 5172; *luxurious; Tryphæna*, a Christian woman:—Tryphena.

5171. τρυφάω, truphaō, *troo-fah´-o*; from 5172; to *indulge in luxury*:—live in pleasure.

From *truphḗ* (5172), luxury. To live luxuriously, in pleasure. Used only in Jas 5:5.

Deriv.: *entrupháō* (1792), to revel luxuriously.

Syn.: *spataláō* (4684), to live in pleasure; *strēniáō* (4763), to live riotously or wantonly.

5172. τρυφή, truphē, *troo-fay´*; from **θρύπτω,** ***thruptō*** (to *break* up or [figurative] *enfeeble*, especially the mind and body by indulgence); *effeminacy*, i.e. *luxury* or *debauchery*:—delicately, riot.

5173. Τρυφῶσα, Truphōsa, *troo-fo´-sah*; from 5172; *luxuriating; Tryphosa*, a Christian female:—Tryphosa.

5174. Τρωάς, Trōas, *tro-as´*; from **Τρός,** ***Tros*** (a *Trojan*); the *Troad* (or plain of Troy), i.e. *Troas*, a place in Asia Minor:—Troas.

5175. Τρωγύλλιον, Trōgullion, *tro-gool´-lee-on*; of uncertain derivative; *Trogyllium*, a place in Asia Minor:—Trogyllium.

5176. τρώγω, trōgō, *tro´-go*; probably strengthened from a collateral form of the base of 5134 and 5147 through the idea of *corrosion* or *wear*; or perhaps rather of a base of 5167 and 5149 through the idea of a *craunching* sound; to *gnaw* or *chew*, i.e. (genitive) to *eat*:—eat.

5177. τυγχάνω, tugchanō, *toong-khan´-o*; probably for an obsolete **τύχω,** ***tuchō*** (for which the middle of another alternate **τεύχω,** ***teuchō***; [to *make ready* or *bring to pass*] is used in certain tenses); akin to the base of 5088 through the idea of *effecting*; properly to *affect*; or (special) to *hit* or *light upon* (as a mark to be reached), i.e. (transitive) to *attain* or *secure* an object or end, or (intransitive) to *happen* (as if *meeting* with); but in the latter application only impersonal (with 1487), i.e. *perchance*; or (presumed participle) as adjective *usual* (as if commonly *met with*, with 3756, *extraordinary*), neuter (as adverb) *perhaps*; or (with another verb) as adverb by *accident* (*as it were*):—be, chance, enjoy, little, obtain, × refresh … self, + special. Compare 5180.

5178. τυμπανίζω, tumpanizō, *toom-pan-id´-zo*; from a derivative of 5180 (meaning a *drum*, "*tympanum*"); to stretch on an instrument of *torture* resembling a drum, and thus *beat* to death:—torture.

5179. τύπος, tupos, *too´-pos*; from 5180; a *die* (as *struck*), i.e. (by implication) a *stamp* or *scar*; (by analogy) a *shape*, i.e. a *statue*, (figurative) *style* or *resemblance*; specially a *sampler* ("*type*"), i.e. a *model* (for imitation) or *instance* (for warning):—en- (ex-) ample, fashion, figure, form, manner, pattern, print.

Noun from *túptō* (5180), to strike, smite with repeated strokes. A type, i.e. something caused by strokes or blows.

(I) A mark, print, impression (Jn 20:25).

(II) A figure, form.

(A) Of an image, statue (Ac 7:43).

(B) Of the form, manner, or contents of a letter (Ac 23:25); of a doctrine (Ro 6:17).

(C) Spoken figuratively of a person as bearing the form and figure of another, a type, as having a certain resemblance in relations and circumstances (Ro 5:14).

(III) A prototype, pattern.

(A) Spoken particularly of a pattern or model after which something is to be made (Ac 7:44; Heb 8:5).

(B) Spoken figuratively of an example, pattern to be imitated, followed (Php 3:17; 1Th 1:7; 2Th 3:9; 1Ti 4:12; Tit 2:7; 1Pe 5:3). Hence also for admonition, warning (1Co 10:6, 11).

Deriv.: *antítupos* (499), that which corresponds to a type, which represents the real thing; *entupóō* (1795), to impress, stamp.

Syn.: *hupotúpōsis* (5296), a sketch, pattern for imitation.

5180. τύπτω, tuptō, *toop´-to*; a primary verb (in a strengthened form); to "*thump*," i.e. *cudgel* or *pummel* (properly with a stick or *bastinado*), but in any case by *repeated* blows; thus differing from 3817 and 3960, which denote a [usually single] blow with the hand or any instrument, or 4141 with the *fist* [or a *hammer*], or 4474 with the *palm*; as well as from 5177, an *accidental* collision); by implication to *punish*; (figurative) to *offend* (the conscience):—beat, smite, strike, wound.

To strike, smite with the hand, stick, or other instrument repeatedly.

(I) Particularly and generally.

(A) To smite in enmity with a stick, club, or the fist (Mt 24:49; Lk

12:45; Ac 18:17; 21:32; 23:3); on the cheek (Lk 6:29); on the head (Mt 27:30; Mk 15:19); on the face (Lk 22:64); on the mouth (Ac 23:2).

(B) To beat upon one's chest in strong emotion (Lk 18:13; 23:48).

(C) Figuratively, to smite meaning to punish, inflict evil, afflict with disease, calamity, and spoken only as being done by God (Ac 23:3).

(II) Figuratively, to strike against, meaning to offend, to wound the conscience of someone (1Co 8:12).

Deriv.: *túpos* (5179), stroke, the impression left by striking, a trace or print.

Syn.: *dérō* (1194), to flay, beat, thrash, strike; *paíō* (3817), to strike, sting; *patássō* (3960), to hit, strike, with the hand, fist, or weapon; *plḗssō* (4141), to strike as with a plague; *rhabdízō* (4463), to beat with a rod or stick; *rhapízō* (4474), to slap, strike.

5181. Τύραννος, Turannos, *too´-ran-nos*; a provincial form of the derivative of the base of 2962; a "*tyrant*"; *Tyrannus*, an Ephesian:—Tyrannus.

5182. τυρβάζω, turbazō, *toor-bad´-zo*; from **τύρβη,** ***turbē*** (Latin *turba*, a *crowd*; akin to 2351); to *make* "*turbid*," i.e. *disturb*:—trouble.

5183. Τύριος, Turios, *too´-ree-os*; from 5184; a *Tyrian*, i.e. inhabitant of Tyrus:—of Tyre.

5184. Τύρος, Turos, *too´-ros*; of Hebrew origin [6865]; *Tyrus* (i.e. *Tsor*), a place in Palestine:—Tyre.

5185. τυφλός, tuphlos, *toof-los´*; from 5187; *opaque* (as if *smoky*), i.e. (by analogy) *blind* (physical or mental):—blind.

5186. τυφλόω, tuphloō, *toof-lo´-o*; from 5185; to *make blind*, i.e. (figurative) to *obscure*:—blind.

5187. τυφόω, tuphoō, *toof-o´-o*; from a derivative of 5188; to envelop with *smoke*, i.e. (figurative) to *inflate* with self-conceit:—high-minded, be lifted up with pride, be proud.

From *túphos* (n.f.), smoke. To smoke, to fume, to surround with smoke. Figuratively, to make conceited, proud, to inflate. In the NT, only in the passive, to be conceited, proud, arrogant (1Ti 3:6; 6:4; 2Ti 3:4).

Deriv.: *tuphlós* (5185), blind.

Syn.: *epaíromai* (1869), to exalt self; *huperaíromai* (5229), to become haughty, proud; *hupsēlophronéō* (5309), to be high-minded; *phusióō* (5448), to inflate, make proud, puff up.

5188. τυφώ, tuphō, *too´-fo*; apparently a primary verb; to make a *smoke*, i.e. slowly *consume* without flame:—smoke.

5189. τυφωνικός, tuphōnikos, *too-fo-nee-kos´*; from a derivative of 5188; *stormy* (as if *smoky*):—tempestuous.

5190. Τυχικός, Tuchikos, *too-khee-kos´*; from a derivative of 5177; *fortuitous*, i.e. *fortunate; Tychicus*, a Christian:—Tychicus.

5191. ὑακίνθινος, huakinthinos, *hoo-ak-in´-thee-nos*; from 5192; "*hyacinthine*" or "*jacinthine*," i.e. deep *blue*:—jacinth.

5192. ὑάκινθος, huakinthos, *hoo-ak´-in-thos*; of uncertain derivative; the "*hyacinth*" or "*jacinth*," i.e. some gem of a deep *blue* colour, probably the *zirkon*:—jacinth.

5193. ὑάλινος, hualinos, *hoo-al´-ee-nos*; from 5194; *glassy*, i.e. *transparent*:—of glass.

5194. ὕαλος, hualos, *hoo´-al-os*; perhaps from the same as 5205 (as being transparent like *rain*); *glass*:—glass.

5195. ὑβρίζω, hubrizō, *hoo-brid´-zo*; from 5196; to *exercise violence*, i.e. *abuse*:—use despitefully, reproach, entreat shamefully (spitefully).

5196. ὕβρις, hubris, *hoo´-bris*; from 5228; *insolence* (as *overbearing*), i.e. *insult, injury*:—harm, hurt, reproach.

5197. ὑβριστής, hubristēs, *hoo-bris-tace´*; from 5195; an *insulter*, i.e. *maltreater*:—despiteful, injurious.

Noun from *húbris* (5196), arrogance. One who is insolent, contemptuous, injurious. Combines the idea of arrogance and violence against others (Ro 1:30; 1Ti 1:13).

Syn.: *loídoros* (3060), reviler.

5198. ὑγιαίνω, hugiainō, *hoog-ee-ah´ee-no*; from 5199; to *have* sound *health*, i.e. *be well* (in body); (figurative) to be *uncorrupt* (*true* in doctrine):—be in health, (be safe and) sound, (be) whole (-some).

From *hugiḗs* (5199), sound, healthy. To be healthy, sound, in good health.

(I) Particularly, to be healthy (Lk 5:31; 7:10; 3Jn 2). With the meaning to be safe and sound (Lk 15:27).

(II) Metaphorically of persons, to be sound in the faith, meaning sound, pure in respect to Christian doctrine and life (Tit 1:13; 2:2). Of doctrine, meaning sound doctrine, i.e. true, pure, uncorrupted (1Ti 1:10; 6:3; 2Ti 1:13; 4:3; Tit 1:9; 2:1).

5199. ὑγιής, hugiēs, *hoog-ee-ace´*; from the base of 837; *healthy*, i.e. *well* (in body); (figurative) *true* (in doctrine):—sound, whole.

An adjective meaning sound, healthy, in good health.

(I) Particularly of the body or its parts. In the NT always with the idea of becoming whole, being healed of disease and infirmity (Mt 12:13; 15:31; Mk 3:5; 5:34; Lk 6:10; Jn 5:4, 6, 9, 11, 14, 15; 7:23; Ac 4:10).

(II) Figuratively of sound speech or doctrine, in the sense of being true, pure, unadulterated (Tit 2:8).

Deriv.: *hugiaínō* (5198), to be healthy.

Syn.: *hólos* (3650), whole, healthy.

5200. ὑγρός, hugros, *hoo-gros´*; from the base of 5205; *wet* (as if with *rain*), i.e. (by implication) *sappy* (*fresh*):—green.

5201. ὑδριά, hudria, *hoo-dree-ah´*; from 5204; a *water-jar*, i.e. *receptacle* for family supply:—waterpot.

5202. ὑδροποτέω, hudropoteō, *hoo-drop-ot-eh´-o*; from a compound of 5204 and a derivative of 4095; to *be* a *water-drinker*, i.e. to *abstain from vinous beverages*:—drink water.

5203. ὑδρωπικός, hudrōpikos, *hoo-dro-pik-os´*; from a compound of 5204 and a derivative of 3700 (as if *looking watery*); to *be* "*dropsical*":—have the dropsy.

5204. ὕδωρ, hudōr, *hoo´-dor*; genitive **ὕδατος,** ***hudatos***, *hoo´-dat-os*, etc.; from the base of 5205; *water* (as if *rainy*) literal or figurative:—water.

5205. ὑετός, huetos, *hoo-et-os´*; from a primary **ὕω,** ***huō*** (to *rain*); *rain*, especially a *shower*:—rain.

5206. υἱοθεσία, uihothesia, *hwee-oth-es-ee´-ah*; from a presumed compound of 5207 and a derivative of 5087; the *placing* as a *son*, i.e. *adoption* (figurative, Christian *sonship* in respect to God):— adoption (of children, of sons).

Noun from *huiós* (5207), son, and *títhēmi* (5087), to place. Adoption, the placing as a son or daughter. In the NT, figuratively meaning adoption, sonship, spoken of the state of those whom God through Christ adopts as His sons and thus makes heirs of His covenanted salvation. See *huiós* (5207, II, B). Of the true Israel, the spiritual descendants of Abraham (Ro 9:4 [cf. 6, 7]), especially of Christians, the followers of the Lord Jesus (Ro 8:15, 23; Gal 4:5; Eph 1:5).

5207. υἱός, uihos, *hwee-os´*; apparently a primary word; a "*son*" (sometimes of animals), used very widely of immediate, remote or figurative kinship:—child, foal, son.

A noun meaning son.

(I) Generally.

(A) A male offspring: **(1)** Strictly spoken only of man (Mt 1:21, 25; 7:9; Mk 6:3; 9:17; Rev 12:5). In Heb 12:8 it is presented emphatically as the opposite of *nóthos* (3541), illegitimate son. Spoken of one who fills the place of a son (Jn 19:26); of an adopted son (Ac 7:21; Heb 11:24). **(2)** Of the young of animals, "foal of an ass" (Mt 21:5).

(B) Spoken in a wider sense of a descendant, in the plural of descendants, posterity; cf. *téknon* (5043, II), child. **(1)** Singular. Spoken of Joseph as a son of David (Mt 1:1, 20; Lk 19:9). Spoken of the Messiah as descended from the line of David (Mt 22:42, 45; Mk 12:35, 37; Lk 20:41, 44). Spoken of Jesus as the "son of David" meaning the Messiah (Mt 1:1; 9:27; 12:23; 15:22; 20:30, 31; 21:9, 15; Mk 10:47, 48; Lk 18:38, 39). **(2)** Plural (Ac 7:16; Heb 7:5); especially the posterity of

Abraham, the sons or descendants of Israel, the Israelites (Mt 27:9; Lk 1:16; Ac 5:21; 7:23, 37; Ro 9:27; 2Co 3:7, 13; Gal 3:7; Rev 21:12). **(3)** Spoken in the title, the Son of Man, in reference to Jesus as the Messiah. See *ánthrōpos* (444, IV), man.

(C) Figuratively, spoken of one who is the object of parental love and care or who yields filial love and reverence toward another, a pupil, disciple, follower, the spiritual child of someone (Heb 2:10; 12:5; 1Pe 5:13; cf. *téknon* [5043, III, B], child). Spoken of the disciples and followers of the Pharisees (Mt 12:27; Lk 11:19).

(D) Figuratively, spoken with a genitive, the son of something as one connected with, partaking of, or exposed to that thing, often used instead of an adjective. **(1)** Followed by a genitive of place, condition, or connectivity; e.g., sons of the bridal chamber, bridesmen (Mt 9:15; Mk 2:19; Lk 5:34). Also spoken of the sons of the kingdom (Mt 8:12; 13:38); the sons of the evil one (Mt 13:38); the son of the devil (Ac 13:10); the sons of this world (Lk 16:8; 20:34). **(2)** Followed by a genitive implying quality, character: e.g., sons of thunder (Mk 3:17). See also Lk 10:6; 16:8; Jn 12:36; Ac 4:36; Eph 2:2; 5:6; Col 3:6; 1Th 5:5. **(3)** Followed by a genitive of that in which one partakes, to which one is exposed: e.g., "children of the resurrection" meaning partakers in it (Lk 20:36). See also Mt 23:15; Jn 17:12; Ac 3:25.

(II) Specifically *huiós toú Theoú* (gen. of *Theós* [2316], God) son of God, and *huioí toú Theoú*, sons of God. Spoken of:

(A) One who derives his human nature directly from God, and not by ordinary generation: spoken of Jesus (Lk 1:35); implied of Adam (Lk 3:38).

(B) Those whom God loves and cherishes as a father. **(1)** Generally of pious worshippers of God, the righteous, the saints (Mt 5:9, 45; Lk 6:35; 20:36). **(2)** Specifically of the Israelites (Ro 9:26; 2Co 6:18). **(3)** Of Christians (Ro 8:14, 19; Gal 3:26; 4:6, 7; Heb 12:6; Rev 21:7).

(C) Jesus Christ as the Son of God, the Son of the Most High (Mt 27:54; Mk 15:39; Lk 1:32). **(1)** In the Jewish sense as the Messiah, the Anointed, the Christ, the expected King of the Jewish nation, constituted of God, and ruling in the world (Mt 2:15; 4:3; 8:29; 14:33; 27:40, 43; Mk 3:11; 5:7; Lk 4:3; 8:28; 22:70; Jn 1:34, 49; 9:35). As joined with *ho Christós* (5547), Christ, in explanation (Mt 16:16; 26:63; Mk 14:61; Lk 4:41; Jn 6:69; 11:27; 20:31). **(2)** In the gospel sense as the Messiah, the Saviour, the Head of the gospel dispensation, as proceeding and sent forth from God, as partaking of the divine nature and being in intimate union with God the Father (Mt 3:17; 11:27; 17:5; 28:19; Mk 13:32; Lk 10:22; Jn 1:18; 3:16–18; 5:26; 10:36; 17:1; Ac 13:33; Ro 1:3, 4, 9; 5:10; 8:3, 29, 32; 1Co 1:9; 15:28; 2Co 1:19; Gal 1:16; 2:20; Eph 4:13; Col 1:13; 1Th 1:10; Heb 1:2, 5; 3:6; 5:5; 6:6; 2Pe 1:17; 1Jn 1:3, 7; 2:22; 4:14; 5:5; 2Jn 3, 9; Rev 2:18).

Deriv.: *huiothesía* (5206), adoption.

Syn.: *nḗpios* (3516), an infant; *paidárion* (3808), a lad; *paidíon* (3813), a young child; *país* (3816), a child or servant; *teknion* (5040), a little child; *téknon* (5043), a child.

5208. ὕλη, hulē, *hoo´-lay*; perhaps akin to 3586; a *forest*, i.e. (by implication) *fuel*:—matter.

5209. ὑμᾶς, humas, *hoo-mas´*; accusative of 5210; *you* (as the object of a verb or preposition):—ye, you (+ -ward), your (+ own).

5210. ὑμεῖς, humeis, *hoo-mice´*; irregular plural of 4771; *you* (as subject of verb):—ye (yourselves), you.

5211. Ὑμεναῖος, Humenaios, *hoo-men-ah´-yos*; from **Ὑμήν, *Humēn*** (the god of *weddings*); "*hymenæal*"; *Hymenæus*, an opponent of Christianity:—Hymenæus.

5212. ὑμέτερος, humeteros, *hoo-met´-er-os*; from 5210; *yours*, i.e. *pertaining to you*:—your (own).

5213. ὑμῖν, humin, *hoo-min´*; irregular dative of 5210; *to* (*with* or *by*) *you*:—ye, you, your (-selves).

5214. ὑμνέω, humneō, *hoom-neh´-o*; from 5215; to *hymn*, i.e. sing a religious ode; by implication to *celebrate* (God) in song:—sing an hymn (praise unto).

5215. ὕμνος, humnos, *hoom´-nos*; apparently from a simpler (obsolete) form of **ὕδέω, *hudeō*** (to *celebrate*; probably akin to 103; compare 5567); a "*hymn*" or religious ode, one of the Psalms):—hymn.

A noun meaning hymn or song of praise. It is used only in Eph 5:19; Col 3:16, where it occurs with *psalmós* (5568), psalm, and *hōdḗ* (5603), spiritual song.

Deriv.: *humnéō* (5214), to sing a hymn.

Syn.: *aínos* (136), praise; *épainos* (1868), commendable thing, praise; *eulogía* (2129), fair speech, blessing, eulogy; *euphēmía* (2162), praise, good report.

5216. ὑμῶν, humōn, *hoo-mone´*; generic of 5210; *of* (*from* or *concerning*) *you*:—ye, you, your (own, -selves).

5217. ὑπάγω, hupagō, *hoop-ag´-o*; from 5259 and 71; to *lead* (oneself) *under*, i.e. *withdraw* or *retire* (as if *sinking* out of sight), literal or figurative:—depart, get hence, go (a-) way.

5218. ὑπακοή, hupakoē, *hoop-ak-o-ay´*; from 5219; *attentive hearkening*, i.e. (by implication) *compliance* or *submission*:—obedience, (make) obedient, obey (-ing).

Noun from *hupakoúō* (5219), to obey. A hearing attentively, a listening, an audience. In the NT, obedience (Ro 1:5; 5:19; 6:16; 15:18; 16:19, 26; 2Co 7:15; 10:5, 6; Phm 21; Heb 5:8; 1Pe 1:2, 14, 22).

Syn.: *hupotagḗ* (5292), subjection, obedience.

5219. ὑπακούω, hupakouō, *hoop-ak-oo´-o*; from 5259 and 191; to *hear under* (as a *subordinate*), i.e. to *listen attentively*; by implication to *heed* or *conform* to a command or authority:—hearken, be obedient to, obey.

From *hupó* (5259), and *akoúō* (191), to hear. To hearken, obey.

(I) Particularly, to listen to something, hearken with stillness or attention, as a doorkeeper would, in order to answer (Ac 12:13).

(II) To yield to a superior command or force.

(A) Spoken of things (Mt 8:27; Mk 4:41; Lk 8:25; 17:6).

(B) Spoken of unclean spirits (Mk 1:27).

(III) To obey one in authority.

(A) Spoken of children obeying parents (Eph 6:1; Col 3:20).

(B) Spoken of slaves obeying their masters (Eph 6:5; Col 3:22).

(C) Spoken of a wife obeying her husband (1Pe 3:6).

(IV) In a spiritual sense, to obey God (Heb 5:9; 11:8); to obey the gospel (Ac 6:7; Ro 10:16; 2Th 1:8); to obey a spiritual leader (Php 2:12; 2Th 3:14).

(V) To obey one's passions, thus becoming enslaved by them (Ro 6:12, 16).

Deriv.: *hupakoḗ* (5218), obedience; *hupḗkoos* (5255), obedient.

Syn.: *peitharchéō* (3980), to be submitted to a ruler, to hearken, obey one in authority; *summorphóō* (4833), to conform oneself to.

5220. ὕπανδρος, hupandros, *hoop´-an-dros*; from 5259 and 435; in subjection *under a man*, i.e. a *married* woman:—which hath an husband.

5221. ὑπαντάω, hupantaō, *hoop-an-tah´-o*; from 5259 and a derivative of 473; to *go opposite* (*meet*) *under* (*quietly*), i.e. to *encounter*, *fall in with*:—(go to) meet.

5222. ὑπάντησις, hupantēsis, *hoop-an´-tay-sis*; from 5221; an *encounter* or *concurrence* (with 1519 for infinite, in order to *fall in with*):—meeting.

5223. ὕπαρξις, huparxis, *hoop´-arx-is*; from 5225; *existency* or *proprietorship*, i.e. (concrete) *property*, *wealth*:—goods, substance.

5224. ὑπάρχοντα, huparchonta, *hoop-ar´-khon-tah*; neuter plural of presumed participle active of 5225 as noun; things *extant* or *in hand*, i.e. *property* or *possessions*:—goods, that which one has, things which (one) possesseth, substance, that hast.

5225. ὑπάρχω, huparchō, *hoop-ar´-kho*; from 5259 and 756; to *begin under* (*quietly*), i.e. *come into existence* (*be present* or *at hand*); expletively, to *exist* (as copula or subordinate to an adjective, participle, adverb or preposition, or as auxiliary to principal verb):—after, behave, live.

From *hupó* (5259), and *árchomai* (756), to begin. To begin to be, to come into existence. In the NT, to exist, to be present (Lk 7:25; 16:23; 27:34).

(I) Generally and in an absolute sense, to exist (Ac 19:40; 27:21; 28:18; 1Co 11:18). Used with an adverbial modifier: e.g., the prepositional phrase "in heaven" (Php 3:20). See also Lk 7:25; 16:23; Ac 5:4; 10:12; 17:27; 27:34; Php 2:6). Followed by the dative of person, to be present with someone, implying possession, property (Ac 3:6; 4:37; 28:7; 2Pe 1:8). The participle used as a substantive: things present, in hand, possessions.

(II) To be, the same as *eimí* (1510), to be, logically connecting the subj. and predicate: e.g., his father was a Greek (Ac 16:3). See also (Lk 8:41; 9:48; 11:13; 16:14; 23:50; Ac 2:30; 3:2; 4:34; 7:55; 14:8; 16:20, 37; 17:24, 29; 21:20; 22:3; 27:12; Ro 4:19; 1Co 7:26; 11:7; 12:22; 2Co 8:17; 12:16; Gal 1:14; 2:14; Jas 2:15; 2Pe 2:19; 3:11). As forming a periphrasis for a finite tense of the same verb: they were baptized (Ac 8:16).

Deriv.: *proüpárchō* (4391), to exist before; *húparxis* (5223), possessions, property.

Syn.: *gínomai* (1096), to become; *eimí* (1510), to be. Also *anastréphō* (390), to live, behave, conduct one's life; *záō* (2198), to live.

5226. ὑπείκω, hupeikō, *hoop-i´-ko*; from 5259 and **εἴκω,** ***eikō*** (to *yield*, be "*weak*"); to *surrender*:—submit self.

5227. ὑπεναντίος, hupenantios, *hoop-en-an-tee´-os*; from 5259 and 1727; *under* (*covertly*) *contrary* to, i.e. *opposed* or (as noun) an *opponent*:—adversary, against.

5228. ὑπέρ, huper, *hoop-er´*; a primary preposition; "*over*," i.e. (with the generic) of place, *above, beyond, across*, or causal, *for* the sake of, *instead, regarding*; with the accusative *superior to*, more *than*:—(+ exceeding abundantly) above, in (on) behalf of, beyond, by, + very chiefest, concerning, exceeding (above, -ly), for, + very highly, more (than), of, over, on the part of, for sake of, in stead, than, to (-ward), very. In comparative it retains many of the above applications.

A preposition governing the genitive and accusative with the primary meaning of over.

(I) With the gen. particularly of place meaning over, above, across or beyond. In the NT, used only figuratively:

(A) Meaning for, in behalf of, for the sake of, in the sense of protection, care, favour, benefit. **(1)** Generally (Mk 9:40; Lk 9:50; Jn 17:19; Ac 21:26; Ro 8:31; 1Co 12:25; 2Co 7:7, 12; 8:16; 13:8; Eph 6:20; Php 4:10; Col 1:7; 4:12, 13; Heb 6:20; 13:17). After verbs implying speaking, praying, pleading, or intercession for someone (Mt 5:44; Lk 6:28; Ac 8:24; 12:5; 26:1; Ro 8:26, 27, 34; 10:1; 15:30; 2Co 9:14; Eph 6:19, 20; Php 1:4; Col 1:9; 1Ti 2:1, 2; Heb 7:25; 9:24; Jas 5:16). Often after words implying suffering or even dying on behalf of someone (Lk 22:19, 20; Jn 6:51; 10:11, 15; 11:50–52; 13:37–38; 15:13; 18:14; Ro 5:6–8; 8:32; 9:3; 14:15; 16:4; 1Co 1:13; 5:7; 11:24; 2Co 5:14–15, 21; 12:15; Gal 2:20; Eph 5:2, 25; 1Th 5:10; 1Ti 2:6; Tit 2:14; Heb 2:9; 1Pe 2:21; 3:18; 4:1; 1Jn 3:16). **(2)** Closely allied to the above is the meaning for, in the stead of someone, in place of (2Co 5:20).

(B) For, because of, on account of, meaning the aim, purpose or objective of an action and implying the ground, motive, occasion of an action: e.g., "for the glory of God," i.e. in order to manifest His glory (Jn 11:4); "for his name" in the sense of for his honour (Ac 5:41; 9:16; 15:26; 21:13; Ro 1:5; 3Jn 7). See also Ro 15:8, 9; 1Co 10:30; 15:3, 29; 2Co 1:6, 11; 12:10, 19; Gal 1:4; Eph 1:16; 3:1, 13; 5:20; Php 1:29; Col 1:24; 2Th 1:5; Heb 5:1, 3; 7:27; 9:7; 10:12).

(C) Over, used with verbs such as speaking or boasting meaning upon, about, concerning (Ro 9:27; 2Co 1:6, 8; 5:12; 7:4, 14; 8:23, 24; 9:2, 3; 12:5, 8; Php 1:7; 2Th 1:4; 2:1).

(II) With the accusative, particularly of place whither, implying motion or direction over or above a place, beyond. In the NT, only figuratively, over, beyond.

(A) Implying superiority in rank, dignity, worth (Mt 10:24; Lk 6:40; Eph 1:22; Phm 16).

(B) Implying excess above a certain measure or standard and spoken comparatively meaning more than (Mt 10:37; Lk 16:8; Ac 26:13; 1Co 4:6; 10:13; 2Co 1:8; 8:3; 12:6, 13; Gal 1:14; Phm 21; Heb 4:12).

(III) In composition, *hupér* implies:

(A) Motion or rest over, above, beyond a place, as *huperaíromai* (5229), to exalt oneself; *huperbaínō* (5233), to transcend, overreach; *huperéchō* (5242), to hold oneself above, to excel.

(B) Protection, aid, for or in behalf of, as *huperentugchánō* (5241), to intercede in behalf of.

(C) Exceeding or surpassing, often with the idea of exaggeration, as *huperbállō* (5235), to throw beyond the usual mark, surpass. Also *huperauxánō* (5232), to grow extraordinarily; *huperekteínō* (5239), to overdo, carry too far; *hupernikáō* (5245), to completely conquer; *huperperisseúō* (5248), to superabound.

Syn.: In the sense of instead of (I, A, 2): *antí* (473), in place of. In the sense of concerning (I, C): *perí* (4012), concerning; *prós* (4314), pertaining to in respect to, in respect to. In the sense of beyond, more than: *epánō* (1883), over; *lían* (3029), exceeding, great, very; *mállon* (3123), more, rather; *meízon* (3185), in a greater degree; *meizóteros* (3186), still larger, greater; *meízōn* (3187), greater; *pámpolus* (3827), very great, immense; *pará* (3844), more than; *pleíōn, pleion* (4119), more; *péran* (4008), beyond, across; *perissós* (4053), superior, beyond measure, more; *perissóteron* (4054), more abundantly; *perissóteros* (4055), more abundant, greater; *perissotérōs* (4056), more abundantly; *perissōs* (4057), exceedingly; *pró* (4253), above, before; *sphódra* (4970), much, very; *huperánō* (5231), far above, over.

5229. ὑπεραίρομαι, huperairomai, *hoop-er-ah´ee-rom-ahee*; middle from 5228 and 142; to *raise* oneself *over*, i.e. (figurative) to *become haughty*:—exalt self, be exalted above measure.

5230. ὑπέρακμος, huperakmos, *hoop-er´-ak-mos*; from 5228 and the base of 188; *beyond* the "*acme*," i.e. figurative (of a daughter) *past* the *bloom* (*prime*) of youth:— + pass the flower of (her) age.

5231. ὑπεράνω, huperanō, *hoop-er-an´-o*; from 5228 and 507; *above upward*, i.e. *greatly higher* (in place or rank):—far above, over.

5232. ὑπεραυξάνω, huperauxanō, *hoop-er-owx-an´-o*; from 5228 and 837; to *increase above* ordinary degree:—grow exceedingly.

5233. ὑπερβαίνω, huperbainō, *hoop-er-bah´ee-no*; from 5228 and the base of 939; to *transcend*, i.e. (figurative) to *overreach*:—go beyond.

From *hupér* (5228), beyond, and *bainō* (n.f., see *anabainō* [305]), to go. To go or pass over something: e.g., a wall or mountains. Figuratively, to overstep certain limits, to transgress, to go too far, to go beyond what is right. Used only in 1Th 4:6.

Syn.: *parabainō* (3845), to transgress.

5234. ὑπερβαλλόντως, huperballontōs, *hoop-er-bal-lon´-toce*; adverb from presumed participle active of 5235; *excessively*:—beyond measure.

5235. ὑπερβάλλω, huperballō, *hoop-er-bal´-lo*; from 5228 and 906; to *throw beyond* the usual mark, i.e. (figurative) to *surpass* (only active participle *supereminent*):—exceeding, excel, pass.

5236. ὑπερβολή, huperbolē, *hoop-er-bol-ay´*; from 5235; a *throwing beyond* others, i.e. (figurative) *supereminence*; adverb (with 1519 or 2596) *pre-eminently*:—abundance, (far more) exceeding, excellency, more excellent, beyond (out of) measure.

5237. ὑπερείδω, hupereidō, *hoop-er-i´-do*; from 5228 and 1492; to *overlook*, i.e. *not punish*:—wink at.

5238. ὑπερέκεινα, huperekeina, *hoop-er-ek´-i-nah*; from 5228 and the neuter plural of 1565; *above those* parts, i.e. *still farther*:—beyond.

5239. ὑπερεκτείνω, huperekteinō, *hoop-er-ek-ti´-no*; from 5228 and 1614; to *extend inordinately*:—stretch beyond.

5240. ὑπερεκχύνω, huperekchunō, *hoop-er-ek-khoo´-no*; from 5228 and the alternate form of 1632; to *pour out over*, i.e. (passive) to *overflow*:—run over.

5241. ὑπερεντυγχάνω, huperentugchanō, *hoop-er-en-toong-khan´-o*; from 5228 and 1793; to *intercede in behalf of*:—make intercession for.

5242. ὑπερέχω, huperechō, *hoop-er-ekh´-o*; from 5228 and 2192; to *hold* oneself *above*, i.e. (figurative) to *excel*; participle (as adjective, or neuter as noun) *superior, superiority*:—better, excellency, higher, pass, supreme.

5243. ὑπερηφανία, huperēphania, *hoop-er-ay-fan-ee´-ah*; from 5244; *haughtiness*:—pride.

5244. ὑπερήφανος, huperēphanos, *hoop-er-ay´-fan-os*; from 5228 and 5316; *appearing above* others (*conspicuous*), i.e. (figurative) *haughty*:—proud.

Adjective from *hupér* (5228), over, above, and *phaínō* (5316), to shine, show. Appearing over, conspicuous above other persons or things. In the NT, only in the sense of arrogant, haughty, proud. Often associated with those who despise God (Lk 1:51; Ro 1:30; 2Ti 3:2; Jas 4:6; 1Pe 5:5).

Deriv.: *huperēphanía* (5243), arrogance, pride.

5245. ὑπερνικάω, hupernikaō, *hoop-er-nik-ah´-o*; from 5228 and 3528; to *vanquish beyond*, i.e. *gain* a decisive *victory*:—more than conquer.

5246. ὑπέρογκος, huperogkos, *hoop-er´-ong-kos*; from 5228 and 3591; *bulging over*, i.e. (figurative) *insolent*:—great swelling.

5247. ὑπεροχή, huperochē, *hoop-er-okh-ay´*; from 5242; *prominence*, i.e. (figurative) *superiority* (in rank or character):—authority, excellency.

5248. ὑπερπερισσεύω, huperperisseuō, *hoop-er-per-is-syoo´-o*; from 5228 and 4052; to *superabound*:—abound much more, exceeding.

5249. ὑπερπερισσῶς, huperperissōs, *hoop-er-per-is-soce´*; from 5228 and 4057; *superabundantly*, i.e. *exceedingly*:—beyond measure.

5250. ὑπερπλεονάζω, huperpleonazō, *hoop-er-pleh-on-ad´-zo*; from 5228 and 4121; to *superabound*:—be exceeding abundant.

5251. ὑπερυψόω, huperupsoō, *hoop-er-oop-so´-o*; from 5228 and 5312; to *elevate above* others, i.e. *raise* to the *highest* position:—highly exalt.

5252. ὑπερφρονέω, huperphroneō, *hoop-er-fron-eh´-o*; from 5228 and 5426; to *esteem* oneself *overmuch*, i.e. *be vain* or *arrogant*:—think more highly.

5253. ὑπερῷον, huperōion, *hoop-er-o´-on*; neuter of a derivative of 5228; a *higher* part of the house, i.e. apartment in the *third story*:—upper chamber (room).

5254. ὑπέχω, hupechō, *hoop-ekh´-o*; from 5259 and 2192; to *hold* oneself *under*, i.e. *endure* with patience:—suffer.

5255. ὑπήκοος, hupēkoos, *hoop-ay´-ko-os*; from 5219; *attentively listening*, i.e. (by implication) *submissive*:—obedient.

Adjective from *hupakoúō* (5219), to submit to, obey. Listening, obedient (Ac 7:39; 2Co 2:9). Spoken also of Christ being obedient even to death (Php 2:8).

Syn.: *eupeithḗs* (2138), easy to be persuaded, compliant.

5256. ὑπηρετέω, hupēreteō, *hoop-ay-ret-eh´-o*; from 5257; to *be a subordinate*, i.e. (by implication) *subserve*:—minister (unto), serve.

5257. ὑπηρέτης, hupēretēs, *hoop-ay-ret´-ace*; from 5259 and a derivative of **ἐρέσσω, eressō** (to *row*); an *under-oarsman*, i.e. (general) *subordinate* (*assistant, sexton, constable*):—minister, officer, servant.

Noun from *hupó* (5259), under, beneath and *erétēs* (n.f.), a rower. A subordinate, servant, attendant, or assistant in general. In Class. Gr., a common sailor or hired hand as distinguished from *naútēs* (3492), a shipman, seaman. In the NT:

(I) Of those who wait on magistrates or public officials and execute their decrees, a constable or officer, as the attendant on a judge (Mt 5:25). Of the attendants of the Sanhedrin (Mt 26:58; Mk 14:54, 65; Jn 7:32, 45, 46; 18:3, 12, 18, 22; 19:6; Ac 5:22, 26).

(II) Of the attendant in a synagogue who handed the volume to the reader and returned it to its place (Lk 4:20).

(III) Generally, a minister, attendant, associate in any work (Jn 18:36; Ac 13:5). Of a minister of the Word of Christ (Lk 1:2; Ac 26:16; 1Co 4:1).

Deriv.: *hupēretéō* (5256), to serve under the direction of someone else.

Syn.: *diákonos* (1249), a servant, attendant, minister, deacon; *doúlos* (1401), slave, servant; *therápōn* (2324), a servant, attendant; *leitourgós* (3011), a public servant; *místhios* (3407) or *misthōtós* (3411), one who is hired to do a certain task, a hired servant; *oikétēs* (3610), a domestic servant; *pais* (3816), servant.

5258. ὕπνος, hupnos, *hoop´-nos*; from an obsolete primary (perhaps akin to 5259 through the idea of *subsilience*); *sleep*, i.e. (figurative) spiritual *torpor*:—sleep.

5259. ὑπό, hupo, *hoop-o´*; a primary prep.; *under*, i.e. (with the generic) of place (*beneath*), or with verbs (the agency or means, *through*); (with the accusative) of place (whither [*underneath*] or where [*below*]) or time (when [*at*]):—among, by, from, in, of, under, with. In comparative it retains the same genitive applications, especially of *inferior* position or condition, and specially *covertly* or *moderately*.

Preposition meaning under, beneath, through.

(I) With the genitive particularly of place meaning whence, from which something comes forth. In the NT, only used in the sense of by, through, from, indicating the agent or the one doing a passive voice action, always indicated in English with the preposition, "by": e.g., that which was spoken by the Lord (Mt 1:22). See also Mt 2:16; 3:6; 4:1; 5:13; 8:24; Lk 7:24; 9:7; 13:17; 14:8; 21:20; Ac 2:24; 4:36; 12:5; 20:3; 23:27; Ro 12:21; 15:15; 1Co 7:25; 10:9; 2Co 1:16; 5:4; 8:19; Gal 1:11; Jas 3:4, 6; 2Pe 2:7, 17; Jude 12; Rev 6:13; et al.). In the same way *hupó* is used after some transitive verbs, where a passive sense is implied: e.g., with *pascho* (3958), to suffer, in the sense of suffering something from someone's hand (Mt 17:12; Mk 5:26; 1Th 2:14). See also Ac 23:30; 2Co 2:6; 11:24; Heb 12:3; Rev 6:8.

(II) With the accusative particularly of place meaning from which; of motion or direction meaning under a place; also of place where something is placed to rest under.

(A) Particularly of place, after verbs of motion or direction meaning under, beneath: e.g., to place something under a bushel (Mt 5:15; Mk 4:21; Lk 11:33). See also Mt 8:8; 23:37; Mk 4:32; Lk 13:34; Jas 2:3).

(B) Of place where, after verbs implying a being or remaining under a place or condition: e.g., to be under heaven (Lk 17:24; Ac 2:5; 4:12; Col 1:23). See also Ro 3:13; 1Co 10:1; Jude 6. Spoken figuratively of what is under the power or authority of any person or thing: e.g., under the Law (Ro 6:14–15; 1Co 9:20; Gal 4:3–5, 21; 5:18). See also Mt 8:9; Lk 7:8; Ro 3:9; 7:14; 16:20; 1Co 15:25, 27; Gal 3:10, 22–23, 25; 4:2–3; Eph 1:22; 1Ti 6:1; 1Pe 5:6).

(C) Of time, meaning at, during (Ac 5:21).

(III) In composition *hupó* implies:

(A) Place, motion or rest meaning under, beneath, as *hupobállō* (5260), to throw under, bribe secretly; *hupodéō* (5265), to bind under one's feet, put on shoes; *hupopódion* (5286), something under the feet, as a footstool.

(B) Subjection, dependence, the state of being under any person or thing as *húpandros* (5220), under a husband or subject to a husband; *hupotássō* (5293), to subordinate.

(C) Succession, being behind or after, as *hupoleípō* (5275), to leave behind, remain; *hupoménō* (5278), to endure.

(D) *Hupó* in composition also implies something done or happening underhandedly, covertly, by stealth, unperceived, without noise or notice; also by degrees: *huponoéō* (5282), to think privately, surmise, conjecture, oppose; *hupopnéō* (5285), to breathe inaudibly.

5260. ὑποβάλλω, hupoballō, *hoop-ob-al´-lo*; from 5259 and 906; to *throw* in *stealthily*, i.e. *introduce* by collusion:—suborn.

5261. ὑπογραμμός, hupogrammos, *hoop-og-ram-mos´*; from a compound of 5259 and 1125; an *underwriting*, i.e. *copy* for imitation (figurative):—example.

Noun from *hupográphō* (n.f.), to undersign, from *hupó* (5259), before, and *gráphō* (1125), to write. Particularly, a writing example to be copied or imitated by beginning students. In the NT, used figuratively of Christ's suffering as a pattern for us to follow. Used only in 1Pe 2:2.

Syn.: *deigma* (1164), a specimen, example; *homoiōma* (3667), a form, likeness; *túpos* (5179), a type, model, pattern; *hupódeigma* (5262), an example.

5262. ὑπόδειγμα, hupodeigma, *hoop-od´-igue-mah*; from 5263; an *exhibit* for imitation or warning (figurative, *specimen, adumbration*):—en- (ex-) ample, pattern.

5263. ὑποδείκνυμι, hupodeiknumi, *hoop-od-ike´-noo-mee*; from 5259 and 1166; to *exhibit under* the eyes, i.e. (figurative) to *exemplify* (*instruct, admonish*):—show, (fore-) warn.

5264. ὑποδέχομαι, hupodechomai, *hoop-od-ekh´-om-ahee*; from 5259 and 1209; to *admit under* one's roof, i.e. *entertain* hospitably:—receive.

From *hupó* (5259), under, and *déchomai* (1209), to receive. To take to oneself, as if placing the hands or arms under a person or thing, to receive hospitably and kindly. In the NT to receive guests hospitably or to welcome, entertain (Lk 10:38; 19:6; Ac 17:7; Jas 2:25).

Syn.: *apodéchomai* (588), to welcome, receive gladly.

5265. ὑποδέω, hupodeō, *hoop-od-eh´-o*; from 5259 and 1210; to *bind under* one's feet, i.e. *put on* shoes or sandals:—bind on, (be) shod.

5266. ὑπόδημα, hupodēma, *hoop-od´-ah-mah*; from 5265; something *bound under* the feet, i.e. a *shoe* or *sandal*:—shoe.

5267. ὑπόδικος, hupodikos, *hoop-od´-ee-kos*; from 5259 and 1349; *under sentence*, i.e. (by implication) *condemned*:—guilty.

Adjective from *hupó* (5259), under, and *díkē* (1349), judgement, justice. Under sentence, condemned, liable, or subject to prosecution. Used only in Ro 3:19.

Syn.: *énochos* (1777), liable, guilty.

5268. ὑποζύγιον, hupozugion, *hoop-od-zoog´-ee-on*; neuter of a compound of 5259 and 2218; an animal *under* the *yoke* (*draught-beast*), i.e. (special) a *donkey*:—ass.

5269. ὑποζώννυμι, hupozōnnumi, *hoop-od-zone´-noo-mee*; from 5259 and 2224; to *gird under*, i.e. *frap* (a vessel with cables across the keel, sides and deck):—undergirt.

5270. ὑποκάτω, hupokatō, *hoop-ok-at´-o*; from 5259 and 2736; *down under*, i.e. *beneath*:—under.

5271. ὑποκρίνομαι, hupokrinomai, *hoop-ok-rin´-om-ahee*; middle from 5259 and 2919; to *decide* (*speak* or *act*) *under* a false part, i.e. (figurative) *dissemble* (*pretend*):—feign.

From *hupó* (5259), under, indicating secrecy, and *krínō* (2919), to judge. To pretend to be what one is not, to act hypocritically. Originally synonymous with *apokrínomai* (611), to answer, reply. Later, it acquired the meaning to answer upon a stage, to play a part, to act. In the NT, to be a hypocrite, to attempt to fool others. Used only in Lk 20:20.

Deriv.: *anupókritos* (505), one without hypocrisy; *sunupokrínomai* (4942), to play the role of a hypocrite together with; *hupókrisis* (5272), hypocrisy; *hupokritḗs* (5273), hypocrite.

Syn.: *prospoiéomai* (4364), to pretend.

5272. ὑπόκρισις, hupokrisis, *hoop-ok´-ree-sis*; from 5271; *acting under* a feigned participle i.e. (figurative) *deceit* ("*hypocrisy*"):—condemnation, dissimulation, hypocrisy.

5273. ὑποκριτής, hupokritēs, *hoop-ok-ree-tace´*; from 5271; an *actor under* an assumed character (*stage-player*), i.e. (figurative) a *dissembler* ("*hypocrite*"):—hypocrite.

Noun from *hupokrínomai* (5271), to act as a hypocrite. A stage-player, actor. In the NT, a hypocrite, specifically in respect to religion (Mt 6:2, 5, 16; 7:5; 15:7; 16:3; 22:18; 23:13–15, 23, 25, 27, 29; 24:51; Mk 7:6; Lk 6:42; 11:44; 12:56; 13:15).

5274. ὑπολαμβάνω, hupolambanō, *hoop-ol-am-ban´-o*; from 5259 and 2983; to *take* from *below*, i.e. *carry upward*; (figurative) to *take up*, i.e. *continue* a discourse or topic; mentally to *assume* (*presume*):—answer, receive, suppose.

5275. ὑπολείπω, hupoleipō, *hoop-ol-i´-po*; from 5295 and 3007; to *leave under* (*behind*), i.e. (passive) to *remain* (*survive*):—be left.

5276. ὑπολήνιον, hupolēnion, *hoop-ol-ah´-nee-on*; neuter of a presumed compound of 5259 and 3025; vessel or receptacle *under* the *press*, i.e. lower *winevat*:—winefat.

5277. ὑπολιμπάνω, hupolimpanō, *hoop-ol-im-pan´-o*; a prolonged form for 5275; to *leave behind*, i.e. *bequeath*:—leave.

5278. ὑπομένω, hupomenō, *hoop-om-en´-o*; from 5259 and 3306; to *stay under* (*behind*), i.e. *remain*; (figurative) to *undergo*, i.e. *bear* (trials), *have fortitude, persevere*:—abide, endure, (take) patient (-ly), suffer, tarry behind.

From *hupó* (5259), under, and *ménō* (3306), to remain.

(I) Intransitive, to remain behind after others are gone (Lk 2:43; Ac 17:14).

(I) Transitive, to remain under the approach or presence of any person or thing, in the sense of to await. Hence, in the NT, figuratively, to bear up under, to be patient under, to endure, to suffer (1Co 13:7; 2Ti 2:10; Heb 10:32; 12:2–3, 7; Jas 1:12). Absolute, to endure in the sense of to hold out, to persevere (Mt 10:22; 24:13; Mk 13:13; Ro 12:12; 2Ti 2:12; Jas 5:11; 1Pe 2:20).

Deriv.: *hupomonḗ* (5281), patience, endurance.

Syn.: *anéchomai* (430), to put up with; *bastázō* (941), to bear; *karteréō* (2594), to be steadfast, patient, to endure; *makrothuméō* (3114), to be long-suffering, patient; *hupéchō* (5254), to endure; *hupophérō* (5297), to bear, endure.

5279. ὑπομιμνήσκω, hupomimnēskō, *hoop-om-im-nace´-ko*; from 5259 and 3403; to *remind quietly*, i.e. *suggest* to the (middle, one's own) memory:—put in mind, remember, bring to (put in) remembrance.

5280. ὑπόμνησις, hupomnēsis, *hoop-om´-nay-sis*; from 5279; a *reminding* or (reflexive) *recollection*:—remembrance.

Noun from *hupomimnḗskō* (5279), to recall to one's mind. A putting in mind, a reminding, remembrance, recollection (2Ti 1:5; 2Pe 1:13; 3:1).

Syn.: *anámnēsis* (364), a remembering, recollection; *mneía* (3417), remembrance, mention; *mnḗmē* (3420), memory, remembrance; *mnēmósunon* (3422), a reminder, memorial.

5281. ὑπομονή, hupomonē, *hoop-om-on-ay´*; from 5278; cheerful (or hopeful) *endurance, constancy*:—enduring, patience, patient continuance (waiting).

Noun from *hupoménō* (5278), to persevere, remain under. A bearing up under, patience, endurance as to things or circumstances. Particularly, with the genitive of thing borne, as evils (2Co 1:6). Generally meaning endurance, patience, perseverance or constancy under suffering in faith and duty (Lk 8:15; 21:19; Ro 2:7; 8:25; 2Co 1:6; 6:4; 12:12; Col 1:11; 1Th 1:3; 2Th 1:4; 3:5; Heb 10:36; 12:1; Jas 1:3, 4; 5:11; 2Pe 1:6; Rev 1:9; 2:2, 3, 19; 3:10; 13:10; 14:12). Specifically patience as a quality of mind, the bearing of evils and suffering with tranquil mind (Ro 5:3, 4; 15:4, 5; 1Ti 6:11; 2Ti 3:10; Tit 2:2).

Syn.: *anochḗ* (463), forbearance, tolerance; *epieíkeia* (1932), clemency, gentleness.

5282. ὑπονοέω, huponoeō, *hoop-on-o-eh´-o*; from 5259 and 3539; to *think under* (*privately*), i.e. to *surmise* or *conjecture*:—think, suppose, deem.

From *hupó* (5259), under, denoting diminution, and *noéō* (3539), to think. To suppose, theorize, suspect. In the NT, in the sense of to conjecture, to suppose, to deem (Ac 13:25; 25:18; 27:27).

Deriv.: *hupónoia* (5283), suspicion, conjecture.

Syn.: *dialogízomai* (1260), to reason, think; *dokéō* (1380), to be of opinion, suppose; *hēgéomai* (2233), to reckon, suppose; *krínō* (2919), to judge, reckon; *logízomai* (3049), to reckon; *nomízō* (3543), to suppose, consider, think; *oíomai* (3633), imagine, suppose; *hupolambánō* (5274), to suppose; *phronéō* (5426), to think.

5283. ὑπόνοια, huponoia, *hoop-on´-oy-ah*; from 5282; *suspicion*:—surmising.

Noun from *huponoéō* (5282), to suspect. Suspicion, surmising, conjecture. Used only in 1Ti 6:4.

5284. ὑποπλέω, hupopleō, *hoop-op-leh´-o*; from 5259 and 4126; to *sail under* the lee of:—sail under.

5285. ὑποπνέω, hupopneō, *hoop-op-neh´-o*; from 5259 and 4154; to *breathe gently*, i.e. *breeze*:—blow softly.

5286. ὑποπόδιον, hupopodion, *hoop-op-od´-ee-on*; neuter of a compound of 5259 and 4228; something *under* the *feet*, i.e. a *foot-rest* (figurative):—footstool.

5287. ὑπόστασις, hupostasis, *hoop-os´-tas-is*; from a compound of 5259 and 2476; a *setting under* (*support*), i.e. (figurative) concrete *essence*, or abstract *assurance* (object or subject):—confidence, confident, person, substance.

Noun from *huphístēmi* (n.f.), to place or set under. That which is set under or stands under, the foundation, origin, beginning. In the NT:

(I) The ground of confidence, assurance, guarantee or proof (Heb 3:14; 11:1).

(II) By metonymy, that quality which leads one to stand under, endure, or undertake something, firmness, boldness, confidence (2Co 9:4; 11:17).

(III) Substance, what really exists under any appearance, reality, essential nature. Spoken of God's essence or nature (Heb 1:3).

Syn.: *élegchos* (1650), certainty, proof, demonstration; *phúsis* (5449), nature.

5288. ὑποστέλλω, hupostellō, *hoop-os-tel´-lo*; from 5259 and 4724; to *withhold under* (*out of sight*), i.e. (reflexive) to *cower* or *shrink*, (figurative) to *conceal* (*reserve*):—draw (keep) back, shun, withdraw.

5289. ὑποστολή, hupostolē, *hoop-os-tol-ay´*; from 5288; *shrinkage* (*timidity*), i.e. (by implication) *apostasy*:—draw back.

5290. ὑποστρέφω, hupostrephō, *hoop-os-tref´-o*; from 5259 and 4762; to *turn under* (*behind*), i.e. to *return* (literal or figurative):—come again, return (again, back again), turn back (again).

5291. ὑποστρώννυμι, hupostrōnnumi, *hoop-os-trone´-noo-mee*; from 5259 and 4766; to *strew underneath* (the feet as a carpet):—spread.

5292. ὑποταγή, hupotagē, *hoop-ot-ag-ay´*; from 5293; *subordination*:—subjection.

5293. ὑποτάσσω, hupotassō, *hoop-ot-as´-so*; from 5259 and 5021; to *subordinate*; reflexive to *obey*:—be under obedience (obedient), put under, subdue unto, (be, make) subject (to, unto), be (put) in subjection (to, under), submit self unto.

From *hupó* (5259) and *tássō* (5021), to place in order. To place under, to subordinate, to make subject.

(I) In the active voice, to make others subject, to subordinate, to force others to be subject. Spoken of God bringing all things under the control of Christ (1Co 15:27–28; Eph 1:22; Heb 2:5, 8). Spoken once of Christ bringing all things under His own control (Php 3:21).

(II) In the passive voice, to be brought under the control of someone else (Lk 10:17, 20; Ro 8:20; 1Co 14:32, 34; 15:27, 28; Eph 5:24; Heb 2:8; 1Pe 3:22).

(III) In the middle voice, to submit oneself, to be subject, to be obedient (Lk 2:51; Ro 8:7; 13:1, 5; 1Co 16:16; Eph 5:21, 22; Col 3:18; Tit 2:5, 9; 3:1; Jas 4:7; 1Pe 2:18; 3:1, 5). Passive voice imperatives have a similar force, to allow oneself to be in subjection, to be obedient (1Pe 2:13). See also 1Pe 5:5, where the passive participle is used with an imperative verb understood. Until God forces the subjection of all, the passive voice in other moods can also signify voluntary submission. For example, the Jews in Paul's day, because of ignorance, were refusing to be submissive (Ro 10:3); and we are encouraged in Heb 12:9 to submit ourselves to God's control.

Deriv.: *anupótaktos* (506), unsubdued; *hupotagḗ* (5292), submission, dependent position.

5294. ὑποτίθημι, hupotithēmi, *hoop-ot-ith´-ay-mee*; from 5259 and 5087; to *place underneath*, i.e. (figurative) to *hazard*, (reflexive) to *suggest*:—lay down, put in remembrance.

5295. ὑποτρέχω, hupotrechō, *hoop-ot-rekh´-o*; from 5259 and 5143 (including its alternate); to *run under*, i.e. (special) to *sail past*:—run under.

5296. ὑποτύπωσις, hupotupōsis, *hoop-ot-oop´-o-sis*; from a compound of 5259 and a derivative of 5179; *typification under* (*after*), i.e. (concrete) a *sketch* (figurative) for imitation:—form, pattern.

Noun from *hupotupóō* (n.f.), to form or copy slightly, to sketch. Figuratively, a form, sketch, imperfect delineation (2Ti 1:13). By metonymy, a sketch, a pattern for imitation(1Ti 1:16).

Syn.: *eikṓn* (1504), profile, resemblance, image; *hupogrammós* (5261), an underwriting, writing copy, example; *hupódeigma* (5262), copy, example, pattern.

5297. ὑποφέρω, hupopherō, *hoop-of-er´-o*; from 5259 and 5342; to *bear* from *underneath*, i.e. (figurative) to *undergo* hardship:—bear, endure.

5298. ὑποχωρέω, hupochōreō, *hoop-okh-o-reh´-o*; from 5259 and 5562; to *vacate down*, i.e. *retire* quietly:—go aside, withdraw self.

5299. ὑπωπιάζω, hupōpiazō, *hoop-o-pee-ad´-zo*; from a compound of 5259 and a derivative of 3700; to hit *under* the *eye* (*buffet* or *disable* an antagonist as a pugilist), i.e. (figurative) to *tease* or *annoy* (into compliance), *subdue* (one's passions):—keep under, weary.

5300. ὗς, us, *hoos*; apparently a primary word; a *hog* ("*swine*"):—sow.

5301. ὕσσωπος, hussōpos, *hoos´-so-pos*; of foreign origin [231]; "*hyssop*":—hyssop.

5302. ὑστερέω, hustereō, *hoos-ter-eh´-o*; from 5306; to *be later*, i.e. (by implication) to be *inferior;* genitive to *fall short (be deficient)*:—come behind (short), be destitute, fail, lack, suffer need, (be in) want, be the worse.

5303. ὑστέρημα, husterēma, *hoos-ter´-ay-mah;* from 5302; a *deficit*; specially *poverty*:—that which is behind, (that which was) lack (-ing), penury, want.

5304. ὑστέρησις, husterēsis, *hoos-ter´-ay-sis*; from 5302; a *falling short*, i.e. (special) *penury*:—want.

5305. ὕστερον, husteron, *hoos´-ter-on*; neuter of 5306 as adverb; *more lately*, i.e. *eventually*:—afterward, (at the) last (of all).

5306. ὕστερος, husteros, *hoos´-ter-os*; comparative from 5259 (in the sense of *behind*); *later*:—latter.

5307. ὑφαντός, huphantos, *hoo-fan-tos´*; from **ὑφαίνω, huphainō** (to *weave*); *woven*, i.e. (perhaps) *knitted*:—woven.

5308. ὑψηλός, hupsēlos, *hoop-say-los´*; from 5311; *lofty* (in place or character):—high (-er, -ly) (esteemed).

5309. ὑψηλοφρονέω, hupsēlophroneō, *hoop-say-lo-fron-eh´-o*; from a compound of 5308 and 5424; to *be lofty in mind*, i.e. *arrogant*:—be high-minded.

5310. ὕψιστος, hupsistos, *hoop´-sis-tos*; superlative from the base of 5311; *highest*, i.e. (masculine singular) the *Supreme* (God), or (neuter plural) the *heavens*:—most high, highest.

5311. ὕψος, hupsos, *hoop´-sos*; from a derivative of 5228; *elevation*, i.e. (abstract) *altitude*, (special) the *sky*, or (figurative) *dignity*:—be exalted, height, (on) high.

5312. ὑψόω, hupsoō, *hoop-so´-o*; from 5311; to *elevate* (literal or figurative):—exalt, lift up.

5313. ὕψωμα, hupsōma, *hoop´-so-mah;* from 5312; an *elevated* place or thing, i.e. (abstract) *altitude,* or (by implication) a *barrier* (figurative):—height, high thing.

5314. φάγος, phagos, *fag´-os;* from 5315; a *glutton:*—gluttonous.

5315. φάγω, phagō, *fag´-o;* a primary verb (used as an alternate of 2068 in certain tenses); to *eat* (literal or figurative):—eat, meat.

5316. φαίνω, phainō, *fah´ee-no;* prolonged for the base of 5457; to *lighten* (*shine*), i.e. *show* (transitive or intransitive, literal or figurative):—appear, seem, be seen, shine, × think.

From *phṓs* (5457), light. To give light, illuminate.

(I) To shine or give light, shine forth as a luminous body (2:16; 8:12; 18:23; 21:23); figuratively, of spiritual light and truth (Jn 1:5; 5:35; Php 2:15; 1Jn 2:8).

(II) To come to light, to appear, be conspicuous, become visible.

(A) Generally to appear, be seen. **(1)** Of persons (Mt 1:20; 2:13, 19; Mk 16:9; Lk 9:8; 1Pe 4:18). With a participle or adjective as predicate in the nominative: e.g., with *díkaios* (1342), righteous, ye appear … righteous (Mt 23:28). See also Mt 6:16, 18; 2Co 13:7. **(2)** Of things (Mt 9:33; 13:26; Heb 11:3); with a predicate adjective as **(1)** above (Mt 23:27; Ro 7:13). Especially of things appearing in the sky or air, meaning phenomena (Mt 2:7; 24:27, 30; Jas 4:14).

(B) Figuratively as referring to the mental eye, to appear, seem (Mk 14:64; Lk 24:11).

Deriv.: *anaphaínō* (398), to be shown or appear openly, to show openly; *aphanḗs* (852), hidden, concealed; *áphantos* (855), invisible; *epiphaínō* (2014), to shine over or upon, to give light, in the pass. to appear; *sukophantéō* (4811), to accuse wrongfully; *huperḗphanos* (5244), one who is conspicuous; *phanerós* (5318), apparent, manifest; *phanós* (5322), lantern; *phantázō* (5324), to cause to appear.

Syn.: *astráptō* (797), to shine forth like lightning; *augázō* (826), to irradiate; *eklámpō* (1584), to shine forth; *lámpō* (2989), to shine; *periastráptō* (4015), to shine round about; *perilámpō* (4034), to shine around; *stílbō* (4744), to glitter.

5317. Φάλεκ, Phalek, *fal´-ek;* of Hebrew origin [6389]; *Phalek* (i.e. *Peleg*), a patriarch:—Phalec.

5318. φανερός, phaneros, *fan-er-os´;* from 5316; *shining,* i.e. *apparent* (literal or figurative); neuter (as adverb) *publicly, externally:*—abroad, + appear, known, manifest, open [+ -ly], outward ([+ -ly]).

Adjective from *phaínō* (5316), to shine, to make to shine or to cause to appear. Apparent, manifest, plain (Ac 4:16; Ro 1:19; Gal 5:19; 1Ti 4:15; 1Jn 3:10); with the verbs *gínomai* (1096), to become, and *érchomai* (2064), to come, to become known, well known, manifest (Mk 4:22; 6:14; Lk 8:17; Ac 7:13; 1Co 3:13; 11:19; 14:25; Php 1:13); with the verb *poiéō* (4160), to make, to make one known or manifest (Mt 12:16; Mk 3:12). With the preposition *en* (1722), in, in the open, openly (Mt 6:4, 6, 18). Also with *en*, in the open in the sense of outwardly, on the outside as opposed to what is on the inside (Ro 2:28).

Deriv.: *phaneróō* (5319), to make manifest or known, show; *phanerṓs* (5320), apparently.

Syn.: *gnōstós* (1110), known; *dḗlos* (1212), evident; *dēmósios* (1219), public, open; *ékdēlos* (1552), wholly evident, manifest; *emphanḗs* (1717), manifest; *éxōthen* (1855), outward; *katádēlos* (2612), quite manifest, evident; *pródēlos* (4271), evident, manifest beforehand, clearly evident.

5319. φανερόω, phaneroō, *fan-er-o´-o;* from 5318; to *render apparent* (literal or figurative):—appear, manifestly declare, (make) manifest (forth), shew (self).

From *phanerós* (5318), manifest, visible, conspicuous. To make apparent, manifest, known, to show openly. Transitively:

(I) Of things (Jn 17:6; Ro 1:19). In the passive (Mk 4:22; Jn 2:11; 3:21; 9:3; 17:6; Ro 1:19; 3:21; 16:26; 1Co 4:5; 2Co 2:14; 4:10, 11; 7:12; Eph 5:13; Col 1:26; 4:4; 2Ti 1:10; Heb 9:8; 1Jn 3:2; 4:9; Rev 3:18; 15:4).

(II) Of persons.

(A) Reflexively with *heautón* (1438), oneself, or with the middle or aorist passive used as middle, to manifest oneself, show oneself openly, to appear (Mk 16:12, 14; Jn 7:4; 21:1, 14; 2Co 5:10; Col 3:4; 1Ti 3:16; Heb 9:26; 1Pe 1:20; 5:4; 1Jn 1:2; 2:28; 3:2, 5, 8).

(B) In the passive to be manifested, become or be made manifest, known (Jn 1:31; 2Co 3:3; 5:11; 1Jn 2:19).

Deriv.: *phanérōsis* (5321), manifestation, making known.

Syn.: *anaggéllō* (312) and *apaggéllō* (518), to announce or report; *apokalúptō* (601), to reveal; *gnōrízō* (1107), to make known; *dēlóō* (1213), to make plain; *diaggéllō* (1229), to announce throughout; *diagnōrízō* (1232), to make fully known, reassert; *emphanízō* (1718), to declare plainly, make manifest; *kataggéllō* (2605), to declare; *phrázō* (5419), to declare.

5320. φανερῶς, phanerōs, *fan-er-oce´;* adverb from 5318; *plainly,* i.e. *clearly* or *publicly:*—evidently, openly.

5321. φανερωσις, phanerōsis, *fan-er´-o-sis;* from 5319; *exhibition,* i.e. (figurative) *expression,* (by extension) a *bestowment:*—manifestation.

Noun from *phaneróō* (5319), to make manifest. A manifestation, a making visible or observable (1Co 12:7; 2Co 4:2).

Syn.: *apokálupsis* (602), revelation.

5322. φανός, phanos, *fan-os´;* from 5316; a *lightener,* i.e. *light; lantern:*—lantern.

5323. Φανουήλ, Phanouēl, *fan-oo-ale´;* of Hebrew origin [6439]; *Phanuël* (i.e. *Penuël*), an Israelite:—Phanuel.

5324. φαντάζω, phantazō, *fan-tad´-zo;* from a derivative of 5316; to *make apparent,* i.e. (passive) to *appear* (neuter participle as noun, a *spectacle*):—sight.

5325. φαντασία, phantasia, *fan-tas-ee´-ah;* from a derivative of 5324; (properly abstract) a (vain) *show* ("fantasy"):—pomp.

5326. φάντασμα, phantasma, *fan´-tas-mah;* from 5324; (properly concrete) a (mere) *show* ("phantasm"), i.e. *spectre:*—spirit.

5327. φάραγξ, pharagx, *far´-anx;* properly strengthened from the base of 4008 or rather of 4486; a *gap* or *chasm,* i.e. *ravine* (*winter-torrent*):—valley.

5328. Φαραώ, Pharaō, *far-ah-o´;* of foreign origin [6547]; *Pharaö* (i.e. *Pharoh*), an Egyptian king:—Pharaoh.

5329. Φαρές, Phares, *far-es´;* of Hebrew origin [6557]; *Phares* (i.e. *Perets*), an Israelite:—Phares.

5330. Φαρισαῖος, Pharisaios, *far-is-ah´-yos;* of Hebrew origin [compare 6567]; a *separatist,* i.e. exclusively *religious;* a *Pharisæan,* i.e. Jewish sectary:—Pharisee.

5331. φαρμακεία, pharmakeia, *far-mak-i´-ah;* from 5332; *medication* ("pharmacy"), i.e. (by extension) *magic* (literal or figurative):—sorcery, witchcraft.

5332. φαρμακεύς, pharmakeus, *far-mak-yoos´;* from **φάρμακον**, ***pharmakon*** (a *drug,* i.e. spell-giving *potion*); a *druggist* ("pharmacist") or *poisoner,* i.e. (by extension) a *magician:*—sorcerer.

5333. φαρμακός, pharmakos, *far-mak-os´;* the same as 5332:—sorcerer.

5334. φάσις, phasis, *fas´-is;* from 5346 (not the same as "phase," which is from 5316); a *saying,* i.e. *report:*—tidings.

5335. φάσκω, phaskō, *fas´-ko;* prolonged from the same as 5346; to *assert:*—affirm, profess, say.

5336. φάτνη, phatnē, *fat´-nay;* from **πατέομαι**, ***pateomai*** (to *eat*); a *crib* (for fodder):—manger, stall.

5337. φαῦλος, phaulos, *fow´-los;* apparently a primary word; "*foul*" or "*flawy,*" i.e. (figurative) *wicked:*—evil.

Adjective meaning bad, worthless, as of food or a garment. In the NT, morally, bad, evil, wicked. Spoken of evil deeds (Jn 3:20; 5:29; Jas 3:16); spoken of wicked statements (Tit 2:8).

Syn.: *kakós* (2556), bad; *ponērós* (4190), malevolent.

5338. φέγγος, pheggos, *feng´-gos*; probably akin to the base of 5457 [compare 5350]; *brilliancy*:—light.

A noun meaning light or brightness, shining. Spoken of the moon (Mt 24:29; Mk 13:24). Spoken of a lamp (Lk 11:33).

Syn.: *phōstḗr* (5458), luminary, light, light-giving; *phōtismós* (5462), an illumination, light.

5339. φείδομαι, pheidomai, *fi´-dom-ahee*; of uncertain affinity; to *be chary* of, i.e. (subject) to *abstain* or (object) to *treat leniently*:—forbear, spare.

5340. φειδομένως, pheidomenōs, *fi-dom-en´-oce*; adverb from participle of 5339; *abstemiously*, i.e. *stingily*:—sparingly.

5341. φελόνης, phelonēs, *fel-on´-ace*; by transposed for a derivative probably of 5316 (as *showing* outside the other garments); a *mantle* (*surtout*):—cloke.

5342. φέρω, pherō, *fer´-o*; a primary verb (for which other and apparently not cognate ones are used in certain tenses only; namely, **οἴω**, ***oiō***, *oy´-o*; and **ἐνέγκω**, ***enegkō***, *en-eng´-ko*); to "*bear*" or *carry* (in a very wide application, literal and figurative, as follows):—be, bear, bring (forth), carry, come, + let her drive, be driven, endure, go on, lay, lead, move, reach, rushing, uphold.

To bear, bring.

(I) Particularly to bear as a burden, bear up, have or take upon oneself. In the NT, only figuratively.

(A) To bear up under or with, to endure, e.g., evils (Ro 9:22; Heb 12:20; 13:13).

(B) To bear up something, uphold, have in charge, to direct, govern (Heb 1:3).

(II) To bear with the idea of motion, bear along, carry (Lk 23:26). In the passive, to be borne along, as a ship before the wind, to be driven (Ac 27:15, 17). Figuratively to be moved, incited (2Pe 1:21). In the middle, to bear oneself along, move along, rush as a wind (Ac 2:2). Figuratively to go on, advance in teaching (Heb 6:1).

(III) To bear, with the idea of motion to a place, bear onward, to bring.

(A) Used of things. Generally (Mt 14:11, 18; Mk 6:27, 28; 12:15, 16; Lk 24:1; Jn 2:8; 4:33; 19:39; 20:27; 21:10; 2Ti 4:13; Rev 21:24, 26). Figuratively: of a voice or declaration, in the passive, to be borne, brought, to come (2Pe 1:17, 18); of good brought to or bestowed on someone (1Pe 1:13); of accusations, charges, to bring forward, present (Jn 18:29; Ac 25:7; 2Pe 2:11); of a doctrine, prophecy, to announce, make known (2Pe 1:21; 2Jn 10). Of a fact or event as reported or testified, to adduce, show, prove (Heb 9:16).

(B) Used of persons, to bear, bring, e.g., the sick or afflicted (Mt 17:17; Mk 1:32; 2:3; 7:32; 8:25; 9:17, 19, 20; Lk 5:18; Ac 5:16). See also Mk 15:22; Jn 21:28.

(IV) To bear as trees or fields bear their fruits, to yield fruit (Mk 4:8; Jn 12:24; 15:2, 4, 5, 8, 16).

Deriv.: *anaphérō* (399), to carry or bring up, offer up; *apophérō* (667), to carry away; *diaphérō* (1308), to bear through, differ; *eisphérō* (1533), to bring to or into; *ekphérō* (1627), to carry something out, to carry out to burial; *epiphérō* (2018), to bring upon, inflict; *thanatēphóros* (2287), deadly; *karpophóros* (2593), fruitful; *kataphérō* (2702), to bring down; *paraphérō* (3911), to bear along, carry off; *periphérō* (4064), to carry about or around; *prosphérō* (4374), to bring to or before, to offer; *prophérō* (4393), bring forth, produce; *sumphérō* (4851), to bear together, contribute; *telesphoréō* (5052), to bring to an intended perfection or goal; *tropophoréō* (5159), mode or style, deportment, character; *hupophérō* (5297), to bear up under, endure; *phoréō* (5409), to have a burden, bear; *phóros* (5411), a tax; *phórtos* (5414), the freight of a ship.

Syn.: *apokuéō* (616), to bring forth, give birth to, beget; *bastázō* (941), to bear, take up, carry; *gennáō* (1080), to bring forth, give birth to, beget; *tíktō* (5088), to give birth to, beget. Also *paréchō* (3930), to offer, furnish, supply.

5343. φεύγω, pheugō, *fyoo´-go*; apparently a primary verb; to *run away* (literal or figurative); by implication to *shun*; (by analogy) to *vanish*:—escape, flee (away).

5344. Φῆλιξ, Phēlix, *fay´-lix*; of Latin origin; *happy; Phelix* (i.e. *Felix*), a Roman:—Felix.

5345. φήμη, phēmē, *fay´-may*; from 5346; a *saying*, i.e. *rumour* ("fame"):—fame.

5346. φημί, phēmi, *fay-mee´*; properly the same as the base of 5457 and 5316; to *show* or *make known* one's thoughts, i.e. *speak* or *say*:—affirm, say. Compare 3004.

From the obsolete *pháō* (n.f.), to shine. Particularly to bring to light by speech; generally to say, speak, utter.

(I) Generally, usually followed by the words that are spoken (Mt 14:8; 26:34, 61; Lk 7:44; Ac 8:36; 10:28, 30, 31; 23:25; 25:5, 22; Ro 3:8; 1Co 6:16; 10:15; 2Co 10:10; Heb 8:5).

(II) As modified by the context, where the sense often lies not so much in *phēmí* as in the adjuncts.

(A) Before interrogations, meaning to ask, inquire (Mt 27:23; Ac 16:30; 21:37).

(B) Before replies, meaning to answer, reply (Mt 4:7; 8:8; 13:29; Lk 23:3; Jn 1:23; Ac 2:38).

(C) Emphatically, meaning to affirm, assert (1Co 7:29; 10:19; 15:50).

Deriv.: *súmphēmi* (4852), to agree with; *phásis* (5334), information; *phḗmē* (5345), fame, rumour.

Syn.: *laléō* (2980), to utter; *légō* (3004), to speak. Also *apophthéggomai* (669), to speak clearly, articulate, give utterance; *diabebaióomai* (1226), to affirm confidently; *diïschurízomai* (1340), to assert vehemently; *eréō* (2046), to say, speak; *homologéō* (3670), to profess, confess; *phthéggomai* (5350), to enunciate clearly.

5347. Φῆστος, Phēstos, *face´-tos*; of Latin derivative; *festal; Phestus* (i.e. *Festus*), a Roman:—Festus.

5348. φθάνω, phthanō, *fthan´-o*; apparently a primary verb; to *be beforehand*, i.e. *anticipate* or *precede*; by extension to *have arrived* at:—(already) attain, come, prevent.

5349. φθαρτός, phthartos, *fthar-tos´*; from 5351; *decayed*, i.e. (by implication) *perishable*:—corruptible.

Adjective from *phtheírō* (5351), to corrupt. Subject to corruption, corruptible, perishable. Spoken of things; corruptible, perishable: e.g., a crown (1Co 9:25); silver or gold (1Pe 1:18); a seed (1Pe 1:23). Spoken of man and the present earthly body (Ro 1:23; 1Co 15:53, 54).

Der.: *áphthartos* (862), incorruptible.

5350. φθέγγομαι, phtheggomai, *ftheng´-gom-ahee*; probably akin to 5338 and thus to 5346; to *utter* a clear sound, i.e. (genitive) to *proclaim*:—speak.

5351. φθείρω, phtheirō, *fthi´-ro*; probably strengthened from **φθίω**, ***phthiō*** (to *pine* or *waste*); properly to *shrivel* or *wither*, i.e. to *spoil* (by any process) or (genitive) to *ruin* (especially figurative by moral influences, to *deprave*):—corrupt (self), defile, destroy.

From *phthíō* or *phthínō* (n.f.), to waste, pine. To corrupt, destroy. Generally, to bring to a worse state (1Co 3:17). Figuratively, in a moral sense, to corrupt, to make depraved (1Co 15:33; Eph 4:22; Jude 10; Rev 19:2). To corrupt, with the meaning of to subvert or corrupt opinions (2Co 7:2; 11:3).

Deriv.: *diaptheírō* (1311), to corrupt, destroy; *kataphtheírō* (2704), to corrupt, destroy, spoil, deprave; *phthartós* (5349), corruptible; *phthorá* (5356), corruption, both physical and spiritual.

Syn.: *sḗpō* (4595), to rot.

5352. φθινοπωρινός, phthinopōrinos, *fthin-op-o-ree-nos´*; from a derivative of **φθίνω**, ***phthinō*** (to *wane*; akin to the base of 5351) and 3703 (meaning *late autumn*); *autumnal* (as *stripped* of leaves):—whose fruit withereth.

5353. φθόγγος, phthoggos, *fthong´-gos*; from 5350; *utterance*, i.e. a *musical* note (vocal or instrumental):—sound.

5354. φθονέω, phthoneō, *fthon-eh´-o*; from 5355; to *be jealous* of:—envy.

5355. φθόνος, phthonos, *fthon´-os*; probably akin to the base of 5351; *ill-will* (as *detraction*), i.e. *jealousy* (*spite*):—envy.

A noun meaning envy. Spoken as the motivation for the delivering of Jesus to be crucified (Mt 27:18; Mk 15:10); spoken as characteristic of the old man (Ro 1:29; 1Ti 6:4; Tit 3:3; Jas 4:5). Spoken as the motivation for some to preach the gospel mockingly (Php 1:15). Used in the plural to indicate bursts of envy (Gal 5:21; 1Pe 2:1). While *zḗlos* (2205), zeal, and *epithumía* (1939), lust, desire, can have a good connotation, *phthónos* seems to be used only with an evil connotation. However, Jas 4:5 in the NASB Bible seems to denote a good connotation for the word: "God jealously desires the Spirit which He has made to dwell in us." The difference in interpretation is whether one takes the word "spirit" as referring to God or as referring to our spirit, in which case the rest of the verse speaks to our own spirits lusting in envy (see *pneúma* [4151], spirit).

Deriv.: *phthonéō* (5354), to envy.

5356. φθορά, phthora, *fthor-ah´*; from 5351; *decay*, i.e. *ruin* (spontaneous or inflicted, literal or figurative):—corruption, destroy, perish.

5357. φιάλη, phialē, *fee-al´-ay*; of uncertain affinity; a broad shallow *cup* ("phial"):—vial.

5358. φιλάγαθος, philagathos, *fil-ag´-ath-os*; from 5384 and 18; *fond to good*, i.e. a *promoter of virtue*:—love of good men.

Adjective from *phílos* (5384), friend, and *agathós* (18), benevolent. Loving good, a lover of what is good, upright. Used only in Tit 1:8.

Deriv.: *aphilágathos* (865), not loving good.

5359. Φιλαδέλφεια, Philadelpheia, *fil-ad-el´-fee-ah*; from **Φιλάδελφος**, ***Philadelphos*** (the same as 5361), a king of Pergamos; *Philadelphia*, a place in Asia Minor:—Philadelphia.

5360. φιλαδελφία, philadelphia, *fil-ad-el-fee´-ah*; from 5361; *fraternal affection*:—brotherly love (kindness), love of the brethren.

Noun from *philádelphos* (5361), one who loves his brother. Brotherly love. In the NT, used only of the love of Christians one to another, brotherly love out of a common spiritual life (Ro 12:10; 1Th 4:9; Heb 13:1; 1Pe 1:22; 2Pe 1:7).

Syn.: *eúnoia* (2133), kindness, goodwill, benevolence; *philanthrōpía* (5363), benevolence, philanthropy; *philía* (5373), friendship.

5361. φιλάδελφος, philadelphos, *fil-ad´-el-fos*; from 5384 and 80; *fond of brethren*, i.e. *fraternal*:—love as brethren.

Adjective from *phílos* (5384), friend, and *adelphós* (80), brother. Loving one's brother, brotherly affectionate. In the NT, only in the strictly Christian sense of loving each other as Christian brothers. Used only in 1Pe 3:8.

Deriv.: *Philadélpheia* (5359), Philadelphia; *philadelphía* (5360), brotherly love.

Syn.: *philóstorgos* (5387), having natural love.

5362. φίλανδρος, philandros, *fil´-an-dros*; from 5384 and 435; *fond of man*, i.e. *affectionate* as a wife:—love their husbands.

5363. φιλανθρωπία, philanthrōpia, *fil-an-thro-pee´-ah*; from the same as 5364; *fondness of mankind*, i.e. *benevolence* ("*philanthropy*"):—kindness, love toward man.

Noun from *philánthrōpos* (n.f.), a lover of mankind, which is from *phílos* (5384), friend, and *ánthrōpos* (444), human being. Human friendship, philanthropy, benevolence, kindness. Used twice in the NT (Ac 28:2; Tit 3:4).

Syn.: *éleos* (1656), compassion, mercy; *oiktirmós* (3628), compassion; *splágchna* (pl. of *splágchon* [4698]), bowels of compassion.

5364. φιλανθρώπως, philanthrōpōs, *fil-an-thro´-poce*; adverb from a compound of 5384 and 444; *fondly to man* ("philanthropically"), i.e. *humanely*:—courteously.

5365. φιλαργυρία, philarguria, *fil-ar-goo-ree´-ah*; from 5366; *avarice*:—love of money.

Noun from *philárguros* (5366), a lover of money, which is from *phílos* (5384), friend, and *árguros* (696), silver. The love of money, covetousness. Used only in 1Ti 6:10.

Syn.: *pleonexía* (4124), covetousness.

5366. φιλάργυρος, philarguros, *fil-ar´-goo-ros*; from 5384 and 696; *fond of silver* (*money*), i.e. *avaricious*:—covetous.

5367. φίλαυτος, philautos, *fil´-ow-tos*; from 5384 and 846; *fond of self*, i.e. *selfish*:—lover of own self.

Adjective from *phílos* (5384), loving or friend, and *autós* (846), oneself. Self-centered or selfish. Used only in 2Ti 3:2.

5368. φιλέω, phileō, *fil-eh´-o*; from 5384; to *be a friend to* (*fond of* [an individual or an object]), i.e. *have affection* for (denoting *personal* attachment, as a matter of sentiment or feeling; while 25 is wider, embracing especially the judgement and the *deliberate* assent of the will as a matter of principle, duty and propriety: the two thus stand related very much as 2309 and 1014, or as 2372 and 3563 respectively; the former being chiefly of the *heart* and the latter of the *head*); specially to *kiss* (as a mark of tenderness):—kiss, love.

From *phílos* (5384), loved, dear, friend. To love.

(I) Generally, to have affection for someone (Mt 10:37; Jn 5:20; 11:3, 36; 15:19; 16:27; 20:2; 21:15–17; 1Co 16:22; Tit 3:15; Rev 3:19). Of things, to be fond of, to like (Mt 23:6; Lk 20:46; Jn 12:25; Rev 22:15).

(II) Specifically, to kiss (Mt 26:48; Mk 14:44; Lk 22:47).

(III) Followed by the infinitive with the meaning to love to do something (Mt 6:5).

Deriv.: *kataphiléō* (2705), to kiss affectionately; *phílēma* (5370), a kiss; *philía* (5373), friendship, love.

5369. φιλήδονος, philēdonos, *fil-ay´-don-os*; from 5384 and 2237; *fond of pleasure*, i.e. *voluptuous*:—lover of pleasure.

5370. φίλημα, philēma, *fil´-ay-mah*; from 5368; a *kiss*:—kiss.

5371. Φιλήμων, Philēmōn, *fil-ah´-mone*; from 5368; *friendly; Philemon*, a Christian:—Philemon.

5372. Φιλητός, Philētos, *fil-ay-tos´*; from 5368; *amiable; Philetus*, an opposer of Christianity:—Philetus.

5373. φιλία, philia, *fil-ee´-ah*; from 5384; *fondness*:—friendship.

Noun from *philéō* (5368), to befriend, love, kiss. Love, friendship, fondness. Used only in Jas 4:4.

Syn.: *agápē* (26), love.

5374. Φιλιππήσιος, Philippēsios, *fil-ip-pay´-see-os*; from 5375; a *Philippesian* (*Philippian*), i.e. native of Philippi:—Philippian.

5375. Φίλιπποι, Philippoi, *fil´-ip-poy*; plural of 5376; *Philippi*, a place in Macedonia:—Philippi.

5376. Φίλιππος, Philippos, *fil´-ip-pos*; from 5384 and 2462; *fond of horses; Philippus*, the name of four Israelites:—Philip.

5377. φιλόθεος, philotheos, *fil-oth´-eh-os*; from 5384 and 2316; *fond of God*, i.e. *pious*:—lover of God.

5378. Φιλόλογος, Philologos, *fil-ol´-og-os*; from 5384 and 3056; *fond of words*, i.e. *talkative* (*argumentative, learned*, "*philological*"); *Philologus*, a Christian:—Philologus.

5379. φιλονεικία, philoneikia, *fil-on-i-kee´-ah*; from 5380; *quarrelsomeness*, i.e. a *dispute*:—strife.

5380. φιλόνεικος, philoneikos, *fil-on´-i-kos*; from 5384 and **νεῖκος**, *neikos* (a *quarrel*; probably akin to 3534); *fond of strife*, i.e. *disputatious*:—contentious.

5381. φιλονεξία, philonexia, *fil-on-ex-ee´-ah*; from 5382; *hospitableness*:—entertain strangers, hospitality.

5382. φιλόξενος, philoxenos, *fil-ox´-en-os*; from 5384 and 3581; *fond of guests*, i.e. *hospitable*:—given to (lover of, use) hospitality.

5383. φιλοπρωτεύω, philoprōteuō, *fil-op-rot-yoo´-o*; from a compound of 5384 and 4413; to *be fond of being first*, i.e. *ambitious* of distinction:—love to have the preeminence.

5384. φίλος, philos, *fee´-los*; properly *dear*, i.e. a *friend*; active *fond*, i.e. *friendly* (still as a noun, an *associate, neighbour*, etc.):—friend.

5385. φιλοσοφία, philosophia, *fil-os-of-ee´-ah*; from 5386; "*philosophy*," i.e. (special) Jewish *sophistry*:—philosophy.

5386. φιλόσοφος, philosophos, *fil-os´-of-os*; from 5384 and 4680; *fond of wise* things, i.e. a "*philosopher*":—philosopher.

5387. φιλόστοργος, philostorgos, *fil-os´-tor-gos*; from 5384 and **στοργή,** ***torgē*** (*cherishing* one's kindred, especially parents or children); *fond of* natural *relatives*, i.e. *fraternal* toward fellow Christian:—kindly affectioned.

5388. φιλότεκνος, philoteknos, *fil-ot´-ek-nos*; from 5384 and 5043; *fond of* one's *children*, i.e. *maternal*:—love their children.

5389. φιλοτιμέομαι, philotimeomai, *fil-ot-im-eh´-om-ahee*; middle from a compound of 5384 and 5092; to be *fond of honour*, i.e. *emulous* (*eager* or *earnest* to do something):—labour, strive, study.

5390. φιλοφρόνως, philophronōs, *fil-of-ron´-oce*; adverb from 5391; *with friendliness of mind*, i.e. *kindly*:—courteously.

5391. φιλόφρων, philophrōn, *fil-of´-rone*; from 5384 and 5424; *friendly of mind*, i.e. *kind*:—courteous.

5392. φιμόω, phimoō, *fee-mo´-o*; from **φιμός,** ***phimos*** (a *muzzle*); to *muzzle*:—muzzle.

5393. Φλέγων, Phlegōn, *fleg´-one*; active participle of the base of 5395; *blazing*; *Phlegon*, a Christian:—Phlegon.

5394. φλογίζω, phlogizō, *flog-id´-zo*; from 5395; to *cause a blaze*, i.e. *ignite* (figurative, to *inflame* with passion):—set on fire.

5395. φλόξ, phlox, *flox*; from a primary **φλέγω,** ***phlegō*** (to "*flash*" or "*flame*"); a *blaze*:—flame (-ing).

5396. φλυαρέω, phluareō, *floo-ar-eh´-o*; from 5397; to *be a babbler* or *trifler*, i.e. (by implication) to *berate* idly or mischievously:—prate against.

5397. φλύαρος, phluaros, *floo´-ar-os*; from **φλύω,** ***phluō*** (to *bubble*); a *garrulous* person, i.e. *prater*:—tattler.

5398. φοβερός, phoberos, *fob-er-os´*; from 5401; *frightful*, i.e. (object) *formidable*:—fearful, terrible.

5399. φοβέω, phobeō, *fob-eh´-o*; from 5401; to *frighten*, i.e. (passive) to *be alarmed*; (by analogy) to *be in awe* of, i.e. *revere*:—be (+ sore) afraid, fear (exceedingly), reverence.

From *phóbos* (5401), fear. To put in fear, terrify, frighten. In the Classical Greek, to cause to run away. In the NT, used only in the passive, to become fearful, afraid, terrified.

(I) Particularly:

(A) Intransitively, to be fearful in a certain situation. Used in a command not to fear (Mt 14:27; Mk 5:36; 6:50; Lk 1:13, 30; Ro 13:4). Used generally (Mt 14:30; 17:6; 27:54; Mk 4:41; 10:32; 16:8; Lk 2:9; 1Pe 3:14).

(B) Transitively, to fear someone (Mt 10:26, 28; 14:5; Mk 12:12; Lk 12:4; 20:19; Jn 9:22; Ac 9:26; Ro 13:3; Gal 2:12); to fear something (Heb 11:23, 27; Rev 2:10).

(C) Followed by a negative clause expressing what is feared: e.g., lest "any of you should seem to come short of it [a promise of rest]" (Heb 4:1). See also Ac 27:17, 29; 2Co 11:3; 12:20; Gal 4:11.

(D) Followed by the infinitive, to fear to do something, hesitate (Mt 1:20; 2:22; Mk 9:32; Lk 9:45).

(II) Morally, to fear, reverence, honour.

(A) Generally (Mk 6:20; Eph 5:33).

(B) In regard to the Lord, meaning to reverence God, to stand in awe of God (Lk 18:2, 4; 23:40; Col 3:22; 1Pe 2:17); expressing piety, equivalent to worship, adoration of God (Lk 1:50; Ac 10:22, 35; 13:16, 26; Rev 11:18; 14:7; 15:4; 19:5).

Deriv.: *ékphobos* (1630), very frightened; *phoberós* (5398), fearful; *phóbētron* (5400), that which causes fear, terror.

Syn.: *sébomai* (4576), to revere; *trémō* (5141), to tremble.

5400. φόβητρον, phobētron, *fob´-ay-tron*; neuter of a derivative of 5399; a *frightening* thing, i.e. *terrific* portent:—fearful sight.

5401. φόβος, phobos, *fob´-os*; from a primary **φέβομαι,** ***phebomai*** (to *be* put in *fear*); *alarm* or *fright*:—be afraid, + exceedingly, fear, terror.

Noun from *phébomai* (n.f.), to flee in fear. Fear, terror, reverence, respect, honour.

(I) Particularly and generally (Mt 14:26; Lk 1:12; 2:9; 8:37; 21:26; Ro 8:15; 2Co 7:5, 11; 1Ti 5:20; 1Jn 4:18; Rev 11:11). Followed by the genitive of person or thing feared meaning that which inspires fear (Mt 28:4; Jn 7:13; 19:38; 20:19; Heb 2:15; 1Pe 3:14; Rev 18:10, 15). By metonymy, a terror, object of fear (Ro 13:3). Including the idea of astonishment, amazement (Mt 28:8; Mk 4:41; Lk 1:65; 5:26; 7:16; Ac 2:43; 5:5, 11; 19:17).

(II) In a moral sense, fear, reverence, respect, honour (1Pe 1:17; 3:2, 15). Of persons (Ro 13:7); of God or Christ, the fear of God or the Lord meaning a deep and reverential sense of accountability to God or Christ (Ac 9:31; Ro 3:18; 2Co 5:11; 7:1; Eph 5:21; 1Pe 2:18; Jude 23). Used intensively, with *trómos* (5156), trembling, in fear and trembling (1Co 2:3; 2Co 7:15; Eph 6:5; Php 2:12).

Deriv.: *émphobos* (1719), afraid; *phobéō* (5399), to terrify, frighten.

Syn.: *deilía* (1167), timidity, fear; *eulábeia* (2124), fear, reverence, piety; *trómos* (5156), trembling.

5402. Φοίβη, Phoibē, *foy´-bay*; feminine of **Φοῖβος,** ***Phoibos*** (*bright*; probably akin to the base of 5457); *Phoebe*, a Christian woman:—Phebe.

5403. Φοινίκη, Phoinikē, *foy-nee´-kay*; from 5404; *palm*-country; *Phoenice* (or *Phoenicia*), a region of Palestine:—Phenice, Phenicia.

5404. φοῖνιξ, phoinix, *foy´-nix*; of uncertain derivative; a *palm*-tree:—palm (tree).

5405. Φοῖνιξ, Phoinix, *foy´-nix*; probably the same as 5404; *Phoenix*, a place in Crete:—Phenice.

5406. φονεύς, phoneus, *fon-yooce´*; from 5408; a *murderer* (always of *criminal* [or at least *intentional*] homicide; which 443 does not necessarily imply; while 4607 is a special term for a *public* bandit):—murderer.

Noun from *phoneúō* (5407), to kill. A manslayer, murderer (Mt 22:7; Ac 3:14; 7:52; 28:4; 1Pe 4:15; Rev 21:8; 22:15).

Syn.: *anthrōpoktónos* (443), manslayer; *sikários* (4607), assassin, murderer.

5407. φονεύω, phoneuō, *fon-yoo´-o*; from 5406; to *be a murderer* (of):—kill, do murder, slay.

5408. φόνος, phonos, *fon´-os*; from an obsolete primary **φένω,** ***phenō*** (to *slay*); *murder*:—murder, + be slain with, slaughter.

5409. φορέω, phoreō, *for-eh´-o*; from 5411; to *have a burden*, i.e. (by analogy) to *wear* as clothing or a constant accompaniment:—bear, wear.

5410. Φόρον, Phoron, *for´-on*; of Latin origin; a *forum* or market-place; only in compound with 675; a *station* on the Appian road:—forum.

5411. φόρος, phoros, *for´-os*; from 5342; a *load* (as *borne*), i.e. (figurative) a *tax* (properly an individual *assessment* on persons or property; whereas 5056 is usually a generic *toll* on goods or travel):—tribute.

Noun from *phérō* (5342), to bring. Particularly what is borne, brought; hence a tax or tribute imposed upon persons and their property annually, in distinction from *télos* (5056), toll, which was usually levied on merchandise and travelers (Lk 20:22; 23:2; Ro 13:6, 7).

Syn.: *dídrachmon* (1323), two (or a double) drachmae, the equivalent of a half-shekel, which was the amount of the tribute in the first century A.D., due from every adult Jew for the maintenance of the temple services; *kē̂nsos* (2778), a poll tax.

5412. φορτίζω, phortizō, *for-tid´-zo*; from 5414; to *load* up (properly as a vessel or animal), i.e. (figurative) to *overburden* with ceremony (or spiritual anxiety):—lade, be heavy laden.

5413. φορτίον, phortion, *for-tee´-on*; diminitive of 5414; an *invoice* (as part of *freight*), i.e. (figurative) a *task* or *service*:—burden.

Noun from *phórtos* (5414), a burden, load. A diminutive in form but not in sense. The goods or merchandise carried by a ship, freight, cargo. In the NT, used figuratively: spoken of the burden of ceremonial observances rigorously exacted and increased by human traditions (Mt 23:4; Lk 11:46); spoken of the precepts and requirements of Christ in antithesis to these burdens (Mt 11:30); spoken of the burden of one's own responsibilities and failures (Gal 6:5).

Syn.: *báros* (922), a weight, something pressing on one physically or emotionally; *gómos* (1117), the freight of a ship.

5414. φόρτος, phortos, *for´-tos*; from 5342; something *carried*, i.e. the *cargo* of a ship:—lading.

5415. Φορτουνάτος, Phortounatos, *for-too-nat´-os*; of Latin origin; "*fortunate*"; *Fortunatus*, a Christian:—Fortunatus.

5416. φραγέλλιον, phragellion, *frag-el´-le-on*; neuter of a derivative from the base of 5417; a *whip*, i.e. Roman *lash* as a public punishment:—scourge.

5417. φραγελλόω, phragelloō, *frag-el-lo´-o*; from a presumed equivalent of the Latin *flagellum*; to *whip*, i.e. *lash* as a public punishment:—scourge.

5418. φραγμός, phragmos, *frag-mos´*; from 5420; a *fence*, or inclosing *barrier* (literal or figurative):—hedge (+ round about), partition.

5419. φράζω, phrazō, *frad´-zo*; probably akin to 5420 through the idea of *defining*; to *indicate* (by word or act), i.e. (special) to *expound*:—declare.

5420. φράσσω, phrassō, *fras´-so*; apparently a strengthened form of the base of 5424; to *fence* or enclose, i.e. (special) to *block* up (figurative, to *silence*):—stop.

5421. φρέαρ, phrear, *freh´-ar*; of uncertain derivative; a *hole* in the ground (dug for obtaining or holding water or other purposes), i.e. a *cistern* or *well*; (figurative) an *abyss* (as a *prison*):—well, pit.

A noun meaning well or pit dug in the earth for water, and thus strictly distinguished from *pēgḗ* (4077), fountain, though a well may also be called a fountain. Generally (Lk 14:5; Jn 4:11, 12). Figuratively of any pit, abyss: e.g., in Hades, the bottomless pit (Rev 9:1, 2).

Syn.: *bóthunos* (999), pit, ditch, cistern.

5422. φρεναπατάω, phrenapataō, *fren-ap-at-ah´-o*; from 5423; to *be a mind-misleader*, i.e. *delude*:—deceive.

5423. φρεναπάτης, phrenapatēs, *fren-ap-at´-ace*; from 5424 and 539; a *mind-misleader*, i.e. *seducer*:—deceiver.

5424. φρήν, phrēn, *frane*; probably from an obsolete **φράω, *phraō*** (to *rein* in or *curb*; compare 5420); the *midrif* (as a *partition* of the body), i.e. (figurative and by implication of sympathy) the *feelings* (or sensitive nature; by extension [also in the plural] the *mind* or cognitive faculties):—understanding.

Literally the diaphragm, the midriff. Figuratively, the supposed seat of all mental and emotional activity. In the NT, by metonymy, meaning the mind, intellect, disposition, feelings. Used only in 1Co 14:20.

Deriv.: *áphrōn* (878), a fool; *homóphrōn* (3675), of the same mind; *sṓphrōn* (4998), of sound mind; *phrenapatáō* (5422), to deceive; *phronéō* (5426), to think.

Syn.: *diánoia* (1271), intellect, mind; *noús* (3563), mind; *súnesis* (4907), discernment, the ability to understand the relationships between ideas.

5425. φρίσσω, phrissō, *fris´-so*; apparently a primary verb; to "*bristle*" or *chill*, i.e. *shudder* (*fear*):—tremble.

5426. φρονέω, phroneō, *fron-eh´-o*; from 5424; to *exercise* the *mind*, i.e. *entertain* or *have a sentiment* or *opinion*; by implication to *be* (mentally) *disposed* (more or less earnestly in a certain direction); intensive to *interest oneself* in (with concern or obedience):—set the affection on, (be) care (-ful), (be like-, + be of one, + be of the same, + let this) mind (-ed), regard, savour, think.

From *phrḗn* (5424), mind. To think, have a mind-set, be minded. The activity represented by *phronéō* involves the will, affections, and conscience.

(I) Generally, to be of an opinion, to consider (Ac 28:22; Ro 12:3, 16; 1Co 4:6; 13:11; Gal 5:10; Php 1:7). Used of time, to regard, keep (Ro 14:6).

(II) To think, in the sense of having a particular mind-set or attitude. Generally (Php 2:5; 3:15). Used with *autós* (846), same, to be of one mind, one accord, to think the same thing (Ro 15:5; 2Co 13:11; Php 2:2; 3:16; 4:2).

(III) To set one's mind on, to be devoted to (Mt 16:23; Mk 8:33; Ro 8:5; Php 3:19; 4:10; Col 3:2).

Deriv.: *kataphronéō* (2706), to despise; *paraphronéō* (3912), to be foolhardy; *periphronéō* (4065), to despise; *huperphronéō* (5252), to think highly of one's self, to be vain, arrogant; *hupsēlophronéō* (5309), to be proud, arrogant; *philóphrōn* (5391), friendly; *phrónēma* (5427), thought; *phrónēsis* (5428), understanding, prudence; *phrónimos* (5429), thoughtful.

Syn.: *aisthánomai* (143), to perceive, understand; *dokéō* (1380), to think, form an opinion; *epístamai* (1987), to know well; *hēgéomai* (2233), to think; *katanoéō* (2657), to perceive fully, comprehend; *katalambánō* (2638), to apprehend, comprehend; *logízomai* (3049), to reckon, think; *noéō* (3539), to perceive, understand; *nomízō* (3543), to think; *oíomai* (3633) or *oímai*, to suppose, think; *punthánomai* (4441), to ascertain; *suniēmi* (4920), to perceive, understand; *huponoéō* (5282), to suppose; *phrontízō* (5431), to think, consider, be careful.

5427. φρόνημα, phronēma, *fron´-ay-mah*; from 5426; (mental) *inclination* or *purpose*:—(be, + be carnally, + be spiritually) mind (-ed).

5428. φρόνησις, phronēsis, *fron´-ay-sis*; from 5426; mental *action* or *activity*, i.e. intellectual or moral *insight*:—prudence, wisdom.

Noun from *phronéō* (5426), to think, have a mind-set. Mind, thought, thinking.

(I) A mode of thinking and feeling (Lk 1:17).

(II) Understanding, prudence (Eph 1:8, where it occurs with the noun *sophía* [4678], wisdom).

Syn.: *súnesis* (4907), perception, discernment.

5429. φρόνιμος, phronimos, *fron´-ee-mos*; from 5424; *thoughtful*, i.e. *sagacious* or *discreet* (implying a *cautious* character; while 4680 denotes *practical* skill or acumen; and 4908 indicates rather *intelligence* or mental acquirement); in a bad sense *conceited* (also in the comparative):—wise (-r).

Adjective from *phronéō* (5426), to think, have a mind-set. Prudent, sensible, practically wise in relationships with others (Mt 7:24; 10:16; 24:45; 25:2, 4, 8, 9; Lk 12:42; 16:8; 1Co 10:15). In an evil sense, thinking oneself to be prudent or wise because of self-complacency (Ro 11:25; 12:16; used ironically in 1Co 4:10; 2Co 11:19).

Deriv.: *phronímōs* (5430), prudently.

Syn.: *sophós* (4680), wise; *sunetós* (4908), sagacious, understanding, able to reason; *sṓphrōn* (4998), of sound mind.

5430. φρονίμως, phronimōs, *fron-im´-oce*; adverb from 5429; *prudently*:—wisely.

5431. φροντίζω, phrontizō, *fron-tid´-zo*; from a derivative of 5424; to *exercise thought*, i.e. *be anxious*:—be careful.

5432. φρουρέω, phroureō, *froo-reh´-o;* from a compound of 4253 and 3708; to *be a watcher in advance*, i.e. to *mount guard* as a sentinel (*post spies* at gates); (figurative) to *hem in*, *protect*:—keep (with a garrison). Compare 5083.

5433. φρυάσσω, phruassō, *froo-as´-so*; akin to 1032, 1031; to *snort* (as a spirited horse), i.e. (figurative) to *make a tumult*:—rage.

5434. φρύγανον, phruganon, *froo´-gan-on*; neuter of a presumed derivative of **φρύγω,** ***phrugō*** (to *roast* or *parch*; akin to the base of 5395); something *desiccated,* i.e. a dry *twig:*—stick.

5435. Φρυγία, Phrugia, *froog-ee´-ah*; probably of foreign origin; *Phrygia,* a region of Asia Minor:—Phrygia.

5436. Φύγελλος, Phugellos, *foog´-el-los*; probably from 5343; *fugitive; Phygellus,* an apostate Christian:—Phygellus.

5437. φυγή, phugē, *foog-ay´*; from 5343; a *fleeing,* i.e. *escape:*—flight.

5438. φυλακή, phulakē, *foo-lak-ay´*; from 5442; a *guarding* or (concrete *guard*), the act, the person; figurative the place, the condition, or (special) the time (as a division of day or night), literal or figurative:—cage, hold, (im-) prison (-ment), ward, watch.

Noun from *phulássō* (5442), to keep. A watching, a guarding.

(I) The act of keeping watch, guarding (Lk 2:8).

(II) By metonymy, persons set to watch, a watch, guard or guards (Ac 12:10).

(III) By metonymy, the place where a watch is kept. In the NT figuratively of Babylon as the dwelling place, station, haunt of demons and unclean birds where they resort and hold their vigils or where they are kept in prison (Rev 18:2).

(IV) Spoken by metonymy of the place where someone is watched, guarded, kept in custody, a prison. Generally (Mt 5:25; 14:3, 10; 18:30; 25:36, 39, 43, 44; Mk 6:17, 24; Lk 3:20; 12:58; 21:12; 22:33; 23:19, 25; Jn 3:24; Ac 5:19, 22, 25; 8:3; 12:4–6, 17; 16:23, 24, 27, 37, 40; 22:4; 26:10; Rev 2:10). In the sense of imprisonment (2Co 6:5; 11:23; Heb 11:36). Poetically of the bottomless pit, abyss, Tartarus, as the prison of demons and the souls of wicked men (1Pe 3:19; Rev 20:7). See *tartaróō* (5020), to consign to Tartarus.

(V) By metonymy, the time for a watch of the night, a period of the night during which one watch of soldiers kept guard and were then relieved (Mt 14:25; 24:43; Mk 6:48; Lk 12:38). The ancient Jews, and probably the Greeks, divided the night into three watches of four hours each (Sept.: Jgs 7:19; Ps 90:4). But after the Jews came under the dominion of the Romans, they made four watches of about three hours each as the Romans had. These were either numbered first, second, third, fourth, and were also called *opsé* (3796), late in the day, after the close of the day, evening; *mesonúktion* (3317), midnight; *alektorophōnía* (219), the time of the cock crowing; and *prōḯ* (4404), morning (cf. Mk 13:35).

Deriv.: *gazophulákion* (1049), a treasury; *phulakízō* (5439), to imprison.

Syn.: *desmōtḗrion* (1201), a prison; *koustōdía* (2892), watch, guard; *tḗrēsis* (5084), a watching, guarding, imprisonment.

5439. φυλακίζω, phulakizō, *foo-lak-id´-zo*; from 5441; to *incarcerate:*—imprison.

5440. φυλακτήριον, phulaktērion, *foo-lak-tay´-ree-on*; neuter of a derivative of 5442; a *guard-case,* i.e. "*phylactery*" for wearing slips of Scripture texts:—phylactery.

5441. φύλαξ, phulax, *foo´-lax*; from 5442; a *watcher* or *sentry:*—keeper.

5442. φυλάσσω, phulassō, *foo-las´-so*; probably from 5443 through the idea of *isolation*; to *watch,* i.e. *be on guard* (literal or figurative); by implication to *preserve, obey, avoid:*—beware, keep (self), observe, save. Compare 5083.

To watch, keep watch.

(I) To watch, guard, keep:

(A) Persons or things from escape or violence (Lk 8:29; 11:21; Ac 12:4; 22:20; 23:35; 28:16).

(B) Of persons or things kept in safety, to keep, preserve (Lk 2:8; Jn 12:25; 17:12; 2Th 3:3; 1Ti 6:20; 2Ti 1:12, 14; 2Pe 2:5; 1Jn 5:21; Jude 24).

(C) In the middle: to protect oneself, to be on one's guard, to beware of, avoid (Lk 12:15; Ac 21:25; 2Ti 4:15; 2Pe 3:17).

(II) Figuratively, to keep, observe, not to violate, e.g., precepts, laws. With the accusative (Mt 19:20; Mk 10:20; Lk 11:28; 18:21; Ac 7:53; 16:4; 21:24; Ro 2:26; Gal 6:13; 1Ti 5:21).

Deriv.: *diaphulássō* (1314), to guard carefully, protect; *phulakḗ* (5438), the act of guarding; *phulaktḗrion* (5440), phylactery; *phúlax* (5441), a keeper, guard.

Syn.: *blépō* (991), to take heed; *diatēréō* (1301), to keep carefully; *epéchō* (1907), to take heed; *kratéō* (2902), to hold fast; *proséchō* (4337), to be on guard, to beware; *skopéō* (4648), to mark, heed, consider; *suntēréō* (4933), to preserve, keep safe; *tēréō* (5083), to watch over, preserve, keep; *phrouréō* (5432), to guard.

5443. φυλή, phulē, *foo-lay´*; from 5453 (compare 5444); an *offshoot,* i.e. *race* or *clan:*—kindred, tribe.

5444. φύλλον, phullon, *fool´-lon*; from the same as 5443; a *sprout,* i.e. *leaf:*—leaf.

5445. φύραμα, phurama, *foo´-ram-ah*; from a prolonged form of **φύρω,** ***phurō*** (to *mix* a liquid with a solid; perhaps akin to 5453 through the idea of *swelling* in bulk), meaning to *knead*; a *mass* of dough:—lump.

5446. φυσικός, phusikos, *foo-see-kos´*; from 5449; "*physical,*" i.e. (by implication) *instinctive:*—natural. Compare 5591.

5447. φυσικῶς, phusikōs, *foo-see-koce´*; adverb from 5446; "*physically,*" i.e. (by implication) *instinctively:*—naturally.

5448. φυσιόω, phusioō, *foo-see-o´-o*; from 5449 in the primary sense of *blowing*; to *inflate,* i.e. (figurative) *make proud* (*haughty*):—puff up.

5449. φύσις, phusis, *foo´-sis*; from 5453; *growth* (by *germination* or *expansion*), i.e. (by implication) natural *production* (lineal *descent*); by extension a *genus* or *sort*; (figurative) native *disposition, constitution* or *usage:*—([man-]) kind, nature ([-al]).

5450. φυσίωσις, phusiōsis, *foo-see´-o-sis*; from 5448; *inflation,* i.e. (figurative) *haughtiness:*—swelling.

5451. φυτεία, phuteia, *foo-ti´-ah*; from 5452; trans-*planting,* i.e. (concrete) a *shrub* or *vegetable:*—plant.

5452. φυτεύω, phuteuō, *foot-yoo´-o*; from a derivative of 5453; to *set out* in the earth, i.e. *implant*; (figurative) to *instill* doctrine:—plant.

5453. φύω, phuō, *foo´-o*; a primary verb; probably original to "*puff*" or *blow,* i.e. to *swell* up; but only used in the implication sense, to *germinate* or *grow* (*sprout, produce*), literal or figurative:—spring (up).

To generate, produce, bring forth, let grow, of plants, fruit, or persons. Usages in the NT:

(I) Particularly, to spring up or grow as a plant (Lk 8:6, 8).

(II) Figuratively, to spring up, grow up within a person. Spoken of a root of bitterness (Heb 12:15).

Deriv.: *ekphúō* (1631), to produce; *neóphutos* (3504), newly planted, novice; *sumphúō* (4855), to bring forth together; *phulḗ* (5443), tribe; *phúllon* (5444), a leaf; *phúsis* (5449), nature, natural birth or condition.

Syn.: *auxánō* (837), to grow or increase.

5454. φωλεός, phōleos, *fo-leh-os´*; of uncertain derivative; a *burrow* or *lurking-place:*—hole.

5455. φωνέω, phōneō, *fo-neh´-o*; from 5456; to emit a *sound* (animal, human or instrumental); by implication to *address* in words or by name, also in imitation:—call (for), crow, cry.

5456. φωνή, phōnē, *fo-nay´*; probably akin to 5316 through the idea of *disclosure*; a *tone* (articulate, bestial or artificial); by implication an *address* (for any purpose), *saying* or *language:*—noise, sound, voice.

Noun from *pháō* (n.f.), to shine. A sound or tone made or given forth.

(I) Generally, spoken of things: of a trumpet or other instrument (Mt 24:31; 1Co 14:7, 8; Rev 18:22); the wind (Jn 3:8; Ac 2:6); rushing wings, chariots, waters (Rev 9:9; 14:2; 19:6); of thunder (Rev 4:5; 6:1; 8:5; 11:19; 14:2; 19:6). See also Heb 12:19.

(II) Specifically, the voice or cry of a person.

(A) Particularly and generally as in phrases with verbs of speaking, calling, crying out: e.g., used with *mégas* (3173), great, in the sense of a loud voice (Mt 27:46, 50; Mk 5:7; 15:34, 37; Lk 8:28; 17:15; 23:23; Jn 11:43; Ac 8:7; Rev 1:10; 6:10; 14:15); used with *akoúō* (191), to hear or hear one's voice, in the sense of obeying one's voice or obeying the person himself (Jn 10:16, 27; Heb 3:7, 15; 4:7). Used figuratively, "to change my voice," meaning to change one's tone, to speak in a different manner and spirit (Gal 4:20).

(B) By metonymy, what is uttered by the voice, a word, saying (Ac 13:27; 24:21).

(C) By metonymy, in the sense of the meaning of the voice, language, dialect (1Co 14:10, 11).

Deriv.: *alektorophōnía* (219), crowing of a rooster; *áphōnos* (880), voiceless, mute; *kenophōnía* (2757), empty speaking; *súmphōnos* (4859), agreeable, sounding together, harmonious; *phōnéō* (5455), to address, speak.

Syn.: *boḗ* (995), a cry; *ḗchos* (2279), a loud noise, roar, echo, sound; *kraugḗ* (2906), clamor, crying; *laliá* (2981), talk, speech, saying, prattle; *lógos* (3056), word, speech, discourse; *phthóggos* (5353), utterance, musical note, sound.

5457. φῶς, phōs, *foce*; from an obsolete **φάω, *phaō*** (to *shine* or make *manifest*, especially by *rays*; compare 5316, 5346); *luminousness* (in the widest application, natural or artificial, abstract or concrete, literal or figurative):—fire light.

Noun from *pháō* (n.f.), to shine. Light.

(I) Particularly and generally, spoken:

(A) Of light in itself (Mt 17:2; 2Co 4:6).

(B) Of light as emitted from a luminous body: e.g., of a lamp (Lk 8:16; Rev 18:23); of the sun (Rev 22:5).

(C) Of daylight (Mt 10:27; Lk 12:3; Jn 3:20, 21; 11:9, 10; Eph 5:13).

(D) Of the dazzling light, splendour or glory which surrounds the throne of God in which He dwells (1Ti 6:16; Rev 21:24). Hence, also as surrounding the Lord Jesus Christ in His appearances after His ascension (Ac 9:3; 22:6, 9, 11; 26:13); of angels (Ac 12:7; 2Co 11:14); of glorified saints (Col 1:12).

(II) By metonymy, a light, a luminous body.

(A) A lamp or torch (Ac 16:29).

(B) A fire (Mk 14:54; Lk 22:56).

(C) Spoken of the heavenly luminaries, the sun, moon, and stars of which God is figuratively called the father (Jas 1:17).

(III) Figuratively, moral and spiritual light and knowledge which enlightens the mind, soul or conscience; including also the idea of moral goodness, purity and holiness, and of consequent reward and happiness.

(A) Generally, true knowledge of God and spiritual things, Christian piety (Mt 4:16; Jn 3:19; 8:12; Ac 26:18, 23; Ro 13:12; 2Co 6:14; Eph 5:8; 1Pe 2:9; 1Jn 1:7; 2:8, 10). Hence, true Christians are spoken of as the sons of light or the children of light (Lk 16:8; Jn 12:36; Eph 5:8; 1Th 5:5). Spoken of as exhibited in the life and teaching of someone (Mt 5:16; Jn 5:35).

(B) By metonymy, the author or dispenser of moral and spiritual light, a moral teacher: spoken generally (Ro 2:19) and of the disciples (Mt 5:14; Ac 13:47). Spoken of God (1Jn 1:5). Used especially of Jesus as the great Teacher and Saviour of the world who brought life and immortality to light in His gospel (see Lk 2:32; Jn 1:4, 5, 7–9; 3:19; 8:12; 9:5; 12:35, 36, 46).

(C) By metonymy, the mind or conscience (Mt 6:23; Lk 11:35).

Deriv.: *phaínō* (5316), to give light, illuminate; *phōstḗr* (5458), light, brightness; *phōsphóros* (5459), bearing light, morning star; *phōteinós* (5460), bright, radiant; *phōtízō* (5461), to shine, make known.

Syn.: *apaúgasma* (541), brightness; *lamprótēs* (2987), brilliancy, brightness.

5458. φωστήρ, phōstēr, *foce-tare´*; from 5457; an *illuminator*, i.e. (concretely) a *luminary*, or (abstract) *brilliancy*:—light.

From *phṓs* (5457), light. A light, light-giver. In Classical Greek, a window. In the NT, spoken figuratively of a person who gives light to those about him (Php 2:15). By metonymy, also spoken of the radiance of the holy Jerusalem that came from the divine glory (Rev 21:11).

5459. φωσφόρος, phōsphoros, *foce-for´-os*; from 5457 and 5342; *light-bearing* ("phosphorus"), i.e. (special) the *morning-star* (figurative):—day star.

5460. φωτεινός, phōteinos, *fo-ti-nos´*; from 5457; *lustrous*, i.e. *transparent* or *well-illuminated* (figurative):—bright, full of light.

5461. φωτίζω, phōtizō, *fo-tid´-zo*; from 5457; to *shed rays*, i.e. to *shine* or (transitive) to *brighten* up (literal or figurative):—enlighten, illuminate, (bring to, give) light, make to see.

Related to *phṓs* (5457), light. To give light to.

(I) Particularly (Lk 11:36; Rev 18:1).

(II) Figuratively, to enlighten, shine light upon, to impart moral and spiritual light (Jn 1:9; Eph 1:18; Heb 6:4; 10:32); to illuminate, make one see or understand (Eph 3:9); to bring to light, make known (1Co 4:5; 2Ti 1:10).

Deriv.: *phōtismós* (5462), a shining, illumination.

Syn.: *anáptō* (381), to enkindle, light; *apokalúptō* (601), to take off the cover, disclose, reveal; *dēlóō* (1213), to show, declare; *dialaléō* (1255), to declare publicly; *diasaphéō* (1285), to make clear, declare; *diaugázō* (1306), to shine through, dawn; *diaphēmízō* (1310), to report thoroughly, spread abroad; *diermēneúō* (1329), to explain thoroughly, expound; *exēgéō* (1834), to explain; *hermēneúō* (2059), to interpret; *plērophoréō* (4135), to inform fully, completely assure; *phaneróō* (5319), to make apparent, show, manifest, declare.

5462. φωτισμός, phōtismos, *fo-tis-mos´*; from 5461; *illumination* (figurative):—light.

Noun from *phōtízō* (5461), to lighten. Illumination, light, a bringing to light. In the NT, figuratively of moral and spiritual light (2Co 4:4, 6).

Syn.: *apaúgasma* (541), radiance, brightness; *lamprótēs* (2987), brilliancy, brightness.

5463. χαίρω, chairō, *khah´ee-ro*; a primary verb; to *be "cheer"ful*, i.e. calmly *happy* or well-off; impersonal especially as salutation (on meeting or parting), *be well*:—farewell, be glad, God speed, greeting, hail, joy (-fully), rejoice.

To rejoice, be glad.

(I) Particularly, to rejoice, be glad (Mt 2:10; 18:13; Mk 14:11; Lk 6:23; 10:20; Jn 3:29; 11:15; 14:28; Php 1:18; 2:17, 18, 28; 3:1; 4:4, 10; 1Pe 4:13).

(II) The infinitive can be used as a brief formula, similar to the English word "greetings," especially at the beginning of a conversation or of an epistle (Ac 15:23; 23:26; Jas 1:1). The Apostle John commands his readers not to even give a greeting to false teachers (2Jn 10).

Deriv.: *sugchaírō* (4796), to rejoice with; *chará* (5479), joy, delight, gladness; *cháris* (5485), grace.

Syn.: *agalliáō* (21), to exult, rejoice greatly; *euthuméō* (2114), to cheer up, make merry; *euphraínō* (2165), to cheer, gladden; *onínēmi* (3685), to gratify; *skirtáō* (4640), to leap for joy.

5464. χάλαζα, chalaza, *khal´-ad-zah*; probably from 5465; *hail*:—hail.

5465. χαλάω, chalaō, *khal-ah´-o*; from the base of 5490; to *lower* (as into a *void*):—let down, strike.

5466. Χαλδαῖος, Chaldaios, *khal-dah´-yos*; probably of Hebrew origin [3778]; a *Chaldæan* (i.e. *Kasdi*), or native of the region of the lower Euphrates:—Chaldæan.

5467. χαλεπός, chalepos, *khal-ep-os´*; perhaps from 5465 through the idea of *reducing* the strength; *difficult*, i.e. *dangerous*, or (by implication) *furious*:—fierce, perilous.

5468. χαλιναγωγέω, chalinagōgeō, *khal-in-ag-ogue-eh´-o*; from a compound of 5469 and the reduplicated form of 71; to *be* a *bit-leader*, i.e. to *curb* (figurative):—bridle.

5469. χαλινός, chalinos, *khal-ee-nos´*; from 5465; a *curb* or *head-stall* (as *curbing* the spirit):—bit, bridle.

5470. χάλκεος, chalkeos, *khal´-key-os*; from 5475; *coppery*:—brass.

5471. χαλκεύς, chalkeus, *khalk-yooce´*; from 5475; a *copper-worker* or *brazier*:—coppersmith.

5472. χαλκηδών, chalkēdōn, *khal-kay-dohn´*; from 5475 and perhaps 1491; *copper-like*, i.e. "*chalcedony*":—chalcedony.

5473. χαλκίον, chalkion, *khal-kee´-on*; diminutive from 5475; a *copper dish*:—brazen vessel.

5474. χαλκαλίβανον, chalkalibanon, *khal-kol-ib´-an-on*; neuter of a compound of 5475 and 3030 (in the implication mean of *whiteness* or *brilliancy*); *burnished copper*, an alloy of copper (or gold) and silver having a brilliant lustre:—fine brass.

5475. χαλκός, chalkos, *khal-kos´*; perhaps from 5465 through the idea of *hollowing* out as a vessel (this metal being chiefly used for that purpose); *copper* (the substance, or some implement or coin made of it):—brass, money.

5476. χαμαί, chamai, *kham-ah´ee*; adverb perhaps from the base of 5490 through the idea of a *fissure* in the soil; *earthward*, i.e. *prostrate*:—on (to) the ground.

5477. Χαναάν, Chanaan, *khan-ah-an´*; of Hebrew origin [3667]; *Chanaan* (i.e. *Kenaan*), the early name of Palestine:—Chanaan.

5478. Χαναναῖος, Chanaanaios, *khan-ah-an-ah´-yos*; from 5477; a *Chanaanæan* (i.e. *Kenaanite*), or native of Gentile Palestine:—of Canaan.

5479. χαρά, chara, *khar-ah´*; from 5463; *cheerfulness*, i.e. calm *delight*:—gladness, × greatly, (× be exceeding) joy (-ful, -fully, -fulness, -ous).

Noun from *chaírō* (5463), to rejoice. Joy, rejoicing, gladness.

(I) Generally (Mt 2:10; 13:20, 44; 28:8; Mk 4:16; Lk 1:14; 8:13; 15:7, 10; Jn 15:11; 16:20; 17:13; Php 2:2; 1Pe 1:8; 1Jn 1:4; 2Jn 12).

(II) By metonymy, of the cause, ground, occasion of joy (Lk 2:10; Php 4:1; 1Th 2:19, 20; Jas 1:2; 3Jn 4).

(III) By metonymy, of enjoyment, fruition of joy, bliss (Mt 25:21, 23; Heb 12:2).

Syn.: *agallíasis* (20), exultation, exuberant joy; *euphrosúnē* (2167), good cheer, mirth, gladness of heart.

5480. χάραγμα, charagma, *khar´-ag-mah*; from the same as 5482; a *scratch* or *etching*, i.e. *stamp* (as a *badge* of servitude), or *sculptured* figure (*statue*):—graven, mark.

Noun from *charássō* (n.f.), to engrave. An engraving, something engraved or sculptured.

(I) An engraving or sculptured work such as images or idols (Ac 17:29).

(II) A mark cut in or stamped on, a sign: e.g., "the mark of the beast" (Rev 13:16, 17; 14:9, 11; 15:2; 16:2; 19:20; 20:4).

Deriv. of *charássō* (n.f.), to carve: *charaktḗr* (5481), something engraved, an impression; *chárax* (5482), a strong stake used in fortification; *chártēs* (5489), paper.

Syn.: *stígma* (4742), mark, brand; *sphragís* (4973), mark, seal.

5481. χαρακτήρ, charaktēr, *khar-ak-tar´*; from the same as 5482; a *graver* (the tool or the person), i.e. (by implication) *engraving* (["*character*"], the *figure* stamped, i.e. an exact *copy* or [figurative] *representation*):—express image.

Noun from *charássō* (n.f.), to carve. Originally an engraving tool. Later, the impression itself, usually something engraved, cut in, or stamped, a character, letter, mark, or sign. In the NT, an impression, image. Used only in Heb 1:3, where Jesus is described as the *charaktḗr* or the express image of God's nature.

Syn.: *eikṓn* (1504), image; *homoíōsis* (3669), likeness; *homoíōma* (3667), likeness.

5482. χάραξ, charax, *khar´-ax*; from **χαράσσω** ***charassō*** (to *sharpen* to a point; akin to 1125 through the idea of *scratching*); a *stake*, i.e. (by implication) a *palisade* or *rampart* (military *mound* for circumvallation in a siege):—trench.

5483. χαρίζομαι, charizomai, *khar-id´-zom-ahee*; middle from 5485; to grant as a *favour*, i.e. gratuitously, in kindness, pardon or rescue:—deliver, (frankly) forgive, (freely) give, grant.

From *cháris* (5485), grace. To show someone a favour, be kind to.

(I) To give or bestow a thing willingly (Lk 7:21; Ro 8:32; 1Co 2:12; Gal 3:18; Php 1:29; 2:9).

(II) Of persons, to deliver up or over in answer to demands (Ac 3:14; 25:11, 16) or in answer to prayer (Ac 27:24; Phm 22).

(III) Of things, to remit, forgive, not to exact (Lk 7:42, 43). Generally of wrong, sin, to forgive, not to punish (2Co 2:7, 10; 12:13; Eph 4:32; Col 2:13; 5:13).

Deriv.: *chárisma* (5486), a gift of grace.

Syn.: *apolúō* (630), to loose from; *aphíēmi* (863), to send forth, remit; *dídōmi* (1325), to give, bestow; *dōréomai* (1433), to give, make a gift; *paréchō* (3930), to provide, supply; *chorēgéō* (5524), to supply, give.

5484. χάριν, charin, *khar´-in*; accusative of 5485 as prep.; through *favour* of, i.e. *on account* of:—be (for) cause of, for sake of, + … fore, × reproachfully.

5485. χάρις, charis, *khar´-ece*; from 5463; *graciousness* (as *gratifying*), of manner or act (abstract or concrete; literal, figurative or spiritual; especially the divine influence upon the heart, and its reflection in the life; including *gratitude*):—acceptable, benefit, favour, gift, grace (-ious), joy, liberality, pleasure, thank (-s, -worthy).

Noun from *chaírō* (5463), to rejoice. Grace, particularly that which causes joy, pleasure, gratification.

(I) Grace in reference to the external form or manner, particularly of persons meaning gracefulness, elegance. In the NT only of words or discourses as graciousness, agreeableness, acceptableness (Lk 4:22; Eph 4:29; Col 4:6).

(II) Grace in reference to disposition, attitude toward another, favour, goodwill, benevolence.

(A) Generally favour, goodwill (Lk 1:30; 2:40, 52; Ac 2:47; 4:33; 7:10, 46; 24:27; 25:9; Heb 4:16). Spoken by metonymy of the object of favour, something acceptable (1Pe 2:19, 20).

(B) Spoken of the grace, favour and goodwill of God and Christ as exercised toward men: where *cháris* is joined with *eirḗnē* (1515), peace, *éleos* (1656), mercy, and the like in salutations and in the introduction to most of the epistles, including the idea of every kind of favour, blessing, good, as proceeding from God the Father and the Lord Jesus Christ (Ro 1:7; 1Co 1:3; 2Co 1:2; Gal 1:3; Eph 1:2; Php 1:2; Col 1:2; 1Th 1:1; 2Th 1:2; 1Ti 1:2; 2Ti 1:2; Tit 1:4; Phm 3; 1Pe 1:2; 2Pe 1:2; 2Jn 3; Rev 1:4). Also spoken of the grace of the Lord Jesus Christ in the benedictions at the close of most of the epistles (Ro 16:20, 24; 1Co 16:23; 2Co 13:14; Gal 6:18). Simply with the definite article with equal meaning (Eph 6:24; Col 4:18; 1Ti 6:21; 2Ti 4:22; Tit 3:15; Heb 13:25). Spoken of the grace of Christ in providing salvation for us (Ac 15:11). Also spoken of the grace which God exercises toward us, the unmerited favour which he shows in saving us from sin (Ac 20:24; Ro 3:24; 5:2; 1Co 15:10; 2Co 1:12; 9:14; 12:9; Gal 1:15; Eph 1:6; Heb 2:9; 1Pe 4:10).

(C) Specifically of the divine grace and favour as exercised in conferring gifts, graces and benefits on man. Particularly as manifested in the benefits bestowed in and through Christ and His gospel (Ac 13:43; 2Co 4:15; 6:1; 8:1; Eph 4:7; Php 1:7; Heb 12:15; 13:9; Jas 4:6; 1Pe 1:10, 13; 5:5). Specifically of the grace or gift of the apostleship, the apostolic office (Ro 12:3; 15:15; 1Co 3:10; Gal 2:9; Eph 3:2, 8; 2Ti 2:1). Also of the grace exhibited in the pardon of sins and admission to the divine kingdom, saving grace (Ro 5:15; Gal 2:21; Tit 2:11; 3:7; 1Pe 3:7, "the grace of life"; 5:12).

(III) Gratitude, appreciation, thankfulness in return for favors and benefits. With the verb *échō* (2192), to have, to have thankfulness, to give thanks (Lk 17:9; 1Ti 1:12; 2Ti 1:3; Heb 12:28). Followed by the dative of *Theos* (2316), God, with an understood verb, thanks be given to God (Ro 6:17; 1Co 15:57; 2Co 2:14; 8:16; 9:15). In a question with the verb *estí* (2076), to be, what thanks is it, i.e. what thanks do you deserve (Lk 6:32–34). Used adverbially in the sense of with thankfulness, thankfully (1Co 10:30; Col 3:16).

Deriv.: *charízomai* (5483), to be kind to; *charitóō* (5487), to bestow grace on, highly honour.

Syn.: *dóma* (1390), a gift; *dósis* (1394), a gift or the act of giving; *dōreá* (1431), a free gift; *dṓrēma* (1434), a favour; *dṓron* (1435), a gift; *euergesía* (2108), a benefit; *eulogía* (2129), a blessing; *eucharistía* (2169), thankfulness, gratitude; *chárisma* (5486), a gift.

5486. χάρισμα, charisma, *char´-is-mah*; from 5483; a (divine) *gratuity*, i.e. *deliverance* (from danger or passion); (special) a (spiritual) *endowment*, i.e. (subject) religious *qualification*, or (objective) miraculous *faculty*:—(free) gift.

Noun from *charízomai* (5483), to show favour. A gift of grace, an undeserved benefit. In the NT used only of gifts and graces imparted from God, e.g., deliverance from peril (2Co 1:11); the gift of self-control (1Co 7:7); gifts of Christian knowledge, consolation, confidence (Ro 1:11; 1Co 1:7); redemption, salvation through Christ (Ro 5:15, 16; 6:23; 11:29). Specifically of the gifts and abilities imparted to the early Christians and particularly to Christian teachers by the Holy Spirit (Ro 12:6; 1Co 12:4, 9, 28, 30, 31; 1Pe 4:10). As communicated with the laying on of hands (1Ti 4:14; 2Ti 1:6).

Syn.: *dóma* (1390), a gift; *dósis* (1394), a gift; *dōreá* (1431), a free gift; *dṓrēma* (1434), a favour, something given; *dṓron* (1435), a gift.

5487. χαριτόω, charitoō, *khar-ee-to´-o*; from 5485; to *grace*, i.e. indue with special *honour*:—make accepted, be highly favoured.

From *cháris* (5485), grace. To bestow grace, highly honour or greatly favour. In the NT spoken only of the divine favour: to the virgin Mary (Lk 1:28); to all believers (Eph 1:6).

5488. Χαῤῥάν, Charrhan, *khar-hran´*; of Hebrew origin [2771]; *Charrhan* (i.e. *Charan*), a place in Mesopotamia:—Charran.

5489. χάρτης, chartēs, *khar´-tace*; from the same as 5482; a *sheet* ("chart") of writing-material (as to be *scribbled* over):—paper.

5490. χάσμα, chasma, *khas´-mah*; from a form of an obsolete primary **χάω** *chaō* (to "*gape*" or "*yawn*"); a "*chasm*" or *vacancy* (impassable *interval*):—gulf.

5491. χεῖλος, cheilos, *khi´-los*; from a form of the same as 5490; a *lip* (as a *pouring* place); (figurative) a *margin* (of water):—lip, shore.

5492. χειμάζω, cheimazō, *khi-mad´-zo*; from the same as 5494; to *storm*, i.e. (passive) to *labour under a gale*:—be tossed with tempest.

5493. χείμαῤῥος, cheimarrhos, *khi´-mar-hros*; from the base of 5494 and 4482; a *storm-runlet*, i.e. *winter-torrent*:—brook.

5494. χειμών, cheimōn, *khi-mone´*; from a derivative of **χέω**, ***cheō*** (to *pour*; akin to the base of 5490 through the idea of a *channel*), meaning a *storm* (as *pouring* rain); by implication the *rainy* season, i.e. *winter*:—tempest, foul weather, winter.

5495. χείρ, cheir, *khire*; perhaps from the base of 5494 in the sense of its congener the base of 5490 (through the idea of *hollowness* for grasping); the *hand* (literal or figurative [*power*]; especially [by Hebrew] a *means* or *instrument*):—hand.

5496. χειραγωγέω, cheiragōgeō, *khi-rag-ogue-eh´-o*; from 5497; to be a *hand-leader*, i.e. to *guide* (a blind person):—lead by the hand.

5497. χειραγωγός, cheiragōgos, *khi-rag-o-gos´*; from 5495 and a reduplicated form of 71; a *hand-leader*, i.e. personal *conductor* (of a blind person):—some to lead by the hand.

5498. χειρόγραφον, cheirographon, *khi-rog´-raf-on*; neuter of a compound of 5495 and 1125; something *hand-written* ("*chirograph*"), i.e. a *manuscript* (specially a legal *document* or *bond* [figurative]):—handwriting.

5499. χειροποίητος, cheiropoiētos, *khi-rop-oy´-ay-tos*; from 5495 and a derivative of 4160; *manufactured*, i.e. *of human construction*:—made by (make with) hands.

5500. χειροτονέω, cheirotoneō, *khi-rot-on-eh´-o*; from a compound of 5495 and **τείνω**, ***teinō*** (to *stretch*); to be a *hand-reacher* or *voter* (by raising the hand), i.e. (genitive) to *select* or *appoint*:—choose, ordain.

From *cheirotónos* (n.f.), stretching out the hands. To stretch out the hand, hold up the hand, as in voting; hence to vote, to give one's vote by holding up the hand. In the NT, to choose by vote, to appoint (Ac 14:23; 2Co 8:19).

Deriv.: *procheirontonéō* (4401), to choose beforehand.

Syn.: *tássō* (5021), to assign; *horízō* (3724), to mark out, specify, ordain; *apostéllō* (649), to set apart; *eklégomai* (1586), to choose.

5501. χείρων, cheirōn, *khi´-rone*; irregular comparative of 2556; from an obsolete equivalent **χέρης**, ***cherēs*** (of uncertain derivative); *more evil* or *aggravated* (physical, mental or moral):—sorer, worse.

5502. χερουβίμ, cheroubim, *kher-oo-beem´*; plural of Hebrew origin [3742]; "*cherubim*" (i.e. *cherubs* or *kerubim*):—cherubims.

5503. χήρα, chēra, *khay´-rah*; feminine of a presumed derivative apparently from the base of 5490 through the idea of *deficiency*; a *widow* (as *lacking* a husband), literal or figurative:—widow.

5504. χθές, chthes, *khthes*; of uncertain derivative; "*yesterday*"; by extension *in time past* or *hitherto*:—yesterday.

5505. χιλιάς, chilias, *khil-ee-as´*; from 5507; one *thousand* ("*chiliad*"):—thousand.

5506. χιλίαρχος, chiliarchos, *khil-ee´-ar-khos*; from 5507 and 757; the *commander of a thousand* soldiers ("*chiliarch*"), i.e. *colonel*:—(chief, high) captain.

5507. χίλιοι, chilioi, *khil´-ee-oy*; plural of uncertain affinity; a *thousand*:—thousand.

5508. Χίος, Chios, *khee´-os*; of uncertain derivative; *Chios*, an island in the Mediterranean:—Chios.

5509. χιτών, chitōn, *khee-tone´*; of foreign origin [3801]; a *tunic* or *shirt*:—clothes, coat, garment.

A noun meaning close-fitting inner vest, an inner garment (Mt 5:40; Jn 19:23; Ac 9:39; Jude 23). At times two tunics seem to have been worn, probably of different materials for ornament or luxury (Mt 10:10; Mk 6:9; Lk 3:11; 9:3). Hence it is said of the high priest that he rent his clothes (*chitṓnas*) or garments (Mk 14:63 where it is used in the plural; Sept.: Ge 37:3; 2Sa 15:32). In Lk 6:29 it is used with *himátion* (2440), an outer cloak as equivalent to *himátia* (Mt 26:65).

Syn.: For a list of various types of clothing, see the synonyms under *himátion* (2440), garment.

5510. χιών, chiōn, *khee-one´*; perhaps akin to the base of 5490 (5465) or 5494 (as *descending* or *empty*); *snow*:—snow.

5511. χλαμύς, chlamus, *khlam-ooce´*; of uncertain derivative; a military *cloak*:—robe.

A feminine noun meaning garment of dignity and office. The purple robe with which our Lord was arrayed in scorn by the mockers in Pilate's judgement hall (Mt 27:28–31). When put over the shoulders of someone, it was an indication that he was assuming a magistracy. It may have been the cast-off cloak of some high Roman officer which they put over the body of Jesus to mock Him as if He were an official person.

Syn.: For a list of various types of clothing, see the synonyms under *himátion* (2440), garment.

5512. χλευάζω, chleuazō, *khlyoo-ad´-zo*; from a derivative probably of 5491; to *throw out* the *lip*, i.e. *jeer* at:—mock.

5513. χλιαρός, chliaros, *khlee-ar-os´*; from **χλίω**, ***chliō*** (to *warm*); *tepid*:—lukewarm.

5514. Χλόη, Chloē, *khlo´-ay*; feminine of apparently a primary word; "*green*"; *Chloë*, a Christian female:—Chloe.

5515. χλωρός, chlōros, *khlo-ros´*; from the same as 5514; *greenish*, i.e. *verdant*, *dun-coloured*:—green, pale.

5516. χξς, chi xi stigma, *khee xee stig´-ma*; the twenty-second, fourteenth and an obsolete letter (4742 as a *cross*) of the Greek alphabet (intermediate between the fifth and sixth), used as numbers; denoting respectively six hundred, sixty and six; six hundred sixty-six as a numeral:—six hundred threescore and six.

5517. χοϊκός, choïkos, *kho-ik-os´*; from 5522; *dusty* or *dirty* (*soil*-like), i.e. (by implication) *terrene*:—earthy.

Adjective from *chóos* (5522), earth, dust. Earthy, made of earth or dust (1Co 15:47–49).

Syn.: *ostrákinos* (3749), of earthenware or clay, earthen; *epígeios* (1919), earthly; *katachthónios* (2709), subterranean.

5518. χοῖνιξ, choinix, *khoy´-nix*; of uncertain derivative; a *choenix* or certain dry measure:—measure.

5519. χοῖρος, choiros, *khoy-´ros*; of uncertain derivative; a *hog*:—swine.

5520. χολάω, cholaō, *khol-ah´-o*; from 5521; to *be bilious*, i.e. (by implication) *irritable* (*enraged*, "choleric"):—be angry.

5521. χολή, cholē, *khol-ay´*; feminine of an equivalent perhaps akin to the same as 5514 (from the *greenish* hue); "*gall*" or *bile*, i.e. (by analogy) *poison* or an *anodyne* (wormwood, poppy, etc.):—gall.

5522. χόος, choos, *kho´-os*; from the base of 5494; a *heap* (as *poured* out), i.e. *rubbish*; loose *dirt*:—dust.

5523. Χοραζίν, Chorazin, *khor-ad-zin´*; of uncertain derivative; *Chorazin*, a place in Palestine:—Chorazin.

5524. χορηγέω, chorēgeō, *khor-ayg-eh´-o*; from a compound of 5525 and 71; to be a *dance-leader*, i.e. (genitive) to *furnish*:—give, minister.

5525. χορός, choros, *khor-os´*; of uncertain derivative; a *ring*, i.e. round *dance* ("choir"):—dancing.

5526. χορτάζω, chortazō, *khor-tad´-zo*; from 5528; to *fodder*, i.e. (genitive) to *gorge* (*supply food* in abundance):—feed, fill, satisfy.

5527. χόρτασμα, chortasma, *khor´-tas-mah*; from 5526; *forage*, i.e. *food*:—sustenance.

5528. χόρτος, chortos, *khor´-tos*; apparently a primary word; a "*court*" or "*garden*," i.e. (by implication of *pasture*) *herbage* or *vegetation*:—blade, grass, hay.

5529. Χουζᾶς, Chouzas, *khood-zas´*; of uncertain origin; *Chuzas*, an officer of Herod:—Chuza.

5530. χράομαι, chraomai, *khrah´-om-ahee*; middle of a primary verb (perhaps rather from 5495, to *handle*); to *furnish* what is needed; (give an *oracle*, "*graze*" [touch slightly], *light* upon, etc.), i.e. (by implication) to *employ* or (by extension) to *act toward* one in a given manner:—entreat, use. Compare 5531, 5534.

Middle deponent of *chráō* (5531), to lend. To use, make use of, make the most of, followed by the dat. of things (Ac 27:17; 1Co 7:21, 31; 9:12, 15; 2Co 1:17; 3:12; 1Ti 1:8; 5:23). Of persons meaning to treat well or badly, with the dat. (Ac 27:3; implied 2Co 13:10; Sept.: Ge 16:6; 19:8).

Deriv.: *eúchrēstos* (2173), useful; *katachráomai* (2710), to abuse; *sugchráomai* (4798), to share usage with someone; *chrḗma* (5536), something usable as wealth, money; *chrḗsimos* (5539), useful, profitable; *chrḗsis* (5540), use; *chrēstós* (5543), profitable, good for any use.

Syn.: *apaitéō* (523), to demand back.

5531. χράω, chraō, *khrah´-o*; probably the same as the base of 5530; to *loan*:—lend.

To lend, furnish as a loan (Lk 11:5); the middle voice, *chráomai* (5530), to borrow, receive for use.

5532. χρεία, chreia, *khri´-ah*; from the base of 5530 or 5534; *employment*, i.e. an *affair*; also (by implication) *occasion, demand, requirement* or *destitution*:—business, lack, necessary (-ity), need (-ful), use, want.

Noun from *chréos* (n.f.), debt. Also from *chréos* (n.f.): *chreōpheilétēs* (5533), one who owes a debt.

(I) Use, usage, employment, act of using. In the NT metonymically, that in which one is employed, an employment, affair, business (Ac 6:3).

(II) Need, necessity, want.

(A) Generally (Eph 4:29 meaning merciful, needful edification). With *estí* (2076), is, and the gen. (Lk 10:42, "one thing is needful"). With the inf. (Heb 7:11).

(B) Of personal need, necessity, want (Ac 20:34; 28:10, "such things as were necessary"; Ro 12:13; Php 2:25; 4:16, for one's need or wants; 4:19; Tit 3:14).

(C) Elsewhere only in the phrase *chreían échō* (2192), I have need. **(1)** Generally and followed by the gen. meaning to have need of (Mt 9:12; 21:3; 26:65; Mk 2:17; 11:3; 14:63; Lk 5:31; 9:11; 15:7; 19:31, 34; 22:71; Jn 13:29; 1Co 12:21, 24; Heb 5:12; 10:36; Rev 21:23; 22:5). **(2)** Of personal need, want, with the gen. (Mt 6:8; 1Th 4:12; Rev 3:17). Used in an absolute sense, meaning to have need, to be in need or want (Mk 2:25; Ac 2:45; 4:35; Eph 4:28; 1Jn 3:17). Followed by the inf. act. (Mt 14:16; 1Th 1:8; 4:9); also the inf. pass. (Mt 3:14; 1Th 5:1); by *hína* (2443), so that (Jn 2:25; 16:30; 1Jn 2:27). In the Sept. with the gen. (Pr 18:2; Isa 13:17).

Deriv.: *achreíos* (888), unprofitable; *chrḗzō* (5535), to have need of, want, desire.

Syn.: *anágkē* (318), necessity, need; *hustérēsis* (5304), need; *anagkaíon* (316), necessary, needful; *epánagkes* (1876), necessary; *tó déon*, that which is needful, from *deí* (1163), necessary; *tó prépon* (from *prépō* [4241]), that which is necessary.

5533. χρεωφειλέτης, chreōpheiletēs, *khreh-o-fi-let´-ace*; from a derivative of 5531 and 3781; a *loan-ower*, i.e. *indebted* person:—debtor.

5534. χρή, chrē, *khray*; third person singular of the same as 5530 or 5531 used impersonally; it *needs* (*must* or *should*) be:—ought.

An impersonal verb from *chreía* (5532), need, necessity. It is necessary, it needs to be, ought to be; translated "it is becoming" or "it is appropriate" (Jas 3:10 with the neg. *ou* [3756], not).

5535. χρῄζω, chrēizō, *khrade´-zo*; from 5532; to *make* (i.e. *have*) *necessity*, i.e. *be in want* of:—(have) need.

From *chreía* (5532), need, necessity. Governing a gen., to have need of, want, desire (Mt 6:32; Lk 11:8; 12:30; Ro 16:2).

5536. χρῆμα, chrēma, *khray´-mah*; something *useful* or *needed*, i.e. *wealth, price*:—money, riches.

Noun from *chráomai* (5530), to use, need. Something useful or capable of being used. In both the sing. and plural it means money (Lk 18:24; Ac 4:37; 8:18; 24:26; Sept.: Job 27:17). In Gr. writings it also means thing, matter, business, equal to *prágma* (4229), business, matter, thing, from which is derived *pragmateúomai* (4231), to trade.

Deriv.: *parachrḗma* (3916), at the very moment, immediately; *chrēmatízō* (5537), to manage a business.

Syn.: *argúrion* (694), silver, money; *chalkós* (5475), copper, as used for money; *kérma* (2772), a coin, change; *nómisma* (3546), money; *statḗr* (4715), a coin, equivalent to four drachmae; *drachmaí* (1406), drachmae, the Greek money; *ploútos* (4149), wealth; *porismós* (4200), gain, a means of gain.

5537. χρηματίζω, chrēmatizō, *khray-mat-id´-zo*; from 5536; to *utter an oracle* (compare the original sense of 5530), i.e. divinely *intimate*; by implication (compare the secular sense of 5532) to constitute a *firm* for business, i.e. (generic) *bear* as a *title*:—be called, be admonished (warned) of God, reveal, speak.

From *chrḗma* (5536), an affair, business. To have a business affair or dealings, manage a business (Sept.: 1Ki 18:27), especially in trade and money affairs. In the middle *chrēmatízomai*, to do good business, make a profit, gain. Of kings and magistrates, to do business publicly, to give audience; to answer as to ambassadors, petitioners, to warn, advise, give a response or decision. Hence in the NT:

(I) Spoken in respect to a divine response, oracle, or declaration, to give response, speak as an oracle, warn from God, used in an absolute sense (Heb 12:25 of Moses who consulted God and delivered to the people the divine response, precepts, warnings, and the like). Used of a prophet (Sept.: Jer 26:2); of God (Sept.: Jer 30:2; 36:4). In the pass. of persons, to receive a divine response, warning, to be warned or admonished of God, used in an absolute sense (Heb 8:5 speaking of Moses); followed by *perí* (4012), concerning, with the gen. (Heb 11:7); with *kat' ónar* (*katá* [2596], according, in; *ónar* [3677], dream), in a dream (Mt 2:12, 22). Of things, to be given in response, be revealed (Lk 2:26, by the Holy Spirit).

(II) In later Gr. usage it means to do business under someone's name; hence generally, to take or bear a name, to be named, called, constructed with the name in apposition (Ac 11:26, "named [or called] Christians for the first time" [a.t.]; Ro 7:3, "named an adulteress" [a.t.]).

Deriv.: *chrēmatismós* (5538), an oracle, response or decision.

Syn.: *kaléō* (2564), to call; *onomázō* (3687), to name; *eponomázō* (2028), to surname, call; *apokalúptō* (601), to unveil, reveal; *légō* (3004), to say, speak; *laléō* (2980), to say; *eréō* (2046), to utter, speak, say, tell.

5538. χρηματισμός, chrēmatismos, *khray-mat-is-mos´*; from 5537; a divine *response* or *revelation*:—answer of God.

Noun from *chrēmatízō* (5537), to do business, utter an oracle, to be warned of God as by an oracle. An oracle, a reply, response or decision (Ro 11:4).

Syn.: *apókrisis* (612), answer; *apókrima* (610), a judicial sentence, answer of God.

5539. χρήσιμος, chrēsimos, *khray´-see-mos*; from 5540; *serviceable*:—profit.

Adjective from *chráomai* (5530), to use, need. Useful, profitable (2Ti 2:14).

Syn.: *eúchrēstos* (2173), useful; *ōphélimos* (5624), useful, profitable; *lusiteleí* (3081), is advantageous, profitable.

5540. χρῆσις, chrēsis, *khray´-sis*; from 5530; *employment*, i.e. (special) sexual *intercourse* (as an *occupation* of the body):—use.

Noun from *chráomai* (5530), to use. Use, the act (usage) or manner (use) of using (Ro 1:26, 27 of the use of the body in sexual intercourse).

5541. χρηστεύομαι, chrēsteuomai, *khraste-yoo´-om-ahee*; middle from 5543; to *show oneself useful*, i.e. *act benevolently*:—be kind.

5542. χρηστολογία, chrēstologia, *khrase-tol-og-ee´-ah*; from a compound of 5543 and 3004; *fair speech*, i.e. *plausibility*:—good words.

5543. χρηστός, chrēstos, *khrase-tos´*; from 5530; *employed*, i.e. (by implication) *useful* (in manner or morals):—better, easy, good (-ness), gracious, kind.

Adjective from *chráomai* (5530), to furnish what is needed. Profitable, fit, good for any use.

(I) Of things (Lk 5:39, better for drinking; Sept.: Jer 24:2, 5, good for eating). Figuratively, good, gentle, easy to use or bear; Christ's yoke is *chrēstós*, as having nothing harsh or galling about it (Mt 11:30). In a moral sense, moral, useful, good, virtuous (in the proverb in 1Co 15:33 quoted from Menander).

(II) Of persons, useful toward others, hence good-natured, good, gentle, kind (Lk 6:35 of God; Eph 4:32; 1Pe 2:3); *tó chrēstón* (neuter with the article), goodness, kindness, equal to *he chrēstótēs* (5544) (Ro 2:4; Sept.: Ps 86:5).

Deriv.: *áchrēstos* (890), unprofitable, useless; *chrēsteúomai* (5541), to be kind, willing to help; *chrēstótēs* (5544), kindness, usefulness.

Syn.: *epieikḗs* (1933), seemly, equitable, fair, forbearing, tolerant; *anexíkakos* (420), one who patiently forbears evil; *ḗpios* (2261), mild, gentle; *kalós* (2570), good; *agathós* (18), benevolent; *akéraios* (185), harmless.

5544. χρηστότης, chrēstotēs, *khray-stot´-ace*; from 5543; *usefulness*, i.e. moral *excellence* (in character or demeanour):—gentleness, good (-ness), kindness.

Noun from *chrēstós* (5543), useful, profitable. Benignity, kindness, usefulness. It often occurs with *philanthrōpía* (5363), philanthropy; *anochḗ* (463), forbearance (Ro 2:4), and is the opposite of *apotomía* (663), severity or cutting something short and quickly (Ro 11:22). *Chrēstótēs* is translated "good" (Ro 3:12); "kindness" (2Co 6:6; Eph 2:7; Col 3:12; Tit 3:4); "gentleness" (Gal 5:22). It is the grace which pervades the whole nature, mellowing all which would be harsh and austere. Thus, wine is *chrēstós* (5543), mellowed with age (Lk 5:39). The word is descriptive of one's disposition and does not necessarily entail acts of goodness as does the word *agathōsúnē* (19), active benignity. *Chrēstótēs* has the harmlessness of the dove but not the wisdom of the serpent which *agathōsúnē* shows in sharpness and rebuke.

Syn.: *epieíkeia* (1932), fairness, moderation, clemency, an active dealing with others involving equity and justice; *praǘtēs* (4240), meekness; *eupoiḯa* (2140), beneficence, doing that which is good.

5545. χρίσμα, chrisma, *khris´-mah*; from 5548; an *unguent* or *smearing*, i.e. (figurative) the special *endowment* ("chrism") of the Holy Spirit:—anointing, unction.

Noun from *chríō* (5548), to anoint. The anointing (Ex 29:7; 30:25). The specially prepared anointing oil was called *chrísma hágion* (*hágion* [39], holy). By metonymy used of the Holy Spirit in 1Jn 2:20, 27 where it signifies an anointing which had been experienced, a communication and reception of the Spirit (cf. Jn 16:13). The allusion is to the anointing and consecration of kings and priests (Ex 28:41; 1Sa 10:1). This was emblematic of a divine spirit descending and abiding upon them from God, as was afterwards the laying on of hands (Dt 34:9). In Da 9:26 *chrísma* stands for the Anointed One, Christ (*christós* [5547]), as it stands for the Holy Spirit in 1Jn 2. *Chrísma* is not merely a figurative name for the Spirit as seen from the expressions *chrísma échete* ("you have an anointing" [a.t.], 2:20) and *elábete* ("you received" [a.t.], 2:27). The word seems chosen on the one hand, to give prominence to what the readers had experienced, and on the other hand, by referring to the OT practice, and especially to Christ, to remind them of their calling and mark (1Pe 2:5, 9).

5546. Χριστιανός, Christianos, *khris-tee-an-os´*; from 5547; a *Christian*, i.e. follower of Christ:—Christian.

Noun from *Christós* (5547), Christ. A name given to the disciples or followers of Christ, first adopted at Antioch. It does not occur in the NT as a name commonly used by Christians themselves (Ac 11:26; 26:28; 1Pe 4:16). The believers first became known as Christians as an appellation of ridicule.

Syn.: *mathētḗs* (3101), a learner; *pistós* (4103), faithful (one); *adelphós* (80), a brother; *hágios* (40), a saint.

5547. Χριστός, Christos, *khris-tos´*; from 5548; *anointed*, i.e. the *Messiah*, an epithet of Jesus:—Christ.

Adjective from *chríō* (5548), to anoint. Anointed, a term used in the OT applied to everyone anointed with the holy oil, primarily to the high priesthood (Le 4:5, 16). Also a name applied to others acting as redeemers.

(I) As an appellative and with the article *ho*, the, *Christós*, Christ, it occurs chiefly in the Gospels and means the Messiah (Mk 15:32, "the King of Israel"; Jn 1:41; 4:42 "the Christ, the Saviour of the world"; Ac 2:36; 9:22; 18:28. Also see Mt 1:17; 2:4; 16:16; Mk 12:35; 13:21; Lk 2:11, 26, "the Christ of the Lord" [a.t.]; 4:41; 23:2; Jn 1:20, 25; Ac 2:30; 3:18; Ro 8:11; 1Jn 2:22; 5:1, 6; Rev 11:15; 12:10; Sept.: Ps 2:2 [cf. Da 9:25]). Joined with *Iēsoús* (2424), Jesus, *Iēsoús ho Christós*, Jesus the Christ (Ac 5:42; 9:34; 1Co 3:11), *Iēsoús Christós* (Jn 17:3; Ac 2:38; 3:20; 1Jn 4:2, 3; 2Jn 7), *ho Christós Iēsoús*, the Christ Jesus (Ac 17:3; 18:5, 28; 19:4).

(II) As a proper noun, Christ.

(A) Used in an absolute sense, *Christós* or *ho Christós* chiefly in the epistles referring to the Messiah (Ro 5:6, 8; 8:10; 1Co 1:12; 3:23; Gal 1:6, 7; 2:20; Eph 4:12; Heb 3:6; 5:5; 1Pe 1:11; 4:14).

(B) More often joined with *Iēsoús* (Mt 1:16, "Jesus the One called Christ" [a.t.]); *Iēsoús Christós* in the Gospels (Mt 1:1, 18; Mk 1:1; Jn 1:17; Ac 3:6, "In the name of Jesus Christ"; 4:10; 8:12; 10:36; 28:31; Ro 1:1, 6, 8; 1Co 1:1; 5:4). *Christós Iēsoús*, stressing the deity of Christ first and then His humanity only after His resurrection beginning with Ac 19:4 and often in the epistles (Ro 3:24; 8:2, 39; 15:5; 1Co 1:2, 30; Gal 3:26; 4:14; Php 2:5; 3:3, 8; Col 1:4; Heb 3:1). For the use of *ho Kúrios* (2962), the Lord, in connection with the names *Iēsoús* and *Christós*, see *Kúrios* (2962), Lord (cf. II, B, 2).

(C) Other designations attributed to Christ: **(1)** The servant of God (*paḯs* [3816], child, servant; Ac 3:13, 26); *tón hágion paída sou* (*hágion* [40], holy; *paída* [3816], child, servant; Ac 4:27, 30). This is a Messianic title of our Lord indicative of humility, submission, vicarious suffering and death (see Ac 8:35; Isa 53:7). **(2)** Prince and Saviour (*archēgós* [747], chief leader, author or captain; *sōtḗr* [4990], Saviour; Ac 5:31 [cf. Ac 3:15; Heb 2:10; 12:2]). The word *archēgós* reflects the meaning of author or originator as expressed in Ac 3:15, *archēgón tḗs zōḗs* (*zōḗs* [2222], of life), the Originator, Author, and Sustainer of life or the one who inaugurates and controls the Messianic experience of salvation here called *zōḗ*, life (Isa 60:16).

(3) Son of Man, *ho Huiós toú anthrṓpou* (*Huiós* [5207], son; *anthrṓpou* [444], of man). This expression occurs eighty-one times in the Gospels, thirty times in Matthew, of which nine passages have direct parallels in both Mark and Luke, four have parallels in Mark only, eight in Luke only, and the remaining nine are peculiar to Matthew.

5548. χρίω, chriō, *khree´-o;* probably akin to 5530 through the idea of *contact;* to *smear* or *rub* with oil, i.e. (by implication) to *consecrate* to an office or religious service:—anoint.

To daub, smear, anoint with oil or ointment, to rub oneself with oil. The practice of anointing is found throughout the biblical record. The following paragraphs discuss its practice and are based upon passages either referring to the concept or employing the key verbs *chríō* or *aleíphō* (218). It was a mark of luxury to use specially scented oils (Am 6:6) such as those Hezekiah kept in his treasure house (2Ki 20:13). The use of ointment was a sign of joy (Pr 27:9), and was discontinued during times of mourning (Da 10:3); thus Joab instructed the woman of Tekoa to appear unanointed before David (2Sa 14:2). On the death of Bathsheba's child, David anointed himself to show that his mourning had ended (2Sa 12:20). The cessation of anointing was to be a mark of God's displeasure if Israel proved rebellious (Dt 28:40; Mic 6:15), and the restoration of the custom was to be a sign of God's returning favor (Isa 61:3). Anointing is used as a symbol of prosperity in Ps 92:10; Ecc 9:8.

Before paying visits of ceremony, the head was anointed. So Naomi told Ruth to anoint herself before visiting Boaz (Ru 3:3). Oil of myrrh was used for this purpose in the harem of Ahasuerus (Est 2:12). This must have been a custom in Palestine as Simon's failure to show hospitality in this respect is commented upon by our Lord in Lk 7:46. Mary's anointing of our Lord was according to this custom.

Rubbing with oil was practiced among the Jews in pre-Christian times as well as by the Apostles (Mk 6:13), recommended by James (Jas 5:14), mentioned in the parable of the Good Samaritan (Lk 10:34), and used as a type of God's forgiving grace when healing the sin-sick soul (Isa 1:6; Eze 16:9). In Egypt and Palestine the application of ointment and spices to the dead body was customary (Mk 16:1; Lk 23:56; Jn 19:40). They were externally applied and did not prevent decomposition (Jn 11:39).

Anointing had the significance of dedication to God. Jacob consecrated the stones at Bethel by pouring oil upon them (Ge 28:18; 35:14), and God recognized the action (Ge 31:13). The tabernacle and its furniture were thus consecrated (Ex 30:26; 40:10; Le 8:11), and the altar of burnt offering was reconsecrated after the sin offering (Ex 29:36). Other offerings, however, were anointed with oil (Le 2:1ff.), but no oil was to be poured on the sin offering (Le 5:11; Nu 5:15).

Priests were set apart by anointing. In the case of Aaron and probably all high priests, this was done twice, first by pouring the holy oil on his head after his robing, but before the sacrifice of consecration (Le 8:12; Ps 133:2), and next by sprinkling after the sacrifice (Le 8:30). The ordinary priests were only sprinkled with oil after the application of the blood of the sacrifice. Hence the high priest is called the anointed priest (Le 4:3, 5).

Kings were designated by anointing, such as Saul (1Sa 10:1) and David (1Sa 16:13). This act was accompanied by the gift of the Spirit. So when David was anointed, the Spirit descended on him and departed from Saul. Also Hazael was anointed over Syria by God's command (1Ki 19:15). Kings thus designated were called the Lord's anointed. David thus speaks of Saul (1Sa 26:11) and of himself (Ps 2:2). This passage is used by the apostles as prophetic of Christ (Ac 4:26). By anointing, kings were installed into office. David was anointed when made king of Judah and a third time when made king of united Israel (2Sa 2:4; 5:3).

Anointing also was used metaphorically to mean setting apart for the prophetic office. Elijah was told to anoint Elisha although the actual event is left unrecorded in Scripture (1Ki 19:16). In Ps 105:15 the words "anointed" and "prophets" are used as synonyms. The servant of the Lord says that he is anointed to preach (Isa 61:1), and Christ tells the people of Nazareth that this prophecy is fulfilled in Him (Lk 4:18).

Similarly in a metaphorical sense someone chosen of God is called an anointed one. Thus Israel as a nation is called God's anointed (Ps 84:9; 89:38, 51; Hab 3:13) being promised deliverance on this account (1Sa 2:10). The name Christ comes from *chríō*, to anoint, equivalent to Messiah. The anointing of Ps 45:7 is taken in Heb 1:9 as prophetic of the Savior's anointing.

Before battle, shields were oiled so that their surfaces might be slippery and shining (Isa 21:5), as was done to the shield of Saul (2Sa 1:21).

NT uses:

(I) Of Jesus as the Messiah, the anointed King (cf. *Christós* [5547], Christ; Ac 4:27, as a prophet; Lk 4:18 from Isa 61:1). With the accusative (Heb 1:9 quoted from Psa 45:7).

(II) Of Christians as anointed or consecrated, set apart to the service and ministry of Christ and His gospel by the gift of the Holy Spirit (cf. *chrísma* [5545], anointing; 2Co 1:21).

Confusion arises in the NT when two distinct words, *chríō* which has a sacred or religious meaning, and *aleíphō* (218), to oil or rub with oil, are translated with the same English word "anoint," without any distinction between the meanings of the words. *Chríō* is consistently translated "anoint" in Lk 4:18; Ac 4:27; 10:38; 2Co 1:21; Heb 1:9. *Aleíphō*, which means to besmear, rub, oil, with a mundane, non-sacred meaning, is also translated "anoint" in every instance of its occurrence (Mt 6:17; Mk 6:13; 16:1; Lk 7:38, 46; Jn 11:2; 12:3; Jas 5:14). Since the English translation "anoint" also bears the connotation of sacredness, dedication, and *aleíphō* does not, and since both words are translated by the same word, much confusion has arisen in the exegesis of the passages (especially where *aleíphō* occurs). Because of the distinction that exists between these two words, it is necessary for us to examine the passages where each occurs.

The verb *aleíphō*, meaning to besmear or oil, is found in Mt 6:17: "But thou when thou fastest, anoint [*áleipsai*, the aor. imper. sing. of *aleíphō*] thine head, and wash thy face." The meaning here is evidently that the person who was fasting should use ointment so that his face would look refreshed and not express a sad countenance. The word here has nothing to do with ceremonial anointing. In Mk 6:13, "and they cast out many devils [demons], and anointed [*ḗleiphon*, the imperfect of *aleíphō*, they were rubbing with oil as a medicinal means] with oil many that were sick, and healed them." Some have argued that because the works performed here were undoubtedly supernatural then the anointing must have been sacral in nature. Two problems hamper this position. First of all, in sacral anointings, the oil is viewed largely as a visible symbol along with which divine activity occurs. No efficacy is attached to the element itself. God works, we might say, supranaturally (above nature) and coordinately with the human action. However, in the case at hand, the application of oil was an instance of a common medical procedure of that day and was looked upon as the immediate agent of healing. That the healings were instantaneous and thoroughly effectual indeed required a special work by God to accelerate the process and exaggerate the results of the oil's healing power. Yet here God's work was not supranatural (above nature) but supernatural (within nature but extending the normal limits) operating through the oil and not simply alongside it. Lastly, the ritual mode in which sacral anointings were usually administered and the mystery in which they were shrouded are conspicuously absent from this scene. The disciples here are not priestly officials performing cultic ritual; they are the representatives of Jesus sent out to proclaim in word and deed the gospel. In fact, the significance of Jesus' circumventing the Levitical body and its work is critical in understanding the import of the disciples' action. Such a gesture was in effect invalidating or treating as obsolete the OT order and signaling the inception of the NT. In this new economy, all men are priests and all things are sacred. In this light, it would be possible to speak of these healings as quasi-sacramental. Nevertheless, the context of the passage and the teaching of Scripture on the subject would not allow one to classify the disciples' deed as strictly sacral.

Elsewhere, we see that oil was used for medicinal means as in the parable of the Good Samaritan (Lk 10:34) and also in Jas 5:14 where "anointing him with oil" is *aleípsantes* (aor. act. participle of *aleíphō*) which means "having rubbed the sick person with oil" (a.t.). The injunction by James is that medicinal means should be applied prior to prayer. It is to be remembered that as priests were to show concern for the body, so also the elders of the local church. In Mk 16:1: "And when the Sabbath was passed, Mary Magdalene, and Mary the mother of James, and Salome, had brought sweet spices, that they might come and anoint [*aleípsōsin*, aor. act. subjunctive 3d person plural] him," which clearly meant the application of ointments and spices to the dead body as was customary in Palestine (Lk 23:56; Jn 19:40). Such an application of ointment did not have any resurrection power, nor was it meant to prevent decomposition (Jn 11:39).

However, the distinction between *chríō* and *aleíphō*, while consistently drawn within the NT, is not as clear in the Sept. (Ex 40:15) and especially in patristic writings.

Deriv.: *egchríō* (1472), to anoint, rub in, besmear; *epichríō* (2025), to anoint; *chrísma* (5545), an anointing; *Christós* (5547), Anointed, the Christ.

5549. χρονίζω, chronizō, *khron-id´-zo*; from 5550; to take time, i.e. linger:—delay, tarry.

Of uncertain derivation; a space of *time* (in general, and thus properly distinguished from 2540, which designates a *fixed* or special occasion; and from 165, which denotes a particular *period*) or *interval*; by extensive an individual *opportunity*; by implication *delay*:— + years old, season, space, (× often-) time (-s), (a) while.

5550. χρόνος, chronos, *khron´-os*; of uncertain derivative; a space of time (in general, and thus properly distinguished from 2540, which designates a fixed or special occasion; and from 165, which denotes a particular period) or interval; by extensive an individual opportunity; by implication delay:— + years old, season, space, (5 often-) time (-s), (a) while.

This word perceives time quantitatively as a period measured by the succession of objects and events and denotes the passing of moments. Another word, *kairós* (2540), season, the time of accomplishment, considers time qualitatively as a period characterized by the influence or prevalence of something. *Chrónos* is a period of measured time, not a period of accomplishment as *kairós*. *Chrónos* embraces all possible *kairoí* (pl.), and is often used as the larger and more inclusive term, but not the converse. In the NT:

(I) Time, particularly and generally.

(A) Mk 9:21; Lk 4:5; Ac 7:23; 14:3, 28; 15:33; 18:23; 27:9; Gal 4:4; Heb 11:32; Rev 2:21; 10:6. With the prep.: *diá* (1223), for (Heb 5:12); *ek* (1537), from (Lk 8:27, "from long times" [a.t.]); *en* (1722), in (Ac 1:21, "at all times" [a.t.]; Sept.: Jos 4:24); *epí* (1909), upon (Lk 18:4, "for a time" [a.t.]; Ac 18:20; Ro 7:1; 1Co 7:39; Gal 4:1); *metá* (3326), after (Mt 25:19, "after a long time"; Heb 4:7).

(B) In the accusative *chrónon*, sing.; *chrónous*, plural, marking duration, time, how long (Mk 2:19; Lk 20:9; Jn 5:6; 7:33; 12:35; 14:9; Ac 13:18; 19:22; 20:18; 1Co 16:7; Rev 6:11; 20:3; Sept.: Dt 12:19; 22:19; Jos 4:14; Isa 54:7.

(C) Dat. *chrónō*, sing.; *chrónois*, plural, marking time meaning when, in, or during which (Lk 8:29, "oftentimes," in, during, since long time; Ac 8:11; Ro 16:25).

(II) Specifically by the force of adjuncts *chrónos* sometimes stands for a time, season, period, like *kairós* (Ac 1:7; 1Th 5:1). Followed by the gen. of event or the like (Mt 2:7; Lk 1:57; Ac 3:21; 7:17; 17:30; 1Pe 1:17; 4:3); with an adj. pron. (Mt 2:16; 2Ti 1:9; Tit 1:2; 1Pe 1:20).

Deriv.: *makrochrónios* (3118), long-lived; *chronízō* (5549), to while away time; *chronotribéō* (5551), to spend time.

Syn.: *hṓra* (5610), hour; *hēméra* (2250), day as referring to a period of time; *diástēma* (1292), an interval, space; *étos* (2094) and *eniautós* (1763), a year; *stigmḗ* (4743), moment.

5551. χρονοτριβέω, chronotribeō, *khron-ot-rib-eh´-o*; from a presumed compound of 5550 and the base of 5147; to be a *time-wearer*, i.e. to *procrastinate* (*linger*):—spend time.

5552. χρύσεος, chruseos, *khroo´-seh-os*; from 5557; made *of gold*:—of gold, golden.

5553. χρυσίον, chrusiŏn, *khroo-see´-on*; diminutive of 5557; a *golden* article, i.e. gold plating, ornament, or coin:—gold.

5554. χρυσοδακτύλιος, chrusodaktulios, *khroo-sod-ak-too´-lee-os*; from 5557 and 1146; *gold-ringed*, i.e. *wearing* a golden finger-ring or similar *jewelry*:—with a gold ring.

5555. χρυσόλιθος, chrusolithos, *khroo-sol´-ee-thos*; from 5557 and 3037; *gold-stone*, i.e. a *yellow gem* ("*chrysolite*"):—chrysolite.

5556. χρυσόπρασος, chrusoprasos, *khroo-sop´-ras-os*; from 5557 and **πράσον, *prason*** (a *leek*); a *greenish-yellow* gem ("*chrysoprase*"):—chrysoprase.

5557. χρυσός, chrusos, *khroo-sos´*; perhaps from the base of 5530 (through the idea of the *utility* of the metal); *gold*; by extensive a *golden* article, as an ornament or coin:—gold.

5558. χρυσόω, chrusoō, *khroo-so´-o*; from 5557; to *gild*, i.e. *bespangle* with golden ornaments:—deck.

5559. χρώς, chrōs, *khroce*; probably akin to the base of 5530 through the idea of *handling*; the *body* (properly its *surface* or *skin*):—body.

5560. χωλός, chōlos, *kho-los´*; apparently a primary word; "*halt*", i.e. *limping*:—cripple, halt, lame.

5561. χώρα, chōra, *kho´-rah*; feminine of a derivative of the base of 5490 through the idea of *empty* expanse; *room*, i.e. a space of *territory* (more or less extensive; often including its inhabitant):—coast, county, fields, ground, land, region. Compare 5117.

5562. χωρέω, chōreō, *kho-reh´-o*; from 5561; to *be* in (*give*) *space*, i.e. (intransitive) to *pass, enter*, or (transitive) to *hold, admit* (literal or figurative):—come, contain, go, have place, (can, be room to) receive.

5563. χωρίζω, chōrizō, *kho-rid´-zo*; from 5561; to *place room* between, i.e. *part*; reflexive to *go away*:—depart, put asunder, separate.

5564. χωρίον, chōrion, *kho-ree´-on*; diminutive of 5561; a *spot* or *plot* of ground:—field, land, parcel of ground, place, possession.

5565. χωρίς, chōris, *kho-rece´*; adverb from 5561; *at a space*, i.e. *separately* or *apart* from (often as preposition):—beside, by itself, without.

5566. χῶρος, chōros, *kho´-ros*; of Latin origin; the *north-west* wind:—north west.

5567. ψάλλω, psallō, *psal´-lo*; probably strengthened from **ψάω, *psaō*** (to *rub* or *touch* the surface; compare 5597); to *twitch* or *twang*, i.e. to *play* on a stringed instrument (*celebrate* the divine worship *with music* and accompanying odes):—make melody, sing (psalms).

5568. ψαλμός, psalmos, *psal-mos´*; from 5567; a set piece of *music*, i.e. a sacred *ode* (accompanied with the voice, harp or other instrument; a "*psalm*"); collective the book of the *Psalms*:—psalm. Compare 5603.

A noun from *psállō* (5567), to sing, chant. Originally a touching, and then a touching of the harp or other stringed instruments with the finger or with the plectrum; later known as the instrument itself, and finally it became known as the song sung with musical accompaniment. This latest stage of its meaning was adopted in the Sept. In all probability the psalms of Eph 5:19; Col 3:16 are the inspired Psalms of the Hebrew Canon (Sept.: Ps 95:1. In superscripts, Ps 3; 4; 5). Specifically of the Psalms as a part of the OT (Lk 20:42; 24:44; Ac 1:20; 13:33). The word certainly designates these on all other occasions when it occurs in the NT, with the one possible exception of 1Co 14:26. These are the old songs to which new hymns and praises are added (Rev 5:9).

Syn.: *húmnos* (5215), a hymn, religious ode; *ōdḗ* (5603) song of praise.

5569. ψευδάδελφος, pseudadelphos, *psyoo-dad´-el-fos*; from 5571 and 80; a *spurious brother*, i.e. *pretended associate*:—false brethren.

A noun from *pseudḗs* (5571), false, and *adelphós* (80), brother. A false brother. In Gal 2:4 it denotes those who had become outwardly members of the Christian church, sharers in its fellowship of life and love, but in reality were not so inwardly. Therefore, they had no right to be counted as brothers. They had the companionship of the brothers but the real kinship of spiritual life was missing (see 2Co 11:26).

5570. ψευδαπόστολος, pseudapostolos, *psyoo-dap-os´-tol-os*; from 5571 and 652; a *spurious apostle*, i.e. *pretended preacher*:—false teacher.

5571. ψευδής, pseudēs, *psyoo-dace´*; from 5574; *untrue*, i.e. *erroneous, deceitful; wicked*:—false, liar.

5572. ψευδοδιδάσκαλος, pseudodidaskalos, *psyoo-dod-id-as´-kal-os*; from 5571 and 1320; a *spurious teacher*, i.e. *propagator* of *erroneous* Christian *doctrine*:—false teacher.

A noun from *pseudḗs* (5571), false, and *didáskalos* (1320), a teacher. A false teacher or one who pretends to be a Christian teacher but teaches false doctrine (2Pe 2:1).

5573. ψευδολόγος, pseudologos, *psyoo-dol-og´-os*; from 5571 and 3004; *mendacious*, i.e. *promulgating erroneous* Christian *doctrine*:—speaking lies.

5574. ψεύδομαι, pseudomai, *psyoo´-dom-ahee*; middle of an apparently primary verb; to *utter an untruth* or attempt to *deceive* by falsehood:—falsely, lie.

5575. ψευδομάρτυρ, pseudomartur, *psyoo-dom-ar´-toor*; from 5571 and a kindred form of 3144; a *spurious witness*, i.e. *bearer of untrue testimony*:—false witness.

5576. ψευδομαρτυρέω, pseudomartureō, *psyoo-dom-ar-too-reh´-o*; from 5575; to *be an untrue testifier*, i.e. offer *falsehood in evidence*:—be a false witness.

5577. ψευδομαρτυρία, pseudomarturia, *psyoo-dom-ar-too-ree´-ah*; from 5575; *untrue testimony*:—false witness.

5578. ψευδοπροφήτης, pseudoprophētēs, *psyoo-dop-rof-ay´-tace*; from 5571 and 4396; a *spurious prophet*, i.e. *pretended foreteller* or religious *impostor*:—false prophet.

5579. ψεῦδος, pseudos, *psyoo´-dos*; from 5574; a *falsehood*:—lie, lying.

5580. ψευδόχριστος, pseudochristos, *psyoo-dokh´-ris-tos*; from 5571 and 5547; a *spurious Messiah*:—false Christ.

A noun from *pseudḗs* (5571), false, and *Christós* (5547), Christ. False christ (Mt 24:24; Mk 13:22). The false christ does not necessarily deny the existence of Christ. On the contrary, he builds on the world's expectations of such a person, while he blasphemously appropriates these to himself and affirms that he is the foretold One in whom God's promises and the saint's expectations are fulfilled. He is of the same character as the *antíchristos* (500), antichrist, who opposes the true Christ (1Jn 4:3). The *pseudóchristos* affirms himself to be the Christ. Both are against the Christ of God. The final antichrist will also be a pseudochrist as well. He will usurp to himself Christ's offices, presenting himself to the world as the true center of its hopes, the satisfier of all its needs, and the healer of all its ills. He will be a pseudochrist and antichrist in one.

5581. ψευδώνυμος, pseudōnumos, *psyoo-do´-noo-mos*; from 5571 and 3686; *untruly named*:—falsely so called.

5582. ψεῦσμα, pseusma, *psyoos´-mah*; from 5574; a *fabrication*, i.e. *falsehood*:—lie.

5583. ψεύστης, pseustēs, *psyoos-tace´*; from 5574; a *falsifier*:—liar.

5584. ψηλαφάω, psēlaphaō, *psay-laf-ah´-o*; from the base of 5567 (compare 5586); to *manipulate*, i.e. *verify* by contact; (figurative) to *search* for:—feel after, handle, touch.

To feel an object or to feel for or after an object (Lk 24:39; Ac 17:27; Heb 12:18; 1Jn 1:1; Sept.: Ge 27:12, 21, 22).

Deriv.: of *psáō* (n.f.), to touch lightly: *psállō* (5567), to play a stringed instrument; *psḗphos* (5586), a small stone; *psichíon* (5589), a crumb; *psōmíon* (5596), a sop; *psṓchō* (5597), to rub.

Syn.: *háptomai* (680), to touch, cling to, lay hold of; *thiggánō* (2345), to touch by way of inquiry, to handle.

5585. ψηφίζω, psēphizō, *psay-fid´-zo*; from 5586; to *use pebbles* in enumeration, i.e. (genitive) to *compute*:—count.

5586. ψῆφος, psēphos, *psay´-fos*; from the same as 5584; a *pebble* (as worn smooth by *handling*), i.e. (by implication of use as a *counter* or *ballot*) a *verdict* (of acquittal) or *ticket* (of admission); a *vote*:—stone, voice.

5587. ψιθυρισμός, psithurismos, *psith-oo-ris-mos´*; from a derivative of **ψίθος**, ***psithŏs*** (a *whisper*; by implication a *slander*; probably akin to 5574); *whispering*, i.e. secret *detraction*:—whispering.

5588. ψιθυριστής, psithuristēs, *psith-oo-ris-tace´*; from the same as 5587; a secret *calumniator*:—whisperer.

A noun from *psithurízō* (n.f.), to whisper. A whisperer, a secret slanderer. It is similar to *katálalos* (2637), an accuser, a backbiter who does his slandering openly (Ro 1:29). Also from *psithurízō* (n.f.): *psithurismós* (5587), a whispering.

5589. ψιχίον, psichion, *psikh-ee´-on*; diminutive from a derivative of the base of 5567 (meaning a *crumb*); a *little bit* or *morsel*:—crumb.

5590. ψυχή, psuchē, *psoo-khay´*; from 5594; *breath*, i.e. (by implication) *spirit*, abstract or concrete (the *animal* sentient principle only; thus distinguished on the one hand from 4151, which is the rational and immortal *soul*; and on the other from 2222, which is mere *vitality*, even of plants: these terms thus exactly correspond respectively to the Hebrew 5315, 7307 and 2416):—heart (+ -ily), life, mind, soul, + us, + you.

The soul, that immaterial part of man held in common with animals. One's understanding of this word's relationship to related terms is contingent upon his position regarding biblical anthropology. Dichotomists view man as consisting of two parts (or substances), material and immaterial, with spirit and soul denoting the immaterial and bearing only a functional and not a metaphysical difference. Trichotomists also view man as consisting of two parts (or substances), but with spirit and soul representing in some contexts a real subdivision of the immaterial. This latter view is here adopted. Accordingly, *psuchḗ* is contrasted to *sṓma* (4983), body, and *pneúma* (4151), spirit (1Th 5:23). The *psuchḗ*, no less than the *sárx* (4561), flesh, belongs to the lower region of man's being. Sometimes *psuchḗ* stands for the immaterial part of man made up of the soul (*psuchḗ* in the restrictive sense of the life element), and the spirit *pneúma*. However, animals are not said to possess a spirit; this is only in man, giving him the ability to communicate with God. Also breath (Sept.: Ge 1:30; Job 41:12), and in the NT, usually meaning the vital breath, the life element through which the body lives and feels, the principle of life manifested in the breath.

(I) The soul as the vital principle, the animating element in men and animals.

(A) Generally (Lk 12:20; Ac 20:10; Sept.: Ge 35:18; 1Ki 17:21). Of beasts (Rev 8:9).

(B) Metonymically, for life itself (Mt 6:25; 20:28; Mk 3:4; 10:45; Lk 6:9; 12:22, 23; 14:26; 21:19; Ac 15:26; 20:24; 27:10, 22; Ro 16:4; Php 2:30; 1Th 2:8; Rev 12:11). To lay down one's life (Jn 10:11, 15, 17; 13:37, 38; 15:13; 1Jn 3:16). To seek one's life (Mt 2:20; Ro 11:3; Sept.: Ex 4:19). Including the idea of life or the spirit, both natural and eternal (Mt 16:26; Mk 8:36, 37 [cf. Lk 9:25]). In antithetic declarations of the Lord Jesus, *psuchḗ* refers not only to natural life, but also to life as continued beyond the grave (Mt 10:39; 16:25; Mk 8:35; Lk 9:24; 17:33; Jn 12:25). Generally, the soul of man, his spiritual and immortal nature with its higher and lower powers, its rational and natural faculties (Mt 10:28; 2Co 1:23; Heb 6:19; 10:39; 13:17; Jas 1:21; 5:20; 1Pe 1:9; 2:11, 25; 4:19). Generally the soul (1Co 15:45, a living soul in allusion to Ge 2:7; Rev 16:3; Sept.: Ge 1:24; 2:19; 9:10, 12, 15).

(C) Of a departed soul, separate from the body; spoken in Greek mythology of the ghosts inhabiting Hades (Ac 2:27, 31, quoted from Ps 16:10; Rev 6:9; 20:4).

(II) Specifically the soul as the sentient principle, the seat of the senses, desires, affections, appetites, passions, the lower aspect of one's nature. Distinguished in Pythagorean and Platonic philosophy from the higher rational nature, expressed by *noús* (3563), mind, and *pneúma* (4151), spirit belonging to man only. This distinction is also followed by the Sept. and sometimes in the NT (cf. *pneúma* [4151], spirit, II, B). In 1Th 5:23 the whole man is indicated as consisting of spirit, soul, and body; soul and spirit, the immaterial part of man upon which the word of God is operative (Heb 4:12); "my soul . . . and my spirit," the immaterial part of personality with which Mary could magnify the Lord (Lk 1:46, 47). Distinguished from *diánoia* (1271), understanding or mind, because soul is related to the affections (Mt 22:37; Mk 12:30; Lk 10:27). From *súnesis* (4907), the ability to put facts together, knowledge, understanding, intellect (Mk 12:33). Sometimes the soul means the mind, feelings (Mt 11:29; Lk 2:35; Jn 10:24; Ac 14:2, 22; 15:24; Heb 12:3; 1Pe 1:22; 2Pe 2:8, 14; Sept.: Ex 23:9; 1Sa 1:15; Isa 44:19). "With all one's soul" (a.t.) means with his entire affection (Mt 22:37; Mk 12:30, 33; Lk 10:27; Sept.: Dt 26:16; 30:2, 6, 10; 2Ch 15:15; 31:21); *Ek psuchḗs* (*ek* [1537], out of), "from the soul" (a.t.), meaning heartily (Eph 6:6; Col 3:23). To be of one soul means to be unanimous, united in affection and will (Ac 4:32; Php 1:27). That which strictly belongs to the person himself, often ascribed to the soul as the seat of the desires, affections, and appetites (Mt 12:18; 26:38; Mk 14:34; Lk 1:46; 12:19; Jn 12:27; Heb 10:38; 3Jn 2; Rev 18:14; Sept.: Ge 27:4, 19; Isa 1:14; 33:18).

(III) Metonymically, a soul, a living thing in which is *hē psuchḗ*, life.

(A) More often of a man, a soul, a living person, *pása psuchḗ* (*pás* [3956], every), every soul, every person, everyone (Ac 2:43; 3:23; Ro 13:1). In a periphrasis, *pása psuchḗ anthrṓpou* ([444], man), "every soul of man" meaning every man (Ro 2:9); *psuchás anthrṓpōn*, "souls of men" (a.t. [Lk 9:56 {TR}; simply *psuchḗ*, Sept.: Ge 17:14; Le 5:1, 2; Dt 24:8]). *Psuchḗ anthrṓpou*, soul of man (Num. 19:11, 13). In enumerations (Ac 2:41, "about three thousand souls"; 7:14; 27:37; 1Pe 3:20; Sept.: Ge 46:15, 18, 26, 27; Ex 1:5; Dt 10:22).

(B) Specifically for a servant, slave (Rev 18:13), probably female slaves in distinction from the preceding *sṓmata* (4983), bodies (cf. *ánthrōpos* [444], man, I, C, 5); Sept.: Ge 12:5.

Deriv.: *ápsuchos* (895), lifeless, inanimate, without life; *dípsuchos* (1374), two-souled, double minded; *isópsuchos* (2473), like-minded; *oligópsuchos* (3642), little-souled, of little spirit, fainthearted, fearful; *súmpsuchos* (4861), joint-souled, agreeing with one accord; *psuchikós* (5591), natural, physical, pertaining to the animal instinct in man.

Syn.: *kardía* (2588), the heart as the seat of life; *diánoia* (1271), understanding; *zōḗ* (2222), life as a principle; *bíos* (979), possessions of life; *bíōsis* (981), the spending of one's life; *agōgḗ* (72), conduct; *noús* (3563), mind, the seat of reflective consciousness; *pneúma* (4151), spirit, only in man as the means of communication with God while soul is held in common with animals as the consciousness of one's environment.

5591. ψυχικός, psuchikos, *psoo-khee-kos´*; from 5590; *sensitive*, i.e. *animate* (in distinction on the one hand from 4152, which is the higher or *renovated* nature; and on the other from 5446, which is the lower or *bestial* nature):—natural, sensual.

An adjective meaning soul, the part of the immaterial life held in common with the animals, as contrasted with spirit (*pneúma* [4151]), only in man, enabling him to communicate with God. Natural, pertaining to the natural as distinguished from the spiritual or glorified nature of man. First Corinthians 15:44 refers to a body *psuchikón*, a body governed by the soul or natural and fallen instinct of man, and a body *pneumatikón* (4152), spiritual, governed by the divine quality in man, the spirit. Rendered as "natural" in 1Co 2:14; 15:44, 46 and sensual in Jas 3:15; Jude 19. The term *psuchikós* is not a word of honor even as *sarkikós* (4559), carnal, is not.

5592. ψύχος, psuchos, *psoo´-khos*; from 5594; *coolness*:—cold.

5593. ψυχρός, psuchros, *psoo-chros´*; from 5592; *chilly* (literal or figurative):—cold.

5594. ψύχω, psuchō, *psoo´-kho*; a primary verb; to *breathe* (*voluntarily* but *gently*; thus differing on the one hand from 4154, which denotes properly a *forcible* respiration; and on the other from the base of 109, which refers properly to an inanimate *breeze*), i.e. (by implication of reduction of temperature by evaporation) to *chill* (figurative):—wax cold.

To breathe, blow, refresh with cool air, or breathe naturally. It is from this verb that *psuchḗ* (5590), soul, is derived. Hence *psuchḗ* is the breath of a living creature, animal life, and *psúchō* in the pass. *psúchomai*, means to be cool, to grow cool or cold in a spiritual sense, as in Christian love (Mt 24:12).

Deriv.: *anapsúchō* (404), to make cool, refresh; *apopsúchō* (674), to be faint of heart; *ekpsúchō* (1634), to expire, die; *katapsúchō* (2711), to cool off; *psuchḗ* (5590), soul; *psúchos* (5592), cold; *psuchrós* (5593), cool, fresh, chilly.

5595. ψωμίζω, psōmizō, *pso-mid´-zo*; from the base of 5596; to *supply* with *bits*, i.e. (genitive) to *nourish*:—(bestow to) feed.

5596. ψωμίον, psōmion, *pso-mee´-on*; diminutive from a derivative of the base of 5597; a *crumb* or *morsel* (as if *rubbed* off), i.e. a *mouthful*:—sop.

5597. ψώχω, psōchō, *pso´-kho*; prolonged from the same base as 5567; to *triturate*, i.e. (by analogy) to *rub* out (kernels from husks with the fingers or hand):—rub.

5598. Ω, Ō, *o´-meg-ah*; the last letter of the Greek alphabet, i.e. (figurative) the *finality*:—Omega.

5599. ὦ, ō, *o*; a primary interjection; as a sign of the vocative *O*; as a note of exclamation, *oh*:—O.

5600. ὦ, ō, *o*; including the oblique forms, as well as **ἦς**, *ēs, ace*; **ἦ**, *ē, ay*; etc.; the subjunctive of 1510; (*may, might, can, could, would, should, must*, etc.; also with 1487 and its comparative, as well as with other particles) *be*:— + appear, are, (may, might, should) be, × have, is, + pass the flower of her age, should stand, were.

5601. Ὠβήδ, Ōbēd, *o-bade´*; of Hebrew origin [5744]; *Obed*, an Israelite:—Obed.

5602. ὧδε, hōde, *ho´-deh*; from an adverbial form of 3592; *in this* same spot, i.e. *here* or *hither*:—here, hither, (in) this place, there.

5603. ᾠδή, ōidē, *o-day´*; from 103; a *chant* or "*ode*" (the genitive term for any words sung; while 5215 denotes especially a *religious* metrical composition, and 5568 still more specially a *Hebrew* cantillation):—song.

The original use of singing among both believers and idolaters was in the confessions and praises of the respective gods. Paul qualifies it in Eph 5:19; Col 3:16 as spiritual songs in association with psalms and hymns, because *ōdḗ* by itself might mean any kind of song, as of battle, harvest, festal, whereas *psalmós* (5568), psalm, from its Hebrew use, and *húmnos* (5215), hymn, from its Greek use, did not require any such qualifying adj. In Rev 5:9; 14:3 *ōdḗ* is designated as *kainḗ* (2537), qualitatively new; in Rev 15:3 as the *ōdḗ* of Moses as celebrating the deliverance of God's people, and the *ōdḗ* of the Lamb as celebrating redemption by atoning sacrifice (Sept.: Jgs 5:12; 1Ki 4:32; Ps 42:8).

Syn.: *húmnos* (5215), hymn; *psalmós* (5568), psalm.

5604. ὠδίν, ōdin, *o-deen´*; akin to 3601; a *pang* or *throe*, especially of childbirth:—pain, sorrow, travail.

A noun meaning pain, sorrow. Used in the sing. when referring to the pain of childbirth (1Th 5:3). Used in the plural when warning of the sorrows that would follow wars, famines and other catastrophes (Mt 24:8; Mk 13:8; Sept.: Job 21:17; Na 2:10). In Ac 2:24 the *ōdínas thanátou*, the cords or snares of death in allusion to Ps 18:4, 5.

Deriv.: *sunōdínō* (4944), to be in travail together; *ōdínō* (5605), to be in pain, travail.

Syn.: *pónos* (4192), pain of any kind; *lúpē* (3077), sorrow; *móchthos* (3449), labor, travail; *stenochōría* (4730), anguish; *sunochḗ* (4928), pressure, anguish; *thlípsis* (2347), affliction.

5605. ὠδίνω, ōdinō, *o-dee´-no*; from 5604; to *experience* the *pains* of parturition (literal or figurative):—travail in (birth).

A noun denoting labor pain at the birth of a child. Intransitively, to be in pain as when a woman is in travail (Gal 4:27; Rev 12:2, in both cases applied spiritually to the Church; see Sept.: SS 8:5; Isa 23:4; 26:18; 66:7, 8); transitively with an accusative, to travail in birth of, to be in labor with (Gal 4:19 where Paul applies it in a spiritual sense to himself with respect to the Galatian converts).

Deriv.: *sunōdínō* (4944), to travail together.

Syn.: *tíktō* (5088), to bear, produce, give birth; *basanízō* (928), torture, torment; *skúllō* (4660), to vex, annoy, trouble; *stenochōréō* (4729), to anguish; *kataponéō* (2669), to toil, afflict, oppress.

5606. ὦμος, ōmos, *o´-mos*; perhaps from the alternant of 5342; the *shoulder* (as that on which burdens are *borne*):—shoulder.

5607. ὤν, ōn, *oan*; including the feminine **οὖσα, ŏusa,** *oo´-sah*; and the neuter **ὄν, ŏn,** *on*; presumed participle of 1510; *being*:—be, come, have.

5608. ὠνέομαι, ōneomai, *o-neh´-om-ahee*; middle from an apparently primary **ὦνος, ōnos** (a *sum* or *price*); to *purchase* (synonym with the earlier 4092):—buy.

5609. ὠόν, ōon, *o-on´*; apparently a primary word; an "*egg*":—egg.

5610. ὥρα, hōra, *ho´-rah*; apparently a primary word; an "*hour*" (literal or figurative):—day, hour, instant, season, × short, [even-]tide, (high) time.

A noun meaning hour, a time, season, a definite space or division of time recurring at fixed intervals, as marked by natural or conventional limits. Figuratively, of a season of life, the fresh, full bloom and beauty of youth, the ripeness and vigor of manhood meaning bloom, beauty. In the NT, of shorter intervals, a time, season, hour.

(I) Of the day generally, daytime (Mt 14:15; Mk 6:35; 11:11).

(II) Of a definite part or division of the day, in earlier writers used only of the greater divisions as morning, noon, evening, night. In the NT, an hour, one of the twelve equal parts into which the natural day and also the night were divided, and which of course, were of different lengths at different seasons of the year.

(A) Particularly and generally (Mt 24:36; 25:13; Mk 13:32; Lk 22:59; Jn 4:52; 11:9; Ac 5:7; 10:30; Rev 9:15). Dat. with *én* (1722), in, of time, when (Mt 8:13; 10:19; 24:50; Lk 12:46; Jn 4:53). Accusative of time, meaning how long (Mt 26:40; Mk 14:37; Ac 19:34). With a numeral marking the hour of the day, as counted from sunrise (Mt 20:3, 5, 6, 9; 27:45, 46; Mk 15:25, 33, 34; Lk 23:44; Jn 1:39; 4:6; 19:14; Ac 2:15; 3:1; 10:3, 9, 30). Of the hours of the nights as counted from sunset (Ac 23:23).

(B) Figuratively meaning a short time, a brief interval, in the accusative (Rev 17:12); dat. (Rev 18:10, 17, 19). With *prós* (4314), toward (Jn 5:35; 2Co 7:8; Gal 2:5; 1Th 2:17; Phm 15).

(III) Metonymically and generally, an hour meaning a time or period as spoken of any definite point or space of time.

(A) With adjuncts such as an adj. or pron. as *apó tḗs hṓras ekeínēs* (*apó* [575], from; *ekeínēs* [gen. fem. of *ekeínos* {1565}, that]), from that hour or that period (Mt 9:22; 15:28; 17:18; Jn 19:27); with *autḗ* (fem. dat. of *autós* [846], this one, *autḗ tḗ hṓra*), at this time. Dat. of time, when (Lk 2:38; 24:33; Ac 16:18; 22:13; Sept.: Da 3:6, 15); with the interrogative *poía* the fem dat. of *poíos* (4169), which (*Poía hṓra* or *hḗ hṓra* [dat. fem. of *hós* {3739}, which], what hour [Mt 24:42, 44; Lk 12:39, 40]); with *en* ([1722], in; *en autḗ tḗ hṓra*), in that same hour (Lk 7:21; 10:21; 12:12; 20:19); with *en ekeínē tḗ hṓra*, at that time (Mt 10:19; 18:1; 26:55; Mk 13:11; Rev 11:13). With *áchri* (891), until, *áchri tḗs árti* ([*árti* {737}, the present]), until the present time (1Co 4:11). With *pásan* (3956), every, *pásan hṓran*, every hour meaning all the time (1Co 15:30; Sept.: Ex 18:22, 26). With an adverb or relative pron.; *érchetai hṓra hóte* (*érchetai* [2064] the present indic. 3d person sing. of *érchomai*, I come; *hóte* [3753], when), there comes an hour when (Jn 4:21, 23; 5:25; 16:25); followed by *en* and the relative pron. (Jn 5:28). With *hína* (2443), so that (Jn 12:23; 13:1; 16:2, 32). With the gen. of thing, to be done or to happen (Sept.: Da 9:21, *tḗ hṓra toú deípnou* (*deípnou* [gen. sing. of *deípnon* {1173}, dinner, supper]), at the time of the supper or feast (Lk 1:10; 14:17); temptation (Rev 3:10); judgment (Rev 14:7, 15); one's own (time) (Lk 22:14). With the inf. (Ro 13:11; Sept.: Ge 29:7); the gen. of person, one's time, appointed to him in which he is to do or suffer (Lk 22:53; Jn 16:21), elsewhere of Christ (Jn 2:4; 7:30; 8:20; 13:1).

(B) Simply meaning the time spoken of or otherwise understood (Mt 26:45; Mk 14:41; Jn 16:4; 1Jn 2:18). Emphatically (Jn 17:1); by implication meaning time or hour of trial, sorrow, suffering (Mk 14:35; Jn 12:27).

Deriv.: *hēmiṓrion* (2256), a half hour; *hōraíos* (5611), attractive, comely.

Syn.: *hēméra* (2250), day, the period of natural light; *kairós* (2540), season, time, opportunity; *chrónos* (5550), time duration; *stigmḗ* (4743), instant, moment.

5611. ὡραῖος, hōraios, *ho-rah´-yos*; from 5610; *belonging* to the right *hour* or *season* (*timely*), i.e. (by implication) *flourishing* (*beauteous* [figurative]):—beautiful.

An adjective from *hṓra* (5610), hour, meaning attractive, comely. Figuratively of a virgin ready for marriage. In the NT only figuratively meaning fair, comely, beautiful, spoken of things (Mt 23:27; Ro 10:15; Sept.: Ge 2:9; 3:6). Of persons (Ge 29:17; 39:6); of a gate of the temple (Ac 3:2, 10), the Beautiful Gate supposed by some to have been the large gate leading from the court of the Gentiles to the court of the Israelites over against the eastern side of the temple, otherwise called the Gate of Nicanor. It was described by Josephus as covered with plates of gold and silver, and was very splendid and massive. However, from Ac 3:3, 8, it would seem rather to have been one of the external gates leading from without into the court of the Gentiles in which also was Solomon's porch (Ac 3:11).

Syn.: *kalós* (2570), beautiful, good; *kósmios* (2887), decorous.

5612. ὠρύομαι, ōruomai, *o-roo´-om-ahee*; middle of an apparently primary verb; to "*roar*":—roar.

5613. ὡς, hōs, *hoce*; probably adverb of comparative from 3739; *which how*, i.e. *in that manner* (very variously used, as follows):—about, after (that), (according) as (it had been, it were), as soon (as), even as (like), for, how (greatly), like (as, unto), since, so (that), that, to wit, unto, when ([-soever]), while, × with all speed.

A relative adverb from *hós* (3739), who, correlative to *pṓs* (4459), how, in what manner or way. As, so as, how, sometimes equivalent to a conjunction (cf. IV). For *hōs án*, as if, see *án* ([302], cf. II, A, 1, and B, 3).

(I) In comparisons. In Attic writers *hṓsper* (5618), just as, is the prevailing word in this usage.

(A) Particularly, fully, with the corresponding demonstrative adverb as *hoútōs* (3779), thus, or the like, either preceding or following, *hoútōs . . . hōs*, so . . . as (Mk 4:26; Jn 7:46, so as if; 1Co 3:15); *hōs amnós . . . hoútōs*, as . . . so (Ac 8:32 quoted from Isa 53:7; Ac 23:11); *hōs gár . . . oútō* (*gár* [1063], and, but, for, therefore; *oútō* [3779], thus), as therefore, "as . . . so also"; Ro 5:15, 18; 2Co 7:14; 11:3; 1Th 2:7; 5:2); *ísos . . . hōs*, (*ísos* [2470], similar, equal), the like, similar, equal gift . . . as (Ac 11:17). *Homoíōs kaí hṓs* (*homoíōs* [3668], similarly, likewise; *kaí* [2532], and), likewise also as (Lk 17:28); *hōs . . . kaí*, where *hoútōs* ([3779], thus) is strictly implied (cf. *kai* [2532], and, II, B). *Hōs en ouranṓ, kaí epí tḗs gḗs* (*ouranṓ* [3772], heaven; *gḗs* [1063], earth), as in heaven, also on earth (Mt 6:10; Ac 7:51; Gal 1:9). Frequently *hoútōs* is omitted and then *hōs* may often be rendered "so as" or simply "as" (Ac 7:37; Ro 4:17; 5:16). Sometimes the whole clause to which *hōs* refers is omitted as in Mk 4:31, "the kingdom of God" is omitted, which, however, occurs in 4:30.

(B) Generally before a noun or adj. in the nom. or accusative meaning as, like as, like (Mt 6:29; 10:25; Mk 1:22; 6:15; Lk 6:10, 40; 21:35; 10:3, 16; 13:43; 28:3; 22:31; Jn 15:6; Ac 11:5; 1Co 3:10; 14:33; Gal 4:12; 1Th 5:6; Heb 1:11; Heb 6:19; Jas 1:10; 1Pe 2:25; 1Jn 1:7; Jude 10; Rev 1:14; 8:1, 10; 10:1; 20:8; 22:1; Sept.: Jgs 8:18; 1Sa 25:36). Here, too, the construction is often elliptical, e.g., where a part. belonging to the noun before *hōs* is also implied with the noun after *hōs*, as in Lk 10:18 (cf. Mt 3:16; Mk 1:10). Also where the noun before *hōs* is also implied after it, as in Rev 1:10, "as [the voice] of a trumpet"; 16:3; Sept.: Jer 4:31. Sometimes the noun after *hōs* is implied before it (Rev 6:1, "saying with a voice, as it were, the voice of a thunder" [a.t.]). A noun preceded by *hōs* often denotes something like itself, a person or thing like that which the noun refers to, with the meaning "as it were" (Rev 4:6 [UBS], something like a sea of glass, as it were a sea of glass; 8:8, "as it were a great mountain"; 9:7, "as it were crowns like gold" or as if they were golden crowns; 15:2; Sept.: Da 10:18); accusative (Rev 19:1 [UBS], a sound like the voice; 9:6).

(II) Implying quality, character, circumstances as known or supposed to exist in any personal thing; something which is matter of belief or opinion, whether true or false.

(A) Before a part. referring to a preceding noun and expressing a quality or circumstance belonging to that noun, either real or supposed, meaning as, as if, as though. **(1)** Before a nom. as referring to a preceding subject (Lk 16:1, as wasting his goods, being so accounted; Ac 23:20, "as though they would inquire"; 28:19, "not as having" [a.t.], meaning not supposing that I have; 1Co 4:7; 5:3; 7:25; 2Co 6:9, 10; 10:14; 13:2; Col 2:20; 1Th 2:4; Heb 11:27; 13:3, 17; Jas 2:12; Sept.: Ge 27:12). With a part. implied (Eph 6:7; 1Pe 4:11). **(2)** Before a gen. referring to a preceding noun (Heb 12:27). Elliptically (Jn 1:14). Often with a gen. absolute (1Co 4:18, "they, supposing that I shall not come" [a.t.]; 2Co

5:20; 1Pe 4:12; 2Pe 1:3). After *prophásei*, the dat. of *próphasis* (4392), pretense (Ac 27:30, as though they would have cast). **(3)** Before a dat. referring to a preceding noun (Ac 3:12; 1Pe 2:14). **(4)** Before an accusative referring to a preceding object (Ac 23:15; Ro 6:13; 15:15; 2Co 10:2; Rev 5:6). **(5)** Once before an inf. apparently with a part. implied or perhaps instead of the part. construction (2Co 10:9).

(B) Before a substantive or adj. either as predicate or obj. expressing a quality or circumstance known or supposed to belong to a preceding noun, meaning as, as if, as though. Here the part. *ṓn* ([5607] masc., *oúsa* fem., *ón* neuter) or the like, may always be supplied, and the construction is then the same as in section II A above. **(1)** Before the nom. as referring to a preceding subject (Ro 3:7, "as though I were a sinner" [a.t.]; 2Co 6:4, 8, 10; 11:15; 13:7; Eph 5:1, 8, as it becomes children of the light, as they are supposed to walk; 6:6; Col 3:12, 22; Heb 3:5, 6; Jas 2:9; 1Pe 1:14; 2:2, 5, 16; 4:10, 15, 16). Once preceded by *toioútos* (5108), such a one (Phm 9, "being such a one as Paul the aged," such a one as you know Paul to be, your aged teacher and friend). **(2)** Before the gen. as referring to a preceding noun (1Pe 2:12; 3:16 [cf. II, A, 2 in text on word *hōs*]). **(3)** Before the dat. as referring to a preceding noun (1Co 3:1, "as unto spiritual"; 10:15; 2Co 6:13; Heb 12:5, 7; 1Pe 2:13; 3:7; 4:19; 2Pe 1:19), implied (1Pe 1:19). **(4)** Before the accusative as referring to another object (Mt 14:5; Lk 6:22; 15:19; Ro 1:21; 1Co 4:9, 14; 8:7; 2Co 11:16; Heb 11:9). Preceded by *hoútōs* (3779), thus, *hoútōs hōs*, thus as (2Co 9:5).

(C) Before prep. with their cases in the same manner as before part. (cf. II, A). **(1)** With *diá* (1223), through (2Th 2:2); *en* (1722), in (Jn 7:10; Ro 13:13); *ek* (1537), out of, of (Ro 9:32 [cf. 9:31]; 2Co 2:17; 3:5; 1Pe 4:11); *epí* (1909), upon (Mt 26:55, "as though against a robber" [a.t.]; Gal 3:16). **(2)** Before a prep. implying motion to a place, *hōs* qualifies the force of the prep. meaning as if to, toward, in the direction of, leaving it undetermined whether one arrives at the place or not. Used in the NT only once with *epí* (Ac 17:14, "as toward the sea" [a.t.]).

(D) Before numerals meaning as if it were, about, marking a supposed or conjectural number (Mk 5:13, about two thousand; 8:9; Lk 2:37; 8:42; Jn 6:19; 21:8; Ac 1:15; 5:7; 19:34; Sept.: Ru 1:4).

(E) Intensive meaning how! how very! how much! expressing admiration. In the NT only before adj., see below III, C (Ro 10:15, how beautiful the feet; 11:33). Once before the comparative (Ac 17:22, how much more religiously inclined do I behold you than other cities or nations; Sept.: Ps 73:1).

(III) Implying manner before a dependent clause qualifying or defining the action of a preceding verb or one that follows.

(A) Generally, meaning as, according as (Mt 1:24; 8:13; 20:14; Lk 14:22; Ro 12:3; 1Co 3:5; Col 2:6; 4:4; Tit 1:5; Rev 9:3; 18:6; 22:12). Once with *hoútō* (3779), thus, corresponding (1Co 7:17). Here in a somewhat more less restrictive *hōs kaí* ([2532], and), like the relative *hós* (3739), he who, serves as a connective particle (Ac 13:33; 17:28; 22:5; 25:10; Ro 9:25).

(B) Before a minor or parenthetic clause which then serves to modify or restrict the general proposition (Mt 27:65; Mk 4:27; 10:1; Lk 3:23; Ac 2:15; 1Co 12:2; 1Pe 5:12; 2Pe 3:9; Rev 2:24).

(C) Before a superlative used as an intensive meaning most speedily, as speedily as possible (Ac 17:15).

(IV) Before dependent clauses expressing the obj. or reference of a preceding verb or word, the nature of the action, the circumstances under which it takes place, and so forth, meaning in what way, how, as, often equivalent to a conjunction.

(A) Generally, meaning how, equivalent to *hópōs* (3704), in the manner that. With the aor. indic. (Mk 12:26; Lk 8:47; 23:55; 24:35; Ac 11:16; Ro 11:2; 2Co 7:15). Pleonastically (Lk 22:61). Once with *toúto* (5124), this, preceding (Lk 6:3, 4). Also followed by *hóti* (3754), that, meaning how that, *hōs hóti*, as that, to wit that. In the NT subjoined to a noun for fuller explanation, usually regarded as pleonastic, but not so in strictness (2Co 5:19; 11:21, "I speak as to the reproach [cast upon us] how that [*hōs hóti*] we are weak, although we were weak" (a.t.); 2Th 2:2, "nor by letter . . . as that."

(B) Before an obj. clause in a more restrictive sense meaning how, how that, that, with the indic. equivalent to *hóti*, that (cf. *hóti* [3754] I, C) (Ac 10:28, 38; Ro 1:9; 1Th 2:10; 2Ti 1:3; Sept.: 1Sa 13:11).

(C) Before a clause expressing end or purpose meaning as that, so that, equivalent to that, to the end that, like *hína* (2443), so that, or *hópōs* (3704), so that. Followed by the inf. expressing the purpose of a preceding verb meaning so as to, in order to (Ac 20:24, "I count not my life dear so that I may finish" [a.t.]; Heb 7:9, "so to speak" [a.t.], "that I may so speak" [a.t.]).

(D) Before a clause expressing result or consequence, so as that, so that, like *hṓste* (5620), so to, so that; with the indic. (Heb 3:11; 4:3 quoted from Ps 95:11).

(E) Before a clause expressing a cause or reason meaning as, that, equivalent to since, because, like *epeí* (1893), thereupon, since, because; *hóti* (3754), that (Gal 6:10, "since we now have opportunity" [a.t.]; perhaps Mt 6:12 [cf. Lk 11:4]).

(F) Before a clause implying time, as when, like *epeí* (1893), thereupon. **(1)** Generally meaning when, in that, while. With the indic. (Mt 28:9; Lk 1:41, 44; 4:25; 19:5; Jn 2:9; Ac 5:24; 28:4). By implication meaning whenever, as often as (Lk 12:58; Sept.: 2Ch 24:11). Also when, with the indic. (Lk 1:23; 2:15, 39; 11:1; Jn 4:1; 6:12, 16; Ac 7:23; 10:7; 13:18, 29). Followed by *tóte* (5119), then, at that time (Jn 7:10). From when, since (Mk 9:21). **(2)** Followed by *án* (302), a particle denoting a supposition, wish, possibility, *hōs án* meaning whensoever, as soon as, with the aor. subjunctive (Ro 15:24 [UBS]; 1Co 11:34, as soon as I come; Php 2:23).

Deriv.: *hōsaútōs* (5615), likewise; *hōseí* (5616), about; *hṓsper* (5618), just as; *hṓste* (5620), therefore.

Syn.: *katá* (2596), according to, as; *katháper* (2509), exactly as; *hoíos* (3739), in the neuter *hoíon*, with a neg., not so, such as; *áchri* (891), until; *méchri* (3360), till (a reference to a space of time).

5614. ὡσαννά, hōsanna, *ho-san-nah´*; of Hebrew origin [3467 and 4994]; *oh save!; hosanna* (i.e. *hoshiana*), an exclamation of adoration:—hosanna.

5615. ὡσαύτως, hōsautōs, *ho-sow´-toce*; from 5613 and an adverb from 846; *as thus*, i.e. *in the same way*:—even so, likewise, after the same (in like) manner.

5616. ὡσεί, hōsei, *ho-si´*; from 5613 and 1487; *as if*:—about, as (it had been, it were), like (as).

A conditional adverb from *hōs* (5613), as, and *ei* (1487), if. As if, as though, followed by the opt. In the NT only before a noun or adj.

(I) In comparisons, as if, as it were, as, like as (cf. *hōs* [5613] I, B) (Mt 9:36; 28:3, 4; Mk 9:26; Lk 22:44; 24:11; Ac 2:3; 6:15; 9:18; Heb 1:12; 11:12; Rev 1:14; Sept.: Job 28:5; 29:25). Elliptically where a part. or inf. belonging to the noun before *hōseí* is also implied with the noun after *hōseí* (Mt 3:16, "as a dove descending" [a.t.]; Mk 1:10; Jn 1:32; inf. Lk 3:22).

(II) Before words of number and measure, as if, as it were, meaning about, approximately (cf. *hōs* [5613] II, D). Before numerals (Mt 14:21, "about five thousand"; Mk 6:44; Lk 1:56; 3:23; 9:14, 28; 22:59; 23:44; Jn 4:6; 6:10; 19:14, 39; Ac 2:41; 4:4; 5:36; 10:3; 19:7; Sept.: Jgs 3:29). Of measure (Lk 22:41).

5617. Ὡσηέ, Hōsēe, *ho-say-eh´*; of Hebrew origin [1954]; *Hoseë* (i.e. *Hosheä*), an Israelite:—Osee.

5618. ὥσπερ, hōsper, *hoce´-per*; from 5613 and 4007; *just as*, i.e. *exactly like*:—(even, like) as.

5619. ὡσπερεί, hōsperei, *hoce-per-i´*; from 5618 and 1487; *just as if*, i.e. *as it were*:—as.

5620. ὥστε, hōste, *hoce´-teh*; from 5613 and 5037; *so too*, i.e. *thus therefore* (in various relations of *consecution*, as follow):—(insomuch) as, so that (then), (insomuch) that, therefore, to, wherefore.

5621. ὠτίον, ōtion, *o-tee´-on*; diminutive of 3775; an *earlet*, i.e. *one* of the ears, or perhaps the *lobe* of the ear:—ear.

5622. ὠφέλεια, ōpheleia, *o-fel´-i-ah*; from a derivative of the base of 5624; *usefulness*, i.e. *benefit*:—advantage, profit.

5623. ὠφελέω, ōpheleō, *o-fel-eh´-o*; from the same as 5622; to *be useful*, i.e. to *benefit*:—advantage, better, prevail, profit.

5624. ὠφέλιμος, ōphelimos, *o-fel´-ee-mos*; from a form of 3786; *helpful* or *serviceable*, i.e. *advantageous*:—profit (-able).